HBJ SCHOOL DICTIONARY

THIRD EDITION

Advisory Board

HBJ SCHOOL DICTIONARY

THIRD EDITION

HBJ

HARCOURT BRACE JOVANOVICH, PUBLISHERS

Orlando San Diego Chicago Dallas

Printed in the United States of America

ISBN 0-15-321132-6

Picture Credits

Definition Sections ***Illustrations:*** Diamond Art Studio, Fred Irvin except for **bar graph, cutlass, cuttlefish, dulcimer,** and **isthmus,** from HBJ Art Department; the following, by Ed Malsberg: **Adam's apple, adjustable, archery, backstroke, breast stroke, butterfly, buttress, clipboard, corsage, creel, crook, crossbow, curtsy, defaced, demijohn, devilfish, dike, distorted, easel, escapement, exercise, fedora, flippers, frog, gas mask, goggles, gown, granny knot, haversack, heart, helmets, ideograms, inflate, jack-in-the-box, jet plane, juggler, leg, mandible, mercator projection, middy, monarch, muff, mushroom, oar, obscure, octopus, outline, overalls, phaeton, pincers, poison sumac, pose, prescription, prime meridian, profile, quiver, rake, relay race, remote control, renovations, robe, rudder, salute, scepter, seatbelt, seine, shadow, sling, spear, stethoscope, stole, surplices, takeoff, theodolite, tombone, walker, waterskiing, yarmulke.**

Photographs: **abacus** Rosario Oddo Productions; **abstract** © Sotheby Parke-Bernet/Art Resource; **acorn** HBJ Photo; **acrobats** David Burnett/Leo de Wys, Inc.; **afghan** Rosario Oddo Productions; **agave** © 1979 Stephen J. Krasemann/Photo Researchers, Inc.; **amphitheater** R. Gates/Frederic Lewis; **aster** HBJ Photo; **automat** HBJ Photo; **backhand** HBJ Photo; **bangs** Rosario Oddo Productions; **bassoon** © 1984 Edie Bresler; **belfry** Rosario Oddo Productions; **bill** Rosario Oddo Productions; **blackbird** © Karl H. Maslowski/Photo Researchers, Inc.: **bloodhound** Percy T. Jones/Frederic Lewis; **bow** HBJ Photo; **bowline** HBJ Photo; **brocade** Dean/ Frederic Lewis; **Byzantine** Klaus Francke/Peter Arnold, Inc., **Canada goose** © Leonard Lee Rue/National Audubon Society/Photo Researchers, Inc.; **caribou** © Leonard Lee Rue/Monkmeyer; **casque** Alinari/Art Resource; **chamois** Toni Angermayer/Photo Researchers, Inc.; **collie** © Mary Eleanor Browning/ Photo Researchers, Inc.; **Colosseum** Cyril Morris/DPI; **comforter** HBJ Photo; **conch** HBJ Photo; **court** Lynn McLaren/Photo Researchers, Inc.; **crèche** Rosario Oddo Productions; **cricket** © Jack Dermid/Photo Researchers, Inc.; **cross section** HBJ Photo; **crown** The Granger Collection; **cruet** HBJ Photo; **crutches** HBJ Photo; **cubist painting** Collection, The Museum of Modern Art, New York. Gift of Edgar Kaufmann, Jr.; **cuirass** The Granger Collection; **cupola** © Jane Latta; **dandelion** © Jerome Wexler/Photo Researchers, Inc.; **dashboard** Rosario Oddo Productions; **date palm** Frank E. Gunnell/Frederic Lewis; **delft plate** © Sotheby Parke-Bernet/Art Resource; **destroyer** Wide World Photos; **dhow** Lynn McLaren/Rapho/Photo Researchers, Inc.; **disk harrow** Grant Heilman; **display** HBJ Photo; **doberman pincher** Joyce R. Wilson/Photo Researchers, Inc.; **donkey** Frederic Lewis; **eagle** Leonard Lee Rue/Monkmeyer; **earphone** HBJ Photo; **echidna** Australian News and Information Bureau/Photo Researchers, Inc.; **eland** © Mark Boulton/National Audubon Society/Photo Researchers, Inc.; **elk** © Richard N. Rife/National Audubon Society/Photo Researchers, Inc.; **English horn** © 1984 Edie Bresler; **ensign** Kathryn Dudek/Photo News; **ermine** © Ed Cesar/National Audubon Society/Photo Researchers, Inc.; **Etruscan vase** Alinari/Art Resource; **extinguisher** Rosario Oddo Productions; **fawn** Hal H. Harrison/Monkmeyer; **fingerprints** HBJ Photo; **fireplace** Rosario Oddo Productions; **flume** UPI/Bettmann; **flute** © 1984 Edie Bresler; **fort** Fritz Henle/Photo Researchers, Inc.; **French horn** The Lattimer Studios; **grand piano** Steinway and Sons; **greyhound** © Walter Chandoha; **grizzly bear** © W. J. Schoonmaker/National Audubon Society/Photo Researchers, Inc.; **gymnast** © Myron Wood/Photo Researchers, Inc.; **gyrfalcon** © Tom McHugh/National Audubon Society/Photo Researchers, Inc.; **gyroscope** HBJ Photo; **hare** © Leonard Lee Rue/National Audubon Society/Photo Researchers, Inc.; **harrow** Grant Heilman; **hawk** © G. Ronald Austing/National Audubon Society/Photo Researchers, Inc.; **hem** HBJ Photo; **hermit crab** Hal H. Harrison/Monkmeyer; **hibachi** Rosario Oddo Productions; **hippopotamus** Leonard Lee Rue/Monkmeyer; **hollyhock** © Henry M. Mayer/National Audubon Society/Photo Researchers, Inc.; **husky** Percy Jones/Frederic Lewis; **icon** The Granger Collection; **impala** Jen and Des Bartlett/Photo Researchers, Inc.; **impressionism** Service de Documentation Photographique, Les Musées Nationaux; **inlay** Art Resource; **insect** HBJ Photo; **insignia** Alon Reininger/Leo de Wys, Inc.; **iris** © F. E. Westlake/National Audubon Society/Photo Researchers, Inc.; **janus** Culver Pictures; **jockey** Kathryn Dudek/Photo News; **kinkajou** Jen and Des Bartlett/Photo Researchers, Inc.; **knocker** Rosario Oddo Productions; **lamp** Rosario Oddo Productions; **lapwing** Russ Kinne/Photo Researchers, Inc.; **lectern** HBJ Photo; **lei** HBJ Photo; **leopard** © Leonard Lee Rue/Photo Researchers, Inc.; **Liberty Bell** Monkmeyer; **lichen** © Jack Dermid/Photo Researchers, Inc.; **longhorn** Grant Heilman; **lure** HBJ Photo; **macaw** Rosario Oddo Productions; **marimba** Deagan-Slingerland; **marlin** © Richard Ellis/Photo Researchers, Inc.; **mask** HBJ Photo; **mesa** Glyn Cloyd; **microfiche** Carroll Morgan Photography; **microscope** HBJ Photo; **mission** © Bruce Roberts/Rapho/Photo Researchers, Inc.; **molds** HBJ Photo; **morning glory** © Russ Kinne/Photo Researchers, Inc.; **mustang** Hope Ryden; **muzzle** Rosario Oddo Productions; **narcissus** HBJ Photo; **newel** Rosario Oddo Productions; **nightshade** Grant Heilman; **nimbus** © Sotheby Parke-Bernet/Art Resource; **nuthatch** © G. Ronald Austing/Photo Researchers, Inc.; **nutria** © Allan D. Cruickshank/National Audubon Society/Photo Researchers, Inc.; **nymph** Stan Schroeder/Animals, Animals; **oboe** Knepp Studio; **observatory** Leo de Wys, Inc.; **old English sheepdog** © Walter Chandoha; **orangutan** © Ylla/Photo Researchers, Inc.; **orchid** Grant Heilman: **organ** J. L. Hamar/Frederic Lewis; **pachyderm** © Leonard Lee Rue/Animals, Animals; **paisley** HBJ Photo; **panther** © S. Nagendra/Photo Researchers, Inc.; **passionflower** Grant Heilman; **Persian cat** © Walter Chandoha; **piggyback** HBJ Photo; **pole vault** H. Armstrong Roberts; **pompon** HBJ Photo; **poncho** HBJ Photo; **post** Rosario Oddo Productions; **poster** Culver Pictures; **pouter** © Yilla/Photo Researchers, Inc.; **press** Wine and the People; **projector** HBJ Photo; **psaltery** © 1984 Edie Bresler; **pulpit** HBJ Photo; **quilt** The Shelbourne Museum; **Quonset hut** American Stock Photos/Frederic Lewis; **racetrack** © M. E. Warren/Photo Researchers, Inc.; **recorder** HBJ Photo; **redwood** William Graham/Photo Researchers, Inc.; **ragalia** British Tourist Authority; **reindeer** © Ylla/Photo Researchers, Inc; **relief** Rosario Oddo Productions; **Renaissance** Russell Thompson/Taurus Photos; **reptile** Grant Heilman; **rhea** © A. W. Ambler/National Audubon Society/Photo Researchers, Inc.; **ripple** HBJ Photo; **rococo** Rapho/Photo Researchers, Inc.; **ruff** Culver Pictures; **rumble seat** Culver Pictures; **saddle** Rosario Oddo Productions; **sarcophagus** Anderson/Art Resource; **sculpture** Alinari/Art Resource; **sentry** Glyn Cloyd; **sheep** © Leonard Lee Rue/Photo Researchers, Inc.; **shield** Art Resource; **sitar** J. Jay Hirz/Frederic Lewis; **slalom** © Peter Arnold; **snout** Grant Heilman; **sofa** Rosario Oddo Productions; **sphinx** George Holton/Photo Researchers, Inc.; **springbok** © Clem Haagner/Photo Researchers, Inc.; **stagecoach** Culver Pictures; **stalactites and stalagmites** Grant Heilman; **starfish** Grant Heilman; **sulky** Martin Vanderwall/Leo de Wys, Inc.; **swan** © A. W. Ambler/National Audubon Society/Photo Researchers, Inc,; **tabard** Culver Pictures; **tarsier** Ron Garrison/Photo Researchers, Inc.; **telescope** HBJ Photo; **terrier** © Walter Chandoha; **thatched roof** George Whiteley/Photo Researchers, Inc.; **thermometer** HBJ

Photo; **thrush** © Karl H. Maslowski/Photo Researchers, Inc.; **timber wolf** © A. W. Ambler/National Audubon Society/Photo Researchers, Inc.; **timpani** Deagan-Slingerland; **toga** Culver Pictures; **tractor** International Harvestor; **turret** © J. Allan Cash/Rapho/Photo Researchers, Inc.; **Uncle Sam** HBJ Photo; **underpass** Rosario Oddo Productions; **unicorn** Alinari/Art Resources; **Union Jack** Carroll Morgan Photography; **upright piano** Steinway and Sons; **vault** Silberstein/Monkmeyer; **Venus's-flytrap** Grant Heilman; **vicuna** © Leonard Lee Rue/National Audubon Society/Photo Researchers, Inc.; **violin** © 1984 Edie Bresler; **vulture** Leonard Lee Rue/Monkmeyer; **walrus** © Leonard Lee Rue/Photo Researchers, Inc.; **wapiti** Leonard Lee Rue/Monkmeyer; **water buffalo** © Leonard Lee Rue/Animals, Animals; **weasel** Karl H. Maslowski/Photo Researchers, Inc.; **Welsh corgi** © Mary Eleanor Browning/National Audubon Society/Photo Researchers, Inc.; **whale** © Frank Stevens/National Audubon Society/Photo Researchers, Inc.; **whirligig** © Rafael Macia/Photo Researchers, Inc.; **wigwam** Culver Pictures; **wolf** © A. W. Ambler/National Audubon Society/Photo Researchers, inc.; **wrought iron** Rosario Oddo Productions; **yellow jacket** Grant Heilman; **yew** Grant Heilman; **zeppelin** Culver Pictures

Appendix

Illustrations: **Solar System** Tom Powers; **U.S. Time Zones** Blaise Zito Associates, Inc.

Photographs: **White House** Bill Berech/Frederick Lewis; **Signers of the Declaration of Independence** the Bettman Archive; **Signature of John Hancock** the Granger Collection.

Biographical Section

Photographs: **Kobo Abe** Wide World Photos; **Ralph Abernathy** Wide World Photos; **Abigail Adams** The Granger Collection; **John Adams** The Granger Collection; **Jane Addams** The Granger Collection; **Konrad Adenauer** Wide World Photos; **Emilio Aguinaldo** Wide World Photos; **Louisa May Alcott** The Granger Collection; **Luis Alvarez** UPI/Bettmann; Roald Amundson UPI/Bettmann; **Marion Anderson** The Granger Collection; **Maya Angelou** Wide World Photos; **Susan B. Anthony** The Granger Collection; **Hannah Arendt** Wide World Photos; **Louis Armstrong** Culver Pictures; **Neil Armstrong** Wide World Photos; **Arthur Ashe** Wide World Photos; **Isaac Asimov** Wide World Photos; **John Jacob Astor** The Granger Collection; **John James Audubon** The Granger Collection; **Jane Austen** The Granger Collection; **Johann Sebastian Bach** The Granter Collection; **Francis Bacon** Culver Pictures; **Enid Bagnold** Wide World Photos; **George Balanchine** Wide World Photos; **Vasco de Balboa** Culver Pictures; **James Baldwin** Wide World Photos; **Sirimavo Bandaranaike** UPI/Bettmann; **Romana Bañuelos** Wide World Photos; **Clara Barton** The Granger Collection; **Charles Beard** The Bettman Archive; **Alexander Graham Bell** The Granger Collection; **Sarah Bernhardt** The Granger Collection; **Mary McLeod Bethune** The Granger Collection; **Otto von Bismarck** The Granger Collection; **Elizabeth Blackwell** The Granger Collection; **Nellie Bly** Culver Pictures; **Simon Bolivar** The Granger Collection; **Napoleon Bonaparte** Brown Brothers; **Daniel Boone** Culver Pictures; **Jorge Luis Borges** UPI/Bettmann; **Nadia Boulanger** Wide World Photos; **Margaret Bourke-White** UPI/Bettmann; **Johannes Brahms** Brown Brothers; **Gwendolyn Brooks** The Granger Collection; **Elizabeth Barrett Browning** The Granger Collection; **Robert Browning** The Granger Collection; **Blanche Bruce** Culver Pictures; **Pearl Buck** Wide World Photos; **Ralph Bunche** The Granger Collection; **Richard E. Byrd** Wide World Photos; **George Gordon Byron** Brown Brothers; **Mother Cabrini** Culver Pictures; **Julius Caesar** Culver Pictures; **Calamity Jane** The Granger Collection; **Sarah Caldwell** Wide World Photos; **Hattie Caraway** Wide World Photos; **Rachel Carson** Wide World Photos; **Jimmy Carter** Wide World Photos; **George Washington Carver** The Granger Collection; **Willa Cather** The Granger Collection; **Catherine the Great** The Granger Collection; **Carrie Chapman Catt** Wide World Photos; **Edith Cavell** The Granger Collection; **Mary Ellen Chase** Culver Pictures; **Carlos Chávez** Wide World Photos; **Chiang Kai-shek** Wide World Photos; **Chiang Kai-shek** Wide World Photos; **Julia Child** UPI/Bettmann; **Shirley Chisholm** UPI/Bettmann; **Agatha Christie** The Granger Collection; **Winston Churchill** Culver Pictures; **Kenneth Clark** Wide World Photos; **Cochise** The Bettmann Archive; **Jacqueline Cochran** Brown Brothers; **Colette** Wide World Photos; **Joan Cooney** UPI/Bettmann; **Nicholaus Copernicus** The Granger Collection; **Hernando Cortés** The Granger Collection; **Marie Curie** The Granger Collection; **Pierre Curie** The Granger Collection; **Salvador Dali** Wide World Photos; **Leonardo da Vinci** The Granger Collection; **Benjamin Davis** Wide World Photos; **Dorothy Day** Wide World Photos; **Charles de Gaulle** Wide World Photos; **Vine Deloria, Jr.,** Wide World Photos; **Agnes De Mille** Wide World Photos; **Hernando de Soto** The Granger Collection; **Emily Dickinson** The Granger Collection; **Babe Didrikson** UPI/Bettmann; **Walt Disney** Wide World Photos; **Helen Gahagan Douglas** Wide World Photos; **Frederick Douglass** The Granger Collection; **Alfred Dreyfus** Brown Brothers; **W.E.B. Du Bois** The Granger Collection; **Isadora Duncan** The Granger Collection; **Amelia Earhart** Culver Pictures; **Charles Eastman** The Granger Collection; **Gertrude Ederle** Culver Pictures; **Albert Einstein** The Granger Collection; **Dwight D. Eisenhower** The Granger Collection; **El Greco** Culver Pictures; **Duke Ellington** The Granger Collection; **Ralph Waldo Emerson** The Granger Collection; **Medgar Evers** UPI/Bettman; **Michael Faraday** The Granger Collection; **Fanny Farmer** Wide World Photos; **Edna Ferber** Wide World Photos; **Kirsten Flagstad** Wide World Photos; **Alexander Fleming** The Granger Collection; **Margot Fonteyn** UPI/Bettmann; **Gerald Ford** Wide World Photos; **Anne Frank** Wide World Photos; **Benjamin Franklin** The Granger Collection; **Anna Freud** Wide World Photos; **Sigmund Freud** The Granger Collection; **Betty Friedan** Wide World Photos; **Yuri Gagarin** Sovfoto; **Galileo** The Granger Collection; **Mahatma Gandhi** The Granger Collection; **Gabriel García Marquez** Columbia Information Service; **William Lloyd Garrison** The Granger Collection; **Marcus Garvey** Culver Pictures; **Geronimo** The Granger Collection; **George Gershwin** The Granger Collection; **Althea Gigson** Wide World Photos; **Nikki Giovanni** Wide World Photos; **George Goethals** The Granger Collection; **Francisco de Goya** Culver Pictures; **Martha Graham** Culver Pictures; **Ella Grasso** Wide World Photos; **Hetty Green** Culver Pictures; **Texas Guinan** Culver Pictures; **José Gutierrez** Wide World Photos; **Haile Selassie** UPI/Bettmann; **Alexander Hamilton** The Granger Collection; **W.C. Handy** The Granger Collection; **Lorraine Hansberry** UPI/Bettmann; **Warren G. Harding** The Granger Collection; **Patricia Harris** Wide World Photos; **William Hastie** Wide World Photos; **Helen Hayes** UPI/Bettmann; **William Randolph Hearst** The Granger Collection; **Ernest Hemingway** Culver Pictures; **Matthew Henson** The Granger Collection; **Barbara Hepworth** Wide World Photos; **Myra Hess** Wide World Photos; **Hirohito** Wide World Photos; **Ho Chi Minh** Culver Pictures; **Helen Hokinson** UPI/Bettmann; **Herbert Hoover** The Granger Collection; **Karen Horney** Culver Pictures; **Samuel Houston** Culver Pictures; **Julia Ward Howe** The Granger Collection; **Delores Huerta** UPI/Bettmann; **Victor Hugo** The Granger Collection; **Marjorie Husted** Wide World Photos; **Fusae Ichikawa** Wide World Photos; **Isabella I** Culver Pictures; **Ivan The Terrible** The Bettmann Archive; **Henry James** The Granger Collection; **William James** The Granger Collection; **Thomas Jefferson** The Granger Collection; **Jiang Zing** Eastfoto/Sovfoto; **Lady Bird Johnson** UPI/Bettmann; **Lyndon B. Johnson** Wide World Photos; **John Paul Jones** The Granger Collection; **Scott Joplin** UPI/Bettmann; **Chief Joseph** The Granger Collection; **Benito Juárez,** The Granger Collection; **Kamehameha I** Culver Pictures; **Helen Keller** The Granger Collection; **John F. Kennedy** The Granger Collection; **Robert F. Kennedy** UPI/Bettmann; **Kathleen Kenyon** UPI/Bettmann; **Martin Luther King, Jr.** Wide World Photos; **Thaddeus Kosciusko** The Granger Collection; **Juanita Kreps** Wide World Photos; **Marquis de Lafayette** The Granger Collection; **Selma Lagerlöf** The Granger Collection; **Louis Leakey** Culver Pictures; **Mary Leakey** Wide World Photos; **Richard Leakey** Wide World Photos; **Robert E. Lee** The Granger Collection; **Nikolai Lenin** Culver Pictures; Liliuokalani The Granger Collection; **Abraham Lincoln** The Granger Collection; **Jenny Lind** Culver Pictures; **Anne Morrow Lindbergh** Culver Pictures; **Charles Lindbergh** The Granger Collection; **Henry Wadsworth Longfellow** Culver Pictures; **Alice Roosevelt Longworth** Culver Pictures; **Amy Lowell** UPI/Bettmann; **Claire Booth Luce** The Granger Collection; **Martin Luther** Culver Pictures; **Douglas MacArthur** Wide World Photos; **Dolley Madison** The Granger Collection; **James Madison** The Granger Collection; **Ferdinand Magellan** The Granger Collection; **Mao Zedong** Wide World Photos; **Marie Antoinette** The Granger Collection; **Thurgood Marshall** UPI/Bettmann; **Maria Martinez** Susan Peterson; **Mary, Queen of Scots** The Granger Collection; **Massasoit** The Bettman Archive; **Henri Matisse** UPI/Bettmann; **Marjorie Matthews** UPI/Bettmann; **Margaret Mead** Wide World Photos; **Golda Meir** UPI/Bettmann; **Felix Mendelssohn** The Granger Collection; **Michelangelo** The Granger Collection; **John Milton** The Granger Collection; **Gabriela Mistral** Wide World Photos; **Maria Mitchell** The Granger Collection; **Scott N. Momaday** UPI/Bettmann; **Constance Baker Motley** Wide World Photos; **Bess Myerson** Wide World Photos; **Ralph Nader** UPI/Bettmann; **Nefertiti** The Granger Collection; **Pablo Neruda** The Granger Collection; **Louise Nevelson** UPI/Bettmann; **Richard Nixon** The Granger Collection; **Alfred Nobel** The Granger Collection; **Isamu Noguchi** Wide World Photos; **Annie Oakley** The Granger Collection; **Sandra Day O'Connor** Wide World Photos; **Georgia O'Keeffe** The Granger

Picture Credits

Collection; **Eugene O'Neill** The Granger Collection; **José Orozco** Wide World Photos; **Jesse Owens** Wide World Photos; **Vijaya Lakshmi Pandit** Culver Pictures; **Ely Samuel Parker** The Granger Collection; **Louis Pasteur** The Granger Collection; **Anna Pavlova** The Granger Collection; **I.M. Pei** Wide World Photos; **Frances Perkins** Wide World Photos; **Pablo Picasso** UPI/Bettmann; **Peter Pitseolak** Notman Photographic Archives, McCord Museum, McGill University; **Francisco Pizarro** The Granger Collection; **Pocahonatas** Culver Pictures; **Emily Post** Wide World Photos; **Beatrix Potter** The Granger Collection; **Marcel Proust** The Granger Collection; **Joseph Pulitzer** Culver Pictures; **Manuel Luis Quezon** Wide World Photos, **Sir Walter Raleigh** The Granger Collection; **A. Phillip Randolph** Wide World Photos; **Jeannette Rankin** Culver Pictures; **Ronald Reagan** Wide World Photos; **Red Jacket** UPI/Bettmann; **Walter Reed** The Granger Collection; **Hiram Revels** Culver Pictures; **Paul Revere** The Granger Collection; **Sally Ride** Wide World Photos; **Jackie Robinson** Wide World Photos; **John D. Rockefeller** The Granger Collection; **Auguste Rodin** Wide World Photos; **Will Rogers** Culver Pictures; **Eleanor Roosevelt** The Granger Collection; **Franklin D. Roosevelt** The Granger Collection; **Margaret Rudkin** Wide World Photos; **Bayard Rustin** © A. Philip Randolph Educational Fund; **Eero Saarinen** Wide World Photos; **Anwar el Sadat** Wide World Photos; **Jonas Salk** UPI/Bettmann; **Dorothy Schiff** UPI/Bettmann; **Albert Schweitzer** The Granger Collection; **Mother Seton** Culver Pictures; **William Shakespeare** The Granger Collection; **Ntozake Shange** Wide World Photos; **George Bernard Shaw** The Granger Collection; **Allan Shepard** Wide World Photos; **Dimitri Shostakovich** Wide World Photos; **Sitting Bull** The Granger Collection; **Margaret Chase Smith** The Granger Collection; **Ching-ling Soong** Wide World Photos; **John Philip Sousa** The Granger Collection; **Joseph Stalin** Culver Pictures; **Elizabeth Cady Stanton** The Granger Collection; **Gertrude Stein** Culver Pictures; **Gloria Steinem** Wide World Photos; **Charles Steinmetz** The Granger Collection; **Adlai Stevenson** The Granger Collection; **Harriet Beecher Stowe** The Granger Collection; **Sun Yat-sen** The Granger Collection; **Junko Tabei** Wide World Photos; **William Howard Taft** The Granger Collection; **Maria Tallchief** Wide World Photos; **Valentina Tereshkova** Wide World Photos; **Margaret Thatcher** Wide World Photos; **Dorothy Thompson** Culver Pictures; **Jim Thorpe** Culver Pictures; **Marshall Tito** Culver Pictures; **Leo Tolstoy** The Granger Collection; **Harry S Truman** The Granger Collection; **Sojourner Truth** The Granger Collection; **Tutankhamen** Wide World Photos; **Mark Twain** The Granger Collection; **Sigird Undset** Wide World Photos; **Vincent van Gogh** Culver Pictures; **Diego Velazquez** Culver Pictures; **Queen Victoria** Culver Pictures; **Voltaire** The Granger Collection; **Richard Wagner** The Granger Collection; **Barbara Ward** Wide World Photos; **Mercy Otis Warren** The Granger Collection; **George Washington** The Granger Collection; **Martha Washington** The Granger Collection; **Robert Weaver** Wide World Photos; **Noah Webster** The Granger Collection; **Edith Wharton** The Granger Collection; **Walt Whitman** The Granger Collection; **Oscar Wilde** The Granger Collection; **Queen Wihlemina** Wide World Photos; **Roy Wilkins** Wide World Photos; **Victoria Woodhull** The Granger Collection; **Virginia Woolf** The Granger Collection; **Frank Lloyd Wright** Wide World Photos; **Richard Wright** The Granger Collection; **Chien-Shiung Wu** Wide World Photos; **Rosalyn Yalow** Wide World Photos; **Chen Ning Yang** Wide World Photos; **William Butler Yeats** The Granger Collection; **Andrew Young** Wide World Photos; **Whitney M. Young Jr.** UPI/Bettmann; **Hideki Yukawa** The Granger Collection; **Emiliano Zapata** Wide World Photos; **Zhou Enlai** Eastfoto/Sovfoto

Geographical Section ***Photographs:*** **Agra** © F. Lisa Beebe/DPI; **Albany** J. Alex Langley/DPI: **Albuquerque** © Shirley Richards/Photo Researchers, Inc.; **Alsace-Lorraine** © Robert Clark/Photo Researchers, Inc.; **Amazon** S. Vidler/Leo de Wys, Inc.; **Amsterdam** Andy Bernhaut/Photo Researchers, Inc.; **Andorra** Dick Huffman/Monkmeyer; **Annapolis** © M. E. Warren/Kay Reese; **Antarctica** DPI; **Argentina** HBJ Photo; **Arizona** © D. Zirinsky/Photo Researchers, Inc.; **Arlington** Shostal Associates; **Athens** DPI; **Atlas Mountains** Gianni Tortoli/Photo Researchers Inc.; **Australia** Gleasner/The Stock Market; **Baghdad** Shostal Associates; **Banaras** © Bernard Wolff/Photo Researchers, Inc.; **Bangkok** Lawrence Smith/Photo Researchers, Inc.; **Beijing** © Brian Brake/Photo Researchers, Inc.; **Berlin** Zefa/Leo deWys, Inc.; **Blue Ridge Mountains** Monkmeyer; **Boston** © Larry D. Doell/The Stock Market; **British Columbia** T. Fujihira/Monkmeyer; **Brittany** Bernard G. Silberstein/Monkmeyer; **Brussels** J. Alex Langley/DPI; **Burma** Slim Aarons/Photo Researchers, Inc., **Cambridge** © Pierre Berger/Photo Researchers, Inc.; **Canada** © Franke Keating/Photo Researchers, Inc.; **Cape Canaveral** Hank Morgan/Photo Researchers, Inc.; **Carlsbad Caverns National Park** © Francis Current/Photo Researchers, Inc.; **Carthage** © Brian Brake/Photo Researchers, Inc.; **Chad** J. Alex Langley/DPI; **Charleston** © Luis Villota/The Stock Market; **Chartres** © Suzanne Brookens/The Stock Market; **China** © Lenore Weber/Omni Photo Communications; **Corfu** Winston H. Sutter/Photo Researchers, Inc.; **Cornwall** T. Hollyman/Photo Researchers, Inc.; **Damascus** © Richard Steedman/The Stock Shop; **Death Valley** Rosalind Joseph/Omni Photo Communications; **Delhi** J. Alex Langely/DPI; **Easter Island** © George Holton/Photo Researchers, Inc.; **Egypt** J. Alex Langley/DPI; **Florence** © Max Tortel/DPI; **Fuji** Herbert Lanks/Monkmeyer; **Galápagos Islands** Jerry Frank/DPI; **Gaspé Peninsula** © Townsend P. Dickinson/Photo Researchers, Inc.; **Georgia** © Tom McHugh/Photo Researchers, Inc.; **Granada** HBJ Photo; **Grand Canyon** © Lowell Georgia/ Photo Researchers, Inc.; **Greece** © Helen Marcus/Photo Researchers, Inc.; **Greenwich** Hays/Monkmeyer; **Hawaii** J. Alex Langley/DPI; **Himalayas** © George Holton/Photo Researchers, Inc.; **Hong Kong** © F. Lisa Beebe/DPI; **Hoover Dam** © L. T. Rhodes/ Taurus Photos; **Indonesia** © George Holton/Photo Researchers, Inc.; **Istanbul** J. Alex Langley/DPI; **Jakarta** Jules Bucher, Photo Researchers; **Jerusalem** Alon Reininger/DPI; **Kampuchea** P. W. Holzgraf/Monkmeyer; **Kashmir** John Stewart/The Stock Shop; **Kentucky** © Frank J. Miller/Photo Researchers, Inc.; **Kilimanjaro** Herbert Lanks/Monkmeyer; **Kyoto** Gerald Hachey/DPI; **Lapland** © George Holton/Photo Researchers, Inc.; **Leningrad** © George Holton/Photo Researchers, Inc.; **London** J. Alex Langley/DPI; **Long Island** Leo de Wys, Inc.; **Luxor** © John G. Ross/Photo Researchers, Inc.; **Machu Picchu** DPI; **Madrid** Bernard Pierre Wolff/Photo Researchers, Inc.; **Manhattan** J. Alex Langley/DPI; **Manila** S. Vidler/Leo de Wys, Inc.; **Marseilles** Starck-Rapho/Kay Reese; **Massachusetts** © Michael Philip Manheim/Photo Researchers, Inc.; **Mecca** © Mehmet Biber/Photo Researchers, Inc.; **Mesa Verde National Park** Bob and Ira Spring; **Mexico** Joel Gordon/DPI; **Mississippi** Shostal Associates; **Monaco** © Jeanne Strongm/The Stock Market; **Mont-Saint-Michel** Bob and Ira Spring; **Moscow** © Luis Villota/The Stock Market; **Nairobi** Shostal Associates; **Naples** F. Damm/Leo de Wys, Inc.; **Netherlands** © Vance Henry/Taurus Photos; **Niagara** © Kasz Maciag/The Stock Market; **Nile** © Richard Steedman/The Stock Market; **Normandy** © Paolo Koch/Photo Researchers, Inc.; **Norway** G. R. Richardson/Taurus Photos; **Nuremberg** V. Lefteroff/Leo de Wys, Inc.; **Oporto** Dick Huffman/Monkmeyer; **Ottawa** © Frank Grant/International Stock Photo; **Pago Pago** David Moore/Black Star; **Panama Canal** © Goode/Photo Researchers, Inc.; **Paris** © Frances Bannett/DPI; **Pisa** Larry Mulvehill/Photo Researchers, Inc.; **Portugal** © Dick Davis/Photo Researchers, Inc.; **Prague** Susan McCartney/Photo Researchers, Inc.; **Rangoon** Slim Aarons/Photo Researchers, Inc.; **Rhine** Messerschmidt/Leo de Wys, Inc.; **Rio de Janeiro** J. Alex Langley/DPI; **Rome** © M. Reichenthal/The Stock Market; **Mount Rushmore** Richard Guches/DPI; **Salzburg** S. Vidler/Leo de Wys, Inc.; **San Francisco** © Richard Steedman/The Stock Market; **San Juan** © Luis Villota/The Stock Market: **São Paolo** © John Moss/Photo Researchers, Inc.; **Scotland** Herbert Lanks/Monkmeyer; **Sicily** © John Snyder/The Stock Market; **Sierra Nevada** Shostal Associates; **South Carolina** Shostal Associates; **South Dakota** © Francis Current/Photo Researchers, Inc.; **Spain** Bernard Pierre Wolff/Photo Researchers, Inc.; **Sweden** Messerschmidt/ Leo de Wys, Inc.; **Syndney** © Luis Villota/The Stock Market; **Tahiti** S. Vidler/Leo de Wys, Inc.; **Tanzania** von Meiss-Teuffen/Photo Researchers, Inc.; **Thames** G. R. Richardson/Taurus Photos; **Thebes** © George Holton/Photo Researchers, Inc.; **Tiber** Bob and Ira Spring; **Tibet** © Marion Patterson/Photo Researchers, Inc.; **Tokyo** Geoffrey Hiller/Leo de Wys, Inc.; **Toronto** E. Otto/Miller Services; **Tunisia** © Suzanne Brookens/The Stock Market; **Turkey** © Fred Maroon/Photo Researchers, Inc.; **Tyrol** Herbert Lanks/Monkmeyer; **Utah** © Leonard Lee Rue/Monkmeyer; **Vatican City** Bob and Ira Spring; **Venice** Bob and Ira Spring; **Versailles** © Jerry Frank/DPI; **Vienna** © LBMLF, Vienna, Andy Bernhaut Archive/Photo Researchers, Inc.; **Wales** Herbert Lanks/Monkmeyer; **Washington** J. Alex Langley/DPI; **West Point** Shostal Associates; **Williamsburg** © Eric Kroll/Taurus Photos; **Wisconsin** © Russ Kinne/Photo Researchers, Inc.; **Yellowstone** Bob and Ira Spring; **Yorkshire** Zefa/Leo de Wys, Inc.; **Yucatán** John Curtis/Taurus Photos; **Yugoslavia** Susan McCarntey/Photo Researchers, Inc.; **Zambezi** © George Holton/Photo Researchers, Inc.; **Zurich** Van Phillips/Leo de Wys, Inc.

Map Section and Geographical Section Opener HBJ Art Department

Cover: Fred Marcellino

Contents

(Contents, continued)

Contents

To Teachers and Parents

An elementary school dictionary should be both a useful reference book and a textbook. As a reference work, it must answer clearly the questions children have about words. As a textbook, a school dictionary must provide ample material for the study of words and usage. The HBJ School Dictionary, Third Edition satisfies both requirements.

The most important feature of a dictionary is its word list. The approximately 60,000 entries in the HBJ School Dictionary, Third Edition have been gathered from many sources. Among these sources are textbooks in all the subject areas, popular juvenile literature, and magazines and newspapers. The HBJ School Dictionary, Third Edition contains many words that have come quite recently into our language. Some of these words have been contributed by computer and space technology; others have been created to express new concepts in the worlds of politics and economics.

Each dictionary entry comes in its natural place in a single alphabetical list. Within an entry, facts about a word also come in a regular order that soon becomes familiar. The system of showing pronunciation uses only a few easily recognizable diacritical marks, and it is simple to learn and use. Irregular or easily confused inflectional forms are shown early in the entry where they cannot be mistaken for idioms or run-on derivatives. Illustrative phrases or sentences follow definitions whenever they are helpful.

Particular care has been taken with the definitions, which have been written for the understanding of the elementary student, both in the presentation of facts and in the wording. In addition, the HBJ School Dictionary, Third Edition contains many features once thought too advanced for the elementary level. Etymologies, for instance, have been expressed in simple words, with no technical terms or abbreviations. Usage notes, cross-references, and subject labels add to the student's understanding of language.

The page on which each letter of the alphabet begins features a history of that letter, starting with its most ancient forms and tracing its development into the modern letter we use today.

The HBJ School Dictionary, Third Edition also contains an informative Appendix with charts, lists, and tables from the fields of social studies, science, mathematics, and language arts. In addition, there is a biographical section with hundreds of entries and a photo gallery of famous faces. The beautiful, full-color geographical section provides the student with information about nations, cities, and geographical features throughout the world.

Dictionary Overview

Main Entry — **cab** [kab] *n.* **1** A taxicab. **2** A one-horse carriage for public hire. **3** An enclosed compartment, as in a locomotive for the engineer, or in a truck or crane for the operator.

Syllable Division — **ca·bal** [kə·bal′] *n.* **1** A group of persons who are secretly engaged in some scheme or plot. **2** The scheme or plot of such a group.

Pronunciation — **cab·al·le·ro** [kab′əl·yâr′ō] *n., pl.* **cab·al·le·ros** A Spanish gentleman; cavalier.

Part of Speech — **ca·ban·a** [kə·ban′ə] *n.* **1** A small cabin. **2** A small bathhouse for changing clothes at the beach.

Definition — **cab·a·ret** [kab′ə·rā′] *n.* A restaurant that provides entertainment for its customers.

Subentry — **cab·i·net** [kab′ə·nit] *n.* **1** A piece of furniture fitted with shelves and drawers. **2** (*often written* **Cab-inet**) A group of official advisers and assistants of a head of state.

Usage Label — **ca·boose** [kə·bo͞os′] *n.* *U.S.* A car, usually the rear car of a freight train, used by the crew.

Inflectional Forms — **cac·tus** [kak′təs] *n., pl.* **cac·tus·es** or **cac·ti** [kak′tī] A plant of hot desert regions having a green pulpy trunk covered with spines or prickles instead of leaves and often bearing showy flowers.

Usage Note — **cai·tiff** [kā′tif] **1** *n.* A low scoundrel. **2** *adj.* Base. ◆ This word is seldom used today.

Homographs — **calf**[1] [kaf] *n., pl.* **calves** [kavz] **1** The young of the cow or other bovine animals. **2** The young of some other mammals, as the seal or whale. **3** Calfskin.

calf[2] [kaf] *n., pl.* **calves** [kavz] The muscular back part of the human leg below the knee.

Variant Spelling Cross-Reference — **ca·lif** [kā′lif] *n.* Another spelling of CALIPH.

Illustration — **cap·stan** [kap′stən] *n.* An upright cylinder resembling a large spool, turned by hand or motor-driven, and around which cables or ropes are wound to lift a weight, as an anchor.

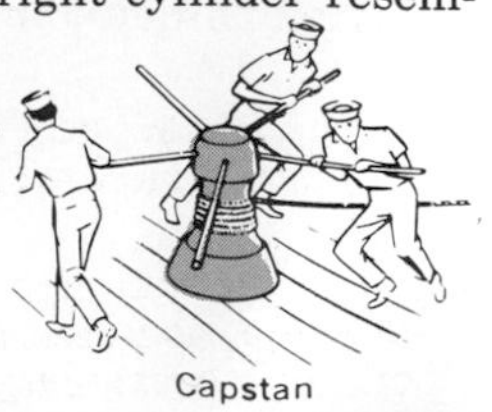

Capstan

Abbreviation — **capt.** or **Capt.** captain.

car·mine [kär'min *or* kär'mīn'] *n., adj.* Deep red or purplish red. — **Variant Pronunciation**

car pool 1 An arrangement made by a group of car owners who take turns driving each other or their children to work or school. **2** The members of such a group. — **Compound Entry**

car·rou·sel [kar'ə·sel'] *n.* Another word for MERRY-GO-ROUND. — **Variant Term Cross-Reference**

car·ry·all[1] [kar'ē·ôl] *n.* A light, one-horse carriage with a top, holding several people. ◆ *Carryall* comes from the French word *cariole.* Apparently the sound and spelling of *cariole* were too un-English, because *carryall,* with its familiar English elements, *carry* and *all*, replaced it. — **Etymology**

cen·sure [sen'shər] *n., v.* **cen·sured, cen·sur·ing** 1 *n.* Blame or criticism; reprimand. **2** *v.* To blame or criticize. ◆ See CENSOR. — **Cross-Reference**

cer·e·mo·ny [ser'ə·mō'nē] *n., pl.* **cer·e·mo·nies** 1 Any formal act or series of actions performed in a definite, set manner: a graduation *ceremony.* **2** A formal or extremely polite manner of acting: to serve tea with *ceremony.* **—stand on ceremony** To act or insist that others act in a formal manner. — **Idiom**

Cha·ryb·dis [kə·rib'dis] *n.* In Greek myths, a whirlpool opposite the rock of Scylla. Ships going between Italy and Sicily had to avoid both. — **Subject Reference**

chill·y [chil'ē] *adj.* **chill·i·er, chill·i·est** 1 Causing coldness or chill: a *chilly* rain. **2** Feeling cold: I am *chilly.* **3** Not friendly or warm: a *chilly* greeting. **—chill'i·ness** *n.* — **Illustrative Sentence**

clas·si·fy [klas'ə·fī] *v.* **clas·si·fied, clas·si·fy·ing** To put or divide into classes or groups: to *classify* books. **—clas'si·fi'er** *n.* — **Run-on Entry**

clerk [klûrk] **1** *n.* An office worker whose tasks include keeping records or accounts and attending to files. **2** *n.* An official or employee, as of a court or government, who keeps records and performs other duties. **3** *n. U.S.* A person who sells goods in a store. **4** *v.* To work as a clerk. — **Multiple Definitions**

co- A prefix meaning: 1 Together, as in *coexist.* **2** With another; joint, as in *coauthor.* — **Prefix**

coel- or **coelo-** or **cel-** or **celo-** A combining form meaning: Hollow; cavity, as in *coelenterate.* — **Combining Form**

-cy A suffix meaning: **1** Quality, state, or condition of being, as in *secrecy.* **2** Rank, grade, or position of, as in *presidency.* — **Suffix**

Introduction for Students

Why do you use a dictionary? If you ask most people that question, they will say that a dictionary is used to find the meaning of a word. If that were its only use, a dictionary would certainly be a very valuable tool. However, a dictionary contains much more than just the meanings of words. You can find how to spell words and how to pronounce them. You can learn how to use a word properly and discover its history. This is just the beginning. There are many other kinds of information in a dictionary.

As you read the following pages, you will learn how to use the dictionary well. The practice exercises will help you develop the skills you need to find the information you want quickly and accurately.

Main Entry — **cab** [kab] *n.* **1** A taxicab. **2** A one-horse carriage for public hire. **3** An enclosed compartment, as in a locomotive for the engineer, or in a truck or crane for the operator.

If you look through the dictionary, you will see words in **dark print** on each page. The words in dark print at the left-hand margin of each column are **main entry** words. They are printed slightly to the left of the rest of the entry. These are the words the dictionary explains.

Below are samples of main entries of this dictionary. Note that sometimes two or more words that go together, such as *junior high school*, are explained together.

blob [blob] *n.* A lump or drop of soft or sticky matter: a *blob* of paint.

Fal·staff [fôl′staff′] *n.* A boastful, cowardly, but witty old knight in Shakespeare's *Henry the Fourth* and *The Merry Wives of Windsor.* **—Fal·staff′i·an** *adj.*

junior high school In the U.S., a school coming between elementary and high school, and usually covering grades 7, 8, and 9.

leak·y [lē′kē] *adj.* **leak·i·er, leak·i·est** Having a leak: a *leaky* roof. **—leak′i·ness** *n.*

mem·o·rize [mem′ə·riz] *v.* **mem·o·rized, mem·o·riz·ing** To commit to memory; learn by heart. **—mem·o·ri·za·tion** [mem′ə·rə·zā′shən] *n.*

plo·ver [pluv′ər *or* plō′vər] *n.* A bird that lives on the shore, having long pointed wings and a short tail.

re·ply [ri·plī′] *v.* **re·plied, re·ply·ing,** *n., pl.* **re·plies** **1** *v.* To give an answer or response. **2** *n.* An answer or response.

sta. or **Sta.** station

Exercise

Use the sample main entries to answer the following questions.

1. Which word might describe a faucet?
2. Where would you go to study?
3. What could you do to a poem?
4. Which word is a short form of another word?
5. What do you do when someone asks you a question?
6. Which word is a character you might see on a stage?
7. Which word is the name of a bird?
8. Which word could you use in place of the word *lump*?

Alphabetical Order

Have you ever used a telephone book to find someone's telephone number? Do you remember how you found the person's name? It was probably very easy if you knew that a telephone book is arranged in **alphabetical order** by last names. Imagine how hard it would be to find someone's telephone number if the names were printed in no particular order. It might be quicker to write a letter and mail it.

Alphabetical order is used in many other places too. Perhaps you have used an encyclopedia at some time. The subjects are arranged in alphabetical order. In the library, fiction books are arranged alphabetically by the author's last name. Look in the index of any of your textbooks. The entries there are arranged in alphabetical order too. Can you think of any other places where alphabetical order is used? Did you think of the dictionary?

The usefulness of a dictionary also depends on its organization in alphabetical order. The main entry words in a dictionary are listed in alphabetical order under each letter.

All the *a* entries are listed alphabetically under *a*.

a or **A** [ā] *n., pl.* **a's** or **A's** 1 The first letter of the English alphabet. 2 *U.S.* The highest or best grade for school work. 3 In music, the sixth note of the scale of C major.

a [ə *or* ā] an indefinite article used before nouns or noun phrases. It means: 1 One: I bought *a* dozen eggs today. 2 One kind of: Sugar is *a* carbohydrate 3 Any; each: *A* burned-out fuse should be replaced. 4 For each: two dollars *a* pound. 5 In each: once *a* week. ◆ See AN.

a. 1 about. 2 acre(s). 3 area(s). 4 In sports, assist.

A 1 acre. 2 angstrom. 3 argon. 4 answer. 5 area.

AA 1 Alcoholics Anonymous. 2 antiaircraft.

AAA American Automobile Association.

aard·vark [ärd'värk'] *n.* A burrowing animal of southern Africa having powerful claws and a long, sticky tongue. It feeds on termites and ants.

aard·wolf [ärd'wŏŏlf] *n., pl.* **aard·wolves** [ärd'·woolvz] A hyenalike mammal of the African plains that feeds on insects and small animals.

Aar·on [âr'ən *or* ar'ən] *n.* In the Bible, the first Hebrew high priest, the brother of Moses.

AAU Amateur Athletic Union.

A.B. Bachelor of Arts.

ABA 1 American Bar Association. 2 American Basketball Association.

ab·a·ca [ab'ə·kä'] *n.* 1 A large tropical plant that grows in the Phillipines. The stalks of its leaves are used to make Manila hemp. 2 Another word for MANILA HEMP.

a·back [ə·bak'] *adv.* Backward: behind. **—taken aback** Surprised; suddenly confused; upset.

ab·a·cus [ab'ə·kəs] *n.* A device using beads that slide on rods for adding, subtracting, multiplying, and dividing.

a·baft [ə·baft'] 1 *adv.* Toward the stern; aft. 2 *prep.* Farther aft than: *abaft* the mainmast.

ab·a·lo·ne [ab'ə·lō'nē] *n.* An edible shellfish having a flat shell lined with mother-of-pearl.

All the *b* entries are listed alphabetically under *b*.

b or **B** [bē] *n., pl.* **b's** or **B's** 1 The second letter of the English alphabet. 2 In music, the seventh note of the scale of C major.

b or b. 1 base. 2 base hit. 3 baseman. 4 bass (music). 5 book. 6 born.

B The symbol for the element boron.

B. 1 bacillus. 2 bay. 3 Bible. 4 British.

Ba The symbol for the element barium.

B.A. Bachelor of Arts.

baa [bä] *n., v.* **baaed, baa·ing** 1 *n.* The natural cry of a sheep or goat. 2 *v.* To make this cry; bleat.

Ba·al [bā'(ə)l] *n., pl.* **Ba·al·im** [bā'(ə)l·im] 1 The sun god of the Phoenicians. 2 A false idol or god.

Bab·bitt metal [bab'ət] Any of a number of soft alloys of tin, copper, and antimony, used to reduce friction in bearings.

bab·ble [bab'əl] *v.* **bab·bled, bab·bling,** *n.* 1 *v.* To make meaningless speech sounds: The baby *babbled* happily. 2 *n.* Meaningless speech sounds. 3 *v.* To talk or say very fast or without thinking: to *babble* to a friend; to *babble* a secret. 4 *n.* Foolish or fast talk. 5 *v.* To make a murmuring or rippling sound, as a brook. 6 *n.* A rippling or bubbling sound; murmur. **—bab'bler** *n.*

babe [bāb] *n.* An infant; baby.

Ba·bel [bā'bəl *or* bab'əl] *n.* 1 In the Bible, a city where people tried to reach heaven by building the **Tower of Babel.** God stopped their work by suddenly causing them to speak different languages so they could not understand one another. 2 (*often written* **babel**) Noise and confusion, as when many people talk at once.

Imagine you are looking for the words *fire, fan,* and *feast* in a dictionary. You know that they will be listed with other words beginning with *f*. But which word will be first? You will have to look at the second letter of each word. Now you can see that *fan* is first, and *feast* and *fire* follow it. If the words you were looking up were *fry, friend,* and *fresh,* you would have to look at the third letter. Sometimes it may be necessary to look at the fourth or even fifth letter of a word.

Exercise 1

Arrange the words in each group in the order they would be found in a dictionary.

1.	**2.**	**3.**	**4.**
desk	napkin	pen	mitten
ranch	fist	paper	mirror
music	weep	plate	milk
thunder	lion	pony	misspell
hug	tree	pear	mistake
bear	time	pride	missile
store	seam	puppy	mite
wretch	elk	pillow	million
clear	dream	puddle	mint
family	pair	peony	minnow

Exercise 2

To find a definition of each word on the left, arrange each group of words on the right in alphabetical order.

5.	Latin	Rome/language/of/ancient/an
6.	forge	metal/fireplace/a/heating/for
7.	herring	fish/in/found/a/ocean/common/waters/northern
8.	overshoe	an/shoe/outer/rubber
9.	slime	soft/moist/clinging/any/stuff/sticky
10.	panacea	ills/for/pains/a/or/cure-all
11.	salary	white-collar/money/to/paid/workers/regularly
12.	mash	stuff/soft/of/mass/pulpy
13.	grisly	fear/causing/terror/or
14.	matzo	Passover/eaten/a/for/bread
15.	man-of-war	naval/armed/vessel/an
16.	abyss	chasm/a/pit/or/bottomless
17.	fang	tooth/pointed/long/a
18.	jewel	stone/or/precious/a/gem
19.	blight	disease/destructive/a/plants/of
20.	pibroch	piece/musical/sounding/bagpipe/a/warlike/very

Division into Thirds and Use of Tab Letters

Imagine that you are going to look up the word *zither* in the dictionary. Where in the dictionary would you look? In the back, of course, because *z* is the last letter in the alphabet. Suppose you want to find the meaning of the word *armor*. You would look in the front of the dictionary because *a* is the first letter of the alphabet. But where would you look to find words like *gopher, karate,* and *rejoice*? Try this. Think of the dictionary as being divided into **thirds.** The words beginning with the letters *a* to *f* are in the first third, or front, of the dictionary. The words beginning with *g* to *p* are in the second third, or middle, of the dictionary. The words beginning with *q* to *z* are in the last third, or back, of the dictionary.

FRONT	a b c d e f
MIDDLE	g h i j k l m n o p
BACK	q r s t u v w x y z

Which part of the dictionary contains the word *karate*? Since *karate* begins with *k*, you should open the dictionary to the middle third. On the right-hand side of each right-hand page is a black box with a letter in it. This is the **tab letter**. The entry words on the page you open to begin with the tab letter in the box. Suppose the tab letter is *g*. You then know you must look further on in the book since *k* comes after *g*. Suppose the tab letter on the page is *p*. You will have to turn toward the front of the book since *k* comes before *p*. By thinking that the dictionary is divided into thirds and by using the tab letters, you can find words quickly.

Exercise 1

Copy the three groups of words. In the first group, circle the words that would be found in the first third of the dictionary. In the second group, circle the words that would be found in the second third. In the third group, circle the words that would be found in the last third of the dictionary.

1. apple, lap, zebra, carport, exit, pencil, mountain, diamond, lame, inside
2. flock, machine, trust, violet, nightgown, pocket, oatmeal, library, know, glove
3. victory, teeth, nail, round, family, sister, brother, yacht, necktie, window

Exercise 2

Each word represents a word you are looking up in the dictionary. The letter next to each word represents the tab letter on the page you opened to. Copy the words and the letters. Next to each letter write whether you should turn to the part of the dictionary that comes before the letter or after it to find the word.

4. barber / D	**5.** sit / Q	**6.** morning / N	**7.** ground / F
8. yard / W	**9.** evergreen / G	**10.** under / R	**11.** opera / P
12. icicle / H	**13.** very / U	**14.** love / J	**15.** quiet / P

dough **235** downstream

dough [dō] *n.* 1 A soft, thick mass of flour and a liquid mixed together with other ingredients, used for making such foods as bread, biscuits, and pastry. 2 *slang* Money.
dough·nut [dō′nut′] *n.* A small cake, usually shaped like a ring, of sweetened dough fried in deep fat.
dough·ty [dou′tē] *adj.* **dough·ti·er, dough·ti·est** Strong and brave: now rarely used except humorously. **—dough′ti·ly** *adv.*
dough·y [dō′ē] *adj.* **dough·i·er, dough·i·est** 1 Like dough. 2 Not fully baked; *doughy* bread.
Doug·las fir [dug′ləs] A tall evergreen tree of western North America grown for its valuable timber.
downs [dounz] *n.pl.* Small, rolling hills usually covered with grass.
down·stage [doun′stāj′] *adj., adv.* On or toward the front part of a stage.
down·stairs [*adv.* doun′stârz′, *adj., n.* doun′stârz′] 1 *adv.* On or to a lower floor: to go *downstairs.* 2 *adj.* Situated on a lower or main floor: a *downstairs* room. 3 *n.* The ground or main floor of a house of building.
down·state [doun′stāt′] *adj., adv.* In or toward the southern part of a U.S. state.
down·stream [*adv.* doun′strēm′, *adj.* doun′strēm′] *adv., adj.* In the direction of the current of a stream: to row *downstream.*

Look at the sample section of a dictionary page. At the top, there are two **guide words.** The guide words help you find the dictionary page you want.

The guide word on the left is *dough.* Notice that the same word, *dough,* is the first main entry word on the page. The guide word on the right is *downstream.* The last word on the page is *downstream.* The guide word on the left shows the first main entry word on the page. The guide word on the right shows the last main entry word on the page. The other main entry words on the page are in alphabetical order between the two guide words. If a word does not fall in alphabetical order between the two guide words, it will not be on the page.

Both guide words on the page begin with the letters *do.* Do the words *dorsal, dovetail,* and *dozen* belong on a dictionary page with the guide words *dough* and *downstream*? The first two letters of all the words are the same. You will have to look at the third letters. The *r* in *dorsal* comes before the *u* in *dough.* The word *dorsal* cannot be on the page. The *v* in *dovetail* comes after the *u* in *dough* and before the *w* in *downstream.* The word *dovetail* would appear on the page. The letter *z* comes after the letter *w* in the alphabet. The word *dozen* cannot be on the page.

Suppose the guide words on a page were *fun* and *furnishings.* The word *fund* could be on that page. The words *fudge* and *furrier* could not. Would *fudge* be on the page with the guide words *fryer* and *fumigate*? Yes, because *fudge* comes between *fryer* and *fumigate* in alphabetical order.

Exercise 1

Write the numbers 1 to 10 on your paper. Write YES or NO next to each number to tell whether the main entry word would be found between the two guide words.

Main Entry Words	**Guide Words**
1. aviator	**a.** autumnal equinox/awakening
2. briefcase	**b.** brigand/broadax

3. cinnamon
4. chamois
5. emerald
6. gibbous
7. hearing aid
8. heritage
9. honeydew
10. initial

c. CIA/circulate
d. challis/channel
e. embay/emigrant
f. ghoul/gin rummy
g. heart/heaven
h. hermetic/hex
i. honesty/hookworm
j. infrared/inhuman

Exercise 2

Copy the main entry words. Look the words up in the dictionary. Beside each word, write the guide words for each page on which you found the main entry words.

11. breakfast
12. dizzy
13. glassful
14. jack o'lantern
15. leviathan
16. onyx
17. newsprint
18. organ grinder
19. perjury
20. reach
21. tunnel
22. work

Exercise 3

On your paper, match the number of each main entry word with the letter of the correct guide words.

Main Entry Word

23. forage
24. flytrap
25. fort
26. fresco
27. forehead
28. fragmentary
29. forfeit
30. freight
31. flummox
32. floppy disk
33. foundation
34. frazzle
35. fold
36. foolscap
37. frosty

Guide Word

a. formulation/foster
b. forced/forensic
c. frontage/fry
d. fought/foxtail
e. floodlight/flowering plant
f. foreordain/forget
g. frenzied/frightful
h. frankfurter/free lance
i. flute/foci
j. fo'c's'le/follow
k. follower/footing
l. fox terrier/Frankenstein
m. footless/force
n. flowerpot/fluster
o. freeman/frenetic

Definition ______ **cab·a·ret** [kab′ə·rā′] *n.* A restaurant that provides entertainment for its customers.

Suppose you received a note from a friend. The note said, "Please help me find my creel." Would you know what to look for? If not, you could find out quickly by looking in the dictionary.

> **creel** [krēl] *n.* A wicker basket used to hold newly caught fish.

Sometimes you may not understand every word in a definition. Suppose the word *wicker* is unfamiliar. You should look up the meaning of *wicker* to help you understand the meaning of *creel.*

> **wicker** [wik′ər] **1** *n.* A pliant young branch or twig, as of osier. **2** *n.* Such branches or twigs woven into a kind of fabric used in making baskets, light furniture, and other items. **3** *adj. use:* a *wicker* chair. **4** *n.* Objects made of wicker.

You now know that a wicker basket is a basket made of woven branches or twigs. The definition of *wicker* has given you more information about the word *creel.*

Looking up the word *creel* led you to another word. You might even want to look up some other words in the definition of *wicker*, words such as *pliant* or *osier*, for example. Use your dictionary in this way. You will learn many new words.

Exercise ______

Copy the words below. Look up the meaning of each. Write the meaning next to the word. Look up any words in the meanings that you do not understand. Write their meanings also.

1. cactus
2. hanger
3. macaroon
4. legible
5. dextrose
6. ladyslipper
7. salubrious
8. crux
9. farina
10. pekoe
11. kiln
12. aileron
13. hardtack
14. ecru
15. zeal
16. flivver
17. thesaurus
18. flagship
19. doubloon
20. googol
21. lorgnette
22. urbane
23. peccary
24. geode
25. pangram
26. ufology
27. spoor
28. thole
29. vermiform
30. ugli
31. jubilant
32. kilter
33. valise
34. theodolite
35. rusticate
36. palanquin

Multiple Definitions —— **clerk** [klûrk] **1** *n.* An office worker whose tasks include keeping records or accounts and attending to files. **2** *n.* An official or employee, as of a court or government, who keeps records and performs other duties. **3** *n. U.S.* A person who sells goods in a store. **4** *v.* To work as a clerk.

Many main entry words have more than one meaning, or **definition.** When a word has more than one meaning, each meaning in the entry is numbered. The meaning that is used most often is listed first. You must be careful when you are looking up a word with more than one meaning. In order to choose the right meaning, it often helps to look closely at the sentence or paragraph in which you found the word. The sentence or paragraph may contain important clues to help you find the right meaning.

Look at the definition of *clerk* at the top of the page. Then read this sentence.

The clerk talked to me.

Can you tell which meaning of *clerk* is being used in the sentence? Of course not. There are no clues in the sentence that tell you which meaning fits best.

Now read this sentence.

The clerk talked to me about organizing the files.

You can tell by the phrase "about organizing the files" that definition 1 fits the sentence.

Suppose the sentence was this one.

The clerk talked to me about several new brands.

You could tell by the phrase "about several new brands" that definition 3 fits the sentence.

Read the following sentence.

The clerk talked to me about recording the verdict.

By now you should be able to recognize the clue that tells you that definition 2 fits the sentence.

Sometimes you may have a problem telling which meaning fits best. A good way to help yourself is to substitute the different meanings of a word, one at a time, for the word itself. The word *tank*, for example, has three meanings listed in the dictionary.

tank [tangk] *n.* **1** A large container used to store fluids: a gasoline *tank.* **2** An armored military vehicle which carries guns and moves on two endless metal tracks. **3** A swimming pool.

Which meaning would fit the following sentence?

They are swimming in the tank.

To find out, look at the numbered definitions of *tank*. Try each meaning in place of the word *tank* in this sentence. Which meaning makes sense?

> They are swimming in "a large container used to store fluids."
> They are swimming in "an armored military vehicle."
> They are swimming in "a swimming pool."

The third meaning of *tank* fits best.

Exercise 1

Write the numbers of the sentences on your paper. Beside the number, write the number of the meaning of each word that fits the sentence.

> **groom** [grōōm] **1** *v.* To attend to the feeding, cleaning, and brushing of (a horse). **2** *n.* A person who tends to horses. **3** *v.* To make neat and tidy: Cats *groom* themselves daily. **4** *v.* To prepare by giving special training to. **5** *n.* A bridegroom.

1. Margo grooms her horse every day.
2. The bride and groom cut the wedding cake.
3. The groom is in the stable.
4. Donna is being groomed for a leadership position.
5. Monkeys groom each other.

> **pis·ta·chi·o** [pis·tä′shē·ō *or* pis·tash′ē·ō] *n., pl.* **pis·ta·chi·os,** *adj.* **1** *n.* An edible green nut. **2** *n.* The small tree it grows on, native of western Asia and the Levant. **3** *n.* The flavor of the nut or a food flavored with it, as ice cream. **4** *n., adj.* Light, yellowish green.

6. I had a scoop of pistachio in a cone.
7. They were sitting under the pistachio.
8. The cheese was rolled in ground pistachios.
9. The room was painted pistachio.

> **re·spon·si·ble** [ri·spon′sə·bəl] *adj.* 1 Obliged to carry out or take care of a duty, trust or debt. 2 Being the cause or reason; accountable: Warm weather is *responsible* for the crowded beaches. 3 Involving trust or important duties: a *responsible* job. 4 Reliable; trustworthy: a *responsible* mechanic. **—re·spon′si·bly** *adv.*

10. You can depend on a responsible employee.
11. That woman holds a responsible position with the bank.
12. He is responsible for all the money.
13. A terrible accident is responsible for this traffic jam.

Multiple Definitions

Exercise 2

Look up the underlined word in each sentence. Write the definition of each underlined word as it is used in the sentence.

14. The battle was lost on the very first day.
15. The old man wandered, dazed and lost, through the park.
16. The technique of making those arrowheads is now lost.
17. The lost golfball was found in a sand trap.
18. The jeweler set the lapis lazuli in the gold brooch.
19. I recognized Roger by the jaunty set of his sombrero.
20. What is the relationship in this set of numbers?
21. Dr. Amos set Nan's broken arm.
22. Last year Amanda won an award for her set for a Broadway musical comedy.
23. Is there a certain set way to address an envelope?
24. Thelma set her hopes on an acting career.
25. Arnie set the time machine on 1880, but he found himself in the year 2050 instead.
26. Connie cleared the fence in an amazing leap.
27. The water is so clear that I can see shells on the sea floor.
28. "How could you make a mistake, Richard?" said Cathy. "The directions were perfectly clear!"
29. Our fund drive cleared $500 for the animal shelter.
30. Susan had a clear idea of what her future would be.
31. We cleared 15 bushels of leaves from the driveway.
32. When the sky is clear, I can see all the way to Long Island from my home in Connecticut.
33. "Shana hit the baseball clear into the next county!" shouted the announcer.
34. Ron's evidence cleared the defendant of the charge.
35. The highway was clear again only an hour after the accident.

Exercise 3

Use your dictionary to find each word below. Write an original sentence for the meaning of the word that is given in parentheses ( ) next to each word.

36. determine (3)
37. operation (3)
38. pulse (1)
39. puff (8)
40. grand (4)
41. burn (3)
42. answer (3)
43. standard (3)
44. stampede (2)
45. stake (9)
46. pepper (3)
47. measure (14)
48. land (9)
49. grade (7)
50. match (10)
51. act (12)
52. cast (9)
53. hand (10)
54. tone (6)
55. balance (5)
56. draft (6)

chill·y [chil′ē] *adj.* **chill·i·er, chill·i·est** 1 Causing coldness or chill: a *chilly* rain. 2 Feeling cold: I am *chilly.* 3 Not friendly or warm: a *chilly* greeting. **—chill′i·ness** *n.*

Illustrative Sentence

Look at the definition of *chilly* above. In the entry you will see the sentence: I am *chilly.* This sentence illustrates, or shows, the meaning and use of the main entry word *chilly.* Many words in this dictionary are followed by **illustrative sentences** or **illustrative phrases.** They make the meaning and use of main entry words easier to understand. The examples also help you choose the correct meaning of a word with more than one meaning. Look at the illustrative phrases in the following entry.

del·i·cate [del′ə·kit] *adj.* 1 Fine, as in structure, design, or shape: a *delicate* snowflake. 2 Pleasing, as in taste, aroma, or color: a *delicate* shade of blue. 3 Weak or easily injured: a *delicate* child; a *delicate* vase. 4 Requiring cautious, tactful treatment: *delicate* diplomatic relations. 5 Barely felt or seen; subtle; slight: a *delicate* distinction. 6 Reacting quickly to slight differences or changes: a *delicate* thermometer. **—del′i·cate·ly** *adv.* **—del′i·cate·ness** *n.*

The illustrative phrases make many meanings of the word *delicate* easier to understand.

Exercise 1

1.–6. Write a sentence using each of the meanings of the word *delicate* shown above.

Exercise 2

Write an illustrative sentence for each of these words.

7. eat	**8.** street	**9.** farmer	**10.** summer
11. wet	**12.** eye	**13.** radio	**14.** socks
15. restaurant	**16.** unfortunate	**17.** thank	**18.** S O S
19. beautiful	**20.** remain	**21.** recognize	**22.** incur
23. quartermaster	**24.** ankle	**25.** mention	**26.** right of way

Exercise 3

The following sentences illustrate one of the meanings of each underlined word. Write the word and the number of the meaning that fits in the sentence.

27. That dress is not <u>proper</u> for a formal wedding.
28. By his <u>grave</u> manner, we could tell that he had bad news for us.
29. In this case you must obey the <u>letter</u> of the law.

Using Illustrations

Illustration

cap·stan [kap′stən] *n.* An upright cylinder resembling a large spool, turned by hand or motor-driven, and around which cables or ropes are wound to lift a weight, as an anchor.

Capstan

On nearly every page of the dictionary, you will find illustrations to help you understand the meanings of words. There are several different kinds of illustrations. They include photographs and drawings. Each illustration adds information and fills out the meaning of an entry.

Read the definitions of *dromedary* and *llama* below.

drom·e·dar·y [drom′ə·der·ē] *n., pl.* **drom·e·dar·ies** A swift camel of Arabia, having only one hump, used for riding.

lla·ma [lä′mə] *n.* A South American beast of burden, like a small camel with no hump.

Now compare the two animals. The dromedary is an Arabian camel, used for riding. The llama from South America has no hump and is used as a beast of burden. There is nothing else you can tell about the differences between the two animals without more information.

Now look at the pictures of the two animals that are included in the dictionary. Think about what other information you could include in a comparison of the dromedary and the llama.

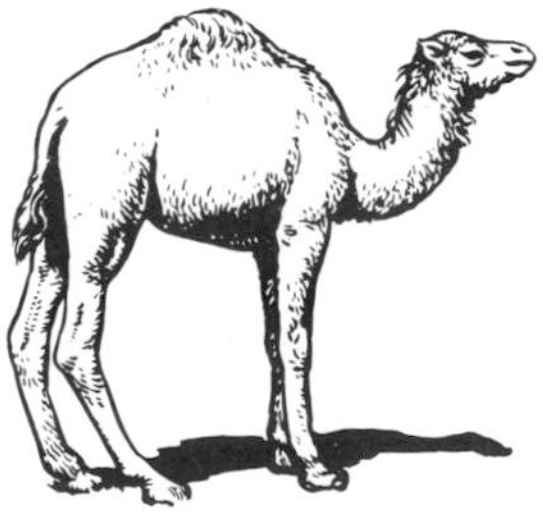
Dromedary

Llama

Exercise

Use the illustrations on the opposite page to answer the following questions.

1. What is a poncho used for?
2. Which planet is farthest from the sun?
3. What two kinds of fans are illustrated?
4. How many horns does a unicorn have?
5. What are davits used for?

1. Poncho

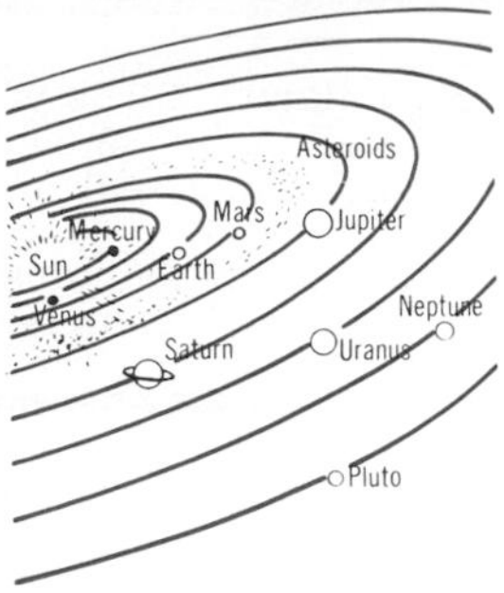

2. Solar system

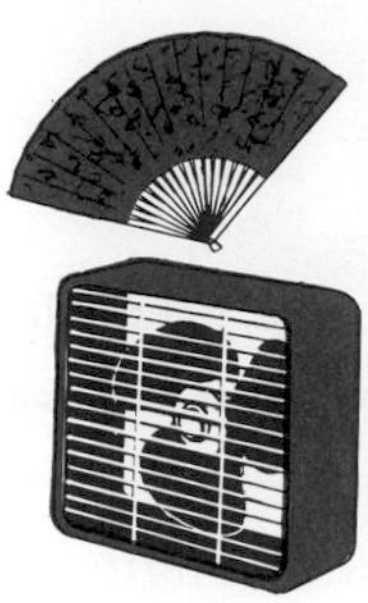

3. Fans

4. Unicorn

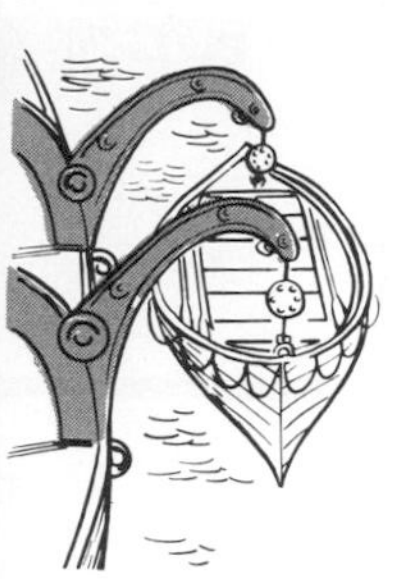

5. Davits

6. In a hibachi, what keeps the food from falling into the fire?
7. Is a satellite at apogee or perigee when it is farthest from the earth?
8. How does a musician get tones from an organ?
9. What was a battering ram used for?

6. Hibachi

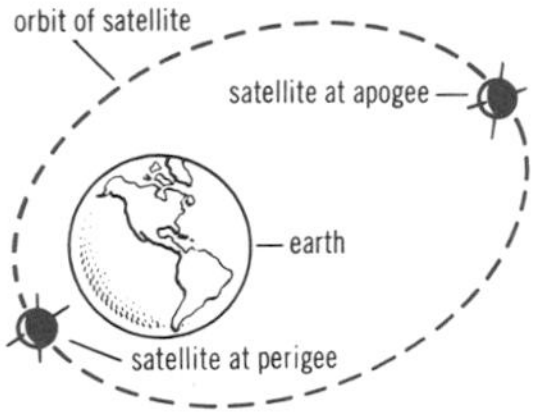

7. Apogee, perigee

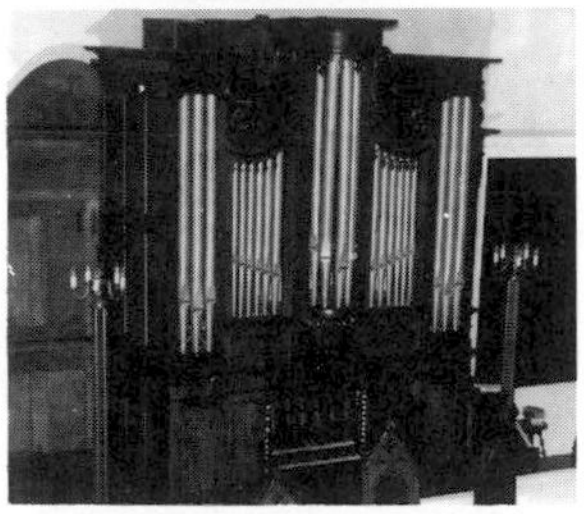

8. Organ

9. Battering ram

10. How many beads are on each column of an abacus?
11. Where does the water from a geyser come from? Where does it go?
12. What was a ruff used for?
13. Where is the bell in a belfry?
14. Which are longer, the front or back legs of a ring-tailed lemur?

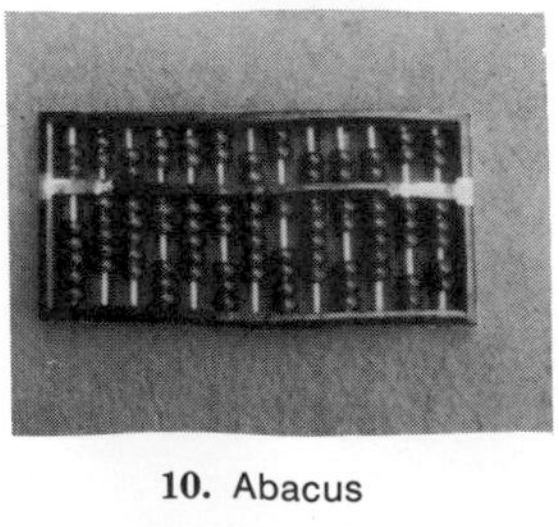

10. Abacus

11. Geyser

12. Ruff

13. Belfry

14. Ring tailed lemur

Homographs

Homographs ——— **calf**[1] [kaf] *n., pl.* **calves** [kavz] **1** The young of the cow or other bovine animals. **2** The young of some other mammals, as the seal or whale. **3** Calfskin.
calf[2] [kaf] *n., pl.* **calves** [kavz] The muscular back part of the human leg below the knee.

Homographs are words that look alike but do not have the same meaning. They have come into our language in different ways. Most have come from different languages and at different times. There are many homographs in the dictionary. As you can see in the sample at the top of the page, homographs are listed as separate main entries. Each homograph is numbered with a small number up and to the right of the word. These numbers are called **superscripts.**

Suppose you are looking up a word that has a superscript. You should look for and read each main entry that is spelled the same way. This will help you find the right meaning of the word you want.

Look at the following sentence.

The king would brook no opposition.

If you look up the word *brook*, you will see this definition.

brook[1] [brŏŏk] *n.* A natural stream smaller than a river.

Suppose you substitute the definition of *brook*[1] for the word *brook* in the sentence. You would have this sentence.

The king would natural stream no opposition.

The sentence makes no sense at all. But if you noticed the superscript, you would know that there is more than one word spelled b-r-o-o-k. Look below *brook*[1] in the dictionary and you will see *brook*[2].

brook[2] [brŏŏk] *v.* To put up with; stand for: The mayor would *brook* no interference with the plan.

Now substitute the meaning of *brook*[2] for the word *brook* in the sentence.

The king would put up with no opposition.

By looking at both homographs spelled b-r-o-o-k, you have found the meaning that fits correctly in your sentence.

Pairs of homographs are spelled alike, but they may not be pronounced the same way. In English you cannot be sure that words that look alike sound alike. In fact, later you will learn about words that are spelled differently but sound the same.

Exercise 1

Write the words on the left of your paper. Look up their meanings. Beside each word write the correct definition from the column on the right.

1. school
2. till
3. well
4. tow
5. limp
6. jade
7. fair
8. fell
9. bow
10. box
11. chap
12. tire

a. following the right rules
b. the forward part of a ship
c. to make weary
d. lacking strength
e. a green mineral
f. to make rough or reddened
g. to pull or drag by a chain
h. thoroughly, completely
i. small evergreen trees used for hedges
j. a large number of fish
k. cruel, vicious
l. a drawer in which valuables are kept

Exercise 2

Write two original sentences for each of these words. Each sentence should show a different meaning of the word.

13. fine
14. mold
15. palm
16. tag
17. page
18. ply
19. firm
20. pike

Exercise 3

Write the definition of each underlined word as it is used in the sentence.

21. That music is to be played forte.
22. His lowering look warned everyone to stay away.
23. Tony pinked the material so that it would not ravel.
24. The blacksmith pounded the metal into a horseshoe.
25. Alicia donned the costume she would wear in the play.
26. Alex decided to fast for four hours between each meal.
27. To free the car from the mud, Sheila had to rock it.
28. Gold is still legal tender in many countries.
29. Roberta cleaved to the principle that all people are equal.
30. Sir Andrew always played cricket when he attended Eton.
31. Chiang sailed the junk up the Yangtze River.
32. Too little watering had stunted the growth of the tree.
33. The roast sizzled and spattered on the spit.
34. The thieves had rifled the refrigerator as well as the safe.
35. I always root for the underdog.
36. Three pales were missing from the fence.
37. Both sailors had been pressed into service at an early age.

Compound Entries

Compound Entry — **car pool** 1 An arrangement made by a group of car owners who take turns driving each other or their children, to work or school. 2 The members of such a group.

Compound entries are main entries made up of more than one word. They are arranged in alphabetical order with the other main entries.

In compound entries, the combination of words has a special meaning. You cannot tell the meaning of the combination by looking up each separate word. If you look up the meaning of *car* and *pool*, you will not find the meaning of the entry *car pool*. You may know the meaning of *sea* and *lion*, but you will not know the meaning of *sea lion*.

sea [sē] *n.* The large body of salt water that covers most of the earth's surface; ocean.

li·on [lī′ən] *n.* A large, tawny, powerful animal related to the cat, found in Africa and sw Asia. The adult male lion has a shaggy mane.

sea lion A very large seal of the Pacific coast of North America.

Compound entries are not needed for every combination of words. You could find the meaning of combinations like *shoe polish*, *library book*, and *bus stop* by looking up each word.

Exercise 1

Copy the following pairs of words. Circle the compound entry in each pair. Use your dictionary if necessary.

1. nail polish/spelling bee
2. piggy bank/orange juice
3. after school/high school
4. piece of pie/ice cream
5. totem pole/blue paper
6. square root/chocolate cake
7. square dance/chair cushion
8. motor oil/sponge cake
9. bird cage/peanut butter
10. potato chip/baked potato

Exercise 2

Write an original sentence using each of these compound entries.

11. comic strip
12. neon sign
13. fine arts
14. beast of burden
15. control tower
16. stock exchange
17. salt lick
18. round trip
19. top hat
20. Russian dressing
21. nervous system
22. rush hour
23. common sense
24. magnifying glass
25. lip reading
26. pup tent
27. cottage cheese
28. car pool

Subentry — **cab·i·net** [kab′ə·nit] *n.* 1 A piece of furniture fitted with shelves and drawers. 2 (*often written* **Cabi-net**) A group of official advisers and assistants of a head of state.

Subentries are capitalized or lowercase forms of main entries. A sub-entry is printed in **dark type** and enclosed in parentheses ( ). It appears within the entry.

Read the following sentences:

The people fought in the Crusade.
The people fought a crusade for cleaner air.

Now look at the entry for crusade:

cru·sade [kro͞o·sād′] *n., v.* **cru·sad·ed, cru·sad·ing** 1 *n.* (*often written* **Crusade**) One of a series of wars fought by European Christians during the Middle Ages in an attempt to capture the Holy Land from the Muslims. 2 *n.* A vigorous struggle against an evil or in favor of a cause. 3 *v.* To take part in a crusade. **—cru·sad′er** *n.*

The lowercase form of *crusade* is the main entry. The capitalized form is the subentry. The capitalized form refers to a particular series of wars fought during the Middle Ages. The lowercase form refers to any struggle for a particular cause.

Look at the following entry:

arc·tic [är(k)′tik] 1 *n.* (*usually written* **Arctic**) The region about the North Pole. 2 *adj.* (*usually writ-ten* **Arctic**) Of or living in this region: an *Arctic* plant. 3 *adj.* Extremely cold; freezing.

Which form of the word *arctic* should be used in the following sentence?

The cold wind blew down from the (arctic, Arctic).

The wind must have blown from somewhere. Definition 1 refers to "the region of the North Pole." Therefore, *Arctic* is the correct choice. Suppose the sentence read:

The freezer keeps the food at (arctic, Arctic) temperatures.

Definition 3 is "extremely cold, or freezing." This definition fits the meaning of the sentence. Since definition 3 uses the lowercase form of the word, *arctic* is the correct choice.

Subentries

Exercise 1

Choose the correct form of the words in parentheses to complete the sentences. Write the completed sentences on your paper.

1. The city of (babel, Babel) is in the Bible.
2. The (moguls, Moguls) live in Asia.
3. The (continental, Continental) soldier fought for the independence of the American colonies.
4. The state legislature meets in the (capitol, Capitol).
5. The book is printed in (roman, Roman).
6. The baby has a healthy (constitution, Constitution).
7. The leaders of the revolt encouraged the people to wage a (civil war, Civil War).
8. The lawmaking body in Britain is the (parliament, Parliament).
9. The only flower we could find was a (narcissus, Narcissus).
10. The firefighters held a (congress, Congress) to talk about new methods of fire prevention.

Exercise 2

Copy each word and its correct definition.

11. creole	**a.**	a descendent of the original French settlers in Louisiana
	b.	cooked with tomatoes, pepper, and spices
12. Scripture	**a.**	the Bible or a passage from the Bible
	b.	any writing considered sacred
13. Secret Service	**a.**	secret investigation done by the government
	b.	a branch of the U.S. Treasury Department
14. senate	**a.**	a governing or lawmaking body
	b.	the upper house of the Congress of the United States
15. treasury	**a.**	a place where funds of the government are kept and paid out
	b.	a department of the United States government
16. Tricolor	**a.**	having three colors
	b.	the French flag
17. Diaspora	**a.**	the dispersion of the Jews into colonies outside Palestine after the Babylonian exile
	b.	the dispersion or migration of any homogeneous people
18. english	**a.**	having to do with England, its people, or its language and customs
	b.	a spinning motion given to a ball, as in billiards

Run-on Entry — **clas·si·fy** [klas′ə·fī] *v.* **clas·si·fied, clas·si·fy·ing** To put or divide into classes or groups: to *classify* books. **—clas′si·fi′er** *n.*

Many new words are made by adding suffixes to base words. You will find many of these new words printed in **dark type** at the end of the main entry of the base word. They are called **run-on entries.**

No definitions follow run-on entries. The meaning of a run-on entry is a combination of the meaning of the base word and the meaning of the suffix. When a suffix has more than one meaning, you must be careful to choose the correct one.

In some cases, words formed by the addition of a suffix to a base word are listed as main entries instead of as run-on entries. One such case occurrs when the suffixed word is used as commonly as the base word from which it is formed. *Kindness* is an example of such a word, and you will find it listed as a main entry in this book. Another case occurrs when a word that starts out with a general meaning later develops a specialized meaning of more importance. The word *silencer,* for example, originally meant "a person or thing which silences." Later it took on a specialized meaning: "a device attached to the muzzle of a gun to muffle the sound when fired." *Silencer,* therefore, is listed as a main entry instead of as a run-on.

Exercise 1

Arrange the following words in two lists. In one list put the words that are run-on entries. In the second list put the words that are separate main entries.

1. examiner **2.** lonely **3.** plotter **4.** harassment
5. flatness **6.** filterable **7.** filler **8.** croupy
9. allowable **10.** bumper **11.** blindness **12.** angrily

Exercise 2

13.–19. Write an original sentence for each of the words in Exercise 1 that is a main entry.

Exercise 3

Match each of these words with a suffix that will make a run-on word. Write the new words. The spelling of the base word may change.

20. cytology **21.** impair **a.** ence **b.** ness
22. sincere **23.** interdependent **c.** ist **d.** er
24. daydream **25.** gruff **e.** ment **f.** ly

Cross-References

Cross-Reference — **cen·sure** [sen'shər] *n., v.* **cen·sured, cen·sur·ing** 1 *n.* Blame or criticism; reprimand. 2 *v.* To blame or criticize. ◆ See CENSOR.

Cross-references are directions to look up further information about an entry under another main entry. Cross-references are printed in SMALL CAPITALS. They appear in a number of ways in this book. They can appear following the symbol ◆ , as in the sample at the top of this page and in the sample below.

as·tro·nau·tics [as'trə·nô'tiks] *n.* The science and art of flight in space. ◆ See -ICS.
-ics A suffix meaning: 1 An art, science, or field of study, as in *mathematics.* 2 Methods, systems, or activities, as in *acrobatics, athletics.* ◆ Nouns ending in *-ics* that refer to arts, sciences, or fields of activity were originally plural, meaning things relating to a field. Later they came to mean all such things relating to a field, taken as a single collection, and they became singular: *Politics* is exciting; *Physics* is my favorite subject. Such words seldom take *a, an,* or *the.* Nouns ending in *-ics* that refer to specific details, qualities, or methods within a field are plural and often take articles: The *acoustics* in this hall are bad; These *statistics* are from the last census.

Cross-references also appear in other ways. Here are several types you will encounter frequently.

built [bilt] Past tense of BUILD.

fal·de·ral [fal'də·ral'] *n.* Another spelling of FOLDEROL.

feet [fēt] Plural of FOOT.

eg·lan·tine [eg'lən·tin *or* eg'lən·ten] *n.* Another name for SWEETBRIER.

Exercise 1

Look up the following entries. Find the cross-reference for each.

1. imply
2. elderly
3. barely
4. foretold
5. further
6. various
7. grade school
8. guardian
9. abaca
10. been
11. hindmost
12. hostel

Exercise 2

Each of the words in the following sets has a similar meaning. Look up each pair of words. On your own paper write a comparison of their meanings.

13. stubborn—obstinate
14. effectual—effective
15. continuous—continual
16. contraction—abbreviation
17. several—few
18. scorn—contempt
19. credulous—credible
20. motive—reason
21. roam—wander
22. prefix *semi-* —prefix *bi-*
23. fashion—custom
24. confidence—trust

Idiom

cer·e·mo·ny [ser′ə·mō′nē] *n., pl.* **cer·e·mo·nies** 1 Any formal act or series of actions performed in a definite, set manner: a graduation *ceremony.* 2 A formal or extremely polite manner of acting: to serve tea with *ceremony.* **—stand on ceremony** To act or insist that others act in a formal manner.

An **idiom** is a group of words that has a special meaning. Look at these sentences:

They *ran out of* the room.
They *ran out of* milk.

In the first sentence, the words *ran out of* mean what they say. If you looked up the definition of each word, you would learn the correct meaning of the sentence. In the second sentence, however, the words *ran out of* cannot have the same meaning. In the second sentence, the words *ran out of* are an idiom meaning "to come to the end of one's supply."

Idioms are printed in **dark type** after the definitions. If you cannot find a meaning that makes sense in a sentence, look for an idiom following the definition.

Exercise

On your paper, copy the sentence with the idiom from each pair.

1. This is a ring for my wife.
   Did you ring for the nurse?
2. They are rolling in money.
   The car's wheels are rolling in mud.
3. She acts on the stage, in the movies, and on television.
   Did the police act on the information provided by the witnesses?
4. This greasy food does not agree with me.
   I cannot agree with what you say.
5. Did the child run across the street?
   Did you run across any of your friends at the beach?
6. Put the salt down on the counter.
   The colonists would salt down fish and meat.
7. The cook moved the pan off and on the burner several times.
   He comes to work off and on.
8. She is out to get a promotion.
   He went out to the movies.
9. The children played out in the yard.
   After the race, the horses were played out.
10. Will you pull up all the weeds in the flower bed?
    The taxi pulled up to the curb.

Variant Term Cross-References

Variant Term

car·rou·sel [kar′ə·sel′] *n.* Another word for MERRY-GO-ROUND.

Many things are known by more than one name. Sometimes both names are included in the dictionary as main entries. The name used most often is followed by the definition. The other name, or **variant term,** is followed by the cross-reference "Another word for . . ." or "Another name for . . ." To find the meaning of the variant term, you must look up the meaning of its more common name. Look at the entry for *carrousel* at the top of the page. To find the meaning of *carrousel*, you must look up the meaning of *merry-go-round.*

Exercise 1

The following words are variant terms. Each has another name. Copy the words on your paper. Beside each, write the more common name by which it is known.

1. baking soda	**2.** codfish	**3.** crayfish
4. Decoration Day	**5.** grammar school	**6.** spun glass
7. infantile paralysis	**8.** nuclear energy	**9.** Roentgen ray
10. rowlock	**11.** vacuum bottle	**12.** flautist
13. large calorie	**14.** manioc	**15.** jessamine
16. duckbill	**17.** cyclopedia	**18.** riata
19. mouth organ	**20.** lending library	**21.** heat rash
22. kittycorner	**23.** scaly anteater	**24.** darning needle
25. leafstalk	**26.** milk sugar	**27.** lightning bug
28. deadly nightshade	**29.** tenantry	**30.** wolfram
31. nerve cell	**32.** adjutant stork	**33.** lawn tennis
34. halite	**35.** septicemia	**36.** green onion

Exercise 2

On your paper, match each term in Column A with its variant form in Column B.

A	B
37. alligator pear	**a.** hand organ
38. windflower	**b.** avocado
39. rooftree	**c.** anemone
40. slide fastener	**d.** cougar
41. painter	**e.** zipper
42. hurdy-gurdy	**f.** ridgepole

Abbreviation ________ **capt.** or **Capt.** captain.

Abbreviations are shortened forms of words or phrases. You see them in many places, including street signs, addresses, and headlines. Some abbreviations are very familiar. You see examples such as *Ms.* Clark, *Dr.* Martin, Willow *St.,* and Police *Dept.* every day. You probably know the meaning of these abbreviations already. Other abbreviations are less common. You may have to look in the dictionary to find their meaning.

You can find abbreviations as main entries in the dictionary. The entry tells you what the abbreviation stands for. As you can see in the sample at the top of the page, the entry does not include a definition. To find the meaning of *captain*, you would have to look up the main entry for the word.

Abbreviations are alphabetized like other main entries in the dictionary. The abbreviation *DST* appears between the words *dry measure* and *dual*. The entry *NATO* comes between *nativity* and *natty*.

Sometimes abbreviations are used as the name of something. When the letters are pronounced as a word, the abbreviation is called an **acronym.** The pronunciation of the acronym appears in the dictionary in brackets [ ].

CARE [kâr] Cooperative for American Relief Everywhere.

Exercise 1

Copy the abbreviations below. Next to each abbreviation, write the words or phrases for which it stands.

1. A.M.	**2.** ch.	**3.** Dec.	**4.** Eng.
5. bldg.	**6.** ct.	**7.** d.	**8.** Al
9. SA	**10.** S.A.	**11.** D.A.	**12.** c.
13. Amb.	**14.** c.g.	**15.** dz.	**16.** etc.
17. D.D.S.	**18.** t.	**19.** Mon.	**20.** Dr.
21. sc.	**22.** SC	**23.** Sc.	**24.** S.C.

Exercise 2

Find the abbreviations in the dictionary. Copy the abbreviations that are pronounced as words.

25. NATO	**26.** BMOC	**27.** UNESCO	**28.** USSR
29. ACTH	**30.** SEATO	**31.** ASCAP	**32.** vhf
33. UNICEF	**34.** UAW	**35.** TV	**36.** awol

Biographical Entries

Biographical Entry — **Car·roll** [kar′əl], **Lewis,** 1832–1898, English mathematician and author of *Alice in Wonderland.* His real name was Charles Lutwidge Dodgson.

The dictionary includes brief biographical information about famous people. Fictional characters and people who may or may not have really existed are listed in the **A** to **Z** section. The Biographical Section on pages 983–1023 contains a listing of people. Entries are in alphabetical order by last name.

Biographical entries usually include the dates of the person's birth and death, the person's nationality, and what the person is known for. Entries for rulers include the years they reigned. Entries for people who have held political office, such as presidents and prime ministers, include the years they held office. Some dates are followed by question marks. The question mark means that there is a question about whether or not the date is exactly right.

Po·lo [pō·lō], **Marco,** 1254?–1324? Venetian traveler who wrote about his travels in Asia.

Exercise

Number your paper from 1 to 17. Using information from the biographical section, answer the following questions TRUE or FALSE.

1. Elizabeth II became Queen of Great Britain and Northern Ireland in 1952.
2. Richard Wagner, a German composer, was known for his operas.
3. Marie Antoinette was a Spanish queen.
4. George Washington was born in 1732 and died in 1799.
5. William Howard Taft served as Chief Justice of the Supreme Court after he was President of the United States.
6. Robert Frost was an American painter.
7. Jean Jacques Rousseau was a French author.
8. James Polk was the eleventh President of the United States.
9. No one is sure of the exact date of Sir Walter Raleigh's birth.
10. Edward Kennedy Ellington, U.S. composer, pianist, and bandleader, was popularly known as "King."
11. William I was also known as William the Conqueror.
12. Julius Caesar, a famous Roman, died in 44 B.C.
13. Jane Austen was a Scottish novelist.
14. Edna St. Vincent Millay wrote mystery novels.
15. Herman Melville was born in 1819 and died in 1891.
16. Leif Ericson, Norwegian sailor, may have landed in North America around the year 1000.
17. Fanny Farmer was an author of cookbooks.

Geographical Entry

Cas·pi·an Sea [kas′pē·ən] The largest salt-water lake in the world. It lies between SE Europe and SW Asia.

Do you know what Europe and the dictionary have in common? You can find France in both of them, along with the Alps and the Danube. **Geographical entries** such as countries, cities, rivers, mountains, and deserts are listed in the Geographical Section on pages 1025–1074. They are found in alphabetical order according to name. The Rocky Mountains will be found among the *R* entries. Lake Erie and Mount Everest will both be among the *E* entries. The People's Republic of China will be found with the *C* entries. Following the Geographical Section is a series of maps. The maps are located on pages 1076–1088.

Fictional places, such as those found in myths or works of literature, are listed alphabetically in the **A** to **Z** section of the dictionary. Thus, El dorado and Lilliput would appear as main entries in the **A** to **Z** section.

Exercise 1

Using information from your dictionary, answer the following questions. Write the answers on your paper.

1. Into which body of water does the Euphrates flow?
2. Which two bodies of water does the Bering Strait connect?
3. Which important sites are located on Oahu?
4. Lake Champlain lies between which two states?
5. In which country is Damascus?
6. What is the Great Barrier Reef ?
7. Why was Mount Olympus important in Greek myths?
8. Where is Cape Horn?
9. Where is Hoover Dam?
10. Where is Walden Pond and for what is it famous?

Exercise 2

Match the city on the left with the state or country on the right.

11. San Diego	**19.** Budapest	**a.** Michigan	**i.** England
12. Milan	**20.** Marseilles	**b.** Australia	**j.** Greece
13. Greenwich	**21.** Brussels	**c.** Switzerland	**k.** Belgium
14. Tulsa	**22.** Copenhagen	**d.** Hungary	**l.** Italy
15. Geneva	**23.** Stockholm	**e.** Denmark	**m.** California
16. Providence	**24.** Corinth	**f.** Cuba	**n.** Canada
17. Detroit	**25.** Quebec	**g.** Rhode Island	**o.** Oklahoma
18. Queensland	**26.** Havana	**h.** France	**p.** Sweden

Prefix ______________________ **co-** A prefix meaning: 1 Together, as in *coexist.* 2 With another; joint, as in *coauthor.*

A **prefix** is a word part that is added to the beginning of a word. The prefix changes the meaning of the word to which it is added. Prefixes are main entries in the dictionary. They are listed in alphabetical order along with all the other main entries.

Because prefixes are not whole words, they are followed in the dictionary by a hyphen to show that they do not stand alone. Most of the time the hyphen is dropped when a prefix is added to a word. When the hyphen is kept, it is only to avoid confusion with the word to which it is joined. For example, the word *recover* means "to get well again." The prefix *re-* means "again." But suppose you wanted to form a word that means "to cover again." You would add the prefix *re-* to the word *cover.* The new word would be spelled *re-cover* so that it would not be confused with *recover.*

Knowing the prefix of a word can help you find the meaning of a word that is not listed in the dictionary. Suppose you were shopping for a pair of jeans. The label on the ones you wanted said "This garment has been prewashed." The word *prewash* is not in the dictionary. But you could find the meaning by looking up the meaning of the prefix *pre-* and the word *wash.*

pre- A prefix meaning: Before in time or order, as in *preschool.*

wash [wäsh *or* wôsh] 1 *v.* To free of dirt or other unwanted material by the action of a liquid, as water, and usually a soap.

You can now figure out that the word *prewashed* means "washed before."

Can you work out the meaning of the word *disharmony*?

dis- A prefix meaning: 1 Not, as in *disloyal.* 2 Opposite of, as in *disadvantaged.* 3 Do the opposite of, as in *disentangle.* 4 Absence or lack of, as in *disinterest.* 5 Exclude from, as in *disbar.* 6 Deprive of, as in *disfranchise.*

harmony [här′mə·nē] *n., pl.* **har·mo·nies** 1 An orderly and pleasing arrangement of simultaneous musical sounds. 2 The method of arranging music into harmony. 3 Any orderly and pleasing arrangement, as of colors or parts. 4 Agreement; accord: to live in *harmony* with neighbors.

If you combine the meaning of the prefix and the base word, you will find that one meaning of *disharmony* is "a lack of pleasing arrangement or order."

Exercise 1

Write the numbers of the prefixes on your paper. Write the letter from the matching definition next to the number.

1. un-	**a.** under; beneath
2. anti-	**b.** together
3. semi-	**c.** before in time or order
4. post-	**d.** again
5. pre-	**e.** opposed to; against
6. re-	**f.** not; the opposite of
7. sub-	**g.** having or containing three parts
8. en-	**h.** after or later in time
9. tri-	**i.** in; within
10. co-	**j.** not fully; exactly half

Exercise 2

Copy these words. Draw a line between the prefix and the base word.

11. unilateral	**12.** biannual	**13.** insensitive
14. preexist	**15.** midsummer	**16.** recollect
17. reestablish	**18.** submarine	**19.** interplanetary
20. counterclockwise	**21.** triangle	**22.** unleash
23. intermarriage	**24.** antibiotic	**25.** discoloration
26. intramural	**27.** dicotyledon	**28.** semitropical
29. archenemy	**30.** foreground	**31.** superabundant
32. ingratitude	**33.** antechamber	**34.** overcharge
35. ultrasonic	**36.** coexistence	**37.** misfortune
38. hypercritical	**39.** outbid	**40.** subcommittee
41. transcontinental	**42.** nonresident	**43.** entangle

Exercise 3

Using the prefixes and base words in this dictionary, write a definition for each of these prefixed words.

44. semipermanent	**45.** prepackage	**46.** encyst
47. bipolar	**48.** transship	**49.** resurface
50. overachieve	**51.** outshout	**52.** unidirectional
53. trisyllabic	**54.** disintoxicate	**55.** supereminent
56. subbasement	**57.** de-emphasize	**58.** forehoof

Exercise 4

59.—68. Choose ten words from the list in Exercise 2. Write an original sentence using each of the words you chose.

Suffixes

Suffix

-cy A suffix meaning: **1** Quality, state, or condition of being, as in *secrecy.* **2** Rank, grade, or position of, as in *presidency.*

A **suffix** is a word part that is added to the end of a word. Like a prefix, a suffix changes the meaning of a word. It can also change the part of speech of a word. It is possible to add more than one suffix to a word.

job [job] *n., v.* **jobbed, job·bing,** *adj.* **1** *n.* Anything that is to be done; piece of work; task. **2** *v.* To perform work that is undertaken and paid for by the job; do piecework. **3** *adj.* Of or doing work that is undertaken and paid for by the job: a *job* printer. **4** *n.* A position or situation of employment. **5** *v.* To buy (merchandise) from manufacturers and sell to retailers.

-less A suffix meaning: **1** Not having; without, as in *motherless* or *harmless.* **2** Not able to do or not capable of being, as in *restless* or *countless.*

Thus the adjective *jobless* means "to be without a position or situation of employment."

-ness A suffix meaning: **1** A condition or quality of being, as in *darkness.* **2** An instance of being, as in *kindness.* **-ness** is a suffix that may be attached to many adjectives to form nouns.

Joblessness is the noun form of the adjective *jobless.* It is the condition or state of being jobless.

Suffixes are dictionary main entries. A hyphen appears before a suffix in the dictionary. The hyphen is always dropped when a suffix is added to a word.

Exercise 1

Copy the suffixes listed below. Next to each suffix write a word using that suffix.

1. -ness	**2.** -ly	**3.** -able	**4.** -er
5. -ed	**6.** -ist	**7.** -tion	**8.** -ism
9. -ic	**10.** -ful	**11.** -ous	**12.** -est
13. -age	**14.** -dom	**15.** -al	**16.** -ish
17. -ize	**18.** -ive	**19.** -ance	**20.** -hood

Exercise 2

21.–30. Write an original sentence using ten of the words you wrote for Exercise 1.

Combining Form **coel-** or **coelo-** or **cel-** or **celo-** A combining form meaning: Hollow; cavity, as in *coelenterate.*

A **combining form** is another kind of word part. It can be joined with one or more prefixes or suffixes, with full words, or with other combining forms to make words. *Biology,* for instance, consists of two combining forms, *bio-* (meaning "life") and *-logy* (meaning "study or science of"). *Biological* results from the addition of two suffixes, *-ic* and *-al.* In the word *nonbiological,* the prefix *non-* is added. The word *photocopy* is formed of the combining form *photo-* and the word *copy.*

Combining forms, like prefixes and suffixes, are main entries in the dictionary. Those that generally appear at the beginning or in the middle of a word are followed by a hyphen (*photo-*). Those that generally appear only at the end of a word are preceded by a hyphen (*-logy*). Sometimes a combining form has more than one form. Both are found in the dictionary. When a new word is formed using a combining form, the hyphen is dropped.

Exercise 1

Find these combining forms in your dictionary. For each combining form write the meaning or meanings and an example word for each meaning.

1. astro-, astr-
2. mega-, meg-
3. -graph
4. tele-, tel-
5. electro-
6. kilo-
7. multi-
8. phon-, phono-
9. therm-, thermo-
10. poly-
11. hom-, homo-
12. hydro-
13. bio-
14. -gram
15. micro-, micr-
16. audio-
17. aut-, auto-
18. -scope
19. phot-, photo-
20. -graphy
21. deca-, dec-
22. geo-, ge-
23. -logy
24. -meter

Exercise 2

Each of the following words contains from one to three of the combining forms listed in Exercise 1. Copy the words on your paper. Circle each of the combining forms you find.

25. microcomputer
26. monogram
27. telecommunication
28. autobiography
29. megastructure
30. biotechnology
31. decahedron
32. geothermal
33. homograph
34. polyunsaturated
35. multimillionaire
36. microwave
37. astrodome
38. electromagnet
39. phonograph
40. photosensitive
41. kilocycle
42. hydrocarbon
43. megaphone
44. autism
45. geography
46. autoimmune
47. thermometer
48. microbiology

Division of Words into Syllables

Syllable Division **ca·bal** [kə·bal′] *n.* 1 A group of persons who are secretly engaged in some scheme or plot. 2 The scheme or plot of such a group.

A **syllable** is a word or part of a word treated as a single unit. The word *pep* is a one-syllable word. *Pepper* is a two-syllable word. *Peppermint* has three syllables. In the dictionary, black dots are used to show the division of words into syllables.

pep·per·mint [pep′ər·mint′] *n.* A fragrant herb related to the mint, yielding an oil that tastes sweet.

When you are writing, it is useful to know how to divide words into syllables. Sometimes an entire word will not fit on a line. You may put part of the word on one line and the rest on the next. You should break a word only between syllables. Be sure to use the syllable divisions in the main entry and not in the pronunciation respelling in brackets [ ]. The part of the word that is written at the end of the line must be followed by a hyphen (-). The hyphen shows the reader that the rest of the word follows on the next line. You should not leave a single letter of a word on either line. For example, the one-syllable word *idea* should not be divided. You should not put *i*- on one line and *dea* on the next. Nor should you put *ide*- on one line and *a* on the next. You should never divide a one-syllable word, no matter how long it is.

Exercise 1

Find each word in the dictionary. On your paper, write the number of syllables in each word.

1. letter	**2.** locomotive	**3.** portfolio	**4.** possession
5. potentiality	**6.** racism	**7.** raft	**8.** really
9. resignation	**10.** salaried	**11.** screech	**12.** telegraphic
13. tornado	**14.** totalitarian	**15.** tower	**16.** tragedy
17. trapezoid	**18.** triplet	**19.** unlearned	**20.** variegated

Exercise 2

Find each word in your dictionary. Copy the words onto your paper. Use black dots to show the division of the words into syllables.

21. chapter	**22.** count	**23.** countdown	**24.** daylight
25. floppy	**26.** gravitation	**27.** activate	**28.** hippopotamus
29. icy	**30.** lesson	**31.** match	**32.** material

Pronunciation ______________ **cab·al·le·ro** [kab′əl·yâr′ō] *n.*, *pl.* **cab·al·le·ros** A Spanish gentleman; cavalier.

The dictionary can help you pronounce unfamiliar words. Look at the sample main entry above. You may not have seen the word *caballero* before. Suppose you tried to sound out the word using words you already know. You know how to pronounce *cab*, *al*, *ler*, and *o*. If you put the sounds together, will you get the pronunciation of *caballero*? No, it is not quite that easy. The English language has 26 letters for writing words. The 26 letters can make 43 sounds. A system of symbols has been developed to represent the sounds. The chart below shows which symbol stands for which sound. The symbols are used to respell the words. This phonetic respelling is printed in brackets [ ] next to the main entry word. Compare the phonetic respelling of *caballero* with the symbols on the Pronunciation Key. You will then be able to sound out the pronunciation of *caballero*.

Pronunciation Key

a	add, map	ī	ice, write	o͞o	pool, food	y	yet, yearn
ā	ace, rate	j	joy, ledge	p	pit, stop	z	zest, muse
â(r)	care, air	k	cool, take	r	run, poor	zh	vision, pleasure
ä	palm, father	l	look, rule	s	see, pass	ə	the schwa,
b	bat, rub	m	move, seem	sh	sure, rush		an unstressed
ch	check, catch	n	nice, tin	t	talk, sit		vowel representing
d	dog, rod	ng	ring, song	th	thin, both		the sound spelled
e	end, pet	o	odd, hot	t͟h	this, bathe		a in *above*
ē	equal, tree	ō	open, so	u	up, done		e in *sicken*
f	fit, half	ô	order, jaw	û(r)	burn, term		i in *possible*
g	go, log	oi	oil, boy	yo͞o	fuse, few		o in *melon*
h	hope, hate	ou	pout, now	v	vain, eve		u in *circus*
i	it, give	o͝o	took, full	w	win, away		

How do you use the chart? On the right-hand side of each column are common words that use the sound represented by the symbol. These words show the sound used in different positions in the words. For example, *r* is shown in *run* and *poor*. Now look at the first respelled syllable of *caballero* [kab]. The word *caballero* starts with the same *k* sound found in *cool*. The *a* sound is the same as in *map*. The *b* sounds like the *b* in *rub*. The second phonetic syllable [əl] starts with ə. This symbol represents the same sound as the *a* in *above*. The *l* sounds like the *l* in *rule*. Now look at the third syllable [yâr]. There is no letter *y* in the word *caballero*, but there *is* in the pronunciation. The second *l* in *caballero* makes the sound of the *y* in *yet*. The *e* makes the sound of [â(r)] in *air*. The *r* makes the sound of the *r* in *poor*. The final letter (ō) sounds like the *o* in *so*. Now put all the sounds together without stopping. You will pronounce *caballero*.

Now try to decode the pronunciation of this word.

[ri·ses′]

Look at the symbols in the Pronunciation Key on page 33. Do you think the word is *rice*, *rises*, or *recess*? Check the words in your dictionary to see if you are right.

There is one symbol that appears very frequently in respelled words. It looks like an upside down *e*. This symbol (ə) is the schwa [shwä]. You have already seen the schwa in the phonetic respelling of *caballero*. The schwa sound can be spelled with any vowel, *a*, *e*, *i*, *o*, or *u*. Practice the following words until you recognize the sound the schwa makes.

about [ə·bout′]	wat**er** [wô′tər]	penc**i**l [pen′səl]
wom**a**n [wo͝om′ən]	eas**e**l [ē′zəl]	horr**i**ble [hôr′ə·bəl]

pers**o**n [pûr′sən]	capt**u**re [kap′chər]
hon**o**r**a**ble [on′ər·ə·bəl]	murm**u**r [mûr′mər]

Exercise

Copy the numbers 1–20 on your paper. Beside each number write the letter of the correct pronunciation of the word on the left.

1. gracious	**a.** grä′zhus	**b.** grā′shəs	**c.** grâ′shōs
2. hawk	**a.** hôk	**b.** hoik	**c.** houk
3. journey	**a.** jûr′nē	**b.** gûr′nē	**c.** jûr′ny
4. discover	**a.** dīs·kōv′ēr	**b.** dīs·kov′ər	**c.** dis·kuv′ər
5. pleasure	**a.** plezh′ər	**b.** plesh′ər	**c.** ple′shər
6. overalls	**a.** ov′·ə·rōls	**b.** ov′ər·ōls	**c.** ō′vər·ôlz
7. actor	**a.** akt′ōr	**b.** ak′tər	**c.** akt′ēr
8. berry	**a.** bē′rē	**b.** bir′e	**c.** ber′ē
9. citizen	**a.** sit′ə·zən	**b.** kit′ə·sən	**c.** sīt′īz in
10. equator	**a.** ek·wə·ter	**b.** i·kwā′tər	**c.** ē·kwat·ər
11. gravitate	**a.** grav′ə·tāt′	**b.** grā′və·tāt	**c.** jrav′ə·tāt
12. stalactite	**a.** stā·lāc′tīt	**b.** stə·lak′tīt′	**c.** stə·lāc′tit
13. unique	**a.** yu·nēk′	**b.** yo͞o·nēk′	**c.** yū′nək
14. dynamo	**a.** dī′nə·mō	**b.** din·ā′mō	**c.** dīn′ə·mo͞o
15. caddie	**a.** kā·dī′	**b.** kəd′ī	**c.** kad′ē
16. cornea	**a.** kôr′nē·ə	**b.** kôr·nē′â	**c.** kər′ni·ə
17. knead	**a.** nēd	**b.** kēd	**c.** kəd
18. premium	**a.** pri′mə·um	**b.** prē′mē·əm	**c.** prə·mi·əm
19. benefit	**a.** ben′ə·fit	**b.** ben′i·fit	**c.** be′nə·fət
20. toxin	**a.** tek′zin	**b.** tok·sīn′	**c.** tok′sin

The Short Key

The Short Key

a	add	**i**	it	**o͝o**	took	**oi**	oil
ā	ace	**ī**	ice	**o͞o**	pool	**ou**	pout
â	care	**o**	odd	**u**	up	**ng**	ring
ä	palm	**ō**	open	**û**	burn	**th**	thin
e	end	**ô**	order	**yo͞o**	fuse	**t͟h**	this
ē	equal					**zh**	vision

ə = { a in *above* e in *sicken* i in *possible*; o in *melon* u in *circus* }

The Pronunciation Key on page 33 includes 43 symbols. As you become more familiar with it, you will have to refer to it less often. You can probably pronounce the following words without referring to the key at all.

krib	gär′dən	ī′təm
mith	pōst′märk′	tab′lit

Some symbols and the sounds they represent may take time to learn. For this reason, a short form of the pronunciation key is printed at the bottom of each right-hand page. A model is printed at the top of this page.

The Short Key is different from the full Pronunciation Key. Only 23 of the 43 symbols are listed. Notice that the symbols are printed in **dark type.** If you consult the Short Key and still have difficulty pronouncing a word, refer to the full Pronunciation Key.

Exercise

Use the Short Key to work out the pronunciation of each of the following words. Write what you think is the original word on your paper. Check in the dictionary to see if you have identified each correctly.

1. dûr′tē
2. dōs
3. in·tīr′
4. wel
5. dō
6. drān
7. bēd
8. wēv
9. trī′pod′
10. vel′vit
11. sûr′kəs
12. di·vīd′
13. ri·kuv′ər
14. ī·lənd
15. gōl
16. un·ā′bəl
17. frun·tir′
18. kub′ərd
19. lô′yər
20. ôr·nāt′
21. fôl′tē
22. nā′shən
23. gi·tär′
24. pri·fûr′
25. līt′ər
26. prin′sə·pəl
27. hap′ē
28. nā′vē
29. bad′lē
30. elvz
31. im·pôr′təns
32. kôrn′stärch′
33. dam′ij
34. blō′pīp′
35. sen·sā′shən
36. wel′kəm
37. thred′bâr′
38. rav′əl
39. bə·lō′nē
40. kang′gə·ro͞o′
41. op′ti·kəl
42. prov′ərb
43. lem′ən·ād′
44. bēt′nik
45. bō′leg′id
46. fik′sə·bəl
47. kol′ə·nist
48. här′mə·nē

Accent Marks

Accent marks indicate which syllable of a word should be stressed. The dictionary uses two marks to show accent. The primary accent (′) is used in words that have only one accented syllable.

Read the sentences below.

They bought their son a present. [prez′ənt]
Did the principal present [pri·zent′] the awards at graduation?

Now quietly repeat to yourself the word *present* as it is pronounced in each sentence. You should hear a difference. The primary accent marks are on different syllables.

Both primary and secondary accents are used with words having more than one accented syllable. The primary accent (′) shows which syllable receives the greatest stress. The secondary accent (′) shows which syllable or syllables receive somewhat less stress. Accent marks are shown on the respelled entry as well as on run-on entries.

pre·his·tor·ic [prē′his·tôr′ik] *adj.* Of or belonging to the period before the start of written history: *prehistoric* reptiles. **—pre′his·tor′i·cal·ly** *adv.*

Exercise 1

Say the following words quietly to yourself. Copy each respelled word and mark it with the accent on the correct syllable.

1. per·fect·ly [pûr fikt lē]
2. cot·ton [kot (ə)n]
3. de·light [di līt]
4. ju·ry [jŏŏr ē]
5. vil·lage [vil ij]
6. fin·ger [fing gər]
7. out-doors [out dôrz]
8. pa·rade [pə rād]
9. dis·cov·er [dis kuv ər]
10. fur·ni·ture [fûr nə chər]

Exercise 2

Copy these respelled words. Mark both the primary and secondary accents on each.

11. sec·re·tar·y [sek rə ter ē]
12. grape·fruit [grāp frŏŏt]
13. com·pe·ti·tion [kom pə tish ən]
14. gin·ger-bread [jin jər bred]
15. tooth·paste [tŏŏth pāst]
16. san·i·ta·tion [san ə tā shən]
17. ad·mi·rā·tion [ad mə rā shən]
18. free·style [frē stīl]
19. re·u·nite [rē yŏŏ nīt]
20. un·der·take [un dər tāk]

Variant Pronunciation ______ **car·mine** [kär′min *or* kär′mīn′] *n., adj.* Deep red or purplish red.

There is more than one correct way to pronounce some words. As you can see below, both pronunciations for *tomato* and *either* are shown in brackets. They follow the main entry word.

to·ma·to [tə·mā′tō *or* tə·mä′tō] **ei·ther** [ē′thər *or* ī′thər]

You may use either pronunciation. The first one is usually used more often.

Sometimes a symbol appears in parentheses in a respelled word. This is another way of showing variant pronunciation.

du·et [d(y)ōō·et′] **i·dol** [ī′d(ə)l] **while** [(h)wīl]

You may pronounce the word *with* the sound the symbol represents or *without* that sound.

Exercise

Pronounce the words below quietly to yourself. On your paper, copy the pronunciation you use.

1. dual [d(y)ōō′əl]
2. neither [nē′thər *or* nī′thər]
3. new [n(y)ōō]
4. adult [ə·dult′ *or* ad′ult]
5. white [(h)wīt]
6. scaffold [skaf′əld *or* skaf′ōld′]
7. inverse [in·vûrs′ *or* in′vûrs]
8. forehead [fôr′id *or* fôr′hed′]
9. percentile [pər·sen′tīl′ *or* pər·sen′til]
10. ratio [rā′shō *or* rā′shē·ō]
11. sandwich [sand′wich *or* san′wich]
12. species [spē′shēz *or* spē′sēz]
13. decoy [dē′koi′ *or* di·koi′]
14. defect [dē′fekt′ *or* di·fekt′]
15. tutor [t(y)ōō′tər]
16. Celtic [sel′tik *or* kel′tik]
17. feudal [fyōōd′(ə)l]
18. wharf [(h)wôrf]
19. ill-humored [il′(h)yōō′mərd]
20. lava [lä′və *or* lav′ə]
21. cod·i·fy [kod′ə·fī′ *or* kō′də·fī′]
22. pre·tense [pri·tens′ *or* prē′tens]

Sometimes you will hear a word that you do not know how to spell. If you are taking notes in class, you may have to write it down the way it sounds. Later, when you go over your notes, you can look the word up in your dictionary. But how? If you cannot spell a word, how can you look it up? The answer is to use the Spelling Chart. Do you remember how the Pronunciation Key helps you to say a word that you can spell? The Spelling Chart on this page and the next page helps you to spell a word that you can say.

Look at the chart. Notice that in some ways it resembles the Pronunciation Key. The first column has a symbol representing a sound. The second column contains a common word in which that sound is heard. The third column has the possible spellings of the sound. The letters used to spell that sound are in *italics*.

Spelling Chart

SOUND	AS IN	POSSIBLE SPELLING
a	add	c*a*t, pl*ai*d, c*al*f, l*au*gh
ā	ace	m*a*te, b*ai*t, g*ao*l, g*au*ge, p*ay*, st*ea*k, sk*ei*n, w*eigh*, pr*ey*
â(r)	care	d*a*re, f*ai*r, pr*ay*er, wh*e*re, b*ea*r, th*ei*r
ä	palm	d*a*rt, *ah*, s*e*rgeant, h*ea*rt
b	bat	*b*oy, ru*bb*er
ch	check	*ch*ip, bat*ch*, righ*te*ous, bas*ti*on, struc*tu*re
d	dog	*d*ay, la*dd*er, call*ed*
e	end	m*a*ny, *ae*sthete, s*ai*d, s*ay*s, b*e*t, st*ea*dy, h*ei*fer, l*eo*pard, fr*ie*nd, *Oe*dipus
ē	equal	C*ae*sar, qu*ay*, sc*e*ne, m*ea*t, s*ee*, s*ei*ze, p*eo*ple, k*ey*, rav*i*ne, gr*ie*f, pho*e*be, cit*y*
f	fit	*f*ake, co*ff*in, cou*gh*, hal*f*, *ph*ase
g	go	*g*ate, be*gg*ar, *gh*oul, *gu*ard, va*gue*
h	hope	*h*ot, *wh*om
hw	where	*wh*ale, *wh*eel
i	it	pr*e*tty, b*ee*n, t*i*n, s*ie*ve, w*o*men, b*u*sy, g*ui*lt, l*y*nch
ī	ice	*ai*sle, *aye*, sl*eigh*t, *eye*, d*i*me, p*ie*, s*igh*, g*ui*le, b*uy*, tr*y*, l*ye*
j	joy	e*dg*e, sol*di*er, mo*du*late, ra*g*e, exa*gg*erate, *j*am
k	cool	*c*an, a*cc*ost, sa*cch*arine, *ch*ord, ta*ck*, a*cq*uit, *k*ing, tal*k*, li*qu*or
l	look	*l*et, ga*ll*
m	move	phle*gm*, pa*lm*, *m*ake, li*mb*, gra*mm*ar, conde*mn*

SOUND	AS IN	POSSIBLE SPELLING
n	nice	*gn*ome, *kn*ow, *mn*emonic, *n*ote, ba*nn*er, *pn*eumatic
ng	ring	si*n*k, so*ng*, meri*ngue*
o	odd	w*a*tch, p*o*t
ō	open	b*eau*, ye*o*man, s*ew*, *o*ver, s*oa*p, r*oe*, *oh*, br*oo*ch, s*ou*l, th*ough*, gr*ow*
ô	order	b*a*ll, b*a*lk, f*au*lt, d*aw*n, c*o*rd, br*oa*d, *ough*t
oi	oil	p*oi*son, t*oy*
ou	pout	*ou*nce, b*ough*, c*ow*
o͝o	took	w*o*lf, f*oo*t, c*ou*ld, p*u*ll
o͞o	pool	rh*eu*m, dr*ew*, m*o*ve, can*oe*, m*oo*d, gr*ou*p, thr*ough*, fl*u*ke, s*ue*, fr*ui*t
p	pit	ma*p*, ha*pp*en, *p*ocket
r	run	*r*ose, *rh*ubarb, ma*rr*y, dia*rrh*ea, *wr*iggle
s	see	*c*ite, di*c*e, *ps*yche, *s*aw, *sc*ene, *sch*ism, ma*ss*
sh	rush	o*c*ean, *ch*ivalry, vi*ci*ous, *psh*aw, *s*ure, *sch*ist, pre*sc*ience, nau*se*ous, *sh*all, pen*si*on, ti*ss*ue, fi*ss*ion, po*ti*on
t	talk	walk*ed*, though*t*, *pt*armigan, *t*one, *Th*omas, bu*tt*er
th	thin	*th*ick, *th*istle
t̶h̶	mother	*th*is, ba*the*
u	up	s*o*me, d*oe*s, bl*oo*d, y*ou*ng, s*u*n
û(r)	burn	y*ear*n, f*er*n, *err*, g*ir*l, w*or*m, j*our*nal, b*ur*n, Gu*er*nsey, m*yr*tle
yo͞o	fuse	b*eau*ty, *eu*logy, qu*eue*, p*ew*, *ewe*, ad*ieu*, v*iew*, c*ue*, *you*th, *yu*le
v	eve	o*f*, Ste*ph*en, *v*ise, fli*vv*er
w	win	ch*o*ir, q*u*ilt, *w*ill
y	yet	on*i*on, hallelu*j*ah, *y*earn
z	zoo	wa*s*, sci*ss*ors, *x*ylophone, *z*est, mu*zz*le
zh	vision	rou*ge*, plea*s*ure, inci*s*ion, sei*z*ure, gla*z*ier
ə		*a*bove, fount*ai*n, dark*e*n, clar*i*ty, parl*ia*ment, cann*o*n, porp*oi*se, vici*ou*s, loc*u*st

Here is how you can use the Spelling Chart to help you to spell a word. Suppose you heard a word that sounded like *naw*. You looked it up in the dictionary under the *N* entries but could not find it. Your next step would be to look at the Spelling Chart for possible spellings of the sound *n*.

n nice *gn*ome, *kn*ow, *mn*emonic, *n*ote, ba*nn*er, *pn*eumatic

As you can see, there are six different ways of spelling the *n* sound. Sometimes you will not have to look any further. You will see a spelling that looks familiar. Perhaps you already recognize *gnaw* as the correct spelling.

You are now ready to look up the meaning of the word in the correct place in the dictionary.

Suppose that you heard a word that sounded like *fōny*, but you could not find it in the dictionary. You would have to look at the Spelling Chart to see ways of spelling the *f* sound.

f fit *f*ake, co*ff*in, cou*gh*, ha*lf*, *ph*ase

Since you have already tried to spell the word with the *f* in fake, you will have to look further. Is *ffony* the correct spelling? No words in the English language start with *ff*, so that cannot be right. Could it be *ghony*? Or *lfony*? Or *phony*? If you have no idea, you will have to look up each one. You will find the word when you come to *phony*.

Exercise

The underlined words in the following sentences are misspelled. Use the Spelling Chart to find the correct spelling. Copy the sentences, using the correct spelling.

1. They can rap the package in the brown paper.
2. I need a new telefone for my office.
3. Whair did you put my sneakers?
4. He exajerates when he talks about the fish he has caught.
5. This is a very brawd avenue.
6. They put the chord around the box before they carried it to the truck.
7. Nice is a rock similar to granite.
8. She has suffered from rhoomatism for many years.
9. Do you have any hand loshun here?
10. I am sure that you have never seen a terodactyl.
11. You must study for many years to become a sikiatrist.
12. The church kwire sang beautifully.
13. I wonder how much this melon ways.
14. The jury akwitted the young man of the crime.
15. That lovely shatow is so picturesk.
16. He seezed the reins of his horse and rode away.
17. She drove with cawshun on the icy road.
18. They often went to the beach at low tide to study mareen life.
19. A plow is used to make furroughs in the soil.
20. The plumber fixed the leaky fawset.
21. The captain sailed the skooner out of the harbor.
22. An arkitekt dezined that unusual house.
23. She supported her opinion with rashunal arguments.
24. The sinking of the *Titanic* was a terrible trajidy.
25. The frayter unloaded its cargo.

Homophones are groups of words that sound alike but are spelled differently. Look at the samples below. Note that in each case the phonetic respelling of the words is the same. The main entry spelling and the meanings, however, are different.

> **pair** [pâr] *n.* **pairs** or **pair,** *v.* **1** *n.* A set of two people or things that match, are alike, or belong together: a *pair* of socks. **2** *v.* To arrange in a pair or pairs; match or couple.
>
> **pare** [pâr] *v.* **pared, paring** **1** To remove the outer layer or skin of (a fruit or a vegetable). **2** To make less or smaller, little by little: to *pare* costs.
>
> **pear** [pâr] *n.* **1** A sweet, juicy fruit, round at the outer end and tapering toward the stem. **2** The tree on which it grows.

Homophones can cause trouble for you when you are using the Spelling Chart. Suppose you have to find the spelling of an unfamiliar word. Your sentence reads "How long did King Richard __________?" The word you want sounds like *rain*, but you know that the spelling of the word is not right. Therefore, you have to look at the Spelling Chart for another way to spell the word.

When you check the chart, you find that the sound *rān* could be spelled *rein.* So you look up *rein*, but you realize that the meaning of *rein* does not make sense in the sentence. You have to go back again to the Spelling Chart. Finally you find that another way to spell the sound *rān* is *reign.* When you read the definition of *reign*, you know you have the right word at last.

Exercise

Copy the following sentences on your paper. Use the correct homophone.

1. Laura gave them (to, too, two) much ice cream.
2. Marge washed every (pain, pane) of glass.
3. Will Gilda come (hear, here) tomorrow?
4. We hope you can go (their, there) with us.
5. The (sun, son) is shining today.
6. I have a jar of (thyme, time) in the kitchen cabinet.
7. Would you like a (peace, piece) of cake?
8. Mike has a tack in the (sole, soul) of his shoe.
9. The choir often sings that (him, hymn).
10. The bride is wearing a white (vale, veil).
11. Jack and Jan took a (slay, sleigh) ride through the snowy countryside.
12. The highest (bough, bow) of that apple tree has delicious fruit on it.
13. The (some, sum) of 15 and 10 is 25.
14. Cora (threw, through) the baseball (threw, through) the open window.
15. I once (knew, new) someone who wore (knew, new) clothes every day.

Inflectional Forms ________

cac·tus [kak′təs] *n., pl.* **cac·tus·es** or **cac·ti** [kak′tī] A plant of hot desert regions having a green pulpy trunk covered with spines or prickles instead of leaves and often bearing showy flowers.

Many words change form depending on the way they are used. A noun, for example, is the name of a person, place, thing, or quality. A noun that means *one* person, place, thing, or quality is a singular noun. You can change it to mean more than one, however, by making it plural. A verb is a word that shows action or being. A verb that shows action happening *now* is in the present tense. It can be changed to show past or future action. An adjective is a word that modifies a noun. An adverb is a word that modifies a verb, an adjective, or another adverb. Both adjectives and adverbs can be changed to show comparison. In each part of speech, the original word is called a *base word.* The new forms are called **inflectional forms.** In this dictionary, inflectional forms are printed in **dark type** following the abbreviation for their part of speech.

The plurals of most nouns are formed by adding *-s* to the base word:

book, books car, cars desk, desks sofa, sofas

The plurals of nouns ending in *s, ch, sh, x,* or *z* are formed by adding *-es.*

bus, buses church, churches dish, dishes
mix, mixes buzz, buzzes

These inflectional forms are not entered in your dictionary. If you look up the base word and add the common ending, you can make the inflectional form.

Sometimes inflectional forms are not made in the usual way. These forms will be printed in **dark type** in the entry. Look at the sample at the beginning of this lesson. One plural form of the word *cactus* is *cacti.* If the only plural of *cactus* were *cactuses,* the inflectional form would not have to be included because it follows a common rule. But *cacti* changes the form of the base word, so it is included in the entry. Look at the sample of other nouns that have uncommon plural forms.

genus, genera woman, women
child, children mouse, mice
deer, deer lily, lilies

Sometimes the plural forms are very different from the base word. If this occurs, the plural form will be listed as a separate main entry.

The inflectional forms of verbs have similar entries. For example, you form the past tense and past participle of most verbs by adding *-ed* to the base word. You form the present participle by adding *-ing*.

walk	walked	walked	walking
fill	filled	filled	filling

These common inflectional forms are not printed in your dictionary. In many cases, however, the base word changes in its inflectional form. When this happens, the inflectional form is printed in the dictionary. If the past tense and past participle are the same, only one is shown. Study these examples.

like	liked	liked	liking
trot	trotted	trotted	trotting
go	went	gone	going
teach	taught	taught	teaching

The *e* is dropped from the verb *like* before *-ed* or *-ing* is added. The *t* in *trot* is doubled before *-ed* or *-ing* is added. The inflectional forms of irregular verbs like *go* and *teach* are also printed as separate main entries.

taught [tôt] Past tense and past participle of TEACH.

The base forms of adjectives and adverbs, called the positive forms, are changed to show comparison. Suppose you want to say that Alex is *more tall* than Carol. You would say that Alex is *taller* than Carol. You add *-er* to the base word to compare two people or things. This is called the comparative form. Suppose no one is taller than Alex. In this case you would say that Alex is the *tallest* person in the class. You add *-est* to the base word to compare more than two people or things. This is called the superlative form. These inflected forms are not included in the dictionary. The base word does not change, and *-er* and *-est* are common endings. Sometimes, however, the inflectional forms are included. Study these examples.

big	bigger	biggest
tiny	tinier	tiniest
well	better	best

In each of these examples the base word is changed. The *g* in *big* was doubled before the endings were added. The *y* in *tiny* was changed to *i* before the endings. In the case of *well*, the entire word was changed. Inflectional forms like these are always included in the dictionary entry. The comparative and superlative forms of irregularly composed adjectives and adverbs appear also as main entries.

One other inflectional form must be mentioned here. Words like *beautiful* and *valuable* are not followed by inflectional forms. This would seem to mean that you can form the comparative and superlative in the ordinary way, by adding *-er* and *-est*. But if you do, you will have words like *beauti-*

fuller and *valuablest*. Such words, particularly long ones, sound strange. If the word you form does not sound right, use *more* or *most* instead of *-er* or *-est*. The correct comparative and superlative forms for *beautiful* and *valuable* are *more beautiful* and *most beautiful* and *more valuable* and *most valuable*.

Exercise 1

Write the plural form of the following nouns on a separate sheet of paper. Check your dictionary if you have any questions.

1. house	**2.** sheep	**3.** leaf	**4.** roof
5. spoonful	**6.** sister-in-law	**7.** ox	**8.** tomato
9. switch	**10.** man	**11.** index	**12.** branch
13. baby	**14.** focus	**15.** fish	**16.** cry
17. fox	**18.** wish	**19.** daisy	**20.** merry-go-round

Exercise 2

Write the past tense and present participle of the following verbs on your paper. Write the past participle also if it is different from the past tense.

21. wash	**22.** break	**23.** bring	**24.** put
25. stir	**26.** carry	**27.** swim	**28.** ring
29. talk	**30.** spell	**31.** take	**32.** fly
33. smile	**34.** dip	**35.** speak	**36.** recognize
37. fall	**38.** believe	**39.** swing	**40.** buy

Exercise 3

Write the comparative and superlative forms of the following adjectives and adverbs.

41. small	**42.** shiny	**43.** long	**44.** fat
45. good	**46.** well	**47.** lovely	**48.** quickly
49. different	**50.** ill	**51.** odd	**52.** funny
53. timely	**54.** slowly	**55.** sad	**56.** anxious
57. angry	**58.** secretly	**59.** bright	**60.** mischievous

Exercise 4

Copy these sentences. Write the plural form of each noun shown in parentheses ( ).

61. Did ____________ live near the lakes in ancient Egypt? (ibex)
62. Helga looked out over the ____________ of the town. (roof)
63. During the winter only two mountain ____________ are clear. (pass)

64. I'm hungry enough to eat three ____________ . (sandwich)
65. The week had been full of ____________ . (crisis)
66. Each evening they played several games of ____________ . (domino)
67. He had been the victim of two ____________ . (hoax)
68. How many ____________ are in a billion? (zero)
69. Toni built some ____________ for her books. (shelf)

Exercise 5

Complete each sentence with the form of each verb shown in parentheses ( ).

70. The prince ____________ the answer to the magic question for three years before finding it. (*seek*—past)
71. Paul had ____________ himself ragged in the marathon after only five miles. (*run*—past participle)
72. "Michael hasn't ____________ that loudly since he ____________ on a beehive!" remarked Aunt Sally. (*speak*—past participle, *sit*—past)
73. "I ____________ advanced math to prepare for college," explained Mary. (*take*—past)
74. "Marie ____________ great promise," remarked Mrs. Tibbs. "I hope she is ____________ a career in science." (*show*—present, *consider*—present participle)
75. Naomi had ____________ for over an hour. (*swim*—past participle)
76. Clyde had ____________ Tim at table tennis earlier that day. (*beat*—past participle)
77. Friends ____________ flowers to Mrs. Grayson. (*bring*—past)
78. The class ____________ to the museum last week. (*go*—past)

Exercise 6

Complete these sentences with the correct form of the adjective or adverb shown in parentheses ( ).

79. Thelma is usually ____________ than Ned. (*thoughtful*—comparative)
80. Alfred ____________ offends people by acting ____________ . (*often*—positive, *unfriendly*—positive)
81. Diane surprised Sam by making the ____________ speech of all. (*brief*—superlative)
82. Cara calculated the weight of the potatoes ____________ than Don. (*carefully*—comparative)
83. Sara had ____________ pocket change than Nick. (*little*—comparative)
84. Ron had rowed ____________ of all the campers. (*far*—superlative)
85. Jiro was a ____________ artist than I. (*good*—comparative)

Variant Spelling Cross-References

Variant Spelling ______________ **ca·lif** [kā′lif] *n.* Another spelling of CALIPH.

Sometimes words have more than one acceptable spelling. The dictionary shows these different spellings in two ways. Sometimes, both spellings are included in the dictionary as main entries. The spelling most often used is followed by the definition. The other spelling, or **variant spelling,** is followed by the cross-reference "Another spelling of . . ." Look at the entry *calif* above. The entry *calif* is not followed by the definition. This tells you that *calif* is the less common spelling. The entry *caliph* includes the definition of the word. This is a sign that *caliph* is the more common spelling.

Now look at this entry from the Geographical Section. It demonstrates the other way in which variant spellings are listed in the dictionary.

> **Cape Town** or **Cape·town** [kāp′toun′] *n.* The legislative capital of the Republic of South Africa, in the sw part of the Atlantic. Pop. 698,000.

In this sample, either Cape Town or Capetown is a correct spelling. The spelling that appears first is the more widely used one, but either is correct.

Of course, if you are writing a composition, you must choose one spelling and stay with it. You cannot use one spelling the first time and the other spelling somewhere else in the same composition. Most people choose, and stick to, the more common spelling.

Exercise 1

Find the more common spelling for each of the following words. Write the more common spelling on your paper.

1. jailor	**2.** catchup	**3.** rime	**4.** encyclopaedia
5. archeology	**6.** omelette	**7.** amoeba	**8.** axe
9. gage	**10.** idyl	**11.** grey	**12.** practised
13. metre	**14.** enthral	**15.** plough	**16.** hiccough
17. lollypop	**18.** sulphur	**19.** fledgeling	**20.** gryphon
21. loveable	**22.** cauldron	**23.** fjord	**24.** amok
25. jibe	**26.** advisor	**27.** forbear	**28.** nosey
29. loadstone	**30.** esthetic	**31.** gantlet	**32.** catalogue

Exercise 2

Look in the Geographical Section to find the more common spelling of each of the following place names. Write the more common spelling on your paper.

33. Djakarta	**34.** Szechwan	**35.** Peiping	**36.** Lanchow
37. Bagdad	**38.** Archangel	**39.** Cusco	**40.** Berne
41. Cameroun	**42.** Belorussia	**43.** Nanking	**44.** Rheims

Spelling Reference ______ **cheque** [chek] *n. British* A spelling of CHECK (def. 11).

Although the Americans and the British pronounce many words differently, most words are spelled the same. However, there are some words and groups of words to look out for.

In this dictionary you will find separate main entries for British words such as these.

> **gaol** [jāl] *n. British* A jail. **—gaol′er** *n.*
>
> **py·ja·mas** [pə·jä′məz] *n.pl.* A British spelling of PAJAMAS.

Other entries include a variant spelling such as this.

> **trav·el** [trav′əl] *v.* **trav·eled** or **trav·elled, trav·el·ing** or **trav·el·ling,** *n.* **1** *v.* To go from one place to another; make a journey or tour: to *travel* through France; to *travel* as a tourist. **2** *n.* The act of traveling.

In British spelling, words that end in a single *l* in an unaccented syllable must have the final *l* doubled before *-er*, *-ed*, or *-ing* is added. Doubling the final *l* is acceptable in American spelling, but the single *l* is preferred.

Other differences in American and British spelling are summarized below. Generally, only the American spellings are found as separate entries.

1. In American spelling, words such as *neighbor*, *color*, and *honor* end in *or*. The British spell these words *neighbour*, *colour*, and *honour.*
2. Words such as *center* and *fiber* end in *er* in American spelling. The British spelling of these words is *centre* and *fibre.*
3. Words such as *nationalize* and *generalize* always end in *-ize* in American spelling. The British use *-ise* or *-ize,* though *-ise* is more common.
4. When adding prefixes to words, Americans often drop the hyphen, as in *nonpartisan.* The British retain the hyphen. Thus, they write *non-partisan.*

Exercise ______

The following words use British spelling. Rewrite them using American spelling.

1. rumour	**2.** patronise	**3.** unravelled	**4.** honoured
5. sombre	**6.** pyjamas	**7.** gaol	**8.** sympathise
9. harbour	**10.** centre	**11.** steriliser	**12.** neighbour
13. metre	**14.** savour	**15.** favourite	**16.** theatre
17. realise	**18.** ochre	**19.** flavour	**20.** capitalise

Parts of Speech

Part of Speech ———— **ca·ban·a** [kə·ban′ə] *n.* 1 A small cabin. 2 A small bathhouse for changing clothes at the beach.

The part-of-speech labels tell you how a word can be used in a sentence. In this dictionary the parts of speech are labeled with the following abbreviations.

n.	noun	*adv.*	adverb
pron.	pronoun	*prep.*	preposition
v.	verb	*conj.*	conjunction
adj.	adjective	*interj.*	interjection

The abbreviations can be found after the phonetic respelling if a word is used as only one part of speech. If a word can be used as more than one part of speech, the abbreviation can be found before each definition. Read these examples.

bank·er [bangk′ər] *n.* A person who owns or runs a bank.

cal·i·co [kal′i·kō] *n., pl.* **cal·i·coes** or **cal·i·cos** 1 *n.* Cotton cloth printed with a figured design. 2 *adj. use*: a *calico* curtain. 3 *adj.* Like calico; spotted or streaked: a *calico* cat.

The first example, *banker*, is used only as a noun. The second example, *calico,* can be used as a noun and an adjective (definitions 1 and 3). In this entry you will notice another abbreviation, *adj. use*, standing for "adjective use." This label lets you know that the word used as a noun in the preceeding definition can be used as an adjective with the same meaning. For this reason, no definition is needed. An illustrative phrase shows you the use and meaning.

In very much the same way, an adjective can sometimes be used as a noun. Such instances are labeled *n. use,* for "noun use." You can see an example of this abbreviation in the second definition of *rich.* Words that are identified with this label are defined briefly.

rich [rich] *adj.* 1 Having a lot of money, goods, or property; wealthy. 2 *n. use*: Rich people: *The rich* are sometimes generous.

In a few entries you will find a definition of a noun immediately followed by a ◆ sign. This sign indicates an adjective related to the noun but spelled differently.

cat [kat] *n.* 1 A small domestic animal of various colors. ◆ *Adj., feline.* 2 Any larger animal related to the cat, as the tiger, lion, leopard, and bobcat.

Exercise 1

Copy the following words. Look them up in your dictionary. Label each one according to its part or parts of speech.

1. alert	**2.** below	**3.** calendar	**4.** deaf
5. equal	**6.** firewood	**7.** glow	**8.** huge
9. isle	**10.** jell	**11.** look	**12.** nod

Exercise 2

Copy the following sentences on your paper. After each sentence, write the part of speech of the underlined word.

13. We went to the preview of a new movie.
14. The teacher previewed the movie before showing it to the class.
15. Did you fold the laundry before you put it away?
16. The kitten is hiding in the folds of the drapes.
17. Give him a lift with that package.
18. Lift the end of his bookcase.
19. The pilot must refer to the instrument panel.
20. A scalpel is a surgical instrument.
21. It started to rain during the picnic.
22. The guard must be alert.
23. The witness alerted the police.
24. The firefighter sounded an alert.
25. On the field trip Dot saw a crane in the water.
26. Joe craned his neck to see what she was looking at.
27. The center beam for this house is 30 feet long.
28. Alyson beamed when her teacher praised her work.
29. Rachel glanced at the stranger but said nothing.
30. Harry gave her a glance that meant "be quiet."
31. Johnelle received a government grant to study city housing.
32. Dr. Frogg will grant three acres of land to the city for a new playground.
33. Mr. Adipose is beginning a new diet this week.
34. Jeanne has been in the lead since the beginning of the race.
35. Bertram will soon break his own track record.
36. Carl considered finding his new job a lucky break.
37. Dorothy was an excellent match for Donald in the tennis tournament.
38. Dorothy matches Donald's ability and exceeds him in enthusiasm.
39. The guard silenced the unruly crowd.
40. Nothing compares to the silence of a sandy beach at sunset.
41. The candidate patterned his speeches on those of a famous orator from his home state.
42. Gigi ordered a pattern for the model ship she wished to make.

Subject References

Subject Reference — **Cha·ryb·dis** [kə·rib′dis] *n.* In Greek myths, a whirlpool opposite the rock of Scylla. Ships going between Italy and Sicily had to avoid both.

Some definitions in this book are identified as pertaining to a particular subject, such as a science, a sport, or a work of literature. Look at the definitions below. You will see the phrases "In physics," "In football," "In Greek and Roman myths," and "In the Bible." Each such reference identifies the subject area of the definition that follows.

grav·i·ta·tion [grav′ə·tā′shən] *n.* **1** In physics, the force by which any two bodies attract each other. **2** The act or process of gravitating. **3** A movement, as to a source of attraction.

half·back [haf′bak′] *n.* In football, either of two players who play behind the line of scrimmage.

Her·cu·les [hûr′kyə·lēz] *n.* In Greek and Roman myths, a hero of great strength who successfully performed gigantic tasks.

Ruth [rōōth] *n.* **1** In the Bible, a widow who left her own people and went to live with her mother-in-law, Naomi. **2** The book of the Old Testament in which this story is told.

These references tell you where to look for more information about the entry. If you wanted more information on gravitation, you should look in a physics book. If you wanted more information about Hercules, you should look in a book about mythology, and so on.

Exercise

Copy the following words. Look in your dictionary to find in what particular area or areas the words have special meanings. Write the field or fields of interest next to each word.

1. love	**2.** Helios	**3.** John	**4.** goal
5. Romulus	**6.** Romeo	**7.** force	**8.** center
9. field	**10.** note	**11.** equation	**12.** family
13. scale	**14.** phoenix	**15.** phrase	**16.** point
17. relief	**18.** accent	**19.** pin	**20.** guard
21. brief	**22.** Valkyrie	**23.** spare	**24.** Hector
25. Penelope	**26.** binomial	**27.** aegis	**28.** foot
29. aureole	**30.** back	**31.** filter	**32.** Lancelot
33. Torah	**34.** pirouette	**35.** focus	**36.** Demeter
37. Zechariah	**38.** transform	**39.** Juno	**40.** crown

Usage Label ______ **ca·boose** [kə·bo͞os′] *n.* *U.S.* A car, usually the rear car of a freight train, used by the crew.

Most of the words printed in this dictionary are considered part of our formal English vocabulary. You can use the words anywhere and be sure that they are correct. Formal English is used in term papers, scholarly works, legal documents, and speeches.

Some entries, not a part of our formal English vocabulary, have special labels. These labels tell you that the use of the word is limited to certain situations. Look at the entries *cop, ornery,* and *outsmart* below. These words are acceptable in conversation with friends and family. You hear them in everyday speech, but you rarely see them in printed material. They are labeled *informal*.

cop [kop] *n.* *informal* A police officer.

or·ner·y [ôr′nər·ē *or* ōrn′rē] *adj.* *U.S. informal* 1 Hard to manage; stubborn: an *ornery* mule. 2 Mean; low: an *ornery* trick.

out·smart [out·smärt′] *v.* *informal* To fool or trick; outwit.

Entries labeled *slang* have even less acceptance in formal English than *informal* entries.

lid [lid] *n.* 1 A hinged or removable cover, as for a box or pot. 2 An eyelid. 3 *slang* A hat.

nut·ty [nut′ē] *adj.* **nut·ti·er, nut·ti·est** 1 Having the flavor of nuts. 2 Containing nuts: *nutty* candy. 3 *slang* Crazy or foolish.

Some labels show that a word is more common in the United States or in Britain.

loan [lōn] 1 *n.* The act of lending: a *loan* of a book. 2 *n.* Something lent, especially a sum of money. 3 *v.* *U.S.* To lend.

trea·cle [trē′kəl] *n.* *British* Molasses.

Exercise

Copy the following words. Look them up in your dictionary. Label each *informal*, *slang*, *U.S.*, or *British*, depending on how it is used.

1. jitters	**2.** lorry	**3.** lobby	**4.** fraud
5. good and	**6.** outside of	**7.** frame-up	**8.** petrol
9. own up	**10.** cotillion	**11.** wireless	**12.** notch
13. cricket	**14.** crib	**15.** folksy	**16.** boss
17. cheapskate	**18.** traipse	**19.** snippy	**20.** cunning
21. picayune	**22.** form	**23.** worship	**24.** ride
25. queue	**26.** cut up	**27.** slew	**28.** snap

Usage Notes

Usage Note — **cai·tiff** [kā'tif] **1** *n.* A low scoundrel. **2** *adj.* Base. ◆ This word is seldom used today.

Usage notes help you to use the English language properly. The notes go beyond giving the definitions of words. They explain which words are seldom used today. They explain the correct grammatical use of other words. Some usage notes eliminate confusion among words that have similar but slightly different meanings. Other notes draw attention to words that are spelled nearly the same but have different meanings. Usage notes are introduced by the symbol ◆ .

ain't [ānt] A contraction of: Am not: I *ain't* going. *Ain't* is also used for *are not, is not, has not,* and *have not.* ◆ *Ain't* is not considered acceptable English today, although speakers and writers sometimes use it for humorous effect.

de·ceive [di·sēv'] *v.* **de·ceived, de·ceiv·ing** To cause to take as true something that is not true; fool or mislead, as by lying: They *deceived* us about the true purpose of their visit. **—de·ceiv'er** *n.* ◆ *Deceive, mislead,* and *delude* all refer to making someone believe as true something that is false or accept as worthwhile something that is without value. *Mislead* is the most general of these words. It can be used to describe a simple error in judgment: A warm day in February *misled* us into thinking we would have an early spring. It can refer to a deception that is innocent and unplanned: Directions in a foreign language can easily *mislead* you. It can also suggest something deliberate and tricky: The advertiser's false claims *misled* customers into paying high prices for third-rate merchandise. There is never anything innocent about an attempt to *deceive.* Anyone who deceives another is always deliberate in the distortion of truth or reality: The candidate's speech *deceived* voters about the seriousness of the recession. *Delude* is close in meaning to *deceive* but suggests an attempt to make a fool or victim out of the person who is deluded: The computer school *deluded* many young people about their abilities, leading them to take more courses than necessary for their future careers. **—de·ceiv'·er** *n.* **—de·ceiv'ing·ly** *adv.*

Exercise

Copy the following sentences. Look up the underlined word in the dictionary. Next to the sentence indicate whether the underlined word is used correctly by writing YES or NO. If the word is used incorrectly, write the correct word.

1. The decent from the mountain was very difficult.
2. The data is very accurate.
3. She is a brunet.
4. George sat among his mother and father.
5. I hope you have learned your lesson.
6. We have less people here today.
7. The painter fell off of the ladder.
8. We went passed this street before.
9. They wandered all over the West looking for gold.
10. The waiter wanted to know if everything was alright.
11. Angelina excepted the invitation to Jed's party.

Etymology

car·ry·all[1] [kar′e·ôl′] *n.* A light, one-horse carriage with a top, holding several people. ◆ *Carryall* comes from the French word *cariole.* Apparently the sound and spelling of *cariole* were too un-English, because *carryall,* with its familiar English elements, *carry* and *all,* replaced it.

The **etymology** of a word is its history. It tells how the word came into the English language. The etymology of particular words follows this symbol ◆ in your dictionary entries. By reading the history of words you can understand how language changes over time. There was no need for the word *astronaut* until this century. However, the word itself is not really new. The roots of the word go back to ancient times.

as·tro·naut [as′trə·nôt′] *n.* A person who travels in space. ◆ *Astronaut* is parallel to *aeronaut,* a balloon pilot, and is formed from the Greek roots *nautes,* meaning *sailor,* and *astro-* meaning (*between* or *among*) *stars.*

Many English words come from the Greek and Latin languages. But these are by no means the only languages that have contributed to English. The following are examples of others.

bun·ga·low [bung′gə·lō′] *n.* A small house or cottage, usually with one, or one and a half stories. ◆ *Bungalow* comes from a word in Hindustani meaning *of Bengal,* because it described a type of house found in Bengal.

cof·fee [kôf′ē] **1** *n.* A beverage made from the roasted and ground seeds or beans of a tropical shrub. **2** *n.* These seeds or beans. **3** *n.* The shrub on which they grow. **4** *n., adj.* Brown, as the color of coffee with cream. ◆ *Coffee* comes from an Arabic word.

del·i·ca·tes·sen [del′ə·kə·tes′(ə)n] *n.* **1** A store selling prepared foods, such as cooked meats, salads, and cheese. **2** The food which such a store sells. ◆ *Delicatessen* comes from a German word meaning *delicacies.*

Exercise

Copy these words on your paper. Next to each word write the name of the language from which it came.

1. alfalfa	**2.** advertiser	**3.** tutti-frutti	**4.** hominy
5. orange	**6.** paper	**7.** ukulele	**8.** pentagon
9. voodoo	**10.** plaid	**11.** pretzel	**12.** racket
13. record	**14.** rendezvous	**15.** school	**16.** toboggan
17. zero	**18.** skunk	**19.** sky	**20.** flamboyant
21. chiffon	**22.** corduroy	**23.** trigonometry	**24.** starboard
25. muscle	**26.** quinine	**27.** rune	**28.** algebra
29. goulash	**30.** kindergarten	**31.** kangaroo	**32.** turnpike
33. book	**34.** idea	**35.** borscht	**36.** dismal
37. yoga	**38.** nasturtium	**39.** curfew	**40.** boomerang

A is the first letter of the alphabet. The sign for it originated among Semitic people in the Near East, in the region of Palestine and Syria, probably in the middle of the second millennium B.C. Little is known about the sign until around 1000 B.C., when the Phoenicians began using it. They named the sign *aleph* and used it not for a vowel but for a breathing sound.

When the Greeks adopted the Phoenician sign around the ninth century B.C., they had no need to use it for a breathing sound. They used the sign for the vowel *A* and called the sign *alpha.* The Greeks gradually refined the shape of the letter until it looked like the sign we use for our capital *A* today. The name of the letter became the first half of the word *alphabet.*

As early as the eighth century B.C., the Etruscans adopted the Greek alphabet. It is from the Etruscans that the Romans took the sign for *A*. Around the time of the Caesars, the Romans made the shape of the letter more graceful. The model of the letter found on the base of Trajan's column, erected in Rome in 114, is considered a masterpiece of letter design. A Trajan-style *majuscule,* or capital letter, *A* can be found at the beginning of this essay.

The *minuscule,* or small letter, *a* developed gradually, between the third and ninth centuries, in the handwriting that scribes used for copying books. Contributing to its shape were the Roman *uncials* of the fourth to the eighth centuries and the *half uncials* of the fifth to the ninth centuries. The true ancestor of the lowercase *a*, however, was the script that evolved under the encouragement of Charlemagne (742-814). This letter was one of the letters known as the *Caroline minuscules*, which became the principal handwriting system used on the medieval manuscripts of the ninth and tenth centuries.

Today the lowercase *a* has two forms, an italic style ( ) and a roman style (a). Having two different forms for *a* was a development of the fifteenth century.

Aa

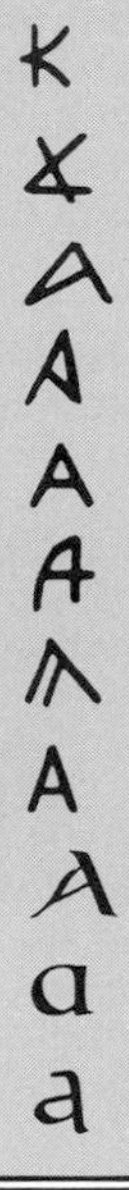

Early Phoenician (late 2nd millennium B.C.)
Phoenician (8th century B.C.)
Early Greek (9th-7th centuries B.C.)
Western Greek (6th century B.C.)
Classical Greek (403 B.C. onward)
Early Etruscan (8th century B.C.)
Monumental Latin (4th century B.C.)
Classical Latin
Uncial
Half uncial
Caroline minuscule

a or **A** [ā] *n., pl.* **a's** or **A's** 1 The first letter of the English alphabet. 2 *U.S.* The highest or best grade for school work. 3 In music, the sixth note of the scale of C major.

a [ə *or* ā] An indefinite article used before nouns or noun phrases. It means: 1 One: I bought *a* dozen eggs today. 2 One kind of: Sugar is *a* carbohydrate. 3 Any; each: *A* burned-out fuse should be replaced. 4 For each: two dollars *a* pound. 5 In each: once *a* week. ◆ See AN.

a. 1 about. 2 acre(s). 3 area(s). 4 In sports, assist.

A 1 acre. 2 angstrom. 3 argon. 4 answer. 5 area.

AA 1 Alcoholics Anonymous. 2 antiaircraft.

AAA American Automobile Association.

aard·vark [ärd′värk′] *n.* A burrowing animal of southern Africa having powerful claws and a long, sticky tongue. It feeds on termites and ants.

aard·wolf [ärd′wo͝olf′] *n., pl.*, **aard·wolves** [ärd′·wo͝olvz′] A hyenalike mammal of the African plains that feeds on insects and small animals.

Aar·on [âr′ən *or* ar′ən] *n.* In the Bible, the first Hebrew high priest, the brother of Moses.

AAU Amateur Athletic Union.

A.B. Bachelor of Arts.

ABA 1 American Bar Association. 2 American Basketball Association.

ab·a·ca [ab′ə·kä′] *n.* 1 A large tropical plant that grows in the Philippines. The stalks of its leaves are used to make Manila hemp. 2 Another word for MANILA HEMP.

a·back [ə·bak′] *adv.* Backward; behind. **—taken aback** Surprised; suddenly confused; upset.

ab·a·cus [ab′ə·kəs] *n.* A device using beads that slide on rods for adding, subtracting, multiplying, and dividing.

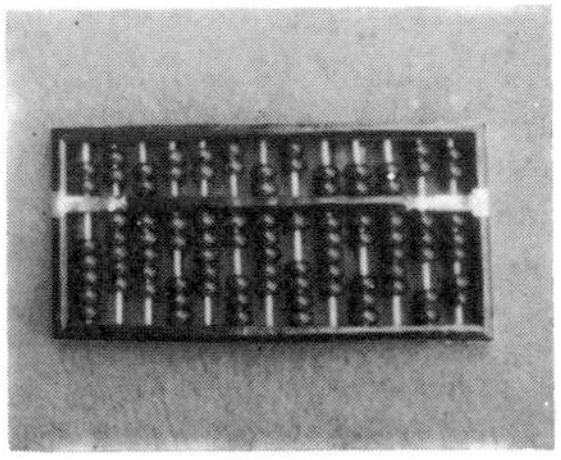

Abacus

a·baft [ə·baft′] 1 *adv.* Toward the stern; aft. 2 *prep.* Farther aft than: *abaft* the mainmast.

ab·a·lo·ne [ab′ə·lō′nē] *n.* An edible shellfish having a flat shell lined with mother-of-pearl.

a·ban·don [ə·ban′dən] 1 *v.* To give up wholly; forfeit: *abandon* all hope. 2 *v.* To leave; desert; forsake. 3 *n.* A giving up of self-control: to dance with *abandon.* 4 *v.* To yield (oneself) to feeling or impulse. **—a·ban′don·ment** *n.*

a·ban·doned [ə·ban′dənd] *adj.* 1 Deserted; left behind; forsaken. 2 Evil; shameless: an *abandoned* rascal.

a	add	**i**	it	**o͝o**	took	**oi**	oil
ā	ace	**ī**	ice	**o͞o**	pool	**ou**	pout
â	care	**o**	odd	**u**	up	**ng**	ring
ä	palm	**ō**	open	**û**	burn	**th**	thin
e	end	**ô**	order	**yo͞o**	fuse	**th**	this
ē	equal					**zh**	vision

ə = { a in *above* e in *sicken* i in *possible*; o in *melon* u in *circus* }

a·base [ə·bās′] *v.* **a·based, a·bas·ing** To lower in rank or position; humble: A cowardly act *abases* a person. **—a·base′ment** *n.*

a·bash [ə·bash′] *v.* To confuse or embarrass; shame: The child was *abashed* by the applause.

a·bate [ə·bāt′] *v.* **a·bat·ed, a·bat·ing** To make or become less, as in value, force, or intensity: to *abate* one's efforts; The wind *abated.* **—a·bate′ment** *n.*

ab·at·toir [ab′ə·twär′] *n.* Another word for SLAUGHTERHOUSE.

ab·bess [ab′is] *n.* A woman who heads a group of nuns connected with an abbey.

ab·bey [ab′ē] *n., pl.* **ab·beys** 1 A community of monks or nuns ruled by an abbot or an abbess; monastery or convent. 2 A church or building connected with a monastery or convent.

ab·bot [ab′ət] *n.* A man who heads a group of monks connected with an abbey.

abbr. or **abbrev.** abbreviation.

ab·bre·vi·ate [ə·brē′vē·āt′] *v.* **ab·bre·vi·at·ed, ab·bre·vi·at·ing** 1 To reduce (a word or phrase) to a short form standing for the whole. 2 To cut short or condense: to *abbreviate* an answer.

ab·bre·vi·a·tion [ə·brē′vē·ā′shən] *n.* 1 The act or process of abbreviating. 2 A shortened form of a word or phrase. ◆ *Abbreviation, contraction,* and *acronym* all mean a shortened form, as of a word, phrase, or name. An *abbreviation* uses the first letter or letters of a word or phrase, and is a space-saving replacement for the fuller form, as *U.S.* for *U*nited *S*tates. A *contraction* is made by leaving out something in the middle and closing up what is left, as *can't* for *cannot.* An *acronym* is an abbreviation that has become a fully pronounced word by itself, as *scuba* for *s*elf-*c*ontained *u*nderwater *b*reathing *a*pparatus.

ABC [ā′bē′sē′] *n., pl.* **ABC's** *usually pl.* 1 The alphabet. 2 The basic or elementary part, as of a subject: the *ABC* of arithmetic.

ABC American Broadcasting Company.

ab·di·cate [ab′də·kāt′] *v.* **ab·di·cat·ed, ab·di·cat·ing** 1 To give up (a throne or other high office). 2 To give up a high office. **—ab′di·ca′tion** *n.*

ab·do·men [ab′də·mən *or* ab·dō′mən] *n.* 1 In animals with backbones, the part of the body that contains the digestive tract, in mammals below the chest and above the pelvis; belly. 2 In insects, the hindmost section of the body.

ab·dom·i·nal [ab·dom′ə·nəl] *adj.* Of, in, or having to do with the abdomen.

ab·dom·i·nal thrust A first-aid technique used to dislodge an object that has stuck in the throat and prevented the victim's breathing.

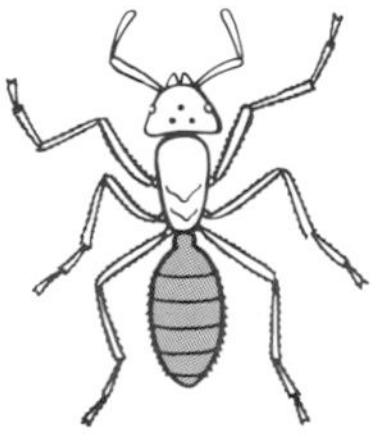
Abdomen of an ant

ab·duct [ab·dukt′] *v.* To carry off or lead away (a person) unlawfully; kidnap: She was *abducted* and held for ransom. **—ab·duc′tion** *n.* **—ab·duc′tor** *n.*

a·beam [ə·bēm′] *adv.* 1 Across a ship at right angles. 2 At one side about even with a ship: The tugboat came *abeam* of the freighter.

a·bed [ə·bed′] *adv.* In bed.

A·bel [ā′bəl] *n.* In the Bible, the second son of Adam, killed by his older brother Cain.

Ab·er·deen An·gus [ab′ər·dēn′ ang′gəs] One of a breed of black, hornless beef cattle that originated in Scotland.

ab·er·rant [ə·ber′ənt *or* ab′ər·ənt] *adj.* Differing from the expected, normal, or typical: The heart defect showed up as an *aberrant* pattern in the heartbeat.

ab·er·ra·tion [ab′ə·rā′shən] *n.* 1 A departure from what is right, correct, or natural. 2 A mild mental disorder. 3 The failure of a lens or mirror to bring all light rays to a single focus.

a·bet [ə·bet′] *v.* **a·bet·ted, a·bet·ting** To encourage and help, especially in doing wrong: to *abet* a bank robber. **—a·bet′tor** *n.* **—a·bet′ter** *n.*

a·bey·ance [ə·bā′əns] *n.* A state of being held up or put aside for future action: The question was held in *abeyance* until a study was made.

ab·hor [ab·hôr′] *v.* **ab·horred, ab·hor·ring** To feel hatred or disgust for; loathe. ◆ See HATE.

ab·hor·rence [ab·hôr′əns] *n.* 1 A feeling of disgust, repulsion, or loathing. 2 Something that causes this feeling: Filth is an *abhorrence.*

ab·hor·rent [ab·hôr′ənt] *adj.* Causing abhorrence; repulsive; disgusting: *abhorrent* crimes.

a·bide [ə·bīd′] *v.* **a·bode** [ə·bōd′] or **a·bid·ed, a·bid·ing** 1 To continue in a place; remain: to *abide* at home. 2 To last a long time: Evil shall not *abide.* 3 To wait for. 4 To put up with; endure: I can't *abide* noise. **—abide by** 1 To submit to and follow. 2 To fulfill: to *abide by* an agreement.

a·bid·ing [ə·bī′ding] *adj.* Continuing without changing or growing less: *abiding* love.

a·bil·i·ty [ə·bil′ə·tē] *n., pl.* **a·bil·i·ties** 1 The quality or state of being able; power to do or perform. 2 (*pl.*) Talents. 3 Skill; craft: natural *ability* developed by coaching.

-ability A suffix meaning: Capacity or inclination to be, as in *adaptability.*

ab·ject [ab′jekt *or* ab·jekt′] *adj.* 1 Contemptible; low: an *abject* coward. 2 Hopelessly bad; crushing: *abject* poverty. **—ab′ject·ly** *adv.*

ab·jure [ab·jŏŏr′] *v.* **ab·jured, ab·jur·ing** To take an oath publicly to give up, as a religion or a belief.

ab·la·tion [a·blā′shən] *n.* The melting away of a protective coating on the front of a spacecraft reentering Earth's atmosphere. Ablation uses up friction-generated heat that might otherwise damage vital parts of the craft.

ab·la·tive [ab′lə·tiv] 1 *n.* A grammatical case in Latin, Finnish, and some other languages that is used to show direction, means, movement, or source. 2 *adj.* Of or indicating the ablative.

a·blaze [ə·blāz′] *adj.* 1 In flames; blazing. 2 Very bright; brilliant: The lights were *ablaze.* 3 Excited; ardent: The lawyer's anger was *ablaze.*

a·ble [ā′bəl] *adj.* **a·bler, a·blest** 1 Having the power or whatever is needed to do something: A race horse is *able* to run fast. 2 Skillful; competent: an *able* surgeon; an *able* performance.

-able A suffix meaning: 1 Capable of being, as in *adjustable.* 2 Inclined or likely to, as in *changeable.* 3 Fit to be, as in *lovable.*

a·ble-bod·ied [ā′bəl·bod′ēd] *adj.* Strong and healthy; physically fit.

able-bodied seaman A highly skilled sailor.

a·bloom [ə·blŏŏm′] *adj.* Flowering; in bloom.

ab·lu·tion [ə·blŏŏ′shən] *n.* (*often pl.*) A washing or cleaning of the body, as in a religious ceremony.

a·bly [ā′blē] *adv.* With ability; skillfully.

ABM antiballistic missile.

ab·ne·ga·tion [ab′nə·gā′shən] *n.* The giving up of things that are necessary or wanted.

ab·nor·mal [ab·nôr′məl] *adj.* Not normal or average; unusual; irregular. **—ab·nor′mal·ly** *adv.*

ab·nor·mal·i·ty [ab′nôr·mal′ə·tē] *n., pl.* **ab·nor·mal·i·ties** An abnormal thing or condition.

a·board [ə·bôrd′] **1** *adv.* On, in, or into a train, ship, etc.: Get *aboard.* **2** *prep.* On, in, or into: We played checkers while *aboard* the bus.

a·bode [ə·bōd′] **1** Past tense and past participle of ABIDE. **2** *n.* The place where one lives or stays; home; dwelling; residence.

a·bol·ish [ə·bol′ish] *v.* To do away with; put an end to; nullify: Bad laws should be *abolished.*

ab·o·li·tion [ab′ə·lish′ən] *n.* **1** The act of abolishing. **2** The state of being abolished. **3** The ending of slavery in the U.S.

ab·o·li·tion·ist [ab′ə·lish′ə·nist] *n.* **1** (*sometimes written* **Abolitionist**) One of the people who wanted to end slavery in the U.S. **2** A person who wants to abolish something.

A–bomb [ā′bom′] *n.* An atomic bomb.

a·bom·i·na·ble [ə·bom′in·ə·bəl] *adj.* **1** Very bad or disgusting. **2** Hateful. **—a·bom′i·na·bly** *adv.*

abominable snowman A hairy, apelike or bearlike animal that is said to live high in the mountains of Tibet. No proof of its existence acceptable to scientists has yet been found.

a·bom·i·nate [ə·bom′ə·nāt′] *v.* **a·bom·i·nat·ed, a·bom·i·nat·ing** To think of with hate, loathing, or strong dislike.

a·bom·i·na·tion [ə·bom′ə·nā′shən] *n.* **1** Something abominable. **2** Strong loathing.

ab·o·rig·i·nal [ab′ə·rij′ə·nəl] *adj.* Of or having to do with aborigines; primitive.

ab·o·rig·i·ne [ab′ə·rij′ə·nē] *n.* (*often pl.*) One of the earliest people, plants, or animals known to have lived in a particular area.

a·bort [ə·bôrt′] **1** *v.* To give birth to a fetus before it has developed enough to survive. **2** *v.* To be born before enough development has occurred to allow survival. **3** *v.* To end (the project or mission of a space vehicle or missile) before it is completed. **4** *v.* To cause an abortion.

a·bor·tion [ə·bôr′shən] *n.* **1** Birth before a fetus has developed enough to live. **2** A failure to grow or develop. **3** The result of such a failure.

a·bor·tive [ə·bôr′tiv] *adj.* **1** Coming to nothing; failing; futile: an *abortive* revolt. **2** Born while too undeveloped to live.

a·bound [ə·bound′] *v.* **1** To be abundant or in plentiful supply: Pigeons *abound* in some cities. **2** To teem or be filled: The world *abounds* with trees. **3** To be rich: Alaska *abounded* in gold.

a·bout [ə·bout′] **1** *prep.* Having to do with: a book *about* dogs. **2** *adv.* Close to; almost; approximately: *about* five dollars. **3** *adv.* Here and there: to wander *about.* **4** *prep.* Here and there in or on: to move *about* the room. **5** *prep.* Around; encircling: to spin *about* an axis; a wall *about* the city. **6** *adv.* Halfway around: Turn *about.* **7** *prep.* Just ready; on the point of: I was *about* to say that.

a·bout-face [*n.* ə·bout′fās′, *v.* ə·bout′fās′] *n., v.* **a·bout-faced, a·bout-fac·ing** **1** *n.* A turn halfway around, to the rear. **2** *v.* To face or go in the opposite direction.

a·bove [ə·buv′] **1** *adv.* In a higher place; farther up: the sky *above.* **2** *prep.* Higher than; over: a shelf *above* the stove; Her grades are *above* average. **3** *prep.* Beyond; past: Turn left *above* the church. **4** *adv.* Earlier in a book, article, or chapter: mentioned *above.* **5** *adj.* Already mentioned: the *above* instructions. **6** *prep.* Too good to stoop to; superior to: He's *above* lying. **—above all** Most important; first of all.

a·bove·board [ə·buv′bôrd′] *adv., adj.* Without deceit, fraud, or trickery; in open sight.

ab·ra·ca·dab·ra [ab′rə·kə·da′brə] *n.* **1** A word that is supposed to have magical power. **2** A magic spell or formula. **3** Meaningless words; gibberish.

a·brade [ə·brād′] *v.* **a·brad·ed, a·brad·ing** To rub off; wear away: to *abrade* shoe soles.

A·bra·ham [ā′brə·ham] *n.* In the Bible, the ancestor and founder of the Hebrew people.

a·bra·sion [ə·brā′zhən] *n.* **1** A scraped area, as a skinned place. **2** The process of wearing or rubbing something away.

a·bra·sive [ə·brā′siv] **1** *adj.* Causing or tending to cause abrasion. **2** *n.* A hard material, as sand, used to rub or wear softer materials away.

a·breast [ə·brest′] *adv., adj.* Side by side: to walk three *abreast.* **—abreast of** or **abreast with** Even with; not behind: *abreast* of events.

a·bridge [ə·brij′] *v.* **a·bridged, a·bridg·ing** **1** To put into fewer words, as a book or speech. **2** To shorten, as in time: to *abridge* a lesson. **3** To deprive of or lessen: to *abridge* a right.

a·bridg·ment [ə·brij′mənt] *n.* **1** A reduction in length; an abridging. **2** A shortened or condensed version, as of a book or play. **3** A curtailment, as of rights.

a·broad [ə·brôd′] *adv.* **1** Out of one's country; in or into foreign lands: to live *abroad.* **2** Out of one's home; outdoors: to stroll *abroad.* **3** At large; all around: Rumors are *abroad.*

ab·ro·gate [ab′rə·gāt′] *v.* **ab·ro·gat·ed, ab·ro·gat·ing** To put an end to; annul; repeal: to *abrogate* a treaty. **—ab′ro·ga′tion** *n.*

a·brupt [ə·brupt′] *adj.* **1** Sudden: an *abrupt* turn. **2** Steep: an *abrupt* cliff. **3** Sudden; hasty: an *abrupt* departure. **4** Rude or curt, as in speech; brusque. **—a·brupt′ly** *adv.* **—a·brupt′ness** *n.*

ab·scess [ab′ses] *n.* A collection of pus in some part of the body, resulting from an infection.

ab·scessed [ab′sest] *adj.* Having an abscess.

ab·scis·sa [ab·sis′ə] *n., pl.* **ab·scis·sas** or **ab·scis·sae** [ab·sis′ē] On a graph, the distance of a point from the vertical axis.

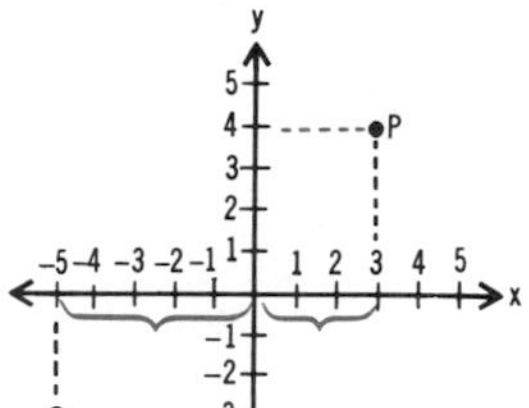

The abscissa of *p* is 3.
The abscissa of *q* is −5.

ab·scond [ab·skond′] *v.* To go away suddenly and hide: Fearing arrest, the racketeer *absconded.*

ab·sence [ab′səns] *n.* **1** The state of being away or not present: *absence* from home. **2** A period of being away: a week's *absence.* **3** Lack: an *absence* of vitamins in the diet.

a	add	**i**	it	**o͝o**	took	**oi**	oil
ā	ace	**ī**	ice	**o͞o**	pool	**ou**	pout
â	care	**o**	odd	**u**	up	**ng**	ring
ä	palm	**ō**	open	**û**	burn	**th**	thin
e	end	**ô**	order	**yo͞o**	fuse	**th**	this
ē	equal					**zh**	vision

ə = a in *above*, e in *sicken*, i in *possible*, o in *melon*, u in *circus*

ab·sent [*adj.* ab′sənt, *v.* ab·sent′] 1 *adj.* Not present; away: The electrician was *absent* from work. 2 *v.* To take or keep (oneself) away: The president *absented* herself from the meeting. 3 *adj.* Lacking; missing: If vitamin C is *absent,* scurvy is likely. 4 *adj.* Showing a lack of attention; preoccupied: an *absent* stare. **—ab′sent·ly** *adv.*

ab·sen·tee [ab′sən·tē′] *n.* A person who is absent, as from a job.

absentee ballot A ballot marked and mailed in by a voter who cannot get to the polls in person.

ab·sen·tee·ism [ab′sən·tē′iz′əm] *n.* Repeated failure to appear, especially at work or at school.

absentee landlord A person who owns and rents out land or buildings where he or she does not live.

ab·sent-mind·ed [ab′sənt·mīn′did] *adj.* Not paying attention to what is happening around one; forgetful. **—ab′sent-mind′ed·ly** *adv.* **—ab′sent-mind′ed·ness** *n.*

ab·sinthe [ab′sinth′] *n.* A green, toxic liqueur that tastes like bitter licorice. It is flavored with wormwood and anise.

ab·so·lute [ab′sə·lo͞ot] *adj.* 1 Having no restrictions; unlimited; unconditional: an *absolute* monarch. 2 Complete; perfect: *absolute* order. 3 Pure; unmixed. 4 Not relative to anything else. 5 Positive; sure: *absolute* certainty.

absolute alcohol Ethyl alcohol containing no more than 1 percent water.

ab·so·lute·ly [ab′sə·lo͞ot′lē *or* ab′sə·lo͞ot′lē] *adv.* 1 Completely. 2 Positively.

absolute temperature Temperature measured from absolute zero, usually on the Kelvin scale.

absolute value On a number line, the distance from zero to any point (+ or −): The *absolute value* of −37 is 37; this can also be written |−37| = 37.

absolute zero In theory, the temperature at which molecular motion stops and all heat disappears, −459.7° F. or −273° C.

ab·so·lu·tion [ab′sə·lo͞o′shən] *n.* A release from guilt or punishment for sin; forgiveness.

ab·so·lut·ism [ab′sə·lo͞o′tiz′əm] *n.* A system of government where the ruler has unlimited power. **—ab′so·lut′ist** *n., adj.*

ab·solve [ab·zolv′] *v.* **ab·solved, ab·solv·ing** 1 To declare (a sinner) free from sin, guilt, or penalty: The priest *absolved* him. 2 To release, as from a promise, obligation, or debt.

ab·sorb [ab·sôrb′ *or* ab·zôrb′] *v.* 1 To take in and hold; suck in: Towels *absorb* water. 2 To take the full attention of; occupy fully: Music *absorbs* the listener. 3 To take in without reflecting back: Felt *absorbs* sound. 4 To take in and make part of itself: The city *absorbs* the suburbs.

ab·sorb·en·cy [ab·sôr′bən·sē *or* ab·zôr′bən·sē] *n.* The quality of being absorbent.

ab·sor·bent [ab·sôr′bənt *or* ab·zôr′bənt] *adj.* Able to or tending to absorb.

ab·sor·bing [ab·sôr′bing *or* ab·zôr′bing] *adj.* Capturing and holding one's attention.

ab·sorp·tion [ab·sôrp′shən *or* ab·zôrp′shən] *n.* 1 An absorbing. 2 Complete attention.

ab·stain [ab·stān′] *v.* 1 To keep oneself back; refrain by choice: They *abstain* from sweets. 2 To keep oneself back from voting. **—ab·stain′er** *n.*

ab·ste·mi·ous [ab·stē′mē·əs] *adj.* Eating and drinking sparingly; temperate.

ab·sten·tion [ab·sten′shən] *n.* An abstaining or refraining, especially from voting.

ab·sti·nence [ab′stə·nəns] *n.* The doing without, fully or partly, as of certain drinks or foods.

ab·stract [*adj., n.* ab′strakt, *v.* ab·strakt′] 1 *adj.* Not dealing with anything specific or particular; general: an *abstract* idea of truth. 2 *adj.* Expressing a quality thought of as separated from any object possessing the quality: "Redness" is an *abstract* word. 3 *adj.* Made to offer a form or pattern rather than to represent real objects: *abstract* art. 4 *adj.* Hard to understand: Nuclear physics is very *abstract.* 5 *n.* A summary or outline covering the main points, as of a book, article, or speech. 6 *v.* [*sometimes* ab′strakt] To make an abstract of; summarize. 7 *v.* To remove or take away, especially in secret. **—ab·stract′ly** *adv.*

Abstract art

ab·stract·ed [ab·strak′tid] *adj.* Not paying attention; absent-minded. **—ab·stract′ed·ly** *adv.*

ab·strac·tion [ab·strak′shən] *n.* 1 Something abstract, as an idea, word, or quality: Mathematics deals with *abstractions.* 2 Absent-mindedness. 3 An abstract work of art, such as a drawing, painting, or sculpture.

ab·struse [ab·stro͞os′] *adj.* Hard to understand.

ab·surd [ab·sûrd′ *or* ab·zûrd′] *adj.* Unreasonable; ridiculous: What an *absurd* tale!; The hat looks *absurd* on the dog. **—ab·surd′ly** *adv.*

ab·surd·i·ty [ab·sûr′də·tē *or* ab·zûr′də·tē] *n., pl.* **ab·surd·i·ties** 1 Foolishness; stupidity; nonsense. 2 Something absurd, as a statement or action.

a·bun·dance [ə·bun′dəns] *n.* A full or plentiful supply; more than enough.

a·bun·dant [ə·bun′dənt] *adj.* 1 Existing in plentiful supply; ample. 2 Rich; abounding: marshes *abundant* in wildfowl. **—a·bun′dant·ly** *adv.*

a·buse [*v.* ə·byo͞oz′, *n.* ə·byo͞os′] *v.* **a·bused, a·bus·ing,** *n.* 1 *v.* To make wrong or improper use of: to *abuse* a privilege. 2 *n.* A wrong or improper use. 3 *v.* To treat harshly or cruelly. 4 *v.* To talk to or of harshly or scornfully. 5 *n.* Harsh or cruel treatment or words. 6 *n.* Something improper or harmful, as a practice or habit.

a·bu·sive [ə·byo͞o′siv] *adj.* 1 Cruel or harsh: *abusive* treatment. 2 Harsh or insulting; scolding: *abusive* words. **—a·bu′sive·ly** *adv.*

a·but [ə·but′] *v.* **a·but·ted, a·but·ting** To end or border: Our lot *abuts* on the park.

a·but·ment [ə·but′mənt] *n.* A supporting structure for an arch or the end of a structure such as a bridge or wall.

a·bys·mal [ə·biz′məl] *adj.* Too deep to measure; bottomless; immeasurable: *abysmal* stupidity. **—a·bys′mal·ly** *adv.*

a·byss [ə·bis′] *n.* 1 A bottomless space, as a crack in the earth; chasm. 2 The lowest depth, too deep to measure: an *abyss* of shame.

Abutments

ac, a.c., AC, or **A.C.** alternating current.

Ac The symbol for the element actinium.

a·ca·cia [ə·kā′shə] *n.* 1 A tree or shrub found in warm regions, having feathery leaves and small, usually yellow flowers. 2 The locust tree.

ac·a·dem·ic [ak′ə·dem′ik] *adj.* 1 Of or having to do with schools, colleges, or studies; scholarly. 2 *U.S.* Having to do with general or liberal rather than technical education. 3 Having little or no practical use; theoretical: It is *academic* to discuss the distant future. **—ac′a·dem′i·cal·ly** *adv.*

a·cad·e·my [ə·kad′ə·mē] *n., pl.* **a·cad·e·mies** 1 A private high school or preparatory school. 2 A school for a particular field of study: a military *academy.* 3 An association of learned people working to promote the arts or sciences.

A·ca·di·an [ə·kā′dē·ən] 1 *adj.* Of Acadia, its people, or their French dialect. 2 *n.* One of the early French settlers of Acadia in eastern Canada, or a descendant of these settlers.

a·can·thus [ə·kan′thəs] *n., pl.* **a·can·thus·es** or **a·can·thi** [ə·kan′thī′] 1 A plant native to southern Europe, having large, segmented, spiny leaves and clustered flowers. 2 A decorative design representing the leaf of this plant, found especially on the capitals of Corinthian columns.

a cap·pel·la [ä′kə·pel′ə] Sung without instrumental accompaniment.

acc. 1 account. 2 accountant. 3 accusative.

ac·cede [ak·sēd′] *v.* **ac·ced·ed, ac·ced·ing** 1 To give consent or agreement; say yes: to *accede* to a plea. 2 To come or enter, as to a high office: to *accede* to the throne.

ac·cel·er·an·do [ak·sel′ə·rän′dō] *adj., adv., n., pl.* **ac·cel·er·an·dos** 1 *adj.* In music, gradually faster. 2 *adv.* Gradually faster. 3 *n.* A gradual speeding up of tempo.

ac·cel·er·ate [ak·sel′ə·rāt′] *v.* **ac·cel·er·at·ed, ac·cel·er·at·ing** 1 To increase speed or the speed of: The car *accelerated.* 2 To cause to happen sooner: Using zip codes *accelerates* delivery. 3 To undergo or cause to undergo acceleration.

ac·cel·er·a·tion [ak·sel′ə·rā′shən] *n.* 1 An increase in speed or velocity. 2 Any change in velocity. 3 The rate of such change at any instant.

ac·cel·er·a·tor [ak·sel′ə·rā′tər] *n.* 1 Something that accelerates, especially a machine that gives very high speeds to atomic particles. 2 The pedal controlling the speed of an automobile engine.

ac·cel·er·om·e·ter [ak·sel′ə·rom′ə·tər] *n.* An instrument that measures the rate at which speed is increasing. ◆ The *accelerometer* should not be confused with the *speedometer,* which measures the speed at which something is moving.

ac·cent [*n.* ak′sent, *v.* ak′sent *or* ak·sent′] 1 *n.* The additional force given to some words or syllables in speech; stress. 2 *v.* To pronounce with force: *Accent* the first syllable of "every." 3 *n.* A mark showing where the stress is located in a word, often (′) for a strong stress and (′) for a weaker one. 4 *v.* To provide with marks showing stressed syllables. 5 *n.* In some languages, a mark placed over or under a letter to show a special pronunciation. 6 *n.* A manner of speaking characteristic of a region or foreign country: a French *accent.* 7 *n.* In music, the stress given to a tone or chord by position, loudness, etc. 8 *n.* Emphasis. 9 *v.* To emphasize: to *accent* the horror of war.

accent mark An accent (def. 3).

ac·cen·tu·ate [ak·sen′cho͞o·āt′] *v.* **ac·cen·tu·at·ed, ac·cen·tu·at·ing** 1 To strengthen the effect of; emphasize; stress: The bareness of the room *accentuated* its size. 2 To mark or pronounce with an accent. **—ac·cen′tu·a′tion** *n.*

ac·cept [ak·sept′] *v.* 1 To take (something offered or given): to *accept* a gift. 2 To agree to; answer with a yes: to *accept* an offer. 3 To receive with warmth, as a person; approve. 4 To take as truth: to *accept* a theory. 5 To adjust to; submit to: to *accept* reality. 6 To agree to, as an offer or invitation. ◆ See EXCEPT.

ac·cept·a·ble [ak·sep′tə·bəl] *adj.* Good enough to be accepted; pleasing; welcome. 2 Capable of being tolerated; bearable: an *acceptable* noise level. **—ac·cept′a·bil′i·ty** *n.* **—ac·cept′a·bly** *adv.*

ac·cep·tance [ak·sep′təns] *n.* 1 The act of accepting: The union's *acceptance* of the wage offer ended the strike. 2 The condition of being accepted. 3 Recognition or approval.

ac·cept·ed [ak·sep′tid] *adj.* 1 Generally believed: an *accepted* scientific theory. 2 Generally approved, recognized, or used: The kilometer is an *accepted* unit of length.

ac·cess [ak′ses] 1 *n.* The opportunity to approach, get, or enter: *access* to court records. 2 *n.* A means of entrance; passage; path. 3 *v* To enter, control, or use information in a computer.

ac·ces·si·ble [ak·ses′ə·bəl] *adj.* 1 Possible to reach; obtainable. 2 Easily reached or got at. **—ac·ces′si·bil′i·ty** *n.*

ac·ces·sion [ak·sesh′ən] *n.* 1 An attaining of an office, dignity, or right: *accession* to power. 2 An increase by something added: an *accession* of land. 3 An addition, as a book to a library.

ac·ces·so·ry [ak·ses′ə·rē] *n., pl.* **ac·ces·so·ries,** *adj.* 1 *n.* Something added for looks, comfort, or convenience, as a belt, gloves, and hat to go with a uniform. 2 *adj.* Added to a main thing; helping: an *accessory* benefit. 3 *n.* A person who knowingly helps or encourages another to commit a crime, or who helps or hides the criminal after the crime.

access time 1 The time a computer takes to find information and move it from a storage area. 2 The time a computer takes to move information it is given to a storage area.

ac·ci·dent [ak′sə·dənt] *n.* 1 Something that happens unexpectedly or without plan or design. 2 An unlucky event that causes damage or harm, such as a collision or fall. 3 Chance luck: It happened by *accident.*

An automobile accident

ac·ci·den·tal [ak′sə·den′təl] 1 *adj.* Occurring unexpectedly and without plan; chance. 2 *n.* In music, a sharp, flat, or natural that applies in only one measure. **—ac′ci·den′tal·ly** *adv.*

a add	**i** it	**o͝o** took	**oi** oil
ā ace	**ī** ice	**o͞o** pool	**ou** pout
â care	**o** odd	**u** up	**ng** ring
ä palm	**ō** open	**û** burn	**th** thin
e end	**ô** order	**yo͞o** fuse	**t̶h̶** this
ē equal			**zh** vision

ə = { a in *above* e in *sicken* i in *possible*
o in *melon* u in *circus* }

ac·claim [ə·klām′] 1 *v.* To hail and declare by acclamation: They *acclaimed* Pat the winner. 2 *v.* To show approval of; applaud: They *acclaimed* the plan. 3 *n.* Praise; applause; approval.

ac·cla·ma·tion [ak′lə·mā′shən] *n.* 1 A shout or some other indication of general approval or welcome: to vote by *acclamation.* 2 Acclaim or the act of acclaiming.

ac·cli·mate [ak′lə·māt′ *or* e·klī′mit] *v.* **ac·cli·mat·ed, ac·cli·mat·ing** To adapt or become adapted to new surroundings or a new climate: The plant *acclimated* to cold weather.

ac·cli·ma·tize [ə·klī′mə·tīz′] *v.* **ac·cli·ma·tized, ac·cli·ma·tiz·ing** To acclimate. **—ac·cli′ma·ti·za′tion** *n.*

ac·co·lade [ak′ə·lād′] *n.* 1 A light blow on the shoulder with the flat side of a sword, given during the ceremony of knighthood. 2 Any great honor or praise.

ac·com·mo·date [ə·kom′ə·dāt′] *v.* **ac·com·mo·dat·ed, ac·com·mo·dat·ing** 1 To hold comfortably; be suitable for: The cage *accommodates* two birds. 2 To provide for; lodge: to *accommodate* a guest. 3 To do a favor for; help. 4 To change so as to be fit; acclimate; adjust: to *accommodate* oneself to a new climate.

ac·com·mo·dat·ing [ə·kom′ə·dā′ting] *adj.* Helpful and eager to please; obliging; willing.

ac·com·mo·da·tion [ə·kom′ə·dā′shən] *n.* 1 An adjustment. 2 Anything that supplies a need; convenience. 3 (*usually pl.*) *U.S.* Room and board; lodgings. 4 A compromise or agreement: The two sides made an *accommodation.* 5 A favor; good turn. 6 Willingness to help or oblige.

ac·com·pa·ni·ment [ə·kum′pə·ni·mənt] *n.* 1 Something going along with something else: rice with beans as an *accompaniment.* 2 Music played or sung along with the main part to enrich and support it.

ac·com·pa·nist [ə·kum′pə·nist] *n.* A person, usually a pianist, who plays accompaniments.

ac·com·pa·ny [ə·kum′pə·nē] *v.* **ac·com·pa·nied, ac·com·pa·ny·ing** 1 To come or go along with; escort: *Accompany* me home. 2 To happen or occur with: Lightning *accompanied* the thunder. 3 To play a musical accompaniment to or for.

ac·com·plice [ə·kom′plis] *n.* A helper or partner in committing a crime.

ac·com·plish [ə·kom′plish] *v.* 1 To carry out; effect: to *accomplish* a change. 2 To finish.

ac·com·plished [ə·kom′plisht] *adj.* 1 Completed; effected: an *accomplished* fact. 2 Skillful, as in an art or in social graces; well-trained.

ac·com·plish·ment [ə·kom′plish·mənt] *n.* 1 The act of accomplishing; completion. 2 Something done or completed; achievement. 3 A skill or ability, especially a social grace.

ac·cord [ə·kôrd′] 1 *v.* To give as due or earned; grant: *Accord* honor to the winner. 2 *v.* To be or cause to be in agreement: to *accord* with the facts. 3 *n.* A state of agreement or concord; harmony: After discussion they reached an *accord.* **—of one's own accord** By one's own choice; voluntarily.

ac·cord·ance [ə·kôr′dəns] *n.* Agreement, especially in the expression **in accordance with.**

ac·cord·ing [ə·kôr′ding] *adj.* In accord or agreement; harmonizing. **—according to** 1 As told by or in: *according to* the book. 2 In agreement with: *according to* law. 3 In proportion or relation to: to dress *according to* the season.

ac·cord·ing·ly [ə·kôr′ding·lē] *adv.* 1 In a fitting manner: Seeing danger, she acted *accordingly.* 2 Therefore; thus; so.

ac·cor·di·on [ə·kôr′dē·ən] 1 *n.* A portable musical instrument in which wind from a bellows, controlled by keys or buttons, causes metal reeds to sound. 2 *adj.* Looking like the folds in the bellows of an accordion: *accordion* pleats.

Accordion

ac·cost [ə·kôst′ *or* ə·kost′] *v.* To stop and speak to; speak to first: A stranger *accosted* him.

ac·count [ə·kount′] 1 *v.* To hold to be; consider: I *account* that a lie. 2 *n.* A statement, narrative, or explanation. 3 *n.* A record of money paid out, received, or owing. 4 *n.* Worth; importance: That shirt is of no *account.* **—account for** 1 To give an explanation of: Shooting stars are easy to *account for.* 2 To be responsible for; answer for: to *account* for a decision. **—call to account** To insist on an explanation from: The editor was *called to account* for the errors. **—on account of** Because of; for the sake of: The airport was closed *on account of* fog. **—on no account** Under no conditions; never. **—on one's account** For one's sake: Don't go to any trouble *on my account.* **—take into account** or **take account of** To make allowance for; take into consideration. **—turn to account** To use to get profit or advantage.

ac·count·a·ble [ə·kount′ə·bəl] *adj.* 1 Liable to be called to account; responsible: to be *accountable* for damage. 2 Capable of being explained. **—ac·count·bil·i·ty** [ə·kount′ə·bil′ə·tē] *n.*

ac·count·ant [ə·koun′tənt] *n.* A person whose work is to keep or go over records of money received or paid out: My *accountant* figures my income tax.

ac·count·ing [ə·koun′ting] *n.* 1 The practice or methods of recording financial dealings. 2 A statement or examination, as of finances.

ac·cou·ter [ə·ko͞o′tər] *v.* To provide with clothing or equipment; outfit.

ac·cou·ter·ments [ə·ko͞o′tər·mənts] *n.pl.* 1 The equipment of a soldier except for weapons and uniforms. 2 Trappings; outfit.

ac·cou·tre [ə·ko͞o′tər] *v.* **ac·cou·tred, ac·cou·tring** Another spelling of ACCOUTER.

ac·cou·tre·ments [ə·ko͞o′tər·mənts] *n.pl.* Another spelling of ACCOUTERMENTS.

ac·cred·it [ə·kred′it] *v.* 1 To give official authority or credentials to: to *accredit* an ambassador. 2 To take as true; believe in: to *accredit* a report. 3 To accept as meeting official standards, as a college, school, or hospital.

ac·cre·tion [ə·krē′shən] *n.* 1 Growth or increase, especially by external addition or accumulation. 2 An increase or addition; something additional.

ac·cru·al [ə·kro͞o′əl] *n.* 1 The process of accruing; accumulation: the *accrual* of interest in a bank. 2 Something that accrues or the amount accrued.

ac·crue [ə·kro͞o′] *v.* **ac·crued, ac·cru·ing** To come about as a natural growth, addition, or result; accumulate: Interest *accrues* rapidly.

acct. 1 account. 2 accountant.

ac·cu·mu·late [ə·kyo͞om′yə·lāt′] *v.* **ac·cu·mu·lat·ed, ac·cu·mu·lat·ing** To heap or pile up; gather together; collect.

ac·cu·mu·la·tion [ə·kyo͞om′yə·lā′shən] *n.* 1 Material gathered together. 2 A collecting or gathering together.

ac·cu·ra·cy [ak′yər·ə·sē] *n.* Freedom from all errors or mistakes; exactness; precision.
ac·cu·rate [ak′yər·it] *adj.* Having or making no error; exact; true. **—ac′cu·rate·ly** *adv.*
ac·curs·ed [ə·kûr′sid *or* ə·kûrst′] *adj.* **1** Deserving a curse; damnable. **2** Cursed; doomed.
accus. accusative.
ac·cu·sa·tion [ak′yōō·zā′shən] *n.* **1** A charge of having done something wrong or illegal or of being something bad. **2** The offense charged.
ac·cu·sa·tive [ə·kyōō′zə·tiv] **1** *adj.* In grammar, showing a direct object or a word agreeing with one. *Him, them,* and *whom* are in the accusative, or objective, case. **2** *n.* The accusative case. **3** *n.* A word in this case.
ac·cuse [ə·kyōōz′] *v.* **ac·cused, ac·cus·ing** To charge with having done something wrong or illegal or with being bad. **—ac·cus′er** *n.*
ac·cused [ə·kyōōzd′] *n., pl.* **accused** A person charged with an offense, especially the defendant in a criminal case.
ac·cus·tom [ə·kus′təm] *v.* To make familiar or adapted by habit: to *accustom* oneself to noise.
ac·cus·tomed [ə·kus′təmd] *adj.* Habitual; usual. **—accustomed to** In the habit of; used to.
ace [ās] *n., adj., v.* **aced, ac·ing** **1** *n.* A single spot, as on a playing card, domino, etc. **2** *n.* A playing card, etc., marked with a single spot. **3** *n.* A person who is an expert at something. **4** *adj.* Expert: an *ace* ballplayer. **5** *n.* In tennis, etc., a point won by a single stroke. **6** *v. slang* To earn an A on: She *aced* the physics test. **—within an ace of** Very close to; on the brink of: She was *within an ace of* winning when her car broke down.
ac·et·an·i·lide [as′ə·tan′(ə)l·īd] *n.* A crystalline chemical compound used as a drug to reduce fever and pain.
ac·e·tate [as′ə·tāt′] *n.* **1** A chemical compound made from acetic acid, as one of its salts. **2** Cellulose acetate, a compound made from acetic acid and cellulose, used in making rayon.
a·ce·tic [ə·sē′tik] *adj.* Of, containing, or producing acetic acid or vinegar.
acetic acid A weak, sharp-smelling acid that is found in vinegar.
a·cet·y·lene [ə·set′ə·lən *or* ə·set′ə·lēn′] *n.* A colorless gas, burned in air to make light, and with oxygen to produce heat for such processes as welding.
a·ce·tyl·sal·i·cyl·ic acid [ə·sēt′(ə)l·sal′ə·sil′ik] The chemical name for aspirin.
ache [āk] *v.* **ached, ach·ing,** *n.* **1** *v.* To hurt with a dull, steady pain: My eyes *ache.* **2** *n.* A dull, steady pain. **3** *v.* To want very much: I'm *aching* to go.
a·chieve [ə·chēv′] *v.* **a·chieved, a·chiev·ing** **1** To accomplish; do well: Flight was *achieved* in 1903. **2** To get or reach by effort: to *achieve* a goal. **—a·chiev′er** *n.*
a·chieve·ment [ə·chēv′mənt] *n.* **1** Something accomplished; a feat. **2** The act of achieving.
achievement test A test that measures skills acquired in a particular subject or class.
A·chil·les [ə·kil′ēz] *n.* In Greek myths, the greatest Greek hero of the Trojan war, killed by an arrow shot into his right heel, the only place where he could be wounded.
Achilles' heel One's weak point: Spelling has always been my *Achilles' heel.*
Achilles tendon The tendon that joins the calf muscle to the heel bone.
ach·ro·mat·ic [ak′rə·mat′ik] *adj.* **1** In physics, refracting white light without separating it into wavelengths of different colors. **2** In music, of or using a major or minor scale with no accidentals or added tones; diatonic.
ach·y [ā′kē] *adj.* **ach·i·er, ach·i·est** Having an ache or aches. **—ach·i·ness** *n.*
ac·id [as′id] **1** *n.* A chemical compound having a sour taste and the ability to react with a base, forming water and a salt. Acids corrode most metals and some destroy living tissue. **2** *adj.* Of, like, producing, or containing an acid. **3** *adj.* Biting; sharp; bad-tempered. **—ac′id·ly** *adv.*
a·cid·ic [ə·sid′ik] *adj.* Acid (def. 2).
a·cid·i·fy [ə·sid′ə·fī′] *v.* **a·cid·i·fied, a·cid·i·fy·ing** To make or become acid.
a·cid·i·ty [ə·sid′ə·tē] *n.* The state, degree, or quality of being acid: high *acidity.*
acid rain Rain containing high levels of sulfuric and nitric acid. It is caused mainly by smoke from the burning of fossil fuels.
acid test A decisive test of value or quality: The *acid test* of her skill at roping calves will come at the state fair. ◆ *Acid test* comes from the use of nitric acid to test the quality of gold.
ac·knowl·edge [ak·nol′ij] *v.* **ac·knowl·edged, ac·knowl·edg·ing** **1** To admit the truth or reality of: He *acknowledged* the difficulty of the problem. **2** To recognize the authority or claims of: They *acknowledged* Dr. Fielding as their leader. **3** To show that one has received or is thankful for: to *acknowledge* a letter or gift.
ac·knowl·edg·ment [ak·nol′ij·mənt] *n.* **1** The act of acknowledging; recognition; acceptance. **2** Something done or given to show that one has received something or is thankful for something.
ACLU American Civil Liberties Union.
ac·me [ak′mē] *n.* The highest point; peak; summit.
ac·ne [ak′nē] *n.* A skin disease due to clogged oil glands and causing pimples on the face and upper body.
ac·o·lyte [ak′ə·līt′] *n.* A helper or assistant, especially an altar boy who assists at Mass.
ac·o·nite [ak′ə·nīt′] *n.* **1** The monkshood or any of several related plants, some poisonous. **2** A sedative drug obtained from these plants.
a·corn [ā′kôrn] *n.* The fruit of the oak tree, a nut containing a single seed.

Acorn

a·cous·tic [ə·kōōs′tik] *adj.* **1** Of or having to do with sound or hearing. **2** Serving to deaden or absorb sound: *acoustic* tile. **3** Of or being an instrument that does not have electronic modification or amplification: an *acoustic* guitar; an *acoustic* bass. **—a·cous′ti·cal·ly** *adv.*

a	add	**i**	it	**ŏŏ**	took	**oi**	oil
ā	ace	**ī**	ice	**ōō**	pool	**ou**	pout
â	care	**o**	odd	**u**	up	**ng**	ring
ä	palm	**ō**	open	**û**	burn	**th**	thin
e	end	**ô**	order	**yōō**	fuse	**th**	this
ē	equal					**zh**	vision

ə = {a in *above* e in *sicken* i in *possible* / o in *melon* u in *circus*}

a·cous·tics [ə·kōōs′tiks] *n.* 1 The science that deals with sound. 2 The qualities of a room that affect sounds. ◆ See -ICS.
ac·quaint [ə·kwānt′] *v.* 1 To make familiar: to *acquaint* oneself with the facts. 2 To cause to know personally: Are you *acquainted* with her?
ac·quain·tance [ə·kwān′təns] *n.* 1 Personal knowledge of a person or thing. 2 A person with whom one is slightly familiar. **—make someone's acquaintance** To get to know someone.
ac·quain·tance·ship [ə·kwān′təns·ship′] *n.* The condition of being acquainted: Our *acquaintanceship* dated back many years.
ac·qui·esce [ak′wē·es′] *v.* **ac·qui·esced, ac·qui·esc·ing** To give in or consent quietly: to *acquiesce* to a demand; to *acquiesce* in a plan.
ac·qui·es·cent [ak′wē·es′ənt] *adj.* Giving in or consenting quietly. **—ac′qui·es′cence** *n.*
ac·quire [ə·kwīr′] *v.* **ac·quired, ac·quir·ing** To come into possession of; get; obtain: to *acquire* wealth; to *acquire* fluency in a foreign language.
ac·quire·ment [ə·kwīr′mənt] *n.* 1 The act of acquiring. 2 Something acquired, especially a skill or ability gained after much effort.
ac·qui·si·tion [ak′wə·zish′ən] *n.* 1 The act of acquiring. 2 Something that is acquired.
ac·quis·i·tive [ə·kwiz′ə·tiv] *adj.* Anxious to acquire things. **—ac·quis′i·tive·ness** *n.*
ac·quit [ə·kwit′] *v.* **ac·quit·ted, ac·quit·ting** 1 To free from blame; declare not guilty: to be *acquitted* of a crime. 2 To conduct (oneself); do one's part.
ac·quit·tal [ə·kwit′(ə)l] *n.* A setting free from a criminal charge by a verdict of not guilty.
a·cre [ā′kər] *n.* 1 A measure of area equal to 43,560 square feet. 2 (*pl.*) Lands; estate: Our country *acres* give us great pleasure. 3 (*pl.*) *informal* A great quantity or expanse: *acres* of parking space. ◆ This word comes from an Old English word meaning *field.*
a·cre·age [ā′kər·ij] *n.* The number of acres in an area: The campus has an *acreage* of 400.
ac·rid [ak′rid] *adj.* 1 Burning; bitter; irritating, as a taste or odor. 2 Sharp; biting; acid, as a remark.
ac·ri·mo·ni·ous [ak′rə·mō′nē·əs] *adj.* Full of bitterness and hard feelings; sharp; caustic.
ac·ri·mo·ny [ak′rə·mō′nē] *n.* Bitterness or hard feeling, especially in speech or manner.
ac·ro·bat [ak′rə·bat′] *n.* A person skilled in tumbling, stunts on a trapeze, rings, or other equipment.

Acrobats

ac·ro·bat·ic [ak′rə·bat′ik] *n.* Of or like an acrobat: an *acrobatic* stunt. **—ac′ro·bat′i·cal·ly** *adv.*
ac·ro·bat·ics [ak′rə·bat′iks] *n.pl.* Stunts performed by or as if by an acrobat; gymnastics. ◆ See -ICS.
ac·ro·nym [ak′rə·nim′] A word made by combining the first letter or letters of a series of other words. **—ac′ro·nym′ic** *adj.* ◆ See ABBREVIATION.
a·crop·o·lis [ə·krop′ə·lis] *n.* 1 A high part of an ancient Greek city, fortified in case of attack. 2 (*written* **Acropolis**) The high, fortified part of ancient Athens.
a·cross [ə·krôs′ *or* ə·kros′] 1 *adv.* From one side to the other: five feet *across.* 2 *adv.* On or at the other side: We soon will be *across.* 3 *prep.* On the other side of; beyond. 4 *prep.* From one side or part of to the other: to ride *across* a field. 5 *prep.* So as to meet or happen on: to come *across* a lost glove.
a·cros·tic [ə·krôs′tik] *n.* 1 A poem or series of written lines in which the first or last letters of each line, when read from top to bottom, form a word or words. 2 Another word for WORD SQUARE.
act [akt] 1 *n.* Something done; deed; action. 2 *n.* A process; activity: in the *act* of eating. 3 *v.* To do something; function; perform: to *act* in an emergency. 4 *v.* To behave; acquit oneself: to *act* bravely. 5 *n.* A pretense; sham: The child's shyness was an *act.* 6 *v.* To pretend; make believe: She's only *acting.* 7 *v.* To imitate; behave like: Don't *act* the fool. 8 *v.* To perform, as in a drama or play: to *act* Hamlet. 9 *n.* A large division of a play or opera. 10 *n.* One of a number of performances on a program: a comedy *act.* 11 *v.* To have an effect: Sunlight *acts* on plants. 12 *n.* A law; statute: an *act* of the legislature. **—act as** To function in particular way: to *act as* a control. **—act for** To substitute for; work on behalf of. **—act on** To do something because of: to *act on* someone's advice. **—act up** *informal* To behave mischievously or playfully.
ACT 1 Action for Children's Television. 2 American College Test.
ACTH A hormone from the pituitary gland that causes the adrenal glands to produce cortisone. ACTH from hogs makes human beings produce cortisone.
act·ing [ak′ting] 1 *adj.* Holding office temporarily or in someone's place: the *acting* mayor. 2 *n.* The occupation, performance, or art of an actor.
ac·tin·ic [ak·tin′ik] *adj.* Of, involving, or having actinism.
actinic ray A form of radiation, as an ultraviolet ray or an X ray, that produces chemical changes in a substance upon which it falls or is directed, as in photography.
ac·ti·nism [ak′tə·niz′əm] The capability of electromagnetic radiation to cause chemical changes.
ac·tin·i·um [ak·tin′ē·əm] *n.* A radioactive metallic element found in association with uranium in pitchblende.
ac·tion [ak′shən] *n.* 1 The process of acting, doing, or working. 2 A deed; act. 3 (*pl.*) Habitual behavior; conduct: the *actions* of an idiot. 4 Vigor; energy; initiative: a man of *action.* 5 Influence: the *action* of sunlight on colors. 6 The way a mechanism moves or works: The spring's *action* is fast. 7 A battle; combat: killed in *action.* 8 A lawsuit. **—take action** 1 To start to do something; begin to operate. 2 To start a lawsuit.
ac·ti·vate [ak′tə·vāt′] *v.* **ac·ti·vat·ed, ac·ti·vat·ing** 1 To make active. 2 To cause or speed up a chemical reaction. 3 To cause to become radioactive. **—ac′ti·va′tion** *n.*
ac·tive [ak′tiv] 1 *adj.* Showing action; busy: an *active* person. 2 *adj.* Working; in action: an *active* volcano. 3 *adj.* In grammar, being or of the voice indicating that a verb expresses an action performed by its subject. In the sentence "I threw the ball" *threw* is active. 4 *n.* The form of a verb that is active; active voice. **—ac′tive·ly** *adv.*
active duty Full-time military service.
ac·tiv·ist [ak′tə·vist] *n.* A person who participates in public action in support of a cause.

ac·tiv·i·ty [ak·tiv′ə·tē] *n., pl.* **ac·tiv·i·ties** 1 The state of being active; action; movement. 2 An action: the *activities* of the chef in the kitchen. 3 An occupation or pastime.

act of God An event, such as an earthquake or a hurricane, that is caused by natural forces and cannot be prevented or foreseen.

ac·tor [ak′tər] *n.* 1 A person who performs, as in plays or motion pictures or on television. 2 A person who acts; doer.

ac·tress [ak′tris] *n.* A woman who performs, as in plays or motion pictures or on television.

Acts of the Apostles The fifth book of the New Testament, relating the beginnings of the Christian church.

ac·tu·al [ak′cho͞o·əl] *adj.* Existing in fact; real.

ac·tu·al·i·ty [ak′cho͞o·al′ə·tē] *n.* The condition of being actual; reality.

ac·tu·al·ly [ak′cho͞o·əl·ē] *adv.* As a matter of fact; really: The bear *actually* walked on its hind legs.

ac·tu·ate [ak′cho͞o·āt′] *v.* **ac·tu·at·ed, ac·tu·at·ing** 1 To put into action: valves *actuated* by cams. 2 To impel to act: He was *actuated* by honor.

a·cu·men [ə·kyo͞o′mən] *n.* Quickness and sharpness of mind; shrewdness: business *acumen.*

ac·u·punc·ture [ak′yo͞o·pungk′chər] *n.* The practice of inserting needles into the body at specific points to relieve pain, cure illness, or induce anesthesia. It is part of traditional Chinese medicine.

a·cute [ə·kyo͞ot′] *adj.* 1 Coming to a sharp point. 2 Reaching a crisis quickly; severe, as a disease. 3 Sharp; intense: *acute* pain. 4 Extremely important; critical; grave: *acute* problems. 5 Very perceptive or sensitive; keen: an *acute* ear. 6 High in pitch; shrill. **—a·cute′ly** *adv.* **—a·cute′ness** *n.*

acute accent A mark (′) used in some languages over a vowel to show its length or quality or to show stress.

acute angle An angle of less than 90 degrees.

ad [ad] *n. informal* An advertisement.

A.D. anno Domini. ◆ *Anno Domini* is a Latin phrase meaning *in the year of [our] Lord.* It indicates dates after the birth of Christ.

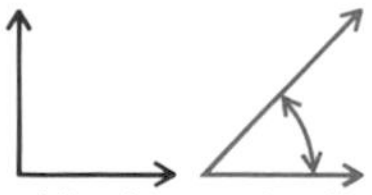

right angle acute angle

ADA 1 American Dental Association. 2 Americans for Democratic Action.

ad·age [ad′ij] *n.* An old, much-used saying generally thought to be true; proverb: "Out of sight, out of mind" is an *adage.*

a·da·gio [ə·dä′jō *or* ə·dä′zhē·ō] *adj., adv., n., pl.* **a·da·gios** 1 *adj.* In music, slow. 2 *adv.* Slowly. 3 *n.* A piece or section of music in an adagio tempo.

Ad·am [ad′əm] *n.* In the Bible, the first man.

ad·a·mant [ad′ə·mənt] 1 *n.* A stone or material too hard to be broken. 2 *adj.* Unyielding; stubborn.

Ad·am's apple [ad′əmz] A lump at the front of the throat, formed by the thyroid cartilage, often prominent in men.

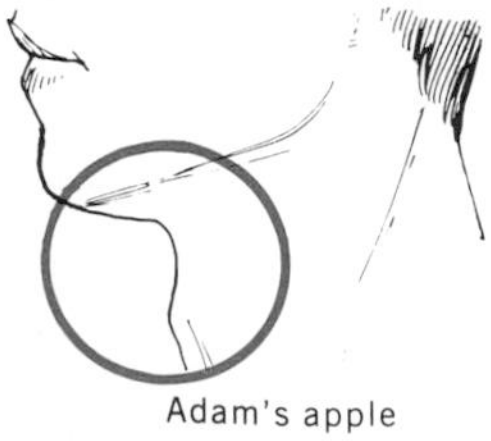

Adam's apple

a·dapt [ə·dapt′] *v.* 1 To change and make suitable for a new use: to *adapt* a play for television. 2 To adjust to certain conditions: The polar bear has *adapted* itself to the Arctic climate; the effort to *adapt* to a new employer.

a·dapt·a·ble [ə·dap′tə·bəl] *adj.* Changed or changing easily to fit conditions. **—a·dapt′a·bil′i·ty** *n.*

ad·ap·ta·tion [ad′əp·tā′shən] *n.* 1 A change made or the process of changing, so as to fit or meet new conditions, uses, or surroundings. 2 Something made by adapting: The play is an *adaptation* of the book.

a·dapt·er or **a·dap·tor** [ə·dap′tər] *n.* 1 Someone or something that adapts. 2 A device used to connect two pieces of equipment in such a way that they can operate together. 3 A device that modifies a piece of equipment for a new use.

a·dap·tive [ə·dap′tiv] *adj.* Capable of, tending toward, or resulting from adaptation: *adaptive* organisms; *adaptive* color changes in butterflies.

add [ad] *v.* 1 To find a number equal to (two or more other numbers taken together). 2 To put on or in so as to change size, characteristics, etc.: to *add* a room to a house; to *add* sugar to a dessert. 3 To say further: "Don't be late," I *added.* **—add to** To increase; make larger. **—add up to** 1 To make a total of: Five and five *add up to* ten. 2 To combine to signify; mean: The facts *add up to* a vindication of the accused.

ad·dend [ad′ənd *or* ə·dend′] *n.* A number that is added or to be added.

ad·den·dum [ə·den′dəm] *n., pl.* **ad·den·da** [ə·den′də] Something that is added; an appendix or supplement: an *addendum* to a book.

ad·der [ad′ər] *n.* 1 A small, poisonous, European snake; viper. 2 A small, nonpoisonous North American snake. ◆ This word was originally *nadder,* but people saying *a nadder* began to attach the *n* to the article, not the noun, which became *an adder.*

ad·dict [*n.* ad′ikt, *v.* ə·dikt′] 1 *n.* A person who feels a strong, uncontrollable need to take a harmful substance, especially a narcotic drug. 2 *v.* To cause to feel such a need: Continued use of sleeping pills can *addict* one. 3 *n.* A devoted user or enjoyer of something who would find it hard to quit: a television *addict.*

ad·dict·ed [ə·dik′tid] *adj.* 1 Uncontrollably dependent on something, especially a narcotic drug. 2 Devoted, as to a habit or activity: *addicted* to card playing.

ad·dic·tion [ə·dik′shən] *n.* The condition of being addicted, especially to a harmful substance; uncontrollable dependence.

ad·dic·tive [ə·dik′tiv] *adj.* Leading to addiction; habit-forming.

adding machine A machine, having a keyboard, that can perform addition and sometimes subtraction, multiplication, and division.

ad·di·tion [ə·dish′ən] *n.* 1 The act or process of adding: the *addition* of several numbers. 2 Something that is added; an annex. **—in addition** or **in addition to** Besides; also. ◆ *Addition,* something

a	add	**i**	it	**o͝o**	took	**oi**	oil
ā	ace	**ī**	ice	**o͞o**	pool	**ou**	pout
â	care	**o**	odd	**u**	up	**ng**	ring
ä	palm	**ō**	open	**û**	burn	**th**	thin
e	end	**ô**	order	**yo͞o**	fuse	**th**	this
ē	equal					**zh**	vision

ə = {a in *above* e in *sicken* i in *possible* / o in *melon* u in *circus*}

added, and *edition,* something published, are sometimes confused. *Addition* is from the Latin word *addere,* meaning *to give to,* while *edition* is from Latin *edere,* meaning *to give out.*

ad·di·tion·al [ə·dish′ən·əl] *adj.* Added or to be added; extra. **—ad·di′tion·al·ly** *adv.*

ad·di·tive [ad′ə·tiv] **1** *adj.* Involving, characterized by, or produced by addition: an *additive* process. **2** *n.* A substance added in small quantities to improve a product in some way: *Additives* make gasoline burn better. **—ad′di·tive·ly** *adv.*

additive identity Zero, the number that leaves another number unchanged when added to it.

additive inverse Either of a pair of numbers whose sum is zero: The number 2 is the *additive inverse* of the number −2.

ad·dle [ad′(ə)l] *v.* **ad·dled, ad·dling** **1** To become or cause to become confused or muddled. **2** To become rotten; spoil, as eggs.

ad·dle·brained [ad′(ə)l·brānd′] *adj.* Having a confused or muddled brain.

ad·dress [ə·dres′] **1** *v.* To speak to or deliver a speech to: The speaker *addressed* the audience. **2** *n.* A speech. **3** *n.* [*also* ad′res] The writing on an envelope or package telling where it is to go, or the place thus indicated. **4** *v.* To write on (as a letter or package) where it is to go. **5** *v.* To direct or send: to *address* a plea. **6** *v.* To direct the force or attention of (oneself): Let us *address* ourselves to the problem. **7** *n.* A label, as a number or character, that identifies the exact place in computer memory where a piece of information is stored.

ad·dress·ee [ad′res·ē′] *n.* The person to whom something (as mail or a package) is addressed.

ad·duce [ə·d(y)o͞os′] *v.* **ad·duced, ad·duc·ing** To offer as proof or as an example.

-ade A suffix meaning: **1** The act or action of, as in *blockade.* **2** A sweet drink made with a particular fruit, as in *lemonade.*

ad·e·noid·al [ad′ə·noid′(ə)l] *adj.* **1** Of or relating to the adenoids. **2** Having a nasal or constricted tone: an *adenoidal* speaking voice.

ad·e·noids [ad′ə·noidz] *n.pl.* Growths of glandular tissue in the passage from the nose to the throat. When swollen they make breathing and speaking difficult.

a·dept [ə·dept′] **1** *adj.* Skillful; adroit: *adept* at tennis. **2** [*also* ad′ept] *n.* A person highly skilled or expert. **—a·dept′ly** *adv.* **—a·dept′ness** *n.*

ad·e·qua·cy [ad′ə·kwə·sē] *n.* The state or quality of being sufficient or good enough.

ad·e·quate [ad′ə·kwit] *adj.* Equal to what is needed; good enough or sufficient: *adequate* food for the dinner. **—ad′e·quate·ly** *adv.* **—ad′e·quate·ness** *n.*

ad·here [ad·hir′] *v.* **ad·hered, ad·her·ing** **1** To stick fast or stick together: Gum makes a stamp *adhere.* **2** To hold or remain devoted: to *adhere* to one's principles. **3** To follow closely: to *adhere* to a plan.

ad·her·ence [ad·hir′əns] *n.* The act or state of adhering; attachment; faithfulness.

ad·her·ent [ad·hir′ənt] **1** *n.* A loyal supporter; faithful follower. **2** *adj.* Sticking tightly; firmly attached.

ad·he·sion [ad·hē′zhən] *n.* **1** A sticking together. **2** Firm attachment, as to a cause.

ad·he·sive [ad·hē′siv] **1** *adj.* Designed or tending to stick fast; sticky: I used *adhesive* paper to cover my shelves. **2** *n.* An adhesive substance, as glue. **—ad·he′sive·ly** *adv.* **—ad·he′sive·ness** *n.*

adhesive tape A tape that is covered on one side with a sticky substance. It is used to hold bandages in place.

ad hoc [ad hok′] For a particular purpose or situation: an *ad hoc* committee to investigate pollution of the town's water supply. ◆ This Latin phrase literally means *for this.*

a·dieu [ə·d(y)o͞o′] *interj., n., pl.* **a·dieus** or **a·dieux** [ə·d(y)o͞oz′] Good-by.

ad in·fi·ni·tum [ad in′fə·nī′təm] A Latin phrase meaning: To infinity; without stopping; endlessly: The speaker talked *ad infinitum.*

a·di·os [ä′dē·ōs′ *or* ad′ē·ōs′] *interj.* Good-by.

ad·i·pose [ad′ə·pōs] *adj.* Of or having to do with animal fat; fatty: *adipose* tissue.

adj. **1** adjective. **2** adjectival. **3** (*also written* **Adj.**) adjutant.

ad·ja·cent [ə·jā′sənt] *adj.* Lying near or close by; adjoining: *adjacent* countries.

adjacent angle Either of two angles that have the same vertex, a side in common, and their second rays on opposite sides of the common ray.

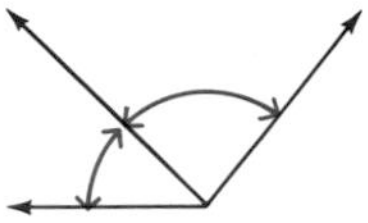

Adjacent angles

ad·jec·ti·val [aj′ik·tī′vəl] *adj.* Having to do with or used as an adjective. **—ad′jec·ti′val·ly** *adv.*

ad·jec·tive [aj′ik·tiv] *n.* A word that is used to modify a noun or pronoun. In the sentences "The black jacket is Don's" and "The brown one is mine" *black* and *brown* are adjectives.

ad·join [ə·join′] *v.* **1** To be next to; border on: Our yard *adjoins* our neighbor's lawn. **2** To be close together or in contact: The two houses *adjoin.*

ad·journ [ə·jûrn′] *v.* **1** To stop with the intention of beginning again later, as a meeting: The court was *adjourned.* **2** To reach the end of a session or time of meeting: The legislature *adjourned* for the year.

ad·journ·ment [ə·jûrn′mənt] *n.* **1** The act or process of adjourning or the state of being adjourned. **2** A period of time during which a court, legislature, or other official body is not in session.

ad·judge [ə·juj′] *v.* **ad·judged, ad·judg·ing** **1** To determine or declare, especially legally or formally: The defendant was *adjudged* insane. **2** To award by law. **3** To consider; deem.

ad·ju·di·cate [ad·jo͞o′di·kāt′] *v.* **ad·ju·di·cat·ed, ad·ju·di·cat·ing** To consider and settle (a case) according to judicial procedures.

ad·junct [aj′ungkt] *n.* Something added to a main thing, less important and not needed, but helpful.

ad·jure [ə·jo͝or′] *v.* **ad·jured, ad·jur·ing** **1** To ask earnestly; entreat: They *adjured* the children to be careful. **2** To command or charge solemnly. **—ad′ju·ra′tion** *n.*

ad·just [ə·just′] *v.* **1** To arrange so as to fit or match: to *adjust* stirrups for a tall rider. **2** To regulate for a desired result: to *adjust* a thermostat. **3** To arrange in a satisfactory way; settle: to *adjust* a claim for insurance. **4** To adapt oneself; get accustomed: to *adjust* to the climate. **—ad·just′ive** *adj.*

ad·just·a·ble [ə·jus′tə·bəl] *adj.* Capable of being changed or regulated: an *adjustable* focus. **—ad·just′a·bly** *adv.*

ad·just·er or **ad·jus·tor** [ə·jus′tər] *n.* **1** A person who adjusts, especially one who adjusts insurance claims. **2** Any device that is used to make adjustments.

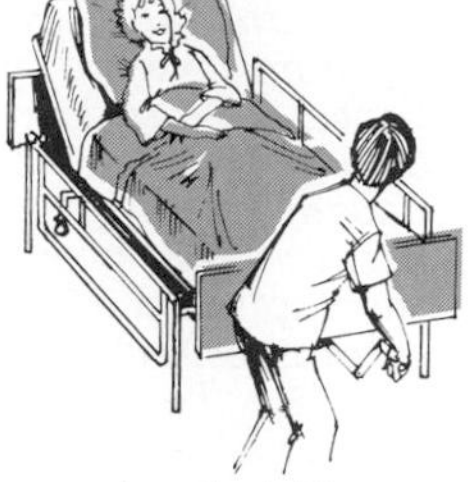

An adjustable hospital bed

ad·just·ment [ə·just′mənt] *n.* **1** The act or process of adjusting or the state of being adjusted; regulation; arrangement. **2** A means of adjusting; a control. **3** A settlement or reconciling, as of a disagreement, claim, or debt.

ad·ju·tant [aj′o͞o·tənt] *n.* An officer who helps a commanding officer by such duties as preparing orders, writing letters, and keeping records.

adjutant stork Another word for MARABOU (def. 1).

ad-lib [ad′lib′] *v.* **ad-libbed, ad-lib·bing,** *n. informal* **1** To make up (as lines or music) on the spot. **2** *n.* Something, as lines or music, made up on the spot. **—ad-lib′ber** *n.*

adm. or **Adm.** admiral.

ad·min·is·ter [ad·min′is·tər] *v.* **1** To be in charge of; manage: The committee *administers* the hospital. **2** To give, as a medicine: to *administer* aspirin for a headache. **3** To give out, as a punishment: to *administer* the death penalty. **4** To give, as an oath or sacrament: to *administer* baptism. **5** To be of service: to *administer* to the poor.

ad·min·is·trate [ad·min′ə·strāt′] *v.* **ad·min·is·trat·ed, ad·min·is·trat·ing** To administer.

ad·min·is·tra·tion [ad·min′is·trā′shən] *n.* **1** The managing of, as a business, bureau, or office. **2** (*sometimes written* **Administration**) A group of people in charge of a government, especially, in the U.S., the President and the Cabinet. **3** The term of office of a government official: The Civil War began during Lincoln's *administration.* **4** A group of people who manage something: the school *administration.*

ad·min·is·tra·tive [ad·min′is·trā′tiv] *adj.* Having to do with administration; executive: the *administrative* department. **—ad·min′is·tra′tive·ly** *adv.*

ad·min·is·tra·tor [ad·min′is·trā′tər] *n.* **1** A person who administers something; executive; manager. **2** A person selected by a court to manage the estate of a dead person.

ad·mi·ra·ble [ad′mər·ə·bəl] *adj.* Worthy of being admired; excellent. **—ad′mi·ra·bly** *adv.*

ad·mi·ral [ad′mər·əl] *n.* **1** A person who commands a navy or a fleet of ships. **2** A naval rank. In the U.S. Navy, an admiral is an office of the second highest rank.

Admiral of the Fleet In the U.S. Navy, the highest ranking officer.

ad·mi·ral·ty [ad′mər·əl·tē] *n., pl.* **ad·mi·ral·ties** **1** (*written* **Admiralty**) The branch of the British government that deals with the navy and naval affairs. **2** A branch of law dealing with matters related to the sea and ships.

ad·mi·ra·tion [ad′mə·rā′shən] *n.* **1** A feeling of wonder, approval, and satisfaction for someone or something of quality: We had great *admiration* for the pilot's courage. **2** A person or thing that causes this feeling.

ad·mire [ad·mīr′] *v.* **ad·mired, ad·mir·ing** To regard or look upon with wonder, pleasure, and approval: I *admire* the photograph. **—ad·mir′er** *n.*

ad·mis·si·ble [ad·mis′ə·bəl] *adj.* Capable or worthy of being allowed, considered, or admitted: an *admissible* theory; no dogs *admissible.*

ad·mis·sion [ad·mish′ən] *n.* **1** The act of admitting or the condition of being admitted: A locked door prevented *admission* to the house. **2** Permission to enter: to allow someone *admission.* **3** The price charged for being admitted: *Admission* is 50 cents. **4** A confession or acknowledgment that something is true: an *admission* of defeat.

ad·mit [ad·mit′] *v.* **ad·mit·ted, ad·mit·ting** **1** To allow to enter or join: This key will *admit* you; They were *admitted* to the club. **2** To have room for; contain: This theater *admits* only 400 people. **3** To confess or acknowledge: We *admitted* our error. **4** To permit or give a chance: This problem *admits* of several answers.

ad·mit·tance [ad·mit′(ə)ns] *n.* The right or permission to enter: *Admittance* was denied.

ad·mit·ted·ly [ad·mit′id·lē] *adv.* By admission or agreement: *Admittedly,* it is hard work.

ad·mix·ture [ad·miks′chər] *n.* **1** A mixture. **2** Anything added to something else to make a mixture.

ad·mon·ish [ad·mon′ish] *v.* **1** To criticize mildly or tell of a fault: The students were *admonished* about their spelling. **2** To warn: The minister *admonished* the congregation to avoid evil. **—ad·mon′ish·ment** *n.*

ad·mo·ni·tion [ad′mə·nish′ən] *n.* A mild criticism, warning, or reminder: an *admonition* to be on time.

ad·mon·i·to·ry [ad·mon′ə·tôr′ē] *adj.* Serving to admonish or give warning: The teacher raised an *admonitory* finger for silence.

a·do [ə·do͞o′] *n.* Activity; fuss; bustle: Much *ado* was made over their leaving for camp.

a·do·be [ə·dō′bē] *n.* **1** A brick that is dried in the sun instead of in an oven or kiln. **2** The earth or clay of which such brick is made. **3** *adj. use:* an *adobe* house.

Adobe house

ad·o·les·cence [ad′ə·les′əns] *n.* The period of life during which a person grows from a child to an adult, roughly from about 12 to 21.

ad·o·les·cent [ad′ə·les′ənt] **1** *adj.* Growing up from a child to an adult. **2** *adj.* Having to do with or characteristic of adolescence. **3** *n.* A person between the ages of 12 or 13 and 21.

A·don·is [ə·don′is] *n.* **1** In Greek myths, a young man loved by Aphrodite because he was extremely handsome. **2** Any very handsome man.

a add	**i** it	**o͝o** took	**oi** oil
ā ace	**ī** ice	**o͞o** pool	**ou** pout
â care	**o** odd	**u** up	**ng** ring
ä palm	**ō** open	**û** burn	**th** thin
e end	**ô** order	**yo͞o** fuse	**th** this
ē equal			**zh** vision

ə = {a in *above*, e in *sicken*, i in *possible*, o in *melon*, u in *circus*}

a·dopt [ə·dopt′] *v.* 1 To take (a child of other parents) by legal means into one's family to be raised as one's own child. 2 *adj. use:* an *adopted* son. 3 To take and have or use as one's own: to *adopt* a new hair style. 4 To choose or vote to accept: to *adopt* a new law. **—a·dop′tion** *n.*

a·dop·tive [ə·dop′tiv] *adj.* Related by adoption: his *adoptive* family. **—a·dop′tive·ly** *adv.*

a·dor·a·ble [ə·dôr′ə·bəl] *adj.* 1 Worthy of love or adoration. 2 *informal* Charming; lovable: an *adorable* child. **—a·dor′a·ble·ness** *n.* **—a·dor′a·bly** *adv.*

ad·o·ra·tion [ad′ə·rā′shən] *n.* 1 The act of adoring. 2 A feeling of great love or admiration.

a·dore [ə·dôr′] *v.* **a·dored, a·dor·ing** 1 To worship. 2 To love and honor with great devotion: to *adore* one's parents. 3 *informal* To like very much: She *adored* riding and hunting. **—a·dor′er** *n.*

a·dorn [ə·dôrn′] *v.* To decorate or increase the beauty of: We *adorned* the table with flowers.

a·dorn·ment [ə·dôrn′mənt] *n.* 1 The act of adorning something. 2 Something that adorns, as jewelry or a decoration.

ad·re·nal [ə·drē′nəl] 1 *adj.* On or near the kidney. 2 *adj.* Of or from the adrenal glands. 3 *n.* An adrenal gland.

adrenal gland One of a pair of small glands resting on top of the kidneys. They secrete many substances needed by the body, especially adrenaline.

Ad·ren·a·lin [ə·dren′ə·lin] *n.* A brand of adrenaline, or epinephrine: a trademark.

ad·ren·a·line or **ad·ren·a·lin** [ə·dren′ə·lin] *n.* A hormone produced by the adrenal glands that raises blood pressure, quickens breathing, and otherwise prepares the body for activity or defense. Fear or anger stimulates its secretion.

a·drift [ə·drift′] *adj., adv.* Loose and moving with wind or current, as a boat.

a·droit [ə·droit′] *adj.* Skillful; clever; expert: *adroit* in acrobatics. **—a·droit′ly** *adv.* **—a·droit′ness** *n.*

ad·sorb [ad·sôrb′ *or* ad·zôrb′] *v.* To take up and hold (a gas, liquid, etc.) in a thin layer on a surface: Charcoal *adsorbs* gas.

ad·sorp·tion [ad·sôrp′shən *or* ad·zôrp′shən] *n.* The process of adsorbing or being adsorbed.

ad·u·la·tion [aj′o͞o·lā′shən] *n.* Too great or hypocritical praise; flattery: *adulation* of a singer.

ad·u·la·to·ry [aj′o͞o·lə·tôr′ē] *adj.* Greatly praising or flattering: The emcee introduced the star performer with *adulatory* phrases.

a·dult [ə·dult′ *or* ad′ult] 1 *n.* A person, animal, or plant that is fully grown. 2 *adj.* Grown-up; mature. 3 *n.* A person who has come of age, usually one 21 or more. 4 *adj.* Of or for adults.

a·dul·ter·ant [ə·dul′tər·ənt] *n.* Something that adulterates.

a·dul·ter·ate [ə·dul′tə·rāt′] *v.* **a·dul·ter·at·ed, a·dul·ter·at·ing** To reduce the quality of by adding cheap or impure materials: to *adulterate* hamburger with fat. **—a·dul′ter·a′tion** *n.*

a·dul·ter·er [ə·dul′tər·ər] *n.* A person, especially a man, who commits adultery.

a·dul·ter·ess [ə·dul′tər·əs] *n.* A woman who commits adultery.

a·dul·ter·ous [ə·dul′tər·əs] *adj.* Having to do with or committing adultery.

a·dul·ter·y [ə·dul′tər·ē] *n., pl.* **a·dul·ter·ies** Unfaithfulness to one's husband or wife.

a·dult·hood [ə·dult′ho͝od] *n.* The condition or time of being an adult.

adv. 1 adverb. 2 adverbial. 3 advertisement.

ad·vance [ad·vans′] *v.* **ad·vanced, ad·vanc·ing,** *n., adj.* 1 *v.* To move forward or upward: The army *advanced.* 2 *v.* To help onward; further; promote: to *advance* the progress of science. 3 *n.* The act of going forward; progress: to stop an army's *advance.* 4 *adj.* Located in front; going before: an *advance* guard. 5 *v.* To offer or put forward: to *advance* a suggestion. 6 *v.* To put in a better or higher rank, position, or situation: We *advanced* the pupil to the fifth grade. 7 *n.* An improvement or promotion: She was given an *advance* in her job. 8 *v.* To make happen earlier: to *advance* the date of a party. 9 *v.* To lend: The bank *advanced* us money. 10 *n.* A loan. 11 *n.* Payment of money before it is due: an *advance* on one's salary. 12 *adj.* Made or done ahead of time: an *advance* payment. 13 *v.* To increase; rise: The cost of living *advanced* a great deal last year. 14 *n.* An increase or rise: an *advance* in price. 15 *n.* (*pl.*) Attempts to gain someone's friendship or favor. — **in advance** 1 In front: We drove *in advance* of the truck. 2 Before due; beforehand.

ad·vanced [ad·vanst′] *adj.* 1 Ahead of or more difficult than others, as in progress or thought: an *advanced* class; an *advanced* book. 2 At a later stage of life or time: My grandparents are *advanced* in years. 3 Located in front or ahead.

advance man An aide who travels ahead of a politician, entertainer, or other employer and makes arrangements for the employer's reception, safety, and public appearances.

ad·vance·ment [ad·vans′mənt] *n.* 1 The act of advancing. 2 Progress: the *advancement* of science. 3 A promotion.

ad·van·tage [ad·van′tij] *n.* 1 Any circumstance or condition that benefits someone or helps toward success: The heavier wrestler had the *advantage* over his opponent. 2 Benefit or gain; profit: It is to your *advantage* to be there. **—take advantage of** 1 To use for one's own benefit or gain: *Take advantage of* our good library. 2 To use selfishly or unfairly: By not behaving, we *took advantage of* their good nature. **—to advantage** For benefit or profit; to good effect.

ad·van·ta·geous [ad′vən·tā′jəs] *adj.* Giving an advantage; favorable; profitable: an *advantageous* offer. **—ad′van·ta′geous·ly** *adv.*

ad·vent [ad′vent] *n.* 1 The coming or arrival of a person or thing: the *advent* of winter. 2 (*written* **Advent**) The birth of Christ. 3 (*written* **Advent**) A season including the four Sundays before Christmas.

Ad·vent·ist [ad·vent′əst *or* ad′vent·əst] *n.* A member of any of a number of fundamentalist Christian denominations that believe that Christ will return soon.

ad·ven·ti·tious [ad′ven·tish′əs] *adj.* Accidentally acquired or added. **—ad′ven·ti′tious·ly** *adv.*

ad·ven·ture [ad·ven′chər] *n., v.* **ad·ven·tured, ad·ven·tur·ing** 1 *n.* An unusual or thrilling experience: a day full of *adventures.* 2 *n.* A dangerous or difficult undertaking: the *adventure* of climbing mountains. 3 *v.* To do difficult, dangerous, or exciting things: to *adventure* on the moon. 4 *v.* To risk: to *adventure* one's life. ◆ This word comes through French from Latin *adventura,* meaning (an event) *about to happen.*

ad·ven·tur·er [ad·ven′chər·ər] *n.* 1 A person who looks for or takes part in adventures. 2 A person who tries to get ahead or become rich by dishonest or shady methods.

ad·ven·ture·some [ad·ven′chər·səm] *adj.* Adventurous; daring.

ad·ven·tur·ess [ad·ven′chər·əs] *n.* A woman who tries to advance herself or become rich by dishonest methods.

ad·ven·tur·ous [ad·ven′chər·əs] *adj.* **1** Liking or seeking adventure; fond of taking risks: an *adventurous* explorer. **2** Full of risk: an *adventurous* climb. **—ad·ven′tur·ous·ly** *adv.*

ad·verb [ad′vûrb] *n.* A word used to modify a verb, an adjective, or another adverb. In the sentence "I sleep here" *here* modifies the verb *sleep.* In the sentence "You are strangely silent" *strangely* modifies the adjective *silent.* In the sentence "They had met long before" *long* modifies the adverb *before.* ◆ See -LY[1].

ad·ver·bi·al [ad·vûr′bē·əl] *adj.* **1** Of or having to do with an adverb: an *adverbial* use. **2** Used like an adverb: an *adverbial* phrase.

ad·ver·sar·y [ad′vər·ser′ē] *n., pl.* **ad·ver·sar·ies** An opponent, as in a contest; enemy.

ad·verse [ad·vûrs′ *or* ad′vûrs] *adj.* **1** Acting against; opposing: *adverse* winds. **2** Unfavorable: *adverse* reviews of a book. **3** Harmful: an *adverse* effect. **—ad·verse′ly** *adv.*

ad·ver·si·ty [ad·vûr′sə·tē] *n., pl.* **ad·ver·si·ties** Great hardship, misfortune, or trouble.

ad·vert [ad·vûrt′] *v.* To make reference; call attention: She *adverted* to those who helped her in her research.

ad·ver·tise [ad′vər·tīz′] *v.* **ad·ver·tised, ad·ver·tis·ing** **1** To make known or praise publicly, usually in order to sell: to *advertise* cars on TV. **2** To ask for or about something, as in a newspaper: to *advertise* for a lost dog. **—ad′ver·tis′er** *n.* ◆ This word comes from a Latin word meaning *to turn toward,* and now has the sense of turning the public's attention to something in order to sell it.

ad·ver·tise·ment [ad′vər·tīz′mənt *or* ad·vûr′tis·mənt] *n.* A public notice that advertises something, as in a newspaper or on television.

ad·ver·tis·ing [ad′vûr·tī′zing] *n.* **1** The process or business of bringing public attention to something for the purpose of selling or promoting it. **2** Advertisements in general.

ad·vice [ad·vīs′] *n.* A suggestion or opinion on what one ought to do or how to do it: The carpenter gave us *advice* on how to build a bookcase.

ad·vis·a·bil·i·ty [ad·vī′zə·bil′ə·tē] *n.* The quality of being advisable; wisdom: I questioned the *advisability* of driving in a snowstorm.

ad·vis·a·ble [ad·vī′zə·bəl] *adj.* Worth advising; sensible; wise.

ad·vise [ad·vīz′] *v.* **ad·vised, ad·vis·ing** **1** To give advice to. **2** To recommend. **3** To tell or inform: *Advise* the staff of the new plan.

ad·vis·ed·ly [ad·vī′zid·lē] *adv.* After careful thought; deliberately: to use a word *advisedly.*

ad·vise·ment [ad·vīz′mənt] *n.* Careful and deliberate thought or consideration: He said he would take the matter under *advisement.*

ad·vis·er or **ad·vis·or** [ad·vī′zər] *n.* **1** A person who advises. **2** A teacher in a school who advises students about such matters as studies and careers.

ad·vi·so·ry [ad·vī′zər·ē] *adj.* **1** Having the right or ability to advise: an *advisory* council. **2** Containing advice: an *advisory* report.

ad·vo·ca·cy [ad′və·kə·sē] *n.* The act of defending or supporting a person, an idea, or a cause: The Senator's *advocacy* of the new law was a great help.

ad·vo·cate [*v.* ad′və·kāt′, *n.* ad′və·kit] *v.* **ad·vo·cat·ed, ad·vo·cat·ing,** *n.* **1** *v.* To speak or write in favor of; defend; support: The coach *advocates* plenty of exercise. **2** *n.* A person who argues for or favors publicly: an *advocate* of physical fitness. **3** *n.* A person, especially a lawyer, who pleads another's case before a court.

advt. advertisement.

adz or **adze** [adz] *n.* A tool like a broad chisel on an ax handle, its edge set crosswise.

Adz

AEC Atomic Energy Commission.

ae·gis [ē′jis] *n.* **1** In Greek mythology, a breastplate or shield used by Zeus and by Athena. **2** Protection, support, or sponsorship: a lifesaving course under the *aegis* of the Red Cross.

Ae·ne·as [i·nē′əs] *n.* In Roman legend, the Trojan warrior who wandered for seven years after the destruction of Troy. He is the hero of the Aeneid.

Ae·ne·id [i·nē′id] *n.* A Latin epic poem by Vergil, telling of the adventures of Aeneas.

Ae·o·li·an [ē·ō′lē·ən] *adj.* **1** Of or relating to Aeolus. **2** Sounding like or played by the wind.

Ae·o·lus [ē′ə·ləs] *n.* In Greek myths, the god of the winds.

ae·on [ē′ən] *n.* Another spelling of EON.

aer·ate [âr′āt′] *v.* **aer·at·ed, aer·at·ing** **1** To put air or gas into. **2** To make fresh by passing air through: to *aerate* water. **3** To supply with oxygen: to *aerate* the blood by respiration. **—aer·a′·tion** *n.*

aer·i·al [âr′ē·əl] **1** *adj.* Of or in the air. **2** *adj.* Light as air; airy. **3** *adj.* Of, by, or for aircraft or flying: an *aerial* maneuver. **4** *n.* An antenna, as for a radio or television set.

aer·i·al·ist [âr′ē·əl·ist] *n.* A person who performs acrobatic stunts, as on a tightrope or a trapeze.

aer·ie [âr′ē] *n.* **1** The nest of a bird of prey, as an eagle, built on a crag or other high place. **2** The brood or young of such a bird. **3** A house or fortress built on a high place.

aero- A combining form meaning: Air or atmosphere, as in *aerodynamics.*

aer·obe [âr′ōb′] *n.* An aerobic microorganism.

aer·o·bic [âr·ō′bik] *adj.* **1** Living or occurring only in the presence of oxygen, as certain microorganisms: *aerobic* bacteria. **2** Designed to increase the body's capacity to take in and utilize oxygen: *aerobic* dancing exercises.

aer·o·bics [âr·ō′biks] *n.pl.* Vigorous physical exercises designed to increase the body's capacity to take in and utilize oxygen. ◆ See -ICS.

a	add	**i**	it	**o͝o**	took	**oi**	oil
ā	ace	**ī**	ice	**o͞o**	pool	**ou**	pout
â	care	**o**	odd	**u**	up	**ng**	ring
ä	palm	**ō**	open	**û**	burn	**th**	thin
e	end	**ô**	order	**yo͞o**	fuse	**t͟h**	this
ē	equal					**zh**	vision

ə = a in *above*, e in *sicken*, i in *possible*, o in *melon*, u in *circus*

aer·o·drome [âr′ə·drōm′] *n. British* A spelling of AIRDROME.
aer·o·dy·nam·ics [âr′ō·dī·nam′iks] *n.* The study of the motions of air and other gases when acted upon by various forces, especially forces produced by moving objects. ◆ See -ICS.
aer·ol·o·gy [âr·ol′ə·jē] *n.* The study of how the air, especially in the upper atmosphere, creates and affects weather conditions.
aer·o·naut [âr′ə·nôt′] *n.* A person who flies an aircraft, especially a balloon.
aer·o·nau·tic [âr·ə·nô′tik] *adj.* Aeronautical.
aer·o·nau·ti·cal [âr′ə·nô′ti·kəl] *adj.* Of or having to do with aeronautics: an *aeronautical* chart.
aer·o·nau·tics [âr′ə·nô′tiks] *n.* The science and art of designing, making, and flying aircraft. ◆ See -ICS.
aer·o·pause [âr′ə·pôz′] *n.* The region of the upper atmosphere above which aircraft cannot fly.
aer·o·plane [âr′ə·plān′] *n. British.* A spelling of AIRPLANE.
aer·o·sol [âr′ə·sôl] *n.* A mass of extremely small liquid or solid particles suspended in a gas, as a fog or an insecticide.
aerosol bomb A pressurized container, usually hand-operated, from which an aerosol is dispensed.
aer·o·space [âr′ō·spās′] **1** *n.* The earth's atmosphere and outer space, considered as a single region. **2** *n.* A branch of science that is concerned with aerospace. **3** *n.* The industry that manufactures vehicles and equipment for use in aerospace. **4** *adj.* Of or having to do with aerospace or the vehicles used in aerospace.
Aes·cu·la·pi·us [es′kyo͞o·lā′pē·əs] *n.* In Roman myths, the god of medicine.
aes·thete [es′thēt′] *n.* A person who is especially interested in, sensitive to, and appreciative of art and beauty.
aes·thet·ic [es·thet′ik] *adj.* **1** Of or having to do with beauty in several areas, as in art or nature: an *aesthetic* view. **2** Very fond of or sensitive to beauty: an *aesthetic* person. **3** Of or relating to aesthetics. **—aes·thet′i·cal·ly** *adv.*
aes·thet·ics [es·thet′iks] *n.* A branch of philosophy that attempts to explain the nature of beauty or of beautiful things. ◆ See -ICS.
AF or **A.F.** **1** Air Force. **2** audio frequency.
a·far [ə·fär′] *adv.* At, from, or to a distance. **—from afar** From a long distance: We saw the mountain *from afar.*
AFB Air Force Base.
af·fa·ble [af′ə·bəl] *adj.* Very pleasant, friendly, and courteous. **—af′fa·bil′i·ty** *n.* **—af′fa·bly** *adv.*
af·fair [ə·fâr′] *n.* **1** An action or occasion: The dance was quite an *affair.* **2** Concern: What you do is your own *affair.* **3** (*pl.*) Important matters or concerns: *affairs* of state. **4** An object or thing: The raft was a crude *affair.* **5** A love affair.
af·fect¹ [*v.* ə·fekt′, *n.* af′ekt′] **1** *v.* To act on; have an effect on; influence; alter: What we eat *affects* our health. **2** *v.* To have an emotional or intellectual effect on, as to make someone sad or thoughtful: The play was so powerfully written that it *affected* us a great deal. **3** *n.* In psychology, feeling or emotion, in contrast to action, thought, or behavior: The patient showed little *affect.* **—af·fect·a·ble** [ə·fek′tə·bəl] ◆ See EFFECT.
af·fect² [ə·fekt′] *v.* **1** To like to have, wear, or use; prefer: He *affects* large sunglasses. **2** To imitate or pretend to have in order to create an effect: She *affects* a British accent.
af·fec·ta·tion [af′ek·tā′shən] *n.* An artificial way of acting or talking meant to create an effect: Their interest in sports is an *affectation.*
af·fect·ed [ə·fek′tid] *adj.* Not natural; artificial: an *affected* voice. **—af·fect′ed·ly** *adv.*
af·fec·tion [ə·fek′shən] *n.* **1** A feeling of kindness, fondness, or love for someone or something. **2** A diseased or unhealthy condition: an *affection* of the eye.
af·fec·tion·ate [ə·fek′shən·it] *adj.* Having or expressing affection; loving; fond.
af·fer·ent [af′ər·ənt] *adj.* Leading inward or toward the center: an *afferent* nerve.
af·fi·ance [ə·fī′əns] *v.* **af·fi·anced, af·fi·anc·ing** To promise in marriage; betroth: Last year Ann Marie was *affianced* to Timothy.
af·fi·da·vit [af′ə·dā′vit] *n.* A written statement sworn to be true.
af·fil·i·ate [ə·fil′ē·āt′] *v.* **af·fil·i·at·ed, af·fil·i·at·ing** To join or unite, as with a larger body: Our club is *affiliated* with a national club. **—af·fil′i·a′tion** *n.* ◆ This word comes from a Latin word meaning *to adopt,* related to the Latin word *filius,* meaning *son.*
af·fin·i·ty [ə·fin′ə·tē] *n., pl.* **af·fin·i·ties** **1** A natural attraction or liking: The teacher has an *affinity* for children. **2** A person to whom one is strongly drawn, especially a person of the opposite sex. **3** A likeness or similarity based on relationship. **4** In chemistry, the attractive force that causes atoms of different elements to form compounds and remain as compounds.
af·firm [ə·fûrm′] *v.* **1** To insist or maintain to be true; say positively. **2** To give formal approval to; validate; ratify; confirm.
af·fir·ma·tion [af′ər·mā′shən] *n.* **1** The act of declaring something to be true. **2** Something declared to be true. **3** Ratification; validation.
af·firm·a·tive [ə·fûr′mə·tiv] **1** *adj.* Saying that something is true; saying yes: an *affirmative* reply. **2** *n.* A word or gesture that shows agreement or approval: To answer yes is to answer in the *affirmative.* **3** *n.* In a debate, the side in favor of the proposition being debated.
affirmative action Action to reverse the effects of prior discrimination against a group: The company took *affirmative action* to increase the number of Blacks and women that it employs.
af·fix [*v.* ə·fiks′, *n.* af′iks] **1** *v.* To attach or fasten to something: to *affix* a label to a box. **2** *v.* To add at the end: to *affix* one's signature. **3** *n.* Something added or attached, as a prefix or suffix to a word.
af·flict [ə·flikt′] *v.* To give pain or trouble to: to be *afflicted* with an aching back.
af·flic·tion [ə·flik′shən] *n.* **1** Any suffering or distress of body or mind. **2** The cause of such suffering: Deafness is an *affliction.*
af·flu·ence [af′lo͞o·əns] *n.* **1** Plenty of money or property; wealth. **2** A plentiful supply; abundance.
af·flu·ent [af′lo͞o·ənt] *adj.* **1** Wealthy. **2** In plentiful supply; abundant.
af·ford [ə·fôrd′] *v.* **1** To be able to pay for: Can you *afford* the trip? **2** To be able to do or be, without risk or harm: They can *afford* to be kind. **3** To give; provide: Good books *afford* knowledge.
af·fray [ə·frā′] *n.* A public brawl or fight.

af·fright [ə·frīt′] *v.* To frighten: seldom used today.

af·front [ə·frunt′] 1 *v.* To insult or offend openly: You *affronted* the class by laughing. 2 *n.* An insult or a rude act done in public: Your laughter was an *affront* to us all.

Af·ghan [af′gən *or* af′gan] 1 *adj.* Of or from Afghanistan. 2 *n.* A person born in or a citizen of Afghanistan. 3 *n.* (*written* **afghan**) A wool blanket or shawl, knitted or crocheted in colorful patterns. 4 *n.* A large dog of a breed native to the Near East, having a long head and a coat of long, silky hair.

Afghan

a·fi·ci·o·na·do [ə·fish′·ē·ə·nä′dō *or* ə·fē′sē·ə·nä′dō] *n., pl.* **a·fi·ci·o·na·dos** An enthusiastic and well-informed admirer; devotee.

a·field [ə·fēld′] *adv.* 1 Off the regular or usual route or track. 2 Away from home; abroad. 3 In, on, or to the field. 4 Away from what is pertinent.

a·fire [ə·fīr′] *adj., adv.* On fire.

AFL 1 American Federation of Labor. 2 American Football League.

a·flame [ə·flām′] *adj.* 1 Flaming; on fire. 2 Colored like flames: with cheeks *aflame.*

AFL–CIO An organization of labor unions, formed when the American Federation of Labor and the Congress of Industrial Organizations merged in 1955.

a·float [ə·flōt′] *adj., adv.* 1 Floating, as on water or air. 2 At sea: We were *afloat* over a month. 3 In circulation; rumored: Stories were *afloat.* 4 Flooded: The leak left the floor *afloat.*

a·flut·ter [ə·flut′ər] *adj.* 1 Fluttering. 2 Disturbed; excited: The runner's heart was *aflutter.*

a·foot [ə·fo͝ot′] *adv., adj.* 1 On foot: to travel *afoot.* 2 In progress; about: dirty work *afoot.*

a·fore [ə·fôr′] *adv., prep., conj.* Before: seldom used today.

a·fore·men·tioned [ə·fôr′men′shənd] *adj.* Mentioned before: the *aforementioned* papers.

a·fore·said [ə·fôr′sed′] *adj.* Said before.

a·fore·thought [ə·fôr′thôt′] *adj.* Thought of or planned beforehand, especially in the phrase **malice aforethought:** There was no *malice aforethought* in the actions.

a·foul [ə·foul′] *adj.* In a tangle; entangled. **—run afoul of** To get into difficulties with: to run *afoul of* the law.

Afr. 1 Africa. 2 African.

a·fraid [ə·frād′] *adj.* 1 Full of fear or dread: to be *afraid* of heights. 2 Mildly concerned or distressed: I am *afraid* we're late.

a·fresh [ə·fresh′] *adv.* Once more; again: To do all our work *afresh.*

Af·ri·can [af′ri·kən] 1 *adj.* Of or having to do with Africa, its peoples, or languages. 2 *n.* A person born or living in Africa, especially a member of one of the indigenous peoples of Africa.

African American [af′ri·kən ə·mer′ə·kən] *n.* A black American of African descent. **African-American** *adj.*

Af·ri·kaans [af′ri·käns′] *n.* One of the two official languages of South Africa today. It developed from the language spoken by the 17th-century Dutch settlers.

Af·ri·kan·er [af′ri·kä′nər] *n.* A white descendant of the Dutch settlers of South Africa.

Af·ro [af′rō] *n., pl.* **Af·ros** A rounded, bushy hairstyle worn by people with tightly curled hair.

Af·ro-A·mer·i·can [af′rō·ə·mer′ə·kən] 1 *adj.* Of or having to do with Afro-Americans or their culture. 2 *n.* A black American of African descent.

aft [aft] *adv.* At, near, or toward the stern or rear part of a ship.

af·ter [af′tər] 1 *prep.* In the rear of; further back than; following: They marched *after* me. 2 *adv.* In the rear; behind: to follow *after.* 3 *prep.* In search of: Strive *after* wisdom. 4 *prep.* In relation to; concerning; about: The guests asked *after* your aunt. 5 *prep.* At a later time than: It is *after* five o'clock. 6 *adv.* Afterward; later: They arrived shortly *after.* 7 *adj.* Later: In *after* years they lived as friends. 8 *prep.* Following repeatedly: day *after* day. 9 *prep.* Next below in rank or importance: The vice president is *after* the president in power. 10 *prep.* According to the nature, wishes, or customs of: a gift *after* my own heart. 11 *prep.* In imitation of; in the manner of: a painting *after* Rembrant. 12 *prep.* In honor or remembrance of: He is named *after* his father. 13 *conj.* Following the time that: I went to bed *after* I got home.

af·ter·birth [af′tər·bûrth′] *n.* The placenta and fetal membranes expelled from the uterus after the birth of offspring.

af·ter·burn·er [af′tər·bûr′nər] *n.* 1 A device that creates additional thrust for a jet engine by injecting fuel into the hot exhaust gases. 2 An antipollution device for burning up unburned fuel in automobile exhaust.

af·ter·deck [af′tər·dek′] *n.* The part of a deck at or near the stern of a ship.

af·ter·ef·fect [af′tər·ə·fekt′] *n.* An effect that follows or results from a main effect: This medicine often has an unpleasant *aftereffect.*

af·ter·glow [af′tər·glō′] *n.* 1 The light that remains after a source of illumination is gone, as in the sky after sunset. 2 The good feeling that remains after a pleasing experience.

af·ter·im·age [af′tər·im′ij] *n.* The image of an object that is still perceived after the object has been removed from view.

af·ter·life [af′tər·līf′] *n., pl.* **af·ter·lives** [af′tər·līvz′] An existence that is believed to follow death.

af·ter·math [af′tər·math] *n.* 1 A result or consequence, especially if it is bad or injurious: the *aftermath* of the storm. 2 The second crop or mowing of grass to come from the original planting.

af·ter·noon [af′tər·no͞on′] *n.* The part of the day between noon and sunset.

a	add	**i**	it	**o͝o**	took	**oi**	oil
ā	ace	**ī**	ice	**o͞o**	pool	**ou**	pout
â	care	**o**	odd	**u**	up	**ng**	ring
ä	palm	**ō**	open	**û**	burn	**th**	thin
e	end	**ô**	order	**yo͞o**	fuse	**t͟h**	this
ē	equal					**zh**	vision

ə = a in *above* e in *sicken* i in *possible* o in *melon* u in *circus*

af·ter·taste [af′tər·tāst′] *n.* A taste that lingers in the mouth after the substance causing it has been swallowed.

af·ter·thought [af′tər·thôt′] *n.* A thought that comes after rather than before an action or a decision, and is thus too late to be useful.

af·ter·ward [af′tər·wərd] *adv.* At a later time: This is what happened *afterward.*

af·ter·wards [af′tər·wərdz] *adv.* Afterward.

af·ter·world [af′tər·wûrld′] *n.* A world believed to be inhabited by the spirits of the dead.

Ag The symbol for the element silver. ◆ The Latin name for silver is *argentum.*

a·gain [ə·gen′] *adv.* **1** Another time; once more: The ball bounced *again.* **2** To, at, or in the same place or condition as before: Here we go *again.* **3** In addition: half as much *again.* **4** On the other hand: I may go, and *again* I may not.

a·gainst [ə·genst′] *prep.* **1** In the opposite direction to; opposing: We sailed *against* the wind. **2** In contact with; upon: The boat was dashed *against* the rocks. **3** In opposition to; contrary to: The class acted *against* her wishes. **4** In contrast to: The trees were seen *against* the sky. **5** In preparation for.

Ag·a·mem·non [ag′ə·mem′non] *n.* In Greek myths, the leader of the Greek armies in the Trojan War.

a·gape [ə·gāp′] *adv., adj.* **1** Wide open; gaping: My mouth was *agape.* **2** In a condition of wonder, surprise, or excitement: We were *agape* at the news.

a·gar-a·gar [ä′gär·ä′gär *or* ā′gär·ā′gär] *n.* A jelly-like substance obtained from certain kinds of seaweeds, and used in the artificial cultivation of bacteria.

ag·ate [ag′it] *n.* **1** A type of quartz that is streaked with colored bands. **2** A playing marble that looks like this.

a·ga·ve [ə·gä′vē *or* ə·gā′vē] *n.* A plant of tropical America, Mexico, and the sw U.S., having stiff, thick leaves and a tall stalk that bears flowers. Some kinds yield a fiber used for making rope.

Agave

age [āj] *n., v.* **aged, ag·ing** or **age·ing** **1** *n.* The length of time any person or thing has been in existence: the *age* of six. **2** *n.* The last part of one's life: *Age* had bent the worker's back. **3** *n.* A stage or period of life: middle *age.* **4** *v.* To make or become old or mature: The French *age* wine very carefully; My grandfather *aged* a lot last year. **5** *n.* A particular period in the history of humanity or of the earth: the Middle *Ages;* the *age* of the dinosaur. **6** *n.* (*usually pl.*) A generation: This artwork will be appreciated by future *ages.* **7** *n.* (*usually pl.*) *informal* A long time: She's been gone for *ages.* **—of age** Being of an age, usually 18 or 21, when one has the legal rights of an adult. **—under age** Not of the age when one has the legal rights of an adult.

-age A suffix meaning: **1** The act or condition of, as in *marriage.* **2** A collection or group of, as in *fruitage.* **3** The cost of, as in *postage.* **4** The amount of, as in *dosage.* **5** The home of, as in *orphanage.*

a·ged *adj.* **1** [ā′jid] Old: His mother is quite *aged.* **2** [ājd] Of the age of: a child *aged* six. ◆ See OLD.

age·ism or **ag·ism** [ā′jiz′əm] *n.* Discrimination or prejudice against a particular age group, especially against the elderly. **—age′ist** or **ag′ist** *n.*

age·less [āj′lis] *adj.* **1** Seeming never to grow old: an *ageless* person. **2** Eternal; timeless.

a·gen·cy [ā′jən·sē] *n., pl.,* **a·gen·cies** **1** The power or means by which something is done: Through the *agency* of water we ground our grain. **2** A firm or establishment where business is carried on for others: an employment *agency.*

a·gen·da [ə·jen′də] *n.* A list of things to be done or discussed: Here is the *agenda* for today's meeting. ◆ *Agenda* was originally the plural form of the Latin word *agendum.* It is now often taken as a singular noun and has a regular plural, *agendas.*

a·gent [ā′jənt] *n.* **1** A person or organization that has the authority to act for someone else: He is the singer's business *agent.* **2** A person or thing that produces a certain effect or result: Oxygen is the *agent* that causes rust.

agent pro·voc·a·teur [ā′jənt prə·vok′ə·to͞or′] *n., pl.* **agents pro·voc·a·teurs** [ā′jənts prə·vok′ə·to͞or′] A person who joins an organization in order to encourage its members to perform illegal acts for which the organization will be punished.

age-old [āj′ōld′] *adj.* Ancient; long-standing: *age-old* customs.

ag·glom·er·ate [*v.* ə·glom′ə·rāt′, *n., adj.* ə·glom′ə·rit] *v.* **ag·glom·er·at·ed, ag·glom·er·at·ing,** *n., adj.* **1** *v.* To cluster or cause to cluster in a mass. **2** *n.* A mass or collection of things clustered together. **3** *adj.* Clustered or jumbled together. **4** *n.* A rock made up of volcanic fragments fused together under pressure.

ag·glom·er·a·tion [ə·glom′ə·ra′shən] *n.* **1** The act or process of forming into a mass. **2** A cluster or jumble of different elements.

ag·glu·ti·nate [*v.* ə·glo͞ot′ən·āt′, *adj.* ə·glo͞ot′ən·ət] *v.* **ag·glu·ti·nat·ed, ag·glu·ti·nat·ing,** *adj.* **1** *v.* To clump or stick together in a mass. **2** *adj.* Stuck or clumped together. **—ag·glu′ti·na′tive** *adj.*

ag·glu·ti·na·tion [ə·glo͞ot′ən·ā′shən] *n.* **1** The act or process of clumping or sticking together. **2** A clump, as of blood cells.

ag·glu·tin·in [ə·glo͞ot·ən·in] *n.* A substance, such as an antibody, that causes agglutination.

ag·gran·dize [ə·gran′dīz′ *or* ag′rən·dīz′] *v.* **ag·gran·dized, ag·gran·diz·ing** **1** To increase, as the power, rank, or wealth, of: The party *aggrandized* itself by taking in reform groups. **2** To make great or greater, as in size. **—ag·gran·dize·ment** [ə·gran′diz·mənt] *n.*

ag·gra·vate [ag′rə·vāt′] *v.* **ag·gra·vat·ed, ag·gra·vat·ing** **1** To make worse, more serious, or more unpleasant: The smart of iodine *aggravated* the pain of the cut. **2** *informal* To make angry; provoke: The noisy audience *aggravated* the pianist so much that she cut short her concert. ◆ *Aggravate* may be used informally (def. 2) as a synonym for *annoy.* Many writers, however, restrict its meaning to "make worse" (def. 1).

ag·gra·va·tion [ag′rə·vā′shən] *n.* **1** The act of aggravating. **2** Something that aggravates. **3** *informal* Anger: irritation.

ag·gre·gate [*v.* ag′rə·gāt′, *adj., n.* ag′rə·git] *v.* **ag·gre·gat·ed, ag·gre·gat·ing,** *adj., n.* **1** *v.* To gather together; collect: The wet sand was *aggregated* into one hard lump. **2** *adj.* Gathered into a whole; total: The *aggregate* number of baseball fans was tremendous. **3** *v.* To amount to; add up to: The tickets sold will *aggregate* above 10,000. **4** *n.* The entire amount; total. **—in the aggregate** Collectively; as a whole.

ag·gre·ga·tion [ag′rə·gā′shən] *n.* A gathering of separate things: a huge *aggregation* of people.

ag·gres·sion [ə·gresh′ən] *n.* **1** An attack, especially an unprovoked attack: That country was accused of *aggression.* **2** A tendency to attack or fight.

ag·gres·sive [ə·gres′iv] *adj.* **1** Quick to attack or start a fight: an *aggressive* country. **2** Very active; vigorous; energetic: an *aggressive* player.

ag·gres·sor [ə·gres′ər] *n.* A person or nation that attacks first or starts a quarrel.

ag·grieve [ə·grēv′] *v.* **ag·grieved, ag·griev·ing** **1** To cause grief or sorrow to; distress: His constant lies *aggrieved* his parents. **2** To injure unjustly; wrong.

ag·grieved [ə·grēvd′] *adj.* Having cause for complaint; ill-treated; wronged: The *aggrieved* tenants complained to their landlord.

a·ghast [ə·gast′] *adj.* Shocked or horrified: We were *aghast* at such rude behavior.

ag·ile [aj′əl] *adj.* Able to move or do something quickly and easily: *agile* fingers; an *agile* mind. **—ag′ile·ly** *adv.*

a·gil·i·ty [ə·jil′ə·tē] *n.* Quickness and easiness in the use of body or mind: Most sports test both physical and mental *agility.*

ag·i·tate [aj′ə·tāt′] *v.* **ag·i·tat·ed, ag·i·tat·ing** **1** To disturb or move: The wind *agitates* the lake. **2** To excite or stir up: News of the crash *agitated* us. **3** To try to arouse interest in changing something, as by speaking or writing: Women *agitated* a long time for the vote.

ag·i·ta·tion [aj′ə·tā′shən] *n.* **1** The act of moving or shaking. **2** Excitement or nervousness: Their *agitation* at the bad news was seen by all. **3** The arousing of public interest in order to change something: *agitation* for equal rights.

ag·i·ta·tor [aj′ə·tā′tər] *n.* **1** A person who stirs up discontent in order to change things. **2** A thing that agitates: the *agitator* of a machine.

a·gleam [ə·glēm′] *adj.* Faintly lit; gleaming: Their eyes were *agleam* with excitement.

a·glit·ter [ə·glit′ər] *adj.* Sparkling; glittering: a sky *aglitter* with stars.

a·glow [ə·glō′] *adj.* In a glow; glowing.

ag·nos·tic [ag·nos′tik] *n.* A person who believes that we can never know for certain whether God does or does not exist. **—ag·nos·ti·cism** [ag·nos′tə·siz′·əm] *n.*

a·go [ə·gō′] **1** *adj.* Gone by; past: a year *ago.* **2** *adv.* In the past: It happened long *ago.*

a·gog [ə·gog′] *adj.* Full of eager curiosity; excited: to be all *agog* about something.

ag·o·nize [ag′ə·nīz′] *v.* **ag·o·nized, ag·o·niz·ing** To suffer or cause to suffer terrible physical or mental pain.

ag·o·ny [ag′ə·nē] *n., pl.* **ag·on·ies** **1** Terrible suffering of body or mind; anguish. **2** The struggle that often comes just before death.

a·gou·ti [ə·gōō′tē] *n., pl.* **a·gou·tis** or **a·gou·ties** A Central and South American rodent about the size of a rabbit. It has a short tail and three toes on its hind feet.

a·grar·i·an [ə·grâr′ē·ən] *adj.* Having to do with land, especially farm land, and how it is owned, distributed, and used: a plan for *agrarian* reform.

a·gree [ə·grē′] *v.* **a·greed, a·gree·ing** **1** To consent: The group *agreed* to go. **2** To admit the truth of; grant: We *agreed* that we had not worked hard enough. **3** To have the same opinions or ideas; concur: I *agree* with that viewpoint. **4** To come to terms: They *agreed* on a settlement. **5** In grammar, to correspond in person, number, case, or gender. **—agree with** To be good for; suit: Spices do not *agree with* me.

a·gree·a·ble [ə·grē′ə·bəl] *adj.* **1** Giving pleasure; pleasing: an *agreeable* companion. **2** Ready or willing to agree: I am *agreeable* to your plan. **3** Suitable; conforming: clothes *agreeable* to the weather. **—a·gree′a·bly** *adv.*

a·gree·ment [ə·grē′mənt] *n.* **1** A sameness or harmony of opinion: We were in *agreement* on many questions. **2** A contract, treaty, or understanding, as between people or nations: a trade *agreement* between England and Canada. **3** Correspondence between words as to person, number, case, or gender.

ag·ri·cul·tur·al [ag′rə·kul′chər·əl] *adj.* Of, having to do with, or used in agriculture.

ag·ri·cul·ture [ag′rə·kul′chər] *n.* The art or science of cultivating the soil; the raising of crops, livestock, or both; farming. **—ag′ri·cul′tur·ist** *n.* **—ag′·ri·cul′tur·al·ist** *n.*

a·gron·o·my [ə·gron′ə·mē] *n.* The science of farming; scientific agriculture. **—a·gron′o·mist** *n.*

a·ground [ə·ground′] *adj., adv.* On or onto a shoal or bottom; stranded.

agt. agent.

a·gue [ā′gyōō] *n.* **1** A fever, as malaria, marked by alternating periods of chills, fever, and sweating. **2** A chill accompanied by shivering.

ah [ä] *interj.* An exclamation expressing by the way it is said such emotions as surprise, disgust, satisfaction, and joy.

a·ha [ä·hä′] *interj.* An exclamation expressing such emotions as surprise, joy, and triumph.

a·head [ə·hed′] **1** *adv.* In front; to the front; before: March *ahead* of us. **2** *adv.* In advance: They telephoned *ahead* for rooms. **3** *adv.* Onward; forward: Go *ahead* with your plans. **4** *adj.* Better or more advanced in some respect: This car is *ahead* of that one in looks.

a·hem [ə·hem] *interj.* A sound used to attract attention or give warning, made by clearing the throat.

a·hoy [ə·hoi′] *interj.* A sailor's call, used to hail a person or ship.

aid [ād] **1** *v.* To help or assist. **2** *n.* Help or assistance: *Aid* came just in time. **3** *n.* A person or thing that helps: a visual *aid* used in teaching.

aide [ād] *n.* An assistant, as an aide-de-camp or an executive who helps to run a business.

a	add	**i**	it	**ŏŏ**	took	**oi**	oil		
ā	ace	**ī**	ice	**ōō**	pool	**ou**	pout		
â	care	**o**	odd	**u**	up	**ng**	ring		
ä	palm	**ō**	open	**û**	burn	**th**	thin		
e	end	**ô**	order	**yōō**	fuse	**th**	this		
ē	equal					**zh**	vision		

ə = a in *above*, e in *sicken*, i in *possible*, o in *melon*, u in *circus*

aide-de-camp [ād′də·kamp′] *n., pl.* **aides-de-camp** An officer who serves as a personal assistant to a high military or naval officer.

AIDS [ādz] *n.* A disease that destroys the body's ability to fight off other diseases. ◆ *AIDS* is an acronym for "*a*cquired *i*mmune *d*eficiency *s*yndrome."

ai·grette [ā·gret′ *or* ā′gret′] *n.* **1** A tuft of feathers, as from the tail of an egret. **2** A headdress of jewels in the shape of a plume.

ai·ki·do [ī·kē′dō] *n.* A Japanese art of self-defense in which the momentum of an opponent's attack is used to one's advantage.

ail [āl] *v.* **1** To cause pain or discomfort to; trouble: His back was *ailing* him. **2** To be ill.

ai·lan·thus [ā·lan′thəs] *n.* A shade tree native to China but now commonly found in urban areas of North America and Europe. It has featherlike, compound leaves and clusters of greenish, strong-smelling flowers.

ai·le·ron [ā′lə·ron′] *n.* A movable surface hinged to the back edge of each wing of an airplane. The pilot tilts the ailerons to bank the plane.

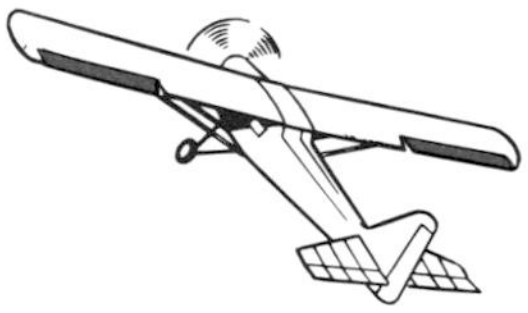

When the right aileron is up and the left down, the airplane banks to the right.

ail·ment [āl′mənt] *n.* An illness, usually not too severe but often chronic.

aim [ām] **1** *v.* To direct (as a weapon or a remark) at some object or person: The gun was *aimed* at us; I *aimed* my remarks at the whole class. **2** *n.* The act of aiming: to have a deadly *aim.* **3** *v.* To have as a purpose or goal; try: She *aimed* to make the team this year. **4** *n.* A purpose or goal: My *aim* was to become a doctor. **—take aim** To point a gun at some target.

aim·less [ām′lis] *adj.* Having no aim or purpose: an *aimless* life. **—aim′less·ly** *adv.*

ain't [ānt] A contraction of: Am not: I *ain't* going. *Ain't* is also used for *are not, is not, has not,* and *have not.* ◆ *Ain't* is not considered acceptable English today, although speakers and writers sometimes use it for humorous effect.

Ai·nu [ī′nōō] *n., pl.* **Ai·nu** or **Ai·nus** **1** A member of a Caucasian people native to northern Japan. **2** The language spoken by these people.

air [âr] **1** *n.* The mixture of invisible, odorless, and tasteless gases that forms the atmosphere of the earth, consisting chiefly of nitrogen and oxygen. **2** *n.* The open space around and above the earth; sky: The *air* was full of birds flying. **3** *adj. use*: an *air* filter; an *air* drill; an *air* current; *air* travel; an *air* attack. **4** *n.* A slight wind or breeze. **5** *v.* To expose to the air so as to ventilate, dry, or make fresh: *Air* the blankets. **6** *n.* The general look or manner of a person or thing: They had an honest *air* about them. **7** *n.* (*pl.*) An affected, unnatural, or haughty way of acting: Don't put on *airs.* **8** *v.* To make known or make public: The people *aired* their troubles to the mayor. **9** *n.* A melody or tune: an old Irish *air.* **—in the air** **1** Going around; abroad: Something is *in the air.* **2** Unsettled. **—on the air** Broadcasting or being broadcast, as by radio. **—walk** (or **float**) **on air** To be very happy; feel elated.

air base A base for military aircraft.

air bladder **1** An air-filled, saclike structure in bony fishes that helps maintain buoyancy. **2** Any air-filled sac.

air·borne [âr′bôrn′] *adj.* **1** Carried by air: *airborne* pollen. **2** Transported by aircraft: *airborne* cargo. **3** In flight; aloft: After a three-hour delay, we were finally *airborne.*

air brake A brake operated by compressed air.

air·brush [âr′brush′] *n.* A device that sprays by compressed air a fine stream of paint droplets.

air-con·di·tion [âr′kən·dish′ən] *v.* To equip with or ventilate by air conditioning.

air conditioner A machine that regulates the air temperature and humidity of an enclosed space, such as a room or a car.

air conditioning A system for treating the air in buildings, rooms, and other enclosed places in order to keep the air clean, dry, and at a comfortable temperature.

air-cool [âr′kōōl′] *v.* To cool by means of circulating air: to *air-cool* an engine.

air·craft [âr′kraft′] *n., pl.* **air·craft** Any machine or vehicle designed to travel from place to place through the air, as airplanes, balloons, and helicopters.

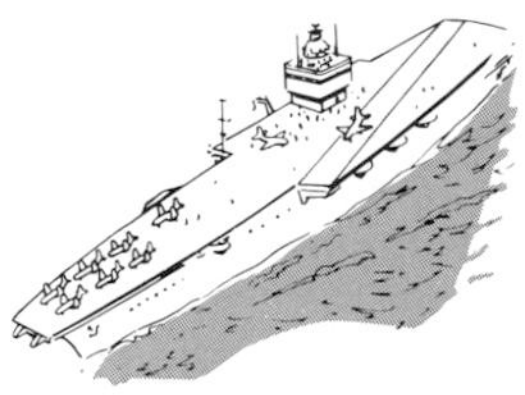

Aircraft carrier

aircraft carrier A warship that serves as a base for aircraft which take off from and land on its long, level, open deck.

air·drome [âr′drōm′] *n.* **1** Another word for AIRPORT. **2** An airplane hanger. **3** A landing field.

air·drop [âr′drop′] *v.* **air·dropped, air·drop·ping,** *n.* **1** *v.* To drop by parachute from a flying aircraft: **2** *n.* An act of airdropping.

Aire·dale [âr′dāl] *n.* A large terrier with a short, wiry tan coat and black markings.

Airedale

air·field [âr′fēld′] *n.* A field equipped for the landing and take-off of aircraft.

air·foil [âr′foil′] *n.* An exposed aircraft part, such as a wing, rudder, or propeller, designed to interact with the flow of air in such a way as to help lift or control the aircraft.

air force The branch of a country's armed forces equipped to wage war in or from the air.

air gun A gun that uses compressed air to propel its bullet or projectile.

air hole **1** A hole that allows air or other gases to pass in and out of an enclosed space: *Air holes* in the cardboard box allowed the cat to breathe. **2** A hole in the frozen surface of a body of water. **3** Another word for AIR POCKET.

air·i·ly [âr′ə·lē] *adv.* In a light, high-spirited manner; jauntily; gaily: They waved *airily* to us.

air·i·ness [âr′ē·nis] *n.* **1** The quality of being light and airy. **2** Delicacy.

air·ing [âr′ing] *n.* **1** An exposure to air in order to dry or freshen. **2** Exercise in the outdoors.

air lane A route of travel for aircraft; airway.

air·less [âr′lis] *adj.* Lacking air, especially fresh air; stuffy: an *airless* room.

air letter **1** A sheet of very lightweight paper that folds on itself to make its own envelope. **2** Any letter sent by air mail.

air·lift [âr′lift′] **1** *n.* The carrying of passengers and cargo by air, especially when other means of

access are closed off. **2** *v.* To carry or transport by this method: to *airlift* supplies.
air·line [âr′līn′] *n.* **1** A system for transporting people and freight by air. **2** A company operating such a transportation system. **3** A regular route flown by aircraft.
air·lin·er [âr′lī′nər] *n.* A large airplane capable of carrying many passengers.
air lock An airtight chamber connecting two areas with different air pressures.
air·mail [âr′māl′] *n., adj., adv., v.* **air·mailed, air·mail·ing** **1** *n.* Mail carried by airplanes. **2** *n.* A system for carrying such mail. **3** *adj.* Of, having to do with, or used with airmail: an *airmail* stamp. **4** *adv.* By airmail: to send a package *airmail.* **5** *v.* To send by airmail: to *airmail* a letter.
air·man [âr′mən] *n., pl.* **air·men** [âr′mən] An enlisted man in the U.S. Air Force.
air mass A large body of air having a generally uniform temperature and humidity.
air mile A unit of distance used in air navigation, equal to about 6,076 feet.
air piracy The hijacking of an airplane while it is in flight; skyjacking.
air·plane [âr′plān′] *n.* A vehicle that flies through the air. It is able to remain aloft by means of the lift produced when air moves over its wing as it is driven forward by the action of propellers or by jet propulsion.
air plant A plant, as certain mosses or orchids, that grows on another plant. The air plant gets its nutrients and moisture directly from the air.
air pocket A strong downward current of air that sometimes causes an airplane to drop sharply from a level course.
air·port [âr′pôrt′] *n.* A large area equipped for aircraft to land and take off and for the loading and unloading, as of passengers and freight.
air pressure **1** The pressure of air in a confined space. The pressure increases as the space grows less. **2** Atmospheric pressure.
air pump A pump for compressing air, removing air, or for forcing a flow of air through pipes.
air raid An attack or raid by aircraft.
air rifle Another name for AIR GUN.
air rights The legal ownership of the space above a piece of property.
air sac **1** One of the many small pouches connected to a bird's lungs that fill with air and help the bird to breathe. **2** An alveolus in a mammal's lungs.
air shaft A passage that lets fresh air into a mine or other closed space.
air·ship [âr′ship′] *n.* A balloon that can be driven and steered; dirigible.
air·sick [âr′sik′] *adj.* Sick at one's stomach from riding in an aircraft. **—air′sick′ness** *n.*
air·space [âr′spās′] *n.* The space located above a nation and governed by the laws of that nation: violations of British airspace.
air speed The speed of an aircraft relative to the air through which it travels rather than its speed in relation to the ground below.
air·strip [âr′strip′] *n.* A flat, smooth surface on land, snow, or ice that can be used for the take-off or landing of aircraft.
air·tight [âr′tīt′] *adj.* **1** Able to hold air or gas in or out: an *airtight* cover. **2** Having no weak spots; flawless: an *airtight* argument.
air-to-air [âr′tə·âr′] *adj.* **1** Involving two or more aircrafts in flight: *air-to-air* communication. **2** Launched from an airborne aircraft and aimed at an airborne target: *air-to-air* missiles.
air·waves [âr·wāvz′] *n.pl.* Radio or television broadcasting: During the holiday season, Christmas carols dominated the *airwaves.*
air·way [âr′wā′] *n.* **1** A route traveled by aircraft. **2** Another word for AIR SHAFT.
air·wor·thy [âr′wûr′t͟hē] *adj.* In good condition to fly; safe for flying. **—air′worth′i·ness** *n.*
air·y [âr′ē] *adj.* **air·i·er, air·i·est** **1** Of, having to do with, or in the air. **2** Open to the air: an *airy* porch. **3** Thin or light as air; delicate: *airy* curtains. **4** Lighthearted or gay in manner: *airy* music. **5** Not real or practical; fanciful.
aisle [īl] *n.* **1** A passageway, as in a theater or church, that separates one section of seats from another section: the center *aisle.* **2** A passageway along the inside wall of a church, separated from the main section by pillars.
a·jar[1] [ə·jär′] *adj., adv.* Partly open, as a door.
a·jar[2] [ə·jär′] *adj., adv.* Not in harmony; on edge: The loud noises set her nerves *ajar.*
A·jax [ā′jaks] *n.* In Greek myths, a Greek hero of the Trojan War, second in bravery only to Achilles.
AK Postal Service abbreviation of Alaska.
AKA also known as.
AKC American Kennel Club.
a·kim·bo [ə·kim′bō] *adj., adv.* With hands on the hips and elbows outward: to stand with arms *akimbo.*
a·kin [ə·kin′] *adj.* **1** Having the same family; related. **2** Similar or alike in certain ways: Our feelings were more *akin* to joy than sorrow.
-al A suffix meaning: **1** Of or having to do with something, as in *musical.* **2** The act or process of doing something, as in *refusal.*

Arms akimbo

Al The symbol for the element aluminum.
AL Postal Service abbreviation of Alabama.
Ala. Alabama.
al·a·bas·ter [al′ə·bas′tər] **1** *n.* A smooth white or tinted stone, often carved into vases or small statues. **2** *adj. use:* an *alabaster* vase.
à la carte or **a la carte** [ä′lə kärt′] With a separate price for each dish on the menu rather than one price for the entire meal. ◆ In French, *à la carte* literally means "by the menu."
a·lack [ə·lak′] *interj.* An exclamation expressing regret or sorrow: seldom used today.
a·lac·ri·ty [ə·lak′rə·tē] *n.* A willingness and promptness: to help someone with *alacrity.*
A·lad·din [ə·lad′(ə)n] *n.* In the Arabian Nights, a boy who was able to summon a genie by rubbing a magic lamp or a magic ring.

a add	**i** it	**o͝o** took	**oi** oil
ā ace	**ī** ice	**o͞o** pool	**ou** pout
â care	**o** odd	**u** up	**ng** ring
ä palm	**ō** open	**û** burn	**th** thin
e end	**ô** order	**yo͞o** fuse	**t͟h** this
ē equal			**zh** vision

ə = a in *above* e in *sicken* i in *possible* o in *melon* u in *circus*

à la king or **a la king** [ä′lə·king′] Prepared by cooking in a cream sauce with peppers and mushrooms: turkey *à la king.*

al·a·me·da [al′ə·me′də *or* al′ə·mā′də] *n.* A public promenade lined with shade trees. ◆ *Alameda* comes from a Spanish word derived from *alamo,* meaning "poplar," a tree frequently planted for shade in the southwestern U.S.

Al·a·mo [al′ə·mō] *n.* A vacant mission building made into a fort in San Antonio, Texas, that was attacked and taken by Mexicans in 1836.

à la mode or **a la mode** [ä′lə mōd′] **1** With ice cream: I like pie *à la mode.* **2** Stylish; fashionable.

a·larm [ə·lärm′] **1** *n.* A sudden feeling of fear: We were filled with *alarm* at the noise. **2** *v.* To fill with fear; frighten: The noise was so loud that it *alarmed* people and caused them to panic. **3** *n.* Any signal or sound used to warn others of danger. **4** *n.* A device, as a bell or siren, used to give such a signal. **5** *n.* A call to arms or to be ready in an emergency, as a flood or fire.

alarm clock A clock that can be set in advance to ring or buzz at a particular time.

a·larm·ist [ə·lär′mist] *n.* A person too ready to be alarmed or to alarm others.

a·las [ə·las′] *interj.* An exclamation expressing such emotions as sorrow, regret, and disappointment.

Alas. Alaska.

Alaskan malamute A malamute.

Alaska standard time (*sometimes written* **Alaska Standard Time**) The standard time observed throughout most of Alaska. It is nine hours earlier than Greenwich time.

alb [alb] *n.* A long, white linen vestment, or robe, worn by a priest while celebrating Mass.

al·ba·core [al·bə·kôr′] *n., pl.* **al·ba·core** or **al·ba·cores** A large ocean fish of the tuna family that is often canned.

Al·ba·ni·an [al·bā′nē·ən] **1** *adj.* Of or from Albania. **2** *n.* A person born in or a citizen of Albania. **3** *n.* The language of Albania.

al·ba·tross [al′bə·trôs] *n.* A large, webfooted sea bird with a hooked beak. It is capable of flying for long distances over the sea.

Albatross

al·be·it [ôl·bē′it] *conj.* Even though; although: a strong, *albeit* slender, support.

al·bin·ism [al′bə·niz′əm] *n.* The absence of normal pigmentation in a plant or animal; the condition of being an albino.

al·bi·no [al·bī′nō] *n., pl.* **al·bi·nos** A person or animal having very pale or white skin and hair and often pink or light blue eyes, due to a lack of normal coloring matter.

Al·bi·on [al′bē·ən] *n.* Another name for ENGLAND: used mostly in poems.

al·bum [al′bəm] *n.* **1** A book or booklike container, used for keeping such items as stamps, pictures, and autographs. **2** A long-playing record or records.

al·bu·men [al·byōō′mən] *n.* **1** The white of an egg. **2** Albumin.

al·bu·min [al·byōō′mən] *n.* A protein found in many plant and animal juices and tissues, as in the whites of eggs, blood serum, muscle, and milk.

al·che·mist [al′kə·mist] *n.* A person who practiced alchemy in the Middle Ages.

al·che·my [al′kə·mē] *n.* **1** An early form of chemistry practiced in the Middle Ages that tried to find a way to change common metals into gold and to discover a substance that could keep a person forever young. **2** Any power that changes or transforms.

al·co·hol [al′kə·hôl] *n.* **1** A clear, colorless, flammable liquid with a pungent taste, formed from fermented sugars in grain and grapes. It is the intoxicating agent in beverages such as wine and gin, and is used in medicine and as a fuel. **2** Any liquor containing alcohol. **3** A chemically related but poisonous liquid distilled from wood. **4** Any similar chemical compound. ◆ This word comes originally from an Arabic word for a fine powder used to paint the eyelids.

al·co·hol·ic [al′kə·hôl′ik] **1** *adj.* Of, containing, or caused by alcohol: an *alcoholic* drink. **2** *n.* A person who suffers from alcoholism.

al·co·hol·ism [al′kə·hôl′iz·əm] *n.* A chronic psychological and nutritional disease characterized by a compulsion to drink alcoholic beverages.

al·cove [al′kōv] *n.* **1** A recess or small section of a room opening out from the main section: a dining *alcove.* **2** A small, often arched hollow place, as in a wall: Put the vase in the *alcove.*

Alcove

Al·deb·a·ran [al·deb′ə·rən] *n.* A red star, one of the brightest in the sky, in the constellation Taurus.

al·der [ôl′dər] *n.* A shrub or small tree that resembles the birch and grows best in wet soil.

al·der·man [ôl′dər·mən] *n., pl.* **al·der·men** [ôl′dər·mən]. In some cities and towns, a member of the local government or city council.

ale [āl] *n.* An alcoholic drink that is similar in taste to beer, made from malt and hops.

a·lee [ə·lē′] *adj., adv.* At, on, or to the side of a ship that faces away from the wind.

a·lert [ə·lûrt′] **1** *adj.* Very watchful and ready, as for sudden action: an *alert* little dog. **2** *adj.* Mentally quick and intelligent. **3** *n.* A warning or signal against attack or danger. **4** *n.* The time during which such a warning is in effect. **5** *v.* To warn or prepare, as for danger or attack. **—on the alert** Very watchful and ready: Keep *on the alert* for trouble. **—a·lert′ly** *adv.* **—a·lert′ness** *n.*

A·leut [ə·lōōt′] *n., pl.* **A·leuts** or **Al·eut** **1** A member of a people native to the Aleutian Islands. **2** The language spoken by the Aleuts. **—A·leu·tian** [ə·lōō′shən] *adj.*

ale·wife [āl′wīf′] *n., pl.* **ale·wives** [āl′wīvz′] **1** A small fish of the North American Atlantic coast, closely related to the herring. **2** Another name for MENHADEN.

Al·ex·an·dri·an [al′ig·zan′drē·ən] **1** *adj.* Of or relating to Alexander the Great or his reign. **2** *adj.* Of or related to the ancient city of Alexandria, Egypt. **3** *n.* A person born in or a citizen of Alexandria.

al·fal·fa [al·fal′fə] *n.* A cloverlike plant having deep roots and purple flowers. It is grown as a food for horses and cattle. ◆ This word comes directly from Spanish. The origin of it was an Arabic word meaning *the best kind of fodder.*

al·fres·co [al·fres′kō] 1 *adj.* Outdoor: an *alfresco* lunch. 2 *adv.* Outdoors: to dine *alfresco.*

alg. algebra.

al·gae [al′jē] *n.pl.* A large group of simple plants growing in water or damp places and lacking true roots, stems, or leaves. Many algae are seaweeds. ◆ This word comes from the Latin word *algae,* which is the plural of *alga,* meaning *seaweed.*

al·ge·bra [al′jə·brə] *n.* A branch of mathematics that deals with the relations between numbers. Actual numbers are often replaced by letters so that these relations may be determined; for instance, if $2a + b = 10$, and $b = 4$, then $a = 3$. ◆ This word comes from an Arabic word meaning *the reunion of broken parts,* such as broken bones. It came to have the meaning of setting up and solving an equation.

al·ge·bra·ic [al′jə·brā′ik] *adj.* 1 Of or having to do with algebra. 2 Used in algebra.

Al·ge·ri·an [al·jir′ē·ən] 1 *adj.* Of or from Algeria. 2 *n.* A person born in or a citizen of Algeria.

Al·gon·qui·an [al·gong′kwē·ən *or* al·gong′kē·ən] 1 *n.* A family of languages spoken by many tribes of North American Indians. 2 *adj.* Of or having to do with this family of languages.

Al·gon·quin [al·gong′kwin *or* al·gong′kin] *n.* A North American Indian who belongs to any of certain tribes that speak an Algonquian language.

al·go·rithm [al′gə·rith′əm] *n.* A procedure for solving a mathematical problem by following a definite series of steps.

Al·ham·bra [al·ham′brə] *n.* The walled palace of the Moorish kings of Spain, built in Granada in the 13th and 14th centuries.

a·li·as [ā′lē·əs] 1 *n.* A false name taken so as to hide one's real name: Criminals often have many *aliases.* 2 *conj.* Otherwise called or known as: Jones *alias* Smith.

al·i·bi [al′ə·bī] *n., pl.* **al·i·bis,** *v.* **al·i·bied, al·i·bi·ing** 1 *n.* The fact or the defense that a person suspected of a crime was in another place when it was committed. 2 *n. informal* An excuse for any fault or failure. 3 *v. informal* To offer excuses.

al·ien [āl′yən *or* ā′lē·ən] 1 *adj.* Of or belonging to another country; foreign. 2 *adj.* Not natural; strange: Such an outburst of anger was *alien* to his nature. 3 *n.* A person who is not a citizen of the country in which he or she is living; a foreigner.

al·ien·ate [āl′yən·āt′ *or* ā′lē·ən·āt′] *v.* **al·ien·at·ed, al·ien·at·ing** To make unfriendly; lose the friendship of: to *alienate* an old friend. **—al′ien·a′tion** *n.*

a·light[1] [ə·līt′] *v.* **a·light·ed** or **a·lit, a·light·ing** 1 To descend and come to rest; settle: The bird *alighted* on the branch. 2 To get off or dismount: to *alight* from a horse. 3 To come upon by accident: to *alight* upon an answer.

a·light[2] [ə·līt′] *adj.* Lighted; on fire: The sky was all *alight* with the blaze.

a·lign [ə·līn′] *v.* 1 To arrange or form into or as if into a line: Please *align* the glasses on the shelf. 2 To join with others for or against something: Several nations *aligned* themselves against the use of force. 3 To adjust or bring into a proper working position, as a machine or parts of a machine: to *align* the wheels of an automobile.

a·lign·ment [ə·līn′mənt] *n.* 1 The act of aligning. 2 A being aligned. 3 Position, place, or arrangement in a line: to be out of *alignment.* 4 An adjustment of views to match those of others.

The black arrow is out of alignment.

a·like [ə·līk′] 1 *adj.* Like or similar to one another: The pattern on these plates is not *alike.* 2 *adv.* In the same way or manner: The twins even talk *alike* now.

al·i·men·ta·ry [al′ə·men′trē *or* al′·ə·men′tə·rē] *adj.* Of or having to do with food or nourishment.

alimentary canal The passage that extends from the mouth through the esophagus, stomach, and intestines to the anus. Food is digested as it passes through this canal.

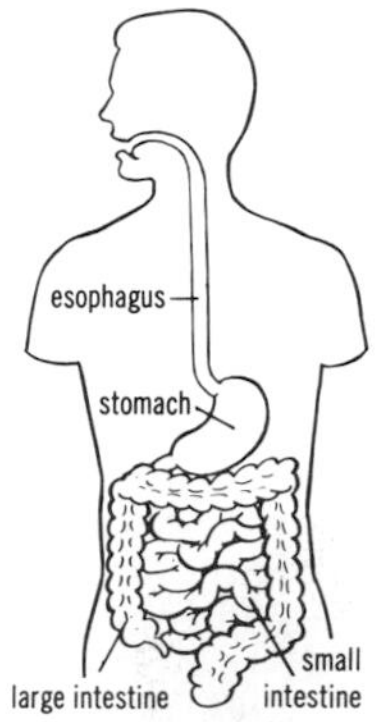

Alimentary canal

al·i·mony [al′ə·mō′nē] *n.* Money that a court orders a man or woman to pay to the divorced or separated wife or husband.

a·line [ə·līn′] *v.* **a·lined, a·lin·ing** Another spelling of ALIGN.

A-line [ā′līn′] *adj.* Having a close-fitting top and a flared skirt: an *A-line* dress.

a·line·ment [ə·līn′mənt] *n.* Another spelling of ALIGNMENT.

a·lit [ə·lit′] Alternative past tense and past participle of ALIGHT[1]: They *alit* from the bus.

a·live [ə·līv′] *adj.* 1 Living; possessing life. 2 In existence or operation; active: to keep hope *alive.* 3 Lively; brisk; alert: very much *alive.* **—alive to** Sensitive to; aware of: *alive to* the needs of the poor. **—alive with** Full of living things or signs of life.

al·ka·li [al′kə·lī] *n., pl.* **al·ka·lis** or **al·ka·lies** A substance, as potash, soda, or ammonia, that neutralizes acids by combining with them to form salts. Alkalis turn pink litmus paper blue, and many of them are used to make soap.

alkali metal Any of a group of soft, white, low-density metallic elements that includes lithium, sodium, potassium, rubidium, cesium, and francium.

al·ka·line [al′kə·līn′ *or* al′kə·lin] *adj.* Of, like, or containing an alkali. **—al·ka·lin·i·ty** [al′kə·lin′ə·tē] *n.*

a·ka·line-earth metal [al′kə·līn′ûrth′] Any of a group of metallic elements that includes beryllium, magnesium, calcium, strontium, barium, and radium.

a	add	**i**	it	**o͝o**	took	**oi**	oil
ā	ace	**ī**	ice	**o͞o**	pool	**ou**	pout
â	care	**o**	odd	**u**	up	**ng**	ring
ä	palm	**ō**	open	**û**	burn	**th**	thin
e	end	**ô**	order	**yo͞o**	fuse	**th**	this
ē	equal					**zh**	vision

ə = {a in *above* e in *sicken* i in *possible* / o in *melon* u in *circus*}

al·ka·lize [al′kə·līz′] *v.* **al·ka·lized, al·ka·liz·ing** To make or become alkaline.
al·ka·loid [al′kə·loid] *n.* Any of a large number of bitter, often poisonous substances found chiefly in plants. Many of them, like quinine and morphine, are used in medicine.
all [ôl] **1** *adj.* The entire quantity or whole of: *All* the audience stood. **2** *adj.* The entire number of; every one of: *All* humans are mortal. **3** *adv.* Wholly; entirely: The toys fell *all* apart. **4** *n.* Everything that one has; the whole: to give one's *all.* **5** *pron.* Everything: *All* is lost; *All* is over. **6** *pron.* Everyone: *All* were invited. **7** *adv.* For each; on each side: a score of three *all.* **8** *adj.* The greatest possible: in *all* haste. **9** *adj.* Any whatever: The situation was beyond *all* help. **10** *adj.* Nothing except; only: The sickly child was *all* skin and bones. **—above all** Most important: *Above all* don't miss the train. **—after all** In spite of everything; nevertheless. **—all at once** Suddenly. **—all in** *informal* Tired; exhausted. **—all in all** Everything considered; on the whole. **—at all** **1** In any way: I can't do it *at all.* **2** To any degree, amount, or extent: We had no luck *at all.* **—in all** Altogether.
Al·lah [al′ə *or* ä′lə] *n.* In the Muslim religion, the name for God.
all-A·mer·i·can [ôl′ə·mer′ə·kən] **1** *adj.* Typically American: *all-American* teen-agers. **2** *adj.* Being or consisting of the best in the U.S. according to a poll of sportswriters or other judges: the *all-American* swimming team. **3** *n.* A member of an all-American team. **4** *adj.* Composed entirely of Americans or of American elements.
all-a·round [ôl′ə·round′] *adj.* **1** Able to do many things; versatile: an *all-around* athlete. **2** Having many uses: an *all-around* knife. **3** Broad; complete: an *all-around* education.
al·lay [ə·lā′] *v.* **al·layed, al·lay·ing** To quiet, soothe, or reduce: to *allay* hunger and fear.
all clear A signal that an air raid or other period of danger is over.
al·le·ga·tion [al′ə·gā′shən] *n.* **1** Something declared to be true but without any proof: Who could take such *allegations* seriously? **2** The act of alleging.
al·lege [ə·lej′] *v.* **al·leged, al·leg·ing** **1** To declare to be true but without proving it: It was *alleged* that he was not the real heir. **2** To give as an argument or reason: The workers *alleged* illness in order to leave early.
al·leged [ə·lejd′ *or* ə·lej′id] *adj.* Declared to be true but without proof; supposed: an *alleged* ability to see into the future. **—al·leg·ed·ly** [ə·lej′id·lē] *adv.*
al·le·giance [ə·lē′jəns] *n.* **1** Loyalty to a government or ruler. **2** Devotion or loyalty, as to a person or cause.
al·le·gor·i·cal [al′ə·gôr′ə·kəl] *adj.* Having to do with or using allegory.
al·le·go·ry [al′ə·gôr′ē] *n., pl.* **al·le·go·ries** A story that uses the surface meaning figuratively to teach a lesson or explain something about life.
al·le·gret·to [al′ə·gret′ō] *adj., adv., n., pl.* **al·le·gret·tos** **1** *adj., adv.* In music, slightly slower than allegro; moderately fast and lively. **2** *n.* A musical composition or a section of one in an allegretto tempo.
al·le·gro [ə·lā′grō *or* ə·leg′rō] *adj., adv., n., pl.* **al·le·gros** **1** *adj., adv.* In music, fast and lively in tempo. **2** *n.* A musical composition or a section of one in an allegro tempo.
al·le·lu·ia [al′ə·lo͞o′yə] *n., interj.* Another spelling of HALLELUJAH.
al·ler·gen [al′ər·jən] *n.* A substance that causes an allergic reaction. **—al′ler·gen′ic** *adj.*
al·ler·gic [ə·lûr′jik] *adj.* **1** Resulting from or having to do with an allergy. **2** Having an allergy.
al·ler·gy [al′ər·jē] *n., pl.* **al·ler·gies** A condition of abnormal sensitiveness, as to certain foods, pollens, or dust. Hives and hay fever are commonly caused by allergies.
al·le·vi·ate [ə·lē′vē·āt′] *v.* **al·le·vi·at·ed, al·le·vi·at·ing** To make lighter or easier to bear; relieve: to *alleviate* pain. **—al·le′vi·a′tion** *n.*
al·ley¹ [al′ē] *n., pl.* **al·leys** **1** A narrow street or passageway between or behind buildings. **2** A bowling alley.
al·ley² [al′ē] *n., pl.* **al·leys** A large marble used to shoot at other marbles in a game.
al·ley·way [al′ē·wā′] *n.* An ALLEY¹ (def. 1).
All Fools' Day Another name for APRIL FOOLS' DAY.

An alley

All·hal·lows [ôl·hal′ōz] *n.* Another name for ALL SAINTS' DAY.
al·li·ance [ə·lī′əns] *n.* **1** A formal agreement or union made between nations, states, or individuals: A treaty is an *alliance* between nations just as a marriage is an *alliance* between individuals. **2** The people or nations who make such an agreement.
al·lied [ə·līd′ *or* al′īd] *adj.* **1** United, joined, or combined: *allied* armies. **2** Closely related: *allied* subjects.
Al·lies [al′īz *or* ə·līz′] *n.pl.* All of the nations, including England, Russia, France, and the U.S., who fought against the Axis powers of Germany, Italy, and Japan in World War II.
al·li·ga·tor [al′ə·gā′tər] *n.* A large reptile found mainly along rivers of the SE U.S., much like a crocodile but with a broader snout.
alligator pear Another name for AVOCADO.
all-im·por·tant [ôl′im·pôr′tənt] *adj.* Extremely important; crucial: Water and sunlight are *all-important* for successful crop production.

Alligator

all-in·clu·sive [ôl′in·klo͞o′·siv] *adj.* Including everything: an *all-inclusive* list.
al·lit·er·a·tion [ə·lit′ə·rā′shən] *n.* The use of the same sound at the beginnings of stressed words in a group or line of verse, as the f's in the phrase "A fair field full of folk."
al·lit·er·a·tive [ə·lit′ə·rā′tiv *or* ə·lit′ər·ə·tiv] *adj.* Characterized by alliteration: *alliterative* verse. **—al·lit′er·a′tive·ly** *adv.*
al·li·um [al′ē·əm] *n.* Any of a group of strong-smelling plants including the onion, leek, chive, garlic, and shallot.
al·lo·cate [al′ə·kāt′] *v.* **al·lo·cat·ed, al·lo·cat·ing** **1** To set apart for a special purpose: to *allocate* money for a birthday gift. **2** To distribute or divide: to

allocate one's energy among several jobs. **—al'lo·ca'tion** *n.*
al·lot [ə·lot'] *v.* **al·lot·ted, al·lot·ting** To give out or assign as a share or portion: to *allot* chores.
al·lot·ment [ə·lot'mənt] *n.* **1** The act of allotting. **2** A share or portion.
al·lo·trope [al'ə·trōp'] *n.* One of two or more different forms that certain chemical elements can exist in under the same conditions: Diamond, charcoal, and graphite are *allotropes* of carbon. **—al'lo·trop'·ic** *adj.*
al·lot·ro·py [ə·lot'rə·pē] *n.* The existence of a chemical element in two or more different forms under the same conditions.
all-out [ôl'out'] *adj.* Complete and entire; total.
all·o·ver [ôl'ō'vər] *adj.* Covering the entire surface: an *allover* print.
al·low [ə·lou'] *v.* **1** To permit: Talking is not *allowed* here. **2** To give or assign; allot: We were *allowed* five dollars for expenses. **3** To admit or concede: to *allow* a point in an argument. **4** To count on, as an addition or deduction: *Allow* more space on this page for your signature. **—allow for** To consider or take into account: In flying to Europe, *allow for* the difference in time.
al·low·a·ble [ə·lou'ə·bəl] *adj.* That can be allowed; permitted; admissible.
al·low·ance [ə·lou'əns] *n.* **1** An amount or portion of something given at more or less regular intervals: a weekly *allowance* of money; a daily *allowance* of food. **2** An amount added or subtracted for some reason: We'll give an *allowance* of $200.00 for your old car. **—make allowances for** To take into account; allow for: We had to *make allowances for* the number of guests.
al·loy [*n.* al'oi *or* ə·loi', *v.* ə·loi'] **1** *n.* A mixture of two or more metals or of a metal and some other substance: Brass is an *alloy* of copper and zinc. **2** *n.* A cheaper metal mixed with a valuable metal. **3** *v.* To mix so as to form an alloy. **4** *v.* To lessen or decrease; mar: The fun of our trip was *alloyed* by many little mishaps.
all right **1** Correct or satisfactory: Your answers are *all right.* **2** Well or well enough: The fan is working *all right.* **3** Healthy; not hurt: His arm is *all right.* **4** Yes. **5** Certainly: I'll be there *all right!* ◆ *Alright* is a spelling of *all right* which is not yet acceptable.
all-round [ôl'round'] *adj.* All-around.
All Saints' Day November 1, a Christian feast in memory of all saints and martyrs.
All Souls' Day November 2, a day when Roman Catholic churches hold services and say masses for all the souls that are believed to be in purgatory.
all·spice [ôl'spīs'] *n.* **1** The dried, aromatic berry of the pimento, a West Indian tree. **2** A spice made from this berry, having a flavor like that of many spices mixed together.
all-star [ôl'stär'] *adj.* Made up of the best players: an *all-star* baseball team.
al·lude [ə·lo͞od'] *v.* **al·lud·ed, al·lud·ing** To refer to something indirectly; just mention: She only *alluded* to last summer's trip.
al·lure [ə·lo͝or'] *v.* **al·lured, al·lur·ing,** *n.* **1** *v.* To draw or entice by something tempting. **2** *v.* To fascinate: India *allured* us. **3** *n.* The power of fascination or attraction; charm.
al·lure·ment [ə·lo͝or'mənt] *n.* **1** The act of alluring. **2** An attractive or fascinating quality or thing.
al·lu·sion [ə·lo͞o'zhən] *n.* A slight or casual mention or suggestion of something: to make an *allusion* to our arrival. ◆ Because the two words sound alike, *allusion* is sometimes confused with *illusion* (which means "a false idea or belief; a deceiving appearance").
al·lu·vi·al [ə·lo͞o'vē·əl] *adj.* Composed of earth or sand left or deposited by running water.
al·lu·vi·um [ə·lo͞o'vē·əm] *n., pl.* **al·lu·vi·ums** or **al·lu·vi·a** [ə·lo͞o'vē·ə] Matter, especially mud and sand, that is deposited by a river or other flowing water.
al·ly [*v.* ə·lī' *or* al'ī, *n.* al'ī *or* ə·lī'] *v.* **al·lied, al·ly·ing,** *n., pl.* **al·lies** **1** *v.* To join or unite for a particular purpose, as for defense: England *allied* herself with France. **2** *n.* A person or country joined with another for a particular purpose. **3** *n.* (*usually written* **Ally**) One of the Allies. ◆ See ALLIES. **4** *n.* A close friend or helper.
al·ma ma·ter [al'mə mā'tər *or* äl'mə mä'tər] The school or college where one is being or has been educated. ◆ *Alma mater* comes from a Latin phrase meaning *fostering mother.*
al·ma·nac [ôl'mə·nak] *n.* A yearly calendar giving the days, weeks, and months of the year with facts about the weather, sun, moon, and other aspects of nature.
al·might·y [ôl·mīt'ē] *adj.* Able to do all things. **—the Almighty** God, the Supreme Being.
al·mond [ä'mənd *or* am'ənd] *n.* **1** A small tree that grows in warm temperate regions. **2** The oval-shaped, edible nut of this tree.
al·mon·er [al'mən·ər *or* ä'mən·ər] *n.* A person who distributes alms, as for a church or wealthy person.
al·most [ôl'mōst *or* ôl·mōst'] *adv.* Very nearly; all but: We are *almost* finished.
alms [ämz] *n.pl.* (*used with a singular or plural verb*) A gift or gifts, usually money, for the poor.
alms·house [ämz'hous'] *n.* A house in which poor persons are taken care of; poorhouse.
al·oe [al'ō] *n., pl.* **al·oes** **1** A South African plant with thick, fleshy leaves and showy red or yellow flowers. **2** (*pl.*) (*used with a singular verb*) A bitter-tasting medicine made from the leaves of this plant, used as a laxative.
a·loft [ə·lôft'] *adv.* **1** In or to a high or higher place; on high; high up. **2** At, to, or toward the masthead of a ship.
a·lo·ha [ə·lō'ə *or* ä·lō'hä] *n., interj.* Love: Hawaiian word used as a greeting and a farewell.
a·lone [ə·lōn'] **1** *adj.* Without anyone or anything near or about: The horse was *alone* in the meadow. **2** *adv.* Without the presence or support of anyone else: to live *alone*; to work *alone.* **3** *adj.* With nothing more: The pictures *alone* are worth the price. **4** *adj.* Only: I *alone* understood. **—let alone** **1** To not disturb or tamper with. **2** And certainly not; not to say: He can't float, *let alone* swim.

a add		**i** it		**o͝o** took		**oi** oil	
ā ace		**ī** ice		**o͞o** pool		**ou** pout	
â care		**o** odd		**u** up		**ng** ring	
ä palm		**ō** open		**û** burn		**th** thin	
e end		**ô** order		**yo͞o** fuse		**th** this	
ē equal						**zh** vision	

ə = a in *above* e in *sicken* i in *possible* / o in *melon* u in *circus*

a·long [ə·long′] 1 *prep.* Through or over the length of; by the side of: to walk *along* the shore. 2 *adv.* Onward; forward: The years roll *along*. 3 *adv.* By the side; near: a brook running *along* by the hedge. 4 *adv.* With one: Bring a friend *along*. 5 *adv.* Advanced: The afternoon is well *along*. **—all along** From the beginning: I expected trouble *all along*. **—along with** 1 Together with. 2 As well as: There are some poor players *along with* some good ones.

a·long·side [ə·long′sīd′] 1 *adv.* Close to or along the side. 2 *prep.* Side by side with; at the side of: The truck pulled in *alongside* my car.

a·loof [ə·lōōf′] 1 *adj.* Cool or distant in manner or action; unsympathetic. 2 *adv.* At a distance; apart: to stay *aloof* from the crowd.

a·loud [ə·loud′] *adv.* 1 Loud enough to be heard. 2 With the voice: Read it *aloud*.

alp [alp] *n.* A high mountain.

al·pac·a [al·pak′ə] *n.* 1 An animal of South America resembling a sheep and related to the llama. 2 Its long, silky wool, or a kind of cloth made from it. 3 A glossy fabric made of cotton and sheep's wool.

Alpaca

al·pen·stock [al′pən·stok′] *n.* A long iron-pointed staff used by mountain climbers.

al·pha [al′fə] *n.* 1 The first letter in the Greek alphabet. 2 The beginning or first of anything.

alpha and omega Both the first and the last; beginning and end; sum total.

al·pha·bet [al′fə·bet] *n.* 1 The letters that form the separate parts or elements of a written language, arranged in a fixed order. 2 Any system of characters or symbols representing the sounds of speech.

al·pha·bet·ic [al′fə·bet′ik] *adj.* Alphabetical.

al·pha·bet·i·cal [al′fə·bet′i·kəl] *adj.* 1 Arranged in the order of the alphabet. 2 Of or having to do with an alphabet. **—al′pha·bet′i·cal·ly** *adv.*

al·pha·bet·ize [al′fə·bə·tīz′] *v.* **al·pha·bet·ized, al·pha·bet·iz·ing** To put in alphabetical order. **—al·pha·bet·i·za·tion** [al′fə·bet′ə·zā′shən] *n.*

al·pha·nu·mer·ic [al′fə·n(y)ōō·mer′ik] *adj.* Consisting of or using letters of the alphabet, numbers, and special characters such as punctuation marks: an *alphanumeric* code.

alpha particle A positively charged particle consisting of two protons and two neutrons, the same as the nucleus of a helium atom, emitted by a radioactive substance.

alpha ray A stream of alpha particles.

alpha rhythm An electrical current emitted by the cortex of the human brain having a frequency between 8 and 13 pulses per second. This frequency is associated with being awake and in a state of relaxation.

al·pine [al′pīn] *adj.* 1 Of or like a mountain. 2 (*written* **Alpine**) Of or having to do with the Alps or the people living there.

al·read·y [ôl·red′ē] *adv.* Before or by this time or a time previously mentioned: We have *already* seen the show. ◆ *Already* should not be confused with *all ready,* which means *completely ready.*

al·right [ôl·rīt′] See ALL RIGHT.

Al·sa·tian [al·sā′shən] *n.* Another name for GERMAN SHEPHERD.

al·so [ôl′sō] *adv.* Besides; too; in addition; as well.

al·so-ran [ôl′sō·ran′] *n.* 1 A person who is defeated in an election or other competition by a wide margin. 2 A horse that fails to come in first, second, or third in a race.

Alta. Alberta.

al·tar [ôl′tər] *n.* 1 A raised table used in most Christian churches in celebrating Mass or Communion. 2 Any raised place or structure on which sacrifices may be offered to a god.

altar boy A boy who assists at the altar; an acolyte.

al·tar·piece [ôl′tər·pēs′] *n.* A painting, carving, or other decoration placed above or behind a church altar.

al·ter [ôl′tər] *v.* To make or become different; change: The coat will have to be *altered*.

al·ter·a·tion [ôl′tə·rā′shən] *n.* 1 The act of changing something. 2 A change made.

al·ter·ca·tion [ôl′tər·kā′shən] *n.* An angry, noisy dispute or quarrel.

al·ter ego [ôl′tər ē′gō] 1 Another aspect of oneself; second self. 2 A best friend or constant companion. ◆ This is a Latin phrase meaning literally "another I."

al·ter·nate [*v.* ôl′tər·nāt′; *adj., n.* ôl′tər·nit] *v.* **al·ter·nat·ed, al·ter·nat·ing,** *adj., n.* 1 *v.* To follow or cause to follow one after another by turns: Day *alternates* with night; *Alternate* the two colors. 2 *v.* To take turns: We *alternated* in mowing the lawn. 3 *adj.* Existing, happening, or following by turns: *alternate* periods of work and study. 4 *adj.* Every other or every second: The dances took place on *alternate* nights. 5 *n.* A substitute, especially a person chosen to take over for another if needed. **—al′ter·nate·ly** *adv.* **—al′ter·na′tion** *n.*

Brown and black beads alternate in the necklace.

alternate angles A pair of nonadjacent angles on opposite sides of a line that intersects two other lines. **Alternate interior angles** are inside the two intersected lines. **Alternate exterior angles** are outside the two intersected lines.

alternating current An electric current that reverses its direction of flow regularly and rapidly.

al·ter·na·tive [ôl·tûr′nə·tiv] 1 *n.* A choice between two or sometimes more things. 2 *n.* Either of the two or more things to be chosen. 3 *adj.* Offering a choice of two or more things: *alternative* plans. **—al·ter′na·tive·ly** *adv.*

al·ter·na·tor [ôl′tər·nā·tər] *n.* 1 Something that alternates. 2 An electrical generator that supplies alternating current.

al·tho [ôl·thō′] *conj.* Another spelling of ALTHOUGH.

al·though [ôl·thō′] *conj.* In spite of the fact that; even if; though.

al·tim·e·ter [al·tim′ə·tər *or* al′tə·mē′tər] *n.* An instrument for measuring height, used in aviation to determine how high a plane is flying.

al·ti·tude [al′tə·t(y)ōōd] *n.* 1 The height above any given point, especially above sea level: a balloon at an *altitude* of 1,500 feet. 2 A high place or rank. 3 In geometry, the perpendicular distance from the base of a figure to the opposite vertex. 4 In astronomy, the angular distance of a celestial body above the horizon.

al·to [al′tō] *n., pl.* **al·tos** 1 The lowest female voice; contralto. 2 A very high male voice. 3 A person with such a voice. 4 The part or range sung by such a voice. 5 An instrument that has such a range.

al·to·cu·mu·lus [al′tō·kyōō′myə·ləs] *n.* A formation of white or gray rounded fleecy clouds typically found at intermediate altitudes.

al·to·geth·er [ôl′tə·geth′ər] *adv.* 1 Completely; wholly; entirely: He was not *altogether* happy. 2 With everything considered or included; in all: *Altogether,* the bill came to $20. ◆ *Altogether* is sometimes confused with *all together* (which means "in one group").

al·to·stra·tus [al′tō·strā′təs *or* al′tō·strat′əs] *n.* A formation of gray or bluish clouds that appears as a layer or sheet, typically found at intermediate altitudes.

al·tru·ism [al′trōō·iz′əm] *n.* Unselfish regard for the welfare of others. **—al′tru·ist** *n.*

al·tru·is·tic [al′trōō·is′tik] *adj.* Concerned with the welfare of others; unselfish.

al·um [al′əm] *n.* A compound of mineral salts, used as an astringent, a styptic, and an emetic.

al·u·min·i·um [al′yə·min′ē·əm] *n.* The British spelling of ALUMINUM.

a·lu·mi·num [ə·lōō′mə·nəm] *n.* A lightweight, bluish white metallic element that does not tarnish easily. It has a wide range of uses.

a·lum·na [ə·lum′nə] *n., pl.* **a·lum·nae** [ə·lum′nē] A female graduate or former student of a college or school.

a·lum·nus [ə·lum′nəs] *n., pl.* **a·lum·ni** [ə·lum′nī] A male graduate or former student of a school or college. ◆ The plural form *alumni* often refers to persons of both sexes.

al·ve·o·lus [al·vē′ə·ləs] *n., pl.* **al·ve·o·li** [al·vē′ə·lī] 1 A small pit or cavity in the body, as a tooth socket in the jaw. 2 One of the many tiny air sacs in the lungs of mammals. **—al·ve′o·lar** *adj.*

al·ways [ôl′wāz *or* ôl′wēz] *adv.* 1 For all time; forever: We will *always* be friends. 2 Every time; on all occasions: You *always* say that.

am [am] The first person singular form of the verb BE in the present tense: I *am* here.

am, AM, or **A.M.** amplitude modulation.

Am The symbol for the element americium.

Am. 1 America. 2 American.

A.M. 1 (also written **a.m.**) ante meridiem. 2 Master of Arts.

AMA or **A.M.A.** American Medical Association.

a·mal·gam [ə·mal′gəm] *n.* 1 An alloy of mercury and another metal or metals. 2 Any mixture or combination of things.

a·mal·ga·mate [ə·mal′gə·māt′] *v.* **a·mal·ga·mat·ed, a·mal·ga·mat·ing** 1 To form an amalgam. 2 To unite or combine: The two companies voted to *amalgamate.* **—a·mal′ga·ma′tion** *n.*

am·a·ni·ta [am′ə·nē′tə] Any of several related mushrooms, some of which are extremely poisonous.

a·man·u·en·sis [ə·man′yōō·en′sis] *n., pl.* **a·man·u·en·ses** [ə·man′yōō·en′sēz] A person who is hired to write down what others say or to copy written material; secretary.

am·a·ryl·lis [am′ə·ril′is] *n.* A plant having large flowers that look something like lilies.

a·mass [ə·mas′] *v.* To heap up; accumulate, especially as wealth or possessions for oneself.

am·a·teur [am′ə·chŏŏr *or* am′ə·t(y)ŏŏr] *n.* 1 A person who practices any art, study, or sport for enjoyment but not for money. 2 A person who does something without sound training or skill. 3 *adj. use:* an *amateur* cast. ◆ *Amateur* and *connoisseur* both come from the French and have Latin roots, *amateur* from a word meaning *to love, connoisseur* from a word meaning *to know.* Thus an *amateur* literally means "one who loves," and a *connoisseur* "one who knows," although in actual everyday use this distinction is not always maintained. An *amateur* may have a great deal of knowledge as well as enthusiasm, and a *connoisseur,* who knows enough to make sharp critical judgments in a certain field, would be odd indeed not to love that field.

am·a·teur·ish [am′ə·chŏŏr′ish *or* am′ə·t(y)ŏŏr′ish] *adj.* Done as by an amateur; not expert. **—am′a·teur′ish·ly** *adv.*

am·a·to·ry [am′ə·tôr′ē] *adj.* Expressing or characterized by love: *amatory* poetry.

a·maze [ə·māz′] *v.* **a·mazed, a·maz·ing** To bewilder with wonder or surprise; astonish; perplex.

a·maze·ment [ə·māz′mənt] *n.* Bewilderment resulting from surprise; astonishment.

a·maz·ing [ə·mā′zing] *adj.* Causing amazement; astonishing; wonderful. **—a·maz′ing·ly** *adv.*

Am·a·zon [am′ə·zon] *n.* 1 In Greek mythology, one of a race of female warriors. 2 (*usually written* **amazon**) Any large, strong, or athletic woman.

Am·a·zo·ni·an [am′ə·zō′nē·ən] *adj.* 1 Of or having to do with an Amazon. 2 Of or having to do with the Amazon River or its valley.

am·bas·sa·dor [am·bas′ə·dər *or* am·bas′ə·dôr] *n.* 1 An official of the highest rank sent as a government representative to another country. 2 Any representative or messenger. **—am·bas′sa·dor·ship** *n.*

am·bas·sa·dor-at-large [am·bas′ə·dər-ət-lärj′] *n., pl.* **am·bas·sa·dors-at-large** An ambassador who is not assigned to a particular foreign country.

am·ber [am′bər] 1 *n.* A hard, brittle, brownish yellow or reddish yellow fossil resin found in the earth, used for such items as jewelry and varnish. 2 *n., adj.* Dark yellowish orange.

am·ber·gris [am′bər·gris *or* am′bər·grēs] *n.* A grayish, waxy substance from the intestines of the sperm whale, used in making perfume.

am·bi·dex·trous [am′bə·dek′strəs] *adj.* Able to use both hands equally well: Being *ambidextrous,* the artist could draw with either hand. **—am′bi·dex′trous·ly** *adv.* **—am′bi·dex′trous·ness** *n.*

am·bi·ence or **am·bi·ance** [am′bē·əns] *n.* A surrounding atmosphere; aura: The artist's studio had an *ambience* of relaxed creativity.

am·bi·ent [am′bē·ənt] *adj.* Surrounding; encompassing: in the *ambient* spaces of the sky.

am·bi·gu·i·ty [am′bə·gyōō′ə·tē] *n., pl.* **am·bi·gu·i·ties** 1 A possibility of more than one meaning. 2 Something ambiguous, as an expression or a situation: Writers should avoid *ambiguities.*

a	add	**i**	it	**ŏŏ**	took	**oi**	oil
ā	ace	**ī**	ice	**ōō**	pool	**ou**	pout
â	care	**o**	odd	**u**	up	**ng**	ring
ä	palm	**ō**	open	**û**	burn	**th**	thin
e	end	**ô**	order	**yōō**	fuse	**th**	this
ē	equal					**zh**	vision

ə = a in *above*, e in *sicken*, i in *possible*, o in *melon*, u in *circus*

am·big·u·ous [am·big′yo͞o·əs] *adj.* 1 Capable of being understood in more senses than one; having more than one possible meaning: an *ambiguous* reply. 2 Doubtful or uncertain: an *ambiguous* position. **—am·big′u·ous·ly** *adv.*

am·bi·tion [am·bish′ən] *n.* 1 An eager desire to succeed or to achieve something, as wealth or power. 2 The object of such a desire: to achieve one's *ambition.*

am·bi·tious [am·bish′əs] *adj.* 1 Moved by or possessing ambition; eager to succeed. 2 Requiring great skill or much effort for success; challenging; difficult: an *ambitious* undertaking. **—am·bi′tious·ly** *adv.*

am·biv·a·lence [am·biv′ə·ləns] *n.* Conflicting or opposite feelings, such as love and hate, toward a person or thing. **—am·biv′a·lent** *adj.*

am·ble [am′bəl] *v.* **am·bled, am·bling,** *n.* 1 *v.* To move at an easy, leisurely pace: to *amble* down a country lane. 2 *v.* To move, as a horse, by lifting and putting down first the two legs on one side and then the two legs on the other side. 3 *n.* The gait of a horse when ambling. 4 *n.* Any leisurely movement or pace.

am·bro·sia [am·brō′zhə *or* am·brō′zhē·ə] *n.* 1 The food of the old Greek and Roman gods, supposed to give eternal life. 2 Any delicious food or drink.

am·bu·lance [am′byə·ləns] *n.* A specially equipped vehicle for carrying the sick and wounded.

am·bu·la·tion [am′byə·lā′shən] *n.* The act or power of walking.

am·bu·la·to·ry [am′byə·lə·tôr′ē] *adj.* 1 Of or relating to walking. 2 Capable of walking; not bedridden: *ambulatory* patients.

am·bus·cade [am′bəs·kād′] *n., v.* **am·bus·cad·ed, am·bus·cad·ing** 1 *n.* An ambush. 2 *v.* To ambush.

am·bush [am′bo͝osh] 1 *n.* A concealed place where troops, or others, lie hidden waiting to attack. 2 *n.* Those who are waiting to attack. 3 *v.* To hide in order to attack. 4 *v.* To attack from a concealed place; waylay.

a·me·ba [ə·mē′bə] *n., pl.* **a·me·bas** or **a·me·bae** [ə·mē′bē] A very small, simple form of animal life, consisting of a single cell and visible only through a microscope.

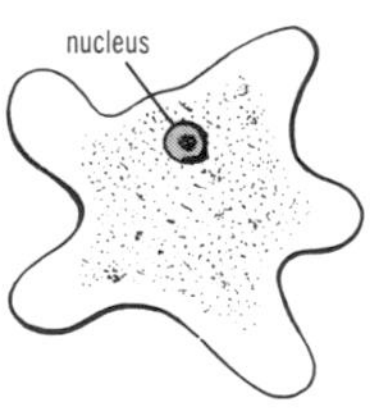

Ameba

a·me·bic [ə·mē′bik] *adj.* 1 Of or relating to an ameba. 2 Caused by an ameba: *amebic* dysentery.

a·mel·io·rate [ə·mēl′yə·rāt′] *v.* **a·mel·io·rat·ed, a·mel·io·rat·ing** To make or become better; improve: to *ameliorate* slum conditions. **—a·mel′io·ra′tion** *n.*

a·men [ā′men′ *or* ä′men′] 1 *interj.* So it is; so be it: a word used at the end of a prayer. 2 *n. informal* Any expression of hearty agreement or conviction: *Amen* to that!

a·me·na·ble [ə·mē′nə·bəl *or* ə·men′ə·bəl] *adj.* 1 Willing to yield or submit; responsive: The children proved *amenable* to our suggestion. 2 Answerable: All citizens are *amenable* to the law. **—a·men′a·bly** *adv.*

a·mend [ə·mend′] *v.* 1 To change for the better; correct; reform: You must *amend* your ways. 2 To change or alter: to *amend* the rules.

a·mend·ment [ə·mend′mənt] *n.* 1 A change for the better. 2 A removal of faults; correction. 3 A change, as of a law or bill.

a·mends [ə·mendz′] *n.pl.* Something done or given to compensate for a wrong, a loss, or an injury.

a·men·i·ty [ə·men′ə·tē] *n., pl.* **a·men·i·ties** 1 The quality of being pleasant or agreeable: the *amenity* of a warm tropical night. 2 (*pl.*) Things, such as good manners, that make life pleasant and comfortable: to practice the *amenities.*

Amer. 1 America. 2 American.

Am·er·a·sian [am′ər·ā′zhən] 1 *n.* A person of mixed American and Asian parentage. 2 *adj.* Of or relating to Amerasians.

A·mer·i·can [ə·mer′ə·kən] 1 *adj.* Of or from the U.S. 2 *n.* A person born in or a citizen of the U.S. 3 *adj.* Of or from the Western Hemisphere. 4 *n.* A person born or living in the Western Hemisphere.

A·mer·i·ca·na [ə·mer′ə·kän′ə *or* ə·mer′ə·kan′ə] *n. pl.* Things such as books, documents, and photographs that relate to American history or culture.

American Beauty A type of long-stemmed rose having large purplish-red flowers.

American cheese A mild-tasting, smooth, yellow or white cheese.

American eagle Another name for BALD EAGLE.

American English English as it is spoken and written in the U.S.

American Indian An Indian (def. 1).

A·mer·i·can·ism [ə·mer′ə·kən·iz′əm] *n.* 1 A trait, custom, or tradition of the people of the U.S. 2 A word, phrase, or usage peculiar to or originating in the U.S.: The words "hot dog" and "OK" are examples of *Americanisms.* 3 Devotion to the U.S., its institutions, and traditions.

A·mer·i·can·ize [ə·mer′ə·kən·īz′] *v.* **A·mer·i·can·ized, A·mer·i·can·iz·ing** To make or become American, as in ideals, customs, or speech. **—A·mer′i·can·i·za′tion** *n.*

American plan A system of charging a single hotel rate that includes a room and three meals a day.

American Revolution The war for independence carried on by the thirteen American Colonies against Great Britain, 1775–1783. It is also called the Revolutionary War.

am·er·i·ci·um [am′ə·rish′ē·əm] *n.* A synthetic, intensely radioactive metallic element produced in nuclear reactors.

Am·er·ind [am′ə·rind′] *n.* An American Indian or Eskimo. **—Am·er·in·di·an** [am′ə·rin′dē·ən] *adj., n.*

am·e·thyst [am′ə·thist] 1 *n.* A variety of quartz having a purple or violet color, used as a gem. 2 *n., adj.* Purplish violet.

a·mi·a·ble [ā′mē·ə·bəl] *adj.* Pleasing in disposition; agreeable; friendly. **—a′mi·a·bil′i·ty** *n.* **—a′mi·a·bly** *adv.*

am·i·ca·ble [am′i·kə·bəl] *adj.* Showing or promoting good will; friendly; peaceable: an *amicable* settlement. **—am′i·ca·bly** *adv.*

a·mid [ə·mid′] *prep.* In the midst of; among.

a·mid·ships [ə·mid′ships′] *adv.* In or at the middle of a ship: The torpedo struck *amidships.*

a·midst [ə·midst′] *prep.* Amid.

a·mi·go [ə·mē′gō] *n., pl.* **a·mi·gos** A friend; comrade: a Spanish word.

a·mi·no acid [ə·mē′nō *or* am′ə·nō] Any of a group of about twenty organic compounds containing nitrogen which have both acid and basic properties and which combine in various proportions to form proteins. When proteins in the diet are digested, they break down into amino acids which are then combined again in different proportions to form the particular proteins needed by the body.

Am·ish [ä′mish *or* am·ish *or* ām′ish] 1 *n., pl.* A strict Mennonite religious sect whose members live mostly in Pennsylvania and Ohio. The Amish live and dress very simply and refuse to take oaths or fight in wars. 2 *adj.* Of or relating to the Amish or their religion.

a·miss [ə·mis′] 1 *adv.* In a wrong or defective way; improperly; erroneously: Have I spoken *amiss*? 2 *adj.* Out of order; wrong; imperfect.

am·i·ty [am′ə·tē] *n., pl.* **am·i·ties** Peaceful relations, as between governments; friendship.

am·me·ter [am′mē′tər] *n.* An instrument for measuring the strength of an electrical current.

am·mo·nia [ə·mōn′yə] *n.* 1 A colorless, suffocating gas formed from nitrogen and hydrogen. 2 Ammonia gas dissolved in water, used for cleaning.

am·mu·ni·tion [am′yə·nish′ən] *n.* 1 Any missiles fired from guns or launched as rockets, or explosive weapons such as bombs, mines, or grenades. 2 Anything used for attack or defense, as of a position or point of view.

am·ne·sia [am·nē·zhə *or* am·nē′zhē·ə] *n.* A partial or complete loss of memory caused by injury, sickness, or severe shock. **—am·ne·si·ac** [am·nē′zhē·ak′ *or* am·nē′zē·ak′] *n., adj.*

am·nes·ty [am′nəs·tē] *n., pl.* **am·nes·ties** An official pardon for offenses committed against a government.

am·ni·on [am′nē·ən *or* am′nē·on′] *n., pl.* **am·ni·ons** or **am·ni·a** [am′nē·ə] The thin, tough membrane forming the fluid-filled sac in which the embryo of a reptile, bird, or mammal is suspended.

am·ni·ot·ic fluid [am′nē·ot′ik] The watery liquid that fills the amnion and cushions the embryo against shock.

a·moe·ba [ə·mē′bə] *n., pl.* **a·moe·bas** or **a·moe·bae** [ə·mē′bē] Another spelling of AMEBA.

a·moe·bic [ə·mē′bik] Another spelling of AMEBIC.

a·mok [ə·muk′ *or* ə·mok′] *adv.* Another spelling of AMUCK.

a·mong [ə·mung′] *prep.* 1 In or through the midst of: He lived *among* the Eskimos; She walked *among* us. 2 By the combined efforts of: *Among* us, we ought to finish the work. 3 In the class, group, or number of: to be *among* the living. 4 In portions for each of: The food was divided *among* them. 5 Mutually between: to have quarrels *among* friends. ◆ See BETWEEN.

a·mongst [ə·mungst′] *prep.* Among.

a·mor·al [ā·môr′əl] *adj.* Lacking standards of right and wrong; neither moral nor immoral.

am·o·rous [am′ər·əs] *adj.* 1 Inclined to fall in love: an *amorous* nature. 2 Of or arising from love: an *amorous* sigh. **—am′o·rous·ly** *adv.* **—am′o·rous·ness** *n.*

a·mor·phous [ə·môr′fəs] *adj.* 1 Not crystallized, though solid: Glass is *amorphous.* 2 Without definite form or shape: *amorphous* clouds. **—a·mor′·phous·ly** *adv.* **—a·mor′phous·ness** *n.*

am·or·tize [am′ər·tīz′ *or* ə·môr′tīz′] *v.* **am·or·tized, am·or·tiz·ing** To pay off (a debt) in installments over time. **—am′or·tiz′a·ble** *adj.* **—am·or·ti·za·tion** [am′ər·tə·zā′shən *or* ə·môr′tə·zā′shən] *n.*

A·mos [ā′məs] *n.* 1 In the Bible, a Hebrew prophet who lived during the eighth century B.C. 2 A book of the Old Testament.

a·mount [ə·mount′] 1 *v.* To reach or add up in number or quantity: Your bill *amounts* to $10. 2 *n.* A sum total: The *amount* due is $10. 3 *n.* Quantity: a small *amount* of flour. 4 *v.* To be equal in effect or importance: Not taking the test *amounts* to failing it.

a·mour [ə·mo͝or′] *n.* A love affair, especially a secret or unlawful one.

amp. 1 amperage. 2 ampere(s).

am·per·age [am′pər·ij] *n.* The strength of an electric current, measured in amperes.

am·pere [am′pir *or* am·pir′] *n.* The unit for measuring the strength of an electric current. It is equal to the current that flows through a resistance of one ohm under an electromotive force of one volt.

am·per·sand [am′pər·sand *or* am′pər·sand′] *n.* The character (&) meaning *and:* Jones & Company.

am·phet·a·mine [am·fet′ə·mēn′ *or* am·fet′ə·mən] *n.* 1 A colorless, liquid compound from which a number of drugs affecting the central nervous system are derived. 2 Any of the drugs derived from this compound.

am·phib·i·an [am·fib′ē·ən] 1 *adj.* Of or having to do with a class of cold-blooded animals adapted for life both on land and in water. 2 *n.* Any amphibian animal, such as frogs and salamanders, whose young have gills and develop through a larval or tadpole stage into animals that breathe with lungs. 3 *n.* Any animal, as a seal or sea lion, that breeds and raises young on land but lives and hunts largely in the water. 4 *adj.* Amphibious. 5 *n.* An airplane that can take off from or alight on land or water. 6 *n.* A vehicle that can be driven on land or on water.

am·phib·i·ous [am·fib′ē·əs] *adj.* 1 Living or adapted to life on land or in water. 2 Capable of operating or landing on either land or water.

am·phi·the·a·ter or **am·phi·the·a·tre** [am′fə·thē′ə·tər] *n.* 1 An oval or circular building with seats in tiers rising from a central open space. 2 Anything resembling this, as a hollow surrounded by sloping hills.

Amphitheater

am·pho·ra [am′fə·rə] *n., pl.* **am·pho·rae** [am′fə·rē] or **am·pho·ras** A narrow-necked jar with two handles, used by the Greeks and Romans to carry and store oil and wine.

am·ple [am′pəl] *adj.* **am·pler, am·plest** 1 Large; spacious. 2 Abundant; liberal. 3 Sufficient; adequate.

am·pli·fi·ca·tion [am′plə·fi·kā′shən] *n.* 1 An extending or enlarging by adding or increasing something. 2 Something that is used to amplify. 3 The creation of a strong electric current that is an enlarged copy of a weaker one, in effect making a weak one strong.

a	add	**i**	it	**o͝o**	took	**oi**	oil		
ā	ace	**ī**	ice	**o͞o**	pool	**ou**	pout		
â	care	**o**	odd	**u**	up	**ng**	ring		
ä	palm	**ō**	open	**û**	burn	**th**	thin		
e	end	**ô**	order	**yo͞o**	fuse	**th**	this		
ē	equal					**zh**	vision		

ə = a in *above* e in *sicken* i in *possible* o in *melon* u in *circus*

am·pli·fi·er [am′plə·fī′ər] *n.* 1 A person or thing that amplifies. 2 Any of various electronic devices that produce amplification, as in a radio.

am·pli·fy [am′plə·fī] *v.* **am·pli·fied, am·pli·fy·ing** 1 To enlarge or increase, as in power or capacity. 2 To make more full or complete: *Amplify* your essay by giving more details. 3 To produce amplification of: to *amplify* an electric current.

am·pli·tude [am′plə·t(y)o͞od′] *n.* 1 The quality of being ample; fullness; abundance. 2 The amount of swing to either side of a middle position made by a wave, as of water, sound, or light, or by an object, as a pendulum.

amplitude modulation The changing of the amplitude of a radio wave in a way that corresponds with the sound or other signal to be broadcast.

am·ply [am′plē] *adv.* In an ample manner; liberally; sufficiently: She was *amply* repaid.

am·pu·tate [am′pyo͞o·tāt′] *v.* **am·pu·tat·ed, am·pu·tat·ing** To cut off, as a limb, by using surgery. **—am′·pu·ta′tion** *n.*

am·pu·tee [am′pyo͞o·tē′] *n.* A person who has had a limb surgically removed.

amt. amount.

a·muck [ə·muk′] *adv.* In a murderous or violent state or manner, especially in the phrase **run amuck,** to become murderous or violent.

am·u·let [am′yə·lit] *n.* An object worn as a charm to keep off evil or bad luck.

a·muse [ə·myo͞oz′] *v.* **a·mused, a·mus·ing** 1 To occupy pleasingly; entertain: to *amuse* a child with a toy. 2 To cause to laugh or smile: I *amused* him with a joke. ◆ See ENTERTAIN.

a·mused [ə·myo͞ozd′] *adj.* 1 Happy or diverted. 2 Showing happiness or amusement: an *amused* expression.

a·muse·ment [ə·myo͞oz′mənt] *n.* 1 The condition of being amused. 2 Something that amuses.

amusement park A commercially operated park offering various games and rides, such as a Ferris wheel and a roller coaster.

a·mus·ing [ə·myo͞o′zing] *adj.* Causing amusement, fun, laughter, or merriment: an *amusing* sitcom. **—a·mus′ing·ly** *adv.*

am·y·lase [am′ə·lās′] *n.* Any of various enzymes that convert starches into sugar.

an [ən *or* an] An indefinite article that is used instead of the article *a* before words beginning with a vowel sound, as *an* owl but *a* dog, *an* honor but *a* house, *an* automobile but *a* universe.

-an A suffix meaning: 1 Of or having to do with, as in *Elizabethan.* 2 A person born or living in or having to do with, as in *Italian* or in *librarian.*

An anachronism

a·nach·ro·nism [ə·nak′rə·niz′əm] *n.* 1 An error that places, shows, or mentions something in a time when it was not known or did not exist. 2 A person or thing existing or occurring out of its proper time.

a·nach·ro·nis·tic [ə·nak′rə·nis′tik] *adj.* Characterized by or containing an anachronism or anachronisms.

an·a·con·da [an′ə·kon′də] *n.* A very large, nonpoisonous snake of South America that crushes its victims in its coils.

a·nae·mi·a [ə·nē′mē·ə] *n.* Another spelling of ANEMIA.

a·nae·mic [ə·nē′mik] *adj.* Another spelling of ANEMIC.

an·aer·obe [an′ə·rōb′ *or* an·âr′ōb′] *n.* An organism, especially a microorganism, that can live in an environment that has no free oxygen.

an·aer·o·bic [an′âr·ō′bik] *adj.* Living or flourishing where there is no free oxygen: *Anaerobic* bacteria cause gangrene. **—an′aer·o′bic·al·ly** *adv.*

an·aes·the·sia [an′is·thē′zhə] *n.* Another spelling of ANESTHESIA.

an·aes·the·si·ol·o·gist [an′is·thē′zē·ol′ə·jist] *n.* Another spelling of ANESTHESIOLOGIST.

an·aes·the·si·ol·o·gy [an′is·thē′zē·ol′ə·jē] *n.* Another spelling of ANESTHESIOLOGY.

an·aes·thet·ic [an′is·thet′ik] *n., adj.* Another spelling of ANESTHETIC.

an·aes·the·tist [ə·nes′thə·tist] *n.* Another spelling of ANESTHETIST.

an·aes·the·tize [ə·nes′thə·tīz′] *v.* **an·aes·the·tized, an·aes·the·tiz·ing** Another spelling of ANESTHETIZE.

an·a·gram [an′ə·gram′] *n.* 1 A word or phrase formed by changing the order of the letters of another word or phrase: "Rate" is an *anagram* of "tear." 2 (*pl.*) A game in which the players make words by changing or adding letters.

a·nal [ā′nəl] *adj.* Of, near, or having to do with the anus.

an·al·ge·si·a [an′əl·jē′zē·ə *or* an′əl·jē′zhə] *n.* The condition of being insensible to pain although fully conscious.

an·al·ge·sic [an′əl·jē′zik *or* an′əl·jē′sik] 1 *n.* A drug or medicine that relieves pain: Aspirin is an *analgesic.* 2 *adj.* Relieving or lessening pain.

an·a·log [an′ə·log′ *or* an′ə·lôg′] *adj.* Of or having to do with an analog computer.

analog computer A computer that solves problems by using continuously measureable quantities, such as voltages or currents, to represent data.

a·nal·o·gous [ə·nal′ə·gəs] *adj.* Alike or similar in certain respects.

a·nal·o·gy [ə·nal′ə·jē] *n., pl.* **a·nal·o·gies** A likeness that exists between two objects that are in other respects not the same: There is an *analogy* between the wings of a bird and the wings of an insect.

a·nal·y·sand [ə·nal′ə·sand′] *n.* A person who is undergoing psychoanalysis.

a·nal·y·sis [ə·nal′ə·sis] *n., pl.* **a·nal·y·ses** [ə·nal′ə·sēz] 1 The separation or breaking up of something into its smaller parts or elements so as to be able to examine or describe the thing more closely: *Analysis* of air shows more than six gases. 2 A written statement of such an analysis. 3 Psychoanalysis.

an·a·lyst [an′ə·list] *n.* 1 A person who analyzes. 2 A psychoanalyst.

an·a·lyt·ic [an′ə·lit′ik] *adj.* Analytical.

an·a·lyt·i·cal [an′ə·lit′ə·kəl] *adj.* 1 Having to do with or using analysis: *analytical* chemistry. 2 Inclined to examine critically or closely: an *analytical* mind. **—an′a·lyt′i·cal·ly** *adv.*

analytic geometry A branch of mathematics in which geometric figures are described by algebraic equations and plotted on coordinate systems.

an·a·lyze [an′ə·līz′] *v.* **an·a·lyzed, an·a·lyz·ing** 1 To make an analysis of: to *analyze* the results of an election. 2 To examine critically or closely.

an·a·pest [an′ə·pest′] *n.* 1 A metrical foot in poetry consisting of two unaccented or short syllables followed by one accented or long one. 2 A line of verse in this rhythm: " 'Twas the night before

Christmas and all through the house" is probably the most widely known *anapest* in the English language.

an·ar·chic [an·är′kik] *adj.* 1 Relating to or promoting anarchy: *anarchic* terrorism. 2 Without control or order; lawless.

an·ar·chi·cal [an·är′ki·kəl] *adj.* Anarchic. —**an·ar′·chi·cal·ly** *adv.*

an·ar·chism [an′ər·kiz′əm] *n.* 1 The political theory that all government should be abolished. 2 Rejection of authority or principles of order. —**an′ar·chis′tic** *adj.*

an·ar·chist [an′ər·kist] *n.* 1 A person who believes all governments should be abolished. 2 A person who rebels against authority and encourages the breaking of all laws or rules.

an·ar·chy [an′ər·kē] *n., pl.* **an·ar·chies** 1 The total absence of government. 2 A condition of lawless confusion and disorder.

a·nath·e·ma [ə·nath′ə·mə] *n.* 1 A very serious ban or curse, especially one placed by a church, as upon a person, book, or doctrine. 2 A person or thing that is banned or cursed. 3 A person or thing that is extremely disliked.

a·nath·e·ma·tize [ə·nath′ə·mə·tīz′] *v.* **a·nath·e·ma·tized, a·nath·e·ma·tiz·ing** To pronounce an anathema against; curse.

an·a·tom·i·cal [an′ə·tom′i·kəl] *adj.* Of or having to do with anatomy or dissection.

a·nat·o·mist [ə·nat′ə·mist] *n.* A person who is an expert in anatomy.

a·nat·o·mize [ə·nat′ə·mīz′] *v.* **a·nat·o·mized, a·nat·o·miz·ing** 1 To dissect (an animal or plant). 2 To examine critically; analyze.

a·nat·o·my [ə·nat′ə·mē] *n., pl.* **a·nat·o·mies** 1 The structure of a person, plant, or animal. 2 The human body or skeleton. 3 The study of the structure of the body. 4 The cutting apart of a body in order to study its separate parts and how they are put together.

-ance A suffix meaning: 1 The act or fact of, as in *resistance.* 2 The quality or condition of being, as in *tolerance.* 3 A thing that, as in *insurance.*

an·ces·tor [an′ses·tər] *n.* 1 A person from whom one is descended, generally a person further back than a grandparent; forebear. 2 An animal of an earlier type from which later animals have developed: The wolf is an *ancestor* of the dog.

an·ces·tral [an·ses′trəl] *adj.* Of, having to do with, or inherited from ancestors: an *ancestral* estate; *ancestral* traits.

an·ces·try [an′ses·trē] *n., pl.* **an·ces·tries** 1 All of one's ancestors. 2 Line of descent; birth: The ruler's family is of noble *ancestry.*

an·chor [ang′kər] 1 *n.* A metal implement with hooks that grip the bottom, lowered into the water by a chain or rope to keep a ship from drifting. 2 *v.* To keep (a ship or boat) secure or held in place by means of an anchor. 3 *v.* To lower the anchor; stay, held by an anchor. 4 *n.* Something that gives security or support: Reading was often an *anchor* for her in times of trouble. 5 *v.* To fix firmly; make secure: to *anchor* the table to the floor. 6 *n.* An anchorman (def. 1). 7 *n.* An anchorwoman.

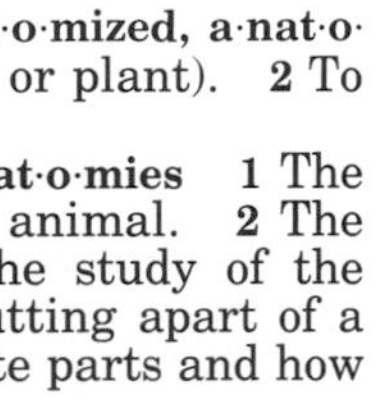

Anchor

an·chor·age [ang′kər·ij] *n.* 1 A place for anchoring. 2 The act of anchoring. 3 The condition of being anchored. 4 Something that gives support, security, or steadiness: an *anchorage* for the tent.

an·cho·rite [ang′kə·rīt′] *n.* 1 A person who has withdrawn from the world for religious reasons. 2 A hermit.

an·chor·man [ang′kər·mən′] *n., pl.* **an·chor·men** [ang′kər·mən] 1 A person who coordinates and narrates a news broadcast in which a number of different newscasters give reports. 2 The last runner for a team in a relay race.

an·chor·wo·man [ang′kər·wŏŏm′ən] *n., pl.* **an·chor·women** [ang′kər·wim′in] A woman who coordinates and narrates a news broadcast in which a number of newscasters give reports.

an·cho·vy [an′chō·vē *or* an·chō′vē] *n., pl.* **an·cho·vies** A very small saltwater fish resembling the herring, eaten as an appetizer.

an·cient [ān′shənt] 1 *adj.* Existing or occurring in times long past, especially in times before the fall of the western Roman Empire in 476. 2 *adj.* Of great age; very old. 3 *n.* (*often pl.*) The people who lived in ancient times.

ancient history 1 History from the earliest recorded events to the fall of the western Roman Empire in 476. 2 *informal* Any fact or event that is no longer interesting or pertinent.

an·cil·lar·y [an′sə·ler′ē] *adj.* 1 Secondary in importance; subordinate. 2 Auxiliary; helping.

-ancy Another form of -ANCE.

and [ənd *or* and] *conj.* 1 As well as; added to; also: eggs *and* butter *and* cheese. 2 As a result: He got his feet wet *and* caught a cold. 3 *informal* To: She'll come *and* get me at six.

an·dan·te [än·dän′tā *or* an·dan′tē] 1 *adj., adv.* In music, moderately slow in tempo. 2 *n.* A musical composition or passage in an andante tempo.

and·i·ron [and′ī′ərn] *n.* One of a pair of metal supports for holding wood in an open fireplace.

Andirons

and/or [and′ôr′] *conj.* A term used mainly in writing to indicate that either or both of two alternatives are to be taken, as in *Fill the pastry with custard and/or whipped cream.*

An·dor·ran [an·dôr′ən] 1 *adj.* Of or from Andorra. 2 *n.* A person born in or a citizen of Andorra.

an·dro·gen [an′drə·jən] *n.* Any of various hormones that are necessary for the development and maintenance of masculine physical characteristics, such as growth of facial hair. —**an·dro·gen·ic** [an′·drə·jen′ik] *adj.*

an·droid [an′droid′] *n.* In science fiction, an artificially created human being.

a	add	**i**	it	**ŏŏ**	took	**oi**	oil		
ā	ace	**ī**	ice	**ōō**	pool	**ou**	pout		
â	care	**o**	odd	**u**	up	**ng**	ring		
ä	palm	**ō**	open	**û**	burn	**th**	thin		
e	end	**ô**	order	**yōō**	fuse	**th̶**	this		
ē	equal					**zh**	vision		

ə = {a in *above* e in *sicken* i in *possible*
o in *melon* u in *circus*

An·drom·e·da [an·drom′ə·də] *n.* 1 In Greek myths, a maiden rescued from a sea monster by Perseus, who then married her. 2 A northern constellation.

an·ec·do·tal [an′ik·dōt′(ə)l] *adj.* Characterized by or consisting of anecdotes.

an·ec·dote [an′ik·dōt] *n.* A brief account or story, usually of an interesting or entertaining nature.

a·ne·mi·a [ə·nē′mē·ə] *n.* A condition in which the blood has too few red corpuscles or too little hemoglobin, resulting in a loss of energy, a pale appearance, and other symptoms.

a·ne·mic [ə·nē′mik] *adj.* Of or having anemia.

an·e·mom·e·ter [an′ə·mom′ə·tər] *n.* An instrument for measuring the speed of the wind.

a·nem·o·ne [ə·nem′ə·nē] *n.* 1 A perennial plant having flowers with no petals but sepals in various colors. 2 The sea anemone.

a·nent [ə·nent′] *prep.* Concerning; in regard to: seldom used today.

an·er·oid barometer [an′ə·roid] An instrument for measuring atmospheric pressure. The flexible top of a box with all air removed bends in or flattens as pressure changes, moving a pointer.

an·es·the·sia [an′is·thē′zhə *or* an′is·thē′zhē·ə] *n.* A local or general loss of sensation, especially of pain, as produced by various drugs or ether.

an·es·the·si·ol·o·gist [an′is·thē′zē·ol′ə·jist] *n.* A physician who specializes in anesthesiology.

an·es·the·si·ol·o·gy [an′is·thē′zē·ol′ə·jē] *n.* A branch of medicine dealing with the study and administration of anesthetics.

an·es·thet·ic [an′is·thet′ik] 1 *n.* Something, as a drug or gas, that causes unconsciousness or deadens sensation, as ether. 2 *adj.* Having to do with or producing anesthesia.

an·es·the·tist [ə·nes′thə·tist] *n.* A person trained to administer anesthetics.

an·es·the·tize [ə·nes′thə·tīz] *v.* **an·es·the·tized, an·es·the·tiz·ing** To cause to be insensible, especially to pain, by means of an anesthetic.

an·eu·rysm [an′yə·riz′əm] *n.* A blood-filled bubble formed in the wall of a weakened blood vessel.

a·new [ə·n(y)ōō′] *adv.* 1 Again: Begin *anew.* 2 Over again in a different way: Write the play *anew.*

an·gel [ān′jəl] *v.* 1 A heavenly being who serves God as a messenger or attendant. 2 A person thought of as like an angel in goodness, purity, or beauty. 3 Any spirit, especially one that guards or protects. 4 *informal* A person who puts up money, as for a theatrical production. ◆ This word comes from the Latin word *angelus,* which in turn came from a Greek word meaning *messenger* (of God).

an·gel·fish [ān′jəl·fish′] *n., pl.* **an·gel·fish** or **an·gel·fish·es** 1 A type of shark having winglike fins. 2 A brightly colored tropical fish.

angel food cake A delicate, spongy cake made without shortening or egg yolks.

an·gel·ic [an·jel′ik] *adj.* 1 Of or having to do with angels. 2 Like an angel; pure; beautiful.

An·ge·lus [an′jə·ləs] *n.* 1 A prayer celebrating the Annunciation. 2 A bell rung morning, noon, and evening as a call to recite this prayer.

an·ger [ang′gər] 1 *n.* The feeling aroused against a person or thing that annoys, offends, opposes, or injures one. 2 *v.* To make or become angry: He *angered* us all; She *angers* easily.

an·gi·o·sperm [an′jē·ə·spûrm′] *n.* Any of a very large group of plants that produce flowers and bear seeds enclosed in an ovary.

an·gle[1] [ang′gəl] *n., v.* **an·gled, an·gling** 1 *n.* A geometric figure formed by two rays that have the same end point. 2 *n.* The space between such rays or surfaces, measured in degrees. 3 *v.* To move or turn at an angle: The halfback *angled* down the field. 4 *n.* A point of view; standpoint: The problem was discussed from all *angles.*

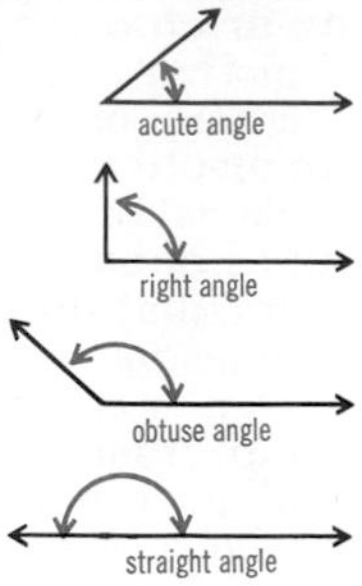

an·gle[2] [ang′gəl] *v.* **an·gled, an·gling** 1 To fish with a hook and line. 2 To try to gain something by using schemes or tricks.

angle of incidence The acute angle formed by the path of a ray striking a surface and a perpendicular line drawn from the surface at the point of impact. When a ray of light strikes a smooth reflecting surface, such as a mirror, the *angle of incidence* is always equal to the *angle of reflection.*

angle of reflection The acute angle formed by the path of a ray reflected from a surface and a perpendicular line drawn from the surface at the point of impact.

angle of refraction The acute angle formed by the path of a refracted ray and a perpendicular line drawn from the refracting surface at the point of refraction.

an·gler [ang′glər] *n.* 1 A person who angles for fish. 2 A large-mouthed saltwater fish having long flexible filaments attached to its head with which it attracts smaller fish.

An·gles [ang′gəlz] *n.pl.* A Germanic people that migrated to Britain in the fifth century.

an·gle·worm [ang′gəl·wûrm′] *n.* An earthworm.

An·gli·can [ang′glə·kən] 1 *adj.* Of or having to do with the Church of England. 2 *n.* A member of the Church of England. **—An′gli·can·ism** *n.*

An·gli·cize [ang′glə·sīz′] *v.* **An·gli·cized, An·gli·ciz·ing** To make English, as in form, pronunciation, or characteristics: to *Anglicize* the pronunciation of a foreign word.

an·gling [ang′gling] *n.* Fishing with a hook and line.

An·glo [ang′glō′] *n., pl.* **An·glos** A white North American who is not of Hispanic descent.

Anglo- A combining form meaning: English, as in *Anglo-American.*

An·glo-Sax·on [ang′glō·sak′sən] 1 *n.* A member of the Germanic people living in England who were conquered by the Normans in 1066. 2 *n.* Their language; Old English. 3 *adj.* Of or having to do with these people or their language. 4 *adj.* Of or having to do with the English people.

An·go·lan [an·gō′lən] 1 *adj.* Of or from Angola. 2 *n.* A person born in or a citizen of Angola.

An·go·ra [ang·gôr′ə] *n.* 1 A kind of cat with long silky hair, also called **Angora cat.** 2 A kind of goat with long silky hair, also called **Angora goat.** 3 A kind of rabbit with long, soft hair, also called **Angora rabbit.** 4 The hair of the Angora goat or the Angora rabbit, also called **Angora wool.** 5 A yarn or fabric made from Angora wool.

an·go·stu·ra bark [ang′gəs·t(y)ŏŏr′ə] *n.* The bitter, aromatic bark of either of two South American trees.

an·gry [ang′grē] *adj.* **an·gri·er, an·gri·est** 1 Feeling or showing anger: an *angry* person; an *angry* tone of voice. 2 Stormy: an *angry* sky or sea. 3 Badly inflamed: an *angry* sore. **—an′gri·ly** *adv.*

ang·strom [ang′strəm] *n.* A unit for measuring extremely small lengths or sizes, especially wavelengths of light. It is often called an **angstrom unit.** In one inch there are 254 million angstroms.

an·guish [ang′gwish] *n.* Great suffering of mind or body; agony: the *anguish* of parents whose child has been killed in an accident.

an·guished [ang′gwisht] *adj.* Feeling, showing, or caused by anguish: an *anguished* cry.

an·gu·lar [ang′gyə·lər] *adj* 1 Having or describing an angle or angles; sharp-cornered: an *angular* outline. 2 Measured by an angle: *angular* distance. 3 Bony; gaunt: an *angular* jaw.

an·gu·lar·i·ty [ang′gyə·lar′ə·tē] *n., pl.* **an·gu·lar·i·ties** 1 The condition of being angular. 2 An angle or sharp corner.

An·gus [ang′gəs] *n.* Another name for ABERDEEN ANGUS.

an·hy·dride [an·hī′drīd′] *n.* 1 A chemical compound derived from another by removing water. 2 A chemical compound that forms an acid or a base when combined with water.

an·hy·drous [an·hī′drəs] *adj.* In chemistry, lacking water, especially water of crystallization.

an·i·line [an′ə·lin] *n.* An oily, poisonous compound derived from benzene and much used for making such items as dyes and plastics.

aniline dye 1 A dye made from aniline. 2 Any of various synthetic dyes.

an·i·mad·ver·sion [an′ə·mad·vûr′zhən] 1 A critical, especially unfavorable remark. 2 Unfavorable, often hostile criticism.

an·i·mal [an′ə·məl] 1 *n.* A living being typically differing from plants in being able to move voluntarily, in having a nervous system, and in being unable to make food by photosynthesis. 2 *n.* Any such creature other than a human being. 3 *adj.* Of or having to do with animals: *animal* life. 4 *n.* A person who acts like a beast or brute. 5 *adj.* Like a beast or a beast's: *animal* desires. ◆ This word comes directly from Latin, where it meant a *living being.*

an·i·mal·cule [an′ə·mal′kyōōl] *n.* Any very small or microscopic animal, as an ameba.

animal husbandry The study and practice of breeding and tending domestic livestock.

animal kingdom One of the three great divisions of nature, including all animals.

an·i·mate [*v.* an′ə·māt′, *adj.* an′ə·mit] *v.* **an·i·mat·ed, an·i·mat·ing,** *adj.* 1 *v.* To give life to. 2 *adj.* Living. Animate nature includes both animals and plants. 3 *v.* To fill with zest and spirit: Spirited tunes *animated* the marchers. 4 *v.* To inspire: to be *animated* by love.

an·i·mat·ed [an′ə·mā′tid] *adj.* Having spirit or zest; lively. **—an′i·mat′ed·ly** *adv.*

animated cartoon A series of drawings shown as a motion picture with moving figures. Each drawing is slightly changed from the one before to make the movement.

an·i·ma·tion [an′ə·mā′shən] *n.* 1 Life. 2 Liveliness; spirit.

an·i·ma·to [ä′nē·mä′tō] *adj., adv.* In music, in a lively manner.

an·i·mism [an′ə·miz′əm] *n.* The belief that natural objects and forces, as mountains, rivers, and wind, have spirits and powers. **—an′i·mist** *n.* **—an′i·mis·tic** *adj.*

an·i·mos·i·ty [an′ə·mos′ə·tē] *n., pl.* **an·i·mos·i·ties** Strong dislike or hatred; enmity.

an·i·mus [an′ə·məs] *n.* 1 Animosity. 2 The animating spirit or purpose; guiding force.

an·i·on [an′ī′ən] *n.* A negatively charged ion.

an·ise [an′is] *n.* 1 A small plant, related to the carrot, grown for its seed. 2 Another word for ANISEED.

an·i·seed [an′ə·sēd′] *n.* The seed of the anise. It tastes like licorice and is used as a flavoring in food, liqueurs, and medicines.

an·kle [ang′kəl] *n.* The joint connecting the foot and the leg.

an·kle·bone [ang′kəl·bōn′] *n.* Another word for TALUS.

an·klet [ang′klit] *n.* 1 A band worn around the ankle as an ornament or fetter. 2 A short sock.

an·nals [an′əlz] *n.pl.* 1 A record of events year by year. 2 History or records: the *annals* of exploration.

an·neal [ə·nēl′] *v.* To make (glass or metal) tougher and less brittle by heating and then slowly cooling.

an·ne·lid [an′ə·lid] *n.* A worm whose body is made up of segments like rings, as the earthworm and leech.

an·nex [*v.* ə·neks′, *n.* an′eks] 1 *v.* To add as an additional part: The U.S. *annexed* Texas in 1845. 2 *n.* Something annexed, 3 *n.* An addition to a building, or another building used along with the main one. **—an′nex·a′tion** *n.*

an·ni·hi·late [ə·nī′ə·lāt′] *v.* **an·ni·hi·lat·ed, an·ni·hi·lat·ing** To destroy completely. **—an·ni′hi·la′tion** *n.*

an·ni·ver·sa·ry [an′ə·vûr′sə·rē] *n., pl.* **an·ni·ver·sa·ries** 1 The day of the year on which an event took place in some preceding year: the *anniversary* of the founding of the U.N. 2 A celebration on such a day. 3 *adj. use:* an *anniversary* celebration. ◆ This word comes from two Latin words meaning *to turn the year.*

an·no Dom·i·ni [an′ō dom′ə·nē] In the year of our Lord: a Latin phrase. ◆ See A.D.

an·no·tate [an′ō·tāt′] *v.* **an·no·tat·ed, an·no·tat·ing** To furnish with notes explaining or commenting on: Homer's epics have been fully *annotated.*

an·no·ta·tion [an′ō·tā′shən] *n.* 1 The act of annotating. 2 An explanatory note or comment.

an·nounce [ə·nouns′] *v.* **an·nounced, an·nounc·ing** 1 To give public notice of; proclaim. 2 To declare the arrival of: to *announce* guests. 3 To make known to the senses.

an·nounce·ment [ə·nouns′mənt] *n.* 1 The act of announcing. 2 Something announced. 3 An often formal public or private notice of an event.

an·nounc·er [ə·noun′sər] *n.* A person who announces, especially one who gives the news or introduces performers, on radio or TV.

an·noy [ə·noi′] *v.* To bother; irritate.

a	add	**i**	it	**ŏŏ**	took	**oi**	oil
ā	ace	**ī**	ice	**ōō**	pool	**ou**	pout
â	care	**o**	odd	**u**	up	**ng**	ring
ä	palm	**ō**	open	**û**	burn	**th**	thin
e	end	**ô**	order	**yōō**	fuse	**t̶h̶**	this
ē	equal					**zh**	vision

ə = {a in *above* e in *sicken* i in *possible* / o in *melon* u in *circus*}

an·noy·ance [ə·noi′əns] *n.* 1 An annoying or being annoyed. 2 The angry feeling caused by being annoyed. 3 Something that annoys.

an·noy·ing [ə·noi′ing] *adj.* Irritating: an *annoying* habit. **—an·noy′ing·ly** *adv.*

an·nu·al [an′yōō·əl] 1 *adj.* Coming or happening once each year, especially at or around the same time: *annual* elections. 2 *adj.* Taking a year: the *annual* cycle of the seasons. 3 *adj.* For a year: *annual* income. 4 *adj.* Of a plant, living or lasting only a year or a season. 5 *n.* An annual plant. 6 *n.* A book or magazine that is published once a year. **—an′nu·al·ly** *adv.*

annual ring One of a series of concentric rings, each representing one year's growth, that can be seen in the cross section of a tree trunk.

an·nu·i·ty [ə·n(y)ōō′ə·tē] *n.* 1 A sum of money paid each year. 2 The right to receive such yearly payments.

an·nul [ə·nul′] *v.* **an·nulled, an·nul·ling** To do away with; declare to be void and canceled: to *annul* a law or marriage. **—an·nul′ment** *n.*

an·nu·lar [an′yə·lər] *adj.* In the shape of or forming a ring.

annular eclipse An eclipse of the sun in which a narrow ring of the sun is visible around the dark circle of the moon.

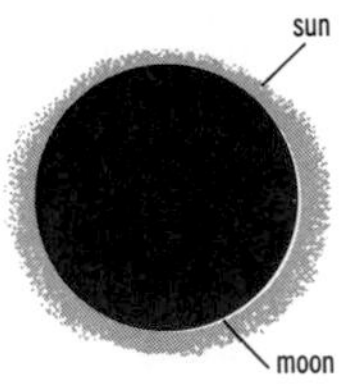

Annular eclipse

an·num [an′əm] *n.* The Latin word for *year,* often used in the phrase *per annum.*

An·nun·ci·a·tion [ə·nun′sē·ā′·shən] *n.* 1 The angel Gabriel's announcement to Mary that she was to be the mother of Jesus. 2 The Christian festival on March 25 commemorating this event.

an·ode [an′ōd′] *n.* The positive terminal of a battery, an electrolytic cell, a diode, or an electron tube.

an·o·dyne [an′ə·dīn′] *n.* 1 A drug that relieves pain. 2 Anything that soothes or comforts: Music and meditation were his *anodynes.*

a·noint [ə·noint′] *v.* To apply oil or ointment to, often as part of a religious ceremony. **—a·noint′·ment** *n.*

a·nom·a·lous [ə·nom′ə·ləs] *adj.* Different from the usual; irregular or abnormal.

a·nom·a·ly [ə·nom′ə·lē] *n., pl.* **a·nom·a·lies** 1 A deviation from the common rule; irregularity. 2 Something anomalous: A wingless bird is an *anomaly.*

a·non [ə·non′] *adv.* 1 In a little while; soon. 2 At another time.

anon. anonymous.

an·o·nym·i·ty [an′ə·nim′ə·tē] *n.* A being anonymous.

a·non·y·mous [ə·non′ə·məs] *adj.* 1 By or from a person not named or not identified: an *anonymous* gift or poem. 2 Whose name is unknown: *anonymous* victims of war. **—a·non′y·mous·ly** *adv.*

a·noph·e·les [ə·nof′ə·lēz] *n.* A kind of mosquito that can transmit the malaria parasite.

an·or·ak [an′ə·rak′] *n.* Another word for PARKA. ◆ This word is the Greenland Eskimo name for this garment.

an·o·rex·i·a [an′ə·rek′sē·ə] *n.* Loss of appetite, especially as a symptom of illness.

anorexia ner·vo·sa [nûr·vō′sə] A serious medical disorder, chiefly in young women, marked by avoidance of food and by dangerous weight loss.

an·oth·er [ə·nuth′ər] 1 *adj., pron.* One more: *another* day; Let me have *another.* 2 *adj.* Not the same; different: *another* page. 3 *pron.* A different one: I would prefer *another.* 4 *adj.* Of the same kind as: *another* Einstein.

an·ox·i·a [an·ok′sē·ə] *n.* A condition in which insufficient oxygen is supplied to the cells of the body.

ans. answer.

an·swer [an′sər] 1 *n.* A reply or response by word or action, as to a letter or question. 2 *v.* To reply or respond to: to *answer* a question; to *answer* the telephone. 3 *n.* A solution to a problem. 4 *v.* To be sufficient; serve: The soft earth *answered* for a bed. 5 *v.* To be responsible or accountable: to *answer* for someone's safety or honesty. 6 *v.* To correspond or match: to *answer* to a description. **—answer back** To reply rudely or defiantly.

an·swer·a·ble [an′sər·ə·bəl] *adj.* 1 Responsible: The clerk is *answerable* to the company for all receipts. 2 That can be answered or refuted.

answering service A company that intercepts and answers telephone calls and takes messages for its clients.

ant [ant] *n.* A small crawling insect belonging to an order that includes bees and wasps. Ants live in tunnels in wood or in the ground in well-organized colonies.

-ant A suffix meaning: 1 In the act of doing, as in *defiant.* 2 A person or thing that does something, as in *servant.*

ant. 1 antenna. 2 antonym.

ant·ac·id [ant′as′id] 1 *n.* A substance used to neutralize acidity, as in the stomach. 2 *adj.* Neutralizing acids.

an·tag·o·nism [an·tag′ə·niz′əm] *n.* Mutual opposition, especially with hostile feelings.

an·tag·o·nist [an·tag′ə·nist] *n.* A person who fights or contends with another; adversary.

an·tag·o·nis·tic [an·tag′ə·nis′tik] *adj.* Opposed; hostile. **—an·tag′o·nis′ti·cal·ly** *adv.*

an·tag·o·nize [an·tag′ə·nīz′] *v.* **an·tag·o·nized; an·tag·o·niz·ing** To make an enemy of.

Ant·arc·tic [ant·ärk′tik] *adj.* (*sometimes written* **antarctic**) Of or having to do with the Antarctic.

Antarctic Circle An imaginary circle at about 66° 33′ south latitude, beyond which the sun cannot be seen in the depth of winter, taken as the boundary of the south frigid zone.

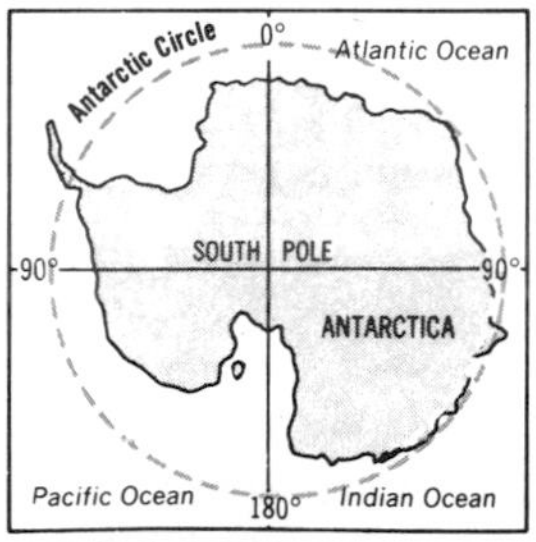

Antarctic circle

ant bear A large, gray-furred anteater of Central and South America.

an·te [an′tē] *n., v.* **an·ted** or **an·teed, an·te·ing** 1 *n.* An amount that each player in a game of poker must put into the pot before a hand is dealt. 2 *v.* To pay an ante. 3 *n. slang.* One's share of a joint expense.

ante- A prefix meaning: Before, in time or space, as in *antediluvian* or *anteroom.*

ant·eat·er [ant′ē′tər] *n.* Any of several mammals that have long, sticky tongues and feed mainly on ants and termites.

an·te·bel·lum [an′tē·bel′əm] *adj.* Of the period before the American Civil War.

an·te·ce·dent [an′tə·sēd′(ə)nt] 1 *adj.* Coming earlier; happening before; previous. **2** *n.* A person, thing, or event that comes or happens earlier. **3** *n.* In grammar, the word, phrase, or clause to which a pronoun refers. In "The song that he sang is very old," *song* is the antecedent of *that.* **4** *n.* (*pl.*) A person's past life or ancestry.

an·te·cham·ber [an′ti·chām′bər] *n.* An anteroom.

an·te·date [an′ti·dāt′] *v.* **an·te·dat·ed, an·te·dat·ing** **1** To come or happen before: The bow *antedates* the crossbow. **2** To give a date to earlier than the actual date: The document was signed on June 5 but was *antedated* to June 1.

an·te·di·lu·vi·an [an′ti·di·lo͞o′vē·ən] **1** *adj.* Before the Flood. **2** *n.* A person, animal, or plant that lived before the Flood. **3** *adj.* Very old or old-fashioned. **4** *n.* A very old or old-fashioned person.

an·te·lope [an′tə·lōp′] *n., pl.* **an·te·lope** or **an·te·lopes** **1** A small, graceful animal with spiral horns, like a deer but related to the goat. **2** The pronghorn of the U.S. and Canada.

an·te me·rid·i·em [an′tə mə·rid′ē·əm] Between 12 o'clock midnight and 11:59 in the morning. ◆ This Latin term for "before noon" is used in its abbreviated form A.M. to designate time.

an·ten·na [an·ten′ə] *n.* **1** *pl.* **an·ten·nae** [an·ten′ē] One of a pair of jointed, sensitive feelers on the head of various insects and such animals as crabs and lobsters. **2** *pl.* **an·ten·nas** A system of wires, rods, or reflecting surfaces for transmitting or receiving radio waves.

Butterfly antennae

an·te·pe·nult [an′tē·pē′nult′] *n.* The third-to-last syllable in a word. In the word "horsefeathers," the syllable *horse-* is the antepenult. **—an·te·pen·ul·ti·mate** [an′tē·pi·nul′tə·mit] *adj., n.*

an·te·ri·or [an·tir′ē·ər] *adj.* **1** At, near, or toward the front; fore. **2** Earlier in time.

an·te·room [an′ti·ro͞om′] *n.* A room leading to a more important or main room; waiting room.

an·them [an′thəm] *n.* **1** A song or hymn of praise, patriotism, or devotion: a national *anthem.* **2** A piece of sacred music, often with words taken from the Bible.

an·ther [an′thər] *n.* A slender stem at the center of a flower that bears the pollen.

Anthers

ant·hill [ant′hil′] *n.* A mound of earth piled up by ants in building their underground nest.

an·thol·o·gy [an·thol′ə·jē] *n., pl.* **an·thol·o·gies** A collection of selected poems or other writings by various authors.

an·thra·cite [an′thrə·sīt′] *n.* Coal that burns slowly and with little flame; hard coal.

an·thrax [an′thraks] *n.* An infectious and often fatal bacterial disease, chiefly of cattle, sheep, and goats, and sometimes transmitted to humans.

an·thro·poid [an′thrə·poid′] **1** *adj.* Like a human being; humanlike: said of certain apes. **2** *n.* A humanlike ape, such as the gorilla.

an·thro·pol·o·gist [an′thrə·pol′ə·jist] *n.* An expert in anthropology.

an·thro·pol·o·gy [an′thrə·pol′ə·jē] *n.* The science that studies the physical, social, and cultural development of human beings. **—an·thro·pol·og·ic** [an′thrə·pə·loj′ik] or **an·thro·po·log·i·cal** [an′thrə·pə·loj′i·kəl] *adj.* **—an′thro·po·log′i·cal·ly** *adv.*

anti- A prefix meaning: **1** Opposed to; against, as in *antislavery.* **2** An opposite of, as in *anticlimax.* **3** Working or counteracting, as in *antiseptic.*

an·ti·air·craft [an′tē·âr′kraft] *adj.* Used or directed against enemy aircraft.

an·ti·at·om [an′tē·at′əm] *n.* An atom made up of antiparticles.

an·ti·bal·lis·tic missile [an′ti·bə·lis′tik] A missile designed to intercept and destroy an airborne ballistic missile.

an·ti·bi·ot·ic [an′ti·bī·ot′ik] *n.* A substance such as penicillin, produced by a microorganism or fungus, that kills or weakens microorganisms harmful to people.

an·ti·black [an′tē·blak′] *adj.* Having or exhibiting hostility and prejudice against Blacks.

an·ti·bod·y [an′ti·bod′ē] *n., pl.* **an·ti·bod·ies** A substance formed in the body that immunizes it against a specific invading agent, as a particular virus or poison.

an·tic [an′tik] **1** *n.* (*usually pl.*) A prank or funny act. **2** *adj.* Odd; ludicrous: *antic* behavior.

An·ti·christ [an′ti·krīst′] *n.* The great enemy or adversary of Christ.

an·tic·i·pate [an·tis′ə·pāt′] *v.* **an·tic·i·pat·ed, an·tic·i·pat·ing** **1** To look forward to; expect: to *anticipate* a happy time. **2** To foresee and act on beforehand: to *anticipate* someone's wishes. **3** To invent, discover, or do in advance of: Leonardo *anticipated* the flying machine. **4** To be ahead of in doing: Russia *anticipated* the United States in orbiting a satellite.

an·tic·i·pa·tion [an·tis′ə·pā′shən] *n.* **1** The act of anticipating. **2** Expectation: People fled in *anticipation* of a flood.

an·ti·cli·mac·tic [an′ti·klī·mak′tik] *adj.* Of, having to do with, or characterized by an anticlimax. **—an′ti·cli·mac′ti·cal·ly** *adv.*

an·ti·cli·max [an′ti·klī′maks] *n.* A sudden descent from the important to the unimportant or silly. Example: The disaster destroyed a great ship, its cargo, 917 people, and a kitten.

an·ti·cline [an′ti·klīn′] *n.* An arched geological formation in which layers of rock slope down on opposite sides of a crest. **—an′ti·cli′nal** *adj.*

an·ti·co·ag·u·lant [an′tē·kō·ag′yə·lənt] **1** *n.* A substance that prevents or slows down the clotting of blood. **2** *adj.* Acting to prevent blood clotting.

an·ti·con·vul·sant [an′tē·kən·vul′sənt] *n.* A drug used to prevent convulsions. **—an′ti·con·vul′sive** *adj.*

an·ti·cy·clone [an′tē·sī′klōn′] *n.* A weather system in which winds, moving clockwise in the Northern Hemisphere and counterclockwise in the Southern Hemisphere, rotate around a center of high atmospheric pressure.

a	add	**i**	it	**o͝o**	took	**oi**	oil
ā	ace	**ī**	ice	**o͞o**	pool	**ou**	pout
â	care	**o**	odd	**u**	up	**ng**	ring
ä	palm	**ō**	open	**û**	burn	**th**	thin
e	end	**ô**	order	**yo͞o**	fuse	**t͟h**	this
ē	equal					**zh**	vision

ə = {a in *above* e in *sicken* i in *possible* / o in *melon* u in *circus*}

an·ti·dote [an′ti·dōt′] *n.* Anything that will counteract or remove the effects of a poison, disease, or any evil.

an·ti·fem·i·nist [an′tē·fem′ə·nist] **1** *adj.* Opposed to feminism. **2** *n.* A person who is opposed to feminism.

an·ti·freeze [an′ti·frēz′] *n.* A substance put into a liquid to keep it from freezing, as in an automobile radiator.

an·ti·gen [an′ti·jən] *n.* A substance that, when introduced into the body, helps it produce antibodies.

An·tig·o·ne [an·tig′ə·ne] *n.* In Greek legends, the daughter of Oedipus, who was put to death by her uncle, Creon, for disobeying his order not to bury her brother.

an·ti·grav·i·ty [an′tē·grav′i·tē] **1** *adj.* Having the power to reduce or cancel the effects of gravity. **2** *n.* The effect that would be produced if a gravitation field were canceled or reduced.

an·ti·his·ta·mine [an′ti·his′tə·mēn′] *n.* Any of several drugs used to treat colds and allergic conditions, as asthma and hay fever.

an·ti·knock [an′ti·nok′] *n.* A substance added to gasoline to keep an engine from making a knocking noise.

an·ti·log·a·rithm [an′tē·lôg′ə·rith′əm *or* an′tē·log′ə·rith′əm] *n.* A number generated when another number called the base is raised to a power called the logarithm.

an·ti·ma·cas·sar [an′tē·mə·kas′ər] *n.* A piece of material placed over the arms and the upper back of a chair as protection against wear and dirt.

an·ti·mat·ter [an′ti·mat′ər] *n.* Matter composed of antiparticles. If antimatter were to come into contact with matter, an explosion would result.

an·ti·mis·sile [an′tē·mis′əl] *adj.* Designed for or used as a defense against missiles.

an·ti·mo·ny [an′tə·mō′nē] *n.* A brittle silver-white metallic element, used in making alloys and in medicine.

an·ti·neu·tri·no [an′tē·n(y)o͞o·trē′nō] *n., pl.* **an·ti·neu·tri·nos** The antiparticle of a neutrino.

an·ti·neu·tron [an′tē·n(y)o͞o′tron′] *n.* The antiparticle of a neutron.

an·ti·par·ti·cle [an′tē·par′ti·kəl] *n.* Any subatomic particle identical in mass to another subatomic particle but having magnetic, electrical, and other properties that are exactly opposite.

an·ti·pas·to [än′ti·päs′tō] *n., pl.* **an·ti·pas·tos** *or* **an·ti·pas·ti** [än′ti·päs′tē] An Italian dish of various appetizers, served before lunch or dinner.

an·tip·a·thy [an·tip′ə·thē] *n., pl.* **an·tip·a·thies** **1** A strong feeling of dislike or aversion. **2** A person or thing so disliked.

an·ti·per·spi·rant [an′tē·pûr′spər·ənt] *n.* A substance applied to the skin to reduce sweating.

an·tip·o·des [an·tip′ə·dēz′] *n.* (*used with singular or plural verb*) A place or region at the other end of a line through the center of the earth. —**an·tip′o·dal** *adj.*

an·ti·pol·lu·tion [an′tē·pə·lo͞o′shən] *adj.* Designed to reduce, counteract, or eliminate pollution: an *antipollution* device.

an·ti·pov·er·ty [an′tē·pov′ər·tē] *adj.* Designed to relieve or eliminate poverty: an *antipoverty* program.

an·ti·pro·ton [an′tē·prō′ton′] *n.* The antiparticle of a proton.

an·ti·quar·i·an [an′ti·kwâr′ē·ən] **1** *adj.* Of or having to do with antiques or antiquities. **2** *n.* A person who studies, collects, or deals in relics from ancient times.

an·ti·quar·y [an′ti·kwer′ē] *n., pl.* **an·ti·quar·ies** An antiquarian.

an·ti·quat·ed [an′ti·kwā′tid] *adj.* Old-fashioned; out-of-date.

an·tique [an·tēk′] **1** *adj.* Of or from early times; very old: an *antique* car over 70 years old. **2** *n.* Something made long ago. **3** *n.* Something that has value because of its age, especially a work of art or handicraft more than a hundred years old. **4** *adj.* Old-fashioned; out-of-date: an *antique* vacuum cleaner.

an·tiq·ui·ty [an·tik′wə·tē] *n., pl.* **an·tiq·ui·ties** **1** The quality of being very old. **2** Ancient times, especially before the Middle Ages. **3** The people of ancient times. **4** (*usually pl.*) Relics of ancient times.

an·ti-Sem·ite [an′ti·sem′īt′] *n.* A person who is hostile toward or prejudiced against Jews.

an·ti-Sem·i·tism [an′ti·sem′ə·tiz′əm] *n.* Hostility, discrimination, or prejudice against Jews. —**an·ti-Se·mit·ic** [an′ti-sə·mit′ik] *adj.*

an·ti·sep·tic [an′ti·sep′tik] **1** *adj.* Preventing infection by killing or stopping the growth of germs. **2** *n.* A substance, such as iodine or alcohol, that does this.

an·ti·slav·er·y [an′ti·slā′vər·ē] *n.* Against slavery.

an·ti·so·cial [an′ti·sō′shəl] *adj.* **1** Not sociable; aloof. **2** Harmful to society, as is crime.

an·tith·e·sis [an·tith′ə·sis] *n., pl.* **an·tith·e·ses** [an·tith′ə·sēz] **1** A direct opposite: Love is the *antithesis* of hate. **2** A contrasting of two opposite words, ideas, or phrases. Example: My hopes soar; my feet stay on the ground. **3** Opposition; contrast: the *antithesis* of war and peace.

an·ti·thet·i·cal [an′ti·thet′i·kəl] *adj.* **1** Marked by or using antithesis. **2** Directly opposing; contradictory: *antithetical* beliefs.

an·ti·tox·in [an′ti·tok′sin] *n.* **1** A substance produced in the body to counteract a specific bacterial poison. **2** A serum containing this substance, injected to prevent a disease such as tetanus.

an·ti·trades [an′ti·trādz′] *n.pl.* Winds that blow from the west in the middle latitudes.

an·ti·trust [an′ti·trust′] *adj.* Opposed to corporations or groups that form monopolies: an *antitrust* law.

an·ti·war [an′tē·wôr′] *adj.* Opposed to war or military preparations.

an·ti·white [an′tē·wīt′] *adj.* Having or exhibiting prejudice against Caucasians.

ant·ler [ant′lər] *n.* **1** A horn, usually branched, grown and shed each year by a deer or related animal. **2** Any branch of such a horn.

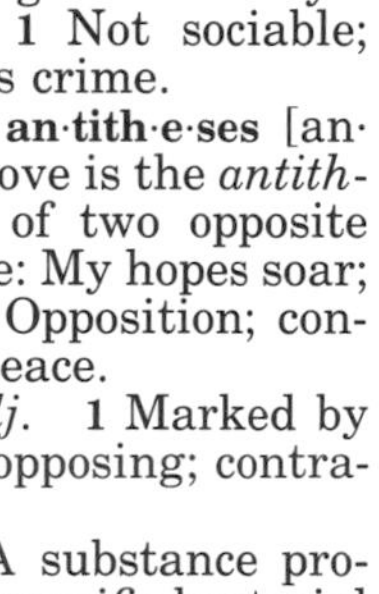
Antlers

ant·lered [ant′lərd] *adj.* Having antlers.

an·to·nym [an′tə·nim] *n.* A word opposite to another in meaning. "Good" and "bad" are antonyms.

A·nu·bis [ə·nyo͞o′bis] *n.* In Egyptian myths, the god who leads the dead to judgment. He is represented as a man with the head of a jackal.

a·nus [ā′nəs] *n.* The opening at the extreme lower end of the alimentary canal through which solid waste matter leaves the body.

an·vil [an′vil] *n.* 1 A heavy block of iron or steel on which heated metal is hammered into shape. 2 A bone of the inner ear; incus.

Anvil

anx·i·e·ty [ang·zī′ə·tē] *n., pl.* **anx·i·e·ties** 1 An uneasy, worried feeling about what may happen; concern. 2 A great or too great desire: an *anxiety* to be popular.

anx·ious [angk′shəs] *adj.* 1 Worried; uneasy. 2 Causing or marked by anxiety; worrying: an *anxious* matter; *anxious* days. 3 Very eager: *anxious* to please. **—anx′ious·ly** *adv.* ◆ Some critics hold that "eager" is a new meaning of *anxious* and thus incorrect; but *anxious* has been used to mean "eager" since the 1700's.

an·y [en′ē] 1 *adj.* One of a group, no matter which: Take *any* piece. 2 *pron.* One or more or a part: Will *any* of the girls go? 3 *adj.* Some, however much or little: Did they eat *any* supper? 4 *adj.* Every: *Any* sports fan knows that! 5 *adv.* At all; to any extent: Are they *any* nearer? 6 *adj.* Enough to count: hardly *any* noise. ◆ Both *any* and *one* come from the Old English word *ān,* meaning *one.* ◆ *Any,* meaning *at all*, is sometimes used informally to end a question or a negative statement: Did you hurt yourself *any*?

an·y·body [en′ē·bod′ē *or* en′ē·bud′ē] *pron.* Any person; anyone.

an·y·how [en′ē·hou′] *adv.* 1 In any way whatever; by any means: *anyhow* you look at it; Plan it *anyhow* you choose. 2 In any event: He's the smartest, *anyhow.* 3 Carelessly; haphazardly.

an·y·one [en′ĕ·wun′] *pron.* Any person; anybody. ◆ *Anyone* is a singular pronoun, so it takes a singular referent: *Anyone* who wants to come on the trip should bring *his* lunch. Some people think that this usage is unfair to females and that the sentence should read "*his or her* lunch." To avoid this awkward wording, it's preferable to rearrange the sentence: If *you* want to come on the trip, bring *your* lunch.

any one 1 Any single: *Any one* person can do it alone. 2 Any single person or thing of a group or class: *Any one* of these wires may be live. ◆ *Anyone* and *any one* may mean any single person. *Anyone* means any person at all: Can *anyone* identify the criminal? *Any one* means any individual from a group or class: *Any one* of these men may be guilty.

an·y·place [en′ē·plās′] *adv.* To, at, or in any place; anywhere: Set it down *anyplace.*

an·y·thing [en′ē·thing′] 1 *pron.* Any thing, event, or matter whatever: Did *anything* happen? 2 *n.* A thing of any kind: She grabbed *anything* and everything she could find. 3 *adv.* In the least; at all: Your hat isn't *anything* like mine.

an·y·time [en′ē·tīm′] *adv.* At any time; whenever.

an·y·way [en′ē·wā′] *adv.* Anyhow.

an·y·where [en′ē·(h)wâr′] *adv.* In, at, or to any place.

an·y·wise [en′ē·wīz′] *adv.* In any way or manner; at all.

A-OK or **A-O.K.** or **A-o·kay** [ā′ō·kā′] *adj., adv.* 1 Excellent; in first-rate condition. 2 Without flaws or problems.

A-1 or **A-one** [ā′wun′] *adj. informal* Of the highest quality; first-rate; an *A-one* movie.

a·or·ta [ā·ôr′tə] *n., pl.* **a·or·tas** or **a·or·tae** [ā·ôr′tē] The great artery rising from the left side of the heart, through which blood passes to all parts of the body except the lungs.

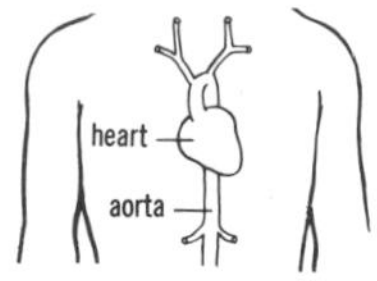

AP or **A.P.** Associated Press.

a·pace [ə·pās′] *adv.* Swiftly: We hurried on *apace.*

A·pach·e [ə·pach′e] *n., pl.* **A·pach·e** or **A·pach·es** 1 A group of tribes of North American Indians now living in the sw U.S. and northern Mexico. 2 A member of any of these tribes. 3 Any of the languages of these tribes.

a·part [ə·pärt′] 1 *adv.* In pieces or to pieces: to take something *apart;* The ship broke *apart.* 2 *adv.* Separated away from each other: Keep them *apart.* 3 *adv.* Aside: We stood *apart* from the crowd. 4 *adj.* Separate; distinct: a breed *apart.* 5 *adv.* One from another: No one can tell the twins *apart.* **—apart from** Except for.

a·part·heid [ə·pär′tīt *or* ə·pärt′hāt′] *n.* The governmental policy of racial segregation and social, economic, and educational discrimination in the Republic of South Africa.

a·part·ment [ə·pärt′mənt] *n.* A suite of rooms, or a single room, to live in.

apartment house A building with apartments.

ap·a·thet·ic [ap′ə·thet′ik] *adj.* Lacking interest or concern; indifferent. **—ap′a·thet′i·cal·ly** *adv.*

ap·a·thy [ap′ə·thē] *n.* 1 Lack of feeling. 2 Lack of interest or concern; indifference.

ape [āp] *n., v.* **aped, ap·ing** 1 *n.* A large monkey with no tail, that can stand and walk almost erect. The chimpanzee, gorilla, and gibbon are apes. 2 *n.* Any monkey. 3 *n.* A mimic. 4 *v.* To mimic.

a·per·i·tif [ä·per′i·tēf′] *n.* An alcoholic drink served before dinner to stimulate the appetite.

ap·er·ture [ap′ər·chər] *n.* 1 An opening or hole. 2 The opening in a photographic lens or other optical instrument through which light passes.

a·pex [ā′peks] *n., pl.* **a·pex·es** or **ap·i·ces** [ap′ə·sēz] 1 The highest point; tip; top. 2 A climax.

a·pha·sia [ə·fā′zhə] *n.* Total or partial damage or loss of the ability to use or understand written or spoken language. This condition is frequently due to lesions in the brain, sometimes as a result of a stroke. **—a·pha′sic** *n., adj.*

a·phe·li·on [ə·fē′lē·ən] *n.* The point farthest from the sun in the orbit of a planet or other body moving around the sun.

a·phid [ā′fid *or* af′id] *n.* A tiny insect that sucks the juices of plants.

aph·o·rism [af′ə·riz′əm] *n.* A brief statement of a general truth; maxim. "Cowards don't win battles" is an aphorism.

aph·ro·dis·i·ac [af′rə·diz′ē·ak′] 1 *n.* A drug or other agent that stimulates sexual desire. 2 *adj.* Stimulating or increasing sexual desire.

a	add	**i**	it	**o͝o**	took	**oi**	oil		
ā	ace	**ī**	ice	**o͞o**	pool	**ou**	pout		
â	care	**o**	odd	**u**	up	**ng**	ring		
ä	palm	**ō**	open	**û**	burn	**th**	thin		
e	end	**ô**	order	**yo͞o**	fuse	**th̸**	this		
ē	equal					**zh**	vision		

ə = { a in *above* e in *sicken* i in *possible*
o in *melon* u in *circus* }

Aph·ro·di·te [af′rə·dī′tē] *n.* In Greek myths, the goddess of love and beauty.
a·pi·ar·y [ā′pē·er′ē] *n., pl.* **a·pi·ar·ies** A place where bees are kept.
ap·i·ces [ap′ə·sēz] A plural of APEX.
a·piece [ə·pēs′] *adv.* For or to each one; each: Give them a dime *apiece.*
a·pish [ā′pish] *adj.* 1 Resembling an ape. 2 Imitative in a slavish or unthinking way. 3 Very foolish or affected.
a·plomb [ə·plom′] *n.* Poise or self-possession; self-confidence.
APO Army Post Office.
a·poc·a·lypse [ə·pok′ə·lips′] *n.* 1 A prophecy or revelation. 2 (*written* **Apocalypse**) The book of Revelation, the last book in the Bible.
A·poc·ry·pha [ə·pok′rə·fə] *n.pl.* Books included in some versions of the Old Testament but not accepted by all as fully genuine or inspired.
a·poc·ry·phal [ə·pok′rə·fəl] *adj.* Having little or no authenticity; probably untrue.
ap·o·gee [ap′ə·jē] *n.* The point farthest from the earth in the orbit of the moon or other satellite of the earth. ◆ See APHELION.

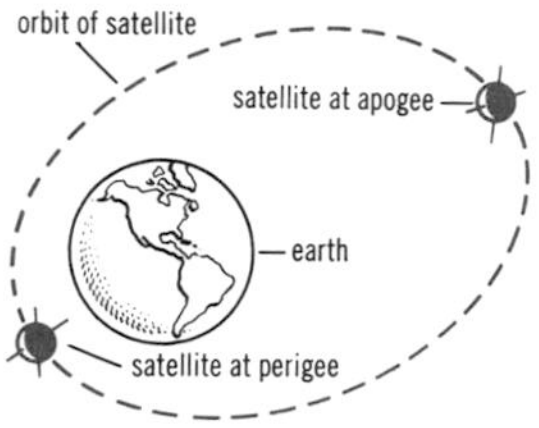

A·pol·lo [ə·pol′ō] *n.* In Greek and Roman myths, the god of the sun, music, poetry, prophecy, and medicine.
a·pol·o·get·ic [ə·pol′ə·jet′·ik] *adj.* Having to do with or expressing apology; showing regret for something; admitting a fault or failure. **—a·pol′o·get′i·cal·ly** *adv.*
a·pol·o·gist [ə·pol′ə·jist] *n.* A person who speaks or writes in defense of something, as a faith, idea, or cause.
a·pol·o·gize [ə·pol′ə·jīz′] *v.* **a·pol·o·gized, a·pol·o·giz·ing** 1 To make an apology; ask pardon or express regret for something: to *apologize* for an insult. 2 To defend something in writing or speech.
a·pol·o·gy [ə·pol′ə·jē] *n., pl.* **a·pol·o·gies** 1 Words saying that one is sorry or asking pardon for a fault, offense, or mistake. 2 A defense or justification in writing or speech. 3 A bad substitute: a poor *apology* for an omelet.
ap·o·plec·tic [ap′ə·plek′tik] 1 *adj.* Of, having, or tending toward apoplexy: an *apoplectic* fit. 2 *n.* A person subject to apoplexy.
ap·o·plex·y [ap′ə·plek′sē] *n.* Sudden loss of the ability to feel, think, or move. It is caused by the bursting or blocking of a blood vessel in the brain.
a·pos·ta·sy [ə·pos′tə·sē] *n.* Desertion of a previous loyalty, as to one's religion, country, or party.
a·pos·tate [ə·pos′tāt′] *n.* A person who deserts a faith, country, party, or the like.
a·pos·tle [ə·pos′əl] *n.* 1 (*often written* **Apostle**) One of the twelve disciples of Christ sent out to preach the gospel. 2 A missionary or preacher in the early Christian Church. 3 A missionary who first brings Christianity to a nation or region: The *apostle* to Ireland was St. Patrick. 4 A leader of any reform or belief: an *apostle* of civil rights.
Apostles' Creed A Christian statement of beliefs, traditionally attributed to the twelve Apostles.
ap·os·tol·ic [ap′ə·stol′ik] *adj.* 1 Of or having to do with the Apostles or apostles: *apostolic* writings; *apostolic* faith. 2 (*often written* **Apostolic**) Papal: an *Apostolic* letter.
a·pos·tro·phe[1] [ə·pos′trə·fē] *n.* A symbol (') used: 1 To mark the omission of a letter or letters, as *I'm* for *I am* or *can't* for *cannot.* 2 To show the possessive case: *Jane's* dog; the *girls'* hats. 3 To form certain plurals: three *5's;* crossed *t's.*
a·pos·tro·phe[2] [ə·pos′trə·fē] *n.* A speech addressed to someone absent or dead, or to a thing.
apothecaries' measure A system for measuring liquid volume used by pharmacists.
apothecaries' weight A system for measuring weight used by pharmacists. An apothecaries' pound equals 12 ounces, and one apothecaries' ounce is equal to 1.097 avoirdupois ounces.
a·poth·e·car·y [ə·poth′ə·ker′ē] *n., pl.* **a·poth·e·car·ies** A druggist or pharmacist.
ap·o·thegm [ap′ə·them′] *n.* A brief and witty instructive saying; a maxim or proverb. "Good fences make good neighbors" is an apothegm.
a·poth·e·o·sis [ə·poth′ē·ō′sis *or* ap′ə·thē′ə·sis] *n., pl.* **a·poth·e·o·ses** [ə·poth′ē·ō′sēz *or* ap′ə·thē′ə·sēz] 1 The raising of a person to the level of a god; deification: the *apotheosis* of a monarch. 2 Glorification.
app. 1 apparatus. 2 apparent. 3 apparently. 4 appendix. 5 appointed.
ap·pall or **ap·pal** [ə·pôl′] *v.* **ap·palled, ap·pall·ing** To fill with dismay or horror: They were *appalled* by the sight.
ap·pall·ing [ə·pôl′ing] *adj.* Causing horror or dismay; frightful. **—ap·pall′ing·ly** *adv.*
Ap·pa·loo·sa [ap′ə·lo͞o′sə] *n.* One of a breed of saddle horses developed in northwestern North America, having black and white spots on the rump and flanks.
ap·pa·ra·tus [ap′ə·rā′təs *or* ap′ə·rat′əs] *n., pl.* **ap·pa·ra·tus** or **ap·pa·ra·tus·es** 1 A device or machine for a particular purpose: an X-ray *apparatus.* 2 All of the devices, tools, and equipment for a particular use.
ap·par·el [ə·par′əl] *n., v.* **ap·par·eled** or **ap·par·elled, ap·par·el·ing** or **ap·par·el·ling** 1 *n.* Clothing. 2 *v.* To clothe, dress, or dress up: a band *appareled* in red.
ap·par·ent [ə·par′ənt] *adj.* 1 Obvious: It's *apparent* he is not well. 2 That only appears to be; seeming: The navigator's *apparent* courage is only a bluff. **—ap·par′ent·ly** *adv.*
ap·pa·ri·tion [ap′ə·rish′ən] *n.* 1 A ghost; spirit; phantom. 2 Anything remarkable that appears.
ap·peal [ə·pēl′] 1 *v.* To ask earnestly for something: to *appeal* for help. 2 *n.* An earnest request. 3 *v.* To call on someone for a decision in one's favor: Denied the car by one parent, she *appealed* to the other. 4 *n.* Such a call. 5 *v.* To be attractive or interesting: Does this *appeal* to you? 6 *adj. use:* an *appealing* smile. 7 *n.* Power to attract or interest: Chess has lost its *appeal.* 8 *v.* To ask to have (a case) tried again by a higher court. 9 *n.* Such a request.
ap·pear [ə·pir′] *v.* 1 To come into sight; become visible: The royal family *appeared* on the balcony. 2 To seem or seem likely: The report *appears* to be true. 3 To come before the public: to *appear* on television. 4 To come formally into court. 5 To be published.
ap·pear·ance [ə·pir′əns] *n.* 1 The act of appearing. 2 A coming before a court or an audience. 3 The outward look of a person or thing: a well-kept *appearance.* 4 A pretense: an *appearance* of working hard. 5 An apparition.

ap·pease [ə·pēz′] *v.* **ap·peased, ap·peas·ing** 1 To satisfy: to *appease* hunger. 2 To calm or soothe, especially by giving in to demands.

ap·pease·ment [ə·pēz′mənt] *n.* 1 The act of appeasing. 2 The policy of making concessions in order to maintain peace.

ap·pel·lant [ə·pel′ənt] 1 *n.* A person who appeals a legal decision to a higher court. 2 *adj.* Of or having to do with legal appeals; appellate.

ap·pel·late [ə·pel′it] *adj.* 1 Of or having to do with legal appeals. 2 Having the power to hear and decide legal appeals: an *appellate* court.

ap·pel·la·tion [ap′ə·lā′shən] *n.* An added name or title. William the Conqueror's *appellation* was "the Conqueror."

ap·pend [ə·pend′] *v.* To add or attach: to *append* a footnote.

ap·pend·age [ə·pen′dij] *n.* Something attached to a larger or main part. Legs, tails, fins, and wings are appendages.

ap·pen·dec·to·my [ap′ən·dek′tə·mē] *n., pl.* **ap·pen·dec·to·mies** The removal of a person's appendix by surgery.

ap·pen·di·ci·tis [ə·pen′di·sī′tis] *n.* Inflammation of the appendix.

ap·pen·dix [ə·pen′diks] *n., pl.* **ap·pen·dix·es** or **ap·pen·di·ces** [ə·pen′də·sēz] 1 An addition or appendage, as of supplementary matter at the end of a book. 2 A narrow, closed tube extending out from the large intestine, in the lower right side of the abdomen. It has no known use.

ap·per·tain [ap′ər·tān′] *v.* To have to do with; belong; relate: problems *appertaining* to fair taxation.

ap·pe·tite [ap′ə·tīt′] *n.* 1 A desire for food. 2 Any strong desire or liking: an *appetite* for sports.

ap·pe·tiz·er [ap′ə·tīz′ər] *n.* A small portion of food or drink served before a meal to stimulate the appetite.

ap·pe·tiz·ing [ap′ə·tī′zing] *adj.* Pleasing or stimulating to the appetite. **—ap′pe·tī′zing·ly** *adv.*

ap·plaud [ə·plôd′] *v.* 1 To show approval, as by clapping the hands, shouting, or cheering: The audience *applauded.* 2 To commend; praise.

ap·plause [ə·plôz′] *n.* A show of approval, as by clapping the hands, shouting, or cheering.

ap·ple [ap′əl] *n.* 1 A round, fleshy, edible fruit having a thin skin of a green, red, or yellow color and a hard core enclosing seeds. 2 Any of the trees bearing this fruit.

ap·ple·jack [ap′əl·jak′] *n.* A type of brandy made by distilling fermented apple cider.

ap·ple·sauce [ap′əl·sôs′] *n.* 1 Apples cut up, sweetened, and stewed to a soft pulp. 2 *informal* Nonsense; foolish talk.

ap·pli·ance [ə·plī′əns] *n.* A machine for doing a task in home or office, as an air conditioner, washer, or toaster.

ap·pli·ca·ble [ap′li·kə·bəl] *adj.* That can be applied; suitable: a dye not *applicable* to leather. **—ap′pli·ca·bil′i·ty** *n.*

ap·pli·cant [ap′li·kənt] *n.* A person who applies for something, such as a job.

ap·pli·ca·tion [ap′li·kā′shən] *n.* 1 The act of applying. 2 Something applied: an *application* to relieve sunburn. 3 A particular way of being applied or used: A single word may have many different *applications.* 4 A request, especially a formal written request, as for a job. 5 Close attention and real work: *application* to one's studies.

ap·pli·ca·tor [ap′lə·kā′tər] *n.* An instrument or device for applying a substance, as a medicine, shoe polish, or glue.

ap·plied [ə·plīd′] *adj.* Put to practical use. An applied science's aim is to put scientific facts and theories to practical use.

ap·pli·qué [ap′li·kā′] *n., adj., v.* **ap·pli·quéd, ap·pli·qué·ing** 1 *n.* Ornaments made by sewing or fastening one material on another. 2 *adj.* Trimmed or decorated with appliqué. 3 *v.* To trim or decorate with appliqué.

ap·ply [ə·plī′] *v.* **ap·plied, ap·ply·ing** 1 To put on: to *apply* paint to a wall or cream to the face. 2 To put to a particular use: to *apply* pressure to fruit to squeeze out the juice. 3 To devote (oneself) with effort: He *applied* himself to his studies. 4 To make a formal request or petition: to *apply* for a job. 5 To be suitable or appropriate; relate: This rule *applies* to you.

ap·point [ə·point′] *v.* 1 To select for a position, office, or duty; designate. 2 To decide on (a time or place); fix or set: The session opened at the hour *appointed.* 3 To equip; furnish: a room *appointed* with antiques.

ap·point·ee [ə·poin′tē′] *n.* A person appointed to some office or position.

ap·poin·tive [ə·poin′tiv] *adj.* Filled by appointment, not by election: an *appointive* office.

ap·point·ment [ə·point′mənt] *n.* 1 Selection for, or a placing in, an office or position not filled by election. 2 Such an office or position. 3 The person chosen. 4 An agreement to meet someone at a certain place and time. 5 (*usually pl.*) Furniture or equipment.

ap·por·tion [ə·pôr′shən] *v.* To divide and give out in proportional shares or according to some rule.

ap·por·tion·ment [ə·pôr′shən·mənt] *n.* 1 The act or an instance of apportioning. 2 The distribution of legislative representatives among state or districts in proportion to population.

ap·po·site [ap′ə·zit] *adj.* Appropriate; to the point: an *apposite* remark.

ap·po·si·tion [ap′ə·zish′ən] *n.* 1 The placing of a noun or noun phrase after another to explain it, both having the same grammatical form. 2 The relation existing between such a pair. In "Mars, the god of war, was worshiped in Rome," *Mars* and *the god of war* are in apposition.

ap·pos·i·tive [ə·poz′ə·tiv] 1 *adj.* Having to do with or in apposition. 2 *n.* A noun or noun phrase placed after another in apposition.

ap·prais·al [ə·prā′z(ə)l] *n.* 1 The act of appraising. 2 The estimate, as of value, quality, or quantity, reached by appraising.

ap·praise [ə·prāz′] *v.* **ap·praised, ap·prais·ing** 1 To decide the value of; set a price on: to *appraise* a house. 2 To estimate the amount, quality, or worth of. **—ap·prais′er** *n.*

a	add	**i**	it	**o͝o**	took	**oi**	oil
ā	ace	**ī**	ice	**o͞o**	pool	**ou**	pout
â	care	**o**	odd	**u**	up	**ng**	ring
ä	palm	**ō**	open	**û**	burn	**th**	thin
e	end	**ô**	order	**yo͞o**	fuse	**th̶**	this
ē	equal					**zh**	vision

ə = a in *above*, e in *sicken*, i in *possible*, o in *melon*, u in *circus*

ap·pre·ci·a·ble [ə·prē′shē·ə·bəl *or* ə·prē′shə·bəl] *adj.* Enough to be noticed or estimated: an *appreciable* angle. **—ap·pre′ci·a·bly** *adv.*

ap·pre·ci·ate [ə·prē′shē·āt′] *v.* **ap·pre·ci·at·ed, ap·pre·ci·at·ing** 1 To recognize the merit of; understand and value or enjoy: to *appreciate* good literature. 2 To be aware of or sensitive to: to *appreciate* someone else's problems. 3 To be grateful for: We *appreciate* your help. 4 To make or become more valuable: Fine homes *appreciate* a neighborhood.

ap·pre·ci·a·tion [ə·prē′shē·ā′shən] *n.* 1 Recognition of value or excellence, especially a favorable criticism. 2 Awareness or sensitivity. 3 Gratitude. 4 Increase in value or amount.

ap·pre·ci·a·tive [ə·prē′shē·ā′tiv *or* ə·prē′shə·tiv] *adj.* Having or showing appreciation. **—ap·pre′ci·a′tive·ly** *adv.*

ap·pre·hend [ap′rə·hend′] *v.* 1 To capture; arrest: to *apprehend* a criminal. 2 To grasp mentally; understand: to *apprehend* a problem. 3 To look forward to, as with anxiety or fear.

ap·pre·hen·sion [ap′rə·hen′shən] *n.* 1 A worried expectation of something bad; dread or fear. 2 An arrest or capture. 3 Understanding; mental grasp.

ap·pre·hen·sive [ap′rə·hen′siv] *adj.* Fearful; worried. **—ap′pre·hen′sive·ly** *adv.*

ap·pren·tice [ə·pren′tis] *n., v.* **ap·pren·ticed, ap·pren·tic·ing** 1 *n.* A person who works for another in order to learn a trade or business. Formerly, an apprentice had to work for several years without pay. 2 *v.* To bind by legal agreement as an apprentice. 3 *n.* Any learner or beginner. **—ap·pren′tice·ship** *n.*

ap·prise [ə·prīz′] *v.* **ap·prised, ap·pris·ing** To notify; inform: to be *apprised* of a coming event.

ap·proach [ə·prōch′] 1 *v.* To come nearer in space or time: Christmas is *approaching.* 2 *v.* To be or become almost; resemble: Her ability *approached* genius. 3 *n.* A coming near or close. 4 *n.* A way or means of reaching a person or thing: the *approach* to a bridge. 5 *n.* A method of beginning or doing something: a new *approach* to purifying salt water. 6 *v.* To come to with a request or proposal: to *approach* someone about a job.

ap·proach·a·ble [ə·prō′chə·bəl] *adj.* 1 Easy to talk to; friendly. 2 Capable of being reached; accessible. **—ap·proach′a·bil′i·ty** *n.*

ap·pro·ba·tion [ap′rə·bā′shən] *n.* 1 Approval. 2 Support and approval.

ap·pro·pri·ate [*adj.* ə·prō′prē·it, *v.* ə·prō′prē·āt′] *adj., v.* **ap·pro·pri·at·ed, ap·pro·pri·at·ing** 1 *adj.* Suitable; fitting. 2 *v.* To set apart for a particular purpose: to *appropriate* money for defense. 3 *v.* To take for one's own use: The thief *appropriated* the necklace. **—ap·pro′pri·ate·ly** *adv.* **—ap·pro′pri·ate·ness** *n.*

ap·pro·pri·a·tion [ə·prō′prē·ā′shən] *n.* 1 Money set aside and made available for a particular use. 2 The act of appropriating.

ap·prov·al [ə·pro͞o′vəl] *n.* 1 A favorable feeling or opinion. 2 Consent as a result of such opinion: They left with the doctor's *approval.* **—on approval** For a customer to try or examine, then decide about buying.

ap·prove [ə·pro͞ov′] *v.* **ap·proved, ap·prov·ing** 1 To have a good opinion: I *approve* of your idea. 2 To accept as good; think well of: The inspector *approved* the work. 3 To consent to; authorize: The mayor *approved* the plan.

ap·prox·i·mate [*adj.* ə·prok′sə·mit, *v.* ə·prok′sə·māt′] *adj., v.* **ap·prox·i·mat·ed, ap·prox·i·mat·ing** 1 *adj.* Almost exact, correct, or like. 2 *v.* To come close to: Speed will *approximate* 650 mph.

ap·prox·i·mate·ly [ə·prok′sə·mit·lē] *adv.* About; around: *approximately* an inch of rain.

ap·prox·i·ma·tion [ə·prok′sə·mā′shən] *n.* 1 The act of approximating. 2 An amount or estimate nearly exact or correct.

ap·pur·te·nance [ə·pûr′tə·nəns] *n.* Something that goes with a more important or main thing.

Apr. April.

a·pri·cot [ā′pri·kot *or* ap′ri·kot] 1 *n.* A juicy, orange-colored fruit similar to a small peach. 2 *n.* The tree bearing this small fruit. 3 *n., adj.* Yellowish orange.

A·pril [ā′prəl] *n.* The fourth month of the year, having 30 days.

April Fools' Day April 1, a day when it is customary to play practical jokes. The victim of such a joke is called an **April fool.**

a·pron [ā′prən] *n.* 1 A garment worn to protect the skirt or trousers in front, often with a bib above. 2 An area in front of a building such as a garage or a hangar. 3 The part of a theater stage in front of the curtain.

ap·ro·pos [ap′rə·pō′] 1 *adj.* Timely; fitting; appropriate: an *apropos* remark. 2 *adv.* Fittingly; at the right time. **—apropos of** In connection with or regard to.

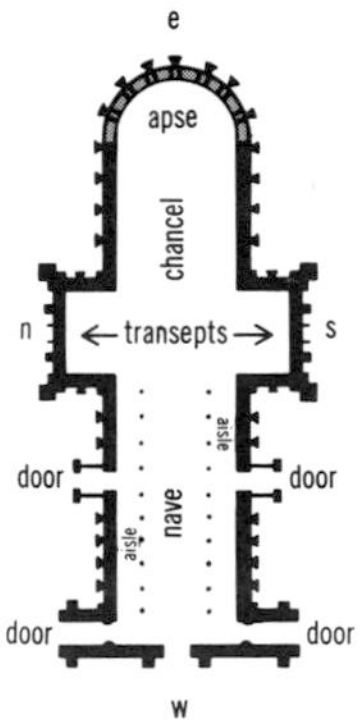

apse [aps] *n.* A semicircular recess with an arched or domed ceiling, at the east end of a church.

apt [apt] *adj.* 1 Having a natural tendency; likely: Fish are *apt* to be biting then. 2 Quick to learn: an *apt* pupil. 3 To the point; fitting: an *apt* suggestion. **—apt′ly** *adv.* **—apt′ness** *n.*

apt. apartment.

ap·ti·tude [ap′tə·t(y)o͞od′] *n.* 1 Natural ability or capacity. 2 Fitness; suitability.

aq·ua [ak′wə] *n., adj.* Bluish green.

aq·ua·cul·ture [ak′wə·kul′chər *or* ä′kwə·kul′chər] *n.* Another spelling of AQUICULTURE.

aq·ua·lung [ak′wə·lung′] *n.* A diver's portable breathing apparatus. Tanks of compressed air on the back supply air through a mask.

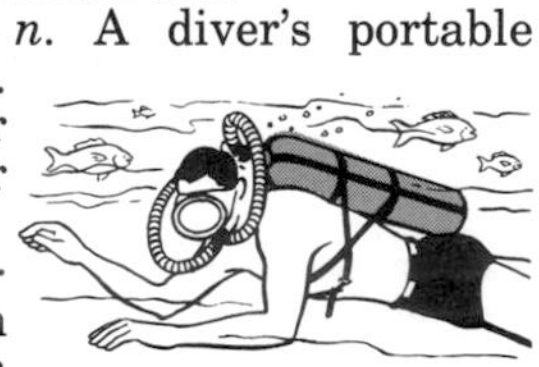
Diver wearing an aqualung

aq·ua·ma·rine [ak′wə·mə·rēn′] 1 *n.* A bluish green variety of beryl. It is a precious stone. 2 *n., adj.* Bluish green.

aq·ua·naut [ak′wə·nôt′ *or* ä′kwə·nôt] *n.* A person who is trained to live in an underwater installation for scientific research.

aq·ua·plane [ak′wə·plān′] *n., v.* **aq·ua·planed, aq·ua·plan·ing** 1 *n.* A board on which a person rides for sport while being towed by a motorboat. 2 *v.* To ride an aquaplane.

a·quar·i·um [ə·kwâr′ē·əm] *n., pl.* **a·quar·i·ums** or **a·quar·i·a** [ə·kwâr′ē·ə] 1 A container, as a bowl or tank, for keeping a collection of fish or other water animals, and often water plants. 2 A building where a collection of water animals and plants is displayed.

A·quar·i·us [ə·kwer′ē·əs] *n.* 1 A constellation in the Southern Hemisphere. 2 The eleventh sign of the zodiac. 3 A person born under this sign. —**A·quar′i·an** *adj.*
a·quat·ic [ə·kwat′ik] *adj.* 1 Living or growing in or near water. 2 Performed on or in water.
a·quat·ics [ə·kwat′iks] *n.pl.* Sports and games performed in or on water. See -ICS.
a·que·duct [ak′wə·dukt′] *n.* 1 A pipeline or artificial channel for carrying water from a distance. 2 A bridgelike structure used, where needed, to bear such a channel.
a·que·ous [ā′kwē·əs *or* ak′wē·əs] *adj.* 1 Of, like, or containing water; watery. 2 Composed of matter deposited by water: *aqueous* rocks.
aqueous humor A clear fluid filling the space in the eye between the cornea and the lens.
aq·ui·cul·ture [ak′wi·kul′chər *or* ä′kwi·kul′chər] *n.* 1 The raising of fish in artificial ponds for commercial markets. 2 Another name for HYDROPONICS. —**aq′ui·cul′tur·al** *adj.*
aq·ui·fer [ak′wə·fər *or* ä′kwə·fər] *n.* An underground layer of water-bearing rock, gravel, or sand that yields groundwater to wells and natural springs. —**a·qui·fer·ous** [ə·kwif′ər·əs] *adj.*
aq·ui·line [ak′wə·līn′ *or* ak′wə·lin] *adj.* 1 Of or like an eagle. 2 Curving or hooked, like an eagle's beak: an *aquiline* nose.
Ar The symbol for the element argon.
AR Postal Service abbreviation of Arkansas.
Ar·ab [ar′əb] 1 *n.* A person born or living in Arabia. 2 *n.* A member of a people spread from Arabia through sw Asia and parts of Africa. 3 *n.* A swift, graceful horse of a breed first developed in Arabia. 4 *adj.* Arabian.
Arab 1 Arabia. 2 Arabian. 3 Arabic.
ar·a·besque [ar′ə·besk′] 1 *n.* A fanciful design using geometric figures, leaves, flowers, and other elements, intertwined. 2 *adj.* Of, having to do with, or done in the style of arabesque.
A·ra·bi·an [ə·rā′bē·ən] 1 *adj.* Of or from Arabia. 2 *n.* An Arab.
Arabian Nights A collection of stories from the area including Arabia, India, and Persia, dating from the tenth century.
Ar·a·bic [ar′ə·bik] 1 *n.* The language of the Arabs. 2 *adj.* Of the Arabs or their language.
Arabic numerals The symbols 1, 2, 3, 4, 5, 6, 7, 8, 9, and 0.
ar·a·ble [ar′ə·bəl] *adj.* Fit for cultivating.
a·rach·nid [ə·rak′nid] *n.* Any of a class of animals including spiders, mites, and scorpions, with four pairs of legs but no antennae.
Ar·a·ma·ic [ar·ə·mā′ik] *n.* A Semitic language spoken in sw Asia in Biblical times.
A·rap·a·ho [ə·rap′ə·hō′] *n., pl.* **A·rap·a·ho** or **A·rap·a·hoes** 1 A tribe of North American Indians now living in Oklahoma and Wyoming. 2 A member of this tribe. 3 The language of this tribe.
ar·bi·ter [är′bə·tər] *n.* 1 A person chosen to settle a dispute; arbitrator; umpire. 2 A person with full power to decide or judge.
ar·bi·trage [ar′bə·trazh′] *n.* Buying and selling the same or similar stocks so as to take advantage of price differences in different financial markets. —**ar′bi·trag′eur** *n.* A person (such as a stockbroker) who engages in arbitrage.
ar·bi·trar·y [är′bə·trer′ē] *adj.* 1 Based only on one's own will, feelings, or notions: an *arbitrary* decision. 2 Not guided by rules or law: an *arbitrary* ruler. —**ar′bi·trar′i·ly** *adv.*
ar·bi·trate [är′bə·trāt′] *v.* **ar·bi·trat·ed, ar·bi·trat·ing** 1 To act as an arbitrator: to *arbitrate* between two nations. 2 To submit (a dispute) to arbitration. 3 To settle by arbitration.
ar·bi·tra·tion [är′bə·trā′shən] *n.* The settling of a dispute by the decision of someone accepted by both sides as umpire or arbiter.
ar·bi·tra·tor [ar′bə·trā′tər] *n.* A person with full power to decide or judge; arbiter.
ar·bor [är′bər] *n.* A place shaded by trees or by latticework covered with vines; bower.
Arbor Day A day selected for the public planting of trees. The date varies from state to state but is usually in the spring.
ar·bo·re·al [är·bôr′ē·əl *or* är·bō′rē·əl] *adj.* 1 Of or like a tree. 2 Living in trees.
ar·bo·re·tum [är′bə·rē′təm] *n., pl.* **ar·bo·re·tums** or **ar·bo·re·ta** [ar′bə·rē′tə] A garden or small forest preserve for the study and display of rare trees and shrubs.
ar·bor·vi·tae [är′bər·vī′tē] *n.* A small evergreen tree, often used for hedges.
ar·bu·tus [är·byōō′təs] *n.* A trailing evergreen plant that bears clusters of fragrant pink or white flowers in very early spring.
arc [ärk] *n., v.* **arced** [ärkt], **arc·ing** [är′king] 1 *n.* A part of a curve, especially of a circle. 2 *v.* To make an arc: The rocket *arced* across the sky. 3 *n.* The bright glow made by an electric current as it passes through a gas, across the gap between two electrodes.

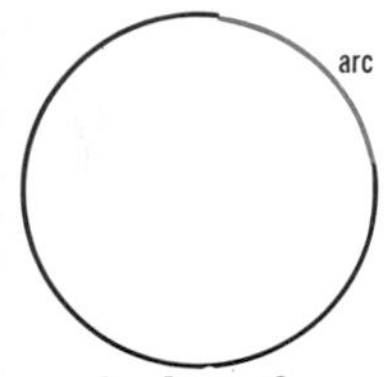

ar·cade [är·kād′] *n.* 1 A covered passage or street, often with an arched roof, especially one lined with small stores. 2 A row of arches held up by columns.
Ar·ca·di·a [är·kā′dē·ə] *n.* A region of ideal rustic simplicity and complete contentment.
arch[1] [ärch] 1 *n.* A curved structure over an opening, capable of holding up material above it. Arches are used in windows, gateways, and bridges. 2 *n.* Anything shaped like an arch: the *arch* of a rainbow. 3 *v.* To bend or curve into an arch: to *arch* an eyebrow. 4 *v.* To make an arch: The bridge *arched* over the river.

Arch

arch[2] [ärch] *adj.* 1 Playful and sly; roguish: an *arch* look. 2 Chief; main. —**arch′ly** *adv.*
arch- A prefix meaning: Chief or main, as in *archbishop.*
ar·chae·o·log·i·cal [är′kē·ə·loj′i·kəl] *adj.* Of or having to do with archaeology.
ar·chae·ol·o·gist [är′kē·ol′ə·jist] *n.* An expert in archaeology.

a	add	**i**	it	**o͝o**	took	**oi**	oil
ā	ace	**ī**	ice	**o͞o**	pool	**ou**	pout
â	care	**o**	odd	**u**	up	**ng**	ring
ä	palm	**ō**	open	**û**	burn	**th**	thin
e	end	**ô**	order	**yo͞o**	fuse	**t͟h**	this
ē	equal					**zh**	vision

ə = a in *above* e in *sicken* i in *possible* o in *melon* u in *circus*

ar·chae·ol·o·gy [är′kē·ol′ə·jē] *n.* The study of past times and cultures, mainly carried on by digging up and examining remains, as of the cities or tombs of ancient cultures.

ar·chae·op·ter·yx [är′kē·op′tər·iks] *n.* One of the first primitive birds, found as a fossil. It had some reptile features.

ar·cha·ic [är·kā′ik] *adj.* 1 No longer in ordinary use: Words or phrases such as "methinks," "soothly," and "I ween" are *archaic.* 2 Belonging to an earlier time; ancient: *archaic* armor. —**ar·cha′i·cal·ly** *adv.*

ar·cha·ism [är′kē·is′əm *or* är′kā·iz′əm] *n.* 1 An archaic word or phrase, such as "methinks" or "God wot." 2 An archaic style, fashion, or quality.

arch·an·gel [ärk′ān′jəl] *n.* A chief angel; angel of a high rank.

arch·bish·op [ärch′bish′əp] *n.* A bishop of the highest station.

arch·dea·con [ärch′dē′kən] *n.* 1 Chief deacon. 2 A priest in the Episcopalian church who assists a bishop in supervising the clergy.

arch·di·o·cese [arch·di′ə·sis *or* arch·di′ə·sēz] *n.* A church district under the jurisdiction of an archbishop.

arch·duch·ess [arch·duch′is] *n.* 1 The wife or widow of an archduke. 2 A royal princess of the former ruling house of Austria.

arch·duke [arch′d(y)ook′] *n.* A prince of the former ruling house of Austria.

arched [ärcht] *adj.* Having an arch or arches.

arch·en·e·my [ärch′en′ə·mē] *n., pl.* **arch·en·e·mies** A chief or major enemy.

ar·che·o·log·i·cal [är′kē·ə·loj′i·kəl] *adj.* Another spelling of ARCHAEOLOGICAL.

ar·che·ol·o·gist [är′kē·ol′ə·jist] *n.* Another spelling of ARCHAEOLOGIST.

ar·che·ol·o·gy [är′kē·ol′ə·jē] *n.* Another spelling of ARCHAEOLOGY.

Ar·che·o·zo·ic [är′kē·ə·zō′ik] 1 *n.* The earlier part of the Precambrian era. The Archeozoic is sometimes considered a geological era itself. 2 *adj.* Of the Archeozoic.

arch·er [är′chər] *n.* A person who shoots with a bow and arrow.

arch·er·y [är′chər·ē] *n.* The art or sport of shooting with a bow and arrow.

Archery

ar·che·type [är′kə·tīp′] *n.* A first model from which others are derived or copied: The Iliad was regarded as the *archetype* of epic poetry.

ar·chi·pel·a·go [är′kə·pel′ə·gō] *n., pl.* **ar·chi·pel·a·goes** or **ar·chi·pel·a·gos** 1 A group of many islands. 2 A sea with many islands in it.

An archipelago

ar·chi·tect [är′kə·tekt] *n.* A person who designs and draws up plans for buildings or other structures, and sees that the plans are carried through by the builders.

ar·chi·tec·tur·al [är′kə·tek′chər·əl] *adj.* Of or having to do with architecture: *architectural* designs. —**ar′chi·tec′tur·al·ly** *adv.*

ar·chi·tec·ture [är′kə·tek′chər] *n.* 1 The science or profession of designing and putting up buildings or other structures. 2 Style or special method of building.

ar·chi·trave [är′kə·trāv′] *n.* The beam or stone that rests directly on top of a column.

ar·chi·val [är·kī′vəl] *adj.* Of, having to do with, or kept in archives.

ar·chives [är′kīvz] *n.pl.* 1 A place for keeping public records and historical papers. 2 Such public records or papers.

ar·chi·vist [är′kə·vist] *n.* A person who is in charge of archives.

arch·way [ärch′wā′] *n.* An entrance or passage under an arch.

-archy A combining form meaning: Rule; government, as in *oligarchy.*

arc lamp A high-intensity electric lamp in which light is produced by an arc made when current flows through ionized gas between two carbon or metal electrodes.

arc light Another name for ARC LAMP.

arc·tic [är(k)′tik] 1 *n.* (*usually written* **Arctic**) The region about the North Pole. 2 *adj.* (*usually written* **Arctic**) Of or living in this region: an *Arctic* plant. 3 *adj.* Extremely cold; freezing.

Arctic Circle An imaginary circle at about 66°33′ north latitude, beyond which the sun cannot be seen in the depth of winter, taken as the boundary of the north frigid zone.

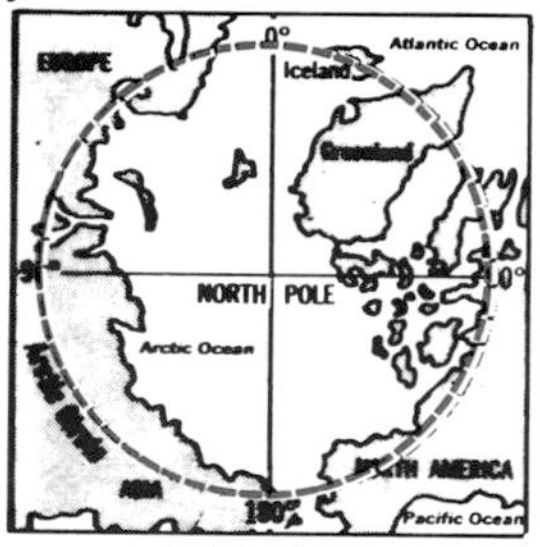

Arctic circle

Arc·tu·rus [ärk·t(y)ŏŏr′əs] *n.* A very bright, orange-red star in the northern sky.

ar·dent [är′dənt] *adj.* Very enthusiastic and eager; fervent: an *ardent* fan. —**ar′dent·ly** *adv.*

ar·dor [är′dər] *n.* Great enthusiasm; strong feeling of warmth or passion.

ar·du·ous [är′jōō·əs] *adj.* 1 Difficult to do; hard: an *arduous* task. 2 Taking much energy; strenuous: *arduous* efforts to climb the fence. —**ar′du·uous·ly** *adv.*

are¹ [är] *v.* A form of the verb BE, in the present tense, used with *we, you, they,* and plural nouns: You *are* right; *Are* we going?

are² [är *or* âr] *n.* A metric unit of area equal to 100 square meters. ◆ Also spelled **ar.**

ar·e·a [âr′ē·ə] *n.* 1 The amount or size of a surface: The *area* of a floor 10 feet by 10 feet is 100 square feet. 2 Region; section: the Chicago *area;* a tropical *area.* 3 An open space devoted to a special purpose: a parking *area;* a camping *area.*

area code A three-digit number designating a geographic region, used when telephoning long distance from one area to another.

ar·e·a·way [âr′ē·ə·wā′] *n.* 1 A small, sunken space leading to or providing air and light for a basement. 2 A passageway, as between buildings.

a·re·na [ə·rē′nə] *n.* 1 The open space in a Roman stadium where combats were held, as between gladiators. 2 Any area of conflict or action: the political *arena.*

aren't [ärnt] A contraction of: Are not: *Aren't* you glad to see me? ◆ *Aren't I* is used to avoid both *ain't I* and *am I not.* It is ungrammatical, but sounds more correct than *ain't I* and less stuffy than *am I not*. It is best to reword an idea so none of the three is needed.

Ar·es [âr′ēz] *n.* The Greek god of war. He was called Mars by the Romans.

Arg. 1 Argentina. 2 Argentine.

Ar·gen·tine [är′jən·tēn′] 1 *adj.* Of or from Argentina. 2 *n.* A person born in or a citizen of Argentina.

Ar·gen·tin·e·an or **Ar·gen·tin·i·an** [är′jən·tin′ē·ən] 1 *adj.* Of or from Argentina. 2 *n.* A person born in or a citizen of Argentina.

ar·gon [är′gon] *n.* A colorless, odorless, gaseous element making up almost one percent of the atmosphere. It is used especially in electric bulbs and electron tubes. ◆ *Argon* comes from a Greek word meaning *lazy*. The name is fitting because argon seems to be totally inert.

Ar·go·naut [är′gə·nôt] *n.* In Greek legend, any of the men who sailed with Jason to find the Golden Fleece.

ar·go·sy [är′gə·sē] *n., pl.* **ar·go·sies** 1 A large ship with a rich cargo. 2 A fleet of such ships.

ar·got [är′gō *or* är′gət] *n.* The special vocabulary and phrases used by a particular group of people, especially criminals.

ar·gue [är′gyōō] *v.* **ar·gued, ar·gu·ing** 1 To give reasons for or against something: We *argued* against going to the beach. 2 To dispute; disagree: They always *argue* about baseball. 3 To show; suggest: The big car *argued* a large family. 4 To convince by giving reasons: The salesperson *argued* me into buying a more expensive car.

ar·gu·ment [är′gyə·mənt] *n.* 1 The act of arguing; an angry discussion; dispute. 2 A reason or reasons offered for or against something. 3 A short statement telling what a story or poem is about.

ar·gu·men·ta·tive [är′gyə·men′tə·tiv] *adj.* 1 Liking argument; ready to argue. 2 Full of arguments. —**ar′gu·men′ta·tive·ly** *adv.*

Ar·gus [är′gəs] *n.* 1 In Greek myths, a giant with a hundred eyes. 2 A very watchful person.

ar·gyle or **Ar·gyle** [är′gīl] *n.* 1 A pattern of diamonds in one or several contrasting colors knitted on a solid background color. 2 A sock knitted in this pattern.

a·ri·a [ä′rē·ə *or* âr′ē·ə] *n.* A song, usually in an opera or oratorio, sung by a single person to musical accompaniment.

Ar·i·ad·ne [ar′ē·ad′nē] *n.* In Greek legends, the daugher of King Minos of Crete. She gave Theseus the ball of yarn that enabled him to find his way out of the Minotaur's labyrinth.

ar·id [ar′id] *adj.* 1 Without enough rainfall to grow things; dry; parched. 2 Dull; dry: an *arid* speech. —**a·rid·i·ty** [ə·rid′ə·tē] *n.*

Ar·ies [âr′ēs] *n.* 1 A constellation in the Northern Hemisphere, thought to look like a ram. 2 The first sign of the zodiac. 3 A person born under this sign.

a·right [ə·rīt′] *adv.* Correctly; rightly: I don't remember *aright*.

a·rise [ə·rīz′] *v.* **a·rose, a·ris·en** [ə·riz′(ə)n], **a·ris·ing** 1 To get up: The speaker *arose* and began to talk. 2 To rise up; ascend: Wild duck *arose* from the lake. 3 To start; come into being: New problems always *arise*. 4 To result: The argument *arose* from their stubbornness.

ar·is·toc·ra·cy [ar′is·tok′rə·sē] *n., pl.* **ar·is·toc·ra·cies** 1 A class of society inheriting by birth a high position or rank, certain powers and privileges, and usually wealth. 2 Government by this upper class. 3 Any group of those thought to be the best: an *aristocracy* of rich families.

a·ris·to·crat [ə·ris′tə·krat′] *n.* 1 A member of an aristocracy; nobleman or noblewoman. 2 A person with the opinions, manners, or appearance of the upper class. 3 A person who prefers an aristocratic form of government.

a·ris·to·crat·ic [ə·ris′tə·krat′ik] *adj.* 1 Fit for an aristocrat; superior; exclusive; snobbish. 2 Belonging to, having the characteristics of, or favoring an aristocracy: *aristocratic* government. —**a·ris′to·crat′i·cal·ly** *adv.*

Ar·is·to·te·li·an [ar′ə·stə·tēl′yən] 1 *adj.* Of or having to do with Aristotle or his philosophy. 2 *n.* A follower of Aristotle or his philosophy.

a·rith·me·tic [*n.* ə·rith′mə·tik, *adj.* ar′ith·met′ik] 1 *n.* A branch of mathematics that deals with numbers, the relations between numbers, and the operations of addition, subtraction, multiplication, division, raising to powers, and the extraction of roots. 2 *n.* Computation or calculation using numbers: a mistake in your *arithmetic*. 3 *adj.* Of or having to do with arithmetic.

ar·ith·met·i·cal [ar′ith·met′i·kəl] *adj.* Arithmetic.

ar·ith·met·ic mean [ar′ith·met′ik] The numerical value of the sum of a set of quantities divided by the number of quantities in the set.

arithmetic progression A sequence of numbers such that the difference between any two successive numbers is the same, as, 3, 7, 11, 15.

Ariz. Arizona.

ark [ärk] *n.* 1 In the Bible, the ship Noah built to save himself, his family, and two of every kind of animal from the Flood. 2 A chest in the ancient Jewish Temple that held the stone tablets on which the Ten Commandments were inscribed: also called **ark of the covenant.**

Ark. Arkansas.

Ark of the Covenant 1 The sacred chest in which the ancient Hebrews carried the stone tablets on which were written the Ten Commandments. 2 A chest in a synagogue in which the Torah and other sacred writings are kept.

arm¹ [ärm] *n.* 1 The part of the body from the shoulder to the hand, or the forelimb of an animal. 2 Something for or like an arm: the *arm* of a coat; the *arm* of a crane.

arm² [ärm] 1 *n.* A weapon of any sort. 2 *v.* To supply with a weapon or weapons. 3 *v.* To supply with anything that strengthens or protects: to be *armed* with the facts.

ar·ma·da [är·mä′də] *n.* (*sometimes written* **Armada**) A fleet of warships: The Spanish *Armada* was defeated by the English in 1588. ◆ This word comes directly from a Spanish word, which in turn came from a Latin word meaning *armed*. It is closely related to the word *army*.

a	add	**i**	it	**o͝o**	took	**oi**	oil		
ā	ace	**ī**	ice	**o͞o**	pool	**ou**	pout		
â	care	**o**	odd	**u**	up	**ng**	ring		
ä	palm	**ō**	open	**û**	burn	**th**	thin		
e	end	**ô**	order	**yo͞o**	fuse	**t͟h**	this		
ē	equal					**zh**	vision		

ə = {a in *above* e in *sicken* i in *possible* / o in *melon* u in *circus*}

ar·ma·dil·lo [är′mə·dil′ō] *n., pl.* **ar·ma·dil·los** A small burrowing mammal found from South America north to Texas, having an armorlike shell of jointed plates. Some kinds can roll up, shell and all, into a ball when attacked.

Armadillo

Ar·ma·ged·don [ar′mə·ged′(ə)n] *n.* **1** According to the New Testament, the place where the final and conclusive battle between the forces of good and evil will take place. **2** Any conclusive or very destructive battle.

ar·ma·ment [är′mə·mənt] *n.* **1** (*often pl.*) The military equipment, as guns, ships, and bombs, used in war. **2** The armed forces of a nation, equipped for war.

ar·ma·ture [är′mə·chŏŏr′] *n.* **1** The rotating part of an electric motor or generator, having a soft-iron core surrounded by coils of insulated wire. **2** The part of an electric relay, buzzer, or bell that is moved by the electromagnet.

arm·chair [ärm′châr′] *n.* A chair with supports on both sides for the arms or elbows.

armed forces [ärmd] All the military, naval, and air forces of a nation.

Ar·me·ni·an [âr·mē′nē·ən *or* âr·mēn′yən] **1** *adj.* Of or from Armenia. **2** *n.* A person born or living in Armenia. **3** *n.* The language of Armenia.

arm·ful [ärm′fŏŏl′] *n., pl.* **arm·fuls** As much as can be held by one or both arms.

arm·hole [ärm′hōl′] *n.* An opening for the arm in clothes.

ar·mi·stice [är′mə·stis] *n.* An agreement to stop fighting for a short time; truce.

Armistice Day The former name for VETERANS DAY.

ar·mor [är′mər] *n.* **1** A covering worn when fighting, to protect the body. **2** Any protective covering, as the shell of a turtle or plates of a tank.

ar·mored [är′mərd] *adj.* **1** Protected by armor. **2** Equipped with tanks and other armored vehicles: an *armored* division.

ar·mor·er [är′mər·ər] *n.* A maker or repairer of arms, especially a soldier or sailor who takes care of the small arms of a company or ship.

Armor of a mounted knight

ar·mo·ri·al [är·môr′ē·əl] *adj.* Of or having to do with coats of arms or heraldry.

armor plate A specially hardened steel, used as protective shielding on warships, tanks, and fortifications.

ar·mor·y [är′mər·ē] *n., pl.* **ar·mor·ies** **1** A place where arms are kept; arsenal. **2** A building where military units, as the National Guard, drill. **3** A factory for making weapons.

arm·pit [ärm′pit′] *n.* The hollow place under the arm at the shoulder.

arms [ärmz] *n.pl.* **1** Weapons. **2** Warfare; fighting. **3** The designs or emblems used in a coat of arms. **—up in arms** Excited and ready to fight.

ar·my [är′mē] *n., pl.* **ar·mies** **1** A large group of soldiers, organized, trained, and armed to fight. **2** All the soldiers in the land forces of a country. **3** Any group of people organized to advance a cause. **4** A great number of persons or things: an *army* of insects.

ar·ni·ca [är′ni·kə] *n.* **1** A perennial plant having large, yellow, daisylike flowers on tall stalks. **2** A medicine prepared from the flower heads of this plant, used for sprains and bruises.

a·ro·ma [ə·rō′mə] *n.* A pleasant fragrance or smell, as of food or a plant.

ar·o·mat·ic [ar′ə·mat′ik] *adj.* Having a pleasant smell; fragrant; spicy: *aromatic* gingerbread.

a·rose [ə·rōz′] Past tense of ARISE.

a·round [ə·round′] **1** *adv.* In a circle: The top spun *around.* **2** *prep.* About the circumference of: *around* the world. **3** *adv.* On all sides: The people crowded *around* to look. **4** *prep.* On all sides of; surrounding: The flowers grew *around* the pond. **5** *adv.* In the opposite direction; about: to turn *around.* **6** *adv.* Here and there; from place to place: to walk *around.* **7** *prep.* Here and there in: to wander *around* the house. **8** *adv.* Nearby; in the neighborhood: Stay *around* until he calls. **9** *prep.* Somewhere near or within: I'll be *around* the house. **10** *prep.* About; near: *around* midnight.

a·rous·al [ə·rouz′əl] *n.* **1** The act of awakening. **2** The act or process of exciting or provoking, or the condition of being excited or provoked.

a·rouse [ə·rouz′] *v.* **a·roused, a·rous·ing** **1** To stir up; awaken. **2** To excite or provoke: The cruel deed *aroused* our anger.

ar·peg·gi·o [är·pej′ē·ō′ *or* är·pej′ō] *n., pl.* **ar·peg·gi·os** **1** The playing of the notes of a chord in rapid succession rather than all at once. **2** A chord played in this manner.

ar·que·bus [är′kwə·bəs] *n.* Another name for HARQUEBUS.

ar·raign [ə·rān′] *v.* **1** To call into court to answer "guilty" or "not guilty" to a charge. **2** To accuse; call in question.

ar·raign·ment [ə·rān′mənt] *n.* The formal act or process of arraigning.

ar·range [ə·rānj′] *v.* **ar·ranged, ar·rang·ing** **1** To put into a certain order; to *arrange* the books on the shelf. **2** To make plans; prepare: Did she *arrange* to meet you here? **3** To come or bring to an agreement about: We can easily *arrange* terms. **4** To adapt (music) to a style or for performers not originally intended.

ar·range·ment [ə·rānj′mənt] *n.* **1** An arranging or placing in order. **2** The way in which something is arranged: the *arrangement* of pictures in an art gallery. **3** (*usually pl.*) A plan or preparation: the *arrangements* for the wedding. **4** Music changed to fit certain performers or a style of performance.

ar·rant [ar′ənt] *adj.* Out-and-out; thorough: an *arrant* coward.

ar·ras [ar′əs] *n.* A decorative wall hanging, especially a tapestry.

ar·ray [ə·rā′] **1** *n.* Regular or proper order; orderly arrangement. **2** *v.* To set in proper order: The soldiers were *arrayed* for an attack. **3** *n.* A large or impressive display: an *array* of gems. **4** *n.* Clothing; fine dress. **5** *v.* To dress; adorn: to be *arrayed* in silks.

ar·ray·al [ə·rā′əl] *n.* **1** The act or process of arraying. **2** An array; orderly arrangement.

ar·rears [ə·rirz′] *n.pl.* **1** A debt overdue and still unpaid. **2** Work already late but not finished: *arrears* of unanswered mail. **—in arrears** Behind in payment of a debt, or in one's work.

ar·rest [ə·rest′] **1** *v.* To stop suddenly; check: The medicine *arrested* his cold. **2** *v.* To attract and hold: The bright signs *arrested* our attention. **3** *v.* To capture by legal authority; take to jail or court. **4** *n.* The act of arresting. **—under arrest** Arrested; in custody.

ar·rest·ing [ə·res′ting] *adj.* Attracting and holding the attention; impressive; striking.

ar·ri·val [ə·rī′vəl] *n.* **1** The act of arriving: the *arrival* of a train. **2** A person or thing that arrives: new *arrivals* to the country.

ar·rive [ə·rīv′] *v.* **ar·rived, ar·riv·ing** **1** To reach a place after a journey: The boat *arrives* in London tomorrow. **2** To come: The hour has finally *arrived.* **3** To achieve success or fame: In this play she has *arrived.*

ar·ri·ve·der·ci [a′rē·və·der′chē] An Italian expression for "until we meet again."

ar·ro·gance [ar′ə·gəns] *n.* Too much pride and too little regard for others.

ar·ro·gant [ar′ə·gənt] *adj.* Too proud and disdainful of others: an *arrogant* manner. **—ar′ro·gant·ly** *adv.*

ar·ro·gate [ar′ə·gāt′] *v.* **ar·ro·gat·ed, ar·ro·gat·ing** To take or claim for oneself, without having a right to do so: In declaring war, the President *arrogated* a power belonging to Congress. **—ar·ro·ga′tion** *n.*

ar·row [ar′ō] *n.* **1** A thin, straight rod, usually with a point at one end and feathers at the other. Arrows are used in shooting with a bow. **2** Anything shaped like an arrow. **3** A sign (→) used to indicate a direction, as in maps or road signs.

ar·row·head [ar′ō·hed′] *n.* The pointed tip or head of an arrow.

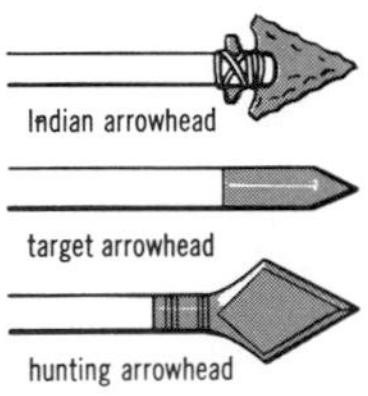

ar·row·root [ar′ō·ro͞ot′] *n.* **1** A nutritious starch from the roots of a tropical American plant. **2** This plant.

ar·roy·o [ə·roi′ō] *n., pl.* **ar·roy·os** A small gulch cut out by a creek, usually dry.

ar·se·nal [är′sə·nəl] *n.* A public building for making or keeping such supplies as guns and ammunition.

ar·se·nic [är′sə·nik] *n.* **1** A gray, poisonous, very brittle crystalline element having some metallic properties. **2** A poisonous compound of arsenic and oxygen used as an insecticide and a weed killer.

ar·son [är′sən] *n.* The crime of setting a building or other property afire on purpose.

ar·son·ist [ar′sə·nist] *n.* A person who commits arson.

art¹ [ärt] *n.* **1** Painting, drawing, or sculpture. **2** The making of arrangements of colors, lines, shapes, sounds, words, and other elements, that appeal to the taste and give pleasure through beauty or form. **3** Such an arrangement itself, as a piece of music or literature, or a painting. **4** (*usually pl.*) Fields of study including literature, philosophy, and languages, but not the sciences. **5** Rules or methods needed to make or do something; skill: the *art* of cooking. **6** Occupation; craft: the mariner's *art.* **7** (*usually pl.*) A sly trick; cunning or wile: the dark *arts* of magic.

art² [ärt] *v.* The old form of ARE used with "thou": Thou *art* right.

Ar·te·mis [är′tə·mis] *n.* In Greek myths, the goddess of hunting and of the moon. Her Roman name is Diana.

ar·te·ri·al [är·tir′ē·əl] *adj.* **1** Of, having to do with, or carried in arteries or an artery. **2** Like an artery: an *arterial* highway.

ar·te·ri·ole [är·tir′ē·ōl] *n.* A small blood vessel at the end of an artery.

ar·te·ri·o·scle·ro·sis [är·tir′ē·ō·sklə·rō′sis] *n.* A hardening of the walls of the arteries, making it hard for the blood to pass through. **—ar·te·ri·o·scle·rot·ic** [är·tir′ē·ō·sklə·rot′ik] *adj.*

ar·ter·y [är′tər·ē] *n., pl.* **ar·ter·ies** Any of the blood vessels that carry blood away from the heart to every part of the body.

ar·te·sian well [är·tē′zhən] A deep well so placed that underground pressure forces water to gush out of it.

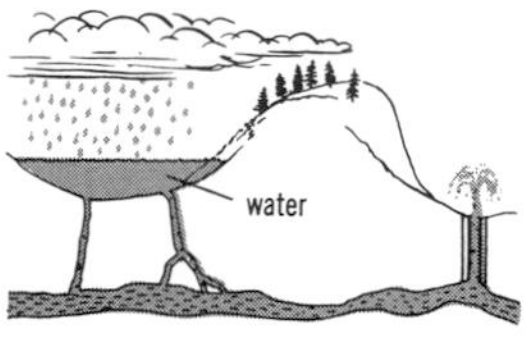

Artesian well

art·ful [ärt′fəl] *adj.* **1** Cunning; crafty: the *artful* dodges of the fox. **2** Skillful: an *artful* writer. **—art′ful·ly** *adv.* **—art′ful·ness** *n.*

ar·thrit·ic [är·thrit′ik] *adj.* Of or brought about by arthritis: *arthritic* pains.

ar·thri·tis [är·thrī′tis] *n.* An inflammation of one or more joints.

ar·thro·pod [är′thrə·pod] *n.* Any of a large group of animals without backbones, having jointed legs and bodies, as insects, spiders, and crabs.

Ar·thur [är′thər] *n.* In many legends, a king of ancient Britain who gathered famous knights at his court in Camelot.

ar·ti·choke [är′tə·chōk′] *n.* **1** A garden plant that looks like a large thistle. **2** Its flowering head, that is eaten as a vegetable.

Artichoke

ar·ti·cle [är′ti·kəl] *n.* **1** A particular thing; an individual item: an *article* of food. **2** A separate, often numbered, section or clause, as in a law, constitution, or contract. **3** A complete piece of writing on a single topic, forming part of a magazine, newspaper, or book: an *article* on folk songs. **4** In English, any of the words *the, a,* or *an. The* is often used to make a noun definite and particular, as in *the* boy; *a* or *an* to make a noun indefinite and general, as in *a* boy.

Articles of Confederation The first constitution of the United States, in force from 1781 until 1788.

ar·tic·u·late [*adj.* är·tik′yə·lit, *v.* är·tik′yə·lāt′] *adj., v.* **ar·tic·u·lat·ed, ar·tic·u·lat·ing** **1** *adj.* Using clear and distinct syllables or words: *articulate* speech. **2** *v.* To speak clearly and distinctly; enunciate. **3** *adj.* Having the power of speech; able to speak

a	add	**i**	it	**o͝o**	took	**oi**	oil
ā	ace	**ī**	ice	**o͞o**	pool	**ou**	pout
â	care	**o**	odd	**u**	up	**ng**	ring
ä	palm	**ō**	open	**û**	burn	**th**	thin
e	end	**ô**	order	**yo͞o**	fuse	**t͟h**	this
ē	equal					**zh**	vision

ə = {a in *above* e in *sicken* i in *possible* / o in *melon* u in *circus*}

one's thoughts clearly: an *articulate* speaker. 4 *v.* To say or tell in words: We tried to *articulate* our gratitude. 5 *adj.* Having joints or segments: The arm is an *articulate* limb. 6 *v.* To connect by a joint: The leg is *articulated* to the body at the hip. **—ar·tic′u·late·ly** *adv.*

ar·tic·u·la·tion [är·tik′yə·lā′shən] *n.* 1 Manner of speaking or pronouncing. 2 The manner in which parts are joined together. 3 A joint.

ar·ti·fact [är′tə·fakt′] *n.* Anything made by human work or art.

ar·ti·fice [är′tə·fis] *n.* 1 A sly or clever trick or expedient: I used every *artifice* to get my way. 2 Ingenuity or skill.

ar·ti·fic·er [är·tif′ə·sər] *n.* 1 A skillful craftsman. 2 A person who plans or invents.

ar·ti·fi·cial [är′tə·fish′əl] *adj.* 1 Made by a person or persons; not natural: *artificial* flowers. 2 Not genuine; false: an *artificial* manner. **—ar·ti·fi·ci·al·i·ty** [är′tə·fish·ē·al′ə·tē] *n.* **—ar′ti·fi′cial·ly** *adv.*

artificial intelligence The capacity of a machine, such as a computer, to perform certain functions of human intelligence, as learning or reasoning.

artificial respiration The act or method of making a person breathe by forcing air in and out of the lungs, as after suffocation or shock.

ar·til·ler·y [är·til′ə·rē] *n.* 1 Large mounted guns; cannon. 2 A part of an army that makes use of such guns.

ar·til·ler·y·man [är·til′ə·rē·mən] *n., pl.* **ar·til·ler·y·men** [är·til′ə·rē·mən] A soldier in the artillery.

ar·ti·san [är′tə·zən] *n.* A worker, such as a plumber or carpenter, trained or skilled in some trade; craftsman or craftswoman.

ar·tist [är′tist] *n.* 1 A person who is skilled in any of the fine arts, as painting or sculpture. 2 A person who works with skill and originality: She is an *artist* at diplomatic negotiations.

ar·tis·tic [är·tis′tik] *adj.* 1 Of art or artists. 2 Showing skill and good design, color, or form: an *artistic* job of decorating. 3 Showing or having a sense for the beautiful. **—ar·tis′ti·cal·ly** *adv.*

art·is·try [är′tis·trē] *n.* Artistic work or ability.

art·less [ärt′lis] *adj.* 1 Without cunning; simple; natural: the *artless* questions of children. 2 Not having skill or ability; clumsy. **—art′less·ly** *adv.* **—art′less·ness** *n.*

art·y [är′tē] *adj.* **art′i·er, art′i·est** Artistic in a phony or pretentious way. **—art′i·ly** *adj.* **—art′i·ness** *n.*

-ary A suffix meaning: 1 Having to do with, as in *parliamentary.* 2 A person or thing connected with or engaged in, as in *revolutionary.*

Ar·y·an [ar′ē·ən] 1 *n.* A member of a prehistoric people who lived in southern Asia and spoke an Indo-European language. 2 *adj.* Of or having to do with this or other prehistoric people who spoke Indo-European. 3 *n.* In Nazi ideology, any non-Jewish Caucasian, especially a Nordic one. 4 *adj.* Of or having to do with non-Jewish Caucasians.

as [az] 1 *adv.* To the same degree; equally: Can you swim *as* well as your friend? 2 *conj.* To the same degree that: as fair *as* the sun. 3 *conj.* In the way that: Sing *as* I am singing. 4 *conj.* To the degree in which: He became wiser *as* he grew older. 5 *conj.* At the same time that; while: They waved *as* we sailed away. 6 *conj.* Because; since: *As* it rained, we stayed at home. 7 *conj.* That the result is, or was: Speak louder, so *as* to be heard. 8 *conj.* Though: Hungry *as* he was, he couldn't eat. 9 *conj.* For instance: We enjoy many sports, *as* tennis and swimming. 10 *pron.* That; who; which (used after *same* and *such*): He has the same mitt *as* I. 11 *pron.* A fact that: A day has 24 hours, *as* everyone knows. 12 *prep.* In the role or character of: to act *as* umpire. **—as for** or **as to** Concerning. **—as if** or **as though** The way it would be if: They looked *as though* they wanted to leave. ◆ *As* used in place of "since" or "because" can cause confusion. The sentence *As it was raining, we covered our heads* can mean either that we covered our heads *because* it was raining or that we simply happened to cover our heads *while* it was raining. ◆ See LIKE.

As The symbol for the element arsenic.

As. 1 Asia. 2 Asian.

AS or **A.S.** Anglo-Saxon.

as·a·fet·i·da or **as·a·foet·i·da** [as′ə·fet′ə·də] *n.* A brownish, bitter resin with a garlicky odor, obtained from the roots of certain Asian plants and formerly used as a medicine.

ASAP as soon as possible.

as·bes·tos [as·bes′təs] *n.* A grayish white mineral that will not burn nor let much heat through. Mats of asbestos are used as insulation, as for furnace pipes or to protect tables against hot dishes.

ASCAP [as′kap′] American Society of Composers, Authors, and Publishers.

as·cend [ə·send′] *v.* 1 To go upward; rise. 2 To climb: The climbers *ascended* the mountain.

as·cen·dan·cy or **as·cen·den·cy** [ə·sen′dən·sē] *n.* The quality or condition of having a position of power or control; domination: The tyrant lost *ascendancy* over the people.

as·cen·dant or **as·cen·dent** [ə·sen′dənt] *adj.* 1 Rising; moving upward. 2 Dominant; in power. **—in the ascendant** Gaining in power or influence; on the rise.

as·cen·sion [ə·sen′shən] *n.* 1 An ascending; rise. 2 (*written* **Ascension**) In the Bible, the ascent of Jesus into heaven after the Resurrection.

as·cent [ə·sent′] *n.* 1 The act of rising or climbing: the *ascent* of a balloon. 2 Advancement; rise: *ascent* to the presidency. 3 A way going up; upward slope. ◆ *Ascent* and *assent* sound and look alike but are unrelated. *Ascent* comes from a Latin verb meaning *to climb to* and still means an upward climb: The *ascent* of the space rocket was shown on TV. *Assent* comes from Latin roots meaning *to feel* and it now means agreement or consent: Congress gave its *assent* to the policy outlined. You will come on both words in rather formal articles but you probably won't hear them often in conversation.

as·cer·tain [as′ər·tān′] *v.* To find out for certain; make sure of: She examined the book to *ascertain* its contents.

as·cet·ic [ə·set′ik] 1 *n.* A person who chooses not to have pleasures or comforts, as wealth or fine clothes, but prefers living plainly, usually for religious reasons. 2 *adj.* Holding back from pleasures or comforts; austere: *ascetic* life. **—as·cet·i·cism** [ə·set′ə·siz′əm] *n.*

As·clep·i·us [ə·sklep′ē·əs] In Greek myths, the god of medicine.

a·scor·bic acid [ə·skôr′bik] Vitamin C. It is found in such foods as oranges, lemons, and tomatoes.

as·cot [as′kət *or* as′kot′] *n.* A kind of neck scarf knotted so that one broad end covers the other at the throat.

as·cribe [ə·skrīb′] *v.* **as·cribed, as·crib·ing** 1 To think of as coming from a cause or source: He *ascribes* his headache to too much television. 2 To think of as belonging; attribute: The work is *ascribed* to Shakespeare.

as·crip·tion [ə·skrip′shən] *n.* 1 The act of ascribing. 2 A sentence or statement that ascribes.

a·sep·sis [ə·sep′sis] The state or condition of being free from microorganisms that cause disease or decay.

a·sep·tic [ə·sep′tik] *adj.* Free from microorganisms that cause disease or decay. **—a·sep′ti·cal·ly** *adv.*

a·sex·u·al [ā·sek′sho͞o·əl] *adj.* 1 Lacking sex. 2 Without union of male and female reproductive cells: *asexual* reproduction. **—a·sex′u·al·ly** *adv.*

ash[1] [ash] *n.* The fine, grayish white powder left after a substance has been burned. See also ASHES.

ash[2] [ash] *n.* A shade tree related to the olive, having tough, springy wood, used for timber.

a·shamed [ə·shāmd′] *adj.* 1 Feeling shame; upset because something bad, silly, or improper was done: Their parents were *ashamed* of their behavior. 2 Not willing because of a fear of shame: I was *ashamed* to tell my poor grades.

ash can 1 A large receptacle for ashes or garbage. 2 *slang* Another name for DEPTH CHARGE.

ash·en [ash′ən] *adj.* Of, like, or pale as ashes; gray: an *ashen* appearance.

ash·es [ash′iz] *n.pl.* 1 The grayish white particles and powder that remain after a substance has been burned. 2 A dead body, especially the remains of a body after cremation.

a·shore [ə·shôr′] *adj., adv.* 1 To or on the shore: A sailor *ashore* is homesick; to come *ashore.* 2 On land; aground.

ash tray A small receptacle for tobacco ashes and for cigarette and cigar butts.

Ash Wednesday The first day of Lent; seventh Wednesday before Easter.

ash·y [ash′ē] *adj.* **ash·i·er, ash·i·est** 1 Of or covered with ashes. 2 Like ashes; pale: an *ashy* complexion.

A·sian [ā′zhən] 1 *adj.* Of or from Asia. 2 *n.* A person born or living in Asia.

Asian flu An acute pulmonary influenza caused by a strain of virus first isolated in Singapore in 1957.

A·si·at·ic [ā′zhē·at′ik] 1 *adj.* Of or from Asia. 2 *n.* An Asian.

a·side [ə·sīd′] 1 *adv.* To or on one side; away: Stand *aside!* 2 *adv.* Apart; away: Put some fruit *aside* for later. 3 *adv.* Out of thought: Put your worries *aside.* 4 *n.* Remarks spoken aside, as those of an actor not supposed to be heard by the other actors. 5 *adv.* Away from the general company; in seclusion. **—aside from** Apart from; excepting: *Aside from* one small bag, I carried no luggage.

as·i·nine [as′ə·nīn′] *adj.* Stupid; foolish: an *asinine* remark. **—as·i·nin·i·ty** [as′ə·nin′ə·tē] *n.*

ask [ask] *v.* 1 To put a question to: *Ask* about their vacation. 2 To use words to try to find out: to *ask* what time it is; to *ask* the price; I'll *ask* about it. 3 To say aloud: to *ask* questions. 4 To request or make a request: to *ask* permission. 5 To demand as a price; require: They are *asking* five dollars for the sweater. 6 To invite: Her aunt was *asked* to tea.

a·skance [ə·skans′] *adv.* 1 With distrust or doubt: They looked *askance* at the new plan. 2 With a look to the side; sidewise.

a·skew [ə·skyo͞o′] *adj., adv.* On or to one side; out of line: The gate hung *askew.*

Picture set askew

a·slant [ə·slant′] 1 *adj.* Slanting. 2 *adv.* At a slant. 3 *prep.* Across or over on a slant.

a·sleep [ə·slēp′] 1 *adj.* Sleeping. 2 *adj.* Numb: My foot is *asleep.* 3 *adv.* Into a sleep: to fall *asleep.*

asp [asp] *n.* A small venomous snake of Africa and Europe; viper.

as·par·a·gus [ə·spar′ə·gəs] *n.* 1 A perennial plant related to the lily. 2 Its young shoots, eaten as a vegetable.

ASPCA American Society for the Prevention of Cruelty to Animals.

as·pect [as′pekt] *n.* 1 Appearance; look: Sunlight gave the room a cheerful *aspect.* 2 One way of looking at or approaching something, as a subject or a problem: There are many *aspects* to the problem. 3 The side or surface facing in a certain direction: the southern *aspect* of a house.

asp·en [as′pən] *n.* A poplar tree with leaves that tremble in the slightest breeze.

as·per·i·ty [as′per′ə·tē] *n., pl.* **as·per·i·ties** 1 Roughness or harshness, as of weather or a surface. 2 Bitterness or sharpness of temper: The *asperity* in the officer's voice surprised me.

as·per·sion [ə·spûr′zhən] *n.* A false or damaging remark or report; slander: to cast *aspersions* on their honesty.

as·phalt [as′fôlt] *n.* 1 A substance like tar, brown to black, found in natural beds or left over when petroleum is refined. 2 A mixture of this with crushed rock or sand used for pavement or roofing.

asphalt jungle A big city or an area of one seen as a dangerous and crowded place.

as·phyx·i·a [as·fik′sē·ə] *n.* Unconsciousness caused by a lack of oxygen or an excess of carbon dioxide.

as·phyx·i·ate [as·fik′sē·āt′] *v.* **as·phyx·i·at·ed, as·phyx·i·at·ing** To undergo or cause to undergo asphyxia. **—as·phyx′i·a′tion** *n.*

as·pic [as′pik] *n.* A jelly of meat or vegetable juices, used in molded salads, as of meat or fish.

as·pi·dis·tra [as′pə·dis′trə] *n.* Any of several Asian evergreen plants having tough, wide, and long leaves, often with white stripes.

as·pir·ant [ə·spīr′ənt *or* as′pər·ənt] *n.* A person who aspires, or tries to achieve honors or high position: an *aspirant* to the governorship.

as·pi·rate [*v.* as′pə·rāt′, *n., adj.* as′pər·it] *v.* **as·pi·rat·ed, as·pi·rat·ing,** *n., adj.* 1 *v.* To start a word or a vowel sound with the sound of *h:* You *aspirate* "hot" but not "honest." 2 *n.* This sound of *h.* 3 *adj.* Pronounced with this sound of *h.* 4 *v.* To remove (fluid) from a body cavity by suction.

as·pi·ra·tion [as′pə·rā′shən] *n.* 1 A great hope or desire; ambition: to have *aspirations* to become a

a	add	**i**	it	**o͝o**	took	**oi**	oil
ā	ace	**ī**	ice	**o͞o**	pool	**ou**	pout
â	care	**o**	odd	**u**	up	**ng**	ring
ä	palm	**ō**	open	**û**	burn	**th**	thin
e	end	**ô**	order	**yo͞o**	fuse	**th**	this
ē	equal					**zh**	vision

ə = { a in *above*, e in *sicken*, i in *possible*, o in *melon*, u in *circus* }

lawyer. **2** The act of breathing; breath. **3** An aspirating of a sound.

as·pi·ra·tor [as′pə·rā′tər] *n.* **1** A medical instrument that uses suction to remove fluids from a body cavity, such as the lungs. **2** Any device that causes suction to pick up or move materials.

as·pire [ə·spīr′] *v.* **as·pired, as·pir·ing** To have great hope or ambition for something; seek: She *aspired* to a career in politics.

as·pi·rin [as′pər·in] *n.* A drug used to relieve headaches, pains, colds, or fever. ◆ The word *aspirin* was formed from an old chemical name and was at one time a trademark.

ass [as] *n.* **1** A donkey. **2** A stupid person; fool.

as·sa·gai [as′ə·gī′] *n.* Another spelling of ASSEGAI.

as·sail [ə·sāl′] *v.* **1** To attack violently, as with blows, weapons, or soldiers; assault. **2** To attack with words, arguments, or questions: to be *assailed* by doubts.

as·sail·ant [ə·sā′lənt] *n.* A person who assails; an attacker.

as·sas·sin [ə·sas′in] *n.* A murderer, especially a fanatic or a person hired to kill someone.

as·sas·si·nate [ə·sas′ə·nāt′] *v.* **as·sas·si·nat·ed, as·sas·si·nat·ing** To murder by a secret or surprise attack. **—as·sas′si·na′tion** *n.*

as·sault [ə·sôlt′] **1** *n.* Any sudden, violent attack, either physical or verbal. **2** *n.* In law, a threat or attempt to inflict physical harm on another person. **3** *v.* To attack with violence.

assault and battery In law, an act in which a threat or attempt of violence against another person is carried out.

as·say [ə·sā′] **1** *v.* To analyze (an alloy or ore) to find out how much of a certain metal is in it. **2** *n.* An analysis such as this. **3** *v.* To estimate; evaluate. **4** *v.* To attempt; try. **—as·say′er** *n.*

as·se·gai [as′ə·gī′] *n.* A lightweight throwing spear used by some tribes in southern Africa.

as·sem·blage [ə·sem′blij] *n.* **1** Any gathering of persons or things; collection; assembly: an *assemblage* of junk in the garage. **2** A fitting together, as of the parts of a machine.

as·sem·ble [ə·sem′bəl] *v.* **as·sem·bled, as·sem·bling** **1** To come or bring together; collect: The team *assembled* for practice. **2** To fit together the parts of: We *assembled* the model airplane.

as·sem·bly [ə·sem′blē] *n., pl.* **as·sem·blies** **1** A gathering or meeting together of persons: right of peaceful *assembly.* **2** A group of persons gathered together for a common purpose; meeting. **3** (*written* **Assembly**) The lower house of the legislature in some states. **4** A putting together of parts, as of a machine. **5** These parts put together. **6** The signal on a bugle or drum calling soldiers to fall into rank.

assembly language A set of alphabetic symbols used to represent computer instructions and commands when programming. It is easier for a human being to remember and use than machine language.

assembly line A line of factory workers and equipment along which a product being put together passes from step to step until it is completed.

as·sem·bly·man [ə·sem′blē·mən] *n., pl.* **as·sem·bly·men** [ə·sem′blē·mən] A member of a legislative assembly.

as·sem·bly·wom·an [ə·sem′blē·wo͝om′ən] *n., pl.* **as·sem·bly·wom·en** [ə·sem′blē·wim′in] A woman who is a member of a legislative assembly.

as·sent [ə·sent′] **1** *v.* To agree or consent: He *assented* to our plan. **2** *n.* Consent or agreement. ◆ See ASCENT.

as·sert [ə·sûrt′] *v.* **1** To say in a clear, firm way; declare: The guide *asserted* that this was the spot. **2** To claim; insist on: She *asserted* her right to speak. **—assert oneself** **1** To insist on one's rights. **2** To put oneself forward; demand attention.

as·ser·tion [ə·sûr′shən] *n.* **1** The asserting of something. **2** A firm, positive statement; claim.

as·ser·tive [ə·sûr′tiv] *adj.* Very bold and self-confident; aggressive. **—as·ser′tive·ly** *adv.* **—as·ser′tive·ness** *n.*

as·sess [ə·ses′] *v.* **1** To set a value on property as a basis for taxes. **2** To place a tax, fine, or other payment on: Each member was *assessed* five dollars. **3** To fix the amount of, as a tax or fine.

as·sess·ment [ə·ses′mənt] *n.* **1** The act of assessing. **2** The amount that is assessed.

as·ses·sor [ə·ses′ər] *n.* An official who makes assessments, especially of property, for taxation.

as·set [as′et] *n.* **1** (*often pl.*) Any item of property having value, as land or money: The business has *assets* of buildings, stocks, and machinery. **2** A valuable thing or quality: Florida's warm winters are one of its *assests.*

as·sev·er·ate [ə·sev′ə·rāt′] *v.* **as·sev·er·at·ed, as·sev·er·at·ing** To declare or say in a firm, positive manner. **—as·sev′er·a′tion** *n.*

as·si·du·i·ty [as′ə·d(y)o͞o′ə·tē] *n., pl.* **as·si·du·i·ties** Hard and constant effort; diligence: to study with *assiduity.*

as·sid·u·ous [ə·sij′o͞o·əs] *adj.* Showing constant, steady attention and effort: *assiduous* work. **—as·sid′u·ous·ly** *adv.* **—as·sid′u·ous·ness** *n.*

as·sign [ə·sīn′] *v.* **1** To give as a task or share: to *assign* homework. **2** To put at some task or job: She was *assigned* to parking cars. **3** To fix, name, or specify: Limits were *assigned* to the debate. **4** To transfer to another; hand over: Rights to the oil field were *assigned* by the owner.

as·sign·ee [as′ə·nē′ *or* ə·sī′nē′] *n.* The person to whom property, interest, or a right is legally transferred.

as·sign·ment [ə·sīn′mənt] *n.* **1** The act of assigning. **2** Something assigned, as a lesson: I spent two hours on the homework *assignment.*

as·sim·i·late [ə·sim′ə·lāt′] *v.* **as·sim·i·lat·ed, as·sim·i·lat·ing** **1** To take in and make part of itself; absorb: His body cannot *assimilate* sugar. **2** To take in and understand: Have you *assimilated* all that data? **3** To make or become part of the cultural tradition of a community or population: New York has *assimilated* many immigrants.

as·sim·i·la·tion [ə·sim′ə·lā′shən] *n.* **1** The process of assimilating or the condition of being assimilated. **2** The conversion of nutrients from digested or absorbed food into living tissue. **3** The process by which a minority social group gradually loses its identity and becomes like a larger or more dominant group with which it lives. **4** In linguistics, the process by which a speech sound changes to become like a neighboring sound: In "handkerchief" [hang′kər·chif], the original *d* sound became *ng* by *assimilation.*

as·sist [ə·sist′] **1** *v.* To give help or aid to: We *assisted* her in laying the carpet. **2** *n.* Help given, as in scoring a goal in hockey.

as·sis·tance [ə·sis′təns] *n.* Help; aid; support.

as·sis·tant [ə·sis′tənt] **1** *n.* A person who assists; a helper. **2** *adj.* Aiding or assisting the person under whom one is employed: an *assistant* editor.

as·siz·es [ə·sīz′əz] *n.pl.* Court sessions held regularly in each county of England.

assn. association.

assoc. **1** associate. **2** association.

as·so·ci·ate [*v.* ə·sō′s(h)ē·āt′, *n., adj.* ə·sō′s(h)ē·it *or* ə·sō′s(h)ē·āt′] *v.* **as·so·ci·at·ed, as·so·ci·at·ing,** *n., adj.* **1** *v.* To make or see a connection between; connect in one's mind: to *associate* mealtime with hunger. **2** *n.* A person connected with another, as a fellow worker, companion, or partner. **3** *adj.* Joined with another or others in some common way: *associate* justices. **4** *v.* To combine with others for a common purpose. **5** *v.* To have dealings; keep company: to *associate* with the other students. **6** *adj.* Having a lower position; with less than full status: an *associate* professor.

as·so·ci·a·tion [ə·sō′s(h)ē·ā′shən] *n.* **1** The act of associating. **2** The state of being associated; fellowship; partnership. **3** An organization of persons with a common purpose; society. **4** The connection in the mind between two ideas or feelings: the *association* of joy with laughter.

as·so·ci·a·tive [ə·sō′shē·ā′tiv] *adj.* **1** Of or having to do with association. **2** Caused by association: an *associative* response. **3** Indicating an operation that can be performed on a set of three numbers by beginning with either of two pairs, as addition or multiplication: $2 + (3 + 4) = (2 + 3) + 4$, or $2 \times (3 \times 4) = (2 \times 3) \times 4$.

as·so·nance [as′ə·nəns] *n.* **1** A resemblance in sounds, especially in vowel sounds of words. **2** A kind of rhyming, in which consonants differ but vowel sounds are the same. **—as′so·nant** *adj.*

as·sort [ə·sôrt′] *v.* To put into groups, as by type, size, or color; classify; sort.

as·sort·ed [ə·sôr′tid] *adj.* Of various sorts; of different kinds of varieties: a box of *assorted* chocolates.

as·sort·ment [ə·sôrt′mənt] *n.* **1** A collection or group of various things; variety: an *assortment* of sweaters. **2** A sorting into groups; classification.

asst. assistant.

as·suage [ə·swāj′] *v.* **as·suaged, as·suag·ing** **1** To make less; mitigate; calm: Time will *assuage* their sorrow. **2** To satisfy, as thirst: Two hamburgers *assuaged* my hunger.

as·sume [ə·sōōm′] *v.* **as·sumed, as·sum·ing** **1** To take as or as if true; suppose: *Assume* that tides will be normal. **2** To take on as a shape, role, or look: The cloud *assumed* the shape of a duck. **3** To take on or over: The new boss has *assumed* control. **4** To pretend; simulate; put on: The child *assumed* an innocent look.

as·sumed [ə·sōōmd′] *adj.* **1** Fictitious; pretended: an *assumed* name. **2** Taken for granted.

as·sum·ing [ə·sōō′ming] *adj.* Arrogant; presumptuous.

as·sump·tion [ə·sump′shən] *n.* **1** The act of assuming. **2** Something supposed or taken for granted: a false *assumption.* **3** (*written* **Assumption**) The taking up of the Virgin Mary bodily into heaven, or a church festival on August 15 in honor of it.

as·sur·ance [ə·shŏŏr′əns] *n.* **1** A positive statement intended to give confidence: We had his *assurance* you would pay us. **2** Certainty; guarantee: Ability gives her *assurance* of success. **3** Self-confidence: to recite a poem with *assurance.* **4** Too much boldness; impudence. **5** The British word for INSURANCE.

as·sure [ə·shŏŏr′] *v.* **as·sured, as·sur·ing** **1** To make (a person) feel sure; convince: They *assured* us of their ability. **2** To tell or declare to; promise: He *assures* us he is happy. **3** To make certain; guarantee: These filters *assure* dust-free air.

as·sured [ə·shŏŏrd′] *adj.* **1** Guaranteed; sure: an *assured* salary. **2** Confident: The mayor was *assured* at her press conference.

as·sur·ed·ly [ə·shŏŏr′id·lē] *adv.* **1** Surely; unquestionably. **2** With assurance; confidently.

as·ta·tine [as′tə·tēn′] *n.* A radioactive halogen element that exists in nature but is so rare that it was not discovered until it was made artificially.

as·ter [as′tər] *n.* A plant with flowers like daisies, having white, pink, or purple petals and yellow centers.

Asters

as·ter·isk [as′tər·isk] *n.* A mark shaped like a star (*), used in printing and writing to indicate a note or show that something has been left out.

a·stern [ə·stûrn′] *adv.* **1** Behind a ship. **2** In or toward its rear end. **3** Backward.

as·ter·oid [as′tə·roid] *n.* Any of thousands of small celestial bodies orbiting the sun, mostly between the orbits of Mars and Jupiter.

asth·ma [az′mə] *n.* A chronic illness that makes breathing difficult and causes wheezing and sometimes coughing.

asth·mat·ic [az·mat′ik] **1** *adj.* Of asthma: an *asthmatic* attack. **2** *adj.* Having asthma. **3** *n.* A person having asthma.

a·stig·ma·tism [ə·stig′mə·tiz′əm] *n.* A defect of an eye or a lens which makes objects look out of shape or blurred. It prevents light rays from coming to a sharp focus.

If any of these lines look thin or blurred, you may have astigmatism.

a·stir [ə·stûr′] *adj., adv.* Stirring; in motion: The forest was *astir* with life.

as·ton·ish [ə·ston′ish] *v.* To surprise very much; fill with wonder; amaze. **—as·ton′ish·ment** *n.*

as·ton·ish·ing [ə·ston′ish·ing] *adj.* Amazing: an *astonishing* scientific breakthrough. **—as·ton′ish·ing·ly** *adv.*

as·tound [ə·stound′] *v.* To stun with amazement: News of his defeat in the election *astounded* the overconfident candidate.

a·strad·dle [ə·strad′(ə)l] *prep.* Astride.

as·tra·khan [as′trə·kan′] *n.* **1** The curly, furlike,

a	add	**i**	it	**ŏŏ**	took	**oi**	oil		
ā	ace	**ī**	ice	**ōō**	pool	**ou**	pout		
â	care	**o**	odd	**u**	up	**ng**	ring		
ä	palm	**ō**	open	**û**	burn	**th**	thin		
e	end	**ô**	order	**yōō**	fuse	**th**	this		
ē	equal					**zh**	vision		

ə = { a in *above* e in *sicken* i in *possible* / o in *melon* u in *circus* }

black or gray wool of young lambs raised in the region of Astrakhan, a city in the Soviet Union. 2 A fabric looking like this.
a·stray [ə·strā′] *adj., adv.* Away from the right path: The guide led the group *astray.*
a·stride [ə·strīd′] 1 *adj., adv.* With one leg on each side: I prefer to ride *astride.* 2 *prep.* With one leg on each side of: She rode *astride* the horse.

Child astride a fence

as·trin·gen·cy [ə·strin′jən·sē] *n.* The quality of being astringent.
as·trin·gent [ə·strin′jənt] 1 *n.* A substance that shrinks body tissues. It tightens skin and checks bleeding. 2 *adj.* Able to shrink body tissue. **—as·trin′·gent·ly** *adv.*
astro- or **astr-** A combining form meaning: 1 Star, as in *astrophysics.* 2 Outer space, as in *astrogate.*
as·tro·dome [as′trə·dōm′] *n.* A transparent dome on the top of an aircraft through which the navigator measures the positions of the stars.
as·tro·gate [as′trə·gāt′] *v.* **as·tro·gat·ed, as·tro·gat·ing** To navigate a spacecraft in outer space. **—as′·tro·ga′tion** *n.* **—as′tro·ga′tor** *n.*
as·tro·labe [as′trə·lāb′] *n.* A medieval instrument for measuring the height of the sun, the stars, and the planets. It was used as an aid to navigation until the invention of the sextant in the 18th century.
as·trol·o·ger [ə·strol′ə·jər] *n.* A person who studies or practices astrology.
as·trol·o·gy [ə·strol′ə·jē] *n.* The study of the supposed influence of stars and planets on human lives. **—as·tro·log·i·cal** [as′trə·loj′i·kəl] *adj.* **—as′·tro·log′i·cal·ly** *v.*
astron. 1 astronomer. 2 astronomy.
as·tro·naut [as′trə·nôt′] *n.* A person who travels in space. ◆ *Astronaut* is parallel to *aeronaut,* a balloon pilot, and is formed from the Greek roots *nautes,* meaning *sailor,* and *astro-,* meaning *(between or among) stars.*
as·tro·nau·tics [as′trə·nô′tiks] *n.* The science and art of flight in space. ◆ See -ICS.
as·tron·o·mer [ə·stron′ə·mər] *n.* A person who is an expert in astronomy.
as·tro·nom·i·cal [as′trə·nom′i·kəl] *adj.* 1 Of or having to do with astronomy. 2 Almost too large to imagine, like the numbers in astronomy; enormous: *astronomical* costs. **—as′tro·nom′i·cal·ly** *adv.*
astronomical unit A unit of length equal to the average distance between the earth and the sun, approximately 93 million miles. It is used in measuring the vast distances between bodies in the solar system.
astronomical year Another term for TROPICAL YEAR.
as·tron·o·my [ə·stron′ə·mē] *n.* The study of the stars, planets, and other heavenly bodies, including information on their makeup, positions, and motions.
as·tro·phys·ics [as′trō·fiz′iks] *n.* The science dealing with the physical properties and chemical composition of celestial bodies. ◆ See -ICS.
As·tro·turf [as′trō·tûrf′] *n.* An artificial outdoor ground covering that looks like grass, used especially in certain sports: a trademark.
as·tute [ə·st(y)o͞ot′] *adj.* Having a keen mind; shrewd. **—as·tute′ly** *adv.* **—as·tute′ness** *n.*
a·sun·der [ə·sun′dər] *adv.* Into separate pieces.
a·sy·lum [ə·sī′ləm] *n.* 1 An institution for sheltering and taking care of orphans, the mentally ill, or other groups of unfortunate people. 2 A place of refuge or safety; shelter.
a·sym·met·ric [ā′si·met′rik] *adj.* Lacking symmetry or balance; not symmetric.
a·sym·met·ri·cal [ā′si·met′ri·kəl] *adj.* Asymmetric. **—a′sym·met′ri·cal·ly** *adv.*
a·sym·me·try [a′sim′ə·trē] *n.* Lack of symmetry or balance.
at [at] *prep.* 1 On; in; by: *at* sea; *at* home; *at* the door. 2 To or toward: Look *at* that sunset. 3 Engaged or occupied in: farmers *at* work. 4 In the condition or position of: countries *at* peace; *at* an angle. 5 In the manner of: He rode *at* a trot. 6 Because of: She was pleased *at* the thought of staying. 7 Amounting to; for: *at* two percent; *at* a dime apiece. 8 On the time or age of: *at* noon; The playwright was still active *at* 60. 9 According to: proceed *at* your own pace. ◆ Never use *at* after *where* (as in "Where is the library at?").
At The symbol for the element astatine.
at·a·vism [at′ə·viz′əm] *n.* The reappearance of a hereditary characteristic after several generations of absence.
at·a·vis·tic [at′ə·vis′tik] *adj.* Reappearing as a trait from one's ancestors after an absence of several generations: the *atavistic* urge to hunt and gather food.
a·tax·i·a [ə·tak′sē·ə] *n.* A lack of muscle coordination due to a disease of the nervous system. **—a·tax′ic** *n., adj.*
ATC all-terrain cycle: a motorcycle designed for travel off roadways and on rugged terrain.
ate [āt] Past tense of EAT.
-ate A suffix meaning: 1 To expose to or treat with, as in *oxygenate.* 2 Something acted upon or brought about, as in *precipitate.* 3 To become or cause to become, as in *differentiate.* 4 Having or characterized by, as in *chordate.*
at·el·ier [at′(ə)l·yā′] *n.* The studio or workshop of an artist.
a tem·po [ä tem′pō] In music, an instruction meaning "return to original tempo."
Ath·a·pas·kan or **Ath·a·pas·can** [ath′ə·pas′kən] 1 *n.* A family of North American Indian languages spoken in the western U.S. and northwest Canada. 2 *adj.* Of, having to do with, or belonging to this family of languages. 3 *n.* A member of an Athapaskan-speaking tribe.
a·the·ism [ā′thē·iz′əm] *n.* The belief that there is no God. **—a′the·ist** *n.* **—a′the·is′tic** *adj.*
A·the·na [ə·thē′nə] *n.* Athene.
A·the·ne [ə·thē·nē] *n.* In Greek myths, the goddess of wisdom and the arts.
A·the·ni·an [ə·thē′nē·ən] 1 *adj.* Of or from Athens. 2 *n.* A person born or living in Athens, or a citizen of Athens.
a·thirst [ə·thûrst′] *adj.* 1 Eager: *athirst* for power. 2 Thirsty: seldom used today.
ath·lete [ath′lēt′] *n.* A person with skill in sports or games that take strength, speed, or dexterity, as football, tennis, or running.
athlete's foot A contagious disease caused by a fungus attacking the skin of the feet.
ath·let·ic [ath·let′ik] *adj.* 1 Of, for, or having to do with athletics or an athlete. 2 Strong and vigorous; active. **—ath·let′i·cal·ly** *adv.*
ath·let·ics [ath·let′iks] *n.pl.* Sports and games that

take strength, speed, or dexterity, as basketball or wrestling. See -ICS.

athletic supporter Another name for JOCK STRAP.

a·thwart [ə·thwôrt′] **1** *adv.* From side to side; across. **2** *prep.* From side to side of; across: A ferry passed *athwart* our course. **3** *prep.* Contrary to; against: music *athwart* popular taste.

-ation A suffix meaning: **1** The act or process of, as in *creation.* **2** The condition or quality of, as in *affectation.* **3** The result of, as in *reformation.*

-ative A suffix meaning: **1** Having to do with, as in *quantitative.* **2** Tending to, as in *talkative.*

At·lan·tic [at·lan′tik] *adj.* Of, on, in, near, or having to do with the Atlantic Ocean.

Atlantic Charter A statement issued by Winston Churchill and Franklin D. Roosevelt in August, 1941, setting forth the basic aims for peace of the Allies after World War II.

Atlantic standard time (*sometimes written* **Atlantic Standard Time**) The standard time observed in eastern Quebec, the Canadian Maritime Provinces, Bermuda, Puerto Rico, and the Virgin Islands. It is four hours earlier than Greenwich time.

At·lan·tis [at·lan′tis] *n.* In Greek myths, an island that was engulfed by the sea.

at·las [at′ləs] *n.* A book of maps.

At·las [at′ləs] *n.* In Greek myths, a giant who supported the heavens on his shoulders.

at·mos·phere [at′məs·fir] *n.* **1** The air surrounding the earth. **2** The gases surrounding a heavenly body. **3** The air or climate in a place. **4** Surrounding influence; background: an *atmosphere* of friendliness. **5** A unit of pressure, the pressure of the atmosphere at sea level, approximately 14.7 pounds per inch. ◆ This word comes from Greek words meaning *vapor sphere.*

at·mos·pher·ic [at′məs·fir′ik] *adj.* Occurring in, caused by, or having to do with the atmosphere.

atmospheric pressure The pressure exerted by the weight of the atmosphere, approximately 14.7 pounds per square inch at sea level, decreasing as one goes higher.

at no or **at. no.** atomic number.

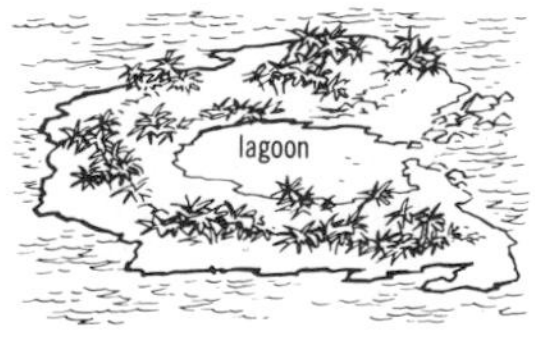

An atoll

at·oll [at′ôl] *n.* An island of coral shaped something like a doughnut and enclosing a lagoon.

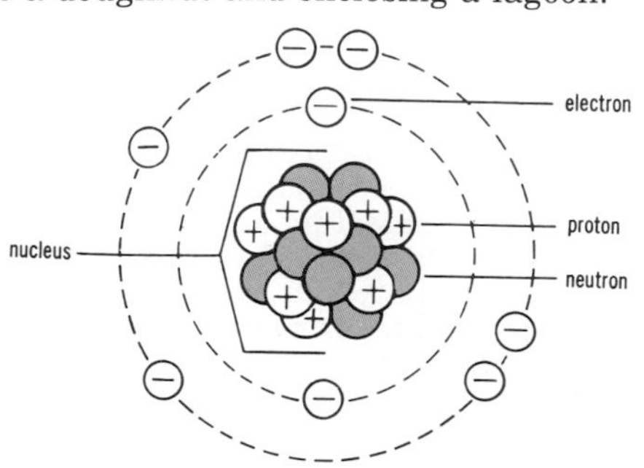

Diagram of one atom of oxygen. The nucleus contains 8 protons, shown as white circles with plus signs, and 8 neutrons, shown as brown circles. The 8 electrons are shown as white circles with minus signs.

at·om [at′əm] *n.* **1** The smallest unit of an element that is able to take part in chemical reactions. It is made up of smaller particles whose number and arrangement are different for each element. **2** A very small amount; least bit. *Atom* comes from a Greek word meaning *indivisible.*

atom bomb An atomic bomb.

a·tom·ic [ə·tom′ik] *adj.* **1** Of or having to do with an atom or atoms. **2** Very small; minute; tiny.

atomic age or **Atomic Age** The current period of history, characterized by the development and use of atomic energy.

atomic bomb A powerful bomb using the energy suddenly released when the nuclei of atoms of uranium or plutonium are split.

atomic clock A very exact timekeeping device that is governed by oscillations or radiation from atoms.

atomic energy The energy released by the splitting of heavy atoms or the fusion of light atoms.

atomic mass The mass of an atom, expressed in atomic mass units.

atomic mass unit A unit of mass equal to one-twelfth of the mass of the most frequently occurring carbon isotope, carbon 12.

atomic number The number of protons in the nucleus of an atom of each element.

atomic pile Another name for NUCLEAR REACTOR.

atomic power Atomic energy used as a source of power.

atomic reactor Another name for NUCLEAR REACTOR.

atomic theory **1** The theory that all matter is composed of atoms. **2** The body of knowledge about the structure, characteristics, and behavior of atoms and subatomic particles.

atomic weight The weight of an atom of any element in relation to that of some standard element. Formerly, the standard was oxygen, taken as 16; now it is carbon, taken as 12.

at·om·ize [at′əm·īz′] *v.* **at·om·ized, at·om·iz·ing** To reduce into tiny bits or into a spray.

at·om·iz·er [at′əm·ī′zər] *n.* A device that reduces liquid, as perfume, to a fine spray.

Atomizer

atom smasher An atomic particle accelerator.

a·ton·al [ā′tō′nəl] *adj.* Being in no apparent key or mode: *atonal* music. **—a′ton′al·ly** *adv.*

a·to·nal·i·ty [ā′tō·nal′i·tē] *n.* In music, the lack of a key or tonal center: The *atonality* of his most recent composition was unexpected.

a·tone [ə·tōn′] *v.* **a·toned, a·ton·ing** To make amends or make up: to *atone* for one's sins with prayer and good works; Willingness to help can often *atone* for lack of skill.

a·tone·ment [ə·tōn′mənt] *n.* **1** The act of atoning,

a	add	**i**	it	**o͝o**	took	**oi**	oil
ā	ace	**ī**	ice	**o͞o**	pool	**ou**	pout
â	care	**o**	odd	**u**	up	**ng**	ring
ä	palm	**ō**	open	**û**	burn	**th**	thin
e	end	**ô**	order	**yo͞o**	fuse	**t̶h̶**	this
ē	equal					**zh**	vision

ə = { a in *above* e in *sicken* i in *possible* / o in *melon* u in *circus* }

as for a sin or crime; amends made. 2 (*written* **Atonement**) The reconciliation between God and man through Christ's suffering and death.

a·ton·ic [ə·ton′ik *or* ā·ton′ik] *adj.* Not accented, as a word or syllable.

a·top [ə·top′] 1 *adj., adv.* On or at the top. 2 *prep.* On the top of: snow *atop* a mountain.

a·tri·um [ā′trē·əm] *n., pl.* **a·tri·a** [ā′trē·ə] 1 One of the upper chambers of the heart, through which blood from the veins passes to the lower chambers. See picture at HEART. 2 The entrance hall or central court of an ancient Roman house.

a·tro·cious [ə·trō′shəs] *adj.* 1 Terribly wicked, criminal, vile, or cruel; barbaric. 2 Horrifying or revolting. 3 *informal* Very bad: an *atrocious* book. **—a·tro′cious·ly** *adv.*

a·troc·i·ty [ə·tros′ə·tē] *n., pl.* **a·troc·i·ties** 1 The quality or condition of being atrocious. 2 An atrocious thing, act, or condition.

at·ro·phy [at′rə·fē] *v.* **at·ro·phied, at·ro·phy·ing,** *n.* 1 *v.* To waste away or wither: Lack of exercise can cause muscles to *atrophy.* 2 *n.* A wasting away of a part of the body. 3 Any wasting away; decline; degeneration.

at·ro·pine [at′rə·pēn′] *n.* A very poisonous, bitter chemical compound, used in minute quantities to dilate the pupils or relieve spasms.

att. 1 attached. 2 attention. 3 attorney.

at·tach [ə·tach′] *v.* 1 To make fast; fasten; connect: to *attach* a button to a coat. 2 To add on, as a signature. 3 To connect in one's mind; ascribe: to *attach* importance to an event. 4 To seize by legal means: to *attach* an employee's pay in collecting a debt. 5 To bind by feelings of love: Parents are *attached* to their children. 6 To assign: to be *attached* to the general's staff.

at·ta·ché [at′ə·shā′] *n.* A person who is officially attached to the staff of a diplomatic mission.

attaché case A briefcase that resembles a small, slim suitcase.

at·tach·ment [ə·tach′mənt] *n.* 1 The act of attaching. 2 An attached condition. 3 Something that attaches or joins; connection. 4 A part that fastens to or on something else, as on a machine. 5 Affection; fondness. 6 The legal seizure of a person or property.

at·tack [ə·tak′] 1 *v.* To set upon with violence; begin battle with: The cavalry *attacked* the fort. 2 *v.* To criticize harshly; condemn: to *attack* a policy. 3 *n.* The act of attacking; assault: an air *attack.* 4 *v.* To affect destructively: Acid *attacks* metal. 5 *v.* To begin work on; set about: to *attack* a problem. 6 *n.* A sudden onset of illness: an *attack* of fever.

at·tain [ə·tān′] *v.* 1 To gain or arrive at by hard work; achieve, as a desired end: to *attain* wealth. 2 To come to: to *attain* an old age.

at·tain·a·ble [ə·tā′nə·bəl] *adj.* Capable of being attained: Peace is an *attainable* goal.

at·tain·der [ə·tān′dər] *n.* The removal of all civil rights from a person who has been sentenced to death or declared an outlaw.

at·tain·ment [ə·tān′mənt] *n.* 1 The act of attaining. 2 Something attained, as a goal or a skill; achievement.

at·taint [ə·tānt′] *v.* To condemn and punish by a sentence of attainder.

at·tar [at′ər] *n.* A fragrant oil from the petals of flowers, especially roses, used in perfume.

at·tempt [ə·tempt′] 1 *v.* To make an effort; try: They *attempted* to lift the trunk. 2 *n.* A putting forth of effort; a try. 3 *n.* An attack; assault: an *attempt* on the bystander's life. 4 *v.* To attack. — **at·tempt′a·ble** *adj.*

at·tend [ə·tend′] *v.* 1 To be present at; go to: I *attended* the party. 2 To go with or be useful to as a servant or helper: The aide *attends* the officer. 3 To take care of: The nurse *attends* the sick and injured. 4 To follow or result from: Danger *attends* careless driving. **—attend to** 1 To give careful attention to. 2 To do or carry out: to *attend to* the sweeping. 3 To dispose of or see to, as a problem. **—at·tend′er** *n.*

at·ten·dance [ə·ten′dəns] *n.* 1 The act of attending. 2 The number of people attending: The *attendance* was over 500. **—dance attendance on** Be at someone's beck and call; wait on constantly. **—take attendance** Call the roll.

at·ten·dant [ə·ten′dənt] 1 *n.* A person who attends, especially a servant or caretaker. 2 *adj.* Serving or attending: an *attendant* desk clerk. 3 *adj.* Following or accompanying: the *attendant* risks of having so many cars on our highways.

at·ten·dee [ə·ten′dē′] *n.* A person who is present on a certain occasion or at a certain place: *attendees* at the wedding.

at·ten·tion [ə·ten′shən] *n.* 1 The act or power of directing the mind, as in noticing or concentrating on something: After listening for four hours, our *attention* began to falter. 2 Thought or care: to give *attention* to one's manners. 3 An act of courtesy or regard: the *attentions* of a thoughtful friend. 4 The military position of readiness: to stand at *attention.*

attention span The span of time during which a person is able to pay attention or concentrate.

at·ten·tive [ə·ten′tiv] *adj.* 1 Giving or showing attention: an *attentive* listener. 2 Courteous; thoughtful: an *attentive* escort. **—at·ten′tive·ly** *adv.* **—at·ten′tive·ness** *n.*

at·ten·u·ate [ə·ten′yōō·āt′] *v.* **at·ten·u·at·ed, at·ten·u·at·ing** 1 To make or become thin, small, or fine; draw out, as a wire. 2 To reduce in size or strength; weaken: to *attenuate* sound; The company's power was *attenuated* by the new court ruling. **—at·ten′u·a′tion** *n.*

at·test [ə·test′] *v.* 1 To state that something is true or genuine; vouch for: to *attest* to the quality of a new product. 2 To be proof of; confirm: The dog's coat *attests* the care it is given. 3 To bear witness; testify.

at·tic [at′ik] *n.* The uppermost story of a house, just under the roof; garret.

at·tire [ə·tīr′] *v.* **at·tired, at·tir·ing,** *n.* 1 *v.* To dress; clothe: *attired* in woolen garments. 2 *n.* Dress; apparel: rich *attire.*

at·ti·tude [at′ə·t(y)ōōd′] *n.* 1 A position of the body, often suggesting some action: an *attitude* of thought. 2 A way of feeling or regarding; a mental view: a stubborn *attitude;* a humble *attitude.* 3 The position of an aircraft or a spacecraft relative to some given line or plane, as the earth on the horizon.

attn. attention.

at·tor·ney [ə·tûr′nē] *n., pl.* **at·tor·neys** 1 A person who has power to act in behalf of another person. 2 A lawyer.

attorney at law A lawyer.

attorney general *pl.* **attorneys general** or **attorney generals** The chief law officer of a government.

at·tract [ə·trakt′] *v.* **1** To cause to come near without visible connection: Magnets *attract* iron. **2** To draw or invite: Parades *attract* crowds.
at·trac·tion [ə·trak′shən] *n.* **1** The act or power of attracting. **2** Something that attracts: The main *attraction* was a juggler's act.
at·trac·tive [ə·trak′tiv] *adj.* **1** Attracting interest; tempting; pleasing: an *attractive* offer; an *attractive* child. **2** Able to attract. **—at·trac′tive·ly** *adv.* **—at·trac′tive·ness** *n.*
at·trib·ut·a·ble [ə·trib′yo͞ot·ə·bəl] *adj.* Capable of being attributed: The team's victory was *attributable* to the skill of the players.
at·trib·ute [*v.* ə·trib′yo͞ot, *n.* at′rə·byo͞ot′] *v.* **at·trib·ut·ed, at·trib·ut·ing,** *n.* **1** *v.* To consider as belonging to or caused by: Many folk stories *attribute* slyness to foxes and wisdom to owls. **2** *n.* A quality or characteristic of a person or thing: Enthusiasm is an *attribute* of youth. **3** *n.* In art and mythology, a mark or symbol belonging to one character: The trident is considered to be an *attribute* of Neptune. **—at′tri·bu′tion** *n.*
at·trib·u·tive [ə·trib′yə·tiv] **1** *adj.* Modifying a noun and placed immediately before it: In "high school students" the phrase "high school" is *attributive.* **2** *n.* An attributive word or phrase: In "book store," the word "book" is an *attributive.*
at·tri·tion [ə·trish′ən] *n.* A gradual wearing down or wearing away; weakening: a disease of *attrition;* a war of *attrition.*
at·tune [ə·t(y)o͞on′] *v.* **at·tuned, at·tun·ing** **1** To bring into accord or harmony: They soon became *attuned* to city life. **2** To tune.
atty. attorney.
Atty. Gen. **1** attorney general. **2** Attorney General.
ATV all-terrain vehicle: a vehicle designed for travel off roadways and on rugged terrain.
a·twit·ter [ə·twit′ər] *adj.* Excited in a nervous or concerned way.
at wt or **at. wt.** atomic weight.
a·typ·i·cal [ā·tip′i·kəl] *adj.* Not typical; without typical character; irregular.
Au The symbol for the element gold. ◆ The Latin word for gold is *aurum.*
au·burn [ô′bûrn] *n., adj.* Reddish brown.
auc·tion [ôk′shən] **1** *n.* A public sale at which each item is sold to the person offering the highest price for it. **2** *v.* To sell by or at an auction.
auc·tion·eer [ôk′shən·ir′] *n.* A person who conducts auctions as a business.
aud. **1** audit. **2** auditor.
au·da·cious [ô·dā′shəs] *adj.* **1** Showing no fear; daring; bold. **2** Too daring or bold; impudent: an *audacious* child. **3** Inventive or original: an *audacious* new talent. **—au·da′cious·ly** *adv.*
au·dac·i·ty [ô·das′ə·tē] *n., pl.* **au·dac·i·ties** **1** Boldness; daring. **2** Impudence; indecency: He had the *audacity* to make excuses for being late. **3** An audacious act.
au·di·ble [ô′də·bəl] *adj.* Heard or capable of being heard. **—au′di·bly** *adv.*
au·di·ence [ô′dē·əns] *n.* **1** A group of listeners or watchers, as at a concert or play. **2** The people who are reached by a book, television program, or other mass medium. **3** A formal hearing; interview: The president granted the ambassador an *audience.* **4** An opportunity to be heard.
au·di·o [ô′dē·ō] **1** *adj.* Of or having to do with sound **2** *adj.* Of, having to do with, or used for the production, reproduction, or broadcasting of sound: Phonographs are *audio* equipment. **3** *n.* Sound. **4** *n.* The production, reproduction, or broadcasting of sound, especially as part of television. **5** *n.* Television and motion picture equipment that has to do with sound.
audio- A combining form meaning: **1** Hearing, as in *audiometer.* **2** Sound, as in *audiophile.*
audio frequency The range of wave frequencies from 20 cycles to 20,000 cycles per second. These are, respectively, the lowest-pitched and highest-pitched sound waves that can be heard by a person with normal hearing.
au·di·om·e·ter [ô′dē·om′ə·tər] *n.* An instrument to gauge and record the acuteness of hearing.
au·di·o·phile [ô′dē·ō·fīl′] *n.* A person who is very interested and knowledgeable about the reproduction of high-fidelity sound.
au·di·o·vis·u·al [ô′dē·ō·vizh′o͞o·əl] **1** *adj.* Of, using, or perceptible to both hearing and sight. **2** *adj.* Of or having to do with educational materials, such as sound movies or slide shows, that are designed to be seen and listened to. **3** *n.* (*pl.*) Such educational materials.
au·dit [ô′dit] **1** *v.* To examine for correctness, as the accounts of a business. **2** *n.* An examination of accounts, as of a business.
au·di·tion [ô·dish′ən] **1** *n.* A trial hearing to test the skill or suitability, as of an actor or singer, for a job or role. **2** *v.* To give an audition to.
au·di·tor [ô′də·tər] *n.* **1** A person who examines accounts, as of a business. **2** A listener.
au·di·to·ri·um [ô′də·tôr′ē·əm] *n.* A building or a large room in a building such as a school or a church, in which an audience can assemble.
au·di·to·ry [ô′də·tôr′ē] *adj.* Of or having to do with hearing.
auditory nerve The nerve that carries signals from the inner ear to the brain, where these impulses are interpreted as sound.
auf Wie·der·seh·en [ouf vē′dər·zā′ən] A German expression for "good-by for now" or "until we meet again."
Aug. August.
au·ger [ô′gər] *n.* A tool for boring holes in the earth or in wood.
aught[1] [ôt] **1** *n.* Anything at all: Have you *aught* to say? **2** *adv.* By any chance at all.
aught[2] [ôt] *n.* The figure zero; naught.
aug·ment [ôg·ment′] *v.* To make or become greater as in size or amount: increase: The chorus was *augmented* by adding more singers.
aug·men·ta·tion [ôg′men·tā′shən] *n.* **1** The act of augmenting. **2**

Auger

a add	**i** it	**o͝o** took	**oi** oil
ā ace	**ī** ice	**o͞o** pool	**ou** pout
â care	**o** odd	**u** up	**ng** ring
ä palm	**ō** open	**û** burn	**th** thin
e end	**ô** order	**yo͞o** fuse	**th** this
ē equal			**zh** vision

ə = { a in *above* e in *sicken* i in *possible* / o in *melon* u in *circus* }

A being augmented. 3 The amount by which something is increased.

au gra·tin [ō grä′tən] Sprinkled with bread crumbs or grated cheese and baked until brown.

au·gur [ô′gər] 1 *n.* In ancient Rome, an official who foretold the future by means of omens. 2 *n.* Anyone who foretells the future. 3 *v.* To foretell (the future). 4 *v.* To be a sign of; give promise of. **—augur ill** To be a bad omen. **—augur well** To be a good omen.

au·gu·ry [ô′gyə·rē] *n., pl.* **au·gu·ries** 1 The art or practice of predicting the future by omens. 2 An omen or a prediction made from an omen.

au·gust [ô·gust′] *adj.* 1 Inspiring such feelings as awe or admiration; majestic; imposing: an *august* spectacle. 2 Of high birth or rank; eminent: an *august* dignitary. **—au·gust′ly** *adv.* **—au·gust′·ness** *n.*

Au·gust [ô′gəst] *n.* The eighth month of the year, having 31 days.

au jus [ō zhōō′] A French phrase meaning "served in the natural juices": beef *au jus.*

auk [ôk] *n.* A diving bird having short wings and webbed feet, found in the northern seas.

Auk

au lait [ō lā′] A French phrase meaning "with milk."

auld lang syne [ōld′lang·zīn′] The good old days. This is a Scottish phrase that literally means "old long since."

aunt [ant] *n.* The sister or sister-in-law of one's father or mother.

au·ra [ôr′ə] *n.* A special air or quality that seems to surround or come from a particular source: There is an *aura* of kindness and humor about this poetry. ◆ *Aura* comes from the Greek word for *breath.*

au·ral [ôr′əl] *adj.* Of or having to do with the ear or the sense of hearing.

au·re·ole [ôr′ē·ōl] *n.* In art, a light shining around the head of a holy figure; halo.

Au·re·o·my·cin [ôr′ē·ō·mī′sin] *n.* The trade name of a strong antibiotic obtained from a soil bacillus, used against bacteria and viruses.

au re·voir [ō′ rə·vwär′] A French expression for "good-by" or "until we meet again."

au·ric [ôr′ik] *adj.* Of, having to do with, or containing gold, especially gold having a valence of three.

au·ri·cle [ôr′i·kəl] *n.* 1 An atrium of the heart. 2 The outside part of the ear.

au·ri·cu·lar [ô·rik′yə·lər] *adj.* 1 Aural. 2 Of or having to do with an auricle of the heart.

au·ro·ra [ô·rôr′ə] *n.,pl.* **au·ro·ras** or **au·ro·rae** [ô·rôr′ē] 1 A richly colored display of lights seen in the night sky, especially close to the North and South Poles, caused by electrical disturbances in the air. 2 The dawn. 3 Aurora australis. 4 Aurora borealis.

Au·ro·ra [ô·rôr′ə] *n.* In Roman myths, the goddess of the dawn.

aurora aus·tra·lis [ôs·trā′lis] The aurora seen near the South Pole.

aurora bo·re·al·is [bôr′ē·al′is] The aurora seen near the North Pole; northern lights.

Aus. 1 Australia. 2 Austria.

aus·pi·ces [ôs′pə·siz] *n.pl.* 1 Helpful or guiding influence; sponsorship: under the *auspices* of a church. 2 Omens; signs.

aus·pi·cious [ôs·pish′əs] *adj.* Showing the likelihood of success in the future; favorable: an *auspicious* beginning. **—aus·pi′cious·ly** *adv.* **—aus·pi′cious·ness** *n.*

Aus·sie [ô′sē] *n. informal* An Australian.

Aust. 1 Australia. 2 Austria.

aus·tere [ô·stir′] *adj.* 1 Stern, as in appearance or conduct; severe; strick. 2 Very plain and simple; without luxury or ornament: *austere* dress. **—aus·tere′ly** *adv.* **—aus·tere′ness** *n.*

aus·ter·i·ty [ôs·ter′ə·tē] *n., pl.* **aus·ter·i·ties** 1 The quality of being austere. 2 (*usually pl.*) Severe acts or practices of self-denial, as doing without food, water, sleep, or comfort.

Austl. 1 Australia. 2 Australian.

Aus·tral·a·sian [ôs′trə·lā′zhən] 1 *adj.* Of or from Australasia. 2 *n.* A person born or living in Australasia.

Aus·tral·ian [ôs·trāl′yən] 1 *adj.* Of or from Australia. 2 *n.* A person born in or a citizen of Australia. 3 *n.* An Australian aborigine. 4 *n.* One of the languages of the Australian aborigines.

Australian ballot A ballot listing all candidates of all parties, voted on in secret.

Aus·tri·an [ôs′trē·ən] 1 *adj.* Of or from Austria. 2 *n.* A person born in or a citizen of Austria.

aut- or **auto-** A combining form meaning: 1 Self; same, as in *autobiography.* 2 Automatic, as in *autopilot.*

au·tar·chy [ô′tär′kē] *n., pl.* **au·tar·chies** 1 Absolute rule; autocracy. 2 A country under such rule.

au·then·tic [ô·then′tik] *adj.* 1 Worthy of belief; trustworthy; reliable: an *authentic* record of events. 2 Genuine: an *authentic* Greek vase.

au·then·ti·cate [ô·then′ti·kāt′] *v.* **au·then·ti·cat·ed, au·then·ti·cat·ing** To prove to be true or show to be genuine. **—au·then′ti·ca′tion** *n.*

au·then·tic·i·ty [ô′thən·tis′ə·tē] *n.* The condition of being genuine or true; authentic nature.

au·thor [ô′thər] *n.* 1 A person who has written something, as a book, story, or article. 2 A person who creates or originates: the *author* of a theory. ◆ The use of *author* as a verb (as in "She authored a novel") is incorrect and unnecessary. Use *write* instead: She *wrote* a novel.

au·thor·i·tar·i·an [ə·thôr′ə·târ′ē·ən] 1 *adj.* Favoring rule by authority rather than individual freedom: an *authoritarian* society. 2 *n.* A person who is authoritarian. **—au·thor′i·tar′i·an·ism** *n.*

au·thor·i·ta·tive [ə·thôr′ə·tā′tiv] *adj.* 1 Having or coming from proper authority. 2 Showing authority; commanding: an *authoritative* way of speaking. 3 Reliable, as if from an authority; trustworthy: an *authoritative* book. **—au·thor′i·ta′·tive·ly** *adv.*

au·thor·i·ty [ə·thôr′ə·tē] *n., pl.* **au·thor·i·ties** 1 The right to command, act, or make decisions: the *authority* to make arrests. 2 (*usually pl.*) A person who governs and enforces laws: The offender was brought before the *authorities.* 3 Personal influence that creates respect or confidence: to speak with *authority.* 4 A person who has special knowledge; expert: an *authority* on old coins.

au·thor·i·za·tion [ô′thər·ə·zā′shən] *n.* 1 The act of authorizing. 2 Legal right granted by someone who has authority.

au·thor·ize [ô′thə·rīz′] *v.* **au·thor·ized, au·thor·izing** 1 To give authority or power to: The broker was *authorized* to sell the house. 2 To give permission for; approve: to *authorize* a loan.

Authorized Version A version of the Bible translated into English at the order of King James I and published in 1611.

au·thor·ship [ô′thər·ship′] *n.* 1 Origin or source, as of a book or an idea. 2 The profession or work of a writer.

au·tism [ô′tiz′əm] A form of childhood schizophrenia characterized by extreme withdrawal from people and almost no contact with reality. **—au·tis′tic** *adj.*

au·to [ô′tō] *n., pl.* **au·tos** *informal* An automobile.

auto- See AUT.

auto. 1 automatic. 2 automotive.

au·to·an·ti·bod·y [ô′tō·an′ti·bod′ē] *n., pl.* **au·to·an·ti·bod·ies** An antibody formed in reaction to a person's own body tissue.

au·to·bi·o·graph·i·cal [ô′tə·bī′ə·graf′i·kəl] *adj.* Of, having to do with, or in the manner of an autobiography: an *autobiographical* story.

au·to·bi·og·ra·phy [ô′tə·bī·og′rə·fē] *n., pl.* **au·to·bi·og·ra·phies** The story of a person's life written by that person.

au·to·clave [ô′tō·klāv′] *n., v.* **au·to·claved, au·to·clav·ing** 1 *n.* An airtight vessel for heating and sterilizing objects under very high steam pressure, used especially for medical or surgical use. 2 *v.* To heat or sterilize in such a vessel.

au·toc·ra·cy [ô·tok′rə·sē] *n., pl.* **au·toc·ra·cies** A government or country ruled by one person with absolute authority.

au·to·crat [ô′tə·krat′] *n.* 1 A ruler with absolute power. 2 A person who dictates to others in an arrogant manner.

au·to·crat·ic [ô′tə·krat′ik] *adj.* 1 Of or like an autocrat: His *autocratic* manner made him difficult to work with. 2 Having absolute power: an *autocratic* government.

au·to·di·dact [ô′tō·dī′dakt′] *n.* A person who is self-taught.

au·to·graph [ô′tə·graf′] 1 *n.* A person's name written in that person's own handwriting. 2 *v.* To write one's name on. 3 *n.* Something written in a person's own handwriting. ◆ *Autograph* comes from a Greek word meaning *self-written.*

au·to·harp [ô′tō·härp′] *n.* A musical instrument resembling a zither, but having an arrangement of mutes enabling the player to produce the correct chords easily.

au·to·im·mune [ô′tō·i·myo͞on′] *adj.* Of or caused by autoantibodies: *autoimmune* disease.

au·to·im·mun·i·ty [ô′tō·i·myo͞on′i·tē] *n.* A condition in which antibodies are formed in reaction to a person's own body tissues.

au·to·mak·er [ô′tō·mā′kər] *n.* A manufacturer of automobiles.

au·to·mat [ô′tə·mat′] *n.* A cafeteria in which servings of certain foods are obtained from small, glass-walled compartments that open when coins are inserted in a slot.

Automat

au·to·mate [ô′tə·māt′] *v.* **au·to·mat·ed, au·to·mat·ing** To convert or adapt to automatic operation, as a factory or process: Computers have fully *automated* the processing of checks. ◆ See AUTOMATION.

au·to·mat·ic [ô′tə·mat′ik] 1 *adj.* Acting and regulated by itself, as machinery. 2 *adj.* Done without conscious thought or attention: Most of the movements in driving a car are *automatic.* 3 *n.* A pistol that fires, throws out the used cartridge, and puts in a new one when the trigger is pulled. **—au′to·mat′i·cal·ly** *adv.*

automatic pilot A device, as on an aircraft, that automatically maintains a predetermined course and altitude.

au·to·ma·tion [ô′tə·mā′shən] *n.* The automatic operation, as of a process or machine, under the control of electronic or mechanical devices instead of human beings. ◆ This word comes from *autom(atic oper)ation.* The verb *automate* was formed from *automation.*

au·tom·a·ti·za·tion [ô·tom′ə·ti·zā′shən] *n.* Automation.

au·tom·a·tize [ô·tom′ə·tīz′] *v.* **au·tom·a·tized, au·tom·a·tiz·ing** To make automatic.

au·tom·a·ton [ô·tom′ə·ton′] *n.* 1 A machine that operates by itself. 2 A person or animal whose actions seem too mechanical to be lifelike.

au·to·mo·bile [ô′tə·mə·bēl′] *n.* A four-wheeled vehicle propelled by its own engine, commonly designed to carry up to about six people. ◆ This word was formed in French from a Greek word meaning *self* and a Latin word meaning *moving.*

au·to·mo·tive [ô′tə·mō′tiv] *adj.* 1 Of or for vehicles such as automobiles or trucks. 2 Moving under its own power.

au·to·nom·ic [ô′tə·nom′ik] *adj.* 1 Acting or occurring independent of conscious will; automatic. 2 Of, having to do with, or under the control of the autonomic nervous system. **—au′to·nom′i·cal′ly** *adv.*

autonomic nervous system The part of the nervous system that regulates the involuntary action of the heart, the digestive system, and other functions of the body.

au·ton·o·mous [ô·ton′ə·məs] *adj.* Independent; self-governing: The Confederate States wanted to become an *autonomous* nation. **—au·ton′o·mous·ly** *adv.*

au·ton·o·my [ô·ton′ə·mē] *n., pl.* **au·ton·o·mies** 1 An autonomous condition; self-government: to seek *autonomy.* 2 An autonomous state. **—au·ton′o·mist** *n.*

au·to·pi·lot [ô′tō·pī′lət] *n.* An automatic pilot.

au·top·sy [ô′top·sē] *n., pl.* **au·top·sies** The examination of a human body after death, especially to find the cause of death.

au·tumn [ô′təm] *n.* 1 The season of the year between summer and winter. 2 *adj. use: autumn* leaves.

au·tum·nal [ô·tum′nəl] *adj.* Of, having to do with, or characteristic of autumn: brisk *autumnal* weather.

a	add	**i**	it	**o͝o**	took	**oi**	oil
ā	ace	**ī**	ice	**o͞o**	pool	**ou**	pout
â	care	**o**	odd	**u**	up	**ng**	ring
ä	palm	**ō**	open	**û**	burn	**th**	thin
e	end	**ô**	order	**yo͞o**	fuse	**th**	this
ē	equal					**zh**	vision

ə = {a in *above* e in *sicken* i in *possible*; o in *melon* u in *circus*}

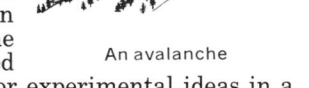

autumnal equinox The equinox that takes place around September 23. It marks the beginning of fall in the Northern Hemisphere and the beginning of spring in the Southern Hemisphere.
aux·il·ia·ry [ôg·zil′yər·ē] *adj., n., pl.* **aux·il·ia·ries** 1 *adj.* Giving help. 2 *adj.* Available if needed; extra: An *auxiliary* engine may be used if the power fails. 3 *adj.* Less important; not major. 4 *n.* Something auxiliary, as a subsidiary group attached to a larger organization.
auxiliary verb Another name for HELPING VERB.
av. 1 avenue. 2 average. 3 avoirdupois.
AV or **A.V.** 1 audiovisual. 2 Authorized Version (of the Bible).
a·vail [ə·vāl′] 1 *v.* To be of use to; help or profit: All our cunning *availed* us nothing. 2 *n.* Usefulness; help; benefit: Their efforts were of no *avail.* **—avail oneself of** To take advantage of; use: to *avail oneself of* an opportunity.
a·vail·a·bil·i·ty [ə·vā′lə·bil′ə·tē] *n., pl.* **a·vail·a·bil·i·ties** 1 The quality or condition of being available. 2 A person or thing that is available.
a·vail·a·ble [ə·vā′lə·bəl] *adj.* That can be used or had: *available* theater seats.
av·a·lanche [av′ə·lanch′] *n.* 1 The falling of a large mass of snow, ice, or rock down a slope. 2 The mass of snow, ice, or rock that so falls. 3 Something that suggests an avalanche: an *avalanche* of work.

An avalanche

a·vant-garde [ä′vänt·gärd′] 1 *n.* The people who are trying out new or experimental ideas in a field, especially in the arts. 2 *adj.* Of, based on, or advancing new or experimental ideas in a field: *avant-garde* music.
av·a·rice [av′ə·ris] *n.* Too much eagerness for riches; greed. ◆ This word comes from the French.
av·a·ri·cious [av′ə·rish′əs] *adj.* Desiring wealth too much; greedy; grasping; miserly. **—av′a·ri′cious·ly** *adv.* **—av′a·ri′cious·ness** *n.*
a·vast [ə·vast′] *interj.* Stop!; hold!; used by sailors.
a·vaunt [ə·vônt′] *interj.* Go away!: seldom used today.
ave. or **Ave.** avenue.
A·ve Ma·ri·a [ä′vā mə·rē′ə] A Roman Catholic prayer to the Virgin Mary. ◆ The first words of this Latin prayer are *Ave Maria,* which mean *Hail, Mary.*
a·venge [ə·venj′] *v.* **a·venged, a·veng·ing** To get revenge for: They *avenged* the insult.
av·e·nue [av′ə·n(y)o͞o′] *n.* 1 A street, especially a broad one. 2 A road or path with trees along its borders. 3 A way of reaching or achieving something: an *avenue* of escape.
a·ver [ə·vûr′] *v.* **a·verred, a·ver·ring** To declare to be true; state positively.
av·er·age [av′rij] *adj., n., v.* **av·er·aged, av·er·ag·ing** 1 *adj.* Of or like the ordinary or usual type; medium: an *average* day; an *average* football team. 2 *n.* Someone or something that is average. 3 *n.* The sum of the elements in a set of numbers divided by the number of elements in the set: The *average* of 4, 6, and 5 is 5. 4 *n.* A point between two extremes that shows a standing of accomplishment: a B *average.* 5 *v.* To calculate an average. 6 *v.* To amount to or get an average of: He *averages* three dollars an hour. **—on the average** As an average.
a·ver·ment [ə·vûr′mənt] *n.* 1 The act of averring. 2 Something that is averred; an affirmation or positive statement.
a·verse [ə·vûrs′] *adj.* Opposed by nature; not disposed: I was *averse* to staying up late.
a·ver·sion [ə·vûr′zhən] *n.* 1 Extreme dislike: an *aversion* to homework. 2 Something disliked.
a·vert [ə·vûrt′] *v.* 1 To turn or direct away: to *avert* the eyes. 2 To prevent or ward off, as a danger: A fight was narrowly *averted.*
a·vi·an [ā′vē·ən] *adj.* Of, having to do with, or characteristic of birds.
a·vi·ar·y [ā′vē·er′ē] *n., pl.* **a·vi·ar·ies** A large cage or other enclosure for birds.
a·vi·ate [ā′vē·āt′ *or* av′ē·āt′] *v.* **a·vi·at·ed, a·vi·a·ting** To fly through the air in an aircraft.
a·vi·a·tion [ā′vē·ā′shən] *n.* The science or techniques of building and flying aircraft.
a·vi·a·tor [ā′vē·ā′tər] *n.* A person who flies airplanes or other aircraft; pilot.
a·vi·a·trix [ā′vē·ā′triks] *n.* A woman who flies airplanes or other aircraft; pilot.
a·vi·cul·ture [ā′və·kul′chər *or* a′və·kul′chər] *n.* The raising and care of birds. **—a·vi·cul′tur·ist** *n.*
av·id [av′id] *adj.* 1 Enthusiastic; eager: an *avid* stamp collector. 2 Greedy: *avid* for food. **—av′id·ly** *adv.*
a·vid·i·ty [ə·vid′ə·tē] *n.* Extreme eagerness; greediness.
av·i·ga·tion [av′ə·gā′shən] *n.* The navigation of aircraft. **—av′i·ga′tor** *n.*
av·o·ca·do [av′ə·kä′dō] *n., pl.* **av·o·ca·dos** The pear-shaped fruit of a West Indian tree, having a green skin and fleshy, edible pulp enclosing a single, large seed.
av·o·ca·tion [av′ə·kā′shən] *n.* An occupation that is not one's regular work; hobby: My teacher's *avocation* is mountain climbing.
a·void [ə·void′] *v.* To keep away from; stay at a distance from; shun: Ever since the argument we have *avoided* each other. **—a·void′ance** *n.*
av·oir·du·pois weight [av′ər·də·poiz′] The ordinary system of weights in the U.S. and Great Britain in which 16 ounces make a pound.
a·vow [ə·vou′] *v.* To say openly as a fact; own up to; acknowledge: to *avow* one's guilt.
a·vow·al [ə·vou′əl] *n.* An open declaration; frank admission or acknowledgment.
a·vowed [ə·voud′] *adj.* Openly acknowledged or admitted; plainly declared: an *avowed* communist. **—a·vow·ed·ly** [ə·vou′id·lē] *adv.*
a·vun·cu·lar [ə·vung′kyə·lər] *adj.* 1 Of or having to do with an uncle. 2 Like an uncle, as in kindliness and generosity.
a·wait [ə·wāt′] *v.* 1 To wait for; expect: to *await* the mail eagerly. 2 To be waiting or in store for: Final exams *await* you in June.
a·wake [ə·wāk′] *adj., v.* **a·woke** or **a·waked, a·wak·ing** 1 *adj.* Not asleep; alert. 2 *v.* To stop sleeping; wake up. 3 *v.* To stir up; excite: to *awake* an interest in history. ◆ See WAKE.
a·wak·en [ə·wā′kən] *v.* To awake.
a·wak·en·ing [ə·wā′kən·ing] 1 *n.* The act of waking. 2 *n.* A stirring up of interest or attention. 3 *adj.* Coming into being: to feel an *awakening* love of music when one first hears the classics.

a·ward [ə·wôrd′] 1 *n.* Something given for merit; prize. 2 *v.* To give after judging, as in a contest: 3 *v.* To judge to be due, as by legal decision. 4 *n.* A legal decision that something is owed.

a·ware [ə·wâr′] *adj.* Realizing or knowing fully; conscious: I am *aware* of the difficulty. **—a·ware′·ness** *n.*

a·wash [ə·wäsh′ *or* ə·wôsh′] *adj.* 1 Covered or overflowing with water. 2 Characterized by an abundance: a store *awash* with holiday shoppers.

a·way [ə·wā′] 1 *adv.* To a different place; off; forth: to drive *away.* 2 *adj.* In a different place; absent: to be *away.* 3 *adv.* To one side; aside: Put your books *away.* 4 *adv.* At or to a distance; far: The road stretches *away.* 5 *adj.* At a distance: many miles *away.* 6 *adv.* Out of existence; at or to an end: to waste *away.* 7 *adv.* On and on; continuously: to work *away* at a task. 8 *adv.* Without hesitating or holding back: to swing *away.* 9 *adv.* Out of one's keeping: They took his hat *away.* 10 *adv.* Off from the whole: to cut the extra fabric *away.* **—do away with** 1 To kill. 2 To put an end to: The store will *do away with* its delivery service.

awe [ô] *n., v.* **awed, aw·ing** 1 *n.* A feeling of fear and wonder, as at the size, power, or majesty of something. 2 *v.* To fill or inspire with awe: We were *awed* by the violence of the thunderstorm.

awe·some [ô′səm] *adj.* 1 Causng awe: an *awesome* sight. 2 Full of awe: an *awesome* look. ◆ The use of *awesome* to mean "outstanding" or "impressive" is a weakened sense of the word and should be avoided.

awe·strick·en [ô′strik′ən] *adj.* Awestruck.

awe·struck [ô′struck′] *adj.* Filled with awe.

aw·ful [ô′fəl] *adj.* 1 *informal* Very bad or unpleasant: an *awful* mess. 2 Causing awe; very striking: the *awful* destruction of a tornado.

aw·ful·ly *adv.* 1 [ô′fəl·ē] In an awful way. 2 [ô′flē] *informal* Very: *awfully* rich.

a·while [ə (h)wil′] *adv.* For a short time. ◆ *Awhile,* an adverb, cannot be the object of a preposition. Compare: I rested *awhile;* I rested *for a while.*

awk·ward [ôk′wərd] *adj.* 1 Not graceful; clumsy; ungainly: an *awkward* movement. 2 Embarrassing: an *awkward* question. 3 Inconvenient or hard to use: an *awkward* place to reach. 4 Uncomfortable: an *awkward* position. **—awk′ward·ly** *adv.* **—awk′ward·ness** *n.*

awl [ôl] *n.* A pointed tool for making small holes, as in wood or leather.

awn·ing [ô′ning] *n.* A cover often made of canvas on a frame used for protection from sun or rain over a window or door.

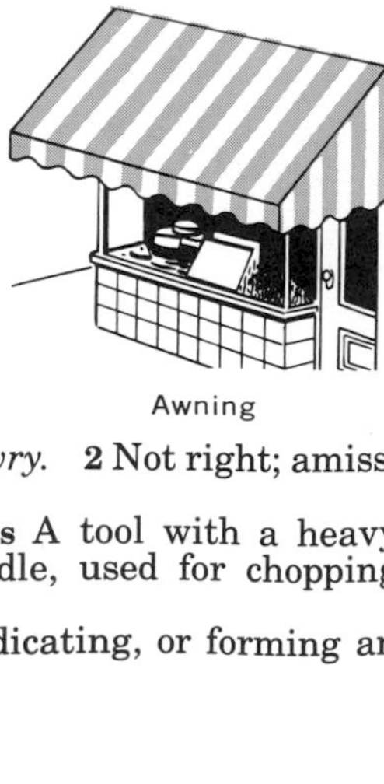
Awning

a·woke [ə·wōk] Past tense of AWAKE.

awol or **AWOL** [ā′wôl] 1 *adj.* Absent without leave. 2 *n.* A person who is absent without leave.

a·wry [ə·rī′] *adj., adv.* 1 Leaning or turned to one side; askew: Your cap is *awry.* 2 Not right; amiss: plans gone *awry.*

ax or **axe** [aks] *n., pl.* **ax·es** A tool with a heavy blade mounted on a handle, used for chopping wood, etc.

ax·i·al [ak′sē·əl] *adj.* Of, indicating, or forming an axis.

ax·i·om [ak′sē·əm] *n.* A self-evident statement whose truth is assumed without proof: "Things equal to the same thing are equal to each other" is an *axiom.*

ax·i·o·mat·ic [ak′sē·ə·mat′ik] *adj.* 1 Like an axiom; self-evident. 2 Full of or using axioms.

ax·is [ak′sis] *n., pl.* **ax·es** [ak′sēz] 1 The line around which a body turns or is imagined to turn. The earth's axis is a line connecting the North and South Poles. 2 A line around which an object is balanced or evenly divided. 3 A line on a graph along which distances are measured and in terms of which points are located. 4 (*written* **Axis**) The alliance of Germany, Italy, Japan, and other nations in World War II.

Earth's axis

ax·le [ak′səl] *n.* A bar or spindle on or with which a wheel or wheels turn.

ax·le·tree [ak′səl·trē′] *n.* A fixed bar on which the opposite wheels of a car or wagon are mounted.

ax·on [ak′son] *n.* The long, slender part of a nerve cell that carries impulses away from the central body of the cell.

Axle

ay[1] [ā] *adv.* Ever; always: used mostly in poems.

ay[2] [ī] *n., adv.* Another spelling of AYE[1].

a·ya·tol·lah [ī′ə·tō′lə *or* ī′ə·tol′ə] A religious leader in one of the sects of Islam.

aye[1] [ī] 1 *n.* A vote of yes or a person who votes yes: The *ayes* win. 2 *adv.* Yes.

aye[2] [ā] *adv.* Another spelling of AY[1].

Ay·ma·ra [ī′mə·rä′] *n., pl.* **Ay·ma·ra** or **Ay·ma·ras** 1 An Indian people of Bolivia and Peru. 2 A member of this people. 3 The language of this people.

Ayr·shire [âr′shir *or* âr′shər] 1 *n.* One of a hardy breed of dairy cattle, brown and white or red and white. 2 *adj.* Of or having to do with this breed.

AZ Postal Service abbreviation of Arizona.

a·zal·ea [ə·zāl′yə] *n.* A shrub having pointed leaves and showy scarlet or orange flowers.

Az·tec [az′tek] 1 *n.* One of a nation of Mexican Indians, noted for their advanced civilization. The Aztecs were conquered by the Spanish under Cortés in 1519. 2 *n.* The language of the Aztecs. 3 *adj.* Of or having to do with the Aztecs, their language, culture, or empire.

az·ure [azh′ər] *n., adj.* Sky blue.

a	add	**i**	it	**o͝o**	took	**oi**	oil
ā	ace	**ī**	ice	**o͞o**	pool	**ou**	pout
â	care	**o**	odd	**u**	up	**ng**	ring
ä	palm	**ō**	open	**û**	burn	**th**	thin
e	end	**ô**	order	**yo͞o**	fuse	**t͟h**	this
ē	equal					**zh**	vision

ə = { a in *above* e in *sicken* i in *possible* / o in *melon* u in *circus* }

Bb

B is the second letter of the alphabet. It has held that position since the very earliest times. The sign for *B* originated among Semitic people in the Near East, in the region of Palestine and Syria, probably in the middle of the second millennium B.C. Little is known about the sign until around 1000 B.C., when the Phoenicians began using it. The Phoenicians named the sign *beth* and used it for the sound of the consonant *b*.

When the Greeks adopted the Phoenician sign around the ninth century B.C., they called it *beta* and changed its shape by adding a second loop. Later they reversed the direction of the sign. The name of the letter became the second half of the word *alphabet*.

As early as the eighth century B.C., the Etruscans adopted the Greek alphabet. Although the Etruscans later dropped the *B* sign because they had no *b* sound, it was from them that the Romans took the letter. Around the time of the Caesars, the Romans made the shape of the letter more graceful. The model of the letter found on the base of Trajan's column, erected in Rome in 114, is considered a masterpiece of letter design. A Trajan-style *majuscule,* or capital letter, *B* opens this essay.

The *minuscule,* or small letter, *b* developed between the third and ninth centuries in the handwriting that scribes used for copying books. *B* was still shaped with two loops in the Roman *uncials* of the fourth to the eighth centuries. It first appeared as a single loop on the base line with a stem ascending above the loop in the *half uncial* script of the fifth to the ninth centuries. It became even more like our present-day lowercase letter in the script that evolved under the encouragement of Charlemagne (742-814). This *b* was one of the letters known as the *Caroline minuscules,* which became the principal handwriting system used on the medieval manuscripts of the ninth and tenth centuries.

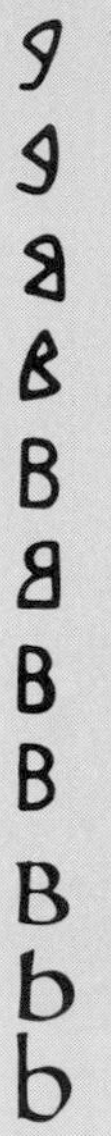

Early Phoenician (late 2nd millennium B.C.)
Phoenician (8th century B.C.)
Early Greek (9th-7th centuries B.C.)
Western Greek (6th century B.C.)
Classical Greek (403 B.C. onward)
Early Etruscan (8th century B.C.)
Monumental Latin (4th century B.C.)
Classical Latin
Uncial
Half uncial
Caroline minuscule

b or **B** [bē] *n., pl.* **b's** or **B's** 1 The second letter of the English alphabet. 2 In music, the seventh note of the scale of C major.

b or **b.** 1 base. 2 base hit. 3 baseman. 4 bass (music). 5 book. 6 born.

B The symbol for the element boron.

B. 1 bacillus. 2 bay. 3 Bible. 4 British.

Ba The symbol for the element barium.

B.A. Bachelor of Arts.

baa [bä] *n., v.* **baaed, baa·ing** 1 *n.* The natural cry of a sheep or goat. 2 *v.* To make this cry; bleat.

Ba·al [bā′(ə)l] *n., pl.* **Ba·al·im** [bā′(ə)l·im] 1 The sun god of the Phoenicians. 2 A false idol or god.

Bab·bitt metal [bab′ət] Any of a number of soft alloys of tin, copper, and antimony, used to reduce friction in bearings.

bab·ble [bab′əl] *v.* **bab·bled, bab·bling,** *n.* 1 *v.* To make meaningless speech sounds: The baby *babbled* happily. 2 *n.* Meaningless speech sounds. 3 *v.* To talk or say very fast or without thinking: to *babble* to a friend; to *babble* a secret. 4 *n.* Foolish or fast talk. 5 *v.* To make a murmuring or rippling sound, as a brook. 6 *n.* A rippling or bubbling sound; murmur. **—bab′bler** *n.*

babe [bāb] *n.* An infant; baby.

Ba·bel [bā′bəl *or* bab′əl] *n.* 1 In the Bible, a city where people tried to reach heaven by building the **Tower of Babel.** God stopped their work by suddenly causing them to speak different languages so they could not understand one another. 2 (*often written* **babel**) Noise and confusion, as when many people talk at once.

ba·boon [ba·bo͞on′] *n.* A large, fierce monkey of Africa and Asia, with a doglike head and a short tail.

Baboon

ba·bush·ka [bə·bo͞osh′kə] *n.* A woman's scarf, usually folded into a triangle, worn on the head and tied under the chin. ◆ *Babushka* comes from the Russian word for *grandmother.*

ba·by [bā′bē] *n., pl.* **ba·bies,** *v.* **ba·bied, ba·by·ing,** *adj.* 1 *n.* A very young child; infant. 2 *adj. use:* *baby* shoes; *baby* talk. 3 *v.* To treat like a baby; be gentle with; pamper. 4 *n.* A person who acts like a baby. 5 *adj.* Very small or young: a *baby* monkey. 6 *n.* The youngest or smallest member, as of a family.

ba·by·hood [bā′bē·ho͝od′] *n.* 1 The condition of being a baby. 2 The time when one is a baby.

ba·by·ish [bā′bē·ish] *adj.* Like a baby; childish.

Bab·y·lo·ni·an [bab′ə·lō′nē·ən] 1 *adj.* Of or from Babylon or Babylonia. 2 *n.* A person who was born or lived in Babylonia. 3 *n.* The language of Babylonia.

baby's breath A plant with clusters of delicate, small white or pink flowers.

ba·by-sit [bā′bē·sit′] *v.* **ba·by-sat, ba·by-sit·ting** To take care of a child while its parents are away for a short time.

baby sit·ter [sit′ər] *n.* A person who baby-sits.

bac·ca·lau·re·ate [bak′ə·lôr′ē·it] *n.* 1 A bachelor's degree granted by a college or university. 2 A speech given to a graduating class at commencement.

Bac·chus [bak′əs] *n.* In Greek and Roman myths, the god of wine. His early Greek name was Dionysus.

bach·e·lor [bach′(ə·)lər] *n.* 1 A man who has not married. 2 A person who has received a first college or university degree, such as a **Bachelor of Arts** or a **Bachelor of Science.**

bach·e·lor's-but·ton [bach′(ə·)lərz·but′(ə)n] *n.* Any of several plants having flowers shaped somewhat like buttons, as the cornflower.

ba·cil·lus [bə·sil′əs] *n., pl.* **ba·cil·li** [bə·sil′ī] Any of a class of bacteria shaped like rods. Some cause serious diseases, such as tetanus and tuberculosis. ◆ *Bacillus* comes from a Latin word meaning *a little rod* or *staff,* the shape of the organism.

back [bak] 1 *n.* The section of the body that extends from the neck to the end of the spine and is opposite to the chest and abdomen. 2 *n.* The spine; backbone. 3 *n.* The section of a seat or chair that supports a person's back. 4 *v.* To support; aid: to *back* a plan. 5 *v.* To provide with a back, as a mirror. 6 *n.* The rear part: the *back* of the car. 7 *adj.* In the rear: a *back* room. 8 *adv.* At, to, or toward the rear: Slide *back* in your seat. 9 *v.* To move or cause to move backward: to *back* away from the fire; *Back* the car into the garage. 10 *n.* The reverse side; other side: the *back* of the door. 11 *adj.* In a backward direction: a *back* flip. 12 *n.* In football, a player whose position is behind the line. 13 *adv.* In, to, or toward a former place, time, or condition: Put it *back* on the shelf; to look *back* in history. 14 *adj.* Of or for a time earlier than the present: a *back* issue of a magazine. 15 *adv.* In return: Give me *back* my pencil. 16 *adv.* In reserve or concealment: to keep something *back.* **—back and forth** First in one direction and then in the opposite direction. **—back down** To abandon or retreat, as from an opinion. **—back out** To withdraw from: to *back out* of a contract.

back·ache [bak′āk′] *n.* A pain in the back, especially one along or near the spine.

back·bite [bak′bīt′] *v.* **back·bit** [bak′bit′], **back·bit·ten** [bak′bit·(ə)n], **back·bit·ing** To tell lies or say mean things about (a person who is not present).

back·board [bak′bôrd′] *n.* In basketball, an elevated, upright board to which the basket is attached.

back·bone [bak′bōn′] *n.* 1 The column of interlocking bones running down the middle of the back in human beings and many other animals; spine. 2 The main or strongest part: She was the *backbone* of the team. 3 Strength of character; courage.

back·break·ing [bak′brā′king] *n.* Requiring very hard physical work; exhausting.

back·drop [bak′drop′] *n.* A curtain, usually having a scene painted on it, that is hung at the back of a stage.

back·er [bak′ər] *n.* A person who supports another person's plan or idea, usually by giving or investing money.

back·field [bak′fēld′] *n.* In football, the players whose regular positions are behind the line of scrimmage.

back·fire [bak′fīr′] *n., v.* **back·fired, back·fir·ing** 1 *n.* An explosion of fuel that occurs too early or in the wrong place in an engine, making a loud bang. 2 *v.* To have such an explosion: The engine *backfired.* 3 *v.* To have an effect opposite to the expected or desired effect: The plot *backfired.* 4 *n.* A fire set to halt an advancing fire by clearing the area in front of it.

back·gam·mon [bak′gam′ən] *n.* A game played by two persons on a special board. Each player has 15 disks or counters, and a throw of the dice determines how they may be moved.

back·ground [bak′ground′] *n.* 1 An area or surface against which something is seen or represented: red polka dots on a dull, gray *background.* 2 The part of a picture or landscape that appears distant. 3 A position that does not attract notice: He stayed in the *background* at the party. 4 A person's education and experience: Her *background* is well suited for newspaper work. 5 The events leading up to or causing a situation: the *background* of the Revolutionary War.

back·hand [bak′hand′] 1 *n.* A stroke, as in tennis, made with the back of the hand turned forward. 2 *adj. use:* a *backhand* stroke. 3 *adv.* With a backhand stroke. 4 *n.* Handwriting that slopes to the left.

A backhand stroke

back·hand·ed [bak′han′·did] *adj.* 1 Done or made with the back of the hand moving forward, as a tennis stroke or a slap. 2 Ambiguous, insincere, or sarcastic: "You didn't do such a terribly bad job for a beginner" is a *backhanded* compliment.

back·ing [bak′ing] *n.* 1 Help or support: The plan has the *backing* of the government. 2 Anything added at the back for strength or support: The rug has a *backing* of rubber.

back·lash [bak′lash′] *n.* 1 A sudden, forceful backward movement. 2 A strong hostile reaction, especially to a social or political development.

back·log [bak′lôg′ *or* bak′log] *n.* 1 An accumulation, as of business orders or unfinished work. 2 A large log at the back of a fireplace.

back·pack [bak′pak′] 1 *n.* A large pack for carrying camping supplies on the back, usually supported by a metal frame. 2 *v.* To hike while carrying camping supplies in a backpack.

back·pe·dal [bak′ped′(ə)l] *v.* 1 To move backward rapidly. 2 To retreat or withdraw, as from a position or argument.

back·rest [bak′rest′] *n.* A rest for the back.

back·seat driver [bak′sēt′] A person who gives unasked for advice and criticism, as to the driver of a car.

back·side [bak′sīd′] *n.* 1 The rear or back part. 2 The buttocks.

a	add	**i**	it	**o͝o**	took	**oi**	oil
ā	ace	**ī**	ice	**o͞o**	pool	**ou**	pout
â	care	**o**	odd	**u**	up	**ng**	ring
ä	palm	**ō**	open	**û**	burn	**th**	thin
e	end	**ô**	order	**yo͞o**	fuse	**t͟h**	this
ē	equal					**zh**	vision

ə = {a in *above*, e in *sicken*, i in *possible*, o in *melon*, u in *circus*}

back·slide [bak′slīd′] *v.* **back·slid** [bak′slid′], **back·slid** or **back·slid·den** [bak′slid′(ə)n], **back·slid·ing** To slip from good behavior to bad or into indifference to religion. **—back′slid′er** *n.*

back·spin [bak′spin′] *n.* A spin that tends to slow down or reverse the direction of a ball once it bounces.

back·stage [bak′stāj′] **1** *adv.* In or toward the part of a theater behind and to the sides of the stage. **2** *adj.* Situated or happening backstage.

back·stitch [bak′stich′] *n.* An overlapping stitch made by starting each new stitch in the middle of the preceding one.

back·stop [bak′stop′] *n.* In baseball and softball, a fence or net behind home plate.

back·stroke [bak′strōk′] *n.* **1** In swimming, a stroke made while on one's back. **2** A backhanded stroke.

Backstroke

back talk *informal* Rude or disrespectful answers.

back·track [bak′trak′] *v.* **1** To turn around and go back along the route by which one has come. **2** To reverse an opinion or policy.

back·up [bak′up′] *n.* **1** A substitute ready in case of need. **2** A reserve supply.

back·ward [bak′wərd] **1** *adv.* Toward the back; to the rear: Go *backward.* **2** *adv.* With the back facing forward: The old clock hung *backward,* its face toward the wall. **3** *adv.* In a reverse order or direction: Movies run *backward* are funny. **4** *adv.* From better to worse: His health is going *backward* lately. **5** *adv.* To time past: to look *backward* into history. **6** *adj.* Turned or directed toward the rear: a *backward* look; a *backward* step. **7** *adj.* Slow in development; retarded. **8** *adj.* Hesitant; shy. **—back′ward·ness** *n.* ◆ Use *backwards* only as an adverb: Move one step *backwards.*

back·wards [bak′wərdz] *adv.* Backward.

back·wash [bak′wäsh′ *or* bak′wôsh′] *n.* **1** A backward movement of air or water, as caused by propellors or oars. **2** An aftereffect or result.

back·wa·ter [bak′wô′tər] *n.* **1** Water turned or held back, as by a dam or an opposing current. **2** An isolated, backward place.

back·woods [bak′wo͝odz′] *n.pl.* Forest or country untouched by city customs, comforts, or ideas.

back·woods·man [bak′wo͝odz′mən] *n., pl.* **back·woods·men** [bak′wo͝odz′mən] A person who lives in the backwoods.

ba·con [bā′kən] *n.* The salted and smoked back and sides of a hog.

bac·te·ria [bak·tir′ē·ə] *n.pl.* Organisms having only one cell each and visible only through a microscope. Some bacteria do such helpful things as enriching the soil and ripening cheese; others cause serious diseases. **—bac·te′ri·al** *adj.*

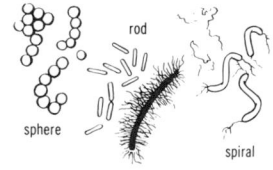

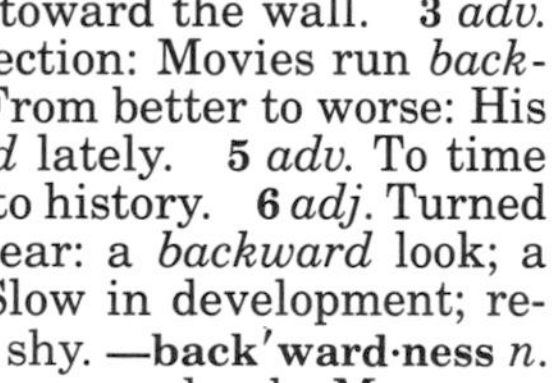

Bacteria, three main shapes

bac·te·ri·ol·o·gy [bak·tir′·ē·ol′ə·jē] *n.* The branch of science that deals with bacteria, especially in relation to medicine and agriculture.

bac·te·ri·um [bak·tir′ē·əm] *n.* Singular of BACTERIA.

Bac·tri·an camel [bak′trē·ən] A camel of SW Asia, having two humps. See picture at CAMEL.

bad [bad] *adj.* **worse, worst,** *n.* **1** *adj.* Not good; below standard: a *bad* road; *bad* marks. **2** *adj.* Evil; wicked: *bad* actions. **3** *adj.* Faulty or incorrect: *bad* grammar. **4** *adj.* Unwelcome; unpleasant: a *bad* odor; *bad* news. **5** *adj.* Harmful: Candy is *bad* for your teeth. **6** *adj.* Spoiled; decayed: *bad* meat. **7** *adj.* Severe: a *bad* cold. **8** *adj.* Sorry; regretful: I felt *bad* about hurting their feelings. **9** *adj.* Sick; in ill health: I feel *bad* today. **10** *n.* People, things, or conditions that are bad: Separate the good from the *bad.* **—be in bad** *informal* To be in disfavor or trouble. **—not bad, not half bad,** or **not so bad** Reasonably good; acceptable. **—too bad** Unfortunate; regrettable; disappointing. **—bad′ness** *n.*

bad blood A feeling of hatred or bitterness.

bade [bad] A past tense of BID.

badge [baj] *n.* **1** An emblem, pin, or other symbol, worn to show that a person belongs to a certain group or has received an award. **2** Any symbol: A doctor's bag is a *badge* of the medical profession.

badg·er [baj′ər] **1** *n.* A small animal with a broad back, short legs, and thick fur. Badgers live in burrows that they dig with the long claws on their forefeet. **2** *n.* The fur of the badger. **3** *v.* To nag at; pester; tease.

bad·i·nage [bad′ə·näzh′] *n.* Playful talk.

bad·ly [bad′lē] *adv.* **1** In a bad way: to dance *badly;* to behave *badly.* ◆ The adjective *bad,* not the adverb *badly,* is the preferred term in contexts such as "I feel *bad* about what happened" and "Things looked *bad* for the home team." **2** *informal* Very much: I need it *badly.*

bad·min·ton [bad′min·tən] *n.* A game in which a shuttlecock is hit back and forth over a high net with light rackets.

bad-mouth [bad′mouth′ *or* bad′mouth′] *v. slang* To criticize harshly and often unfairly.

bad-tem·pered [bad′tem′pərd] *adj.* Easily angered; irritable; cross.

baf·fle [baf′əl] *v.* **baf·fled, baf·fling,** *n.* **1** *v.* To confuse; bewilder; perplex: The question *baffled* me. **2** *n.* A screen or partition used to control a flow, as of gases, liquids, or sound waves. **3** *v.* To control or slow the flow of, as with a baffle; hinder.

bag [bag] *n., v.* **bagged, bag·ging** **1** *n.* A soft container, usually made of paper, cloth, or plastic, used to carry or hold something. **2** *v.* To put into a bag. **3** *n.* A suitcase, a handbag, or other container. **4** *n.* A sag or bulge in the shape of a bag. **5** *v.* To sag or bulge like a bag. **6** *n.* The amount of game caught or killed in hunting. **7** *v.* To catch or kill, as game. **8** *n.* In baseball, a base.

bag·a·telle [bag′ə·tel′] *n.* Something that is of little importance or value; trifle.

ba·gel [bā′gəl] *n.* A doughnut-shaped roll with a tough, glazed crust. ◆ *Bagel* comes directly from a Yiddish word, which in turn came from a word in an older German language meaning *ring.*

bag·gage [bag′ij] *n.* **1** The trunks, suitcases, and packages, of a person traveling; luggage. **2** An army's movable equipment.

bag·gy [bag′ē] *adj.* **bag·gi·er, bag·gi·est** Sagging or bulging like a bag; loose. **—bag′gi·ness** *n.*

bag lady A homeless woman who lives on the streets and in the public places of a city and carries her possessions about in shopping bags.

bag·pipe [bag′pīp′] *n.* A shrill-toned musical instrument consisting of a leather bag and several pipes with reeds in them, played by blowing air into the bag and squeezing it.

Bagpipe

bah [bä *or* ba] *interj.* An exclamation of contempt or disgust.
Ba·ha'i [bä·hī′] *n., pl.* **Ba·ha'is,** *adj.* **1** *n.* A member of an international religious movement stressing the unity of all religions and the importance of world peace and the equality of men and women. **2** *adj.* Of or having to do with this religious movement. **—Ba·ha'ism** *n.* ◆ *Baha'i* is named for the founder of Bahaism, *Baha Ullah* (1817–1892), an Iranian religious leader.
Ba·ha·mi·an [bə·hā′mē·ən *or* bə·hä′mē·ən] **1** *adj.* Of or from the Bahamas. **2** *n.* A person born in or a citizen of the Bahamas.
Bah·rain·i or **Bah·rein·i** [bä·rā′nē] **1** *adj.* Of or from Bahrain. **2** *n.* A person born in or a citizen of Bahrain.
bail[1] [bāl] **1** *n.* Money put up as a guarantee that an accused person will appear for trial, securing the person's release from jail pending the trial. **2** *v.* To provide bail for (an arrested person). **—jump bail** *informal* To run away and fail to appear for trial after being released on bail.
bail[2] [bāl] *v.* **1** To scoop (water) out of a boat, as with a bucket or pail. **2** To scoop the water out of. **—bail out** To parachute from an aircraft that is in danger of crashing.
bail[3] [bāl] *n.* The curved handle of a bucket, kettle, or other receptacle.
bai·liff [bā′lif] *n.* **1** A court officer who is in charge of prisoners while they are in a courtroom. **2** A sheriff's deputy. **3** A person who manages an estate; steward.
bai·li·wick [bā′lə·wik′] *n.* **1** The office, district, or jurisdiction of a bailiff. **2** A field in which someone has special authority or familiarity; domain.
bails·man [bālz′mən] *n., pl.* **bails·men** [bālz′mən] A person who provides bail or surety for another.
bairn [bârn] *n.* A young child: a Scottish word.
bait [bāt] **1** *n.* Something, usually food, placed on a hook or in a trap to lure fish or animals. **2** *v.* To put food or some other lure in or on: to *bait* a trap. **3** *n.* Anything used as a lure or temptation. **4** *v.* To set dogs to attack: *Baiting* bulls was a cruel sport. **5** *v.* To torment or annoy; tease: They *baited* him by calling him names.
baize [bāz] *n.* A thick, fuzzy wool or cotton cloth.
bake [bāk] *v.* **baked, bak·ing** **1** To cook in an oven: to *bake* a cake; The bread is *baking.* **2** To harden by heating: Bricks are *baked* in kilns.
bak·er [bā′kər] *n.* A person whose work is baking foods such as bread, cake, and cookies.
baker's dozen Thirteen. ◆ Bakers used to add an extra roll to every dozen they sold.
bak·er·y [bāk′(ə·)rē] *n., pl.* **bak·er·ies** A place where bread and cake are baked or sold.
bak·ing [bāk′ing] *n.* **1** Cooking or hardening by dry heat, as in an oven. **2** The amount baked at one time.
baking powder A powdered mixture of baking soda and acid salt used to make bread or cake rise.
baking soda Another name for SODIUM BICARBONATE.
ba·kla·va [bä′klə·vä] *n.* A pastry made of thin layers of dough filled with honey and chopped nuts.
bal. balance.
Ba·laam [bā′ləm] *n.* In the Bible, a prophet who was reprimanded by the ass that he rode.
bal·a·lai·ka [bal′ə·lī′kə] *n.* A guitarlike musical instrument with a triangular body and three strings, used especially in Russia.
bal·ance [bal′əns] *n., v.* **bal·anced, bal·anc·ing** **1** *n.* An instrument for weighing, especially a bar with two matched pans suspended from its ends, that pivots on a central point. **2** *n.* A condition of equality, as between opposing forces, amounts, or values: the *balance* of power between two countries. **3** *v.* To bring into or keep in balance: He *balanced* the board by holding it up at its center. **4** *v.* To weigh or compare in a balance or as if in a balance: to *balance* two suggested ways of doing something. **5** *v.* To offset or counteract: The trip's inconvenience was *balanced* by the pleasure of seeing my old friends. **6** *n.* The ability to keep one's body in a desired position without falling: It takes *balance* to walk a tightrope. **7** *n.* A person's normal mental or emotional condition. **8** *n.* An arrangement in harmony and proportion. **9** *v.* To arrange in harmony and proportion: to *balance* colors in a room. **10** *n.* The amount of money in a bank account. **11** *n.* The amount a person still owes after a bill has been partly paid. **12** *n.* An amount left over; remainder. **13** *n.* The difference in an account between the amount a person owes and the amount that the person is owed. **14** *v.* To compute such a difference. **15** *v.* To adjust such a difference, as by paying a bill. **16** *n.* A wheel that regulates motion, as in a watch. **—in the balance** Undecided; not settled.

Balance

balance of power A distribution of power among nations such that no one nation is strong enough to overpower other nations.
balance of trade The difference in value between the exports and imports of a country.
bal·anc·er [bal′ən·sər] *n.* **1** A person or thing that balances. **2** An acrobat.
balance wheel A wheel that vibrates back and forth against a spring at a fixed rate and regulates the motion of a clock or other mechanism.
bal·co·ny [bal′kə·nē] *n., pl.* **bal·co·nies** **1** A platform that projects from the side of a building and has a low wall or railing around it. **2** An upper floor with seats, as in a theater.
bald [bôld] *adj.* **1** Without hair on all or part of the head. **2** Lacking a natural covering. **3** Simple; plain: the *bald* facts. **—bald′ness** *n.*
bald eagle A large, dark brown North American

a	add	**i**	it	**o͝o**	took	**oi**	oil
ā	ace	**ī**	ice	**o͞o**	pool	**ou**	pout
â	care	**o**	odd	**u**	up	**ng**	ring
ä	palm	**ō**	open	**û**	burn	**th**	thin
e	end	**ô**	order	**yo͞o**	fuse	**th**	this
ē	equal					**zh**	vision

ə = {a in *above* e in *sicken* i in *possible* / o in *melon* u in *circus*}

eagle that has white feathers on its head, neck, and tail.

bal·der·dash [bôl′dər·dash′] *n.* Nonsense.

bal·dric [bôl′drik] *n.* A belt used to hold a sword, bugle, or other piece of equipment. It is worn over one shoulder and across the chest.

bale [bāl] *n., v.* **baled, bal·ing** 1 *n.* A large, tightly packed bundle of hay, cotton, or other bulky material. 2 *v.* To gather together and tie into bales: to *bale* cotton.

Bales

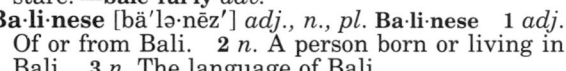

ba·leen [bə·lēn′] *n.* Another word for WHALEBONE.

bale·ful [bāl′fəl] *adj.* Evil or threatening; malicious: a *baleful* stare. **—bale′ful·ly** *adv.*

Ba·li·nese [bä′lə·nēz′] *adj., n., pl.* **Ba·li·nese** 1 *adj.* Of or from Bali. 2 *n.* A person born or living in Bali. 3 *n.* The language of Bali.

balk [bôk] 1 *v.* To stop and refuse to move or act. 2 *v.* To cause to stop; thwart; hinder: Their efforts were *balked* by the difficulty of the task. 3 *n.* Something that checks or hinders. 4 *n.* In baseball, an illegal breaking off of a pitching motion when there are runners on base.

Bal·kan [bôl′kən] *adj.* Of or from the Balkans.

balk·y [bô′kē] *adj.* **balk·i·er, balk·i·est** Given to balking: a *balky* engine.

ball[1] [bôl] 1 *n.* Any round body; sphere: a *ball* of twine; a snow*ball.* 2 *n.* A round or oval object, often hollow, used in a number of games: a tennis *ball;* a foot*ball.* 3 *n.* A game played with a ball, as baseball. 4 *n.* A ball that has been thrown or hit so that it moves in a special way: a curve *ball*; a bouncing *ball.* 5 *n.* In baseball, a pitch that is not struck at by the batter and is not a strike. 6 *n.* A round bullet or a cannon ball. 7 *v.* To make into a ball.

ball[2] [bôl] *n.* A large, formal dance.

bal·lad [bal′əd] *n.* 1 A poem or song that tells a story in a series of short stanzas. 2 A sentimental song of two or more stanzas.

ball-and-sock·et joint [bôl′ən·sok′it] A joint made of a ball in a socket, as the hip.

bal·last [bal′əst] 1 *n.* Anything heavy, as sand, stone, or water carried in a ship, balloon, or other container, to steady it. 2 *n.* Gravel or broken stone used as a bed for railroad tracks. 3 *n.* Something that gives steadiness to character or conduct. 4 *v.* To steady or supply with ballast.

ball bearing 1 A bearing in which a shaft or revolving part is borne by hard metal balls that roll easily in a groove. 2 One of these balls.

bal·le·ri·na [bal′ə·rē′nə] *n.* A woman who dances ballets.

bal·let [bal′ā′ *or* ba·lā′] *n.* 1 A dance in which formal steps and movements are performed by costumed dancers. A ballet often tells a story. 2 A group that performs ballets.

bal·lis·tic [bə·lis′tik] *adj.* Of or having to do with projectiles or ballistics.

ballistic missile A rocket guided while its fuel lasts but descending as any freely falling body.

bal·lis·tics [bə·lis′tiks] *n.* The science that deals with the motion of projectiles, missiles, and other objects propelled by force. ◆ See -ICS.

ball lightning A rarely seen kind of lightning consisting of shining balls that move along surfaces or float in the air during a thunderstorm.

bal·loon [bə·lo͞on′] 1 *n.* A large bag that rises and floats high in the air when filled with a gas lighter than air, often with a car or basket attached, for carrying people. 2 *n.* A small rubber bag that can be inflated and used as a toy. 3 *v.* To swell up like a balloon being filled.

bal·loon·ist [bə·lo͞on′ist] *n.* A person who rides in or operates a balloon.

bal·lot [bal′ət] 1 *n.* A piece of paper used to cast a secret vote. 2 *n.* The total number of votes cast in an election. 3 *n.* The action or method of voting secretly. 4 *v.* To vote or decide by ballot.

ball park A park or stadium in which baseball is played.

ball·play·er [bôl′plā′ər] *n.* A person who plays ball, especially a professional baseball player.

ball-point pen [bôl′point′] A pen having as its point a tiny ball that transfers ink from a cartridge to the paper against which it is pressed.

ball·room [bôl′ro͞om′ *or* bôl′ro͝om′] *n.* A large room for dancing.

bal·ly·hoo [bal′ē·ho͞o′] *n., v.* **bal·ly·hooed, bal·ly·hoo·ing** *U.S. informal* 1 *n.* Sensational, noisy advertising or propaganda. 2 *v.* To advocate or promote by ballyhoo.

balm [bäm] *n.* 1 An oily substance taken from certain trees and used as a salve or ointment. 2 Anything that soothes or heals: Darkness was *balm* to my tired eyes.

balm·y [bä′mē] *adj.* **balm·i·er, balm·i·est** 1 Mild and soothing; pleasant: *balmy* weather. 2 Fragrant; aromatic. **—balm′i·ness** *n.*

ba·lo·ney [bə·lō′nē] *n.* 1 Another spelling of BOLOGNA. 2 *slang* Nonsense.

bal·sa [bôl′sə] *n.* 1 A tree of tropical America and the West Indies that has a soft, lightweight wood. 2 The wood, used in rafts and model airplanes.

bal·sam [bôl′səm] *n.* 1 A fragrant, oily substance obtained from certain trees and used in making varnishes, perfumes, and ointments. 2 Any tree from which balsam is obtained.

balsam fir A resinous North American evergreen tree used widely as a Christmas tree.

Baltimore oriole A North American songbird, the male of which has bright black, orange, and white plumage.

bal·us·ter [bal′əs·tər] *n.* One of the small posts that supports the handrail, as of a staircase.

bal·us·trade [bal′ə·strād′] *n.* A handrail supported by small posts, as on a staircase or balcony.

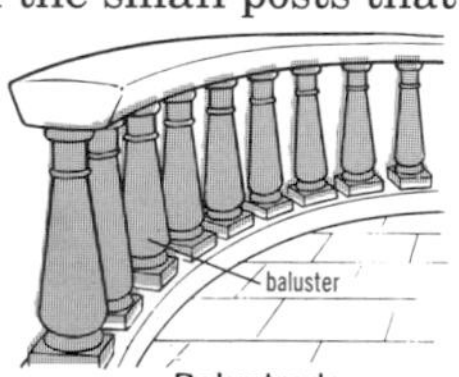

Balustrade

bam·boo [bam·bo͞o′] *n.* A tall, treelike, tropical grass with hollow, jointed stems that are used in building and in making things, as furniture and utensils. ◆ *Bamboo* comes from a Malay word.

bam·boo·zle [bam·bo͞o′zəl] *v.* **bam·boo·zled, bam·boo·zling** *informal* 1 To trick; hoodwink; cheat. 2 To puzzle or confuse: Card tricks *bamboozle* me.

ban [ban] *v.* **banned, ban·ning,** *n.* 1 *v.* To forbid, especially by law; prohibit: to *ban* the sale of a book. 2 *n.* A law or order forbidding something. 3 *n.* A curse: seldom used today.

ba·nal [bə·näl′ *or* bə·nal′] *adj.* Boring or meaningless because it has been used too much; trite.

ba·nal·i·ty [bə·nal′ə·tē] *n., pl.* **ba·nal·i·ties** 1 The quality of being banal; triteness. 2 Something that is banal, as a trite remark or idea.

ba·nan·a [bə·nan′ə] *n.* 1 The fruit of a large, tropical plant. It has a red or yellow skin, sweet, creamy flesh, and grows in clusters on a stalk. **2** The plant. ◆ *Banana* comes from a Spanish or Portuguese word taken from an African language.

band[1] [band] **1** *n.* A group of persons united for a purpose: a *band* of strolling players. **2** *v.* To unite in a band. **3** *n.* A group of musicians organized to play together.

band[2] [band] **1** *n.* A flat, flexible strip of any material, often used to bind or secure something: A barrel has iron *bands* around it. **2** *n.* A stripe: The flag was white with a blue *band.* **3** *v.* To put a band on or identify with a band, as a bird. **4** *n.* A specific range of radio frequencies: the shortwave *band.*

band·age [ban′dij] *n., v.* **band·aged, band·ag·ing** **1** *n.* A strip of soft cloth or other material used to cover or bind up a wound or injury. **2** *v.* To cover or support with a bandage.

Band-Aid [band′ād′] *n.* A small adhesive bandage with a gauze pad in the middle for covering a cut or sore: a trademark.

ban·dan·na or **ban·dan·a** [ban·dan′ə] *n.* A large, brightly colored, patterned handkerchief.

band·box [band′boks′] *n.* A round or oval box used to hold things, as collars or hats.

ban·deau [ban·dō′] *n., pl.* **ban·deaux** [ban·dōz′] A narrow band worn by women to hold their hair in place.

ban·di·coot [ban′di·ko͞ot′] *n.* **1** A very large rat of India and Ceylon. **2** A ratlike Australian marsupial with a long tapering snout and long hind legs.

ban·dit [ban′dit] *n., pl.* **ban·dits** or **ban·dit·ti** [ban·dit′ē] A robber or outlaw; highwayman.

ban·dit·ry [ban′di·trē] *n.* The actions or behavior of a bandit.

band·mas·ter [band′mas′tər] *n.* The leader of a musical band; conductor.

ban·do·lier or **ban·do·leer** [ban′də·lēr′] *n.* A wide military belt with loops and pockets for ammunition, worn over the shoulder and across the chest.

band saw A saw whose blade is a toothed steel band that forms a loop around a pair of motor-driven wheels.

band shell A bandstand with a large, overhanging, concave wall behind it to reflect sound toward the audience.

band·stand [band′stand′] *n.* A platform for a musical band, often roofed when out of doors.

band·wag·on [band′wag′ən] *n.* A decorated wagon used to carry a band in a parade. **—on the bandwagon** *informal* On the side that is popular or winning, as in an election: Get *on the bandwagon.*

ban·dy [ban′dē] *v.* **ban·died, ban·dy·ing,** *adj.* **1** *v.* To give and take; exchange: to *bandy* stories. **2** *adj.* Bent outward; bowed, as legs.

ban·dy-legged [ban′dē·legd′] *adj.* Bow-legged.

bane [bān] *n.* A cause of worry, ruin, or death.

bane·ful [bān′fəl] *adj.* Destructive; harmful.

bang[1] [bang] **1** *n.* A hard, noisy blow or thump. **2** *v.* To beat or hit hard and noisily: Who's *banging* on the door? **3** *n.* A sudden, loud sound: the *bang* of a gun. **4** *v.* To make a loud sound: I wish that drum would stop *banging.* **5** *v.* To knock or thrust forcefully so as to make a sharp noise: to *bang* a door shut. **6** *adv.* Suddenly and loudly: The dog ran *bang* into the door. ◆ *Bang* comes from an old Scandinavian word meaning *to hammer.*

bang[2] [bang] *n.* (*often pl.*) A fringe of hair cut so that it hangs squarely across the forehead.

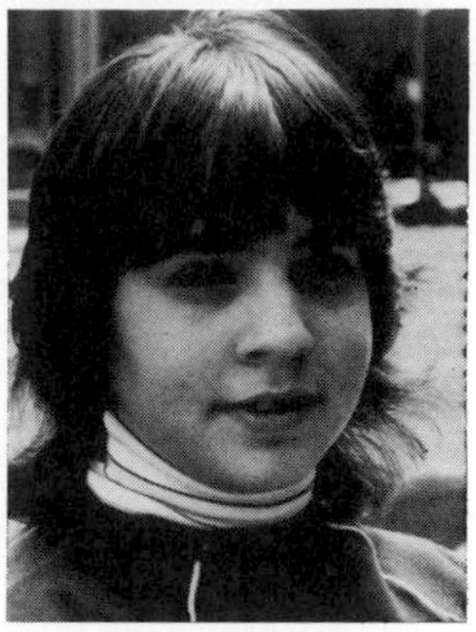

Child with bangs

Ban·gla·desh·i [bäng′glə·desh′ē *or* bang′glə·desh′ē] **1** *adj.* Of or from Bangladesh. **2** *n.* A person born in or a citizen of Bangladesh.

ban·gle [bang′gəl] *n.* Something, as a hoop or chain, worn around the wrist or ankle as jewelry.

bang-up [bang′up′] *adj. informal* Excellent; great; first-rate: a *bang-up* job of clearing out the attic.

ban·ish [ban′ish] *v.* **1** To compel to leave a country, as by political decree. **2** To drive away; get rid of; dispel; dismiss. **—ban′ish·ment** *n.*

ban·is·ter [ban′is·tər] *n.* **1** A post that supports a railing, as along a staircase. **2** A balustrade.

ban·jo [ban′jō] *n., pl.* **ban·jos** or **ban·joes** A stringed musical instrument that has a long neck attached to a shallow drum with a skin stretched over the top. It has four or five strings and is played by strumming or plucking.

Banjo

bank[1] [bangk] **1** *n.* A pile, mass, or mound: a cloud *bank.* **2** *v.* To heap up into a bank: The plow *banked* the snow at the side of the road. **3** *n.* The land along the edge of a river or stream. **4** *n.* A shallow place in a body of water: a sand *bank.* **5** *v.* To slant (a road or track on a curve) so the outer edge is higher. **6** *v.* To tilt an airplane so that one wing is higher than the other, as when turning. **7** *v.* To cover (a fire), as with ashes so that it will burn more slowly.

bank[2] [bangk] **1** *n.* A place whose business is the lending, exchanging, and safeguarding of money. **2** *v.* To put or keep money in a bank. **3** *n.* A place where a supply of something is kept for future use: Many hospitals have blood *banks.* **—bank on** *informal* To rely on; be sure about.

bank[3] [bangk] *n.* **1** A set of like objects in a row: a *bank* of organ keys. **2** A tier of oars in a galley.

bank·book [bangk′bo͝ok′] *n.* A booklet containing a record of amounts deposited in and withdrawn from a depositor's bank account.

bank·er [bangk′ər] *n.* A person who owns or runs a bank.

bank·ing [bangk′ing] *n.* The business of a bank or banker.

a	add	**i**	it	**o͝o**	took	**oi**	oil		
ā	ace	**ī**	ice	**o͞o**	pool	**ou**	pout		
â	care	**o**	odd	**u**	up	**ng**	ring		
ä	palm	**ō**	open	**û**	burn	**th**	thin		
e	end	**ô**	order	**yo͞o**	fuse	**th̶**	this		
ē	equal					**zh**	vision		

ə = a in *above*, e in *sicken*, i in *possible*, o in *melon*, u in *circus*

bank note A piece of paper issued by an authorized bank rather than a government and usable as money.
bank·roll [bangk′rōl′] **1** *n.* An available supply of money. **2** *v.* To supply money for; finance.
bank·rupt [bangk′rupt] **1** *n.* A person who has been declared by a court unable to pay debts and whose property has been taken away and distributed among the creditors. **2** *adj.* Declared a bankrupt by a court. **3** *v.* To make bankrupt.
bank·rupt·cy [bangk′rupt·sē] *n., pl.* **bank·rupt·cies** The condition of being bankrupt.
ban·ner [ban′ər] **1** *n.* A flag. **2** *n.* A piece of cloth with a motto or emblem on it. **3** *n.* A headline extending across a newspaper page. **4** *adj.* Leading; outstanding: a *banner* year.
ban·nock [ban′ək] *n.* A thin cake of meal baked on a griddle.
banns [banz] *n.pl.* An announcement in church that a man and woman are to be married.
ban·quet [bang′kwit] **1** *n.* A lavish feast. **2** *v.* To eat well; feast. **3** *n.* A formal dinner, often followed by speeches. **4** *v.* To give a banquet for.
ban·quette [bang′ket′] *n.* An upholstered bench along a wall or built into a wall, as in a restaurant.
ban·shee [ban′shē] *n.* In Gaelic myths, a female spirit whose wailing was supposed to warn that someone was going to die.
ban·tam [ban′təm] *n.* **1** (*often written* **Bantam**) A breed of small chickens, known for their fighting ability. **2** A small, aggressive person.
ban·tam·weight [ban′təm·wāt′] *n.* A boxer who weighs 118 pounds or less.
ban·ter [ban′tər] **1** *n.* Playful teasing; good-natured joking. **2** *v.* To tease or joke playfully.
Ban·tu [ban′to͞o] *n., pl.* **Ban·tu** or **Ban·tus** [ban′to͞oz], *adj.* **1** *n.* A member of any of a group of Negro tribes of central and southern Africa. **2** *n.* Any of the languages spoken by these tribes. **3** *adj.* Of or having to do with the Bantu or their languages.
ban·yan [ban′yən] *n.* A fig tree of the East Indies whose branches send down roots that develop into new trunks, producing a thick, shady grove.

Banyan

ban·zai [bän′zī′] *interj.* A Japanese patriotic cheer or battle cry meaning "May you live ten thousand years."
ba·o·bab [bā′ō·bab′ *or* bä′ō·bab] *n.* A tropical African tree with a thick trunk, large, gourdlike fruit, and bark used in making rope and cloth.
bap·tism [bap′tiz·əm] *n.* **1** A sacrament or rite in which a person is sprinkled with or dipped in water, used by most Christian churches when taking in a new member. **2** A first and often difficult experience: She received her *baptism* as a performer last night.
bap·tis·mal [bap·tiz′məl] *adj.* Of or having to do with baptism: a *baptismal* ceremony.
Bap·tist [bap′tist] **1** *n.* A member of a Christian church that baptizes only professed believers and only by immersing them in water. **2** *adj.* Of or having to do with Baptists or their church. **3** *n.* A person who baptizes: John the *Baptist*.
bap·tis·ter·y or **bap·tis·try** [bap′tis·trē] *n., pl.* **bap·tis·ter·ies** or **bap·tis·tries** A place where baptisms are performed.
bap·tize [bap′tīz′] *v.* **1** To admit someone into a Christian church by baptism. **2** To give a name to at baptism: He was *baptized* Thomas.
bar [bär] *n., v.* **barred, bar·ring,** *prep.* **1** *n.* A straight, evenly shaped piece, as of wood or metal, that is longer than it is wide or thick. Bars are used for such things as levers and barriers. **2** *v.* To fasten or shut off with a bar: to *bar* a door. **3** *n.* A solid, bar-shaped block: a *bar* of butter. **4** *n.* Something that blocks the way; obstacle: The toys on the floor were a *bar* to the stairs. **5** *v.* To block the way; obstruct: The stalled car *barred* the road. **6** *v.* To exclude; prevent; forbid: Nonunion members are *barred* from the job. **7** *n.* A band or stripe, as of color. **8** *v.* To mark with a band or stripe. **9** *n.* A court of law. **10** *n.* Something that acts like a court of law; an authority that passes judgment: the *bar* of conscience. **11** *n.* The railing around the place where a prisoner stands in court. **12** *n.* The legal profession: to be admitted to the *bar.* **13** *n.* Lawyers as a group. **14** *n.* Any of the vertical lines that divide a musical staff into measures. **15** *n.* The unit of music between two bars; measure. **16** *n.* A counter or room where drinks are served. **17** *prep.* Excepting, especially in the expression **bar none,** with no exceptions.
bar- or **baro-** A combining form meaning: Weight; pressure, as in *barometer*.
barb [bärb] **1** *n.* A point, as on an arrow or fishhook, that sticks out and back from the main point. **2** *v.* To provide with a barb or barbs.

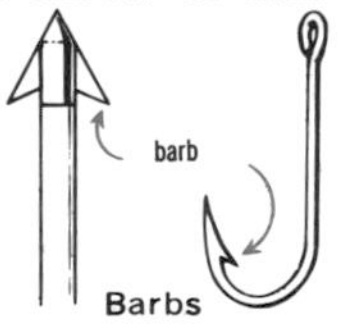

Barbs

Bar·ba·di·an [bär·bā′dē·ən] **1** *adj.* Of or from Barbados. **2** *n.* A person born in or a citizen of Barbados.
bar·bar·i·an [bär·bâr′ē·ən] **1** *n.* A member of a nation, group, or tribe whose way of life is considered primitive or backward. **2** *adj.* Of or like barbarians: *barbarian* manners. **3** *n.* A crude or brutal person. **4** *adj.* Brutal; crude. ◆ *Barbarian* and *barbarous* come from a Latin word taken from a Greek word meaning *foreign*. The ancient Greeks thought all foreigners uncivilized.
bar·bar·ic [bär·bar′ik] *adj.* **1** Of or like barbarians; uncivilized. **2** Wild; cruel.
bar·ba·rism [bär′bə·riz′əm] *n.* **1** An uncivilized condition. **2** Uncivilized action; brutality. **3** A word or phrase considered incorrect: "They is" is a *barbarism* for "they are."
bar·bar·i·ty [bär·bar′ə·tē] *n., pl.* **bar·bar·i·ties** **1** Barbaric conduct. **2** A barbaric act. **3** Crudity or coarseness in style or taste.
bar·ba·rize [bär′bə·rīz′] *v.* **bar·ba·rized, bar·ba·riz·ing** To make or become barbarous. **—bar′ba·ri·za′·tion** *n.*
bar·ba·rous [bär′bər·əs] *adj.* **1** Uncivilized. **2** Crude or coarse. **3** Cruel; brutal. **4** Using incorrect words or phrases. **—bar′ba·rous·ly** *adv.* ◆ See BARBARIAN.
bar·be·cue [bär′bə·kyo͞o′] *n., v.* **bar·be·cued, bar·be·cu·ing** **1** *n. U.S.* A picnic or party at which food, especially meat, is roasted over an open fire. **2** *n.* Meat roasted over an open fire, especially a whole animal carcass. **3** *n.* A grill, stove, or pit for outdoor cooking. **4** *v.* To roast over an open fire. **5** *v.* To cook (meat) with a highly seasoned sauce.

B

barbed [bärbd] *adj.* **1** Having a barb or barbs. **2** Pointed; wounding; painful: a *barbed* reply.

barbed wire Wire that has barbs on it, used for fences.

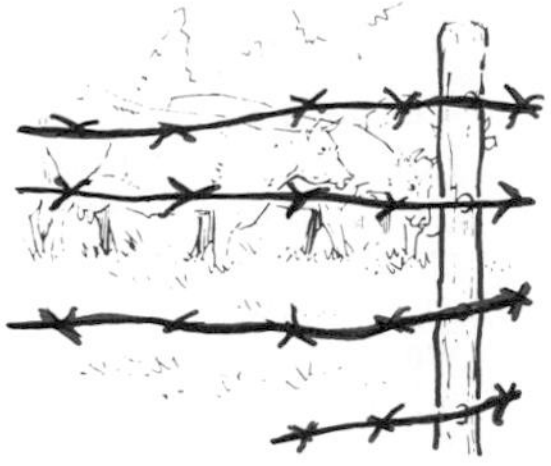
Barbed wire

bar·bel [bär′bəl] *n.* **1** A feeler growing like a whisker from the head of a catfish or certain other fishes. **2** Any of several freshwater fish with such feelers.

bar·bell [bär′bel′] *n.* A bar several feet long with weights at each end, used in exercising and weight lifting.

bar·ber [bär′bər] **1** *n.* A person whose work includes giving haircuts and shaves. **2** *v.* To cut the hair of, shave, or trim the beard of.

bar·ber·ry [bär′ber′ē] *n., pl.* **bar·ber·ries** **1** A shrub that has yellow flowers and red berries. **2** Its berry.

bar·bi·can [bär′bi·kən] *n.* A defensive tower next to a gate or bridge, as at the entrance to a castle.

bar·bit·u·rate [bär·bich′ər·it] *n.* Any of several drugs used to relieve pain and insomnia and to treat certain nervous conditions.

bar·ca·role or **bar·ca·rolle** [bär′kə·rōl′] *n.* A Venetian gondolier's song or a melody imitating such a song.

bard [bärd] *n.* **1** A writer or singer of narrative poems in ancient times. **2** A poet.

bare [bâr] *adj.* **bar·er, bar·est,** *v.* **bared, bar·ing** **1** *adj.* Without clothing or covering; naked. **2** *adj.* Lacking the usual furnishings or supplies; empty: The cupboard is *bare.* **3** *adj.* Plain; unadorned: the *bare* truth. **4** *adj.* Nothing more than; mere: the *bare* necessities of life. **5** *v.* To make bare; uncover: He *bared* his head. **—lay bare** To expose; reveal. **—bare′ness** *n.*

bare·back [bâr′bak′] **1** *adj.* Riding a horse without a saddle. **2** *adv.* Without a saddle.

bare·faced [bâr′fāst′] *adj.* Shameless; bold.

bare·foot [bâr′fo͝ot′] *adj., adv.* With bare feet.

bare·foot·ed [bâr′fo͝ot′id] *adj.* Barefoot.

bare-hand·ed [bâr′han′dəd] *adj., adv.* With the hands alone, unaided by a glove, tool, or weapon.

bare·head·ed [bâr′hed′id] *adj., adv.* With the head uncovered or bare; without a hat.

bare·ly [bâr′lē] *adv.* **1** Only just; scarcely: We have *barely* enough food to last a week. **2** Plainly; openly. See HARDLY.

bar·gain [bär′gən] **1** *n.* An agreement between people, as about something to be done or traded: We made a *bargain* to trade flute lessons for swimming instructions. **2** *n.* Something bought or offered for sale at less than its usual price. **3** *v.* To discuss a trade, sale, or other transaction in order to get a better price or better terms. **—bargain for** To expect; be prepared for: The work was harder than I had *bargained for.* **—into the bargain** In addition; besides: She's intelligent, and hardworking *into the bargain.*

barge [bärj] *n., v.* **barged, barg·ing** **1** *n.* A large, flat-bottomed boat used to carry freight in harbors, rivers, and other inland waters. **2** *n.* Any large boat like this. **3** *v. informal* To enter or intrude quickly and rudely: We were angry when three strangers *barged* into our meeting.

bar graph A graph using rectangles with lengths proportional to the numbers they represent.

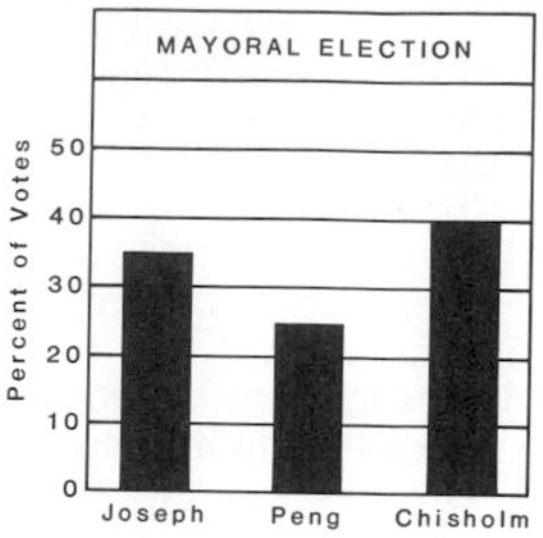

Bar graph

bar·ite [bâr′īt′] *n.* A mineral of barium sulfate that is the main source of barium chemicals.

bar·i·tone [bar′ə·tōn′] *n.* **1** A male voice with a range higher than bass and lower than tenor. **2** A person having such a voice. **3** An instrument with this range.

bar·i·um [bâr′ē·əm] *n.* A soft, silver-white metallic element. Many of its compounds are used in chemistry, industry, and medicine.

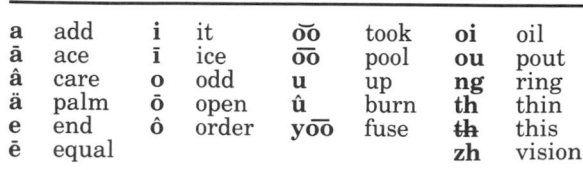

bark[1] [bärk] **1** *n.* The short, abrupt, explosive cry of a dog. **2** *n.* Any sound like this: the *bark* of a rifle. **3** *v.* To utter a bark or a sound like a bark. **4** *v.* To say roughly and curtly: to *bark* a command. **5** *v. informal* To work as a barker.

bark[2] [bärk] **1** *n.* The rind or covering of a tree or other plant. **2** *v.* To remove the bark from. **3** *v.* To rub off the skin of: to fall off a bicycle and *bark* one's shins.

bark[3] [bärk] *n.* **1** A sailing vessel with three masts, all square-rigged except the mast farthest aft, which is fore-and-aft rigged. **2** In poetry, any sailing vessel.

Bark

bar·keep·er [bär′kē′pər] *n.* Another name for BARTENDER.

bar·ken·tine [bär′kən·tēn′] *n.* A sailing vessel having three masts, square-rigged on the foremast and fore-and-aft rigged on the other masts.

bark·er [bär′kər] *n. U.S. informal* A person who stands outside a show, carnival, or other event, and gives a talk urging people to go in.

bar·ley [bär′lē] *n.* **1** A cereal grass whose grain is used in such items as malt beverages, breakfast foods, and food for stock. **2** This grain.

bar·ley·corn [bär′lē·kôrn′] *n.* Barley or grain of barley.

bar mitz·vah [bär mits′və] In the Jewish religion, a ceremony in which a boy who is thirteen is publicly recognized as having reached the age of religious duty and responsibility.

barn [bärn] *n.* A farm building that is used for such purposes as storing hay and stabling livestock.

bar·na·cle [bär′nə·kəl] *n.* A sea shellfish that attaches itself to such things as rocks and ship bottoms.

barn dance A social gathering, originally held in

a	add	**i**	it	**o͝o**	took	**oi**	oil
ā	ace	**ī**	ice	**o͞o**	pool	**ou**	pout
â	care	**o**	odd	**u**	up	**ng**	ring
ä	palm	**ō**	open	**û**	burn	**th**	thin
e	end	**ô**	order	**yo͞o**	fuse	**t͟h**	this
ē	equal					**zh**	vision

ə = a in *above*, e in *sicken*, i in *possible*, o in *melon*, u in *circus*

a barn, with square dances and traditional music.

barn·storm [bärn'stôrm'] *v. U.S. informal* To tour rural districts giving shows, making speeches, or giving exhibitions of stunt flying.

barn·yard [bärn'yärd'] *n.* A yard around a barn.

bar·o·gram [bar'ə·gram'] *n.* A record traced by a barograph.

bar·o·graph [bar'ə·graf'] *n.* A barometer that automatically makes a graph of its air pressure measurements.

ba·rom·e·ter [bə·rom'ə·tər] *n.* **1** An instrument for measuring air pressure, used for such purposes as forecasting weather and determining height above sea level. **2** Something that indicates changes, as of public opinion and business conditions.

bar·o·met·ric [bar'ə·met'rik] *adj.* Of, having to do with, or measured by a barometer.

bar·on [bar'ən] *n.* The lowest ranking member of the nobility in many European countries.

bar·on·ess [bar'ən·is] *n.* **1** The wife or widow of a baron. **2** A woman who holds the rank of baron in her own right.

bar·on·et [bar'ən·it] *n.* **1** An English title, below that of baron and above that of knight. **2** A person who holds such a title.

ba·ro·ni·al [bə·rō'nē·əl] *adj.* Having to do with or suitable for a baron or his estate.

bar·o·ny [bar'ə·nē] *n., pl.* **bar·o·nies** The rank or land of a baron.

ba·roque [bə·rōk'] *adj.* **1** Much ornamented, massive, and sometimes grotesque: *baroque* architecture. **2** Irregular in shape: said of pearls. ◆ This word comes from a Portuguese word meaning *rough or imperfect pearl.*

ba·rouche [bə·ro͞osh'] *n.* A four-wheeled carriage with a folding top, two seats facing each other, and an outside seat for the driver.

barque [bärk] Another spelling of BARK^{3}.

bar·racks [bar'əks] *n.pl.* (*sometimes used with singular verb*) A building or group of buildings where soldiers are housed.

bar·ra·cu·da [bar'ə·ko͞o'də] *n., pl.* **bar·ra·cu·da** or **bar·ra·cu·das** A fierce, powerful fish of warm seas.

bar·rage [bə·räzh'] *n.* **1** A heavy curtain of gunfire to keep enemy troops from moving or to protect one's own. **2** Any overwhelming attack, as of words or blows.

bar·rel [bar'əl] *n., v.* **bar·reled** or **bar·relled, bar·rel·ing** or **bar·rel·ling** **1** *n.* A round container, flat at the top and base and bulging slightly in the middle, usually made of wood. **2** *n.* As much as a barrel will hold. The standard U.S. barrel contains 3.28 bushels dry measure or 31.5 gallons liquid measure. **3** *v.* To put or pack in barrels. **4** *n.* In a gun, the tube through which the bullet or shell is shot.

Man hammering bung into the bunghole of a barrel

bar·rel-chest·ed [bar'əl·ches'tid] *adj.* Having a broad, well-developed chest: a *barrel-chested* piano mover.

barrel organ Another name for HAND ORGAN.

bar·ren [bar'ən] **1** *adj.* Unable to produce offspring; sterile. **2** *adj.* Not yielding fruit or crops: *barren* soil. **3** *adj.* Not producing, as results or profit: a *barren* plan. **4** *adj.* Empty; lacking: *barren* of ideas. **5** *n.* (*usually pl.*) A tract of barren land. —**bar'ren·ness** *n.*

bar·rette [bə·ret'] *n.* A small bar with a clasp used for holding hair in place.

bar·ri·cade [bar'ə·kād' *or* bar'ə·kād'] *n., v.* **bar·ri·cad·ed, bar·ri·cad·ing** **1** *n.* An obstruction hastily built to bar passage or for defense. **2** *n.* Something that blocks passage; barrier. **3** *v.* To enclose, obstruct, or defend with a barricade.

bar·ri·er [bar'ē·ər] *n.* **1** Something that blocks the way or stops movement, as a wall, fence, or dam. **2** Something that acts as a barrier: Bad roads are a *barrier* to an efficient trasportation system.

barrier reef A long coral reef near a shore and parallel to it.

bar·ring [bär'ing] *prep.* Excepting; apart from: *Barring* snow, we will arrive at noon.

bar·ri·o [bär'rē·ō] *n., pl.* **bar·ri·os** A Spanish-speaking neighborhood in a U.S. city.

bar·ris·ter [bar'is·tər] *n. British* A lawyer who argues cases in court.

bar·room [bär'ro͞om' *or* bär'ro͝om'] *n.* A room or other place where alcoholic drinks are served at a bar.

bar·row^{1} [bar'ō] *n.* **1** A wheelbarrow. **2** A frame or tray with handles at each end by which it is carried, used for transporting loads.

bar·row^{2} [bar'ō] *n.* A mound of earth and stones erected in early times to make a grave.

Bart. baronet.

bar·tend·er [bär'ten·dər] *n.* A person who mixes and serves alcoholic drinks over a bar.

bar·ter [bär'tər] **1** *v.* To trade by exchanging goods or services without using money. **2** *v.* To trade or exchange: The trapper *bartered* fish for supplies. **3** *n.* The act of bartering.

ba·sal [bā'səl] *adj.* **1** Of, at, or forming the base. **2** Basic; fundamental.

basal metabolism The smallest amount of energy required by a plant or animal at rest to maintain essential life activities.

bas·alt [bə·sôlt' *or* bā'sôlt] *n.* A dark, hard, fine-grained rock of volcanic origin.

bas·cule [bas'kyo͞ol] *n.* A structure that is balanced on a fulcrum like a seesaw, so that one end is raised when the other is lowered with weights. A **bascule bridge,** a kind of drawbridge, uses a pair of bascules that meet at the center when lowered. ◆ *Bascule* comes from a French word meaning *seesaw.*

base^{1} [bās] *n., v.* **based, bas·ing** **1** *n.* The lowest supporting part of anything; bottom: the *base* of a monument. **2** *v.* To place on a foundation or on something serving as a support: They *based* their hopes on the peace treaty. **3** *n.* A headquarters, especially one from which the members of an armed force, planes, ships, and other equipment, are sent forth and in which supplies are stored. **4** *n.* The chief or fundamental part of something: Meat is the *base* of this stew. **5** *n.* A goal or stopping place in certain sports. **6** *n.* In mathematics, the number on which a system of numeration is based. The base of the decimal system is 10; computers use the binary system, which has the base 2. **7** *n.* In mathematics, a number that is to be multiplied by itself the number of times indicated by an exponent or logarithm. In 2^4, 2 is the base and 4 is the exponent. Where 2 is the base, the logarithm of 16 is 4, since $2^4 = 16$. **8**

n. In mathematics, the side of a polygon or face of a three-dimensional figure by which the figure is measured or named. **9** *n.* In chemistry, a substance that can combine with an acid to form a salt. **10** *n.* In grammar, a word to which affixes and inflectional endings may by added.

base[2] [bās] *adj.* **bas·er, bas·est** **1** Dishonorable or cowardly; mean; low: a *base* act. **2** Suiting or typical of an unworthy person: *base* flattery. **3** Low in value: Lead is a *base* metal. **—base′ly** *adv.* **—base′ness** *n.*

base·ball [bās′bôl′] *n.* **1** A game played with a wooden bat and a hard ball by two teams of nine players each. To score, a player must run a diamond-shaped course, touching four bases. **2** The ball used in this game.

base·board [bās′bôrd′] *n.* A board running along the wall of a room, next to the floor.

base·born [bās′bôrn′] *adj.* Of humble birth.

base hit In baseball, a batted ball that enables the batter to reach a base safely, not helped by an error or the putout of another runner.

base·less [bās′lis] *adj.* Without reason; groundless; unfounded: *baseless* fears.

base·man [bās′mən] *n., pl.* **base·men** [bās′mən] Any of three baseball players whose fielding position is near one of the bases. They are the **first baseman,** the **second baseman,** and the **third baseman.**

base·ment [bās′mənt] *n.* The lowest floor of a building, usually completely or partly underground.

base on balls In baseball, a walk (def. 10).

bash [bash] *v. informal* To strike heavily.

bash·ful [bash′fəl] *adj.* Timid or uncomfortable with strangers; shy. **—bash′ful·ly** *adv.* **—bash′ful·ness** *n.*

ba·sic [bā′sik] *adj.* **1** Of, at, or forming a base or basis; fundamental: *basic* ingredients. **2** In chemistry, of, like, or producing a base. **—ba·si·cal·ly** [bā′sik·lē] *adv.* ◆ Many writers overwork *basically.* Use it only when it truly adds meaning to the sentence. Avoid uses such as "Summer weather here is *basically* hot and dry."

BA·SIC [bā′sik] *n.* A simple, popular programming language, widely used for small computers and in timesharing systems. ◆ *BASIC* comes from *B(eginner's) A(ll-purpose) S(ymbolic) I(nstructional) C(ode).*

bas·il [baz′(ə)l *or* bās′(ə)l] *n.* A plant with a sweet smell. Its leaves are used in cooking.

ba·sil·i·ca [bə·sil′i·kə] *n.* **1** A rectangular hall with a row of columns along each side and a semicircular section at one end. **2** An early Christian church in this style.

bas·i·lisk [bas′ə·lisk] *n.* **1** In myths, a lizardlike monster whose breath and look were said to kill. **2** A crested tropical American lizard with a pouch on its head that it can inflate.

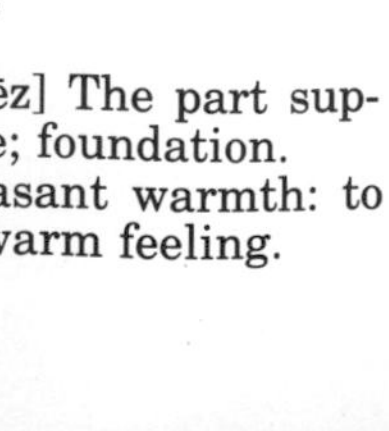
Basilisk

ba·sin [bā′sən] *n.* **1** A wide, shallow bowl used for holding liquids. **2** The amount a basin will hold. **3** A sink or a bowl for washing. **4** A hollow containing water, as a bay. **5** The region drained by a river and its branches.

ba·sis [bā′sis] *n., pl.* **ba·ses** [bā′sēz] The part supporting or essential to the whole; foundation.

bask [bask] *v.* **1** To enjoy a pleasant warmth: to *bask* in the sun. **2** To enjoy a warm feeling.

bas·ket [bas′kit] *n.* **1** A container made of an interwoven material, as rushes, cane, or strips of wood. **2** Something like a basket in shape or use. **3** The amount a basket will hold. **4** In basketball, the circular net through which the ball is thrown. **5** A goal scored in basketball.

bas·ket·ball [bas′kit·bôl′] *n.* **1** A game played with a large, inflated round ball by two teams of five players each. The object of the game is to toss the ball through the open net, or basket, at the opposing team's end of the court. **2** The round ball used in this game.

basket case *informal* A person who is disabled or unable to function.

bas·ket·ry [bas′kə·trē] *n.* **1** The craft of making baskets. **2** Baskets.

basket weave A way of weaving cloth in which double threads are interlaced to produce the checkered effect of a woven basket.

bas mitz·vah [bäs mits′və] Another spelling of BAT MITZVAH.

Basque [bask] **1** *n.* A member of a people living in northern Spain and SW France. **2** *n.* The language of the Basques, which is apparently unrelated to any other language. **3** *adj.* Of or having to do with the Basques or their language.

bas-re·lief [bä′ri·lēf′] *n.* A type of sculpture in which the figures stand out only slightly from the background.

bass[1] [bās] *n.* **1** The lowest pitched male singing voice. **2** A man with such a voice. **3** An instrument having the range of such a voice.

bass[2] [bas] *n., pl.* **bass** or **bass·es** Any of various food fishes found in salt and fresh water.

bass clef [bās] The clef used in writing the notes for low-pitched instruments and voices.

bass drum [bās] A large drum having two surfaces for beating. It makes a deep sound.

bas·set [bas′it] *n.* A hound with a long body, long head and ears, and short, heavy legs.

bas·si·net [bas′ə·net′] *n.* A basket, often with a hood at one end, used as a baby's bed.

bas·soon [ba·so͞on′ *or* bə·so͞on′] *n.* A large, low-pitched woodwind instrument with a double reed.

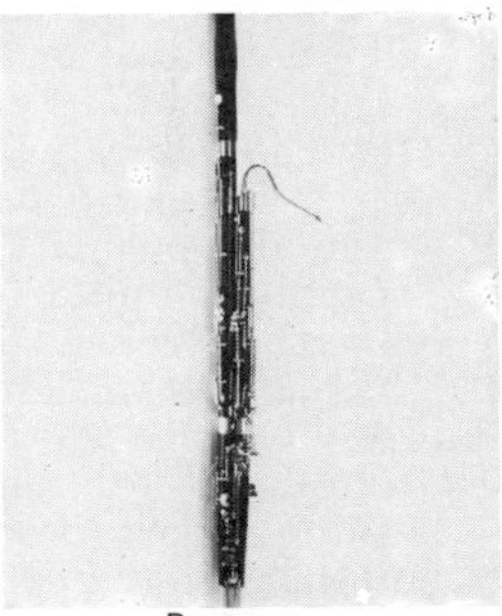
Bassoon

bass viol [bās] Another name for DOUBLE BASS.

bass·wood [bas′wo͝od′] *n.* **1** The American linden tree. **2** The wood of this tree.

bast [bast] *n.* Strong fibers from the stems and bark of certain plants, used in making cord, cloth, and other products.

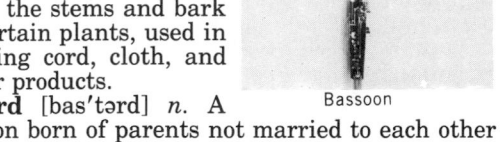

bas·tard [bas′tərd] *n.* A person born of parents not married to each other

a	add	**i**	it	**o͝o**	took	**oi**	oil
ā	ace	**ī**	ice	**o͞o**	pool	**ou**	pout
â	care	**o**	odd	**u**	up	**ng**	ring
ä	palm	**ō**	open	**û**	burn	**th**	thin
e	end	**ô**	order	**yo͞o**	fuse	**t͟h**	this
ē	equal					**zh**	vision

ə = a in *above* e in *sicken* i in *possible* / o in *melon* u in *circus*

at the time of the birth: usually an insulting term.
baste[1] [bāst] *v.* **bast·ed, bast·ing** To sew temporarily with long, loose stitches.
baste[2] [bāst] *v.* **bast·ed, bast·ing** To moisten (as meat) while roasting, as by pouring drippings or melted butter over it.
Bas·tille [bas·tēl′] *n.* A fortress in Paris once used as a prison. It was attacked and destroyed during the French Revolution on July 14, 1789.
bas·ti·na·do [bas′tə·nā′dō] *n., pl.* **bas·ti·na·does** 1 A beating with a stick, especially on the soles of the feet, as a punishment. 2 A stick or cudgel.
bas·tion [bas′chən] *n.* 1 In fortifications, a part of the rampart that juts out so that the main rampart can be protected. 2 A stronghold.
bat[1] [bat] *n., v.* **bat·ted, bat·ting** 1 *n.* A sturdy stick or a club, especially one used for hitting a ball. 2 *v.* To hit with or as if with a bat. 3 *n. informal* A sharp blow. 4 *v.* To use a bat. 5 *n.* In baseball, a turn at batting. 6 *v.* To take a turn at batting. **—at bat** In the act or position of batting: She sat on the bench until it was her turn *at bat.*
bat[2] [bat] *n.* A small, mouselike animal with wings of thin skin supported by bones of the forelimbs. Bats fly at night.
bat[3] [bat] *v.* **bat·ted, bat·ting** *informal* To wink, as in surprise.
bat·boy [bat′boi′] *n.* A boy who takes care of the bats and other equipment of a baseball team during games.

Big brown bat

batch [bach] *n.* 1 A quantity or number taken together: a *batch* of newspapers. 2 An amount of something produced at one time: a *batch* of bread.
bat·ed [bāt′id] *adj.* Held in; restrained, especially in the phrase **with bated breath,** barely breathing because of excitement or fear.
bath [bath] *n., pl.* **baths** [bat͟hz] 1 A washing of the body with water. 2 The water used for this: Run my *bath.* 3 A bathtub or bathroom. 4 A public building for bathing. 5 A liquid in which something is treated by dipping or soaking, as metals or camera film.
bathe [bāt͟h] *v.* **bathed, bath·ing** 1 To give a bath to. 2 To take a bath. 3 To go into a body of water, as a pool or the sea, to swim or cool off. 4 To apply a liquid to for healing or soothing: to *bathe* the forehead. 5 To cover as with a liquid: a hill *bathed* in light. **—bath′er** *n.*
ba·thet·ic [bə·thet′ik] *adj.* Characterized by bathos.
bath·house [bath′hous′] *n.* 1 A building at a bathing resort used as a dressing room. 2 A building where people may take baths.
bathing suit A garment worn for swimming.
ba·thos [bā′thos′] *n.* The sudden, often comic change from a lofty style to the ordinary or commonplace in speech or writing.
bath·robe [bath′rōb′] *n.* A long, loose garment worn before and after bathing and for lounging.
bath·room [bath′ro͞om′ *or* bath′ro͝om′] *n.* 1 A room in which to bathe. 2 A toilet.
bath·tub [bath′tub′] *n.* A tub to take baths in, usually a permanent fixture in a bathroom.
bath·y·scaph [bath′ə·skaf′] *n.* A kind of submarine capable of propelling itself and designed for scientific explorations at great depths in the sea. It has a spherical cabin underneath.
bath·y·sphere [bath′ə·sfir′] *n.* A hollow spherical steel structure with windows, used in underwater diving for deep-sea observations.
ba·tik [bə·tēk′] *n.* 1 A method of dyeing designs on cloth by putting wax on the parts not to be dyed. 2 Cloth dyed in this way.
ba·tiste [bə·tēst′] *n.* A very fine linen or cotton fabric.
bat mitz·vah [bät mits′və] 1 A Jewish religious ceremony in which a thirteen-year-old girl is recognized as having reached the age of religious responsibility. It is less common than the bar mitzvah ceremony for boys. 2 A girl for whom such a ceremony is conducted.
ba·ton [bə·ton′] *n.* 1 A slender stick or rod used by a conductor in leading an orchestra. 2 A short staff or rod carried as a symbol of authority. 3 A hollow, metal staff twirled rapidly for display, as by a drum majorette.
bats·man [bats′mən] *n., pl.* **bats·men** [bats′mən] A batter, especially in cricket.
bat·tal·ion [bə·tal′yən] *n.* 1 Two or more companies of soldiers led by a lieutenant colonel or major. 2 A large group of persons doing the same thing: a *battalion* of photographers.
bat·ten[1] [bat′(ə)n] 1 *n.* A narrow strip of wood, as one used to fasten canvas over a ship's hatch in rough weather. 2 *v.* To fasten with such strips: *Batten* down the hatches!
bat·ten[2] [bat′(ə)n] *v.* To make or become fat by feeding well.
bat·ter[1] [bat′ər] *n.* In baseball or cricket, a player who bats or whose turn it is to bat.
bat·ter[2] [bat′ər] *n.* A thick liquid mixture, as of milk, eggs, and flour, beaten up for making biscuits, cakes, and other foods.
bat·ter[3] [bat′ər] *v.* 1 To strike repeatedly; beat. 2 To break down by striking hard again and again: The storm *battered* down the door. 3 To damage with hard blows or by rough use.
bat·ter·ing ram A long, thick wooden beam, used in ancient and medieval times in war for breaking down walls, gates, or doors. A battering ram sometimes had a ram's head of iron at one end.

Battering ram

bat·ter·y [bat′ər·ē] *n., pl.* **bat·ter·ies** 1 Several electric cells operating together to give a required current or voltage. 2 An electric cell, as used in a flashlight. 3 A group of big guns used together in battle. 4 Any group of things or people connected or working together: a *battery* of typists. 5 In baseball, the pitcher and catcher together. 6 The illegal beating or touching of another person: assault and *battery.*
battery jar A squarish glass container open at the top, used in science laboratories.
bat·ting [bat′ing] *n.* 1 Sheets or rolls of wadded cotton or wool, as used in quilts or as bandages. 2 The act of a person who bats.
batting average The number of hits that a baseball player has made divided by the number of official times the player has been at bat, expressed as a three-digit decimal: A player who has made 100 hits in 400 times at bat has a *batting average* of .250.
bat·tle [bat′(ə)l] *n., v.* **bat·tled, bat·tling** 1 *n.* A com-

bat between enemy armies or fleets. **2** *n.* Any fight, conflict, or struggle. **3** *v.* To fight or struggle. **4** *v.* To force or attain by battling.

bat·tle-ax or **bat·tle-axe** [bat′(ə)l·aks′] *n.* A large ax used long ago in battle.

battle cry **1** A shout of self-encouragement made by troops in battle. **2** A slogan or motto repeated by the supporters of a cause.

bat·tle·dore [bat′(ə)l·dôr′] *n.* A paddle or racket used to hit a shuttlecock over a net.

battledore and shuttlecock An ancient form of the game of badminton.

bat·tle·field [bat′(ə)l·fēld′] *n.* The land on which a battle is fought or has been fought.

bat·tle·front [bat′(ə)l·frunt′] *n.* An area where the front lines of opposing armies meet and fight.

bat·tle·ground [bat′(ə)l·ground′] *n.* A battlefield.

bat·tle·ment [bat′(ə)l·mənt] *n.* **1** A wall with indented openings built at the top of a fort or tower, used for the defense of soldiers during warfare. **2** A low wall like this used to decorate a building.

Soldiers shooting from a battlement

battle royal **1** A big, confused fight in which many people are involved. **2** A heated or unrestrained quarrel or argument.

bat·tle·ship [bat′(ə)l·ship′] *n.* A large, armored warship equipped with heavy guns.

bat·ty [bat′ē] *adj.* **bat·ti·er, bat·ti·est** *slang* Insane; crazy.

bau·ble [bô′bəl] *n.* A worthless, showy trinket.

baux·ite [bôk′sīt′] *n.* A white to red claylike substance that is the main source of aluminum.

bawd·y [bô′dē] *adj.* **bawd·i·er, bawd·i·est** Indecent; immoral; improper: a *bawdy* song.

bawl [bôl] *v.* **1** To cry or sob noisily. **2** To call out loudly and harshly; shout; bellow. **—bawl out** *U.S. slang* To scold severely.

bay[1] [bā] *n.* A body of water partly enclosed by land; an inlet of the sea or of a lake.

bay[2] [bā] *n.* **1** A recess, nook, or alcove of a room. **2** A bay window. **3** A main part or division of a structure, set off, as by columns or pillars.

bay[3] [bā] **1** *n.* A deep, prolonged bark or cry, as of dogs in hunting. **2** *v.* To utter such a bark or cry. **3** *n.* The position of a hunted animal or person forced to turn and fight its attackers. **4** *n.* The position of an animal or person that is being held back or kept at a safe distance.

bay[4] [bā] *n.* **1** An evergreen tree with shiny, sweet-smelling leaves; laurel. **2** (*often pl.*) A laurel wreath with which poets and victors were once crowned as a sign of honor or fame. **3** (*usually pl.*) Honor; distinction.

bay[5] [bā] **1** *n., adj.* Reddish brown. **2** *n.* A reddish brown horse.

bay·ber·ry [bā′ber′ē] *n., pl.* **bay·ber·ries** **1** A shrub with sweet-smelling, waxy berries used in making a type of candle. **2** The berry itself.

bay leaf The dried leaf of a laurel, used as a spice in cooking.

bay·o·net [bā′ə·nit *or* bā′ə·net′] **1** *n.* A daggerlike weapon that may be attached to the muzzle of a rifle. **2** *v.* To stab with this weapon.

bay·ou [bī′o͞o] *n.* In the southern U.S., a marshy inlet or outlet, as of a lake or river.

bay rum A fragrant lotion made from various oils, alcohol, and water. It was originally distilled from bayberry leaves.

bay window A window or set of windows jutting out from the wall of a building and forming a recess or alcove in the room within.

Bay window

ba·zaar or **ba·zar** [bə·zär′] *n.* **1** An Oriental marketplace or street of shops. **2** A store for the sale of many kinds of goods. **3** A fair to raise money for some purpose: a school *bazaar.*

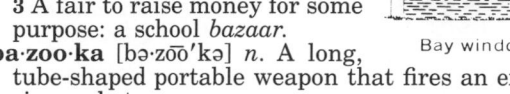

ba·zoo·ka [bə·zo͞o′kə] *n.* A long, tube-shaped portable weapon that fires an explosive rocket.

bb or **b.b.** ball bearing.

BB [bē′bē] *n., pl.* **BB's** A lead ball that is shot from a **BB gun,** a type of air gun.

BBC or **B.B.C.** British Broadcasting Corporation.

bbl. **1** barrel. **2** (*often written* **bbls.**) barrels.

B.C. **1** before Christ. It indicates dates before the birth of Christ. **2** British Columbia.

bd. **1** board. **2** bond.

bd. ft. **1** board foot. **2** board feet.

bdl. or **bdle.** bundle.

be [bē] *v.* **was** or **were, been, be·ing** **1** To have existence: Can such things *be?*; There *are* bears in the zoo. **2** To take place; happen: The parade *was* yesterday; Her birthday will *be* next month. **3** To stay or continue: I *was* in school all day. ◆ In addition to its use as a main verb, *be* is also a helping verb to show continuous action: I *am* working; She has *been* sleeping. It is also used with the past participle of transitive verbs to form the passive voice, and with the past participle of intransitive verbs to form the perfect tense: He *was* promoted, I *am* finished. *Be* also may join a subject with an adjective, noun, or pronoun: You *were* late; We *are* friends; What *is* it? To show that something is expected to happen in the future, *be* is used with an infinitive or a present participle: He *is* to leave soon; They *are* returning Monday.

be- A prefix meaning: **1** Around; all over, as in *bestrew.* **2** Completely; thoroughly, as in *befuddle.* **3** Off; away from, as in *behead.* **4** To provide or cover with, as in *bejewel.* **5** To make; cause to be, as in *befoul.* **6** About; because of, as in *bemoan.*

Be The symbol for the element beryllium.

beach [bēch] **1** *n.* The sloping shore of a body of water, especially a sandy or pebbly shore. **2** *v.* To drive or haul up (a boat) on a beach.

beach buggy Another name for DUNE BUGGY.

beach·comb·er [bēch′kō′mər] *n.* **1** A person who lives on a beach or wharf, especially a beach in

a	add	**i**	it	**o͝o**	took	**oi**	oil
ā	ace	**ī**	ice	**o͞o**	pool	**ou**	pout
â	care	**o**	odd	**u**	up	**ng**	ring
ä	palm	**ō**	open	**û**	burn	**th**	thin
e	end	**ô**	order	**yo͞o**	fuse	**t͟h**	this
ē	equal					**zh**	vision

ə = {a in *above* e in *sicken* i in *possible* / o in *melon* u in *circus*}

the South Seas, existing by digging or searching for things to eat or sell. 2 A person who roams beaches and shorelines, collecting things of value or utility. 3 A long ocean wave rolling in toward a beach.

beach·head [bēch′hed′] *n.* An area on a shore seized and held by an invading force.

bea·con [bē′kən] *n.* 1 A signal meant to warn or guide, as a light or fire. 2 A lighthouse. 3 Any place or height from which signals may be given. 4 A radio transmitter that sends out signals to guide ships and aircraft.

bead [bēd] 1 *n.* A small, usually round, piece of a material such as glass or wood, with a hole in it to draw a thread through. 2 *v.* To decorate with beads. 3 *n.* (*pl.*) A string of beads. 4 *n.* (*pl.*) A rosary. 5 *n.* A bubble or a drop of moisture, as sweat. 6 *n.* A small knob on a gun used in aiming. **—draw a bead on** To aim at.

bead·ing [bē′ding] *n.* 1 A trimming made of beads. 2 Material of or covered with beads.

bea·dle [bēd′(ə)l] *n.* A church officer who keeps order during the services.

bead·y [bē′dē] *adj.* **bead·i·er, bead·i·est** Small and glittering: *beady* eyes.

bea·gle [bē′gəl] *n.* A small hound with short legs and drooping ears, used in hunting.

beak [bēk] *n.* 1 The hooked bill of a bird of prey. 2 Any bird's bill. 3 Anything that looks like a bird's beak.

beak·er [bē′kər] *n.* 1 A large, wide-mouthed cup or goblet. 2 A glass or metal container with a lip for pouring, used by chemists.

Beakers

beam [bēm] 1 *n.* A long, horizontal piece of wood or metal shaped for use, as in the frame of a building or ship. 2 *n.* The part where a ship is the widest. 3 *n.* The crossbar of a balance. 4 *n.* A ray of light. 5 *v.* To send out rays of light; shine. 6 *n.* A radiant, happy look; smile. 7 *v.* To smile very warmly: I *beamed* when I heard the good news. 8 *n.* A continuous radio signal along a course to guide pilots. 9 *v.* To aim or transmit (a signal or broadcast) in a specific direction.

bean [bēn] *n.* 1 The oval seed of certain plants, used as food: lima *beans.* 2 The pod containing such seeds. Both the beans and pod of the string bean are used as a vegetable. 3 A plant bearing beans. 4 A seed or plant resembling a bean or bean plant: a vanilla *bean.*

bean·bag [bēn′bag′] *n.* A cloth bag filled with dried beans and used in games.

bean curd A light, cheeselike Oriental food made from puréed soybeans and shaped into small cakes.

bean·ie [bē′nē] *n.* A small, brimless cap worn on the back of the head.

bean sprout A young sprout of a bean seed, used as food.

bean·stalk [bēn′stôk′] *n.* The main stem of a bean plant.

bear[1] [bâr] *v.* **bore, borne** (or **born** for def. 5), **bear·ing** 1 To hold up; support: The swing couldn't *bear* my weight. 2 To focus or exert force: to bring one's influence to *bear* on a case. 3 To show; display: to *bear* a scar. 4 To endure: to *bear* pain. 5 To give birth to: She had *borne* a son; He was *born* today. 6 To produce: The farm *bore* good crops. 7 To carry or convey: The horse *bore* two riders. 8 To take on: to *bear* all the costs. 9 To conduct or behave (oneself): He *bore* himself with confidence. 10 To go in a certain direction: *Bear* to the right. 11 To keep in the mind: to *bear* a grudge. 12 To require: The experiments *bear* repeating. 13 To have: What relation does he *bear* to you? 14 To relate or apply to: This does not *bear* on the matter at hand. **—bear down** 1 To apply pressure. 2 To try very hard. **—bear out** To confirm as true; prove. **—bear up** To keep up strength or spirits when under a strain. **—bear with** To endure patiently.

bear[2] [bâr] *n.* 1 A large, very strong mammal with a heavy, thickly furred body and a very short tail, as the grizzly bear, brown bear, or polar bear. 2 A gruff, clumsy person.

bear·a·ble [bâr′ə·bəl] *adj.* Endurable.

beard [bird] 1 *n.* The hair that grows on a man's face. 2 *n.* Any similar growth, as the tuft of hairs on a goat's chin or the slender, stiff bristles on some spikes of wheat. 3 *v.* To defy courageously.

beard·ed [bir′did] *adj.* Having a beard.

bear·er [bâr′ər] *n.* 1 A person or thing that bears, carries, or upholds. 2 A person who presents a check, money order, or other document, for payment.

bear hug A vigorous, tight hug.

bear·ing [bâr′ing] *n.* 1 The way a person moves or behaves; posture, carriage, or manner: a regal *bearing.* 2 (*often pl.*) Position in relation to other, known points; direction: to lose one's *bearings.* 3 Relation; application: Their remarks had no *bearing* on the subject. 4 A part of a machine on or in which another part slides or turns.

bear·ish [bâr′ish] *adj.* 1 Like a bear, as in being rough, clumsy, or rude: *bearish* manners. 2 Characterized by, tending to cause, or expecting a decline in prices: *bearish* about the stock market. 3 Pessimistic.

bear·skin [bâr′skin′] *n.* 1 The skin of a bear, or a rug or coat made from it. 2 A tall, bushy, black fur cap worn with some uniforms.

beast [bēst] *n.* 1 Any animal except a human being, especially a large, four-footed animal. 2 A cruel, rude, or filthy person.

beast·ly [bēst′lē] *adj.* **beast·li·er, beast·li·est** 1 Like a savage beast; cruel. 2 *informal* Disagreeable: *beastly* weather.

beast of burden An animal used to carry loads.

beat [bēt] *v.* **beat, beat·en** or **beat, beat·ing,** *n., adj.* 1 *v.* To strike over and over; pound. 2 *n.* A stroke or blow. 3 *v.* To punish by hitting again and again; thrash. 4 *v.* To defeat, as in a fight or contest. 5 *v.* To stir or mix rapidly: to *beat* eggs. 6 *v.* To flap or flutter, as wings. 7 *v.* To make, as one's way, by hitting or shoving. 8 *v.* To make flat by tramping or treading: to *beat* a path through the woods. 9 *n.* A route regularly walked or covered, as by a police officer or reporter. 10 *v.* To hunt, as through underbrush, as for game. 11 *n.* A regular stroke, or its sound. 12 *n.* The basic unit of musical time. 13 *n.* Rhythm. 14 *v.* To give forth sound, as drums do when struck. 15 *n.* A throbbing, as of the heart. 16 *v.* To throb. 17 *adj. U.S. informal* Extremely tired. 18 *v. informal* To baffle; puzzle: It *beats* me. **—beat a retreat** To turn back; flee. **—beat time** To measure time in music, as by tapping the foot.

beat·en [bēt′(ə)n] **1** Past participle of BEAT. **2** *adj.* Shaped or made thin by hammering: *beaten* gold. **3** *adj.* Mixed by beating: *beaten* eggs. **4** *adj.* Much traveled; commonly used: off the *beaten* track. **5** *adj.* Whipped or defeated.

beat·er [bē′tər] *n.* A person or thing that beats, as a utensil for stirring foods rapidly or a person who drives hunted game from hiding.

be·a·tif·ic [bē′ə·tif′ik] *adj.* Giving or expressing bliss or blessedness: a *beatific* smile.

be·at·i·fy [bē·at′ə·fī] *v.* **be·at·i·fied, be·at·i·fy·ing** **1** To make supremely happy or blessed. **2** In the Roman Catholic Church, to declare publicly that (a certain dead person) is among the blessed in heaven. **—be·at·i·fi·ca·tion** [bē·at′ə·fi·kā′shən] *n.*

beat·ing [bē′ting] *n.* A whipping or defeat.

be·at·i·tude [bē·at′ə·t(y)o͞od′] *n.* **1** Supreme blessedness; bliss. **2** (*written* **the Beatitudes**) In the Bible, the verses naming the kinds of people who are blessed.

beat·nik [bēt′nik] *n.* A person whose behavior and clothing show a defiance of conventional values. ◆ The word *beatnik* is used to describe unconventional young people of the 1950's, members of what is referred to as the Beat Generation.

beat-up [bēt′up′] *adj. informal* Worn out; broken down, as from overuse.

beau [bō] *n., pl.* **beaus** or **beaux** [bōz] **1** A man courting a woman; lover. **2** A dandy.

Beau Brum·mell [bō′brum′əl] A well-dressed, fashionable man; dandy. ◆ The first *Beau Brummel* was George Bryan Brummell (1778–1840), an English dandy.

Beau·fort scale [bō′fərt] An internationally accepted scale of wind speeds, ranging from 0 (calm) to 12 (hurricane).

beaut [byo͞ot] *n. slang* A remarkable or extreme one: When I make a mistake, it's a real *beaut.*

beau·te·ous [byo͞o′tē·əs] *adj.* Beautiful.

beau·ti·cian [byo͞o·tish′ən] *n.* A person who works in a beauty parlor, especially one who cuts and styles hair.

beau·ti·ful [byo͞o′tə·fəl] *adj.* Giving pleasure or delight to the senses or the mind; very lovely.

beau·ti·fy [byo͞o′tə·fī] *v.* **beau·ti·fied, beau·ti·fy·ing** To make beautiful or lovelier. **—beau·ti·fi·ca·tion** [byo͞o′tə·fə·kā′shən] *n.*

beau·ty [byo͞o′tē] *n., pl.* **beau·ties** **1** The quality in a person or thing that delights the eye, the ear, or the mind. **2** A person or thing that is beautiful.

beauty parlor or **beauty shop** A place of business where women have their hair dressed, nails manicured, and complexion cared for.

bea·ver[1] [bē′vər] *n.* **1** A large rodent that can live on land or in water and has soft, brown fur and a broad, flat tail. It builds dams across streams from trees which it cuts down with its teeth. **2** The valuable fur of the beaver.

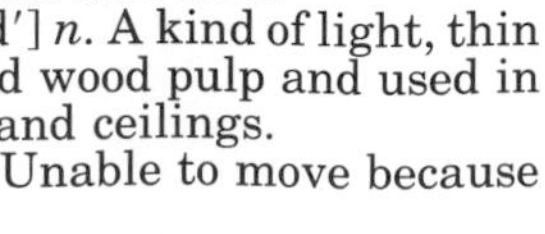

Beaver

bea·ver[2] [bē′vər] *n.* The lower part of a knight's helmet, covering the mouth and chin.

bea·ver·board [bē′vər·bôrd′] *n.* A kind of light, thin board made of compressed wood pulp and used in construction, as of walls and ceilings.

be·calmed [bi·kämd′] *adj.* Unable to move because of a lack of wind.

be·came [bi·kām′] Past tense of BECOME.

be·cause [bi·kôz′] *conj.* For the reason that; since. **—because of** On account of: The game was canceled *because of* rain. ◆ *Because* and *since* are often given identical meanings, but there is a distinction. *Because* introduces a direct cause: *Because* the day was cold, the snow did not melt. *Since* usually introduces only one step toward a reason, not the whole reason: *Since* it was raining hard, I did my homework.

beck [bek] *n.* A motion of the hand or head used to call someone closer. **—at one's beck and call** Subject to one's every order or wish.

beck·on [bek′ən] *v.* **1** To summon or signal by a movement of the hand or head. **2** To entice.

be·cloud [bi·kloud′] *v.* **1** To cover with clouds; darken. **2** To confuse, as an issue.

be·come [bi·kum′] *v.* **be·came, be·come, be·com·ing** **1** To come to be or grow to be: The caterpillar *became* a butterfly. **2** To be suitable to or look nice on: Blue *becomes* you. **—become of** To happen to.

be·com·ing [bi·kum′ing] *adj.* Appropriate or suitable and attractive: a *becoming* style.

bed [bed] *n., v.* **bed·ded, bed·ding** **1** *n.* An article of furniture to rest or sleep on. **2** *n.* Any place or thing used for resting or sleeping. **3** *v.* To go to bed, put to bed, or prepare a place to sleep or lie: *Bed* down by the trail. **4** *n.* Sleep or sleeping: time for *bed.* **5** *n.* A place to stay: *bed* and board. **6** *n.* A layer in the earth, as of rock. **7** *n.* The ground beneath a body of water: a river *bed.* **8** *n.* A plot of ground for growing plants or flowers. **9** *n.* A level foundation: a driveway built on a *bed* of gravel. **—get up on the wrong side of the bed** To be grouchy.

be·daub [bi·dôb′] *v.* **1** To smear or daub; besmirch; soil. **2** To ornament vulgarly or excessively.

be·daz·zle [bi·daz′əl] *v.* **be·daz·zled, be·daz·zling** **1** To confuse or blind by dazzling, as with a strong light. **2** To impress greatly; overwhelm: I was *bedazzled* by the paintings in the museum.

bed·bug [bed′bug′] *n.* A small, flat insect that bites. They sometimes get into beds.

bed·cham·ber [bed′chām′bər] *n.* A bedroom.

bed·clothes [bed′klō(t͟h)z′] *n.pl.* Bed coverings, as blankets, sheets, and spreads.

bed·ding [bed′ing] *n.* **1** Bedclothes and mattresses. **2** Straw as a bed for animals.

be·deck [bi·dek′] *v.* To ornament; adorn.

be·dev·il [bi·dev′əl] *v.* **be·dev·iled** or **be·dev·illed, be·dev·il·ing** or **be·dev·il·ling** **1** To trouble very much; torment: *bedeviled* by mosquitoes and gnats. **2** To possess with or as with a devil; bewitch.

be·dew [bi·d(y)o͞o′] *v.* To wet, as with dew.

bed·fast [bed′fast′] *adj.* Bedridden.

bed·fel·low [bed′fel′ō] *n.* **1** A person who shares a bed with another. **2** An associate.

a	add	**i**	it	**o͝o**	took	**oi**	oil
ā	ace	**ī**	ice	**o͞o**	pool	**ou**	pout
â	care	**o**	odd	**u**	up	**ng**	ring
ä	palm	**ō**	open	**û**	burn	**th**	thin
e	end	**ô**	order	**yo͞o**	fuse	**t͟h**	this
ē	equal					**zh**	vision

ə = a in *above* e in *sicken* i in *possible* o in *melon* u in *circus*

be·dim [bi·dim′] *v.* **be·dimmed, be·dim·ming** To make dim or indistinct; darken, obscure.
be·diz·en [bi·dī′zən] *v.* To dress or adorn with cheap, flashy splendor.
bed·lam [bed′ləm] *n.* 1 A place or scene of noisy confusion. 2 A lunatic asylum; madhouse. ◆ This word comes from *Bedlam,* a popular name for *St. Mary of Bethlehem,* an old hospital in London for the insane.
Bed·ou·in [bed′o͞o·in] *n.* 1 One of the wandering Arabs living in the desert areas of Syria, Arabia, and northern Africa. 2 Any nomad or vagabond.
bed·pan [bed′pan′] *n.* A pan used instead of a toilet by a person confined to bed.
bed·post [ped′pōst′] *n.* An upright post at the corner of a bed.
be·drag·gled [bi·drag′əld] *adj* Wet, dirty, and messy, as though dragged through mud.
bed·rid·den [bed′rid′(ə)n] *adj.* Confined to bed for a long time by sickness or injury.
bed·rock [bed′rok′] *n.* The solid rock under the looser materials of the earth's surface.
bed·roll [bed′rōl′] *n.* Bedding or a sleeping bag rolled up for carrying, as by a camper.
bed·room [bed′ro͞om′ *or* bed′ro͝om′] *n.* A room for sleeping.
bed·side [bed′sīd′] *n.* 1 The space beside a bed, especially a sick person's bed: The patient's family remained at the *bedside* all day. 2 *adj. use:* a doctor with a cheerful *bedside* manner.
bed·sore [bed′sôr′] *n.* A sore on the skin caused by prolonged pressure at the same place. Persons who are confined to bed for a long time may get bedsores.
bed·spread [bed′spred′] *n.* A cover spread over a bed to hide the sheets or blankets.
bed·stead [bed′sted′] *n.* A framework for supporting the springs and mattress of a bed.
bed·time [bed′tīm′] *n.* Time to go to bed.
bed-wet·ting [bed′wet′ing] *n.* Involuntary urination while in bed.
bee [bē] *n.* 1 An insect with four wings, a hairy body, and usually a sting. Some bees live and work together in large groups. People raise honeybees in hives because they make honey from the nectar of flowers. 2 *U.S.* A social gathering, as of people for work or a contest: a sewing *bee.*

Bee gathering pollen

bee·bread [bē′bred′] *n.* A mixture of pollen and certain proteins stored by bees for food.
beech [bēch] *n.* 1 A tree with smooth, gray bark, dark green leaves, and small, sweet nuts that are good to eat. 2 The wood of this tree.
beech·nut [bēch′nut′] *n.* The edible, triangular nut of the beech tree.
beef [bēf] 1 *n.* The flesh of a cow, steer, or bull. 2 *n., pl.* **beeves** [bēvz] or **beefs** A full-grown cow, steer, or bull fattened for food. 3 *n., pl.* **beefs** *U.S. slang* A complaint. 4 *v. U.S. slang* To complain. **—beef up** *informal* To strengthen or reinforce: to *beef up* a team with new players. ◆ *Beef* comes from the French word *boeuf. Beef up* comes from the idea of supplying with more beef or muscle, as by giving a thin steer more to eat.
beef·steak [bēf′stāk′] *n.* A slice of beef suitable for broiling or frying.
beef·y [bē′fē] *adj.* **beef·i·er, beef·i·est** Muscular and heavy: a *beefy* arm.
bee·hive [bē′hīv′] *n.* 1 A shelter or container for a colony of honeybees, in which they live and store honey. 2 A place full of activity.
bee·keep·er [bē′kē′pər] *n.* A person who raises bees.
bee·line [bē′līn′] *n.* The shortest course from one place to another, as of a bee to its hive.
Be·el·ze·bub [bē·el′zə·bub′] *n.* The Devil.
been [bin] Past participle of BE.
beep [bēp] 1 *n.* A short sound, as made by the horn of a car. 2 *v.* To sound a horn. 3 *n.* A short, high-pitched sound coming at intervals, as in radio devices to help boats keep on course.
beep·er [bē′pər] *n.* A signaling device that makes a beeping noise, especially an electronic one used to signal the person who carries it to telephone his or her home or office.
beer [bir] *n.* 1 An alcoholic drink made from malt and hops. 2 A soft drink made from the roots or leaves of various plants, as ginger.
bees·wax [bēz′waks′] *n.* The yellow, fatty substance of which honeybees make their honeycombs. It is used in such products as polishes and cosmetics.
beet [bēt] *n.* The fleshy, edible root of a leafy plant. Red beets are used as vegetables and white beets are used to make sugar.
bee·tle[1] [bēt′(ə)l] *n.* Any of a large group of insects having biting mouth parts and two pairs of wings, of which the outside pair is hard and horny.
bee·tle[2] [bēt′(ə)l] *v.* **bee·tled, bee·tling** 1 To jut out; overhang. 2 *adj. use: beetling* brows.
bee·tle-browed [bēt′(ə)l·broud′] *adj.* 1 Having eyebrows that jut out. 2 Scowling.

Japanese beetle

beet sugar Sugar obtained from sugar beets.
beeves [bēvz] A plural of BEEF.
be·fall [bi·fôl′] *v.* **be·fell, be·fall·en, be·fall·ing** 1 To happen, as though by destiny. 2 To happen to: Some trouble had *befallen* them.
be·fit [bi·fit′] *v.* **be·fit·ted, be·fit·ting** To be suited to; be appropriate for.
be·fit·ting [bi·fit′ing] *adj.* Suitable; proper: received the guest with *befitting* courtesy. **—be·fit·ting·ly** *adv.*
be·fog [bi·fog′] *v.* **be·fogged, be·fog·ging** 1 To wrap or envelop in fog. 2 To confuse; bewilder: My mind was *befogged* from fatigue.
be·fore [bi·fôr′] 1 *prep.* In front of; ahead of: She was *before* me in line. 2 *adv.* In front; ahead: The musicians followed while the band leader strode *before.* 3 *prep.* Earlier or sooner than: *before* daybreak. 4 *adv.* Earlier; sooner: Go at noon, not *before.* 5 *adv.* In the past; previously: *Before,* things were different. 6 *conj.* Previous to the time when: They got there *before* we did. 7 *prep.* In preference to: They will go hungry *before* eating here. 8 *conj.* Rather than; sooner than: I will take the case to the highest court *before* I accept this verdict.
be·fore·hand [bi·fôr′hand′] *adv., adj.* In advance; ahead of time.
be·foul [bi·foul′] *v.* To make foul or dirty: to *befoul* the air with sooty smoke.

be·friend [bi·frend′] *v.* To act as a friend to; help: You should *befriend* the new arrivals.

be·fud·dle [bi·fud′(ə)l] *v.* **be·fud·dled, be·fud·dling** To confuse or cloud the mind of: The rapid questions *befuddled* the applicant. **—be·fud′dle·ment** *n.*

beg [beg] *v.* **begged, beg·ging** 1 To ask for as money or food as a charity, especially to live as a beggar. 2 To ask for or of earnestly; beseech: We *begged* him to keep his promise. 3 To ask for politely: I *beg* your pardon. **—beg off** To ask to be excused from. **—beg the question** To take for granted the very matter in dispute. **—go begging** To be unnoticed or unwanted.

be·gan [bi·gan′] Past tense of BEGIN.

be·get [bi·get′] *v.* **be·got** (or **be·gat:** seldom used today), **be·got·ten** or **be·got, be·get·ting** 1 To be the father of; produce. 2 To result in: Careful work *begets* excellence. **—be·get′ter** *n.*

beg·gar [beg′ər] 1 *n.* A person who asks for charity or lives by begging. 2 *n.* A poor person; pauper. 3 *v.* To make poor; impoverish. 4 *v.* To make seem inadequate or useless: The scene that met our eyes *beggars* description.

beg·gar·ly [beg′ər·lē] *adj.* Appropriate for a beggar; extremely poor; miserable.

be·gin [bi·gin′] *v.* **be·gan, be·gun, be·gin·ning** 1 To take the first step in; start: to *begin* reading a new book. 2 To come or bring into being; originate: The river *begins* in the mountains; Two chemists *began* the company.

be·gin·ner [bi·gin′ər] *n.* 1 A person who has little experience or is doing something for the first time. 2 A person who begins something.

be·gin·ning [bi·gin′ing] *n.* 1 The first or earliest part: the *beginning* of a chapter; toward the *beginning* of her career. 2 The act of starting: *Beginning* is the hardest part. 3 Source; origin.

be·gone [bi·gôn′ *or* bi·gon′] *interj.* Go away! Leave!: seldom used today.

be·gon·ia [bi·gōn′yə] *n.* A plant with large, brightly colored leaves and small waxy flowers.

be·got [bi·got′] Past tense and alternative past participle of BEGET.

be·got·ten [bi·got′(ə)n] Alternative past participle of BEGET: Jacob was *begotten* by Isaac.

be·grime [bi·grīm′] *v.* **be·grimed, be·grim·ing** To make dirty with grime; soil.

be·grudge [bi·gruj′] *v.* **be·grudged, be·grudg·ing** 1 To envy another's enjoyment or possession of: to *begrudge* a neighbor's good luck. 2 To give or grant unwillingly: I *begrudged* every second away from my work.

be·guile [bi·gīl′] *v.* **be·guiled, be·guil·ing** 1 To mislead or trick; deceive; The government was *beguiled* into trusting the traitor. 2 To pass pleasantly; while away: to *beguile* the lonely hours with good books. 3 To charm; please: The puppy's tricks *beguiled* the children.

be·gun [bi·gun′] Past participle of BEGIN.

be·half [bi·haf′] *n.* Interest, part, or defense: My lawyer will act in my *behalf.* **—in behalf of** or **on behalf of** In the interest of; representing.

be·have [bi·hāv′] *v.* **be·haved, be·hav·ing** 1 To act; conduct oneself: to *behave* a certain way. 2 To conduct oneself properly: The children *behaved* well all afternoon.

be·hav·ior [bi·hāv′yər] *n.* 1 Manner of conducting oneself; deportment. 2 The way a person or thing acts under certain conditions: to test the *behavior* of the new drug.

be·head [bi·hed′] *v.* To cut off the head of; decapitate.

be·held [bi·held′] Past tense and past participle of BEHOLD.

be·he·moth [bi·hē′məth] *n.* 1 In the Bible, a huge animal. 2 Any huge thing.

be·hest [bi·hest′] *n.* A formal command: We are here at the *behest* of the government.

be·hind [bi·hīnd′] 1 *adv.* In, at, or toward the rear: to *lag* behind. 2 *prep.* At the back of; to the rear of: Nobody sits *behind* me; Look *behind* you. 3 *adv.* To a position that is too slow or lagging: to fall *behind* in paying the rent. 4 *prep.* Later than or not up to the normal or expected time or position: The mail arrived *behind* schedule. 5 *adv.* In a former place or time: He left his keys *behind.* 6 *prep.* Backing; supporting: We're *behind* the team 100 percent. 7 *n. informal* The part of the body one sits on; rump.

be·hind·hand [bi·hīnd′hand′] *adv., adj.* 1 Behind time; late. 2 Behind in development.

be·hold [bi·hōld′] *v.* **be·held, be·hold·ing** To look at or upon; view; see: to *behold* the Promised Land.

be·hold·en [bi·hōl′dən] *adj.* Under obligation; indebted: We are *beholden* to you for your kindness.

be·hoove [bi·hōōv′] *v.* **be·hooved, be·hoov·ing** To be right or proper for; be expected of: It *behooves* all citizens to accept their responsibilities.

beige [bāzh] *n., adj.* Grayish tan.

be·ing [bē′ing] 1 Present participle of BE. 2 *n.* Existence: The company came into *being* during the war. 3 *n.* A living thing, especially a person. ◆ Avoid the expressions *being as* and *being that.* Use *since* or *because* instead.

be·jew·el [bi·jōō′əl] *v.* **be·jew·eled** or **be·jew·elled, be·jew·el·ing** or **be·jew·el·ling** To cover or ornament with jewels.

bel [bel] *n.* A unit of measure for sounds, radio signals, or the like, equal to 10 decibels.

be·la·bor [bi·lā′bər] *v.* 1 To hit hard again and again. 2 To criticize severely; scold.

be·lat·ed [bi·lā′tid] *adj.* Late, or too late: a *belated* apology. **—be·lat′ed·ly** *adv.*

be·lay [bi·lā′] *v.* **be·layed, be·lay·ing,** *interj.* 1 *v.* To secure (a rope) by winding around a pin. 2 *interj.* Stop!: used mostly by sailors.

belaying pin A metal or wooden pin fitting in a hole, used on ships for making ropes secure.

Sailor belaying a rope around a belaying pin

belch [belch] 1 *v.* To let out wind from the stomach through the mouth. 2 *n.* The act of belching. 3 *v.* To throw out violently: The furnace *belched* smoke. 4 *v.* To gush; spurt.

a	add	**i**	it	**ŏŏ**	took	**oi**	oil
ā	ace	**ī**	ice	**ōō**	pool	**ou**	pout
â	care	**o**	odd	**u**	up	**ng**	ring
ä	palm	**ō**	open	**û**	burn	**th**	thin
e	end	**ô**	order	**yōō**	fuse	**th̶**	this
ē	equal					**zh**	vision

ə = { a in *above* e in *sicken* i in *possible* / o in *melon* u in *circus* }

bel·dam or **bel·dame** [bel′dəm] *n.* An old woman, especially one who is ugly or mean.
be·lea·guer [bi·lē′gər] *v.* **1** To surround or shut in with an armed force; besiege. **2** To beset; surround: *beleaguered* with problems.
bel·fry [bel′frē] *n., pl.* **bel·fries** **1** A tower in which a bell is hung. **2** The part of a tower or steeple containing a bell. ◆ *Belfry* comes from the old French word *berfrei,* meaning *tower.* Because bells were associated with towers, and *belfrei* was easier for English-speaking people to pronounce, the word came to have its present sound and spelling.

Belfry

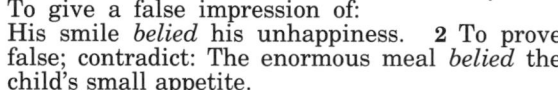

Bel·gian [bel′jən] **1** *adj.* Of or from Belgium. **2** *n.* A person born in or a citizen of Belgium.
be·lie [bi·lī′] *v.* **be·lied, be·ly·ing** **1** To give a false impression of: His smile *belied* his unhappiness. **2** To prove false; contradict: The enormous meal *belied* the child's small appetite.
be·lief [bi·lēf′] *n.* **1** Acceptance of the truth or reality of something without certain proof. **2** Something believed: to defend one's *belief* in democracy. **3** Trust or faith; confidence.
be·liev·a·ble [bi·lēv′ə·bəl] *adj.* Capable of being believed: a *believable* story.
be·lieve [bi·lēv′] *v.* **be·lieved, be·liev·ing** **1** To accept as true or real: I *believe* your story. **2** To trust as having told the truth: I *believe* you. **3** To have faith or confidence; trust: I *believe* in my doctor's ability. **4** To have religious faith. **5** To think; suppose: I *believe* he's away. **—be·liev′er** *n.*
be·like [bi·līk′] *adv.* Perhaps; probably: seldom used today.
be·lit·tle [bi·lit′(ə)l] *v.* **be·lit·tled, be·lit·tling** To make seem small or less important: Jealous people *belittle* the success of others.
Be·liz·e·an [bə·lē′zē·ən] **1** *adj.* Of or from Belize. **2** *n.* A person born in or a citizen of Belize.
bell [bel] **1** *n.* A hollow, cup-shaped metal instrument that makes a ringing sound when its side is struck by a clapper or hammer. **2** *n.* The sound of a bell. **3** *v.* To put a bell on: to *bell* a cow. **4** *n.* Anything shaped like a bell, as the flaring end of a wind instrument. **5** *v.* To take the shape of a bell. **6** *v.* The time told by the striking of a ship's bell.
bel·la·don·na [bel′ə·don′ə] *n.* **1** A poisonous plant having black berries and purple-red flowers. **2** A drug made from this plant.
bell-bot·tom [bel′bot′əm] *adj.* Flaring out at the bottom of each leg: *bell-bottom* trousers.
bell-bot·toms [bel′bot′əmz] *n.pl.* Trousers that flare out at the bottom of each leg.
bell·boy [bel′boi′] *n. U.S.* A boy or man employed to serve hotel guests, as by carrying luggage.
belle [bel] *n.* An attractive woman or girl, especially one most admired in a social group.
Bel·ler·o·phon [bə·ler′ə·fon′] *n.* In Greek myths, the rider of the winged horse, Pegasus.
belles let·tres [bel′let′rə] *n.pl.* (*used with singular verb*) Literature meant primarily to give pleasure to the reader, not to inform or teach lessons.
bell·flow·er [bel′flou′ər] *n.* A plant with bell-shaped, usually blue flowers.
bell·hop [bel′hop′] *n. informal* A bellboy.
bel·li·cose [bel′ə·kōs′] *adj.* Inclined to fight; warlike; belligerent. **—bel′li·cose·ly** *adv.* **—bel′li·cose·ness** *n.* **—bel·li·cos·i·ty** [bel′ə·kos′ə·tē] *n.*
bel·lig·er·ent [bə·lij′ər·ənt] **1** *adj.* Inclined to fight; warlike: a *belligerent* attitude. **2** *adj.* Engaged in war. **3** *n.* A person or nation engaged in warfare or fighting. **—bel·lig′er·ence** *n.* **—bel·lig′er·ent·ly** *adv.*
bell jar A bell-shaped glass container used as a cover for fragile articles, or in scientific experiments with gases and vacuums.
bel·low [bel′ō] **1** *v.* To utter a loud, hollow cry like that of a bull. **2** *n.* A loud cry or roar. **3** *v.* To cry out loudly; roar: to *bellow* orders.
bel·lows [bel′ōz] *n.pl.* (*used with singular or plural verb*) **1** An instrument that sucks in air when its sides are spread and blows it out, as to fan fires, when its sides are brought together. **2** The folding part of some cameras.

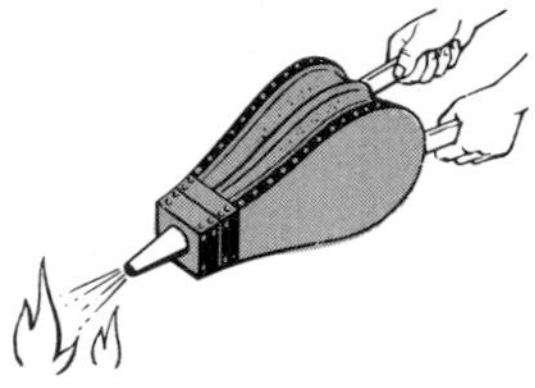
Bellows blowing into a fire

bell·weth·er [bel′weth′ər] *n.* **1** A male sheep that wears a bell around its neck and leads a flock. **2** Someone or something that leads or takes the initiative: New York, *bellwether* of the theater in the U.S. ◆ The *wether* in *bellwether* is an old word for "male sheep."
bel·ly [bel′ē] *n., pl.* **bel·lies,** *v.* **bel·lied, bel·ly·ing** **1** *n.* The part of the human body just below the ribs, containing the stomach and bowels; abdomen. **2** *n.* The under part of an animal. **3** *n.* The stomach. **4** *n.* Something that bulges out. **5** *v.* To swell out or fill, as a sail. **6** *n.* A deep, interior part: the *belly* of a ship.
bel·ly·ache [bel′ē·āk′] *n., v.* **bel·ly·ached, bel·ly·ach·ing** **1** *n.* A pain in the abdomen. **2** *v. slang* To complain whiningly; grumble.
bel·ly·band [bel′ē·band′] *n.* A strap that goes under an animal's belly as part of a harness or saddle; girth.
belly button *informal* The navel.
belly flop A dive in which the front of the body hits flat against the water surface.
bel·ly-land [bel′ē·land′] *v.* To land an airplane on its undersurface without using the landing gear. **—belly landing**
belly laugh A deep, loud laugh.
be·long [bi·lông′] *v.* To have a proper place: The clean laundry *belongs* on this shelf. **—belong to** **1** To be the property of: This book *belongs to* me. **2** To be a part of: This cup *belongs to* the new set of dishes. **3** To be a member of: to *belong to* a club.
be·long·ings [bi·lông′ingz] *n.pl.* The things a person owns; possessions.
be·lov·ed [bi·luv′id *or* bi·luvd′] **1** *adj.* Greatly loved. **2** *n.* A person who is greatly loved.
be·low [bi·lō′] **1** *adv.* In or to a lower place: During the storm at sea, the sailors went *below.* **2** *prep.* Lower than in place, amount, or degree; under: The subway runs *below* the streets; a body temperature *below* normal.
belt [belt] **1** *n.* A strap or band worn around the waist to support clothing or weapons, or as an ornament. **2** *v.* To put a belt on, or fasten with a belt. **3** *v. informal* To strike or hit, as with a belt. **4** *n.* An endless band for turning two or more

wheels, as in a machine. **5** *n.* A broad area or region: the wheat *belt.*
belt highway A highway that skirts a big city.
belt·ing [bel′ting] *n.* **1** Material for belts. **2** *informal* A beating, as with a belt; thrashing.
be·lu·ga [bə·lo͞o′gə] *n.* **1** A kind of sturgeon of the Black and Caspian seas whose eggs are eaten as caviar. **2** A small white whale of northern coastal waters.
be·moan [bi·mōn′] *v.* To moan about; lament.
be·mused [bi·myo͞ozd′] *adj.* **1** Confused; dazed. **2** Lost in thought.
bench [bench] **1** *n.* A long seat of wood, stone, or metal, with or without a back. **2** *n.* A sturdy table for doing carpentry or other work with tools. **3** *n.* The seat for a judge in a courtroom. **4** *n.* The judge or judges in a courtroom. **5** *n.* The profession of a judge. **6** *n.* The substitute players on an athletic team. **7** *v.* To remove (a player) from a game, as for poor play.
bench mark or **bench·mark** [bench′märk′] *n.* **1** A mark on a rock or other stationary object that indicates elevation and is used as a reference point in surveying and tidal observation. **2** (*usually written* **benchmark**) A standard used in making comparisons or judgments: The unemployment rate is an economic *benchmark.*
bend [bend] *v.* **bent** (or **bend·ed:** seldom used today), **bend·ing,** *n.* **1** *v.* To cause to take the form of a curve: to *bend* a wire. **2** *v.* To become curved. **3** *n.* A curve or crook: a *bend* in the road. **4** *v.* To stoop or bow: He *bent* over to tie his shoelaces. **5** *v.* To yield or make yield: I *bent* my opponent to my will. **6** *v.* To move or turn in a certain direction: to *bend* one's steps toward home. **7** *n.pl.* (**the bends**) Another name for CAISSON DISEASE.
be·neath [bi·nēth′] **1** *prep.* Under; below or directly below: *beneath* the stars; Put the coaster *beneath* the glass. **2** *adv.* In a lower place: Look *beneath.* **3** *prep.* Lower than, as in place or rank: Nobody ranks *beneath* a private. **4** *prep.* Unworthy of: That rude remark was *beneath* you.
Ben·e·dic·tine [ben′ə·dik′tin] **1** *n.* A member of a religious order founded by St. Benedict, an Italian monk. **2** *adj.* Of or having to do with St. Benedict or his order.
ben·e·dic·tion [ben′ə·dik′shən] *n.* **1** An asking of God's blessing at the end of a religious service. **2** A blessing.
ben·e·fac·tion [ben′ə·fak′shən] *n.* A kindly or generous act, especially a gift or endowment.
ben·e·fac·tor [ben′ə·fak′tər] *n.* A person who has given help or money.
ben·e·fice [ben′ə·fis] *n.* *British* A position in the church, and the income attached to it.
be·nef·i·cence [bə·nef′ə·səns] *n.* **1** The doing of good; kindness. **2** A charitable act; gift.
be·nef·i·cent [bə·nef′ə·sənt] *adj.* Bringing about or doing good; charitable.
ben·e·fi·cial [ben′ə·fish′əl] *adj.* Tending to help or benefit; useful or helpful: The treaty was *beneficial* to us because it increased our security.
ben·e·fi·ci·ar·y [ben′ə·fish′ē·er′ē *or* ben′ə·fish′ər·ē] *n., pl.* **ben·e·fi·ci·ar·ies** **1** A person who receives benefits or advantages. **2** A person entitled to receive an inheritance by a will or money from an insurance policy.
ben·e·fit [ben′ə·fit] *n., v.* **ben·e·fit·ed, ben·e·fit·ing** **1** *n.* Something that is helpful; help; advantage: Give me the *benefit* of your advice. **2** *v.* To be helpful or useful to: Schools *benefit* the entire community. **3** *v.* To receive help or benefit; profit: to *benefit* from experience. **4** *n.* A public entertainment to raise money, especially for a charitable cause: The concert was a *benefit* for the flood victims. **5** *n.* (*usually pl.*) Money, such as is paid by insurance companies or welfare agencies.
Ben·e·lux [ben′ə·luks′] *n.* The economic union of Belgium, the Netherlands, and Luxembourg.
be·nev·o·lence [bə·nev′ə·ləns] *n.* **1** The desire to do good; kindliness. **2** An act of kindness. **3** A charitable gift.
be·nev·o·lent [bə·nev′ə·lənt] *adj.* Desiring or showing the desire to do good; kindly: a *benevolent* look. **—be·nev′o·lent·ly** *adv.*
be·night·ed [bi·nī′tid] *adj.* Mentally or morally ignorant; not enlightened.
be·nign [bi·nīn′] *adj.* **1** Pleasant and friendly; kind: a *benign* smile. **2** Not seriously harmful: a *benign* tumor. **3** Favorable to health; mild: a *benign* climate. **—be·nign′ly** *adv.*
be·nig·nant [bi·nig′nənt] *adj.* **1** Kind; gracious. **2** Favorable; mild.
be·nig·ni·ty [bi·nig′nə·tē] *n., pl.* **be·nig·ni·ties** **1** Kindliness. **2** A kind action; favor.
ben·i·son [ben′ə·zən] *n.* A blessing.
Ben·ja·min [ben′jə·mən] *n.* **1** In the Bible, the youngest son of Jacob and Rachel. **2** The tribe of Israel descended from him.
bent [bent] **1** Past tense and past participle of BEND. **2** *adj.* Made crooked by bending: a *bent* nail. **3** *adj.* Set in purpose; determined: a man *bent* on success. **4** *n.* A liking or talent: She has a decided *bent* for music.
be·numb [bi·num′] *v.* To make numb; deaden.
Ben·ze·drine [ben′zi·drēn′] *n.* A drug that stimulates the central nervous system: a trademark.
ben·zene [ben′zēn′ *or* ben·zēn′] *n.* A colorless liquid compound of carbon and hydrogen, derived from petroleum and used in making other chemicals or as a solvent or fuel.
ben·zine [ben′zēn′ *or* ben·zēn′] *n.* **1** A mixture of hydrocarbon compounds distilled from petroleum, used as a solvent and as a fuel. **2** Benzene.
ben·zo·ic acid [ben·zō′ik] An organic acid obtained from plants or synthesized and used as a food preservative and in cosmetics and medicines.
ben·zol [ben′zôl′] *n.* Benzene.
Be·o·wulf [bā′ə·wo͝olf′] *n.* The hero of the Old English epic poem *Beowulf.*
be·queath [bi·kwēth′ *or* bi·kwēth′] *v.* **1** To leave (property) to another when one dies, by means of a will. **2** To pass on; hand down: to *bequeath* a love for music to one's children.
be·quest [bi·kwest′] *n.* **1** Something bequeathed; legacy. **2** The act of bequeathing.
be·rate [bi·rāt′] *v.* **be·rat·ed, be·rat·ing** To scold sharply and severely.

a add	**i** it	**o͝o** took	**oi** oil
ā ace	**ī** ice	**o͞o** pool	**ou** pout
â care	**o** odd	**u** up	**ng** ring
ä palm	**ō** open	**û** burn	**th** thin
e end	**ô** order	**yo͞o** fuse	**th** this
ē equal			**zh** vision

ə = a in *above* e in *sicken* i in *possible* o in *melon* u in *circus*

Ber·ber [bûr′bər] 1 *adj.* Of the Berbers or their languages. 2 *n.* A member of a Muslim people living in NW Africa. 3 *n.* Any of several languages spoken by this people.

be·reave [bi·rēv′] *v.* **be·reaved** or **be·reft, be·reav·ing** To deprive, especially by death: War *bereaved* the boy of his parents.

be·reave·ment [bi·rēv′mənt] *n.* 1 A bereaved condition: lonely in their *bereavement.* 2 Loss by death, as of a relative.

be·reft [bi·reft′] 1 A past tense and past participle of BEREAVE. 2 *adj.* Deprived: refugees *bereft* of homes and property.

be·ret [bə·rā′ *or* ber′ā] *n.* A soft, flat cap without a visor, usually made of wool.

Beret

berg [bûrg] *n.* Another name for ICEBERG.

ber·i·ber·i [ber′ē·ber′ē] *n.* A disabling disease caused by lack of thiamine in the diet.

ber·ga·mot [bûr′gə·mot′] *n.* 1 A small tree whose pear-shaped fruit has a rind that yields a fragrant oil. 2 The oil extracted from the rind, widely used in perfumery.

ber·ke·li·um [bər·kē′lē·əm] *n.* A radioactive metallic element first identified when made artificially but existing in nature in very small amounts.

Bermuda shorts Shorts that reach down to just above the knees, worn by men and women.

ber·ry [ber′ē] *n., pl.* **ber·ries,** *v.* **ber·ried, ber·ry·ing** 1 *n.* A small, pulpy fruit containing many seeds, as the raspberry. 2 *v.* To gather berries. 3 *n.* Any fleshy fruit enclosed in a soft skin, as the banana.

ber·serk [bûr′sûrk *or* bər·sûrk′] *adj.* In a frenzy of wild rage: The wounded elephant was *berserk.*

berth [bûrth] 1 *n.* A space for sleeping on a ship, train, or airplane. 2 *n.* A place in which a ship may anchor or dock. 3 *v.* To put into or provide with a berth. 4 *n.* A job or position: She found a *berth* as a TV announcer. **—give a wide berth to** To keep safely out of the way of: to *give a wide berth to* a passing truck.

ber·yl [ber′əl] *n.* A mineral of great hardness. Some varieties, as the aquamarine and emerald, are used as gems.

be·ryl·li·um [bə·ril′ē·əm] *n.* A very light and brittle toxic metallic element. It is used mainly in nuclear reactors, where it is useful because neutrons and other kinds of radiation pass through it easily.

be·seech [bi·sēch′] *v.* **be·sought** or **be·seeched, be·seeching** To ask in a very serious way; beg: I *beseech* mercy of the court.

be·seem [bi·sēm′] *v.* To be suitable; be fitting: It ill *beseems* you to act like that.

be·set [bi·set′] *v.* **be·set, be·set·ting** 1 To attack on all sides: *beset* by dozens of angry wasps. 2 *adj. use: besetting* sin. 3 To hem in; surround: The ship was *beset* by fields of ice.

be·shrew [bi·shrōō′] *v.* To curse: seldom used today.

be·side [bi·sīd′] *prep.* 1 At the side of; near: a chair *beside* the desk. 2 In comparison with: These roses look poor *beside* those. 3 Away or apart from: This discussion is *beside* the point. 4 Other than; over and above: I have no money with me *beside* this. **—beside oneself** Out of one's senses, as from anger or fear.

be·sides [bi·sīdz′] 1 *adv.* In addition; as well: My friend has a scooter and a bicycle *besides.* 2 *prep.* In addition to: My friend has a bicycle *besides* a scooter. 3 *adv.* Moreover; furthermore: Fresh fruit is good to eat, and *besides* it's good for you. 4 *prep.* Other than; apart from: I care for nothing *besides* this. ◆ Don't confuse *besides* with *beside,* as in "The plane will hold 15 people, beside the two pilots." The correct word here is *besides.*

be·siege [bi·sēj′] *v.* **be·sieged, be·sieg·ing** 1 To seek to capture by surrounding and wearing down resistance: to *besiege* the castle. 2 To crowd around: to *besiege* a movie star. 3 To bother; harass: to *besiege* a teacher with questions. **—be·sieg′er** *n.*

be·smear [bi·smir′] *v.* To smear over; sully.

be·smirch [bi·smûrch′] *v.* To soil; stain.

be·som [bē′zəm] *n.* A bundle of twigs used as a broom.

be·sot·ted [bi·sot′id] *adj.* Dull or stupefied, as from being foolishly in love or drunk.

be·sought [bi·sôt′] Alternative past tense and past participle of BESEECH.

be·span·gle [bi·spang′gəl] *v.* **be·span·gled, be·span·gling** To decorate with or as with spangles.

be·spat·ter [bi·spat′ər] *v.* To cover or soil by spattering, as with mud or paint.

be·speak [bi·spēk′] *v.* **be·spoke** [bi·spōk′] or **be·spo·ken** [bi·spō′kən], **be·speak·ing** 1 To ask for or order in advance: *Bespoke* clothing is specially made to order. 2 To show or indicate, signify: The sculpture *bespeaks* a strong talent.

be·spec·ta·cled [bi·spek′tə·kəld] *adj.* Wearing eyeglasses.

be·sprin·kle [bi·spring′kəl] *v.* **be·sprin·kled, be·sprin·kling** To sprinkle widely or all over: a lawn *besprinkled* with dew.

Bes·se·mer process [bes′ə·mər] A process of making steel, in which a blast of air is forced through molten iron to burn out carbon and impurities.

best [best] 1 Superlative of GOOD, WELL. 2 *adj.* Superior to all others; most excellent: the *best* wrist watch in the store. 3 *adv.* In the most excellent way: Which watch keeps time *best?* 4 *n.* The best, whether a person, thing, or part: If this watch is the *best,* I'll buy it. 5 *adj.* Most favorable; advantageous: Noon will be the *best* time to start our trip. 6 *adj.* Most; largest: He spent the *best* part of his lunch hour reading. 7 *adv.* To the greatest degree; most completely: Who is *best* able to finish this math problem? 8 *n.* Finest condition or quality: Be at your *best.* 9 *n.* Utmost: Do your *best.* 10 *v.* To do better than; defeat. **—at best** Under the most favorable circumstances: *At best* we can't get there before two o'clock. **—get the best of** To defeat. **—make the best of** To do as well as one can in spite of: To *make the best of* a handicap.

bes·tial [bes′chəl *or* best′yəl] *adj.* Having low, animal qualities; brutal; cruel. **—bes·ti·al·i·ty** [bes′·chē·al′ə·tē *or* bes′tē·al′ə·tē] *n.*

bes·ti·ar·y [bes′chē·er′ē] *n., pl.* **bes·ti·ar·ies** A medieval collection of fables about animals.

be·stir [bi·stûr′] *v.* **be·stirred, be·stir·ring** To make (oneself) active: I *bestirred* myself and cleaned the house.

best man A friend chosen by the bridegroom to be his chief attendant at a wedding.

be·stow [bi·stō′] *v.* To present as a gift: to *bestow* money on a charity.

be·strew [bi·strōō′] *v.* **be·strewed, be·strewed** or **be·strewn, be·strew·ing** To spread at random; scatter.

be·stride [bi·strīd′] *v.* **be·strode** [bi·strōd′], **be·strid·den** [bi·strid′(ə)n], **be·strid·ing** To sit or stand with one leg on each side of; straddle: He *bestrode* his horse.

best-seller [best′sel′ər] *n.* An article in stores, especially a book, that is selling in large quantities. **—best′-sell′ing** *adj.*

bet [bet] *v.* **bet** (or **bet·ted**: seldom used today), **bet·ting,** *n.* **1** *v.* To risk or pledge (something), as on the outcome of a contest or uncertain issue: I *bet* him a dollar that my team would win. **2** *n.* The agreement made when one risks or pledges something in this way. **3** *n.* Something risked in a bet, as money: My *bet* was a nickel against a dime. **4** *n.* The person, thing, or event on which a bet is made: Which runner is the best *bet* in the 100-yard dash? **5** *v.* To say positively as in a bet: I *bet* she doesn't come.

be·ta [bā′tə *or* bē′tə] *n.* The second letter of the Greek alphabet.

be·take [bi·tāk′] *v.* **be·took, be·tak·en, be·tak·ing** To take (oneself); go: They *betook* themselves to bed.

beta particle An electron or a positron emitted from an atomic nucleus during radioative decay.

beta ray A stream of beta particles.

be·ta·tron [bā′tə·tron′] *n.* A device that uses a changing magnetic field to accelerate electrons.

be·tel [bēt′(ə)l] *n.* A pepper plant of Asia whose leaves are mixed with **betel nut,** the seed of an unrelated Asian palm tree. The mixture is chewed by SE Asians for its stimulating effect.

Be·tel·geuse [bēt′(ə)l·jo͞oz] *n.* A very bright, reddish, giant star in the constellation Orion.

bête noire [bet′nwär′] A person or thing that is particularly detested or dreaded. ◆ *Bête noire* comes directly from the French and literally means *black beast.*

be·think [bi·thingk′] *v.* **be·thought** [bi·thôt′], **be·think·ing** To cause (oneself) to think or remember.

be·tide [be·tīd′] *v.* **be·tid·ed, be·tid·ing** To happen to or befall: Woe *betide* a lawbreaker.

be·times [bi·tīmz′] *adv.* Early: We'll rise *betimes* and start out.

be·to·ken [bi·tō′kən] *v.* To be a sign of; indicate: My pale color *betokened* my troubled state.

be·took [bi·to͝ok′] Past tense of BETAKE.

be·tray [bi·trā′] *v.* **1** To aid an enemy of; be a traitor to: Benedict Arnold *betrayed* his country. **2** To fail, desert, or be unfaithful to: Never *betray* a friend. **3** To give away; disclose: to *betray* secrets. **4** To reveal without meaning to: To *betray* nervousness by stammering. **5** To indicate; show: Laugher *betrayed* their presence. **—be·tray′er** *n.*

be·tray·al [bi·trā′əl] *n.* **1** The act of betraying. **2** A being betrayed.

be·troth [bi·trō*th*′ *or* bi·trôth′] *v.* To promise in marriage: It used to be the custom for a woman's parents to *betroth* her to a man.

be·troth·al [bi·trō′*th*əl *or* bi·trôth′əl] *n.* An engagement or mutual promise to marry.

be·trothed [bi·trō*th*d′ *or* bi·trôtht′] **1** *adj.* Engaged to be married. **2** *n.* A person engaged to be married.

bet·ter[1] [bet′ər] **1** Comparative of GOOD, WELL. **2** *adj.* Superior, as in quality, excellence, usefulness, or operation: This coat is *better* than that one. **3** *adv.* In a more excellent manner: Which coat will wear *better?* **4** *n.* The better person or thing: Who is the *better* of the two runners? **5** *v.* To make better; improve: A good night's sleep *bettered* my disposition. **6** *v.* To improve on; surpass: to *better* the old record by two seconds. **7** *adj.* Larger; greater: I ate the *better* part of the cake. **8** *adj.* Improved in health: She feels *better* today. **9** *adv.* To a larger degree; more thoroughly: Pat is *better* informed than Henry. **10** *adv.* More: We spent *better* than a week traveling. **11** *n.* (*usually pl.*) One's superiors, as in ability or position: They are my *betters* in math. **—better off** In an improved condition. **—get the better of** To defeat. **—had better** Ought to; should: We *had better* leave.

bet·ter[2] [bet′ər] *n.* Another spelling of BETTOR.

bet·ter·ment [bet′ər·mənt] *n.* Improvement.

bet·tor [bet′ər] *n.* A person who bets.

be·tween [bi·twēn′] **1** *prep.* Within the time, space, range, or amount separating two things: *between* New York and Chicago; *between* the chair and the table; *between* noon and one o'clock. **2** *adv.* In a position or relation between two things: two classes with a study period *between.* **3** *prep.* Connecting: the plane *between* London and Paris. **4** *prep.* Involving: an agreement *between* nations. **5** *prep.* By the joint action of: *Between* them they finished the job. **6** *prep.* In the joint possession of: two dollars *between* them. **7** *prep.* After comparing: We must judge *between* right and wrong. **—between you and me** Confidentially. **—in between** In an intermediate position or condition. ◆ Although *between* is usually limited to two people or things and *among* is used for more than two, *between* is often used for more than two objects or persons, especially when they are considered as separate and individual: a choice *between* three candidates. *Among* suggests a group whose members are not necessarily considered individually: We lived *among* the villagers.

be·twixt [bi·twikst′] *prep.* Between: seldom used today. **—betwixt and between** Neither one thing nor the other; in a middle position.

Bev or **bev** [bev] *n., pl.* **Bev** or **bev** In physics, a unit of energy equal to one billion electron volts.

bev·a·tron [bev′ə·tron′] *n.* A machine used by physicists for accelerating atomic particles to energy levels in the billions of electron volts.

bev·el [bev′əl] *n., v.* **bev·eled** or **bev·elled, bev·el·ing** or **bev·el·ling** **1** *n.* A slanted or sloping edge, as on a mirror, chisel, or ruler. **2** *v.* To cut on a slant or angle other than a right angle: to *bevel* a printing plate.

bev·er·age [bev′rij *or* bev′ər·ij] *n.* Any drink: Milk, coffee, and water are *beverages.*

bev·y [bev′ē] *n., pl.* **bev·ies** A group or flock, as of quail.

be·wail [bi·wāl′] *v.* To express sorrow for; mourn; weep over: to *bewail* one's bad luck.

be·ware [bi·wâr′] *v.* **be·wared, be·war·ing** **1** To be

a	add	**i**	it	**o͝o**	took	**oi**	oil
ā	ace	**ī**	ice	**o͞o**	pool	**ou**	pout
â	care	**o**	odd	**u**	up	**ng**	ring
ä	palm	**ō**	open	**û**	burn	**th**	thin
e	end	**ô**	order	**yo͞o**	fuse	***th***	this
ē	equal					**zh**	vision

ə = {a in *above*, e in *sicken*, i in *possible*, o in *melon*, u in *circus*}

careful: to *beware* of the dog. 2 To be on guard against: *Beware* the ides of March.
be·wil·der [bi·wil′dər] *v.* To puzzle and confuse; baffle. **—be·wil′der·ment** *n.*
be·witch [bi·wich′] *v.* 1 To gain power over by the use of magic or a spell. 2 To attract; charm; fascinate.
bey [bā] *n.* A governor of a Turkish province during the Ottoman Empire.
be·yond [bi·yond′] 1 *prep.* On or to the far side of; farther on than: the hill *beyond* the forest. 2 *adv.* Farther on or away; at a distance: The hill lies *beyond.* 3 *prep.* Later than; past: to stay *beyond* noon. 4 *prep.* Outside the reach or scope of: *beyond* help. 5 *prep.* In an amount that surpasses: *beyond* belief. 6 *prep.* More than: *Beyond* that, we know nothing.
B.F.A. Bachelor of Fine Arts.
Bhu·ta·nese [bo͞o′tə·nēz′] *adj., n., pl.* **Bhu·ta·nese** 1 *adj.* Of or from Bhutan. 2 *n.* A person born in or a citizen of Bhutan. 3 *n.* The language of Bhutan.
bi- A prefix meaning: 1 Twice; doubly; two; having two, as in *bilingual.* 2 Once every two, as in *biennial.* 3 Twice a, as in *biannual.* ◆ *Bi-* in words like *bimonthly* may mean twice a (as month or year) but more often means once every two (months or years). *Semi-* in words like *semimonthly* always means twice a (month or year). Use *semi-* for twice a ___, and use *bi-* for once every two ___.
Bi The symbol for the element bismuth.
B.I.A. Bureau of Indian Affairs.
bi·a·ly [bē·ä′lē] *n., pl.* **bi·a·lys** A chewy, flat roll sprinkled with onion flakes.
bi·an·nu·al [bī·an′yo͞o·əl] *adj.* Occurring twice a year; semiannual. **—bi·an′nu·al·ly** *adv.* ◆ Notice that *biannual* means twice a year, four times as often as *biennial,* once every two years.
bi·as [bī′əs] *n., pl.* **bi·as·es,** *v.* **bi·ased** or **bi·assed, bi·as·ing** or **bi·as·sing** 1 *n.* A line slanting across the weave of a fabric. 2 *n.* A leaning of the mind for or against a person or thing; prejudice. 3 *v.* To prejudice: A series of lies *biased* the jury against the defendant. **—on the bias** On a slanting line across a fabric: The material is cut *on the bias.* ◆ See PREJUDICE.

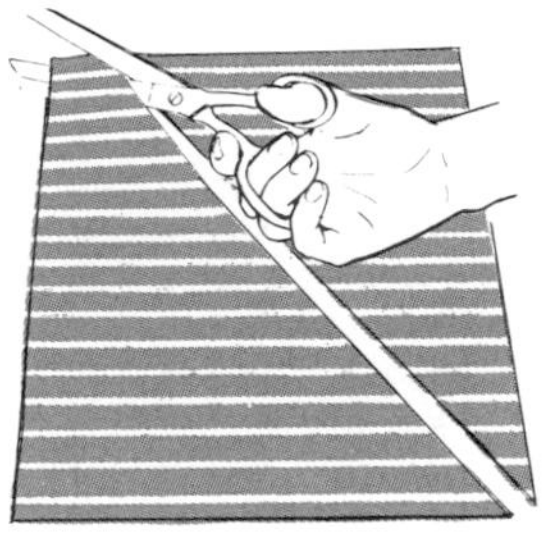
Cutting on the bias

bib [bib] *n.* 1 A cloth tied under a child's chin at meals to protect the clothing. 2 The upper front part of an apron or of overalls.

Bib

Bi·ble [bī′bəl] *n.* 1 The collection of writings which make up the Old Testament and the New Testament, held sacred in Christianity. 2 The Old Testament, held sacred in Judaism. 3 The sacred book or writings of any religion. ◆ *Bible* comes from the Greek word for *book* which came from a word for *papyrus.* The ancient Greeks wrote on a kind of paper made from papyrus. *Bibliography* comes from the same root as *Bible* plus a Greek word meaning *a writing about.*
Bib·li·cal [bib′li·kəl] *adj.* (*sometimes written* **biblical**) Of or having to do with the Bible.
bib·li·o·graph·i·cal [bib′lē·ə·graf′ə·kəl] *adj.* Of or having to do with bibliography.
bib·li·og·ra·phy [bib′lē·og′rə·fē] *n., pl.* **bib·li·og·ra·phies** 1 A list of the writings of an author, or of the writings about a certain subject. 2 The description and history of writings or books, including details, as of editions, dates, and typography. ◆ See BIBLE.
bib·li·o·phile [bib′lē·ə·fīl′] *n.* A person who loves or collects books.
bi·cam·er·al [bī·kam′ər·əl] *adj.* Consisting of two chambers, houses, or branches: The U.S. Congress is a *bicameral* legislative body made up of the Senate and the House of Representatives.
bi·car·bo·nate [bī·kär′bə·nāt′ *or* bī·kär′bə·nit] *n.* An acid carbonate, as sodium bicarbonate.
bicarbonate of soda Another name for SODIUM BICARBONATE. It is used in cooking and as a medicine.
bi·cen·ten·ni·al [bī′sen·ten′ē·əl] 1 *n.* A 200th anniversary or its celebration. 2 *adj.* Of or having to do with a 200th anniversary. 3 *adj.* Occurring once in a period of 200 years. 4 *adj.* Lasting for 200 years.
bi·ceps [bī′seps] *n., pl.* **bi·ceps** A large muscle in the front part of the arm above the elbow.
bi·chlo·ride [bī·klôr′īd] *n.* A chemical compound whose molecules contain two atoms of chlorine along with atoms of one other element.
bick·er [bik′ər] *v.* To argue in a mean way over a matter of little importance.
bi·con·cave [bī′kon·kāv′ *or* bī·kon′kāv′] *adj.* Curving inward on both sides: a *biconcave* lens.
bi·con·vex [bī′kon·veks′ *or* bī·kon′veks′] *adj.* Curving outward on both sides: a *biconvex* lens.
bi·cus·pid [bī·kus′pid] *n.* A tooth with two points on its biting surface. Adults have eight, two on each side of the upper and lower jaws.
bi·cy·cle [bī′sik·əl] *n., v.* **bi·cy·cled, bi·cy·cling** 1 *n.* A vehicle with two large wheels, one behind the other. A rider moves it by foot pedals and steers with handlebars. 2 *v.* To ride a bicycle. **—bi′cy·clist** *n.*
bid [bid] *n., v.* **bade** or **bid, bid·den** or **bid, bid·ding** 1 *n.* An offer to pay or accept a price: She made a number of *bids* at the auction. 2 *v.* To make an offer of (a price): I *bid* $20 for an antique sofa. 3 *n.* The amount offered: a $20 *bid.* 4 *v.* In some card games, to declare (the amount one proposes to win or make under specified conditions). 5 *n.* In some card games, the amount proposed. 6 *n.* An effort to obtain: The head of the council made a *bid* for the governorship. 7 *v.* To command; order: Do as I *bid* you. 8 *v.* To invite: They *bade* the guests come to dinner. 9 *v.* To tell, as a greeting or farewell: I *bid* you good night. **—bid fair** To seem likely.
bid·da·ble [bid′ə·bəl] *adj.* 1 Capable of being bid, as in a card game. 2 Eager to obey or follow; docile.
bid·der [bid′ər] *n.* A person who makes a bid, as at an auction or in a card game.
bid·ding [bid′ing] *n.* 1 Command; order: At the dentist's *bidding,* he opened his mouth. 2 Invitation: At their *bidding,* I accepted the tickets. 3 The making of a bid or bids, as at an auction or in a card game.
bide [bīd] *v.* **bid·ed** or **bode, bid·ed, bid·ing** To wait;

stay: seldom used today except in the phrase **bide one's time,** to wait for the best opportunity.
bi·en·ni·al [bī·en′ē·əl] 1 *adj.* Occurring every second year. 2 *n.* An event occurring every second year. 3 *adj.* Lasting or living for two years. 4 *n.* A plant that produces flowers and fruit in its second year, and then dies. ◆ See BIANNUAL.
bier [bir] *n.* A framework on which a corpse or coffin is placed or carried to the grave.
bi·fo·cal [bī·fō′kəl] 1 *adj.* Having one part for seeing objects close up, and one for distant objects: said of eyeglass lenses. 2 *n.* (*pl.*) A pair of eyeglasses with bifocal lenses.

Bifocals

big [big] *adj.* **big·ger, big·gest,** *adv.* 1 *adj.* Of great size or amount; large: a *big* car. 2 *adj.* Full of self-importance; pompous: a *big* talker. 3 *adv. informal* Self-importantly; pompously: They talked *big.* 4 *adj.* Important; prominent: a *big* event. 5 *adj.* Loud: a *big* voice. **—big′ness** *n.*
big·a·my [big′ə·mē] *n.* The criminal act of marrying someone while legally married to another person. **—big′a·mist** *n.*
big bang theory The theory, held by many scientists, that the beginning of the universe occurred billions of years ago with the explosion of a single dense mass of matter.
Big Dipper Seven stars in the constellation Ursa Major so situated as to resemble a dipper.
Bigfoot [big′foot] *n.* A large, hairy humanlike creature said to live in the Pacific Northwest, supposedly identified by its huge footprints.
big game Large wild animals hunted for sport, such as lions and tigers.
big·heart·ed [big′här′tid] *adj.* Generous.
big·horn [big′hôrn′] *n., pl.* **big·horns** or **big·horn** A large wild sheep of the Rocky Mountains, remarkable for its big, downward-curving horns.
bight [bīt] *n.* 1 A loop in a rope or cable. 2 A bend or curve, as in a shoreline. 3 A bay.
big·ot [big′ət] *n.* A person who has narrow-minded and intolerant attitudes, especially toward religion, politics, or race.
big·ot·ed [big′ət·id] *adj.* Having the characteristics of a bigot; narrow-minded; intolerant.
big·ot·ry [big′ə·trē] *n., pl.* **big·ot·ries** An attitude, belief, or action characteristic of a bigot.
big shot *slang* A very important or powerful person.
big time *slang* The highest level of achievement or fame: an actor who hit the *big time.*
big tree One of two California sequoias, the giant sequoia, which grows in the Sierra Nevada, often attaining a height of over 300 feet.
big·wig [big′wig′] *n. informal* A person of importance.
bike [bīk] *n., v.* **biked, bik·ing** *informal* 1 *n.* A bicycle. 2 *v.* To ride a bicycle.
bi·ki·ni [bi·kē′nē] *n., pl.* **bi·ki·nis** A very brief bathing suit.
bi·lat·er·al [bī·lat′ər·əl] *adj.* 1 Of or having two sides. 2 Arranged on opposite sides of an axis, often symmetrically. 3 Affecting two sides. **—bi·lat′er·al·ly** *adv.* **—bi·lat′er·al·ness** *n.*
bile [bīl] *n.* A bitter yellow or greenish liquid secreted by the liver. It aids digestion.
bilge [bilj] *n.* 1 A ship's bottom, inside or out. 2 The bulge of a barrel. 3 Bilge water.
bilge water Foul, dirty water that collects in the bilge of a ship.
bi·lin·gual [bī·ling′gwəl] *adj.* 1 Written or expressed in two languages. 2 Able to speak two languages: a *bilingual* person. **—bi·lin′gual·ism** *n.*
bil·ious [bil′yəs] *adj.* 1 Having or caused by trouble with the bile or liver. 2 Ill-tempered.
bilk [bilk] *v.* To cheat, especially by evading payment of money owed.
bill[1] [bil] *n.* A statement of money owed for work done or things supplied. 2 *v.* To send such a statement to: The store *billed* me for my purchases. 3 *n.* A list of items. 4 *n.* A piece of paper money: a dollar *bill.* 5 *n.* A proposed law offered to a legislative body. 6 *n.* A printed advertisement or notice. 7 *v.* To advertise by such bills. 8 *n.* The program of a theatrical performance, or the performance itself. **—fill the bill** To be what is wanted.
bill[2] [bil] 1 *n.* The horny mouth parts of a bird; beak. 2 *v.* To join beaks, as doves. **—bill and coo** To caress and speak in a loving way.

Bill

bill·board [bil′bôrd′] *n.* A large outdoor panel for notices or advertisements.
bil·let[1] [bil′it] *n.* 1 A short, thick stick, as of firewood. 2 A bar of iron or steel.
bil·let[2] [bil′it] 1 *n.* An order to lodge troops, as in private homes. 2 *n.* A lodging assigned to a person. 3 *v.* To order lodging for.
bil·let-doux [bil′ē·do͞o′] *n., pl.* **bil·lets-doux** [bil′ē·do͞oz′] A love letter.
bill·fold [bil′fōld′] *n.* A wallet or pocketbook, as for holding paper money, or papers.
bil·liards [bil′yərdz] *n.pl.* A game in which hard balls are hit by long, tapering rods called cues. Billiards is played on an oblong, cloth-covered table with cushioned edges.

Billiards

bil·lings·gate [bil′ingz·gāt′] *n.* Vulgar, abusive language. ◆ *Billingsgate* comes from the name of a London fish market where such language was used.
bil·lion [bil′yən] *n., adj.* 1 In the U.S., a thousand million, written as 1,000,000,000. 2 In Great Britain, a million million, written as 1,000,000,000,000. **—bil·lionth** [bil′yənth] *n., adj.*
bil·lion·aire [bil′yən·âr′] n. A person whose wealth is valued at a billion or more dollars, pounds, or other kind of currency.
bill of exchange A written order to pay a sum of money to a certain person.

a	add	**i**	it	**o͝o**	took	**oi**	oil
ā	ace	**ī**	ice	**o͞o**	pool	**ou**	pout
â	care	**o**	odd	**u**	up	**ng**	ring
ä	palm	**ō**	open	**û**	burn	**th**	thin
e	end	**ô**	order	**yo͞o**	fuse	**th**	this
ē	equal					**zh**	vision

ə = a in *above*, e in *sicken*, i in *possible*, o in *melon*, u in *circus*

bill of fare A list of the dishes provided at a meal; menu.
bill of goods A shipment of goods. **—sell a bill of goods** *informal* To cheat or hoodwink.
Bill of Rights The first ten amendments to the U.S. Constitution, guaranteeing certain rights to the people.
bill of sale A paper transferring ownership of something from seller to buyer.
bil·low [bil′ō] 1 *n.* A great wave or swell of the sea. 2 *n.* Anything that swells or surges like a wave: *billows* of sound. 3 *v.* To rise or roll in waves; surge; swell. **—bil′low·y** *adj.*
bil·ly [bil′ē] *n., pl.* **bil·lies** A short club, such as those carried by some police officers.
billy club A billy.
billy goat *informal* A male goat.
bi·me·tal·lic [bī′mə·tal′ik] *adj.* 1 Composed of two metals, often two metals with different rates of expansion bonded together: a *bimetallic* strip in a toaster's timing device. 2 Of, having to do with, or using bimetallism.
bi·met·al·lism [bī·met′(ə)l·iz′əm] *n.* The use of two metals, especially gold and silver, as a standard of value in a system of money.
bi·month·ly [bī·munth′lē] *adj., adv., n., pl.* **bi·month·lies** 1 *adj.* Occurring every second month. 2 *adv.* Every second month. 3 *adj.* Occurring twice a month. 4 *adv.* Twice a month. 5 *n.* A bimonthly publication. ◆ See BI-.
bin [bin] *n.* An enclosed storage space for such things as grain or coal.
bi·na·ry [bī′nər·ē] *adj.* Made up of or having to do with two parts or elements: A *binary* number system uses two as a base and therefore has two numerals, 0 and 1.
binary star Two stars that are held close to each other by gravity and revolve about a common center between them.
bin·au·ral [bī·nôr′əl] *adj.* 1 Of, for, or hearing with two ears. 2 Of, having to do with, or characterized by a system of sound transmission or reproduction in which two sources are utilized to provide a stereophonic effect.
bind [bīnd] *v.* **bound, bind·ing** 1 To tie or fasten, as with a band or cord. 2 To bandage. 3 To make stick together: gravel *bound* by tar. 4 To unite or hold together, as by love or duty. 5 To force, as by legal or moral authority: The witness is *bound* by law to testify. 6 To fasten in a cover, as a book. 7 To cover the edge of, as with tape, for strength or decoration. 8 To constipate.
bind·er [bīn′dər] *n.* 1 A person who binds books. 2 Anything used to bind or tie, as a cord, or to hold together, as cement. 3 A cover in which sheets of paper may be fastened. 4 A machine that cuts and ties grain.
bind·er·y [bīn′dər·ē] *n., pl.* **bind·er·ies** A place where books are bound.
bind·ing [bīn′ding] 1 n. The act of tying or joining. 2 *n.* Anything that binds; binder. 3 *adj.* Having the force to bind or oblige: a *binding* agreement. 4 *n.* The cover holding together and enclosing the pages of a book. 5 *n.* A strip sewed over an edge for protection.

Binding of a book

bind·weed [bīnd′wēd′] *n.* A twining plant with trumpet-shaped flowers.
binge [binj] *n. informal.* A period of unrestrained indulgence, as in eating or spending; spree.
bin·go [bing′gō] *n.* A game of chance in which players use markers to cover numbers on a card as numbers are drawn and called out.
bin·na·cle [bin′ə·kəl] *n.* A stand or case for a ship's compass, near the steering wheel.
bin·oc·u·lar [bə·nok′yə·lər] 1 *adj.* Having to do with, using, or used by both eyes at once. 2 *n. (pl.)* Two short telescopes fastened together, for seeing distant objects with both eyes. Field glasses are binoculars.

Binoculars

bi·no·mi·al [bī·nō′mē·əl] *n.* 1 In algebra, an expression made up of two terms joined by a plus or minus sign, as $a + b$ or $x - y$. 2 In biology, a name made up of two terms, one indicating the genus, the other indicating the species of some plant or animal, as *Homo sapiens,* human being.
bio- A combining form meaning: Life or living things, as in *biology.*
bi·o·chem·i·cal [bī′ō·kem′i·kəl] *adj.* Of or having to do with biochemistry. **—bi′o·chem′i·cal·ly** *adv.*
bi·o·chem·ist [bī′ō·kem′ist] *n.* A person trained in biochemistry.
bi·o·chem·is·try [bī′ō·kem′is·trē] *n.* The science that studies the chemical processes that take place in living things, plant and animal.
bi·o·de·grad·a·ble [bī′ō·di·grā′də·bəl] *adj.* Capable of being broken down into simpler or harmless substances by the action of living things, especially bacteria: *biodegradable* food containers.
bi·o·e·lec·tric·i·ty [bī′ō·i·lek′tris′ə·tē] *n.* Electricity produced by living things, such as certain eels.
bi·o·en·gi·neer·ing [bī′ō·en′jə·nir′ing] *n.* The application of engineering principles or technology to biology and medicine, as in the making of artificial organs.
bi·o·feed·back [bī′ō·fēd′bak′] *n.* A technique for learning to control involuntary body processes, as blood pressure or heartbeat, with the aid of an electronic device that monitors the processes.
bi·og·ra·pher [bī·og′rə·fər] *n.* A writer of biography.
bi·o·graph·i·cal [bī′ə·graf′i·kəl] *adj.* 1 Of or having to do with a person's life. 2 Of or having to do with biography.
bi·og·ra·phy [bī·og′rə·fē] *n., pl.* **bi·og·ra·phies** An account of a person's life.
bi·o·log·i·cal [bī′ə·loj′i·kəl] *adj.* Of or having to do with biology. **—bi′o·log′i·cal·ly** *adv.*
biological clock A timing mechanism in living things that regulates cycles, such as waking and sleeping.
biological magnification The gathering of huge amounts of a harmful substance such as DDT in a large animal. All of it in the plants and animals eaten in a food chain finally funnels into the top animal.
biological warfare The use in war of destructive organisms or poisons they produce against human beings, livestock, or crops.
bi·ol·o·gy [bī·ol′ə·jē] *n.* The science of life and of the ways in which living things grow, develop, and reproduce. Its two chief divisions are zoology and botany. **—bi·ol′o·gist** *n.* ◆ This word comes from two Greek words meaning *study of life.*
bi·o·lu·mi·nes·cence [bī′ō·lōō′mə·nes′əns] *n.* The

giving off of light by living things, such as fireflies.

bi·on·ic [bī·on′ik] *adj.* 1 Composed of or strengthened by an electronic or mechanical device: a *bionic* arm. 2 Of or having to do with bionics.

bi·on·ics [bī·on′iks] *n.* The study of the structure and function of living things in order to learn principles that can be applied to the making of machines and machine parts. ◆ See -ICS.

bi·o·phys·ics [bī′ō·fiz′iks] *n.* The study of living things and biological processes using the principles and methods of physics. **—bi′o·phys′i·cist** *n.* ◆ See -ICS.

bi·op·sy [bī′op′sē] *n., pl.* **bi·op·sies** The removal and examination of cells or tissue from a living body.

bi·o·rhythm [bī′ō·rith′əm] *n.* 1 A biological function or process that recurs according to an innate rhythm, such as menstruation in women. 2 The rhythm that determines such a function or process.

bi·o·sphere [bī′ə·sfir′] *n.* The part of the earth and its atmosphere in which life exists.

bi·o·tech·nol·o·gy [bī′ō·tek·nol′ə·jē] *n.* The study of the relationship between people and machines. It emphasizes the biological and technological requirements and problems of this relationship.

bi·ot·ic [bī·ot′ik] *adj.* Of or having to do with life or living things.

bi·o·tin [bī′ə·tin] *n.* An organic compound that is necessary for the growth of yeast organisms and for the health of some experimental animals. It is present in many plants and animal tissues; vitamin H.

bi·par·ti·san [bī·pär′tə·zən] *adj.* Of or supported by two parties: a *bipartisan* committee.

bi·par·tite [bī·pär′tīt′] *adj.* 1 Having two parts. 2 Having two parts that correspond, as for two parties who sign a contract. 3 Sides.

bi·ped [bī′ped′] *n.* An animal having two feet.

bi·plane [bī′plān′] *n.* A type of airplane having two wings, one above the other.

Biplane

birch [bûrch] 1 *n.* A tree with thin bark that may be peeled off easily. Its wood is hard and is used in making furniture and other articles. 2 *n.* A rod from this tree, used as a whip. 3 *v.* To whip with a birch rod.

bird [bûrd] *n.* 1 A warm-blooded, feathered animal with two feet and wings. 2 A rounded piece of cork with a crown of feathers, used in badminton. 3 *slang* A person, especially one who is peculiar or remarkable. ◆ In Old English, this word was pronounced [brid] and spelled *bridd;* later on people began to pronounce it [bird] and the word came to be spelled *bird.*

bird·bath [bûrd′bath′] *n.* A shallow basin of water on a stand for birds to bathe in.

bird call 1 The song or sound of a bird. 2 An imitation of this song or sound. 3 A device that imitates this song or sound.

bird dog A dog trained to hunt and retrieve game birds.

bird·ie [bûr′dē] *n.* 1 *informal* A little bird. 2 In golf, a score of one stroke under par on a hole.

bird of paradise A bird of New Guinea noted for the brilliant colors of its feathers.

bird of prey Any of various birds, as the eagle or vulture, that feed on the flesh of other animals.

bird's-eye [bûrdz′ī′] *adj.* Marked with spots like birds' eyes. 2 Seen from above or afar.

bird watcher A person who observes or identifies wild birds in their natural surroundings as a hobby.

bi·ret·ta [bi·ret′ə] *n.* A stiff, square cap worn by Roman Catholic clergymen.

birth [bûrth] *n.* 1 The coming out from its mother's body of a new person or animal. 2 Beginning; origin: the *birth* of an idea. 3 Ancestry or descent: a person of humble *birth.* **—give birth to** 1 To bear: She *gave birth to* twins. 2 To create or originate, as an idea.

birth control The control of the number and timing of the children a woman has, especially by the use of techniques to prevent conception.

birth·day [bûrth′dā′] *n.* The day of one's birth or its anniversary.

birth·mark [bûrth′märk′] *n.* A mark or spot existing on the body from birth.

birth·place [bûrth′plās′] *n.* 1 Place of a person's birth. 2 Place where something originates.

birth·rate [bûrth′rāt′] *n.* The number of births in proportion to a given number of persons in a certain area or group during a given time, commonly the number of births per thousand persons per year.

birth·right [bûrth′rīt′] *n.* A privilege or right a person has because of birth.

birth·stone [bûrth′stōn′] *n.* A jewel identified with a particular month of the year and thought to bring good luck when worn by a person whose birthday falls in that month.

bis·cuit [bis′kit] *n., pl.* **bis·cuits** or **bis·cuit** 1 A kind of bread baked in small cakes, raised with baking powder or soda. 2 The British word for a cracker.

bi·sect [bī·sekt′] *v.* To cut into two parts, especially of equal size.

bi·sec·tor [bī·sek′tər] *n.* 1 Something that bisects. 2 A line that divides an angle or a line segment into two equal parts.

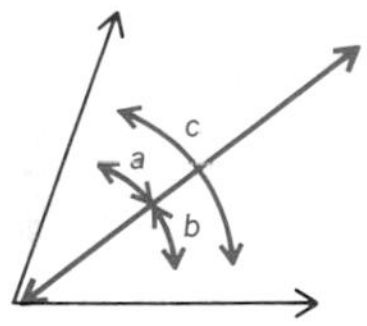

The blue line bisects the angle.

bi·sex·u·al [bī·sek′shōō·əl] *adj.* 1 Having both male and female reproductive organs, as certain plants and animals. 2 Of, for, or involving both sexes.

bish·op [bish′əp] *n.* 1 A priest or minister of high position, usually in charge of a diocese or church district. 2 A piece that moves diagonally in the game of chess.

bish·op·ric [bish′əp·rik] *n.* 1 The diocese of a bishop. 2 The position or rank of bishop.

bis·muth [biz′məth] *n.* A pinkish white, brittle metallic element. It is used in making alloys and in medicine.

a	add	**i**	it	**o͝o**	took	**oi**	oil
ā	ace	**ī**	ice	**o͞o**	pool	**ou**	pout
â	care	**o**	odd	**u**	up	**ng**	ring
ä	palm	**ō**	open	**û**	burn	**th**	thin
e	end	**ô**	order	**yo͞o**	fuse	**t͟h**	this
ē	equal					**zh**	vision

ə = { a in *above* e in *sicken* i in *possible* / o in *melon* u in *circus* }

bi·son [bī'sən *or* bī'zən] *n., pl.* **bi·son** A large wild animal related to the ox, having a big, shaggy head, short horns, and a humped back. The North American bison is called a buffalo.

Bison

bisque [bisk] *n.* A thick, creamy soup, as of puréed shellfish.

bi·state [bī'stāt'] *adj.* Of, having to do with, or involving two states.

bis·tro [bē'strō *or* bis'trō] *n., pl.* **bis·tros** 1 In Europe, a small tavern or restaurant where wine is served. 2 A small restaurant, bar, or nightclub.

bit[1] [bit] *n.* 1 A metal part of a bridle that fits in a horse's mouth, used to control its movements. 2 A tool for boring or drilling, used with a brace or drill. 3 The cutting part of a tool, as the blade of an ax. 4 That part of a key that enters a lock and moves the bolt.

bit[2] [bit] 1 *n.* A small quantity; a little: a *bit* of cake. 2 *n.* A short time: Wait a *bit.* 3 *n.* A small part, as in a play or movie. 4 *adj.* Small, unimportant; a *bit* part in a movie. 5 *n.* Twelve and one-half cents, used only in expressions like **two bits,** twenty-five cents. **—a bit** To a certain extent; somewhat: a *bit* tired.

bit[3] [bit] The past tense and a past participle of BITE.

bit[4] [bit] *n.* The smallest unit of information a computer can use for processing; either of the binary digits 0 and 1. ◆ *Bit* comes from *b(inary) (dig)it.*

bitch [bich] *n.* A female dog, fox, coyote, or other related animal.

bite [bīt] *v.* **bit** [bit], **bit·ten** or **bit, bit·ing,** *n.* 1 *v.* To seize, cut, or wound with the teeth: *Bite* the orange; The dog *bites.* 2 *n.* The act of biting. 3 *n.* A wound inflicted by biting. 4 *v.* To sting, or have the effect of stinging: Mustard *bites* the tongue. 5 *n.* A painful sensation; sting: mosquito *bites.* 6 *v.* To take firm hold of; grip: The anchor *bit* the ground. 7 *v.* To take a bait, as fish. 8 *n.* A small bit of food; mouthful. 9 *n.* A light meal; snack. **—bit the hand that feeds one** To mistreat or injure someone who has been kind.

bite·wing [bīt'wing'] *n.* In dentistry, an X-ray film plate with a flap that the patient bites to hold it in place.

bit·ing [bī'ting] *adj.* 1 Sharp; stinging: *biting* weather. 2 Sarcastic. **—bit'ing·ly** *adv.*

bit·ten [bit'(ə)n] Past participle of BITE.

bit·ter [bit'ər] *adj.* 1 Having a sharp, disagreeable taste. 2 Difficult to accept or bear: the *bitter* truth. 3 Painful to body or mind: a *bitter* wind. 4 Feeling, showing, or caused by intense dislike: a *bitter* enemy; a *bitter* argument. 5 Stinging; sharp: *bitter* criticism. 6 Resentful, as because of a disappointment: *bitter* about not getting a raise. **—bit'ter·ly** *adv.* **—bit'ter·ness** *n.*

bit·tern [bit'ərn] *n.* A long-legged bird related to the heron. It lives in marshy places and has a harsh, deep cry.

bit·ter·root [bit'ər·rōōt' *or* bit'ər·rōōt'] *n.* A succulent plant of the Rocky Mountain region that has an edible root and showy, pink or white flowers.

bit·ters [bit'ərz] *n.pl.* A bitter, usually alcoholic liquid made by steeping plant parts, used to flavor drinks and as a tonic.

bit·ter·sweet [bit'ər·swēt'] 1 *n.* A poisonous plant with purple flowers and red berries whose taste is first bitter, then sweet. 2 *n.* A vine with green flowers and orange seedcases that open to show red seeds. 3 *adj.* Bitter and sweet. 4 *adj.* Pleasant and unpleasant.

bi·tu·men [bi·t(y)ōō'mən] *n.* Any of various mixtures of hydrocarbons, as naphtha, tar, or asphalt.

bi·tu·mi·nous coal [bi·t(y)ōō'mə·nəs] A soft coal containing bitumen but low in carbon. It burns with a yellow flame and much smoke.

bi·va·lent [bī·vā'lənt] *adj.* Having a valence of two.

bi·valve [bī'valv'] *n.* A mollusk having a soft body enclosed in two half shells hinged to open and close like doors. Clams are bivalves.

biv·ou·ac [biv'ōō·ak *or* biv'wak] *n., v.* **biv·ou·acked, biv·ou·ack·ing** 1 *n.* A temporary camp, usually without shelter, especially for soldiers. 2 *v.* To camp out in a bivouac.

bi·week·ly [bī·wēk'lē] *adj., adv., n., pl.* **bi·week·lies** 1 *adj.* Occurring once every two weeks. 2 *adv.* Once in two weeks. 3 *adj., adv.* Semiweekly. 4 *n.* A biweekly publication. ◆ See BI-.

bi·zarre [bi·zär'] *adj.* Very different from the usual style or manner; odd; fantastic.

bk. 1 bank. 2 book.

Bk The symbol for the element berkelium.

bkg. banking.

bkgd. background.

bl. 1 bale(s). 2 barrel(s). 3 black.

blab [blab] *v.* **blabbed, blab·bing** 1 To give away by talking too freely: to *blab* secrets. 2 To go on and on talking foolishly.

blab·ber [blab'ər] 1 *v.* To chatter foolishly; babble. 2 *n.* Foolish talk; babble. 3 *n.* A person who blabbers.

blab·ber·mouth [blab'ər·mouth'] *n., pl.* **blab·ber·mouths** [blab'ər·mouthz'] A person who talks too much or gives away secrets.

black [blak] 1 *n.* The opposite of white; the darkest of all colors. Black is the color of the printing on this page. 2 *adj.* Having the color black. 3 *adj.* Without light; in total darkness. 4 *v.* To make black; blacken. 5 *adj.* Gloomy; dismal: a *black* future. 6 *adj.* Angry; threatening: *black* looks. 7 *adj.* Evil; wicked: a *black* heart. 8 *v.* To put on blacking. **—black out** 1 To lose vision or consciousness temporarily. 2 To put out or cover all lights. **—black'ish** *adj.* **—black'ness** *n.*

Black [blak] 1 *n.* (*also written* **black**) A member of an ethnic division of human beings indigenous to Africa and now widespread; Negro. 2 *n.* Those desirable traits or qualities thought of as characteristic of Blacks or of their culture: *Black* is beautiful. 3 *adj.* (*usually written* **black**) Of, being, or having to do with a Black or Blacks: *black* history: Newark's *black* Mayor; Liberia is a *black* republic.

black-and-blue [blak'ən·blōō'] *adj.* Discolored by a bruise.

black·ball [blak'bôl'] 1 *v.* To vote against, especially to vote to keep out, as from a club. 2 *n.* A vote against; formerly, a small black ball placed in a ballot box to indicate such a vote.

black belt 1 The rank of expert awarded in an art of self-defense, as karate or judo. 2 The black sash or belt that is the symbol of such a rank. 3 A person having such a rank.

black·ber·ry [blak'ber'ē] *n., pl.* **black·ber·ries** 1 The small, edible, black or dark purple fruit of certain prickly shrubs. 2 Any of the shrubs producing it.

black·bird [blak′bûrd′] *n.* **1** A common European thrush, the male of which is black with a yellow bill. **2** Any of several North American birds that have black or dark feathers.

Blackbird

black·board [blak′bôrd′] *n.* A dark surface for drawing and writing on with chalk.

black·bod·y [blak′bod′ē] *n., pl.* **black·bod·ies** A hypothetical body or surface that can completely absorb all radiation that falls on it and reflect none. At any given absolute temperature, a blackbody is a theoretically perfect emitter of radiation.

black·damp [blak′damp′] *n.* A gas low in oxygen, a mixture of carbon dioxide and nitrogen, found in mines after fires or explosions.

Black Death A very destructive plague that was widespread in Europe and Asia during the 14th century.

black·en [blak′ən] *v.* **1** To make or become black or dark. **2** To hurt by evil talk or gossip.

black eye The flesh around an eye discolored by a bruise.

black-eyed pea [blak′īd′] Another name for COWPEA. (def. 2).

black-eyed Su·san [blak′īd′ so͞o′z(ə)n] A North American plant that has yellow flowers with dark centers. It resembles the daisy.

black·face [blak′fās′] *n.* Makeup worn by entertainers disguised as Blacks, especially in a minstrel show.

black flag Another name for JOLLY ROGER.

Black·foot [blak′fo͝ot′] *n., pl.* **Black·feet** [blak′fēt′] or **Black·foot** **1** A tribe of North American Indians once living on the Great Plains, now in Montana, Alberta, and Saskatchewan. **2** A member of this tribe. **3** The language of this tribe.

black·guard [blag′ərd *or* blag′ärd] *n.* A person who has no principles; scoundrel; villain.

black·head [blak′hed′] *n.* A small piece of dried, fatty matter clogging a pore of the skin.

black hole A star that has contracted under its own gravitation and become so dense that nothing, not even light, can escape its gravitational field. Black holes have not yet been proved conclusively to exist, but there is strong evidence that they do.

black·ing [blak′ing] *n.* A polish used to blacken or shine such items as shoes or stoves.

black·jack [blak′jak′] **1** *n.* A very short club with a flexible handle, used as a weapon. **2** *v.* To strike with a blackjack. **3** *n.* A large drinking cup. **4** *n.* A card game in which players try to get cards with a value under 22 and closer to 21 than the dealer's.

black·list [blak′list′] **1** *n.* A list of persons or organizations regarded as bad or dangerous. **2** *v.* To place on a blacklist.

black lung A disease of miners caused by breathing in coal dust over a long period.

black magic Magic that has an evil purpose.

black·mail [blak′māl′] **1** *v.* To get money or a service from, by threatening to tell something damaging. **2** *n.* The act of threatening for this purpose. **3** *n.* The money or service demanded: to pay *blackmail*. **—black′mail′er** *n.*

black mark A sign of something shameful or adverse on a person's record; demerit.

black market Illegal trade that violates regulations such as rationing or price controls.

Black Muslim A member of a group of black Americans that believes in the religious and ethical principles of Islam and supports a separate, independent black community.

black·out [blak′out′] *n.* **1** The putting out or covering of all lights, especially during an air raid. **2** Temporary unconsciousness, blindness, or failure of memory. **3** A ban, as on news.

black sheep A person regarded as a disgrace by his or her family or group: the *black sheep* of an illustrious family.

black·smith [blak′smith′] *n.* **1** A person who works with iron by heating it in a forge and then hammering it into shape. **2** A person who makes, fits, and puts on horseshoes.

Blacksmith

black·snake [blak′snāk′] *n.* **1** A harmless, dark-colored snake of the eastern U.S. **2** A heavy whip of braided leather or rawhide.

black studies The study of the history and culture of Afro-Americans.

black·thorn [blak′thôrn′] *n.* **1** A thorny European shrub having white flowers and a small fruit that looks like a plum and is called a sloe. **2** A cane made from its wood.

black·top [blak′top′] *n.* **1** Asphalt or a similar black material used to pave roads and driveways. **2** A surface paved with blacktop.

black widow A poisonous female spider, black with red markings on her belly, so named because she has the habit of eating her mate.

blad·der [blad′ər] *n.* **1** A baglike organ in the body that collects urine from the kidneys. **2** A bag, usually of rubber, that fits inside a ball, as a football or basketball, and holds the air.

blade [blād] *n.* **1** The flat, sharp-edged part of a tool such as a knife, hoe, saw, or saber. **2** The thin, flat part of something: the *blade* of an oar. **3** The leaf of grasses or grains. **4** A sword. **5** A dashing young man. **6** The broad, flat part of a leaf or petal.

blam·a·ble [blā′mə·bəl] *adj.* Deserving blame; blameworthy. **—blam′a·bly** *adv.*

blame [blām] *v.* **blamed, blam·ing,** *n.* **1** *v.* To hold responsible; accuse: I *blame* you for this mistake. **2** *n.* Responsibility: You deserve the *blame* for this mistake. **3** *v.* To find fault with: Don't *blame* me if your plan fails. **4** *n.* The act of finding fault. **—be to blame** To deserve to be criticized.

blame·less [blām′lis] *adj.* Not deserving blame; innocent. **—blame′less·ly** *adv.*

a	add	**i**	it	**o͝o**	took	**oi**	oil
ā	ace	**ī**	ice	**o͞o**	pool	**ou**	pout
â	care	**o**	odd	**u**	up	**ng**	ring
ä	palm	**ō**	open	**û**	burn	**th**	thin
e	end	**ô**	order	**yo͞o**	fuse	**th**	this
ē	equal					**zh**	vision

ə = a in *above* e in *sicken* i in *possible* / o in *melon* u in *circus*

blame·wor·thy [blām′wûr′thē] *adj.* Deserving of blame; at fault.
blanch [blanch] *v.* **1** To remove the color from; bleach: to *blanch* linen. **2** To turn pale. **3** To remove the skin of by scalding.
bland [bland] *adj.* **1** Gentle and pleasant: a *bland* smile. **2** Not irritating; soothing; mild: a *bland* diet. **—bland′ly** *adv.* **—bland′ness** *n.*
blan·dish [blan′dish] *v.* To urge with flattery or charm; coax.
blan·dish·ment [blan′dish·mənt] *n.* Flattering speech or action; coaxing.
blank [blangk] **1** *adj.* Free from writing or printing: a *blank* page. **2** *adj.* Not completed or filled out: a *blank* check. **3** *n.* A space left empty in a printed form, to be filled in. **4** *n.* A paper or form with such spaces. **5** *adj.* Without expression; vacant: a *blank* stare. **6** *adj.* Without variety or interest: a *blank* prospect. **7** *adj.* Empty or void: a *blank* mind. **8** *n.* An empty space; void. **9** *n.* A cartridge loaded with powder but not having a bullet. **—blank′ly** *adv.* **—blank′ness** *n.*

An application blank

blank check **1** A signed check with the amount left blank. **2** Freedom to spend or act as one thinks best.
blan·ket [blang′kit] **1** *n.* A large piece of soft, warm cloth, mainly used as a covering in bed. **2** *n.* Anything that covers, conceals, or protects: a *blanket* of fog. **3** *v.* To cover with or as if with a blanket: Snow *blanketed* the city. **4** *adj.* Covering many things: to issue a *blanket* order.
blank verse Poetry that is not rhymed, each line having five iambic feet.
blare [blâr] *v.* **blared, blar·ing,** *n.* **1** *v.* To sound loudly, as a trumpet. **2** *n.* A loud, brassy sound: the *blare* of a trumpet. **3** *v.* To speak loudly.
blar·ney [blär′nē] *n., v.* **blar·neyed, blar·ney·ing** **1** *n.* Flattery. **2** *v.* To coax or wheedle. ◆ This word comes from *Blarney Stone,* a stone in a castle in Blarney, Ireland. Legend has it that people who kiss the stone gain skill in flattery.
bla·sé [blä·zā′ *or* blä′zā] *adj.* Wearied or bored, as from too much pleasure.
blas·pheme [blas·fēm′] *v.* **blas·phemed, blas·phem·ing** To speak with a lack of respect for (God or sacred things). **—blas·phem′er** *n.*
blas·phe·mous [blas′fə·məs] *adj.* Showing lack of respect for God or sacred things.
blas·phe·my [blas′fə·mē] *n., pl.* **blas·phe·mies** Words or actions showing a lack of respect for God or sacred things.
blast [blast] **1** *n.* A strong wind or sudden rush of air. **2** *n.* A strong current, as of air or steam, as in a furnace or from a tool for grinding or cleaning. **3** *n.* A loud, sudden sound, as of a trumpet. **4** *n.* An explosion, as of dynamite. **5** *n.* The charge of dynamite or other explosive used. **6** *v.* To blow up or blow apart with an explosive. **7** *v.* To cause to wither or shrivel; blight; ruin: Age *blasted* their hopes. **—at full blast** In full operation or at top speed. **—blast off** To take off by means of a rocket.
blast furnace A furnace for separating iron from its ores, in which blasts of air blown through the fuel from the bottom make a very high heat.
blas·to·coel or **blas·to·coele** [blas′tə·sēl′] *n.* The cavity of a blastula.
blas·to·derm [blas′tə·dûrm′] *n.* The layer of cells that forms the wall of a blastula.
blast-off [blast′ôf′] *n.* The launching of a rocket-propelled spacecraft or missile.
blas·tu·la [blas′chə·lə] *n., pl.* **blas·tu·las** or **blas·tu·lae** [blas′chə·lē′] A very young animal embryo in a form consisting of a single layer of cells around a hollow center. ◆ *Blastula* comes through Latin from the Greek word *blastos,* meaning *bud.*
bla·tant [blā′tənt] *adj.* **1** Loud or noisy in an offensive way. **2** Impossible to overlook: *blatant* stupidity. **—bla′tant·ly** *adv.*
blaze[1] [blāz] *n., v.* **blazed, blaz·ing** **1** *n.* A bright, glowing flame; fire. **2** *v.* To burn with a bright, glowing flame. **3** *n.* A sudden outburst: a *blaze* of anger. **4** *v.* To burn, as with feeling: Her eyes *blazed.* **5** *n.* Brightness; glow: the *blaze* of many lights. **6** *v.* To shine; glow: The painting *blazed* with color.
blaze[2] [blāz] *n., v.* **blazed, blaz·ing** **1** *n.* A white spot on the face of a horse or other animal. **2** *n.* A mark chipped on a tree to indicate a trail. **3** *v.* To make such a mark. **4** *v.* To indicate, as a trail, by such marks.
blaze[3] [blāz] *v.* **blazed, blaz·ing** To make known: It was *blazed* on billboards everywhere.
blaz·er [blā′zər] *n.* A light sport jacket in solid colors or bright stripes.
bla·zon [blā′zən] **1** *v.* To display publicly; proclaim: A sign *blazoned* the names of the actors. **2** *v.* To describe or picture (a coat of arms) in its proper form. **3** *n.* A coat of arms.
bldg. building.
bleach [blēch] **1** *v.* To make or become colorless or white by the use of chemicals or by the sun's action. **2** *n.* A fluid or powder used for bleaching.
bleach·ers [blē′chərz] *n.pl.* A section of seats, usually without a roof, for spectators at outdoor sports events.

Bleachers

bleak [blēk] *adj.* **1** Exposed to wind and weather; bare: *bleak* hills. **2** Cold; harsh; raw: *bleak* weather. **3** Gloomy; dismal: a *bleak* future. **—bleak′ly** *adv.* **—bleak′ness** *n.*
blear [blir] **1** *v.* To make dim by or as if by tears; blur. **2** *adj.* Blurred; bleary.
blear·y [blir′ē] *adj.* **blear·i·er, blear·i·est** **1** Made dim by or as if by tears: *bleary* eyes. **2** Blurred; dimmed; indistinct: *bleary* images.
bleat [blēt] **1** *v.* To utter the cry of a sheep, goat, or calf. **2** *v.* To speak in a voice like this. **3** *n.* Such a cry or sound.
bleed [blēd] *v.* **bled** [bled], **bleed·ing** **1** To lose or shed blood. **2** To draw blood from: Doctors used to *bleed* their patients. **3** To exude sap or other fluid. **4** To feel great grief for: My heart *bleeds* for those poor children.
bleed·er [blē′dər] *n.* A person, such as a hemophiliac, who bleeds a lot even from small wounds.
blem·ish [blem′ish] **1** *n.* A mark or defect, especially of the skin. **2** *n.* A moral fault or defect. **3** *v.* To spoil or mar the perfection of.

blench [blench] *v.* To shrink back; flinch.
blend [blend] *v.* **blend·ed** (or **blent**: seldom used today), **blend·ing,** *n.* **1** *v.* To combine or mix so that the separate parts cannot be distinguished: to *blend* two colors; These six kinds of tea *blend* well. **2** *v.* To pass or shade into each other, as the sky and sea at the horizon. **3** *n.* The result of blending; mixture. **4** *v.* To harmonize: These colors *blend* well together.
blend·er [blen′dər] *n.* A person or thing that blends, especially an electrical appliance for chopping, mixing, and blending foods and drinks.
bless [bles] *v.* **blessed** or **blest, bless·ing** **1** To bring happiness or prosperity to: The Lord *bless* thee. **2** To ask God's favor for: The priest *blessed* the congregation. **3** To make holy; consecrate: This food has been *blessed.* **4** To endow: *blessed* with a great talent. **5** To glorify: *Bless* the Lord. **6** To guard; protect: used as an exclamation: *Bless* me!
bless·ed [bles′id *or* blest] *adj.* **1** Holy; sacred. **2** Blissful; happy. **—bless′ed·ness** *n.*
bless·ing [bles′ing] *n.* **1** A prayer or request for God's favor on someone or something. **2** Approval or favor: Give me your *blessing.* **3** Something that gives happiness or satisfaction: The harvest feast was a *blessing* for everyone.
blest [blest] An alternative past tense and past participle of BLESS.
blew [blo͞o] Past tense of BLOW[1].
blight [blīt] **1** *n.* Any disease that harms or destroys plants. **2** *n.* Anything that harms or destroys: Litter is a *blight* on our highways. **3** *v.* To ruin, harm, or destroy: to *blight* one's prospects of success.
blimp [blimp] *n. informal* A small dirigible whose shape is not formed by a rigid framework.
blind [blīnd] **1** *adj.* Unable to see. **2** *v.* To make blind. **3** *n.* A thing to shut out light or hinder seeing, as a shutter or window shade. **4** *adj.* Done with instruments alone: *blind* flying. **5** *adj.* Hidden: a *blind* driveway. **6** *adj.* Lacking the ability to see or know the truth: to be *blind* to a person's faults. **7** *v.* To make unable to see or know the truth about someone or something: Her clever words *blinded* him to her real intent. **8** *n.* A thing or person intended to deceive or mislead. **9** *adj.* Having no opening: a *blind* wall. **—blind′ly** *adv.* **—blind′ness** *n.*
blind alley A course of action that turns out to be fruitless or mistaken.
blind date **1** A date between two persons who have not met before. **2** Either of the two persons who take part in a blind date.
blind·er [blīn′dər] *n.* A flap, one of a pair, on the side of a horse's bridle, used to prevent the horse from looking sideways.
blind·fold [blīnd′fōld′] **1** *v.* To cover the eyes of with a cloth. **2** *adj.* Having the eyes so covered. **3** *n.* A cloth that is used to cover the eyes.
blind·man's buff [blīnd′manz′ buf′] A game in which a player who is blindfolded tries to catch and identify any one of the other players.
blind spot A small spot at the back of the eyeball where the optic nerve enters. It is insensitive to light.
blink [blingk] **1** *v.* To wink rapidly. **2** *n.* A blinking; wink. **3** *v.* To flash on and off. **4** *n.* A brief flash of light. **5** *v.* To ignore: You can't *blink* at that evidence! **—on the blink** *informal* Not working or not working right: The radio's *on the blink.*
blink·er [blingk′ər] *n.* A light that blinks, as in warning or for sending messages.
blintz [blints] *n.* A thin, rolled pancake with a filling, as of cheese or fruit.
blip [blip] *n.* One of the luminous signals recorded on a radar screen.
bliss [blis] *n.* Great happiness or joy.
bliss·ful [blis′fəl] *adj.* Full of bliss. **—bliss′ful·ly** *adv.*
blis·ter [blis′tər] **1** *n.* A small swelling on the skin full of watery matter. Blisters often result from burning or from rubbing. **2** *n.* A similar swelling on a plant, on steel, or on a painted surface. **3** *v.* To raise a blister or blisters on. **4** *v.* To develop a blister or blisters.
blis·ter·ing [blis′tər·ing] *adj.* Extremely strong or intense: *blistering* heat; *blistering* criticism.
blithe [blīth] *adj.* **1** Joyous; gay; cheerful. **2** Showing no interest or concern; heedless; indifferent. **—blithe′ly** *adv.*
blitz [blits] **1** *n.* A blitzkreig. **2** *n.* Any swift or overwhelming attack or campaign. **3** *n.* In football, a sudden rush across the line by a linebacker or defensive back. **4** *v.* To attack with a blitz.
blitz·krieg [blits′krēg′] *n.* A sudden, overwhelming military attack, especially by closely coordinated air and ground forces. ◆ This word comes from the German *Blitzkrieg,* literally meaning *lightning war.*
bliz·zard [bliz′ərd] *n.* A heavy snowstorm accompanied by strong, freezing wind.
bloat [blōt] *v.* To puff up; swell.
blob [blob] *n.* A lump or drop of soft or sticky matter: a *blob* of paint.
bloc [blok] *n.* A group, as of nations, united in promoting certain interests.
block [blok] **1** *n.* A solid piece of material, as wood or metal, usually with one or more flat surfaces. **2** *n.* A stand from which articles are sold at auction. **3** *n.* A support or form on which something is shaped or displayed: a hat *block.* **4** *v.* To shape with a block: to *block* a hat. **5** *n.* A set or section, as of tickets or seats, considered as a unit. **6** *n. U.S.* The square or rectangular area enclosed by four streets, or the buildings in this area. **7** *n. U.S.* One side of such an area. **8** *n.* An obstacle or hindrance: a road *block.* **9** *v.* To hinder or obstruct: to *block* progress. **10** *n.* A pulley or set of pulleys in a frame with a hook or the like at one end. **—block out** To plan or sketch quickly and without great detail.

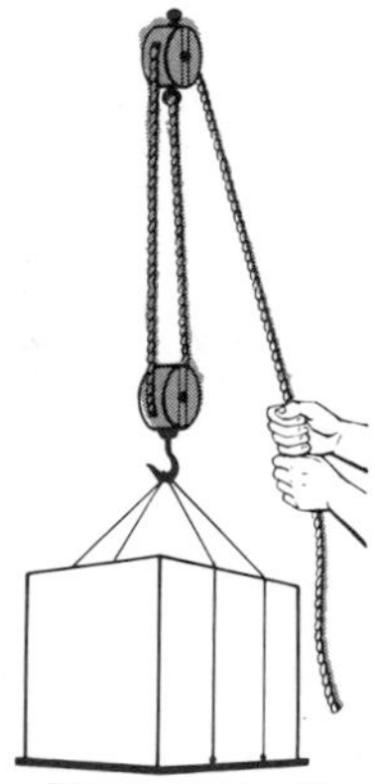
Block and tackle

a	add	**i**	it	**o͝o**	took	**oi**	oil		
ā	ace	**ī**	ice	**o͞o**	pool	**ou**	pout		
â	care	**o**	odd	**u**	up	**ng**	ring		
ä	palm	**ō**	open	**û**	burn	**th**	thin		
e	end	**ô**	order	**yo͞o**	fuse	**th**	this		
ē	equal					**zh**	vision		

ə = a in *above* e in *sicken* i in *possible* o in *melon* u in *circus*

block·ade [blo·kād′] *n., v.* **block·ad·ed, block·ad·ing** 1 *n.* The shutting off of a place, as a coast city, by enemy ships or troops. 2 *v.* To subject to a blockade. 3 *n.* Anything that hinders or obstructs. 4 *v.* To obstruct or hinder. **—run the blockade** To get through a blockade.

block and tackle A set of pulley blocks and ropes for pulling or hoisting something.

block·bust·er [blok′bus′tər] *n. informal* 1 A bomb that can destroy a large area, as a city block. 2 A person or thing that has a tremendous impact, effect, or success.

block·head [blok′hed′] *n.* A stupid person.

block·house [blok′hous′] *n.* A small fortification with loopholes to shoot from.

Blockhouse

bloke [blōk] *n. British slang* A fellow; guy.

blond or **blonde** [blond] 1 *adj.* Having light-colored hair, especially golden yellow hair, and a light skin. 2 *n.* A blond person. 3 *adj.* Light-colored: a chair of *blond* wood. **—blond′·ness** *n.* ◆ The spelling *blond* is always used for the adjective, and the noun *blond* can mean a blond person of either sex. *Blonde,* however, can only refer to a blond woman or girl.

blood [blud] *n.* 1 The dark red liquid that is pumped by the heart to every part of the body, bringing oxygen and digested food and carrying away waste materials. 2 *adj. use: blood* transfusions; a *blood* clot. 3 Descent from a common ancestor; kinship. 4 *adj. use:* a *blood* relative. 5 Temper; disposition: hot *blood.* 6 A dashing man: a young *blood.* **—in cold blood** Deliberately and without emotion: to kill *in cold blood.*

blood bank A place where human blood is stored for use in transfusions.

blood bath A massacre.

blood count 1 A medical test in which the red and white cells in a sample of a person's blood are counted. 2 The number of cells counted in such a test.

blood·cur·dling [blud′kûrd′ling] *adj.* Terrifying; horrifying.

blood·ed [blud′id] *adj.* 1 Having a certain blood, disposition, or character: often used in combination, as in *hot-blooded.* 2 Thoroughbred: *blooded* horses.

blood group One of several classes into which individuals are placed on the basis of chemical differences in the makeup of their blood.

blood·hound [blud′hound′] *n.* A large, smooth-coated hound with a keen sense of smell, often used to track escaped prisoners.

Bloodhound

blood·less [blud′lis] *adj.* 1 Without blood or with little blood; pale. 2 Without vigor; listless. 3 Without bloodshed: a short, *bloodless* revolution. **—blood′less·ly** *adv.*

blood·let·ting [blud′let′·ing] *n.* 1 The opening of a vein to let out blood. 2 Bloodshed.

blood·line [blud′līn′] A series of ancestors in a record of descent, especially of an animal.

blood·mo·bile [blud′mō·bēl′] *n.* A small, specially equipped truck used to collect blood from donors.

blood poisoning A diseased condition of the blood caused by toxins or bacteria.

blood pressure The pressure of the blood on the walls of the arteries. It varies in different people and in the same person at different times.

blood·shed [blud′shed′] *n.* The shedding of blood; killing; slaughter: the *bloodshed* of war.

blood·shot [blud′shot′] *adj.* Red, inflamed, and irritated: *bloodshot* eyes.

blood·stain [blud′stān′] *n.* A stain or spot caused by blood.

blood·stone [blud′stōn′] *n.* A green variety of quartz flecked with red, used as a gemstone.

blood·stream [blud′strēm′] *n.* The blood flowing through a living body.

blood·suck·er [blud′suk′ər] *n.* 1 A small animal, as the leech, that sucks blood. 2 *informal* A person who sponges on others.

blood test An examination and analysis of a sample of blood.

blood·thirst·y [blud′thûrs′tē] *adj.* Eager to kill or shed blood; murderous; cruel.

blood type Another name for BLOOD GROUP.

blood vessel An artery, vein, or capillary through which the blood circulates.

blood·y [blud′ē] *adj.* **blood·i·er, blood·i·est,** *v.* **blood·ied, blood·y·ing** 1 *adj.* Full of, containing, or stained with blood: a *bloody* shirt. 2 *v.* To make bloody. 3 *adj.* Involving much bloodshed: a *bloody* fight. 4 *adj.* Bloodthirsty.

bloom [blo͞om] 1 *n.* A flower; blossom. 2 *n.* The condition or time of being in flower: lilacs in *bloom.* 3 *v.* To bear flowers. 4 *v.* To spring up; appear suddenly. 5 *n.* A condition or time of freshness and vigor: the *bloom* of youth. 6 *v.* To glow with freshness or health. 7 *n.* A healthy, youthful glow, as of the cheeks. 8 *n.* A powdery coating covering some fruits and leaves.

bloom·ers [blo͞o′mərz] *n.pl.* 1 Loose, wide trousers gathered at the knee, formerly worn by women for sports. 2 An undergarment like these.

blos·som [blos′əm] 1 *n.* A flower, especially one of a plant or tree that bears edible fruit. 2 *n.* The condition or time of being in flower: cherry trees in *blossom.* 3 *v.* To bear blossoms; bloom. 4 *v.* To develop or grow.

blot [blot] *n., v.* **blot·ted, blot·ting** 1 *n.* A spot or stain, as of ink. 2 *v.* To spot or stain. 3 *v.* To dry by absorbing: to *blot* ink with a blotter. 4 *v.* To erase or do away with: to *blot* out a memory. 5 *n.* A blemish or disgrace: These slums are a *blot* on our city.

blotch [bloch] 1 *n.* A spot or mark, especially on the skin. 2 *v.* To mark or cover with blotches. 3 *v.* To become blotched. **—blotch′y** *adj.*

blot·ter [blot′ər] *n.* 1 A sheet or pad of soft thick paper used to absorb wet ink. 2 A book for keeping temporary records, especially records of arrests in a police station.

blouse [blous *or* blouz] *n.* 1 A loose outer garment, extending from the neck to the waist. 2 A U.S. Army jacket.

blow[1] [blō] *v.* **blew, blown, blow·ing,** *n.* 1 *v.* To move rather strongly or forcefully, as wind or air. 2 *v.* To send out or emit (air or another gas), as from the mouth: *Blow* your breath on the hot coals. 3 *v.* To drive or move by blowing: The wind *blew* down the telephone lines. 4 *v.* To be carried or swept by the wind: My hat *blew* off. **5** *v.* To produce or cause to produce sound by blowing or being blown: to *blow* a horn; The whistle *blew.* **6** *v.* To clear by forcing air into or through: to *blow* the nose. **7** *v.* To form by filling with air: to *blow* bubbles. **8** *n.* The act of blowing. **9** *n.* A windstorm or gale. **10** *v.* To melt or cause to melt: to *blow* a fuse. **—blow hot and cold** *informal* To be uncertain; vacillate. **—blow out** **1** To extinguish or become extinguished by blowing. **2** To burst, as a tire. **3** To melt, as a fuse, from too much current. **—blow over** To pass by or away. **—blow up** **1** To inflate. **2** To explode. **3** *informal* To lose one's temper. **4** To arise, as a storm.

blow[2] [blō] *n.* **1** A hard hit with the fist, a weapon, or the like. **2** A sudden and shocking event. **3** A sudden attack: a *blow* at the enemy. **—come to blows** To start fighting.

blow-dry [blō′drī′] *v.* **blow-dried, blow-dry·ing** To dry and often style (wet hair) with hot air blown from an electric device. **—blow′-dry′er** *n.*

blow·er [blō′ər] *n.* **1** A person or thing that blows. **2** A fan or other device for creating a current of air.

blow·fly [blō′flī′] *n., pl.* **blow·flies** Any of various flies that deposit their eggs on meat, carrion, or in animals' wounds.

blow·gun [blō′gun′] *n.* A long tube through which darts or other missiles can be blown.

blow·hard [blō′härd′] *n. slang* A braggart; boaster.

blow·hole [blō′hōl′] *n.* **1** A nostril at the top of the head of a whale and other related marine animals. **2** A hole in the ice to which seals and certain other marine animals come for air. **3** A vent for releasing air or gas.

blown [blōn] Past participle of BLOW[1].

blow·out [blō′out′] *n.* **1** A blowing out, as of a tire. **2** The melting of an electric fuse. **3** *slang* A big, lavish party.

blow·pipe [blō′pīp′] *n.* A tube used to blow a jet of air or gas into a flame to increase its heat and direct it to a point.

blow·sy [blou′zē] *adj.* **blow·si·er, blow·si·est** **1** Ruddy, coarse, and bloated in appearance. **2** Sloppy in appearance, messy.

blow·torch [blō′tôrch′] *n.* An apparatus that burns a liquid fuel and shoots out a jet of very hot flame, used in such activities as soldering or removing paint.

Blowtorch

blow·up [blō′up′] *n.* **1** An explosion. **2** An outburst of anger. **3** An enlargement of a photograph.

blow·y [blō′ē] *adj.* **blow·i·er, blow·i·est** Windy.

blow·zy [blou′zē] *adj.* **blow·si·er, blow·zi·est** Another spelling of BLOWSY.

blub·ber [blub′ər] **1** *n.* The layer of fat beneath the skin of a whale or other sea mammal, used as a source of oil. **2** *v.* To weep noisily.

bludg·eon [bluj′ən] **1** *n.* A short club, usually heavy at one end, used as a weapon. **2** *v.* To strike with or as if with a bludgeon. **3** *v.* To use force on; bully.

blue [blo͞o] *n., adj.* **blu·er, blu·est** **1** *n.* The color of the clear sky in the daytime. **2** *adj.* Having this color. **3** *n.* Any blue dye or paint. **4** *n.* Something having a blue color, as the sea or sky. **5** *adj.* Sad and melancholy. **—out of the blue** Very suddenly and unexpectedly. **—the blues** (*used with a singular or plural verb*) **1** Low spirits; melancholy. **2** A song, or songs, of a type originated by American Blacks and typically having a mournful melody, minor harmonies, and sad words.

blue·bell [blo͞o′bel′] *n.* Any of various plants with blue, bell-shaped flowers.

blue·ber·ry [blo͞o′ber′ē] *n., pl.* **blue·ber·ries** **1** A blue or black berry that is good to eat. **2** The shrub it grows on.

blue·bird [blo͞o′bûrd′] *n.* A small songbird with a blue back and wings, found in North America.

blue blood **1** Membership in a noble or aristocratic family. **2** A member of a noble or aristocratic family.

blue·bon·net [blo͞o′bon′it] *n.* A plant of Texas and adjacent regions that bears clusters of small blue flowers.

blue·bot·tle [blo͞o′bot′(ə)l] *n.* Any of various flies having large, hairy bodies of a metallic blue or greenish color.

blue cheese A sharp-tasting cheese streaked with greenish-blue mold.

blue-col·lar [blo͞o′kol′ər] *adj.* Of, having to do with, or being the class of workers whose jobs are performed in work clothes and usually involve physical or manual labor.

blue·fish [blo͞o′fish′] *n., pl.* **blue·fish** or **blue·fish·es** A blue and silver food fish common along the Atlantic coast of the U.S.

blue·grass [blo͞o′gras′] *n.* A grass with bluish-green stems, such as is found in Kentucky.

blue jay or **blue·jay** [blo͞o′jā′] *n.* A North American bird with a blue back, a crest on its head, and a noisy call.

blue jeans Pants made of blue denim or a similar cloth.

blue law A law that forbids or strictly limits sports, motion pictures, and other activities, on Sunday.

blue·print [blo͞o′print′] *n.* A photographic print, as of an architectural plan, that shows white lines on a blue background.

blue ribbon The first prize in a contest.

blue whale A whale with a gray or blue-gray back and a yellowish underside. It is the largest animal that has ever lived, growing to a length of 100 feet and a weight of over 100 tons.

bluff[1] [bluf] **1** *v.* To fool or frighten, usually by acting in a bold or confident manner. **2** *n.* The act or an instance of bluffing. **3** *n.* A person who bluffs. **—bluff′er** *n.*

bluff[2] [bluf] **1** *n.* A broad, steep bank or cliff. **2** *adj.* Having a broad, steep appearance: a *bluff* seacoast. **3** *adj.* Gruff but kindly.

blu·ing or **blue·ing** [blo͞o′ing] *n.* A blue liquid or powder added to water when rinsing clothes to keep white fabrics from turning yellow.

blu·ish [blo͞o′ish] *adj.* Somewhat blue.

a add	**i** it	**o͝o** took	**oi** oil
ā ace	**ī** ice	**o͞o** pool	**ou** pout
â care	**o** odd	**u** up	**ng** ring
ä palm	**ō** open	**û** burn	**th** thin
e end	**ô** order	**yo͞o** fuse	**th** this
ē equal			**zh** vision

ə = a in *above*, e in *sicken*, i in *possible*, o in *melon*, u in *circus*

blun·der [blun′dər] **1** *n.* A stupid mistake. **2** *v.* To make a blunder. **3** *v.* To act or move blindly, awkwardly, or stupidly; stumble.

blun·der·buss [blun′dər·bus′] *n.* A short gun with a wide muzzle for scattering shot at close range, now no longer used.

Blunderbuss

blunt [blunt] **1** *adj.* Having a dull edge or end; not sharp: a *blunt* knife. **2** *v.* To make or become blunt or dull. **3** *adj.* Extremely frank and outspoken. **—blunt′ly** *adv.* **—blunt′ness** *n.*

blur [blûr] *v.* **blurred, blur·ring,** *n.* **1** *v.* To make less clear or distinct in form or outline: to *blur* a drawing. **2** *n.* A blurred condition or appearance. **3** *v.* To smudge; smear: The manuscript was *blurred* with ink. **4** *n.* A smudge; smear. **—blur′ry** *adv.*

blurb [blûrb] *n.* A brief piece of writing used to publicize or advertise something, as on a book jacket.

blurt [blûrt] *v.* To say abruptly or without thinking.

blush [blush] **1** *v.* To become red in the face, as from embarrassment or confusion. **2** *n.* Such a reddening of the face. **3** *n.* A red or rosy tint: the first *blush* of a rose. **—at first blush** At first sight; without thinking.

blush·er [blush′ər] *n.* **1** A person who blushes. **2** A makeup that gives a rosy tint to the face.

blus·ter [blus′tər] **1** *v.* To blow with a lot of force and noise, as the wind. **2** *n.* A noisy, blustering wind. **3** *v.* To speak in a noisy, boastful, or threatening manner. **4** *n.* Noisy, boastful, or hostile talk. **—blus′ter·y** *adj.*

blvd. boulevard.

BMOC big man on campus.

bo·a [bō′ə] *n.* **1** Any of several very large, nonpoisonous, tropical snakes that kill their prey by crushing it in their coils. **2** A long scarf of feathers or fur.

boa constrictor A kind of boa found in South and Central America.

boar [bôr] *n., pl.* **boars** or **boar** **1** A male swine. **2** A wild hog.

board [bôrd] **1** *n.* A flat, thin slab of sawed wood much longer than it is wide. **2** *v.* To cover or enclose with boards: to *board* up windows. **3** *n.* A thin slab of wood or other material having a specific purpose: an ironing *board.* **4** *n.* A table set for serving food. **5** *n.* Food or meals, especially meals furnished for pay: room and *board.* **6** *v.* To give or get meals, especially for pay. **7** *v.* To enter (as a ship, train, or bus). **8** *n.* A group of people who control or direct something: a school *board.* **9** *n.* The side of a ship. **—on board** On or in a vehicle such as a ship or bus.

board·er [bôr′dər] *n.* A person who pays for meals, lodging, or both at another's house.

board foot *pl.* **board feet** A unit of measure for lumber, equal to the volume of a board one foot square and one inch thick.

boarding house or **board·ing·house** [bôr′ding·hous′] *n.* A house where board, and usually lodging, is provided for pay.

boarding school A school which furnishes board and lodging to its students for pay.

board·walk [bôrd′wôk′] *n.* A walk make of boards or planks, especially along a beach.

boast [bōst] **1** *v.* To talk in a vain or bragging manner; brag. **2** *n.* Boastful talk; bragging. **3** *v.* To take pride in having. **4** *n.* Something that a person boasts about. **—boast′er** *n.*

boast·ful [bōst′fəl] *adj.* Given to boasting or bragging. **—boast′ful·ly** *adv.*

boat [bōt] **1** *n.* A small vessel for traveling on water by oars, sails, or an engine. **2** *n. informal* A ship of any size. **3** *v.* To travel by boat. **4** *v.* To transport in a boat. **5** *n.* Something, such as a dish, resembling a small boat in shape.

boat·house [bōt′hous′] *n., pl.* **boat·houses** [bōt′·hou′zəz] A building in which boats are kept.

boat·ing [bōt′ing] *n.* The activity of sailing, rowing, and driving boats.

boat·man [bōt′mən] *n., pl.* **boat·men** [bōt′mən] A person who rents boats, or is paid to operate or take care of a boat or boats.

boat·swain [bō′sən *or* bōt′swān′] *n.* The officer of a ship who supervises the crew in the care and maintenance of the hull, rigging, and other equipment.

bob [bob] *v.* **bobbed, bob·bing,** *n.* **1** *v.* To move up and down or to and fro with short, jerky motions: to *bob* the head; The bottle *bobbed* on the waves. **2** *n.* A short, jerky motion up and down or to and fro. **3** *v.* To try to snatch with the teeth: to *bob* for apples. **4** *v.* To cut short, as hair. **5** *n.* A short haircut. **6** *n.* A small weight at the end of a line, as on a plumb line. **7** *n.* A cork or float on a fishing line.

bob·bin [bob′in] *n.* A reel or spool around which thread, yarn, or the like is wound for use in spinning, weaving, or sewing with a machine.

bob·ble [bob′(ə)l] *v.* **bob·bled, bob·bling** *informal* **1** *v.* To fumble (a ball). **2** *v.* To make an error. **3** *n.* An error.

bob·by [bob′ē] *n., pl.* **bob·bies** *British informal* A police officer.

bobby pin A metal hairpin shaped so as to clasp and hold the hair tightly.

bobby socks Thick, ribbed socks that reach just above the ankle, worn especially by teenage girls.

bob·cat [bob′kat′] *n.* A wildcat of North America. It is also called a lynx.

bob·o·link [bob′ə·lingk′] *n.* A North American songbird, named from the sound of its call.

bob·sled [bob′sled′] *n., v.* **bob·sled·ded, bob·sled·ding** **1** *n.* A long sled having two sets of runners, the front set pivoted so that the sled can be steered. **2** *v.* To ride on a bobsled.

Bobsled

bob·tail [bob′tāl′] *n.* **1** A short tail, or a tail cut short. **2** An animal, as a dog or cat, having such a tail. **3** *adj. use:* a *bobtail* cat.

bob·white [bob′(h)wīt′] *n.* A North American quail that is gray with brown and white markings, named from the sound of its call.

bode¹ [bōd] *v.* **bod·ed, bod·ing** To be an omen or sign of: Thunder *bodes* a storm. **—bode ill** To be a bad sign. **—bode well** To be a good sign.

bode² [bōd] An alternative past tense and past participle of BIDE: seldom used today.

bo·de·ga [bō·dā′gə] *n.* A small grocery store, especially in a Spanish-speaking neighborhood.

bod·ice [bod′is] *n.* **1** The upper portion of a dress. **2** An ornamental vest, held together by laces in front.

Bodice

bod·i·less [bod′i·lis] *adj.* Having no body.

bod·i·ly [bod′ə·lē] **1** *adj.* Of or having to do with the body: *bodily* needs. **2** *adv.* In the flesh; in person: to appear *bodily.* **3** *adv.* All together; as a whole: The house was moved *bodily* to another town. ◆ See PHYSICAL.

bod·kin [bod′kin] *n.* **1** A blunt needle for drawing tape through a hem or loop. **2** A stiletto: seldom used today.

bod·y [bod′ē] *n., pl.* **bod·ies** **1** The entire physical part of a person, animal, or plant. **2** The main portion of a person or animal, not including the head and limbs; the trunk. **3** The principal part of anything: the *body* of a letter. **4** A distinct mass or portion of matter: a *body* of water; a heavenly *body.* **5** Density or substance: a soup with real *body.* **6** A group or collection of people or things taken as a whole: a student *body.* **7** *informal* A person.

bod·y·guard [bod′ē·gärd′] *n.* A guard whose job is to protect a particular person from harm.

body language Body postures, movements, gestures, and facial expressions that communicate attitudes and feelings, often without the communicator intending it.

body politic The people of a nation, considered as a political unit.

body shirt A woman's close-fitting shirt that extends below the waist and snaps or is sewn closed at the crotch.

body stocking A tight-fitting one-piece garment that covers the torso and sometimes the arms, legs, and feet.

Boer [bôr] *n.* **1** A South African of Dutch descent. **2** *adj. use:* the *Boer* War, a war between the Boers and Great Britain, 1899–1902.

bog [bog *or* bôg] *n., v.* **bogged, bog·ging** **1** *n.* Wet and spongy ground, such as a marsh or swamp. **2** *v.* To sink or cause to sink in or as if in a bog: to *bog* down in difficulties. **—bog′gy** *adv.*

bo·gey [bō′gē] *n., pl.* **bo·geys** A bogy.

bo·gey·man [bŏŏg′ē·man′ *or* bō′gē·man′] *n., pl.* **bo·gey·men** [bŏŏg′ē·men′ *or* bō′gē·men′] A frightening imaginary man.

bog·gle [bog′(ə)l] *v.* **bog·gled, bog·gling** **1** To overwhelm or be overwhelmed with a feeling of amazement, fright, or helplessness: These complications *boggle* the mind; We *boggled* at the mountain of snow still to be shoveled. **2** To hesitate from doubt or disapproval: Even criminals *boggle* at certain crimes.

bo·gie [bō′gē] *n.* **1** A bogy. **2** One of the small rollers or wheels that support the weight of a tractor or tank, located inside the treads.

bo·gus [bō′gəs] *adj.* Counterfeit; fake; sham: a *bogus* ten-dollar bill.

bo·gy [bō′gē] *n., pl.* **bo·gies** Someone or something that startles or frightens, especially something imaginary, as a goblin.

Bo·he·mi·an [bō·hē′mē·ən] **1** *adj.* Of or from Bohemia. **2** *n.* A person born or living in Bohemia. **3** *n.* The Czech language of Bohemia. **4** *n.* A person, usually an artist, musician, or writer, who lives in a very free, unconventional way. **5** *adj.* Of, having to do with, or leading the life of a Bohemian. **6** *n.* A gypsy.

boil[1] [boil] **1** *v.* To heat (a liquid) until bubbles are formed within it and rise to the surface as steam or vapor. **2** *v.* To become heated so as to form bubbles in this way: At sea level water *boils* at 212° F. **3** *n.* The condition of boiling. **4** *v.* To cook or cleanse by boiling: to *boil* rice; to *boil* surgical instruments. **5** *v.* To be stirred up; be agitated: to *boil* with anger. **—boil away** To evaporate in boiling. **—boil down** **1** To reduce the bulk of by boiling. **2** To shorten; summarize.

boil[2] [boil] *n.* A red, painful swelling on the skin enclosing a hard core surrounded by pus.

boil·er [boi′lər] *n.* **1** A container in which something is boiled. **2** A tank for hot water. **3** A large tank in which hot water is converted into steam for heating or power.

boiling point The temperature at which a liquid begins to boil.

bois·ter·ous [bois′tər·əs] *adj.* **1** Noisy and wild: a *boisterous* party. **2** Stormy: *boisterous* weather. **—bois′ter·ous·ly** *adv.*

bo·la [bō′lə] *n.* A weapon consisting of a cord with heavy balls attached to its ends, used in South America to catch animals by entangling their legs.

bold [bōld] *adj.* **1** Having or requiring courage; daring: a *bold* warrior; a *bold* plan. **2** Very free or impudent in manner or character: a *bold* reply. **3** Distinct or striking, as in outline or color. **4** Steep: a *bold* cliff. **—bold′ly** *adv.* **—bold′ness** *n.*

bold·face [bōld′fās′] *n.* A printing type in which the lines have been thickened to give a very black impression, like **this.**

bole [bōl] *n.* The trunk of a tree.

bo·le·ro [bō·lâr′ō] *n., pl.* **bo·le·ros** **1** A Spanish dance usually accompanied by castanets. **2** The music for this dance. **3** A kind of short, vestlike jacket, open at the front.

Bo·liv·i·an [bə·liv′ē·ən] **1** *adj.* Of or from Bolivia. **2** *n.* A person born in or a citizen of Bolivia.

boll [bōl] *n.* The seed pod of cotton, flax, and certain other plants.

boll weevil A small grayish beetle that lays its eggs in cotton bolls, thereby causing great damage to the cotton.

bo·lo·gna [bə·lō′nē *or* bə·lō′n(y)ə] *n.* A big sausage made of pork, beef, and veal.

Bol·she·vik [bōl′shə·vik] *n.* (*often written* **bolshevik**) **1** A member of the radical wing of the socialist party in Russia that seized power late in 1917, becoming the Communist Party in 1918. **2** A member of any Communist party. **3** Loosely, any radical.

a	add	**i**	it	**ŏŏ**	took	**oi**	oil
ā	ace	**ī**	ice	**ōō**	pool	**ou**	pout
â	care	**o**	odd	**u**	up	**ng**	ring
ä	palm	**ō**	open	**û**	burn	**th**	thin
e	end	**ô**	order	**yōō**	fuse	**th̶**	this
ē	equal					**zh**	vision

ə = a in *above* e in *sicken* i in *possible* o in *melon* u in *circus*

Bol·she·vism [bōl′shə·viz′(ə)m] *n.* (*often written* **bolshevism**) The doctrine and policies of the Bolsheviks. —**Bol′she·vist** *adj., n.*
bol·ster [bōl·stər] **1** *n.* A long, narrow pillow. **2** *v.* To support, prop, or make stronger: to *bolster* up someone's courage.
bolt [bōlt] **1** *n.* A pin or rod for holding something in place. It has a head at one end and a screw thread at the other for a nut. **2** *n.* A sliding bar or rod for fastening a door. **3** *n.* The part of a lock that shoots out or withdraws when the key is turned. **4** *v.* To fasten with a bolt. **5** *n.* A short arrow which was shot from a crossbow. **6** *n.* A stroke of lightning. **7** *n.* A sudden start or spring: He made a *bolt* for the door. **8** *v.* To move, go, or spring suddenly: The horse *bolted.* **9** *v.* To break away from (a political party or its candidates). **10** *v.* To gulp down (food or a meal). **11** *n.* A roll of cloth, wallpaper, or other material. —**bolt upright** Stiff and erect: to stand *bolt upright.*

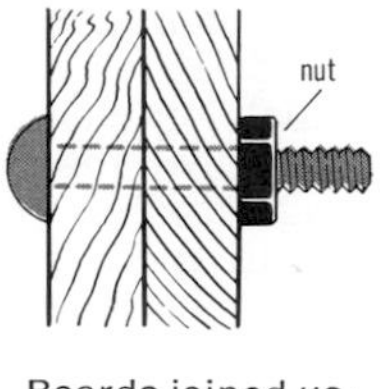

Boards joined using a bolt and nut

bomb [bom] **1** *n.* A container filled with a material that explodes or burns violently when set off, as by a time fuse. **2** *v.* To attack with a bomb or bombs. **3** *n.* A receptacle containing a liquid under pressure: an insecticide *bomb.*
bom·bard [bom·bärd′] *v.* **1** To shell or bomb. **2** To attack, as with questions or requests. **3** To subject (substances) to high-energy radiation or atomic particles. —**bom·bard′ment** *n.*
bom·bar·dier [bom′bər·dir′] *n.* The member of a bomber's crew who releases the bombs.
bom·bast [bom′bast′] *n.* Talk or writing that sounds impressive but means little; pompous language. —**bom·bas′tic** *adj.* —**bom·bas′ti·cal·ly** *adv.*
bomb bay The compartment on the underside of a bomber in which bombs are carried and from which they are dropped.
bomb·er [bom′ər] *n.* **1** A person who bombs. **2** An airplane designed to carry and drop bombs.
bomb·shell [bom′shel′] *n.* **1** A bomb (def. 1). **2** A complete surprise.
bomb·sight [bom′sīt′] *n.* A device in a bomber used in aiming bombs.
bo·na fide [bō′nə·fīd′ *or* bō′nə·fī′dē] Made, being, or acting in good faith; genuine; sincere. ◆ This expression comes directly from the Latin.
bo·nan·za [bə·nan′zə] *n.* **1** A rich deposit of ore. **2** Something that provides great wealth.
bon·bon [bon′bon′] *n.* A small sugared candy.
bond [bond] **1** *n.* Something that binds or holds together. **2** *n.* A uniting force or influence: the *bonds* of friendship. **3** *n.* In chemistry, the force that holds atoms or groups of atoms together in a molecule. **4** *n.* A written agreement to pay a sum of money at a specified time, subject to certain conditions. **5** *n.* A certificate, issued by a government or company, the purchase of which will pay for some project, job, or cause. The buyer is later paid back with interest. **6** *v.* To issue bonds on. **7** *n.* Bail. **8** *v.* To furnish bond for. **9** *n.* The way in which bricks or stones are overlapped in a building. **10** *v.* To lay (as brick or stones) in interlocking patterns for strength.
bond·age [bon′dij] *n.* Slavery; serfdom.
bond·hold·er [bond′hōl′dər] *n.* The owner of a bond or bonds issued by a government or company.
bond·man [bond′mən] *n., pl.* **bond·men** [bond′mən] A male slave or serf.
bond·ser·vant [bond′sûr′vənt] *n.* **1** A person who is bound to service without pay. **2** A slave or serf.
bonds·man [bondz′mən] *n., pl.* **bonds·men** [bondz′·mən] **1** A person who provides bail or bond for someone. **2** A bondman.
bone [bōn] *n., v.* **boned, bon·ing** **1** *n.* One of the hard pieces that form the skeleton of a person or any vertebrate animal. **2** *n.* The hard, porous material of which a bone is made. **3** *v.* To remove the bones from: to *bone* fish. **4** *n.* A substance like bone, as whalebone.
bone meal Ground or powdered bones, used as animal feed or fertilizer.
bon·er [bō′nər] *n. slang* An error; blunder.
bon·fire [bon′fīr′] *n.* A fire built outdoors.
bon·go drums [bong′gō] A pair of joined drums held between the knees and played with the hands.
bo·ni·to [bə·nē′tō] *n., pl.* **bo·ni·to** or **bo·ni·toes** A saltwater fish related to the mackerel and tuna. Its flesh is canned for eating.
bon·net [bon′it] *n.* **1** A hat covering most of the hair and held in place by ribbons tied under the chin. **2** A cap worn in Scotland by men and boys.

Bongo drums

bon·ny or **bon·nie** [bon′ē] *adj.* **bon·ni·er, bon·ni·est** **1** Good-looking, healthy, and cheerful: a *bonny* child. **2** Fine; good. ◆ This word is used in Scotland and parts of England.
bon·sai [bōn·sī′ *or* bōn′sī *or* bon′sī] *n., pl.* **bon·sai** **1** A dwarfed and shaped tree or shrub grown in a pot. **2** The Japanese art of growing such dwarfed and shaped plants. ◆ *Bonsai* comes directly from a Japanese word meaning "potted plant."

Bonnet

bo·nus [bō′nəs] *n.* Something extra given in addition to what is due or usual, as money given in addition to regular wages.
bon vo·yage [bôn vwä·yäzh′] Pleasant journey: a French expression often used as a farewell to someone going on a trip.
bon·y [bō′nē] *adj.* **bon·i·er, bon·i·est** **1** Of or like bone: a *bony* material. **2** Full of bones. **3** Having prominent bones; thin: *bony* arms.
boo [bōō] *interj., n., v.* **booed, boo·ing** **1** *interj., n.* A vocal sound made to show dislike or disapproval. **2** *v.* To shout this sound at (someone or something): to *boo* a play. **3** *interj., n.* A short sound made to frighten someone.
boob [bōōb] *n. slang* A stupid or uncultured person.
boo-boo [bōō′bōō] *n., pl.* **boo·boos** *slang* A mistake; blunder.
boo·by [bōō′bē] *n., pl.* **boo·bies** **1** A stupid person; dunce. **2** A large sea bird; gannet.
booby prize An award for the worst score or performance, as in a game or contest.
booby trap **1** Something concealed, as a bomb or mine, set to explode when some harmless-looking object to which it is attached is moved or touched. **2** Any trap for an unsuspecting person.
boo·gie-woo·gie [bŏŏg′ē·wŏŏg′ē *or* bōōg′ē·wōōg′ē] *n.* **1** A style of playing jazz on the piano in which a distinctive rhythmic and melodic pattern in the bass is repeated as an accompaniment to often

B

simple melodic variations in the treble. **2** Any music written or performed in this style.

book [bo͝ok] **1** *n.* A bound set of printed sheets of paper, usually between covers. **2** *n.* A written work of some length, such as a novel or biography, that has been or will be published as a book. **3** *n.* (*written* **Book**) The Bible. **4** *n.* A main division of a long literary work: a *book* of the Bible. **5** *n.* A volume of blank pages for entering things in writing, such as a notebook or ledger. **6** *v.* To list charges against in a police register: to *book* a suspect for robbery. **7** *v.* To arrange for beforehand, as seats or reservations. **8** *n.* Something like a book in shape, as a packet of matches or stamps. **—by the book** Strictly according to the rules. **—keep books** To keep business records or accounts. ◆ This word comes from an Old English word meaning *beech,* probably because letters and words were at one time carved on its wood.

book·bind·er [bo͝ok′bīn′dər] *n.* A person whose business is binding books.

book·case [bo͝ok′kās′] *n.* A cabinet containing shelves for books.

book club A mail-order business that periodically sells books to subscribers, who choose from a list of selections and pay a reduced rate.

book end A support to hold books upright.

book·ie [bo͝ok′ē] *n., informal* A bookmaker (def. 2).

book·ish [bo͝ok′ish] *adj.* **1** Fond of reading and studying. **2** Knowing only what can be read in books. **3** Formal or literary.

book·keep·ing [bo͝ok′kē′ping] *n.* The work or system of recording business accounts and transactions. **—book′keep′er** *n.*

book·let [bo͝ok′lit] *n.* A small book or pamphlet.

book·mak·er [bo͝ok′mā′kər] *n.* **1** A printer or binder of books. **2** A person whose business is accepting, recording, and paying off bets, as on horse races.

book·mark [bo͝ok′märk′] *n.* An object, as a ribbon, inserted in a book to mark a place.

book·mo·bile [bo͝ok′mō·bēl′] *n.* A truck equipped to serve as a traveling library.

book·plate [bo͝ok′plāt′] *n.* A label pasted in a book, identifying its owner.

book·stall [bo͝ok′stôl′] *n.* A stall, usually outdoors, where books are sold.

book·store [bo͝ok′stôr′] *n.* A store that sells books.

book·worm [bo͝ok′wûrm′] *n.* **1** A small worm that gnaws through books. **2** A person who is very fond of reading or studying.

boom[1] [bo͞om] **1** *n.* A deep, reverberating sound, as of a supersonic airplane or a cannon. **2** *v.* To make this sound. **3** *n. U.S.* A sudden increase, as in growth or prosperity. **4** *v. U.S.* To grow rapidly; flourish: The western towns *boomed.* **5** *v. U.S.* To praise or advertise vigorously.

boom[2] [bo͞om] *n.* **1** The long pole or beam of a crane or derrick from which the objects to be lifted are suspended. **2** A long pole used to hold or extend the bottom of certain sails. **3** An object, as a chain or string of logs, stretched across a body of water to keep things in or out. ◆ This word comes from the Dutch word *boom,* meaning *tree* or *beam.*

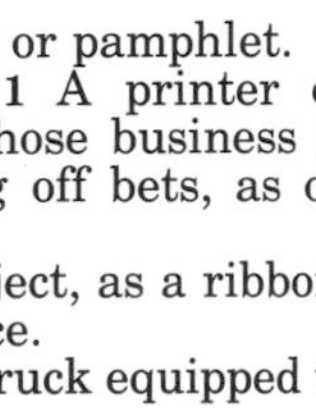

boom·e·rang [bo͞o′mə·rang′] **1** *n.* A curved wooden weapon used by the natives of Australia. Some forms of it, when thrown, will return to the thrower. **2** *n.* Something said or done against someone else which turns out to hurt the originator. **3** *v.* To return in this way: His plot *boomeranged.* ◆ This word comes from an Australian aborigine name for the weapon.

boon[1] [bo͞on] *n.* **1** A blessing: Rain is a *boon* to farmers. **2** A request: seldom used today.

boon[2] [bo͞on] *adj.* Jolly; merry: now used only in the expression **boon companion.**

boon·docks [bo͞on′doks′] *n.pl. slang* **1** A rough, densely wooded area: usually preceded by *the.* **2** Remote, rural country; the sticks: usually preceded by *the.*

boon·dog·gle [bo͞on′dog′(ə)l] *n., v.* **boon·dog·gled, boon·dog·gling** *informal* **1** *n.* An impractical or unnecessary project. **2** *v.* To work on an impractical or unnecessary project.

boon·ies [bo͞o′nēz] *n.pl.* Boondocks: usually preceded by *the.*

boor [bo͝or] *n.* A crude, ill-mannered person. **—boor′ish** *adj.* **—boor′ish·ness** *n.*

boost [bo͞ost] **1** *v.* To raise by pushing from beneath or behind. **2** *n.* A lift; help: to give someone a *boost.* **3** *v.* To give support to: to *boost* a candidate or a team. **4** *v.* To increase: to *boost* prices. **5** *n.* An increase.

boost·er [bo͞os′tər] *n.* **1** Anything used to increase or extend the force or operation of something, as an additional dose of a vaccine or serum or the first stage of a rocket which lifts and propels it in its early flight. **2** *informal* A person who gives enthusiastic support, as to a cause or an organization.

boot[1] [bo͞ot] **1** *n.* A covering, usually of leather, for the foot and part of the leg. **2** *v.* To put boots on. **3** *v.* To kick. **4** *n.* A kick. **5** *n.* A thick patch on the inside of an automobile tire.

boot[2] [bo͞ot] *n.* To benefit or avail: seldom used today. **—to boot** In addition: a turkey dinner and apple pie *to boot.*

boot·black [bo͞ot′blak′] *n.* A person whose business is shining boots and shoes.

boot camp A military camp for basic training of recruits to the navy or marines.

Bo·ö·tes [bō·ō′tēz] *n.* A northern constellation near the Big Dipper.

booth [bo͞oth] *n.* **1** A small compartment or space for privacy or keeping out sound: a voting *booth;* a telephone *booth.* **2** A place where goods are displayed or sold at an exhibition or fair.

boot·jack [bo͞ot′jak′] *n.* A V-shaped device for holding a boot while the foot is being pulled out.

boot·leg [bo͞ot′leg′] *v.* **boot·legged, boot·leg·ging** To make, sell, or transport illegally: to *bootleg* liquor. **—boot′leg′ger** *n.*

boot·less [bo͞ot′lis] *adj.* Useless; futile.

a	add	**i**	it	**o͝o**	took	**oi**	oil		
ā	ace	**ī**	ice	**o͞o**	pool	**ou**	pout		
â	care	**o**	odd	**u**	up	**ng**	ring		
ä	palm	**ō**	open	**û**	burn	**th**	thin		
e	end	**ô**	order	**yo͞o**	fuse	**th̶**	this		
ē	equal					**zh**	vision		

ə = { a in *above* e in *sicken* i in *possible*
o in *melon* u in *circus* }

boot·lick [bo͞ot′lik′] *v.* To flatter or obey slavishly in order to gain favor. **—boot′lick′er** *n.*
boo·ty [bo͞o′tē] *n., pl.* **boo·ties** 1 Goods taken from an enemy in war. 2 Goods taken by violence or robbery. 3 Any prize or gain.
booze [bo͞oz] *n. informal* Alcoholic drink. ◆ This word was probably taken from an old Dutch word meaning *to drink.*
bop [bop] *v.* **bopped, bop·ping,** *n. informal* 1 *v.* To hit sharply. 2 *n.* A sharp blow.
bo·rax [bôr′aks] *n.* A white crystalline mineral, used in cleaning and making glass.
Bor·deaux [bôr·dō′] *n., pl.* **Bor·deaux** [bôr·dōz′] A red or white wine from the Bordeaux region of sw France.
bor·der [bôr′dər] 1 *n.* A margin or edge. 2 *v.* To put a border on: to *border* a handkerchief. 3 *n.* The boundary line dividing one country or state from another. 4 *v.* To lie along the border of; bound: The park *borders* the lake. **—border on** or **border upon** 1 To be next to. 2 To come close to being.
bor·der·land [bôr′dər·land′] *n.* 1 Land on or near the border of two adjoining countries. 2 A vague or uncertain area or condition.
bor·der·line [bôr′dər·līn′] 1 *n.* The boundary line between two countries or states; border. 2 *adj.* On a border: a *borderline* village. 3 *adj.* Hard to classify or rank; uncertain; doubtful: a *borderline* case.
bore[1] [bôr] *v.* **bored, bor·ing,** *n.* 1 *v.* To make a hole in or through, as with a drill. 2 *v.* To make (a hole or tunnel) by or as if by drilling. 3 *n.* A hole made by boring. 4 *n.* The hollow space inside a tube or pipe, such as a gun barrel. 5 *n.* The inside diameter of a tube.
bore[2] [bôr] *v.* **bored, bor·ing,** *n.* 1 *v.* To make weary, as by being dull or tedious: This book *bores* me. 2 *n.* A boring person or thing.
bore[3] [bôr] The past tense of BEAR[1].
bore[4] [bôr] *n.* A very high wave caused by the rush of an incoming tide.
Bo·re·as [bôr′ē·əs] *n.* In Greek myths, the north wind.
bore·dom [bôr′dəm] *n.* The condition of being bored by something dull or tiresome.
bor·er [bôr′ər] *n.* 1 A tool used for boring, such as an auger or bit. 2 A beetle, moth, or worm that burrows in plants, wood, and other materials.
bo·ric acid [bôr′ik] A white, crystalline compound of hydrogen, boron, and oxygen. It is poisonous and slightly antiseptic.
born [bôrn] 1 An alternative past participle of BEAR[1] meaning *given birth to:* a lamb *born* in May. 2 *adj.* Brought forth or into being: A nation was *born.* 3 *adj.* Natural; by birth: a *born* painter.
born-a·gain [bôrn′ə·gen′] *adj.* 1 Having experienced a birth or awakening of faith in Jesus Christ as one's personal savior. 2 Evangelical (def. 2). 3 Having or characterized by a strong, renewed interest or commitment: a *born-again* political worker.
borne [bôrn] Past participle of BEAR[1]: The large crate was *borne* by two assistants.
bo·ron [bôr′on′] *n.* A nonmetallic element that in pure form exists either as a hard, crystalline solid with a metallic sheen or as a brownish black powder. It is found only in compounds such as borax and has various technological uses.
bor·ough [bûr′ō] *n.* 1 A village or town with a charter granting it the right of self-government. 2 One of the five administrative divisions of New York City.
bor·row [bôr′ō *or* bor′ō] *v.* 1 To take (something) from somebody else with the promise or understanding of returning it. 2 In a subtraction problem, to take away 1 from a digit in the top number and add it as 10 to the digit in the place to the right so as to make subtraction possible. 3 To take or adopt for one's own use, as words or ideas. **—borrow trouble** To worry before there is any need to. **—bor′row·er** *n.*
borsch [bôrsh] *n.* Borscht.
borscht [bôrsht] *n.* A Russian beet soup, eaten hot or cold. ◆ This word comes from the Russian word *borshch.*
bor·zoi [bôr′zoi] *n.* A large, slender-bodied dog with a narrow, pointed head and long, silky hair. ◆ *Borzoi* comes from a Russian word meaning "swift." These dogs were bred in Russia for speed so that they could hunt wolves.
bosh [bosh] *n. informal* Nonsense; rubbish.
bosk·y [bos′kē] *adj.* 1 Wooded; shady. 2 Shaded by or as by trees.
bo's'n [bō′sən] *n.* Another word for BOATSWAIN.
bos·om [bo͝oz′əm *or* bo͞o′zəm] 1 *n.* The breast of a human being, especially of a woman. 2 *n.* The portion of a dress or other garment covering the breast. 3 *n.* The breast as the seat of thought and emotion: Within his *bosom,* Philip felt he was right. 4 *n.* Inner circle; midst: in the *bosom* of my family. 5 *adj.* Close; intimate: a *bosom* friend.
boss[1] [bôs] *informal* 1 *n.* A person who employs or is in charge of workers. 2 *n.* A person who controls a political organization. 3 *v.* To supervise; direct: to *boss* a project. ◆ This word comes from the Dutch word *baas,* meaning *master.*
boss[2] [bôs] *n.* An ornamental knob or stud.
boss·y [bôs′ē] *adj.* **boss·i·er, boss·i·est** *informal* Tending to boss or be domineering.
bo·sun [bō′sən] *n.* Another word for BOATSWAIN.
bo·tan·i·cal [bə·tan′i·kəl] *adj.* Having to do with plants or with botany.
botanical garden A place where many different plants and trees are grown and exhibited.
bot·a·ny [bot′ə·nē] *n.* The scientific study of the origin, development, life, structure, and classification of plants. **—bot′an·ist** *n.*
botch [boch] 1 *v.* To spoil by carelessness or clumsiness; bungle: to *botch* a job. 2 *n.* A bungled piece of work; a bad job.
both [bōth] 1 *adj., pron.* The two together; one and the other: *Both* children laughed; *Both* were there. 2 *adv., conj.* Equally; alike; as well: He is *both* kind and intelligent.
both·er [both′ər] 1 *v.* To annoy or trouble. 2 *n.* A person or thing that bothers. 3 *v.* To trouble or concern oneself.
both·er·some [both′ər·səm] *adj.* Annoying or troublesome: a very *bothersome* problem.
Bot·swa·nan [bot·swä′nən] 1 *adj.* Of or from Botswana. 2 *n.* A person born in or a citizen of Botswana.
bot·tle [bot′(ə)l] *n., v.* **bot·tled, bot·tling** 1 *n.* A vessel, usually of glass, for holding liquids, having a neck and a narrow mouth that can be stopped. 2 *n.* As much as a bottle will hold: a *bottle* of milk. 3 *v.* To put into a bottle or bottles. **—bottle up** To hold in check or under control: to *bottle up* one's temper.

bot·tle·neck [bot′(ə)l·nek′] *n.* 1 Something narrow or congested, as a passageway or road. 2 A hindrance.

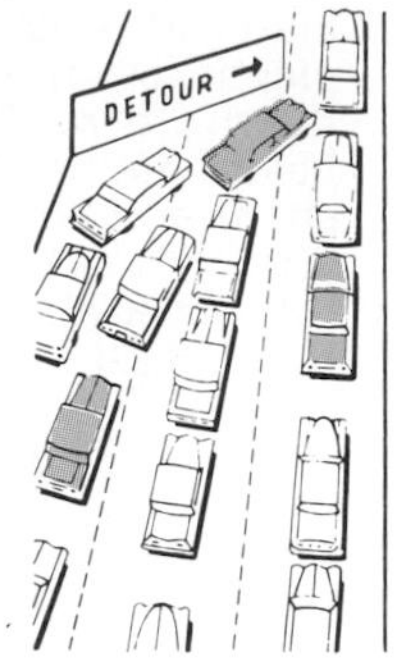

Traffic bottleneck

bot·tom [bot′əm] 1 *n.* The lowest part: the *bottom* of the page. 2 *adj.* Lowest: the *bottom* rung of the ladder. 3 *n.* The underside or under surface: the *bottom* of a box. 4 *n.* The ground beneath a body of water: The box fell into the lake and sank to the *bottom.* 5 *n.* (*often pl.*) Lowland along a river. 6 *n.* The seat of a chair. 7 *n.* The basic facts, source, or cause: to get to the *bottom* of a matter.
bot·tom·less [bot′əm·lis] *adj.* 1 Having no bottom. 2 Infinitely deep, or so deep the distance can't be measured: a *bottomless* pit.
bottom line 1 The final entry in a financial report, showing net profit or loss. 2 *informal* Final result; outcome: The team has improved, but the *bottom line* is they're still not good enough to win the pennant. ◆ This term has been overworked, especially in its figurative sense (def. 2).
bot·u·lism [boch′o͞o·liz′əm] *n.* Poisoning caused by bacteria sometimes found in spoiled food.
bou·doir [bo͞od′wär′ *or* bo͞od′wär′] *n.* A woman's private dressing room or bedroom.
bouf·fant [bo͞o·fänt′] *adj.* Puffed out, as a skirt or hairdo. ◆ This word comes directly from the French.
bou·gain·vil·le·a [bo͞o′gən·vil′yə *or* bo͞o′gən·vil′ē·ə] *n.* A tropical American vine with small flowers surrounded by bright purple or red bracts. ◆ This plant was named for Louis Antoine de *Bougainville* (1729–1811), a French explorer who brought specimens of it back from a voyage.
bough [bou] *n.* A large branch of a tree.
bought [bôt] Past tense and past participle of BUY.
bouil·la·baisse [bo͞o′yə·bās′] *n.* A strongly seasoned soup made of fish and shellfish.
bouil·lon [bo͝ol′yon] *n.* A clear soup made from beef, chicken, or other meat.
boul·der [bōl′dər] *n.* A large, detached rock or stone, worn or rounded as by water.
boul·e·vard [bo͝ol′ə·värd′] *n.* A broad city avenue or main road, often lined with trees.
bounce [bouns] *v.* **bounced, bounc·ing,** *n.* 1 *v.* To strike or hit and spring back from a surface; rebound: to *bounce* on a sofa. 2 *v.* To cause to bounce: to *bounce* a ball. 3 *n.* A bound or rebound. 4 *n.* Ability or capacity to bounce or spring: a ball with *bounce.* 5 *v.* To jump or leap suddenly: to *bounce* out of bed. 6 *n.* A sudden jump or leap. 7 *n. informal* Pep and vitality.
bounc·er [boun′sər] *n. slang* A person employed to eject disorderly persons, as from a night club.
bounc·ing [boun′sing] *adj.* Healthy; robust.
bound[1] [bound] 1 *v.* To strike and spring back from a surface; bounce. 2 *v.* To move by a series of leaps. 3 *n.* A bounce, leap, or spring.
bound[2] [bound] 1 Past tense and past participle of BIND. 2 *adj.* Having a cover or binding. 3 *adj.* Certain; sure: It's *bound* to rain. 4 *adj. informal* Resolved; determined: I'm *bound* on finishing this.
bound[3] [bound] *adj.* On the way; headed; going: *bound* for home.
bound[4] [bound] 1 *n.* (*usually pl.*) A boundary, edge, or limit: the *bounds* of space; Keep within the *bounds* of reason. 2 *v.* To form the boundary of; enclose: The jungle *bounds* the village. 3 *v.* To give the boundaries of. **—out of bounds** 1 Beyond the limits of a playing area, as in basketball. 2 Not to be entered, done, or considered.
bound·a·ry [boun′də·rē *or* boun′drē] *n., pl.* **bound·a·ries** Something, as a line or mark, that forms an outer limit, edge, or extent.
bound·en [boun′d(ə)n] *adj.* Required: seldom used today: our *bounden* duty.
bound·less [bound′lis] *adj.* Having no bounds or limits: *boundless* space; *boundless* sympathy.
boun·te·ous [boun′tē·əs] *adj.* Bountiful.
boun·ti·ful [boun′tə·fəl] *adj.* 1 Generous and free in giving; liberal: a *bountiful* ruler. 2 Abundant; plentiful: a *bountiful* harvest. **—boun′ti·ful·ly** *adv.*
boun·ty [boun′tē] *n., pl.* **boun·ties** 1 Generosity in giving. 2 Something given freely and generously. 3 A reward from a government, as for killing a dangerous animal.
bou·quet *n.* 1 [bō·kā′ *or* bo͞o·kā′] A bunch of flowers; nosegay. 2 [bo͞o·kā′] A delicate odor, especially the odor of a good wine.
Bour·bon *n.* 1 [bo͝or′bən] A family that formerly ruled France and Spain. 2 [bûr′bən] (*written* **bourbon**) A kind of whiskey made chiefly of corn.
bour·geois [bo͝or′zhwä *or* bo͝or·zhwä′] *n., pl.* **bour·geois,** *adj.* 1 *n.* A member of the middle class. 2 *n.* The middle class. 3 *adj.* Of or like the ways or habits of the middle class.
bour·geoi·sie [bo͝or′zhwä·zē′] *n.* The middle class, falling between the laboring class and the wealthy or noble class.
bourn[1] or **bourne**[1] [bôrn] *n.* 1 A goal or destination. 2 A boundary or limit. 3 A place.
bourne[2] or **bourne**[2] [bôrn] *n.* A brook.
bout [bout] *n.* 1 A contest or trial: a boxing *bout.* 2 A fit or spell, as of illness.
bou·tique [bo͞o·tēk′] *n.* A small shop or shoplike department in a department store, especially one that sells fashionable clothing, accessories, and gifts. ◆ *Boutique* comes from the French word for *shop,* and ultimately goes back to the Greek word *apothēkē,* meaning *storehouse. Apothecary* and *bodega* also come from this Greek word.
bou·ton·niere [bo͞ot′(ə)n·ir′ *or* bo͞ot′(ə)n·yâr′] *n.* A flower worn in the buttonhole of a coat lapel.
bo·vine [bō′vīn′] 1 *adj.* Of or like a cow or ox. 2 *n.* A cow or ox. 3 *adj.* Dull, slow, or stupid.
bow[1] [bou] *v.* **bowed, bow·ing,** *n.* 1 *v.* To bend the head or body, as in greeting, worship, or saying yes. 2 *n.* A bending of the head or body, as in greeting or worship. 3 *v.* To give up; yield: They *bowed* to the dictator's wishes. 4 *v.* To bend or curve: He was *bowed* by arthritis. **—bow out** To withdraw; resign. **—take a bow** To acknowledge the applause of an audience by returning to a stage after a performance.

a	add	**i**	it	**o͝o**	took	**oi**	oil
ā	ace	**ī**	ice	**o͞o**	pool	**ou**	pout
â	care	**o**	odd	**u**	up	**ng**	ring
ä	palm	**ō**	open	**û**	burn	**th**	thin
e	end	**ô**	order	**yo͞o**	fuse	**th̶**	this
ē	equal					**zh**	vision

ə = { a in *above* e in *sicken* i in *possible* / o in *melon* u in *circus* }

bow[2] [bō] **1** *n.* A strip of springy wood bent by a string, used for shooting arrows. **2** *n.* A knot with loops in it. **3** *n.* Anything bent or curved, as a rainbow. **4** *v.* To bend into a curve. **5** *n.* A rod holding tightly stretched horsehair, used to play a violin or related instruments. **6** *v.* To play with a bow.

A violin bow

bow[3] [bou] *n.* The forward part, as of a ship or boat.

bowd·ler·ize [boud′lə·rīz′] *v.* **bowd·ler·ized, bowd·ler·iz·ing** To edit, as a book or play, by taking out or changing parts considered obscene or improper. ◆ This word comes from Thomas *Bowdler* (1754–1825), an English editor who published a prudish *Family Shakespeare* and even expurgated the Bible.

bow·el [bou′əl] *n.* **1** (*often pl.*) The part of the alimentary canal below the stomach; intestines. **2** (*pl.*) The inner part of anything: *bowels* of the earth.

bow·er [bou′ər] *n.* **1** A shady spot, as in a garden. **2** A bedroom or other private room.

bow·front [bō′frunt′] *adj.* Having an outward curving front, as certain pieces of furniture.

bow·head [bō′hed′] *n.* A large-headed whale of northern waters.

bow·ie knife [bō′ē *or* bo͞o′ē] A long, single-edged hunting knife.

bow·ing [bō′ing] *n.* In music, the technique of using the bow in playing a stringed instrument.

bowl[1] [bōl] *n.* **1** A rounded, rather deep dish. **2** The amount a bowl will hold: a *bowl* of water. **3** Anything shaped like a bowl: the *bowl* of a pipe. **—bowl′ful′** *n.*

bowl[2] [bōl] **1** *v.* To play at bowling or bowls. **2** *n.* The ball used in bowls. **3** *v.* To move swiftly: to *bowl* along. **—bowl′er** *n.*

bowl·der [bōl′dər] *n.* Another spelling of BOULDER.

bow·leg [bō′leg′] *n.* A leg that bows out at the knee or just below.

bow·leg·ged [bō′leg′id] *adj.* Having legs that are bowed out at the knee or just below.

Bowline

bow·line [bō′lin *or* bō′līn′] *n.* A knot tied so as to make a loop. One type will slip; another won't.

bowl·ing [bō′ling] *n.* A game in which each player rolls a heavy ball down a wooden path to try to knock down ten wooden pins at the other end.

bowling alley A long narrow wooden lane for bowling, or a building containing such lanes.

bowls [bōlz] *n.pl.* **1** A game played on a smooth lawn with slightly flattened balls. **2** A game of tenpins, ninepins, or skittles.

bow·man [bō′mən] *n., pl.* **bow·men** [bō′mən] An archer.

bow·sprit [bou′sprit′] *n.* A spar reaching forward from the bow of a sailing vessel. Wires from it brace the mast and hold jibs.

bow·string [bō′string′] *n.* A strong cord stretched between the two ends of an archer's bow: My nerves are as taut as a *bowstring*.

bow tie [bō] A short necktie that is tied in a bow.

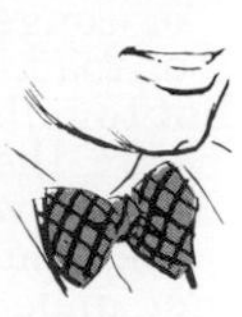
Bow tie

box[1] [boks] **1** *n.* A container made of a material such as wood, leather, or plastic, often with a lid, to hold something. **2** *n.* The amount a box will hold: I ate half a *box* of candy. **3** *v.* To put into a box. **4** *n.* Anything like a box, as a separate seating area in a theater or a marked space for a batter in baseball.

box[2] [boks] **1** *v.* To fight with one's fists. **2** *v.* To strike or slap with the hand; cuff: John *boxed* Tom's ear. **3** *n.* A blow given with the hand, especially on the ear.

box[3] [boks] *n.* Any of a family of evergreen shrubs or small trees, as those used for hedges.

box·car [boks′kär′] *n.* A freight car with a roof and its sides closed in.

box elder A North American tree of the maple family, having compound leaves.

box·er[1] [bok′sər] *n.* A person who fights with his or her fists.

box·er[2] [bok′sər] *n.* A sturdy dog related to the bulldog, usually fawn or brindled in color.

Box·er [bok′sər] *n.* A member of a Chinese secret society whose violent opposition to the spread of foreign influence in China culminated in an unsuccessful uprising, the **Boxer Rebellion,** in 1900.

boxer shorts Men's loose-fitting shorts, worn as underpants.

box·ing [bok′sing] *n.* The sport or skill of fighting according to certain rules with the fists, using padded gloves.

boxing glove One of a pair of padded leather mitts used for fighting.

box office The place, as in a theater or stadium, where tickets are sold.

box seat A seat in a box, as of a theater or stadium.

box spring A cloth-covered frame containing rows of coiled springs, placed on a bedstead underneath the mattress.

box·wood [boks′wo͝od′] *n.* **1** The hard, tough wood of the box. **2** The shrub.

boy [boi] *n.* **1** A male child; lad; youth. **2** *informal* Any man: The *boys* at the office have formed a sports club. **3** A male servant.

boy·cott [boi′kot] **1** *v.* To unite in refusing to buy from, sell to, use, or deal or associate with: The nationalist party *boycotted* all imported goods. **2** *n.* The act of boycotting.

boy·friend [boi′frend′] *n. informal* **1** A male friend. **2** A male with whom one has a romantic relationship; sweetheart.

boy·hood [boi′ho͝od′] *n.* The condition or time of being a boy.

boy·ish [boi′ish] *adj.* Of, having to do with, like, or fit for a boy. **—boy′ish·ly** *adv.* **—boy′ish·ness** *n.*

boy scout A member of the Boy Scouts.

Boy Scouts An organization for boys that trains them in self-reliance, camping skills, and good citizenship.

boy·sen·ber·ry [boi′zən·ber′ē] *n., pl.* **boy·sen·ber·ries** **1** A large, purplish berry from a plant related to the blackberry, raspberry, and loganberry. **2** The plant on which it grows.

BPOE or **B.P.O.E.** Benevolent and Protective Order of Elks.

Br The symbol for the element bromine.

Br. **1** Britain. **2** British. **3** brother (religious).

bra [brä] *n. informal* A brassiere.

brace [brās] *v.* **braced, brac·ing,** *n.* 1 *v.* To strengthen, support, or make firm: to *brace* a shelf with a bracket. 2 *n.* Something used to support, strengthen, or hold in place. 3 *v.* To prepare for a jerk, bump, or pressure: *Brace* yourself for a sharp turn. 4 *v.* To stimulate or refresh: A cold shower *braced* the tired athlete. 5 *n.* A pair; couple: a *brace* of deer. 6 *n.* A tool like a handle, used to hold and turn a bit or drill. 7 *n.* Either of two marks { }, used to show that the words or numbers enclosed between them should be taken together. 8 *n.* (*pl.*) *British* Suspenders. **—brace up** To regain lost courage and confidence.

brace·let [brās′lit] *n.* A band or chain worn as an ornament around the wrist or arm.

brac·ing [brā′sing] *adj.* Giving energy; invigorating: a *bracing* wind.

brack·en [brak′ən] *n.* 1 A large hardy fern. 2 A clump of such ferns.

brack·et [brak′it] 1 *n.* A support, often a wooden triangle or a metal right angle, for a shelf or other weight sticking out from a wall. 2 *n.* A shelf supported by brackets. 3 *v.* To support with a bracket or brackets. 4 *n.* Either of two marks, [ ], used to enclose and separate inserted words or figures, or in mathematics, to enclose numbers or symbols that are to be treated as a single element. 5 *v.* To put between brackets. 6 *n.* A section of a numbered or graded series: the 18–25 age *bracket.* 7 *v.* To group together; associate: Radar and sonar are often *bracketed.*

Brackets

brack·ish [brak′ish] *adj.* 1 Somewhat salty. 2 Tasting unpleasant.

bract [brakt] *n.* A specialized leaf growing at the base of a flower or on the stem.

brad [brad] *n.* A thin nail with a small head.

brae [brā] *n.* The Scottish word for a hillside.

brag [brag] *v.* **bragged, brag·ging,** *n.* 1 *v.* To boast too much about what one has, has done, or can do: They *brag* constantly. 2 *n.* A boasting. 3 *n.* A person who brags; braggart.

brag·ga·do·ci·o [brag′ə·dō′s(h)ē·ō′ *or* brag′ə·dō′·shō′] *n., pl.* **brag·ga·do·ci·os** 1 Empty, boastful talk. 2 A braggart.

brag·gart [brag′ərt] *n.* A person who brags.

Brah·ma [brä′mə] *n.* In the Hindu religion, the creator of the universe.

Brah·man [brä′mən] *n.* 1 A member of the highest caste or social level in India. 2 A breed of humped cattle.

Brah·man·ism [brä′mən·iz′əm] *n.* 1 The strict, traditional form of Hinduism practiced by Brahmans. 2 The system of social castes of the Brahmans.

Brah·min [brä′mən] *n.* 1 Another spelling of BRAHMAN. 2 A well-educated, cultivated member of an old, upper-class family: a Boston *Brahmin.*

braid [brād] 1 *v.* To weave together three or more strands of; plait: to *braid* the hair. 2 *n.* Anything braided. 3 *v.* To ornament, as with braided cloth or ribbon. 4 *n.* A strip of something braided, used for trimming.

Braille [brāl] *n.* (*sometimes written* **braille**) A system of printing and writing for blind people in which the letters are indicated by raised dots read by touch with the fingers.

brain [brān] 1 *n.* The complex mass of nerve tissue in the skull of human beings and vertebrate animals. It is the chief nerve center, controls voluntary movements, thinks, and remembers. 2 *n.* (*pl.*) Intelligence; intellect: They have *brains.* 3 *v. slang* To hit hard on the head.

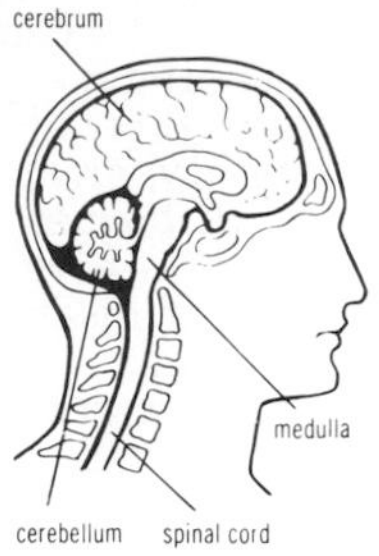

Brain

brain·child [brān′chīld′] *n.* Something that is the result of one's creativity, as an original idea or an invention.

brain·less [brān′lis] *adj.* Lacking intelligence; stupid; foolish.

brain scan A series of diagnostic images of the brain made by a CAT scanner or similar device.

brain·storm [brān′stôrm′] *n. informal* A sudden inspiration; brilliant idea.

brain·wash [brān′wäsh′ *or* brān′wôsh′] *v.* 1 To forcibly change the basic beliefs of a person by psychological or physical means, as intensive indoctrination, drugs, or torture. 2 To persuade, as by cajolery, deception, or propaganda.

brain wave 1 A small, rhythmic change of voltage between parts of the brain that arises from electrical activity of nerve cells. Brain waves can be measured by placing electrodes on the scalp. 2 *informal* A brainstorm.

brain·y [brā′nē] *adj.* **brain·i·er, brain·i·est** *informal* Having great intelligence; clever.

braise [brāz] *v.* To cook by first browning in fat and then simmering in a covered pan with a little liquid.

brake[1] [brāk] *n., v.* **braked, brak·ing** 1 *n.* A device for slowing or stopping a turning wheel or a moving vehicle, as a car, or truck, usually by friction. 2 *v.* To slow or stop by applying a brake.

brake[2] [brāk] *n.* Bracken.

brake[3] [brāk] *n.* An area covered with bushes, tall grass, or briers; thicket.

brake·man [brāk′mən] *n., pl.* **brake·men** [brāk′·mən] A person who helps the conductor manage a train. The brakeman used to put on the brakes.

bram·ble [bram′bəl] *n.* A prickly shrub, especially the blackberry.

bran [bran] *n.* The husks left when grains like wheat or rye are ground and the flour sifted out.

branch [branch] 1 *n.* A woody part of a tree growing out from the trunk or from a limb. 2 *n.* A part coming out like a branch of a tree from a main part: a *branch* of a railroad. 3 *v.* To separate or divide into branches: The highway *branches* here. 4 *n.* Any part or division, as of a system or subject: Geometry is a *branch* of mathematics; the Ohio *branch* of our family. 5 *n.* A part, as a store or office, away from the main unit: Our bank has 18 branches. 6 *adj. use*: a *branch* office. **—branch**

a	add	**i**	it	**o͝o**	took	**oi**	oil
ā	ace	**ī**	ice	**o͞o**	pool	**ou**	pout
â	care	**o**	odd	**u**	up	**ng**	ring
ä	palm	**ō**	open	**û**	burn	**th**	thin
e	end	**ô**	order	**yo͞o**	fuse	**t͟h**	this
ē	equal					**zh**	vision

ə = {a in *above* e in *sicken* i in *possible*; o in *melon* u in *circus*}

out To widen or add to one's activities or interests: The agency has *branched out* with a line of foreign cars. ◆ This word comes from a Latin word meaning *paw*.

brand [brand] 1 *n.* A trademark. 2 *n.* A kind, quality, or make: a good *brand* of tires. 3 *n.* A mark burned on with a hot iron, as on cattle to show ownership or, long ago, on criminals as a sign of disgrace. 4 *v.* To put a mark on with a hot iron. 5 *n.* The iron used to make the mark. 6 *n.* A mark of disgrace or shame. 7 *v.* To mark or set apart as shameful or disgraced: He was *branded* a thief. 8 *n.* A burning stick of wood.

bran·dish [bran'dish] *v.* To wave triumphantly or threateningly: to *brandish* a knife.

brand name Another term for TRADE NAME (def. 1).

brand-new [bran(d)'n(y)o͞o'] *adj.* Very new; not used.

bran·dy [bran'dē] *n., pl.* **bran·dies,** *v.* **bran·died, bran·dy·ing** 1 *n.* An alcoholic drink distilled from wine or other fermented fruit juice. 2 *v.* To mix or flavor with brandy.

brant [brant] *n.* A small wild goose.

brash [brash] *adj.* 1 Acting too hastily; rash. 2 Impudent and pert.

brass [bras] *n.* 1 An alloy of copper and zinc. 2 Such items as ornaments or dishes made of this yellow metal. 3 (*sometimes pl.*) The brass instruments of an orchestra, taken together. 4 *informal* Barefaced boldness or impudence. 5 *informal* High-ranking officers in the armed forces.

brass band A band that is made up chiefly or totally of brass and percussion instruments.

bras·siere or **bras·sière** [brə·zir'] *n.* A woman's undergarment to support the breasts.

brass instrument A musical instrument consisting of a long, bent tube with a flare at one end, as a trumpet or tuba.

brass·y [bras'ē] *adj.* **brass·i·er, brass·i·est** 1 Made of or decorated with brass. 2 Looking or sounding like brass. 3 *informal* Too bold.

brat [brat] *n.* An annoying or unpleasant child.

bra·va [brä'vä *or* brä·vä'] *interj., n., pl.* **bra·vas** Bravo: used when cheering a woman.

bra·va·do [brə·vä'dō] *n.* A show of bravery without much courage or confidence underneath.

brave [brāv] *adj.* **brav·er, brav·est,** *v.* **braved, brav·ing,** *n.* 1 *adj.* Having or showing courage; not afraid. 2 *v.* To meet or face with courage; defy: to *brave* danger. 3 *adj.* Making a fine show; splendid: band members in *brave* apparel. 4 *n.* A North American Indian warrior. —**brave'ly** *adv.*

brav·er·y [brā'vər·ē] *n., pl.* **brav·er·ies** 1 Valor; courage; fearlessness. 2 Fine appearance or showy display: to parade with a *bravery* of banners.

bra·vo [brä'vō *or* brä·vō'] *interj., n., pl.* **bra·vos,** *v.* **bra·voed, bra·vo·ing** 1 *interj.* Well done. 2 *n.* A shout of "bravo." 3 *v.* To shout "bravo."

bra·vu·ra [brə·v(y)o͝or'ə] *n.* 1 Great technical skill in artistic performance, or a musical passage requiring it. 2 A display of brilliance or daring.

brawl [brôl] 1 *n.* A noisy argument or fight. 2 *v.* To fight roughly and noisily. —**brawl'er** *n.*

brawn [brôn] *n.* 1 Strong, well-developed muscles. 2 Power of muscles; strength.

brawn·y [brô'nē] *adj.* **brawn·i·er, brawn·i·est** Muscular; strong.

bray [brā] 1 *n.* The loud, harsh call of a donkey or a sound like it. 2 *v.* To make such a sound.

bra·zen [brā'z(ə)n] *adj.* 1 Made of or like brass. 2 Too bold; impudent; shameless: a *brazen* manner. —**brazen it out** To face something boldly as if not ashamed or afraid. —**bra'zen·ly** *adv.*

bra·zier [brā'zhər] *n.* An open pan for holding hot coals or burning charcoal.

Bra·zil·ian [brə·zil'yən] 1 *adj.* Of or from Brazil. 2 *n.* A person born in or a citizen of Brazil.

Brazil nut An edible South American nut with a white kernel and dark shell.

breach [brēch] 1 *n.* A hole; gap. 2 *v.* To make a hole in; break through: The flood *breached* the dam. 3 *n.* A breaking, as of a law, obligation, or promise: a *breach* of contract. 4 *n.* A breaking up of friendship; quarrel.

breach of promise The act of breaking a promise, especially a promise to marry someone.

bread [bred] 1 *n.* A baked food made of flour or meal, a liquid, and usually yeast. 2 *v.* To coat with bread crumbs before cooking: to *bread* veal cutlets. 3 *n.* Food or the needs of life. —**know which side one's bread is buttered on** To know where one's best interests lie.

bread-and-butter [bred'(ə)n·but'ər] *adj.* 1 Having to do with basic needs, such as making a living. 2 Expressing gratitude for hospitality: a *bread-and-butter* letter.

bread·bas·ket [bred'bas'kit] *n.* 1 A farm region that produces much grain. 2 *slang* The stomach.

bread·fruit [bred'fro͞ot'] *n.* A round, starchy fruit grown in the South Sea Islands. It tastes like bread when roasted.

bread line A line of poor people waiting to receive free food from the government or a charitable organization.

breadth [bredth] *n.* 1 Distance from side to side; width. 2 Freedom from narrowness; broadness: *breadth* of vision.

bread·win·ner [bred'win'ər] *n.* A person who supports a family or other group by his or her earnings.

break [brāk] *v.* **broke, brok·en, break·ing,** *n.* 1 *v.* To separate or crack into pieces, as by a blow or pull: Don't *break* the cup; The rope *broke.* 2 *n.* The act of breaking. 3 *n.* A gap, crack, or broken place. 4 *v.* To open the surface of, as with a plow; pierce: to *break* ground. 5 *v.* To put or get out of order; make or become useless: The clock *broke.* 6 *v.* To lessen the force or effect of: The snow *broke* my fall. 7 *v.* To overcome or defeat: to *break* a deadlock. 8 *n.* A stopping; interruption: to take a *break* from work. 9 *v.* To end or stop: to *break* a silence. 10 *v.* To fail to keep or obey; violate: to *break* a promise; to *break* the law. 11 *v.* To teach to obey; tame: to *break* a horse. 12 *v.* To lower in rank; demote: To be *broken* from corporal to private. 13 *v.* To give or get smaller units of money: to *break* a dollar. 14 *v.* To make or become poor; put or go into debt: Taxes will *break* me. 15 *v.* To make or become known: There may be trouble when the story *breaks.* 16 *v.* To do better than; exceed: The snowfall *broke* all records. 17 *v.* To change suddenly in tone or quality, as a singer's voice. 18 *v.* To dissolve and go away: The clouds *broke.* 19 *v.* To come into being; appear suddenly: The storm *broke;* Dawn is *breaking.* 20 *v.* To force one's way out of; escape from: They *broke* jail. 21 *n.* An escape, as from prison. 22 *n. informal* A chance or opportunity: a lucky *break.* 23 *v.* To change or fall off suddenly: The fever *broke.* 24

n. A sudden change: a *break* in a fever. **25** *v.* In baseball, to curve sharply near the plate: said of a pitch. **—break away** To leave or go away. **—break down** **1** To stop working; undergo mechanical failure. **2** To have a physical or nervous collapse. **3** To lose one's self-control, as to begin to cry: The prisoners *broke down* under questioning. **4** To divide into smaller parts for study: Let us *break down* the problem. **—break in** **1** To make ready for use; train. **2** To interrupt, as a conversation. **3** To enter by force. **—break into** **1** To enter by force. **2** To interrupt. **—break off** **1** To stop friendly relations. **2** To end suddenly: The diary *breaks off* here. **—break out** **1** To have a rash, as on the skin. **2** To begin or appear suddenly, as a fire, riot, or epidemic. **3** To escape. **—break up** **1** To spread out; scatter: to *break up* a crowd. **2** To take or fall to pieces. **3** To put an end to; stop. **—break with** To end relations with: It is sad to *break with* an old friend.

break·a·ble [brā′kə·bəl] *adj.* That can be or is easily broken: a *breakable* dish.

break·age [brā′kij] *n.* **1** A breaking or being broken; break. **2** Damage due to breaking. **3** The cost of or payment for such damage: The restaurant expected to have a certain amount of *breakage.*

break·down [brāk′doun′] *n.* **1** A collapse or failure, as of a machine or one's health. **2** A separation into parts, as of facts or statistics; analysis. **3** The separation of a chemical compound into simpler compounds or elements.

break·er [brā′kər] *n.* **1** A person or thing that breaks. **2** A wave that breaks into foam, as on a shore or reef.

break·fast [brek′fəst] **1** *n.* The first meal of the day. **2** *v.* To eat breakfast. ◆ This word was formed by combining *break* and *fast,* because the first meal of the day breaks the fast which has lasted all night.

break·neck [brāk′nek′] *adj.* Likely to break the neck; dangerous: to drive a car at *breakneck* speed.

break·through [brāk′thro͞o′] *n.* An important discovery or advance, as in science or diplomacy.

break·up [brāk′up′] *n.* **1** A breaking into pieces: the *breakup* of the ice in spring. **2** An ending of a union; separation: the *breakup* of a marriage.

break·wa·ter [brāk′wô′tər] *n.* A barrier or wall for protecting a harbor or beach from the force of waves.

Breakwater

bream [brēm] *n., pl.* **bream** or **breams** **1** Any of several freshwater fish commonly found in Europe. **2** Any of several freshwater sunfishes.

breast [brest] **1** *n.* The front of the chest, from the neck to the belly. **2** *n.* One of the glands from which mothers give milk to babies. **3** *n.* The breast as the seat of emotions; heart: Joy filled my *breast.* **4** *v.* To face boldly; oppose: to *breast* the waves. **—make a clean breast of** To make a full confession of.

breast·bone [brest′bōn′] *n.* The long narrow bone in front of the chest, to which most of the ribs are attached.

breast·plate [brest′plāt′] *n.* A piece of armor to protect the breast.

breast stroke A swimming stroke made while lying face down by moving the hands forward together, then sweeping them outward and backward.

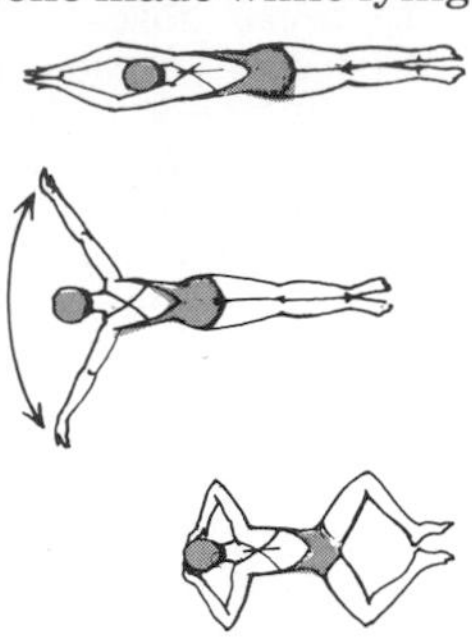

Breast stroke

breast·work [brest′wûrk′] *n.* A low, temporary wall put up as a defense.

breath [breth] *n.* **1** Air drawn into and sent out from the lungs. **2** Ability to breathe freely: I lost my *breath.* **3** Life; existence: We hope while *breath* remains. **4** A slight movement of air. **5** Air carrying a fragrance; hint: a *breath* of spring. **—in the same breath** At the same moment. **—under one's breath** In a whisper or mutter.

breathe [brēth̶] *v.* **breathed, breath·ing** **1** To draw air into and let it out from the lungs; respire. **2** To be alive; live. **3** To stop for breath; rest. **4** To whisper: He *breathed* a secret in my ear. **5** To move gently, as a breeze. **6** To put into: to *breathe* life into a statue.

breath·er [brē′th̶ər] *n.* **1** A person who breathes, especially in a certain manner: a heavy *breather.* **2** *informal* A short rest; rest period.

breathing space **1** Enough space to allow ease of breathing, movement, or work-related activities. **2** A period of time free from activity in which one can rest or think.

breathing spell Another term for BREATHING SPACE (def. 2).

breath·less [breth′lis] *adj.* **1** Out of breath; panting. **2** Holding the breath, as from fear or excitement. **3** Taking the breath away: *breathless* speed. **—breath′less·ly** *adv.*

breath·tak·ing [breth′tā′king] *adj.* Thrilling; exciting: a *breathtaking* trapeze act.

bred [bred] Past tense and past participle of BREED.

breech [brēch] *n.* **1** The part, as of a gun or cannon, that is behind the barrel. **2** The lower, rear part of the body.

breech·cloth [brēch′klôth′] *n.* A loincloth.

breech·clout [brēch′klout′] *n.* Another word for BREECHCLOTH.

breech·es [brich′iz] *n.pl.* **1** Short trousers that fasten below the knees. **2** Any trousers.

breeches buoy A device for transferring persons from ship to ship or from ship to shore. It consists of a canvas seat similar to a pair of breeches that is suspended under a life preserver attached to a pulley that slides along a line.

breech·load·er [brēch′lō′dər] *n.* A firearm that is loaded at the breech.

breed [brēd] *v.* **bred, breed·ing,** *n.* **1** *v.* To produce young; propagate. **2** *v.* To raise (plants or ani-

a	add	**i**	it	**o͝o**	took	**oi**	oil
ā	ace	**ī**	ice	**o͞o**	pool	**ou**	pout
â	care	**o**	odd	**u**	up	**ng**	ring
ä	palm	**ō**	open	**û**	burn	**th**	thin
e	end	**ô**	order	**yo͞o**	fuse	**th̶**	this
ē	equal					**zh**	vision

ə = a in *above* e in *sicken* i in *possible* o in *melon* u in *circus*

mals) to sell or to develop a new variety or strain: to *breed* roses. **3** *v.* To give rise to; produce: Speeding *breeds* accidents. **4** *v.* To bring up; train: She was *bred* to be a lawyer. **5** *n.* A particular kind, variety, or race of animals or plants. **—breed′er** *n.*

breeder reactor A nuclear reactor that produces more fissionable material than it uses.

breed·ing [brē′ding] *n.* **1** The producing of young. **2** Training or upbringing as displayed in one's manners and behavior. **3** The raising of plants or animals, especially to get new or better kinds.

breeze [brēz] *n., v.* **breezed, breez·ing** **1** *n.* A light, gentle wind. **2** *v. informal* To move quickly and easily: She *breezed* through the door.

breeze·way [brēz′wā′] *n.* A passageway between two buildings, as a house and a garage, having a roof but no walls.

breez·y [brē′zē] *adj.* **breez·i·er, breez·i·est** **1** Having breezes blowing. **2** Gay; lively: a *breezy* attitude. **—breez′i·ly** *adv.* **—breez′i·ness** *n.*

breth·ren [bret͟h′rən] *n.pl.* **1** Brothers. **2** Members of the same church or society.

Bret·on [bret′(ə)n] **1** *adj.* Of or from Brittany. **2** *n.* A person from Brittany. **3** *n.* The language of Brittany.

breve [brev *or* brēv] *n.* A mark (˘) sometimes put over a vowel to indicate that it has a short sound or put over an unstressed syllable in verse.

bre·vi·ar·y [brē′vē·er′ē] *n., pl.* **bre·vi·ar·ies** In the Roman Catholic and Eastern Orthodox churches, a book containing the prayers that are to be said every day by priests.

brev·i·ty [brev′ə·tē] *n.* Briefness; shortness.

brew [bro͞o] **1** *v.* To make, as beer or ale, by soaking, boiling, and fermenting malt or hops. **2** *n.* Something brewed, as beer or ale. **3** *v.* To prepare, as by boiling or soaking: to *brew* tea. **4** *n.* The amount brewed at one time. **5** *v.* To make up; devise: to *brew* mischief. **6** *v.* To be coming up; gather, as a storm or trouble. **—brew′er** *n.*

brew·er·y [bro͞o′ər·ē] *n., pl.* **brew·er·ies** A place for brewing beer and ale.

bri·ar [brī′ər] *n.* **1** A tobacco pipe made from the root of a European shrub. **2** Another spelling of BRIER[1] and BRIER[2].

bribe [brīb] *n., v.* **bribed, brib·ing** **1** *n.* A gift offered or given to persuade someone to do something wrong. **2** *v.* To give or offer a bribe.

brib·er·y [brī′bər·ē] *n.* The giving, offering, or taking of a bribe.

bric-a-brac [brik′ə·brak′] *n.* Small objects, rare or beautiful, used to decorate a room.

brick [brik] **1** *n.* A block of clay that has been baked by the sun or in a kiln, as used for building or paving. **2** *n.* Bricks thought of together: a wall made of *brick.* **3** *adj. use:* a *brick* house. **4** *v.* To build with bricks. **5** *v.* To cover or wall up with bricks. **6** *n.* Any object shaped like a brick.

brick·bat [brik′bat′] *n.* **1** A piece of brick used for throwing at someone or something. **2** *informal* An insulting remark.

brick·lay·er [brik′lā′ər] *n.* A person skilled in building with brick. **—brick′lay′ing** *n.*

brick·work [brik′wûrk′] *n.* Something that is made of or with bricks.

brick·yard [brik′yärd′] *n.* A place where bricks are made or sold.

bri·dal [brīd′(ə)l] *adj.* Of or having to do with a bride or wedding: *bridal* flowers.

bride [brīd] *n.* A woman who is being married or who has been recently married.

bride·groom [brīd′gro͞om′] *n.* A man who is being married or who has been recently married. ◆ This word was formed by combining two Old English words meaning *bride* and *man.* Thus the word meant *the bride's man.*

brides·maid [brīdz′mād′] *n.* A young woman who attends a bride at her wedding.

bridge[1] [brij] *n., v.* **bridged, bridg·ing** **1** *n.* A structure built across something, as water, a ravine, or a road, on which people, cars, or other items cross over. **2** *v.* To build a bridge across: Engineers *bridged* the strait. **3** *v.* To extend across; span: A plank *bridged* the creek. **4** *n.* A platform raised above the deck of a ship, as for the officer in command or the pilot. **5** *n.* The upper, bony ridge of the nose. **6** *n.* The part of a pair of eyeglasses that rests on the nose. **7** *n.* A thin piece of wood that supports the strings of an instrument such as a violin or cello. **8** *n.* A mounting for false teeth attached to real teeth.

bridge[2] [brij] *n.* A card game played by two pairs of partners.

bridge·head [brij′hed′] *n.* A position on the enemy's side of a river made or taken by advance troops of an attacking force.

bridge·work [brij′wûrk′] *n.* False teeth mounted and attached on each side to real teeth.

bri·dle [brīd′(ə)l] *n., v.* **bri·dled, bri·dling** **1** *n.* The part of a harness for the head of a horse, including the bit and reins. **2** *v.* To put a bridle on. **3** *v.* To check or control: She *bridled* her anger. **4** *v.* To raise the head and draw in the chin as a way of showing an emotion, as anger or pride.

Bridle

bridle path A path for horseback riding.

brief [brēf] **1** *adj.* Not long; short: a *brief* holiday. **2** *adj.* Of few words; concise: a *brief* talk. **3** *n.* In law, a summary, as of the facts or points of law, of a case, for the use of lawyers in court. **4** *v.* To prepare in advance by instructing or advising: to *brief* salespeople. **—hold a brief for** To be on the side of; argue for. **—in brief** In short; briefly. **—brief′ly** *adv.*

brief·case [brēf′kās′] *n.* A flexible case or bag, usually of leather, for carrying books, papers, and other items.

bri·er[1] [brī′ər] *n.* A prickly bush or shrub, as the sweetbrier.

bri·er[2] [brī′ər] *n.* A European shrub from whose roots briar pipes for tobacco are made.

brig [brig] *n.* **1** A square-rigged sailing vessel having two masts. **2** A prison on a ship.

brig. **1** brigade. **2** brigadier.

bri·gade [bri·gād′] *n.* **1** A unit of troops smaller than a division but rather large. **2** A group of people organized for a purpose: a fire *brigade.*

brig·a·dier [brig′ə·dir′] *n.* A brigadier general.

Brig

brigadier general A military officer ranking next above a colonel and next below a major general.

B

brig·and [brig′ənd] *n.* A robber or bandit, especially one of a band of outlaws.
brig·an·tine [brig′ən·tēn′] *n.* A sailing vessel with the foremast square-rigged and the mainmast fore-and-aft-rigged.
bright [brīt] **1** *adj.* Giving off or reflecting much light; shining: a *bright* lamp. **2** *adj.* Vivid in color or sound; glowing: *bright* green. **3** *adj.* Having a quick, clever mind. **4** *adj.* Full of gladness or hope: a *bright* future. **5** *adj.* Splendid; glorious: *bright* fame. **6** *adv.* In a bright way; brightly: The sun shone *bright.* **—bright′ly** *adv.* **—bright′ness** *n.*
bright·en [brīt′(ə)n] *v.* To make or become bright or brighter.
bril·liance [bril′yəns] *n.* **1** Intense brightness or sparkle. **2** Very great intelligence. **3** Magnificence; excellence.
bril·lian·cy [bril′yən·sē] *n.* Brilliance.
bril·liant [bril′yənt] **1** *adj.* Sparkling or glowing with light; very bright. **2** *adj.* Very intelligent or able: a *brilliant* scientist. **3** *adj.* Splendid; illustrious: a *brilliant* performance. **4** *n.* A diamond or other gem cut so as to sparkle. **—bril′liant·ly** *adv.* **—bril′liant·ness** *n.*
brim [brim] *n., v.* **brimmed, brim·ming** **1** *n.* The upper edge of a container, as a cup; rim. **2** *n.* A rim that sticks out, as on a hat. **3** *n.* An edge or margin. **4** *v.* To fill or be filled to the brim.
brim·ful [brim′fo͝ol′] *adj.* Full to the brim.
brim·stone [brim′stōn′] *n.* Sulfur.
brin·dle [brin′dəl] **1** *n.* A brindled color. **2** *adj.* Brindled.
brin·dled [brin′dəld] *adj.* Tawny or grayish with darker streaks or spots: a *brindled* horse.
brine [brīn] *n.* **1** Water that has a great deal of salt in it, often used for pickling. **2** The ocean.
bring [bring] *v.* **brought, bring·ing** **1** To carry or cause to come with oneself or to or toward a place: *Bring* some milk home; *Bring* the dog. **2** To cause to happen or come about: War *brings* destruction. **3** To attract or draw; fetch: The knocking *brought* us to the door. **4** To sell for: The house *brought* a good price. **5** To influence or persuade: We *brought* them to our point of view. **6** To put before a court; start: to *bring* suit for damages. **—bring about** To make happen; cause; accomplish. **—bring around** or **bring round** **1** To win over gradually; persuade. **2** To bring back to consciousness; revive. **—bring forth** **1** To give birth to. **2** To produce: to *bring forth* an opinion. **—bring off** To do successfully. **—bring on** To cause; lead to. **—bring out** **1** To make known, as the truth. **2** To bring before the public; introduce, as a person, play, or book. **—bring to** To bring back to consciousness; revive. **—bring up** **1** To take care of through childhood; rear. **2** To introduce, as into a discussion or conversation; raise: *Bring up* the subject at the next meeting. **3** To cough or vomit up. **4** To stop or make stop suddenly. ◆ There is a slight difference between the words *bring* and *take.* You generally bring things to a place and take things away: *Bring* in the mail and *take* out the garbage.
brink [bringk] *n.* The edge of a steep place, as a cliff. **—on the brink of** Very close to: *on the brink of* war.
brin·y [brī′nē] *adj.* **brin·i·er, brin·i·est** Of or like brine; salty.
bri·quette or **bri·quet** [bri·ket′] *n.* A block, as of compressed coal dust, used as fuel.
brisk [brisk] *adj.* **1** Acting or moving quickly; lively: a *brisk* walk; Business is *brisk.* **2** Cool and stimulating. **—brisk′ly** *adv.* **—brisk′ness** *n.*
bris·ket [bris′kit] *n.* Meat on or cut from the breast of an animal.
bris·ling [bris′ling] *n.* A small herring.
bris·tle [bris′(ə)l] *n., v.* **bris·tled, bris·tling** **1** *n.* A coarse, stiff hair on the back of a hog. **2** *n.* Any similar real or artificial hair, often used for brushes. **3** *v.* To stand on end, like bristles. **4** *v.* To make the bristles stand up, as in anger. **5** *v.* To show anger or annoyance. **6** *v.* To be thickly set, filled, or covered: The fort *bristled* with cannon.

A cat bristling

bris·tly [bris′lē] *adj.* **bris·tli·er, bris·tli·est** **1** Of, like, or covered with bristles. **2** Easily angered or annoyed.
Brit. **1** Britain. **2** British.
Bri·tan·ni·a [bri·tan′ē·ə] *n.* **1** The ancient Roman name for Britain. **2** In poetry, Britain.
britch·es [brich′iz] *n.pl.* Another spelling of BREECHES.
Brit·i·cism [brit′i·siz′əm] *n.* A word, phrase, or usage peculiar to British English.
Brit·ish [brit′ish] **1** *adj.* Of, from, or having to do with Great Britain or its people. **2** *n.* **(the British)** The people of Great Britain.
British English English as it is spoken and written in Great Britain.
Brit·ish·er [brit′ish·ər] *n.* A person born in or a subject of Great Britain.
British thermal unit The quantity of heat needed to raise the temperature of one pound of water one degree Fahrenheit.
Brit·on [brit′(ə)n] *n.* **1** A member of a Celtic people who used to live in England before the Anglo-Saxon invasions. **2** A Britisher.
brit·tle [brit′(ə)l] **1** *adj.* Likely to break or snap; fragile: *brittle* bones. **2** *n.* A hard, crunchy kind of candy made with nuts.
bro. brother(s).
broach [brōch] *v.* **1** To mention for the first time; introduce: to *broach* a subject in a conversation. **2** To make a hole in so as to withdraw liquid.
broad [brôd] *adj.* **1** Large in width; wide. **2** Of considerable size; large and spacious: a *broad* plain. **3** Open and clear: *broad* daylight. **4** Wide in scope; not narrow or limited: a *broad* rule. **5** Liberal; tolerant. **6** General; main: a *broad* outline. **7** Easy to understand; obvious: a *broad* hint. **8** Vulgar: a *broad* joke. **—broad′ly** *adv.*
broad·ax or **broad·axe** [brôd′aks′] *n., pl.* **broad·ax·es** An ax with a broad head, used as a tool or weapon.

a	add	**i**	it	**o͝o**	took	**oi**	oil
ā	ace	**ī**	ice	**o͞o**	pool	**ou**	pout
â	care	**o**	odd	**u**	up	**ng**	ring
ä	palm	**ō**	open	**û**	burn	**th**	thin
e	end	**ô**	order	**yo͞o**	fuse	**th**	this
ē	equal					**zh**	vision

ə = a in *above*, e in *sicken*, i in *possible*, o in *melon*, u in *circus*

broad·cast [brôd′kast′] *v.* **broad·cast** or **broad·cast·ed, broad·cast·ing,** *n., adj., adv.* **1** *v.* To send by radio or television; transmit. **2** *n.* A sending by radio or television; transmission. **3** *n.* The material, as music or words, sent out by radio or television; program: Did you see last night's *broadcast?* **4** *adj.* Of, having to do with, or sent by radio or television. **5** *v.* To scatter, as seed, over a wide area. **6** *n.* A scattering or sowing over a wide area. **7** *adj.* Scattered, as seed. **8** *adv.* So as to scatter over a wide area: to sow wheat *broadcast.* **—broad′cast·er** *n.*

broad·cloth [brôd′klôth′] *n.* **1** A fine woolen cloth. **2** A closely woven, fine cloth of cotton, silk, or other fabric, used for clothing.

broad·en [brôd′(ə)n] *v.* To make or become broad or broader; widen.

broad jump In athletics, a contest to see who can jump the farthest, rather than the highest.

broad·loom [brôd′lo͞om′] **1** *adj.* Of, having to do with, or being carpet woven on a wide loom: a *broadloom* carpet. **2** *n.* A broadloom carpet.

broad-mind·ed [brôd′mīn′did] *adj.* Without prejudice; tolerant. **—broad′mind′ed·ness** *n.*

broad·side [brôd′sīd′] **1** *n.* The side of a ship above the water line. **2** *n.* The firing of all the guns on one side of a ship at once, or the guns themselves. **3** *adv.* With the side turned or exposed: The car was hit *broadside.* **4** *n.* A sheet of paper printed on one side: a *broadside* advertising a sale.

broad·sword [brôd′sôrd′] *n.* A sword with a broad blade for cutting and slashing.

Broad·way [brôd′wā′] *n.* **1** A street that runs through New York City, on or near which were once located most of the city's legitimate theaters. **2** The district of New York City noted for its theaters. **3** The American theater industry.

bro·cade [brō·kād′] *n.* A fabric woven with a raised design, often in gold or silver threads.

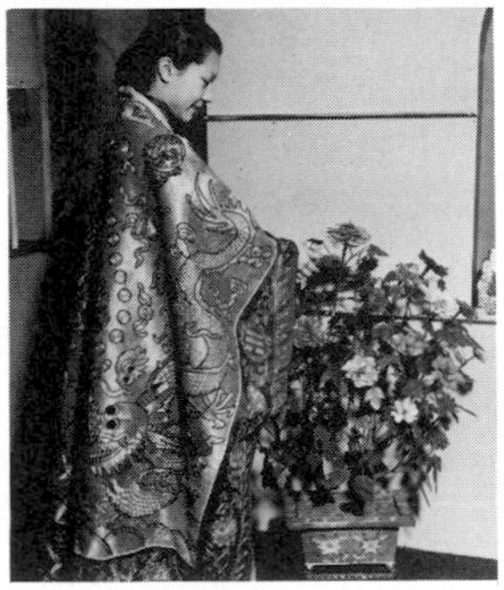

Brocade

broc·co·li [brok′ə·lē] *n.* A variety of cauliflower. Its green stalks and tiny green flowers are eaten as a vegetable.

bro·chure [brō·sho͝or′] *n.* A pamphlet or booklet.

bro·gan [brō′gən] *n.* A heavy shoe.

brogue[1] [brōg] *n.* Speech characteristic of a certain accent in the pronunciation of English.

brogue[2] [brōg] *n.* A heavy oxford shoe, decorated with stitches and rows of holes.

broil [broil] *v.* **1** To cook, as meat, close to a flame or other source of heat. **2** To make or become very hot.

broil·er [broi′lər] *n.* **1** A pan, rack, or grill for broiling. **2** A tender young chicken for broiling.

broke [brōk] **1** Past tense of BREAK. **2** *adj. informal* Without money.

bro·ken [brō′kən] **1** Past participle of BREAK. **2** *adj.* Cracked or shattered into pieces; fractured. **3** *adj.* Out of order; damaged: a *broken* radio. **4** *adj.* Not kept or followed; violated: a *broken* law. **5** *adj.* Interrupted: *broken* sleep. **6** *adj.* Rough; uneven, as ground. **7** *adj.* Humbled; beaten: a *broken* creature. **8** *adj.* Not properly spoken: It is difficult to understand *broken* English.

bro·ken-down [brō′kən·doun′] *adj.* **1** Out of order; not working: a *broken-down* machine. **2** Sick or disabled: a *broken-down* horse.

bro·ken·heart·ed [brō′kən·här′tid] *adj.* Full of grief or sorrow.

broken home A family in which the parents are divorced or separated.

bro·ker [brō′kər] *n.* A person who buys and sells for others, as stocks or real estate.

bro·ker·age [brō′kər·ij] *n.* The business of a broker, or the fee paid to a broker.

bro·mide [brō′mīd′] *n.* **1** A compound of bromine with another element or group of elements. Some bromides are used as drugs to calm the nerves. **2** A dull, often heard remark, as "Keep smiling."

bro·mine [brō′mēn′] *n.* A dark reddish brown liquid element that gives off suffocating fumes. Its chemical properties resemble those of chlorine and iodine.

bron·chi·al [brong′kē·əl] *adj.* Of or having to do with the bronchi or any of their smaller tubes or branches within the lungs.

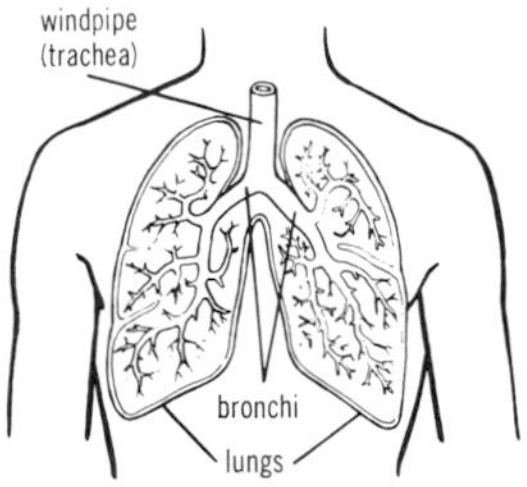

bronchial tube A bronchus or any of the tubes branching from it.

bron·chi·ole [brong′kē·ōl′] A minute branch of a bronchus.

bron·chi·tis [brong·kī′tis] *n.* Acute inflammation of the bronchial tubes, marked by coughing.

bron·chus [brong′kəs] *n., pl.* **bron·chi** [brong′kī] Either of the two main branches of the trachea, or windpipe, that lead to the lungs.

bron·co or **bron·cho** [brong′kō] *n., pl.* **bron·cos** or **bron·chos** A small, wild or partly broken horse of the western U.S.

bron·to·sau·rus [bron′tə·sôr′əs] *n.* An extinct, very large dinosaur of North America.

bronze [bronz] *n., v.* **bronzed, bronz·ing,** *adj.* **1** *n.* A hard, reddish brown alloy of copper and tin. **2** *adj. use:* a *bronze* vase. **3** *v.* To coat with bronze. **4** *n., adj.* Reddish brown. **5** *v.* To make or become such a color. **6** *n.* A statue of bronze.

Bronze Age A time before history was written, after the Stone Age and before the Iron Age, when weapons and tools were made of bronze.

brooch [brōch] *n.* An ornamental pin secured by a catch, worn near the neck of a garment.

brood [bro͞od] **1** *n.* All of the young produced at one time by a bird. **2** *v.* To hatch by sitting on, as eggs. **3** *n.* All of the young of the same mother. **4** *v.* To think deeply in a worried manner.

brood·er [bro͞o′dər] *n.* **1** A heated shelter for raising young fowl, as chickens or ducks. **2** A person or animal that broods.

brood·y [bro͞o′dē] *adj.* **brood·i·er, brood·i·est** **1** Inclined to sit on eggs: a *broody* hen. **2** Brooding; thoughtful.

brook[1] [bro͝ok] *n.* A natural stream smaller than a river.

brook[2] [bro͝ok] *v.* To put up with; stand for: The mayor would *brook* no interference with the plan.

brook trout A speckled game fish of eastern North America.

broom [bro͞om] *n.* **1** A brush for sweeping, with a long handle. **2** A shrub with yellow flowers, small leaves, and stiff green branches.

broom·stick [bro͞om′stik′] *n.* The handle of a broom.

bros. brothers.

broth [brôth] *n.* A soup made by boiling meat, vegetables, or other foods in water and then straining.

broth·er [brut͟h′ər] *n., pl.* **broth·ers** or, *less frequently,* **breth·ren** 1 A boy or man having the same parents as another person of either sex. 2 A fellow member, as of the same organization or profession. 3 A member of a religious order who is not a priest.

broth·er·hood [brut͟h′ər·ho͝od′] *n.* 1 The condition of being brothers. 2 A group of men organized for some purpose, as fellowship.

broth·er-in-law [brut͟h′ər·in·lô′] *n., pl.* **broth·ers-in-law** 1 A brother of one's husband or wife. 2 The husband of one's sister or of one's wife's or husband's sister.

broth·er·ly [brut͟h′ər·lē] *adj.* 1 Of or like a brother. 2 Affectionate; kindly.

brougham [bro͞om *or* bro͞o′əm] *n.* A closed carriage or automobile with the driver's seat outside.

Brougham

brought [brôt] Past tense and past participle of BRING.

brou·ha·ha [bro͞o′hä·hä′] *n.* An uproar.

brow [brou] *n.* 1 The front, upper part of the head; forehead. 2 The eyebrow. 3 The upper edge of a steep place: the *brow* of a hill.

brow·beat [brou′bēt′] *v.* **brow·beat, brow·beat·en, brow·beat·ing** To bully or frighten by a stern or rough manner.

brown [broun] 1 *n.* The color of coffee, toast, or milk chocolate; a mixture of red, yellow, and black. 2 *adj.* Of this color. 3 *v.* To make or become brown. **—brown′ish** *adj.*

brown Bet·ty [bet′ē] A baked dessert of apples, bread crumbs, brown sugar, butter, and spices.

brown coal Another name for LIGNITE.

brown·ie [brou′nē] *n.* 1 In folk tales, an elf or sprite who does good, useful deeds at night. 2 (*written* **Brownie**) A junior Girl Scout. 3 A small, flat chocolate cake with nuts.

brown·ish [broun′ish] *adj.* Somewhat brown.

brown·out [broun′out′] *n.* 1 A curtailment of electric power in an area. 2 The period during which such a curtailment is in effect.

brown rice Unpolished rice.

brown·stone [broun′stōn′] *n.* A reddish brown sandstone used for buildings.

brown study A state of deep thought or daydreaming.

brown sugar Unrefined sugar, brown in color.

browse [brouz] *v.* **browsed, brows·ing** 1 To feed on or nibble at leaves, shoots, or other vegetation: Giraffes *browse* on trees. 2 To glance at a book or books, reading a little at one place or another.

bru·in [bro͞o′in] *n.* A bear, especially a brown bear.

bruise [bro͞oz] *v.* **bruised, bruis·ing,** *n.* 1 *v.* To injure a part of the body without breaking the skin, as by a blow. 2 *n.* An injury caused by bruising, as a black-and-blue mark. 3 *v.* To dent or hurt the outside of. 4 *v.* To hurt or offend, as feelings.

bruit [bro͞ot] *v.* To make known by talking, especially in the phrase **bruit about:** The rumor was *bruited about.*

brunch [brunch] *n.* A meal, usually in the late morning, combining breakfast and lunch. ◆ This word is a blend of *br(eakfast)* and *(l)unch.*

bru·nette or **bru·net** [bro͞o·net′] 1 *adj.* Having more or less dark skin, hair, and eyes. 2 *n.* A brunette person. ◆ *Brunette* usually refers to a girl or woman, whereas *brunet* is used only of a boy or man.

brunt [brunt] *n.* The main shock or force, as of a blow or attack; heaviest part: I bore the *brunt* of their accusations.

brush[1] [brush] 1 *n.* A tool having bristles, hairs, or wires, fastened to a back or handle, used for sweeping, scrubbing, painting, or grooming. 2 *v.* To use a brush on; paint, sweep, or polish, with a brush. 3 *n.* The act of brushing. 4 *n.* A light, grazing touch: a *brush* of the lips. 5 *v.* To touch lightly in passing. 6 *v.* To remove with or as if with a brush: She *brushed* the papers from the desk. 7 *n.* A brief encounter, especially a fight or skirmish: a *brush* with the law. 8 *n.* A conductor making contact between moving and stationary parts of an electric motor or generator. **—brush off** *informal* To dismiss or refuse abruptly. **—brush up** To refresh one's memory of; review.

brush[2] [brush] *n.* 1 A growth of small trees and shrubs. 2 Wooded country where few people live. 3 Branches that have been cut off; brushwood.

brush·off [brush′ôf′] *n. informal* A rude dismissal or cold refusal.

brush·wood [brush′wo͝od′] *n.* 1 Branches chopped or broken off. 2 A growth of small trees or shrubs.

brusque [brusk] *adj.* Blunt and abrupt in manner; curt: a *brusque* refusal. **—brusque′ly** *adv.*

Brussels sprouts 1 A plant with heads like little cabbages along the stalk. 2 The small, edible heads on this plant.

bru·tal [bro͞ot′(ə)l] *adj.* 1 Of or like a brute; cruel; savage. 2 Unfeeling; rude; coarse. **—bru′tal·ly** *adv.*

bru·tal·i·ty [bro͞o·tal′ə·tē] *n., pl.* **bru·tal·i·ties** 1 A being brutal. 2 A brutal act.

bru·tal·ize [bro͞ot′(ə)l·īz′] *v.* **bru·tal·ized, bru·tal·iz·ing** 1 To make cruel, savage, or unfeeling: The castaway was *brutalized* by years of solitude. 2 To treat brutally; abuse.

brute [bro͞ot] 1 *n.* An animal. 2 *n.* A person who is stupid and cruel or coarse. 3 *adj.* Without mind or feeling: the *brute* force of the gale. **—brut′ish** *adj.*

b.s. bill of sale.

B.S. or **B.Sc.** Bachelor of Science.

BSA or **B.S.A.** Boy Scouts of America.

btl. bottle.

btry. battery.

Btu, BTU, or **B.T.U.** British thermal unit.

bu. 1 bureau. 2 bushel(s).

a add	**i** it	**o͝o** took	**oi** oil
ā ace	**ī** ice	**o͞o** pool	**ou** pout
â care	**o** odd	**u** up	**ng** ring
ä palm	**ō** open	**û** burn	**th** thin
e end	**ô** order	**yo͞o** fuse	**t͟h** this
ē equal			**zh** vision

ə = {a in *above* e in *sicken* i in *possible* / o in *melon* u in *circus*}

bub·ble [bub′əl] *n., v.* **bub·bled, bub·bling** 1 *n.* A film of liquid in the form of a ball, filled with air or other gas. 2 *n.* A round space filled with air or other gas, as in a liquid or solid such as ice. 3 *v.* To form or give off bubbles; rise in bubbles, as boiling water. 4 *v.* To flow with a gurgling sound, as a brook. 5 *n.* An idea or plan that seems fine but turns out worthless and unsubstantial. 6 *v.* To express an emotion such as joy or delight, in a happy way: They *bubbled* with glee. **—bubble over** To be unable to keep in one's excitement, joy, or other feeling.

bubble chamber An apparatus in which movement of atomic particles leaves trails of bubbles.

bubble gum A kind of chewing gum that can be blown into large bubbles.

bu·bon·ic plague [byo͞o·bon′ik] A deadly contagious disease with fever, chills, and swollen lymph glands, spread by fleas mainly from rats.

buc·ca·neer [buk′ə·nir′] *n.* A pirate.

buck[1] [buk] 1 *n.* The male of certain animals, as of antelope, deer, rabbits, or goats. 2 *v.* To jump suddenly with back arched up, as a horse trying to throw off its rider. 3 *n.* Such a jump by a horse. 4 *v.* To throw off (a rider) by bucking. 5 *v.* To charge or butt with the head lowered, as a football player, or an animal such as a goat. **—buck up** To take courage or cheer up.

A bucking horse

buck[2] [buk] *n. slang* A dollar.

buck·board [buk′bôrd′] *n.* A light, open carriage having, instead of springs, a flexible frame of long, springy boards.

buck·et [buk′it] *n.* 1 A deep, round container with a flat bottom and curved handle, used for carrying things, as water or coal; pail. 2 As much as a bucket will hold: Add two *buckets* of water. 3 Something like a bucket, as the scoop on a dredge or steam shovel. **—buck′et·ful′** *n.*

bucket seat A single seat with a rounded back, used in racing and sports cars and some aircraft.

buck·eye [buk′ī′] *n.* 1 The horse chestnut tree. 2 Its glossy, brown seed or nut.

buck·le [buk′əl] *n., v.* **buck·led, buck·ling** 1 *n.* A clasp for fastening together two loose ends, as of a strap or belt. 2 *n.* Anything that looks like a buckle, as an ornament on a shoe. 3 *v.* To fasten with or as if with a buckle. 4 *v.* To bend under pressure; crumple; warp: The dam *buckled*, then collapsed. 5 *n.* A bend, kink, or twist. **—buckle down** To work hard; apply oneself vigorously.

buck·ler [buk′lər] *n.* A small, round shield for defense.

buck·ram [buk′rəm] *n.* A coarse, stiffened fabric used for such purposes as binding books and lining garments.

buck·saw [buk′sô′] *n.* A saw set in an adjustable frame, used for cutting wood.

buck·shot [buk′shot′] *n.* A large size of lead shot, used in a shotgun for big game.

buck·skin [buk′skin′] *n.* 1 A soft, strong, grayish yellow leather made from skins of deer or sheep. 2 (*pl.*) Clothing made of such leather.

buck·tooth [buk′to͞oth′] *n., pl.* **buck·teeth** [buk′·tēth′] A large, projecting front tooth.

buck·wheat [buk′(h)wēt′] *n.* 1 A plant with three-sided brown seeds, ground into flour or fed to animals. 2 The flour, used to make pancakes.

bu·col·ic [byo͞o·kol′ik] *adj.* 1 Of or about shepherds; pastoral. 2 Of the country; rural; rustic: a *bucolic* scene.

bud [bud] *n., v.* **bud·ded, bud·ding** 1 *n.* A small swelling on a plant, that will grow into a flower, branch, or leaf. 2 *n.* A half-opened blossom. 3 *v.* To put forth buds. 4 *v.* To begin to grow or develop: Her talents *budded* in her youth. **—nip in the bud** To stop in the early stages: to *nip* a rebellion *in the bud.*

Bud·dhism [bo͞o′diz′əm *or* bo͝od′iz′əm] *n.* An Asian religion, founded by Buddha, that holds that freedom from pain, suffering, and desire can be reached by right living, meditation, and self-control. **—Bud′dhist** *adj., n.*

bud·dy [bud′ē] *n., pl.* **bud·dies** *informal* Chum; pal; partner.

budge [buj] *v.* **budged, budg·ing** To move even slightly: The mule refused to *budge.*

budg·et [buj′it] 1 *n.* A plan for spending the money received for a given period: a household *budget.* 2 *v.* To draw up a budget. 3 *v.* To plan carefully for the use of: to *budget* time.

buff [buf] 1 *n.* A thick, soft, brownish yellow leather, made from the skin of a buffalo or ox. 2 *n., adj.* Brownish yellow. 3 *n.* A stick or wheel covered with leather, used for polishing. 4 *v.* To clean or polish, as with a buff.

buf·fa·lo [buf′ə·lō] *n., pl.* **buf·fa·loes** or **buf·fa·los** 1 A wild ox of Europe, Africa, and Asia, having a thick body and curved horns. Some are tamed to serve as work animals. 2 The bison of North America.

Cape buffalo

buff·er[1] [buf′ər] *n.* A person or thing that polishes or buffs, as a leather-covered stick.

buff·er[2] [buf′ər] *n.* 1 Anything that lessens or cushions the shock of a blow. 2 An area in a computer that holds information temporarily. For example, if a computer's output is too fast for a printer, the data can be held in a buffer until the printer is ready to accept it.

buffer state A small country between two larger enemy countries, that serves as a barrier between them.

buf·fet[1] [bo͞o·fā′] *n.* 1 A piece of dining-room furniture for holding silver, glassware, or table linen. 2 A meal at which guests serve themselves from platters of food.

buf·fet[2] [buf′it] 1 *n.* A blow or slap with the hand. 2 *n.* Any blow or upset: the *buffets* of fortune. 3 *v.* To strike over and over: The shore was *buffeted* by the waves.

buf·foon [bu·fo͞on′] *n.* 1 A clown. 2 A person who tries to be funny and plays practical jokes. **—buf·foon′er·y** *n.*

bug [bug] *n., v.* **bugged, bug·ging** 1 *n.* Any of a group of insects with biting and sucking mouth parts, usually wingless, but some having two pairs of wings. 2 *n. informal* Any insect. 3 *n. informal* A germ that causes disease. 4 *n. slang* A defect, error, or malfunction, as in a machine. 5 *n.* A concealed electronic device for recording private conversations. **6** *v.* To conceal such a device in. **7** *n. slang* A person who is very enthusiastic, as about a hobby. **8** *v.* To bulge or protrude. **9** *v. slang* To bother; pester; annoy.

bug·a·boo [bug'ə·bo͞o'] *n., pl.* **bug·a·boos** A bugbear.

bug·bear [bug'bâr'] *n.* **1** A make-believe person or thing, used in stories to frighten children. **2** Anything used to cause fear without good reason.

bug·gy [bug'ē] *n., pl.* **bug·gies** **1** A light carriage with one large seat, drawn by one horse. **2** A baby's carriage.

bu·gle [byo͞o'gəl] *n., v.* **bu·gled, bu·gling** **1** *n.* A kind of small trumpet, usually not having keys or valves. It is used to sound out orders and signals, as to soldiers. **2** *v.* To sound or call on a bugle. **—bu'gler** *n.* ◆ *Bugles* were originally made from the horns of oxen, and the word *bugle* comes from a Latin word for *ox.*

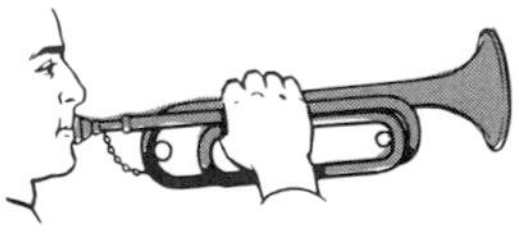

Bugle

build [bild] *v.* **built** (or **build·ed:** seldom used today), **build·ing,** *n.* **1** *v.* To make by putting parts or materials together; construct; erect: to *build* a house. **2** *v.* To make; create: to *build* a business. **3** *n.* The way a person or thing is constructed; form; figure: to have the *build* of an athlete.

build·er [bil'dər] *n.* A person who builds, especially one in charge of putting up houses or other buildings.

build·ing [bil'ding] *n.* **1** Something that is built; a structure, as a house, barn, or factory. **2** The act or business of someone who builds.

building block **1** One of a set of children's blocks used for building. **2** A basic or supporting unit: Atoms are the *building blocks* of matter.

build·up [bild'up'] *n.* **1** A steady increase: a *buildup* of suspense. **2** An accumulation: the *buildup* of lava at the foot of a volcano. **3** Praise intended to make someone or something more respected or popular, especially when it is part of a publicity or advertising campaign.

built [bilt] Past tense of BUILD.

built-in [bilt'in'] *adj.* That cannot be taken out or removed: a *built-in* bookcase.

built-up [bilt'up'] *adj.* Having many buildings: *built-up* urban areas.

bulb [bulb] *n.* **1** The enlarged spherical underground bud of certain plants, as the lily and onion, from which the roots and upper parts grow. **2** Anything in the form of a bulb: an electric light *bulb.*

Onion bulb

bul·bous [bul'bəs] *adj.* **1** Of or growing from bulbs. **2** Shaped like a bulb: a *bulbous* nose.

Bul·gar·i·an [bul·gâr'ē·ən *or* bo͝ol·gâr'·ē·ən] **1** *adj.* Of or from Bulgaria. **2** *n.* A person born in or a citizen of Bulgaria. **3** *n.* The language of Bulgaria.

bulge [bulj] *n., v.* **bulged, bulg·ing** **1** *n.* A part that swells out. **2** *v.* To swell out.

bu·lim·ia [byo͞o·lim'ē·ə] *n.* An eating disorder characterized by overeating and vomiting.

bulk [bulk] **1** *n.* Great size or mass: The package's *bulk* made it hard to carry. **2** *n.* A greater or main part: The *bulk* of the work is finished. **3** *v.* To appear large or important; loom. **—in bulk** **1** Not packaged; loose. **2** In large amounts.

bulk·head [bulk'hed'] *n.* Any of several upright partitions dividing a ship into watertight sections.

bulk·y [bul'kē] *adj.* **bulk·i·er, bulk·i·est** Having great size, especially so big and clumsy as to be hard to handle.

bull[1] [bo͝ol] *n.* **1** The full-grown male of domestic cattle. **2** The male of certain other animals, as the elephant or whale.

bull[2] [bo͝ol] *n.* An official pronouncement or order from a pope: a papal *bull.*

bull[3] [bo͝ol] *n.* A funny mistake in language, as in "The kitchen and dining room are the same size, especially the kitchen."

bull·dog [bo͝ol'dôg'] *n., v.* **bull·dogged, bull·dog·ging** **1** *n.* A stocky dog with a large head and jaws that grip and hold. **2** *v. informal* To throw (a steer) down by gripping its horns and twisting its head.

bull·doze [bo͝ol'dōz'] *v.* **bull·dozed, bull·doz·ing** **1** *slang* To frighten by using force or threats; bully. **2** To dig, level, scrape, or otherwise use a bulldozer.

bull·doz·er [bo͝ol'dō'zər] *n.* **1** A tractor with a broad, heavy steel blade in front, used for moving earth and rubble. **2** *informal* A person who bulldozes.

Bulldozer

bul·let [bo͝ol'it] *n.* A metal ball or shaped cone, for shooting from a firearm.

bul·le·tin [bo͝ol'ə·tən] *n.* **1** A short account of the latest news. **2** A magazine or paper put out at regular times, especially by a group for its members.

bulletin board **1** A board, hung on a wall, on which announcements or notices are posted. **2** A message center that operates by computer, so that someone can leave messages which other people can read on their own computer screens.

bul·let·proof [bo͝ol'it·pro͞of'] **1** *adj.* Capable of keeping a bullet from passing through. **2** *v.* To make bulletproof.

bullet train A high-speed passenger train.

bull·fight [bo͝ol'fīt'] *n.* A contest in which a matador, using a cape and sword, shows skill at handling and killing a bull. **—bull'fight'er** *n.* **—bull'·fight'ing** *n.*

bull·finch [bo͝ol'finch'] *n.* A songbird of Europe with a short beak and red breast.

bull·frog [bo͝ol'frog'] *n.* A large frog with a deep, low croak.

bull·head [bo͝ol'hed'] *n.* Any of various American fishes with a broad head, as the catfish.

bull·head·ed [bo͝ol'hed'id] *adj.* Stubborn.

bul·lion [bo͝ol'yən] *n.* Bars of gold or silver, often later made into coins.

a	add	**i**	it	**o͝o**	took	**oi**	oil
ā	ace	**ī**	ice	**o͞o**	pool	**ou**	pout
â	care	**o**	odd	**u**	up	**ng**	ring
ä	palm	**ō**	open	**û**	burn	**th**	thin
e	end	**ô**	order	**yo͞o**	fuse	**th**	this
ē	equal					**zh**	vision

ə = { a in *above* e in *sicken* i in *possible* / o in *melon* u in *circus* }

bull·ish [bo͝ol′ish] *adj.* 1 Like a bull. 2 Characterized by, tending to cause, or expecting a rise in prices: *bullish* about the stock market. 3 Optimistic.
bul·lock [bo͝ol′ək] *n.* A steer or ox.
bull's-eye [bo͝olz′ī′] *n.* 1 The round, usually colored center of a target. 2 A shot that hits this center. 3 A small lantern with a lens formed like a half-sphere for making a stronger light.
bull·ter·ri·er [bo͝ol′ter′ē·ər] *n.* A strong, compactly built dog with a short, white coat, developed by crossing the bulldog with the terrier.
bul·ly [bo͝ol′ē] *n., pl.* **bul·lies,** *v.* **bul·lied, bul·ly·ing,** *adj., interj.* 1 *n.* A person who likes frightening or hurting weaker people. 2 *v.* To act like a bully. 3 *adj. informal* Excellent; very good: a *bully* dinner. 4 *interj.* Excellent!
bul·rush [bo͝ol′rush′] *n.* A tall plant growing in shallow water or damp ground.
bul·wark [bo͝ol′wərk] *n.* 1 A sturdy wall of stone or earth, raised for defense against an enemy. 2 Any strong defense or safeguard: Democracy is a *bulwark* of liberty. 3 (*pl.*) The side of a ship above the deck.
bum [bum] *n., v.* **bummed, bum·ming,** *adj. informal* 1 *n.* A person who lives as a loafer and does no work; a worthless person; tramp. 2 *v.* To pass time idly; loaf. 3 *v.* To get by begging: to *bum* lunch. 4 *adj.* Bad: a *bum* knee; a *bum* check.
bum·ble·bee [bum′bəl·bē′] *n.* A large hairy type of bee, with a loud buzz.
bum·bling [bum′bling] *adj.* Stumbling or clumsy in speech or action; faltering.
bump [bump] 1 *v.* To strike or knock, often heavily or with force: The ball *bumped* the player on the head. 2 *n.* A sudden blow or jolt; knock. 3 *v.* To move with jerks or jolts: The car *bumped* down the road. 4 *n.* A part that sticks out, making an uneven surface; bulge: a road full of *bumps.* 5 *n.* A swelling caused by a blow or knock. —**bump into** *informal* To meet by chance.
bump·er[1] [bum′pər] *n.* Something that protects against bumps, as the metal bar across the front or back of a car.
bump·er[2] [bum′pər] 1 *n.* A cup or glass filled to the brim. 2 *adj.* Unusually large or full: a *bumper* crop of tomatoes.
bump·kin [bump′kin] *n.* An awkward or unsophisticated person from the country.
bump·tious [bump′shəs] *adj.* Rudely asserting oneself; forward; obtrusive.
bump·y [bum′pē] *adj.* **bump·i·er, bump·i·est** Having or causing bumps; rough: a *bumpy* ride. —**bump′·i·ly** *adv.*
bun [bun] *n.* 1 A small bread roll, sometimes sweetened. 2 Hair twisted into a coil on the back of the head.
bunch [bunch] 1 *n.* A number of things of the same kind, growing or placed together: a *bunch* of bananas; a *bunch* of letters. 2 *n. informal* A group: a *bunch* of teenagers. 3 *v.* To gather in or form into a bunch: The flowers were *bunched* to make a bouquet.
bun·dle [bun′dəl] *n., v.* **bun·dled, bun·dling** 1 *n.* A number of things bound or wrapped up together. 2 *n.* A package or parcel. 3 *v.* To make into a bundle: *Bundle* my old clothes together. 4 *v.* To send or put quickly: The children were *bundled* into bed. —**bundle up** To dress in lots of warm clothing.
bung [bung] 1 *n.* A stopper for the hole in a cask or barrel. 2 *n.* The hole in a cask or barrel; bunghole. 3 *v.* To close or stop with a bung.

Man hammering bung into the bunghole of a barrel

bun·ga·low [bung′gə·lō′] *n.* A small house or cottage, usually with one, or one and a half stories. ◆ *Bungalow* comes from a word in Hindustani meaning *of Bengal,* because it described a type of house found in Bengal.
bung·hole [bung′hōl′] *n.* A hole in a cask or barrel, through which liquid is drawn out.
bun·gle [bung′gəl] *v.* **bun·gled, bun·gling,** *n.* 1 *v.* To make or do clumsily or badly; botch: The nervous singer *bungled* the first song. 2 *n.* The act of bungling. 3 *n.* Something that is done or made in a bad or clumsy way. —**bun′gler** *n.*
bun·ion [bun′yən] *n.* A painful, inflamed swelling at the base of the big toe.
bunk[1] [bungk] 1 *n.* A narrow bed, built-in or set against a wall like a shelf. 2 *n. informal* Any narrow bed. 3 *v. informal* To sleep in a bunk. 4 *v. informal* To go to bed; sleep.
bunk[2] [bungk] *n. slang* Silly talk; nonsense. ◆ *Bunk* is short for *buncombe,* meaning *empty talk,* from the habit of a 19th-century congressman from North Carolina, of making windy, pointless speeches "for Buncombe," the name of the county he represented.
bunk bed 1 A narrow bed, one of two placed one above the other. 2 The two beds together, considered as a unit.
bun·ker [bung′kər] 1 *n.* A large bin, as for storing coal on a ship. 2 *n.* A hollow or a mound of earth serving as an obstacle on a golf course. 3 *v.* To provide (a ship) with fuel.
bunk·house [bungk′hous′] *n.* A building having bunks, used as sleeping quarters by groups, as of miners or ranch hands.
bun·ny [bun′ē] *n., pl.* **bun·nies** A rabbit, especially a young rabbit.
Bun·sen burner [bun′sən] A type of burner in which a mixture of gas and air is burned at the top of a short metal tube. It produces a very hot flame.
bunt [bunt] 1 *v.* To strike or push as with horns; butt. 2 *n.* A push or shove; a butt. 3 *v.* To bat (a baseball) very lightly so that the ball rolls in front of the infielders. 4 *n.* A ball that has been bunted.
bunt·ing[1] [bun′ting] *n.* 1 Light, thin material, used for making flags. 2 Strips of material in the colors or designs of the flag, used as holiday decorations. 3 A blanket for a baby made like a sleeping bag with a hood.

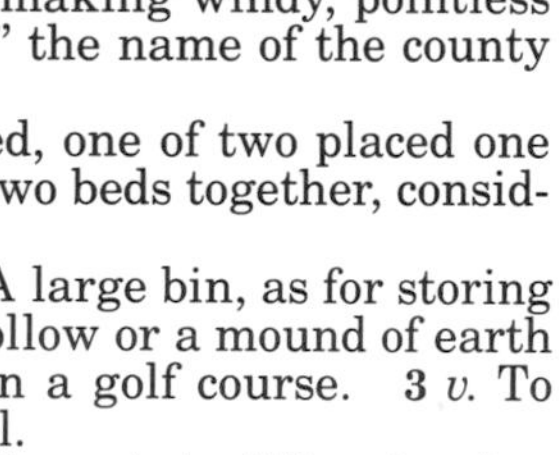
Bunting

bunt·ing[2] [bun′ting] *n.* A type of bird related to finches and sparrows.
Bun·yan [bun′yən], **Paul** In American folklore, a huge lumberjack, famous for his amazing deeds of strength.

B

buoy [boi *or* bo͞o′ē] **1** *n.* A floating object, held in place by an anchor, used to mark a channel or dangerous spot in the water. It sometimes carries a bell or light. **2** *n.* A life preserver; life buoy. **3** *v.* To keep afloat. **4** *v.* To hold up or raise the spirits of: The good news *buoyed* him up.

A bell buoy and a light buoy

buoy·an·cy [boi′ən·sē *or* bo͞o′yən·sē] *n.* **1** The ability to keep afloat: Using a life preserver gives you *buoyancy* in the water. **2** The power to keep an object afloat. **3** Lightness of spirits; cheerfulness.
buoy·ant [boi′ənt *or* bo͞o′yənt] *adj.* **1** Able to keep afloat or rise in liquid or air. **2** Able to keep an object afloat. **3** Cheerful and lighthearted: a *buoyant* wave of the hand. **—buoy′ant·ly** *adv.*
bur [bûr] *n.* **1** A rough or prickly flower head or seedcase, as of the chestnut. **2** A plant that bears burs. **3** A person or thing that clings like a bur.
bur·ble [bûr′bəl] *v.* **bur·bled, bur·bling** **1** To bubble; gurgle: The brooks *burbled.* **2** To talk with excitement and confusion.
bur·den[1] [bûr′dən] **1** *n.* Something carried; a load. **2** *n.* Something difficult to carry or bear: the *burden* of debts. **3** *v.* To load or overload; trouble: I won't *burden* you with my difficulties.
bur·den[2] [bûr′dən] *n.* **1** The chorus or refrain of a song. **2** The main idea or topic.
burden of proof The obligation of proving a disputed allegation or charge.
bur·den·some [bûr′dən·səm] *adj.* Hard to bear; heavy: a *burdensome* task.
bur·dock [bûr′dok] *n.* A plant with large, roundish leaves and round burs.
bu·reau [byo͝or′ō] *n., pl.* **bu·reaus** or **bu·reaux** [byo͝or′ōz] **1** A chest of drawers, usually with a mirror. **2** A government department: the Federal *Bureau* of Investigation. **3** An office or division of a business: a travel *bureau.*
bu·reauc·ra·cy [byo͝o·rok′rə·sē] *n., pl.* **bu·reauc·ra·cies** **1** Government with many departments made up of appointed officials, who follow set rules and regulations. **2** These departments and officials as a group. **3** Any system in which there are mix-ups and delays because of a too strict following of rules.
bu·reau·crat [byo͝or′ə·krat′] *n.* **1** A member of a bureaucracy. **2** An official who follows the rules strictly and rigidly.
bu·reau·crat·ic [byo͝or′ə·krat′ik] *adj.* Of or like a bureaucrat or bureaucracy.
burg [bûrg] *n. informal* A city or town, especially a small or unexciting one.
bur·geon [bûr′jən] *v.* To grow or flourish; blossom.
burg·er [bûr′gər] *n., informal* A hamburger.
bur·gess [bûr′jis] *n.* **1** A citizen or officer of a borough. **2** During colonial times, a member of the lower house of the legislature of Virginia or Maryland.
burgh [bûrg] *n.* In Scotland, a town or borough.
burgh·er [bûr′gər] *n.* A citizen of a burgh or town.
bur·glar [bûr′glər] *n.* A person who breaks into a building or house to commit a theft or other crime.
bur·glar·ize [bûr′glə·rīz′] *v.,* **bur·glar·ized, bur·glar·iz·ing** To break into, as a home or office, in order to steal.
bur·gla·ry [bûr′glər·ē] *n., pl.* **bur·gla·ries** The breaking into a building, especially in order to steal.
bur·go·mas·ter [bûr′gə·mas′tər] *n.* A mayor of a town in some European countries, as Germany.
bur·i·al [ber′ē·əl] *n.* The burying of a dead body.
bur·lap [bûr′lap] *n.* A coarse material, usually made of jute or hemp, used for making such items as bags or wrappings.
bur·lesque [bər·lesk′] *n., v.* **bur·lesqued, bur·les·quing** **1** *n.* A comic or sarcastic imitation of something serious, usually in the form of a play or book. **2** *v.* To imitate in a comic or sarcastic way. **3** *n.* A stage show with singing, dancing, and vulgar comedy.
bur·ly [bûr′lē] *adj.* **bur·li·er, bur·li·est** Big and sturdy; husky: a *burly* football player.
Bur·mese [bər·mēz′] *adj., n., pl.* **Bur·mese** **1** *adj.* Of, having to do with, or from Burma. **2** *n.* A person born in or a citizen of Burma. **3** *n.* The language of Burma.
burn[1] [bûrn] *v.* **burned** or **burnt, burn·ing,** *n.* **1** *v.* To be on fire or undergo combustion. **2** *v.* To set on fire or subject to combustion so as to produce heat or light. **3** *v.* To give off light or heat: The lamp *burns* in the window. **4** *v.* To destroy or be destroyed by fire. **5** *v.* To hurt or damage, as by fire, steam, acid, or wind. **6** *n.* An injury or damage from burning. **7** *v.* To produce by fire: The match *burned* a hole in the paper. **8** *v.* To cause to feel hot: Pepper *burns* my tongue. **9** *v.* To appear or feel hot. **10** *v.* To excite or be excited. **11** *n.* In a spacecraft, the firing of a rocket while in flight.
burn[2] [bûrn] *n.* A Scottish word for a brook.
burn·er [bûr′nər] *n.* **1** A person whose job is to burn something. **2** A device for burning something; incinerator. **3** The part of a stove, lamp, or furnace from which the flame comes.
bur·nish [bûr′nish] **1** *v.* To polish by rubbing: to *burnish* metal. **2** *n.* Polish; luster.
bur·noose or **bur·nous** [bər·no͞os′ *or* bûr′no͞os] *n.* A long, hooded cloak work by Arabs.
burn·out [bûrn′out′] *n.* **1** The end of the operation of a jet engine or rocket when its fuel has been used up or cut off. **2** A state of physical or mental exhaustion, particularly when caused by stress from work or other responsibilities.
burnt [bûrnt] **1** An alternative past tense and past participle of BURN. **2** *adj.* Injured or charred by fire: *burnt* fingers; *burnt* toast.
burp [bûrp] *informal* **1** *v.* To belch. **2** *v.* To cause to belch: to *burp* a baby. **3** *n.* A belch.
burr[1] [bûr] *n.* Another spelling of BUR.
burr[2] [bûr] *n.* **1** A rough edge left on metal in drilling or cutting. **2** A cutting or drilling tool, as a dental drill. **3** The rough, trilled sound of "r," used by some Scots. **4** A whirring sound; a buzz.

a add	**i** it	**o͝o** took	**oi** oil				
ā ace	**ī** ice	**o͞o** pool	**ou** pout				
â care	**o** odd	**u** up	**ng** ring				
ä palm	**ō** open	**û** burn	**th** thin				
e end	**ô** order	**yo͞o** fuse	**th** this				
ē equal			**zh** vision				

ə = a in *above*, e in *sicken*, i in *possible*, o in *melon*, u in *circus*

bur·ro [bûr′ō] *n., pl.* **bur·ros** A small donkey, used for riding or for carrying packs in the sw U.S.

Burro

bur·row [bûr′ō] **1** *n.* A hole made in the ground by certain animals: Rabbits live in *burrows.* **2** *v.* To dig a burrow. **3** *v.* To live or hide in a burrow. **4** *v.* To search deeply: The clerk *burrowed* into the pile of reports.

bur·sa [bûr′sə] *n., pl.* **bur·sae** [bûr′sē] or **bur·sas** A pouch or saclike cavity in the body, especially one between the parts of a joint. It is filled with lubricating fluid to lessen friction.

bur·sar [bûr′sər] *n.* A treasurer, as of a college.

bur·si·tis [bər·sī′tis] *n.* Inflammation of a bursa.

burst [bûrst] *v.* **burst, burst·ing,** *n.* **1** *v.* To break open or apart suddenly; explode from a force inside: The balloon *burst* with a bang. **2** *v.* To give way to a sudden, strong feeling: to *burst* into tears. **3** *n.* A sudden explosion or outbreak: a *burst* of gunfire; a *burst* of laughter. **4** *v.* To be filled to overflowing: Our house is *bursting* with children. **5** *v.* To appear or enter suddenly: They *burst* into the hall. **6** *n.* A sudden rush or spurt: a *burst* of speed. ◆ Careful writers and speakers should avoid using *bust* when they mean *burst.*

Bu·run·di·an [bə·run′dē·ən *or* bŏŏ·rōōn′dē·ən] **1** *adj.* Of or from Burundi. **2** *n.* A person born in or a citizen of Burundi.

bur·y [ber′ē] *v.* **bur·ied, bur·y·ing** **1** To put (a dead body) in a grave, tomb, or the sea. **2** To hide or cover from view: He *buried* his face in his hands. **3** To put out of mind and forget: to *bury* a disagreement. **4** To absorb (oneself) deeply; engross: She *buried* herself in her studies.

bus [bus] *n., pl.* **bus·es** or **bus·ses,** *v.* **bused** or **bussed, bus·ing** or **bus·sing** **1** *n.* A large, long motor vehicle with seats for carrying many passengers. **2** *v.* To bring or transport by bus. **3** *n.* A wire or set of wires that sends information or instructions in the form of electrical signals from one part of a computer to another. ◆ Originally *buses* were called *omnibuses,* because *omnibus* in Latin means "for all," and buses hold large numbers of passengers and are for the use of all. Later *omnibus* was shortened to *bus.*

bus·boy [bus′boi′] *n.* A restaurant employee who helps waiters, as by clearing and setting tables.

bush [bŏŏsh] **1** *n.* A low, treelike shrub with many branches or stems. **2** *v.* To grow or branch out like a bush. **3** *n.* Wild, uncleared land, with few settlers on it. **—beat about the bush** or **beat around the bush** To talk around a subject to avoid getting to the point.

bush·el [bŏŏsh′əl] *n.* **1** A unit of volume used to measure fruits, vegetables, or other dry things. It is equal to 4 pecks or 32 quarts. **2** A container, as a basket, holding this amount.

bush·ing [bŏŏsh′ing] *n.* A detachable metal lining used in a machine to prevent wearing down of parts.

Bush·man [bŏŏsh′mən] *n., pl.* **Bush·men** [bŏŏsh′·mən] A member of a people of South Africa, who move from place to place and are related to the Pygmies.

bush·mas·ter [bŏŏsh′mas′tər] *n.* A large, very poisonous snake of tropical America.

bush·whack [bŏŏsh′(h)wak′] *v. informal* **1** To make one's way through thick woods without a trail, especially by cutting away bushes and branches. **2** To attack from a hiding place; ambush.

bush·y [bŏŏsh′ē] *adj.* **bush·i·er, bush·i·est** **1** Covered with or full of bushes. **2** Thick like a bush; shaggy: *bushy* hair and eyebrows.

bus·i·ly [biz′ə·lē] *adv.* In a busy manner.

busi·ness [biz′nis] *n.* **1** A trade or occupation: Their *business* is selling cars. **2** The buying, selling, and other details of trade or industry. **3** A commercial or industrial enterprise: My father's clothing *business* is uptown. **4** *adj. use:* a *business* suit; a *business* card. **5** Matter or affair: Climbing mountains is a risky *business.* **6** Right; concern: It's not your *business* to tell me what to do. **—mean business** To be serious or determined. ◆ See OCCUPATION.

busi·ness·like [biz′nis·līk′] *adj.* Systematic and methodical; practical.

busi·ness·man [biz′nis·man′] *n., pl.* **busi·ness·men** [biz′nis·men′] A man who owns or manages a business.

busi·ness·wom·an [biz′nis·wŏŏm′ən] *n., pl.* **busi·ness·wom·en** [biz′nis·wim′in] A woman who owns or manages a business.

bus·kin [bus′kin] *n.* A type of boot worn long ago by Greek and Roman actors as a symbol of tragedy.

buss [bus] *n., v.* An old-fashioned word for KISS.

bust[1] [bust] *n.* **1** A piece of sculpture of the head, shoulders, and upper chest of a person. **2** The chest of a person, especially the bosom of a woman.

Bust of Lincoln

bust[2] [bust] *v. slang* **1** To burst or break. **2** To put under arrest. ◆ See BURST.

bus·tard [bus′tərd] *n.* A large, heavy bird with a long neck and long legs. ◆ *Bustard* can be traced back to a Latin name, *avis tarda,* which literally means *slow bird.*

bus·tle[1] [bus′(ə)l] *v.* **bus·tled, bus·tling,** *n.* **1** *v.* To move or hurry with much fuss and excitement. **2** *n.* Noisy activity and motion.

bus·tle[2] [bus′(ə)l] *n.* A pad or frame formerly worn by women at the back of a long skirt to puff it out.

bus·y [biz′ē] *adj.* **bus·i·er, bus·i·est,** *v.* **bus·ied, bus·y·ing** **1** *adj.* Occupied; working: We were *busy* in the kitchen. **2** *adj.* Filled with activity: a *busy* morning. **3** *adj.* In use: The phone line is *busy.* **4** *v.* To keep or make busy: She *busied* herself working on the report.

bus·y·bod·y [biz′ē·bod′ē] *n., pl.* **bus·y·bod·ies** A person who pries into other people's affairs.

Bustle

but [but] **1** *conj.* On the other hand: Your desk is large, *but* mine is small. **2** *conj.* Other than; except: I have no choice *but* to listen. **3** *prep.* With the exception of: hearing nothing *but* praise. **4** *conj.* Yet; nevertheless: They were poor *but* honest. **5** *conj.* Without the result that: It never rains *but* it pours. **6** *conj.* That: We don't doubt *but* he'll be there. **7** *adv.* Only; just: You are *but* a child. **—all but** Almost. ◆ In writing, avoid colloquial double negatives with *but* (such as "no doubt but that" or "couldn't help but").

bu·ta·di·ene [byōō'tə·dī'ēn'] *n.* A colorless, flammable gas used chiefly in the manufacture of synthetic rubber.

bu·tane [byōō'tān' *or* byōō·tān'] *n.* A flammable gas made from petroleum or natural gas.

butch·er [bŏŏch'ər] **1** *n.* A person who kills animals for market. **2** *n.* A person who cuts up and sells meat. **3** *v.* To kill or prepare for market. **4** *n.* A person who kills in a brutal way. **5** *v.* To kill in a brutal, bloody way; slaughter. **6** *v.* To ruin; botch.

butch·er·y [bŏŏch'ər·ē] *n., pl.* **butch·er·ies** Senseless and cruel killing; slaughter.

but·ler [but'lər] *n.* A manservant who directs other servants and is in charge of the dining room.

butt[1] [but] *n.* **1** The thicker or larger end of a weapon or tool: a rifle *butt.* **2** An unused end, as of a cigarette. **3** Someone who is ridiculed: to be the *butt* of the joke.

butt[2] [but] *n.* A large cask, especially for wine, beer, or water.

butt[3] [but] **1** *v.* To strike, push, or bump with the head or horns; ram. **2** *n.* A blow or push with the head. **—butt in** or **butt into** To interrupt, or meddle in someone else's affairs.

butte [byōōt] *n.* A hill, standing alone, that has steep sides and sometimes a flat top.

but·ter [but'ər] **1** *n.* The yellowish fat that becomes separated from milk during churning. It is used as a spread and in cooking. **2** *v.* To spread butter on. **3** *n.* Something with the same use as butter: peanut *butter.* **4** *v. informal* To flatter: They *buttered* up the teacher. **—but'ter·y** *adj.*

but·ter·cup [but'ər·kup'] *n.* A plant with small, yellow, cup-shaped flowers.

but·ter·fat [but'ər·fat'] *n.* The fatty substance in milk, from which butter is made.

but·ter·fin·gers [but'ər·fing'gərz] *n.pl.* (*used with singular verb*) *slang* A person who is always dropping things.

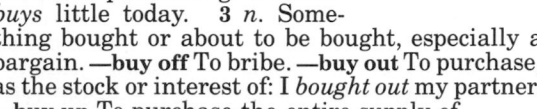

but·ter·fly [but'ər·flī'] *n., pl.* **but·ter·flies** **1** A four-winged insect related to the moth, but having clubbed antennae and usually a more slender body and more brightly colored wings. **2** A type of swimming stroke.

Butterfly

but·ter·milk [but'ər·milk'] *n.* The sour liquid left after the butterfat is removed from milk.

but·ter·nut [but'ər·nut'] *n.* **1** The oily nut of a certain walnut tree. **2** This tree.

but·ter·scotch [but'ər·skoch'] **1** *n.* A hard, sticky candy, made with brown sugar and butter. **2** *adj.* Made of or flavored with butterscotch.

but·tock [but'ək] *n.* Either of the two fleshy parts at the back of the hip, upon which human beings sit; rump.

but·ton [but'(ə)n] **1** *n.* A disk or knob sewn to a garment, serving as a fastening when passed through a narrow opening or buttonhole, or used simply for decoration. **2** *v.* To fasten or enclose with buttons. **3** *n.* Anything like a button, as a small knob operating an electric bell.

but·ton-down [but'(ə)n·doun'] *adj.* Having collar tips that button to the front of the shirt.

but·ton·hole [but'(ə)n·hōl'] *n., v.* **but·ton·hol·ed, but·ton·hol·ing** **1** *n.* A slit to receive and hold a button. **2** *v.* To detain (a person) by or as if by holding on to the buttonhole of the person's coat so that he or she is forced to listen to what one says.

but·ton·wood [but'(ə)n·wŏŏd'] *n.* **1** The sycamore tree of North America. **2** Its wood.

but·tress [but'tris] **1** *n.* A structure built against a wall to strengthen it. **2** *v.* To prop up or sustain; support: to *buttress* a wall; to *buttress* one's hopes.

Buttress

bux·om [buk'səm] *adj.* Plump and pleasant to look at. ◆ *Buxom* is used only of women.

buy [bī] *v.* **bought, buy·ing,** *n.* **1** *v.* To obtain in exchange for money or some other thing; purchase: The child *bought* a balloon for a dime. **2** *v.* To be a means of purchasing: A dollar *buys* little today. **3** *n.* Something bought or about to be bought, especially a bargain. **—buy off** To bribe. **—buy out** To purchase, as the stock or interest of: I *bought out* my partner. **—buy up** To purchase the entire supply of.

buy·er [bī'ər] *n.* **1** A person who buys. **2** A person whose work is buying merchandise for a store.

buy·out [bī'out] *n.* The purchase of large quantities of stock so as to gain control of a company.

buzz [buz] **1** *v.* To make the steady, humming sound of a bee. **2** *n.* The steady, humming sound made by a bee. **3** *v.* To talk with quiet excitement: The town *buzzed* with gossip. **4** *n.* A low, confused murmur, as of many voices. **5** *v.* To signal with a buzzer: The manager *buzzed* for the secretary. **6** *v.* To fly an airplane low over: to *buzz* a ship.

buz·zard [buz'ərd] *n.* **1** A kind of large, slow-flying hawk. **2** Another name for TURKEY BUZZARD. **3** A contemptible or avaricious person.

Turkey buzzard

buzz·er [buz'ər] *n.* An electrical device that makes a buzzing sound.

buzz saw A circular saw rotated by a motor.

buzz·word [buz'wûrd'] *n.* *slang* An important-sounding word used by members of a particular group or field to impress listeners or readers.

by [bī] **1** *prep.* Next to; near: the tree *by* the river. **2** *adv.* At hand; near: Stay close *by*! **3** *prep.* Past and beyond: The train roared *by* us. **4** *adv.* Past:

a	add	**i**	it	**ŏŏ**	took	**oi**	oil
ā	ace	**ī**	ice	**ōō**	pool	**ou**	pout
â	care	**o**	odd	**u**	up	**ng**	ring
ä	palm	**ō**	open	**û**	burn	**th**	thin
e	end	**ô**	order	**yōō**	fuse	**th**	this
ē	equal					**zh**	vision

ə = a in *above* e in *sicken* i in *possible* o in *melon* u in *circus*

The years go *by.* **5** *prep.* By way of; through: Come *by* the nearest road. **6** *prep.* In the course of; during: to travel *by* night. **7** *prep.* According to a standard or fixed rate: to work *by* the day. **8** *prep.* Not later than: Be here *by* noon. **9** *prep.* After: day *by* day. **10** *prep.* Through the work of; by means of: to travel *by* plane. **11** *prep.* Regarding; for: to do well *by* one's friends. **12** *prep.* According to: *by* law. **13** *prep.* In accordance with: *by* your leave. **14** *prep.* In multiplication with: Multiply 6 *by* 8. **15** *prep.* In or to the amount of: insects *by* the hundreds. **16** *adv.* Aside, apart: to lay money *by.* **—by and by** After a time. **—by and large** On the whole; generally. **—by the by** or **by the bye** By the way; incidentally. ◆ In writing, avoid using *by* informally to mean "with" (as in "It's all right by me").

by-and-by [bī′ən·bī′] *n.* A future time: We shall meet in the *by-and-by.*

by-e·lec·tion [bī′i·lek′shən] *n.* A special election held to fill a vacancy in a legislature.

Bye·lo·rus·sian [b(y)el′ō·rush′ən] **1** *adj.* Of or from Byelorussia. **2** *n.* A person born or living in Byelorussia. **3** *n.* The language of Byelorussia.

by·gone [bī′gôn′ *or* bī′gon′] **1** *adj.* Gone by; past: *bygone* days. **2** *n.* Something past or gone by. —**let bygones be bygones** To let past disagreements be forgotten.

by·law [bī′lô′] *n.* **1** A rule passed by a club or corporation for governing its own meetings and affairs. **2** A law that is secondary to the main set of laws.

by-line [bī′līn′] *n.* The line at the head of a newspaper article giving the writer's name.

by·pass [bī′pas′] **1** *n.* A road, route, or pipe that goes off the main course, so as to pass around an obstacle: We took a *bypass* to avoid the traffic jam. **2** *n.* An operation to allow blood to pass around a damaged blood vessel: a coronary *bypass.* **3** *v.* To go around or avoid: We *bypassed* the towns to save time.

by·path [bī′path′] *n.* A side or indirect path.

by·play [bī′plā′] *n.* Action or talking apart from the main action, as in a stage scene.

by-prod·uct [bī′prod′əkt] *n.* Anything else resulting from making a main product.

byre [bīr] *n. British* A cow stable.

by·road [bī′rōd′] *n.* A back or side road.

by·stand·er [bī′stan′dər] *n.* A person who is present but not taking part; onlooker.

byte [bīt] *n.* A memory unit in a digital computer, usually made up of eight bits. ◆ *Byte* may come from *bite,* meaning a morsel.

by·way [bī′wā′] *n.* A side path; a path not often used.

by·word [bī′wûrd′] *n.* **1** A common saying or proverb. **2** An object of scorn: Your dishonesty will make you the *byword* of the whole school.

Byz·an·tine [biz′ən·tēn′ *or* biz′ən·tīn′] **1** *adj.* Of or from the ancient city of Byzantium. **2** *adj.* Of or designating the eastern part of the later Roman Empire, the capital of which was Byzantium, renamed Constantinople. **3** *adj.* Of, having to do with, or having the characteristics of the style of architecture developed in this city, which used round arches, rich mosaic art work, and many domes. **4** *n.* A native or inhabitant of Byzantium.

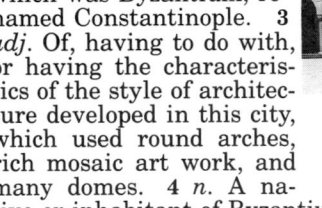

Byzantine architecture

C is the third letter of the alphabet. The sign for it originated among Semitic people in the Near East, in the region of Palestine and Syria, probably in the middle of the second millennium B.C. Little was known about the sign until around 1000 B.C., when the Phoenicians began using it. The Phoenicians named the sign *gimel* and used it for the sound of the consonant *g*.

When the Greeks adopted the Phoenician sign around the ninth century B.C., they called it *gamma* and used it, too, for the sound of *g*. Throughout the early centuries, the shape of the letter changed several times. Most of the shapes were angular, with the letter facing first to the left and in later years to the right.

As early as the eighth century B.C., the Etruscans adopted the Greek alphabet. Since the Etruscan language made no distinction between the *g* and the *k* sounds, the Etruscans used the letter for the sound of *k*. It was from the Etruscans that the Romans took the letter. At first the Romans, too, used the sign for both the *g* and the *k* sounds. Eventually, however, the Romans formed a new letter for the *g* sound (see *G*). They retained the *C* symbol for the sound of *k*, limiting its use to words in which the *k* sound preceded an *E* or an *I* (see also *K* and *Q*).

Both the Etruscans and the Romans had contributed to the rounding of the shape of the *majuscule,* or capital letter, *C*.

The *minuscule,* or small letter, *c* had little separate development and is a small version of the capital letter. Shown are some major versions: the Roman *uncial c* of the fourth to the eighth centuries, the *half uncial c* of the fifth to the ninth centuries, and the *Caroline minuscule c*. The Caroline minuscules—a script that evolved under the encouragement of Charlemagne (742-814)—became the principal handwriting system used on the medieval manuscripts of the ninth and tenth centuries.

Cc

Early Phoenician (late 2nd millennium B.C.)

Phoenician (8th century B.C.)

Early Greek (9th-7th centuries B.C.)

Western Greek (6th century B.C.)

Classical Greek (403 B.C. onward)

Early Etruscan (8th century B.C.)

Monumental Latin (4th century B.C.)

Classical Latin

Uncial

Half uncial

Caroline minuscule

c or **C** [sē] *n., pl.* **c's** or **C's** **1** The third letter of the English alphabet. **2** (*written* **C**) The Roman numeral for 100. **3** In music, the first and last notes in the scale of C major.

c or **c.** **1** centimeter. **2** cubic.

c. **1** approximately. ◆ *c.* is an abbreviation of Latin *circa,* meaning *around.* **2** carat. **3** cent(s). **4** centigrade. **5** century. **6** copyright.

C The symbol for the element carbon.

C **1** Celsius. **2** centigrade. **3** coulomb.

C. **1** calorie. **2** Catholic. **3** In Britain, Conservative.

Ca The symbol for the element calcium.

CA Postal Service abbreviation of California.

cab [kab] *n.* **1** A taxicab. **2** A one-horse carriage for public hire. **3** An enclosed compartment, as in a locomotive for the engineer, or in a truck or crane for the operator.

CAB Civil Aeronautics Board.

ca·bal [kə·bal′] *n.* **1** A group of persons who are secretly engaged in some scheme or plot. **2** The scheme or plot of such a group.

ca·ba·la or **cab·ba·la** [kab′ə·lə *or* ka·bäl′ə] *n.* A system of mystical Jewish philosophy developed by rabbis, especially in the Middle Ages. **—cab′a·lism** *n.* **—cab′a·list** *n.*

cab·al·le·ro [kab′əl·yâr′ō] *n., pl.* **cab·al·le·ros** A Spanish gentleman; cavalier.

ca·ban·a [kə·ban′ə] *n.* **1** A small cabin. **2** A small bathhouse for changing clothes at the beach.

cab·a·ret [kab′ə·rā′] *n.* A restaurant that provides entertainment for its customers.

cab·bage [kab′ij] *n.* A vegetable with closely folded leaves forming a hard, round head.

cab·by or **cab·bie** [kab′ē] *n., pl.* **cab·bies** *informal* A cab driver.

cab·driv·er [kab′drī′vər] *n.* A person who drives a cab, especially a taxicab.

cab·in [kab′in] *n.* **1** A small, roughly built wooden house or hut. **2** A room equipped for sleeping on a ship. **3** The passengers' section in an aircraft.

cabin boy A boy who serves the officers and passengers on a ship.

cab·i·net [kab′ə·nit] *n.* **1** A piece of furniture fitted with shelves and drawers. **2** (*often written* **Cabinet**) A group of official advisers and assistants of a head of state.

cab·i·net·mak·er [kab′ə·nit·mā′kər] *n.* A person who makes fine wooden furniture and woodwork.

ca·ble [kā′bəl] *n., v.* **ca·bled, ca·bling** **1** *n.* A heavy rope, now usually made of steel wire. **2** *n.* An insulated electric wire or group of wires, espe-

a	add	**i**	it	**o͝o**	took	**oi**	oil
ā	ace	**ī**	ice	**o͞o**	pool	**ou**	pout
â	care	**o**	odd	**u**	up	**ng**	ring
ä	palm	**ō**	open	**û**	burn	**th**	thin
e	end	**ô**	order	**yo͞o**	fuse	**t͟h**	this
ē	equal					**zh**	vision

ə = { a in *above* e in *sicken* i in *possible* / o in *melon* u in *circus* }

cially used to carry telephone and telegraph messages. **3** *n.* A cablegram. **4** *v.* To send a cablegram.

cable car A car moving along an overhead cable or pulled along tracks by an underground cable.

ca·ble·gram [kā′bəl·gram′] *n.* A message sent across an ocean by a cable laid under the water.

cable television **1** A system in which television programs are delivered by cable from a tall or elevated antenna to the sets of subscribers. **2** A system in which television programs are delivered by cable to subscribers who view the programs on channels other than those regularly used for television transmission.

ca·boose [kə·bo͞os′] *n. U.S.* A car, usually the rear car, of a freight train, used by the crew.

ca·ca·o [kə·kā′ō] *n., pl.* **ca·ca·os** **1** A tropical tree having large seeds from which cocoa and chocolate are made. **2** The seeds of this tree.

cach·a·lot [kash′ə·lot′] *n.* Another name for SPERM WHALE.

cache [kash] *n., v.* **cached, cach·ing** **1** *n.* A place for concealing or storing something. **2** *n.* The goods concealed or stored. **3** *v.* To hide or store away, as in a cache.

ca·chet [ka·shā′] *n.* **1** A mark of official approval. **2** A mark, quality, or characteristic that confers prestige.

cack·le [kak′əl] *n., v.* **cack·led, cack·ling** **1** *n.* A shrill, broken cry, as of a hen laying eggs. **2** *v.* To make such a cry. **3** *n.* A short, shrill laugh. **4** *v.* To utter such a laugh. **5** *n.* Idle, loud chatter: the *cackle* of the gossipers.

ca·coph·o·ny [kə·kof′ə·nē] *n., pl.* **ca·coph·o·nies** A harsh or displeasing mixture of sounds; dissonance.

cac·tus [kak′təs] *n., pl.* **cac·tus·es** or **cac·ti** [kak′tī] A plant of hot desert regions having a green pulpy trunk covered with spines or prickles instead of leaves and often bearing showy flowers.

Saguaro cactus

cad [kad] *n.* An ill-bred, dishonorable man.

ca·dav·er [kə·dav′ər] *n.* A dead body, especially one awaiting dissection.

ca·dav·er·ous [kə·dav′ər·əs] *adj.* Resembling a dead person; pale, thin, and gloomy looking.

cad·die [kad′ē] *n., v.* **cad·died, cad·dy·ing** **1** *n.* A person who carries clubs for golf players, usually for money. **2** *v.* To act as a caddie.

Cad·do [kad′ō] *n., pl.* **Cad·do** or **Cad·dos** **1** A group of tribes of North American Indians once living in Texas, Louisiana, Arkansas, and Kansas, now in Oklahoma. **2** A member of any of these tribes.

Cad·do·an [kad′ō·ən] *n.* A family of Indian languages spoken by the Caddo.

cad·dy[1] [kad′ē] *n., pl.* **cad·dies** A small box or case, especially one in which to keep tea.

cad·dy[2] [kad′ē] *n., pl.* **cad·dies,** *v.* **cad·died, cad·dy·ing** Another spelling of CADDIE.

ca·dence [kād′əns] *n.* **1** A rhythmic flow or movement: the *cadence* of words in poetry. **2** The rise or fall in a speaker's voice. **3** A succession of harmonies ending a piece of music.

ca·den·za [kə·den′zə] *n.* A solo musical passage, usually near the end of a composition, intended to allow a performer to display his or her skill.

ca·det [kə·det′] *n.* A person in training to become an officer in any of the armed forces. **2** A student attending a military school.

cadge [kaj] *v.* **cadged, cadg·ing** To beg or obtain by begging.

cad·mi·um [kad′mē·əm] *n.* A soft, bluish white toxic metallic element having numerous industrial uses.

ca·du·ce·us [kə·d(y)o͞o′sē·əs] *n.* A staff with snakes twined around it and wings at the top, carried by the Greek god Hermes. It is the emblem of the medical profession.

Cae·sar [sē′zər] *n.* **1** The title of any of the Roman emperors succeeding Augustus. **2** Any dictator or tyrant.

Cae·sar·e·an section [si·zâr′ē·ən] Another spelling of CESAREAN SECTION.

cae·su·ra [si·zho͝or′ə] *n., pl.* **cae·su·ras** or **cae·su·rae** [si·zho͝or′ē] A pause or break in a line of poetry, usually near the middle.

ca·fé [ka·fā′] *n.* **1** A restaurant or barroom. **2** Coffee.

caf·e·te·ri·a [kaf′ə·tir′ē·ə] *n.* A restaurant in which customers select food that is displayed and served at counters and then carry it to tables to eat.

caf·feine [ka·fēn′] *n.* A substance with a slightly bitter taste found in tea and coffee. It is used in medicine as a heart and nerve stimulant.

caf·tan [kaf′tən *or* kaf·tan′] *n.* An ankle-length robe with long sleeves, worn in the Middle East and northern Africa.

cage [kāj] *n., v.* **caged, cag·ing** **1** *n.* A boxlike structure closed in with wire or bars for confining animals or birds. **2** *n.* Any cagelike structure, as an elevator car. **3** *v.* To shut up in or as if in a cage; imprison.

cage·y [kā′jē] *adj.* **cag·i·er, cag·i·est** *informal* Shrewd, sly, and careful. **—cag′i·ly** *adv.*

ca·hoots [kə·ho͞ots′] *n. slang* Secret or dishonest partnership: in *cahoots* with a robber.

cai·man [kā′mən] *n., pl.* **cai·mans** A large reptile of tropical America, like the alligator but having bony scales on its belly.

Cain [kān] *n.* In the Bible, the eldest son of Adam. He killed his brother Abel. **—raise Cain** *slang* To cause trouble, make noise, or otherwise create a disturbance.

cairn [kârn] *n.* A mound or heap of stones set up as a memorial or a marker.

cais·son [kā′sən] *n.* **1** A two-wheeled cart used to carry ammunition for a gun. **2** A large, watertight chamber in which people can work under water.

caisson disease A disease caused by too rapid a change from a high to a normal air pressure, often affecting divers; the bends.

cai·tiff [kā′tif] **1** *n.* A low scoundrel. **2** *adj.* Base. ◆ This word is seldom used today.

ca·jole [kə·jōl′] *v.* **ca·joled, ca·jol·ing** To coax or persuade by flattery or deceit; wheedle.

ca·jol·er·y [kə·jō′lər·ē] *n., pl.* **ca·jol·er·ies** The act of cajoling; coaxing.

Ca·jun [kā′jən] *n.* A person whose ancestors were among the French-speaking people who were expelled from eastern Canada and settled in Louisiana in the 18th century.

cake [kāk] *n., v.* **caked, cak·ing** **1** *n.* A baked mixture, including flour, eggs, and butter, usually sweeter than bread. **2** *n.* A small, usually thin mass of dough or other food, baked or fried: a fish

cake. **3** *n.* A mass of material compressed or hardened into a compact form: a *cake* of soap. **4** *v.* To form or harden into a cake.
cake·walk [kāk′wôk′] **1** *n.* Originally, an elaborate walk or promenade performed by American Blacks. A cake was awarded to the person or persons who used the most original and accomplished steps in performing the cakewalk. **2** *n.* A dance based on this. **3** *n.* The music used for this dance. **4** *v.* To do a cakewalk.
cal small calorie.
Cal large calorie.
Cal. California.
cal·a·bash [kal′ə·bash′] *n.* **1** Either of two tropical American trees bearing a hard-shelled, gourdlike fruit. **2** This fruit. **3** A utensil made from this fruit, as a bowl or tobacco pipe.
cal·a·mine [kal′ə·mīn′] *n.* A pink powder prepared from a zinc compound, used in ointments or lotions for skin treatment.
ca·lam·i·tous [kə·lam′ə·təs] *adj.* Causing or resulting in a calamity; disastrous.
ca·lam·i·ty [kə·lam′ə·tē] *n., pl.* **ca·lam·i·ties** **1** Any happening that causes great distress; a disaster. **2** A condition or time of suffering or disaster.
cal·car·e·ous [kal·kâr′ē·əs] *adj.* Of or containing calcium, calcium carbonate, or limestone.
cal·ci·fi·ca·tion [kal′sə·fi·kā′shən] *n.* **1** The process of calcifying, especially the depositing of insoluble lime salts in living tissue. **2** A calcified structure or formation.
cal·ci·fy [kal′sə·fī] *v.* **cal·ci·fied, cal·ci·fy·ing** To make or become hard or bony by the deposit of lime salts.
cal·ci·mine [kal′sə·mīn′] *n., v.* **cal·ci·mined, cal·ci·min·ing** **1** *n.* A watery mixture of chalk and glue, white or tinted, as used to paint plastered walls. **2** *v.* To apply calcimine to.
cal·cine [kal′sīn′] *v.* **cal·cined, cal·cin·ing** **1** To change into lime by prolonged heating. **2** To burn to ashes.
cal·cite [kal′sīt′] *n.* A mineral composed of calcium carbonate. It is the main component of chalk, limestone, and marble.
cal·ci·um [kal′sē·əm] *n.* A soft, silver-white, metallic element. It is an essential part of bones and is found in such materials as marble and chalk.
calcium carbonate A compound forming the principal part of certain rocks and minerals, as marble. It is used in making lime.
cal·cu·la·ble [kal′kyə·lə·bəl] *adj.* That can be calculated. **—cal′cu·la·bly** *adv.*
cal·cu·late [kal′kyə·lāt′] *v.* **cal·cu·lat·ed, cal·cu·lat·ing** **1** To figure by using mathematics: to *calculate* expenses. **2** To think out; form an estimate of: to *calculate* the chance of success. **3** To plan or design: a move *calculated* to confuse the foe.
cal·cu·lat·ed [kal′kyə·lā′tid] *adj.* **1** Accomplished by mathematical calculation. **2** Attempted or accomplished after considering the probable chances of success or failure: a *calculated* assault on the guerrillas' camp.
cal·cu·lat·ing [kal′kyə·lā′ting] *adj.* Very sly and cautious; shrewd; scheming.
cal·cu·la·tion [kal′kyə·lā′shən] *n.* **1** The act of calculating. **2** The answer arrived at by calculating. **3** A forecast. **4** Careful planning.
cal·cu·la·tor [kal′kyə·lā′tər] *n.* **1** A person who calculates. **2** A machine that does mathematical problems, as an adding machine or computer.
cal·cu·lus [kal′kyə·ləs] *n.* An advanced form of algebra used to solve problems involving things that are changing at varying rates.
cal·dron [kôl′drən] *n.* A large kettle or pot.
cal·en·dar [kal′ən·dər] *n.* **1** An arrangement of time into years, months, weeks, and days. **2** A table showing the days, weeks, and months of a year. **3** A schedule or list of events or appointments: a social *calendar.*
calendar month A month (def. 1).
calendar year A year (def. 1).
cal·en·der [kal′ən·dər] **1** *n.* A machine for giving a gloss to cloth, paper, and other items, by pressing between rollers. **2** *v.* To press in a calender.
calf[1] [kaf] *n., pl.* **calves** [kavz] **1** The young of the cow or other bovine animals. **2** The young of some other mammals, as the seal or whale. **3** Calfskin.
calf[2] [kaf] *n., pl.* **calves** [kavz] The muscular back part of the human leg below the knee.
calf·skin [kaf′skin′] *n.* **1** The skin or hide of young cattle. **2** Leather made from this.
Cal·i·ban [kal′ə·ban′] *n.* A deformed, savage slave in Shakespeare's play *The Tempest.*
cal·i·ber or **cal·i·bre** [kal′ə·bər] *n.* **1** The diameter of the inside of a tube, especially of the barrel of a gun, as a revolver or rifle: a .38 *caliber* pistol. **2** The diameter of a cartridge, shell, or other projectile fired from a gun. **3** Excellence or ability.
cal·i·brate [kal′ə·brāt′] *v.* **cal·i·brat·ed, cal·i·brat·ing** **1** To mark, check, or adjust the scale of (a measuring instrument). **2** To determine the caliber of. **—cal′i·bra′tion** *n.*
cal·i·co [kal′i·kō] *n., pl.* **cal·i·coes** or **cal·i·cos,** *adj.* **1** *n.* Cotton cloth printed with a figured design. **2** *adj. use*: a *calico* curtain. **3** *adj.* Like calico; spotted or streaked: a *calico* cat.
ca·lif [kā′lif] *n.* Another spelling of CALIPH.
Calif. California.
cal·i·for·ni·um [kal′ə·fôr′nē·əm] *n.* An artificially produced radioactive chemical element.
cal·i·pers [kal′ə·pərz] *n. pl.* An instrument with two movable, hinged legs, used for measuring the diameter or thickness of an object.

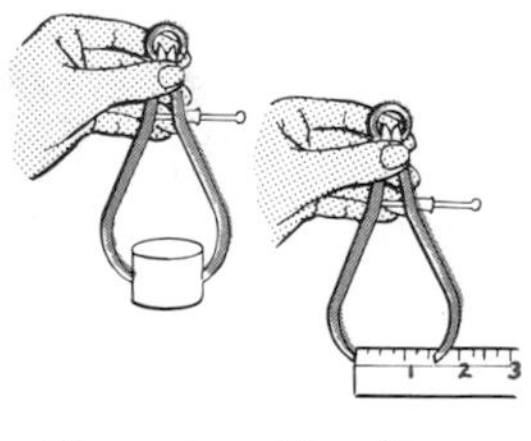
Measuring with calipers

ca·liph [kā′lif] *n.* Successor of Muhammad, a title of a Muslim ruler.
cal·iph·ate [ka′li·fāt′] *n.* The office, government, reign, or territory of a caliph.
cal·is·then·ics [kal′is·then′iks] *n.pl.* Exercises done to promote grace and health.
calk[1] [kôk] *v.* Another spelling of CAULK.
calk[2] [kôk] *n.* **1** A pointed piece of metal on a horse's

a	add	**i**	it	**o͝o**	took	**oi**	oil
ā	ace	**ī**	ice	**o͞o**	pool	**ou**	pout
â	care	**o**	odd	**u**	up	**ng**	ring
ä	palm	**ō**	open	**û**	burn	**th**	thin
e	end	**ô**	order	**yo͞o**	fuse	**th**	this
ē	equal					**zh**	vision

ə = a in *above*, e in *sicken*, i in *possible*, o in *melon*, u in *circus*

shoe to prevent slipping. **2** A device like this worn on the sole of a shoe or boot.

call [kôl] **1** *v.* To speak in a loud voice; shout: to *call* the roll. **2** *n.* A shout or cry: a *call* for help. **3** *v.* To summon: The principal *called* me to the office. **4** *n.* A summons or invitation. **5** *v.* To make a brief visit. **6** *n.* A brief visit. **7** *v.* To arouse, as from sleep: *Call* me early. **8** *v.* To make a telephone call to (someone). **9** *n.* A telephone message. **10** *v.* To name: They *called* the dog Tex. **11** *v.* To consider or regard: I *call* such behavior disgraceful. **12** *v.* To insist upon payment of: to *call* a loan. **13** *v.* To stop or suspend: to *call* a baseball game. **14** *n.* A demand; claim: the *call* of duty. **15** *n.* An inward urge or attraction: a *call* to the stage. **16** *n.* A need, occasion: You've no *call* to do that. **17** *n.* The special cry of an animal or bird. **—call for** **1** To require; need. **2** To order. **—call off** **1** To summon away. **2** To say or read aloud. **3** To cancel. **—call on** **1** To visit. **2** To invite; request; ask. **—call up** **1** To telephone. **2** To remember; recall. **3** To summon, especially for service in the armed forces. **—on call** Available when called for. ◆ *Call* comes from a Scandinavian word, *kalla.*

cal·la [kal′ə] *n.* A plant having a large milk-white leaf that resembles a flower. It is often called a **calla lily.**

call·er [kô′lər] *n.* **1** A person making a brief visit. **2** A person who calls out the steps in a square dance.

cal·lig·ra·phy [kə·lig′rə·fē] *n.* The art of handwriting.

call·ing [kô′ling] *n.* **1** The act of speaking or crying aloud. **2** A profession; occupation. **3** A summons.

calling card A small card with the name and sometimes the address of a person, used when making a social call.

cal·li·o·pe [kə·lī′ə·pē *or* kal′ē·ōp] *n.* A musical instrument consisting of a series of steam whistles played by means of a keyboard.

cal·li·pers [kal′ə·pərz] *n.pl.* Another spelling for CALIPERS.

cal·lis·then·ics [kal′is·then′iks] *n.pl.* Another spelling of CALISTHENICS.

call letters The letter or letters and numbers that form the name of a radio or television station.

call number A number given to a library book to indicate its general subject matter and its place on a shelf.

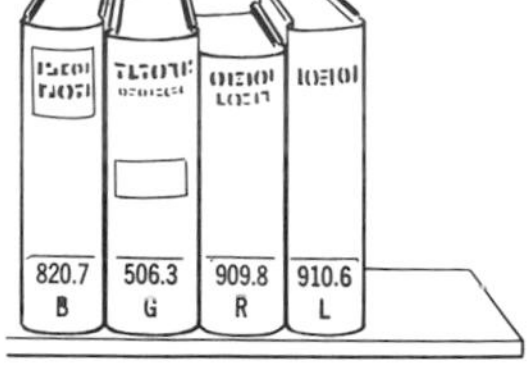

Call numbers

cal·los·i·ty [kə·los′ə·tē] *n., pl.* **cal·los·i·ties** **1** A callus. **2** The condition of being thickened or hardened. **3** Lack of sensitivity; callousness.

cal·lous [kal′əs] *adj.* **1** Thickened and hardened, as a callus. **2** Unfeeling; hardhearted: a *callous* remark. **—cal′lous·ly** *adv.* **—cal′lous·ness** *n.*

cal·low [kal′ō] *adj.* Without experience; immature: a *callow* youth. **—cal′low·ness** *n.*

call-up [côl′up] *n.* An order to report for active military duty.

cal·lus [kal′əs] *n., pl.* **cal·lus·es** A thickened and hardened part of the skin, as on the foot.

calm [käm] **1** *adj.* Quiet; peaceful; still: a *calm* sea; a *calm* manner. **2** *n.* Lack of wind or motion: the *calm* before a storm. **3** *v.* To make or become calm. **—calm′ly** *adv.* **—calm′ness** *n.*

cal·o·mel [kal′ə·mel] *n.* A heavy, white, tasteless compound of mercury and chlorine, formerly used as an antiseptic and laxative.

ca·lor·ic [kə·lôr′ik] *adj.* Of or having to do with heat or calories.

cal·o·rie [kal′ə·rē] *n.* **1** The amount of heat needed to raise one gram of water one degree centigrade. This is also called a **small calorie.** **2** (*often written* **Calorie**) The amount of heat needed to raise one kilogram of water one degree centigrade. This is also called a **large calorie.** **3** A unit equivalent to the large calorie, used in measuring the energy-producing value of food when it is oxidized in the body. **4** A quantity of food that has the energy-producing value of one large calorie.

cal·o·rif·ic [kal′ə·rif′ik] *adj.* Of or giving off heat.

cal·o·rim·e·ter [kal′ə·rim′ə·tər] *n.* A device for measuring amounts of heat.

cal·u·met [kal′yə·met′] *n.* A pipe smoked by American Indians when talking peace.

ca·lum·ni·ate [kə·lum′nē·āt′] *v.* **ca·lum·ni·at·ed, ca·lum·ni·at·ing** To accuse falsely.

ca·lum·ni·ous [kə·lum′nē·əs] *adj.* Characterized by or containing calumny; defamatory; slanderous. **—ca·lum′ni·ous·ly** *adv.*

cal·um·ny [kal′əm·nē] *n., pl.* **cal·um·nies** A false and spiteful accusation or report intended to harm another; slander.

calve [kav] *v.* **calved, calv·ing** To give birth to (a calf): Our cow *calved* this morning.

calves [kavz] Plural of CALF[1] and CALF[2].

Cal·vin·ism [kal′vin·iz′əm] *n.* The teachings of John Calvin, especially that salvation comes only by God's grace, and only those He has chosen will receive it. **—Cal′vin·ist** *adj., n.*

ca·lyp·so [kə·lip′sō] *n., pl.* **ca·lyp·sos** A type of West Indian song with improvised lyrics that are usually of a humorous or timely nature.

ca·lyx [kā′liks *or* kal′iks] *n., pl.* **ca·lyx·es** or **cal·y·ces** [kal′ə·sēz *or* kā′lə·sēz] The outer ring of leaves or sepals, usually green in color, which hold the petals of a flower.

cam [kam] *n.* A revolving part in a machine so shaped that its motion gives a to-and-fro or irregular motion to the part or parts it touches.

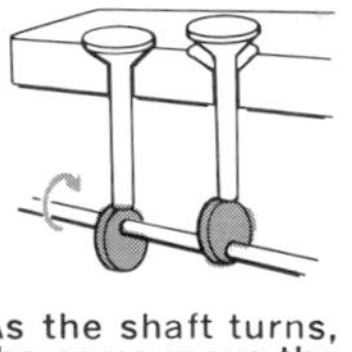
As the shaft turns, the cams move the valves up and down.

ca·ma·ra·de·rie [kä′mə·rä′dər·ē] *n.* The spirit of loyalty and friendship among comrades.

cam·ber [kam′bər] **1** *n.* A slight arching or bulging in the middle, as of the surface of a road or deck. **2** *v.* To give a camber to; arch slightly.

cam·bi·um [kam′bē·əm] *n.* A layer of tissue between the bark and wood of trees and woody plants, from which new bark and wood grow.

Cam·bo·di·an [kam·bō′dē·ən] **1** *adj.* Of or from Cambodia. **2** *n.* A person born in or a citizen of Cambodia. **3** *n.* The language of Cambodia.

Cam·bri·an [kam′brē·ən] **1** *n.* The earliest geological period of the Paleozoic era. Rocks of this period yield fossils of many primitive forms of life. **2** *adj.* Of the Cambrian. ◆ *Cambrian* is a Latin word for "Welsh." Some of the first rocks identified from the Cambrian period were found in Wales. Most of the names of early geological periods were derived in this way from old names for British regions and peoples.

cam·bric [kām′brik] *n.* 1 A fine white linen. 2 A cotton cloth made to look like linen.

cambric tea A drink made of sweetened hot water and milk and sometimes a little tea.

came [kām] The past tense of COME.

cam·el [kam′əl] *n.* A large beast of burden of Asia and Africa that chews its cud and has one or two humps on its back. The **Arabian camel,** or dromedary, has one hump; the **Bactrian camel** has two humps. The camel has great powers of endurance in desert regions.

Bactrian camel

ca·mel·lia [kə·mēl′yə] *n.* A tropical plant with green leaves and white, pink, or red flowers.

Cam·e·lot [kam′ə·lot′] *n.* In English legend, the place where King Arthur had his court.

camel's hair A soft, heavy, usually tan cloth made mainly from the hair of a camel or a mixture of this hair and wool.

Cam·em·bert [kam′əm·bâr′] *n.* A soft, creamy cheese. ◆ *Camembert* cheese was first made in Camembert, a village in northwestern France.

cam·e·o [kam′ē·ō] *n., pl.* **cam·e·os** A gem of sometimes differently colored layers, having a design carved in relief on the top layer with a lower layer serving as a background.

cam·er·a [kam′(ə·)rə] *n.* 1 A device for taking pictures in which light passes through a lens to form an image which is recorded on a film or plate. 2 An electronic device that forms an image and converts it into electrical impulses for television. ◆ Modern *camera* and *chamber* both came from Latin *camera,* which meant a room, as *chamber* still does.

cam·er·a·man [kam′(ə·)rə·man′] *n., pl.* **cam·er·a·men** [kam′(ə·)rə·men′] A person whose job is operating a camera, as for motion pictures or television.

Cam·e·roo·ni·an or **Cam·e·rou·ni·an** [kam′ə·rōō′·nē·ən] 1 *adj.* Of or from Cameroon. 2 *n.* A person born in or a citizen of Cameroon.

cam·i·sole [kam′ə·sōl′] *n.* A type of woman's undergarment with a fancy top.

cam·o·mile [kam′ə·mīl′] *n.* A strongly scented plant from whose leaves and daisylike flowers a medicinal tea is brewed.

cam·ou·flage [kam′ə·fläzh′] *n., v.* **cam·ou·flaged, cam·ou·flag·ing** 1 *n.* The act or technique of using such materials as paint or leaves to change the appearance, as of guns or troops, so as to conceal them from the enemy. 2 *n.* The material used to do this. 3 *n.* Any disguise that hides or protects: Chameleons change color as a *camouflage.* 4 *v.* To change the appearance of, so as to hide.

camp [kamp] 1 *n.* A group of tents, cabins, or other structures, usually in the country, used for vacations or outings: a summer *camp.* 2 *n.* A similar place where soldiers and sailors live, usually used for training purposes. 3 *v.* To set up or live in a tent or camp: We'll *camp* by the river. —**break camp** To take down tents or other structures, and move on.

cam·paign [kam·pān′] 1 *n.* A series of connected military operations made to gain some special objective. 2 *n.* An organized series of activities designed to obtain a definite result. 3 *v.* To take part in, or go on, a campaign. —**cam·paign′er** *n.*

cam·pa·ni·le [kam′pə·nē′lē] *n.* A tower with bells in it, especially one that is not part of another building.

Campanile

camp·er [kam′pər] *n.* 1 A person who camps. 2 A girl or boy who goes to a summer camp. 3 A vehicle outfitted as a dwelling place, used especially on camping trips.

camp·fire [kamp′fīr′] *n.* A fire in an outdoor camp, used for cooking or warmth.

Camp Fire Girls An organization for girls, the purpose of which is to improve their health and welfare, as by encouraging outdoor life.

cam·phor [kam′fər] *n.* A white, crystalline substance with a strong odor, obtained from an Asian tree or made synthetically. It is used in medicine, plastics, lacquers, and mothballs.

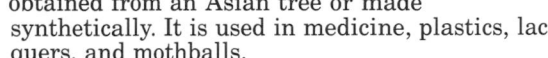

camp meeting A religious gathering held outdoors or in a large tent.

camp·site [kamp′sīt′] *n.* An area set aside or suitable for camping.

cam·pus [kam′pəs] *n.* The grounds of a school, college, or university.

can[1] [kan *or* kən] *v. Present tense for all subjects* **can,** *past tense* **could.** *Can* is a helping verb having the following senses. 1 To be able to: She *can* win the race. 2 To know how to: I *can* find my way. 3 To have the right to: You *can* drive in this state at eighteen. 4 *informal* To be permitted to: You *can* leave the room.

can[2] [kan] *n., v.* **canned, can·ning** 1 *n.* A metal container for holding, carrying, or preserving liquids or solids. 2 *n.* The contents of such a container: Add one *can* of corn. 3 *v.* To put in sealed cans or jars; preserve, as fruit. —**can′ner** *n.*

can. 1 cancelled. 2 canon. 3 canto.

Can. 1 Canada. 2 Canadian.

Ca·naan [kā′nən] *n.* In the Bible, the name given by the Israelites to that part of Palestine between the Jordan River and the Mediterranean Sea; the Promised Land.

Ca·naan·ite [kā′nən·īt′] *n.* A person who lived in Canaan before its conquest by the Israelites.

Canada goose The common wild goose of North America, brownish gray with black head and neck.

Canada goose

a	add	**i**	it	**ŏŏ**	took	**oi**	oil
ā	ace	**ī**	ice	**ōō**	pool	**ou**	pout
â	care	**o**	odd	**u**	up	**ng**	ring
ä	palm	**ō**	open	**û**	burn	**th**	thin
e	end	**ô**	order	**yōō**	fuse	**t͟h**	this
ē	equal					**zh**	vision

ə = {a in *above* e in *sicken* i in *possible* / o in *melon* u in *circus*}

Ca·na·di·an [kə·nā′dē·ən] 1 *adj.* Of, having to do with, or from Canada. 2 *n.* A person born in or a citizen of Canada.

ca·nal [kə·nal′] *n.* 1 A waterway constructed across land, used by ships or boats or for supplying water to dry areas. 2 A passage, duct, or tube in the body: the alimentary *canal.* 3 A long, narrow arm of the sea.

can·a·pé [kan′ə·pē *or* kan′ə·pā′] *n.* A cracker or thin piece of toasted bread spread with cheese, fish, or other food, and served as an appetizer.

ca·nard [kə·närd′] *n.* A false story; rumor.

ca·nar·y [kə·nâr′ē] *n., pl.* **ca·nar·ies,** *adj.* 1 *n.* A small, yellow songbird, popular as a pet. 2 *n., adj.* Light yellow. ◆ This word comes from the Canary Islands, from which canaries originally came.

ca·nas·ta [kə·nas′tə] *n.* A card game based on rummy and using two decks of cards.

can·can [kan′kan′] *n.* A dance for female performers, characterized by high kicking.

can·cel [kan′səl] *v.* **can·celed** or **can·celled, can·cel·ing** or **can·cel·ling** 1 To cross out or mark (as a postage stamp or check) to show it has been used or noted. 2 To call off, make impossible, or do away with: to *cancel* a trip; to *cancel* an order. 3 To have the same force, value, or importance as; make up for: A good deed can often *cancel* a bad one. 4 In mathematics, to indicate division of the numerator and denominator of a fraction or both sides of an equation or inequality by a (common factor) that is crossed out in both. 5 To subtract (a common term) from both sides of an equation or inequality in the same way.

can·cel·la·tion [kan′sə·lā′shən] *n.* 1 The act or process of canceling. 2 The marks used in canceling. 3 The thing that is canceled: Are there any *cancellations* for that flight?

can·cer [kan′sər] *n.* A serious, often fatal growth of abnormal cells in the body. It can destroy normal tissue and often spreads from its original location to other parts of the body. **—can′cer·ous** *adj.*

Can·cer [kan′sər] *n.* 1 A constellation north of the equator. 2 The fourth sign of the zodiac. 3 A person born under this sign.

can·del·a [kan·del′ə] *n.* A unit for measuring the brightness or intensity of light.

can·de·la·brum [kan′də·lä′brəm] *n., pl.* **can·de·la·bra** [kan′də·lä′brə] or **can·de·la·brums** A candlestick branched to hold more than one candle.

Candelabrum

can·did [kan′did] *adj.* 1 Honest and direct; frank: a *candid* statement. 2 Not posed; informal: a *candid* photograph. **—can′did·ly** *adv.*

can·di·da·cy [kan′də·də·sē] *n., pl.* **can·di·da·cies** The fact or condition of being a candidate.

can·di·date [kan′də·dāt′] *n.* A person who seeks, or is proposed for, an office or honor. ◆ This word comes from a Latin word meaning *wearing white* because candidates for office in ancient Rome wore white togas.

can·died [kan′dēd] *adj.* 1 Cooked in or coated with sugar: *candied* yams. 2 That has turned into sugar; crystallized: *candied* maple syrup.

can·dle [kan′dəl] *n., v.* **can·dled, can·dling** 1 *n.* A stick of wax, tallow, or other solid fat, containing a wick that gives light when burning. 2 *v.* To examine, as eggs, by holding between the eye and a light. 3 *n.* A candela. ◆ This word comes originally from the Latin verb *to gleam.*

can·dle·light [kan′dəl·līt′] *n.* 1 The light given by a candle. 2 The time for lighting candles; twilight.

can·dle·pow·er [kan′dəl·pou′ər] *n.* A standard measure of the strength of a light, based on a comparison with a standard light.

can·dle·stick [kan′dəl·stik′] *n.* A utensil with a socket on top for holding a candle.

can·dor [kan′dər] *n.* 1 Honesty; openness; frankness. 2 Fairness; impartiality.

can·dy [kan′dē] *n., pl.* **can·dies,** *v.* **can·died, can·dy·ing** 1 *n.* A sweet food made of sugar or syrup, usually with flavorings, nuts, or fruits added. 2 *v.* To form or cause to form into sugar. 3 *v.* To preserve by cooking in sugar. ◆ This word comes from an Arabic word meaning *made of sugar.*

cane [kān] *n., v.* **caned, can·ing** 1 *n.* A walking stick. 2 *n.* Any rod, especially one used for flogging. 3 *v.* To strike or beat with a cane. 4 *n.* The slender, woody stem of certain plants, as bamboo and rattan, that is easily bent and is used as a weaving material in making such items as baskets or furniture. 5 *n.* A plant having such a stem. 6 *adj. use: cane* furniture. 7 *v.* To make or repair with cane, as furniture. 8 *n.* Sugar cane.

cane·brake [kān′brāk′] *n.* A thick growth of cane.

cane sugar Sugar that is obtained from sugarcane.

ca·nine [kā′nīn′] 1 *adj.* Of, like, or having to do with the family of animals that includes dogs, wolves, and foxes. 2 *n.* A dog or other canine animal. 3 *n.* In humans, any of the four pointed teeth situated on either side of the upper and lower incisors.

can·is·ter [kan′is·tər] *n.* A container, usually metal, for coffee, tea, spices, and other items.

can·ker [kang′kər] *n.* 1 An open sore, especially of the mouth and lips. 2 Anything that gradually decays and destroys: the *canker* of corrupt politics.

can·ker·ous [kang′kər·əs] *adj.* 1 Of, like, or having a canker. 2 Causing or caused by a canker.

can·ker·worm [kang′kər·wûrm′] *n.* Any of several caterpillars that destroy fruit trees and other plants.

can·na [kan′ə] *n.* A tropical plant with large leaves and red or yellow flowers.

canned [kand] *adj.* 1 Preserved in a sealed can or jar: *canned* tomatoes. 2 *informal* Recorded: *canned* music.

can·ner·y [kan′ər·ē] *n., pl.* **can·ner·ies** A factory where foods are canned.

can·ni·bal [kan′ə·bəl] *n.* 1 A human being who eats human flesh. 2 An animal that eats its own kind. ◆ This word comes through Spanish from a South American Indian word for *strong men.*

can·ni·bal·ism [kan′ə·bəl·iz′əm] *n.* The act or practice of eating the flesh of one's own kind. **—can′·ni·bal·is′tic** *adj.*

can·ni·bal·ize [kan′ə·bəl·īz′] *v.* **can·ni·bal·ized, can·ni·bal·iz·ing** To take parts from (damaged equipment) for use in making or repairing other things. **—can′ni·bal·i·za′tion** *n.*

can·ning [kan′ing] *n.*The preserving of foods in tightly sealed cans and jars.

can·non [kan′ən] *n., pl.* **can·nons** or **can·non** A large gun mounted on a fixed or movable base.

C

can·non·ade [kan′ən·ād′] *n., v.* **can·non·ad·ed, can·non·ad·ing** 1 *n.* A steady firing of cannons. 2 *v.* To fire cannons repeatedly, as in an attack.

cannon ball A solid metal ball that formerly was used as ammunition for a cannon.

can·not [kan′ot *or* ka·not′] Can not. ◆ *Cannot* is usually preferred to *can not,* unless the writer wants to put a strong emphasis on the *not.*

can·ny [kan′ē] *adj.* **can·ni·er, can·ni·est** Careful; cautious; shrewd. **—can′ni·ly** *adv.*

ca·noe [kə·noo͞′] *n., v.* **ca·noed, ca·noe·ing** 1 *n.* A small, lightweight boat, pointed at both ends and moved by paddles. 2 *v.* To paddle, sail, or travel in a canoe.

Canoe

can·on[1] [kan′ən] *n.* 1 A rule or law, especially a rule of faith and practice enacted by a church. 2 An established rule; an accepted principle. 3 A standard for judgment; criterion. 4 The sacred books of any sect or religion. 5 A list of such books. 6 The list of canonized saints.

can·on[2] [kan′ən] *n.* A member of the clergy who is on the staff of a cathedral or collegiate church.

ca·ñon [kan′yən] *n.* Another spelling of CANYON.

ca·non·i·cal [kə·non′i·kəl] *adj.* According to, or accepted by, church rule or law.

can·on·ize [kan′ən·īz′] *v.* **can·on·ized, can·on·iz·ing** To declare (a dead person) to be a saint. **—can′on·i·za′tion** *n.*

canon law The body of laws governing a Christian church, especially the Roman Catholic Church.

can·o·py [kan′ə·pē] *n., pl.* **can·o·pies,** *v.* **can·o·pied, can·o·py·ing** 1 *n.* A covering, as hung over a throne, bed, or entrance, or carried on poles over high officials or sacred objects. 2 *n.* Any covering overhead, as the sky or a tree. 3 *v.* To cover with or as with a canopy.

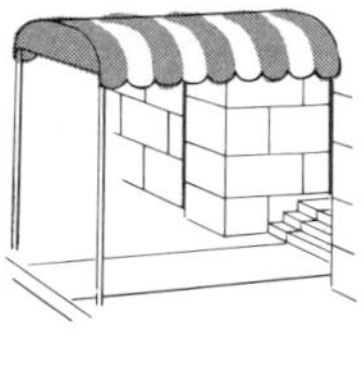

Canopy

canst [kanst] A form of the verb CAN, used with *thou:* seldom used today.

cant[1] [kant] 1 *n.* A slope or tilt; incline. 2 *v.* To slant or tilt; tip.

cant[2] [kant] *n.* 1 Talk or statements that are insincere or stale; trite words or phrases. 2 Insincere religious talk. 3 Special words or phrases used by a particular group or profession; jargon: legal *cant;* political *cant.*

can't [kant] Cannot. ◆ *Can't* should not be used with negative words such as *hardly* or *scarcely.*

can·ta·loupe or **can·ta·loup** [kan′tə·lōp′] *n.* A variety of muskmelon having a sweet, juicy, orange-colored pulp.

can·tank·er·ous [kan·tang′kər·əs] *adj.* Stubborn and contrary; troublesome. **—can·tank′er·ous·ly** *adv.*

can·ta·ta [kən·tä′tə] *n.* A large musical composition to be sung. It often tells a story.

can·teen [kan·tēn′] *n.* 1 A small, usually metal container for carrying water or other liquids. 2 A store at a military post where military personnel can buy personal supplies, food, drink, and other items.

can·ter [kan′tər] 1 *n.* A slow, gentle gallop. 2 *v.* To ride or go at a canter.

can·ti·cle [kan′ti·kəl] *n.* A short hymn with words taken directly from the Bible.

can·ti·lev·er [kan′tə·lē′vər *or* kan′tə·lev′ər] *n.* A beam, slab, or similar structure firmly anchored at one end to a pier or wall, the other end extended free in space. A **cantilever bridge** is constructed of two cantilever arms, each supported on piers at one end and meeting at the center to complete the span.

can·tle [kan′təl] *n.* The hind part of a saddle that sticks up.

can·to [kan′tō] *n., pl.* **can·tos** A division of a long poem, similar to a chapter of a novel.

can·ton [kan′tən] *n.* A small division or district of a country, as of Switzerland.

Can·ton·ese [kan′tə·nēz′] *adj., n., pl.* **Can·ton·ese** 1 *adj.* Of or from Canton, China. 2 *n.* A person born or living in Canton. 3 *n.* The Chinese dialect spoken in and around Canton.

can·ton·ment [kan·tōn′mənt *or* kan·ton′mənt] *n.* A place for the temporary housing of troops.

can·tor [kan′tər] *n.* The chief singer in a synagogue.

can·vas [kan′vəs] 1 *n.* A heavy, strong cloth made of cotton, hemp, or flax, as used for sails or tents. 2 *adj. use: canvas* shoes. 3 *n.* A piece of canvas on which to paint, especially in oils. 4 *n.* A painting on canvas. **—under canvas** 1 With sails set, as a ship. 2 In tents.

can·vas·back [kan′vəs·bak′] *n.* A wild duck having a grayish white back.

can·vass [kan′vəs] 1 *v.* To go about (a district) or among (persons) seeking votes, orders, or opinions. 2 *v.* To examine, discuss, or debate (as questions or plans). 3 *n.* The act of canvassing. **—can′vass·er** *n.*

can·yon [kan′yən] *n.* A deep, narrow valley or gorge with very steep sides.

caout·chouc [kou′cho͝ok′ *or* kou′cho͞ok′] *n.* Raw, natural rubber as it comes from the tree.

cap [kap] *n., v.* **capped, cap·ping** 1 *n.* A close-fitting covering for the head, made of a soft material without a brim but sometimes with a visor. 2 *n.* Any headgear designed to show one's rank or profession: a nurse's *cap.* 3 *n.* Something like a cap in appearance, position, or use: a *radiator* cap. 4 *v.* To put a cap on; cover. 5 *v.* To serve as a cap or cover to; lie on top of: Snow *capped* the trees. 6 *v.* To match or do better than: to *cap* a teammate's record. 7 *n.* A small amount of explosive material in a piece of paper, used in toy pistols.

cap. 1 capital (city). 2 capital letter.

ca·pa·bil·i·ty [kā′pə·bil′ə·tē] *n., pl.* **ca·pa·bil·i·ties** The quality of being capable; ability.

ca·pa·ble [kā′pə·bəl] *adj.* Having ability or skill; efficient; competent. **—capable of** In possession of the capacity, qualities, or nature needed for. **—ca′pa·bly** *adv.*

ca·pa·cious [kə·pā′shəs] *adj.* Able to contain much; roomy; large: a *capacious* closet.

ca·pac·i·tance [kə·pas′ə·təns] *n.* The ability of an

a	add	**i**	it	**o͝o**	took	**oi**	oil
ā	ace	**ī**	ice	**o͞o**	pool	**ou**	pout
â	care	**o**	odd	**u**	up	**ng**	ring
ä	palm	**ō**	open	**û**	burn	**th**	thin
e	end	**ô**	order	**yo͞o**	fuse	**th̶**	this
ē	equal					**zh**	vision

ə = {a in *above* e in *sicken* i in *possible* / o in *melon* u in *circus*}

electric circuit to store energy in the form of a charge built up across two points that are at different voltages.

ca·pac·i·tor [kə·pas′ə·tər] *n.* A device made of two electrical conductors with an insulator between them across which a charge builds up when they are at different voltages.

ca·pac·i·ty [kə·pas′ə·tē] *n., pl.* **ca·pac·i·ties** 1 The ability, room, or space to contain or hold. 2 The most something can contain, hold, or do. 3 Ability, talent, or skill. 4 A specific function, occupation, or position.

ca·par·i·son [kə·par′ə·sən] 1 *n.* A richly ornamented covering for a horse. 2 *n.* Showy or expensive clothing or ornaments. 3 *v.* To adorn with rich or showy clothing.

cape[1] [kāp] *n.* A sleeveless outer garment fastened at the neck and hanging loosely from the shoulders.

cape[2] [kāp] *n.* A point of land extending into the sea or a lake.

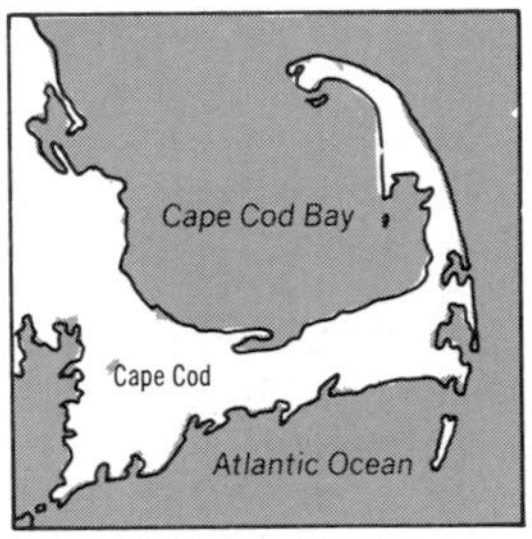

ca·per[1] [kā′pər] 1 *n.* A playful leap, skip, or jump. 2 *v.* To leap or skip playfully; frolic. 3 *n.* A wild, silly prank or trick. **—cut a caper** To caper, frolic, or play tricks.

ca·per[2] [kā′pər] *n.* (*usually pl.*) The green flower bud of a Mediterranean shrub, pickled and used as a relish or seasoning.

cap·il·lar·y [kap′ə·ler′ē] *adj., n., pl.* **cap·il·lar·ies** 1 *adj.* Like a hair; extremely fine. 2 *n.* Any very narrow tube, as the inside of a thermometer. 3 *n.* One of the very narrow, threadlike blood vessels that connect the arteries with the veins.

capillary attraction A force that causes a liquid to rise against gravity when enclosed in a very narrow tube or in contact with an absorbent material, as a blotter.

cap·i·tal[1] [kap′ə·təl] 1 *n.* The city or town in a country or state which is the seat of government. 2 *adj. use:* a *capital* city. 3 *n.* A capital letter. 4 *n.* The total amount of wealth, as money, property, or stock, owned or used by an individual or corporation. 5 *n.* Wealth, as money or property, used or available for the production of more wealth. 6 *n.* People who have wealth, as a group: *capital* and labor. 7 *adj.* Of the first quality; chief; most important. 8 *adj.* Excellent: a *capital* idea. 9 *adj.* Punishable by or involving the penalty of death: a *capital* crime. **—make capital of** To turn to advantage. **—cap′i·tal·ly** *adv.* ◆ (def. 1) *Capital* and *capitol* both mean a seat of government, but a *capital* is a city, and a *capitol* is a building in which a legislature meets.

cap·i·tal[2] [kap′ə·təl] *n.* The top of a column.

A Corinthian capital

cap·i·tal·ism [kap′ə·təl·iz′əm] *n.* A system in which the factories, materials, and equipment for making and distributing goods are privately owned and operated for private profit rather than being owned or controlled by a state or government.

cap·i·tal·ist [kap′ə·təl·ist] *n.* 1 A person who has a great deal of capital. 2 A person who believes in capitalism. **—cap′i·tal·is′tic** *adj.* **—cap′i·tal·is′ti·cal·ly** *adv.*

cap·i·tal·i·za·tion [kap′ə·təl·ə·zā′shən] *n.* 1 The act or process of capitalizing. 2 The total capital employed in a business.

cap·i·tal·ize [kap′ə·təl·īz′] *v.* **cap·i·tal·ized, cap·i·tal·iz·ing** 1 To begin with or write in capital letters. 2 To provide capital for, as for a business. 3 To change into capital. 4 To profit or gain by turning something to one's own advantage: The children *capitalized* on their parents' fame.

capital letter The form of a letter used to begin a sentence, a proper name, and certain other words.

cap·i·tal·ly [kap′ə·təl·ē] *adv.* 1 In a manner that involves capital punishment. 2 In a capital manner; excellently; very well.

capital punishment A penalty of death for a crime.

capital ship A warship of large size, as a battleship or aircraft carrier.

Cap·i·tol [kap′ə·təl] *n.* 1 The official building of the U.S. Congress in Washington, D.C. 2 (*written* **capitol**) The building in which a state legislature meets. ◆ See CAPITAL[1].

U.S. Capitol

ca·pit·u·late [kə·pich′o͞o·lāt′] *v.* **ca·pit·u·lat·ed, ca·pit·u·lat·ing** To surrender, especially on certain terms. **—ca·pit′u·la′tion.** *n.*

ca·pon [kā′pon] *n.* A rooster from which the sex glands have been removed to improve its flesh for eating.

ca·price [kə·prēs′] *n.* A sudden, unreasonable change of mind, mood, or opinion; whim.

ca·pri·cious [kə·prish′əs] *adj.* Likely to change without warning; fickle. **—ca·pri′cious·ly** *adv.*

Cap·ri·corn [kap′rə·kôrn′] *n.* 1 A constellation south of the equator. 2 The tenth sign of the zodiac. 3 A person born under this sign.

caps. capital letters.

cap·size [kap′sīz′ *or* kap·sīz′] *v.* **cap·sized, cap·siz·ing** To upset; tip over; overturn.

cap·stan [kap′stən] *n.* An upright cylinder resembling a large spool, turned by hand or motor-driven, and around which cables or ropes are wound to lift a weight, as an anchor.

Capstan

cap·stone [kap′stōn′] *n.* The top stone of a structure.

cap·su·lar [kap′sə·lər] *adj.* Of, having to do with, like, or enclosed in a capsule.

cap·sule [kap′səl *or* kap′s(y)o͞ol] 1 *n.* A small container made of gelatine, which is easily dissolved, used to hold one dose of medicine. 2 *n.* A covering or case for the seeds of some plants. 3 *adj.* Condensed; concise: a *capsule* summary. 4 *n.* A compartment of a spacecraft designed to separate from the rocket during flight. Astronauts often travel and return to earth in a space capsule.

capt. or **Capt.** captain.

cap·tain [kap′tən] 1 *n.* A military rank. In the U.S. Army, Air Force, and Marine Corps, a captain is an officer ranking above a first lieutenant and below a major. In the U.S. Navy and Coast Guard, a captain is an officer ranking above a commander and below a rear admiral. 2 *n.* A person at the head or in command; leader. **3** *n.* The master or commander of a vessel. **4** *n.* A member of a team acting as leader. **5** *v.* To act as captain to; command; lead: to *captain* the team to victory.

cap·tain·cy [kap′tən·sē] *n., pl.* **cap·tain·cies** The position, rank, or term of office of a captain.

cap·tion [kap′shən] **1** *n.* A heading, as of a chapter of a book or an article in a newspaper. **2** *n.* The title and written matter describing a picture. **3** *v.* To furnish with a caption.

cap·tious [kap′shəs] *adj.* **1** Apt or eager to find fault; critical: a *captious* teacher. **2** Intended only to stir up arguments: *captious* remarks.

cap·ti·vate [kap′tə·vāt′] *v.* **cap·ti·vat·ed, cap·ti·vat·ing** To fascinate or charm, as by beauty or excellence: The play *captivated* the audience.

cap·tive [kap′tiv] **1** *n.* A person or thing captured and held in confinement; prisoner. **2** *adj.* Held prisoner; not allowed to escape.

cap·tiv·i·ty [kap·tiv′ə·tē] *n., pl.* **cap·tiv·i·ties** The condition of being held captive; confinement; imprisonment.

cap·tor [kap′tər] *n.* A person who takes or holds another captive.

cap·ture [kap′chər] *v.* **cap·tured, cap·tur·ing,** *n.* **1** *v.* To take captive, as by force or cleverness: to *capture* a lion; to *capture* a ship. **2** *n.* The act of capturing. **3** *n.* A being captured. **4** *n.* A person or thing captured.

cap·u·chin [kap′yə·shən *or* ka·pyōō′shən] *n.* **1** (*written* **Capuchin**) A monk belonging to an order that is a branch of the Franciscans and whose members wear brown, hooded cloaks. **2** A long-tailed monkey of Central and South America. Some have dark hair on their head that looks like a monk's hood.

cap·y·ba·ra [kap′i·bä′rə] *n.* A rodent of South America, about four feet long and having a stubby tail, often found near lakes and rivers.

car [kär] *n.* **1** Any vehicle used to carry people or goods, especially an automobile. **2** A vehicle for use on rails, as a railroad car or streetcar. **3** The enclosed platform on which people or things are carried in an elevator.

car·a·bao [kar′ə·bou′] *n., pl.* **car·a·baos** Another name for WATER BUFFALO.

car·a·cal [kar′ə·kal′] *n.* A wild cat of Africa and southern Asia related to the lynx.

car·a·cul [kar′ə·kəl] *n.* **1** The black or gray, loosely curled fur made from the skin of an Asian lamb. **2** The animal producing this fur.

ca·rafe [kə·raf′] *n.* A bottle, usually of glass, used to hold water, hot coffee, or other drinks.

car·a·mel [kar′ə·mel′] *n.* **1** A candy, usually cut in small cubes. **2** Burnt sugar, used to color and flavor foods.

car·a·pace [kar′ə·pās′] *n.* The hard, bony covering of certain animals, as the turtle or lobster.

car·at [kar′ət] *n.* **1** A unit of weight for gems, equal to one fifth of a gram. **2** Karat.

car·a·van [kar′ə·van′] *n.* **1** A group of traders, pilgrims, or nomads traveling together, especially through a desert. **2** A covered wagon or truck, especially one used as a house on wheels.

car·a·van·sa·ry [kar′ə·van′sə·rē] *n., pl.* **car·a·van·sa·ries** **1** In countries of the Near East or the Far East, a large inn with a central courtyard in which caravans can be accomodated. **2** Any large hotel or inn.

car·a·vel [kar′ə·vel′] *n.* A small, fast sailing ship of the 15th and 16th centuries.

Caravel

car·a·way [kar′ə·wā′] *n.* A plant related to parsley, having small, spicy seeds.

car·bide [kär′bīd′] *n.* A compound of carbon with another element.

car·bine [kär′bīn′ *or* kär′·bēn′] *n.* A light rifle with a short barrel.

car·bo·hy·drate [kär′bō·hī′drāt′] *n.* Any of a large group of compounds of carbon, hydrogen, and oxygen. Green plants make them out of carbon dioxide and water. Sugars and starches are carbohydrates.

car·bo·la·ted [kär′bə·lā′tid] *adj.* Containing carbolic acid.

car·bol·ic acid [kär·bol′ik] A poisonous compound obtained from coal tar.

car·bon [kär′bən] *n.* **1** A nonmetallic element found in all living things, and also in coal, charcoal, and petroleum. It occurs in pure form as diamond and graphite. **2** A piece of carbon paper, or a copy made with it.

carbon 14 A radioactive isotope of carbon whose presence in very old bones, fossils, and other items, helps to determine their age.

car·bon·ate [kär′bə·nāt′] *v.* **car·bon·at·ed, car·bon·at·ing,** *n.* **1** *v.* To charge with carbon dioxide: Ginger ale is *carbonated* so that it fizzes. **2** *n.* A salt of carbonic acid. **—car′bon·a′tion** *n.*

carbon copy **1** A copy of something written or typed made with carbon paper. **2** Something closely resembling something else: This vase is a *carbon copy* of the one I broke.

carbon dioxide An odorless, colorless, gaseous compound of carbon and oxygen. Formula: CO_2. It is breathed out by animals and taken up as food by plants.

car·bon·ic acid [kär·bon′ik] A compound formed from carbon dioxide and water. It produces a sharp taste in carbonated water.

Car·bon·if·er·ous [kär′bə·nif′ər·əs] **1** *adj.* (*written* **carboniferous**) Containing or yielding carbon, especially in the form of coal. **2** *n.* The fifth geological period of the Paleozoic era, in which large coal beds were formed. It is sometimes divided into the **Lower Carboniferous** and the **Upper Carboniferous.** **3** *adj.* Of the Carboniferous.

car·bon·i·za·tion [kär′bə·nə·zā′shən] *n.* The act or process of carbonizing.

car·bon·ize [kär′bən·īz′] *v.* **car·bon·ized, car·bon·iz·ing** **1** To reduce to carbon, as by burning or charring. **2** To overlay or coat with carbon.

carbon monoxide A colorless, odorless, very poi-

a	add	**i**	it	**o͝o**	took	**oi**	oil
ā	ace	**ī**	ice	**ōō**	pool	**ou**	pout
â	care	**o**	odd	**u**	up	**ng**	ring
ä	palm	**ō**	open	**û**	burn	**th**	thin
e	end	**ô**	order	**yōō**	fuse	**th**	this
ē	equal					**zh**	vision

ə = { a in *above*   e in *sicken*   i in *possible*
      o in *melon*   u in *circus*

sonous gas given off in the exhaust fumes of automobile engines.

carbon paper Thin paper coated with a waxy carbon substance. It is placed between sheets of paper so as to reproduce on the bottom sheets what has been typed or written on the top sheet.

carbon tet·ra·chlo·ride [tet′rə·klôr′īd′] A clear liquid compound composed of carbon and chlorine, used as a solvent and in fire extinguishers. It evaporates easily and its fumes are poisonous.

Car·bo·run·dum [kär′bə·run′dəm] *n.* Any of various abrasives: a trademark.

car·bun·cle [kär′bung·kəl] *n.* **1** A painful, inflamed sore beneath the skin, larger than a boil. **2** A deep red precious stone, especially a garnet cut with a smooth surface.

car·bu·re·tor [kär′bə·rā′tər] *n.* A device for mixing air with the fuel of an internal combustion engine, as in an automobile.

car·cass or **car·case** [kär′kəs] *n.* **1** The dead body of an animal. **2** The human body: used in a joking way.

car·cin·o·gen [kär·sin′ə·jin] *n.* A substance that causes cancer. **—car·cin·o·gen·ic** [kär′sə·nə·jen′ik] *adj.*

car coat A short overcoat.

card[1] [kärd] *n.* **1** A small, usually rectangular piece of thin cardboard or stiff paper with something written or printed on it: a business *card;* a greeting *card;* a library *card;* a membership *card;* an index *card.* **2** A PLAYING CARD. **3** A POSTCARD. **4** *informal* A witty or funny person.

card[2] [kärd] **1** *n.* A tool with bent wire points used for combing and cleansing wool and other fibers. **2** *v.* To comb or cleanse with a card.

card·board [kärd′bôrd′] *n.* Thick, stiff paper used for making such things as boxes and cards.

card-car·ry·ing [kärd′kar′ē·ing] *adj.* Being a fully enrolled or devoted member of a certain group: a *card-carrying* Communist.

card catalogue A card file, as of library books or other items, with a separate card for each item, the cards being arranged in alphabetical order.

cardi- or **cardio** A combining form meaning: **1** Of the heart, as in *cardiogram.* **2** Cardiac; cardiac and, as in *cardiopulmonary.*

car·di·ac [kär′dē·ak] *adj.* Of, having to do with, or near the heart: a *cardiac* patient.

car·di·gan [kär′də·gən] *n.* A jacket or sweater without a collar, and with long sleeves, that opens down the front. ◆ The garment was named after the Earl of *Cardigan.*

car·di·nal [kär′də·nəl] **1** *adj.* Of first importance; chief: the *cardinal* virtues. **2** *adj., n.* Deep, rich red. **3** *n.* One of the high officials in the Roman Catholic Church who are appointed by the pope. Cardinals wear scarlet robes and hats. **4** *n.* A red songbird.

Cardinal

cardinal number A number (as *six*) used to count how many. An ORDINAL NUMBER (as *sixth*) shows order in a series.

cardinal point Any of the four principal points of the compass, north, south, east, and west.

card·ing [kär′ding] *n.* The cleaning and combing of wool, flax, or cotton fibers.

The carding of wool

car·di·o·gram [kär′dē·ə·gram′] *n.* Another name for ELECTROCARDIOGRAM.

car·di·o·graph [kär′dē·ə·graf′] *n.* Another name for ELECTROCARDIOGRAPH.

car·di·ol·o·gy [kär′dē·ol′ə·jē] *n.* The study of the heart, its diseases, and their treatment. **—car′di·ol′o·gist** *n.*

car·di·o·pul·mo·nar·y [kär′dē·ō·po͝ol′mə·ner′ē] *adj.* Of or having to do with the heart and the blood vessels.

cards [kärdz] *n.pl.* (*often used with singular verb*) **1** Any game played with playing cards. **2** The act of playing games with cards.

care [kâr] *n., v.* **cared, car·ing** **1** *n.* A feeling of concern; worry: With the harvest in, the family felt free from *care.* **2** *v.* To have or show interest and concern: Sue *cares* about her career and works hard. **3** *n.* A cause to worry: They don't seem to have a *care* in the world. **4** *n.* Watchful attention; heed: Always handle matches with *care.* **5** *n.* A looking after; tending: The farmer has the *care* of forty cows. **6** *v.* To feel inclined; like: Would you *care* to go to the movies? **—care for** **1** To look after; provide for: Children should learn to *care for* their own pets. **2** To have a fondness for; like: Some people don't *care* for oysters. **—take care of** **1** To look after; protect: Can you *take care of* my cat for a week? **2** To attend to; do: He *takes care of* the shopping.

CARE [kâr] Cooperative for American Relief Everywhere.

ca·reen [kə·rēn′] *v.* **1** To lurch from side to side while moving, as if out of control: The truck *careened* around the curve. **2** To lean or cause to lean to one side, as a sailboat in the wind.

ca·reer [kə·rir′] **1** *n.* The course of a person's life, especially the part having to do with important activities: Marie Curie had an interesting *career.* **2** *n.* A person's lifework; profession: Engineering is a good *career.* **3** *adj. U.S.* Planning to spend one's life in a certain kind of work: a *career* diplomat. **4** *n.* Great speed: The motorcycle passed in full *career.* **5** *v.* To move along at great speed: The bus *careered* down the highway, out of control.

care·free [kâr′frē′] *adj.* Free of troubles or worry; happy; lighthearted.

care·ful [kâr′fəl] *adj.* **1** Giving close attention to one's work or to what one is doing; painstaking: a *careful* typist. **2** Cautious: Be *careful* not to slip on the ice. **3** Done with care: a *careful* piece of work. **—care′ful·ly** *adv.* **—care′ful·ness** *n.*

care·less [kâr′lis] *adj.* **1** Not giving close attention to what one is doing or saying: a *careless* worker. **2** Due to or done with lack of care; thoughtless: a *careless* mistake; a *careless* remark. **3** Carefree; happy: a *careless* life. **—care′less·ly** *adv.* **—care′less·ness** *n.*

ca·ress [kə·res′] **1** *n.* A gentle, loving touch, as a kiss, embrace, or pat. **2** *v.* To touch or embrace gently and lovingly: to *caress* a kitten.

car·et [kar′ət] *n.* A sign (^) placed below a line of writing or printing to show where something is to be inserted.

care·tak·er [kâr′tā′kər] *n.* A person employed to take care of and watch over a place or building, as an unoccupied house or a church.
care·worn [kâr′wôrn′] *adj.* Showing the effects of much care or worry: *careworn* eyes.
car·fare [kär′fâr′] *n.* The money a person pays to ride on public transportation, as a bus or subway.
car·go [kär′gō] *n., pl.* **car·goes** or **car·gos** Freight carried by a vehicle such as a ship or aircraft.
Car·ib [kar′ib] *n.* **1** A group of American Indian peoples of NE South America and the Lesser Antilles. **2** A member of this group of peoples. **3** The language of these peoples.
car·i·bou [kar′ə·bōō′] *n., pl.* **car·i·bou** or **car·i·bous** Any of several kinds of reindeer found in North America. ◆ *Caribou* comes directly from Canadian French and goes back to an Algonquian Indian word meaning *a creature that paws or scratches.*

Caribou

car·i·ca·ture [kar′i·kə·chŏŏr] *n., v.* **car·i·ca·tured, car·i·ca·tur·ing** **1** *n.* A picture or description in which certain features or qualities are exaggerated or distorted so as to produce an absurd effect. **2** *n.* The art of caricaturing. **3** *v.* To make a caricature of.
car·ies [kâr′ēz] *n.* Decay of a bone or of a tooth.
car·il·lon [kar′ə·lon′] *n.* A set of bells on which a melody can be played, often by hammers operated from a keyboard.
car·load [kär′lōd′] *n.* The amount that will fill a car, especially a railroad freight car.
car·mine [kär′min *or* kär′mīn′] *n., adj.* Deep red or purplish red.
car·nage [kär′nij] *n.* A bloody killing of great numbers of people, as in war.
car·nal [kär′nəl] *adj.* **1** Of the body and bodily appetites. **2** Worldly; not spiritual.
car·na·tion [kär·nā′shən] *n.* **1** A white, yellow, or pink garden flower with a strong, spicy smell. **2** Its plant. **3** A pink or red color.
car·nel·i·an [kär·nēl′yən] *n.* A clear, red stone.
car·ni·val [kär′nə·vəl] *n.* **1** An amusement show, typically having a merry-go-round, Ferris wheel, and side shows. **2** Any festival or celebration, including parades, dancing, and masquerades. **3** In some countries, the week of festivity just before Lent.
car·ni·vore [kär′nə·vôr′] *n.* A carnivorous animal.
car·niv·o·rous [kär·niv′ə·rəs] *adj.* Eating or living on meat: Cats and dogs are *carnivorous.*
car·ol [kar′əl] *n., v.* **car·oled** or **car·olled, car·ol·ing** or **car·ol·ling** **1** *n.* A song of joy or praise, especially a Christmas song. **2** *v.* To sing or praise with carols. **—car′ol·er** or **car′ol·ler** *n.*
car·om [kar′əm] **1** *n.* In billiards, a shot in which the cue ball strikes against two balls, one after the other. **2** *n.* A similar shot in other games. **3** *v.* To make a carom. **4** *v.* To strike and bounce off: The car *caromed* off the wall.
car·o·tene [kar′ə·tēn′] *n.* Any of several related pigments found in yellow and dark green vegetables which can be converted to vitamin A in the liver. ◆ *Carotene* is from *carota,* the Latin word for *carrot.* Carrots are very rich in carotene.
ca·rou·sal [kə·rou′zəl] *n.* A noisy, merry drinking party or banquet.
ca·rouse [kə·rouz′] *n., v.* **ca·roused, ca·rous·ing** **1** *n.* A noisy, jolly party with much drinking and eating; carousal. **2** *v.* To join in such a party.
car·ou·sel [kar′ə·sel′] *n.* A merry-go-round.
carp[1] [kärp] *v.* To find fault in an unpleasant or nagging way; keep grumbling or whining.
carp[2] [kärp] *n., pl.* **carp** or **carps** An edible freshwater fish, found in lakes and slow streams.
car·pal [kär′pəl] **1** *adj.* Of or having to do with the wrist or with the bones in the wrist. **2** *n.* Any of the bones in the wrist.
car·pel [kär′pəl] *n.* A simple pistil, or seed-bearing organ of a flower.
car·pen·ter [kär′pən·tər] *n.* A worker whose trade is to cut and put in place the wood used in constructing buildings, ships, and other structures.
car·pen·try [kär′pən·trē] *n.* The work of a carpenter.
car·pet [kär′pit] **1** *n.* A covering for floors, usually made of a heavy, woven fabric. **2** *n.* Anything that covers like a carpet: a *carpet* of pine needles. **3** *v.* To cover with a carpet: to *carpet* a flight of stairs. **—on the carpet** Being scolded or criticized by someone in authority.
car·pet·bag [kär′pit·bag′] *n.* An old-fashioned suitcase or bag made of carpeting.
car·pet·bag·ger [kär′pit·bag′ər] *n.* One of the Northerners who went South right after the Civil War in order to profit financially from the confused, unsettled conditions there.
car·pet·ing [kär′pit·ing] *n.* **1** The act of covering with a carpet. **2** Material used for carpets. **3** Carpets: new *carpeting* for the halls.
carpet sweeper A hand-pushed cleaning device on small wheels that picks up dirt from rugs by means of a revolving brush.
car pool **1** An arrangement made by a group of car owners who take turns driving each other or their children to work or school. **2** The members of such a group.
car·port [kär′pôrt′] *n.* A shelter for a car, built against a building. It has a roof but is open at the sides.

Carport

car·pus [kär′pəs] *n., pl.* **car·pi** [kär′pī] The wrist or the bones of the wrist.
car·riage [kar′ij; *for def. 7 also* kar′ē·ij] *n.* **1** A wheeled vehicle for carrying people. It is usually drawn by horses. **2** A perambulator; baby carriage. **3** A moving part of a machine for carrying along another part or an object: a typewriter *carriage.* **4** A wheeled frame for carrying something heavy, as a gun. **5**

a	add	**i**	it	**ŏŏ**	took	**oi**	oil
ā	ace	**ī**	ice	**ōō**	pool	**ou**	pout
â	care	**o**	odd	**u**	up	**ng**	ring
ä	palm	**ō**	open	**û**	burn	**th**	thin
e	end	**ô**	order	**yōō**	fuse	**th̸**	this
ē	equal					**zh**	vision

ə = { a in *above* e in *sicken* i in *possible*
o in *melon* u in *circus* }

The manner of carrying one's head and limbs; posture: a graceful *carriage.* **6** The act of carrying or transporting persons or goods. **7** The cost of transporting something.

car·ri·er [kar′ē·ər] *n.* **1** A person or thing that carries. **2** A person or company that carries persons or goods for a fee. **3** An aircraft carrier. **4** A person who is immune to a disease but carries the germs and may infect others.

carrier pigeon A homing pigeon that is used for carrying messages.

carrier wave The radio wave produced by a broadcasting station or other radio transmitter. When modulated, it carries the program or message.

car·ri·on [kar′ē·ən] **1** *n.* Dead and decaying flesh; meat not fit to be eaten by people: Buzzards live on *carrion.* **2** *adj.* Feeding on carrion: a *carrion* crow. **3** *adj.* Like carrion; dead and decaying.

car·rot [kar′ət] *n.* **1** The long, reddish yellow root of a plant related to parsley. It is eaten as a vegetable. **2** The plant itself.

car·rou·sel [kar′ə·sel′] *n.* Another word for MERRY-GO-ROUND.

car·ry [kar′ē] *v.* **car·ried, car·ry·ing** **1** To bear from one place to another; transport: *Carry* the dishes to the sink; This pipe *carries* gas. **2** To hold up; support: The columns in this room *carry* the weight of the ceiling. **3** To wear on or about one's person: Police officers *carry* guns. **4** To bear (the body or part of it) in a certain way: *Carry* your shoulders straight. **5** To cause to go or come: A love of animals *carries* them to the zoo every Sunday. **6** To reach to a distance: The sound *carried* for ten miles. **7** To win: Our candidate *carried* the election. **8** To have or keep for sale: A hardware store *carries* tools. **9** To bear in mind: to *carry* the memory of the experience. **10** To sing or play (a part or melody). **11** In adding up a row of figures, to transfer (a figure) from one column to the next. **12** To contain; include: The guard's voice *carried* a note of warning. **—carry away** To move the feelings greatly: We were *carried away* by the music. **—carry out** To accomplish.

car·ry·all[1] [kar′ē·ôl′] *n.* A light, one-horse carriage with a top, holding several people. ◆ *Carryall* comes from the French word *cariole.* Apparently the sound and spelling of *cariole* were too un-English, because *carryall,* with its familiar English elements, *carry* and *all,* replaced it.

car·ry·all[2] [kar′ē·ôl′] *n.* A large bag or handbag.

car·ry-o·ver [kar′ē·ō′vər] *n.* Something carried over or remaining from an earlier place or time.

car·sick [kär′sik′] *adj.* Dizzy or sick at one's stomach from riding in a car.

cart [kärt] **1** *n.* A heavy, two-wheeled vehicle for carrying heavy loads, usually pulled by a horse. **2** *n.* A light, usually two-wheeled vehicle for small loads or for riding: a pony *cart;* a grocery *cart.* **3** *v.* To carry in a cart.

carte blanche [kärt′blänsh′] Freedom to act as one thinks best; full authority.

car·tel [kär·tel′] *n.* **1** A large group of companies that are joined together to control the prices and production of certain goods. **2** An agreement between nations that are at war, especially for the exchange of prisoners.

Car·te·sian coordinate system [kär·tē′zhən] **1** A system for locating a point in a plane by means of its distances from each of two lines or axes that intersect at right angles. The numbers that locate a point are called **Cartesian coordinates.** **2** A similar system for locating a point in three-dimensional space by means of its distances from each of three intersecting planes.

Car·tha·gin·i·an [kär′thə·jin′ē·ən] **1** *adj.* Of or from Carthage. **2** *n.* A person who was born or lived in Carthage.

car·ti·lage [kär′tə·lij] *n.* A tough, elastic tissue that connects some bones and forms part of the skeleton; gristle.

car·ti·lag·i·nous [kär′tə·laj′ə·nəs] *adj.* **1** Of or like cartilage. **2** Having a supporting structure made mainly of cartilage.

car·tog·ra·phy [kär·tog′rə·fē] *n.* The art of making maps and charts. **—car·tog′ra·pher** *n.*

car·ton [kär′tən] *n.* A cardboard container.

car·toon [kär·to͞on′] *n.* **1** A satirical drawing, as in a newspaper or magazine, that pokes fun at personal foibles or comments on public and often political issues. **2** A comic strip. **3** A motion picture made by photographing a series of slightly different drawings so that the figures seem to move.

car·toon·ist [kär·to͞on′ist] *n.* A person who draws cartoons.

car·tridge [kär′trij] *n.* **1** A casing of metal or cardboard containing a charge of powder for a gun and usually the bullet or shot. **2** A small container, often shaped like a cylinder, made to be inserted into a larger instrument or mechanism: the ink *cartridge* of a pen. **3** A case in the pickup of a phonograph that contains the needle. **4** A case containing a roll of camera film that is loaded as a unit directly into a camera.

cart·wheel [kärt′(h)wēl′] *n.* A sideways handspring, in which the body is supported first on one hand and then the other.

carve [kärv] *v.* **carved, carv·ing** **1** To make by cutting or as if by cutting: to *carve* a statue; to *carve* one's name in history. **2** To cut figures or designs upon: to *carve* a table. **3** To cut up, as a piece of roasted meat. **—carv′er** *n.*

carv·ing [kär′ving] *n.* **1** The act of a person who carves. **2** A carved figure or design.

car·y·at·id [kar′ē·at′id] *n., pl.* **car·y·at·ids** or **car·y·at·i·des** [kar′ē·at′ə·dēz] A supporting column made in the form of a sculptured woman.

ca·sa·ba [kə·sä′bə] *n.* A sweet melon with a yellow rind and whitish flesh.

cas·cade [kas·kād′] *n., v.* **cas·cad·ed, cas·cad·ing** **1** *n.* A small waterfall over steep rocks. **2** *n.* Something that looks like a waterfall. **3** *v.* To fall in or as if in a cascade.

case[1] [kās] *n.* **1** A particular instance or example: a clear *case* of robbery. **2** The actual facts or state of affairs: Louise now loves to read, which was not the *case* last year. **3** An action or lawsuit in a court of law. **4** Someone being cared for, as by a doctor; patient. **5** In grammar, the form of a noun, pronoun, or adjective that expresses its relationship to the other words in a sentence. In "The cat scratched me with its sharp claws," *cat* is in the nominative *case, me* is in the objective *case,* and *its* is in the possessive *case.* **—in any case** No matter what. **—in case** In the event that.

case[2] [kās] *n., v.* **cased, cas·ing** **1** *n.* A box, bag, or other container for carrying or keeping things in. **2** *n.* A box and the containers or bottles it holds: a *case* of pop. **3** *v.* To put into or cover with a case. **4** *n.* A frame for a window or door.

case history A set of facts describing the history of a person or thing under study, as in medicine or sociology.

ca·se·in [kā′sēn′ *or* kā′sē·in] *n.* A protein found in milk, used in making products such as cheese and plastics.

case·ment [kās′mənt] *n.* A window hung on side hinges and opening as a door does.

Casement

case study A detailed study of a person or thing considered a good example of its kind.

case·work [kās′wûrk′] *n.* Social work in which individuals or families with problems are interviewed and given guidance. **—case′work′er** *n.*

cash [kash] **1** *n.* Money in the form of bills and coins which a person has on hand. **2** *v.* To give or receive coins and bills for: to *cash* a check. **3** *n.* Money or its equivalent, such as a check, used when one makes a purchase: a store that accepts only *cash*, not credit cards.

cash·ew [kash′o͞o *or* kə·sho͞o′] *n.* **1** A soft, kidney-shaped nut that is good to eat. It is grown on a tropical tree. **2** The tree itself.

cash·ier[1] [ka·shir′] *n.* A person who is employed to handle the money, as in a restaurant, store, or bank.

cash·ier[2] [ka·shir′] *v.* To dismiss from service in disgrace, especially a military officer.

cash·mere [kash′mir *or* kazh′mir] **1** *n.* A fine, soft wool obtained from a goat originally native in Kashmir. **2** *n.* A soft fabric woven from this wool. **3** *adj. use:* a *cashmere* sweater.

cash register A machine in a store that records the amount of each sale and usually has a drawer for keeping money received from customers.

cas·ing [kā′sing] *n.* **1** A protective case or covering, as the outer part of an automobile tire. **2** The intestines of hogs and other animals that are cleaned and used as sausage skins. **3** A framework, as around a door or window.

ca·si·no [kə·sē′nō] *n., pl.* **ca·si·nos** **1** A room or building for public amusement, especially for dancing or gambling. **2** A card game.

cask [kask] *n.* **1** A barrel-shaped wooden container for liquids. **2** The amount a cask will hold.

cas·ket [kas′kit] *n.* **1** A small box or chest, as for jewelry. **2** A coffin.

casque [kask] *n.* A large helmet worn with armor.

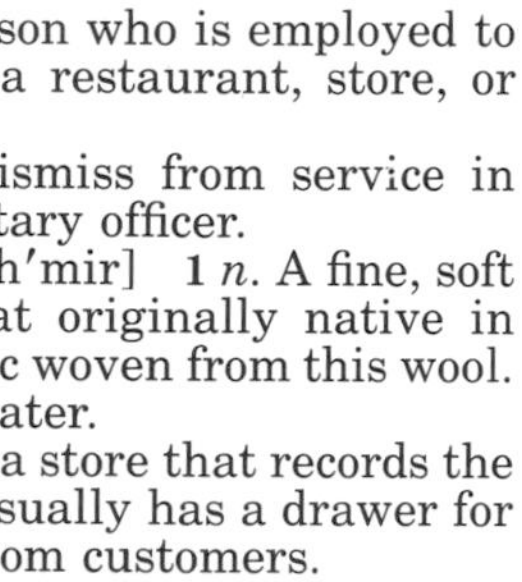

Casque

Cas·san·dra [kə·san′drə] *n.* **1** In Greek myths, a daughter of the king of Troy whose prophecies, although true, were never believed by anyone. **2** A person who predicts disaster or misfortune.

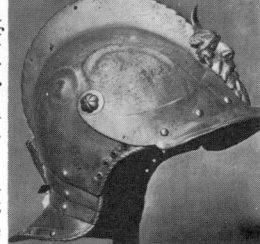

cas·sa·va [kə·sä′və] *n.* **1** A tropical American plant with starchy roots. **2** The starch made from this plant, used to make tapioca.

cas·se·role [kas′ə·rōl′] *n.* **1** A dish, often with a cover, in which food may be baked and served. **2** Any food so prepared and served.

cas·sette [kə·set′] *n.* **1** A case holding a spool of magnetic tape for easy insertion into a tape recorder or player. **2** A film cartridge for a camera. ◆ *Cassette* was borrowed from French, in which it means *small box.*

cas·si·no [kə·sē′nō] *n.* Casino (def. 2).

Cas·si·o·pe·ia [kas′ē·ə·pē′ə] *n.* A northern constellation.

cas·sock [kas′ək] *n.* A close-fitting, usually black robe reaching to the feet. It is worn by the clergy of some churches.

cas·so·war·y [kas′ə·wer′ē] *n., pl.* **cas·so·war·ies** A large flightless bird of New Guinea and neighboring areas. It is like an ostrich, but smaller, and has a bony ridge on the top of its head.

cast [kast] *v.* **cast, cast·ing,** *n.* **1** *v.* To throw or hurl with force; fling: to *cast* a spear; to *cast* a fishing line. **2** *n.* The act of casting or throwing: a *cast* of the dice. **3** *n.* The distance to which a thing may be thrown: a stone's *cast.* **4** *v.* To throw off; shed: Grasshoppers *cast* their hard shells as they grow. **5** *v.* To cause to fall upon or over something: to *cast* a shadow. **6** *v.* To let down; drop: to *cast* anchor. **7** *v.* To select actors, as for a play or motion picture: In the school play, the youngest children were *cast* as elves. **8** *n.* All of the actors appearing in a play or motion picture. **9** *v.* To pour into a mold and let harden: to *cast* molten iron. **10** *v.* To shape in a mold: to *cast* a statue in bronze. **11** *n.* Something shaped or formed in a mold, as of metal or plaster; casting. **12** *n.* The appearance or form of something: a face with an Oriental *cast.* **13** *n.* A heavy bandage stiffened with plaster. It is wrapped around a broken bone to keep it from moving until it has healed. **14** *v.* To direct; cause to turn: to *cast* a glance up the street. **15** *v.* To deposit; give: to *cast* a vote. **16** *n.* A twist or turn of an eye to one side; squint. **17** *n.* A tinge or shade: a bluish *cast.* **—cast down** **1** To overthrow; defeat. **2** To make discouraged; depress: to be *cast down* over a failure. **3** To throw or turn downward: *Cast down* your weapons.

cas·ta·nets [kas′tə·nets′] *n.pl.* A pair of small, shell-shaped disks of wood or ivory, clapped together with the fingers to beat time to music, especially to Spanish music or dances.

cast·a·way [kast′ə·wā′] **1** *adj.* Shipwrecked. **2** *adj.* Thrown away; discarded. **3** *n.* A person who has been shipwrecked.

caste [kast] *n.* **1** In India, one of the social classes into which Hindus are born. Formerly, Hindus of higher castes were forbidden to mix with or touch those of a lower caste. **2** Any social class to which a person belongs because of money, occupation, rank, or other criterion. **—lose caste** To lose one's social position.

cas·tel·lat·ed [kas′tə·lā′tid] *adj.* Having tower-

a	add	**i**	it	**o͝o**	took	**oi**	oil
ā	ace	**ī**	ice	**o͞o**	pool	**ou**	pout
â	care	**o**	odd	**u**	up	**ng**	ring
ä	palm	**ō**	open	**û**	burn	**th**	thin
e	end	**ô**	order	**yo͞o**	fuse	**th̶**	this
ē	equal					**zh**	vision

ə = {a in *above* e in *sicken* i in *possible* / o in *melon* u in *circus*}

C

shaped projections and battlements, like a castle.

cast·er [kas′tər] *n.* **1** A person or thing that casts. **2** One of a set of small, swiveling wheels fastened under each leg or corner of a piece of furniture to make it easier to move about. **3** A small container for vinegar, mustard, or other seasoning that is used at the table.

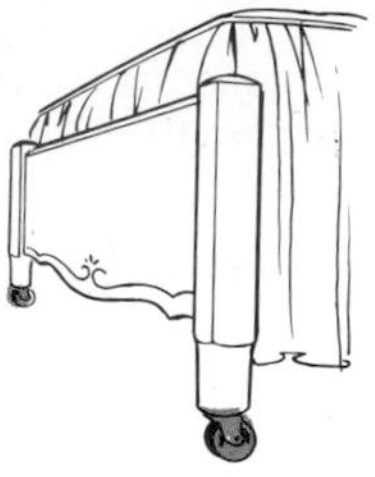
Casters

cas·ti·gate [kas′tə·gāt′] *v.* **cas·ti·gat·ed, cas·ti·gat·ing** To scold or criticize harshly or severely; rebuke. **—cas′ti·ga′tion** *n.*

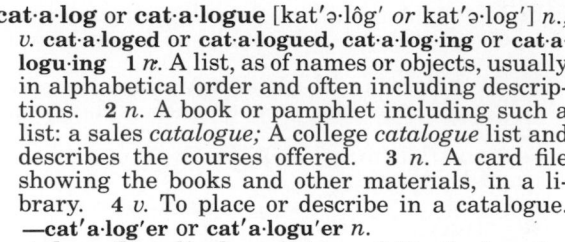

Castile soap A pure soap made from olive oil.

Cas·til·ian [kas·til′yən] **1** *n.* A person born or living in Castile. **2** *n.* The standard and literary language of Spain. **3** *adj.* Of or from Castile.

cast·ing [kas′ting] *n.* **1** The act of a person or thing that casts. **2** Something that is cast, as a statue or other article formed in a mold.

cast-i·ron [kast′ī′ərn] *adj.* **1** Made of cast iron. **2** Like cast iron; strong and unyielding: to have a *cast-iron* will.

cast iron A hard, brittle kind of iron cast in molds. It contains a large amount of carbon.

cas·tle [kas′əl] *n.* **1** A large, fortified building or set of buildings, usually having a moat around it for defense. During the Middle Ages, rulers and nobles lived in castles. **2** Any large, elegant house. **3** In chess, a rook. **—castle in the air** or **castle in Spain** A pleasing thought or daydream.

cast·off [kast′ôf′] **1** *adj.* Thrown away or laid aside because no longer wanted: a *castoff* coat. **2** *n.* A person or thing no longer wanted.

cas·tor [kas′tər] *n.* Another spelling for CASTER (*defs. 2 and 3*).

castor oil A thick, pale yellow oil extracted from the bean of a shrubby tropical tree. It is taken as a laxative and used to oil machinery.

cas·trate [kas′trāt′] *v.* **cas·trat·ed, cas·trat·ing** **1** To remove the testes of; geld. **2** To remove the ovaries of; spay. **—cas·tra′tion** *n.*

cas·u·al [kazh′ōō·əl] **1** *adj.* Happening by chance; unexpected: a *casual* meeting. **2** *adj.* Done without thinking; not planned: a *casual* comment. **3** *adj.* Happening once in a while; not regular: a *casual* visit. **4** *n.* A person who works only occasionally. **5** *adj.* Not dressy; informal: *casual* clothes. **—cas′u·al·ly** *adv.*

cas·u·al·ty [kazh′ōō·əl·tē] *n., pl.* **cas·u·al·ties** **1** A serious accident, especially one in which someone is killed. **2** Anyone who is injured or killed in an accident. **3** A soldier who is killed, wounded, or missing during a battle.

cas·u·ist [kazh′ōō·ist] *n.* A person who is skillful at reasoning but uses subtly false arguments.

cas·u·ist·ry [kazh′ōō·is·trē] *n., pl.* **cas·u·ist·ries** Subtle but false reasoning; sophistry.

cat [kat] *n.* **1** A small domestic animal of various colors. ◆ Adj., *feline.* **2** Any larger animal related to the cat, as the tiger, lion, leopard, and bobcat. **3** A woman who makes spiteful, mean remarks. **4** A cat-o'-nine-tails.

CAT [kat] computerized axial tomography.

cat·a·clysm [kat′ə·kliz′əm] *n.* Any violent change or disturbance, as a war or flood.

cat·a·comb [kat′ə·kōm′] *n.* (*usually pl.*) An underground place of burial made up of passages and small rooms for tombs.

cat·a·log or **cat·a·logue** [kat′ə·lôg′ *or* kat′ə·log′] *n., v.* **cat·a·loged** or **cat·a·logued, cat·a·log·ing** or **cat·a·logu·ing** **1** *n.* A list, as of names or objects, usually in alphabetical order and often including descriptions. **2** *n.* A book or pamphlet including such a list: a sales *catalogue;* A college *catalogue* list and describes the courses offered. **3** *n.* A card file showing the books and other materials, in a library. **4** *v.* To place or describe in a catalogue. **—cat′a·log′er** or **cat′a·logu′er** *n.*

ca·tal·pa [kə·tal′pə] *n.* A tree of North America having large, heart-shaped leaves and long pods that look like string beans.

ca·tal·y·sis [kə·tal′ə·sis] *n., pl.* **ca·tal·y·ses** [kə·tal′ə·sez] The speeding up or slowing down of a chemical reaction by a substance that does not itself undergo permanent change; the action of a catalyst.

cat·a·lyst [kat′ə·list] *n.* A substance that speeds up a chemical reaction without itself appearing to undergo permanent change.

cat·a·lyt·ic [kat′ə·lit′ik] *adj.* Of, using, or being a catalyst. A **catalytic converter** in an automobile exhaust system speeds up the conversion of carbon monoxide to carbon dioxide.

cat·a·ma·ran [kat′ə·mə·ran′] *n.* **1** A long, narrow raft of logs. **2** A boat having twin hulls, side by side.

cat·a·mount [kat′ə·mount′] *n.* Any of several wild cats, especially the puma or lynx.

cat·a·pult [kat′ə·pult′] **1** *n.* An ancient military machine for throwing arrows, spears, or rocks with great force. **2** *n.* A device for helping an airplane to take off quickly into the air, as from the deck of a ship. **3** *v.* To hurl or be hurled from or as if from a catapult.

Catamaran

cat·a·ract [kat′ə·rakt′] *n.* **1** A very large waterfall. **2** A heavy downpour or flood of water. **3** A disease in which the lens of the eye clouds over, causing partial or total blindness.

ca·tarrh [kə·tär′] *n.* An old-fashioned name for an inflammation of the nose and throat.

ca·tas·tro·phe [kə·tas′trə·fē] *n.* A sudden and widespread misfortune, calamity, or disaster.

cat·a·stroph·ic [kat′ə·strof′ik] *adj.* Caused by, resulting in, or like a catastrophe.

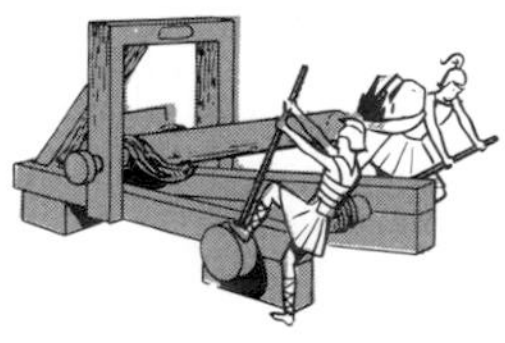
Catapult

cat·bird [kat′bûrd′] *n.* A small North American songbird whose cry is like the meow of a cat.

cat·boat [kat′bōt′] *n.* A sailboat that has a single mast set forward in the bow and only a single sail, with no jib.

cat·call [kat′kôl′] **1** *n.* A shrill call or whistle made in public to show dislike or impatience. **2** *v.* To make catcalls.

catch [kach] *v.* **caught, catch·ing,** *n.* **1** *v.* To seize or capture after pursuing: to *catch* a runaway dog. **2** *v.* To take in a trap or by means of a hook; ensnare: to *catch* rats; to *catch* fish. **3** *n.* Something that is caught: a fine *catch* of trout. **4** *v.* To entangle or become entangled: The thorns *caught* my sleeve. **5** *n.* Something that fastens or holds closed: a window *catch.* **6** *v.* To stop the motion of, as by grasping with the hands or arms: to *catch* a ball. **7** *n.*The act of catching, especially in baseball: a difficult *catch.* **8** *v.* In baseball, to act as a catcher. **9** *v.* To overtake: I *caught* them before they had gone very far. **10** *v.* To reach in time to board: to *catch* a bus at the corner. **11** *v.* To strike suddenly: The cat *caught* the kitten a blow on the ear. **12** *v.* To get (an infectious disease): to *catch* cold. **13** *v.* To become aware of through hearing, seeing, or understanding: I *caught* what my two friends were whispering. **14** *v.* To please or captivate: The puppy *caught* their fancy. **15** *v.* To start to burn: The house *caught* fire. **16** *v.* To surprise in the act; detect: The storekeeper *caught* them stealing. **17** *v.* To check suddenly: He *caught* himself just before blurting out the secret. **18** *n.* A break, as in the voice or breath from fear or strong feeling. **19** *n.* In music, a round. **20** *n. informal* A hidden trick or difficulty: There is a *catch* in this arithmetic problem. **—catch on** *informal* **1** To become popular or fashionable: Folk music has *caught on.* **2** To understand: to *catch on* to a new idea. **—catch up** **1** To overtake: I *caught up* with her in the hall. **2** To pick up suddenly: He *caught up* his hat and left. ◆ See CHASE.

catch·all [kach′ôl′] *n.* **1** A place or container for storing odds and ends. **2** A word, phrase, or subject heading that covers many different things.

catch·er [kach′ər] *n.* **1** A person or thing that catches. **2** In baseball, the player behind home plate who catches balls that pass the batter.

catch·ing [kach′ing] *adj.* **1** Passing from person to person; contagious. **2** Attractive; charming.

catch·up [kach′əp *or* kech′əp] *n.* Another spelling of KETCHUP.

catch·word [kach′wûrd′] *n.* **1** An often repeated word or phrase; slogan. **2** Another name for GUIDE WORD.

catch·y [kach′ē] *adj.* **catch·i·er, catch·i·est** **1** Easily remembered because pleasing: a *catchy* song. **2** Catching the fancy; attractive. **3** Likely to confuse; tricky. **4** Fitful; gusty: *catchy* winds.

cat·e·chism [kat′ə·kiz′əm] *n.* **1** A short book in the form of questions and answers for teaching the principles of a religion. **2** Any list of questions like this used for teaching.

cat·e·chize [kat′ə·kīz′] *v.* **cat·e·chized, cat·e·chiz·ing** **1** To teach, as by questions and answers. **2** To question at length.

cat·e·gor·i·cal [kat′ə·gôr′i·kəl] *adj.* Positive and definite; without any question or condition: a *categorical* refusal. **—cat′e·gor′i·cal·ly** *adv.*

cat·e·go·ry [kat′ə·gôr′ē] *n., pl.* **cat·e·go·ries** A division, class, or group in any system of classification: Drama is a *category* of literature.

ca·ter [kā′tər] *v.* **1** To furnish prepared food, drink, and services: to *cater* for a wedding. **2** To please by furnishing what is needed or wanted: That restaurant *caters* to families.

cat·er·cor·ner [kat′ər·kôr′nər] **1** *adj.* Diagonal: a *catercorner* line. **2** *adv.* Diagonally: to walk *catercorner* across a street.

cat·er-cor·nered [kat′ər·kôr′nərd] *adj., adv.* Catercorner.

ca·ter·er [kā′tər·ər] *n.* A person who caters, especially one whose business is providing food and services, as for parties and banquets.

cat·er·pil·lar [kat′ər·pil′ər] *n.* The wormlike form of certain insects, such as the butterfly or moth, after they hatch from the egg; larva.

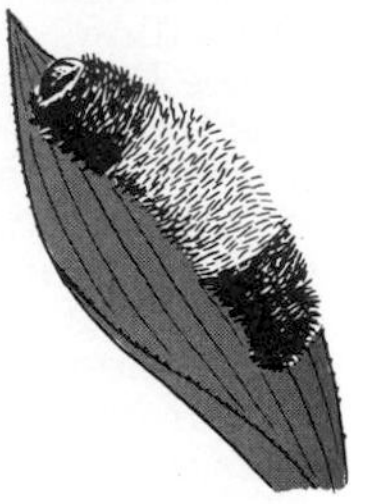

Caterpillar

Cat·er·pil·lar Tractor [kat′ər·pil′ər] A tractor that moves by means of two endless metal tracks running along each side, enabling it to be used on soft or rough ground: a trademark.

cat·er·waul [kat′ər·wôl′] **1** *v.* To make a shrill yowl or shriek like that of a cat when fighting. **2** *n.* A sound like that of cats fighting.

cat·fish [kat′fish′] *n., pl.* **cat·fish** or **cat·fish·es** Any of several fish having feelers about the mouth that look like a cat's whiskers.

cat·gut [kat′gut′] *n.* A tough cord made from the intestines of certain animals, as sheep, and used as strings for musical instruments and thread for sewing up surgical wounds.

ca·thar·tic [kə·thär′tik] **1** *n.* A strong medicine, such as castor oil, used to empty the bowels. **2** *adj.* Cleansing; purifying.

ca·the·dral [kə·thē′drəl] *n.* **1** The main church of a diocese of some Christian churches, containing the bishop's throne. **2** Any large church.

A Gothic cathedral

cath·e·ter [kath′i·tər] *n.* A thin tube inserted into the body for a medical purpose, as to drain away a fluid or to keep a passageway open.

cath·ode [kath′ōd′] *n.* **1** The negative terminal of a battery, electrolytic cell, diode, or electron tube. **2** The positive terminal of a battery that is supplying current.

cath·ode-ray tube [kath′ōd·rā′] A special vacuum tube in which a beam of electrons strikes a fluorescent screen and makes it glow, as the picture tube of a television set.

Cath·o·lic [kath′ə·lik] **1** *adj.* Of or indicating the ancient Christian church or a church directly descended from it, especially the Roman Catholic Church. **2** *n.* A member of such a church, especially a Roman Catholic. **3** *adj.* (*written* **catholic**) Broad; extensive: a *catholic* taste in books.

Ca·thol·i·cism [kə·thol′ə·siz′əm] *n.* The beliefs and practices of the Roman Catholic Church.

cath·o·lic·i·ty [kath′ə·lis′ə·tē] *n.* The quality or condition of including many things; breadth.

cat·i·on [kat′ī′ən] *n.* An ion with a positive charge. Cations move toward the negatively charged electrode during electrolysis.

a	add	**i**	it	**o͝o**	took	**oi**	oil
ā	ace	**ī**	ice	**o͞o**	pool	**ou**	pout
â	care	**o**	odd	**u**	up	**ng**	ring
ä	palm	**ō**	open	**û**	burn	**th**	thin
e	end	**ô**	order	**yo͞o**	fuse	**th̶**	this
ē	equal					**zh**	vision

ə = { a in *above* e in *sicken* i in *possible*
o in *melon* u in *circus* }

cat·kin [kat′kin] *n.* A cluster of small flowers arranged like scales along a drooping spike, as in the willow.
cat·like [kat′līk′] *adj.* Like a cat: the burglar's *catlike* tread.
cat·nap [kat′nap′] *n., v.* **cat·napped, cat·nap·ping** 1 *n.* A short nap. 2 *v.* To take a short nap.
cat·nip [kat′nip] *n.* A fragrant herb of the mint family. Cats love to sniff and nibble at it.
cat-o'-nine-tails [kat′ə·nīn′tālz′] *n., pl.* **cat-o'-nine-tails** A whip with nine knotted lines and a handle, once used to inflict punishment.
CAT scan A picture produced by a CAT scanner that is a combination of X rays, each showing a different cross section of the body or part of the body. ◆ The *CAT* in *CAT scan* stands for *computerized axial tomography*.
CAT scanner A specialized X-ray machine that can scan a part of the body in search of disease or abnormality.
cat's cradle A game played with a loop of string stretched in various arrangements over the fingers of both hands.
cat's-paw or **cat's·paw** [kats′pô′] *n.* A person tricked by another into doing something dangerous or wrong.
cat·sup [kat′səp *or* kech′əp] *n.* Another spelling of KETCHUP.
cat·tail [kat′tāl′] *n.* A marsh plant with long leaves and long, round, velvety spikes.
cat·tle [kat′(ə)l] *n.pl.* Domesticated cows, bulls, and steers; oxen.
cat·tle·man [kat′(ə)l·mən] *n., pl.* **cat·tle·men** [kat′·(ə)l·mən] A person who raises cattle.
cat·ty [kat′ē] *adj.* **cat·ti·er, cat·ti·est** 1 Having to do with or like a cat. 2 Spiteful.
cat·ty-cor·ner [kat′ē·kôr′nər] *adj., adv.* Another word for CATERCORNER.
cat·ty-cor·nered [kat′ē·kôr′nərd] *adj., adv.* Another word for CATERCORNER.
cat·walk [kat′wôk′] *n.* Any narrow walk, as along the side of a bridge.
Cau·ca·sian [kô·kā′zhən] 1 *n.* A member of the division of human beings that is the so-called white race. 2 *adj.* Of or having to do with this group. 3 *adj.* Of the Caucasus region.
cau·cus [kô′kəs] 1 *n.* A meeting of the leading members of a political party to choose candidates or to make plans, as for a campaign. 2 *v.* To meet in or hold a caucus.
cau·dal [kôd′(ə)l] *adj.* 1 Of or near the tail or hind part of the body. 2 Like a tail.
caught [kôt] Past tense of CATCH.
caul·dron [kôl′drən] *n.* Another spelling of CALDRON.
cau·li·flow·er [kô′lə·flou′ər] *n.* A variety of cabbage with a solid white head made up of clusters of flowers pressed tightly together.
caulk [kôk] *v.* To make tight, as the seams of a boat, by plugging with tar, putty, or other material.
caus·al [kô′zəl] *adj.* 1 Of, having to do with, or being a cause. 2 Indicating or expressing cause.
cause [kôz] *n., v.* **caused, caus·ing** 1 *n.* A person or thing that makes something happen: The driver was the *cause* of the accident. 2 *v.* To make happen; bring about: Fear *caused* my voice to tremble. 3 *n.* A reason for feeling or acting in a certain way: a *cause* for celebrating. 4 *n.* A movement or idea supported by an individual or group: the *cause* of freedom.
cause·way [kôz′wā′] *n.* 1 A raised road across marshy ground or shallow water. 2 A highway.
caus·tic [kôs′tik] 1 *adj.* Capable of eating or burning away living tissue, as lye or certain acids. 2 *n.* A caustic substance. 3 *adj.* Sarcastic; biting: *caustic* remarks.
caustic soda Another name for SODIUM HYDROXIDE.
cau·ter·ize [kô′tə·rīz′] *v.* **cau·ter·ized, cau·ter·iz·ing** To burn (living tissue) with a hot iron or a caustic substance.
cau·tion [kô′shən] 1 *n.* Care to avoid injury or other mishaps; watchfulness: to use *caution* when walking on icy pavements. 2 *n.* A warning. 3 *v.* To advise to be careful; warn.
cau·tious [kô′shəs] *adj.* Using care; careful not to take chances or make mistakes; watchful: a *cautious* diplomat; a *cautious* statement. **—cau′tious·ly** *adv.* **—cau′tious·ness** *n.*
cav·al·cade [kav′əl·kād′] *n.* 1 A procession of people on horseback or in carriages. 2 Any procession or series, as of shows.
cav·a·lier [kav′ə·lir′] 1 *n.* A horseman or knight. 2 *n.* A courtly or dashing gentleman. 3 *n.* A lady's escort. 4 *adj.* Free and easy; offhand: a *cavalier* attitude toward work. 5 *adj.* Haughty; scornful. **—cav′a·lier′ly** *adv.*
cav·al·ry [kav′əl·rē] *n., pl.* **cav·al·ries** 1 In the past, soldiers who were trained to fight on horseback. 2 In recent times, soldiers who fight and maneuver in armored motor vehicles.
cav·al·ry·man [kav′əl·rē·mən] *n., pl.* **cav·al·ry·men** [kav′əl·rē·mən] A soldier who fights on horseback.
cave [kāv] *n., v.* **caved, cav·ing** 1 *n.* A natural hollow beneath the surface of the earth, having an opening to the outside. 2 *v.* To hollow out. **—cave in** To fall in or collapse, as when undermined: The mine *caved in* on the men.
cave-in [kāv′in′] *n.* A collapse or falling in, as of a tunnel or mine.
cave man 1 A human being who lived in a cave in prehistoric times. 2 A person who is rough and brutal.
cav·ern [kav′ərn] *n.* A large cave.
cav·ern·ous [kav′ər·nəs] *adj.* 1 Like a cavern; deeply hollowed out: a *cavernous* cellar. 2 Full of caverns or caves.
cav·i·ar or **cav·i·are** [kav′ē·är] *n.* A salty appetizer made of the eggs, or roe, of the sturgeon or certain other fishes.
cav·il [kav′əl] *v.* **cav·iled** or **cav·illed, cav·il·ing** or **cav·il·ling,** *n.* 1 *v.* To find fault unnecessarily; pick flaws: to *cavil* at school rules instead of obeying them. 2 *n.* A strong objection about something unimportant.
cav·i·ty [kav′ə·tē] *n., pl.* **cav·i·ties** 1 A hollow or sunken place; hole. 2 A natural hollow in the body: the abdominal *cavity.* 3 A hollow place in a tooth caused by decay.
ca·vort [kə·vôrt′] *v.* To prance about; caper.
caw [kô] 1 *v.* To make the high, harsh cry of a crow or raven. 2 *n.* This cry.
cay·enne [kī·en′] *n.* A hot, biting red pepper made by grinding up certain pepper plants.
cay·man [kā′mən] *n., pl.* **cay·mans** Another spelling of CAIMAN.
Ca·yu·ga [kā·yōō′gə *or* kī·yōō′gə] *n., pl.* **Ca·yu·ga** or **Ca·yu·gas** 1 A tribe of North American Indians once living in New York, now in Ontario, Canada. 2 A member of this tribe. 3 The language of this tribe.

cay·use [kī·yo͞os′] *n.* A pony of the western U.S.
CB citizens band (radio).
CBS Columbia Broadcasting System.
cc cubic centimeter(s).
C clef In music, a symbol placed on the line of the staff that represents middle C.
Cd The symbol for the element cadmium.
CD 1 certificate of deposit. 2 compact disc.
CDC Center for Disease Control.
Ce The symbol for the element cerium.
cease [sēs] *v.* **ceased, ceas·ing** To bring or come to an end: *Cease* that noise.
cease-fire [sēs′fīr′] *n.* 1 A military order to stop shooting at the enemy. 2 An armistice.
cease·less [sēs′lis] *adj.* Going on without pause; continual. **—cease′less·ly** *adv.*
ce·cro·pi·a moth [sə·krō′pē·ə] A large, colorful moth of eastern North America.
ce·dar [sē′dər] *n.* 1 A large, broad evergreen tree of the pine family, with a fragrant, reddish wood. 2 This wood. 3 *adj. use:* a *cedar* chest.
cede [sēd] *v.* **ced·ed, ced·ing** To yield or give up; transfer the ownership of, as territory.
ce·dil·la [si·dil′ə] *n.* A hooklike mark placed under the letter *c* (ç) in some French words to show that the *c* is to be pronounced as an *s*.
ceil·ing [sē′ling] *n.* 1 The lining of the top side of a room. 2 The upper limit set, as on wages or prices. 3 The height of the lowest layers of clouds. 4 The greatest height at which a given type of airplane can fly.
cel·e·brant [sel′ə·brənt] *n.* 1 A person who celebrates something. 2 The priest who performs the main part of the Mass.
cel·e·brate [sel′ə·brāt′] *v.* **cel·e·brat·ed, cel·e·brat·ing** 1 To observe or honor in a special manner: to *celebrate* a holiday. 2 To make known or famous; praise: to *celebrate* an astronaut. 3 To perform the ceremony of in a solemn manner: A priest *celebrates* Mass. **—cel′e·bra′tion** *n.*
cel·e·brat·ed [sel′ə·brā′tid] *adj.* Well-known; spoken of by many people: a *celebrated* artist.
ce·leb·ri·ty [sə·leb′rə·tē] *n., pl.* **ce·leb·ri·ties** 1 A famous or celebrated person. 2 The condition of being celebrated; fame.
ce·ler·i·ty [sə·ler′ə·tē] *n.* Quickness of motion or action; speed: to work with *celerity.*
cel·er·y [sel′ər·ē] *n.* A plant whose long, crisp stalks are eaten as a vegetable or in salads.
ce·les·ta [sə·les′tə] *n.* A small keyboard instrument with hammers that strike steel plates.
ce·les·tial [sə·les′chəl] *adj.* 1 Of or having to do with the sky or heavens. 2 Very beautiful; exquisite: *celestial* music.
celestial equator A great circle on the celestial sphere in the same place as Earth's equator and midway between the celestial poles.
celestial pole Either of the points on the celestial sphere intersected by an extension of Earth's axis.
celestial sphere An imaginary sphere formed by the entire sky, with the earth at its center. Such a device is a convenient way of mapping the stars and planets, which appear as points on the surface of the sphere.
cel·i·ba·cy [sel′ə·bə·sē] *n.* The state of being and remaining unmarried, especially by a religious vow: the *celibacy* of monks.
cel·i·bate [sel′ə·bit] 1 *n.* A person who remains unmarried, especially by a religious vow. 2 *adj.* Unmarried.
cell [sel] *n.* 1 The tiny basic structural unit of all living matter. Cells are usually enclosed by a membrane or wall and consist mostly of protoplasm with a nucleus in the middle. 2 A device that changes chemical energy into electricity. Several cells connected together make up a battery. 3 A small room, as for a prisoner or monk. 4 Any small space or cavity.

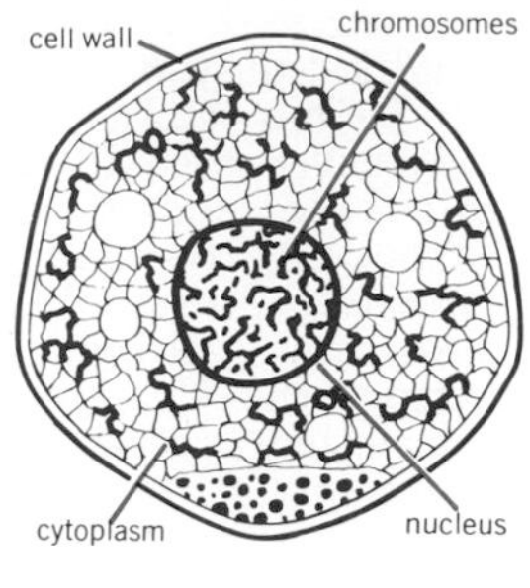

Cell

cel·lar [sel′ər] *n.* A room or several rooms completely or partly underground, usually beneath a building.
cel·list [chel′ist] *n.* A person who plays the cello.
cel·lo or **'cel·lo** [chel′ō] *n., pl.* **cel·los** or **'cel·los** A large instrument like a violin but bigger, with a deep tone. It is held between the performer's knees when played.

Cello

cel·lo·phane [sel′ə·fān′] *n.* A thin, transparent, waterproof substance made from cellulose, used as a wrapping or covering.
cel·lu·lar [sel′yə·lər] *adj.* Of, having to do with, or made up of cells: *cellular* tissue.
cellular phone A mobile telephone linked to a computerized system in which a limited area is served by a low-power radio transmitter.
cel·lu·loid [sel′yə loid′] *n.* 1 A hard plastic material made from cellulose combined with nitrogen and camphor. 2 Motion-picture film.
cel·lu·lose [sel′yə·lōs′] *n.* A carbohydrate forming the main part of cell walls of plants, widely used in making explosives, paper, and other products.
Cel·si·us [sel′sē·əs] *adj.* Of, having to do with, or according to the Celsius scale.
Celsius scale A temperature scale with 0 degrees at the freezing point of water and 100 degrees at its boiling point, used by scientists in most countries throughout the world.
Celt [selt *or* kelt] *n.* A person belonging to a people who speak a Celtic language.
Celt·ic [sel′tik *or* kel′tik] 1 *n.* A family of European languages that include those now spoken by the Irish, the Welsh, the Scottish Highlanders, and the Bretons. 2 *adj.* Of or having to do with the Celts or their languages.
Celtic cross An upright cross having a circle behind the crossbeam.
ce·ment [si·ment′] 1 *n.* A substance made from

a	add	**i**	it	**o͝o**	took	**oi**	oil
ā	ace	**ī**	ice	**o͞o**	pool	**ou**	pout
â	care	**o**	odd	**u**	up	**ng**	ring
ä	palm	**ō**	open	**û**	burn	**th**	thin
e	end	**ô**	order	**yo͞o**	fuse	**th**	this
ē	equal					**zh**	vision

ə = { a in *above* e in *sicken* i in *possible* / o in *melon* u in *circus* }

limestone and clay burned together. **2** *n.* This substance mixed with water and sometimes sand, used in making mortar or concrete. **3** *n.* Any gluelike substance that will bind objects together. **4** *v.* To join or bind with or as if with cement. **5** *v.* To cover or coat with cement.

cem·e·ter·y [sem′ə·ter′ē] *n., pl.* **cem·e·ter·ies** A place for burying the dead; graveyard.

Ce·no·zo·ic [sē′nə·zō′ik *or* sen′ə·zō′ik] **1** *n.* The most recent geological era, including the present. During the Cenozoic the continents moved to where they now are, and mammals have been the dominant forms of life. **2** *adj.* Of, having to do with, or like the Cenozoic. ◆ *Cenozoic* comes from two Greek words meaning "new life."

cen·ser [sen′sər] *n.* A container for burning incense, especially in religious ceremonies.

cen·sor [sen′sər] **1** *n.* A person empowered to examine such materials as letters, books, and plays, and to suppress what he or she deems harmful to morals or to security. **2** *v.* To examine so as to cut out parts; act as a censor. **3** *n.* Any person who is very critical of what others do or say. **4** *n.* In ancient Rome, an official who took the census and supervised the manners and morals of the people. ◆ Both *censor* [sen′sər] and *censure* [sen′shər] come from the same Latin word, *censere,* meaning *to judge,* and both words as used today involve acts of judgment. To *censor* is to prevent something from being seen or heard. To *censure* is to blame someone formally for wrongdoing: Congress *censured* the controversial senator for improper conduct.

cen·so·ri·al [sen·sôr′ē·əl] *adj.* Of or having to do with censors.

cen·so·ri·ous [sen·sôr′ē·əs] *adj.* **1** Very critical: a *censorious* person. **2** Full of criticism: a *censorious* article. **—cen·so′ri·ous·ly** *adv.* **—cen·so′ri·ous·ness** *n.*

cen·sor·ship [sen′sər·ship′] *n.* **1** The act, method, or system of censoring: strict *censorship* during a war. **2** The position or occupation of a censor.

cen·sure [sen′shər] *n., v.* **cen·sured, cen·sur·ing** **1** *n.* Blame or criticism; a reprimand. **2** *v.* To blame or criticize. ◆ See CENSOR.

cen·sus [sen′səs] *n.* An official count of all the people in an entire country, a district, or a city, with additional information about each person, including age, sex, and occupation.

cent [sent] *n.* The hundredth part of a dollar; also, a coin of this value. Symbol: ¢.

cent. **1** centigrade. **2** central. **3** century.

cen·taur [sen′tôr] *n.* In Greek myths, one of a race of monsters having the head, arms, and upper body of a man united to the body and legs of a horse.

Centaur

cen·ta·vo [sen·tä′vō] *n., pl.* **cen·ta·vos** A small coin of the Philippines and various Spanish-American countries.

cen·te·nar·i·an [sen′tə·nâr′ē·ən] *n.* A person who has reached the age of 100 years.

cen·te·nar·y [sen′tə·ner′ē *or* sen·ten′ə·rē] *n., pl.* **cen·te·nar·ies** **1** A period of 100 years. **2** A centennial.

cen·ten·ni·al [sen·ten′ē·əl] **1** *adj.* Lasting or having an age of 100 years. **2** *adj.* Happening every 100 years. **3** *adj.* Having to do with a 100th anniversary. **4** *n.* A 100th anniversary or its celebration.

cen·ter [sen′tər] **1** *n.* In geometry, the point of a circle or sphere that is equally distant from every point on the circumference or surface. **2** *n.* The middle part or point of something: the *center* of a lake. **3** *v.* To place in or at the center. **4** *n.* A place or point where there is something special to see or do: a tourist *center.* **5** *v.* To direct toward one place; concentrate: *Center* your energy on your schoolbooks. **6** *n.* In some sports, a player stationed in the middle.

cen·ter·board [sen′tər·bôrd′] *n.* In certain sailboats, a keel that can be lowered through a watertight slot to prevent drifting to leeward.

center of gravity The point in an object around which its weight is equally distributed.

cen·ter·piece [sen′tər·pēs′] *n.* A decorative object, as a bowl of flowers, placed at the center of a dining table.

centi- A combining form meaning: **1** Hundred, as in *centipede.* **2** Hundredth part, as in *centimeter.*

cen·ti·grade [sen′tə·grād′] *adj.* Another name for CELSIUS.

cen·ti·gram [sen′tə·gram′] *n.* In the metric system, a unit of weight equal to one hundredth of a gram.

cen·time [sän′tēm′] *n.* A coin, equal to one hundredth of a franc, used in France, Switzerland, and other countries.

cen·ti·me·ter [sen′tə·mē′tər] *n.* A measure of length, equal to 1/100 of a meter. One inch is about 2.54 centimeters.

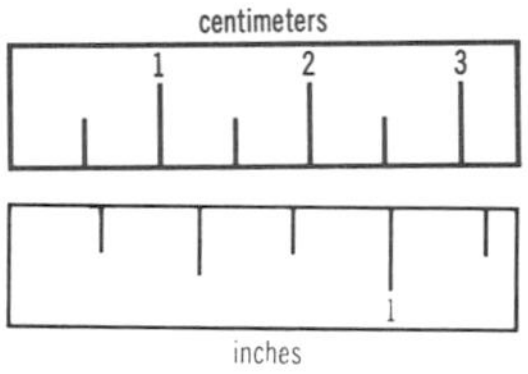

cen·ti·pede [sen′tə·pēd′] *n.* Any of various wormlike animals having many pairs of legs and two poison fangs on the head.

cen·tral [sen′trəl] *adj.* **1** At, in, or near the center: the *central* part of the city. **2** Most important; principal; chief: the *central* character in a play. **3** Of or being the center. **—cen′tral·ly** *adv.*

Central American **1** Of or from Central America. **2** A person born or living in Central America.

central heating A system for heating a building in which one source, such as a basement boiler, provides heat that is circulated to individual rooms.

cen·tral·ize [sen′trəl·īz′] *v.* **cen·tral·ized, cen·tral·iz·ing** **1** To bring or come to a center; make central. **2** To bring under one central authority: to *centralize* a government. **—cen′tral·i·za′tion** *n.*

central nervous system That part of the nervous system consisting of the brain and spinal cord.

central processing unit The main part, or brain, of a computer, where information is interpreted and instructions are executed.

Central Standard Time The standard time observed in the central United States and east central Canada. It is six hours earlier than Greenwich time.

cen·tre [sen′tər] *n., v.* **cen·tred, cen·tring** *British* Center.

cen·trif·u·gal [sen·trif′(y)ə·gəl] *adj.* **1** Moving away from a center. **2** Using centrifugal force.

centrifugal force The force tending to pull an object outward from a center about which it is rotating.

cen·tri·fuge [sen′trə·fyōōj′] 1 *n.* A machine that spins its contents, using centrifugal force to remove moisture, separate liquids of different densities, or for other purposes. 2 *n.* A machine designed to simulate the effects of gravity, as on an astronaut. 3 *v.* To subject to the action of a centrifuge.

cen·trip·e·tal [sen·trip′ə·təl] *adj.* 1 Going toward a center. 2 Using centripetal force.

centripetal force The force that tends to pull an object inward toward the center about which it is rotating.

cen·trist [sen′trist] *n.* A person whose political views avoid both left-wing and right-wing extremes.

cen·tu·ri·on [sen·t(y)ŏŏr′ē·ən] *n.* In ancient Rome, a captain of about 100 foot soldiers.

cen·tu·ry [sen′chə·rē] *n., pl.* **cen·tu·ries** 1 A period of 100 years, counting from some particular time, such as the birth of Christ. From A.D. 1 to 100 was the first century; from 1901 to 2000 is the twentieth. 2 Any period of 100 years. 3 In ancient Rome, a group of 100 foot soldiers.

century plant A desert plant that is wrongly believed to bloom once every 100 years.

ce·phal·ic [si·fal′ik] *adj.* Of or having to do with the head.

ceph·a·lo·pod [sef′ə·lə·pod′] *n.* Any of a class of sea animals, including the octopus and the squid, that have a beaked head and strong tentacles.

ce·ram·ic [sə·ram′ik] 1 *n.* Clay or a similar material that has been fired. 2 *n.* (*often pl.*) An object of such material. 3 *adj.* Of or having to do with such material. 4 *adj.* Of or having to do with ceramics.

ce·ram·ics [sə·ram′iks] *n.* The art or process of making such things as pottery or porcelain, of fired clay or a similar material. ◆ See -ICS.

ce·ram·ist [sə·ram′ist *or* ser′ə·mist] *n.* An artist who specializes in ceramics.

Cer·ber·us [sûr′bər·əs] *n.* In Greek and Roman myths, the three-headed dog that guarded the door to Hades.

ce·re·al [sir′ē·əl] 1 *n.* Any edible grain that comes from certain grasses, as rice, wheat, rye, and oats. 2 *n.* The plants from which these grains come. 3 *adj.* Of or having to do with such edible grains or the plants that produce them. 4 *n.* A breakfast food made from grain.

cer·e·bel·lum [ser′ə·bel′əm] *n., pl.* **cer·e·bel·lums** or **cer·e·bel·la** [ser′ə·bel′ə] The part of the brain that is at the back of the head and that controls coordination of the muscles.

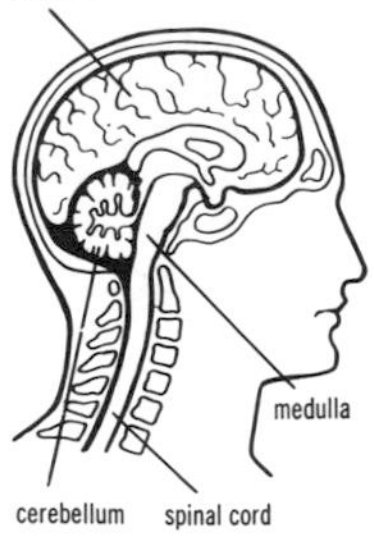

cer·e·bral [ser′ə·brəl *or* sə·rē′brəl] *adj.* 1 Of or having to do with the brain or the cerebrum. 2 Having or requiring great intelligence.

cerebral palsy An inability to control one's movement and speech, caused by damage to the brain before or during birth.

cer·e·bro·spi·nal [ser′ə·brō·spī′nəl] *adj.* Of, having to do with, or affecting the brain and spinal cord.

cer·e·brum [ser′ə·brəm *or* sə·rē′brəm] *n., pl.* **cer·e·brums** or **cer·e·bra** [ser′ə·brə *or* sə·rē′brə] The largest and most highly developed part of the brain. It controls voluntary movement and all conscious mental activities.

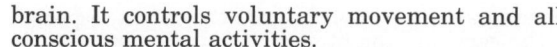

cere·ment [ser′ə·mənt *or* sir′mənt] *n.* A cloth used to wrap a dead body.

cer·e·mo·ni·al [ser′ə·mō′nē·əl] 1 *adj.* Of, like, or used in a ceremony: a *ceremonial* robe. 2 *adj.* Very elaborate or formal: a *ceremonial* dinner. 3 *n.* A set of rules or actions for performing a particular ceremony.

cer·e·mo·ni·ous [ser′ə·mō′nē·əs] *adj.* 1 Full of or done with ceremony. 2 Extremely polite or formal. **—cer′e·mo′ni·ous·ly** *adv.*

cer·e·mo·ny [ser′ə·mō′nē] *n., pl.* **cer·e·mo·nies** 1 Any formal act or series of actions performed in a definite, set manner: a graduation *ceremony.* 2 A formal or extremely polite manner of acting: to serve tea with *ceremony.* **—stand on ceremony** To act or insist that others act in a formal manner.

Ce·res [sir′ēz] *n.* 1 In Roman myths, the goddess of grain and harvests. Her Greek name was Demeter. 2 The largest of the asteroids, orbiting the sun between Mars and Saturn. It was discovered in 1801.

ce·rise [sə·rēs′] *n., adj.* Very bright red.

ce·ri·um [sir′ē·əm] *n.* A metallic element occurring in rare earths. ◆ See RARE-EARTH ELEMENT.

cer·tain [sûr′tən] *adj.* 1 Completely sure, confident, or convinced: She is *certain* of success. 2 Sure as to results: To drive that way means *certain* disaster. 3 Not named or stated, but known: I saw a *certain* person buying you a gift. 4 Some, but not much: a *certain* improvement in their work. **—for certain** Without doubt; surely.

cer·tain·ly [sûr′tən·lē] *adv.* Without doubt; surely.

cer·tain·ty [sûr′tən·tē] *n., pl.* **cer·tain·ties** 1 The condition or fact of being certain: There is no *certainty* of our winning the game. 2 Something that is positively true; a known fact.

cer·tif·i·cate [sər·tif′ə·kit] *n.* 1 An official document containing facts about a person or persons: a birth *certificate*; a marriage *certificate.* 2 An official document certifying to the truth of something: a *certificate* indicating that a person had fulfilled a state's requirements for teaching. 3 A document indicating ownership or debt.

certified public accountant An accountant who has been granted a certificate indicating that he or she has met state requirements for the accounting profession.

cer·ti·fy [sûr′tə·fī] *v.* **cer·ti·fied, cer·ti·fy·ing** 1 To testify, usually in writing, as to the truth or correctness of; vouch for; verify: Your statement will *certify* his correct age. 2 To guarantee the quality or worth of: to *certify* a check. 3 To furnish with a certificate. **—cer′ti·fi·ca′tion** *n.*

cer·ti·tude [sûr′tə·t(y)ōōd′] *n.* Freedom from any doubt; complete confidence and certainty.

ce·ru·le·an [sə·rōō′lē·ən] *n., adj.* Sky blue.

a	add	**i**	it	**ŏŏ**	took	**oi**	oil
ā	ace	**ī**	ice	**ōō**	pool	**ou**	pout
â	care	**o**	odd	**u**	up	**ng**	ring
ä	palm	**ō**	open	**û**	burn	**th**	thin
e	end	**ô**	order	**yōō**	fuse	**th**	this
ē	equal					**zh**	vision

ə = a in *above* e in *sicken* i in *possible* o in *melon* u in *circus*

cer·vi·cal [sûr′vi·kəl] *adj.* Of the cervix, especially the cervix of the uterus.
cer·vix [sûr′viks] *n., pl.* **cer·vix·es** or **cer·vi·ces** [sûr′·vi·sēz] **1** The neck. **2** A neck-shaped body part, especially the outer end of the uterus.
Ce·sar·e·an section [si·zâr′ē·ən] A surgical incision made through the abdomen and the uterus to deliver a baby. It is performed when an obstruction or other condition prevents a normal birth. ◆ This term comes from the belief that Julius Caesar was thus delivered.
ce·si·um [sē′zē·əm] *n.* A soft, grayish metallic element. Because it is very sensitive to light, it is used in photoelectric cells.
ces·sa·tion [se·sā′shən] *n.* A ceasing; stopping.
ces·sion [sesh′ən] *n.* The act of ceding or giving up to another: a *cession* of territory.
cess·pool [ses′pōōl′] *n.* A deep, covered pit for drainage, as from sinks or toilets.
ce·ta·cean [si·tā′shən] **1** *n.* Any of a group of fish-shaped, aquatic mammals, as whales and dolphins. **2** *adj.* Of or having to do with such mammals.
cf. compare. ◆ *cf.* is an abbreviation of the Latin word *conferre,* meaning *to compare.*
Cf The symbol for the element californium.
cg or **cgm** centigram(s).
c.g. center of gravity.
C.G. Coast Guard.
ch. **1** chapter. **2** church.
Ch. **1** China. **2** Chinese.
cha-cha [chä′chä′] *n.* A rhythmic dance that originated in Latin America.
Chad·i·an [chad′ē·ən] **1** *adj.* Of or from Chad. **2** *n.* A person born in or a citizen of Chad.
chafe [chāf] *v.* **chafed, chaf·ing** **1** To make or become rough or sore by rubbing. **2** To make warm by rubbing: to *chafe* one's hands. **3** To make or become irritated or annoyed.
chaff¹ [chaf] **1** *v.* To tease good-naturedly. **2** *n.* Good-natured teasing or banter.
chaff² [chaf] *n.* **1** The outside husks or coverings of grain that are removed by threshing. **2** Any worthless or unimportant thing.
chaf·finch [chaf′inch] *n.* A songbird of Europe, popular as a pet and kept in a cage.
chafing dish A pan with a heating unit under it, to cook food or keep it warm at the table.

Chafing dish

cha·grin [shə·grin′] *n., v.* **cha·grined** [shə·grind′], **cha·grin·ing** [shə·grin′ing] **1** *n.* A feeling of embarrassment or distress caused by a disappointment or failure. **2** *v.* To annoy, embarrass, or distress.
chain [chān] **1** *n.* A series of connected rings or links, usually of metal, used to bind, drag, or hold something, or often as an ornament. **2** *v.* To fasten or connect with a chain. **3** *n.(pl.)* Anything that binds or restrains. **4** *v.* To bind or restrain: Her work *chains* her to a desk. **5** *n.* A series of connected things: a *chain* of lakes. **6** *n.* A measuring line like a chain: An engineer's *chain* is 100 feet long.
chain gang A group of convicts chained together while working.
chain letter A letter sent to a number of persons requesting that each of them send a copy of it to an equal number of other persons.
chain mail Very flexible armor that is made of small metal rings linked together.
chain reaction Any series of reactions or events, each of which develops from a preceding one. Atomic energy is produced by a chain reaction in which particles from the nuclei of certain atoms are set free, some of them striking the nuclei of other atoms, until the whole mass is used up.
chain saw A power saw with teeth linked together in a circular chain.
chain store One of a number of retail stores all owned and run by the same company.
chair [châr] **1** *n.* A seat for one person, usually having four legs and a back. **2** *n.* A position of importance or authority, as the position of a bishop or professor. **3** *n.* A chairman or chairwoman. **4** *v.* To act as chairman or chairwoman of.
chair·man [châr′mən] *n., pl.* **chair·men** [châr′mən] **1** A person who presides over or is the head of a meeting, committee, board, department, or the like.
chair·per·son [châr′pûr′sən] *n.* A chairman or chairwoman.
chair·wom·an [châr′wŏŏm′ən] *n., pl.* **chair·wom·en** [châr′wim′in] A woman who presides over or is the head of a meeting, committee, board, department, or the like.
chaise [shāz] *n.* A two-wheeled carriage, having a folding top and seating two persons.
chaise longue [shāz′lông′] A chair that has a long, couchlike seat on which one can sit and stretch one's legs.

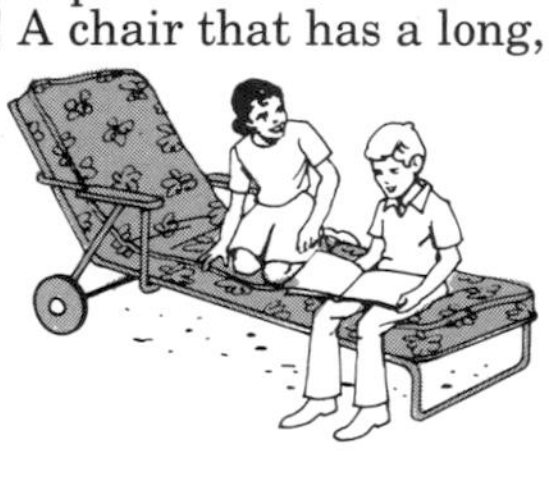
Chaise longue

chal·ced·o·ny [kal·ced′ən·ē] *n.* A type of milky, lustrous quartz used as a gemstone.
Chal·de·a [kal·dē′ə] *n.* In Biblical times, a region on the Tigris and Euphrates rivers in SW Asia. **—Chal·de′an** *adj., n.*
cha·let [sha·lā′ *or* shal′ā] *n.* **1** A Swiss cottage with very wide eaves. **2** Any house built like this.
chal·ice [chal′is] *n.* **1** A goblet. **2** The cup used in the Communion service.
chalk [chôk] **1** *n.* A soft, grayish or yellowish limestone, largely made up of very small sea shells. **2** *n.* A stick of this or a similar material used for marking or drawing, as on a chalkboard. **3** *v.* To write, draw, or mark with chalk. **—chalk up** **1** To give as a score: *Chalk up* four points. **2** To give as a reason; credit: I *chalk up* the student's failure to laziness.
chalk·board [chôk′bôrd′] *n.* A board for writing on with chalk.
chalk·y [chôk′ē] *adj.* **chalk·i·er, chalk·i·est** **1** Like chalk in color or texture: a *chalky* powder. **2** Made or full of chalk: *chalky* soil.
chal·lah [hä′lə] *n.* A white bread, often baked in the shape of a braid, traditionally served by Jews on the Sabbath.
chal·lenge [chal′ənj] *v.* **chal·lenged, chal·leng·ing,** *n.* **1** *v.* To ask for a contest, duel, or fight with: They *challenged* us to a game. **2** *n.* An invitation or dare to do something, usually difficult or dangerous. **3** *v.* To question or dispute the truth or correctness of: I *challenge* your answer. **4** *n.* A questioning of the truth or correctness of something. **5** *v.* To dare or defy. **6** *v.* To stop and ask for

identification: The guards *challenged* us at every border. **7** *n.* A stopping in order to question, examine, or make certain. **—chal′leng·er** *n.*

chal·lis or **chal·lie** [shal′ē] *n.* A lightweight fabric, usually of printed wool, rayon, or cotton.

cham·ber [chām′bər] *n.* **1** A room in a house, especially a bedroom. **2** (*pl.*) The office of a judge or of a lawyer: a judge's *chambers.* **3** A hall where a group of lawmakers meet. **4** One house of a legislature or congress. **5** A group of people who meet together for a common purpose: a *chamber* of commerce. **6** A hollow or enclosed space, as in the body of an animal or plant. **7** An enclosed space in a gun or revolver for the shell or the cartridge. ◆ See CAMERA.

cham·ber·lain [chām′bər·lin] *n.* **1** A person who has charge of the household of a ruler or noble. **2** A very high officer in a royal court.

cham·ber·maid [chām′bər·mād′] *n.* A person who takes care of bedrooms, as in a hotel.

chamber music Music composed for a small group of instruments, as for a string quartet.

chamber of commerce A group of merchants and business people who meet regularly to promote business in their city or area.

cham·bray [sham′brā′] *n.* A lightweight fabric having a glistening surface created by the interweaving of white and colored threads.

cha·me·le·on [kə·mē′lē·ən] *n.* **1** A lizard having the ability to change color. **2** A person who often changes opinions or habits.

cham·ois [sham′ē] *n., pl.* **cham·ois** **1** An antelope found in the mountains of Europe and SW Asia. **2** A very soft leather originally made from the skin of the chamois but now from sheep, goats, or deer.

Chamois

cham·o·mile [kam′ə·mīl′] *n.* Another spelling of CAMOMILE.

champ[1] [champ] *v.* **1** To chew or bite noisily or impatiently: a horse *champing* its bit; a nervous child *champing* a pencil. **2** To make restless biting motions. **—champ at the bit** To show signs of impatience; act restless.

champ[2] [champ] *n. informal* Champion.

cham·pagne [sham·pān′] *n.* A fine white wine that sparkles and bubbles.

cham·paign [sham·pān′] *n.* An expanse of flat, open country; plain.

cham·pi·on [cham′pē·ən] **1** *n.* A person who comes out ahead of all rivals, as in a sport. **2** *n.* Anything awarded first place. **3** *adj.* Having won first place; better than all others: a *champion* dog. **4** *n.* A person who fights for another person or for a cause. **5** *v.* To fight for; defend: to *champion* the cause of peace.

cham·pi·on·ship [cham′pē·ən·ship′] *n.* **1** The condition or honor of being champion: The *championship* meant much to the team. **2** The act of defending or supporting.

chance [chans] *n., v.* **chanced, chanc·ing,** *adj.* **1** *n.* The unknown cause of the way things often turn out; fate; luck. **2** *v.* To happen accidentally or by chance: I *chanced* to look down and there was my ring. **3** *adj.* Not planned or expected: a *chance* trip. **4** *n.* A possibility: There is a *chance* they won't come. **5** *n.* An opportunity: Now is your *chance* to study. **6** *n.* A risk or gamble: They'll take a *chance* on anything. **7** *v.* To take the chance of; risk: Let's *chance* it. **—chance on** or **chance upon** To find or meet unexpectedly or by chance: We *chanced* on a quiet, deserted park.

chan·cel [chan′səl] *n.* The area around the altar of a church, used by the clergy and choir.

chan·cel·lor [chan′s(ə·)lər] *n.* **1** In some European countries, a chief minister of state. **2** The head of certain universities. **3** A judge of certain courts in the U.S.

chan·cer·y [chan′sə·rē] *n., pl.* **chan·cer·ies** **1** A law court dealing with people's rights and duties in cases not covered by common law or statute law. **2** An office where official records are kept. **3** A chancellor's office or court.

chanc·y [chan′sē] *adj.* **chanc·i·er, chanc·i·est** Of uncertain outcome; risky.

chan·de·lier [shan′də·lir′] *n.* A lighting fixture that hangs from the ceiling and has supports or branches for a number of lights: a crystal *chandelier.*

Chandelier

chan·dler [chan′dlər] *n.* A dealer in groceries or supplies, especially for ships.

change [chānj] *v.* **changed, chang·ing,** *n.* **1** *v.* To make or become different; alter; vary: His facial expression *changed* when he saw us. **2** *n.* The act or result of changing: a *change* in the temperature. **3** *n.* Something new or different: Everyone likes a *change* now and then. **4** *v.* To exchange or substitute one thing for another: to *change* places. **5** *v.* To put other coverings or linens on: to *change* a bed. **6** *v.* To put on other clothes: It will take me only a minute to *change.* **7** *n.* A clean or different set, as of clothes or coverings. **8** *v.* To transfer from one vehicle, as a train or bus, to another. **9** *v.* To give or receive the equivalent of, usually in a different form: Can you *change* a dollar for me? **10** *n.* Money of smaller denominations given in exchange for the same amount of money in a higher denomination. **11** *n.* The amount returned when a person pays more than is owed. **12** *n.* Small coins. **—chang′er** *n.*

change·a·ble [chān′jə·bəl] *adj.* **1** Likely to change or vary: a *changeable* person. **2** Having different colors in different lights; iridescent: the *changeable* feathers of certain birds. **—change′a·ble·ness** *n.* **—change′a·bly** *adv.*

change·less [chānj′lis] *adj.* Free from change; constant; enduring.

change·ling [chānj′ling] *n.* A child secretly left in place of another who has been carried off.

chan·nel [chan′əl] *n., v.* **chan·neled** or **chan·nelled, chan·nel·ing** or **chan·nel·ling** **1** *n.* The bed of a

a	add	**i**	it	**o͝o**	took	**oi**	oil
ā	ace	**ī**	ice	**o͞o**	pool	**ou**	pout
â	care	**o**	odd	**u**	up	**ng**	ring
ä	palm	**ō**	open	**û**	burn	**th**	thin
e	end	**ô**	order	**yo͞o**	fuse	**th**	this
ē	equal					**zh**	vision

ə = { a in *above* e in *sicken* i in *possible* / o in *melon* u in *circus* }

river or stream. **2** *n.* A body of water connecting two larger bodies of water: the English *Channel.* **3** *n.* The deep part, as of a river or harbor. **4** *n.* A tubelike passage through which liquids can flow. **5** *v.* To cut or wear a channel in. **6** *n.* The way or route through which anything moves or passes: *channels* of information. **7** *n.* A path for communicating something by electronic means, as a band of frequencies assigned to a radio or television station by the government. **8** *v.* To send through or as if through a channel.

chant [chant] **1** *n.* A very simple melody in which many words or syllables are sung on each note. Chants are used in the services of some churches. **2** *v.* To sing to a chant: to *chant* a psalm. **3** *v.* To recite or say in the manner of a chant: to *chant* a poem. **4** *n.* Any monotonous, rhythmic singing or shouting. **—chant′er** *n.*

chant·ey or **chant·y** [shan′tē *or* chan′tē] *n., pl.* **chant·eys** or **chant·ies** A rhythmical song for sailors working together.

chan·ti·cleer [chan′tə·klir′ *or* shan′tə·klir] *n.* A rooster: used as a proper name in animal stories.

Cha·nu·kah [hä′no͝o·kə] *n.* Another spelling of HANUKKAH.

cha·os [kā′os] *n.* Complete disorder and confusion.

cha·ot·ic [kā·ot′ik] *adj.* Completely disordered and confused. **—cha·ot′i·cal·ly** *adv.*

chap[1] [chap] *v.* **chapped, chap·ping** To make or become rough, reddened, or cracked: The cold has *chapped* my hands.

chap[2] [chap] *n. informal* A man or boy.

chap. chapter.

chap·ar·ral [shap′ə·ral′] *n.* A dense growth of shrubs or small trees, especially in the SW United States.

chap·el [chap′əl] *n.* **1** A building or place of Christian worship, usually smaller than a church. **2** A separate room or enclosed area in a larger building, used for religious services.

chap·er·on or **chap·er·one** [shap′ə·rōn′] *n., v.* **chap·er·oned, chap·er·on·ing** **1** *n.* An older person who goes with a group of young people, as to a party, to see that they behave. **2** *v.* To act as a chaperon for.

chap·lain [chap′lin] *n.* A priest, minister, or rabbi who conducts religious services, as for the armed forces, Congress, a hospital, or royal court.

chap·let [chap′lit] *n.* **1** A wreath for the head. **2** A short rosary. **3** A string of beads.

chaps [chaps] *n., pl.* Leather trousers without any backs or seat, worn over regular trousers to protect the legs.

Chaps

chap·ter [chap′tər] *n.* **1** Any of the main divisions of a book, usually numbered. **2** Any period of time or experience: School began a happy *chapter* in her life. **3** A branch of a society.

char [chär] *v.* **charred, char·ring** **1** To burn or scorch slightly. **2** To change into charcoal by incomplete burning.

char·ac·ter [kar′ik·tər] *n.* **1** All of the good as well as the bad qualities, habits, and traits that go to make up the nature or worth of a particular person. **2** Good and noble qualities, habits, and traits: She is a person of *character.* **3** Any special quality, look, or thing that makes one person, group, or thing different from all others: The jungle has a sinister *character.* **4** A person in a play, novel, poem, or other literary work. **5** *informal* An odd, humorous, or unusual person: He's a *character.* **6** Any letter, figure, or mark used in writing or printing.

char·ac·ter·is·tic [kar′ik·tə·ris′tik] **1** *adj.* Indicating a special quality or character of a person or thing; typical: Sadness is the *characteristic* expression of a basset hound. **2** *n.* A very special feature, quality, or trait: Curiosity was one of the child's *characteristics.* **3** *n.* The part of a logarithm that is an integer. For example, if 2.345 is a logarithm, 2 is the characteristic. **—char′ac·ter·is′ti·cal·ly** *adv.*

char·ac·ter·ize [kar′ik·tə·rīz′] *v.* **char·ac·ter·ized, char·ac·ter·iz·ing** **1** To describe the character or qualities of: to *characterize* someone as a hard worker. **2** To be a quality or characteristic of: Courage *characterizes* most explorers. **—char′ac·ter·i·za′tion** *n.*

cha·rades [shə·rādz′] *n.pl.* (*often used with singular verb*) A game in which the players try to guess what words or phrases are being acted out in pantomime, often syllable by syllable.

char·coal [chär′kōl′] *n.* A black substance made by heating wood in a container from which most of the air has been removed. Charcoal is used in many ways, including as a filter, drawing crayon, and fuel.

chard [chärd] *n.* A plant related to the beet whose spinachlike leaves and stalks are eaten as a vegetable.

charge [chärj] *v.* **charged, charg·ing,** *n.* **1** *v.* To ask for as a price: to *charge* two dollars for tickets; Do you *charge* for checking the tires? **2** *n.* Cost; price: a *charge* for repairs. **3** *v.* To set down and record as a debt to be paid: to *charge* groceries. **4** *n.* A purchase that will be paid for later. **5** *v.* To attack or rush upon violently: to *charge* a fort. **6** *n.* An attack. **7** *v.* To load (a weapon). **8** *n.* Something used to load or fill: The gun's *charge* went off. **9** *v.* To fill with electricity, as a battery. **10** *n.* An amount of stored electricity, as in a battery or capacitor. **11** *v.* To accuse: to be *charged* with a crime. **12** *n.* Something of which one is accused: a burglary *charge.* **13** *v.* To command or instruct: I *charge* you to tell the truth; The judge *charged* the jury. **14** *n.* An order, command, or instruction. **15** *v.* To entrust, as with a duty or task: The teacher *charged* us to take care of the new student. **16** *n.* A person or thing under one's care: The children are in our *charge.* **17** *n.* Care and custody: to have *charge* of supplies. **—charge off** **1** To look upon as a loss. **2** To think of as belonging: We *charged off* their behavior to their enthusiasm. **—in charge** Having the care or control of: Who is *in charge* of this classroom?

charge·a·ble [chär′jə·bəl] *adj.* **1** That may be charged: This lunch is *chargeable* to my account. **2** Liable to be charged, as with a crime.

charge account A plan by which a store or business allows a customer to purchase and receive goods, but pay for them later.

char·gé d'af·faires [shär·zhā′ də·fâr′] *pl.* **char·gés d'affaires** [shär·zhā′ də·fâr′ *or* shär·zhāz′ də·fâr′] A diplomat who temporarily substitutes for an absent ambassador or minister.

charg·er[1] [chär′jər] *n.* **1** An apparatus for charging batteries. **2** A horse trained for battle.

charg·er[2] [chär′jər] *n.* A large, shallow dish or platter: seldom used today.

char·i·ly [châr′ə·lē] *adv.* **1** In a cautious or careful manner. **2** Sparingly; stingily.

char·i·ot [char′ē·ət] *n.* A two-wheeled vehicle pulled by horses, used in ancient times for racing, in war, and in processions.

Egyptian chariot

char·i·o·teer [char′ē·ə·tir′] *n.* A person who drives a chariot.

cha·ris·ma [kə·riz′mə] *n.* A personal quality that attracts many devoted followers; strong personal magnetism. ◆ *Charisma,* which was originally a theological term, comes from a Greek word meaning *divine gift* or *power.*

char·is·mat·ic [kar′iz·mat′ik] *adj.* Having or showing charisma.

char·i·ta·ble [char′ə·tə·bəl] *adj.* **1** Generous in giving help of any kind to the poor and unfortunate. **2** Kind and understanding in judging others; lenient. **3** Of or concerned with charity: a *charitable* institution. **—char′i·ta·bly** *adv.*

char·i·ty [char′ə·tē] *n., pl.* **char·i·ties** **1** A feeling of love or good will toward others. **2** Kindness and tolerance in judging others; forgiveness. **3** The giving of help, usually money, to the poor and unfortunate. **4** An organization, institution, or fund for helping those in need.

char·la·tan [shär′lə·tən] *n.* A person who claims to have knowledge and skill but who really doesn't; a fake; quack.

Charles·ton [chärl′stən] *n.* A fast dance, very popular in the 1920's.

char·ley horse [chär′lē] *informal* A severe cramp or pain in the muscles of the arm or leg.

charm [chärm] **1** *n.* A pleasing or fascinating quality or feature: Their conversation has such *charm.* **2** *v.* To delight or fascinate. **3** *n.* Any word, phrase, action, or object supposed to bring good luck or keep away evil. **4** *v.* To protect, as if by magic. **5** *n.* A small ornament worn on a bracelet, necklace, or chain. **—charmed life** A life that seems protected as if by a charm. **—charm′er** *n.*

charm·ing [chär′ming] *adj.* Very attractive, pleasing, or delightful: a *charming* person. **—charm′·ing·ly** *adv.*

char·nel house [chär′nəl] A place where the bodies or bones of the dead are kept.

Char·on [kâr′ən] *n.* In Greek myths, the man who ferried the dead across the river Styx to Hades.

chart [chärt] **1** *n.* A map, especially one used by sailors, showing coastlines, lighthouses, currents, depth of water, and other features. **2** *n.* A sheet or graph that shows facts such as the changes in temperature, population, prices, or wages. **3** *v.* To show, record, or map out on a chart: We *charted* the progress of the class in spelling.

char·ter [chär′tər] **1** *n.* An official document or paper given by a government and granting special rights or privileges to a person or company. **2** *n.* A document that states the laws and the purposes of an organization or government; constitution. **3** *n.* A document giving the right to form a branch or chapter of a larger organization. **4** *v.* To give a charter to. **5** *v.* To hire (as a bus or airplane) for some special purpose.

char·treuse [shär·tro͞oz′] *n., adj.* Pale, yellowish green.

char·wom·an [chär′wo͝om′ən] *n., pl.* **char·wom·en** [chär′wim′in] *British* A woman who is hired to clean, as a house or office building.

char·y [châr′ē] *adj.* **char·i·er, char·i·est** **1** Cautious; careful; wary: *chary* of strangers. **2** Not generous; stingy: *chary* of praise.

Cha·ryb·dis [kə·rib′dis] *n.* In Greek myths, a whirlpool opposite the rock of Scylla. Ships going between Italy and Sicily had to avoid both.

chase [chās] *v.* **chased, chas·ing,** *n.* **1** *v.* To go after or follow, as to catch, overtake, or harm. **2** *n.* The act of chasing or running after. **3** *n.* The sport of hunting, usually with dogs and horses. **4** *n.* That which is hunted; prey. **5** *v.* To put to flight; drive away: to *chase* mosquitoes. **—give chase** To go after; pursue. ◆ Both *chase* and *catch* go back to the Latin word *captiare,* meaning *to strive after* or *seize.*

chas·er [chā′sər] *n.* **1** A person or thing that chases. **2** A drink, as of water, soda, or beer, taken after a drink of liquor.

Cha·sid [hä′sid] *n., pl.* **Cha·si·dim** [hä·sē′dim] Another spelling of HASID. **—Cha·sid·ic** [hä·sid′ik] *adj.*

chasm [kaz′əm] *n.* **1** A deep crack or gorge in the surface of the earth. **2** A great difference, as of opinion or feeling.

chas·sis [shas′ē *or* chas′ē] *n., pl.* **chas·sis** [shas′ēz *or* chas′ēz] **1** The frame that supports the body of an automobile and includes such parts as the wheels, springs, and motor. **2** The metal framework of a radio or television set to which the tubes and other working parts are attached. **3** The frame that supports the main body of an airplane.

Chassis of an automobile

chaste [chāst] *adj.* **1** Pure or virtuous; moral. **2** Very simple or pure in style. **—chaste′ly** *adv.*

chas·ten [chā′sən] *v.* **1** To discipline or correct by some form of punishment: Those parents never *chastened* their unruly children. **2** To make more simple; purify; refine.

chas·tise [chas·tīz′] *v.* **chas·tised, chas·tis·ing** To punish, especially by beating. **—chas·tise·ment** [chas′·tiz·mənt *or* chas·tīz′mənt] *n.*

chas·ti·ty [chas′tə·tē] *n.* The condition of being chaste or pure.

chas·u·ble [chaz′yə·bəl] *n.* A sleeveless outer robe worn by a priest at Mass.

chat [chat] *v.* **chat·ted, chat·ting,** *n.* **1** *v.* To talk in a relaxed, informal manner. **2** *n.* A relaxed, informal conversation. **3** *n.* Any of several singing birds.

a	add	**i**	it	**o͝o**	took	**oi**	oil
ā	ace	**ī**	ice	**o͞o**	pool	**ou**	pout
â	care	**o**	odd	**u**	up	**ng**	ring
ä	palm	**ō**	open	**û**	burn	**th**	thin
e	end	**ô**	order	**yo͞o**	fuse	**th**	this
ē	equal					**zh**	vision

ə = {a in *above* e in *sicken* i in *possible*; o in *melon* u in *circus*}

châ·teau or **cha·teau** [sha·tō′] *n., pl.* **châ·teaux** or **cha·teaux** [sha·tōz′] **1** A French castle. **2** A large country house resembling a French castle.

Chateau

chat·e·laine [shat′ə·lān′] *n.* **1** A woman who is the mistress of a castle or large estate. **2** A clasp or chain worn at the waist to hold such items as keys, a purse, or a watch.

chat·tel [chat′(ə)l] *n.* In law, any personal possession that can be moved. Furniture, clothing, and automobiles are chattels.

chat·ter [chat′ər] **1** *v.* To click together rapidly, as the teeth when one is cold. **2** *n.* A rattling of the teeth. **3** *v.* To talk about nothing of any importance. **4** *n.* Foolish, unimportant talk. **5** *v.* To make many quick, sharp sounds, as a squirrel or monkey. **6** *n.* The sounds made by a squirrel or monkey. **—chat′ter·er** *n.*

chat·ter·box [chat′ər·boks′] *n.* A person who talks often and in a silly way.

chat·ty [chat′ē] *adj.* **chat·ti·er, chat·ti·est** **1** Fond of talking and chatting: a *chatty* person. **2** Relaxed and informal: a *chatty* style of writing. **—chat′ti·ly** *adv.* **—chat′ti·ness** *n.*

chauf·feur [shō′fər *or* shō·fûr′] **1** *n.* A person employed as driver of a car. **2** *v.* To act as chauffeur for: I'll *chauffeur* you there.

chau·vin·ism [shō′və·niz′əm] *n.* **1** Biased belief that one's own group, race, or sex is superior. **2** Militant, fanatical patriotism. **—chau′vin·ist** *n.*

cheap [chēp] **1** *adj.* Not costing much money; inexpensive: a *cheap* car. **2** *adj.* Charging low prices: a *cheap* store. **3** *adj.* Lower in price than it is worth: During the sale, this ring is *cheap.* **4** *adv.* At a low price: to sell *cheap.* **5** *adj.* Easily obtained: to gain a *cheap* victory. **6** *adj.* Of little value; poor; inferior: a toy made of *cheap* metal. **7** *adj.* Vulgar; common; tasteless: a TV sitcom full of *cheap* humor. **8** *adj.* Not generous; stingy. **—cheap′ly** *adv.* **—cheap′ness** *n.* ◆ *Cheap* was once used in the expression *good cheap,* meanig a *bargain,* and came from the Old English word *cēap,* meaning *trade* or *business.*

cheap·en [chē′pən] *v.* To make or become cheap or cheaper.

cheap·skate [chēp′skāt′] *n. slang* A person who is stingy or miserly.

cheat [chēt] **1** *v.* To act in a dishonest way; defraud. **2** *v.* To get away from; escape: to *cheat* the gallows. **3** *n.* A person who cheats. **4** *n.* A cheating act; swindle. **—cheat′er** *n.*

check [chek] **1** *v.* To bring to a stop; halt: to *check* careless spending. **2** *n.* A sudden stop. **3** *v.* To hold back; curb: to *check* angry words. **4** *n.* A person, thing, or event that holds back. **5** *v.* To test or examine, as for accuracy or completeness: to *check* a column of addition. **6** *n.* A comparison or examination, as to prove right or true. **7** *v.* To agree or correspond: Does your list *check* with mine? **8** *n.* A mark (√) to show that something is accurate or needs attention. **9** *v.* To mark with a check. **10** *adj.* Used to verify or check: a *check* list. **11** *n.* An order in writing to a bank asking that a certain sum of money be paid out of one's account. **12** *v.* To deposit or put in temporary safekeeping: to *check* one's luggage. **13** *n.* A ticket given to a person who has checked something for safekeeping. **14** *n.* A slip of paper listing the items one has bought and the amount one owes: a *check* for a meal. **15** *n.* A single, small square in a pattern or design made up of many small squares. **16** *n.* A fabric having a pattern or design of small squares. **17** *adj. use:* a *check* suit. **18** *n.* In chess, the position of a king that makes it possible for the piece to be captured on the next opposing move. **19** *v.* In chess, to put (an opponent's king) in danger. **20** *interj.* In chess, a call warning that an opponent's king is in check. **—check in** To register and become a guest, as at a hotel or motel. **—check out** **1** To pay one's bill and leave, as from a hotel. **2** *informal* To investigate: to *check out* a rumor. **3** To total or have totaled the prices of. **—in check** Under control: Keep your temper *in check.*

check·book [chek′bŏŏk′] *n.* A book of forms furnished by a bank for writing checks.

checked [chekt] *adj.* Marked with a pattern of small squares.

check·er [chek′ər] **1** *n.* One of the pieces used in the game of checkers. **2** *n.* One of the squares in a pattern or design made up of many squares. **3** *n.* A pattern or design of squares. **4** *v.* To mark with squares or patches.

check·er·board [chek′ər·bôrd′] *n.* A board divided into 64 squares in alternating colors, used in playing checkers or chess.

check·ered [chek′ərd] *adj.* **1** Divided into squares. **2** Marked by light and dark patches: the *checkered* shade of the trees. **3** Full of ups and downs; often changing: a *checkered* career.

check·ers [chek′ərz] *n.pl.* (*used with singular verb*) A game played on a checkerboard by two players, each starting with 12 pieces.

checking account A bank account that allows the depositor to make payments by checks drawn against the amount in the account.

check·mate [chek′māt′] *v.* **check·mat·ed, check·mat·ing,** *n.* **1** *v.* In chess, to put (an opponent's king) in a position from which no escape is possible, thus winning the game. **2** *n.* In chess, the move that ends the game. **3** *v.* To defeat by some skillful action. **4** *n.* Total defeat.

check·out [chek′out′] *n.* **1** The act of checking out. **2** A place where checking out is done.

check·point [chek′point′] *n.* A place at which a check is made, as of people, vehicles, or baggage.

check·room [chek′rōōm′] *n.* A room in which packages, coats, and other items may be temporarily left for safekeeping.

check·up [chek′up′] *n.* A thorough examination or test, especially a medical examination.

Ched·dar or **ched·dar** [ched′ər] *n.* A hard, yellowish cheese with a flavor varying from mild to sharp.

cheek [chēk] *n.* **1** Either side of one's face below the eyes and above the mouth. **2** *informal* Impudent boldness or self-confidence.

cheek·bone [chēk′bōn′] *n.* A bone of the side of the face, just below the eye.

cheek·y [chē′kē] *adj.* **cheek·i·er, cheek·i·est** *informal* Impudent; saucy: a *cheeky* reply.

cheep [chēp] **1** *n.* A faint, shrill sound, as that made by a young bird. **2** *v.* To make this sound.

cheer [chir] **1** *n.* A shout, as of encouragement or approval. **2** *n.* A set form of words or phrases shouted in a rhythmical manner as encouragement to the players in a sports contest. **3** *v.* To urge, encourage, or greet with cheers: We *cheered* them on. **4** *n.* Gladness and joy; happiness. **5** *v.* To make or become happy and cheerful. **—be of good cheer** To be happy, hopeful, or courageous.

cheer·ful [chir′fəl] *adj.* **1** Happy; joyous: a *cheerful* mood. **2** Bright and pleasant: a *cheerful* color. **3** Willing; ready: a *cheerful* helper. **—cheer′ful·ly** *adv.* **—cheer′ful·ness** *n.*

cheer·lead·er [chir′lē′dər] *n.* A person who directs the shouting of cheers at a sports contest.

cheer·less [chir′lis] *adj.* Sad and gloomy. **—cheer′·less·ly** *adv.* **—cheer′less·ness** *n.*

cheer·y [chir′ē] *adj.* **cheer·i·er, cheer·i·est** Bright, gay, and cheerful: a *cheery* laugh. **—cheer′i·ly** *adv.* **—cheer′i·ness** *n.*

cheese [chēz] *n.* A food made of the curds of sour milk or cream that have been pressed into a more or less solid mold.

cheese·burg·er [chēz′bûr′gər] *n.* A hamburger with melted cheese on top of the meat.

cheese·cloth [chēz′klôth′] *n.* A very thin, loosely woven cotton cloth.

chees·y [chē′zē] *adj.* **chees·i·er, chees·i·est** **1** Of or like cheese. **2** *slang* Of poor quality; cheap; shabby. **—chees′i·ness** *n.*

chee·tah [chē′tə] *n.* An animal like the leopard but smaller, often trained to hunt.

Cheetah

chef [shef] *n.* **1** A cook in charge of other cooks or of a kitchen. **2** Any cook.

chef-d'oeu·vre [shā·do͞o′·vrə] *n., pl.* **chefs-d'oeu·vre** [shā·do͞o′vrə] A masterpiece, as in literature or art.

che·la [kē′lə] *n., pl.* **che·lae** [kē′lē] A claw or clawlike organ on a limb, as of a lobster, crab, or scorpion.

chem. **1** chemical. **2** chemist. **3** chemistry.

chem·i·cal [kem′i·kəl] **1** *adj.* Of, used in, or having to do with chemistry. **2** *n.* A substance made by or used in a chemical process.

chemical engineering The science or profession concerned with the application of chemical processes to large-scale industrial production.

chemical warfare Warfare conducted with chemicals or chemical products, such as incendiary bombs and poison gases.

che·mise [shə·mēz′] *n.* **1** A loose undergarment resembling a short slip. **2** A dress that hangs straight from the shoulder. ◆ *Chemise* comes directly from French.

chem·ist [kem′ist] *n.* **1** A person trained in chemistry. **2** *British* A druggist.

chem·is·try [kem′is·trē] *n.* The science that deals with the structure, composition, and properties of substances and with the ways in which they react or interact under various conditions.

chemistry set A set of equipment and materials for performing simple chemistry experiments at home.

che·mo·ther·a·py [kē′mō·ther′ə·pē *or* kem′ō·ther′ə·pē] *n.* The use of chemicals, such as medicines, to treat disease.

chem·ur·gy [kem′ər·jē] *n.* The development of new chemicals for industrial use from farm products and other organic materials.

che·nille [shə·nēl′] *n.* **1** A yarn with a velvety pile made of one of several fibers, as cotton or silk. **2** Fabric woven with this yarn.

cheque [chek] *n. British* A spelling of CHECK (def. 11).

cher·ish [cher′ish] *v.* **1** To hold dear; treat tenderly: to *cherish* a dear friend. **2** To think about with fondness and hope: a *cherished* hope.

Cher·o·kee [cher′ə·kē] *n., pl.* **Cher·o·kee** or **Cher·o·kees** **1** A tribe of North American Indians once living in the SE U.S., now in Oklahoma. **2** A member of this tribe. **3** The language of this tribe.

che·root [shə·ro͞ot′] *n.* A cigar with squared ends.

cher·ry [cher′ē] *n., pl.* **cher·ries** **1** A small, round, edible fruit, red, yellow, or nearly black in color, and having a single pit. **2** The tree bearing this fruit. **3** The wood of this tree. **4** *adj. use:* a *cherry* table. **5** A bright red color.

cherry picker A movable crane equipped to carry a passenger at the end of a long boom.

cher·ry·stone [cher′ē·stōn′] *n.* A quahog, not fully grown and small in size.

cher·ub [cher′əb] *n.* **1** *pl.* **cher·ubs** or **cher·u·bim** [cher′(y)ə·bim] An angel usually pictured as a beautiful child with wings. **2** *pl.* **cher·ubs** Any beautiful child.

che·ru·bic [chə·ro͞o′bik] *adj.* Beautiful, sweet, or plump, like a cherub: a *cherubic* face.

chess [ches] *n.* A game of skill played on a checkerboard by two players. Each player has 16 pieces and the winner of the game is the one who is first to checkmate the other's king.

Chess

chess·board [ches′bôrd′] *n.* A checkerboard.

chess·man [ches′man′ *or* ches′mən] *n., pl.* **chess·men** [ches′men′ *or* ches′·mən] Any of the pieces used in the game of chess.

chest [chest] *n.* **1** The part of the body that is enclosed by the ribs; thorax. **2** The front of this part of the body: to be tattooed on the *chest.* **3** A box with a lid, in which to keep or store things. **4** A chest of drawers.

chest·nut [ches′nut] **1** *n.* An edible nut that grows in a prickly bur. **2** *n.* The tree that bears it. **3** *n., adj.* Reddish brown. **4** *n.* A horse of this color. **5** *n.* An old joke.

chest of drawers A piece of furniture having several drawers and used for storing, as clothing or linens; bureau.

chev·a·lier [shev′ə·lir′] *n.* **1** A member of an honorary society, especially in France. **2** A knight or cavalier: seldom used today.

chev·i·ot [shev′ē·ət] *n.* A rough cloth, usually having raised diagonal ribs or lines on its surface, used for clothing, as suits or overcoats.

a	add	**i**	it	**o͝o**	took	**oi**	oil
ā	ace	**ī**	ice	**o͞o**	pool	**ou**	pout
â	care	**o**	odd	**u**	up	**ng**	ring
ä	palm	**ō**	open	**û**	burn	**th**	thin
e	end	**ô**	order	**yo͞o**	fuse	**th**	this
ē	equal					**zh**	vision

ə = { a in *above* e in *sicken* i in *possible* / o in *melon* u in *circus* }

chev·ron [shev′rən] *n.* An emblem made up of one or more stripes meeting at an angle, worn on the sleeve of a military, naval, or police uniform.

Chevron

chew [cho͞o] **1** *v.* To crush or grind with the teeth: I can't *chew* this gristle. **2** *n.* Something that is chewed: a *chew* of tobacco.

chew·ing gum [cho͞o′ing] A gum, usually chicle, that is flavored and sweetened for chewing.

che·wink [chi·wingk′] *n.* Another name for TOWHEE.

chew·y [cho͞o′ē] *adj.* **chew·i·er, chew·i·est** Soft, thick, and needing much chewing: *chewy* candy.

Chey·enne [shī·an′ *or* shī·en′] *n., pl.* **Chey·enne** or **Chey·ennes** **1** A tribe of North American Indians now living in Montana and Oklahoma. **2** A member of this tribe. **3** The language of this tribe.

chg. **1** change. **2** charge.

chi [kī] *n.* The twenty-second letter of the Greek alphabet.

chic [shēk] **1** *adj.* Stylish; elegant: a *chic* suit. **2** *n.* Style, elegance, and taste, especially in dress: The movie star dresses with great *chic.*

chi·can·er·y [shi·kā′nər·ē] *n., pl.* **chi·can·er·ies** The use of tricky actions or clever arguing and quibbling, in order to deceive or outwit.

Chi·ca·na [chi·kä′nä] *n.* A Mexican-American woman or girl.

Chi·ca·no [chi·kä′nō] *n., pl.* **Chi·ca·nos** A Mexican-American.

chick [chik] *n.* **1** A young chicken. **2** Any young bird.

chick·a·dee [chik′ə·dē] *n.* A small bird having the top of its head and its throat of a darker color than the body.

Chick·a·saw [chik′ə·sô′] *n., pl.* **Chick·a·saw** or **Chick·a·saws** **1** A tribe of North American Indians once living in Mississippi and Tennessee, now living in Oklahoma. **2** A member of this tribe. **3** The language of this tribe.

chick·en [chik′ən] **1** *n.* The common domestic fowl. **2** *n.* The flesh of this fowl used as food. **3** *n.* Any young bird. **4** *adj. slang* Cowardly.

chick·en-heart·ed [chik′ən·här′tid] *adj.* Timid or cowardly.

chicken pox A contagious disease, especially of children, in which there is a slight fever and small blisters on the skin.

chicken wire A netlike material made of crisscrossed wires and used especially to make fences and chicken coops.

chick·pea [chik′pē′] *n.* The round, pealike seed of a bushy plant, eaten as a vegetable.

chick·weed [chik′wēd′] *n.* A plant whose seeds are used for feeding caged birds.

chic·le [chik′əl] *n.* The milky, gummy juice of a large, tropical evergreen tree. It is used as the main ingredient of chewing gum.

chic·o·ry [chik′ər·ē] *n., pl.* **chic·o·ries** **1** A plant whose leaves are often used in salads. **2** The roasted root of this plant which is often mixed with coffee or used in place of coffee.

chide [chīd] *v.* **chid·ed** or **chid** [chid], **chid·ed** or **chid** or **chid·den** [chid′ən], **chid·ing** To scold: He *chided* me for laughing.

chief [chēf] **1** *n.* The person who is highest in rank or authority, as the leader of a tribe or police force. **2** *adj.* Having the highest authority or rank: the *chief* officer. **3** *adj.* Most significant or important; principal. **—in chief** Having the highest rank or authority: commander *in chief.*

chief justice The judge who presides over a court composed of several judges.

chief·ly [chēf′lē] *adv.* **1** Most of all; above all: *Chiefly* she told us of the town. **2** Principally; mostly; mainly: a club *chiefly* of young people.

chief·tain [chēf′tən] *n.* **1** The head of a clan or tribe: an Aztec *chieftain.* **2** Any chief or leader.

chif·fon [shi·fon′ *or* shif′on] **1** *n.* A very thin silk or rayon cloth, as used in dresses or scarves. **2** *adj.* In cooking, light and fluffy: a *chiffon* custard. ◆ *Chiffon* comes directly from French and was formed from *chiffe,* meaning a *rag.*

chif·fo·nier [shif′ə·nir′] *n.* A narrow chest of drawers, often with a mirror on it.

chig·ger [chig′ər] *n.* The larva of certain mites. It attaches itself to the skin and causes great itching.

chi·gnon [shēn′yon′] *n.* A tight ball or roll of hair worn at the back of the head by women.

Chi·hua·hua [chi·wä′wä] *n.* A small Mexican dog having a smooth coat and large ears.

chil·blain [chil′blān′] *n.* A painful itching, swelling, and redness of the hands or feet, caused by exposure to extreme cold.

child [chīld] *n., pl.* **chil·dren** [chil′drən] **1** A baby. **2** A young boy or girl. **3** A son or daughter. **4** A person from a certain family or country: the *children* of Israel. **—with child** Pregnant.

child·bear·ing [chīld′bâr′ing] **1** *n.* The act of giving birth to a child or children. **2** *adj.* Having to do with or capable of bearing a child or children: the *childbearing* years.

child·birth [chīld′bûrth′] *n.* The act of giving birth to a child or children.

child·hood [chīld′ho͝od′] *n.* **1** The time during which one is a child. **2** The condition of being a child.

child·ish [chīl′dish] *adj.* **1** Of, like, or proper for a child. **2** Not proper to an adult, as foolish or thoughtless: a *childish* temper tantrum. **—child′·ish·ly** *adv.* **—child′ish·ness** *n.*

child·less [chīld′lis] *adj.* Having no children.

child·like [chīld′līk′] *adj.* Having certain of the best qualities of a child, as trusting, lovable, or refreshing: a *childlike* simplicity.

chil·dren [chil′drən] Plural of CHILD.

child's play [chīldz] Something that is very easy to do.

Chil·e·an [chil′ē·ən] **1** *adj.* Of or from Chile. **2** *n.* A person born in or a citizen of Chile.

chil·i or **chil·e** or **chil·li** [chil′ē] *n., pl.* **chil·ies** or **chil·es** or **chil·lies** **1** A very hot and spicy red pepper, used as a seasoning. **2** Chili con carne.

chili con car·ne [kon kär′nē] A dish that includes meat, chilies, other seasonings, and often beans.

chili sauce A thick sauce with ingredients that include tomatoes, peppers, onions, and spices.

chill [chil] **1** *n.* A feeling of being cold, often with shivering. **2** *v.* To have a chill. **3** *n.* A moderate but uncomfortable coldness: There is a *chill* in this room. **4** *adj.* Moderately or unpleasantly cold: a *chill* wind. **5** *v.* To make or become cold: to *chill* food. **6** *v.* To harden (metal) by sudden cooling. **7** *adj.* Not friendly.

chill·y [chil'ē] *adj.* **chill·i·er, chill·i·est** 1 Causing coldness or chill: a *chilly* rain. 2 Feeling cold: I am *chilly.* 3 Not friendly or warm: a *chilly* greeting. —**chill'i·ness** *n.*

chi·mae·ra [kə·mir'ə *or* kī·mir'ə] *n.* Another spelling of CHIMERA.

chime [chīm] *n., v.* **chimed, chim·ing** 1 *n.* (*often pl.*) A set of bells each of which has a different pitch. 2 *n.* The sounds or music produced by chimes. 3 *v.* To sound or ring: The bells *chimed* all over town. 4 *v.* To indicate (the time of day) by chiming: The clock *chimed* three. 5 *n.* A metal tube or set of tubes making bell-like sounds when struck. —**chime in** 1 To interrupt. 2 To agree or be in harmony.

chi·me·ra [kə·mir'ə *or* kī·mir'ə] *n.* 1 (*written* **Chimera**) In Greek myths, a fire-breathing monster, part lion, part goat, and part serpent. 2 Any horrible idea or fancy. 3 An absurd, impractical, or impossible idea.

chi·mer·i·cal [kə·mer'i·kəl *or* kī·mer'i·kəl] *adj.* 1 Fantastic; imaginary. 2 Wildly impossible.

chim·ney [chim'nē] *n., pl.* **chim·neys** 1 A tall, hollow structure that carries away smoke or fumes, as from fireplaces, stoves, or furnaces. 2 A glass tube for enclosing the flame of a lamp.

chimney sweep A person who makes a living by cleaning away the soot from inside chimneys.

chimney swift A bird that looks like a swallow and often builds its nest in an unused chimney.

chimp [chimp] *n. informal* A chimpanzee.

chim·pan·zee [chim'pan·zē' *or* chim·pan'zē] *n.* An ape of Africa that lives in trees, has large ears and dark brown hair, and is smaller and more intelligent than the gorilla. ◆ *Chimpanzee* comes from a native African name.

Chimpanzee

chin [chin] *n., v.* **chinned, chin·ning** 1 *n.* The part of the face just below the mouth. 2 *v.* To hang by the hands and lift (oneself) until the chin is level with or above the hands.

Chin. Chinese.

chi·na [chī'nə] *n.* 1 A fine kind of glasslike porcelain, baked twice. 2 Items, as dishes, vases, or figurines, made of china or porcelain. 3 Any earthenware dishes.

Chi·na·town [chī'nə·town'] *n.* A neighborhood, as in a U.S. city, inhabited mainly by people of Chinese descent.

chi·na·ware [chī'nə·wâr'] *n.* China (def. 2, 3).

chinch [chinch] *n.* 1 A chinch bug. 2 A bedbug.

chinch bug A small black and white bug that is very destructive to grain.

chin·chil·la [chin·chil'ə] *n.* 1 A small rodent of the Andes, about the size of a squirrel. 2 Its soft, valuable fur. 3 A heavy woolen cloth with a tufted surface.

chine [chīn] *n.* 1 The backbone or back. 2 A piece of meat including all or part of the backbone.

Chi·nese [chī·nēz'] *adj., n., pl.* **Chi·nese** 1 *adj.* Of or from China. 2 *n.* A person born in or a citizen of China. 3 *n.* A person of Chinese ancestry. 4 *n.* The language of China.

Chinese checkers A game in which players move marbles from hole to hole across a star-shaped board.

Chinese lantern A lantern made of thin paper, that can be folded flat.

Chinese lantern

Chinese puzzle 1 An intricate puzzle that is hard to solve. 2 Anything that is intricate or difficult.

chink[1] [chingk] 1 *n.* A crack: a *chink* in armor. 2 *v.* To fill the cracks of: to *chink* the walls with sticks and mud.

chink[2] [chingk] 1 *n.* A short, sharp metallic sound, as of coins hitting each other. 2 *v.* To make or cause to make this sound.

chi·no [chē'nō] *n.* 1 A strong cotton cloth. 2 (*pl.*) Trousers, usually khaki-colored, made of this cloth.

chi·nook [chi·no͝ok'] *n.* 1 A warm, moist southwest wind that blows in from the sea along the coast of Oregon, Washington, and British Columbia. 2 A warm, dry wind blowing down the eastern slopes of the Rocky Mountains.

chintz [chints] *n.* A cotton fabric, usually glazed and printed in bright colors: The slipcovers were made of flowered *chintz.*

chin-up [chin'up'] *n.* An act of chinning on an exercise bar.

chip [chip] *n., v.* **chipped, chip·ping** 1 *n.* A small piece cut or broken off. 2 *v.* To break off a small piece or pieces of: to *chip* china. 3 *v.* To become chipped: This china *chips* easily. 4 *n.* A place where something has been chipped off: a *chip* on a glass. 5 *n.* A thinly sliced piece or morsel: a potato *chip.* 6 *n.* A small disk or counter used in certain games, as poker. 7 *v.* To chop or cut as with an ax. 8 *v.* To shape by cutting off pieces. 9 *n.* A thin square piece of a semiconductor, as silicon, often as small as a fingernail, containing thousands of tiny wires and circuits that can operate a computer. —**chip in** To go along with others in giving money or help: We all *chipped in* to buy a new basketball. —**chip off the old block** A son or daughter who closely resembles either parent, as in behavior or looks.

chip·munk [chip'mungk'] *n.* A small North American ground squirrel with stripes down its back. ◆ *Chipmunk* comes from an Algonquian Indian word, *chitmunk.* Perhaps it was changed because the animal's sharp, scolding call sounds like *chip, chip, chip,* or perhaps only because *chip* is easier for us to say before the sound of *m.*

Chipmunk

chipped beef Dried beef sliced into small, thin pieces.

chip·per [chip'ər] *adj. U.S. informal* Feeling fine and spry or cheerful.

Chip·pe·wa [chip'ə·wä', chip'ə·wô', *or* chip'ə·wə]

a	add	**i**	it	**o͝o**	took	**oi**	oil
ā	ace	**ī**	ice	**o͞o**	pool	**ou**	pout
â	care	**o**	odd	**u**	up	**ng**	ring
ä	palm	**ō**	open	**û**	burn	**th**	thin
e	end	**ô**	order	**yo͞o**	fuse	**t͟h**	this
ē	equal					**zh**	vision

ə = {a in *above* e in *sicken* i in *possible*
o in *melon* u in *circus*}

n., pl. **Chip·pe·wa** or **Chip·pe·was** Another name for OJIBWA.

chi·rop·o·dist [kə·rop′ə·dist] *n.* A person who treats corns and other ailments of the feet.

chi·ro·prac·tic [kī′rə·prak′tik] *n.* A method of treating disease and pain by manipulating the spine and other body structures by hand.

chi·ro·prac·tor [kī′rə·prak′tər] *n.* A person who practices chiropractic.

chirp [chûrp] **1** *n.* A short, sharp sound like that made by a sparrow or cricket. **2** *v.* To make such a sound.

chir·rup [chir′əp] *v.* **1** To chirp continuously, as a bird. **2** To make a chirping sound with the lips, as in urging a horse.

chis·el [chiz′(ə)l] *n., v.* **chis·eled** or **chis·elled, chis·el·ing** or **chis·el·ling** **1** *n.* A cutting tool with a sharp, beveled edge, used to cut or shape wood, metal, or stone. **2** *v.* To cut or shape with or as if with a chisel. **3** *v. slang* To cheat; swindle. **—chis′el·er** or **chis′·el·ler** *n.*

Chisel

chit·chat [chit′chat′] *n.* **1** Light conversation. **2** Gossip. ◆ *Chitchat* was formed when another syllable sounding like *chat* was put in front of it.

chi·tin [kī′tin] *n.* A tough, colorless, horny substance forming the main part of the hard covering of insects and crustaceans. **—chi′tin·ous** *adj.*

chit·ter·lings or **chit·lings** or **chit·lins** [chit′linz] *n.pl.* The small intestines of pigs, fried and used as food.

chiv·al·rous [shiv′əl·rəs] *adj.* **1** Gallant and brave, as an ideal knight; kind, courteous, and generous. **2** Of or having to do with chivalry. **—chiv′al·rous·ly** *adv.* **—chiv′al·rous·ness** *n.*

chiv·al·ry [shiv′əl·rē] *n.* **1** The beliefs and code of life of knights in the Middle Ages. **2** The ideal qualities of knighthood, as gallantry, courtesy, bravery, and kindness.

chive [chīv] *n.* A plant of the onion family whose long, slender leaves are chopped up and used for seasoning

chlo·ride [klôr′īd′] *n.* A compound of chlorine with another element or group of elements. Common salt is sodium chloride.

chlo·rin·ate [klôr′ə·nāt′] *v.* **chlo·rin·at·ed, chlo·rin·at·ing** **1** To add chlorine or a compound of chlorine, as in treating water to make it safe to drink. **2** To change a chemical compound by introducing atoms of chlorine into its molecules. **—chlo′rin·a′tion** *n.*

chlo·rine [klôr′ēn′] *n.* A greenish yellow poisonous gaseous element with a penetrating odor, obtained chiefly from common salt. Chlorine never occurs naturally as a gas but only in compounds, some of which are essential to all plant and animal life.

chlo·ro·form [klôr′ə·fôrm′] **1** *n.* A colorless, volatile liquid used as an anesthetic and solvent. **2** *v.* To make unconscious or kill with an overdose of chloroform.

Chlo·ro·my·ce·tin [klôr′ə·mī·sē′tən] *n.* An antibiotic obtained from certain soil microorganisms or made synthetically, used to treat a wide variety of infections: a trademark.

chlo·ro·phyll or **chlo·ro·phyl** [klôr′ə·fil] *n.* The green substance found in most plants. In the presence of sunlight it converts water and carbon dioxide from the air into sugars and starches.

chlo·ro·plast [klôr′ə·plast′] *n.* A part of a plant cell where chlorophyll is found.

chock [chok] **1** *n.* A block or wedge placed to prevent something from moving or rolling. **2** *v.* To hold in position with a chock or chocks.

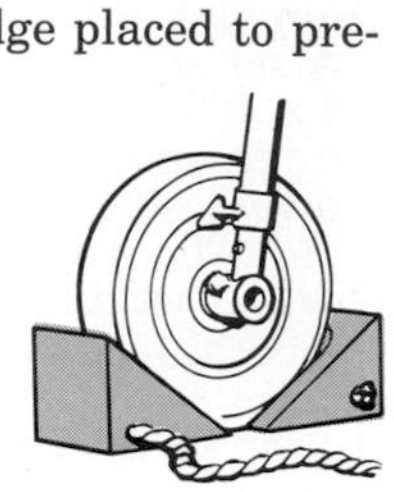

Chocks holding an airplane wheel

chock-full [chok′fŏŏl′] *adj.* Completely full.

choc·o·late [chôk′(ə·)lit *or* chok′·(ə·)lit] **1** *n.* Cacao nuts that have been roasted and ground. **2** *n.* A drink or candy made from this. **3** *adj.* Made or flavored with chocolate: a *chocolate* cake. **4** *n., adj.* Dark, reddish brown. ◆ This word comes from a Mexican Indian word. Indians introduced chocolate to Spanish explorers in South America and Mexico.

Choc·taw [chok′tô] *n., pl.* **Choc·taw** or **Choc·taws** **1** A tribe of North American Indians once living in Mississippi, Alabama, Georgia, and Louisiana, now in Oklahoma. **2** A member of this tribe. **3** The language of this tribe.

choice [chois] *n., adj.* **choic·er, choic·est** **1** *n.* The act of choosing; selection. **2** *n.* The right or privilege of choosing; option. **3** *n.* The person or thing chosen: the people's *choice.* **4** *n.* A number or variety from which to choose: a large *choice* of articles. **5** *n.* An alternative: We had no *choice.* **6** *adj.* Of very good quality; excellent: *choice* food.

choir [kwīr] *n.* **1** A trained group of singers, especially in a religious service. **2** The part of a church occupied by the choir.

choke [chōk] *v.* **choked, chok·ing,** *n.* **1** *v.* To stop the breathing of by squeezing or blocking the windpipe. **2** *v.* To become suffocated or stifled: to *choke* from smoke. **3** *n.* The act or sound of choking. **4** *v.* To keep back; suppress: to *choke* down anger. **5** *v.* To clog or become clogged: Leaves *choked* the pipes. **6** *v.* To stop or hold back the progress, growth, or action of: to *choke* a fire. **7** *v.* To lessen the intake of air of (a gasoline engine). **8** *n.* A device that does this. **9** *v. slang* To lose one's nerve in a critical situation and perform badly. **—choke up** To be overcome, as by emotion or nervousness.

choke·cher·ry [chōk′cher′ē] *n., pl.* **choke·cher·ries** **1** A wild North American cherry with a bitter taste. **2** The tree it grows on.

chok·er [chō′kər] *n.* **1** A necklace worn high on the neck. **2** A person or thing that chokes.

chol·er [kol′ər] *n.* An excitable temper; anger.

chol·er·a [kol′ər·ə] *n.* An infectious bacterial disease that attacks the intestines, often causing death.

chol·er·ic [kol′ər·ik] *adj.* Easily made angry.

cho·les·ter·ol [kə·les′tə·rōl′] *n.* A fatty crystalline substance present in animal fats, gallstones, and bile. It plays a part in metabolism.

choose [chōōz] *v.* **chose, cho·sen, choos·ing** **1** To select from a group: to *choose* a library book; I *chose* in haste. **2** To decide or prefer (to do something): They *chose* to remain. **—choos′er** *n.*

choos·y [chōō′zē] *adj.* **choos·i·er, choos·i·est** *informal* Very fussy in choosing.

chop[1] [chop] *v.* **chopped, chop·ping,** *n.* **1** *v.* To cut by hitting with a sharp tool: to *chop* a tree down. **2** *n.* A cutting blow. **3** *v.* To cut into small pieces: to *chop* onions. **4** *n.* A slice, as of lamb or pork, with part of its bone. **5** *v.* To make by cutting: to *chop* a hole in ice. **6** *v.* To hit a ball with a downward slice, as in tennis.

chop^2 [chop] *v.* **chopped, chop·ping** To shift suddenly; veer, as the wind.

chop^3 [chop] *n.* (*usually pl.*) The jaw, or the part of the face that includes it.

chop·per [chop′ər] *n.* **1** A person or thing that chops. **2** *slang* A helicopter.

chop·py^1 [chop′ē] *adj.* **chop·pi·er, chop·pi·est** Full of short, rough waves: a *choppy* sea.

chop·py^2 [chop′ē] *adj.* **chop·pi·er, chop·pi·est** Variable; changing, as the wind.

chop·sticks [chop′stiks′] *n.pl.* Slender rods of ivory or wood used in pairs, as by the Chinese and Japanese, to lift food to the mouth.

Chopsticks

chop su·ey [sōō′ē] A Chinese-American dish that includes bits of meat, bean sprouts, onions, celery, and mushrooms, cooked in a sauce and served with rice. ◆ *Chop suey* is an American pronunciation and spelling of a Chinese term meaning *odds and ends.*

cho·ral [*adj.* kôr′əl, *n.* kə·ral′ *or* kô·ral′] **1** *adj.* Of, for, by, or in the manner of a chorus. **2** *n.* Another spelling of CHORALE.

cho·rale [kə·ral′ *or* kô·ral′] *n.* A hymn having a simple melody and firm rhythm.

chord^1 [kôrd] *n.* **1** A combination of three or more musical tones sounded together.

chord^2 [kôrd] *n.* **1** A straight line joining any two points of an arc. **2** A string of a musical instrument. **3** An emotional response or reaction: to touch a sympathetic *chord.*

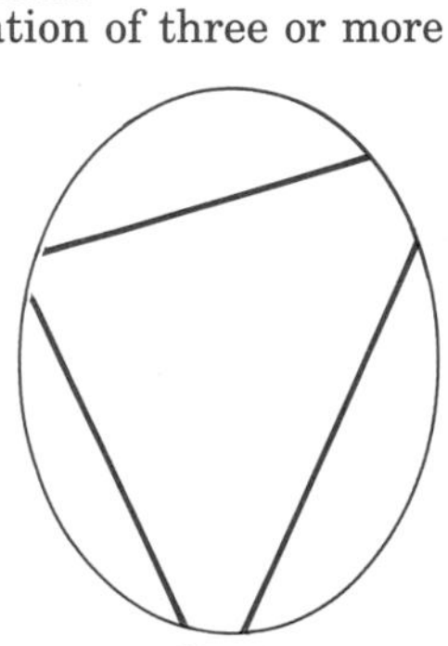

Chords

chor·date [kôr′dāt′] *n.* Any of the animals having backbones or having breathing organs and nervous systems placed as in vertebrates.

chore [chôr] *n. U.S.* **1** A routine task, as in housework. **2** An unpleasant or hard task.

cho·re·a [kə·rē′ə] *n.* A disease most often found in children that affects the nervous system, causing involuntary movements of the limbs and facial muscles.

cho·re·o·graph [kôr′ē·ə·graf′] *v.* To make up dance movements for: to *choreograph* a ballet. **—cho·re·og·ra·pher** [kôr′ē·og′rə·fər] *n.*

cho·re·og·ra·phy [kôr′ē·og′rə·fē] *n.* The planning of movements for dance performances. **—cho·re·o·graph·ic** [kôr′ē·ə·graf′ik] *adj.*

chor·is·ter [kôr′is·tər] *n.* A member of a choir, especially a boy singer.

cho·roid [kôr′oid′] **1** *n.* A membrane full of blood vessels between the retina and outer cover of the eye. **2** *adj.* Of or like this membrane.

chor·tle [chôr′təl] *v.* **chor·tled, chor·tling** To chuckle loudly or gleefully.

cho·rus [kôr′əs] **1** *n.* A group of singers, speakers, or dancers that perform together. **2** *n.* A musical or dramatic composition to be sung or spoken by a chorus. **3** *n.* A part of a song sung after each stanza; refrain. **4** *n.* Any group singing or speaking all at once. **5** *n.* A saying or shouting of something by many at once. **6** *v.* To sing or speak all at once. **—in chorus** All together.

chose [chōz] Past tense of CHOOSE.

cho·sen [chō′zən] Past participle of CHOOSE.

chow [chou] *n.* **1** A medium-sized dog native to China, having a thick brown or black coat and a blue-black tongue. **2** *slang* Food.

chow·der [chou′dər] *n.* A dish made of clams or fish stewed with vegetables, often in milk. ◆ *Chowder* comes from the French word *chaudière* [shō·dyâr′] meaning a *kettle or its contents.* People in New England changed it into *chowder.*

chow mein [chou′ mān′] A Chinese-American dish that includes meat, onions, and bean sprouts, stewed and served with fried noodles.

Christ [krīst] *n.* **1** The promised savior of Israel, foretold by the prophets. **2** Jesus, regarded as fulfilling this prophecy. ◆ The name *Christ* comes from a Greek word meaning the *Anointed.* It is a translation of a Hebrew word.

chris·ten [kris′(ə)n] *v.* **1** To baptize or name in baptism. **2** To give a name to: to *christen* a boat.

Chris·ten·dom [kris′(ə)n·dəm] *n.* **1** Christian lands. **2** All Christians, as a group.

chris·ten·ing [kris′(ə)n·ing] *n.* A Christian baptism, especially of a baby.

Chris·tian [kris′chən] **1** *n.* A person who believes in Jesus, his teachings, or his example. **2** *adj.* Of, having to do with, or believing in Jesus or his teachings. **3** *adj.* In keeping with the teachings of Jesus: *Christian* behavior.

Chris·ti·an·i·ty [kris′chē·an′ə·tē] *n.* **1** The religion taught by Jesus and his followers. **2** All Christians as a group.

Chris·tian·ize [kris′chən·īz′] *v.* **Chris·tian·ized, Chris·tian·iz·ing** To make Christian.

Christian name A given name, or first name.

Christian Science A religion and system of healing founded in 1866 by Mary Baker Eddy and based on her interpretation of the Bible.

Christian Scientist A person who believes in Christian Science.

Christ·like [krīst′līk′] *adj.* Like Christ; having the spirit of Christ.

Christ·mas [kris′məs] *n.* The celebration on December 25 of the birth of Jesus.

Christ·mas·tide [kris′məs·tīd′] *n.* The festival of Christmas, often thought of as extending from Christmas Eve through New Year's Day or to Epiphany.

a	add	**i**	it	**o͝o**	took	**oi**	oil
ā	ace	**ī**	ice	**o͞o**	pool	**ou**	pout
â	care	**o**	odd	**u**	up	**ng**	ring
ä	palm	**ō**	open	**û**	burn	**th**	thin
e	end	**ô**	order	**yo͞o**	fuse	**t̶h̶**	this
ē	equal					**zh**	vision

ə = a in *above*, e in *sicken*, i in *possible*, o in *melon*, u in *circus*

Christmas tree An evergreen tree decorated with ornaments and lights at Christmas.

Christmas tree

chro·mat·ic [krō·mat′ik] *adj.* 1 Of, having, or having to do with color. 2 Of, using, or built on semitones: a *chromatic* scale.
chro·ma·tin [krō′mə·tin] *n.* The easily stained material of a cell nucleus in which the genes are located.
chro·ma·tog·ra·phy [krō′mə·tog′·rə·fē] *n.* A method for separating and analyzing the parts of a fluid mixture by adsorption.
chrome [krōm] *n.* Chromium, especially when used to plate another metal.
chro·mic [krō′mik] *adj.* Of, having to do with, or containing chromium.
chro·mi·um [krō′mē·əm] *n.* A grayish white, very hard metallic element that does not tarnish easily, much used in making alloys and pigments.
chro·mo·some [krō′mə·sōm′] *n.* One of the rod-shaped or loop-shaped bodies that carry the genes in the cells of plants and animals.
chro·mo·sphere [krō′mə·sfir′] *n.* A flaming red gaseous envelope that surrounds the sun, visible during a total eclipse.
chron. 1 chronicle. 2 chronological. 3 chronology.
chron·ic [kron′ik] *adj.* 1 Continuing for a long time: *chronic* discontent. 2 Lasting or coming back again and again: *chronic* illness. 3 Long affected; habitual: a *chronic* complainer.
chron·i·cle [kron′i·kəl] *n., v.* **chron·i·cled, chron·i·cling** 1 *n.* A record of events as they happened in time. 2 *v.* To make a chronicle of.
Chron·i·cles [kron′i·kəlz] *n.pl.* (*used with singular verb*) Either of two historical books of the Old Testament.
chron·o·log·i·cal [kron′ə·loj′i·kəl] *adj.* 1 Arranged according to the order in which things happened. 2 Of or having to do with chronology. —**chron′o·log′i·cal·ly** *adv.*
chro·nol·o·gy [krə·nol′ə·jē] *n., pl.* **chro·nol·o·gies** 1 The science of determining the proper sequence and dating of historical events. 2 Something chronological, as a list or an arrangement.
chro·nom·e·ter [krə·nom′ə·tər] *n.* A very precise clock, used in science, navigation, and other fields.
chrys·a·lid [kris′ə·lid] *n.,* A chrysalis.
chrys·a·lis [kris′ə·lis] *n., pl.* **chrys·a·lis·es** or **chry·sal·i·des** [kri·sal′ə·dēz] The form of an insect such as a butterfly when it is enclosed in a cocoon and before it becomes an adult.

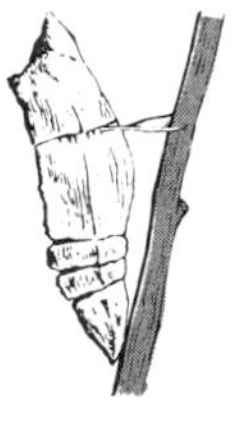
Chrysalis

chrys·an·the·mum [kri·san′thə·məm] *n.* Any of a group of plants cultivated in many varieties for their large, round, showy flowers.
chub [chub] *n., pl.* **chub** or **chubs** Any of various small freshwater fish related to the carp and the minnow.
chub·by [chub′ē] *adj.* **chub·bi·er, chub·bi·est** Plump; rounded. —**chub′bi·ness** *n.*
chuck[1] [chuk] 1 *v.* To pat or tap playfully, as under the chin. 2 *n.* Such a pat or tap. 3 *v.* To throw or pitch: to *chuck* a baseball. 4 *n.* A throw; toss.
chuck[2] [chuk] *n.* 1 The cut of beef extending from the neck to the shoulder blade. 2 A clamp to hold a tool in a machine.
chuck-full [chuk′fo͝ol′] *adj.* Another word for CHOCK-FULL.
chuck·le [chuk′əl] *v.* **chuck·led, chuck·ling,** *n.* 1 *v.* To laugh softly. 2 *n.* A soft laugh.
chuck wagon A wagon equipped to cook food for outdoor workers.
chug [chug] *n., v.* **chugged, chug·ging** 1 *n.* A dull explosive sound, as of the exhaust of an engine. 2 *v.* To move while making a series of such sounds: The old car *chugged* by.
chug·a·lug [chug′ə·lug′] *v.* **chug·a·lugged, chug·a·lug·ging** *slang* To drink the entire contents of a container of (a liquid) without stopping.
chum [chum] *n., v.* **chummed, chum·ming** 1 *n.* A close friend; buddy. 2 *v.* To have a close friendship with someone. 3 *n.* A roommate.
chum·my [chum′ē] *adj.* **chum·mi·er, chum·mi·est** *informal* Very friendly; intimate.
chump [chump] *n. informal* A foolish person.
chunk [chungk] *n.* A short thick piece or lump.
chunk·y [chung′kē] *adj.* **chunk·i·er, chunk·i·est** Short and thickset; stocky.
church [chûrch] *n.* 1 A building for Christian worship. 2 Christian religious services. 3 (*usually written* **Church**) A distinct body of Christians having the same faith and discipline: the Lutheran *Church.* 4 (*usually written* **Church**) Christians, as a group. ◆ *Church* comes originally from a Greek word meaning *of the Lord.*
church·go·er [chûrch′gō′ər] *n.* A person who goes to church regularly.
church·man [chûrch′mən] *n., pl.* **church·men** [chûrch′mən] 1 A supporter or member of a church. 2 A member of the clergy.
Church of Christ, Scientist The official name of the Christian Science Church.
Church of England The national church of England, established in the 16th century.
Church of Jesus Christ of Latter-day Saints The official name of the Mormon Church.
church·war·den [chûrch′wôr′dən] *n.* In the Episcopal Church, or the Church of England, a layperson who helps to manage church property.
church·yard [chûrch′yärd′] *n.* The ground around a church, often used as a cemetery.
churl [chûrl] *n.* 1 In early England, a freeman of low birth. 2 A rude or surly person; boor. ◆ *Churl* comes from an Old English word meaning *man.* At first a *churl* was a free man, but after the Norman Conquest most of the common people were made serfs and *churl* began to mean *peasant of a low class.*
churl·ish [chûr′lish] *adj.* Rude; boorish. —**churl′ish·ly** *adv.* —**churl′ish·ness** *n.*
churn [chûrn] 1 *n.* A container or machine in which milk or cream is beaten to make butter. 2 *v.* To beat (milk or cream) in or as if in a churn. 3 *v.* To move or stir about violently.
chute [sho͞ot] *n.* 1 An inclined trough or vertical passage down which water, coal, laundry, and other items may pass. 2 A slide, as for toboggans. 3 A waterfall or rapid. 4 *informal* A parachute.
chut·ney [chut′nē] *n., pl.* **chut·neys** A spicy relish that includes fruit and spices.
chutz·pah or **chutz·pa** [ho͝ot′spə] *n. slang* Brazen audacity; nerve; impudence.
chyme [kīm] *n.* Partly digested food, in the form of

a thick, soft mass, on its way from the stomach to the small intestine.

CIA Central Intelligence Agency.

ciao [chou] *interj.* An Italian expression of greeting or farewell.

ci·ca·da [si·kā'də] *n.* A large insect with four transparent wings. The male makes a shrill sound by rubbing its legs against a vibrating membrane on its abdomen.

-cide A combining form meaning: **1** Killer, as in *insecticide.* **2** Killing, as in *infanticide.*

ci·der [sī'dər] *n.* The juice of apples, used for drinking and for making vinegar.

ci·gar [si·gär'] *n.* A roll of tobacco leaves prepared and shaped for smoking.

cig·a·rette [sig'ə·ret' *or* sig'ə·ret'] *n.* A paper tube filled with shredded tobacco for smoking.

cil·i·a [sil'ē·ə] *n.pl., sing.* **cil·i·um** [sil'ē·əm] **1** Tiny hairlike outgrowths on some plant and animal cells. Some small water animals use them to move about or to set up currents. **2** The eyebrows.

cinch [sinch] *U.S.* **1** *n.* A strap that holds a pack or saddle on an animal. **2** *v.* To put a cinch on. **3** *v.* To tighten a cinch. **4** *n. informal* A strong grip. **5** *n. slang* Something easy or certain. **6** *v. slang* To make certain of.

cin·cho·na [sin·kō'nə] *n.* **1** A tree, originally of Peru, now cultivated in India and Java. **2** The bitter-tasting bark of this tree, from which quinine and related substances are obtained.

cin·der [sin'dər] *n.* **1** A piece of partly burned material, as wood or coal, that is not flaming. **2** (*pl.*) Charred bits and ashes from a fire.

cinder block A block, usually hollow, of cement and pressed cinders, used in building.

Cin·der·el·la [sin'də·rel'ə] *n.* A girl in a fairy tale, treated cruelly by her stepmother and stepsisters, who finally marries a prince.

cin·e·ma [sin'ə·mə] *n.* **1** A motion picture. **2** A motion picture theater. **3** Motion pictures in general. ◆ *Cinema* comes from a Greek word meaning *movement.*

cin·e·mat·ic [sin'ə·mat'ik] *adj.* Of, having to do with, or suitable for motion pictures or the filming of them.

cin·e·ma·tog·ra·phy [sin'ə·mə·tog'rə·fē] *n.* The art or technique of motion picture photography. **—cin'e·ma·tog'ra·pher** *n.*

cin·na·bar [sin'ə·bär'] *n.* A heavy red mineral, the principal ore of mercury.

cin·na·mon [sin'ə·mən] **1** *n.* The inner bark of various tropical trees, used as a spice. **2** *n.* Any of these trees. **3** *adj., n.* Reddish brown.

CIO Congress of Industrial Organizations.

ci·on [sī'ən] *n.* A twig or shoot cut from a plant or tree, especially for grafting.

ciph·er [sī'fər] **1** *n.* Zero; naught. Symbol: 0. **2** *n.* An unimportant person or thing. **3** *v.* To work out (a problem), using arithmetic. **4** *n.* A system for writing secret messages; code. **5** *n.* A message in cipher. ◆ See ZERO.

cir·ca [sûr'kə] *prep.* About; around: a Latin word used before an approximate date or figure.

cir·ca·di·an [sər·kā'dē·ən *or* sər·kad'ē·ən] *adj.* Being, happening in, or characterized by periods of about 24 hours: the *circadian* rhythm of sleeping and waking.

Cir·ce [sûr'sē] *n.* In Homer's *Odyssey,* an enchantress who changed Odysseus's companions into pigs by a magic drink.

cir·cle [sûr'kəl] *n., v.* **cir·cled, cir·cling** **1** *n.* A plane curve all of whose points are equally distant from a point in the plane, called the center. **2** *n.* The area enclosed by this curve. **3** *n.* Something resembling a circle, as a ring. **4** *v.* To make or put a closed curve around: The fence *circled* the field. **5** *v.* To move about in or nearly in a circle: The lion *circled* its prey. **6** *n.* A complete series that repeats over and over: the *circle* of seasons. **7** *n.* A group of people with a common interest or purpose: a literary *circle.*

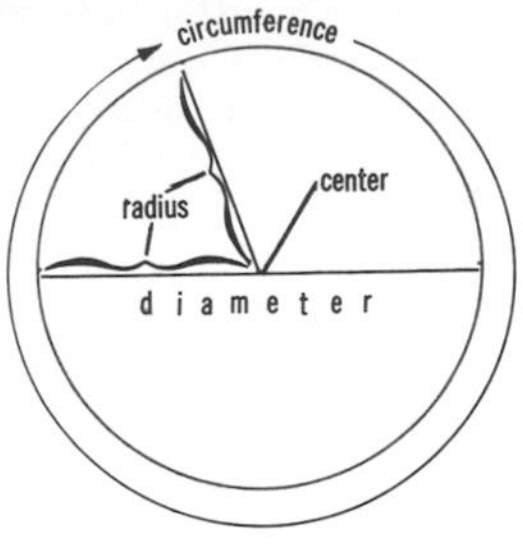

Circle

cir·clet [sûr'klit] *n.* **1** A small circle. **2** A small circular object, as a ring.

cir·cuit [sûr'kit] *n.* **1** A route or path that turns back to where it began. **2** The line or distance around an area. **3** A periodic trip through a set of places, usually in a fixed order and in connection with one's work. **4** The route traveled in such a trip. **5** The path taken by an electric current. **6** The arrangement of parts in an electrical or electronic device or system. **7** A group of theaters under the same mangement.

circuit breaker A switch that automatically cuts off the current in an electric circuit when the current gets too strong.

circuit court A court that holds sessions in several places within its district.

circuit judge A judge in a circuit court.

cir·cu·i·tous [sər·kyoo͞'ə·təs] *adj.* Roundabout; indirect. **—cir·cu'i·tous·ly** *adv.*

circuit rider A minister who preaches at places on a circuit.

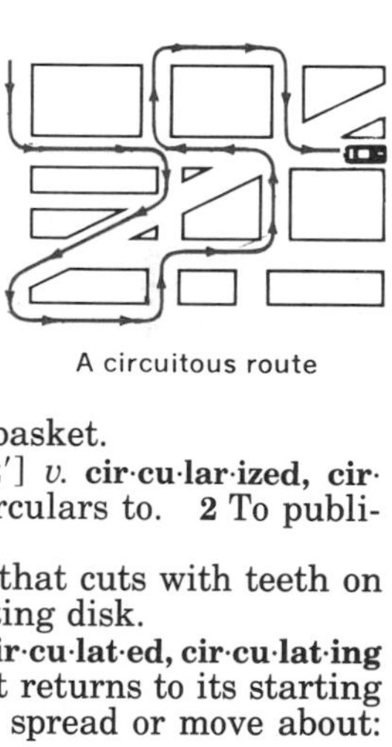
A circuitous route

cir·cu·lar [sûr'kyə·lər] **1** *adj.* Shaped like, moving in, or forming a circle. **2** *adj.* Of or having to do with circles. **3** *n.* A notice or advertisement sent to many people.

circular file *slang* A wastebasket.

cir·cu·lar·ize [sûr'kyə·lə·rīz'] *v.* **cir·cu·lar·ized, cir·cu·lar·iz·ing** **1** To send circulars to. **2** To publicize by sending circulars.

circular saw A power saw that cuts with teeth on the edge of a rapidly rotating disk.

cir·cu·late [sûr'kyə·lāt'] *v.* **cir·cu·lat·ed, cir·cu·lat·ing** **1** To move in a course that returns to its starting point, as the blood. **2** To spread or move about: Rumors *circulate.*

a	add	**i**	it	**o͝o**	took	**oi**	oil
ā	ace	**ī**	ice	**o͞o**	pool	**ou**	pout
â	care	**o**	odd	**u**	up	**ng**	ring
ä	palm	**ō**	open	**û**	burn	**th**	thin
e	end	**ô**	order	**yo͞o**	fuse	**t͟h**	this
ē	equal					**zh**	vision

ə = a in *above*, e in *sicken*, i in *possible*, o in *melon*, u in *circus*

circulating library A library from which books can be borrowed or rented.

cir·cu·la·tion [sûr′kyə·lā′shən] *n.* 1 A moving around or through something back to the starting point. 2 The movement of the blood through the body. 3 A passing or spreading from one person or place to another. 4 The average number of copies of a publication, as a magazine or newspaper, distributed within a certain period of time.

cir·cu·la·to·ry [sûr′kyə·lə·tôr′ē] *adj.* Of or having to do with circulation, as of the blood.

circum- A prefix meaning: Around, as in *circumnavigate.*

cir·cum·cise [sûr′kəm·sīz′] *v.* **cir·cum·cised, cir·cum·cis·ing** To cut off the foreskin of. **—cir·cum·ci·sion** [sûr′kəm·sizh′ən] *n.*

cir·cum·fer·ence [sər·kum′fər·əns] *n.* 1 The boundary of any closed curve, especially a circle. 2 The length of such a boundary.

cir·cum·flex [sûr′kəm·fleks′] *n.* A mark (ˆ) used over a vowel to show how to pronounce it.

cir·cum·lo·cu·tion [sûr′kəm·lō·kyōō′shən] *n.* A roundabout use of words: "to move from this place" is a *circumlocution* for "to go."

cir·cum·nav·i·gate [sûr′kəm·nav′ə·gāt′] *v.* **cir·cum·nav·i·gat·ed, cir·cum·nav·i·gat·ing** To sail around. **—cir′cum·nav′i·ga′tion** *n.*

cir·cum·po·lar [sûr′kəm·pō′lər] *adj.* 1 Near or around one of the earth's poles. 2 Seeming to circle one of the earth's poles, as a star.

cir·cum·scribe [sûr′kəm·skrīb′] *v.* **cir·cum·scribed, cir·cum·scrib·ing** 1 To limit; confine: The committee's powers were *circumscribed.* 2 To draw a line around; encircle. 3 To draw a circle so that it passes through each vertex of (a polygon). 4 To draw a polygon so that all its sides are tangent to (a circle).

cir·cum·scrip·tion [sûr′kəm·skrip′shən] *n.* 1 The act of circumscribing. 2 The state of being circumscribed. 3 Something that circumscribes. 4 An area or space that is circumscribed.

cir·cum·spect [sûr′kəm·spekt′] *adj.* Watchful and cautious; prudent.

cir·cum·spec·tion [sûr′kəm·spek′shən] *n.* Watchful caution; prudence.

cir·cum·stance [sûr′kəm·stans′] *n.* 1 Something connected with an act or event: the *circumstances* of a crime. 2 An event, fact, or detail. 3 (*pl.*) Condition in life: a person in poor financial *circumstances.* 4 Formal display: pomp and *circumstance.* **—under the circumstances** Since such is the case.

cir·cum·stan·tial [sûr′kəm·stan′shəl] *adj.* 1 Having to do with or dependent on circumstances: *circumstantial* evidence. 2 Full of detail. 3 Not essential; incidental.

cir·cum·vent [sûr′kəm·vent′] *v.* 1 To trap or get the better of by cleverness or slyness. 2 To avoid or go around. **—cir′cum·ven′tion** *n.*

cir·cus [sûr′kəs] *n.* 1 A traveling show, as of acrobats, clowns, or trained animals. 2 *informal* A funny, entertaining person or thing. 3 In ancient Rome, a stadium for sports and other events.

cirque [sûrk] *n.* A half basin with steep walls, cut by a glacier at the head of a valley.

cir·rho·sis [si·rō′sis] *n.* A disease in which the healthy cells in a body organ are gradually destroyed and replaced by scar tissue. Cirrhosis of the liver, the most common form, often strikes chronic alcoholics.

cir·rus [sir′əs] *n., pl.* **cir·ri** [sir′ī] A kind of cloud seen as feathery bands in the sky.

Cirrus clouds

cis·tern [sis′tərn] *n.* A tank for storing water or other liquids.

cit·a·del [sit′ə·dəl] *n.* A fortress overlooking a town or city.

ci·ta·tion [sī·tā′shən] *n.* 1 The act of quoting or mentioning someone or something. 2 A person or thing quoted or mentioned. 3 A public commendation or award. 4 A summons.

cite [sīt] *v.* **cit·ed, cit·ing** 1 To quote or mention as an example or authority. 2 To mention in a report, as for bravery. 3 To summon to a court of law. ◆ See SITE.

cit·i·zen [sit′ə·zən] *n.* 1 A person who is born in or made a member of a country or nation. A citizen has certain rights and owes certain duties. 2 A resident of a city or town.

cit·i·zen·ry [sit′ə·zən·rē] *n.* Citizens as a group: an aroused local *citizenry.*

citizens band A range of radio frequencies used for short-distance communication by private citizens.

cit·i·zen·ship [sit′ə·zən·ship′] *n.* The condition of being a citizen, with its rights and duties.

cit·rate [sit′rāt′] *n.* A salt of citric acid.

cit·ric [sit′rik] *adj.* Of or obtained from citrus fruit.

citric acid A weak acid found in citrus fruit.

cit·ron [sit′rən] *n.* 1 A fruit like a lemon, but larger and less acid. 2 The tree it grows on. 3 The rind of this fruit, candied and used in foods such as cakes and puddings.

cit·ron·el·la [sit′rə·nel′ə] *n.* 1 An oil used in making perfumes, in cooking, and to keep mosquitoes away. 2 The grass it comes from.

cit·rus [sit′rəs] *n.* 1 Any tree that bears oranges, lemons, grapefruit, limes, or related fruit. 2 The fruit of any such tree. 3 *adj. use: citrus* fruit.

cit·y [sit′ē] *n., pl.* **cit·ies** 1 A large town that takes care of its own affairs. 2 In the U.S., a local government organized and operated on the basis of a charter from its state. 3 The people of a city, as a group. 4 *adj. use: city* politics.

city hall The building where the government of a city is located.

city manager A person appointed by a city government to take charge of managing the city.

city-state [sit′ē·stāt′] *n.* An independent political unit consisting of a city and its surrounding territory. Ancient Athens and Sparta were city-states.

civ·et [siv′it] *n.* 1 A small, spotted animal of Africa and Asia, often called **civet cat.** 2 A musky substance secreted by the civet, used in making perfume.

civ·ic [siv′ik] *adj.* Of or having to do with a city, a citizen, or citizenship.

civ·ics [siv′iks] *n.pl.* The study of citizenship and government. ◆ See -ICS.

civ·il [siv′əl] *adj.* 1 Of or having to do with citizens or citizenship. 2 Not connected with the armed forces or the church. 3 Within a state or nation: a *civil* war. 4 Civilized; polite; courteous: a *civil* answer. **—civ′il·ly** *adv.*

civil defense Plans and facilities for protecting people and property in case of enemy attack or natural disasters.

civil disobedience The refusal to obey laws that one considers unjust or wrong, especially as a means of publicly protesting against these laws.

civil engineer An engineer trained to plan and build roads, harbors, bridges, tunnels, dams, and other structures. **—civil engineering**

ci·vil·ian [sə·vil′yən] *n.* 1 A person who is not in active military service. 2 *adj. use: civilian* life; *civilian* clothes.

ci·vil·i·ty [sə·vil′ə·tē] *n., pl.* **ci·vil·i·ties** 1 Courtesy; politeness. 2 A polite action.

civ·i·li·za·tion [siv′ə·lə·zā′shən] *n.* 1 A stage of human society in which there is a high level of culture and well-developed industry and science. 2 Civilized countries or peoples. 3 The society and culture of a particular people, place, or period.

civ·i·lize [siv′ə·līz′] *v.* **civ·i·lized, civ·i·liz·ing** To bring from a primitive way of life into a state of civilization.

civil law The body of laws dealing with the private rights of citizens of a state or nation.

civil liberties Freedom within the law to think, speak, and act as one likes.

civil marriage A marriage ceremony performed by a government official.

civil rights The rights and privileges of a citizen, especially, in the U.S., the rights guaranteed by the 13th, 14th, 15th, and 19th amendments to the Constitution.

civil service The administrative services of a government, excluding the armed forces, the courts, and the legislature.

Civil War 1 The war between the Union and the Confederacy from 1861 to 1865. 2 (*written* **civil war**) A war between groups of citizens of the same country.

cl or **cl.** centiliter(s).

cl. 1 claim. 2 class. 3 clause. 4 clearance.

Cl The symbol for the element chlorine.

clab·ber [klab′ər] 1 *n.* Curdled milk. 2 *v.* To form clots when souring; curdle.

clack [klak] 1 *v.* To make or cause to make a sharp, dry sound. 2 *n.* Such a sound.

clad [klad] An alternative past tense and past participle of CLOTHE: The graduate was *clad* in white.

claim [klām] 1 *v.* To demand what is one's own or one's right: to *claim* one's wages. 2 *n.* A demand for what is rightfully due to one. 3 *n.* A basis for claiming something: a *claim* to greatness. 4 *n.* Something that is claimed, as a piece of land. 5 *v.* To declare or maintain: to *claim* the truth of a report. 6 *n.* A declaration or statement: a *claim* of innocence. 7 *v.* To require or deserve: The problem *claims* our careful attention.

claim·ant [klā′mənt] *n.* A person who makes a claim.

clair·voy·ance [klâr·voi′əns] *n.* The supposed ability to see things that are out of sight.

clair·voy·ant [klâr·voi′ənt] 1 *adj.* Having clairvoyance. 2 *n.* A clairvoyant person.

clam [klam] *n., v.* **clammed, clam·ming** 1 *n.* A soft-bodied animal something like an oyster, having a shell in two hinged halves. Clams live in sand along the shore of the ocean or rivers and lakes. Some are good to eat. 2 *v.* To hunt or dig for clams. **—clam up** *informal* To refuse to speak.

clam·bake [klam′bāk′] *n.* *U.S.* A picnic where clams and other foods are baked.

clam·ber [klam′bər] *v.* To climb up or down with effort, using both hands and feet.

clam·my [klam′ē] *adj.* **clam·mi·er, clam·mi·est** Stickily soft and damp, and usually cold. **—clam·mi·ly** [klam′ə·lē] *adv.* **—clam′mi·ness** *n.*

clam·or [klam′ər] 1 *n.* A loud and continuous noise, especially a loud protest or outcry. 2 *v.* To make a clamor.

clam·or·ous [klam′ər·əs] *adj.* 1 Full of clamor; noisy. 2 Loudly insistent or complaining. **—clam′or·ous·ly** *adv.* **—clam′or·ous·ness** *n.*

clamp [klamp] 1 *n.* A device having parts that can be brought together by a screw or spring to hold something. 2 *v.* To hold or bind with or as if with a clamp. **—clamp down** *U.S. informal* To become more strict.

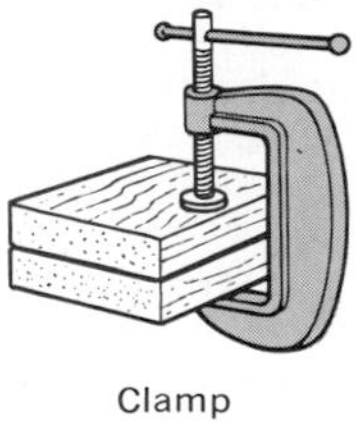
Clamp

clan [klan] *n.* 1 A group of families claiming descent from a common ancestor. 2 A group of people bound by a common interest.

clan·des·tine [klan·des′tin] *adj.* Kept secret, often for an evil reason: a *clandestine* plot. **—clan·des′tine·ly** *adv.* **—clan·des′tine·ness** *n.*

clang [klang] 1 *v.* To make or cause to make a loud, ringing, metallic sound. 2 *n.* This sound.

clan·gor [klang′(g)ər] *n.* 1 A clang. 2 Repeated clanging. **—clan′gor·ous** *adj.*

clank [klangk] 1 *v.* To make or cause to make a short, harsh, metallic sound. 2 *n.* This sound.

clan·nish [klan′ish] *adj.* 1 Of or having to do with a clan. 2 Closely united, like a family; bound by family traditions, prejudices, and other shared feelings.

clans·man [klanz′mən] *n., pl.* **clans·men** [klanz′·mən] A member of a clan.

clap [klap] *v.* **clapped, clap·ping,** *n.* 1 *v.* To strike (the hands) together with a sharp sound. 2 *n.* A loud, sharp sound: a *clap* of thunder. 3 *v.* To make or cause to make a clap by striking: to *clap* books together. 4 *v.* To slap with the palm of the hand: to *clap* someone on the back. 5 *n.* A slap. 6 *v.* To put or place quickly: They *clapped* them into jail.

clap·board [klab′ərd *or* klap′bôrd′] *n.* A thin board having one edge thinner than the other, used as siding on wooden buildings.

clap·per [klap′ər] *n.* 1 The tongue of a bell. 2 A person or thing that claps.

clap·trap [klap′trap′] *n.* Nonsense.

claque [klak] *n.* A group hired to applaud a performance.

clar·et [klar′ət] *n.* 1 A dry, red wine. 2 *adj., n.* Deep purplish red.

clar·i·fi·ca·tion [klar′ə·fə·kā′shən] *n.* The act or process of clarifying.

clar·i·fy [klar′ə·fī] *v.* **clar·i·fied, clar·i·fy·ing** 1 To make or become clear or pure, as a liquid. 2 To make or become understandable.

a add	**i** it	**o͝o** took	**oi** oil
ā ace	**ī** ice	**o͞o** pool	**ou** pout
â care	**o** odd	**u** up	**ng** ring
ä palm	**ō** open	**û** burn	**th** thin
e end	**ô** order	**yo͞o** fuse	**th** this
ē equal			**zh** vision

ə = a in *above*, e in *sicken*, i in *possible*, o in *melon*, u in *circus*

clar·i·net [klar′ə·net′] *n.* A high-pitched woodwind musical instrument having a cylindrical body and a single-reed mouthpiece.

Clarinet

clar·i·on [klar′ē·ən] **1** *n.* An old-fashioned kind of trumpet. **2** *n.* The sound of a clarion. **3** *adj.* Clear and piercing, as a trumpet sound.

clar·i·ty [klar′ə·tē] *n.* Clearness.

clash [klash] **1** *v.* To hit or cause to hit with a harsh, metallic sound: The cymbals *clashed.* **2** *n.* A harsh, metallic sound. **3** *v.* To be in opposition; conflict. **4** *n.* A conflict.

clasp [klasp] **1** *n.* A fastening, as a hook, by which things or parts are held together. **2** *v.* To fasten with or as if with a clasp. **3** *n.* A firm grasp or embrace. **4** *v.* To grasp or embrace.

class [klas] **1** *n.* A group of persons or things that have something in common: the working *class*; the *class* of odd numbers. **2** *v.* To put in a class; classify. **3** *n.* A division, as of people or objects, according to quality or rank: to travel in first *class.* **4** *n.* A group of students who are taught or who graduate together. **5** *n.* A meeting at which a group of students is taught. **6** *n. slang* High quality or elegance; excellence: an outfit with *class.*

clas·sic [klas′ik] **1** *adj.* Being in the first class or highest rank, as in literature or art. **2** *n.* A novel, symphony, or other work, of such quality. **3** *n.* A person who creates work of such quality. **4** *adj.* Following strict or formal rules, principles, or conditions. **5** *adj.* Of or characteristic of the art, literature, or culture of ancient Greece and Rome. **6** *adj.* Customary; traditional: a *classic* holiday meal. **7** *n.* A well-known or traditional event: a football *classic.* **—the classics** Ancient Greek and Roman literature.

clas·si·cal [klas′i·kəl] *adj.* **1** Of or characteristic of the arts or culture of ancient Greece and Rome. **2** Following a strict, established form, as a fugue. **3** Formal or serious, as in nature or form. **4** High in quality; first-rate. **—clas′si·cal·ly** *adv.*

clas·si·cism [klas′ə·siz′əm] *n.* **1** The principles, as of simplicity and balance, found in classical art. **2** Observance of these principles. **—clas′si·cist** *n.*

clas·si·fi·ca·tion [klas′ə·fə·kā′shən] *n.* The act, process, or result of classifying.

clas·si·fied [klas′ə·fīd′] *adj.* **1** Arranged or placed in a class. **2** Secret; confidential: *classified* information. **3** Consisting of classified advertisements: the *classified* section of a newspaper.

classified advertisement A brief advertisement printed in a newspaper.

clas·si·fy [klas′ə·fī] *v.* **clas·si·fied, clas·si·fy·ing** To put or divide into classes or groups: to *classify* books. **—clas′si·fi′er** *n.*

class·mate [klas′māt′] *n.* A member of the same class in school or college.

class·room [klas′rōōm′ *or* klas′rŏŏm′] *n.* A room in a school or college where classes are held.

class·y [klas′ē] *adj.* **class·i·er, class·i·est** *slang* Stylish; elegant.

clat·ter [klat′ər] **1** *v.* To move with or make a clashing noise. **2** *n.* A clashing noise, as of horses' hoofs on pavement. **3** *v.* To talk or chatter noisily. **4** *n.* Noisy chatter.

clause [klôz] *n.* **1** A group of words having a subject and predicate and forming part of a sentence. Some clauses can stand alone; others cannot. **2** A single point or article of a law, will, treaty, or contract.

claus·tro·pho·bi·a [klôs′trə·fō′bē·ə] *n.* An abnormal fear of being in a small or enclosed space. **—claus′·tro·pho′bic** *adj.*

clav·i·chord [klav′ə·kôrd′] *n.* An early keyboard musical instrument like the piano but smaller and not as loud. Its keys were directly attached to metal wedges that struck the strings. ◆ *Clavichord, clavier,* and *clavicle* all go back to the Latin word *clavis,* key. *Clavichords* and *claviers* are instruments played with keys, and the *clavicle* bone is shaped somewhat like an old-fashioned door key.

clav·i·cle [klav′ə·kəl] *n.* The bone connecting the shoulder blade and breastbone; collarbone. ◆ See CLAVICHORD.

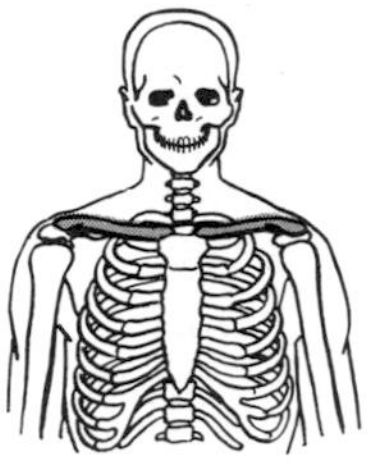
Clavicles

clav·ier [klə·vir′] *n.* **1** A musical keyboard. **2** An early type of keyboard instrument. ◆ See CLAVICHORD.

claw [klô] **1** *n.* A sharp, hooked nail on the toe of an animal or bird. **2** *n.* A foot with claws. **3** *v.* To tear, scratch, dig, or pull, with or as if with claws. **4** *n.* A pincer of a lobster, crab, scorpion, or similar animal. **5** *n.* Something shaped like a claw, as the forked end of a hammer.

clay [klā] *n.* **1** A fine-grained earth that can be molded when wet, used in making such things as bricks, tiles, and pottery. **2** The human body: used in this sense in the Bible.

clay·ey [klā′ē] *adj.* **clay·i·er, clay·i·est** Of, like, full of, or covered with clay.

clay pigeon A clay disk hurled into the air as a target in trapshooting.

clean [klēn] **1** *adj.* Free from dirt or stain. **2** *v.* To make clean. **3** *v.* To do cleaning: We *clean* on Saturdays. **4** *adv.* To a condition of cleanness: to wash a cup *clean.* **5** *adj.* Complete: a *clean* miss. **6** *adv.* Wholly; completely: You're *clean* wrong. **7** *adj.* Wholesome; virtuous: a *clean* life. **8** *adj.* Free of faults or flaws: a *clean* record. **9** *adj.* Neat in habits or work. **10** *adj.* Skillfully or properly made or done: a *clean* hit. **11** *adj.* Of pleasing proportions: *clean* features. **—clean out** **1** To empty, as of contents or occupants. **2** *informal* To use up all the money of. **—clean up** **1** To clean completely. **2** *informal* To finish. **3** *slang* To make a large profit. **—clean′ness** *n.*

clean-cut [klēn′kut′] *adj.* **1** Sharply outlined; distinct. **2** Neat and wholesome in appearance.

clean·er [klē′nər] *n.* **1** A person whose work is cleaning. **2** A substance or machine used for cleaning.

clean·ly [*adv.* klēn′lē, *adj.* klen′lē] *adv., adj.* **clean·li·er, clean·li·est** **1** *adv.* In a clean way. **2** *adj.* Clean and neat by habit: a *cleanly* person. **—clean·li·ness** [klen′lē·nis] *n.*

cleanse [klenz] *v.* **cleansed, cleans·ing** To make clean or pure.

cleans·er [klen′zər] *n.* A cleaning substance, as a detergent.

clear [klir] **1** *adj.* Easily seen through; transparent:

a *clear* glass. **2** *adj.* Not blocked: a *clear* road. **3** *adj.* Free of clouds or fog: a *clear* day. **4** *adj.* With no blemish: a *clear* skin. **5** *adj.* Distinct and without blurs: a *clear* picture. **6** *v.* To make clear. **7** *v.* To become clear. **8** *adj.* Plain and understandable: *clear* instructions. **9** *adv.* In a clear way: Shout loud and *clear.* **10** *adj.* Obvious; plain: a *clear* case of fraud. **11** *adj.* Keen and alert: a *clear* head. **12** *v.* To remove; get rid of: to *clear* away junk. **13** *v.* To get by, under, or over without touching: The ball *cleared* the fence. **14** *adv. informal* Completely: to go *clear* over a fence. **15** *adj.* Free from guilt or shame: a *clear* conscience. **16** *v.* To free of blame or suspicion: to *clear* a defendant. **17** *adj.* Net: a *clear* profit of $500. **18** *v.* To receive after all expenses have been deducted: to *clear* $50. **—clear up** **1** To make clear. **2** To become clear, as weather. **3** To free from confusion or mystery. **—in the clear** **1** In the open; not blocked or confined. **2** Free from guilt or suspicion. **3** Not in code. **—clear′ly** *adv.* **—clear′·ness** *n.*

clear·ance [klir′əns] *n.* **1** The act of clearing. **2** A clear space, especially between a moving thing and a stationary thing. **3** Disposal of goods, as in a sale. **4** Permission or approval.

Clearance

clear-cut [klir′kut′] *adj.* **1** Sharply outlined. **2** Plain; obvious.

clear·ing [klir′ing] *n.* An area that is free of trees but surrounded by them.

clear·ing·house [klir′ing·hous′] *n.* **1** An office where banks exchange checks and settle accounts and claims. **2** A central location or agency for receiving, classifying, and giving out information.

cleat [klēt] *n.* **1** A piece of wood or metal, fastened to a surface to provide strength or secure footing. **2** A wood or metal fixture with arms to which a rope may be fastened.

cleav·age [klē′vij] *n.* **1** A cleaving. **2** A split. **3** A tendency in some rocks or crystals to split in certain planes.

cleave[1] [klēv] *v.* **cleft** or **cleaved** or **clove, cleft** or **cleaved** or **clo·ven, cleav·ing** **1** To split, as with an ax or wedge. **2** To cut through; penetrate.

cleave[2] [klēv] *v.* **cleaved, cleav·ing** To stick fast; cling: to *cleave* to a principle.

cleav·er [klē′vər] *n.* A butcher's chopper, with a broad, heavy blade and short handle.

clef [klef] *n.* In music, a sign that indicates the pitch of the notes written on each of the lines and spaces of a staff.

cleft [kleft] **1** Past tense and past participle of CLEAVE[1]. **2** *adj.* Divided or split, wholly or partly. **3** *n.* A division between two parts; crack or dent, as in the chin.

cleft palate A lengthwise split in the roof of the mouth. It is a birth defect that can be corrected by surgery.

clem·a·tis [klem′ə·tis] *n.* A climbing vine usually having purple or white flowers.

clem·en·cy [klem′ən·sē] *n.* **1** Mildness in judging; mercy. **2** Mildness, as of weather.

clem·ent [klem′ənt] *adj.* **1** Merciful or lenient; not harsh. **2** Mild: said about weather.

clench [klench] **1** *v.* To grasp or grip firmly. **2** *n.* A tight grip. **3** *v.* To close tightly or lock, as the fist or teeth.

cler·gy [klûr′jē] *n., pl.* **cler·gies** All the people ordained for the service of God, as ministers, priests, and rabbis.

cler·gy·man [klûr′jē·mən] *n., pl.* **cler·gy·men** [klûr′·jē·mən] A member of the clergy.

cler·gy·wom·an [klûr′jē·wo͝om′ən] *n., pl.* **cler·gy·wom·en** [klûr′jē·wim′in] A woman member of the clergy.

cler·ic [kler′ik] *n.* A member of the clergy.

cler·i·cal [kler′i·kəl] *adj.* **1** Of or related to clerks in offices or their work: a *clerical* error. **2** Having to do with the clergy.

clerk [klûrk] **1** *n.* An office worker whose tasks include keeping records or accounts and attending to files. **2** *n.* An official or employee, as of a court or government, who keeps records and performs other duties. **3** *n. U.S.* A person who sells goods in a store. **4** *v.* To work as a clerk.

clev·er [klev′ər] *adj.* **1** Good at learning and solving problems; bright; ingenious. **2** Skillful, as in work with the hands. **3** Exhibiting skill, wit, or sharp thinking: a *clever* remark. **—clev′er·ly** *adv.* **—clev′er·ness** *n.*

clew [klo͞o] *n.* **1** A ball of yarn, thread, or cord. **2** Another spelling of CLUE. **3** A lower corner of a sail or a loop at the corner.

cli·ché [klē·shā′] *n.* An expression that has lost its original point and freshness from too much use. *As busy as a bee* is a cliché.

click [klik] **1** *n.* A short, sharp sound: the *click* of knitting needles. **2** *v.* To make or cause to make a click or clicks: heels *clicking* across the floor. **3** *v. slang* To succeed.

cli·ent [klī′ənt] *n.* **1** A person consulting a professional, as a lawyer. **2** A customer.

cli·en·tele [klī′ən·tel′] *n.* One's group of clients or customers: an exclusive *clientele.*

cliff [klif] *n.* A high, steep face of rock rising sharply above the ground or water below.

cliff dweller **1** A member of a prehistoric American Indian people of the sw U.S. who made their homes on ledges or in caves along the walls of cliffs. **2** A person who lives in a large, tall apartment house, especially in a city.

cliff-hang·er [klif′hang′ər] *n.* An exciting story or contest whose outcome is in doubt until the very end.

cli·mac·tic [kli·mak′tik] *adj.* Of having to do with, or forming a climax.

cli·mate [klī′mit] *n.* **1** The kind of weather a place usually has over a long period. **2** A region having given weather conditions: to go to a cool, dry *climate.* **3** An atmosphere or trend among people.

cli·mat·ic [klī·mat′ik] *adj.* Of or having to do with climate.

a	add	**i**	it	**o͝o**	took	**oi**	oil
ā	ace	**ī**	ice	**o͞o**	pool	**ou**	pout
â	care	**o**	odd	**u**	up	**ng**	ring
ä	palm	**ō**	open	**û**	burn	**th**	thin
e	end	**ô**	order	**yo͞o**	fuse	**th̶**	this
ē	equal					**zh**	vision

ə = {a in *above* e in *sicken* i in *possible* / o in *melon* u in *circus*}

cli·ma·tol·o·gy [klī′mə·tol′ə·gē] *n.* The science dealing with climates. **—cli′ma·tol′o·gist** *n.*
cli·max [klī′maks′] *n.* The point of highest interest or greatest effect, coming at or near the end, as of an action or a series of events.
climb [klīm] 1 *v.* To go up or down by means of the feet and sometimes the hands: to *climb* a mountain; to *climb* down from a ledge. 2 *n.* The action of climbing. 3 *n.* A place to be climbed: a steep *climb.* 4 *v.* To rise in position: The kite *climbed* higher. 5 *v.* To grow up, as certain vines, by twining around or clinging to a support.
climb·er [klī′mər] *n.* 1 A person or thing that climbs. 2 A plant that climbs, as a vine.
clime [klīm] *n.* A country, region, or climate: used mostly in poems.
clinch [klinch] 1 *v.* To fix firmly in place, as a driven nail or staple, by bending over the part that sticks out. 2 *v.* To make sure; settle: Our offer to reduce the price *clinched* the sale. 3 *v.* To grip an opponent closely, as in boxing. 4 *n.* The act of clinching.
clinch·er [klinch′ər] *n.* 1 A person or thing that clinches. 2 A fact or point that decides an issue or settles an argument.
cling [kling] *v.* **clung, cling·ing** To hold tight; stick: His wet coat *clung* to his back.
cling·stone [kling′stōn′] *n.* A fruit, especially a peach, having a stone that clings to its flesh.
clin·ic [klin′ik] *n.* 1 A special department of a hospital or medical school where people can come in for medical treatment, often at little or no cost. 2 A place where patients are studied and treated by specialists. 3 The teaching of medicine by treating patients in front of a class. 4 A place where advice on specific problems is given: a sales *clinic.*
clin·i·cal [klin′i·kəl] *adj.* 1 Of, like, or having to do with a clinic. 2 Used for sick people. 3 Coldly objective. **—clin′i·cal·ly** *adv.*
clink [klingk] 1 *v.* To make or cause to make a short, ringing sound, as of glasses struck together lightly. 2 *n.* A clinking sound.
clink·er [kling′kər] *n.* A stony mass of rough cinder sometimes left after coal burns.
clip[1] [klip] *v.* **clipped, clip·ping,** *n.* 1 *v.* To cut, cut short, or cut out, as with scissors or shears: to *clip* hair; to *clip* a coupon. 2 *v.* To trim the wool, hair, or excess growth of: to *clip* a sheep; to *clip* a hedge. 3 *n.* The act of clipping. 4 *v. informal* To strike with a quick, sharp blow: I was *clipped* on the chin. 5 *n. informal* A quick, sharp blow. 6 *v. informal* To move swiftly. 7 *n. informal* A quick pace: to go at a good *clip.*
clip[2] [klip] *n., v.* **clipped, clip·ping** 1 *n.* A device that clasps or holds things together, especially papers. 2 *v.* To fasten with a clip: *Clip* the check to the letter.
clip·board [klip′bôrd′] *n.* A board with a clip at the top, used to hold papers for writing.

Clipboard

clip·per [klip′ər] *n.* 1 (*usually pl.*) A tool for clipping. 2 A person who clips. 3 A sailing ship of the 19th century, built for speed, having slender lines and an overhanging bow.
clip·ping [klip′ing] *n.* A part clipped off or out, as an article cut from a newspaper or a branch of a plant to form a new plant.
clique [klēk *or* klik] *n.* A small group whose members stick together and shut out outsiders.
cli·quish [klē′kish *or* kli′kish] *adj.* 1 Forming or apt to form cliques. 2 Like a clique: *cliquish* office workers.
clo·a·ca [klō·ā′kə] *n., pl.* **clo·a·cae** [klō·ā′sē] A small saclike part at the lower end of the digestive tract of birds, frogs, and some other animals. It holds and discharges eggs and sperm as well as body wastes. ◆ *Cloaca* comes from a Latin word meaning *sewer.*
cloak [klōk] 1 *n.* A loose outer garment, usually without sleeves. 2 *v.* To cover with a cloak. 3 *n.* Something that covers or hides: Darkness is a *cloak* for thieves. 4 *v.* To conceal: She *cloaked* her disappointment under a smile.
cloak·room [klōk′ro͞om′ *or* klōk′ro͝om′] *n.* A room where such items as coats, hats, and luggage are left for a short time.
clob·ber [klob′ər] *v. slang* 1 To hit very hard; smash. 2 To defeat by a wide margin.
clock[1] [klok] 1 *n.* An instrument for measuring and telling the time, usually by pointers, or hands, moving around a dial. A clock is not made to be worn or carried on the person as a watch is. 2 *v.* To measure the speed or time of: to *clock* a race.
clock[2] [klok] *n.* An ornamental design on the side of a sock or stocking at the ankle.
clock·wise [klok′wīz′] *adv., adj.* In the direction traveled by the hands of a clock: We skated around the pond *clockwise.*
clock·work [klok′wûrk′] *n.* A machine driven by a spring, such as that used to run a clock or a mechanical toy. **—like clockwork** In a regular, precise, orderly way: The convention was well planned and everything went off *like clockwork.*
clod [klod] *n.* 1 A lump, as of earth or clay. 2 A dull, stupid person; dolt.
clod·hop·per [klod′hop′ər] *n.* 1 *informal* A rustic person; hick. 2 (*pl.*) Big, heavy shoes.
clog [klog] *v.* **clogged, clog·ging,** *n.* 1 *v.* To make or become stopped up or blocked up: Hair had *clogged* the drain. 2 *v.* To slow down or hold back; hinder. 3 *n.* Anything interfering with movement. 4 *n.* A shoe with a wooden sole.
clois·ter [klois′tər] 1 *n.* A covered walk, often around a courtyard, as of a monastery or college. 2 *n.* A place of religious retirement; monastery or convent. 3 *v.* To put away from the world, as in a convent or monastery. 4 *n.* Any quiet, solitary place.

Cloister

clone [klōn] *n., v.* **cloned, clon·ing** 1 *n.* An organism or a group of organisms produced asexually from a single ancestor. A clone has exactly the same genes as its one parent. 2 *v.* To make a genetic duplicate of; reproduce asexually. 3 *n.* An exact copy or duplicate.
close [*adj., adv.* klōs, *v., n.* klōz] *adj.* **clos·er, clos·est,** *adv., v.* **closed, clos·ing,** *n.* 1 *adj.* Near or near together in space, time, or relationship: *close* as-

sociates. 2 *adv.* Near: Stay *close* to home. 3 *adv.* In a close way; closely: following too *close.* 4 *v.* To bring together; join, as parts of an electric circuit. 5 *adj.* Having the parts near to each other; compact: a *close* weave. 6 *adj.* Lacking extra space; cramped: *close* quarters. 7 *adj.* Stuffy, stifling, or muggy, as a room or the weather. 8 *n.* [klōs] An enclosed place. 9 *v.* To shut, as a door. 10 *v.* To fill or block up: to *close* a gap. 11 *v.* To bring or come to an end: to *close* a chapter. 12 *n.* The end: the *close* of day. 13 *adj.* Near to the surface, as a shave or haircut. 14 *adj.* Very near to an original: a *close* resemblance. 15 *adj.* Near and dear: a *close* friend. 16 *adj.* Almost even: said about contests. 17 *adj.* Strict or careful: *close* attention. 18 *adj.* Stingy, as with money. 19 *adj.* Strictly guarded or hidden: *close* secrecy. 20 *adj.* Secretive: to be *close* about one's personal life. **—close down** To stop operating; shut down. **—close in** To advance from all sides so as to prevent escape. **—close out** *U.S.* To sell all of, as merchandise, at reduced prices. **—close·ly** [klōs'lē] *adv.* **—close·ness** [klōs'nis] *n.*

close call [klōs] *informal* A narrow escape.

closed circuit 1 An electric circuit that forms a path through which current can flow without interruption. 2 A television system for transmitting signals by cable to sets. Closed-circuit television is used in schools, factories, and building security systems. **—closed'-cir'cuit** *adj.*

closed shop A place of employment hiring only union members.

close-fisted [klōs'fis'təd] *adj.* Stingy; ungenerous.

close-mouthed [klōs'mou~~th~~d' *or* klōs'moutht'] *adj.* Cautious about talking; reticent or secretive.

close·out [klōs'out'] *n.* A sale of merchandise at reduced prices.

clos·et [kloz'it] 1 *n. U.S.* A small room or alcove for storing things, as clothes or linens. 2 *n.* A small, private room. 3 *v.* To shut up in a room for a talk in private: The candidate was *closeted* with her campaign manager.

close-up [klōs'up'] *n.* 1 A picture or movie shot taken with the camera close to the subject. 2 A close look or view.

clo·sure [klō'zhər] *n.* 1 A closing or shutting up. 2 A way of putting an end to debate in a legislature in order to get a vote on an issue.

clot [klot] *n., v.* **clot·ted, clot·ting** 1 *n.* A mass resulting from a thickening of a liquid, as blood. 2 *v.* To form into clots or a clot.

cloth [klôth] *n., pl.* **cloths** [klô~~th~~z *or* klôths] 1 A fabric made of fibers, as wool, cotton, or rayon. 2 A piece of such material for a special use, as a tablecloth. 3 *adj. use:* a *cloth* coat. **—the cloth** The clergy.

clothe [klō~~th~~] *v.* **clothed** or **clad, cloth·ing** 1 To cover or provide with clothes; dress. 2 To cover: Spring *clothed* the trees in blossoms.

clothes [klō(~~th~~)z] *n.pl.* 1 The articles of dress worn by people, as dresses, suits, and shirts; garments. 2 Bedclothes.

clothes·horse [klō(~~th~~)z'hôrs'] *n.* 1 A frame on which to hang clothes, as for airing out or drying. 2 A person who has an interest in and wears fashionable clothing.

clothes·line [klō(~~th~~)z'līn'] *n.* A cord, rope, or wire on which to hang clothes to dry.

clothes·pin [klō(~~th~~)z'pin'] *n.* A forked peg or clamp used to fasten clothes on a line.

clothes tree An upright pole with hooks or pegs at the top on which garments can be hung.

cloth·ier [klō~~th~~'yər] *n.* A person who makes or sells clothes or cloths.

cloth·ing [klō'~~th~~ing] *n.* Clothes in general.

clo·ture [klō'chər] *n.* Closure (def. 2).

cloud [kloud] 1 *n.* A white or dark mass floating up in the air, made up of tiny particles of water or ice. 2 *n.* A visible mass of dust, smoke, or steam. 3 *n.* A cloudlike mass of things in motion: a *cloud* of gnats. 4 *n.* Something that darkens or threatens: a *cloud* of gloom. 5 *v.* To cover or become covered with or as if with clouds; dim or darken. 6 *n.* A dark vein, as in marble. 7 *n.* A milkiness, as in liquids.

cloud·burst [kloud'bûrst'] *n.* A sudden, heavy downpour of rain.

cloud chamber A closed vessel containing air or gas overloaded with water vapor that forms dense fog along the paths taken by charged particles. Cloud chambers are used for observing the behavior of atomic radiation.

cloud·less [kloud'lis] *adj.* Free of clouds.

cloud·y [klou'dē] *adj.* **cloud·i·er, cloud·i·est** 1 Overcast with clouds. 2 Of or like clouds. 3 Not clear; misty or murky. 4 Streaked, as marble. 5 Gloomy. **—cloud'i·ness** *n.*

clout [klout] *informal* 1 *n.* A heavy blow. 2 *n.* In baseball, a long hit. 3 *v.* To hit hard.

clove[1] [klōv] *n.* A dried flower bud of a tropical evergreen tree, used as a spice in cookery.

clove[2] [klōv] *n.* One of the small inner sections of a large plant bulb, as of garlic.

clove[3] [klōv] An alternative past tense of CLEAVE[1].

clo·ven [klō'vən] 1 An alternative past participle of CLEAVE[1]. 2 *adj.* Split, as a hoof.

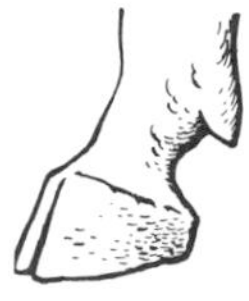
Cloven hoof

clo·ver [klō'vər] *n.* A low-growing plant with leaves normally having three leaflets but on rare occasions, four. It has fragrant white, red, yellow, or purple blossoms. It is grown as rich food for horses and cattle. **—in clover** Enjoying prosperity or luxuries without working.

clo·ver·leaf [klō'vər·lēf'] *n., pl.* **clo·ver·leafs** An intersection in which two highways crossing at different levels are connected by a system of curving ramps that allow a vehicle to change roads without interference.

Cloverleaf

clown [kloun] 1 *n.* A performer in a circus or pantomime who entertains, as by jokes or tricks; jester; buffoon. 2 *v.* To behave like a clown, as by acting silly. 3 *n.* A coarse or rude person; boor. **—clown'ish** *adj.*

a	add	**i**	it	**o͝o**	took	**oi**	oil
ā	ace	**ī**	ice	**o͞o**	pool	**ou**	pout
â	care	**o**	odd	**u**	up	**ng**	ring
ä	palm	**ō**	open	**û**	burn	**th**	thin
e	end	**ô**	order	**yo͞o**	fuse	**~~th~~**	this
ē	equal					**zh**	vision

ə = { a in *above*   e in *sicken*   i in *possible*   o in *melon*   u in *circus* }

cloy [kloi] *v.* To displease with too much of a good thing: appetites *cloyed* with sweets.

club [klub] *n., v.* **clubbed, club·bing** 1 *n.* A heavy wooden stick for use as a weapon, generally thicker at one end. 2 *v.* To beat, as with a club. 3 *n.* A stick or bat used to hit a ball: a golf *club.* 4 *n.* A figure like this: ♣. 5 *n.* A playing card of the suit marked with black club figures. 6 *n.* (*pl.*) The suit so marked. 7 *n.* A group of people organized for enjoyment or for some purpose: a social *club.* 8 *n.* The building or room where such a group meets. 9 *v.* To unite for some purpose.

club car A railroad passenger car equipped with lounge chairs and other facilities such as card tables and a bar.

club·foot [klub′fo͝ot′] *n., pl.* **club·feet** [klub′fēt′] A deformity, usually present from birth, in which the foot is twisted out of shape.

club·house [klub′hous′] *n.* 1 A building used by a club. 2 The locker room of a sports team.

club moss Any of various low-growing evergreen plants with small, needlelike leaves and no flowers.

club sandwich A sandwich with many layers.

club soda Another name for SODA WATER.

cluck [kluk] 1 *v.* To make a low, throaty, clicking sound such as a hen makes when calling her chicks. 2 *n.* Such a sound.

clue [klo͞o] *n.* A hint or piece of evidence, helpful in solving a problem or mystery.

clump [klump] 1 *n.* A group of similar things very close together; tight cluster: a *clump* of bushes. 2 *n.* An irregular mass; lump: a *clump* of earth. 3 *n.* A compact mass, as of bacteria. 4 *v.* To form or cause to form clumps. 5 *n.* A heavy, dull sound, as of tramping. 6 *v.* To walk heavily and noisily.

clumsy [klum′zē] *adj.* **clum·si·er, clum·si·est** 1 Lacking control; not graceful; awkward: a *clumsy* puppy. 2 Not well made, said, or done: *clumsy* excuses. **—clum′si·ly** *adv.* **—clum′si·ness** *n.*

clung [klung] Past tense and past participle of CLING: The monkey *clung* to the cage.

clus·ter [klus′tər] 1 *n.* A group of things of the same kind growing or found together: a flower *cluster.* 2 *v.* To form into a cluster or clusters: The campers *clustered* around the fire.

clutch[1] [kluch] 1 *v.* To grasp and hold firmly. 2 *n.* A tight grip or grasp. 3 *n.* (*pl.*) Power or control: in the *clutches* of the police. 4 *v.* To seize or reach for eagerly or desperately; snatch. 5 *n.* A device in a machine for connecting or disconnecting driving and driven parts. Many cars have clutches to permit the shifting of gears or stopping. 6 *n.* The pedal or lever operating this device.

clutch[2] [kluch] *n.* 1 A number of eggs laid at one time. 2 A brood of chickens hatched together.

clut·ter [klut′ər] 1 *n.* A collection of things scattered without order; litter. 2 *v.* To fill or cover with disordered or worthless things: to *clutter* up a closet or a shelf.

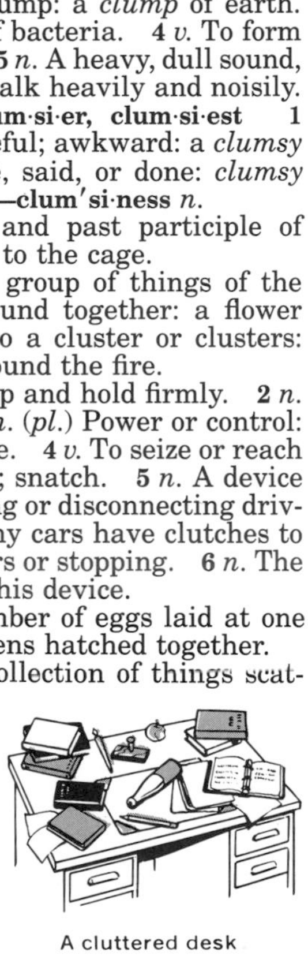

A cluttered desk

Cly·tem·nes·tra [klī′təm·nes′trə] *n.* In Greek myths, the wife of Agamemnon and the mother of Electra and Orestes. She killed her husband and was later killed by Orestes.

cm or **cm.** centimeter(s).

Cm The symbol for the element curium.

cmdr. or **Cmdr.** commander.

CNS or **C.N.S.** central nervous system.

co- A prefix meaning: 1 Together, as in *coexist.* 2 With another; joint, as in *coauthor.*

co. or **Co.** 1 company. 2 county.

c.o. or **c/o** in care of.

Co The symbol for the element cobalt.

CO 1 Postal Service abbreviation of Colorado. 2 commanding officer. 3 conscientious objector.

coach [kōch] 1 *n.* An old-fashioned, closed carriage pulled by horses. 2 *n.* A bus or railroad car in which passengers sit. 3 *n.* A teacher or trainer, as for pupils, athletes, or actors. 4 *v.* To instruct, train, or direct. 5 *v.* To tutor, as for a test.

coach·man [kōch′mən] *n., pl.* **coach·men** [kōch′·mən] A person who drives a coach.

co·ad·ju·tor [kō·aj′ə·tər *or* kō′ə·jo͞o′tər] *n.* 1 A person who assists another; helper. 2 An assistant to a bishop, often another bishop.

co·ag·u·lant [kō·ag′yə·lənt] *n.* A substance that causes a liquid, especially blood, to coagulate.

co·ag·u·late [kō·ag′yə·lāt′] *v.* **co·ag·u·lat·ed, co·ag·u·lat·ing** To change from a liquid to a thick mass; clot. **—co·ag′u·la′tion** *n.*

coal [kōl] 1 *n.* A black or dark brown mineral, mostly carbon, which gives off heat when burned. Coal was formed by decaying plants covered by land or water and under great pressure. 2 *n.* A glowing piece, as of coal or wood; ember. 3 *v.* To supply with or take on coal.

co·a·lesce [kō′ə·les′] *v.* **co·a·lesced, co·a·lesc·ing** To grow or come together into one; fuse, blend, or unite: Five groups of wagons *coalesced* to make a big train.

coal gas 1 Gas given off by burning coal. 2 A mixture of gases produced by heating bituminous coal without air, used as a fuel.

co·a·li·tion [kō′ə·lish′ən] *n.* A temporary alliance of leaders, parties, or nations.

coal oil Another term for KEROSENE.

coal·scut·tle [kōl′skut′(ə)l] *n.* A pail for carrying coal.

coal tar A black, gummy substance produced by the distillation of soft coal. It is the raw material for products such as dyes, explosives, and drugs.

coarse [kôrs] *adj.* **coars·er, coars·est** 1 Composed of large particles; not fine: *coarse* salt. 2 Rough: *coarse* skin. 3 Not refined; vulgar: *coarse* talk. 4 Inferior in quality: *coarse* food. **—coarse′ly** *adv.* **—coarse′ness** *n.*

coars·en [kôr′sən] *v.* To make or become coarse.

coast [kōst] 1 *n.* The land next to the sea; seashore. 2 *v.* To sail along a coast or the coast of. 3 *n.* A region near the sea. 4 *v.* To slide or ride down a slope, as on a sled or bicycle, with no force applied.

coast·al [kōs′təl] *adj.* Of, on, or near a coast: *coastal* waters.

coast·er [kōs′tər] *n.* 1 A person or ship that trades along a coast. 2 Something, as a sled or toboggan, used for coasting. 3 A small tray set under a glass to protect the surface, as of a table.

coast guard 1 A naval or military group whose duties include patrolling coasts, saving lives, and preventing smuggling. 2 (*written* **Coast Guard**) In the U.S., such a group that operates in peacetime under the Treasury Department and in wartime under the U.S. Navy.

coast·line [kōst′līn′] *n.* The outline or boundary of a coast.

coast·wise [kōst′wīz′] *adj., adv.* Along the coast.
coat [kōt] 1 *n.* An outer garment with sleeves as the jacket of a suit or an overcoat. 2 *n.* A natural covering or skin, as the fur of an animal. 3 *n.* Any layer covering a surface, as paint or ice. 4 *v.* To cover with a layer: *Coat* the walls with paint.
co·a·ti [kō·ä′tē] *n., pl.* **co·a·tis** An animal of tropical America related to and resembling the raccoon but having a longer body and tail and a long snout.
co·a·ti·mun·di [kō·ä′tē·mun′dē] *n., pl.* **co·a·ti·mun·dis** Another word for COATI.
coat·ing [kō′ting] *n.* 1 A covering; layer; coat. 2 Cloth for coats.
coat of arms A design, as on a shield, used as the symbol, as of a family or nation.
coat of mail *pl.* **coats of mail** A suit of armor made of metal chain or plates.
coat·room [kōt′ro͞om *or* kōt′ro͝om] *n.* Another word for CLOAKROOM.
coat·tail [kōt′tāl′] *n.* The loose lower part of a coat at the back, often split into two parts. **—on someone's coattails** By profiting from someone else's success.
co·au·thor [kō·ô′thər] 1 *n.* An author who writes in conjunction with another author. 2 *v.* To be a coauthor of.

Coat of arms

coax [kōks] *v.* 1 To ask or persuade in a gentle, flattering manner; wheedle: They *coaxed* me to bake a cake. 2 To obtain by coaxing: to *coax* a promise from someone.
co·ax·i·al cable [kō·ak′sē·əl] An electrical cable made up of pairs of conductors arranged so that one of each pair surrounds the other and is separated from it by an insulator, used to carry radio and television signals.
cob [kob] *n.* 1 The center of an ear of corn, on which the kernels grow. 2 A male swan. 3 A heavy horse with short legs.
co·balt [kō′bôlt′] *n.* A hard, brittle metallic element resembling nickel, used in alloys. Brilliant blues in porcelain and glass are often due to cobalt compounds.
cobalt blue 1 A greenish blue pigment made from a mixture of cobalt and aluminum oxides. 2 Dark blue or greenish blue.
cobalt 60 A radioactive isotope of cobalt used in medicine and industry.
cob·ble[1] [kob′əl] *n.* A cobblestone.
cob·ble[2] [kob′əl] *v.* **cob·bled, cob·bling** To make or repair, as boots or shoes.
cob·bler[1] [kob′lər] *n.* A shoemaker.
cob·bler[2] [kob′lər] *n.* A fruit pie baked in a deep dish, with no bottom crust.
cob·ble·stone [kob′əl·stōn′] *n.* A rounded stone formerly used for paving streets.
co·bel·lig·er·ent [kō′bə·lij′ər·ənt] *n.* A nation fighting or cooperating with another nation in a war against a common enemy, often with no formal alliance.
CO·BOL [kō′bôl] *n.* The most widely used computer programming language for solving business problems. ◆ *COBOL* comes from *CO(mmon) B(usiness) O(riented) L(anguage).*
co·bra [kō′brə] *n.* A very poisonous snake of Asia and Africa that can swell its neck into a hood when excited.
cob·web [kob′web′] *n.* 1 The delicate web spun by a spider. 2 Anything delicate like a cobweb.
co·caine [kō·kān′ *or* kō′kān′] *n.* A white, bitter substance, used as a drug to deaden pain.
coc·cus [kok′əs] *n., pl.* **coc·ci** [kok′sī] Any of a large group of bacteria having an oval shape.
coc·cyx [kok′siks] *n., pl.* **coc·cy·ges** [kok′si·jez′] A small, triangular bone at the lower end of the human spinal column. ◆ *Coccyx* comes from the Greek word meaning *cuckoo,* because early students of anatomy thought the bone resembled this bird's beak.
coch·i·neal [koch′ə·nēl′ *or* koch′ə·nēl′] *n.* A bright red dye made by drying and powdering the bodies of female cochineal insects.
cochineal insect A small insect found primarily in Mexico that has a bright red body.
coch·le·a [kok′lē·ə] *n., pl.* **coch·le·ae** [kok′lē·ē′] A small, hollow organ in the inner ear shaped like a snail shell, containing the sensory ends of the auditory nerve.
cock[1] [kok] 1 *n.* A male bird, especially a rooster. 2 *n.* A faucet or tap. 3 *n.* The hammer of a gun or its position when set for firing. 4 *v.* To put the cock of (a gun) into firing position. 5 *v.* To put into a ready position: He *cocked* his fists. 6 *v.* To turn up or to one side alertly or inquisitively: to *cock* the head. 7 *n.* A tipping or turning up, as of a hat brim: a jaunty *cock.*
cock[2] [kok] *n.* A cone-shaped pile of hay or straw.
cock·ade [kok·ād′] *n.* A rosette or decoration, as worn on the hat or lapel.
cock·a·too [kok′ə·to͞o′] *n., pl.* **cock·a·toos** Any of several brightly colored parrots with crests, found in Australasia.
cock·a·trice [kok′ə·tris *or* kok′ə·trīs′] *n.* In folk tales, a serpent hatched from a bird's egg, whose look was said to be deadly.
cocked hat A hat with the brim turned up in such a way that it has a three-cornered look.
cock·er·el [kok′ər·əl] *n.* A young rooster.
cock·er spaniel [kok′ər] A small dog with long ears and silky hair, used as a house pet and for hunting. It is also called a **cocker.**
cock·eyed [kok′īd′] *adj.* 1 Cross-eyed. 2 *slang* Off center; crooked. 3 *slang* Ridiculous.
cock·fight [kok′fīt′] *n.* A fight between gamecocks, usually with spurs attached to their legs.

Cocker spaniel

cock·le[1] [kok′əl] *n.* 1 An edible shellfish with ridged shells. 2 A cockleshell. 3 A wrinkle; pucker. **—warm the cockles of one's heart** To give heartfelt joy or pleasure.
cock·le[2] [kok′əl] *n.* A weed that grows among grain.
cock·le·bur [kok′əl·bûr′] *n.* A coarse weed having prickly burs.

a	add	**i**	it	**o͝o**	took	**oi**	oil
ā	ace	**ī**	ice	**o͞o**	pool	**ou**	pout
â	care	**o**	odd	**u**	up	**ng**	ring
ä	palm	**ō**	open	**û**	burn	**th**	thin
e	end	**ô**	order	**yo͞o**	fuse	**th**	this
ē	equal					**zh**	vision

ə = a in *above* e in *sicken* i in *possible* o in *melon* u in *circus*

cock·le·shell [kok′əl·shel′] *n.* 1 The shell of a cockle. 2 A frail, light boat.
cock·ney [kok′nē] *n., pl* **cock·neys** *(often written* **Cockney**) 1 *n.* A person born or living in the East End of London, England. 2 *n.* The dialect of this section of London. 3 *adj.* Of or having to do with cockneys or their dialect.
cock·pit [kok′pit′] *n.* 1 A compartment in some airplanes where the pilot and others sit. 2 A low part aft of the decked area of a sailboat or motorboat. 3 A pit or enclosure for cockfights.
cock·roach [kok′rōch′] *n.* An insect with a flat, oval, dark brown body that is a household pest.
cocks·comb [koks′kōm′] *n.* 1 The fleshy, red growth on a rooster's head. 2 A plant with showy red or yellowish flowers. 3 A jester's cap.
cock·sure [kok′shŏŏr′] *adj.* 1 Absolutely sure. 2 Too sure of oneself; too self-confident.
cock·tail [kok′tāl′] *n.* 1 Any of various mixed alcoholic drinks. 2 An appetizer served at the start of a meal, as seafood in a sauce.
cock·y [kok′ē] *adj.* **cock·i·er, cock·i·est** *informal* Too sure of oneself; boldly conceited. **—cock′i·ly** *adv.*
co·co [kō′kō] *n., pl.* **co·cos** 1 The coconut palm. 2 Its fruit, the coconut.
co·coa [kō′kō] *n.* 1 A powder made from the seeds of the cacao; chocolate. 2 A beverage made from cocoa. 3 *adj., n.* Light, reddish brown.
cocoa butter A yellowish-white, waxy substance obtained from cacao seeds and used to make candy, soap, and medicines.
co·co·nut [kō′kə·nut′] *n.* The large fruit of the coconut palm with a hard shell, white meat, and a center filled with a sweet liquid.
coconut palm A tropical palm bearing coconuts.
co·coon [kə·kōōn′] *n.* The envelope spun by the larvae of certain insects for protection while they are undergoing changes, as from a caterpillar to a moth.
coco palm Another name for the COCONUT PALM.
cod [kod] *n., pl.* **cod** or **cods** An important food fish of the northern Atlantic.
c.o.d. or **C.O.D.** 1 cash on delivery. 2 collect on delivery.
co·da [kō′də] *n.* A separate passage at the end of a musical composition or movement. ◆ *Coda* comes from an Italian word meaning *tail.*
cod·dle [kod′(ə)l] *v.* **cod·dled, cod·dling** 1 To treat gently, as a baby or sick person; pamper. 2 To cook in hot water, as eggs.
code [kōd] *n., v.* **cod·ed, cod·ing** 1 *n.* A body of laws, arranged in a systematic way. 2 *n.* Any set of rules or principles: the *code* of honor. 3 *v.* To arrange, as laws, in an orderly way. 4 *n.* A set of signals used in communication: the Morse *code.* 5 *n.* A set of letters, words, or symbols that has a secret meaning, used in transmitting messages. 6 *v.* To put (as a message) into code.
co·deine [kō′dēn′] *n.* A drug obtained from opium and used as a mild narcotic to deaden pain.
cod·fish [kod′fish′] *n., pl.* **cod·fish** or **cod·fish·es** Another word for COD.
codg·er [koj′ər] *n. informal* An odd or grouchy person, especially an old man.
cod·i·cil [kod′ə·sil] *n.* An addition to a will that changes it in some way.
cod·i·fy [kod′ə·fī′ *or* kō′də·fī′] *v.* **cod·i·fied, cod·i·fy·ing** To put into a code, as laws. **—cod′i·fi·ca′tion** *n.*
cod·ling moth [kod′ling] A moth whose larvae feed on the insides of fruits, particularly apples.
cod·liv·er oil [kod′liv′ər] Oil from the livers of cod, used as a source of vitamins A and D.
co·ed or **co-ed** [kō′ed′] *n. informal* A female student at a coeducational college.
co·ed·u·ca·tion [kō′ej·ōō·kā′shən] *n.* The system of education in which both male and female students go to the same school.
co·ed·u·ca·tion·al [kō′ej·ōō·kā′shən·əl] *adj.* Indicating a school or college to which both males and females are admitted and allowed to attend classes together.
co·ef·fi·cient [kō′ə·fish′ənt] *n.* A number placed in front of an algebraic expression and multiplying it; factor: In the expression $3y = 9$, 3 is the *coefficient* of *y.*
coel- or **coelo-** or **cel-** or **celo-** A combining form meaning: Hollow; cavity, as in *coelenterate.*
coe·la·canth [sē′lə·kanth′] *n.* A large, primitive fish with broad fins. It was thought to be extinct until a live specimen was caught off the coast of SE Africa in 1938.
coe·len·ter·ate [si·len′tə·rāt′] *n.* Any of a large group of invertebrate sea animals having a hollow, saclike body and tentacles encircling a central mouth. The jellyfish, hydra, and sea anemone are coelenterates.
co·erce [kō·ûrs′] *v.* **co·erced, co·erc·ing** To force or compel into doing something, as by threats or violence: They *coerced* us into paying. **—co·er·cion** [kō·ûr′shən] *n.*
co·er·cive [kō·ûr′siv] *adj.* Tending to coerce.
co·ex·ist [kō′ig·zist′] *v.* To live or exist together in the same place or at the same time.
co·ex·ist·ence [kō′ig·zis′təns] *n.* 1 The state of coexisting. 2 The living together in peace of nations with different political systems or ways of thinking.
cof·fee [kôf′ē] 1 *n.* A beverage made from the roasted and ground seeds or beans of a tropical shrub. 2 *n.* These seeds or beans. 3 *n.* The shrub on which they grow. 4 *n., adj.* Brown, as the color of coffee with cream. ◆ *Coffee* comes from an Arabic word.
coffee bean The berry or seed of a tropical shrub from which coffee is made.
coffee cake A sweet cake, often topped with nuts and raisins, to be eaten with coffee.
cof·fee·house [kôf′ē·hous′] *n., pl.* **cof·fee·houses** [kôf′e·hou′zəz] An establishment that serves coffee and other refreshments and where people gather to socialize.
cof·fee·pot [kôf′ē·pot′] *n.* A utensil used to brew and serve coffee.
coffee shop A small restaurant, often with a counter, where light meals are served.
coffee table A low table usually placed in front of a sofa in a living room.
cof·fer [kôf′ər] *n.* 1 A chest or box, especially one for keeping money or valuables. 2 (*pl.*) Financial resources; a treasury.
cof·fer·dam [kô′fər·dam′ *or* ko′fər·dam′] *n.* 1 A temporary watertight structure at the bottom of a body of water. Water is pumped from the structure so that work, as pier construction, can be done inside it. 2 A watertight chamber used in making repairs below the waterline of a ship.
cof·fin [kôf′in] *n.* The box or case in which a dead body is buried.
cog [kog] *n.* 1 A tooth or one of a series of teeth on the edge of a wheel, used to transmit or receive

motion or power. 2 A cogwheel. 3 A person who plays a small but necessary part in a large process or business.

co·gent [kō′jənt] *adj.* Causing belief, agreement, or action; forceful; convincing: a *cogent* speech. **—co′gen·cy** *n.* **—co′gent·ly** *adv.*

cog·i·tate [koj′ə·tāt′] *v.* **cog·i·tat·ed, cog·i·tat·ing** To think with care; ponder; reflect; meditate. **—cog′i·ta′tion** *n.*

co·gnac [kōn′yak *or* kon′yak] *n.* 1 A kind of brandy from western France. 2 Any brandy.

cog·nate [kog′nāt′] *adj.* Related, as by blood or by common source: French and Spanish are *cognate* languages since both come from Latin.

cog·ni·tion [kog·nish′ən] *n.* The act or process of acquiring knowledge.

cog·ni·zance [kog′nə·zəns] *n.* The knowing or understanding of something; attention. **—take cognizance of** To notice; perceive.

cog·ni·zant [kog′nə·zənt] *adj.* Having knowledge; aware: Are you *cognizant* of the situation?

cog·no·men [kog·nō′mən] *n.* 1 A surname. 2 Any name, especially a nickname.

cog·wheel [kog′(h)wēl′] *n.* A wheel with cogs or teeth, used to transmit or receive motion.

Cogwheels

co·here [kō·hir′] *v.* **co·hered, co·her·ing** 1 To stick or hold together: Grains of salt often *cohere* into a lump. 2 To show a logical connection, as among the parts: the story *coheres.*

co·her·ent [kō·hir′ənt] *adj.* 1 Having logical order or connection; consistent: a *coherent* essay. 2 Sticking or holding together, as particles of the same substance. **—co·her′ence** *n.* **—co·her′ent·ly** *adv.*

co·he·sion [kō·hē′zhən] *n.* 1 The act or condition of cohering. 2 In physics, the force by which similar molecules are held together.

co·he·sive [kō·hē′siv] *adj.* Having or showing cohesion. **—co·he′sive·ness** *n.*

co·hort [kō′hôrt] *n.* 1 The tenth part of an ancient Roman legion of soldiers, from 300 to 600 men. 2 A band or group, especially of warriors. 3 A companion or follower: He was led in by his *cohorts.*

coif [koif] *n.* A close-fitting cap or hood, as worn by certain nuns under the veil.

coif·fure [kwä·fyŏŏr′] *n.* A hair style.

coil [koil] 1 *n.* A ring or spiral formed by twisting or winding: I caught my leg in a *coil* of the rope. 2 *n.* A series of coils: to wind the rope into a *coil.* 3 *v.* To wind into a coil. 4 *n.* A wire wound in a spiral, usually used for an electromagnetic effect.

coin [koin] 1 *n.* A piece of metal stamped by a government for use as money. 2 *v.* To make (coins) of metal. 3 *n.* Metal money as a whole: the *coin* of the realm. 4 *v.* To make up or invent, as a word or phrase.

coin·age [koi′nij] *n.* 1 The act or right of making coins. 2 The coins made. 3 Something newly invented or created, as a word or phrase.

co·in·cide [kō′in·sīd′] *v.* **co·in·cid·ed, co·in·cid·ing** 1 To be the same size and take up the same space: If one of these two circles ○○ were placed on the other, the two would coincide. 2 To occur at the same time: The holiday *coincides* with my vacation. 3 To agree exactly: Your idea *coincided* with mine.

co·in·ci·dence [kō·in′sə·dəns] *n.* 1 A seemingly remarkable chance occurrence or appearance of two things at the same place or time. 2 The act of condition of coinciding.

co·in·ci·dent [kō·in′sə·dənt] *adj.* 1 Occupying the same time or space; coinciding. 2 In agreement; corresponding: an alibi *coincident* with the facts.

co·in·ci·den·tal [kō·in′sə·den′təl] *adj.* Involving coincidence; happening at the same time purely by chance. **—co·in′ci·den′tal·ly** *adv.*

coke [kōk] *n.* A solid fuel made from coal that has been heated to remove gases.

col- A prefix meaning: With; together; in association with, as in *collateral.*

col. 1 color. 2 colored. 3 colony. 4 column.

Col. 1 Columbia. 2 Columbian. 3 (*sometimes written* **col.**) colonel. 4 Colorado.

col·an·der [kul′ən·dər *or* kol′ən·dər] *n.* A kitchen utensil with holes, for draining off liquids from foods.

Colander

cold [kōld] 1 *adj.* Having little heat or a low temperature: a *cold* night; a *cold* iron; *cold* hands. 2 *n.* The lack of heat: The *cold* invigorates me. 3 *adj.* Feeling cold or chilled: I'm *cold.* 4 *adj.* Lacking the usual heat: Eat your soup before it gets *cold.* 5 *adj.* Lacking affection or sympathy: a *cold* person. 6 *adj.* Not new or fresh; stale: a *cold* trail. 7 *n.* A mild illness with symptoms of sneezing, running nose, coughing, and sometimes fever. **—catch cold** To become ill with a cold. **—cold′ly** *adv.* **—cold′ness** *n.*

cold-blood·ed [kōld′blud′id] *adj.* 1 Heartless and cruel: a *cold-blooded* crime. 2 Having blood whose temperature changes with that of the surrounding air or water: Snakes and fish are *cold-blooded* creatures. **—cold′blood′ed·ly** *adv.* **—cold′·blood′ed·ness** *n.*

cold cream A cleansing salve for the skin.

cold cuts Slices of various cold cooked meats.

cold front The forward edge of a cold mass of air coming forward against a warm air mass.

cold fusion An experimental technique for carrying out nuclear fusion at low temperatures.

cold·heart·ed [kōld′här′tid] *adj.* Having no sympathy or compassion; unfeeling; insensitive. **—cold′heart′ed·ly** *adv.* **—cold′heart′ed·ness** *n.*

cold shoulder *informal* A snub or show of indifference.

cold sore A blister or sore on the mouth that often comes with a cold or fever.

cold storage The storage, as of food or clothing, in a refrigerated place.

cold war An international conflict expressed in diplomatic and economic rivalry rather than war.

cold wave A period of unusually cold weather.

a	add	**i**	it	**ŏŏ**	took	**oi**	oil
ā	ace	**ī**	ice	**ōō**	pool	**ou**	pout
â	care	**o**	odd	**u**	up	**ng**	ring
ä	palm	**ō**	open	**û**	burn	**th**	thin
e	end	**ô**	order	**yōō**	fuse	**th̶**	this
ē	equal					**zh**	vision

ə = a in *above* e in *sicken* i in *possible* o in *melon* u in *circus*

cole·slaw [kōl′slô′] *n.* A salad made of finely shredded raw cabbage.
co·le·us [kō′lē·əs] *n.* A plant of the mint family grown for its showy leaves.
col·ic [kol′ik] *n.* A pain in the abdomen that comes from muscular spasms. **—col′ick·y** *adj.*
col·i·se·um [kol′ə·sē′əm] *n.* 1 A building or stadium, as one used for exhibitions and sports events. 2 (*written* **Coliseum**) A spelling of COLOSSEUM.
co·li·tis [kō·lī′təs *or* kə·lī′təs] *n.* Inflammation of the colon.
col·lab·o·rate [kə·lab′ə·rāt′] *v.* **col·lab·o·rat·ed, col·lab·o·rat·ing** 1 To work together, as on literary or scientific efforts: They *collaborated* on the play. 2 To work against one's country by helping the enemy. **—col·lab′o·ra′tion** *n.* **—col·lab′o·ra′tor** *n.*
col·lage [kə·läzh′] *n.* A decorative composition of bits of paper, cloth, or other materials attached to a surface.

A collage

col·lapse [kə·laps′] *v.* **col·lapsed, col·laps·ing,** *n.* 1 *v.* To give way; cave in: The old barn *collapsed.* 2 *v.* To fail completely: Our plans *collapsed.* 3 *v.* To lose health or strength: to *collapse* from overwork. 4 *n.* The act of collapsing. 5 *n.* A collapsed condition: a mental *collapse.* 6 *v.* To fold together compactly: She *collapsed* the table.
col·laps·i·ble [kə·lap′sə·bəl] *adj.* Capable of being folded: a *collapsible* chair.
col·lar [kol′ər] 1 *n.* A part of a garment or a separate piece of fabric worn at the neck. 2 *v.* To put a collar on. 3 *v.* To grab by the collar. 4 *n.* A metal or leather piece placed around an animal's neck: a dog *collar.* 5 *n.* The part of a harness that fits over a horse's neck. 6 *n.* A ring-shaped part in a machine encircling a rod or a shaft and used to limit motion.
col·lar·bone [kol′ər·bōn′] *n.* The clavicle.
col·lard [kol′ərd] *n.* A leafy, dark green vegetable.
col·late [kə·lāt′ *or* kōl′āt′] *v.* **col·lat·ed, col·lat·ing** 1 To put into proper order. 2 To examine and compare carefully.
col·lat·er·al [kə·lat′ər·əl] 1 *adj.* Aside from the main subject; secondary: a *collateral* argument. 2 *adj.* Going with the main part; parallel. 3 *adj.* Additional; supporting: *collateral* evidence. 4 *n.* Money or property used as security for a loan. 5 *adj.* Descended from the same ancestors but in a different line or branch, as a cousin is.
col·la·tion [kə·lā′shən] *n.* A light meal.
col·league [kol′ēg] *n.* A fellow worker in a profession or organization; associate.
col·lect [kə·lekt′] 1 *v.* To gather; assemble: *Collect* all the papers; A crowd *collected.* 2 *v.* To accumulate, as sand or dust. 3 *v.* To bring together, as for study or as a hobby. 4 *v.* To seek and receive as payments: to *collect* taxes. 5 *adv., adj.* To be paid for by the receiver: a *collect* call. 6 *v.* To regain control of: to *collect* one's wits. **—col·lect′i·ble** or **col·lect′a·ble** *adj.*
col·lect·ed [kə·lek′tid] *adj.* Calm and composed.
col·lec·tion [kə·lek′shən] *n.* 1 The act of collecting. 2 The things collected: a *collection* of stamps. 3 A pile that has gathered: a *collection* of dirt. 4 An asking for and collecting of money, as for a church or charity. 5 The money so collected.
col·lec·tive [kə·lek′tiv] 1 *adj.* Formed or gathered together by collecting: the *collective* result of wear. 2 *adj.* Of, having to do with, run by, or coming from a group: a *collective* effort; a *collective* farm. 3 *n.* An enterprise in which a group works together, especially a farm. 4 *adj.* In grammar, indicating a group of persons or things that is thought of as a unit: "Audience" is a *collective* noun. **—col·lec′tive·ly** *adv.*
collective bargaining Negotiation between an employer and the representatives of organized workers about wages and other issues.
col·lec·tiv·ism [kə·lek′ti·viz′əm] *n.* 1 The theory that the production and distribution of goods should be controlled by the people as a whole. 2 A political and economic system based on this theory. **—col·lec′tiv·ist** *adj., n.*
col·lec·tiv·ize [kə·lek′tə·vīz′] *v.* **col·lec·tiv·ized, col·lec·tiv·iz·ing** To organize according to the theory of collectivism.
col·lec·tor [kə·lek′tər] *n.* A person or thing that collects: The government is the *collector* of taxes.
col·leen [kə·lēn′ *or* kol′ēn′] *n.* An Irish girl.
col·lege [kol′ij] *n.* 1 A school of higher learning that gives a bachelor's degree to students who have completed a course of study. 2 A school for instruction in a special field or profession, often attached to a university: a *college* of medicine. 3 A group of people who have certain duties and rights: the electoral *college.*
col·le·gian [kə·lē′jən] *n.* A college student or a recent graduate of a college.
col·le·giate [kə·lē′jit] *adj.* 1 Of, like, or having to do with a college. 2 Of or for college students.
col·lide [kə·līd′] *v.* **col·lid·ed, col·lid·ing** 1 To come together with a strong or violent impact; crash. 2 To come into conflict; disagree; clash.
col·lie [kol′ē] *n.* A breed of large dog, sometimes used to herd sheep. It has a long head and a heavy coat.

Collie

col·lier [kol′yər] *n. British* 1 A coal miner. 2 A ship used to carry coal.
col·lier·y [kol′yər·ē] *n., pl.* **col·lier·ies** A coal mine.
col·li·sion [kə·lizh′ən] *n.* 1 A violent colliding: The *collision* involved four cars. 2 A clash of views; conflict.
col·loid [kol′oid′] *n.* A substance formed when small particles are suspended in a liquid or gas, neither dissolved nor sinking, as blood or gelatin. **—col·loi·dal** [kə·loid′(ə)l] *n.*
col·lo·qui·al [kə·lō′kwē·əl] *adj.* Used in or appropriate to informal speech or to writing that seeks to be like such speech. **—col·lo′qui·al·ly** *adv.*
col·lo·qui·al·ism [kə·lō′kwē·əl·iz′əm] *n.* A word or phrase used in conversation but not in formal speech or writing.
col·lo·quy [kol′ə·kwē] *n., pl.* **col·lo·quies** A talk or conference, especially a formal one.
col·lu·sion [kə·lo͞o′zhən] *n.* A secret agreement for a wrongful purpose, as to cheat or deceive.
Colo. Colorado.
co·logne [kə·lōn′] *n.* A scented toilet water.
Co·lom·bi·an [kə·lum′bē·ən] 1 *adj.* Of or from Colombia. 2 *n.* A person born in or a citizen of Colombia.

co·lon[1] [kō'lən] *n.* The largest part of the large intestine, above the rectum.

co·lon[2] [kō'lən] *n.* A punctuation mark (:), as used to introduce a long quotation, a series, or an example.

colo·nel [kûr'nəl] *n.* A military rank. In the U.S. Army, a colonel is a commissioned officer ranking below a brigadier general.

co·lo·ni·al [kə·lō'nē·əl] 1 *adj.* Of, having to do with, or living in a colony or colonies, especially the 13 British colonies that became the U.S. 2 *n.* A person who lives in a colony. 3 *adj.* Of a style of architecture or furniture used originally in the American colonies.

co·lo·ni·al·ism [kə·lō'nē·əl·iz'əm] *n.* A national policy based on the control of a dependent territory or people.

col·o·nist [kol'ə·nist] *n.* 1 A person who lives in a colony. 2 A settler or founder of a colony.

col·o·nize [kol'ə·nīz'] *v.* **col·o·nized, col·o·niz·ing** 1 To set up a colony in; settle. 2 To settle in colonies. **—col'o·ni·za'tion** *n.* **—col'o·niz'er** *n.*

col·on·nade [kol'ə·nād'] *n.* A row of regularly spaced columns.

Colonnade

col·o·ny [kol'ə·nē] *n., pl.* **col·o·nies** 1 A group of people who live in a land separate from, but under the control of, the country from which they came. 2 The region where they settle. 3 Any territory governed by a distant state. 4 A group of people from the same country or who have the same occupation, living together in one area: a writers' *colony.* 5 A group of organisms of the same kind that live or grow together.

col·or [kul'er] 1 *n.* The visual sensation produced when light of particular wavelengths strikes the retina of the eye. It ranges from bright red for the longest to deep violet for the shortest wavelength, and includes all tones from white to black. 2 *n.* Something, as paint or dye, capable of giving color. 3 *v.* To apply or give color to. 4 *v.* To take on or change color, as fruit. 5 *n.* The hue of the skin; complexion. 6 *v.* To blush. 7 *n.* Appearance: Their story had the clear *color* of truth. 8 *v.* To change or distort: Enthusiasm *colored* our words. 9 *n.* (*pl.*) Nature; beliefs, especially in the expression **show one's true colors.** 10 *n.* Liveliness: to speak with *color.* 11 *n.* (*pl.*) The flag, as of a country or military unit. **—change color** 1 To turn pale. 2 To blush. **—with flying colors.**

col·or·a·tion [kul'ə·rā'shən] *n.* The arrangement of colors, as of an animal or plant; coloring.

col·or·a·tur·a [kul'ər·ə·t(y)ŏŏr'ə] *n.* 1 Trills, runs, and other musical ornaments designed to show off a voice. 2 Music having such ornaments. 3 A singer, especially a high soprano, who specializes in performing such music. 4 *adj. use:* a *coloratura* soprano.

col·or·blind [kul'ər·blīnd'] *adj.* Incapable of telling the difference between two or more colors because of some defect in the eyes.

col·or·cast [kul'ər·kast'] *v.* **col·or·cast** or **col·or·cast·ed, col·or·cast·ing,** *n.* 1 *v.* To televise in color. 2 *n.* A television broadcast in color.

col·ored [kul'ərd] *adj.* 1 Having color. 2 Of a race not white: sometimes used to mean BLACK. 3 Influenced, as by prejudice; biased; distorted: a *colored* report.

col·or·fast [kul'ər·fast'] *adj.*Having color that will not run or fade when washed or worn.

col·or·ful [kul'ər·fəl] *adj.* 1 Full of colors. 2 Full of interest or variety: a *colorful* story. **—col'or·ful·ly** *adv.* **—col'or·ful·ness** *n.*

col·or·ing [kul'ər·ing] *n.* 1 The act or style of applying colors. 2 Something that gives color, as a dye or paint: food *coloring.* 3 The appearance of something in respect to its color.

col·or·ize [kul'ər īz'] *v.* To create a color motion picture by using a computer to analyze the color values in a film that was originally made in black and white. **—col'or·i·za'tion** *n.*

col·or·less [kul'ər·lis] *adj.* 1 Without color. 2 Dull; monotonous: a *colorless* voice.

co·los·sal [kə·los'əl] *adj.* 1 Of enormous size; huge. 2 *informal* Beyond belief: *colossal* nerve. **—co·los'·sal·ly** *adv.*

Col·os·se·um [kol'ə·sē'əm] *n.* A stadium built in Rome A.D. 75–80 and still partly standing.

The Roman Colosseum

co·los·sus [kə·los'əs] *n., pl.* **co·los·si** [kə·los'ī] or **co·los·sus·es** 1 A gigantic statue. 2 Anything large or great.

Colossus of Rhodes A gigantic statue of Apollo that was set at the entrance to the harbor of Rhodes about 285 B.C.

colt [kōlt] *n.* A young horse or donkey, especially a male.

Co·lum·bi·a [kə·lum'bē·ə] *n.* The U.S.: used only in poems.

col·um·bine [kol'əm·bīn'] *n.* 1 A plant with variously colored flowers of five petals. 2 (*written* **Columbine**) A stock character in pantomimes, the sweetheart of Harlequin.

co·lum·bi·um [kə·lum'bē·əm] *n.* Another name for NIOBIUM.

col·umn [kol'əm] *n.* 1 A tall post or pillar shaped like a cylinder, used as a support in or around a building or for decoration. 2 Something shaped like a column: the spinal *column.* 3 A tall, narrow section of a page, set off by a line or space at the side: This page has two *columns.* 4 A feature article, usually by one person, that appears regularly in a newspaper or magazine: a society *column;* a bridge *column.* 5 A military or naval formation consisting of rows, as of people or ships, one behind another.

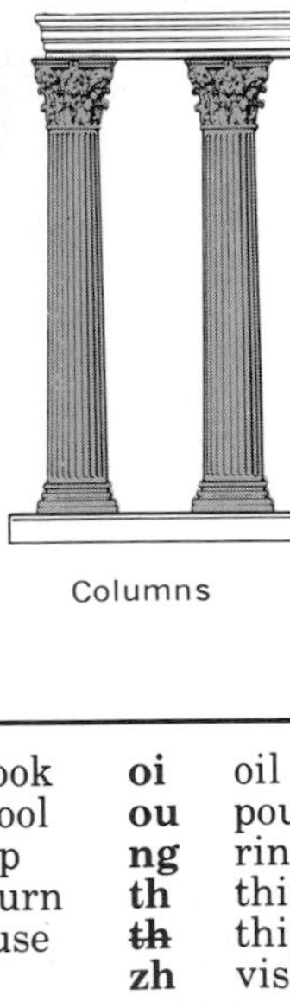
Columns

a	add	**i**	it	**ŏŏ**	took	**oi**	oil
ā	ace	**ī**	ice	**ōō**	pool	**ou**	pout
â	care	**o**	odd	**u**	up	**ng**	ring
ä	palm	**ō**	open	**û**	burn	**th**	thin
e	end	**ô**	order	**yōō**	fuse	**th**	this
ē	equal					**zh**	vision

ə = a in *above* e in *sicken* i in *possible* o in *melon* u in *circus*

co·lum·nar [kə·lum′nər] *adj.* 1 Of, having to do with, or like a column. 2 Characterized by or built with columns.
col·um·nist [kol′əm·nist] *n.* A person who writes a column in a newspaper or magazine.
com- A prefix meaning: With; together; in association with, as in *commingle.*
com. 1 comedy. 2 commerce. 3 committee. 4 common. 5 communication. 6 communist.
Com. 1 Commander. 2 Commission. 3 Commissioner. 4 Committee. 5 Commodore. 6 Communist.
co·ma[1] [kō′mə] *n.* A state of deep and lasting unconsciousness, caused by injury, disease, or poison.
co·ma[2] [kō′mə] *n., pl.* **co·mae** [kō′mē] The shining mass of gases that surrounds the nucleus of a comet and makes up most of the comet's head.
Co·man·che [kə·man′chē] *n., pl.* **Co·man·che** or **Co·man·ches** 1 A tribe of North American Indians once living on the plains from Wyoming to Texas, now in Oklahoma. 2 A member of this tribe. 3 The language of this tribe.
co·ma·tose [kō′mə·tōs′ *or* kom′ə·tōs′] *adj.* Of, having to do with, or in a coma.
comb [kōm] 1 *n.* A strip of hard material with teeth, used to arrange or clean hair, or to keep it neat. 2 *n.* A thing like this used to clean and straighten wool or other fibers. 3 *v.* To arrange or clean, as hair or wool, with a comb. 4 *v.* To search carefully: We all *combed* the area until we found our missing dog. 5 *n.* The fleshy, red outgrowth on the head of a fowl. 6 *n.* Something like a fowl's comb in shape or position, as the top of a breaking wave. 7 *n.* A honeycomb.
com·bat [*n.* kom′bat′, *v.* kəm·bat′ *or* kom′bat′] *n., v.* **com·bat·ed** or **com·bat·ted, com·bat·ing** or **com·bat·ting** 1 *n.* A battle or fight: *combat* between soldiers. 2 *v.* To battle or fight with: Doctors are *combating* cancer. 3 *v.* To fight or struggle: The candidates *combated* fiercely for the election.
com·bat·ant [kəm·bat′ənt *or* kom′bə·tənt] 1 *n.* A person fighting or prepared to fight: The *combatants* entered the ring. 2 *adj.* Fighting: *combatant* troops. 3 *adj.* Combative.
com·bat·ive [kəm·bat′iv] *adj.* Eager or ready to fight: Those two are rivals, but friendly, not *combative.*
comb·er [kō′mər] *n.* 1 A person or thing that combs wool or other fibers. 2 A wave that breaks or is topped with foam.
com·bi·na·tion [kom′bə·nā′shən] *n.* 1 The act of joining: *Combination* of oil with water is impossible. 2 A combined condition: Working in *combination,* tiny tugs dock the big ship easily. 3 The thing that is formed by combining. 4 A series of numbers or letters used in opening certain locks. 5 In mathematics, one or more elements selected from a set without regard to order.
combination lock A lock that is opened by turning its dial or dials to a particular series of positions in a fixed order and in fixed directions.
com·bine [*v.* kəm·bīn′, *n.* kom′bīn′] *v.* **com·bined, com·bin·ing,** *n.* 1 *v.* To bring together; unite; join. 2 *v.* To come together: Oxygen and carbon *combine* readily. 3 *n.* A combination.
combining form A word part that can be joined with one or more prefixes or suffixes, with full words, or with other combining forms to create words. *Tele-* and *-phone* are combining forms.
com·bus·ti·ble [kəm·bus′tə·bəl] 1 *adj.* Capable of catching fire; easily burned: Magnesium is highly *combustible.* 2 *n.* Any substance that will burn easily. 3 *adj.* Excitable; fiery. —**com·bus′ti·bil′i·ty** *n.* —**com·bus′ti·bly** *adv.*
com·bus·tion [kəm·bus′chən] *n.* 1 The action or process of burning. 2 A chemical reaction, especially a rapid oxidation that is accompanied by heat and, usually, light.
Comdr. Commander.
come [kum] *v.* **came, come, com·ing** 1 To approach the speaker; move toward where the speaker is or is going: *Come* here. 2 To arrive: We *came* yesterday. 3 To happen; occur: Labor Day *came* late last year. 4 To originate; be born: to *come* from a large family. 5 To result: Nothing *comes* of wasting time. 6 To become: The wheel *came* loose. 7 To be obtainable: The shirt *comes* in four colors. 8 To turn out to be: The prediction *came* true. 9 To reach or extend: The waves *came* up to the dunes. 10 To amount; add up: The bill *comes* to $10. 11 To arrive at some state or condition: to *come* to one's senses. —**come about** To take place; occur; happen: How did this *come about*? —**come around** To recover; revive: I fainted but soon *came around.* —**come back** 1 To return: *Come back* soon. 2 To return to a former state or position: After a bad season, the pitcher *came back.* —**come by** To get: How did you *come by* that beautiful sweater? —**come into** To inherit: I *came into* some money from my grandparents. —**come off** 1 To happen; occur: What time does the race *come off*? 2 To act so as to be judged: In the contest I *came off* as a second-rate speller. —**come out** 1 To be made known: Wait till the inside story *comes out.* 2 To be published: My book *came out* last week. 3 To make one's debut. 4 To speak out in support: Whom did you *come out* for in the school election? 5 To try out: Did you *come out* for the debating team? 6 To end: How did the movie *come out*? —**come to** To recover; revive: How soon did the patient *come to*? —**come up** To come into discussion.
come·back [kum′bak′] *n. informal* 1 A return to former success, health, or achievement after a decline. 2 A quick, clever reply; retort.
co·me·di·an [kə·mē′dē·ən] *n.* An actor or entertainer who tries, by performing, to make people laugh.
co·me·di·enne [kə·mē′dē·en′] *n.* A female actor or entertainer who tries, by performing, to make people laugh.
come·down [kum′doun′] *n. informal* 1 A decline in status or position. 2 A disappointment.
com·e·dy [kom′ə·dē] *n., pl.* **com·e·dies** 1 An entertainment, as a play or movie, that tells a story in a light and humorous way, and has a happy ending. 2 The branch of drama that tells such stories. 3 Any writing that tells such stories. 4 Any happening in real life that is like the happenings in such stories.
come·ly [kum′lē] *adj.* **come·li·er, come·li·est** 1 Pleasant looking; handsome: *comely* men and women. 2 Suitable; proper. —**come′li·ness** *n.*
come-on [kum′on′] *n. informal* Something used to attract or entice others; attraction; inducement.
com·er [kum′ər] *n.* 1 A person who comes or arrives. 2 *informal* A person who gives signs of future success.
com·et [kom′it] *n.* A bright celestial body moving in elliptical orbit around the sun, usually having

a tail of luminous gaseous matter pointing away from the sun.

come·up·pance [kum′up′əns] *n. informal* A punishment or misfortune that a person deserves.

com·fit [kum′fit] *n.* A piece of candy.

com·fort [kum′fərt] **1** *v.* To make feel better in time of grief or trouble: My friends *comforted* me after the accident. **2** *n.* Anything that eases grief or trouble: A kind word can give *comfort* when you are sad. **3** *n.* A pleasant condition, free from pain, want, or worry: Everyone likes to live in *comfort.* **4** *n.* A person or thing that gives ease or freedom from pain or worry.

com·fort·a·ble [kum′fər·tə·bəl *or* kumf′tə·bəl] *adj.* **1** Giving comfort and satisfaction: Is that hat *comfortable,* or is it too small? **2** Free from physical or mental trouble; at ease: Are you *comfortable*? **—com′fort·a·bly** *adv.*

com·fort·er [kum′fər·tər] *n.* **1** A person who comforts. **2** A thick, quilted cover for a bed.

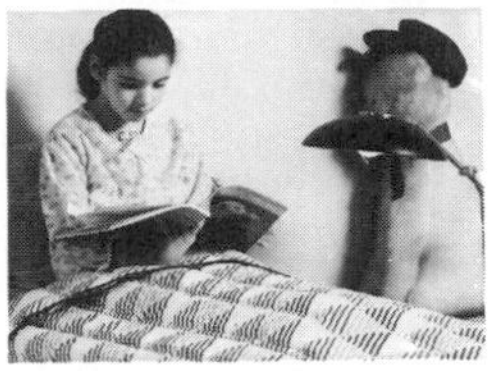

Comforter

com·fort·less [kum′fərt·lis] *adj.* **1** Giving no comfort: Their advice was *comfortless.* **2** Having no comfort: a hard and *comfortless* life.

com·ic [kom′ik] **1** *adj.* Of, having to do with, or characterized by comedy. **2** *adj.* Funny; entertaining: I just heard a *comic* story. **3** *n.* A funny person, especially an actor. **4** *n.* (*pl.*) Comic strips.

com·i·cal [kom′i·kəl] *adj.* Causing laughter; funny: Punch and Judy's quarrel was *comical.* **—com′i·cal·ly** *adv.* **—com′i·cal·ness** *n.*

comic book A booklet of comic strips.

comic opera A humorous or sentimental opera characterized by some spoken dialogue and, usually, a happy ending.

comic strip A group of drawings that tell a story which is comical or adventurous.

com·ing [kum′ing] **1** *adj.* Approaching, especially in time: the *coming* year. **2** *adj.* On the way to success: a *coming* writer. **3** *n.* Approach; arrival.

coming-out [kum′ing·out′] *n. informal* **1** A debut (def. 2). **2** *adj. use:* a *coming-out* party.

com·i·ty [kom′ə·tē] *n., pl.* **com·i·ties** Mutual recognition, respect, and courtesy.

comm. **1** commerce. **2** commission. **3** committee. **4** communication.

com·ma [kom′ə] *n.* A punctuation mark (,) that indicates a short pause between words, phrases, or clauses in a sentence.

com·mand [kə·mand′] **1** *v.* To order; direct: to *command* planes to search the area. **2** *n.* An order: a *command* to march. **3** *v.* To be in control of or authority over: to *command* a ship. **4** *n.* The power or authority to give orders. **5** *n.* The people or area under a commander. **6** *v.* To overlook and dominate: These hills *command* the town. **7** *v.* To deserve and call for: The scientist's knowledge *commands* our respect. **8** *v.* To have or surely get for use: The mayor can *command* the support of city voters. **9** *n.* The ability to make use: a good *command* of English. **10** *n.* An electronic signal to a computer.

com·man·dant [kom′ən·dant′] *n.* The officer in charge, as of a navy yard or military school.

com·man·deer [kom′ən·dir′] *v.* **1** To take control of for public use, especially because of military necessity: The army *commandeered* all trucks in the city. **2** To force into military service.

com·man·der [kə·man′dər] *n.* **1** A person who is in command, as of a ship or military force. **2** A naval rank. In the U.S. Navy, a commander is a commissioned officer ranking next above a lieutenant commander and next below a captain.

commander in chief *pl.* **commanders in chief** **1** (*often written* **Commander in Chief**) The person who is in command of all the armed forces of a nation. In the U.S., the President is the Commander in Chief. **2** The officer who is in command of a major military force, as an army or a fleet.

com·mand·ing [kə·man′ding] *adj.* **1** In charge or control: the *commanding* general. **2** That must be obeyed; powerful: *Commanding* necessity forces this step. **3** Authoritative: a *commanding* manner. **4** Dominating, as from a height: a *commanding* view.

com·mand·ment [kə·mand′mənt] *n.* **1** A command or law. **2** (*sometimes written* **Commandment**) One of the Ten Commandments.

com·man·do [kə·man′dō] *n., pl.* **com·man·dos** or **com·man·does** **1** A soldier trained for quick raids and hand-to-hand fighting. **2** A group of such soldiers.

com·mem·o·rate [kə·mem′ə·rāt′] *v.* **com·mem·o·rat·ed, com·mem·o·rat·ing** To honor or keep fresh the memory of: The monument *commemorates* the landing of the Pilgrims.

com·mem·o·ra·tion [kə·mem′ə·rā′shən] *n.* **1** The act of commemorating. **2** Something that commemorates, as a ceremony or service in honor of someone or something. **—in commemoration of** As a reminder of; in honor of.

com·mem·o·ra·tive [kə·mem′ə·rā′tiv *or* kə·mem′ə·rə·tiv] *adj.* Serving to commemorate.

com·mence [kə·mens′] *v.* **com·menced, com·menc·ing** To start; initiate; begin.

com·mence·ment [kə·mens′mənt] *n.* **1** A commencing; beginning. **2** The ceremony at a school or college of giving out diplomas or degrees to graduating students. **3** The day on which such a ceremony takes place.

com·mend [kə·mend′] *v.* **1** To speak highly of; praise: The teacher *commended* the pupils on their homework. **2** To mention with approval; recommend. **3** To give over with confidence: The director *commended* the assignment to an assistant.

com·mend·a·ble [kə·men′də·bəl] *adj.* Deserving credit or approval: a *commendable* job.

com·men·da·tion [kom′ən·dā′shən] *n.* **1** Praise or recommendation. **2** The entrusting of something to another.

com·men·sal [kə·men′səl] *adj.* **1** Of, having to do with, or living in commensalism. **2** *n.* A plant or animal that lives in such a relationship. ◆

a	add	**i**	it	**o͝o**	took	**oi**	oil
ā	ace	**ī**	ice	**o͞o**	pool	**ou**	pout
â	care	**o**	odd	**u**	up	**ng**	ring
ä	palm	**ō**	open	**û**	burn	**th**	thin
e	end	**ô**	order	**yo͞o**	fuse	**t͟h**	this
ē	equal					**zh**	vision

ə = {a in *above* e in *sicken* i in *possible* / o in *melon* u in *circus*}

Commensal is derived from the Latin *com-*, together, and *mensa*, table. It originally meant "eating at the same table."

com·men·sal·ism [kə·men′səl·iz′əm] *n.* A relationship of close association in which one organism benefits and another organism of a different kind is not harmed.

com·men·su·rate [kə·men′shə·rit *or* kə·men′sə·rit] *adj.* 1 Having the same measure or size. 2 In proper proportion: The result is not *commensurate* with the effort. —**com·men′su·rate·ly** *adv.*

com·ment [kom′ent] 1 *n.* A note or remark explaining or giving an opinion of a person or thing, as a play or book. 2 *v.* To give an opinion or explanation. 3 *n.* Talk; conversation; gossip: The speaker's position caused much *comment.*

com·men·tar·y [kom′ən·ter′ē] *n., pl.* **com·men·tar·ies** 1 A series of notes that explain a book or other writing. 2 A description, with comment and explanation, of some event while it is going on, as a political convention. 3 A comment.

com·men·ta·tor [kom′ən·tā′tər] *n.* 1 A person who writes or reads commentaries. 2 A person who reports, analyzes, and explains the news on radio or television.

com·merce [kom′ərs] *n.* The buying and selling of goods, especially on a large scale between different places or nations; trade.

com·mer·cial [kə·mûr′shəl] 1 *adj.* Of or having to do with commerce. 2 *adj.* Created or made to be sold, with profit as the object: He wrote a *commercial* novel. 3 *n.* An advertisement on radio or television. 4 *adj.* Paid for or supported by an advertiser or advertisers.

com·mer·cial·ism [kə·mûr′shəl·iz′əm] *n.* 1 The tendency in commercial enterprises to put great emphasis on making a profit. 2 The principles, methods, or institutions of commerce.

com·mer·cial·ize [kə·mûr′shəl·īz′] *v.* **com·mer·cial·ized, com·mer·cial·iz·ing** To put on a commercial basis for profit; treat as a business: Some art galleries are *commercialized.*

com·min·gle [kə·ming′əl] *v.* **com·min·gled, com·min·gling** To mix or blend together: Nine scents are *commingled* in this perfume.

com·mis·er·ate [kə·miz′ə·rāt′] *v.* **com·mis·er·at·ed, com·mis·er·at·ing** 1 To feel or express sympathy for; pity: to *commiserate* the condition of the poor and needy. 2 To sympathize: to *commiserate* with a worried parent.

com·mis·er·a·tion [kə·miz′ə·rā′shən] *n.* A feeling or expression of sympathy; pity.

com·mis·sar [kom′ə·sär′] *n.* A Communist official assigned to a Soviet military unit to teach Communist principles and check on loyalty.

com·mis·sar·i·at [kom′ə·sâr′ē·ət] *n.* The department of an army that is responsible for providing food and daily supplies.

com·mis·sar·y [kom′ə·ser′ē] *n., pl.* **com·mis·sar·ies** A store that sells food and daily supplies, as at a camp or military post.

com·mis·sion [kə·mish′ən] 1 *n.* A written paper giving certain powers, rights, and duties. 2 *n.* A written order giving a certain rank to an officer in any of the armed services. 3 *n.* The rank and powers given by such an order. 4 *v.* To give a specified rank and powers to by such an order. 5 *v.* To authorize, appoint, or hire to do something: The museum *commissioned* a dealer in London to buy a painting for the new gallery. 6 *n.* The authority to do something for another. 7 *n.* The thing which a person is authorized and trusted to do. 8 *n.* A group of people chosen to do certain things: a *commission* to study air pollution. 9 *n.* Pay consisting of a percentage of the business done or arranged by an agent or salesperson. 10 *n.* A performance or doing: the *commission* of a crime. 11 *v.* To order to be created: The concerto was *commissioned* by a famous violinist. 12 *v.* To put into active service, as a ship. —**in commission** In active use, or ready for use, as a ship or an aircraft; usable. —**out of commission** Not in active use; not usable.

commissioned officer In the U.S., a member of the armed forces who has received a commission.

com·mis·sion·er [kə·mish′ən·ər] *n.* 1 A member of a commission. 2 A public official in charge of a department: a fire *commissioner.* 3 One of a group chosen to govern in some cities or counties.

com·mit [kə·mit′] *v.* **com·mit·ted, com·mit·ting** 1 To do; perform: to *commit* a crime. 2 To give over for safekeeping; entrust: to *commit* the Presidential papers to the university. 3 To hand over for custody, as to a prison or mental institution. 4 To pledge (oneself); make known one's view: The senators have *committed* themselves in favor of the bill. 5 To refer, as to a committee, for consideration. —**commit to memory** To learn by heart; memorize. —**commit to writing** To write down.

com·mit·ment [kə·mit′mənt] *n.* 1 A committing or being committed. 2 An order sending someone to prison or a mental hospital. 3 A sending to or placement in a prison or mental hospital. 4 A pledge; promise.

com·mit·tee [kə·mit′ē] *n.* A group of people chosen to do certain specified things.

com·mode [kə·mōd′] *n.* 1 A low chest of drawers. 2 A movable washstand with a bowl and pitcher.

com·mo·di·ous [kə·mō′dē·əs] *adj.* Having plenty of room; spacious: a *commodious* house.

com·mod·i·ty [kə·mod′ə·tē] *n., pl.* **com·mod·i·ties** 1 Something that is bought and sold: Corn, steel, and lumber are *commodities.* 2 Anything useful.

com·mo·dore [kom′ə·dôr′] *n.* 1 A naval rank. In the U.S. Navy, an officer next above a captain and next below a rear admiral: no longer used. 2 A title given to the chief officer of a yacht club.

com·mon [kom′ən] 1 *adj.* Frequent or usual: a *common* happening. 2 *adj.* Widespread; general: *common* knowledge. 3 *adj.* Shared equally by each or by all: Cousins have a *common* ancestor. 4 *adj.* Of, for, from, by, or to all; general: the *common* welfare. 5 *n.* Land owned or used by all the people of a community. 6 *adj.* Of low rank: a *common* soldier. 7 *adj.* Vulgar; low; coarse. —**in common** Equally with another or others: We have tastes *in common.* —**com′mon·ness** *n.*

com·mon·al·ty [kom′ən·əl·tē] *n., pl.* **com·mon·al·ties** The common or ordinary people.

common carrier A person or company that transports people or goods for a fee.

common denominator A number that may be evenly divided by each of the denominators of a given group of fractions: 6, 12, and 18 are all *common denominators* of ⅓ and ½.

common divisor A number or quantity that can evenly divide two or more other numbers or quantities: 4 is a *common divisor* of 12 and 20.

com·mon·er [kom′ən·ər] *n.* One of the common people; a person who is not a noble.

common factor Another name for COMMON DIVISOR.
common fraction A fraction having a whole number as a numerator and a whole number as a denominator.
common law Law based on past court decisions and on custom and precedent rather than on written and enacted laws.
common logarithm A logarithm using the base 10.
com·mon·ly [kom′ən·lē] *adv.* Ordinarily; usually: The word "street" is *commonly* abbreviated.
Common Market A group of European nations that is working toward freer trade among its members.
common multiple A number or quantity that is a multiple of two or more other numbers or quantities: 16 is a *common multiple* of 2, 4, and 8.
common noun A noun that names any one of a group of persons, places, or things, and is not capitalized. In the sentence "My niece bought a house in the country," *niece, house,* and *country* are common nouns.
com·mon·place [kom′ən·plās′] **1** *adj.* Not remarkable or interesting; ordinary. **2** *n.* Something ordinary and familiar: A traffic jam is considered a *commonplace* in a large city. **3** *n.* A flat or ordinary remark.
com·mons [kom′ənz] *n.pl.* **1** The common people; those not of a noble class. **2** (*written* **The Commons**) The House of Commons. **3** (*often used with singular verb*) A dining hall where food is provided at a common table, as in a college. **4** Food; rations.
common sense Ordinary intelligence; the understanding a person gets from practical experience.
com·mon·weal [kom′ən·wēl′] *n.* The general welfare.
com·mon·wealth [kom′ən·welth′] *n.* **1** The whole people of a state or nation. **2** A democratic state or nation; republic. **3** A group of states or nations linked by common ties and interests.
com·mo·tion [kə·mō′shən] *n.* Great confusion; excitement; disturbance: Boos and *commotion* interrupted the speech.
com·mu·nal [kom′yə·nəl *or* kə·myōō′nəl] *adj.* Of, having to do with, or belonging to a community; public: a *communal* playground.
com·mune[1] [kə·myōōn′] *v.* **com·muned, com·mun·ing** **1** To talk privately or intimately. **2** To be close to. **3** To receive Holy Communion.
com·mune[2] [kom′yōōn′] *n.* **1** A group of people working or living closely together and often sharing property and tasks. **2** The smallest political division that is locally governed in several European countries.
com·mu·ni·ca·ble [kə·myōō′ni·kə·bəl] *adj.* That can be passed on or communicated from person to person, as a contagious disease.
com·mu·ni·cant [kə·myōō′nə·kənt] *n.* **1** A person who receives or has a right to receive Holy Communion. **2** A person who communicates.
com·mu·ni·cate [kə·myōō′nə·kāt′] *v.* **com·mu·ni·cat·ed, com·mu·ni·cat·ing** **1** To give or exchange thoughts, information, or messages. **2** To express or exchange (as ideas or information). **3** To pass on; transmit: to *communicate* a disease. **4** To be joined; connect: The den *communicates* with the living room. **5** To receive Holy Communion.
com·mu·ni·ca·tion [kə·myōō′nə·kā′shən] *n.* **1** The act of passing on; transmitting. **2** The giving or exchange of ideas or information, as by speech or writing: All our *communication* was by mail. **3** The ideas or information given. **4** A message or letter carrying information. **5** A connection or means of passage from one place to another. **6** (*pl.*) A system for sending and receiving information or messages, as by telephone, radio, and television.

C

communications satellite An artificial satellite that aids communications, as by relaying radio and other signals between stations on Earth.
com·mu·ni·ca·tive [kə·myōō′nə·kā′tiv *or* kə·myōō′·nə·kə·tiv] *adj.* Tending to talk freely.
com·mun·ion [kə·myōōn′yən] *n.* **1** A having or sharing in common: a *communion* of ideas. **2** A fellowship or intimate association: In the mountains we felt a *communion* with nature. **3** A body of people having common religious beliefs. **4** (*written* **Communion**) A Christian ceremony in which bread and wine are blessed and consumed in memory of the death of Christ. **5** (*written* **Communion**) The consecrated bread and wine used in the ceremony. **6** (*written* **Communion**) *adj. use:* a *Communion* service.
com·mu·ni·qué [kə·myōō′nə·kā′] *n.* An official announcement or bulletin.
com·mu·nism [kom′yə·niz′əm] *n.* **1** A social system in which the means for producing economic goods belong to the entire community or the state, not to individuals. **2** (*written* **Communism**) A political organization in which a single political party controls the state and manages the production and distribution of goods, as in the Soviet Union.
com·mu·nist [kom′yə·nist] **1** *n.* A person who supports or is in favor of communism. **2** *n.* (*written* **Communist**) A member of a political party that advocates Communism. **3** *adj.* Communistic.
com·mu·nis·tic [kom′yə·nis′tik] *adj.* Having to do with or favoring communism.
Communist Party A political party based on and supporting the principles of communism.
com·mu·ni·ty [kə·myōō′nə·tē] *n., pl.* **com·mu·ni·ties** **1** A group of people living together in one locality: a rural *community.* **2** A group of people living together who share common interests: a religious *community.* **3** The public; society in general: The *community* votes for the laws it supports. **4** Sameness or likeness: a *community* of interests.
community chest A fund made up of individual contributions to help local welfare organizations.
community college A nonresidential junior college designed to serve a particular community and usually supported by that community.
com·mu·ta·tion [kom′yə·tā′shən] *n.* **1** A substitution, as of one kind of payment for another. **2** A reduction or lightening of punishment: a *commutation* of life imprisonment to 12 years in jail. **3** Regular travel to and from work, usually of some distance.

a	add	**i**	it	**ŏŏ**	took	**oi**	oil		
ā	ace	**ī**	ice	**ōō**	pool	**ou**	pout		
â	care	**o**	odd	**u**	up	**ng**	ring		
ä	palm	**ō**	open	**û**	burn	**th**	thin		
e	end	**ô**	order	**yōō**	fuse	**th**	this		
ē	equal					**zh**	vision		

ə = { a in *above*, e in *sicken*, i in *possible*, o in *melon*, u in *circus* }

com·mu·ta·tive [kom′yə·tā′tiv *or* kə·myōō′tə·tiv] *adj.* Indicating a mathematical operation in which the order of the numbers or quantities does not affect the result, as addition, a + b = b + a, or multiplication, a × b = b × a.

com·mu·ta·tor [kom′yə·tā′tər] *n.* A device, as in an electric motor or generator, that makes the current flow in the right direction at the right time.

com·mute [kə·myōōt′] *v.* **com·mut·ed, com·mut·ing** 1 To change for something less severe: to *commute* a prison term. 2 To make regular, rather long trips to and from work.

com·mut·er [kə·myōō′tər] *n.* A person who makes regular trips of some distance to and from work.

com·pact[1] [*adj.* kəm·pakt′ *or* kom′pakt′, *v.* kəm·pakt′, *n.* kom′pakt′] 1 *adj.* Closely and firmly put together: The magazines were stacked in a *compact* pile. 2 *v.* To pack or press closely and firmly. 3 *adj.* Brief and to the point: a *compact* speech. 4 *n.* A small box for carrying face powder. 5 *n.* A small automobile. **—com·pact′ly** *adv.* **—com·pact′ness** *n.*

A compact car

com·pact[2] [kom′pakt] *n.* An agreement or contract: a *compact* between two nations to promote trade.

compact disc A digital disc on which music or information is recorded, to be played back on a device that uses a laser beam to read the data.

com·pac·tor [kəm·pak′tər] *n.* A device that compresses refuse or other material into tight bundles.

com·pan·ion [kəm·pan′yən] *n.* 1 A person who goes with another person; comrade; associate. 2 A person employed to live or travel with and help another. 3 One of a pair of things that match: These two chairs are *companions.* ◆ *Companion* comes from the Latin *com-,* meaning *together,* and *panis,* meaning *bread,* because *companions* "break bread"—that is, share meals—together.

com·pan·ion·a·ble [kəm·pan′yən·ə·bəl] *adj.* Fitted to be a companion; friendly. **—com·pan′ion·a·bly** *adv.*

com·pan·ion·ship [kəm·pan′yən·ship′] *n.* A being companions; fellowship.

com·pan·ion·way [kəm·pan′yən·wā′] *n.* A staircase leading from the deck of a ship to the area below.

com·pa·ny [kum′pə·nē] *n., pl.* **com·pa·nies** 1 A group of people. 2 A group of people who have come together because of some common purpose or interest: an insurance *company.* 3 Companionship: We always enjoy their *company.* 4 Companions: Don't associate with bad *company.* 5 A guest or guests: We're having *company* tonight. 6 A body of soldiers commanded by a captain. 7 The officers and sailors of a ship. **—keep company** 1 To be with or go with: *Keep* me *company* at the movies. 2 To go together, as an engaged couple; court. **—part company** To end friendship or association: After vacation, they *parted company.*

com·pa·ra·ble [kom′pər·ə·bəl] *adj.* 1 Similar enough to be compared: Are the boats *comparable* in size? 2 Fit to be compared: A bow is not *comparable* to a rifle. **—com′pa·ra·bly** *adv.*

com·par·a·tive [kəm·par′ə·tiv] 1 *adj.* Having to do with or using comparison: *comparative* studies. 2 *adj.* Estimated by comparison; relative: The work is of *comparative* importance. 3 *adj.* In grammar, designating the form of an adjective or adverb used to express a greater or lesser quantity, quality, or relation. 4 *n.* The comparative degree of an adjective or adverb. **—com·par′a·tive·ly** *adv.*

com·pare [kəm·pâr′] *v.* **com·pared, com·par·ing,** *n.* 1 *v.* To describe as similar; liken: to *compare* a laugh to music. 2 *v.* To examine so as to find similarities or differences: to *compare* one student's work with another's. 3 *n.* Comparison. 4 *v.* To be suitable for comparison: Few composers can be *compared* with Beethoven. 5 *v.* To form or state the degrees of comparison of (an adjective or adverb). **—beyond compare** Above comparison; without equal.

com·par·i·son [kəm·par′ə·sən] *n.* 1 A comparing or being compared: Would you make a *comparison* between the two books? 2 Enough likeness to make things worth comparing: There's no *comparison* between the two books. 3 In grammar, the change in form of an adjective or adverb that indicates differences of degree. There are three degrees of comparison, the positive, the comparative, and the superlative: The *comparison* of *new* is *new, newer, newest.* **—in comparison with** Compared with.

com·part·ment [kəm·pärt′mənt] *n.* Any one of the separate sections into which an enclosed area is divided: a *compartment* in a desk drawer.

com·part·men·tal·ize [kəm·pärt′men′təl·īz′] *v.* **com·part·men·tal·ized, com·part·men·tal·iz·ing** To divide into compartments or separate sections.

com·pass [kum′pəs *or* kom′pəs] 1 *n.* An instrument that shows direction, usually by a magnetic needle that always points to magnetic north. 2 *n.* The reach or extent; scope: the *compass* of a lifetime. 3 *n.* The limits: Stay within the *compass* of the school playground. 4 *n.* The range of tones of a voice or instrument. 5 *n.* (*sometimes pl.*) An instrument with two legs that are hinged at one end, used for taking measurements and drawing circles. 6 *v.* To go round; circle: to *compass* the schoolyard. 7 *v.* To surround; encircle; encompass. 8 *v.* To grasp mentally; understand: to *compass* a problem. 9 *v.* To attain or accomplish: to *compass* one's wishes.

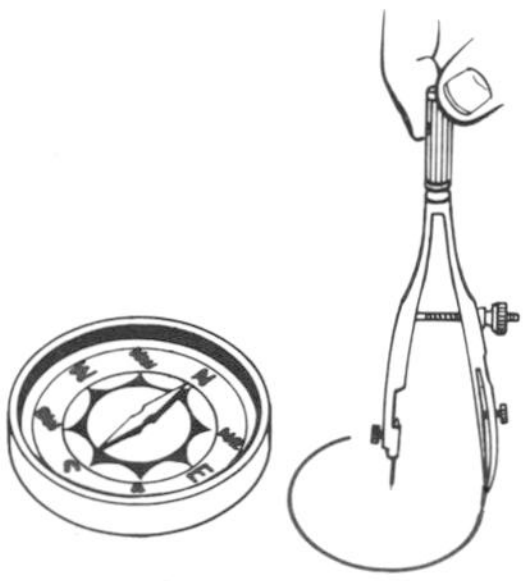
Compasses

com·pas·sion [kəm·pash′ən] *n.* Pity for the suffering or distress of another and the desire to help.

com·pas·sion·ate [kəm·pash′ən·it] *adj.* Feeling compassion or pity; sympathetic; merciful. **—com·pas′sion·ate·ly** *adv.*

com·pat·i·ble [kəm·pat′ə·bəl] *adj.* Able to get along together; agreeable. **—com·pat′i·bil′i·ty** *n.* **—com·pat′i·bly** *adv.*

com·pa·tri·ot [kəm·pā′trē·ət] *n.* Someone from one's own country.

com·peer [kom′pir′ *or* kəm·pir′] *n.* An equal, peer, or companion.

com·pel [kəm·pel′] *v.* **com·pelled, com·pel·ling** 1 To force; drive: The flood *compelled* us to seek high ground. 2 To obtain by force; demand: The law *compels* obedience.

com·pen·di·ous [kəm·pen'dē·əs] *adj.* Giving much information in a small space; concise and complete.
com·pen·di·um [kəm·pen'dē·əm] *n., pl.* **com·pen·di·ums** or **com·pen·di·a** [kəm·pen'dē·ə] A summary giving much information in a small space.
com·pen·sate [kom'pən·sāt'] *v.* **com·pen·sat·ed, com·pen·sat·ing** 1 To make suitable payment or reward to or for: to *compensate* a person for work. 2 To be a balance; make up: Your hard work *compensated* for your late arrival.
com·pen·sa·tion [kom'pən·sā'shən] *n.* 1 The act of compensating. 2 Something paid, given, or done to balance something else.
com·pete [kəm·pēt'] *v.* **com·pet·ed, com·pet·ing** 1 To take part in a contest. 2 To be a rival or contender: Six teams *competed* in all.
com·pe·tence [kom'pə·təns] *n.* 1 Ability; capability: They have the *competence* to do the work. 2 Enough money to live comfortably.
com·pe·ten·cy [kom'pə·tən·sē] *n.* Competence.
com·pe·tent [kom'pə·tənt] Having enough ability; capable: a *competent* teacher. **—com'pe·tent·ly** *adv.*
com·pe·ti·tion [kom'pə·tish'ən] *n.* 1 Effort to get something wanted by others or to excel others: Do you think that *competition* in the classroom is good for most students? 2 A contest: a swimming *competition.*
com·pet·i·tive [kəm·pet'ə·tiv] *adj.* Having to do with or decided by competition. **—com·pet'i·tive·ly** *adv.*
com·pet·i·tor [kəm·pet'ə·tər] *n.* A person who competes, as in games or in business.
com·pi·la·tion [kom'pə·lā'shən] *n.* 1 The act of compiling. 2 Something that is compiled, as an encyclopedia.
com·pile [kəm·pīl'] *v.* **com·piled, com·pil·ing** 1 To put together in a list, book, or account: to *compile* statistics of population. 2 To make or compose (a book) from various materials.
com·pil·er [kəm·pī'lər] *n.* A computer program that changes a higher-level language such as BASIC into machine language.
com·pla·cence [kəm·plā'səns] *n.* Complacency.
com·pla·cen·cy [kəm·plā'sən·sē] *n.* A being pleased or satisfied with oneself; smugness.
com·pla·cent [kəm·plā'sənt] *adj.* Satisfied with oneself, one's possessions, or one's accomplishments.
com·plain [kəm·plān'] *v.* 1 To find fault or say that something is bad, wrong, or uncomfortable: to *complain* about bad weather. 2 To make a charge or report of something bad: to *complain* to the neighbors about their noisy party.
com·plain·ant [kəm·plā'nənt] *n.* A person who starts a lawsuit against another.
com·plaint [kəm·plānt'] *n.* 1 An expression of dissatisfaction or discomfort; a finding fault. 2 The thing complained about: "No hot water" is a common *complaint.* 3 A sickness or physical disorder. 4 A charge or accusation.
com·plai·sant [kəm·plā'sənt *or* kəm·plā'zənt] *adj.* Showing a desire to please. **—com·plai'sance** *n.*
com·ple·ment [*n.* kom'plə·mənt, *v.* kom'plə·ment'] 1 *n.* Something that completes or perfects. 2 *n.* Full or complete number, allowance, or amount: The team has its *complement* of players. 3 *v.* To make complete; supply a lack in: The artist's drawings *complement* the poet's funny verses. 4 *n.* In grammar, a word or group of words used to complete a predicate. *Gray* in "The sky was gray" is a complement. ◆ See COMPLIMENT.
com·ple·men·ta·ry [kom'plə·men'tər·ē *or* kom'plə·men'trē] *adj.* Serving to fill up or complete.
complementary angle Either one of two angles whose sum is a right angle.

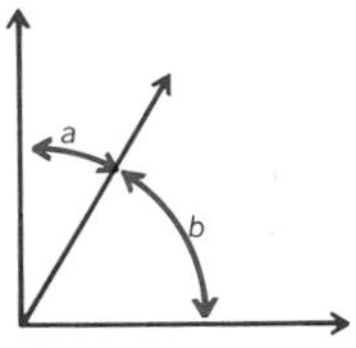

a + b = 90°
a and b are complementary angles

complementary color Any one of a pair of contrasting colors of the spectrum that produce gray or white when mixed in the right proportions: Green and red are *complementary* colors.
com·plete [kəm·plēt'] *adj., v.* **com·plet·ed, com·plet·ing** 1 *adj.* Having all needed or normal parts; entire; whole: a *complete* set of dishes. 2 *v.* To make whole, with no part missing: A viola *completed* the quartet. 3 *adj.* Wholly finished; ended: My review for the test is *complete.* 4 *v.* To finish; end: I'll *complete* the housework at noon. 5 *adj.* Full; thorough: She has a *complete* command of French.
com·plete·ly [kəm·plēt'lē] *adv.* In a complete manner or degree; entirely; wholly.
com·ple·tion [kəm·plē'shən] *n.* 1 The act of completing. 2 A completed condition; finish: At the *completion* of the school year we go on vacation.
com·plex [*adj.* kəm·pleks' *or* kom'pleks', *n.* kom'·pleks'] 1 *adj.* Complicated; intricate; not simple: a *complex* mathematical problem. 2 *adj.* Made up of a number of parts. 3 *n.* A complicated or intricate whole: The railroad yard is a *complex* of tracks. 4 *n.* An unreasonable dislike or fear caused by memories and emotions which a person may not be aware of. **—com·plex'ly** *adv.*
complex fraction A fraction containing a fraction or mixed number in the numerator or the denominator or both.
com·plex·ion [kəm·plek'shən] *n.* 1 The color and appearance of the skin, especially of the face. 2 Character; quality: The *complexion* of our friendship was changed by an argument.
com·plex·i·ty [kəm·plek'sə·tē] *n., pl.* **com·plex·i·ties** 1 The state of being complex. 2 A complex thing.
complex sentence A sentence that is made up of an independent clause and one or more subordinate clauses. "Recess ends when the bell rings" is a complex sentence.
com·pli·ance [kəm·plī'əns] *n.* 1 The act of yielding or giving in: The law demands *compliance.* 2 A tendency to yield or give in. **—in compliance with** In agreement with.
com·pli·ant [kəm·plī'ənt] *adj.* Complying; yielding.
com·pli·cate [kom'plə·kāt'] *v.* **com·pli·cat·ed, com·pli·cat·ing** To make or become hard to understand, use, or solve: Problems *complicate* a person's life.
com·pli·cat·ed [kom'plə·kā'tid] *adj.* Involved; complex; not simple: a *complicated* engine.

a add	**i** it	**o͝o** took	**oi** oil
ā ace	**ī** ice	**o͞o** pool	**ou** pout
â care	**o** odd	**u** up	**ng** ring
ä palm	**ō** open	**û** burn	**th** thin
e end	**ô** order	**yo͞o** fuse	**th** this
ē equal			**zh** vision

ə = a in *above*, e in *sicken*, i in *possible*, o in *melon*, u in *circus*

com·pli·ca·tion [kom′plə·kā′shən] *n.* 1 An involved, difficult, or confusing state. 2 Anything that complicates: Our trip turned out to be full of annoying *complications.* 3 The act of complicating.

com·plic·i·ty [kəm·plis′ə·tē] *n., pl.* **com·plic·i·ties** Connection in a wrongful act as a partner or accomplice.

com·pli·ment [*n.* kom′plə·mənt, *v.* kom′plə·ment′] 1 *n.* An expression of admiration, praise, or congratulation: They paid me a *compliment* on my report. 2 *n.* An expression of courtesy: The students paid the teacher the *compliment* of complete silence during the lecture. 3 *n.* (*usually pl.*) A formal greeting. 4 *v.* To pay a compliment. ◆ Originally a *compliment* was thought of as completing or fulfilling an act of courtesy. Now it refers to any expression of praise or admiration. *Complement* is a part added to something else to make it complete: This novel is the *complement* to my set of Virginia Woolf's works.

com·pli·men·ta·ry [kom′plə·men′tər·ē *or* kom′plə·men′trē] *adj.* 1 Paying or like a compliment. 2 Given free: a *complimentary* copy of a book.

com·ply [kəm·plī′] *v.* **com·plied, com·ply·ing** To act in agreement: *Comply* with my request.

com·po·nent [kəm·pō′nənt] 1 *n.* One main part, ingredient, or constituent of a whole: Tuner, amplifier, and speaker are major *components* of a radio. 2 *adj.* Helping to form: *component* parts.

com·port [kəm·pôrt′] *v.* 1 To conduct or behave: The judges *comported* themselves with great dignity. 2 To agree; suit: Your solemn look did not *comport* with the gaiety of the occasion.

com·port·ment [kəm·pôrt′mənt] *n.* Behavior or bearing.

com·pose [kəm·pōz′] *v.* **com·posed, com·pos·ing** 1 To make up; form: Water is *composed* of hydrogen and oxygen. 2 To create: to *compose* music. 3 To make calm: *Compose* yourself before you speak. 4 To settle, as differences. 5 To arrange, as elements in a painting. 6 To arrange; set: to *compose* type.

com·posed [kəm·pōzd′] *adj.* Not disturbed or agitated; calm; self-possessed.

com·pos·er [kəm·pō′zər] *n.* A person who composes, especially one who composes music.

com·pos·ite [kəm·poz′it] 1 *adj.* Made up of separate parts; compound. 2 *adj.* Belonging to a group of plants that have heads made up of many tiny flowers, as asters and dandelions. 3 *n.* Something that is made up of parts.

composite number A number that is evenly divisible by one or more whole numbers besides itself and 1. 6, 8, and 9 are composite numbers.

com·po·si·tion [kom′pə·zish′ən] *n.* 1 The makeup of something. 2 The act of putting together: The *composition* of the symphony took two years. 3 The thing that is put together, as a piece of music. 4 A short essay, especially one written as an exercise for school. 5 A mixture, as of metals.

com·pos·i·tor [kəm·poz′ə·tər] *n.* Another word for TYPESETTER.

com·post [kom′pōst′] *n.* 1 A mixture of rotted materials, as leaves, grass, and manure, used for fertilizing. 2 A mixture; compound.

com·po·sure [kəm·pō′zhər] *n.* Calmness; self-control.

com·pote [kom′pōt′] *n.* 1 Fruit stewed in syrup and served as a dessert. 2 A dish or bowl, usually with a stem, for holding fruit, sweets, or nuts.

com·pound[1] [*n., adj.* kom′pound′, *v.* kom·pound′ *or* kəm·pound′] 1 *n.* A combination or mixture of two or more ingredients or parts. 2 *adj.* Having or made up of more than one part. 3 *v.* To mix; put together: to *compound* a medicine. 4 *n.* A word formed by combining two or more words. The words that are combined are sometimes joined by a hyphen or hyphens, as in *first-class* or *forget-me-not.* They are sometimes written in solid form, as in *shoestring.* They also are sometimes written separately, if their combination has its own special meaning, as in *high school.* 5 *n.* A substance formed by chemical combination of two or more elements: Salt is a *compound* of sodium and chlorine. 6 *v.* To settle by compromise, as a debt.

com·pound[2] [kom′pound′] *n.* A fenced or walled yard with buildings in it.

compound eye An eye, as of an insect, having many small sections, each with its own lens.

compound fraction Another term for COMPLEX FRACTION.

compound fracture A fracture in which part of the broken bone is visible through skin that it has pierced.

compound interest Interest on both the original sum of money and the accumulated interest.

compound leaf A leaf, as of an ash or locust tree, made of several leaflets attached to a common stalk.

compound sentence A sentence that has two or more independent clauses but no subordinate clauses.

compound word A compound (def. 4).

com·pre·hend [kom′pri·hend′] *v.* 1 To understand; grasp: I don't *comprehend* spoken German. 2 To take in; include: The list *comprehends* all the dealers in the city.

com·pre·hen·si·ble [kom′pri·hen′sə·bəl] *adj.* Understandable: a *comprehensible* problem.

com·pre·hen·sion [kom′pri·hen′shən] *n.* 1 The act of understanding. 2 The power to understand: His *comprehension* of foreign languages was excellent.

com·pre·hen·sive [kom′pri·hen′siv] *adj.* 1 Of wide scope; including much: a *comprehensive* study of literature. 2 Having a broad understanding. —**com′pre·hen′sive·ly** *adv.*

com·press [*v.* kəm·pres′, *n.* kom′pres′] 1 *v.* To press together; condense; squeeze: to *compress* gas. 2 *n.* A folded cloth or pad, used to stop bleeding or to apply moisture, heat, or cold.

compressed air Air reduced in volume by pressure greater than atmospheric pressure.

com·press·i·ble [kəm·pres′ə·bəl] *adj.* Capable of being compressed. —**com·press′i·bil′i·ty** *n.*

com·pres·sion [kəm·presh′ən] *n.* 1 The act of compressing. 2 The state of being compressed.

com·press·ive [kəm·pres′iv] *adj.* Compressing or tending to compress.

com·pres·sor [kəm·pres′ər] *n.* 1 A person or thing that compresses. 2 A machine for compressing a gas or air.

com·prise [kəm·prīz′] *v.* **com·prised, com·pris·ing** To consist of; contain; include: The state *comprises* 29 counties.

com·pro·mise [kom′prə·mīz′] *n., v.* **com·pro·mised, com·pro·mis·ing** 1 *n.* An adjustment or settlement in which each side gives up part of its demands: I offered $20.00. The dealer asked for $30.00, but accepted $25.00 as a *compromise.* **2** *v.* To settle a dispute by such an adjustment. **3** *v.* To expose to risk, suspicion, or disgrace: to *compromise* one's reputation.

comp·trol·ler [kən·trō'lər] *n.* Another spelling of CONTROLLER (def. 1). ◆ *Comptroller* is a word based on the French word *compte,* meaning *an account,* because a *comptroller* managed the accounts and expenditures of a large household.

com·pul·sion [kəm·pul'shən] *n.* **1** The act of compelling. **2** A being compelled: Under *compulsion* they went into exile. **3** An irresistible, sometimes irrational, urge: a *compulsion* to eat sweets.

com·pul·sive [kəm·pul'siv] *adj.* Of, having to do with, or caused by compulsion.

com·pul·so·ry [kəm·pul'sər·ē] *adj.* **1** Required; enforced: *compulsory* education. **2** Using force.

com·punc·tion [kəm·pungk'shən] *n.* A feeling of guilt or regret: to have a slight *compunction* about missing a class.

com·pu·ta·tion [kom'pyə·tā'shən] *n.* **1** The act or method of computing; calculation; reckoning. **2** The amount or number arrived at by computing.

com·pute [kəm·pyo͞ot'] *v.* **com·put·ed, com·put·ing** To figure by using mathematics; calculate; reckon.

com·put·er [kəm·pyo͞o'tər] *n.* An electronic device that can compile, store, process, and retrieve data. Computers are widely used to solve mathematical and logical problems quickly and accurately.

com·put·er·ize [kəm·pyo͞o'tər·īz'] *v.* **com·put·er·ized, com·put·er·iz·ing** **1** To equip with an electronic computer or computers: to *computerize* an industry. **2** To store or process in an electronic computer: to *computerize* the records of a bank. **3** To accomplish or operate by means of a computer: *computerized* axial tomography.

computerized axial tomography Tomography in which a computerized combination of tomograms forms a three-dimensional image.

computer language A code used to give instructions to, store information in, or retrieve information from a computer.

computer literacy The ability to use computers, including a basic, nontechnical understanding of how they work.

com·rade [kom'rad *or* kom'rəd] *n.* **1** A close companion or friend. **2** A person who shares one's occupation or interests. **—com'rade·ship** *n.*

con[1] [kon] *v.* **conned, con·ning** To study with care; learn: to *con* a book.

con[2] [kon] **1** *n.* A vote, argument, or person against something. **2** *adv.* Against: to discuss a matter pro and *con.*

con[3] [kon] *n., v.* **conned, con·ning** *slang* **1** To swindle (someone) after first gaining his or her confidence. **2** To fool or trick, as by flattery or deceit.

con- A prefix meaning: With; together, in association with, as in *concentrate.*

con·cave [kon·kāv' *or* kon'kāv'] *adj.* Hollow and curved like the inner curve of a crescent or bowl. **—con·cav·i·ty** [kon·kav'·ə·tē] *n.*

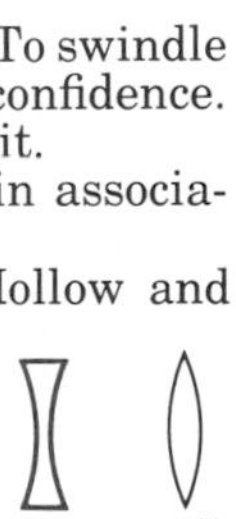
concave lens convex lens

con·ceal [kən·sēl'] *v.* To keep secret or out of sight; hide.

con·ceal·ment [kən·sēl'mənt] *n.* **1** The act of concealing. **2** A place or means of hiding.

con·cede [kən·sēd'] *v.* **con·ced·ed, con·ced·ing** **1** To admit as true; acknowledge: to *concede* a point in an argument. **2** To grant; yield: I'll *concede* you the extra point.

con·ceit [kən·sēt'] *n.* **1** Too high an opinion of oneself or one's accomplishments: Your *conceit* about your intelligence is ridiculous. **2** A fanciful idea; a clever thought or expression. ◆ *Conceit* was formed from *conceive* in imitation of *deceit* and *deceive.*

con·ceit·ed [kən·sē'tid] *adj.* Having too high an opinion of oneself or one's accomplishments; vain. **—con·ceit'ed·ly** *adv.* **—con·ceit'ed·ness** *n.*

con·ceiv·a·ble [kən·sē'və·bəl] *adj.* Capable of being thought of; imaginable: the best plan *conceivable.* **—con·ceiv'a·bly** *adv.*

con·ceive [kən·sēv'] *v.* **con·ceived, con·ceiv·ing** **1** To form or develop as an idea; imagine: a new nation, *conceived* in liberty; to *conceive* a solution to the problem. **2** To understand; grasp: It is hard to *conceive* a million years. **3** To become pregnant with.

con·cen·trate [kon'sən·trāt'] *v.* **con·cen·trat·ed, con·cen·trat·ing,** *n.* **1** *v.* To gather or focus one's entire attention: to *concentrate* on a book. **2** *v.* To gather or collect closely together: to *concentrate* our troops. **3** *v.* To make less diluted or mixed: to *concentrate* a solution by boiling off water. **4** *n.* A concentrated substance, as frozen juice.

con·cen·tra·tion [kon'sən·trā'shən] *n.* **1** The act of concentrating. **2** A concentrated condition. **3** Complete attention: Odd noises broke our *concentration.* **4** Strength, as of a solution.

concentration camp A fenced and guarded camp for confining political enemies, aliens, or prisoners of war.

con·cen·tric [kən·sen'trik] *adj.* Having a common center: *concentric* circles.

concentric circles concentric triangles

con·cen·tri·cal [kən·sen'·tri·kəl] *adj.* Concentric.

con·cept [kon'sept'] *n.* A general idea or notion: the *concept* of natural rights.

con·cep·tion [kən·sep'shən] *n.* **1** The act of forming an idea. **2** An idea, notion, or concept: They have no *conception* of punctuality. **3** The beginning of pregnancy.

con·cep·tu·al [kən·sep'cho͞o·əl] *adj.* Of, having to do with, or made up of concepts: *conceptual* thought.

con·cern [kən·sûrn'] **1** *v.* To relate to; be the business of: This situation *concerns* everyone. **2** *n.* Anything that relates to one; affair; business. **3** *v.* To engage, involve, or interest (oneself): Doctors *concern* themselves with medical matters. **4** *v.* To worry; trouble: The child's poor health *concerns* me. **5** *n.* Interest; worry. **6** *n.* A business firm.

con·cerned [kən·sûrnd'] *adj.* **1** Interested or involved: As a pianist, Mary is more *concerned* with

a	add	**i**	it	**o͝o**	took	**oi**	oil
ā	ace	**ī**	ice	**o͞o**	pool	**ou**	pout
â	care	**o**	odd	**u**	up	**ng**	ring
ä	palm	**ō**	open	**û**	burn	**th**	thin
e	end	**ô**	order	**yo͞o**	fuse	**t͟h**	this
ē	equal					**zh**	vision

ə = { a in *above* e in *sicken* i in *possible* / o in *melon* u in *circus* }

music than with painting. 2 Uneasy; worried: I'm *concerned* about the future of our project.
con·cern·ing [kən·sûr′ning] *prep.* Relating to; about; regarding: a book *concerning* dinosaurs.
con·cert [*n.* kon′sûrt, *v.* kən·sûrt′] 1 *n.* A musical program or performance. 2 *n.* Agreement; harmony; unity; accord. 3 *v.* To arrange or work out by agreement: Plans were *concerted* for the next season. **—in concert** In unison; all together.
con·cer·ted [kən·sûr′tid] *adj.* Planned or done together: Theirs was a *concerted* effort.
con·cer·ti·na [kon′sər·tē′nə] *n.* A small musical instrument like an accordion.
con·cer·tize [kon′sər·tīz′] *v.* **con·cer·tized, con·cer·tiz·ing** To perform in professional concerts.
con·cer·to [kən·cher′tō] *n., pl.* **con·cer·tos** or **con·cer·ti** [kən·cher′tē] A musical composition, usually of three movements, for a solo instrument or instruments accompanied by an orchestra.

Concertina

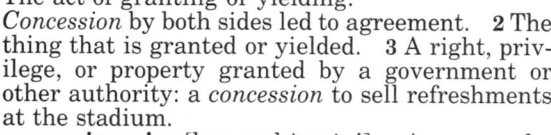

con·ces·sion [kən·sesh′ən] *n.* 1 The act of granting or yielding: *Concession* by both sides led to agreement. 2 The thing that is granted or yielded. 3 A right, privilege, or property granted by a government or other authority: a *concession* to sell refreshments at the stadium.
con·ces·sion·aire [kən·sesh′ə·nâr′] *n.* A person who holds or runs a business concession, as at a public park or stadium.
conch [kongk *or* konch] *n., pl.* **conchs** [kongks] or **conch·es** [kon′chiz] 1 A marine animal that lives in a large, spiral shell. 2 The shell itself.

Conch

con·cil·i·ate [kən·sil′ē·āt′] *v.* **con·cil·i·at·ed, con·cil·i·at·ing** 1 To overcome the unfriendliness of; win over; soothe: to *conciliate* an enemy. 2 To reconcile; make compatible: to *conciliate* conflicting stories. **—con·cil′i·a′tion** *n.*
con·cil·i·a·to·ry [kən·sil′ē·ə·tôr′ē] *adj.* Tending to soothe or win over.
con·cise [kən·sīs′] *adj.* Expressing much in brief form; short: a *concise* summary. **—con·cise′ly** *adv.* **—con·cise′ness** *n.*
con·clave [kon′klāv′] *n.* A private or secret meeting, especially a private meeting held by Roman Catholic cardinals to elect a pope.
con·clude [kən·klōōd′] *v.* **con·clud·ed, con·clud·ing** 1 To end; finish: How did the orator *conclude* the speech? 2 To arrange or settle finally: to *conclude* a treaty. 3 To form an opinion; infer.
con·clu·sion [kən·klōō′zhən] *n.* 1 The end of something; finish; close: the *conclusion* of a play. 2 A closing part, as the summing up of a speech. 3 The result of an act or process; outcome. 4 A judgment or opinion reached by reasoning: My *conclusion* is that a tube is weak. 5 A final arrangement; settlement. **—in conclusion** In closing; finally.
con·clu·sive [kən·klōō′siv] *adj.* Putting an end to doubt; decisive: The debating team's reasons were *conclusive* and sound.
con·coct [kən·kokt′ *or* kon·kokt′] *v.* 1 To make by mixing ingredients, as food. 2 To make up; devise: to *concoct* a plan.
con·coc·tion [kən·kok′shən *or* kon·kok′shən] *n.* 1 The act of concocting. 2 Something concocted: a *concoction* of ice cream and fruit juice.
con·com·i·tant [kən·kom′ə·tənt *or* kon·kom′ə·tənt] 1 *adj.* Going along with; accompanying: hotel service and *concomitant* comforts. 2 *n.* Something that goes along with something else.
con·cord [kon′kôrd′ *or* kong′kôrd′] *n.* 1 Peace; harmonious agreement. 2 A treaty establishing this: a *concord* between nations.
con·cor·dance [kən·kôr′dəns *or* kon·kôr′dəns] *n.* 1 Agreement; concord. 2 An alphabetical index of the important words in a book with references to the places where they occur: a *concordance* to the Bible.
con·cor·dant [kən·kôr′dənt *or* kon·kôr′dənt] *adj.* In agreement; harmonious.
con·cor·dat [kən·kôr′dat] *n.* 1 A formal agreement; covenant. 2 An agreement between a pope and a sovereign or government regarding ecclesiastical matters.
con·course [kon′kôrs′ *or* kong′kôrs′] *n.* 1 A coming or moving together; confluence: a *concourse* of waterways. 2 A crowd; assembly. 3 An open place where crowds gather or through which they pass, as in a railroad station.
con·crete [kon′krēt′ *or* kon·krēt′] 1 *n.* A hard substance formed of cement, sand, gravel, and water, used as a building and paving material. 2 *adj. use:* a *concrete* floor. 3 *adj.* Actually existing; real: A chair is *concrete,* but a dream is not. 4 *adj.* Specific; particular: Give me a *concrete* example. **—con·crete′ness** *n.*
con·cu·bine [kong′kyə·bīn′ *or* kon′kyə·bīn′] *n.* 1 A woman who lives with a man without being married to him. 2 A secondary wife, in certain countries where a man is allowed to have more than one wife.
con·cur [kən·kûr′] *v.* **con·curred, con·cur·ring** 1 To agree or approve: I *concur* with you in your decision. 2 To cooperate; work together: Reading, study, and reflection had *concurred* to make him wise. 3 To happen at the same time.
con·cur·rence [kən·kûr′əns] *n.* 1 Agreement: Both sides are in *concurrence* on this matter. 2 A working or happening together.
con·cur·rent [kən·kûr′ənt] *adj.* 1 Happening at the same time; existing in close association: The earliest birds and mammals had *concurrent* developments. 2 In agreement; consistent: The views brought out were not identical but *concurrent.* **—con·cur′rent·ly** *adv.*
con·cus·sion [kən·kush′ən] *n.* 1 A violent shaking; a shock, as an earthquake. 2 A violent shock to some organ, especially to the brain, by a fall, blow, or blast.
con·demn [kən·dem′] *v.* 1 To speak against as being wrong: to *condemn* dishonesty. 2 To declare the guilt of; convict: to *condemn* a prisoner. 3 To pass sentence on: to *condemn* someone to prison. 4 To declare unfit or unsafe for use: to *condemn* a building. 5 To take over for public use: to *condemn* land for a highway.
con·dem·na·tion [kon′dem·nā′shən] *n.* 1 The act of condemning. 2 The state of being condemned. 3 Great disapproval; blame; censure. 4 A reason or cause for condemning: The criminals' behavior

upon their arrest was sufficient *condemnation.*

con·dem·na·to·ry [kon·dem′nə·tôr′ē] *adj.* Imposing or containing condemnation; condemning; a *condemnatory* sentence.

con·den·sate [kon′dən·sāt′ *or* kən·den′sāt′] *n.* Something produced by condensation, especially a liquid obtained by condensing a gas or vapor.

con·den·sa·tion [kon′den·sā′shən] *n.* **1** The act of condensing. **2** A being condensed. **3** Any product of condensing: Dew is a *condensation* of water vapor from the air. **4** The changing of a vapor or gas to a liquid, or of a liquid to a solid.

Condensation on a glass

con·dense [kən·dens′] *v.* **con·densed, con·dens·ing** **1** To make or become denser, thicker, or more compressed, as by removing water: to *condense* orange juice before freezing it. **2** To shorten; make concise, as a speech or essay. **3** To change (a gas or vapor) into a liquid, or (a liquid) into a solid.

condensed milk Cow's milk that has been sweetened and thickened by evaporation.

con·dens·er [kən·den′sər] *n.* **1** A person or thing that condenses. **2** Any device for reducing a vapor to liquid or solid form. **3** A capacitor.

con·de·scend [kon′di·send′] *v.* **1** To come down willingly to the status of one's inferiors or show kindness to them: The star pitcher *condescended* to talk to our ball club. **2** To behave as if superior; patronize.

con·de·scend·ing [kon′di·sen′ding] *adj.* Showing condescension.

con·de·scen·sion [kon′di·sen′shən] *n.* **1** A willing descent to the status of one's inferiors. **2** Proud, patronizing behavior.

con·di·ment [kon′də·mənt] *n.* Something used to season food, as a sauce, pepper, or spice.

con·di·tion [kən·dish′ən] **1** *n.* The state of being of a person or thing: This book is in good *condition.* **2** *n.* Physical fitness; healthy state: The team is in *condition* for a hard game. **3** *v.* To put into a good state; make fit: Running two miles a day *conditioned* the jogger's legs. **4** *n.* Rank in life; social status: A serf had a low *condition.* **5** *n.* Something on which another thing depends: A dry track is a *condition* of a fast race. **6** *v.* To be a necessary factor of: A fast or slow track *conditions* the speed of a race. **7** *n.* A requirement or stipulation: Each side set up *conditions* before the meeting could begin. **8** *v.* To make conditional or dependent. **9** *v.* To accustom or train: The teacher *conditioned* the students to work hard. **10** *v.* To cause to develop a conditioned response. **—on condition that** Provided that; if.

con·di·tion·al [kən·dish′ən·əl] *adj.* **1** Dependent on or subject to a condition. **2** Expressing or implying a condition: *If I can come* in "If I can come, I will" is a *conditional* clause.

con·di·tioned [kən·dish′ənd] *adj.* **1** Subject to or dependent on a condition or conditions; conditional. **2** Of, having to do with, or resulting from conditioning.

conditioned reflex A conditioned response.

conditioned response A response to a secondary stimulus that has become associated over a period of time with a primary stimulus. An example of a conditioned response would be the salivating of a dog at the sound of a bell (the secondary stimulus) after it has been trained to associate the sound of the bell with the sight and smell of meat (the primary stimulus).

con·do [kon′dō] *n., pl.* **con·dos** *informal* A condominium (defs. 1, 2).

C

con·dole [kən·dōl′] *v.* **con·doled, con·dol·ing** To grieve or express sympathy.

con·do·lence [kən·dō′ləns] *n.* An expression of sympathy.

con·do·min·i·um [kon′də·min′ē·əm] *n.* **1** An apartment building or group of buildings in which the apartments are owned individually. **2** An apartment in such a building or group of buildings. **3** The contractual arrangement under which such an apartment is owned.

con·done [kən·dōn′] *v.* **con·doned, con·don·ing** To forgive or pass over: Many parents *condone* the mistakes of their children.

con·dor [kon′dôr′ *or* kon′dər] *n.* A large vulture having no feathers on its head and neck. Condors are found in the mountains of South America and California. ◆ *Condor* comes from a South American Indian name.

Condor

con·duce [kən·d(y)o͞os′] *v.* **con·duced, con·duc·ing** To help or tend toward a result; contribute: Fresh air *conduces* to good health.

con·du·cive [kən·d(y)o͞o′siv] *adj.* Helpful: Good lighting is *conducive* to good vision.

con·duct [*n.* kon′dukt, *v.* kən·dukt′] **1** *n.* The way a person acts or lives; behavior. **2** *v.* To act or behave: They *conduct* themselves well. **3** *n.* Management, as of a business; direction; control. **4** *v.* To manage; direct; control: How does she *conduct* her staff? **5** *v.* To guide or lead: to *conduct* an orchestra brilliantly. **6** *v.* To pass on; carry (as heat or electricity): Wood *conducts* heat badly.

con·duc·tion [kən·duk′shən] *n.* **1** A carrying: the *conduction* of water through a pipe. **2** The passage of heat, light, sound, or electricity through a material that does not appear to move.

con·duc·tive [kən·duk′tiv] *adj.* Able to conduct, as heat or electricity.

con·duc·tiv·i·ty [kon′duk·tiv′ə·tē] *n.* The ability of a substance to act as a conductor.

con·duc·tor [kən·duk′tər] *n.* **1** A person who leads or guides. **2** A person in charge of a railroad train, streetcar, or bus. **3** The director of an orchestra or chorus. **4** A material that allows light, heat, sound, or electricity to pass through.

con·duit [kon′do͞o·it *or* kon′dit] *n.* **1** A channel or pipe for carrying water or other liquid. **2** A covered passage or tube for electric wires.

a	add	**i**	it	**o͝o**	took	**oi**	oil
ā	ace	**ī**	ice	**o͞o**	pool	**ou**	pout
â	care	**o**	odd	**u**	up	**ng**	ring
ä	palm	**ō**	open	**û**	burn	**th**	thin
e	end	**ô**	order	**yo͞o**	fuse	**t͟h**	this
ē	equal					**zh**	vision

ə = a in *above*, e in *sicken*, i in *possible*, o in *melon*, u in *circus*

cone [kōn] *n.* 1 A surface formed by the set of points on all the lines joining the points of a given curve to a fixed point. 2 A figure consisting of such a surface bounded by two planes that intersect all its lines and form closed curves. 3 Any object having such a shape. 4 A dry, scaly fruit, as of the pine tree.

cone pine cone ice cream cone

Con·es·to·ga wagon [kon′is·tō′gə] A heavy covered wagon with broad wheels, used by early American freight haulers and pioneers. ◆ These wagons were named for the *Conestoga* region of SE Pennsylvania, where they were first built in the 1700s.

con·ey [kō′nē] *n., pl.* **con·eys** 1 A rabbit, especially the European rabbit. 2 Rabbit fur.

con·fec·tion [kən·fek′shən] *n.* Any of various sweet preparations, as candy or preserves.

con·fec·tion·er [kən·fek′shən·ər] *n.* A person who makes or has to do with confectionery.

con·fec·tion·er·y [kən·fek′shən·er′ē] *n., pl.* **con·fec·tion·er·ies** 1 All kinds of sweets, as ice cream, candies, and cakes. 2 The shop or business of a confectioner.

con·fed·er·a·cy [kən·fed′ər·ə·sē] *n., pl.* **con·fed·er·a·cies** 1 A union or league of persons or states who have joined together for mutual support or action. 2 An unlawful combination; conspiracy. 3 (*written* **the Confederacy**) The Confederate States of America.

con·fed·er·ate [*n., adj.* kən·fed′ər·it, *v.* kən·fed′ə·rāt′] *n., adj., v.* **con·fed·er·at·ed, con·fed·er·at·ing** 1 *n.* A partner or accomplice, as in a crime. 2 *adj.* Joined or allied for some purpose. 3 *v.* To bring together or join in a league or alliance. 4 *n.* (*written* **Confederate**) A supporter of the Confederate States of America. 5 *adj.* (*written* **Confederate**) Having to do with the Confederate States of America.

Confederate States of America A league of 11 southern states that seceded from the United States in 1860 and 1861.

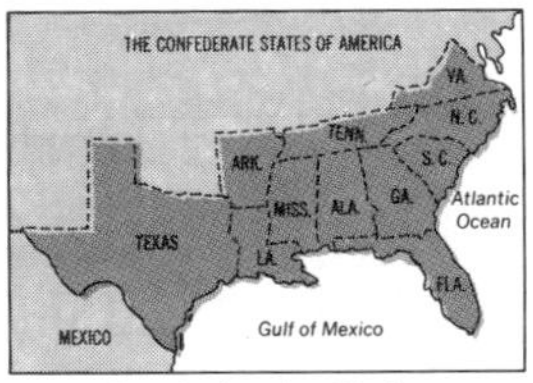

Confederate States of America

con·fed·er·a·tion [kən·fed′ə·rā′shən] *n.* 1 The act of confederating. 2 A being confederated. 3 A union or league of states or nations.

con·fer [kən·fûr′] *v.* **con·ferred, con·fer·ring** 1 To grant, bestow, or award: to *confer* a diploma. 2 To hold a discussion; talk together: The two students *conferred* in the lunchroom.

con·fer·ence [kon′fər·əns *or* kon′frəns] *n.* 1 A discussion or consultation on a particular subject. 2 A meeting at which such a discussion is held: The teachers are in an important *conference* in the principal's office. 3 A league or association, as of athletic teams.

con·fess [kən·fes′] *v.* 1 To admit, concede, or acknowledge: I *confess* I wasn't listening. 2 To admit guilt or error: Will you *confess*? 3 To declare; profess: to *confess* one's belief in God. 4 To admit or make known (one's sins) to a priest. 5 To hear the confession of: The priest *confessed* the members of the congregation.

con·fess·ed·ly [kən·fes′id·lē] *adv.* By confession; admittedly.

con·fes·sion [kən·fesh′ən] *n.* 1 The act of confessing; acknowledgment; admission, especially of faults or guilt. 2 The thing that is admitted.

con·fes·sion·al [kən·fesh′ən·əl] *n.* A booth or stall where a priest hears confessions.

con·fes·sor [kən·fes′ər] *n.* 1 A priest who hears confessions. 2 A person who confesses.

con·fet·ti [kən·fet′ē] *n.pl.* (*used with singular verb*) Small pieces of colored paper thrown at events such as weddings and carnivals: *Confetti* is colorful.

con·fi·dant [kon′fə·dant′ *or* kon′fə·dant′] *n.* A friend whom one trusts with one's secrets.

con·fi·dante [kon′fə·dant′ *or* kon′fə·dant′] *n.* A woman whom one trusts with one's secrets.

con·fide [kən·fīd′] *v.* **con·fid·ed, con·fid·ing** 1 To tell in trust or confidence: I *confided* my secret to my best friend. 2 To have trust; place confidence: I *confided* in my closest friend. 3 To hand over for safekeeping; entrust: The will had been *confided* to a lawyer.

con·fi·dence [kon′fə·dəns] *n.* 1 A feeling of trust; reliance; faith: I have *confidence* in my parents. 2 A relationship of trust and intimacy: We spoke in *confidence.* 3 Faith in oneself; self-reliance: They have *confidence* in their ability. 4 Something told in trust; a secret: The two children exchanged *confidences.* ◆ See TRUST.

con·fi·dent [kon′fə·dənt] *adj.* Having confidence; assured: *confident* of success. **—con′fi·dent·ly** *adv.*

con·fi·den·tial [kon′fə·den′shəl] *adj.* 1 Given in confidence; secret: *confidential* information. 2 Having another's confidence; trusted. 3 Showing readiness to confide: a *confidential* tone. **—con′fi·den′tial·ly** *adv.*

con·fig·u·ra·tion [kən·fig′yə·rā′shən] *n.* The form, shape, and arrangement of parts of a thing: the *configuration* of a leaf.

con·fine [*v.* kən·fīn′, *n.* kon′fīn′] *v.* **con·fined, con·fin·ing,** *n.* 1 *v.* To shut in or keep shut in: I won't *confine* a wild bird; Rain *confined* us to the house all day. 2 *v.* To limit: to *confine* a telephone call to five minutes. 3 *n.* (*usually pl.*) A boundary or border; limit: Keep within the *confines* of your subject.

con·fine·ment [kən·fīn′mənt] *n.* 1 The act of confining. 2 A being confined.

con·firm [kən·fûrm′] *v.* 1 To make certain of; verify: to *confirm* a report. 2 To approve; ratify: to *confirm* a treaty. 3 To receive into the church by confirmation.

con·fir·ma·tion [kon′fər·mā′shən] *n.* 1 The act of confirming. 2 Something that proves or makes certain. 3 A ceremony in which a person is admitted to full membership in a church.

con·firmed [kən·fûrmd′] *adj.* 1 Fixed; firmly established. 2 Habitual: a *confirmed* sports fan.

con·fis·cate [kon′fis·kāt′] *v.* **con·fis·cat·ed, con·fis·cat·ing** 1 To take or seize for the public treasury: The new government *confiscated* properties owned abroad. 2 To take by authority: The smuggled watches were *confiscated.* **—con′fis·ca′tion** *n.*

con·fla·gra·tion [kon′flə·grā′shən] *n.* A great fire.

con·flict [*n.* kon′flikt, *v.* kən·flikt′] 1 *n.* A struggle, fight, or battle. 2 *v.* To be opposed; clash; disagree: The views of Elizabeth I and her advisers often *conflicted.* 3 *n.* An opposition or disagreement, as of ideas or interests.

con·flu·ence [kon′flo͞o·əns] *n.* 1 A flowing together: a *confluence* of streams. 2 A flocking together; crowd: a *confluence* of people.

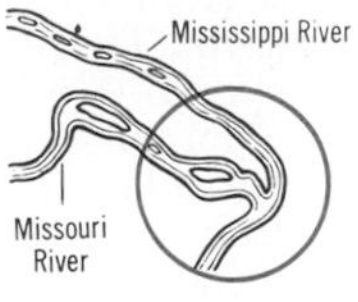

Confluence of the Mississippi and Missouri rivers

con·flu·ent [kon′flo͞o·ənt] *adj.* Running together.

con·form [kən·fôrm′] *v.* 1 To make similar; adapt: *Conform* your behavior to that of the other students. 2 To be or act in accord with customs, rules, or accepted ideas: *Conform* to the rules. **—con·form′·ist** *n.*

con·form·a·ble [kən·fôr′mə·bəl] *adj.* 1 Similar; corresponding; adapted: a schedule *conformable* to your wishes. 2 Obedient; submissive.

con·for·mance [kən·fôr′məns] *n.* Another word for CONFORMITY.

con·for·ma·tion [kon′fôr·mā′shən] *n.* The structure, shape, or way in which a thing is formed: the *conformation* of a glacier.

con·form·i·ty [kən·fôr′mə·tē] *n., pl.* **con·form·i·ties** 1 Similarity or correspondence: the *conformity* of the jacket to the pattern. 2 The following of the customs, fashions, tastes, and ideas of others.

con·found [kon·found′] *v.* 1 To confuse, amaze, or bewilder: This kind of riddle *confounds* me. 2 To mix up; not to know apart: to *confound* fact and fancy.

con·front [kən·frunt′] *v.* 1 To stand face to face with; face boldly: to *confront* a storm at sea. 2 To put face to face: to *confront* a liar with the truth. **—con′fron·ta′tion** *n.*

Con·fu·cian·ism [kən·fyo͞o′shə·niz′əm] *n.* The philosophy of Confucius and his followers, who stressed personal good conduct, devotion to one's family and ancestors, social harmony, justice, and peace. **—Con·fu′cian** *adj., n.*

con·fuse [kən·fyo͞oz′] *v.* **con·fused, con·fus·ing** 1 To perplex; mix up: The traffic *confused* me. 2 To mix up; jumble: Don't *confuse* the papers on my desk. 3 To fail to distinguish; mistake: You are *confusing* me with someone else.

con·fu·sion [kən·fyo͞o′zhən] *n.* 1 A mixed-up or disordered state of mind or of things: thoughts in *confusion*. 2 The taking of one thing for another by mistake; failure to distinguish: Our *confusion* of the chemicals caused an explosion. 3 Commotion; turmoil.

con·fute [kən·fyo͞ot′] *v.* **con·fut·ed, con·fut·ing** 1 To prove (as an argument or statement) wrong or false. 2 To prove (a person) wrong: to *confute* one's critics. **—con′fu·ta′tion** *n.*

Cong. 1 Congregational. 2 Congress. 3 Congressional.

con·ga [kong′gə] *n., v.* **con·gaed, con·ga·ing** 1 *n.* A Cuban dance performed by a group of dancers in a line. 2 *n.* The music for this dance. 3 *v.* To perform this dance. 4 *n.* A narrow, tall bass drum played by beating with the hands.

con·geal [kən·jēl′] *v.* To thicken or change to a solid condition, as by growing cooler: The melted candle wax *congealed*.

con·gen·ial [kən·jēn′yəl] *adj.* 1 Getting along well with one another: *congenial* associates. 2 Suited to one's nature; agreeable: a *congenial* job. **—con·gen′ial·ly** *adv.*

con·gen·i·tal [kən·jen′ə·təl] *adj.* Existing at or before the time of birth but not hereditary. **—con·gen′i·tal·ly** *adv.*

con·ger [kong′gər] *n.* A large eel of warm ocean waters.

conger eel A conger.

con·gest [kən·jest′] *v.* 1 To make too full or very crowded: Planes *congested* the airport. 2 To cause an excessive amount of blood to accumulate in the blood vessels of (an organ or body part). 3 To become congested. **—con·ges′tion** *n.*

con·glom·er·ate [*v.* kən·glom′ə·rāt′, *adj., n.* kən·glom′ər·it] *v.* **con·glom·er·at·ed, con·glom·er·at·ing,** *adj., n.* 1 *v.* To gather into a mass that holds together; cluster. 2 *adj.* Made up of various materials or parts gathered into a whole: a *conglomerate* mass. 3 *n.* A collection of things that are not alike. 4 *n.* Rock made of pebbles or the like stuck together, as by hardened clay. 5 *n.* A corporation made up of companies in unrelated, diversified industries. **—con·glom′er·a′tion** *n.*

Con·go·lese [kong′gə·lēz′] *adj., n., pl.* **Con·go·lese** 1 *adj.* Of or from the Congo or Zaire. 2 *n.* A person born in or a citizen of the Congo or Zaire.

con·grat·u·late [kən·grach′ə·lāt′] *v.* **con·grat·u·lat·ed, con·grat·u·lat·ing** To express one's pleasure at the success or good fortune of: We *congratulated* her on her promotion.

con·grat·u·la·tion [kən·grach′ə·lā′shən] *n.* 1 The act of congratulating. 2 (*pl.*) Good wishes expressing pleasure at another's good fortune or success: to offer *congratulations*.

con·grat·u·la·to·ry [kən·grach′ə·lə·tôr′ē] *adj.* Expressing congratulation.

con·gre·gate [kong′grə·gāt′] *v.* **con·gre·gat·ed, con·gre·gat·ing** To bring or come together into a crowd; assemble: A group of tourists *congregated* around the statue.

con·gre·ga·tion [kong′grə·gā′shən] *n.* 1 A group of people, especially those who meet together for worship. 2 A collection of things. 3 A collecting together into one group or mass.

con·gre·ga·tion·al [kong′grə·gā′shən·əl] *adj.* 1 Of or done by a congregation. 2 (*written* **Congregational**) Of a Protestant denomination in which each congregation governs itself.

con·gress [kong′gris] *n.* 1 An assembly or conference, especially a formal meeting of representatives. 2 (*written* **Congress**) In the U.S., the assembly of elected representatives that meets to make the laws for the nation. It is divided into the Senate and the House of Representatives. 3 A coming together; meeting.

con·gres·sion·al [kən·gresh′ən·əl] *adj.* Having to do with Congress or with a congress.

con·gress·man [kong′gris·mən] *n., pl.* **con·gress·men** [kong′gris·mən] A person who is a Representative in Congress.

con·gress·wom·an [kong′gris·wo͝om′ən] *n., pl.* **con·gress·wom·en** [kong′gris·wim′·in] A woman who is a Representative in Congress.

a	add	**i**	it	**o͝o**	took	**oi**	oil
ā	ace	**ī**	ice	**o͞o**	pool	**ou**	pout
â	care	**o**	odd	**u**	up	**ng**	ring
ä	palm	**ō**	open	**û**	burn	**th**	thin
e	end	**ô**	order	**yo͞o**	fuse	**t͟h**	this
ē	equal					**zh**	vision

ə = { a in *above* e in *sicken* i in *possible* / o in *melon* u in *circus* }

con·gru·ent [kong′groo͞·ənt] *adj.* Having the exact same size and shape, as the triangles illustrated here. **—con′gru·ence** *n.*

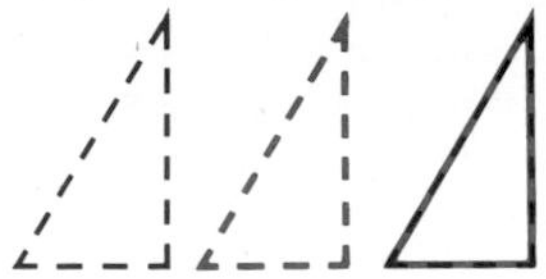
Congruent triangles

con·gru·i·ty [kən·groo͞′i·tē] *n., pl.* **con·gru·i·ties** The condition of being congruous; harmony.

con·gru·ous [kong′groo͞·əs] *adj.* Fitting or working well together; harmonious.

con·ic [kon′ik] *adj.* Conical.

con·i·cal [kon′i·kəl] *adj.* Of or like a cone, as in shape. **—con′i·cal·ly** *adv.*

con·i·fer [kon′ə·fər *or* kō′nə·fər] *n.* Any tree or shrub that bears cones, as the pine, fir, and spruce. **—co·nif·er·ous** [kō·nif′ər·əs] *adj.*

conj. Abbreviation of CONJUNCTION.

con·jec·ture [kən·jek′chər] *n., v.* **con·jec·tured, con·jec·tur·ing** 1 *n.* A guess made when there is not enough evidence to be sure. 2 *v.* To guess: The major *conjectured* that the missing soldiers were alive. 3 *n.* The making of conjectures. **—con·jec′·tur·al** *adj.*

con·join [kən·join′] *v.* To join together; associate: Wit and memory are often *conjoined.*

con·joint·ly [kən·joint′lē] *adv.* In association: together: They acted *conjointly.*

con·ju·gal [kon′jo͝o·gəl] *adj.* Having to do with marriage: *conjugal* bliss.

con·ju·gate [kon′jo͝o·gāt′] *v.* **con·ju·gat·ed, con·ju·gat·ing** To list in regular order the various forms of (a verb): To conjugate *to have,* begin with "I have, you have, she has, or he has."

con·ju·ga·tion [kon′jo͝o·gā′shən] *n.* 1 A listing or arrangement in regular order of the various forms of a verb. 2 A joining together; union.

con·junc·tion [kən·jungk′shən] *n.* 1 Combination; association: The FBI worked in *conjunction* with local police. 2 In grammar, a word that is used to join other words or groups of words, as *or* in "day or night," *and* in "over the hill and across the bridge," and *when* in "He waved when he saw me."

con·junc·ti·va [kon′jungk·tī′və] *n., pl.* **con·junc·ti·vas** or **con·junc·ti·vae** [kon′jungk·tī′vē] The membrane that lines the inside surface of the eyelid and covers the front of the eyeball.

con·junc·tive [kən·jungk′tiv] *adj.* 1 Joining things or parts together; connecting. 2 Joined; connected.

con·junc·ti·vi·tis [kən·jungk′ti·vī′tis] *n.* Inflammation of the conjunctiva.

con·jure [kon′jər *or* kun′jər] *v.* **con·jured, con·jur·ing** 1 To summon (a spirit) by magic words or spells: to *conjure* up a devil. 2 To perform a magician's puzzling tricks. 3 To bring to mind as if by magic: She *conjured* up a scene. 4 [kən·jo͝or′] To appeal to seriously: I *conjure* you to heed my advice.

con·jur·er or **con·jur·or** [kon′jər·ər *or* kun′jər·ər] *n.* A magician.

Conn. Connecticut.

con·nect [kə·nekt′] *v.* 1 To join together; link: A canal *connects* the lake with Puget Sound. 2 To join by association or relationship: A broker is *connected* with insurance. 3 To place in an electric circuit: to *connect* a telephone.

con·nec·tion [kə·nek′shən] *n.* 1 The act of connecting. 2 The condition of being connected; union. 3 A thing or part that connects, or a means for connecting; link; bond: The hose *connection* was bent. 4 An association or relationship: There is no *connection* between the two events. 5 (*usually pl.*) A group of persons with whom one is associated: to have good *connections.* 6 A relative, especially by marriage. 7 A transfer from one means of transportation, as a train or bus, to another.

con·nec·tive [kə·nek′tiv] 1 *adj.* Serving to connect: *Connective* tissue unites and supports the various parts of the body. 2 *n.* A thing or word that connects, as a conjunction.

con·ning tower [kon′ing] A low, raised structure on the deck of a submarine, used for observation and as an entrance to the interior of the ship.

con·niv·ance [kə·nī′vəns] *n.* The act of conniving, as silent consent to wrongdoing.

con·nive [kə·nīv′] *v.* **con·nived, con·niv·ing** 1 To allow something wrong to go on by pretending not to see it or by not telling about it. 2 To join secretly in wrongdoing. **—con·niv′er** *n.* ◆ *Connive* comes from a Latin word meaning *to wink* or *shut the eyes.*

con·nois·seur [kon′ə·sûr′] *n.* An expert qualified to judge in some field of art or taste: a *connoisseur* of old china. ◆ See AMATEUR.

con·no·ta·tion [kon′ə·tā′shən] *n.* What a word or expression suggests or may be associated with, not what it actually means. ◆ See DENOTATION.

con·note [kə·nōt′] *v.* **con·not·ed, con·not·ing** To suggest or imply along with the actual meaning: The word "summer" may *connote* swimming.

con·nu·bi·al [kə·n(y)o͞o′bē·əl] *adj.* Having to do with marriage; matrimonial.

con·quer [kong′kər] *v.* 1 To defeat or win control of by use of force, as in war: to *conquer* an enemy nation. 2 To be victorious. 3 To overcome by effort: to *conquer* a bad habit. **—con′quer·or** *n.*

con·quest [kon(g)′kwest′] *n.* 1 The act of winning over or defeating by force. 2 Something conquered, as territory.

con·quis·ta·dor [kon·k(w)is′tə·dôr′] *n., pl.* **con·quis·ta·dors** or **con·quis·ta·do·res** [kon·k(w)is′tə·dôr′ās] Any of the Spanish conquerors of Mexico and Peru in the 16th century.

con·san·guin·i·ty [kon′sang·gwin′ə·tē] *n.* The state of being descended from a common ancestor; blood relationship.

con·science [kon′shəns] *n.* The inner understanding that lets a person know when an action is right and when it is wrong: A guilty *conscience* led the wrongdoer to confess. ◆ See *conscious.*

con·sci·en·tious [kon′shē·en′shəs] *adj.* 1 Trying to do right; guided by conscience: a *conscientious* student. 2 Done carefully and thoroughly: *conscientious* work. **—con′sci·en′tious·ly** *adv.* **—con′·sci·en′tious·ness** *n.*

conscientious objector A person who refuses to serve in the armed forces because of religious or moral beliefs that war is wrong.

con·scious [kon′shəs] *adj.* 1 Able to hear, see, or feel; awake: Is the patient *conscious*? 2 Aware of some object, fact, or feeling: *conscious* of a low hum. 3 Felt or known by oneself: *conscious* superiority. 4 Deliberate; intended: a *conscious* rebuke. **—con′scious·ly** *adv.* ◆ Distinguish the adjective *conscious* from the noun *conscience:* When I became *conscious* of my guilt, my *conscience* started bothering me. See CONSCIENCE.

con·scious·ness [kon′shəs·nis] *n.* 1 A conscious

condition; awareness: to regain *consciousness*; *consciousness* of danger. **2** One's conscious thoughts or feelings.

con·script [*v.* kən·skript′, *adj., n.* kon′skript′] **1** *v.* To force into military, naval, or other service; draft. **2** *adj.* Forced into service. **3** *n.* A person drafted into the armed forces or forced to do some job. **—con·scrip′tion** *n.*

con·se·crate [kon′sə·krāt′] *v.* **con·se·crat·ed, con·se·crat·ing** **1** To dedicate to sacred uses: to *consecrate* a church. **2** To devote to a special purpose: to *consecrate* one's life to caring for the sick. **—con′·se·cra′tion** *n.*

con·sec·u·tive [kən·sek′yə·tiv] *adj.* Following each other without a break: for five *consecutive* months. **—con·sec′u·tive·ly** *adv.*

con·sen·sus [kən·sen′səs] *n.* Agreement of a majority or of everyone; general opinion. ◆ The phrase *consensus of opinion* is widely used, although it is actually repetitious, since *consensus* by itself means *general opinion.*

con·sent [kən·sent′] **1** *v.* To give approval; agree: I *consented* to the appointment. **2** *n.* Permission or approval; agreement: You may not go without your parents' *consent.*

con·se·quence [kon′sə·kwens′] *n.* **1** A result or effect: Consider the *consequences* of your acts. **2** Importance: an event of no *consequence.*

con·se·quent [kon′sə·kwent′] *adj.* Following as a result; excitement and *consequent* confusion.

con·se·quen·tial [kon′sə·kwen′shəl] *adj.* **1** Important. **2** Self-important. **3** Consequent.

con·se·quent·ly [kon′sə·kwent′lē] *adv.* As a result; therefore.

con·ser·va·tion [kon′sər·vā′shən] *n.* The protecting or preserving from waste, injury, or loss: the *conservation* of natural resources such as forests. **—con′ser·va′tion·ist** *n.*

conservation of energy The principle in physics that energy can be changed in form or converted to mass but never created or destroyed.

conservation of mass The principle in physics that mass can be converted to or from energy but not created or destroyed.

con·ser·va·tism [kən·sûr′və·tiz′əm] *n.* Opposition to change; the desire to keep things as they have been: political *conservatism.*

con·ser·va·tive [kən·sûr′və·tiv] **1** *adj.* Wishing to keep things as they have been; opposed to change: a *conservative* politician. **2** *n.* (*often written* **Conservative**) A member of a conservative political party. **3** *adj.* Moderate; cautious: a *conservative* estimate. **4** *n.* A conservative person. **5** *adj.* Conserving. **6** *adj.* (*written* **Conservative**) Of, having to do with, or being a member of that branch of Judaism that adheres to most principles of the Torah and the Talmud but that accepts some changes in keeping with contemporary life.

con·ser·va·to·ry [kən·sûr′və·tôr′ē] *n., pl.* **con·ser·va·to·ries** **1** A small greenhouse for growing plants. **2** A school of music.

con·serve [*v.* kən·sûrv′, *n.* kon′sûrv′] *v.* **con·served, con·serv·ing,** *n.* **1** *v.* To keep from becoming lost, spoiled, or used up: to *conserve* water. **2** *n.* (*often pl.*) A jam made of fruits stewed with sugar.

con·sid·er [kən·sid′ər] *v.* **1** To think about carefully: I will *consider* your request. **2** To believe to be: They *consider* her a genius. **3** To take into account; make allowance for: The cake is good, if you *consider* the lack of icing. **4** To be thoughtful of; respect: to *consider* other people's feelings.

con·sid·er·a·ble [kən·sid′ər·ə·bəl] *adj.* Rather large; worth noticing: *considerable* talent.

con·sid·er·a·bly [kən·sid′ər·ə·blē] *adv.* Much.

con·sid·er·ate [kən·sid′ər·it] *adj.* Thoughtful of others; kind. **—con·sid′er·ate·ly** *adv.*

con·sid·er·a·tion [kən·sid′ə·rā′shən] *n.* **1** The act of thinking carefully: After long *consideration,* he refused the job offer. **2** Thoughtful concern, as for the feelings or interests of others. **3** A reason, as for an action: Your safety was my major *consideration* in refusing to let you go. **4** A payment given for a service; fee. **—in consideration of** **1** Because of. **2** In return for. **—take into consideration** To take into account; allow for. **—under consideration** Being thought about or discussed.

con·sid·ered [kən·sid′ərd] *adj.* Carefully thought about: a *considered* opinion.

con·sid·er·ing [kən·sid′ər·ing] *prep.* In view of; taking into account: *Considering* its length, the movie was very enjoyable.

con·sign [kən·sīn′] *v.* **1** To give or hand over: The artist *consigned* the pictures to a museum. **2** To send: to *consign* goods to an agent.

con·sign·ment [kən·sīn′mənt] *n.* **1** The act of consigning. **2** Something consigned, as goods.

con·sist [kən·sist′] *v.* **1** To be made up or composed: The program *consisted* of folk songs. **2** To be found or contained; lie: For them, happiness *consisted* in helping others.

con·sis·ten·cy [kən·sis′tən·sē] *n., pl.* **con·sis·ten·cies** **1** The degree of firmness or stiffness: egg whites beaten to the *consistency* of whipped cream. **2** A sticking to the same principles or ways of acting: The council voted with *consistency* against all taxes. **3** Agreement or accord.

con·sis·tent [kən·sis′tənt] *adj.* **1** Sticking to the same principles or ways of acting: a *consistent* supporter of higher pay for teachers. **2** In agreement or accord: actions *consistent* with promises. **—con·sis′tent·ly** *adv.*

con·sis·to·ry [kən·sis′tər·ē] *n., pl.* **con·sis·to·ries** A court or council of a church.

con·so·la·tion [kon′sə·lā′shən] *n.* **1** The act of consoling. **2** A person or thing that consoles. **3** The condition of being consoled.

con·sole[1] [kən·sōl′] *v.* **con·soled, con·sol·ing** To comfort in sorrow or disappointment; cheer.

con·sole[2] [kon′sōl′] *n.* **1** The part of an organ containing the keyboards, pedals, and stops. **2** A radio, phonograph, or television cabinet made to stand on the floor.

con·sol·i·date [kən·sol′ə·dāt′] *v.* **con·sol·i·dat·ed, con·sol·i·dat·ing** **1** To combine or unite: to *consolidate* three school districts. **2** To make or become firm; strengthen: The prize *consolidated* the singer's rating as a star. **—con·sol′i·da′tion** *n.*

a	add	**i**	it	**o͝o**	took	**oi**	oil
ā	ace	**ī**	ice	**o͞o**	pool	**ou**	pout
â	care	**o**	odd	**u**	up	**ng**	ring
ä	palm	**ō**	open	**û**	burn	**th**	thin
e	end	**ô**	order	**yo͞o**	fuse	**t͟h**	this
ē	equal					**zh**	vision

ə = { a in *above* e in *sicken* i in *possible* / o in *melon* u in *circus* }

C

con·som·mé [kon′sə·mā′] *n.* A clear soup made of meat boiled in water.

con·so·nance [kon′sə·nəns] *n.* **1** Agreement. **2** Harmony of sounds, especially of consonants.

con·so·nant [kon′sə·nənt] **1** *n.* A speech sound made when the breath is partly or completely blocked by the teeth, tongue, or lips. **2** *n.* A letter representing such a sound, as *b, f, k, s;* any letter that is not a vowel. **3** *adj.* In agreement or accord: His acts are *consonant* with his character.

con·so·nan·tal [kon′sə·nant′əl] *adj.* Of, having to do with, being, or characterized by one or more consonants.

con·sort [*n.* kon′sôrt, *v.* kən·sôrt′] **1** *n.* A husband or wife, especially of a ruler. **2** *v.* To associate: Don't *consort* with strangers. **3** *n.* A ship sailing with another.

con·spic·u·ous [kən·spik′yo͞o·əs] *adj.* **1** Easily or clearly seen: a *conspicuous* poster. **2** Attracting attention because remarkable: *conspicuous* courage. **—con·spic′·u·ous·ly** *adv.* **—con·spic′·u·ous·ness** *n.*

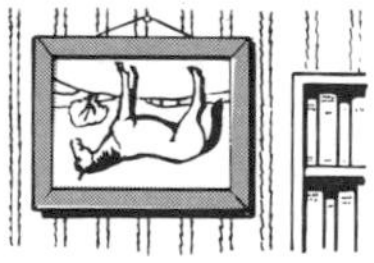

This is a conspicuous error.

con·spir·a·cy [kən·spir′ə·sē] *n., pl.* **con·spir·a·cies** A secret plan of two or more persons to do an evil or unlawful act; plot.

con·spir·a·tor [kən·spir′ə·tər] *n.* A person involved in a conspiracy; plotter.

con·spire [kən·spīr′] *v.* **con·spired, con·spir·ing** **1** To plan with one another secretly to commit an evil or unlawful act; plot. **2** To act together: Winds and currents *conspired* to speed the voyage.

con·sta·ble [kon′stə·bəl] *n.* A police officer.

con·stab·u·lar·y [kən·stab′yə·ler′ē] *n., pl.* **con·stab·u·lar·ies** **1** The total number of constables, as of a district or city. **2** An armed police force set up on a military basis but not part of a regular army.

con·stan·cy [kon′stən·sē] *n.* Faithfulness or firmness in purpose, action, or affections.

con·stant [kon′stənt] **1** *adj.* Remaining the same; not changing: a *constant* factor. **2** *n.* A number or other thing that never changes: The speed of light is a *constant.* **3** *adj.* Faithful; true: a *constant* friend. **4** *adj.* Happening over and over; endless; continual: *constant* interruptions. **—con′·stant·ly** *adv.*

con·stel·la·tion [kon′stə·lā′shən] *n.* A group of stars to which a definite name has been assigned, as Orion or Ursa Major.

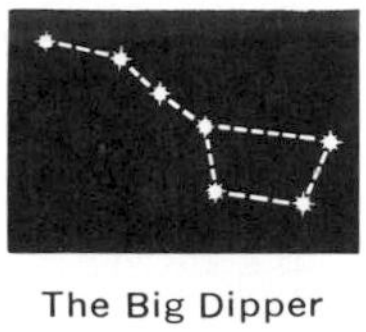

The Big Dipper

con·ster·na·tion [kon′stər·nā′·shən] *n.* Great fear or dismay that makes one feel helpless.

con·sti·pate [kon′stə·pāt′] *v.* **con·sti·pat·ed, con·sti·pat·ing** To cause constipation in.

con·sti·pa·tion [kon′stə·pā′shən] *n.* A condition in which bowel movements are difficult or do not occur often enough.

con·stit·u·en·cy [kən·stich′o͞o·ən·sē] *n., pl.* **con·stit·u·en·cies** **1** All of the voters in an election district. **2** The district itself.

con·stit·u·ent [kən·stich′o͞o·ənt] **1** *adj.* Necessary in making up a whole: a *constituent* part or element. **2** *n.* A necessary part or element: Hydrogen is a *constituent* of water. **3** *n.* A voter represented by an elected representative. **4** *adj.* Entitled to vote for a representative or to make or change a constitution: a *constituent* assembly.

con·sti·tute [kon′stə·t(y)o͞ot′] *v.* **con·sti·tut·ed, con·sti·tut·ing** **1** To make up; compose: Two pints *constitute* a quart. **2** To set up; establish: a government *constituted* by the people. **3** To select or appoint.

con·sti·tu·tion [kon′stə·t(y)o͞o′shən] *n.* **1** The fundamental laws and principles set up to govern a nation, state, or association. **2** (*written* **the Constitution**) The fundamental law of the U.S. **3** The way in which a person or thing is put together; makeup: She attributes her strong *constitution* to daily exercise. **4** The act of constituting.

con·sti·tu·tion·al [kon′stə·t(y)o͞o′shən·əl] **1** *adj.* Of, in agreement with, or subject to the constitution of a nation or state: a *constitutional* right; a *constitutional* monarchy. **2** *adj.* Of or found in the makeup of a person or thing: a *constitutional* weakness. **3** *n.* A walk taken for the benefit of one's health. **—con′sti·tu′tion·al·ly** *adv.*

con·sti·tu·tion·al·i·ty [kon′stə·t(y)o͞o′shən·al′ə·tē] *n.* Agreement with a constitution: to question a law's *constitutionality.*

con·strain [kən·strān′] *v.* **1** To force; compel: Honesty *constrained* us to agree. **2** To hold back; restrain.

con·straint [kən·strānt′] *n.* **1** Force, either to compel or to hold back and restrain. **2** The holding back of feelings.

con·strict [kən·strikt′] *v.* To draw together; make narrower; squeeze: A frown *constricted* my brow. **—con·stric′tion** *n.*

con·stric·tor [kən·strik′tər] *n.* A snake that coils about and crushes its prey.

con·struct [kən·strukt′] *v.* To make by putting parts together; build: to *construct* a garage.

con·struc·tion [kən·struk′shən] *n.* **1** The act of constructing: The *construction* of a house takes time. **2** The business of building. **3** Something built or put together; structure. **4** The way in which a thing is formed or built: a table of sturdy *construction.* **5** Explanation; interpretation: What *construction* do you put on such behavior? **6** The arrangement of words in a sentence.

con·struc·tive [kən·struk′tiv] *adj.* **1** Helping to build up or improve: *constructive* criticism. **2** Having to do with construction. **—con·struc′tive·ly** *adv.*

con·strue [kən·stro͞o′] *v.* **con·strued, con·stru·ing** **1** To interpret; explain: We *construed* the gesture as a signal. **2** To show how the parts of (a clause or sentence) are arranged.

con·sul [kon′səl] *n.* **1** An official living in a foreign city to protect the people and business interests of the country represented. **2** Either of the two chief magistrates ruling the ancient Roman republic. **—con·su·lar** [kon′sə·lər] *adj.* **—con′sul·ship** *n.* ◆ See COUNCIL.

con·su·late [kon′sə·lit] *n.* **1** The official place of business of a consul. **2** The position or term of office of a consul.

con·sult [kən·sult′] *v.* **1** To turn to for advice, aid, or information: to *consult* a doctor or a dictionary. **2** To compare views: to *consult* with others. **3** To take into account; consider: to *consult* one's best interests.

con·sult·ant [kən·sul′tənt] *n.* A person who provides expert or professional advice.

con·sul·ta·tion [kon′səl·tā′shən] *n.* 1 A meeting to discuss something or to share opinions; conference. 2 The act of consulting.
con·sume [kən·so͞om′] *v.* **con·sumed, con·sum·ing** 1 To destroy, as by burning. 2 To use up or waste, as money or time. 3 To eat or drink. 4 To take up all the attention or interest of: Curiosity *consumed* all the listeners.
con·sum·er [kən·so͞o′mər] *n.* A person who uses goods or services.
con·sum·er·ism [kən·so͞o′mər·iz′əm] *n.* 1 Advancement of the interests of consumers, as by making products safer and requiring honest advertising. 2 The theory that it is economically beneficial to produce and sell more goods. **—con·sum′er·ist** *n.*
con·sum·mate [*adj.* kən·sum′it, *v.* kon′sə·māt′] *adj., v.* **con·sum·mat·ed, con·sum·mat·ing** 1 *adj.* Of the highest degree; perfect; complete: *consummate* wisdom. 2 *v.* To make complete or perfect; fulfill: The award *consummated* the actor's career. **—con′sum·ma′tion** *n.*
con·sump·tion [kən·sump′shən] *n.* 1 The act of using up or destroying. 2 The amount used up: a rise in the *consumption* of fuel. 3 An old-fashioned word for tuberculosis of the lungs.
con·sump·tive [kən·sump′tiv] 1 *adj.* Suffering from tuberculosis of the lungs. 2 *n.* A person suffering from this disease. 3 *adj.* Of or like consumption. 4 *adj.* Wasteful; destructive.
cont. 1 containing. 2 contents. 3 continent. 4 continue. 5 continued. 6 contrast.
con·tact [kon′takt] 1 *n.* A coming together, touching, or meeting: The bomb exploded on *contact.* 2 *n.* The relation of touching or being in touch: They kept in *contact* by writing. 3 *v. informal* To get in touch with: Try to *contact* them at the office. 4 *n.* Connection: to maintain radio *contact* with an astronaut. 5 *n.* The connection of two electric conductors, as in a switch or relay.
contact lens A thin lens worn directly on the eyeball to aid vision.
con·ta·gion [kən·tā′jən] *n.* 1 The passing on of disease from person to person by contact. 2 A disease spread in this manner. 3 The passing on of an influence: the *contagion* of laughter.
con·ta·gious [kən·tā′jəs] *adj.* Easily spread from person to person, as by contact; catching: a *contagious* disease; Laughter is *contagious.*
con·tain [kən·tān′] *v.* 1 To have inside; hold or include: Each carton *contains* 12 cans. 2 To be able to hold: This basket *contains* a bushel. 3 To be equal to: A pound *contains* 16 ounces. 4 To hold back; restrain: We could not *contain* our laughter.
con·tain·er [kən·tā′nər] *n.* Something, as a box, jar, cup, or can, used to hold something.
con·tain·ment [kən·tān′mənt] *n.* The act or policy of keeping something from growing or expanding, as the power of a hostile nation or ideology.
con·tam·i·nate [kən·tam′ə·nāt′] *v.* **con·tam·i·nat·ed, con·tam·i·nat·ing** To make impure or spoil by mixing with or getting into: Smoke *contaminates* city air. **—con·tam′i·na′tion** *n.*
contd. continued.
con·temn [kən·tem′] *v.* To feel or express contempt for; despise.
con·tem·plate [kon′təm·plāt′] *v.* **con·tem·plat·ed, con·tem·plat·ing** 1 To look at or consider thoughtfully for a long time: to *contemplate* a painting. 2 To intend or plan; expect: We don't *contemplate* moving before next fall. 3 To meditate. **—con′tem·pla′tion** *n.*
con·tem·pla·tive [kən·tem′plə·tiv *or* kon′təm·plā′·tiv] *adj.* Given to meditation, especially religious; thoughtful: a *contemplative* mind.
con·tem·po·ra·ne·ous [kən·tem′pə·rā′nē·əs] *adj.* Living or happening at the same time: *contemporaneous* discoveries.
con·tem·po·rar·y [kən·tem′pə·rer′ē] *adj., n., pl.* **con·tem·po·rar·ies** 1 *adj.* Living or happening during the same period of time. 2 *n.* A person living at the same time as another: Byron and Keats were *contemporaries.* 3 *adj.* Modern; current.
con·tempt [kən·tempt′] *n.* 1 The feeling that a person, act, or thing is low, dishonorable, or disgusting: to have *contempt* for a traitor. 2 The condition of being despised; disgrace: to hold a liar in *contempt.* 3 Disrespect for or disregard of the rules or orders of a court or legislature: jailed for *contempt* of Congress. ◆ *Contempt, disdain,* and *scorn* all suggest a looking down on others. *Contempt* is the strongest term, and is reserved for those whom, if we regarded them as equals, we would loathe or hate. *Disdain* suggests more an unwillingness to touch or get involved with than a feeling as intense as hate: the *disdain* of an aristocrat for a beggar. *Scorn* is closer to ridicule: The *scorn* with which my request was greeted made me ashamed.
con·tempt·i·ble [kən·temp′tə·bəl] *adj.* Deserving contempt or scorn: a *contemptible* bully.
con·temp·tu·ous [kən·temp′cho͞o·əs] *adj.* Full of contempt or scorn; disdainful: a *contemptuous* attitude. **—con·temp′tu·ous·ly** *adv.*
con·tend [kən·tend′] *v.* 1 To struggle; fight: to *contend* with prejudice. 2 To engage in a contest or competition; compete: to *contend* for a trophy. 3 To argue; maintain: I *contend* that you are wrong. **—con·tend′er** *n.*
con·tent[1] [kon′tent] *n.* 1 (*usually pl.*) All that a thing contains: the *contents* of a box; a book's table of *contents.* 2 The amount of a particular substance contained: the silver *content* of ore. 3 Facts, ideas, or meaning expressed in speaking or writing: the style and *content* of a novel.
con·tent[2] [kən·tent′] 1 *adj.* Happy enough not to complain or to want something else; satisfied: They were *content* to stay at home. 2 *v.* To satisfy: *Content* yourself with what you have. 3 *n.* Ease of mind; satisfaction.
con·tent·ed [kən·ten′tid] *adj.* Satisfied with things as they are. **—con·tent′ed·ly** *adv.*
con·ten·tion [kən·ten′shən] *n.* 1 Argument, strife, or dispute. 2 A point or belief for which someone argues: It was their *contention* that I was at fault.
con·ten·tious [kən·ten′shəs] *adj.* Liking to argue; quarrelsome. **—con·ten′tious·ly** *adv.*

a	add	**i**	it	**o͝o**	took	**oi**	oil
ā	ace	**ī**	ice	**o͞o**	pool	**ou**	pout
â	care	**o**	odd	**u**	up	**ng**	ring
ä	palm	**ō**	open	**û**	burn	**th**	thin
e	end	**ô**	order	**yo͞o**	fuse	**th**	this
ē	equal					**zh**	vision

ə = a in *above*, e in *sicken*, i in *possible*, o in *melon*, u in *circus*

con·tent·ment [kən·tent'mənt] *n.* Calm satisfaction; peaceful happiness.

con·test [*n.* kon'test, *v.* kən·test'] 1 *n.* A game, race, or competition that is to be won or lost. 2 *v.* To fight for: The two teams *contested* every yard. 3 *n.* A struggle, fight, or quarrel. 4 *v.* To question or challenge: to *contest* a decision.

con·test·ant [kən·tes'tənt] *n.* A person who enters a contest or who contests something.

con·text [kon'tekst'] *n.* The phrase or passage in which a word or group of words is found and which affects or suggests its meaning.

con·tex·tu·al [kən·teks'cho͞o·əl] *adj.* Of, having to do with, or depending on the context.

con·tig·u·ous [kən·tig'yo͞o·əs] *adj.* 1 Touching at the edge: *contiguous* backyards. 2 Close, but not touching: *contiguous* buildings.

con·ti·nence [kon'tə·nəns] *n.* Self-restraint.

con·ti·nent¹ [kon'tə·nənt] 1 *n.* One of the major land areas of the earth. Europe, Asia, Africa, Australia, North America, South America, and Antarctica are the continents. 2 *n.* (*written* **the Continent**) Europe, apart from the British Isles.

con·ti·nent² [kon'tə·nənt] *adj.* Practicing continence; moderate.

con·ti·nen·tal [kon'tə·nen'təl] 1 *adj.* Of or resembling a continent. 2 *adj.* (*often written* **Continental**) Of, on, or having to do with the European continent. 3 *n.* (*usually written* **Continental**) A European. 4 *adj.* (*written* **Continental**) Having to do with the 13 American colonies during and just after the Revolutionary War. 5 *n.* (*written* **Continental**) An American soldier in the Revolutionary War.

con·tin·gen·cy [kən·tin'jən·sē] *n., pl.* **con·tin·gen·cies** 1 A possible happening or chance event: equipped for every *contingency.* 2 The condition of being subject to chance or accident.

con·tin·gent [kən·tin'jənt] 1 *adj.* Likely, but not sure, to happen; possible: a *contingent* result. 2 *adj.* Occurring by chance; accidental. 3 *adj.* Dependent upon an uncertain event or condition: A good crop is *contingent* on summer rains. 4 *n.* A possible happening or accident; contingency. 5 *n.* A group making up part of a larger group. 6 *n.* A share or quota, as of troops or workers: a *contingent* of uniformed troops.

con·tin·u·al [kən·tin'yo͞o·əl] *adj.* 1 Repeated very often; frequent: *continual* complaints. 2 Going on without a pause; continuous. **—con·tin'u·al·ly** *adv.* ◆ Something *continual* starts and stops, as the dripping of a faucet. Something *continuous,* however, continues without any interruptions: a *continuous* flow of water.

con·tin·u·ance [kən·tin'yo͞o·əns] *n.* 1 A continuing, lasting, or remaining: The *continuance* of this privilege depends on how you behave. 2 A putting off of a legal action to a future time.

con·tin·u·a·tion [kən·tin'yo͞o·ā'shən] *n.* 1 The act of going on, keeping up, or carrying further, as after a break: the *continuation* of our studies after lunch. 2 An added part: Look for a *continuation* of this story next month.

con·tin·ue [kən·tin'yo͞o] *v.* **con·tin·ued, con·tin·u·ing** 1 To go on or persist in an action or condition: They *continued* to try. 2 To go on or begin again after a break; resume: The story *continues* on the next page. 3 To go or carry further; extend: to *continue* a history. 4 To remain in the same place or condition: He will *continue* in this present job. 5 To keep on; retain: The mayor was *continued* in office. 6 To postpone, as a case for trial.

con·ti·nu·i·ty [kon'tə·no͞o'ə·tē *or* kon'tə·nyo͞o'ə·tē] *n., pl.* **con·ti·nu·i·ties** 1 The condition or quality of being continuous. 2 An unbroken sequence, as of thoughts or actions.

con·tin·u·ous [kən·tin'yo͞o·əs] *adj.* Going on without any pause or interruption: a *continuous* flow. **—con·tin'u·ous·ly** *adv.* ◆ See CONTINUAL.

con·tort [kən·tôrt'] *v.* To twist or wrench out of the normal shape: Rage *contorted* my face.

con·tor·tion [kən·tôr'shən] *n.* 1 The act of twisting. 2 A twisted condition. 3 A twisted shape or position, as one taken by an acrobat.

con·tor·tion·ist [kən·tôr'shə·nist] *n.* An acrobat who specializes in twisting his or her body into unusual positions.

con·tour [kon'to͝or] 1 *n.* The outline of a figure or body, or a line representing it. 2 *adj.* Following a line crosswise to any slope, as in plowing, to prevent erosion: *contour* farming.

contour map A map showing altitudes in a region by use of **contour lines** which connect points of equal altitude.

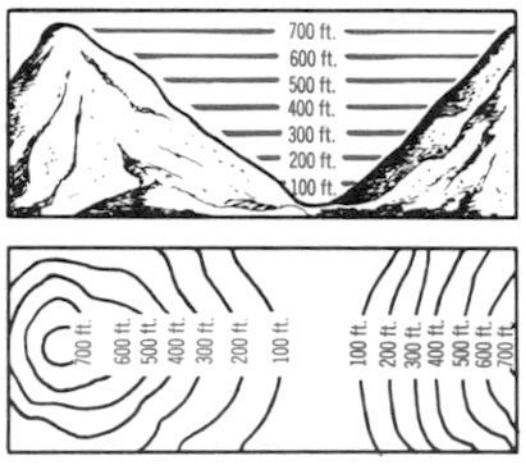

Contour map

contra- A prefix meaning: Against; contrary; opposed to, as in *contradistinction.*

con·tra·band [kon'trə·band'] 1 *n.* Goods that cannot legally be imported or exported; smuggled goods. 2 *adj. use:* *contraband* goods. 3 *n.* Illegal trade; smuggling. 4 *n.* Goods such as arms, called **contraband of war,** that can be legally seized by either party in a war if they are shipped to the other.

con·tra·bas·soon [kon'trə·bə·so͞on'] *n.* A large bassoon pitched an octave lower than a standard bassoon.

con·tra·cep·tion [kon'trə·sep'shən] *n.* The prevention of conception.

con·tra·cep·tive [kon'trə·sep'tiv] 1 *adj.* Of, having to do with, or used to prevent conception: a *contraceptive* device. 2 *n.* A device or substance used to prevent conception.

con·tract [*n.* kon'trakt, *v.* kən·trakt' *or in def. 2* kon'trakt] 1 *n.* A binding agreement between two or more parties, especially a written one. 2 *v.* To enter into or arrange by such an agreement: She *contracted* to do the work; to *contract* marriage. 3 *v.* To acquire or catch: to *contract* debts; to *contract* a disease. 4 *v.* To draw together into a smaller space: to *contract* a muscle; When cooled, metals *contract.* 5 *n.* A form of the game of bridge.

con·trac·tile [kən·trak'təl] *adj.* Capable of contracting or of causing contraction.

con·trac·tion [kən·trak'shən] *n.* 1 The action of drawing together or contracting: *Contraction* of the heart drives blood to the arteries. 2 A contracted condition. 3 In grammar, a shortened form of a word, figure, or group of words. *Can't* is a contraction for *cannot, '64* for *1964,* and *let's* for *let us.* ◆ See ABBREVIATION.

con·trac·tor [kon'trak·tər] *n.* A person or firm that agrees to supply materials or perform services for a stated price.

con·trac·tu·al [kən·trak'cho͞o·əl] *adj.* Of, having to

do with, or making up a contract: *contractual* rights.

con·tra·dict [kon′trə·dikt′] *v.* 1 To deny (a statement); state the opposite of. 2 To deny what is stated by: Don't *contradict* me. 3 To be opposite or contrary to: Her testimony *contradicted* his.

con·tra·dic·tion [kon′trə·dik′shən] *n.* 1 Denial of a statement. 2 A statement or action contradicting another. 3 Lack of agreement.

con·tra·dic·to·ry [kon′trə·dik′tər·ē] *adj.* Expressing the opposite; contradicting. ◆ Two statements are *contradictory* if one must be true and the other false. *I am an American* and *I am not an American* are *contradictory* statements. *Contrary* statements cannot both be true, but they can both be false. *I am an American* and *I am a Spaniard* are *contrary* statements.

con·tra·dis·tinc·tion [kon′trə·dis·tingk′shən] *n.* Distinction by contrast: poetry in *contradistinction* to prose.

con·tral·to [kən·tral′tō] *n., pl.* **con·tral·tos** 1 The lowest female singing voice. 2 *adj. use:* a *contralto* voice. 3 A singer having a contralto voice.

con·trap·tion [kən·trap′shən] *n. informal* An odd or puzzling device or gadget.

con·tra·ri·wise [kon′trer·ē·wīz′] *adv.* 1 In a contrary direction, order, or manner. 2 On the contrary.

con·trar·y [kon′trer·ē *or for def. 5* kən·trâr′ē] *adj., n., pl.* **con·trar·ies** 1 *adj.* Entirely different; opposite: *contrary* beliefs. 2 *n.* The opposite: The *contrary* is true. 3 *adj.* Opposite in position or direction. 4 *adj.* Opposed: a claim *contrary* to the facts. 5 *adj.* Stubbornly determined to oppose or contradict: *contrary* children. **—on the contrary** The reverse is true. ◆ See CONTRADICTORY.

con·trast [*v.* kən·trast′, *n.* kon′trast] 1 *v.* To compare in order to show differences: *Contrast* city life with country life. 2 *n.* A difference revealed when things are compared: the sharp *contrast* between light and shadow. 3 *v.* To show differences when compared: Blue and white *contrast* attractively. 4 *n.* A person or thing showing such differences: This antique car is quite a *contrast* to a new one.

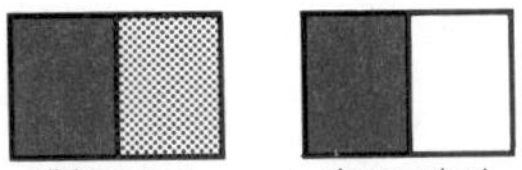
slight contrast strong contrast

con·trib·ute [kən·trib′yo͞ot′] *v.* **con·trib·ut·ed, con·trib·ut·ing** 1 To join others in giving to some cause: to *contribute* to a charity. 2 To furnish (as an article or story) to a newspaper or magazine. **—contribute to** To share in bringing about: Many causes *contribute to* the growth of suburbs. **—con·trib′u·tor** *n.*

con·tri·bu·tion [kon′trə·byo͞o′shən] *n.* 1 The act of contributing. 2 Anything contributed, as money to a fund or a story to a magazine.

con·trib·u·to·ry [kən·trib′yə·tôr′ē] *adj.* Helping toward a result; contributing: Poor diet can be a *contributory* cause of illness.

con·trite [kən·trīt′ *or* kon′trīt′] *adj.* 1 Deeply and humbly sorry for having done wrong. 2 Resulting from such a feeling: *contrite* tears.

con·tri·tion [kən·trish′ən] *n.* Sincere sorrow for sin or wrongdoing; repentance; penitence.

con·triv·ance [kən·trī′vəns] *n.* 1 A mechanical device, clever plan, or other invention: That new can opener is an odd-looking *contrivance.* 2 The act, power, or manner of contriving.

con·trive [kən·trīv′] *v.* **con·trived, con·triv·ing** 1 To figure out; plan or plot: We *contrived* a way to get the information. 2 To manage, as by a plan: We *contrived* to leave early. 3 To design; invent.

con·trived [kən·trīvd′] *adj.* Too obviously planned; artificial: a *contrived* reconciliation.

con·trol [kən·trōl′] *v.* **con·trolled, con·trol·ling,** *n.* 1 *v.* To have power or authority to direct or manage: Each principal *controls* one school. 2 *n.* Power or authority to direct or manage: to win *control* of a company. 3 *v.* To hold back; restrain; check: Try to *control* your temper. 4 *n.* A controlled or guided condition; restraint: Everything is under *control;* a car out of *control.* 5 *n.* (*often pl.*) A device used to operate a machine: The copilot took the *controls.* 6 *n.* A standard of comparison used in checking the results of a scientific experiment.

con·trol·ler [kən·trō′lər] *n.* 1 An official who decides about making proposed expenditures. 2 A person or thing that controls or regulates.

control tower A building at an airport where take-offs and landings are directed.

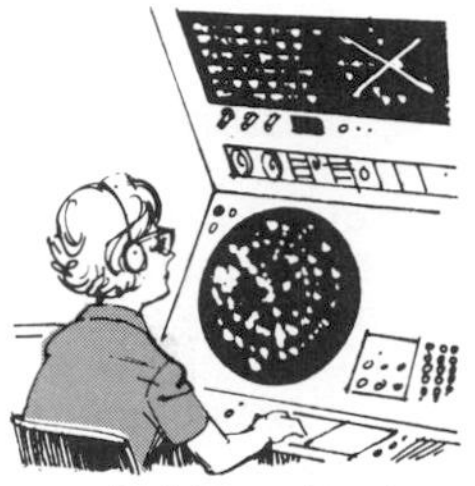
Inside an airport control tower

con·tro·ver·sial [kon′trə·vûr′shəl] *adj.* 1 Tending to stir up argument: a *controversial* issue. 2 Fond of arguing.

con·tro·ver·sy [kon′trə·vûr′·sē] *n., pl.* **con·tro·ver·sies** 1 Argument or debate on a matter about which opinions differ. 2 A dispute.

con·tro·vert [kon′trə·vûrt′ *or* kon′trə·vûrt′] *v.* 1 To argue against; contradict; deny. 2 To argue about.

con·tu·ma·cious [kon′t(y)ə·mā′shəs] *adj.* Stubbornly disobedient or rebellious.

con·tu·me·ly [kon′t(y)o͞o·mə·lē] *n.* 1 Insulting rudeness; scorn. 2 An insult.

con·tu·sion [kən·to͞o′zhən] *n.* A bruise.

co·nun·drum [kə·nun′drəm] *n.* A riddle whose answer depends on a pun. Example: "When is a horse not a horse?" "When it's turned into a pasture."

A black eye is a contusion.

con·va·lesce [kon′və·les′] *v.* **con·va·lesced, con·va·lesc·ing** To get well gradually: The invalid *convalesced* at the seashore after a long illness.

con·va·les·cence [kon′və·les′əns] *n.* Gradual recovery from illness, or the recovery period.

con·va·les·cent [kon′və·les′ənt] 1 *adj.* Recovering from illness. 2 *n.* A person recovering from illness. 3 *adj.* Of convalescence.

con·vec·tion [kən·vek′shən] *n.* 1 The transfer of

a add	**i** it	**o͝o** took	**oi** oil
ā ace	**ī** ice	**o͞o** pool	**ou** pout
â care	**o** odd	**u** up	**ng** ring
ä palm	**ō** open	**û** burn	**th** thin
e end	**ô** order	**yo͞o** fuse	**th** this
ē equal			**zh** vision

ə = a in *above* e in *sicken* i in *possible* o in *melon* u in *circus*

heat within a gas or liquid by means of movement of warmer parts. **2** The act of conveying.

con·vene [kən·vēn′] *v.* **con·vened, con·ven·ing** **1** To come together; assemble: Congress *convenes* every year. **2** To summon to meet: The governor *convened* the legislature.

con·ven·ience [kən·vēn′yəns] *n.* **1** Personal comfort; benefit: The motel has a restaurant for the *convenience* of guests. **2** Anything that increases comfort or saves work: Television sets and freezers are modern *conveniences.* **3** The condition of being convenient: the *convenience* of the arrangement. **—at one's convenience** At a time that suits one's plans or preference.

convenience store A small market, generally open longer hours than a supermarket, where packaged foods and other basic items are sold.

con·ven·ient [kən·vēn′yənt] *adj.* **1** Suited to one's purpose, plans, or comfort: We went at a *convenient* hour. **2** Within easy reach; handy: a *convenient* store. **—con·ven′ient·ly** *adv.*

con·vent [kon′vent] *n.* **1** A group of nuns who live together, following set religious rules. **2** The house or buildings which they occupy.

con·ven·tion [kən·ven′shən] *n.* **1** A meeting or assembly for some purpose: a *convention* of the Democratic Party. **2** The established way of doing things; accepted custom: The artist defied *convention* and produced new and exciting paintings. **3** An established practice, rule, or form; a custom. **4** An agreement on minor matters, as between nations.

con·ven·tion·al [kən·ven′shən·əl] *adj.* **1** Established by custom; customary; usual: It is *conventional* to say "Hello" when answering the telephone. **2** Behaving in an expected way: a highly *conventional* person. **3** Not original; commonplace: a *conventional* painting. **4** In accordance with set rules rather than with nature: In early Egyptian art, it was *conventional* to paint the king larger than his subjects. **—con·ven′tion·al·ly** *adv.*

con·ven·tion·al·i·ty [kən·ven′shən·al′ə·tē] *n., pl.* **con·ven·tion·al·i·ties** **1** The condition of being conventional; allegiance to custom. **2** A rule, custom, or conventional practice.

con·verge [kən·vûrj′] *v.* **con·verged, con·verg·ing** To move toward one point or place; draw together: The rails seemed to *converge* in the distance.

con·ver·gence [kən·vûr′jəns] *n.* **1** The act or fact of converging. **2** The point at which things come together. **—con·ver′gent** *adj.*

con·ver·sant [kən·vûr′sənt *or* kon′vər·sənt] *adj.* Well acquainted or familiar, as by study: to be *conversant* with American history.

con·ver·sa·tion [kon′vər·sā′shən] *n.* An exchange of ideas by informal talk; talk. **—con′ver·sa′tion·al** *adj.*

con·ver·sa·tion·al·ist [kon′vər·sā′shən·əl·ist] *n.* A person who converses: a good *conversationalist.*

con·verse[1] [*v.* kən·vûrs′, *n.* kon′vûrs] *v.* **con·versed, con·vers·ing,** *n.* **1** *v.* To take part in conversation; talk. **2** *n.* A conversation.

con·verse[2] [kon′vûrs] **1** *adj.* Turned about or reversed; opposite; contrary. **2** *n.* The opposite or contrary: "Happy" is the *converse* of "sad." **—con·verse′ly** *adv.*

con·ver·sion [kən·vûr′zhən] *n.* **1** A changing into another form or substance: the *conversion* of ice into water. **2** A winning over or changing to a new religion or belief.

con·vert [*v.* kən·vûrt′, *n.* kon′vûrt] **1** *v.* To change, turn, or transform: to *convert* wool into yarn; to *convert* a garage into an apartment. **2** *v.* To exchange for equal value: to *convert* merchandise into cash. **3** *v.* To win over or change to a new religion or belief: to *convert* the nonbelievers. **4** *n.* A person who has been won over to a new religion or belief. **5** *v.* In football, to score one or two extra points after a touchdown.

con·vert·er [kən·vûr′tər] *n.* **1** A person or thing that converts. **2** A device that changes electric current from alternating current to direct current or vice versa. **3** A device that changes one radio frequency to another.

con·vert·i·ble [kən·vûr′tə·bəl] **1** *adj.* Capable of being changed into something else: Fuel is *convertible* into heat. **2** *n.* Something convertible, as a car with a folding top.

con·vex [kon·veks′ *or* kon′veks] *adj.* Curving outward, as the outside of a globe: a *convex* surface. **—con·vex′i·ty** *n.*

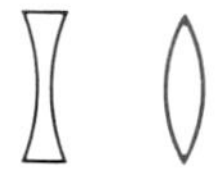
concave lens convex lens

con·vey [kən·vā′] *v.* **1** To carry from one place to another; transport: Trucks *convey* supplies to a city. **2** To serve as a medium or path for; transmit: Pipes *convey* water and gas. **3** To make known; communicate: to *convey* ideas. **4** To transfer ownership of, as land.

con·vey·ance [kən·vā′əns] *n.* **1** The act of conveying. **2** Something used for conveying, as a truck or bus.

con·vey·er or **con·vey·or** [kən·vā′ər] *n.* A person or thing that conveys.

conveyor belt or **conveyer belt** A continuously moving surface on which things are put to be carried from one place to another, as in a factory.

Conveyor belt

con·vict [*v.* kən·vikt′, *n.* kon′vikt] **1** *v.* To prove or find guilty, as in a trial: The defendant was *convicted* of the crime. **2** *n.* A person found guilty of a crime and serving a prison sentence.

con·vic·tion [kən·vik′shən] *n.* **1** A strong, firm belief. **2** The condition of being judged guilty. **3** The act of proving or declaring guilt.

con·vince [kən·vins′] *v.* **con·vinced, con·vinc·ing** To make feel certain; cause to believe, as by proof or persuasion: Her smile *convinced* me that all was well.

con·vinc·ing [kən·vin′sing] *adj.* Serving to convince; producing belief or certainty; persuasive: a *convincing* story. **—con·vinc′ing·ly** *adv.*

con·viv·i·al [kən·viv′ē·əl] *adj.* **1** Fond of feasting and good company; sociable. **2** Festive. **—con·viv′i·al·ly** *adv.*

con·vo·ca·tion [kon′vō·kā′shən] *n.* **1** An assembly; meeting: a religious *convocation.* **2** The act of calling together for a meeting.

con·voke [kən·vōk′] *v.* **con·voked, con·vok·ing** To summon to meet; cause to assemble.

con·vol·ut·ed [kon′və·lo͞o′tid] *adj.* **1** Twisted or coiled. **2** Very complicated.

con·vo·lu·tion [kon′və·lo͞o′shən] *n.* **1** A winding or coiling together. **2** A fold or twist, as one of the folds or ridges of the surface of the brain.

con·voy [*v.* kon′voi *or* kən·voi′, *n.* kon′voi] 1 *v.* To go with to protect; escort: Destroyers were *convoying* the freighters. 2 *n.* A protecting escort. 3 *n.* A group, as of ships or trucks, traveling with an escort. 4 *n.* The act of convoying. 5 *n.* The condition of being convoyed.

A naval convoy

con·vulse [kən·vuls′] *v.* **con·vulsed, con·vuls·ing** 1 To disturb with violent movements; shake: a world *convulsed* by war. 2 To cause to jerk or shake, as in a fit: A spasm of coughing *convulsed* the speaker. 3 To cause to shake with laughter.

con·vul·sion [kən·vul′shən] *n.* 1 (*often pl.*) A sudden, violent drawing up or jerking of the muscles that a person cannot stop: epileptic *convulsions.* 2 A violent disturbance, as an earthquake. 3 A violent fit of laughter.

con·vul·sive [kən·vul′siv] *adj.* 1 Like a convulsion: *convulsive* rage. 2 Causing or marked by convulsions. **—con·vul′sive·ly** *adv.*

co·ny [kō′nē] *n., pl.* **co·nies** Another spelling for CONEY.

coo [ko͞o] *v.* **cooed, coo·ing,** *n., pl.* **coos** 1 *v.* To make the soft, murmuring sound of a dove: The baby *cooed.* 2 *n.* The sound itself. 3 *v.* To talk or say in low, loving murmurs.

cook [ko͝ok] 1 *v.* To use heat to prepare (food) to be eaten. Boiling, frying, and baking are ways of cooking. 2 *n.* A person who cooks or otherwise prepares food for eating. 3 *v.* To undergo cooking: The turkey *cooked* all morning. **—cook up** *informal* To make up; invent.

cook·book [ko͝ok′bo͝ok′] *n.* A book containing recipes, instructions for cooking, and other information on cookery.

cook·er [ko͝ok′ər] *n.* A person or thing that cooks, especially an appliance or utensil used for cooking: a popcorn *cooker.*

cook·er·y [ko͝ok′ər·ē] *n.* The art of cooking.

cook·ie or **cook·y** [ko͝ok′ē] *n., pl.* **cook·ies** *U.S.* A small, thin, dry, sweet cake.

cook·out [ko͝ok′out′] *n.* 1 An outdoor gathering for cooking and eating a meal. 2 The meal eaten at such a gathering.

cool [ko͞ol] 1 *adj.* Slightly cold; lacking warmth: a *cool* breeze. 2 *v.* To make or become less warm: to *cool* drinks with ice; The hot chocolate *cooled.* 3 *n.* Something cool, as a time, thing, or place: the *cool* of dawn. 4 *adj.* Comfortable and not heating in hot weather: a *cool* suit. 5 *adj.* Suggesting coolness: Blue, green, and violet are *cool* colors. 6 *adj.* Not excited; calm: The referee remained *cool* and collected. 7 *v.* To make or become less excited; calm down. 8 *adj.* Calmly bold or daring. 9 *adj.* Not enthusiastic; unfriendly: a *cool* answer. 10 *adj. informal* Actual: a *cool* million. **—cool′ly** *adv.* **—cool′ness** *n.*

cool·ant [ko͞o′lənt] *n.* A substance, usually a liquid, that is circulated over machine parts to carry heat away.

cool·er [ko͞o′lər] *n.* A container, device, or room used for cooling something: a water *cooler.*

cool·head·ed [ko͞ol′hed′id] *adj.* Not easily flustered or disturbed; calm; collected.

coo·lie or **coo·ly** [ko͞o′lē] *n., pl.* **coo·lies** A poorly paid, unskilled Oriental worker.

coon [ko͞on] *n.* A raccoon.

coop [ko͞op] 1 *n.* A cage or enclosed house for keeping fowl or small animals: a chicken *coop.* 2 *v.* To shut up in or as if in a coop: Because of the storm, we were *cooped* up inside all day.

A chicken coop

co-op [kō′op] *n. informal* A cooperative.

coop·er [ko͞o′pər *or* ko͝op′ər] *n.* A person who makes or mends such things as barrels and casks.

co·op·er·ate [kō·op′ə·rāt′] *v.* **co·op·er·at·ed, co·op·er·at·ing** To work together or with others for a common purpose: The fifth and sixth grades *cooperated* in giving the play.

co·op·er·a·tion [kō·op′ə·rā′shən] *n.* 1 A working together for a common purpose; joint action. 2 Assistance: I need your *cooperation.*

co·op·er·a·tive [kō·op′(ə·)rə·tiv *or* kō·op′ə·rā′tiv] 1 *adj.* Acting or willing to act with others; giving help. 2 *n.* Something, as a store or an apartment house, owned and managed by an association of people. 3 *adj.* Owned and operated as a cooperative: a *cooperative* store. **—co·op′er·a·tive·ly** *adv.* **—co·op′er·a·tive·ness** *n.*

co-opt [kō·opt′ *or* kō′opt′] *v.* To take in and make part of an established group: to *co-opt* student troublemakers by making them hallway guards.

co·or·di·nate [*v.* kō·ôr′də·nāt′, *adj., n.* kō·ôr′də·nit] *v.* **co·or·di·nat·ed, co·or·di·nat·ing,** *adj., n.* 1 *v.* To bring or come into the right relation for working together: to *coordinate* the plans of four groups. 2 *adj.* Of equal importance or rank: *coordinate* branches of the armed forces. 3 *v.* To put or be in the same rank or order. 4 *n.* A person or thing of the same rank; an equal. 5 *n.* One of a set of numbers used to locate a point or line in space, as on a graph.

coordinating conjunction A word such as *and, but,* or *or,* used to join words or groups of words of equal rank.

co·or·di·na·tion [kō·ôr′də·nā′shən] *n.* 1 The act of coordinating. 2 A being coordinated. 3 A smooth working together, as of parts of the body.

coot [ko͞ot] *n.* A web-footed water bird having short wings.

cop [kop] *n. informal* A police officer.

cope[1] [kōp] *v.* **coped, cop·ing** To deal successfully; handle: to *cope* with a problem.

cope[2] [kōp] *n.* 1 A cape worn by bishops or priests on ceremonial occasions. 2 Something that arches overhead; canopy: the *cope* of heaven.

Co·per·ni·can [kə·pûr′nə·kən *or* kō·pûr′nə·kən] *adj.* Of or having to do with Copernicus or his

a	add	**i**	it	**o͝o**	took	**oi**	oil
ā	ace	**ī**	ice	**o͞o**	pool	**ou**	pout
â	care	**o**	odd	**u**	up	**ng**	ring
ä	palm	**ō**	open	**û**	burn	**th**	thin
e	end	**ô**	order	**yo͞o**	fuse	**th**	this
ē	equal					**zh**	vision

ə = {a in *above* e in *sicken* i in *possible* / o in *melon* u in *circus*}

C

theory that Earth and the other planets revolve around the sun, and Earth rotates on its axis.

cop·ied [kop′ēd] Past tense and past participle of COPY.

co·pi·lot [kō′pī′lət] *n.* The assistant pilot of an aircraft.

cop·ing [kō′ping] *n.* The top layer of a brick or stone wall, usually sloping so as to shed water.

coping saw A narrow blade in a U-shaped frame, used to saw curves.

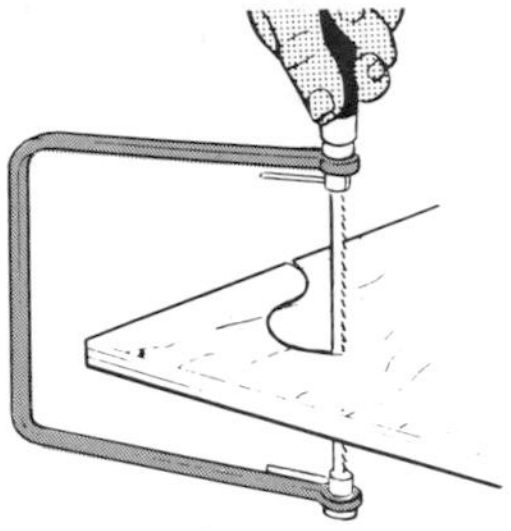

Coping saw

co·pi·ous [kō′pē·əs] *adj.* **1** Abundant; plentiful: a *copious* harvest. **2** Wordy; not brief: a *copious* apology. **—co′pi·ous·ly** *adv.*

cop·per [kop′ər] **1** *n.* A reddish brown metal, one of the chemical elements. It is easy to work and is a good conductor of electricity. **2** *adj. use: copper* wire. **3** *v.* To cover or coat with copper. **4** *n.* A coin of copper or bronze. **5** *n., adj.* Reddish brown.

cop·per·head [kop′ər·hed′] *n.* A poisonous snake of North America, with copper-colored markings on its head and body.

cop·per·smith [kop′ər·smith′] *n.* A person who makes things of copper.

cop·pice [kop′is] *n.* A copse.

cop·ra [kop′rə *or* kō′prə] *n.* Dried coconut meat. It yields coconut oil.

copse [kops] *n.* A thicket of bushes and small trees.

Copt [kopt] *n.* **1** A member of a people descended from ancient inhabitants of Egypt. **2** A member of the Coptic Church.

cop·ter [kop′tər] *n. informal* A helicopter.

Cop·tic [kop′tik] **1** *adj.* Of or having to do with the Copts or their language. **2** *adj.* Of or having to do with the Coptic Church. **3** *n.* A language once spoken by the ancient Egyptians and their descendants and now used only in the services of the Coptic Church.

Coptic Church The Christian Church of Egypt.

cop·u·la [kop′yə·lə] *n.* Another word for LINKING VERB.

cop·u·la·tive [kop′yə·lāt′iv *or* kop′yə·lə·tiv] *adj.* **1** Joining together coordinate words or groups of words. **2** Functioning as a copula: a *copulative* verb.

cop·y [kop′ē] *n., pl.* **cop·ies**, *v.* **cop·ied, cop·y·ing** **1** *n.* A likeness or reproduction of something: a *copy* of a drawing; Make two *copies* of this letter. **2** *v.* To make a copy or copies of. **3** *v.* To follow as a model. **4** *n.* A model or pattern to be imitated, especially a sample of penmanship. **5** *n.* A single specimen of an issue, as of a newspaper, magazine, or book. **6** *n.* Written material to be set in type and printed.

cop·y·book [kop′ē·bo͝ok′] *n.* A book containing models of good handwriting for students to imitate.

copy boy A young man employed in a newspaper office to carry copy and run errands.

cop·y·cat [kop′ē·kat′] *n. slang* An imitator.

copy girl A young woman employed in a newspaper office to carry copy and run errands.

cop·y·ist [kop′ē·əst] *n.* A person who makes written copies, as of documents.

cop·y·right [kop′ē·rīt′] **1** *n.* The exclusive right to publish or sell any part or all of a literary, musical, or art work. **2** *v.* To protect by copyright.

cop·y·writ·er [kop′ē·rī′tər] *n.* A person who writes copy for advertisements.

co·quet·ry [kō′kə·trē *or* kō·ket′rē] *n., pl.* **co·quet·ries** **1** Flirtation. **2** A flirtatious act.

co·quette [kō·ket′] *n.* A woman who flirts with men. **—co·quet′tish** *adj.*

co·qui·na [kō·kē′nə] *n.* A soft limestone formed from sea shells, used as a building material.

cor·a·cle [kôr′ə·kəl] *n.* A small, rounded boat made of wickerwork covered with a waterproof material, used in some parts of the British Isles.

cor·al [kor′əl *or* kôr′əl] **1** *n.* A stony substance formed by great numbers of the skeletons of tiny sea animals. **2** *adj. use:* a *coral* reef. **3** *n.* Coral, especially red coral, made into jewelry. **4** *adj. use:* a *coral* necklace. **5** *n.* The animal whose skeleton forms coral. **6** *n., adj.* Pinkish or yellowish red.

Coral

coral snake A poisonous snake with brilliant red, black, and yellow rings, found in Mexico and the SW and southern U.S.

cord [kôrd] **1** *n.* A thick string or very thin rope made of several strands twisted together. **2** *v.* To bind with a cord or cords: to *cord* a box for shipping. **3** *n.* A part of the body that is like a cord: the spinal *cord.* **4** *n.* A pair of insulated wires used to connect a lamp or an appliance to an electric outlet. **5** *n.* A ridge or rib in a cloth such as corduroy. **6** *n.* A cloth having ridges or ribs. **7** *n.* A measure for a pile of cut firewood. A cord is 8 feet long, 4 feet wide, and 4 feet high. **8** *v.* To pile wood into cords.

cord·age [kôr′dij] *n.* **1** The ropes and cords of a ship's rigging. **2** An amount of wood, in cords.

cor·dial [kôr′jəl] **1** *adj.* Warm and hearty; sincere. **2** *n.* A liqueur. **—cor′dial·ly** *adv.*

cor·dial·i·ty [kôr·jal′ə·tē] *n., pl.* **cor·dial·i·ties** Cordial quality; warm, friendly feeling.

cor·dil·le·ra [kôr′dil·yâr′ə] *n.* A very long mountain chain, such as the one that includes the Rocky Mountains and the Andes.

cor·don [kôr′dən] *n.* **1** A line, as of people, ships, or fortresses, enclosing an area to guard it. **2** A cord or ribbon worn as an emblem of honor or rank.

cor·do·van [kôr′də·vən] **1** *n.* A fine, soft leather, now usually made of split horsehide. **2** *adj. use: cordovan* shoes.

cor·du·roy [kôr′də·roi] *n., pl.* **cor·du·roys** **1** *n.* A strong cloth, usually made of cotton, having raised, velvety ridges or ribs. **2** *adj. use:* a *corduroy* suit. **3** *n.* (*pl.*) Trousers made of corduroy. ◆ *Corduroy* may come from the French *corde du roi* meaning *king's cord,* "cord" being a ribbed fabric.

corduroy road A road made from logs laid crosswise over wet or muddy ground.

cord·wood [kôrd′wo͝od′] *n.* Wood cut in 4-foot lengths, to be sold by the cord.

core [kôr] *n., v.* **cored, cor·ing** **1** *n.* The hard central part of certain fruits, such as apples or pears. The core contains seeds. **2** *v.* To remove the core from. **3** *n.* The central or innermost part of anything. **4** *n.* The most important part of anything.

CORE [kôr] Congress of Racial Equality.

Co·rin·thi·an [kə·rin′thē·ən] 1 *adj.* Of or from ancient Corinth. 2 *n.* A person born or living in Corinth. 3 *adj.* Of or having to do with a highly ornamented style of Greek architecture.

Co·rin·thi·ans [kə·rin′thē·ənz] *n.* In the New Testament, either of two letters of Paul to the Christians at Corinth.

cork [kôrk] 1 *n.* The thick but light outer bark of a type of oak tree that grows in the Mediterranean region. Cork has many uses. 2 *n.* A stopper made of cork for a container, as a bottle or barrel. 3 *n.* A stopper made of other material, as glass or rubber. 4 *v.* To stop with a cork, as a bottle. 5 *n.* A small float used on a fishing net or line.

cork·er [kôr′kər] *n. slang* A remarkable or excellent person or thing.

cork·screw [kôrk′skro͞o′] 1 *n.* A tool, basically a pointed metal spiral attached to a handle, for drawing corks from bottles. 2 *adj.* Spiral; twisted: *corkscrew* curls. 3 *v.* To move or cause to move in a winding or spiral course.

Corkscrew

cork·y [kôr′kē] *adj.* **cork·i·er, cork·i·est** Of, having to do with, or like cork.

corm [kôrm] *n.* A bulblike swelling of the underground stem of certain plants, as the crocus.

cor·mo·rant [kôr′mər·ənt] *n.* A large web-footed sea bird having a hooked beak with a pouch under it for holding fish.

corn[1] [kôrn] 1 *n.* A tall, cultivated plant bearing kernels on a large ear. It is also called maize or Indian corn. 2 *n.* The kernels, an important food for people and domestic animals. 3 *n.* In Great Britain, any grain or grain plant, especially wheat or oats. 4 *v.* To preserve (as beef or tongue) in dry salt or brine.

corn[2] [kôrn] *n.* A painful growth of hard, thick skin, as on a toe, usually caused by a shoe that rubs or binds.

corn bread Bread made from cornmeal.

corn·cob [kôrn′kob′] *n.* The woody part of an ear of corn, on which the kernels grow.

corn·crib [kôrn′krib′] *n.* A bin or small building for storing ears of corn.

cor·ne·a [kôr′nē·ə] *n.* The transparent outer layer of the eyeball covering the iris and pupil.

corned [kôrnd] *adj.* Preserved and kept from spoiling in salt or salt water: *corned* beef.

cor·ner [kôr′nər] 1 *n.* The place where two lines or surfaces meet and form an angle. 2 *n.* The area around such a place: Put your name in the upper right-hand *corner* of the page. 3 *n.* The place where two or more streets meet. 4 *adj.* Located in or on a corner: the *corner* grocery store. 5 *n.* A difficult or embarrassing position. 6 *v.* To drive into a corner or into a position hard to get out of: They *cornered* the escaped lion in an alley. 7 *n.* A place that is far from the center of things: the far *corners* of the earth. 8 *n.* The buying of all or most of a certain stock or product in order to control its price: a *corner* in cotton. 9 *v.* To buy such control: to *corner* rye. **—cut corners** 1 To take a short cut by going across corners instead of around them. 2 To economize; reduce expenses. **—turn a corner** To pass a critical point and begin to get better.

cor·ner·stone [kôr′nər·stōn′] *n.* 1 A stone at the corner of a building, especially one laid during a ceremony to mark the start of construction. 2 The main support; foundation: Free speech is the *cornerstone* of liberty.

cor·net [kôr·net′] *n.* A brass musical instrument like a trumpet. **—cor·net′ist** or **cor·net′tist** *n.*

corn·field [kôrn′fēld′] *n.* A field used for growing corn.

corn·flow·er [kôrn′flou′ər] *n.* Any of several plants with blue, purple, pink, or white flowers, especially the bachelor's-button.

corn·husk [kôrn′husk′] *n.* The tough leaves or husk enclosing an ear of corn.

cor·nice [kôr′nis] *n.* 1 The molding that juts out from the top of a building or pillar. 2 A molding high on the walls of a room.

Cor·nish [kôr′nish] 1 *adj.* Of or from Cornwall. 2 *n.* The old Celtic language of Cornwall, now no longer spoken.

corn·meal [kôrn′mēl′] *n.* Meal ground from corn.

corn pone [pōn] Corn bread made without milk or eggs and baked or fried in patties.

corn·stalk [kôrn′stôk′] *n.* The stalk, or stem, of the corn plant.

corn·starch [kôrn′stärch′] *n.* A floury starch made from corn, used in cooking.

cor·nu·co·pi·a [kôr′nə·kō′pē·ə] *n.* 1 A curved goat's horn overflowing with fruits and flowers, symbolizing abundance. It is also called horn of plenty. 2 Any horn-shaped container.

Cornucopia

corn·y [kôr′nē] *adj.* **corn·i·er, corn·i·est** *slang* Trite, silly, or sentimental.

co·rol·la [kə·rol′ə] *n.* The petals of a flower.

cor·ol·lar·y [kôr′ə·ler′ē] *n., pl.* **cor·ol·lar·ies** 1 Something that clearly follows once something else is shown to be true. 2 Something that is a natural consequence or result.

co·ro·na [kə·rō′nə] *n., pl.* **co·ro·nas** or **co·ro·nae** [kə·rō′nē] A luminous ring surrounding the sun, seen during a total eclipse of the sun.

cor·o·nar·y [kôr′ə·nər′ē] *adj., n., pl.* **cor·o·nar·ies** 1 *adj.* Having to do with either of the two main arteries (**coronary arteries**) that supply blood to the heart muscle. 2 *n.* Coronary thrombosis.

coronary thrombosis A blocking of the flow of blood to the heart muscle. It is caused by a clot in a coronary artery.

cor·o·na·tion [kôr′ə·nā′shən] *n.* The crowning of a king or queen.

cor·o·ner [kôr′ə·nər] *n.* An official in charge of investigating the cause of any death not clearly due to natural causes.

cor·o·net [kôr′ə·net] *n.* 1 A small crown worn by

a	add	**i**	it	**o͝o**	took	**oi**	oil
ā	ace	**ī**	ice	**o͞o**	pool	**ou**	pout
â	care	**o**	odd	**u**	up	**ng**	ring
ä	palm	**ō**	open	**û**	burn	**th**	thin
e	end	**ô**	order	**yo͞o**	fuse	**th**	this
ē	equal					**zh**	vision

ə = a in *above*, e in *sicken*, i in *possible*, o in *melon*, u in *circus*

princes, princesses, and nobles. 2 A circlet of jewels, flowers, or the like, worn on the head.

corp. or **Corp.** 1 corporal. 2 corporation.

cor·po·ral[1] [kôr′pə·rəl] *n.* A military rank. In the U.S. Army, a corporal is the lowest ranking noncommissioned officer, below a sergeant.

cor·po·ral[2] [kôr′pə·rəl] *adj.* Of the body; bodily: Spanking is *corporal* punishment.

cor·po·rate [kôr′pə·rit] *adj.* 1 Formed by law into one body, as a business; incorporated. 2 Of or related to a corporation. 3 United; collective: *corporate* efforts.

cor·po·ra·tion [kôr′pə·rā′shən] *n.* A group of people who have been given the legal power to act as one person. Such groups as businesses, universities, and towns, may all be organized as corporations.

cor·po·re·al [kôr·pôr′ē·əl] *adj.* 1 Of, for, or related to the body; bodily. 2 Tangible; real: Land is *corporeal* property.

corps [kôr] *n., pl.* **corps** [kôrz] 1 A branch of the armed forces having some special function: the Marine *Corps;* a medical *corps.* 2 A large military unit made up of two or more divisions. 3 A group of people working or acting together; team: a *corps* of accountants.

corpse [kôrps] *n.* The dead body of a human being.

cor·pu·lent [kôr′pyə·lənt] *adj.* Having a fleshy body; fat. **—cor′pu·lence** *n.*

cor·pus·cle [kôr′pəs·əl] *n.* One of the red or white cells forming part of the blood.

cor·ral [kə·ral′] *n., v.* **cor·ralled, cor·ral·ling** 1 *n.* An enclosed space or pen for livestock. 2 *v.* To drive into a corral: to *corral* horses. 3 *v. U.S. informal* To seize or capture. 4 *n.* A circle of covered wagons surrounding a camp to protect it from attack. 5 *v.* To arrange (wagons) in the form of a corral.

cor·rect [kə·rekt′] 1 *adj.* Exact; right: the *correct* amount of change. 2 *adj.* Proper: *correct* behavior. 3 *v.* To change so as to make right; eliminate faults or errors from: *Correct* your spelling. 4 *v.* To mark for errors: to *correct* tests. 5 *v.* To punish or rebuke so as to improve: to *correct* a child for misbehaving. 6 *v.* To adjust, alter, or set right: contact lenses to *correct* myopia. **—cor·rect′ly** *adv.* **—cor·rect′ness** *n.*

cor·rec·tion [kə·rek′shən] *n.* 1 The act of correcting. 2 A change, made or suggested, that removes an error or makes an improvement. 3 Punishment or rebuke.

cor·rec·tive [kə·rek′tiv] 1 *adj.* That corrects or tends to correct: *corrective* measures. 2 *n.* Something that corrects: Exercise can be a *corrective* for poor posture.

cor·re·late [kôr′ə·lāt′] *v.* **cor·re·lat·ed, cor·re·lat·ing** 1 To place or put in relation one to the other: to *correlate* art with history. 2 To be mutually related: Crime and poverty often *correlate.* **—cor′re·la′tion** *n.*

cor·rel·a·tive [kə·rel′ə·tiv] 1 *adj.* Mutually related, as a pair of words: *Either* and *or* are *correlative* conjunctions. 2 *n.* Either of two mutually related things.

cor·re·spond [kôr′ə·spond′] *v.* 1 To be in agreement with each other: Their answers *correspond.* 2 To be similar in function or character: A bird's beak *corresponds* to a human being's mouth. 3 To write or exchange letters.

cor·re·spon·dence [kôr′ə·spon′dəns] *n.* 1 A being alike or in agreement. 2 Letter writing, or letters written.

cor·re·spon·dent [kôr′ə·spon′dənt] 1 *n.* A person who writes letters to someone else and receives letters in return. 2 *n.* A reporter who regularly sends news back to a newspaper or magazine, often from a distant place. 3 *n.* A person or company that carries on business with another at a distance. 4 *adj.* Corresponding; agreeing.

cor·re·spond·ing [kôr′ə·spon′ding] *adj.* Similar or equivalent. **—cor′re·spond′ing·ly** *adv.*

cor·ri·dor [kôr′ə·dər] *n.* A long hallway or passageway with rooms opening onto it.

cor·rob·o·rate [kə·rob′ə·rāt′] *v.* **cor·rob·o·rat·ed, cor·rob·o·rat·ing** To bear out; confirm: His friends *corroborated* his story. **—cor·rob′o·ra′tion** *n.*

cor·rode [kə·rōd′] *v.* **cor·rod·ed, cor·rod·ing** 1 To eat away or destroy gradually: Rust and acid *corrode* metal. 2 To become eaten away; rust: Iron *corrodes* in damp air.

cor·ro·sion [kə·rō′zhən] *n.* A corroding; eating or wearing away.

cor·ro·sive [kə·rō′siv] 1 *adj.* That corrodes; corroding. 2 *n.* A corrosive substance.

cor·ru·gate [kôr′ə·gāt′] *v.* **cor·ru·gat·ed, cor·ru·gat·ing** To shape or bend into ridges and hollows like waves. **—cor′ru·ga′tion** *n.*

cor·ru·gat·ed [kôr′ə·gā′tid] *adj.* Having a ridged or wrinkled surface: *Corrugated* cardboard is used in making cartons; *Corrugated* iron is used for roofs.

A corrugated roof

cor·rupt [kə·rupt′] 1 *adj.* Depraved, wicked, or dishonest: the *corrupt* government of a city. 2 *v.* To make wicked or dishonest, as by bribery. 3 *adj.* Rotten; decayed. 4 *v.* To make or become rotten or decayed. 5 *v.* To change from the original; debase: to *corrupt* a language by adding words from other languages. 6 *adj.* Made worse by changes or errors: a *corrupt* translation of Homer's *Odyssey.* **—cor·rupt′ly** *adv.*

cor·rupt·i·ble [kə·rup′tə·bəl] *adj.* Capable of being corrupted.

cor·rup·tion [kə·rup′shən] *n.* 1 Evil or dishonest behavior. 2 Bribery. 3 Decay; rottenness. 4 The changing of a text or language.

cor·sage [kôr·säzh′] *n.* A small bouquet of flowers worn especially at the shoulder or waist.

Corsage

cor·sair [kôr′sâr′] *n.* 1 A privateer. 2 A pirate. 3 A pirate ship.

corse·let *n.* 1 [kôrs′lit] A type of armor worn on the upper part of the body. 2 [kôr′sə·let′] A light corset.

cor·set [kôr′sit] *n.* A close-fitting undergarment worn to give support and shape to the hips and waist.

cor·tege or **cor·tège** [kôr·tezh′ *or* kôr·tāzh′] *n.* 1 A ceremonial procession: a funeral *cortege.* 2 A train of attendants; retinue.

cor·tex [kôr′teks] *n., pl.* **cor·ti·ces** [kôr′tə·sēz′] 1 The bark of a tree. 2 The outer layers of an organ or gland. 3 The layer of gray matter covering most of the surface of the brain.

cor·ti·cal [kôr′tə·kəl] *adj.* Of or having to do with a cortex, especially of the brain.

cor·ti·sone [kôr′tə·sōn′] *n.* A powerful hormone

from the adrenal glands, sometimes used in treating arthritis, rheumatic fever, and other illnesses.

co·run·dum [kə·run′dəm] *n.* A very hard mineral used for grinding. Transparent varieties include the ruby and the sapphire.

cor·vette [kôr·vet′] *n.* A small warship used against submarines and to escort other ships.

cos. cosine.

co·se·cant [kō·sē′kant′] *n.* In a right triangle, the length of the hypotenuse divided by the length of the side opposite an acute angle. This quotient changes with the size of the angle and is a function of the angle.

co·sine [kō′sīn′] *n.* In a right triangle, the length of the shorter side next to an acute angle divided by the length of the hypotenuse. This quotient changes with the size of the angle and is a function of the angle.

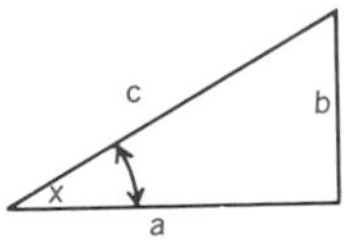

Cosine $x = \frac{a}{c}$

cos·met·ic [koz·met′ik] 1 *n.* A preparation for beautifying the complexion, hair, eyes, or nails. Lipstick, powder, and nail polish are cosmetics. 2 *adj.* Used to beautify.

cos·mic [koz′mik] *adj.* 1 Of or having to do with the universe or cosmos. 2 Vast; tremendous.

cosmic dust Fine particles of matter in outer space.

cosmic rays Very powerful rays that hit the earth from outer space.

cos·mol·ogy [koz·mol′ə·jē] *n., pl.* **cos·mol·o·gies** The study, whether by philosophers or astronomers, of the origin and structure of the universe. **—cos·mol′o·gist** *n.*

cos·mo·naut [koz′mə·nôt′] *n.* An astronaut.

cos·mo·pol·i·tan [koz′mə·pol′ə·tən] 1 *adj.* Common to all the world; not local or limited. 2 *adj.* At home in all parts of the world. 3 *n.* A person who feels at home anywhere.

cos·mos [koz′məs *or* koz′mōs′] *n.* 1 The universe thought of as a complete and harmonious system. 2 Any complete and ordered system. 3 A tall, flowering garden plant, related to the dahlia.

Cos·sack [kos′ak] *n.* One of a people of southern Russia noted as horsemen and soldiers.

cost [kôst] *n., v.* **cost, cost·ing** 1 *n.* Price: The *cost* of this suit includes alterations. 2 *v.* To have as its price; be sold for: How much does popcorn *cost* a bag? 3 *n.* Loss; sacrifice: We won the war at the *cost* of many lives. 4 *v.* To cause to lose: Your lateness will *cost* you your job. 5 *n.* (*pl.*) The expenses of conducting a lawsuit, usually paid by the loser. **—at all costs** or **at any cost** Regardless of cost or trouble.

Cos·ta Ri·can [kos′tə *or* kô′stə rē′kən] 1 Of or from Costa Rica. 2 A person born in or a citizen of Costa Rica.

cost-ef·fec·tive [kôst′i·fek′tiv] *adj.* Worth the money spent, judging by the benefits gained.

cos·ter·mon·ger [kos′tər·mung′gər] *n. British* A street vendor, as of vegetables or fruits.

cost·ly [kôst′lē] *adj.* **cost·li·er, cost·li·est** Costing very much; expensive.

cost of living The average cost of food, housing, and other necessities over a period of time.

cos·tume [*n.* kos′t(y)o͞om, *v.* kos·t(y)o͞om′] *n. v.* **cos·tumed, cos·tum·ing** 1 *n.* The clothing, ornaments, and arrangement of hair worn in a particular time or place or by a certain group of people: an Arab *costume.* 2 *n.* Clothing worn by an actor or a masquerader. 3 *n.* A special set of clothes for a certain time or activity: a summer *costume;* a riding *costume.* 4 *v.* To furnish with costumes.

costume jewelry Relatively inexpensive jewelry made of materials such as nonprecious metals and stones.

cos·tum·er [kos·t(y)o͞o′mər] *n.* A person who makes, sells, or rents costumes.

co·sy [kō′zē] *adj., n.* Another spelling of COZY.

cot[1] [kot] *n.* A light, narrow bed usually made of a piece of canvas stretched on a folding frame.

cot[2] [kot] *n.* 1 A cottage: used mostly in poems. 2 A cote. 3 A covering for an injured finger.

co·tan·gent [kō·tan′jənt] *n.* In a right triangle, the length of the shorter side next to an acute angle divided by the length of the side opposite the acute angle. This quotient changes with the size of the angle and is a function of the angle.

cote [kōt] *n.* A shelter for birds or small animals.

co·te·rie [kō′tə·rē] *n.* A small circle of people who share the same interests or activities.

co·til·lion [kə·til′yən] *n.* 1 An elaborate dance in which the dancers change partners often. 2 *U.S.* A formal ball.

cot·tage [kot′ij] *n.* 1 A small house. 2 A house, as at a beach, for use on a vacation.

cottage cheese A soft white cheese made of strained milk curds.

cottage industry An industry whose labor force consists of people who work at home using their own tools or machines.

cot·tag·er [kot′i·jər] *n.* A person who lives in a cottage.

cot·ter or **cot·tar** [kot′ər] *n.* A Scottish worker on a farm, allowed the use of a cottage and plot of land there.

cot·ter pin [kot′ər] A metal pin inserted to hold machinery parts together. It is split lengthwise so that the ends may be spread apart to keep it in its hole.

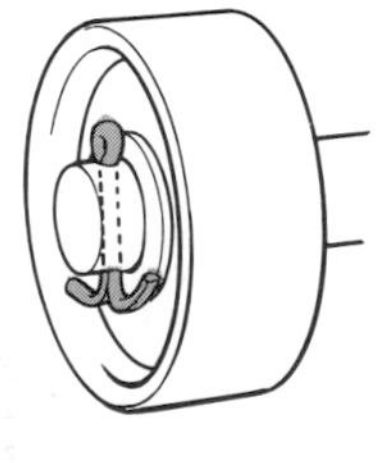

Cotter pin

cot·ton [kot′(ə)n] *n.* 1 The soft white fibers that surround the seeds of the cotton plant. 2 The plant itself. It is a low shrub. 3 Cloth or thread made from cotton fibers. 4 *adj. use:* *cotton* socks. 5 A crop of cotton plants.

cotton candy A candy made by boiling sugar, drawing it into long threads, and winding it around a stick or cone.

cotton gin A machine that separates the seeds from the fibers of cotton.

cot·ton·mouth [kot′(ə)n·mouth′] *n., pl.* **cot·ton·mouths** [kot′(ə)n·mouth̶z′] Another name for WATER MOCCASIN.

cot·ton·seed [kot′(ə)n·sēd′] *n.* The seed of the cotton plant. It yields an oil and is used as fodder or fertilizer.

a	add	**i**	it	**o͝o**	took	**oi**	oil
ā	ace	**ī**	ice	**o͞o**	pool	**ou**	pout
â	care	**o**	odd	**u**	up	**ng**	ring
ä	palm	**ō**	open	**û**	burn	**th**	thin
e	end	**ô**	order	**yo͞o**	fuse	**th̶**	this
ē	equal					**zh**	vision

ə = a in *above*, e in *sicken*, i in *possible*, o in *melon*, u in *circus*

cottonseed oil A yellow oil pressed from cottonseed, used for cooking and in soaps and other products.

cot·ton·tail [kot′(ə)n·tāl′] *n.* The common rabbit of America, having a little white tail.

cot·ton·wood [kot′(ə)n·wo͝od′] *n.* **1** An American poplar tree having seeds covered with cottony tufts of hair. **2** The wood of this tree.

cot·ton·y [kot′(ə)n·ē] *adj.* Of or like cotton; soft and downy.

cot·y·le·don [kot′ə·lēd′(ə)n] *n.* The first leaf, or either one of the first pair of leaves, sprouting from a seed.

couch [kouch] **1** *n.* A sofa or upholstered bed. **2** *n.* Any place for resting or sleeping, as the burrow of an animal. **3** *v.* To lie down or cause to lie down, as on a bed. **4** *v.* To put into words: Millay *couched* her thoughts in poetry.

cou·gar [ko͞o′gər] *n.* A large wildcat of North and South America.

cough [kôf] **1** *v.* To force air from the lungs with a sudden harsh noise. **2** *n.* The act of coughing. **3** *n.* Frequent coughing as an ailment: a bad *cough.* **4** *v.* To expel by coughing: to *cough* up phlegm.

could [ko͝od] Past tense of CAN. ◆ *Could have* sounds like *could of.* Use *have,* not *of,* with the helping verb *could:* Muriel *could have* gone with us.

could·n't [ko͝od′(ə)nt] Could not.

couldst [ko͝odst] *v.* A form of the verb CAN, used with *thou*: seldom used today.

cou·lee [ko͞o′lē] *n.* **1** A ravine or gulch, often dry in summer. **2** A sheet of solidified lava.

cou·lomb [ko͞o′lom *or* ko͞o′lōm] *n.* A unit of electric charge equal to the amount of charge transferred by a current of one ampere in one second. ◆ This unit is named for Charles A. Coulomb (1736–1806), a French scientist known for his work on electricity.

coun·cil [koun′səl] *n.* **1** A group of people called together for discussion. A council makes plans or decisions or gives advice. **2** A group of people elected to make laws for a city or town. ◆ *Council, counsel,* and *consul* are pronounced similarly, but their meanings are different. A *council* is a group of people meeting to discuss something or make decisions: a city *council. Counsel* may mean either *advice* or *a lawyer* (because you hire a lawyer to give you advice): In the U.S. every person accused of a crime has the right to *counsel.* A *consul* [kon′səl] is a person who lives in a foreign city to protect the people and business interests of the country represented.

coun·cil·man [koun′səl·mən] *n., pl.* **coun·cil·men** [koun′səl·mən] A member of a council, especially of a city or town council.

coun·cil·or or **coun·cil·lor** [koun′səl·ər *or* koun′slər] *n.* A member of a council.

coun·cil·wom·an [koun′səl·wo͝om′ən] *n., pl.* **coun·cil·wom·en** [koun′səl·wim′in] A woman who is a member of a council, especially of a city or town council.

coun·sel [koun′səl] *n., v.* **coun·seled** or **coun·selled, coun·sel·ing** or **coun·sel·ling** **1** *n.* Talk and exchange of ideas between or among people. **2** *n.* Advice: wise *counsel.* **3** *n.* A lawyer or group of lawyers handling one side of a case. **4** *v.* To give advice to: to *counsel* a child. **5** *v.* To recommend; advise in favor of. ◆ See COUNCIL.

coun·sel·or or **coun·sel·lor** [koun′səl·ər *or* koun′·slər] *n.* **1** An adviser. **2** A lawyer. **3** A children's supervisor in a camp.

count[1] [kount] **1** *v.* To list or call off numbers in a regular order: to *count* to 100. **2** *v.* To add up; find the total of: I *counted* 20 pencils in the box. **3** *n.* The act of counting or reckoning. **4** *n.* The amount found by counting; total: a *count* of 50. **5** *v.* To include: *Counting* the driver, there were nine people on the bus. **6** *v.* To be taken into account: The mark in this test will *count* toward your final grade. **7** *v.* To be important: Every vote *counts.* **8** *v.* To consider to be; judge: I *count* myself fortunate. **9** *n.* A separate charge against an accused person: guilty on two *counts* of forgery. **—count off** To divide into equal groups by counting: to *count off* in groups of three. **—count on** To rely on.

count[2] [kount] *n.* In some European countries, a noble having a rank equal to that of an earl in England.

count·down [kount′doun′] *n.* A downward counting of the time left before a scheduled act, as the firing of a rocket. Zero marks the doing of the act.

coun·te·nance [koun′tə·nəns] *n., v.* **coun·te·nanced, coun·te·nanc·ing** **1** *n.* The expression of the face: a sad *countenance.* **2** *n.* A face. **3** *n.* Approval; encouragement: John's parents gave *countenance* to his playing football. **4** *v.* To approve; encourage: I will not *countenance* bad manners. **5** *n.* Self-control; calmness. **—out of countenance** Embarrassed; abashed: The laughter put the child *out of countenance.*

coun·ter[1] [koun′tər] **1** *adv.* In an opposite manner or direction; contrary: to act *counter* to orders. **2** *adj.* Opposing; contrary: a *counter* proposal. **3** *v.* To oppose: They *countered* my suggestions with some of their own. **4** *n.* In boxing, a blow given while receiving or blocking another. **5** *v.* To give such a blow.

coun·ter[2] [koun′tər] *n.* **1** A long board or table, as in a restaurant or store, on which meals are served or goods sold: a lunch *counter.* **2** Something used for counting or keeping score in games, as a disk or chip.

count·er[3] [koun′tər] *n.* A person or thing that counts.

counter- A prefix meaning: **1** Opposite; contrary, as in *counterbalance.* **2** In return, as in *counterattack.* **3** Corresponding; being duplicate or parallel, as in *counterpart.*

coun·ter·act [koun′tər·akt′] *v.* To act against; check: Penicillin *counteracts* infection.

coun·ter·at·tack [koun′tər·ə·tak′] **1** *n.* An attack made in return for or to stop an enemy's attack. **2** *v.* To make a counterattack.

coun·ter·bal·ance [*n.* koun′tər·bal′əns, *v.* koun′tər·bal′əns] *n., v.* **coun·ter·bal·anced, coun·ter·bal·anc·ing** **1** *n.* A power or force that balances and offsets another. **2** *n.* A weight that balances another. **3** *v.* To act as a counterbalance to; offset.

coun·ter·claim [koun′tər·klām′] *n.* A claim that opposes another claim, as in a lawsuit.

coun·ter·clock·wise [koun′tər·klok′wīz′] *adj., adv.* In the opposite direction from that in which the hands of a clock turn.

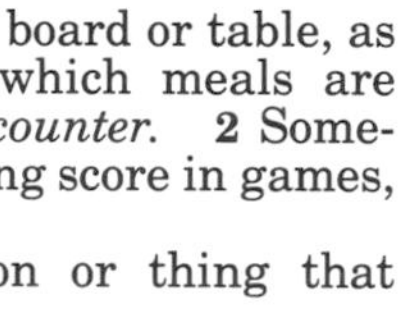

coun·ter·es·pi·o·nage [koun′tər·es′pē·ə·näzh′ *or* koun′tər·es′pē·ə·nij′] *n.* Spying done to uncover and counteract enemy spies.

coun·ter·feit [koun′tər·fit] **1** *adj.* Copied to look like and pass as something genuine; false: a *counterfeit* ten-dollar bill. **2** *n.* Something that is counterfeit. **3** *v.* To copy or imitate, especially in order to deceive: to *counterfeit* money. **4** *v.* To sham: to *counterfeit* sympathy. **—coun′ter·feit′er** *n.* ◆ *Counterfeit* once meant simply an imitation. Now, however, it almost always implies an evil motive.

coun·ter·in·tel·li·gence [koun′tər·in·tel′ə·jəns] *n.* Work done to find out military and political information about an enemy, to keep information from an enemy, to counteract the enemy's espionage, and to prevent sabotage.

coun·ter·man [koun′tər·man′] *n., pl.* **coun·ter·men** [koun′tər·men′] A person who serves food at a counter, as in a restaurant.

coun·ter·mand [koun′tər·mand′] *v.* To cancel (an order), often by giving a contrary one.

coun·ter·meas·ure [koun′tər·mezh′ər] *n.* An action taken to oppose or counteract another action.

coun·ter·of·fen·sive [koun′tər·ə·fen′siv] *n.* An offensive undertaken by a military force to repel the attack of an enemy.

coun·ter·pane [koun′tər·pān′] *n.* A bedspread or quilt.

coun·ter·part [koun′tər·pärt′] *n.* **1** A person or thing that closely resembles another: Tokyo is a *counterpart* of New York. **2** Something that goes with or completes another, as one of a pair of gloves. **3** A copy or duplicate.

coun·ter·point [koun′tər·point′] *n.* **1** Music in which two or more parts or voices contribute melodic material at the same time. **2** Any of these parts. **3** The art of writing counterpoint.

coun·ter·poise [koun′tər·poiz′] *n., v.* **coun·ter·poised, coun·ter·pois·ing** **1** *n.* A weight that balances another weight. **2** *n.* A counterbalancing force or power. **3** *n.* A being in balance. **4** *v.* To offset.

coun·ter·rev·o·lu·tion [koun′tər·rev′ə·lo͞o′shən] *n.* A revolution to overthrow the government set up by a previous revolution.

coun·ter·sign [koun′tər·sīn′] **1** *n.* A password or signal that must be given to a sentry in order to pass. **2** *n.* A person's signature showing that someone else's signature is confirmed. **3** *v.* To put a countersign on: to *countersign* a check. **4** *n.* A secret sign or signal, especially one given in answer to another.

coun·ter·sink [koun′tər·singk′] *v.* **coun·ter·sunk, coun·ter·sink·ing** **1** To widen the top of a hole so the head of a screw or bolt will lie flush with or below the surface. **2** To sink (a screw or bolt) into such a hole.

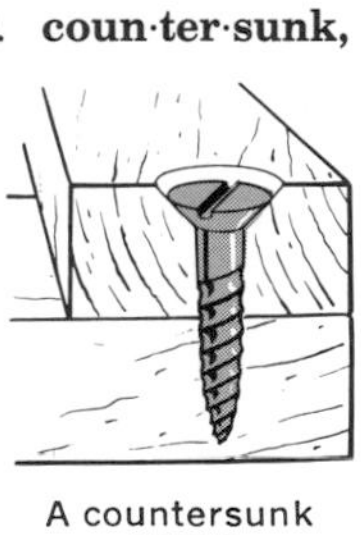

A countersunk screw

coun·ter·spy [koun′tər·spī′] *n., pl.* **coun·ter·spies** A spy whose job is to uncover and counteract enemy spies.

coun·ter·vail [koun′tər·vāl′] *v.* **1** To make up for; offset. **2** To act against; counteract.

coun·ter·weight [koun′tər·wāt′] *n.* A weight that offsets another; counterpoise.

count·ess [koun′tis] *n.* **1** The wife or widow of a count or earl. **2** A woman equal in rank to a count or an earl.

count·ing·house [koun′ting·hous′] An office or building in which a firm keeps its accounts and transacts business.

counting number Any whole number but zero. 24 and 231 are counting numbers but ½ is not.

count·less [kount′lis] *adj.* Too numerous to be counted: *countless* centuries.

coun·tri·fied [kun′tri·fīd′] *adj.* Looking or behaving like simple country people.

coun·try [kun′trē] *n., pl.* **coun·tries,** *adj.* **1** *n.* An area, district, or region: mountain *country*; farm *country*. **2** *n.* The land of a nation: France is a beautiful *country*. **3** *n.* A nation: the *countries* of Europe. **4** *n.* The people of a nation. **5** *n.* The land of one's birth or allegiance. **6** *n.* The land outside cities and towns. **7** *adj.* Of or having to do with the country; rural: *country* dances.

country club A private club, usually in the country, with facilities for sports and social activities.

coun·try·man [kun′trē·mən] *n., pl.* **coun·try·men** [kun′trē·mən] **1** A person of one's own country. **2** A person who lives in the country.

country music A style of popular music based on folk songs of the southern and sw U.S.

coun·try·seat [kun′trē·sēt′] *n.* A mansion or estate in the country.

coun·try·side [kun′trē·sīd′] *n.* **1** A rural area. **2** The people living in it.

coun·try·wom·an [kun′trē·wo͝om′ən] *n., pl.* **coun·try·wom·en** [kun′trē·wim′in] **1** A woman of one's own country. **2** A woman living in the country.

coun·ty [koun′tē] *n., pl.* **coun·ties** **1** One of the sections into which a country or, in the U.S., a state is divided. A county has its own local government, courts, roads, and other facilities. **2** The people living in it.

county seat A town where the government of a county is located.

coup [ko͞o] *n., pl.* **coups** [ko͞oz] A sudden and brilliant maneuver; a clever or lucky move.

coup d'état [ko͞o′dā·tä′] A sudden change in the political affairs of a country, often involving the seizing of the government by force.

coupe [ko͞op] *n.* A closed automobile with two doors, seating up to six people.

cou·pé [ko͞o·pā′] *n.* **1** A coupe. **2** A low, closed carriage having a seat for two persons and a seat outside for the driver.

A coupe

cou·ple [kup′əl] *n., v.* **cou·pled, cou·pling** **1** *n.* Two things of the same kind; a pair. **2** *n.* A man and woman who are married, engaged, or considered partners, as in a dance. **3** *v.* To join two things together: to *couple* two railroad cars; talent *coupled* with hard work.

cou·plet [kup′lit] *n.* Two successive lines of verse that go together, usually rhymed and having the same meter.

coup·ling [kup′ling] *n.* **1** A joining together of two

a add	**i** it	**o͝o** took	**oi** oil
ā ace	**ī** ice	**o͞o** pool	**ou** pout
â care	**o** odd	**u** up	**ng** ring
ä palm	**ō** open	**û** burn	**th** thin
e end	**ô** order	**yo͞o** fuse	**th** this
ē equal			**zh** vision

ə = a in *above*, e in *sicken*, i in *possible*, o in *melon*, u in *circus*

things. **2** A device that connects parts together, as one that links one railroad car to another.

cou·pon [k(y)ōō′pon] *n.* **1** A ticket, certificate, or advertisement, that entitles the holder to something: They are saving cereal *coupons* for a kite. **2** One of the parts of a bond that are clipped off at regular times and turned in for interest payments.

cour·age [kûr′ij] *n.* The ability to meet danger or pain without giving in to fear; bravery.

cou·ra·geous [kə·rā′jəs] *adj.* Having or showing courage. **—cou·ra′geous·ly** *adv.*

cou·ri·er [kŏŏr′ē·ər *or* kûr′ē·ər] *n.* **1** A messenger required to deliver a message quickly. **2** A person who accompanies travelers to take care of travel arrangements, as tickets and reservations.

course [kôrs] *n., v.* **coursed, cours·ing** **1** *n.* A moving onward in space or time: the *course* of a journey; the *course* of time. **2** *v.* To move swiftly: The blood *coursed* through the runner's veins. **3** *n.* Something, as a path or ground, passed over: the *course* of a river; a golf *course.* **4** *n.* Line of motion; direction: The ship's *course* was due west. **5** *n.* A way of proceeding: What *course* should we take? **6** *n.* A series of like things having a certain order: a *course* of exercises. **7** *n.* A program of study leading to a degree or diploma: a high school *course.* **8** *n.* A particular subject or study: a history *course.* **9** *n.* A part of a meal served by itself: the dessert *course.* **10** *n.* A horizontal row, as of brick or stones in a wall. **11** *v.* To hunt with hounds. **—of course** Naturally; certainly.

cours·er [kôr′sər] *n.* A swift, spirited horse: used mostly in poems.

court [kôrt] **1** *n.* An open space surrounded by buildings or walls; courtyard. **2** *n.* A short street open at only one end. **3** *n.* A space laid out for a game: a tennis *court.* **4** *n.* A palace. **5** *n.* Those who serve or attend a ruler. **6** *n.* A group of persons made up of a ruler and the ruler's council. **7** *n.* A formal meeting held by a ruler. **8** *n.* A place where law cases are tried. **9** *n.* A person or group of persons who lawfully decide cases; a judge or judges. **10** *n.* A meeting in which a law case is conducted: *Court* is adjourned until two o'clock. **11** *adj. use: court* sessions; *court* fees. **12** *n.* An attempt to win someone's affections or to gain someone's favor; courtship. **13** *v.* To seek the love of; woo. **14** *v.* To try to gain the favor of: to *court* voters in an election. **15** *v.* To act in such a way that one will probably get: to *court* disaster.

Court

cour·te·ous [kûr′tē·əs] *adj.* Polite and considerate. **—cour′te·ous·ly** *adv.*

cour·te·san [kôr′tə·zən *or* kōr′tə·zən] *n.* A prostitute, especially one with wealthy, socially prominent, or courtly clients.

cour·te·sy [kûr′tə·sē] *n., pl.* **cour·te·sies** **1** Politeness and consideration for others; good manners. **2** A courteous act. **3** A curtsy.

court·house [kôrt′hous′] *n., pl.* **court·hous·es** [kôrt′·hou′zəz] **1** A building occupied by courts of law. **2** The main building used for the offices of a county government.

cour·ti·er [kôr′tē·ər] *n.* **1** A member of a ruler's court. **2** A person who seeks favor by flattering or trying to please.

court·ly [kôrt′lē] *adj.* **court·li·er, court·li·est** **1** Having elegant, polished manners: a *courtly* diplomat. **2** Of, having to do with, or suitable for a sovereign's court. **—court′li·ness** *n.*

court-mar·tial [kôrt′mär′shəl] *n., pl.* **courts-mar·tial,** *v.* **court-mar·tialed** or **court-mar·tialled, court-mar·tial·ing** or **court-mar·tial·ling** **1** *n.* A military court that tries soldiers, sailors, or others coming under military law. **2** *n.* A trial by such a court. **3** *v.* To try by court-martial.

court·room [kôrt′rōōm′] *n.* A room in which the sessions of a law court are held.

court·ship [kôrt′ship′] *n.* A seeking of a person in marriage; wooing.

court·yard [kôrt′yärd′] *n.* An open space surrounded by buildings or walls; a court.

cous·in [kuz′(ə)n] *n.* **1** A son or daughter of one's uncle or aunt. **2** A less close relative.

cou·ture [kōō·tŏŏr′] *n.* The business of designing, making, and selling women's high-fashion clothing.

co·va·lent bond [kō·vā′lənt] A bond between the atoms of a molecule formed when the atoms share one or more electrons, especially pairs of electrons.

cove [kōv] *n.* A small, sheltered bay or inlet in a shoreline.

cov·en [kuv′ən *or* kōv′ən] *n.* A group or gathering of witches.

cov·e·nant [kuv′ə·nənt] **1** *n.* An agreement entered into by two or more persons; pact. **2** *v.* To promise by or in such an agreement.

Cov·en·try [kuv′ən·trē] *n.* A state of ostracism or banishment. **—send to Coventry** To ostracize, as by refusing to talk to or associate with.

cov·er [kuv′ər] **1** *v.* To place over or upon something else so as to protect or hide: to *cover* a person with a blanket. **2** *v.* To lie over or upon: Snow *covered* the ground. **3** *v.* To hide: to *cover* an error. **4** *v.* To protect, as against loss: Their family is *covered* by insurance. **5** *n.* Anything that covers, conceals, or protects: a *cover* of topsoil. **6** *n.* The binding of a book or magazine. **7** *v.* To travel or pass over: to *cover* 300 miles a day. **8** *v.* To include or deal with: This book *covers* the Civil War. **9** *v.* To get news of or photograph, as for a newspaper: to *cover* a trial. **10** *v.* To provide for: Is this *covered* by the rules? **11** *v.* To keep a gun pointed at: to *cover* a prisoner. **12** *v.* In sports, to guard (an opponent). **13** *v.* In sports, to defend (as a position or base). **—under cover** In secret; secretly.

cov·er·age [kuv′ər·ij] *n.* The extent or amount to which anything is covered: the *coverage* of an insurance policy.

cov·er·all [kuv′ər·ôl′] *n.* (*usually pl.*) A one-piece work garment combining pants and a shirt with long sleeves.

cover crop A crop planted to protect the soil during the winter and to enrich it.

covered wagon A large wagon covered with canvas stretched over hoops, used especially by American pioneers.

cover glass A thin piece of glass put over a specimen on a slide for examination under a microscope.

cov·er·ing [kuv′ər·ing] *n.* Anything that covers.

cov·er·let [kuv′ər·lit] *n.* A bedspread.

cov·ert [kuv′ərt *or* kō′vərt] 1 *adj.* Secret; concealed: a *covert* smile. 2 *n.* A shelter or hiding place, especially underbrush where wild animals are likely to hide. **—cov′ert·ly** *adv.*

cov·er-up [kuv′ər·up′] *n.* 1 The concealment of something, such as a mistake or a crime, that could be embarrassing or harmful if revealed. 2 A device or strategy used to effect such a concealment.

cov·et [kuv′it] *v.* To desire strongly (something belonging to someone else).

cov·et·ous [kuv′ə·təs] *adj.* Strongly desiring what belongs to someone else. **—cov′et·ous·ly** *adv.* **—cov′et·ous·ness** *n.*

cov·ey [kuv′ē] *n., pl.* **cov·eys** 1 A flock of quail or partridge. 2 A small group of people.

cow[1] [kou] *n.* 1 A full-grown female of domestic cattle. Cows are kept for their milk, have cloven hoofs, and chew their cud. 2 A full-grown female of certain other animals, as the elephant, moose, seal, and whale.

cow[2] [kou] *v.* To make afraid or timid.

cow·ard [kou′ərd] *n.* A person who lacks the courage to meet pain, danger, or difficulty.

cow·ard·ice [kou′ər·dis] *n.* Lack of courage when facing pain, danger, or difficulty.

cow·ard·ly [kou′ərd·lē] 1 *adj.* Of or like a coward. 2 *adv.* In a cowardly way.

cow·bell [kou′bel′] *n.* A bell hung around a cow's neck to make her easy to find.

cow·bird [kou′bûrd′] *n.* A small American blackbird often found with cattle. It lays its eggs in smaller birds' nests.

cow·boy [kou′boi′] *n. U.S.* A man, usually working on horseback, who handles cattle on a ranch.

cow·catch·er [kou′kach′ər] *n.* An iron frame on the front of a locomotive or streetcar to clear off anything on the track.

Cowcatcher

cow·er [kou′ər] *v.* To crouch, as in fear or shame; tremble.

cow·girl [kou′gûrl′] *n.* A woman, usually working on horseback, who handles cattle on a ranch.

cow·hand [kou′hand′] *n.* A cowboy or cowgirl.

cow·herd [kou′hûrd′] *n.* A person who tends cattle.

cow·hide [kou′hīd′] *n.* 1 The skin of a cow. 2 Leather made from it. 3 A heavy, flexible whip, usually of braided leather.

cowl [koul] *n.* 1 A monk's robe having a hood. 2 The hood itself. 3 The part of an automobile that holds the windshield and dashboard. 4 A cowling.

cow·lick [kou′lik′] *n.* A tuft of hair that sticks up and will not easily lie flat.

Cowlick

cowl·ing [kou′ling] *n.* A metal covering for an engine of an aircraft.

co-work·er [kō′wûrk′ər] *n.* A fellow worker.

cow·pea [kou′pē′] *n.* 1 A plant related to the bean, widely cultivated in the southern U.S. 2 The seed of this plant.

cow·poke [kou′pōk′] *n. informal* A cowboy.

cow·pox [kou′poks′] *n.* A mild contagious disease of cattle. The virus of cowpox is used to make smallpox vaccine.

cow·punch·er [kou′pun′chər] *n. informal* A cowboy.

cow·rie or **cow·ry** [kou′rē] *n., pl.* **cow·ries** A small mollusk found in warm seas with a glossy, brightly marked, oval shell.

cow·slip [kou′slip′] *n.* A wild marigold with yellow flowers, found in swampy places.

cox·comb [koks′kōm′] *n.* A conceited, foolish person, often vain about personal appearance.

cox·swain [kok′sən *or* kok′swān′] *n.* A person who steers a racing shell or other boat.

coy [koi] *adj.* 1 Shy; bashful. 2 Pretending to be shy in order to be flirtatious. **—coy′ly** *adv.* **—coy′·ness** *n.*

coy·o·te [kī·ō′tē] *n., pl.* **coy·o·tes** or **coy·o·te** A small wolf of the western prairies of North America. ◆ *Coyote* comes directly from a Mexican Spanish word, which in turn came from a Mexican Indian word for the animal, *coyotl.*

Coyote

coz·en [kuz′ən] *v.* To cheat or deceive, especially in small ways.

co·zy [kō′zē] *adj.* **co·zi·er, co·zi·est,** *n., pl.* **co·zies** 1 *adj.* Warm and comfortable; snug: to be *cozy* in bed on a cold night. 2 *n.* A padded cover for a teapot to keep the tea warm. **—co′zi·ly** *adv.* **—co′·zi·ness** *n.*

cp. 1 compare. 2 coupon.

c.p. candlepower.

C.P. Communist Party.

C.P.A. Certified Public Accountant.

cpd. compound.

cpl. or **Cpl.** corporal.

CPR cardiopulmonary resuscitation.

CPU central processing unit.

Cr The symbol for the element chromium.

crab[1] [krab] *n., v.* **crabbed, crab·bing** 1 *n.* A sea animal related to the lobster, having a flat shell, eight legs, and two pincerlike front claws. Crabs usually move sideways. 2 *v.* To catch or try to catch crabs.

Blue crab

crab[2] [krab] *n., v.* **crabbed, crab·bing** 1 *n. informal* A cross, disagreeable person. 2 *v. informal* To complain ill-naturedly. 3 *n.* A crab apple.

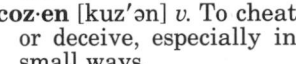

crab apple 1 A small, sour apple usually used for making jelly or preserves. 2 The small tree on which these apples grow.

crab·bed [krab′id] *adj.* 1 Complaining; surly; dis-

a	add	**i**	it	**o͝o**	took	**oi**	oil
ā	ace	**ī**	ice	**o͞o**	pool	**ou**	pout
â	care	**o**	odd	**u**	up	**ng**	ring
ä	palm	**ō**	open	**û**	burn	**th**	thin
e	end	**ô**	order	**yo͞o**	fuse	**t͟h**	this
ē	equal					**zh**	vision

ə = {a in *above* e in *sicken* i in *possible* / o in *melon* u in *circus*}

agreeable. 2 Crowded, uneven, and difficult to figure out, as handwriting.

crab·by [krab'ē] *adj.* **crab·bi·er, crab·bi·est** Ill-tempered; peevish; cross.

crab grass A rapidly spreading grass with broad leaves, considered a pest in lawns.

crack [krak] 1 *n.* A break that shows as a fine line or narrow opening in a surface. 2 *v.* To break so as to form such lines or split apart: to *crack* an egg; The dish *cracked* when it fell. 3 *n.* A narrow space: Open the door a *crack.* 4 *n.* A sharp, snapping sound: the *crack* of a rifle. 5 *v.* To make or cause to make such a sound: to *crack* one's knuckles. 6 *v.* To change abruptly in tone: The singer's voice *cracked* on a high note. 7 *v. informal* To strike sharply or with a sharp sound: She *cracked* her elbow against the wall. 8 *n. informal* A sudden, sharp blow: a *crack* on the nose. 9 *v. informal* To tell or say humorously: to *crack* jokes. 10 *n. informal* A funny or sarcastic remark. 11 *v. informal* To find the solution of: to *crack* a code. 12 *n. informal* A try; chance: Let me have a *crack* at pitching. 13 *adj. informal* Very good; first-class: a *crack* regiment. 14 *v.* To break down mentally or physically: to *crack* under pressure. 15 *v.* To break up (petroleum) into simpler compounds. 16 *n.* The crystallized form of COCAINE, a highly dangerous drug. **—crack down** *informal* To become harsh or strict, especially to enforce discipline. **—cracked up to be** *slang* Said or believed to be: The movie we saw yesterday was not what it was *cracked up to be.* **—crack up** *informal* 1 To be in a crash or collision, as of an airplane. 2 To have a nervous breakdown. 3 To praise.

crack·down [krak'doun'] *n.* A sudden strictness, as in enforcing rules or laws: a *crackdown* on talking in class.

cracked [krakt] *adj.* 1 Having a crack or cracks. 2 Broken apart or into pieces: *cracked* ice. 3 Harsh and uneven in tone: a high, *cracked* voice. 4 *informal* Crazy.

crack·er [krak'ər] *n.* 1 A thin, brittle biscuit, usually unsweetened. 2 A firecracker.

crack·er·jack [krak'ər·jak'] *informal* 1 *adj.* Of exceptional quality; excellent. 2 *n.* A person or thing of exceptional merit or skill.

crack·ing [krak'ing] 1 *n.* A process in which the molecules of petroleum are changed by heat and pressure into smaller ones. It is used in making gasoline. 2 *adj. informal* Extremely good; excellent: You did a *cracking* repair job on your bicycle. 3 *adv. informal* Extremely; very: We heard a *cracking* good concert last night.

crack·le [krak'əl] *v.* **crack·led, crack·ling,** *n.* 1 *v.* To make sudden, snapping sounds: The twigs *crackled* as they burned. 2 *n.* A snapping or rustling sound: the *crackle* of dry leaves under our feet. 3 *n.* A network of fine cracks in the surface, as of china or porcelain.

crack·ling [krak'ling] *n.* 1 The crisp, browned skin of roasted pork. 2 The sound of something that crackles.

crack·ly [krak'lē] *adj.* **crack·li·er, crack·li·est** Tending or likely to crackle.

crack·pot [krak'pot'] *slang* 1 *n.* A crazy, eccentric, or very foolish person. 2 *adj.* Crazy, eccentric, or very foolish: a *crackpot* scheme.

crack-up [krak'up'] *n.* 1 A crash, as of an automobile or an airplane. 2 *informal* A breakdown of the mind or body.

cra·dle [krād'(ə)l] *n., v.* **cra·dled, cra·dling** 1 *n.* A small bed for a baby, that can be rocked from side to side. 2 *v.* To hold or rock as if in a cradle: I *cradled* the frightened child in my arms. 3 *n.* A place where something originated: the *cradle* of freedom. 4 *n.* A rack or framework, as a support for a ship being built or repaired, or a frame attached to a scythe to catch cut grain.

Cradle

craft [kraft] *n.* 1 Skill, especially in work done with the hands. 2 An occupation or trade requiring skillful or artistic work: Making pottery is a *craft.* 3 Cleverness in deceiving others; cunning. 4 *pl.* **craft** A boat, ship, or aircraft.

crafts·man [krafts'mən] *n., pl.* **crafts·men** [krafts'·mən] 1 A person skilled in a craft. 2 Anyone who does skilled work. **—crafts'man·ship** *n.*

crafts·wom·an [krafts'wŏŏm'ən] *n., pl.* **crafts·wom·en** [krafts'wim'in] 1 A woman skilled in a craft. 2 A woman who does skilled work.

craft union A labor union whose members all work in the same craft.

craft·y [kraf'tē] *adj.* **craft·i·er, craft·i·est** Clever at deceiving others; sly; wily. **—craft'i·ly** *adv.* **—craft'i·ness** *n.* ◆ *Crafty* originally meant *able* or *skilled.* A *crafty* workman was a good workman, not a sly one. Only in more recent times has *crafty* come to mean *skillful in deceiving.*

crag [krag] *n.* A rough mass of rock jutting out from a cliff.

crag·gy [krag'ē] *adj.* **crag·gi·er, crag·gi·est** 1 Full of crags. 2 Like a crag; jutting. **—crag'gi·ness** *n.*

cram [kram] *v.* **crammed, cram·ming** 1 To push or stuff into a tight or crowded space: to *cram* papers into a drawer. 2 To fill completely; pack: a closet *crammed* with clothes. 3 To eat fast and greedily. 4 To study hard for a short time: to *cram* before a history test.

cramp [kramp] 1 *n.* A sudden, painful tightening of a muscle, often in the leg or foot. 2 *v.* To hold or confine so as to prevent free action; hamper: Tight shoes *cramp* the toes. 3 *n.* (*pl.*) Twinges of pain in the abdomen.

cram·pon [kram'pən] *n.* 1 One of a hinged pair of iron bars with hooked ends, used for lifting heavy weights. 2 One of a pair of spiked iron plates attached to shoe bottoms to prevent slipping.

cran·ber·ry [kran'ber'ē] *n., pl.* **cran·ber·ries** 1 A glossy, sour, red berry used to make sauce and jelly. 2 The shrub it grows on.

crane [krān] *n., v.* **craned, cran·ing** 1 *n.* A wading bird with long legs, a long neck, and a long, pointed bill. 2 *v.* To stretch out (one's neck), especially to try to see something. 3 *n.* A machine with a long, movable arm, used to lift and move heavy objects. 4 *n.* A swinging metal rod, as one used to hold a pot over a fire.

cra·ni·al [krā'nē·əl] *adj.* Of or having to do with the skull or cranium.

cra·ni·um [krā'nē·əm] *n., pl.* **cra·ni·ums** or **cra·ni·a** [krā'nē·ə] The skull, especially the upper part, in which the brain is enclosed.

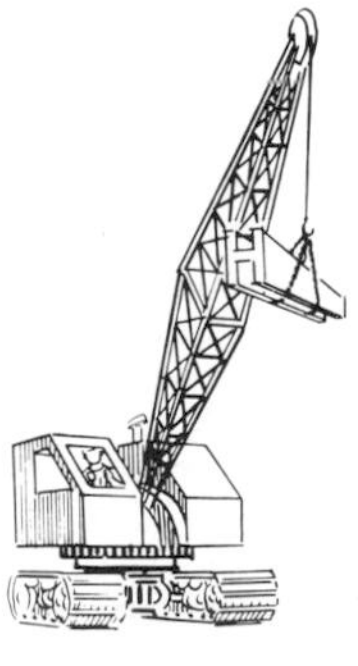
Crane

crank [krangk] 1 *n.* A part or handle that sticks out at a right angle from another part and transmits motion by turning. 2 *v.* To start, move, or turn by means of a crank. 3 *n. informal* A grouchy, ill-tempered person. 4 *n. informal* A person with strong and unreasonable feelings about a particular subject.

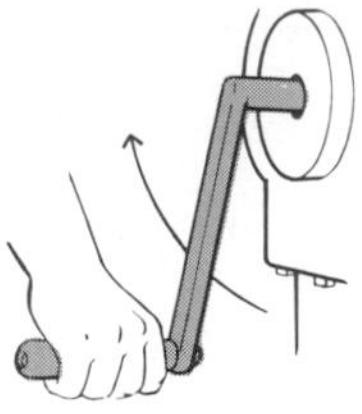
Crank

crank·case [krangk′kās′] *n.* The case enclosing the crankshaft of an engine, as of an automobile.
crank·shaft [krangk′shaft′] *n.* A shaft turned by or turning one or more cranks.
crank·y [krang′kē] *adj.* **crank·i·er, crank·i·est** Peevish; irritable. **—crank′i·ness** *n.*
cran·ny [kran′ē] *n., pl.* **cran·nies** A narrow opening, crack, or chink, as in a wall.
crape [krāp] *n.* Another spelling of CREPE, used chiefly to mean black crepe worn as a sign of mourning.
crap·pie [krap′ē] *n.* A North American freshwater fish caught for food.
craps [kraps] *n.pl.* (*used with singular verb*) A gambling game played with dice.
crash[1] [krash] 1 *n.* A loud noise, as of something being violently broken or struck. 2 *v.* To fall, strike, or break with a loud noise. 3 *v.* To be damaged or destroyed by falling or colliding. 4 *n.* A destructive fall or collision. 5 *v.* To move noisily and violently: Elephants *crashed* through the jungle. 6 *n.* Failure or collapse, as of a business. 7 *v. informal* To come to (as a party or meeting) without being invited.
crash[2] [krash] *n.* Cloth woven from thick, uneven threads, used for towels, curtains, and other goods.
crash-dive [krash′dīv′] *v.* **crash-dived, crash-diving** To make or cause to make a crash dive.
crash dive A rapid dive made by a submarine in an emergency.
crash helmet A padded helmet, as one worn by a pilot or motorcyclist, to protect the head.
crash-land [krash′land′] *v.* To make or cause to make a crash landing.
crash landing The landing of an airplane in an emergency, usually in such a way that the airplane is damaged.
crass [kras] *adj.* Vulgar and ignorant; crude: *crass* stupidity. **—crass′ly** *adv.* **—crass′ness** *n.*
crate [krāt] *n., v.* **crat·ed, crat·ing** 1 *n.* A wooden box or frame for packing goods to be shipped. 2 *v.* To pack in a crate.
cra·ter [krā′tər] *n.* 1 A bowl-shaped hollow around an opening of a volcano. 2 A hole made by an explosion, as of a bomb.
cra·vat [krə·vat′] *n.* An old-fashioned word for a necktie.
crave [krāv] *v.* **craved, crav·ing** 1 To need or want very much; long for: The starving animal *craved* food. 2 To ask for earnestly; beg: to *crave* forgiveness.
cra·ven [krā′vən] 1 *adj.* Cowardly. 2 *n.* A coward. **—cra′ven·ly** *adv.*
crav·ing [krā′ving] *n.* A very strong desire; a hankering: a *craving* for candy.
craw [krô] *n.* 1 The enlarged part of a bird's gullet; crop. 2 The stomach of any animal.
craw·fish [krô′fish′] *n., pl.* **craw·fish** or **craw·fish·es** 1 A freshwater animal that looks like a small lobster. 2 Any of several similar saltwater animals. ◆ *Crevice,* from the French, was the earlier English name for *crawfish.* Because the animal lived in the water, people began substituting *fish* for *-vice* [pronounced vēs], and the main stress shifted to the first syllable, changing *cre-* [krə] to *craw-* [krô] or *cray-* [krā].
crawl [krôl] 1 *v.* To move along slowly with the body on or close to the ground; creep. 2 *v.* To move very slowly: Traffic *crawled* on the crowded road. 3 *n.* The action of crawling; a slow or creeping motion. 4 *v.* To be covered with things that crawl. 5 *v.* To feel as if covered with crawling things. 6 *n.* A speedy overhand swimming stroke in which the legs are kicked rapidly.
cray·fish [krā′fish′] *n., pl.* **cray·fish** or **cray·fish·es** Another word for CRAWFISH, used by biologists. ◆ See CRAWFISH.
cray·on [krā′on *or* krā′ən] 1 *n.* A stick, as of colored wax or chalk, used for drawing or writing. 2 *v.* To draw, color, or write with crayons. 3 *n.* A drawing made with crayons.
craze [krāz] *v.* **crazed, craz·ing,** *n.* 1 *v.* To make insane; cause to go mad: *crazed* by fear. 2 *n.* A short-lived fashion or enthusiasm; fad. 3 *v.* To become or cause to become covered with fine, crisscrossing cracks, as in the glaze of pottery.
cra·zy [krā′zē] *adj.* **cra·zi·er, cra·zi·est** 1 Out of one's mind; insane. 2 Foolish; senseless; absurd: *crazy* plans. 3 *informal* Very enthusiastic; extremely fond: He's *crazy* about that singing group. 4 Shaky; rickety. **—cra′zi·ly** *adv.* **—cra′zi·ness** *n.*
crazy bone Another term for FUNNY BONE.

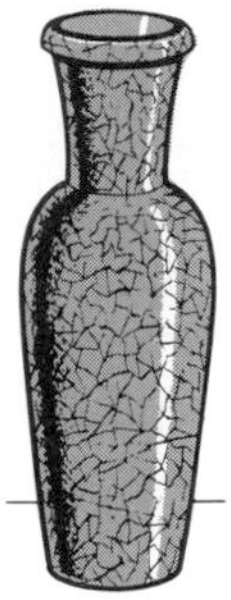
Crazed vase

crazy quilt A patchwork quilt made of pieces of various sizes, colors, and shapes.
creak [krēk] 1 *v.* To make a sharp, squeaking sound: The gate *creaked* in the wind. 2 *n.* A sharp, squeaking sound.
creak·y [krē′kē] *adj.* **creak·i·er, creak·i·est** 1 Likely to creak: a *creaky* door. 2 Creaking.
cream [krēm] 1 *n.* The yellowish, oily part of milk. It can be removed and used separately or churned into butter. 2 *n.* A yellowish white color. 3 *n.* A food that is made from cream or is soft and creamy. 4 *v.* To stir together, as butter and sugar, so as to make soft and creamy. 5 *n.* A soft, oily substance used to clean or protect the skin. 6 *n.* The best part: the *cream* of the senior class. 7 *v.* To remove the cream from. 8 *v.* To add cream to (as coffee or tea).
cream cheese Soft, white cheese made from cream or a mixture of cream and milk.

a	add	**i**	it	**o͝o**	took	**oi**	oil
ā	ace	**ī**	ice	**o͞o**	pool	**ou**	pout
â	care	**o**	odd	**u**	up	**ng**	ring
ä	palm	**ō**	open	**û**	burn	**th**	thin
e	end	**ô**	order	**yo͞o**	fuse	**th̶**	this
ē	equal					**zh**	vision

ə = { a in *above* e in *sicken* i in *possible* / o in *melon* u in *circus* }

cream·er [krē′mər] *n.* A small pitcher used for serving cream.

cream·er·y [krē′mər·ē] *n., pl.* **cream·er·ies** A place where butter and cheese are made, sold, or stored.

cream of tartar A white powder with an acid taste, used as an ingredient of baking powder.

cream puff A rounded shell of very light pastry with a filling of whipped cream or custard.

cream sauce A sauce made of milk or cream cooked with butter and flour.

cream·y [krē′mē] *adj.* **cream·i·er, cream·i·est** 1 Full of cream; rich and moist as cream. 2 Having the color or appearance of cream: a *creamy* complexion. **—cream′i·ness** *n.*

crease [krēs] *n., v.* **creased, creas·ing** 1 *n.* A mark or line made by folding, pressing, or wrinkling. 2 *v.* To form or become marked with a crease or creases.

cre·ate [krē·āt′] *v.* **cre·at·ed, cre·at·ing** 1 To cause to come into existence; originate; make. 2 To be the cause of: The speech *created* much interest.

cre·a·tion [krē·ā′shən] *n.* 1 The act of creating or forming. 2 Anything that is created, especially something that shows great originality. 3 (*written* **Creation**) The act of God in creating the universe. 4 The world or the universe, including all living things.

cre·a·tion·ism [krē·ā′shən·iz·əm] *n.* The belief that the universe, including all living things, was created by God in the exact manner described in Genesis, the first book of the Bible. **—cre·a′tion·ist** *n.* **—cre·a′tion·is′tic** *adj.*

cre·a·tive [krē·ā′tiv] *adj.* 1 Having the power or ability to create. 2 Having or showing originality and imagination: *creative* writing. **—cre·a′tive·ly** *adv.*

cre·a·tiv·i·ty [krē′ā·tiv′ə·tē] *n.* The quality of being creative.

cre·a·tor [krē·ā′tər] *n.* 1 A person or thing that creates. 2 (*written* **Creator**) God.

crea·ture [krē′chər] *n.* 1 A living being, animal or human. 2 A person who is dominated by and carries out the wishes of another.

crèche [kresh *or* krāsh] *n.* A group of figures representing the scene in the stable when Jesus was born.

Creche

cre·dence [krēd′(ə)ns] *n.* Belief in the truth of; trust: to give *credence* to an unlikely story.

cre·den·tials [kri·den′·shəlz] *n.pl.* Something, as a letter or certificate, that identifies the bearer and shows the person's position, authority, or right to be trusted.

cred·i·ble [kred′ə·bəl] *adj.* 1 Believable: a *credible* excuse. 2 Deserving belief or confidence; reliable: a *credible* witness. **—cred·i·bil·i·ty** [kred′ə·bil′ə·tē] *n.* **—cred′i·bly** *adv.* ◆ A *credible* explanation is one that can be believed. It may or may not be true, but there are good grounds for believing it. A *credulous* person is someone who is ready to believe almost anything, no matter how unlikely. Only people can be *credulous,* but both people and statements can be *credible.*

cred·it [kred′it] 1 *n.* Belief in the truth or reliability of; faith; trust: to place *credit* in the story. 2 *v.* To believe to be true or reliable: to *credit* a story. 3 *n.* Admiration and approval; honor: This student deserves *credit* for a job well done. 4 *n.* A source of honor or praise: to be a *credit* to one's family. 5 *n.* Reputation for paying bills or meeting obligations: The company's *credit* is good. 6 *n.* Confidence in a person's ability to pay for something: to extend *credit* for a week's supply of groceries. 7 *n.* Time allowed for payment: a month's *credit.* 8 *n.* A balance in one's favor, as in an account: I have a *credit* of $10.00. 9 *v.* To make a record of money due to: *Credit* me with this amount. 10 *n.* Recognition or certification, as in some official record: to get *credit* for an art course. **—credit with** To believe or declare that (someone) has: to *credit* the employee *with* good intentions. **—on credit** With the agreement to pay later.

cred·it·a·ble [kred′it·ə·bəl] *adj.* Deserving credit or respect: a *creditable* effort.

credit card An identification card that allows its holder to buy goods or services on credit.

cred·i·tor [kred′i·tər] *n.* A person to whom money is owed.

cre·do [krē′dō *or* krā′dō] *n., pl.* **cre·dos** A creed.

cre·du·li·ty [krə·d(y)ōō′lə·tē] *n.* Thoughtless or foolish readiness to believe anything.

cred·u·lous [krej′ŏŏ·ləs] *adj.* Believing without question; easily misled. **—cred′u·lous·ly** *adv.* ◆ See CREDIBLE.

Cree [krē] *n., pl.* **Cree** or **Crees** 1 A tribe of North American Indians of Manitoba and Saskatchewan. 2 A member of this tribe. 3 The language of this tribe.

creed [krēd] *n.* 1 A summary or formal statement of religious beliefs. 2 A set of personal beliefs or principles.

creek [krēk *or* krik] *n.* 1 *U.S.* A stream, especially one smaller than a river and larger than a brook. 2 *British* [krēk] A narrow inlet.

Creek [krēk] *n., pl.* **Creek** or **Creeks** 1 A group of tribes of North American Indians once living in Alabama, Georgia, and upper Florida, now in Oklahoma. 2 A member of any of these tribes. 3 The language of any of these tribes.

creel [krēl] *n.* A wicker basket used to hold newly caught fish.

Creel

creep [krēp] *v.* **crept, creep·ing,** *n.* 1 *v.* To move on hands and knees, or with the body close to or on the ground; crawl. 2 *v.* To move cautiously and slyly; sneak. 3 *v.* To move very slowly: The glacier *crept* down the mountainside. 4 *n.* The action of creeping. 5 *v.* To trail along the ground or cling to something for support, as a vine. 6 *v.* To feel as if covered by creeping things: to make one's flesh *creep.* 7 *n.* (*pl.*) A feeling of horror and disgust: Scary movies give me the *creeps.*

creep·er [krē′pər] *n.* 1 A person or thing that creeps. 2 A trailing or climbing plant, as ivy.

creep·y [krē′pē] *adj.* **creep·i·er, creep·i·est** Having or producing a feeling of horror or disgust. **—creep′·i·ly** *adv.* **—creep′i·ness** *n.*

cre·mate [krē′māt′ *or* kri·māt′] *v.* **cre·mat·ed, cre·mat·ing** To cause (a dead body) to be burned to ashes. **—cre·ma′tion** *n.*
cre·ma·to·ri·um [krē′mə·tôr′ē·əm] *n., pl.* **cre·ma·to·ri·ums** or **cre·ma·to·ri·a** [krē′mə·tôr′ē·ə] A crematory.
cre·ma·to·ry [krē′mə·tôr′ē *or* krem′ə·tôr′ē] *n., pl.* **cre·ma·to·ries** A place where dead bodies are cremated.
Cre·ole [krē′ōl] **1** *n.* A descendant of the original French settlers of Louisiana. **2** *n.* A person of European descent born in the West Indies or Latin America. **3** *n.* The French dialect spoken in Louisiana. **4** *adj.* Having to do with or typical of Creoles: *Creole* manners. **5** *adj.* (*written* **creole**) Cooked with tomatoes, peppers, spices, and other ingredients: shrimp *creole.* ◆ *Creole* comes through the French from the Spanish word *criollo,* meaning a *native.*
cre·o·sote [krē′ə·sōt′] *n.* An oily liquid with a strong odor, used to preserve wood from rot.
crepe or **crêpe** [krāp] *n.* A thin fabric, of silk, rayon, or other fiber, with a crinkled surface.
crepe paper Thin paper with a crinkled texture, used for decorations.
crepe rubber Rubber that has a crinkled surface, used especially for shoe soles.
crept [krept] Past tense of CREEP.
cre·scen·do [krə·shen′dō] *n., pl.* **cre·scen·dos** A gradual increase in loudness or strength: The symphony ended with a *crescendo.*
cres·cent [kres′ənt] *n.* **1** The curved shape of the moon seen in its first or last quarter. **2** *adj. use:* the *crescent* moon. **3** Anything having the curved shape of the crescent moon. ◆ *Crescent* comes from a Latin word meaning *increasing.*

Crescent

cress [kres] *n.* One of several related plants, many of whose leaves have a peppery taste and are used in salads.
cres·set [kres′it] *n.* A metal holder for burning materials, as oil or wood, for illumination.
crest [krest] *n.* **1** A tuft or projection on the head, especially one of feathers on a bird's head. **2** Something resembling this in shape or position: waves with foamy *crests.* **3** A plume or similar decoration on the top of a helmet. **4** The top or highest point of something: the *crest* of the flood. **5** A design or symbol at the top of a coat of arms, as used on stationery and silver.
crest·ed [kres′tid] *adj.* Having a crest.
crest·fall·en [krest′fô′lən] *adj.* Low in spirits; downcast; dejected.
Cre·ta·ceous [kri·tā′shəs] **1** *n.* The third and final geological period of the Mesozoic era, during which flowering plants appeared. At the end of the Cretaceous, all dinosaurs and many other species of life became extinct. **2** *adj.* Of the Cretaceous.
cre·tin [krēt′(ə)n] *n.* A person having cretinism.
cre·tin·ism [krēt′(ə)n·iz·əm] *n.* A condition that is usually congenital and is characterized by mental deficiency and the stoppage of physical development. It is caused by a severe lack of thyroid hormone.
cre·tonne [krē′ton *or* kri·ton′] *n.* A strong cotton or linen fabric printed in colored patterns, used for curtains and covering furniture.
cre·vasse [krə·vas′] *n.* **1** A deep crack or gap, as in a glacier. **2** A break in a levee or dam.
crev·ice [krev′is] *n.* A narrow opening due to a crack or split, as in a rock or wall.
crew[1] [kro͞o] *n.* **1** The company of people who work together on a ship. **2** A group of people working together to do a particular job: a repair *crew.* **3** The oarsmen and coxswain of a racing boat. **4** Any gang, band, or set: a *crew* of pilgrims.
crew[2] [kro͞o] A past tense of CROW[1] (def. 1).
crew cut A very short, bristly haircut.
crew·el [kro͞o′əl] *n.* A loosely twisted worsted yarn used in **crewelwork,** a kind of embroidery done on linen, cotton, or other fabric.
crew·man [kro͞o′mən] *n., pl.* **crew·men** [kro͞o′mən] A member of a crew.
crib [krib] *n., v.* **cribbed, crib·bing** **1** *n.* A small bed enclosed by railings for a baby. **2** *n.* A bin or building for storing grain, corn, and other foods. **3** *n.* A rack or box from which cattle or horses eat. **4** *n.* A supporting wooden or metal framework, as in a mine. **5** *v. informal* To copy someone else's words or ideas and use them as one's own. **6** *n. informal* Something, as a copy or translation, used to cheat in doing school work.
crib·bage [krib′ij] *n.* A card game in which the score is kept by moving pegs in holes on a board.
crick [krik] *n.* A pain or cramp: a *crick* in the neck.
crick·et[1] [krik′it] *n.* An insect related to the grasshopper. The male makes a chirping sound by rubbing its front wings together.
crick·et[2] [krik′it] *n.* **1** An outdoor game popular in the British Commonwealth, played with bats, a ball, and wickets, by two teams of 11 players. **2** *informal* Fair, honest behavior; sportsmanship.

Cricket

cried [krīd] Past tense and past participle of CRY: I *cried* when I stubbed my toe.
cri·er [krī′ər] *n.* In former times, an official who called out news and information.
crime [krīm] *n.* **1** An action that is against the law, especially a serious wrongdoing for which one can be severely punished. Murder and robbery are crimes. **2** Any very wrong or improper act.
crim·i·nal [krim′ə·nəl] **1** *n.* A person who has committed a crime. **2** *adj.* Consisting of or guilty of crime; wicked and unlawful. **3** *adj.* Having to do with crime or enforcement of laws against crime: a *criminal* court. **—crim′i·nal·ly** *adv.*
crim·i·nol·o·gy [krim′ə·nol′ə·jē] *n.* The scientific study of criminals, crime, and crime prevention. **—crim′i·nol′o·gist** *n.*

a	add	**i**	it	**o͝o**	took	**oi**	oil
ā	ace	**ī**	ice	**o͞o**	pool	**ou**	pout
â	care	**o**	odd	**u**	up	**ng**	ring
ä	palm	**ō**	open	**û**	burn	**th**	thin
e	end	**ô**	order	**yo͞o**	fuse	**th**	this
ē	equal					**zh**	vision

ə = { a in *above* e in *sicken* i in *possible* / o in *melon* u in *circus* }

crimp [krimp] **1** *v.* To press or bend into small, regular ridges or folds. **2** *n.* A fold or wavy surface produced by crimping.

crim·py [krim′pē] *adj.* **crimp·i·er, crimp·i·est** Having many small ridges or folds; wavy.

crim·son [krim′zən] **1** *n., adj.* Deep red. **2** *v.* To make or become crimson.

cringe [krinj] *v.* **cringed, cring·ing** **1** To shrink, cower, or crouch in fear or submission. **2** To behave too humbly; fawn.

crin·kle [kring′kəl] *v.* **crin·kled, crin·kling,** *n.* **1** *v.* To form a ridged, wrinkled, or roughened surface: The corners of his eyes *crinkle* when he smiles; The leaves *crinkled* underfoot. **2** *v.* To rustle or crackle. **3** *n.* A wrinkling or crumpling. **—crin′·kly** *adj.*

cri·noid [krī′noid] *n.* One of a group of marine sea animals related to the sea urchin and the starfish, having a body shaped somewhat like a cup with radiating, feathery arms.

crin·o·line [krin′ə·lin] *n.* **1** A stiff material used to line or spread out part of a garment. **2** A petticoat of this material, worn under a full skirt to make it flare. **3** A hoop skirt.

crip·ple [krip′əl] *n., v.* **crip·pled, crip·pling** **1** *n.* Someone unable to move normally because part of the body is lost, damaged, or deformed; a lame person. **2** *v.* To make a cripple of. **3** *v.* To make unable to function well; disable: Ignorance *cripples* the mind.

cri·sis [krī′sis] *n., pl.* **cri·ses** [krī′sēz] **1** A very important or decisive moment in the course of any series of events: The battle at Gettysburg was a *crisis* in the Civil War. **2** The climax of an illness, when a change for better or worse occurs. **3** A time of worry or danger.

crisp [krisp] **1** *adj.* Dry, brittle, and easily broken: *crisp* bacon. **2** *adj.* Fresh and firm: *crisp* vegetables. **3** *adj.* Brisk; fresh: a *crisp* breeze. **4** *adj.* Short and forceful: a *crisp* answer. **5** *adj.* Wiry and waved or curled tightly: *crisp* curls. **6** *v.* To make or become crisp. **—crisp′ly** *adv.* **—crisp′ness** *n.*

crisp·y [kris′pē] *adj.* **crisp·i·er, crisp·i·est** Crisp. **—crisp′i·ness** *n.*

criss·cross [kris′krôs′] **1** *n.* A network or pattern of crossing lines. **2** *adj.* Forming such a pattern: *crisscross* lines. **3** *adv.* In different crossing directions. **4** *v.* To move in or form a pattern of crossing lines.

cri·te·ri·on [krī·tir′ē·ən] *n., pl.* **cri·te·ri·a** [krī·tir′ē·ə] or **cri·te·ri·ons** A standard or rule by which a judgment can be made: Responsibility is a good *criterion* for choosing a public official.

crit·ic [krit′ik] *n.* **1** A person who judges the quality or value of books, art, plays, opera, music, or the like. **2** A person whose occupation is to form or write such judgments: a music *critic.* **3** A person who shows disapproval and finds fault: a *critic* of the mayor.

crit·i·cal [krit′i·kəl] *adj.* **1** Apt to find fault; disapproving. **2** Typical of or suitable for a critic; expressing thoughtful judgment: a *critical* discussion of a new book. **3** Of, related to, or causing a crisis; crucial: a *critical* period in history. **4** Likely to cause trouble or danger; risky: a *critical* water shortage. **—crit′i·cal·ly** *adv.*

crit·i·cism [krit′ə·siz′əm] *n.* **1** The opinions or judgment of a critic: favorable *criticism.* **2** Unfavorable comment; severe judgment of faults. **3** Something, as a book or an article, expressing critical opinion.

crit·i·cize [krit′ə·sīz′] *v.* **crit·i·cized, crit·i·ciz·ing** **1** To find fault with; judge severely. **2** To pass judgment on the qualities of.

cri·tique [kri·tēk′] *n.* A review, as of a work of art or literature, expressing critical judgment.

crit·ter [krit′ər] *n. informal* A creature.

croak [krōk] **1** *v.* To make a hoarse, throaty sound, as a frog or crow does. **2** *v.* To speak in a low, hoarse voice. **3** *n.* The sound made by croaking. **4** *v.* To talk gloomily and predict misfortune.

Croat [krōt *or* krō′at] *n.* A person born in or a citizen of Croatia.

cro·chet [krō·shā′] *v.* **cro·cheted** [krō·shād′], **cro·chet·ing** [krō·shā′ing], *n.* **1** *v.* To make or trim (as sweaters or afghans) by forming connected loops of thread or yarn with a hooked needle. **2** *n.* Something crocheted.

crock [krok] *n.* A pot or jar made of baked clay.

crock·er·y [krok′ər·ē] *n.* Dishes or similar articles made of baked clay; earthenware.

croc·o·dile [krok′ə·dīl′] *n.* A large reptile resembling the alligator, with thick, armorlike skin and a long head. Crocodiles live in and near rivers in warm parts of Africa, the Americas, Asia, and Australia.

Crocodile

crocodile tears Pretended tears; insincere grief. ◆ This expression comes from an old belief that crocodiles pity their prey and cry as they eat it.

cro·cus [krō′kəs] *n.* A small plant having cup-shaped yellow, purple, or white flowers. Crocuses bloom very early in the spring.

Croe·sus [krē′səs] *n.* **1** A very wealthy king who lived in Asia Minor in the sixth century B.C. **2** Any very wealthy person.

croft [krôft] *n. British* **1** A small planted field or pasture near a house. **2** A small farm on rented land.

crois·sant [krwä·sänt′] *n.* A rich, light roll with a flaky crust, shaped like a crescent.

Cro-Mag·non [krō·mag′nən] *adj.* Of or belonging to a race of people who lived in Europe in prehistoric times and were very similar to modern human beings.

crone [krōn] *n.* A withered old witchlike person.

cro·ny [krō′nē] *n., pl.* **cro·nies** A close friend or constant companion.

crook [krŏŏk] **1** *n.* A bend or curve; bent or curved part: to lean on the *crook* of a cane. **2** *n.* A long staff with a crook at the top, as one carried by shepherds. **3** *v.* To bend into a curve or hook: to beckon by *crooking* one's finger. **4** *n. informal* A thief or cheat.

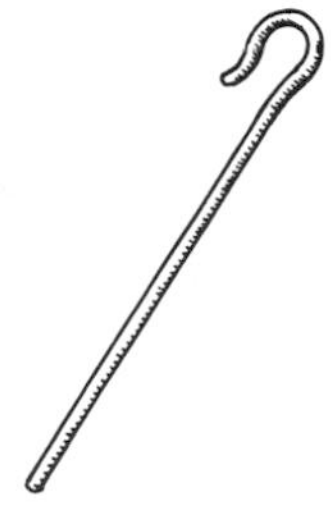
Crook

crook·ed [krŏŏk′id] *adj.* **1** Bent, twisted, or uneven; not straight. **2** Dishonest. **—crook′ed·ly** *adv.* **—crook′·ed·ness** *n.*

croon [krōōn] **1** *v.* To sing or hum in a low, murmuring tone: to *croon* a lullaby. **2** *v.* To sing (popular songs) in a soft, sentimental manner. **3** *v.* To lull by crooning: to *croon* a baby to sleep. **4** *n.* A low, murmuring singing or humming. **—croon'er** *n.*

crop [krop] *n., v.* **cropped, crop·ping** **1** *n.* Any farm product, growing or harvested, as cotton, corn, hay, or apples. **2** *n.* The amount of one product grown in one season: the Minnesota wheat *crop.* **3** *n.* A collection or quantity appearing or occurring at the same time: a new *crop* of school graduates. **4** *v.* To trim the upper or outer parts of: to *crop* one's hair; to *crop* a hedge. **5** *n.* A short haircut. **6** *n.* To bite off or nibble, as grass. **7** *n.* An enlarged part of a bird's digestive tract, where food is partly digested before reaching the stomach. **8** *n.* A short whip with a loop at one end. —**crop out** To appear above the surface, as a rock on the surface of the earth. **—crop up** To appear or come up unexpectedly: That old rumor *cropped up* again.

crop·per [krop'ər] *n.* A bad fall, as from a horse, especially in the expression **come a cropper,** to fail badly or meet with misfortune.

cro·quet [krō·kā'] *n.* An outdoor game in which the players use mallets with long handles to drive wooden balls through a series of wickets.

Croquet

cro·quette [krō·ket'] *n.* A ball or patty consisting chiefly of finely chopped cooked meat, fish, or other food, fried in deep fat.

cro·sier [krō'zhər] *n.* A bishop's staff resembling a shepherd's crook, carried in religious ceremonies.

cross [krôs] **1** *n.* Any mark or object formed by two straight lines or parts across one another. **2** *v.* To place or put crosswise: to *cross* one's legs. **3** *v.* To go or pass across or over: *Cross* the street carefully. **4** *v.* To pass going in different directions: Their planes *crossed* in flight; Our paths *crossed* while we were hiking. **5** *adj.* Going across; crosswise: *cross* currents. **6** *n.* A tall upright post with a shorter horizontal piece near the top. In ancient times a cross was used to crucify those convicted of crime. **7** *n.* (*often written* **Cross**) The symbol of the Christian religion, representing the cross on which Jesus was crucified. **8** *v.* To make motions of forming a cross over, especially as a sign of religious faith: to *cross* oneself; to *cross* one's heart. **9** *n.* Any burdensome trouble or suffering. **10** *v.* To draw a line or lines through or across: *Cross* my name off the list; *Cross* your t's carefully. **11** *adj.* Bad-tempered; irritable. **12** *v.* To interfere with; oppose: No one likes to be *crossed.* **13** *n.* A breeding together of related kinds of animals or plants, or the result of such breeding: A mule is a *cross* between a donkey and a horse. **14** *v.* To breed to produce such a plant or animal. **—cross one's mind** To enter one's thoughts. **—cross'ly** *adv.*

cross·bar [krôs'bär'] *n.* A crosswise bar, strip, or line.

cross·beam [krôs'bēm'] *n.* A beam placed across another or between two walls or posts.

cross·bones [krôs'bōnz'] *n.pl.* A picture of two bones crossed to form an X. ◆ See SKULL AND CROSSBONES.

cross·bow [krôs'bō'] *n.* A weapon consisting of a bow fastened crosswise at the front of a grooved stock, used in the Middle Ages.

Crossbow

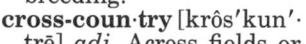

cross·breed [krôs'brēd'] *v.* **cross·bred** [krôs'bred'], **cross·breed·ing** *n.* **1** *v.* To produce (a cross) by breeding related kinds of plants or animals. **2** *n.* The product of such breeding.

cross-coun·try [krôs'kun'·trē] *adj.* Across fields or open countryside rather than by roads or paths: a *cross-country* hike.

cross·cut [krôs'kut'] *v.* **cross·cut, cross·cut·ting,** *adj., n.* **1** *v.* To cut crosswise, as across the grain of wood. **2** *adj.* Used or made for cutting crosswise: a *crosscut* saw. **3** *n.* A crosswise cut. **4** *n.* Something that cuts across. **5** *n.* A short cut.

cross-ex·am·ine [krôs'ig·zam'in] *v.* **cross-ex·am·ined, cross-ex·am·in·ing** To question (a witness called and questioned by the other side), usually to test or discredit answers already given by the witness. **—cross'-ex·am'i·na'tion** *n.*

cross-eyed [krôs'īd'] *adj.* Having one or both eyes turned toward the bridge of the nose.

cross-fer·til·i·za·tion [krôs'fûr'təl·ə·zā'shən] *n.* Fertilization in which the sex cells that unite to form a new plant or animal are from different individuals or from individuals of different kinds.

cross-fer·til·ize [krôs'fûr'təl·īz] *v.* **cross-fer·til·ized, cross-fer·til·iz·ing** To fertilize by cross-fertilization.

cross-grained [krôs'grānd'] *adj.* **1** Having the grain twisted or crosswise: *cross-grained* lumber. **2** Stubborn and contrary: a *cross-grained* person.

cross-hatch [krôs'hach'] *v.* To shade, as part of a drawing or map, with sets of parallel lines that cross each other.

cross·ing [krôs'ing] *n.* **1** A place where something, as a road or a stream, may be crossed. **2** A place where things, such as roads or railroad tracks, cross one another. **3** A going across.

cross-leg·ged [krôs'leg'id *or* krôs'legd'] *adj., adv.* With the legs crossed and the knees wide apart: to sit *cross-legged* on the floor.

cross·piece [krôs'pēs'] *n.* Any piece, as of wood or metal, placed across another.

cross-pol·li·nate [krôs'pol'ə·nāt'] *v.* To fertilize (a plant or flower) with pollen carried from another, as by wind or insects. **—cross'pol'li·na'tion** *n.*

cross-pur·pose [krôs'pûr'pəs] *n.* A purpose or aim in conflict with another, especially in the expres-

a add	**i** it	**o͝o** took	**oi** oil
ā ace	**ī** ice	**o͞o** pool	**ou** pout
â care	**o** odd	**u** up	**ng** ring
ä palm	**ō** open	**û** burn	**th** thin
e end	**ô** order	**yo͞o** fuse	**th** this
ē equal			**zh** vision

ə = a in *above*, e in *sicken*, i in *possible*, o in *melon*, u in *circus*

sion **at cross-purposes,** opposing or blocking each other's aims without meaning to.

cross-ques·tion [krôs′kwes′chən] *v.* To cross-examine.

cross-re·fer [krôs′ri·fûr′] *v.* **cross-re·ferred, cross-re·fer·ring** 1 To refer (a reader) from one place in a piece of reading material to another. 2 To make a cross-reference.

cross-ref·er·ence [krôs′ref′ər·əns *or* krôs′ref′rəns] *n.* A note or statement directing a reader from one place in a piece of reading material to another place for additional information.

cross·road [krôs′rōd′] *n.* 1 A road that connects two main roads or crosses one. 2 *pl.* (*used with singular verb*) A place where roads meet.

cross section 1 A slice or piece cut straight across something: a *cross section* of an airplane wing. 2 A cut made in this way. 3 A sample or selection considered typical of a whole: a *cross section* of public opinion.

Cross section of a grapefruit

cross-stitch [krôs′stich′] 1 *n.* A sewing or embroidery stitch that forms an X. 2 *v.* To sew or embroider with such a stitch.

cross·tie [krôs′tī′] *n.* One of the beams laid crosswise under railroad tracks to support them.

cross·town [krôs′toun′] 1 *adj.* Extending or traveling from one side of a town or city to the other: a *crosstown* street; a *crosstown* bus. 2 *adv.* Across a town or city: This bus runs *crosstown.*

cross·trees [krôs′trēz′] *n.pl.* Two crosswise pieces at the top of a ship's lower mast, for spreading the shrouds of the mast above.

cross·walk [krôs′wôk′] *n.* A lane marked off for people to use when crossing a street on foot.

cross·way [krôs′wā′] *n.* A crossroad.

cross·wise [krôs′wīz′] *adv.* So as to cross; across; athwart.

cross·word puzzle [krôs′wûrd′] A puzzle calling for words to be guessed and spelled out on a pattern of numbered squares, crosswise and downward as specified. For each direction a list of clues suggests the words.

crotch [kroch] *n.* 1 The fork where a trunk or limb divides into two limbs or branches. 2 The place where the body divides into legs.

crotch·et [kroch′it] *n.* An odd notion or whim.

crotch·et·y [kroch′ə·tē] *adj.* 1 Full of odd notions; queer. 2 Cranky; peevish.

crouch [krouch] 1 *v.* To stoop down with the knees bent, as an animal about to spring. 2 *v.* To bend in a shrinking or cowering position. 3 *n.* The action or position of crouching.

croup[1] [kro͞op] *n.* A children's throat disease accompanied by a hoarse cough and difficulty in breathing. **—croup′y** *adj.*

croup[2] [kro͞op] *n.* The part of a horse's back above the hind legs.

crou·ton [kro͞o′ton′ *or* kro͞o·ton′] *n.* A small cube of toasted or fried bread, served on top of soups and salads.

crow[1] [krō] *v.* **crowed** or sometimes for def. 1 **crew, crow·ing,** *n.* 1 *v.* To make the high, shrill cry of a rooster. 2 *n.* The cry itself. 3 *v.* To make cries or squeals of delight, as a baby. 4 *n.* Such a cry of pleasure. 5 *v.* To rejoice loudly and triumphantly; boast.

crow[2] [krō] *n.* A large black bird with a harsh cawing voice. **—eat crow** *informal* To humble oneself, as by publicly admitting a mistake.

Crow [krō] *n., pl.* **Crow** or **Crows** 1 A tribe of North American Indians now living in Montana. 2 A member of this tribe. 3 The language of this tribe.

crow·bar [krō′bär′] *n.* A straight metal bar used as a lever for lifting or prying.

crowd [kroud] 1 *n.* A large number of people gathered closely together. 2 *v.* To gather in large numbers. 3 *n.* People in general, considered as acting or thinking alike. 4 *v.* To fill too full; cram; pack. 5 *v.* To press or force forward. 6 *v.* To shove or push: They *crowded* us to the wall. 7 *n. informal* A group of people who do things together; set: Our friends belong to our *crowd.*

crown [kroun] 1 *n.* An ornament, often of precious metal set with jewels, worn encircling the head as a sign of royal power. 2 *n.* (*often written* **Crown**) The ruling sovereign, or the power of the sovereign. 3 *adj. use:* *crown* jewels; *crown* land. 4 *n.* A wreath or similar object worn on the head, especially as a sign of victory or honor. 5 *v.* To honor or install as a ruler by placing a crown on the head of. 6 *n.* The top part of the head. 7 *n.* The part or place at the top of something: the *crown* of a hat; the *crown* of the hill. 8 *v.* To be at or cover the top of; cap: peaks *crowned* with snow. 9 *v.* To make complete or perfect; climax: a career *crowned* with honors. 10 *n.* A former British coin worth five shillings. 11 *v.* In checkers, to make (a piece) a king by placing another piece upon it. 12 *n.* The part of a tooth covered with enamel, outside the gum, or an artificial substitute for it. 13 *v.* To place an artificial crown on (a tooth).

Crown

crown colony A British colony having a governor appointed by the sovereign.

crown prince A man or boy next in line to inherit the title and rank of king.

crown princess 1 A woman or girl who is the heir to a crown or throne. 2 The wife of a crown prince.

crow's-feet [krōz′fēt′] *n.pl.* The wrinkles spreading from the outer corner of the eye.

crow's-nest [krōz′nest′] *n.* A high, partly sheltered platform on a ship's mast for a lookout.

Crow's-nest

CRT cathode-ray tube.

cru·cial [kro͞o′shəl] *adj.* Likely to have a very important or decisive result or effect; critical: a *crucial* decision. **—cru′cial·ly** *adv.*

cru·ci·ble [kro͞o′sə·bəl] *n.* 1 A container that can withstand great heat, used for melting, as metals or ore. 2 A severely trying test.

cru·ci·fix [kro͞o′sə·fiks′] *n.* A cross with an image of Christ crucified on it, used as a Christian symbol.

cru·ci·fix·ion [kro͞o′sə·fik′shən] *n.* 1 The act of crucifying. 2 A being crucified. 3 (*written* **Crucifix-**

ion) The execution of Jesus on the cross. **4** A painting or sculpture of this.

cru·ci·form [kro͞o′sə·fôrm′] *adj.* Shaped like a cross.

cru·ci·fy [kro͞o′sə·fī′] *v.* **cru·ci·fied, cru·ci·fy·ing** **1** To put to death by nailing the hands and feet to a cross. **2** To cause to suffer greatly.

crude [kro͞od] *adj.* **crud·er, crud·est** **1** In an unrefined state; not processed: *crude* oil. **2** Roughly made; not well finished: a *crude* shack. **3** Lacking refinement or good taste; uncouth. **—crude′ly** *adv.* **—crude′ness** *n.*

cru·di·ty [kro͞o′də·tē] *n., pl.* **cru·di·ties** **1** A crude condition. **2** A crude act or remark.

cru·el [kro͞o′əl] *adj.* **cru·el·er** or **cru·el·ler, cru·el·est** or **cru·el·lest** **1** Eager or willing to give pain to others; brutal. **2** Not caring whether others suffer; pitiless. **3** Resulting in great pain or suffering; harsh: *cruel* neglect. **—cru′el·ly** *adv.* **—cru′el·ness** *n.*

cru·el·ty [kro͞o′əl·tē] *n., pl.* **cru·el·ties** **1** Cruel behavior, feelings, or treatment. **2** Harshness; severity: the *cruelty* of the wind.

cru·et [kro͞o′it] *n.* A small glass bottle with a stopper, for holding a liquid, as oil or vinegar.

Cruet

cruise [kro͞oz] *n., v.* **cruised, cruis·ing** **1** *n.* A sea voyage stopping at several ports, often taken for pleasure. **2** *v.* To sail or ride about, as for pleasure or business. **3** *v.* To go at the speed found most efficient, as for the use of fuel.

cruis·er [kro͞o′zər] *n.* **1** A power boat with a cabin equipped for living aboard. **2** A fast, rather large warship. **3** A person or thing that cruises.

crul·ler [krul′ər] *n.* A cake made from a strip or twist of sweetened dough fried in deep fat.

crumb [krum] **1** *n.* A tiny broken piece, as of bread or cake. **2** *n.* A bit or scrap: *crumbs* of learning. **3** *v.* To break into crumbs; crumble. **4** *v.* To coat with crumbs, as for frying. **5** *n.* The soft part of bread, enclosed by the crust.

crum·ble [krum′bəl] *v.* **crum·bled, crum·bling** **1** To break into crumbs or tiny pieces. **2** To fall apart or into pieces.

crum·bly [krum′blē] *adj.* **crum·bli·er, crum·bli·est** Crumbling easily; likely to crumble.

crum·pet [krum′pit] *n.* A flat, unsweetened cake baked on a griddle, and usually split and toasted.

crum·ple [krum′pəl] *v.* **crum·pled, crum·pling** **1** To crush so as to form wrinkles: to *crumple* paper. **2** *informal* To collapse: to *crumple* with weariness.

crunch [krunch] **1** *v.* To chew with a crushing or crackling sound. **2** *v.* To grind or crush noisily. **3** *v.* To move with or make a crushing or crackling sound: We *crunched* over the gravel; Gravel *crunched* under us. **4** *n.* The sound or act of crunching. **5** *n. informal* A critical situation, as because of pressure or stress. **6** *n. informal* A confrontation between opposing forces. **7** *n. informal* A reduction or shortage, as in the supply of something needed: the energy *crunch.*

crunch·y [krun′chē] *adj.* **crunch·i·er, crunch·i·est** Crisp and easily crunched, as cookies.

crup·per [krup′ər] *n.* One of the straps of a horse's harness, forming a loop under the tail.

cru·sade [kro͞o·sād′] *n., v.* **cru·sad·ed, cru·sad·ing** **1** *n.* (*often written* **Crusade**) One of a series of wars fought by European Christians during the Middle Ages in an attempt to capture the Holy Land from the Muslims. **2** *n.* A vigorous struggle against an evil or in favor of a cause. **3** *v.* To take part in a crusade. **—cru·sad′er** *n.*

C

cruse [kro͞oz *or* kro͞os] *n.* A small pottery jar or jug.

crush [krush] **1** *v.* To press or squeeze so as to break, injure, or force out of shape. **2** *v.* To grind or smash into small pieces: to *crush* ore. **3** *v.* To rumple or wrinkle: Linen *crushes* easily. **4** *v.* To put down; subdue; quell: to *crush* a rebellion. **5** *v.* To press together; cram. **6** *n.* A closely pressed crowd; jam. **7** *n.* The act of crushing; very strong pressure. **8** *n. informal* A strong, often silly liking for another person.

Cru·soe [kro͞o′sō], **Robinson** In Daniel Defoe's novel *Robinson Crusoe,* the hero, a sailor shipwrecked on a desert island.

crust [krust] **1** *n.* The hard outer part of bread. **2** *n.* Any dry, hard piece of bread: Only a few *crusts* were left from the loaf. **3** *n.* A shell or cover of pastry, as for a pie. **4** *n.* Any hard, crisp surface, as of snow. **5** *n.* The solid outer part of the earth. **6** *v.* To have, cover with, or form into a crust: rocks *crusted* with lichens.

crus·ta·cean [krus·tā′shən] **1** *n.* One of a large class of animals having a tough outer shell and generally living in water. Lobsters, crabs, and crawfish are crustaceans. **2** *adj.* Belonging to this class of animals.

crust·y [krus′tē] *adj.* **crust·i·er, crust·i·est** **1** Having a crust: *crusty* rolls. **2** Gruff and irritable in manner: a *crusty* old codger.

crutch [kruch] *n.* **1** A device, usually one of a pair, used to help lame or injured persons walk. It usually has a grip for the hand and either a crosspiece under the armpit or a curved piece that fits around the forearm. **2** Anything used to give support.

Crutches

crux [kruks] *n.* The most important or significant point.

cry [krī] *v.* **cried, cry·ing,** *n., pl.* **cries** **1** *v.* To weep or sob, especially with sounds of unhappiness, pain, or fear. **2** *n.* A spell of weeping: to have a good *cry.* **3** *v.* To call out loudly; shout. **4** *v.* To say loudly; exclaim: "How lovely!" I *cried.* **5** *n.* A shout, call, or exclamation: a *cry* for help. **6** *n.* The characteristic sound made by some ani-

a	add	**i**	it	**o͝o**	took	**oi**	oil
ā	ace	**ī**	ice	**o͞o**	pool	**ou**	pout
â	care	**o**	odd	**u**	up	**ng**	ring
ä	palm	**ō**	open	**û**	burn	**th**	thin
e	end	**ô**	order	**yo͞o**	fuse	**t͟h**	this
ē	equal					**zh**	vision

ə = {a in *above* e in *sicken* i in *possible* / o in *melon* u in *circus*}

mal or bird: the *cry* of the owl. **7** *v.* To make such a sound. **8** *v.* To beg with emotion; plead: to *cry* for mercy. **9** *v.* To need very much; demand: a situation that *cries* for attention. **10** *n.* A strong appeal or demand: a *cry* for justice. **11** *n.* A slogan or rallying call. **12** *v.* To advertise by calling or shouting: to *cry* one's wares. **—a far cry** A long way: It's *a far cry* from New York to Los Angeles. **—in full cry** In noisy pursuit, as a pack of hounds.

cry·ba·by [krī′bā′bē] *n., pl.* **cry·ba·bies** A person who cries or complains often or with little cause.

cry·ing [krī′ing] *adj.* Calling for immediate action or remedy: a *crying* need.

cry·o·gen [krī′ə·jən] *n.* A substance used to produce very low temperatures; refrigerant.

cry·o·gen·ic [krī′ə·jen′ik] *adj.* Of or having to do with very low temperatures.

cry·o·gen·ics [krī′ə·jen′iks] *n.* A branch of physics that deals with matter at very low temperatures.

cry·on·ics [krī·on′iks] *n.* The freezing of a diseased dead body in the hope of reviving it some time in the future when a cure for the disease has been found. ◆ See-ICS.

crypt [kript] *n.* An underground vault or chamber, especially one beneath a church used as a burial place. ◆ *Crypt* and *grotto* both come from Latin *crypta* which comes from a Greek word meaning *hidden. Crypt* came directly from *crypta,* but *grotto* was changed by coming through Italian.

cryp·tic [krip′tik] *adj.* Having a secret or hidden meaning; mysterious: *cryptic* remarks; a *cryptic* message. **—cryp′ti·cal·ly** *adv.*

cryp·to·gram [krip′tə·gram′] *n.* A message or puzzle written in a secret code.

cryp·tog·ra·phy [krip·tog′rə·fē] *n.* The science, study, or use of secret codes. **—cryp·tog′ra·pher** *n.*

crys·tal [kris′təl] **1** *n.* A body formed when a substance solidifies, having flat surfaces and angles in a regular, characteristic pattern: salt *crystals;* ice *crystals.* **2** *n.* Colorless, transparent quartz. **3** *n.* A type of fine, clear glass. **4** *adj. use:* a *crystal* goblet. **5** *adj.* Resembling crystal; very clear: a *crystal* stream. **6** *n.* A transparent covering for the dial of a watch: The jeweler had to replace the *crystal.*

crystal ball A glass globe believed to show the future when gazed into by a fortuneteller.

crys·tal·line [kris′tə·lin] *adj.* **1** Made of crystal. **2** Resembling crystal; transparent; clear. **3** Composed of or typical of crystals.

crys·tal·lize [kris′tə·līz′] *v.* **crys·tal·lized, crys·tal·liz·ing** **1** To form or cause to form into crystals: Diamonds are *crystallized* carbon. **2** To become or cause to become clear and definite: to allow one's plans to *crystallize.* **—crys′tal·li·za′tion** *n.*

crys·tal·log·ra·phy [kris′tə·log′rə·fē] *n.* The scientific study of crystals and crystallization. **—crys′·tal·log′ra·pher** *n.*

Cs The symbol for the element cesium.

CS **1** Civil Service. **2** Christian Science.

CSC Civil Service Commission.

CST or **C.S.T.** central standard time.

ct. **1** carat. **2** cent. **3** court.

Ct. Connecticut.

CT Postal Service abbreviation of Connecticut.

cts. cents.

cu or **cu.** cubic.

Cu The symbol for the element copper. ◆ The Latin word for copper is *cuprum.*

cub [kub] *n.* **1** The young of certain animals, such as the bear, fox, wolf, or lion. **2** A clumsy or ill-mannered young person.

Cu·ban [kyōō′bən] **1** *adj.* Of or from Cuba. **2** *n.* A person born in or a citizen of Cuba.

cub·by·hole [kub′ē·hōl′] *n.* A snug, enclosed space, such as a closet or storage compartment.

cube [kyōōb] *n., v.* **cubed, cub·ing** **1** *n.* A solid object with six equal square sides. **2** *v.* To multiply a number by itself and multiply the result by the original number: Two *cubed* equals eight, or 2 × 2 × 2 = 8. **3** *n.* A number obtained in this way: The *cube* of 4 is 64. **4** *v.* To cut or form into cubes; dice: to *cube* potatoes.

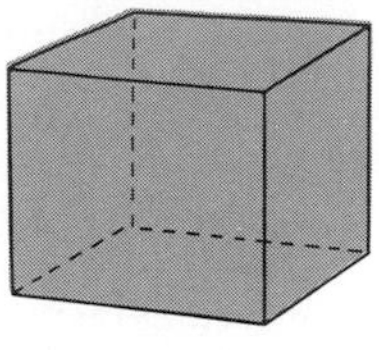
Cube

cube root A number which, cubed, equals the number given: The *cube root* of 125 is 5.

cu·bic [kyōō′bik] *adj.* **1** Shaped like a cube. **2** Having or measured in the three dimensions length, breadth, and thickness: A *cubic* foot is the amount of space in a cube one foot long, one foot broad, and one foot high. **3** Of or raised to the third power.

cu·bi·cal [kyōō′bi·kəl] *adj.* **1** Shaped like a cube; cubic. **2** Of or having to do with volume.

cu·bi·cle [kyōō′bi·kəl] *n.* Any small room or partly enclosed section of a room. ◆ This word comes from the Latin word *cubare,* meaning *to lie down,* and originally meant a bedroom.

cubic measure A unit or system of units used to measure volume.

cub·ism [kyōō′biz′əm] *n.* A style of modern art, especially painting, that uses cubes and other basic geometric forms to represent objects. **—cub′ist** *adj., n.*

cu·bit [kyōō′bit] *n.* An ancient measure of length based on the distance between the elbow and the tip of the middle finger, usually ranging from 18 to 22 inches.

Cubist painting

Cub Scout A member of a junior division of Boy Scouts for boys eight to ten years of age.

cuck·oo [kŏŏk′ōō *or* kōō′kōō] *n., pl.* **cuck·oos,** *adj.* **1** *n.* Any of several birds with a whistle or call that sounds like the word "cuckoo." Some European cuckoos lay their eggs in the nests of other birds. **2** *adj. slang* Crazy; silly.

cuckoo clock A clock with a mechanical cuckoo that announces the hours in a sound resembling a cuckoo's call.

cu cm or **cu. cm.** cubic centimeter(s).

cu·cum·ber [kyōō′kum·bər] *n.* **1** A long vegetable with tough, green skin and crisp, moist, whitish flesh, used in salads and for making pickles. **2** The creeping plant it grows on.

cud [kud] *n.* Food forced back up into the mouth from the first stomach of certain animals, as the cow, and chewed over again.

cud·dle [kud′(ə)l] *v.* **cud·dled, cud·dling** **1** To hold and caress gently in one's arms: to *cuddle* a furry rabbit. **2** To lie or nestle snugly: *Cuddle* up under the covers.

cudg·el [kuj′əl] *n., v.* **cudg·eled** or **cudg·elled, cudg·el·ing** or **cudg·el·ling** **1** *n.* A short, thick club. **2**

v. To beat with a cudgel. **—cudgel one's brains** To think hard, as if trying to remember something.
cue[1] [kyōō] *n., v.* **cued, cu·ing** **1** *n.* In theatrical performances, something, as an action or word, that serves as a signal or reminder to another actor: Wait for your *cue* before you start your speech. **2** *v.* To give a cue to (a performer). **3** *n.* Any signal to begin: The conductor gave the *cue* to the orchestra. **4** *n.* A helpful hint or indication, as when one is uncertain what to do.
cue[2] [kyōō] *n., v.* **cued, cu·ing** **1** *n.* A long, tapering stick used in billiards to strike the ball. **2** *n., v.* Another spelling of QUEUE.
cuff[1] [kuf] *n.* **1** A band or fold at the wrist of a sleeve. **2** A folded piece at the bottom of a trouser leg. **3** A handcuff.
cuff[2] [kuf] **1** *v.* To strike with the open hand; box. **2** *n.* A blow, especially with the open hand.
cuff link One of a pair of fasteners that hold together buttonless shirt cuffs.
cu ft or **cu. ft.** **1** cubic foot. **2** cubic feet.
cu in or **cu. in.** cubic inch(es).
cui·rass [kwi·ras′] *n.* A piece of armor worn to protect the upper part of the body.

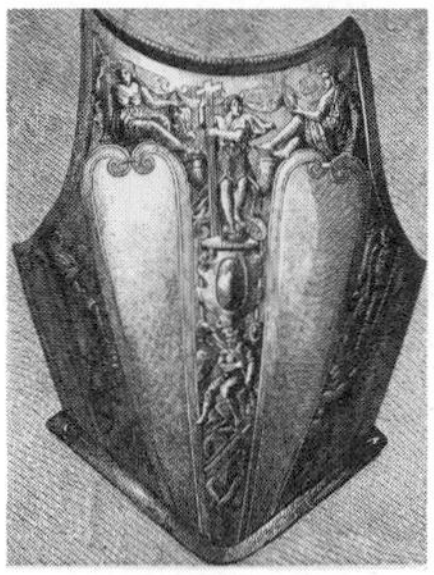
Cuirass

cui·sine [kwi·zēn′] *n.* **1** A style or type of cooking: French *cuisine.* **2** The food prepared: The *cuisine* is excellent. ◆ This word comes from the French word meaning *kitchen.*
cul-de-sac [kul′də·sak′ *or* kōōl′də·sak′] *n., pl.* **cul-de-sacs** or **culs-de-sac** [kulz′də·sak′ *or* kōōlz′də·sak′] **1** A dead-end street or passageway. **2** Any impasse.
cu·li·nar·y [kyōō′lə·ner′ē *or* kul′ə·ner′ē] *adj.* Of or having to do with cooking or the kitchen: *culinary* art.
cull [kul] **1** *v.* To pick out; select: to *cull* the best specimens. **2** *v.* To sort out and take the poor or worthless ones from. **3** *n.* Something of poor quality picked out to be discarded, as damaged fruit or spoiled vegetables.
cul·mi·nate [kul′min·āt′] *v.* **cul·mi·nat·ed, cul·mi·nat·ing** To reach the highest point or climax: The ceremonies *culminated* in the presentation of awards. **—cul′mi·na′tion** *n.*
cu·lotte [k(y)ōō·lot′ *or* k(y)ōō′lot′] *n.* (*often pl.*) Trousers for women, cut full to look like a skirt; a divided skirt.
cul·pa·ble [kul′pə·bəl] *adj.* Deserving blame; at fault: *culpable* negligence. **—cul·pa·bil·i·ty** [kul′pə·bil′ə·tē] *n.* **—cul′pa·bly** *adv.*
cul·prit [kul′prit] *n.* **1** A person guilty of a crime or misdeed; offender. **2** A person accused of a crime, as in court.
cult [kult] *n.* **1** Religious worship of someone or something: a *cult* of the sun. **2** A great liking or enthusiasm, as for an activity, idea, or person: the *cult* of folk singing. **3** The people who share such a liking or enthusiasm.
cul·ti·vate [kul′tə·vāt′] *v.* **cul·ti·vat·ed, cul·ti·vat·ing** **1** To prepare (land) for the growing of plants, as by loosening the soil and putting on fertilizer: to *cultivate* the fields. **2** To plant and care for: to *cultivate* roses. **3** To loosen the soil around (plants) so as to help them grow and kill weeds. **4** To improve and develop by study, exercise, or training: to *cultivate* one's mind. **5** *adj. use:* a *cultivated* mind. **6** To make an effort to get to know or be friendly with.
cul·ti·va·tion [kul′tə·vā′shən] *n.* **1** The work of cultivating plants or the ground around them. **2** The development of something by study or effort. **3** Culture and refinement.
cul·ti·va·tor [kul′tə·vā′tər] *n.* **1** A person who cultivates. **2** A tool or machine used to loosen the soil around plants.
cul·tur·al [kul′chər·əl] *adj.* Having to do with or resulting in culture: *cultural* traditions. **—cul′tur·al·ly** *adv.*
cul·ture [kul′chər] *n., v.* **cul·tured, cul·tur·ing** **1** *n.* The entire way of life of a particular people, including its customs, religions, ideas, inventions, and tools: ancient Egyptian *culture.* **2** *n.* The training or care of the mind or body: physical *culture.* **3** *n.* The knowledge, refinement, and good taste acquired through training the mind and faculties: a person of *culture.* **4** *n.* The growing or improvement of animals or plants: the *culture* of bees. **5** *n.* A colony or growth as of bacteria or viruses, in a prepared medium, as for study. **6** *v.* To grow and improve; cultivate: to *culture* roses. **7** *n.* The cultivation of the soil.
cul·tured [kul′chərd] *adj.* **1** Having or showing culture or refinement: a *cultured* person. **2** Produced by special methods: *cultured* bacteria.
cul·vert [kul′vərt] *n.* A covered channel for water crossing under a road or railroad.

Culvert

cum·ber [kum′bər] *v.* **1** To obstruct; clutter. **2** To burden or weigh down: My aunt was *cumbered* by worries about her health.
cum·ber·some [kum′bər·səm] *adj.* Hard to move or manage; unwieldy: a *cumbersome* package.
cum·brous [kum′brəs] *adj.* Cumbersome.
cum·in [kum′ən] *n.* **1** A plant related to the carrot, grown for its spicy seeds. **2** The seeds of this plant.
cum lau·de [kōōm·lou′də *or* kōōm·lou′dē] With honors: She graduated *cum laude* from the state college.
cum·mer·bund [kum′ər·bund′] *n.* A wide sash worn around the waist, especially with a man's tuxedo.
cum·u·late [kyōōm′yə·lāt′] *v.* **cum·u·lat·ed, cum·u·lat·ing** **1** To gather in a heap; pile up; accumulate. **2** To combine into a single unit; merge. **3** To expand by adding new material.

a	add	**i**	it	**ŏŏ**	took	**oi**	oil
ā	ace	**ī**	ice	**ōō**	pool	**ou**	pout
â	care	**o**	odd	**u**	up	**ng**	ring
ä	palm	**ō**	open	**û**	burn	**th**	thin
e	end	**ô**	order	**yōō**	fuse	**th**	this
ē	equal					**zh**	vision

ə = {a in *above* e in *sicken* i in *possible* / o in *melon* u in *circus*}

cu·mu·la·tive [kyo͞om′yə·lə·tiv *or* kyo͞om′yə·lā′tiv] *adj.* Increasing by being added to: *cumulative* knowledge. **—cu′mu·la′tive·ly** *adv.*

cu·mu·lus [kyo͞om′yə·ləs] *n., pl.* **cu·mu·li** [kyo͞om′yə·lī] **1** A large cloud having a flat base and rounded masses piled up on top. **2** A mass; pile.

cu·ne·i·form [kyo͞o·nē′ə·fôrm′] **1** *adj.* Shaped like a wedge, as the characters used in the writings of ancient Assyria, Babylonia, and Persia. **2** *n.* Ancient writing in cuneiform characters.

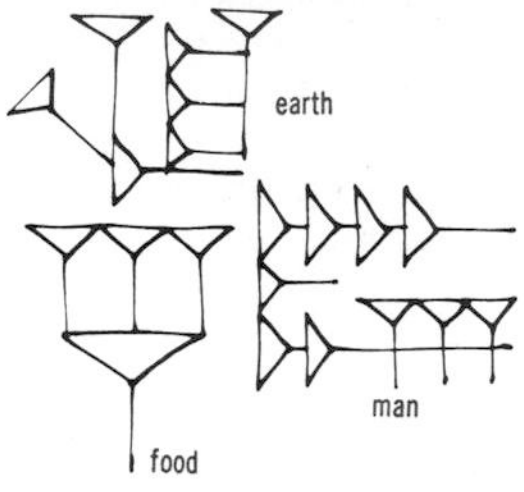

Cuneiform characters

cun·ning [kun′ing] **1** *adj.* Clever or tricky. **2** *n.* Slyness or cleverness in getting something wanted: Cats use great *cunning* to catch their prey. **3** *adj. U.S.* Cute and appealing: a *cunning* toy. **—cun′ning·ly** *adv.* ◆ If you called someone *cunning* today, it would not be appreciated, but in former times it would have been taken as a compliment. A *cunning* craftsman was very skillful.

cup (kup] *n., v.* **cupped, cup·ping** **1** *n.* A small, open bowl, usually with a handle, used mainly for drinking. **2** *n.* The amount a cup will hold; cupful; in measuring, half a pint. **3** *n.* A cuplike bowl or vessel awarded as a prize. **4** *n.* Something shaped like a cup, as certain parts of a flower. **5** *n.* One of the holes, or its metal lining, on a golf course. **6** *v.* To shape like a cup: to *cup* one's hands. **7** *v.* To place in or as if in a cup: He *cupped* his ear with his hand. **8** *n.* One's lot or fate in life: The exile's *cup* is bitter.

cup·bear·er [kup′bâr′ər] *n.* In former times, a person who served cups of wine at banquets.

cup·board [kub′ərd] *n.* A closet or cabinet, usually with shelves, as for dishes or food.

cup·cake [kup′kāk′] *n.* A small cake baked in a cup-shaped container.

cup·ful [kup′fo͝ol′] *n., pl.* **cup·fuls** As much as a cup will hold.

Cu·pid [kyo͞o′pid] *n.* **1** The Roman god of love, usually shown as a winged boy with a bow and arrow. **2** (*usually written* **cupid**) The picture of a winged baby carrying a bow and arrow, often seen on valentines.

cu·pid·i·ty [kyo͞o·pid′ə·tē] *n.* Greedy desire to possess something.

cup of tea **1** A person or thing that one likes or appreciates: Hot summer weather is really not my *cup of tea.* **2** A person or thing to be dealt with; matter: I can understand algebra but calculus is a different *cup of tea.*

cu·po·la [kyo͞o′pə·lə] *n.* **1** A circular, dome-shaped roof. **2** A small tower built on a roof and having a dome-shaped top.

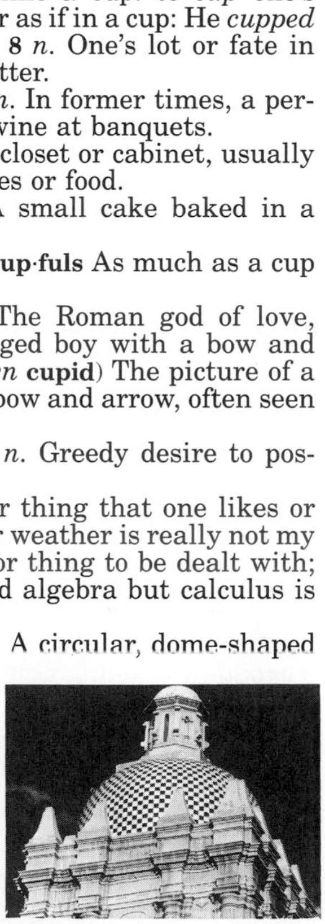
Cupola

cu·pre·ous [k(y)o͞o′prē·əs] *adj.* Of or like copper; coppery.

cu·pric [k(y)o͞o′prik] *adj.* Of, having to do with, or containing copper with a valence of two.

cu·prous [k(y)o͞o′prəs] *adj.* Of, having to do with, or containing copper with a valence of one.

cur [kûr] *n.* **1** A scrubby mongrel dog. **2** A nasty, ill-tempered, or cowardly person.

cur·a·ble [kyo͝or′ə·bəl] *adj.* Capable of being cured: a *curable* disease.

cu·ra·re or **cu·ra·ri** [k(y)o͞o·rä′rē] *n.* An extract of a South American tree, used by some Indians as an arrow poison and in medicine as a muscle relaxer.

cu·rate [kyo͝or′it] *n.* A clergyman who acts as assistant to a parish priest, rector, or vicar.

cur·a·tive [kyo͝or′ə·tiv] **1** *adj.* Having the power or tendency to cure: a *curative* diet. **2** *n.* A remedy: They tried all the known *curatives* for arthritis. **—cur′a·tive·ly** *adv.*

cu·ra·tor [kyo͞o·rā′tər] *n.* A person in charge of a museum, zoo, or other place where things are collected or exhibited.

curb [kûrb] **1** *v.* To control or restrain: to *curb* one's excitement. **2** *n.* Anything that controls or restrains; a check. **3** *n.* A raised border of concrete or stone along the edge of a street or pavement. **4** *n.* A chain or strap connected to the bit of a horse and used to control the horse when the reins are pulled.

curb·ing [kûrb′ing] *n.* **1** The material used to make a curb. **2** A curb (def. 3).

curb service A service, as the provision of food and beverages, to customers seated in parked automobiles at roadside eating places.

curb·stone [kûrb′stōn′] *n.* A stone or a row of stones along the edge of a sidewalk.

curd [kûrd] *n.* (*often pl.*) The thick clots that separate from the watery part when milk sours. Many cheeses are made from curd.

cur·dle [kûr′dəl] *v.* **cur·dled, cur·dling** **1** To turn into or form curds. **2** To thicken; clot: The sauce *curdled.* **—curdle one's blood** To fill with terror; frighten badly.

cure [kyo͝or] *v.,* **cured, cur·ing,** *n.* **1** *v.* To restore to good health; make well: to *cure* a sick person. **2** *v.* To get rid of or correct: to *cure* a sore throat. **3** *n.* A medicine, diet, treatment, or other means of curing; remedy. **4** *n.* A recovery from an illness or harmful condition. **5** *v.* To preserve (meat), as by salting, smoking, or drying.

cu·ré [kyo͞o·rā′ *or* kyo͝or′ā′] *n.* The French word for a parish priest.

cure-all [kyo͝or′ôl′] *n.* A remedy supposed to cure everything.

cur·few [kûr′fyo͞o] *n.* **1** A rule or law requiring certain persons to keep off the streets after a certain hour in the evening. **2** The sounding of a bell or other signal to announce that the curfew is in effect. ◆ This word comes from two French words meaning *to cover the fire.* In a medieval town people had to put out or cover all fires when a bell rang in the evening. Gradually *curfew* came to mean the bell or the hour at which it rang.

cu·rie [kyo͝or′ē *or* kyo͞o·rē′] *n.* A unit used in measuring radioactivity. ◆ This unit was named for Marie Curie.

cu·ri·o [kyo͝or′ē·ō] *n., pl.* **cu·ri·os** Any object that is thought to be rare or unusual.

cu·ri·os·i·ty [kyo͝or′ē·os′ə·tē] *n., pl.* **cu·ri·os·i·ties** **1** Eager desire to know or find out. **2** Too much interest in other people's affairs. **3** Something strange, rare, or unusual.

cu·ri·ous [kyo͝or′ē·əs] *adj.* **1** Eager to know or learn more. **2** Odd or unusual; strange: a *curious* old Chinese coin. **—cu′ri·ous·ly** *adv.*

cu·ri·um [kyo͝or′ē·əm] *n.* An intensely radioactive

metallic element produced artificially in nuclear reactors.

curl [kûrl] **1** *v.* To twist into or form curves or ringlets. **2** *n.* A coiled or rounded lock of hair; ringlet. **3** *v.* To become or cause to become curved or twisted: to *curl* one's lips in scorn. **4** *v.* To move in rings or spirals: The fog *curled* over the town. **5** *n.* Anything having a curled, rounded, or spiral shape.

curl·er [kûr'lər] *n.* A device on which a lock of hair is rolled and fastened for curling.

cur·lew [kûr'lo͞o] *n., pl.* **cur·lews** or **cur·lew** A bird that lives along the shore and has long legs and a very long bill curving downward.

curl·i·cue [kûr'li·kyo͞o'] *n., v.* **curl·i·cued, curl·i·cu·ing** **1** *n.* Any fancy curl or twist: handwriting with many *curlicues.* **2** *v.* To form curlicues or decorate with them.

Curlicues in a signature

curl·ing [kûr'ling] *n.* A game played by two four-person teams who slide heavy disks of stone or iron called **curling stones** toward circular targets at either end of a stretch of ice.

cur·ly [kûr'lē] *adj.* **curl·i·er, curl·i·est** **1** Curling or tending to curl: *curly* hair. **2** Having curls: a *curly* hair style. **3** Having a wavy grain, as certain woods. **—curl'i·ness** *n.*

cur·rant [kûr'ənt] *n.* **1** A small, sour, red, white, or black berry, used for jelly. **2** The bush on which this berry grows. **3** A small seedless raisin used in cooking.

cur·ren·cy [kûr'ən·sē] *n., pl.* **cur·ren·cies** **1** Money in general use. **2** General acceptance or use; popularity: Many new fads lose *currency* quickly. **3** A circulating or spreading from one person to another: That story enjoyed wide *currency.* ◆ *Money* and *currency* have almost the same meaning. *Money* is the common word. *Currency* is likely to mean many people's money, as the money used in another country is foreign *currency.*

cur·rent [kûr'ənt] **1** *n.* That part of any body of water or air that flows more or less in a definite direction: an ocean *current.* **2** *n.* A flow of electricity through a wire or other conductor. **3** *adj.* Belonging to the present time; now in effect: *current* fashions; the *current* year. **4** *adj.* Generally accepted or practiced; common. **5** *n.* Any noticeable course, trend, or tendency: a *current* of revolt. **—cur'rent·ly** *adv.*

cur·ric·u·lum [kə·rik'yə·ləm] *n., pl.* **cur·ric·u·lums** or **cur·ric·u·la** [kə·rik'yə·lə] All of the subjects or courses taught in a school or in any particular grade.

cur·ry[1] [kûr'ē] *v.* **cur·ried, cur·ry·ing** To rub down and clean (a horse or other animal) with a currycomb. **—curry favor** To try to get favors by flattering a person in an insincere way.

cur·ry[2] [kûr'ē] *n., pl.* **cur·ries,** *v.* **cur·ried, cur·ry·ing** **1** *n.* A sauce or powder made of finely ground spices and used to season food. **2** *n.* A dish of meat, fish, or other foods, seasoned with this sauce or powder. **3** *v.* To season food with curry: to *curry* rice and shrimp. ◆ *Curry* comes from a word meaning *sauce* in a language of southern India and Ceylon.

cur·ry·comb [kûr'ē·kōm'] **1** *n.* A comb having rows of metal teeth or ridges used to groom horses. **2** *v.* To groom with a currycomb.

curse [kûrs] *n., v.* **cursed** [kûrst] or **curst, cur·sing** **1** *n.* A wish for evil or harm to befall someone or something, often made by calling on God or gods. **2** *v.* To wish harm or punishment on: The prophet *cursed* the wicked people. **3** *n.* The harm or evil asked for. **4** *v.* To use profane language; swear or swear at. **5** *n.* A word used in cursing or swearing. **6** *n.* A source of harm, evil, or trouble: That ring was always a *curse.* **7** *v.* To cause to suffer; afflict: to be *cursed* with ill health.

curs·ed [kûr'sid *or* kûrst] *adj.* **1** Deserving a curse; wicked; hateful. **2** Under a curse.

cur·sive [kûr'siv] *adj.* Written or printed so that the letters are joined together, as in handwriting.

cur·sor [kûr'sər] *n.* A blinking or movable spot of light used in the display of a computer terminal as an indicator, as of data to be corrected or added or the position of the next data to be entered.

cur·so·ry [kûr'sər·ē] *adj.* Not thorough; hasty: a *cursory* reading. **—cur'so·ri·ly** *adv.*

curt [kûrt] *adj.* Short and somewhat rude in tone or manner: a *curt* nod; a *curt* answer. **—curt'ly** *adv.* **—curt'ness** *n.*

cur·tail [kər·tāl'] *v.* To cut short or cut back; reduce: to *curtail* a meeting. **—cur·tail'ment** *n.*

cur·tain [kûr'tən] **1** *n.* A piece of cloth hung in or over a window, door, or other opening, as a decoration or screen, usually capable of being drawn to the sides or raised. **2** *n.* Such a screen used to hide the stage of a theater from the audience. **3** *n.* Something like a curtain that covers, hides, or screens: a *curtain* of mist. **4** *v.* To cover, hide, or screen with or as if with a curtain: to *curtain* a window.

curt·sey [kûrt'sē] *n., pl.* **curt·seys,** *v.* **curt·seyed, curt·sey·ing** Curtsy.

curt·sy [kûrt'sē] *n., pl.* **curt·sies,** *v.* **curt·sied, curt·sy·ing** **1** *n.* A bow made by bending the knees and inclining the upper part of the body forward, used as a sign of respect. **2** *v.* To make such a bow.

Curtsy

cur·va·ture [kûr'və·chər] *n.* A curve or a curved condition: *curvature* of the earth.

curve [kûrv] *n., v.* **curved, curv·ing** **1** *n.* A continuous line that keeps changing its direction smoothly, without straight parts or angular bends. **2** *n.* Something shaped like a curve: a *curve* in the road. **3** *v.* To bend into or take the form of a curve: One track *curved* off to the west. **4** *n.* In baseball, a ball pitched with a spin that causes it to swerve. **5** *v.* To throw or move in a curve: Smoke *curved* from the chimney. **6** *n.* A

a	add	**i**	it	**o͝o**	took	**oi**	oil
ā	ace	**ī**	ice	**o͞o**	pool	**ou**	pout
â	care	**o**	odd	**u**	up	**ng**	ring
ä	palm	**ō**	open	**û**	burn	**th**	thin
e	end	**ô**	order	**yo͞o**	fuse	**th**	this
ē	equal					**zh**	vision

ə = {a in *above* e in *sicken* i in *possible* / o in *melon* u in *circus*}

connected set of points on a graph, especially a set of points representing possible values of a mathematical function.

cur·vet [kər·vet′] *n., v.* **cur·vet·ted** or **cur·vet·ed, cur·vet·ting** or **cur·vet·ing** **1** *n.* A light, low leap of a horse, made so that, for an instant, all four legs are off the ground at one time. **2** *v.* To make or cause to make a curvet.

cush·ion [kŏŏsh′ən] **1** *n.* A case or bag filled with a soft, springy material and used to sit, kneel, or lie on; pillow. **2** *n.* Anything like a cushion in appearance or use. **3** *v.* To provide or support with or as if with a cushion: She *cushioned* the child's head in her lap. **4** *v.* To absorb the shock or effect of: to *cushion* a blow.

cusp [kusp] *n.* **1** A pointed end formed by the meeting of two curves. Either end of a crescent moon is a cusp. **2** A point on the crown of a tooth.

cus·pid [kus′pid] *n.* A tooth having one cusp; canine tooth.

cus·pi·dor [kus′pə·dôr] *n. U.S.* A container for spitting into; spittoon. ◆ *Cuspidor* comes directly from Portuguese.

cuss [kus] *U.S. informal* **1** *v.* To swear or curse. **2** *n.* A person.

cus·tard [kus′tərd] *n.* A dessert made of sweetened milk and eggs, baked or boiled.

cus·to·di·an [kus·tō′dē·ən] *n.* A guardian or keeper: the *custodian* of a building.

cus·to·dy [kus′tə·dē] *n., pl.* **cus·to·dies** Care and control; guardianship: The foster parents were given *custody* of the child. **—in custody** Under arrest; in prison or jail. **—take into custody** To arrest.

cus·tom [kus′təm] **1** *n.* A usual way of acting or doing something; habit: It was his *custom* to walk to work. **2** *n.* Something that has become an accepted practice by many people: the *custom* of decorating Christmas trees. **3** *n.* Business given by a steady customer: We gave our *custom* to the neighborhood grocery. **4** *n.* (*pl.*) The tax which a government collects on goods brought into a country from abroad; also, the agency of the government that collects such taxes. **5** *adj.* Made specially for an individual customer; made-to-order: *custom* shoes. **6** *adj.* Dealing or specializing in made-to-order goods: a *custom* tailor. ◆ *Custom, habit,* and *fashion* refer to a way of doing or behaving that has become usual. *Custom* is used especially for rules of conduct followed by a group: the Mexican *custom* of taking a midday siesta. *Habit* usually refers to a person's behavior: Brushing your teeth after meals is a good *habit. Fashions* are styles, as of dress, taken up by many but often not for long: Tall silk hats were then the *fashion.*

cus·tom·ar·y [kus′tə·mer′ē] *adj.* Based on custom; usual: at the *customary* time. **—cus′tom·ar′i·ly** *adv.*

cus·tom·er [kus′təm·ər] *n.* **1** A person who buys something, as from a store. **2** *informal* A person unusual in some way: a tough *customer.*

cus·tom·house [kus′təm·hous′] *n.* The government office where customs are collected on goods brought into a country from abroad.

cus·tom-made [kus′təm·mād′] *adj.* Made for an individual customer; made-to-order.

cut [kut] *v.* **cut, cut·ting,** *n.* **1** *v.* To make an opening in (something) with a sharp edge or instrument: to *cut* one's foot. **2** *n.* An opening made with something having a sharp edge: to bandage a *cut.* **3** *n.* A stroke, slice, or blow with something having a sharp edge. **4** *v.* To divide, separate, or break up into parts: to *cut* paper; Tender meat *cuts* easily. **5** *v.* To remove a part or parts by cutting: to *cut* hair. **6** *n.* A part removed by cutting: a *cut* of meat. **7** *v.* To make, shape, or ornament by or as if by cutting: to *cut* a diamond. **8** *adj. use:* finely *cut* features. **9** *v.* To make less; reduce: to *cut* prices. **10** *n.* A reduction: a *cut* in salary. **11** *v.* To take a direct route; go straight: to *cut* through the woods. **12** *n.* A passage or channel made by cutting: The road goes through a *cut* there. **13** *n.* A route or way that is straight and direct: a short *cut.* **14** *v.* To pierce like a knife: The harsh words *cut* me to the heart. **15** *n.* Something that hurts one's feelings. **16** *v.* To pretend not to see or recognize (someone); snub: I nodded to the neighbors, but they *cut* me. **17** *v.* To have (a new tooth) grow through the gum. **18** *n.* The fashion or style of anything: the *cut* of a suit. **19** *n.* An engraved block or plate used in printing; also, the picture made from this. **20** *v.* To hit a ball so that it will spin or swerve to one side. **21** *n. slang* A part; portion; share: a *cut* of the loot. **—cut in** **1** To move or swerve into a line suddenly: to *cut in* ahead of someone. **2** To break in, as on a conversation; interrupt. **—cut off** **1** To remove a part or parts by cutting. **2** To shut off; stop: to *cut off* the water supply. **3** To disinherit: The grandchildren were *cut off* without a cent. **—cut out** **1** To remove or shape by cutting: to *cut out* pictures. **2** Suited: I'm not *cut out* for this kind of work. **3** *slang* To stop doing; cease: *Cut out* that nonsense. **—cut up** **1** To divide or separate into pieces. **2** *informal* To show off; act silly. **3** To upset or distress.

cut-and-dried [kut′(ə)n·drīd′] *adj.* **1** Done according to a plan or formula. **2** Not interesting or different; routine.

cut·a·way [kut′ə·wā′] *n.* A man's formal coat for daytime wear, cut slopingly away from the waist in front down to the tails at the back.

cut·back [kut′bak′] *n.* A sharp reduction: a *cutback* in prices.

cute [kyōōt] *adj.* **cut·er, cut·est** *informal* **1** Charming and appealing: a *cute* puppy. **2** Clever or shrewd. ◆ *Cute* was first used, mostly in the U.S., only with the second meaning, a sense now not common. It is a shortened form of *acute.*

cu·ti·cle [kyōō′ti·kəl] *n.* **1** The hardened skin around the base of a fingernail or toenail. **2** The outer layer of skin.

cut·lass or **cut·las** [kut′ləs] *n.* A short, curved sword, used in former days chiefly by sailors.

Cutlass

cut·ler·y [kut′lər·ē] *n.* **1** Tools or utensils used for cutting: Knives and scissors are *cutlery.* **2** Knives, forks, and spoons used in eating and serving food.

cut·let [kut′lit] *n.* **1** A thin piece of meat, such as veal, for frying or broiling. **2** A flat cake of chopped meat or fish, usually fried.

cut·off [kut′ôf′] **1** *n.* A stopping or shutting off of something: The water *cutoff* will last two hours. **2** *adj. use:* The *cutoff* hour is two o'clock. **3** *n. U.S.* A shorter, more direct way; shortcut.

cut·out [kut′out′] *n.* A figure or design cut out or meant to be cut out.

cut·purse [kut′pûrs′] *n.* A pickpocket.

cut-rate [kut′rāt′] *adj.* **1** Sold or offering goods at reduced prices: a *cut-rate* department store. 2 Cheap; second-rate.

cut·ter [kut′ər] *n.* 1 A person or instrument that cuts: a paper *cutter.* 2 A small, armed ship, especially one used by the Coast Guard. 3 A boat carried by a ship to go to and from a ship. 4 A small sleigh. 5 A sailboat having a single mast.

cut·throat [kut′thrōt′] 1 *n.* A murderer. 2 *adj.* Merciless; ruthless: The *cutthroat* competition forced the corner store out of business.

cut·ting [kut′ing] 1 *adj.* Able to cut; sharp: a *cutting* blade. 2 *adj.* Cold and piercing: a *cutting* wind. 3 *adj.* Able to wound the feelings; sarcastic: a *cutting* reply. 4 *n.* The action of a person or thing that cuts. 5 *n.* An excavation made through a hill or high piece of ground for the construction of a railroad, canal, or other passageway. 6 *n.* A shoot cut from a plant to form a new plant.

cut·tle·bone [kut′(ə)l·bōn′] *n.* The shell of a cuttlefish, used as a polishing powder or as a food supplement for caged birds.

cut·tle·fish [kut′(ə)l·fish′] *n., pl.* **cut·tle·fish** or **cut·tle·fish·es** A sea animal having ten arms with suckers on them and a hard inner shell. Some kinds squirt an inky fluid to hide in when attacked.

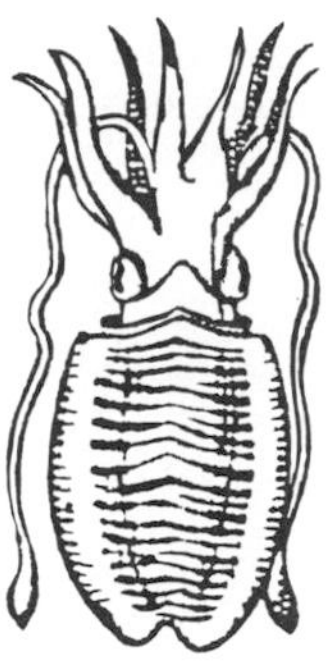
Cuttlefish

cut·up [kut′up′] *n. informal* A person who jokes and plays mischievous tricks; clown.

cut·worm [kut′wûrm′] *n.* A caterpillar that cuts off plants near the surface of the ground.

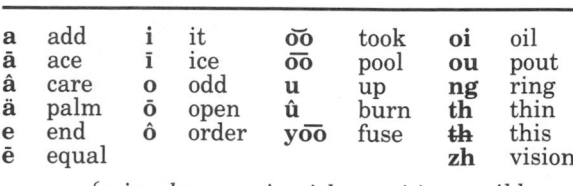

cwt or **cwt.** hundredweight. ◆ This abbreviation comes from the Latin word *centum,* meaning *hundred,* and the English word *weight.*

-cy A suffix meaning: 1 Quality, state, or condition of being, as in *secrecy.* 2 Rank, grade, or position of, as in *presidency.*

cy·a·nide [sī′ə·nīd′] *n.* Any of various very poisonous chemical compounds.

cy·ber·net·ics [sī′bər·net′iks] *n.* The comparative study of machines such as computers and the nervous system of human beings or animals, to gain better understanding of the functioning of the brain. ◆ See -ICS.

cyc·la·mate [sī′klə·māt′] *n.* A very sweet crystalline compound used as a sugar substitute.

cyc·la·men [sik′lə·mən] *n.* A plant having large pink, red, or white flowers.

cy·cle [sī′kəl] *n., v.* **cy·cled, cy·cling** 1 *n.* A series of events that always happen in the same order and return to the original position, as the waxing and waning of the moon. 2 *n.* A series of predictable stages in the growth of a plant or animal or the completion of a process, as the erosion of a river valley. 3 *n.* The time needed for such series. 4 *n.* In physics, one complete occurrence of a process that recurs or varies in magnitude at regular intervals, such as a wave or a current alternation. 5 *n.* A long period of time; an eon. 6 *n.* A collection of poems, songs, or stories handed down about a certain hero, period, or event. 7 *n.* A vehicle, such as a bicycle or motorcycle. 8 *v.* To ride a bicycle, motorcycle, or similar vehicle.

cy·clic [sī′klik *or* sik′lik] *adj.* 1 Of a cycle. 2 Returning or occurring in cycles. 3 Of or having atoms arranged in a ring: *cyclic* compounds.

cy·cli·cal [sī′kli·kəl *or* sik′li·kəl] *adj.* Cyclic.

cy·clist [sī′klist] *n.* A person who rides a bicycle or motorcycle.

cy·clone [sī′klōn] *n.* 1 A storm in which winds whirl spirally in toward a center of low pressure, which also moves. 2 Any violent windstorm; a tornado: used chiefly in the Middle West.

cy·clon·ic [sī·klon′ik] *adj.* 1 Of a cyclone. 2 Like a cyclone; violent; destructive.

cy·clo·pe·di·a [sī′klə·pē′dē·ə] *n.* Another word for ENCYCLOPEDIA.

Cy·clops [sī′klops] *n., pl.* **Cy·clo·pes** [sī·klō′pēz] or **Cy·clops** In Greek legend, any of a race of giants having one eye in the middle of the forehead.

Cyclops

cy·clo·tron [sī′klə·tron′] *n.* An apparatus that whirls charged particles through a strong magnetic field to such high speeds that they can enter and change the nuclei of certain atoms.

cyg·net [sig′nit] *n.* A young swan. ◆ *Cygnet* comes from the French word *cygne,* meaning *swan,* and *-et,* meaning *small.*

cyl. cylinder.

cy·lin·der [sil′in·dər] *n.* 1 A geometric figure bounded by two circles in parallel planes and the parallel lines joining them. The lines may or may not be perpendicular to the planes. 2 Any object or container having this shape.

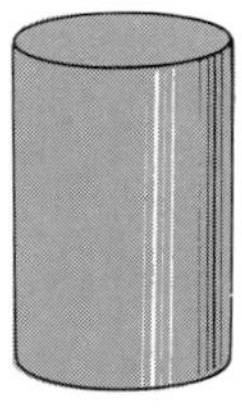
Cylinder

cy·lin·dri·cal [si·lin′dri·kəl] *adj.* Shaped like a cylinder.

cym·bal [sim′bəl] *n.* A round metal plate that makes a ringing sound when struck, often used in pairs in a band or orchestra.

cyn·ic [sin′ik] 1 *n.* A sneering, faultfinding person who distrusts the goodness and sincerity of others. 2 *adj.* Cynical.

cyn·i·cal [sin′i·kəl] *adj.* 1 Having no belief in the goodness and sincerity of others. 2 Sneering; sarcastic. **—cyn′i·cal·ly** *adv.*

cyn·i·cism [sin′ə·siz′əm] *n.* 1 The thoughts and feelings of a cynic. 2 Something cynical, as a remark or an act.

cy·no·sure [sī′nə·shŏŏr *or* sin′ə·shŏŏr] *n.* A person or object that is the center of attention, attraction, or admiration: The winner of the marathon was the *cynosure* of all eyes.

cy·pher [sī′fər] *n.* Another spelling of CIPHER.

cy·press [sī′prəs] *n.* 1 An evergreen tree with hard

a	add	**i**	it	**ŏŏ**	took	**oi**	oil
ā	ace	**ī**	ice	**ōō**	pool	**ou**	pout
â	care	**o**	odd	**u**	up	**ng**	ring
ä	palm	**ō**	open	**û**	burn	**th**	thin
e	end	**ô**	order	**yōō**	fuse	**t͟h**	this
ē	equal					**zh**	vision

ə = {a in *above* e in *sicken* i in *possible* / o in *melon* u in *circus*}

wood and dark, scalelike leaves. **2** The wood of this tree.

Cyp·ri·ot [sip′rē·ət] **1** *adj.* Of or from Cyprus. **2** *n.* A person born in or a citizen of Cyprus. **3** *n.* The ancient or modern Greek dialect of Cyprus.

Cyp·ri·ote [sip′rē·ōt′] *adj., n.* Cypriot.

Cy·ril·lic [si·ril′ik] *adj.* Of or designating an alphabet used in writing Russian and certain other Slavic languages. ◆ *Cyrillic* is derived from St. *Cyril,* a Greek missionary who brought Christianity to the Slavs in the 9th century A.D. According to legend, he invented the alphabet, but historians attribute it to his followers.

cyst [sist] *n.* An abnormal baglike growth in some part of the body, in which liquid or solid material may collect and remain.

cyst- or **cysti-** or **cysto-** A combining form meaning: Bladder, as in *cystitis.*

cys·tic [sis′tik] *adj.* **1** Of, having to do with, or like a cyst. **2** Having, containing, or composed of a cyst or cysts. **3** Of or having to do with the gallbladder or urinary bladder.

cystic fi·bro·sis [fī·brō′səs] An inherited disease of the exocrine glands that usually appears in early childhood and results in disorders of the pancreas, lungs, and sweat glands.

cys·ti·tis [sis·tī′təs] *n.* Inflammation of the urinary bladder.

cyt- or **cyto-** A combining form meaning: Cell, as in *cytology.*

cy·tol·o·gy [sī·tol′ə·jē] *n.* The scientific study of the structure and workings of living cells. **—cy·tol′o·gist** *n.*

cy·to·plasm [sī′tə·plaz′əm] *n.* All of the protoplasm of a cell, except for that in the nucleus.

C.Z. Canal Zone.

czar [zär] *n.* **1** One of the former emperors of Russia. **2** Someone having great power or authority in a certain field or activity: a baseball *czar.* **—czar′dom** *n.*

cza·ri·na [zä·rē′nə] *n.* A former empress of Russia.

czar·ism [zär′iz·əm] *n.* The government of Russia under the czars. **—czar′ist** *adj., n.*

Czech [chek] **1** *adj.* Of or from Czechoslovakia. **2** *n.* A person born in or a citizen of Czechoslovakia, especially one from the western part of the country. **3** *n.* A language of Czechoslovakia.

Czech·o·slo·vak [chek′ə·slō′väk *or* chek′ə·slō′vak] **1** *adj.* Of or from Czechoslovakia. **2** *n.* A person born in or a citizen of Czechoslovakia.

Czech·o·slo·va·ki·an [chek′ə·slə·vä′kē·ən] *adj., n.* Czechoslovak.

Dd

D is the fourth letter of the alphabet. It has held that position since the very earliest times. The sign for *D* originated among Semitic people in the Near East, in the region of Palestine and Syria, probably in the middle of the second millennium B.C. Little is known about the sign until around 1000 B.C., when the Phoenicians began using it. The Phoenicians named the sign *daleth* and used it for the sound of the consonant *d*.

When the Greeks adopted the Phoenician sign around the ninth century B.C., they called it *delta* and gave it various triangular shapes. A rounded variant also appeared. Like the Phoenicians, the Greeks used the sign for the sound of *d*.

As early as the eighth century B.C., the Etruscans adopted the Greek alphabet, including the rounded version of the *D*. The sign was virtually unused by the Etruscans, however, because they made no distinction between the *d* and *t* sounds. The Romans adopted the rounded version of the sign, changed its direction, and used it for their *d* sound. Around the time of the Caesars, the Romans made the shape of the letter more graceful. The model of the letter found on the base of Trajan's column, erected in Rome in 114, is considered a masterpiece of letter design. A Trajan-style *majuscule,* or capital letter, *D* opens this essay.

The *minuscule,* or small letter, *d* developed gradually, between the third and ninth centuries, in the handwriting that scribes used for copying books. Contributing to its shape were the Roman *uncials* of the fourth to the eighth centuries and the *half unicals* of the fifth to the ninth centuries. It became even more like our present-day lowercase letter in the script that evolved under the encouragement of Charlemagne (742-814). This *d* was one of the letters known as the *Caroline minuscules,* which became the principal handwriting system used on the medieval manuscripts of the ninth and tenth centuries.

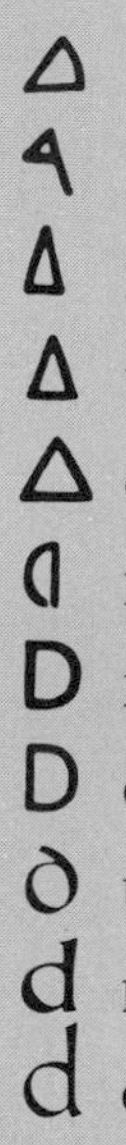

Early Phoenician (late 2nd millennium B.C.)
Phoenician (8th century B.C.)
Early Greek (9th-7th centuries B.C.)
Western Greek (6th century B.C.)
Classical Greek (403 B.C. onward)
Early Etruscan (8th century B.C.)
Monumental Latin (4th century B.C.)
Classical Latin
Uncial
Half uncial
Caroline minuscule

d or **D** [dē] *n., pl,* **d's** or **D's** 1 The fourth letter of the English alphabet. 2 (*written* **D**) The Roman numeral for 500. 3 *U.S.* A school grade indicating the student's work is poor. 4 In music, the second note of the scale of C major.

d. 1 date. 2 daughter. 3 day(s). 4 dead. 5 degree. 6 diameter. 7 died. 8 dime. 9 dollar. 10 pence or penny.

D In physics, density.

D. 1 Democrat. 2 December. 3 Dutch. 4 Department. 5 Doctor.

D.A. District Attorney.

dab[1] [dab] *n., v.* **dabbed, dab·bing** 1 *n.* A quick, gentle stroke; pat. 2 *v* To stroke quickly and gently: to *dab* one's eyes. 3 *n.* A small lump of something soft and moist.

dab[2] [dab] *n.* A flatfish, especially any of several related to and resembling the flounder.

dab·ber [dab′ər] *n.* 1 A person or thing that dabs. 2 In printing and engraving, a cushioned pad used in applying ink.

dab·ble [dab′əl] *v.* **dab·bled, dab·bling** 1 To splash gently, as with the hands: to *dabble* in a brook. 2 To spatter lightly: clothing *dabbled* with mud. 3 To do something but not seriously: to *dabble* at chess. **—dab′bler** *n.*

da ca·po [dä kä′pō] An Italian expression for "from the beginning." It is used in written music to show that a passage should be repeated.

dace [dās] *n., pl.* **dac·es** or **dace** A small freshwater fish related to carp and goldfish.

da·cha [dä′chə] *n.* A small Russian country house.

dachs·hund [däks′ho͝ont′ *or* däk′sənt] *n.* A breed of small hound dog native to Germany, having a long, compact body, very short legs, and short hair, usually red, tan, or black and tan in color.

Dachshund

Da·cron [dā′kron *or* dak′ron] *n.* A synthetic fiber or cloth that does not wrinkle or stretch easily: a trademark. Also written **dacron.**

dac·tyl [dak′təl] *n.* A metrical foot made up of one stressed syllable followed by two unstressed syllables. ◆ The ancient Greeks, who used this metrical unit far more than modern poets do, named it *daktylos,* meaning "finger." Like a finger, a dactyl has one longer segment followed by two shorter ones.

a	add	**i**	it	**o͝o**	took	**oi**	oil		
ā	ace	**ī**	ice	**o͞o**	pool	**ou**	pout		
â	care	**o**	odd	**u**	up	**ng**	ring		
ä	palm	**ō**	open	**û**	burn	**th**	thin		
e	end	**ô**	order	**yo͞o**	fuse	**th̶**	this		
ē	equal					**zh**	vision		

ə = a in *above* e in *sicken* i in *possible* o in *melon* u in *circus*

dad [dad] *n. informal* Father: Where is your *dad*?
dad·dy [dad'ē] *n., pl.* **dad·dies** *informal* Father: used mostly by children: My *daddy* reads to me.
dad·dy-long·legs [dad'ē·lông'legz'] *n., pl.* **dad·dy-long·legs** An animal that looks like a spider with long thin legs and a small body.

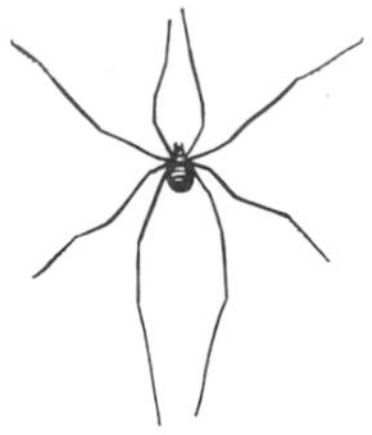
Daddy-longlegs

Daed·a·lus [ded'ə·ləs] *n.* In Greek myths, the architect of the labyrinth at Crete. He and his son Icarus were imprisoned there and escaped by using artificial wings.
daf·fo·dil [daf'ə·dil] *n.* A plant with yellow flowers and long, bladelike leaves. It grows from a bulb.
daf·fy [daf'ē] *adj.* **daf·fi·er, daf·fi·est** *informal* Crazy or silly.
daft [daft] *adj. British* Crazy or foolish. **—daft'ly** *adv.* **—daft'ness** *n.*
dag·ger [dag'ər] *n.* A short, pointed weapon used for stabbing.
da·guerre·o·type [də·ger'ə·tīp'] *n.* An old-fashioned kind of photograph made on a silver-coated metal plate sensitive to light.
dahl·ia [dal'yə] *n.* A plant that has bright, showy flowers in red, purple, yellow, or white.
dai·ly [dā'lē] *adj., adv., n., pl.* **dai·lies** 1 *adj.* Done, occurring, or appearing every day: *daily* exercise; a *daily* newspaper. 2 *adv.* Every day; day after day: to walk *daily* in the park. 3 *n.* A newspaper published every day.
dain·ty [dān'tē] *adj.* **dain·ti·er, dain·ti·est,** *n., pl.* **dain·ties** 1 *adj.* Delicately pretty or graceful: a *dainty* flower. 2 *adj.* Very particular or fussy: a *dainty* eater. 3 *n.* A delicious food; delicacy. 4 *adj.* Delicious; tasty. **—dain'ti·ly** *adv.* **—dain'ti·ness** *n.*
dair·y [dâr'ē] *n., pl.* **dair·ies** 1 A place where milk and cream are stored or made into such products as butter and cheese. 2 A farm or store that specializes in milk products.
dair·y·maid [dâr'ē·mād'] *n.* A woman who works on a dairy farm.
dair·y·man [dâr'ē·mən] *n., pl.* **dair·y·men** [dâr'ē·mən] 1 A person who owns or manages a dairy. 2 A person who works in a dairy.
da·is [dā'is] *n.* A platform in a room or hall for a speaker, a throne, or seats of honor.
dai·sy [dā'zē] *n., pl.* **dai·sies** 1 A flower with a central yellow disk surrounded by white or pink rays. 2 The plant.
daisy wheel The type element of a certain kind of computer printer, consisting of a metal disk with a character embossed on each spoke (or "petal").
Da·ko·ta [də·kō'tə] *n., pl.* **Da·ko·ta** or **Da·ko·tas** 1 A tribe of North American Indians forming the largest division of the Sioux, now living in North Dakota or South Dakota, Montana, and Minnesota. 2 A member of this tribe. 3 The language of this tribe.
dale [dāl] *n.* A small valley.
dal·li·ance [dal'ē·əns] *n.* 1 Trifling or wasting of time. 2 Flirting or playing.
dal·ly [dal'ē] *v.* **dal·lied, dal·ly·ing** 1 To treat lightly or playfully; trifle: to *dally* with danger. 2 To waste time; dawdle; linger. ◆ *Dally* comes from an old French word meaning *to chat.*
Dal·ma·tian [dal·mā'shən] *n.* A large, short-haired dog, white with black spots.
dam[1] [dam] *n., v.* **dammed, dam·ming** 1 *n.* A wall or other barrier to hold back or control flowing water. 2 *v.* To hold back by or as if by a dam: to *dam* a river.

Dam

dam[2] [dam] *n.* The female parent of a horse, sheep, or cow, and of some other animals.
dam·age [dam'ij] *n., v.* **dam·aged, dam·ag·ing** 1 *n.* Injury or harm that reduces value or usefulness: The drought did much *damage* to the crops; *damage* to one's reputation. 2 *n.* The resulting loss: The *damage* was estimated at $750. 3 *v.* To cause injury to: to *damage* a library book. 4 *n.* (*pl.*) Money asked for or paid under law to make up for an injury or wrong.
Damascus steel A hard steel with a surface ornamented with wavy patterns, originally developed in the Near East and used especially for sword blades.
dam·ask [dam'əsk] 1 *n.* A fine table linen with a pattern woven into it. 2 *adj. use:* a *damask* tablecloth. 3 *n.* A rich, reversible silk fabric with an elaborate woven design. 4 *n.* A steel with wavy markings. 5 *n., adj.* Deep pink or rose.
dame [dām] *n.* 1 A lady: seldom used today except as a British title of honor. 2 An old woman. 3 *slang* A woman or girl.
damn [dam] 1 *v.* In some religions, to condemn to eternal punishment. 2 *v.* To pronounce as bad or worthless: to *damn* a book or a movie. 3 *interj.* An exclamation or curse expressing emotions such as annoyance or disappointment. 4 *v.* To curse by saying "damn."
dam·na·ble [dam'nə·bəl] *adj.* That ought to be damned; hateful; detestable. **—dam'na·bly** *adv.*
dam·na·tion [dam·nā'shən] *n.* 1 The act of damning. 2 The condition of being damned.
damned [damd] *adj.* **damned·er** [dam'dər], **damned·est** [dam'dəst], *adv.* 1 *adj.* Detestable; hateful. 2 *adj.* Utter; complete. 3 *adj.* Condemned; accursed. 4 *adv. informal* Very.
Dam·o·cles [dam'ə·klēz'] *n.* In Greek myths, a man who flattered his king and was forced to sit at a banquet table under a sword hung by a single hair to teach him how insecure rulers are.
Da·mon and Pyth·i·as [dā'mən; pith'ē·əs] In Roman myths, two very devoted friends.
damp [damp] 1 *adj.* Slightly wet; moist: a *damp* day; *damp* shoes. 2 *n.* Moisture; vapor: The cellar is full of *damp*. 3 *v.* To dampen; moisten: to *damp* clothes. 4 *v.* To discourage or dull: to *damp* enthusiasm. 5 *n.* A discouragement; check; damper. 6 *n.* Foul air or poisonous gas, especially in a mine. **—damp'ly** *adv.* **—damp'ness** *n.*
damp·en [dam'pən] *v.* 1 To make or become damp; moisten: Dew *dampened* the grass. 2 To check or dull: Nothing could *dampen* our spirits.
damp·er [dam'pər] *n.* 1 A flat plate in the flue, as of a stove or furnace, that can be tilted to control the draft. 2 A person or thing that dulls, depresses, or checks.
dam·sel [dam'zəl] *n.* A young girl; maiden: seldom used today.

dam·son [dam′zən] *n.* 1 A small, oval purple plum. 2 The tree it grows on.
Dan. Danish.
dance [dans] *v.* **danced, danc·ing,** *n.* 1 *v.* To move the body and feet rhythmically, usually to music. 2 *n.* The act of dancing. 3 *n.* A round of dancing: the next *dance.* 4 *n.* A particular form of dance, as the waltz or polka. 5 *v.* To perform (a dance): to *dance* the polka. 6 *n.* A piece of music for dancing. 7 *n.* A gathering of people for dancing; a ball. 8 *v.* To move up and down; leap about: to *dance* for joy. **—dance attendance on** To wait upon (another) constantly and eagerly.
danc·er [dan′sər] *n.* A person who dances, especially a paid performer.
dan·de·li·on [dan′də·lī′ən] *n.* A common weed with a yellow flower and toothed leaves.

Dandelion

dan·der [dan′dər] 1 *n.* Tiny flakes from the hair, skin, or feathers of animals: I am allergic to cat *dander.* 2 *n. informal* Temper. **—get one's dander up** To lose or cause to lose one's temper.
dan·dle [dan′dəl] *v.* **dan·dled, dan·dling** 1 To move up and down lightly on the knee or in the arms: to *dandle* a baby. 2 To pamper; coddle.
dan·druff [dan′drəf] *n.* Small scales of dead skin formed on the scalp.
dan·dy [dan′dē] *n., pl.* **dan·dies,** *adj.* **dan·di·er, dan·di·est** 1 *n.* A person who is greatly interested in fine clothes and an elegant appearance. 2 *n. slang* Something very good. 3 *adj. slang* Very good; excellent.
Dane [dān] *n.* A person born in or a citizen of Denmark.
dan·ger [dān′jər] *n.* 1 A being exposed to harm, trouble, or risk: A firefighter's life is full of *danger.* 2 Something that may cause harm: Icy streets are a *danger* to pedestrians.
dan·ger·ous [dān′jər·əs] *adj.* 1 Full of danger or risk; unsafe. 2 Likely to cause injury; harmful. **—dan′ger·ous·ly** *adv.* **—dan′ger·ous·ness** *n.*
dan·gle [dang′gəl] *v.* **dan·gled, dan·gling** 1 To hang loosely and swing to and fro: The light cord *dangled* from the ceiling. 2 To hold or carry so as to swing loosely: to *dangle* a piece of string in front of a kitten. 3 To follow or hover about: My sister kept the company *dangling* for several weeks before she agreed to accept the job. **—dan′gler** *n.*
dangling participle A participle in a sentence that does not contain a word the participle can sensibly modify. In the sentence "Carrying a heavy pile of books, her foot caught on the step," *carrying* is a dangling participle. It appears to modify *foot,* but it cannot sensibly do so (a foot cannot carry books).
Dan·iel [dan′yəl] *n.* 1 In the Bible, a Hebrew prophet whose faith was so great that he stood in a den of lions and was not harmed. 2 A book of the Old Testament named after him.
Dan·ish [dā′nish] 1 *adj.* Of or from Denmark. 2 *n.* **(the Danish)** The people of Denmark. 3 *n.* The language of the Danes.
Danish pastry A pastry made of leavened dough, often glazed and filled, as with cheese, fruit, or nuts.
dank [dangk] *adj.* Unpleasantly cold and wet: The cellar can be *dank.* **—dank′ly** *adv.* **—dank′ness** *n.*
dap·per [dap′ər] *adj.* 1 Smartly dressed; trim. 2 Small and lively: a *dapper* elf.
dap·ple [dap′əl] *adj., v.* **dap·pled, dap·pling** 1 *adj.* Spotted; mottled. 2 *v.* To make spotted or mottled: Clouds *dappled* the sky. 3 *adj. use:* a *dappled* horse.
DAR or **D.A.R.** Daughters of the American Revolution.
dare [dâr] *v.* **dared** (or **durst**: seldom used today), **dar·ing,** *n.* 1 *v.* To have the courage or boldness to do something: I wouldn't *dare* challenge the expert. 2 *v.* To have the courage to face: The diver *dared* the dangers of the deep. 3 *v.* To challenge to do something: My friend *dared* me to climb the tree. 4 *n.* A challenge: I took the *dare* and climbed the tree. **—I dare say** Very likely; probably. ◆ *Dare,* when used with *he, she,* or *it* in the present tense, sometimes takes the form *dare* rather than *dares*: He *dare* not go; *Dare* he do it?
dare·dev·il [dâr′dev′əl] 1 *n.* A recklessly bold person. 2 *adj.* Reckless; rash.
dar·ing [dâr′ing] 1 *n.* Adventurous courage; bravery; boldness. 2 *adj.* Brave and adventurous; fearless. **—dar′ing·ly** *adv.*
dark [därk] 1 *adj.* Without light, or having little light: a *dark* night; a *dark* cave. 2 *n.* Darkness: The child is afraid of the *dark.* 3 *adj.* Having a deep shade; nearly black: *dark* blue. 4 *adj.* Gloomy: to look on the *dark* side of things. 5 *adj.* Evil: *dark* deeds. 6 *adj.* Having little knowledge or understanding; ignorant. **—in the dark** In ignorance. **—dark′ness** *n.*
Dark Ages A name given to the early Middle Ages because the period was thought to be one of little knowledge or progress.
dark·en [där′kən] *v.* To make or become dark.
dark horse A contestant who wins unexpectedly, especially in a political campaign.
dark·ling [därk′ling] 1 *adj.* Dark, or occurring in the dark. 2 *adv.* In the dark. ◆ This word is used mostly in poems.
dark·ly [därk′lē] *adv.* 1 Gloomily: He looked *darkly* at me. 2 Mysteriously: to hint *darkly.*
dark·room [därk′ro͞om′] *n.* A dark room where film may be processed.
dar·ling [där′ling] 1 *n.* A person very dearly loved: often used as a form of address. 2 *adj.* Dearly loved: my *darling* child.
darn¹ [därn] 1 *v.* To mend (cloth) by filling the hole or tear with crossing stitches. 2 *n.* A place mended by darning.
darn² [därn] *interj. informal* Another word for DAMN, used as a mild exclamation or curse.
darning needle 1 A long needle having a large eye, used in darning. 2 Another word for DRAGONFLY.
dart [därt] 1 *n.* A small, pointed missile that can

a	add	**i**	it	**o͝o**	took	**oi**	oil
ā	ace	**ī**	ice	**o͞o**	pool	**ou**	pout
â	care	**o**	odd	**u**	up	**ng**	ring
ä	palm	**ō**	open	**û**	burn	**th**	thin
e	end	**ô**	order	**yo͞o**	fuse	**th**	this
ē	equal					**zh**	vision

ə = {a in *above* e in *sicken* i in *possible* / o in *melon* u in *circus*}

D

be thrown by hand or blown from a blowgun. It is used in a game, **darts**, or as a weapon. **2** *n.* A sudden, quick movement: The deer made a *dart* across the road. **3** *v.* To move suddenly and swiftly: Fish *dart* through the water. **4** *v.* To throw or send out suddenly or swiftly: We *darted* an angry look at the people talking in the movies.

dash [dash] **1** *v.* To throw violently so as to break or shatter: Angrily he *dashed* the vase to pieces. **2** *v.* To strike; hit: Waves *dashed* against the rocks. **3** *n.* A striking against; blow: the *dash* of rain on a windowpane. **4** *v.* To splash or sprinkle: The coach *dashed* water on the boxer's face. **5** *v.* To destroy; ruin: to *dash* hopes. **6** *v.* To rush: The children *dashed* out onto the playground. **7** *n.* A short race; sprint: a 50-yard *dash.* **8** *n.* A small bit: a *dash* of salt. **9** *n.* Spirit; zest: The Johnsons always add *dash* to a party. **10** *n.* A horizontal line (—) used as a punctuation mark, usually to show a pause or break in a sentence.

dash·board [dash'bôrd'] *n.* The panel below the windshield of an automobile or other vehicle that holds the dials and controls.

Dashboard of an automobile

dash·er [dash'ər] *n.* **1** A person that dashes. **2** A dashing person. **3** The plunger of a churn.

da·shi·ki [də·shē'kē] *n.* A loose-fitting pullover garment of West African origin, usually brightly colored and worn by men.

dash·ing [dash'ing] *adj.* **1** Full of spirit; energetic: a *dashing* actor. **2** Colorful; gay: a *dashing* outfit. **—dash'ing·ly** *adv.*

das·tard [das'tərd] **1** *n.* A mean, sneaky coward. **2** *adj.* Dastardly.

das·tard·ly [das'tərd·lē] *adj.* Cowardly and mean: a *dastardly* act.

da·ta [dā'tə] *n.pl.* Facts or figures; information. ◆ *Data* comes from a plural Latin word meaning *things given.* Its singular form, *datum,* is rarely used today, and *data* is now commonly used with either a plural or a singular verb.

data bank A data base.

data base A collection of information, as about a particular company or subject, usually stored in a computer.

da·ta·ma·tion [dā'tə·mā'shən] *n.* Data processing.

data processing The collection, processing, storage, and distribution of information, especially through the use of electronic computers.

date[1] [dāt] *n., v.* **dat·ed, dat·ing** **1** *n.* The time of some event: The *date* of the landing of the Mayflower was 1620. **2** *n.* The day of the month: What's today's *date*? **3** *n.* A date written or inscribed on something: The *date* is part of the heading of a letter. **4** *v.* To mark with a date: to *date* a painting. **5** *v.* To find out the age of; give a date to: to *date* a fossil. **6** *n.* A certain period of time: At that *date* video games were just becoming popular. **7** *v.* To belong to a certain period: This picture *dates* from the 14th century. **8** *n. informal* A social appointment for a certain time. **9** *n. informal* A person with whom such an appointment is made. **10** *v. informal* To have a date or dates with: The secretary of the class has been *dating* my best friend. **—out of date** Old-fashioned. **—up to date** **1** In fashion; modern. **2** Up to the present time; till now. **—dat'a·ble** or **date'a·ble** *adj.* **—dat'er** *n.*

date[2] [dāt] *n.* **1** The sweet fruit of a type of palm tree. **2** The tree bearing this fruit, often called **date palm.**

Date palm

dat·ed [dā'tid] *adj.* **1** Marked with a date: a *dated* certificate of vaccination. **2** Old-fashioned; out of date: *dated* clothing.

date·less [dāt'lis] *adj.* **1** Bearing no date. **2** Ageless; enduring: a jewel's *dateless* beauty.

date line Another name for INTERNATIONAL DATE LINE.

da·tive [dā'tiv] **1** *adj.* Showing the case of or indicating the indirect object of a verb. In "I gave Linda the book," Linda is in the dative case. **2** *n.* A word in the dative case. **3** *n.* The dative case. ◆ In certain languages, as Latin and Greek, datives have special endings.

da·tum [dā'təm] *n.* Singular of DATA.

daub [dôb] **1** *v.* To smear or coat with a sticky or greasy substance: to *daub* plaster on a wall. **2** *n.* Something daubed on. **3** *v.* To smear on or paint without skill: to *daub* colors on a canvas. **4** *n.* A poor painting. **—daub'er** *n.*

daugh·ter [dô'tər] *n.* **1** A girl or woman, considered in relation to either or both of her parents. **2** A girl or woman regarded as an offspring or descendant: a *daughter* of Spain.

daughter cell Either of the two cells formed when a cell undergoes division.

daugh·ter-in-law [dô'tər·in·lô'] *n., pl.* **daugh·ters-in-law** The wife of one's son.

daugh·ter·ly [dô'tər·lē] *adj.* Of, having to do with, or appropriate for a daughter.

daunt [dônt] *v.* To frighten or discourage.

daunt·less [dônt'lis] *adj.* Fearless; brave; daring. **—daunt'less·ly** *adv.* **—daunt'less·ness** *n.*

dau·phin [dô'fin] *n.* The eldest son of the king of France: a title no longer used.

DAV Disabled American Veterans.

dav·en·port [dav'ən·pôrt'] *n. U.S.* A large upholstered sofa. Some open out to form beds.

Da·vid [dā'vid] *n.* In the Bible, the second king of Israel, father of Solomon.

dav·it [dav'it] *n.* One of a pair of small cranes on a ship's side for raising and lowering small boats.

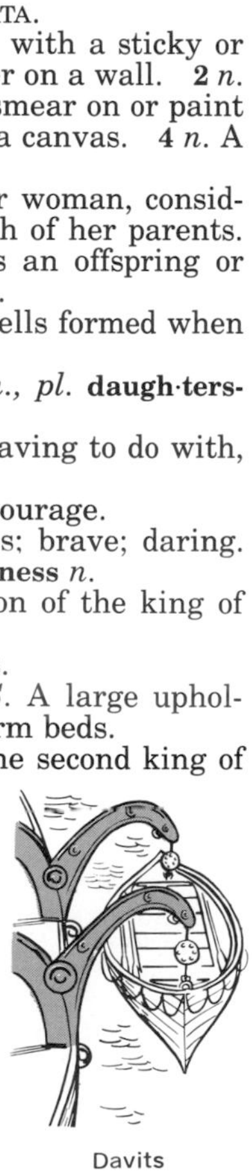
Davits

Da·vy Jones [dā'vē jōnz'] The spirit of the sea: a humorous name used by sailors. **—Davy Jones's locker** The bottom of the sea, especially as the graveyard of those drowned or buried at sea.

daw [dô] *n.* Another name for JACKDAW.

daw·dle [dôd'(ə)l] *v.* **daw·dled, daw·dling** To waste time; idle. **—daw'dler** *n.*

dawn [dôn] 1 *n.* The first appearance of light in the morning. 2 *v.* To begin to grow light in the morning. 3 *n.* An awakening; beginning: the *dawn* of a new period in history. 4 *v.* To begin to appear or develop: New hope *dawned* on his face. 5 *v.* To begin to be clear to the mind: The truth just *dawned* on me.

day [dā] *n.* 1 The time between sunrise and sunset. 2 The period of 24 hours from one midnight to the next. 3 The time of the day a person spends at work: an eight-hour *day.* 4 A time or period; age: the present *day*; in Caesar's *day.* 5 (*pl.*) A lifetime, or part of one: Doctors spend their *days* treating the sick.

day·bed [dā'bed'] *n.* A couch that can be turned into a bed.

day·book [dā'bo͝ok'] *n.* 1 A diary. 2 An old-fashioned kind of book for keeping records of accounts.

day·break [dā'brāk'] *n.* Dawn: The farmer was up at *daybreak* to milk the cows.

day-care center [da'kâr'] 1 A place where children of preschool age are looked after during the daytime when their parents are at work. 2 A social and medical center for the elderly.

day·dream [dā'drēm'] 1 *n.* A pleasant, dreamlike thought, as of something one wishes would happen. 2 *v.* To have daydreams. **—day'dream'er** *n.*

day·light [dā'līt'] *n.* 1 Light from the sun; light of day. 2 Dawn; daybreak.

day·light-sav·ing time [dā'līt'sā'ving] Time which is an hour ahead of standard time, usually used in the summer. Nine o'clock standard time is 10 o'clock daylight-saving time.

Day of Atonement Another name for YOM KIPPUR.

day school A school that has classes only during the day and does not board its pupils.

day·star [dā'stär'] *n.* 1 Another name for MORNING STAR. 2 The sun: seldom used today.

day·time [dā'tīm'] *n.* The time of the day between sunrise and sunset.

day-to-day [dā'tə·dā'] *adj.* 1 Of or occurring every day; daily: the *day-to-day* routine. 2 Concerned with the needs and pleasures of the present, not with the future.

daze [dāz] *v.* **dazed, daz·ing,** *n.* 1 *v.* To confuse or bewilder; stun: to be *dazed* by a blow on the head. 2 *n.* A dazed condition.

daz·zle [daz'(ə)l] *v.* **daz·zled, daz·zling,** *n.* 1 *v.* To blind or dim the vision of by too much light: to be *dazzled* by intense sunshine. 2 *v.* To charm, bewilder, or overpower, as with a brilliant display: The violinist *dazzled* the audience with her skill. 3 *n.* The act of dazzling. 4 *n.* Something that dazzles. **—daz'zler** *n.* **—daz'zling·ly** *adv.*

db or **dB** decibel.

D. Bib. Douay Bible.

dc, d.c., DC, or **D.C.** direct current.

DC Postal Service abbreviation of District of Columbia.

D.C. District of Columbia.

D.D. Doctor of Divinity.

D.D.S. Doctor of Dental Surgery.

DDT Dichloro-diphenyl-trichloro-ethane, a toxic organic chemical that tends to accumulate in plant and animal tissues, formerly widely used as an insecticide.

de- A prefix meaning: 1 To remove from, as in *dethrone.* 2 To remove, as in *debug.* 3 To reduce, as in *devalue.* 4 To do the opposite of; reverse, as in *decriminalize.* 5 To get off of, as in *deplane.*

DE Postal Service abbreviation of Delaware.

dea·con [dē'kən] *n.* 1 A clergyman who is next below a priest in rank. 2 A church official who helps a clergyman in things not connected with actual worship.

dea·con·ess [dē'kə·nis] *n.* A woman who serves as an assistant in a church.

de·ac·ti·vate [de·ak'tə·vāt'] *v.* **de·ac·ti·vat·ed, de·ac·ti·vat·ing** 1 To make inactive. 2 To remove from active military duty.

dead [ded] 1 *adj.* Without life: *dead* leaves. 2 *n. use:* Dead people: The *dead* are remembered on Memorial Day. 3 *adj.* Not having interest or excitement; dull: a *dead* town. 4 *adj.* Not working or operating: a *dead* battery. 5 *adj.* No longer used: a *dead* language. 6 *n.* The coldest or darkest part: the *dead* of night. 7 *adj.* Sure; accurate: a *dead* shot. 8 *adj.* Absolute; complete: a *dead* certainty. 9 *adv.* Absolutely: You are *dead* right. 10 *adv.* Directly: *dead* ahead. **—dead'ness** *n.*

dead·beat [ded'bēt'] *n. slang* 1 A person who does not pay his debts or pay for what he is getting. 2 A loafer; idler.

dead·en [ded'(ə)n] *v.* 1 To take away the sensation of; make numb: to *deaden* a nerve with anesthetic. 2 To lessen the force of; weaken: Thick carpets *deaden* noise.

dead-end [ded'end'] *adj.* Being or like a dead end.

dead end 1 A passageway, as a street, having no exit at one end. 2 A position or situation from which there is no possibility of progress.

dead heat A race in which two or more finish together; tie.

dead letter 1 A letter that is not claimed or cannot be delivered because of an incorrect address. 2 A law that is not enforced.

dead·line [ded'līn'] *n.* A date or time by which something must be done or finished.

dead·lock [ded'lok'] 1 *n.* A stopping of activity because opposing sides are equally strong and neither one will give in. 2 *v.* To cause or reach a deadlock.

dead·ly [ded'lē] *adj.* **dead·li·er, dead·li·est,** *adv.* 1 *adj.* Likely or certain to cause death: a *deadly* poison. 2 *adj.* Filled with enough hatred and violence to kill: a *deadly* fight; a *deadly* enemy. 3 *adj.* Deathlike: The patient had a *deadly* pallor. 4 *adj. informal* Very boring or lifeless. 5 *adv. informal* Very: *deadly* dull. **—dead'li·ness** *n.*

deadly nightshade Another name for BELLADONNA (def. 1).

dead·pan [ded'pan'] *informal* 1 *adj.* Showing or expressing no emotion. 2 *adv.* In a deadpan manner.

dead reckoning The locating of a ship's position without observing the sun or stars, by charting the direction and distance traveled.

dead·weight [ded'wāt'] *n.* 1 The weight of some-

a	add	**i**	it	**o͝o**	took	**oi**	oil
ā	ace	**ī**	ice	**o͞o**	pool	**ou**	pout
â	care	**o**	odd	**u**	up	**ng**	ring
ä	palm	**ō**	open	**û**	burn	**th**	thin
e	end	**ô**	order	**yo͞o**	fuse	**t͟h**	this
ē	equal					**zh**	vision

ə = { a in *above* e in *sicken* i in *possible*
o in *melon* u in *circus* }

thing heavy and unmoving. **2** Any heavy or unnecessary burden.
dead·wood [ded′wŏŏd′] *n., pl.* **deadwood** A useless or worthless person or thing.
deaf [def] *adj.* **1** Completely or partially unable to hear. **2** Unwilling to listen: Some people are *deaf* to good advice. **—deaf′ly** *adv.* **—deaf′ness** *n.*
deaf·en [def′ən] *v.* **1** To make deaf. **2** To confuse or overwhelm with noise: The noise of the truck *deafened* everyone on the street.
deaf-mute [def′myŏŏt′] *n.* A person who can neither hear nor speak.
deal [dēl] *v.* **dealt, deal·ing,** *n.* **1** *v.* To be concerned with; have to do with: Biology *deals* with plants and animals. **2** *v.* To consider, discuss, or take action: to *deal* with a problem; to *deal* justly with a criminal. **3** *v.* To do business; trade: This store *deals* in furniture. **4** *n. informal* A bargain or transaction: a business *deal.* **5** *v.* To give: The cat *dealt* the dog a sharp blow on the nose. **6** *v.* To distribute among a number of persons: to *deal* playing cards. **7** *n.* A distributing of cards, or the cards dealt. **—a good deal** or **a great deal** **1** A large amount; a lot. **2** Much; a lot: Go *a good deal* faster.
deal·er [dē′lər] *n.* **1** A person whose business it is to buy and sell; a trader. **2** In card games, the player who deals the cards.
deal·ing [dē′ling] *n.* **1** (*usually pl.*) Relations with others: business *dealings.* **2** A way of acting: honest *dealing.*
dealt [delt] Past tense and past participle of DEAL.
dean [dēn] *n.* **1** A person in a college or university who is in charge of students, teachers, or a division of study: *dean* of student affairs; *dean* of the law school. **2** A clergyman who has charge of a cathedral. **3** The person who has been a member of a class or group the longest.
dear [dir] **1** *adj.* Beloved; precious: my *dear* child. **2** *n.* A loved person: *Dear,* will you help me make a cake? **3** *adj.* Highly regarded: used at the opening of letters: *Dear* Sir. **4** *adj.* Expensive: Food is *dear* during wartime. **5** *adv.* At great cost; dearly. **6** *interj.* An exclamation, as of surprise or regret: Oh, *dear*! **—dear′ness** *n.*
dear·ly [dir′lē] *adv.* **1** With much affection. **2** At great cost: I paid *dearly* for my inattention.
dearth [dûrth] *n.* **1** A great scarcity; inadequate supply; lack. **2** Famine.
death [deth] *n.* **1** The ending of life. **2** The condition of being dead. **3** A cause of death: This blizzard will be the *death* of us. **4** A wiping out; destruction: the *death* of a city. **—put to death** To kill; execute.
death·bed [deth′bed′] **1** *n.* The bed on which a person dies or has died. **2** *adj.* Made or done while dying: a *deathbed* confession.
death·blow [deth′blō′] *n.* **1** A blow that causes death. **2** An event that brings final destruction or defeat: The injury was the *deathblow* to my athletic career.
death·less [deth′lis] *adj.* That will live forever; immortal: *deathless* poetry.
death·like [deth′līk′] *adj.* Like or characteristic of death: a *deathlike* pallor.
death·ly [deth′lē] **1** *adj.* Like death: a *deathly* silence. **2** *adv.* As in death: *deathly* pale. **3** *adj.* Deadly; fatal. **4** *adv.* Very: *deathly* ill.
death rate The number of persons per thousand of population who die within a given time.
death row A row or block of cells reserved for prisoners who have been condemned to death.
death's-head [deths′hed′] *n.* A human skull, thought of as a symbol of death.

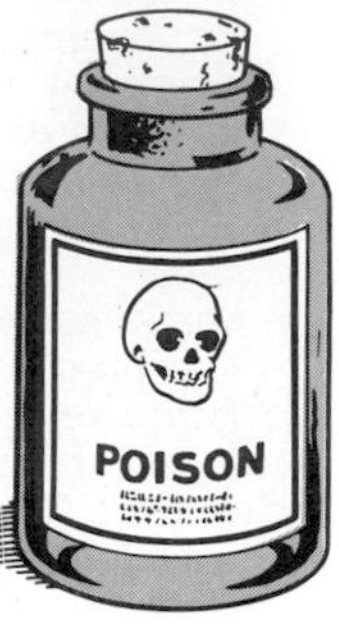

Death's-head

de·ba·cle [di·bäk′əl *or* di·bak′əl] *n.* A sudden, complete disaster or collapse; downfall: the *debacle* of the stock market in 1929.
de·bar [di·bär′] *v.* **de·barred, de·bar·ring** To bar; exclude: A person under 35 is *debarred* from being President.
de·bark [di·bärk′] *v.* To disembark.
de·base [di·bās′] *v.* **de·based, de·bas·ing** To lower in character or worth: Cheating *debases* a person; High prices cut down what a dollar will buy, and thus they *debase* it. **—de·base′ment** *n.*
de·bat·a·ble [di·bā′tə·bəl] *adj.* Open to doubt or disagreement: The wisdom of your plan to raise funds is *debatable.*
de·bate [di·bāt′] *v.* **de·bat·ed, de·bat·ing,** *n.* **1** *v.* To discuss or argue for or against, especially in a formal way between persons taking opposite sides of a question. **2** *v.* To try to decide; consider: to *debate* whether to go home. **3** *n.* The act of debating. **—de·bat′er** *n.*
de·bauch [di·bôch′] **1** *v.* To lead away from right and good conduct; corrupt. **2** *n.* An act or period of giving in too much to one's appetites or desires.
de·bauch·er·y [di·bô′chər·ē] *n., pl.* **de·bauch·er·ies** Too much giving in to physical desires and appetites; dissipation.
de·bil·i·tate [di·bil′ə·tāt′] *v.* **de·bil·i·tat·ed, de·bil·i·tat·ing** To weaken; make feeble: A long illness *debilitated* the vigorous athlete.
de·bil·i·ty [di·bil′ə·tē] *n.* Great weakness; feebleness or languor.
deb·it [deb′it] **1** *n.* An entry in an account of an amount owed. **2** *v.* To enter (a debt) in an account. **3** *v.* To charge with a debt. ◆ See DEBT.
deb·o·nair or **deb·o·naire** [deb′ə·nâr′] *adj.* Lively and pleasant; gracious; jaunty: a *debonair* person. **—deb′o·nair′ly** *adv.* **—deb′o·nair′ness** *n.*
de·brief [dē·brēf′] *v.* To question or instruct at the end of a mission or period of service: The commandos were carefully *debriefed* after their patrol behind enemy lines.
de·bris or **dé·bris** [də·brē′ *or* dā·brē′] *n.* Scattered fragments or remains; rubble: The explosion left much *debris.*

Debris

debt [det] *n.* **1** That which a person owes to another: a *debt* of ten dollars; a *debt* of gratitude. **2** The condition of owing; indebtedness: The store is in *debt* to the bank. ◆ *Debt* comes from an Old French word *dette.* The "b" was added later because the Latin word for "something owed" was *debitum,* from which the English word *debit* is also derived.
debt·or [det′ər] *n.* A person who owes something to another, as money or services.
de·bug [dē·bug′] *v.* **de·bugged, de·bug·ging** **1** To find and correct a defect, error, or malfunction in,

as a computer program. 2 To remove a concealed electronic device used for recording private conversations from: to *debug* an office.

de·bunk [di·bungk′] *v.* To expose the nonsense or false sentiment in: to *debunk* witchcraft.

de·but or **dé·but** [dā′byōō′ *or* dā·byōō′] *n.* 1 A first public appearance: an actor's *debut.* 2 A formal entrance into society, made at a party.

deb·u·tante or **dé·bu·tante** [deb′yə·tänt′ *or* dā′·byōō·tänt′] *n.* A young woman making a debut into society.

Dec. December.

deca- or **dec-** A combining form meaning: Ten, as in *decagon.*

dec·ade [dek′ād′] *n.* A period of ten years.

dec·a·dence [dek′ə·dəns *or* di·kād′(ə)ns] *n.* A process or period of decay or decline, especially in morals or art.

dec·a·dent [dek′ə·dənt *or* di·kād′(ə)nt] 1 *adj.* Characterized by or undergoing decadence. 2 *n.* A decadent person. **—dec′a·dent·ly** *adv.*

de·caf·fein·ate [dē·kaf′ə·nāt′] *v.* **de·caf·fein·at·ed, de·caf·fein·at·ing** To remove the caffeine from: to *decaffeinate* coffee.

dec·a·gon [dek′ə·gon′] *n.* A closed plane figure bounded by ten line segments.

dec·a·he·dron [dek′ə·hē′drən] *n.* A solid figure bounded by ten plane surfaces.

de·cal [de′kal′ *or* di·kal′] *n.* A shortened form of DECALCOMANIA.

de·cal·co·ma·ni·a [di·kal′kə·mā′nē·ə] *n.* A design or picture transferred from specially prepared paper to a surface, as glass or porcelain.

Decalcomania

de·ca·li·ter [dek′ə·lē′tər] *n.* Another spelling of DEKALITER.

Dec·a·logue [dek′ə·lôg′] *n.* (*sometimes written* **decalogue**) Another name for the TEN COMMANDMENTS.

de·camp [di·kamp′] *v.* 1 To leave suddenly or secretly. 2 To leave a camping ground.

de·cant [di·kant′] *v.* 1 To pour off (a liquid) without disturbing its sediment: to *decant* vinegar. 2 To pour into another container.

de·cant·er [di·kan′tər] *n.* A decorative, stoppered glass bottle for serving wine or liquor.

de·cap·i·tate [di·kap′ə·tāt′] *v.* **de·cap·i·tat·ed, de·cap·i·tat·ing** To cut off the head of; behead. **—de·cap′i·ta′tion** *n.*

Decanter

de·cath·lon [di·kath′lon] *n.* An athletic contest like a track meet in which each contestant must take part in all ten events.

de·cay [di·kā′] 1 *v.* To rot or cause to rot: Fruit *decays* in a hot room; Too much candy can *decay* teeth. 2 *n.* A rotting. 3 *v.* To decline, as in health, power, or beauty. 4 *n.* A falling into ruin. 5 *n.* A steady, natural decrease in the radioactivity of a substance as unstable atoms disintegrate into stabler forms. 6 *v.* To undergo such a decrease in radioactivity. 7 *n.* A decrease in the altitude of a satellite's orbit. 8 *v.* To move into a lower orbit: The satellite is *decaying* and will soon fall to earth.

de·cease [di·sēs′] *n., v.* **de·ceased, de·ceas·ing** 1 *n.* Death. 2 *v.* To die. ◆ See DECEASED.

de·ceased [di·sēst′] 1 *adj.* Dead. 2 *n. use*: A dead person or persons: The *deceased* left a great deal of money to charity.

de·ce·dent [di·sē′dənt] *n.* In law, a dead person.

de·ceit [di·sēt′] *n.* 1 The act of deceiving; lying or cheating. 2 A lie or a dishonest trick. 3 A tendency or readiness to deceive.

de·ceit·ful [di·sēt′fəl] *adj.* Tending to deceive; lying or treacherous: a *deceitful* person. **—de·ceit′ful·ly** *adv.* **—de·ceit′ful·ness** *n.*

de·ceive [di·sēv′] *v.* **de·ceived, de·ceiv·ing** To cause to take as true something that is not true; fool or mislead, as by lying: They *deceived* us about the true purpose of their visit. **—de·ceiv′er** *n.* ◆ *Deceive, mislead,* and *delude* all refer to making someone believe as true something that is false or accept as worthwhile something that is without value. *Mislead* is the most general of these words. It can be used to describe a simple error in judgment: A warm day in February *misled* us into thinking we would have an early spring. It can refer to a deception that is innocent and unplanned: Directions in a foreign language can easily *mislead* you. It can also suggest something deliberate and tricky: The advertiser's false claims *misled* customers into paying high prices for third-rate merchandise. There is never anything innocent about an attempt to *deceive.* Anyone who deceives another is always deliberate in the distortion of truth or reality: The candidate's speech *deceived* voters about the seriousness of the recession. *Delude* is close in meaning to *deceive* but suggests an attempt to make a fool or victim out of the person who is deluded: The computer school *deluded* many young people about their abilities, leading them to take more courses than necessary for their future careers. **—de·ceiv′·er** *n.* **—de·ceiv′ing·ly** *adv.*

de·cel·er·ate [dē·sel′ə·rāt′] *v.* **de·cel·er·at·ed, de·cel·er·at·ing** To move or cause to move at a lesser speed; slow down. **—de·cel′er·a′tion** *n.* **—de·cel′er·a′tor** *n.*

De·cem·ber [di·sem′bər] *n.* The 12th month of the year, having 31 days.

de·cen·cy [dē′sən·sē] *n., pl.* **de·cen·cies** 1 The quality of being decent; proper character or behavior: They didn't even have the *decency* to thank us. 2 (*usually pl.*) Things needed for a pleasant, proper life.

de·cent [dē′sənt] *adj.* 1 Proper; respectable: *decent* clothes. 2 Reasonably good; fair; adequate: A mechanic makes a *decent* living. 3 Kind or kindhearted; generous: a *decent* person. **—de′cent·ly** *adv.* ◆ *Decent, descent,* and *dissent* look and sound rather alike but are not related. *Decent* [dē′sənt] is from a Latin word meaning *fitting* and still means *fitting* or *proper. Descent* [di·sent′] comes from a Latin verb meaning *to climb down,* and it still means *a coming down. Dissent* [di·

a	add	**i**	it	**o͝o**	took	**oi**	oil
ā	ace	**ī**	ice	**o͞o**	pool	**ou**	pout
â	care	**o**	odd	**u**	up	**ng**	ring
ä	palm	**ō**	open	**û**	burn	**th**	thin
e	end	**ô**	order	**yo͞o**	fuse	**t͟h**	this
ē	equal					**zh**	vision

ə = {a in *above* e in *sicken* i in *possible* / o in *melon* u in *circus*}

sent′] is from a Latin verb meaning *to feel opposed* or *apart.* It is now either a noun meaning *disagreement* or a verb meaning *to disagree.*

de·cen·tral·ize [dē·sen′trəl·īz′] *v.* **de·cen·tral·ized, de·cen·tral·iz·ing** To lessen the central authority, as of a government, by giving local groups more power. **—de·cen′tral·i·za′tion** *n.*

de·cep·tion [di·sep′shən] *n.* **1** The act of deceiving or tricking: a magician's *deception* of an audience. **2** A being deceived. **3** Something that deceives; an illusion; fraud.

de·cep·tive [di·sep′tiv] *adj.* That deceives or is meant to deceive; misleading: Statistics can be *deceptive.* **—de·cep′tive·ly** *adv.* **—de·cep′tive·ness** *n.*

de·cer·ti·fy [dē·sûr′tə·fī′] *v.* **de·cer·ti·fied, de·cer·ti·fy·ing** To revoke the certification of. **—de·cer·ti·fi·ca·tion** [dē·sûr′tə·fə·kā′shən] *n.*

deci- A combining form meaning: One tenth, as in *decigram.*

de·ci·bel [des′ə·bel′ *or* des′ə·bəl] *n.* A unit used in comparing the loudness of sounds, the strength of electrical signals, or the like. When the unit is used for sounds, zero often corresponds to barely audible sounds and 130 to painfully loud ones.

de·cide [di·sīd′] *v.* **de·cid·ed, de·cid·ing** **1** To make up one's mind; come to a decision: She *decided* to become a computer programmer. **2** To determine or settle: The jury will *decide* whether the defendant is guilty.

de·cid·ed [di·sī′did] *adj.* **1** Definite: There is a *decided* improvement in the group's test scores. **2** Resolute; sure; determined: a *decided* manner. **—de·cid′ed·ly** *adv.* **—de·cid′ed·ness** *n.*

de·cid·u·ous [di·sij′ōō·əs] *adj.* **1** Falling off at a certain time of year or when fully developed: *deciduous* leaves; *deciduous* antlers. **2** Shedding leaves every year: *deciduous* trees. ◆ See EVERGREEN.

dec·i·gram [des′ə·gram′] *n.* In the metric system, a unit of mass or weight equal to one tenth of a gram.

dec·i·li·ter [des′ə·lē′tər] *n.* In the metric system, a unit of volume equal to one tenth of a liter.

dec·i·mal [des′ə·məl] **1** *n.* A fraction written using base ten and place values to show 10 or 10 multiplied by itself some number of times as its denominator, as 0.3 (3/10), 0.27 (27/100), 0.034 (34/1000), etc. **2** *adj.* Of or based on the number 10: a *decimal* system; a *decimal* fraction. ◆ *Decimal* comes from a Latin word meaning *tenth.*

decimal fraction A decimal (def. 1).

decimal point A dot used in decimal numbers to separate the whole number part from the decimal fraction, as in 1.37 (1 + 37/100).

dec·i·mate [des′ə·māt′] *v.* **dec·i·mat·ed, dec·i·mat·ing** To destroy or kill a large part of: The gypsy moths *decimated* the forest. **—dec′i·ma′tion** *n.*

dec·i·me·ter [des′ə·mē′tər] *n.* In the metric system, a unit of length equal to one tenth of a meter.

de·ci·pher [di·sī′fər] *v.* **1** To translate from cipher or code into plain language; decode. **2** To determine the meaning of: to *decipher* a garbled telegram; to *decipher* hieroglyphics.

de·ci·sion [di·sizh′ən] *n.* **1** A making up of one's mind. **2** A conclusion or judgment. **3** Firmness; determination: to act with *decision.*

de·ci·sive [di·sī′siv] *adj.* **1** Putting an end to doubt: a *decisive* victory. **2** Showing decision; firm: a *decisive* statement. **3** Very important; crucial: a *decisive* moment. **—de·ci′sive·ly** *adv.*

deck [dek] **1** *n.* Any floor or platform extending from side to side of a ship. It may be open or roofed over by another deck. **2** *n.* A pack of playing cards. **3** *v.* To dress or adorn: They *decked* the room with crepe paper and balloons.

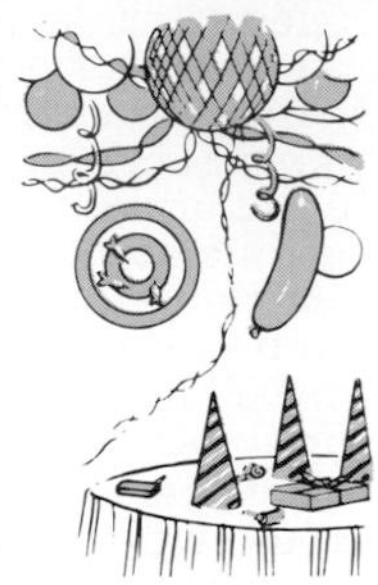

A room decked out for a party

deck chair A folding chair, usually having arms and a leg rest.

deck·hand [dek′hand′] *n.* A sailor who does manual tasks on deck.

de·claim [di·klām′] *v.* To speak loudly and forcefully in the manner of an orator.

dec·la·ma·tion [dek′lə·mā′shən] *n.* **1** The act or art of declaiming. **2** Something that is or may be declaimed, as a formal speech.

de·clam·a·to·ry [di·klam′ə·tôr′ē] *adj.* **1** Having to do with or used for declamation. **2** Loud and forceful: *declamatory* speech.

dec·la·ra·tion [dek′lə·rā′shən] *n.* A formal statement or announcement: a *declaration* of war.

Declaration of Independence The formal proclamation that the 13 American colonies were free and independent of Great Britain. It was adopted on July 4, 1776.

de·clar·a·tive [di·klar′ə·tiv] *adj.* Making a statement: "I'll be home at five o'clock" is a *declarative* sentence.

de·clare [di·klâr′] *v.* **de·clared, de·clar·ing** **1** To make known to be; announce formally; proclaim: to *declare* war; The company was *declared* bankrupt. **2** To say forcefully; assert: All the guests *declared* they had never eaten a better meal. **3** To describe or make a list of (taxable things): We *declared* everything we bought overseas.

de·clas·si·fy [dē·klas′ə·fī] *v.* **de·clas·si·fied, de·clas·si·fy·ing** To remove from the category of classified information.

de·clen·sion [di·klen′shən] *n.* **1** The changing of the forms or endings of nouns, pronouns, or adjectives according to case. The declension of *they* consists of *they, their* or *theirs, them.* **2** A class of words having similar endings or forms in each case.

dec·li·na·tion [dek′lə·nā′shən] *n.* **1** An inclining or bending downward. **2** The deviation of a compass needle from true north or true south. **3** A polite or formal refusal.

de·cline [di·klīn′] *v.* **de·clined, de·clin·ing,** *n.* **1** *v.* To refuse in a polite way: to *decline* an invitation. **2** *v.* To lessen or fail gradually: His health *declined* over the years. **3** *n.* A gradual lessening or failing: the *decline* of a nation's power. **4** *v.* To slope or bend downward: The land gently *declines* to the sea. **5** *n.* A downward slope. **6** *v.* To give the declension of (a noun, pronoun, or adjective).

de·cliv·i·ty [di·kliv′ə·tē] *n., pl.* **de·cliv·i·ties** **1** A surface, as of a hill, that slopes downward. **2** A sloping downward.

de·code [dē·kōd′] *v.* **de·cod·ed, de·cod·ing** To translate from code into plain language.

dé·col·le·té [dā′kol(ə)·tā′] *adj.* Having or wearing a low neckline: a *décolleté* evening dress.

de·com·pose [dē′kəm·pōz′] *v.* **de·com·posed, de·com·pos·ing** **1** To decay; rot. **2** To separate into its basic parts or elements: to *decompose* water into hydrogen and oxygen.

de·com·po·si·tion [dē′kom·pə·zish′ən] *n.* **1** The process or result of decay. **2** A separating into basic parts or elements.

de·com·pres·sion [dē′kəm·presh′ən] *n.* The lowering or removing of pressure, especially of air.

de·con·tam·i·nate [dē′kən·tam′ə·nat′] *v.* To rid of contamination; purify. **—de′con·tam′i·na′tion** *n.*

de·con·trol [dē′kən·trōl′] *v.* **de·con·trolled, de·con·trol·ling,** *n.* **1** *v.* To remove controls from, especially legal controls or limits: to *decontrol* rents. **2** *n.* The act of decontrolling.

de·cor or **dé·cor** [dā·kôr′ *or* dā′kôr] *n.* **1** The style of interior decoration, as of a room or house. **2** Stage scenery.

dec·o·rate [dek′ə·rāt′] *v.* **dec·o·rat·ed, dec·o·rat·ing** **1** To make more fancy, pretty, or attractive by adding ornaments or frills: to *decorate* a street with colored lights. **2** To paint, paper, or add new furnishings to (as a room or house). **3** To honor with a medal or ribbon.

dec·o·ra·tion [dek′ə·rā′shən] *n.* **1** The act of decorating. **2** Something used for decorating; ornament. **3** A medal or other sign given as a mark of honor.

Decoration Day Another name for MEMORIAL DAY.

dec·o·ra·tive [dek′(ə)rə·tiv *or* dek′ə·rā′tiv] *adj.* Serving to decorate; ornamental.

dec·o·ra·tor [dek′ə·rā′tər] **1** *n.* A person who decorates, especially an interior decorator. **2** *adj.* Used in or suitable for interior decoration: *decorator* colors.

dec·o·rous [dek′ə·rəs *or* di·kôr′əs] *adj.* Proper or dignified; decent. **—dec′o·rous·ly** *adv.* **—dec′o·rous·ness** *n.*

de·co·rum [di·kôr′əm] *n.* Something proper, as behavior, speech, dress, or seemliness.

de·coy [*n.* dē′koi′ *or* di·koi′, *v.* di·koi′] **1** *n.* A bird or animal trained to lure game into a trap or into shooting range. **2** *n.* An imitation duck used to lure real ducks. **3** *n.* A person or thing used as a lure. **4** *v.* To lure or entice into danger or a trap.

A decoy duck

de·crease [*v.* di·krēs′, *n.* dē′krēs *or* di·krēs′] *v.* **de·creased, de·creas·ing,** *n.* **1** *v.* To make or become less: to *decrease* the amount of sugar in a recipe for cookies; Their influence *decreased.* **2** *n.* A lessening; reduction: a *decrease* in population. **—de·creas′ing·ly** *adv.*

de·cree [di·krē′] *n., v.* **de·creed, de·cree·ing** **1** *n.* A formal order or decision, as by a government or court. **2** *v.* To proclaim by a decree: The governor *decreed* a state holiday.

dec·re·ment [dek′rə·mənt] *n.* The amount by which a variable decreases.

de·crep·it [di·krep′it] *adj.* Worn out or feeble from old age or much use: a *decrepit* old hound.

de·crep·i·tude [di·krep′ə·t(y)o͞od′] *n.* The condition of being decrepit.

de·cre·scen·do [dā′krə·shen′dō] *n., pl.* **de·cre·scen·dos,** *adj., adv.* **1** *n.* A gradual decrease in loudness in a musical passage; diminuendo. **2** *n.* A musical passage played or sung with a decrescendo. **3** *adj.* With a gradual decrease in loudness. **4** *adv.* With a gradual decrease in loudness.

de·crim·i·nal·ize [dē·krim′ə·nəl·īz′] *v.* **de·crim·i·nal·ized, de·crim·i·nal·iz·ing** To stop treating as criminal or illegal. **—de·crim′i·nal·i·za′tion** *n.*

de·cry [di·krī′] *v.* **de·cried, de·cry·ing** To speak critically of; condemn: to *decry* bribery in government.

ded·i·cate [ded′ə·kāt′] *v.* **ded·i·cat·ed, ded·i·cat·ing** **1** To set apart for or devote to a special purpose: to *dedicate* one's life to science. **2** To write or say publicly that one has written (as a book or symphony) as a sign of affection or respect for a person named.

D

ded·i·ca·tion [ded′ə·kā′shən] *n.* **1** The act of dedicating. **2** A being dedicated. **3** The words dedicating a book or other work to someone.

ded·i·ca·to·ry [ded′ə·kə·tôr′ē] *adj.* That is or serves as a dedication: a *dedicatory* inscription.

de·duce [di·d(y)o͞os′] *v.* **de·duced, de·duc·ing** To arrive at by reasoning; infer.

de·duct [di·dukt′] *v.* To take away; subtract: If you *deduct* 7 from 10, you get 3.

de·duct·i·ble [di·duk′tə·bəl] *adj.* That can be deducted, especially from taxable income.

de·duc·tion [di·duk′shən] *n.* **1** A conclusion based on reasoning; inference: If everyone who took the test passed, and I took the test, then it is a simple *deduction* that I passed. **2** This form of reasoning. **3** An amount deducted: a $30 *deduction.* **4** A taking away; subtraction.

de·duc·tive [di·duk′tiv] *adj.* Of, based on, or reached by deduction. **—de·duc′tive·ly** *adv.*

deed [dēd] **1** *n.* Anything done; an act: a heroic *deed.* **2** *n.* A legal document showing ownership of property. **3** *v.* To give over ownership of by a deed: to *deed* a house to the buyer.

deem [dēm] *v.* To judge; consider: It was *deemed* advisable to accept the offer at once.

deep [dēp] **1** *adj.* Extending far below a surface: *deep* water; a *deep* cut. **2** *adj.* Extending far in or back: a *deep* dresser drawer. **3** *adj.* Being or reaching a certain distance down, in, or back: The hole is four feet *deep.* **4** *adv.* Far down, in, or back: to dig *deep.* **5** *n.* A very deep place, especially the ocean: used mostly in poems. **6** *adj.* Having a low pitch: a *deep* voice. **7** *adj.* Difficult to understand; complicated: a *deep* person. **8** *adj.* Having the mind occupied; absorbed: to be *deep* in thought. **9** *adj.* Intense; great; profound: *deep* feelings; a *deep* sleep. **10** *adj.* Vivid and dark: *deep* red. **11** *n.* The darkest or most intense part: the *deep* of night. **—deep′ly** *adv.* **—deep′ness** *n.*

deep·en [dē′pən] *v.* To make or become deep or deeper: to *deepen* a well; The darkness *deepens.*

deep-root·ed [dēp′ro͞o′tid] *adj.* **1** Rooted deep in the ground. **2** Firmly held: a *deep-rooted* loyalty.

deep-sea [dēp′sē′] *adj.* In or having to do with the deeper parts of the sea: *deep-sea* fish.

deep-seat·ed [dēp′sē′tid] *adj.* Firmly established; hard to root out or change: *deep-seated* prejudice.

deep-set [dēp′set′] *adj.* Placed or appearing as if placed deep in the skull: *deep-set* eyes.

a	add	**i**	it	**o͝o**	took	**oi**	oil
ā	ace	**ī**	ice	**o͞o**	pool	**ou**	pout
â	care	**o**	odd	**u**	up	**ng**	ring
ä	palm	**ō**	open	**û**	burn	**th**	thin
e	end	**ô**	order	**yo͞o**	fuse	**t͟h**	this
ē	equal					**zh**	vision

ə = a in *above* e in *sicken* i in *possible* o in *melon* u in *circus*

deer [dir] *n., pl.* **deer** A swift, graceful wild animal that chews its cud. The male usually has antlers which are shed yearly. ◆ *Deer* comes from an Old English word meaning *beast.* Gradually, over the years, *deer* came to be the name of one special kind of beast.

deer·skin [dir′skin′] *n.* 1 A deer's hide. 2 Leather made from it.

de-es·ca·late [dē-es′kə·lāt′] *v.* **de-es·ca·lat·ed, de-es·ca·lat·ing** To decrease to a lower intensity or smaller scope: to *de-escalate* a war by withdrawing troops. **—de-es′ca·la′tion** *n.*

def. 1 defense. 2 definite. 3 definition.

de·face [di·fās′] *v.* **de·faced, de·fac·ing** To spoil the looks of; mar: to *deface* a statue. **—de·face′ment** *n.*

A defaced statue

de fac·to [dē fak′tō] Actual or functioning, whether legal or not. See DE JURE.

def·a·ma·tion [def′ə·mā′shən] *n.* The act of defaming; slander or libel.

de·fam·a·to·ry [di·fam′·ə·tôr′ē] *adj.* That defames: a *defamatory* newspaper article.

de·fame [di·fām′] *v.* **de·famed, de·fam·ing** To say untrue or harmful things about the character or reputation of; slander or libel. **—de·fam′er** *n.*

de·fault [di·fôlt′] 1 *n.* A failure to do something required or expected, as to appear in court or take part in or finish a game or contest: to lose by *default.* 2 *v.* To fail to pay (money) or fail to do (something expected or required): to *default* a loan. **—de·fault′er** *n.*

de·feat [di·fēt′] 1 *v.* To gain a victory over; conquer; beat: to *defeat* a nation in war. 2 *n.* A defeating: Rutgers' *defeat* of Columbia. 3 *n.* A being defeated: Columbia's *defeat* by Rutgers. 4 *v.* To keep from succeeding; thwart; frustrate.

de·feat·ist [di·fē′tist] 1 *n.* A person who gives up too easily because of the expectation of defeat or failure. 2 *adj.* Of, like, or held by a defeatist: *defeatist* reasoning. **—de·feat′ism** *n.*

def·e·cate [def′ə·cāt′] *v.* **def·e·cat·ed, def·e·cat·ing** To discharge waste matter from the bowels. **—def′e·ca′tion** *n.*

de·fect [*n.* dē′fekt′ *or* di·fekt′, *v.* di·fekt′] 1 *n.* A fault, flaw, or lack of something necessary: a speech *defect.* 2 *v.* To desert, as one's country or side, especially in order to go over to an opposing group.

de·fec·tion [di·fek′shən] *n.* A deserting of one's country or side, especially to go over to an opposing group.

de·fec·tive [di·fek′tiv] *adj.* Having a defect; not perfect. **—de·fec′tive·ly** *adv.* **—de·fec′tive·ness** *n.*

de·fec·tor [di·fek′tər] *n.* A person who deserts a country, cause, or side for an opposing one.

de·fence [di·fens′] *n. British* Another spelling of DEFENSE.

de·fend [di·fend′] *v.* 1 To guard against harm or attack; protect: Learn how to *defend* yourself. 2 To justify: The mayor *defended* the new rule as fair to all. 3 To act as a lawyer for (a person prosecuted in court). 4 To fight (a legal charge, suit, or claim). **—de·fend′er** *n.*

de·fen·dant [di·fen′dənt] *n.* A person who is accused or sued in a court of law.

de·fense [di·fens′] *n.* 1 A defending against danger or attack: the *defense* of one's country. 2 Something that guards, protects, or defends: A levee is a *defense* against floods. 3 An argument that justifies or supports: The people who had received parking tickets gave a *defense* of their actions. 4 The answer to charges or claims brought against a defendant. 5 A defendant and the defendant's lawyers, as a group.

de·fense·less [di·fens′lis] *adj.* Without any defense or means of protection; helpless. **—de·fense′less·ly** *adv.* **—de·fense′less·ness** *n.*

de·fen·si·ble [di·fen′sə·bəl] *adj.* Capable of being defended: a *defensible* castle; a *defensible* action.

de·fen·sive [di·fen′siv] 1 *adj.* Defending or suitable for defense. 2 *n.* A defensive attitude or position. **—de·fen′sive·ly** *adv.* **—de·fen′sive·ness** *n.*

de·fer[1] [di·fûr′] *v.* **de·ferred, de·fer·ring** To put off until later; delay: to *defer* payment of money owed.

de·fer[2] [di·fûr′] *v.* **de·ferred, de·fer·ring** To yield to the opinions, wishes, or decisions of another out of respect.

def·er·ence [def′ər·əns] *n.* Respect and consideration for the wishes and opinions of another. **—in deference to** Out of consideration or respect for.

def·er·en·tial [def′ə·ren′shəl] *adj.* Full of deference; respectful. **—def′er·en′tial·ly** *adv.*

de·fer·ment [di·fûr′mənt] *n.* A putting off, especially of induction into military service.

de·fer·ral [di·fûr′əl] *n.* A putting off; postponement.

de·fi·ance [di·fī′əns] *n.* Bold opposition to power or authority; refusal to submit or obey.

de·fi·ant [di·fī′ənt] *adj.* Full of defiance; resisting. **—de·fi′ant·ly** *adv.*

de·fi·cien·cy [di·fish′ən·sē] *n., pl.* **de·fi·cien·cies** 1 A deficient condition. 2 An amount that is lacking and needed.

deficiency disease A disease, as rickets or scurvy, caused by a lack or shortage in the diet of some substance needed by the body.

de·fi·cient [di·fish′ənt] *adj.* Not sufficient or complete; lacking: mentally *deficient.* **—de·fi′cient·ly** *adv.*

def·i·cit [def′ə·sit] *n.* The amount by which money available falls short of money needed: With $100 on hand and bills for $300, the *deficit* is $200.

de·file[1] [di·fīl′] *v.* **de·filed, de·fil·ing** 1 To make dirty or impure; pollute: to *defile* a clear pond. 2 To spoil the purity or sacredness of; desecrate: to *defile* a temple. **—de·file′ment** *n.* **—de·fil′er** *n.*

de·file[2] [di·fīl′] *v.* **de·filed, de·fil·ing,** *n.* 1 *v.* To march one behind the other in a line. 2 *n.* A long, narrow pass, as between mountains.

de·fine [di·fīn′] *v.* **de·fined, de·fin·ing** 1 To give the exact meaning of (a word or term). 2 To describe; explain: to *define* the duties of a job. 3 To set or mark the limits of: to *define* the area of a farm. **—de·fine′ment** *n.* **—de·fin′er** *n.*

def·i·nite [def′ə·nit] *adj.* 1 Having fixed limits. 2 Known for certain: It is *definite* that our team won. 3 Plain and clear in meaning: *definite* rules. **—def′i·nite·ness** *n.*

definite article The word *the,* put before a noun to show that the noun refers to one or more particular persons or things.

def·i·nite·ly [def′ə·nit·lē] *adv.* 1 Without question; positively. 2 In a definite way.

D

def·i·ni·tion [def′ə·nish′ən] *n.* **1** The act of defining. **2** A being defined. **3** A statement giving the meaning of a word or term. **4** A being clearly or sharply outlined.

de·fin·i·tive [di·fin′ə·tiv] *adj.* Ending uncertainty; conclusive; final: a *definitive* statement. **—de·fin′i·tive·ly** *adv.* **—de·fin′i·tive·ness** *n.*

de·flate [di·flāt′] *v.* **de·flat·ed, de·flat·ing** **1** To let the air or gas out of; collapse: to *deflate* a balloon. **2** To take the conceit or confidence out of: to *deflate* a pompous person. **3** To reduce (the supply of money or amount of spending) so that prices go down.

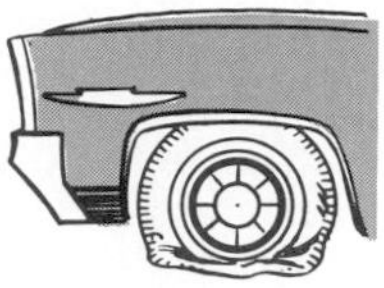
A deflated tire

de·fla·tion [di·flā′shən] *n.* **1** The act of deflating. **2** A deflated condition. **3** A reduction in the amount of available money or of spending, resulting in lower prices.

de·flect [di·flekt′] *v.* To turn aside from its regular course: Wind *deflected* the bullet. **—de·flec′tion** *n.*

de·fo·li·ant [dē·fō′lē·ənt] *n.* A chemical spray or dust used to strip the leaves of a plant or tree.

de·fo·li·ate [dē·fō′lē·āt′] *v.* **de·fo·li·at·ed, de·fo·li·at·ing** To strip the leaves of, as by using a chemical spray or dust.

de·for·est [dē·fôr′ist] *v.* To clear (land) of trees or forests. **—de·for′es·ta′tion** *n.*

de·form [di·fôrm′] *v.* To spoil the shape or appearance of; disfigure: The roof *deformed* the line of the building.

de·formed [di·fôrmd′] *adj.* Distorted in form; misshapen.

de·form·i·ty [di·fôr′mə·tē] *n., pl.* **de·form·i·ties** **1** A deformed condition. **2** A part that is not normal in shape, as a clubfoot.

A deformed tree

de·fraud [di·frôd′] *v.* To take (as money or rights), away from by tricking or deceiving.

de·fray [di·frā′] *v.* To pay or furnish the money for (costs or expenses). **—de·fray′al** *n.*

de·frost [dē·frôst′] *v.* To remove ice or frost from, as a refrigerator.

de·frost·er [dē·frôs′tər] *n.* A device for melting or removing ice, as from a windshield.

deft [deft] *adj.* Quick and skillful: a *deft* tennis stroke. **—deft′ly** *adv.* **—deft′ness** *n.*

de·funct [di·fungkt′] *adj.* No longer in existence; dead or extinct: a *defunct* magazine.

de·fuse [dē·fyo͞oz′] *v.* **de·fused, de·fus·ing** **1** To remove the fuse from: A police squad *defused* the bomb. **2** To make less dangerous, harmful, or tense: to *defuse* a dispute between workers and their employees.

de·fy [di·fī′] *v.* **de·fied, de·fy·ing** **1** To resist openly and boldly; refuse to submit to: to *defy* the doctor's orders. **2** To resist successfully; withstand: a situation so complicated that it *defies* explanation. **3** To challenge (someone) to do something; dare.

deg. degree(s).

de·gen·er·a·cy [di·jen′ər·ə·sē] *n.* **1** The process of degenerating. **2** A being degenerate.

de·gen·er·ate [*v.* di·jen′ə·rāt′, *n., adj.* di·jen′ər·it] *v.* **de·gen·er·at·ed, de·gen·er·at·ing,** *n., adj.* **1** *v.* To become worse, inferior, or lower, as in quality, condition, or character. **2** *n.* A person who has low moral standards and does evil things. **3** *adj.* Having grown worse, inferior, or lower, as in quality, condition, or character. **4** *v.* To go back to a simpler type or earlier stage of development, as some animals, plants, or organs of the body. **—de·gen′·er·a′tion** *n.*

de·gen·er·a·tive [di·jen′ə·rə·tiv] *adj.* Of, having to do with, or tending to cause degeneration.

deg·ra·da·tion [deg′rə·dā′shən] *n.* **1** The act of degrading. **2** A degraded condition.

de·grade [di·grād′] *v.* **de·grad·ed, de·grad·ing** **1** To bring down from a higher to a lower condition; corrupt; debase: Telling lies *degrades* a person. **2** To reduce in rank; demote.

de·gree [di·grē′] *n.* **1** A step in a series or stage in a process. **2** A unit for measuring temperature: The normal temperature of the body is 98.6 *degrees* Fahrenheit. **3** A unit used for measuring arcs and angles: There are 360 *degrees* in a circle. **4** The number of times variables, as x and y, are used as factors in a term, or the largest such number in an equation: x^2, xy, and y^2 are of the second *degree.* **5** A measure of damage done to bodily tissue: a burn of the second *degree.* **6** A measure of guilt as fixed by law: murder in the first *degree.* **7** Amount, extent, or measure: There is only a small *degree* of difference between the twins. **8** Station; rank: a person of high *degree.* **9** A title awarded to a student who has completed a course of study or to a person as an honor: a B.S. *degree.* **10** In grammar, any of the three forms that an adjective or adverb takes in comparison. The adjective *bright* is in the positive degree, *brighter* is in the comparative degree, and *brightest* is in the superlative degree.

de·gree-day [di·grē′dā′] *n.* A unit used to estimate fuel requirements for heating buildings. It is equal to one of the degrees by which the average outdoor temperature on a given day falls below 65°F. or some other standard temperature.

de·his·cent [di·his′ənt] *adj.* Opening at maturity to release seeds or pollen: *dehiscent* plant pods.

de·hu·man·ize [dē·hyo͞o′mə·nīz′] *v.* **de·hu·man·ized, de·hu·man·iz·ing** To make less human or humane: machines that *dehumanize* the workplace. **—de·hu′man·i·za′tion** *n.*

de·hu·mid·i·fy [dē′hyo͞o·mid′ə·fī′] *v.* **de·hu·mid·i·fied, de·hu·mid·i·fy·ing** To lower the humidity of; remove moisture from. **—de′hu·mid′i·fi′er** *n.*

de·hy·drate [dē·hī′drāt′] *v.* **de·hy·drat·ed, de·hy·drat·ing** **1** To take water out of: to *dehydrate* vegetables to preserve them. **2** To lose water; dry up. **—de′hy·dra′tion** *n.*

de·ice [dē·īs′] *v.* **de·iced, de·icing** To free or keep free of ice.

de·ic·er [dē·ī′sər] *n.* A device for removing ice, as from an airplane wing.

a	add	**i**	it	**o͝o**	took	**oi**	oil
ā	ace	**ī**	ice	**o͞o**	pool	**ou**	pout
â	care	**o**	odd	**u**	up	**ng**	ring
ä	palm	**ō**	open	**û**	burn	**th**	thin
e	end	**ô**	order	**yo͞o**	fuse	**th**	this
ē	equal					**zh**	vision

ə = a in *above*, e in *sicken*, i in *possible*, o in *melon*, u in *circus*

de·i·fy [dē′ə·fī] *v.* **de·i·fied, de·i·fy·ing** To make a god of; treat as sacred: to *deify* a ruler. **—de·i·fi·ca·tion** [dē′ə·fə·kā′shən] *n.*

deign [dān] *v.* To lower oneself; think fit: The officer did not *deign* to answer.

de·ism [dē′iz′əm] *n.* The belief, based on reason and not revelation, that God exists and is the creator of the universe.

de·ist [dē′ist] *n.* A person who believes in deism.

de·i·ty [dē′ə·tē] *n., pl.* **de·i·ties** 1 (*written* **the Deity**) God. 2 A god or goddess: Mars was a Roman *deity.* 3 Divine nature: They believed in the *deity* of their emperor.

dé·jà vu [dā′zhä vo͞o′] The illusion that an experience one is having for the first time already occurred in the past. ◆ This odd sensation gets its name from the French phrase for "already seen."

de·ject [di·jekt′] *v.* To make sad or low in spirits; depress: losing the election *dejected* him.

de·jec·ted [di·jek′tid] *adj.* Low in spirits; unhappy; downcast. **—de·ject′ed·ly** *adv.*

de·jec·tion [di·jek′shən] *n.* Lowness of spirits; depression; sadness.

de ju·re [dē jo͝or′ē] According to law. ◆ *De jure* and *de facto,* Latin terms for "in law" and "in fact," are used to describe situations where what the law says exists is different from what really exists. Thus a city can be the *de jure* capital because a nation's constitution says it is, while another city, the *de facto* capital, is actually the site of the government.

deka- or **dek-** Another form of DECA-.

de·ka·li·ter [dek′ə·lē′tər] *n.* In the metric system, a unit of volume equal to 10 liters.

Del. Delaware.

Del·a·ware [del′ə·wâr′] *n., pl.* **Del·a·ware** or **Del·a·wares** 1 A tribe of North American Indians once living in the Delaware River Valley. 2 A member of this tribe. 3 The language of this tribe.

de·lay [di·lā′] 1 *v.* To make late by stopping or slowing up: The traffic jam *delayed* me. 2 *v.* To put off until later: They *delayed* the game because of rain. 3 *v.* To go slow; linger: Don't *delay* along the way. 4 *n.* The act of delaying. 5 *n.* A putting off, waiting, or going slow.

de·lec·ta·ble [di·lek′tə·bəl] *adj.* 1 Giving pleasure; delightful. 2 Delicious: a *delectable* dish. **—de·lec′ta·ble·ness** *n.* **—de·lec′ta·bly** *adv.*

de·lec·ta·tion [dē′lek·tā′shən] *n.* Delight; enjoyment; amusement: They had a concert for the *delectation* of their guests.

del·e·gate [*n.* del′ə·git *or* del′ə·gāt′, *v.* del′ə·gāt′] *n., v.* **del·e·gat·ed, del·e·gat·ing** 1 *n.* A person sent with authority to act for a group; representative. 2 *v.* To choose or send as a representative. 3 *v.* To give or entrust (as duties, authority, or rights) to another.

del·e·ga·tion [del′ə·gā′shən] *n.* 1 The act of delegating. 2 A being delegated. 3 A group of delegates.

de·lete [di·lēt′] *v.* **de·let·ed, de·let·ing** To remove or mark out (something written or printed). **—de·le′tion** *n.*

He wore a blue cloth shirt
The word "cloth" is deleted.

del·e·te·ri·ous [del′ə·tir′ē·əs] *adj.* Causing injury; physically or morally harmful: Dieting can have a *deleterious* effect. **—del′e·ter′i·ous·ly** *adv.* **—del′e·ter′i·ous·ness** *n.*

delft [delft] *n.* A style of dishes and pottery made of glazed, baked clay and decorated with delicate, usually blue patterns on a white background. ◆ Such earthenware gets its name from *Delft,* Netherlands, where it was first made.

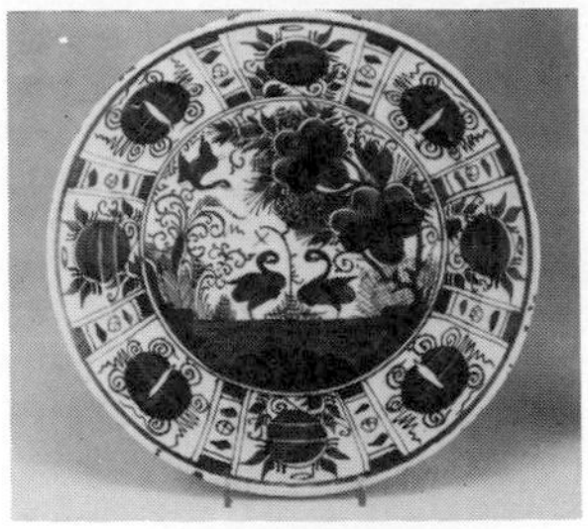
Delft plate

del·i [del′ē] *n., pl.* **del·is** *informal* A delicatessen (def. 1).

de·lib·er·ate [*adj.* di·lib′ər·it, *v.* di·lib′ə·rāt′] *adj., v.* **de·lib·er·at·ed, de·lib·er·at·ing** 1 *adj.* Thought about and intended: a *deliberate* insult. 2 *adj.* Slow and careful about deciding: The driver was *deliberate,* not reckless. 3 *v.* To consider carefully; ponder: The committee always *deliberates* before taking action. 4 *v.* To talk things over in order to reach a decision: They have been *deliberating* for hours. 5 *adj.* Not hurried; slow and steady: the horse's *deliberate* trot. **—de·lib′er·ate·ly** *adv.* **—de·lib′er·ate·ness** *n.*

de·lib·er·a·tion [di·lib′ə·rā′shən] *n.* 1 Long and careful thought: The guide decided at once, without *deliberation.* 2 (*often pl.*) Discussion of the arguments for and against an action: The jury interrupted its *deliberations* to have lunch. 3 Slowness and care: He climbed the stairs with *deliberation.*

de·lib·er·a·tive [di·lib′ə·rā′tiv *or* di·lib′ə·rə·tiv] *adj.* Involved in or concerned with the careful consideration of issues. **—de·lib′er·a′tive·ly** *adv.*

del·i·ca·cy [del′ə·kə·sē] *n., pl.* **del·i·ca·cies** 1 Fineness of structure, design, or make: the *delicacy* of a butterfly's wing. 2 Refinement, as of feeling or manner; sensitivity. 3 Weakness of body or health. 4 Need of careful, tactful treatment: a situation of great *delicacy.* 5 Ability to appreciate fine differences: a *delicacy* of taste. 6 A choice food: Fine cheese is a *delicacy.* 7 Consideration for other people's feeling.

del·i·cate [del′ə·kit] *adj.* 1 Fine, as in structure, design, or shape: a *delicate* snowflake. 2 Pleasing, as in taste, aroma, or color: a *delicate* shade of blue. 3 Weak or easily injured: a *delicate* child; a *delicate* vase. 4 Requiring cautious, tactful treatment: *delicate* diplomatic relations. 5 Barely felt or seen; subtle; slight: a *delicate* distinction. 6 Reacting quickly to slight differences or changes: a *delicate* thermometer. **—del′i·cate·ly** *adv.* **—del′i·cate·ness** *n.*

del·i·ca·tes·sen [del′ə·kə·tes′(ə)n] *n.* 1 A store selling prepared foods, such as cooked meats, salads, and cheese. 2 The food which such a store sells. ◆ *Delicatessen* comes from a German word meaning *delicacies.*

de·li·cious [di·lish′əs] *adj.* Highly pleasing, especially to the taste; extremely good. **—de·li′cious·ly** *adv.* **—de·li′cious·ness** *n.*

de·light [di·līt′] 1 *n.* Great pleasure or joy: full of *delight* at hearing the good news. 2 *v.* To please extremely: The teacher's praise *delighted* the class. 3 *v.* To take great pleasure: They *delighted* in their victory. 4 *n.* Something that gives great joy or pleasure.

de·light·ful [di·līt′fəl] *adj.* Giving joy or pleasure. **—de·light′ful·ly** *adv.* **—de·light′ful·ness** *n.*

de·lim·it [di·lim′it] *v.* To fix the limits or boundaries of.

de·lin·e·ate [di·lin′ē·āt′] *v.* **de·lin·e·at·ed, de·lin·e·at·ing** 1 To outline, sketch, or draw; portray: The artist faithfully *delineated* the scene. 2 To describe or show in words: to *delineate* character in a novel. —**de·lin′e·a′tion** *n.*

de·lin·quen·cy [di·ling′kwən·sē] *n., pl.* **de·lin·quen·cies** 1 The doing of things that are wrong or that break the law: juvenile *delinquency.* 2 Failure to do what is required; neglect of duty. 3 A fault; offense.

de·lin·quent [di·ling′kwənt] 1 *n.* A person who neglects what should be done, who does wrong things, or who breaks the law: a juvenile *delinquent.* 2 *adj.* Guilty of doing wrong or of breaking the law: a *delinquent* person. 3 *adj.* Guilty of neglect or lateness: *delinquent* in payment of a debt. 4 *adj.* Due but not paid: *delinquent* taxes.

del·i·quesce [del′i·kwes′] *v.* **del·i·quesced, del·i·quesc·ing** 1 To melt away. 2 To become liquid by absorbing water vapor from the air. —**del′i·ques′cence** *n.*

de·lir·i·ous [di·lir′ē·əs] *adj.* 1 Temporarily out of one's mind; wild and raving. 2 Extremely excited. —**de·lir′i·ous·ly** *adv.* —**de·lir′i·ous·ness** *n.*

de·lir·i·um [di·lir′ē·əm] *n.* 1 A disturbance of the mind marked by restlessness, excitement, and wild, confused thoughts and speech. It occurs only at times, as during fever or drunkenness. 2 Extreme excitement.

de·liv·er [di·liv′ər] *v.* 1 To hand over; give up; transfer: to *deliver* a message. 2 To carry and distribute: to *deliver* groceries. 3 To speak or utter: to *deliver* a speech. 4 To give forth; strike: The fighter *delivered* a blow. 5 To throw. 6 To set free; rescue, as from danger. 7 To aid in the birth of, or in childbirth. —**de·liv′er·er** *n.*

de·liv·er·ance [di·liv′ər·əns] *n.* Freedom; rescue: thankful for their *deliverance.*

de·liv·er·y [di·liv′ər·ē] *n., pl.* **de·liv·er·ies** 1 The action of handing over or distributing: the *delivery* of mail. 2 Way of speaking: The comedian's *delivery* made the jokes funny. 3 The action or manner, as of throwing or striking: a fast *delivery.* 4 Rescue or release: The captives still hoped for *delivery.* 5 The act of giving birth.

dell [del] *n.* A small, protected valley, usually full of trees; dale; glen.

Del·phic [del′fik] *adj.* 1 Having to do with Delphi or the oracle there. 2 Having more than one possible meaning; puzzling.

del·phin·i·um [del·fin′ē·əm] *n.* A garden plant having small, usually blue flowers on long spikes.

del·ta [del′tə] *n.* 1 The fourth letter of the Greek alphabet (Δ or δ). 2 A piece of low land shaped like a Greek delta or like a fan, formed at the mouths of some rivers by deposits of soil or sand.

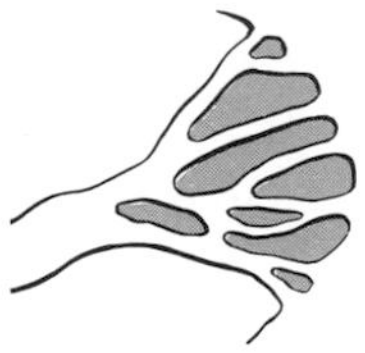

A river delta

delta wing A triangular, swept-back wing of certain supersonic airplanes.

de·lude [di·lo͞od′] *v.* **de·lud·ed, de·lud·ing** To mislead the mind or judgment of; deceive; fool. ◆ See DECEIVE.

del·uge [del′yo͞oj] *v.* **del·uged, del·ug·ing,** *n.* 1 *v.* To flood with water: Rain *deluged* the area. 2 *n.* A great flood or fall of rain. 3 *v.* To swamp or overwhelm: The television station was *deluged* with mail. 4 *n.* A very great number or amount. —**the Deluge** The great flood in the time of Noah.

de·lu·sion [di·lo͞o′zhən] *n.* 1 A false, fixed belief, especially one held by a person who is mentally ill. 2 The act of deluding or deceiving.

de·lu·sive [di·lo͞o′siv] *adj.* Apt to delude; misleading: a *delusive* promise of help. —**de·lu′sive·ly** *adv.*

de luxe [di lo͝oks′ *or* di luks′] Of the very highest quality; elegant and expensive.

delve [delv] *v.* **delved, delv·ing** To make a careful search for information: to *delve* into a crime.

Dem. 1 Democrat. 2 Democratic.

de·mag·net·ize [dē·mag′nə·tīz′] *v.* **de·mag·net·ized, de·mag·net·iz·ing** To treat (a magnetized object) so that it is no longer a magnet.

dem·a·gog·ic [dem′ə·goj′ik] *adj.* Of, having to do with, or characteristic of a demagogue.

dem·a·gogue [dem′ə·gôg′] *n.* A leader or politician who stirs up the feelings and fears of people in order to gain personal power.

dem·a·gogu·er·y [dem′ə·gô′gə·rē] *n.* The methods or style of speaking used by a demagogue.

dem·a·go·gy [dem′ə·gô′jē *or* dem′ə·gō′jē] *n.* Demagoguery.

de·mand [di·mand′] 1 *v.* To ask for boldly; claim as a right: The suspect *demanded* a lawyer. 2 *v.* To ask for forcefully: The teacher *demanded* an answer. 3 *n.* The act of demanding: a *demand* for silence. 4 *v.* To need; require: This job *demands* skill. 5 *n.* A claim or requirement: The work made great *demands* on the miner's health. —**in demand** Sought after; wanted.

de·mand·ing [di·man′ding] *adj.* Requiring or expecting effort or excellence: a *demanding* job; a *demanding* teacher. —**de·mand′ing·ly** *adv.*

de·mar·ca·tion [dē′mär·kā′shən] *n.* 1 The fixing or marking of boundaries or limits. 2 A setting apart; separation.

de·mean[1] [di·mēn′] *v.* To lower in dignity or worth; degrade: to *demean* oneself by lying.

de·mean[2] [di·mēn′] *v.* To behave or conduct (oneself): The school chorus *demeaned* itself like a professional group.

de·mean·or [di·mē′nər] *n.* Behavior or bearing; manner: a meek *demeanor.*

de·ment·ed [di·men′tid] *adj.* Out of one's mind; crazy; insane.

de·mer·it [di·mer′it] *n.* 1 A fault or weakness. 2 A mark set down against someone for poor work or bad conduct.

de·mesne [di·mān′ *or* di·mēn′] *n.* 1 A house and land on an estate kept for the owner's use. 2 A region or district; domain.

De·me·ter [di·mē′tər] *n.* In Greek myths, the goddess of agriculture and marriage. Her Roman name was Ceres.

dem·i·god [dem′ē·god′] *n.* In myths, a lesser god who is half god and half human.

a	add	**i**	it	**o͝o**	took	**oi**	oil
ā	ace	**ī**	ice	**o͞o**	pool	**ou**	pout
â	care	**o**	odd	**u**	up	**ng**	ring
ä	palm	**ō**	open	**û**	burn	**th**	thin
e	end	**ô**	order	**yo͞o**	fuse	**th**	this
ē	equal					**zh**	vision

ə = a in *above*, e in *sicken*, i in *possible*, o in *melon*, u in *circus*

D

dem·i·john [dem′ē·jon′] *n.* A large jug with a narrow neck. It is often enclosed in wicker.

Demijohn

de·mil·i·ta·rize [dē·mil′ə·tə·rīz′] *v.* **de·mil·i·ta·rized, de·mil·i·ta·riz·ing** To remove or do away with the military personnel and weapons of: to *demilitarize* a zone. **—de·mil·i·ta·ri·za·tion** [dē·mil′ə·tə·rə·zā′·shən] *n.*

de·mise [di·mīz′] *n.* Death.

dem·i·tasse [dem′ē·tas′ *or* dem′ē·täs′] *n.* **1** A small cup in which coffee is served after dinner. **2** Such a cup of coffee.

A demitasse

de·mo·bi·lize [dē·mō′bə·līz′] *v.* **de·mo·bi·lized, de·mo·bi·liz·ing** **1** To break up or disband (an army or troops), as after a war. **2** To discharge from the armed forces. **—de·mo·bi·li·za·tion** [dē·mō′bə·lə·zā′shən] *n.*

de·moc·ra·cy [di·mok′rə·sē] *n., pl.* **de·moc·ra·cies** **1** A form of government in which the people rule, either by voting directly or by electing representatives to manage the government and make the laws. **2** A country, state, or community with such a government. **3** Equal rights, treatment, and opportunity for everyone. ◆ *Democracy* comes from a Greek word meaning *rule of the people.*

dem·o·crat [dem′ə·krat′] *n.* **1** A person who believes in government by the people. **2** A person who holds that all people should have equal rights and social treatment. **3** (*written* **Democrat**) A member of the Democratic Party.

dem·o·crat·ic [dem′ə·krat′ik] *adj.* **1** Of, favoring, or like a democracy. **2** Treating all people the same way: a *democratic* school system. **3** (*written* **Democratic**) Of or belonging to the Democratic Party. **—dem′o·crat′i·cal·ly** *adv.*

Democratic Party One of the two major political parties in the U.S., dating from 1828.

de·moc·ra·tize [di·mok′rə·tīz′] *v.* **de·moc·ra·tized, de·moc·ra·tiz·ing** To make or become democratic.

de·mo·graph·ic [dem′ə·graf′ik] *adj.* Of or having to do with demography.

de·mog·ra·phy [di·mog′rə·fē] *n.* The statistical study of human populations and their characteristics. **—de·mog′ra·pher** *n.*

de·mol·ish [di·mol′ish] *v.* To tear down completely; wreck; ruin.

dem·o·li·tion [dem′ə·lish′ən] *n.* The act or result of demolishing; destruction.

de·mon [dē′mən] *n.* **1** An evil spirit; devil. **2** A person or thing that is very cruel or evil. **3** A person having great energy or skill. **4** A lesser Greek god or guardian spirit.

de·mo·ni·ac [di·mō′nē·ak] **1** *adj.* Of or like a demon or evil spirit. **2** *n.* A person thought to be possessed by an evil spirit. **3** *adj.* Violent, furious, or frantic.

de·mo·ni·a·cal [dē′mə·nī′ə·kəl] *adj.* Demoniac.

de·mon·stra·ble [di·mon′strə·bəl] *adj.* That can be demonstrated, shown, or proved: a *demonstrable* error. **—de·mon′stra·bly** *adv.*

dem·on·strate [dem′ən·strāt′] *v.* **dem·on·strat·ed, dem·on·strat·ing** **1** To show clearly; exhibit. **2** To explain or prove by reasoning or by the use of examples or experiments: Our teacher *demonstrated* that helium does not burn. **3** To show how a product works: to *demonstrate* a new car. **4** To make a public show of feeling, as by meeting, marching, or picketing.

dem·on·stra·tion [dem′ən·strā′shən] *n.* **1** A showing or expressing outwardly: a *demonstration* of anger. **2** An explanation or proof, as by the use of reasoning, examples, or experiments: a *demonstration* of the weight of air. **3** A public showing of how a product works: a *demonstration* of a sewing machine. **4** Expression of public feeling by a meeting, march, or other gathering.

Demonstration for a lower voting age

de·mon·stra·tive [di·mon′strə·tiv] **1** *adj.* In grammar, serving to point out a person or thing. In the sentence "This is my book," *this* is a demonstrative pronoun. **2** *n.* A demonstrative pronoun or adjective. **3** *adj.* Freely and openly showing one's feelings, especially love: a *demonstrative* parent.

dem·on·stra·tor [dem′ən·strā′tər] *n.* A person or thing that demonstrates.

de·mor·al·ize [di·môr′əl·īz′] *v.* **de·mor·al·ized, de·mor·al·iz·ing** **1** To destroy the morals of; corrupt. **2** To weaken or destroy the spirit or discipline of: Hunger *demoralized* the explorers. **—de·mor′al·i·za′tion** *n.*

de·mote [di·mōt′] *v.* **de·mot·ed, de·mot·ing** To reduce to a lower grade, rank, or position. **—de·mo′tion** *n.*

de·mur [di·mûr′] *v.* **de·murred, de·mur·ring,** *n.* **1** *v.* To raise an objection: to *demur* at being sent to bed. **2** *n.* An objection or protest.

de·mure [di·myo͝or′] *adj.* **de·mur·er, de·mur·est** Quiet, modest, and shy, or seeming so.

de·mur·ral [di·mûr′əl] *n.* Demur.

de·mys·ti·fy [dē·mis′tə·fī] *v.* **de·mys·ti·fied, de·mys·ti·fy·ing** To make less mysterious or puzzling; clarify.

den [den] *n.* **1** The cave or resting place of a wild animal; lair. **2** A place where criminals gather secretly. **3** A private room to relax or study in. **4** A patrol of Cub Scouts.

Den. Denmark.

de·na·tured [dē·nā′chərd] *adj.* **1** Changed in nature. **2** Made unfit for drinking or eating, although not spoiled for other purposes.

den·drite [den′drīt′] *n.* One of the long, branching filaments that conduct impulses to the body of a nerve cell.

den·dro·chro·nol·o·gy [den′drō·krə·nol′ə·jē] *n.* The science of dating objects, sites, and events in the distant past by comparing the growth rings in trees and ancient wood.

den·gue [deng′gē *or* deng′gā] *n.* A severe infectious disease of warm regions, caused by a virus transmitted by mosquitoes. It is also called **dengue fever.**

de·ni·al [di·nī′əl] *n.* **1** A saying that something is false: The newspaper issued a *denial* of the charges against the governor. 2 A refusal to grant or allow: *denial* of a permit. 3 A refusal to recognize or claim a connection with: their *denial* of their ancestors.

de·ni·grate [den′ə·grāt′] *v.* **de·ni·grat·ed, de·ni·grat·ing** 1 To say harmful things about the character of; defame. 2 To deny the importance of; belittle. **—de′ni·gra′tion** *n.*

den·im [den′əm] *n.* 1 A strong twilled cotton cloth, used for overalls and play clothes. 2 (*pl.*) Clothes made of this material.

den·i·zen [den′ə·zən] *n.* 1 A person, plant, or animal that lives or is found in a particular place: A bird is a *denizen* of the air. 2 A person, animal, or thing at home in a place not native to it.

de·nom·i·nate [*v.* di·nom′ə·nāt′, *adj.* di·nom′ə·nit] *v.* **de·nom·i·nat·ed, de·nom·i·nat·ing,** *adj.* 1 *v.* To give a name to; call. 2 *adj.* Made up of units of a specified kind: Three pounds and 25 feet are *denominate* numbers.

de·nom·i·na·tion [di·nom′ə·nā′shən] *n.* 1 The name by which a thing or class of things is known. 2 A particular religious group; sect. 3 A specific class of units, as in a system of measures, weights, or money. **—de·nom′i·na′tion·al** *adj.*

de·nom·i·na·tor [di·nom′ə·nā′tər] *n.* In a fraction the number by which another number is to be divided; divisor.

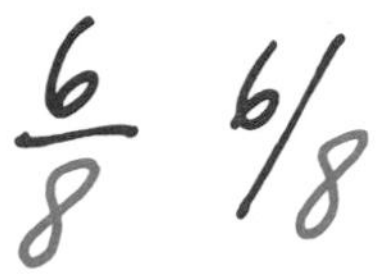

The denominator is in blue

de·no·ta·tion [dē′nō·tā′shən] *n.* 1 What a word or statement actually means or says, not what it suggests or may be associated with. 2 The act of denoting; indication. ◆ *Denotation* and *connotation* both have to do with meaning. The *denotation* of a word is its exact, literal meaning. The *connotation* is what it suggests in one's mind. The *denotation* of *book* is a bound set of pages, whereas its *connotations* may include a whole world of excitement and adventure.

de·note [di·nōt′] *v.* **de·not·ed, de·not·ing** 1 To be a sign or symbol of; show; indicate: Red spots on the face may *denote* measles. 2 To be the name for; mean: The word "dell" *denotes* a small, sheltered valley.

de·noue·ment [dā′no͞o·män′] *n.* 1 The way in which the problems or complications in a plot are solved; outcome. 2 The outcome of any complicated situation. ◆ *Denouement* comes for the French word *dénouement* (literally, *the untying of a knot*), and it is still pronounced and sometimes spelled in the French way.

de·nounce [di·nouns′] *v.* **de·nounced, de·nounc·ing** 1 To speak against openly and strongly; call bad; condemn. 2 To inform against; tell on: The arrested robbers *denounced* their partners. 3 To give formal notice of the ending of (a treaty or pact).

dense [dens] *adj.* **dens·er, dens·est** 1 Having its parts crowded together; thick: a *dense* jungle. 2 Stupid; dull. 3 In mathematics, indicating a set that always has a member between any two other members. **—dense′ly** *adv.*

den·si·ty [den′sə·tē] *n., pl.* **den·si·ties** 1 A dense condition; closeness; compactness: the *density* of the fog 2 The amount of something per unit of volume or area: the *density* of population. 3 The mass of a substance per unit of its volume: the *density* of a gas. 4 Stupidity.

dent [dent] 1 *n.* A small hollow made in a hard surface by a blow or by pressure. 2 *v.* To make or become dented: Tin *dents* easily.

den·tal [den′təl] *adj.* 1 Of, for, or having to do with the teeth or with a dentist's work: *dental* hygiene. 2 Pronounced with the tip of the tongue against or near the upper front teeth. **—den′tal·ly** *adv.*

dental floss Strong, usually waxed thread for cleaning between the teeth.

den·ti·frice [den′tə·fris] *n.* A substance, such as toothpaste, used to clean the teeth.

den·tin [den′tin] *n.* Dentine.

den·tine [den′tēn′] *n.* The hard, bony substance that makes up the main part of a tooth. It is under the enamel.

den·tist [den′tist] *n.* A doctor whose job is caring for and treating the teeth. A dentist cleans teeth, fills cavities, fits braces, pulls diseased teeth, and fits false teeth.

den·tist·ry [den′tis·trē] *n.* The profession or work of a dentist.

den·ti·tion [den·tish′ən] *n.* 1 The number, type, and arrangement of teeth, as in animals. 2 The process of cutting teeth; teething.

den·ture [den′chər] *n.* A full or partial set of false teeth; plate.

de·nude [di·n(y)o͞od′] *v.* **de·nud·ed, de·nud·ing** To strip the covering from; make bare: The garden is *denuded* of flowers.

de·nun·ci·a·tion [di·nun′sē·ā′shən] *n.* An act or instance of denouncing.

de·ny [di·nī′] *v.* **de·nied, de·ny·ing** 1 To declare to be untrue or not right: Columbus *denied* that the world was flat. 2 To refuse to give, grant, or allow: They *denied* us our rights. 3 To refuse (someone) a request: It is hard to *deny* a sick friend. 4 To refuse to recognize or claim a connection with: to *deny* one's background. **—deny oneself** To make oneself do without things one wants.

de·o·dor·ant [dē·ō′dər·ənt] *n.* Any substance used to prevent or cover up bad odors.

de·o·dor·ize [dē·ō′dər·īz′] *v.* **de·o·dor·ized, de·o·dor·iz·ing** To take away or prevent the smell of.

de·ox·y·dize [dē·ok′sə·dīz′] *v.* **de·ox·y·dized, de·ox·y·diz·ing** To remove oxygen from, especially oxygen that is chemically combined.

de·ox·y·gen·ate [dē·ok′sə·jən·āt′] *v.* **de·ox·y·gen·at·ed, de·ox·y·gen·at·ing** To remove oxygen from.

de·ox·y·ri·bo·nu·cle·ic acid [dē·ok′sē·rī′bō·no͞o·klē′·ik] See DNA.

de·part [di·pärt′] *v.* 1 To go away; leave: The expedition *departed* in early May. 2 To turn away or aside; change: to *depart* from the usual custom. 3 To die.

de·part·ed [di·pär′tid] 1 *adj.* Gone; past: *departed* time. 2 *n. use:* A dead person or persons: to mourn the *departed.*

a	add	**i**	it	**o͝o**	took	**oi**	oil		
ā	ace	**ī**	ice	**o͞o**	pool	**ou**	pout		
â	care	**o**	odd	**u**	up	**ng**	ring		
ä	palm	**ō**	open	**û**	burn	**th**	thin		
e	end	**ô**	order	**yo͞o**	fuse	**th**	this		
ē	equal					**zh**	vision		

ə = {a in *above* e in *sicken* i in *possible* / o in *melon* u in *circus*}

de·part·ment [di·pärt′mənt] *n.* A separate part or division, as of a business, government, or school. **—de′part·men′tal** *adj.*

de·part·men·tal·ize [di·pärt′ment′əl·īz′] *v.* **de·part·men·tal·ized, de·part·men·tal·iz·ing** To divide or organize into departments.

department store A large store having separate sections for selling different kinds of goods.

de·par·ture [di·pär′chər] *n.* 1 A going away; leaving: a *departure* for unknown regions. 2 A change or turning away, as from an accepted thought, practice, or pattern, to a new one: Taking care of a new baby will be a *departure* for them. 3 Death: seldom used today.

de·pend [di·pend′] *v.* 1 To trust; rely: You can *depend* on me to do it. 2 To rely for support or aid: The organization *depends* on contributions. 3 To be controlled or determined by: Crops here *depend* on the amount of rain. 4 To hang down: Lanterns *depended* from the ceiling.

de·pend·a·bil·i·ty [di·pen′də·bil′ə·tē] *n.* The quality of being dependable; reliability.

de·pend·a·ble [di·pen′də·bəl] *adj.* Worthy of trust; reliable. **—de·pend′a·bly** *adv.*

de·pen·dant [di·pen′dənt] *adj., n.* Dependent.

de·pen·dence [di·pen′dəns] *n.* 1 A depending on someone or something, as for support, help, or direction. 2 Trust or reliance: He put his *dependence* in his teacher. 3 A being determined by something else: Safe speed varies because of its *dependence* on traffic conditions.

de·pen·den·cy [di·pen′dən·sē] *n., pl.* **de·pen·den·cies** 1 A dependent condition; dependence. 2 A territory or state governed by another country geographically separated from it.

de·pen·dent [di·pen′dənt] 1 *adj.* Depending on someone or something for support or aid: *dependent* children. 2 *n.* A person who depends on another for support. 3 *adj.* Determined or controlled by something else: How soon you finish is *dependent* upon how fast you go. 4 *adj.* Subject to outside control: *dependent* territories.

dependent clause A clause that cannot stand alone and that is used as a noun, adjective, or adverb. In the sentence "I know what the score is," the dependent clause *what the score is* functions as a noun, the object of a verb.

de·pict [di·pikt′] *v.* 1 To show by a picture; portray. 2 To describe in words: The poet *depicted* a sunset. **—de·pic′tion** *n.*

de·pil·a·to·ry [di·pil′ə·tôr′ē] *n., pl.* **de·pil·a·to·ries,** *adj.* 1 *n.* A substance, as a cream or liquid, used to remove body hair. 2 *adj.* Used to remove body hair.

de·plane [dē·plān′] *v.* **de·planed, de·plan·ing** To get off an airplane.

de·plete [di·plēt′] *v.* **de·plet·ed, de·plet·ing** 1 To make less; reduce: The fever *depleted* the patient's strength. 2 To empty: to *deplete* a club's treasury. **—de·ple′tion** *n.*

de·plor·a·ble [di·plôr′ə·bəl] *adj.* 1 That causes or should cause regret: a *deplorable* temper. 2 Wretched. **—de·plor′a·bly** *adv.*

de·plore [di·plôr′] *v.* **de·plored, de·plor·ing** To feel or express strong regret over; be extremely sorry about: The mayor *deplored* the shortage of water.

de·ploy [di·ploi′] *v.* 1 To spread out in or as if in battle formation. 2 To put in appropriate positions for use. **—de·ploy′ment** *n.*

de·pop·u·late [dē·pop′yə·lāt′] *v.* **de·pop·u·lat·ed, de·pop·u·lat·ing** To remove many or all of the people from. **—de·pop′u·la′tion** *n.*

de·port [di·pôrt′] *v.* 1 To expel (a person, usually an alien) from a country by legal order; banish. 2 To behave (oneself) in a particular way: to *deport* oneself like a soldier.

de·por·ta·tion [dē′pôr·tā′shən] *n.* The expulsion of a person from a country.

de·port·ment [di·pôrt′mənt] *n.* The way a person acts or behaves; conduct.

de·pose [di·pōz′] *v.* **de·posed, de·pos·ing** 1 To remove or oust from high office. 2 To give testimony under oath, especially in writing.

de·pos·it [di·poz′it] 1 *v.* To set down; place; put: to *deposit* the silverware on the table. 2 *v.* To put down in the form of a layer: The river had *deposited* soil and sand to form a delta. 3 *n.* Material laid down by natural forces: a *deposit* of silt; a mineral *deposit.* 4 *v.* To give over or entrust for safekeeping: to *deposit* money in a savings account. 5 *n.* Something given over or entrusted for safekeeping, especially money in a bank. 6 *v.* To put down money as partial payment or as a pledge: She *deposited* $10 on a new radio. 7 *n.* The money put down as a partial payment for something, or as a pledge.

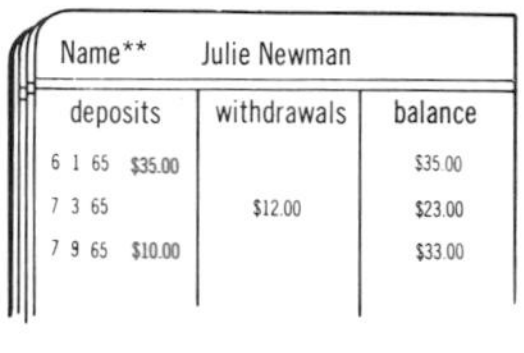
Name** Julie Newman
deposits
withdrawals
balance
6 1 65 $35.00
$35.00
7 3 65
$12.00
$23.00
7 9 65 $10.00
$33.00
A record of bank deposits

dep·o·si·tion [dep′ə·zish′ən] *n.* 1 The action of removing from high office or rank. 2 The giving of testimony before a court. 3 The testimony given by a witness under oath, especially written testimony. 4 The action of depositing, or the material deposited.

de·pos·i·tor [di·poz′ə·tər] *n.* A person who makes a deposit, especially in a bank.

de·pos·i·to·ry [di·poz′ə·tôr′ē] *n., pl.* **de·pos·i·to·ries** A place where something is put for safekeeping or storage.

de·pot [dē′pō *for defs. 1, 2,* dep′ō *for def. 3*] *n.* 1 *U.S.* A railroad station. 2 A place for storing things; warehouse. 3 A place for storing military equipment and supplies, or for receiving and training troops.

de·praved [di·prāvd′] *adj.* Completely wicked.

de·prav·i·ty [di·prav′ə·tē] *n., pl.* **de·prav·i·ties** A wicked and corrupt condition, action, or habit; sin or vice.

dep·re·cate [dep′rə·kāt′] *v.* **dep·re·cat·ed, dep·re·cat·ing** 1 To express disapproval of. 2 To depreciate; belittle. **—dep′re·ca′tion** *n.*

dep·re·ca·to·ry [dep′rə·kə·tôr′ē] *adj.* Expressing disapproval, deprecating.

de·pre·ci·ate [di·prē′shē·āt′] *v.* **de·pre·ci·at·ed, de·pre·ci·at·ing** 1 To lessen the value of: to *depreciate* currency. 2 To become less valuable: Fruit *depreciates* quickly. 3 To make seem small; belittle: Envious friends *depreciated* the prize I won. **—de·pre′ci·a′tion** *n.*

de·pre·cia·to·ry [di·prē′shə·tôr′ē] *adj.* Tending to make something seem small or unimportant; belittling.

dep·re·da·tion [dep′rə·dā′shən] *n.* An act of robbing or plundering, as in war.

de·press [di·pres′] *v.* 1 To lower the spirits of; make gloomy or sad: Loneliness *depresses* many people. 2 To make less active or strong: The highway has *depressed* travel on the railroad. **3** To press or push down; lower.

de·pres·sant [di·pres′ənt] *n.* A drug or other substance which calms or soothes; a sedative.

de·pressed [di·prest′] *adj.* **1** Gloomy or sad: a *depressed* person. **2** Suffering from unemployment and a low standard of living: a *depressed* area. **3** Reduced in activity, energy, power, amount, or value. **4** Pressed down; lowered or flattened, especially below the general surface.

de·pres·sion [di·presh′ən] *n.* **1** Low spirits; gloom or sadness. **2** A pressing down: the *depression* of a piano key. **3** A low or sunken place in a surface; hollow. **4** A time when business is sharply cut down and many people are out of work.

dep·ri·va·tion [dep′rə·vā′shən] *n.* **1** The action of depriving or taking away. **2** The condition of being deprived, as of something needed or wanted: the *deprivation* of civil rights.

de·prive [di·prīv′] *v.* **de·prived, de·priv·ing** **1** To take away from: to *deprive* a child of a favorite toy. **2** To keep from getting, having, or enjoying: to *deprive* them of rest.

dept. department.

depth [depth] *n.* **1** Distance to the bottom or to the back; deepness: the *depth* of a pool; the *depth* of a cave. **2** (*usually pl.*) The part deepest down or farthest in: the *depths* of the sea. **3** (*sometimes pl.*) The part of anything that is most intense: the *depth* of night. **4** Deepness of thought: This book has great *depth.* **5** Lowness of pitch. **6** Understanding or ability: Calculus is beyond my *depth.*

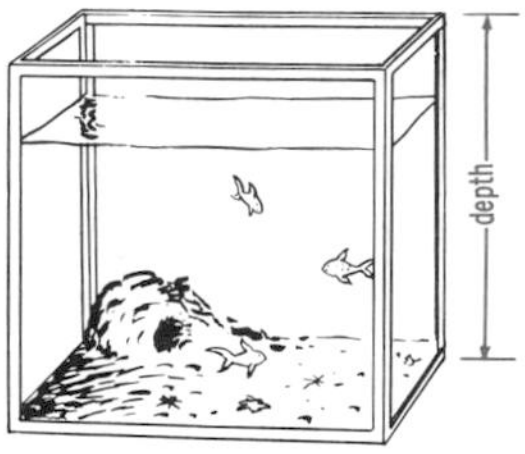

depth charge An explosive charge designed to go off underwater, usually launched from a ship or dropped from an aircraft and aimed at submarines.

depth perception **1** The ability to perceive the distance between oneself and objects one is looking at. **2** The ability to perceive the spatial relationship of objects at different distances.

dep·u·ta·tion [dep′yə·tā′shən] *n.* **1** The act of deputing. **2** A group of persons sent to act for a larger group; delegation: A *deputation* of tenants demanded lower rents.

de·pute [di·pyo͞ot′] *v.* **de·put·ed, de·put·ing** **1** To appoint to act for one or to do one's work: The leader *deputed* an assistant to serve in her absence. **2** To transfer (duties, powers, or authority) to another.

dep·u·tize [dep′yə·tīz′] *v.* **dep·u·tized, dep·u·tiz·ing** **1** To appoint as a deputy: to *deputize* a helper. **2** To act as a deputy.

dep·u·ty [dep′yə·tē] *n., pl.* **dep·u·ties** A person given the power to do another's job or to act in another's place: a sheriff's *deputy.*

de·rail [dē·rāl′] *v.* To run or cause to run off a track: to *derail* a train. **—de·rail′ment** *n.*

de·rail·leur [di·rā′lər] *n.* A mechanism on a bicycle that shifts gears by moving the chain from one set of gearwheels to another.

de·range [di·rānj′] *v.* **de·ranged, de·rang·ing** **1** To upset, confuse, or disturb the arrangement of: The delay *deranged* the schedule. **2** To cause to go crazy; make insane. **—de·range′ment** *n.*

der·by [dûr′bē] *n., pl.* **der·bies** A stiff felt hat having a curved, narrow brim and a round crown.

derby

Der·by *n.* **1** [där′bē] A famous horse race run each year in England, founded in 1780 by the Earl of Derby. **2** [dûr′bē] Any similar horse race, as the Kentucky Derby.

de·reg·u·late [dē·reg′yə·lāt′] *v.* **de·reg·u·lat·ed, de·reg·u·la·ting** To remove controlling regulations from: After the airline industry was *deregulated,* prices and routes began to vary. **—de·reg′·u·la′tion** *n.*

der·e·lict [der′ə·likt] **1** *n.* A ship left abandoned at sea. **2** *adj.* Abandoned; deserted. **3** *n.* A poor, homeless person; bum. **4** *adj.* Guilty of neglect or carelessness.

der·e·lic·tion [der′ə·lik′shən] *n.* **1** Failure to do what is required; neglect of duty: The guard's *dereliction* allowed the prisoner to escape. **2** A deliberate abandonment; desertion.

de·ride [di·rīd′] *v.* **de·rid·ed, de·rid·ing** To laugh at with contempt; make fun of.

de·ri·sion [di·rizh′ən] *n.* Mocking laughter; ridicule: to greet someone with *derision.*

de·ri·sive [di·rī′siv] *adj.* Full of contempt; mocking: a *derisive* smile. **—de·ri′sive·ly** *adv.*

der·i·va·tion [der′ə·vā′shən] *n.* **1** A getting from a source. **2** Descent or origin: to be of Spanish *derivation.* **3** The history of a word, showing how it was formed and how it developed. **4** The formation of a word from an existing word, chiefly by the addition of an affix.

de·riv·a·tive [di·riv′ə·tiv] **1** *adj.* That is derived from something else. **2** *n.* Something that is derived: The word "functional" is a *derivative* of "function." **3** *n.* A chemical compound formed from another compound by certain chemical processes: a benzine *derivative.*

de·rive [di·rīv′] *v.* **de·rived, de·riv·ing** **1** To get or receive: to *derive* satisfaction from one's work. **2** To trace or come from a particular source: The word "zoo" *derives* from the Greek.

der·ma [dûr′mə] *n.* Another word for DERMIS.

der·mal [dûr′məl] *adj.* Of or having to do with the skin.

der·ma·tol·o·gist [dûr′mə·tol′ə·jist] *n.* A doctor who specializes in dermatology. ◆ See EPIDERMIS.

der·ma·tol·o·gy [dûr′mə·tol′ə·jē] *n.* The branch of medicine that deals with the skin and its diseases.

der·mis [dûr′mis] *n.* The sensitive layer of skin lying under the outer skin.

der·o·gate [der′ə·gāt′] *v.* **der·o·gat·ed, der·o·gat·ing** **1** To make seem bad, wrong, or inferior; disparage: to *derogate* her political opponents. **2** To take away; detract: Their criticism of the government

a	add	**i**	it	**o͝o**	took	**oi**	oil
ā	ace	**ī**	ice	**o͞o**	pool	**ou**	pout
â	care	**o**	odd	**u**	up	**ng**	ring
ä	palm	**ō**	open	**û**	burn	**th**	thin
e	end	**ô**	order	**yo͞o**	fuse	**th̶**	this
ē	equal					**zh**	vision

ə = { a in *above* e in *sicken* i in *possible*; o in *melon* u in *circus* }

does not *derogate* from their patriotism. **—der′o·ga′tion** *n.*

de·rog·a·to·ry [di·rog′ə·tôr′ē] *adj.* Meant to lessen the value or merit of someone or something; belittling: a *derogatory* remark.

der·rick [der′ik] *n.* **1** A machine for lifting heavy weights and swinging them into place. It has a long arm hinged at an angle from the foot of an upright pole and is raised or lowered by ropes or cables. **2** The framework over the mouth of an oil well or similar deep hole made by drilling. It holds machinery for drilling, hoisting, and pumping. ◆ *Derrick* comes from the name of *Derrick,* a London hangman in the 1600's.

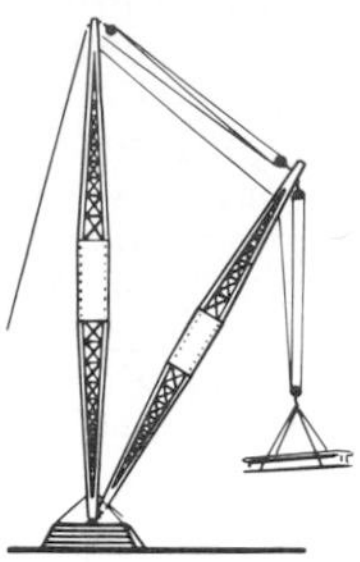
Derrick

der·ring-do [der′ing·dōō′] *n.* Brave or daring action: a deed of *derring-do.*

der·rin·ger [der′in·jər] *n.* A small pistol with a short, wide barrel. ◆ The *derringer* is named after Henry Deringer (1806–1868), an American gunsmith who invented it.

der·vish [dûr′vish] *n.* A member of any of various Muslim religious orders. Some dervishes worship by whirling or howling.

de·sa·li·nate [dē·sal′ə·nāt′] *v.* **de·sa·li·nat·ed, de·sa·li·nat·ing** To desalt. **—de·sa′li·na′tion** *n.*

de·sa·li·nize [dē·sal′ə·nīz′] *v.* **de·sa·li·nized, de·sa·li·niz·ing** To desalt. **—de·sa·li·ni·za·tion** [dē·sal′ə·nə·zā′shən] *n.*

de·salt [dē·sôlt′] *v.* To remove salt from, as sea water.

des·cant [des′kant′ *or* des·kant′] *v.* To talk at length; hold forth: to *descant* upon baseball.

de·scend [di·send′] *v.* **1** To go or move from a higher to a lower point; go down: to *descend* a stairway; to *descend* to the town. **2** To lower oneself; stoop: to *descend* to lying. **3** To come or derive by birth from a certain source: The painter is *descended* from a family of artists. **4** To be passed down by inheritance: Their property will *descend* to their children. **5** To make a sudden attack; swoop.

de·scen·dant [di·sen′dənt] *n.* The child or grandchild of an ancestor; offspring.

de·scent [di·sent′] *n.* **1** The action of going or coming down to a lower point: the *descent* of an airplane. **2** A slope or way going down: a steep *descent.* **3** Family origin; ancestry: She is of Italian *descent.* **4** A sudden attack; assault. ◆ See DECENT.

de·scribe [di·skrīb′] *v.* **de·scribed, de·scrib·ing** **1** To tell about in words, either in speaking or writing: to *describe* a house; to *describe* one's emotions. **2** To draw or form the outline of: His arm *described* an arc.

de·scrip·tion [di·skrip′shən] *n.* **1** The act of describing. **2** An account given in words: the *description* of the accident. **3** Sort, kind, or variety: birds of every *description.*

de·scrip·tive [di·skrip′tiv] *adj.* Telling what a person or thing is like; describing: a *descriptive* passage. **—de·scrip′tive·ly** *adv.*

de·scry [di·skrī′] *v.* **de·scried, de·scry·ing** To catch sight of, as something far off or hard to make out: to *descry* a boat.

des·e·crate [des′ə·krāt′] *v.* **des·e·crat·ed, des·e·crat·ing** To treat something sacred without reverence, or use it in an unworthy way: to *desecrate* an altar. **—des′e·cra′tion** *n.*

de·seg·re·gate [dē·seg′rə·gāt′] *v.* **de·seg·re·gat·ed, de·seg·re·gat·ing** To abolish the separation of races in: to *desegregate* a school. **—de′seg·re·ga′tion** *n.* ◆ *Desegregate* was formed from the word *segregate* and the prefix *de-,* which means *do the opposite of.*

des·ert[1] [dez′ərt] **1** *n.* An extremely dry region, often covered with sand, where few or no plants will grow: the Gobi *Desert.* **2** *adj.* Of or like a desert; barren or remote.

de·sert[2] [di·zûrt′] *v.* **1** To leave a person, place, or thing, especially if one has a duty to stay; abandon: to *desert* one's family. **2** To leave one's military duty or post without leave and without intending to return. **—de·sert′er** *n.* ◆ See DESSERT.

de·sert[3] [di·zûrt′] *n.* (*often pl.*) Reward or punishment that is deserved, especially in the phrase **just deserts:** They got their *just deserts.*

de·ser·tion [di·zûr′shən] *n.* **1** The action of deserting. **2** A deliberate abandoning of a person or persons toward whom one has a duty, as one's family. **3** The leaving of one's military duty without permission and without intending to return. **4** A being deserted.

de·serve [di·zûrv′] *v.* **de·served, de·serv·ing** To be worthy of or entitled to; merit: We *deserve* a second chance.

de·serv·ed·ly [di·zûr′vid·lē] *adv.* According to what is fair and right; justly: That scientist is *deservedly* famous.

de·serv·ing [di·zûr′ving] *adj.* Worthy of help, praise, or reward: a *deserving* composer.

des·ic·cate [des′ə·kāt′] *v.* **des·ic·cat·ed, des·ic·cat·ing** **1** To dry completely; dry up. **2** To dry (a food) in order to preserve. **—des′ic·ca′tion** *n.*

de·sign [di·zīn′] **1** *n.* A plan or sketch to be used as a pattern for making something: a *design* for a theater. **2** *v.* To work out and draw plans or sketches for: to *design* a costume. **3** *n.* The arrangement, as of the parts, features, or shape, of something: The new *design* has two carburetors. **4** *n.* A visible pattern or arrangement: cloth having a floral *design.* **5** *n.* The art of making designs. **6** *v.* To plan or set aside, as for a certain purpose: clothes *designed* for skiing. **7** *n.* (*often pl.*) A sly and wicked plot or scheme to get or take something: My assistant has *designs* on my job. **8** *v.* To form (plans or schemes) in the mind.

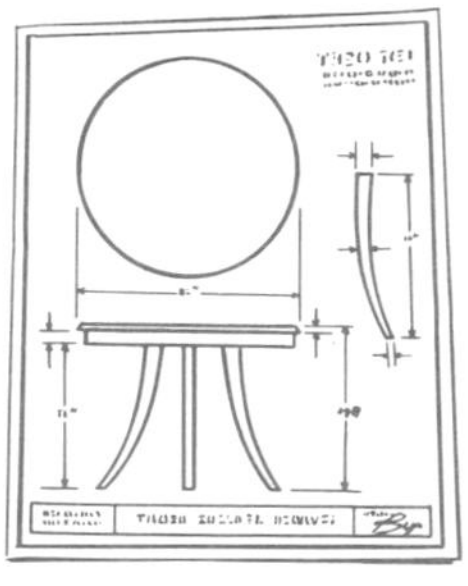
Design for a table

des·ig·nate [dez′ig·nāt′] *v.* **des·ig·nat·ed, des·ig·nat·ing** **1** To point out; indicate: Signs *designate* the places where you may park. **2** To stand for; represent: Names *designate* persons, places, or things. **3** To choose or appoint for a definite duty or purpose: Jones was *designated* to pitch. **—des′ig·na′tion** *n.*

designated hitter A baseball player named at the start of a game to bat in place of the pitcher.

de·sign·ed·ly [di·zī′nid·lē] *adv.* By design; on purpose; purposely.

de·sign·er [di·zī′nər] *n.* A person who creates designs, as for dresses or machinery.

de·sign·ing [di·zī′ning] **1** *n.* The act or art of making designs. **2** *adj.* Scheming; crafty: a *designing* person.

de·sir·a·ble [di·zīr′ə·bəl] *adj.* Worth wanting because good, helpful, or very pleasing: a *desirable* job. **—de·sir·a·bil·i·ty** [di·zī′rə·bil′ə·tē] *n.*

de·sire [di·zīr′] *v.* **de·sired, de·sir·ing,** *n.* **1** *v.* To long for; want very badly: to *desire* freedom. **2** *n.* A longing or craving: a *desire* for gold. **3** *v.* To express a wish for; request: You may have milk if you *desire* it. **4** *n.* A request or wish. **5** *n.* The thing one wishes.

de·sir·ous [di·zīr′əs] *adj.* Having a desire; wanting; eager: to be *desirous* of sleep. **—de·sir′ous·ly** *adv.*

de·sist [di·zist′] *v.* To stop what one is doing; cease.

desk [desk] *n.* **1** A piece of furniture at which a person sits to study, read, or write. Many desks have drawers or a compartment for storage. **2** A division or department in an organization: the copy *desk* of a newspaper.

desktop publishing The use of a personal computer to produce printed newsletters, book pages, etc.

des·o·late [*adj.* des′ə·lit, *v.* des′ə·lāt′] *adj., v.* **des·o·lat·ed, des·o·lat·ing** **1** *adj.* Dreary; barren: a *desolate* prairie. **2** *v.* To ruin or destroy: The flood *desolated* the valley. **3** *adj.* Laid waste; ruined: a *desolate* tangle of fallen trees. **4** *adj.* Lacking people; deserted. **5** *v.* To empty of inhabitants. **6** *adj.* Lonely; miserable: The lost dog looked hungry and *desolate.* **7** *v.* To make sorrowful.

des·o·la·tion [des′ə·lā′shən] *n.* **1** A lonely or deserted condition: the *desolation* of the moors. **2** Destruction; ruin: The army left *desolation* in its wake. **3** Sorrow that comes from loss or loneliness. **4** A desolate region.

de·spair [di·spâr′] **1** *n.* The heavy feeling that comes when all hope is lost or given up: to feel *despair.* **2** *v.* To lose or give up all one's hopes: The survivors of the crash *despaired* of being rescued. **3** *n.* A person or thing that causes a feeling of hopelessness: The attitude of the class is the *despair* of the teacher.

de·spair·ing [di·spâr′ing] *adj.* Caused by, given to, or characterized by despair; hopeless. **—de·spair′·ing·ly** *adv.*

des·patch [di·spach′] *v., n.* Another spelling of DISPATCH.

des·per·a·do [des′pə·rä′dō *or* des′pə·rā′dō] *n., pl.* **des·per·a·does** or **des·per·a·dos** A reckless or violent criminal; outlaw.

des·per·ate [des′pər·it] *adj.* **1** Reckless because all hope or choice seems gone: a *desperate* effort to escape. **2** Considered almost hopeless; dangerous; critical: a *desperate* illness. **3** Very great; extreme: in *desperate* need of money. **—des′per·ate·ly** *adv.*

des·per·a·tion [des′pə·rā′shən] *n.* A state of despair that causes reckless behavior.

des·pi·ca·ble [des′pi·kə·bəl *or* di·spik′ə·bəl] *adj.* Deserving to be despised; mean; contemptible: a *despicable* liar. **—des′pi·ca·bly** *adv.*

de·spise [di·spīz′] *v.* **de·spised, de·spis·ing** To look on with contempt; to dislike and scorn: The rest of the crew *despised* the lazy workers.

de·spite [di·spīt′] **1** *prep.* In spite of; notwithstanding: They kept cheerful *despite* hardships. **2** *n.* A harmful or defiant act.

de·spoil [di·spoil′] *v.* To strip of possessions or things of value; plunder; rob; pillage: Bands of pirates *despoiled* many undefended coastal cities. **—de·spoiler** *n.* **—de·spoil·ment** *n.*

de·spond [di·spond′] **1** *v.* To become discouraged or depressed. **2** *n.* Despondency.

de·spon·dence [di·spon′dəns] *n.* Despondency.

de·spon·den·cy [di·spon′dən·sē] *n.* A state of discouragement or depression.

de·spon·dent [di·spon′dənt] *adj.* Discouraged or depressed: *despondent* over one's bad health. **—de·spon′dent·ly** *adv.*

des·pot [des′pət] *n.* A person, especially a ruler, with absolute power over people; tyrant.

des·pot·ic [di·spot′ik] *adj.* Exercising power in a harsh or bullying way; tyrannical: a *despotic* ruler. **—des·pot′i·cal·ly** *adv.*

des·pot·ism [des′pə·tiz′əm] *n.* **1** Absolute authority; unlimited power; tyranny. **2** A state ruled by a despot.

des·sert [di·zûrt′] *n.* A sweet food, such as pie, cake, pudding, or fruit, served at the end of a meal. ◆ *Dessert* is frequently misspelled as *desert*—and vice versa.

de·sta·bi·lize [dē·stā′bə·līz′] *v.* **de·sta·bi·lized, de·sta·bi·liz·ing** To impair or destroy the stability of.

des·ti·na·tion [des′tə·nā′shən] *n.* The place towards which someone or something is traveling; goal.

des·tine [des′tin] *v.* **des·tined, des·tin·ing** **1** To intend, as if by fate, for some special purpose: to be *destined* to become a performer. **2** To cause by fate. **—destined for** Bound or intended for.

des·ti·ny [des′tə·nē] *n., pl.* **des·ti·nies** **1** The outcome or fate that is bound to come; one's lot: It was Amy Lowell's *destiny* to be a poet. **2** The power which is believed to decide the course of events in advance; fate.

des·ti·tute [des′tə·t(y)o͞ot′] *adj.* **1** Without the necessities of life; in great need; extremely poor. **2** Not having; lacking: a pond *destitute* of fish.

des·ti·tu·tion [des′tə·t(y)o͞o′shən] *n.* **1** The condition of being without the necessities of life; extreme poverty. **2** Lack; deficiency.

de·stroy [di·stroi′] *v.* **1** To ruin completely; wreck; smash: A tornado *destroyed* five houses. **2** To put an end to; kill: Frost *destroyed* the plants.

de·stroy·er [di·stroi′ər] *n.* **1** A person or thing that destroys. **2** A small warship equipped with guns, depth charges, and other weapons.

Destroyer

de·struct [di·strukt′] **1** *n.* The deliberate destruction of a missile after it has been launched. **2** *v.* To destroy.

a	add	**i**	it	**o͝o**	took	**oi**	oil
ā	ace	**ī**	ice	**o͞o**	pool	**ou**	pout
â	care	**o**	odd	**u**	up	**ng**	ring
ä	palm	**ō**	open	**û**	burn	**th**	thin
e	end	**ô**	order	**yo͞o**	fuse	**t̶h̶**	this
ē	equal					**zh**	vision

ə = { a in *above* e in *sicken* i in *possible* / o in *melon* u in *circus* }

de·struc·tion [di·struk′shən] *n.* 1 The action of destroying. 2 Ruin or great damage.

de·struc·tive [di·struk′tiv] *adj.* 1 Causing destruction or apt to destroy: *destructive* floods. 2 Intended to tear down or discredit: *destructive* criticism. **—de·struc′tive·ly** *adv.*

destructive distillation The heating of a substance such as coal or wood in an airtight chamber, so that it decomposes rather than burns and turns into materials that are collected for various later uses.

des·ue·tude [des′wi·t(y)o͞od′] *n.* The condition of not being used; disuse.

des·ul·to·ry [des′əl·tôr′ē] *adj.* Passing abruptly from one thing to another; lacking order or purpose: *desultory* conversation.

de·tach [di·tach′] *v.* 1 To unfasten and remove; disconnect: *Detach* and mail the coupon. 2 To send off for special duty: A squad of soldiers was *detached* to blow up the bridge.

de·tach·a·ble [di·tach′ə·bəl] *adj.* That can be unfastened and taken off or out: a *detachable* hood on a coat.

de·tached [di·tacht′] *adj.* 1 Not connected to something else; standing alone; separate: a *detached* house. 2 Not favoring a certain side; impartial: a *detached* attitude.

de·tach·ment [di·tach′mənt] *n.* 1 The act of detaching or separating. 2 Troops or ships sent off for special duty. 3 A permanent military unit that serves a specific purpose: a medical *detachment.* 4 A feeling of not being personally involved; freedom from prejudice: *Detachment* is necessary for a judge. 5 Aloofness.

de·tail [di·tāl′ *or* dē′tāl *for defs. 1, 2, 4,* di·tāl′ *for def. 3,* dē′tāl *for defs. 5, 6*] 1 *n.* A small, secondary part of something: The artist paid attention to *details.* 2 *n.* A minor piece of information; particular: Please write and give further *details.* 3 *v.* To tell item by item; give particulars about: The union *detailed* its demands. 4 *n.* A dealing with small items one by one: Avoid going into *detail.* 5 *n.* A small group, as of soldiers or police officers, selected for a special duty. 6 *v.* To select for special duty: to *detail* soldiers to guard the prisoners. **—in detail** Item by item.

de·tailed [di·tāld′ *or* dē′tāld] *adj.* 1 Including many details: *detailed* information. 2 Thorough in the treatment of details; exhaustive.

de·tain [di·tān′] *v.* 1 To keep from going ahead or leaving; hold back; delay: A phone call *detained* our friends. 2 To hold in custody; confine.

de·tect [di·tekt′] *v.* To discover, as something hidden or hard to perceive: to *detect* a slight movement in the bushes. **—de·tec′tion** *n.*

de·tec·tive [di·tek′tiv] 1 *n.* A person, often a police officer, whose work is to investigate crimes, find out hidden information, and watch suspected persons. 2 *adj.* Of, for, or about detectives and their work: a *detective* story.

de·tec·tor [di·tek′tər] *n.* 1 A person or device that detects or discovers something: a lie *detector.* 2 In a radio or television receiver, a device that separates the sound or other signal from the carrier wave.

de·ten·tion [di·ten′shən] *n.* 1 The act of detaining or confining: the police's *detention* of the suspect. 2 A being detained, delayed, or held: a suspected spy's *detention* for questioning. 3 Forced legal confinement, as in a jail: a house of *detention.*

de·ter [di·tûr′] *v.* **de·terred, de·ter·ring** To prevent from doing something through fear or doubt; discourage. **—de·ter′ment** *n.* **—de·ter′rer** *n.*

de·ter·gent [di·tûr′jənt] 1 *n.* A synthetic cleansing substance, like soap, used for washing and cleaning. 2 *adj.* Having cleansing qualities.

de·te·ri·o·rate [di·tir′ē·ə·rāt′] *v.* **de·te·ri·o·rat·ed, de·te·ri·o·rat·ing** To make or become worse or less valuable: The building *deteriorated* **—de·te′ri·o·ra′tion** *n.*

de·ter·mi·nant [di·tûr′mi·nənt] *n.* Something that decides the nature or outcome of something else; determining factor.

de·ter·mi·na·tion [di·tûr′mə·nā′shən] *n.* 1 The act of deciding or settling finally: the *determination* of a new government policy. 2 Firmness of purpose; courage: Her *determination* never wavered. 3 A decision reached on the basis of judgment or analysis. 4 The act or result of finding out exactly, as by measuring or calculating: a *determination* of the position of an aircraft.

de·ter·mine [di·tûr′min] *v.* **de·ter·mined, de·ter·min·ing** 1 To decide firmly; resolve: He *determined* to do far better in school. 2 To settle or decide: The court *determined* the case in their favor. 3 To find out by investigation; discover: to *determine* the salt content of sea water. 4 To have a direct effect on; define the limits of: Hereditary factors *determine* the color of one's eyes. 5 To fix in advance: to *determine* the date for a parade.

de·ter·mined [di·tûr′mind] *adj.* Firmly decided; resolute: a *determined* effort to win.

de·ter·min·er [di·tûr′min·ər] *n.* A word such as *a, his, six,* or *that,* used before a noun and descriptive adjectives modifying it.

de·ter·rence [di·tûr′əns] *n.* 1 The act of deterring. 2 The maintenance of powerful military forces and weapons to discourage another nation from starting a war.

de·ter·rent [di·tûr′ənt] 1 *n.* Something that deters. 2 *adj.* Serving to deter.

de·test [di·test′] *v.* To dislike strongly; hate. **—de·tes·ta·tion** [dē′tes·tā′shən] *n.* ◆ *See* HATE.

de·test·a·ble [di·tes′tə·bəl] *adj.* Deserving to be strongly disliked or disapproved; abominable.

de·throne [dē·thrōn′] *v.* **de·throned, de·thron·ing** To remove from the throne or from any high position. **—de·throne′ment** *n.*

det·o·nate [det′ə·nāt′] *v.* **det·o·nat·ed, det·o·nat·ing** To explode suddenly and violently: A clockwork *detonated* the bomb. **—det′o·na′tion** *n.* **—det′o·na′·tor** *n.*

de·tour [dē′to͝or *or* di·to͝or′] 1 *n.* A roundabout way, as a road used temporarily when a more direct route is closed off. 2 *v.* To follow or direct to follow a detour: to *detour* incoming traffic.

de·tox·i·fy [dē·tok′sə·fī′] *v.* **de·tox·i·fied, de·tox·i·fy·ing** To remove a poison or the effects of poison from.

de·tract [di·trakt′] *v.* To take away a part; withdraw something: Losing a game does not *detract* from the fun of playing. **—de·trac′tion** *n.*

de·trac·tor [di·trak′tər] *n.* A person who speaks ill of or belittles someone.

det·ri·ment [det′rə·mənt] *n.* 1 Damage; loss; impairment: To the *detriment* of her health, the director worked seven days a week. **2** Something that injures or damages.

det·ri·men·tal [det′rə·men′təl] *adj.* Causing damage, loss, or impairment; harmful; injurious.

de·tri·tus [di·trī′təs] *n.* **1** Loose particles of rock separated, as by erosion, from masses of rock. **2** Any mass of crumbly material; debris.

deuce[1] [d(y)o͞os] *n.* **1** Something standing for the number two, as a playing card having two spots. **2** In tennis, the score when both sides are tied after having won three or more points each in a game, or five or more games each in a set.

deuce[2] [d(y)o͞os] *n. informal* The devil or bad luck: used as a mild oath: What the *deuce* is that?

deu·te·ri·um [d(y)o͞o·tir′ē·əm] *n.* An isotope of hydrogen in which each atom contains a neutron. Deuterium is about twice as heavy as ordinary hydrogen.

Deu·ter·on·o·my [d(y)o͞o′tə·ron′ə·mē] *n.* The fifth book of the Old Testament.

deut·sche mark [doi′chə märk] The basic unit of money in West Germany.

de·val·u·ate [dē·val′yo͞o·āt′] *v.* **de·val·u·at·ed, de·val·u·at·ing** **1** To lessen the value of. **2** To lower the exchange value of (a currency). **—de·val′u·a′tion** *n.*

de·val·ue [dē·val′yo͞o] *v.* **de·val·ued, de·val·u·ing** To devaluate.

dev·as·tate [dev′ə·stāt′] *v.* **dev·as·tat·ed, dev·as·tat·ing** To leave in ruins; destroy: An earthquake *devastated* Tokyo. **—dev′as·ta′tion** *n.*

de·vel·op [di·vel′əp] *v.* **1** To expand or increase gradually, as if by natural growth: to *develop* one's talent; The cold *developed* into pneumonia. **2** To start having: to *develop* good manners. **3** To work out in detail: unfold: to *develop* a sentence into a paragraph. **4** To bring or come into existence: to *develop* a TV program; Some tastes *develop* slowly. **5** In photography, to treat (as a film or plate) with chemicals to bring out a picture.

de·vel·op·er [di·vel′əp·ər] *n.* **1** A person or thing that develops. **2** A chemical solution used to develop photographs.

de·vel·op·ment [di·vel′əp·mənt] *n.* **1** A growing or causing to grow larger or better: the *development* of one's mind. **2** The result of such growth: a fine muscular *development.* **3** A stage in the developing of something; event: a political *development.* **—de·vel·op·men·tal** [di·vel′əp·men′təl] *adj.*

de·vi·ant [dē′vē·ənt] **1** *adj.* Differing from what is normal or accepted; abnormal. **2** *n.* Something that is deviant, especially a person whose behavior differs from what society considers normal or accepted.

de·vi·ate [dē′vē·āt′] *v.* **de·vi·at·ed, de·vi·at·ing** To turn aside or away from, as a course or rule: The scientists' research *deviated* from all earlier studies. **—de′vi·a′tion** *n.*

de·vice [di·vīs′] *n.* **1** Something built for a specific purpose; an instrument or tool: A thermometer is a *device* for measuring temperature. **2** A scheme or plan: a *device* to bring in customers. **—leave someone to his or her own devices** To let someone do as he or she pleases.

dev·il [dev′əl] *n., v.* **dev·iled** or **dev·illed, dev·il·ing** or **dev·il·ling** **1** *n.* An evil spirit; demon. **2** *n.* A mean or wicked person. **3** *n.* An unfortunate person: poor *devil.* **4** *n.* A person who is bold, lively, and carefree. **5** *v.* To bother or annoy. **—the Devil** or **the devil** In the Jewish and Christian religions, the prince and ruler of the kingdom of evil; Satan.

dev·iled [dev′əld] *adj.* Highly seasoned and usually chopped fine: *deviled* eggs.

dev·il·fish [dev′əl·fish′] *n., pl.* **dev·il·fish** or **dev·il·fish·es** **1** A large ray having a flat body and wide pectoral fins. **2** An octopus.

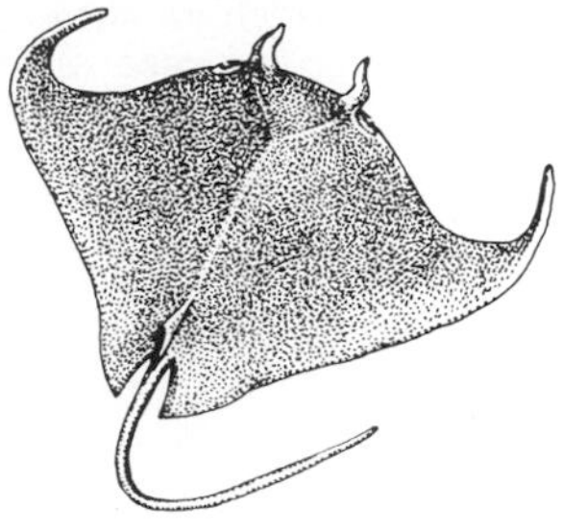
Devilfish

dev·il·ish [dev′əl·ish] *adj.* Of or like a devil; evil: a *devilish* plot. **—dev′il·ish·ly** *adv.*

dev·il-may-care [dev′·əl·mā·kâr′] *adj.* Reckless; careless.

dev·il·ment [dev′əl·mənt] *adj.* Prankish behavior; mischief.

devil's advocate A person who upholds an unpopular cause or defends a questionable position so that arguments for and against the cause or position are both fairly presented. ◆ *Devil's advocate* is a translation of the Latin phrase *advocatus diaboli.* It originally meant the Roman Catholic official who is appointed to argue against a proposed beatification or canonization.

devil's food cake A rich chocolate cake.

dev·il·try [dev′əl·trē] *n., pl.* **dev·il·tries** **1** Reckless and spiteful mischief: to be up to some *deviltry.* **2** Wickedness or cruelty.

de·vi·ous [dē′vē·əs] *adj.* **1** Not direct, straight, or simple; roundabout: a *devious* route. **2** Untrustworthy; dishonest: *devious* conduct. **—de′vi·ous·ly** *adv.* **—de′vi·ous·ness** *n.*

de·vise [di·vīz′] *v.* **de·vised, de·vis·ing** **1** To figure out; invent; plan: to *devise* a means of escape. **2** To pass on (real estate) by will.

de·void [di·void′] *adj.* Entirely without; empty: a situation *devoid* of hope; a sea *devoid* of fish.

de·vo·lu·tion [dev′ə·lo͞o′shən] *n.* **1** A transferring, as of a right, from one person to another. **2** The transfer of powers from a central government to local governing units.

de·volve [di·volv′] *v.* **de·volved, de·volv·ing** **1** To pass over; be transferred: Direction of meetings *devolves* on a student committee. **2** To hand over, as to a successor; transfer.

De·von·i·an [di·vō′nē·ən] **1** *n.* The fourth geological period of the Paleozoic era, during which amphibians appeared and land plants evolved. **2** *adj.* Of the Devonian.

de·vote [di·vōt′] *v.* **de·vot·ed, de·vot·ing** To give over (as oneself or one's time) to a person or activity: to *devote* hours to music.

de·vot·ed [di·vō′tid] *adj.* Feeling or showing love or devotion; true: a *devoted* friend. **—de·vot′ed·ly** *adv.*

dev·o·tee [dev′ə·tē′] *n.* A person who is deeply in-

a	add	**i**	it	**o͝o**	took	**oi**	oil
ā	ace	**ī**	ice	**o͞o**	pool	**ou**	pout
â	care	**o**	odd	**u**	up	**ng**	ring
ä	palm	**ō**	open	**û**	burn	**th**	thin
e	end	**ô**	order	**yo͞o**	fuse	**th**	this
ē	equal					**zh**	vision

ə = a in *above*, e in *sicken*, i in *possible*, o in *melon*, u in *circus*

terested in or devoted to something: a *devotee* of the theater.

de·vo·tion [di·vō′shən] *n.* 1 A strong, loyal affection. 2 Dedication: a lifelong *devotion* to the arts. 3 (*pl.*) Prayers; worship.

de·vo·tion·al [di·vō′shən·əl] *adj.* Of or having to do with devotion; used in worship: *devotional* music.

de·vour [di·vour′] *v.* 1 To eat up greedily. 2 To eat away, consume, or destroy: Fire *devoured* the house. 3 To take in eagerly, as by reading: The politician *devours* the paper each day.

de·vout [di·vout′] *adj.* 1 Religious; pious. 2 Heartfelt; sincere: a *devout* hope. —**de·vout′ly** *adv.*

dew [d(y)o͞o] 1 *n.* Moisture condensed from the air in small drops upon cool surfaces. Dew forms overnight on grass and trees. 2 *v.* To wet with or as if with dew. 3 *n.* Anything fresh, pure, or young.

dew·ber·ry [d(y)o͞o′ber′ē] *n., pl.* **dew·ber·ries** 1 A sweet, edible berry, similar to a blackberry. 2 The plant on which it grows.

dew·claw [d(y)o͞o′klô′] *n.* A vestigial toe or hoof that does not reach the ground on the foot of some mammals.

dew·drop [d(y)o͞o′drop′] *n.* A drop of dew.

Dew·ey Decimal System [d(y)o͞o′ē] A code of numbers used to classify books by subject.

dew·lap [d(y)o͞o′lap′] *n.* The loose skin hanging under the throat of some animals, as cattle.

dew point The temperature at which dew forms or vapor condenses to drops of liquid.

dew·y [d(y)o͞o′ē] *adj.* **dew·i·er, dew·i·est** 1 Moist with or as if with dew: *dewy* eyes. 2 Fresh; clear: a *dewy* complexion.

dex·ter·i·ty [dek·ster′ə·tē] *n.* 1 Skill in using the hands or body; agility. 2 Mental quickness.

dex·ter·ous [dek′strəs *or* dek′stər·əs] *adj.* 1 Skillful in using the hands or body; adroit: a *dexterous* billiards player. 2 Mentally quick; keen. —**dex′·ter·ous·ly** *adv.* ◆ *Dexterous* comes from a Latin word meaning *skillful,* which in turn comes from a Latin root meaning *on the right* or *right-handed.*

dex·trin [dek′strin] *n.* A powder made from starch and used, when dissolved in liquid, as a glue and as a coating for paper and fabrics.

dex·trine [dek′strēn′ *or* dek′strin] *n.* Another spelling of DEXTRIN.

dex·trose [dek′strōs′] *n.* A natural sugar found in plants and animals; glucose.

dex·trous [dek′strəs] *adj.* Another spelling of DEXTEROUS.

dg or **dg.** decigram.

DH designated hitter.

dho·ti [dōt′e] *n., pl.* **dho·tis** 1 A loincloth worn by Hindu men in India. 2 The fabric used to make dhotis.

dhow [dou] *n.* An Arabian boat having lateen sails.

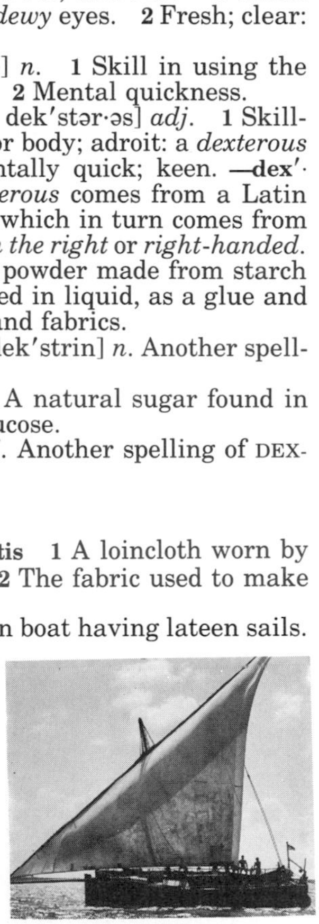

Dhow

di- A prefix meaning: Two; twice; double; twofold, as in *dicotyledon.*

di·a·be·tes [dī′ə·bē′tis *or* dī′ə·bē′tēz′] *n.* A disease in which carbohydrates that have been eaten cannot be absorbed into the system because of too little natural insulin.

di·a·bet·ic [dī′ə·bet′ik] 1 *adj.* Of or having to do with diabetes. 2 *adj.* Having diabetes. 3 *n.* A person who has diabetes.

di·a·bol·ic [dī′ə·bol′ik] *adj.* Diabolical.

di·a·bol·i·cal [dī′ə·bol′ə·kəl] *adj.* Of or like the devil; fiendish; wicked: a *diabolical* plot. —**di′a·bol′i·cal·ly** *adv.*

di·a·crit·ic [dī′ə·krit′ik] 1 *n.* A diacritical mark. 2 *adj.* Diacritical.

di·a·crit·i·cal [dī′ə·krit′i·kəl] *adj.* Used to indicate a difference: *diacritical* marks.

diacritical mark A mark, point, or sign placed near or attached to a letter or letters to indicate special pronunciation, as ē, o͞o, ô, ä.

di·a·dem [dī′ə·dem] *n.* A crown or band worn on the head as a sign of royalty or honor.

di·ag·nose [dī′əg·nōs′ *or* dī′əg·nōz′] *v.* **di·ag·nosed, di·ag·nos·ing** To determine by diagnosis.

di·ag·no·sis [dī′əg·nō′sis] *n., pl.* **di·ag·no·ses** [dī′əg·nō′sēz] 1 The act or process of recognizing a disease by its symptoms. Diagnosis begins with examination of the patient, and often includes tests of the blood and urine, and X rays. 2 A conclusion reached as to the nature of a disease: The tests confirmed the doctor's *diagnosis.* 3 A critical study of any condition or situation; conclusion based on analysis: a *diagnosis* of the country's economic troubles.

di·ag·nos·tic [dī′əg·nos′tik] 1 *adj.* Of, having to do with, or used in diagnosis. 2 *n.* (*often pl.*) The art or practice of diagnosis, especially medical diagnosis. 3 *n.* A sign useful in recognizing a disease.

di·ag·nos·ti·cian [dī′əg·no·stish′ən] *n.* A person, especially a physician, who specializes in making diagnoses.

di·ag·o·nal [dī·ag′ə·nəl] 1 *adj.* Crossing in a slanting direction from corner to corner or from side to side. 2 *adj.* In geometry, connecting any two vertices of a closed plane figure that do not have a common side. 3 *n.* A diagonal line. —**di·ag′o·nal·ly** *adv.*

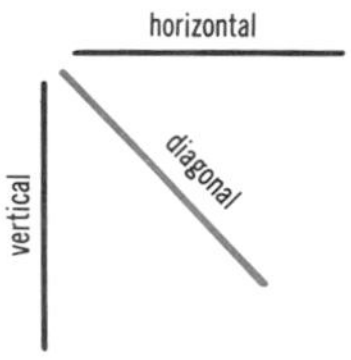

diagonal cloth A fabric with diagonal ridges or lines.

di·a·gram [dī′ə·gram′] *n., v.* **di·a·gramed** or **di·a·grammed, di·a·gram·ing** or **di·a·gram·ming** 1 *n.* An outline or drawing of something, not intended to look like it but to explain how its parts are arranged or how it works: a *diagram* of an internal-combustion engine. 2 *n.* A graph or chart: a *diagram* showing population growth. 3 *v.* To show by diagram; make a diagram of.

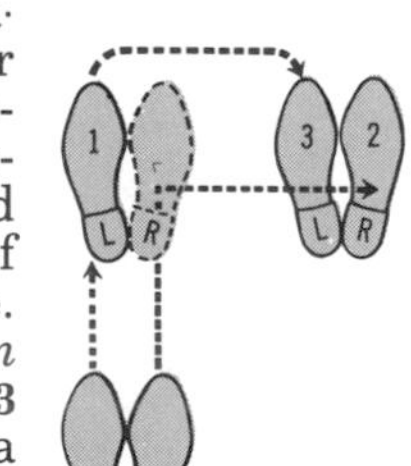

Diagram of a dance

di·a·gram·mat·ic [dī′ə·grə·mat′·ik] *adj.* 1 Having the form of a diagram. 2 Lacking detail; sketchy.

di·a·gram·mat·i·cal [dī′ə·grə·mat′i·kəl] *adj.* Diagrammatic. —**di′a·gram·mat·i·cal·ly** *adv.*

di·al [dī′(ə)l] *n., v.* **di·aled** or **di·alled, di·al·ing** or **di·al·ling** 1 *n.* A flat surface marked with numbers or other signs so that a movable pointer can indicate certain information, as time, pressure, or temperature. The face of a watch or clock is a dial. 2 *n.* Something, as a knob or disk, on a radio or television set for turning it on and off or regulating its operation. 3 *v.* To turn to or indicate by means of a dial: *Dial* the station you like best. **4** *n.* A disk on some telephones that can be rotated over a numbered or lettered guide in making a call. **5** *v.* To call by means of the dial on a telephone: I *dialed* my sister. **6** *v.* To use a dial, as in telephoning. **7** *n.* A sundial.

di·a·lect [dī′ə·lekt′] *n.* A form of speech characteristic of a particular region or class, different in some of its words, idioms, and pronunciations from the standard language: "Auld lang syne" is Scottish *dialect* for "long ago."

di·a·lec·tal [dī′ə·lek′təl] *adj.* Of, having to do with, or characteristic of a speech dialect.

di·a·lec·ti·cian [di′ə·lek′tish′ən] *n.* A person who studies or specializes in dialects.

di·a·logue [dī′ə·lôg′ *or* dī′ə·log′] *n.* **1** A conversation in which two or more speakers take part. **2** The conversation, as in a play or novel: The *dialogue* didn't sound natural to me. ◆ *Dialogue* comes originally from two Greek roots that mean *across* or *between* and *word* or *speech*.

dial tone A low, steady, humming sound indicating to the user of a telephone that a call may be made.

di·al·y·sis [dī·al′ə·sis] *n., pl.* **di·al·y·ses** [dī·al′ə·sēz′] The removal of relatively large colloidal particles from a solution by means of a thin membrane through which only smaller particles can pass.

di·am·e·ter [dī·am′ə·tər] *n.* **1** A line segment joining two points on a circle or sphere and passing through its center. **2** The length of such a segment, especially when used to measure something: The *diameter* of the tube was 16 inches.

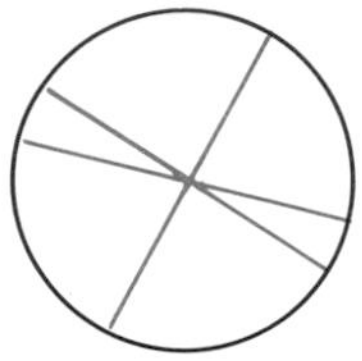
Diameters

di·a·met·ric [dī′ə·met′rik] *adj.* Diametrical.

di·a·met·ri·cal [dī′ə·met′ri·kəl] *adj.* **1** Of a diameter: *diametrical* distance. **2** Directly opposite: *diametrical* opinions.

di·a·met·ri·cal·ly [dī′ə·met′rik·lē] *adv.* **1** Completely; exactly: *diametrically* opposed points of view. **2** Along a diameter.

dia·mond [dī′(ə·)mənd] *n.* **1** A mineral consisting of carbon in crystal form, which when cut and polished is highly valued as a gem. Because of their great hardness, diamonds are used in industry in cutting tools and for grinding. **2** A figure like this ♦. **3** A playing card of the suit marked with red diamond figures. **4** (*pl.*) The suit so marked. **5** The infield of a baseball field. **6** The entire field.

dia·mond·back [dī′(ə·)mənd·bak′] *n.* A large rattlesnake of the SE U.S. having diamond-shaped marks on its back.

Di·an·a [dī·an′ə] *n.* In Roman myths, the goddess of hunting and of the moon. Her Greek name was Artemis.

di·a·pa·son [dī′ə·pā′zən *or* dī′ə·pā′sən] *n.* **1** Either of two principal stops in an organ. **2** A fixed standard of musical pitch. **3** The entire range of a voice or instument. **4** A great rush of sound or harmony.

di·a·per [dī′(ə·)pər] **1** *n.* A piece of cloth or other absorbent material pinned around the loins of a baby, worn as an undergarment. **2** *v.* To put a diaper on. **3** *n.* A decorative pattern of repeated designs. **4** *n.* A silk or linen cloth having such a pattern.

di·aph·a·nous [dī·af′ə·nəs] *adj.* Thin enough to be seen through; transparent: a *diaphanous* veil.

di·a·phragm [dī′ə·fram′] *n.* **1** A muscular wall separating the chest and abdominal cavities in mammals. **2** Any partition or membrane that divides. **3** A disk with an adjustable opening that can control the amount of light passing through the lens of a camera. **4** A disk that responds to sound by vibrating, as used in telephones.

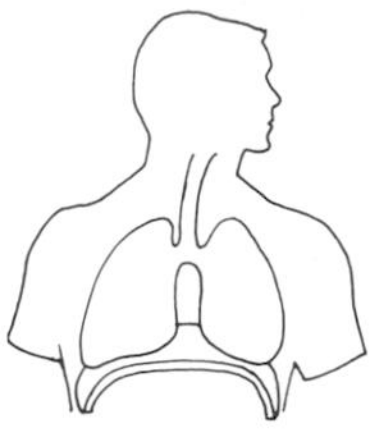
Diaphragm

di·a·rist [dī′ə·rəst] *n.* A person who keeps a diary.

di·ar·rhe·a [dī′ə·rē′ə] *n.* A condition in which the bowels move very often and very loosely.

di·a·ry [dī′(ə·)rē] *n., pl.* **di·a·ries** **1** A personal record kept day by day of what happens or what one thinks about each day. **2** A book with space for writing down each day's record: The traveler kept a *diary* of the summer's trip. ◆ *Diary* comes from a Latin word meaning *day*.

Di·as·po·ra [dī·as′pə·rə] *n.* **1** The dispersion of the Jews into colonies outside Palestine after the Babylonian exile. **2** The Jews that were dispersed or the areas in which they settled. **3** The Jews who live outside Palestine or modern Israel. **4** (*written* **diaspora**) The dispersion or migration of any homogeneous people.

di·as·to·le [dī·as′tə·lē′] *n.* The rhythmic expansion of the heart that draws the blood into its chambers. ◆ See SYSTOLE.

di·a·stol·ic [dī′ə·stol′ik] *adj.* Of, having to do with, or during diastole: *diastolic* blood pressure.

di·a·tom [dī′ə·tom′ *or* dī′ə·təm] *n.* Any of various tiny, single-celled plants with hard cell walls, largely of silica, found in fresh or salt water.

di·a·ton·ic [dī′ə·ton′ik] *adj.* Using or having to do with the tones of an ordinary major or minor scale without alteration or added tones.

di·a·tribe [dī′ə·trīb′] *n.* A very strong spoken or written criticism, often bitter or malicious: The speech turned out to be a *diatribe* against the tax bill.

dib·ble [dib′əl] *n.* A pointed tool that makes holes in soil for seeding and planting.

Dibble

dibs [dibz] *n.pl. slang* A claim: I have *dibs* on whatever's left.

dice [dīs] *n.pl. of* **die**, *v.* **diced, dic·ing** **1** *n.* Small cubes marked on each side with from one to six spots, used in games of chance. **2** *n.* A game played with dice. **3** *v.* To cut into cubes: to *dice* potatoes.

dic·ey [dī′sē] *adj.* **dic·i·er, dic·i·est** *slang* Involving danger or uncertainty; risky.

di·chot·o·my [dī·kot′ə·mē] *n., pl.* **di·chot·o·mies** Di-

a add	**i** it	**o͝o** took	**oi** oil
ā ace	**ī** ice	**o͞o** pool	**ou** pout
â care	**o** odd	**u** up	**ng** ring
ä palm	**ō** open	**û** burn	**th** thin
e end	**ô** order	**yo͞o** fuse	**t͟h** this
ē equal			**zh** vision

ə = a in *above*, e in *sicken*, i in *possible*, o in *melon*, u in *circus*

vision into two usually opposite or contradictory parts, groups, opinions, or sides.

dick·er [dik′ər] 1 *v.* To bargain, especially over a petty trade: to *dicker* over the price of a dozen eggs. 2 *n.* A petty agreement or deal.

dick·ey [dik′ē] *n., pl.* **dick·eys** An article of clothing that circles the neck and sometimes covers part of the chest, worn under a shirt, blouse, or jacket.

Dickey

di·cot·y·le·don [dī′kot·ə·lēd′(ə)n] *n.* A plant having two cotyledons, or first leaves sprouting from a seed. **—di′cot·y·le′do·nous** *adj.*

dict. 1 dictation. 2 dictionary.

Dic·ta·phone [dik′tə·fōn′] *n.* An office machine on which dictation may be recorded and played back to be typed: a trademark.

dic·tate [dik′tāt′] *v.* **dic·tat·ed, dic·tat·ing,** *n.* 1 *v.* To say or read aloud (something to be written down or recorded): to *dictate* a long letter. 2 *v.* To order or require with authority: Fog *dictated* postponement of the flight. 3 *v.* To give orders. 4 *n.* (*often pl.*) Something established with authority; rule or order: the *dictates* of the heart.

dic·ta·tion [dik·tā′shən] *n.* 1 The act of speaking or reading something aloud to be written down or recorded. 2 Whatever is so spoken or read; dictated material: Do you take *dictation*? 3 The giving of orders that must be obeyed.

dic·ta·tor [dik′tā·tər *or* dik·tā′tər] *n.* 1 A person who rules a country with absolute power. 2 Any person who rules with authority: a *dictator* of fashion. 3 A person who dictates words to be written down or recorded. **—dic·ta′tor·ship′** *n.*

dic·ta·to·ri·al [dik′tə·tôr′ē·əl] *adj.* 1 Of or suited to a dictator: a *dictatorial* policy. 2 Overbearing; bossy. **—dic′ta·to′ri·al·ly** *adv.*

dic·tion [dik′shən] *n.* 1 The way in which one expresses oneself in words; the use, choice, and arrangement of words in talking and writing. "I ain't got none" is an example of poor diction. 2 A manner of saying or pronouncing words; enunciation: clear *diction.*

dic·tion·ar·y [dik′shən·er′ē] *n., pl.* **dic·tion·ar·ies** A reference book that lists words in a language or languages in alphabetical order and that gives information about the words, including what they mean and how they are pronounced. This dictionary, a general English-language dictionary, explains its words with other words in the same language. Bilingual dictionaries translate words of one language into those of another. Specialized dictionaries include only words that are related to a particular subject, like sports, cooking, or chemistry.

dic·tum [dik′təm] *n., pl.* **dic·tums** or **dic·ta** [dik′tə] Something said with authority; formal pronouncement: the *dicta* of the Church.

did [did] Past tense of DO[1].

di·dac·tic [dī·dak′tik *or* di·dak′tik] *adj.* 1 Suitable or intended for teaching or for guiding moral conduct: a *didactic* story. 2 Inclined to teach or lecture: The professor had a *didactic* nature.

did·n't [did′(ə)nt] Did not.

Di·do [dī′dō] *n.* In Roman legend, a queen of Carthage who fell in love with Aeneas.

die[1] [dī] *v.* **died, dy·ing** 1 To stop living; suffer death. 2 To lose force or power; fade away: The fire *died* out; The noise *died* down. 3 To stop working: The engine *died.* 4 To fail or be defeated: The bill *died* in Congress.

die[2] [dī] *n.* 1 *pl.* **dies** A hard metal block or plate for stamping, shaping, or cutting out some object. Dies cut the threads on nuts and bolts, stamp designs on coins, and shape wire. 2 *pl.* **dice** A small marked cube used in games. ◆ See DICE. **—the die is cast** The choice has been made and cannot be undone.

Die for stamping nickels

die-hard [dī′härd′] 1 *adj.* Refusing to give up or change one's views: a *die-hard* optimist. 2 *n.* A person who resists to the end.

di·er·e·sis [dī·er′ə·sis] *n., pl.* **di·er·e·ses** [dī·er′ə·sēz] Two dots (¨) placed over the second of two vowels that are next to one another to indicate that two separate vowel sounds are to be pronounced, as in *naïve.*

die·sel [dē′zəl] *n.* (*sometimes written* **Diesel**) 1 An internal-combustion engine used in vehicles, as ships, locomotives, and trucks, burning oil injected into hot compressed air. 2 *adj. use:* a *diesel* engine. 3 A vehicle powered by a diesel, as a locomotive. 4 *adj. use:* a *diesel* locomotive. ◆ *Diesel* comes from the name of *Rudolf Diesel,* the inventor of the *diesel* engine.

di·et[1] [dī′ət] 1 *n.* The food and drink that a person or animal is used to; daily fare: Does your *diet* include fruits and vegetables? 2 *n.* Food and drink specially selected, as for someone's health or appearance: a salt-free *diet;* a *diet* of liquids. 3 *v.* To eat and drink according to a special diet: They *dieted* to lose weight.

di·et[2] [dī′ət] *n.* 1 In some countries, the national legislature: the Japanese *Diet.* 2 An official meeting or assembly.

di·e·tar·y [dī′ə·ter′ē] *adj.* Having to do with diet: *dietary* rules; *dietary* habits.

di·e·tet·ic [dī′ə·tet′ik] *adj.* 1 Suitable for use in special diets: *dietetic* recipes. 2 Having to do with diet.

di·e·tet·ics [dī′ə·tet′iks] *n.* The science that deals with how much and what kinds of food a person or group needs to maintain health. ◆ See -ICS.

di·e·ti·tian or **di·e·ti·cian** [dī′ə·tish′ən] *n.* A person who is trained in the planning of meals or diets necessary for good health.

dif·fer [dif′ər] *v.* 1 To be unlike; have different content or form: His version of the story *differed* from ours. 2 To have a difference of opinion; disagree: They *differed* over who was the best teacher.

dif·fer·ence [dif′(ə·)rəns] *n.* 1 A being unlike or different: the *difference* between right and wrong; a *difference* in price. 2 A particular way in which things are different: The only *difference* between our cars is color. 3 The amount by which things are different, as the amount remaining after subtracting one number from another: The *difference* between 22 and 8 is 14. 4 A disagreement; quarrel. **—make a difference** To be important; matter: Having a seat in the front row *made a* big *difference* in my enjoyment of the movie.

dif·fer·ent [dif′(ə·)rənt] *adj.* 1 Not the same; separate; distinct: We went to two *different* parties on the same day. 2 Not similar; not alike: The U.S. has citizens of many *different* backgrounds. 3 Out of the ordinary; unusual: You may not like this painting, but you must admit it's *different*. —**dif′fer·ent·ly** *adv.* ◆ *Different* is usually followed by *from* in American speech and writing: This book is *different from* that one. *Different than,* when a clause follows, is also widely used, but is best avoided in formal writing: The weather was *different than* what we had expected. In Great Britain *different to* is sometimes used as a substitute for *different from:* This soup is *different to* most dishes I've tasted.

dif·fer·en·tial [dif′ə·ren′shəl] 1 *adj.* Indicating, showing, or based on a difference: *differential* tax rates. 2 *n.* An arrangement of gears, as in an automobile or bus, that lets one wheel powered by the engine turn faster than its opposite, as on curves.

dif·fer·en·ti·ate [dif′ə·ren′shē·āt′] *v.* **dif·fer·en·ti·at·ed, dif·fer·en·ti·at·ing** 1 To recognize a difference: to *differentiate* between common sense and intelligence. 2 To distinguish from something similar: Color of skin, eyes, and hair *differentiates* albinos from other people. 3 To become different or specialized, as cells when they are developing into organs. —**dif′fer·en′ti·a′tion** *n.*

dif·fi·cult [dif′ə·kult′ *or* dif′ə·kəlt] *adj.* 1 Hard to do: a *difficult* job. 2 Not easy to understand: a *difficult* chapter. 3 Hard to please, handle, or get along with: a *difficult* person. ◆ *Difficult* was formed from the noun *difficulty,* which comes from a Latin word meaning *not easy to do.*

dif·fi·cul·ty [dif′ə·kul′tē *or* dif′ə·kəl·tē] *n., pl.* **dif·fi·cul·ties** 1 A being difficult; difficult nature: the *difficulty* of a problem. 2 Something that is not easy to do, understand, or overcome; obstacle: to face many *difficulties.* 3 A good deal of effort: to walk with *difficulty.* 4 Trouble or worry, especially involving money.

dif·fi·dence [dif′ə·dəns] *n.* The quality or condition of being diffident.

dif·fi·dent [dif′ə·dənt] *adj.* Lacking confidence in oneself; timid; shy. —**dif′fi·dent·ly** *adv.*

dif·fract [di·frakt′] *v.* To undergo or cause to undergo diffraction.

dif·frac·tion [di·frak′shən] *n.* 1 A breaking up of light rays into light and dark or colored bands, caused by interference. 2 A similar breaking up, as of sound waves or X rays.

dif·fuse [*v.* di·fyōōz′, *adj.* di·fyōōs′] *v.* **dif·fused, dif·fus·ing,** *adj.* 1 *v.* To spread out in all directions; circulate in a wider area: The heat *diffused* throughout the house. 2 *adj.* Spread out; dispersed: a *diffuse* light. 3 *v.* To mix together or spread by mixing: said about gases and liquids. 4 *adj.* Using more words than necessary; wordy. —**dif·fu′sion** *n.*

dig [dig] *v.* **dug** (or **digged:** seldom used today), **dig·ging,** *n.* 1 *v.* To break up, turn over, or remove (as earth), as with a spade, claws, or the hands: They *dug* for gold; to *dig* the ground. 2 *v.* To make or form by digging: to *dig* a trench. 3 *v.* To make a way by digging: to *dig* through a mountain. 4 *v.* To find and remove by digging: to *dig* clams. 5 *v.* To discover by painstaking effort or study: to *dig* up the facts. 6 *v.* To stick or thrust; jab: He *dug* his finger into my chest. 7 *n.* A thrust; poke. 8 *n. informal* A sarcastic remark; gibe. 9 *v. U.S. informal* To study hard.

di·gest [*v.* di·jest′ *or* dī·jest′, *n.* dī′jest] 1 *v.* To change (food) chemically in the stomach and intestines into a form that can be absorbed by the body. 2 *v.* To become changed into a form usable by the body. 3 *v.* To take in by the mind; let sink in. 4 *n.* A summary or condensed account of what is in one or more books, articles, or other sources: a *digest* of recent discoveries in medicine.

di·gest·i·ble [di·jes′tə·bəl *or* dī·jes′tə·bəl] *adj.* Capable of being digested; easy to digest.

di·ges·tion [di·jes′chən *or* dī·jes′chən] *n.* 1 The act or process of digesting, as food. 2 The ability or power to digest: a good *digestion.*

di·ges·tive [di·jes′tiv *or* dī·jes′tiv] *adj.* Having to do with digestion: the *digestive* system.

dig·ger [dig′ər] *n.* A person or thing that digs.

dig·gings [dig′ingz] *n.pl.* 1 Materials dug out, as from a mine. 2 A mining region.

dig·it [dij′it] *n.* 1 A finger or toe. 2 Any of the numerals from 0 through 9, so named from counting on the fingers.

dig·i·tal [dij′i·təl] 1 *adj.* Of, having to do with, or like a finger or toe. 2 *adj.* Of, having, or expressed in numerical digits. 3 *adj.* Representing information as a series of numerical digits: a *digital* clock. 4 *n.* A key struck by a finger, as on an organ. —**dig′i·tal·ly** *adv.*

digital computer A computer that uses binary digits, or bits, to process data.

di·gi·tal·is [dij′i·tal′is] *n.* A strong medicine prepared from the dried leaves of the foxglove and used to stimulate the heart.

dig·ni·fied [dig′nə·fīd′] *adj.* Having dignity; proud; calm and stately: a *dignified* manner.

dig·ni·fy [dig′nə·fī′] *v.* **dig·ni·fied, dig·ni·fy·ing** To give dignity to; make or make seem more honorable or worthy.

dig·ni·tar·y [dig′nə·ter′ē] *n., pl.* **dig·ni·tar·ies** A person having a high position, as in a government, church, or university.

dig·ni·ty [dig′nə·tē] *n., pl.* **dig·ni·ties** 1 The quality of character, worth, or nobility that commands respect: Queen Victoria had great *dignity.* 2 Proper pride in one's worth or position: beneath one's *dignity* to complain. 3 A grave, stately manner: The official's *dignity* was unruffled. 4 High position, rank, or office.

di·graph [dī′graf′] *n.* A combination of two letters having one sound, as *oa* in *boat.*

di·gress [di·gres′ *or* dī·gres′] *v.* To turn aside from the main subject. —**di·gres′sion** *n.*

di·gres·sive [di·gres′iv *or* dī·gres′iv] *adj.* 1 Tending to digress. 2 Characterized by digression.

di·he·dral [dī·hē′drəl] 1 *adj.* Formed by two intersecting planes: a *dihedral* angle. 2 *n.* A dihedral angle.

a	add	**i**	it	**ŏŏ**	took	**oi**	oil
ā	ace	**ī**	ice	**ōō**	pool	**ou**	pout
â	care	**o**	odd	**u**	up	**ng**	ring
ä	palm	**ō**	open	**û**	burn	**th**	thin
e	end	**ô**	order	**yōō**	fuse	**th**	this
ē	equal					**zh**	vision

ə = a in *above*, e in *sicken*, i in *possible*, o in *melon*, u in *circus*

D

dike [dīk] *n., v.* **diked, dik·ing** 1 *n.* A dam or wall to keep back a river or sea from low land. 2 *v.* To provide with a dike.

Dike

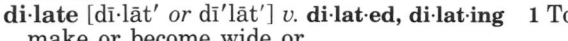

di·lap·i·dat·ed [di·lap′·ə·dā′tid] *adj.* Half ruined by neglect; falling to pieces: a *dilapidated* old farmhouse.
di·lap·i·da·tion [di·lap′ə·dā′shən] *n.* A run-down or ruined condition.
di·late [dī·lāt′ *or* dī′lāt′] *v.* **di·lat·ed, di·lat·ing** 1 To make or become wide or larger: Fear causes a person's eyes to *dilate.* 2 To enlarge in all directions; swell: to *dilate* the heart muscle. **—di·la′tion** *n.*

The pupil dilates in the dark.

dil·a·to·ry [dil′ə·tôr′ē] *adj.* 1 Inclined to delay or put off; not prompt: *dilatory* in making payments. 2 Intended to cause delay: a *dilatory* legal measure.
di·lem·ma [di·lem′ə] *n.* A position where either of two choices is as bad and unpleasant as the other.
dil·et·tante [dil′ə·tänt′ *or* dil′ə·tän′te] *n., pl.* **dil·et·tantes** or **dil·et·tan·ti** [dil′ə·tän′tē] A person whose interest in an art or science is not serious; dabbler.
dil·i·gence[1] [dil′ə·jəns] *n.* 1 Hard, careful work. 2 Willingness or ability to work steadily and carefully.
dil·i·gence[2] [dil′ə·jəns] *n.* A public stagecoach used in France in the 18th century.
dil·i·gent [dil′ə·jənt] *adj.* Hard working: a *diligent* worker. **—dil′i·gent·ly** *adv.*
dill [dill] *n.* An herb whose spicy seeds are used as a seasoning.
dill pickle A cucumber pickled in vinegar and seasoned with dill.
dil·ly-dal·ly [dil′ē·dal′ē] *v.* **dil·ly-dal·lied, dil·ly-dal·ly·ing** To take one's time; dawdle; loiter: Don't *dilly-dally* over your lunch.
di·lute [di·lo͞ot′ *or* dī·lo͞ot′] *v.* **di·lut·ed, di·lut·ing,** *adj.* 1 *v.* To make weaker or thinner by adding a liquid, as water. 2 *v.* To weaken by adding something else: The candidate *diluted* a strong speech with too many jokes. 3 *adj.* Weak; diluted: a *dilute* solution. **—di·lu′tion** *n.*
dim [dim] *adj.* **dim·mer, dim·mest,** *v.* **dimmed, dim·ming** 1 *adj.* Lacking enough light; not bright: a *dim* lamp. 2 *adj.* Not clearly seen; shadowy: a *dim* figure in the distance. 3 *adj.* Not clearly understood or remembered; vague: a *dim* recollection. 4 *adj.* Lacking brilliance; faint: a *dim* sound; a *dim* yellow. 5 *v.* To make or grow dim. **—dim′ly** *adv.* **—dim′ness** *n.*
dime [dīm] *n.* A coin of the United States or Canada worth ten cents.
di·men·sion [di·men′shən] *n.* 1 A measurement along a straight line of the length, width, or thickness of a thing. 2 (*usually pl.*) Size, bulk, or importance: a project of large *dimensions.*
di·men·sion·al [di·men′shən·əl] *adj.* Having dimensions: a three-*dimensional* figure.
dime store Another term for FIVE-AND-TEN.
di·min·ish [di·min′ish] *v.* 1 To make smaller or less; decrease: A sandwich *diminished* his hunger. 2 To grow smaller or weaker; lessen; dwindle: The winds *diminished.*
di·min·u·en·do [di·min′yo͞o·en′dō] *n., pl.* **di·min·u·en·dos,** *adj., adv.* Another word for DECRESCENDO.
dim·i·nu·tion [dim′ə·n(y)o͞o′shən] *n.* A lessening or reduction in size, amount, or degree.
di·min·u·tive [di·min′yə·tiv] *adj.* 1 Of very small size; tiny. 2 Expressing diminished size: said of certain suffixes as *-ette* or *-let.*
dim·i·ty [dim′ə·tē] *n., pl.* **dim·i·ties** A sheer cotton cloth with raised stripes or patterns, used to make curtains and dresses.
dim·mer [dim′ər] *n.* A device for reducing the brightness of an electric light.
dim·ple [dim′pəl] *n., v.* **dim·pled, dim·pling** 1 *n.* A slight hollow on the cheek or chin or on any smooth surface. 2 *v.* To mark with or form dimples: A smile *dimpled* my face.

Dimple

dim sum [dim′ so͝om′ *or* dim′ sum′] In Chinese cookery, a variety of small dishes of food, including steamed and fried dumplings that are stuffed with seasoned meat, fish, or vegetables.
din [din] *n., v.* **dinned, din·ning** 1 *n.* A loud, harsh, confused noise or clamor; uproar: the *din* of the machine shop. 2 *v.* To make a din. 3 *v.* To keep saying over and over: The rules were *dinned* into our ears.
di·nar [di·när′] *n.* The basic unit of money in Algeria, Bahrain, Iraq, Jordan, Kuwait, Libya, Southern Yemen, Tunisia, and Yugoslavia.
dine [dīn] *v.* **dined, din·ing** To eat the principal meal of the day: to *dine* out.
din·er [dī′nər] *n.* 1 A person who dines. 2 A railroad dining car. 3 Any restaurant resembling a dining car.
din·ette [dī·net′] *n.* An alcove or a small room used as a dining room.
ding [ding] *v.* 1 To sound, as a bell; ring. 2 To keep saying over and over.
ding-dong [ding′dông′ *or* ding′dong′] *n.* The sound of a bell when it is struck repeatedly.
din·ghy [ding′ē *or* ding′gē] *n., pl.* **din·ghies** A small boat used with oars as a tender for a larger craft or with jib and mainsail for sailing.
din·gle [ding′gəl] *n.* A narrow, wooded valley; dell.
din·go [ding′gō] *n., pl.* **din·goes** A wild dog native to Australia.
din·gus [ding′əs] *n. slang* Something, as a device or gadget, the name of which is forgotten or not known.
din·gy [din′jē] *adj.* **din·gi·er, din·gi·est** Looking dirty; dull; shabby: *dingy* wallpaper. **—din′gi·ness** *n.*
dining car A railway car in which meals are served while the train is moving.
dining room A room designed and furnished for serving and eating meals.
dink·y [ding′kē] *adj.* **dink·i·er, dink·i·est** *informal* Small and unimportant.
din·ner [din′ər] *n.* 1 The principal meal of the day. 2 A banquet given in honor of a person or event: a *dinner* for the astronauts.
dinner jacket A man's formal jacket; tuxedo (def. 1).
din·ner·ware [din′ər·wâr′] *n.* The dishes, platters, and other tableware, sometimes excluding table utensils, used in serving a meal.

di·no·saur [dī′nə·sôr′] *n.* Any of a large group of reptiles that died off millions of years ago. They had four limbs. They were of all sizes, some being the largest land animals ever known.

Dinosaur

dint [dint] **1** *n.* Means; force: The spy escaped by *dint* of trickery. **2** *n.* A dent. **3** *v.* To make a dent in.

di·oc·e·san [dī·os′ə·sən] **1** *adj.* Of or having to do with a diocese. **2** *n.* A bishop with authority over a diocese.

di·o·cese [dī′ə·sis *or* dī′ə·sēs′] *n.* The district under a bishop's authority.

di·ode [dī′ōd′] *n.* An electronic device that allows current to flow in only one direction.

Di·o·ny·sus [dī′ə·nī′səs] *n.* In Greek myths, the god of wine. He was later called Bacchus.

di·o·ra·ma [dī′ə·rä′mə *or* dī′ə·ram′ə] *n.* An exhibit made up of lifelike figures in natural surroundings in the foreground with a painting for the background.

di·ox·ide [dī·ok′sīd′] *n.* An oxide containing two atoms of oxygen to the molecule.

di·ox·in [dī·ok′sin] *n.* Any of a group of similar organic compounds formed as unwanted by-products in the manufacture of various chlorinated derivatives of hydrocarbons and found as dangerous contaminants in some chemical dumps.

dip [dip] *v.* **dipped, dip·ping,** *n.* **1** *v.* To put into a liquid and take out again at once: to *dip* a foot in hot water. **2** *v.* To lower and then raise: to *dip* a flag. **3** *v.* To dye by immersion. **4** *n.* A brief plunge into water: a *dip* in the pool. **5** *n.* A liquid or sauce into which something is dipped: a cream cheese *dip.* **6** *n.* A hollow or depression: a *dip* in the road. **7** *v.* To make by dipping into tallow or wax: to *dip* candles.

diph·the·ri·a [dif·thir′ē·ə *or* dip·thir′ē·ə] *n.* A serious contagious disease of the throat, usually with high fever, caused by a bacillus. It blocks air passages and makes breathing difficult.

diph·thong [dif′thông′ *or* dip′thông′] *n.* A blend of two vowel sounds in one syllable, as *oi* in *coil.*

di·plo·ma [di·plō′mə] *n.* A certificate given by a school or college to a student who has successfully completed a course of study.

di·plo·ma·cy [di·plō′mə·sē] *n., pl.* **di·plo·ma·cies** **1** The handling of relations, friendly or unfriendly, short of war, between nations. **2** Skill or tact in dealing with others.

dip·lo·mat [dip′lə·mat′] *n.* **1** A person engaged in diplomacy. **2** A person having skill and tact in dealing with others.

dip·lo·mat·ic [dip′lə·mat′ik] *adj.* **1** Of or having to do with diplomacy: a *diplomatic* mission. **2** Tactful: to be *diplomatic* and efficient. **—dip′lo·mat′i·cal·ly** *adv.*

di·plo·mat·tist [di·plō′·mə·tist] *n.* A diplomat.

dip·per [dip′ər] *n.* **1** A long-handled cup used to dip liquids. **2** Either of two northern groups of stars (the **Big Dipper** and the **Little Dipper**) so situated as to resemble dippers.

A dipper and the Big Dipper

dip·ter·ous [dip′tər·əs] *adj.* Of, having to do with, or belonging to an order of insects having a single pair of wings: The fly and the mosquito are *dipterous* insects.

dip·tych [dip′tik] *n.* A picture or pictures, often of a religious subject, painted or carved on two panels that are hinged together.

dire [dīr] *adj.* **dir·er, dir·est** Dreadful; terrible: *dire* distress; *dire* poverty.

di·rect [di·rekt′ *or* dī·rekt′] **1** *v.* To control; manage: to *direct* a company's affairs. **2** *v.* To instruct; order; command: to *direct* soldiers to attack. **3** *v.* To tell or show the way: *Direct* me to the office. **4** *adj.* Straight; shortest: a *direct* road. **5** *adj.* Straightforward; clear: a speech that was *direct* and to the point. **6** *adj.* Having nothing between; immediate: a *direct* plea to the president. **7** *adj.* From parent to child to grandchild, in unbroken line: a *direct* descendant. **8** *adv.* In a direct line or manner; directly. **—di·rect′ness** *n.*

direct current An electrical current flowing in one direction at all times.

di·rec·tion [di·rek′shən *or* dī·rek′shən] *n.* **1** Control or management: research under the *direction* of Dr. Black. **2** A command or order. **3** (*usually pl.*) Instructions on how to do something, operate something, or reach a place: *directions* for knitting a sock. **4** The line along which something moves or the point toward which it faces. South, east, and down are directions. **5** A tendency or line of development: to change the *direction* of a discussion.

di·rec·tion·al [di·rek′shən·əl *or* dī·rek′shən·əl] *adj.* **1** Of or having to do with a direction. **2** Sending or receiving radio waves mainly in or from one direction. **—di·rec′tion·al·ly** *adv.*

directional signal Any of the flashing lights on an automobile that the driver uses to show an intention to turn.

di·rec·tive [di·rek′tiv *or* dī·rek′tiv] *n.* An order or regulation.

di·rect·ly [di·rekt′lē *or* dī·rekt′lē] *adv.* **1** In a direct line or manner; straight: *directly* west; Go *directly* to the shelter. **2** Without anything or anyone between: I am *directly* responsible to the captain. **3** Exactly: *directly* opposite.

direct object The person or thing that receives the action of the verb or shows the result of the action. In the sentence "I wrote a poem," *poem* is a direct object.

di·rec·tor [di·rek′tər *or* dī·rek′tər] *n.* **1** A person who directs, as one in charge of the production of a play or movie. **2** One of a group chosen to direct the affairs, as of a corporation or society. **—di·rec′·tor·ship** *n.*

di·rec·tor·ate [di·rek′tər·ət *or* dī·rek′tər·ət] *n.* **1** The position of director. **2** A board of directors.

di·rec·to·ri·al [di·rek′tôr′ē·əl *or* dī′rek′tôr′ē·əl] *adj.*

a	add	**i**	it	**o͝o**	took	**oi**	oil
ā	ace	**ī**	ice	**o͞o**	pool	**ou**	pout
â	care	**o**	odd	**u**	up	**ng**	ring
ä	palm	**ō**	open	**û**	burn	**th**	thin
e	end	**ô**	order	**yo͞o**	fuse	**t͟h**	this
ē	equal					**zh**	vision

ə = { a in *above* e in *sicken* i in *possible* / o in *melon* u in *circus* }

1 Of or having to do with a director or directorate. 2 Giving directions; instructive.

di·rec·to·ry [di·rek′tər·ē *or* dī·rek′tər·ē] *n., pl.* **di·rec·to·ries** An alphabetical list of names and addresses: a telephone *directory.*

dire·ful [dīr·fəl] *adj.* Dreadful; terrible. **—dire′ful·ly** *adv.*

dirge [dûrj] *n.* A slow, sad song or piece of music, as for a funeral.

dir·i·gi·ble [dir′ə·jə·bəl *or* di·rij′ə·bəl] *n.* A cigar-shaped balloon driven by motors and steered by rudders.

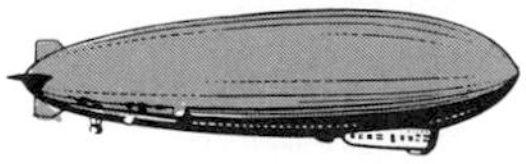
Dirigible

dirk [dûrk] *n.* A dagger.

dirn·dl [dûrn′dəl] *n.* 1 A dress having a full, gathered skirt and a close-fitting bodice. 2 A full, gathered skirt.

dirt [dûrt] *n.* 1 Loose earth. 2 Anything filthy or unclean; anything that soils. 3 Something despised or of little value.

dirt-cheap [dûrt′chēp′] *adj., adv. informal* Very inexpensive.

dirt farmer *informal* A farmer who does his own farm work.

dirt·y [dûr′tē] *adj.* **dirt·i·er, dirt·i·est,** *v.* **dirt·ied, dirt·y·ing** 1 *adj.* Unclean; soiled: *dirty* hands. 2 *adj.* Unpleasant; stormy: a *dirty* job; *dirty* weather. 3 *adj.* Despicable; mean: a *dirty* trick. 4 *adj.* Lacking brightness; muddy: a *dirty* yellow. 5 *v.* To make or become dirty. **—dirt′i·ness** *n.*

dis- A prefix meaning: 1 Not, as in *disloyal.* 2 Opposite of, as in *disadvantaged.* 3 Do the opposite of, as in *disentangle.* 4 Absence or lack of, as in *disinterest.* 5 Exclude from, as in *disbar.* 6 Deprive of, as in *disfranchise.*

dis·a·bil·i·ty [dis′ə·bil′ə·tē] *n., pl.* **dis·a·bil·i·ties** 1 Something that disables. 2 Lack of ability to function normally.

dis·a·ble [dis·ā′bəl] *v.* **dis·a·bled, dis·a·bling** To make unfit or unable; incapacitate; cripple.

dis·a·buse [dis′ə·byo͞oz′] *v.* **dis·a·bused, dis·a·bus·ing** To free from false or mistaken ideas.

dis·ad·van·tage [dis′əd·van′tij] *n.* 1 Something that hinders success; handicap: A poor education is a *disadvantage.* 2 An unfavorable condition or situation: Weak ankles put the runner at a *disadvantage* in the race.

dis·ad·van·taged [dis′əd·van′tijd] *adj.* 1 Lacking advantages; underprivileged. 2 *n. use:* Disadvantaged people: Try to help the *disadvantaged.*

dis·ad·van·ta·geous [dis′ad·vən·tā′jəs] *adj.* Creating a disadvantage; detrimental; unfavorable: in a *disadvantageous* position.

dis·af·fect [dis′ə·fekt′] *v.* To destroy the affection of; cause to be disloyal, discontented, or unfriendly. **—dis′af·fec′tion** *n.*

dis·af·fect·ed [dis′ə·fek′tid] *adj.* No longer contented or friendly; disloyal: spies hidden by *disaffected* farmers.

dis·a·gree [dis′ə·grē′] *v.* **dis·a·greed, dis·a·gree·ing** 1 To have a different opinion; differ: I *disagree* with the speaker. 2 To quarrel; argue. 3 To be unsuitable or upsetting: The medicine *disagreed* with the patient.

dis·a·gree·a·ble [dis′ə·grē′ə·bəl] *adj.* 1 Not agreeable; unpleasant. 2 Having a bad temper; irritable. **—dis′a·gree′a·bly** *adv.*

dis·a·gree·ment [dis′ə·grē′mənt] *n.* 1 A difference in views; failure to agree. 2 An angry dispute; quarrel. 3 A difference; discrepancy: a *disagreement* between your answer and mine.

dis·al·low [dis′ə·lou′] *v.* 1 To refuse to allow or permit. 2 To reject or deny, as a petition.

dis·ap·pear [dis′ə·pir′] *v.* 1 To pass from sight; fade away; vanish. 2 To pass out of existence: The snow *disappeared.* **—dis′ap·pear′ance** *n.*

dis·ap·point [dis′ə·point′] *v.* 1 To fail to meet the hope, expectation, or wishes of: The movie *disappointed* me. 2 To fail to do something promised to: You promised to sing; don't *disappoint* us.

dis·ap·point·ment [dis′ə·point′mənt] *n.* 1 The state or feeling of being disappointed: The children's *disappointment* was hard to forget. 2 Something that disappoints: The new house was a *disappointment.*

dis·ap·pro·ba·tion [dis′ap·rə·bā′shən] *n.* Disapproval.

dis·ap·prov·al [dis′ə·pro͞o′vəl] *n.* A feeling, judgment, or opinion against something; refusal to approve: a look of *disapproval.*

dis·ap·prove [dis′ə·pro͞ov′] *v.* **dis·ap·proved, dis·ap·prov·ing** To have feeling, judgment, or opinion against; think of as bad or wrong: to *disapprove* of a child's behavior.

dis·arm [dis·ärm′] *v.* 1 To take away the weapons of: to *disarm* a soldier. 2 To lay aside weapons: We agreed to *disarm.* 3 To reduce fighting forces and equipment: said about nations. 4 To overcome or reduce the unfriendliness or suspicion in; win over: Their charming manner *disarmed* us.

dis·arm·a·ment [dis·är′mə·mənt] *n.* The cutting down, limiting, or getting rid of a nation's fighting forces and equipment.

dis·arm·ing [dis·är′ming] *adj.* Tending to overcome or reduce unfriendliness or suspicion. **—dis·arm′·ing·ly** *adv.*

dis·ar·range [dis′ə·rānj′] *v.* **dis·ar·ranged, dis·ar·rang·ing** To disturb the order or arrangement of; disorder: to *disarrange* hair.

dis·ar·ray [dis′ə·rā′] 1 *n.* A very untidy state; confusion; disorder. 2 *v.* To put out of orderly arrangement; throw into confusion. 3 *n.* Disordered or incomplete clothing: to escape from a fire in *disarray.*

dis·as·sem·ble [dis′ə·sem′bəl] *v.* **dis·as·sembled, dis·as·sem·bling** To take apart: to *disassemble* a big tent.

dis·as·so·ci·ate [dis′ə·sō′s(h)ē·āt′] *v.* **dis·as·so·ci·at·ed, dis·as·so·ci·at·ing** To stop having a connection; separate: She *disassociated* herself from her former friends.

dis·as·ter [di·zas′tər] *n.* An event causing great distress or ruin, as fires or floods.

dis·as·trous [di·zas′trəs] *adj.* Causing great distress or damage: a *disastrous* fire. **—dis·as′trous·ly** *adv.*

dis·a·vow [dis′ə·vou′] *v.* To say that one does not know about, approve of, or have any responsibility for: The representative *disavowed* the statement quoted as hers.

dis·a·vow·al [dis′ə·vou′əl] *n.* The act of disavowing; denial of responsibility or knowledge.

dis·band [dis·band′] *v.* To break up as an organization; scatter or become scattered: The club *disbanded*; The army was *disbanded.*

dis·bar [dis·bär′] *v.* **dis·barred, dis·bar·ring** To take away the right to practice law from: to *disbar* a dishonest lawyer. **—dis·bar′ment** *n.*

dis·be·lief [dis′bi·lēf′] *n.* A conviction that something is untrue.

dis·be·lieve [dis′bi·lēv′] *v.* **dis·be·lieved, dis·be·liev·ing** To refuse to believe; consider untrue.
dis·bur·den [dis·bûr′dən] *v.* To relieve of a burden.
dis·burse [dis·bûrs′] *v.* **dis·bursed, dis·burs·ing** To pay out or spend.
dis·burse·ment [dis·bûrs′mənt] *n.* **1** The act of disbursing. **2** Money paid out.
disc [disk] *n.* **1** A phonograph record. **2** Another spelling of DISK. ◆ *Disc* and *disk* are a rare pair in English: two spellings of the same word that are equally correct. *Disk* is more common, largely because it is the spelling preferred by the computer industry.
dis·card [*v.* dis·kärd′, *n.* dis′kärd] **1** *v.* To throw away or get rid of as useless or not wanted. **2** *n.* A person or thing that is discarded. **3** *v.* To play (a card not a trump and not of the suit led). **4** *v.* To lay aside from one's hand (one or more unwanted cards).
dis·cern [di·sûrn′ *or* di·zûrn′] *v.* To pick out or recognize with the eye or the mind: to *discern* a deer; to *discern* the truth. **—dis·cern′i·ble** *adj.*
dis·cern·ing [di·sûr′ning *or* di·zûr′ning] *adj.* Quick to discern; discriminating.
dis·cern·ment [di·sûrn′mənt *or* dis·zûrn′mənt] *n.* **1** Keenness of judgment; insight. **2** The act of discerning.
dis·charge [*v.* dis·chärj′, *n.* dis′chärj *or* dis·chärj′] *v.* **dis·charged, dis·charg·ing** *n.* **1** *v.* To shoot or fire, as a weapon. **2** *v.* To remove; unload: to *discharge* a cargo. **3** *v.* To dismiss: to *discharge* an employee. **4** *v.* To release or set free: to *discharge* a soldier or a patient. **5** *n.* A certificate of release: a military *discharge.* **6** *v.* To fulfill the requirements of: to *discharge* a duty. **7** *v.* To give or send forth contents: The wound *discharges* constantly. **8** *n.* Something that is discharged, as pus. **9** *v.* To pay (a debt). **10** *n.* Payment.
dis·ci·ple [di·sī′pəl] *n.* **1** A person who accepts and follows a teacher. **2** A follower of Jesus.
dis·ci·pli·nar·i·an [dis′ə·plə·nâr′ē·ən] *n.* A person who disciplines or believes in the use of discipline.
dis·ci·pli·nar·y [dis′ə·plə·ner′ē] *adj.* Of or for discipline: *disciplinary* training.
dis·ci·pline [dis′ə·plin] *n., v.* **dis·ci·plined, dis·ci·plin·ing** **1** *n.* Strict, systematic training that teaches obedience and orderly conduct. **2** *n.* The obedience, self-control, and orderly conduct that result from such training. **3** *v.* To train to obedience, self-control, and order: to *discipline* a squad of recruits. **4** *n.* Punishment for the sake of training or correcting. **5** *v.* To punish.
disc jockey **1** A person who conducts a radio program that features recorded music along with announcements and informal talk. **2** A person who plays records at a disco.
dis·claim [dis·klām′] *v.* **1** To deny any knowledge of or connection with; disavow. **2** To give up any right or claim to: to *disclaim* a share in the inheritance.
dis·close [dis·klōz′] *v.* **dis·closed, dis·clos·ing** **1** To expose to sight; uncover. **2** To make known: to *disclose* a secret.
dis·clo·sure [dis·klō′zhər] *n.* **1** The act of disclosing. **2** The thing that is disclosed.
dis·co [dis′kō] *n., pl.* **dis·cos** **1** A nightclub that features dancing to popular, usually recorded music. **2** A style of popular dance music having a strong steady beat. ◆ See DISCOTHEQUE.
dis·cog·ra·phy [dis·kog′rə·fē] *n., pl.* **dis·cog·ra·phies** A list of all the recordings, as of a performer, a composer, or a musical composition.
dis·col·or [dis·kul′ər] *v.* **1** To change or harm the color of: Dampness *discolored* the walls. **2** To become changed, as spoiled or faded, in color.
dis·col·or·a·tion [dis·kul′ə·rā′shən] *n.* **1** The act of discoloring. **2** A stain or discolored spot.
dis·com·bob·u·late [dis′kəm·bob′yə·lāt′] *v.* **dis·com·bob·u·lat·ed, dis·com·bob·u·lat·ing** To throw into confusion; upset completely. ◆ *Discombobulate* is a humorous word made up to sound like Latin, but not derived from any real Latin word.
dis·com·fit [dis·kum′fit] *v.* To frustrate, confuse, or embarrass, as by thwarting plans. **—dis·com·fi·ture** [dis·kum′fi·chər] *n.*
dis·com·fort [dis·kum′fərt] *n.* **1** An uncomfortable condition; distress. **2** Something that causes discomfort.
dis·com·mode [dis′kə·mōd′] *v.* **dis·com·mod·ed, dis·com·mod·ing** To inconvenience; trouble.
dis·com·pose [dis′kəm·pōz′] *v.* **dis·com·posed, dis·com·pos·ing** To make uneasy and nervous; upset the calmness of: The pianist was *discomposed* by the loud whispers of the audience. **—dis·com·po·sure** [dis′kəm·pō′zhər] *n.*
dis·con·cert [dis′kən·sûrt′] *v.* To upset or embarrass, as by unexpected difficulty or unfriendliness: Your rude stare *disconcerted* me.
dis·con·nect [dis′kə·nekt′] *v.* To break or undo the connection of or between.
dis·con·nect·ed [dis′kə·nek′tid] *adj.* **1** Not connected. **2** Not in logical order; wandering: *disconnected* ideas. **—dis′con·nect′ed·ly** *adv.*
dis·con·so·late [dis·kon′sə·lit] *adj.* Full of sadness or despair; unhappy; forlorn. **—dis·con′so·late·ly** *adv.* **—dis·con′so·late·ness** *n.*
dis·con·tent [dis′kən·tent′] **1** *n.* An unhappy, dissatisfied feeling: *discontent* over the new rules. **2** *v.* To cause to become discontented. **—dis′con·tent′·ment** *n.*
dis·con·tent·ed [dis′kən·ten′tid] *adj.* Unhappy and dissatisfied. **—dis′con·tent′ed·ly** *adv.*
dis·con·tin·ue [dis′kən·tin′yōō] *v.* **dis·con·tin·ued, dis·con·tin·u·ing** To stop having, using, or making; break off or end: to *discontinue* weekly meetings.
dis·con·ti·nu·i·ty [dis·kon′tə·n(y)ōō′ə·tē] *n., pl.* **dis·con·ti·nu·i·ties** **1** Lack of continuity. **2** A break or gap.
dis·con·tin·u·ous [dis′kən·tin′yōō·əs] *adj.* Not continuous; having breaks or interruptions. **—dis′con·tin′u·ous·ly** *adv.*
dis·cord [dis′kôrd] *n.* **1** Angry or quarrelsome disagreement; lack of harmony: *discord* between North and South. **2** A combination of clashing or disagreeable sounds. **3** In music, a sounding together of notes that do not seem to harmonize. ◆ *Discord* comes from a Latin word whose elements mean literally *apart from the heart.*

D

a add	**i** it	**ŏŏ** took	**oi** oil
ā ace	**ī** ice	**ōō** pool	**ou** pout
â care	**o** odd	**u** up	**ng** ring
ä palm	**ō** open	**û** burn	**th** thin
e end	**ô** order	**yōō** fuse	**th** this
ē equal			**zh** vision

ə = {a in *above* e in *sicken* i in *possible* / o in *melon* u in *circus*}

dis·cor·dance [dis·kôr′dəns] *n.* 1 The condition of being discordant; discord. 2 A harsh or displeasing combination of sounds; dissonance.

dis·cor·dant [dis·kôr′dənt] *adj.* 1 Not agreeing or fitting together; clashing: *discordant* opinions. 2 Not in harmony; disagreeable; jarring: *discordant* tones. **—dis·cor′dant·ly** *adv.*

dis·co·theque [dis′kə·tek′] *n.* A disco (def. 1). ◆ *Discotheque* comes from the French *discothèque,* which was coined from *disque,* meaning *record,* and the *-othèque* part of *bibliothèque,* meaning *library. Disco* is a shortened form of *discotheque.*

dis·count [*n.* dis′kount′, *v.* dis′kount′ *or* dis·kount′] 1 *n.* A reduction in an amount charged: Students get a *discount* on tickets. 2 *v.* To deduct (a part), as of a bill or price. 3 *v.* To disregard, doubt, or consider exaggerated: *Discount* the stories of their adventures.

dis·coun·te·nance [dis·koun′tə·nəns] *v.* **dis·coun·te·nanced, dis·coun·te·nanc·ing** 1 To disapprove of; frown on: to *discountenance* lateness. 2 To make uneasy; embarrass.

dis·cour·age [dis·kûr′ij] *v.* **dis·cour·aged, dis·cour·ag·ing** 1 To cause to lose courage or confidence: Harsh criticism can *discourage* one. 2 To try to prevent, as by expressing disapproval: Their parents *discourage* late hours. 3 To interfere with; hinder: Poor eating habits can *discourage* growth. **—dis·cour′age·ment** *n.*

dis·course [*n.* dis′kôrs, *v.* dis·kôrs′] *n., v.* **dis·coursed, dis·cours·ing** 1 *n.* A formal speech or written treatment of a subject. 2 *v.* To speak at length; make a long, formal speech. 3 *n.* Conversation or talk. 4 *v.* To talk.

dis·cour·te·ous [dis·kûr′tē·əs] *adj.* Impolite; rude. **—dis·cour′te·ous·ly** *adv.*

dis·cour·te·sy [dis·kûr′tə·sē] *n., pl.* **dis·cour·te·sies** 1 Lack of courtesy; rudeness. 2 Something discourteous, as an act or remark.

dis·cov·er [dis·kuv′ər] *v.* 1 To find out, get knowledge of, or come upon before anyone else: Balboa *discovered* the Pacific; Roentgen *discovered* X rays. 2 To learn or find out, especially for the first time: We *discovered* that reading can be fun. **—dis·cov′er·er** *n.* ◆ Contrast *discover* with INVENT. To *discover* means to find something that already exists; to *invent* means to bring something new into existence.

dis·cov·er·y [dis·kuv′ər·ē] *n., pl.* **dis·cov·er·ies** 1 The act of discovering: the *discovery* of an ancient city. 2 Something discovered.

dis·cred·it [dis·kred′it] 1 *v.* To cause to be doubted; consider unacceptable or untrustworthy: to *discredit* a rumor. 2 *n.* Doubt; disbelief: a theory fallen into *discredit.* 3 *n.* Loss of reputation or honor; disgrace. 4 *n.* A cause of disgrace or loss of honor: A traitor is a *discredit* to the country. 5 *v.* To harm the reputation of; bring dishonor to.

dis·cred·it·a·ble [dis·kred′it·ə·bəl] *adj.* Resulting in or causing discredit.

dis·creet [dis·krēt′] *adj.* Tactful, cautious, and wise: *discreet* inquiries. **—dis·creet′ly** *adv.*

dis·crep·an·cy [dis·krep′ən·sē] *n., pl.* **dis·crep·an·cies** A difference or inconsistency; contradiction: a *discrepancy* between two answers to the same problem.

dis·cre·pant [dis·krep′ənt] *adj.* Differing; disagreeing: witnesses with *discrepant* accounts of the crime.

dis·crete [dis·krēt′] *adj.* Separate from others; distinct: A molecule is a *discrete* particle of matter. **—dis·crete′ness** *n.*

dis·cre·tion [dis·kresh′ən] *n.* 1 Good judgment; prudence: Use *discretion* in confiding secrets. 2 Individual judgment, or freedom to use it: Use your own *discretion* in choosing.

dis·cre·tion·ar·y [dis·kresh′ən·er′ē] *adj.* Left to one's own judgment or discretion.

dis·crim·i·nate [dis·krim′ə·nāt′] *v.* **dis·crim·i·nat·ed, dis·crim·i·nat·ing** 1 To recognize a difference between; distinguish: to *discriminate* between right and wrong. 2 To show prejudice or partiality: The store owner *discriminated* against all goods that were not handmade.

dis·crim·i·nat·ing [dis·krim′ə·nā′ting] *adj.* 1 Noticing small differences or making fine distinctions: a moviegoer of *discriminating* taste. 2 Serving to identify; distinguishing. 3 Showing prejudice; discriminatory.

dis·crim·i·na·tion [dis·krim′ə·nā′shən] *n.* 1 Prejudice in one's attitude or actions: to show *discrimination* against foreigners. 2 The noticing of differences or the making of distinctions. 3 The ability to note small differences.

dis·crim·i·na·to·ry [dis·krim′ə·nə·tôr′ē] *adj.* Showing prejudice or partiality.

dis·cur·sive [dis·kûr′siv] *adj.* Going from subject to subject and often wandering from the main point: a *discursive* lecture.

dis·cus [dis′kəs] *n.* A heavy disk, now usually of metal and wood, used in athletic contests to see who can throw it the greatest distance.

Woman throwing a discus

dis·cuss [dis·kus′] *v.* 1 To talk over or consider; exchange ideas or opinions about: to *discuss* a proposed law. 2 To have or treat as a subject: This chapter *discusses* the American Revolution.

dis·cus·sion [dis·kush′ən] *n.* Argument on or consideration of a subject.

dis·dain [dis·dān′] 1 *n.* Scorn or haughty contempt, especially toward someone or something considered inferior. 2 *v.* To regard as beneath one; scorn; spurn: an intellectual who *disdains* novels. ◆ See CONTEMPT.

dis·dain·ful [dis·dān′fəl] *adj.* Filled with or expressing disdain; scornful. **—dis·dain′ful·ly** *adv.*

dis·ease [di·zēz′] *n.* A sickness or illness, usually of a particular kind. People, animals, and plants may have diseases: Chicken pox is a contagious *disease;* elm trees dying of *disease.*

dis·eased [di·zēzd′] *adj.* 1 Having or affected by a disease. 2 Seriously disordered: a *diseased* mind.

dis·em·bark [dis′im·bärk′] *v.* To go or put ashore from a ship; land: The Pilgrims *disembarked* at Plymouth Rock; to *disembark* troops.

dis·em·bod·ied [dis′im·bod′ēd] *adj.* Existing apart from a body: a *disembodied* spirit.

dis·em·bow·el [dis′im·bou′əl] *v.* To remove the bowels or entrails of. **—dis′em·bow′el·ment** *n.*

dis·en·chant [dis′in·chant′] *v.* To free from a pleasant but false belief; disillusion: The travelers were expecting luxury, but their first meal *disenchanted* them. **—dis′en·chant′ment** *n.*

dis·en·cum·ber [dis′in·kum′bər] *v.* To free from a heavy or hampering burden: She *disencumbered* herself from her backpack.
dis·en·fran·chise [dis′in·fran′chīz′] *v.* **dis·en·fran·chised, dis·en·fran·chis·ing** To disfranchise. **—dis′·en·fran′chise·ment** *n.*
dis·en·gage [dis′in·gāj′] *v.* **dis·en·gaged, dis·en·gag·ing** **1** To loosen, detach, or free from something that holds: She *disengaged* the clutch of the car; to *disengage* a scarf from a thorn. **2** To free oneself, as from an obligation.
dis·en·tan·gle [dis′in·tang′gəl] *v.* **dis·en·tan·gled, dis·en·tan·gling** To make or become free from a tangled or confused condition; unravel. **—dis′en·tan′gle·ment** *n.*
dis·es·teem [dis′ə·stēm′] **1** *v.* To look upon with disfavor. **2** *n.* A lack of esteem; disfavor; disapproval.
dis·fa·vor [dis·fā′vər] **1** *n.* Disapproval; dislike: to regard someone with *disfavor.* **2** *n.* A being disapproved of or opposed: a theory now in *disfavor.* **3** *v.* To disapprove of; oppose.
dis·fig·ure [dis·fig′yər] *v.* **dis·fig·ured, dis·fig·ur·ing** To mar or destroy the appearance of; make unattractive; deface: A broken nose *disfigured* the statue. **—dis·fig′ure·ment** *n.*
dis·fran·chise [dis·fran′chīz′] *v.* **dis·fran·chised, dis·fran·chis·ing** To take a right or privilege away from, especially the right to vote. **—dis·fran′chise·ment** *n.*
dis·gorge [dis·gôrj′] *v.* **dis·gorged, dis·gorg·ing** To throw out; vomit forth: a volcano *disgorging* streams of lava.
dis·grace [dis·grās′] *n., v.* **dis·graced, dis·grac·ing** **1** *n.* A condition of shame or dishonor: The child is in *disgrace* for teasing the dog. **2** *n.* A person or thing that causes shame or dishonor: That untidy room is a *disgrace*! **3** *v.* To bring shame or dishonor to: to *disgrace* one's family by cheating.
dis·grace·ful [dis·grās′fəl] *adj.* Causing, deserving, or involving disgrace. **—dis·grace′ful·ly** *adv.* **—dis·grace′ful·ness** *n.*
dis·grun·tle [dis·grun′təl] *v.* To make resentful and dissatisfied; cause discontent in: The employees were *disgruntled* with their working conditions.
dis·guise [dis·gīz′] *v.* **dis·guised, dis·guis·ing,** *n.* **1** *v.* To change in appearance or manner so as not to be known or to appear as someone else: a soldier *disguised* as a civilian. **2** *n.* Something that disguises, as a costume. **3** *v.* To conceal or give a false idea of: to *disguise* one's voice. **4** *n.* The condition of being disguised: Great clowns are masters of *disguise.*
dis·gust [dis·gust′] **1** *v.* To fill with a sickening feeling of intense distaste or dislike: The sight of blood *disgusts* some people. **2** *n.* Strong dislike caused by something offensive.
dis·gust·ed [dis·gus′tid] *adj.* Filled with or indicating disgust. **—dis·gust′ed·ly** *adv.*
dis·gust·ful [dis·gust′fəl] *adj.* **1** Causing disgust; offensive. **2** Full of or characterized by disgust.
dis·gust·ing [dis·gus′ting] *adj.* Arousing disgust; offensive. **—dis·gust′ing·ly** *adv.*
dish [dish] **1** *n.* A flat or concave container for serving or holding food, as a plate or a bowl. **2** *n.* The amount held or served in a dish: The six diners shared four *dishes* of pudding. **3** *n.* A food prepared for eating: Peach pie is a delicious *dish.* **4** *v.* To put (food to be served) in a dish or dishes: to *dish* out scrambled eggs. **5** *n.* Something shaped like a dish, as the concave reflector of a radar, radio, or television antenna.
dish·cloth [dish′klôth′] *n.* A cloth for washing dishes.
dis·heart·en [dis·här′tən] *v.* To cause to lose one's hope or confidence; discourage.
di·shev·eled or **di·shev·elled** [di·shev′əld] *adj.* Rumpled and untidy, as hair or clothing.

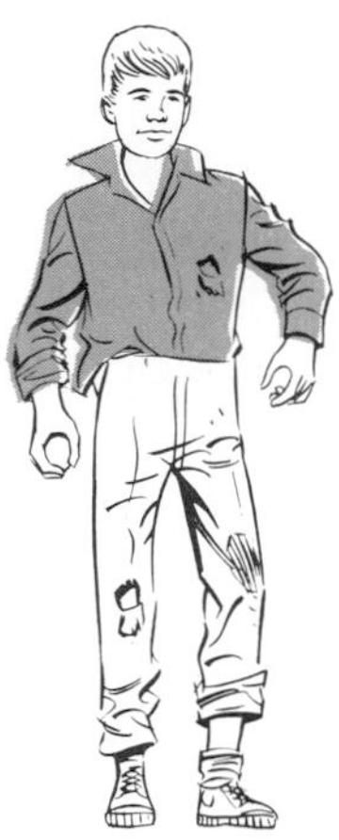

A disheveled boy

dis·hon·est [dis·on′ist] *adj.* **1** Not honest, as a person who lies, steals, or cheats. **2** Showing a lack of honesty: a *dishonest* act. **—dis·hon′est·ly** *adv.*
dis·hon·es·ty [dis·on′ə·stē] *n., pl.* **dis·hon·es·ties** **1** A lack of honesty or probity. **2** A dishonest action or statement.
dis·hon·or [dis·on′ər] **1** *n.* Loss of honor, respect, or good reputation; disgrace or humiliation. **2** *n.* Something that causes loss of honor or respect. **3** *v.* To bring shame to; disgrace. **4** *v.* To treat shamefully; insult.
dis·hon·or·a·ble [dis·on′ər·ə·bəl] *adj.* Not honorable; dishonest or deceitful. **—dis·hon′or·a·bly** *adv.*
dish rag A dishcloth.
dish towel A towel for drying dishes.
dish·wash·er [dish′wäsh′ər *or* dish′wôsh′ər] *n.* **1** A machine for washing dishes. **2** A person hired to wash dishes.
dis·il·lu·sion [dis′i·lo͞o′zhən] **1** *v.* To free from or deprive of illusion; disenchant: We were *disillusioned* to discover that the cake didn't taste as good as it looked. **2** *n.* The condition of being free from or deprived of illusion. **—dis′il·lu′sion·ment** *n.*
dis·in·cli·na·tion [dis·in′klə·nā′shən] *n.* A lack of inclination; unwillingness; aversion.
dis·in·clined [dis′in·klīnd′] *adj.* Not inclined; not willing: *disinclined* to talk.
dis·in·fect [dis′in·fekt′] *v.* To destroy or prevent the growth of disease germs in or on.
dis·in·fec·tant [dis′in·fek′tənt] *n.* A substance used to destroy disease germs.
dis·in·her·it [dis′in·her′it] *v.* To keep from inheriting; deprive of an inheritance: She *disinherited* her children, leaving her money to charity.
dis·in·te·grate [dis·in′tə·grāt′] *v.* **dis·in·te·grat·ed, dis·in·te·grat·ing** To break apart into small pieces or fragments; crumble: Rain *disintegrated* the children's mud pies; Their alibi began to *disintegrate* after questioning. **—dis·in′te·gra′tion** *n.*
dis·in·ter [dis′in·tûr′] *v.* **dis·in·terred, dis·in·ter·ring** **1** To remove from a grave. **2** To bring to light; dig up; unearth. **—dis′in·ter′ment** *n.*

a	add	**i**	it	**o͝o**	took	**oi**	oil
ā	ace	**ī**	ice	**o͞o**	pool	**ou**	pout
â	care	**o**	odd	**u**	up	**ng**	ring
ä	palm	**ō**	open	**û**	burn	**th**	thin
e	end	**ô**	order	**yo͞o**	fuse	**t͟h**	this
ē	equal					**zh**	vision

ə = {a in *above* e in *sicken* i in *possible* / o in *melon* u in *circus*}

dis·in·ter·est [dis·in′tər·ist *or* dis·in′trist] *n.* **1** Lack of interest. **2** Lack of self-interest; impartiality.

dis·in·ter·est·ed [dis·in′tər·is·tid *or* dis·in′tris·tid] *adj.* Free from prejudice or a desire for personal advantage; impartial: *disinterested* advice. **—dis·in′ter·est·ed·ly** *adv.* **—dis·in′ter·est·ed·ness** *n.* ◆ *Disinterested* is sometimes inaccurately used to mean *not interested* or *indifferent.*

dis·joint [dis·joint′] **1** *v.* To take apart or separate at the joints: to *disjoint* a roasted turkey. **2** *adj.* In mathematics, indicating or describing sets in which none of the members of one set appear in any other: 1, 3, 5, 7 and 2, 4, 6, 8 and 1/10, 1/11, 1/12 are *disjoint* sets.

dis·joint·ed [dis·join′tid] *adj.* Rambling and disorganized: This composition is full of *disjointed* ideas. **—dis·joint′ed·ly** *adv.*

disk [disk] *n.* **1** Any flat, circular object, such as a plate or coin. **2** Something appearing to have this form: The *disk* of the moon darkens the sun in an eclipse. **3** (*written* **disc**) A phonograph record. **4** A flat, circular plate with a magnetic coating on which information for a computer can be stored.

disk drive The device that reads and writes information stored on computer disks.

dis·kette [dis·ket′] *n.* Another name for FLOPPY DISK.

disk harrow A harrow that breaks up soil with a row of disks set at an angle on a rotating shaft.

Disk harrow

disk jockey Another spelling of DISC JOCKEY.

dis·like [dis·līk′] *v.* **dis·liked, dis·lik·ing,** *n.* **1** *v.* To have no liking for; consider disagreeable: We are fond of cats, but *dislike* dogs. **2** *n.* A feeling of not liking; distaste.

dis·lo·cate [dis′lō·kāt′] *v.* **dis·lo·cat·ed, dis·lo·cat·ing** **1** To put or force out of joint, as a bone: The fall *dislocated* my shoulder. **2** To throw into disorder: to *dislocate* the nation's economy. **—dis′lo·ca′tion** *n.*

dis·lodge [dis·loj′] *v.* **dis·lodged, dis·lodg·ing** To move or force out from a firm or settled position.

dis·loy·al [dis·loi′əl] *adj.* Not loyal; betraying one's allegiance.

dis·loy·al·ty [dis·loi′əl·tē] *n., pl.* **dis·loy·al·ties** **1** A lack of loyalty or faithfulness. **2** A disloyal act.

dis·mal [diz′məl] *adj.* **1** Dark, gloomy, and depressing: a *dismal* day. **2** Sad and miserable. **3** Very bad: a *dismal* failure. **—dis′mal·ly** *adv.* ◆ *Dismal* comes from the Latin words *dies mali,* meaning *evil days,* from the days that were marked as unlucky on medieval calendars.

dis·man·tle [dis·man′təl] *v.* **dis·man·tled, dis·man·tling** **1** To remove all equipment or furnishings from; strip bare: to *dismantle* a battleship. **2** To take apart: to *dismantle* a stove in order to clean it. **—dis·man′tle·ment** *n.*

dis·may [dis·mā′] **1** *n.* A feeling of alarm, uneasiness, and confusion: The children squealed in *dismay* when the lights went out. **2** *v.* To fill with uneasiness and alarm: a teacher *dismayed* by the students' lack of discipline.

dis·mem·ber [dis·mem′bər] *v.* **1** To cut into pieces or separate limb from limb: to *dismember* a chicken. **2** To divide into separate parts, as a conquered nation. **—dis·mem′ber·ment** *n.*

dis·miss [dis·mis′] *v.* **1** To tell or permit to leave: to *dismiss* a class. **2** To discharge from a job; fire. **3** To put aside or refuse to consider: to *dismiss* a suggestion. **4** To get rid of; forget: *Dismiss* your fears. **5** To put out of a law court without further hearing: The judge *dismissed* the case.

dis·miss·al [dis·mis′əl] *n.* **1** The act of dismissing. **2** The condition of being dismissed. **3** A notification of discharge.

dis·mount [dis·mount′] *v.* **1** To get off or get down, as from a horse. **2** To knock off or throw down; unseat: to *dismount* an enemy horseman. **3** To take apart or remove from a support: to *dismount* a gun.

dis·o·be·di·ence [dis′ə·bē′dē·əns] *n.* A refusal or failure to obey.

dis·o·be·di·ent [dis′ə·bē′dē·ənt] *adj.* Not obedient; refusing or failing to obey: a *disobedient* dog. **—dis′o·be′di·ent·ly** *adv.*

dis·o·bey [dis′ə·bā′] *v.* To refuse or fail to obey.

dis·o·blige [dis′ə·blīj′] *v.* **dis·o·bliged, dis·o·blig·ing** **1** To fail to oblige; act against the wishes of. **2** To inconvenience.

dis·or·der [dis·ôr′dər] **1** *n.* A condition of untidiness or confusion: a room left in *disorder.* **2** *n.* Unhealthy or unsound condition; illness: a digestive *disorder.* **3** *n.* Disturbance of the peace; riot; uproar. **4** *v.* To cause disorder in; upset or disarrange.

dis·or·der·ly [dis·ôr′dər·lē] *adj.* **1** Lacking neatness or order; a *disorderly* bed. **2** Undisciplined, unruly, and likely to cause trouble: *disorderly* conduct. **—dis·or′der·li·ness** *n.*

dis·or·gan·ize [dis·ôr′gə·nīz′] *v.* **dis·or·gan·ized, dis·or·gan·iz·ing** To throw into disorder; upset the arrangement or working of: Fog *disorganized* plane schedules. **—dis·or′gan·i·za′tion** *n.*

dis·or·gan·ized [dis·ôr′gə·nīzd′] *adj.* Not organized; lacking order, arrangement, or management: a *disorganized* report; a *disorganized* project.

dis·or·i·ent [dis·ôr′ē·ent] *v.* To cause (a person) to lose his or her sense of time, location, or identity.

dis·own [dis·ōn′] *v.* To refuse to regard as one's own; deny responsibility for: The man *disowned* his only son; to *disown* one's former beliefs.

dis·par·age [dis·par′ij] *v.* **dis·par·aged, dis·par·ag·ing** To speak of as having little value or importance; belittle: to *disparage* a rival's success. **—dis·par′·age·ment** *n.*

dis·par·ate [dis′pər·it *or* dis·par′it] *adj.* Distinctly different; dissimilar.

dis·par·i·ty [dis·par′ə·tē] *n., pl.* **dis·par·i·ties** A noticeable difference; inequality: a *disparity* between the wrestlers' weights.

dis·pas·sion·ate [dis·pash′ən·it] *adj.* Not affected by strong feelings or prejudices; calm and impartial. **—dis·pas′sion·ate·ly** *adv.*

dis·patch [dis·pach′] **1** *v.* To send off, as on a route or errand, to a destination: to *dispatch* a messenger; to *dispatch* buses; to *dispatch* mail. **2** *n.* A message or report, especially from an official source: a news *dispatch.* **3** *v.* To finish or get rid of quickly: to *dispatch* one's business for the day. **4** *n.* Speed and efficiency: to finish a job with *dispatch.* **5** *n.* The act or process of dispatching. **6** *v.* To kill quickly.

dis·patch·er [dis·pach′ər] *n.* A person who sends out scheduled trains or buses.

dis·pel [dis·pel′] *v.* **dis·pelled, dis·pel·ling** To drive away by or as if by scattering: to *dispel* fears.

dis·pen·sa·ble [dis·pen′sə·bəl] *adj.* Capable of being done without; unnecessary. **—dis·pen·sa·bil·i·ty** [dis·pen′sə·bil′ə·tē] *n.*

dis·pen·sa·ry [dis·pen′sər·ē] *n., pl.* **dis·pen·sa·ries** A place where medicine or first-aid treatment is given free or at a low cost.

dis·pen·sa·tion [dis′pən·sā′shən] *n.* **1** The act of dispensing or dealing out; distribution: the *dispensation* of funds. **2** What is given out or distributed. **3** An official permission to disregard a rule in a particular case. **4** Management or rule, especially the ordering of earthly affairs by nature or God. **5** A system of religious laws: the Christan *dispensation.*

dis·pense [dis·pens′] *v.* **dis·pensed, dis·pens·ing** **1** To give out, especially in separate portions; distribute: a machine that *dispenses* candy bars. **2** To carry out; administer: to *dispense* justice. **3** To prepare and distribute (medicines). **—dispense with** To do without. **—dis·pen′ser** *n.*

dis·perse [dis·pûrs′] *v.* **dis·persed, dis·pers·ing** **1** To scatter or spread in many directions: The guests *dispersed* after the party. **2** To drive away: The sun *dispersed* the mist. **—dis·per′sal** *n.* **—dis·per·sion** [dis·pûr′zhən] *n.*

dis·pir·it [dis·pir′it] *v.* To make discouraged or depressed: Early election returns *dispirited* the candidate.

dis·pir·it·ed [dis·pir′ə·tid] *adj:* Discouraged; depressed; disheartened.

dis·place [dis·plās′] *v.* **dis·placed, dis·plac·ing** **1** To remove or shift from the usual or proper place: to *displace* a lock of hair. **2** To take the place of; supplant: Electric lights have *displaced* candles and oil lamps.

The brick has displaced the water colored brown.

displaced person A person forced to leave home and country because of war, famine, persecution, or other disasters.

dis·place·ment [dis·plās′mənt] *n.* **1** The act of displacing. **2** A being displaced. **3** The amount of fluid displaced by a floating object, as by a ship in water, equal to the weight of the object itself.

dis·play [dis·plā′] **1** *v.* To show in a way that attracts notice; exhibit: to *display* goods. **2** *n.* An arrangement for public viewing: a floral *display.* **3** *n.* In communications, a device that provides data in visual form, as a cathode-ray tube. **4** *n.* A visual representation of data, as that shown on a cathode-ray tube. **5** *n.* A show of something simply to attract notice: an elaborate *display* of courtesy. **6** *v.* To show openly; reveal: to *display* skill. **7** *n.* A show or exhibition: a *display* of anger. **—on display** Exhibited for people to see; on view.

Display

dis·please [dis·plēz′] *v.* **dis·pleased, dis·pleas·ing** To annoy, vex, or offend.

dis·pleas·ure [dis·plezh′ər] *n.* Disapproval, dislike, or an annoyed or angry feeling.

dis·port [dis·pôrt′] *v.* To amuse (oneself) or play: a kitten *disporting* itself on the rug.

dis·pos·a·ble [dis·pō′zə·bəl] *adj.* Made to be thrown away after use: *disposable* napkins.

dis·po·sal [dis·pō′zəl] *n.* **1** A getting rid of something, as by throwing away or selling: the *disposal* of garbage. **2** A settling of something: the *disposal* of a case by a judge. **3** A particular arrangement: the *disposal* of the pictures on the wall. **—at one's disposal** Freely available for one's use or service: During vacation, we had time *at our disposal.*

dis·pose [dis·pōz′] *v.* **dis·posed, dis·pos·ing** **1** To put in the mood or condition for; make inclined: Your apology *disposes* me to forgive you. **2** To set in a certain order; arrange: to *dispose* books about the room. **—dispose of** **1** To get rid of, as by throwing away or selling: to *dispose of* property. **2** To attend to or settle: Let's *dispose of* this matter first.

dis·po·si·tion [dis′pə·zish′ən] *n.* **1** A person's usual mood or spirit; nature; temperament: a sweet *disposition.* **2** A tendency or inclination: a *disposition* to loaf. **3** A particular arrangement: the *disposition* of troops in the field. **4** Settlement: *disposition* of a case in court. **5** Transfer of something to another, as by gift or sale.

dis·pos·sess [dis′pə·zes′] *v.* To deprive of possession: The debtors were *dispossessed* of their house and land. **—dis′pos·ses′sion** *n.*

dis·proof [dis·proof′] *n.* **1** The act of disproving. **2** Evidence that disproves something.

dis·pro·por·tion [dis′prə·pôr′shən] *n.* Lack of proportion or balance.

dis·pro·por·tion·ate [dis′prə·pôr′shən·it] *adj.* Out of proportion to something else, as in size. **—dis′·pro·por′tion·ate·ly** *adv.*

dis·prove [dis·proov′] *v.* **dis·proved, dis·prov·ing** To prove to be false or wrong: The theory was *disproved* by the evidence.

dis·put·a·ble [dis′pyə·tə·bəl *or* dis·pyoo′tə·bəl] *adj.* Capable of being disputed; debatable; undecided.

dis·pu·tant [dis′pyoo·tənt *or* dis·pyoo′tənt] *n.* A person engaged in a dispute or argument.

dis·pu·ta·tion [dis′pyoo·tā′shən] *n.* **1** The act of disputing. **2** A formal debate.

dis·pu·ta·tious [dis′pyoo·tā′shəs] *adj.* Inclined to dispute. **—dis′pu·ta′tious·ly** *adv.* **—dis′pu·ta′tious·ness** *n.*

dis·pute [dis·pyoot′] *v.* **dis·put·ed, dis·put·ing,** *n.* **1** *v.* To argue or challenge in debate: to *dispute* a point; to *dispute* over one's legal rights. **2** *v.* To quarrel: to *dispute* over a boundary. **3** *n.* An argument, debate, or quarrel. **4** *v.* To question the truth or justice of, as a claim. **5** *v.* To fight or struggle

D

a	add	**i**	it	**oo**	took	**oi**	oil
ā	ace	**ī**	ice	**oo**	pool	**ou**	pout
â	care	**o**	odd	**u**	up	**ng**	ring
ä	palm	**ō**	open	**û**	burn	**th**	thin
e	end	**ô**	order	**yoo**	fuse	**th**	this
ē	equal					**zh**	vision

ə = a in *above*, e in *sicken*, i in *possible*, o in *melon*, u in *circus*

against: to *dispute* the advance of enemy troops.

dis·qual·i·fi·ca·tion [dis·kwol′ə·fi·kā′shən] *n.* **1** The act of disqualifying. **2** A being disqualified. **3** Something that disqualifies: Holding one school office is usually a *disqualification* for holding another.

dis·qual·i·fy [dis·kwol′ə·fī′] *v.* **dis·qual·i·fied, dis·qual·i·fy·ing** **1** To make unqualified or unfit: Lack of education *disqualified* the applicant for the job. **2** To declare not qualified, as to exercise a right or to receive a prize: to *disqualify* a winner for breaking rules.

dis·qui·et [dis·kwī′ət] **1** *v.* To make uneasy; disturb; worry: Our suspicions *disquieted* us. **2** *n.* An anxious or uneasy feeling.

dis·qui·e·tude [dis·kwī′ə·t(y)o͞od′] *n.* Disquiet.

dis·qui·si·tion [dis′kwi·zish′ən] *n.* A long formal writing or speech about some subject.

dis·re·gard [dis′ri·gärd′] **1** *v.* To pay no attention to; ignore: People who *disregard* traffic regulations endanger the lives of others. **2** *n.* Lack of attention or regard, especially when deliberate; neglect.

dis·re·pair [dis′ri·pâr′] *n.* A run-down condition due to neglect: The deserted house fell into *disrepair.*

dis·rep·u·ta·ble [dis·rep′yə·tə·bəl] *adj.* Having or giving a bad reputation; not respectable or decent: a *disreputable* character. **—dis·rep′u·ta·ble·ness** *n.* **—dis·rep′u·ta·bly** *adv.*

dis·re·pute [dis′ri·pyo͞ot′] *n.* Low regard; disfavor: That idea is now in *disrepute.*

dis·re·spect [dis′ri·spekt′] *n.* A lack of proper respect or courtesy: to show *disrespect* for your elders.

dis·re·spect·ful [dis′ri·spekt′fəl] *adj.* Lacking in proper respect or politeness; rude. **—dis′re·spect′·ful·ly** *adv.*

dis·robe [dis·rōb′] *v.* **dis·robed, dis·rob·ing** To undress.

dis·rupt [dis·rupt′] *v.* To break up or interfere with: The accident *disrupted* railway service. **—dis·rup′·tion** *n.* **—dis·rup′tive** *adj.*

dis·sat·is·fac·tion [dis′sat·is·fak′shən] *n.* A displeased feeling; discontent.

dis·sat·is·fac·to·ry [dis′sat·is·fak′tər·ē] *adj.* Not satisfying; causing displeasure or discontent.

dis·sat·is·fy [dis·sat′is·fī′] *v.* **dis·sat·is·fied, dis·sat·is·fy·ing** To fail to satisfy or suit; leave discontented.

dis·sect [di·sekt′ *or* dī·sekt′] *v.* **1** To cut apart so as to study the structure: to *dissect* an earthworm. **2** To examine or analyze part by part: to *dissect* a problem. **—dis·sec′tion** *n.*

dis·sem·ble [di·sem′bəl] *v.* **dis·sem·bled, dis·sem·bling** **1** To cover or disguise (true thoughts, feelings, or intentions): They *dissembled* their displeasure with an easy laugh. **2** To be a hypocrite. **3** To pretend in order to deceive; feign. **—dis·sem′·bler** *n.*

dis·sem·i·nate [di·sem′ə·nāt′] *v.* **dis·sem·i·nat·ed, dis·sem·i·nat·ing** **1** To scatter, as seeds. **2** To spread widely, as ideas, news, or knowledge. **—dis·sem′i·na′tion** *n.*

dis·sen·sion [di·sen′shən] *n.* Quarrelsome disagreement, often within a group; conflict.

dis·sent [di·sent′] **1** *v.* To hold or express a different opinion or belief; disagree: One justice *dissented* from the Supreme Court decision. **2** *n.* Difference of opinion; disagreement: religious *dissent.* **—dis·sent′er** *n.* ◆ *See* DECENT.

dis·sen·tient [di·sen′shənt] **1** *adj.* Dissenting, especially from the ideas of the majority. **2** *n.* A person who dissents.

dis·ser·ta·tion [dis′ər·tā′shən] *n.* **1** A long, formal treatment of some subject. **2** A thesis written for the university degree of doctor.

dis·ser·vice [dis·sûr′vis] *n.* A bad turn, especially where a service was intended; harm: You did the team a *disservice* by playing with an injury.

dis·sev·er [di·sev′ər] *v.* To separate into parts; divide; sever.

dis·si·dence [dis′ə·dəns] *n.* Conflicting opinion or belief; dissent.

dis·si·dent [dis′ə·dənt] **1** *adj.* Disagreeing in opinion or belief; dissenting. **2** *n.* A person who disagrees with prevailing or official opinions or beliefs; dissenter.

dis·sim·i·lar [di·sim′ə·lər] *adj.* Not similar or alike; different: *dissimilar* styles. **—dis·sim·i·lar·i·ty** [di·sim′ə·lar′ə·tē] *n.* **—dis·sim′i·lar·ly** *adv.*

dis·sim·i·late [di·sim′ə·lāt′] *v.* **dis·sim·i·lat·ed, dis·sim·i·lat·ing** To make dissimilar or unlike.

dis·sim·u·late [di·sim′yə·lāt′] *v.* **dis·sim·u·lat·ed, dis·sim·u·lat·ing** To conceal (one's true thoughts, feelings, or intentions).

dis·sim·u·la·tion [di·sim′yə·lā′shən] *n.* False pretense; hypocrisy.

dis·si·pate [dis′ə·pāt′] *v.* **dis·si·pat·ed, dis·si·pat·ing** **1** To break up and scatter or dissolve: The sun *dissipated* the mist; The mourner's grief gradually *dissipated.* **2** To use up or spend foolishly; waste, as one's energies or money. **3** To indulge in harmful pleasures.

dis·si·pat·ed [dis′ə·pā′tid] *adj.* Given to or characterized by dissipation; dissolute.

dis·si·pa·tion [dis′ə·pā′shən] *n.* **1** Too much indulgence in harmful pleasures. **2** Useless or foolish waste. **3** A scattering or dissolving.

dis·so·ci·ate [di·sō′s(h)ē·āt′] *v.* **dis·so·ci·at·ed, dis·so·ci·at·ing** To break the connection with; separate: to *dissociate* oneself from a club. **—dis·so′ci·a′tion** [di′sō·s(h)ē·ā′shən] *n.*

dis·sol·u·ble [di·sol′yə·bəl] *adj.* Capable of being dissolved or decomposed.

dis·so·lute [dis′ə·lo͞ot′] *adj.* Lacking moral principles or restraint: a *dissolute* life.

dis·so·lu·tion [dis′ə·lo͞o′shən] *n.* **1** A breaking up, ending, or dissolving: the *dissolution* of a marriage. **2** Separation into parts; disintegration. **3** Decay or death.

dis·solve [di·zolv′] *v.* **dis·solved, dis·solv·ing** **1** To pass into or cause to pass into solution: Salt *dissolves* in water; *Dissolve* the medicine in alcohol. **2** To make or become liquid; melt. **3** To seem to melt from emotion: to *dissolve* in tears. **4** To break up or end: to *dissolve* parliament. **5** To fade away or vanish.

dis·so·nance [dis′ə·nəns] *n.* **1** A mingling together or combination of sounds that are not in harmony; discord. **2** Any lack of agreement.

dis·so·nant [dis′ə·nənt] *adj.* **1** Not in harmony; clashing: *dissonant* sounds. **2** Not in agreement; conflicting. **—dis′so·nant·ly** *adv.*

dis·suade [di·swād′] *v.* **dis·suad·ed, dis·suad·ing** To persuade not to take some step or do something: The librarian was *dissuaded* from quitting by the promise of a raise.

dis·sua·sion [di·swā′zhən] *n.* The act of dissuading.

dis·sua·sive [di·swā′siv] *adj.* Tending or seeking to dissuade.

dist. **1** distance. **2** district.

dis·taff [dis′taf] *n.* A stick from which flax or wool was drawn off in spinning by hand or using an old-fashioned spinning wheel.

Twisting fibers from a distaff onto a spindle

distaff side The maternal or female side of a family.

dis·tance [dis′təns] *n., v.* **dis·tanced, dis·tanc·ing** 1 *n.* The extent of space between two points: to walk a *distance* of three miles. 2 *n.* A point or place far away: We could barely make out a steeple in the *distance.* 3 *n.* The condition of being far off. 4 *n.* The interval between points of time. 5 *v.* To leave behind, as in a race; excel. **—keep one's distance** To be unfriendly; hold aloof.

dis·tant [dis′tənt] 1 *adj.* Far off or remote in space or time: a *distant* star; a *distant* era. 2 *adv.* Away: She lives 15 miles *distant.* 3 *adj.* Not closely related: *distant* cousins. 4 *adj.* Unfriendly or reserved; aloof. **—dis′tant·ly** *adv.*

dis·taste [dis·tāst′] *n.* Dislike.

dis·taste·ful [dis·tāst′fəl] *adj.* Unpleasant, disagreeable, or offensive: a *distasteful* duty. **—dis·taste′ful·ly** *adv.* **—dis′taste′ful·ness** *n.*

dis·tem·per [dis·tem′pər] *n.* A contagious disease of dogs and other animals.

dis·tend [dis·tend′] *v.* To stretch out; expand.

dis·ten·sion or **dis·ten·tion** [dis·ten′shən] *n.* 1 The act of distending. 2 A being distended.

dis·till or **dis·til** [dis·til′] *v.* **dis·tilled, dis·till·ing** 1 To heat (a liquid or solid) until it gives off a vapor that is then condensed by cooling into a purer liquid form. Distilled water is produced in this way. 2 To obtain by distilling: to *distill* whisky from fermented rye. 3 To find and draw out, as if by distilling: to *distill* the moral from a fable.

dis·til·late [dis′tə·lit *or* dis′tə·lāt′ *or* di·stil′it] *n.* A substance obtained by distilling.

dis·til·la·tion [dis′tə·lā′shən] *n.* 1 The act or process of distilling. 2 Anything obtained by distilling.

dis·til·ler [dis·til′ər] *n.* A person or firm that makes alcoholic liquors by distilling.

dis·til·ler·y [dis·til′ər·ē] *n., pl.* **dis·til·ler·ies** A place where alcoholic liquors are made by distilling.

dis·tinct [dis·tingkt′] *adj.* 1 Not alike or not the same; clearly different; separate: The chapter dealt with four *distinct* topics. 2 Easy to perceive or understand; sharp and clear: a *distinct* outline or scent; a *distinct* difference. 3 Definite: a *distinct* possibility. **—dis·tinct′ly** *adv.* **—dis·tinct′ness** *n.*

dis·tinc·tion [dis·tingk′shən] *n.* 1 A difference that may be distinguished: a *distinction* between two brands of soap. 2 Attention to differences: All are invited without *distinction.* 3 The act of distinguishing. 4 Exceptional merit; honor: to serve one's country with *distinction.* 5 A mark of honor, as a medal.

dis·tinc·tive [dis·tingk′tiv] *adj.* Serving to mark out as different or special; characteristic: a *distinctive* style of writing. **—dis·tinc′tive·ly** *adv.*

dis·tin·guish [dis·ting′gwish] *v.* 1 To mark as different, or characterize: A very long neck *distinguishes* the giraffe. 2 To recognize as different: to *distinguish* one twin from the other. 3 To recognize or point out a difference: to *distinguish* between truth and falsehood. 4 To perceive clearly or make out: The sailor could not *distinguish* the shape in the fog. 5 To bring fame or honor upon: Our school *distinguished* itself in the sports program. **—dis·tin′guish·a·ble** *adj.*

dis·tin·guished [dis·ting′gwisht] *adj.* 1 Famous; prominent: a *distinguished* author. 2 Having the look of a notable person; dignified.

D

dis·tort [dis·tôrt′] *v.* 1 To twist or bend out of the normal shape: Rage *distorted* his features. 2 To alter in a way that creates a false impression: to *distort* the facts.

A distorted image

dis·tor·tion [dis·tôr′·shən] *n.* 1 The act of distorting: a *distortion* of the facts. 2 A distorted condition. 3 Something distorted.

dis·tract [dis·trakt′] *v.* 1 To draw (as the mind) from something claiming attention: Does the radio *distract* you from your homework? 2 To confuse or bother, as by dividing the attention. 3 To amuse; entertain; divert. **—dis·trac′tive** *adj.*

dis·trac·tion [dis·trak′shən] *n.* 1 The act of distracting. 2 A being distracted. 3 Something that draws the attention away, as an amusement: The movie was a pleasant *distraction* after the test. 4 A condition of being extremely upset; mental distress: Pain can drive a person to *distraction.*

dis·traught [dis·trôt′] *adj.* Extremely upset; crazed: *distraught* with fear and worry.

dis·tress [dis·tres′] 1 *n.* Extreme suffering or its cause; pain; trouble. 2 *v.* To cause to suffer, worry, or be sorry: The child's illness *distressed* the doctors. 3 *n.* A condition of needing help badly: a ship in *distress.*

dis·tress·ful [dis·tres′fəl] *adj.* Causing or showing distress. **—dis·tress′ful·ly** *adv.*

dis·trib·u·tar·y [dis·trib′yə·ter′ē] *n., pl.* **dis·trib·u·tar·ies** A branch of a river that flows away from the main stream and does not rejoin it.

dis·trib·ute [dis·trib′yōōt] *v.* **dis·trib·ut·ed, dis·trib·ut·ing** 1 To divide and deal out in shares; hand out: *Distribute* the drawing materials to the class. 2 To scatter or spread out: Animals are *distributed* over the earth. 3 To divide and classify or arrange: to *distribute* letters throughout a file.

dis·tri·bu·tion [dis′trə·byōō′shən] *n.* 1 The act of distributing: the *distribution* of gifts. 2 The way in which something is distributed: an even *distribution.* 3 Something distributed.

dis·trib·u·tive [dis·trib′yə·tiv] *adj.* 1 Having to do

a	add	**i**	it	**o͝o**	took	**oi**	oil
ā	ace	**ī**	ice	**ōō**	pool	**ou**	pout
â	care	**o**	odd	**u**	up	**ng**	ring
ä	palm	**ō**	open	**û**	burn	**th**	thin
e	end	**ô**	order	**yōō**	fuse	**t̶h̶**	this
ē	equal					**zh**	vision

ə = a in *above* e in *sicken* i in *possible* o in *melon* u in *circus*

with distribution. **2** Singling out separate individuals. *Each* in "Each contestant gets a gift" is a distributive adjective. **3** Indicating an operation that when performed on the sum of a set of numbers gives a result equal to the sum of the results of performing the operation on each member of the set. Multiplication is distributive in respect to addition, since $2 \times (3 + 4) = (2 \times 3) + (2 \times 4)$.

dis·trib·u·tor [dis·trib′yə·tər] *n.* **1** A person, thing, or group that distributes something or sells merchandise. **2** In a gasoline engine, a device that connects each of the spark plugs into an electric circuit in turn.

dis·trict [dis′trikt] *n.* **1** A particular region or locality. **2** An area, as within a city or state, marked out for a particular purpose: a school *district*; an election *district*.

district attorney A lawyer who acts for the government in a district. A district attorney prosecutes persons accused of crime.

dis·trust [dis·trust′] **1** *n.* Lack of trust or confidence; suspicion; doubt. **2** *v.* To feel no trust for; suspect.

dis·trust·ful [dis·trust′fəl] *adj.* Feeling or showing distrust; suspicious; doubtful. **—dis·trust′ful·ly** *adv.*

dis·turb [dis·tûrb′] *v.* **1** To break in on or interrupt, especially with noise or disorder: to *disturb* someone's rest. **2** To bother or annoy. **3** To worry, trouble, or upset: The bad news *disturbed* the leaders. **4** To upset the order of: A leaping trout *disturbed* the calm pool.

dis·tur·bance [dis·tûr′bəns] *n.* **1** The act of disturbing. **2** A being disturbed. **3** Something that disturbs. **4** Confusion; tumult; commotion.

di·sul·fide [dī·sul′fīd′] *n.* A compound that contains two atoms of sulfur in combination with another element or radical.

dis·un·ion [dis·yo͞on′yən] *n.* **1** Division or separation. **2** Disagreement or conflict.

dis·u·nite [dis′yo͞o·nīt′] *v.* **dis·u·nit·ed, dis·u·nit·ing** To break the union or harmony of; divide; separate.

dis·u·ni·ty [dis·yo͞o′ni·tē] *n., pl.* **dis·u·ni·ties** Lack of unity; dissension.

dis·use [dis·yo͞os′] *n.* A condition of not being used; lack of use: Some words fall into *disuse.*

ditch [dich] **1** *n.* A long, narrow hole dug in the ground, often used as a channel for water; trench. **2** *v.* To dig a ditch around or in. **3** *v.* To run, send, or drive into a ditch. **4** *v. slang* To get rid of.

dith·er [dith′ər] *n.* A condition of nervous excitement or agitation: to be in a *dither.*

dit·to [dit′ō] *n., pl.* **dit·tos,** *adv.* **1** *n.* The same thing (as something just mentioned). **2** *n.* A mark (″) placed beneath something written to show that it is to be repeated.
Example:
2 dozen notebooks sent to 35 Grove St.
4 ″ pencils ″ ″ ″ ″ ″
3 *adv.* As written above or as mentioned before. ◆ *Ditto* comes directly from an Italian word meaning *said.*

dit·ty [dit′ē] *n., pl.* **dit·ties** A short, simple song or poem meant for singing.

di·ur·nal [dī·ûrn′əl] *adj.* **1** Happening every day; daily: the *diurnal* rotation of the earth. **2** Visible or active during the daytime: *diurnal* and nocturnal animals. **3** Open during the day and closed at night: a *diurnal* flower. **—di·ur′nal·ly** *adv.*

di·va [dē′və] *n.* A leading female opera singer; prima donna.

di·van [di·van′ *or* dī′van′] *n.* A long, low sofa or couch, often without arm rests or back.

dive [dīv] *v.* **dived** or **dove, dived, div·ing,** *n.* **1** *v.* To plunge into water, especially headfirst. **2** *n.* A plunge, as into water. **3** *v.* To plunge into something suddenly or deeply, as with the body or mind: to *dive* into bed. **4** *v.* To plunge sharply downward, as an airplane. **5** *n.* A sudden, steep descent. **6** *n. informal* A place, as a tavern or nightclub, considered cheap and vulgar.

dive-bomb·er [dīv′bom′ər] *n.* A bomber that dives steeply toward the target before releasing its bombs.

div·er [dī′vər] *n.* **1** A person who dives into water. **2** Someone who works under water, often wearing a waterproof suit and a helmet supplied with air. **3** A bird that dives, as a loon.

di·verge [di·vûrj′ *or* dī·vûrj′] *v.* **di·verged, di·verg·ing** **1** To branch off, lie, or move in different directions from a common point: Two paths *diverged* in a forest. **2** To depart from a given or normal course. **3** To differ, as in opinion.

Diverging roads

di·ver·gence [di·vûr′jəns *or* dī·vûr′jəns] *n.* **1** A moving apart; difference: a serious *divergence* of opinion. **2** Departure from a set course or standard. **—di·ver′·gent** *adj.*

di·ver·gen·cy [di·vûr′jən·sē *or* dī·vûr′jən·sē] *n., pl.* **di·ver·gen·cies** Divergence.

di·vers [dī′vərz] *adj.* Several or various.

di·verse [di·vûrs′ *or* dī′vûrs] *adj.* Distinctly different; not alike. **—di·verse′ly** *adv.*

di·ver·si·fi·ca·tion [di·vûr·sə·fə·kā′shən] *n.* **1** The act of diversifying. **2** The condition of being diversified.

di·ver·si·fy [di·vûr′sə·fī′] *v.* **di·ver·si·fied, di·ver·si·fy·ing** To give variety to, as by adding different things or changing; vary: to *diversify* one's meals with new foods.

di·ver·sion [di·vûr′zhən] *n.* **1** The act of diverting or turning aside: the *diversion* of a stream into a new channel. **2** An amusement, game, or pastime as a change or relaxation.

di·ver·si·ty [di·vûr′sə·tē] *n., pl.* **di·ver·si·ties** **1** A being unlike; difference: The two talked despite *diversity* of language. **2** Variety: The teacher has a *diversity* of interests.

di·vert [di·vûrt′] *v.* **1** To turn aside: to *divert* someone from a purpose or goal. **2** To amuse or entertain: The game *diverted* us.

di·vest [di·vest′] *v.* **1** To strip, as of clothing. **2** To deprive, as of rights, possessions, or authority; dispossess.

di·vide [di·vīd′] *v.* **di·vid·ed, di·vid·ing,** *n.* **1** *v.* To split or separate into parts: to *divide* a room with a partition. **2** *v.* To find a number by which one given number must be multiplied to get (a second given number). Thus, 6 divided by 2 equals 3 because $3 \times 2 = 6$. **3** *v.* To cause to be or keep apart: A hedge *divides* the two yards. **4** *n.* A ridge or area of high land between two regions drained by separate river systems. **5** *v.* To split up into opposed sides: The jury *divided* on the question of the defendant's guilt. **6** *v.* To separate into groups; classify: These jewels are *divided* into two kinds, the real ones and the false ones. **7** *v.* To give out portions of; distribute: to *divide* food.

div·i·dend [div′ə·dend] *n.* **1** In mathematics, a number that is to be divided by another number. In 9 ÷ 3, 9 is the dividend. **2** A sum of money to be distributed, as profits to be divided among the owners of a company. **3** One share of such a sum.

di·vid·er [di·vī′dər] *n.* **1** A person or thing that divides. **2** (*pl.*) A pair of compasses used for measuring or marking off short intervals.

A room divider

div·i·na·tion [div′ə·nā′·shən] *n.* **1** The act of foretelling the future or finding out secret knowledge, as by interpreting omens or using magic. **2** A prophecy. **3** A clever guess.

di·vine [di·vīn′] *adj., n., v.* **di·vined, di·vin·ing** **1** *adj.* Of, coming from, or having to do with God or a god: *divine* might; *divine* inspiration. **2** *adj.* Devoted to God or a god; religious: *divine* worship. **3** *n.* A clergyman or theologian. **4** *adj.* Almost godlike in excellence or perfection: *divine* singing. **5** *v.* To foretell or discover, as through magic or the interpretation of omens. **6** *v.* To know instinctively; guess: From my guilty behavior, my friends *divined* the truth. **—di·vine′ly** *adv.* **—di·vin′er** *n.*

diving bell A large, hollow container open only at the bottom and supplied with compressed air, used to carry persons working underwater.

diving board A flexible board attached at one end and extending out over a swimming pool. Divers gain momentum for their dives by springing from the end of it.

diving suit A heavy waterproof suit and helmet, worn by persons working underwater. Air is pumped into the helmet through a tube.

divining rod A forked twig believed to bend down when carried over water, oil, or ore.

Divining rod

di·vin·i·ty [di·vin′ə·tē] *n., pl.* **di·vin·i·ties** **1** The quality of being divine; divine nature. **2** (*written* **the Divinity**) God. **3** A god or goddess; deity. **4** The study of religion; theology.

di·vis·i·ble [di·viz′ə·bəl] *adj.* **1** Capable of being divided. **2** That can be divided by a certain number and leave no remainder: 9 is *divisible* by 3. **—di·vis·i·bil·i·ty** [di·viz′ə·bil′ə·tē] *n.*

di·vi·sion [di·vizh′ən] *n.* **1** The act of dividing; separation. **2** A divided condition. **3** In mathematics, the process of determining the number which, used as a multiplier of a given number, will lead to another given number. When 15 is divided by 3, division determines the number 5, for 5 × 3 = 15. **4** Something that divides, as a boundary line. **5** A separate part, section, or unit: the research *division* of a company. **6** A major unit of an army, larger than a regiment. **7** A difference in opinion or interest; disagreement. **—di·vi′sion·al** *adj.*

division sign The sign (÷) placed between two numbers or quantities to show that the first is to be divided by the second, as 8 ÷ 2 = 4.

di·vi·sive [di·vī′siv] *adj.* Causing people to disagree sharply: School busing is a *divisive* issue. **—di·vi′·sive·ly** *adv.* **—di·vi′sive·ness** *n.*

di·vi·sor [di·vī′zər] *n.* A number by which another number is divided. In 8 ÷ 2, 2 is the divisor.

di·vorce [di·vôrs′] *n., v.* **di·vorced, di·vorc·ing** **1** *n.* The ending of a marriage by process of law. **2** *v.* To free legally from the marriage relationship: They were *divorced.* **3** *v.* To free oneself from (one's husband or wife) by divorce. **4** *v.* To separate: He could not *divorce* his mind from his emotions. **5** *n.* Total separation: the *divorce* of body and soul at death.

di·vor·cé [di·vôr′sā′ *or* di·vôr′sē′] *n.* A divorced man.

di·vor·cée [di·vôr′sā′ *or* di·vôr′sē′] *n.* A divorced woman.

di·vot [div′ət] *n.* A piece of turf torn from the sod by the stroke of a golf club.

di·vulge [di·vulj′] *v.* **di·vulged, di·vulg·ing** To tell; reveal; disclose: to *divulge* secrets.

Dix·ie·land [dik′sē·land′] *n.* A traditional style of jazz music originating in New Orleans. It is characterized by a relatively fast tempo, a steady rhythm, and improvisation by the musicians.

diz·zy [diz′ē] *adj.* **diz·zi·er, diz·zi·est,** *v.* **diz·zied, diz·zy·ing** **1** *adj.* Affected by a whirling sensation in the head and apt to weave about or fall; giddy: Swinging makes me *dizzy.* **2** *adj.* Causing a dizzy feeling: a *dizzy* height. **3** *v.* To make dizzy: Dancing around the room *dizzied* the children. **—diz′·zi·ly** *adv.* **—diz′zi·ness** *n.*

dl or **dl.** deciliter.

dm or **dm.** decimeter.

DMZ demilitarized zone.

DNA A complex substance found in the genes of plants and animals and having much to do with the passing on of inherited characteristics; deoxyribonucleic acid.

do[1] [do͞o] *v.* **did, done, do·ing** **1** To carry out in action; perform: The staff *did* its duty. **2** To work at: What does she *do* for a living? **3** To deal with or take care of: Who's going to *do* the dishes? **4** To finish or complete: The students have *done* the exercises. **5** To cause or produce; bring about: The volunteers went about *doing* good. **6** To put forth: We *did* our best. **7** To get along or behave oneself: How did you *do* at school? **8** To give; render: You aren't *doing* this job justice. **9** To be enough or be right; serve: Two pounds of apples will *do.* **—do away with** **1** To get rid of; throw away. **2** To kill. **—do up** **1** To wrap up, as a package. **2** To put in order or arrange. **—have to do with** To deal with or concern. **—make do** To get along with whatever is available. ◆ Apart from its use as a main verb, *do* is often used as a

a	add	**i**	it	**o͝o**	took	**oi**	oil
ā	ace	**ī**	ice	**o͞o**	pool	**ou**	pout
â	care	**o**	odd	**u**	up	**ng**	ring
ä	palm	**ō**	open	**û**	burn	**th**	thin
e	end	**ô**	order	**yo͞o**	fuse	**th**	this
ē	equal					**zh**	vision

ə = a in *above* e in *sicken* i in *possible*; o in *melon* u in *circus* helping verb in questions and negative statements: *Do* you *want* it? I *did*n't *want* it. It is also sometimes used in affirmative statements, where it is usually spoken with extra heavy stress: I *did* want it! *Do* may also substitute for another verb: They will go home when I *do*.

do[2] [dō] *n.* In music, a syllable used to represent the first tone of a major scale or the third tone of a minor scale, or in a fixed system the tone C.

do. ditto.

DOA dead on arrival.

dob·bin [dob'in] *n.* A slow, good-natured horse.

Do·ber·man pin·scher [dō'bər·mən pin'chər] *n.* A large, slender dog of a breed first developed in Germany, having a long head and neck and a short, smooth coat. ◆ This dog was named for the German dog breeder Ludwig Dobermann, who developed it in about 1890. *Pinscher* is the German word for *terrier.*

Doberman pinscher

do·cent [dōs'ənt *or* dō·sent'] *n.* **1** In some colleges and universities, a teacher or lecturer who is not a member of the regular faculty. **2** A guide or lecturer in a museum or art gallery.

doc·ile [dos'(ə)l] *adj.* Easy to teach, manage, or handle; obedient: a *docile* pupil. **—doc'ile·ly** *adj.* **—do·cil·i·ty** [do·sil'ə·tē] *n.*

dock[1] [dok] **1** *n.* A platform built beside or out from a shore where ships or boats tie up; wharf; pier. **2** *n.* The water between two wharves. **3** *v.* To bring or come into a dock: to *dock* a ship; The ship *docked* at the pier. **4** *n.* Short for DRY DOCK. **5** *n.* A raised platform for loading vehicles, as trucks or freight cars.

Dock

dock[2] [dok] *v.* **1** To cut off the end of (a tail). **2** To take away from: to *dock* one's wages.

dock[3] [dok] *n.* A weed with bitter or sour leaves, sometimes used as a food or seasoning.

dock[4] [dok] *n.* An enclosed space in a law court where an accused person stands or sits.

dock·age [dok'ij] *n.* **1** A charge for docking a ship. **2** Facilities for docking a ship.

dock·et [dok'it] **1** *n.* A schedule listing cases to be tried in court. **2** *n.* Any schedule of things to be done or dealt with; agenda. **3** *v.* To enter in a docket. **4** *n.* A tag or label put on a package, listing contents, directions, and other information. **5** *v.* To put such a tag or label on.

dock·yard [dok'yärd'] *n.* A waterfront area where ships are built, repaired, or fitted out.

doc·tor [dok'tər] **1** *n.* A person trained and licensed to treat disease, illness, or injury, and to preserve health. **2** *v. informal* To try to cure or heal by treatment: to *doctor* a cut. **3** *n.* A person who holds one of the highest degrees awarded by a university. **Doctor of Philosophy** is such a degree. **4** *v. informal* To tamper with or alter.

doc·tor·al [dok'tər·əl] *adj.* Of, having to do with, or characteristic of a doctor or doctorate.

doc·tor·ate [dok'tər·it] *n.* The university degree or status of a doctor.

doc·tri·naire [dok'trə·nâr'] **1** *n.* A person who stubbornly sticks to a theory whether it is working or not. **2** *adj.* Of or characteristic of a doctrinaire; dogmatic.

doc·trine [dok'trin] *n.* **1** Something that is taught. **2** A principle or belief, or a set of principles or beliefs, as of a religious or political group. **—doc·tri·nal** [dok'trə·nəl] *adj.*

doc·u·ment [*n.* dok'yə·mənt, *v.* dok'yə·ment'] **1** *n.* A written or printed paper that gives information or serves as evidence of something. Licenses and maps are documents. **2** *v.* To prove by documents. **—doc'u·men·ta'tion** *n.*

doc·u·men·ta·ry [dok'yə·men'tər·ē] *adj., n., pl.* **doc·u·men·ta·ries** **1** *adj.* Consisting of or based on documents: *documentary* proof. **2** *adj.* Dealing with facts rather than telling an invented story. **3** *n.* A presentation, as a movie or novel, that deals with factual rather than invented material.

dod·der [dod'ər] *v.* To tremble or walk in a feeble, unsteady way, as from old age.

dodge [doj] *v.* **dodged, dodg·ing,** *n.* **1** *v.* To move aside suddenly. **2** *v.* To get out of the path of: Jaywalkers *dodged* the cars. **3** *n.* An act of dodging. **4** *v.* To avoid by tricks or cunning: to *dodge* a duty. **5** *n.* A trick used to avoid something or deceive someone. **—dodg'er** *n.*

do·do [dō'dō] *n., pl.* **do·does** or **do·dos** **1** A large, heavy, pigeonlike bird that could not fly and no longer exists. **2** *informal* A silly, stupid, or senile person. ◆ *Dodo* comes from a Portuguese word meaning *silly* or *stupid.*

doe [dō] *n.* The female of the deer, antelope, rabbit, kangaroo, and certain other animals.

do·er [dōō'ər] *n.* A person who does or acts: a *doer* of deeds; Our leader is a *doer,* not a thinker.

does [duz] *v.* The third person form of DO, in the present tense, used with *he, she, it,* and singular nouns: *Does* your dog bite?

doe·skin [dō'skin'] *n.* **1** The skin of the female deer. **2** Soft leather made from this. **3** A heavy, smooth, woolen cloth.

does·n't [duz'ənt] Does not.

doff [dof] *v.* **1** To take off (the hat) as a greeting. **2** To take off, as clothing.

Man doffing his hat

dog [dôg] *n., v.* **dogged, dog·ging** **1** *n.* A tame, flesh-eating animal kept as a pet or used to guard, guide, hunt, or herd. ◆ Adj., *canine.* **2** *v.* To follow like a hunting dog; hound: Misfortune *dogged* their steps. **3** *n.* A device, as for gripping or holding logs.

dog·bane [dôg'bān'] *n.* A plant with milky sap and small, bell-shaped white or pink flowers.

dog·cart [dôg'kärt'] *n.* **1** A small cart drawn by dogs. **2** An open, two-wheeled, horse-drawn cart with two seats set back-to-back.

dog·catch·er [dôg'kach'ər] *n.* An official whose job is to catch stray dogs.

dog days The hot, sultry days of July and early August when the heat causes discomfort.

doge [dōj] *n.* The elected chief magistrate in the former republics of Venice and Genoa.

dog-eared [dôg′ird′] *adj.* Having the corners of the pages turned down: said about a book.

A dog-eared book

dog-eat-dog [dôg′ēt·dôg′] *adj.* With everyone looking out for their own interests; ruthlessly competitive.

dog·fight [dôg′fīt′] *n.* **1** A fight between dogs. **2** A violent, disorderly fight. **3** A battle in the sky between fighter planes.

dog·fish [dôg′fish′] *n., pl.* **dog·fish** or **dog·fish·es** A type of small shark.

dog·ged [dôg′id] *adj.* Continuing stubbornly despite difficulties; persistent: *dogged* efforts. **—dog′ged·ly** *adv.* **—dog′ged·ness** *n.*

dog·ger·el [dôg′ər·əl] *n.* Badly-written verse, often having singsong rhythm.

dog·gy or **dog·gie** [dô′gē] *n., pl.* **dog·gies** A dog, especially a small dog.

dog·house [dôg′hous′] *n., pl.* **dog·hous·es** [dôg′hou′·zəz] A small shelter for a dog. **—in the doghouse** *slang* In disfavor or disrepute.

do·gie [dō′gē] *n.* A motherless or stray calf: used chiefly in the western U.S.

dog·ma [dôg′mə] *n., pl.* **dog·mas** **1** Teaching to be taken as true on the word of one's church or other authority. **2** Any unquestioned belief.

dog·mat·ic [dôg·mat′ik] *adj.* **1** Holding or asserting opinions as if one were the final authority. **2** Stated without proof or evidence. **3** Having to do with dogma. **—dog·mat′i·cal·ly** *adv.*

dog·ma·tism [dôg′mə·tiz′əm] *n.* Undue positiveness and rigidity in asserting one's opinions.

do-good·er [do͞o′go͝od′ər] *n.* A person who eagerly seeks to help people and reform society, especially with schemes that are impractical or not well thought out.

dog·pad·dle [dôg′pad′əl] *v.* **dog·pad·dled, dog·pad·dling** To swim by using the dog paddle.

dog paddle A simple way to swim or keep afloat by paddling with the hands near the surface of the water and churning with the legs below.

Dog Star Another name for the star SIRIUS.

dog·trot [dôg′trot′] *n.* A regular, easy trot.

dog·wood [dôg′wo͝od′] *n.* A tree whose small flower is enclosed by four white or pink petallike leaves, notched at the tips.

doi·ly [doi′lē] *n., pl.* **doi·lies** A thin, ornamental mat, often lace, used under a dish or vase.

Doily

do·ings [do͞o′ingz] *n.pl.* Activities; events.

do-it-your·self [do͞o′it·yər·self′] *adj.* Of, having to do with, or designed to be used by an amateur: a *do-it-yourself* wallpapering kit.

dol·drums [dōl′drəmz *or* dol′·drəmz] *n.pl.* **1** The parts of the ocean near the equator where there is often little or no wind. **2** A dull, sad, or bored condition of mind: in the *doldrums.*

dole [dōl] *n., v.* **doled, dol·ing** **1** *n.* The giving or distributing of money, food, or clothing to the poor. **2** *n.* Anything given out or distributed, as money or food for the poor. In Great Britain, government relief for the poor and unemployed is called *dole.* **3** *v.* To distribute in small quantities: to *dole* out cookies.

dole·ful [dōl′fəl] *adj.* Sorrowful; mournful. **—dole′·ful·ly** *adv.* **—dole′ful·ness** *n.*

doll [dol] *n.* **1** A toy made to look like a baby or a human being of any age. **2** A pretty or adorable child. **—doll up** *informal* To dress stylishly or formally: We all *dolled up* for the wedding. ◆ *Doll* comes from a nickname for Dorothy.

dol·lar [dol′ər] *n.* **1** 100 cents, the basic unit of money in the United States. Symbol: $. **2** A silver coin or a piece of paper currency equal to 100 cents. **3** A similar unit of money in certain other countries: the Canadian or Australian *dollar.*

dol·ly [dol′ē] *n.* **1** A doll: a child's term. **2** A low, flat frame set on small wheels or rollers, used for moving heavy loads.

dol·men [dōl′mən *or* dol′mən] *n.* A prehistoric structure made of two or more upright stones supporting a large horizontal stone slab.

do·lo·mite [dō′lə·mīt′ *or* dol′ə·mīt′] *n.* **1** A pale-colored, crystalline mineral consisting mostly of a carbonate of calcium and magnesium. **2** A rock similar to dolomite in composition.

do·lor [dō′lər] *n.* Sorrow; grief.

do·lor·ous [dō′lər·əs *or* dol′ər·əs] *adj.* **1** Very sad or mournful: *dolorous* moaning. **2** Wretched and painful: a *dolorous* condition. **—do′lor·ous·ly** *adv.* **—do′lor·ous·ness** *n.*

dol·phin [dol′fin] *n.* **1** A saltwater mammal, related to the whale but smaller, having a snout like a bird's beak. **2** A large, edible, oceanic fish which changes colors when taken from the water.

Dolphin

dolt [dōlt] *n.* A stupid person; dunce. **—dolt′ish** *adj.* **—dolt′ish·ly** *adv.* **—dolt′ish·ness** *n.*

-dom A suffix meaning: **1** The realm of, as in *kingdom.* **2** The position or rank of, as in *earldom.* **3** The state or condition of being, as in *freedom.* **4** The whole group or class of, as in *officialdom.*

do·main [dō·mān′] *n.* **1** A land or territory owned or controlled by a government or ruler: the state's *domain.* **2** Any field of action, interest, or knowledge: the *domain* of chemistry.

dome [dōm] *n.* **1** A round roof shaped somewhat like an upside-down cup or hemisphere. **2** Something like a dome in shape: the *dome* of a hill.

Dome

domed [dōmd] *adj.* Having or shaped like a dome: a *domed* capitol.

do·mes·tic [də·mes′tik] **1** *adj.* Of or having to do with the home or family: *domestic* affairs. **2**

a add	**i** it	**o͝o** took	**oi** oil
ā ace	**ī** ice	**o͞o** pool	**ou** pout
â care	**o** odd	**u** up	**ng** ring
ä palm	**ō** open	**û** burn	**th** thin
e end	**ô** order	**yo͞o** fuse	**th** this
ē equal			**zh** vision

ə = a in *above*, e in *sicken*, i in *possible*, o in *melon*, u in *circus*

adj. Fond of home and family affairs: a *domestic* person. **3** *n.* A household servant. **4** *adj.* Tame: *domestic* animals. **5** *adj.* Produced in or having to do with one's own country: *domestic* goods; *domestic* laws.

do·mes·ti·cate [də·mes′tə·kāt′] *v.* **do·mes·ti·cat·ed, do·mes·ti·cat·ing** **1** To tame or cultivate for domestic use: to *domesticate* a wild animal or plant. **2** To make happy with domestic life: to *domesticate* a family member. **3** To make feel at ease or at home: to *domesticate* a foreigner.

do·mes·tic·i·ty [dō′mes·tis′ə·tē] *n., pl.* **do·mes·tic·i·ties** **1** Life at home or with one's family. **2** Devotion to home and family. **3** (*pl.*) Domestic matters: They found the *domesticities* of their new life very tiring.

dom·i·cile [dom′ə·sīl′ *or* dom′ə·səl] *n., v.* **dom·i·ciled, dom·i·cil·ing** **1** *n.* A person's home or residence. **2** *n.* A person's legal residence. **3** *v.* To provide with a home or residence: The soldiers were *domiciled* in that old castle.

dom·i·nance [dom′ə·nəns] *n.* The state or condition of being dominant; authority; control.

dom·i·nant [dom′ə·nənt] **1** *adj.* Most powerful, influential, or important: a *dominant* nation. **2** *adj.* Higher than or rising above its surroundings: a *dominant* cliff. **3** *n.* The fifth note of a musical scale: D is the *dominant* in the key of G.

dom·i·nate [dom′ə·nāt′] *v.* **dom·i·nat·ed, dom·i·nat·ing** **1** To control or rule over: to *dominate* one's students. **2** To tower over; loom above. **—dom′i·na′tion** *n.*

dom·i·neer [dom′ə·nir′] *v.* To rule in an arrogant or insolent manner; bully.

dom·i·neer·ing [dom′ə·nir′ing] *adj.* Overbearing; tyrannical; bullying.

Do·min·i·can [də·min′i·kən] **1** *adj.* Of or from the Dominican Republic. **2** *n.* A person born in or a citizen of the Dominican Republic.

dom·i·nie [dom′ə·nē] *n.* **1** *U.S. informal* A clergyman. **2** A Scottish word for a schoolmaster.

do·min·ion [də·min′yən] *n.* **1** Supreme power or authority; rule. **2** A country under a particular government. **3** (*often written* **Dominion**) A self-governing member of the British Commonwealth of Nations. **—the Dominion** Canada.

Dominion Day July 1, a national holiday in Canada, commemorating the formation of the Dominion in 1867.

dom·i·no [dom′ə·nō] *n., pl.* **dom·i·noes** or **dom·i·nos** **1** A small, rectangular piece of wood, plastic, or other material, one side of which is either blank or marked with dots. **2** (*pl., used with a singular verb*) A game played with a set of these pieces. **3** A small, half mask worn over the eyes.

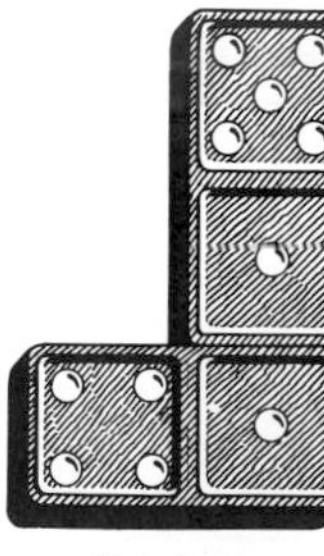

Dominoes

don[1] [don] *v.* **donned, don·ning** To put on (a piece or pieces of clothing).

don[2] [don] *n.* **1** (*written* **Don**) A Spanish title of respect used before a man's first name, equivalent to *Sir.* **2** A Spanish gentleman or nobleman. **3** *informal* In Great Britain, the head of a college or a tutor in one.

do·ña [dōn′yə] *n.* **1** (*written* **Doña**) A Spanish title of respect used before a married woman's first name, equivalent to *Lady.* **2** A Spanish lady.

do·nate [dō′nāt′ *or* dō·nāt′] *v.* **do·nat·ed, do·nat·ing** To give, as to a charity. ◆ *Donate* comes from the noun *donation.*

do·na·tion [dō·nā′shən] *n.* **1** The act of giving, as to a charity. **2** A gift or contribution.

done [dun] **1** Past participle of DO: We have *done* the job. **2** *adj.* Completed; finished. **3** *adj.* Cooked enough. **4** *adj. informal* Tired out; exhausted.

dong [dong] *n.* The basic unit of money in Vietnam.

don·jon [dun′jən *or* don′jən] *n.* The main tower inside the walls of a castle; keep. ◆ Both *donjon* and *dungeon* (originally a room deep in a castle keep) come by way of Old French from the Latin word *dominus,* meaning *lord.* The lord of a castle lived in its donjon.

Don Juan [don hwän′] In Spanish legend, a nobleman famous for his many love affairs.

don·key [dong′kē *or* dung′kē] *n., pl.* **don·keys** **1** A long-eared animal related to the horse but smaller and used throughout the world as a beast of burden. It is also called an ass. **2** A stupid or stubborn person.

Donkey

donkey engine A small steam engine for pumping or hoisting, as on board a ship.

don·na [don′ə *or* dōn′ə] *n.* **1** (*written* **Donna**) An Italian title of courtesy used before a married woman's first name, equivalent to *Lady.* **2** An Italian woman, especially a gentlewoman or one of rank.

don·nish [don′ish] *adj.* Of, having to do with, or like a university don; bookish and academic in manner. **—don′nish·ly** *adv.* **—don′nish·ness** *n.*

don·ny·brook [don′ē·bro͝ok′] *n.* A wild brawl; free-for-all.

do·nor [dō′nər] *n.* A person who gives or donates something.

do-noth·ing [do͞o′nuth′ing] **1** *adj.* Not active; having no initiative, especially in regard to change or improvement: a *do-nothing* governor. **2** A lazy person.

Don Quix·ote [don kē·hō′tē *or* don kwik′sət] The hero of a Spanish novel by Cervantes. He is an idealistic but often foolish knight.

don't [dōnt] Do not. ◆ *Don't* is not correct with singular nouns or with *he/she/it;* use *doesn't* instead: I *don't* like spinach; he *doesn't* either.

doo·dad [do͞o′dad′] *n. informal* A small object, as a trinket or gadget.

doo·dle [do͞od′(ə)l] *v.* **doo·dled, doo·dling,** *n.* **1** *v.* To draw or scribble aimlessly, without thinking of what one is doing. **2** *n.* Something drawn or scribbled in this manner. **—doo′dler** *n.*

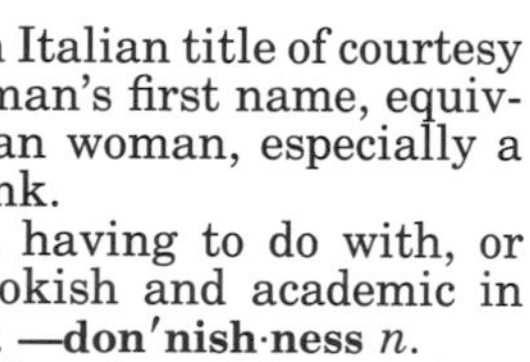

Doodles on a letter

doo·hick·ey [do͞o′hik′ē] *n. informal* A doodad.

doom [do͞om] **1** *n.* A terrible or tragic fate or destiny: It was the writer's *doom* to die young. **2** *n.* Death or ruin: A sense of *doom* came over us.

3 *n.* A severe judgment or punishment: The judge pronounced the prisoner's *doom.* 4 *v.* To condemn to a terrible fate: to be *doomed* from birth. 5 *adj. use:* a *doomed* person. ◆ *Doom* comes from an Old English word meaning *judgment.*

doom·say·er [do͞om′sā′ər] *n.* A person who often foresees failure or predicts disaster.

dooms·day [do͞omz′dā′] *n.* 1 Another name for JUDGMENT DAY. 2 Any dreaded day, as of judgment, punishment, or extinction.

door [dôr] *n.* 1 A hinged, sliding, folding, or rotating structure, as of wood, used for closing or opening an entrance, as to a house, room, or car. 2 A doorway. 3 A house or building: three *doors* down the street. 4 A way or means of achieving something: the *door* to success.

door·jamb [dôr′jam′] *n.* Either of the two vertical pieces that form the side of a doorway.

door·knob [dôr′nob′] *n.* A handle for opening a door.

door·man [dôr′man′] *n., pl.* **door·men** [dôr′men′] A person at the entrance of a building, as a hotel or an apartment house, to guard it or to help people coming in or going out.

Doorman

door mat A mat at an entrance for wiping the shoes.

door·nail [dôr′nāl′] *n.* A large-headed nail once used to decorate doors. **—dead as a doornail** Dead beyond any doubt.

door·step [dôr′step′] *n.* A step up to an outside door.

door·stop [dôr′stop′] *n.* 1 A device, as a wedge or spring, used to hold a door open. 2 A small, usually rubber-tipped device attached to a wall or floor to keep an opened door from striking the wall.

door·way [dôr′wā′] *n.* 1 An opening, as into a room or building, that a door closes. 2 Any means of getting into or to: the *doorway* to fame.

door·yard [dôr′yärd′] *n.* A yard in front of or about the door of a house.

dope [dōp] *n., v.* **doped, dop·ing** 1 *n. slang* A stupid person. 2 *n. slang* A drug or narcotic. 3 *v. slang* To give a drug or narcotic to. 4 *n.* A thick lubricant or varnish. 5 *n. slang* Information; news: to get the inside *dope.* **—dope out** *slang* To plan or figure out: to *dope out* a new idea for the party.

dope·ster [dōp′stər] *n.* A person who makes predictions about future events, as elections or sports events.

dopey or **dopy** [dō′pē] *adj.* **dop·i·er, dop·i·est** *slang* 1 Dazed or dulled, as by alcohol or a drug; stupified: a *dopey* look in his eyes. 2 Stupid; inane; foolish: What a *dopey* thing to do!

Dop·pler effect [dop′lər] The change in the frequency of a sound wave or light wave as the distance between the source of the waves and the observer increases or decreases.

Dor·ic [dôr′ik] *adj.* Of or having to do with the oldest and simplest of the three types of ancient Greek architecture.

dorm [dôrm] *n. informal* A dormitory.

dor·man·cy [dôr′mən·cē] *n.* The condition of being dormant.

dor·mant [dôr′mənt] *adj.* 1 Asleep or as if asleep. 2 Inactive: a *dormant* volcano.

dor·mer [dôr′mər] *n.* 1 A small, roofed structure extending out from a sloping roof and containing an upright window. 2 The window. It is often called a **dormer window.**

Dormer window

dor·mi·to·ry [dôr′mə·tôr′ē] *n., pl.* **dor·mi·to·ries** 1 A building, as at a school or college, that has many rooms for sleeping. 2 A large room with many beds for sleeping.

dor·mouse [dôr′mous′] *n., pl.* **dor·mice** [dôr′mīs′] A small European animal that is related to the mouse but lives in trees like a squirrel.

dor·sal [dôr′səl] *adj.* Having to do with, on, or near the back.

do·ry [dôr′ē] *n., pl.* **do·ries** A flat-bottomed rowboat having high sides and well adapted to rough weather, used by fishermen.

DOS [dos] A computer program that governs how information is stored on a disk and how it can be retrieved and used. ◆ DOS is an acronym for *D*isk *O*perating *S*ystem.

dos·age [dō′sij] *n.* 1 A specified amount of medicine to be given or taken. 2 The giving of medicine in certain quantities or doses.

dose [dōs] *n., v.* **dosed, dos·ing** 1 *n.* A specified amount of medicine or other treatment to be given at one time. 2 *v.* To give a dose or doses to. 3 *n.* An amount of anything, especially something that is unpleasant: a large *dose* of criticism.

do·sim·e·ter [dō·sim′ə·tər] *n.* A device for measuring the amount of radioactivity or X rays to which a person has been exposed.

dos·si·er [dôs′ē·ā *or* dos′ē·ā] *n.* A collection of papers containing detailed, sometimes confidential information about a person or subject.

dost [dust] A form of DO used with *thou:* seldom used today.

dot [dot] *n., v.* **dot·ted, dot·ting** 1 *n.* A round, usually very small mark or spot. 2 *v.* To mark with or as with a dot or dots. 3 *n.* A very short, clicklike sound used in Morse code to form letters. **—on the dot** *informal* At exactly the specified time.

do·tage [dō′tij] *n.* The condition of being feeble-minded or childish as the result of old age.

dote [dōt] *v.* **dot·ed, dot·ing** 1 To lavish or show too much love or affection: They *doted* on their pets. 2 To be feeble-minded as a result of old age.

doth [duth] A form of DOES: seldom used today.

dot·ted swiss [dot′id] A thin, crisp cotton fabric, having a pattern of dots.

dou·ble [dub′əl] *adj., v.* **dou·bled, dou·bling,** *n., adv.* 1 *adj.* Twice as large, as many, or as much: a *double* portion; *double* fare. 2 *v.* To make or become twice as much or as great: to *double* an amount; The membership *doubled.* 3 *n.* Some-

a	add	**i**	it	**o͝o**	took	**oi**	oil
ā	ace	**ī**	ice	**o͞o**	pool	**ou**	pout
â	care	**o**	odd	**u**	up	**ng**	ring
ä	palm	**ō**	open	**û**	burn	**th**	thin
e	end	**ô**	order	**yo͞o**	fuse	**th**	this
ē	equal					**zh**	vision

ə = {a in *above* e in *sicken* i in *possible* / o in *melon* u in *circus*}

thing that is twice as much: 18 is the *double* of 9. **4** *adv.* Twice as much, as in amount or size: We paid *double* what we did before. **5** *adj.* Having or made of two parts, like or unlike: a *double* yolk in an egg; a *double* meaning. **6** *n.* A person or thing that closely resembles another: She is my *double.* **7** *v.* To have or serve two purposes: This sofa *doubles* as a bed. **8** *adv.* Two at a time; in pairs: to march *double.* **9** *adj.* Made for two: a *double* bed. **10** *v.* To bend or fold: to *double* the blanket back over the bed. **11** *v.* To clench (the fist). **12** *v.* To turn and go back on one's course: Scared by a bear, we *doubled* back fast. **13** *v.* To sail around: to *double* a cape. **14** *n.* In baseball, a hit that enables a batter to get to second base. **15** *v.* In baseball, to hit a double. **16** *n.* (*pl.*) A game, as of tennis, in which each side has two players. **—double up** **1** To bend over or cause to bend over, as from pain or laughter. **2** *U.S. informal* To share, as a room or a bed, with someone else. **—on the double** *informal* Quickly.

double agent A spy who pretends to work for one government while actually working for another.

double bass [bās] The largest stringed instrument, having a deep bass tone. It is also called a BASS VIOL.

Double bass

double bassoon Another term for CONTRABASSOON.

double boiler Two pots, one fitting into the other. Food in the upper pot is cooked by the heat from water boiling in the lower pot.

dou·ble-breast·ed [dub′əl·bres′·tid] *adj.* Of a coat or vest, with sides overlapping clear across the breast, usually with two rows of buttons.

dou·ble-check [dub′əl·chek′] *v.* To test or examine a second time, as for accuracy.

double chin A fold of loose flesh under the chin.

dou·ble-cross [*v.* dub′əl·krôs′, *n.* dub′əl·krôs′] *slang* **1** *v.* To betray by failing to act as promised. **2** *n.* An act that betrays or cheats someone. **—dou′·ble-cross′er** *n.*

double date A social engagement in which two couples go out together.

dou·ble-deal·ing [dub′əl·dē′ling] **1** *n.* A dishonest or treacherous way of dealing with others. **2** *adj.* Dishonest; deceitful. **—dou′ble-deal′er** *n.*

dou·ble-deck·er [dub′əl·dek′ər] *n.* **1** A bus or other vehicle having two decks for passengers. **2** A pair of beds, one built above the other. **3** A sandwich having two separate layers of fillings.

dou·ble-dig·it [dub′əl·dij′it] *adj.* Between 10 and 99 percent: *double-digit* inflation.

dou·ble-edged [dub′əl·ejd′] *adj.* **1** Having two cutting edges. **2** Capable of being understood in two different ways: a *double-edged* compliment.

dou·ble-head·er [dub′əl·hed′ər] *n.* In sports, two games played one after the other on the same day, usually by the same two teams.

double jeopardy The trying of a person twice for the same offense.

dou·ble-joint·ed [dub′əl·join′tid] *adj.* Having joints so flexible that the arms, legs, fingers, and other joints can be bent in unusual ways.

double knit **1** A fabric having two thicknesses joined by interlocking stitches, knitted on a machine with a double set of needles. **2** *adj. use:* a *double-knit* suit.

double negative A construction using two negatives to express a single negative meaning, as in *I don't know nothing.* Double negatives are considered ungrammatical in modern English.

dou·ble-park [dub′əl·pärk′] *v.* To park (a motor vehicle) alongside another vehicle that is already parked parallel to the curb.

double play In baseball, a play in which two base runners are put out.

double pneumonia Pneumonia affecting both lungs.

dou·ble-quick [dub′əl·kwik′] **1** *adj.* Very quick. **2** *adv.* Very quickly: to run *double-quick.* **3** *n.* A very fast marching step. **4** *v.* To march or run or cause to march or run very quickly.

double star Two stars that look like one unless viewed through a telescope: Sirius is a *double star.*

dou·blet [dub′lit] *n.* A short, tight-fitting jacket, with or without long sleeves, worn from about 1400 to 1660.

Doublet

double take *informal* A delayed reaction, as to an unusual person or situation.

dou·ble-talk [dub′əl·tôk′] *n.* Speech that mixes meaningless syllables with real words.

double time **1** A very fast marching pace. **2** A rate of pay that is twice the usual rate.

dou·bloon [du·blo͞on′] *n.* A former Spanish gold coin, originally worth about 16 dollars.

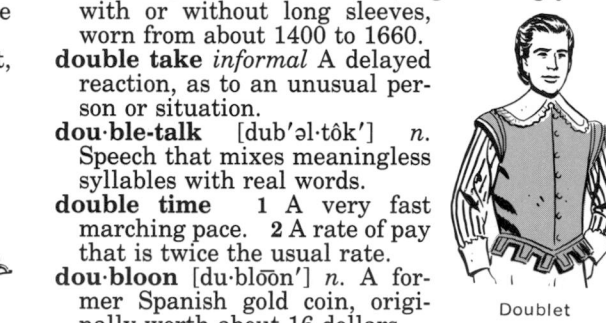

dou·bly [dub′lē] *adv.* In twice the quantity or degree: *doubly* successful.

doubt [dout] **1** *v.* To feel uncertain about the truthfulness or rightness of (someone or something): We *doubted* the speaker; I *doubt* that it will fit. **2** *n.* A lack of trust, confidence, or certainty: to have many *doubts.* **3** *n.* The state or condition of being uncertain or undecided: The exact date is in *doubt.* **—no doubt** **1** Most likely; probably: *No doubt* she went home. **2** Certainly. **—without doubt** or **beyond doubt** Surely; certainly: It is *without doubt* the worst play I've seen. **—doubt′·er** *n.* ◆ *Doubt* comes from a French word, *douter,* meaning *to doubt.* The "b" was added later because the Latin word for *doubt* has a "b" in it.

doubt·ful [dout′fəl] *adj.* **1** Uncertain or undecided: It is *doubtful* whether or not we'll go. **2** Open to doubt: a *doubtful* reputation. **—doubt′ful·ly** *adv.* **—doubt′ful·ness** *n.*

doubting Thom·as [tom′əs] A person who is not willing to believe anything without proof; a skeptic. ◆ This term comes from St. *Thomas,* the apostle in the Bible who would not believe in the Resurrection until he had actually touched Jesus' wounds.

doubt·less [dout′lis] **1** *adv.* Probably: The train will *doubtless* arrive late. **2** *adv.* Without doubt; certainly: *Doubtless* it arrived late yesterday. **3** *adj.* Free from uncertainty; sure. **—doubt′less·ly** *adv.* **—doubt·less·ness** *n.*

douche [do͞osh] *n., v.* **douched, douch·ing** **1** *n.* A stream of liquid applied to a body part or a body cavity in order to cleanse or treat it. **2** *v.* To cleanse or treat with a douche. **3** *n.* A device for applying a douche.

dough [dō] *n.* 1 A soft, thick mass of flour and a liquid mixed together with other ingredients, used for making such foods as bread, biscuits, and pastry. 2 *slang* Money.
dough·nut [dō′nut′] *n.* A small cake, usually shaped like a ring, of sweetened dough fried in deep fat.
dough·ty [dou′tē] *adj.* **dough·ti·er, dough·ti·est** Strong and brave: now rarely used except humorously. **—dough′ti·ly** *adv.*
dough·y [dō′ē] *adj.* **dough·i·er, dough·i·est** 1 Like dough. 2 Not fully baked: *doughy* bread.
Doug·las fir [dug′ləs] A tall evergreen tree of western North America grown for its valuable timber.
dour [dŏŏr *or* dour] *adj.* 1 Gloomy and sullen: a *dour* nature. 2 Severe; stern: a *dour* look.
douse [dous] *v.* **doused, dous·ing** 1 To thrust into water or other liquid. 2 To throw water or other liquid on: We *doused* the campfire with water. 3 *informal* To put out: *Douse* the light.
dove[1] [duv] *n.* A pigeon, especially any of a number of small, usually wild pigeons.
dove[2] [dōv] A past tense of DIVE.
dove·cote [duv′kōt′ *or* duv′kot′] *n.* A house or box for pigeons or doves.
dove·tail [duv′tāl′] 1 *v.* To join (as two boards) by fitting wedge-shaped projections on one into corresponding openings in the other. 2 *n.* One of these projections. 3 *n.* A joint formed by this method. 4 *v.* To fit together perfectly: Our schedules *dovetailed.*

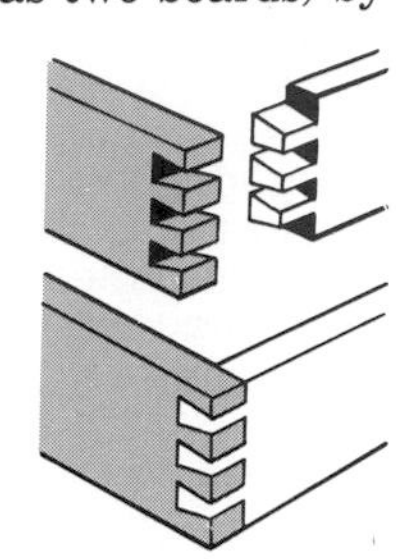
Dovetail joint

dow·a·ger [dou′ə·jər] *n.* 1 A widow who holds a title or property from her dead husband. 2 *informal* Any dignified old woman.
dow·dy [dou′dē] *adj.* **dow·di·er, dow·di·est,** *n., pl.* **dow·dies** 1 *adj.* Lacking style; unfashionable. 2 *adj.* Sloppy; untidy. 3 *n.* A dowdy person. **—dow′di·ly** *adv.*
dow·el [dou′əl] *n.* A peg that fits tightly into corresponding holes in two pieces of wood or metal to hold them together.

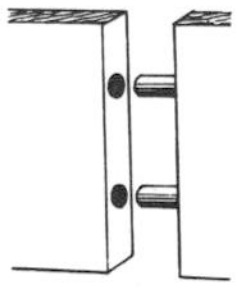
Dowels

dow·er [dou′ər] 1 *n.* The part of a dead man's estate given by law to his widow for life. 2 *n.* A dowry. 3 *n.* A natural or inborn talent or gift. 4 *v.* To give a dower to.
down[1] [doun] 1 *adv.* In, on, or to a lower place, level, or position: Come *down*; Sit *down.* 2 *adv.* To or in a place or position regarded as lower or more distant: The sun went *down.* 3 *adj.* Directed, going, or brought downward: a *down* curve; The champion is *down*! 4 *prep.* In a descending direction along, upon, through, or in: The store is *down* the street. 5 *v.* To knock, throw, shoot, or put down: to *down* a plane. 6 *v. informal* To swallow: *Down* your milk. 7 *adv.* To a smaller or lower amount, size, or rate: The swelling went *down*; to boil *down* syrup; Prices have gone *down.* 8 *adv.* Actually; seriously: Let's get *down* to work. 9 *n.* (*usually pl.*) Bad luck, used chiefly in the phrase **have ups and downs,** to have both good and bad luck. 10 *adj.* Ill: to be *down* with a cold. 11 *adj. informal* Downcast; depressed: to be *down.* 12 *adj.* Unable to be used, as a computer. 13 *adv.* From an earlier time or individual: This sword came *down* from my ancestors. 14 *adv.* Completely; fully: loaded *down* with work. 15 *adv.* When something is bought: to pay five dollars *down.* 16 *adj.* Made when something is bought: a *down* payment. 17 *adv.* In writing: Take *down* the taxi driver's name. 18 *adj.* In football, not in play. 19 *n.* In football, an opportunity to move the ball forward, one of a series of four in which a team must advance the ball at least ten yards or give it to the other team. **—down and out** In a miserable state, as of poverty or ill health. **—down on** *informal* Angry with: to be *down on* someone. **—down with** (Let's) do away with; overthrow: *Down with* the party!
down[2] [doun] *n.* 1 The fine, soft feathers of birds, especially of young birds. 2 Fine, soft hair, as on a baby's head.
down·beat [doun′bēt′] *n.* 1 A downward stroke of the hand, made by a conductor to indicate the first beat of each measure of music. 2 The first beat in a musical measure.
down·cast [doun′kast′] *adj.* 1 Directed downward: *downcast* eyes. 2 Low in spirits; sad.
down·fall [doun′fôl′] *n.* 1 Ruin; collapse: the *downfall* of a government. 2 A heavy, usually sudden fall of rain or snow.
down·grade [doun′grād′] *n., v.* **down·grad·ed, down·grad·ing** 1 *n.* A descending slope, as of a hill or road. 2 *v.* To make less in amount or importance: to *downgrade* wages; to *downgrade* a person's work. **—on the downgrade** Becoming less or worse: The patient's health is *on the downgrade.*
down·heart·ed [doun′här′tid] *adj.* Sad; dejected; discouraged.
down·hill [*adv.* doun′hil′, *adj.* doun′hil′] 1 *adv.* Down a hill: to run *downhill.* 2 *adj.* Downward: a *downhill* path. **—go downhill** To become worse: The town has *gone downhill.*
down·play [doun′plā′] *v.* To treat lightly; play down.
down·pour [doun′pôr′] *n.* A heavy fall of rain.
down·right [doun′rīt′] 1 *adj.* Absolute; complete; utter: *downright* nonsense. 2 *adv.* Thoroughly; extremely: *downright* scared. 3 *adj.* Straightforward; frank: a *downright* answer.
downs [dounz] *n.pl.* Small, rolling hills usually covered with grass.
down·stage [doun′stāj′] *adj., adv.* On or toward the front part of a stage.
down·stairs [*adv.* doun′stârz′, *adj., n.* doun′stârz′] 1 *adv.* On or to a lower floor: to go *downstairs.* 2 *adj.* Situated on a lower or main floor: a *downstairs* room. 3 *n.* The ground or main floor of a house or building.
down·state [doun′stāt′] *adj., adv.* In or toward the southern part of a U.S. state.
down·stream [*adv.* doun′strēm′, *adj.* doun′strēm′] *adv., adj.* In the direction of the current of a stream: to row *downstream.*

a	add	**i**	it	**o͝o**	took	**oi**	oil
ā	ace	**ī**	ice	**o͞o**	pool	**ou**	pout
â	care	**o**	odd	**u**	up	**ng**	ring
ä	palm	**ō**	open	**û**	burn	**th**	thin
e	end	**ô**	order	**yo͞o**	fuse	**th**	this
ē	equal					**zh**	vision

ə = { a in *above*   e in *sicken*   i in *possible*
  o in *melon*   u in *circus* }

down·time [doun′tīm′] *n.* The time when something, as a machine or a manufacturing plant, is inactive.

down-to-earth [doun′to͞o·ûrth′] *adj. informal* Sensible and realistic: Imaginative people should have *down-to-earth* advisers.

down·town [*adv.* doun′toun′, *adj.* doun′toun′] *adv., adj.* To, toward, or in the lower or the chief business section of a town or city: to move *downtown*; a *downtown* store.

down·trod·den [doun′trod′(ə)n] *adj.* Abused or oppressed by those in power.

down·turn [doun′tûrn′] *n.* A downward turn, especially in business activity.

down under *informal* Australia or New Zealand.

down·ward [doun′wərd] **1** *adv., adj.* From a higher to a lower place or position: to fly *downward*; a *downward* movement. **2** *adv.* From an earlier to a more recent time: to go *downward* in history.

down·wards [doun′wərdz] *adv.* Downward.

down·wind [doun′wind′] *adj., adv.* In the direction in which the wind is blowing: We hid *downwind* of our prey, so that it couldn't smell us.

down·y [dou′nē] *adj.* **down·i·er. down·i·est** **1** Of or covered with down. **2** Soft like down.

dow·ry [dou′rē] *n., pl.* **dow·ries** The money or property a wife brings to her husband when they marry.

dowse [douz] *v.* **dowsed, dows·ing** To use a divining rod to try to find something, as underground water or a mineral.

dox·ol·o·gy [dok·sol′ə·jē] *n., pl.* **dox·ol·o·gies** A hymn or verse praising God.

doz. dozen(s).

doze [dōz] *v.* **dozed, doz·ing,** *n.* **1** *v.* To sleep lightly; nap. **2** *n.* A brief, light sleep; nap.

doz·en [duz′ən] *n., pl.* **doz·ens** or, after a number, **doz·en** **1** A group or set of twelve: two *dozen* eggs. **2** (*pl.*) A fairly large number: *Dozens* of people attended the show.

doz·enth [duz′ənth] *adj.* Another word for TWELFTH.

DP **1** data processing. **2** (*also written* **D.P.**) displaced person.

dpt. department.

Dr. **1** Doctor. **2** drive.

drab [drab] *adj.* **drab·ber, drab·best,** *n.* **1** *adj.* Dull and monotonous in appearance or quality: a *drab* painting; a *drab* city. **2** *adj., n.* Dull, yellowish or grayish brown.

drach·ma [drak′mə] *n., pl.* **drach·mas** or **drach·mae** [drak′mē] **1** The basic unit of money in modern Greece. **2** An ancient Greek silver coin. **3** An ancient Greek unit of weight about equal to the weight of the silver coin. ◆ *Drachma* comes from a Greek word meaning *handful.*

dra·co·ni·an [drə·kō′nē·ən *or* drā·kō′nē·ən] *adj.* Very harsh or severe: a *draconian* penalty. ◆ *Draconian* comes from *Draco,* an ancient Greek lawgiver whose code of laws for Athens prescribed death for almost all offenses.

draft [draft] **1** *v.* To select for service in the armed forces or for some other purpose or job: to *draft* recruits into the Army; to *draft* baseball players. **2** *n.* The act of selecting an individual for service in the armed forces or for some other purpose or job. **3** *n.* The persons so selected. **4** *n.* A current of air: There is a *draft* coming in the window. **5** *n.* A device for controlling the flow of air, as in a furnace. **6** *n.* A sketch, plan, or design of something that is to be made or written: a *draft* of a speech. **7** *v.* To make a plan, outline, or rough copy of: to *draft* a sermon. **8** *n.* A written order, as made by an individual or bank, directing the payment of money to a person, bank, or business: a *draft* for $100.00. **9** *n.* The pulling or drawing of a load. **10** *adj.* Used for pulling heavy loads: a *draft* animal. **11** *n.* The drawing in of a fishing net, or the amount of fish drawn in. **12** *n.* The depth of water needed for a ship to float, or the depth reached by the lowest part of a fully loaded ship. **13** *n.* The act of drinking or inhaling something. **14** *n.* The amount drunk or inhaled. **15** *n.* A drink: a *draft* of ale.

draft·ee [draf·tē′] *n.* A person who is drafted for military service.

drafts·man [drafts′mən] *n., pl.* **drafts·men** [drafts′·mən] **1** A person who draws designs or sketches, as of buildings or machinery. **2** A person who draws up documents.

drafts·man·ship [drafts′mən·ship′] *n.* Skill in drawing sketches or designs.

drafts·wom·an [drafts′wo͝om′ən] *n., pl.* **drafts·wom·en** [drafts′wim′in] **1** A woman who draws designs or sketches, as of buildings or machinery. **2** A woman who draws up documents.

draft·y [draf′tē] *adj.* **draft·i·er, draft·i·est** Having or being exposed to drafts of air: a *drafty* apartment. **—draft′i·ness** *n.*

drag [drag] *v.* **dragged, drag·ging,** *n.* **1** *v.* To haul or pull along: to *drag* a log through the water. **2** *v.* To be pulled or hauled along: His coat *dragged* behind him. **3** *n.* Some device or tool that works by being dragged or pulled along, as a harrow. **4** *v.* To search the bottom of with a net or hooklike device: We *dragged* the lake for old tires. **5** *v.* To go or continue too slowly: Time *drags* at a dull party. **6** *n.* Any person or thing that hinders or slows down something: War is a *drag* on civilization's progress.

drag·gle [drag′əl] *v.* **drag·gled, drag·gling** **1** To make or become soiled or wet by dragging. **2** To follow slowly; lag.

drag·net [drag′net′] *n.* **1** A net for dragging along the bottom of the water or along the ground in order to find or capture something. **2** Any device or plan for catching or gathering: The *dragnet* caught a gang of thieves.

drag·on [drag′ən] *n.* In old legends, a huge monster, shaped like a serpent with claws and wings, often said to breathe out fire.

drag·on·fly [drag′ən·flī′] *n., pl.* **drag·on·flies** An insect having a long, slender body and four long, very thin wings. It eats flies and mosquitoes.

Dragonfly

dra·goon [drə·go͞on′] **1** *n.* In former times, a soldier who served on horseback. **2** *v.* To force or browbeat: We *dragooned* the farmers into helping us.

drag race A race on a straight course between cars that accelerate from a standstill. The winning car is the one that accelerates the fastest.

drain [drān] **1** *v.* To draw off (a liquid) gradually: to *drain* water from a pool. **2** *v.* To draw water or other liquid from: to *drain* a pool. **3** *v.* To flow off: The water in our new sink *drains* very quickly. **4** *v.* To let liquid flow off; become empty or dry: Many rivers *drain* into the sea. **5** *n.* A pipe, ditch, or other device for draining: The basement *drain* is clogged up. **6** *v.* To use up gradually; exhaust: Hunger *drained* our strength. **7** *n.* Something that gradually uses up or exhausts another thing.

drain·age [drā′nij] *n.* **1** The act or method of draining. **2** A system of drains: The town's *drainage* is bad. **3** Something drained off.

drain·pipe [drān′pīp′] *n.* A pipe used for draining.

drake [drāk] *n.* A male duck.

dram [dram] *n.* **1** A small weight equaling 1/8 of an ounce in apothecaries' weight or 1/16 of an ounce in avoirdupois weight. **2** A small drink.

dra·ma [drä′mə *or* dram′ə] *n.* **1** A play written to be performed by actors. **2** The art or profession of writing or putting on plays. **3** A series of exciting actions or events: the *drama* of exploring outer space.

Dram·a·mine [dram′ə·mēn′] *n.* A medicine used to prevent motion sickness: a trademark.

dra·mat·ic [drə·mat′ik] *adj.* **1** Of or having to do with plays or with the theater. **2** Exciting; thrilling: a *dramatic* race. **—dra·mat′i·cal·ly** *adv.*

dra·mat·ics [drə·mat′iks] *n.* **1** The art or study of acting or of putting on plays. **2** An exaggerated or dramatic manner of behaving or of expressing oneself. ◆ See -ICS.

dram·a·tist [dram′ə·tist] *n.* A person who writes plays.

dram·a·tize [dram′ə·tīz′] *v.* **dram·a·tized, dram·a·tiz·ing** **1** To make a play or movie out of: to *dramatize* the life of Helen Keller. **2** To make seem exciting or unusual: to *dramatize* one's troubles. **—dram′a·ti·za′tion** *n.*

drank [drangk] Past tense of DRINK. ◆ In speech, *drank* is sometimes used with *had:* Joe didn't stop till he'd *drank* the whole quart of milk. This usage should be avoided in writing.

drape [drāp] *v.* **draped, drap·ing,** *n.* **1** *v.* To cover or decorate with cloth or clothing: to *drape* a window or statue. **2** *v.* To arrange in graceful folds: to *drape* a cloth. **3** *n.* (*usually pl.*) Cloth arranged in long, loose folds, especially when used as a curtain; drapery.

drap·er [drā′pər] *n. British* A person who deals in cloth and, sometimes, clothing and dry goods.

dra·per·y [drā′pər·ē] *n., pl.* **dra·per·ies** **1** (*usually pl.*) Curtains or other hangings arranged in loose folds. **2** Cloth that hangs in loose folds, especially as seen in painting or sculpture.

dras·tic [dras′tik] *adj.* Very forceful or severe; extreme: *drastic* methods. **—dras′ti·cal·ly** *adv.*

draught [draft] *n., v., adj.* Another spelling of DRAFT.

draughts [drafts] *n.pl.* (*used with a singular verb*) *British* The game of checkers.

draught·y [draf′tē] *adj.* **draught·i·er, draught·i·est** Another spelling of DRAFTY.

draw [drô] *v.* **drew, drawn, draw·ing,** *n.* **1** *v.* To pull; drag: to *draw* a cart. **2** *v.* To pull off, on, down, out, together, or back: to *draw* a gun; to *draw* the curtains; to *draw* gloves on. **3** *v.* To pull tight; stretch: to *draw* a bowstring taut. **4** *v.* To inhale: to *draw* a breath. **5** *v.* To obtain or get: to *draw* money from the bank; to *draw* water from a well; to *draw* an audience. **6** *v.* To result in: Their exciting acts *drew* praise from the audience. **7** *v.* To move: to *draw* near. **8** *v.* To create a linear representation of (someone or something): to *draw* a child's face; to *draw* a circle. **9** *v.* To create (a picture or sketch): to *draw* a cartoon; to *draw* well. **10** *v.* To describe: A novelist must *draw* characters well. **11** *v.* To write (a check). **12** *v.* To produce a current of air: The chimney *draws* well. **13** *v.* To sink to when floating: This ship *draws* 25 feet. **14** *n.* The act or action of drawing, especially the act of pulling out a weapon: to be quick on the *draw.* **15** *n.* The part of a drawbridge that is moved out of the way. **16** *n.* Something pulled or drawn, as a ticket in a lottery. **17** *n.* A tie in a game or contest: to end in a *draw.* **18** *n.* *U.S.* A gully or ravine. **—draw out** **1** To make longer; prolong: You must *draw out* the ending of your story. **2** To cause to talk freely: A newspaper reporter must be able to *draw* people *out.* **—draw up** **1** To write out in a correct or legal form, as a will. **2** To stop: The car *drew up* near us.

draw·back [drô′bak′] *n.* Any unpleasant or objectionable feature or characteristic: Heat is one *drawback* to living in the tropics.

draw·bridge [drô′brij′] *n.* A bridge so built that all or part of it can be raised, lowered, or drawn aside. Now, opened, it lets ships pass; formerly, it kept enemies from crossing over it.

Drawbridge

draw·er [drô′ər *for def. 1,* drôr *for def. 2*] *n.* **1** A person who draws. **2** A sliding, boxlike container, as in a bureau or desk, that can be drawn out and pushed back.

draw·ers [drôrz] *n.pl.* An undergarment covering the lower part of the body and having either long or short legs.

draw·ing [drô′ing] *n.* **1** The act or art of making a picture, sketch, or design, by means of lines and sometimes shading. **2** The picture, design, or sketch made by this method. **3** A lottery.

drawing board **1** A board for holding paper on which drawings are made. **2** *informal* The planning or designing stage of a project: When the engine failed, we went back to the *drawing board.*

drawing room A room in which visitors are received and entertained; parlor. ◆ *Drawing room* is short for *withdrawing room,* which was so called because people withdrew to it from another room, as from a dining room after dinner.

draw·knife [drô′nīf′] *n., pl.* **draw·knives** [drô′nīvz′] A tool for shaving wood surfaces, having a blade with a handle at each end.

drawl [drôl] **1** *v.* To speak or pronounce slowly, especially by making the vowel sounds long. **2** *n.* A drawling manner of speaking.

drawn [drôn] Past participle of DRAW.

a	add	**i**	it	**o͝o**	took	**oi**	oil
ā	ace	**ī**	ice	**o͞o**	pool	**ou**	pout
â	care	**o**	odd	**u**	up	**ng**	ring
ä	palm	**ō**	open	**û**	burn	**th**	thin
e	end	**ô**	order	**yo͞o**	fuse	**t͟h**	this
ē	equal					**zh**	vision

ə = {a in *above* e in *sicken* i in *possible* / o in *melon* u in *circus*}

drawn butter Melted butter, often seasoned and used as a sauce.
draw·string [drô'string'] *n.* A string, cord, ribbon, or tape run through a hem, casing, or set of eyelets, as in a bag, garment, or curtain, and pulled to close an opening or make something tighter.
dray [drā] *n.* A low, strong cart with removable sides, used for carrying heavy loads.
dread [dred] **1** *v.* To look forward to with fear or uneasiness. **2** *n.* Great fear or uneasiness, especially over something in the future: Some people have a *dread* of the dentist. **3** *adj.* Dreadful.
dread·ful [dred'fəl] *adj.* **1** Causing dread or awe; terrible: a *dreadful* threat. **2** *informal* Very bad; shocking; awful: a *dreadful* book. **—dread'ful·ly** *adv.* **—dread'ful·ness** *n.*
dread·nought or **dread·naught** [dred'nôt'] *n.* A type of large battleship having many big guns and much used in World War I.
dream [drēm] *n., v.* **dreamed** or **dreamt, dream·ing** **1** *n.* A series of thoughts or pictures passing through the mind during sleep. **2** *v.* To see or imagine in a dream. **3** *v.* To have a dream. **4** *n.* An imaginary and usually pleasant thought or reverie one has while awake; daydream. **5** *v.* To have daydreams or imaginary reveries: They *dream* too much in class. **—dream of** To think or consider possible; imagine: Our ancestors never *dreamed of* such things. **—dream up** To invent; devise: to *dream up* a TV plot. **—dream'er** *n.*
dream·land [drēm'land'] *n.* An imaginary land that exists in dreams.
dreamt [drem(p)t] Alternative past tense and past participle of DREAM: I *dreamt* I was flying.
dream·y [drē'mē] *adj.* **dream·i·er, dream·i·est** **1** Like a dream; vague; dim. **2** Given to daydreaming: a *dreamy* child. **3** Soothing; soft: *dreamy* music. **—dream'i·ly** *adv.* **—dream'i·ness** *n.*
drear [drir] *adj.* Dreary: used mostly in poems.
drear·y [drir'ē] *adj.* **drear·i·er, drear·i·est** Full of or causing sadness or gloom: a *dreary* day. **—drear'i·ly** *adv.* **—drear'i·ness** *n.*
dredge[1] [drej] *n., v.* **dredged, dredg·ing** **1** *n.* A large machine used to scoop out or suck up materials, as mud or sand, from the bottom of a body of water. **2** *n.* Something like a net that is used to gather shellfish and other creatures from under the water. **3** *v.* To clear, widen, or remove with a dredge: to *dredge* a harbor. **—dredg'er** *n.*

Dredge

dredge[2] [drej] *v.* **dredged, dredg·ing** To sprinkle or dust (food), as with flour or sugar.
dregs [dregz] *n.pl.* **1** Bits of solid matter that settle to the bottom of a liquid, as coffee grounds. **2** The most undesirable part of anything: the *dregs* of society.
drench [drench] *v.* **1** To saturate by or as if by soaking: a fruit cake *drenched* with rum; a brain *drenched* with advanced mathematics. **2** To wet completely with liquid that falls: dry land *drenched* by a sudden downpour.
dress [dres] **1** *n.* The outer garment worn by a woman or girl, usually in one piece; frock. **2** *n.* Clothes; apparel. **3** *v.* To put clothes on: to *dress* a baby; We must *dress* quickly. **4** *v.* To trim or decorate: to *dress* a store window. **5** *v.* To comb and arrange (hair). **6** *v.* To clean or prepare for use or sale: to *dress* a chicken; to *dress* leather. **7** *v.* To treat with medicine and bandages: to *dress* a wound. **8** *v.* To line up in a straight line, as soldiers.
dress circle A tier of seats, usually the first above the main floor, in a theater or opera house.
dress·er[1] [dres'ər] *n.* **1** A person who dresses something or someone. **2** A tool for dressing leather, stone, and other materials.
dress·er[2] [dres'ər] *n.* A chest of drawers for clothing, usually with a mirror above it.
dress·ing [dres'ing] *n.* **1** Bandages and medicine put on a wound or sore. **2** A sauce, as for salads or vegetables. **3** A mixture of bread crumbs and seasonings, used for stuffing chickens, turkeys, and other fowl, before roasting.
dressing gown A loose gown or robe worn while resting at home or before dressing.
dressing room A room for dressing, as backstage in a theater.
dressing table A small table with a mirror and usually drawers, used when putting on makeup or arranging the hair.
dress·mak·er [dres'mā'kər] *n.* A person who makes dresses or other articles of clothing for women.
dress·mak·ing [dres'mā'king] *n.* The occupation or craft of a dressmaker.
dress rehearsal A final rehearsal, as of a play or opera, done with all the costumes, properties, and the lighting to be used in the actual performance.
dress·y [dres'ē] *adj.* **dress·i·er, dress·i·est** *informal* **1** Very stylish or fancy: a *dressy* jacket. **2** Fond of dressing up: a *dressy* crowd. **—dresss'i·ly** *adv.* **—dress'i·ness** *n.*
drew [drōō] Past tense of DRAW.
drib·ble [drib'əl] *v.* **drib·bled, drib·bling,** *n.* **1** *v.* To fall or let fall in drops; drip: The faucets *dribbled* water. **2** *v.* To come in small amounts: Contributions *dribbled* in slowly. **3** *n.* A small quantity of water, usually falling in drops. **4** *v.* To drool: The baby *dribbled* saliva. **5** *v.* To move (a ball) either by bouncing or by short kicks: In both basketball and soccer the ball is *dribbled.* **6** *n.* The act of dribbling a ball. **—drib'bler** *n.*
drib·let [drib'lit] *n.* A small amount or bit.
dried [drīd] Past tense and past participle of DRY: The clothes were *dried* by the wind.
dri·er [drī'ər] **1** Comparative of DRY: This sheet is *drier* than that one. **2** *n.* A person or thing that dries. **3** *n.* Another spelling of DRYER.
dri·est [drī'ist] Superlative of DRY.
drift [drift] **1** *v.* To move or float along in a current of water or air: We let the boat *drift;* Leaves *drifted* down. **2** *v.* To become piled up by water or wind: The snow *drifted* as high as the door. **3** *n.* Something piled or heaped up by the wind or water: a *drift* of snow. **4** *v.* To move or live without any particular goal or purpose: The traveler *drifted* from city to city. **5** *n.* The act of drifting, or the direction or speed of drifting: a westward *drift.* **6** *n.* The meaning of something: the *drift* of a speech.
drift·er [drif'tər] *n.* A person or thing that drifts, especially a person who moves without purpose, as from one place to another.
drift·wood [drift'wood'] *n.* Wood drifting in water or washed up on the shore.

drill[1] [dril] **1** *n.* A tool or machine used for boring holes. **2** *v.* To make (a hole) with or as with a drill: We *drilled* holes for rivets. **3** *v.* To make a hole in with a drill: The dentist *drilled* my tooth. **4** *n.* A kind of instruction based on the repetition of physical or mental exercises. **5** *n.* Such an exercise, aimed at perfecting a skill or kind of knowledge: a piano *drill.* **6** *v.* To teach or learn by this method: to *drill* recruits. **—drill′er** *n.* ◆ *See* PRACTICE.

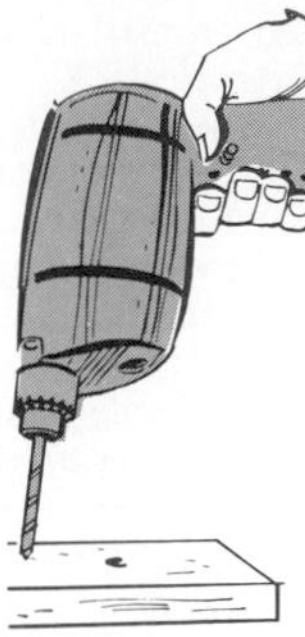

Electric drill

drill[2] [dril] *n.* A machine that plants seeds in rows by digging holes, dropping the seed, and then covering the seeds with soil.

dri·ly [drī′lē] *adv.* Another spelling of DRYLY.

drink [dringk] *v.* **drank, drunk, drink·ing,** *n.* **1** *v.* To swallow (a liquid): We have *drunk* too much pop. **2** *n.* Any liquid that one can drink. **3** *n.* A portion of liquid for drinking, as a glassful. **4** *n.* Alcoholic liquor. **5** *v.* To drink alcoholic liquor. **—drink in** To take in eagerly with the senses or the mind. **—drink to** To drink a toast to. **—drink′er** *n.*

drink·a·ble [dring′kə·bəl] *adj.* Safe or fit for drinking.

drip [drip] *v.* **dripped, drip·ping,** *n.* **1** *v.* To fall or cause to fall in drops: Rain *dripped* from the trees; The faucet *drips* water. **2** *n.* The forming and falling of drops of liquid, or the sound made by this. **3** *n.* Liquid that falls in drops. **4** *n. slang* A stupid and irritating person.

drip-dry [drip′drī′] *v.* **drip-dried, drip-dry·ing,** *adj.* **1** *v.* To dry quickly when hung up dripping wet and need little or no ironing when dry: to let a dress *drip-dry.* **2** *adj.* Made of a fabric that drip-dries: a *drip-dry* shirt.

drip·pings [drip′ingz] *n.pl.* The fat and juices that drip from meat when it is roasted or broiled.

drive [drīv] *v.* **drove, driv·en, driv·ing,** *n.* **1** *v.* To direct and control the movement of (a car or other vehicle). **2** *v.* To go or carry in a car or other vehicle: to *drive* to town; to *drive* someone home. **3** *n.* A trip in a car or other vehicle. **4** *n.* A road, street, or driveway. **5** *v.* To move or cause to move: The car *drove* slowly; We *drove* cattle all day. **6** *n.* Something that is being driven along, as a herd of cattle. **7** *n.* The means by which the power of a machine is passed on to where it takes effect, as in an automobile. **8** *v.* To move by striking: to *drive* a nail or a ball. **9** *n.* In certain games, the act of hitting a ball or the flight of a ball when hit: a hard *drive;* a *drive* to center field. **10** *v.* To produce or form by drilling: to *drive* a well. **11** *v.* To force into some act or condition: to *drive* someone mad. **12** *v.* To force to work hard: The boss *drove* them all day. **13** *v.* To bring about with force and energy: The merchant *drives* a hard bargain. **14** *n. informal* Energy: The head of the organization has a lot of *drive.* **15** *n.* A planned effort of a group for getting something done: a *drive* for charity. **16** *n.* A strong, instinctual, or basic need: the self-preservation *drive.* **—drive at** To mean: What are you *driving at*? **—let drive** To aim or hit: to *let drive* with both fists.

drive-in [drīv′in′] *n.* **1** Any establishment serving or entertaining people seated in their cars, as a bank, restaurant, or motion-picture theater. **2** *adj. use:* a *drive-in* movie.

driv·el [driv′əl] *v.* **driv·eled** or **driv·elled, driv·el·ing** or **driv·el·ling,** *n.* **1** *v.* To drool; slobber. **2** *n.* A flow of saliva from the mouth. **3** *v.* To talk or write foolishly. **4** *n.* Foolish talk or writing. **—driv′el·er** or **driv′el·ler** *n.*

driv·en [driv′ən] Past participle of DRIVE.

driv·er [drī′vər] *n.* **1** A person or thing that drives. **2** A golf club having a wooden head, used to drive the ball from the tee.

drive shaft A shaft that transmits mechanical power, as to the rear axle of an automobile.

drive·way [drīv′wā′] *n.* A private road leading from a street or highway to a house, garage, or other building.

driz·zle [driz′əl] *v.* **driz·zled, driz·zling,** *n.* **1** *v.* To rain steadily in tiny drops like mist. **2** *n.* A mistlike rain: It's only a light *drizzle.* **—driz′zly** *adj.*

drogue [drōg] *n.* A parachute released to slow down or stabilize something, as a space vehicle during reentry. It is also called a **drogue parachute.**

droll [drōl] *adj.* Comically strange, odd, or quaint: a *droll* little elf.

droll·er·y [drō′lər·ē] *n., pl.* **droll·er·ies** **1** An amusing way of acting or talking. **2** Something droll, as a story.

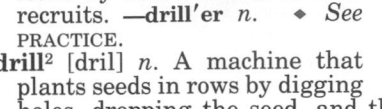

drom·e·dar·y [drom′ə·der′ē] *n., pl.* **drom·e·dar·ies** A swift camel of Arabia, having only one hump, used for riding.

Dromedary

drone[1] [drōn] *v.* **droned, dron·ing,** *n.* **1** *v.* To make a deep humming or buzzing sound. **2** *n.* Such a sound: the *drone* of bees. **3** *v.* To speak in a dull, monotonous manner: The lecturer *droned* on.

drone[2] [drōn] *n.* **1** A male bee. Drones have no sting and do no work. **2** A person who won't work but lives by the work of others.

drool [dro͞ol] **1** *v.* To let saliva flow from the mouth. **2** *n. informal* Foolish talk; drivel.

droop [dro͞op] **1** *v.* To sink or hang down: The flowers *drooped* in the sun. **2** *n.* A drooping condition or position. **3** *v.* To become tired, sad, or discouraged.

droop·y [dro͞o′pē] *adj.* **droop·i·er, droop·i·est** **1** Drooping or tending to droop. **2** Sad; gloomy.

drop [drop] *n., v.* **dropped** or **dropt, drop·ping** **1** *n.* A small amount of liquid shaped like a tiny ball or pear. **2** *n.* Something like this in size or shape: a chocolate *drop.* **3** *v.* To fall in drops, as a liquid. **4** *n.* A very small amount of anything, especially of a liquid: a *drop* of coffee. **5** *n.* A sudden or

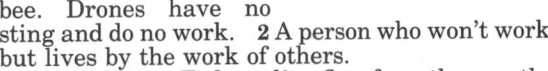

a	add	**i**	it	**o͝o**	took	**oi**	oil
ā	ace	**ī**	ice	**o͞o**	pool	**ou**	pout
â	care	**o**	odd	**u**	up	**ng**	ring
ä	palm	**ō**	open	**û**	burn	**th**	thin
e	end	**ô**	order	**yo͞o**	fuse	**th̸**	this
ē	equal					**zh**	vision

ə = { a in *above* e in *sicken* i in *possible* / o in *melon* u in *circus* }

quick fall or downward movement. **6** *n.* The distance straight down from a higher place to a lower place: a 50-foot *drop.* **7** *v.* To fall or let fall: We *dropped* to the ground; Don't *drop* your books. **8** *n.* A sudden decrease or decline: a *drop* in prices. **9** *v.* To decline or decrease, as in amount or volume: His voice *dropped* to a whisper. **10** *v.* To fall down dead, injured, or exhausted: After the race, the sprinter *dropped* to the ground. **11** *v.* To cause to fall: to *drop* a deer. **12** *v.* To fall into some state or condition: to *drop* into a sound sleep. **13** *v.* To have no more to do with: to *drop* a friend or an argument. **14** *v.* To fire (a worker): used chiefly in the U.S. and Canada. **15** *v.* To send, give, or say casually: to *drop* a hint; to *drop* a letter to a friend. **16** *v.* To leave out or omit. **17** *v.* To let out or leave: *Drop* me off at my house. **—drop back** or **drop behind** To fall or lag behind. **—drop in** or **drop over** To make an informal or surprise visit. **—drop out** To leave or quit some activity: to *drop out* of a game.

drop cloth A cloth used to cover and protect floors and furniture in a room being painted.

drop kick In football, a kick made by dropping the ball and kicking it just as it starts to bounce up from the ground.

drop·let [drop′lit] *n.* A tiny drop.

drop·out [drop′out′] *n.* A person who drops out, especially a student who leaves school before graduating or who leaves a course of study before finishing it.

drop·per [drop′ər] *n.* A glass tube with one narrowed end from which a rubber bulb at the other end, when squeezed, releases a liquid drop by drop.

Dropper

drop·sy [drop′sē] *n.* A diseased condition in which too much liquid collects in certain parts of the body.

dropt [dropt] A past tense and past participle of DROP.

drosh·ky [drosh′kē] *n., pl.* **drosh·kies** An open, four-wheeled Russian carriage.

dro·soph·i·la [drə·sof′ə·lə *or* drō·sof′ə·lə] *n.* A kind of small fruit fly used in scientific studies of heredity.

dross [drôs] *n.* **1** Scum that rises to the surface of melted metal. **2** Any worthless matter; rubbish.

drought [drout] *n.* A lack of rain for a long period; severe dry spell.

drouth [drouth] *n.* Another word for DROUGHT.

drove[1] [drōv] Past tense of DRIVE.

drove[2] [drōv] *n.* **1** A herd or flock of animals driven or moving along together. **2** A crowd of people moving along together.

drov·er [drō′vər] *n.* **1** A person who drives cattle, sheep, or other animals to market in droves. **2** A cattle or sheep dealer.

drown [droun] *v.* **1** To die or kill by suffocation in water or other liquid. **2** To cover with or as if with a liquid: The cook *drowned* the potatoes in butter. **3** To overwhelm the sound of by a louder sound; keep from being heard.

drowse [drouz] *v.* **drowsed, drows·ing,** *n.* **1** *v.* To be only half asleep; doze. **2** *n.* A nap or doze.

drow·sy [drou′zē] *adj.* **drow·si·er, drow·si·est** **1** Sleepy. **2** Causing sleepiness: a *drowsy* summer day. **—drow′si·ly** *adv.* **—drow′si·ness** *n.*

drub [drub] *v.* **drubbed, drub·bing** **1** To beat, as with a stick. **2** To defeat thoroughly.

drudge [druj] *n., v.* **drudged, drudg·ing** **1** *n.* A person whose work is hard and boring. **2** *v.* To do hard, tiresome work.

drudg·er·y [druj′ər·ē] *n., pl.* **drudg·er·ies** Dull, hard, unpleasant work.

drug [drug] *n., v.* **drugged, drug·ging** **1** *n.* Any substance, other than food, used as a medicine or in the preparation of medicines. **2** *n.* A substance that relieves pain or makes one sleep; narcotic. **3** *v.* To give a drug to. **4** *v.* To add drugs to: They *drugged* our food. **5** *v.* To make sleepy or unconscious: The talk seemed to *drug* the dinner guests. **—drug on the market** A product that nobody wants to buy.

drug·gist [drug′ist] *n.* **1** A person who sells drugs, medicines, toilet articles, and other items. **2** A pharmacist.

drug·store [drug′stôr′] *n.* Formerly, a place where drugs and medicines were sold. In modern drugstores, however, a person can buy many other things.

dru·id [dro͞o′id] *n.* (*often written* **Druid**) A priest of a Celtic religion that was formerly practiced in ancient Britain, Ireland, and Gaul.

drum [drum] *n., v.* **drummed, drum·ming** **1** *n.* A hollow musical instrument, usually shaped like a cylinder or hemisphere with skin or other material stretched tightly over one or both ends. It is played by striking with sticks or with the hands. **2** *n.* A thumping or tapping sound made by or as if by a drum. **3** *v.* To beat a drum. **4** *v.* To tap or thump over and over again: to *drum* on the table with one's fingers. **5** *v.* To force a person to learn or remember by constant repetition: to *drum* rules into a person's head. **6** *n.* Something shaped like a drum, as a large, cylindrical container for oil. **—drum up** **1** To try to get: to *drum up* business. **2** To bring together: We couldn't *drum up* enough people for the game.

Drum(s)

drum·beat [drum′bēt′] *n.* A stroke on a drum or the sound of it.

drum·head [drum′hed′] *n.* The skin or other material stretched over the end or ends of a drum.

drum·lin [drum′lin] *n.* A long or oval hill made up of dirt and stones left behind by glaciers.

drum major The person who leads a marching band, usually twirling a baton.

drum ma·jor·ette [mā′jə·ret′] A female who leads a marching band or marches with such a band, twirls a baton, and does acrobatics.

drum·mer [drum′ər] *n.* **1** A person who plays a drum. **2** *U.S. informal* A traveling salesperson.

drum·stick [drum′stik′] *n.* **1** A stick used for beating a drum. **2** The lower half of the leg of a cooked chicken, turkey, or other fowl.

drunk [drungk] **1** Past participle of DRINK: We have *drunk* our last toast. **2** *adj.* Having alcohol enough in the body to make mental and physical reactions less accurate than normal; intoxicated. **3** *n. informal* A drunkard.

drunk·ard [drungk′ərd] *n.* A person who is drunk a great part of the time.

drunk·en [drungk′ən] *adj.* **1** Drunk; intoxicated. **2** Resulting from or showing the effects of being drunk: a *drunken* act; a *drunken* look. **—drunk′·en·ly** *adv.* **—drunk′en·ness** *n.*

drunk·o·me·ter [drung·kom′ə·tər] *n.* A device that estimates the amount of alcohol in a person's blood by analysis of the breath.

drupe [dro͞op] *n.* A fleshy fruit with a single hard pit, such as a cherry or peach.

dry [drī] *adj.* **dri·er, dri·est,** *v.* **dried, dry·ing** **1** *adj.* Not wet or damp. **2** *v.* To make or become dry: *Dry* your hands; The clothes will *dry* quickly today. **3** *adj.* Not lying under water: *dry* land. **4** *adj.* Having little or no water or moisture: a *dry* stream; a *dry* well. **5** *adj.* Having little or no rain: a *dry* season. **6** *adj.* Shriveled or withered from lack of water: The plants are *dry.* **7** *adj.* No longer giving milk: a *dry* cow. **8** *adj.* Thirsty: to feel *dry.* **9** *adj.* Having no tears: *dry* eyes. **10** *adj.* Eaten or served without butter, jam, or other spread: *dry* toast. **11** *adj.* Dull and boring: a *dry* lecture. **12** *adj.* Having no warmth, excitement, or feeling: a *dry* welcome. **13** *adj.* Plain and bare: the *dry* facts. **14** *adj.* Not sweet: said about wine. **15** *adj. informal* Not allowing the sale of alcoholic liquor: a *dry* country. **—dry′ness** *n.*

dry·ad [drī′əd] *n.* (*often written* **Dryad**) In mythology, a nymph that lives in the woods or in trees.

dry cell A battery cell that produces an electric current, as for a flashlight. Its electrolyte is a paste rather than a liquid.

dry-clean [drī′klēn′] *v.* To subject to or undergo dry cleaning.

dry cleaner **1** A person who dry-cleans. **2** An establishment whose business is dry cleaning.

dry cleaning **1** The cleaning of clothes or other cloth articles with a liquid that contains little or no water, as gasoline or naptha. **2** Clothes or other cloth articles that are dry-cleaned.

dry dock A floating or stationary dock from which the water can be emptied, used for rebuilding, repairing, or cleaning ships.

Dry dock

dry·er [drī′ər] *n.* **1** A mechanical device used for drying, as by heat or whirling: a clothes *dryer.* **2** Another spelling of DRIER.

dry goods Such items as clothing, cloth, ribbon, needles, and thread.

dry ice Solidified carbon dioxide, used to keep things cold.

dry·ly [drī′lē] *adv.* In a dry manner.

dry measure A system for measuring the volume of dry commodities, such as fruits or grains.

dry rot A decay of timber caused by a fungus and making it brittle and powdery.

dry run A practice exercise before the actual event; rehearsal.

DST or **D.S.T.** daylight saving time.

du·al [d(y)o͞o′əl] *adj.* Of, having, or consisting of two parts or sets; double: a car with *dual* controls.

du·al·i·ty [d(y)o͞o·al′ə·tē] *n., pl.* **du·al·i·ties** The quality or condition of having two parts or natures.

dub[1] [dub] *v.* **dubbed, dub·bing** **1** To make (someone) a knight by tapping the person's shoulder with a sword. **2** To give a name or nickname to: They *dubbed* the largest player "Tiny." **3** To make smooth, usually by rubbing: to *dub* wood.

dub[2] [dub] *v.* **dubbed, dub·bing** To substitute or add sound or language to, as a motion picture or phonograph record.

du·bi·ous [d(y)o͞o′bē·əs] *adj.* **1** Not sure or certain; doubtful: I was *dubious* about going out without permission. **2** Causing doubt, question, or suspicion: a *dubious* answer. **3** Questionable as to quality, validity, integrity, or propriety: a person of *dubious* character; a *dubious* business strategy. **—du′bi·ous·ly** *adv.* **—du′bi·ous·ness** *n.*

du·cal [d(y)o͞o′kəl] *adj.* Of or having to do with a duke or a duchy.

duc·at [duk′ət] *n.* Any of several gold or silver coins formerly used in Europe.

duch·ess [duch′is] *n.* **1** The wife or widow of a duke. **2** A woman holding rank equal to that of a duke; female ruler of a duchy.

duch·y [duch′ē] *n., pl.* **duch·ies** The territory that a duke or duchess rules; dukedom.

duck[1] [duk] *n.* **1** A swimming bird, either wild or tame, having short legs, webbed feet, and a broad bill. **2** The female of this bird. The male is called a drake. **3** The flesh of the duck used as food.

Mallard

duck[2] [duk] **1** *v.* To thrust or plunge under water suddenly and briefly: to *duck* someone in a swimming pool. **2** *v.* To lower the head or stoop down quickly. **3** *n.* The act of ducking. **4** *v.* To dodge, as by lowering the head or bending the body: to *duck* a punch.

duck[3] [duk] *n.* A strong, tightly woven linen or cotton cloth similar to canvas but of a lighter weight: slacks made of *duck.*

duck[4] [duk] *n.* A military truck which can travel on land and on water.

duck·bill [duk′bil′] *n.* Another name for the PLATYPUS.

duck hawk A swift falcon of North and South America.

duck·ling [duk′ling] *n.* A young duck.

duck·pins [duk′pinz′] *n.pl.* (*used with singular verb*) **1** A game like bowling but played with smaller pins and balls. **2** A pin used in this game.

duck·weed [duk′wēd′] *n.* A small, stemless water plant that floats on the surface of ponds and streams.

duct [dukt] *n.* **1** A tube, channel, or other passage through which fluid, gas, electric cables, or other material, can pass. **2** A tube in the body that carries fluid: tear *ducts.*

duc·tile [duk′təl] *adj.* **1** Capable of being ham-

a	add	**i**	it	**o͝o**	took	**oi**	oil
ā	ace	**ī**	ice	**o͞o**	pool	**ou**	pout
â	care	**o**	odd	**u**	up	**ng**	ring
ä	palm	**ō**	open	**û**	burn	**th**	thin
e	end	**ô**	order	**yo͞o**	fuse	**th̶**	this
ē	equal					**zh**	vision

ə = {a in *above* e in *sicken* i in *possible*
o in *melon* u in *circus*}

mered into thin layers or drawn out into wire, as certain metals. **2** Easily molded or shaped, as plastic. **3** Easily led or managed.

duct·less gland [dukt′lis] A gland that has no duct but releases its fluids directly into the blood or lymph, as the thyroid gland.

dud [dud] *n.* **1** A bomb or shell that fails to explode. **2** *informal* A person, thing, or event that proves a failure.

dude [d(y)o͞od] *n.* **1** A person whose clothes are always too dressy or showy. **2** *informal* A city dweller in the country, especially in the West.

dude ranch A vacation resort that entertains guests with horseback riding and the activities of a cattle ranch.

dudg·eon [duj′ən] *n.* Anger or resentment, now used mainly in the phrase **in high dudgeon,** in a very angry or resentful mood.

duds [dudz] *n.pl. informal* Clothes.

due [d(y)o͞o] **1** *adj.* Owed and expected to be paid: The rent is *due* May 1st. **2** *n.* Something that is owed or should be given; a right: Respect is their rightful *due.* **3** *adj.* Proper or sufficient: *due* caution; in *due* time. **4** *n.* (*pl.*) Money charged or paid for belonging to a union, club, or other group: We pay *dues* twice a year. **5** *adj.* Expected to arrive or to be ready: When is the bus *due*? **6** *adv.* Directly; exactly: *due* east. **—due to** Caused by: Her success was *due to* hard work. ◆ Careful writers avoid *due to* as a substitute for *because of* or *on account of:* We were delayed *because of* (or *on account of*) rain, NOT *due to* rain. It is, however, correct to use *due* as an adjective: The delay was *due* to rain.

du·el [d(y)o͞o′əl] *n., v.* **du·eled** or **du·elled, du·el·ing** or **du·el·ling** **1** *n.* A combat between two persons, fought with deadly weapons according to set rules and before witnesses. **2** *n.* Any conflict or contest: a *duel* of words. **3** *v.* To fight in a duel. **—du′el·ist** or **du′el·list** *n.*

du·en·na [d(y)o͞o·en′ə] *n.* **1** An elderly woman who is governess and companion of the girls in a Spanish family. **2** A chaperon.

du·et [d(y)o͞o·et′] *n., v.* **du·et·ted, du·et·ting** **1** *n.* A piece of music to be played or sung by two performers. **2** *v.* To perform a duet.

duf·fel [duf′əl] *n.* **1** A coarse woolen fabric napped on both sides. **2** Equipment or supplies, especially for camping.

duffel bag A sack, usually made of canvas or duck, used to carry clothing and personal possessions.

dug[1] [dug] Past tense and past participle of DIG.

dug[2] [dug] *n.* A breast, udder, or nipple of a female animal.

du·gong [do͞o′gong′] *n.* A plant-eating tropical sea mammal having a blunt snout, flipperlike forelimbs, and a flat tail. ◆ *Dugong* comes from a Malay word for *sea cow.*

dug·out [dug′out′] *n.* **1** A boat made by hollowing out a log. **2** A shelter hollowed out in the earth. **3** A low, covered shelter at a baseball diamond, in which players sit when not on the field.

duke [d(y)o͞ok] *n.* **1** A person in the highest rank of the British nobility. **2** The male ruler of a duchy in continental Europe. **3** (*usually pl.*) *slang* Fist; hand.

duke·dom [d(y)o͞ok′dəm] *n.* **1** A duchy. **2** The rank or title of a duke.

dul·cet [dul′sit] *adj.* Pleasing to the ear; sweet, melodious, or soothing: *dulcet* tones. **—dul′cet·ly** *adv.*

dul·ci·mer [dul′sə·mər] *n.* A musical instrument having wire strings that are struck with two padded hammers held in the hands.

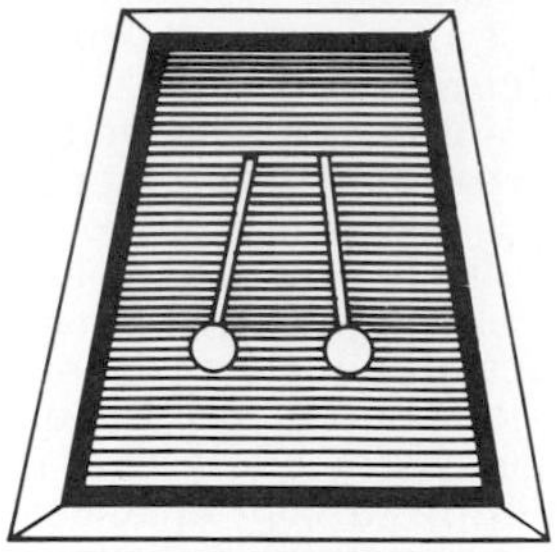

Dulcimer

dull [dul] **1** *adj.* Not sharp or piercing: a *dull* blade; a *dull* pain. **2** *adj.* Not bright or clear: *dull* colors; a *dull* sound. **3** *adj.* Slow to learn; stupid: a *dull* student. **4** *adj.* Not interesting; tedious; boring: a *dull* book. **5** *adj.* Not active; slow: Trade is *dull.* **6** *v.* To make or become dull: to *dull* the appetite; The old man's eyesight *dulled.* **—dul′ly** *adv.* **—dull′ness** *n.*

dull·ard [dul′ərd] *n.* A stupid person.

du·ly [d(y)o͞o′lē] *adv.* **1** In the proper manner or degree: *duly* respectful. **2** At the proper time: bills *duly* paid.

dumb [dum] *adj.* **1** Lacking the power of speech: a *dumb* animal. **2** Speechless for a time; silent: to be *dumb* with horror. **3** *U.S. informal* Stupid; obtuse. **—dumb′ly** *adv.* **—dumb′ness** *n.*

dumb·bell [dum′bel′] *n.* **1** A wood or metal bar with a heavy knob at each end, used in pairs to exercise the muscles. **2** *U.S. slang* A stupid person.

Dumbbells

dumb·found [dum′found′] *v.* Another spelling of DUMFOUND.

dumb show Gestures without words; pantomime: The mime acted it out in *dumb show.*

dumb·wait·er [dum′wā′tər] *n.* **1** A small elevator used to hoist things, as food or dishes, from one floor to another. **2** A movable stand for serving food.

dum·found [dum′found′] *v.* To strike speechless with surprise; astonish; amaze: I was *dumfounded* when I heard of it. ◆ *Dumfound* comes from the blending of parts of the two words *dum(b)* and *(con)found.*

dum·my [dum′ē] *n., pl.* **dum·mies,** *adj.* **1** *n.* A figure made to look like a real person, used for several purposes, including displaying clothing and tackling in football practice. **2** *n.* Any imitation object made to look like the real thing, as a false drawer or a model of a book. **3** *adj.* Imitation; artificial: a *dummy* door. **4** *n. slang* A stupid person. **5** *n.* In bridge, the inactive player who lays a hand of cards face up for his or her partner to play; also, the hand of cards. **6** *adj.* Acting for another while seeming to act for oneself: a *dummy* stockholder.

dump [dump] **1** *v.* To throw down or away: to *dump* packages on the bed; to *dump* trash. **2** *v.* To empty out; unload: to *dump* gravel on the road. **3** *n.* A place used for dumping: a garbage *dump.* **4** *n.* A temporary storage place for military supplies: a munitions *dump.* **5** *n. U.S. slang* A shabby, poorly kept place.

dump·ling [dump′ling] *n.* **1** A ball of dough filled with fruit and baked. **2** A small mass of dough cooked in soup or stew.

dumps [dumps] *n.pl.* A gloomy state of mind, es-

pecially in the phrase **in the dumps,** sad and gloomy.
dump truck A truck with a back part that tilts to slide out the load at the rear.
dump·y [dump′ē] *adj.* **dump·i·er, dump·i·est** Short and plump: a *dumpy* figure.
dun[1] [dun] *v.* **dunned, dun·ning,** *n.* 1 *v.* To ask over and over for payment of a debt: The agency *dunned* me for the money I owed. 2 *n.* A repeated demand for payment of a debt.
dun[2] [dun] *n., adj.* Grayish or reddish brown.
dunce [duns] *n.* A dull, slow student; stupid person.
dune [d(y)o͞on] *n.* A hill or bank of loose sand heaped up by the wind.
dune buggy A small, usually roofless automobile with oversize tires for driving on sand dunes and beaches.
dung [dung] *n.* The solid waste matter eliminated from the body by animals; manure.
dun·ga·ree [dung′gə·rē′] *n.* 1 (*pl.*) Trousers or overalls made from a coarse, heavy, usually blue, cotton cloth. 2 This kind of cloth.
dun·geon [dun′jən] *n.* A dark underground prison or cell: the *dungeon* of a castle.
dung·hill [dung′hil′] *n.* A heap of manure.
dunk [dungk] *v.* To dip or soak (as doughnuts or bread) in a liquid, as coffee or soup. 2 To push a basketball down through the basket from above the rim.

Dunking a doughnut

du·o [d(y)o͞o′ō] *n., pl.* **du·os** 1 A duet, especially instrumental. 2 A pair.
du·o·dec·i·mal system [do͞o′ō·des′ə·məl] A system of counting and of arithmetic based on 12. Each successive digit tells the number of ones, twelves, 144's, and so forth, instead of a system of ones, tens, and hundreds.
du·o·de·nal [d(y)o͞o′ə·dē′nəl *or* d(y)o͞o·od′ə·nəl] *adj.* Of, having to do with, or located in the duodenum.
du·o·de·num [d(y)o͞o′ə·dē′nəm *or* d(y)o͞o·od′ə·nəm] *n., pl.* **du·o·de·na** [d(y)o͞o′ə·dē′nə *or* d(y)o͞o·od′ə·nə] The part of the small intestine that connects with the stomach.
dupe [d(y)o͞op] *n., v.* **duped, dup·ing** 1 *n.* A person who is easily deceived or made a fool of. 2 *v.* To make a fool of; deceive, trick, or cheat.
du·ple [d(y)o͞o′pəl] *adj.* 1 Double. 2 Having two beats to the measure, as music: *duple* time.
du·plex [d(y)o͞o′pleks] 1 *adj.* Double; twofold. 2 *n.* A duplex apartment. 3 *n.* A duplex house.
duplex apartment An apartment having rooms on two floors.
duplex house A house having separate dwelling units for two families.
du·pli·cate [*v.* d(y)o͞o′plə·kāt′, *n., adj.* d(y)o͞o′plə·kit] *v.* **du·pli·cat·ed, du·pli·cat·ing,** *n., adj.* 1 *v.* To copy exactly or do again: That work of art could not be *duplicated.* 2 *n.* An exact copy. 3 *adj.* Made like or exactly corresponding to something else: a *duplicate* key. 4 *adj.* In pairs; double. **—in duplicate** In two identical copies: Submit the application forms *in duplicate.* **—du′pli·ca′tion** *n.*
du·pli·ca·tor [d(y)o͞o′plə·kā′tər] *n.* A machine that makes copies of printed or written matter.
du·plic·i·ty [d(y)o͞o·plis′ə·tē] *n., pl.* **du·plic·i·ties** An acting contrary to one's real feelings and beliefs in order to deceive; deceitfulness.
du·ra·bil·i·ty [d(y)o͝or′ə·bil′ə·tē] *n.* The quality of being durable.
du·ra·ble [d(y)o͝or′ə·bəl] *adj.* Lasting a long time without wearing out: a *durable* material. **—du′ra·ble·ness** *n.* **—du′ra·bly** *adv.*
dur·ance [d(y)o͝or′əns] *n.* Imprisonment, especially in the phrase **in durance vile,** in confinement.
du·ra·tion [d(y)o͞o·rā′shən] *n.* The time during which anything goes on or lasts: the *duration* of the winter.
du·ress [d(y)o͞o·res′] *n.* The use of threats or force to compel a person to do something: to confess under *duress.*
dur·ing [d(y)o͝or′ing] *prep.* 1 Throughout the time of: That school is closed *during* the summer. 2 In the course of: *During* today's game she hit a home run. ◆ *During* comes from the present participle of the verb *dure,* seldom used today, meaning *to last. During* thus meant *lasting.*
durst [dûrst] Past tense of DARE: seldom used today.
du·rum [d(y)o͝or′əm] *n.* A kind of wheat with hard kernels, used mainly for making spaghetti and macaroni. It is also called **durum wheat.**
dusk [dusk] *n.* The darkest part of twilight, just before night falls.
dusk·y [dus′kē] *adj.* **dusk·i·er, dusk·i·est** 1 Dim or gloomy: The room grew *dusky.* 2 Somewhat dark in color or complexion. **—dusk′i·ly** *adv.* **—dusk′i·ness** *n.*
dust [dust] 1 *n.* Any substance, as earth, that is in the form of very fine, light, dry particles: *dust* in the air; gold *dust.* 2 *v.* To wipe dust from (as furniture): to *dust* a table; *Dust* well today. 3 *v.* To sprinkle, as with powder or insecticide: to *dust* crops. 4 *n.* A dead human body or the earth in which it is buried: used in the Bible and in literary works. **—bite the dust** To fall down dead or injured. **—throw dust in someone's eyes** To deceive or mislead on purpose.
dust bowl A very dry region where the topsoil is blown away in clouds of dust.
dust·er [dus′tər] *n.* 1 A cloth or brush for removing dust. 2 A dress-length housecoat. 3 A lightweight, loose-fitting coat. 4 A lightweight jacket or coat to protect one's clothes from dust. 5 A device for sprinkling powder or insecticide.
dust jacket The removable paper cover that comes on new books.
dust·pan [dust′pan′] *n.* A shovel-shaped pan with a short handle, used for collecting dust swept from a floor.
dust storm A windstorm of dry regions that carries clouds of dust with it.
dust·y [dus′tē] *adj.* **dust·i·er, dust·i·est** 1 Full of or covered with dust: a *dusty* room. 2 Like dust; powdery: a light, *dusty* snow. 3 Grayish or dull, as a color. **—dust′i·ness** *n.*
Dutch [duch] 1 *adj.* Of or from the Netherlands.

a	add	**i**	it	**o͝o**	took	**oi**	oil		
ā	ace	**ī**	ice	**o͞o**	pool	**ou**	pout		
â	care	**o**	odd	**u**	up	**ng**	ring		
ä	palm	**ō**	open	**û**	burn	**th**	thin		
e	end	**ô**	order	**yo͞o**	fuse	**th**	this		
ē	equal					**zh**	vision		

ə = {a in *above* e in *sicken* i in *possible* / o in *melon* u in *circus*}

D

2 *n.* **(the Dutch)** The people of the Netherlands. **3** *n.* The language of the Netherlands. **—go Dutch** *U.S. informal* To have each person pay his or her own expenses, as on a date. **—in Dutch** *U.S. informal* In trouble, disfavor, or disgrace.

Dutch door A door divided across the middle so that the upper and lower parts can be opened and closed independently.

Dutch·man [duch′mən] *n., pl.* **Dutch·men** [duch′·mən] **1** A person who was born in or is a citizen of the Netherlands. **2** A German. ◆ The German word for *German* is *Deutsch.* Perhaps this is why Germans are sometimes called "Dutchmen."

Dutch·man's-breech·es [duch′mənz·brich′iz] *n. pl.* (*used with singular or plural verb*) A woodland plant of eastern North America having small, whitish, two-pointed flowers.

Dutch oven **1** A heavy pot or kettle with a tight-fitting lid, used for slow baking and stewing. **2** An oven with brick walls that are preheated to furnish heat for cooking.

Dutch treat *U.S. informal* A meal or entertainment at which each person pays his or her own bill.

du·te·ous [d(y)o͞o′tē·əs] *adj.* Dutiful; obedient. **—du′te·ous·ly** *adv.*

du·ti·a·ble [d(y)o͞o′tē·ə·bəl] *adj.* Subject to a customs duty or tax: *dutiable* imported goods.

du·ti·ful [d(y)o͞o′ti·fəl] *adj.* Having or showing a sense of duty; obedient or respectful: a *dutiful* child. **—du′ti·ful·ly** *adv.* **—du′ti·ful·ness** *n.*

du·ty [d(y)o͞o′tē] *n., pl.* **du·ties** **1** That which a person ought to do because it is right or required: It is your *duty* to obey. **2** Any work or task that is part of a particular job or occupation: the *duty* of a doctor. **3** A tax on goods brought into a country and sometimes on goods sent out.

D.V.M. Doctor of Veterinary Medicine.

dwarf [dwôrf] **1** *n.* A person, animal, or plant that is much less than normal size. **2** *n.* In fairy tales, a tiny person having some special skill or magical power. **3** *v.* To keep from growing to normal size; stunt the growth of: to *dwarf* trees. **4** *v.* To cause to appear small or less by comparison: That great hill *dwarfs* all the others around it. **5** *adj.* Small; stunted: a *dwarf* tree. **6** *n.* A star of medium or less than medium brightness and mass. Astronomers class the sun as a dwarf.

dwarf·ish [dwôr′fish] *adj.* Like a dwarf; small; stunted. **—dwarf′ish·ly** *adv.* **—dwarf′ish·ness** *n.*

dwarf star A relatively small star that gives off an average or below average amount of light: The sun is a *dwarf star.*

dwell [dwel] *v.* **dwelt** or **dwelled, dwell·ing** **1** To live; reside: to *dwell* by the sea. **2** To talk, write, or think about something for a long time: Don't *dwell* too much on your mistakes. **—dwell′er** *n.*

dwell·ing [dwel′ing] *n.* A place where someone lives; a house or other home: Some American Indians live in adobe *dwellings.*

dwelt [dwelt] A past tense and past participle of DWELL.

dwin·dle [dwin′dəl] *v.* **dwin·dled, dwin·dling** To grow steadily smaller or less; shrink; diminish: Hope of rescue *dwindled.*

dwt. pennyweight.

Dy The symbol for the element dysprosium.

dyb·buk [dib′ək] *n.* In Jewish folklore, the spirit of a dead person that enters and controls the body of a living person.

dye [dī] *v.* **dyed, dye·ing,** *n.* **1** *v.* To give lasting color to by soaking in liquid coloring matter: to *dye* a dress. **2** *n.* A colored preparation, often dissolved in a liquid, used for dyeing. **3** *n.* The color produced by dyeing. **4** *v.* To take color: Wool *dyes* well. **5** *v.* To color or stain. **—dy′er** *n.*

dyed-in-the-wool [dīd′in·t͟hə·wo͝ol′] *adj.* Complete; thoroughgoing: a *dyed-in-the-wool* scoundrel.

dye·stuff [dī′stuf′] *n.* A natural or artificial substance used for dyeing or making dye.

dy·ing [dī′ing] Present participle of DIE[1].

dyke [dīk] *n., v.* **dyked, dyk·ing** Another spelling of DIKE.

dy·nam·ic [dī·nam′ik] *adj.* **1** Having to do with physical force or energy. **2** Causing or marked by change or action: a *dynamic* period in history. **3** Full of energy and forcefulness: a *dynamic* leader.

dy·nam·ics [dī·nam′iks] *n.* **1** The science concerned with things in motion and how forces act to cause or change this motion. **2** The forces causing or controlling activity of any kind: the *dynamics* of progress. ◆ See -ICS.

dy·na·mism [dī′nə·miz′əm] *n.* The quality of being dynamic; energy; vigor.

dy·na·mite [dī′nə·mīt′] *n., v.* **dy·na·mit·ed, dy·na·mit·ing** **1** *n.* A powerful explosive made from nitroglycerin, used for blasting. **2** *v.* To blow up with dynamite; blast. **3** *n.* Anything having an explosive effect.

dy·na·mo [dī′nə·mō] *n., pl.* **dy·na·mos** A machine used to change mechanical energy into electricity; generator.

dy·na·mom·e·ter [dī′nə·mom′ə·tər] *n.* An instrument for measuring mechanical force or power.

dy·nast [dī′nast *or* dī′nəst] *n.* A ruler, especially a member of a dynasty.

dy·nas·tic [dī·nas′tik] *adj.* Of or having to do with a dynasty: *dynastic* power.

dy·nas·ty [dī′nəs·tē] *n., pl.* **dy·nas·ties** **1** A ruling family whose members reign one after another over a long period of time. **2** The period during which one ruling family is in power: the Ming *dynasty* of China.

dyne [dīn] *n.* In physics, a unit of force equal to the force needed to accelerate a mass of one gram at the rate of one centimeter per second per second.

dys·en·ter·y [dis′ən·ter′ē] *n.* A disease of the intestines, marked by the passing of blood and mucus in loose bowel movements.

dys·func·tion [dis·fungk′shən] *n.* A disorder or abnormality in functioning.

dys·gen·ic [dis·jen′ik] *adj.* Damaging to offspring or to their genes; genetically harmful: a *dysgenic* mutation.

dys·lex·i·a [dis·lek′sē·ə] *n.* An impairment of the ability to read or to learn to read.

dys·pep·sia [dis·pep′shə *or* dis·pep′sē·ə] *n.* Difficulty in digesting food; indigestion. ◆ *Dyspepsia* comes from a Greek word meaning *bad* or *hard to digest.*

dys·pep·tic [dis·pep′tik] **1** *adj.* Suffering from indigestion. **2** *n.* A person suffering from indigestion. **3** *adj.* Cross; irritable.

dys·pha·sia [dis·fā′zhə *or* dis·fā′zhē·ə] *n.* The loss or impairment of the ability to use or understand language as a result of brain injury.

dys·pro·si·um [dis·prō′s(h)ē·əm] *n.* A metallic element occurring in rare earths. ◆ See RARE-EARTH ELEMENT.

dz. dozen(s).

E is the fifth letter of the alphabet. The sign for it originated among Semitic people in the Near East, in the region of Palestine and Syria, probably in the middle of the second millennium B.C. Little is known about the sign until around 1000 B.C., when the Phoenicians began using it. They named it *he* and used it for the sound of the consonant *h*.

When the Greeks adopted the Phoenician sign around the ninth century B.C., they used it for the vowel *e* and called it *epsilon,* meaning "the short *e*," to distinguish it from another *e* sign called *eta,* meaning "the long *e*." The Greeks reversed the original direction of the sign. They also gradually refined its shape until it became like the sign we use for our capital *E* today.

As early as the eighth century B.C., the Etruscans adopted the Greek alphabet. It is from the Etruscans that the Romans took the sign for *E,* forming it crudely at first and then refining it into its present-day shape. The Romans used the letter for all *e* sounds, long and short. Around the time of the Caesars, the Romans made the shape of the letter more graceful. The model of the letter *E* found on the base of Trajan's column, erected in Rome in 114, is considered a masterpiece of letter design. A Trajan-style *majuscule,* or capital letter, *E* opens this essay.

The *minuscule,* or small letter, *e* developed gradually, between the third and the ninth centuries, in the handwriting that scribes used for copying books. At first the letter merely became rounded in the Roman *uncials* of the fourth to the eighth centuries. It then began to take its present-day shape in the *half uncials* of the fifth to the ninth centuries. This trend was continued in the script that evolved under the encouragement of Charlemagne (742-814). These letters were known as the *Caroline minuscules,* which became the principal handwriting system used on the medieval manuscripts of the ninth and tenth centuries.

Ee

Early Phoenician (late 2nd millennium B.C.)

Phoenician (8th century B.C.)

Early Greek (9th-7th centuries B.C.)

Western Greek (6th century B.C.)

Classical Greek (403 B.C. onward)

Early Etruscan (8th century B.C.)

Monumental Latin (4th century B.C.)

Classical Latin

Uncial

Half uncial

Caroline minuscule

e or **E** [ē] *n., pl.* **e's** or **E's** **1** The fifth letter of the English alphabet. **2** In music, the third note of the scale of C major.

e, e., E, or **E.** **1** east. **2** eastern.

E In physics, energy.

ea. each.

each [ēch] **1** *adj.* Being one of two or more persons or things, considered as separate from the others; every: *Each* child had a pencil. **2** *pron.* Every one of any group or number taken singly: *Each* of them printed her name. **3** *adv.* For or to each person or thing; apiece: The toys cost a dollar *each.* **—each other** One another. ◆ See ONE.

ea·ger [ē′gər] *adj.* **1** Impatiently anxious: *eager* for a chance; I am *eager* to go. **2** Extremely interested. **—ea′ger·ly** *adv.* **—ea′ger·ness** *n.*

ea·gle [ē′gəl] *n.* **1** A very large bird of prey with powerful wings and sharp eyesight. **2** A design or picture of an eagle used as an emblem or symbol. **3** A former gold coin of the U.S.

Eagle

eagle-eyed [ē′gəl·īd′] *adj.* Very sharp-sighted and alert to details.

ea·glet [ē′glit] *n.* A young eagle.

ea·gre [ē′gər] *n.* A tide that rises on shore in one high, often dangerous, wave; tidal bore.

ear[1] [ir] *n.* **1** The organ of hearing in people and animals, especially the outer part of the ear on either side of the head. **2** The ability to hear: to have a good *ear.* **3** An ability to distinguish sounds or tunes with accuracy: an *ear* for music. **4** Careful attention. **5** Something like an ear in shape. **—be all ears** To be eagerly attentive.

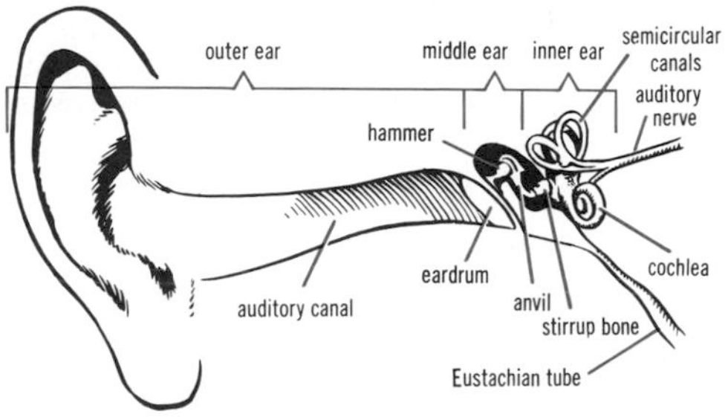

a add	**i** it	**o͝o** took	**oi** oil
ā ace	**ī** ice	**o͞o** pool	**ou** pout
â care	**o** odd	**u** up	**ng** ring
ä palm	**ō** open	**û** burn	**th** thin
e end	**ô** order	**yo͞o** fuse	**th** this
ē equal			**zh** vision

ə = { a in *above* e in *sicken* i in *possible* / o in *melon* u in *circus* }

ear² [ir] 1 *n.* The part of a cereal plant, as corn, rice, or wheat, on which the edible grains grow. 2 *v.* To form ears: This corn will *ear* late.
ear·ache [ir'āk'] *n.* Pain in the middle or inner part of the ear.
ear·drum [ir'drum'] *n.* A thin membrane stretched tight inside the ear, which transmits sound waves to the inner part of the ear.
ear·ful [ir'fo͞ol'] *n.* 1 A sharp reprimand; scolding. 2 A surprising bit of interesting news or gossip.
earl [ûrl] *n.* A member of the British nobility next above a viscount, and below a marquis.
earl·dom [ûrl'dəm] *n.* 1 The lands of an earl or countess. 2 The rank or title of an earl.
ear·lobe [ir'lōb'] *n.* The lowest, fleshy part of the outer ear.
ear·ly [ûr'lē] *adj.* **ear·li·er, ear·li·est,** *adv.* 1 *adj.* Coming or happening near the beginning: The *early* reports were better than the later ones; *early* evening. 2 *adv.* At or near the beginning: It happened *early* in the century. 3 *adv., adj.* Before the usual or arranged time: The guests came *early*; an *early* dinner. 4 *adj.* About to be; soon to occur: An *early* truce is expected.
early bird 1 A person who gets up early in the morning. 2 A person who arrives early for any occasion. ◆ *Early bird* comes from the proverb "The early bird catches the worm."
ear·mark [ir'märk'] 1 *n.* A mark on the ear of an animal that tells who the owner is. 2 *v.* To put an earmark on: to *earmark* cattle. 3 *n.* Any quality, sign, or feature that tells something about a person or thing: It has all the *earmarks* of a good car. 4 *v.* To set aside: to *earmark* money for a college education.
ear·muff [ir'muf'] *n.* A covering for the ear to protect it from cold or noise, usually worn in a pair attached to a headband.
earn [ûrn] *v.* 1 To receive in payment of work or service done: to *earn* a good salary. 2 To gain through effort; win or deserve: She *earned* fame by her success at tennis.
ear·nest¹ [ûr'nist] *adj.* Very serious, determined, or sincere: an *earnest* apology. **—in earnest** 1 With great determination. 2 Serious; sincere: You can't be *in earnest* when you say that. **—ear'·nest·ly** *adv.* **—ear'nest·ness** *n.* ◆ See SERIOUS.
ear·nest² [ûr'nist] *n.* Anything given as a pledge or token of something more to come later: Money is a good *earnest* to bind a bargain.
earn·ings [ûr'ningz] *n.pl.* Money earned, as wages or profits.
ear·phone [ir'fōn'] *n.* A listening device, as a telephone receiver, held against the ear.

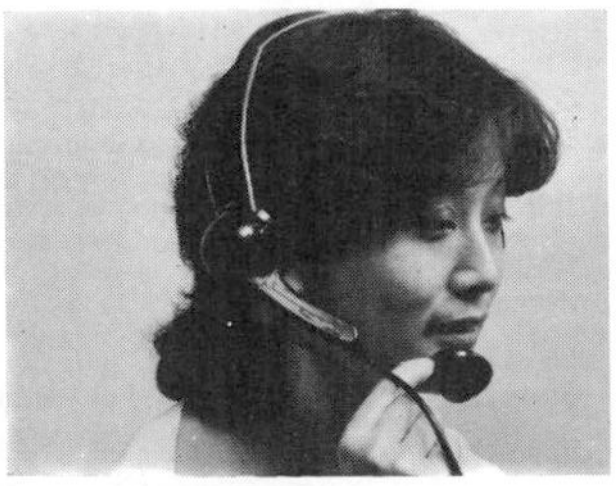
Earphone

ear·plug [ir'plug'] *n.* A plug designed to be fitted into the ear to stop noise or water.
ear·ring [ir'ring'] *n.* An ornament worn at the lobe of the ear.
ear·shot [ir'shot'] *n.* The distance at which sounds may be heard: Stay within *earshot* of the camp.
ear·split·ting [ir'split'ing] *adj.* Painfully loud; deafening: an *earsplitting* shriek.
earth [ûrth] *n.* 1 (*often written* **Earth**) The planet of the solar system on which we live, the fifth in size and third in distance from the sun. 2 The dry land of the earth, considered as separate from the oceans, lakes, and rivers. 3 The softer, loose part of land; soil; dirt. **—down to earth** Simple and natural in behavior.
earth·en [ûr'thən] *adj.* Made of earth or baked clay.
earth·en·ware [ûrth'ən·wâr'] *n.* Dishes, pots, pans, and the like, made of baked clay.
earth·light [ûrth'līt'] *n.* Another word for EARTHSHINE.
earth·ling [ûrth'ling] *n.* 1 A human being. 2 Any creature whose natural home is the planet Earth.
earth·ly [ûrth'lē] *adj.* 1 Of or having to do with the earth and this present life rather than with heaven or some imaginary world. 2 Possible: of no *earthly* use. **—earth'li·ness** *n.*
earth·quake [ûrth'kwāk'] *n.* A shaking or vibration of a part of the earth's surface, caused by an underground shift, volcanic action, or other movement.
earth science Any of the sciences that deal with the planet Earth or part of it, such as geology, oceanography, and meteorology.
earth·shak·ing [ûrth'shā'king] *adj.* Extremely important. **—earth'shak'ing·ly** *adv.*
earth·shine [ûrth'shīn'] *n.* Sunlight reflected from the earth that illuminates the part of the moon not directly illuminated by the sun.
earth·ward [ûrth'wərd] 1 *adv.* Toward the earth: The rocket plunged *earthward.* 2 *adj.* Directed toward the earth: The rocket took an *earthward* course.
earth·wards [ûrth'wərdz] *adv.* Earthward.
earth·work [ûrth'wûrk'] *n.* A wall or high earthen bank, used for protection or defense.
earth·worm [ûrth'wûrm'] *n.* A very common worm that lives and burrows in the earth, loosening up the soil; angleworm.
earth·y [ûr'thē] *adj.* **earth·i·er, earth·i·est** 1 Of or like earth or soil: an *earthy* color. 2 Natural and simple; not refined: an *earthy* dance.
ear·wig [ir'wig'] *n.* One of several related insects with a pair of appendages like pincers at the end of a stiff, slender body. ◆ *Earwig* comes from a mistaken belief that these insects sometimes crawl into a sleeping person's ears.
ease [ēz] *n., v.* **eased, eas·ing** 1 *n.* Freedom from discomfort or worry: a life of *ease.* 2 *v.* To relieve of mental or physical pain: to *ease* a person of suffering. 3 *v.* To make less painful: to *ease* a toothache. 4 *n.* Freedom from effort or difficulty: to jump with *ease.* 5 *n.* Freedom from embarrassment or nervousness. 6 *v.* To lessen the pressure or strain on: We must *ease* the chain before it breaks. 7 *v.* To move or put in place slowly and carefully: to *ease* a car into a parking space. **—at ease** 1 In a relaxed position: Stand *at ease.* 2 Free from nervousness; relaxed: *at ease* before an audience.

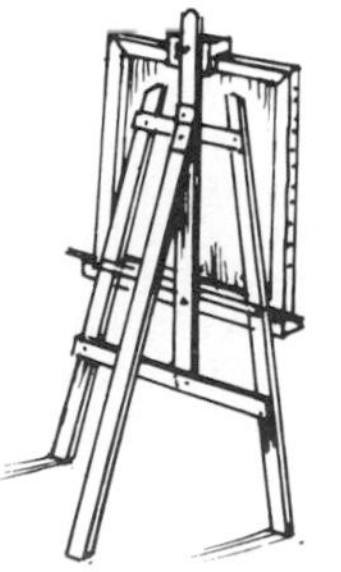
Easel

ea·sel [ē'zəl] *n.* A folding frame resting on three legs, used for holding an artist's canvas, a chart, or other items.
eas·i·ly [ē'zə·lē] *adv.* 1 Without effort, difficulty,

or discomfort: to do something *easily.* **2** Without a doubt; certainly: This is *easily* your best work. **3** Very possibly: The answer may *easily* be correct.

east [ēst] **1** *n.* The direction of the Earth's rotation and one of the four cardinal points of the compass, being 90 degrees clockwise from due north. If you face the sun at sunrise, you are facing east. **2** *adj.* To, toward, or in the east. **3** *adj.* Coming from the east. **4** *adv.* In or toward the east. **—east of** Farther east than: Illinois is *east of* Iowa. **—the East** **1** Asia and its neighboring lands; the Orient. **2** The eastern part of the U.S., especially the part east of the Allegheny Mountains and north of Maryland.

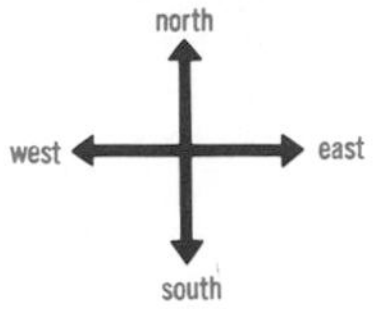

east·bound [ēst′bound′] *adj.* Moving or headed eastward.

east by north The direction or compass point midway between east and east-northeast; 11 degrees 15 minutes north of due east.

east by south The direction or compass point midway between east and east-southeast; 11 degrees 15 minutes south of due east.

East·er [ēs′tər] *n.* A Christian festival commemorating the resurrection of Christ. It is celebrated on the first Sunday (**Easter Sunday**) after the first full moon that occurs on or after March 21st.

east·er·ly [ēs′tər·lē] **1** *adj.* In or of the east. **2** *adj., adv.* Toward or from the east.

east·ern [ēs′tərn] *adj.* **1** Of, to, or in the east: an *eastern* bird. **2** From the east: an *eastern* wind. **3** (*often written* **Eastern**) Of or in the Orient or the eastern part of the U.S.

Eastern Church **1** The official Christian church of the Byzantine Empire. **2** Another name for the EASTERN ORTHODOX CHURCH.

east·ern·er [ēs′tərn·ər] *n.* **1** A person born or living in the east. **2** (*usually written* **Easterner**) A person born or living in the East, especially in the eastern U.S.

east·ern·most [ēs′tərn·mōst′] *adj.* Farthest east.

Eastern Orthodox Church A group of modern Christian churches, including the Greek Orthodox, that are derived from the Eastern Church of the Byzantine Empire.

Eastern Roman Empire The Byzantine Empire.

eastern standard time (*sometimes written* **Eastern Standard Time**) The standard time observed in the eastern United States and in most sections of the provinces of Quebec and Ontario in Canada. It is five hours earlier than Greenwich time.

East German **1** Of or from East Germany. **2** A person born in or a citizen of East Germany.

East Indian **1** Of or from the East Indies. **2** A person born or living in the East Indies.

east-north·east [ēst′nôrth′ēst′] **1** *n.* The direction or compass point midway between east and northeast; 22 degrees 30 minutes north of due east. **2** *adj.* To, toward, or in the east-northeast. **3** *adv.* In or toward the east-northeast.

east-south·east [ēst′south′ēst′] **1** *n.* The direction or compass point midway between east and southeast; 22 degrees 30 minutes south of due east. **2** *adj.* To, toward, or in the east-southeast. **3** *adv.* In or toward the east-southeast.

east·ward [ēst′wərd] **1** *adj., adv.* To or toward the east. **2** *n.* An eastward direction or point.

east·wards [ēst′wərdz] *adv.* Eastward.

eas·y [ē′zē] *adj.* **eas·i·er, eas·i·est,** *adv.* **1** *adj.* Requiring little work or effort; not difficult: an *easy* task. **2** *adj.* Free from worry or trouble: an *easy* mind. **3** *adj.* Comfortable: an *easy* chair. **4** *adj.* Not strict; lenient: an *easy* boss. **5** *adj.* Not stiff or formal; relaxed: an *easy* manner. **6** *adj.* Not strained or rushed; unhurried: an *easy* pace. **7** *adv. informal* Easily or slowly: Go *easy.* **—take it easy** *informal* To avoid haste, anger, or too much effort. **—eas′i·ness** *n.* ◆ Use *easy* as an adverb only in idiomatic expressions such as *take it easy* and *easy come, easy go.* Otherwise, use the adverb *easily* to modify verbs. See EASILY.

easy chair A large, comfortable chair with cushions or padding.

eas·y·go·ing [ē′zē·gō′ing] *adj.* Not hurried, strained, or upset about things; relaxed.

easy mark *slang* A person who is easily deceived, made fun of, or taken advantage of; patsy.

easy street The condition of having no financial worries.

eat [ēt] *v.* **ate, eat·en, eat·ing** **1** To take in as nourishment; chew and swallow: to *eat* fruit. **2** To have a meal: to *eat* three times a day. **3** To destroy or wear away: The lock had been *eaten* away by rust. **4** To use up: His stamp collection *ate* up his allowance. **—eat′er** *n.*

eat·a·ble [ēt′ə·bəl] **1** *n.* (*often pl.*) Food: to have good *eatables.* **2** *adj.* Fit to be eaten.

eat·ery [ēt′ə·rē] *n., pl.* **eat·er·ies** *informal* A restaurant.

eats [ēts] *n.pl. slang* Food.

eau de cologne [ō′də·kə·lōn′] *n.,pl.* **eaux de cologne** [ō′də·kə·lōn′ *or* ōz′də·kə·lōn′] Scented toilet water; COLOGNE. ◆ French for *water from Cologne.*

eaves [ēvz] *n.pl.* The lower border or edge of a roof that hangs over the side of the building.

Eaves

eaves·drop [ēvz′drop′] *v.* **eaves·dropped, eaves·drop·ping** To listen secretly to things being said in private. **—eaves′·drop′per** *n.*

ebb [eb] **1** *v.* To flow out or recede, as the tide. **2** *n.* The flowing back of the tide to the ocean. **3** *v.* To decline or weaken: Their courage *ebbed.* **4** *n.* A condition or period of decline or decay.

ebb tide The tide that flows back to the sea.

EbN east by north.

eb·on [eb′ən] *n., adj.* Ebony: used mostly in poems.

eb·o·nite [eb′ə·nīt′] *n.* A hard, usually black form of rubber.

eb·o·nize [eb′ə·nīz′] *v.* **eb·o·nize, eb·o·niz·ing** To stain black to look like ebony.

a	add	**i**	it	**o͝o**	took	**oi**	oil		
ā	ace	**ī**	ice	**o͞o**	pool	**ou**	pout		
â	care	**o**	odd	**u**	up	**ng**	ring		
ä	palm	**ō**	open	**û**	burn	**th**	thin		
e	end	**ô**	order	**yo͞o**	fuse	**t͟h**	this		
ē	equal					**zh**	vision		

ə = {a in *above* e in *sicken* i in *possible* / o in *melon* u in *circus*}

eb·on·y [eb′ə·nē] *n., pl.* **eb·on·ies,** *adj.* **1** *n.* A hard, heavy wood, usually black. **2** *adj. use:* An *ebony* cabinet. **3** *adj.* Black, like ebony.

EbS east by south.

e·bul·lient [i·bo͝ol′yənt] *adj.* Bubbling over with high spirits and enthusiasm. ◆ *Ebullient* comes from the Latin word for *boiling* or *bubbling.* — **e·bul′lience** *n.* —**e·bul′lient·ly** *adv.*

ec·cen·tric [ik·sen′trik] **1** *adj.* Very different in behavior, appearance, or opinions; odd; peculiar. **2** *n.* An eccentric person. **3** *adj.* Not having the same center, as two circles, one within the other. **4** *n.* A wheel set off center turning within a ring or collar to change circular motion into motion up and down. —**ec·cen′tri·cal·ly** *adv.*

ec·cen·tric·i·ty [ek′sen·tris′ə·tē] *n., pl.* **ec·cen·tric·i·ties** **1** Something that is odd, peculiar, or eccentric, as a manner of speaking or dressing. **2** The condition of being eccentric: My neighbor's *eccentricity* caused comment.

Ec·cle·si·as·tes [i·klē′zē·as′tēz] *n.* A book of the Old Testament.

ec·cle·si·as·tic [i·klē′zē·as′tik] **1** *adj.* Ecclesiastical. **2** *n.* A clergyman.

ec·cle·si·as·ti·cal [i·klē′zē·as′ti·kəl] *adj.* Of, having to do with, or suitable for a church.

ECG electrocardiogram.

ech·e·lon [esh′ə·lon] *n.* **1** A steplike formation of troops, ships, or airplanes in which each unit is behind and slightly to one side of the one in front. **2** A level or grade of command: the top *echelon.* **3** A section of a military unit: the rear *echelon.* ◆ *Echelon* comes from a French word meaning *ladder.*

e·chid·na [i·kid′nə] *n.* A small, toothless, egg-laying mammal with a spiny coat, strong claws for digging, a long snout, and a very long, sticky tongue with which it catches ants. Echidnas are a kind of anteater found in Australia and neighboring islands.

Echidna

e·chi·no·derm [i·kī′·nə·dûrm′] *n.* Any of a class of sea animals having a radial arrangement of its parts and often a spiny shell.

ech·o [ek′ō] *n., pl.* **echoes,** *v.* **ech·oed, ech·o·ing** **1** *n.* The repetition of a sound caused by sound waves striking an obstacle and being thrown back toward their starting point. **2** *v.* To repeat or send back the sound of: The walls *echoed* the shot. **3** *v.* To be sounded again as an echo: The shouts *echoed* throughout the house. **4** *v.* To repeat the words, opinions, or actions of: to *echo* great thinkers.

Ech·o [ek′ō] *n.* In Greek legend, a nymph who pined away for love of Narcissus until all that remained was the sound of her voice.

ech·o·lo·ca·tion [ek′ō·lō·kā′shən] *n.* A method used, as by a bat or a submarine, to locate unseen obstacles and moving objects in the surroundings by emitting sounds and noting the direction and extent of the area from which the echoes are reflected.

echo sounder A device for calculating the depth of water or of underwater objects by measuring the time it takes for emitted sounds to return as echoes.

é·clair [ā·klâr′ *or* ā′klâr′] *n.* A rich, finger-shaped pastry with a whipped cream or custard filling and usually a chocolate topping.

é·clat [ā·klä′] *n.* **1** Brilliance of action or effect: The musicians performed with *éclat.* **2** Fame; renown; glory.

ec·lec·tic [e·klek′tik] **1** *adj.* Choosing or composed of material from various sources: an *eclectic* teacher; an *eclectic* style of dress. **2** *n.* A person who uses eclectic methods or ideas in some pursuit. —**ec·lec′ti·cal·ly** *adv.* —**ec·lec′ti·cism** *n.*

e·clipse [i·klips′] *n., v.* **e·clipsed, e·clips·ing** **1** *n.* A complete or partial hiding of the sun (**solar eclipse**) as the moon passes between the sun and an observer on the earth. **2** *n.* A complete or partial hiding of the moon (**lunar eclipse**) as the moon passes through the earth's shadow. **3** *v.* To cause an eclipse of; darken. **4** *v.* To surpass; outshine: The team members *eclipsed* their coach in skill.

Progress of a solar eclipse

e·clip·tic[1] [i·klip′tik] *n.* The great circular path the sun seems to travel among the stars during one revolution of the earth around it.

e·clip·tic[2] [i·klip′tik] *adj.* Of or having to do with an eclipse or the ecliptic. —**e·clip′tic·al·ly** *adv.*

e·co·cide [ek′ō·sīd′ *or* ē′kō·sīd′] *n.* Destruction of an ecosystem by reckless damage to some vital feature of the environment. —**e′co·ci′dal** *adj.*

ec·o·log·ic [ek′ə·loj′ik *or* ē′kə·loj′ik] *adj.* Ecological.

ec·o·log·i·cal [ek′ə·loj′i·kəl *or* ē′kə·loj′i·kəl] *adj.* Of or having to do with ecology.

e·col·o·gy [i·kol′ə·jē *or* ē·kol′ə·jē] *n.* **1** The study of the relationships between living things and their surroundings. **2** The pattern or balance of relationships between living things and their surroundings: The volcanic eruption disturbed the *ecology* of the entire region. —**e·col′o·gist** *n.*

e·con·o·met·rics [i·kon′ə·met′riks] *n.* The application of statistical methods to the study of economic theories, data, and problems. ◆ See -ICS.

ec·o·nom·ic [ek′ə·nom′ik *or* ē′kə·nom′ik] *adj.* **1** Of or having to do with the science of economics. **2** Of or having to do with money or with the managing of money: Underdeveloped nations have many *economic* problems.

ec·o·nom·i·cal [ek′ə·nom′i·kəl *or* ē′kə·nom′i·kəl] *adj.* Not wasteful; thrifty: an *economical* little car to operate. —**ec′o·nom′i·cal·ly** *adv.*

ec·o·nom·ics [ek′ə·nom′iks *or* ē′kə·nom′iks] *n.* The science that deals with the production, distribution, and use of goods and services. It includes the study of such matters as money, wages, and taxes. ◆ See -ICS.

e·con·o·mist [i·kon′ə·mist] *n.* A student of or a specialist in economics.

e·con·o·mize [i·kon′ə·mīz′] *v.* **e·con·o·mized, e·con·o·miz·ing** **1** To be thrifty and sparing: In the desert, one must *economize* on water. **2** To spend or use with care and thrift.

e·con·o·my [i·kon′ə·mē] *n., pl.* **e·con·o·mies** **1** Careful and thrifty use, as of money, food, or resources, to avoid waste. **2** The management of the resources or finances of a country, business, home, or other organization.

e·co·sys·tem [ek'ō·sis'təm] *n.* An ecological community along with its nonliving environment thought of as a functioning unit.
ec·ru [ek'rōō] *n., adj.* Light, yellowish brown.
ec·sta·sy [ek'stə·sē] *n., pl.* **ec·sta·sies** A feeling of great happiness or delight; rapture.
ec·stat·ic [ek·stat'ik] *adj.* Full of or marked by ecstasy. **—ec·stat'i·cal·ly** *adv.*
ect- or **ecto-** A combining form meaning: External; outer; outside, as in *ectoparasite.*
ec·to·derm [ek'tə·dûrm'] *n.* The outermost of the three primary layers of cells of the embryo, from which are developed the skin, the brain and spinal cord, and the sense organs. **—ec'to·der'mal** *adj.*
ec·tog·e·nous [ek·toj'ə·nəs] *adj.* Able to develop outside a host, as certain pathogenic bacteria.
ec·to·par·a·site [ek'tō·par'ə·sīt'] *n.* A parasite that lives outside the body of its host. **—ec·to·par·a·sit·ic** [ek'tō·par'ə·sit'ik] *adj.*
ec·to·plasm [ek'tə·plaz'əm] *n.* The relatively rigid, clear cytoplasm near the outer boundaries of some cells.
Ec·ua·do·ri·an [ek'wə·dôr'ē·ən] **1** *adj.* Of or from Ecuador. **2** *n.* A person born in or a citizen of Ecuador.
Ec·ua·dor·an [ek'wə·dôr'ən] *adj., n.* Ecuadorian.
ec·u·men·i·cal [ek'yōō·men'i·kəl] *adj.* Universal; all-inclusive. ◆ *Ecumenical* is most often used to describe a modern movement toward unity and cooperation between the Roman Catholic and Protestant branches of Christianity, or sometimes between Christianity and other religions.
ec·ze·ma [ek'sə·mə *or* eg·zē'mə] *n.* A skin condition marked by red, scaly pimples and severe itching.
-ed A suffix meaning: **1** Taking place in the past, and used to form the past tense and past participle of regular verbs, as in *walked, washed, mended, clothed.* **2** Having, as in *bearded.* **3** Like, as in *bigoted.*
ed. **1** edited. **2** edition. **3** editor. **4** education.
e·da·cious [i·dā'shəs] *adj.* Voracious.
E·dam cheese [ē'dəm *or* ē'dam] A mild, yellow Dutch cheese usually pressed into balls and covered with red wax. ◆ *Edam* is the name of a town in the Netherlands where this cheese was first made.
ed·dy [ed'ē] *n., pl.* **ed·dies,** *v.* **ed·died, ed·dy·ing** **1** *n.* A current of water or air moving against a main current, often in circles; a whirlpool or whirlwind. **2** *v.* To move or cause to move in an eddy.
e·del·weiss [ād'(ə)l·wīs' *or* ād'(ə)l·vīs'] *n.* A small plant growing high in the Alps. Its small flowers are surrounded by downy white leaves that look like petals.
e·de·ma [i·dē'mə] *n.* An excess accumulation of fluid in body tissues or cavities, resulting in swelling.
E·den [ēd'(ə)n] *n.* **1** In the Bible, the garden that was the first home of Adam and Eve. **2** Any place of joy and happiness; paradise.
edge [ej] *n., v.* **edged, edg·ing** **1** *n.* The line or place where an object or area ends; margin: the *edge* of a table. **2** *v.* To put an edge or border on: to *edge* a collar with lace. **3** *n.* A brink or rim: the *edge* of a cup; the *edge* of a cliff. **4** *n.* The thin, sharp, cutting side of a blade. **5** *v.* To sharpen: to *edge* an ax. **6** *v.* To move sideways or little by little: to *edge* into a crowded room. **—on edge** Too nervous or impatient to sit still; jumpy.
edge·wise [ej'wīz'] *adv.* **1** With the edge forward. **2** On or in the direction of the edge.
edg·ing [ej'ing] *n.* Something that forms an edge or is attached to an edge: an *edging* of lace.

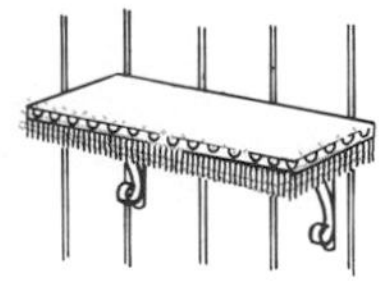
Edging on a shelf

edg·y [ej'ē] *adj.* **edg·i·er, edg·i·est** Tense, nervous, or irritable; on edge.
ed·i·ble [ed'ə·bəl] **1** *adj.* Suitable for food; fit to eat. **2** *n.* (*usually pl.*) Something fit to eat. **—ed·i·bil·i·ty** [ed'ə·bil'ə·tē] *n.* **—ed'·i·ble·ness** *n.*
e·dict [ē'dikt] *n.* An official order, rule, or law that is made known to the public by a formal announcement; decree.
ed·i·fi·ca·tion [ed'ə·fi·kā'shən] *n.* The process or result of being edified; moral or spiritual enlightenment.
ed·i·fice [ed'ə·fis] *n.* A building, especially a large and impressive structure.
ed·i·fy [ed'ə·fī'] *v.* **ed·i·fied, ed·i·fy·ing** To instruct or improve, especially morally or spiritually: A good book *edifies* the mind.
ed·it [ed'it] *v.* **1** To arrange, correct, or in any way prepare for publication: to *edit* a new novel. **2** To direct the publication of: to *edit* a paper.
edit. **1** edition. **2** editor.
e·di·tion [i·dish'ən] *n.* **1** The particular form in which a literary work is published: a three-volume *edition.* **2** The total number of copies of a publication issued at any one time and printed from the same plates. **3** A copy belonging to this printing: a first *edition.* ◆ See ADDITION.
ed·i·tor [ed'i·tər] *n.* **1** A person who edits. **2** A person in charge of a newspaper or magazine or of one of its departments: a sports *editor.* **3** A writer of editorials. **—ed'i·tor·ship'** *n.*
ed·i·to·ri·al [ed'i·tôr'ē·əl] **1** *n.* An article in a newspaper or magazine expressing an opinion held by the editor or publisher. **2** *adj.* Of or having to do with an editor or editing: *editorial* policy.
ed·u·ca·ble [ej'ōō·kə·bəl] *adj.* Capable of learning; teachable. **—ed·u·ca·bil·i·ty** [ej'ōō·kə·bil'ə·tē] *n.*
ed·u·cate [ej'ōō·kāt'] *v.* **ed·u·cat·ed, ed·u·cat·ing** **1** To teach, develop, or train: to *educate* one's ear to appreciate good music. **2** To provide schooling for: to *educate* one's children.
ed·u·ca·tion [ej'ōō·kā'shən] *n.* **1** The development of a person's mind, body, or natural talents through study and training: *Education* ought not to end with school. **2** Instruction or training: a college *education.* **3** All of the things a person learns by study or training.
ed·u·ca·tion·al [ej'ōō·kā'shən·əl] *adj.* **1** Of or having to do with education: an *educational* meeting. **2** That instructs or gives information: an *educational* trip. **—ed'u·ca'tion·al·ly** *adv.*
ed·u·ca·tive [ej'ōō·kā'tiv] *adj.* **1** Giving education or information. **2** Having to do with education.

a	add	**i**	it	**ŏŏ**	took	**oi**	oil
ā	ace	**ī**	ice	**ōō**	pool	**ou**	pout
â	care	**o**	odd	**u**	up	**ng**	ring
ä	palm	**ō**	open	**û**	burn	**th**	thin
e	end	**ô**	order	**yōō**	fuse	**th**	this
ē	equal					**zh**	vision

ə = a in *above*, e in *sicken*, i in *possible*, o in *melon*, u in *circus*

ed·u·ca·tor [ej′ōō·kā′tər] *n.* **1** A teacher. **2** A person skilled in the field of education.

e·duce [i·d(y)ōōs′] *v.* **e·duced, e·duc·ing** **1** To draw out; elicit. **2** To form an opinion from the facts shown; deduce.

Ed·war·di·an [ed·wär′dē·ən *or* ed·wôr′dē·ən] **1** *adj.* Of or suggestive of the period of Edward VII of Great Britain. **2** *n.* A person living in or typifying the Edwardian period.

-ee A suffix meaning: **1** A person who undergoes or benefits from an action, as in *payee.* **2** A person who is or does something, as in *absentee* or *standee.*

eel [ēl] *n., pl.* **eels** or **eel** A fish having a long, snakelike body and a smooth skin.

eel·grass [ēl′gras′] *n.* An aquatic plant growing under water with long, narrow leaves resembling grass.

Eel

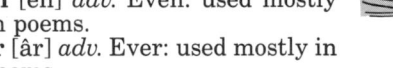

e'en [ēn] *adv.* Even: used mostly in poems.

e'er [âr] *adv.* Ever: used mostly in poems.

ee·rie or **ee·ry** [ir′ē] *adj.* **ee·ri·er, ee·ri·est** Causing or arousing fear; weird; strange.

ef·face [i·fās′] *v.* **ef·faced, ef·fac·ing** **1** To rub or blot out; get rid of; destroy: Time had *effaced* the words carved on the ancient pillar; to *efface* old memories. **2** To hide or keep (oneself) from the notice or attention of others. **—ef·face′a·ble** *adj.* **—ef·face′ment** *n.* **—ef·fac′er** *n.*

ef·fect [i·fekt′] **1** *n.* Something brought about by some action or cause; result: the *effect* of an explosion. **2** *n.* The ability or power to produce some result: The hot soup had a warming *effect.* **3** *v.* To bring about or cause; accomplish: to *effect* a change in government. **4** *n.* An impression or reaction made on the mind or body: the *effect* of music; the *effect* of drugs. **5** *n.* (*pl.*) Personal goods or belongings. **—for effect** In order to be noticed or make an impression. **—in effect** **1** In actual fact; really: *In effect* she refused the offer. **2** In active force or operation: The law is now *in effect.* **—take effect** To begin to act upon something or bring about a result. ◆ *Effect* and *affect* are often confused because they sound alike, but their meanings are different. *To effect* means *to bring about* or *cause to happen:* Good treatment should *effect* a cure. *To affect* means *to influence* or *have an effect upon:* Early experiences *affect* one's outlook on life. Both words are based on the Latin word for *to do,* but *effect* comes from elements meaning *to do out,* and *affect* from elements meaning *to do to.*

ef·fec·tive [i·fek′tiv] *adj.* **1** Producing or able to produce the proper result; efficient: an *effective* machine. **2** Producing a great impression; impressive: an *effective* speaker. **3** In effect or in force: This law is only *effective* in July. **—ef·fec′tive·ly** *adv.* **—ef·fec′tive·ness** *n.* ◆ *Effective* and *effectual* both refer to the ability to achieve a desired result. *Effective* is the more general term, and may apply to both persons and things: an *effective* leader; an *effective* strategy. *Effectual* is usually limited to things: an *effectual* remedy; an *effectual* plan.

ef·fec·tu·al [i·fek′chōō·əl] *adj.* Producing or able to produce a desired result or effect. **—ef·fec′tu·al·ly** *adv.* ◆ See EFFECTIVE.

ef·fec·tu·ate [i·fek′chōō·āt′] *v.* **ef·fec·tu·at·ed, ef·fec·tu·at·ing** To cause to happen; bring about; effect.

ef·fem·i·na·cy [i·fem′ə·nə·sē] *n.* The quality in a boy or man of being like a girl or woman.

ef·fem·i·nate [i·fem′ə·nit] *adj.* Having qualities, traits, or ways usually found in a woman and not characteristic of a man.

ef·fer·ent [ef′ər·ənt] *adj.* Carrying or carried outward. Efferent nerves carry impulses from the brain or spinal cord to the muscles.

ef·fer·vesce [ef′ər·ves′] *v.* **ef·fer·vesced, ef·fer·vesc·ing** **1** To give off bubbles, as soda water. **2** To be lively and enthusiastic. **—ef′fer·ves′cence** *n.*

ef·fer·ves·cent [ef′ər·ves′ənt] *adj.* **1** Bubbling up. **2** Full of life and high spirits; lively.

ef·fete [i·fēt′] *adj.* **1** Having lost strength and vigor; worn-out. **2** Unable to produce anything new or original; decadent: an *effete* society. **—ef·fete′ly** *adv.* **—ef·fete′ness** *n.*

ef·fi·ca·cious [ef′ə·kā′shəs] *adj.* Producing the desired effect or result; effective: an *efficacious* medicine. **—ef′fi·ca′cious·ly** *adv.* **—ef′fi·ca′cious·ness** *n.*

ef·fi·ca·cy [ef′ə·kə·sē] *n.* Power to produce an effect wanted; effectiveness: I doubted the *efficacy* of the new medicine.

ef·fi·cien·cy [i·fish′ən·sē] *n.* The ability to produce results without any waste, as of time, effort, or money.

efficiency apartment Self-contained living quarters, usually furnished, consisting of one room with a kitchenette and small bathroom.

ef·fi·cient [i·fish′ənt] *adj.* Producing results with the least effort or waste; capable: an *efficient* motor. **—ef·fi′cient·ly** *adv.*

ef·fi·gy [ef′ə·jē] *n., pl.* **ef·fi·gies** **1** A painting or statue of a person. **2** A crude, often stuffed figure of a person who is disliked: The dictator was burnt in *effigy.*

ef·flo·resce [ef′lə·res′] *v.* **ef·flo·resced, ef·flo·res·cing** **1** To blossom; flower; bloom. **2** In chemistry, to become a powder through loss of water of crystallization.

ef·flo·res·cence [ef′lə·res′əns] *n.* **1** The process or period of producing blossoms. **2** Any process or result of fruitful development. **3** The act, process, or product of chemically efflorescing.

ef·flu·ent [ef′lōō·ənt] **1** *adj.* Flowing forth. **2** *n.* A stream of any fluid flowing from a source. **3** *n.* Industrial waste or sewage discharging into the environment.

ef·fort [ef′ərt] *n.* **1** The use of physical or mental energy or power to get something done: Playing tennis requires *effort.* **2** Something produced by work and effort: A new play is a theatrical *effort.* **3** An attempt: I made an *effort* to finish the work on time.

ef·fort·less [ef′ərt·lis] *adj.* Requiring or showing little or no effort: His *effortless* playing of the violin is amazing. **—ef′fort·less·ly** *adv.* **—ef′fort·less·ness** *n.*

ef·front·er·y [i·frun′tər·ē] *n.* Shameless or insolent boldness; audacity; impudence: The child had the *effrontery* to criticize the teacher in front of the class.

ef·ful·gence [i·ful′jəns] *n.* Great brightness or radiance of light.

ef·ful·gent [i·ful′jənt] *adj.* Shining brilliantly; radiant; splendid.

ef·fu·sion [i·fyōō′zhən] *n.* **1** The action of pouring forth or out: The *effusion* of blood was finally checked. **2** An unrestrained outpouring of emotion or words: The old friends greeted each other with effusion.

ef·fu·sive [i·fyo͞o′siv] *adj.* Overly emotional and enthusiastic; gushing: an *effusive* greeting. **—ef·fu′·sive·ly** *adv.* **—ef·fu′sive·ness** *n.*

EFL *E*nglish as a *F*oreign *L*anguage: The teaching of English to speakers of other languages.

eft [eft] *n.* A newt or small lizard.

e.g. for example. ◆ *e.g.* is an abbreviation of the Latin phrase *exempli gratia,* meaning *for example.*

e·gal·i·tar·i·an [i·gal′ə·ter′ē·ən] **1** *n.* A person who advocates equal treatment for all classes and conditions of people. **2** *adj.* Unbiased; not influenced by rank or wealth.

egg[1] [eg] *n.* **1** The round or oval body produced by female birds, insects, and most reptiles and fishes, and containing the material from which the offspring develops. An egg is covered by a thin shell or skin, and usually hatches outside the mother's body. **2** The egg of the domestic hen, raw or cooked.

egg[2] [eg] *v.* To urge or coax into doing something.

egg·beat·er [eg′bē′tər] *n.* A cooking utensil having blades that whirl, used to beat eggs and whip cream.

egg·cup [eg′kup′] *n.* A small cup for serving a boiled egg.

egg·head [eg′hed′] *n. informal* A person mostly interested in intellectual things; a highbrow.

egg·nog [eg′nog′] *n.* A drink made of beaten eggs, milk, sugar, and sometimes liquor or wine.

egg·plant [eg′plant′] *n.* A plant bearing a large egg-shaped, usually purple-skinned fruit that is cooked and eaten as a vegetable.

egg·shell [eg′shel′] **1** *n.* The hard, brittle covering of the egg of a bird. **2** *adj.* Thin and easily broken. **3** *adj.* Pale yellow or ivory: *eggshell* satin.

egg white The transparent, viscid substance that surrounds the yolk of an egg and turns white and firm on heating; albumen.

e·gis [ē′jis] *n.* Another spelling of AEGIS.

eg·lan·tine [eg′lən·tīn′ *or* eg′lən·tēn′] *n.* Another name for SWEETBRIER.

e·go [ē′gō] *n., pl.* **e·gos** **1** The part of a person's mind or self by which the person is aware that he or she is different from all other people in thoughts, feelings, and actions. **2** *informal* Egotism. **3** Self-esteem. ◆ *Ego* comes from the Latin word for *I.*

e·go·ism [ē′gō·iz′əm] *n.* **1** The tendency to think mainly of one's own welfare; selfishness. **2** Egotism.

e·go·ist [ē′gō·ist] *n.* A person who is self-centered or conceited. **—e′go·is′tic** *adj.* **—e′go·is′ti·cal** *adj.* **—e′go·is′ti·cal·ly** *adv.*

e·go·ma·ni·a [ē′gō·mā′nē·ə] *n.* An excessive, abnormal preoccupation with oneself; self-centeredness. **—e′go·ma′ni·ac′** *n.* **—e·go·ma·ni·a·cal** [ē′gō·mə·nī′ə·kəl] *adj.*

e·go·tism [ē′gə·tiz′əm] *n.* **1** The habit of talking or writing about oneself, often boastfully; conceit. **2** Egoism. **—e′go·tist** *n.*

e·go·tis·ti·cal [ē′gə·tis′ti·kəl] *adj.* Inclined to think too highly of oneself; conceited. **—e′go·tis′ti·cal·ly** *adv.*

e·go·trip [ē′gō·trip′] *v.* **e·go·tripped, e·go·trip·ping** slang To indulge in AN EGO TRIP.

ego trip *slang* An action or experience that gratifies and enhances one's self-esteem.

e·gre·gious [i·grē′jəs *or* i·grē′jē·əs] *adj.* Outstandingly bad; glaring; flagrant; an *egregious* error.

e·gress [ē′gres′] *n.* **1** A way of getting out; exit. **2** The act of going out. **3** The right to go out.

e·gret [ē′grit] *n.* **1** A white heron, valued for its long, beautiful white plumes. **2** One of its plumes; aigrette.

Egret

E·gyp·tian [ē·jip′shən] **1** *adj.* Of or from Egypt. **2** *n.* A person born in or a citizen of Egypt. **3** *n.* The language of ancient Egypt.

Egyptian cotton A cotton of high quality with long, fine fibers, grown chiefly in northern Africa.

eh [ā *or* e] *interj.* What; isn't that so: usually spoken with the voice rising: You had a bad fall, *eh?*

ei·der [ī′dər] *n.* A large sea duck found in northern waters.

ei·der·down [ī′dər·doun′] *n.* **1** The soft feathers of the eider duck, used for stuffing pillows and quilts. **2** A quilt stuffed with eiderdown.

eight or **8** [āt] *n., adj.* One more than seven.

eight·een or **18** [ā′tēn′] *n., adj.* One more than seventeen.

eight·eenth or **18th** [ā′tēnth′] **1** *adj.* Next after the seventeenth. **2** *n.* The eighteenth one. **3** *adj.* Being one of eighteen equal parts. **4** *n.* An eighteenth part.

eight·fold [āt′fōld′] **1** *adj.* Consisting of eight parts: an *eightfold* program. **2** *adj.* Being eight times greater in size or number: an *eightfold* gain. **3** *adv.* By eight times: It has multiplied *eightfold.*

eighth or **8th** [ātth *or* āth] **1** *adj.* Next after the seventh. **2** *n.* The eighth one. **3** *adj.* Being one of eight equal parts. **4** *n.* An eighth part.

eighth note In music, a note having one eighth the time value of a whole note.

Eighth notes

eight·i·eth or **80th** [ā′tē·ith] **1** *adj.* Tenth in order after the seventieth. **2** *n.* The eightieth one. **3** *adj.* Being one of eighty equal parts. **4** *n.* An eightieth part.

eight·y or **80** [ā′tē] *n., pl.* **eight·ies** **1** *n., adj.* Ten more than seventy. **2** *n.* (*pl.*) The years between the age of 80 and the age of 90.

ein·stei·ni·um [īn·stīn′ē·əm] *n.* A synthetic radioactive element first discovered in fallout from a hydrogen bomb explosion.

ei·ther [ē′*th*ər *or* ī′*th*ər] **1** *adj.* One or the other of two: Use *either* hand. **2** *pron.* One or the other;

a add	**i** it	**o͝o** took	**oi** oil
ā ace	**ī** ice	**o͞o** pool	**ou** pout
â care	**o** odd	**u** up	**ng** ring
ä palm	**ō** open	**û** burn	**th** thin
e end	**ô** order	**yo͞o** fuse	***th*** this
ē equal			**zh** vision

ə = { a in *above* e in *sicken* i in *possible*
  o in *melon* u in *circus* }

one of two: *Either* will do. **3** *adj.* Each of two; one and the other: They sat on *either* side of the couch. **4** *conj.* In one of two or more cases: used before two or more choices joined by *or: Either* you will buy it *or* you won't. **5** *adv.* Any more so; in addition; besides: If you can't speak, I won't *either.* ◆ *Either* and *neither* in formal writing both take a singular verb: *Either* team *has* a chance to win. In informal speech and writing, a plural verb is often used: *Are either* of them going to the party?

e·jac·u·late [i·jak′yə·lāt′] *v.* **e·jac·u·lat·ed, e·jac·u·lat·ing** To say or utter suddenly: "No!" he *ejaculated.*

e·jac·u·la·tion [i·jak′yə·lā′shən] *n.* A brief utterance or exclamation.

e·ject [i·jekt′] *v.* To throw or put out; expel: to *eject* steam; The police *ejected* the unruly people at the fair. **—e·ject′a·ble** *adj.* **—e·jec′tion** *n.* **—e·jec′tive** *adj.*

ejection seat A seat fitted with an explosive propelling device and a parachute to carry the occupant safely free of an airplane and to earth in case of emergency.

e·jec·tor [i·jek′tər] *n.* **1** A person or thing that ejects. **2** A device that ejects used material, as shells or cartridges from a gun.

eke [ēk] *v.* **eked, ek·ing** **1** To make with difficulty and effort: to *eke* out a living. **2** To add to; supplement: to *eke* out one's income by working at a second job.

EKG **1** electrocardiogram. **2** electrocardiograph.

el [el] *n. informal* An elevated railway.

e·lab·o·rate [*v.* i·lab′ə·rāt′, *adj.* i·lab′ər·it] *v.* **e·lab·o·rat·ed, e·lab·o·rat·ing,** *adj.* **1** *v.* To work out or develop very carefully: to *elaborate* an idea. **2** *adj.* Worked out or developed carefully and thoroughly: an *elaborate* plan. **3** *adj.* Fancy and usually costly or luxurious in its details or parts: an *elaborate* dress; an *elaborate* dinner. **4** *v.* To add more details: A letter *elaborated* on the phone message. **—e·lab′o·rate·ly** *adv.* **—e·lab′o·ra′tion** *n.*

é·lan [ā·län′] *n.* Verve combined with talent and style. ◆ *Élan* is a French word with the same meaning as in English, except that in French it also means a forward leap or dash.

e·land [ē′lənd] *n.* A large, oxlike antelope of Africa, having short spirally twisted horns.

Eland

e·lapse [i·laps′] *v.* **e·lapsed, e·laps·ing** To slip by; pass away: Months *elapsed* before we met again.

e·las·tic [i·las′tik] **1** *adj.* Able to return to a former size or shape after being pulled or pressed: an *elastic* rubber ball. **2** *n.* Any elastic material or fabric. **3** *adj.* Springy; lively: an *elastic* stride. **4** *adj.* Easily adaptable or adjustable, so as to fit changes or new circumstances: an *elastic* schedule.

e·las·tic·i·ty [i·las′tis′ə·tē] *n.* The quality of being elastic.

e·late [i·lāt′] *v.* **e·lat·ed, e·lat·ing** To cause to feel full of joy or pride.

e·lat·ed [i·lā′tid] *adj.* Filled with joy or pride, as over success or good fortune. **—e·lat′ed·ly** *adv.*

e·la·tion [i·lā′shən] *n.* A feeling of joy or triumph.

el·bow [el′bō] **1** *n.* The joint at the bend of the arm between the forearm and the upper arm. **2** *n.* Something having an angle or bend like an elbow, as a curved length of pipe. **3** *v.* To push or jostle, as if with the elbows: to *elbow* one's way through a crowd.

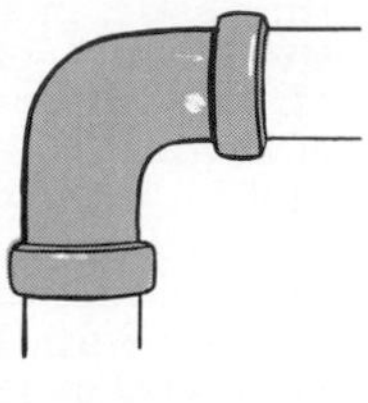
Elbow joint

elbow grease *informal* Physical effort; hard work: Use some *elbow grease* on that dirty pan.

el·bow·room [el′bō·rōōm′ *or* el′bō·rŏŏm′] *n.* Enough room to work or move about in.

eld·er[1] [el′dər] **1** *adj.* Older: an *elder* sister. **2** *n.* An older person. **3** *n.* A church official.

el·der[2] [el′dər] *n.* A shrub with white flowers and dark purple or red berries.

el·der·ber·ry [el′dər·ber′ē] *n., pl.* **el·der·ber·ries** **1** The berry of the elder, used to make wine. **2** Another name for ELDER[2].

eld·er·ly [el′dər·lē] *adj.* Approaching old age; rather old. ◆ See OLD.

elder statesman A prominent person of long experience in public affairs who acts in the role of adviser only.

eld·est [el′dist] *adj., n.* Oldest.

El Do·ra·do or **El·do·ra·do** [el′də·rä′dō] *n.* **1** An imaginary South American city long sought by early Spanish explorers because it was believed to be rich in gold and jewels. **2** Any region that is rich in gold or in opportunities.

e·lect [i·lekt′] **1** *v.* To choose for an office by vote; select: to *elect* a mayor. **2** *adj.* Elected to office but not yet sworn in: a president *elect.* **3** *v.* To choose; decide: to *elect* to remain behind. **—the elect** A specially favored group: Members of the Honor Society belong to *the elect.*

e·lec·tion [i·lek′shən] *n.* **1** The selecting of a person or persons for any position or honor, especially by voting. **2** A choice.

e·lec·tion·eer [i·lek′shən·ir′] *v.* To work to get votes for a candidate or political party.

e·lec·tive [i·lek′tiv] **1** *adj.* Settled by an election: an *elective* position. **2** *adj.* Selected by vote: an *elective* official. **3** *n.* A school subject that may be chosen or not as the student prefers. **4** *adj.* Left to choice; optional: an *elective* course.

e·lec·tor [i·lek′tər] *n.* **1** A person who is qualified to vote in an election. **2** *U.S.* A member of the electoral college.

e·lec·tor·al [i·lek′tər·əl] *adj.* Having to do with an election or electors.

electoral college In the U.S., a group of persons chosen by the voters of each state to elect formally the president and vice-president.

e·lec·tor·ate [i·lek′tər·it] *n.* Those persons who are eligible to vote in an election.

E·lec·tra [i·lek′trə] *n.* In Greek myths, the daughter of Agamemnon and Clytemnestra and the sister of Orestes. She encouraged Orestes to kill their mother and her lover because they had killed Agamemnon.

e·lec·tric [i·lek′trik] *adj.* **1** Consisting of or having to do with electricity. **2** Producing or carrying electricity: an *electric* generator; *electric* cable. **3** Operated by electricity: an *electric* train. **4** Thrilling; exciting: an *electric* personality. **—e·lec′tri·cal·ly** *adv.*

e·lec·tri·cal [i·lek′tri·kəl] *adj.* Electric.

electric chair 1 A chair used to electrocute persons who are sentenced to death. 2 Electrocution.

electric current A flow of electrons through a conductor, as through a wire.

electric eel An eellike, freshwater fish found in South America, capable of delivering powerful electric shocks.

electric eye Another name for PHOTOELECTRIC CELL.

e·lec·tri·cian [i·lek′trish′ən] *n.* A person who designs, installs, operates, or repairs electrical equipment or machinery.

e·lec·tric·i·ty [i·lek′tris′ə·tē] *n.* 1 A property of matter by which some atomic particles (electrons and protons) attract and repel each other and by their movements create magnetic fields. 2 Energy in the form of an excess or shortage of electrons, as caused by rubbing glass with silk. 3 Energy in the form of electrons flowing through a conductor; an electric current. 4 A very strong feeling, as of excitement or tension.

e·lec·tri·fi·ca·tion [i·lek′trə·fi·kā′shən] *n.* 1 The act of electrifying. 2 The installation of wiring for electricity.

e·lec·tri·fy [i·lek′trə·fī] *v.* **e·lec·tri·fied, e·lec·tri·fy·ing** 1 To charge with or expose to electricity: to *electrify* steel. 2 To equip for using electricity: to *electrify* a barn. 3 To arouse; startle; thrill: to *electrify* a crowd.

electro- A combining form meaning: Electric; by, with, or of electricity, as in *electroplate.* ◆ *See* ELECTROMAGNET.

e·lec·tro·car·di·o·gram [i·lek′trō·kär′dē·ə·gram′] *n.* A record of the performance of a person's heart made automatically by a device that responds to changes in electrical activity in the heartbeat.

e·lec·tro·car·di·o·graph [i·lek′trō·kär′dē·ə·graf′] *n.* The device by which an electrocardiogram is recorded.

e·lec·tro·cute [i·lek′trə·kyōōt′] *v.* **e·lec·tro·cut·ed, e·lec·tro·cut·ing** To execute or kill with a charge of electricity. **—e·lec′tro·cu′tion** *n.*

e·lec·trode [i·lek′trōd′] *n.* Any of the points at which current enters or leaves an electrical device; terminal.

e·lec·trol·y·sis [i·lek′trol′ə·sis] *n.* The process of separating an electrolyte into its elements by passing an electric current through it. Electrolysis deposits a metal in electroplating.

e·lec·tro·lyte [i·lek′trə·līt′] *n.* A substance that, when dissolved in a suitable medium or when fused, separates into ions and becomes a conductor of electricity. **—e·lec·tro·lyt·ic** [i·lek′trə·lit′ik] *adj.*

e·lec·tro·lyze [i·lek′trə·līz′] *v.* **elec·tro·lyzed, elec·tro·lyz·ing** To decompose by means of electrolysis.

e·lec·tro·mag·net [i·lek′trō·mag′nit] *n.* A device made of a soft iron core surrounded by a coil of insulated wire. The core becomes a magnet while an electric current is passing through the wire. ◆ *Electromagnet* is formed by combining *electro-,* meaning *electric,* with *magnet. Electro-* comes from a Greek word meaning *amber.*

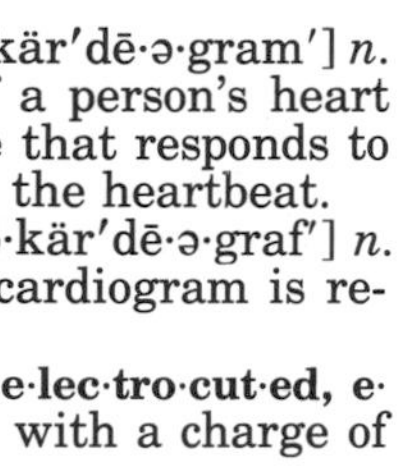

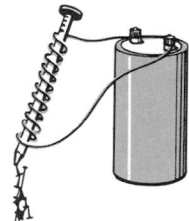

An electromagnet made from a nail and a coil of wire.

e·lec·tro·mag·net·ic [i·lek′trō·mag·net′ik] *adj.* Of, having to do with, or resulting from electromagnetism.

electromagnetic wave Any wave made up of electrical and magnetic pulsations moving through space at about 186,000 miles per second. Light, radio waves, X rays, and cosmic rays are electromagnetic waves.

e·lec·tro·mag·net·ism [i·lek′trō·mag′nə·tiz′əm] *n.* 1 Magnetism that is developed by a current of electricity. 2 A branch of science that deals with the relationship between electricity and magnetism.

e·lec·tro·mo·tive [i·lek′trə·mō′tiv] *adj.* Producing or tending to produce an electric current.

E

electromotive force The force that moves or tends to move electrons through a conductor. It is usually measured in volts.

e·lec·tron [i·lek′tron′] *n.* One of the negatively charged particles that surround the central core (nucleus) of an atom.

electron gun In an electron tube, the electron-emitting electrode together with an assembly that focuses and directs the beam of electrons.

e·lec·tron·ic [i·lek′tron′ik] *adj.* Of or having to do with electrons or electronics. **—e·lec′tron′i·cal·ly** *adv.*

e·lec·tron·ics [i·lek′tron′iks] *n.* The branch of engineering that deals with the design and manufacture of radios, television sets, and other devices that use electron tubes, transistors, and similar parts. ◆ See -ICS.

electron microscope An instrument that uses a beam of electrons instead of light rays to magnify very tiny objects.

electron tube A glass or metal tube containing a vacuum or a small amount of gas, in which electrons are emitted by a heated cathode and their flow to the anode is controlled.

electron volt In physics, a unit of energy equal to the energy gained by an electron accelerated by a potential difference of one volt.

e·lec·tro·plate [i·lek′trə·plāt′] *v.* **e·lec·tro·plat·ed, e·lec·tro·plat·ing** To deposit a metal film or coating upon by means of an electric current.

e·lec·tro·scope [i·lek′trə·skōp′] *n.* A mechanical instrument that indicates the presence of an electric charge and shows whether the charge is positive or negative.

e·lec·tro·ther·a·py [i·lek′trō·ther′ə·pē] *n.* The treatment of a disorder or disease by means of electricity.

e·lec·tro·type [i·lek′trə·tīp′] *n.* A metallic copy of something to be printed, made by electroplating a wax or plastic mold of the original page of type.

el·e·gance [el′ə·gəns] *n.* Good taste and luxuriousness, as in clothes, household furnishings, or decorations.

el·e·gant [el′ə·gənt] *adj.* 1 Tasteful, luxurious, and beautiful: an *elegant* living room. 2 Graceful and refined in style, manners, or taste: an *elegant* host. **—el′e·gant·ly** *adv.*

a	add	**i**	it	**ŏŏ**	took	**oi**	oil		
ā	ace	**ī**	ice	**ōō**	pool	**ou**	pout		
â	care	**o**	odd	**u**	up	**ng**	ring		
ä	palm	**ō**	open	**û**	burn	**th**	thin		
e	end	**ô**	order	**yōō**	fuse	**th**	this		
ē	equal					**zh**	vision		

ə = {a in *above*   e in *sicken*   i in *possible*
     o in *melon*   u in *circus*

el·e·gi·ac [el′ə·jī′ək *or* i·lē′jē·ak′] *adj.* Sad; mournful. **—el′e·gi′a·cal·ly** *adv.*

el·e·gize [el′ə·jīz′] *v.* **el·e·gized, el·e·giz·ing** To compose an elegy in memory of; mourn for in verse.

el·e·gy [el′ə·jē] *n., pl.* **el·e·gies** A melancholy or sad poem, often expressing sorrow for a dead person.

el·e·ment [el′ə·mənt] *n.* **1** Any of a limited number of substances of which all matter is made. An element is made up of atoms that have the same number of protons in their nucleus, that have characteristic properties, and that cannot be changed by chemical means. Some elements are gold, silver, carbon, oxygen, and iron. **2** A necessary or basic part of anything: Hard work is an *element* of success; the *elements* of French. **3** A quality or trait: an *element* of mischief. **4** A condition or environment that is natural or pleasing to a person or thing: to be out of one's *element.* **5** (*pl.*) Weather conditions, especially if violent or severe. **6** One of the four substances (earth, air, fire, water) which the ancients believed made up the universe.

el·e·men·tal [el′ə·men′təl] *adj.* **1** Of, having to do with, or being an element; not combined chemically with another element: Gold is found in the *elemental* state. **2** Simple; basic; fundamental: an *elemental* principle. **3** Of or having to do with the powerful forces at work in nature: The storm broke with *elemental* fury.

el·e·men·ta·ry [el′ə·men′tər·ē] *adj.* **1** Of or dealing with simple, beginning rules or principles: an *elementary* course in arithmetic. **2** Simple and undeveloped: an *elementary* knowledge of chemistry.

elementary particle A unit of matter or energy that is thought not to be divisible into smaller units.

elementary school A school having six or eight grades, where elementary subjects such as reading, writing, spelling, and arithmetic are taught.

el·e·phant [el′ə·fənt] *n.* The largest of all animals that live on land, having a long, tubelike snout or trunk and two ivory tusks. It is found in both Africa and Asia.

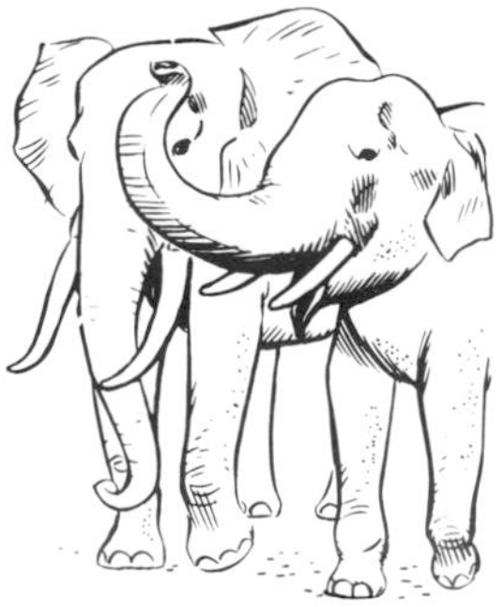

An African elephant and an Indian elephant

el·e·phan·tine [el′ə·fan′·tēn′ *or* el′ə·fan′tīn′ *or* el′ə·fən·tēn′ *or* el′ə·fən·tīn′] *adj.* **1** Of an elephant or elephants. **2** Huge, clumsy, and heavy, like an elephant.

el·e·vate [el′ə·vāt′] *v.* **el·e·vat·ed, el·e·vat·ing** **1** To raise; lift up: a building *elevated* on stilts. **2** To raise to a higher position: The vice president was *elevated* to the presidency. **3** To raise the spirits or improve the quality of: to *elevate* the mind.

elevated railway A railroad that runs mainly on an elevated framework.

el·e·va·tion [el′ə·vā′shən] *n.* **1** The act of elevating. **2** An elevated place, as a hill. **3** Height above the ground or above sea level.

el·e·va·tor [el′ə·vā′tər] *n.* **1** A movable, usually enclosed platform or cage for carrying passengers or freight up and down, as inside a building. **2** A large warehouse for storing grain. **3** A movable flat piece attached to the tail of an airplane, used to make the airplane go up or down.

e·lev·en or **11** [i·lev′ən] *n., adj.* One more than ten.

e·lev·enth or **11th** [i·lev′ənth] **1** *adj.* Next after the tenth. **2** *n.* The eleventh one. **3** *adj.* Being one of eleven equal parts. **4** *n.* An eleventh part.

eleventh hour The last moments before the end of a period of time; the latest time possible for something to be done.

elf [elf] *n., pl.* **elves** A small, usually mischievous fairy. **—elf′ish** *adj.* **—elf′ish·ly** *adv.*

elf·in [el′fin] *adj.* Of or like an elf; mischievous; impish: an *elfin* smile. ◆ *Elfin* and *elfish* are very similar in meaning, but *elfin* is used mostly in a favorable way and *elfish* for less attractive qualities: *elfin* charm; *elfish* malice.

e·lic·it [i·lis′it] *v.* To draw out or call forth: to *elicit* a reply; to *elicit* the truth. ◆ *Elicit* and *illicit,* although pronounced alike, have different meanings. *Elicit* is a verb meaning *to draw out:* The cross-examination of the attorney *elicited* a confession. *Illicit* is an adjective meaning *not legal* or *not allowed:* an *illicit* trade in smuggled goods.

el·i·gi·ble [el′ə·jə·bəl] *adj.* **1** Capable of or legally qualified for something: Minors are not *eligible* to vote. **2** Fit; suitable; desirable, as for marriage. **—el′i·gi·bil′i·ty** *n.* **—el′i·gi·bly** *adv.*

e·lim·i·nate [i·lim′ə·nāt′] *v.* **e·lim·i·nat·ed, e·lim·i·nat·ing** **1** To get rid of: Sunglasses *eliminate* glare. **2** To take out or omit: to *eliminate* a sentence. **3** To remove from competition, as by defeating: to be *eliminated* from a tennis tournament. **—e·lim′·i·na′tion** *n.* **—e·lim′i·na′tor** *n.*

e·li·sion [i·lizh′ən] *n.* The slurring or omission of certain sounds in speaking or certain letters in writing. *We're* in "We're here" is an example of elision in which *a* is omitted from *are.*

e·lite or **é·lite** [i·lēt′ *or* ā·lēt′] *n.* **1** The social or professional group considered to be the best: Only the *elite* were invited. **2** *adj.* Superior socially or professionally. **3** *n.* A size of type on typewriters. Twelve characters of elite occupy one inch.

e·lit·ism or **é·lit·ism** [i·lē′tiz·əm *or* ā·lē′tiz·əm] *n.* An attitude or a policy that admits only the elite in some activity or role. **—e·lit′ist** *adj., n.*

e·lix·ir [i·lik′sər] *n.* **1** An imaginary substance sought by medieval alchemists, who believed it could change ordinary metals to gold, restore youth, and prolong life indefinitely. **2** A sweetened liquid containing alcohol and drugs or herbs, used as a medicine and as a flavoring.

E·liz·a·be·than [i·liz′ə·bē′thən *or* i·liz′ə·beth′ən] **1** *adj.* Of or having to do with Queen Elizabeth I or the time during which she reigned. **2** *n.* An English person who lived during the reign of Elizabeth I.

elk [elk] *n., pl.* **elks** or **elk** **1** A large deer of North America. It is also called a wapiti. **2** A large deer of Europe and Asia, similar to the moose of North America.

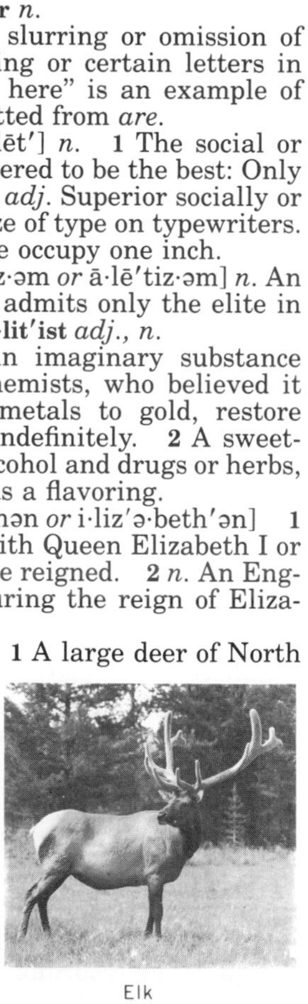

Elk

ell¹ [el] *n.* A wing extending at a right angle from the end of a rectangular building. ◆ *Ell* is for *L,* because an ell gives a building the shape of a capital L.

ell² [el] *n.* A unit of length formerly used in England, equal to 45 inches.

el·lipse [i·lips′] *n.* A closed curve which is a set of points so located that the sum of the distances from any point to two interior points, called the foci, is constant.

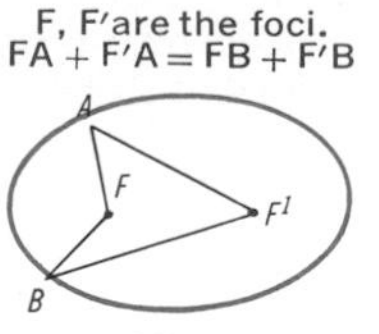

Ellipse

el·lip·sis [i·lip′sis] *n., pl.* **el·lip·ses** [i·lip′sēz] **1** The omission of a word or words that are essential to the meaning but are implied in the context: The sentence "I go this way and you that" has been shortened by the ellipsis of two words. The complete sentence would be "I go this way and you go that way." **2** A mark or series of marks (. . .) inserted to indicate where material has been omitted from a printed or written quotation.

el·lip·tic [i·lip′tik] *adj.* Elliptical.

el·lip·ti·cal [i·lip′tə·kəl] *adj.* Shaped like an ellipse. **—el·lip′ti·cal·ly** *adv.*

elm [elm] *n.* **1** A large shade tree having arching branches. **2** The wood of this tree.

el·o·cu·tion [el′ə·kyōō′shən] *n.* A way or style of making speeches or reciting, especially an old-fashioned style.

e·lon·gate [i·lông′gāt′] *v.* **e·lon·gat·ed, e·lon·gat·ing** To increase in length; lengthen; stretch out: The mirror *elongated* my image. **—e′lon·ga′tion** *n.*

e·lope [i·lōp′] *v.* **e·loped, e·lop·ing** To run away in secret, especially to get married. **—e·lope′ment** *n.*

el·o·quence [el′ə·kwəns] *n.* **1** A moving and skillful use of language, especially in speaking: The orator's *eloquence* stirred us all. **2** Expressiveness: the *eloquence* of a smile.

el·o·quent [el′ə·kwənt] *adj.* **1** Effective or skillful in expressing feelings or ideas; moving: an *eloquent* speaker. **2** Showing much feeling; expressive. **—el′o·quent·ly** *adv.*

else [els] **1** *adj.* Other; different or more: I want something *else;* What *else* could I do? **2** *adv.* In a different place, time, or manner: How *else* can I do it? **3** *adv.* If not; otherwise: Run fast or *else* you'll miss the bus. ◆ Today, such expressions as *someone else* and *anyone else* are usually treated as compound pronouns. This means that the possessive, instead of being *anyone's else,* is *anyone else's:* Let's go to *someone else's* house.

else·where [els′(h)wâr′] *adv.* In or to another place or places.

e·lu·ci·date [i·lōō′sə·dāt′] *v.* **e·lu·ci·dat·ed, e·lu·ci·dat·ing** To explain; clarify. **—e·lu′ci·da′tion** *n.*

e·lude [i·lōōd′] *v.* **e·lud·ed, e·lud·ing** **1** To escape from or avoid by quickness or cleverness: The fugitive *eluded* the police. **2** To escape the understanding of: The meaning *eludes* me.

e·lu·sion [i·lōō′zhən] *n.* An escape or avoidance of capture.

e·lu·sive [i·lōō′siv] *adj.* **1** Escaping or avoiding capture. **2** Hard to understand, remember, or recognize. **—e·lu′sive·ly** *adv.* **—e·lu′sive·ness** *n.*

e·lute [ē·lōōt′] *v.* **e·lut·ed, e·lut·ing** To extract (adsorbed substances) by dissolving. **—e·lu′tion** *n.*

el·ver [el′vər] *n.* An immature eel.

elves [elvz] The plural of ELF.

E·ly·sian [i·lizh′ən] *adj.* **1** Of or like Elysium. **2** Heavenly; delightful.

E·ly·si·um [i·lizh′ē·əm *or* i·liz′ē·əm] *n.* **1** In Greek myths, a pleasant region of the underworld where the souls of good people went after death. It is often called the **Elysian Fields.** **2** Any heavenly or delightful place or condition.

'em [əm] *pron. informal* Them: Look at 'em go!

EM **1** enlisted man. **2** electromagnetic.

e·ma·ci·ate [i·mā′shē·āt′] *v.* **e·ma·ci·at·ed, e·ma·ci·at·ing** **1** To make abnormally thin: *emaciated* by hunger or disease. **2** *adj. use:* an *emaciated* person. **—e·ma′ci·a′tion** *n.*

em·a·nate [em′ə·nāt′] *v.* **em·a·nat·ed, em·a·nat·ing** To come or flow forth from a source; issue: Heat *emanated* from the lighted stove; News *emanates* from Washington.

em·a·na·tion [em′ə·nā′shən] *n.* **1** The action of emanating. **2** Something that emanates.

e·man·ci·pate [i·man′sə·pāt′] *v.* **e·man·ci·pat·ed, e·man·ci·pat·ing** To set free, as from slavery or oppression. **—e·man′ci·pa′tion** *n.* **—e·man′ci·pa′tor** *n.*

Emancipation Proclamation An order issued by President Lincoln on January 1, 1863, abolishing slavery in the areas still at war with the Union.

e·mas·cu·late [*v.* i·mas′kyə·lāt′, *adj.* i·mas′kyə·lət] *v.,* **e·mas·cu·lated, e·mas·cu·lat·ing,** *adj.* **1** *v.* To castrate. **2** *v.* To deprive of strength or force; make weak: The amendments to the bill *emasculated* it. **3** *adv.* Castrated. **4** *adj.* Weakened; deprived of force. **—e·mas′cu·la′tion** *n.*

em·balm [im·bäm′] *v.* To preserve (a dead body) from decay by treatment with chemicals and other steps. **—em·balm′er** *n.*

em·bank [im·bangk′] *v.* To support or protect behind an embankment.

em·bank·ment [im·bangk′mənt] *n.* A mound or bank, as of stone, cement, or earth, built usually to hold back water or support a roadway.

em·bar·go [im·bär′gō] *n., pl.* **em·bar·goes,** *v.* **em·bar·goed, em·bar·go·ing** **1** *n.* An order by a government that prohibits certain ships from entering or leaving its ports. **2** *n.* Any official restriction or rule that prevents or interferes with trade. **3** *v.* To place an embargo on.

em·bark [im·bärk′] *v.* **1** To go or put on board a ship for a voyage. **2** To begin, as an adventure or project; set forth: to *embark* upon a new career. **—em′bar·ka′tion** *n.*

em·bar·rass [im·bar′əs] *v.* **1** To make self-conscious and uneasy or confused. **2** To hinder; hamper: *embarrassed* by lack of funds.

em·bar·rass·ment [im·bar′əs·mənt] *n.* **1** An embarrassed condition or feeling. **2** Something that embarrasses.

em·bas·sy [em′bə·sē] *n., pl.* **em·bas·sies** **1** The official home or headquarters of an ambassador in a foreign country. **2** An ambassador and the embassy staff. **3** The assignment or duties entrusted to an ambassador.

em·bat·tled [im·bat′(ə)ld] *adj.* **1** Prepared for and awaiting battle. **2** Fortified against attack.

em·bat·tle·ment [im·bat′(ə)l·mənt] *n.* Another word for BATTLEMENT.

a	add	**i**	it	**ŏŏ**	took	**oi**	oil
ā	ace	**ī**	ice	**ōō**	pool	**ou**	pout
â	care	**o**	odd	**u**	up	**ng**	ring
ä	palm	**ō**	open	**û**	burn	**th**	thin
e	end	**ô**	order	**yōō**	fuse	**th**	this
ē	equal					**zh**	vision

ə = { a in *above* e in *sicken* i in *possible* / o in *melon* u in *circus* }

em·bay [im·bā′] *v.* To shelter or confine in a bay.
em·bed [im·bed′] *v.* **em·bed·ded, em·bed·ding** To set firmly in a surrounding substance.
em·bel·lish [im·bel′ish] *v.* To make more attractive by adding something; decorate: to *embellish* a cake with icing; to *embellish* a story with vivid details. **—em·bel′lish·ment** *n.*
em·ber [em′bər] *n.* 1 Something, as a coal or piece of wood, no longer in flames but still glowing. 2 (*pl.*) A fire that has died down but is still glowing.
em·bez·zle [im·bez′əl] *v.* **em·bez·zled, em·bez·zling** To take (as someone else's money) that has been entrusted to one's care: The treasurer *embezzled* large sums from the company. **—em·bez′zle·ment** *n.* **—em·bez′zler** *n.*
em·bit·ter [im·bit′ər] *v.* To make bitter or resentful: a person *embittered* by hardships.
em·bla·zon [im·blā′zən] *v.* 1 To mark or decorate with brilliant colors or designs: The title was *emblazoned* in gold on the cover; a banner *emblazoned* with the royal arms. 2 To honor with praise; celebrate: events *emblazoned* in history.
em·blem [em′bləm] *n.* 1 Something that stands for something else, as an idea, belief, or nation; symbol: The lily is the *emblem* of purity. 2 A seal or badge: We wore our club's *emblem* proudly.
em·blem·at·ic [em′blə·mat′ik] *adj.* Used or considered as an emblem; symbolic. **—em′blem·at′i·cal·ly** *adv.*
em·bod·i·ment [im·bod′i·mənt] *n.* 1 A person or thing thought of as representing an idea or quality: You are the *embodiment* of kindness. 2 The act of embodying. 3 A being embodied.
em·bod·y [im·bod′ē] *v.* **em·bod·ied, em·bod·y·ing** 1 To put or represent (as an idea, belief, or quality) in real or definite form: The Bill of Rights *embodies* our individual freedoms. 2 To bring together in a single form or system; incorporate: The information you need is *embodied* in this leaflet.
em·bold·en [im·bōl′dən] *v.* To make bold or bolder; encourage: A series of early successes *emboldened* the young reporter.
em·bo·lism [em′bə·liz′əm] *n.* The blocking of the flow of blood in a vein or artery, as by a clot.
em·bo·lus [em′bə·ləs] *n., pl.* **em·bo·li** [em′bə·lī′] An obstacle, such as a clot or an air bubble, circulating in the blood and obstructing its flow through a vein or an artery.
em·bo·som [im·bo͝oz′əm] *v.* To shelter by or as if by enclosing; embrace or cherish.
em·boss [im·bôs′] *v.* To form or decorate with raised designs: a gold bracelet *embossed* with birds and butterflies.
em·bow [im·bō′] *v.* To bend or curve like a bow; arch. **—em·bow′ment** *n.*
em·bow·er [im·bou′ər] *v.* To enclose in a bower.
em·brace [im·bras′] *v.* **em·braced, em·brac·ing,** *n.* 1 *v.* To clasp or enfold in the arms; hug. 2 *n.* The act of embracing. 3 *v.* To hug each other. 4 *v.* To surround or encircle: Dense woods *embraced* the village. 5 *v.* To include; contain: Astronomy *embraces* the study of all the heavenly bodies. 6 *v.* To accept or take up willingly: They discarded the old theory and *embraced* the new one.
em·bra·sure [im·brā′zhər] *n.* 1 An opening for a window or door in a thick wall, having slanted sides that make it wider on the inside. 2 An opening, as in the wall of a fort, through which a gun may be fired.
em·broi·der [im·broi′dər] *v.* 1 To decorate with or make designs in needlework: to *embroider* flowers on a pillow. 2 To add fanciful details to (as a description or story).
em·broi·der·y [im·broi′dər·ē] *n., pl.* **em·broi·der·ies** 1 Stitches or decoration made by embroidering. 2 The art of embroidering.
em·broil [im·broil′] *v.* To involve in disagreement or conflict: *embroiled* in a war; *embroiled* in a struggle for political power.
em·bry·o [em′brē·ō] *n., pl.* **em·bry·os** 1 A plant or animal in its earliest stages, as a plant within its seed, a mammal not yet born, or a bird within an egg. 2 An early, undeveloped stage of anything: The committee's report is still in *embryo*.

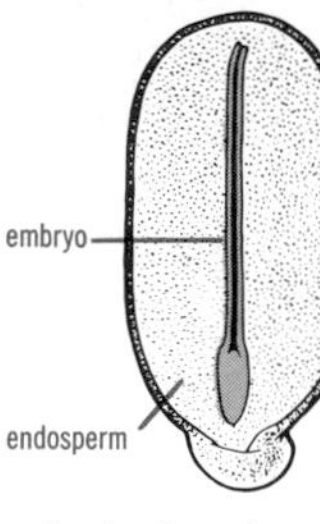

A plant embryo

em·bry·ol·o·gy [em′brē·ol′ə·jē] *n.* A branch of biology concerned with the structure and development of embryos. **—em·bry·o·log·i·cal** [em′brē·ə·loj′ə·kəl] *adj.* **—em′bry·ol′o·gist** *n.*
em·bry·on·ic [em′brē·on′ik] *adj.* 1 Just beginning to develop. 2 Of an embryo.
em·cee [em′sē′] *n., v.* **em·ceed, em·cee·ing** *informal* 1 *n.* A master of ceremonies. 2 *v.* To act as a master of ceremonies. 3 *v.* To conduct or preside over: to *emcee* a contest.
e·mend [i·mend′] *v.* To correct and polish: to *emend* an essay. ◆ *Emend* and *amend* both involve making improvements, but *emend* applies only to verbal corrections, whether of fact or of style.
e·men·da·tion [ē′men·dā′shən *or* em′ən·dā′shən] *n.* 1 A correction or improvement in wording. 2 The process of emending.
em·er·ald [em′ər·əld *or* em′rəld] 1 *n.* A bright green precious stone. 2 *n., adj.* Bright green.
e·merge [i·mûrj′] *v.* **e·merged, e·merg·ing** 1 To come forth or come out, especially so as to be visible: The woodchuck *emerged* from its burrow. 2 To become known; come to light: New facts *emerged* during the trial.
e·mer·gence [i·mûr′jəns] *n.* A coming out or becoming known; appearance.
e·mer·gen·cy [i·mûr′jən·sē] *n., pl.* **e·mer·gen·cies** A sudden and unexpected turn of events calling for immediate action.
e·mer·gent [i·mûr′jənt] *adj.* 1 Arising unexpectedly: an *emergent* crisis. 2 Just coming into being: *emergent* nations.
e·mer·i·ta [i·mer′ə·tə] *adj., n., pl.* **e·mer·i·tae** [i·mer′·ə·tē′] 1 *adj.* Being a woman who is retired but retains her rank or title as an honor: a professor *emerita*. 2 *n.* A woman who is emerita.
e·mer·i·tus [i·mer′ə·təs] *adj., n., pl.* **e·mer·i·ti** [i·mer′ə·tī′] 1 *adj.* Retired from active work but still retaining one's rank or title as an honor: a professor *emeritus*. 2 *n.* A person who is emeritus.
em·er·y [em′ər·ē *or* em′rē] *n.* A very hard mineral used, usually in powdered form, for polishing, smoothing, or sharpening metal or stone.
emery board A small, flat stick coated with emery powder, used to file the nails.
e·met·ic [i·met′ik] 1 *n.* Something that causes vomiting, as a medicine given to someone who has swallowed poison. 2 *adj.* Causing vomiting.
em·i·grant [em′ə·grənt] *n.* A person who leaves a place or country to settle in another.

em·i·grate [em′ə·grāt′] *v.* **em·i·grat·ed, em·i·grat·ing** To move from one country or section of a country to settle in another: to *emigrate* from Italy to the U.S. **—em′i gra′tion** *n.* ◆ Avoid confusing *emigrate* and *immigrate* by noting their prefixes: *e-* (like *ex-*) means "out of"; *im-* (like *in-*) means "into." Thus to *emigrate* is to move *out of* a country; to *immigrate* is to move *into* a country.

é·mi·gré [em′i·grā′] *n.* A person who has emigrated for political reasons.

em·i·nence [em′ə·nəns] *n.* 1 Superiority or importance because of high rank or great achievement. 2 A high place, as a hill. 3 (*written* **Eminence**) A title of honor used when formally addressing or speaking of a cardinal of the Roman Catholic Church: Your *Eminence*.

em·i·nent [em′ə·nənt] *adj.* Important or respected because of high rank or quality; outstanding: an *eminent* musician. ◆ *Eminent* and *imminent* have completely different meanings, although they come from similar Latin roots. An *eminent* person is one who stands out above others, and the Latin roots of *eminent* literally mean *to stand out. Imminent* was formed from elements that mean *to lean over,* and *imminent* means *hanging over* or *threatening to happen at any moment.*

eminent domain The right of a government to take over private property for public use.

em·i·nent·ly [em′ə·nənt·lē] *adv.* Notably; outstandingly: She is *eminently* suited to the job.

e·mir [i·mir′ *or* ā·mir′] *n.* A Muslim prince or chief, especially in the Middle East.

em·is·sar·y [em′ə·ser′ē] *n., pl.* **em·is·sar·ies** 1 A person sent as a special representative or to carry out special orders. 2 A spy.

e·mis·sion [i·mish′ən] *n.* 1 The act or process of emitting. 2 Something emitted. **—e·mis′sive** *adj.*

e·mit [i·mit′] *v.* **e·mit·ted, e·mit·ting** To send forth or give off: Fireflies *emit* light. ◆ See TRANSMIT.

Em·my [em′ē] *n., pl.* **Em·mys** One of the awards made annually for notable achievement in television.

e·mol·lient [i·mol′yənt] 1 *adj.* Soothing and softening, especially to the skin: an *emollient* lotion. 2 *n.* A preparation that softens or soothes the skin.

e·mol·u·ment [i·mol′yə·mənt] *n.* The salary or fees connected with one's occupation or position.

e·mote [i·mōt′] *v.* **e·mot·ed, e·mot·ing** *informal* To express emotion in a theatrical or exaggerated manner.

e·mo·tion [i·mō′shən] *n.* A strong feeling, such as love, anger, fear, sorrow, or joy.

e·mo·tion·al [i·mō′shən·əl] *adj.* 1 Of or related to the emotions: an *emotional* problem. 2 Having one's emotions easily aroused: an *emotional* child. 3 Expressing or arousing emotion: an *emotional* appeal. **—e·mo′tion·al·ly** *adv.*

e·mo·tion·al·ism [i·mō′shən·əl·iz′əm] *n.* 1 A tendency to be swayed too easily by emotion. 2 An appeal to the emotions that goes beyond a proper limit: campaign speeches full of *emotionalism.*

e·mo·tive [i·mō′tiv] *adj.* 1 Having to do with feeling rather than with reasoning. 2 Arousing or expressing emotion. **—e·mo′tive·ly** *adj.*

em·pan·el [im·pan′əl] *v.* **em·pan·eled** or **em·pan·elled, em·pan·el·ing** or **em·pan·el·ling** Another word for IMPANEL.

em·pa·thize [em′pə·thīz′] *v.* **em·pa·thized, em·pa·thiz·ing** To experience or show evidence of empathy: to *empathize* with another's happiness.

em·pa·thy [em′pə·thē] *n.* The capacity to share another person's feelings or thoughts.

em·per·or [em′pər·ər] *n.* A person who reigns over an empire or has the title of ruler of an empire.

em·pha·sis [em′fə·sis] *n., pl.* **em·pha·ses** [em′fə·sēz] 1 A stressing by the voice of a particular syllable, word, or phrase. 2 Special significance or importance given to something; stress: The *emphasis* here is on achievement.

em·pha·size [em′fə·sīz′] *v.* **em·pha·sized, em·pha·siz·ing** To point out for special notice; stress: to *emphasize* the value of education.

em·phat·ic [em·fat′ik] *adj.* 1 Spoken or done with emphasis. 2 Striking; decisive: an *emphatic* success. **—em·phat′i·cal·ly** *adv.*

em·phy·se·ma [em′fə·sē′mə *or* em′fə·zē′mə] *n.* A condition in which the lungs contain distended pockets of air that prevent normal functioning and thus cause labored breathing and an inadequate supply of oxygen to the body.

em·pire [em′pīr] *n.* 1 A group of different, often widespread states, nations, or territories under a single ruler or government: the Roman *Empire.* 2 A country reigned over by an emperor or empress. 3 Wide power or range of influence, as of a person or industry.

em·pir·ic [em·pir′ik] 1 *n.* A person who relies on practical experience rather than theory. 2 *adj.* Empirical.

em·pir·i·cal [em·pir′i·kəl] *adj.* Based on direct experience or observation rather than theory. **—em·pir′i·cal·ly** *adv.*

em·pir·i·cism [em·pir′ə·siz′əm] *n.* 1 Reliance on practical experience rather than on theory. 2 A philosophical theory that knowledge is arrived at through experience alone. **—em·pir′i·cist** *n.*

em·place·ment [im·plās′mənt] *n.* 1 The act of putting something into a designated position. 2 A position or location, especially a location prepared for military equipment such as heavy guns.

em·ploy [im·ploi′] 1 *v.* To give work and payment to; hire: This store *employs* six clerks. 2 *n.* Paid service; employment: in the *employ* of the government. 3 *v.* To make use of: to *employ* force. 4 *v.* To keep occupied: to *employ* oneself in a hobby.

em·ploy·able [im·ploi′ə·bəl] 1 *adj.* Having the qualities or skill required to work for hire. 2 *n.* A person who is capable of being employed.

em·ploy·ee or **em·ploy·e** [im·ploi′ē *or* im′ploi·ē′] *n.* A person who is employed for pay.

em·ploy·er [im·ploi′ər] *n.* A person or business firm that employs a person or people.

em·ploy·ment [im·ploi′mənt] *n.* 1 A person's job or occupation. 2 The condition of being employed. 3 The act of employing; use.

em·po·ri·um [em·pôr′ē·əm] *n., pl.* **em·po·ri·ums** or **em·po·ri·a** [em·pôr′ē·ə] A large store selling many different kinds of merchandise.

a	add	**i**	it	**o͝o**	took	**oi**	oil
ā	ace	**ī**	ice	**o͞o**	pool	**ou**	pout
â	care	**o**	odd	**u**	up	**ng**	ring
ä	palm	**ō**	open	**û**	burn	**th**	thin
e	end	**ô**	order	**yo͞o**	fuse	**th̸**	this
ē	equal					**zh**	vision

ə = a in *above*, e in *sicken*, i in *possible*, o in *melon*, u in *circus*

em·pow·er [im·pou′ər] *v.* To give the power or right to do something; authorize: The President is *empowered* to appoint judges.

em·press [em′pris] *n.* **1** A woman who reigns over an empire. **2** The wife of an emperor.

emp·ty [emp′tē] *adj.* **emp·ti·er, emp·ti·est,** *n., pl.* **emp·ties,** *v.* **emp·tied, emp·ty·ing** **1** *adj.* Containing or holding nothing: an *empty* jar; *empty* hands. **2** *n.* Something empty, as a bottle or freight car. **3** *adj.* Not filled; vacant: an *empty* seat. **4** *v.* To make or become empty. **5** *v.* To pour out; drain: *Empty* the milk from the pitcher; The Mississippi River *empties* into the Gulf of Mexico. **6** *adj.* Having no real value or significance; idle: *empty* boasts. **—emp′ti·ness** *n.*

emp·ty-hand·ed [emp′tē·han′did] *adj.* Without something sought or needed: to go fishing and come home *empty-handed.*

emp·ty-head·ed [emp′tē·hed′id] *adj.* Lacking sense; silly; scatterbrained. **—emp′ty-head′ed·ness** *n.*

em·pyr·e·al [em′pi·rē′əl *or* em·pir′ē·əl] *adj.* Of or from the heavens; celestial.

em·py·re·an [em′pi·rē′ən *or* em′pi·rē′ən] **1** *n.* The highest heaven. **2** *adj.* Empyreal.

e·mu [ē′myōō] *n.* An Australian bird similar to the ostrich, but somewhat smaller.

Emu

em·u·late [em′yə·lāt′] *v.* **em·u·lat·ed, em·u·lat·ing** To try to equal or surpass; imitate so as to excel: to *emulate* the success of great writers.

em·u·la·tion [em′yə·lā′·shən] *n.* **1** A striving to equal or surpass. **2** Imitation.

em·u·la·tor [em′yə·lā′tər] *n.* A person who emulates.

em·u·lous [em′yə·ləs] *adj.* Eager to equal or surpass the performance of another person: *emulous* of my rival's success. **—em′u·lous·ly** *adv.* **—em′u·lous·ness** *n.*

e·mul·si·fy [i·mul′sə·fī′] *v.* **e·mul·si·fied, e·mul·si·fy·ing** To make into an emulsion.

e·mul·sion [i·mul′shən] *n.* A mixture in which many small droplets or globules of one liquid remain evenly distributed throughout another, as cream in milk.

en- A prefix meaning: **1** In, into, or within, as in *entrap.* **2** To make, as in *enrich.* **3** Very much or completely, as in *entangle.* ◆ Many words beginning with *en-* can also be written with the prefix *in-*[1], as *incase* for *encase.*

-en[1] A suffix meaning: Made of, as in *earthen.*

-en[2] A suffix meaning: **1** To cause to have, as in *lengthen.* **2** To cause to be, as in *shorten.*

en·a·ble [in·ā′bəl] *v.* **en·a·bled, en·a·bling** To give the means, ability, or opportunity to; make able: Telescopes *enable* us to see far into space.

en·act [in·akt′] *v.* **1** To make into or approve officially, as a statute or edict: Congress *enacts* laws. **2** To act or perform, as a part in a play.

en·act·ment [in·akt′mənt] *n.* **1** The act or process of enacting into law. **2** A law.

en·am·el [in·am′əl] *n., v.* **en·am·eled** or **en·am·elled, en·am·el·ing** or **en·am·el·ling** **1** *n.* A glassy, often colorful substance that is fused by heat to a surface, as of metal or porcelain, for protection or decoration. **2** *n.* A paint or varnish that dries to form a hard, glossy surface. **3** *v.* To cover or inlay with enamel. **4** *n.* The hard, outer layer of the teeth.

en·am·el·ware [in·am′əl·wâr′] *n.* Metal kitchen utensils coated with enamel, often in bright colors.

en·am·ored [in·am′ərd] *adj.* In love, especially in the phrase **enamored of,** in love with: The audience was *enamored* of the star.

en·camp [in·kamp′] *v.* To set up and move into a camp: The scouts *encamped* near the river.

en·camp·ment [in·kamp′mənt] *n.* **1** The act of encamping. **2** A camp or the people in it.

en·cap·su·late [in·kap′sə·lāt′] *v.* **en·cap·su·lat·ed, en·cap·su·lat·ing** **1** To enclose in a capsule or other small container. **2** To contain in a condensed form; to put in a nutshell: This brief account *encapsulates* a lifetime of experience. **—en·cap′su·la′tion** *n.*

en·case [in·kās′] *v.* **en·cased, en·cas·ing** To enclose in or as if in a case: a caterpillar *encased* in a cocoon.

-ence A suffix meaning: **1** The condition or quality of being, as in *independence.* **2** The act of, as in *emergence.*

en·ceph·a·li·tis [in·sef′ə·lī′tis] *n., pl.* **en·ceph·a·lit·i·des** [in·sef′ə·lī′tə·dēz] Inflammation of the brain. **—en·ceph·a·lit·ic** [in·sef′ə·lit′ik] *adj.*

en·ceph·a·lo·gram [en·sef′ə·lə·gram′] *n.* A photograph of the brain of a living person, usually made with X rays.

en·ceph·a·lon [en·sef′ə·lon′] *n., pl.* **en·ceph·a·la** [en·sef′ə·lə] The brain of a human or any vertebrate.

en·chain [in·chān′] *v.* To restrain with or as if with chains. **—en·chain′ment** *n.*

en·chant [in·chant′] *v.* **1** To put under a magic spell; bewitch: A wave of the magic wand *enchanted* the royal court. **2** To charm; delight. **3** *adj. use:* an *enchanting* smile. **—en·chant′er** *n.*

en·chant·ment [in·chant′mənt] *n.* **1** The use or effect of charms or spells; magic. **2** Something enchanting. **3** Great charm or fascination.

en·chant·ress [in·chant′ris] *n.* **1** A witch or sorceress. **2** A charming, fascinating woman.

en·chase [in·chās′] *v.* **en·chased, en·chas·ing** **1** To mount (a gem) in a setting. **2** To ornament, as with an inlay or carving.

en·chi·la·da [en′chə·lä′də] *n.* A tortilla wrapped around a meat filling and covered wih a spicy tomato sauce.

en·ci·pher [in·sī′fər] *v.* To convert into cipher, as a message; encode. **—en·ci′pher·er** *n.* **—en·ci′pher·ment** *n.*

en·cir·cle [in·sûr′kəl] *v.* **en·cir·cled, en·cir·cling** **1** To form a circle around; surround: A belt *encircled* the waist of the pants. **2** To move in a circle around; go around: We *encircled* the lake on our hike. **—en·cir′cle·ment** *n.*

en·clave [en′klāv *or* än′klāv] *n.* A distinctly separate community or area lying within another: the United Nations *enclave.*

en·close [in·klōz′] *v.* **en·closed, en·clos·ing** **1** To close in on all sides; surround: A fence *enclosed* the yard. **2** To put in an envelope or container along with whatever is being sent.

en·clo·sure [in·klō′zhər] *n.* **1** An enclosed area, as a yard or pen. **2** Something that encloses, as a fence. **3** Something enclosed in an envelope or container. **4** The act or process of enclosing. **5** A being enclosed.

en·code [in·kōd′] *v.* **en·cod·ed, en·cod·ing** **1** To put into code, as a message: I can't decode what you have *encoded.* **2** To prepare a series of instructions for a computer. **—en·cod′er** *n.*

en·co·mi·um [en·kō′mē·əm] *n.* High praise, especially when expressed formally; tribute.

en·com·pass [in·kum′pəs] *v.* **1** To encircle; surround. **2** To include; contain: The social sciences *encompass* psychology and sociology.

en·core [än(g)′kor′] **1** *interj.* Once more! Again! **2** *n.* A call by an audience to perform again, as by shouting "Encore!" or applauding steadily. **3** *n.* A performance in response to such a call.

en·coun·ter [in·koun′tər] **1** *v.* To meet unexpectedly; come upon: to *encounter* an old friend at a party. **2** *n.* A meeting, especially when unexpected. **3** *v.* To be faced with; have to contend with: to *encounter* difficulties. **4** *v.* To face in battle. **5** *n.* A battle; contest.

en·cour·age [in·kûr′ij] *v.* **en·cour·aged, en·cour·ag·ing** **1** To give courage or hope to; inspire with confidence or the wish to do well. **2** To be favorable for; help or foster: Watering *encourages* plant growth.

en·cour·age·ment [in·kûr′ij·ment] *n.* **1** Something that encourages: The teacher's praise served as *encouragement.* **2** The act of encouraging. **3** An encouraged condition.

en·croach [in·krōch′] *v.* **1** To advance beyond the usual or proper limits; overrun: Weeds *encroached* upon the garden. **2** To intrude upon the rights or property of another; trespass: troops *encroaching* upon the territory of a neighboring country. **—en·croach′ment** *n.*

en·crust [in·krust′] *v.* **1** To cover with a crust or hard coating: dirty dishes *encrusted* with food. **2** To decorate or cover with jewels or other ornamentation: a scepter *encrusted* with rubies. **—en′·crust·ta′tion** *n.*

en·cryp·tion [in·krip′shən] *n.* The process of devising and employing a code or secret word that prevents access by unauthorized persons to a computer and the information stored in it.

en·cum·ber [in·kum′bər] *v.* **1** To weigh down with or as if with a burden: a horse *encumbered* with a heavy load; a person *encumbered* with troubles. **2** To interfere with; hinder: *encumbered* with galoshes and an umbrella. **3** To crowd or fill with obstacles: a staircase *encumbered* with scattered toys.

en·cum·brance [in·kum′brəns] *n.* Something that encumbers, as a burden or added difficulty.

-ency A suffix meaning: The condition or quality of being, as in *decency.*

en·cyc·li·cal [in·sik′li·kəl] *n.* A letter about important religious matters, sent by the Pope to bishops of the Roman Catholic Church.

en·cy·clo·pe·di·a or **en·cy·clo·pae·di·a** [in·sī′klə·pē′dē·ə] *n.* A book or set of books containing information arranged in alphabetical order according to subjects, and covering a wide range of knowledge. Some encyclopedias are limited to one field, as science or art.

en·cy·clo·pe·dic [in·sī′klə·pē′dik] *adj.* **1** Having or covering information on a wide range of subjects: an *encyclopedic* mind. **2** Of, like, or suitable for an encyclopedia.

end [end] **1** *n.* The last or outermost part of something long: the *end* of the road; the *end* of a log. **2** *n.* The last or final part: the *end* of a story; the *end* of October. **3** *v.* To come or bring to an end; terminate: *End* a sentence with a period. **4** *n.* Final state or condition. **5** *adj. use:* the *end* result; an *end* product. **6** *n.* Aim; purpose: to work toward good *ends.* **7** *n.* Death: Their *end* was swift and painless. **8** *n.* A leftover part; remnant: odds and *ends.* **9** *n.* In football, either of the two outermost players in the line. **—make ends meet** To manage to get along on the money one has or earns. **—on end** In an upright position.

end- or **endo-** A combining form meaning: Inner; inside; within, as in *endoskeleton.*

en·dan·ger [in·dān′jər] *v.* To expose to danger: Faulty breaks *endanger* people's lives.

en·dan·gered [in·dān′jərd] *adj.* In danger of extinction: an *endangered* species.

en·dear [in·dir′] *v.* To make dear; cause to be well liked: Their kindness and generosity *endears* them to everyone.

en·dear·ment [in·dir′mənt] *n.* An expressing of love or affection, as by a word or action.

en·deav·or [in·dev′ər] **1** *v.* To try hard; make an earnest effort; attempt: to *endeavor* to succeed. **2** *n.* An earnest effort.

en·dem·ic [en·dem′ik] *adj.* Usually found in a certain region or among certain people: an *endemic* disease.

end game The final, decisive state of a game or contest. ◆ *End game* is a chess term.

end·ing [end′ing] *n.* The last part; conclusion.

en·dive [en′dīv′ *or* än′dēv′] *n.* A plant with crisp white or green leaves used in salads.

Endive

end·less [end′lis] *adj.* **1** Having no end; lasting or going on forever. **2** Seeming to have no end; going on too long: *endless* complaints. **3** Forming a closed loop or circle: the *endless* chain on a bicycle. **—end′less·ly** *adv.*

end·most [end′mōst′] *adj.* Occupying the extreme end; last.

endo- See END-.

en·do·car·di·um [en′dō·kär′dē·əm] *n., pl.* **en·do·car·di·a** [en′dō·kär′de·ə] A thin membrane that lines the chambers of the heart. **—en′do·car′di·al** *adj.*

en·do·crine [en′də·krin *or* en′də·krīn′ *or* en′də·krēn′] **1** *adj.* Producing secretions that pass directly into the bloodstream. **2** *adj.* Having to do with or caused by a hormone. **3** *n.* Another name for HORMONE. **4** *n.* An endocrine gland.

a	add	**i**	it	**o͝o**	took	**oi**	oil
ā	ace	**ī**	ice	**o͞o**	pool	**ou**	pout
â	care	**o**	odd	**u**	up	**ng**	ring
ä	palm	**ō**	open	**û**	burn	**th**	thin
e	end	**ô**	order	**yo͞o**	fuse	**th**	this
ē	equal					**zh**	vision

ə = {a in *above* e in *sicken* i in *possible* / o in *melon* u in *circus*}

endocrine gland *n.* Any of several glands, as the pituitary or thyroid, whose secretions enter the blood or lymph directly instead of through a duct.

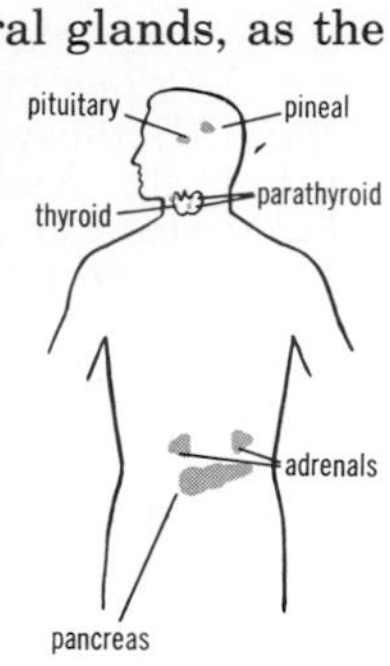

Endocrine glands

en·do·cri·nol·o·gy [en′də·krə·nol′ə·jē] *n.* The study of the endocrine glands and the secretion, functions, and effects of hormones.
en·do·derm [en′də·dûrm′] *n.* The innermost of the three primary layers of cells of the embryo, from which are developed certain internal organs and the lining of the digestive system.
en·dog·e·nous [en·doj′ə·nəs] *adj.* 1 Arising from an interior source. 2 Growing on or toward the inside. **—en·dog′e·nous·ly** *adv.*
en·do·par·a·site [en′dō·par′ə·sīt′] *n.* A parasite that lives inside the body of its host. **—en·do·par·a·sit·ic** [en′dō·par′ə·sit′ik] *adj.*
en·do·plasm [en′də·plaz′əm] *n.* The fluid, granular cytoplasm surrounding the nucleus of some cells.
en·dor·phin [en·dôr′fin] *n.* A hormone originating in the brain and acting as a natural tranquilizer and painkiller.
en·dorse [in·dôrs′] *v.* **en·dorsed, en·dors·ing** 1 To sign the back of (a check or similar paper), especially so that it may be cashed. 2 To give support or approval to: to *endorse* a party's political opinions.
en·dorse·ment [in·dôrs′mənt] *n.* 1 A signature or note written on the back of a check or similar paper. 2 Approval, especially formal approval. 3 The act or process of endorsing.
en·do·scope [en′də·skōp′] *n.* An instrument that makes it possible to see the inside of a hollow organ in the body, such as the stomach or bladder.
en·do·scop·ic [en′də·skop′ik] *adj.* Performed or made possible by means of an endoscope: an *endoscopic* examination of the bronchi. **—en′do·scop′i·cal·ly** *adv.*
en·do·skel·e·ton [en′dō·skel′ə·tən] *n.* The supporting framework of bone inside the body of a vertebrate animal.
en·do·sperm [en′də·spûrm′] *n.* The substance within a seed that nourishes a plant embryo.
en·dow [in·dou′] *v.* 1 To equip or supply, as with talents or natural gifts: Nature *endowed* her with genius. 2 To provide money or property to earn income for (as a college or hospital).
en·dow·ment [in·dou′mənt] *n.* 1 Something with which a person is endowed, such as beauty or talent. 2 A fund to earn income, as for a college or museum. 3 The act of endowing.
end·point [end′point′] *n.* 1 The point at either end of a line segment. 2 The stage at which a chemical reaction is complete. A chemical endpoint can sometimes be pinpointed by using an indicator such as litmus that changes color at the endpoint.
end table A small low table placed usually at either end of a sofa or in any position convenient to persons seated nearby.
en·due [in·d(y)ōō′] *v.* **en·dued, en·du·ing** 1 To provide or endow with some power or quality: His education *endued* him with skill and wisdom. 2 To clothe; garb.
en·dur·a·ble [in·d(y)ŏŏr′ə·bəl] *adj.* Capable of being endured; bearable.
en·dur·ance [in·d(y)ŏŏr′əns] *n.* The ability or power to bear up or last under continued effort, hardship, or strain.
en·dure [in·d(y)ŏŏr′] *v.* **en·dured, en·dur·ing** 1 To bear up under; stand firm against: to *endure* pain or suffering. 2 To put up with; bear; tolerate. 3 To last for a long time; continue to exist.
en·dur·ing [in·d(y)oor′ing] *adj.* Lasting for a long time; durable; permanent.
end·ways [end′wāz′] *adv.* 1 On end: logs stacked *endways.* 2 With the end forward or toward something else: a table placed *endways* against a wall. 3 End to end; lengthwise.
end·wise [end′wiz′] *adv.* Endways.
end zone An area that extends ten yards beyond the goal line at either end of a football field.
ENE east-northeast.
en·e·ma [en′ə·mə] *n.* The injection of a liquid by means of a tube or nozzle into the rectum, especially to empty the bowels.
en·e·my [en′ə·mē] *n., pl.* **en·e·mies** 1 A person, nation, or group who hates and tries to harm, destroy, or triumph over another. 2 Anyone strongly opposed to or trying to combat something: The police force is an *enemy* of crime. 3 Anything harmful or destructive.
en·er·get·ic [en′ər·jet′ik] *adj.* Full of energy; forceful; vigorous.
en·er·get·i·cal·ly [en′ər·jet′ik·lē] *adv.* In an energetic manner; vigorously.
en·er·gize [en′ər·jīz′] *v.* **en·er·gized, en·er·giz·ing** To give energy, force, or strength to; make active or effective. **—en′er·giz′er** *n.*
en·er·gy [en′ər·jē] *n., pl.* **en·er·gies** 1 Lively force or activity; vigor; vitality. 2 (*often pl.*) Power forcefully and effectively used: All their *energies* were thrown into the campaign. 3 The capacity for doing work or supplying power: the *energy* of electricity. 4 Usable electric or heat power.
en·er·vate [en′ər·vāt′] *v.* **en·er·vat·ed, en·er·vat·ing** To drain the strength or vigor of; weaken: The heat *enervated* the players. **—en′er·va′tion** *n.* **—en′er·va′tive** *adj.*
en·fee·ble [in·fē′bəl] *v.* **en·fee·bled, en·fee·bling** To make feeble.
en·fold [in·fōld′] *v.* 1 To wrap in or as if in folds; envelop. 2 To hug; embrace.
en·force [in·fôrs′] *v.* **en·forced, en·forc·ing** 1 To require to be obeyed: to *enforce* rules. 2 To impose by the use of force or severity: to *enforce* discipline.
en·force·a·ble [in·fôr′sə·bəl] *adj.* Capable of being enforced: Some rules are not *enforceable.*
en·force·ment [in·fôrs′mənt] *n.* A putting into force: *Enforcement* of the new tax law has begun.
en·fran·chise [in·fran′chīz′] *v.* **en·fran·chised, en·fran·chis·ing** 1 To allow to vote. 2 To set free, as from slavery. **—en·fran·chise·ment** [in·fran′chiz·mənt *or* in·fran′chīz·mənt] *n.*
eng. 1 engine. 2 engineer. 3 engineering.
Eng. 1 England. 2 English.
en·gage [in·gāj′] *v.* **en·gaged, en·gag·ing** 1 To hire; employ: to *engage* a piano teacher. 2 To occupy; keep busy: to be *engaged* in doing one's homework. 3 To take part; enter into: to *engage* in conversation or battle. 4 To attract; gain: to *engage* someone's attention. 5 To reserve the use of: to *engage* a room at a hotel. 6 To pledge oneself; promise: to *engage* to do certain chores. 7 To meet in battle; attack: to *engage* the enemy. 8 To fit together or interlock, as gear wheels.

en·gaged [in·gājd′] *adj.* 1 Pledged to marry; betrothed: The couple is *engaged.* 2 Busy; occupied: The doctor is *engaged.*
en·gage·ment [in·gāj′mənt] *n.* 1 A promise to marry; betrothal. 2 The period of being engaged to be married: a long *engagement.* 3 An arrangement to meet someone; appointment. 4 A pledge or obligation. 5 A job or employment, as an appearance in a theater. 6 A battle. 7 The act of engaging. 8 A being engaged.
en·gag·ing [in·gā′jing] *adj.* Pleasing; charming: *engaging* manners. **—en·gag′ing·ly** *adv.*
en·gen·der [in·jen′dər] *v.* To be the cause or source of; produce: Poverty can *engender* crime.
en·gine [en′jin] *n.* 1 A machine that uses energy, such as that produced by burning fuel, to do work, as by causing wheels or other mechanical parts to move. 2 A locomotive. 3 Any device or apparatus used for a special purpose: an *engine* of war.
en·gi·neer [en′jə·nir′] 1 *n.* A person who works or is trained in any branch of engineering. 2 *n.* A person who operates an engine, such as the driver of a locomotive. 3 *n.* A soldier who builds or repairs bridges, roads, and other structures. 4 *v.* To manage or accomplish cleverly or skillfully: to *engineer* a scheme. 5 *v.* To plan, build, or supervise as an engineer.
en·gi·neer·ing [en′jə·nir′ing] *n.* The work, skill, or profession in which scientific knowledge is put to practical use, as in the planning, designing, and building of roads, bridges, and machinery.
en·gir·dle [in·gûr′dəl] *v.* **en·gir·dled, en·gir·dling** To encircle as with a belt or girdle: The moon's orbit *engirdles* Earth.
Eng·lish [ing′glish] 1 *adj.* Of or having to do with England, its people, or its language and customs. 2 *n.* **(the English)** The people of England. 3 *n.* The language of Great Britain and also of the United States and many parts of the British Commonwealth of Nations. 4 *n.* A course of study dealing with the English language or English literature. 5 *n.* (*sometimes written* **english**) A spinning motion given to a ball, as in billiards.
English horn A musical instrument resembling the oboe, but larger and lower in pitch.

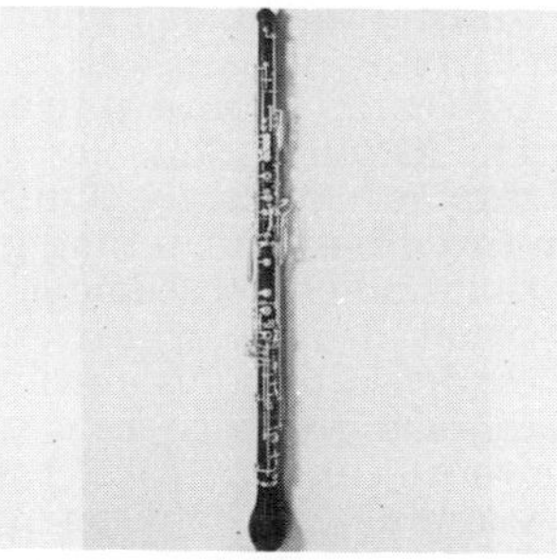
English horn

Eng·lish·man [ing′glish·mən] *n., pl.* **Eng·lish·men** [ing′glish·mən] A person born in or a citizen of England.
English muffin A round flat bun leavened with yeast, usually split and eaten toasted with butter.
Eng·lish·wom·an [ing′glish·wŏŏm′ən] *n., pl.* **Eng·lish·wom·en** [ing′glish·wim′in] A woman born in or a citizen of England.
en·gorge [in·gôrj′] *v.* **en·gorged, en·gorg·ing** 1 To eat greedily or stuff with food. 2 To swell or make swollen with blood or other fluid. **—en·gorge′ment** *n.*
en·graft [in·graft′] *v.* 1 To graft (a shoot or branch) onto a tree or plant. 2 To add as if by grafting; implant.
en·grave [in·grāv′] *v.* **en·graved, en·grav·ing** 1 To carve or cut letters or designs into: to *engrave* a ring. 2 To print with a block or plate of metal, stone, or wood, into which pictures, letters, or marks have been cut: to *engrave* invitations. 3 To fix or impress deeply, as in the memory. **—en·grav′er** *n.*
en·grav·ing [in·grā′ving] *n.* 1 A picture or print made from an engraved plate or surface. 2 The art or process of making engraved designs or printing plates. 3 An engraved design.

Printing from an engraving

en·gross [in·grōs′] *v.* To occupy completely; take up the attention of: to be *engrossed* by a novel.
en·gross·ing [in·grō′sing] *adj.* Absorbing.
en·gulf [in·gulf′] *v.* To swallow up; overwhelm completely: Night *engulfed* the city.
en·hance [in·hans′] *v.* **en·hanced, en·hanc·ing** To add to; increase: Good grooming *enhances* good looks. **—en·hance′ment** *n.*
e·nig·ma [i·nig′mə] *n.* Something or someone that is baffling, mysterious, or hard to understand.
en·ig·mat·ic [en′ig·mat′ik] *adj.* Puzzling; baffling: *enigmatic* answers. **—en′ig·mat′i·cal·ly** *adv.*
en·join [in·join′] *v.* 1 To order or direct, especially officially: The police *enjoined* the crowd to leave. 2 To forbid or prohibit: They were *enjoined* from trespassing.
en·joy [in·joi′] *v.* 1 To receive pleasure or delight from: I *enjoy* a good book. 2 To have the benefit or satisfaction of: to *enjoy* good health. **—enjoy oneself** To have a pleasant time.
en·joy·a·ble [in·joi′ə·bəl] *adj.* Giving pleasure; pleasant; satisfying: an *enjoyable* dinner. **—en·joy′a·ble·ness** *n.* **—en·joy′a·bly** *adv.*
en·joy·ment [in·joi′mənt] *n.* 1 The act of enjoying something. 2 The condition of enjoying something. 3 The possession or use of something.
en·kin·dle [in·kin′dəl] *v.* **en·kin·dled, en·kin·dling** 1 To set on fire: Flying sparks may *enkindle* the roof. 2 To begin to glow; catch fire.
en·lace [in·lās′] *v.* **en·laced, en·lac·ing** Another word for ENTWINE.
en·large [in·lärj′] *v.* **en·larged, en·larg·ing** To make or become larger; expand. **—enlarge on** or **enlarge upon** To tell about in great detail. **—en·larg′er** *n.*
en·large·ment [in·lärj′mənt] *n.* 1 A making or becoming larger. 2 Something enlarged, especially a photograph made larger than its negative.
en·light·en [in·līt′(ə)n] *v.* To give knowledge and understanding to; inform.
en·light·en·ment [in·līt′(ə)n·mənt] *n.* 1 The condition of being enlightened; knowledge. 2 The act of enlightening; instruction.

a	add	**i**	it	**ŏŏ**	took	**oi**	oil		
ā	ace	**ī**	ice	**ōō**	pool	**ou**	pout		
â	care	**o**	odd	**u**	up	**ng**	ring		
ä	palm	**ō**	open	**û**	burn	**th**	thin		
e	end	**ô**	order	**yōō**	fuse	**t͟h**	this		
ē	equal					**zh**	vision		

ə = { a in *above* e in *sicken* i in *possible*
o in *melon* u in *circus* }

E

en·list [in·list′] *v.* 1 To join or cause to join a branch of the armed forces without being drafted. 2 To join any activity or cause: to *enlist* in the fight against poverty. 3 To obtain (as help, support, or aid). —**en·list′ment** *n.*
en·list·ed [in·lis′tid] *adj.* Of or having to do with members of the armed forces below the rank of commissioned or warrant officers.
enlisted man A person in the armed forces who is not a commissioned officer or a warrant officer.
en·li·ven [in·lī′vən] *v.* To make lively, cheerful, or more spirited: to *enliven* a speech.
en masse [än mas′ *or* en mas′] In a group or mass; all together: They marched *en masse* to the auditorium.
en·mesh [in·mesh′] *v.* To entangle in or as if in a net: to be *enmeshed* in difficulties.
en·mi·ty [en′mə·tē] *n., pl.* **en·mi·ties** Deep hatred, mistrust, or dislike.
en·no·ble [i·nō′bəl] *v.* **en·no·bled, en·no·bling** 1 To make noble; give greatness, honor, or dignity to. 2 To raise to the rank of the nobility.
en·nui [än′wē′] *n.* A feeling of discontented weariness or boredom.
e·nor·mi·ty [i·nôr′mə·tē] *n., pl.* **e·nor·mi·ties** 1 Tremendous wickedness: the *enormity* of the crime. 2 An exceedingly wicked act or crime.
e·nor·mous [i·nôr′məs] *adj.* Unusually large or great; immense. —**e·nor′mous·ly** *adv.*
e·nough [i·nuf′] 1 *adj.* Sufficient for what is needed or wanted: There is *enough* cake for everyone. 2 *n.* As much as is required: You've had *enough.* 3 *adv.* Sufficiently: Are you well *enough* to go? 4 *adv.* Fairly; quite; somewhat: Strangely *enough,* we had no rain last month.
en·quire [in·kwīr′] *v.* **en·quired, en·quir·ing** Another spelling of INQUIRE.
en·quir·y [in·kwīr′ē *or* in′kwər·ē] *n., pl.* **en·quir·ies** Another spelling of INQUIRY.
en·rage [in·rāj′] *v.* **en·raged, en·rag·ing** To fill with rage; make angry or furious.
en·rapt [in·rapt′] *adj.* 1 Enraptured; delighted. 2 Completely absorbed; spellbound.
en·rap·ture [in·rap′chər] *v.* **en·rap·tured, en·rap·tur·ing** To fill with rapture; delight greatly: *enraptured* by the sound of the singer's voice.
en·rich [in·rich′] *v.* 1 To make wealthy. 2 To improve by adding something: to *enrich* flour with extra vitamins. —**en·rich′ment** *n.*
en·robe [in·rōb′] *v.* **en·robed, en·rob·ing** To swathe in a robe or similar garment.
en·roll or **en·rol** [in·rōl′] *v.* **en·rolled, en·roll·ing** 1 To put one's name on a list, as for membership; register. 2 To join as a member; enlist: to *enroll* in an art class.
en·roll·ment or **en·rol·ment** [in·rōl′mənt] *n.* 1 The act or process of enrolling. 2 A being enrolled. 3 The number of people enrolled.
en route [än ro͞ot′ *or* en ro͞ot′] On the way: I pass the police station *en route* to school.
ens. or **Ens.** ensign.
en·sconce [in·skons′] *v.* **en·sconced, en·sconc·ing** To settle or place firmly or snugly: The baby was *ensconced* among the cushions.
en·sem·ble [än·säm′bəl] *n.* 1 All the parts of a thing considered as a whole. 2 A costume made up of parts that match or harmonize. 3 A group, as of players, or singers, performing together.
en·shrine [in·shrīn′] *v.* **en·shrined, en·shrin·ing** 1 To place in or as if in a shrine. 2 To cherish as precious or sacred: The stirring words are *enshrined* in our hearts.
en·shroud [in·shroud′] *v.* To wrap or enclose in or as if in a shroud.
en·sign [en′sīn′ *or* en′sən] *n.* 1 A flag or banner, especially a national banner or naval flag. 2 [en′sən] In the U.S. Navy, a commissioned officer of the lowest rank. 3 Any badge or symbol.

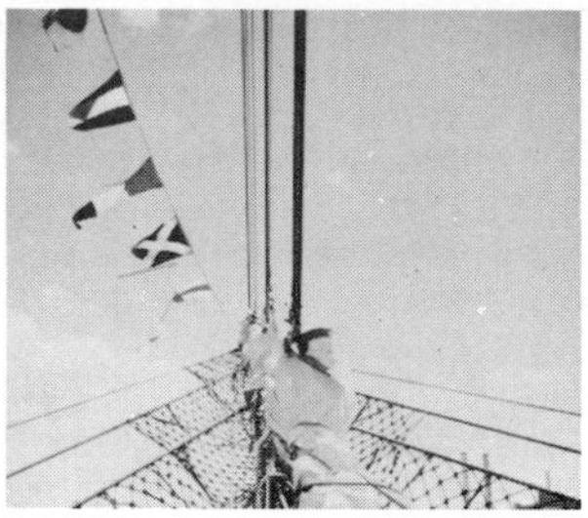
Ensign

en·si·lage [en′sə·lij] *n.* Fodder made from green plants stored in a silo.
en·slave [in·slāv′] *v.* **en·slaved, en·slav·ing** 1 To force into slavery. 2 To dominate or control completely. —**en·slave′ment** *n.*
en·snare [in·snâr′ *v.* **en·snared, en·snar·ing** To catch in or as if in a snare; trap.
en·sue [in·so͞o′] *v.* **en·sued, en·su·ing** 1 To follow in time; come next: A long correspondence *ensued* after their trip. 2 To follow as a consequence: We disagreed, and an argument *ensued.*
en·sure [in·sho͝or′] *v.* **en·sured, en·sur·ing** 1 To make sure or certain; guarantee: Winning this game will *ensure* our final victory. 2 To make safe or secure: to *ensure* liberty.
-ent A suffix meaning: 1 Showing, having, or doing something, as in *independent.* 2 A person or thing that does something, as in *superintendent.*
en·tab·la·ture [in·tab′lə·chər] *n.* In classical styles of architecture, the upper part of an outer wall above the supporting columns, usually comprising the architrave, frieze, and cornice.
en·tail [in·tāl′] 1 *v.* To require or necessitate: This project will *entail* much research. 2 *v.* To restrict the inheritance of (property) to a certain succession of heirs, thus preventing its being willed or disposed of in any other way. 3 *n.* A legal restriction by which property is entailed. 4 *n.* Something entailed, as property.
en·tan·gle [in·tang′gəl] *v.* **en·tan·gled, en·tan·gling** 1 To catch in or as if in something tangled; snarl: The kitten became *entangled* in the yarn. 2 To trap or involve, as in difficulties.
en·tan·gle·ment [in·tang′gəl·mənt] *n.* 1 Anything that hampers freedom of action. 2 A complicated situation from which escape is difficult. 3 The condition of being involved in a complicated and confusing situation.
en·tente [än·tänt′] *n.* 1 An agreement or understanding, as between nations. 2 The alliance formed by such an agreement.
en·ter [en′tər] *v.* 1 To come or go in or into: to *enter* a building. 2 To pierce; penetrate: The nail *entered* his shoe. 3 To join; take part in: to *enter* a discussion. 4 To cause to join or be admitted: to *enter* a child in school. 5 To write down; record: to *enter* one's name on a list. 6 To list or offer for competition in a contest. 7 To cause to be recorded, as evidence in a law court. —**enter on** or **enter upon** To start out on; begin: to *enter on* a new career.
en·ter·i·tis [en′tə·rī′təs] *n.* Inflammation of the intestines, especially of the small intestine.
en·ter·prise [en′tər·prīz′] *n.* 1 A project, undertak-

ing, or venture requiring effort, ability, or daring. **2** Energy and spirit for starting new or difficult undertakings.

en·ter·pris·ing [en′tər·prīz′ing] *adj.* Full of energy, daring, and willingness to embark on new undertakings.

en·ter·tain [en′tər·tān′] *v.* **1** To hold the attention of and give enjoyment to: to *entertain* an audience. **2** To have as a guest or guests: to *entertain* friends. **3** To have guests: They rarely *entertain.* **4** To take into or have in one's mind: to *entertain* doubts. ◆ *Entertain* and *amuse* both mean to hold the attention of others in an enjoyable way, but *amuse* often adds the idea of being funny. A musician and a comedian both like to *entertain* an audience, but the musician might be displeased if the listeners were *amused.*

en·ter·tain·er [en′tər·tān′ər] *n.* A person who entertains, especially one who earns money by entertaining audiences.

en·ter·tain·ing [en′tər·tā′ning] *adj.* Holding the attention and giving enjoyment; diverting: an *entertaining* book. **—en′ter·tain′ing·ly** *adv.*

en·ter·tain·ment [en′tər·tān′mənt] *n.* **1** Something that entertains, as a performance for an audience. **2** The act of entertaining. **3** A being entertained; amusement.

en·thrall or **en·thral** [in·thrôl′] *v.* **en·thralled, en·thrall·ing** **1** To keep spellbound; fascinate. **2** To enslave. **—en·thrall′ment** or **en·thral′ment** *n.*

en·throne [in·thrōn′] *v.* **en·throned, en·thron·ing** **1** To place on a throne. **2** To place in a position of very high rank or esteem.

en·thuse [in·thōōz′] *v.* **en·thused, en·thus·ing** *informal* **1** To make or become very enthusiastic. **2** To say with enthusiasm; gush.

en·thu·si·asm [in·thōō′zē·az′əm] *n.* Keen interest or liking: *enthusiasm* for a hobby.

en·thu·si·ast [in·thōō′zē·ast′] *n.* A person filled with enthusiasm.

en·thu·si·as·tic [in·thōō′zē·as′tik] *adj.* Full of enthusiasm; expressing eager interest or approval. **—en·thu′si·as′ti·cal·ly** *adv.*

en·tice [in·tīs′] *v.* **en·ticed, en·tic·ing** To attract or lure by offering or tempting with something attractive or desirable. **—en·tice′ment** *n.*

en·tire [in·tīr′] *adj.* **1** All the members or parts of; whole: The *entire* family was there. **2** Complete; full; total: The manager has *entire* control of the business. **3** Not divided, broken, or in parts: Put the *entire* mass of dough in one pan.

en·tire·ly [in·tīr′lē] *adv.* **1** Completely: The sky was *entirely* overcast. **2** Only; exclusively: The choice is *entirely* up to you.

en·tire·ty [in·tīr′tē] *n., pl.* **en·tire·ties** **1** Complete state, with nothing missing or omitted. **2** Something entire; a whole.

en·ti·tle [in·tīt′(ə)l] *v.* **en·ti·tled, en·ti·tling** **1** To give the right to receive, demand, or do something: Your ticket *entitles* you to a seat. **2** To give a title to: The novel was *entitled* "Treasure Island."

en·ti·tle·ment [in·tīt′(ə)l·mənt] *n.* **1** Something that someone has a right to have or receive. **2** A payment, such as a pension or a social security benefit, that a government is obligated to make by law or legal contract.

en·ti·ty [en′tə·tē] *n., pl.* **en·ti·ties** Something that exists or can be thought of as a real and recognizable thing, individual, or whole, such as a person, a building, or an orchestra.

en·tomb [in·tōōm′] *v.* To place or confine in or as if in a tomb; bury. **—en·tomb′ment** *n.*

en·to·mol·o·gy [en′tə·mol′ə·jē] *n.* The scientific study of insects. **—en·to·mo·log·i·cal** [en′tə·mə·loj′·ə·kəl] *adj.* **—en·to·mol·o·gist** [en′tə·mol′ə·jist] *n.*

en·tour·age [än′tōō·räzh′] *n.* **1** The group of aides and attendants accompanying a person of importance or high rank. **2** A person's surroundings.

en·tr'acte [än′trakt′] *n.* **1** A short pause between two acts of a play; intermission. **2** A piece of music or other incidental entertainment performed during an intermission. ◆ *Entr'acte* (literally, *between* acts) is one of many French theatrical words borrowed into English.

en·trails [en′trālz] *n. pl.* The inner parts of the body, especially the intestines.

en·train [in·trān′] *v.* To board or put on board a train.

en·trance[1] [en′trəns] *n.* **1** A passageway, as a doorway, used for entering something. **2** The act of entering: No one noticed our late *entrance.* **3** The right, privilege, or ability to enter.

en·trance[2] [in·trans′] *v.* **en·tranced, en·tranc·ing** **1** To fill with wonder or delight; charm; fascinate. **2** To put in a trance.

en·trant [en′trənt] *n.* A person who enters or is entered, especially in a race or contest.

en·trap [in·trap′] *v.* **en·trapped, en·trap·ping** **1** To catch in or as if in a trap. **2** To lure or trick into a troublesome situation.

en·treat [in·trēt′] *v.* To ask earnestly; implore; beg: I *entreat* you to forgive me.

en·treat·y [in·trē′tē] *n., pl.* **en·treat·ies** An earnest request or plea.

en·tre·chat [än′trə·shä′] *n.* A ballet leap in which the feet are repeatedly tapped against each other or crossed while the dancer is in the air.

en·trée or **en·tree** [än′trā] *n.* **1** A dish served as the main course of a meal. **2** The means or privilege of entering or visiting: to have *entrée* to a private club.

en·trench [in·trench′] *v.* **1** To protect in a trench, or surround with trenches for defense: The soldiers were *entrenched* on the battlefield. **2** To establish firmly: The idea was *entrenched* in my mind. **—en·trench′ment** *n.*

en·tre·pre·neur [än′trə·prə·nûr′] *n.* A person who organizes and runs a business venture. **—en′tre·pre·neur′i·al** *adj.*

en·trust [in·trust′] *v.* **1** To give or turn over, as for care or safekeeping: to *entrust* money to someone. **2** To make responsible for something: to *entrust* a pilot with one's safety.

en·try [en′trē] *n., pl.* **en·tries** **1** The act of entering. **2** A place for entering, as a hallway. **3** A word, phrase, or number entered in a list or series, as in a dictionary or ledger. **4** A person or thing entered in a contest or race.

a	add	**i**	it	**ŏŏ**	took	**oi**	oil		
ā	ace	**ī**	ice	**ōō**	pool	**ou**	pout		
â	care	**o**	odd	**u**	up	**ng**	ring		
ä	palm	**ō**	open	**û**	burn	**th**	thin		
e	end	**ô**	order	**yōō**	fuse	**t͟h**	this		
ē	equal					**zh**	vision		

ə = {a in *above* e in *sicken* i in *possible* / o in *melon* u in *circus*}

E

en·twine [in·twīn'] *v.* **en·twined, en·twin·ing** To twine around; twist or twine together.

e·nu·mer·ate [i·n(y)ōō'mər·āt'] *v.* **e·nu·mer·at·ed, e·nu·mer·at·ing** 1 To name one by one: to *enumerate* the presidents of the United States. 2 To count. **—e·nu'mer·a'tion** *n.* **—e·nu'mer·a'·tor** *n.*

e·nun·ci·ate [i·nun'sē·āt'] *v.* **e·nun·ci·at·ed, e·nun·ci·at·ing** 1 To pronounce words; speak: *Enunciate* clearly. 2 To state in precise language: to *enunciate* a theory. **—e·nun'ci·a'tion** *n.* **—e·nun'ci·a'tor** *n.*

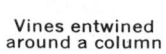

Vines entwined around a column

en·vel·op [in·vel'əp] *v.* To wrap, cover, or surround: Clouds *enveloped* the mountain peak. **—en·vel'op·ment** *n.*

en·ve·lope [en'və·lōp' *or* än'və·lōp'] *n.* 1 A flat paper case or wrapper, usually with a flap that folds over and is sealed at the back, used chiefly to mail letters. 2 Something that envelops.

en·ven·om [in·ven'əm] *v.* 1 To put poison in or on: to *envenom* arrows. 2 To fill with hatred or resentment: a mind *envenomed* by misfortune.

en·vi·a·ble [en'vē·ə·bəl] *adj.* So excellent as to be envied or much desired: *enviable* talent.

en·vi·er [en'vē·ər] *n.* A person who has feelings of envy.

en·vi·ous [en'vē·əs] *adj.* Full of envy: an *envious* rival. **—en'vi·ous·ly** *adv.* **—en'vi·ous·ness** *n.*

en·vi·ron·ment [in·vī'rən·mənt] *n.* The conditions and surroundings that have an effect on the development of a person, animal, or plant. **—en·vi·ron·men·tal** [in·vī'rən·men'təl] *adj.* **—en·vi'ron·men'tal·ly** *adv.*

en·vi·ron·men·tal·ist [in·vī'rən·men'təl·ist] *n.* 1 A person who supports efforts to prevent pollution and preserve the healthfulness and beauty of the natural environment. 2 A person who argues that the social and material environment rather than heredity determines the nature of an individual or a group of people.

en·vi·rons [in·vī'rənz] *n.pl.* Surrounding area or neighborhoods: Chicago and its *environs.*

en·vis·age [in·viz'ij] *v.* **en·vis·aged, en·vis·ag·ing** To form a mental image of; visualize: to *envisage* oneself as a pilot.

en·vi·sion [in·vizh'ən] *v.* To see or predict in the imagination: to *envision* the future.

en·voy [en'voi *or* än'voi] *n.* 1 A government representative sent to a foreign country, ranking just below an ambassador. 2 A messenger on a special mission.

en·vy [en'vē] *n., pl.* **en·vies,** *v.* **en·vied, en·vy·ing** 1 *n.* A feeling of discontent or jealousy aroused by the good fortune or superior abilities of another. 2 *n.* A desire to have in equal amount or degree what someone else has. 3 *v.* To have a feeling of envy toward or because of: I *envied* you because of your high marks. 4 *n.* A person or thing that is envied: The captain is the *envy* of the team. ◆ *Envy* comes from a Latin word meaning *to look at in a bad way.*

en·wrap [in·rap'] *v.* **en·wrapped, en·wrap·ping** To wrap up; envelop.

en·wreathe [in·rēth'] *v.* **en·wreathed, en·wreath·ing** To wind around with or as if with a wreath.

en·zy·mat·ic [en'zə·mat'ik] *adj.* Of, caused by, or having to do with an enzyme. **—en'zy·mat'i·cal·ly** *adv.*

en·zyme [en'zīm'] *n.* A protein substance produced by living cells, and capable of causing a specific chemical reaction in the body without being changed itself. Some enzymes play an important part in the digestion of food.

EO executive order.

E·o·cene [ē'ə·sēn'] 1 *n.* The second geological epoch of the Tertiary period of the Cenozoic era. During the Eocene mammals continued to develop. 2 *adj.* Of the Eocene.

eo·hip·pus [ē'ō·hip'əs] *n.* A primitive ancestor of the horse that lived and became extinct during the Eocene epoch. It was less than 20 inches high and had toes instead of hoofs. ◆ *Eohippus* comes from the Greek words *eos,* meaning *dawn,* and *hippus,* meaning *horse.*

e·on [ē'ən *or* ē'on] *n.* An extremely long time; hundreds of thousands of years: Dinosaurs lived *eons* ago.

EPA Environmental Protection Agency.

ep·au·let or **ep·au·lette** [ep'ə·let'] *n.* An ornament worn on each shoulder of a naval or military officer's uniform.

Epaulets

e·phed·rine [i·fed'rin] *n.* A drug used to relieve swollen nasal passages and allergic symptoms such as sneezing and wheezing.

e·phem·e·ra [i·fem'ər·ə] *n.pl.* Things, especially printed matter, of temporary interest that are soon forgotten. ◆ *Ephemera* is the plural of *ephemeron,* the Greek name of the mayfly, an insect that has a very short life in the adult stage.

e·phem·er·al [i·fem'ər·əl] *adj.* Living or lasting for a brief time only: *ephemeral* sorrows.

E·phe·sians [i·fē'zhənz] *n.* A book of the New Testament, a letter written in the name of St. Paul to Christians in Asia Minor.

ep·ic [ep'ik] 1 *n.* A long poem that tells of the wanderings and adventures of a great person or persons: The *Iliad* by Homer is an ancient Greek *epic.* 2 *n.* Something, as a novel or play, that resembles an epic. 3 *adj.* Heroic; impressive: *epic* courage.

ep·i·cal [ep'i·kəl] *adj.* Epic. **—ep'i·cal·ly** *adv.*

ep·i·cot·yl [ep'ə·kot'əl] *n.* The part of a young plant stem that emerges just above the cotyledons and reaches as far as the first leaves.

ep·i·cure [ep'ə·kyŏŏr] *n.* A person who is very interested in good and often unusual food and drink; a gourmet. ◆ *Epicure* comes from the name of *Epicurus,* an ancient Greek philosopher.

ep·i·cu·re·an [ep'ə·kyŏŏ·rē'ən] 1 *adj.* Of or suitable for an epicure: Some people would consider this meal an *epicurean* delight. 2 *n.* An epicure.

ep·i·dem·ic [ep'ə·dem'ik] 1 *n.* The sudden spread of a disease among many people: a measles *epidemic.* 2 *adj.* Occurring in many places at once.

ep·i·der·mis [ep'ə·dûr'mis] *n.* The outer, protective layer of the skin. ◆ The Greek word for *skin* is *derma,* and many English words, such as *epidermis, pachyderm,* and *dermatology,* are derived partly from it. *Epidermis* literally means *upon the skin, pachyderm* means *thick skin,* and *dermatology* means *the science or study of the skin.*

ep·i·glot·tis [ep′ə·glot′is] *n.* A lidlike piece of cartilage that keeps food from entering the windpipe during swallowing.
ep·i·gram [ep′ə·gram′] *n.* A brief, witty verse or statement that makes a clever point: "I can resist everything except temptation" is an *epigram.*
ep·i·gram·mat·ic [ep′i·grə·mat′ik] *adj.* 1 Brief and witty, like an epigram. 2 Full of or using epigrams: an *epigrammatic* speaker.
ep·i·lep·sy [ep′ə·lep′sē] *n.* A disorder of the nervous system, attacks of which sometimes cause loss of consciousness and convulsions.
ep·i·lep·tic [ep′ə·lep′tik] 1 *n.* A person who suffers from epilepsy. 2 *adj.* Of, like, or having epilepsy.
ep·i·logue or **ep·i·log** [ep′ə·lôg *or* ep′ə·log′] *n.* 1 A short section at the end of a book, poem, or other written piece. 2 A speech to the audience by an actor at the end of a play.
ep·i·neph·rine [ep′ə·nef′rin *or* ep′ə·nef′rēn′] *n.* The correct scientific name for ADRENALINE.
E·piph·a·ny [i·pif′ə·nē] *n.* January 6th, the day Christians celebrate the visit of the Wise Men to adore the infant Jesus.
ep·i·phyte [ep′ə·fīt′] *n.* Another name for AIR PLANT.
Epis. 1 Episcopal. 2 Episcopalian.
e·pis·co·pal [i·pis′kə·pəl] *adj.* 1 (*written* **Episcopal**) Of or having to do with the Protestant Episcopal Church. 2 Having to do with or ruled by bishops.
E·pis·co·pa·li·an [i·pis′kə·pā′lē·ən *or* i·pis′kə·pāl′·yən] 1 *n.* A member of the Protestant Episcopal Church. 2 *adj.* Of or having to do with Episcopalians or their church.
ep·i·sode [ep′ə·sōd′] *n.* Any incident or event that is part of something continuous, as a story or a person's life.
ep·i·sod·ic [ep′ə·sod′ik] *adj.* 1 Made up of separate episodes. 2 Occurring for brief periods and at irregular times: an *episodic* disease. **—ep′i·sod′i·cal·ly** *adv.*
e·pis·tle [i·pis′əl] *n.* 1 A long, formal letter. 2 (*written* **Epistle**) Any of the books of the New Testament that are written in the form of a letter by one of the Apostles.
ep·i·taph [ep′ə·taf′] *n.* The writing on a monument or gravestone in remembrance of the person who has died.

John Hale
1879-1939
May he rest
in peace
Epitaph

ep·i·the·li·um [ep′ə·thē′lē·əm] *n., pl.* **ep·i·the·li·ums** *or* **ep·i·the·li·a** [ep′ə·thē′lē·ə] A tissue consisting of a very thin layer of cells covering the outer surface and most of the inner surfaces of an animal's body.
ep·i·thet [ep′ə·thet′] *n.* A descriptive word or phrase used to indicate some outstanding characteristic or feature of a person or thing, as "the Great" in Alexander the Great.
e·pit·o·me [i·pit′ə·mē] *n.* 1 A person or thing that possesses all of the qualities or characteristics of something: Our class president is the *epitome* of good citizenship. 2 A short summary or statement of something; condensed account: the *epitome* of a speech.
e·pit·o·mize [i·pit′ə·mīz′] *v.* **e·pit·o·mized, e·pit·o·miz·ing** 1 To have or represent the chief qualities of. 2 To summarize briefly.
e plu·ri·bus u·num [ē plo͝or′ə·bəs yo͞o′nəm] One out of many: a Latin expression used as a motto of the United States.
ep·och [ep′ək] *n.* 1 A period of time especially remembered, as for great events or new discoveries: Recent years may be remembered as the atomic *epoch.* 2 A period that is part of a longer period of the earth's history: a geological *epoch.*
ep·och-mak·ing [ep′ək·mā′king] *adj.* 1 Bringing in a new period of knowledge or discovery: The airplane was an *epoch-making* invention. 2 Having important results: an *epoch-making* decision to go to war.
ep·o·nym [ep′ə·nim′] *n.* A person or imaginary character whose name is used to identify something else: George Washington became the *eponym* of a state, a city, and a bridge.
e·pon·y·mous [i·pon′ə·məs] *adj.* Of or being the person after whom something is named.
ep·ox·y [ep′ok′sē *or* i·pok′sē] *n., pl.* **ep·ox·ies,** *v.* **ep·ox·ied, ep·ox·y·ing** 1 *n.* A tough synthetic resin used to make strong glue and coatings. 2 *v.* To glue with epoxy.
epoxy resin Epoxy.
ep·si·lon [ep′sə·lon′] *n.* The fifth letter of the Greek alphabet.
Ep·som salts [ep′səm] A compound found in certain mineral springs, used as a laxative or to reduce swelling.
eq. 1 equal. 2 equation. 3 equator. 4 equivalent.
eq·ua·ble [ek′wə·bəl *or* ē′kwə·bəl] *adj.* 1 Not changing or varying greatly: *equable* temperature. 2 Not easily upset; peaceful; calm: an *equable* nature. **—eq′ua·bly** *adv.*
e·qual [ē′kwəl] *adj., v.* **e·qualed** or **e·qualled, e·qual·ing** or **e·qual·ling,** *n.* 1 *adj.* Having the same measure, amount, or extent as another: *equal* portions. 2 *adj.* Having the same rights, privileges, or rank. 3 *v.* To be equal to: 10 × 2 *equals* 20; Your swimming speed *equaled* mine. 4 *n.* A person or thing equal to another: She is his *equal* in ability. 5 *v.* To do or produce something equal to. **—be equal to** To have the necessary strength or ability for: The contestant *is equal to* the race.
e·qual·i·ty [i·kwol′ə·tē] *n., pl.* **e·qual·i·ties** The condition or quality of being equal: an *equality* of size or amount.
e·qual·ize [ē′kwəl·īz′] *v.* **e·qual·ized, e·qual·iz·ing** To make equal, uniform, or even.
e·qual·iz·er [ē′kwəl·ī′zər] *n.* 1 A person or thing that equalizes. 2 A device for equalizing pressure or strain between parts of a structure.
e·qual·ly [ē′kwəl·ē] *adv.* 1 In equal amounts or parts: Divide the gold *equally.* 2 To the same extent: You and I are *equally* wrong.
equal sign In mathematics, a sign (=) that means "is equal to," as in 4 + 3 = 7.
e·qua·nim·i·ty [ē′kwə·nim′ə·tē *or* ek′wə·nim′ə·tē] *n.* Evenness of mind and disposition.
e·quate [i·kwāt′] *v.* **e·quat·ed, e·quat·ing** 1 To consider or treat as equal: Some people *equate* old age with wisdom. 2 To make or set equal.
e·qua·tion [i·kwā′zhən] *n.* 1 In mathematics, a

a	add	**i**	it	**o͝o**	took	**oi**	oil
ā	ace	**ī**	ice	**o͞o**	pool	**ou**	pout
â	care	**o**	odd	**u**	up	**ng**	ring
ä	palm	**ō**	open	**û**	burn	**th**	thin
e	end	**ô**	order	**yo͞o**	fuse	**t͟h**	this
ē	equal					**zh**	vision

ə = {a in *above* e in *sicken* i in *possible*
o in *melon* u in *circus*}

statement that two or more quantities or groups of quantities are equal, usually made with an equal sign: "$9 \times 3 - 1 = 26$" and "$a + b = c$" are *equations.* **2** In chemistry, a way of showing results of chemical reaction, as $CO_2 + H_2O \rightarrow H_2CO_3$. **3** The act of making things equal.

e·qua·tor [i·kwā'tər] *n.* An imaginary line that encircles the earth exactly halfway between the North Pole and the South Pole.

The equator

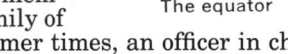

e·qua·to·ri·al [ē'kwə·tôr'·ē·əl] *adj.* **1** Of or close to the equator. **2** Like or related to conditions at the equator: *equatorial* heat.

eq·uer·ry [ek'wər·ē] *n., pl.* **eq·uer·ries** **1** An officer who works for any member of the royal family of England. **2** In former times, an officer in charge of the horses of a prince or nobleman.

e·ques·tri·an [i·kwes'trē·ən] **1** *n.* A skilled rider of horses. **2** *adj.* Having to do with horses or with the riding of horses. **3** *adj.* Showing a person mounted on horseback: an *equestrian* portrait.

e·ques·tri·enne [i·kwes'trē·en'] *n.* A woman who is a skilled rider of horses.

equi- A prefix meaning: Equal or equally, as in *equidistant.*

e·qui·dis·tant [ē'kwə·dis'tənt] *adj.* Equally distant: The midpoint of a line is *equidistant* from either end.

e·qui·lat·er·al [ē'kwə·lat'ər·əl] *adj.* Having all the sides of the same length: an *equilateral* triangle.

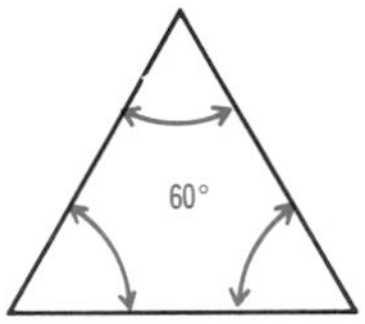

Equilateral triangle

e·qui·lib·ri·um [ē'kwə·lib'rē·əm] *n.* A state of balance: Beginning skaters find it hard to keep their *equilibrium;* Identical weights on each side of a scale will be in *equilibrium.*

e·quine [ē'kwīn'] *adj.* Of, related to, or like a horse: The zebra is an *equine* animal.

equi·noc·tial [ē'kwə·nok'shəl] **1** *adj.* Of or occurring at the time of an equinox. **2** *n.,* An equinoctial storm.

e·qui·nox [ē'kwə·nok'] *n.* Either of two times of the year when the sun crosses the celestial equator, so that the days and the nights are of equal length. The **vernal equinox** takes place about March 21, the **autumnal equinox** about September 21. ◆ *Equinox* comes from a Latin word meaning *equal night.*

Weights in equilibrium

e·quip [i·kwip'] *v.* **e·quipped, e·quip·ping** To supply or fit out with something needed: to *equip* an automobile with seat belts.

eq·ui·page [ek'wə·pij] *n.* **1** A carriage, especially a showy one with horses, equipment, and servants. **2** The equipment, as for a camp or army.

e·quip·ment [i·kwip'mənt] *n.* **1** A thing or things needed for some special use or purpose: football *equipment.* **2** The act of equipping.

e·qui·poise [ek'wə·poiz' *or* ē'kwə·poiz'] *n.* **1** Equal weight or balance; equilibrium. **2** A thing that balances another in weight or force.

eq·ui·ta·ble [ek'wə·tə·bəl] *adj.* Just, fair, and reasonable: *equitable* laws. **—eq'ui·ta·bly** *adv.*

eq·ui·ty [ek'wə·tē] *n., pl.* **eq·ui·ties** **1** Fairness; justice. **2** Something that is fair or just.

e·quiv·a·lence [i·kwiv'ə·ləns] *n.* **1** The relation that exists between equivalent things. **2** The condition of being equivalent.

e·quiv·a·lent [i·kwiv'ə·lənt] **1** *adj.* Equal, as in worth, force, or amount. **2** *n.* Something that is equivalent. **—e·quiv'a·lent·ly** *adv.*

e·quiv·o·cal [i·kwiv'ə·kəl] *adj.* **1** Having a double meaning; puzzling: Her *equivocal* reply left me confused. **2** Uncertain or unreliable, as in value or results: Our *equivocal* findings did not solve the mystery at all. **3** Causing suspicion; not to be trusted: *equivocal* politeness.

e·quiv·o·cate [i·kwiv'ə·kāt'] *v.* **e·quiv·o·cat·ed, e·quiv·o·cat·ing** To use language that can have two or more meanings, so as to mislead, confuse, or deceive. **—e·quiv'o·ca'tion** *n.* **—e·quiv'o·ca'tor** *n.*

-er[1] A suffix meaning: **1** A person or thing that does something, as in *runner* or *grater.* **2** A person who lives in or comes from, as in *Northerner.* **3** A person practicing a trade or profession, as in *geographer.*

-er[2] A suffix meaning: More, as in *larger* or *faster.* It is added to adjectives and adverbs to form the comparative.

Er The symbol for the element erbium.

e·ra [ir'ə *or* ē'rə] *n.* **1** A period of time that dates from some important event or discovery: the atomic *era.* **2** A period of time noted for certain characteristics or accomplishments: the Elizabethan *era.* **3** One of the major divisions of geological time.

ERA Equal Rights Amendment.

e·rad·i·cate [i·rad'ə·kāt'] *v.* **e·rad·i·cat·ed, e·rad·i·cat·ing** To remove or get rid of completely: to *eradicate* a disease; to *eradicate* stains. **—e·rad'i·ca'tion** *n.*

e·rase [i·rās'] *v.* **e·rased, e·ras·ing** **1** To remove (as writing or drawing), especially by rubbing or scraping. **2** To remove written or recorded matter from, as a tape. **—e·ras'a·ble** *adj.*

e·ras·er [i·rā'sər] *n.* Something used for erasing, as a small piece of rubber for removing pencil or ink marks.

e·ra·sure [i·rā'shər] *n.* **1** The act of erasing. **2** Something erased, as a word or letter. **3** The place where something has been erased.

er·bi·um [ûr'bē·əm] *n.* A metallic element occurring in rare earths and sometimes used to give a pink color to glass or porcelain. See RARE-EARTH ELEMENT.

ere [âr] *prep., conj.* Before: seldom used today.

e·rect [i·rekt'] **1** *adj.* Upright; not stooping or leaning: an *erect* posture; The tree remained *erect* in the wind. **2** *v.* To put or raise into an upright position: to *erect* a flagpole. **3** *v.* To build or construct: to *erect* a hospital.

e·rec·tion [i·rek'shən] *n.* **1** The act or process of erecting something. **2** Something erected, as a building.

erg [ûrg] *n.* In physics, a unit of work and energy equal to the work done by one dyne acting through a distance of one centimeter. ◆ *Erg* comes from a Greek word meaning *work.*

er·go [ûr'gō] *conj., adv.* Hence; therefore: a Latin word.

er·go·nom·ics [ûr'gə·nom'iks] *n.pl.* Another word for BIOTECHNOLOGY.

er·got [ûr′gət] *n.* A fungus that causes a disease in rye and other grains.
Er·in [âr′in] *n.* Ireland: used mostly in poems.
er·mine [ûr′min] *n.* 1 A weasel having brown fur that in winter turns white with a black tip on the tail. 2 The white fur of the ermine, used for garments and, in Europe, for trimming on certain royal and judicial ceremonial robes.

Ermine

e·rode [i·rōd′] *v.* **e·rod·ed, e·rod·ing** To wear away or gradually destroy by constant action, as of water, wind, friction, or acid.
Er·os [er′os *or* ir′os] *n.* In Greek myths, the god of love. His Roman name was Cupid.
e·ro·sion [i·rō′zhən] *n.* The wearing away or gradual destruction of something, as by the action of wind, water, or acid: the *erosion* of land.
e·ro·sive [i·rō′siv] *adj.* Capable of eroding or causing erosion. **—e·ro′sive·ness** *n.*
err [ûr *or* er] *v.* **erred, err·ing** 1 To make an error; be wrong. 2 To do what is not right; sin.
er·rand [er′ənd] *n.* 1 A short trip made to carry out some task, usually for someone else. 2 The purpose of such a trip.
er·rant [er′ənt] *adj.* 1 Roving or wandering in search of adventure: an *errant* knight. 2 Straying from what is right or correct: *errant* behavior.
er·rat·ic [i·rat′ik] *adj.* 1 Uneven or irregular, as in action or progress: *erratic* growth. 2 Unusual; odd: *erratic* behavior. **—er·rat′i·cal·ly** *adv.*
er·ro·ne·ous [ə·rō′nē·əs] *adj.* Not correct or true; mistaken; false: *erroneous* opinions. **—er·ro′ne·ous·ly** *adv.* **—er·ro′ne·ous·ness** *n.*
er·ror [er′ər] *n.* 1 Something done, said, or believed incorrectly; a mistake: an *error* in addition. 2 The condition of being incorrect or mistaken: to be in *error.* 3 In baseball, a misplay, such as a fumble or wild throw, that allows a runner to reach base or to advance safely.
er·ror-prone [er′ər·prōn′] *adj.* Having a tendency to make many errors.
erst·while [ûrst′(h)wīl′] *adj.* Previous; former: an *erstwhile* companion.
e·ruct [i·rukt′] *v.* To belch.
e·ruc·ta·tion [i·ruk·tā′shən] *n.* The act or an instance of belching.
er·u·dite [er′yo͝o·dīt′] *adj.* Having or displaying much knowledge; scholarly: an *erudite* teacher.
er·u·di·tion [er′yo͝o·dish′ən] *n.* Great knowledge or learning: The author's *erudition* impressed us.
e·rupt [i·rupt′] *v.* 1 To cast forth, as lava or steam: Mount Etna *erupts* frequently. 2 To cast forth (as lava or steam). 3 To become covered with pimples or a rash. 4 Of new teeth, to break through the gums.
e·rup·tion [i·rup′shən] *n.* 1 The act or process of erupting. 2 A breaking out in a rash.

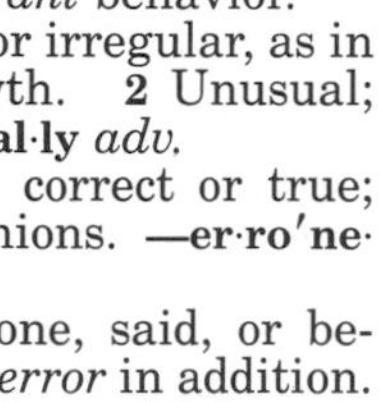
Volcano erupting

e·rup·tive [i·rup′tiv] *adj.* 1 Tending to discharge matter violently: an *eruptive* geyser. 2 Of or relating to volcanic eruptions. 3 Characterized by a skin rash.
-ery A suffix meaning: 1 A business or place where something is done, as in *bakery.* 2 A place or residence for, as in *nunnery.* 3 A collection of things, as in *finery.* 4 The actions or attitudes of, as in *snobbery.* 5 An act, art, trade, or profession, as in *cookery.* 6 A state of being, as in *bravery.*
e·ryth·ro·cyte [i·rith′rə·sīt′] *n.* The hemoglobin-carrying cell that is formed in the bone marrow and released into the circulating blood when mature. Erythrocytes are responsible for the red color of blood.

Es The symbol for the element einsteinium.
E·sau [ē′sô] *n.* In the Bible, the oldest son of Isaac.
es·ca·late [es′kə·lāt′] *v.* **es·ca·lat·ed, es·ca·lat·ing** To develop, increase, or expand, especially by stages: to *escalate* a conflict. **—es′ca·la′tion** *n.*
es·ca·la·tor [es′kə·lā′tər] *n.* A moving stairway for carrying people from one floor to another.

Escalator

es·cal·lop [es·kol′əp *or* es·kal′əp] *n., v.* Another word for SCALLOP.
es·ca·pade [es′kə·pād′] *n.* A reckless or mischievous act or prank; fling; spree.
es·cape [i·skāp′] *v.* **es·caped, es·cap·ing,** *n.* 1 *v.* To break out or get free. 2 *v.* To get or keep free from: to *escape* notice. 3 *v.* To avoid or remain untouched by: to *escape* chicken pox. 4 *n.* The act of escaping. 5 *n.* A way of escaping. 6 *v.* To leak out little by little: Fumes *escaped* from the pipe. 7 *v.* To fail to be noticed, understood, or remembered by: Your meaning *escapes* me. 8 *v.* To slip out from unintentionally: A groan *escaped* his lips. 9 *n.* A means of forgetting, as troubles or boredom: TV is a popular *escape.* **—es·cap′er** *n.*
es·cap·ee [i·skā′pē′ *or* es′kā·pē′] *n.* A person who has escaped, as from prison.
es·cape·ment [i·skāp′mənt] *n.* 1 A device in clocks and watches that keeps the movement regular. It consists of a wheel having notches around its rim, each notch of which is held back briefly by a catch and then alowed to escape at regular intervals. 2 A device in a typewriter that controls the sideways movement of the carriage.

Escapement

a	add	**i**	it	**o͝o**	took	**oi**	oil
ā	ace	**ī**	ice	**o͞o**	pool	**ou**	pout
â	care	**o**	odd	**u**	up	**ng**	ring
ä	palm	**ō**	open	**û**	burn	**th**	thin
e	end	**ô**	order	**yo͞o**	fuse	**t͟h**	this
ē	equal					**zh**	vision

ə = {a in *above* e in *sicken* i in *possible* / o in *melon* u in *circus*}

escape velocity The velocity that an object, as a rocket, must reach in order to escape the pull of gravity of Earth or another body.

es·cap·ism [i·skā′piz·əm] *n.* A desire or tendency to escape something unpleasant by daydreaming or by some form of entertainment.

es·ca·role [es′kə·rōl′] *n.* A plant with curly green leaves, used in salads.

es·carp·ment [is·kärp′mənt] *n.* 1 A steep, constructed slope that surrounds a fortification. 2 Any steep slope or cliff.

es·chew [is·chōō′] *v.* To avoid on principle; shun: to *eschew* evil. **—es·chew·al** [is·chōō′əl] *n.*

es·cort [*n.* es′kôrt′, *v.* is·kôrt′] 1 *n.* A person or group of persons attending someone so as to protect, guide, or honor: The president was given a military *escort.* 2 *n.* A person who takes someone to a party, dance, or other event. 3 *n.* One or more planes, ships, or cars, moving along with another so as to protect, guide, or honor. 4 *v.* To accompany as an escort.

es·crow [es′krō′] *n.* The legal condition of something that is put in the keeping of a third party until the intended recipient has met certain conditions: He put the rent money in *escrow* at a bank until his landlord repaired the plumbing.

es·cutch·eon [i·skuch′ən] *n.* A shield on whose surface there is a coat of arms.

Escutcheon

-ese A suffix meaning: 1 A native or inhabitant of, as in *Japanese.* 2 The language of, as in *Portuguese.*

ESE east-southeast.

Es·ki·mo [es′kə·mō] *n., pl.* **Es·ki·mos** or **Es·ki·mo** 1 A member of a people living along the Arctic coasts of North America, Greenland, and NE Siberia. 2 The language of these people. Compare INUIT.

Eskimo dog Another name for HUSKY.

ESL *E*nglish as a *S*econd *L*anguage: the teaching of English to speakers of other languages.

e·soph·a·gus [i·sof′ə·gəs] *n., pl.* **e·soph·a·gi** [i·sof′ə·jī′] The tube through which food passes from the throat to the stomach.

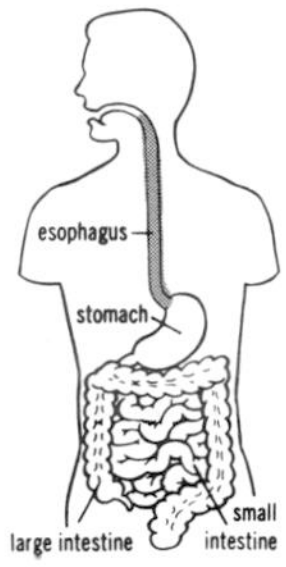

es·o·ter·ic [es′ə·ter′ik] *adj.* 1 Known or understood by only a few special people: *esoteric* religious doctrines. 2 Private; confidential.

esp. especially.

ESP extrasensory perception.

es·pa·drille [es′pə·dril′] *n.* A sandal consisting of a flexible sole, usually made of rope, and uppers made of strips of fabric, leather, or other material.

es·pal·ier [i·spal′yər] 1 *n.* A tree or shrub trained to grow flat against a wall or trellis. 2 *n.* A structure for supporting such plants. 3 *v.* To train (a plant) to grow as an espalier.

es·pe·cial [is·pesh′əl] *adj.* Very special or particular: It is of *especial* importance. **—in especial** In particular; especially.

es·pe·cial·ly [is·pesh′əl·ē] *adv.* To a very special degree; particularly: an *especially* good pie.

Es·pe·ran·to [es′pə·rän′tō *or* es′pə·ran′tō] *n.* An artificial language based on various European languages.

es·pi·o·nage [es′pē·ə·nij′ *or* es′pē·ə·näzh′] *n.* 1 The act of spying. 2 The work of a spy, especially the attempt to learn the military or political secrets of other nations.

es·pla·nade [es′plə·näd′ *or* es′plə·nād′] *n.* An open, level area of grass or pavement used as a promenade or driveway, especially along the shore.

es·pou·sal [is·pou′zəl] *n.* 1 The taking up or support, as of a cause or idea. 2 An engagement to marry. 3 (*usually pl.*) A marriage ceremony.

es·pouse [is·pouz′] *v.* **es·poused, es·pous·ing** 1 To take up or back a cause or idea; support: to *espouse* civil rights. 2 To marry.

es·prit [is·prē′] *n.* Spirit; wit: a French word.

esprit de corps [is·prē′ də kôr′] A sense of pride in and devotion to a group to which one belongs: a French phrase.

es·py [is·pī′] *v.* **es·pied, es·py·ing** To catch sight of (something hidden or distant); see.

Esq. Esquire.

es·quire [es′kwīr′ *or* is·kwīr′] *n.* 1 (*written* **Esquire**) A polite title, more common in Great Britain than the U.S., sometimes used instead of "Mr." When written, it is abbreviated, and placed after the name: Lloyd Jones, *Esq.* 2 In England, a person ranking just below a knight. 3 An attendant to a knight.

-ess A suffix meaning: Female, as in *tigress.*

es·say 1 *n.* [es′ā] A short composition, in which the writer gives his or her own ideas on a single subject. 2 *n.* [es′ā *or* e·sā′] An attempt; endeavor. 3 *v.* [e·sā′] To attempt; try.

es·say·ist [es′ā·ist] *n.* A writer of essays.

es·sence [es′əns] *n.* 1 That which makes something what it is; basic quality: The *essence* of mercy is love. 2 A substance that has in concentrated form the special qualities, as of smell and taste, of the plant or drug from which it was taken: *essence* of peppermint. 3 A perfume.

es·sen·tial [i·sen′shəl] 1 *adj.* Of, having to do with, or forming a basis or foundation; basic: Learning to read is an *essential* part of education. 2 *adj.* Extremely important or necessary; vital: It is *essential* to keep alert while driving. 3 *n.* Something extremely important or basic: Good balance is an *essential* in bicycling. **—es·sen′tial·ly** *adv.*

essential oil An oil that contains in concentrated form the characteristic odor or taste of the plant from which it was obtained, used in perfumes and flavorings. ◆ *Essential* in this case is the adjectival form of *essence,* referring to a plant's essence. It does not have the usual sense of *necessary* or *basic.*

-est[1] A suffix meaning: Most, as in *softest.* It is used with many adjectives and adverbs for the superlative form.

-est[2] An ending once used for the present tense of verbs with "thou": "Thou *singest*" is the old form of "you sing."

est. 1 established. 2 estate. 3 estimate. 4 estimated.

EST or **E.S.T.** eastern standard time.

es·tab·lish [i·stab′lish] *v.* 1 To set up, found, or institute on a firm or lasting basis: to *establish* a government, colony, or business. 2 To put or settle permanently or securely, as in a particular place or business: to *establish* oneself as a lawyer.

3 To introduce and cause to last (as a law, custom, or habit). 4 To show to be true; prove: The lawyer sought to *establish* her client's innocence.

established church A church set up as the official church of a nation, and supported by the government.

es·tab·lish·ment [i·stab′lish·mənt] *n.* 1 The act of establishing. 2 A being established. 3 Something established, as a company, store, household, or church.

es·tate [is·tāt′] *n.* 1 A large piece of land, usually with a home on it. 2 Everything a person possesses, as money, land, or property. 3 A stage in life: to reach an adult's *estate* at 21 years.

es·teem [is·tēm′] 1 *v.* To have a high opinion of; value: We *esteem* bravery. 2 *n.* Respect; high regard: to be held in *esteem*. 3 *v.* To consider; deem: We *esteem* it an honor.

es·ter [es′tər] *n.* Any of a large group of organic compounds that are formed by the chemical union of an alcohol and a fatty acid.

Es·ther [es′tər] *n.* 1 In the Bible, the Jewish wife of a Persian king. She saved her people from being slaughtered. 2 A book of the Old Testament containing her story.

es·thete [es′thēt′] *n.* Another spelling of AESTHETE.

es·thet·ic [es·thet′ik] *adj.* Another spelling of AESTHETIC. **—es·thet′i·cal·ly** *adv.*

es·thet·ics [es·thet′iks] *n.pl.* Another spelling of AESTHETICS.

es·ti·ma·ble [es′tə·mə·bəl] *adj.* Worthy of respect and esteem: an *estimable* deed. **—es′ti·ma·ble·ness** *n.* **—es′ti·ma·bly** *adv.*

es·ti·mate [*v.* es′tə·māt′, *n.* es′tə·mit] *v.* **es·ti·mat·ed, es·ti·mat·ing,** *n.* 1 *v.* To make a close guess about (as size, number, or cost): He *estimates* the cost to be $20.00. 2 *n.* A general but careful guess, as about size, value, or cost. 3 *n.* A judgment or opinion.

es·ti·ma·tion [es′tə·mā′shən] *n.* 1 The act of estimating. 2 Opinion; judgment. 3 Esteem; regard.

Es·to·ni·an [es·tō′nē·ən] 1 *adj.* Of or from Estonia. 2 A person born or living in Estonia. 3 The language of Estonia.

es·trange [is·trānj′] *v.* **es·tranged, es·trang·ing** To make (someone once friendly) unfriendly or hostile. **—es·trange′ment** *n.*

es·tu·ar·y [es′cho͞o·er′ē] *n., pl.* **es·tu·ar·ies** 1 The broad meeting place of a river and sea, where the tide flows in. 2 An arm of the sea.

-et A suffix meaning: 1 Small, as in *islet.* 2 Group, as in *octet.*

e·ta [ā′tə *or* ē′tə] *n.* The seventh letter of the Greek alphabet.

ETA estimated time of arrival.

et al. and others. ◆ *Et al.* is an abbreviation of the Latin *et alii,* meaning *and the other people.*

etc. et cetera.

et cet·er·a [et set′ər·ə] And other things; and so on: a Latin phrase.

etch [ech] *v.* To engrave (a design) on a metal plate. The surface of the plate is coated with a substance, as wax, and the desired design is drawn on the wax with a sharp instrument. Acid is then used to eat into the parts of the metal not protected by the wax.

etch·ing [ech′ing] *n.* 1 A process of engraving a design, as on metal or glass. 2 A plate that is etched. 3 An etched design. 4 A print that is made from an etched plate.

ETD estimated time of departure.

e·ter·nal [i·tûr′nəl] *adj.* 1 Having no beginning or end; lasting forever. 2 Unchanging; always the same: *eternal* truths. 3 Seeming to last forever; continual: *eternal* bickering. **—e·ter′nal·ly** *adv.*

e·ter·ni·ty [i·tûr′nə·tē] *n., pl.* **e·ter·ni·ties** 1 All time, with no beginning or ending. 2 A seemingly endless period of time: It was an *eternity* before my pen pal answered my letter. 3 The unending time that follows death.

-eth[1] A suffix used after a vowel to form an ordinal number, as in *twentieth.*

E

-eth[2] A suffix once used in the third person singular for the present tense of some verbs. "He *goeth*" is an old-fashioned way of saying "He goes."

eth·a·nol [eth′ə·nôl′ *or* eth′ə·nōl′] Alcohol (def. 1).

e·ther [ē′thər] *n.* 1 A colorless liquid whose fumes, when inhaled, can make a person unconscious, as before an operation. 2 An elastic substance once believed to fill all space. 3 The upper, clear regions of the sky.

e·the·re·al [i·thir′ē·əl] *adj.* 1 Like air or ether; light; delicate: *ethereal* beauty. 2 Not belonging to earth; heavenly: *ethereal* spirits.

eth·i·cal [eth′i·kəl] *adj.* 1 Of or having to do with ethics and morality. 2 Conforming to certain rules of behavior. **—eth′i·cal·ly** *adv.*

eth·ics [eth′iks] *n.pl* 1 The study of right and wrong in human behavior. 2 Rules of right behavior, especially with reference to a particular profession or way of life. ◆ See -ICS.

E·thi·o·pi·an [ē′thē·ō′pē·ən] 1 *adj.* Of or from Ethiopia. 2 *n.* A person born in or living in Ethiopia.

eth·nic [eth′nik] 1 *adj.* Having to do with or belonging to a specific group of people who share a language or culture. 2 *adj.* Having to do with or belonging to a distinct cultural group within a larger society: The city had many *ethnic* neighborhoods where Italians, Irish, and other immigrants lived. 3 *n.* A member of an ethnic group.

eth·nol·o·gy [eth·nol′ə·jē] *n.* The science that deals with the racial and ethnic groups of human beings, their origins, characteristics, distribution, and cultures. **—eth·no·log·i·cal** [eth′nə·loj′ə·kəl] *adj.* **—eth·nol·o·gist** [eth·nol′ə·jist] *n.*

e·thol·o·gy [ē·thol′ə·jē] *n.* A branch of biology concerned with animal behavior. **—e·thol′o·gist** *n.*

eth·yl [eth′əl] *adj.* In chemistry, indicating the radical C_2H_5, found only as a part of some chemical compounds: *ethyl* ether.

ethyl alcohol Alcohol (def. 1).

eth·yl·ene gly·col [eth′ə·lēn′ glī′kol′] A thick, colorless alcohol used as an antifreeze.

et·i·quette [et′ə·kət] *n.* The rules established for behavior in polite society or in official or professional life.

E·ton [ē′t(ə)n] *n.* A boys' school in England.

a	add	**i**	it	**o͝o**	took	**oi**	oil
ā	ace	**ī**	ice	**o͞o**	pool	**ou**	pout
â	care	**o**	odd	**u**	up	**ng**	ring
ä	palm	**ō**	open	**û**	burn	**th**	thin
e	end	**ô**	order	**yo͞o**	fuse	**t͟h**	this
ē	equal					**zh**	vision

ə = { a in *above* e in *sicken* i in *possible*
o in *melon* u in *circus* }

E·trus·can [i·trus′kən] 1 *adj.* Of or from Etruria. 2 *n.* A person who was born or lived in Etruria. 3 *n.* The extinct language of Etruria.

Etruscan vase

-ette A suffix meaning: 1 Little; small, as in *kitchenette.* 2 Female, as in *drum majorette.* 3 Imitation, as in *leatherette.*

é·tude [ā′t(y)o͞od′] *n.* A piece of music, used for developing or showing off certain skills on an instrument.

et·y·mol·o·gist [et′ə·mol′ə·jist] *n.* A person who specializes in etymology.

et·y·mol·o·gy [et′ə·mol′ə·jē] *n., pl.* **et·y·mol·o·gies** 1 The history of a word, showing how the word developed into its present form and meaning. 2 The science that deals with the history of words. **—et·y·mo·log·i·cal** [et′ə·mə·loj′i·kəl] *adj.*

Eu The symbol for the element europium.

eu·ca·lyp·tus [yo͞o′kə·lip′təs] *n., pl.* **eu·ca·lyp·tus·es** or **eu·ca·lyp·ti** [yo͞o′kə·lip′tī] An evergreen tree, common in Australia, that is valuable for its oil and wood.

Eu·char·ist [yo͞o′kə·rist] *n.* 1 Another name for HOLY COMMUNION. 2 The consecrated bread and wine used in this. **—Eu′cha·ris′tic** *adj.*

Eu·clid·e·an [yo͞o·klid′ē·ən] *adj.* Of or based on Euclid's system of geometry.

eu·gen·ic [yo͞o·jen′ik] *adj.* 1 Favorable to the production of good offspring. 2 Having to do with eugenics. **—eu·gen′i·cal·ly** *adv.*

eu·gen·ics [yo͞o·jen′iks] *n.pl.* The science that deals with improving the human race through control of the factors influencing heredity, as by careful selection of parents. ◆ See -ICS.

eu·gle·na [yo͞o·glē′nə] *n.* A microscopic green organism with a flagellum at one end and a red eyespot, often found in fresh water.

eu·lo·gist [yo͞o′lə·jist] *n.* A person who eulogizes.

eu·lo·gize [yo͞o′lə·jīz′] *v.* **eu·lo·gized, eu·lo·giz·ing** To praise highly; extol.

eu·lo·gy [yo͞o′lə·jē] *n., pl.* **eu·lo·gies** A speech or writing in praise of a person or thing, especially when presented formally and in public. **—eu′lo·gis′tic** *adj.*

eu·nuch [yo͞o′nək] *n.* 1 A castrated man employed as an attendant in an Oriental harem. 2 Any castrated man or boy.

eu·pep·tic [yo͞o·pep′tik] *adj.* 1 Having good digestion. 2 Cheerful and happy.

eu·phe·mism [yo͞o′fə·miz′əm] *n.* 1 An inoffensive word or term used in place of another felt to be offensive: "The departed" is a *euphemism* for "the dead." 2 The use of such words or terms. **—eu′phe·mis′tic** *adj.* **—eu′phe·mis′ti·cal·ly** *adv.*

eu·pho·ni·ous [yo͞o·fō′nē·əs] *adj.* Having an agreeable sound; pleasant to the ear. **—eu·pho′ni·ous·ly** *adv.* **—eu·pho′ni·ous·ness** *n.*

eu·pho·ny [yo͞o′fə·nē] *n., pl.* **eu·pho·nies** Pleasant sound or combination of sounds.

eu·pho·ria [yo͞o·fôr′ē·ə] *n.* A strong feeling of happiness and well-being; elation. **—eu·phor′ic** *adj.*

Eur. 1 Europe. 2 European.

Eur·a·sian [yo͞o·rā′zhən] 1 *adj.* Of or from Eurasia. 2 *adj.* Of mixed European and Asian ancestry. 3 *n.* A person of mixed European and Asian ancestry.

EURATOM European Atomic Energy Community.

eu·re·ka [yo͞o·rē′kə] *interj.* I have found it!: a cry of joy upon making a discovery.

Eu·ro·pe·an [yo͞or′ə·pē′ən] 1 *adj.* Of or from Europe. 2 *n.* A person born or living in Europe.

European plan A method of reckoning hotel rates based on charges for the room and services but excluding meals. ◆ See AMERICAN PLAN.

eu·ro·pi·um [yo͞o·rō′pē·əm] *n.* A metallic element found in rare earths. It is one of the costliest and least abundant of the rare-earth elements. See RARE-EARTH ELEMENT.

Eu·sta·chi·an tube [yo͞o·stā′kē·ən *or* yo͞o·stā′shən] A narrow canal between the pharynx and middle ear, that helps make the air pressure equal on both sides of the eardrum.

eu·tha·na·sia [yo͞o′thə·nā′zhə] *n.* The merciful killing of a person or an animal suffering severely from a condition that cannot be cured or relieved.

eu·tro·phi·ca·tion [yo͞o′trə·fə·kā′shən] *n.* A natural or pollution-caused increase of dissolved nutrients in a lake, causing excessive plant growth and often also shortages of the free oxygen needed for animal life.

EVA extravehicular activity.

e·vac·u·ate [i·vak′yo͞o·āt′] *v.* **e·vac·u·at·ed, e·vac·u·at·ing** 1 To remove; withdraw: to *evacuate* troops from the besieged town. 2 To move out of; vacate: to *evacuate* a firetrap. 3 To remove the contents of; empty: to *evacuate* the stomach. **—e·vac′u·a′·tion** *n.*

e·vac·u·ee [i·vak′yo͞o·ē′] *n.* A person who has been evacuated from a place, especially because of dangerous conditions there.

e·vade [i·vād′] *v.* **e·vad·ed, e·vad·ing** To get or keep away from by tricks or cleverness; avoid; elude: to *evade* a bill collector.

e·val·u·ate [i·val′yo͞o·āt′] *v.* **e·val·u·at·ed, e·val·u·at·ing** To judge the value of; appraise: to *evaluate* a student's essay. **—e·val′u·a′tion** *n.*

ev·a·nesce [ev′ə·nes′] *v.* **ev·a·nesced, ev·a·nesc·ing** To melt away like mist; vanish quickly.

ev·a·nes·cence [ev′ə·nes′əns] *n.* The quality of quickly fading away; fleetingness.

ev·a·nes·cent [ev′ə·nes′ənt] *adj.* Soon passing away; not lasting; fleeting: Their anger was *evanescent.* **—ev′a·nes′cence** *n.*

e·van·gel·i·cal [ē′van·jel′i·kəl] *adj.* 1 Of, having to do with, or according to the New Testament, especially the four Gospels. 2 Of, related to, or holding the belief that the Bible is the most important rule of faith and that the soul is saved only through faith in Jesus. 3 Of, having to do with, or being a Protestant group holding this belief.

e·van·gel·ism [i·van′jə·liz′əm] *n.* Enthusiastic preaching or spreading of the gospel.

e·van·gel·ist [i·van′jə·list] *n.* 1 (*usually written* **Evangelist**) One of the four writers of the Gospels: Matthew, Mark, Luke, or John. 2 A person who preaches the gospel, especially a traveling preacher or minister. **—e·van′gel·is′tic** *adj.*

e·vap·o·rate [i·vap′ə·rāt′] *v.* **e·vap·o·rat·ed, e·vap·o·rat·ing** 1 To turn into vapor: Boiling *evaporates* water. 2 To remove moisture from: to *evaporate* fruit. 3 To give off vapor. 4 To vanish; disappear: My embarrassment *evaporated* in the friendly atmosphere. **—e·vap′o·ra′tion** *n.* **—e·vap′·o·ra′tor** *n.*

evaporated milk Milk, in cans, that has been made thick by removal of some of its water.

e·va·sion [i·vā′zhən] *n.* The act of evading, especially the avoiding of something unpleasant or difficult by cleverness or tricks.

e·va·sive [i·vā′siv] *adj.* Tending to evade; not direct or frank: an *evasive* reply. **—e·va′sive·ly** *adv.* **—e·va′sive·ness** *n.*

eve [ēv] *n.* 1 The evening or day before a holiday or festival: Chrstmas *Eve.* 2 The time just before some event: on the *eve* of the election. 3 Evening: used mostly in poems.

Eve [ēv] *n.* In the Bible, the first woman, Adam's wife. ◆ The name *Eve* comes from a Hebrew word meaning *life.*

e·ven[1] [ē′vən] 1 *adj.* Flat and smooth: an *even* sheet of ice. 2 *adj.* Steady; not changing: to hold an *even* speed. 3 *v.* To make or become even: to *even* up accounts; The road *evens* off here. 4 *adj.* The same, as in quantity, number, or measure; equal: *even* portions. 5 *adj.* On the same line or level: The speeding cars were *even.* 6 *adj.* Not easily excited; calm: an *even* disposition. 7 *adj.* Not owing or being owed anything: You owe me a dime and I owe you a dime, so we're *even.* 8 *adj.* Precise; exact: to walk an *even* mile. 9 *adv.* Precisely; exactly; just: Do *even* as I say. 10 *adj.* Exactly divisible by 2: 6, 8, and 10 are *even* numbers. 11 *adv.* Still: an *even* better plan. 12 *adv.* At the very same time; while: *Even* as they watched, the ship sank. 13 *adv.* Indeed; in fact: to feel glad, *even* delighted. 14 *adv.* Unlikely as it may seem: to be kind *even* to one's enemies. 15 *adv.* All the same; notwithstanding: *Even* on a limited budget, they served us delicious meals. **—even if** Although; notwithstanding. **—get even with** To get revenge upon. **—e′ven·ly** *adv.* **—e′ven·ness** *n.*

e·ven[2] [ē′vən] *n.* Evening: seldom used today.

e·ven·hand·ed [ē′vən·han′did] *adj.* Not favoring one side over another; impartial. **—e′ven·hand′ed·ly** *adv.* **—e′ven·hand′ed·ness** *n.*

eve·ning [ēv′ning] *n.* The end of the day and the first part of night, or the time from sunset until bedtime.

evening star A bright planet, as Venus, visible in the western sky just after sunset.

even·song [ē′vən·sông′] *n.* A service in some churches, said or sung in the evening.

e·vent [i·vent′] *n.* 1 A happening; occurrence, especially an important one: historical *events.* 2 One of the items that make up a sports program. 3 Final outcome; result. **—in any event** In any case; anyhow. **—in the event of** If there should be; in case of.

e·ven-tem·pered [ē′vən·tem′pərd] *adj.* Not easily angered, excited, or depressed; peaceful; calm.

e·vent·ful [i·vent′fəl] *adj.* 1 Full of events, usually important ones: an *eventful* day. 2 Having significant results; important: an *eventful* decision.

e·ven·tide [ē′vən·tīd′] *n.* Evening: used mostly in poems.

e·ven·tu·al [i·ven′chōō·əl] *adj.* Happening or resulting in the future: *eventual* victory.

e·ven·tu·al·i·ty [i·ven′chōō·al′ə·tē] *n., pl.* **e·ven·tu·al·i·ties** Something that may or may not take place; a possible occurrence.

e·ven·tu·al·ly [i·ven′chōō·əl·ē] *adv.* In the course of time; in the end; ultimately.

ev·er [ev′ər] *adv.* 1 At any time: Did you *ever* see it? 2 At all times; always: They remained *ever* on guard. ◆ *Ever* is often used in informal talk to make what is being said more forceful: How did you *ever* manage it? **—ever so** *informal* So very; extremely.

ev·er·glade [ev′ər·glād′] *n.* A swamp covered with tall grass.

ev·er·green [ev′ər·grēn′] 1 *adj.* Having leaves that stay green all through the year. 2 *n.* An evergreen tree or plant, as ivy.

ev·er·last·ing [ev′ər·las′ting] 1 *adj.* Lasting forever; eternal. 2 *adj.* Seeming to last forever; constant: *everlasting* chatter. 3 *n.* Eternity. **—the Everlasting** God.

ev·er·more [ev′ər·môr′] *adv.* Always: used mostly in poems. **—for evermore** Forever.

eve·ry [ev′rē] *adj.* 1 Each of all that form a group: *Every* guest is here now. 2 All that is possible; each possible: She had *every* chance to succeed. 3 Each: *every* tenth person; *every* four hours. **—every now and then** or **every so often** From time to time; occasionally. **—every other** Skipping one each time; as first, third, or fifth, in a series: They won *every other* game. **—every which way** 1 In every direction at once. 2 In an irregular manner; disorderly.

eve·ry·bod·y [ev′rē·bod′ē] *pron.* Every person; everyone.

eve·ry·day [ev′rē·dā′] *adj.* 1 Happening each day; daily. 2 Suitable for ordinary or common use: *everyday* clothes.

eve·ry·one [ev′rē·wun′] *pron.* Every person; everybody.

ev·ery·place [ev′rē·plās′] *adv.* *informal* Everywhere.

eve·ry·thing [ev′rē·thing′] *n.* 1 All things: to have *everything* one needs. 2 The only thing that matters: Tennis was *everything* to him.

eve·ry·where [ev′rē·(h)wâr′] *adv.* In or at all places; all about: The grass grew *everywhere.*

e·vict [i·vikt′] *v.* To make (a person) by law move out from a building or house: They were *evicted* for not having paid the rent. **—e·vic′tion** *n.*

ev·i·dence [ev′ə·dəns] *n., v.* **ev·i·denced, ev·i·denc·ing** 1 *n.* Something that proves what is true or not true or that provides reason or support for believing the truth or falsity of something: Good grades are usually *evidence* that one has studied. 2 *v.* To show clearly or unmistakably: Their laughter *evidenced* their joy. **—in evidence** Readily seen; in plain view.

ev·i·dent [ev′ə·dənt] *adj.* Easily seen or understood; apparent: an *evident* error.

ev·i·den·tial [ev′ə·den′shəl] *adj.* Of or constituting evidence.

a add	**i** it	**ŏŏ** took	**oi** oil
ā ace	**ī** ice	**ōō** pool	**ou** pout
â care	**o** odd	**u** up	**ng** ring
ä palm	**ō** open	**û** burn	**th** thin
e end	**ô** order	**yōō** fuse	**th** this
ē equal			**zh** vision

ə = a in *above*, e in *sicken*, i in *possible*, o in *melon*, u in *circus*

E

ev·i·dent·ly [ev′ə·dənt·lē *or* ev′ə·dent′lē] *adv.* So far as can be seen; apparently: *Evidently* the ballots are deposited here.
e·vil [ē′vəl] **1** *adj.* Bad; depraved; wicked: to say *evil* things. **2** *n.* Something that is wicked or bad. **3** *adj.* Causing pain or misfortune: *evil* times. **4** *n.* Anything that causes harm or suffering: Poverty is an *evil.* **—e′vil·ly** *adv.* **—e′vil·ness** *n.*
e·vil·do·er [ē′vəl·dōō′ər] *n.* A person who does evil.
e·vil-mind·ed [ē′vəl·mīn′did] *adj.* Having evil thoughts or ideas.
e·vince [i·vins′] *v.* **e·vinced, e·vinc·ing** To show clearly; make plain: The outcome of the election *evinced* the voters' preference.
e·vis·cer·ate [i·vis′ə·rāt′] *v.* **e·vis·cer·at·ed, e·vis·cer·at·ing** **1** To remove the intestines of; gut. **2** To remove the essential part of. **—e·vis′cer·a′tion** *n.*
e·vo·ca·tion [ev′ə·kā′shən] *n.* The act of evoking; summoning.
e·voc·a·tive [i·vok′ə·tiv] *adj.* Tending to call to mind certain ideas or memories: a scent *evocative* of spring flowers. **—e·voc′a·tive·ly** *adv.*
e·voke [i·vōk′] *v.* **e·voked, e·vok·ing** To bring forth; call up: This photograph *evokes* pleasant memories.
ev·o·lu·tion [ev′ə·lōō′shən] *n.* **1** The changes that take place in the gradual development of something: the *evolution* of the seed into a plant. **2** The theory that all living things developed from earlier, simpler forms, through changes that were passed through generations over long periods of time. **3** One of a series of movements, as in dancing. **—ev′o·lu′tion·ar′y** *adj.*
ev·o·lu·tion·ist [ev′ə·lōō′shə·nist] *n.* A person who believes in biological evolution.
e·volve [i·volv′] *v.* **e·volved, e·volv·ing** To work out; develop gradually: to *evolve* a new theory in psychology.
EVR electronic video recorder.
EW enlisted woman.
ewe [yōō] *n.* A female sheep.
ew·er [yōō′ər] *n.* A large water pitcher with a wide mouth.
ex-[1] A prefix meaning: **1** Out, as in *exit.* **2** Former, written with a hyphen, as in *ex-president.*
ex-[2] See EXO-.
ex. **1** examined. **2** example. **3** exchange. **4** executive. **5** extra.

Ewer

ex·ac·er·bate [ig·zas′ər·bāt′] *v.* **ex·ac·er·bat·ed, ex·ac·er·bat·ing** To make worse; aggravate: His answer *exacerbated* their anger. **—ex·ac′er·ba′tion** *n.*
ex·act [ig·zakt′] **1** *adj.* Completely accurate; precise: the *exact* amount necessary. **2** *v.* To insist upon and get: to *exact* obedience. **3** *adj.* Very strict and correct: to be *exact* about one's behavior. **—ex·act′ness** *n.*
ex·act·ing [ig·zak′ting] *adj.* **1** Strict; demanding a lot: an *exacting* teacher. **2** Requiring hard work and attention: an *exacting* profession.
ex·ac·tion [ig·zak′shən] *n.* **1** The exacting or requiring of something, especially by wrongful means. **2** Something required or exacted.
ex·act·i·tude [ig·zak′tə·t(y)ōōd′] *n.* Exactness.
ex·act·ly [ig·zakt′lē] *adv.* **1** In an exact manner; precisely: to cut a cake *exactly* in half. **2** Precisely right; just so.
ex·ag·ger·ate [ig·zaj′ə·rāt′] *v.* **ex·ag·ger·at·ed, ex·ag·ger·at·ing** **1** To make appear greater than is really true; overstate: to *exaggerate* one's own importance. **2** To make greater in size than is normal or expected: The actors *exaggerated* their eyebrows by blackening them heavily.
ex·ag·ger·a·tion [ig·zaj′ə·rā′shən] *n.* **1** The act of exaggerating. **2** The condition of being exaggerated. **3** Something, as a statement or story, that is exaggerated.
ex·alt [ig·zôlt′] *v.* **1** To praise or honor: to *exalt* the glory of one's nation. **2** To raise up in position, power, or honor. **3** To fill with delight or pride; elate: I was *exalted* by the singing. **—ex·al·ta·tion** [eg′zôl·tā′shən] *n.*
ex·alt·ed [ig·zôl′tid] *adj.* **1** High in position or rank. **2** Lofty or noble: an *exalted* ideal.
ex·am [ig·zam′] *n. informal* An examination.
ex·am·i·na·tion [ig·zam′ə·nā′shən] *n.* **1** The act of examining; careful inspection. **2** A formal test of what a person has learned or has the skill to do.
ex·am·ine [ig·zam′in] *v.* **ex·am·ined, ex·am·in·ing** **1** To look at with care and attention: to *examine* an injured leg; to *examine* fruit for spots. **2** To ask questions of in order to get information or to test a person's knowledge or skill. **—ex·am′in·er** *n.*
ex·am·ple [ig·zam′pəl] *n.* **1** Something used to show what others of the same kind or group are like; sample: an *example* of modern art. **2** A model or pattern deserving to be imitated: Parents should set a good *example* for their children. **3** A warning: Let this be an *example* to you. **4** A problem, as in arithmetic, that is to be worked out. **—for example** For instance.
ex·as·per·ate [ig·zas′pə·rāt′] *v.* **ex·as·per·at·ed, ex·as·per·at·ing** To annoy or irritate almost to the point of anger.
ex·as·per·a·tion [ig·zas′pə·rā′shən] *n.* **1** The feeling of being exasperated. **2** Something that exasperates.
exc. **1** excellent. **2** except. **3** exception.
Ex·cal·i·bur [eks·kal′ə·bər] *n.* In legend, the name of King Arthur's sword.
ex·ca·vate [eks′kə·vāt′] *v.* **ex·ca·vat·ed, ex·ca·vat·ing** **1** To make a hole or cavity in by digging: to *excavate* the side of a mountain. **2** To make by digging out: to *excavate* a tunnel. **3** To remove by digging or scooping out. **4** To uncover by digging: Archaeologists *excavate* ancient ruins.
ex·ca·va·tion [eks′kə·vā′shən] *n.* **1** The act or process of excavating. **2** A hole or hollow made by digging.
ex·ca·va·tor [eks′kə·vā′·tər] *n.* A person or a machine that excavates.
ex·ceed [ik·sēd′] *v.* **1** To be greater or better than: Crops *exceeded* estimates. **2** To go beyond the limits of: The task *exceeds* our abilities.
ex·ceed·ing [ik·sē′ding] **1** *adj.* Unusual; very great; extreme. **2** *adv.* Exceedingly: seldom used today.

An excavation

ex·ceed·ing·ly [ik·sē′ding·lē] *adv.* Extremely; very: The clerk is *exceedingly* busy.
ex·cel [ik·sel′] *v.* **ex·celled, ex·cel·ling** To be better than; surpass: Our club *excels* theirs in sports.

ex·cel·lence [ek′sə·ləns] *n.* Very high quality; great goodness or superiority.

ex·cel·len·cy [ek′sə·lən·sē] *n., pl.* **ex·cel·len·cies** 1 (*usually written* **Excellency**) A title of honor used when formally addressing or speaking of certain high officials, as governors, ambassadors, or bishops: Your *Excellency.* 2 Excellence.

ex·cel·lent [ek′sə·lənt] *adj.* Extremely good; superior. **—ex′cel·lent·ly** *adv.*

ex·cel·si·or [*n.* ik·sel′sē·ər, *interj.* ek·sel′sē·ôr] 1 *n.* Fine shavings of wood used for packing breakable goods, as dishes or glassware. 2 *interj.* (*usually written* **Excelsior**) Ever higher; upward: a Latin word used as a motto.

ex·cept [ik·sept′] 1 *prep.* With the exception of; leaving out; but: any color *except* blue. 2 *v.* To leave out; exclude: Medicines are *excepted* from the tax. 3 *conj.* Only; but: I would write *except* I have no paper. ◆ *Except* and *accept* are often confused. Though they have the same root, from a Latin verb meaning *to take,* the prefixes are different. Latin *ex-* means *out,* and Latin *ac-* (or *ad-*) means *to. Except* is often a preposition meaning *taking out* or *leaving out,* less often a verb meaning *to take out. Accept* is a verb meaning *to take to oneself,* or *receive.*

ex·cept·ing [ik·sep′ting] *prep.* Except.

ex·cep·tion [ik·sep′shən] *n.* 1 A leaving out; exclusion: With the *exception* of the recording secretary, everyone was at the meeting. 2 A person or thing that is different in some way from others of its class; an instance that does not fit the general rule: Auks, not able to fly, are *exceptions* among sea birds. 3 An objection or complaint: a statement open to *exception.* **—take exception** To feel angry or resentful; object.

ex·cep·tion·a·ble [ik·sep′shə·nə·bəl] *adj.* Deserving opposition or complaint; objectionable.

ex·cep·tion·al [ik·sep′shən·əl] *adj.* Not ordinary; unusual. **—ex·cep′tion·al·ly** *adv.*

ex·cerpt [*n.* ek′sûrpt, *v.* ik·sûrpt′] 1 *n.* A passage or section taken from a piece of writing: They acted out *excerpts* from several plays. 2 *v.* To pick out and quote (as a passage from a book).

ex·cess [*n.* ik·ses′ *or* ek′ses, *adj.* ek′ses] 1 *n.* An amount or degree of something over what is needed, wanted, used, or proper: an *excess* of rain; an *excess* of emotion. 2 *adj.* Over the usual, allowed, or necessary amount; extra: *excess* baggage. 3 *n.* The amount by which one thing is more than another: The *excess* of 25 over 13 is 12. **—in excess of** Over; above: weight *in excess of* five pounds. **—to excess** More than is proper: Don't eat *to excess.*

ex·ces·sive [ik·ses′iv] *adj.* Too great or too much: It took an *excessive* amount of time. **—ex·ces′sive·ly** *adv.*

ex·change [iks·chānj′] *v.* **ex·changed, ex·chang·ing,** *n.* 1 *v.* To give and receive in return; interchange: to *exchange* gifts. 2 *n.* The act of giving and receiving in return: an *exchange* of compliments. 3 *v.* To give one thing for something else; trade; swap: to *exchange* a red shirt for a blue one. 4 *n.* A trade or substitution: What will you give me in *exchange* for this marble? 5 *n.* A place where people, as brokers or merchants, buy, sell, or trade: a stock *exchange.* 6 *n.* A central office in a telephone system. **—ex·change′a·bil′i·ty** *n.* **—ex·change′a·ble** *adj.*

ex·cheq·uer [eks′chek·ər *or* iks·chek′ər] *n.* 1 The treasury, as of a state or nation. 2 (*written* **Exchequer**) The department of the British government that has charge of all public revenue and finance. 3 *informal* The amount of money a person has for everyday use.

ex·cise[1] [ek′sīz *or* ik·sīz′] *n.* A tax within a country on the production, sale, or use of certain goods, such as tobacco.

ex·cise[2] [ik·sīz′] *v.* **ex·cised, ex·cis·ing** To remove by or as if by cutting out or off: to *excise* a tumor. **—ex·ci·sion** [ik·sizh′ən] *n.*

ex·cit·a·ble [ik·sī′tə·bəl] *adj.* Easily excited: An *excitable* horse may be dangerous. **—ex·cit′a·bil′i·ty** *n.* **—ex·cit′a·bly** *adv.*

ex·cite [ik·sīt′] *v.* **ex·cit·ed, ex·cit·ing** 1 To stir up strong or lively feelings in: The fireworks *excited* them. 2 To stir up (as a feeling or reaction); arouse: That story *excited* our interest. 3 To arouse to activity or motion: The loud noise *excited* the horse.

ex·cit·ed [ik·sī′tid] *adj.* Full of strong or lively feelings; stirred up; aroused: I'm so *excited* about the trip! **—ex·cit′ed·ly** *adv.*

ex·cite·ment [ik·sīt′mənt] *n.* 1 The condition of being excited: to be full of *excitement.* 2 The act of exciting. 3 Something that excites.

ex·cit·ing [ik·sī′ting] *adj.* Causing excitement; thrilling: an *exciting* movie.

ex·claim [iks·klām′] *v.* To cry out suddenly or speak with force, as in surprise or anger: "The supper's burning!" we *exclaimed.*

ex·cla·ma·tion [eks′klə·mā′shən] *n.* 1 The act of exclaiming. 2 A word or words cried out suddenly or said with force.

exclamation point or **exclamation mark** A punctuation mark (!) used to show that the word, phrase, or sentence which it follows is an exclamation.

ex·clam·a·to·ry [iks·klam′ə·tôr′ē] *adj.* Expressing, using, containing, or having to do with exclamation: an *exclamatory* phrase.

ex·clude [iks·klo͞od′] *v.* **ex·clud·ed, ex·clud·ing** 1 To keep out or shut out: heavy draperies to *exclude* the glare of the sun. 2 To bar, as from inclusion, participation, or consideration: Don't *exclude* the possibility of coming back.

ex·clu·sion [iks·klo͞o′zhən] *n.* 1 An act or instance of excluding. 2 The condition of being excluded: *Exclusion* from a group can cause hurt feelings.

ex·clu·sive [iks·klo͞o′siv] *adj.* 1 Very particular about admitting or including people, as friends or members: an *exclusive* club. 2 Not shared with any other; belonging to only one: That magazine has *exclusive* rights to the story. 3 Complete and undivided: my *exclusive* attention. 4 Excluding all others: Work is their *exclusive* concern. **—exclusive of** Not including: The price *exclusive of* tax is $2.00. **—ex·clu′sive·ly** *adv.* **—ex·clu′sive·ness** *n.*

a	add	**i**	it	**o͝o**	took	**oi**	oil
ā	ace	**ī**	ice	**o͞o**	pool	**ou**	pout
â	care	**o**	odd	**u**	up	**ng**	ring
ä	palm	**ō**	open	**û**	burn	**th**	thin
e	end	**ô**	order	**yo͞o**	fuse	**th**	this
ē	equal					**zh**	vision

ə = {a in *above* e in *sicken* i in *possible* / o in *melon* u in *circus*}

ex·com·mu·ni·cate [*v.* eks′kə·myōō′nə·kāt′; *n., adj.* eks′kə·myōō′ni·kət] *v.* **ex·com·mu·ni·cat·ed, ex·com·mu·ni·cat·ing,** *n., adj.* 1 *v.* To expel officially from membership in a church; cut off from the sacraments of a church. 2 *v.* To deprive of membership or participation in a community or group. 3 *n.* A person who has been excommunicated. 4 *adj.* Excommunicated. **—ex′com·mu′ni·ca′tion** *n.*

ex·co·ri·ate [iks·kôr′ē·āt′] *v.* **ex·co·ri·at·ed, ex·co·ri·at·ing** 1 To remove skin from, as by rubbing. 2 To blame or criticize harshly. **—ex·co′ri·a′tion** *n.*

ex·cre·ment [eks′krə·mənt] *n.* Waste matter eliminated from the body, especially solid waste matter.

ex·cres·cence [iks·kres′əns] *n.* An unnatural growth, as a wart or corn.

ex·crete [iks·krēt′] *v.* **ex·cret·ed, ex·cret·ing** To throw off or eliminate (waste matter) from the body: to *excrete* sweat.

ex·cre·tion [iks·krē′shən] *n.* 1 Elimination of waste matter, as from the body. 2 Waste matter eliminated, as sweat and urine.

ex·cre·to·ry [eks′krə·tôr′ē] *adj.* Of, having to do with, or adapted for excreting: an *excretory* organ.

ex·cru·ci·at·ing [iks·krōō′shē·ā′ting] *adj.* 1 Causing great pain or anguish. 2 Of great intensity; extreme. **—ex·cru′ci·at′ing·ly** *adv.*

ex·cul·pate [eks′kəl·pāt′] *v.* **ex·cul·pat·ed, ex·cul·pat·ing** To free of blame or suspicion; show to be innocent. **—ex′cul·pa′tion** *n.*

ex·cur·sion [ik·skûr′zhən] *n.* 1 A short pleasure trip or outing. 2 A short trip, as on a boat or train, at reduced prices. 3 *adj. use:* an *excursion* boat.

ex·cus·a·ble [ik·skyōō′zə·bəl] *adj.* That can be excused; pardonable: an *excusable* error.

ex·cuse [*v.* ik·skyōōz′, *n.* ik·skyōōs′] *v.* **ex·cused, ex·cus·ing,** *n.* 1 *v.* To pardon or forgive: *Excuse* me, would you let me by? 2 *v.* To offer an apology for (oneself): I *excused* myself for being late. 3 *v.* To understand and overlook: to *excuse* a mistake. 4 *v.* To serve as a reason for; explain: Nothing can *excuse* such rude behavior. 5 *n.* A reason given to explain or justify: What is your *excuse* for this mistake? 6 *v.* To free from some duty or obligation: to *excuse* a sick pupil from homework. 7 *n.* A note or statement explaining an absence or freeing someone from a duty: The student brought an *excuse* from home. 8 *v.* To allow to leave: She asked to be *excused* from the room.

ex·e·cra·ble [ek′sə·krə·bəl] *adj.* 1 Extremely wicked; hateful: an *execrable* crime. 2 Extremely bad or poor: an *execrable* speller. **—ex′e·cra·ble·ness** *n.* **—ex′e·cra·bly** *adv.*

ex·e·crate [ek′sə·krāt′] *v.* **ex·e·crat·ed, ex·e·crat·ing** 1 To hate; detest; abominate. 2 To curse; denounce.

ex·e·cra·tion [ek′sə·krā′shən] *n.* 1 The act of cursing or denouncing. 2 A curse. 3 A person or thing that is cursed or hated.

ex·e·cute [ek′sə·kyōōt′] *v.* **ex·e·cut·ed, ex·e·cut·ing** 1 To follow or carry out; do: to *execute* an order. 2 To put into force or effect; administer: to *execute* a law. 3 To put to death by legal order: to *execute* a condemned criminal. 4 To produce, following a plan or design: to *execute* a portrait. 5 To make (as a will or deed) legal by signing and meeting other requirements.

ex·e·cu·tion [ek′sə·kyōō′shən] *n.* 1 The act of doing or carrying out something: the *execution* of plans. 2 The act of putting to death as legally ordered. 3 The manner in which something is done or performed: Their *execution* of the dance was wonderful. 4 The act of making something legal: the *execution* of a will.

ex·e·cu·tion·er [ek′sə·kyōō′shən·ər] *n.* A person who puts to death those sentenced to die.

ex·ec·u·tive [ig·zek′yə·tiv] 1 *n.* One of the persons responsible for directing and managing a business or institution. 2 *adj.* Of, for, or having to do with an executive: an *executive* decision. 3 *n.* A person or group responsible for directing a government and putting its laws into effect. 4 *adj.* Having the authority and the duty of managing the affairs of a nation and of putting its laws into effect.

ex·ec·u·tor [ig·zek′yə·tər] *n.* Someone appointed to carry out the directions of another person's will after that person has died.

ex·em·plar [ig·zem′plär′ *or* ig·zem′plər] *n.* An ideal example or model.

ex·em·pla·ry [ig·zem′plər·ē] *adj.* 1 Deserving to be imitated; model: an *exemplary* career. 2 Serving as a warning: *exemplary* discipline. 3 Serving as a typical example.

ex·em·pli·fi·ca·tion [ig·zem′plə·fi·kā′shən] *n.* 1 An example or illustration. 2 The act of exemplifying.

ex·em·pli·fy [ig·zem′plə·fī] *v.* **ex·em·pli·fied, ex·em·pli·fy·ing** To show by example; illustrate: This article *exemplifies* the writer's style.

ex·empt [ig·zempt′] 1 *v.* To free or excuse, as from a duty or obligation: Teachers are usually *exempted* from jury duty. 2 *adj.* Freed or excused, as from a duty or obligation: bonds *exempt* from taxes.

ex·emp·tion [ig·zemp′shən] *n.* 1 The act of exempting. 2 The condition of being exempted. 3 A portion of a person's income that is not taxed. 4 Someone claimed as a dependent.

ex·er·cise [ek′sər·sīz′] *v.* **ex·er·cised, ex·er·cis·ing,** *n.* 1 *v.* To develop or train by active use or repeated movement: Running *exercises* the legs. 2 *n.* Active movement of the body to improve health or strength. 3 *n.* (*usually pl.*) A series, as of movements or problems, that gives training, skill, or strength: to play *exercises* on the piano; arithmetic *exercises.* 4 *v.* To use; employ: to *exercise* a right; to *exercise* patience. 5 *n.* The act of using: the *exercise* of authority. 6 *n.* (*usually pl.*) A ceremony or program: A song opened the *exercises.* ◆ See PRACTICE.

Exercise

ex·ert [ig·zûrt′] *v.* To put forth or use: to *exert* one's influence. **—exert oneself** To put forth effort; try hard.

ex·er·tion [ig·zûr′shən] *n.* 1 Active use or employment: the *exertion* of will power. 2 Great effort: The *exertions* of the UN stopped the war.

ex·ha·la·tion [eks′hə·lā′shən] *n.* 1 Something exhaled; a vapor or an odor. 2 The process of breathing out.

ex·hale [eks·hāl′] *v.* **ex·haled, ex·hal·ing** 1 To breathe out. 2 To give off, as air, vapor, or an odor: The woods *exhaled* a musty odor.

ex·haust [ig·zôst′] 1 *v.* To make extremely tired: to *exhaust* oneself. 2 *v.* To use up entirely: We *exhausted* our supply of wood. 3 *v.* To draw off; empty: to *exhaust* the air from a jar. 4 *n.* The escape of waste gases or fumes from an engine, or the waste gases or fumes that escape. 5 *n.* In an engine, a pipe or opening through which waste gases or fumes escape. 6 *v.* To study, treat, or discuss thoroughly and completely. **—ex·haust′er** *n.* **—ex·haust′i·bil′i·ty** *n.* **—ex·haust′i·ble** *adj.*

Exhaust from a car

ex·haus·tion [ig·zôs′chən] *n.* 1 Extreme weariness or fatigue. 2 The act of exhausting. 3 The condition of being exhausted.

ex·haus·tive [ig·zôs′tiv] *adj.* Thoroughly covering all details or possibilities; complete: an *exhaustive* study. **—ex·haus′tive·ly** *adv.*

ex·haust·less [ig·zôst′lis] *adj.* Inexhaustible.

ex·hib·it [ig·zib′it] 1 *v.* To display or show publicly; put on view: to *exhibit* art. 2 *n.* A public showing; display. 3 *n.* A thing or things put on display: Their *exhibit* was a 1908 car. 4 *v.* To show signs of; reveal: to *exhibit* patience. 5 *n.* Something submitted as evidence in a court of law.

Outdoor art exhibit

ex·hib·it·er [ig·zib′ə·tər] *n.* Another spelling of EXHIBITOR.

ex·hi·bi·tion [ek′sə·bish′·ən] *n.* 1 An open showing; display: an *exhibition* of bad temper. 2 A public display, as of art. 3 Something displayed; exhibit.

ex·hi·bi·tion·ism [ek′sə·bish′ə·niz′əm] *n.* An effort or tendency to make oneself the center of attention. **—ex′hi·bi′tion·ist** *n., adj.*

ex·hib·i·tor [ig·zib′ə·tər] *n.* A person or group that exhibits: an *exhibitor* of motion pictures.

ex·hil·a·rate [ig·zil′ə·rāt′] *v.* **ex·hil·a·rat·ed, ex·hil·a·rat·ing** To fill with happiness or high spirits; stimulate.

ex·hil·a·ra·tion [ig·zil′ə·rā′shən] *n.* 1 High spirits; the feeling of being exhilarated. 2 The process of exhilarating.

ex·hort [ig·zôrt′] *v.* To advise or urge earnestly: to *exhort* a team to play better.

ex·hor·ta·tion [eg′zôr·tā′shən *or* ek′sôr·tā′shən] *n.* A very earnest plea or request: The principal's talk was an *exhortation* to do better.

ex·hor·ta·tive [ig·zôr′tə·tiv] *adj.* Earnestly pleading.

ex·hume [ig·zyōōm′ *or* iks·hyōōm′] *v.* **ex·humed, ex·hum·ing** 1 To dig up from a grave. 2 To bring to light; reveal. **—ex′hum·a′tion** *n.*

ex·i·gen·cy [ek′sə·jən·sē] *n., pl.* **ex·i·gen·cies** 1 A situation requiring immediate action; emergency. 2 (*usually pl.*) An urgent need or demand: The *exigencies* of feeding their young took all the birds' attention.

ex·i·gent [ek′sə·jənt] *adj.* 1 Demanding immediate aid or action; urgent: an *exigent* situation. 2 Hard to satisfy or meet: *exigent* demands.

ex·ile [eg′zīl *or* ek′sīl] *v.* **ex·iled, ex·il·ing,** *n.* 1 *v.* To send (someone) away from his or her native land and forbid a return; banish. 2 *n.* A person who is exiled. 3 *n.* The condition of an exile: to be driven into *exile.*

ex·ist [ig·zist′] *v.* 1 To have actual being or reality; be: Dinosaurs once *existed.* 2 To continue to live: People can't *exist* without oxygen. 3 To be present; be found: Does life *exist* on Mars?

ex·is·tence [ig·zis′təns] *n.* 1 The fact or condition of being. 2 Life: a fight for *existence.* 3 Manner of living: a lonely *existence.* 4 Presence; occurrence: the *existence* of life on Mars.

ex·is·tent [ig·zis′tənt] *adj.* 1 Having existence. 2 Now existing; present.

ex·it [eg′zit *or* ek′sit] *n.* 1 A way out, as a door or passage: Leave by the nearest *exit.* 2 A departure, especially the departure of an actor from the stage.

ex li·bris [eks lē′brəs] A Latin expression for "from the books," used on a bookplate before the owner's name.

exo- A combining form meaning: Outer; outside, as in *exoskeleton.*

ex·o·bi·ol·o·gy [ek′sō·bī·ol′ə·jē] *n.* A branch of biology concerned with extraterrestrial life. **—ex′o·bi·ol′o·gist** *n.*

ex·o·crine [ek′sə·krin *or* ek′sə·krēn′] *adj.* Producing secretions that are sent directly to a specific area of the body, usually through a duct.

ex·o·dus [ek′sə·dəs] *n.* 1 A departure or going away: a mass *exodus* from the flooded city. 2 (*written* **Exodus**) The second book of the Old Testament, describing the departure of Moses and the Israelites from Egypt. **—the Exodus** This departure.

ex of·fi·ci·o [eks ə·fish′ē·ō] Because of one's office or position: a Latin term: The mayor is, *ex officio,* on the committee.

ex·og·e·nous [ek·soj′ə·nəs] *adj.* 1 Originating from an exterior source: The doctor prescribed injections of an *exogenous* hormone. 2 Growing on or from the outside. **—ex·og′e·nous·ly** *adv.*

ex·on·er·ate [ig·zon′ə·rāt′] *v.* **ex·on·er·at·ed, ex·on·er·at·ing** To free from blame; find innocent: Witnesses *exonerated* the driver. **—ex·on′er·a′tion** *n.*

ex·or·bi·tance [ig·zôr′bə·təns] *n.* The quality of being exorbitant.

ex·or·bi·tant [ig·zôr′bə·tənt] *adj.* Much greater than is usual or proper; unreasonably excessive: *exorbitant* prices; *exorbitant* demands.

ex·or·cise [ek′sôr·sīz′] *v.* **ex·or·cised, ex·or·cis·ing** 1 To get rid of (an evil spirit) by religious or magical rites. 2 To rid (as a person or place) of an evil spirit.

ex·or·cism [ek′sôr·siz′əm] *n.* 1 The expulsion of an evil spirit from a person or place. 2 A formula used in exorcising. **—ex′or·cist** *n.*

a	add	**i**	it	**ŏŏ**	took	**oi**	oil
ā	ace	**ī**	ice	**ōō**	pool	**ou**	pout
â	care	**o**	odd	**u**	up	**ng**	ring
ä	palm	**ō**	open	**û**	burn	**th**	thin
e	end	**ô**	order	**yōō**	fuse	**th̸**	this
ē	equal					**zh**	vision

ə = { a in *above* e in *sicken* i in *possible*; o in *melon* u in *circus* }

ex·o·skel·e·ton [ek′sō·skel′ə·tən] *n.* The tough, stiff covering of chitin surrounding and supporting the soft tissues of insects and certain other invertebrate animals.

ex·o·sphere [ek′sō·sfir′] *n.* The outer part of the atmosphere of the earth or another celestial body. **—ex′o·spher′ic** *adj.*

ex·o·ther·mic [ek′sō·thûr′mik] *adj.* Producing heat: Combustion is an *exothermic* process.

ex·ot·ic [ig·zot′ik] **1** *adj.* Belonging to or growing in another part of the world; foreign: an *exotic* fruit. **2** *adj.* Strangely different and fascinating: an *exotic* custom. **3** *n.* Anything exotic. **—ex·ot′i·cal·ly** *adv.*

ex·pand [ik·spand′] *v.* **1** To make or become larger: Heat makes air *expand.* **2** To spread out by unfolding: The eagle *expanded* its wings. **3** To make longer or more complete: to *expand* a speech.

ex·panse [ik·spans′] *n.* A wide and open area or space: a blue *expanse* of sky.

ex·pan·si·ble [ik·span′sə·bəl] *adj.* Capable of being expanded. **—ex·pan·si·bil·i·ty** [ik·span′sə·bil′ə·tē] *n.*

ex·pan·sion [ik·span′shən] *n.* **1** The act of expanding: *expansion* due to heat. **2** An expanded condition. **3** Something, as a part or surface, that results from expanding.

ex·pan·sive [ik·span′siv] *adj.* **1** Able or tending to expand: Air is *expansive.* **2** Wide; broad; extensive: an *expansive* view. **3** Very friendly and outgoing: an *expansive* personality. **—ex·pan′sive·ly** *adj.* **—ex·pan′sive·ness** *n.*

ex·pa·ti·ate [ik·spā′shē·āt′] *v.* **ex·pa·ti·at·ed, ex·pa·ti·at·ing** To speak or write at length; hold forth: to *expatiate* upon a topic.

ex·pa·tri·ate [*v.* eks·pā′trē·āt′, *n.* eks·pā′trē·it] *v.* **ex·pa·tri·at·ed, ex·pa·tri·at·ing,** *n.* **1** *v.* To drive (a person) from his or her native land; exile. **2** *v.* To withdraw (oneself) from one's native land to live in another country. **3** *n.* An expatriated person. **—ex·pa′tri·a′tion** *n.*

ex·pect [ik·spekt′] *v.* **1** To be sure or almost sure of the coming or happening of: We *expect* them tonight. **2** To look for as right, proper, or necessary; require: Our teacher *expects* the best from us. **3** *informal* To suppose; imagine: I *expect* so.

ex·pec·tan·cy [ik·spek′tən·sē] *n., pl.* **ex·pec·tan·cies** Expectation.

ex·pec·tant [ik·spek′tənt] *adj.* Feeling or showing expectation; looking forward to something: an *expectant* look. **—ex·pec′tant·ly** *adv.*

ex·pec·ta·tion [ek′spek·tā′shən] *n.* **1** A looking forward to something; anticipation: to wait in *expectation.* **2** Something expected. **3** (*often pl.*) A reason or ground for expecting something.

ex·pec·to·rate [ik·spek′tə·rāt′] *v.* **ex·pec·to·rat·ed, ex·pec·to·rat·ing** To spit. **—ex·pec′to·ra′tion** *n.*

ex·pe·di·ence [ik·spē′dē·əns] *n.* Expediency.

ex·pe·di·en·cy [ik·spē′dē·ən·sē] *n., pl.* **ex·pe·di·en·cies** **1** The usefulness or suitability of an action or plan: the *expediency* of returning to port before a storm. **2** Selfishness or self-interest in one's thoughts, actions, or plans: The politician was guided only by *expediency.*

ex·pe·di·ent [ik·spē′dē·ənt] **1** *adj.* Helpful; useful; suitable: It is *expedient* to be early. **2** *n.* A way of doing or achieving something: We tried various *expedients* before one worked. **3** *adj.* Selfish or easy rather than right or proper: purely *expedient* plans. **—ex·pe′di·ent·ly** *adv.*

ex·pe·dite [ek′spə·dīt′] *v.* **ex·pe·dit·ed, ex·pe·dit·ing** To make go faster or more easily; speed up: Please *expedite* this order.

ex·pe·dit·er or **ex·pe·dit·or** [ek′spə·dī′tər] *n.* A person in charge of eliminating obstacles and delays in a service or process.

ex·pe·di·tion [ek′spə·dish′ən] *n.* **1** A journey, march, or voyage made for a definite purpose: a scientific *expedition.* **2** The group of people making such a journey, or their ships or planes. **3** Speed: with great *expedition.*

ex·pe·di·tion·ar·y [ek′spə·dish′ən·er′ē] *adj.* Of, for, or going on an expedition: *expeditionary* forces sent abroad to fight.

ex·pe·di·tious [ek′spə·dish′əs] *adj.* Quick and efficient; prompt: *expeditious* handling of a complaint. **—ex′pe·di′tious·ly** *adv.* **—ex′pe·di′tious·ness** *n.*

ex·pel [ik·spel′] *v.* **ex·pelled, ex·pel·ling** **1** To drive out or force out: to *expel* air from the lungs. **2** To put out permanently; dismiss: to *expel* a student from school.

ex·pend [ik·spend′] *v.* To use up; spend.

ex·pend·a·ble [ik·spen′də·bəl] *adj.* **1** Available for spending: *expendable* funds. **2** Worth giving up or losing to gain some end or military objective: *expendable* equipment.

ex·pen·di·ture [ik·spen′də·chər] *n.* **1** The act of spending or using up: *expenditure* of energy. **2** The amount spent or used.

ex·pense [ik·spens′] *n.* **1** Cost; price: at the *expense* of a phone call. **2** (*pl.*) Money needed or spent to cover costs or charges: traveling *expenses.* **3** A cause or reason for spending: A car is an *expense.* **4** Loss, cost, or sacrifice: at the *expense* of one's health.

expense account A record of an employee's expenses, to be turned in with a claim for repayment.

ex·pen·sive [ik·spen′siv] *adj.* Costing a great deal; costly: an *expensive* purchase; an *expensive* mistake. **—ex·pen′sive·ly** *adv.* **—ex·pen′sive·ness** *n.*

ex·pe·ri·ence [ik·spir′ē·əns] *n., v.* **ex·pe·ri·enced, ex·pe·ri·enc·ing** **1** *n.* The actual doing or undergoing of something: to learn from *experience.* **2** *n.* Something one has actually done or gone through: Our trip was a most unusual *experience.* **3** *n.* Knowledge or skill gained by doing or undergoing something: This job requires no previous *experience.* **4** *v.* To feel or undergo: to *experience* fear.

ex·pe·ri·enced [ik·spir′ē·ənst] *adj.* **1** Having had experience: an *experienced* worker. **2** Skilled or able through experience: an *experienced* guide.

ex·per·i·ment [*n.* ik·sper′ə·mənt, *v.* ik·sper′ə·ment′] **1** *n.* Any test or trial that one makes in order to gain knowledge or try out a theory: a chemical *experiment.* **2** *v.* To make experiments: to *experiment* with the equipment. **—ex·per′i·ment′er** *n.*

ex·per·i·men·tal [ik·sper′ə·men′təl] *adj.* **1** Having to do with, based on, or using experiment: an *experimental* vaccine. **2** Like an experiment; early; tentative: His first attempts were *experimental.* **—ex·per′i·men′tal·ly** *adv.*

ex·per·i·men·ta·tion [ik·sper′ə·men·tā′shən] *n.* The act or practice of experimenting: to learn through *experimentation.*

ex·pert [*n.* ek′spûrt, *adj.* ek′spûrt *or* ik·spûrt′] **1** *n.* A person who has special skill or knowledge in a certain field: an *expert* in chemistry. **2** *adj.* Highly skillful: an *expert* skater. **3** *adj.* Of or done by an expert: *expert* cooking. **—ex′pert·ly** *adv.* **—ex′pert·ness** *n.*

ex·per·tise [ek′spər·tēz′] *n.* The special skill or knowledge of an expert; know-how.

ex·pi·a·ble [ek′spē·ə·bəl] *adj.* Capable of being expiated.

ex·pi·ate [ek′spē·āt′] *v.* **ex·pi·at·ed, ex·pi·at·ing** To make up for (as a sin, offense, or failure); atone for. **—ex′pi·a′tor** *n.*

ex·pi·a·tion [ek′spē·ā′shən] *n.* The act of expiating or the condition of being expiated; atonement.

ex·pi·ra·tion [ek′spə·rā′shən] *n.* **1** The running out of something; ending: the *expiration* of a license. **2** The breathing out of air from the lungs.

ex·pire [ik·spīr′] *v.* **ex·pired, ex·pir·ing** **1** To end its term; run out: When does your driver's license *expire*? **2** To die. **3** To breathe out; exhale.

ex·plain [ik·splān′] *v.* **1** To make plain or understandable: The teacher *explained* the problem to us. **2** To give the meaning of; interpret: to *explain* a poem. **3** To give reasons for: *Explain* your conduct.

ex·pla·na·tion [ek′splə·nā′shən] *n.* **1** The act or process of explaining something: Is an *explanation* needed? **2** A reason that explains: A slow leak is the *explanation* of the flat tire.

ex·plan·a·to·ry [ik·splan′ə·tôr′ē] *adj.* That explains: a brief, *explanatory* statement.

ex·ple·tive [eks′plə·tiv] **1** *n.* An exclamation or an oath. *Gee!* and *Darn!* are expletives. **2** *n.* A word having no particular meaning of its own used to fill out the pattern of a clause. *It* in "It is cold today," and *there* in "Upstairs there are five rooms" are expletives.

ex·pli·ca·ble [ik·splik′ə·bəl *or* eks′pli·kə·bəl] *adj.* Capable of being explained. **—ex·pli′ca·bly** *adv.*

ex·pli·cate [ek′spli·kāt′] *v.* **ex·pli·cat·ed, ex·pli·cat·ing** To explain clearly and in detail. **—ex′pli·ca′·tion** *n.*

ex·plic·it [ik·splis′it] *adj.* Clearly and plainly expressed; definite: I was given *explicit* orders not to go out. **—ex·plic′it·ly** *adv.* **—ex·plic′it·ness** *n.*

ex·plode [ik·splōd′] *v.* **ex·plod·ed, ex·plod·ing** **1** To burst or cause to burst violently and with noise: to watch fireworks *explode;* to *explode* a bomb. **2** To prove completely wrong: The experiment *exploded* the existing theory. **3** To burst out suddenly: to *explode* with laughter.

ex·ploit [*n.* eks′ploit, *v.* ik·sploit′] **1** *n.* A brave or daring act: the *exploits* of Robin Hood. **2** *v.* To make good use of: to *exploit* a coal mine. **3** *v.* To use selfishly or unfairly: Have the natural resources of this area been *exploited*?

ex·ploi·ta·tion [eks′ploi·tā′shən] *n.* **1** A using or utilizing. **2** Improper or selfish use.

ex·plo·ra·tion [eks′plə·rā′shən] *n.* **1** The exploring of a new or strange region in order to learn about it: *exploration* of outer space. **2** A careful examination or study: *exploration* of various solutions to a problem.

ex·plor·a·to·ry [ik·splôr′ə·tôr′ē] *adj.* Of, for, or having to do with exploration: an *exploratory* voyage.

ex·plore [ik·splôr′] *v.* **ex·plored, ex·plor·ing** **1** To travel in or through in order to learn or discover something: to *explore* an island. **2** To look through or examine closely: to *explore* the contents of a drawer.

ex·plor·er [ik·splôr′ər] *n.* A person who explores, especially one who goes into unknown territory in search of geographic or scientific knowledge.

ex·plo·sion [ik·splō′zhən] *n.* **1** A sudden blowing up or bursting: the *explosion* of dynamite. **2** The loud noise caused by exploding: a deafening *explosion.* **3** A sudden noisy outburst: an *explosion* of laughter. **4** A sudden expansion or increase: the population *explosion.*

An explosion

ex·plo·sive [ik·splō′siv] **1** *adj.* Able to explode or to cause an explosion: an *explosive* charge. **2** *n.* A substance that explodes: TNT is an *explosive.* **3** *adj.* Apt to burst out suddenly in noise or violence: The quarrel created an *explosive* atmosphere. **—ex·plo′sive·ly** *adv.* **—ex·plo′sive·ness** *n.*

ex·po·nent [ik·spō′nənt] *n.* **1** A person who explains or interprets something: an *exponent* of modern art. **2** A person or thing that represents or is an example of something: an *exponent* of fair play. **3** A number placed as a superscript to show how many times another number is to be used as a factor. In $a^2 = a \times a$ and $4^3 = 4 \times 4 \times 4 = 64$, 2 and 3 are exponents.

ex·port [*v.* ik·spôrt′ *or* eks′pôrt, *n., adj.* eks′pôrt] **1** *v.* To send to other countries for sale or trade: Germany *exports* many cars. **2** *n.* Something that is exported: Brazil's chief *export* is coffee. **3** *adj.* Of or having to do with exports or exportation. **4** *n.* The act of exporting: These goods are for *export.* **—ex·port′er** *n.*

ex·por·ta·tion [ek′spôr·tā′shən] *n.* **1** The act of exporting. **2** Something that is exported.

ex·pose [ik·spōz′] *v.* **ex·posed, ex·pos·ing** **1** To put in an open or unprotected position: to *expose* oneself, as to danger or laughter. **2** To display or uncover: I opened the box and *exposed* the birthday cake. **3** To make known or reveal: to *expose* a crime. **4** To bring into contact with something; subject: to *expose* a child to good music. **5** To let light come into contact with (a sensitive photographic film).

ex·po·sé [ek′spō·zā′] *n.* The making known to the public of a crime, fraud, or scandal.

ex·po·si·tion [eks′pə·zish′ən] *n.* **1** A large public display or exhibition: an *exposition* of farm products. **2** A written or spoken explanation of an idea or process.

ex·pos·i·tor [ik·spoz′ə·tər] *n.* A person who explains and describes.

ex·pos·i·to·ry [ik·spoz′ə·tôr′ē] *adj.* That explains; explanatory: *expository* writing.

ex·pos·tu·late [ik·spos′cho͝o·lāt′] *v.* **ex·pos·tu·lat·ed, ex·pos·tu·lat·ing** To argue earnestly in objection to a person's plans, opinions, or actions: The supervisor *expostulated* with the employee about the

a	add	**i**	it	**o͝o**	took	**oi**	oil
ā	ace	**ī**	ice	**o͞o**	pool	**ou**	pout
â	care	**o**	odd	**u**	up	**ng**	ring
ä	palm	**ō**	open	**û**	burn	**th**	thin
e	end	**ô**	order	**yo͞o**	fuse	**t͟h**	this
ē	equal					**zh**	vision

ə = { a in *above* e in *sicken* i in *possible* / o in *melon* u in *circus* }

work he'd left unfinished. **—ex·pos'tu·la'tion** *n.*

ex·po·sure [ik·spō'zhər] *n.* 1 The act of exposing. 2 The condition of being exposed: to suffer from *exposure* to the cold. 3 The position of something with regard to the sun, weather, or points of a compass: a room with a northern *exposure.* 4 The time required for light to produce the desired effect on a photographic film: Astronomers often use long *exposures.* 5 A section of film that makes a single picture: There are 12 *exposures* on this roll.

exposure meter Another name for a LIGHT METER.

ex·pound [ik·spound'] *v.* To explain or interpret; set forth in detail: to *expound* a theory.

ex·press [ik·spres'] 1 *v.* To tell in words; state: to *express* an opinion. 2 *v.* To show without words, as by a look or sign: A frown *expresses* disapproval. 3 *adj.* Clearly stated or expressed; explicit: Her *express* request was to wake her at seven. 4 *n.* A fast train, bus, or other means of transportation that takes a direct route and makes few stops. 5 *adj.* Designed for fast travel: an *express* highway. 6 *adj.* Operating at a fast speed: an *express* train. 7 *n.* A system for moving things, as goods, parcels, or money, very rapidly from one point to another. 8 *n.* Something sent by this system. 9 *adj.* Rapid; quick: to send goods by *express* delivery. 10 *v.* To send by rapid delivery: to *express* a parcel. 11 *adv.* By express: The package went *express.* **—express oneself** To say or communicate what one thinks or feels.

ex·pres·sion [ik·spresh'ən] *n.* 1 The saying or putting into words of something: the *expression* of an opinion. 2 A word or group of words used together: "Ahoy" is a sailors' *expression.* 3 In mathematics, a set of symbols that represents a quantity or operation. 4 Something that indicates what one is thinking or feeling: We sent flowers as an *expression* of sympathy. 5 A look on the face that shows a feeling or mood: a sad *expression.* 6 Emotional warmth and feeling: The opera star sang with great *expression.*

Helpless expression

ex·pres·sion·less [ik·spresh'ən·lis] *adj.* 1 Lacking any indication of what one is thinking or feeling: His face was *expressionless* as he heard the news. 2 Monotonous: an *expressionless* speaker.

ex·pres·sive [ik·spres'iv] *adj.* 1 Serving to express: a frown *expressive* of anger. 2 Full of feeling or special meaning; significant: an *expressive* sigh. **—ex·pres'sive·ly** *adv.* **—ex·pres'sive·ness** *n.*

ex·press·ly [ik·spres'lē] *adv.* 1 With the definite purpose; particularly: I came here *expressly* to see the show. 2 Clearly and plainly: We were *expressly* warned against going.

ex·press·man [ik·spres'mən] *n., pl.* **ex·press·men** [ik·spres'mən] A person who works for an express system, especially one who delivers parcels.

ex·press·way [ik·spres'wā'] *n.* A highway designed for rapid travel.

ex·pro·pri·ate [eks·prō'prē·āt'] *v.* **ex·pro·pri·at·ed, ex·pro·pri·at·ing** To take (private property) away from the owner, by or as if by government authority. **—ex·pro'pri·a'tion** *n.*

ex·pul·sion [ik·spul'shən] *n.* 1 The act of expelling: the *expulsion* of a student. 2 A being forced or driven out: Gases on *expulsion* from a jet engine are very hot.

ex·punge [ik·spunj'] *v.* **ex·punged, ex·pung·ing** To remove (something written); delete: to *expunge* a paragraph from a speech.

ex·pur·gate [eks'pər·gāt'] *v.* **ex·pur·gat·ed, ex·pur·gat·ing** To remove from (as a book) words or passages thought to be improper. **—ex'pur·ga'tion** *n.* **—ex'pur·ga'tor** *n.*

ex·qui·site [eks'kwi·zit *or* ik·skwiz'it] *adj.* 1 Finely and delicately made: an *exquisite* bracelet. 2 Extremely beautiful: an *exquisite* painting. 3 Of great excellence; admirable: *exquisite* skill; *exquisite* taste. 4 Very sharp; keen: *exquisite* pain. **—ex'qui·site·ly** *adv.*

ex·tant [ek'stənt *or* ik·stant'] *adj.* Still in existence: All of her works are *extant.*

ex·tem·po·ra·ne·ous [ik·stem'pə·rā'nē·əs] *adj.* Done, made, or given with little or no advance preparation: *extemporaneous* verses. **—ex·tem'po·ra'ne·ous·ly** *adv.*

ex·tem·po·re [ik·stem'pə·rē] *adv.* With little or no advance preparation; offhand: to speak *extempore.*

ex·tem·po·ri·za·tion [ik·stem'pə·rə·zā'shən] *n.* 1 The act of extemporizing. 2 Something that is invented or made up on the spot.

ex·tem·po·rize [ik·stem'pə·rīz'] *v.* **ex·tem·po·rized, ex·tem·po·riz·ing** To make up as one goes along; improvise: She *extemporized* a graceful speech of thanks.

ex·tend [ik·stend'] *v.* 1 To stretch out: *Extend* your arm. 2 To lengthen or prolong in time or space: to *extend* a lease; to *extend* a pier. 3 To stretch, reach, or last: The desert *extends* for miles; The trial *extended* over five weeks. 4 To make greater or broader; increase: to *extend* one's knowledge. 5 To give or offer: to *extend* hospitality.

ex·tend·ed [ik·sten'did] *adj.* 1 Stretched out: *extended* arms. 2 Made long or longer; lengthy: an *extended* journey. 3 Extensive; broad.

extended family A group of relatives who live together, including others besides parents and their children.

ex·ten·sion [ik·sten'shən] *n.* 1 The act of extending. 2 The condition of being extended. 3 That which extends something: an *extension* to a house; a telephone *extension.* 4 *adj. use:* an *extension* cord. 5 Additional time allowed in which to do something: We got an *extension* on the payment of our loan.

ex·ten·sive [ik·sten'siv] *adj.* 1 Spreading over a wide area: *extensive* damage. 2 Large in amount: *extensive* funds. 3 Wide or far-reaching: *extensive* reading. **—ex·ten'sive·ly** *adv.* **—ex·ten'sive·ness** *n.*

ex·ten·sor [ik·sten'sər *or* ik·sten'sôr] *n.* A muscle that straightens out a limb, as an arm, leg, or wing.

ex·tent [ik·stent'] *n.* 1 The size, amount, or degree to which something extends: the *extent* of the damage; To what *extent* can their opinion be trusted? 2 An extended space; expanse.

ex·ten·u·ate [ik·sten'yoo·āt'] *v.* **ex·ten·u·at·ed, ex·ten·u·at·ing** To make (a fault or bad action) seem less serious; partially excuse: I couldn't forgive his rudeness, though fatigue and the late hour *extenuated* it. **—ex·ten'u·a'tion** *n.*

ex·te·ri·or [ik·stir'ē·ər] 1 *n.* The outside: the *exterior* of the building. 2 *adj.* Being on the outside or on an outside surface: *exterior* damage to a house. 3 *n.* Outward appearance: a meek *exterior.* 4 *adj.* Suitable for use outside or on an outside surface: *exterior* paint.

ex·ter·mi·nate [ik·stûr′mə·nāt′] *v.* **ex·ter·mi·nat·ed, ex·ter·mi·nat·ing** To destroy (living things) entirely; kill: to *exterminate* harmful insects. **—ex·ter′mi·na′tion** *n.* **—ex·ter′mi·na′tor** *n.*

ex·ter·nal [ik·stûr′nəl] 1 *adj.* Of, on, or for the outside: Weeping is an *external* sign of grief; an *external* covering of paint. 2 *adj.* Of or for the outside part of the body: for *external* use only. 3 *adj.* Coming from the outside: *external* causes. 4 *adj.* Not real or genuine; on the surface only: an *external* appearance of amusement. 5 *n.* (*usually pl.*) An outer appearance or act: Don't judge a person by *externals.* **—ex·ter′nal·ly** *adv.*

external ear The visible parts of the ear and the short passage leading to the eardrum.

ex·tinct [ik·stingkt′] *adj.* 1 No longer in existence: an *extinct* animal. 2 No longer active; extinguished: an *extinct* volcano.

ex·tinc·tion [ik·stingk′shən] *n.* 1 The condition of no longer existing: The bald eagle is in danger of *extinction.* 2 The destruction or wiping out of something: the *extinction* of all one's hopes. 3 The act of extinguishing something: the *extinction* of a flame.

ex·tin·guish [ik·sting′gwish] *v.* 1 To put out: *Extinguish* the lights. 2 To wipe out; destroy: to *extinguish* life. ◆ *Extinguish* comes from a Latin word meaning *to quench completely.*

ex·tin·guish·er [ik·sting′gwish·ər] *n.* A fire extinguisher.

Fire extinguisher

ex·tir·pate [ek′stûr·pāt′] *v.* **ex·tir·pat·ed, ex·tir·pat·ing** 1 To root out; get rid of completely. 2 To cut out in a surgical operation.

ex·tol or **ex·toll** [ik·stōl′] *v.* **ex·tolled, ex·tol·ling** To praise highly: to *extol* a new play.

ex·tort [ik·stôrt′] *v.* To get (as money or a confession) from a person by force or threats.

ex·tor·tion [ik·stôr′shən] *n.* 1 The getting of something, as money or a confession, by force or threats. 2 Something extorted. **—ex·tor′tion·ist** *n.*

ex·tor·tion·ate [ik·stôr′shə·nət] *adj.* 1 Practicing or having to do with extortion. 2 Far too much; exorbitant.

ex·tra [ek′strə] 1 *adj.* In addition to what is usual, required, or expected; additional: an *extra* phone. 2 *n.* A person, thing, or charge in addition to what is needed or expected: We need six, but get an *extra.* 3 *adv.* Extremely; unusually: *extra* good. 4 *n.* A special edition of a newspaper telling of some important event. 5 *n.* An actor hired by the day to play in a motion picture, as part of a crowd, army, or other group.

extra- A prefix meaning: Outside; besides; beyond, as in *extraordinary.*

ex·tract [*v.* ik·strakt′, *n.* eks′trakt] 1 *v.* To take out, as by pulling or squeezing: to *extract* a tooth; to *extract* juice. 2 *n.* A concentrated preparation, as taken from a plant or drug: Vanilla *extract* is used as flavoring. 3 *v.* To get by using force or effort: to *extract* the truth from a prisoner. 4 *v.* To draw or derive; get: to *extract* satisfaction from one's work. 5 *v.* To figure out; deduce: to *extract* a principle. 6 *v.* To calculate (a root of a number). 7 *v.* To choose or copy for quoting: to *extract* a passage from a poem. 8 *n.* A passage taken from a piece of writing. **—ex·tract′a·ble** or **ex·tract′i·ble** *adj.* **—ex·trac′tor** *n.*

ex·trac·tion [ik·strak′shən] *n.* 1 The act of extracting: the *extraction* of a tooth. 2 Origin or descent; ancestry: a person of German *extraction.*

ex·tra·cur·ric·u·lar [ek′strə·kə·rik′yə·lər] *adj.* Connected with a school but not part of its regular course of study.

ex·tra·dite [ek′strə·dīt′] *v.* **ex·tra·dit·ed, ex·tra·dit·ing** 1 To hand over (a prisoner or fugitive) to the authorities of another state or country. 2 To obtain the transfer of (a prisoner). **—ex·tra·di·tion** [eks′·trə·dish′ən] *n.*

ex·tra·ga·lac·tic [ek′strə·gə·lak′tik] *adj.* Taking place, located, or coming from beyond the Milky Way.

ex·tra·mu·ral [ek′strə·myo͝or′əl] *adj.* Outside of the physical limits of a particular school or organization: *extramural* sports. **—ex′tra·mu′ral·ly** *adv.*

ex·tra·ne·ous [ik·strā′nē·əs] *adj.* Coming from without; foreign: Static and *extraneous* noises spoiled the broadcast.

ex·traor·di·nar·y [ik·strôr′də·ner′ē *or* ek′strə·ôr′də·ner′ē] *adj.* 1 Remarkable; unusual; surprising: *extraordinary* strength. 2 Employed for a special purpose or mission: an envoy *extraordinary.* **—ex·traor′di·nar′i·ly** *adv.*

ex·trap·o·late [ik·strap′ə·lāt′] *v.* **ex·trap·o·lat·ed, ex·trap·o·lat·ing** 1 To make a prediction based on the present direction of events. 2 To use the familiar as the basis for guesses about the unknown. 3 In mathematics, to infer (a value of a function not within the observed range) from known values. **—ex·trap′o·la′tion** *n.*

ex·tra·sen·so·ry [ek′strə·sen′sə·rē] *adj.* Not due to the ordinary senses, as of sight, hearing, touch, smell, or taste: *extrasensory* awareness of danger.

extrasensory perception Knowledge of external objects apparently gained without using any of the senses of sight, sound, smell, taste, or touch.

ex·tra·ter·res·tri·al [ek′strə·tə·res′trē·əl] 1 *adj.* Of, relating to, or originating beyond the Earth: Asteroids are *extraterrestrial* bodies. 2 *n.* A creature from or inhabiting outer space.

ex·tra·ter·ri·to·ri·al [ek′strə·ter′ə·tôr′ē·əl] *adj.* Situated outside of the geographic limits of a nation or other authority.

ex·trav·a·gance [ik·strav′ə·gəns] *n.* 1 Wasteful spending of money. 2 A great lack of reason or moderation in one's behavior, speech, or dress. 3 Anything extravagant, as an action or purpose.

ex·trav·a·gant [ik·strav′ə·gənt] *adj.* 1 Spending too much; wasteful: an *extravagant* person. 2 Going beyond reason or proper limits: *extravagant* praise. **—ex·trav′a·gant·ly** *adv.*

ex·trav·a·gan·za [ik·strav′ə·gan′zə] *n.* A theatrical

a	add	**i**	it	**o͝o**	took	**oi**	oil
ā	ace	**ī**	ice	**o͞o**	pool	**ou**	pout
â	care	**o**	odd	**u**	up	**ng**	ring
ä	palm	**ō**	open	**û**	burn	**th**	thin
e	end	**ô**	order	**yo͞o**	fuse	**t͟h**	this
ē	equal					**zh**	vision

ə = a in *above*, e in *sicken*, i in *possible*, o in *melon*, u in *circus*

presentation done in an elaborate, spectacular style.

ex·tra·ve·hic·u·lar [ek′strə·vē·hik′yə·lər] *adj.* Taking place outside of a vehicle: an *extravehicular* walk in space.

ex·tra·vert [ek′strə·vûrt] *n.* Another spelling of EXTROVERT.

ex·tra·vert·ed [ek′strə·vûr′tid] *adj.* Another spelling of EXTROVERTED.

ex·treme [ik·strēm′] **1** *adj.* Very great or severe: *extreme* weakness; *extreme* danger. **2** *n.* The greatest or highest degree: They were ambitious to the *extreme.* **3** *adj.* Far beyond the usual or average; exaggerated: to take *extreme* measures; *extreme* opinions. **4** *n.* One of two things that are completely different from each other: the *extremes* of joy and sorrow. **5** *adj.* Most distant; farthest out: the *extreme* frontier outposts. **—go to extremes** To do or say more than is usual or expected.

ex·treme·ly [ik·strēm′lē] *adv.* Much more than usual or common; very: Be *extremely* careful.

extremely high frequency A radio wave frequency in the range of 30,000 to 300,000 megahertz.

ex·trem·ist [ik·strē′mist] *n.* A person who holds extreme opinions, favors extreme measures, or goes to extremes in actions or behavior.

ex·trem·i·ty [ik·strem′ə·tē] *n., pl.* **ex·trem·i·ties** **1** The most distant point or part; end or edge: the western *extremity* of the state. **2** The utmost degree: the *extremity* of despair. **3** Something extreme, as distress, need, or danger: to be in *extremity.* **4** An extreme action or measure: *Extremities* such as blowing up buildings failed to halt the fire. **5** (*pl.*) The hands or feet.

ex·tri·cate [ek′strə·kāt′] *v.* **ex·tri·cat·ed, ex·tri·cat·ing** To free from something that tangles, holds back, endangers, or embarrasses: to *extricate* a car stuck in sand. **—ex′tri·ca′tion** *n.*

ex·trin·sic [ik·strin′sik] *adj.* Not belonging as an essential part; extraneous: Try to keep *extrinsic* details out of your story. **—ex·trin′si·cal·ly** *adv.*

ex·tro·vert [ek′strə·vûrt] *n.* A person chiefly interested in other things or people rather than in his or her own thoughts and feelings.

ex·tro·vert·ed [ek′strə·vûr′tid] *adj.* Having an outgoing disposition.

ex·trude [ik·strōōd′] *v.* **ex·trud·ed, ex·trud·ing** **1** To push or thrust out. **2** To shape (as plastic or metal) by forcing through special openings. **3** To stick out.

ex·tru·sion [ik·strōō′zhən] *n.* The act or process of extruding, especially the shaping of plastic or metal by forcing it through special openings.

ex·u·ber·ance [ig·zōō′bər·əns] *n.* Joy and energy; high spirits: to greet with *exuberance.*

ex·u·ber·ant [ig·zōō′bər·ənt] *adj.* **1** Full of high spirits, joy, and energy. **2** Growing in great abundance: *exuberant* foliage. **—ex·u′ber·ant·ly** *adv.*

ex·u·da·tion [ek′syōō·dā′shən] *n.* **1** The process of exuding. **2** Exuded matter.

ex·ude [ig·zōōd′ *or* ik·syōōd′] *v.* **ex·ud·ed, ex·ud·ing** **1** To discharge or cause to discharge in small amounts or in drops, as through pores: The skin *exudes* sweat; The ground *exuded* oil. **2** To give forth or show; radiate: to *exude* confidence.

ex·ult [ig·zult′] *v.* To be extremely joyful; rejoice greatly: to *exult* in victory. **—ex·ult′ing·ly** *adv.*

ex·ul·tant [ig·zul′tənt] *adj.* Full of great joy, as in triumph; jubilant: The home team gave an *exultant* cheer. **—ex·ul′tant·ly** *adv.*

ex·ul·ta·tion [eg′zul·tā′shən] *n.* Great joy and jubilation: The crowd yelled in *exultation.*

eye [ī] *n., v.* **eyed, ey·ing** or **eye·ing** **1** *n.* The organ of the body with which human beings and other animals see. In humans it includes the cornea, iris, pupil, lens, and retina. **2** *n.* The area around the eye: a black *eye.* **3** *n.* The colored part of the eye; iris: brown *eyes.* **4** *n.* The power of sight; eyesight; vision: Making models requires good *eyes.* **5** *v.* To look at or watch carefully: They *eyed* each other with distrust. **6** *n.* A gaze or glance; look: Cast an *eye* in this direction. **7** *n.* Sight; view: in the public *eye.* **8** *n.* Attention; notice: to try to catch a waiter's *eye.* **9** *n.* The ability to recognize, judge, or appreciate: to have an *eye* for beauty. **10** *n.* (*often pl.*) A way of regarding something; judgment; opinion: That is a sin in the *eyes* of the church. **11** *n.* Anything resembling a human eye in some way, as the hole in a needle, a bud on a potato, or a loop through which a hook fits. **12** *n.* A calm area of low pressure in the center of a cyclone: the *eye* of the storm. **—keep an eye on** To watch closely or tend carefully: *Keep an eye on* the baby. **—lay eyes on** or **set eyes on** To see: I've never *laid eyes on* her. **—make eyes at** To look at in an admiring or flirting way. **—see eye to eye** To agree in all respects: He and I don't *see eye to eye.*

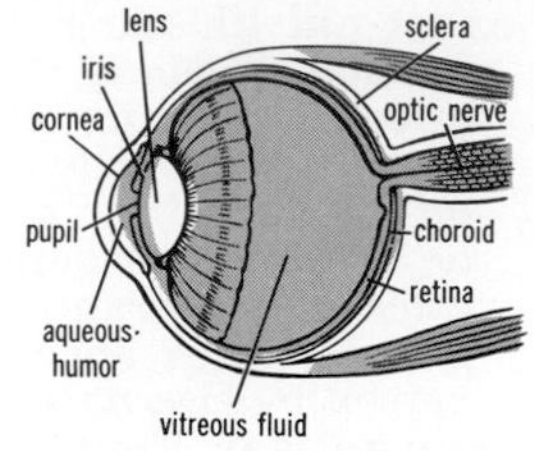

Diagram of a human eye

eye·ball [ī′bôl′] *n.* The entire globe or ball of the eye.

eye bank A place where corneas from the eyes of persons who have just died are kept in readiness for transplanting to the eyes of the blind.

eye·brow [ī′brou′] *n.* The bony ridge above each eye or the arch of small hairs growing on it.

eye·cup [ī′kup′] *n.* A small cup with a rim curved to fit the eye socket, used for bathing or applying a medicine to the eye.

eyed [īd] *adj.* Having a certain kind or number of eyes: often used in combination, as in *bleary-eyed.*

eye·drop·per [ī′drop′ər] *n.* A small dropper for applying a soothing or medicated liquid to the eyeball drop by drop.

eye·glass [ī′glas′] *n., pl.* **eye·glass·es** **1** (*pl.*) A pair of glass lenses fitted into a frame and worn over the eyes to help a person see more clearly. **2** Any lens used to aid the vision, as a monocle.

eye·lash [ī′lash′] *n.* One of the stiff, curved hairs growing from the edge of the eyelids. ◆ *Eyelash* was formed by combining the words *eye* and *lash.*

eye·less [ī′lis] *adj.* Lacking eyes.

eye·let [ī′lit] *n.* **1** A small hole to hold a cord, lace, or other fastening: Shoelaces are put through the *eyelets* of a shoe. **2** A metal ring that lines and strengthens such a hole. **3** A small opening in embroidery edged with fancy stitches.

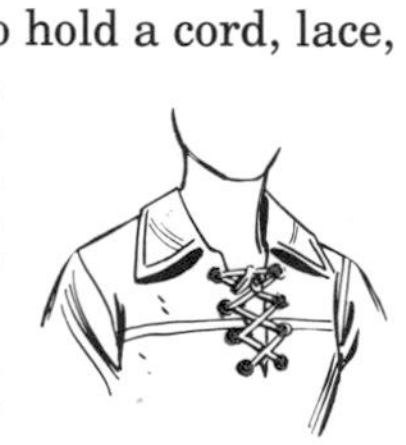
Eyelets

eye·lid [ī′lid′] *n.* Either of the folds of skin that move to cover or uncover the eyes.

eye-o·pen·er [ī′ō′pən·ər] *n.* An event or a piece of information that makes a person aware of something previously ignored.

eye·piece [ī′pēs′] *n.* The lens or lenses nearest the eye of someone looking through a telescope, microscope, or similar piece of equipment.
eye·shade [ī′shād′] *n.* A visor, often made of translucent green plastic, attached to a headband and worn to protect the eyes from overhead glare.
eye shadow A cosmetic for coloring and accenting the eyelids.
eye·sight [ī′sīt′] *n.* **1** The power of seeing; vision: weak *eyesight.* **2** The distance that the eye can see: to be within *eyesight.*
eye socket Either of the two hollows in the skull that hold the eyeballs.
eye·sore [ī′sôr′] *n.* A disagreeable or ugly thing to see: That billboard is an *eyesore.*
eye·spot [ī′spot′] *n.* **1** A small colored spot that is sensitive to light, seen in many microscopic organisms. **2** A circular, brightly colored marking, as on a peacock's tail feather.
eye·stalk [ī′stôk′] *n.* In crabs and similar crustaceans, one of a pair of movable cylindrical projections bearing an eye or a spot sensitive to light.
eye·strain [ī′strān′] *n.* A tired or uncomfortable condition of the eyes caused by using them too much or in the wrong way.
eye·tooth [ī′tŏŏth′] *n., pl.* **eye·teeth** [ī′tēth′] One of the two canine teeth of the upper jaw. It is the third tooth from the middle on either side.
eye·wash [ī′wäsh′ *or* ī′wôsh′] *n.* **1** A liquid for bathing the eyes. **2** *slang* Deceptive or falsely reassuring language or actions.
eye·wit·ness [ī′wit′nis] *n.* **1** A person who sees something happen, as a crime or accident, especially such a person who reports on what he or she has seen. **2** *adj. use:* an *eyewitness* account.
ey·rie [âr′ē *or* ir′ē] *n.* Another spelling of AERIE.
E·ze·ki·el [i·zē′kē·əl] *n.* **1** In the Bible, a Hebrew prophet who lived during the sixth century B.C. **2** A book of the Old Testament.
Ez·ra [ez′rə] *n.* **1** In the Bible, a Hebrew priest who lived during the fifth century B.C. **2** A book of the Old Testament.

E

a	add	**i**	it	**ŏŏ**	took	**oi**	oil
ā	ace	**ī**	ice	**ōō**	pool	**ou**	pout
â	care	**o**	odd	**u**	up	**ng**	ring
ä	palm	**ō**	open	**û**	burn	**th**	thin
e	end	**ô**	order	**yōō**	fuse	**th**	this
ē	equal					**zh**	vision

ə = a in *above*, e in *sicken*, i in *possible*, o in *melon*, u in *circus*

Ff

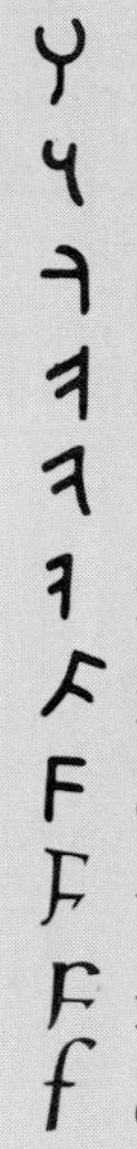

Early Phoenician (late 2nd millennium B.C.)

Phoenician (8th century B.C.)

Early Greek (9th-7th centuries B.C.)

Early Etruscan (8th century B.C.)

Classical Etruscan (around 400 B.C.)

Early Latin (around 7th century B.C.)

Monumental Latin (4th century B.C.)

Classical Latin

Uncial

Half uncial

Caroline minuscule

F is the sixth letter of the alphabet. The sign for it originated among Semitic people in the Near East, in the region of Palestine and Syria, probably in the middle of the second millennium B.C. Little is known about the sign until around 1000 B.C., when the Phoenicians began using it. They named it *waw* and used it for a *w*-like sound.

When the Greeks adopted the Phoenician sign around the ninth century B.C., they developed two signs of their own from it. For the history of the primary sign, see *V.* The Greeks called the lesser form of the letter *digamma* and used it as a consonantal *u* and a *w*-like sound. The sound had died out in most Greek dialects by classical times, and the letter was eventually discontinued in Greek.

As early as the eighth century B.C., the Etruscans adopted the Greek alphabet. They retained the *digamma,* giving it the sound of *v* or *w.* The Etruscan language contained an *f* sound, which the Etruscans expressed by combining their sign for the *digamma*—shaped like a reversed *F*—with that for the sound of *h.* The *f* sound thus was written as the equivalent of *WH.* When the Romans adopted the Etruscan alphabet, they, too, expressed the *f* sound at first as the equivalent of *WH.* Later, however, the Romans adopted a reversed digamma sign—shaped like our letter *F*—to express the sound of *f.*

The *minuscule,* or small letter, *f* developed gradually, between the third and the ninth centuries, in the handwriting that scribes used for copying books. Contributing to the shape were the Roman *uncials* of the fourth to the eighth centuries and the *half uncials* of the fifth to the ninth centuries. The true ancestor of the lowercase letter, however, was the script that evolved under the encouragement of Charlemagne (742-814). This letter was one of the letters known as the *Caroline minuscules,* which became the principal handwriting system used on the medieval manuscripts of the ninth and tenth centuries.

f or **F** [ef] *n., pl.* **f's** or **F's** 1 The sixth letter of the English alphabet. 2 In music, the fourth note of the scale of C major.

f. 1 fathom. 2 female. 3 feminine. 4 fluid. 5 folio. 6 forte. 7 franc.

F The symbol for the element fluorine.

F. 1 Fahrenheit. 2 February. 3 French. 4 Friday.

fa [fä] *n.* In music, a syllable used to represent the fourth tone in a major scale, the sixth tone in a minor scale, or in a fixed system the tone F.

FAA or **F.A.A.** Federal Aviation Agency.

fa·ble [fā′bəl] *n.* 1 A short story teaching a lesson. It is often about animals who behave like people. 2 A story that is not true, as a lie or falsehood.

fa·bled [fā′bəld] *adj.* 1 Told of in legends or stories: *fabled* sea monsters. 2 Not real.

fab·ric [fab′rik] *n.* 1 A material, as cloth, lace, or felt, made of woven, knitted, or matted fibers. 2 A thing formed of different parts, or its structure: the social *fabric.*

fab·ri·cate [fab′rə·kāt′] *v.* **fab·ri·cat·ed, fab·ri·cat·ing** 1 To make or build by joining parts; construct; manufacture. 2 To make up; invent: to try to *fabricate* a clever excuse. ◆ *Fabricate* comes from a Latin word meaning *to construct* or *build,* and this was once its only meaning in English. Nowadays, it usually refers to making up or "constructing" a story or a lie. **—fab′ri·ca′tion** *n.*

fab·u·list [fab′yə·list] *n.* 1 A person who invents fables. 2 A liar.

fab·u·lous [fab′yə·ləs] *adj.* 1 Unbelievable; astonishing: a *fabulous* fortune. 2 Of, like, or found in fables; imaginary: The unicorn is a *fabulous* animal. **—fab′u·lous·ly** *adv.*

fa·çade or **fa·cade** [fə·säd′] *n.* The front of a building, especially if more impressive than the rest.

face [fās] *n., v.* **faced, fac·ing** 1 *n.* The front of the head, extending from the forehead to the chin and from ear to ear. 2 *n.* A look or expression: happy *faces.* 3 *n.* An exaggerated expression made by twisting or pulling at the features: The clown made a *face.* 4 *n.* Outward appearance; look: The claim seems false on the *face* of it. 5 *n.* The front, top, outer, or most important side or surface: to turn a card *face* up; the *face* of a clock or watch. 6 *v.* To cover with another material: to *face* a lapel with velvet. 7 *v.* To turn or be turned with the front side toward: *Face* the flag. 8 *v.* To confront: to be *faced* with a problem. 9 *v.* To meet with courage: to *face* the fact of defeat. 10 *n.* Respect, dignity, or reputation: to lose *face.* 11 *n. informal* Shameless or disrespectful boldness. **—face to face** 1 Turned toward each other at close range. 2 In the presence of: *face to face* with danger. **—in the face of** 1 In the presence of. 2 In spite of.

face card Any playing card with a picture; a king, queen, or jack.

face·cloth [fās′klôth′] *n., pl.* **face·cloths** [fās′klôthz′ *or* fās′klôths′] Another name for WASHCLOTH.

face-lift [fās′lift′] *n.* Another word for FACE-LIFTING.

face-lift·ing [fās′lif′ting] *n.* 1 Plastic surgery that tightens the skin of the face and removes wrinkles. 2 A superficial renovation, as of a house.

fac·et [fas′it] *n.* 1 One of the small, smooth surfaces cut upon a gem. 2 A side or aspect: the many *facets* of the artist's talent.

Facets of a jewel

fa·ce·tious [fə·sē′shəs] *adj.* Meant or trying to be funny or flippant. **—fa·ce′tious·ly** *adv.* **—fa·ce′tious·ness** *n.*

face value 1 The value indicated on the face of a stamp, bill, or certificate. 2 The apparent meaning of something spoken or written: Don't take their excuses at *face value.*

fa·cial [fā′shəl] 1 *adj.* Of, near, or for the face: a *facial* expression. 2 *n. informal* A massage or other treatment for the face.

fac·ile [fas′(ə)l] *adj.* 1 Requiring little effort; easy: *facile* work. 2 Too easy; superficial: a *facile* solution. 3 Quick and skillful in performance: a *facile* speaker.

fa·cil·i·tate [fə·sil′ə·tāt′] *v.* **fa·cil·i·tat·ed, fa·cil·i·tat·ing** To make easier or more convenient.

fa·cil·i·ty [fə·sil′ə·tē] *n., pl.* **fa·cil·i·ties** 1 Ease or skill in performance: to write with *facility.* 2 (*usually pl.*) A thing that makes some action or work easier: good library *facilities.* 3 (*often pl.*) A place used by or serving people, as a school or restaurant.

fac·ing [fā′sing] *n.* 1 A covering in front, as for decoration or protection: a brick house with a stucco *facing.* 2 (*sometimes pl.*) The lining of a garment on parts exposed by being turned back, as the collar and cuffs.

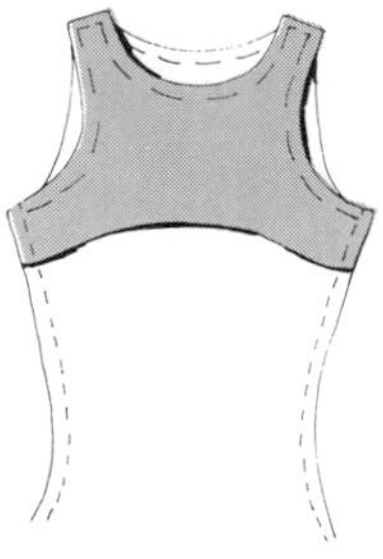
Facing

fac·sim·i·le [fak·sim′ə·lē] *n.* An exact copy: a *facsimile* of an old manuscript.

fact [fakt] *n.* 1 Something known to be true, to exist, or to have happened: a scientific *fact.* 2 Something claimed to be true or supposed to have happened: I have my *facts* wrong. 3 Reality or truth. **—as a matter of fact** or **in fact** Actually. ◆ It is always wise to distinguish between *facts* and *opinions.* A *fact* is either true or false; it can be proved or disproved. An *opinion,* though it may be based upon *facts,* is a judgment or conclusion. The statement "The vine is six feet tall" is a *fact,* but the conclusion that the vine is tall is an *opinion.*

fac·tion [fak′shən] *n.* 1 A distinct group of people within a larger group, working against other parts of the main group to gain its own ends. 2 Angry disagreement or strife among group or party members. **—fac′tion·al** *adj.*

fac·tious [fak′shəs] *adj.* Characterized by or promoting disagreement or conflict within a group. **—fac′tious·ness** *n.*

fac·ti·tious [fak·tish′əs] *adj.* Artificially created rather than occurring naturally; sham. **—fac·ti′tious·ly** *adv.* **—fac·ti′tious·ness** *n.*

fac·tor [fak′tər] 1 *n.* One of the elements or causes that help to produce a result: Luck was a *factor* in our victory. 2 *n.* A number that when multiplied by one or more other numbers gives a certain result. 3 is a factor of 18; *a* is a factor of *ab* + *ac.* 3 *v.* To find the factors of. 4 *n.* A business agent.

fac·to·ri·al [fak·tôr′ē·əl] *n.* The product of all the positive whole numbers from 1 to a given number. The factorial of 4 (written 4!) equals 1 × 2 × 3 × 4 = 24.

fac·to·ry [fak′tər·ē] *n., pl.* **fac·to·ries** A building or group of buildings where goods are manufactured or assembled: a shoe *factory.*

fac·to·tum [fak·tō′təm] *n.* A person employed to take care of extra work or do odd jobs.

fac·tu·al [fak′cho͞o·əl] *adj.* Based on or made up of facts; literal. **—fac′tu·al·ly** *adv.*

fac·ul·ty [fak′əl·tē] *n., pl.* **fac·ul·ties** 1 *U.S.* The entire teaching staff at a college or school. 2 A department of learning at a university: the English *faculty.* 3 A natural or acquired ability or talent: a *faculty* for writing. 4 *n.* An ability or power of the body or mind: the *faculties* of seeing and reasoning.

fad [fad] *n.* A style, amusement, or fashion that is very popular for a short time; craze.

fad·dish [fad′ish] *adj.* 1 Being a fad; temporarily popular. 2 Fond of fads. **—fad′dish·ness** *n.*

fade [fād] *v.* **fad·ed, fad·ing** 1 To lose or cause to lose brightness or color: The yellow rug *faded;* Washing *faded* the blouse. 2 To lose freshness; wither. 3 To grow dimmer and slowly disappear: His smile *faded.*

fade-in [fād′in′] *n.* 1 A gradual appearance and coming into focus of a picture on a television or motion-picture screen. 2 A gradually increasing volume of sound from silence to full audibility. ◆ *Fade-in* was invented when a word was needed to complement *fade-out,* a word long in use for the opposite process. Thus *fade* became a part of a word for something that is the exact opposite of fading.

fade-out [fād′out′] *n.* The gradual disappearance or fading away of a motion-picture, television, or radio scene.

fa·er·ie or **fa·er·y** [fā′(ə·)rē] *n., pl.* **fa·er·ies** 1 The domain of fairies; fairyland. 2 Another spelling of FAIRY: seldom used today.

fag [fag] *v.* **fagged, fag·ging** To tire out by hard work: By evening the crew was *fagged* out.

fag end 1 The frayed or untwisted end of a piece of cloth or rope. 2 A last part or remnant of anything, almost worthless in itself.

fag·ot or **fag·got** [fag′ət] *n.* A bound bundle of sticks or twigs, as used for fuel.

Fahr·en·heit [far′ən·hīt′] *adj.* Of or indicating the temperature scale used for ordinary purposes in the U.S. and Great Britain. In this system water freezes at 32 degrees and boils at 212 degrees.

Woman holding fagot

fail [fāl] 1 *v.* To turn out to be unsuccessful or not good enough: to *fail* in an effort. 2 *v.* To be lacking, missing, or too little: The electricity *failed.* 3 *v.* To neglect or omit: Don't *fail*

a	add	**i**	it	**o͝o**	took	**oi**	oil		
ā	ace	**ī**	ice	**o͞o**	pool	**ou**	pout		
â	care	**o**	odd	**u**	up	**ng**	ring		
ä	palm	**ō**	open	**û**	burn	**th**	thin		
e	end	**ô**	order	**yo͞o**	fuse	**th**	this		
ē	equal					**zh**	vision		

ə = {a in *above* e in *sicken* i in *possible* / o in *melon* u in *circus*}

to return my book. 4 *n.* Failure, especially in the phrase **without fail:** Be here *without fail.* 5 *v.* To prove of no help to when needed: My courage *failed* me. 6 *v.* To receive a grade too low to pass (as a test or course). 7 *v.* To give (a student) such a grade. 8 *v.* To weaken or decline: Her health was *failing.* 9 *v.* To become bankrupt, as a business.

fail·ing [fā′ling] 1 *n.* A minor fault; weakness. 2 *n.* Failure. 3 *prep.* In the absence of; lacking: *Failing* your reply, we left.

faille [fīl] *n.* A very finely ribbed silk or rayon fabric used mainly to make dresses.

fail-safe [fāl′sāf′] *adj.* 1 Designed in case of failure or malfunction, as of some system, to insure safety or continued operation: An electrical fuse is a *fail-safe* device. 2 Of, having to do with, or being a system of controls designed to prevent unauthorized actions by nuclear-armed aircraft.

fail·ure [fāl′yər] *n.* 1 A turning out to be unsuccessful. 2 A person or thing that has failed. 3 A failing to pass in school work. 4 Neglect, as of something expected: *failure* to obey the law. 5 A falling short or giving out: *failure* of the food supply. 6 A breaking down or weakening: the *failure* of communications. 7 A becoming bankrupt, as a business or bank.

fain [fān] 1 *adv.* Gladly: *Fain* would he depart. 2 *adj.* Willing, glad, or eager: *fain* to go. ◆ This word is used mostly in poems.

faint [fānt] 1 *n.* A condition in which one suddenly loses consciousness and is unaware of things for a time. 2 *v.* To fall into such a condition; swoon. 3 *adj.* Weak enough to faint: I felt *faint.* 4 *adj.* Weak, slight, or dim: a *faint* glow; a *faint* noise. 5 *adj.* Timid: a *faint* heart. **—faint′ly** *adv.*

faint·heart·ed [fānt′här′tid] *adj.* Cowardly or undecided; timid; a *fainthearted* effort.

fair[1] [fâr] 1 *adj.* Not favoring one above another; just. 2 *adj.* Following the right rules; honest: *fair* play. 3 *adv.* In a fair manner: Play *fair* with me. 4 *adj.* Less than good but better than poor; average: a *fair* student. 5 *adj.* Clear and bright; sunny: a *fair* day. 6 *adj.* Light in coloring: *fair* hair. 7 *adj.* Beautiful: a *fair* face. 8 *adj.* Gracious and pleasant: *fair* words. 9 *adj.* Not soiled or spoiled; clean: Write a *fair* paper. 10 *adj.* Not foul: a *fair* bunt. 11 *adj.* Properly open to attack: Your position is *fair* game. **—bid fair** To appear likely. **—fair′ness** *n.*

fair[2] [fâr] *n.* 1 An exhibition, as of goods, products, or machinery. 2 A regularly held gathering of buyers and sellers. 3 A sale of articles, often with entertainment, as to benefit a charity.

fair ball In baseball, a batted ball that lands within the foul lines or that bounces past first or third base within the foul line.

fair copy A final, corrected version of a document or a manuscript in neatly typed or written form.

fair·ground [fâr′ground′] *n.* A piece of ground set aside for fairs and exhibitions, often having a grandstand and other permanent structures.

fair-haired [fâr′hârd′] *adj.* Having hair of a light color.

fair·ish [fâr′ish] *adj.* Moderately good; so-so. **—fair′·ish·ly** *adv.*

fair·ly [fâr′lē] *adv.* 1 In a fair, just way: My employer dealt *fairly* with me. 2 Not extremely; somewhat: a *fairly* fast trip. 3 Positively; really: They *fairly* raced for the door.

fair-mind·ed [fâr′mīn′did] *adj.* Not prejudiced; impartial. **—fair′mind′ed·ness** *n.*

fair·way [fâr′wā′] *n.* In golf, a strip from tee to green where the grass is kept short.

fair-weather [fâr′weth′ər] *adj.* 1 Suited for or done in fair weather: *fair-weather* sports. 2 Dependable only in prosperous times: a *fair-weather* friend.

fair·y [fâr′ē] *n., pl.* **fair·ies,** *adj.* 1 *n.* An imaginary being, often tiny with a graceful human form, able to work magic. 2 *adj.* Of fairies. 3 *adj.* Like a fairy, as in delicacy.

fair·y·land [fâr′ē·land′] *n.* 1 The place where the fairies are supposed to live. 2 Any delightful and enchanting place.

fairy tale 1 A story involving fairies. 2 A story that is or sounds made up; lie or fib.

fait ac·com·pli [fā′tä·kôm·plē′] *n., pl.* **faits ac·com·plis** [fā′tä·kôm·plē′] Something done that cannot easily be undone; accomplished deed. ◆ *Fait accompli* comes directly from French.

faith [fāth] 1 *n.* Confidence, trust, or belief: I have *faith* in you. 2 *n.* Belief in God or in religious teachings. 3 *n.* A system of religious belief: the Christian *faith.* 4 *n.* A promise, as of loyalty: The rest of the group broke *faith* with us. 5 *n.* Allegiance: a pledge of *faith.* 6 *interj.* In truth; indeed. **—bad faith** Dishonesty or falseness. **—good faith** Honesty, sincerity, or loyalty. ◆ See TRUST.

faith·ful [fāth′fəl] *adj.* 1 Loyal, true, and constant: a *faithful* friend. 2 *n. use*: The followers of a religion or loyal members of any group: The officers of our club are among *the faithful.* 3 True in detail; accurate: Give a *faithful* account. **—faith′·ful·ly** *adv.* **—faith′ful·ness** *n.*

faith·less [fāth′lis] *adj.* 1 Not true to one's word or duty. 2 Lacking religious faith.

fake [fāk] *n., adj., v.* **faked, fak·ing** *informal* 1 *n.* A person or thing passed off as something it is not; fraud. 2 *adj.* Not genuine; false: *fake* jewels. 3 *v.* To try to pass off as genuine: to *fake* a painting; to *fake* gratitude. **—fak′er** *n.*

fak·er·y [fā′kə·rē] *n., pl.* **fak·er·ies** The act or an example of faking; fraud.

fa·kir [fə·kir′ *or* fā′kər] *n.* A Muslim or Hindu holy person who is a beggar.

fa·la·fel [fə·lä′fəl] *n.* Ground and spiced chick-peas shaped into balls and fried, often eaten as a sandwich filling.

fal·chion [fôl′chən] *n.* A broad, slightly curved sword used in the Middle Ages.

fal·con [fal′kən *or* fô(l)′kən] *n.* 1 A swift hawk trained to hunt and kill other birds and small animals. 2 Any of various related hawks with long, pointed wings and a notched bill.

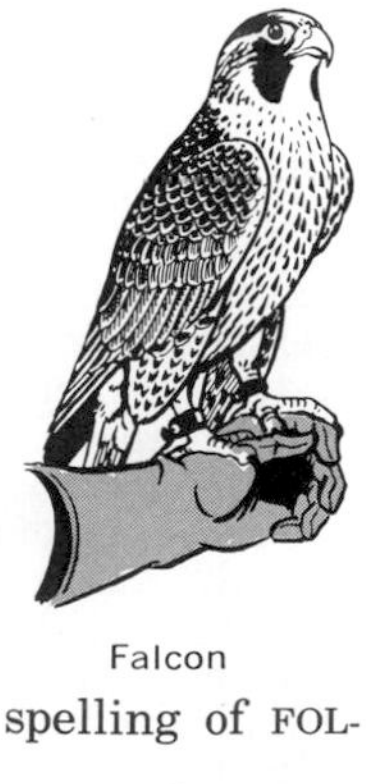
Falcon

fal·con·er [fal′kən·ər *or* fô(l)′kən·ər] *n.* 1 A person who breeds falcons or trains them to hunt. 2 A person who hunts with falcons.

fal·con·ry [fal′kən·rē *or* fô(l)′kən·rē] *n.* 1 The art of training falcons to hunt small game. 2 The sport of hunting with falcons.

fal·de·ral [fal′də·ral′] *n.* Another spelling of FOLDEROL.

fall [fôl] *v.* **fell, fall·en, fall·ing,** *n.* 1 *v.* To drop to a lower place, position, or level: A tear *fell* from my eye; to *fall* off a horse. **2** *v.* To drop suddenly from an erect position: to slip and *fall.* **3** *n.* The act of falling or dropping down: the silent *fall* of snow; injured in a *fall.* **4** *n.* Something that falls, or the amount that falls: a light *fall* of rain. **5** *n.* The distance anything falls: a long *fall.* **6** *n. U.S.* The season when leaves fall; autumn. **7** *adj. use: fall* weather. **8** *n.* (*usually pl.*) A waterfall. **9** *v.* To slope downward: The land *falls* away gradually eastward. **10** *n.* A downward slope. **11** *v.* To hang down: The drapes *fell* to the floor. **12** *v.* To become lower or less: Prices *fell;* The wind has *fallen.* **13** *n.* A lowering or lessening; decrease: a sudden *fall* in temperature. **14** *v.* To hit; land: Snow *fell* on the city. **15** *v.* To be wounded or killed, as in combat. **16** *v.* To be taken, captured, or overthrown: The fort *fell.* **17** *n.* Overthrow or collapse: the *fall* of the Roman Empire. **18** *v.* To collapse: The bridge *fell.* **19** *n.* Loss of innocence through wrongdoing: the *fall* of humanity. **20** *v.* To pass into a given condition: to *fall* asleep. **21** *v.* To show or experience sadness: The child's face *fell.* **22** *v.* To happen or come: The holiday *falls* on a Monday. **23** *v.* To come as though descending: Night *fell.* **24** *v.* To come by chance or right: Suspicion *fell* on the staff; The estate *fell* to the oldest child. **25** *v.* To be divided: The speech *fell* into three parts. **26** *n.* A woman's hairpiece, usually long and straight. **—fall back** To move back; retreat. **—fall back on** To turn to for help or security. **—fall behind** To fail to keep up, as in work or meeting payments. **—fall in** **1** To get into a military line. **2** To meet or go along, as with others. **—fall off** To become less, as attendance. **—fall on** or **fall upon** To attack. **—fall out** **1** To quarrel. **2** To drop out of a military line. **—fall short** To fail, as in reaching a goal. **—fall through** To come to nothing; fail. **—fall to** **1** To begin. **2** To begin eating or fighting. **—fall under** To come under.

fal·la·cious [fə·lā'shəs] *adj.* **1** Not logical or correct: a *fallacious* conclusion. **2** Deceptive or misleading: *fallacious* evidence. **—fal·la'cious·ly** *adv.* **—fal·la'cious·ness** *n.*

fal·la·cy [fal'ə·sē] *n., pl.* **fal·la·cies** **1** A false or misleading notion: the *fallacy* that age always brings wisdom. **2** Faulty reasoning.

fall·en [fô'lən] **1** Past participle of FALL. **2** *adj.* Having dropped down: *fallen* leaves. **3** *adj.* Overthrown, captured, or ruined: a *fallen* empire. **4** *adj.* Killed: a *fallen* soldier.

fall guy *slang* A person who is made to take the blame, as for a crime.

fal·li·ble [fal'ə·bəl] *adj.* Liable to make errors or to be wrong. **—fal·li·bil·i·ty** [fal'ə·bil'ə·tē] *n.*

fall·ing-out [fô'ling·out'] *n., pl.* **fall·ings-out** or **fall·ing-outs** A break in friendly relations; quarrel.

falling star Another name for METEOR.

fall line **1** An imaginary line connecting waterfalls on a number of roughly parallel rivers. A fall line forms the boundary between regions of different elevation. **2** The natural course of descent between two points on a slope, as in skiing.

fall·off [fôl'ôf'] *n.* A downward trend in quantity or quality: a *falloff* in production at a factory.

fall·out [fôl'out'] *n.* **1** Radioactive dust that falls from the atmosphere as a result of a nuclear explosion. **2** Any particles that are sent high into the atmosphere and that eventually fall to earth: harmful *fallout* of ash from a volcanic eruption.

fal·low [fal'ō] **1** *adj.* Plowed but not planted for a season: *fallow* land. **2** *n.* Land allowed to lie unplanted so as to make it more fertile.

fallow deer A small European deer whose yellowish coat has white spots on it in summer.

Fallow deer

false [fôls] **1** *adj.* Not true, right, or correct; wrong. **2** *adj.* Based on mistaken ideas: *false* economy. **3** *adj.* Not real or genuine; artificial: *false* teeth. **4** *adj.* Meant to deceive or trick: *false* pretenses. **5** *adj.* Not truthful; lying: a *false* witness. **6** *adj.* Not faithful; disloyal: *false* friends. **7** *adv.* In a false manner. **—play (someone) false** To mislead, cheat, or betray (someone). **—false'ly** *adv.* **—false'ness** *n.*

false colors **1** The flag of another country flown as though one's own: The ship was sailing under *false colors.* **2** False pretenses.

false·hood [fôls'hŏŏd'] *n.* **1** A lie or act of lying. **2** Untruthfulness. **3** An untrue belief.

false teeth **1** Artificial teeth made to replace real ones. **2** A set of artificial teeth.

fal·set·to [fôl·set'ō] *n., pl.* **fal·set·tos,** *adv., adj.* **1** *n.* A way of singing that makes the voice high but thin: The high notes in a yodel are in *falsetto.* **2** *adv.* In falsetto. **3** *adj.* Sung or to be sung in falsetto.

fal·si·fy [fôl'sə·fī] *v.* **fal·si·fied, fal·si·fy·ing** **1** To change or give a wrong idea of so as to deceive: to *falsify* results. **2** To tell lies. **3** To prove to be false; disprove. **—fal·si·fi·ca·tion** [fôl'sə·fə·kā'shən] *n.*

fal·si·ty [fôl'sə·tē] *n., pl.* **fal·si·ties** **1** The quality of being false. **2** A lie.

Fal·staff [fôl'staf'] *n.* A boastful, cowardly, but witty old knight in Shakespeare's *Henry the Fourth* and *The Merry Wives of Windsor.* **—Fal·staff'i·an** *adj.*

fal·ter [fôl'tər] **1** *v.* To hesitate, be uncertain, or give way: His determination never *faltered.* **2** *v.* To move or speak in an unsteady or stumbling way. **3** *n.* An uncertainty or hesitation in voice or action. **—fal'ter·er** *n.* **—fal'ter·ing·ly** *adv.*

fame [fām] *n.* **1** The act or condition of being well known and highly regarded; renown. **2** Reputation: of ill *fame.*

famed [fāmd] *adj.* Widely known; famous.

fa·mil·ial [fə·mil'yəl] *adj.* Of, characteristic of, or having to do with a family.

a	add	**i**	it	**ŏŏ**	took	**oi**	oil
ā	ace	**ī**	ice	**ōō**	pool	**ou**	pout
â	care	**o**	odd	**u**	up	**ng**	ring
ä	palm	**ō**	open	**û**	burn	**th**	thin
e	end	**ô**	order	**yōō**	fuse	**th**	this
ē	equal					**zh**	vision

ə = a in *above* e in *sicken* i in *possible* o in *melon* u in *circus*

fa·mil·iar [fə·mil′yər] 1 *adj.* Well acquainted, as through experience or study: *familiar* with modern art. 2 *adj.* Well-known because often encountered: a *familiar* voice. 3 *adj.* Intimate or friendly: We are on *familiar* terms. 4 *n.* A good friend. 5 *adj.* Improperly friendly; forward: Don't be *familiar* with strangers. 6 *n.* A spirit said to take animal form to serve a witch: A black cat was thought of as a witch's *familiar.* **—fa·mil′iar·ly** *adv.*

fa·mil·i·ar·i·ty [fə·mil′ē·ar′ə·tē *or* fə·mil′yar′ə·tē] *n., pl.* **fa·mil·i·ar·i·ties** 1 Thorough acquaintance, as with a subject. 2 Absence of formality. 3 Friendly closeness. 4 (*often pl.*) Impertinent speech or manner.

fa·mil·iar·ize [fə·mil′yə·rīz′] *v.* **fa·mil·iar·ized, fa·mil·iar·iz·ing** 1 To make well acquainted: *Familiarize* yourself with the traffic laws. 2 To make (something) well known. **—fa·mil′iar·i·za′tion** *n.*

fam·i·ly [fam′ə·lē *or* fam′lē] *n., pl.* **fam·i·lies** 1 A unit consisting of parents and their children. 2 One's group of children: They reared a large *family.* 3 A group of persons forming a household. 4 One's entire group of relatives. 5 A group of people descended from the same ancestor. 6 In biology, a group of related animals or plants: The wolf belongs to the dog *family.* 7 Any class or group of related things: a *family* of languages.

family name Another term for SURNAME.

family tree A diagram giving the ancestors of a family and showing all their descendants.

fam·ine [fam′in] *n.* 1 A widespread lack of food which causes many to starve. 2 Starvation. 3 Any serious scarcity: a water *famine.*

fam·ished [fam′isht] *adj.* Extremely hungry.

fa·mous [fā′məs] *adj.* 1 Very well known and often mentioned or praised; celebrated; renowned. 2 *informal* Excellent; splendid. **—fa′mous·ly** *adv.*

fan[1] [fan] *n., v.* **fanned, fan·ning** 1 *n.* A device for stirring the air, so as to create a cool breeze. A hand fan folds up and opens out into a wedge-like shape, while an electric fan has revolving blades. 2 *v.* To stir (the air) with or as if with a fan. 3 *v.* To direct air upon, as by using a fan: to *fan* the face. 4 *v.* To stir to action: to *fan* the flames of hatred. 5 *n.* Anything like an open fan, as a peacock's tail. 6 *v.* To spread like a fan.

Fans

fan[2] [fan] *n.* 1 A person very enthusiastic about some sport or entertainment. 2 A devoted admirer, as of an actor or sports star.

fa·nat·ic [fə·nat′ik] *n.* A person whose exaggerated enthusiasm or zeal leads to unreasonable beliefs.

fa·nat·i·cal [fə·nat′i·kəl] *adj.* Unreasonably enthusiastic. **—fa·nat′i·cal·ly** *adv.*

fa·nat·i·cism [fə·nat′ə·siz′əm] *n.* Devotion or zeal that goes beyond the bounds of reason.

fan·cied [fan′sēd] *adj.* Imagined; unreal: *fancied* insults.

fan·ci·er [fan′sē·ər] *n.* A person with a special interest in something, as in breeding a certain kind of animal: a poodle *fancier.*

fan·ci·ful [fan′si·fəl] *adj.* 1 Full of pleasantly odd, imaginative ideas: a *fanciful* mind. 2 Created by the fancy; not real: *fanciful* notions. 3 Pleasantly odd in appearance; quaint; whimsical: a *fanciful* costume. **—fan′ci·ful·ly** *adv.* **—fan′ci·ful·ness** *n.*

fan·ci·ly [fan′sə·lē] *adv.* In a fancy way; finely or showily.

fan·ci·ness [fan′sē·nis] *n.* Fancy appearance or quality.

fan·cy [fan′sē] *n., pl.* **fan·cies,** *v.* **fan·cied, fan·cy·ing,** *adj.* **fan·ci·er, fan·ci·est** 1 *n.* The ability to picture odd, whimsical, or unreal things in the mind; imagination. 2 *v.* To imagine or picture: *Fancy* that! 3 *n.* Something imagined, as an idea or notion: Was it a fact or a *fancy?* 4 *v.* To believe without being positive; suppose: I *fancy* they are tired. 5 *n.* A liking: He took a *fancy* to the child. 6 *v.* To like; enjoy: to *fancy* special foods. 7 *adj.* Decorated or elegant: a *fancy* shirt. 8 *adj.* Of unusually high quality; choice: *fancy* peaches. 9 *adj.* Extremely high: *fancy* prices. 10 *adj.* Showy and elaborate: a dancer's *fancy* footwork.

fancy dress A costume of the kind worn at a masquerade.

fan·cy-free [fan′sē·frē′] *adj.* Free from commitments or obligations; carefree.

fan·cy·work [fan′sē·wûrk′] *n.* Ornamental needlework, as embroidery.

fan·dan·go [fan·dang′gō] *n., pl.* **fan·dan·gos** A lively Spanish dance or the music for it.

fan·fare [fan′fâr′] *n.* 1 A lively phrase of music played on trumpets or bugles to attract attention. 2 Any noisy or showy display: The candidate slipped into town without *fanfare.*

Fangs

fang [fang] *n.* 1 A long, pointed tooth by which an animal seizes and tears its prey. 2 One of the long, hollow or grooved teeth with which a poisonous snake injects its poison.

fan·light [fan′līt′] *n.* A semicircular window resembling an open fan, as over a door.

Fanlight

fan mail The mail an entertainer or other celebrity receives from admirers.

fan·tail [fan′tāl′] *n.* 1 Any end, tail, or part shaped like an open fan. 2 A domestic pigeon or fancy goldfish with a fanlike tail.

fan·tas·tic [fan·tas′tik] *adj.* 1 Odd, original, weird, or unreal, like a creation of the fancy: *fantastic* shapes and forms. 2 Amazing; unbelievable: He told a *fantastic* story about how he was kidnapped by invaders from Mars. ◆ *Fantastic* has its roots in *fantasy.* Save this word for amazing things; don't overuse it to describe things that are merely "very good."

fan·tas·ti·cal [fan·tas′ti·kəl] *adj.* Fantastic or eccentric. **—fan·tas′ti·cal·ly** *adv.*

fan·ta·sy [fan′tə·sē] *n., pl.* **fan·ta·sies** 1 Imagination or wild fancy. 2 A creation of the imagination, as a story or daydream very different from reality.

far [fär] *adv., adj.* **far·ther** or **fur·ther, far·thest** or **fur·thest** 1 *adv.* At, to, or from a great distance: *far* from town; to come *far.* **2** *adj.* Very distant in space or time: a *far* country. **3** *adj.* More distant: the *far* side of the moon. **4** *adv.* To or at a particular distance, point, or degree: How *far* will they go to help us? **5** *adv.* Very much: *far* wiser. **—as far as** To the extent, distance, or degree that. **—by far** To a considerable degree; very much. **—far and away** Without a doubt; decidedly. **—far and wide** Over a considerable area; everywhere. **—so far** **1** To that extent; up to that point. **2** Up to now.

far·ad [far′ad′ *or* far′əd] *n.* A unit of capacitance equal to the capacitance of an object on which one coulomb of charge accumulates when it is subject to a potential difference of one volt.

faraday [far′ə·dā′] *n.* The quantity of electric charge needed to dissolve or deposit by electrolysis a number of grams of a substance equal to its molecular weight. One faraday is equal to 96,487 coulombs. ◆ Both *farad* and *faraday* are named for the English scientist Michael Faraday.

far·a·way [fär′ə·wā′] *adj.* **1** Distant: *faraway* islands. **2** Absentminded: a *faraway* look.

farce [färs] *n.* **1** A comedy using exaggeration and ridiculous situations to be funny. **2** A ridiculous action or empty pretense that deceives no one: The investigation was a *farce.*

far·ci·cal [fär′si·kəl] *adj.* **1** Like a farce; laughable; absurd; ridiculous. **2** Of farce. **—far′ci·cal′i·ty** *n.* **—far′ci·cal·ly** *adv.*

far cry A long way.

fare [fâr] *n., v.* **fared, far·ing** **1** *n.* The money charged or paid to ride in a bus, train, or other means of transportation. **2** *n.* A passenger who pays a fare. **3** *v.* To get along; manage; do: Their team *fared* poorly in the race. **4** *v.* To turn out; happen or go: Things *fared* well with us. **5** *n.* Food and drink.

fare-thee-well [fâr′~~th~~ē·wel′] *n.* The greatest or best possible degree or condition; the utmost: polished his shoes to a *fare-thee-well.*

fare·well [fâr′wel′] **1** *interj.* Good-by and may you get on well. **2** *n.* A saying good-by. **3** *adj.* Parting: a *farewell* speech.

far·fetched [fär′fecht′] *adj.* Not natural or probable: a *farfetched* excuse.

far-flung [fär′flung′] *adj.* Extending over great distances: *far-flung* business interests.

fa·ri·na [fə·rē′nə] *n.* Finely ground grain, especially wheat, used as a breakfast cereal and in puddings.

farm [färm] **1** *n.* An area of land used for growing crops or raising animals, as cattle, sheep, pigs, and chickens. **2** *v.* To grow crops or raise livestock. **3** *v.* To prepare or use (land) for crops: to *farm* 80 acres. **4** *n.* Land or water used to grow other products: an oyster *farm.* **—farm out** **1** To send (an athlete) to a minor league for experience. **2** To send out (work) from an office or shop to be done by others.

farm·er [fär′mər] *n.* A person who works on, manages, or owns a farm.

farmer cheese A white cheese made from milk curds, similar to but more solid than cottage cheese.

farm·hand [färm′hand′] *n.* A laborer who works for wages on a farm.

farm·house [färm′hous′] *n.* A home on a farm.

farm·ing [fär′ming] *n.* The business of running a farm and raising crops or livestock.

farm·stead [färm′sted′] *n.* A farm and the buildings on it: a beautiful, old *farmstead* in Massachusetts.

farm·yard [färm′yärd′] *n.* The yard around farm buildings; barnyard.

far-off [fär′ôf′] *adj.* Distant; remote.

far-out [fär′out′] *adj. slang* Very unconventional or unusual; extreme.

far·ra·go [fə·rä′gō] *n., pl.* **far·ra·goes** A confused mixture; hodgepodge.

far-reach·ing [fär′rē′ching] *adj.* Having a wide influence or range: *far-reaching* changes.

far·ri·er [far′ē·ər] *n.* **1** A person who shoes horses; blacksmith. **2** A doctor for animals.

far·row [far′ō] **1** *n.* A litter of pigs. **2** *v.* To give birth to (young): said about pigs.

far·see·ing [fär′sē′ing] *adj.* **1** Able to see far. **2** Good at planning ahead for the future.

far·sight·ed [fär′sī′tid] *adj.* **1** Able to see distant things more clearly than things near at hand. **2** Showing good judgment in looking and planning ahead. **—far′sight′ed·ly** *adv.* **—far′sight′ed·ness** *n.*

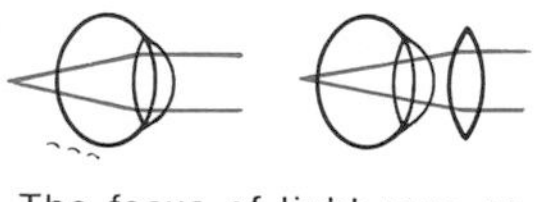

The focus of light rays entering a farsighted eye is behind the retina. A convex lens corrects this.

far·ther [fär′~~th~~ər] **1** Comparative of FAR. **2** *adv.* At or to a more distant point: *farther* down the road; I can go no *farther.* **3** *adj.* More distant: the *farther* end of the avenue. **4** *adj.* Additional; more; further. ◆ *Farther* is preferred for distance in space: ten miles *farther;* Don't go any *farther* away. *Further* is preferred in relation to time, degree, or quantity: *further* information; My memory goes back no *further.*

far·ther·most [fär′~~th~~ər·mōst′] *adj.* Most distant; farthest: the *farthermost* point.

far·thest [fär′~~th~~ist] **1** Superlative of FAR. **2** *adv.* At or to the most distant point: Who jumped *farthest?* **3** *adj.* Most distant: the *farthest* island in the chain.

far·thing [fär′~~th~~ing] *n.* A small coin once used in England, worth about 1/4 of a penny.

far·thin·gale [fär′~~th~~ən·gāl′ *or* fär′thing·gāl′] *n.* A hooplike frame worn under a skirt to hold it out from the hips, popular in the 16th century.

fas·ci·nate [fas′ə·nāt′] *v.* **fas·ci·nat·ed, fas·ci·nat·ing** **1** To attract and interest extremely, as by novelty, mystery, or charm: The magician's tricks *fascinated* us. **2** To hold paralyzed and helpless, as by a strange influence: a bird *fascinated* by a snake.

fas·ci·na·ting [fas′ə·nā′ting] *adj.* Strongly attracting and holding the attention of others; extremely interesting. **—fas ci·na′ting·ly** *adv.*

fas·ci·na·tion [fas′ə·nā′shən] *n.* **1** The act of fascinating. **2** Great interest or charm.

fas·ci·na·tor [fas′ə·nā′tər] *n.* **1** A person or thing that fascinates. **2** A woman's lightweight, decorative scarf, worn on the head.

a	add	**i**	it	**o͝o**	took	**oi**	oil
ā	ace	**ī**	ice	**o͞o**	pool	**ou**	pout
â	care	**o**	odd	**u**	up	**ng**	ring
ä	palm	**ō**	open	**û**	burn	**th**	thin
e	end	**ô**	order	**yo͞o**	fuse	**~~th~~**	this
ē	equal					**zh**	vision

ə = a in *above* e in *sicken* i in *possible* o in *melon* u in *circus*

fas·cism [fash′iz·əm] *n.* A form of government in which a dictator and the dictator's party support private property but strictly control industry and labor, and ruthlessly suppress criticism or opposition. **—fas′cist** *adj., n.*

fash·ion [fash′ən] **1** *n.* The style, as of dress or behavior, popular at any given time: new spring *fashions.* **2** *n.* A current practice. **3** *n.* Manner; way: The lecturer spoke in a forceful *fashion.* **4** *v.* To make, shape, or form: to *fashion* a snowman. **5** *n.* Outward appearance. **—after a fashion** In a way; not well. ◆ See CUSTOM.

fash·ion·a·ble [fash′ən·ə·bəl] *adj.* **1** In style; stylish: a *fashionable* coat. **2** Of or attracting socially prominent people: a *fashionable* part of the city. **—fash′ion·a·bly** *adv.*

fashion plate **1** An illustration of a style of dress. **2** A person who dresses in the latest styles.

fast[1] [fast] **1** *adj.* Moving or acting with speed; quick; swift; rapid: a *fast* worker. **2** *adv.* Quickly; swiftly; rapidly: to walk *fast.* **3** *adj.* Ahead of the correct time: The clock is *fast.* **4** *adj.* Devoted to harmful pleasures; wild: a *fast* life. **5** *adv.* In a firm manner; firmly: Stand *fast* and don't yield. **6** *adj.* Firmly fastened, attached, or fixed: a boat made *fast* to the dock. **7** *adj.* Faithful; loyal: *fast* friends. **8** *adj.* Not apt to fade: *fast* colors. **9** *adv.* Soundly: *fast* asleep.

fast[2] [fast] **1** *v.* To go without food or avoid certain foods, as for religious reasons. **2** *n.* The act of fasting. **3** *n.* A period of fasting.

fast·back [fast′bak′] *n.* An automobile with a long, gradual slope to the rear from the top of the roof.

fas·ten [fas′(ə)n] *v.* **1** To close up or make secure: *Fasten* my dress; *Fasten* the door. **2** To attach, as by tying or pinning: *Fasten* the boat to the dock. **3** To direct steadily: The audience *fastened* its gaze on the stage.

fas·ten·er [fas′(ə)n·ər] *n.* A fastening.

fas·ten·ing [fas′(ə)n·ing] *n.* Something used to fasten, as a bolt, zipper, or clasp.

fast-food [fast′fo͞od′] *adj.* Specializing in a small selection of food that is quickly prepared and informally served: We had a snack at a *fast-food* counter.

fas·tid·i·ous [fas·tid′ē·əs] *adj.* Extremely particular; hard to suit or please: My boss is a *fastidious* person. **—fas·tid′i·ous·ly** *adv.* **—fas·tid′i·ous·ness** *n.*

fast·ness [fast′nis] *n.* **1** A fortress; stronghold. **2** A firm or fixed condition. **3** Swiftness.

fast-talk [fast′tôk′] *v. informal* To talk glibly and deceptively in order to gain an advantage or escape blame. **—fast′-talk′er** *n.*

fat [fat] *n., adj.* **fat·ter, fat·test** **1** *n.* Any of a large class of yellowish to white, greasy substances found in plant and animal tissues. **2** *n.* Any such substance used in cooking, as butter, oil, or lard. **3** *adj.* Containing much oil or grease: *fat* meat. **4** *adj.* Rounded in body from having more flesh than is needed. **5** *adj.* Profitable: a *fat* job. **6** *n.* The richest or most desirable part: the *fat* of the land. **—fat′ness** *n.*

fa·tal [fāt′(ə)l] *adj.* **1** Causing death: a *fatal* illness. **2** Causing ruin or disaster: a *fatal* mistake. **3** Having important consequences: the *fatal* meeting. **—fa′tal·ly** *adv.*

fa·tal·ism [fāt′(ə)l·iz′əm] *n.* **1** The belief that all events are determined by fate, not by one's efforts. **2** Resigned acceptance of fate. **—fa′tal·ist** *n.* **—fa′·tal·is′tic** *adj.* **—fa′tal·is′ti·cal·ly** *adv.*

fa·tal·i·ty [fā·tal′ə·tē] *n., pl.* **fa·tal·i·ties** **1** A death brought about through some disaster or accident: Reduce traffic *fatalities.* **2** The capability of causing death or disaster; deadliness: the *fatality* of cancer.

fat·back [fat′bak′] *n.* Fat from the back of a hog, usually cured like bacon.

fat cat *slang* **1** A very rich and highly privileged person. **2** A very influential or powerful person. **3** A very rich person who makes large contributions to a political party.

fate [fāt] *n.* **1** A power supposed to determine in advance the way things happen; destiny: to defy *fate.* **2** What happens to a person; fortune; lot: It was the author's *fate* to write a best seller. **3** Final outcome; end: The jury will decide the *fate* of the accused. **—the Fates** In Greek myths, the three goddesses who controlled human destiny.

fat·ed [fā′tid] *adj.* Destined, doomed, or marked by fate: They were *fated* never to meet.

fate·ful [fāt′fəl] *adj.* **1** Having a serious effect on the future: a *fateful* choice. **2** Warning about the future; ominous: a prophet's *fateful* words. **3** Bringing death or disaster: the *fateful* shot. **4** Brought about by fate.

fa·ther [fä′thər] **1** *n.* The male parent of a child. **2** *v.* To become the father of: He *fathered* twin sons. **3** *n.* Any male ancestor. **4** *n.* A man or a thing to which something else owes its existence; creator or source: the founding *fathers* of our nation. **5** *v.* To originate, create, or claim as one's own: to *father* new legislation. **6** *n.* (*written* **Father**) God. **7** *n.* (*usually written* **Father**) A priest. **8** *n.* (*usually pl.*) A leader: the city *fathers.*

father figure A person regarded as a benevolent source of protection and authority.

fa·ther·hood [fä′thər·ho͝od′] *n.* The condition of being a father.

fa·ther-in-law [fä′thər·in·lô′] *n., pl.* **fathers-in-law** The father of one's husband or wife.

fa·ther·land [fä′thər·land′] *n.* The land of one's birth; one's native country.

fa·ther·less [fä′thər·lis] *adj.* **1** Having no father living. **2** Not having a known father.

fa·ther·ly [fä′thər·lē] *adj.* Of or like a father: *fatherly* pride. **—fa′ther·li·ness** *n.*

Father's Day A day for honoring fathers, observed on the third Sunday in June.

fath·om [fath′əm] **1** *n.* A measure of length equal to six feet, used mainly in measuring the depth of water. **2** *v.* To find the depth of. **3** *v.* To understand; puzzle out. **—fath′om·a·ble** *adj.*

fath·om·less [fath′əm·lis] *adj.* Too deep to measure or to understand; unfathomable.

fa·tigue [fə·tēg′] *n., v.* **fa·tigued, fa·ti·guing** **1** *n.* A tired condition resulting from hard work, effort, or strain; weariness. **2** *v.* To tire out; weary.

fat·ten [fat′(ə)n] *v.* To make or become fat.

fat·ty [fat′ē] *adj.* **fat·ti·er, fat·ti·est** **1** Made of fat. **2** Containing fat or too much fat, as bodily tissues. **3** Like fat; greasy.

fatty acid Any of a group of organic compounds with acidic properties that occur in animals and plant fats.

fa·tu·i·ty [fə·t(y)o͞o′ə·tē] *n., pl.* **fa·tu·i·ties** **1** Self-satisfied stupidity; fatuousness. **2** Something, especially a remark, that is fatuous.

fat·u·ous [fach′o͞o·əs] *adj.* Foolish or stupid in a self-satisfied way. **—fat′u·ous·ly** *adv.* **—fat′u·ous·ness** *n.*

fau·cet [fô′sit] *n.* A device with an adjustable valve

used to start, stop, or regulate the flow of a liquid, as from a pipe; spigot.

faugh [fô] *interj.* An expression of distaste or contempt.

fault [fôlt] *n.* 1 Something that makes a person or thing less than perfect; defect, weakness, or flaw. 2 A mistake or blunder. 3 Responsibility for wrongdoing or neglect; blame. 4 A break in the earth's crust causing rock layers to shift. **—at fault** In the wrong. **—find fault** To look for and complain about mistakes. **—find fault with** To criticize.

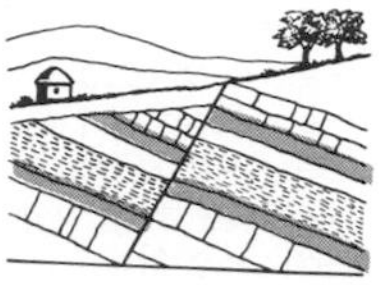

Fault

fault·find·er [fôlt'fīn'dər] *n.* A person who is always looking for and complaining about mistakes.

fault·find·ing [fôlt'fīn'ding] 1 *adj.* Always looking for faults; unduly critical. 2 *n.* Petty and persistent criticism.

fault·less [fôlt'lis] *adj.* Free from any fault or flaw; perfect. **—fault'less·ly** *adv.*

fault·y [fôl'tē] *adj.* **fault·i·er, fault·i·est** Having faults; imperfect. **—fault'i·ly** *adv.*

faun [fôn] *n.* In Roman myths, a woodland god represented as a man having the ears, horns, tail, and hind legs of a goat.

fau·na [fô'nə] *n.* The animals living within a certain area or during a certain period.

Faust [foust] *n.* In German legend, a magician who made a bargain with the devil and received power and knowledge in exchange for his soul. **—Faust'·i·an** *adj.*

Faus·tus [fou'stəs] *n.* Another name for FAUST.

fau·vism [fō'viz·əm] *n.* (*often written* **Fauvism**) A movement in painting of the early 20th century characterized by the use of vivid colors and a treatment of form that resulted in bold, often distorted images. **—fau'vist** (*often written* **Fauvist**) *n., adj.*

faux pas [fō' pä'] *pl.* **faux pas** [fō' pä(z)'] An embarrassing blunder, especially in etiquette or conduct. ◆ *Faux pas* comes from a French term meaning *false step.*

fa·vor [fā'vər] 1 *n.* A kind act or service: My friend did me a *favor.* 2 *v.* To oblige. 3 *v.* To help along; aid: The thick fog *favored* their escape. 4 *v.* To approve of or support: I *favor* your suggestion. 5 *n.* Good will, liking, or approval. 6 *v.* To prefer in a prejudiced way: The reviewer *favors* novels over biographies. 7 *n.* A little gift; keepsake: party *favors.* 8 *v.* To look like: Which side of the family do you *favor*? 9 *v.* To treat gently; spare: to *favor* a hurt foot. **—in favor of** 1 On the side of; for. 2 To the advantage of. **—in one's favor** To one's advantage or profit.

fa·vor·a·ble [fā'vər·ə·bəl] *adj.* 1 Helping: a *favorable* wind. 2 Encouraging or supporting: a *favorable* reply. **—fa'vor·a·bly** *adv.* **—fa'vor·a·ble·ness** *n.*

fa·vored [fā'vərd] *adj.* 1 Having special gifts or advantages. 2 Looked upon or treated with special favor. 3 Having an appearance of a specified kind: to be ill-*favored.*

fa·vor·ite [fā'vər·it] 1 *n.* A person or thing preferred over others. 2 *adj.* Best loved.

fa·vor·it·ism [fā'vər·ə·tiz'əm] *n.* An unfair favoring of one or a few out of a group.

fawn[1] [fôn] *v.* 1 To show affection as a dog does by crouching or licking the hands. 2 To seek favor or advantage by humbling oneself and flattering.

fawn[2] [fôn] *n.* 1 A young deer not yet a year old. 2 Its color, a light yellowish brown.

FAX [faks] 1 *n.* A machine that sends printed documents over telephone lines and then reproduces them at another location. 2 *v.* To send by means of a FAX machine.

Fawn

fay [fā] *n.* A fairy.

faze [fāz] *v.* **fased, faz·ing** *informal* To disturb or upset.

FBI Federal Bureau of Investigation.

FCC Federal Communications Commission.

FDA Food and Drug Administration.

FDIC or **F.D.I.C.** Federal Deposit Insurance Corporation.

FDR or **F.D.R.** Franklin Delano Roosevelt.

Fe The symbol for the element iron. ◆ The Latin word for iron is *ferrum.*

fe·al·ty [fē'əl·tē] *n.* 1 The loyalty owed to a feudal lord by a vassal. 2 Faithfulness; allegiance; loyalty.

fear [fir] 1 *n.* A frightening feeling that danger or trouble is close; dread; terror. 2 *v.* To feel dread or terror. 3 *v.* To be frightened of: to *fear* the dark. 4 *n.* A cause of dread: My worst *fear* is failure. 5 *v.* To be uneasy or worried: I *fear* that they won't come. 6 *n.* An uneasy feeling.

fear·ful [fir'fəl] *adj.* 1 Full of fear; frightened: *fearful* of strangers; a *fearful* look. 2 Causing fear; frightening: a *fearful* storm. 3 *informal* Extremely bad. **—fear'ful·ly** *adv.* **—fear'ful·ness** *n.*

fear·less [fir'lis] *adj.* Without fear; not at all afraid; brave. **—fear'less·ly** *adv.*

fear·some [fir'səm] *adj.* Causing fear; alarming. **—fear'some·ly** *adv.* **—fear'some·ness** *n.*

fea·si·ble [fē'ze·bəl] *adj.* 1 Capable of being done or put into effect: a *feasible* plan. 2 Fairly probable; likely: a *feasible* explanation. **—fea·si·bil·i·ty** [fē'zə·bil'ə·tē] *n.* **—fea'si·bly** *adv.*

feast [fēst] 1 *n.* A great meal at which there is an abundance of food; banquet. 2 *v.* To entertain with such a meal: To celebrate, we *feasted* our friends. 3 *v.* To eat heartily. 4 *v.* To delight; gratify: to *feast* the eyes on a loved one. 5 *n.* A joyous religious celebration.

feat [fēt] *n.* A remarkable act or deed, as one showing great skill, endurance, or daring.

feath·er [feth'ər] 1 *n.* One of the growths that cover a bird's skin, made up of a hollow quill with fanlike webs of light, soft filaments growing out on each side of it. 2 *n.* A thing like a feather. 3 *v.* To furnish or cover with feathers. 4 *v.* To grow

a	add	**i**	it	**ŏŏ**	took	**oi**	oil
ā	ace	**ī**	ice	**ōō**	pool	**ou**	pout
â	care	**o**	odd	**u**	up	**ng**	ring
ä	palm	**ō**	open	**û**	burn	**th**	thin
e	end	**ô**	order	**yōō**	fuse	**th**	this
ē	equal					**zh**	vision

ə = a in *above* e in *sicken* i in *possible* o in *melon* u in *circus*

feathers. **5** *n.* The same class or sort; kind: birds of a *feather.* **6** *v.* To turn edgewise, or flat: to *feather* an oar; to *feather* propeller blades. **—a feather in one's cap** An achievement to be proud of.

feather bed A soft mattress stuffed with feathers and used on a bed or as a bed.

feath·er·bed·ding [feth'ər·bed'ing] *n.* The practice, used by some labor unions, of requiring employers to hire more workers than are actually needed. ◆ *Featherbedding* was made up, or "coined," from a bed of feathers to describe the soft life of the workers involved.

feath·er·weight [feth'ər·wāt'] *n.* **1** A boxer whose weight is between 118 and 127 pounds. **2** A person or thing of very light weight or small importance.

feath·er·y [feth'ər·ē] *adj.* **1** Provided with or suggesting feathers. **2** Light as a feather.

fea·ture [fē'chər] *n., v.* **fea·tured, fea·tur·ing** **1** *n.* A part of the face, as the eyes, nose, or mouth. **2** *n.* A prominent characteristic or quality: The snow was the worst *feature* of our trip. **3** *n.* A special attraction, as at a sale or exhibit. **4** *n.* A full-length motion picture. **5** *n.* A special article, story, or column, as in a newspaper. **6** *v.* To present as worthy of special attention: to *feature* a story on page one.

Feb. February.

feb·ri·fuge [feb'rə·fyōōj'] **1** *n.* Something that relieves a fever. **2** *adj.* Effective in reducing fever.

fe·brile [feb'rəl] *adj.* Of, caused by, or having fever; feverish.

Feb·ru·ar·y [feb'rōō·er'ē *or* feb'yōō·er'ē] *n.* The second month of the year, having 28, or, in leap years, 29 days.

fe·cal [fē'səl] *adj.* Consisting of or resembling feces.

fe·ces [fē'sēz] *n.pl.* Solid waste matter discharged from the intestines.

feck·less [fek'lis] *adj.* **1** Careless; irresponsible. **2** Weak; useless. **—feck'less·ly** *adv.* **—feck'less·ness** *n.* ◆ *Feckless* was first a Scottish word meaning *effectless* or *futile.* It was borrowed by English speakers in the 1500's along with *feckful,* meaning *effective,* but *feckful* eventually fell out of use.

fe·cund [fē'kənd *or* fek'ənd] *adj.* **1** Fruitful; fertile. **2** Intellectually creative or productive. **—fe·cun·di·ty** [fi·kun'də·tē] *n.*

fed [fed] Past tense and past participle of FEED.

fed·er·al [fed'ər·əl] **1** *adj.* Of, having to do with, or based on an agreement between two or more states to unite under one central government: a *federal* union. **2** *adj.* (*often written* **Federal**) Of, having, or belonging to such a union of states: *federal* troops; the *Federal* government. **3** *adj.* (*written* **Federal**) Of, having to do with, or loyal to the Union cause in the Civil War. **4** *n.* (*written* **Federal**) A supporter of the Union during the Civil War. **5** *adj.* (*written* **Federal**) Of or supporting the Federalist Party.

Federal Bureau of Investigation A division of the Department of Justice charged with the investigation of violations of federal law.

fed·er·al·ism [fed'ər·ə·liz'əm] *n.* **1** A political system or theory favoring federal control. **2** (*usually written* **Federalism**) The doctrines or activities of the Federalist Party.

fed·er·al·ist [fed'ər·əl·ist] **1** *n.* A person who favors a federal government. **2** *n.* (*written* **Federalist**) A member of the Federalist Party. **3** *adj.* (*often written* **Federalist**) Of or having to do with a federal government or the Federalist Party.

Federalist Party A political party (1787–1830) that favored the adoption of the U.S. Constitution and a strong central government.

fed·er·al·ize [fed'ər·ə·līz'] *v.* **fed·er·al·ized, fed·er·al·iz·ing** **1** To bring (separate political units) together under a central authority. **2** To put under the control of a federal government.

fed·er·ate [fed'ə·rāt'] *v.* **fed·er·at·ed, fed·er·at·ing** To unite in a federation.

fed·er·a·tion [fed'ə·rā'shən] *n.* The union of two or more states or groups under one governing body.

fe·do·ra [fə·dôr'ə] *n.* A soft hat, usually of felt, with a curved brim and a low crown creased lengthwise.

Fedora

fee [fē] *n.* **1** A charge, as for services or rights: a membership *fee;* a doctor's *fee.* **2** A piece of land or an estate that has been or can be inherited.

fee·ble [fē'bəl] *adj.* **fee·bler, fee·blest** **1** Lacking strength; weak. **2** Not adequate or effective: *feeble* efforts. **—fee'ble·ness** *n.* **—fee'bly** *adv.*

fee·ble·mind·ed [fē'bəl·mīn'did] *adj.* Lacking normal mental ability; mentally deficient. **—fee'ble·mind'ed·ly** *adv.* **—fee'ble·mind'ed·ness** *n.*

feed [fēd] *v.* **fed, feed·ing,** *n.* **1** *v.* To give food to: to *feed* the family. **2** *v.* To give as food: to *feed* carrots to rabbits. **3** *v.* To eat: goats *feed* on grass. **4** *n.* Food, especially for animals: chicken *feed.* **5** *n. informal* A meal. **6** *v.* To supply or furnish with something: to *feed* a fire with fuel; to *feed* suspicions. **—fed up** *slang* Bored, tired, or annoyed.

feed·back [fēd'bak'] *n.* A sample of or information about what a machine or system is producing, returned to it in a way that modifies operation.

feed·bag [fēd'bag'] *n.* A bag that holds feed and fits over a horse's muzzle.

feed·er [fē'dər] *n.* **1** A person or animal that either consumes or supplies food. **2** Anything that contributes material to a system or process.

feed·lot [fēd'lot'] *n.* A plot of land on which livestock are grazed to fatten them for market.

feel [fēl] *v.* **felt, feel·ing,** *n.* **1** *v.* To get an impression of by touching: *Feel* the material. **2** *n.* Quality as perceived by touch: a soft *feel.* **3** *v.* To be aware of: to *feel* sweat on one's forehead. **4** *n.* A sense or impression. **5** *v.* To be or seem to be to the body, touch, or mind: The room *feels* cold. **6** *v.* To move along or explore by touching: to *feel* one's way in the dark. **7** *v.* To have the sensation of being: He *feels* cold. **8** *v.* To experience: to *feel* joy. **9** *v.* To experience sympathy: I *feel* for you. **10** *v.* To believe or be convinced: I *feel* that I should go. **—feel like** *informal* To have an inclination for: I *feel like* swimming. **—feel (like) oneself** To seem to oneself to be in one's usual or normal state of health or spirits. **—feel out** **1** To try to learn indirectly and cautiously the viewpoint or opinions of (a person). **2** To try to find out about (a situation) in a cautious way. **—feel up to** *informal* To think one is capable of.

feel·er [fē′lər] *n.* 1 A special part of an animal for touching, as a tentacle or an insect's antenna. 2 A question or remark made in order to find out the opinions, attitudes, or plans of others.

Feelers

feel·ing [fē′ling] 1 *n.* The sense of touch, through which one experiences heat, cold, and contact. 2 *n.* A sensation or awareness of something: a *feeling* of dizziness. 3 *n.* An emotion: the *feeling* of joy or sadness. 4 *n.* Sympathy or compassion. 5 *n.* (*pl.*) The sensitive or emotional side of a person's nature: The remark hurt my *feelings.* 6 *adj.* Full of emotion or sympathy: a *feeling* reply. 7 *n.* An opinion: I have a *feeling* that this answer is wrong. **—feel′ing·ly** *adv.*

fee simple *pl.* **fees simple** A piece of land that the owner is legally free to will or dispose of without restriction.

feet [fēt] Plural of FOOT.

feign [fān] *v.* To pretend: to *feign* interest.

feigned [fānd] *adj.* 1 Purely imaginary; made up: *feigned* illness. 2 Meant to deceive; false: *feigned* sympathy.

feint [fānt] 1 *n.* A pretended blow or attack made in order to distract an opponent from the real blow or attack. 2 *n.* An appearance or action meant to deceive or mislead. 3 *v.* To make a feint.

fe·la·fel [fə·lä′fəl] *n.* Another spelling of FALAFEL.

feld·spar [feld′spär′] *n.* A hard, crystalline mineral containing silicon and aluminum.

fe·lic·i·tate [fə·lis′ə·tāt′] *v.* **fe·lic·i·tat·ed, fe·lic·i·tat·ing** To congratulate. **—fe·lic′i·ta′tion** *n.* **—fe·lic′i·ta·tor** *n.*

fe·lic·i·tous [fə·lis′ə·təs] *adj.* Particularly well chosen; apt: a *felicitous* phrase. **—fe·lic′i·tous·ly** *adv.* **—fe·lic′i·tous·ness** *adj.*

fe·lic·i·ty [fə·lis′ə·tē] *n., pl.* **fe·lic·i·ties** 1 Very great happiness; bliss. 2 A pleasant or effective manner or style: a *felicity* of phrasing. 3 A pleasant and appropriate remark.

fe·line [fē′līn′] 1 *n.* An animal of the cat family, which also includes lions, tigers, and leopards. 2 *adj.* Of the cat family. 3 *adj.* Like a cat: *feline* grace.

fell[1] [fel] Past tense of FALL.

fell[2] [fel] *v.* 1 To knock down: to *fell* an opponent. 2 To cut down (timber). 3 To hem one edge of (a seam) down flat over another.

fell[3] [fel] *adj.* Cruel; vicious; fierce: to kill with one *fell* blow.

fell[4] [fel] *n.* The skin of an animal; hide.

fel·lah [fel′ə] *n., pl.* **fel·la·hin** or **fel·la·heen** [fel′ə·hēn′] A small farmer or farm laborer in Egypt and some other Arab countries.

fel·loe [fel′ō] *n.* Another word for FELLY.

fel·low [fel′ō] 1 *n.* A man or boy. 2 *n.* A companion, associate, or equal: *fellows* in misery. 3 *adj.* Joined through some common condition: one's *fellow* workers. 4 *n.* A member of certain scholarly societies. 5 *n.* A graduate student awarded a fellowship. 6 *n.* Either one of a pair; mate: the *fellow* to a boot. ◆ *Fellow* goes back to a Scandinavian word meaning *a business partner.*

fel·low·man [fel′ō·man′] *n., pl.* **fel·low·men** [fel′ō·men′] A fellow human being.

fel·low·ship [fel′ō·ship′] *n.* 1 Warm companionship; friendship. 2 Association, as with others. 3 A group sharing the same interests. 4 A position or sum of money given to a student to finance graduate study.

fel·ly [fel′ē] *n., pl.* **fel·lies** A section of the rim of a spoked wheel.

fel·on[1] [fel′ən] *n.* A person guilty of a serious crime, such as murder or burglary.

fel·on[2] [fel′ən] *n.* A painful inflammation of a finger or toe, generally near the nail.

fe·lo·ni·ous [fə·lō′nē·əs] *adj.* Having to do with a felony; criminal: *felonious* assault. **—fe·lo′ni·ous·ly** *adv.* **—fe·lo′ni·ous·ness** *n.*

fel·o·ny [fel′ə·nē] *n., pl.* **fel·o·nies** A very serious crime, as murder, which is punishable by long imprisonment or even death.

felt[1] [felt] Past tense and past participle of FEEL: I *felt* better after resting.

felt[2] [felt] *n.* 1 A fabric made by matting a material, as wool or fur, by pressure under heat. 2 *adj. use:* a *felt* hat.

fem. 1 female. 2 feminine.

fe·male [fē′māl] 1 *adj.* Of the sex that brings forth children or young. 2 *n.* A person or animal of the female sex. 3 *adj.* Of or having to do with women: the *female* population.

fem·i·nine [fem′ə·nin] *adj.* 1 Of or having to do with the female sex. 2 Like, typical of, or appropriate to women. 3 In grammar, of the gender that includes words for females: *She, duchess,* and *mare* are in the *feminine* gender.

fem·i·nism [fem′ə·niz′əm] *n.* 1 The principle that women should have the same political, social, and economic rights and opportunities as men. 2 Activity to equalize the status of female and male members of a society. **—fem′i·nist** *n., adj.* **—fem′i·nis′tic** *adj.*

fem·i·nin·i·ty [fem′ə·nin′i·tē] *n.* 1 The characteristics possessed by or associated with women; the quality of being female. 2 Women in general.

fe·mur [fē′mər] *n.* The long bone of the thigh, extending from the pelvis to the knee.

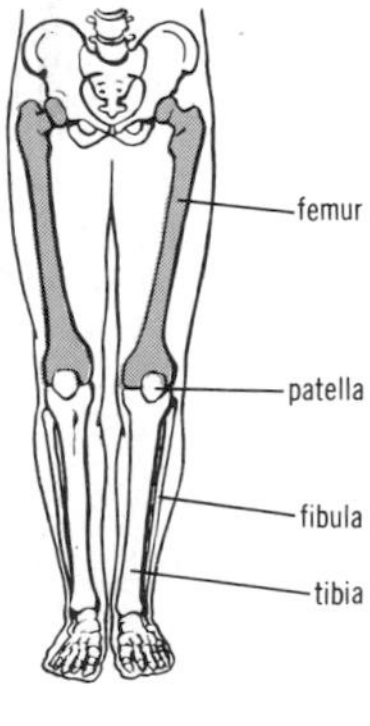

fen [fen] *n.* A swamp; marsh; bog.

fence [fens] *n., v.* **fenced, fenc·ing** 1 *n.* A structure, as of wooden rails, steel mesh, or wire, built as an enclosure, barrier, or boundary. 2 *v.* To enclose with a fence: to *fence* in cattle; to *fence* off a garden. 3 *v.* To practice the art of fencing with foils or swords. 4 *n.* A person who receives and disposes of stolen goods. **—on the fence** Undecided on some issue; not committed to one side or the other.

F

a	add	**i**	it	**o͝o**	took	**oi**	oil
ā	ace	**ī**	ice	**o͞o**	pool	**ou**	pout
â	care	**o**	odd	**u**	up	**ng**	ring
ä	palm	**ō**	open	**û**	burn	**th**	thin
e	end	**ô**	order	**yo͞o**	fuse	**t͟h**	this
ē	equal					**zh**	vision

ə = { a in *above* e in *sicken* i in *possible* / o in *melon* u in *circus* }

fence·mend·ing [fens′men′ding] *n.* The improvement of relations with former opponents.

fenc·er [fen′sər] *n.* A person who fences with a foil or sword.

fenc·ing [fen′sing] *n.* 1 The art or sport of using a foil or sword in attack and defense. 2 Material used in making or repairing fences. 3 Fences.

Fencing

fend [fend] *v.* To ward off: to *fend* off a blow or an attack. **—fend for oneself** To get along on one's own: An alley cat *fends for itself.*

fend·er [fen′dər] *n.* 1 A metal part projecting over each wheel, as of a car, to keep mud from being thrown upwards. 2 A part on the front of a locomotive to push away objects blocking the tracks. 3 A metal frame or screen set in front of a fireplace to keep in sparks or hot coals.

fen·nel [fen′əl] *n.* A tall herb with bright yellow flowers. Its seeds are used in medicines and as a flavoring in cooking.

FEPC or **F.E.P.C.** Fair Employment Practices Commission.

fe·ral [fir′əl *or* fer′əl] *adj.* 1 Wild; savage: a *feral* snarl. 2 Having escaped from a domesticated state and become wild: *feral* herds of horses.

fer-de-lance [fer′də·lans′] *n., pl.* **fer-de-lance** A large, extremely venomous snake of tropical America and the West Indies. ◆ French settlers in the West Indies named this dreaded snake *fer-de-lance,* or *spearhead,* because it has a horny spike on its tail like the metal tip of a spear.

fer·ment [*v.* fər·ment′, *n.* fûr′ment] 1 *v.* To undergo or bring about the slow decomposition of organic substances by the action of yeast, bacteria, or enzymes: Wine is formed when grape juice *ferments.* 2 *n.* Any substance that is used to bring about fermenting. 3 *n.* Fermentation. 4 *v.* To excite or be excited with emotion. 5 *n.* Agitation; excitement: the *ferment* of a battle.

fer·men·ta·tion [fûr′mən·tā′shən] *n.* The chemical change brought about in a substance by the action of a ferment, such as yeast, bacteria, or enzymes.

fer·mi·um [fûr′mē·əm] *n.* An artificially produced radioactive metallic element first discovered in fallout from a hydrogen bomb test.

fern [fûrn] *n.* Any of a large class of plants that have no flowers or seeds. They reproduce by means of spores growing on the undersides of their featherlike leaves, or fronds.

Fern

fe·ro·cious [fə·rō′shəs] *adj.* 1 Extremely fierce or savage. 2 *informal* Very intense or great: *ferocious* heat. **—fe·ro′cious·ly** *adv.* **—fe·ro′cious·ness** *n.*

fe·roc·i·ty [fə·ros′ə·tē] *n.* Extreme fierceness; savagery; cruelty.

fer·ret [fer′it] 1 *n.* A small animal related to the weasel that is sometimes tamed and used in hunting rabbits, rats, and other animals. 2 *v.* To drive out of hiding or to hunt with a ferret. 3 *v.* To uncover with difficulty by determined investigation: to *ferret* out a secret.

fer·ric [fer′ik] *adj.* Containing or having to do with iron in its higher valence.

Fer·ris wheel [fer′is] A giant wheel that revolves around a fixed axle and has seats in which passengers ride for amusement.

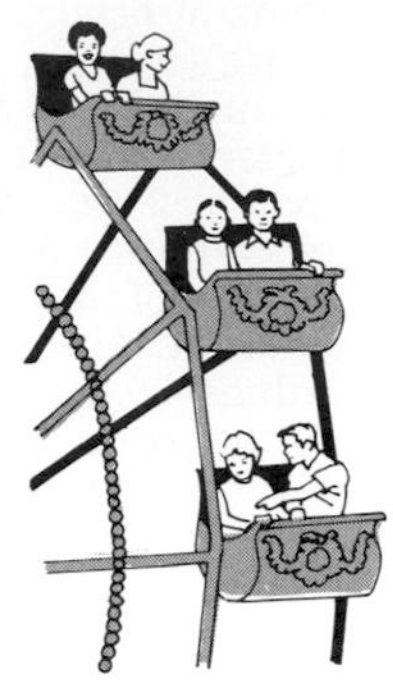
Ferris wheel

fer·ro·mag·net·ic [fer′ō·mag·net′·ik] *adj.* Having the property of readily becoming magnetic in the presence of a magnetic field. **—fer′ro·mag′ne·tism** *n.* ◆ *Ferromagnetic* contains the Latin root *ferrum,* meaning *iron,* because iron was the first substance known to be magnetic. As other metals, such as cobalt, nickel, and various alloys, were discovered, it was natural to liken their magnetic properties to those of iron.

fer·rous [fer′əs] *adj.* Containing or having to do with iron in its lower valence.

fer·rule [fer′əl *or* fer′o͞ol] *n.* A metal ring or cap put around the end of something, as a cane or handle, to strengthen it or to prevent splitting.

fer·ry [fer′ē] *v.* **fer·ried, fer·ry·ing,** *n., pl.* **fer·ries** 1 *v.* To transport (people, cars, or goods) across a river or other narrow body of water by boat or other craft. 2 *n.* A boat or other craft used for ferrying. 3 *n.* A place where a ferry docks or crosses a body of water. 4 *v.* To deliver (as an airplane or boat) under its own power to the place where it is needed or wanted.

fer·ry·boat [fer′ē·bōt′] *n.* A boat used as a ferry.

fer·ry·man [fer′ē·mən] *n., pl.* **fer·ry·men** [fer′ē·mən] A person who operates a ferry.

fer·tile [fûr′təl] *adj.* 1 Producing or able to produce abundant crops or vegetation: *fertile* soil. 2 Capable of producing, as seeds, fruit, or young; not sterile. 3 Able to grow into a new animal or plant: *fertile* eggs; *fertile* seeds. 4 Able to produce many ideas or thoughts: a *fertile* mind.

fer·til·i·ty [fûr·til′i·tē] *n.* 1 The characteristic or condition of being fertile. 2 Another word for BIRTHRATE.

fer·til·i·za·tion [fûr′təl·ə·zā′shən] *n.* 1 The application of fertilizer to soil. 2 Impregnation. 3 Pollination. 4 The union of a sperm cell with an egg cell.

fer·til·ize [fûr′təl·īz′] *v.* **fer·til·ized, fer·til·iz·ing** 1 To make (soil) more fertile by applying fertilizer. 2 To cause (a female cell) to start growing into a new animal or plant by union with a male cell: to *fertilize* an egg; Bumblebees *fertilize* clover by carrying pollen from one blossom to another. 3 To impregnate.

fer·til·iz·er [fûr′təl·ī′zər] *n.* A substance, such as manure or certain chemicals, applied to soil to furnish food for plants.

fer·ule[1] [fer′əl *or* fer′o͞ol] *n., v.* **fer·uled, fer·ul·ing** 1 *n.* A flat stick or ruler sometimes used for punishing children, usually by hitting them on the hand. 2 *v.* To punish with a ferule.

fer·ule[2] [fer′əl *or* fer′o͞ol] *n.* Another spelling of FERRULE.

fer·ven·cy [fûr′vən·sē] *n.* Fervor.

fer·vent [fûr′vənt] *adj.* 1 Very eager and earnest; ardent: a *fervent* hope of winning. 2 Very hot;

burning or glowing: *fervent* heat: used mostly in poems. **—fer′vent·ly** *adv.*

fer·vid [fûr′vid] *adj.* Afire with feeling; fiery: a *fervid* speech. **—fer′vid·ly** *adv.* **—fer′vid·ness** *n.*

fer·vor [fûr′vər] *n.* Very strong emotion or enthusiasm; zeal.

fes·tal [fes′təl] *adj.* Of or having to do with a feast or a festival: *festal* songs.

fes·ter [fes′tər] **1** *v.* To become full of pus: A neglected wound or cut may *fester.* **2** *n.* A festering sore or wound. **3** *v.* To remain or grow in the mind as a constant source of bad feeling: Jealousy *festered* within the other contestants.

fes·ti·val [fes′tə·vəl] *n.* **1** A time or occasion for rejoicing or feasting. **2** A particular feast, holiday, or celebration, especially an annual one: a spring *festival.* **3** A special series of performances: a drama *festival.*

fes·tive [fes′tiv] *adj.* Of, having to do with, or suitable for a joyous celebration; gay. **—fes′tive·ly** *adv.* **—fes′tive·ness** *n.*

fes·tiv·i·ty [fes·tiv′ə·tē] *n., pl.* **fes·tiv·i·ties** **1** Gladness and rejoicing typical of a joyous occasion. **2** (*pl.*) The activities accompanying such an occasion: birthday *festivities.*

fes·toon [fes·to͞on′] **1** *n.* A length of flowers, leaves, colored paper, or other material hung in a curve as a decoration. **2** *v.* To decorate with festoons. **3** *v.* To fashion into festoons.

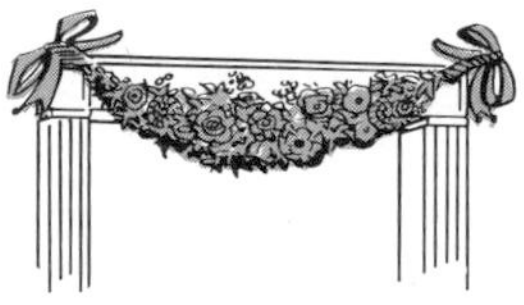
A festoon

fe·tal [fē′təl] *adj.* Of, belonging to, or having to do with a fetus: *fetal* heartbeat.

fetch [fech] *v.* **1** To go for, get, and bring back: to *fetch* a package from the post office. **2** To draw forth: The announcement of the test *fetched* a groan from the class. **3** To give forth (as a sigh or groan). **4** To cost or sell for: The material will *fetch* a good price.

fetch·ing [fech′ing] *adj. informal* Very attractive or pleasing: a *fetching* smile.

fete or **fête** [fāt *or* fet] *n., v.* **fet·ed** or **fêt·ed, fet·ing** or **fêt·ing** **1** *n.* A festival, party, or entertainment, often held outdoors. **2** *v.* To honor, as with a party or dinner; entertain: to *fete* a visiting celebrity.

fet·id [fet′id] *adj.* Having a bad odor, as of rot or decay; stinking. **—fet′id·ly** *adv.* **—fet′id·ness** *n.*

fet·ish [fet′ish *or* fē′tish] *n.* **1** An object worshiped by primitive peoples as being the dwelling place of a spirit or having magical powers to protect its owner. **2** Anything to which a person is excessively and unreasonably devoted: Don't make a *fetish* of being on time.

fet·ish·ism [fet′ish·iz′əm *or* fē′tish·iz′əm] *n.* **1** The worship of fetishes. **2** An abnormal attachment to an object. **—fet′ish·ist** *n.* **—fet′ish·is′tic** *adj.*

fet·lock [fet′lok′] *n.* **1** A tuft of hair growing at the back of the leg of a horse or similar animal just above the hoof. **2** The part or joint of the leg where this tuft grows.

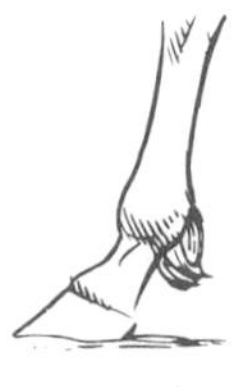
Fetlock

fet·ter [fet′ər] **1** *n.* A chain or other bond put about the ankles to restrain movement. **2** *n.* (*usually pl.*) Anything that checks freedom of movement or expression. **3** *v.* To bind with fetters or as if with fetters; shackle.

fet·tle [fet′(ə)l] *n.* Condition of health and spirits.

fet·tuc·ci·ne or **fet·tuc·ci·ni** [fet′ə·chē′nē] *n.pl.* (*used with a sing. or pl. verb*) A pasta in the form of long, thin strips.

fe·tus [fē′təs] *n., pl.* **fe·tus·es** An unborn baby or animal in the later stages of its development in the womb.

feud [fyo͞od] **1** *n.* A long, bitter quarrel between families, sometimes leading to bloodshed. **2** *n.* A lasting quarrel between two or more people or groups. **3** *v.* To take part in a feud.

feu·dal [fyo͞od′(ə)l] *adj.* Of or having to do with feudalism.

feu·dal·ism [fyo͞od′(ə)l·iz′əm] *n.* An economic and political system of medieval Europe in which vassals were given land and protection by their lords in return for military service or the performance of other duties. **—feu′dal·ist** *n.* **—feu′dal·is′tic** *adj.*

feu·dal·ize [fyo͞od′(ə)l·īz′] *v.* **feu·dal·ized, feu·dal·iz·ing** To make feudal.

feudal system Feudalism.

feu·da·to·ry [fyo͞o′də·tôr′ē] *n., pl.* **feu·da·to·ries,** *adj.* **1** *n.* A person occupying land under a lord in the feudal system. **2** *n.* An estate held under a feudal lord. **3** *adj.* Under the protection of and owing allegiance to a feudal lord.

feud·ist [fyo͞o′dist] *n.* A person who feuds.

fe·ver [fē′vər] *n.* **1** A body temperature higher than normal, usually indicating illness. **2** A sickness characterized by high fever. **3** A highly excited condition: in a *fever* of anticipation.

fever blister Another term for COLD SORE.

fe·vered [fē′vərd] *adj.* **1** Affected by fever. **2** Overly excited: a *fevered* imagination.

fe·ver·ish [fē′vər·ish] *adj.* **1** Having a fever, especially a low fever. **2** Showing signs of fever: *feverish* eyes. **3** Tending to cause fever: a *feverish* swamp. **4** Excited; restless: a *feverish* desire for speed. **—fe′ver·ish·ly** *adv.* **—fe′ver·ish·ness** *n.*

fever pitch A condition of intense excitement or activity: working at *fever pitch.*

fever sore Another term for COLD SORE.

few [fyo͞o] *adj.* **few·er, few·est,** *n., pron.* **1** *adj.* Small in number; not many: a *few* books. **2** *n., pron.* A small number; not very many: Many applied for jobs, but only a *few* were chosen. **—quite a few** A fairly large number. ◆ *Few, several,* and *various* all indicate a quantity that is not large. *Few* stresses *not many,* whereas *several* stresses *more than two.* Note the difference in emphasis between "Only a *few* good apples were left out of the entire bushel" and "*Several* good apples were left." *Various* refers mainly to things that are not alike: *various* duties. ◆ See LESS.

fey [fā] *adj.* **1** Having the power to foresee the future; visionary. **2** Strange or unusual in some way; eccentric, otherworldly, bewitched, or touched.

a	add	**i**	it	**o͝o**	took	**oi**	oil
ā	ace	**ī**	ice	**o͞o**	pool	**ou**	pout
â	care	**o**	odd	**u**	up	**ng**	ring
ä	palm	**ō**	open	**û**	burn	**th**	thin
e	end	**ô**	order	**yo͞o**	fuse	**t͟h**	this
ē	equal					**zh**	vision

ə = {a in *above* e in *sicken* i in *possible* / o in *melon* u in *circus*}

fez [fez] *n., pl.* **fez·zes** A felt cap worn by Egyptians and formerly by Turks, usually red and having a black tassel.

Fez

ff. and those that follow. Pages 56 *ff.* means page 56 and following pages.
f.g. field goal.
FHA or **F.H.A.** Federal Housing Authority.
fi·an·cé [fē′än·sā′] *n.* A man to whom a woman is engaged to be married.
fi·an·cée [fē′än·sā′] *n.* A woman to whom a man is engaged to be married.
fi·as·co [fē·as′kō] *n., pl.* **fi·as·coes** or **fi·as·cos** A complete or humiliating failure: The hoarse singer's recital was a *fiasco.*
fi·at [fī′at] *n.* An official order; decree.
fib [fib] *n., v.* **fibbed, fib·bing** 1 *n.* A lie about something of little importance told without any bad intention. 2 *v.* To tell a fib. **—fib′ber** *n.*
fi·ber [fī′bər] *n.* 1 A thread or threadlike part, as of a fabric or of animal or plant tissue: silk *fibers;* muscle *fibers.* 2 A material made up of fibers, or the fibers themselves as a group: hemp *fiber.* 3 Character; nature: a person of weak moral *fiber.*
fi·ber·board [fī′bər·bôrd′] *n.* A tough, flexible building material made of wood or plant fiber pressed into sheets.
fi·ber·fill [fī′bər·fil′] *n.* A resilient mass of fibers used as a filling for upholstery, cushions, and quilts.
fi·ber·glass [fī′bər·glas′] *n.* 1 A tough, flexible material made of glass spun into filaments and bound together in a resin, used as lightweight building material. 2 Glass fibers spun into thread, woven into cloth, or used as padding or insulation.
fiber optics The technique of sending light through long, very thin clear tubes of glass or plastic.
fi·brin [fī′brin] *n.* A strong, elastic substance in the blood. It promotes clotting by becoming a network of fibers.
fi·brin·o·gen [fī·brin′ə·jən] *n.* A substance present in blood plasma that changes to fibrin when a blood clot is formed.
fi·broid [fī′broid′] 1 *adj.* Resembling or consisting of fibrous material. 2 *n.* A kind of benign tumor consisting of fibrous tissue.
fi·brous [fī′brəs] *adj.* Made up of, having, or resembling fiber: *fibrous* tissue.
fib·u·la [fib′yŏŏ·lə] *n., pl.* **fib·u·lae** [fib′yŏŏ·lē] or **fib·u·las** The outer and smaller of the two bones forming the lower part of the human leg between the knee and the ankle.

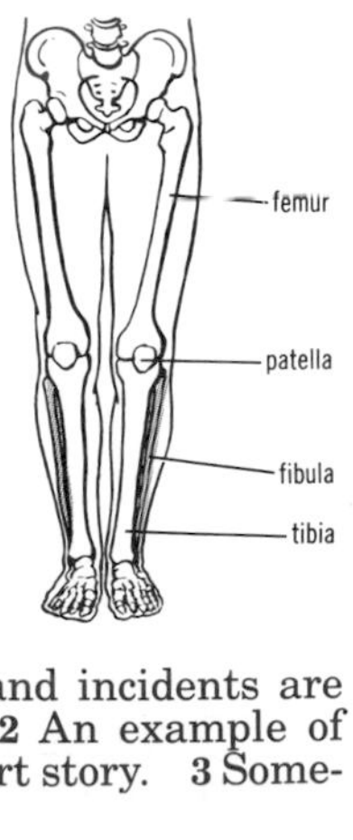

-fic A suffix meaning: Making; causing, as in *pacific.*
-fication A suffix meaning: The act of or the condition of being. It is added to some verbs ending in *-fy* to form nouns, as in *glorification.*
fick·le [fik′əl] *adj.* Not constant in feeling, purpose, or nature; apt to change without warning: a *fickle* person. **—fick′le·ness** *n.*
fic·tion [fik′shən] *n.* 1 A form of literature whose characters and incidents are entirely or partly imaginary. 2 An example of such literature, as a novel or short story. 3 Something made up; an invention or lie: That excuse is a *fiction.*
fic·tion·al [fik′shə·nəl] *adj.* 1 Of, constituting, or used in fiction. 2 Imaginary; made-up. **—fic′tion·al·ly** *adv.*
fic·tion·al·ize [fik′shə·nəl·īze′] *v.* **fic·tion·al·ized, fic·tion·al·iz·ing** To turn into fiction; make an imaginative story of: to *fictionalize* one's experience as a factory worker. **—fic′tion·al·i·za′tion** *n.*
fic·ti·tious [fik·tish′əs] *adj.* Not real; made-up: a *fictitious* name. **—fic·ti′tious·ly** *adv.* **—fic·ti′tious·ness** *n.*
fic·tive [fik′tiv] *adj.* 1 Consisting of or resembling fiction. 2 Fictitious; made-up. **—fic′tive·ly** *adv.*
fid·dle [fid′(ə)l] *n., v.* **fid·dled, fid·dling** 1 *n. informal* A violin. 2 *v. informal* To play a violin. 3 *v.* To make restless movements with the fingers; fidget or play: to *fiddle* with a rubber band. **—fid·dler** [fid′lər] *n.*
fiddler crab A small crab found mostly off the Atlantic coast of the U.S. One of the claws in the male is much larger than the other.

Fiddler crab

fid·dle·sticks [fid′(ə)l·stiks′] *interj.* Nonsense!
fi·del·i·ty [fə·del′ə·tē *or* fī·del′ə·tē] *n.* 1 Faithfulness in carrying out one's duties or responsibilities; loyalty. 2 Accuracy; correctness: a translation done with *fidelity.*
fidg·et [fij′it] 1 *v.* To stir about in an impatient, nervous, or restless way: Children often *fidget* on rainy days. 2 *n.* (*usually pl.*) A restless condition causing constant impatient or nervous movements: I had the *fidgets* and couldn't sit still.
fidg·et·y [fij′i·tē] *adj.* Restless; impatient; nervously active. **—fidg′et·i·ness** *n.*
fie [fī] *interj.* Shame! For shame!: rarely used today except humorously.
fief [fēf] *n.* In the feudal system, land held by a vassal from a lord.
field [fēld] 1 *n.* A large stretch of land with few or no trees, especially one set aside for crops or as a pasture. 2 *n.* An area or region yielding a natural resource: coal *fields.* 3 *n.* A piece of land used for sports, or a part of this: a baseball *field;* left *field.* 4 *v.* To catch or pick up (a batted baseball) and throw it to the proper player. 5 *v.* To send (a player or group of players) to a field position. 6 *n.* All of the competitors entered in a contest. 7 *n.* At a track meet, the playing area in which such events as the high jump, running broad jump, pole vault, and shot-put, are held. 8 *adj.* Of, in, used in, or taking place in a field: *field* flowers; *field* events. 9 *n.* Any wide or open expanse: a *field* of snow. 10 *n.* An airfield. 11 *n.* A battlefield. 12 *n.* The part, as of a painting, flag, or shield, that serves as a background: a red cross on a white *field.* 13 *n.* Range or extent: within my *field* of vision. 14 *n.* A sphere or branch of knowledge, study, or activity: the *field* of medicine; well-known in her *field.* 15 *n.* In physics, a region of space where a force can be detected: a magnetic *field;* a gravitational *field.*
field day 1 A day spent outdoors, as for athletic contests or military maneuvers. 2 A time of or chance for great enjoyment or success.
field·er [fēl′dər] *n.* In baseball or cricket, a player in the field.

field glasses Two small, portable telescopes fastened together for use outdoors; binoculars.
field goal In football, a goal worth three points, scored by kicking the ball over the crossbar of the goal post during regular play.
field hockey A kind of hockey played on a field with a ball.
field hospital A mobile hospital serving an area of disaster or combat.
field house A building on a playing field providing facilities for athletes and sometimes indoor tracks and courts.
field magnet The magnet used to create a magnetic field in a generator or electric motor.
field marshal In some European armies, an officer ranking just below the commander in chief.
field mouse **1** Any of various kinds of mice that frequent open fields, often destroying crops. **2** Another name for VOLE.
field officer A major, lieutenant colonel, or colonel in the army, air force, or marine corps.
field test A trial of a new procedure or product in a limited area before its introduction on a large scale.
field trip An educational trip by a class to a place away from school.
fiend [fēnd] *n.* **1** An evil spirit; demon; devil. **2** A terribly wicked or cruel person. **3** *informal* A person very much devoted or addicted to a thing: a tennis *fiend.*
fiend·ish [fēn′dish] *adj.* **1** Exceedingly wicked or cruel. **2** Abnormally difficult or devious: a *fiendish* puzzle.
fierce [firs] *adj.* **fierc·er, fierc·est** Frighteningly savage, cruel, violent, or intense: a *fierce* tiger; *fierce* anger. **—fierce′ly** *adv.* **—fierce′ness** *n.*
fier·y [fīr′ē *or* fī′ər·ē] *adj.* **fier·i·er, fier·i·est** **1** Containing or composed of fire: a *fiery* furnace. **2** Hot as fire; burning: the *fiery* sun. **3** Very passionate; intense: a *fiery* speech; a *fiery* temper. **—fier′i·ly** *adv.* **—fier′i·ness** *n.*
fi·es·ta [fē·es′tə] *n.* A festival, especially a religious one in Spain and Latin America.
fife [fīf] *n., v.* **fifed, fif·ing** **1** *n.* A small flute having a shrill tone, used with drums in military music. **2** *v.* To play on a fife.
fif·teen or **15** [fif′tēn′] *n., adj.* One more than fourteen.
fif·teenth or **15th** [fif′tēnth′] **1** *adj.* Next after the fourteenth. **2** *n.* The fifteenth one. **3** *adj.* Being one of fifteen equal parts. **4** *n.* A fifteenth part.
fifth or **5th** [fifth] **1** *adj.* Next after the fourth. **2** *n.* The fifth one. **3** *adj.* Being one of five equal parts. **4** *n.* A fifth part.
fifth column In war, a civilian group working secretly within their country for the enemy.
fifth disease A mild epidemic disease affecting young children with a reddish rash on the face. ◆ *Fifth disease* got its name from being the fifth of five childhood diseases accompanied by a rash in an old system of classification.
fifth wheel **1** An extra wheel carried as a spare. **2** An ineffective and unnecessary member of a group.
fif·ti·eth or **50th** [fif′tē·ith] **1** *adj.* Tenth in order after the fortieth. **2** *n.* The fiftieth one. **3** *adj.* Being one of fifty equal parts. **4** *n.* A fiftieth part.
fif·ty or **50** [fif′tē] *n., pl.* **fif·ties** or **50's,** *adj.* **1** *n., adj.* Ten more than forty. **2** *n.* (*pl.*) The years between the age of 50 and the age of 60: He's in his *fifties.*
fif·ty-fif·ty [fif′tē·fif′tē] *informal* **1** *adj.* Equal. **2** *adv.* Equally. **3** *adj.* Half favorable and half not favorable.
fig [fig] *n.* **1** A small, sweet, pear-shaped fruit, often dried or canned but also eaten fresh. **2** The tree that bears this fruit. **3** The least bit; trifle: I don't care a *fig.*

Figs

fig. figure (illustration).
fight [fīt] *v.* **fought, fight·ing,** *n.* **1** *v.* To try to beat or conquer, as by struggling with or hitting. **2** *v.* To take part in angry, violent, or determined struggle. **3** *n.* A struggle or battle involving physical combat or weapons. **4** *v.* To carry on or engage in (as a war or duel). **5** *v.* To make (one's way) by struggling. **6** *v.* To put forth efforts in order to overcome: to *fight* crime. **7** *n.* Any struggle or contest. **8** *n.* Power or willingness to fight: The wounded dog still had *fight* in it.
fight·er [fī′tər] *n.* **1** A person or animal that fights. **2** A person who boxes. **3** A person who struggles hard against opposition or does not give up easily. **4** An airplane designed for combat in war.
fighting chance A chance of success dependent on great effort.
fig·ment [fig′mənt] *n.* An unreal creation of the mind: only a *figment* of your imagination.
fig·ur·a·tive [fig′yər·ə·tiv] *adj.* Departing from the actual, or literal, meaning of a word to create a vivid effect. *Blazing* in "The tiger had blazing eyes" is a word used in a figurative way. **—fig′ur·a·tive·ly** *adv.* **—fig′ur·a·tive·ness** *n.*
fig·ure [fig′yər] *n., v.* **fig·ured, fig·ur·ing** **1** *n.* A character or symbol representing a number: the *figure* 4. **2** *n.* (*pl.*) The use of numbers in arithmetic: a good head for *figures.* **3** *n.* An amount expressed in numbers, as a price: The paintings sold at a high *figure.* **4** *v.* To use arithmetic to find; calculate: Given the distance and the rate of speed, *figure* the time. **5** *v. informal* To think or predict: I *figure* that conditions will improve. **6** *n.* A visible outline or form; shape: A rectangle is a four-sided *figure;* a person with a good *figure.* **7** *n.* A human form: to glimpse a ghostly *figure.* **8** *n.* A person in terms of appearance, conduct, or impression conveyed: a fine *figure* of a leader. **9** *n.* A personage or character: a well-known *figure* in the theater. **10** *v.* To have a part: Determination as well as talent *figured* in the inventor's success. **11** *n.* A pattern or design, as on a fabric. **12** *v.* To decorate or mark with a design. **13** *n.* A movement or series of movements in dancing or skating, or a pattern traced by such movements: a *figure* 8. **14** *n.* A picture, drawing, or diagram, as in a textbook; illustration. **15** *n.* A figure of speech. **—figure on** *U.S. informal* To rely on or

a	add	**i**	it	**o͝o**	took	**oi**	oil
ā	ace	**ī**	ice	**o͞o**	pool	**ou**	pout
â	care	**o**	odd	**u**	up	**ng**	ring
ä	palm	**ō**	open	**û**	burn	**th**	thin
e	end	**ô**	order	**yo͞o**	fuse	**th**	this
ē	equal					**zh**	vision

ə = {a in *above* e in *sicken* i in *possible* / o in *melon* u in *circus*}

plan on. **—figure out** To solve or understand: I can't *figure* it *out*.

figure eight Anything that resembles the form of an 8, as a kind of knot or a movement in figure skating.

fig·ure·head [fig′yər·hed′] *n.* 1 A carved figure decorating the prow of a sailing ship. 2 A leader in name only, with no real power.

Figurehead

figure of speech An expression, as a metaphor, which cannot be taken literally but is used to create a vivid picture or striking effect, as in "The fog crept in" or "Lightning streaked the sky."

figure skating Skating in which a series of standard patterns is traced out on the ice.

fig·u·rine [fig′yə·rēn′] *n.* A small molded or carved statue; statuette.

Fi·ji·an [fē′jē·ən *or* fi·jē′ən] 1 *adj.* Of or from Fiji. 2 *n.* A person born in or a citizen of Fiji. 3 *n.* The language of Fiji.

fil·a·gree [fil′ə·grē] *n.* Another spelling of FILIGREE.

fil·a·ment [fil′ə·mənt] *n.* A very thin thread or a threadlike structure, as the fine wire that produces light in an electric bulb.

fil·bert [fil′bərt] *n.* Another name for HAZELNUT.

filch [filch] *v.* To steal slyly and in small amounts; pilfer: to *filch* cookies from a jar.

file[1] [fīl] *n., v.* **filed, fil·ing** 1 *n.* A cabinet, drawer, box, or folder in which papers are systematically arranged. 2 *n.* The papers, cards, or other documents so arranged. 3 *v.* To arrange and put in a file. 4 *v.* To enter or have entered in an official record: to *file* a complaint. 5 *n.* In a computer, a collection of records or facts that have to do with the same subject. 6 *n.* A line of persons, animals, or things, one behind the other. 7 *v.* To move in a file: the players *filed* onto the field. **—on file** Stored in a file for quick reference.

file[2] [fīl] *n., v.* **filed, fil·ing** 1 *n.* A tool of hard steel with rough teeth or ridges used to grind, smooth, or polish. 2 *v.* To cut, smooth, sharpen, or remove with a file.

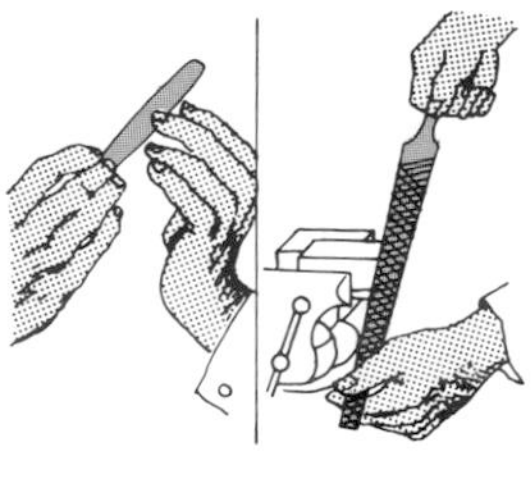

Files

file clerk A person employed to keep the papers and records of a business in accessible order.

fi·let [fi·lā′ *or* fil′ā] *n.* 1 Net lace having a square mesh. 2 A fish or meat fillet.

fi·let mi·gnon [fi·lā′ min·yon′] *pl.* **fi·lets mi·gnons** [fi·lā′ min·yonz′] A small, choice cut of steak from the end of a beef tenderloin. ◆ *Filet mignon* is a French term that literally means *dainty fillet.*

fil·i·al [fil′ē·əl] *adj.* Suitable to or expected of a son or daughter: *filial* respect. **—fil′i·al·ly** *adv.*

fil·i·bus·ter [fil′ə·bus′tər] *U.S.* 1 *n.* In a legislative body, the making of long, often pointless speeches or the use of other delaying tactics in order to prevent a bill from being passed. 2 *v.* To block passage of (legislation) by means of long speeches and delay. **—fil′i·bus′ter·er** *n.* ◆ *Filibuster* comes from a Spanish word, which in turn came from the Dutch word for *freebooter.* Originally a *filibuster* was a person who organized an attack in a foreign country. Later the word came to mean a person in a legislature who tried to obstruct the will of the majority, and finally switched from the person to the actions or methods.

fil·i·gree [fil′ə·grē] *n.* Delicate ornamental work, as of intertwined gold or silver wire.

Filigree

fil·ings [fī′lingz] *n.pl.* Bits or particles rubbed off with a file: brass *filings.*

Fil·i·pi·no [fil′ə·pē′nō] *adj., n., pl.* **Fil·i·pi·nos** 1 *adj.* Philippine. 2 *n.* A person born in or a citizen of the Philippines.

fill [fil] 1 *v.* To put as much into (as a space or container) as it can hold; make full: to *fill* a pitcher with lemonade. 2 *v.* To become full: Soon the dry ravine will *fill* with water. 3 *v.* To occupy the whole of: Guests *filled* the ballroom. 4 *v.* To stop up; plug: to *fill* a cavity in a tooth. 5 *v.* To satisfy or meet, as a need or requirement. 6 *n.* An amount sufficient to fill or satisfy: to eat one's *fill.* 7 *n.* Material used to fill, as gravel or dirt used to build up low ground. 8 *v.* To supply what is called for in: to *fill* a prescription. 9 *v.* To occupy or put someone into (an office or position): to *fill* the governorship. 10 *v.* To cause (a sail) to swell out: said about wind. **—fill in** 1 To insert: *Fill in* the answer. 2 To complete or fill by putting in something: *Fill in* the blanks. 3 To substitute. **—fill out** 1 To make or become fuller or more rounded. 2 To complete by adding the requested information: to *fill out* a form. **—fill up** To make or become full.

fill·er [fil′ər] *n.* 1 A person who fills. 2 A thing that fills, as a brief piece of writing used to fill space in a newspaper, or paper packaged for use in loose-leaf notebooks.

fil·let [fil′it *for defs. 1, 2,* fil′ā *or* fi·lā′ *for defs. 3, 4*] 1 *n.* A narrow band or ribbon for binding the hair. 2 *v.* To bind or adorn with a fillet. 3 *n.* A slice of boneless meat or fish. 4 *v.* To cut into fillets.

fill·ing [fil′ing] *n.* A substance used to fill something: a custard *filling* for a pie; a silver *filling* for a cavity in a tooth.

filling station A gas station.

fil·lip [fil′ip] 1 *n.* An outward snap of a finger that has been pressed against the thumb and suddenly released. 2 *v.* To strike or toss with a fillip. 3 *n.* Something that arouses or stirs up: The sight of a deer gave a *fillip* to our hike

fil·ly [fil′ē] *n., pl.* **fil·lies** A young mare.

film [film] 1 *n.* A thin coating or layer: a *film* of dust on the table. 2 *v.* To cover or become covered with a film. 3 *n.* A sheet, roll, or strip of material having a thin coating of a chemical substance that is sensitive to light, used for making photographs. 4 *n.* A motion picture. 5 *v.* To make or take motion pictures of: to *film* a novel. 6 *n.* A thin haze or blur: a *film* of mist.

film badge A device containing a packet of photographic film that indicates the wearer's exposure to radiation.

film·dom [film′dəm] *n.* 1 The motion-picture industry. 2 The people engaged in the production of motion pictures.

film·ic [fil′mik] *adj.* Of, concerning, or resembling motion pictures. **—film′i·cal·ly** *adv.*

film·mak·er [film′mā′kər] *n.* A person who makes motion pictures.

film·strip [film′strip′] *n.* A series of still pictures on film that are projected on a screen, often used as an aid in teaching.

film·y [fil′mē] *adj.* **film·i·er, film·i·est** 1 Made up of or like a film; gauzy. 2 Covered with a film; clouded; dim. **—film′i·ly** *adv.* **—film′i·ness** *n.*

fil·ter [fil′tər] 1 *n.* Any device containing a porous substance, as paper, charcoal, or sand, used to strain out impurities from a liquid or gas. 2 *n.* The porous substances used in such a device. 3 *v.* To pass or cause to pass through a filter. 4 *v.* To act as a filter for: Charcoal *filters* air. 5 *n.* In physics, any of various devices that allow waves or electric currents of certain frequencies to pass through while stopping all others. 6 *v.* To leak out slowly.

fil·ter·a·ble [fil′tər·ə·bəl] *adj.* 1 Capable of being filtered. 2 Small enough to pass through a filter: A *filterable* virus passes through a filter that stops bacteria.

filter paper A porous paper that remains strong when wet, used especially for filtering liquids.

filth [filth] *n.* 1 Anything that soils or makes foul; disgusting dirt. 2 Something indecent, as dirty words, pictures, or books.

filth·y [fil′thē] *adj.* **filth·i·er, filth·i·est** 1 Covered with filth; foul; dirty. 2 Indecent or obscene. 3 Contemptible; vile: a *filthy* cheat. **—filth′i·ly** *adv.* **—filth′i·ness** *n.*

fil·trate [fil′trāt′] *v.* **fil·trat·ed, fil·trat·ing,** *n.* 1 *v.* To filter. 2 *n.* Liquid that has been passed through a filter. **—fil·tra′tion** *n.*

fin [fin] *n.* 1 A fanlike or winglike part sticking out on a fish's body, used as a balance or to propel the fish. 2 A similar structure on the body of a whale, seal, or other water animal. 3 Any finlike part, as on an aircraft or missile, used for steadiness in flight.

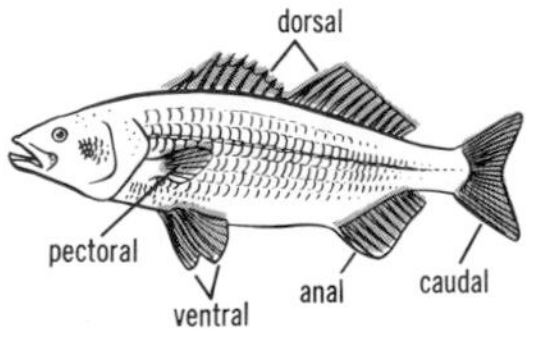

Fins

Fin. 1 Finland. 2 Finnish.

fi·na·gle [fi·nā′gəl] *v.* **fi·na·gled, fi·na·gling** *informal* 1 To obtain by scheming or trickery. 2 To cheat; deceive. **—fi·na′gler** *n.*

fi·nal [fī′nəl] 1 *adj.* Coming at the end; last: the *final* page of a newspaper. 2 *adj.* That cannot be changed; definite: a *final* decision. 3 *n.* (*pl.*) The last examinations in a school term. 4 *n.* (*pl.*) The last competitive event or events in a series of such events: to reach the *finals* in a statewide soccer competition.

fi·na·le [fə·nä′lē] *n.* The last part of something, as the final scene of a play or the concluding section of a musical composition.

fi·nal·ist [fī′nəl·ist] *n.* A contestant who has reached the finals of a contest.

fi·nal·i·ty [fī·nal′ə·tē] *n., pl.* **fi·nal·i·ties** 1 A final or definite condition or quality: to speak with *finality.* 2 Something final or definite, as an act, remark, or decision.

fi·nal·ize [fī′nə·līz′] *v.* **fi·nal·ized, fi·nal·iz·ing** To bring to completion; put into final form: to *finalize* a business deal. **—fi′nal·i·za′tion** *n.*

fi·nal·ly [fī′nə·lē] *adv.* 1 At last; at the end; in conclusion: We *finally* finished our homework. 2 In a decisive or conclusive way; definitely: I'm reluctant to say *finally* whether I'll go to the school prom or not.

fi·nance [fi·nans′ *or* fī′nans] *n., v.* **fi·nanced, fi·nanc·ing** 1 *n.* (*pl.*) Available money; funds: family *finances;* government *finances.* 2 *n.* The use or management of money, especially in large amounts. 3 *v.* To provide or get the necessary money for: to *finance* a new car.

fi·nan·cial [fi·nan′shəl *or* fī·nan′shəl] *adj.* Of or having to do with money or the use or management of money. **—fi·nan′cial·ly** *adv.*

fin·an·cier [fin′ən·sir′] *n.* A person who is an expert in financial affairs, as a banker.

finch [finch] *n.* Any of a large group of small songbirds, having a short bill adapted for eating seeds. Sparrows and canaries are finches.

find [fīnd] *v.* **found, find·ing,** *n.* 1 *v.* To come upon unexpectedly: to *find* a ring. 2 *v.* To search for and discover: Please *find* my glasses. 3 *v.* To recover or get back (something lost): I *found* my wallet. 4 *n.* Something found, especially something valuable. 5 *v.* To learn; discover: We *found* that the new horse was a good jumper. 6 *v.* To reach a decision and declare: The jury *found* for the defendant. 7 *v.* To arrive at; reach: The bullet *found* its mark. **—find oneself** 1 To discover one's special abilities. 2 To discover that one is in a certain place or condition: He *found himself* alone. **—find out** To learn with certainty: to *find out* the truth.

find·er [fīn′dər] *n.* 1 A person or thing that finds. 2 An attachment on a camera that shows the user what will appear in the picture.

find·ing [fīn′ding] *n.* 1 The action of finding; discovery. 2 Something found. 3 (*usually pl.*) A conclusion arrived at, as by a law court, after careful investigation of the facts.

fine[1] [fīn] *adj.* **fin·er, fin·est,** *adv.* 1 *adj.* Very good; excellent: a *fine* dinner. 2 *adv. informal* Very well: Cold weather suits me *fine.* 3 *adj.* Free from impurities; pure: *fine* gold. 4 *adj.* Not cloudy; clear: *fine* weather. 5 *adj.* Made up of very small particles: *fine* powder. 6 *adj.* Very thin; slender: a *fine* thread. 7 *adj.* Keen; sharp: a sword with a *fine* edge. 8 *adj.* Delicate: *fine* lace. 9 *adj.* Very refined; elegant: *fine* manners. 10 *adj.* Not obvious; subtle; clever: a *fine* point in an argument. 11 *adv.* Finely. **—fine′ness** *n.*

fine[2] [fīn] *n., v.* **fined, fin·ing** 1 *n.* A sum of money that has to be paid as a penalty for breaking a law or rule. 2 *v.* To punish by a fine.

fine arts The arts having to do with the creation of beautiful things, as painting, drawing, sculpture, and architecture. Fine arts may include music, literature, drama, and dancing.

a	add	**i**	it	**o͝o**	took	**oi**	oil
ā	ace	**ī**	ice	**o͞o**	pool	**ou**	pout
â	care	**o**	odd	**u**	up	**ng**	ring
ä	palm	**ō**	open	**û**	burn	**th**	thin
e	end	**ô**	order	**yo͞o**	fuse	**th̶**	this
ē	equal					**zh**	vision

ə = {a in *above*, e in *sicken*, i in *possible*, o in *melon*, u in *circus*}

fine·ly [fīn′lē] *adv.* 1 Very well; excellently. 2 In a very precise or subtle way: The distinction is *finely* drawn. 3 In small pieces.

fin·er·y [fī′nər·ē] *n., pl.* **fin·er·ies** Fine or showy clothes or decorations.

fine·spun [fīn′spun′] *adj.* 1 Extremely thin: *finespun* thread. 2 Very subtle: *finespun* reasoning.

fi·nesse [fi·nes′] *n.* 1 Delicate skill: The pianist plays with *finesse.* 2 Skill in handling a difficult situation without offending anyone.

fin·ger [fing′gər] 1 *n.* Any of the five separate parts forming the end of the hand, especially the four other than the thumb. 2 *n.* The part of a glove that covers a finger. 3 *v.* To touch or handle with the fingers: to *finger* a bracelet. 4 *v.* To play (music) by using the fingers on a musical instrument in a certain way: to *finger* a scale. 5 *n.* Anything that looks like or serves as a finger. 6 *n.* The width of a finger, about 3/4 of an inch. 7 *v. slang* To betray by identifying.

fin·ger·board [fing′gər·bôrd′] *n.* A strip of wood on the neck of a stringed musical instrument against which the fingers press the strings.

finger bowl A small bowl holding water to be used to rinse the fingers at a formal meal.

finger food Any food that is usually picked up and eaten without utensils.

fin·ger·ing [fing′gər·ing] *n.* 1 The way that the fingers are used in playing a musical instrument. 2 An indication on a musical score of which fingers should play which notes.

fin·ger·nail [fing′gər·nāl′] *n.* The horny plate at the end of each finger.

finger painting 1 The act of painting pictures on wet paper using the fingers and palms rather than a brush. 2 A picture made in this way.

fin·ger·post [fing′gər·pōst′] *n.* A directional sign consisting of a diagram of a hand with a pointing index finger.

fin·ger·print [fing′gər·print′] 1 *n.* An impression of the skin pattern on the inner side of a finger, at the tip, very commonly used for identification. 2 *v.* To take the fingerprints of: to *fingerprint* a suspected robber.

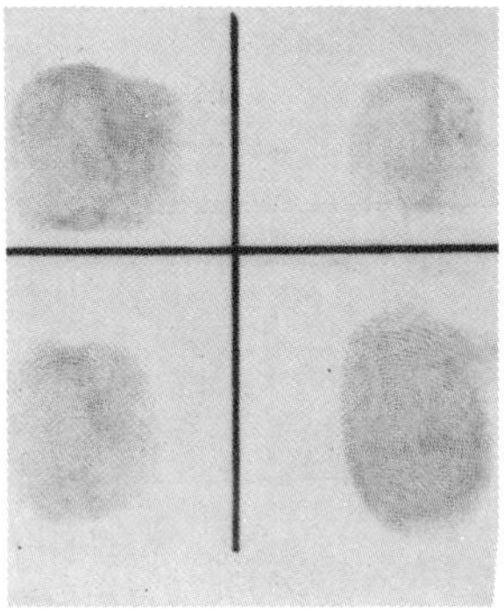
Fingerprints

fin·ger·tip [fing′gər·tip′] *n.* 1 The tip of a finger. 2 A protective covering for a finger; cot. **—at one's fingertips** Immediately available.

fin·i·cal [fin′i·kəl] *adj.* Finicky. **—fin′i·cal·ly** *adv.* **—fin′i·cal·ness** *n.*

fin·ick·y [fin′i·kē] *adj.* Hard to please; fussy. **—fin′·ick·i·ness** *n.*

fi·nis [fin′əs *or* fī′nəs] *n.* The end. ◆ *Finis* is a Latin word used to mark the end of a written work or a motion picture. Like any Latin noun, it does not take an article.

fin·ish [fin′ish] 1 *v.* To bring to or reach an end: The poet finally *finished* the poem; The movie *finished* at midnight. 2 *v. informal* To kill, destroy, or defeat. 3 *v.* To use or consume completely: to *finish* the cake. 4 *n.* The last stage of anything; end: the *finish* of a race. 5 *v.* To give a particular kind of surface to: to *finish* a table with shellac. 6 *n.* The type of surface something has: a bright *finish.* 7 *n.* A material or substance used in finishing: an oil *finish* on a painting. 8 *n.* Perfection or polish in speech, manners, or education.

fin·ished [fin′isht] *adj.* 1 Ended; completed. 2 Perfected; polished: a *finished* work of art. 3 Highly skilled: a *finished* musician.

finish line 1 A line marking the end of a racecourse. 2 The end of any contest: The campaign is near the *finish line.*

fi·nite [fī′nīt′] *adj.* Having a limit or boundary; not infinite: a *finite* quantity.

Finn [fin] *n.* A person born in or a citizen of Finland.

fin·nan had·die [fin′ən had′ē] Smoked haddock.

Finn·ish [fin′ish] 1 *adj.* Of or from Finland. 2 *n.* **(the Finnish)** The people of Finland. 3 *n.* The language of Finland.

fin·ny [fin′ē] *adj.* **fin·ni·er, fin·ni·est** 1 Having fins. 2 Being or having to do with fish: *finny* inhabitants of the deep.

fiord [fyôrd] *n.* In Norway, a long, narrow inlet of the sea between high cliffs or banks.

Fiord

fir [fûr] *n.* 1 Any of several kinds of evergreen trees related to the pine, often used as Christmas trees. 2 The wood of a fir tree.

fire [fīr] *n., v.* **fired, fir·ing** 1 *n.* The flame and heat caused by something burning. 2 *n.* A burning mass of fuel, as in a fireplace. 3 *n.* A destructive burning, as of a building. 4 *v.* To cause to burn; kindle or ignite. 5 *v.* To feed or tend the fire of. 6 *v.* To bake in a kiln: to *fire* a piece of pottery. 7 *n.* Strong feeling; excitement; ardor: Her eyes were full of *fire.* 8 *v.* To inspire or excite: to *fire* the child's imagination with adventure stories. 9 *v.* To shoot, as a gun. 10 *n.* Shooting: enemy *fire*; Cease *fire*! 11 *v.* To launch, as a rocket. 12 *v. informal* To hurl: to *fire* stones; to *fire* questions. 13 *n.* A rapid series or an outburst of something: a *fire* of questions. 14 *v. informal* To discharge from a job; dismiss. **—between two fires** Under attack or criticism from both sides. **—catch fire** To start to burn. **—hang fire** To be delayed or undecided, as an event or decision. **—on fire** 1 Burning. 2 Full of fervor or excitement. **—under fire** 1 Exposed to gunfire. 2 Being severely criticized.

fire alarm A device that emits a loud signal intended to warn people of a fire.

fire·arm [fīr′ärm′] *n.* A weapon, especially one small enough to be carried, that shoots a bullet or other missile.

fire·ball [fīr′bôl′] *n.* 1 A mass of matter hot enough to emit light. 2 The very bright sphere of gases and dust formed by a nuclear or other powerful explosion. 3 A brilliant meteor. 4 *informal* A busy, energetic person; go-getter.

fire·bird [fīr′bûrd′] *n.* 1 Any bird with bright red plumage, as the male scarlet tanager. 2 The phoenix.

fire·boat [fīr′bōt′] *n.* A boat fitted with pumps, hoses, and other apparatus to fight fires.

fire·brand [fīr′brand′] *n.* **1** A piece of burning wood. **2** A person who stirs others to strife.
fire·break [fīr′brāk′] *n.* A strip of land that has been plowed or cleared to stop the spread of a forest or brush fire.
fire·brick [fīr′brik′] *n.* A type of brick able to withstand great heat, used for lining fireplaces and some types of furnaces.
fire brigade A company of firefighters trained to work together.
fire·bug [fīr′bug′] *n. informal* A person who purposely sets fire to property.
fire·crack·er [fīr′krak′ər] *n.* A paper cylinder containing an explosive and used as a noisemaker, as on the Fourth of July.
fire·damp [fīr′damp′] *n.* A dangerous gas that collects in coal mines and is explosive when mixed with certain proportions of air.
fire·dog [fīr′dôg′] *n.* Another word for ANDIRON.
fire drill A rehearsal of what to do and where to go in case of fire.
fire-eat·er [fīr′ē′tər] *n.* **1** A performer, as at a circus, who pretends to swallow fire. **2** A person who is eager to fight or to take aggressive action.
fire-eat·ing [fīr′ē′ting] *adj.* Belligerent; militant.
fire engine A truck with special equipment for putting out fires, especially one having powerful pumps for throwing water or chemicals.
fire escape A metal stairway, ladder, or chute along the outside of a building to be used as a means of escape in case of fire.
fire extinguisher A portable metal container from which a chemical may be sprayed to put out a fire.
fire·fight·er [fīr′fī′tər] *n.* A person who puts out fires.
fire·fly [fīr′flī′] *n., pl.* **fire·flies** An insect having, in the lower part of its body, a phosphorescent substance that glows on and off as it flies at night.
fire·guard [fīr′gärd′] *n.* A fire screen.
fire·house [fīr′hous′] *n.* A building where firefighters are stationed and fire engines are kept.
fire·light [fīr′līt′] *n.* The light cast from a fire, as from a campfire or a fireplace.
fire·man [fīr′mən] *n., pl.* **fire·men** [fīr′mən] **1** A member of a group of firefighters. **2** A person who tends the fire, as in a furnace, steam boiler, or locomotive.
fire·place [fīr′plās′] *n.* A structure or opening in which a fire is built, especially one connected with a chimney and opening into a room.

Fireplace

fire·plug [fīr′plug′] *n.* A hydrant.
fire·pow·er [fīr′pou′·ər] *n.* The capacity for sending bullets and other missiles at a target.
fire·proof [fīr′pro͞of′] **1** *adj.* Protecting against or resistant to damage from fire: The documents are kept in a *fireproof* vault. **2** *v.* To protect against fire.
fire screen A fireproof screen to stop sparks that are ejected from a fireplace.
fire·side [fīr′sīd′] *n.* **1** The hearth or space about a fireplace. **2** Home or home life.
fire station A firehouse.
fire tower A watchtower in which a lookout is stationed to watch for forest fires.
fire·trap [fīr′trap′] *n.* A building which can easily burn down or which does not have adequate means of escape or protection from fire.
fire·wa·ter [fīr′wô′tər] *n.* Whisky or other strong alcoholic drink: a term first used by North American Indian groups.
fire·wood [fīr′wo͝od′] *n.* Wood suitable for making a fire, as in a fireplace.
fire·works [fīr′wûrks′] *n.pl.* Things that burn brightly or explode with a loud noise, as firecrackers, rockets, or sparklers.
firing pin The part of a gun that strikes the primer when the gun is fired.
firm[1] [fûrm] *adj.* **1** That does not readily give in to touch or pressure; solid or unyielding: *firm* snow; *firm* muscle. **2** Difficult to move or loosen: a *firm* structure; a *firm* fastening. **3** Constant; steadfast: a *firm* friend. **4** Strong; vigorous; steady: a *firm* friendship. **—firm′ly** *adv.* **—firm′ness** *n.*
firm[2] [fûrm] *n.* A partnership of two or more persons for conducting business.
fir·ma·ment [fûr′mə·mənt] *n.* The expanse of the heavens; sky: used mostly in poems.
first [fûrst] **1** *adj.* (*sometimes written* **1st**) Coming before another or all others in time, position, or quality: a *first* child; to be *first* in one's class. **2** *adv.* Before all others or anything else: to go *first*; *First* put your books away. **3** *n.* A person or thing that is first. **4** *n.* The beginning: from the *first.* **5** *n.* (*sometimes written* **1st**) The first day of the month. **6** *adv.* For the first time: I met her *first* ten years ago. **7** *adv.* In preference to anything else; sooner; rather: Pat would die *first.* **8** *adj.* In music, playing or singing the higher or principal part: *first* violin.
first-aid [fûrst′ād′] *adj.* Of, having to do with, or for first aid.
first aid Treatment given in an emergency to an injured person before full medical attention can be had.
first-born [fûrst′bôrn′] **1** *adj.* Born before any other children in the family; oldest. **2** *n.* A first-born child.
first-class [fûrst′klas′] **1** *adj.* Of the highest, best, or most expensive group in a category: a *first-class* store. **2** *adj.* Of or having to do with a class of mail that includes letters, postcards, and other mailable material sealed against inspection. **3** *adv.* By first-class means: to travel *first-class;* to mail a package *first-class.*
first class **1** First-class travel accomodations, as on an airplane or ship. **2** First-class mail.
first cousin A daughter or son of one's aunt or uncle.
first-de·gree burn [fûrst′di·grē′] A mild burn that reddens the skin.

a	add	**i**	it	**o͝o**	took	**oi**	oil
ā	ace	**ī**	ice	**o͞o**	pool	**ou**	pout
â	care	**o**	odd	**u**	up	**ng**	ring
ä	palm	**ō**	open	**û**	burn	**th**	thin
e	end	**ô**	order	**yo͞o**	fuse	**t͟h**	this
ē	equal					**zh**	vision

ə = {a in *above* e in *sicken* i in *possible*
o in *melon* u in *circus*}

first·hand [fûrst′hand′] *adj., adv.* Directly from the person involved: a *firsthand* report.
first lady (*often written* **First Lady**) The wife of the chief executive, as of a nation or state.
first lieutenant A military rank. In the U.S. Army, a first lieutenant is a commissioned officer ranking next above a second lieutenant and next below a captain.
first·ly [fûrst′lē] *adv.* In the first place; to begin with.
first name The name that comes first in a person's full name. Using a person's first name usually implies that you know that person fairly well.
first person The form of a pronoun or verb used in referring to the speaker. *I, me, we, us,* and *am* are words in the first person.
first-rate [fûrst′rāt′] 1 *adj.* Of the finest class, quality, or character; excellent. 2 *adv. informal* Excellently; very well: He sings *first-rate.*
firth [fûrth] *n.* An inlet of the sea.
fis·cal [fis′kəl] *adj.* Of or having to do with money matters; financial. **—fis′cal·ly** *adv.*
fiscal year Any twelve-month period at the end of which financial accounts are balanced. Each *fiscal year* of the U.S. government begins on October 1 and is named for the following year.
fish [fish] *n., pl.* **fish** or **fish·es,** *v.* 1 *n.* Any of a group of animals that have backbones, live in water, and have gills to breathe with. Fish are usually covered with scales and have fins for moving themselves. 2 *n.* The flesh of a fish used as food. 3 *v.* To catch or try to catch fish. 4 *v.* To grope for and bring out: to *fish* money out of one's pockets. 5 *v.* To try to get or uncover in an indirect manner: to *fish* for information. ◆ *Fish* is the usual plural: There are many *fish* in the stream. However, when different kinds are meant, *fishes* is often used: We saw many freshwater *fishes* in the market.
fish cake A fried patty made of ground fish mixed with potato and seasonings.
fish·er [fish′ər] *n.* 1 A person or animal that fishes. 2 A kind of marten found in North America. 3 The dark brown fur of this animal.

Fisher

fish·er·man [fish′ər·mən] *n., pl.* **fish·er·men** [fish′·ər·mən] A person who fishes for sport or as work.
fish·er·y [fish′ə·rē] *n., pl.* **fish·er·ies** 1 The business of catching fish. 2 A place where this is done. 3 A place where fish are bred.
fish-eye [fish′ī′] *adj.* Being or having to do with a camera lens that covers a very wide angle and produces a circular image.
fish hatchery A system of tanks in which fish are hatched, fed, and protected from natural enemies until they are of a size suitable for transfer to a natural environment.
fish hawk Another name for OSPREY.
fish·hook [fish′ho͝ok′] *n.* A hook, usually barbed, for catching fish.
fish·ing [fish′ing] *n.* The catching of fish, either for a living or for pleasure.
fishing rod A slender pole with a hook, a line, and often a reel, used to catch fish.
fishing tackle The gear used for catching fish, such as rods, reels, lines, and lures.
fish·mon·ger [fish′mung′gər] *n. British* A person who deals in fish.
fish·pond [fish′pond′] *n.* A small pond in which live fish are maintained for food or for the pleasure of watching them.
fish·wife [fish′wīf′] *n., pl.* **fish·wives** [fish′wīvz′] 1 A woman who sells fish. 2 A woman who uses loud, abusive language.
fish·y [fish′ē] *adj.* **fish·i·er, fish·i·est** 1 Having to do with or like fish: a *fishy* smell. 2 Abounding in fish. 3 *informal* Unlikely; improbable; doubtful: a *fishy* story. 4 Without expression; vacant: *fishy* eyes. **—fish′i·ness** *n.*
fis·sion [fish′ən] *n.* 1 A splitting or breaking apart. 2 The division of a cell or small organism into new cells or organisms, especially as a means of reproduction. 3 In physics, nuclear fission.
fis·sion·a·ble [fish′ən·ə·bəl] *adj.* Capable of undergoing nuclear fission.
fis·sure [fish′ər] *n.* A narrow split or crack, as in a rock.
fist [fist] *n.* A hand that is tightly closed.
fist·ful [fist′fo͝ol′] *n., pl.* **fist·fuls** As much or as many as can be grasped in the fist.
fist·ic [fis′tik] *adj.* Of or having to do with boxing.
fist·i·cuffs [fis′ti·kufs′] *n.pl.* 1 A fight with the fists. 2 The art of boxing.
fis·tu·la [fis′chə·lə] *n., pl.* **fis·tu·las** or **fis·tu·lae** [fis′·chə·lē′] An abnormal passage connecting an abscess or a hollow organ inside the body to the outside of the body or to another abscess or cavity within the body.
fit[1] [fit] *adj.* **fit·ter, fit·test,** *v.* **fit·ted** or **fit, fit·ting,** *n.* 1 *adj.* Right or satisfactory; suitable: This house isn't *fit* to live in. 2 *adj.* Proper or appropriate: It is not *fit* for people to make fun of others. 3 *v.* To be proper or suitable for: The tune of this song *fits* the words. 4 *v.* To provide with what is suitable or necessary: to *fit* a library with good lighting. 5 *v.* To be the right size and shape for: Does this suit *fit* well? Yes, it *fits* you perfectly. 6 *v.* To cause to fit by altering or adjusting: to *fit* a coat. 7 *n.* The way something fits: a loose *fit.* 8 *v.* To put in place carefully or exactly: to *fit* an arrow to a bow. 9 *adj.* In good physical condition; healthy: to be *fit* enough to travel. **—fit′ly** *adv.* **—fit′ness** *n.*
fit[2] [fit] *n.* 1 A sudden attack marked by convulsions or unconsciousness. 2 A sudden attack of something such as coughing or sneezing. 3 A sudden show of feeling that is too strong to be held back.
fitch [fich] *n.* 1 The fur or pelt of a European polecat. 2 A European polecat.
fit·ful [fit′fəl] *adj.* Ceasing from time to time; not steady; irregular: a *fitful* breeze. **—fit′ful·ly** *adv.* **—fit′ful·ness** *n.*
fit·ter [fit′ər] *n.* 1 A person who checks and adjusts the fit of a garment. 2 A person who puts together pipes or parts of a machine.
fit·ting [fit′ing] 1 *adj.* Suitable; proper: a *fitting* answer. 2 *n.* A trying on of clothes to find out how much altering has to be done to make them fit. **—fit′ting·ly** *adv.* **—fit′ting·ness** *n.*
fit·tings [fit′ingz] *n.pl* Furnishings, fixtures, or decorations, as for a house.
five or **5** [fīv] *n., adj.* One more than four.

five-and-dime [fīv'ən·dīm'] *n.* Another term for FIVE-AND-TEN.

five-and-ten [fīv'ən·ten'] *n.* A retail store that sells a large variety of inexpensive items. ◆ *Five-and-ten* refers to the prices in the original stores of this kind, where everything sold for five or ten cents.

five·fold [*adj.* fīv'fōld', *adv.* fīv'fōld'] **1** *adj.* Composed of five parts. **2** *adj.* Being five times greater or five times as many. **3** *adv.* By five times: increased *fivefold.*

Five Nations A confederation of North American Iroquois Indian tribes: Cayuga, Mohawk, Oneida, Onondaga, and Seneca.

fiv·er [fī'vər] *n. informal* A five-dollar bill.

fix [fiks] **1** *v.* To make or become firm or secure: to *fix* a picture to the wall. **2** *v.* To hold or direct steadily: to *fix* one's eyes on someone. **3** *v.* To settle or decide definitely: to *fix* a date for a party. **4** *v.* To arrange properly; put in order: to *fix* one's hair. **5** *v.* To restore to good condition; repair: to *fix* a rickety table. **6** *v.* To prepare: to *fix* breakfast. **7** *v. informal* To use bribery or other dishonest methods to get a certain result: to *fix* a basketball game. **8** *v. informal* To punish or get even with: I'll *fix* you if you bother me again. **9** *v.* To place (as blame or responsibility) on a person. **10** *v.* In photography, to bathe (a film) in chemicals so as to prevent fading. **11** *n. informal* An embarrassing or difficult situation: When I lost my money, I was in a *fix.* —**fix on** To decide upon: We *fixed on* $20.00 as a salary for the job. —**fix up** *informal* **1** To repair. **2** To arrange; put in order: We *fixed up* the room for the party. **3** To supply the needs of: The manager will *fix* you *up* with a uniform. —**fix'er** *n.*

fix·a·ble [fik'sə·bəl] *adj.* Capable of being fixed.

fix·a·tion [fik·sā'shən] *n.* **1** The act of fixing. **2** The condition of being fixed or unchanging. **3** An obsession.

fix·a·tive [fik'sə·tiv] **1** *n.* A substance that fixes or makes permanent. Varnish sprayed on a pastel or crayon drawing to prevent smudging is called a fixative. **2** *adj.* Making permanent.

fixed [fikst] *adj.* **1** Firm; steady: a *fixed* gaze. **2** Agreed upon; set: a *fixed* price. —**fix·ed·ly** [fik'sid·lē] *adv.* —**fix·ed·ness** [fik'sid·nis] *n.*

fixed star Any star so far away that it seems to keep the same position in relation to the stars around it.

fix·ings [fik'singz] *n.pl. informal* The things that usually go with a more important thing; trimmings: a turkey dinner with all the *fixings.*

fix·ture [fiks'chər] *n.* **1** Anything securely fixed or fastened into a permanent position, especially in a building: light *fixtures.* **2** A person or thing thought of as being fixed in a particular place because of having been there so long: The music teacher has become a *fixture* at school.

Light fixtures

fizz [fiz] **1** *n.* A hissing or bubbling sound. **2** *v.* To bubble and hiss like soda water. —**fizz'y** *adj.*

fiz·zle [fiz'əl] *v.* **fiz·zled, fiz·zling,** *n.* **1** *v.* To make a hissing or sputtering sound. **2** *n.* Such a sound. **3** *v. informal* To fail, especially after a good start: The artist's attempt to sell pictures *fizzled* out. **4** *n. informal* A failure.

fjord [fyôrd] *n.* Another spelling of FIORD.

fl or **fl.** fluid.

Fl A symbol for the element fluorine.

FL Postal Service abbreviation of Florida.

Fla. Florida.

flab [flab] *n.* Soft, flabby flesh. ◆ *Flab* comes from the adjective *flabby* by dropping the *-by.* This process is backwards from the more usual method of forming adjectives by adding a *y* to a noun.

flab·ber·gast [flab'ər·gast] *v. informal* To amaze greatly; astound.

flab·by [flab'ē] *adj.* **flab·bi·er, flab·bi·est** Lacking strength or firmness; soft: Exercise will tone up *flabby* muscles. —**flab'bi·ly** *adv.* —**flab'bi·ness** *n.*

flac·cid [flak'sid] *adj.* Lacking firmness or elasticity; flabby. —**flac·cid'i·ty** *n.* —**flac'cid·ly** *adv.*

fla·con [flak'ən] *n.* A small, often ornamented bottle with a tight stopper; vial.

flag[1] [flag] *n., v.* **flagged, flag·ging** **1** *n.* A piece of cloth, usually rectangular, having certain colors and designs on it. A flag is used as a symbol, as of a country or state, or as a signal. **2** *v.* To cause to stop by signaling with or as if with a flag: to *flag* a taxi. **3** *v.* To send (information) by signals.

flag[2] [flag] *v.* **flagged, flag·ging** To grow tired or weak; lose vigor; droop: Their spirits *flagged* when no one came to rescue them.

flag[3] [flag] *n.* Either of two plants with sword-shaped leaves, an iris or a marsh plant.

flag[4] [flag] *n., v.* **flagged, flag·ging** **1** *n.* A kind of stone that splits in layers suitable for paving. **2** *n.* A paving stone of flag; flagstone. **3** *v.* To pave with flagstone.

Flag Day June 14th, the anniversary of the day in 1777 when Congress made the Stars and Stripes the flag of the United States.

flag·el·late [flaj'ə·lāt'] *v.* **flag·el·lat·ed, flag·el·lat·ing,** *adj.* **1** *v.* To whip; flog; scourge. **2** *adj.* Shaped like a flagellum or whip. —**flag'el·la'tion** *n.*

fla·gel·lum [flə·jel'əm] *n., pl.* **fla·gel·la** [flə·jel'ə] or **fla·gel·lums** **1** A whiplike part, such as one on a one-celled animal or bacterium, which it uses for moving about. **2** A whip.

flag·eo·let [flaj'ə·let'] *n.* A small musical instrument resembling a flute or recorder.

flag·man [flag'mən] *n., pl.* **flag·men** [flag'mən] A person who sends signals with a flag or flags.

flag officer Any officer in the navy or coast guard above the rank of captain. Flag officers are entitled to display a flag with their insignia of rank.

flag·on [flag'ən] *n.* **1** A container with a handle and spout and often a lid on hinges, used for serving liquids. **2** A large wine bottle.

flag·pole [flag'pōl'] *n.* A pole on which a flag is

a	add	**i**	it	**o͝o**	took	**oi**	oil
ā	ace	**ī**	ice	**o͞o**	pool	**ou**	pout
â	care	**o**	odd	**u**	up	**ng**	ring
ä	palm	**ō**	open	**û**	burn	**th**	thin
e	end	**ô**	order	**yo͞o**	fuse	**th̶**	this
ē	equal					**zh**	vision

ə = {a in *above* e in *sicken* i in *possible* / o in *melon* u in *circus*}

displayed and flown. ◆ *Flagpole* was created by putting together as one word what had been written as two: *flag* + *pole*.

fla·grance [flā′grəns] *n.* Flagrancy.

fla·gran·cy [flā′grən·sē] *n.* 1 The quality of being flagrant. 2 An example of flagrant behavior.

fla·grant [flā′grənt] *adj.* Openly disgraceful; shockingly bad: a *flagrant* contempt for the law. **—fla′·grant·ly** *adv.*

A flagrant violation

flag·ship [flag′ship′] *n.* The ship carrying the commander of a fleet and displaying the commander's flag.

flag·staff [flag′staf′] *n., pl.* **flag·staffs** or **flag·staves** [flag′stāvz′] A flagpole.

flag·stone [flag′stōn′] *n.* A broad, flat stone used in paving, as footpaths or terraces.

flail [flāl] 1 *n.* A tool for beating off, or threshing, the heads of ripened grain. It has a long handle to which a shorter, freely swinging bar is attached. 2 *v.* To beat with or as if with a flail.

Flail

flair [flâr] *n.* 1 A natural ability or talent; knack; a *flair* for drawing. 2 Sharp perception.

flak [flak] *n.* 1 Antiaircraft guns or the bursting shells fired from them. 2 *informal* Aggressive criticism, opposition, or dissension. ◆ *Flak* comes from a contraction of the German compound word *fliegerabwehrkanone,* which means *antiaircraft gun*.

flake [flāk] *n., v.* **flaked, flak·ing** 1 *n.* A small thin chip or fluffy bit of a substance: a *flake* of paint; *flakes* of snow. 2 *v.* To form or peel off in flakes: Paint *flaked* from the ceiling.

flak·y [flā′kē] *adj.* **flak·i·er, flak·i·est** 1 Consisting of or like flakes. 2 Easily separated into flakes. 3 *slang* Very odd; eccentric: a *flaky* sense of humor. **—flak′i·ness** *n.*

flam·boy·ance [flam·boi′əns] *n.* The quality of being flamboyant.

flam·boy·ant [flam·boi′ənt] *adj.* 1 Brilliant in color; glowing: a *flamboyant* sunrise. 2 Too gaudy or showy: a *flamboyant* design. ◆ *Flamboyant* comes from a French word that means *flaming* or *blazing*.

flame [flām] *n., v.* **flamed, flam·ing** 1 *n.* The burning gas rising from a fire, usually in glowing orange or yellow tongues. 2 *n.* A single tongue of flame. 3 *v.* To give out flame; blaze. 4 *n.* (*often pl.*) A burning condition: in *flames.* 5 *n.* Something bright, hot, or otherwise like a flame. 6 *v.* To light up or burn as if on fire: to *flame* with rage.

fla·men·co [flə·meng′kō] *n., pl.* **fla·men·cos** 1 A brilliant and noisy style of folk dancing among Spanish gypsies, accompanied by rhythmic stamping of feet and clapping. 2 The guitar or vocal music that accompanies this dancing.

flame·proof [flām′prōōf′] 1 *adj.* Resistant to catching fire. 2 *v.* To make flameproof, as with chemicals.

flame·throw·er [flām′thrō′ər] *n.* A weapon or other device for directing through a nozzle a flaming stream of fluid under pressure.

flam·ing [flā′ming] *adj.* 1 Burning brightly; in flames. 2 Resembling flames in brightness: a *flaming* red dress. 3 Ardent; passionate: *flaming* youth. **—flam′ing·ly** *adv.*

fla·min·go [flə·ming′gō] *n., pl.* **fla·min·gos** or **fla·min·goes** A pink or red wading bird that lives in tropical areas and has a long neck and long legs.

Flamingo

flam·ma·bil·i·ty [flam′ə·bil′ə·tē] *n.* The tendency to catch fire and burn quickly: Dry weather increased the *flammability* of the underbrush.

flam·ma·ble [flam′ə·bəl] *adj.* Likely to catch fire easily and burn quickly.

flan [flan] *n.* 1 An open pie or tart with a filling of custard, cheese, or fruit. 2 A blank metal disk before it is stamped to make a coin.

flange [flanj] *n.* An edge or ridge, as on a wheel, pipe, or girder, used to attach it to something else or to keep it in place.

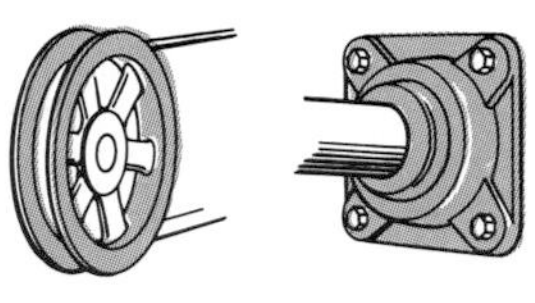
Flanges

flank [flangk] 1 *n.* The side of an animal or person between the ribs and the hip. 2 *n.* The right or left part, as of an army, fleet, or football team. 3 *v.* To be located at the side or sides of: Trees *flanked* the driveway. 4 *v.* To move around the flank of.

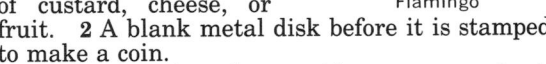

flank·er [flang′kər] *n.* A person positioned at the side of a formation.

flan·nel [flan′əl] 1 *n.* A soft cotton or wool fabric of a plain, loose weave with a slight nap. 2 *adj. use:* a gray *flannel* suit. 3 *n.* (*pl.*) Clothing made of flannel, especially trousers.

flan·nel·ette [flan′ə·let′] *n.* A soft cotton flannel used for infants' wear and pajamas.

flap [flap] *v.* **flapped, flap·ping,** *n.* 1 *v.* To cause to move rapidly up and down: The eagle *flapped* its wings. 2 *v.* To have a waving or fluttering motion, as a flag in the wind. 3 *n.* The action or sound of flapping. 4 *n.* A loosely hanging part, often used to cover an opening: Tuck the *flap* inside the envelope; the *flap* of a pocket.

flap·jack [flap′jak′] *n.* A pancake.

flap·per [flap′ər] *n.* 1 A person or thing that flaps. 2 *informal* A lively young woman of the decade after World War I who behaved and dressed in a daringly unconventional way.

flare [flâr] *v.* **flared, flar·ing,** *n.* 1 *v.* To blaze up suddenly with a glaring, unsteady light: If you fan glowing embers, they will *flare* up. 2 *n.* A bright, flickering light lasting for a short time: the *flare* of a match. 3 *n.* A brilliant light, as one used for signaling or lighting up an airfield. 4 *v.* To burst out in sudden anger: to *flare* up at someone. 5 *v.* To widen out in the shape of a bell. 6 *n.* A widening or spreading outward.

flare-up [flâr′up′] *n.* 1 A sudden increase in intensity, as of a fire or an illness. 2 An outburst of anger or protest.

flash [flash] 1 *n.* A sudden blaze of brilliant light or fire: a *flash* of lightning. 2 *v.* To give out a sudden blaze; gleam brightly: The searchlight *flashed* across the sky. 3 *v.* To cause to shine brightly: to *flash* a lantern. 4 *n.* A sudden feeling or thought: a *flash* of hope. 5 *v.* To move or appear suddenly or quickly: The train *flashed* by; An idea *flashed* into his mind. 6 *n.* A very short time; instant: She had the answer in a *flash.* 7 *n.* A short news report sent by radio or telegraph. 8 *v.* To send at great speed: to *flash* a message by telegraph. 9 *v. informal* To show suddenly or abruptly: The police officer *flashed* her badge.
flash·back [flash′bak′] *n.* An interruption in a natural time sequence to describe earlier events, as in a story or motion picture.
flash·bulb [flash′bulb′] *n.* A light bulb on a camera that flashes a brilliant light as a picture is being taken.
flash burn A burn caused by momentary exposure to very intense heat.
flash card A card bearing a word, letters, numbers, or pictures, shown briefly to a person or group during learning drills.
flash·cube [flash′kyōōb′] *n.* A cubic device designed to revolve and provide a flash from four sides when attached to a camera adapted to use it.
flash flood A sudden, rushing flood of a river, lake, or other body of water, usually caused by heavy rains.
flash·gun [flash′gun′] *n.* A device that holds and triggers a flashbulb.
flash·light [flash′līt′] *n.* 1 A small portable electric light that uses batteries. 2 The burst of bright light from a flashbulb. 3 A bright, flashing light, as in a lighthouse.
flash point 1 The lowest temperature at which vapor rising from a volatile liquid will burn when exposed to a flame. The flash point is a property that serves to identify some liquids. 2 The point at which an outburst of violence, anger, or action occurs.
flash·y [flash′ē] *adj.* **flash·i·er, flash·i·est** 1 Dazzling for a short time. 2 Too showy or gaudy: a *flashy* car. **—flash′i·ly** *adv.* **—flash′i·ness** *n.*
flask [flask] *n.* A small container with a narrow neck, usually made of glass or metal.

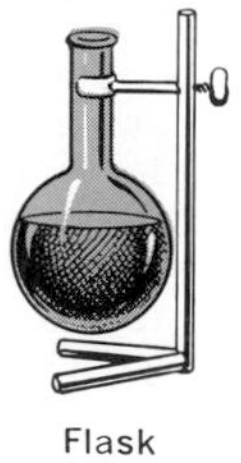
Flask

flat[1] [flat] *adj.* **flat·ter, flat·test,** *n., v.* **flat·ted, flat·ting,** *adv.* 1 *adj.* Having a level surface; smooth: The top of a table is *flat.* 2 *n.* The flat part: the *flat* of a sword. 3 *n.* (*pl.*) A level piece of land, as a marsh. 4 *adj.* Stretched or spread out horizontally: *flat* on one's back. 5 *adj.* Not very deep; shallow: a *flat* dish. 6 *n.* A shallow box of earth for holding young plants. 7 *adj.* Having lost all or most of its air: a *flat* tire. 8 *n.* A flat tire. 9 *adj.* Without much flavor or liveliness: *flat* soda. 10 *adj.* Having little or no gloss: said about paint. 11 *adj.* Not changing; fixed: to charge a *flat* rate. 12 *n.* A musical tone half a step below a natural tone of the same name. 13 *n.* The sign (♭) indicating that the note following is a flat. 14 *adv.* Below the proper pitch: to sing *flat.* 15 *v.* To make or become flat. 16 *adv.* In a flat position or way: to fall *flat.* 17 *adv.* Exactly: ten pounds *flat.* **—flat′ly** *adv.* **—flat′ness** *n.*
flat[2] [flat] *n.* A set of rooms on one floor used as a dwelling; apartment.
flat·boat [flat′bōt′] *n.* A large boat with a flat bottom, used on rivers.
flat·car [flat′kär′] *n.* A railroad car with no sides or roof, used for large pieces of freight.
flat·fish [flat′fish′] *n., pl.* **flat·fish** or **flat·fish·es** A fish having a flattened body and both eyes on the upper side, as a flounder.
flat·foot [flat′fŏŏt′] *n.* 1 *pl.* **flat·feet** [flat′fēt′] The condition of a foot having an unusually flat instep so that most of the sole comes in contact with the ground. 2 A foot affected with flatfoot. 3 *pl.* **flat·foots** *slang* A policeman who patrols on foot.
flat·foot·ed [flat′fŏŏt′id] *adj.* 1 Having flatfeet. 2 Having a firmly balanced stance. 3 *informal* Firm and forthright: a *flatfooted* refusal. 4 Not ready to react; unprepared: The announcement caught him *flatfooted.*
flat·iron [flat′ī′ərn] *n.* Another name for IRON, a device for pressing clothes and other articles.
flat·ten [flat′(ə)n] *v.* To make or become flat.
flat·ter [flat′ər] *v.* 1 To praise insincerely or too much, usually to gain favor. 2 To make appear more attractive than is actually so: That camera angle *flatters* the star. 3 To please: I'm *flattered* that you think so. **—flat′ter·er** *n.*
flat·ter·y [flat′ər·ē] *n., pl.* **flat·ter·ies** 1 The act of flattering. 2 Too much or insincere praise: The new section head used *flattery* to get ahead.
flat·top [flat′top′] *n. informal* 1 An aircraft carrier. 2 A crew cut. 3 Anything with a flat top, as a mesa.
flat·u·lent [flach′ə·lənt] *adj.* 1 Having excessive gas in the stomach or intestines. 2 Puffed up with self-importance; pompous: *flatulent* prose. **—flat′u·lence** *n.*
flat·ware [flat′wâr′] *n.* Tableware that is approximately flat, as knives, forks, spoons, and serving trays.
flat·worm [flat′wûrm′] *n.* Any of several kinds of thin, flat worms. Many live in water, and some, as the tapeworm, live in other animals as parasites.
flaunt [flônt] *v.* 1 To wave or flutter freely, as flags. 2 To call too much attention to; show off: to *flaunt* one's knowledge.
flau·tist [flô′tist *or* flou′tist] *n.* Another word for FLUTIST.
fla·vor [flā′vər] 1 *n.* The special taste and smell of something: the *flavor* of cinnamon. 2 *v.* To give flavor to, as by adding spices. 3 *n.* A distinctive quality; aura: the *flavor* of spring.
fla·vor·ful [flā′vər·fəl] *adj.* Full of good flavor; tasty. **—fla′vor·ful·ly** *adv.*
fla·vor·ing [flā·vər·ing] *n.* Something added, as to food or drink, to give a certain taste.
flaw [flô] 1 *n.* A crack, blemish, or other defect: a *flaw* in a gem; Your plan has one *flaw.* 2 *v.* To make a flaw in: The argument was *flawed* by poor rea-

a add	**i** it	**ŏŏ** took	**oi** oil
ā ace	**ī** ice	**ōō** pool	**ou** pout
â care	**o** odd	**u** up	**ng** ring
ä palm	**ō** open	**û** burn	**th** thin
e end	**ô** order	**yōō** fuse	**th** this
ē equal			**zh** vision

ə = a in *above*, e in *sicken*, i in *possible*, o in *melon*, u in *circus*

soning. 3 *v.* To become defective, as marred or cracked.

flaw·less [flô'lis] *adj.* Having no defects or blemishes; perfect. **—flaw'less·ly** *adv.* **—flaw'less·ness** *n.*

flax [flaks] *n.* 1 A plant with blue flowers and a slender stem that yields the fiber used in making linen. Linseed oil is produced from its seeds. 2 The fibers of this plant when ready to be spun into thread.

flax·en [flak'sən] *adj.* 1 Having the pale yellow color of flax: *flaxen* hair. 2 Of flax.

flax·seed [flaks'sēd' *or* flak'sēd'] *n.* The seeds of flax, used to make linseed oil and in medicines.

flay [flā] *v.* 1 To strip off the skin or hide from. 2 To scold or criticize very harshly.

fl dr or **fl. dr.** fluid dram(s).

flea [flē] *n.* A tiny, leaping insect without wings. Fleas suck the blood of animals and live on their bodies as parasites.

flea·bag [flē'bag'] *n. slang* A cheap, shabby hotel or rooming house.

flea·bite [flē'bīt'] *n.* 1 The bite of a flea. 2 A minor irritator.

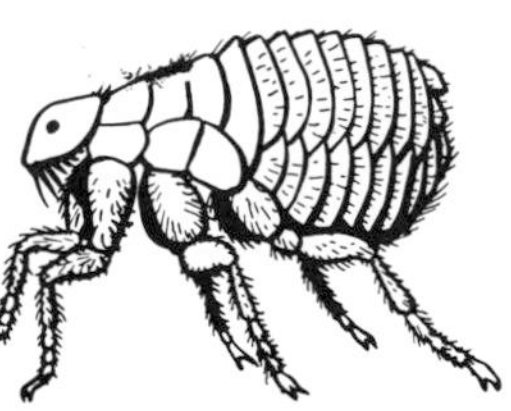

Dog flea

flea collar A collar for a cat or dog containing a substance that kills or repels fleas.

flea market An area containing small booths where secondhand items are displayed for sale.

fleck [flek] 1 *n.* A spot or speck, as of color or dust. 2 *v.* To mark or sprinkle with flecks: Stars *flecked* the evening sky.

flec·tion [flek'shən] *n.* Another spelling of FLEXION.

fled [fled] Past tense and past participle of FLEE.

fledge [flej] *v.* **fledged, fledg·ing** 1 To grow enough feathers for flying: said about a young bird. 2 To furnish with feathers.

fledg·ling or **fledge·ling** [flej'ling] *n.* 1 A young bird just learning to fly. 2 A young, inexperienced person; beginner.

flee [flē] *v.* **fled, flee·ing** 1 To run away, as from danger or enemies: People *fled* to shelters during the air raid. 2 To run away from: When the fire started, they *fled* the house. 3 To move swiftly: cars *fleeing* by.

fleece [flēs] *n., v.* **fleeced, fleec·ing** 1 *n.* The coat of wool covering a sheep or similar animal. 2 *v.* To shear or clip the fleece from. 3 *v. slang* To rob or cheat: to *fleece* a person of money.

fleec·y [flē'sē] *adj.* **fleec·i·er, fleec·i·est** Made of or like fleece; downy and soft.

fleet[1] [flēt] *n.* 1 All of the ships belonging to one country, or sailing under one command: the U.S. *fleet.* 2 A group, as of ships, aircraft, or motor vehicles, used together or belonging to one company: a *fleet* of taxicabs.

fleet[2] [flēt] *adj.* Rapid in movement; swift: to be *fleet* of foot. **—fleet'ness** *n.*

fleet admiral An officer of the highest rank in the navy.

fleet·ing [flēt'ing] *adj.* Passing quickly: a *fleeting* moment. **—fleet'ing·ly** *adv.* **—fleet'ing·ness** *n.*

Flem·ing [flem'ing] *n.* 1 A person born in Flanders. 2 A Belgian who speaks Flemish.

Flem·ish [flem'ish] 1 *adj.* Of or from Flanders. 2 *n.* **(the Flemish)** The people of Flanders. 3 *n.* The language of Flanders.

flesh [flesh] *n.* 1 The soft parts that cover the bones in a human or animal body. 2 The parts of an animal used for food; meat. 3 The human body, as distinguished from the mind or spirit. 4 Humanity: the way of all *flesh.* 5 The pulpy, solid part of fruits or vegetables. **—in the flesh** 1 Actually present; in person. 2 Alive. **—one's own flesh and blood** One's blood relatives.

flesh·ly [flesh'lē] *adj.* **flesh·li·er, flesh·li·est** 1 Of the body; bodily. 2 Sensual.

flesh wound A wound involving outer muscular tissue and not bones or vital organs of the body.

flesh·y [flesh'ē] *adj.* **flesh·i·er, flesh·i·est** Having much flesh; plump or fat.

fleur-de-lis [flo͞or'də·lē'] *n., pl.* **fleurs-de-lis** [flo͞or'də·lēz'] A design that looks like the iris flower. The fleur-de-lis was the emblem of the kings of France.

Fleur-de-lis

flew [flo͞o] Past tense and past participle of FLY: The butterfly *flew* from flower to flower.

flex [fleks] *v.* 1 To bend: to *flex* one's arm. 2 To pull tight; contract: to *flex* a muscle.

flex·i·ble [flek'sə·bəl] *adj.* 1 Capable of being bent or twisted without breaking: Rope is *flexible.* 2 Easily changed; adaptable: *flexible* rules. **—flex'i·bil'i·ty** *n.* **—flex'i·bly** *adv.*

flex·ion [flek'shən] *n.* 1 The act of bending: *Flexion* of the hips and knees creates a lap. 2 A being bent. 3 A bend.

flex·or [flek'sər] *n.* Any muscle that by contracting causes a limb to bend.

flex·time [fleks'tīm] *n.* A system that allows employees some choice in determining the times when they begin and end their working day.

flick [flik] 1 *n.* A light, snapping movement or blow, as of a whip. 2 *n.* A slight, cracking sound. 3 *v.* To strike at or remove with a quick, light snap: to *flick* crumbs from one's lap. 4 *v.* To cause to move with a snap: to *flick* a dust cloth over furniture.

flick·er[1] [flik'ər] 1 *v.* To gleam or burn with an unsteady, wavering light: The moon's reflection *flickered* among the waves. 2 *n.* A fluttering, unsteady light. 3 *v.* To flutter or quiver; wave to and fro: The leaves are *flickering* in the wind. 4 *n.* A quivering motion or feeling: the *flicker* of a cat's ear; a *flicker* of fear.

flick·er[2] [flik'ər] *n.* A large woodpecker of North America with a brown back. The undersides of its wings are brightly colored.

flied [flīd] Alternative past tense and past participle of FLY[1] (def. 7): I *flied* out to left field.

fli·er [flī'ər] *n.* 1 Something that can fly, as a bird or insect. 2 A pilot of an airplane. 3 *U.S.* A leaflet or handbill.

flight[1] [flīt] *n.* 1 The act or manner of flying: the *flight* of a bee. 2 The distance traveled, by an aircraft, bird, or bullet. 3 A trip in an aircraft. 4 A group flying together: a *flight* of gulls. 5 A soaring above or beyond usual bounds: a poetic *flight.* 6 A set of stairs, as between floors of a building.

flight[2] [flīt] *n.* The act of running away. **—put to flight** To cause to run away: Our shouts *put* the dogs *to flight.* **—take flight** To run away.

flight attendant A person whose duties include waiting on passengers in an aircraft.

flight bag A light traveling bag for carrying small personal items, especially on an airplane journey.

flight·less [flīt′lis] *adj.* Unable to fly.

flight·y [flī′tē] *adj.* **flight·i·er, flight·i·est** Unable to keep one's mind or attention fixed on any one thing; whimsical; frivolous; impulsive; fickle. —**flight′i·ness** *n.*

flim·sy [flim′zē] *adj.* **flim·si·er, flim·si·est** 1 Ready to fall apart or tear; easily damaged or broken: a *flimsy* old chair; *flimsy* cloth. 2 Not very convincing; weak: They gave a *flimsy* excuse for being late. —**flim′si·ly** *adv.*

flinch [flinch] 1 *v.* To shrink back, as from anything painful or dangerous; wince: I tried not to *flinch* when the splinter was removed. 2 *n.* The act of drawing back or wincing.

fling [fling] *v.* **flung, fling·ing,** *n.* 1 *v.* To throw, especially with force; hurl: We *flung* fish to the porpoise. 2 *n.* The act of flinging. 3 *v.* To rush headlong: to *fling* out of class after a fight. 4 *n.* A brief time of freedom and fun: We all had a last *fling* before school opened. 5 *n.* A Scottish dance with rapid steps and flinging arm movements. 6 *n. informal* An attempt; try: to have a *fling* at painting.

flint [flint] *n.* A hard, dark stone which produces sparks when struck against steel.

flint·lock [flint′lok′] *n.* 1 A gunlock in which a piece of flint is struck against steel in order to light the gunpowder. 2 An old-fashioned type of gun having such a lock.

flint·y [flin′tē] *adj.* **flint·i·er, flint·i·est** 1 Made of or containing flint: *flinty* soil. 2 Like flint; very hard or cruel: a *flinty* heart.

flip [flip] *v.* **flipped, flip·ping,** *n., adj.* 1 *v.* To move suddenly or jerkily: The fish *flipped* out of the net. 2 *n.* A quick snap or jerk. 3 *v.* To toss up and over, often with a snapping movement of the thumb: to *flip* a coin. 4 *adj. informal* Impertinent; flippant. 5 *n.* A somersault, especially one that is performed in the air.

flip chart A chart in a set that can be flipped over and shown in sequence.

flip-flop [flip′flop′] *n., v.* **flip-flopped, flip-flop·ping** 1 *n.* The sound of something flapping. 2 *v.* To make a flapping sound. 3 *n. informal* A sudden reversal of opinion or decision. 4 *v. informal* To reverse oneself.

flip·pant [flip′ənt] *adj.* Not respectful or serious; too smart or pert: to make a *flippant* remark. —**flip′·pan·cy** *n.* —**flip′pant·ly** *adv.*

flip·per [flip′ər] *n.* 1 A broad, flat limb, as of a seal, adapted for swimming. 2 A broad, flat shoe like a fin, worn by skin divers.

Flippers

flip side The reverse side, especially of a phonograph record.

flirt [flûrt] 1 *v.* To act in an affectionate or loving way without being serious; play at love. 2 *n.* A person who flirts. 3 *v.* To expose oneself to something, often carelessly or not seriously: to *flirt* with danger. 4 *v.* To snap or move quickly; flick: Mockingbirds *flirt* their tails. 5 *n.* A sudden, jerky movement.

flir·ta·tion [flûr·tā′shən] *n.* 1 The act of flirting. 2 A brief and casual romance.

flir·ta·tious [flûr·tā′shəs] *adj.* 1 Of or characteristic of a flirt: a *flirtatious* look. 2 Having the habit of flirting: a *flirtatious* person. —**flir·ta′tious·ly** *adv.* —**flir·ta′tious·ness** *n.*

flirt·y [flûrt′ē] *adj.* **flirt·i·er, flirt·i·est** Tending to flirt; flirtatious.

flit [flit] *v.* **flit·ted, flit·ting** 1 To move or fly rapidly and lightly; dart: Birds *flitted* among the trees. 2 To move or pass quickly or abruptly: My thoughts *flitted* back to my years in high school.

flitch [flich] *n.* A salted and smoked cut of meat from the side of a pig: a *flitch* of bacon.

fliv·ver [fliv′ər] *n.* A small, inexpensive automobile, especially an old one.

float [flōt] 1 *v.* To rest or cause to rest on the surface of a liquid, such as water, without sinking: A life preserver *floats.* 2 *n.* An object that floats or holds up something else in a liquid, as an anchored raft at a beach or a piece of cork attached to a fishing line. 3 *v.* To be carried along gently on the surface of a liquid or through the air; drift: Fog *floated* over the city. 4 *v.* To move lightly and without effort: The skater *floated* across the ice. 5 *n.* A wheeled platform or truck on which an exhibit is carried in a parade.

float·er [flō′tər] *n.* 1 A person or thing that floats. 2 A person who wanders from place to place; vagrant.

floating rib One of the four lower ribs of a human being that are attached to the backbone but not to the breastbone.

flock [flok] 1 *n.* A group of animals of the same kind herded, feeding, or moving together: a *flock* of sheep; a *flock* of pigeons. 2 *n.* A large number or group: a *flock* of people. 3 *v.* To come or move together in a flock or crowd: to *flock* together; People *flock* to the shore in hot weather. 4 *n.* The people belonging to the congregation of a church.

floe [flō] *n.* A large, almost flat field of floating ice.

flog [flog] *v.* **flogged, flog·ging** To beat hard, as with a whip or stick.

flood [flud] 1 *n.* A great flow of water, especially over land not usually covered with water. 2 *v.* To cover, fill, or pour into, as with a flood: The water from the broken dam *flooded* the town; Sunshine *flooded* the porch. 3 *v.* To overflow: After the storm, the lake *flooded.* 4 *n.* The coming in of the tide; high tide. 5 *n.* Any great flow or stream: a *flood* of words. —**the Flood** The deluge in the time of Noah, as told in the Old Testament.

flood·gate [flud′gāt′] *n.* 1 A gate or valve that controls the flow of water in a body of water, as a canal or stream. 2 Anything that restrains or holds back: to open the *floodgates* of anger.

a	add	**i**	it	**o͝o**	took	**oi**	oil
ā	ace	**ī**	ice	**o͞o**	pool	**ou**	pout
â	care	**o**	odd	**u**	up	**ng**	ring
ä	palm	**ō**	open	**û**	burn	**th**	thin
e	end	**ô**	order	**yo͞o**	fuse	**t͟h**	this
ē	equal					**zh**	vision

ə = a in *above* e in *sicken* i in *possible* o in *melon* u in *circus*

flood·light [flud′līt′] *n.* 1 A lamp that gives a very bright, wide beam of light. 2 The light from such a lamp.

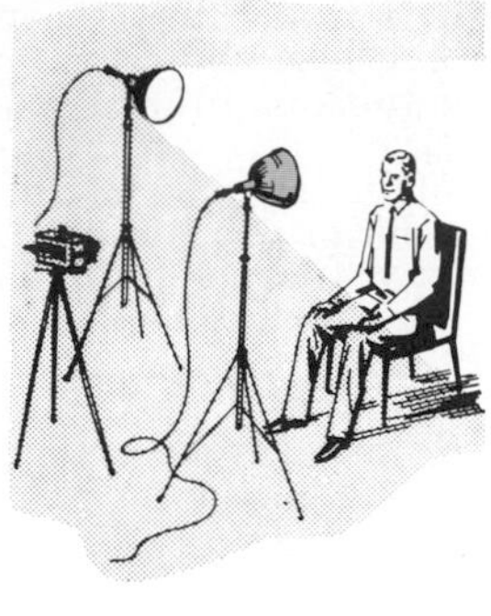
Floodlights

flood·plain [flud′plān′] *n.* Low, flat land along a river that sometimes overflows its banks.

flood tide The incoming tide.

flood·wa·ter [flud′wô′tər] *n.* The water that causes a flood.

floor [flôr] 1 *n.* The surface in a room or building upon which one walks. 2 *v.* To cover or provide with a floor: The kitchen was *floored* with tiles. 3 *n.* A story of a building: We live on the third *floor.* 4 *n.* The lowest surface; bottom: the *floor* of the sea. 5 *n.* The right to speak at a meeting: The opposing side has the *floor* now. 6 *v.* To knock down, as to the floor. 7 *v. informal* To bewilder or surprise; flabbergast.

floor·ing [flôr′ing] *n.* 1 Material for the making of a floor. 2 A floor or floors.

floor-length [flôr′leng(k)th′] *adj.* Extending down to the floor: *floor-length* curtains.

floor show An entertainment by professional performers in a night club.

floor·walk·er [flôr′wôk′ər] *n.* A person who supervises salespeople and assists customers in a department of a large store.

flop [flop] *v.* **flopped, flop·ping,** *n.* 1 *v.* To move about heavily and clumsily. The seal *flopped* across the stage. 2 *v.* To fall or cause to drop heavily: to *flop* into bed. 3 *v.* To flap loosely, as in a wind. 4 *n.* The act or sound of flopping. 5 *n. informal* A total failure.

flop·py [flop′ē] *adj.* **flop·pi·er, flop·pi·est** *informal* Tending or likely to flop: Dachshunds have *floppy* ears. **—flop′pi·ly** *adv.* **—flop′pi·ness** *n.*

floppy disk A small disk made of very thin, flexible plastic and coated with magnetic material on which computer programs and data can be stored.

flo·ra [flôr′ə] *n.* All the plants of a particular place or period of time.

flo·ral [flô′rəl] *adj.* Of, like, or having to do with flowers: a *floral* wreath.

Flor·en·tine [flôr′ən·tēn′] 1 *adj.* Of or coming from Florence. 2 *n.* A person born or living in Florence.

flo·ret [flôr′ət] *n.* A small flower, such as any of the tiny flowers that form the flower head of a dandelion or other composite plant.

flor·id [flôr′id] *adj.* 1 Having a ruddy, flushed color: a *florid* complexion. 2 Decorated very much; flowery: *florid* architecture. **—flor′id·ly** *adv.* **—flor′id·ness** *n.*

flor·in [flôr′in] *n.* Any of several gold or silver coins used at different times in various countries of Europe.

flo·rist [flôr′ist] *n.* A person who sells flowers or raises them to sell.

floss [flôs] *n., v.* **flossed, floss·ing** 1 *n.* Soft, silky fibers, as those produced by the milkweed. 2 *n.* Glossy, untwisted silk thread used in embroidery. 3 *v.* To clean the teeth with dental floss.

floss·y [flôs′ē] *adj.* **floss·i·er, floss·i·est** Resembling or covered with soft, silky fibers.

flo·til·la [flō·til′ə] *n.* 1 A fleet of boats or small ships. 2 A small fleet of ships.

flot·sam [flot′səm] *n.* Parts of a wrecked ship or its cargo drifting on the water.

flounce[1] [flouns] *v.* **flounced, flounc·ing,** *n.* 1 *v.* To move or go with exaggerated tosses of the body. 2 *n.* The act of flouncing.

flounce[2] [flouns] *n., v.* **flounced, flounc·ing** 1 *n.* A gathered or pleated ruffle used for trimming on such items as curtains and slipcovers, sewn on by one edge. 2 *v.* To decorate with a flounce or flounces.

Flounce

floun·der[1] [floun′dər] *v.* 1 To struggle clumsily; move awkwardly, as through mud or snow. 2 To struggle in speech or action as if confused: The actor forgot some lines but *floundered* along.

floun·der[2] [floun′dər] *n., pl.* **floun·der** or **floun·ders** A flatfish valued as food.

flour [flour] 1 *n.* A fine, soft powder made by grinding wheat or other grain, and used in making bread, cake, and other foods. 2 *v.* To cover or sprinkle with flour. **—flour′y** *adj.*

flour·ish [flûr′ish] 1 *v.* To grow vigorously; thrive: Chrysanthemums *flourish* in cool weather. 2 *v.* To be successful; prosper: The business *flourished.* 3 *v.* To wave about or brandish: The lawyer *flourished* the photograph before the jury. 4 *n.* The act of waving about or shaking. 5 *n.* Showy display in doing anything: The chorus sang the song with a *flourish.* 6 *n.* A curve or decorative stroke in handwriting. 7 *n.* A showy, lively passage of music; fanfare.

flout [flout] *v.* To treat with open contempt; scoff at; defy: to *flout* tradition. **—flout′er** *n.* ◆ *Flout* and *flaunt* are often confused, even though they have distinct meanings. See FLAUNT (def. 2).

flow [flō] 1 *v.* To move along or pour steadily and smoothly: said about water or other fluids. 2 *n.* The act or manner of flowing: to stop a *flow* of blood; the elegant *flow* of a long robe. 3 *v.* To move steadily and freely. 4 *v.* To hang or ripple down loosely: The curtain *flowed* at the window. 5 *n.* A smooth outpouring; uninterrupted movement: the *flow* of traffic. 6 *n.* The amount of something that flows: a daily *flow* of 500 barrels of oil. 7 *v.* To be derived; follow; stem.

flow·chart [flō′chärt′] *n.* A diagram showing the successive steps in a process.

flow·er [flou′ər *or* flour] 1 *n.* The part of a plant or tree that encloses the seeds; blossom. A flower usually has brightly colored petals. 2 *n.* Any plant that produces such blossoms. 3 *v.* To produce flowers; bloom: to *flower* in the spring. 4 *n.* The finest part or result of anything: the *flower* of our youth. 5 *n.* The time when something is at its finest: when knighthood was in *flower.* 6 *v.* To reach fullest growth or development: a talent that *flowered* early. **—flow′er·like** *adj.*

flow·ered [flou′ərd] *adj.* Covered or decorated with flowers or a floral pattern: a *flowered* fabric.

flow·er·et [flou′ər·it] *n.* A small flower.

flower girl A young girl who carries flowers in a wedding procession or other ceremonial occasion.

flowering plant Any of the large class of plants that produce seeds enclosed in an ovary.

flow·er·pot [flou′ər·pot′] *n.* A pot to be filled with earth and used for growing plants.

flow·er·y [flou′ər·ē *or* flour′ē] *adj.* **flow·er·i·er, flow·er·i·est** 1 Covered or decorated with flowers. 2 Full of fancy words and showy language: a *flowery* poem. **—flow′er·i·ness** *n.*

flown [flōn] Past participle of FLY[1].

fl oz or **fl. oz.** fluid ounce(s).

flu [flo͞o] *n. informal* Influenza.

flub [flub] *v.* **flubbed, flub·bing,** *n. informal* 1 *v.* To make bad mistakes with or handle clumsily; botch. 2 *n.* An act of flubbing.

fluc·tu·ate [fluk′cho͞o·āt′] *v.* **fluc·tu·at·ed, fluc·tu·at·ing** To change or move in an irregular manner or up and down: The patient's temperature *fluctuated* often. **—fluc′tu·a′tion** *n.*

flue [flo͞o] *n.* A tube, as in a chimney, through which smoke or hot air is drawn off.

flu·en·cy [flo͞o′ən·sē] *n.* Smoothness and ease in speech or writing.

flu·ent [flo͞o′ənt] *adj.* 1 Able to speak or write with smoothness or ease. 2 Spoken or written with smoothness or ease: The interpreter speaks *fluent* German. **—flu′ent·ly** *adv.*

fluff [fluf] 1 *n.* A very soft, light mass of wool, fur, feathers, or other downy substance. 2 *v.* To make something, as pillows, hair, or feathers, soft and light by shaking or patting.

fluff·y [fluf′ē] *adj.* **fluff·i·er, fluff·i·est** 1 Like fluff; light and frothy: Beaten egg whites are *fluffy.* 2 Covered or filled with fluff: *fluffy* kittens; *fluffy* blankets. **—fluff′i·ly** *adv.* **—fluff′i·ness** *n.*

flu·id [flo͞o′id] 1 *n.* Any substance able to flow easily; liquid or gas. Water, air, and steam are fluids. 2 *adj.* Able to flow or pour easily; not solid. 3 *adj.* Changing or flowing, as a fluid: *fluid* opinions. **—flu′id·ly** *adv.* **—flu′id·ness** *n.*

fluid dram A liquid measure equal to one-eighth of a fluid ounce.

flu·i·di·ty [flo͞o·id′ə·tē] *n.* 1 The ability to flow. 2 The condition of being fluid.

fluid ounce A liquid measure equal to one-sixteenth of a pint.

fluke[1] [flo͞ok] *n.* 1 Any of several kinds of flat, parasitic worms living in the livers of some animals. 2 Another name for a FLATFISH or FLOUNDER.

fluke[2] [flo͞ok] *n.* 1 The triangular head at the end of either arm of an anchor. A fluke sticks into the ground to hold the anchor fast. 2 A barb on an arrowhead or harpoon. 3 Either of the two parts of a whale's tail.

fluke[3] [flo͞ok] *n. informal* Any piece of good luck, especially a lucky stroke in a game.

flume [flo͞om] *n.* 1 A narrow gap in a mountain through which a torrent passes. 2 A long, sloping trough filled with running water. It is used to carry logs or supply water.

Flume

flum·mox *v. slang* To baffle; confuse.

flung [flung] Past tense and past participle of FLING: I *flung* my coat on a chair.

flunk [flungk] *informal* 1 *v.* To fail, as a school subject or examination. 2 *v.* To give a failing grade to: to *flunk* a poor student. 3 *n.* A failure in school work. **—flunk out** To leave or cause to leave a class, school, or college because of failure.

flun·ky or **flun·key** [flung′kē] *n., pl.* **flun·kies** or **flun·keys** 1 A manservant or footman: no longer used. 2 A person who fawns upon or flatters others, especially those in authority: a TV producer surrounded by *flunkies.*

flu·o·resce [flo͞o′ə·res′] *v.* **flu·o·resced, flu·o·resc·ing** To be fluorescent.

flu·o·res·cence [flo͞o′ə·res′əns] *n.* 1 The emission of light by an object when it is exposed to certain kinds of radiation. 2 The light so emitted.

flu·o·res·cent [flo͞o′ə·res′ənt] *adj.* Giving off light when acted upon by certain forms of energy, as by ultraviolet rays.

fluorescent lamp A lamp consisting of a glass tube containing mercury vapor and coated on the inside with a fluorescent material. When an electric current passes through the mercury vapor, ultraviolet rays strike the coating and cause it to emit light.

fluor·i·date [flo͝or′ə·dāt′] *v.* **fluor·i·dat·ed, fluor·i·dat·ing** To add a fluoride to (drinking water), especially to prevent tooth decay. **—fluor′i·da′tion** *n.*

flu·o·ride [flo͞o′(ə·)rīd′] *n.* A compound of fluorine and another element.

flu·o·rine [flo͞o′(ə·)rēn′] *n.* A pale yellow, corrosive, extremely reactive gaseous element that forms many compounds. Both the element and its compounds are toxic, although traces are essential to some organisms.

fluor·o·scope [flo͝or′ə·skōp′] *n.* A device for looking at the shadows on a fluorescent screen made by objects put between the screen and a direct beam of X rays. A fluoroscope is often used to examine the bones and inner organs of the body.

flur·ry [flûr′ē] *n., pl.* **flur·ries,** *v.* **flur·ried, flur·ry·ing** 1 *n.* A sudden, brief gust of wind. 2 *n.* A light, brief rain or snowfall, often with wind. 3 *n.* A sudden commotion; stir. 4 *v.* To confuse or excite; fluster: The crowd's noise *flurried* the players.

flush[1] [flush] 1 *v.* To become or cause to become red in the face; redden: to *flush* with embarrassment. 2 *n.* A warm, rosy glow; blush. 3 *v.* To wash out or purify, as a sewer, with a gush of water or other liquid. 4 *v.* To flow or rush suddenly; flood. 5 *n.* A sudden gush, as of water. 6 *v.* To stir with a sudden, strong feeling: The winning team was *flushed* with pride. 7 *n.* A warm feeling of excitement or pleasure.

flush[2] [flush] 1 *adj.* Even or level with another surface: The tiles are all *flush.* 2 *adv.* In a flush manner; on an even level: The door should fit *flush* with the frame. 3 *adj.* Having plenty of money on hand.

flush[3] [flush] *v.* To drive or rush from a cover or hiding place: to *flush* rabbits from their burrows.

flus·ter [flus′tər] 1 *v.* To make confused or upset:

a	add	**i**	it	**o͝o**	took	**oi**	oil
ā	ace	**ī**	ice	**o͞o**	pool	**ou**	pout
â	care	**o**	odd	**u**	up	**ng**	ring
ä	palm	**ō**	open	**û**	burn	**th**	thin
e	end	**ô**	order	**yo͞o**	fuse	**th**	this
ē	equal					**zh**	vision

ə = a in *above*, e in *sicken*, i in *possible*, o in *melon*, u in *circus*

Big crowds *fluster* some people. **2** *n.* A confused or excited condition.

flute [flo͞ot] *n., v.* **flut·ed, flut·ing** **1** *n.* A musical wind instrument having a high, clear pitch and made in the shape of a narrow tube. A flute is played by blowing across a mouthpiece at one end and by opening and closing holes along its length with the fingers or with keys. **2** *v.* To play on the flute. **3** *v.* To make flutelike sounds by whistling or singing. **4** *n.* In architecture, one of the rounded grooves cut from the top to the bottom of a column. **5** *n.* A small ruffle or pleat in cloth. **6** *v.* To make flutes in (columns or cloth).

Flute

flut·ing [flo͞o′ting] *n.* **1** Rounded grooves in a column. **2** Small ruffles or pleats made in cloth.

flut·ist [flo͞o′tist] *n.* A person who plays the flute.

flut·ter [flut′ər] **1** *v.* To wave back and forth irregularly: The line of clothes *fluttered* in the wind. **2** *v.* To flap the wings without really flying; fly clumsily. **3** *v.* To move or cause to move rapidly or unevenly; quiver: The frightened rabbit's heart *fluttered.* **4** *n.* A waving or quivering motion; fluttering. **5** *v.* To excite or fluster. **6** *n.* Excitement; stir: The new pupil caused a *flutter* among the other children. **—flut′ter·er** *n.* **—flut′ter·y** *adj.*

flutter kick In swimming, a rapid alternate kicking of the legs without bending the knees.

flu·vi·al [flo͞o′vē·əl] *adj.* Of or living in a river.

flux [fluks] *n.* **1** A flowing or pouring out. **2** Constant change or movement: in a state of *flux.* **3** An abnormal flow of fluid from the body during an illness. **4** A substance used to help melt or solder metals together.

fly[1] [flī] *v.* **flew** (*for def. 7* **flied**), **flown** (*for def. 7* **flied**), **fly·ing,** *n., pl.* **flies** **1** *v.* To move through the air on wings, as birds or insects. **2** *v.* To move or travel through the air in an aircraft. **3** *v.* To cause to fly in the air: to *fly* a kite. **4** *v.* To move very fast: Summer *flies* by. **5** *v.* To wave or flutter in the air, as a flag. **6** *v.* To run away; flee: to *fly* for one's life. **7** *v.* In baseball, to bat the ball over the field. **8** *n.* Another word for FLY BALL. **9** *n.* A flap covering a zipper or buttons on the opening of a garment, especially on a pair of pants. **—on the fly** **1** While still in the air: to catch a ball *on the fly.* **2** *informal* In motion; very busy.

fly[2] [flī] *n., pl.* **flies** **1** One of a large group of small, two-winged insects, especially the housefly. **2** Any of several other flying insects, as the dragonfly or May fly. **3** A fishhook to which bits of colored cloth or feathers are tied so that it looks like an insect. **—fly in the ointment** Any small, annoying thing that spoils one's enjoyment.

fly ball A baseball batted high over the field.

fly·by [flī′bī′] *n., pl.* **fly·bys** **1** A flight by one or more airplanes past a certain place. **2** A near approach by a spacecraft to a celestial body for the purpose of observation.

fly·catch·er [flī′kach′ər] *n.* A bird that catches and eats insects as it flies.

fly·er [flī′ər] *n.* Another spelling of FLIER.

flying boat A seaplane designed to float in the water rather than on pontoons above the water.

flying buttress An arched support between the wall of a building and a supporting structure, used to help resist outward pressure on the wall.

Flying buttresses

flying field A field with the surface leveled so that planes can land and take off.

flying fish A fish with large, flat, winglike fins that enable it to jump out of the water and glide through the air for short distances.

flying saucer Any of various strange, moving objects shaped like a disk that some people have reported seeing in the sky.

flying squirrel A squirrel having a wide fold of skin connecting its front and back legs on both sides, enabling it to make gliding leaps.

fly·leaf [flī′lēf′] *n., pl.* **fly·leaves** [flī′lēvz′] An extra blank page at the beginning or end of a book.

fly·pa·per [flī′pā′pər] *n.* A strip of paper coated with a sticky, often poisonous substance. It is placed so as to catch and kill flies.

fly·speck [flī′spek′] **1** *n.* A small speck of dirt left by a fly. **2** *n.* Any small speck. **3** *v.* To mark with flyspecks.

fly·swat·ter [flī′swä′tər] *n.* A small, flat piece of rubber, plastic, or wire mesh, attached to a long handle and used to kill insects with a swift blow.

fly·trap [flī′trap′] *n.* **1** A device for trapping flies or other insects. **2** An insectivorous plant, as the Venus's flytrap.

fly·way [flī′wā′] *n.* A route regularly followed by migrating birds.

fly·weight [flī′wāt′] *n.* A boxer who weighs 112 pounds or less.

fly·wheel [flī′(h)wēl′] *n.* A heavy wheel attached to a revolving shaft to keep the speed of the shaft from changing suddenly.

Fm The symbol for the element fermium.

FM or **F.M.** frequency modulation.

f number In photography, a number that shows the effectiveness of a lens in admitting light to a camera. The lower the f number, the more light the lens admits.

foal [fōl] **1** *n.* A young horse, donkey, zebra, or similar animal. **2** *v.* To give birth to (a foal).

foam [fōm] **1** *n.* A white, frothy mass of small bubbles, as that on the crest of a wave. **2** *v.* To form or give off foam; froth.

foam rubber A firm, spongy rubber, used especially in mattresses, pillows, and cushions.

foam·y [fō′mē] *adj.* **foam·i·er, foam·i·est** Full of, consisting of, or like foam. **—foam′i·ness** *n.*

fob[1] [fob] *n.* **1** A small pocket for a watch. **2** A short chain or ribbon attached to a watch and dangling from such a pocket. **3** An ornament worn on the dangling end of such a chain.

fob[2] [fob] *v.* **fobbed, fob·bing** To trick; deceive: seldom used today. **—fob off** **1** To put off or get rid of (a person) by trickery or excuses. **2** To represent falsely; pass off: They *fobbed off* the glass beads as real gems.

f.o.b. or **F.O.B.** free on board.

fo·cal [fō′kəl] *adj.* Of or having to do with a focus. **—fo′cal·ly** *adv.*

focal length The distance from the center of a lens or curved mirror to its focus.

fo·ci [fō′sī′] Plural of FOCUS.

fo'c's'le [fōk'səl] *n.* A contraction of FORECASTLE.

fo·cus [fō'kəs] *n., pl.* **fo·cus·es** or **fo·ci** [fō'sī'], *v.* **fo·cused** or **fo·cussed, fo·cus·ing** or **fo·cus·sing** **1** *n.* In physics, a point at which light rays, sound waves, or radio waves come together after passing through something that bends them, as a lens, or after bouncing off a curved reflector. **2** *v.* To bring something, as light rays or sound waves, to a focus. **3** *n.* Focal distance. **4** *n.* An adjustment, as of the eye or a lens, that produces a clear image: to bring binoculars into *focus.* **5** *v.* To adjust the focus of (as the eye or a lens) to receive a clear image. **6** *n.* The place where a visual image is clearly formed, as in a camera. **7** *v.* To become focused: Our eyes *focused* on the door. **8** *n.* Any central point, as of interest or importance: The mysterious package was the *focus* of attention. **9** *v.* To fix; concentrate: to *focus* one's mind on a problem. **10** *n., pl.* **fo·ci** Either of two points inside an ellipse, the sum of whose distances to any point on the curve is always the same.

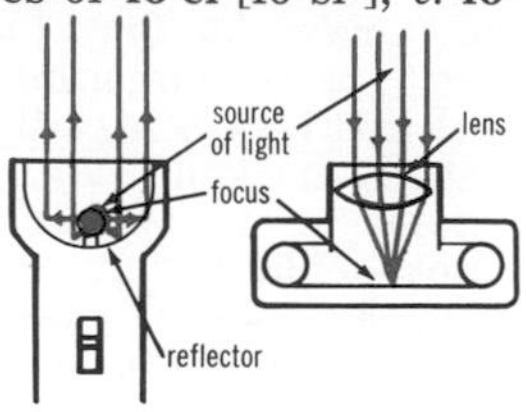

Foci in flashlight and camera

fod·der [fod'ər] *n.* Coarse feed, as hay or stalks of corn, for horses, cattle, and other livestock.

foe [fō] *n.* An enemy: friend or *foe?*

foe·tus [fē'təs] *n.* Another spelling of FETUS.

fog [fog] *n., v.* **fogged, fog·ging** **1** *n.* Condensed, watery vapor suspended in the air; dense mist through which it is hard to see. **2** *v.* To cover or become covered with or as if with fog; cloud or blur: The photograph was *fogged* during development; His glasses *fogged* up. **3** *n.* A bewildered, confused condition. **4** *v.* To make or become confused.

fog·gy [fog'ē] *adj.* **fog·gi·er, fog·gi·est** **1** Full of fog. **2** Dim, cloudy, or confused: not even a *foggy* notion. **—fog'gi·ly** *adv.* **—fog'gi·ness** *n.*

fog·horn [fog'hôrn'] *n.* A horn or loud whistle to warn ships during a fog.

fo·gy [fō'gē] *n., pl.* **fo·gies** A person whose ideas or ways are fussy and old-fashioned.

foi·ble [foi'bəl] *n.* A slight, easily excusable fault or weak point in a person's nature.

foil[1] [foil] *v.* To keep from succeeding in some purpose; outwit and thwart.

foil[2] [foil] *n.* A light, narrow sword used in fencing. It has a button at its tip to prevent injury.

foil[3] [foil] *n.* **1** Metal that has been hammered or rolled into thin, flexible sheets: aluminum *foil.* **2** Something that by contrast shows up the qualities of something else: The clumsy puppy was a *foil* for the graceful kitten.

foist [foist] *v.* To pass off or present wrongfully as being good or genuine: to *foist* a bad check on someone.

fold[1] [fōld] **1** *v.* To turn, bend, or crease so that one part covers another: to *fold* a blanket. **2** *n.* A part of a thing folded over another part: the *folds* of a curtain. **3** *n.* The crease made by folding. **4** *v.* To place or twine together, especially against the body: to *fold* one's arms. **5** *v.* To embrace or hug gently: She *folded* the puppy in her arms. **6** *v.* To wrap up: *Fold* the picture in paper.

fold[2] [fōld] *n.* **1** A pen for sheep. **2** The congregation of a church.

-fold A suffix meaning: **1** Having a certain number of parts: a *threefold* piece of luck. **2** An amount multiplied by a certain number: increased a *hundredfold.*

fold·er [fōl'dər] *n.* **1** A sheet of heavy paper folded double or an envelope for holding loose papers. **2** A booklet made of folded sheets. **3** A person or machine that folds something.

fol·de·rol [fol'də·rol'] *n.* **1** A useless trifle. **2** Senseless talk or activity; nonsense.

fo·li·age [fō'lē·ij *or* fō'lij] *n.* The leaves on a tree or other plant.

fo·li·a·tion [fō'lē·ā'shən] *n.* The process of sprouting leaves.

fo·lic acid [fō'lik] One of the vitamins of the B complex group, found in green plants, mushrooms, and other foods, and used in treating anemia.

fo·li·o [fō'lē·ō] *n., pl.* **fo·li·os,** *adj.* **1** *n.* A sheet of paper folded once to form four pages of a book. **2** *n.* A book of the largest size, with pages made by folding large sheets once. **3** *n.* Any page number of a book. **4** *adj.* Having to do with or being the size of a folio.

folk [fōk] *n., pl.* **folk** or **folks,** *adj.* **1** *n.* A people, nation, or race. **2** *adj.* Having to do with or coming from the common people: *folk* songs. **3** *n.* People in general or as a group: old *folk;* young *folk.* **4** *n.* (*pl.*) *informal* One's family or relatives: All their *folks* came to the reunion.

folk dance A dance that was started among the common people of a region or country.

folk etymology The gradual alteration of words so that they come to resemble more familiar but actually unrelated words: A chaise longue is sometimes called a chaise lounge by *folk etymology.* ◆ See FORLORN HOPE.

folk·lore [fōk'lôr'] *n.* The beliefs, stories, and customs preserved among a people or tribe.

folk music The traditional music of a people, usually transmitted orally in many variations and of unknown or group authorship.

folk singer A person or entertainer who sings folk songs.

folk song A song originating and passed down among the common people of a region or country.

folk·sy [fōk'sē] *adj.* **folk·si·er, folk·si·est** *U.S. informal* Friendly, neighborly, or casual.

folk tale A traditional story handed down by word of mouth among a people.

folk·way [fōk'wā'] *n.* A characteristic practice or belief of a people or social group.

fol·li·cle [fol'i·kəl] *n.* A small cavity or sac in the body. Hair grows from follicles.

fol·low [fol'ō] *v.* **1** To go or come after: The dog *followed* me home; Summer *follows* spring. **2** To keep to the course of: to *follow* a path. **3** To come after as a result: Fresh, cool air *follows* a thunderstorm. **4** To act in accordance with; obey: to

a	add	**i**	it	**o͝o**	took	**oi**	oil
ā	ace	**ī**	ice	**o͞o**	pool	**ou**	pout
â	care	**o**	odd	**u**	up	**ng**	ring
ä	palm	**ō**	open	**û**	burn	**th**	thin
e	end	**ô**	order	**yo͞o**	fuse	**th̶**	this
ē	equal					**zh**	vision

ə = a in *above* e in *sicken* i in *possible* o in *melon* u in *circus*

follow orders. **5** To watch or observe closely: to *follow* a tennis match. **6** To understand clearly: I don't *follow* your line of thought. **7** To engage in as one's work: to *follow* a trade. **—follow through** In games, to continue a stroke after having struck the ball. **—follow up** **1** To pursue closely. **2** To add to the effect of by further action.

fol·low·er [fol′ō·ər] *n.* **1** A person or thing that follows, as a person who follows the beliefs of another. **2** A servant or attendant.

fol·low·ing [fol′ō·ing] **1** *adj.* Coming next in order: the *following* week. **2** *n.* A group of disciples or followers. **—the following** The persons or things about to be mentioned.

fol·low-up [fol′ō·up′] **1** *n.* An instance of following up. **2** *n.* Something that follows up or reinforces previous action: This letter is a *follow-up* of my pledge to help. **3** *adj.* Having to do with following up: a *follow-up* letter.

fol·ly [fol′ē] *n., pl.* **fol·lies** **1** Lack of sense; foolishness. **2** A foolish idea or act.

fo·ment [fō·ment′] *v.* To stir up or promote (trouble): to *foment* rebellion. **—fo·ment′er** *n.*

fo·men·ta·tion [fō′mən·tā′shən] *n.* **1** The act or process of fomenting. **2** A hot poultice.

fond [fond] *adj.* **1** Loving or affectionate: a *fond* parent; a *fond* farewell. **2** Foolishly loving and indulgent. **3** Cherished: *fond* hopes. **—fond of** Having a liking for or love of: I'm *fond of* animals. **—fond′ly** *adv.* **—fond′ness** *n.*

fon·dant [fon′dənt] *n.* A soft, creamy preparation used for icings and candy, made by melting sugar with a little water and flavoring. ◆ *Fondant* comes from the French word *fondre,* to melt. The same word in different forms gave us *fondue,* a melted cheese, and *foundry,* a place where metals are melted.

fon·dle [fon′dəl] *v.* **fon·dled, fon·dling** To handle lovingly; caress: to *fondle* a baby. **—fon′dler** *n.*

Child fondling a kitten

fon·due or **fon·du** [fon·do͞o′] *n.* **1** A dish of melted cheese and wine into which bits of bread are dipped. **2** A dish made with small pieces of food, as meat, that are cooked by dipping them into a hot liquid. ◆ See FONDANT.

font[1] [font] *n.* **1** A basin for holy water or for water used in baptism. **2** A source, as a spring or fountain: a *font* of knowledge.

font[2] [font] *n.* A complete assortment of printing type of a particular size and style.

food [fo͞od] *n.* **1** Anything that is eaten, drunk, or absorbed by plants, animals, or people to make them grow and go on living. **2** Nourishment taken in solid form, as distinguished from drink. **3** Anything that feeds or nourishes: The inspiring speech gave us *food* for thought.

food chain A group of plants and animals connected with each other in such a way that each member of the group feeds upon the one below it and is itself eaten by the one above it. Grass-cattle-human beings is an example of a food chain.

food poisoning Illness caused by eating food contaminated with bacteria.

food stamp A piece of paper somewhat resembling money and issued by the government to needy persons for buying food at a discount.

food·stuff [fo͞od′stuf′] *n.* Any substance suitable for use as food.

foo·fa·raw [fo͞o′fə·rô′] *n.* **1** A flashy ornament; finery. **2** A commotion over a trifle.

fool [fo͞ol] **1** *n.* A silly, stupid person who can be easily tricked. **2** *n.* A clown formerly kept by a noble or a member of royalty to entertain the household; jester. **3** *v.* To behave as a fool; tease or joke. **4** *v.* To make a fool of; deceive.

fool·er·y [fo͞o′lə·rē] *n., pl.* **fool·er·ies** **1** Silly behavior; clowning. **2** An act of clowning.

fool·har·dy [fo͞ol′här′dē] *adj.* **fool·har·di·er, fool·har·di·est** Daring in a foolish, reckless way. **—fool′har′·di·ness** *n.*

fool·ish [fo͞o′lish] *adj.* Showing lack of good sense; unwise; silly. **—fool′ish·ly** *adv.* **—fool′ish·ness** *n.*

fool·proof [fo͞ol′pro͞of′] *adj.* So simple, strong, or trustworthy that even a fool could not cause it to fail: a *foolproof* plan.

fools·cap [fo͞olz′kap′] *n.* **1** A size of writing paper about 13 inches wide and 16 inches long. **2** Another spelling of FOOL'S CAP.

fool's cap A decorated cap traditionally worn by court jesters, usually having several drooping peaks tipped with bells.

fool's gold Iron pyrites, a mineral sometimes mistaken for gold.

fool's paradise A condition of blissful ignorance of impending danger or disappointment.

foot [fo͝ot] *n., pl.* **feet,** *v.* **1** *n.* The end part of the leg of a person or animal, upon which it stands or moves. **2** *v. informal* To walk: They had to *foot* it home. **3** *n.* Infantry. **4** *n.* The part farthest from the top or head; base, bottom, or end: the *foot* of a ladder; the *foot* of a list. **5** *n.* The end of a bed where one's feet go. **6** *n.* The part of a stocking or boot that covers the foot. **7** *n.* A measure of length equal to 12 inches. **8** *n.* In poetry, one of the rhythmic parts into which a line is divided. "Upōn/thŏse bōughs/thăt shāke/ăgāinst/thĕ cōld"/ is a line having five feet. **9** *v. informal* To pay: to *foot* a bill. **10** *v.* To add: *Foot* up the bill. **—on foot** **1** Walking or standing. **2** In progress. **—put one's foot down** *informal* To act firmly.

foot·ball [fo͝ot′bôl′] *n.* **1** An inflated, leather-covered ball used in various games. The U.S. football is oval. **2** A game played in the U.S. by two teams on a field, the object being to carry the ball over the opponent's goal line or kick it over the goal.

foot·bridge [fo͝ot′brij′] *n.* A bridge for persons on foot.

foot-can·dle [fo͝ot′kan′dəl] *n.* A unit used in measuring how well a surface is lighted.

foot·ed [fo͝ot′id] *adj.* **1** Having a foot or feet. **2** Having a certain kind or number of feet: often used in combination: a *flatfooted* person; a *four-footed* animal.

foot·fall [fo͝ot′fôl′] *n.* The sound of a footstep.

foot·hill [fo͝ot′hil′] *n.* A low hill at the base of a mountain or a range of mountains.

foot·hold [fo͝ot′hōld′] *n.* **1** A place on which the foot can rest securely, as in climbing. **2** A firm position from which one can carry forward some action: to get a *foothold* in politics.

foot·ing [fo͝ot′ing] *n.* **1** A secure position or placing of the feet: to lose one's *footing* and slip. **2** A place on which to stand, walk, or climb securely. **3** Any secure position or foundation. **4** Relationship; standing: to be on a friendly *footing* with one's classmates.

foot·less [fo͝ot′lis] *adj.* **1** Lacking feet. **2** Unfounded; groundless: *footless* arguments. **3** Ineffective; inept: *footless* efforts.
foot·lights [fo͝ot′līts′] *n.pl.* Lights in a row along the very front of a stage floor.
foot·lock·er [fo͝ot′lok′ər] *n.* A small chest for keeping personal belongings, as at the foot of a person's bed in a dormitory or barracks.
foot·loose [fo͝ot′lo͞os′] *adj.* Free to wander at will; without obligations or attachments.
foot·man [fo͝ot′mən] *n., pl.* **foot·men** [fo͝ot′mən] A servant who answers the door, waits on table, or attends a rider in a carriage.
foot·note [fo͝ot′nōt′] *n.* A note at the bottom of a page explaining something on the page or telling where the information came from.
foot·pad [fo͝ot′pad′] *n.* A highwayman who goes on foot: seldom used today.
foot·path [fo͝ot′path′] *n.* A path to be used only by persons on foot.
foot-pound [fo͝ot′pound′] *n.* The amount of energy needed to raise a mass of one pound a distance of one foot. This is used as a unit of energy.
foot·print [fo͝ot′print′] *n.* The mark left by a foot or shoe, as in sand, mud, or snow.
foot·rest [fo͝ot′rest′] *n.* A small stool or other support on which the feet may be placed.
foot soldier An infantryman.
foot·sore [fo͝ot′sôr′] *adj.* Having sore or tired feet, as from walking.
foot·step [fo͝ot′step′] *n.* **1** A step made by a foot in walking, or its sound. **2** The distance covered in a single step. **3** A footprint.
foot·stool [fo͝ot′sto͞ol′] *n.* A low stool on which to rest the feet when sitting down.
foot·wear [fo͝ot′wâr′] *n.* Apparel for the feet, such as shoes, boots, and slippers.
foot·work [fo͝ot′wûrk′] *n.* Use or control of the feet, as in boxing, tennis, or dancing.
fop [fop] *n.* A person who is very vain about clothes and looks; dandy. **—fop′pish** *adj.*
fop·per·y [fop′ə·rē] *n., pl.* **fop·per·ies** **1** The manners or clothes of a fop. **2** An act or an article of dress characteristic of a fop.
fop·pish [fop′ish] *adj.* Being or resembling a fop in manner or dress. **—fop′pish·ly** *adv.* **—fop′pish·ness** *n.*
for [fôr] **1** *prep.* To the distance of: The land is flat *for* many miles. **2** *prep.* For the period of time of: We waited *for* an hour. **3** *prep.* To the amount of: a check *for* six dollars. **4** *prep.* At the cost of: to buy a ticket *for* fifty cents. **5** *prep.* As the equivalent of in exchange: You will get ten points *for* each correct answer. **6** *prep.* On account of; because of: We chose the restaurant *for* its reasonable prices. **7** *conj.* Because; as: I am thirsty, *for* the sun is very hot. **8** *prep.* In spite of: I believe in it *for* all your arguments. **9** *prep.* To be used at, in, on, or by: tickets *for* a play; a time *for* work; a collar *for* a dog. **10** *prep.* Appropriate to: It's time *for* a change. **11** *prep.* In favor, support, or approval of: We voted *for* the proposal. **12** *prep.* Directed toward; with regard to: love *for* one's country; an eye *for* bargains. **13** *prep.* As affecting: good *for* your health. **14** *prep.* Sent or given to: a package *for* you. **15** *prep.* In honor of: The baby was named *for* a favorite relative. **16** *prep.* In proportion to: The puppy is big *for* its age. **17** *prep.* Considering the usual qualities of: The box is sturdy *for* cardboard. **18** *prep.* As being: I took him *for* his twin brother. **19** *prep.* In place of: to use a mat on the floor *for* a bed. **20** *prep.* With the purpose of: She reads *for* pleasure. **21** *prep.* In order to go to: to leave *for* school. **22** *prep.* In order to find, get, or keep: He was looking *for* his coat.
for·age [fôr′ij] *n., v.* **for·aged, for·ag·ing** **1** *n.* Food suitable for horses, cattle, and other livestock. **2** *v.* To search about for something, as for food or supplies: Pigs like to *forage* in the farmyard; to *forage* in the closet for a lost shoe. **3** *v.* To plunder in order to get supplies, as soldiers do during war. **—for′ag·er** *n.*
for·ay [fôr′ā] **1** *n.* A raid or expedition, as for plunder or in a war: a brief *foray* behind enemy lines. **2** *v.* To raid.
for·bade or **for·bad** [fər·bad′] Past tense of FORBID.
for·bear[1] [fôr·bâr′] *v.* **for·bore, for·borne, for·bear·ing** **1** To refrain or hold back from (doing something): to *forbear* answering a silly question. **2** To show patience or self-control.
for·bear[2] [fôr′bâr′] *n.* Another spelling of FOREBEAR.
for·bear·ance [fôr·bâr′əns] *n.* **1** The act of forbearing or holding back. **2** Patience; self-control.
for·bid [fər·bid′] *v.* **for·bade** or **for·bad, for·bid·den, for·bid·ding** To refuse to allow; keep from doing or being done: Eating is *forbidden* during class; The crossing guard *forbade* the children to cross the street alone.
for·bid·ding [fər·bid′ing] *adj.* Grim and unfriendly; frightening: a *forbidding* swamp.
for·bode [fôr·bōd′] *v.* **for·bod·ed, for·bod·ing** Another spelling of FOREBODE.
for·bore [fôr·bôr′] Past tense of FORBEAR[1].
for·borne [fôr·bôrn′] Past participle of FORBEAR[1].
force [fôrs] *n., v.* **forced, forc·ing** **1** *n.* Power or energy; strength: the *force* of the waves. **2** *n.* Power used to overcome the resistance of a person or thing: They dragged the unwilling participant in by *force.* **3** *v.* To drive or move in spite of resistance: to *force* the enemy back into the hills. **4** *v.* To bring forth with an effort: to *force* a smile to one's lips. **5** *v.* To compel to do something by using power or persuasion: Fear of the consequences *forced* me to tell the truth. **6** *n.* The quality that affects the thinking or feelings of people: the *force* of one's argument. **7** *v.* To break open, as a door or lock. **8** *n.* A group of people organized to do certain work: a police *force;* the armed *forces.* **9** *n.* Anything that changes or tends to change the state of rest or motion in a body: the *force* of gravitation. **10** *v.* To make grow faster by artificial means, as the plants in a hothouse. **11** *v.* In baseball, to put out (a base runner who must move up to the next base). **—in force** **1** In effect or being applied, as a law. **2** In full strength. **—forc′er** *n.*

a	add	**i**	it	**o͝o**	took	**oi**	oil
ā	ace	**ī**	ice	**o͞o**	pool	**ou**	pout
â	care	**o**	odd	**u**	up	**ng**	ring
ä	palm	**ō**	open	**û**	burn	**th**	thin
e	end	**ô**	order	**yo͞o**	fuse	**th̶**	this
ē	equal					**zh**	vision

ə = { a in *above* e in *sicken* i in *possible* / o in *melon* u in *circus* }

forced [fôrst] *adj.* 1 Compelled or required by force: *forced* labor. 2 Strained; affected: a *forced* smile. 3 Done in an emergency: the *forced* landing of an airplane.

force-feed [fôrs′fēd′] *v.* **force-fed** [fôrs′fed′], **force-feed·ing** To feed (an animal or a person) by force.

force·ful [fôrs′fəl] *adj.* Full of or done with force; vigorous; strong: a *forceful* blow; a *forceful* speech. **—force′ful·ly** *adv.* **—force′ful·ness** *n.*

force·meat [fôrs′mēt′] *n.* Finely chopped meat, poultry, or fish, usually highly seasoned, that is used in cookery as a stuffing or is eaten alone.

for·ceps [fôr′səps] *n., pl.* **for·ceps** Pincers for grasping or handling small or delicate objects. Forceps are used by doctors, dentists, and jewelers.

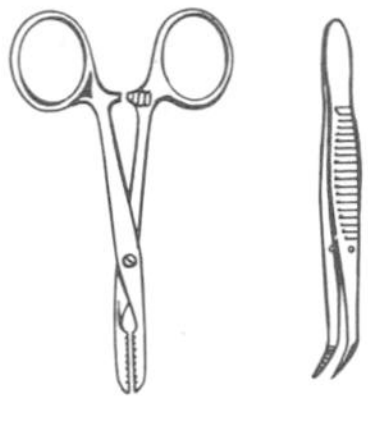

Surgical forceps

for·ci·ble [fôr′sə·bəl] *adj.* 1 Brought about or done by force: the *forcible* removal of demonstrators. 2 Having or displaying force; vigorous; effective: a *forcible* speech. **—for′ci·bly** *adv.*

ford [fôrd] 1 *n.* A shallow place in a stream, river, or other body of water, that can be crossed by wading. 2 *v.* To cross (as a river) at a shallow place. **—ford′a·ble** *adj.*

fore [fôr] 1 *adv.* In or toward the front part or bow of a boat; forward. 2 *adj.* At or toward the front or beginning. 3 *n.* The front part, foremost position, or forefront. 4 *interj.* A call by a golfer warning those ahead to look out.

fore- A prefix meaning: 1 Before, earlier, or in advance, as in *forewarn.* 2 At the front, as in *forepaw.*

fore-and-aft [fôr′ən·aft′] *adj.* Lying or going from bow to stern on a ship; lengthwise.

fore and aft 1 In a line extending from the bow to the stern of a boat. 2 In, at, or toward both the front and the back of a boat.

fore·arm[1] [fôr′ärm′] *n.* The part of the arm between the elbow and the wrist.

fore·arm[2] [fôr·ärm′] *v.* To prepare in advance, as for coming trouble; arm beforehand.

fore·bear [fôr′bâr′] *n.* An ancestor.

fore·bode [fôr·bōd′] *v.* **fore·bod·ed, fore·bod·ing** 1 To be a warning sign of. 2 To sense beforehand, as some coming evil. **—fore·bod′er** *n.*

fore·bod·ing [fôr·bō′ding] *n.* A feeling that something bad is going to happen; premonition.

fore·cast [fôr′kast′] *v.* **fore·cast** or **fore·cast·ed, fore·cast·ing,** *n.* 1 *v.* To predict after studying available facts: to *forecast* the weather on the basis of meteorological observations; to *forecast* an election from polling results. 2 *n.* A prediction, as of coming weather conditions. **—fore′cast′er** *n.*

fore·cas·tle [fōk′səl] *n.* 1 The upper deck of a ship forward of the foremast. 2 Sailors' quarters near the bow of a ship.

fore·close [fôr·klōz′] *v.* **fore·closed, fore·clos·ing** To end a mortgage agreement and claim the mortgaged property, as when payments on the original loan are not met.

fore·clo·sure [fôr·klō′zhər] *n.* A legal procedure to foreclose.

fore·deck [fôr′dek′] *n.* The foreward part of the main deck of a ship.

fore·doom [fôr·dōōm′] *v.* To doom or condemn beforehand.

fore·fa·ther [fôr′fä′thər] *n.* An ancestor.

fore·fin·ger [fôr′fing′gər] *n.* The finger next to the thumb; index finger.

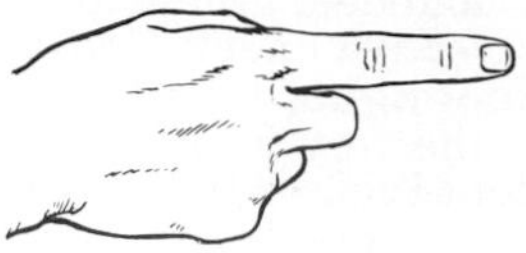

Forefinger

fore·foot [fôr′fŏŏt′] *n., pl.* **fore·feet** [fôr′fēt′] A front foot of an animal or insect.

fore·front [fôr′frunt′] *n.* 1 The very front. 2 The position of most activity or importance: She was in the *forefront* of the debate.

fore·gath·er [fôr·gath′ər] *v.* Another spelling of FORGATHER.

fore·go [fôr·gō′] *v.* **fore·went, fore·gone, fore·go·ing** Another spelling of FORGO.

fore·go·ing [fôr·gō′ing] *adj.* Going before; previous: The *foregoing* statement is correct.

fore·gone [fôr′gôn′ *or* fôr′gon′] *adj.* 1 Certain enough to be known in advance: a *foregone* conclusion. 2 Previous or past: *foregone* eras.

fore·ground [fôr′ground′] *n.* The part of a landscape or picture that is nearest or seems nearest to the person looking at it.

fore·hand [fôr′hand′] 1 *n.* A stroke, as in tennis, made with the palm of the hand that holds the racket faced forward. 2 *adj.* Done with the palm turned forward: a powerful *forehand* stroke.

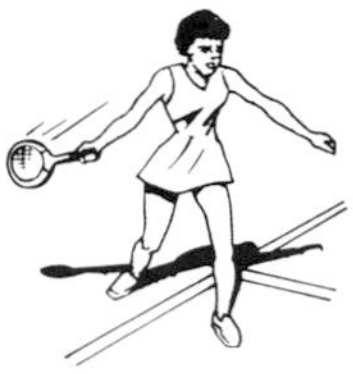

A forehand stroke

fore·head [fôr′id *or* fôr′hed′] *n.* The part of the face between the eyebrows and the natural hairline.

for·eign [fôr′in] *adj.* 1 Located or coming from outside one's own country; not native: a *foreign* city; a *foreign* language. 2 Carried on or concerned with other countries: *foreign* trade; *foreign* affairs. 3 Not belonging naturally or normally: a *foreign* substance in the body; attitudes *foreign* to our traditions. **—for′eign·ness** *n.*

for·eign·er [fôr′in·ər] *n.* 1 A native or citizen of a foreign country. 2 An outsider.

foreign office In some countries, a department of the government that manages foreign affairs.

fore·know [fôr·nō′] *v.* **fore·knew** [fôr·n(y)ōō′], **fore·known** [fôr·nōn′], **fore·know·ing** To know ahead of time, especially by supernatural means.

fore·knowl·edge [fôr′nol′ij] *n.* Knowledge of something before it exists or takes place.

fore·lady [fôr′lā′dē] *n., pl.* **fore·la·dies** Another word for FOREWOMAN.

fore·leg [fôr′leg′] *n.* One of the front legs of an animal or insect.

fore·limb [fôr′lim′] *n.* A front limb, such as the arm of a human being or an animal's foreleg.

fore·lock [fôr′lok′] *n.* A lock of hair growing over the forehead.

fore·man [fôr′mən] *n., pl.* **fore·men** [fôr′mən] 1 A worker in charge of a group of workers. 2 The chairperson of a jury, who announces its verdict.

fore·mast [fôr′mast′] *n.* The mast that is closest to the bow of a ship.

fore·most [fôr′mōst′] 1 *adj.* First in place, time, rank, or order; chief: the *foremost* artist of Venice. 2 *adv.* Before everything else; first: The delegates kept one aim *foremost,* peace.

fore·moth·er [fôr′muth′ər] *n.* A female ancestor.

fore·noon [fôr′nōōn′] *n.* The period of daylight before noon; morning.

fo·ren·sic [fə·ren′sik] *adj.* Of or used in discussions and debates in law courts or public forums. **—fo·ren′si·cal·ly** *adv.*

fore·or·dain [fôr′ôr·dān′] *v.* To order or decide in advance; determine beforehand. **—fore′or·dain′·ment** *n.*

fore·part [fôr′pärt′] *n.* The front or first part of anything.

fore·paw [fôr′pô′] *n.* The paw of a front leg.

fore·quar·ter [fôr′kwôr′tər] *n.* **1** The front half of a side of beef or other meat. **2** A foreleg and shoulder of a live four-footed animal.

fore·run·ner [fôr′run′ər] *n.* **1** A person who goes ahead to tell that another is coming. **2** A sign of some coming thing: The first robin is a *forerunner* of spring. **3** A predecessor.

fore·sail [fôr′sāl′] *n.* **1** The lowest sail on the foremast of a square-rigged vessel. **2** The main fore-and-aft sail on a schooner's foremast.

fore·see [fôr·sē′] *v.* **fore·saw, fore·seen, fore·see·ing** To see, imagine, or know in advance. **—fore·see′a·ble** *adj.* **—fore·se′er** *n.*

fore·shad·ow [fôr·shad′ō] *v.* To give an advance indication or warning of: The first chapter *foreshadowed* the ending of the book.

fore·shock [fôr′shok′] *n.* A minor tremor that indicates a coming earthquake.

fore·shore [fôr′shôr′] *n.* A strip of land along a shore, especially one submerged at high tide.

fore·short·en [fôr·shôr′tən] *v.* To draw (a line) less than true length to create a sense of distance or depth.

Foreshortened legs

fore·sight [fôr′sīt′] *n.* **1** The act or power of foreseeing or looking ahead. **2** Preparation or concern for the future. **—fore′·sight′ed** *adj.* **—fore′sight′ed·ly** *adv.* **—fore′sight′ed·ness** *n.*

fore·skin [fôr′skin′] *n.* A fold of skin that covers the end of the male sex organ.

for·est [fôr′ist] **1** *n.* A thick growth of trees spreading over a large tract of land. **2** *adj.* Of, in, or having to do with a forest. **3** *v.* To plant with many trees: to *forest* a barren tract of land.

fore·stall [fôr·stôl′] *v.* To prevent, keep out, or get ahead of by taking action first: to *forestall* criticism by doing a good job. **—fore·stall′er** *n.* **—fore·stall′ment** *n.*

for·est·a·tion [fôr′is·tā′shən] *n.* The planting or care of forests.

for·est·er [fôr′is·tər] *n.* A person who is trained and skilled in forestry.

forest ranger An officer who patrols and protects a forested area.

for·est·ry [fôr′is·trē] *n.* The science of planting, developing, and managing forests.

fore·taste [fôr′tāst′] *n.* A taste or brief experience of something to come later.

fore·tell [fôr·tel′] *v.* **fore·told, fore·tell·ing** To tell about in advance; predict: A computer *foretold* these figures a year ago.

fore·thought [fôr′thôt′] *n.* Careful planning or attention ahead of time; thought in advance.

fore·told [fôr·tōld′] Past tense and past participle of FORETELL.

fore·top [fôr′top′] *n.* A platform near the top of the foremast of a ship.

for·ev·er [fôr·ev′ər] **1** *adv.* Throughout all time; eternally. **2** *adv.* Again and again; always: My parents are *forever* telling me what to do. **3** *n. informal* An objectionably long time: It takes *forever* to walk there.

for·ev·er·more [fôr·ev′ər·môr′] *adv.* To the end of time; forever.

fore·warn [fôr·wôrn′] *v.* To warn in advance.

fore·went [fôr·went′] Past tense of FOREGO.

fore·wom·an [fôr′wo͝om′ən] *n., pl.* **fore·wom·en** [fôr′·wim′in] **1** A woman who is in charge of a group of workers. **2** A woman appointed to preside over a jury and announce its verdict.

fore·word [fôr′wûrd′] *n.* An introduction to a book; preface.

F

for·feit [fôr′fit] **1** *v.* To lose or give up as a penalty for an offense or mistake: By failing to register, you *forfeited* your right to vote. **2** *n.* The giving up or loss of something as a penalty: the *forfeit* of a privilege. **3** *n.* Something that is forfeited; penalty.

for·fei·ture [fôr′fi·chər] *n.* **1** The act of forfeiting. **2** Something given up as a penalty.

for·gath·er [fôr·gath′ər] *v.* **1** To meet; assemble. **2** To meet by chance. **3** To meet socially.

for·gave [fər·gāv′] Past tense of FORGIVE.

forge[1] [fôrj] *n., v.* **forged, forg·ing** **1** *n.* A fireplace or furnace for heating metal so it can be hammered into shape. **2** *n.* A blacksmith's shop; smithy. **3** *v.* To work (metal) into shape by heating and hammering. **4** *v.* To produce or form; shape: to *forge* armor. **5** *n.* A furnace or factory for melting or refining metals. **6** *v.* To make an imitation of to be passed off as genuine: to *forge* a signature. **7** *v.* To be guilty of forgery.

Colonial forge

forge[2] [fôrj] *v.* **forged, forg·ing** To move slowly but steadily forward, as by effort: to *forge* through the mud.

forg·er [fôr′jər] *n.* **1** A person who commits forgery. **2** A person who forges metal; smith.

for·ger·y [fôr′jər·ē] *n., pl.* **for·ger·ies** **1** The act of making an imitation, as of a signature or document, to be passed off as genuine. **2** An imitation meant to deceive.

for·get [fər·get′] *v.* **for·got, for·got·ten** or **for·got, for·get·ting** **1** To cease or fail to remember; lose from memory: I *forgot* the answer. **2** To neglect (to do something), fail to think of, or leave behind accidentally: You *forgot* to feed the cat; to *forget* your lunch. **—for·get′ter** *n.*

a	add	**i**	it	**o͝o**	took	**oi**	oil
ā	ace	**ī**	ice	**o͞o**	pool	**ou**	pout
â	care	**o**	odd	**u**	up	**ng**	ring
ä	palm	**ō**	open	**û**	burn	**th**	thin
e	end	**ô**	order	**yo͞o**	fuse	**th̸**	this
ē	equal					**zh**	vision

ə = { a in *above* e in *sicken* i in *possible* / o in *melon* u in *circus* }

for·get·ful [fər·get′fəl] *adj.* 1 Inclined to forget easily. 2 Neglectful; careless: *forgetful* of one's duty. **—for·get′ful·ly** *adv.* **—for·get′ful·ness** *n.*

for·get-me-not [fər·get′mē·not′] *n.* A small herb bearing clusters of blue or white flowers.

for·get·ta·ble [fər·get′ə·bəl] *adj.* Easy to forget; not worth remembering.

for·giv·a·ble [fər·giv′ə·bəl] *adj.* Capable of being forgiven: a *forgivable* error. **—for·giv′a·bly** *adv.*

for·give [fər·giv′] *v.* **for·gave, for·giv·en, for·giv·ing** 1 To stop blaming or being angry with: I have *forgiven* you. 2 To excuse; pardon: to *forgive* a mistake. **—for·giv′er** *n.*

for·give·ness [fər·giv′nis] *n.* 1 Pardon, as for an offense. 2 A willingness to forgive.

for·giv·ing [fər·giv′ing] *adj.* 1 Willing or ready to forgive. 2 Showing pardon; pardoning. **—for·giv′ing·ly** *adv.* **—for·giv′ing·ness** *n.*

for·go [fôr·gō′] *v.* **for·went, for·gone, for·go·ing** To give up; go without: to *forgo* watching TV when one is studying. **—for·go′er** *n.*

for·got [fər·got′] Past tense and an alternative past participle of FORGET.

for·got·ten [fər·got′(ə)n] An alternative past participle of FORGET.

fork [fôrk] 1 *n.* A small eating utensil, large farm tool, or other instrument with a handle at one end and two or more prongs at the other. 2 *v.* To lift or toss with a fork: to *fork* hay into a wagon. 3 *n.* A dividing of something, as a road, into branches. 4 *n.* One such branch: Follow the right *fork* at the crossroads. 5 *v.* To divide into branches: The river *forks* upstream.

forked [fôrkt] *adj.* Having a fork or a part that branches: a *forked* road; *forked* lightning.

fork·lift or **fork lift** [fôrk′lift′] *n.* A hoisting machine with fingerlike prongs that slide under heavy objects to lift, move, or stack them.

Fork lift

for·lorn [fôr·lôrn′] *adj.* Sad or pitiful because alone or neglected. **—for·lorn′ly** *adv.* **—for·lorn′ness** *n.*

forlorn hope 1 A small group of people engaged in a dangerous or hopeless task. 2 An extremely difficult or risky undertaking. ◆ *Forlorn hope* comes from the Dutch term *verloren hoop,* meaning *lost band,* as of scouts taken in enemy territory. By the process of folk etymology, the strange Dutch words were transformed into words already familiar in the English language.

form [fôrm] 1 *n.* An outline or outward shape: the shifting *forms* of clouds. 2 *n.* A mold, frame, or model that gives shape to something, as wet cement. 3 *v.* To make, shape, or fashion: to *form* clay into a ball; to *form* a plan. 4 *v.* To shape by training: Education *forms* the mind. 5 *v.* To develop or acquire, as a habit. 6 *v.* To take shape or form; come to be: A scab *formed* over the sore. 7 *n.* Any of the shapes given to a word to show special meaning: "Feet" is the plural *form* of "foot." 8 *n.* A specific type; kind: Democracy is a *form* of government. 9 *n.* Condition of body or mind for performance: an athlete in top *form.* 10 *n.* Arrangement or organization: the sonata *form* in music. 11 *n.* A manner of proceeding or behaving: to show good *form* in diving; Showing anger in public is bad *form.* 12 *n.* Outward ceremony or formality: I nodded as a matter of *form.* 13 *n.* A set arrangement of words, as for a letter; model. 14 *adj. use:* a *form* letter. 15 *n.* A document with blanks to be filled in. 16 *v.* To make up: Guesswork *forms* a part of the inspector's theory. 17 *v.* To combine or organize into: to *form* a club. 18 *n. British* A grade in school. 19 *n. British* A long bench without a back.

for·mal [fôr′məl] 1 *adj.* Strictly or stiffly following set rules or patterns: a *formal* greeting; a *formal* garden; a *formal* agreement. 2 *adj.* Requiring elaborate dress and manners. 3 *n. informal* A formal dance. 4 *adj.* Suiting elaborate occasions. 5 *n. informal* An evening dress. 6 *adj.* Concerning outward form. **—for′mal·ly** *adv.*

for·mal·de·hyde [fôr·mal′də·hīd′] *n.* A colorless gas used in a liquid solution to kill germs and to preserve dead animals for study.

for·mal·ism [fôr′mə·liz′əm] *n.* The strict observance of established forms, as in art. **—for′mal·ist** *n.* **—for′mal·is′tic** *adj.* **—for′mal·is′ti·cal·ly** *adv.*

for·mal·i·ty [fôr·mal′ə·tē] *n., pl.* **for·mal·i·ties** 1 Formal character or quality. 2 Strict politeness; ceremony. 3 A proper or customary act or ceremony: the *formalities* of an interview. 4 A required outward gesture.

for·mal·ize [fôr′mə·līz′] *v.* **for·mal·ized, for·mal·iz·ing** 1 To give form to; structure. 2 To make formal. **—for′mal·i·za′tion** *n.* **—for′mal·iz′er** *n.*

for·mat [fôr′mat′] *n.* The form, size, arrangement, and style of a printed publication.

for·ma·tion [fôr·mā′shən] *n.* 1 The act of forming: the *formation* of rust on iron. 2 Something formed, as a mass of rock. 3 An arrangement, as of troops.

form·a·tive [fôr′mə·tiv] *adj.* Of or related to formation or development: *formative* stages.

for·mer [fôr′mər] *adj.* 1 Belonging to the past; previous; earlier: a *former* mayor; *former* ages. 2 Being the first of two persons or things referred to. 3 *n. use*: The first one referred to: I prefer the *former* to the latter. ◆ Note that *former* (def. 2) always refers to the first of *two.* If more than two items are named, use *first, second,* etc.

for·mer·ly [fôr′mər·lē] *adv.* At an earlier time; in the past; once; previously.

For·mi·ca [fôr·mī′kə] *n.* A durable and glossy laminated plastic used as a surface for the tops of tables and counters: a trademark.

for·mi·da·ble [fôr′mi·də·bəl] *adj.* 1 Causing fear or dread, as because of strength or size: a *formidable* opponent. 2 Extremely difficult: a *formidable* assignment. **—for′mi·da·bil′i·ty** *n.* **—for′mi·da·ble·ness** *n.* **—for′mi·da·bly** *adv.*

form·less [fôrm′lis] *adj.* Lacking form or structure; shapeless. **—form′less·ly** *adv.* **—form′less·ness** *n.*

form letter A letter printed in many copies and sent to a large number of people.

for·mu·la [fôr′myə·lə] *n., pl.* **for·mu·las** or **for·mu·lae** [fôr′myə·lē] 1 A set of words used by custom. "Dear Sir" is a formula for beginning a letter. 2 A statement expressing some belief or principle. 3 An established method or rule. 4 A statement of some fact or relationship in mathematical terms. The formula $d = 16t^2$ gives the distance in feet, *d,* that an object falls in the time, *t,* in seconds. 5 A prescription or recipe. 6 A mixture prepared by prescription. 7 A set of symbols showing the elements making up a chemical compound. The formula for carbon dioxide is CO_2.

for·mu·late [fôr′myə·lāt′] *v.* **for·mu·lat·ed, for·mu·lat·ing** 1 To express in or as a formula. 2 To work out and state in an exact, orderly way. **—for′mu·la′tor** *n.*

for·mu·la·tion [fôr′myə·lā′shən] *n.* 1 The act of formulating. 2 Something that has been formulated.

for·sake [fôr·sāk′] *v.* **for·sook** [fôr·so͝ok′], **for·sak·en, for·sak·ing** To leave completely; desert; give up. **—for·sak′er** *n.*

for·sooth [fôr·so͞oth′] *adv.* In truth; in fact: seldom used today.

for·swear [fôr·swâr′] *v.* **for·swore, for·sworn, for·swear·ing** 1 To swear to give up completely. 2 To swear falsely; commit perjury.

for·syth·i·a [fôr·sith′ē·ə] *n.* A shrub bearing bell-shaped yellow flowers early in spring.

fort [fôrt] *n.* A structure or enclosed area strong enough to be defended against attack.

Fort

forte[1] [fôrt] *n.* Something one does with excellence; strong point: Singing is her *forte.*

for·te[2] [fôr′tā] *adj., adv.* In music, loud.

forth [fôrth] *adv.* 1 Forward; on: from this day *forth.* 2 Out, as from hiding or a place of origin: Come *forth!*; to put *forth* effort.

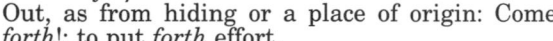

forth·com·ing [fôrth′kum′ing] *adj.* 1 About to appear, arrive, or happen; approaching: our *forthcoming* vacation. 2 Available when expected or needed: Money will be *forthcoming.*

forth·right [fôrth′rīt′] *adj.* Coming straight to the point; frank; direct: *forthright* advice. **—forth′·right′ly** *adv.* **—forth′right′ness** *n.*

forth·with [fôrth′with′] *adv.* Immediately.

for·ti·eth or **40th** [fôr′tē·ith] 1 *adj.* Tenth in order after the thirtieth. 2 *n.* The fortieth one. 3 *adj.* Being one of forty equal parts. 4 *n.* A fortieth part.

for·ti·fi·ca·tion [fôr′tə·fə·kā′shən] *n.* 1 The act of fortifying. 2 Something, as a wall or ditch, used for defense. 3 A military place of defense.

for·ti·fy [fôr′tə·fī] *v.* **for·ti·fied, for·ti·fy·ing** 1 To make strong enough to resist attack, as by building walls and forts. 2 To give added strength to; strengthen: Our support *fortified* the fund raising. 3 To add minerals or vitamins to (a food, as milk).

for·tis·si·mo [fôr·tis′ə·mō] *adj., adv.* In music, very loud.

for·ti·tude [fôr′tə·t(y)o͞od′] *n.* Courage to meet and endure pain, hardship, or danger: the amazing *fortitude* of the pioneers.

fort·night [fôrt′nīt′] *n.* A period of two weeks.

fort·night·ly [fôrt′nīt′lē] 1 *adv.* Once every two weeks. 2 *adj.* Appearing or happening every two weeks. 3 *n.* A paper or magazine that is published once every two weeks.

FOR·TRAN [fôr′tran′] *n.* A computer programming language used chiefly for solving mathematical, scientific, and engineering problems. ◆ *FORTRAN* comes from *FOR(mula) TRAN(slation).*

for·tress [fôr′tris] *n.* A fort, a series of forts, or a fortified town; stronghold.

for·tu·i·tous [fôr·t(y)o͞o′ə·təs] *adj.* 1 Coming about by chance; accidental. 2 Fortunate; lucky. **—for·tu′i·tous·ly** *adv.*

for·tu·nate [fôr′chə·nit] *adj.* Having, happening by, or bringing good luck; lucky: a *fortunate* person or event. **—for′tu·nate·ly** *adv.* **—for′tu·nate·ness** *n.*

for·tune [fôr′chən] *n.* 1 A power supposed to determine the course of one's life; destiny; fate. 2 A person's future fate: to claim to tell *fortunes.* 3 Luck or chance, whether good or bad: *Fortune* favored the successful playwright. 4 Favorable luck; success. 5 A great sum of money; wealth.

fortune cookie A small, hollow cookie containing a slip of paper on which is written a fortune or piece of advice for the eater.

for·tune-tell·er [fôr′chən·tel′ər] *n.* A person claiming to foretell the future.

for·ty or **40** [fôr′tē] *n., pl.* **for·ties** or **40's,** *adj.* 1 *n., adj.* Ten more than thirty. 2 *n.* (*pl.*) The years between the age of 40 and the age of 50.

for·ty-nin·er [fôr′tē·nī′nər] *n.* A pioneer who went to California in the 1849 gold rush.

fo·rum [fôr′əm] *n.* 1 The public market place of an ancient Roman city, where assemblies met and most legal and political business was carried on. 2 A court of law. 3 An assembly for the discussion of public affairs.

for·ward [fôr′wərd] 1 *adj.* At, near, or toward the front. 2 *adv.* To or toward the front or forefront: to move *forward*; to bring *forward* an idea. 3 *n.* A player in the front line or one who leads the offensive play, as in basketball. 4 *v.* To send onward, as to another address: *Forward* my mail. 5 *v.* To help to advance: to *forward* someone's hopes. 6 *adj.* Ahead of the usual; advanced: to be *forward* for one's age. 7 *adv.* To the future: to look *forward* to retirement. 8 *adj.* Ready or prompt: Don't be so *forward* in speaking out. 9 *adj.* Too bold; rude. **—for′ward·ly** *adv.*

for·ward·ness [fôr′wərd·nis] *n.* 1 Improper boldness in behavior. 2 Willing readiness.

for·wards [fôr′wərdz] *adv.* Forward; ahead.

for·went [fôr·went′] Past tense of FORGO.

fos·sil [fos′əl] 1 *n.* The remains of a plant or animal of an earlier age, hardened and preserved in earth or rock. 2 *adj. use*: a *fossil* fern. 3 *n. informal* A person with old-fashioned notions or ways.

A fossil fern

fossil fuel A fuel, such as coal or oil, derived from once living matter preserved and transformed in the earth over long ages.

fos·sil·ize [fos′ə·līz′] *v.* **fos·sil·ized, fos·sil·iz·ing** 1 To change into a fossil. 2 *informal* To resist changing with the times. **—fos′sil·i·za′·tion** *n.*

fos·ter [fôs′tər] 1 *v.* To bring up (a child); rear. 2 *adj.* Providing, receiving, or having to do with care and rearing of children by persons who are

a add	**i** it	**o͝o** took	**oi** oil
ā ace	**ī** ice	**o͞o** pool	**ou** pout
â care	**o** odd	**u** up	**ng** ring
ä palm	**ō** open	**û** burn	**th** thin
e end	**ô** order	**yo͞o** fuse	**th** this
ē equal			**zh** vision

ə = a in *above*, e in *sicken*, i in *possible*, o in *melon*, u in *circus*

F

not their parents by birth or adoption: The *foster* child lives in a *foster* home in the care of *foster* parents. **3** *v.* To promote the growth or development of: to *foster* talent.

fought [fôt] Past tense and past participle of FIGHT.

foul [foul] **1** *adj.* Very dirty, disgusting, stinking, or rotten: *foul* water; *foul* smells. **2** *v.* To make or become foul or dirty: Gasoline fumes *fouled* the air. **3** *v.* To stop up; clog: Dirt *fouled* the gun barrel. **4** *adj.* Clogged or packed, as with dirt: a *foul* chimney. **5** *adj.* Not decent; profane or abusive: *foul* language. **6** *adj.* Evil; wicked: *foul* deeds. **7** *adj.* Not fair; rainy or stormy: *foul* weather. **8** *v.* To tangle or become tangled up: The fishing lines *fouled.* **9** *adj.* Caught or entangled: a *foul* anchor. **10** *v.* To hit against or hit together, as two boats. **11** *adj.* Against the rules; unfair: a *foul* blow. **12** *n.* An action that breaks the rules of a game. **13** *v.* To commit a foul, as against an opponent. **14** *adj.* In baseball, landing first outside the foul lines or passing outside these lines before reaching first or third base: a *foul* ball. **15** *n.* A foul ball. **16** *v.* To bat (a baseball) outside the foul lines. **—foul'ly** *adv.* **—foul'ness** *n.*

fou·lard [fo͞o·lärd'] *n.* A lightweight fabric, as of silk, usually with a printed design.

foul line In baseball, either of the two lines extending from home plate past first and third bases to the limits of the playing field.

foul play **1** Unfair or dishonest action, as in sports. **2** A violent, evil action, as murder.

found[1] [found] *v.* **1** To set up; establish; start: to *found* a school. **2** To base, as for support: suspicions *founded* on rumors.

found[2] [found] Past tense and past participle of FIND.

found[3] [found] *v.* To melt and cast (metal).

foun·da·tion [foun·dā'shən] *n.* **1** A base, as of a building, which supports everything above it. **2** An underlying basis, as for a belief. **3** The act of founding. **4** The condition of being founded. **5** An organization set up and endowed to carry on or pay for some worthy purpose, as charity or research.

found·er[1] [foun'dər] *n.* A person who has established or helped to establish an institution or organization: the school's *founders.*

found·er[2] [foun'dər] *n.* A person who founds metal.

found·er[3] [foun'dər] *v.* **1** To fill with water and sink, as a ship. **2** To fall or cave in. **3** To fail completely. **4** To stumble or go lame.

Founding Father Any of the members of the American Constitutional Convention of 1787.

found·ling [found'ling] *n.* A baby found after having been deserted by its unknown parents.

foun·dry [foun'drē] *n., pl.* **foun·dries** **1** A place where molten metal is shaped in molds. **2** The act of casting metal to make things. ◆ See FONDANT.

fount [fount] *n.* **1** A fountain. **2** Any source.

foun·tain [foun'tən] *n.* **1** A natural spring of water. **2** A jet of water thrown into the air from a pipe and caught in a basin, for ornament or drinking. **3** The basinlike structure in which this water rises and falls. **4** A soda fountain. **5** A source, as of wisdom.

foun·tain·head [foun'tən·hed'] *n.* A source, as a spring from which a stream originates.

fountain pen A pen holding a supply of ink which automatically flows to the writing end.

four or **4** [fôr] *n., adj.* One more than three. **—on all fours** **1** On hands and knees. **2** On all four feet.

four·fold [*adj.* fôr'fōld', *adv.* fôr'fōld'] **1** *adj.* Composed of four parts. **2** *adj.* Being four times greater or four times as many. **3** *adv.* By four times: increased *fourfold.*

four-foot·ed [fôr'fo͝ot'id] *adj.* Having four feet; quadruped: *four-footed* animals.

4-H Club Four-H Club.

Four-H Club [fôr'āch'] A club training boys and girls in farming and home economics.

four-leaf clover A leaf of clover having four leaflets, traditionally considered a lucky omen.

four-poster [fôr'pōs'tər] *n.* A bed with four tall posts at the corners which may be used to support a canopy or curtains.

four·score [fôr'skôr'] *adj.* Four times twenty; eighty.

four·some [fôr'səm] *n.* A group of four, as four persons joining together to play golf.

four·square [fôr'skwâr'] **1** *adj.* Square in shape. **2** *adj.* Frank; direct. **3** *adj.* Not giving way; firm. **4** *adv.* Firmly.

four·teen or **14** [fôr'tēn'] *n., adj.* One more than thirteen.

four·teenth or **14th** [fôr'tēnth'] **1** *adj.* Next after the thirteenth. **2** *n.* The fourteenth one. **3** *adj.* Being one of fourteen equal parts. **4** *n.* A fourteenth part.

fourth or **4th** [fôrth] **1** *adj.* Next after the third. **2** *n.* The fourth one. **3** *adj.* Being one of four equal parts. **4** *n.* A fourth part.

fourth dimension **1** A dimension in addition to those of length, width, and depth. **2** Time, regarded in relativity theory as a coordinate along with the three spatial coordinates in the space-time continuum.

fourth estate The public press; journalists.

Fourth of July Independence Day.

fowl [foul] *n., pl.* **fowl** or **fowls** **1** A hen or rooster. **2** Any similar large bird, as the duck or turkey. **3** The flesh of such birds used as food. **4** Birds as a group: wild *fowl.*

Gray fox

fowl·ing piece [fou'ling] A light gun for shooting birds.

fox [foks] *n.* **1** A small wild animal, kin to the dog and wolf and noted for its cunning. It has a long, pointed muzzle and bushy tail. **2** The fur of the fox. **3** A sly, crafty person.

fox·glove [foks'gluv'] *n.* A tall plant bearing flowers shaped something like a bell.

fox·hole [foks'hōl'] *n.* A shallow pit dug by a soldier for shelter against enemy gunfire.

Soldier in a foxhole

fox·hound [foks'hound'] *n.* A large, swift breed of dog with a keen sense of smell, trained to hunt foxes.

fox·tail [foks'tāl'] *n.* **1** The tail of a fox. **2** Any of several species of grass having brushlike flower heads suggestive of a fox's tail.

fox terrier A small, lively white dog with dark markings, once used to hunt foxes.
fox-trot [foks′trot′] *n., v.* **fox-trot·ted, fox-trot·ting** 1 *n.* A ballroom dance combining fast steps and slow steps. 2 *n.* A piece of music used for this dance. 3 *v.* To dance the fox-trot.
fox·y [fok′sē] *adj.* **fox·i·er, fox·i·est** Having the cunning of a fox; sly; shrewd. **—fox′i·ly** *adv.* **—fox′i·ness** *n.*
foy·er [foi′ər] *n.* 1 A public lobby, as in a hotel or theater. 2 An entrance room or hall.
FPC or **F.P.C.** Federal Power Commission.
fr. 1 father. 2 fragment. 3 franc. 4 from.
Fr The symbol for the element francium.
Fr. 1 Father (clergyman). 2 France. 3 French. 4 Friday.
fra·cas [frā′kəs] *n.* A noisy fight or quarrel.
frac·tion [frak′shən] *n.* 1 A part taken from a whole. 2 A little bit. 3 A rational number that is more than zero and less than 1, or the sum of a whole number and such a quantity. In the fraction 2/3, the 3 tells into how many equal parts a whole is divided, and the 2 tells how many of those parts the fraction contains.
frac·tion·al [frak′shən·əl] *adj.* 1 Having to do with or making up a fraction. 2 Small in size or importance. **—frac′tion·al·ly** *adv.*
fractional distillation The separating of a substance, as petroleum, by boiling off one component of it at a time.
frac·tion·ate [frak′shə·nāt′] *v.* **frac·tion·at·ed, frac·tion·at·ing** 1 To separate the components of, as by fractional distillation. 2 To break up. **—frac′·tion·a′tion** *n.* **—frac′tion·a′tor** *n.*
frac·tious [frak′shəs] *adj.* 1 Hard to control; unruly. 2 Easily annoyed; irritable.
frac·ture [frak′chər] *n., v.* **frac·tured, frac·tur·ing** 1 *n.* The act of breaking, as the breaking or cracking of a bone. 2 *n.* A break, crack, or rupture. 3 *v.* To break or crack: to *fracture* a rib. 4 *n.* A broken condition.
frag·ile [fraj′əl] *adj.* Easily shattered or broken; delicate: *fragile* dishes. **—frag′ile·ly** *adv.* **—fra·gil·i·ty** [frə·jil′ə·tē] *n.* ◆ Both *fragile* and *frail* come from a Latin word meaning *to break.*
frag·ment [*n.* frag′mənt, *v.* frag′ment′] 1 *n.* A part broken off or incomplete: *fragments* of a broken mirror. 2 *v.* To break into fragments.
frag·men·tar·y [frag′mən·ter′ē] *adj.* Made up of fragments; not complete: *fragmentary* pieces of a broken vase; *fragmentary* evidence.
frag·men·ta·tion [frag′mən·tā′shən] *n.* The process or result of breaking into fragments.
fra·grance [frā′grəns] *n.* 1 Sweetness of scent or smell. 2 A sweet or delicate smell.
fra·grant [frā′grənt] *adj.* Sweet in smell. **—fra′·grant·ly** *adv.*
frail [frāl] *adj.* 1 Easily damaged in body or structure; weak: a *frail* person; a *frail* scaffold. 2 Weak in character. **—frail′ly** *adv.* **—frail′ness** *n.* ◆ See FRAGILE.
frail·ty [frāl′tē] *n., pl.* **frail·ties** 1 Weakness. 2 A fault or moral weakness.
frame [frām] *n., v.* **framed, fram·ing** 1 *n.* A basic inner structure which gives support and shape to the thing built around it; framework: the *frame* of a building. 2 *n.* The bone structure or build of the body. 3 *v.* To plan and put together; make or construct: to *frame* a question; to *frame* a law. 4 *n.* The arrangement or structure of a thing. 5 *n.* A case or border made to hold or surround something, as a window. 6 *v.* To put within such a case or border: to *frame* a picture. 7 *v. slang* To cause (an innocent person) to look guilty by furnishing false evidence. 8 *n.* One of the divisions of a game of bowling. 9 Any one of the series of still pictures that make up a motion-picture film. **—frame of mind** Condition of mind or feeling; mood. **—fram′er** *n.*
frame house A house constructed with a wooden framework.
frame of reference The general framework of facts and assumptions in which a subject is considered or an argument presented.
frame-up [frām′up′] *n. slang* 1 A plot to make an innocent person look guilty. 2 A scheme to bring about a dishonest result.
frame·work [frām′wûrk′] *n.* The basic structure around which a thing is built: the *framework* of a ship; the *framework* of society.

Framework of a barn

franc [frangk] *n.* The basic unit of money in countries including France, Belgium, Switzerland, and Luxembourg.
fran·chise [fran′chīz′] *n.* 1 The right to vote. 2 A right or special privilege granted by a government: a *franchise* to operate a bus line. 3 Permission given to a dealer to market a certain company's products or services.
Fran·cis·can [fran·sis′kən] 1 *adj.* Of Saint Francis of Assisi or the religious order that he founded. 2 *n.* A Franciscan friar or nun.
fran·ci·um [fran′sē·əm] *n.* A radioactive metallic element produced in nature by the radioactive decay of actinium but never isolated in weighable amounts, its half-life being only 22 minutes.
Fran·co·phone [frang′kə·fōn′] 1 *adj.* French-speaking: *Francophone* Canadians. 2 *n.* A person who speaks French.
frank[1] [frangk] *adj.* Completely honest in saying or showing what one really thinks or feels. **—frank′·ly** *adv.* **—frank′ness** *n.*
frank[2] [frangk] 1 *n.* The right to send mail free of charge. 2 *n.* The mark used to indicate this right. 3 *v.* To send (mail) without postage by marking it with an official sign.
Frank [frangk] *n.* A member of the Germanic tribes that conquered Gaul in the fifth century A.D. and gave their name to France. **—Frank′ish** *adj., n.*
Fran·ken·stein [frang′kən·stīn′] *n.* A scientist in Mary Shelley's novel *Frankenstein* who creates an artificial man but fails to provide for his happiness and is later tormented by him. ◆ A *Frankenstein's monster* has come to mean a work or invention that gets out of control and threatens its creator. The use of *Frankenstein* in this sense and

a	add	**i**	it	**o͝o**	took	**oi**	oil
ā	ace	**ī**	ice	**o͞o**	pool	**ou**	pout
â	care	**o**	odd	**u**	up	**ng**	ring
ä	palm	**ō**	open	**û**	burn	**th**	thin
e	end	**ô**	order	**yo͞o**	fuse	**t͟h**	this
ē	equal					**zh**	vision

ə = a in *above*, e in *sicken*, i in *possible*, o in *melon*, u in *circus*

in the sense of *a manlike monster* are also common, although the artificial creature in Shelley's novel is neither called *Frankenstein* nor is he a monster.

frank·furt·er [frangk′fər·tər] *n.* A smoked, reddish sausage of beef or of beef and pork.

frank·in·cense [frangk′in·sens′] *n.* A gum or resin from various trees of East Africa, burned as incense for its sweet, spicy smell.

fran·tic [fran′tik] *adj.* Wild with fear, worry, pain, or rage: We were *frantic* until we heard that they had arrived safely. **—fran′ti·cal·ly** or **fran′tic·ly** *adv.* **—fran′tic·ness** *n.*

frap·pé or **frappe** [fra·pā′ *or* frap] *n.* 1 A partly frozen drink, as of fruit juice poured over crushed ice. 2 A milk shake.

fra·ter·nal [frə·tûr′nəl] *adj.* 1 Of or characteristic of brothers; brotherly. 2 Made up of men with mutual interests: *fraternal* organizations. 3 Describing twins of the same or the opposite sex that develop from two separately fertilized egg cells and so are not identical. **—fra·ter′nal·ism** *n.* **—fra·ter′nal·ly** *adv.*

fra·ter·ni·ty [frə·tûr′nə·tē] *n., pl.* **fra·ter·ni·ties** 1 Brotherly unity or affection; brotherhood. 2 A club of men or boys, especially one made up of college students. 3 A group of people sharing the same interests or profession: the legal *fraternity.*

frat·er·nize [frat′ər·nīz′] *v.* **frat·er·nized, frat·er·niz·ing** To associate in a friendly way: Don't *fraternize* with the enemy. **—frat′er·ni·za′tion** *n.* **—frat′·er·niz′er** *n.*

frat·ri·cide [frat′ri·sīd′] *n.* 1 The act of murdering one's own brother or sister. 2 A person who commits fratricide. **—frat′ri·cid′al** *adj.*

Frau [frou] *n., pl.* **Frau·en** (frou′ən) 1 The German title of courtesy for a married woman, equivalent to *Mrs.* 2 A German married woman.

fraud [frôd] *n.* 1 The deceiving of another for one's own gain; dishonest deception. 2 A thing that deceives or is not genuine; trick; deception. 3 *U.S. informal* A person who is not what he or she seems to be.

fraud·u·lence [frô′jə·ləns] *n.* 1 The quality of being fraudulent; deceitfulness. 2 A fraudulent act or acts.

fraud·u·lent [frô′jə·lənt] *adj.* 1 Employing fraud; dishonest. 2 Acquired or done by fraud. 3 Based on fraud; false: *fraudulent* claims. **—fraud′u·lent·ly** *adv.*

fraught [frôt] *adj.* Filled; loaded: Our exploration of space is *fraught* with danger.

Fräu·lein or **Frau·lein** [froi′līn′] *n.* The German title of courtesy for an unmarried woman or girl, equivalent to *Miss.*

fray[1] [frā] *n.* A noisy quarrel; fight; brawl.

fray[2] [frā] *v.* To wear down so that loose threads or fibers show; make or become ragged: The cuffs of the old shirt were *frayed.*

A frayed collar

fraz·zle [fraz′(ə)l] *v.* **fraz·zled, fraz·zling,** *n. informal* 1 *v.* To make or become ragged; fray. 2 *v.* To tire out; exhaust. 3 *n.* A ragged, worn-out, or exhausted condition.

freak [frēk] 1 *n.* A person, animal, or plant that is not normal, as a dog with five legs. 2 *n.* Anything that is unusual or odd. 3 *adj.* Unusual; odd: a *freak* flood.

freak·ish [frē′kish] *adj.* 1 Having the characteristics of a freak; abnormal. 2 Unpredictable; capricious. **—freak′ish·ly** *adv.* **—freak′ish·ness** *n.*

freck·le [frek′əl] *n., v.* **freck·led, freck·ling** 1 *n.* A small brownish spot on the skin. 2 *v.* To mark or become marked with such spots.

free [frē] *adj.* **fre·er, fre·est,** *v.* **freed, free·ing,** *adv.* 1 *adj.* Not under any other's control; enjoying liberty. 2 *adj.* Not tied, held, or shut up; loose: the *free* end of a rope. 3 *v.* To set at liberty; release: to *free* a prisoner. 4 *adv.* In a free manner; without restraint: Let the prisoner go *free.* 5 *adj.* Allowed; permitted: *free* to go. 6 *adj.* Having the right to think, act, vote, express oneself, and worship as one wishes. 7 *adj.* Not influenced by any outside power: to have *free* choice. 8 *adj.* Not held back or slowed down: a *free* fall. 9 *adj.* Not blocked; clear; open: a *free* drain. 10 *v.* To clear or rid: to *free* a drain of grease. 11 *adj.* Having or containing no: used in combination, as in *salt-free,* containing no salt. 12 *adj.* Not restricted, as by taxes or limitations: *free* trade; *free* debate. 13 *adj.* Not following set rules of form: *free* verse. 14 *adj.* Not chemically combined: *free* hydrogen. 15 *adj.* Not occupied or busy: *free* time. 16 *adj.* Costing no money: a *free* sample. 17 *adv.* Without cost or charge: to get tickets *free.* 18 *adj.* Generous in giving; liberal: to be *free* with advice. 19 *adj.* Honest and frank. 20 *adj.* Bold and not polite or proper. **—free from** or **free of** Without any: *free from* care; *free of* infection. **—free on board** Transported and loaded on board a carrier without charge to the buyer. **—set free** To release. **—free′·ly** *adv.* **—free′ness** *n.*

free-and-easy [frē′ən(d)·ē′zē] *adj.* Not bound by convention; casual; informal.

free·bie or **free·bee** [frē′bē] *n. slang* Something handed out free of charge.

free·boot·er [frē′bo͞o′tər] *n.* A person who plunders, as a pirate or buccaneer.

free·born [frē′bôrn′] *adj.* 1 Born free, not in slavery. 2 Of or suiting those born free.

freed·man [frēd′mən] *n., pl.* **freed·men** [frēd′mən] A former slave who has been freed.

free·dom [frē′dəm] *n.* 1 The condition of being free. 2 Frankness or familiarity, often improper: The *freedom* of the salesclerk's manner offended them. 3 Ease, as in acting: The leash hampered the dog's *freedom* of movement. 4 The right to enter or use all parts: to give a cat the *freedom* of one's apartment.

free enterprise An economic system based upon private ownership and operation of business with little or no governmental control.

free-fall [frē′fôl′] *n.* 1 The motion of an object under the sole influence of the force of gravity. 2 The part of a parachutist's fall before the parachute opens.

free-for-all [frē′fər·ôl′] *n.* 1 A noisy or disorderly fight in which anyone can become involved. 2 Something, as a contest or game, open to anyone who wishes to take part.

free·hand [frē′hand′] *adj.* Drawn by hand without the help of instruments, as rulers.

free·hand·ed [frē′han′did] *adj.* Generous.

free-lance [frē′lans′] *v.* **free-lanced, free-lanc·ing,** *adj.* 1 *v.* To work independently, as some artists or writers do, often for different employers. 2 *adj.* Working in this way: a *free-lance* illustrator.

free lance 1 A medieval knight whose services

were available for hire. **2** A person who freelances.
free·man [frē′mən] *n., pl.* **free·men** [frē′mən] A person who is free, not a slave, and who has the rights of a citizen.
Free·ma·son [frē′mā′sən] *n.* A member of a widespread secret order or fraternity; Mason.
free·ma·son·ry [frē′mā′sən·rē] *n.* **1** (written **Freemasonry**) The principles and practices of the Freemasons. **2** A spontaneous feeling of sympathy among people; fellowship.
free-spoken [frē′spō′kən] *adj.* Not hesitating to speak; outspoken.
free·stone [frē′stōn′] **1** *n.* A stone that can be cut in any direction without breaking, as sandstone. **2** *adj.* Having a pit from which the fruit pulp easily separates: a *freestone* peach. **3** *n.* A fruit having a pit or stone like this.
free·style [frē′stīl′] **1** *n.* An event in which a contestant, as a swimmer or skater, may use any style he or she chooses. **2** *adj.* Having no restrictions as to the style used.
free·think·er [frē′thing′kər] *n.* A person who forms his or her own opinions, as about religion, not accepting anything solely on authority.
free trade Trade between nations without restrictive charges on imported or exported goods.
free verse Verse without regular meter or rhyme, having its own special form and rhythm.
free·way [frē′wā′] *n.* A highway for fast travel with no toll charges.
free·wheel·ing [frē′(h)wē′ling] *adj.* **1** Indifferent to consequences; irresponsible. **2** Ignoring rules or restraints.
free·will [frē′wil′] *adj.* Made, done, or given of one's own free choice; voluntary.
free will The power to choose on one's own, free of outside influence or interference: We decided to go of our own *free will.*
freeze [frēz] *v.* **froze, fro·zen, freez·ing,** *n.* **1** *v.* To change into ice by the action of cold: to *freeze* water; The milk *froze.* **2** *v.* To become or cause to be covered or filled with ice: The pond *froze* over; Cold *froze* the water pipes. **3** *n.* A period of weather marked by freezing temperatures. **4** *v.* To be damaged or killed by great cold: The crops *froze* during the night. **5** *v.* To make or be extremely cold. **6** *v.* To stick because of cold or ice: The paper cover *froze* to the ice cream. **7** *v.* To stick or tighten, as by the heat of friction. **8** *v.* To make or become motionless, as with fear, or unfriendly, as with dislike. **9** *v.* To hold (as prices or wages) at a fixed level. **10** *n.* The act of freezing. **11** *n.* A frozen condition.
freeze-dry [frēz′drī′] *v.* **freeze-dried, freeze-dry·ing** To preserve (food) by evaporating water at a freezing temperature and low pressure. **—freeze′-dried′** *adj.*
freeze frame A frame in a motion picture that is repeated, with the effect that the action appears to be frozen.
freez·er [frē′zər] *n.* **1** A refrigerator made to freeze food quickly and preserve frozen food. **2** A device for freezing ice cream.
freezing point The temperature at which a liquid freezes. The freezing point for fresh water at sea level is 32° F. or 0° C.
freight [frāt] **1** *n.* The service of shipping goods by train, truck, ship, or plane at regular rates: Ship it by *freight.* **2** *n.* Goods shipped in this way, or the charge for shipping them: The customer refused to pay the *freight.* **3** *v.* To send or carry as or by freight. **4** *v.* To load, as with goods to be transported. ◆ *Freight* comes from an old Dutch word.
freight car A railroad car designed to carry freight.
freight·er [frā′tər] *n.* A ship used chiefly for carrying loads of goods or cargo.
freight train A train of freight cars.
French [french] **1** *adj.* Of or from France. **2** *n.* (**the French**) The people of France. **3** *n.* The language of France.
French-Ca·na·di·an [french′kə·nā′dē·ən] **1** *n.* A French settler or a descendant of French settlers in Canada. **2** *adj.* Of, concerning, or occupied mainly by Canadians who speak French.
French cuff A wide shirt cuff that is worn doubled back and fastened with a cuff link.
French curve A drawing instrument like a ruler with curved sides and scrolled-shaped cutouts, used to guide the pencil or pen in drawing curved lines.
French door **1** A light door with inset glass panels. **2** A pair of such doors installed with the handles next to each other.
French dressing A dressing for salads made of oil, vinegar, and seasoning.
French fried Cooked by frying crisp in deep fat.
French fries French fried potatoes.
French fry To cut in strips and fry in deep fat, as potatoes.
French horn A brass musical instrument with a long, coiled tube, flaring widely at the end and producing a mellow tone.

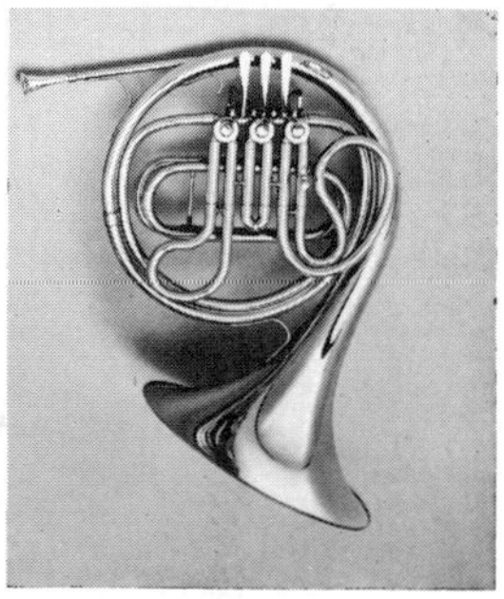
French horn

French leave A stealthy or hurried departure.
French·man [french′·mən] *n., pl.* **French·men** [french′mən] A person born in or a citizen of France.
French Revolution The revolution in France from 1789 to 1799, during which the monarchy was overthrown and replaced by a republic.
French toast Bread sautéed after being dipped in a milk-and-egg mixture.
French window A long window hinged like a door, usually installed in pairs with the latches in the middle.
French·wom·an [french′wo͝om′ən] *n., pl.* **French·wom·en** [french′wim′in] A woman of French birth or citizenship.
fre·net·ic [frə·net′ik] *adj.* Wildly excited; frenzied. **—fre·net′i·cal·ly** *adv.*

a	add	**i**	it	**o͝o**	took	**oi**	oil
ā	ace	**ī**	ice	**o͞o**	pool	**ou**	pout
â	care	**o**	odd	**u**	up	**ng**	ring
ä	palm	**ō**	open	**û**	burn	**th**	thin
e	end	**ô**	order	**yo͞o**	fuse	**t̶h̶**	this
ē	equal					**zh**	vision

ə = { a in *above* e in *sicken* i in *possible* / o in *melon* u in *circus* }

fren·zied [fren′zēd] *adj.* 1 Madly excited; wild: A *frenzied* mob attacked the factory. 2 Very enthusiastic: *frenzied* applause.

fren·zy [fren′zē] *n., pl.* **fren·zies** 1 A wild, excited fit or condition suggesting madness: to be angry to the point of *frenzy.* 2 Very great or intense work or effort: The gardener attacked the weeds with *frenzy.*

fre·quen·cy [frē′kwən·sē] *n., pl.* **fre·quen·cies** 1 The fact of being frequent; repeated occurrence. 2 Rate of occurrence, as within a given time or group. 3 The number of times a recurring event happens in a given time, often expressed in cycles per second.

frequency modulation The changing of the frequency of a radio wave in a way that corresponds with the sound or other signal to be broadcasted.

fre·quent [*adj.* frē′kwənt, *v.* fri·kwent′] 1 *adj.* Happening again and again; often occurring: *frequent* interruptions. 2 *v.* To go to regularly; be often at or in: a person who *frequents* the library. **—fre·quent′er** *n.* **—fre′quent·ly** *adv.*

fres·co [fres′kō] *n., pl.* **fres·coes** or **fres·cos,** *v.* **fres·coed, fres·co·ing** 1 *n.* The art of painting on a surface of moist plaster. 2 *v.* To paint in fresco, as a ceiling. 3 *n.* A picture so painted. ◆ *Fresco* comes directly from an Italian word meaning *fresh,* because a *fresco* is made while the plaster is fresh.

fresh[1] [fresh] *adj.* 1 Newly made, gotten, or gathered: *fresh* orange juice; *fresh* fruit. 2 Having just come: vegetables *fresh* from the garden. 3 Not stale or spoiled: *fresh* rolls; *fresh* cream. 4 Not dirty; clean: *fresh* sheets. 5 Pure and clear: *fresh* air. 6 Free of salt: *fresh* water. 7 New or original: *fresh* ideas. 8 Recent: *fresh* news. 9 Appearing young or healthy. 10 Rested and lively: a *fresh* horse. **—fresh′ly** *adv.* **—fresh′ness** *n.*

fresh[2] [fresh] *adj. U.S. informal* So bold as to offend; rude or disrespectful.

fresh·en [fresh′ən] *v.* To make or become fresh, as by washing oneself: to *freshen* up.

fresh·et [fresh′it] *n.* 1 A sudden overflow of a stream when snow melts or it rains a lot. 2 A freshwater stream emptying into the sea.

fresh·man [fresh′mən] *n., pl.* **fresh·men** [fresh′mən] A student during the first year of studies in a high school or college.

fresh·wa·ter [fresh′wô′tər] *adj.* Of or living in water free of salt: *freshwater* fish.

fret[1] [fret] *v.* **fret·ted, fret·ting,** *n.* 1 *v.* To make or be cross, irritated, or worried: Small cares *fret* us; Don't *fret.* 2 *n.* A cross or worried condition: He is in a *fret* over the delay. 3 *v.* To wear away, as by much rubbing.

fret[2] [fret] *n., v.* **fret·ted, fret·ting** 1 Any of the ridges across the top of the neck of an instrument, as a guitar or ukulele. 2 *v.* To furnish (an instrument) with frets.

Frets on a guitar

fret[3] [fret] *n.* 1 A pattern of bars and lines employed in fretwork. 2 A medieval woman's headdress formed of a net of wire.

fret·ful [fret′fəl] *adj.* Cross, restless, or peevish: a *fretful* baby. **—fret′ful·ly** *adv.* **—fret′ful·ness** *n.*

fret·saw [fret′sô′] *n.* A small, narrow-bladed saw with fine teeth, used for making fretwork.

fret·work [fret′wûrk′] *n.* Ornamental openwork, as in wood, usually composed of bands of lines or bars arranged in balanced patterns.

Freu·di·an [froi′dē·ən] *adj.* Of, having to do with, or following the teachings of Sigmund Freud.

Fri. Friday.

fri·a·ble [frī′ə·bəl] *adj.* Easily crumbled or reduced to powder or dust: Pumice is *friable.* **—fri′a·bil′i·ty** *n.*

fri·ar [frī′ər] *n.* A member of any of certain Roman Catholic religious orders.

fri·ar·y [frī′ə·rē] *n., pl.* **fri·ar·ies** A monastery occupied by friars.

frib·ble [frib′əl] *v.* **frib·bled, frib·bling,** *n.* 1 *v.* To dawdle; waste time on trifles. 2 *n.* A trifle; frivolity. 3 *n.* A person who fribbles.

fric·as·see [frik′ə·sē′] *n., v.* **fric·as·seed, fric·as·see·ing** 1 *n.* A dish of meat, especially chicken, cut up in small pieces, stewed, and served with gravy. 2 *v.* To make (meat) into a fricassee.

fric·tion [frik′shən] *n.* 1 The rubbing of one object against another. 2 The resistance to movement of a body that is in contact with another body. 3 A conflict or disagreement.

fric·tion·al [frik′shə·nəl] *adj.* Of, produced by, or having to do with friction.

friction tape A strong, moisture-resistant adhesive tape used mainly to insulate electrical conductors.

Fri·day [frī′dē] *n.* The sixth day of the week.

fridge [frij] *n.* An informal word for REFRIGERATOR.

fried [frīd] 1 *adj.* Cooked by frying in hot fat. 2 Past tense and past participle of FRY[2].

friend [frend] *n.* 1 A person one knows well, likes, and is willing to help. 2 A person who helps; supporter: *friends* of the college. 3 Someone on the same side, as contrasted with a foe. 4 (*written* **Friend**) A member of the Society of Friends; Quaker.

friend·less [frend′lis] *adj.* Without friends. **—friend′·less·ness** *n.*

friend·ly [frend′lē] *adj.* **friend·li·er, friend·li·est** 1 Of or typical of a friend: a *friendly* suggestion. 2 Showing friendship or kindness: a *friendly* town. 3 Showing no ill will: a *friendly* rival. 4 Favorable. **—friend′li·ness** *n.*

friend·ship [frend′ship′] *n.* 1 The condition or fact of being friends. 2 Mutual liking or friendly relationship. 3 Friendly feelings.

frieze [frēz] *n.* A decorated or sculptured horizontal band, as along the top of a wall.

frig·ate [frig′it] *n.* 1 A fast, square-rigged sailing warship of medium size, in use in the 18th and early 19th centuries. 2 A modern ship used on escort and patrol missions.

Frigate

frigate bird Either of two types of large sea birds noted for great powers of flight.

fright [frīt] *n.* 1 Sudden, violent alarm or fear. 2 *informal* Anything ugly, ridiculous, or shocking: The clown's matted wig was a *fright*!

fright·en [frīt′(ə)n] *v.* 1 To fill with sudden fear; make or become afraid; scare. 2 To force or drive by scaring: to *frighten* someone into agreeing; to *frighten* a thief away. **—fright′en·ing·ly** *adv.*

fright·ful [frīt′fəl] *adj.* 1 Alarming or terrifying: a *frightful* experience. **2** Shocking or horrible: a *frightful* sight. **3** *informal* Very great; excessive: a *frightful* bore. **—fright′ful·ly** *adv.* **—fright′ful·ness** *n.*

frig·id [frij′id] *adj.* **1** Bitterly cold: a *frigid* region. **2** Lacking warmth of feeling; formal and unfriendly: a *frigid* greeting. **—fri·gid′i·ty** *n.* **—frig′·id·ly** *adv.* **—frig′id·ness** *n.*

frigid zone The zone between the North Pole and the Arctic Circle or between the South Pole and the Antarctic Circle.

fri·jol [frē·hōl′ *or* frē′hōl′] *n., pl.* **fri·jo·les** [frē·hō′lēz *or* frē′hō′lēz] Any of several kinds of beans grown for food in Latin America.

frill [fril] **1** *n.* A pleated or gathered strip, as of lace, used as a fancy trimming or edging; ruffle. **2** *v.* To put frills on: to *frill* a pillowcase. **3** *n.* *U.S. informal* An unnecessary thing added because it is fancy: to live simply, without *frills.* **—frill′y** *adj.*

fringe [frinj] *n., v.* **fringed, fring·ing** **1** *n.* An ornamental border or trimming of hanging cords or threads. **2** *n.* Any border, outer edge, or edging: He lives on the *fringe* of town. **3** *v.* To border with or as if with a fringe: Flowers *fringed* the path.

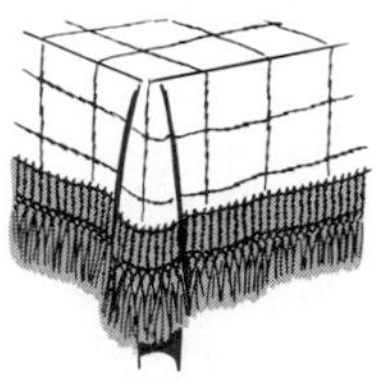
Fringe

fringe benefit A job benefit given in addition to wages, such as sick pay or medical insurance.

frip·per·y [frip′ər·ē] *n., pl.* **frip·per·ies** **1** Cheap, flashy dress or decoration. **2** A showing off or putting on airs, as in speech.

Fris·bee [friz′bē] *n.* A light plastic disk that can sail through the air and is tossed between players for amusement: a trademark.

frisk [frisk] *v.* **1** To move or leap about playfully: Lambs *frisk* in the field. **2** *U.S. slang* To search (someone), as for weapons.

frisk·y [fris′kē] *adj.* **frisk·i·er, frisk·i·est** Lively or playful. **—frisk′i·ly** *adv.* **—frisk′i·ness** *n.*

frit·il·lar·y [frit′(ə)l·er′ē] *n., pl.* **frit·il·lar·ies** Any of various small butterflies having orange wings with black or silver spots.

frit·ter[1] [frit′ər] *v.* To waste or squander little by little: to *fritter* away one's time. **—frit′ter·er** *n.*

frit·ter[2] [frit′ər] *n.* A small, fried cake of batter, often having another food, as corn or fruit, in it.

fri·vol·i·ty [fri·vol′ə·tē] *n., pl.* **fri·vol·i·ties** **1** The quality or condition of being frivolous. **2** A frivolous action or thing.

friv·o·lous [friv′ə·ləs] *adj.* **1** Not important or worthwhile; trivial: *frivolous* comment. **2** Not serious or responsible; silly; giddy: *frivolous* people. **—friv′o·lous·ly** *adv.* **—friv′o·lous·ness** *n.*

frizz [friz] **1** *v.* To curl tightly; frizzle. **2** *n.* A crisp curl.

friz·zle[1] [friz′(ə)l] *v.* **friz·zled, friz·zling** To fry or cook with a sizzling noise.

friz·zle[2] [friz′(ə)l] *v.* **friz·zled, friz·zling,** *n.* **1** *v.* To curl tightly; kink, as the hair. **2** *n.* A crisp curl.

friz·zly [friz′lē] *adj.* **friz·zli·er, friz·zli·est** Frizzy.

frizz·y [friz′ē] *adj.* **frizz·i·er, frizz·i·est** Having tight curls; kinky: *frizzy* hair. **—frizz′i·ly** *adv.* **—frizz′i·ness** *n.*

fro [frō] *adv.* Back again, especially in the phrase **to and fro,** back and forth.

frock [frok] *n.* **1** A dress. **2** A long, loose robe worn by monks.

frock coat A man's coat with knee-length skirts.

frog [frôg *or* frog] *n.* **1** A small, tailless, web-footed animal that lives in water or on land. It has large, strong hind legs for leaping. **2** An ornamental piece of braid or cord, as on a jacket, looped so as to fasten over a button. **3** *informal* Hoarseness in the throat. **4** A device for holding the stems of cut flowers in place at the bottom of a vase.

Frog

frog kick A swimming kick used with the breast stroke, in which the legs are drawn up, thrust outward, and closed.

frog·man [frog′man′] *n., pl.* **frog·men** [frog′men′] A skin diver, often in the armed forces, equipped with an independent supply of air in order to be able to swim and work under water.

frol·ic [frol′ik] *n., v.* **frol·icked, frol·ick·ing** **1** *n.* An occasion full of playful fun. **2** *n.* Merriment. **3** *v.* To play about in a frisky way: The dog *frolicked* in the yard.

frol·ic·some [frol′ik·səm] *adj.* Playful; lively; frisky: a *frolicsome* kitten.

from [frum, from, *or* frəm] *prep.* **1** Beginning at: the plane *from* New York; *from* May to June. **2** Sent, made, or given by: a letter *from* home. **3** Because of: to faint *from* weakness. **4** Out of: I took a coin *from* my pocket; Subtract 3 *from* 8. **5** Out of the control or reach of: to escape *from* one's enemies. **6** At a distance in relation to: far *from* home. **7** Protected against: The rope kept the climber *from* falling. **8** In respect to: An injured ankle prevented the runner *from* competing. **9** As being other than: to know right *from* wrong.

frond [frond] *n.* A large leaf or leaflike part, as of a palm tree or fern.

front [frunt] **1** *n.* The part or side that faces forward. **2** *v.* To face in the direction of: This room *fronts* the ocean. **3** *n.* A position directly ahead: He sits in *front* of me. **4** *n.* The part coming before the rest: I was at the *front* of the line. **5** *adj.* In, at, on, of, or toward the front: a *front* seat. **6** *n.* The forward edge of a moving mass of warm or cold air. **7** *n.* In war, one of the areas where armies are fighting. **8** *n.* Land bordering a place, as a lake or road: a hotel on the ocean *front.* **9** *n.* Look, manner, or attitude: The frightened child put on a bold *front.* **10** *v.* To meet boldly face to face; confront. **11** *n.* *informal* An outward pretense, as of wealth or success: to keep up a *front.* **12** *n.* Something, as a person or business, used as a cloak for hidden actions.

a	add	**i**	it	**o͝o**	took	**oi**	oil
ā	ace	**ī**	ice	**o͞o**	pool	**ou**	pout
â	care	**o**	odd	**u**	up	**ng**	ring
ä	palm	**ō**	open	**û**	burn	**th**	thin
e	end	**ô**	order	**yo͞o**	fuse	**t̶h̶**	this
ē	equal					**zh**	vision

ə = {a in *above* e in *sicken* i in *possible*; o in *melon* u in *circus*}

front·age [frun′tij] *n.* **1** The front part of a lot or building. **2** The length of this part. **3** Land next to a road or body of water. **4** The land lying between the front of a building and a road or river.

fron·tal [frun′təl] *adj.* **1** Of, in, or on the front: a *frontal* assault. **2** Of or for the forehead: the *frontal* bone **—fron′tal·ly** *adv.*

fron·tier [frun·tir′] *n.* **1** The part of a country lying along another country's border. **2** The edge of a settled region that borders on unsettled territory. **3** A new or unexplored area, as of knowledge: the *frontiers* of biology.

fron·tiers·man [frun·tirz′mən] *n., pl.* **fron·tiers·men** [frun·tirz′mən] A person who lives on the frontier, next to the wilderness.

fron·tis·piece [frun′tis·pēs′] *n.* A picture or drawing facing the title page of a book.

front·let [frunt′lit] *n.* **1** Something worn on or across the forehead. **2** An animal's forehead.

front-page [frunt′pāj′] *adj., v.* **front-paged, front-pag·ing** **1** *adj.* Worthy of printing on a newspaper's front page; highly newsworthy. **2** *v.* To print on the front page of a newspaper.

front-run·ner [frunt′run′ər] *n.* A leading contender in any contest: a *front-runner* in the coming election.

frost [frôst] **1** *n.* Dew or water vapor that has frozen into many fine, white ice crystals: *frost* on a window. **2** *n.* Weather cold enough to freeze things: A *frost* in summer ruins fruit trees. **3** *v.* To cover with frost. **4** *v.* To cover with frosting: to *frost* a cake.

frost·bite [frôst′bīt′] *n., v.* **frost·bit, frost·bit·ten, frost·bit·ing** **1** *n.* An injury to some part of the body caused by freezing. **2** *v.* To injure (some part of the body) by freezing: The cold wind *frostbit* our ears.

frost·ed [frôs′tid] *adj.* **1** Covered with frost. **2** Covered with frosting. **3** Having a roughened, frostlike surface, as some glass.

frost·ing [frôs′ting] *n.* A sweet, smooth mixture that may include eggs and sugar, used to decorate cakes; icing.

frost·y [frôs′tē] *adj.* **frost·i·er, frost·i·est** **1** Cold enough to produce frost: *frosty* weather. **2** Covered with frost: *frosty* ground. **3** Cool and unfriendly: a *frosty* look. **—frost′i·ly** *adv.* **—frost′i·ness** *n.*

froth [frôth] **1** *n.* A mass of very small bubbles; foam. **2** *n.* Something light and rather empty: Most of the conversation was *froth.* **3** *v.* To foam or cause to foam: The wind *frothed* the sea.

Froth

froth·y [frô′thē] *adj.* **froth·i·er, froth·i·est** **1** Covered with or full of froth. **2** Light or unimportant: a *frothy* bit of gossip. **—froth′i·ness** *n.*

frot·tage [frô·täzh′] *n.* **1** The process of transferring a design from an object to paper by rubbing with a pencil or charcoal on a piece of paper placed on the object. **2** A design so transferred.

fro·ward [frō′(w)ərd] *adj.* Stubbornly disobedient; contrary. **—fro′ward·ly** *adv.* **—fro′ward·ness** *n.*

frown [froun] **1** *v.* To wrinkle the forehead, as in thought, disapproval, or anger; scowl: The difficult problem made me *frown.* **2** *n.* A wrinkling of the forehead, as in thought, disapproval, or anger. **3** *v.* To be displeased; express disapproval: to *frown* upon eating between meals.

frow·sy or **frow·zy** [frou′zē] *adj.* **frow·si·er** or **frow·zi·er, frow·si·est** or **frow·zi·est** **1** Dirty and messy; slovenly. **2** Having a bad smell; musty. **—frow′·si·ness** or **frow′zi·ness** *n.*

froze [frōz] Past tense of FREEZE.

fro·zen [frō′zən] **1** Past participle of FREEZE. **2** *adj.* Changed into or covered with ice: a *frozen* lake. **3** *adj.* Killed or damaged by great cold: a *frozen* sparrow. **4** *adj.* Describing a place with very cold weather: the *frozen* North Pole. **5** *adj.* Preserved by freezing: *frozen* vegetables. **6** *adj.* Cold and cruel: a *frozen* look. **7** *adj.* Unable to move, as from fright or astonishment.

fruc·tose [fruk′tōs′ *or* fro͝ok′tōs′] *n.* A very sweet sugar found mainly in fruits and honey.

fru·gal [fro͞o′gəl] *adj.* **1** Avoiding waste; using thrift: a *frugal* housekeeper. **2** Costing little money; meager: a *frugal* meal. **—fru·gal·i·ty** [fro͞o·gal′ə·tē] *n.* **—fru′gal·ly** *adv.*

fruit [fro͞ot] **1** *n.* An edible part of a plant that develops from a flower, as a peach, apple, or grape. **2** *n.* The part of a plant that encloses the seeds, as a peach or nut. **3** *v.* To produce fruit. **4** *n.* Any useful plant product. **5** *n.* An outcome or result of some effort: the *fruit* of one's labor.

fruit·age [fro͞o′tij] *n.* **1** The state or process of bearing fruit: the time of *fruitage.* **2** A harvest of fruit; fruits: a season's *fruitage.* **3** An outcome or successful result.

fruit·cake [fro͞ot′kāk′] *n.* A rich, spicy cake filled with nuts, raisins, and candied fruits.

fruit·er·er [fro͞o′tər·ər] *n.* A fruit dealer.

fruit fly A type of fly that in its larval stage of development feeds on fruit.

fruit·ful [fro͞ot′fəl] *adj.* **1** Bearing much fruit. **2** Producing a great deal; abundant. **3** Having useful results; productive: We had a *fruitful* discussion. **—fruit′ful·ly** *adv.* **—fruit′ful·ness** *n.*

fru·i·tion [fro͞o·ish′ən] *n.* **1** The bearing of fruit. **2** An achievement worked or hoped for: The design was the *fruition* of hard work. **3** Enjoyment found in having or using something.

fruit·less [fro͞ot′lis] *adj.* **1** Yielding no fruit; barren. **2** Useless or unsuccessful. **—fruit′less·ly** *adv.* **—fruit′less·ness** *n.*

fruit sugar Another name for FRUCTOSE.

fruit·y [fro͞o′tē] *adj.* **fruit·i·er, fruit·i·est** Tasting or smelling like fruit. **—fruit′i·ness** *n.*

frump [frump] *n.* A drab, dowdy, unattractive person.

frump·y [frum′pē] *adj.* **frump·i·er, frump·i·est** Drab, dowdy, and unattractive. **—frump′i·ness** *n.*

frus·trate [frus′trāt′] *v.* **frus·trat·ed, frus·trat·ing** To baffle the efforts of or bring to nothing; foil: The low grade *frustrated* my goal of being first in the class; The long delay *frustrated* the travelers.

frus·tra·tion [frus·trā′shən] *n.* **1** The act of frustrating. **2** A being frustrated. **3** A feeling of disappointment at wasted effort. **4** Something that frustrates.

fry[1] [frī] *n., pl.* **fry** A very young fish.

fry[2] [frī] *v.* **fried, fry·ing,** *n., pl.* **fries** **1** *v.* To cook in hot fat, usually over direct heat. **2** *n.* An outing at which foods are fried and eaten. **3** *n.* A dish of anything fried.

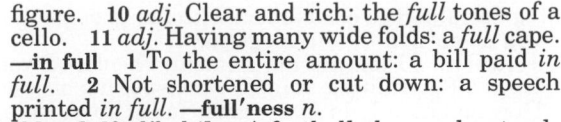

fry·er [frī′ər] *n.* 1 A young chicken suitable for frying. 2 A pot used for frying food.
frying pan Another term for SKILLET.
FSLIC or **F.S.L.I.C.** Federal Savings and Loan Insurance Corporation.
FSP or **F.S.P.** Food Stamp Program.
ft or **ft.** 1 foot. 2 feet.
ft. 1 fort. 2 fortification.
FTC or **F.T.C.** Federal Trade Commission.
fth. fathom.
fuch·sia [fyo͞o′shə] 1 *n., adj.* Bluish red. 2 *n.* A plant with handsome drooping flowers.
fud·dle [fud′(ə)l] *v.* **fud·dled, fud·dling** To make stupid with or as if with liquor; confuse: The glare of the lights *fuddled* the driver.
fudge [fuj] *n.* A rich, soft candy made from butter, chocolate, sugar, and sometimes nuts.
Fuehr·er [fyo͝or′ər] *n.* Another spelling of FÜHRER.
fu·el [fyo͞o′əl] *n., v.* **fu·eled** or **fu·elled, fu·el·ing** or **fu·el·ling** 1 *n.* Something that readily produces energy in the form of heat when burnt, as wood, coal, or oil. 2 *n.* Anything that feeds a desire or emotion: The insult was *fuel* to their anger. 3 *v.* To supply or be supplied with fuel: to *fuel* an engine.
fuel cell A device that makes electricity directly from the reaction of two chemicals.
fuel oil A petroleum product that is heavier than kerosene and has a higher flash point, used in furnaces for heating and for generating electric power.
fu·gi·tive [fyo͞o′jə·tiv] 1 *adj.* Fleeing, as from danger or arrest. 2 *n.* A fugitive person: a *fugitive* from justice. 3 *adj.* Quickly passing; not lasting: a *fugitive* hope.
fugue [fyo͞og] *n.* A musical piece in which elaborate counterpoint is developed from one or sometimes more themes.
Füh·rer [fyo͝or′ər] *n.* Leader: a German word.
-ful A suffix meaning: 1 Full of, as in *hopeful.* 2 Tending to; able to, as in *helpful.* 3 Having the character of, as in *masterful.* 4 The amount or number that will fill, as in *cupful.*
ful·crum [fo͝ol′krəm] *n.* A support on which a lever rests or turns when raising or moving a weight. ◆ *Fulcrum* comes from the Latin word for *bedpost,* which in turn comes from a word meaning *to prop up.*

Fulcrum

ful·fill or **ful·fil** [fo͝ol·fil′] *v.* **ful·filled, ful·fill·ing** 1 To carry out, as a promise or prediction. 2 To do or perform (a duty) or obey (a law or request): to *fulfill* an obligation. 3 To meet or satisfy (as a requirement or quota). 4 To finish up: to *fulfill* a task. **—ful·fill′ment** or **ful·fil′·ment** *n.*
full [fo͝ol] 1 *adj.* Filled with as much as is possible: a *full* barrel. 2 *adj.* Containing much or many: a book *full* of pictures. 3 *adj.* Whole or complete: a *full* day's work. 4 *adv.* To a complete degree: to know *full* well; a *full*-grown lion. 5 *adv.* Directly; straight: I looked him *full* in the eye. 6 *adj.* At the greatest point, as in size or degree: a *full* moon. 7 *n.* The greatest size or degree: the *full* of the moon. 8 *adj.* Having had much food and drink. 9 *adj.* Well-rounded; plump: a *full* figure. 10 *adj.* Clear and rich: the *full* tones of a cello. 11 *adj.* Having many wide folds: a *full* cape. **—in full** 1 To the entire amount: a bill paid *in full.* 2 Not shortened or cut down: a speech printed *in full.* **—full′ness** *n.*
full·back [fo͝ol′bak′] *n.* A football player who stands farthest behind the front line.
full-blood·ed [fo͝ol′blud′id] *adj.* 1 Of unmixed breed; purebred. 2 Having a ruddy appearance. 3 Robust; forceful.
full-blown [fo͝ol′blōn′] *adj.* At the peak of bloom or development: a *full-blown* rose.
full dress The style of dress prescribed for formal occasions.
full-fledged [fo͝ol′flejd′] *adj.* 1 Completely developed or mature: a *full-fledged* bird. 2 Having full standing: a *full-fledged* doctor.
full-grown [fo͝ol′grōn′] *adj.* Having reached full growth: a *full-grown* lion.
full-length [fo͝ol′leng(k)th′] *adj.* 1 Extending or showing the entire length: a *full-length* portrait. 2 Having the customary length: a *full-length* novel.
full moon The phase of the moon when its face appears as a full circle.
full-rigged [fo͝ol′rigd′] *adj.* Having three or more masts with complete rigging: a *full-rigged* sailing ship.
full-scale [fo͝ol′skāl′] *adj.* 1 Of the same size as the original: a *full-scale* drawing of an insect. 2 Not limited or reduced in size or scope: a *full-scale* rehearsal.
ful·ly [fo͝ol′ē] *adv.* 1 Totally and entirely: *fully* proved. 2 Sufficiently; adequately: *fully* fed. 3 At least: *fully* 50 miles away.
ful·mi·nate [ful′mə·nāt′] *v.* **ful·mi·nat·ed, ful·mi·nat·ing** 1 To talk, argue, or utter violently and loudly: to *fulminate* against taxes. 2 To explode noisily. **—ful′mi·na′tion** *n.* ◆ *Fulminate* comes from the Latin word meaning *lightning.*
ful·some [fo͝ol′səm] *adj.* So much or so false as to be offensive. ◆ *Fulsome* once meant *full* or *abundant,* but in time began to mean *too full* or *full in a false or insincere way,* and this is its meaning today. *Fulsome* flattery is so exaggerated that it is offensive.
fu·ma·role [fyo͞o′mə·rōl′] *n.* A hole in the earth emitting hot vapors near a volcano.
fum·ble [fum′bəl] *v.* **fum·bled, fum·bling,** *n.* 1 *v.* To search about blindly or clumsily: to *fumble* for a key. 2 *v.* To handle or let drop clumsily, as a ball. 3 *n.* The act of fumbling. **—fum′bler** *n.* **—fum′bling·ly** *adv.*
fume [fyo͞om] *n., v.* **fumed, fum·ing** 1 *n.* (*usually pl.*) Unpleasant smoke, gas, or vapor. 2 *v.* To give off fumes. 3 *v.* To darken with fumes: *fumed* oak. 4 *n.* A state of rage. 5 *v.* To complain angrily.
fu·mi·gate [fyo͞o′mə·gāt′] *v.* **fu·mi·gat·ed, fu·mi·gat·**

a	add	**i**	it	**o͝o**	took	**oi**	oil
ā	ace	**ī**	ice	**o͞o**	pool	**ou**	pout
â	care	**o**	odd	**u**	up	**ng**	ring
ä	palm	**ō**	open	**û**	burn	**th**	thin
e	end	**ô**	order	**yo͞o**	fuse	**th**	this
ē	equal					**zh**	vision

ə = { a in *above* e in *sicken* i in *possible* / o in *melon* u in *circus* }

ing To subject to or disinfect with fumes or smoke. **—fu'mi·ga'tion** *n.* **—fu'mi·ga'tor** *n.*

fun [fun] *n.* 1 Pleasant amusement: The dance was *fun.* 2 Playfulness: full of *fun.* 3 Joking or jest: They fought only in *fun.* **—make fun of** To ridicule: They *made fun of* my clothes. ◆ In casual speech, *fun* is sometimes used as an adjective: a *fun* person; a *fun* time. In writing, use more precise words: an *enjoyable* time; an *amusing* person.

func·tion [fungk'shən] 1 *n.* The proper action, use, or purpose: The *function* of a clock is to keep time. 2 *v.* To operate or work properly: Oiled machines *function* best. 3 *n.* A social affair. 4 *n.* A set of ordered pairs of numbers *(x, y)* in which there is exactly one value of *y* for each value of *x*.

func·tion·al [fungk'shən·əl] *adj.* 1 Of or having to do with a function. 2 Affecting a physiological or psychological function with no apparent structural or organic changes. 3 Designed, manufactured, or built mainly from the point of view of use: a *functional* office. **—func'tion·al·ly** *adv.*

func·tion·ar·y [fungk'shən·er'ē] *n., pl.* **func·tion·ar·ies** A public official.

function word A word used to indicate grammatical relationship in a sentence or phrase, as a preposition, conjunction, or auxiliary verb.

fund [fund] 1 *n.* A sum of money set aside for a purpose: a building *fund.* 2 *v.* To set up a fund. 3 *v.* To pay off (a debt). 4 *n.* (*pl.*) Money available for use: insufficient *funds.* 5 *n.* A ready supply or stock: a *fund* of jokes.

fun·da·men·tal [fun'də·men'təl] 1 *adj.* Having to do with or serving as a foundation; essential; basic. 2 *n.* Anything basic to a system; essential part. **—fun'da·men'tal·ly** *adv.*

fun·da·men·tal·ism [fun'də·men'təl·iz'əm] *n.* 1 (*often written* **Fundamentalism**) A movement in American Protestantism, that accepts the Bible as being historically accurate and regards a belief in it as fundamental to the faith and morality of a true Christian. 2 The religious beliefs of people in this movement. **—fun'da·men'tal·ist** *n., adj.*

fu·ner·al [fyōō'nər·əl] 1 *n.* The ceremony at a burial or cremation, usually including a religious service and a procession to the cemetery. 2 *adj.* Of or suitable for a funeral.

fu·ne·re·al [fyōō·nir'ē·əl] *adj.* Depressing and sad; gloomy: a *funereal* expression.

fun·gal [fung'gəl] *adj.* Fungous.

fun·gi·cid·al [fun'ji·sī'dəl *or* fung'gi·sī'dəl] *adj.* Destroying or stopping the growth of fungi. **—fun'gi·cid'al·ly** *adv.*

fun·gi·cide [fun'ji·sīd' *or* fung'gi·sīd'] *n.* A substance that kills or prevents the growth of fungi.

fun·gous [fung'gəs] *adj.* 1 Of or like a fungus. 2 Caused by a fungus: a *fungous* disease.

fun·gus [fung'gəs] *n., pl.* **fun·gi** [fun'jī'] or **fun·gus·es** A plant with no chlorophyll, flowers, or leaves, as a mold or mushroom. ◆ *Fungus* comes from the Latin word for *mushroom.*

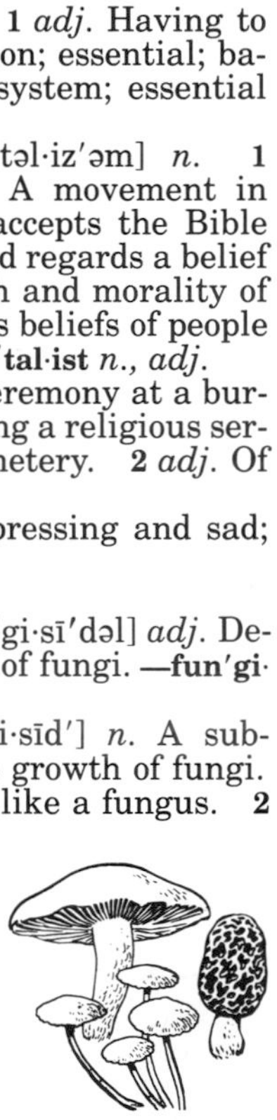

Fungi

funk [fungk] *informal* 1 *n.* A panic; fear. 2 *v.* To shrink from or avoid. 3 *v.* To be afraid of.

funk·y[1] [fung'kē] *adj.* **funk·i·er, funk·i·est** Being in a state of funk; panicky; frightened.

funk·y[2] [fung'kē] *adj.* **funk·i·er, funk·i·est** 1 Having an offensively moldy or musty odor. 2 Having a simple, earthy quality characteristic of the blues: *funky* guitar playing. 3 Offbeat, unconventional, or faddish: *funky* clothes.

fun·nel [fun'əl] *n., v.* **fun·neled** or **fun·nelled, fun·nel·ing** or **fun·nel·ling** 1 *n.* A cone-shaped utensil for pouring liquids, powders, and other materials through a small opening. 2 *v.* To pour through or as if through a funnel. 3 *n.* A smokestack or chimney on a ship or steam locomotive.

Funnel

fun·nic·u·lar [fyōō·nik'yə·lər] 1 *adj.* Hanging from or moved by a cord or cable. 2 *n.* A railway in which the cars are moved by a cable up and down a steep hillside.

fun·nies [fun'ēz] *n.pl. informal* The comic strips in a newspaper.

fun·ny [fun'ē] *adj.* **fun·ni·er, fun·ni·est** 1 Amusing or comical: a *funny* story. 2 *informal* Strange; peculiar: a *funny* look. **—fun'·ni·ly** *adv.* **—fun'ni·ness** *n.*

funny bone The place at the back of the elbow where a nerve is located close to the surface of the skin. When struck, the nerve causes an unpleasant tingling.

fur [fûr] *n., v.* **furred, fur·ring** 1 *n.* The soft, hairy coat of many animals, as foxes, seals, and squirrels. 2 *n.* A cleaned animal skin covered with such a coat. 3 *adj. use:* a *fur* hat. 4 *n.* Something, as a coat, made of fur. 5 *v.* To trim, cover, or line with fur. 6 *n.* A fuzzy layer on the tongue, often accompanying illness. 7 *v.* To coat, as the tongue, with a layer of foul matter. **—fur'less** *adj.*

fur·be·low [fûr'bə·lō'] 1 *n.* A fancy trimming: a coat with frills and *furbelows.* 2 *v.* To trim with ruffles and frills. ◆ Originally the English word for *furbelow* was *falbala,* which comes from the French. Apparently the grouping of sounds seemed too foreign to English ears, because the word came to be pronounced and written as if it were the familiar words *fur* and *below.*

fur·bish [fûr'bish] *v.* 1 To make bright by rubbing; burnish. 2 To renovate: to *furbish* an old bureau. **—fur'bish·er** *n.*

Fu·ries [fyŏŏr'ēz] *n. pl.* In Greek and Roman myths, three goddesses who avenged crimes that had gone unpunished.

fu·ri·ous [fyŏŏr'ē·əs] *adj.* 1 Very angry. 2 Very strong or fierce: a *furious* wind. 3 Very great: a *furious* speed. **—fu'ri·ous·ly** *adv.* **—fu'ri·ous·ness** *n.*

furl [fûrl] 1 *v.* To roll up and fasten: to *furl* a sail to the yard. 2 *n.* Something furled.

fur·long [fûr'lông'] *n.* A measure of length, equal to 1/8 of a mile, or 220 yards.

fur·lough [fûr'lō] 1 *n.* An official leave of absence, especially one granted to a member of the armed forces. 2 *v.* To give a furlough to.

fur·nace [fûr'nis] *n.* A large structure with a chamber in which a fire of such intense heat may be made as to heat a building or melt metals.

fur·nish [fûr'nish] *v.* 1 To provide with furniture, as a room. 2 To provide or supply: to *furnish* each child with a ruler.

fur·nish·ings [fûr'nish·ingz] *n.pl.* 1 Clothing and accessories: men's *furnishings.* 2 Furniture or appliances, as for a room or office.

fur·ni·ture [fûr′nə·chər] *n.* The movable articles in a house or office, as chairs and beds.

fu·ror [fyŏŏr′ôr] *n.* **1** Great rage or fury: the mob's *furor.* **2** Intense enthusiasm or excitement: The movie caused a *furor.* **3** Craze or mania.

fur·ri·er [fûr′ē·ər] *n.* **1** A dealer in furs. **2** A person who makes or restores fur garments.

fur·row [fûr′ō] **1** *n.* A long, deep groove made in land by a plow. **2** *n.* A wrinkle on the face or forehead. **3** *v.* To make furrows in.

Furrows

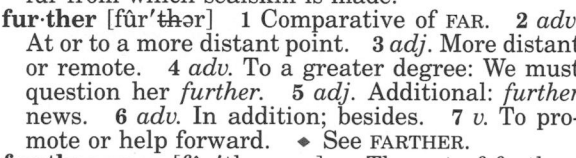

fur·ry [fûr′ē] *adj.* **fur·ri·er, fur·ri·est** **1** Covered with fur. **2** Of or like fur.

fur seal Any of several seals having soft, thick fur from which sealskin is made.

fur·ther [fûr′thər] **1** Comparative of FAR. **2** *adv.* At or to a more distant point. **3** *adj.* More distant or remote. **4** *adv.* To a greater degree: We must question her *further.* **5** *adj.* Additional: *further* news. **6** *adv.* In addition; besides. **7** *v.* To promote or help forward. ◆ See FARTHER.

fur·ther·ance [fûr′thər·əns] *n.* The act of furthering; promotion.

fur·ther·more [fûr′thər·môr′] *adv.* Moreover.

fur·ther·most [fûr′thər·mōst′] *adj.* Furthest and most distant: the *furthermost* point on a map.

fur·thest [fûr′thist] **1** Superlative of FAR. **2** *adv.* At or to the most distant point. **3** *adv.* To the greatest degree. **4** *adj.* Most distant in space, time, or degree.

fur·tive [fûr′tiv] *adj.* **1** Done in secret; stealthy: a *furtive* glance. **2** Sly: a *furtive* manner. **—fur′tive·ly** *adv.* **—fur′tive·ness** *n.* ◆ See STEALTHY.

fu·ry [fyŏŏr′ē] *n., pl.* **fu·ries** **1** Wild or extreme anger; rage. **2** A fit of such anger. **3** Great force or violence. **4** A person with a violent temper.

furze [fûrz] *n.* Another name for GORSE.

fuse[1] [fyōōz] *n.* **1** An enclosed length of combustible material used to set off an explosive charge. **2** Another spelling of FUSE.

fuse[2] [fyōōz] *v.* **fused, fus·ing,** *n.* **1** *v.* To melt or join by melting together. **2** *v.* To unite, as if by melting. **3** *n.* A small, enclosed strip of metal that completes an electrical circuit. If the current in the circuit gets too strong, the fuse melts and breaks the circuit.

fu·see [fyōō·zē′] *n.* **1** A match with a large striking head that will not be blown out easily in a wind. **2** A colored flare used to signal rail or road traffic. **3** A fuse for detonating an explosive charge.

fu·se·lage [fyōō′sə·lij *or* fyōō′sə·läzh′] *n.* The body of an airplane, excluding the wings and tail.

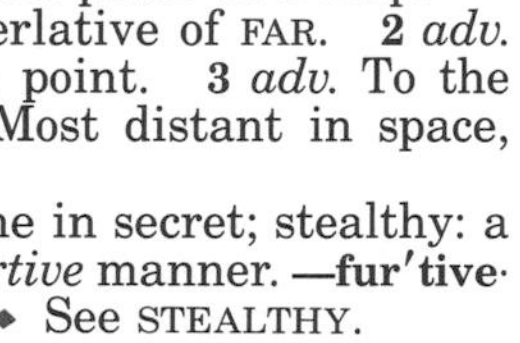

Fuselage

fu·si·ble [fyōō′zə·bəl] *adj.* Capable of being fused or melted by heat: a *fusible* metal.

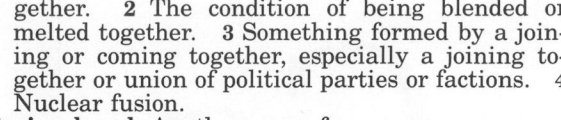

fu·sil·ier [fyōō′zə·lēr′] *n.* A soldier in any of certain British regiments with a long tradition. ◆ *Fusilier* comes from *fusil,* an old kind of light musket.

fu·sil·lade [fyōō′sə·lād′] *n.* **1** A burst of fire, as from guns or cannons. **2** Anything like a fusillade: a *fusillade* of complaints.

fu·sion [fyōō′zhən] *n.* **1** A blending or melting together. **2** The condition of being blended or melted together. **3** Something formed by a joining or coming together, especially a joining together or union of political parties or factions. **4** Nuclear fusion.

fusion bomb Another name for HYDROGEN BOMB.

fuss [fus] **1** *n.* Unnecessary bother over unimportant matters or small details. **2** *v.* To bother unnecessarily with unimportant matters or small details. **3** *n.* A protest or complaint. **4** *v.* To protest or complain. **5** *n.* A quarrel or dispute. **—fuss′er** *n.*

fuss·budg·et [fus′buj′it] *n.* A person who fusses over trivial details.

fuss·y [fus′ē] *adj.* **fuss·i·er, fuss·i·est** **1** Habitually fussing; easily upset. **2** Hard to please; particular; finicky: a *fussy* eater. **3** Elaborate in the way it is made or trimmed: a *fussy* outfit. **4** Requiring or characterized by close attention to details: a *fussy* job. **—fuss′i·ly** *adv.* **—fuss′i·ness** *n.*

fus·tian [fus′chən] *n.* **1** A coarse, twilled, cotton fabric, as corduroy. **2** High-flown speech or writing; bombast.

fust·y [fus′tē] *adj.* **fust·i·er, fust·i·est** **1** Moldy; musty: *fusty* old books. **2** Old-fashioned: a person with *fusty* ideas. **—fust′i·ly** *adv.* **—fust′i·ness** *n.*

fu·tile [fyōō′təl] *adj.* **1** Done in vain; useless: *futile* efforts. **2** Having no importance; trivial: *futile* chatter. **—fu′tile·ly** *adv.*

fu·til·i·ty [fyōō·til′ə·tē] *n., pl.* **fu·til·i·ties** **1** Complete lack of effectiveness; uselessness: the *futility* of our efforts to stop the flood. **2** Unimportance or triviality: the *futility* of arguing over such matters. **3** A futile act, event, or thing.

fu·ture [fyōō′chər] **1** *n.* The time yet to come; time that is to be. **2** *adj.* Occurring in the future: a *future* date. **3** *adj.* Having to do with or expressing time to come. **4** *n.* In grammar, the future tense or a verb form in this tense. **5** *n.* Chance for success; prospect: a job with a *future.*

future perfect tense The tense used to express action or a state of being that will be completed in the future before a specified future time.

future tense The tense used to express action or a state of being in the future.

fu·tu·ri·ty [fyōō·t(y)ŏŏr′ə·tē] *n., pl.* **fu·tu·ri·ties** **1** The future. **2** The state or quality of being future. **3** Something future, as an act or thing.

fuze [fyōōz] *n.* A mechanical or electrical device used to detonate an explosive charge, as a bomb.

fuzz [fuz] *n.* Short light hairs or fibers; fine down: Peaches have *fuzz.*

fuzz·y [fuz′ē] *adj.* **fuzz·i·er, fuzz·i·est** **1** Of, like, or having fuzz. **2** Blurry; not clear: *fuzzy* images. **—fuzz′i·ly** *adv.* **—fuzz′i·ness** *n.*

-fy A suffix meaning: **1** To make or cause to be, as in *simplify.* **2** To become, as in *liquefy.*

FYI or **F.Y.I.** for your information.

a	add	**i**	it	**ŏŏ**	took	**oi**	oil
ā	ace	**ī**	ice	**ōō**	pool	**ou**	pout
â	care	**o**	odd	**u**	up	**ng**	ring
ä	palm	**ō**	open	**û**	burn	**th**	thin
e	end	**ô**	order	**yōō**	fuse	**th**	this
ē	equal					**zh**	vision

ə = a in *above* e in *sicken* i in *possible* / o in *melon* u in *circus*

Gg

Early Phoenician (late 2nd millennium B.C.)

Phoenician (8th century B.C.)

Early Greek (9th-7th centuries B.C.)

Western Greek (6th century B.C.)

Classical Greek (403 B.C. onward)

Early Etruscan (8th century B.C.)

Monumental Latin (4th century B.C.)

Classical Latin

Uncial

Half uncial

Caroline minuscule

G is the seventh letter of the alphabet. The sign for it originated among Semitic people in the Near East, in the region of Palestine and Syria, probably in the middle of the second millennium B.C. Little is known about the sign until around 1000 B.C., when the Phoenicians began using it. They named it *gimel* and used it for the sound of the consonant *g*.

When the Greeks adopted the Phoenician sign around the ninth century B.C., they called it *gamma* and used it, too, for the sound of *g*. Throughout the early centuries the shape of the letter changed several times. Most of the shapes were angular, with the letter facing first to the left and in later years to the right.

As early as the eighth century B.C., the Etruscans adopted the Greek alphabet. The Etruscan language made no distinction between the *g* and the *k* sounds, and the Etruscans used the letter for the sound of *k*. It was from the Etruscans that the Romans took the letter. At first the Romans, too, used the sign for both the *g* and the *k* sounds. In 312 B.C., however, the Latin alphabet was reformed. The sign for the *z* sound, originally the seventh letter of the Greek alphabet, was dropped because it was not needed in Latin. A new letter, a *C* with a bar added to the lower end, was formed to stand for the *g* sound, and *C* was reserved for the *k* sound. (See *C* for that letter's later history.) Thus was born the sign for the *majuscule,* or capital letter, *G* that we know.

The *minuscule,* or small letter, *g* developed gradually, between the third and the ninth centuries, in the handwriting that scribes used for copying books. It changed form many times and looks today very little like the majuscule. Contributing to its shape were the Roman *uncials* of the fourth to the eighth centuries, the *half uncials* of the fifth to the ninth centuries, and the *Caroline minuscules,* a script that evolved under the encouragement of Charlemagne (742-814). The Caroline script was used on the medieval manuscripts of the ninth and tenth centuries.

g or **G** [jē] *n., pl.* **g's** or **G's** 1 The seventh letter of the English alphabet. 2 In music, the fifth note of the scale of C major.

g 1 acceleration of gravity. 2 gram(s).

g. 1 gram(s). 2 gauge.

G gravity.

G. 1 German. 2 Germany. 3 Gulf. 4 specific gravity.

ga gauge.

Ga The symbol for the element gallium.

Ga. Georgia.

GA Postal Service abbreviation of Georgia.

G.A. General Assembly.

gab [gab] *v.* **gabbed, gab·bing,** *n. informal* 1 *v.* To chatter; talk a great deal, especially idly. 2 *n.* Idle talk.

gab·ar·dine [gab′ər·dēn′ *or* gab′ər·dēn′] *n.* 1 A firm, twilled fabric used for coats, suits, and other garments. 2 Another spelling of GABERDINE.

gab·ber [gab′ər] *n.* A person who talks a great deal, especially idly.

gab·ble [gab′əl] *v.* **gab·bled, gab·bling,** *n.* 1 *v.* To talk or utter quickly, making little or no sense; jabber: They *gabbled* away, like so many geese. 2 *n.* Rapid, senseless talk. **—gab′bler** *n.*

gab·by [gab′ē] *adj.* **gab·bi·er, gab·bi·est** *informal* Extremely talkative.

gab·er·dine [gab′ər·dēn′ *or* gab′ər·dēn′] *n.* 1 A long, loose coat worn by men in the Middle Ages. 2 Another spelling of GABARDINE.

gab·fest [gab′fest′] *n. informal* A small get-together for casual chat and gossip.

ga·ble [gā′bəl] *n.* The triangular top part of an outer wall, between the sides of a sloped roof.

Gables

ga·bled [gā′bəld] *adj.* Built with or forming a gable or gables.

gable roof A roof that slopes down on two sides from a common peak and forms a gable at each end.

Gab·o·nese [gab′ə·nēz′] *adj., n., pl.* **Gab·o·nese** 1 *adj.* Of or from Gabon. 2 *n.* A person born in or a citizen of Gabon.

Ga·bri·el [gā′brē·əl] *n.* In the Bible, an archangel, chosen as the special messenger of God.

gad [gad] *v.* **gad·ded, gad·ding** To roam about idly or looking for fun and excitement.

gad·a·bout [gad′ə·bout′] *n.* A person who gads about aimlessly or restlessly.

gad·fly [gad′flī′] *n., pl.* **gad·flies** 1 A large fly that bites cattle, horses, and other animals. 2 An irritating, bothersome person.

gadg·et [gaj′it] *n. informal* A small device or contrivance, especially a mechanical one.

gad·o·lin·i·um [gad′ə·lin′e·əm] *n.* A metallic element found in rare earths and having magnetic properties when below room temperature. ◆ See RARE-EARTH ELEMENT.

Gae·a [jē′ə] *n.* In Greek mythology, the earth goddess and mother of the Titans.

Gael [gāl] *n.* 1 A Gaelic-speaking Celt of Ireland, Scotland, or the Isle of Man. 2 A Celt of the Scottish Highlands.
Gael·ic [gā'lik] 1 *n.* The Celtic language of the Irish, the Scottish Highlanders, or the Manx. 2 *adj.* Of or having to do with these Celts or their language.
gaff [gaf] 1 *n.* A spear or iron hook used to land large fish. 2 *v.* To hook or land with a gaff. 3 *n.* A spar to hold the upper edge of a fore-and-aft sail.
gaffe [gaf] *n.* A social blunder; faux pas.
gaf·fer [gaf'ər] *n.* 1 *informal* An old man. 2 An electrician who does the lighting for a motion-picture or television set. ◆ Gaffer is probably a changed form of *grandfather.*
gag [gag] *n., v.* **gagged, gag·ging** 1 *n.* Something, as a cloth, put in or across the mouth to muffle the voice. 2 *v.* To prevent from speaking by applying a gag to. 3 *v.* To retch or cause to retch. 4 *n. slang* A joke or playful hoax.
gage[1] [gāj] *n.* 1 Something given as security; pledge. 2 Anything offered in challenge, as a glove for a duel. 3 Any challenge.
gage[2] [gāj] *n., v.* Another spelling of GAUGE.
gag·gle [gag'əl] *n.* 1 A flock of geese. 2 Any group or cluster: *gaggle* of teen-agers.
Gai·a [gā'ə] *n.* Another spelling of GAEA.
gai·e·ty [gā'ə·tē] *n., pl.* **gai·e·ties** 1 Gay liveliness. 2 Gay activity. 3 Colorful brightness.
gai·ly [gā'lē] *adv.* In a gay manner.
gain [gān] 1 *v.* To obtain, earn, or win: to *gain* the advantage. 2 *v.* To increase in: to *gain* momentum. 3 *n.* An increase, as in size or amount. 4 *n.* (*often pl.*) Profit or winnings: small *gains.* 5 *v.* To profit or advance: to *gain* by an action. 6 *n.* An advantage or lead: a *gain* of one mile. 7 *v.* To reach or draw nearer: to *gain* port; to *gain* on an opponent. 8 *v.* To put on, as weight. 9 *v.* To grow better or stronger: The invalid was *gaining.* 10 *n.* The act of gaining.
gain·er [gā'nər] *n.* 1 A person who gains. 2 A fancy dive in which the diver leaves the board facing forward, somersaults backward in the air, and hits the water feet first and facing forward.
gain·ful [gān'fəl] *adj.* Yielding or bringing gain; profitable. **—gain'ful·ly** *adv.*
gain·say [gān'sā'] *v.* **gain·said, gain·say·ing** 1 To deny. 2 To contradict. 3 To oppose.
'gainst or **gainst** [genst] *prep.* Against: used mostly in poems.
gait [gāt] *n.* 1 A way of walking, stepping, or running. 2 Any of the ways by which a horse moves, as a trot or gallop.
gai·ter [gā'tər] *n.* 1 A covering, as of cloth or leather, for the lower leg or ankle. 2 A high shoe with an elastic strip in each side.
gal or **gal.** gallon(s).
gal [gal] *n. informal* A girl or woman.
ga·la [gā'lə *or* gal'ə] 1 *adj.* Festive and gay. 2 *n.* A lively celebration; festival.
ga·lac·tic [gə·lak'tik] *adj.* Of or having to do with a galaxy, especially the Milky Way.
Gal·a·had [gal'ə·had'] *n.* The noblest knight of the Round Table, who found the Grail.
Gal·a·te·a [gal'ə·tē'ə] *n.* In Greek mythology, a statue of a young woman sculpted by Pygmalion, who fell in love with his creation. The goddess of love and beauty, Aphrodite, brought the statue to life in answer to his prayers.
Ga·la·tians [gə·lā'shənz] *n.* A book of the New Testament written by Saint Paul.
gal·ax·y [gal'ək·sē] *n., pl.* **gal·ax·ies** 1 (*written* **Galaxy**) The Milky Way. 2 A large system of celestial bodies. 3 Any brilliant group.
gale [gāl] *n.* 1 A strong wind. 2 An outburst, as of laughter.
ga·le·na [gə·lē'nə] *n.* A metallic, dull gray mineral from which lead is extracted.
Gal·i·le·an [gal'ə·lē'ən] 1 *adj.* Of or from Galilee. 2 *n.* A person born or living in Galilee. **—the Galilean** Jesus Christ.
gall[1] [gôl] *n.* 1 The bitter fluid produced by the liver; bile. 2 Bitter feeling; malice. 3 Anything bitter. 4 *U.S. slang* Impudence.
gall[2] [gôl] 1 *n.* A sore made by rubbing. 2 *v.* To make sore by rubbing. 3 *v.* To annoy; vex.
gall[3] [gôl] *n.* A lump or growth on a part of a plant that has been injured by insects, fungi, or bacteria.
gal·lant [gal'ənt *or* gə·lant' *or* gə·länt'] 1 *adj.* [gal'ənt] Bold and courageous; brave. 2 *adj.* [gə·lant' *or* gə·länt'] Courteous and respectful to women; chivalrous. 3 *n.* [gə·lant' *or* gə·länt *or* gal'ənt] A brave or chivalrous man. 4 *n.* [gə·lant' *or* gə·länt *or* gal'ənt] A fashionable young man. **—gal'lant·ly** *adv.*
gal·lant·ry [gal'ən·trē] *n., pl.* **gal·lant·ries** 1 Bravery and nobility. 2 Chivalrous behavior. 3 A courteous act or speech.
gall·blad·der [gôl'blad'ər] *n.* A small, pear-shaped sac beneath the liver, in which excess bile is stored.
gal·le·on [gal'ē·ən] *n.* A large sailing ship of former times, having many decks.

Galleon

gal·ler·y [gal'ər·ē] *n., pl.* **gal·ler·ies** 1 A long corridor or passageway, sometimes with one open side. 2 An indoor balcony, especially the highest one in a theater. 3 The people who sit in this balcony. 4 A place where works of art are displayed. 5 A long room or building used for a special purpose: a shooting *gallery.*
gal·ley [gal'ē] *n., pl.* **gal·leys** 1 In ancient and medieval times, a long, narrow ship with sails and oars, usually rowed by prisoners or slaves. 2 The kitchen of a ship. 3 In printing, a long metal tray used to hold type that has been set. 4 A galley proof.

Galley

a	add	**i**	it	**o͝o**	took	**oi**	oil
ā	ace	**ī**	ice	**o͞o**	pool	**ou**	pout
â	care	**o**	odd	**u**	up	**ng**	ring
ä	palm	**ō**	open	**û**	burn	**th**	thin
e	end	**ô**	order	**yo͞o**	fuse	**t͟h**	this
ē	equal					**zh**	vision

ə = {a in *above* e in *sicken* i in *possible*; o in *melon* u in *circus*}

galley proof A proof taken from type in the galley. It is checked for errors before the type is made up in pages.
galley slave A prisoner or slave who rows on a galley.
gall·fly [gôl′flī′] *n., pl.* **gall·flies** Any of various insects that cause the development of galls in the plants in which they deposit their eggs.
Gal·lic [gal′ik] *adj.* **1** Of or having to do with Gaul or the Gauls. **2** French.
gall·ing [gô′ling] *adj.* Very irritating: It was a *galling* experience to have to ask for help.
gal·li·um [gal′ē·əm] *n.* A rare metallic element that melts at ordinary temperatures.
gal·li·vant [gal′ə·vant′] *v.* To roam about in search of fun and excitement.
gall·nut [gôl′nut′] *n.* A swelling on the trunk of a tree, especially an oak tree, that is shaped like a nut.
gal·lon [gal′ən] *n.* A liquid measure equal to 4 quarts or 8 pints.
gal·lop [gal′əp] **1** *n.* The fastest gait of a four-footed animal. Once in each stride all four feet are off the ground at the same time. **2** *v.* To ride or go at this gait. **3** *n.* Such a ride. **4** *v.* To go at a fast pace. **—gal′lop·er** *n.*

Horse galloping

gal·lows [gal′ōz] *n., pl.* **gal·lows·es** or **gal·lows** **1** A wooden framework with a suspended noose, used for hanging criminals. **2** The punishment of execution by hanging: sentenced to the *gallows.*
gallows humor Humorous treatment of something that is serious or dreadful.
gall·stone [gôl′stōn′] *n.* A hard, stonelike substance sometimes formed in the gallbladder.
ga·lore [gə·lôr′] *adv.* In great abundance.
ga·losh·es [gə·losh′əz] *n.pl.* A pair of high overshoes worn when it rains, sleets, or snows.
ga·lumph [gə·lumf′] *v.* To walk or bound clumsily and noisily.
gal·van·ic [gal·van′ik] *adj.* **1** Of or having to do with electricity produced by chemical action. **2** Sudden or startling: *galvanic* news. **—gal·van′i·cal·ly** *adv.*
gal·va·nism [gal′və·niz′əm] *n.* **1** Direct electrical current, especially when chemically produced. **2** The use of direct electrical current in medicine.
gal·va·nize [gal′və·nīz′] *v.* **gal·va·nized, gal·va·niz·ing** **1** To shock or stimulate with electricity. **2** To rouse; startle. **3** To coat (as iron) with a protective layer of zinc. **—gal·va·ni·za·tion** [gal′və·ni·zā′shən] *n.* **—gal′va·niz′er** *n.*
gal·va·nom·e·ter [gal′və·nom′ə·tər] *n.* A device that measures the strength and direction of an electric current.
gam[1] [gam] *n.* A school of whales.
gam[2] [gam] *n. slang* The leg of a person, especially the well-shaped leg of a woman.
Gam·bi·an [gam′bē·ən] **1** *adj.* Of or from Gambia. **2** *n.* A person born in or a citizen of Gambia.
gam·bit [gam′bit] *n.* In chess, an opening in which a piece is risked to gain an advantage.
gam·ble [gam′bəl] *v.* **gam·bled, gam·bling,** *n.* **1** *v.* To risk (something, as money) by betting on the outcome of an event or game. **2** *v.* To take a risk, as on a chance for gain. **3** *n.* An act of gambling; wager; bet. **4** *n.* A risky or uncertain act or venture. **5** *v.* To lose by gambling. **—gam·bler** *n.*
gam·bol [gam′bəl] *v.* **gam·boled** or **gam·bolled, gam·bol·ing** or **gam·bol·ling,** *n.* **1** *v.* To skip or run about in play: lambs *gamboling* about the field. **2** *n.* A frolic; play.
gam·brel roof [gam′brəl] A ridged roof with its slope broken on each side so that the lower section is steeper than the upper.

Gambrel roof

game[1] [gām] *n., adj.* **gam·er, gam·est,** *v.* **gamed, gam·ing** **1** *n.* A contest or sport involving chance, skill, and endurance, governed by set rules. **2** *n.* A set used in playing a game. **3** *n.* A form of play. **4** *n.* A plan; scheme. **5** *n.* Animals or birds hunted for food or sport. **6** *n.* The flesh of such game used as food. **7** *adj.* Of, having to do with, or being such game. **8** *adj.* Spirited; plucky. **9** *adj. informal* Ready; willing. **10** *v.* To gamble. **11** *n.* A score needed to win, as in tennis. **—make game of** To ridicule. **—game′ly** *adv.*
game[2] [gām] *adj.* Lame: to favor a *game* leg.
game·cock [gām′kok′] *n.* A rooster bred and trained to fight other roosters.
game·keep·er [gām′kē′pər] *n.* A person who tends and protects wild game, as on an estate.
game plan **1** A strategy of play developed before a game, especially a football game. **2** Any strategy developed to achieve an objective.
game·some [gām′səm] *adj.* Playful; sportive; merry. **—game′some·ly** *adv.* **—game′some·ness** *n.*
game·ster [gām′stər] *n.* A gambler.
gam·ete [gam′ēt *or* gə·mēt′] *n.* Either of the two reproductive cells, a sperm or ovum, that unite to form a new plant or animal.
ga·me·to·phyte [gə·mē′tə·fīt′] *n.* In plants in which gametes are produced in alternate generations, the generation that is capable of producing gametes.
game warden An official who enforces fishing and hunting laws on public lands.
gam·in [gam′in] *n.* A homeless, neglected child who wanders about the streets.
gam·ing [gām′ing] *n.* Gambling.
gam·ma [gam′ə] *n.* The third letter of the Greek alphabet.
gamma glob·u·lin [glob′yə·lin] The part of blood plasma that has most of the antibodies.
gamma ray A type of electromagnetic radiation of short wavelength and great penetrating power.
gam·mer [gam·ər] *n.* An old woman. ◆ *Gammer* is probably a changed form of *grandmother.*
gam·mon [gam′ən] **1** *n.* In the game of backgammon, a victory that occurs before the losing player has removed a single disk from the board. **2** *v.* To defeat in backgammon by scoring a gammon.
gam·ut [gam′ət] *n.* **1** The whole range of anything. **2** The entire range of musical tones.
gam·y [gā′mē] *adj.* **gam·i·er, gam·i·est** **1** Having the odor or flavor of game, especially of game that has been kept uncooked so long that it is tainted. **2** Plucky.
gan·der [gan′dər] *n.* A male goose.
gang [gang] **1** *n.* A group of people, as friends, laborers, or criminals, who work or pass the time together. **2** *v.* To form a gang. **3** *n.* A set of

similar tools or machines that work together: a *gang* of saws. **—gang up** or **gang up on** To attack or act against as a group.

gang·bus·ter [gang′bus′tər] *n. slang* An officer of the law who tries to get convictions against members of organized criminal groups. **—like gangbusters** *slang* With great energy and fervor.

gang·land [gang′land′] *n.* The world of organized crime and criminals.

gan·gling [gang′gling] *adj.* Awkward, tall, and lanky: a *gangling* youth.

gan·gli·on [gang′glē·ən] *n., pl.* **gan·gli·ons** or **gan·gli·a** [gang′glē·ə] **1** A collection of nerve cells, located elsewhere than in the brain or spinal cord. **2** A center of activity or strength.

gan·gly [gang′glē] *adj.* **gan·gli·er, gan·gli·est** Gangling.

gang·plank [gang′plangk′] *n.* A movable bridge which persons cross to get on or off a ship.

Gangplank

gan·grene [gang′grēn′] *n., v.* **gan·grened, gan·gren·ing** **1** *n.* The decay of tissue in part of the body, caused by a failure in circulation of the blood, as from injury or disease. **2** *v.* To be or cause to be affected by gangrene. **—gan·gre·nous** [gang′·grə·nəs] *adj.*

gang·ster [gang′stər] *n.* A member of a gang of criminals or racketeers.

gang·way [gang′wā′] **1** *n.* A passageway or gangplank. **2** *interj.* Move aside!

gan·net [gan′it] *n.* Any of several large sea birds related to the pelican.

gant·let[1] [gônt′lit] *n.* Another spelling of GAUNTLET[1].

gant·let[2] [gônt′lit] *n.* Another spelling of GAUNTLET[2].

gan·try [gan′trē] *n., pl.* **gan·tries** **1** A frame erected on side supports that moves on parallel tracks and is used to carry a crane. **2** A bridgelike structure spanning several railroad tracks, used to support signals. **3** A movable scaffold used in the building and servicing of rockets. It has work platforms at various heights from the ground.

Gan·y·mede [gan′ə·mēd′] *n.* In Greek mythology, a very handsome youth who was carried off by Zeus to become the gods' cupbearer.

gaol [jāl] *n. British* A jail. **—gaol′er** *n.*

gap [gap] *n., v.* **gap·ped, gap·ping** **1** *n.* A crack or opening, as in a wall. **2** *n.* A mountain pass. **3** *n.* An empty space. **4** *v.* To make a gap in. **5** *v.* To be or become open. **6** *n.* A difference.

gape [gāp] *v.* **gaped, gap·ing,** *n.* **1** *v.* To stare with the mouth open, as in surprise. **2** *v.* To open the mouth wide, as in yawning. **3** *n.* The act of gaping. **4** *v.* To be or become wide open. **5** *n.* A wide opening; gap.

ga·rage [gə·räzh′] *n.* A place where automobiles are housed or repaired. ◆ When the French word *garage,* meaning *a storing away,* came into use in English, its meaning became narrower, referring only to a place where vehicles were stored.

garage sale Another term for TAG SALE.

garb [gärb] **1** *n.* Clothing; manner of dress: the *garb* of a sailor. **2** *v.* To clothe; dress.

gar·bage [gär′bij] *n.* **1** Food wastes, especially from a kitchen. **2** Anything that is worthless or offensive.

gar·ban·zo [gär·bän′zō] *n., pl.* **gar·ban·zos** Another name for CHICK-PEA.

gar·ble [gär′bəl] *v.* **gar·bled, gar·bling** **1** To mix up or confuse (as a story or facts) by mistake. **2** To deliberately change or leave out, as parts of a story, so that a false or unclear presentation is given. **—gar′bler** *n.*

gar·çon [gär·sôn′] *n., pl.* **gar·çons** [gär·sôn′] A waiter. ◆ This word is French for *servant.*

gar·den [gär′dən] **1** *n.* A plot of land where flowers, vegetables, and other plants are grown. **2** *v.* To work in a garden.

garden apartment **1** A group of low apartment buildings having a good deal of surrounding lawn or garden space. **2** A usually ground-floor apartment that has direct access to an adjoining garden or backyard.

gar·den·er [gärd′nər] *n.* A person who gardens, especially for pay.

gar·de·nia [gär·dēn′yə] *n.* A large, white flower with a very sweet scent.

Garden of Eden In the Old Testament, the original home of Adam and Eve.

gar·gan·tu·an [gär·gan′chōō·ən] *adj.* Of very great size or volume; huge; enormous; gigantic. ◆ *Gargantuan* comes from *Gargantua,* the name of a giant king in *Gargantua and Pantagruel,* a satire by François Rabelais.

gar·gle [gär′gəl] *v.* **gar·gled, gar·gling,** *n.* **1** *v.* To rinse (the throat and mouth) with a liquid kept in motion by expelling air. **2** *n.* A liquid used for gargling.

gar·goyle [gär′goil′] *n.* A carved figure of a grotesque animal or human being that juts out from a building and usually contains a channel for draining off rain water.

Gargoyle

gar·ish [gâr′ish] *adj.* Too showy or bright; gaudy. **—gar′ish·ly** *adv.* **—gar′·ish·ness** *n.*

gar·land [gär′lənd] **1** *n.* A wreath or rope of flowers or leaves. **2** *v.* To decorate with or make into a garland.

gar·lic [gär′lik] *n.* **1** A plant related to the onion. **2** The bulb of this plant, which is divided into sections called cloves. It has a pungent odor and taste, and is used as a seasoning.

gar·ment [gär′mənt] *n.* An article of clothing.

garment bag **1** A long bag that hangs in a closet and is used to store and protect clothing. **2** A long folding bag used to carry clothes when traveling.

gar·ner [gär′nər] **1** *v.* To gather and store: to *gar-*

a	add	**i**	it	**o͝o**	took	**oi**	oil
ā	ace	**ī**	ice	**o͞o**	pool	**ou**	pout
â	care	**o**	odd	**u**	up	**ng**	ring
ä	palm	**ō**	open	**û**	burn	**th**	thin
e	end	**ô**	order	**yo͞o**	fuse	**th**	this
ē	equal					**zh**	vision

ə = a in *above*, e in *sicken*, i in *possible*, o in *melon*, u in *circus*

ner grain. **2** *n.* A place for storing grain; granary. **3** *v.* To earn or acquire.
gar·net [gär′nit] **1** *n.* A hard, deep red mineral, often used as a gem. **2** *adj., n.* Deep red.
gar·nish [gär′nish] **1** *n.* Something, as a small piece of fruit or a bit of spice, added to a main dish to improve its taste or appearance. **2** *n.* A decoration; ornament. **3** *v.* To add garnishes to.
gar·nish·ee [gär′nish·ē′] *v.* **gar·nish·eed, gar·nish·ee·ing** To seize (a person's money or property) by legal means, in payment of the person's debt.
gar·ni·ture [gär′ni·chər] *n.* Something that decorates; ornament; embellishment.
gar·ret [gar′it] *n.* A small room or set of rooms in an attic, under a sloping roof.
gar·ri·son [gar′ə·sən] **1** *n.* The troops stationed in a fort or town. **2** *v.* To station (troops) in a fort or town. **3** *n.* The place where the troops are stationed. **4** *v.* To station troops in (as a town or fort).
gar·ru·li·ty [gə·rōō′lə·tē] *n.* The quality of being garrulous; talkativeness; loquacity.
gar·ru·lous [gar′ə·ləs] *adj.* Talking a lot, especially about trifles. **—gar′ru·lous·ly** *adv.* **—gar′ru·lous·ness** *n.*
gar·ter [gär′tər] **1** *n.* An elastic band or strap, used to hold up a stocking or sock. **2** *v.* To support or fasten with a garter.
Gar·ter [gär′tər], **Order of the** The most honored badge and award of knighthood given in Great Britain.
garter snake A small, harmless American snake with long yellow lines on the back.
gas [gas] *n., pl.* **gas·es,** *v.* **gassed, gas·sing** **1** *n.* A substance that is not solid or liquid but is fluid and able to expand indefinitely: Oxygen and hydrogen are *gases* at normal temperatures. **2** *n.* Any gas, considered with respect to its use, effect, or origin: cooking *gas*; poison *gas*; swamp *gas*. **3** *v.* To kill or injure with poison gas: to *gas* the enemy. **4** *n. informal* Gasoline. **5** *v. informal* To fill with gasoline. **6** *v. slang* To talk idly and boastfully. **7** *n. slang* Someone or something that is especially good fun: The party was a *gas*. ◆ *Gas* was coined about 350 years ago by a Belgian chemist, either from the Dutch word *geest,* meaning *a spirit,* or the Greek word *chaos,* meaning *a formless mass.* Later the suffix *-eous,* a form of *-ous,* was added to *gas* to make *gaseous.*
gas burner A nozzle or burner through which combustible gas is released for burning.
gas chamber A sealed room in which prisoners are executed by exposure to lethal gas.
gas·e·ous [gas′ē·əs *or* gash′əs] *adj.* Of or like gas; in the form of gas. ◆ See GAS.
gas-guz·zler [gas′guz′lər] *n. informal* An automobile that consumes an excessive amount of gasoline in relation to its mileage.
gas-guz·zling [gas′guz′ling] *adj. informal* Consuming excessive gasoline in relation to its mileage.
gash [gash] **1** *v.* To make a long, deep cut in. **2** *n.* A long, deep cut or flesh wound.
gas·ket [gas′kit] *n.* A ring or packing, as of rubber or metal, tightly fitted around the edges of two joined parts to prevent leaking.
gas·light [gas′līt′] *n.* **1** The light emitted when gas is burned. **2** A lighting fixture that burns gas.
gas main A pipe with a large diameter that transports and distributes gas to smaller pipes that deliver it to consumers.
gas mask A protective mask with an air filter worn to prevent poisoning or irritation by such things as harmful gases or radioactive dust.

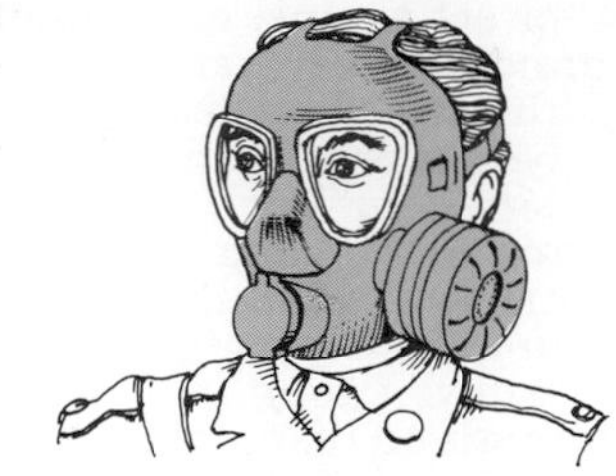
Gas mask

gas·o·hol [gas′ə·hôl′] *n.* A motor fuel that is a mixture of unleaded gasoline and ethyl alcohol, combined in a ratio of at least 9 parts gasoline to 1 part alcohol.
gas·o·line or **gas·o·lene** [gas′ə·lēn′] *n.* An almost colorless liquid made from petroleum, used mainly as a motor fuel.
gasp [gasp] **1** *n.* A sudden catching of the breath; pant. **2** *v.* To breathe in gasps. **3** *v.* To utter (sounds or words) between gasps.
gas·ser [gas′ər] *n.* A gas-producing oil well.
gas station A place where gasoline and other supplies for motor vehicles are sold.
gas·sy [gas′ē] *adj.* **gas·si·er, gas·si·est** Like, full of, or containing gas: a *gassy* substance.
gas·tric [gas′trik] *adj.* Of or having to do with the stomach.
gastric juice Fluid secreted by glands in the lining of the stomach. It contains hydrochloric acid and various enzymes that are important in digestion.
gas·tro·nome [gas′trə·nōm′] *n.* A person who enjoys and is knowledgeable about fine foods and drink; gourmet.
gas·tron·o·my [gas·tron′ə·mē] *n.* The art, science, and lore of fine dining. **gas·tro·nom·ic** [gas′·trə·nom′ik] *adj.* **—gas·tro·nom·i·cal** [gas′trə·nom′·i·kəl] *adj.* **—gas′tro·nom′i·cal·ly** *adv.*
gas·tro·pod [gas′trə·pod′] *n.* Any of various mollusks, as a slug or snail, that characteristically have a single shell, usually spiral, that serves as protection, and a muscular footlike part on the underside of the belly that enables them to creep.
gas·tru·la [gas′trōō·lə] *n., pl.* **gas·tru·las** or **gas·tru·lae** [gas′trōō·lē] A stage in the development of an animal when the embryo is a hollow sac formed by two layers of cells.
gas·works [gas′wûrks′] *n.* A plant that manufactures gas for heating or lighting.
gat[1] [gat] A past tense of GET: seldom used today.
gat[2] [gat] *n. slang* A pistol.
gate [gāt] *n.* **1** A part of a fence or wall that opens and shuts like a door. **2** An opening in a fence or wall with a gate in it. **3** Something that controls a flow, as a valve or sluice. **4** The number of people who pay to attend a play, sporting event, or other public showing. **5** The total amount of money collected from these people.
-gate A combining form meaning: a government scandal, especially one involving a cover-up of covert acts: *Irangate, contragate.* ◆ From the *Watergate* scandal of the 1970's.
gate-crash·er [gāt′krash′ər] *n. slang* A person who attends a party without having been invited or who gains admittance to an event or performance without having purchased a ticket.
gate·house [gāt′hous′] *n., pl.* **gate·hous·es** [gāt′·hou′zəz] A small house over or next to a gate, used to shelter or house the gatekeeper.
gate·keep·er [gāt′kē′pər] *n.* A person who opens and closes or guards a gate.

gate·post [gāt′pōst′] *n.* The sturdy vertical post on which a gate is hung or the one to which it is fastened when closed.
gate·way [gāt′wā′] *n.* **1** An entrance or archway, often fitted with a gate. **2** A way of entering, exiting, or getting at: the *gateway* to wisdom.
gath·er [gath′ər] **1** *v.* To bring together or come together; collect; assemble: *Gather* your books; They *gathered* to celebrate. **2** *v.* To pick or harvest: to *gather* flowers. **3** *v.* To collect over a period of time; accumulate: The storm *gathered* force. **4** *v.* To draw (cloth) into folds. **5** *n.* A pleat or fold in cloth. **6** *v.* To draw as a conclusion: I *gather* that you're unhappy. **7** *v.* To swell and fill with pus: The boil *gathered.* **—gath′er·er** *n.*
gath·er·ing [gath′ər·ing] *n.* **1** The act of a person or thing that gathers or the things that are gathered; collection. **2** A meeting or assembly. **3** A boil or abscess.
Gat·ling gun [gat′ling] A machine gun having a cluster of barrels rotated by means of a hand crank, each barrel being fired in turn. ◆ The gun was named after its inventor, Richard J. Gatling.
gauche [gōsh] *adj.* Awkward or crude. **—gauche′ly** *adv.* **—gauche′ness** *n.*
gau·che·rie [gōsh′ə·rē] *n.* Action or speech that is gauche.
gau·cho [gou′chō] *n., pl.* **gau·chos** A cowhand of the South American pampas.
gaud·y [gô′dē] *adj.* **gaud·i·er, gaud·i·est** Showy or bright in a way that lacks taste. **—gaud′i·ly** *adv.* **—gaud′i·ness** *n.*
gauge [gāj] *v.* **gauged, gaug·ing,** *n.* **1** *v.* To make an accurate measurement of. **2** *n.* Any of various systems or standards for measuring. **3** *n.* A measurement made according to such a system or standard: the *gauge* of a wire. **4** *n.* Any of various instruments for measuring: a pressure *gauge.* **5** *n.* The distance between rails of a railway. **6** *v.* To estimate or judge: to *gauge* a person's character.

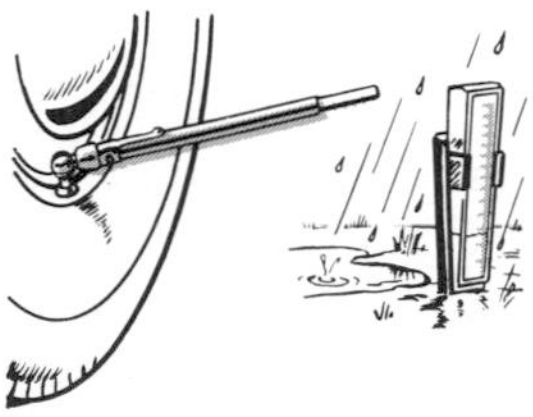
The tire gauge measures air pressure in the tire. The rain gauge measures rainfall.

Gaul [gôl] *n.* **1** A member of one of the Celtic tribes that inhabited Gaul. **2** A native of France.
Gaul·ish [gôl′ish] *n.* The language of the Gauls.
gaunt [gônt] *adj.* **1** Very thin and bony, as from illness or hunger; worn. **2** Gloomy and barren; desolate. **—gaunt′ly** *adv.* **—gaunt′ness** *n.*
gaunt·let[1] [gônt′lit] *n.* **1** A glove covered with metal plates, worn by knights as part of their armor. **2** A heavy glove with a long, wide cuff, flaring past the wrist. **—throw down the gauntlet** To challenge to fight.
gaunt·let[2] [gônt′lit] *n.* A punishment in which the victim runs between and is hit by two lines of people with clubs. **—run the gauntlet** **1** To run between and be hit by two lines of people with clubs. **2** To undergo an ordeal of any kind.
gauze [gôz] *n.* A thin, loosely-woven fabric.
gauz·y [gô′zē] *adj.* **gauz·i·er, gauz·i·est** **1** Of or like gauze. **2** Thin enough to be seen through. **—gauz′i·ly** *adv.* **—gauz′i·ness** *n.*
gave [gāv] Past tense of GIVE.
gav·el [gav′əl] *n.* A small, wooden mallet used by the person in charge of a meeting to call for attention or order.

Gavel

ga·votte [gə·vot′] *n.* A 17th-century French dance, like the minuet, but somewhat quicker.
Ga·wain [gä′win] *n.* One of the knights of the Round Table, nephew of King Arthur.
gawk [gôk] *informal.* **1** *v.* To stare stupidly; gape. **2** *n.* An awkward, stupid person.
gawk·y [gô′kē] *adj.* **gawk·i·er, gawk·i·est** Awkward or clumsy. **—gawk′i·ly** *adv.* **—gawk′i·ness** *n.*
gay [gā] *adj.* **1** Joyful; full of fun. **2** Colorful and bright: *gay* decorations. **—gay′ness** *n.*
gay·e·ty [gā′ə·tē] *n.* Another spelling of GAIETY.
gay·ly [gā′lē] *adv.* Another spelling of GAILY.
gaze [gāz] *v.* **gazed, gaz·ing,** *n.* **1** *v.* To look steadily; stare. **2** *n.* A steady or fixed look. **—gaz′er** *n.*
ga·ze·bo [gə·zē′bō *or* gə·zā′bō] *n., pl.* **ga·ze·bos** or **ga·ze·boes** An outdoor roofed structure, often having no sides, built in a scenic or attractively landscaped location.
ga·zelle [gə·zel′] *n.* A small, graceful antelope of Africa and Arabia with curved horns and large eyes.

Gazelle

ga·zette [gə·zet′] *n., v.* **ga·zet·ted, ga·zet·ting** **1** *n.* A newspaper: used mainly in the names of newspapers. **2** *n.* An official journal. **3** *v.* To publish or announce in a gazette.
gaz·et·teer [gaz′ə·tir′] *n.* A book or part of a dictionary naming and describing geographical features such as countries, mountains, and rivers.
gaz·pa·cho [gə·spä′chō *or* gəz·pä′chō] *n.* A chilled soup whose ingredients may include tomatoes, onions, cucumbers, green peppers, olive oil, bread crumbs, and garlic.
G.B. Great Britain.
G clef Another name for TREBLE CLEF.
Gd The symbol for the element gadolinium.
gds or **gds.** goods.
Ge The symbol for the element germanium.
gear [gir] **1** *n.* A toothed wheel that meshes with another such wheel. A smaller wheel turns faster than a larger one meshed with it. **2** *n.* One of several alternative systems of such wheels in an automobile, each delivering a range of speed and power: low *gear.* **3** *n.* A mechanism to do something: a steering *gear.* **4** *v.* To

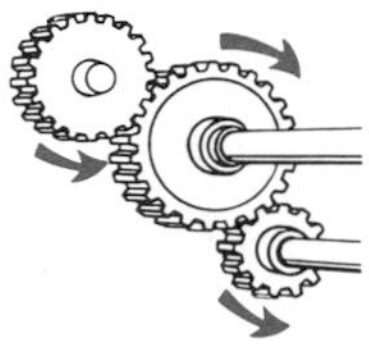
Gears

a	add	**i**	it	**o͝o**	took	**oi**	oil		
ā	ace	**ī**	ice	**o͞o**	pool	**ou**	pout		
â	care	**o**	odd	**u**	up	**ng**	ring		
ä	palm	**ō**	open	**û**	burn	**th**	thin		
e	end	**ô**	order	**yo͞o**	fuse	**th**	this		
ē	equal					**zh**	vision		

ə = { a in *above* e in *sicken* i in *possible*; o in *melon* u in *circus* }

G

connect (machine parts) by gears. **5** *v.* To adjust or regulate: to *gear* a plan to necessity. **6** *n.* Equipment for a special purpose: camping *gear.* **7** *v.* To provide with gear; equip. **—in gear** Connected, as to a motor. **—out of gear 1** Disconnected, as from a motor. **2** Unable to operate correctly; fouled.

gear·ing [gir′ing] *n.* Any system of gears or parts that transmits power or motion.

gear·shift [gir′shift′] *n.* A device that allows speed to be varied by the connection of different sets of gears.

gear·wheel [gir′(h)wēl′] *n.* A toothed wheel in a gear.

geck·o [gek′ō] *n., pl.* **geck·os** or **geck·oes** A small lizard having suction pads on its toes that enable it to walk on walls, ceilings, and other angled surfaces.

gee[1] [jē] *interj.* A command meaning "turn to the right," given to an ox or horse.

gee[2] [jē] *interj.* An exclamation of surprise, sympathy, or wonder.

gee[3] [jē] *n. slang* A thousand dollars: The computer cost two *gees.*

geese [gēs] Plural of GOOSE.

gee whiz *interj.* Gee[2].

gee·zer [gē′zər] *n. slang* An odd, queer, or eccentric old man.

Gei·ger counter [gī′gər] An instrument for detecting and measuring radioactivity.

gei·sha [gā′shə] *n., pl.* **gei·sha** or **gei·shas** A Japanese girl trained to entertain by singing and dancing.

gel·a·tin or **gel·a·tine** [jel′ə·tin] *n.* A protein obtained by boiling the bones, skins, and hooves of animals. It forms a jelly when mixed with hot water and cooled, and is used in foods and photographic films.

ge·lat·i·nous [ji·lat′ə·nəs] *adj.* Of or resembling gelatin or jelly.

geld [geld] *v.* **geld·ed** or **gelt, geld·ing** To castrate (an animal, especially a horse).

geld·ing [gel′ding] *n.* A castrated horse.

gelt[1] [gelt] An alternative past tense and past participle of GELD.

gelt[2] [gelt] *n. slang* Money.

gem [jem] *n., v.* **gemmed, gem·ming 1** *n.* A cut and polished precious or semiprecious stone; jewel. **2** *v.* To decorate or set with or as with gems. **3** *n.* A person or thing that is greatly admired or prized. **4** *n.* A kind of muffin.

Gem·i·ni [jem′ə·nī *or* jem′ə·nē] *n.* **1** A constellation in the Northern Hemisphere. **2** The third sign of the zodiac. **3** A person born under this sign.

gems·bok [gemz′bok′] *n.* An antelope of the dry areas of southern Africa with long, almost perfectly straight horns, prominent striping on the face and legs, and a long tail with a tuft at its end.

gem·stone [jem′stōn′] *n.* Any mineral or petrified substance that can be cut and polished and used to make jewelry.

gen. or **Gen.** general.

gen·darme [zhän′därm′] *n., pl.* **gen·darmes** [zhän′·därmz′] An armed police officer, especially in France.

gen·der [jen′dər] *n.* Any of the classes into which nouns, pronouns, and sometimes adjectives are divided. In English, *boy* and *he* are of the masculine gender, *girl* and *she* are of the feminine gender, *stone* and *it* are of the neuter gender, and *child* and *they* are of the common gender.

gene [jēn] *n.* A segment of chromosomal DNA governing the production of a specific protein.

ge·ne·a·log·i·cal [jē′nē·ə·loj′i·kəl] *adj.* Of or having to do with genealogy. **—ge′ne·a·log′i·cal·ly** *adv.*

ge·ne·al·o·gy [jē′nē·al′ə·jē *or* jē′nē·ol′ə·jē] *n., pl.* **ge·ne·al·o·gies 1** A record of the ancestors and descent of a person or family. **2** Direct descent from an ancestor or ancestors. **3** The study of family descent. **—ge′ne·al′o·gist** *n.*

gen·er·a [jen′ər·ə] Plural of GENUS.

gen·er·al [jen′ər·əl] **1** *adj.* Of, for, from, or having to do with everyone or with the whole: the *general* welfare; a *general* election. **2** *adj.* Common among the majority; prevalent: a *general* opinion. **3** *adj.* Not limited or specialized: a *general* principle. **4** *adj.* Not precise or detailed: a *general* idea. **5** *n.* Any of several military ranks higher than colonel. **—in general** On the whole; usually; commonly.

General Assembly 1 The main body of the United Nations, in which every member nation is represented. **2** The legislature in some states.

general delivery 1 The post office department that handles mail that is to be picked up by, rather than delivered to, the person to whom it is addressed. **2** Mail that is handled by this department.

gen·er·al·is·si·mo [jen′ər·ə·lis′ə·mō′] *n., pl.* **gen·er·al·is·si·mos** In certain countries, the military leader who commands all the armed forces.

gen·er·al·ist [jen′ər·ə·list] *n.* A person who has wide general knowledge in several different fields.

gen·er·al·i·ty [jen′ə·ral′ə·tē] *n., pl.* **gen·er·al·i·ties 1** The condition or quality of being general. **2** A general statement or idea. **3** The greater number; majority.

gen·er·al·i·za·tion [jen′ər·əl·ə·zā′shən] *n.* **1** The act of generalizing. **2** A general statement, rule, or principle.

gen·er·al·ize [jen′ər·əl·īz′] *v.* **gen·er·al·ized, gen·er·al·iz·ing 1** To make (as a statement, conclusion, or rule) general or more general. **2** To form (a general conclusion) from particular facts or data. **3** To make general statements in speaking or writing. **4** To bring into general use; make widespread.

gen·er·al·ly [jen′ər·əl·ē *or* jen′rəl·ē] *adv.* **1** Usually; ordinarily: We *generally* close at six. **2** Widely; commonly: The song became *generally* popular. **3** In a general way.

General of the Air Force An officer of the highest rank in the U.S. Air Force.

General of the Army An officer of the highest rank in the U.S. Army.

general practitioner A doctor who does not specialize in a particular branch of medicine.

gen·er·al·ship [jen′ər·əl·ship′] *n.* **1** The rank, authority, or term of office of a general. **2** The military skill of a general. **3** Leadership; skill in management.

general store A usually rural retail store that sells a variety of merchandise, including groceries, but is not divided into departments.

gen·er·ate [jen′ə·rāt′] *v.* **gen·er·at·ed, gen·er·at·ing** To produce or cause to be: to *generate* offspring; to *generate* electricity.

gen·er·a·tion [jen′ə·rā′shən] *n.* **1** The act or process of generating. **2** One step in the line of descent, as of human beings, animals, or plants. 3 The average time span between the birth of parents and the birth of their offspring. 4 Any group of people born at about the same time. 5 Any group of people of about the same age who share something in common, as ideas or life-style. 6 A stage in development, as of a product, usually marked by improvement over previous stages: a new *generation* of digital watches.

generation gap The difference in attitudes, values, and mores that sometimes exists between members of different generations, especially between teenagers and their parents.

gen·er·a·tive [jen'ə·rā'tiv] *adj.* 1 Of or having to do with generation. 2 Able to generate.

gen·er·a·tor [jen'ə·rā'tər] *n.* 1 A person or thing that generates. 2 A machine that changes mechanical energy to electricity.

ge·ner·ic [ji·ner'ik] *adj.* 1 Characteristic of or indicating a whole group, genus, or class: a *generic* trait. 2 General; not specific. 3 Not sold under a brand name or trademark: *Generic* products usually cost less than brand-name items. **—ge·ner'·i·cal·ly** *adv.*

gen·er·os·i·ty [jen'ə·ros'ə·tē] *n., pl.* **gen·er·os·i·ties** 1 The quality of being generous. 2 A generous act.

gen·er·ous [jen'ər·əs] *adj.* 1 Quick to give or share; unselfish. 2 Large or abundant. 3 Not mean or petty; kind. **—gen'er·ous·ly** *adv.*

gen·e·sis [jen'ə·sis] *n.* Origin; beginning.

Gen·e·sis [jen'ə·sis] *n.* The first book of the Old Testament, describing the creation of the world.

gene-splic·ing [jēn'splī'sing] *n.* The techniques, act, or process of separating bits of DNA from one organism and combining one or more of these bits with strands of DNA in a different organism.

ge·net·ic [jə·net'ik] *adj.* 1 Of or having to do with genetics. 2 Having to do with the origin or genesis of something. 3 Having to do with, consisting of, or caused by genes: a *genetic* defect. **—ge·net'i·cal·ly** *adv.*

genetic code The sequence of structural units in a molecule of DNA or RNA that determines the sequence in which amino acids are assembled to form specific proteins.

genetic engineering The application of the techniques of genetic research to practical uses, as in medicine and industry. An example is the manufacture of insulin by bacterial cells into which the human gene for insulin has been spliced. In medicine, certain hereditary defects may be corrected by replacing a defective gene.

ge·net·i·cist [jə·net'ə·sist] *n.* A person who specializes in the field of genetics.

ge·net·ics [jə·net'iks] *n.* The science that studies heredity and variation, and their causes, in organisms of the same or related kinds. ◆ See -ICS.

Geneva Convention The international agreement that established the rules governing wartime treatment of prisoners of war and of sick, wounded, and dead soldiers.

gen·ial [jēn'yəl] *adj.* 1 Friendly and kind; cheerful: a *genial* smile. 2 Giving warmth and comfort; helping life or growth: the *genial* rays of the sun. **—ge·ni·al·i·ty** [jē'nē·al'ə·tē] *n.* **—gen'ial·ly** *adv.*

gen·ic [jē'nik *or* jen'ik] *adj.* Another word for GENETIC (def. 3). **—gen'i·cal·ly** *adv.*

ge·nie [jē'nē] *n., pl.* **ge·nies** or **ge·ni·i** [jē'nē·ī] In Arabian stories, a supernatural being having great magical powers.

ge·ni·i [jē'nē·ī'] 1 The plural of GENIUS (defs. 4 and 6). 2 A plural of GENIE.

gen·i·tal [jen'ə·təl] *adj.* 1 Of or having to do with the sex organs. 2 Of or having to do with sexual reproduction.

gen·i·ta·li·a [jen'i·tāl'yə *or* jen'i·tā'lē·ə] *n.pl.* The genitals.

gen·i·tals [jen'ə·təlz] *n.pl.* The external sex organs.

gen·i·tive [jen'ə·tiv] 1 *adj.* In grammar, showing possession or origin; possessive. 2 *n.* The genitive case, or a word in the genitive case.

gen·ius [jēn'yəs] *n.* 1 *pl.* **gen·ius·es** An extremely high degree of mental power or talent. 2 *pl.* **gen·ius·es** A person who possesses such talent or mental power. 3 *pl.* **gen·ius·es** A special talent or knack: That salesperson has a *genius* for persuasion. 4 *pl.* **ge·ni·i** [jē'nē·ī] In Roman myths, a spirit that watched over a person or place. 5 *pl.* **gen·ius·es** The spirit, thought, or character of a people, place, or time. 6 *pl.* **ge·ni·i** A person who has great influence over another for good or evil.

genl. general.

gen·o·cide [jen'ə·sīd'] *n.* The extermination of an entire people or cultural or political group.

Gen·o·ese [jen'ō·ēz'] 1 *adj.* Of or from Genoa. 2 *n., pl.* **Gen·o·ese** A person born or living in Genoa.

gen·re [zhän'rə] *n.* 1 Type, kind, sort, or class: I felt ill at ease in conversations of that *genre.* 2 A category of literary, musical, or other artistic endeavor characterized by a particular style or subject matter. 3 A style of painting that realistically depicts intimate scenes from daily life: 17th-century Dutch *genre* painters.

gen·teel [jen·tēl'] *adj.* 1 Polite or well-bred; refined. 2 Making a pretence of elegance. **—gen·teel'ly** *adv.* **—gen·teel'ness** *n.*

gen·tian [jen'shən] *n.* A plant with showy, usually blue flowers.

Gen·tile [jen'tīl] 1 *n.* (*often written* **gentile**) A heathen; pagan. 2 *n.* A person who is not Jewish. 3 *adj.* Of, having to do with, or being a Gentile.

gen·til·i·ty [jen·til'ə·tē] *n.* 1 The condition of being wellborn. 2 Wellborn people as a group. 3 Refinement and good manners.

gen·tle [jen'təl] *adj.* **gen·tler, gen·tlest** 1 Quiet or kindly; mild: a *gentle* manner; a *gentle* nature. 2 Soft or mild: a *gentle* touch; a *gentle* voice. 3 Of or fit for a person of wealth and breeding. 4 Easily managed; tame: a *gentle* animal. 5 Not steep; gradual: a *gentle* slope. **—gen'tle·ness** *n.*

gen·tle·folk [jen'təl·fōk'] *n.pl.* People of good family and good breeding.

gen·tle·man [jen'təl·mən] *n., pl.* **gen·tle·men** [jen'təl·mən] 1 A man of high social standing. 2 A courteous, refined, and honorable man. 3 Any man: a polite term.

gen·tle·man·ly [jen'təl·mən·lē] *adj.* Of, like, or fit for a gentleman.

a	add	**i**	it	**o͝o**	took	**oi**	oil
ā	ace	**ī**	ice	**o͞o**	pool	**ou**	pout
â	care	**o**	odd	**u**	up	**ng**	ring
ä	palm	**ō**	open	**û**	burn	**th**	thin
e	end	**ô**	order	**yo͞o**	fuse	**t͟h**	this
ē	equal					**zh**	vision

ə = { a in *above* e in *sicken* i in *possible* / o in *melon* u in *circus* }

G

gentleman's agreement or **gentlemen's agreement** An agreement that has no force under law and is guaranteed only by the honor of the participants.
gen·tle·wom·an [jen′təl·wŏŏm′ən] *n., pl.* **gen·tle·wom·en** [jen′təl·wim′in] 1 A woman of high social standing. 2 A polite, refined woman; lady.
gen·tly [jen′tlē] *adv.* 1 In a gentle or mild way. 2 Gradually: a *gently* sloping hillside.
gen·tri·fi·ca·tion [jen′tri·fi·kā′shən] *n.* The restoration of run-down, urban, working-class neighborhoods, especially the renovation of housing by middle-class people.
gen·try [jen′trē] *n.* 1 People who are wellborn, but not of the nobility. 2 Persons of a particular area or profession.
gen·u·flect [jen′yə·flekt′] *v.* To bend one knee, as in worship. **—gen′u·flec′tion** *n.*
gen·u·ine [jen′yŏŏ·in] *adj.* 1 Being as it appears; not false: a *genuine* pearl. 2 Sincere; frank: *genuine* pity. **—gen′u·ine·ly** *adv.* **—gen′u·ine·ness** *n.*
ge·nus [jē′nəs] *n., pl.* **gen·e·ra** A group of closely related animals or plants, composed of one or more species.
geo- or **ge-** A combining form meaning: Earth or of the earth, as in *geophysics.*
ge·o·cen·tric [jē′ō·sen′trik] *adj.* 1 As seen or measured from the earth's center: *geocentric* distance. 2 Considering the earth the center of the universe: a *geocentric* theory.
ge·o·chem·is·try [jē′ō·kem′i·strē] *n.* The branch of chemistry concerned with the study of the composition of and changes in the crust of the earth. **—ge′o·chem′i·cal** *adj.* **—ge′o·chem′i·cal·ly** *adv.* **—ge′o·chem′ist** *n.*
ge·ode [jē′ōd′] *n.* A small hollow stone whose inside wall is lined with crystals.
ge·o·de·sic [jē′ə·de′sik *or* je′ə·dē′sik] 1 *n.* The shortest line connecting any two points on a surface, especially a curved surface. 2 *adj.* Of or having to do with these lines. 3 *adj.* Of or having to do with geodesy.
geodesic dome A hollow, domed structure supported by a framework made of lightweight, rigid, straight elements that are connected in a pattern of interlocking polygons.
ge·od·e·sy [jē·od′ə·sē] *n.* The science concerned with determining the size and shape of the earth and the variations in the earth's gravitational field.
geog. 1 geographer. 2 geographical. 3 geography.
ge·og·ra·pher [jē·og′rə·fər] *n.* A person who specializes in geography.
ge·o·graph·ic [jē′ə·graf′ik] *adj.* Geographical.
ge·o·graph·i·cal [jē′ə·graf′i·kəl] *adj.* Of or having to do with geography. **—ge′o·graph′i·cal·ly** *adv.*
geographical mile A measure of distance equal to about 6,076 feet.
ge·og·ra·phy [jē·og′rə·fē] *n.* 1 The study of the features of the earth's surface, sometimes also including its peoples, natural resources, and climates. 2 The natural features of a place.
geol. 1 geologic. 2 geological. 3 geologist. 4 geology.
ge·o·log·ic [jē′ə·loj′ik] *adj.* Geological.
ge·o·log·i·cal [jē′ə·loj′ə·kəl] *adj.* Of or having to do with geology. **—ge′o·log′i·cal·ly** *adv.*
ge·ol·o·gist [jē·ol′ə·jist] *n.* A person who specializes in geology.
ge·ol·o·gy [jē·ol′ə·jē] *n.* 1 The study of the origin, history, and structure of the earth, especially as recorded in rocks. 2 The structure of the earth's surface in a specific area. 3 The study of the history and composition of the solid matter of a celestial body. ◆ *Geology* comes from Greek words meaning *study of the earth.*
geom. 1 geometric. 2 geometrical. 3 geometrician. 4 geometry.
ge·o·met·ric [jē′ə·met′rik] *adj.* 1 Of or according to the principles of geometry. 2 Consisting of straight lines and simple curves: a *geometric* shape. **—ge′o·met′ri·cal·ly** *adv.*
ge·o·met·ri·cal [jē·ə·met′rə·kəl] *adj.* Geometric.
ge·om·e·tri·cian [jē·om′ə·trish′ən] *n.* A person who specializes in geometry.
geometric progression A sequence of terms in which every pair of consecutive terms is in the same ratio, as 2, 4, 8, and 16.
ge·om·e·try [jē·om′ə·trē] *n.* The branch of mathematics that studies the relations among points, lines, angles, surfaces, and solids.
ge·o·mor·phol·o·gy [jē′ō·môr·fol′ə·jē] *n.* The science concerned with the origin, development, and characteristics of the earth's surface. **—ge·o·mor·pho·log·ic** [jē′ō·môr′fə·loj′ik] *or* **ge′o·mor′pho·log′i·cal** *adj.* **—ge′o·mor′pho·log′i·cal·ly** *adv.* **—ge′o·mor·phol′o·gist** *n.*
ge·o·phys·i·cal [jē′ō·fiz′i·kəl] *adj.* Of or having to do with geophysics. **—ge′o·phys′i·cal·ly** *adv.*
ge·o·phys·ics [jē′ō·fiz′iks] *n.pl.* The study of the physics of the earth, including its magnetism, volcanoes, and movements of air and water. **—ge′o·phys′i·cist** *n.* ◆ See -ICS.
Geor·gian [jôr′jən] 1 *adj.* Of or from Georgia. 2 *n.* A person born in or living in Georgia. 3 *n.* The language of the Soviet republic of Georgia. 4 *adj.* Of or having to do with the reigns of the first four King Georges of Great Britain, 1714–1830, or with that of George V, 1910–1936.
ge·o·ther·mal [jē′ō·thûr′məl] *adj.* Of, having to do with, or produced by the earth's internal heat.
ge·o·ther·mic [jē′ō·thûr′mik] *adj.* Geothermal.
ge·ot·ro·pism [jē·ot′rə·piz′əm] *n.* A reaction in response to gravity, especially by a plant.
Ger. 1 German. 2 Germany.
ge·ra·ni·um [ji·rā′nē·əm] *n.* 1 A plant with showy pink, scarlet, or white flowers. 2 A plant related to it, having pink or purple flowers.
ger·bil [jûr′bil] *n.* A small, furry rodent having long hind legs and short forelegs, popular as a pet.
ger·fal·con [jûr′fal′kən *or* jûr′fôl′kən] *n.* Another spelling of GYRFALCON.
ger·i·at·rics [jer′ē·at′riks] *n.pl.* The branch of medicine dealing with old people and their diseases. ◆ See -ICS.
germ [jûrm] *n.* 1 A microscopic animal or plant that can cause disease; microbe, especially one of the bacteria that cause disease. 2 Something, as a seed or bud, that will develop into a plant or animal. 3 Something in its beginning form: the *germ* of an idea.
Ger·man [jûr′mən] 1 *adj.* Of or from Germany. 2 *n.* A person born in or a citizen of Germany. 3 *n.* The Germanic language of Germany, Austria, and part of Switzerland.
ger·mane [jər·mān′] *adj.* Having to do with what is being discussed or considered; pertinent.
Ger·man·ic [jər·man′ik] *adj.* 1 Of or having to do with a large group of people of northern and central Europe, as the Germans, Dutch, Flemings, Scandinavians, Swiss of German descent, and the

English. **2** Of or having to do with the languages these people speak. **3** Of Germany or the people of Germany.

ger·ma·ni·um [jər·mā′nē·əm] *n.* A grayish white metallic element which is used in electronics, metallurgy, and optics.

German measles A contagious disease marked by fever, sore throat, and a skin rash.

German shepherd A breed of dog with a large, strong body, thick, smooth coat, and high intelligence, often used as a guide for the blind.

German silver Another term for NICKEL SILVER.

germ cell **1** A fully developed reproductive cell; ovum or sperm; gamete. **2** One of the antecedent cells from which a gamete develops.

germ·free [jûrm′frē′] *adj.* Free of microorganisms; aseptic.

ger·mi·cide [jûr′mə·sīd′] *n.* Something used to kill germs. **—ger·mi·ci·dal** [jûr′mə·sī′dəl] *adj.*

ger·mi·nate [jûr′mə·nāt′] *v.* **ger·mi·nat·ed, ger·mi·nat·ing** **1** To sprout or cause to sprout: Seeds *germinate* in warm weather. **2** To develop or evolve, as an idea. **—ger′mi·na′tion** *n.*

germ plasm That part of the bodily substance of an organism that is exclusively involved in reproduction.

germ warfare The use of disease-causing microorganisms as weapons of war.

ger·ry·man·der [jer′i·man′dər] **1** *v.* To alter (a voting area) so as to give an unfair advantage to one political party. **2** *n.* The act or result of gerrymandering.

ger·und [jer′ənd] *n.* A form of a verb, ending in *-ing,* that is used as a noun. In "Playing baseball is fun" *playing* is a gerund.

Ge·sta·po [gə·stä′pō *or* gə·shtä′pō] *n.* The secret police in Germany under the Nazis.

ges·ta·tion [jes·tā′shən] *n.* **1** A carrying of the unborn young in the womb; pregnancy: The period of *gestation* for elephants is about 20 months. **2** The development of an idea in the mind.

ges·tic·u·late [jes·tik′yə·lāt′] *v.* **ges·tic·u·lat·ed, ges·tic·u·lat·ing** To make emphatic or expressive gestures. **—ges·tic′u·la′tion** *n.*

ges·ture [jes′chər] *n., v.* **ges·tured, ges·tur·ing** **1** *n.* A motion of the hands, head, or other part of the body expressing or emphasizing some feeling or idea. **2** *v.* To make gestures. **3** *n.* Something done, offered, or said as a formality, courtesy, or for effect: a polite *gesture.*

Ge·sund·heit [gə·zo͝ont′hīt′] *interj.* A German expression used to wish good health, especially to a person who has just sneezed.

get [get] *v.* **got, got** or *U.S.* **got·ten, get·ting** **1** To obtain: to *get* money. **2** To go for and bring back: Please *get* my hat. **3** To arrive: When does the train *get* here? **4** To carry away; take: *Get* this out of the house! **5** To make ready; prepare: to *get* lunch. **6** To cause to be: to *get* the work done. **7** To prevail on; persuade: *Get* the guitarist to play for us. **8** To receive (reward or punishment): to *get* a whipping. **9** To learn, master, or understand: to *get* a lesson. **10** To be or become: to *get* rich. **11** To become sick with: to *get* a cold. **12** To communicate with: I'll *get* the operator on the phone. **13** *informal* To possess: He has *got* quite a temper. **14** *informal* To be obliged or forced: I have *got* to go home. **15** *informal* To strike, hit, or kill: That shot *got* the target. **16** *slang* To puzzle; baffle: The remark *got* me. **17** *slang* To notice; observe: *Get* the new bike! **—get along** **1** To leave; go. **2** To manage or be successful, as in business. **3** To be friendly or compatible. **—get away with** *slang* To do (something) without being caught, criticized, or punished. **—get behind** To support (a person or cause). **—get by** **1** To pass. **2** *informal* To manage to survive or succeed. **—get off** **1** To descend from; come off. **2** To depart. **3** To be relieved or freed, as of a duty. **4** To escape or help to escape, as from a sentence or punishment. **5** To take off; remove. **—get on** **1** To go onto or into. **2** To get along. **3** To put on. **4** To grow older. **5** To upset. **6** To proceed. **—get out** **1** To depart or leave. **2** To escape. **3** To become known, as a secret. **4** To publish. **5** To express or utter with difficulty. **6** To take out. **—get over** **1** To recover from. **2** To get across. **—get up** **1** To rise, as from sleep or from a sitting position. **2** To mount; climb. **3** To plan or organize.

get·a·way [get′ə·wā′] *n.* **1** An escape, as by a criminal. **2** A start, as in a race.

Geth·sem·a·ne [geth·sem′ə·nē] *n.* A garden near Jerusalem where Jesus began his sufferings and was betrayed and arrested.

get-to·geth·er [get′tə·geth′ər] *n. informal* A small social gathering; informal, casual party.

get-up [get′up′] *n. informal* **1** Dress; costume: an actor's *get-up.* **2** Appearance or style.

get-up-and-go [get′up′ən·gō′] *n. informal* Energy and drive.

gew·gaw [gyo͞o′gô′] *n.* A showy, usually worthless trinket or bauble.

gey·ser [gī′zər] *n.* A natural spring which at intervals sends up a fountain of hot water, steam, or mud.

A geyser

Gha·na·ian [gä·nā′ən] or **Gha·ni·an** [gä′nē·ən] **1** *adj.* Of or from Ghana. **2** *n.* A person born in or a citizen of Ghana.

ghast·ly [gast′lē] *adj.* **ghast·li·er, ghast·li·est** **1** Horrible; terrifying. **2** Deathlike in appearance; pale; wan. **3** *informal* Very bad or unpleasant: a truly *ghastly* book. **—ghast′li·ness** *n.*

gher·kin [gûr′kin] *n.* A very small cucumber used for pickling.

ghet·to [get′ō] *n., pl.* **ghet·tos** **1** The section of some cities or towns where, in former times, Jews were forced to live. **2** Any section of a city or town crowded with a minority group or the very poor.

ghost [gōst] *n.* **1** The spirit of a dead person that supposedly appears to the living. **2** A mere trace or suggestion: the *ghost* of a smile.

ghost·ly [gōst′lē] *adj.* **ghost·li·er, ghost·li·est** Of, having to do with, or like a ghost. **—ghost′li·ness** *n.*

ghost town A deserted town, especially an abandoned mining town in the West.

ghost·writ·er [gōst′rī′tər] *n.* A person who writes

a	add	**i**	it	**o͝o**	took	**oi**	oil
ā	ace	**ī**	ice	**o͞o**	pool	**ou**	pout
â	care	**o**	odd	**u**	up	**ng**	ring
ä	palm	**ō**	open	**û**	burn	**th**	thin
e	end	**ô**	order	**yo͞o**	fuse	**t̶h̶**	this
ē	equal					**zh**	vision

ə = { a in *above* e in *sicken* i in *possible* o in *melon* u in *circus* }

material, as articles or speeches, for other people who take credit for the writing.

ghoul [gōōl] *n.* **1** In Muslim legend, an evil spirit who robs graves and eats corpses. **2** A person who robs graves. **3** A person who enjoys disgusting or horrible things. **—ghoul'ish** *adj.* **—ghoul'·ish·ly** *adv.* **—ghoul'ish·ness** *n.*

gi or **gi.** gill(s).

GI [jē'ī'] *n., pl.* **GI's** or **GIs** *adj. informal* **1** *n.* An enlisted member of the U.S. Army. **2** *adj.* Of or issued by the U.S. Army: *GI* rations.

gi·ant [jī'ənt] **1** *n.* An imaginary being in human form but a great deal larger and more powerful than a real person. **2** *n.* Any person, animal, or thing of great size, strength, intelligence or ability. **3** *adj.* Huge or great.

giant panda A panda (def. 2).

giant sequoia Another name for BIG TREE.

giant star A star of great brightness and mass.

gib·ber [jib'ər] **1** *v.* To jabber rapidly and apparently without meaning, as monkeys do. **2** *n.* Gibberish.

gib·ber·ish [jib'ər·ish] *n.* Rapid and senseless talk or chatter.

gib·bet [jib'it] *n., v.* **gib·bet·ed** or **gib·bet·ted, gib·bet·ing** or **gib·bet·ting** **1** *n.* An upright post with a projecting arm at the top, formerly used to hang criminals or to display them after being executed, as a warning to others. **2** *v.* To hang or execute on a gibbet.

gib·bon [gib'ən] *n.* A slender, long-armed ape of SE Asia and the East Indies, that lives in trees.

Gibbon

gib·bous [gib'əs *or* jib'əs] *adj.* Having a nearly circular form, as the moon when it is more than half full but less than full.

gibe [jīb] *v.* **gibed, gib·ing,** *n.* **1** *v.* To make jeering remarks; scoff. **2** *n.* A sneering remark; jeer.

gib·let [jib'lit] *n.* (*usually pl.*) Any of the parts of a fowl that are usually cooked separately, as the heart, liver, or gizzard.

gid·dy [gid'ē] *adj.* **gid·di·er, gid·di·est** **1** Dizzy. **2** Causing or tending to cause dizziness: a *giddy* height. **3** Frivolous; flighty: silly. **—gid'di·ly** *adv.* **—gid'di·ness** *n.*

gift [gift] *n.* **1** Something that is given; present. **2** A natural ability; talent: a *gift* for music.

gift·ed [gif'tid] *adj.* Very talented.

gig[1] [gig] *n., v.* **gigged, gig·ging** **1** *n.* A light, open, two-wheeled carriage drawn by a single horse. **2** *n.* A small boat used by a captain to get to and from the ship. **3** *v.* To ride or travel in a gig.

gig[2] [gig] *n., v.* **gigged, gig·ging** **1** *n.* A lightweight, pronged spear for fishing. **2** *n.* An arrangement of hooks that is dragged through a school of fish. It catches fish by hooking them through their bodies. **3** *v.* To fish with a gig.

giga- A combining form meaning: Billion, as in *gigahertz.*

gi·ga·hertz [jig'ə·hûrts' *or* gig'ə·hûrts'] *n.* A unit of frequency equal to one billion hertz.

gi·gan·tic [jī·gan'tik] *adj.* Like a giant; huge; mighty; powerful.

gig·gle [gig'əl] *v.* **gig·gled, gig·gling,** *n.* **1** *v.* To laugh in a silly or nervous manner with high fluttering sounds. **2** *n.* Such a laugh. **—gig'gler** *n.*

Gi·la monster [hē'lə] A large, poisonous lizard of the SW U.S. and northern Mexico. It is covered with black and orange scales.

Gila monster

gild[1] [gild] *v.* **gild·ed** or **gilt, gild·ing** **1** To cover or coat with a thin layer of gold. **2** To brighten or adorn. **3** To make (something) seem better or more pleasing than it is.

gild[2] [gild] *n.* Another spelling of GUILD.

gill[1] [gil] *n.* **1** An organ for obtaining oxygen in fishes and other animals that live in water. Oxygen is removed from the water that passes through the gills, and carbon dioxide is discharged. **2** One of the many thin, radiating, platelike structures on the underside of the cap of a mushroom.

gill[2] [jil] *n.* A liquid measure equal to $\frac{1}{4}$ pint, or half a cup.

gilt [gilt] **1** Alternative past tense and past participle of GILD. **2** *n.* Gold or a gold-colored material used in gilding. **3** *adj.* Covered with gilt; gilded.

gim·crack [jim'krak'] **1** *n.* A useless, gaudy object; knickknack. **2** *adj.* Cheap and gaudy.

gim·let [gim'lit] **1** *n.* A small, sharp tool with a handle at one end and a pointed spiral tip at the other for boring holes. **2** *adj.* Sharp and piercing: a *gimlet* stare.

gim·mick [gim'ik] *n.* **1** A clever attention-getting innovation, device, or stratagem, especially to promote a product or project: an advertising *gimmick.* **2** Any small object or device; gadget.

gimp [gimp] *n.* **1** A person who is lame or crippled. **2** A limp. **—gimp'y** *adj.*

gin[1] [jin] *n.* A strong alcoholic drink, flavored usually with juniper berries.

gin[2] [jin] *n., v.* **ginned, gin·ning** **1** *n.* Another name for COTTON GIN. **2** *v.* To remove the seeds from (cotton) in a gin.

gin[3] [jin] *n.* Another name for GIN RUMMY.

gin·ger [jin'jər] *n.* **1** A spice made from the root of a tropical plant. Ginger is used in cooking and in medicine. **2** This root. **3** This plant. **4** *informal* Liveliness; pep.

ginger ale A bubbly soft drink flavored with ginger.

ginger beer A carbonated soft drink that is very strongly flavored with ginger.

gin·ger·bread [jin'jər·bred'] *n.* **1** A dark ginger-flavored cake sweetened with molasses, often cut into fancy shapes. **2** Gaudy decoration, as showy carving on furniture.

gin·ger·ly [jin'jər·lē] **1** *adj.* In a cautious, careful, or reluctant manner: to step *gingerly* around the broken pavement. **2** *adj.* Cautious; careful: *gingerly* movements.

gin·ger·snap [jin'jər·snap'] *n.* A small, flat, brittle cookie flavored with ginger and molasses.

ging·ham [ging'əm] *n.* A cotton fabric woven in solid colors, stripes, checks, or plaids. ◆ *Gingham* goes back to a Malay word meaning *striped.*

gin·gi·vi·tis [jin'jə·vī'tis] *n.* Inflammation of the gums.

gink·go [ging'kō *or* jing'kō] *n., pl.* **gink·goes** A large tree with fan-shaped leaves native to China and grown in the U.S.

gin rummy A variation of rummy in which a person can win a hand by matching all his or her cards or by melding with less than 10 points' worth of unmatched cards in her or his hand.

gin·seng [jin′seng′] *n.* 1 A plant native to China and North America, from whose root a bitter medicine is made by the Chinese. 2 This root. 3 The medicine made from it.

gip·sy [jip′sē] *n., pl.* **gip·sies** Another spelling of GYPSY.

gipsy moth Another spelling of GYPSY MOTH.

gi·raffe [jə·raf′] *n.* An African animal that chews its cud. The tallest of all animals living today, it has a very long neck, long slender legs, and a spotted skin.

Giraffe

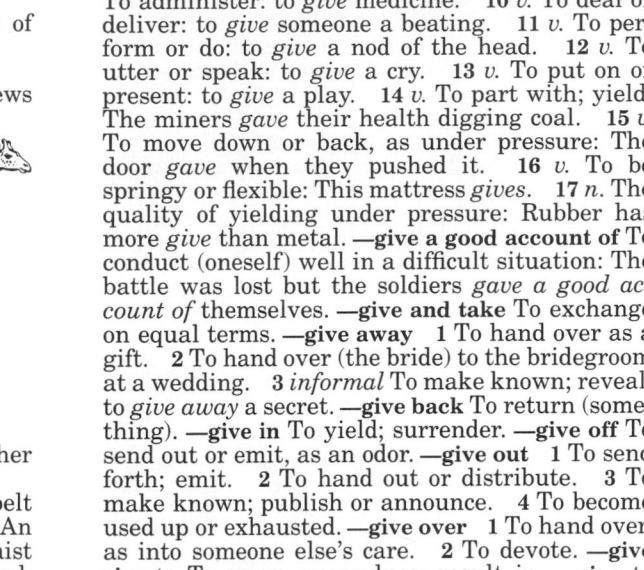

gird [gûrd] *v.* **gird·ed** or **girt, gird·ing** 1 To surround or fasten, as with a belt or girdle. 2 To encircle; surround: Trees *girded* the fields. 3 To get ready for action: The players *girded* themselves for the contest.

gir·der [gûr′dər] *n.* A long heavy beam, as of steel or wood, that acts as a horizontal support for the framework of a bridge, building, or other structure.

gir·dle [gûr′dəl] *n., v.* **gir·dled, gir·dling** 1 *n.* A belt or cord worn around the waist; sash. 2 *n.* An elastic corset worn to support and shape the waist and hips. 3 *v.* To fasten a girdle or belt around: to *girdle* the waist. 4 *n.* Something that encircles like a belt. 5 *v.* To encircle; surround.

girl [gûrl] *n.* 1 A female baby or child. 2 A young unmarried woman. 3 *informal* A sweetheart. 4 *informal* Any woman. 5 A female servant.

girl Friday *informal* A female assistant, usually in an office, who performs a wide variety of jobs and has a number of different responsibilities.

girl·friend [gûrl′frend′] *n.* 1 A female friend. 2 A female with whom one has a romantic relationship; sweetheart.

girl guide A member of the Girl Guides.

Girl Guides A British organization like the Girl Scouts, founded in 1910.

girl·hood [gûrl′ho͝od′] *n.* 1 The condition or time of being a girl. 2 Girls as a group.

girl·ish [gûr′lish] *adj.* Of, like, or proper for a girl. **—girl′ish·ly** *adv.* **—girl′ish·ness** *n.*

girl scout A member of the Girl Scouts.

Girl Scouts An organization founded in the U.S. in 1912 for girls between 7 and 17. Its purpose is to develop character, health, and practical skills.

girt [gûrt] An alternative past tense and past participle of GIRD.

girth [gûrth] 1 *n.* The circumference of anything: the *girth* of a tree. 2 *v.* To measure in girth. 3 *n.* A band or strap around a horse or other animal to hold something, as a saddle or pack, in place. 4 *v.* To bind with a girth. 5 *n.* A girdle or band. 6 *v.* To encircle; girdle.

gis·mo [giz′mō] *n., pl.* **gis·mos** *slang* Another spelling of GIZMO.

gist [jist] *n.* The main idea or substance of an argument, question, or the like.

give [giv] *v.* **gave, giv·en, giv·ing,** *n.* 1 *v.* To hand over freely as a gift or present: I *gave* a jigsaw puzzle to my cousin. 2 *v.* To make donations; make free gifts: to *give* to a charity. 3 *v.* To hand over in exchange for something: I'll *give* you a quarter for this pen. 4 *v.* To hand over freely for a time: *Give* me your newspaper to read. 5 *v.* To put into the grasp of another: *Give* me your hand. 6 *v.* To make available; offer: to *give* help and advice. 7 *v.* To be a source of; yield: Fire *gives* warmth. 8 *v.* To grant: to *give* permission. 9 *v.* To administer: to *give* medicine. 10 *v.* To deal or deliver: to *give* someone a beating. 11 *v.* To perform or do: to *give* a nod of the head. 12 *v.* To utter or speak: to *give* a cry. 13 *v.* To put on or present: to *give* a play. 14 *v.* To part with; yield: The miners *gave* their health digging coal. 15 *v.* To move down or back, as under pressure: The door *gave* when they pushed it. 16 *v.* To be springy or flexible: This mattress *gives.* 17 *n.* The quality of yielding under pressure: Rubber has more *give* than metal. **—give a good account of** To conduct (oneself) well in a difficult situation: The battle was lost but the soldiers *gave a good account of* themselves. **—give and take** To exchange on equal terms. **—give away** 1 To hand over as a gift. 2 To hand over (the bride) to the bridegroom at a wedding. 3 *informal* To make known; reveal: to *give away* a secret. **—give back** To return (something). **—give in** To yield; surrender. **—give off** To send out or emit, as an odor. **—give out** 1 To send forth; emit. 2 To hand out or distribute. 3 To make known; publish or announce. 4 To become used up or exhausted. **—give over** 1 To hand over, as into someone else's care. 2 To devote. **—give rise to** To cause or produce; result in. **—give to understand** To cause to understand or know. **—give up** 1 To yield; surrender. 2 To stop; cease. 3 To stop trying. 4 To lose all hope for. 5 To devote completely: to *give* oneself *up* to art. **—give way** 1 To yield or collapse under pressure. 2 To draw back. **—giv′er** *n.*

give-and-take [giv′ən·tāk′] *n.* A smooth, good-natured exchange, as of ideas or talk.

give·a·way [giv′ə·wā′] *n. informal* 1 Something that one tells, as a secret or clue, usually without meaning to. 2 Something given for nothing or for a very low price.

giv·en [giv′ən] 1 The past participle of GIVE. 2 *adj.* Inclined; disposed: I am *given* to taking short naps. 3 *adj.* Stated; specified: a *given* date or address.

given name A name given to a child in addition to the family name; the first name, as *Ralph* in *Ralph Johnson.*

giz·mo [giz′mō] *n., pl.* **giz·mos** *slang* Any device or item, especially a mechanical one, whose name a person does not know or does not remember.

giz·zard [giz′ərd] *n.* A second stomach in birds, where the food is ground to bits.

Gk. Greek.

gla·cial [glā′shəl] *adj.* 1 Of, having to do with, or marked by the presence of ice or glaciers. 2 Icy; cold; frigid: a *glacial* stare. **—gla′cial·ly** *adv.*

a	add	**i**	it	**o͝o**	took	**oi**	oil
ā	ace	**ī**	ice	**o͞o**	pool	**ou**	pout
â	care	**o**	odd	**u**	up	**ng**	ring
ä	palm	**ō**	open	**û**	burn	**th**	thin
e	end	**ô**	order	**yo͞o**	fuse	**th**	this
ē	equal					**zh**	vision

ə = a in *above*, e in *sicken*, i in *possible*, o in *melon*, u in *circus*

G

glacial epoch Another term for ICE AGE (def. 1).
gla·cier [glā′shər] *n.* A large mass or field of ice that moves very slowly down a mountain valley or across land until it either melts or breaks off in the sea to form icebergs.
glad [glad] *adj.* **glad·der, glad·dest** 1 Having a feeling of joy or pleasure. 2 Giving joy or happiness: *glad* tidings. 3 Bright and cheerful: a *glad* face. 4 More than willing: I'm *glad* to do it. **—glad′ly** *adv.* **—glad′ness** *n.*
glad·den [glad′(ə)n] *v.* To make glad.
glade [glād] *n.* An open place in a forest.
glad-hand [glad′hand′] *v.* 1 To extend a glad hand to: a candidate for the senate *glad-handing* her staff. 2 To extend a glad hand: a sales manager *glad-handing* all day at a convention.
glad hand A greeting or welcome, often effusive or insincere.
glad·i·a·tor [glad′ē·ā′tər] *n.* 1 In ancient Rome, a slave, captive, or paid freeman who fought other men or wild animals with weapons as public entertainment. 2 A person who takes part in any kind of struggle.

Gladiators

glad·i·o·lus [glad′ē·ō′ləs] *n., pl.* **glad·i·o·lus·es** or **glad·i·o·li** [glad′ē·ō′lī] A plant related to the iris, having sword-shaped leaves and spikes of colored flowers.
glad·some [glad′səm] *adj.* Giving or showing joy or pleasure. **—glad′some·ly** *adv.* **—glad′some·ness** *n.*
glam·or [glam′ər] *n. U.S.* Another spelling of GLAMOUR.
glam·or·ize [glam′ər·īz′] *v.* **glam·or·ized, glam·or·iz·ing** To make glamorous.
glam·or·ous [glam′ər·əs] *adj.* Full of glamour: a *glamorous* style. **—glam′or·ous·ly** *adv.* **—glam′or·ous·ness** *n.*
glam·our [glam′ər] *n.* A charm, beauty, or fascination: the *glamour* of Paris; the *glamour* of a movie star.
glance [glans] *v.* **glanced, glanc·ing,** *n.* 1 *v.* To take a quick look: to *glance* around; to *glance* at a building. 2 *n.* A quick look. 3 *v.* To strike slantwise and go off at an angle: Bullets *glanced* off the wall. 4 *n.* A grazing hit and slanting off. 5 *v.* To flash; glint: The water *glanced* in the sun. 6 *n.* A flash or glint.
gland [gland] *n.* Any of several organs of the body that have to do with the production, storage, or secretion of certain substances, either for elimination as waste or for use elsewhere in the body. The liver, pancreas, thyroid, and adrenals are glands.
glan·du·lar [glan′jə·lər] *adj.* Of, like, or affecting a gland or glands.
glare [glâr] *n., v.* **glared, glar·ing** 1 *n.* A bright, blinding light. 2 *v.* To give off such a light. 3 *n.* An angry, hostile stare. 4 *v.* To stare in anger or hostility.
glar·ing [glâr′ing] *adj.* 1 Shining with a glare. 2 Staring with anger or hostility. 3 Showy; gaudy: a *glaring* array of colors. 4 Plainly or unpleasantly conspicuous: a *glaring* mistake. **—glar′ing·ly** *adv.*
glar·y [glâr′ē] *adj.* **glar·i·er, glar·i·est** Harshly bright.
glass [glas] 1 *n.* A hard substance that breaks easily and is usually transparent. Glass is made by melting together sand and other materials, as soda and lime, and then rapidly cooling them. 2 *adj. use:* a *glass* door; a *glass* jar. 3 *n.* Something made of glass, such as a container for drinking, a mirror, or a lens. 4 *n.* (*pl.*) A pair of eyeglasses; spectacles. 5 *n.* The amount a drinking glass holds: a *glass* of water. 6 *v.* To cover or enclose with glass: Last summer we *glassed* in our porch.
glass blowing The technique or art of forming a mass of molten glass into an object by blowing air into it through a tube.
glass·ful [glas′fo͝ol′] *n., pl.* **glass·fuls** The amount a drinking glass holds.
glass·ine [gla·sēn′] *n.* A thin, tough, glazed paper that is transparent or nearly so and is used to make such things as envelope windows and book jackets.
glass snake A limbless, snakelike lizard having a fragile tail that easily breaks off.
glass·ware [glas′wâr′] *n.* Articles made of glass.
glass·y [glas′ē] *adj.* **glass·i·er, glass·i·est** 1 Like glass; clear, shiny, and brittle. 2 Fixed, blank, and lifeless: a *glassy* stare. **—glass′i·ly** *adv.* **—glass′i·ness** *n.*
glau·co·ma [glou·kō′mə *or* glô·kō′mə] *n.* A disease of the eye in which there is increased pressure within and hardening of the eyeball. It can result in partial or total loss of vision.
glaze [glāz] *v.* **glazed, glaz·ing,** *n.* 1 *v.* To fit or cover with glass: to *glaze* a window. 2 *v.* To coat with a glassy surface: to *glaze* pottery. 3 *n.* A glassy surface or coating, or a substance used to produce such a surface or coating. 4 *v.* To make or become covered with or as if with a thin coating or film: His eyes *glazed* with pain. 5 *v.* To cover (food) with a thin coating, as of syrup. 6 *n.* A substance used to coat foods, as syrup or egg white.
gla·zier [glā′zhər] *n.* A person whose job is to put glass in windows or doors.
gleam [glēm] 1 *n.* A ray or beam of light that is faint or that shines for only a short time. 2 *n.* The shine of reflected light upon a surface. 3 *v.* To shine with a gleam. 4 *n.* A faint trace: a *gleam* of hope.
glean [glēn] *v.* 1 To gather (grain) left in a field after it has been reaped: to *glean* corn. 2 To collect (as facts) by patient effort. **—glean′er** *n.*
glean·ings [glē′ningz] *n.pl.* Things that are gleaned: the *gleanings* of research scientists.
glee [glē] *n.* 1 Joy or merriment. 2 A song for three or more voices, usually unaccompanied.
glee club A group organized to sing songs.
glee·ful [glē′fəl] *adj.* Full of glee; mirthful; joyous; merry. **—glee′ful·ly** *adv.* **—glee′ful·ness** *n.*
glen [glen] *n.* A small secluded valley.
Glen·gar·ry [glen·gar′ē] *n., pl.* **Glen·gar·ries** A wool cap worn in Scotland, having straight sides, a creased crown, and often short streamers at the back.
glib [glib] *adj.* **glib·ber, glib·best** Speaking or spoken easily but without much thought or sincerity: a *glib* person; a *glib* answer. **—glib′ly** *adv.* **—glib′·ness** *n.*
glide [glīd] *v.* **glid·ed, glid·ing,** *n.* 1 *v.* To move smoothly and without effort. 2 *v.* To pass quietly and unnoticed, as time. 3 *v.* To move in a downward slant without using power, as an airplane. 4 *n.* A gliding movement. ◆ *Glide* comes from the Old English word *glīdan.*

glid·er [glī′dər] *n.* 1 A person or thing that glides. 2 A light aircraft like an airplane but without an engine. It is kept aloft by air currents. 3 A swing made of a seat hung in a metal frame so it can glide back and forth.

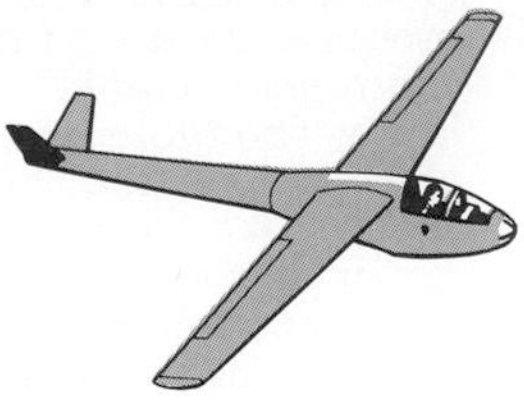
Glider

glim·mer [glim′ər] 1 *v.* To shine with a faint, unsteady light. 2 *n.* A faint, unsteady light. 3 *n.* A faint hint or trace: a *glimmer* of hope.
glimpse [glimps] *n., v.* **glimpsed, glimps·ing** 1 *n.* A momentary view or look. 2 *v.* To see for a moment: to *glimpse* someone in a passing car. 3 *v.* To look for an instant: to *glimpse* at a picture. 4 *n.* A faint hint; inkling.
glint [glint] 1 *n.* A gleam; flash. 2 *v.* To gleam or flash; glitter.
glis·san·do [gli·sän′dō] *n., pl.* **glis·san·di** [gli·sän′dē] or **glis·san·dos** A sliding effect, as that made by running a finger across a group of piano keys.
glis·ten [glis′(ə)n] 1 *v.* To shine or sparkle, as with reflected light. 2 *n.* A shine; sparkle.
glitch [glich], *n.* 1 A malfunction, as of a computer or other machine. 2 A surge of electricity that causes any kind of a machine to malfunction. 3 *informal* Any minor problem, especially one that causes a delay.
glit·ter [glit′ər] 1 *v.* To sparkle brightly, as a diamond. 2 *n.* A bright or brilliant sparkle. 3 *v.* To be showy, attractive, or outstanding. 4 *n.* Showiness; brilliance. **—glit′ter·y** *adj.*
glitz [glits] *n. slang* Excessive gaudiness or flashiness. **—glitz·y** *adj.*
gloam·ing [glō′ming] *n.* Twilight; dusk.
gloat [glōt] *v.* To think about with an intense, often malicious or evil delight: to *gloat* over someone else's misfortune. **—gloat′er** *n.*
glob [glob] *n.* 1 A globule. 2 A usually rounded and large lump or mass: a *glob* of ice cream.
glob·al [glō′bəl] *adj.* 1 Of or having to do with the whole world or a large part of it: a *global* war. 2 Shaped like a globe; spherical. **—glob′al·ly** *adv.*
globe [glōb] *n.* 1 A sphere; ball. 2 Something having a shape like this. 3 The earth. 4 A sphere on which is drawn a map of the earth or the heavens.
globe·trot·ter [glōb′trot′ər] *n.* A person who travels to many faraway places. **—globe′trot′ting** *n.*
glo·bose [glō′bōs′] *adj.* In the shape of a globe; spherical; globular.
glob·u·lar [glob′yə·lər] *adj.* 1 Shaped like a globe; round; spherical. 2 Made up of globules.
glob·ule [glob′yo͞ol] *n.* A tiny sphere of matter or drop of liquid.
glock·en·spiel [glok′ən·spēl′] *n.* A musical instrument made up of a series of metal bars in a frame, each sounding a different note when struck with a small, light hammer.
gloom [glo͞om] 1 *n.* Partial or total darkness; heavy shadow. 2 *n.* Low spirits; dejection; sadness. 3 *v.* To make or become gloomy.
gloom·y [glo͞o′mē] *adj.* **gloom·i·er, gloom·i·est** 1 Dark; dismal. 2 Sad; dejected. 3 Causing gloom. **—gloom′i·ly** *adv.* **—gloom′i·ness** *n.*
glop [glop] *n. informal* A messy mass; jumbled mixture, as of food.
Glo·ri·a [glôr′ē·ə *or* glōr′ē·ə] *n.* 1 Any of various Christian hymns of praise that begin with the Latin word *gloria,* which means *glory.* 2 The music to which any of these hymns has been set.
glo·ri·fy [glôr′ə·fī′] *v.* **glo·ri·fied, glo·ri·fy·ing** 1 To make glorious. 2 To honor or exalt; worship. 3 To make seem more splendid or glorious than is actually so: Movies sometimes *glorify* crime. **—glo′ri·fi·ca′tion** *n.* **—glor′i·fi′er** *n.*
glo·ri·ous [glôr′ē·əs] *adj.* 1 Full of or deserving glory: a *glorious* work. 2 Bringing glory: a *glorious* victory. 3 Magnificently beautiful: a *glorious* sunset. 4 *informal* Very pleasant; delightful. **—glo′ri·ous·ly** *adv.*
glo·ry [glôr′ē] *n., pl.* **glo·ries,** *v.* **glo·ried, glo·ry·ing** 1 *n.* Great honor and praise; very high renown. 2 *n.* A person or thing bringing praise or honor: Shakespeare's plays are his *glory.* 3 *n.* Splendor; magnificence: the *glory* of Rome. 4 *n.* A condition of happiness, prosperity, or pride: to be in one's *glory.* 5 *v.* To rejoice proudly; take pride: to *glory* in one's accomplishments. 6 *n.* Worship; adoration: to give *glory* to God. 7 *n.* The bliss of heaven: to dwell in *glory* with the saints.
gloss[1] [glôs] 1 *n.* The luster or shine of a polished surface. 2 *v.* To make shiny or lustrous. 3 *n.* A nice surface appearance that hides something wrong. 4 *v.* To conceal or make little of: Don't try to *gloss* over your error.
gloss[2] [glôs] 1 *n.* An explanation, as of a difficult word or section in a text. 2 *n.* A glossary. 3 *v.* To provide glosses for a text.
glos·sa·ry [glos′ə·rē] *n., pl.* **glos·sa·ries** A list of difficult or special words of a book or subject, together with their meanings.
gloss·y [glôs′ē] *adj.* **gloss·i·er, gloss·i·est,** *n., pl.* **glos·sies** 1 *adj.* Smooth and shiny; lustrous. 2 *n.* A photograph on smooth, glossy paper. **—gloss′i·ly** *adv.*
glot·tis [glot′is] *n.* The cleft or opening between the vocal cords in the larynx.
glove [gluv] *n., v.* **gloved, glov·ing** 1 *n.* A covering for the hand, having a separate part for each finger and thumb. 2 *n.* Such an article specially padded for protection of the hand: a baseball *glove.* 3 *n.* A boxing glove. 4 *v.* To cover or furnish with gloves.
glove compartment A small storage compartment located in the dashboard of an automobile.
glow [glō] 1 *v.* To shine because of great heat, especially without a flame: An ember *glows.* 2 *v.* To shine without a flame or heat: A glowworm *glows.* 3 *n.* The light from something that glows. 4 *n.* Brightness or warmth of color. 5 *v.* To show a bright, warm color: My cheeks *glowed.* 6 *v.* To be eager, excited, or ardent: to *glow* with love. 7 *n.* Warm emotion.
glow·er [glou′ər] 1 *v.* To stare angrily: to *glower* at someone. 2 *n.* An angry stare.

a	add	**i**	it	**o͝o**	took	**oi**	oil
ā	ace	**ī**	ice	**o͞o**	pool	**ou**	pout
â	care	**o**	odd	**u**	up	**ng**	ring
ä	palm	**ō**	open	**û**	burn	**th**	thin
e	end	**ô**	order	**yo͞o**	fuse	**t͟h**	this
ē	equal					**zh**	vision

ə = {a in *above* e in *sicken* i in *possible*; o in *melon* u in *circus*}

glow·worm [glō′wûrm′] *n.* Any of various insects or insect larvae that emit light, especially the wingless female and the larva of the firefly.
glu·cose [glo͞o′kōs] *n.* **1** A kind of sugar found in fruits, not as sweet as cane sugar. **2** A thick, yellowish syrup made from starch.
glue [glo͞o] *n., v.* **glued, glu·ing** **1** *n.* A substance made from the hoofs, bones, and other parts of animals and used to stick things together. **2** *n.* Any substance like this. **3** *v.* To stick together or attach with glue: to *glue* a notice to a wall. **4** *v.* To fasten or hold as if with glue: We were *glued* to our seats with suspense.
glue·y [glo͞o′ē] *adj.* **glu·i·er, glu·i·est** **1** Like glue; sticky. **2** Covered with glue.
glum [glum] *adj.* **glum·mer, glum·mest** Gloomy and silent. **—glum′ly** *adv.* **—glum′ness** *n.*
glut [glut] *v.* **glut·ted, glut·ting,** *n.* **1** *v.* To stuff, as with food; gorge: to *glut* oneself with pastry. **2** *v.* To supply with too much: The market was *glutted* with dairy products. **3** *n.* A supply that is too great.
glu·ten [glo͞ot′(ə)n] *n.* A sticky substance left in flour after the starch has been removed.
glu·ti·nous [glo͞ot′(ə)n·əs] *adj.* Sticky.
glut·ton [glut′(ə)n] *n.* **1** A person who eats greedily. **2** A person with a great liking or capacity for something: a *glutton* for work. **—glut′ton·ous** *adj.* **—glut′ton·ous·ly** *adv.*
glut·ton·y [glut′(ə)n·ē] *n., pl.* **glut·ton·ies** The habit of eating too much; greediness.
glyc·er·in or **glyc·er·ine** [glis′ər·in] *n.* A clear, sweet, oily liquid obtained from natural fats and used in ointments and explosives.
glyc·er·ol [glis′ə·rôl′ *or* glis′ə·rōl′] *n.* Glycerin.
gly·co·gen [glī′kə·jən] *n.* A white, starchlike substance found in the liver and muscles of animals. Glucose is stored in the form of glycogen.
gm or **gm.** gram(s).
G-man [jē′man′] *n., pl.* **G-men** [jē′men′] An agent of the FBI.
gnarl [närl] **1** *n.* A protruding lump or knot on a tree. **2** *v.* To make twisted or deformed.
gnarled [närld] *adj.* Knotty or twisted: The farmer's hands were *gnarled* from hard work.
gnash [nash] *v.* To grind or strike (the teeth) together, as in rage.
gnat [nat] *n.* A small biting or stinging fly.
gnaw [nô] *v.* **gnawed, gnawed** or **gnawn** [nôn], **gnaw·ing** **1** To bite or eat away little by little with or as if with teeth: to *gnaw* at a bone. **2** To make by gnawing: to *gnaw* a hole. **3** To trouble persistently: Worry *gnawed* at them.
gneiss [nīs] *n.* A rock similar to granite, having a coarse grain.
gnome [nōm] *n.* In folklore, a dwarf who lives in a cave and guards a treasure.
GNP gross national product.
gnu [n(y)o͞o] *n., pl.* **gnus** or **gnu** **1** A large antelope of South Africa with a head like an ox's, curved horns, a mane, and a long tail.
go[1] [gō] *v.* **went, gone, go·ing,** *third person singular present* **goes,** *n., adj.* **1** *v.* To proceed or pass along; move: We *went* on the highway. **2** *v.* To move from a place; pass away; leave; depart: *Go* home!; I wish my toothache would *go.* **3** *v.* To have a regularly scheduled route or specific destination: This train *goes* to Chicago daily. **4** *v.* To move for some specific purpose: The guests *went* to dress for dinner. **5** *v.* To be in motion or operation; work; function: The motor is *going.* **6** *v.* To extend or reach: This pipe *goes* to the cellar. **7** *v.* To produce, as a certain sound or movement: The chain *goes* "clank." **8** *v.* To fail, give way, or collapse: The table legs *went.* **9** *v.* To have a specific place or position; belong: The plates *go* on that shelf. **10** *v.* To pass into someone's possession; be given or sold: Antiques often *go* for high prices at an auction. **11** *v.* To be, continue, or become: to *go* unpunished; to *go* insane. **12** *v.* To proceed, happen, or end in a specific way: The election *went* well for the other party. **13** *v.* To be about or intending: I am *going* to ask them tonight. **14** *v.* To be suitable; fit: These colors *go* well together. **15** *v.* To be phrased; expressed, or sung: How does that tune *go*? **16** *v.* To pass: A weekend *goes* fast. **17** *v.* To put or subject oneself: They *went* to great pains to get the tickets. **18** *n. informal* A try; attempt: to have a *go* at something. **19** *n. informal* A success: to make a *go* of it. **20** *adj.* In working order; ready for use: an announcement that all systems were *go.* **—go around** **1** To enclose; encircle. **2** To satisfy the demand or need. **—go at** **1** To attack. **2** To work at. **—go back on** **1** To break (a promise or the like). **2** To betray or forsake. **—go for** **1** To try to get. **2** *informal* To attack. **3** To favor or support. **4** *informal* To be strongly attracted by. **—go in for** *informal* To take part in or be interested in. **—go into** **1** To investigate. **2** To be contained in: 4 *goes into* 12 three times. **—go off** **1** To leave. **2** To explode. **3** *informal* To happen in a certain way. **—go out** **1** To go to a party, to the theater, or to another social event. **2** To be extinguished. **—go over** **1** To examine. **2** To review or rehearse. **3** To treat or cover again. **4** *informal* To succeed. **—go through** **1** To be accepted or approved. **2** To experience; undergo. **3** To search. **—go together** **1** To suit each other; harmonize. **2** To keep steady company as sweethearts. **—let go** **1** To set free or let escape. **2** To give up a hold. **—let oneself go** To give in to one's feelings or desires; throw off restraint. **—no go** *informal* Hopeless; useless. **—on the go** *informal* Very busy: The tourists were *on the go* every minute.
go[2] [gō] *n.* A Japanese board game for two persons, played with black and white stones on a board ruled with 19 horizontal and 19 vertical lines.
goad [gōd] **1** *n.* A pointed stick for driving oxen or other animals by pricking them. **2** *n.* Something that drives or spurs; incentive: a *goad* to study. **3** *v.* To drive with or as if with a goad.
go-a·head [gō′ə·hed′] *n. informal* A signal or permission to proceed.
goal [gōl] *n.* **1** The end of a race or journey. **2** An end; aim; objective: What is your *goal* in life? **3** In hockey, soccer, and certain other games, a place or structure where a score can be made. **4** A score made in these games.
goal·ie [gō′lē] *n. informal* Another word for GOALKEEPER.
goal·keep·er [gōl′kē′pər] *n.* In hockey, soccer, or other games, a player who guards a team's goal.
goal line A line representing the goal in certain sports, as football.
goal post One of two posts joined by a crosspiece to form a goal, as in football.
goal·tend·er [gōl′ten′dər] *n.* A goalkeeper.
goat [gōt] *n.* **1** An animal, related to the sheep, that chews its cud. It has hollow horns that curve back-

ward, usually straight hair, a lean body, and a short tail. **2** *informal* A person who is the butt of a joke or on whom blame is placed; scapegoat. **—get (someone's) goat** *informal* To annoy or anger.

goat·ee [gō·tē'] *n.* A beard trimmed short to a pointed end below the chin.

Goatee

goat·herd [gōt'hûrd'] *n.* A person who tends goats.

goat·skin [gōt'skin'] *n.* **1** The skin of a goat. **2** Leather made from this. **3** Something made from this leather, as a container for liquid.

gob[1] [gob] *n. informal* A sailor in the U.S. Navy.

gob[2] [gob] *n. informal* A lump or mass, as of something soft or sticky: a *gob* of mud.

gob·ble[1] [gob'əl] *v.* **gob·bled, gob·bling** To eat greedily and in gulps: The children *gobbled* their sandwiches and ran out to play.

gob·ble[2] [gob'əl] *n., v.* **gob·bled, gob·bling** **1** *n.* The throaty sound made by a male turkey. **2** *v.* To make this sound.

gob·ble·dy·gook or **gob·ble·de·gook** [gob'əl·dē·go͝ok'] *n. informal* Speech or writing that is incomprehensible and wordy.

gob·bler [gob'lər] *n.* A male turkey.

go-be·tween [gō'bə·twēn'] *n.* A person who goes back and forth between two people or sides, making arrangements or proposals.

gob·let [gob'lit] *n.* A drinking glass with a base and stem and no handles.

Goblets

gob·lin [gob'lin] *n.* In folklore, an ugly, mischievous, elflike creature.

go-cart [gō'kärt'] *n.* A small carriage or wagon for little children to ride in or pull.

god [god] *n.* **1** (*written* **God**) In certain religions, as Judaism, Christianity, and Islam, the one supreme being, creator, protector, and ruler of the world. **2** In myths and primitive religions, any of various beings whose supposed immortality and supreme powers are or were considered worthy of worship by humans. **3** A statue, image, or symbol of such beings. **4** Any person or thing greatly loved or considered most important: Physical fitness is their *god*.

god·child [god'chīld'] *n., pl.* **god·chil·dren** A baby or child for whom another person is a sponsor, as at baptism.

god·daugh·ter [god'dô'tər] *n.* A female godchild.

god·dess [god'is] *n.* **1** In myths and primitive religions, any of various female beings whose supposed immortality and supreme powers are or were considered worthy of worship by humans. **2** A female of great beauty or charm.

god·fa·ther [god'fä'*th*ər] *n.* A male godparent.

god-fear·ing [god'fir'ing] *adj.* (*often written* **God-fearing**) **1** Having reverence for God. **2** Pious; devout.

god·head [god'hed'] *n.* **1** Divine nature; divinity. **2** (*written* **Godhead**) God (def. 1).

god·less [god'lis] *adj.* **1** Having or believing in no god. **2** Wicked. **—god'less·ness** *n.*

god·like [god'līk'] *adj.* Like or proper for a god or God; very great, holy, or beautiful.

god·ly [god'lē] *adj.* **god·li·er, god·li·est** Filled with reverence and love for God; devout. **—god'li·ness** *n.*

god·moth·er [god'mu*th*'ər] *n.* A female godparent.

god·par·ent [god'pâr'ənt] *n.* A person who is a sponsor for a baby or child, as at baptism.

God's acre Another name for CHURCHYARD.

god·send [god'send'] *n.* Something unexpected that comes or happens when it is badly needed: Your offer to help was a *godsend*.

god·son [god'sun'] *n.* A male godchild.

God·speed [god'spēd'] *n.* An expression used to wish a person a successful journey or undertaking. It is short for *God speed you*.

go·fer [gō'fər] *n. slang* A person employed to do minor tasks, such as running errands: sending the office *gofer* to buy coffee.

G

go-get·ter [gō'get'ər] *n. U.S. informal* A very bold, ambitious, energetic person.

gog·gle [gog'əl] *n., v.* **gog·gled, gog·gling,** *adj.* **1** *n.* (*pl.*) Large glasses that protect the eyes, as from dust, wind, or sparks. **2** *v.* To stare with the eyes wide open and bulging: We all *goggled* as the rocket took off. **3** *adj.* Staring or bulging: *goggle* eyes.

Goggles

gog·gle-eyed [gog'əl·īd'] *adj.* Having or characterized by bulging or rolling eyes.

go·ing [gō'ing] **1** Present participle of GO. **2** *adj.* Moving ahead successfully: a *going* business. **3** *n.* A departing; leaving: one's coming and *going*. **4** *n.* A condition of something as it affects moving or getting along: The *going* was bad on these rutted roads; Adjusting to a new job can be rough *going*.

go·ing-o·ver [gō'ing·ō'vər] *n., pl.* **go·ings-o·ver** *informal* **1** A thorough examination or inspection. **2** A severe scolding or reprimand. **3** A beating.

go·ings-on [gō'ingz·on'] *n.pl. informal* Behavior or actions, especially when looked upon as strange or deserving of criticism.

goi·ter [goi'tər] *n.* An abnormal enlargement of the thyroid gland. It is visible as a swelling in the front of the neck.

gold [gōld] **1** *n.* A soft, heavy, yellow element, the most highly malleable and ductile metal. **2** *adj. use:* a *gold* cup. **3** *adj.* Producing gold: a *gold* mine. **4** *n.* Gold coins. **5** *n.* Wealth; riches. **6** *n., adj.* Bright yellow.

gold·brick [gōld'brik'] *slang* **1** *v.* To evade one's duties or responsibilities. **2** *n.* A person, espe-

a	add	**i**	it	**o͝o**	took	**oi**	oil
ā	ace	**ī**	ice	**o͞o**	pool	**ou**	pout
â	care	**o**	odd	**u**	up	**ng**	ring
ä	palm	**ō**	open	**û**	burn	**th**	thin
e	end	**ô**	order	**yo͞o**	fuse	***th***	this
ē	equal					**zh**	vision

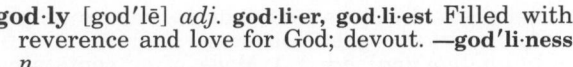

ə = { a in *above* e in *sicken* i in *possible* / o in *melon* u in *circus* }

cially a soldier, who evades duties or responsibilities; shirker. **—gold'brick'er** *n.*

gold·en [gōl'dən] *adj.* 1 Made of or containing gold: a *golden* statue. 2 Having the color of gold. 3 Very good, happy, prosperous, or valuable: a *golden* opportunity.

golden calf 1 In the Old Testament, a gold statue of a calf worshiped as an idol by the Israelites. 2 Money or material goods, considered as something to be worshiped and pursued.

golden eagle A large eagle inhabiting the mountainous regions of the Northern Hemisphere. It is dark brown with yellowish feathers on its head and neck.

Golden Fleece In Greek myth, a fleece of gold guarded by a dragon. It was taken away by Jason and the Argonauts with Medea's help.

golden mean A middle way between extremes; moderation.

gold·en·rod [gōl'dən·rod'] *n.* A North American plant with small, usually yellow flowers that bloom in the late summer or early fall.

golden rule A rule stating that one should treat other people in the way that one would like to be treated by others.

golden wedding The fiftieth anniversary of a wedding.

gold-filled [gōld'fild'] *adj.* Covered over with a layer of gold: *gold-filled* jewelry.

gold·finch [gōld'finch'] *n.* A small American songbird. In the summer the male goldfinch has a yellow body and a black tail.

gold·fish [gōld'fish'] *n., pl.* **gold·fish** or **gold·fish·es** A small fish, usually gold or orange, often kept in ponds or small aquariums.

gold leaf Sheets of gold hammered until they are extremely thin, used in gilding.

gold mine 1 A place where gold ore is mined. 2 *informal* A source of something valuable or desired: a *gold mine* of information.

gold rush A large migration of people to an area where gold has been discovered.

gold·smith [gōld'smith'] *n.* A person who makes or deals in articles of gold.

golf [golf] 1 *n.* An outdoor game played on a large course with a small hard ball and a set of clubs. The object of the game is to hit the ball into a series of holes, 9 or 18, in as few strokes as possible. 2 *v.* To play golf. **—golf'er** *n.*

golf cart 1 A small cart in which to wheel a bag of golf clubs around a golf course. 2 A motorized cart designed to transport a golfer and his or her clubs around a golf course.

golf club 1 Any of a set of clubs having long shafts and wooden or metal heads used to hit the ball in golf. 2 A club made up of golf players. 3 The clubhouse and grounds belonging to such a club.

golf course A large piece of land that has been laid out and landscaped for the game of golf.

Gol·go·tha [gol'gə·thə] *n.* Another name for CALVARY.

Go·li·ath [gə·lī'əth] *n.* In the Bible, a giant killed by David with a stone from a sling.

gol·ly [gol'ē] *interj.* An exclamation, as of mild surprise, concern, or wonder.

Go·mor·rah or **Go·mor·rha** [gə·môr'ə] *n.* In the Bible, a city destroyed by God because of the wickedness of its people.

go·nad [gō'nad'] *n.* An organ that produces gametes; an ovary or testis.

gon·do·la [gon'də·lə] *n.* 1 A long, narrow boat with a high point at each end, used on the canals of Venice. 2 A railroad freight car that has low sides and no top. 3 A cabin attached to the bottom of a dirigible. 4 A basket or enclosure suspended from a balloon. 5 An enclosed car suspended from a cable, used to carry people, as to the top of a ski slope.

Gondola

gondola car A gondola (def. 2).

gon·do·lier [gon'də·lir'] *n.* A person who moves a gondola by rowing or poling.

gone [gôn *or* gon] 1 The past particle of GO. 2 *adj.* Moved away; left. 3 *adj.* Ruined; lost. 4 *adj.* Dead. 5 *adj.* Used up. 6 *adj.* Weak, failing.

gon·er [gôn'ər] *n. informal* A person or thing that is dying, ruined, or beyond help.

gong [gông] *n.* A heavy metal disk giving a deep, resonant tone when struck.

gon·o·coc·cus [gon'ə·kok'əs] *n., pl.* **gon·o·coc·ci** [gon'ə·kok'sī'] A bacterium that causes gonorrhea.

gon·or·rhe·a [gon'ə·rē'ə] *n.* A highly contagious venereal disease caused by the gonococcus, characterized by inflammation of the mucous lining of the genital and urinary tracts.

goo [go͞o] *n. U.S. slang* Any sticky substance.

goo·ber [go͞o'bər] *n. U.S.* A peanut. ◆ *Goober* may come from *nguba,* an African Bantu word for *peanut.*

good [go͝od] *adj.* **bet·ter, best,** *n.* 1 *adj.* Having the proper qualities; admirable. 2 *adj.* Skillful: a *good* pianist. 3 *adj.* Kind: a *good* turn. 4 *adj.* Well-behaved; polite: a *good* child. 5 *adj.* Proper; desirable: *good* manners. 6 *adj.* Favorable: a *good* opinion. 7 *adj.* Pleasant; agreeable: *good* company. 8 *adj.* Beneficial; helpful: *good* advice. 9 *n.* Benefit; advantage: for the *good* of humanity. 10 *adj.* Genuine; valid: a *good* excuse. 11 *adj.* Above the average in quality, degree, or kind: *good* food; a really *good* coat. 12 *adj.* Unspoiled; fresh: *good* meat. 13 *adj.* In a sound or satisfactory condition: *good* eyesight; a *good* chair. 14 *adj.* Satisfactory or appropriate, as for a particular purpose: *good* weather for flying. 15 *adj.* Great or fairly great in amount or extent: a *good* share. 16 *adj.* Thorough; sufficient: a *good* spanking. 17 *adj.* Full: a *good* mile away. 18 *n.* A thing that is good. **—as good as** Almost; nearly; practically. **—for good** For the last time; permanently. **—good and** *informal* Very; extremely: This chili is *good and* hot. **—good for** 1 Capable of lasting or remaining valid or in operation (for a certain period of time). 2 *informal* Able or willing to pay, give, or produce (something). **—make good** 1 To be successful. 2 To replace; repay. 3 To fulfill (as a promise or threat). 4 To prove. **—to the good** To the credit, profit, or advantage of someone or something. ◆ The word *good* is primarily an adjective describing a person or thing, and as such it often follows a verb telling how a person or thing is or appears, as in "This pie tastes *good,*" or "I feel *good* today," or "Your singing sounded *good* to me." However, *good* should not be used adverbially to modify a verb, as in "The band doesn't play *good,*" or "This watch doesn't run *good* any more." In these last two examples, *well* is the proper word to use.

Good Book The Bible.

good-bye or **good-by** [go͝od′bī′] *interj., n., pl.* **good-byes** or **good-bys** [go͝od′bīz′] What a person says at parting; farewell. ◆ *Good-by* is a contraction of *God be with you.*

good day A greeting made during the day.

good evening A greeting made in the evening.

good-for-noth·ing [go͝od′fər·nuth′ing] **1** *n.* A worthless person. **2** *adj.* Worthless.

Good Friday The Friday before Easter, commemorating the crucifixion of Jesus.

good-heart·ed [go͝od′här′tid] *adj.* Kind; generous.

good-hu·mored [go͝od′(h)yo͞o′mərd] *adj.* Cheerful; amiable; pleasant. **—good′-hu′mored·ly** *adv.*

good-look·ing [go͝od′lo͝ok′ing] *adj.* Handsome or pretty; attractive.

good·ly [go͝od′lē] *adj.* **good·li·er, good·li·est** **1** Handsome or pleasing. **2** Excellent. **3** Large; considerable. **—good′li·ness** *n.*

good·man [go͝od′mən] *n., pl.* **good·men** [go͝od′mən] **1** A man who is the head of a household. **2** A title, similar to *Mr.* ◆ This word is seldom used today.

good morning A greeting made in the morning.

good-na·tured [go͝od′nā′chərd] *adj.* Friendly, pleasant, and kindly: a *good-natured* reply; *good-natured* joking. **good′-na′tured·ly** *adv.* **—good′-na′tured·ness** *n.*

good·ness [go͝od′nis] **1** *n.* The condition of being good, especially of being virtuous or generous. **2** *n.* The best or most nourishing part of anything. **3** *interj.* A word used to express surprise or emphasis: *Goodness,* but you're late!

good night A farewell made at night, especially when going to bed.

goods [go͝odz] *n.pl.* **1** Anything made to be sold; merchandise. **2** Cloth; material: dress *goods.* **3** Personal property capable of being moved.

Good Samaritan **1** In a parable of Jesus, a man who helps another man who has been robbed and beaten. **2** Any person who voluntarily helps someone else in trouble.

good-sized [go͝od′sīzd′] *adj.* Quite large.

good-tem·pered [go͝od′tem′pərd] *adj.* Having a good disposition; not easily angered: a *good-tempered,* pleasant person.

good·wife [go͝od′wīf′] *n.* **1** A woman who is the head of a household. **2** A title, similar to *Mrs.* ◆ This word is seldom used today.

good·will [go͝od′wil′] *n.* **1** Good feeling toward others. **2** The advantage a business develops over the years because of its good reputation and its friendly relationship with its customers.

good·y [go͝od′ē] *n., pl.* **good·ies,** *interj. informal* **1** *n.* Something tasty, as a piece of candy or a cooky. **2** *interj.* A word showing delight, which is used mostly by children.

good·y-good·y [go͝od′ē·go͝od′ē] *adj., n., pl.* **good·y-good·ies** **1** *adj.* Excessively and artificially proper and virtuous. **2** *n.* A person who is goody-goody.

goo·ey [go͞o′ē] *adj.* **goo·i·er, goo·i·est** *U.S. slang* Sticky and messy.

goof [go͞of] *slang* **1** *n.* A careless, stupid, or ridiculous mistake; blunder. **2** *v.* To make a careless, stupid, or ridiculous mistake; blunder. **3** *n.* A careless, stupid, or ridiculous person. **—goof around** or **goof off** To waste time or avoid responsibilities. **—goof up** To mishandle or make a mess of; bungle: to *goof up* a really simple task.

goof-off [go͞of′ôf′ *or* go͞of′of′] *n.* A person who habitually wastes time or avoids responsibilities.

goof·y [go͞o′fē] *adj.* **goof·i·er, goof·i·est** *slang* Careless, stupid, or ridiculous. **—goof′i·ness** *n.*

goo·gol [go͞o′gol′] *n.* An enormous number, 1 followed by a hundred zeros.

goon [go͞on] *n. slang* **1** A stupid or clumsy person. **2** A hoodlum; thug, especially one hired to intimidate or eliminate opponents.

goose [go͞os] *n., pl.* **geese** [gēs] **1** A swimming bird, tame or wild, that is like a duck but is larger and has a longer neck. **2** The female of this bird. The male is called a gander. **3** A silly person. **—cook one's goose** *informal* To ruin one's chances or plans.

Canada goose

goose·ber·ry [go͞os′ber′ē] *n., pl.* **goose·ber·ries** **1** A sour berry that grows on a prickly shrub, used in making pies, tarts, and jams. **2** The shrub itself.

goose bumps Goose flesh.

goose egg *slang* Zero; nothing: used especially in reference to a score of zero in a contest or game.

goose flesh A condition of the skin in which many tiny bumps appear. It is caused usually by fear or cold.

goose·neck [go͞os′nek′] *n.* Any of various mechanical devices curved like a goose's neck, as a flexible shaft between the base and the bulb of a desk lamp.

goose pimples Goose flesh.

goose-step [go͞os′step′] *v.* **goose-stepped, goose-step·ping** To walk or march in a goose step.

goose step A marching step in which the leg is kicked high with the knee stiff.

GOP or **G.O.P.** Grand Old Party (Republican Party).

go·pher [gō′fər] *n.* **1** A rodent of North America that burrows into the ground and has large cheek pouches for storing food. **2** Any of various ground squirrels of western North America.

Gor·di·an knot [gôr′dē·ən] **1** In Greek myths, a complicated knot that could only be untied by the future ruler of Asia. Alexander the Great is said to have cut through the knot with his sword. **2** An exceptionally difficult or complicated problem. **—cut the Gordian knot** To find a quick or daring solution to a difficult or complicated problem.

gore¹ [gôr] *n.* Blood that has come from wounds, especially when thick or partly clotted.

gore² [gôr] *n., v.* **gored, gor·ing** **1** *n.* A triangular piece of cloth sewn into a garment or a sail to provide a fuller shape. **2** *v.* To put gores into.

gore³ [gôr] *v.* **gored, gor·ing** To wound or pierce with

a	add	**i**	it	**o͝o**	took	**oi**	oil
ā	ace	**ī**	ice	**o͞o**	pool	**ou**	pout
â	care	**o**	odd	**u**	up	**ng**	ring
ä	palm	**ō**	open	**û**	burn	**th**	thin
e	end	**ô**	order	**yo͞o**	fuse	**t͟h**	this
ē	equal					**zh**	vision

ə = { a in *above* e in *sicken* i in *possible* / o in *melon* u in *circus* }

G

a horn or tusk: The horse was *gored* by the enraged bull.

gorge [gôrj] *n., v.* **gorged, gorg·ing** 1 *n.* A narrow, very deep ravine; canyon. 2 *v.* To stuff (oneself) with food: A hungry dog will *gorge* itself. 3 *n.* The throat; gullet: seldom used today.

Gorge

gor·geous [gôr'jəs] *adj.* 1 Brilliant; dazzling: a *gorgeous* tiara. 2 Very beautiful: a *gorgeous* model. **—gor'geous·ly** *adv.* **—gor'geous·ness** *n.*

gor·get [gôr'jit] *n.* 1 A piece of armor worn to protect the throat. 2 A decorative collar.

Gor·gon [gôr'gən] *n.* In Greek myths, any of the three sisters, with snakes for hair, who were so frightening that the sight of them turned the viewer to stone.

Gor·gon·zo·la [gôr'gən·zō'lə] *n.* A strong, blue-veined cheese of Italian origin.

go·ril·la [gə·ril'ə] *n.* The largest and most powerful of the apes, living in the African jungles.

Gorilla

gor·mand·ize [gôr'mən·dīz'] *v.* **gor·mand·ized, gor·mand·iz·ing** To eat like a glutton. **—gor'·mand·iz'er** *n.*

gorp [gôrp] *n.* A mixture of foods that are high in energy, as nuts and dried fruit.

gorse [gôrs] *n.* A spiny shrub having many branches and yellow flowers, common in Europe.

go·ry [gôr'ē] *adj.* **gor·i·er, gor·i·est** 1 Covered or stained with gore. 2 Like gore. 3 Characterized by bloodshed and violence: a *gory* battle. 4 Unpleasant or grisly: hearing the *gory* details of a murder. **—gor'i·ly** *adv.* **—gor'i·ness** *n.*

gosh [gosh] *interj.* An exclamation, as of surprise, delight, or concern.

gos·hawk [gos'hôk' *or* gôs'hôk'] *n.* A large, short-winged hawk.

Go·shen [gō'shən] *n.* 1 In the Bible, the part of Egypt where the Israelites lived. 2 Any place of peace or plenty.

gos·ling [goz'ling] *n.* A young goose.

gos·pel [gos'pəl] *n.* 1 The teaching of Christ and his apostles. 2 Something thought to be true. 3 (*written* **Gospel**) Any of the first four books of the New Testament. Matthew, Mark, Luke, and John wrote the Gospels. 4 (*written* **Gospel**) A lesson taken from the Gospel, read as part of a church service.

gospel music A kind of evangelical religious music that originated in America. It combines melodies derived from folk tunes with elements of spirituals and jazz.

gos·sa·mer [gos'ə·mər] 1 *n.* The fine strands of a spider's web. 2 *n.* A flimsy, delicate material or fabric. 3 *adj.* Like gossamer; filmy.

gos·sip [gos'əp] *n., v.* **gos·siped, gos·sip·ing** 1 *n.* Idle, often malicious talk about others; chatter or tales. 2 *v.* To spread gossip. 3 *n.* A person who spreads gossip; busybody. **—gos'sip·er** *n.* **—gos'sip·y** *adj.*

got [got] Past tense and past participle of GET. ◆ See GOTTEN.

Goth [goth] *n.* A member of a Germanic tribe that invaded the Roman Empire in the third, fourth, and fifth centuries.

Goth·ic [goth'ik] 1 *adj.* Having to do with the Goths or their language. 2 *n.* The language of the Goths. 3 *adj.* Belonging to a style of architecture marked by pointed arches and flying buttresses, used in Europe from about 1200 to 1500. 4 *n.* Gothic architecture.

Gothic architecture

got·ten [got'(ə)n] Past participle of GET. ◆ *Gotten* is no longer used in Great Britain, but it is still widely used in the U.S.: It has *gotten* cold since last night. With the meaning of "must" or "possess," however, only the past participle *got* is used: I've *got* to go; The school's *got* a fine library.

gouge [gouj] *n., v.* **gouged, goug·ing** 1 *n.* A chisel with a scoop-shaped blade, used to carve wood. 2 *n.* A groove made by or as if by a gouge. 3 *v.* To make a gouge in or scoop out: to *gouge* the eyes. 4 *v. informal* To cheat.

gou·lash [go͞o'läsh] *n.* A stew of beef or veal with vegetables and paprika and other spices. ◆ *Goulash* comes from two Hungarian words meaning *shepherd's meat.*

gourd [gôrd *or* go͝ord] *n.* 1 A fruit related to the pumpkin, with a hard outer shell. 2 A ladle, drinking cup, or other container made from a dried gourd. 3 The plant bearing this fruit.

gour·mand [go͝or'mənd *or* go͝or·män'] *n.* A person who takes great joy in eating. ◆ *Gourmand* comes from a French word meaning *glutton.*

gour·met [go͝or·mā'] 1 *n.* A person who appreciates the finest food and drink. 2 *adj.* Of, having to do with, or fit for a gourmet: *gourmet* cooking. ◆ *Gourmet* comes from an old French word meaning *wine taster.*

gout [gout] *n.* A painful inflammation of the joints, especially of the big toe.

gout·y [gou'tē] *adj.* **gout·i·er, gout·i·est** 1 Of, having to do with, or like gout. 2 Having or subject to gout. 3 Swollen with or as with gout. **—gout'i·ness** *n.*

gov. or **Gov.** governor.

gov·ern [guv'ərn] *v.* To rule or guide; manage.

gov·ern·ess [guv'ər·nis] *n.* A woman who cares for and teaches children in a private home.

gov·ern·ment [guv'ər(n)·mənt] *n.* 1 Control or administration of the affairs of a nation, state, city, or the like. 2 The system of such administration. 3 The officials in a government. **—gov·ern·men·tal** [guv'ər(n)·men'təl] *adj.* **—gov'ern·men'tal·ly** *adv.*

government issue Supplies or clothing issued by the government to soldiers.

gov·er·nor [guv'ər·nər] *n.* 1 The elected chief executive of any state of the U.S. 2 A person who governs, especially an official appointed to govern a colony or territory. 3 A device that regulates the speed of a motor.

gov·er·nor·ship [guv'ər·nər·ship'] *n.* The position, powers, or time of service of a governor.

govt. or **Govt.** government.

gown [goun] **1** *n.* A woman's dress worn mainly on formal occasions. **2** *n.* Any long, flowing garment, as a nightgown. **3** *n.* A flowing outer robe, as worn by a judge. **4** *v.* To dress in a gown.

Gown

G.P. general practitioner.
GPA grade-point average.
GPO or **G.P.O.** **1** General Post Office. **2** Government Printing Office.
gr. **1** grade. **2** grain. **3** gram(s). **4** gross. **5** group.
Gr. **1** Greece. **2** Greek. **3** Grecian.
grab [grab] *v.* **grabbed, grab·bing,** *n.* **1** *v.* To grasp suddenly and forcefully; snatch. **2** *n.* The act of grabbing. **—grab′ber** *n.*
grab bag A bag filled with various objects, as toys, from which one draws without looking.
grab·by [grab′ē] *adj.* **grab·bi·er, grab·bi·est** Inclined or tending to grab; greedy; avaricious. **—grab′bi·ly** *adv.* **—grab′bi·ness** *n.*
grace [grās] *n., v.* **graced, grac·ing** **1** *n.* Beauty or delicacy of movement or form. **2** *n.* Pleasing manners and behavior: social *graces.* **3** *n.* Extra time allowed in which to do something, as pay a debt: ten days of *grace.* **4** *n.* A short prayer of thanks said at a meal. **5** *n.* The love and favor of God: to fall from *grace.* **6** *n.* (*often pl.*) Esteem; regard: They stayed in our good *graces.* **7** *v.* To dignify; honor: The mayor *graced* us with a visit. **8** *v.* To beautify: Flowers *grace* a room. **—Your Grace** A title of honor used in speaking to an archbishop, duke, or duchess. In speaking about the person, **His Grace** or **Her Grace** is used. **—the Graces** In Greek myths, three sister goddesses who gave joy, beauty, charm, and grace to people and nature.
grace·ful [grās′fəl] *adj.* Having or showing grace, especially of form, movement, or manner: a *graceful* dancer. **—grace′ful·ly** *adv.* **—grace′ful·ness** *n.*
grace·less [grās′lis] *adj.* **1** Without grace; clumsy; awkward. **2** Having no sense of good manners or decency: a *graceless* boor. **—grace′less·ly** *adv.* **—grace′less·ness** *n.*
grace note A very short note that embellishes a musical passage but is not essential to its melody or harmony.
grace period Another term for GRACE (def. 3).
gra·cious [grā′shəs] **1** *adj.* Kind and polite. **2** *adj.* Elegant; refined: *gracious* living. **3** *interj.* A cry of surprise. **—gra′cious·ly** *adv.* **—gra′cious·ness** *n.*
grack·le [grak′əl] *n.* A variety of blackbird.
gra·da·tion [grā·dā′shən] *n.* **1** A gradual change by steps: a *gradation* from loud to soft. **2** Any of the steps or degrees in a series: *gradations* between light and dark.
grade [grād] *n., v.* **grad·ed, grad·ing** **1** *n.* A degree or step in a scale, as of quality, rank, or worth: This meat is of a high *grade.* **2** *v.* To divide into groups by quality or size: to *grade* lumber. **3** *n.* *U.S.* Any regular stage of study in a school: the third *grade.* **4** *n.* A group of people or things that are alike in some way. **5** *n.* *U.S.* A mark showing the merit of someone's work, as at school: Good *grades* mean promotion. **6** *v.* To assign a grade or mark to: The teacher *graded* the test. **7** *n.* A slope, as of a road or track. **8** *v.* To adjust or improve the slope of, as a road or track. **9** *v.* To change gradually: Day *grades* into dusk. **—make the grade** *informal* To be successful.
grade crossing A crossing of railroad tracks or of a road and a railroad at the same level.
grade point average An average that is determined by dividing the total number of grade points earned by the total number of credits attempted.
grad·er [grā′dər] *n.* **1** A person or thing that grades. **2** *U.S.* A student in a specified grade in school: a first *grader.*
grade school Another name for ELEMENTARY SCHOOL.
gra·di·ent [grā′dē·ənt] *n.* **1** Degree of slope: a steep *gradient.* **2** A ramp or incline. **3** In physics, the rate at which something changes: a temperature *gradient.*
grad·u·al [graj′o͞o·əl] *adj.* Happening slowly and in small steps; bit by bit: *gradual* changes. **—grad′u·al·ly** *adv.* **—grad′u·al·ness** *n.*
grad·u·ate [*v.* graj′o͞o·āt′, *n., adj.* graj′o͞o·it] *v.* **grad·u·at·ed, grad·u·at·ing,** *n., adj.* **1** *v.* To complete a course of study, as at a school or college; earn a diploma. **2** *n.* A person who has graduated. **3** *adj. use: graduate* students; *graduate* studies. **4** *v.* To mark off for use in measuring: Rulers are *graduated.* ◆ *She graduated from college* is now more usual than the older form, *She was graduated from college. She graduated college* is not considered good usage.
grad·u·a·tion [graj′o͞o·ā′shən] *n.* **1** The act of graduating. **2** The ceremonies performed when students graduate. **3** Any of the marks on a measuring instrument: *graduations* on a ruler.
graf·fi·to [grə·fē′tō] *n., pl.* **graf·fi·ti** [grə·fē′tē] **1** An ancient inscription or drawing on a wall or other surface. **2** (*pl.*) Inscriptions, slogans, drawings, or other graphic images painted or scrawled on a public surface, as on the wall of a building.
graft[1] [graft] **1** *n.* A shoot from a plant joined to the stem and roots of another plant. **2** *n.* A piece of skin or bone transferred from one part of the body to another, or from one person to another. **3** *n.* The joining of a graft to a plant or body. **4** *v.* To transfer as a graft: Some plants *graft* well; to *graft* skin. **—graft′er** *n.*
graft[2] [graft] *U.S.* **1** *n.* The getting of money or unfair advantage by dishonest use of a position, especially in a government. **2** *n.* Money obtained in this way. **3** *v.* To obtain by graft. **—graft′er** *n.*
gra·ham [grā′əm] *adj.* Made of unsifted whole-wheat flour: *graham* crackers.
Grail [grāl] *n.* (*sometimes written* **grail**) In medieval legends, the cup or dish used by Christ at the Last Supper, and in which some of the blood shed at

a	add	**i**	it	**o͝o**	took	**oi**	oil
ā	ace	**ī**	ice	**o͞o**	pool	**ou**	pout
â	care	**o**	odd	**u**	up	**ng**	ring
ä	palm	**ō**	open	**û**	burn	**th**	thin
e	end	**ô**	order	**yo͞o**	fuse	**th**	this
ē	equal					**zh**	vision

ə = a in *above* e in *sicken* i in *possible* / o in *melon* u in *circus*

G

the Crucifixion was caught. It is sometimes called the Holy Grail.

grain [grān] *n.* 1 A small, hard seed, especially from a cereal plant, as wheat or rye. 2 Any cereal plant. 3 A small bit of something: a *grain* of sand; a *grain* of truth. 4 A small unit of weight. There are 7,000 grains in one pound. 5 The arrangement of the fibers or particles in wood and stone: Oak has a fine *grain*. 6 Basic nature; temperament: Having to sit still goes against my *grain*.

Grain

grain alcohol Ethyl alcohol, often made from grain.

grain elevator A building for storing grain.

grain·y [grā′nē] *adj.* **grain·i·er, grain·i·est** 1 Full of or made up of grains. 2 Having many small bumps; rough: a *grainy* surface. 3 Rough in tone and showing details poorly, as a photograph. 4 Like the grain of wood. **—grain′i·ness** *n.*

gram [gram] *n.* In the metric system, a unit often used to measure mass or weight. There are about 28⅓ grams in an ounce.

-gram A combining form meaning: Something written or drawn, as in *telegram* or *diagram.*

gram atom The quantity of an element having a weight, measured in grams, that is equal to the atomic weight of the element.

gram·mar [gram′ər] *n.* 1 The study of the forms, structure, and arrangement of words as used in a language. 2 A set of rules telling how to use words and how to form sentences in a particular language. 3 A way of speaking or writing as judged by how closely it follows these rules: good *grammar.* 4 A book about grammar.

gram·mar·i·an [grə·mâr′ē·ən] *n.* A person who specializes in grammar.

grammar school 1 Another name for an ELEMENTARY SCHOOL. 2 *British* A school similar to a high school, especially one in which Latin and Greek are taught.

gram·mat·i·cal [grə·mat′i·kəl] *adj.* 1 Having to do with grammar: a *grammatical* mistake. 2 Following the rules of grammar; correct: a *grammatical* sentence; *grammatical* speech. **—gram·mat′i·cal·ly** *adv.* **—gram·mat′i·cal·ness** *n.*

gramme [gram] *n.* Another spelling of GRAM.

gram-mo·lec·u·lar weight [gram′mə·lek′yə·lər] Another term for GRAM MOLECULE.

gram molecule The quantity of a substance having a weight, measured in grams, that is equal to the molecular weight of the substance. For example, a gram molecule of water (H_2O) weighs 18.017 grams.

Gram·my [gram′ē] *n., pl.* **Gram·mies** or **Gram·mys** One of the awards made annually for notable achievement in the record industry.

gram·pus [gram′pəs] *n.* 1 A large, dolphinlike creature. 2 A relatively small but ferocious whale, sometimes called the killer whale.

gran·a·ry [gran′ə·rē *or* grā′nə·rē] *n., pl.* **gran·a·ries** A storehouse for grain.

grand [grand] 1 *adj.* Remarkable because of great size or splendor; magnificent; impressive. 2 *adj.* Of high rank or position: a *grand* duke; a *grand* jury. 3 *adj.* First in size or importance: a *grand* ballroom. 4 *adj.* Respected; honored: a *grand* old custom. 5 *adj.* Too conscious of being important; haughty. 6 *adj.* Including everything; complete: the *grand* total. 7 *adj. informal* Very pleasing; excellent. 8 *n.* A grand piano. 9 *n. slang* A thousand dollars. **—grand′ly** *adv.* **—grand′ness** *adj.*

gran·dam [gran′dam′] *n.* 1 A grandmother. 2 An old woman. ◆ This word is seldom used today.

grand·aunt [gran(d)′ant′] *n.* An aunt of either of one's parents.

grand·child [gran(d)′chīld′] *n., pl.* **grand·chil·dren** [gran(d)′chil′drən] A child of one's son or daughter.

grand·dad [gran(d)′dad′] *n. informal* Grandfather.

grand·daugh·ter [gran(d)′dô′tər] *n.* A daughter of one's son or daughter.

grand duchess 1 The wife or widow of a grand duke. 2 A female ruler of a grand duchy. 3 In czarist Russia, a daughter of the czar or of a male descendant of the czar.

grand duchy A territory ruled by a grand duke or grand duchess.

grand duke 1 The male ruler of a grand duchy. 2 In czarist Russia, a son of the czar or of a male descendant of the czar.

gran·dee [gran·dē′] *n.* 1 A Spanish or Portuguese nobleman of the highest rank. 2 A person of high rank or status.

gran·deur [gran′jər] *n.* 1 Largeness and splendor; magnificence. 2 Nobility of character.

grand·fa·ther [gran(d)′fä′t͟hər] *n.* The father of one's father or mother.

grandfather clock A clock having a pendulum and enclosed in a tall cabinet.

grand·fa·ther·ly [gran(d)′fä′t͟hər·lē] *adj.* Having or exhibiting qualities, as indulgence or kindness, considered typical of a grandfather. **—grand′fa′·ther·li·ness** *n.*

gran·dil·o·quent [gran·dil′ə·kwənt] *adj.* Speaking in a very fancy and pretentious way; pompous. **—gran·dil·o·quence** [gran·dil′ə·kwəns] *n.* **—gran·dil′o·quent·ly** *adv.*

gran·di·ose [gran′dē·ōs *or* gran′dē·ōs′] *adj.* 1 Very grand and magnificent; imposing. 2 Making a show of being grand; pompous. **—gran′di·ose′ly** *adv.* **—grand′di·ose′ness** *n.* **—gran·di·os·i·ty** [gran′dē·os′ə·tē] *n.*

grand jury A group of from 12 to 23 persons that hears the evidence of suspected crime and decides if the accused person should be tried.

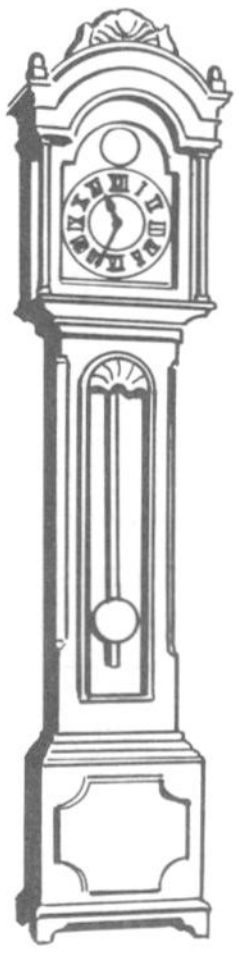

Grandfather clock

grand·ma [gran(d)′mä′] *n. informal* Grandmother.

grand·moth·er [gran(d)′mut͟h′ər] *n.* The mother of one's father or mother.

grand·moth·er·ly [gran(d)′mut͟h′ər·lē] *adj.* Having or exhibiting qualities, as indulgence or kindness, considered typical of a grandmother. **—grand′·moth′er·li·ness** *n.*

grand·neph·ew [gran(d)′nef′yōō] *n.* A son of one's nephew or niece.

grand·niece [gran(d)′nēs′] *n.* A daughter of one's nephew or niece.

grand opera An opera in which the entire libretto is set to music.

grand·pa [gran(d)′pä′ *or* gram′pä′] *n. informal* Grandfather.

grand·par·ent [gran(d)′pâr′ənt] *n.* A grandmother or a grandfather.

grand piano A large piano whose strings extend from the front to the back of its case.

Grand piano

grand·sire [gran(d)′·sīr′] *n.* 1 A grandfather. 2 An ancestor. 3 A respected old man. ◆ This word is seldom used today.

grand slam 1 In bridge, the winning of all thirteen tricks in one hand. 2 In baseball, a home run hit when runners are on all three bases.

grand·son [gran(d)′sun′] *n.* A son of one's son or daughter.

grand·stand [gran(d)′stand′] 1 *n.* The main seating place for spectators at sports events. 2 *n.* The spectators in the grandstand. 3 *v.* To perform an action in a showy, attention-getting manner; show off: a U.S. senator *grandstanding* for her constituency. **—grand′stand′er** *n.*

grand·un·cle [grand′ung′kəl] An uncle of either of one's parents.

grange [grānj] *n.* 1 (*often written* **Grange**) An association of U.S. farmers. 2 *British* A farm and its buildings.

gran·ite [gran′it] *n.* A hard, igneous rock that will take a high polish and is often used as a building material.

gran·ny [gran′ē] *n., pl.* **gran·nies** *informal* 1 Grandmother. 2 An old woman.

granny knot A square knot with the second part crossed the wrong way, so that it often slips and is hard to untie.

Granny knot

gra·no·la [grə·nō′lə] *n.* A nutritious breakfast cereal made of ingredients such as dried rolled oats, wheat germ, nuts, honey or brown sugar, and bits of dried dates or other fruits.

grant [grant] 1 *v.* To give; bestow: We *grant* you pardon; The owner *granted* permission. 2 *v.* To accept as true; concede: I *grant* it will be hard. 3 *n.* Something that is granted, as a sum of money. 4 *n.* The act of granting. **—take for granted** To accept or assume without question, as an idea. **—grant′a·ble** *adj.* **—grant′er** *n.*

grant·ee [gran·tē′] *n.* A person to whom a grant is awarded.

grant·or [gran′tər *or* gran′tôr′] *n.* A person who makes a grant.

gran·u·lar [gran′yə·lər] *adj.* 1 Made up of, like, or containing grains or granules. 2 Having a granulated surface.

gran·u·late [gran′yə·lāt′] *v.* **gran·u·lat·ed, gran·u·lat·ing** To reduce or form into grains or granules.

gran·u·la·tion [gran′yə·lā′shən] *n.* The act or process of granulating.

gran·ule [gran′yo͞ol] *n.* A small grain; particle.

grape [grāp] *n.* 1 A smooth-skinned, juicy berry that grows in bunches on some vines. Grapes are edible, and their juice is used to make wine. 2 A vine that bears grapes. 3 Grapeshot.

grape·fruit [grāp′fro͞ot′] *n.* 1 A large, round citrus fruit having a yellow rind and sour, juicy pulp. 2 The tree that bears this fruit.

grape·shot [grāp′shot′] *n.* A cluster of small iron balls, formerly fired from cannons.

grape sugar Another term for DEXTROSE.

grape·vine [grāp′vīn′] *n.* 1 A vine on which grapes grow. 2 *U.S.* A secret or informal way of passing news from person to person: We heard by the *grapevine* that they were coming.

graph [graf] 1 *n.* A diagram that shows the relation between the elements of two sets by a series of points or by a curve or by lines or bars of different lengths. 2 *v.* To express or present in the form of a graph.

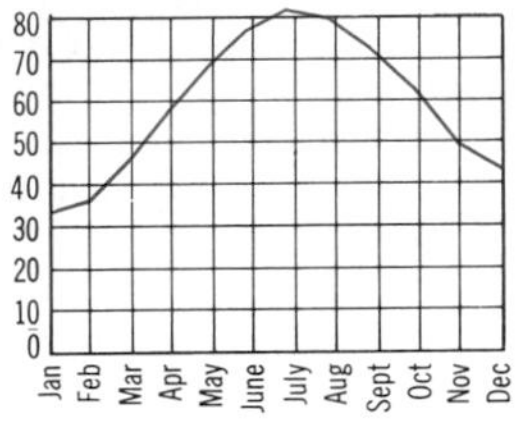

Graph of average temperature in Washington, D.C.

-graph A combining form meaning: 1 Something written, as in *autograph.* 2 An instrument that writes or transmits records, as in *telegraph.*

G

graph·ic [graf′ik] 1 *adj.* Of or having to do with written or drawn representations. 2 *adj.* Of or having to do with graphics or the graphic arts. 3 *n.* A work of graphic art. 4 *n.* A graphic representation generated by a computer. 5 *adj.* Of or having to do with graphs. 6 *adj.* Giving an exact picture or report; vivid; detailed. **—graph′i·cal·ly** *adv.*

graphic arts Any of the many forms of visual representation on a two-dimensional surface, as painting, photography, engraving, or lithography.

graph·ics [graf′iks] *n.pl.* (*used with sing. or pl. verb*) 1 The art and techniques of making drawings according to the rules of mathematics. 2 The process by which a computer generates a display of graphics. 3 The graphics so displayed. 4 The graphic arts.

graph·ite [graf′īt] *n.* A soft, black, slippery form of carbon, used as lead for pencils and to make moving parts of machines slide against each other more easily.

gra·phol·o·gy [grə·fol′ə·jē] *n.* The study of handwriting, especially when it is used in character analysis.

graph paper Paper marked with many intersecting lines, usually into small, equal squares, and used for drawing graphs, curves, and other figures.

-graphy A combining form meaning: 1 Writing or other representation done in a particular way, as in *photography.* 2 The art or science of or the writing on a particular subject, as *oceanography.*

a	add	**i**	it	**o͝o**	took	**oi**	oil
ā	ace	**ī**	ice	**o͞o**	pool	**ou**	pout
â	care	**o**	odd	**u**	up	**ng**	ring
ä	palm	**ō**	open	**û**	burn	**th**	thin
e	end	**ô**	order	**yo͞o**	fuse	**t͟h**	this
ē	equal					**zh**	vision

ə = { a in *above* e in *sicken* i in *possible* / o in *melon* u in *circus* }

grap·nel [grap′nəl] *n.* 1 A shaft with several hooks at one end, often attached to a rope and thrown so as to hook something and pull it closer. 2 A similar object used as an anchor.

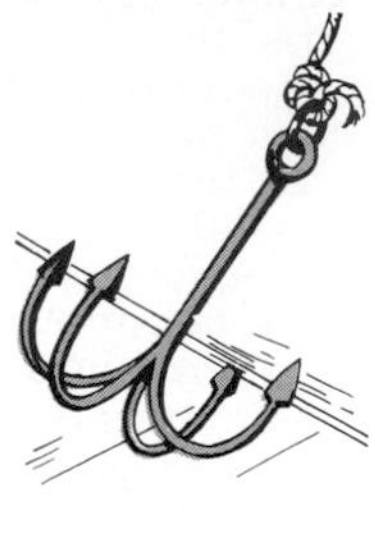

Grapnel

grap·ple [grap′əl] *v.* **grap·pled, grap·pling,** *n.* 1 *v.* To take hold of; grab firmly. 2 *n.* A hold or grip, as in wrestling. 3 *v.* To struggle closely; contend: The wrestlers *grappled;* to *grapple* with a problem. 4 *n.* A grapnel. **—grap′pler** *n.*

grappling iron A type of grapnel used to find sunken objects and pull them from the water.

grasp [grasp] 1 *v.* To take hold of firmly, as with the hand. 2 *n.* A hold, or the ability to hold; grip: Get a good *grasp.* 3 *v.* To understand; comprehend: to be able to *grasp* a problem. 4 *n.* Understanding; comprehension: a good *grasp* of English. 5 *n.* Complete control; domination: the *grasp* of a tyrant. **—grasp at** 1 To try to grab. 2 To accept eagerly: We *grasped at* the chance to spend a week at the beach.

grasp·ing [gras′ping] *adj.* Greedy; acquisitive. **—grasp′ing·ly** *adv.* **—grasp′ing·ness** *n.*

grass [gras] *n.* 1 A green plant with narrow leaves that covers fields and lawns. Cows, sheep, and other grazing animals eat grass. 2 Ground on which grass grows, as a lawn or pasture. 3 Any of various other plants with jointed stems, as grains, bamboo, and sugar cane. 4 *slang* Another name for MARIJUANA.

grass·hop·per [gras′hop′ər] *n.* Any of a large group of insects having strong hind legs for leaping and two pairs of wings. They often destroy plants and crops.

grass·land [gras′land′] *n.* Land with grass growing on it; a pasture or prairie.

grass-roots [gras′ro͞ots′] *adj.* Of, having to do with, or coming from grass roots: The candidate had *grass-roots* support.

grass roots 1 People or society at a local level, especially people in a rural area considered as a political or social group. 2 The source of something; foundation; groundwork.

grass·y [gras′ē] *adj.* **grass·i·er, grass·i·est** 1 Covered with or full of grass. 2 Like or having to do with grass. **—grass′i·ness** *n.*

grate[1] [grāt] *v.* **grat·ed, grat·ing** 1 To reduce to small pieces by rubbing against a rough surface: to *grate* onions; Cheese *grates* easily. 2 To rub together so as to make a scraping sound: The bent fender *grated* on the wheel. 3 To cause irritation: Certain mannerisms *grate* on me.

grate[2] [grāt] *n., v.* **grat·ed, grat·ing** 1 *n.* A framework of crossed or parallel bars placed over a window, door, drain, or other opening. 2 *n.* A metal framework used to hold burning fuel, in a furnace or fireplace. 3 *n.* A fireplace. 4 *v.* To fit with a grate: to *grate* a window.

grate·ful [grāt′fəl] *adj.* 1 Thankful or expressing thanks: a *grateful* person; a *grateful* nod. 2 Giving pleasure; welcome; agreeable: a *grateful* warmth. **—grate′ful·ly** *adv.* **—grate′ful·ness** *n.*

grat·er [grā′tər] *n.* 1 A person or thing that grates. 2 A kitchen utensil with sharp teeth or holes, used to grate food: a cheese *grater.*

grat·i·fi·ca·tion [grat′ə·fi·kā′shən] *n.* 1 The act of gratifying. 2 The condition of being gratified. 3 A source of satisfaction.

grat·i·fy [grat′ə·fī′] *v.* **grat·i·fied, grat·i·fy·ing** 1 To give pleasure or satisfaction to: The child's eagerness to learn *gratified* the teachers. 2 To satisfy, as a want or need; indulge: to *gratify* a friend's wish. **—grat′i·fi′er** *n.*

grat·i·fy·ing [grat′ə·fī′ing] *adj.* Giving pleasure or satisfaction. **—grat′i·fy′ing·ly** *adv.*

grat·ing[1] [grā′ting] *n.* An arrangement of bars or slats, as over a window or opening; grate.

grat·ing[2] [grā′ting] *adj.* 1 Harsh or unpleasant in sound; rasping. 2 Irritating; annoying.

gra·tis [grā′tis *or* gra′tis] *adj., adv.* Free of charge: a dinner *gratis*; Admit them *gratis.*

grat·i·tude [grat′ə·t(y)o͞od′] *n.* Thankfulness for a gift or favor; appreciation.

gra·tu·i·tous [grə·t(y)o͞o′ə·təs] *adj.* 1 Given without payment; free: a *gratuitous* ticket. 2 Lacking cause; needless; uncalled-for: *gratuitous* advice; *gratuitous* insults. **—gra·tu′i·tous·ly** *adv.* **—gra·tu′·i·tous·ness** *n.*

gra·tu·i·ty [grə·t(y)o͞o′ə·tē] *n., pl.* **gra·tu·i·ties** A gift, usually money, given in return for some service; tip: a generous *gratuity.*

grave[1] [grāv] *adj.* **grav·er, grav·est,** *n.* 1 *adj.* Of great importance; weighty: a *grave* responsibility. 2 *adj.* Filled with or showing danger: a *grave* problem. 3 *adj.* Solemn and dignified; sober; heavy: a *grave* mood. 4 *n.* A grave accent. **—grave′ly** *adv.*

grave[2] [grāv] *n.* 1 A burial place for a dead body, usually a hole in the ground. 2 Any final resting place: The ship went down to a watery *grave.* 3 Death.

grave[3] [grāv] *v.* **graved, grav·en** or **graved, grav·ing** 1 To make by carving; sculpture: to *grave* a statue. 2 To engrave or inscribe: to *grave* words in stone.

grave accent [grāv *or* gräv] A mark (`) used in some languages to change the pronunciation of a vowel. In English it is used to indicate that the "e" in the English ending "-ed" is to be pronounced. For example, "markèd" is to be pronounced [mär′kəd] instead of [märkt].

grav·el [grav′əl] *n., v.* **grav·eled** or **grav·elled, gravel·ing** or **grav·el·ling** 1 *n.* A mixture of small, rounded pebbles and pieces of stone. 2 *v.* To put gravel on, as a road.

grav·el·ly [grav′əl·ē] *adj.* 1 Made of or containing gravel. 2 Like gravel. 3 Harsh, as a voice.

grav·en [grāv′ən] An alternative past participle of GRAVE[3].

graven image An image carved of wood or stone that is worshipped as a deity; idol.

grave·stone [grāv′stōn′] *n.* A stone used to mark a grave and tell who the dead person was.

grave·yard [grāv′yärd′]*n.* A burial place; cemetery.

grav·i·tate [grav′ə·tāt′] *v.* **grav·i·tat·ed, grav·i·tat·ing** 1 To move or tend to move as a result of the force of gravity. 2 To move as though pulled by a powerful force; be attracted: Crowds *gravitate* to the exhibit. 3 To sink or settle: Mud *gravitates* to the bottom of a jar of water.

grav·i·ta·tion [grav′ə·tā′shən] *n.* 1 In physics, the force by which any two bodies attract each other. 2 The act or process of gravitating. 3 A movement, as to a source of attraction. **—grav′i·ta′tion·al** *adj.* **—grav′i·ta′tion·al·ly** *adv.*

grav·i·ty [grav′ə·tē] *n., pl.* **grav·i·ties** 1 In physics, gravitation, especially as shown by the tendency of objects to fall toward the center of the earth. 2 Weight; heaviness: the center of *gravity.* 3 Seriousness: the *gravity* of the situation.

gra·vy [grā′vē] *n., pl.* **gra·vies** 1 The juice and melted fat given off by meat while it is cooking. 2 A sauce made from this liquid, often thickened with flour. 3 *slang* Money or another benefit easily obtained, especially something received that is more than what is expected or due.

gravy train Something that provides a source of easy money: government contracts that prove to be a *gravy train* for aircraft manufacturers.

gray [grā] 1 *n.* A shade or color made up of a mixture of white and black. 2 *adj.* Of or having this color or shade. 3 *adj.* Dark or dull; dismal; gloomy: a *gray* day. 4 *adj.* Having gray hair. 5 *v.* To make or become gray. **—gray′ness** *n.*

gray·beard [grā′bird′] *n.* An old man.

gray·ish [grā′ish] *adj.* Somewhat gray.

gray·ling [grā′ling] *n., pl.,* **gray·ling** or **gray·lings** A troutlike fish having a large, colorful dorsal fin.

gray matter 1 The reddish gray nerve tissue of the brain and spinal cord. 2 *informal* Brains; intelligence.

graze[1] [grāz] *v.* **grazed, graz·ing** 1 To feed on growing grass: Cattle *graze* when hungry. 2 To let or put to graze: The farmer *grazed* sheep in the field.

graze[2] [grāz] *v.* **grazed, graz·ing,** *n.* 1 *v.* To brush against or scrape lightly in passing: A truck *grazed* the car. 2 *n.* A light contact. 3 *n.* A mark or scrape made by grazing.

graz·ing [grā′zing] *n.* Land used for feeding livestock; pasturage.

grease [*n.* grēs, *v.* grēs *or* grēz] *n., v.* **greased, greas·ing** 1 *n.* Animal fat in a soft state. 2 *n.* Any thick, fatty, or oily substance; lubricant. 3 *v.* To apply grease to: to *grease* a car.

grease monkey *slang* 1 A person who greases machinery. 2 A mechanic, especially an automobile or aircraft mechanic.

grease paint A waxy substance used for theatrical makeup.

greas·y [grē′sē *or* grē′zē] *adj.* **greas·i·er, greas·i·est** 1 Smeared or spotted with grease. 2 Containing much grease or fat; oily. 3 Like grease; slick; *greasy* mud. **—greas′i·ly** *adv.* **—greas′i·ness** *n.*

great [grāt] *adj.* 1 Very large, as in size, quantity, amount, extent, or expanse; immense; big. 2 More than ordinary; remarkable: *great* pain. 3 Of unusual importance: a *great* writer; a *great* victory. 4 Enthusiastic: a *great* hiker. 5 One generation further away in relationship: used in combination: *great-aunt.* 6 *informal* Excellent; first-rate; fine: a *great* friend. **—great′ness** *n.* ◆ Avoid overworking *great* for more specific words such as *skillful, clever,* or *enthusiastic.*

great ape Any of the various anthropoid apes, as chimpanzees or gorillas.

great-aunt [grāt′ant′] *n.* Another name for GRANDAUNT.

Great Bear A constellation of the northern sky, containing seven bright stars.

great circle 1 In geometry, a circle formed on the surface of a sphere by a plane that passes through the center of the sphere. It is the largest circle that can be drawn on a sphere. 2 In geography, a similar circle on the surface of the earth. The shortest distance between any two places is on a great circle.

great·coat [grāt′kōt′] *n.* A heavy overcoat.

Great Dane One of a breed of large, strong, smooth-haired dogs.

Great Dane

great·er [grāt′ər] 1 Comparative of GREAT. 2 *adj.* (*usually written* **Greater**) Indicating a city and its suburbs: *Greater* London.

great-grand·child [grāt′·gran(d)′chīld] *n., pl.* **great - grand · chil · dren** [grāt′gran(d)′chil′drən] A great-grandson or great-granddaughter.

great-grand·daugh·ter [grāt′gran(d)′dô′tər] *n.* A female, considered in relation to any of her great-grandparents.

great-grand·fa·ther [grāt′gran(d)′fä′thər] *n.* A man, considered in relation to any of the grandchildren of his children.

great-grand·moth·er [grāt′gran(d)′muth′ər] *n.* A woman, considered in relation to any of the grandchildren of her children.

great-grand·par·ent [grāt′gran(d)′pâr′ənt] *n.* A person, considered in relation to any of the grandchildren of his or her children.

great-grand·son [grāt′gran(d)′sun′] *n.* A male, considered in relation to any of his great-grandparents.

great·heart·ed [grāt′här′tid] *adj.* 1 Noble or generous in spirit. 2 Brave; courageous.

great·ly [grāt′lē] *adv.* 1 In or to a great degree; very much. 2 In a great manner.

great-neph·ew [grāt′nef′yōō] *n.* Another word for GRANDNEPHEW.

great-niece [grāt′nēs′] *n.* Another word for GRANDNIECE.

great seal The principal seal of a government, used to stamp official documents.

great-un·cle [grāt′ung′kəl] *n.* Another name for GRANDUNCLE.

greave [grēv] *n.* (*usually pl.*) Armor that protects the leg from knee to ankle.

grebe [grēb] *n.* A swimming and diving bird, having flaps on its toes but not webbed feet.

Gre·cian [grē′shən] *n., adj.* Greek.

Gre·co-Ro·man [grek′ō·rō′mən *or* grē′kō·rō′mən] *adj.* Of, having to do with, or characteristic of both ancient Greece and Rome.

greed [grēd] *n.* A selfish and grasping desire for possessions, especially for money.

greed·y [grē′dē] *adj.* **greed·i·er, greed·i·est** 1 Wanting selfishly to get more, especially more money: a *greedy* landlord. 2 Wanting to eat and drink a lot; gluttonous: *greedy* children at a birthday party. **—greed′i·ly** *adv.* **—greed′i·ness** *n.*

Greek [grēk] 1 *adj.* Of or from Greece. 2 *n.* A

a	add	**i**	it	**o͝o**	took	**oi**	oil
ā	ace	**ī**	ice	**ōō**	pool	**ou**	pout
â	care	**o**	odd	**u**	up	**ng**	ring
ä	palm	**ō**	open	**û**	burn	**th**	thin
e	end	**ô**	order	**yōō**	fuse	**th**	this
ē	equal					**zh**	vision

ə = {a in *above* e in *sicken* i in *possible* / o in *melon* u in *circus*}

G

person born in or a citizen of Greece. **3** *n.* The language of Greece.
Greek cross A cross composed of two bars of equal dimensions that intersect at right angles at their midpoints.
Greek Orthodox Church A branch of the Eastern Orthodox Church.
green [grēn] **1** *n.* The color of growing grass and foliage. **2** *adj.* Of or having this color. **3** *adj.* Not cured or ready for use: *green* lumber. **4** *adj.* Not fully developed; immature; unripe: *green* fruit. **5** *adj.* Not fully trained; inexperienced: *green* troops. **6** *adj.* Thriving; flourishing: a *green* garden. **7** *n.* A plot of land covered with turf: a large putting *green*; the village *green*. **8** *n.* (*pl.*) The leaves and stems of certain plants used as food, such as spinach or beets. **—green′ness** *n.*
green·back [grēn′bak′] *n.* Any U.S. paper money that is printed in green ink on the back.
green bean A string bean (defs. 1 and 2).
green·belt [grēn′belt′] *n.* An area around a community that is reserved for parks, parkways, or farmland.
green·er·y [grē′nər·ē] *n.* Green plants; foliage.
green-eyed [grēn′īd] *adj.* **1** Having green eyes. **2** Jealous.
green·gage [grēn′gāj′] *n.* A type of sweet plum having green skin and flesh.
green·gro·cer [grēn′grō′sər] *n. British* A dealer in fresh fruits and vegetables.
green·horn [grēn′hôrn′] *n.* An inexperienced person; beginner.
green·house [grēn′hous′] *n.* A heated building used for growing delicate plants, having its roof and sides made partly of glass; hothouse.

Greenhouse

green·ing [grē′ning] *n.* Any of several varieties of apples that are green-skinned when ripe. They have a somewhat tart flavor and are used for cooking.
green·ish [grēn′ish] *adj.* Somewhat green.
green light **1** A traffic light that signals permission to proceed. **2** *informal* Any signal to proceed; go-ahead.
green·mail [grēn′māl′] *n. informal* A method of financial speculation where an investor threatens to take over a corporation by buying a large block of its stock, hoping that the company will pay an inflated price to buy back its own stock.
green onion Another term for SCALLION.
green pepper The green, unripe fruit of several of the pepper plants.
green·room [grēn′ro͞om′ *or* grēn′ro͝om′] *n.* A room in some theaters and concert halls where performers can relax when they are offstage.
green soap A soft soap specially formulated for the treatment of certain skin conditions.
green·sward [grēn′swôrd′] *n.* Ground covered with green grass; turf.
green thumb A special knack for making plants grow very well.
Greenwich time (*sometimes written* **Greenwich Time**) The standard time observed along the meridian that passes through Greenwich, England. It is used as the basis for reckoning time in the 24 time zones into which the Earth is divided.
green·wood [grēn′wo͝od′] *n.* A forest during the period when it is green with foliage, as in summer.
greet [grēt] *v.* **1** To show friendly recognition to, as when meeting; welcome: I *greeted* my friends. **2** To meet or receive in a certain way: The child *greeted* us with flowers. **3** To present itself to: The glow of the fire *greeted* us. **—greet′er** *n.*
greet·ing [grē′ting] *n.* **1** The act of a person who greets; welcome. **2** (*sometimes pl.*) A message showing friendship or regard.
greeting card A card, usually illustrated, that has a message printed on it, usually sent or given on a holiday or special occasion.
gre·gar·i·ous [gri·gâr′ē·əs] *adj.* **1** Living together in flocks, herds, or groups: Cattle are *gregarious*. **2** Enjoying the company of others; sociable. **—gre·gar′i·ous·ly** *adv.* **—gre·gar′i·ous·ness** *n.*
Gre·go·ri·an calendar [gri·gôr′ē·ən] The calendar now used in most parts of the world, prescribed by Pope Gregory XIII in 1582.
Gregorian chant A type of music sung in the services of the Roman Catholic and some other churches. It was started by Pope Gregory I.
grem·lin [grem′lin] *n.* An imaginary, elflike creature jokingly said to cause mechanical troubles in airplanes and other devices.
gre·nade [gri·nād′] *n.* **1** A small bomb thrown by hand or fired from a rifle. **2** A glass container that breaks and releases chemicals when thrown, as to put out a fire.
Gre·na·di·an [gri·nā′dē·ən] **1** *adj.* Of or from Grenada. **2** *n.* A person born in or a citizen of Grenada.
gren·a·dier [gren′ə·dir′] *n.* **1** In earlier times, a soldier assigned to throw grenades. **2** A member of a special regiment in the British army.
grew [gro͞o] Past tense of GROW.
grey [grā] *n., adj.* Another spelling of GRAY.
grey·hound [grā′hound′] *n.* One of a breed of tall, slender dogs, used in dog races.

Greyhound

grid [grid] *n.* **1** An arrangement of evenly spaced parallel or intersecting bars, wires, or the like; grate. **2** An arrangement of lines that divides a map into small squares. **3** The metal framework that supports the active material in a storage battery.
grid·dle [grid′(ə)l] *n.* A flat pan, often with no raised rim, used for cooking pancakes and other foods.
grid·dle·cake [grid′(ə)l·kāk′] *n.* A pancake.
grid·i·ron [grid′ī′ərn] *n.* **1** A metal grating in a frame, used to hold meat or other food during broiling. **2** Something that looks like a cooking gridiron, as a structure of beams or pipes. **3** A football field.
grid·lock [grid′lok] *n.* **1** A traffic jam in which cars are packed so closely at an intersection that none can move in any direction. **2** A situation resembling such a traffic jam.
grief [grēf] *n.* **1** Deep sorrow or mental distress. **2** A cause of deep sorrow. **—come to grief** To end badly; meet with disaster; fail.
grief-strick·en [grēf′strik′ən] *adj.* Overcome by grief; deeply sorrowful.

griev·ance [grē′vəns] *n.* A real or imagined wrong thought of as a cause for anger or complaint: Tell your *grievance* to the judge.

grieve [grēv] *v.* **grieved, griev·ing** To feel or cause to feel grief: They *grieved* over their loss; Your absence *grieves* us.

griev·ous [grē′vəs] *adj.* **1** Causing grief, sorrow, or pain: a *grievous* wound. **2** Deserving severe punishment; very bad; grave: a *grievous* crime. **3** Showing grief; mournful: a *grievous* wail. **—griev′·ous·ly** *adv.* **—griev′ous·ness** *n.*

grif·fin [grif′ən] *n.* In Greek myths, a beast with the head and wings of an eagle and the body of a lion.

Griffin

grill [gril] **1** *n.* A gridiron or similar cooking utensil. **2** *v.* To cook, as on a grill. **3** *n.* A meal or serving of grilled food. **4** *n.* A restaurant where grilled food is served. **5** *v.* To torment with great heat. **6** *v.* *U.S. informal* To question hard and thoroughly: The police *grilled* the suspect.

grille [gril] *n.* A grating, often decorative, used as a covering or screen in a door or window.

grill·work [gril′wûrk′] *n.* A grille or any metalwork in the pattern of a grille.

grilse [grils] *n., pl.* **grilse** A young, mature Atlantic salmon on its first return to fresh water, where it will spawn.

grim [grim] *adj.* **grim·mer, grim·mest** **1** Stern or forbidding: a *grim* expression. **2** Unyielding; fixed: *grim* determination. **3** Cruel; fierce: a *grim* war. **4** Repulsive or ghastly: *grim* tales of murder. **—grim′ly** *adv.* **—grim′ness** *n.*

gri·mace [gri·mās′ *or* grim′əs] *n., v.* **gri·maced, gri·mac·ing** **1** *n.* A twisting of the face expressing pain, annoyance, disgust, or other feelings. **2** *v.* To make a grimace; make faces.

grime [grīm] *n., v.* **grimed, grim·ing** **1** *n.* Dirt, especially soot, rubbed into or coating a surface. **2** *v.* To make dirty: to *grime* a floor.

grim·y [grī′mē] *adj.* **grim·i·er, grim·i·est** Full of or covered with grime; dirty. **—grim′i·ness** *n.*

grin [grin] *v.* **grinned, grin·ning,** *n.* **1** *v.* To smile broadly and sometimes foolishly, showing the teeth. **2** *v.* To pull back the lips and show the teeth, as in a snarl or grimace. **3** *n.* An expression made by grinning, especially a broad smile.

grind [grīnd] *v.* **ground, grind·ing,** *n.* **1** *v.* To crush or undergo crushing into small pieces or fine powder: to *grind* coffee; Meat *grinds* easily. **2** *n.* The degree of fineness to which something is ground: a coarse *grind* of hominy. **3** *v.* To sharpen, shape, or polish by rubbing with something rough: to *grind* a chisel. **4** *v.* To press together with a scraping motion; grate: to *grind* the teeth. **5** *v.* To operate by turning a crank. **6** *n.* The act of grinding. **7** *v.* To produce mechanically or with effort: The author *grinds* out bad stories. **8** *v.* To reduce to misery, as by harsh treatment: Injustice *grinds* people down. **9** *v.* *U.S. informal* To work or study hard or long. **10** *n.* *U.S. informal* Long and hard work or study. **11** *n.* *U.S. informal* A student who studies constantly.

grind·er [grīn′dər] *n.* **1** A person who grinds, especially one who sharpens tools. **2** A device that grinds, as a mill for coffee. **3** A tooth that grinds food; molar.

grind·stone [grīnd′stōn′] *n.* A flat, circular stone that is rotated and is used for grinding tools. **—keep one's nose to the grindstone** To work hard and steadily.

Grindstone

grin·go [gring′gō] *n., pl.* **grin·gos** *slang* In Latin America, a foreigner, especially an American or English person: usually considered offensive.

grip [grip] *v.* **gripped** or **gript, grip·ping,** *n.* **1** *v.* To grasp or hold on firmly. **2** *n.* The act of gripping. **3** *n.* The ability to grip: a good *grip.* **4** *n.* Control: in the *grip* of fear. **5** *v.* To capture the imagination of: The story *gripped* us. **6** *n.* Understanding; mastery: a good *grip* of history. **7** *n.* The part of an object to be held in the hand; handle. **8** *n.* The way in which something, as a tool or bat, is held. **9** *n.* The strength of a handshake: a strong *grip.* **10** *n.* A secret handshake, as one used by members of a fraternity or society. **11** *n.* *U.S.* A small suitcase. **—come to grips** **1** To struggle in combat. **2** To face bravely, as a difficulty or problem.

gripe [grīp] *v.* **griped, grip·ing,** *n.* **1** *v.* To cause cramps or sharp pains in the bowels. **2** *n.* (*usually pl.*) Cramps in the bowels. **3** *v.* *U.S. informal* To anger or annoy: Their lies *gripe* me. **4** *v.* *U.S. informal* To complain or grumble: to *gripe* about the weather. **5** *n.* *U.S. informal* A complaint; grievance.

grippe [grip] *n.* Influenza.

gris·ly [griz′lē] *adj.* **gris·li·er, gris·li·est** Causing fear or horror; gruesome: I shivered when I heard the *grisly* story. **—gris′li·ness** *n.*

grist [grist] *n.* **1** Grain that is to be ground. **2** Ground grain; meal.

gris·tle [gris′(ə)l] *n.* A tough, stringy substance found in meat; cartilage.

gris·tly [gris′lē] *adj.* **gris·tli·er, gris·tli·est** Like gristle. **2** Containing gristle.

grist·mill [grist′mil′] *n.* A mill for grinding grain.

grit [grit] *n., v.* **grit·ted, grit·ting** **1** *n.* Small hard particles, as of sand or stone. **2** *n.* A hard, coarse sandstone, used for making grindstones. **3** *n.* Determined courage; pluck. **4** *v.* To grind or press together: To *grit* one's teeth.

grits [grits] *n.pl.* Coarse meal made from grain, especially corn, with the husks removed.

grit·ty [grit′ē] *adj.* **grit·ti·er, grit·ti·est** **1** Like, containing, or made of grit. **2** Bravely determined; plucky: a *gritty* soldier. **—grit′ti·ly** *adv.* **—grit′ti·ness** *n.*

griz·zled [griz′əld] *adj.* **1** Streaked or mixed with gray. **2** Having gray hair.

griz·zly [griz′lē] *adj.* **griz·zli·er, griz·zli·est,** *n., pl.*

a	add	**i**	it	**o͝o**	took	**oi**	oil
ā	ace	**ī**	ice	**o͞o**	pool	**ou**	pout
â	care	**o**	odd	**u**	up	**ng**	ring
ä	palm	**ō**	open	**û**	burn	**th**	thin
e	end	**ô**	order	**yo͞o**	fuse	**th**	this
ē	equal					**zh**	vision

ə = a in *above*, e in *sicken*, i in *possible*, o in *melon*, u in *circus*

griz·zlies 1 *adj.* Grayish; grizzled. 2 *n.* A grizzly bear.

grizzly bear A large, brownish or grayish bear of western North America.

Grizzly bear

groan [grōn] 1 *v.* To make a long, low sound that shows emotion, as pain, anguish, displeasure, or boredom: We *groaned* at the extra homework. 2 *v.* To make a rough, creaking sound, especially from being overloaded: The chair *groaned* under my weight. 3 *n.* Any groaning sound.

groat [grōt] *n.* 1 An old English silver coin worth four pennies. 2 Any very small, trivial sum.

groats [grōts] *n.pl.* (*used with sing. or pl. verb*) Hulled and usually coarsely cracked grain, especially oats.

gro·cer [grō'sər] *n.* A person who deals in foods and other household goods.

gro·cer·y [grō'sər·ē *or* grōs'rē] *n., pl.* **gro·cer·ies** 1 *U.S.* A store selling foods and other household goods. 2 (*pl.*) The food and other goods sold by a grocer.

grog [grog] *n.* 1 Alcoholic liquor, especially rum, mixed with water. 2 Any alcoholic drink.

grog·gy [grog'ē] *adj.* **grog·gi·er, grog·gi·est** 1 Dazed or not fully conscious, as from a blow or exhaustion. 2 Drunk. **—grog'gi·ly** *adv.* **—grog'gi·ness** *n.*

groin [groin] 1 *n.* The fold or crease formed where either of the thighs joins the abdomen. 2 *n.* A curved line formed on a ceiling where two vaults meet. 3 *v.* To build with or form into groins.

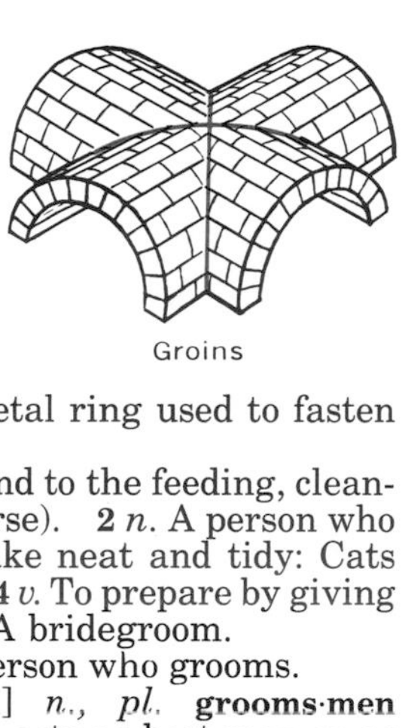
Groins

grom·met [grom'it] *n.* 1 An eyelet or ring, as of metal or plastic, used to reinforce a hole in sailcloth, leather, or other material. 2 A rope or metal ring used to fasten a sail.

groom [grōōm] 1 *v.* To attend to the feeding, cleaning, and brushing of (a horse). 2 *n.* A person who tends horses. 3 *v.* To make neat and tidy: Cats *groom* themselves daily. 4 *v.* To prepare by giving special training to. 5 *n.* A bridegroom.

groom·er [grōōm'ər] *n.* A person who grooms.

grooms·man [grōōmz'mən] *n., pl.* **grooms·men** [grōōmz'mən] A man who acts as best man or as an usher for the bridegroom at his wedding.

groove [grōōv] *n., v.* **grooved, groov·ing** 1 *n.* A long, narrow cut or furrow made in a surface, especially by a tool. 2 *n.* Any long, narrow depression, channel, or rut. 3 *n.* A thin spiral track cut into the surface of a phonograph record. 4 *v.* To make a groove or grooves in: to *groove* wood. 5 *n.* A fixed or habitual routine: to be in the same old *groove.*

grope [grōp] *v.* **groped, grop·ing** 1 To feel or reach around blindly and clumsily. 2 To search in a confused, uncertain way: to *grope* for truth. 3 To find by groping: I *groped* my way in the dark.

gros·beak [grōs'bēk'] *n.* Any of various finchlike birds with a short, stout beak.

gros·grain [grō'grān'] *n.* A strong silk or rayon fabric with horizontal ribs, usually woven as ribbon.

gross [grōs] 1 *adj.* Having nothing subtracted; total: *gross* income. 2 *adj.* Clearly bad or wrong; flagrant: *gross* errors. 3 *adj.* Too large or fat; hulking. 4 *adj.* Coarse or improper; vulgar; obscene: *gross* conduct. 5 *n., pl.* **gross·es** The entire amount; total: 10 percent of the *gross.* 6 *n., pl.* **gross** Twelve dozen; 144. **—gross'ly** *adv.* **—gross'·ness** *n.*

gross national product The total value of all goods and services produced in a nation during a specified time, especially a year.

gro·tesque [grō·tesk'] *adj.* Distorted or very strange or ugly in appearance or style: The hyena is a *grotesque* animal. **—gro·tesque'ly** *adv.* **—gro·tesque'ness** *n.*

grot·to [grot'ō] *n., pl.* **grot·toes** or **grot·tos** 1 A cave. 2 An artificial cavelike structure, as a shrine. ◆ See CRYPT.

grouch [grouch] *U.S. informal* 1 *v.* To complain and find fault. 2 *n.* A discontented, grumbling person. 3 *n.* A sulky, grouchy mood.

grouch·y [grouch'ē] *adj.* **grouch·i·er, grouch·i·est** *U.S. informal* Cross or ill-humored. **—grouch'i·ly** *adv.* **—grouch'i·ness** *n.*

ground[1] [ground] 1 *n.* The part of the earth's surface that is solid; land. 2 *n.* A tract of land used for a particular purpose: a burial *ground.* 3 *n.* (*pl.*) Land surrounding and belonging to a building: a house and *grounds.* 4 *v.* To put or place on the ground. 5 *n.* A connection of an electric circuit with the earth. 6 *v.* To connect with the ground, as an electric circuit. 7 *adj.* On, near, or level with the ground. 8 *v.* To run aground, as a ship. 9 *n.* (*often pl.*) A basic cause, reason, or justification: What were the *grounds* for that accusation? 10 *v.* To base, as on a foundation or idea; establish: to *ground* a theory on facts. 11 *v.* To teach basic principles to: to *ground* students in grammar. 12 *n.* (*pl.*) Sediment, especially if remaining after a beverage has been brewed: coffee *grounds.* 13 *n.* The background or main surface, as of a painting. 14 *v.* To confine to the ground: The airline *grounded* the plane. 15 *v.* In baseball, to hit a ball so that it bounces or rolls on the ground: The batter *grounded* to first base. **—break ground** 1 To dig into the earth, as in plowing or building. 2 To make a start in doing something. **—cover ground** 1 To travel, especially over a long distance. 2 To make progress. **—gain ground** To advance; make headway. **—give ground** To give up a position or advantage; retreat. **—lose ground** To fall behind or weaken.

ground[2] [ground] Past tense and past participle of GRIND.

ground ball A grounder.

ground cover Plants that form a dense and extensive growth close to the ground.

ground crew The group of workers who service and maintain an aircraft before and after a flight.

ground·er [groun'dər] *n.* In baseball, a ball hit so that it bounces or rolls on the ground.

ground floor The floor of a building that is at or nearly at ground level. **—get in on the ground floor** To participate in something, as an investment or project, from the very beginning.

ground·hog [ground'hog' *or* ground'hôg] *n.* The

woodchuck. In popular tradition the animal comes out of hibernation on February 2, or Groundhog Day. If the groundhog sees its shadow, winter remains for another six weeks; and if the animal does not see it, spring comes early.
ground·less [ground′lis] *adj.* Having no reason or cause; baseless.
ground·nut [ground′nut′] *n.* Any of various plants having edible underground parts, as the peanut.
ground pine Any of various creeping evergreens.
ground rule A basic rule of procedure or behavior in a particular situation or field.
ground speed or **ground·speed** [ground′spēd′] *n.* The speed of an aircraft calculated in terms of the ground distance the aircraft flies over in a specified amount of time.
ground squirrel A chipmunk or similar small rodent that lives on or in the ground.
ground swell Broad, deep ocean waves caused by an often distant storm or earthquake.
ground water Water that seeps into the earth and collects, serving to supply wells and springs.
ground·work [ground′wûrk′] *n.* A foundation; basis.
ground zero The point on the earth or water that is directly at, above, or below a nuclear explosion.
group [gro͞op] **1** *n.* A number of persons or things. **2** *n.* A number of people or things that have one or more things in common; class. **3** *v.* To gather or arrange in a group or groups: *Group* yourselves around me. **4** *n.* A radical (def. 6).
group·er [gro͞o′pər] *n., pl.* **group·er** or **group·ers** Any of a number of large, usually tropical saltwater fishes.
group·ing [gro͞o′ping] *n.* **1** The act or process of assigning someone or something to a group, class, or category. **2** A collection of things in a group.
group therapy A form of psychotherapy in which a number of patients meet regularly to discuss their problems and feelings, usually in the presence of a trained psychotherapist.
grouse [grous] *n., pl.* **grouse** A plump bird, often hunted for sport.
grove [grōv] *n.* **1** A small group of trees. **2** An orchard: an orange *grove.*

Ruffed grouse

grov·el [gruv′əl *or* grov′əl] *v.* **grov·eled** or **grov·elled, grov·el·ing** or **grov·el·ling** **1** To kneel, crawl, or lie face downward in fear or humility. **2** To act in a very humble and fearful way; cringe. **—grov′el·er** or **grov′el·ler** *n.*
grow [grō] *v.* **grew, grown, grow·ing** **1** To increase in size, age, or maturity: Our kitten *grew.* **2** To increase in size or amount: The debt *grew* rapidly. **3** To exist in a live or flourishing condition: Bananas *grow* in the tropics. **4** To make grow; cultivate: to *grow* roses. **5** To develop naturally: Our interest in science *grew.* **6** To become: to *grow* angry; to *grow* older. **—grow on** To become increasingly pleasing or necessary to. **—grow out of** **1** To become too big or mature for; outgrow. **2** To result from. **—grow up** To reach full growth; become adult. **—grow′er** *n.*
growl [groul] **1** *n.* A deep, rumbling, threatening sound, as that of an angry dog. **2** *v.* To make a growl. **3** *v.* To speak gruffly and angrily.
grown [grōn] **1** Past participle of GROW. **2** *adj.* Fully developed; mature; adult: not yet a *grown* man.
grown-up [*n.* grōn′up′, *adj.* grōn′up′] **1** *n.* An adult. **2** *adj.* Fully grown; adult. **3** *adj.* Of or suited for adults.
growth [grōth] *n.* **1** The action of growing. **2** The amount grown: a season's *growth.* **3** Something grown or growing: a *growth* of weeds.
grub [grub] *v.* **grubbed, grub·bing,** *n.* **1** *v.* To dig or dig up: to *grub* for food; to *grub* potatoes. **2** *v.* To work hard and live miserably: to *grub* along from day to day. **3** *n.* A fat, wormlike larva of an insect. **4** *n. slang* Food. **—grub′ber** *n.*
grub·by [grub′ē] *adj.* **grub·bi·er, grub·bi·est** Dirty or sloppy. **—grub′bi·ly** *adv.* **—grub′bi·ness** *n.*
grub·stake [grub′stāk′] *n., v.* **grub·staked, grub·stak·ing** **1** *n.* Supplies or funds advanced to a person starting a venture, especially such an advance made to someone prospecting for ore on the promise of a share of future profits. **2** *v.* To supply a grubstake to someone. **—grub′stak′er** *n.*
grudge [gruj] *n., v.* **grudged, grudg·ing** **1** *n.* A feeling of hatred or resentment: I had a *grudge* against a friend who hurt my feelings. **2** *v.* To be envious of or angry at (someone) because of what he or she has: Don't *grudge* the winners their prizes. **3** *v.* To give or allow unwillingly: I *grudged* the time I spent cleaning.
grudg·ing [gruj′ing] *adj.* Reluctant; unwilling: *grudging* admiration. **—grudg′ing·ly** *adv.*
gru·el [gro͞o′əl] *n.* A thin, liquid food made by boiling cereal in water or milk.
gru·el·ing or **gru·el·ling** [gro͞o′əl·ing] *adj.* Very tiring or exhausting: a *grueling* trip.
grue·some [gro͞o′səm] *adj.* Causing disgust or horror; repulsive; frightful. **—grue′some·ly** *adv.* **—grue′some·ness** *n.*
gruff [gruf] *adj.* **1** Harsh or hoarse: a *gruff* voice. **2** Rude or surly; unfriendly: a *gruff* response to a question. **—gruff′ly** *adv.* **—gruff′ness** *n.*
grum·ble [grum′bəl] *v.* **grum·bled, grum·bling,** *n.* **1** *v.* To complain in a grumpy way; mutter unhappily. **2** *n.* A low, muttered complaint. **3** *v.* To make a low, rumbling sound. **4** *n.* A low, rumbling sound: the *grumble* of thunder. **—grum′bler** *n.*
grump [grump] *n.* A cranky or grouchy person.
grump·y [grum′pē] *adj.* **grump·i·er, grump·i·est** Cranky or grouchy: a *grumpy* person. **—grump′i·ly** *adv.* **—grump′i·ness** *n.*
grunt [grunt] **1** *n.* A short, deep, hoarse sound made in the throat. **2** *v.* To make such a sound: The movers *grunted* as they lifted the heavy piano. **3** *v.* To say or express by grunting: to *grunt* one's approval.
gry·phon [grif′ən] *n.* Another spelling of GRIFFIN.
G.S.A. Girl Scouts of America.
Gt. Brit. Great Britain.
gtd. guaranteed.

a	add	**i**	it	**o͝o**	took	**oi**	oil
ā	ace	**ī**	ice	**o͞o**	pool	**ou**	pout
â	care	**o**	odd	**u**	up	**ng**	ring
ä	palm	**ō**	open	**û**	burn	**th**	thin
e	end	**ô**	order	**yo͞o**	fuse	**t͟h**	this
ē	equal					**zh**	vision

ə = a in *above* e in *sicken* i in *possible* o in *melon* u in *circus*

Hh

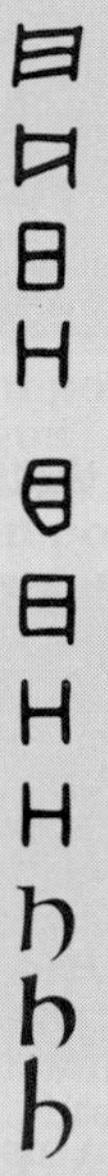

Early Phoenician (late 2nd millennium B.C.)

Phoenician (8th century B.C.)

Early Greek (9th-7th centuries B.C.)

Classical Greek (403 B.C. onward)

Early Etruscan (around 8th century B.C.)

Early Latin (around 7th century B.C.)

Monumental Latin (4th century B.C.)

Classical Latin

Uncial

Half uncial

Caroline minuscule

H is the eighth letter of the alphabet. The sign for it originated among Semitic people in the Near East, in the region of Palestine and Syria, probably in the middle of the second millennium B.C. Little is known about the sign until around 1000 B.C., when the Phoenicians began using it. They named it *kheth* or *heth* and used it for the sound of *kh,* or a throaty *h* sound not found in European languages.

When the Greeks adopted the Phoenician sign around the ninth century B.C., they used the sign in two ways. Eastern Greeks called it *eta* and used it to stand for the long *e* sound. They also simplified the shape of the letter. Western Greeks used the sign for the sound of the consonant *h*.

As early as the eighth century B.C., the Etruscans adopted the Greek alphabet. It is from the Etruscans that the Romans took the sign for *H*. Both the Etruscans and the Romans retained the Western Greek use of the sign for the sound of the consonant *h*. The Romans later accepted the simplified shape of the sign. Around the time of the Caesars, the Romans made the shapes of all their letters more graceful. The models of the letters found on the base of Trajan's column, erected in Rome in 114, are considered masterpieces of letter design. A *majuscule,* or capital letter, *H* in the style of the Trajan capitals opens this essay.

The *minuscule,* or small letter, *h* developed gradually, between the third and the ninth centuries, in the handwriting that scribes used for copying books. It developed as they attempted to write the letter without lifting their pens. Contributing to its shape were the Roman *uncials* of the fourth to the eighth centuries and the *half uncials* of the fifth to the ninth centuries. Its development was continued in the script that evolved under the encouragement of Charlemagne (742-814). This script was known as the *Caroline minuscules,* and it became the principal handwriting system used on the medieval manuscripts of the ninth and tenth centuries.

h or **H** [āch] *n., pl.* **h's** or **H's** The eighth letter of the English alphabet.

h. 1 height. 2 hour(s). 3 hundred.

H The symbol for the element hydrogen.

ha [hä] *interj.* An exclamation expressing surprise, discovery, triumph, or joy.

ha·be·as cor·pus [hā'bē·əs kôr'pəs] A legal order demanding that a prisoner be produced in court to determine if it is lawful to hold him or her. ◆ *Habeas corpus* comes directly from Latin, where it literally means *you shall have the body.*

hab·er·dash·er [hab'ər·dash'ər] *n.* A dealer in men's clothes, as shirts, ties, and hats.

hab·er·dash·er·y [hab'ər·dash'ər·ē] *n., pl.* **hab·er·dash·er·ies** 1 The goods sold by a haberdasher. 2 A haberdasher's shop.

ha·bil·i·ment [hə·bil'ə·mənt] *n. (usually pl.)* Clothing; attire; garb.

hab·it [hab'it] *n.* 1 An act or practice done so often that it becomes almost automatic and is difficult to stop. 2 A usual form or way of developing of a plant or animal: Ivy is of a creeping *habit.* 3 The clothing worn by people in certain activities or religious orders. ◆ See CUSTOM.

hab·it·a·ble [hab'it·ə·bəl] *adj.* Fit to be lived in.

hab·i·tant [hab'ə·tənt] *n.* An inhabitant.

hab·i·tat [hab'ə·tat'] *n.* 1 The place where a plant or animal normally grows or lives. 2 A place where something lives; dwelling.

hab·i·ta·tion [hab'ə·tā'shən] *n.* 1 A dwelling place. 2 The act or state of inhabiting or living in: fit for human *habitation.*

hab·it-form·ing [hab'it·fôr'ming] *adj.* Leading to or causing a habit or physiological addiction.

ha·bit·u·al [hə·bich'ōō·əl] *adj.* 1 Done or happening by habit; customary: *habitual* politeness. 2 Expected from habit; usual: our *habitual* way home. **—ha·bit'u·al·ly** *adv.* **—ha·bit'u·al·ness** *n.*

ha·bit·u·ate [hə·bich'ōō·āt'] *v.* **ha·bit·u·at·ed, ha·bit·u·at·ing** To accustom; make used: to *habituate* oneself to high altitudes.

ha·bit·u·é [hə·bich'ōō·ā'] *n.* A person who frequently visits a particular place or places of a particular nature: a *habitué* of museums.

ha·ci·en·da [hä'sē·en'də] *n.* In Spanish America, a large estate or plantation, or the main house on such an estate.

hack[1] [hak] 1 *v.* To cut or chop crudely or irregularly, as with an ax. 2 *n.* A crude gash or notch. 3 *n.* A short, dry cough. 4 *v.* To give forth such a cough.

hack[2] [hak] 1 *n.* A carriage for hire. 2 *n.* A worn-out horse. 3 *n.* A taxicab. 4 *n.* A person who does dull, tedious work, especially a writer. 5 *adj.* Done only for money: *hack* writing.

hack·ber·ry [hak'ber'ē] *n., pl.* **hack·ber·ries** 1 Any of various trees and shrubs of the elm family that bear small, often edible berries. 2 The fruit of a hackberry.

hack·er [hak'ər] *n.* A person who likes to experiment with computers; someone who is interested in computers as a hobby.

hack·le [hak'əl] *n.* 1 One of the long, narrow feathers on the neck of a rooster, pigeon, or other bird.

2 (*pl.*) The hairs on the neck and back of a dog that stand up when it is angry or attacked.
hack·ney [hak′nē] *n., pl.* **hack·neys** 1 A horse used to ride or drive. 2 A carriage for hire.
hack·neyed [hak′nēd] *adj.* Made ordinary or dull by too much use; trite: a *hackneyed* plot.
hack·saw [hak′sô′] *n.* A saw with a fine-toothed, narrow blade set in a frame, used to cut metal.

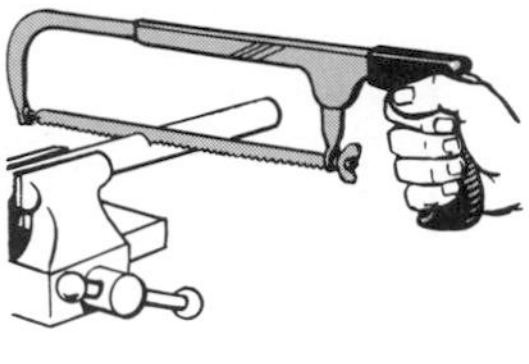
Hacksaw

had [had] The past tense and past participle of HAVE. ◆ *Had* is used in certain phrases showing obligation or preference. "You *had* better hurry" means "You ought to hurry." "I *had* rather stay home" means "I prefer to stay home."
had·dock [had′ək] *n., pl.* **had·dock** or **had·docks** A food fish of the northern Atlantic, related to but not so big as the cod.
Ha·des [hā′dēz] *n.* 1 In Greek myths, the underground kingdom of the dead. 2 *informal* Hell.
had·n't [had′(ə)nt] Had not.
hadst [hadst] *v.* A form of HAD, used with *thou*: seldom used today.
haf·ni·um [haf′nē·əm] *n.* A metallic element similar to and found associated with zirconium in minerals, used in nuclear reactors.
haft [haft] *n.* A handle, especially of a knife, sword, or ax; hilt.
hag [hag] *n.* An ugly and usually spiteful old woman; crone.
hag·fish [hag′fish′] *n., pl.* **hag·fish** or **hag·fish·es** Any of various eel-shaped ocean fishes having a round sucking mouth with no jaws. They fix onto other fishes with their mouths and bore into them.
Hag·ga·dah [hə·gä′də] *n.* In Judaism, the story of the Exodus from Egypt, read at Passover services.
Hag·ga·i [hag′ē·ī′] *n.* In the Bible, a Hebrew prophet who lived during the sixth century B.C.
hag·gard [hag′ərd] *adj.* Looking as if ill, starved, exhausted, or in pain.
hag·gle [hag′əl] *v.* **hag·gled, hag·gling,** *n.* 1 *v.* To bargain in a petty way: to *haggle* over a purchase. 2 *n.* The act of haggling. **—hag′gler** *n.*
hah [hä] *interj.* Another spelling of HA.
ha-ha [hä′hä′] *interj.* A sound made to imitate laughter, usually with a mocking or scornful intent.
hai·ku [hī′ko͞o] *n., pl.* **hai·ku** An unrhymed three-line Japanese poem that follows a strict form. It consists of seventeen syllables—five in the first line, seven in the second, and five in the third—and is usually written on a subject having to do with nature.
hail¹ [hāl] 1 *n.* Drops of ice that fall during a storm; hailstones. 2 *n.* A rapid or heavy showering: a *hail* of bullets. 3 *v.* To fall or shower like hail. 4 *v.* To pour down hail.
hail² [hāl] 1 *n.* A shout to attract attention; greeting. 2 *v.* To call loudly to in greeting; salute. 3 *v.* To call to so as to attract attention: to *hail* a cab. 4 *interj.* An exclamation of greeting or tribute: *Hail* to Caesar! **—hail from** To come from as a birthplace or point of origin: My ancestors *hail from* Arkansas.
Hail Mary A Roman Catholic prayer to the Virgin Mary.
hail·stone [hāl′stōn′] *n.* A pellet of frozen rain.
hail·storm [hāl′stôrm′] *n.* A storm in which hailstones fall.
hair [hâr] *n.* 1 A fine, threadlike structure growing from the skin of most mammals. 2 The thick growth of hairs, as on the human head. 3 A small measure, as of space or degree: to miss by a *hair.* **—split hairs** To search for small differences; raise petty objections.
hair·breadth [hâr′bredth′] 1 *n.* An extremely small space or margin. 2 *adj.* Very narrow or close: a *hairbreadth* escape.
hair·brush [hâr′brush′] *n.* A brush for grooming the hair.
hair·cloth [hâr′klôth′] *n.* A wiry fabric used for stiffening and upholstering.
hair·cut [hâr′kut′] *n.* The act of cutting the hair, or the style in which it is cut.
hair·do [hâr′do͞o′] *n., pl.* **hair·dos** 1 A style of fixing one's hair. 2 The hair thus styled. ◆ The word *hairdo* was made up or "coined" in the 1930's. The two words *hair* and *do* (meaning *to arrange* or *set,* as in "to do one's hair") were simply stuck together to form one word.

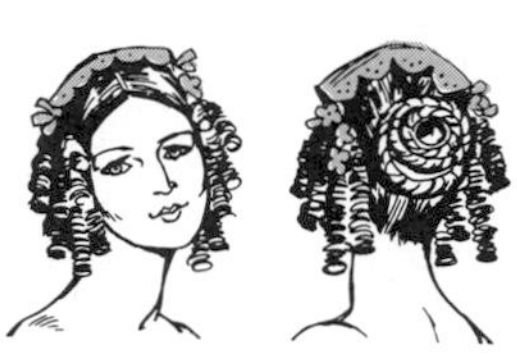
19th-century hairdo

hair·dress·er [hâr′dres′ər] *n.* A person who cuts or arranges hair.
hair·less [hâr′lis] *adj.* Without hair.
hair·line [hâr′līn′] *n.* 1 The edge of the growth of hair on the head, as at the forehead. 2 A very thin line.
hair·piece [hâr′pēs′] *n.* A small removable wig or partial wig, as a toupee or fall, made of real or synthetic hair.
hair·pin [hâr′pin′] 1 *n.* A thin, U-shaped piece of wire, bone, or other material, for holding a hairdo. 2 *adj.* Shaped like a hairpin: a *hairpin* turn.
hair-rais·ing [hâr′rā′zing] *adj.* Causing fright or terror: The leader of the expedition gave a *hair-raising* account of the avalanche.
hairs·breadth [hârz′bredth′] *n., adj.* Another spelling of HAIRBREADTH.
hair·split·ting [hâr′split′ing] 1 *n.* The making of distinctions too fine to matter. 2 *adj.* Inclined to quibble about details.
hair spray A commercial preparation, usually an aerosol, that is sprayed on hair to keep it in place.
hair·spring [hâr′spring′] *n.* The very fine spring that regulates the balance wheel in a watch or clock.
hair·style [hâr′stīl′] *n.* The design of a hairdo.
hair-trig·ger [hâr′trig′ər] *adj.* 1 Responding to the slightest impulse or pressure: *hair-trigger* brakes. 2 Easily provoked: *hair-trigger* rage.
hair trigger The trigger of a firearm that is ad-

a	add	**i**	it	**o͝o**	took	**oi**	oil		
ā	ace	**ī**	ice	**o͞o**	pool	**ou**	pout		
â	care	**o**	odd	**u**	up	**ng**	ring		
ä	palm	**ō**	open	**û**	burn	**th**	thin		
e	end	**ô**	order	**yo͞o**	fuse	**th̶**	this		
ē	equal					**zh**	vision		

ə = { a in *above* e in *sicken* i in *possible* / o in *melon* u in *circus* }

justed in such a way that the gun will fire with very little pressure.

hair·y [hâr′ē] *adj.* **hair·i·er, hair·i·est** 1 Covered with hair; having much hair. 2 Made of or resembling hair. 3 *slang* Dangerous; difficult: a *hairy* situation. **—hair′i·ness** *n.*

Hai·tian [hā′shən *or* hā′tē·ən] 1 *adj.* Of or from Haiti. 2 *n.* A person born in or a citizen of Haiti. 3 *n.* The language of most Haitians, based on French and West African languages.

hake [hāk] *n., pl.* **hake** or **hakes** A food fish related to the cod.

hal·berd [hal′bərd] *n.* A weapon used about 400 years ago, with a spear point and an ax blade on a long shaft.

Halberd

hal·cy·on [hal′sē·ən] *adj.* Calm; peaceful. ◆ In myths, the *halcyon* was a bird that was supposed to build its nest in the water and make the winds become calm while it was nesting.

hale[1] [hāl] *v.* **haled, hal·ing** To compel to go: to *hale* into court.

hale[2] [hāl] *adj.* **hal·er, hal·est** Vigorous and healthy; robust: The hikers felt *hale* and hearty.

half [haf] *n., pl.* **halves** [havz] 1 *n.* Either of two equal or almost equal parts into which a thing may be divided, or a quantity equal to such a part: Give me *half.* 2 *adj.* Having half of a standard value: a *half* teaspoon. 3 *adj.* Not complete; partial. 4 *adv.* To the extent of a half; partially. 5 *adv.* Nearly: I was *half* inclined to refuse. 6 *adv. informal* To any extent at all: not *half* good enough. ◆ In writing, avoid the informal expression *a half a* by deleting one *a*: half a loaf; a half loaf.

half-and-half [haf′ən·haf′] 1 *n.* A mixture of two elements in equal amounts. 2 *adv.* In equal proportions. 3 *adj.* Being half one thing and half another.

half·back [haf′bak′] *n.* In football, either of two players who play behind the line of scrimmage.

half-baked [haf′bākt′] *adj.* 1 Not completely baked. 2 *informal* Badly or insufficiently thought out; poorly planned: a *half-baked* idea.

half-breed [haf′brēd′] *n.* A person having parents of different races, especially a person born of a Caucasian and an American Indian. ◆ This word is often considered offensive.

half brother A brother related through only one parent.

half-caste [haf′kast′] *n.* A person having parents of different races, especially a person born of a European and an Asian. ◆ This word is often considered offensive.

half crown A former British silver coin worth 2½ shillings.

half dollar A U.S. or Canadian coin worth 50 cents.

half gainer A dive in which the diver, facing forward, does half of a back somersault and hits the water headfirst and facing back.

half·heart·ed [haf′här′tid] *adj.* Having or showing little interest or enthusiasm.

half hitch A knot made by passing the end of a rope around itself and then passing it through the loop thus formed. It forms a simple knot that is very easily untied.

half hour 1 A period of time equal to 30 minutes. 2 The point in time that is thirty minutes after any hour: The clock chimes on the *half hour.*

half-life [haf′līf′] *n.* The time taken for half the atoms in a given quantity of a particular radioactive substance to undergo radioactive decay. Every radioactive element or isotope has its own characteristic half-life, which may be anything from a small fraction of a second to millions of years.

half-mast [haf′mast′] *n.* The position of a flag, about halfway up a mast, used to show respect for the dead or to signal distress.

half-moon [haf′mo͞on′] *n.* 1 The moon when only half its visible surface is illuminated. 2 Something in the shape of a crescent.

half nelson A wrestling hold in which an arm is placed under an opponent's armpit from the back and its hand is pressed against the back of the opponent's neck.

half note A note in music having half the time value of a whole note.

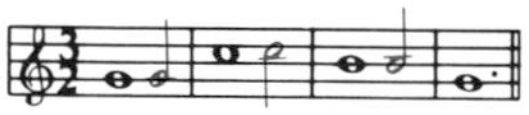
Half notes

half·pen·ny [hā′pən·ē] *n., pl.* **half·pence** [hā′pəns] or **half·pen·nies,** *adj.* 1 *n.* A British bronze coin worth half of a penny. 2 *adj.* Almost worthless.

half sister A sister related through only one parent.

half-staff [haf′staf′] *n.* Half-mast.

half step Another term for SEMITONE.

half·time [haf′tīm′] *n.* In certain sports, as football or basketball, an intermission between two equal amounts of playing time.

half·tone [haf′tōn′] *n.* 1 Any of the tones between the lightest and the darkest, as in a photograph. 2 In photoengraving, a technique for representing the shading in an object by photographing it on a metal plate through a screen and then etching the plate so that details of the image are reproduced as dots. 3 The metal plate made by this technique. 4 A print made from such a plate.

half-track [haf′trak′] *n.* A military vehicle with wheels in front and short endless tracks in the rear.

half-truth [haf′tro͞oth′] *n., pl.* **half·truths** [haf′·tro͞othz′ *or* haf′tro͞oths′] A statement that omits some facts, especially in a deliberate attempt to deceive.

half uncial A style of handwriting that is a combination of uncial letters and cursive forms.

half·way [haf′wā′] 1 *adj.* Midway between two points: the *halfway* mark. 2 *adj.* Partial; incomplete: *halfway* measures. 3 *adv.* At or to half the distance: to go *halfway* home. **—meet halfway** To be willing to give in to on some points so as to reach an agreement.

halfway house A place for formerly institutionalized people, as mental patients or drug addicts, to live while engaged in therapeutic activities designed to prepare them for reentry into society.

half-wit [haf′wit′] *n.* 1 A feebleminded person. 2 A foolish or silly person.

half-wit·ted [haf′wit′id] *adj.* 1 Feebleminded. 2 Foolish; silly.

hal·i·but [hal′ə·bət] *n., pl.* **hal·i·but** or **hal·i·buts** A large flatfish of northern seas, used as a food.

hal·ite [hā′līt′ *or* hal′īt′] *n.* Another name for ROCK SALT.

hal·i·to·sis [hal′ə·tō′sis] *n.* A condition in which the breath has a stale or foul odor; bad breath.

hall [hôl] *n.* 1 A passage or corridor in a building.

2 A room at the entry of a house or building; lobby. 3 A large building or room used for public business or entertainment: a concert *hall.* 4 In England, the main house on the estate of a landowner. 5 A building or dormitory on a college campus.

hal·lah [hä′lə] *n.* Another spelling for CHALLAH.

hal·le·lu·jah or **hal·le·lu·iah** [hal′ə·lo͞o′yə] 1 *interj.* Praise ye the Lord. 2 *n.* A song of praise or thanksgiving. ◆ *Hallelujah* comes from two Hebrew words meaning *Praise Jehovah!*

Hal·ley's comet [hal′ēz] A comet that reappears every 75 or 76 years.

hall·mark [hôl′märk′] 1 *n.* In England, an official mark placed upon articles of gold or silver to indicate purity. 2 *v.* To stamp with a hallmark. 3 *n.* Any mark or proof that something is genuine or of high quality.

hal·loa [hə·lō′] *v.* **hal·loaed, hal·loa·ing,** *n., interj.* Halloo.

Hall of Fame or **hall of fame** 1 A room or building in which there are memorials to outstanding people. 2 A group of individuals in a particular category, as a sport, who have been chosen as outstanding in the category.

hal·loo [hə·lo͞o′] *n., pl.* **hal·loos,** *v.* **hal·looed, hal·loo·ing,** *interj.* 1 *n.* A loud call or shout. 2 *v.* To shout or call. 3 *interj.* An exclamation to attract attention.

hal·low [hal′ō] *v.* To make holy; consecrate.

hal·lowed [hal′ōd] *adj.* 1 Made holy or sacred; consecrated. 2 Regarded as holy or sacred; revered: our *hallowed* freedoms of speech and of the press.

Hal·low·een or **Hal·low·e'en** [hal′ō·ēn′ *or* hôl′ō·ēn′] *n.* The evening of October 31, celebrated by masquerading.

Hal·low·mas [hal′ō·məs] *n.* Another name for ALL SAINTS' DAY.

halls of ivy An institution of higher education; college or university.

hal·lu·ci·nate [hə·lo͞o′sə·nāt′] *v.* **hal·lu·ci·nat·ed, hal·lu·ci·nat·ing** To experience hallucinations.

hal·lu·ci·na·tion [hə·lo͞o′sə·nā′shən] *n.* 1 The impression of seeing or hearing something that is not really present. 2 The thing supposedly seen or heard.

hal·lu·ci·na·to·ry [hə·lo͞o′sə·nə·tôr′ē] *adj.* Of, having to do with, causing, or characterized by hallucinations.

hal·lu·cin·o·gen [hə·lo͞o′sə·nə·jən] *n.* A substance that causes hallucinations. **—hal·lu′cin·o·gen′ic** *adj.*

hall·way [hôl′wā′] *n.* A passageway between rooms; hall; corridor.

ha·lo [hā′lō] *n., pl.* **ha·los** or **ha·loes** 1 A shining circle, as around the moon. 2 In art, a shining circle around the head of a holy person. 3 An aura of glory or splendor.

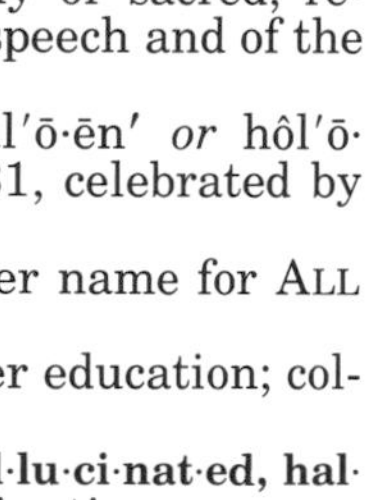
Halo

hal·o·gen [hal′ə·jən] *n.* Any of the group of nonmetallic elements that includes fluorine, chlorine, bromine, iodine, and astatine.

halt¹ [hôlt] 1 *n.* A complete but temporary stop in an activity. 2 *v.* To stop. **—call a halt** To demand that something be stopped.

halt² [hôlt] 1 *v.* To be in doubt; hesitate; waver. 2 *v.* To walk with a limp; hobble. 3 *adj.* Lame; crippled: seldom used today.

hal·ter [hôl′tər] *n.* 1 A strap or rope used to lead or hold a horse or other animal. 2 A hangman's rope. 3 A blouse held up by a band around the neck, leaving the arms and most of the back bare.

Halter

hal·vah or **hal·va** [häl·vä′ *or* häl′vä] *n.* A sweet candy originating in Turkey, made chiefly of crushed sesame seeds and honey.

halve [hav] *v.* **halved, halv·ing** 1 To divide into halves. 2 To lessen by half: to *halve* one's expenses.

halves [havz] Plural of HALF. **—go halves** To share equally: to *go halves* on expenses.

hal·yard [hal′yərd] *n.* A rope used on ships to raise or lower a sail, yard, or flag.

ham [ham] *n.* 1 The upper part of a hog's hind leg, salted and smoked. 2 The back of the thigh and the buttock. 3 *informal* An amateur radio operator. 4 *slang* An actor who overdoes a part and exaggerates feelings.

Ha·man [hā′mən] *n.* In the Bible, a Persian official who persecuted the Jews and was hanged.

ham·burg·er [ham′bûr′gər] *n.* 1 Ground beef. 2 A sandwich made with a broiled or fried patty of this meat.

ham·let [ham′lit] *n.* A small village.

Ham·let [ham′lit] *n.* 1 A play by William Shakespeare. 2 The hero of this play.

ham·mer [ham′ər] 1 *n.* A hand tool with a solid metal head and a handle, used chiefly for driving nails or for pounding or flattening metal. 2 *n.* A mechanical part that strikes or beats: the *hammer* of a gun. 3 *n.* The largest of the three small bones of the middle ear. It is shaped like a hammer. 4 *v.* To strike, beat, or drive with or as if with a hammer. 5 *v.* To form or shape with a hammer; forge. 6 *v.* To form by steady mental labor: to *hammer* out a solution. 7 *v.* To work hard or steadily: to *hammer* away at a job. 8 *v.* To have the sound or feeling of pounding: My heart *hammered* with excitement. 9 *v.* To force or impress by constant repetition.

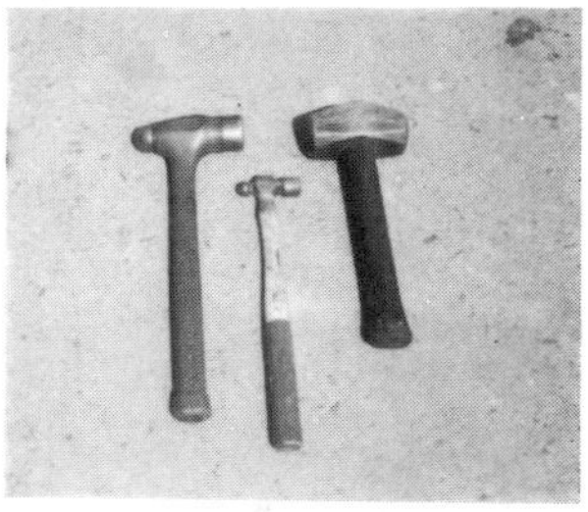
Types of hammers

ham·mer·head [ham′ər·hed′] *n.* A shark with a head resembling a hammer.

ham·mer·lock [ham′ər·lok′] *n.* In wrestling, a hold in which an opponent's arm is pulled behind his or her back and twisted upward.

a	add	**i**	it	**o͝o**	took	**oi**	oil
ā	ace	**ī**	ice	**o͞o**	pool	**ou**	pout
â	care	**o**	odd	**u**	up	**ng**	ring
ä	palm	**ō**	open	**û**	burn	**th**	thin
e	end	**ô**	order	**yo͞o**	fuse	**t͟h**	this
ē	equal					**zh**	vision

ə = {a in *above* e in *sicken* i in *possible* / o in *melon* u in *circus*}

ham·mock[1] [ham′ək] *n.* A bed or couch formed by hanging a strong fabric between two supports.

Hammock

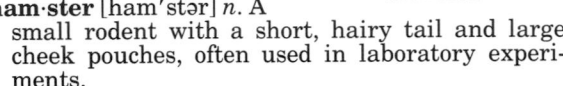

ham·mock[2] [ham′ək] *n.* Another spelling of HUMMOCK.
ham·per[1] [ham′pər] *v.* To interfere with the movements of; hinder; obstruct.
ham·per[2] [ham′pər] *n.* A large covered basket, as for storing laundry or carrying food.
ham·ster [ham′stər] *n.* A small rodent with a short, hairy tail and large cheek pouches, often used in laboratory experiments.
ham·string [ham′string′] *n., v.* **ham·strung, ham·string·ing** 1 *n.* A tendon at the back of the human knee. 2 *n.* In animals with four legs, the large sinew at the back of the hock. 3 *v.* To cut the hamstring of; cripple. 4 *v.* To frustrate: The project was *hamstrung* by a lack of funds.
hand [hand] 1 *n.* The end part of the arm from the wrist down, including the palm, fingers, and thumb. ◆ Adj., *manual.* 2 *adj.* Of or suited for the hand. 3 *n.* The use of the hand: to write a letter by *hand.* 4 *adj.* Worked or done by hand: a *hand* loom; *hand* sewing. 5 *n.* A group or bunch of something: a *hand* of bananas. 6 *n.* One of the pointers on a clock. 7 *v.* To give, pass, or transmit by hand. 8 *v.* To assist or lead with the hand. 9 *n.* Help: to lend a *hand.* 10 *n.* A part or role in doing something: to have a *hand* in the victory. 11 *n.* A laborer: hired *hands.* 12 *n.* A characteristic mark: The painting showed the *hand* of a true artist. 13 *n.* A round of applause. 14 *n.* A style of handwriting: a broad *hand.* 15 *n.* A measure for the height of a horse, equal to four inches: a horse 15 *hands* high. 16 *n.* (*pl.*) Possession; control: a fort in enemy *hands.* 17 *n.* A side: He stood at my left *hand.* 18 *n.* One of two sides, as of an issue or argument: On the one *hand* we felt that we should confront our opposition, on the other we felt we should avoid a confrontation. 19 *n.* A pledge or promise of marriage: to ask for one's *hand.* 20 *n.* One round in a card game. 21 *n.* The cards held by a player during one round of a game. 22 *n.* A player in a card game. **—at hand** 1 Close by. 2 About to happen. **—change hands** To pass from one person to another: The store *changed hands.* **—hand down** To pass along; bequeath. **—hand in glove** In close contact; intimately: to work *hand in glove* with a partner. **—in hand** 1 Under control. 2 In one's possession: to have money *in hand.* **—keep one's hand in** To continue an activity; keep in practice. **—lay hands on** To get hold of; seize. **—on hand** 1 Available for use: enough food *on hand* for a week. 2 Present: Be *on hand* for the speech. **—out of hand** 1 Not under control: The children were cross and *out of hand.* 2 At once; immediately. **—upper hand** The controlling advantage.
hand·bag [hand′bag′] *n.* 1 A purse for holding money and small articles. 2 A small suitcase.
hand·ball [hand′bôl′] *n.* 1 A game in which a ball is hit by hand so as to strike a wall on the fly. 2 The small ball used in this game.
hand·bar·row [hand′bar′ō] *n.* A flat, rectangular frame or litter with handles at both ends, used by two people to carry loads.
hand·bill [hand′bil′] *n.* A small printed notice distributed by hand.
hand·book [hand′bo͝ok′] *n.* A small guidebook, reference book, or book of instructions.
hand·cart [hand′kärt′] *n.* A small cart, usually with two wheels, that is pushed or pulled by hand.
hand·craft·ed [hand′kraf′tid] *adj.* Made by hand.
hand·cuff [hand′kuf′] 1 *n.* (*often pl.*) One of a pair of metal rings joined by a chain, designed to lock around the wrist; manacle. 2 *v.* To put handcuffs on.

Handcuffs

hand·ed [han′did] *adj.* 1 Characterized by, done by, or designed for a special hand or number of hands: used in combinations, as a *left-handed* mitt or a *two-handed* catch. 2 Involving a specified number of persons: used in combination, as a *four-handed* card game.
hand·ful [hand′fo͝ol′] *n., pl.* **hand·fuls** 1 As much or as many as a hand can hold at one time. 2 A small number. 3 *informal* A thing or person hard to control: The cat was a *handful.*
hand grenade A small bomb that is thrown by hand.
hand·gun [hand′gun′] *n.* A firearm, as a pistol, that is designed to be held and fired with one hand.
hand·i·cap [han′dē·kap′] *n., v.* **hand·i·capped, hand·i·cap·ping** 1 *n.* A race or contest in which some competitors are given advantages or disadvantages so that all have an equal chance of winning. 2 *n.* Such an advantage or disadvantage: a twenty-pin *handicap* in a bowling tournament. 3 *v.* To assign handicaps for a race or contest. 4 *n.* Any disadvantage. 5 *v.* To put at a disadvantage: We felt *handicapped* by poor equipment.
hand·i·capped [han′dē·kapt′] *adj.* 1 Afflicted with a handicap; disabled. 2 *n. use:* Handicapped people: Many of the *handicapped* make valuable contributions to our society.
hand·i·craft [han′dē·kraft′] *n.* 1 Skill in working with the hands. 2 A trade, occupation, or art requiring such skill.
hand·i·work [han′dē·wûrk′] *n.* 1 Work done by the hands. 2 Work done personally.
hand·ker·chief [hang′kər·chif] *n.* A square piece of cloth used for wiping the face or nose, or as an ornament.
han·dle [han′dəl] *v.* **han·dled, han·dling,** *n.* 1 *v.* To touch, feel, or hold with the hand. 2 *n.* A part of a tool, cup, pail, or other object, made to be grasped by the hand. 3 *v.* To manage, control, or operate: to *handle* a tractor. 4 *v.* To deal with or treat: to *handle* customers. 5 *v.* To buy and sell; deal in: to *handle* used cars. 6 *v.* To respond to control: This car *handles* well. **—han·dler** [hand′·lər] *n.*
han·dle·bar [han′dəl·bär′] *n.* (*often pl.*) The curved steering bar, as on a bicycle.
handlebar mustache A long, thick mustache that curves upward at the ends like a handlebar.
hand·made [hand′mād′] *adj.* Made by hand or by hand tools.
hand·maid [hand′mād′] *n.* Another word for HANDMAIDEN: seldom used today.

hand·maid·en [hand′mād′(ə)n] *n.* A female servant or attendant: seldom used today.
hand-me-down [hand′mē·doun′] **1** *n.* An item, especially of clothing, that is given by its original owner or user to someone else for additional use. **2** *adj.* Used; secondhand. **3** *adj.* Cheaply made; inferior in quality.
hand organ A large music box with a hand crank, once used by street musicians.
hand·out [hand′out′] *n.* **1** Money or food given to a tramp or beggar. **2** A prepared statement distributed as publicity or information.
hand·rail [hand′rāl′] *n.* A railing used to support or protect, as on a balcony or staircase.
hand·saw [hand′sô′] *n.* A saw used with one hand.
hand·shake [hand′shāk′] *n.* The act of clasping and shaking a person's hand, as in greeting.
hand·some [han′səm] *adj.* **hand·som·er, hand·som·est** **1** Pleasing in appearance, especially in a stately or manly way. **2** Of generous size; ample: a *handsome* gift. **—hand′some·ly** *adv.* **—hand′·some·ness** *n.*
hands-off [handz′ôf′] *adj.* Avoiding intervention or interference: a *hands-off* foreign policy.
hands-on [handz′on′] *adj.* Involving active, personal participation, as with a piece of equipment one is learning to use.
hand·spike [hand′spīk′] *n.* A bar used as a lever, as on a ship.
hand·spring [hand′spring′] *n.* An acrobatic turn like a somersault, but with only one or both hands touching the ground.

Handspring

hand·stand [hand′stand′] *n.* The act of balancing the body on the palms of the hands with the feet held upright in the air.
hand-to-hand [hand′tə·hand′] *adj.* In close contact: *hand-to-hand* combat.
hand-to-mouth [hand′tə·mouth′] *adj.* Having nothing in reserve; using at once whatever is obtained: a *hand-to-mouth* existence.
hand·work [hand′wûrk′] *n.* Work that is done by hand; handiwork. **—hand′work′er** *n.*
hand·writ·ing [hand′rī′ting] *n.* **1** Writing done by hand, not printed or typewritten. **2** The form of writing peculiar to a certain person: I recognized my friend's *handwriting*.
hand·writ·ten [hand′rit′(ə)n] *adj.* Written by hand.
hand·y [han′dē] *adj.* **hand·i·er, hand·i·est** **1** Within easy reach; nearby. **2** Skillful with the hands. **3** Easy to use; useful: a *handy* tool. **—come in handy** To be useful or helpful: Those cooking classes *came in handy* when I was living alone. **—hand′i·ly** *adv.* **—hand′i·ness** *n.*
hand·y·man [hand′dē·man′] *n., pl.* **hand·y·men** [han′dē·men′] A person who is employed to do odd jobs.
hang [hang] *v.* **hung** or **hanged, hang·ing,** *n.* **1** *v.* To fasten or be attached to something above: to *hang* pictures; A lamp *hangs* in the hall. **2** *v.* To attach or be attached, as to hinges, so as to swing freely: to *hang* a door. **3** *v.* To decorate with hangings: a wall *hung* with tapestries. **4** *n.* The manner in which something hangs: the *hang* of a coat. **5** *v.* To die or put to death by hanging with a rope around the neck. **6** *v.* To cause to droop: I *hung* my head. **7** *v.* To fasten (as wallpaper) to walls with paste. **8** *v.* To deadlock: The jury was *hung*. **9** *v.* To depend: The decision *hangs* on your vote. **10** *n. informal* The manner in which something is done or controlled: We soon got the *hang* of sailing. **—hang back** To be unwilling. **—hang on** **1** To keep a hold. **2** To pay close attention to. **3** To linger: My cold *hung* on. **—hang together** **1** To stay united. **2** To remain intact, coherent, or unchanged. **—hang up** **1** To finish using a telephone. **2** To place on a hanger or hook: *Hang up* your clothes. **3** To delay; hold back. ◆ *Hanged* is used when referring to putting to death by hanging: The traitor will be *hanged* at dawn. In the other meanings, *hung* is the more common form: They *hung* the picture from the molding.
han·gar [hang′ər] *n.* A shelter or shed for storing aircraft.
hang·dog [hang′dôg′] *adj.* Guilty, ashamed, or sneaky: a *hangdog* expression.
hang·er [hang′ər] *n.* **1** A device on which or from which something may be hung, as a light frame for hanging garments. **2** A person who hangs something.
hang·er-on [hang′ər·on′] *n., pl.* **hang·ers-on** [hang′·ərz·on′] A person who attaches himself or herself to others in the hope of receiving favors.
hang glider A kitelike device beneath which a rider hangs in a harness while gliding down from a high place, as a cliff.
hang gliding The act of gliding in a hang glider.
hang·ing [hang′ing] **1** *n.* Death by hanging with a rope tight around the neck. **2** *n.* (*often pl.*) Curtains, drapes, or the like. **3** *adj.* Suspended or dangling. **4** *n.* The act of suspending.
hang·man [hang′mən] *n., pl.* **hang·men** [hang′mən] An official who hangs condemned people.
hang·nail [hang′nāl′] *n.* Skin partially torn loose at the side or root of a fingernail.
hang·out [hang′out′] *n. slang* A place where a person or group spends much time.
hang·o·ver [hang′ō′vər] *n.* **1** The aftereffects, as nausea and headache, that frequently follow excessive drinking of alcoholic beverages. **2** Something that remains from an earlier time or situation; holdover.
hang-up [hang′up′] *n. informal* **1** A psychological or emotional problem, as an inhibition or fixation, that interferes with a person's functioning or happiness. **2** Any problem that interferes with or delays something; obstacle.
hank [hangk] *n.* **1** A skein of yarn or thread. **2** A loop or curl: a *hank* of hair.
han·ker [hang′kər] *v.* To have a strong desire; wish: to *hanker* for roast turkey. **—han′ker·er** *n.*
han·ker·ing [hang′kər·ing] *n.* A strong desire; craving: an irresistible *hankering* for sweets.
han·kie or **han·ky** [hang′kē] *n., pl.* **han·kies** *informal* Handkerchief.

H

a	add	**i**	it	**o͝o**	took	**oi**	oil
ā	ace	**ī**	ice	**o͞o**	pool	**ou**	pout
â	care	**o**	odd	**u**	up	**ng**	ring
ä	palm	**ō**	open	**û**	burn	**th**	thin
e	end	**ô**	order	**yo͞o**	fuse	**t͟h**	this
ē	equal					**zh**	vision

ə = { a in *above* e in *sicken* i in *possible*
o in *melon* u in *circus* }

han·ky-pan·ky [hang′kē·pang′kē] *n. informal* Dishonest, improper, or mischievous behavior.
han·som [han′səm] *n.* A low, two-wheeled, one-horse carriage with the driver's seat perched at the rear.

Hansom

Ha·nuk·kah [hä′no͝o·kə] *n.* A Jewish festival lasting eight days, commemorating the rededication of the Temple in Jerusalem in 165 B.C.
hap [hap] *n., v.* **happed, hap·ping** 1 *n.* Chance; fortune. 2 *n.* An occurrence; happening. 3 *v.* To happen.
hap·haz·ard [hap′haz′ərd] 1 *adj.* Happening by chance; accidental. 2 *n.* Mere chance. 3 *adv.* By chance; at random: to choose *haphazard.* **—hap′·haz′ard·ly** *adv.* **—hap′haz′ard·ness** *n.*
hap·less [hap′lis] *adj.* Having no luck; unfortunate. **—hap′less·ly** *adv.* **—hap′less·ness** *n.*
hap·ly [hap′lē] *adv.* By accident or chance; perhaps.
hap·pen [hap′ən] *v.* 1 To come about; occur: What *happened* while I was gone? 2 To occur by chance: Anything can *happen.* 3 To have the fortune: We *happened* to be home. 4 To come or go by chance: My neighbor *happened* by just as we were leaving. **—happen on** (or **upon**) To meet or find by chance.
hap·pen·chance [hap′ən·chans′] *n.* Happenstance.
hap·pen·ing [hap′ən·ing] *n.* Something that happens; event.
hap·pen·stance [hap′ən·stans′] *n.* An accidental circumstance; chance occurrence.
hap·pi·ness [hap′ē·nis] *n.* 1 A being pleased and contented. 2 Good fortune; good luck.
hap·py [hap′ē] *adj.* **hap·pi·er, hap·pi·est** 1 Enjoying or showing pleasure; joyous; contented. 2 Timely; lucky: by some *happy* chance. **—hap′pi·ly** *adv.*
hap·py-go-luck·y [hap′ē·gō·luk′ē] *adj.* Trusting to luck; without a care.
Haps·burg [haps′bûrg] *n.* A German family that once ruled many European countries.
ha·ra·ki·ri [har′i·kir′ē or har′i·kar′ē] *n.* An act of ritual suicide accomplished by slitting open the abdomen with a knife, formerly considered an honorable way to die by high-ranking Japanese.
ha·rangue [hə·rang′] *n., v.* **ha·rangued, ha·rangu·ing** 1 *n.* A long, loud, emotional speech. 2 *v.* To address in or deliver a harangue. **—ha·rangu′er** *n.*
har·ass [har′əs *or* hə·ras′] *v.* 1 To trouble, as with cares or worries: Parents are sometimes *harassed* by their children. 2 To annoy with small, repeated attacks: to *harass* an enemy. **—har·ass·ment** [har′əs·mənt *or* hə·ras′mənt] *n.*
har·bin·ger [här′bin·jər] 1 *n.* A person or thing that goes ahead and announces the coming of something. 2 *v.* To announce; herald.
har·bor [här′bər] 1 *n.* A place or port where ships can anchor or be protected in a storm. 2 *n.* Any place of refuge. 3 *v.* To take shelter in or as if in a harbor. 4 *v.* To give refuge or shelter to: to *harbor* an escaped convict. 5 *v.* To keep in the mind: to *harbor* a grudge.
har·bor·age [här′bər·ij] *n.* 1 A shelter or refuge for ships. 2 Any shelter.
hard [härd] 1 *adj.* Solid and firm; not easily dented or broken; not soft. 2 *adj.* Difficult to solve, do, or understand: a *hard* problem. 3 *adj.* Difficult to manage or deal with: a *hard* person in business. 4 *adj.* Strict; harsh: a *hard* employer. 5 *adj.* Energetic: a *hard* worker. 6 *adv.* With much continued effort: to study *hard.* 7 *adv.* With great vigor: to fight *hard.* 8 *adv.* With difficulty: to breathe *hard.* 9 *adv.* Close; near. 10 *adj.* Describing the sound of *c* and *g* in *car* and *good,* as opposed to soft *c* and *g* in *cent* and *age.* 11 *adj.* Involving suffering; severe: *hard* times. 12 *adj.* Containing much alcohol: *hard* cider. 13 *adj.* Containing minerals that keep soap from working: *hard* water. 14 *adv.* Securely: tightly: to hold on *hard.* **—hard of hearing** Deaf or partially deaf. **—hard up** *informal* 1 Poor; broke. 2 In need of something. **—hard′ness** *n.*
hard-and-fast [härd′(ə)n(d)·fast′] *adj.* Fixed and unchangeable: a *hard-and-fast* rule.
hard·ball [härd′bôl′] *n.* Baseball.
hard-bit·ten [härd′bit′(ə)n] *adj.* Tough; unyielding.
hard-boiled [härd′boild′] *adj.* 1 Boiled until cooked through. 2 *informal* Tough; unfeeling.
hard coal Coal that burns slowly and with little flame; anthracite.
hard copy A printed record, as of computer output.
hard-core or **hard·core** [härd′kôr′] *adj.* 1 Incapable of being changed; stubbornly resistant: *hard-core* gamblers. 2 Considered to be a social problem that is incapable of being changed: *hard-core* poverty. 3 Of, having to do with, or being persons who are continually out of work for reasons over which they have no control, as inferior education or substandard skills: the *hard-core* unemployed. 4 Graphically explicit: *hard-core* pornography.
hard disk A hard plate made from metal or clay and coated with magnetic material, used in a computer to store a large amount of information.
hard·en [här′dən] *v.* To make or become hard or harder.
hard hat 1 A worker's protective hat, made of a hard material. 2 *informal* A construction worker.
hard·head·ed [härd′hed′id] *adj.* 1 Possessing common sense; realistic. 2 Willful; stubborn; obstinate. **—hard′head′ed·ly** *adv.* **—hard′head′ed·ness** *n.*
hard·heart·ed [härd′här′tid] *adj.* Lacking pity or sympathy; unfeeling. **—hard′heart′ed·ly** *adv.* **—hard′heart′ed·ness** *n.*
har·di·hood [här′dē·ho͝od′] *n.* Unflinching courage; boldness; daring.
hard landing A landing, as of a spacecraft on a planet in outer space, made at too high a speed because of the absence or malfunction of devices to slow it down.
hard-line [härd′līn′] *adj.* Characterized by rigidity and persistence, as in principles, policy, or actions; unyielding; uncompromising: a *hard-line* policy on disarmament. **—hard′lin′er** *n.*
hard·ly [härd′lē] *adv.* 1 Only just; scarcely; barely: Because of my cold, I could *hardly* speak. 2 Not quite; probably not: That is *hardly* the true story. 3 In a harsh, cruel, or severe way. ◆ *Hardly, barely,* and *scarcely* all have negative force. "I hardly heard the noise" means "I almost did *not* hear the noise." Therefore, it is not necessary or correct to use another negative with any of the three, as in "I didn't hardly hear the noise."
hard·nosed [härd′nōzd′] *adj.* Hardheaded.
hard palate The hard, bony front part of the palate.
hard·pan [härd′pan′] *n.* 1 A layer of hard subsoil

through which roots cannot grow. **2** Hard, unplowed ground. **3** Any solid foundation; bedrock.

hard sauce An uncooked dessert sauce made of creamed butter and sugar with a flavoring, as of rum or vanilla.

hard sell *informal* Aggressive, insistent sales or promotion techniques.

hard·ship [härd′ship′] *n.* Something that is hard to endure.

hard·tack [härd′tak′] *n.* A hard, unsalted, crackerlike biscuit.

hard·top [härd′top′] *n.* A car with the body design of a convertible, but with a rigid top.

hard·ware [härd′wâr′] *n.* **1** Manufactured articles of metal, as utensils or tools. **2** Weapons, especially heavy military equipment. **3** The mechanical and electronic components, as of a computer.

hard·wood [härd′wo͝od′] *n.* **1** Any hard, heavy wood, as oak. **2** *adj. use: hardwood* floors.

hard·work·ing [härd′wûr′king] *adj.* Industrious.

har·dy [här′dē] *adj.* **har·di·er, har·di·est** **1** Able to endure hardship; robust; tough. **2** Able to endure a winter outdoors, as some plants. **3** Having courage; bold; daring. **—har′di·ly** *adv.* **—har′di·ness** *n.*

hare [hâr] *n., pl.* **hare** or **hares** A timid, rabbitlike animal having a split upper lip, noted for its great speed.

Hare

hare·bell [hâr′bel′] *n.* A slender herb with blue, bell-shaped flowers.

hare·brained [hâr′·brānd′] *adj.* Foolish; flighty; giddy.

hare·lip [hâr′lip′] *n.* A split upper lip, a deformity some people are born with. —**hare′lipped′** *adj.*

har·em [hâr′əm] *n.* **1** The part of a Muslim household reserved for women. **2** The women living there.

ha·ri-ka·ri [har′i·kar′ē *or* har′i·kir′ē] *n.* Another spelling of HARA-KIRI.

hark [härk] *v.* To listen. **—hark back** To go back, as in one's memory, to a previous time.

hark·en [här′kən] *v.* Another spelling of HEARKEN.

har·le·quin [här′lə·kwin] **1** *n.* (*written* **Harlequin**) A pantomime character who wears a mask and a costume of contrasting colors. **2** *adj.* Checkered in many colors. **3** *adj.* Shaped like Harlequin's mask: *harlequin* eyeglasses. **4** *n.* A clown.

Harlequin

har·lot [här′lət] *n.* A prostitute. **—har′lot·ry** *n.*

harm [härm] **1** *n.* Injury; damage: The storm did great *harm.* **2** *v.* To do harm to.

harm·ful [härm′fəl] *adj.* Able to harm; doing harm. **—harm′ful·ly** *adv.* **—harm′ful·ness** *n.*

harm·less [härm′lis] *adj.* Not harmful; meaning no harm: a *harmless* prank. **—harm′less·ly** *adv.* **—harm′less·ness** *n.*

har·mon·ic [här·mon′ik] **1** *adj.* Related to or marked by harmony. **2** *n.* An overtone closely related to its primary or fundamental tone.

har·mon·i·ca [här·mon′i·kə] *n.* A small wind instrument played by blowing in and out on metal reeds fixed within a frame; mouth organ.

har·mon·ics [här·mon′iks] *n.* The science and study of musical sounds. ◆ See -ICS.

har·mo·ni·ous [här·mō′nē·əs] *adj.* **1** Made up of things that harmonize. **2** Free from disagreement; in accord. **3** Pleasing to the senses. **—har·mo′ni·ous·ly** *adv.*

har·mo·nist [här·mə·nist] *n.* A person who is skilled in musical harmony.

har·mo·ni·um [här·mō′nē·əm] *n.* Another name for REED ORGAN.

har·mo·nize [här′mə·nīz′] *v.* **har·mo·nized, har·mo·niz·ing** **1** To arrange or be in musical harmony. **2** To bring into or be in agreement or harmony.

har·mo·ny [här′mə·nē] *n., pl.* **har·mo·nies** **1** An orderly and pleasing arrangement of simultaneous musical sounds. **2** The method of arranging music into harmony. **3** Any orderly and pleasing arrangement, as of colors or parts. **4** Agreement; accord: to live in *harmony* with neighbors.

har·ness [här′nis] **1** *n.* Leather straps or bands, used to hitch a horse or mule to a cart, plow, or other piece of equipment. **2** *v.* To put a harness on. **3** *n.* Any similar arrangement of straps or cords, as one used to attach a parachute to the body. **4** *v.* To make use of the power of: to *harness* a waterfall.

harness racing The sport of racing specially bred horses harnessed to sulkies.

harp [härp] **1** *n.* A stringed musical instrument played by plucking with the fingers. **2** *v.* To play on a harp. **—harp on** To talk or write about in a repetitious or monotonous manner. —**harp′er** *n.*

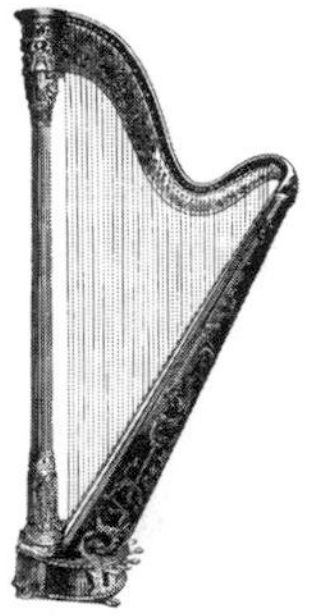
Harp

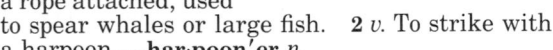

harp·ist [här′pist] *n.* A person who plays the harp.

har·poon [här·po͞on′] **1** *n.* A pointed and barbed weapon with a rope attached, used to spear whales or large fish. **2** *v.* To strike with a harpoon. **—har·poon′er** *n.*

harp·si·chord [härp′sə·kôrd′] *n.* A keyboard instrument resembling a piano but having its strings mechanically plucked instead of struck.

Har·py [här′pē] *n., pl.* **Har·pies** **1** In Greek myths, a greedy, nasty creature, in part a woman, in part a bird. **2** (*written* **harpy**) Any greedy, mean, or shrewish person.

a	add	**i**	it	**o͝o**	took	**oi**	oil		
ā	ace	**ī**	ice	**o͞o**	pool	**ou**	pout		
â	care	**o**	odd	**u**	up	**ng**	ring		
ä	palm	**ō**	open	**û**	burn	**th**	thin		
e	end	**ô**	order	**yo͞o**	fuse	**th**	this		
ē	equal					**zh**	vision		

ə = {a in *above* e in *sicken* i in *possible* / o in *melon* u in *circus*}

H

har·que·bus [här′kwə·bəs] *n.* An early portable gun, fired resting on a hooked stick.
har·ri·dan [har′i·dən] *n.* A mean, nagging woman.
har·ri·er [har′ē·ər] *n.* 1 A small hound used for hunting hares. 2 A cross-country runner.
har·row [har′ō] 1 *n.* A frame with spikes or upright disks used to level or break up soil. 2 *v.* To work (land) with a harrow. 3 *v.* To agitate or distress; torment; vex. —**har′row·er** *n.*

Disk harrow

har·ry [har′ē] *v.* **har·ried, har·ry·ing** 1 To make raids upon; assault. 2 To disturb; agitate; torment.
harsh [härsh] *adj.* 1 Grating, rough, or unpleasant to the senses. 2 Severe; cruel; unfeeling: a *harsh* judgment. —**harsh′ly** *adv.* —**harsh′ness** *n.*
harsh·en [här′shən] *v.* To make or become harsh: a voice *harshening* with anger.
hart [härt] *n., pl.* **hart** or **harts** The male of the red deer, especially after its fifth year.
har·te·beest [här′tə·bēst′ *or* härt′bēst′] *n., pl.* **har·te·beests** or **har·te·beest** An African antelope having a reddish-brown coat and ridged horns that curve backward at the tips.
harts·horn [härts′hôrn′] *n.* A preparation of ammonia used as smelling salts.
har·um-scar·um [hâr′əm·skâr′əm] 1 *adj.* Reckless; wild. 2 *adv.* Wildly. 3 *n.* A reckless, careless person.
har·vest [här′vist] 1 *n.* The gathering and bringing in of a crop. 2 *v.* To gather and bring in a crop of: to *harvest* apples. 3 *n.* The time of year for harvesting. 4 *n.* One season's yield of any product grown. 5 *n.* The consequences or natural outcome: We are enjoying the *harvest* of the good will that our plans created.
har·vest·er [här′vis·tər] *n.* 1 A person who harvests. 2 A machine used in harvesting.
harvest fly Another name for CICADA.
harvest mite Another name for CHIGGER.
harvest moon The full moon occurring closest to the autumnal equinox.
has [haz] The third person form of HAVE, in the present tense, used with *he, she, it,* and singular nouns: The team *has* luck; The worker *has* more work than one person can finish.
has-been [haz′bin] *n. informal* A person who was at one time but is no longer famous, successful, or powerful.
hash [hash] 1 *n.* A dish of cooked meat, potatoes, and other ingredients, chopped fine and fried or baked. 2 *v.* To cut or chop into small pieces. 3 *n.* A jumble; mess: to make a *hash* of a project. 4 *v. informal* To discuss at length and in detail: We'll *hash* the plan over later.
hash·ish or **hash·eesh** [hash′ēsh′ *or* hash′ish] *n.* A drug made from Indian hemp.
hash mark *slang* Another term for SERVICE STRIPE.
Ha·sid or **Has·sid** [hä′sid] *n., pl.* **Ha·si·dim** or **Has·si·dim** [hä·sē′dim] A member of a Jewish sect founded in Poland in the 18th century. Members of this sect seek a mystical union with God, and celebrate Him in song and dance. —**Ha·si·dic** [hä·sid′ik] *adj.*
has·n't [haz′ənt] Has not.
hasp [hasp] *n.* A hinged fastening or flap that fits over a staple and is fastened by a padlock or peg.

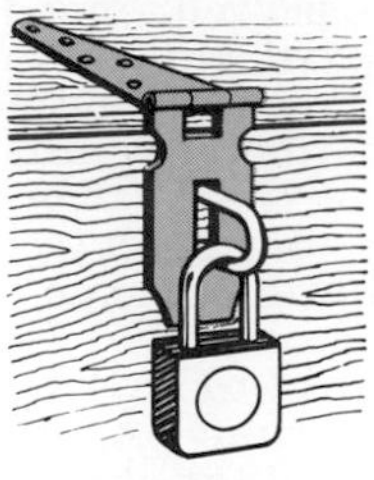
Hasp

has·sle [has′(ə)l] *n. slang* An argument; fight.
has·sock [has′ək] *n.* 1 An upholstered stool or cushion used to sit or kneel on or as a foot rest. 2 A tuft of coarse grass.
hast [hast] A form of HAVE, used with *thou:* seldom used today.
haste [hāst] *n.* 1 Swiftness of movement or action. 2 Reckless hurry: *Haste* makes waste. —**make haste** To hurry.
has·ten [hā′sən] *v.* 1 To move or act with speed; hurry. 2 To cause to hasten: The rain *hastened* our departure.
hast·y [hās′tē] *adj.* **hast·i·er, hast·i·est** 1 Quick: a *hasty* retreat. 2 Acting or done on impulse; rash: a *hasty* decision. 3 Showing impatience: *hasty* words. —**hast′i·ly** *adv.* —**hast′i·ness** *n.*
hasty pudding Porridge made of cornmeal.
hat [hat] *n., v.* **hat·ted, hat·ting** 1 *n.* A covering for the head, usually with a brim. 2 *v.* To supply or cover with a hat. —**pass the hat** To ask for donations. —**under one's hat** *informal* Secret: You must promise to keep what I tell you *under your hat.*
hat·band [hat′band′] *n.* A ribbon or band of cloth around a hat just above the brim.
hat·box [hat′boks′] *n.* A box or piece of luggage for holding a hat or hats.
hatch[1] [hach] *n.* 1 A hatchway. 2 The cover on a hatchway.
hatch[2] [hach] *v.* 1 To produce young from (an egg), or (young) from an egg: Hens *hatch* eggs; The hen *hatched* 11 chicks. 2 To come out of an egg. 3 To think out or invent, as a plot or plan. —**hatch′·able** *adj.* —**hatch′er** *n.*
hatch·er·y [hach′ər·ē] *n., pl.* **hatch·er·ies** A place for hatching eggs of fish or poultry.
hatch·et [hach′it] *n.* 1 A small ax with a short handle, held in one hand. 2 A tomahawk. —**bury the hatchet** To make peace.
hatch·way [hach′wā′] *n.* An opening in a deck, floor, or roof, leading to spaces beneath.
hate [hāt] *n., v.* **hat·ed, hat·ing** 1 *n.* A deep, strong dislike; hostility. 2 *v.* To dislike intensely; detest. 3 *v.* To dislike; want to avoid: I *hate* to bother you. —**hat′er** *n.* ◆ *Hate, detest,* and *abhor* all mean to dislike greatly. *Hate* often refers to a deep, personal feeling that may make someone try to hurt another or be happy at another's misfortune: Cain *hated* Abel. *Detest* is not so strong. It is intense, but often leads to avoiding rather than damaging the person or thing detested: I *detest* people who gossip. *Abhor* suggests a disgust that makes one shrink away from something: Many people who like realistic painting *abhor* abstract art. —**hat′er** *n.*
hate·ful [hāt′fəl] *adj.* 1 Arousing or worthy of hatred. 2 Feeling or showing hate. —**hate′ful·ly** *adv.* —**hate′ful·ness** *n.*
hath [hath] A form of HAS, used with *he, she,* or *it*: seldom used today.
hat·pin [hat′pin′] *n.* A long pin used to attach a hat to one's hair.
ha·tred [hā′trid] *n.* Bitter dislike; hate.
hat·ter [hat′ər] *n.* A person who makes, sells, or otherwise deals in hats.

hau·berk [hô′bûrk] *n.* A long coat of chain mail.

haugh·ty [hô′tē] *adj.* **haugh·ti·er, haugh·ti·est** Satisfied with oneself and scornful of others; arrogant: a *haughty* manner. **—haugh′ti·ly** *adv.* **—haugh′ti·ness** *n.*

Hauberk

haul [hôl] **1** *v.* To pull with force; drag. **2** *n.* A strong pull; tug. **3** *v.* To move or carry, as in a truck. **4** *n.* The load hauled. **5** *n.* The distance over which something is hauled: a short *haul.* **6** *n.* The amount of something caught or taken at one time: a *haul* of fish. **7** *v.* To change the course of (a ship). **—haul off** To draw back the arm to punch.

haunch [hônch] *n.* **1** The fleshy part of the hip and buttock. **2** The leg and loin of an animal, considered as meat: a *haunch* of beef.

haunt [hônt] **1** *v.* To visit often: They *haunted* the library that whole summer. **2** *n.* A place often visited: a favorite *haunt* of students. **3** *v.* To visit or linger in as a ghost: Ghosts and demons *haunted* the house. **4** *v.* To trouble or molest. **5** *v.* To disturb by returning to the mind or memory: The song *haunts* me.

Man on his haunches

haunt·ed [hôn′tid] *adj.* Often visited by ghosts or spirits: The story took place in a *haunted* castle.

haunt·ing [hôn′ting] *adj.* Difficult to forget: a *haunting* tune. **—haunt′ing·ly** *adv.*

haut·boy [hō′boi′] *n.* An oboe.

hau·teur [hō·tûr′] *n.* A haughty manner or spirit; arrogance.

have [hav] *v.* **had, having,** *n.* **1** *v.* To be in possession of; own: to *have* a new car; to *have* blue eyes. **2** *v.* To hold; contain: The well *has* little water; The hotel *has* 200 rooms. **3** *v.* To hold in the mind: to *have* an opinion. **4** *v.* To be obliged or compelled: People *have* to eat. **5** *v.* To get; take: to *have* a nap. **6** *v.* To experience; suffer or enjoy: to *have* a headache. **7** *v.* To allow: I'll *have* no interruptions. **8** *v.* To cause to do or be done: Please *have* my order delivered; *Have* the porter bring up the bags. **9** *v.* To carry on; accomplish: to *have* a talk. **10** *v.* To give birth to: She *had* twins last year. **11** *v.* To possess in some relationship, as in a family: I *have* two brothers. **12** *n. informal* A comparatively rich person or country: the *haves* and the have-nots. **—have at** To attack. **—have done** To stop; desist. **—have it out** To continue a fight or discussion to a final settlement. **—have to do with** To be concerned with; be related to. ◆ *Have* is used as a helping verb with the past participles of other verbs to show that an action is completed: We *have* worked all day; I *had* gone before they arrived.

ha·ven [hā′vən] *n.* **1** A harbor; port. **2** A safe place; refuge; shelter.

have-not [hav′not′] *n. informal* A person or country lacking in wealth.

have·n't [hav′ənt] Have not. ◆ Avoid using with *but* or *only.* Use *have:* We *have* but a moment.

hav·er·sack [hav′ər·sak′] *n.* A bag for carrying provisions on a march or hike.

hav·oc [hav′ək] *n.* Widespread destruction of life and property; ruin; devastation. **—play havoc with** To ruin; destroy; devastate: The war *played havoc with* the country's economy.

Haversack

haw¹ [hô] *n.* **1** The hawthorn tree. **2** The hawthorn's red berry.

haw² [hô] **1** *n., interj.* A word used by a driver to make a horse or ox turn left. **2** *v.* To turn to the left.

haw³ [hô] **1** *v.* To make short, grunting sounds while fumbling for words: to hem and *haw.* **2** *interj.* A word that represents such sounds.

Ha·wai·ian [hə·wä′yən] **1** *adj.* Of or from Hawaii. **2** *n.* A person born or living in Hawaii. **3** *n.* The Polynesian language of Hawaii.

hawk¹ [hôk] **1** *n.* A large bird with a strong, hooked beak, very powerful talons, rounded wings, and a long tail, that captures and eats smaller birds and animals. **2** *v.* To use trained hawks in hunting birds. **—hawk′er** *n.*

Hawk

hawk² [hôk] *v.* To announce (goods) for sale in the streets by shouting; peddle. **—hawk′er** *n.*

hawk³ [hôk] **1** *v.* To cough or cough up, as in clearing the throat. **2** *n.* A loud cough.

hawk-eyed [hôk′īd′] *adj.* Having very keen vision.

haw·ser [hô′zər] *n.* A rope or cable used for mooring or towing ships.

haw·thorn [hô′thôrn′] *n.* A small, thorny tree of the rose family having white or pink flowers and red berries.

hay [hā] **1** *n.* Grass, clover, and the like, that is cut,

a	add	**i**	it	**o͝o**	took	**oi**	oil
ā	ace	**ī**	ice	**o͞o**	pool	**ou**	pout
â	care	**o**	odd	**u**	up	**ng**	ring
ä	palm	**ō**	open	**û**	burn	**th**	thin
e	end	**ô**	order	**yo͞o**	fuse	**t̶h̶**	this
ē	equal					**zh**	vision

ə = {a in *above* e in *sicken* i in *possible* / o in *melon* u in *circus*}

H

dried, and used for animal feed. 2 *v.* To make (grass and the like) into hay: to *hay* for a week; to *hay* clover. 3 *v.* To feed with hay: to *hay* cows.

hay·cock [hā′kok′] *n.* A pile of hay in a field.

hay fever A disease caused by an allergy to certain pollens. Sneezing, a running nose, and itching eyes are common symptoms.

hay·fork [hā′fôrk′] *n.* 1 A tool for pitching hay by hand; pitchfork. 2 A machine-operated device for loading or transporting hay.

hay·loft [hā′lôft′] *n.* An upper section of a barn or stable, used for storing hay.

hay·mow [hā′mou′] *n.* 1 A mass of stored hay. 2 A place in a barn or stable for storing hay.

hay·rack [hā′rak′] *n.* 1 A rack or frame from which livestock feed. 2 A rack (def. 2).

hay·rick [hā′rik′] *n.* A haystack.

hay·ride [hā′rīd′] *n.* A ride taken for pleasure by a group of persons in a wagon partially filled with hay.

hay·seed [hā′sēd′] *n.* 1 Grass seeds and bits of chaff and straw that fall from hay when it is shaken or transported. 2 *slang* Another word for BUMPKIN.

hay·stack [hā′stak′] *n.* A large pile of hay stacked outdoors, sometimes covered.

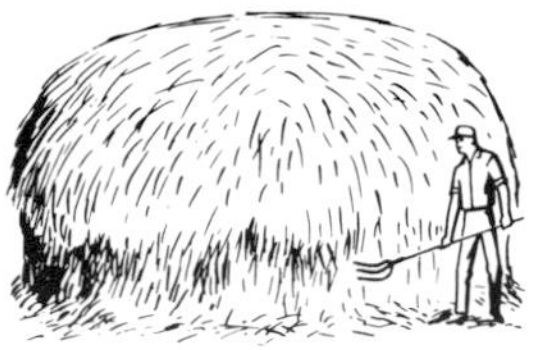
Haystack

hay·wire [hā′wīr′] 1 *n.* Wire for binding hay into bales. 2 *adj. slang* Broken down or messed up. 3 *adj. slang* Confused or crazy.

haz·ard [haz′ərd] 1 *n.* A chance of injury or loss; danger; peril: the *hazards* of war. 2 *v.* To put in danger; risk: to *hazard* one's life. 3 *v.* To take a chance on; venture: to *hazard* an opinion. 4 *n.* Chance; accident. 5 *n.* In golf, an obstacle, as a sand trap.

haz·ard·ous [haz′ər·dəs] *adj.* Full of danger or risk. **—haz′ard·ous·ly** *adv.* **—haz′ard·ous·ness** *n.*

haze[1] [hāz] *n.* 1 Fine droplets, as of water or dust particles, suspended in the air, making seeing difficult. 2 Mental confusion or fogginess; muddle.

haze[2] [hāz] *v.* **hazed, haz·ing** *U.S.* To force (newcomers) to do silly or humiliating things; bully.

ha·zel [hā′zəl] 1 *n.* A small tree or bushy shrub related to the birch. 2 *n., adj.* Light, yellowish brown.

ha·zel·nut [hā′zəl·nut′] *n.* The small, edible nut of the hazel.

haz·y [hā′zē] *adj.* **haz·i·er, haz·i·est** 1 Full of or blurred by haze; misty. 2 Unclear; confused: *hazy* thoughts. **—haz′i·ly** *adv.* **—haz′i·ness** *n.*

H-bomb [āch′bom′] *n.* A hydrogen bomb.

he [hē] *pron., n., pl.* **hes** 1 *pron.* The man, boy, or male animal that has been mentioned: The student knew *he* had passed the test. 2 *pron.* That person; one: *He* who reads learns. 3 *n.* A male: Is it a *he* or a she? ◆ Do not use unnecessary pronouns, as in "My father he works downtown." (This error is known as the *double subject.*)

He The symbol for the element helium.

head [hed] 1 *n.* In animals having a backbone, the part of the body at the top or front of the spinal column, containing the brain, eyes, mouth, and other organs. 2 *n.* A similar part of other animals and organisms. 3 *n.* A sculpture of a head. 4 *n.* The top or front part: the *head* of a nail; Go to the *head* of the line. 5 *adj.* Located at the top or front: the *head* seat. 6 *adj.* Hitting or striking against the front: *head* winds. 7 *n.* The part of a tool or weapon that strikes: the *head* of a hammer. 8 *n.* The skin stretched across a drum, tambourine, or other instrument. 9 *n.* A leader; boss; chief: the *head* of a firm. 10 *adj.* Principal; chief: a *head* waiter. 11 *n.* The most outstanding position: to be at the *head* of the class. 12 *v.* To lead or command: to *head* a scout troop. 13 *v.* To be the first or the most prominent or outstanding on or in: to *head* the class. 14 *n., pl.* **head** A single person or individual: Admission is $5.00 a *head*; ten *head* of cattle. 15 *n.* Something shaped like a head: a *head* of lettuce. 16 *n.* Mind or intelligence: Use your *head!*; a good *head* for figures. 17 *n.* A source, as of a river. 18 *n. (pl.)* The top side of a coin, often bearing a likeness of a person's head. 19 *v.* To move or turn in a specified direction: to *head* toward shore. 20 *n.* Progress against something that opposes: to make *head* against the wind. 21 *n.* The tip of a boil or abscess, where pus may break through. 22 *n.* A climax or crisis: Things came to a *head.* **—head off** To get in front of and block the way; intercept. **—head over heels** Totally and helplessly: I'm *head over heels* in love. **—keep one's head** To remain calm and under self-control in a distressing situation. **—lose one's head** To lose self-control; become excited. **—out of one's head** or **off one's head** Not reasonable; crazy; insane. **—over one's head** 1 Too difficult to understand. 2 Beyond one's ability to control or cope with. **—turn someone's head** To spoil or make vain with praise.

head·ache [hed′āk′] *n.* 1 Discomfort or pain in the head. 2 *U.S. informal* A difficulty or trouble.

head·band [hed′band′] *n.* A band worn around the head.

head·board [hed′bôrd′] *n.* A board or panel that forms the head of a bed.

head cheese A jellied loaf or sausage made with bits of seasoned meat from the head, feet, and sometimes the tongue and heart of an animal, especially a hog.

head·dress [hed′dres′] *n.* A covering or ornament for the head.

head·ed [hed′id] *adj.* 1 Formed or grown into a head, as certain vegetables. 2 Having a specified kind or number of heads: used in combination, as *round-headed* hammer or *two-headed* calf. 3 Having a head or heading: *headed* columns.

head·er [hed′ər] *n. informal* A fall or plunge with the head leading, especially in the expression **take a header,** to fall headfirst.

head·first [hed′fûrst′] *adv.* 1 With the head first. 2 Without caution; recklessly.

head·gear [hed′gir′] *n.* A covering for the head, as a hat or helmet.

head·ing [hed′ing] *n.* 1 Something written or printed at the top of a page, as a name or address. 2 Something serving as the top or front part of anything. 3 A title, as of a chapter or new topic. 4 A direction of travel: The ship took a *heading* ten degrees west of north.

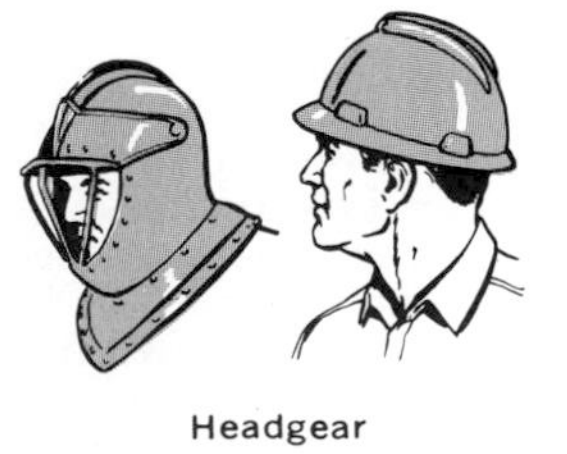
Headgear

head·lamp [hed′lamp′] *n.* A headlight.

head·land [hed′lənd] *n.* A point of high land extending out into water.

head·less [hed′lis] *adj.* **1** Without a head. **2** Without a leader. **3** Stupid; brainless.

head·light [hed′līt′] *n.* A powerful lamp placed at the front of a motor vehicle, train, or other conveyance, to allow the operator to see ahead at night.

head·line [hed′līn′] *n., v.* **head·lined, head·lin·ing** **1** *n.* Several words set in bold type at the top of a newspaper article, serving to introduce it and tell what it is about. **2** *v.* To give a headline to, as a news article. **3** *v.* To be or be listed as the main attraction of a show.

head·lock [hed′lok′] *n.* A wrestling hold in which the head of one wrestler is held under the arm of the other.

head·long [hed′lông′] *adv., adj.* **1** With the head leading: to fall *headlong* from a tree; a *headlong* plunge. **2** With reckless speed or energy: to burst *headlong* into a meeting.

head·man [hed′man′] *n., pl.* **head·men** [hed′men′] A leader in a tribal group; chief.

head·mas·ter [hed′mas′tər] *n.* The principal of a school, especially a private school.

head·mis·tress [hed′mis′tris] *n.* A woman who is principal of a school, especially a private school for girls.

head-on [hed′on′] *adj., adv.* With the front ends striking: a *head-on* crash; to collide *head-on.*

head·phone [hed′fōn′] *n.* An earphone held to the ear by a band that fits over the head.

head·piece [hed′pēs′] *n.* A hat, helmet, or other covering for the head.

head·quar·ter [hed′kwôr′tər] *v.* **1** To set up headquarters. **2** To provide headquarters for.

head·quar·ters [hed′kwôr′tərz] *n.pl. (usually used with singular verb)* **1** The place from which operations, as those of an organization, military unit, or police force, are directed. **2** The person or persons who direct the operations: *Headquarters* says to attack at dawn.

head·rest [hed′rest′] *n.* A support for the head, as a padded frame attached to the top of a car seat.

head·shrink·er [hed′shringk′ər] *n. slang* A psychiatrist or psychoanalyst.

heads·man [hedz′mən′] *n., pl.* **heads·men** [hedz′·mən′] A person who beheads condemned criminals; executioner.

head·stand [hed′stand′] *n.* The act of balancing one's body on the head with one's feet in the air, usually with one's hands on the ground to provide balance and support.

head start **1** A start in advance of other competitors, as in a race. **2** An early start or other advantage in any endeavor.

head·stone [hed′stōn′] *n.* **1** The stone placed at the head of a grave. **2** A cornerstone.

John Hale
1879-1939
May he rest
in peace
Headstone

head·strong [hed′strông′] *adj.* Stubbornly set upon having one's own way; obstinate: The *headstrong* child insisted on going, despite opposition.

head·wait·er [hed′wā′tər] *n.* A waiter who is in charge of the other service personnel in a restaurant.

head·wa·ters [hed′wô′tərz] *n.pl.* The streams or other waters that form the source of a river.

head·way [hed′wā′] *n.* **1** Forward motion or progress: They could make little *headway* in the dark without a lantern; to make *headway* against ignorance. **2** The height clear under a bridge, arch, or other structure; clearance.

head wind A wind in a direction opposite to the course of a ship, airplane, or the like.

head·y [hed′ē] *adj.* **head·i·er, head·i·est** **1** Apt to make one lightheaded or dizzy; intoxicating: a *heady* perfume. **2** Headstrong; rash.

heal [hēl] *v.* **1** To return to soundness or health: The patient's cuts have all *healed*; The ointment *healed* the burn. **2** To remedy, repair, or mend: Time *healed* their quarrel. **—heal′er** *n.*

health [helth] *n.* **1** Freedom in body and mind from any disease, defect, or disorder. **2** General condition of the body and mind: good *health*; poor *health*. **—health′ful·ly** *adv.* **—health′ful·ness** *n.*

health food A food that is believed to be highly nutritious and beneficial to one's health, as one grown without chemical fertilizers and prepared without chemical additives.

health·ful [helth′fəl] *adj.* **1** Promoting health or well-being: a *healthful* sport. **2** Healthy.

health·y [hel′thē] *adj.* **health·i·er, health·i·est** **1** Having or showing good health: a *healthy* person. **2** Promoting good health: to enjoy a *healthy* diet. **—health′i·ly** *adv.* **—health′i·ness** *n.*

heap [hēp] **1** *n.* A collection of things piled up; pile; mound. **2** *v.* To pile or collect into a heap: *Heap* the wood here. **3** *v.* To fill full or more than full: to *heap* a plate with food. **4** *v.* To give or give something to in large amounts: to *heap* abuse on a worker; to *heap* someone with praise. **5** *n. informal* A large amount: to have a *heap* of money.

hear [hir] *v.* **heard** [hûrd], **hear·ing** **1** To experience (sounds) in the ears: The deaf cannot *hear*; I *hear* thunder. **2** To listen to: *Hear* what I say! **3** To learn or come to know: Did you *hear* about the fire? **4** To receive a message: Have you *heard* from your cousin? **5** To listen to officially or legally: to *hear* a case in court. **6** To answer, as a prayer. **—hear′er** *n.*

hearing [hir′ing] *n.* **1** The sense by which sounds are experienced; the ability to hear. **2** The act or process of experiencing sound. **3** A chance to be heard: New ideas deserve a *hearing*. **4** An official examination, as by a court. **5** The range or distance within which a sound may be heard; earshot.

hearing aid A small electronic device that makes sounds strong enough for partially deaf people to hear them.

heark·en [här′kən] *v.* To listen or pay attention: seldom used today: *Hearken* to my words.

hear·say [hir′sā′] *n.* Something heard from others; rumor.

hearse [hûrs] *n.* A vehicle for carrying a dead person to the place of burial.

a	add	**i**	it	**o͝o**	took	**oi**	oil
ā	ace	**ī**	ice	**o͞o**	pool	**ou**	pout
â	care	**o**	odd	**u**	up	**ng**	ring
ä	palm	**ō**	open	**û**	burn	**th**	thin
e	end	**ô**	order	**yo͞o**	fuse	**th̶**	this
ē	equal					**zh**	vision

ə = a in *above*, e in *sicken*, i in *possible*, o in *melon*, u in *circus*

heart [härt] *n.* 1 The hollow muscular organ that by rhythmically contracting and expanding acts as a pump to keep blood flowing through the body. 2 The heart regarded as the source of feelings and emotions, especially of love, affection, or sorrow: to pour out one's *heart*; a heavy *heart.* 3 The ability to be kind and gentle: a good *heart.* 4 Courage or strength: to gain *heart.* 5 Energy or enthusiasm: My *heart* was not in it. 6 Someone loved or respected: a brave *heart.* 7 The central or inner part: the *heart* of the city. 8 The main or essential part: the *heart* of the problem. 9 A figure like this ♥. It is often used as a symbol of love. 10 A playing card of the suit marked with red heart figures. 11 (*pl.*) The suit so marked. **—after one's heart** or **after one's own heart** Exactly to one's liking. **—at heart** By nature; basically. **—by heart** By memory. **—take to heart** To be seriously concerned with. **—with all one's heart** With full sincerity or enthusiasm.

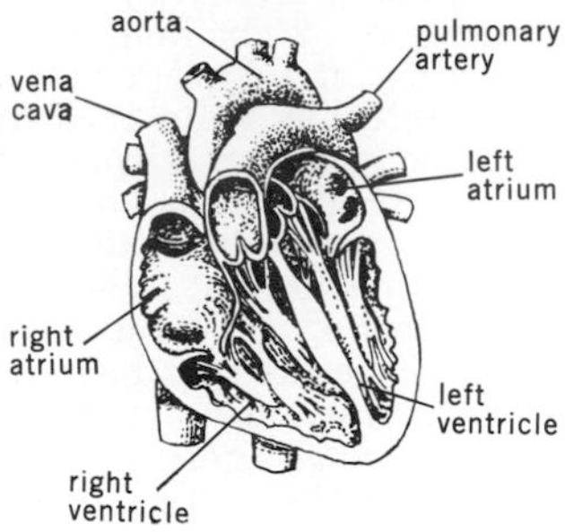

heart·ache [härt'āk'] *n.* Grief or great sorrow.

heart·beat [härt'bēt'] *n.* 1 A single contraction and relaxation of the heart. 2 The rhythmic sound that the heart makes.

heart·break [härt'brāk'] *n.* Great disappointment or sorrow.

heart·break·ing [härt'brā'king] *adj.* Causing great disappointment or sorrow. **—heart'break'ing·ly** *adv.*

heart·bro·ken [härt'brō'kən] *adj.* Overcome by grief or sorrow. **—heart'bro'ken·ly** *adv.*

heart·burn [härt'bûrn'] *n.* Discomfort caused by too much acid in the stomach.

heart·ed [här'tid] *adj.* Having a particular kind of heart: used in combination, as in *heavy-hearted,* having a heart heavy with sadness or grief.

heart·en [här'tən] *v.* To give courage or cheer to: The news *heartened* my listeners.

heart·felt [härt'felt'] *adj.* Deeply felt; sincere: Please accept my *heartfelt* thanks.

hearth [härth] *n.* 1 The floor of a fireplace or furnace. 2 The fireside; home. 3 The bottom of a blast furnace, where molten metal collects.

heart·land [härt'land'] *n.* A vital central area.

hearth·stone [härth'stōn'] *n.* 1 The stone that forms a hearth. 2 The fireside; home.

heart·i·ly [här'tə·lē] *adv.* 1 Sincerely and enthusiastically: to greet friends *heartily.* 2 Eagerly and abundantly: to eat *heartily.* 3 Completely; thoroughly: *heartily* disgusted.

heart·less [härt'lis] *adj.* Without sympathy or kindness; cruel; pitiless: a *heartless* action. **—heart'less·ly** *adv.* **—heart'less·ness** *n.*

heart-rend·ing [härt'ren'ding] *adj.* Causing much grief and sorrow: a *heart-rending* tale.

hearts·ease or **heart's-ease** [hârtz'ēz'] *n.* Mental and emotional peace; tranquillity and serenity.

heart·sick [härt'sik'] *adj.* Very disappointed; depressed: to be *heartsick* over losing one's job.

heart·strings [härt'stringz'] *n.pl.* Deep or strong feelings, as of sympathy or pity: Their sad story touched my *heartstrings.*

heart-to-heart [härt'tə·härt'] *adj.* Frank and sincere; candid: a *heart-to-heart* discussion.

heart·y [här'tē] *adj.* **heart·i·er, heart·i·est,** *n, pl.* **heart·ies** 1 *adj.* Full of warmth; friendly: a *hearty* welcome. 2 *adj.* Strongly felt; intense: *hearty* disgust. 3 *adj.* Healthy and strong: a *hearty* person; a *hearty* appetite. 4 *adj.* Abundant and satisfying: a *hearty* meal. 5 *n.* A hearty fellow or sailor. **—heart'i·ness** *n.*

heat [hēt] 1 *n.* The condition of being hot or the degree to which something is hot. Scientifically, heat is the energy possessed by an object or substance due to the vibration of its molecules. 2 *n.* Warmth supplied to the air in a building, as from a furnace. 3 *v.* To make or become hot or less cold. 4 *n.* Hot weather. 5 *n.* Excitement or intensity of feeling: in the *heat* of debate. 6 *v.* To make or become excited or intense. 7 *n.* A single trial or effort, as in a race.

heat·ed [hē'tid] *adj.* Characterized by anger or excitement: The presidential candidates had a *heated* debate. **—heat'ed·ly** *adv.*

heat·er [hē'tər] *n.* A device that produces heat.

heath [hēth] *n.* 1 A low, hardy evergreen shrub with narrow leaves and small red, white, or yellow flowers. 2 *British* An open area overgrown with heath or coarse plants.

hea·then [hē't͟hən] *n., pl.* **hea·thens** or **hea·then** 1 A member of a tribe of people that is neither Christian, Jewish, nor Islamic, especially a worshiper of idols or spirits. 2 *adj. use: heathen* worship; *heathen* lands; *heathen* tribes. 3 A person whose religion is thought to be false. **—hea'then·ish** *adj.*

hea·then·dom [hē't͟hən·dəm] 1 The beliefs, values, or practices of heathens. 2 Heathen people or countries.

heath·er [het͟h'ər] *n.* A low evergreen shrub related to the heath, having small pinkish flowers.

heat rash Another name for PRICKLY HEAT.

heat shield A barrier of heat-resistant material used to protect a space vehicle as it reenters the atmosphere.

heat·stroke [hēt'strōk'] *n.* A serious condition produced by prolonged exposure to very high temperatures. The symptoms include headache, a cessation of sweating, high temperature, collapse, and coma.

heat wave A period of very hot weather.

heave [hēv] *v.* **heaved** or **hove, heav·ing,** *n.* 1 *v.* To lift or throw with great effort: to *heave* a sack onto a platform. 2 *v.* To pull or haul up or on: *Heave* in the net; to *heave* a rope. 3 *v.* To pitch and toss about: The boat *heaved* in the waves. 4 *v.* To move or proceed, as a ship. 5 *v.* To utter painfully: to *heave* a sigh. 6 *v.* To vomit; retch. 7 *v.* To breathe hard; pant. 8 *v.* To expand and contract rhythmically: My chest *heaved.* 9 *n.* The act of heaving. **—heave to** 1 To bring (a ship) to a halt. 2 To stop.

People heaving a log

heav·en [hev'ən] *n.* 1 In various religions, the place where God, the angels, and the blessed souls are located. 2 (*written* **Heaven**) God: *Heaven* protect you. 3 (*pl.*) The stars, planets, and other celestial bodies, and the apparent background in which they are located. 4 Something very pleasant: Listening to good music is *heaven.*

heav·en·ly [hev′ən·lē] *adj.* 1 Of or belonging to heaven: *heavenly* choirs of angels. 2 Located in the heavens: *heavenly* bodies. 3 Delightful: *heavenly* weather.

heav·en·ward [hev′ən·wərd] *adj., adv.* Towards heaven: The angel flew *heavenward.*

Heav·i·side layer [hev′i·sīd′] A region of the atmosphere about 60 miles above the earth that reflects radio waves of certain frequencies.

heav·y [hev′ē] *adj.* **heav·i·er, heav·i·est,** *adv., n., pl.* **heav·ies** 1 *adj.* Having great weight or mass; hard to move or hold up. 2 *adj.* Having relatively great weight compared to size or volume: a *heavy* oil. 3 *adj.* Greater, as in amount, size, or number, than what is usual: a *heavy* snow; a *heavy* vote. 4 *adj.* Giving an impression of thickness; coarse; broad: *heavy* features. 5 *adj.* Weighted down; burdened: a tree *heavy* with fruit. 6 *adj.* Lacking grace; clumsy: a *heavy* style. 7 *adj.* Forceful and severe: a *heavy* blow. 8 *adj.* Of great importance; serious: a *heavy* discussion. 9 *adj.* Affected by grief or misery: a *heavy* heart. 10 *adj.* Hard to do or bear; oppressive: *heavy* labor; *heavy* taxes. 11 *adj.* Overcast; gloomy: The sky was *heavy.* 12 *adj.* Hard to digest; rich: a *heavy* meal. 13 *adv.* In a heavy or thick manner: The snow lay *heavy* on the ground. 14 *n.* A serious or villainous character or role, as in a play or movie. 15 *n.* An actor who plays such a character. 16 *adj.* Of or having to do with such a character or role. 17 *n.* A villainous person. 18 *n. slang* A person who is very important or significant: a *heavy* in the political arena. **—heav′i·ly** *adv.* **—heav′i·ness** *n.*

heav·y-du·ty [hev′ē·d(y)o͞o′tē] *adj.* Designed and constructed to withstand hard use and wear: *heavy-duty* construction boots.

heav·y-hand·ed [hev′ē·han′did] *adj.* 1 Lacking dexterity or grace; clumsy; awkward. 2 Harsh; cruel; oppressive. **—heav′y-hand′ed·ly** *adv.* **—heav′y-hand′ed·ness** *n.*

heav·y-heart·ed [hev′ē·här′tid] *adj.* Gloomy and sad; depressed; dejected. **—heav′y-heart′ed·ly** *adv.* **—heav′y-heart′ed·ness** *n.*

heavy hydrogen Another name for DEUTERIUM.

heav·y·set [hev′ē·set′] *adj.* Having a stocky and compact build.

heavy water Water in which deuterium constitutes a larger proportion of the hydrogen than occurs naturally.

heav·y·weight [hev′ē·wāt′] *n.* 1 An unusually heavy person or thing. 2 A boxer or wrestler who weighs more than 175 pounds.

He·be [hē′bē] *n.* In greek mythology, the goddess of youth and spring.

He·bra·ic [hi·brā′ik] *adj.* Of, having to do with, or characteristic of the Hebrews, their language, or their culture.

He·brew [hē′bro͞o] 1 *n.* One of the Semitic people that claim descent from Abraham; Jew. 2 *n.* An ancient Semitic language in which most of the Old Testament was first written. 3 *n.* The modern form of this language, used officially in Israel. 4 *adj.* Of or having to do with the Hebrews, their language, or their culture.

Hec·a·te [hek′ə·tē] *n.* In Greek myths, a goddess of the earth, moon, and underworld, associated with witchcraft and magic.

hec·a·tomb [hek′ə·tōm′] *n.* 1 In ancient Greece and Rome, a public sacrifice to the gods during which a hundred oxen or cattle were slaughtered. 2 Any slaughter of many victims.

heck·le [hek′əl] *v.* **heck·led, heck·ling** To try to confuse or annoy with insults or mocking questions: to *heckle* a speaker. **—heck·ler** [hek′lər] *n.*

hect- or **hecto** A combining form meaning: A hundred, as in *hectometer.*

hec·tare [hek′târ′] *n.* In the metric system, a unit of area equal to 100 ares or 2.471 acres.

hec·tic [hec′tik] *adj.* 1 Marked by or full of excitement, confusion, or haste: a *hectic* trip. 2 Flushed and feverish, as if from illness.

hec·to·me·ter [hek′tə·mē′tər] *n.* In the metric system, a unit of length equal to 100 meters.

hec·tor [hek′tər] 1 *v.* To bully, as by ranting or blustering. 2 *n.* A bully; boor.

Hec·tor [hek′tər] *n.* In the *Iliad,* the leading Trojan warrior, killed by Achilles.

he'd [hēd] 1 He had. 2 He would.

hedge [hej] *n., v.* **hedged, hedg·ing** 1 *n.* A fence formed by bushes planted close together. 2 *n.* Any boundary or barrier. 3 *v.* To surround with a hedge: to *hedge* a patio. 4 *v.* To restrict the movement or action of: to *hedge* someone in. 5 *v.* To avoid frank or direct answers: The mayor *hedged* when asked if taxes would be raised. 6 *n.* The act of hedging.

hedge·hog [hej′hog′] *n.* 1 A small European animal with spines on its back. 2 *U.S.* A porcupine.

Hedgehog

hedge·row [hej′rō′] *n.* A dense row of trees or bushes planted as a hedge.

heed [hēd] 1 *v.* To pay close attention to: *Heed* my advice. 2 *n.* Careful attention: Give *heed* to what the teacher says. **—heed′ful** *adj.* **—heed′·ful·ly** *adv.* **—heed′ful·ness** *n.*

heed·less [hēd′lis] *adj.* Not caring or paying attention; reckless: *heedless* of the consequences of their act. **—heed′less·ly** *adv.* **—heed′less·ness** *n.*

hee·haw [hē′hô′] 1 *n.* The braying sound made by a donkey. 2 *v.* To laugh with a similar sound.

heel[1] [hēl] 1 *n.* The rounded back part of the human foot, below the ankle. 2 *n.* The part of a shoe, sock, or stocking that covers the heel. 3 *n.* The built-up part of a shoe or boot on which the heel rests. 4 *v.* To supply (a shoe) with a heel. 5 *n.* Something that suggests a heel, as by shape or position: the *heel* of a golf club. 6 *v.* To follow closely. 7 *n. slang* A low or dishonorable person. **—down at the heel** 1 Having the heels of one's shoes worn down. 2 Shabby; run-down. **—take to one's heels** To run away; flee.

a	add	**i**	it	**o͝o**	took	**oi**	oil
ā	ace	**ī**	ice	**o͞o**	pool	**ou**	pout
â	care	**o**	odd	**u**	up	**ng**	ring
ä	palm	**ō**	open	**û**	burn	**th**	thin
e	end	**ô**	order	**yo͞o**	fuse	**th**	this
ē	equal					**zh**	vision

ə = a in *above*, e in *sicken*, i in *possible*, o in *melon*, u in *circus*

heel² [hēl] 1 *v.* To lean or cause to lean: The boat *heeled.* 2 *n.* The act or extent of heeling.
heft [heft] *informal* 1 *v.* To lift up; heave. 2 *n.* Heaviness. 3 *v.* To test the weight of by lifting.
heft·y [hef′tē] *adj.* **heft·i·er, heft·i·est** *informal* 1 Heavy or weighty. 2 Large and powerful: a *hefty* athlete.
heif·er [hef′ər] *n.* A young cow that has not produced a calf.
heigh-ho [hī′hō′ *or* hā′hō′] *interj.* An expression, as of weariness, disappointment, or surprise.
height [hīt] *n.* 1 The condition of being high. 2 The distance upward from the bottom to the top: the *height* of a tree. 3 (*often pl.*) A high place: to ascend to the *heights.* 4 Distance from the ground or sea level: clouds at a *height* of 20,000 feet. 5 The highest part; summit; peak. 6 The greatest degree: the *height* of stupidity.
height·en [hīt′(ə)n] *v.* 1 To make or become high or higher. 2 To increase or intensify: Seasoning *heightens* the taste of food.
hei·nous [hā′nəs] *adj.* Extremely wicked; terrible: a *heinous* crime.
heir [âr] *n.* A person who inherits or is likely to inherit rank or property upon the death of the person who possesses it: *heir* to the throne.
heir apparent *pl.* **heirs apparent** A person who must by law become the heir to rank or property if the person possessing it dies before he or she does.
heir·ess [âr′is] *n.* A female who inherits or is likely to inherit rank or property upon the death of the person who possesses it.
heir·loom [âr′lo͞om′] *n.* An object that has been passed through several generations of a family.
heir presumptive *pl.* **heirs presumptive** A person who will become heir to rank or property unless someone is born with a closer kinship to the ancestor.
held [held] Past tense and past participle of HOLD: I *held* the pitcher upside down.
Hel·en of Troy [hel′ən] In the *Iliad,* the beautiful wife of the king of Sparta. Her abduction by Paris caused the Trojan War.
hel·i·cal [hel′i·kəl] *adj.* Of, having to do with, or in the shape of a helix. **—hel′i·cal·ly** *adv.*
hel·i·ces [hel′ə·sēz′] A plural of HELIX.
hel·i·con [hel′ə·kon′] *n.* A large tuba that encircles the player's shoulder.
hel·i·cop·ter [hel′ə·kop′tər] *n.* An aircraft that is lifted and propelled by big, motor-driven, horizontal rotors and is able to hover and to fly in any direction. ◆ *Helicopter* comes from two Greek words meaning *spiral wing.*

Helicopter

he·li·o·cen·tric [hē′lē·ə·sen′trik] *adj.* Having or regarding the sun as the center: a *heliocentric* universe; a *heliocentric* theory.
he·li·o·graph [hē′lē·ə·graf′] 1 *n.* A device used in photographing the sun. 2 *n.* A device with a movable mirror, used to signal by reflecting flashes of sunlight. 3 *v.* To signal by heliograph.
He·li·os [hē′lē·ōs] *n.* In Greek myths, the sun god.
he·li·o·trope [hē′lē·ə·trōp′] 1 *n.* A plant with fragrant white or purplish flowers. 2 *adj., n.* Soft, rosy purple.
he·li·ot·ro·pism [hē′lē·ot′rə·piz′əm] *n.* A response to sunlight, especially the tendency of some plants to turn toward it.
hel·i·pad [hel′ə·pad′] *n.* Heliport.
hel·i·port [hel′ə·pôrt′] *n.* An airport for helicopters. ◆ *Heliport* is a combination of *heli(copter)* and *(air)port.*
he·li·um [hē′lē·əm] *n.* A light, odorless, chemically inert gaseous element formed from the alpha particles emitted by radioactive elements in the earth's crust, present only in traces in the atmosphere of the earth, but the second most abundant element in the universe.
he·lix [hē′liks] *n., pl.* **he·lix·es** or **hel·i·ces** [hel′ə·sēz′] 1 A spiral coil, like the thread of a screw. 2 In mathematics, a curve drawn on the surface of a cone or cylinder in such a way that it cuts the figure at the same angle at each turn.
hell [hel] *n.* 1 (*often written* **Hell**) In various religions, the realm of devils and the place where wicked souls are punished after death. 2 Any evil place. 3 A condition of suffering: The patient went through *hell* with an inflamed foot.

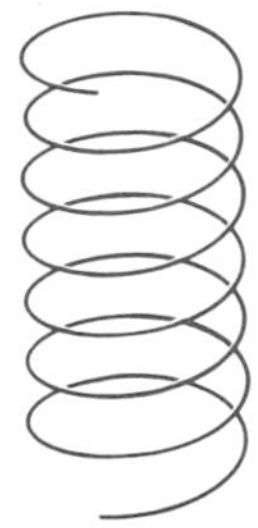
Helix

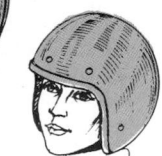

he'll [hēl] 1 He will. 2 He shall.
Hel·las [hel′əs] *n.* Ancient or modern Greece.
hell·bend·er [hel′ben′dər] *n.* A large salamander that lives in streams and rivers in the central and eastern United States.
hel·le·bore [hel′ə·bôr′] *n.* A flowering plant whose roots are used in medicines and in insecticides.
Hel·lene [hel′ēn] *n.* Greek.
Hel·len·ic [he·len′ik *or* he·lē′nik] 1 *adj.* Greek; Grecian. 2 *n.* The family of languages that includes ancient and modern Greek.
Hel·le·nis·tic [hel′ə·nis′tik] *adj.* Of, having to do with, or characteristic of the Greek people, their language, and their culture during the period from the death of Alexander the Great in 323 B.C. on into the 1st century B.C.
hell·ish [hel′ish] *adj.* 1 Of or like hell. 2 Horrible; fiendish: a *hellish* plan.
hel·lo [hə·lō′] *interj., n., pl.* **hel·los,** *v.* **hel·loed, hel·lo·ing** 1 *interj.* An exclamation of greeting. 2 *interj.* An exclamation, as of surprise or interest: "*Hello*! What's happened here?" 3 *n.* A saying or shouting of "hello." 4 *v.* To say or greet with "hello."
helm¹ [helm] *n.* 1 A wheel or lever for steering a vessel. 2 A position of control: The vice president took over the *helm* of the business.
helm² [helm] *n.* A helmet: seldom used today.
hel·met [hel′mit] *n.* A protective covering for the head: a football *helmet.*
helms·man [helmz′·mən] *n., pl.* **helms·men** [helmz′mən] The person who steers a ship.
hel·ot [hel′ət *or* hē′lət] *n.* 1 A slave or serf; bondman. 2 (*usually written* **Helot**) A member of a class of serfs in ancient Sparta.

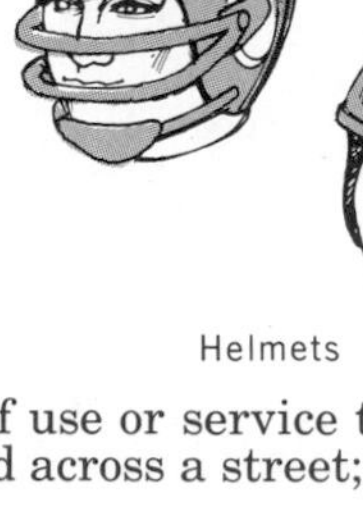
Helmets

help [help] 1 *v.* To be of use or service to; assist or support: to *help* a child across a street; to *help* our country. **2** *v.* To be of use or service; lend a hand: Will you come and *help*?; to *help* with the dishes. **3** *interj.* A cry, as of fear or terror, calling for assistance. **4** *v.* To improve or cure: Rest *helps* a cold. **5** *n.* The act of helping; assistance: Thanks for the *help*. **6** *n.* A person or thing that helps: You were a great *help*. **7** *n.* The condition of being helped. **8** *n.* A hired worker or workers. **—help oneself to** **1** To serve oneself, as with food. **2** To take without requesting or being offered: They *helped themselves to* my books while I was away. **—help′er** *n.*

help·ful [help′fəl] *adj.* Useful or beneficial. **—help′·ful·ly** *adv.* **—help′ful·ness** *n.*

help·ing [help′ing] *n.* A single portion of food.

helping verb A verb that precedes a main verb in a verb phrase. A helping verb forms the tense, mood, or voice of a main verb. In "Jane has completed her novel," *has* is a helping verb.

help·less [help′lis] *adj.* **1** Unable to help oneself; defenseless. **2** Lacking power or effectiveness. **—help′less·ly** *adv.* **—help′less·ness** *n.*

help·mate [help′māt′] *n.* A partner or helper, especially a wife or husband.

hel·ter-skel·ter [hel′tər·skel′tər] **1** *adj.* Hurried and confused. **2** *adv.* In a hurried or confused manner: to run *helter-skelter.*

helve [helv] *n.* The handle of a tool, as of an ax or hatchet.

hem[1] [hem] *n., v.* **hemmed, hem·ming** **1** *n.* A smooth edge on cloth or a garment, made by turning the rough edge under and sewing it down. **2** *v.* To provide with a hem: to *hem* a coat. **3** *v.* To shut in; surround: to *hem* in an enemy.

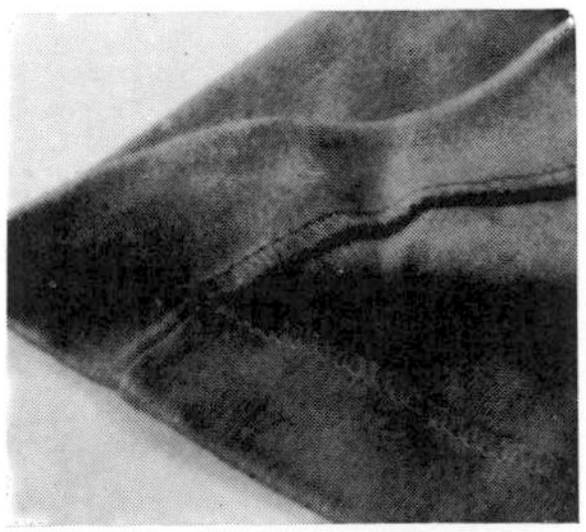

Hem

hem[2] [hem] *interj., n., v.* **hemmed, hem·ming** **1** *interj., n.* A cough-like sound made in clearing the throat. **2** *v.* To make this sound, as in clearing the throat or attracting attention. **—hem and haw** To hesitate in speaking to avoid making a clear statement.

hem·a·tite [hem′ə·tīt′] *n.* A common mineral that is an important ore of iron.

hemi- A prefix meaning: Half, as in *hemisphere.*

hem·i·sphere [hem′ə·sfir′] *n.* **1** A half of a sphere. **2** (*often written* **Hemisphere**) One half of the earth's surface. See EASTERN HEMISPHERE, WESTERN HEMISPHERE, NORTHERN HEMISPHERE, and SOUTHERN HEMISPHERE in Geographical Section. **—hem·i·spher·ic** [hem′i·sfer′ik] *adj.* **—hem·i·spher·i·cal** [hem′i·sfer′i·kəl] *adj.*

hem·line [hem′līn′] *n.* The bottom edge of a skirt, dress, or coat.

hem·lock [hem′lok′] *n.* **1** An evergreen tree with drooping branches, related to the pine. **2** A large plant that yields a poison.

he·mo·glo·bin [hē′mə·glō′bin] *n.* A red pigment that contains iron, found in red blood corpuscles, where it serves to carry oxygen.

he·mo·phil·i·a [hē′mə·fil′ē·ə] *n.* An inherited tendency to bleed without stopping, because the blood does not clot properly.

he·mo·phil·i·ac [hē′mə·fil′ē·ak] *n.* A person who has hemophilia.

hem·or·rhage [hem′ər·ij] *n., v.* **hem·or·rhaged, hem·or·rhag·ing** **1** *n.* A flow of blood, usually a heavy flow from a broken blood vessel. **2** *v.* To lose blood; bleed.

hem·or·rhoids [hem′ə·roidz′] *n.pl.* A condition in which veins in the lower or outer part of the rectum swell up and itch. It can be very painful, and sometimes requires surgery.

hemp [hemp] *n.* **1** A tall plant with small green flowers. **2** The tough, strong fibers of this plant, used to make rope and cloth. **3** A drug from the flowers and leaves of this plant.

hemp·en [hem′pən] *adj.* Having to do with, like, or made of hemp.

hem·stitch [hem′stich′] **1** *n.* A decorative stitch made by pulling out many threads of a fabric and then stitching together in groups the remaining cross threads so as to form a design. **2** *v.* To decorate with a hemstitch.

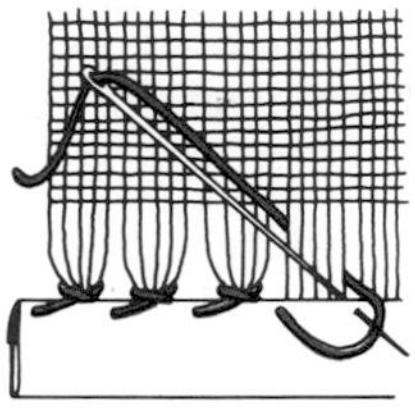

Hemstitching

hen [hen] *n.* The female of various birds, especially of the chicken and related birds.

hence [hens] **1** *adv.* Consequently; therefore: The door is locked, *hence* you can't enter. **2** *adv.* From this time: The group will depart a week *hence.* **3** *adv.* From this place: They live a mile *hence.* **4** *interj.* Go away!: seldom used today.

hence·forth [hens′fôrth′] *adv.* From this time on: *Henceforth* you will be more careful!

hence·for·ward [hens′fôr′wərd] *adv.* Henceforth.

hench·man [hench′mən] *n., pl.* **hench·men** [hench′·mən] A faithful and devoted helper or follower, especially of a wicked person or cause.

hen·e·quen [hen′ə·kin] *n.* **1** A tropical plant native to Mexico from whose thick leaves a coarse reddish fiber is made. **2** The fiber obtained from the henequen, used to make rope and twine.

hen·house [hen′hous′] *n., pl.* **hen·hous·es** [hen′hou′·zəz] A long, usually low, structure in which poultry is housed.

hen·na [hen′ə] *n., v.* **hen·naed, hen·na·ing,** *adj.* **1** *n.* An Oriental shrub with slender leaves and white flowers. **2** *n.* A reddish brown dye made from this plant. **3** *v.* To dye with henna. **4** *adj., n.* Reddish brown.

hen·peck [hen′pek′] *v.* To dominate (one's husband) by nagging or abuse.

hen·ry [hen′rē] *n., pl.* **hen·ries** or **hen·rys** In physics, a unit of measurement used to measure inductance. One henry is the amount of inductance that produces 1 volt of electricity when the current changes at the rate of 1 ampere per second.

he·pat·i·ca [hi·pat′ə·kə] *n.* A small plant having pink, white, or purple flowers and blooming early in the spring.

a	add	**i**	it	**o͝o**	took	**oi**	oil
ā	ace	**ī**	ice	**o͞o**	pool	**ou**	pout
â	care	**o**	odd	**u**	up	**ng**	ring
ä	palm	**ō**	open	**û**	burn	**th**	thin
e	end	**ô**	order	**yo͞o**	fuse	**t͟h**	this
ē	equal					**zh**	vision

ə = {a in *above*, e in *sicken*, i in *possible*, o in *melon*, u in *circus*}

hep·a·ti·tis [hep′ə·tī′tis] *n.* Inflammation of the liver.

hep·ta·gon [hep′tə·gon′] *n.* A two-dimensional geometric figure having seven sides and seven angles. **—hep·tag·o·nal** [hep·tag′ə·nəl] *adj.*

her [hûr] *pron.* 1 The pronoun *she* when used as an object of a verb or preposition: Please tell *her* now; I gave the book to *her.* 2 Of or belonging to her: the possessive form of *she*: *her* job; *her* stamp collection.

He·ra [hir′ə] *n.* In Greek myths, the wife of Zeus and queen of the gods. Her Roman name was Juno.

Her·a·cles or **Her·a·kles** [her′ə·klēz′] *n.* Hercules.

her·ald [her′əld] 1 *n.* A bearer of important news; messenger. 2 *n.* A person or thing that announces something to come. 3 *v.* To announce or foretell: Autumn frosts *herald* winter.

he·ral·dic [hi·ral′dik] *adj.* Of or having to do with heralds or heraldry.

her·ald·ry [her′əl·drē] *n., pl.* **her·ald·ries** 1 The study of coats of arms and family descent. 2 A coat of arms. 3 Formal pageantry and pomp.

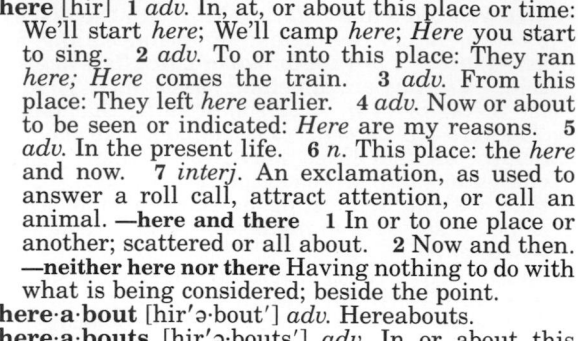

Heraldic emblem

herb [(h)ûrb] *n.* A plant that withers and dies away after its yearly flowering, especially such a plant used as a seasoning or medicine.

her·ba·ceous [(h)ûr·bā′shəs] *adj.* Of, like, or having to do with an herb or herbs.

herb·age [(h)ûr′bij] *n.* Grass and green plants for grazing animals.

herb·al [(h)ûr′bəl] 1 *adj.* Of, having to do with, or consisting of herbs. 2 *n.* A book about herbs or plants, especially about those that are believed to have therapeutic value.

herb·al·ist [(h)ûr′bə·list] *n.* A person who specializes in the cultivation, collection, or use of herbs, especially herbs believed to have therapeutic value.

her·bar·i·um [(h)ûr·bâr′ē·əm] *n., pl.* **her·bar·i·ums** or **her·bar·i·a** [(h)ûr·bâr′ē·ə] 1 A scientifically presented collection of dried plants. 2 A place where such a collection is housed.

her·bi·cide [(h)ûr′bə·sīd′] *n.* A chemical substance used to destroy or inhibit the growth of plants, especially weeds. **—her′bi·cid′al** *adj.*

her·bi·vore [(h)ûr′bə·vôr′] *n.* An animal that feeds on plants, especially an ungulate.

her·biv·o·rous [(h)ûr·biv′ə·rəs] *adj.* Feeding on plants: Cows are *herbivorous* animals.

Her·cu·le·an [hûr·kyo͞o′lē·ən *or* hûr′kyə·lē′ən] *adj.* 1 Of or having to do with Hercules. 2 (*often written* **herculean**) Having or requiring great strength, courage, and endurance: a *herculean* task.

Her·cu·les [hûr′kyə·lēz′] *n.* In Greek and Roman myths, a hero of great strength who successfully performed gigantic tasks.

herd [hûrd] 1 *n.* A large group of animals of one kind, moving about or kept together in a group: a *herd* of cattle. 2 *v.* To take care of in a herd: to *herd* goats. 3 *n.* A person who herds a specified kind of animal: used in combination, as in *swineherd.* 4 *v.* To gather or form into a herd. 5 *n.* The common people; masses. **—herd′er** *n.*

herds·man [hûrdz′mən] *n., pl.* **herds·men** [hûrdz′·mən] A person who breeds or takes care of a herd.

here [hir] 1 *adv.* In, at, or about this place or time: We'll start *here*; We'll camp *here*; *Here* you start to sing. 2 *adv.* To or into this place: They ran *here; Here* comes the train. 3 *adv.* From this place: They left *here* earlier. 4 *adv.* Now or about to be seen or indicated: *Here* are my reasons. 5 *adv.* In the present life. 6 *n.* This place: the *here* and now. 7 *interj.* An exclamation, as used to answer a roll call, attract attention, or call an animal. **—here and there** 1 In or to one place or another; scattered or all about. 2 Now and then. **—neither here nor there** Having nothing to do with what is being considered; beside the point.

here·a·bout [hir′ə·bout′] *adv.* Hereabouts.

here·a·bouts [hir′ə·bouts′] *adv.* In or about this place; in this vicinity.

here·af·ter [hir·af′tər] 1 *adv.* After this time; from now on: *Hereafter* keep silent! 2 *adv.* In the future. 3 *n.* A life after death.

here·by [hir·bī′ *or* hir′bī] *adv.* With or by means of this: You are *hereby* permitted to go.

he·red·i·tar·y [hə·red′ə·ter′ē] *adj.* 1 Left to one by an ancestor; inherited: a *hereditary* title. 2 Holding office by inheritance: a *hereditary* monarch. 3 Transmitted from parents to their offspring: a *hereditary* disease. 4 Of or having to do with heredity or inheritance.

he·red·i·ty [hə·red′ə·tē] *n.* 1 The passing on of characteristics from parents to offspring by means of genes. 2 The total of the qualities passed on in this way.

Here·ford [hûr′fərd *or* her′ə·fərd] *n.* One of a breed of beef cattle having a white face and a red coat with white markings.

here·in [hir·in′ *or* hir′in] *adv.* In or into this place, thing, matter, or case: Payment is included *herein*; *Herein* is your mistake.

here·of [hir·uv′] *adv.* Of or concerning this.

here·on [hir·on′] *adv.* On this.

her·e·sy [her′ə·sē] *n., pl.* **her·e·sies** 1 A belief different from or contrary to an accepted belief of a church, profession, or science. 2 The holding of such a belief.

her·e·tic [her′ə·tik] *n.* A person who believes or teaches heresy.

he·ret·i·cal [hə·ret′i·kəl] *adj.* Made up of, having in it, or having to do with heresy.

here·to [hir·to͞o′] *adv.* To this place, matter, or subject.

here·to·fore [hir′tə·fôr′] *adv.* Before this; up to now.

here·un·to [hir·un′to͞o] *adv.* Hereto.

here·up·on [hir′ə·pon′] *adv.* At this; immediately after this.

here·with [hir·with′] *adv.* 1 Along with this: I am enclosing *herewith* my passport. 2 By means of this.

her·i·ta·ble [her′ə·tə·bəl] *adj.* That can be inherited: a *heritable* trait.

her·i·tage [her′ə·tij] *n.* 1 Inherited things, as property or characteristics. 2 Something, as a tradition, belief, or attitude, handed down from the past.

her·maph·ro·dite [hûr·maf′rə·dīt′] *n.* An animal or plant that shows both male and female physical characteristics.

Her·mes [hûr′mēz] *n.* In Greek myths, the messenger of the gods, and the god of science, commerce, travel, eloquence, and cunning. His Roman name was Mercury.

her·met·ic [hûr·met′ik] *adj.* Preventing gases or liquids from getting in or out; airtight: a *hermetic* seal.
her·met·i·cal [hûr·met′i·kəl] *adj.* Hermetic. **—her·met′i·cal·ly** *adv.*
her·mit [hûr′mit] *n.* A person who lives alone and apart from others, as for religious reasons.
her·mit·age [hûr′mə·tij] *n.* The place where a hermit lives.
hermit crab A crab that has a soft abdomen and lives in abandoned shells of other creatures.
hermit thrush A North American thrush having a spotted breast, red tail, and a lovely song.

Hermit crab

her·ni·a [hûr′nē·ə] *n.* A bulging out of an organ or tissue through a break in its surrounding walls; rupture.
he·ro [hir′ō *or* hē′rō] *n., pl.* **he·roes** 1 A person who is known for such traits as courage and nobility, and for great deeds. 2 The principal male character, as in a story or play. 3 A large sandwich made on a long roll or thin, crusty loaf of bread.
he·ro·ic [hi·rō′ik] *adj.* 1 Of, like, or proper for a hero or heroine: a *heroic* person; a *heroic* attempt to rescue the drowning child. 2 Telling or describing the deeds or lives of heroes or heroines: a *heroic* play. 3 On a scale larger than life: a *heroic* sculpture. **—he·ro′i·cal·ly** *adv.*
he·ro·i·cal [hi·rō′i·kəl] *adj.* Heroic.
he·ro·ics [hi·rō′iks] *n.pl.* Words or deeds not truly grand or noble but meant to seem so.
her·o·in [her′ō·in] *n.* A habit-forming drug, made from morphine, now illegal in the U.S.
her·o·ine [her′ō·in] *n.* 1 A female who is known for such traits as courage and nobility, and for great deeds. 2 The principal female character, as in a story or play.
her·o·ism [her′ō·iz′əm] *n.* 1 The qualities of a hero or heroine. 2 Heroic behavior or deeds.
her·on [her′ən] *n.* Any of several wading birds having a long bill, a long neck, and long legs.
he·ron·ry [her′ən·rē] *n., pl.* **he·ron·ries** A place where herons gather during the breeding season.
her·pes [hûr′pēz′] *n.* Any of several diseases caused by certain viruses. The most common symptom is one or several blisterlike eruptions of the skin or mucous membrane.
her·pe·tol·o·gy [hûr′pə·tol′ə·jē] *n.* The science that studies reptiles. **—her′pe·tol′o·gist** *n.*

Great blue heron

Herr [her] *n., pl.* **Her·ren** [her′ən] The German title of courtesy for a man, equivalent to *Mr.*
her·ring [her′ing] *n., pl.* **her·rings** or **her·ring** A food fish common in the North Atlantic, the young of which are canned as sardines, and the adults of which are eaten cooked, smoked, or salted.
her·ring·bone [her′ing·bōn′] *n.* 1 A design something like the bones of a herring, or like rows of closely spaced v's one above another. This design is often used in fabrics and embroidery. 2 *adj. use: herringbone* tweed.
hers [hûrz] *pron.* 1 The one or ones belonging to her. 2 Of or belonging to her: That book is *hers.*
her·self [hər·self′] *pron.* 1 A form of *her* that refers back to the subject: She taught *herself* to play the piano. 2 A form of *her* that makes the word it goes with stronger or more intense: She *herself* told me. 3 Her normal, healthy, usual, or proper condition: After a long illness, she's *herself* again.
hertz [hûrts] *n., pl.* **hertz** or **hertz·es** A unit of frequency equal to one cycle per second.
hertz·i·an wave [hûr′tsē·ən] An electromagnetic wave, as a radio wave, produced by the oscillation of electricity in a conductor.
he's [hēz] 1 He is. 2 He has.
hes·i·tan·cy [hez′ə·tən·sē] *n.* The act or condition of hesitating; hesitation.
hes·i·tant [hez′ə·tənt] *adj.* Lacking certainty; hesitating; doubtful: The employee appeared *hesitant* in asking for the raise. **—hes′i·tant·ly** *adv.*
hes·i·tate [hez′ə·tāt′] *v.* **hes·i·tat·ed, hes·i·tat·ing** 1 To be slow or doubtful, as in acting or making a decision; pause or falter: We *hesitated* before giving the order; Don't *hesitate* to call me. 2 To be unwilling or reluctant: I *hesitate* to say what's really on my mind. 3 To stammer in speech.
hes·i·ta·tion [hez′ə·tā′shən] *n.* 1 The act of hesitating; wavering or doubt: I answered promptly, without the slightest *hesitation.* 2 A pause or faltering in speech.
Hes·per·i·des [hes·per′ə·dēz′] *n.pl.* In Greek myths, the nymphs who together with a dragon guarded the golden apples of Hera.
Hes·pe·rus [hes′pər·əs] *n.* The evening star.
Hes·sian [hesh′ən] *n.* One of the German soldiers hired to fight for the British in the American Revolution.
heter- or **hetero-** A combining form meaning: Different; other, as in *heterodox.*
het·er·o·dox [het′ə·rə·doks′] *adj.* 1 Different from an accepted view or standard. 2 Rejecting accepted views or standards.
het·er·o·doxy [het′ər·ə·dok′sē] *n., pl.* **het·er·o·dox·ies** 1 The state or condition of being heterodox. 2 A heterodox belief or set of beliefs.
het·er·o·ge·ne·ous [het′ər·ə·jē′nē·əs] *adj.* Consisting of parts or units that are not alike: a *heterogeneous* collection of rubbish; Ours is a *heterogeneous* society. **—het′er·o·ge′ne·ous·ly** *adv.* **—het′er·o·ge′ne·ous·ness** *n.*
hew [hyo͞o] *v.* **hewed, hewed** or **hewn** [hyo͞on], **hew·ing** 1 To cut or strike, as with an ax or sword: to *hew* branches. 2 To make or shape with blows of a knife or ax: to *hew* railings. **—hew′er** *n.*
hex [heks] *U.S. informal* 1 *n.* An evil spell. 2 *v.*

a add	**i** it	**o͝o** took	**oi** oil
ā ace	**ī** ice	**o͞o** pool	**ou** pout
â care	**o** odd	**u** up	**ng** ring
ä palm	**ō** open	**û** burn	**th** thin
e end	**ô** order	**yo͞o** fuse	**th** this
ē equal			**zh** vision

ə = {a in *above* e in *sicken* i in *possible* / o in *melon* u in *circus*}

H

To bewitch. ◆ *Hex* comes from the German word for *witch.*

hex·a·gon [hek′sə·gon′] *n.* A closed plane figure having six sides and six angles.

hex·ag·o·nal [hek·sag′ə·nəl] *adj.* Having the form of a hexagon: a *hexagonal* building.

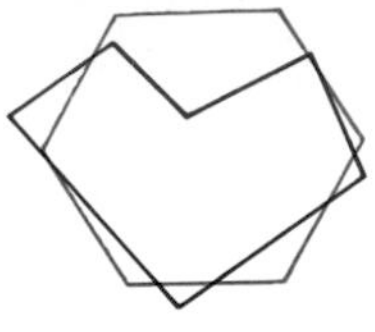

Hexagons (the red one is regular)

hex·a·he·dron [hek′sə·hē′drən] *n., pl.* **hex·a·he·dra** [hek′sə·hē′·drə] or **hex·a·he·drons** A solid figure bounded by six plane faces.

hex·am·e·ter [hek·sam′ə·tər] *n.* A line of verse having six rhythmic feet, as "Thĕn mūl | tĭ tūdes | păssed bȳ | thĕir vōi | cĕs rāised | ĭn sōng."

hey [hā] *interj.* A cry used to attract attention or express an emotion, as one of interest, surprise, or pleasure.

hey·day [hā′dā′] *n.* The time of greatest vigor or power: in the *heyday* of British naval power; in the athlete's *heyday.*

hf or **hf.** 1 half. 2 high frequency.

Hf The symbol for the element hafnium.

hg or **h.g.** hectogram.

Hg The symbol for the element mercury. ◆ The Latin word for mercury is *hydrargyrum.*

H.H. 1 Her Highness. 2 His Highness. 3 His Holiness.

HHS Department of Health and Human Services.

hi [hī] *interj. U.S. informal* Hello.

HI Postal Service abbreviation of Hawaii.

H.I. Hawaiian Islands.

hi·a·tus [hī·ā′təs] *n., pl.* **hi·a·tus·es** or **hi·a·tus** A space where something is missing, as in a manuscript; gap.

Hi·a·wath·a [hī′ə·woth′ə *or* hī′ə·wô′thə] *n.* In Longfellow's poem *The Song of Hiawatha,* the hero, a young Indian brave.

hi·ba·chi [hi·bä′chē] *n.* A portable stove of Japanese origin consisting of a grill set over a deep iron brazier in which charcoal is burned.

Hibachi

hi·ber·nate [hī′bər·nāt′] *v.* **hi·ber·nat·ed, hi·ber·nat·ing** To spend the winter sleeping or dormant, as bears and certain other animals do. —**hi′ber·na′tion** *n.*

Hi·ber·ni·an [hī·bûr′nē·ən] 1 *adj.* Irish. 2 *n.* A person who was born in or is a resident of Ireland. ◆ From *Hibernia,* the Latin name for Ireland.

hi·bis·cus [hī·bis′kəs] *n.* A plant having large showy flowers of various colors.

hic·cough [hik′up] *n., v.* Another spelling of HICCUP.

hic·cup [hik′up] *n., v.* **hic·cuped** or **hic·cupped, hic·cup·ing** or **hic·cup·ping** 1 *n.* A sudden, involuntary gasp of breath which is immediately cut off by a spasm in the throat. 2 *v.* To undergo these gasps and spasms.

hick [hik] *informal* 1 *n.* A naive, unsophisticated person considered typical of rural areas; yokel. 2 *adj.* Rural or unsophisticated.

hick·o·ry [hik′ə·rē] *n., pl.* **hick·o·ries** 1 Any of several North American trees related to the walnut and having a hard wood and edible nuts. 2 The wood of this tree. ◆ *Hickory* comes from an Algonquian word.

hid·den [hid′ən] 1 A past participle of HIDE. 2 *adj.* Not easily seen, found, or discerned; concealed: a *hidden* meaning.

hide[1] [hīd] *v.* **hid** [hid], **hid·den** [hid′(ə)n] or **hid, hid·ing** 1 To put or keep out of sight; conceal: to *hide* a key: Smoke *hid* the building. 2 To go or remain out of sight. 3 To keep secret: The children tried to *hide* their fear of the dark.

hide[2] [hīd] *n.* 1 The skin of an animal, especially when stripped from its carcass. 2 *informal* The human skin: I'll tan your *hide!*

hide-and-seek [hīd′(ə)n·sēk′] *n.* A game in which a person who is "it" has to find others who have hidden and touch home base before they do.

hide·a·way [hīd′ə·wā′] *n.* 1 A secluded place where one can go to be alone. 2 A hideout.

hide·bound [hīd′bound′] *adj.* Narrow-minded, obstinate, and with little imagination.

hid·e·ous [hid′ē·əs] *adj.* Very ugly; horrible. —**hid′·e·ous·ly** *adv.* —**hid′e·ous·ness** *n.*

hide·out [hīd′out′] *n. informal* A hiding place, especially for criminals.

hid·ing[1] [hī′ding] *n.* 1 The act of a person or thing that hides. 2 A place out of sight.

hid·ing[2] [hī′ding] *n. informal* A whipping or flogging.

hie [hī] *v.* **hied, hy·ing** or **hie·ing** To hasten; hurry: I *hied* myself home.

hi·er·ar·chi·cal [hī′ə·rär′ki·kəl] *adj.* Of or having to do with a hierarchy. —**hi′er·ar′chi·cal·ly** *adv.*

hi·er·ar·chy [hī′ə·rär′kē] *n., pl.* **hi·er·ar·chies** 1 A group of persons or things arranged in successive classes, each class subject to or dependent on the ones above it. 2 A group of clergymen organized in this way.

hi·er·o·glyph [hī′ər·ə·glif′ *or* hī′rə·glif′] *n.* A hieroglyphic.

hi·er·o·glyph·ic [hī′ər·ə·glif′ik *or* hī′rə·glif′ik] *n.* 1 A picture or symbol representing an object, idea, or sound. 2 (*pl.*) A system of writing using such pictures or symbols: ancient Egyptian *hieroglyphics.* 3 (*pl.*) Any writing that is hard to read or make out. 4 *adj. use: hieroglyphic* writing. ◆ *Hieroglyphic* comes from Greek words meaning *sacred carved* (writing), because the symbols were originally found on temple walls and in tombs.

Hieroglyphics

hi-fi [hī′fī′] *n., pl.* **hi-fis,** *adj.* 1 *n.* High fidelity. 2 *n.* Equipment for reproducing sound with high fidelity. 3 *adj.* Of or having to do with high fidelity. ◆ *Hi-fi* is a shortened or "clipped" form of *hi(gh) fi(delity).*

hig·gle·dy-pig·gle·dy [hig′əl·dē·pig′əl·dē] 1 *adv.* In great confusion or disorder: things tossed about *higgledy-piggledy.* 2 *adj.* Jumbled.

high [hī] 1 *adj.* Reaching upward a great distance: a *high* mountain. 2 *adj.* At a good distance from the floor or ground: The kite was *high.* 3 *adj.* Having a certain height: 10 feet *high.* 4 *adj.* To or from a great height: a *high* jump; a *high* dive. 5 *adj.* Great or large, as in amount or degree: *high* speeds; *high* voltage. 6 *adj.* Raised in pitch; shrill: a *high* sound. 7 *adj.* Superior, as in rank or quality: a *high* office. 8 *adj.* Very favorable: a *high* opinion of someone. 9 *adj.* Gay and joyful:

high spirits. **10** *n.* A high level, position, or degree: a *high* in prices. **11** *adv.* In or to a high level, position, or degree: The cat jumps *high.* **12** *adj.* Most important; chief: a *high* court. **13** *adj.* Serious or grave: *high* treason. **14** *adj.* Having a bad odor, as spoiled meat. **15** *adj.* Giving the greatest speed, as an arrangement of gears. **16** *n.* Such an arrangement of gears. **—high and dry** **1** Completely out of water, as a stranded ship. **2** Helpless and alone; stranded. **—high and low** All around: to look *high and low.* **—high and mighty** Too proud or arrogant; haughty. **—on high** **1** In or at a high place. **2** In heaven.

high·born [hī′bôrn′] *adj.* Of noble ancestry.

high·boy [hī′boi′] *n.* A tall chest of drawers, usually in two sections, the lower one on legs.

high·brow [hī′brou′] *informal* **1** *n.* A person claiming to be mainly interested in serious ideas and culture. **2** *adj.* Of or suitable for a highbrow.

high chair A baby's chair standing on tall legs and having a tray.

high·er-up [hī′ər·up′] *n. informal* A person who is superior in rank or position.

high·fa·lu·tin [hī′fə·lo͞ot′(ə)n] *adj. informal* Too grand; pompous; pretentious.

high fidelity The reproduction of sound with no noticeable change or distortion from the original. **—high-fi·del·i·ty** [hī′fə·del′ə·tē] *adj.*

high-flown [hī′flōn′] *adj.* Too grand or pretentious; not simple: *high-flown* talk.

high frequency A radio wave frequency between 3 and 30 megahertz.

High German The official and literary form of the German language.

high-grade [hī′grād′] *adj.* Of superior quality.

high-hand·ed [hī′han′did] *adj.* Acting or done in an arrogant manner without any thought for the wishes or desires of other people. **—high-hand′ed·ly** *adv.* **—high-hand′ed·ness** *n.*

high-hat [hī′hat′] *v.* **high-hat·ted, high-hat·ting,** *adj.* **1** *v.* To treat in a snobbish, condescending manner. **2** *adj.* Snobbish; condescending.

high·jack [hī′jak′] *v., n.* Another spelling of HIJACK.

high jinks [jingks] Mischevious but playful and good-natured pranks.

high jump **1** A contest to see who can jump highest. **2** A jump in such a contest.

high·land [hī′lənd] *n.* Land high above sea level.

High·land·er [hī′lən·dər] *n.* A person born or living in the Scottish Highlands.

Highland fling A lively Scottish dance.

high·light [hī′līt′] **1** *n.* A bright area, as in a painting or photograph. **2** *n.* An especially important or excellent part of something. **3** *v.* To have as or make into a highlight.

high·ly [hī′lē] *adv.* **1** Very much; extremely: *highly* agreeable. **2** Very favorably: to think *highly* of someone. **3** In a high position or rank: a *highly* placed diplomat. **4** At a high price or rate: *highly* paid.

High Mass A Mass celebrated with full ceremony.

high-mind·ed [hī′mīn′did] *adj.* Having noble ideals, thoughts, or feelings.

High·ness [hī′nis] *n.* A title used in formally addressing or speaking of a person of royal rank: Your *Highness;* Her *Highness.*

high noon **1** The precise moment of noon. **2** The high point, as in productivity or creativity, of some specified period or stage: the *high noon* of an artist's career.

high-octane [hī′ok′tān′] *adj.* Having a relatively high octane number.

high-pitched [hī′picht′] *adj.* **1** High in pitch, as a musical tone or a sound. **2** Having a steep slope, as a roof. **3** Showing strong feeling; emotional; agitated: a *high-pitched* argument.

high-pres·sure [hī′presh′ər] *adj., v.* **high-pres·sured, high-pres·sur·ing** **1** *adj.* Having, using, or able to withstand high pressure: a *high-pressure* boiler; a *high-pressure* area. **2** *adj. informal* Forceful in trying to persuade. **3** *v. informal* To try to persuade in a forceful way.

high-rise [hī′rīz′] **1** *adj.* Having many stories. **2** *n.* A high-rise building. **3** *adj.* Of, having to do with, or characteristic of high-rise buildings.

high·road [hī′rōd′] *n.* A main road.

high school A school which in the U.S. covers grades 9 or 10 through 12.

high seas The open waters of an ocean or sea that do not belong to any nation.

high-sound·ing [hī′soun′ding] *adj.* Impressive or pretentious.

high-spir·it·ed [hī′spir′it·id] *adj.* Having a courageous, vigorous, or fiery spirit.

high-strung [hī′strung′] *adj.* Very nervous.

high-tech [hī′tek′] *adj.* **1** Using or involving advanced technology, especially related to computers. **2** Using modern industrial materials or design: The restaurant has a *high-tech* decor.

high-ten·sion [hī′ten′shən] *adj.* Carrying, requiring, or having high voltage: *high-tension* cables.

high tide **1** The highest level that the tide reaches. **2** The time when this occurs.

high time So late as to be nearly too late: It's *high time* we did some work.

high treason Treason (def. 1).

high·way [hī′wā′] *n.* A main road; thoroughfare.

high·way·man [hī′wā′mən] *n., pl.* **high·way·men** [hī′wā′mən] A person who holds up and robs travelers on a road.

hi·jack [hī′jak′] **1** *v.* To steal goods from (a vehicle in transit). **2** *v.* To seize control of (a vehicle, especially an airplane) and insist that it go to a destination other than the scheduled one. **3** *n.* The act or an instance of hijacking. **—hi′jack′er** *n.*

hike [hīk] *n., v.* **hiked, hik·ing** **1** *n.* A long walk or march. **2** *v.* To take a hike: We *hiked* through the woods. **3** *v. informal* To raise or rise: to *hike* up prices; My jacket *hiked* up in back. **—hik′er** *n.*

hi·lar·i·ous [hi·lâr′ē·əs] *adj.* **1** Noisily cheerful and gay; merry: a *hilarious* party. **2** Very humorous: a *hilarious* story. **—hi·lar′i·ous·ly** *adv.* **—hi·lar′i·ous·ness** *n.*

hi·lar·i·ty [hi·lar′ə·tē] *n.* Boisterous gaiety or laugh-

a	add	**i**	it	**o͝o**	took	**oi**	oil
ā	ace	**ī**	ice	**o͞o**	pool	**ou**	pout
â	care	**o**	odd	**u**	up	**ng**	ring
ä	palm	**ō**	open	**û**	burn	**th**	thin
e	end	**ô**	order	**yo͞o**	fuse	**th**	this
ē	equal					**zh**	vision

ə = {a in *above* e in *sicken,* i in *possible,* o in *melon,* u in *circus*}

ter: The party had many moments of great *hilarity.*

hill [hil] *n.* **1** A piece of ground higher than the surrounding land, but not as high as a mountain. **2** Any heap or pile. **3** A small mound of earth placed over or around certain plants: a *hill* of corn.

hill·bil·ly [hil′bil′ē] *n., pl.* **hill·bil·lies** *U.S. informal* A person coming from or living in the mountains or backwoods.

hill·ock [hil′ək] *n.* A small hill or mound.

hill·side [hil′sīd′] *n.* The slope of a hill.

hill·top [hil′top′] *n.* The top of a hill.

hill·y [hil′ē] *adj.* **hill·i·er, hill·i·est** **1** Having many hills. **2** Steep: a *hilly* slope. **—hill′i·ness** *n.*

hilt [hilt] *n.* The handle of a sword or dagger. **—to the hilt** To the full extent; thoroughly; fully.

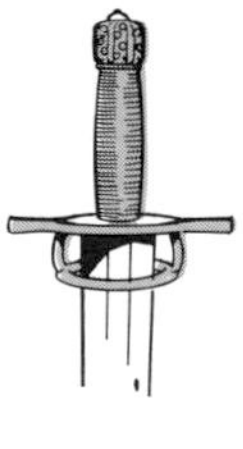
Hilt

hi·lum [hī′ləm] *n., pl.* **hi·la** [hī′lə] or **hi·lums** The scar on a seed at the point where it was attached to the seed vessel.

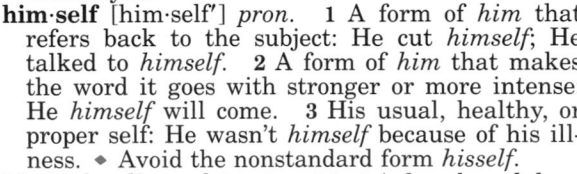

him [him] *pron.* The form of *he* used as the object of a verb or preposition: Help *him*; Give it to *him.*

Hi·ma·la·yan [him′ə·lā′ən *or* hi·mäl′·yən] *adj.* Of or having to do with the Himalayas.

him·self [him·self′] *pron.* **1** A form of *him* that refers back to the subject: He cut *himself*; He talked to *himself.* **2** A form of *him* that makes the word it goes with stronger or more intense: He *himself* will come. **3** His usual, healthy, or proper self: He wasn't *himself* because of his illness. ◆ Avoid the nonstandard form *hisself.*

hind[1] [hīnd] *n., pl.* **hinds** or **hind** A female red deer, especially one fully grown.

hind[2] [hīnd] *adj.* **hind·er, hind·most** or **hind·er·most** Back; rear: a *hind* leg.

hin·der[1] [hin′dər] *v.* To interfere with; retard, obstruct, or thwart: to *hinder* a person's attempts.

hind·er[2] [hīn′dər] Comparative of HIND[2].

hind·er·most [hīn′dər·mōst′] *adj.* Hindmost.

Hin·di [hin′dē] *n.* The main language of northern India.

hind·most [hīnd′mōst′] Superlative of HIND[2].

Hin·doo [hin′do͞o] *n., pl.* **Hin·doos,** *adj.* Another spelling of HINDU.

hind·quar·ter [hīnd′kwôr′tər] *n.* A large cut of meat including a hind leg and loin.

hin·drance [hin′drəns] *n.* **1** A person or thing that hinders; obstacle or impediment: Lack of confidence is a *hindrance* to getting ahead. **2** A hindering or being hindered.

hind·sight [hīn(d)′sīt′] *n.* Realization of what should have been done when it is too late.

Hin·du [hin′do͞o] *n., pl.* **Hin·dus,** *adj.* **1** *n.* A native of India descended from an ancient race that conquered it. **2** *n.* A person whose religion is Hinduism. **3** *adj.* Of, having to do with, or characteristic of Hindus or Hinduism.

Hin·du-Ar·a·bic numerals [hin′do͞o·ar′ə·bik] Arabic numerals.

Hinduism [hin′do͞o·iz′əm] *n.* A religion and a body of cultural beliefs and practices native to India, in which a supreme being of three aspects is worshiped and many other gods are honored.

Hin·du·sta·ni [hin′do͞o·stä′nē] **1** *n.* An important, and probably the commonest, language of India, based on Hindi. **2** *adj.* Of or having to do with India, its people, or Hindustani.

hinge [hinj] *n., v.* **hinged, hing·ing** **1** *n.* A joint on which something, as a door or lid, pivots or turns. **2** *v.* To equip with a hinge or hinges. **3** *v.* To hang or swing on a hinge. **4** *v.* To depend: Success *hinges* on your actions.

Hinge

hint [hint] **1** *n.* A slight suggestion that is made with delicacy or tact. **2** *v.* To make a hint or hints. **3** *n.* A small piece of advice: household *hints.* **4** *n.* A slight bit or trace: Put a *hint* of garlic in the sauce.

hin·ter·land [hin′tər·land′] *n.* **1** A region behind a coast; inland region. **2** A region far from cities and towns.

hip[1] [hip] *n.* **1** The projecting part on either side of the human body where the thigh is jointed to the body. **2** A similar part of an animal where the hind leg is attached.

hip[2] [hip] *n.* The ripened fruit of a rose.

hip[3] [hip] *adj.* **hip·per, hip·pest,** *n. slang* **1** *adj.* Familiar with and interested in the newest trends: *hip* to the latest styles. **2** *adj.* In the latest fashion: a *hip* outfit. **3** *n.* The condition or quality of being hip. **—hip′ness** *n.*

hip·bone [hip′bōn′] *n.* Either of two bones that form the sides of the pelvis.

hip·pie [hip′ē] *n.* A person who adopts an alternative, often rebellious life-style characterized by liberal or radical politics, casual and colorful dress, and indifference to the values of work and career.

Hip·po·crat·ic oath [hip′ə·krat′ik] A code of ethics and professional behavior that new physicians swear to uphold in their medical practice. ◆ This code gets its name from Hippocrates, an early Greek physician and founder of scientific medicine, whose ideals are expressed in it.

hip·po·drome [hip′ə·drōm′] *n.* **1** In ancient Greece and Rome, an oval track for horse and chariot racing surrounded by seats for spectators. **2** An arena for horse shows, circuses, and other events.

hip·po·pot·a·mus [hip′ə·pot′ə·məs] *n., pl.* **hip·po·pot·a·mus·es** or **hip·po·pot·a·mi** [hip′ə·pot′ə·mī] A large four-footed mammal with thick skin that lives in and around African rivers. Its diet consists of plants. ◆ *Hippopotamus* comes from two Greek words meaning *river horse.*

Hippopotamus

hip·py [hip′ē] *n., pl.* **hip·pies** Another spelling of HIPPIE.

hire [hīr] *v.* **hired, hir·ing,** *n.* **1** *v.* To agree to pay for the work or use of; employ or rent: to *hire* a helper; to *hire* a car. **2** *v.* To allow the use of in return for payment: to *hire* out boats. **3** *v.* To accept employment: to *hire* on as a guide. **4** *n.* Payment received for work or services; wages or fee. **—for hire** Available to be hired: The livery stable had some spirited horses *for hire* last year.

hire·ling [hīr′ling] *n.* A person who works for hire and cares for little besides the pay.

hir·sute [hir′so͞ot′ *or* hûr′so͞ot′] *adj.* Covered with hair; hairy. **—hir′sute·ness** *n.*

his [hiz] *pron.* **1** Of or belonging to him: the possessive form of *he*: *his* book; *his* work. **2** The one or ones belonging to or having to do with him: The book is *his*.

His·pan·ic [his·pan′ik] **1** *adj.* Of or having to do with the people, language, or culture of Spain, Portugal, or Latin America. **2** *n.* A person of Spanish, Portuguese, or Latin American descent.

hiss [his] **1** *n.* A prolonged sound like *ss,* or like a gas passing through a small opening. **2** *v.* To make such a sound, often as a sign of anger or dislike: The crowd *hissed* at the umpire.

hist [hist] *interj.* An exclamation meaning: "Be quiet! Listen!"

hist. **1** historian. **2** historical. **3** history.

his·ta·mine [his′tə·mēn′] *n.* A chemical compound found in plant and animal tissue that causes certain physiological responses in humans, as stimulating secretion of gastric juice, lowering blood pressure, and swelling blood vessels during allergic reactions.

his·tol·o·gy [his·tol′ə·jē] *n.* The study of plant and animal tissues by the use of a microscope. **—his·to·log·i·cal** [his′tə·loj′i·kəl] *adj.* **—his·to·log·i·cal·ly** [his′tə·loj′ik(ə)·lē] *adv.* **—his·tol·o·gist** [his·tol′ə·jist] *n.*

his·to·ri·an [his·tôr′ē·ən] *n.* A writer of or authority on history.

his·tor·ic [his·tôr′ik] *adj.* Important or famous in history: a *historic* place or event. ◆ Some people mistakenly use the article *an* with *historic* in the belief that it sounds more formal and correct. But like any other English word that begins with a consonant sound, *historic* takes *a,* not *an.*

his·tor·i·cal [his·tôr′ə·kəl] *adj.* **1** Of, having to do with, or belonging to history: *historical* documents. **2** Historic. **3** That really happened or existed: *historical* characters. **4** Based on people and events in history: a *historical* novel. **—his·tor′·i·cal·ly** *adv.*

his·to·ry [his′tə·rē] *n., pl.* **his·to·ries** **1** Past events or a record of them, often concerning a particular nation, people, or activity: European *history*; the *history* of art. **2** The branch of knowledge that deals with past events. **3** An interesting past: That house has quite a *history.*

his·tri·on·ic [his′trē·on′ik] *adj.* **1** Having to do with actors or acting. **2** Affected; insincere.

his·tri·on·ics [his′trē·on′iks] *n.pl.* Exaggerated display of emotion to gain the attention or sympathy of others.

hit [hit] *v.* **hit, hit·ting,** *n.* **1** *v.* To give a blow to or make forceful contact with; strike: to *hit* a ball; The car *hit* the tree. **2** *v.* To reach or strike, as with a shot from a gun: to *hit* the target. **3** *n.* Something, as a blow or shot, that reaches its target. **4** *v.* To have a bad effect on; cause to suffer: Misfortune *hit* the company hard. **5** *v.* To come upon or discover: to *hit* the main road; to *hit* upon an idea. **6** *n.* A great success: The song was a *hit.* **7** *n.* In baseball, a base hit. **8** *v.* To bat. **—hit it off** To get on well together. **—hit′ter** *n.*

hit-and-run [hit′(ə)n·run′] *adj.* Having to do with or involved in an accident in which the driver of the motor vehicle that caused the accident drives away: a *hit-and-run* victim.

hitch [hich] **1** *v.* To fasten or tie: to *hitch* a rope to a post; to *hitch* up a horse. **2** *n.* A thing used to hitch, as one of various knots. **3** *n.* A coupling; fastening. **4** *v.* To become fastened or snarled: Moorings fouled and *hitched.* **5** *n.* An obstacle or delay: a *hitch* in a plan. **6** *v.* To move, pull, or raise with a jerk: to *hitch* up one's pants. **7** *n.* A quick jerking movement. **8** *v. U.S. slang* To seek or get (a ride or rides) in hitchhiking.

hitch·hike [hich′hīk′] *v.* **hitch·hiked, hitch·hik·ing** To travel by asking for and receiving rides in passing cars. **—hitch′hik′er** *n.*

hitching post A post, stump, or rail to which a horse or other animal is tied.

hith·er [hith′ər] **1** *adv.* To or toward this place. **2** *adj.* Situated toward this side; nearer.

hith·er·to [hith′ər·tōō′ *or* hith′ər·tōō′] *adv.* Up to now: A *hitherto* unknown architect was chosen to develop recreation areas for the city.

hith·er·ward [hith′ər·wərd] *adv.* Toward this place; hither.

hit-or-miss [hit′ər·mis′] *adj.* Haphazard; random; careless.

Hit·tite [hit′īt′] **1** *n.* A member of a people that established a powerful empire in Asia Minor and northern Syria from about 2000 to 1200 B.C. **2** The language of this people. **3** Of or having to do with the Hittites or their language.

hive [hīv] *n., v.* **hived, hiv·ing** **1** *n.* A shelter or container for a colony of honeybees. **2** *n.* A colony of bees living in a hive. **3** *v.* To put or gather into a hive. **4** *v.* To live close together in or as if in a hive. **5** *n.* A place full of people or animals busily working or moving about.

hives [hīvz] *n.* A skin disease caused by an allergy, in which the skin itches and breaks out in swollen patches.

hl or **hl.** hectoliter.

hm or **hm.** hectometer.

H.M.S. Her (*or* His) Majesty's Ship.

ho [hō] *interj.* An exclamation, as one to get attention or to show surprise or joy.

Ho The symbol for the element holmium.

hoa·gie or **hoa·gy** [hō′gē] *n., pl.* **hoa·gies** Another word for HERO (def. 3).

hoar [hôr] *adj.* Hoary.

hoard [hôrd] **1** *v.* To save and store away, often greedily: to *hoard* food. **2** *n.* Something hoarded: a *hoard* of gold. **—hoard′er** *n.*

hoar·frost [hôr′frôst′] *n.* White frost.

hoar·hound [hôr′hound′] *n.* Another spelling of HOREHOUND.

hoarse [hôrs] *adj.* **hoars·er, hoars·est** Rough, deep, and husky in sound: a *hoarse* voice. **—hoarse′ly** *adv.* **—hoarse′ness** *n.*

hoar·y [hôr′ē] *adj.* **hoar·i·er, hoar·i·est** **1** White or whitish. **2** Gray or white with age. **3** Very old; ancient. **—hoar′i·ness** *n.*

hoax [hōks] **1** *n.* A trick or deception, often intended to fool the public: The news of war was a *hoax.* **2** *v.* To fool by a hoax.

hob[1] [hob] *n.* A hobgoblin or elf. **—play hob** To cause mischief or confusion.

a	add	**i**	it	**o͝o**	took	**oi**	oil
ā	ace	**ī**	ice	**o͞o**	pool	**ou**	pout
â	care	**o**	odd	**u**	up	**ng**	ring
ä	palm	**ō**	open	**û**	burn	**th**	thin
e	end	**ô**	order	**yo͞o**	fuse	**th**	this
ē	equal					**zh**	vision

ə = a in *above*, e in *sicken*, i in *possible*, o in *melon*, u in *circus*

hob[2] [hob] *n.* A shelf in the interior of a fireplace for keeping things warm.

hob·ble [hob′əl] *v.* **hob·bled, hob·bling,** *n.* **1** *v.* To walk lamely. **2** *n.* A limping walk. **3** *v.* To tie the legs of (an animal) together to limit movement. **4** *n.* Something used to hobble an animal. **5** *v.* To hinder or hamper.

hob·ble·de·hoy [hob′əl·dē·hoi′] *n.* An adolescent boy, especially an awkward, gawky one.

hob·by [hob′ē] *n., pl.* **hob·bies** Something a person does for pleasure during spare time: My *hobby* is building model airplanes.

hob·by·horse [hob′ē·hôrs′] *n.* **1** A stick with the figure of a horse's head at one end, used as a toy. **2** A rocking horse. **3** A favorite subject of discussion.

hob·gob·lin [hob′gob′lin] *n.* **1** A goblin or imp. **2** An imaginary cause of fear or dread.

hob·nail [hob′nāl′] *n.* A short nail with a large head. Hobnails are put into the soles of heavy shoes so that they won't slip or wear out.

hob·nob [hob′nob′] *v.* **hob·nobbed, hob·nob·bing** To be on friendly terms: to *hobnob* with the neighbors.

ho·bo [hō′bō] *n., pl.* **ho·boes** or **ho·bos** A tramp who lives by odd jobs and begging.

hock[1] [hok] *n.* A joint on the hind leg of a horse, ox, sheep, or other animal, corresponding to the ankle in humans.

Horse's hock

hock[2] [hok] *U.S. informal* **1** *v.* To pawn. **2** *n.* The condition of being pawned: My guitar is in *hock*.

hock·ey [hok′ē] *n.* **1** A game played on ice in which the players wear skates and use large sticks curved at one end to try to drive a small disk or puck into the goal of the opponent. **2** A similar game played on a field with a ball.

hockey stick A long stick that is curved and flattened at one end, used in hockey.

ho·cus-po·cus [hō′kəs·pō′kəs] *n.* **1** An expression used in conjuring and performing magic tricks. **2** Trickery or deception.

hod [hod] *n.* **1** A trough set on a long handle, used to carry bricks, cement, and other materials. **2** A pail or scuttle for carrying coal.

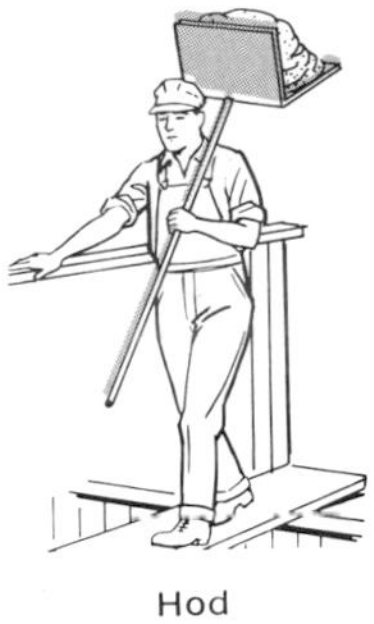
Hod

hodge·podge [hoj′poj′] *n.* A confused mixture.

hoe [hō] *n., v.* **hoed, hoe·ing** **1** *n.* A tool having a flat blade set across the end of a long handle, used to clear weeds and loosen soil. **2** *v.* To use a hoe on (weeds or soil).

hoe·cake [hō′kāk′] *n.* A flat bread made of coarse cornmeal. ◆ This bread was originally baked on a hoe in the fire.

hog [hôg *or* hog] *n., v.* **hogged, hog·ging** **1** *n.* A pig, especially a large one raised for meat. **2** *n. informal* A gluttonous, selfish, or filthy person. **3** *v. slang* To take more than one's proper share of: to *hog* everything in sight.

ho·gan [hō′gən] *n.* A Navaho Indian hut made of sticks and branches covered with earth.

hog·gish [hôg′ish *or* hog′ish] *adj.* **1** Very greedy. **2** Filthy. **—hog′gish·ly** *adv.* **—hog′gish·ness** *n.*

hog·nose snake [hôg′nōz′ *or* hog′nōz′] Any of several nonpoisonous North American snakes having a broadened, upturned snout used for burrowing.

hogs·head [hôgz′hed′ *or* hogz′hed′] *n.* **1** A cask that holds from 63 to 140 gallons. **2** A measure of volume for liquids equal to 63 gallons.

hog-tie [hôg′tī′ *or* hog′tī′] *v.* **hog-tied, hog-ty·ing** **1** To tie together the four limbs of (a hog or other animal). **2** *informal* To prevent from moving or acting; render helpless.

hog·wash [hôg′wôsh′ *or* hog′wäsh′] *n.* **1** Garbage fed to pigs; swill. **2** *informal* Nonsense.

hoist [hoist] **1** *v.* To raise or lift, especially by mechanical means. **2** *n.* A machine that hoists. **3** *n.* A lift or boost.

hold[1] [hōld] *v.* **held, hold·ing,** *n.* **1** *v.* To take and keep in the hands or arms; grip or clasp. **2** *n.* An act or method of holding: a firm *hold*. **3** *v.* To support or keep fixed: The beams *hold* the roof up. **4** *n.* Something grasped for support. **5** *v.* To contain or have room for: The bottle *holds* a quart. **6** *v.* To keep confined: to *hold* someone in jail. **7** *v.* To have or keep in possession or control: to *hold* one's temper; to *hold* someone's attention. **8** *n.* A controlling influence: The music had a *hold* on the audience. **9** *v.* To have the use or responsibility of: to *hold* the office of senator. **10** *v.* To conduct; have: to *hold* a meeting. **11** *v.* To have in the mind or believe, as an idea or opinion. **12** *v.* To regard or consider: to *hold* someone dear. **13** *v.* To remain firm or unbroken: Will the knot *hold*? **14** *v.* To be true or in effect: This rule *holds* in all cases. **15** *v.* To keep to the terms of: to *hold* to a promise; We will *hold* you to our agreement. **16** *v.* To remain or continue: The weather *held* fair. **17** *v.* To prolong or sustain (a musical tone). **—hold forth** **1** To preach or speak for a long time. **2** To offer, as an idea. **—hold off** **1** To keep at a distance: to *hold off* an enemy. **2** To refrain, as from doing something. **—hold on** **1** To keep one's grip or hold. **2** To keep on; continue. **3** *informal* To stop or wait: *Hold on* a moment. **—hold one's own** To maintain one's position; not lose ground. **—hold out** **1** To continue resisting. **2** To last: Our supplies *held out*. **—hold over** **1** To put off until later; postpone. **2** To remain or keep beyond the expected time. **—hold up** **1** To prevent from falling. **2** To show; display. **3** *informal* To last or endure: to *hold up* under wear. **4** To delay or stop: The storm *held* us *up*. **5** To rob by using force or threats. **—hold with** To approve of or support: I don't *hold with* violence in movies. **—on hold** *informal* In a condition of inaction or waiting: The project has been put *on hold* until the new budget is approved.

hold[2] [hōld] *n.* The compartment where cargo is carried in a ship or airplane.

hold·er [hōl′dər] *n.* **1** A person or thing that holds. **2** A device used in holding something.

hold·ing [hōl′ding] *n.* **1** The act of a person or thing that holds. **2** (*often pl.*) Property that is owned, as stocks and bonds.

holding pattern A usually oval flight pattern over an airport for aircraft awaiting permission to land.

hold·o·ver [hōld′ō′vər] *n.* A person or thing kept or left over from an earlier time.

hold·up [hōld′up′] *n.* **1** A stopping or delay. **2** *informal* A robbing by force or threats.

hole [hōl] *n., v.* **holed, hol·ing** **1** *n.* An opening in or through anything: a *hole* in a shoe. **2** *n.* A pit, hollow, or cavity: a *hole* in the sand. **3** *v.* To make a hole or holes in. **4** *n.* An animal's burrow: a rat's *hole.* **5** *n.* A dark, miserable place, as a dungeon. **6** *n.* In golf, a small opening lined with a cup into which the ball is to be hit. **7** *n.* One of the divisions of a golf course. **8** *v.* To putt or hit (a ball) into a hole. **9** *n.* A defect or fault: a *hole* in an argument. **—hole up** **1** To hibernate in a cave. **2** To hide or seclude oneself.

hol·i·day [hol′ə·dā′] *n.* **1** A day on which most business is stopped in remembrance of an important event. **2** A holy day. **3** *adj. use*: *holiday* clothes; *holiday* joy. ◆ *Holiday* once referred only to days set aside to celebrate religious events. They were thus thought of as *holy days,* and it is the latter term that is now used when referring to them.

ho·li·ness [hō′lē·nis] *n.* **1** The condition of being holy. **2** (*written* **Holiness**) A title used in speaking to or of the Pope: his *Holiness.*

ho·lis·tic [hō·lis′tik] *adj.* Concerned with whole systems rather than with their separate parts. *Holistic* medicine focuses on the patient's whole body rather than on individual symptoms.

hol·ler [hol′ər] *U.S. informal* **1** *v.* To shout: We *hollered* for help. **2** *n.* A shout.

hol·low [hol′ō] **1** *adj.* Empty on the inside; not solid: a *hollow* log. **2** *n.* An empty space in something; hole. **3** *adj.* Having the shape of a dish or bowl; concave. **4** *adj.* Sunken or fallen in. **5** *v.* To make or become hollow. **6** *n.* A valley. **7** *adj.* Deep and muffled as though echoing in a cave. **8** *adj.* Meaningless and empty: *hollow* praise. **—hol′low·ly** *adv.* **—hol′low·ness** *n.*

hol·ly [hol′ē] *n., pl.* **hol·lies** An evergreen tree or shrub with shining, dark green, pointed leaves and scarlet berries.

hol·ly·hock [hol′ē·hok′] *n.* A tall plant with large rounded leaves and showy flowers.

Hollyhock

hol·mi·um [hōl′mē·əm] *n.* A metallic element occurring in rare earths. See RARE-EARTH ◆ELEMENTS.

holm oak [hōm] A tree of the beech family native to southern Europe, having evergreen, hollylike leaves.

hol·o·caust [hol′ə·kôst′] *n.* **1** Great destruction and loss of life, especially by fire. **2 the Holocaust** The mass killing of Jews and others in Nazi concentration camps during World War II.

Ho·lo·cene [hō′lə·sēn′ *or* hol′ə·sēn′] **1** *n.* The later of the two geological epochs of the Quaternary period of the Cenozoic era. It began at the end of the Ice Age and continues today. **2** *adj.* Of the Holocene.

hol·o·gram [hol′ə·gram′] *n.* A three-dimensional image produced by holography.

hol·o·graph [hol′ə·graf′] *n.* **1** A document, as a will or deed, written entirely in the handwriting of the signer. **2** Another word for HOLOGRAM. **—hol′o·graph′ic** *adj.* **—hol′o·graph′i·cal** *adj.* **—hol′o·graph′i·cal·ly** *adv.*

ho·log·raph·y [hō·log′rə·fē] *n.* A photographic technique that employs laser light to produce a three-dimensional image without the use of a camera.

Hol·stein [hōl′stīn *or* hōl′stēn] *n.* One of a breed of large black and white dairy cattle.

hol·ster [hōl′stər] *n.* A leather case for a pistol, often worn on a belt.

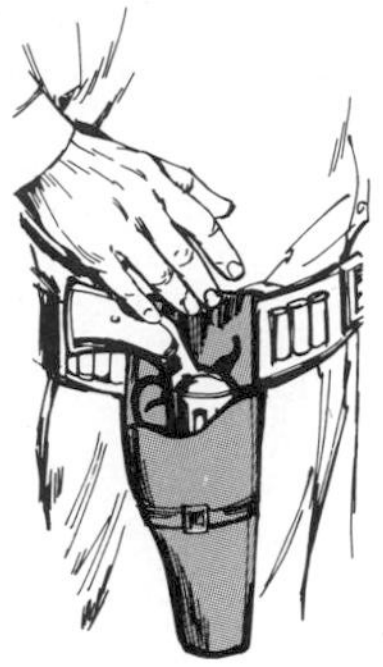
Holster

ho·ly [hō′lē] *adj.* **ho·li·er, ho·li·est** **1** Regarded with reverence because it comes from or has to do with God; sacred: *holy* Scripture. **2** Saintly: a *holy* person; *holy* love. **3** Thought of with devotion and respect: a *holy* cause.

Holy Communion The sacrament in which consecrated bread and wine are eaten and sipped in memory of the death of Christ; the Eucharist.

holy day or **ho·ly·day** [hō′lē·dā′] *n.* A day set aside for a special religious reason. ◆ See HOLIDAY.

Holy Father One of the titles of the Pope.

Holy Ghost Another name for HOLY SPIRIT.

Holy Grail The Grail.

Holy Land Palestine.

holy of holies **1** The most sacred part of the Jewish temple at Jerusalem, where the Ark of the Covenant was kept. **2** Any very holy place.

Holy Roman Empire The empire in central and western Europe from 962 to 1806, whose spiritual head was the Pope.

Holy Scripture The Bible.

Holy See The Pope's office or authority.

Holy Spirit In Christianity, the third person of the Trinity; the spirit of God.

ho·ly·stone [hō′lē·stōn′] *n., v.* **ho·ly·stoned, ho·ly·ston·ing** **1** *n.* A flat piece of soft sandstone used to scrub the wooden decks of a ship. **2** *v.* To scrub with a holystone.

holy water Water that has been blessed by a priest for use in religious ceremonies.

Holy Week The week before Easter.

Holy Writ The Bible.

hom- or **homo-** A combining form meaning: The same or similar, as in *homogeneous.*

hom·age [(h)om′ij] *n.* **1** Respect or honor given or shown: to pay *homage.* **2** In the Middle Ages, the allegiance sworn by a vassal to a lord.

hom·bre [om′brā *or* om′brē] *n. slang* Man; guy.

home [hōm] *n., v.* **homed, hom·ing,** *adv.* **1** *n.* The place where a person or animal lives. **2** *adj. use: home* furnishings. **3** *n.* The place or region where a person was born or raised. **4** *adv.* To, in, or at one's home: to fly *home*; to stay *home.* **5** *v.* To have a home: Deer *home* in the woods. **6** *v.* To return home, as a pigeon. **7** *n.* A family or household. **8** *n.* A shelter, as one for the care of the poor, sick, or aged. **9** *n.* A place of comfort and security. **10** *n.* The place where something orig-

a	add	**i**	it	**o͝o**	took	**oi**	oil
ā	ace	**ī**	ice	**o͞o**	pool	**ou**	pout
â	care	**o**	odd	**u**	up	**ng**	ring
ä	palm	**ō**	open	**û**	burn	**th**	thin
e	end	**ô**	order	**yo͞o**	fuse	**th̶**	this
ē	equal					**zh**	vision

ə = a in *above*, e in *sicken*, i in *possible*, o in *melon*, u in *circus*

inates, develops, or is mainly located. **11** *adj. use*: the *home* office. **12** *adv.* In or at the place intended: to strike *home*. **13** *n.* The goal or base that one must reach in order to score, as in baseball. **14** *v.* To go or be guided toward a destination: The missile *homed* in on its target. **—at home** **1** At or in one's home. **2** At one's ease; in a familiar or comfortable place. **3** Prepared to receive visitors.

home base **1** Another term for HOME PLATE. **2** Headquarters: The company's *home base* is in Toledo.

home·bod·y [hōm′bod′ē] *n., pl.* **home·bod·ies** A person whose interests, energies, and concerns are centered in the home.

home economics The study of how to manage a household.

home·grown [hōm′grōn′] *adj.* **1** Grown in one's own garden: *homegrown* tomatoes. **2** Produced and developed in the place where exhibited: *homegrown* talent.

home·land [hōm′land′] *n.* The country regarded as home, usually one's place of birth.

home·less [hōm′lis] *adj.* Having no home.

home·like [hōm′līk′] *adj.* Like or typical of home; comfortable or familiar.

home·ly [hōm′lē] *adj.* **home·li·er, home·li·est** **1** Not good-looking; plain or ugly. **2** Plain and familiar: *homely* truths. **3** Simple; plain; ordinary: *homely* meals. **—home′li·ness** *n.*

home·made [hōm′mād′] *adj.* Made at home or in a nonprofessional way.

home·mak·er [hōm′mā′kər] *n.* A person who manages a household.

home plate In baseball, the rubber slab beside which a player stands when batting and to which the player must return in order to score.

hom·er [hō′mər] *n. informal* A home run.

Ho·mer·ic [hō·mer′ik] *adj.* **1** Of, having to do with, or characteristic of Homer or his poetry. **2** Epic in scale; heroic.

home·room [hōm′rōōm′ *or* hōm′rŏŏm′] *n.* The schoolroom in which pupils of the same class meet for certain routines, as a check of attendance or dismissal.

home rule Internal self-government by a dependent political unit.

home run In baseball, a hit that allows a batter to circle the bases and score a run.

home·sick [hōm′sik′] *adj.* Unhappy or ill because of longing for home. **—home′sick′ness** *n.*

home·spun [hōm′spun′] **1** *adj.* Spun at home. **2** *n.* Cloth made of homespun yarn or a strong, loose fabric like it. **3** *adj.* Plain; simple: *homespun* humor.

home·stead [hōm′sted′] *n.* **1** A house and its land, used as a home. **2** A piece of land given to a settler by the U.S. government to farm, improve, and eventually own.

home·stretch [hōm′strech′] *n.* **1** The straight section of a racetrack between the final turn and the finish line. **2** The last stage of any journey or effort.

home·town [hōm′toun′] *n.* The town or city in which a person was born or reared or has a home.

home·ward [hōm′wərd] *adv., adj.* Toward home: to go *homeward*; a *homeward* journey.

home·wards [hōm′wərdz] *adv.* Homeward.

home·work [hōm′wûrk′] *n.* Work done at home, especially school work.

home·y [hō′mē] *adj.* **hom·i·er, hom·i·est** **1** Homelike. **2** Plain and simple.

hom·i·ci·dal [hom′ə·sīd′(ə)l] *adj.* **1** Of or having to do with homicide. **2** Murderous: a *homicidal* maniac.

hom·i·cide [hom′ə·sīd′] *n.* **1** The killing of a person by another, on purpose or accidentally. **2** A person who kills someone.

hom·i·ly [hom′ə·lē] *n., pl.* **hom·i·lies** **1** A sermon, especially about something in the Bible. **2** A long lecture on morals and conduct.

homing pigeon A pigeon that can make its way home from great distances, often used for carrying messages.

hom·i·nid [hom′ə·nid] *n.* Any of the family of primates of which human beings constitute the only living species. There are fossil remains of other hominids.

hom·i·ny [hom′ə·nē] *n.* Kernels of dried corn with the hulls removed, usually crushed, and boiled in milk or water. ◆ *Hominy* comes from an Algonquian word meaning *parched corn*.

hominy grits A coarse white meal made by grinding hominy.

hom·mos [hum′əs *or* hom′əs] *n.* Another spelling of HUMMUS.

ho·mo·ge·ne·ous [hō′mə·jē′nē·əs] *adj.* Alike or made of like parts: a *homogeneous* fishing village. **—ho′mo·ge′ne·ous·ly** *adv.* **—ho·mo·ge·ne·i·ty** [hō′·mə·jə·nē′ə·tē *or* hō′mə·jə·nā′ə·tē] *n.* **—ho′mo·ge′ne·ous·ness** *n.*

ho·mog·en·ize [hə·moj′ə·nīz′] *v.* **ho·mog·en·ized, ho·mog·en·iz·ing** **1** To mix the cream throughout (milk) so that it cannot separate. **2** To make homogeneous.

hom·o·graph [hom′ə·graf′] *n.* Any of two or more words that are spelled alike but have different meanings, origins, and, sometimes, pronunciations, as *wind* (moving air) and *wind* (coil around).

ho·mol·o·gous [hə·mol′ə·gəs *or* hō·mol′ə·gəs] *adj.* Similar, as in structure or function.

hom·o·nym [hom′ə·nim] *n.* Any of two or more words that sound and may be spelled alike but have different meanings and origins, as *cleave* (split) and *cleave* (stick to).

hom·o·phone [hom′ə·fōn′] *n.* Any of two or more words that are pronounced alike but have different meanings, origins, and usually spellings, as *sun* and *son*.

Ho·mo sa·pi·ens [hō′mō sā′pē·enz] The scientific name for modern human beings.

Hon. Honorable.

hon·cho [hon′chō] *n., pl.* **hon·chos** *slang* A person who is in charge; boss.

Hon·du·ran [hon·d(y)ŏŏr′ən] **1** *adj.* Of or from Honduras. **2** *n.* A person born in or a citizen of Honduras.

Hon·du·ra·ne·an or **Hon·du·ra·ni·an** [hon′də·rā′·nē·ən] *adj., n.* Honduran.

hone [hōn] *n., v.* **honed, hon·ing** **1** *n.* A stone used for sharpening tools, razors, and other objects. **2** *v.* To sharpen with a hone: to *hone* an ax.

hon·est [on′ist] *adj.* **1** Acting honorably and justly; not lying, stealing, or cheating: an *honest* shopkeeper. **2** Truthful, genuine, or fair: an *honest* answer. **3** Fairly done or earned: *honest* wages. **4** Belonging to or indicating an honest person: an *honest* face; an *honest* manner. **—hon′est·ness** *n.*

hon·est·ly [on′ist·lē] *adv.* **1** In an honest manner. **2** Really; indeed: *Honestly,* that's right.

hon·es·ty [on′is·tē] *n.* The condition or quality of being honest.

hon·ey [hun′ē] *n., pl.* **hon·eys,** *v.* **hon·eyed** or **hon·ied, hon·ey·ing** 1 *n.* A sweet, syruplike substance made by bees from nectar gathered from flowers. 2 *v.* To sweeten with or as if with honey. 3 *n.* Anything like honey. 4 *n.* Sweetness. 5 *n.* Darling; dear. 6 *v.* To speak or speak to in a loving or flattering way.

hon·ey·bee [hun′ē·bē′] *n.* A bee that makes honey.

hon·ey·comb [hun′ē·kōm′] 1 *n.* A wax structure of many six-sided cells made by bees for storing honey and their eggs. 2 *n.* Anything like a honeycomb. 3 *adj. use:* a *honeycomb* pattern. 4 *v.* To fill with many small holes: Termites *honeycombed* the woodwork.

Honeycomb

hon·ey·dew [hun′ē·d(y)ōō′] *n.* 1 A sweet liquid given off by the leaves of certain plants in warm weather. 2 A sweet substance secreted on leaves and stems by aphids.

honeydew melon A kind of melon having a smooth white skin and a sweet greenish pulp.

hon·ey·moon [hun′ē·mōōn′] 1 *n.* A vacation spent by a couple who have just been married. 2 *v.* To have or spend a honeymoon.

hon·ey·suck·le [hun′ē·suk′əl] *n.* A climbing shrub with white, buff, or crimson flowers that give off a fragrant smell.

honk [hôngk *or* hongk] 1 *n.* The sound made by a goose or a sound like it, as that of an automobile horn. 2 *v.* To make such a sound. **—honk′er** *n.*

hon·or [on′ər] 1 *n.* Respect and admiration: to give *honor* to our heroes. 2 *v.* To give or show respect and admiration for: to *honor* a great president. 3 *n.* An act or sign of respect. 4 *n.* Glory, reputation, or credit for fine or heroic acts: The *honor* must go to our leader. 5 *n.* A person or thing that brings honor: This promotion is a great *honor.* 6 *v.* To bring honor to: Good works *honor* one's name. 7 *n.* Fairness, rightness, and honesty: to act with *honor.* 8 *n.* Reputation; standing: Your *honor* is at stake. 9 *n.* (*pl.*) Special mention or credit given to a student for excellent work: to graduate with *honors.* 10 *n.* (*written* **Honor**) A title of respect used in formally addressing or speaking of a judge, mayor, or other official: Your *Honor.* 11 *v.* To accept as good for payment or credit: to *honor* a check. **—do the honors** 1 To act as a host or hostess. 2 To perform a social courtesy, as offering a toast.

hon·or·a·ble [on′ər·ə·bəl] *adj.* 1 Worthy of honor or respect. 2 Fair; honest; upright: an *honorable* person. 3 Bringing honor or credit: *honorable* work. 4 (*written* **Honorable**) A title of respect used in speaking of important officials: the *Honorable* Roberta Hickok. **—hon′or·a·bly** *adv.* **—hon′·or·a·ble·ness** *n.*

hon·o·rar·i·um [on′ə·râr′ē·əm] *n., pl.* **hon·o·rar·i·ums** or **hon·o·rar·i·a** [on′ə·râr′ē·ə] A payment made for a service, as giving a lecture, for which there is no fixed fee.

hon·or·ar·y [on′ə·rer′ē] *adj.* 1 Given as an honor: an *honorary* degree. 2 As an honor, without duties, powers, or pay: an *honorary* chairperson.

hood¹ [hŏŏd] 1 *n.* A covering for the head and back of the neck, often part of a coat or robe. 2 *n.* Something that looks like or is used like a hood, as the cover of an automobile engine. 3 *v.* To cover or furnish with a hood.

hood² [hŏŏd] *n. U.S. slang* A hoodlum.

-hood A suffix meaning: 1 The condition, time, or quality of being, as in *babyhood.* 2 The whole group or class of, as in *priesthood.*

hood·ed [hŏŏd′id] *adj.* 1 Having or covered with a hood. 2 Shaped like a hood.

hood·lum [hŏŏd′ləm] *n. U.S.* A gangster or thug.

hoo·doo [hōō′dōō] *n., pl.* **hoo·doos,** *v.* **hoo·dooed, hoo·doo·ing** 1 *n.* Voodoo. 2 *n. informal* Bad luck. 3 *n. informal* A bringer of bad luck. 4 *v. informal* To bring bad luck to.

hood·wink [hŏŏd′wingk′] *v.* 1 To trick; mislead; deceive. 2 To blindfold.

hoof [hŏŏf *or* hōōf] *n., pl.* **hoofs** or **hooves** [hŏŏvz *or* hōōvz], *v.* 1 *n.* The horny covering of the foot of certain animals, as horses, cattle, and pigs. 2 *n.* A foot of such an animal. 3 *v. informal* To walk or dance. **—on the hoof** Not butchered; alive, as cattle.

hoof·beat [hŏŏf′bēt′ *or* hōōf′bēt′] *n.* The sound made by the hoof of a horse or other hoofed animal when it walks or runs.

hoofed [hŏŏft *or* hōōft] *adj.* Having hoofs.

hook [hŏŏk] 1 *n.* A curved piece of metal, wood, or other material, used to hold up, fasten, catch, or drag things. 2 *v.* To catch or fasten with a hook or hooks: to *hook* a fish. 3 *n.* Something shaped like or suggesting a hook, as a punch thrown with a bent elbow. 4 *v.* To curve or bend like a hook. 5 *v. informal* To swindle; hoodwink; The customer was *hooked* into a bad deal. 6 *v. slang* To steal. **—by hook or by crook** By any means available: to succeed *by hook or by crook.* **—hook up** 1 To put together or connect the parts of: to *hook up* a garment. 2 To connect (a device) to a source, as of power or water. **—off the hook** *informal* Freed from a troublesome obligation or difficulty. **—on one's own hook** *informal* By or for oneself; independently. **—hook′like** *adj.*

hook·ah [hŏŏk′ə] *n.* An Oriental smoking pipe that passes the smoke through water.

hook and eye A fastener for clothing that consists of a small hook that is inserted through a loop.

hook and ladder A fire engine carrying long ladders, axes, hooked poles, and other equipment.

hooked [hŏŏkt] *adj.* 1 Curved like a hook. 2 Having a hook or hooks. 3 Made by looping yarn through canvas or burlap with a hook.

hooked rug A rug made by pulling loops of yarn or other material through a coarse fabric with a hook.

hook·up [hŏŏk′up′] *n.* The arrangement of parts, as those used in a radio or phonograph.

hook·worm [hŏŏk′wûrm′] *n.* A small worm with hooked mouth parts that invades the intestines of humans and some animals and sucks blood.

a add	**i** it	**ŏŏ** took	**oi** oil
ā ace	**ī** ice	**ōō** pool	**ou** pout
â care	**o** odd	**u** up	**ng** ring
ä palm	**ō** open	**û** burn	**th** thin
e end	**ô** order	**yōō** fuse	**th** this
ē equal			**zh** vision

ə = a in *above* e in *sicken* i in *possible* o in *melon* u in *circus*

H

hook·y [ho͝ok'ē] *n. U.S. informal* Absence without permission, especially in the phrase **play hooky,** to be absent from school without permission.
hoo·li·gan [ho͞o'li·gən] *n.* A person who goes about committing violent or destructive acts for little or no purpose; ruffian. **—hoo'li·gan·ism** *n.*
hoop [ho͞op *or* ho͝op] 1 *n.* A circular band of metal, wood, or other material, used to bind barrels, to extend a skirt, or as a toy. 2 *v.* To surround or fasten with a hoop or hoops.
hoop skirt A skirt puffed out with hoops.
hoo·ray [ho͝o·rā'] *interj., n., v.* Another word for HURRAH.
hoot [ho͞ot] 1 *n.* The cry of an owl. 2 *n.* A sound like it. 3 *n.* A loud outcry, especially one showing contempt. 4 *v.* To make a hoot or hoots. 5 *v.* To drive off with hoots: The audience *hooted* the performer from the stage.
hoo·ten·an·ny [ho͞ot'(ə)n·an'ē] *n., pl.* **hoot·en·an·nies** A performance by folksingers, usually involving much audience participation.

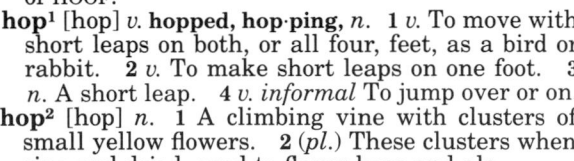

Hoop skirt

hooves [ho͝ovz *or* ho͞ovz] A plural of HOOF.
hop[1] [hop] *v.* **hopped, hop·ping,** *n.* 1 *v.* To move with short leaps on both, or all four, feet, as a bird or rabbit. 2 *v.* To make short leaps on one foot. 3 *n.* A short leap. 4 *v. informal* To jump over or on.
hop[2] [hop] *n.* 1 A climbing vine with clusters of small yellow flowers. 2 (*pl.*) These clusters when ripe and dried, used to flavor beer and ale.
hope [hōp] *n., v.* **hoped, hop·ing** 1 *n.* A feeling that what one wishes for may happen. 2 *v.* To want and expect. 3 *n.* Something that is hoped for. 4 *n.* A person or thing that is a cause for hope.
HOPE Health Opportunity for People Everywhere.
hope·ful [hōp'fəl] *adj.* 1 Having or showing hope: a *hopeful* attitude. 2 Giving or allowing hope: a *hopeful* situation. **—hope'ful·ness** *n.*
hope·ful·ly [hōp'fə·lē] *adv.* 1 In a hopeful way: *Hopefully,* I searched for my dog. 2 *informal* It is hoped; let us hope that: *Hopefully,* I'll find him soon. ◆ Though many critics object to it, the informal usage of *hopefully* is well-established.
hope·less [hōp'lis] *adj.* 1 Without hope: a *hopeless* feeling. 2 Giving or allowing no hope: a *hopeless* situation. **—hope'less·ly** *adv.* **—hope'less·ness** *n.*
Ho·pi [hō'pē] *n., pl.* **Ho·pi** or **Ho·pis** 1 A tribe of American Indians living in NE Arizona. 2 A member of this tribe. 3 The language of this tribe.
hop·per [hop'ər] *n.* 1 A person or thing that hops. 2 A container, as one for coal or grain, that narrows toward the bottom, through which the contents can be dropped or fed slowly.
hop·scotch [hop'skoch'] *n.* A children's game in which a player hops on one foot over the lines of a diagram marked on the ground to pick up something thrown into an area of the diagram.

Hopper

horde [hôrd] *n.* 1 A great crowd; swarm: a *horde* of people. 2 A wandering tribe or clan: *Hordes* from the east swept into Spain.
hore·hound [hôr'hound'] *n.* 1 A plant related to the mint. 2 A substance extracted from it, used to make a candy that helps stop coughing.
ho·ri·zon [hə·rī'zən] *n.* 1 The line where the earth and sky seem to meet. 2 The limits of one's observation, knowledge, or experience.
hor·i·zon·tal [hôr'ə·zon'təl] 1 *adj.* Parallel to the horizon; level. 2 *n.* Something that is horizontal, as a line, plane, or bar. 3 *adj.* Measured parallel to the horizon: *horizontal* distance. **—hor'i·zon'tal·ly** *adv.*

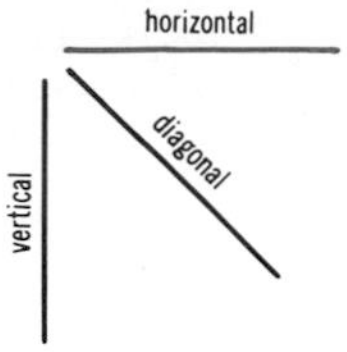

hor·mone [hôr'mōn'] *n.* Any of various substances produced in the body and circulated in the blood, each controlling the activity of a specific organ or of a related group of organs.
horn [hôrn] *n.* 1 One of a pair of hard, hollow, permanent growths, usually curved and pointed, on the heads of certain animals, as cattle, sheep, and goats. 2 One of a pair of branched, solid growths on the heads of deer, shed each year; antler. 3 The material of a horn. 4 Something made from a horn: a powder *horn.* 5 A musical wind instrument, originally made from a horn, now usually of brass. 6 A device for sounding a warning. **—horn in** *slang* To intrude.
horn·bill [hôrn'bil'] *n.* Any of various tropical birds of Africa and Asia, having an extraordinarily large, curving bill and a loud croaking cry.
horn·blende [hôrn'blend'] *n.* A common mineral found in granite and other rocks.
horn·book [hôrn'bo͝ok'] *n.* A leaf or page on which was printed the alphabet and other information, covered with transparent horn and framed, formerly used in teaching reading to children.
horned [hôrnd] *adj.* Having a horn or horns.
horned owl Any of several large, fierce owls having tufts of feathers on the head that resemble horns.
horned toad A small harmless lizard with a flat body and hornlike spines.
hor·net [hôr·nit] *n.* A large wasp with a very severe and painful sting.
horn of plenty Another name for CORNUCOPIA.
horn·pipe [hôrn'pīp'] *n.* 1 A lively English dance for one or more people, originally danced by sailors. 2 Music for it.

Hornet

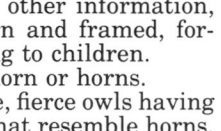

horn·y [hôr'nē] *adj.* **horn·i·er, horn·i·est** 1 Made of horn or a similar substance. 2 Having horns or hornlike projections. 3 Calloused; rough: *horny* hands.
hor·o·scope [hôr'ə·skōp'] *n.* 1 The position of the sun, moon, and planets in the zodiac at a certain time, especially the time of a person's birth. 2 A chart showing this, used in predicting a person's future by astrology.
hor·ren·dous [hô·ren'dəs] *adj.* Horrible; frightful: a *horrendous* sight.
hor·ri·ble [hôr'ə·bəl] *adj.* 1 Causing horror; frightful. 2 *informal* Very unpleasant or very bad: a *horrible* day. **—hor'ri·bly** *adv.* **—hor'ri·ble·ness** *n.*
hor·rid [hôr'id] *adj.* 1 Frightful; horrible. 2 *informal* Very unpleasant or offensive: a *horrid* odor. **—hor'rid·ly** *adv.* **—hor'rid·ness** *n.*

hor·ri·fy [hôr′ə·fī′] *v.* **hor·ri·fied, hor·ri·fy·ing** 1 To fill with horror. 2 *informal* To shock or surprise in an annoying way: The story *horrified* everyone.
hor·ror [hôr′ər] *n.* 1 A feeling of extreme fear, dread, or loathing. 2 Something that causes this feeling. 3 The quality of being horrible: the *horror* of war. 4 A strong dislike or hatred: a *horror* of cats.
hors d'oeuvre [ôr dûrv′] *n., pl.* **hors d'oeuvres** A hot or cold appetizer, generally served before a meal.
horse [hôrs] *n., v.* **horsed, hors·ing** 1 *n.* A large, four-legged animal with hoofs and a long tail and mane, used for riding or to pull loads. ◆ Adj., *equine.* 2 *v.* To mount a horse. 3 *n.* Mounted soldiers: a unit of *horse.* 4 *v.* To supply with a horse or horses. 5 *n.* A frame with four legs, used as a support. 6 *n.* A padded block on legs, used in gymnastics. **—horse around** *slang* To play in a boisterous or rough way.
horse·back [hôrs′bak′] 1 *n.* A horse's back. 2 *adv.* On a horse's back: to ride *horseback.*
horse chestnut 1 A shade tree having large leaves, clusters of white flowers, and large, glossy brown nuts. 2 The nut of this tree.
horse·flesh [hôrs′flesh′] *n.* 1 The flesh of a horse, especially when used as food. 2 Horses as a group.
horse·fly [hôrs′flī′] *n., pl.* **horse·flies** A large fly that bites horses and cattle.
horse·hair [hôrs′hâr′] *n.* 1 The hair from the mane or tail of horses. 2 A cloth made from this. 3 *adj. use*: a *horsehair* mattress.
horse·hide [hôrs′hīd′] *n.* 1 The hide of a horse. 2 Leather made from horsehide.
horse latitudes Either of two ocean regions located between 30° and 35° latitude north and south of the equator. The horse latitudes typically have high atmospheric pressure, very little rain, and few or very light winds. ◆ The term *horse latitudes* is a translation of a nickname used by 18th-century Spanish sailors for this part of the Atlantic. The Spaniards may have been referring to the horselike waywardness of winds there, or to incidents in which horses had to be thrown overboard there because of water shortages on becalmed trading vessels.
horse·laugh [hôrs′laf′] *n.* A loud, scornful laugh; guffaw.
horse·man [hôrs′mən] *n., pl.* **horse·men** [hôrs′mən] 1 A person skilled in riding or handling horses. 2 A person riding a horse.
horse·man·ship [hôrs′mən·ship′] *n.* The skill or riding and managing horses.
horse opera *informal* A movie, play, or serial about the American West.
horse·play [hôrs′plā′] *n.* Rough, boisterous play or fun.
horse·pow·er [hôrs′pou′ər] *n.* A unit of power equal to that needed to lift 550 pounds one foot in one second.
horse·rad·ish [hôrs′rad′ish] *n.* 1 A plant related to mustard. 2 A sharp-tasting relish made from the white, grated root of this plant.
horse sense *informal* Ordinary common sense.
horse·shoe [hôr(s)′shōō′] *n., v.* **horse·shoed, horse·shoe·ing** 1 *n.* A U-shaped piece of metal nailed to the bottom of a horse's hoof for protection. 2 *v.* To furnish with horseshoes. 3 *n.* Something shaped like a horseshoe. 4 *n.* (*pl.*) A game in which the object is to toss horseshoes onto or near a stake. **—horse′sho′er** *n.*
horseshoe crab A crablike sea animal with a spiny tail and a shell shaped like a horseshoe.

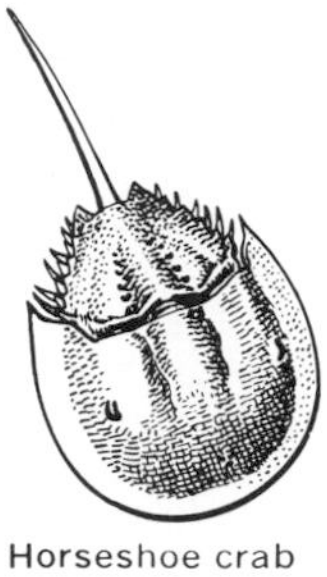
Horseshoe crab

horse·tail [hôrs′tāl′] *n.* 1 The tail of a horse. 2 A flowerless plant with hollow, jointed stems.
horse trade *slang* A bargain agreed on after vigorous negotiations and mutual concessions.
horse·whip [hôrs′(h)wip′] *n., v.* **horse·whipped, horse·whip·ping** 1 *n.* A whip for managing horses. 2 *v.* To flog with a horsewhip.
horse·wom·an [hôrs′wŏŏm′ən] *n., pl.* **horse·wom·en** [hôrs′wim′in] 1 A woman skilled in riding or handling horses. 2 A woman riding a horse.
hors·y [hôr′sē] *adj.* **hors·i·er, hors·i·est** 1 Of or having to do with a horse or horses: a *horsy* odor. 2 Fond of horses, horse racing, fox hunting, and other related activities. 3 Like a horse: *horsy* features.
hor·ta·to·ry [hôr′tə·tôr′ē] *adj.* Expressing encouragement: *hortatory* phrases.
hor·ti·cul·ture [hôr′tə·kul′chər] *n.* 1 The cultivation of a garden. 2 The science of growing garden vegetables, flowers, and other plants. **—hor′ti·cul′·tur·al** *adj.* **—hor′ti·cul′tur·ist** *n.*
ho·san·na [hō·zan′ə] *interj.* A cry of praise and adoration to God.
hose [hōz] *n., v.* **hosed, hos·ing** 1 *n., pl.* **hose** Stockings or socks; hosiery. 2 *n., pl.* **hose** An outer garment once worn by men, fitting like tight trousers. 3 *n., pl.* **hos·es** An easily bent tube, often of rubber, through which water and other materials may be forced. 4 *v.* To water with a hose.
Ho·se·a [hō·zē′ə] *n.* 1 A Hebrew prophet who lived during the 8th century B.C. 2 A book of the Old Testament which he wrote.
ho·sier·y [hō′zhər·ē] *n.* Stockings or socks.
hos·pice [hos′pis] *n.* 1 A place of rest or shelter for travelers, especially one maintained by a religious group or order. 2 An establishment for the care of people who are terminally ill.
hos·pi·ta·ble [hos′pi·tə·bəl *or* hos·pit′ə·bəl] *adj.* 1 Fond of having guests, or showing welcome and generosity toward guests. 2 Showing an open mind: *hospitable* to new ideas. **—hos′pi·ta·bly** *adv.*
hos·pi·tal [hos′pi·təl] *n.* A place where injured or sick people are taken care of. ◆ See HOTEL.
hos·pi·tal·i·ty [hos′pə·tal′ə·tē] *n., pl.* **hos·pi·tal·i·ties** Friendly, welcoming treatment of guests or strangers.
hos·pi·tal·i·za·tion [hos′pi·təl·ə·zā′shən] *n.* 1 The

a	add	**i**	it	**ŏŏ**	took	**oi**	oil
ā	ace	**ī**	ice	**ōō**	pool	**ou**	pout
â	care	**o**	odd	**u**	up	**ng**	ring
ä	palm	**ō**	open	**û**	burn	**th**	thin
e	end	**ô**	order	**yōō**	fuse	**th̶**	this
ē	equal					**zh**	vision

ə = a in *above*, e in *sicken*, i in *possible*, o in *melon*, u in *circus*

H

act or an instance of hospitalizing. **2** A being hospitalized. **3** The period of time during which a person is hospitalized. **4** A form of insurance coverage that pays all or a part of a patient's hospital costs.

hos·pi·tal·ize [hos′pi·təl·īz′] *v.* **hos·pi·tal·ized, hos·pi·tal·iz·ing** To put into a hospital for treatment and care.

host[1] [hōst] *n.* **1** A person who entertains guests. **2** A person in charge of a hotel or inn. **3** A living plant or animal on or in which a parasite lives.

host[2] [hōst] *n.* **1** A large number of people or things: a *host* of children. **2** An army.

host[3] [hōst] *n.* (*often written* **Host**) The bread or wafer used in the Communion services of various Christian churches.

hos·tage [hos′tij] *n.* **1** A person given up to or held by an enemy until certain promises or conditions are fulfilled. **2** A pledge; security.

hos·tel [hos′təl] *n.* A supervised shelter, as for youths on hikes or tours. ◆ See HOTEL.

hos·tel·ry [hos′təl·rē] *n., pl.* **hos·tel·ries** An inn; lodging place: seldom used today.

host·ess [hōs′tis] *n.* **1** A woman who entertains guests. **2** A woman hired to seat people at tables in a restaurant. **3** A woman who runs an inn or hotel.

hos·tile [hos′təl] *adj.* **1** Of, having to do with, or belonging to an enemy: *hostile* acts; *hostile* forces. **2** Showing dislike; unfriendly: a *hostile* glance. **—hos′tile·ly** *adv.*

hos·til·i·ty [hos·til′ə·tē] *n., pl.* **hos·til·i·ties** **1** An unfriendly feeling; dislike or hate. **2** (*pl.*) Warfare, or acts of war. **3** Opposition: *hostility* to a scientific theory.

hos·tler [(h)os′lər] *n.* A person who cares for horses in a stable or at an inn.

hot [hot] *adj.* **hot·ter, hot·test,** *adv.* **1** *adj.* Having a high temperature or great heat; very warm: a *hot* day; a *hot* oven. **2** *adv.* With heat: Desert winds blow *hot.* **3** *adj.* Causing a burning sensation in the mouth: *hot* pepper. **4** *adj.* Showing great activity or feeling: a *hot* battle; *hot* words. **5** *adj.* Not far behind; close: in *hot* pursuit. **6** *adj.* Fresh or strong: a *hot* scent. **7** *adj.* Dangerously radioactive. **—in hot water** *informal* In trouble. **—hot′ly** *adv.* **—hot′ness** *n.*

hot air *informal* Empty, boastful talk.

hot·bed [hot′bed′] *n.* **1** A bed of rich earth, warmed by manure and protected by glass, for growing plants. **2** A place or condition favoring growth, as of something bad: a *hotbed* of disease.

hot-blood·ed [hot′blud′id] *adj.* Easily excited; passionate.

hot·cake [hot′kāk′] *n.* A pancake or griddlecake. **—sell** (or **go**) **like hotcakes** *informal* To be bought up quickly: These tickets are *going like hotcakes.*

hot cross bun A sweet roll made with raisins or other dried fruit and topped with a cross made of white icing, traditionally baked during Lent.

hot dog *informal* A cooked frankfurter, usually served in a long roll.

ho·tel [hō·tel′] *n.* A place where travelers and others go for food and lodging; inn. ◆ *Hotel, hostel,* and *hospital* all refer to places that give lodging to strangers, and all three words come originally from the same Latin word, *hospes,* meaning *guest* or *stranger. Hotels* are usually in cities, and are often large and luxurious, whereas *hostels,* which are for students and others traveling on low budgets, are often small and humble. *Hospitals,* of course, are specially designed for the ill.

hot·foot [hot′fo͝ot′] **1** *v.* To go very quickly; rush; run. **2** *adv.* In great haste.

hot·head [hot′hed′] *n.* A person who is hotheaded.

hot·head·ed [hot′hed′id] *adj.* **1** Quick-tempered; easily angered. **2** Impetuous; rash. **—hot′head′·ed·ly** *adv.* **—hot′head′ed·ness** *n.*

hot·house [hot′hous′] *n., pl.* **hot·hous·es** A heated building with glass roof and sides, in which delicate plants are grown.

hot line *informal* **1** A direct telephone line that is always open for emergency use, as between governments or heads of state. **2** A confidential telephone service staffed by people trained to deal with a particular type of problem or crisis.

hot plate A small, portable gas or electric cooking stove.

hot rod *slang* An automobile, usually old, with an engine that is rebuilt for greater speeds.

A hot rod

hot seat *slang* **1** A highly stressful position or situation. **2** Another name for ELECTRIC CHAIR.

Hot·ten·tot [hot′(ə)n·tot′] **1** *n.* A member of a people of southern Africa. **2** *n.* The language of these people. **3** *adj.* Of or having to do with the Hottentots or their language.

hound [hound] **1** *n.* A dog with droopy ears and short hair, used in hunting because of its keen sense of smell. **2** *v. informal* To follow or pester: The senator was *hounded* by reporters.

hour [our] *n.* **1** Any of the 24 equal periods making up a day; 60 minutes. **2** A definite or particular time of day: The *hour* is 6:15. **3** (*pl.*) A regularly fixed time, as for school or work: office *hours.* **4** The present time: the topic of the *hour.* **5** The distance measured by the time it takes to cover it: to live two *hours* away.

hour·glass [our′glas′] *n.* An old-fashioned device for measuring time. It is made up of two glass bulbs connected by a narrow neck through which a quantity of sand runs from the upper bulb to the lower one during a certain time, usually an hour.

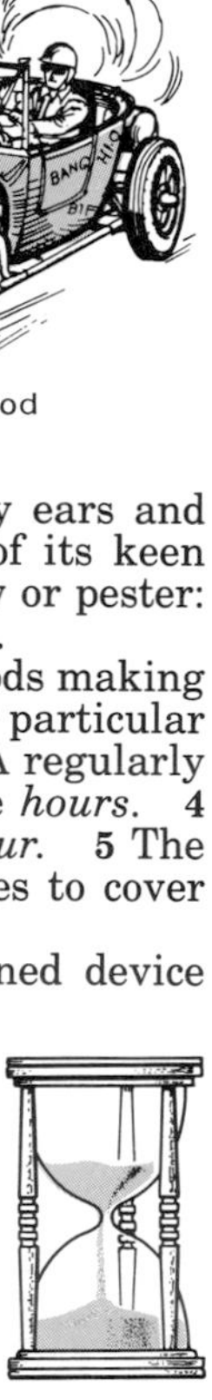
Hourglass

hour hand The hand that indicates the hours on the face of a watch or clock.

hou·ri [ho͞o′rē *or* ho͝or′ē] *n., pl.* **hou·ris** One of the maidens of the Muslim paradise, remaining forever young and beautiful.

hour·ly [our′lē] **1** *adj.* Done, taken, or happening every hour: an *hourly* news report. **2** *adj.* Of or for an hour: an *hourly* wage rate. **3** *adj.* Continual; frequent: *hourly* rumors. **4** *adv.* At or during every hour. **5** *adv.* Frequently: Telephone calls came *hourly.*

house [*n.* hous, *v.* houz] *n., pl.* **hous·es** [hou′zəz], *v.* **housed, hous·ing** **1** *n.* A building for one or a few persons or families to live in. **2** *v.* To give shelter to; lodge: The building *houses* 50 families. **3** *n.* A building for holding anything: a carriage *house.* **4** *v.* To put away; store. **5** *n.* A family, especially of the nobility: a *house* of royal blood. **6** *n.* A building in which people meet for a special purpose: a *house* of worship. **7** *n.* A business firm: a publishing *house.* **8** *n.* An audience, as in a theater. **9** *n.* An assembly of people who make the laws for a country, or the place where they meet. **—keep house** To do housework; manage a home.

house·boat [hous′bōt′] *n.* A boat or barge used as a home.

Houseboat

house·bound [hous′·bound′] *adj.* Confined to the home.

house·break [hous′brāk′] *v.* **house·broke, house·bro·ken, house·break·ing** To train (a pet animal) in habits of excretion for indoor living.

house·break·ing [hous′·brā′king] *n.* The act of breaking into another's home, so as to steal or commit some other crime. **—house′break′er** *n.*

house·bro·ken [hous′bro′kən] *adj.* Trained to excrete outdoors or in a designated place in the home, as in a litter box.

house·clean [hous′klēn′] *v.* **1** To clean, as a house, apartment, or room. **2** To improve, as by getting rid of superfluous or undesirable persons, things, or conditions.

house·coat [hous′kōt′] *n.* A lightweight, loose-fitting garment for informal wear about the house.

house·fly [hous′flī′] *n., pl.* **house·flies** A small, two-winged insect that lives about houses and feeds on garbage.

house·hold [hous′hōld′] *n.* **1** All the persons who live in one house, especially a family. **2** The home and its domestic affairs. **3** *adj. use: household* tasks.

house·hold·er [hous′hōl′dər] *n.* **1** A person dwelling in a house. **2** The head of a family.

house·hus·band [hous′huz′bənd] *n.* A man who manages his family's household while his wife works to earn the family's income.

house·keep·er [hous′kē′pər] *n.* A person hired to manage and take care of a home.

house·keep·ing [hous′kē′ping] *n.* The doing or managing of household tasks; housework.

house·maid [hous′mād′] *n.* A woman servant hired to do housework.

house·mate [hous′māt′] *n.* A person with whom one shares a house.

house·moth·er [hous′mu*th*′ər] *n.* A woman employed as a live-in supervisor in a residence, as a college dormitory, for young people.

House of Commons The lower house of the British Parliament. Its members are elected.

house of correction An institution to which persons who have been convicted of minor offenses are sentenced.

House of Lords The upper house of the British Parliament, made up of members of the nobility and clergymen of high rank. Membership is hereditary.

House of Representatives The lower house of the U.S. Congress and of many state legislatures.

house·plant [hous′plant′] *n.* A plant grown or suitable for growth in a house or apartment.

house sparrow A small brown-and-gray bird native to Europe but now flourishing in North America and Australia as well.

house·top [hous′top′] *n.* The top of a house.

house·wares [hous′wârz′] *n.pl.* Household or kitchen appliances or utensils.

house·warm·ing [hous′wôr′ming] *n.* A party given when a family first moves into a home.

house·wife [hous′wīf′] *n., pl.* **house·wives** [hous′·wīvz′] A woman who manages a household for her family; homemaker.

house·work [hous′wûrk′] *n.* The work done in a home, as cleaning and cooking.

house·work·er [hous′wûr′kər] *n.* A person hired to do housework; servant.

hous·ing[1] [hou′zing] *n.* **1** The providing of shelter or lodgings. **2** Houses or dwellings: low-cost *housing.* **3** Something that protects or shelters, as a cover or casing.

hous·ing[2] [hou′zing] *n.* An ornamental covering or blanket worn by a horse.

hove [hōv] A past tense and past participle of HEAVE.

hov·el [huv′əl *or* hov′əl] *n.* A poor, dirty hut or small house in bad condition.

hov·er [huv′ər *or* hov′ər] *v.* **1** To remain in or near one place in the air, as birds do. **2** To linger or remain nearby: to *hover* over a sick child. **3** To remain in an uncertain condition; waver: to *hover* between laughter and tears.

Hov·er·craft [huv′ər·kraft′ *or* hov′ər·kraft′] *n.* A vehicle that travels over land or water a little above the surface, supported on a cushion of air produced by powerful fans: a trademark.

how [hou] *adv.* **1** In what way: *How* does the tune go? **2** To what degree, amount, or extent: *How* far is it? **3** In what state or condition: *How* are you? **4** For what reason; why: *How* could you have done it? **5** *informal* What: *How* about coming? **—how come** *informal* Why?

how·be·it [hou·bē′it] *adv.* Nevertheless: seldom used today.

how·dah [hou′də] *n.* A seat for people riding on an elephant's back, often with a canopy.

Howdah

how·dy [hou′dē] *interj. informal* A word used as a greeting; hello. ◆ *Howdy,* which is used mainly in the western U.S., is a contraction of the phrase "how do you do."

how·ev·er [hou·ev′ər] **1** *adv.* In whatever way; by whatever means: *However* did you fix that car? **2** *adv.* To whatever degree, amount, or extent: Spend *however* much it costs. **3** *conj.* Nevertheless; yet; but: I agreed; *however,* I wasn't convinced.

a	add	**i**	it	**o͝o**	took	**oi**	oil		
ā	ace	**ī**	ice	**o͞o**	pool	**ou**	pout		
â	care	**o**	odd	**u**	up	**ng**	ring		
ä	palm	**ō**	open	**û**	burn	**th**	thin		
e	end	**ô**	order	**yo͞o**	fuse	***th***	this		
ē	equal					**zh**	vision		

ə = {a in *above* e in *sicken,* i in *possible,* o in *melon,* u in *circus*

H

how·it·zer [hou'it·sər] *n.* A short cannon that fires off shells at a high angle.

Howitzer

howl [houl] **1** *v.* To make one or more loud, drawn-out cries: Dogs and wolves often *howl* at night. **2** *v.* To make sounds like this: The wind *howls.* **3** *n.* A loud, drawn-out cry. **4** *v.* To cry out or shout loudly: to *howl* with laughter. **5** *v.* To force or drive by howling.

how·so·ev·er [hou'sō·ev'ər] *adv.* No matter how; in whatever manner.

hoy·den [hoid'(ə)n] *n.* A bold, boisterous girl; tomboy. **—hoy'den·ish** *adj.*

hp or **h.p., HP** or **H.P.** 1 high pressure. 2 horsepower.

hq or **h.q., HQ** or **H.Q.** headquarters.

hr. 1 hour. 2 (*usually written* **hrs.**) hours.

HR or **H.R.** House of Representatives.

HRH or **H.R.H.** 1 Her Royal Highness. 2 His Royal Highness.

H.S. High School.

HST or **H.S.T.** Hawaiian standard time.

ht or **ht.** height.

hub [hub] *n.* **1** The center part of a wheel, that turns on or with an axle. **2** A center of great activity or interest: Washington, D.C., is the *hub* of U.S. politics.

Hub of a wheel

hub·bub [hub'ub] *n.* A loud, confused noise; uproar.

hub·cap [hub'kap'] *n.* A metal covering that fits tightly over the hub of an automobile wheel.

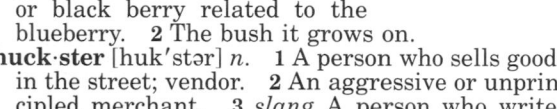

huck·le·ber·ry [huk'əl·ber'ē] *n., pl.* **huck·le·ber·ries 1** A dark blue or black berry related to the blueberry. **2** The bush it grows on.

huck·ster [huk'stər] *n.* **1** A person who sells goods in the street; vendor. **2** An aggressive or unprincipled merchant. **3** *slang* A person who writes advertising copy. **—huck'ster·ism** *n.*

HUD or **H.U.D.** Housing and Urban Development.

hud·dle [hud'(ə)l] *v.* **hud·dled, hud·dling,** *n.* **1** *v.* To crowd or nestle together closely: The puppies *huddled* together for warmth. **2** *v.* To bring, push, or crowd together: The hen *huddled* her chicks under her wings. **3** *n.* A number of persons or things crowded or jumbled together. **4** *n.* A small, private conference, especially the gathering together of a football team to receive instructions for the next play.

hue [hyōō] *n.* A color, or shade of a color.

hue and cry A loud protest or outcry: The mayor joined in the *hue and cry* against crime.

huff [huf] *n.* A fit of anger: Don't leave in a *huff.*

huff·y [huf'ē] *adj.* **huff·i·er, huff·i·est 1** Touchy; quickly offended. **2** Sulky; peevish. **—huff'i·ly** *adv.* **—huf'fi·ness** *n.*

hug [hug] *v.* **hugged, hug·ging,** *n.* **1** *v.* To clasp in the arms; embrace: The children kissed and *hugged* their parents. **2** *n.* A close embrace or tight clasping with the arms. **3** *v.* To keep close to: The ship *hugged* the shore. **4** *v.* To cling to, as a belief or principle.

huge [(h)yōōj] *adj.* **hug·er, hug·est** Very large; vast: a *huge* tree. **—huge'ly** *adv.* **—huge'ness** *n.*

Hu·gue·not [hyōō'gə·not'] *n.* Any French Protestant of the 16th or 17th century.

hu·la [hōō'lə] *n.* A Hawaiian dance characterized by sinuous motions of the arms, hands, and hips, which often pantomine a story.

hulk [hulk] **1** *n.* The hull of an old, broken-down ship. **2** *n.* A large, clumsy person or thing. **3** *v.* To move clumsily; lurch.

hulk·ing [hul'king] *adj.* Large and clumsy: a *hulking* person.

hull [hul] **1** *n.* The outer covering of certain fruits or seeds, as a husk or pod. **2** *n.* The green, leaflike parts around the base of some fruits, as the strawberry; calyx. **3** *v.* To remove the hull of. **4** *n.* The body or frame, as of a ship, seaplane, or dirigible. **5** *n.* Any outer covering.

hul·la·ba·loo [hul'ə·bə·lōō'] *n., pl.* **hul·la·ba·loos** An uproar; tumult.

hul·lo [hə·lō'] *interj., n., pl.* **hul·los,** *v.* **hul·loed, hul·lo·ing** Another spelling of HELLO.

hum [hum] *v.* **hummed, hum·ming,** *n.* **1** *v.* To make a low, steady droning or buzzing sound, as a bee or mosquito. **2** *n.* Such a sound. **3** *v.* To sing with closed lips, using no words. **4** *n.* The act of humming. **5** *n.* The sound made by humming. **6** *v.* To put into a certain condition by humming: to *hum* a child to sleep. **7** *v. informal* To be very busy or active: The office *hummed.*

hu·man [hyōō'mən] **1** *n.* A human being. **2** *adj.* Of, having to do with, or characteristic of human beings.

human being A man, woman, or child; person.

hu·mane [hyōō·mān'] *adj.* Kind; merciful; compassionate: Pets deserve *humane* care. **—hu·mane'ly** *adv.* **—hu·mane'ness** *n.*

hu·man·ism [hyōō'mə·niz'əm] *n.* A philosophy or way of life that focuses on the needs, interests, achievements, and values of human beings. **—hu'·man·ist** *n.*

hu·man·i·tar·i·an [hyōō·man'ə·târ'ē·ən] **1** *n.* A person concerned with or working for human welfare. **2** *adj.* Helpful to people. **—hu·man'i·tar'i·an·ism** *n.*

hu·man·i·ty [hyōō·man'ə·tē] *n., pl.* **hu·man·i·ties 1** The human race. **2** The state or quality of being human; human nature. **3** Kindness: *humanity* to animals. **4** (*pl.*) The study of classical Greek and Roman literature. **5** (*pl.*) The area of learning that includes literature, history, and the arts, as distinguished from the sciences.

hu·man·ize [hyōō'mə·nīz'] *v.* **hu·man·ized, hu·man·iz·ing** To make or become humane, gentle, or kindly. **—hu·man·i·za·tion** [hyōō'mə·nə·zā'shən] *n.*

hu·man·kind [hyōō'mən·kīnd'] *n.* The entire human race; all human beings.

hu·man·ly [hyōō'mən·lē] *adv.* **1** In a human manner. **2** Within human knowledge or power: That's not *humanly* possible.

hu·man·oid [hyōō'mə·noid'] **1** *adj.* Resembling a human being or something human: *humanoid* fossil bones. **2** *n.* A science fiction character who somewhat resembles but is not actually a human being.

hum·ble [hum'bəl] *adj.* **hum·bler, hum·blest,** *v.* **hum·bled, hum·bling 1** *adj.* Not proud or vain; modest; meek. **2** *adj.* Low, as in station or rank. **3** *v.* To lower, as in power or pride; humiliate. **—hum'ble·ness** *n.* **—hum'bly** *adv.*

humble pie In former times, a pie containing the less choice parts of a deer, made for servants after a hunt. It is now used mainly in the phrase **eat humble pie,** to be forced to make apologies or admit that one is wrong.

hum·bug [hum′bug′] *n., v.* **hum·bugged, hum·bug·ging** 1 *n.* A person who seeks to deceive others; fake. 2 *n.* Something used to trick or deceive others; fraud; sham. 3 *v.* To trick or cheat.

hum·drum [hum′drum′] *adj.* Dull; monotonous.

hu·mer·us [hyōō′mər·əs] *n., pl.* **hu·mer·i** [hyōō′mər·ī] or **hu·mer·us·es** 1 The long bone in the upper part of the human arm, extending from the shoulder to the elbow. 2 The part of the arm containing this bone.

hu·mid [hyōō′mid] *adj.* Containing water vapor; damp; moist: *humid* air.

hu·mid·i·fy [hyōō·mid′ə·fī′] *v.* **hu·mid·i·fied, hu·mid·i·fy·ing** To make (the air) moist or humid. **—hu·mid′i·fi′er** *n.*

hu·mid·i·ty [hyōō·mid′ə·tē] *n.* Moisture; dampness, especially of the air.

hu·mi·dor [hyōō′mə·dôr′] *n.* A container for the storage of tobacco products, especially cigars, that has a device inside to control the humidity.

hu·mil·i·ate [hyōō·mil′ē·āt′] *v.* **hu·mil·i·at·ed, hu·mil·i·at·ing** To strip of pride or self-respect; humble; embarrass: Public scolding *humiliated* the child.

hu·mil·i·a·tion [hyōō·mil′ē·ā′shən] *n.* 1 The act or an instance of humiliating. 2 A being humiliated; disgrace.

hu·mil·i·ty [hyōō·mil′ə·tē] *n.* The condition or quality of being humble.

hum·ming·bird [hum′ing·bûrd′] *n.* A tiny, brightly colored bird with a long bill. It moves its wings so rapidly that they hum.

Hummingbird

hum·mock [hum′ək] *n.* 1 A low mound. 2 A ridge or mound in an ice field.

hum·mus [hum′əs] *n.* A thick mixture of puréed chick-peas, tahini, and lemon juice, used in Middle Eastern dishes.

hu·mon·gous [hyōō·mong′gəs] *adj. slang* Enormous; gigantic.

hu·mor [hyōō′mər] 1 *n.* The quality of being funny or amusing: a conversation full of *humor.* 2 *n.* Speech, writing, or actions that are amusing. 3 *n.* The ability to see or bring out the funny side of things: a sense of *humor.* 4 *n.* A state of mind; mood: to be in a good *humor.* 5 *n.* A whim; caprice. 6 *v.* To give in to the whims or caprices of; indulge: Parents sometimes *humor* their children. **—out of humor** Temporarily cross or ill-tempered.

hu·mor·ist [hyōō′mər·ist] *n.* A person who tells or writes funny stories or ancedotes.

hu·mor·less [hyōō′mər·lis] *adj.* Lacking a sense of humor. **—hu′mor·less·ly** *adv.* **—hu′mor·less·ness** *n.*

hu·mor·ous [hyōō′mər·əs] *adj.* Full of or using humor; funny; amusing. **—hu′mor·ous·ly** *adv.* **—hu′·mor·ous·ness** *n.*

hump [hump] 1 *n.* A rounded lump, especially on the bank, as of a buffalo or camel. 2 *n.* A low mound of earth; hummock. 3 *v.* To raise or rise into a hump: Cats *hump* their backs when frightened.

hump·back [hump′bak′] *n.* 1 A hunchback. 2 Another word for HUMPBACK WHALE.

hump·backed [hump′bakt′] *adj.* Hunchbacked.

humpback whale A large whale having very long flippers and the ability to produce prolonged, songlike underwater vocal sounds.

humph [humf] *interj.* An exclamation, as of doubt, annoyance, or contempt.

hu·mus [hyōō′məs] *n.* Rich, dark soil containing decayed plant and animal matter.

Hun [hun] *n.* A member of a warlike Asian tribe that invaded Europe in the fourth and fifth centuries.

hunch [hunch] 1 *n.* A hump. 2 *v.* To bend or draw, as into a hump: to *hunch* one's shoulders. 3 *v.* To move or thrust oneself forward jerkily. 4 *n. informal* A vague feeling or notion: I had a *hunch* that I had done well in the test.

hunch·back [hunch′bak′] *n.* 1 A deformed back with a hump at or just below the shoulders. 2 A person with such a back.

hunch·backed [hunch′bakt′] *adj.* Having a hunchback.

hun·dred or **100** [hun′drid] *n., adj.* Ten more than ninety.

hun·dred·fold [hun′drid·fōld′] 1 *adj.* Being a hundred times as much or as many. 2 *n.* A hundred times as much or as many. 3 *adv.* By a hundred times.

hun·dredth [hun′dridth] 1 *n.* One of a hundred equal parts. 2 *adj.* Being one of a hundred equal parts. 3 *adj.* Next after 99 others; coming after the 99th. 4 *n.* The hundredth person or thing.

hun·dred·weight [hun′drid·wāt′] *n., pl.* **hun·dred·weight** or **hun·dred·weights** A weight of 100 pounds in the U.S., or 112 pounds in England.

hung [hung] A past tense and past participle of HANG: We *hung* the painting on the wall.

Hun·gar·i·an [hung·gâr′ē·ən] 1 *adj.* Of or from Hungary. 2 *n.* A person born in or a citizen of Hungary. 3 *n.* The language of Hungary.

hun·ger [hung′gər] 1 *n.* The discomfort or weakness caused by eating too little or nothing. 2 *n.* A desire or need for food. 3 *n.* Any strong desire or craving: a *hunger* for fame. 4 *v.* To have or experience a hunger.

hunger strike A fast voluntarily undertaken as a protest.

hung jury A jury that cannot agree on a verdict and is consequently dismissed by the judge.

hun·gry [hung′grē] *adj.* **hun·gri·er, hun·gri·est** 1 Wanting or needing food. 2 Having or showing a desire or need: to be *hungry* for fame. **—hun′gri·ly** *adv.* **—hun′gri·ness** *n.*

hunk [hungk] *n. informal* A large piece or lump; chunk: a *hunk* of meat.

hunt [hunt] 1 *v.* To try to find and kill (deer, wild ducks, or other animals). 2 *v.* To chase and try to catch (a fox, coon, or other animal) with dogs and often horses. 3 *n.* A group of huntsmen. 4 *v.* To try to track and catch (a person, as a criminal or

a	add	**i**	it	**ŏŏ**	took	**oi**	oil		
ā	ace	**ī**	ice	**ōō**	pool	**ou**	pout		
â	care	**o**	odd	**u**	up	**ng**	ring		
ä	palm	**ō**	open	**û**	burn	**th**	thin		
e	end	**ô**	order	**yōō**	fuse	**th̶**	this		
ē	equal					**zh**	vision		

ə = a in *above*, e in *sicken*, i in *possible*, o in *melon*, u in *circus*

H

spy). **5** *v.* To look carefully; make a search: to *hunt* for one's glasses. **6** *n.* The act of hunting.

hunt·er [hun'tər] *n.* A person or animal that hunts or takes part in a hunt.

hunt·ing [hun'ting] *n.* The activity of pursuing and killing animals for food or sport.

hunts·man [hunts'mən] *n., pl.* **hunts·men** [hunts'·mən] A person who hunts or directs a hunt.

hur·dle [hûr'dəl] *n., v.* **hur·dled, hur·dling** **1** *n.* A small frame or fence to be jumped over in a race. **2** *n.* (*pl.*) A race in which hurdles are used. **3** *v.* To leap over: to *hurdle* a gate. **4** *n.* A movable fence woven from branches. **5** *v.* To fence in with hurdles. **6** *n.* A difficulty or obstacle to be overcome. **7** *v.* To overcome (a difficulty or obstacle). **—hur'dler** *n.*

Runner going over a hurdle

hur·dy-gur·dy [hûr'dē·gûr'dē] *n., pl.* **hur·dy-gur·dies** Another name for a HAND ORGAN.

hurl [hûrl] *v.* **1** To throw (an object) with force. **2** To say with force: to *hurl* abuse. **—hurl'er** *n.*

hur·ly-bur·ly [hûr'lē·bûr'lē] *n.* Uproar; commotion.

hur·rah [hə·rä'] **1** *n., interj.* A cry of joy or applause. **2** *v.* To applaud by shouts; cheer.

hur·ray [hōō·rā'] *n., interj., v.* Hurrah.

hur·ri·cane [hûr'ə·kān'] *n.* A storm with heavy rains and whirling winds of 75 miles per hour or more, usually beginning in the tropics, often the West Indies. ◆ *Hurricane* comes from a Spanish word taken from an Indian language in the West Indies.

hur·ried [hûr'ēd] *adj.* Made, done, or acting in haste. **—hur'ried·ly** *adv.* **—hur'ried·ness** *n.*

hur·ry [hûr'ē] *v.* **hur·ried, hur·ry·ing,** *n.* **1** *v.* To act or move with haste. **2** *n.* The act of hurrying; haste. **3** *v.* To cause to act or move too hastily: If you *hurry* me, I'll make mistakes. **4** *v.* To move or transport with haste: *Hurry* the wounded to a doctor. **5** *v.* To speed the preparation or completion of; expedite: Please *hurry* lunch. **6** *n.* A state of urgency; rush: I'm in a *hurry* to get home.

hurt [hûrt] *v.* **hurt, hurt·ing,** *n.* **1** *v.* To cause pain, injury, or damage to: The fall *hurt* my back. **2** *v.* To be painful or uncomfortable: My neck *hurts.* **3** *n.* Pain, injury, or damage. **4** *v.* To cause grief or mental suffering to: Being called bad names *hurt* the child.

hurt·ful [hûrt'fəl] *adj.* Causing or tending to cause hurt; harmful; injurious. **—hurt'ful·ly** *adv.* **—hurt'·ful·ness** *n.*

hur·tle [hûr'təl] *v.* **hur·tled, hur·tling** To move or cause to move with great speed or force.

hus·band [huz'bənd] **1** *n.* A man to whom a woman is married; married man. **2** *v.* To manage wisely; save part of: to *husband* energy.

hus·band·man [huz'bənd·mən] *n., pl.* **hus·band·men** [huz'bənd·mən] A farmer: seldom used today.

hus·band·ry [huz'bən·drē] *n.* **1** The business of farming. **2** Careful, efficient management.

hush [hush] **1** *v.* To make or become quiet or silent: to *hush* a noisy dog; At dusk the birds *hushed.* **2** *n.* Stillness; quiet: in the *hush* of the night. **3** *v.* To keep hidden: to *hush* up a scandal.

hush-hush [hush'hush'] *adj. informal* Secret: They managed to keep the information *hush-hush.*

hush·pup·py [hush'pup'ē] *n., pl.* **hush·pup·pies** A cornmeal fritter.

husk [husk] **1** *n.* The dry outer covering of various seeds or fruits. **2** *v.* To strip the husk from: to *husk* corn. **3** *n.* Any outer covering, especially when worthless.

husk·ing [husk'ing] *n.* A gathering, as of families, friends, or neighbors, for the purpose of husking corn. Also **husking bee.**

husk·y[1] [hus'kē] *adj.* **husk·i·er, husk·i·est,** *n., pl.* **husk·ies** **1** *adj.* Full of, like, or made of husks. **2** *adj.* Rough and somewhat hoarse in sound, as a voice. **3** *adj. informal* Large and strong. **4** *n. informal* A strong or powerfully built person. **—husk'i·ly** *adv.* **—husk'i·ness** *n.*

husk·y[2] [hus'kē] *n., pl.* **huskies** (*often written* **Husky**) A large, strong dog with thick fur, used by the Eskimos and others to pull sleds.

Husky

hus·sar [hōō·sär'] *n.* In some European armies, a cavalryman, often wearing a showy uniform.

hus·sy [huz'ē *or* hus'ē] *n., pl.* **hus·sies** **1** An immoral woman. **2** A girl who is too bold or saucy.

hus·tle [hus'(ə)l] *v.* **hus·tled, hus·tling,** *n.* **1** *v.* To force one's way: to *hustle* through a mob. **2** *v.* To push or carry with force: to *hustle* an intruder out. **3** *v. U.S. informal* To work with drive and energy. **4** *n.* Energy and drive. **5** *n.* Great activity: the *hustle* of a bus station. **—hus'tler** *n.*

hut [hut] *n.* A small, crude house or cabin.

hutch [huch] *n.* **1** A pen or coop for keeping small animals: a rabbit *hutch.* **2** A chest, box, or cupboard used for storage.

hutz·pah or **hutz·pa** [hōōt'spə] *n.* Another spelling of CHUTZPAH.

huz·zah or **huz·za** [hə·zä'] *n., interj., v.* Another word for HURRAH.

hwy. highway.

hy·a·cinth [hī'ə·sinth] *n.* A plant related to the lily, having a spikelike cluster of fragrant, bell-shaped flowers.

hy·brid [hī'brid] **1** *n.* The offspring of parents that are of different species or strains. **2** *adj. use: hybrid* corn. **3** *n.* Something that combines elements from different sources. **4** *adj. use*: a *hybrid* word. **—hy'brid·ism** *n.*

hybrid computer A computer that represents data by a combination of the systems used by analog computers and digital computers.

hy·brid·ize [hī'brid·īz'] *v.* **hy·brid·ized, hy·brid·iz·ing** To produce or cause to produce hybrids; crossbreed. **—hy'brid·i·za'tion** *n.* **—hy'brid·iz'er** *n.*

hy·dra [hī'drə] *n., pl.* **hy·dras** or **hy·drae** [hī'drē] **1** (*usually written* **Hydra**) In Greek myths, a serpent with nine heads. It grew two new heads for each one that was cut off. **2** A tiny, tubelike, freshwater animal having a ring of tentacles surrounding its mouth.

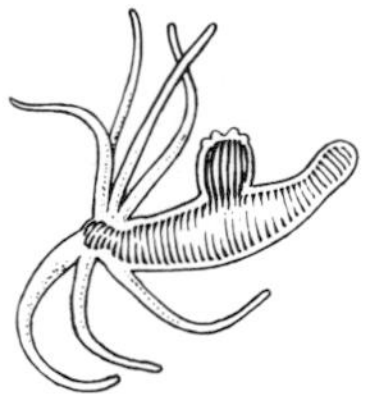
Hydra

hy·dran·gea [hī·drān'jə] *n.* A shrub with large clusters of white, blue, or pink flowers.

hy·drant [hī'drənt] *n.* A large upright pipe coming

from a water main, from which water may be drawn for fighting fires or washing streets.

hy·drate [hī'drāt'] *n., v.* **hy·drat·ed, hy·drat·ing** 1 *n.* A chemical compound that contains water. 2 *v.* To cause (a chemical compound) to combine with water. —**hy·dra'tion** *n.*

hy·drau·lic [hī·drô'lik] *adj.* 1 Of or having to do with a liquid in motion. 2 Operated by the force of a moving liquid: a *hydraulic* jack. 3 Hardening under water, as a cement.

hydraulic ram A pump that uses the energy of running water to force some of this water to a higher level.

hy·drau·lics [hī·drô'liks] *n.* The branch of engineering dealing with the properties and uses of liquids in motion. ◆ See -ICS.

hy·dra·zine [hī'drə·zēn'] *n.* A toxic, colorless, liquid rocket fuel made of hydrogen and nitrogen. It smells like ammonia.

hydro- A combining form meaning: 1 Of or having to do with water, as in *hydrosphere.* 2 Containing hydrogen, as in *hydrocarbon.*

hy·dro·car·bon [hī'drə·kär'bən] *n.* A chemical compound containing only hydrogen and carbon.

hy·dro·chlo·ric acid [hī'drə·klôr'ik] A strong acid composed of hydrogen and chlorine.

hy·dro·cy·an·ic acid [hī'drō·sī·an'ik] A toxic, flammable acid made of carbon, nitrogen, hydrogen, and water. It is used in the manufacture of dyes, pesticides, and plastics.

hy·dro·dy·nam·ic [hī'drō·dī·nam'ik] *adj.* 1 Of, having to do with, or characteristic of fluids in motion. 2 Of or having to do with hydrodynamics. —**hy'dro·dy·nam'i·cal·ly** *adv.*

hy·dro·dy·nam·ics [hī'drō·dī·nam'iks] *n.* The branch of physics dealing with water and other fluids in motion. ◆ See -ICS.

hy·dro·e·lec·tric [hī'drō·i·lek'trik] *adj.* Of or having to do with electricity produced by water power.

hy·dro·foil [hī'drə·foil'] *n.* 1 A device similar to a short airplane wing, attached to a boat below the waterline in order to lift the hull out of the water to allow for greater speeds. 2 A boat equipped with hydrofoils.

Hydrofoils

hy·dro·gen [hī'drə·jən] *n.* The lightest and most abundant of the elements, a colorless, odorless, highly flammable gas, on the earth found mainly in combination with oxygen as water. —**hy·drog·e·nous** [hī·droj'ə·nəs] *adj.*

hy·dro·gen·ate [hī'drə·jə·nāt' *or* hī·droj'ə·nāt'] *v.* **hy·dro·gen·at·ed, hy·dro·gen·at·ing** To combine or treat with hydrogen. —**hy·dro·gen·a·tion** (hī'drə·jə·nā'shən] *n.* —**hy'dro·gen·a'tor** *n.*

hydrogen bomb A very powerful bomb that gets its energy from the fusion of atomic nuclei of light weight, often those of lithium and an isotope of hydrogen.

hydrogen peroxide An unstable, colorless, liquid compound used in diluted form as an antiseptic and as a bleaching agent.

hy·drog·ra·phy [hī·drog'rə·fē] *n.* The study, measuring, and mapping of oceans, rivers, and other bodies of water. —**hy·drog'ra·pher** *n.* —**hy·dro·graph·ic** [hī'drə·graf'ik] *adj.*

hy·drol·y·sis [hī·drol'ə·sis] *n., pl.* **hy·drol·y·ses** [hī·drol'ə·sēz] A chemical reaction in which a molecule of water and another molecule break apart and exchange components to form two new molecules.

hy·drom·e·ter [hī·drom'ə·tər] *n.* An instrument for measuring the density of liquids. —**hy·dro·met·ric** [hī'drə·met'rik] *adj.*

hy·dro·pho·bi·a [hī'drə·fō'bē·ə] *n.* Another name for RABIES.

hy·dro·plane [hī'drə·plān'] *n.* 1 A small motorboat whose hull skims over the water when driven at high speeds. 2 A seaplane.

hy·dro·pon·ics [hī'drə·pon'iks] *n.* The growing of plants in solutions of special salts and water rather than in soil. ◆ See -ICS.

hy·dro·sphere [hī'drə·sfir'] *n.* 1 All of the water, both salt and fresh, on the earth. 2 The moisture in the earth's atmosphere.

hy·dro·stat·ics [hī'drə·stat'iks] *n.* The branch of physics dealing with water and other fluids at rest. —**hy'dro·stat'ic** *adj.* —**hy'dro·stat'i·cal·ly** *adv.* ◆ See -ICS.

hy·dro·ther·a·py [hī'drə·ther'ə·pē] *n., pl.* **hy·dro·ther·a·pies** The medical use of water in treating diseases.

hy·drot·ro·pism [hī·drot'rə·piz'əm] *n.* The tendency of a plant to grow or turn toward water.

hy·drous [hī'drəs] *adj.* In chemistry, containing water, especially water of crystallization or hydration.

hy·drox·ide [hī·drok'sīd'] *n.* A chemical compound that contains the radical made up of one hydrogen atom and one oxygen atom.

hy·drox·yl [hī·drok'sil] *n.* A chemical radical composed of one atom of hydrogen and one atom of oxygen.

hy·dro·zo·an [hī'drə·zō'ən] *n.* Any of a class of invertebrate water animals including corals, polyps, the hydra, and the smaller jellyfish.

hy·e·na [hī·ē'nə] *n.* A wolflike animal of Africa and Asia that feeds on decaying carcasses.

Hyena

hy·giene [hī'jēn'] *n.* 1 The science of maintaining good health and preventing disease. 2 Practices, habits, and conditions that keep people healthy and clean. —**hy'gien'i·cal·ly** *adv.* —**hy·gien'ist** *n.*

hy·gi·en·ic [hī'j(ē·)en'ik] *adj.* 1 Of or having to do with hygiene. 2 Very clean; sanitary. —**hy'gi·en'·i·cal·ly** *adv.*

hy·gi·en·ics [hī'j(ē·)en'iks] *n.* Hygiene (def. 1)

hy·grom·e·ter [hī·grom'ə·tər] *n.* An instrument for measuring the humidity in the air.

hy·grom·e·try [hī·grom'ə·trē] *n.* The measurement

a	add	**i**	it	**o͝o**	took	**oi**	oil
ā	ace	**ī**	ice	**o͞o**	pool	**ou**	pout
â	care	**o**	odd	**u**	up	**ng**	ring
ä	palm	**ō**	open	**û**	burn	**th**	thin
e	end	**ô**	order	**yo͞o**	fuse	**th**	this
ē	equal					**zh**	vision

ə = a in *above* e in *sicken* i in *possible* o in *melon* u in *circus*

H

of atmospheric humidity. **—hy·gro·met·ric** [hī′grə·met′rik] *adj.*

hy·gro·scope [hī′grə·skōp′] *n.* An instrument that measures water vapor in the atmosphere.

hy·gro·scop·ic [hī′grə·skop′ik] *adj.* 1 Of or having to do with a hygroscope. 2 Absorbing or attracting moisture from the atmosphere. **—hy′gro·scop′·i·cal·ly** *adv.* **—hy·gro·scop·ic·i·ty** [hī′grə·skə·pis′ə·tē] *n.*

hy·ing [hī′ing] Present participle of HIE.

Hy·men [hīmən] *n.* In Greek myths, the god of marriage.

hymn [him] *n.* A song of praise, especially to God.

hym·nal [him′nəl] *n.* A book of church hymns.

hymn·book [him′bo͝ok′] *n.* A hymnal.

hyper- A prefix meaning: 1 Overly; too, as in *hypersensitive.* 2 More than normal, as in *hypertension.*

hy·per·ac·tive [hī′pər·ak′tiv] *adj.* Excessively active. **—hy·per·ac·tiv·i·ty** [hī′pər·ak·tiv′ə·tē] *n.*

hy·per·bo·la [hī·pûr′bə·lə] *n.* A set of points whose distances from each of two fixed points equal a constant when subtracted. It forms a symmetrical plane figure consisting of two open curves.

hy·per·bo·le [hī·pûr′bə·lē] *n.* An obviously exaggerated statement made for dramatic effect, as in "The coach is as tough as nails."

hy·per·bol·ic [hī′pər·bol′ik] *adj.* 1 Of or using hyperbole. 2 Of or having the shape of a hyperbola. **—hy′per·bol′i·cal·ly** *adv.*

hy·per·crit·i·cal [hī′pər·krit′i·kəl] *adj.* Too critical; very difficult to please.

hy·per·sen·si·tive [hī′pər·sen′sə·tiv] *adj.* Excessively sensitive. **—hy·per·sen·si·tiv·i·ty** [hī′pər·sen′·sə·tiv′ə·tē], **—hy′per·sen′si·tive·ness** *n.*

hy·per·son·ic [hī′pər·son′ik] *adj.* Of or having to do with speeds at least five times greater than the speed of sound.

hy·per·ten·sion [hī′pər·ten′shən] *n.* Blood pressure that is much higher than normal.

hy·per·tro·phy [hī·pûr′trə·fē] *n.* Abnormal increase in size of an organ or part, due to an increase in the size but not the number of cells.

hy·per·ven·ti·late [hī′pər·ven′tə·lāt′] *v.* **hy·per·ven·ti·lat·ed, hy·per·ven·ti·lat·ing** To take very rapid or deep breaths, causing dizziness, tingling, and sometimes fainting. **—hy′per·ven′ti·la′tion** *n.*

hy·phen [hī′fən] *n.* A mark (-) used between parts of a compound word, as in "full-blown," or to show that a word had been divided at the end of a line.

hy·phen·ate [hī′fən·āt′] *v.* **hy·phen·at·ed, hy·phen·at·ing** To separate or connect by a hyphen. **—hy′·phen·a′tion** *n.*

hyp·no·sis [hip·nō′sis] *n.* An artificially induced condition like sleep in which a person responds to suggestions or instructions made by the person who has induced the condition.

hyp·not·ic [hip·not′ik] 1 *adj.* Of, causing, or having to do with hypnosis. 2 *n.* A hypnotized or easily hypnotized person. 3 *adj.* Tending to cause sleep. 4 *n.* A drug that puts one to sleep. **—hyp·not′ic·al·ly** *adv.*

hyp·no·tism [hip′nə·tiz′əm] *n.* The act or practice of producing hypnosis. **—hyp′no·tist** *n.*

hyp·no·tize [hip′nə·tīz′] *v.* **hyp·no·tized, hyp·no·tiz·ing** 1 To produce hypnosis in. 2 To control the feelings and will of; fascinate or charm: The honeyed words *hypnotized* me. **—hyp·no·tiz·a·ble** [hip′·nə·tī′zə·bəl] *adj.* **—hyp′no·tiz′er** *n.*

hy·po¹ [hī′pō] *n., pl.* **hy·pos** A chemical used as a fixing agent in developing or printing photographs.

hy·po² [hī′pō] *n., pl.* **hy·pos** *informal* A hypodermic injection or syringe.

hy·po·chon·dri·a [hī′pə·kon′drē·ə] *n.* An obsessive, unwarranted concern about one's health, accompanied by anxiety and, frequently, depression.

hy·po·chon·dri·ac [hī′pə·kon′drē·ak′] *n.* A person who suffers from hypochondria. **—hy·po·chon·dri·a·cal** [hī′pə·kon·drī′ə·kəl] *adj.*

hy·po·cot·yl [hī′pə·kot′(ə)l] *n.* The part of the main stem of a plant embryo or seedling below the cotyledon.

hy·poc·ri·sy [hi·pok′rə·sē] *n., pl.* **hy·poc·ri·sies** 1 A pretending to have attitudes or qualities that one really does not have; insincerity. 2 A hypocritical act.

hyp·o·crite [hip′ə·krit] *n.* A person who pretends to have but does not really have certain attitudes or qualities; insincere person.

hyp·o·crit·i·cal [hip′ə·krit′ə·kəl] *adj.* 1 Being a hypocrite. 2 Characteristic of a hypocrite: insincere; deceitful: a *hypocritical* remark. **—hyp′o·crit′i·cal·ly** *adv.*

hy·po·der·mic [hī′pə·dûr′mik] 1 *adj.* Beneath the skin. 2 *n.* An injection of a substance beneath the skin. 3 *n.* A syringe (**hypodermic syringe**) having a sharp, hollow needle for injecting substances beneath the skin.

hy·pot·e·nuse [hī·pot′ə·n(y)o͞os′] *n.* In a right triangle, the side opposite the right angle.

hy·po·thal·a·mus [hī′pō·thal′ə·məs] *n.* A part of the brain located directly below the thalamus that regulates body temperature, heartbeat, and other autonomic functions.

hy·po·ther·mi·a [hī′pō·thûr′mē·ə] *n.* A condition in which the temperature of the body falls abnormally low.

hy·poth·e·sis [hī·poth′ə·sis] *n., pl.* **hy·poth·e·ses** [hī·poth′ə·sēz] An idea assumed to be true for the sake of argument or further study.

hy·poth·e·size [hī·poth′ə·sīz′] *v.* **hy·poth·e·sized, hy·poth·e·siz·ing** To develop or put forward (a hypothesis).

hy·po·thet·i·cal [hī′pə·thet′i·kəl] *adj.* 1 Based on a hypothesis; theoretical: a *hypothetical* question. 2 Based on supposition; imaginary: a *hypothetical* situation. **—hy′po·thet′i·cal·ly** *adv.*

hy·pox·i·a [hī·pok′sē·ə] *n.* An insufficiency in the amount of oxygen that reaches body tissues.

hy·rax [hī′raks′] *n., pl.* **hy·rax·es** *or* **hy·ra·ces** [hī′rə·sēz′] A small mammal of Africa and the Middle East that looks like a woodchuck but has hoofs instead of paws.

hys·sop [his′əp] *n.* 1 A plant of the mint family having blue flower spikes and spicy leaves formerly used in medicines and perfumes. 2 A plant used by the ancient Hebrews in certain purification rituals.

hys·te·ri·a [his·tir′ē·ə *or* his·ter′ē·ə] *n.* 1 Uncontrolled excitement or emotion; frenzy. 2 A mental disease marked by disorders of the body for which no physical causes exist.

hys·ter·ic [his·ter′ik] 1 *n.* A person who suffers from attacks of hysteria. 2 *adj.* Hysterical.

hys·ter·i·cal [his·ter′ə·kəl] *adj.* 1 Showing or caused by hysteria: a *hysterical* symptom. 2 Affected with hysteria. **—hys·ter′i·cal·ly** *adv.*

hys·ter·ics [his·ter′iks] *n.pl.* A fit of uncontrolled, wild laughing and crying. ◆ See -ICS.

Ii

I is the ninth letter of the alphabet. The sign for it originated among Semitic people in the Near East, in the region of Palestine and Syria, probably in the middle of the second millennium B.C. Little is known about the sign until around 1000 B.C., when the Phoenicians began using it. They named it *yodh* and used it for a *y*-like sound.

When the Greeks adopted the Phoenician alphabet around the ninth century B.C., they had no use for the sign because the consonant *y* sound had disappeared from the Greek language long before. The Greeks, therefore, used the sign for the vowel *i*. They renamed it *iota* and simplified its shape.

As early as the eighth century B.C., the Etruscans adopted the Greek alphabet. It is from the Etruscans that the Romans took the sign for *I*. The Romans used the sign for the sounds of long and short *i* and of consonantal *y*. Around the time of the Caesars, the Romans made the shape of the letter more graceful. The model of the letter found on the base of Trajan's column, erected in Rome in 114, is considered a masterpiece of letter design. A Trajan-style *majuscule,* or capital letter, *I* opens this essay.

The *minuscule,* or small letter, *i* developed gradually, between the third and the ninth centuries, in the handwriting that scribes used for copying books. It is essentially a smaller version of the majuscule. Shown are three versions: the Roman *uncial* of the fourth to the eighth centuries, the *half uncial* of the fifth to the ninth centuries, and the *Caroline minuscule.* The Caroline minuscules, a script that evolved under the encouragement of Charlemagne (742-814), became the principal handwriting system used on the medieval manuscripts of the ninth and tenth centuries. The minuscule letter remained undotted until the eleventh century. The dot was added then to clarify the reading of words, especially those that contained lowercase letters such as an *m* or an *n* close to an *i*.

Early Phoenician (late 2nd millennium B.C.)
Phoenician (8th century B.C.)
Early Greek (9th-7th centuries B.C.)
Western Greek (6th century B.C.)
Classical Greek (403 B.C. onward)
Early Etruscan (8th century B.C.)
Monumental Latin (4th century B.C.)
Classical Latin
Uncial
Half uncial
Caroline minuscule

i or **I** [ī] *n., pl.* **i's** or **I's** [īz] **1** The ninth letter of the English alphabet. **2** (*written* **I**) The Roman numeral for 1.
i. intransitive.
I The symbol for the element iodine.
I [ī] *pron., pl.* **we** A speaker or writer when referring to himself or herself: *I* asked them to help me. ◆ *I* is often used incorrectly as part of an object (as in "a great day for Tom and I"). Use *me* instead.
I. **1** Island(s). **2** Isle(s).
Ia. Iowa.
IA Postal Service abbreviation of Iowa.
IAAF International Amateur Athletic Federation.
-ial Another form of the suffix -AL, as in *artificial.*
i·amb [ī'amb'] *n.* In verse, a metrical foot in which an unaccented syllable is followed by an accented one. The line "Hĭs flēēce/ wăs whīte/ ăs snōw" is made up of three iambs.
i·am·bic [ī·am'bik] **1** *adj.* Marked by or written in iambs. **2** *n.* Another word for IAMB. **3** *n.* Verse written in iambs.
-ian Another form of the suffix -AN, as in *Grecian.*
i·bex [ī'beks'] *n., pl.* **i·bex** or **i·bex·es** A wild goat of Europe, Asia, and Africa, with long horns that curve backwards.
ibid. In the same work or on the same line or page as previously quoted. ◆ *Ibid.* is an abbreviation of the Latin word *ibidem,* meaning *in the same place,* and is used in footnotes.
-ibility Another form of the suffix -ABILITY, as in *possibility.*
i·bis [ī'bis] *n., pl.* **i·bis** or **i·bis·es** A wading bird related to the heron, having a long bill that curves downward. The ancient Egyptians looked on it as sacred.

Ibis

-ible A suffix meaning: **1** Capable of being or tending to, as in *flexible.* **2** Worthy of, as in *contemptible.* **3** Full of, as in *forcible.* **4** Causing, as in *horrible.*
-ic A suffix meaning: **1** Of, like, or having to do with, as in *metallic.* **2** Caused or produced by, as in *allergic.* **3** Consisting of or containing, as in *alcoholic.*
-ical Another form of the suffix -IC. ◆ Some twin adjectives ending in *-ic* and *-ical* differ in meaning, as *economic* and *economical.*
Ic·a·rus [ik'ər·əs] *n.* In Greek myths, a youth who, with his father, Daedalus, escaped from Crete us-

a	add	**i**	it	**o͝o**	took	**oi**	oil		
ā	ace	**ī**	ice	**o͞o**	pool	**ou**	pout		
â	care	**o**	odd	**u**	up	**ng**	ring		
ä	palm	**ō**	open	**û**	burn	**th**	thin		
e	end	**ô**	order	**yo͞o**	fuse	**t͟h**	this		
ē	equal					**zh**	vision		

ə = a in *above* e in *sicken* i in *possible* o in *melon* u in *circus*

ing artificial wings held together with wax. When Icarus flew too near the sun, the wax melted and he fell into the sea.

ICBM intercontinental ballistic missile.

ICC or **I.C.C.** Interstate Commerce Commission.

ice [īs] *n., v.* **iced, ic·ing** 1 *n.* Frozen water; water in solid form. 2 *v.* To chill by adding ice. 3 *v.* To cover or become covered with ice: The windshield *iced* up. 4 *v.* To turn to ice; freeze: The pond *iced* over. 5 *n.* The frozen surface of a body of water. 6 *n.* A substance resembling ice in form. 7 *n.* A frozen dessert made of fruit juice, sugar, and water. 8 *n.* Frosting. 9 *v.* To spread icing over.

Ice. 1 Iceland. 2 Icelandic.

ice age 1 A period in the earth's development when icecaps and glaciers covered large parts of the surface of the earth. 2 Another name for PLEISTOCENE.

ice·berg [īs′bûrg′] *n.* 1 A thick mass of ice separated from a glacier and floating in the ocean. 2 *informal* A person who is emotionally cold.

Iceberg

ice·boat [īs′bōt′] *n.* 1 A light framework with skatelike runners and sails for sailing over ice. 2 An icebreaker.

ice·boat·ing [īs′bō′ting] *n.* The sport of sailing over ice in an iceboat. —**ice·boat·er** [īs′bō′tər] *n.*

ice·bound [īs′bound′] *adj.* 1 Held fast in or halted by ice, as a ship. 2 Covered or choked with ice: an *icebound* harbor.

ice·box [īs′boks′] *n.* A cabinet kept cool by putting ice in it, and used for storing food.

ice·break·er [īs′brā′kər] *n.* A boat with a very strong prow and powerful engines, used to open channels through ice for ships.

Icebreaker

ice·cap [īs′kap′] *n.* A field of ice and snow permanently covering an area of land and spreading outward from its center.

ice cream A frozen mixture of sweetened and flavored cream, milk, or custard.

ice cube A small piece of ice frozen in the form of a cube and used to cool drinks and fill ice bags.

ice field 1 A broad mass of floating ice, found mostly in Arctic seas. 2 An icecap.

ice floe 1 A large, level area of floating sea ice. 2 A single piece, any size, of floating ice.

ice hockey Hockey (def. 1).

Ice·land·er [īs′lən·dər] *n.* A person born in or a citizen of Iceland.

Ice·land·ic [īs·lan′dik] 1 *adj.* Of or from Iceland. 2 *n.* The language of Iceland.

ice·man [īs′mən] *n., pl.* **ice·men** [īs′mən] A person who sells or delivers ice.

ice pack 1 A waterproof bag or a folded cloth filled with chipped ice and used on parts of the body to relieve pain or reduce swelling. 2 Another term for PACK ICE.

ice pick A pointed tool similar to an awl, used to crack or chip ice.

ice sheet A field or layer of thick ice covering a vast area of land for a long time.

ice-skate [īs′skāt′] *v.* **ice-skat·ed, ice-skat·ing** To move or slide over ice on ice skates.

ice skate 1 A metal blade or runner mounted on a frame that is attached to a high shoe, used for gliding over ice. 2 The blade alone: to sharpen *ice skates.*

ich·neu·mon [ik·n(y)o͞o′mən] *n.* 1 An ichneumon fly. 2 A type of mongoose.

ichneumon fly A fly whose larvae feed on the larvae of other insects.

ich·thy·ol·o·gy [ik′thē·ol′ə·jē] *n.* The branch of zoology that has to do with the study of fish, their classification, structure, and life history. —**ich′thy·ol′o·gist** *n.*

ich·thy·o·saur [ik′thē·ə·sôr′] *n.* An extinct, fishlike sea reptile having a long head, four limbs resembling paddles, and a long snout.

i·ci·cle [ī′si·kəl] *n.* A hanging rod of ice formed by the freezing of dripping water.

ic·ing [ī′sing] *n.* A smooth mixture of sugar, egg whites, and other ingredients, spread over cakes; frosting.

i·con [ī′kon] *n.* 1 An image; picture. 2 On a computer screen, a symbol for some command or function. 3 In some churches, a picture treated as sacred. 4 An object of devotion; IDOL.

Icon

i·con·o·clast [ī·kon′ə·klast′] *n.* 1 A person who opposes the worship of images. 2 A person who attacks popular beliefs or established customs. —**i·con′o·clas′tic** *adj.*

◆ *Iconoclast* comes from two Greek words meaning *breaker of images.*

-ics A suffix meaning: 1 An art, science, or field of study, as in *mathematics.* 2 Methods, systems, or activities, as in *acrobatics, athletics.* ◆ Nouns ending in *-ics* that refer to arts, sciences, or fields of activity were originally plural, meaning things relating to a field. Later they came to mean all such things relating to a field, taken as a single collection, and they became singular: *Politics* is exciting; *Physics* is my favorite subject. Such words seldom take *a, an,* or *the.* Nouns ending in *-ics* that refer to specific details, qualities, or methods within a field are plural and often take articles: The *acoustics* in this hall are bad; These *statistics* are from the last census.

ICU or **I.C.U.** intensive care unit.

i·cy [ī′sē] *adj.* **i·ci·er, i·ci·est** 1 Covered with or having a lot of ice: *icy* steps. 2 Like ice, as in coldness: *icy* hands; an *icy* greeting. —**i′ci·ly** [ī′sə·lē] *adv.* —**i′ci·ness** *n.*

I'd [īd] 1 I would. 2 I should. 3 I had.

ID 1 Postal Service abbreviation of Idaho. 2 identification.

i·de·a [ī·dē′ə] *n.* 1 A way of seeing, understanding, or solving things that is formed in or grasped by the mind; a thought. 2 An impression or notion: I have no *idea* where the book is. 3 An opinion or belief: What are your *ideas* on the subject? 4 An intention, plan, or purpose: The editor of the school paper has the *idea* of becoming a writer. ❖*Idea* comes from a Greek word meaning *to see.*

i·de·al [ī·dē′əl *or* ī·dēl′] **1** *n.* A standard, principle, or goal of perfection: to live up to high *ideals.* **2** *n.* A perfect model or example. **3** *adj.* Perfect or excellent: an *ideal* pupil; an *ideal* location. **4** *adj.* Existing only in the mind as a concept: an *ideal* government.

i·de·al·ism [ī·dē′əl·iz′əm] *n.* **1** The tendency to see things as one would like to have them rather than as they are. **2** The following of ideals of conduct that one has set up. **3** Any system of philosophy that teaches that things do not exist except as ideas in the mind.

i·de·al·ist [ī·dē′əl·ist] *n.* **1** A person who has high ideals of conduct and tries to live according to them. **2** An impractical dreamer. **3** In philosophy, a believer in idealism. **—i′de·al·is′tic** *adj.*

i·de·al·ize [ī·dē′əl·īz′] *v.* **i·de·al·ized, i·de·al·iz·ing** To regard or represent as perfect: Some people tend to *idealize* the past.

i·de·al·ly [ī·dē′ə·lē] *adv.* **1** In all aspects; completely: Ann is *ideally* suited to her job. **2** Under the best of circumstances; in theory: *Ideally,* everyone should have good health.

i·den·ti·cal [ī·den′ti·kəl] *adj.* **1** The very same: the *identical* spot where it happened. **2** Exactly alike: *identical* notebooks. **3** Describing twins of the same sex that develop from a single fertilized egg cell. **—i·den′ti·cal·ly** *adv.*

i·den·ti·fi·ca·tion [ī·den′tə·fə·kā′shən] *n.* **1** The action of identifying. **2** A being identified. **3** A means of proving identity, as an official card or document telling who one is.

i·den·ti·fy [ī·den′tə·fī′] *v.* **i·den·ti·fied, i·den·ti·fy·ing** **1** To recognize, claim, or prove to be a certain person or thing: to *identify* a lost dog. **2** To regard as the same: to *identify* change with progress. **3** To associate closely: People *identify* Edison with the electric light.

i·den·ti·ty [ī·den′tə·tē] *n., pl.* **i·den·ti·ties** **1** The fact of being a specific person or thing and no other: My passport established my *identity.* **2** Individuality: to lose one's *identity.* **3** Sameness or oneness: the *identity* of the handwriting in two letters. **4** A mathematical statement of equality that is true for all values of the variables involved, shown by the sign ≡, as, $(a + b)^2 \equiv a^2 + 2ab + b^2$.

identity element A mathematical element that, when multiplied by or added to another element, results in that element. In addition, 0 is the identity element, since 4 + 0 = 4; in multiplication, 1 is the identity element, since 4 × 1 = 4.

id·e·o·gram [id′ē·ə·gram′] *n.* In certain languages, such as Chinese, a symbol used to represent an object or idea, rather than a word or phrase for it.

Ideograms

id·e·o·graph [id′ē·ə·graf′] *n.* Another word for IDEOGRAM.

i·de·o·log·i·cal [ī′dē·ə·loj′i·kəl *or* id′ē·ə·loj′ə·kəl] *adj.* **1** Having to do with or arising from ideologies or an ideology. **2** Having to do with ideas. **—i′de·o·log′i·cal·ly** *adv.*

i·de·ol·o·gy [ī′dē·ol′ə·jē] *n., pl.* **i·de·ol·o·gies** The ideas or beliefs held by a class or group.

ides [īdz] *n.pl.* In the ancient Roman calendar, the 15th of March, May, July, and October, and the 13th of the other months.

id·i·o·cy [id′ē·ə·sē] *n., pl.* **i·di·o·cies** **1** The condition of being or acting like an idiot. **2** Extreme stupidity or foolishness.

id·i·om [id′ē·əm] *n.* **1** An expression having a special meaning different from the usual meanings of the words. "To put up with" is an idiom meaning "to tolerate or endure." **2** The language or dialect of a region, profession, or social class: Scottish *idiom;* legal *idiom.*

id·i·o·mat·ic [id′ē·ə·mat′ik] *adj.* **1** Using or containing an idiom or idioms. **2** Showing a language's characteristic way of putting things: *idiomatic* French. **—id′i·o·mat′i·cal·ly** *adv.*

id·i·o·syn·cra·sy [id′ē·ō·sing′krə·sē] *n., pl.* **id·i·o·syn·cra·sies** A way of thinking or behaving that is peculiar to an individual; quirk: Refusing to wait in lines was one of her *idiosyncrasies.*

id·i·ot [id′ē·ət] *n.* **1** A person so feebleminded as to be unable to learn or understand and who needs constant care. **2** A very foolish person.

id·i·ot·ic [id′ē·ot′ik] *adj.* Very foolish.

i·dle [īd′(ə)l] *adj.* **i·dler** [īd′lər], **i·dlest** [īd′list], *v.* **i·dled, i·dling** **1** *adj.* Not busy: *idle* hands; *idle* moments. **2** *adj.* Unwilling to work; lazy. **3** *adj.* Not operating: *idle* machines. **4** *v.* To waste (time) doing nothing: to *idle* away a morning. **5** *v.* To operate without transmitting power: to let the motor *idle* in a car. **6** *adj.* Of no worth or importance; useless; meaningless: *idle* chatter; *idle* threats. **—i′dle·ness** *n.* **—i·dly** [īd′lē] *adv.*

i·dler [īd′lər] *n.* A lazy person; loafer.

i·dol [ī′d(ə)l] *n.* **1** An image of a god that is worshiped as sacred. **2** A person or thing greatly loved or admired: a sports *idol.*

i·dol·a·ter [ī·dol′ə·tər] *n.* **1** A person who worships idols. **2** An overly devoted admirer of a person or thing.

i·dol·a·trous [ī·dol′ə·trəs] *adj.* **1** Having to do with or practicing idolatry. **2** Blindly devoted.

i·dol·a·try [ī·dol′ə·trē] *n., pl.* **i·dol·a·tries** **1** The worship of idols. **2** Extreme admiration or love for a person or thing.

i·dol·ize [īd′(ə)l·īz′] *v.* **i·dol·ized, i·dol·iz·ing** **1** To love or admire blindly or too much. **2** To worship as an idol.

i·dyll or **i·dyl** [īd′(ə)l] *n.* **1** A short work in poetry or prose describing simple, peaceful scenes of country life. **2** Any scene or event whose simple charm might inspire an idyll.

a	add	**i**	it	**o͝o**	took	**oi**	oil
ā	ace	**ī**	ice	**o͞o**	pool	**ou**	pout
â	care	**o**	odd	**u**	up	**ng**	ring
ä	palm	**ō**	open	**û**	burn	**th**	thin
e	end	**ô**	order	**yo͞o**	fuse	**th**	this
ē	equal					**zh**	vision

ə = { a in *above* e in *sicken* i in *possible* / o in *melon* u in *circus* }

I

i·dyl·lic [ī·dil′ik] *adj.* Full of simple charm and contentment: an *idyllic* cruise.
i.e. that is. ◆ *I.e.* is an abbreviation of the Latin phrase *id est,* meaning *that is.*
-ier A suffix meaning: A person who is or does something, as in *gondolier.*
if [if] *conj.* 1 In the event that; in case that: *If* you come home early, call me. 2 Even though; although: an enjoyable *if* rather tiring day. 3 Whether: See *if* I have any mail. **—if only** I wish that: *If only* I could go! ◆ *If* (def. 3) is generally an acceptable synonym for *whether.* But *whether* is preferable in serious writing and whenever more than two choices are listed: I don't know *whether* we'll go to Paris, to London, or to Rome.
ig·loo [ig′lōō] *n., pl.* **ig·loos** A dome-shaped hut built by Eskimos, usually of blocks of hard snow. ◆ *Igloo* comes from an Eskimo word meaning a *house.*

Igloo

ign. ignition.
ig·ne·ous [ig′nē·əs] *adj.* Formed, as rocks, by great heat within the earth: Granite is an *igneous* rock.
ig·nite [ig·nīt′] *v.* **ig·nit·ed, ig·nit·ing** 1 To set on fire; make burn. 2 To catch fire.
ig·ni·tion [ig·nish′ən] *n.* 1 The act of igniting or of being ignited. 2 The electrical system that sets fire to the fuel in a gasoline engine.
ig·no·ble [ig·nō′bəl] *adj.* Dishonorable; shameful: an *ignoble* betrayal. **—ig·no′bly** *adv.*
ig·no·min·i·ous [ig′nə·min′ē·əs] *adj.* Deserving or bringing disgrace; shameful: an *ignominious* defeat. **—ig′no·min′i·ous·ly** *adv.*
ig·no·min·y [ig′nə·min′ē] *n., pl.* **ig·no·min·ies** 1 Public disgrace or dishonor. 2 An action that brings disgrace or dishonor.
ig·no·ra·mus [ig′nə·rā′məs] *n.* An ignorant person.
ig·no·rance [ig′nər·əns] *n.* The condition of being ignorant; lack of knowledge.
ig·no·rant [ig′nər·ənt] *adj.* 1 Having little or no learning or knowledge: an *ignorant* person. 2 Indicating a lack of knowledge: *ignorant* remarks. 3 Not informed; unaware: *ignorant* of what had happened. **—ig′no·rant·ly** *adv.*
ig·nore [ig·nôr′] *v.* **ig·nored, ig·nor·ing** To refuse to notice; pay no attention to.
i·gua·na [i·gwä′nə] *n.* A large, climbing lizard of tropical America, having a ridge of scales along its spine.

Iguana

i·kon [ī′kon] Another spelling of ICON.
il- Another form of the prefix IN-[2], meaning *not,* used before words beginning with *l,* as in *illiterate.*
IL Postal Service abbreviation of Illinois.
il·e·um [il′ē·əm] *n., pl.* **il·e·a** [il′ē·ə] The third and lowest part of the small intestine.
ILGWU or **I.L.G.W.U.** International Ladies' Garment Workers' Union.
Il·i·ad [il′ē·əd] *n.* An ancient Greek epic poem written by Homer, describing the siege of Troy by the Greeks.
il·i·um [il′ē·əm] *n., pl.* **il·e·a** [il′ē·ə] The broad, uppermost bone of the three principal bones that form each side of the human pelvis.
ilk [ilk] *n.* Family; kind; sort; class. **—of that ilk** *informal* 1 Of the same name, place, or estate. 2 Of the same kind or sort.
ill [il] *adj.* **worse, worst,** *n., adv.* 1 *adj.* Not in good health; sick. 2 *n.* A sickness: childhood *ills.* 3 *adj.* Bad or harmful: an *ill* omen; an *ill* wind. 4 *n.* Evil, wrong, injury, or harm: Do good in return for *ill.* 5 *adv.* Badly or wrongly: a job *ill* done. 6 *adv.* Unkindly: Don't speak *ill* of the dead. 7 *adj.* Unfriendly; bitter: *ill* feeling. 8 *adv.* With difficulty; hardly: I can *ill* afford the expense. **—ill at ease** Uncomfortable; nervous.
ill. 1 illustrated. 2 illustration. 3 illustrator.
Ill. Illinois.
I'll [īl] 1 I will. 2 I shall.
ill-ad·vised [il′əd·vīzd′] *adj.* Unwise; rash.
ill-bred [il′bred′] *adj.* Showing a lack of good training in the home; impolite; rude.
il·le·gal [i·lē′gəl] *adj.* Not legal; forbidden by law. **—il·le′gal·ly** *adv.*
il·leg·i·ble [i·lej′ə·bəl] *adj.* Not printed or written clearly enough to be read; hard or impossible to read. **—il·leg′i·bly** *adv.*
il·le·git·i·mate [il′i·jit′ə·mit] *adj.* 1 Born of parents who were not married to each other. 2 Contrary to the law or rules. **—il·le·git·i·ma·cy** [il′i·jit′ə·mə·sē] *n.* **—il′le·git′i·mate·ly** *adv.*
ill-fat·ed [il′fā′tid] *adj.* Doomed to end in or to bring disaster or woe: an *ill-fated* voyage.
ill-fa·vored [il′fā′vərd] *adj.* Ugly.
ill-got·ten [il′got′(ə)n] *adj.* Obtained by dishonest or evil means: *ill-gotten* gains.
ill-hu·mored [il′(h)yōō′mərd] *adj.* Irritable.
il·lib·er·al [i·lib′ər·əl] *adj.* 1 Not generous; stingy. 2 Narrow-minded; intolerant.
il·lic·it [i·lis′it] *adj.* Not permitted; unlawful: *illicit* trading. ◆ See ELICIT.
il·lim·it·a·ble [i·lim′it·ə·bəl] *adj.* Having no limits; limitless: an *illimitable* capacity.
il·lit·er·a·cy [i·lit′ər·ə·sē] *n.* 1 Inability to read and write. 2 Lack of education.
il·lit·er·ate [i·lit′ər·it] 1 *adj.* Lacking the ability to read and write. 2 *n.* A person who cannot read and write. 3 *adj.* Showing lack of education; ignorant: an *illiterate* writer.
ill-man·nered [il′man′ərd] *adj.* Impolite; rude.
ill-na·tured [il′nā′chərd] *adj.* Cross; grumpy.
ill·ness [il′nis] *n.* 1 Poor health; sickness. 2 An ailment; disease.
il·log·i·cal [i·loj′i·kəl] *adj.* Showing a lack of sound reasoning. **—il·log′i·cal·ly** *adv.*
ill-starred [il′stärd′] *adj.* Unlucky.
ill-tem·pered [il′tem′pərd] *adj.* Having a bad temper; ill-natured.
ill-treat [il′trēt′] *v.* To treat cruelly or roughly; abuse. **—ill′-treat′ment** *n.*
il·lu·mi·nate [i·lōō′mə·nāt′] *v.* **il·lu·mi·nat·ed, il·lu·mi·nat·ing** 1 To light up: to *illuminate* a room. 2 To make clear; clarify: to *illuminate* an idea. 3 To decorate, as the first letter or the margin of a page, with designs in gold and colors: to *illuminate* a manuscript.
il·lu·mi·na·tion [i·lōō′mə·nā′shən] *n.* 1 The act of illuminating. 2 An illuminated condition. 3 An amount of light: adequate *illumination* for read-

ing. **4** A public display of lights. **5** Enlightenment. **6** Decoration, as of a manuscript, with designs in gold and colors.

il·lu·mine [i·lo͞o′min] *v.* **il·lu·mined, il·lu·min·ing** To light up.

illus. **1** illustrated. **2** illustration. **3** illustrator.

ill-us·age [il′yo͞o′sij] *n.* Bad treatment.

ill-use [il′yo͞oz′] *v.* **ill-used, ill-us·ing** To treat badly or cruelly; abuse.

il·lu·sion [i·lo͞o′zhən] *n.* **1** A false, mistaken idea or belief: to lose childish *illusions.* **2** A deceiving appearance or the false impression it gives: an optical *illusion.*

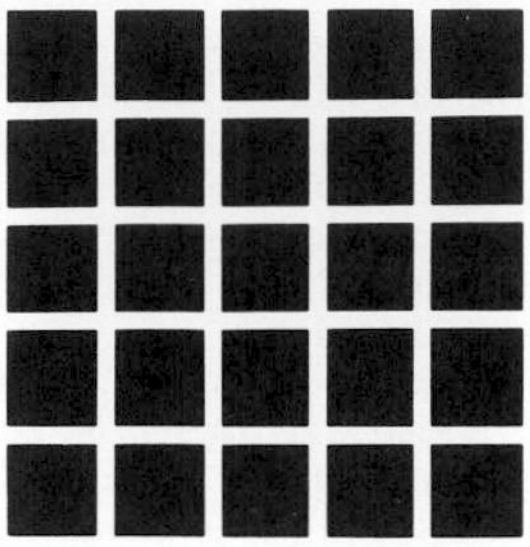

The flickering gray spots at the intersections of the white lines are an illusion.

il·lu·sive [i·lo͞o′siv] *adj.* Illusory.

il·lu·so·ry [i·lo͞o′sər·ē] *adj.* Coming from or causing an illusion; not real; deceptive.

il·lus·trate [il′ə·strāt′ *or* i·lus′trāt′] *v.* **il·lus·trat·ed, il·lus·trat·ing** **1** To explain or make clear, as by examples or comparisons: The speaker told a story to *illustrate* the point. **2** To furnish with pictures or drawings that explain or decorate: to *illustrate* a children's book.

il·lus·tra·tion [il′ə·strā′shən] *n.* **1** A picture, as one in a book, used to explain or decorate. **2** An example or comparison used to explain: The ant was given as an *illustration* of a social insect. **3** The process of illustrating.

il·lus·tra·tive [i·lus′trə·tiv *or* il′ə·strā′tiv] *adj.* Serving to illustrate or explain: An *illustrative* phrase shows how a word is used.

il·lus·tra·tor [il′ə·strā′tər] *n.* An artist who makes illustrations, as for books.

il·lus·tri·ous [i·lus′trē·əs] *adj.* Very famous; distinguished: an *illustrious* statesman.

ill will Unfriendly feeling; hostility.

il·ly [il′lē] *adv.* Wrongly or badly; ill: a job *illy* done.

im-[1] A prefix meaning: In, into, or on, as in *import* or *imprint.*

im-[2] A form of the prefix IN-[2], meaning *not,* used before words beginning with *b, m,* and *p,* as in *imbalance, immoderate,* and *impossible.*

I'm [īm] I am.

im·age [im′ij] *n.* **1** A statue or other likeness of some person or thing: a graven *image.* **2** A picture such as is formed in a mirror or by a lens. **3** A person or thing very much like another: The two cousins are the *image* of each other. **4** A mental picture: *images* in daydreams. **5** An expression, as a metaphor or simile, that calls up a picture or other sense impression to the mind. "The curtain of night" is an image.

im·age·ry [im′ij·rē] *n.* Images, especially word pictures or figures of speech in poetry.

im·ag·i·na·ble [i·maj′ə·nə·bəl] *adj.* Capable of being imagined; conceivable.

im·ag·i·nar·y [i·maj′ə·ner′ē] *adj.* Existing only in the imagination; unreal.

imaginary number A number that generates a negative number when squared.

im·ag·i·na·tion [i·maj′ə·nā′shən] *n.* **1** The power to picture absent, unknown, or unreal things in the mind: In my *imagination,* I had already finished the job I hadn't even started. **2** The power to see things in new ways, form new ideas, or create new things from thought: the *imagination* of an artist.

im·ag·i·na·tive [i·maj′ə·nə·tiv *or* i·maj′ə·nā′tive] *adj.* Full of or showing imagination.

im·ag·ine [i·maj′in] *v.* **im·ag·ined, im·ag·in·ing** **1** To form a mental picture or idea of: Try to *imagine* how the early tribes must have lived; *Imagine* the earth revolving around the sun. **2** To suppose; guess: I *imagine* I'll be able to go.

i·ma·go [i·mā′gō] *n., pl.* **i·ma·goes** or **i·mag·i·nes** [i·maj′ə·nēz] An insect in its adult stage.

i·mam [i·mäm′] *n.* **1** In the Muslim religion, an official prayer leader. **2** (*written* **Imam**) A Muslim leader who claims descent from the prophet Muhammad. **3** (*written* **Imam**) Any of various Muslim leaders.

im·bal·ance [im·bal′əns] *n.* The condition of lacking balance or being out of balance.

im·be·cile [im′bə·səl] *n.* **1** A feebleminded person not quite so helpless as an idiot. **2** A very foolish or stupid person. **—im·be·cil·ic** [im′bə·sil′ik] *adj.*

im·be·cil·i·ty [im′bə·sil′ə·tē] *n., pl.* **im·be·cil·i·ties** **1** The condition of being or acting like an imbecile. **2** Utter stupidity of foolishness. **3** A stupid or foolish action.

im·bed [im·bed′] *v.* **im·bed·ded, im·bed·ding** Another spelling of EMBED.

im·bibe [im·bīb′] *v.* **im·bibed, im·bib·ing** **1** To drink, especially liquor. **2** To take in as if drinking; absorb: soil *imbibing* water. **3** To absorb in the mind: to *imbibe* learning. **—im·bi′ber** *n.*

im·bro·glio [im·brōl′yō] *n., pl.* **im·bro·glios** A confused state of affairs, complicated misunderstanding, or other difficult situation.

im·bue [im·byo͞o′] *v.* **im·bued, im·bu·ing** **1** To fill, as with emotions or ideals: to be *imbued* with the ideals of democracy. **2** To fill or saturate, as with color or moisture.

IMF International Monetary Fund.

im·i·ta·ble [im′ə·tə·bəl] *adj.* Able to be imitated or copied.

im·i·tate [im′ə·tāt′] *v.* **im·i·tat·ed, im·i·tat·ing** **1** To try to act or look the same way as: Children often *imitate* their parents. **2** To copy or mimic: to *imitate* the call of a bird. **3** To have or take on the appearance of: a plastic material made to *imitate* leather. **—im′i·ta′tor** *n.*

im·i·ta·tion [im′ə·tā′shən] *n.* **1** The act of imitating: *Imitation* is a form of flattery. **2** Something made or done by imitating an original; copy: The drawing was an *imitation* of a famous painting. **3** *adj. use: imitation* gems.

im·i·ta·tive [im′ə·tā′tiv] *adj.* Copying or imitating. *Buzz* and *swish* are imitative words.

im·mac·u·late [i·mak′yə·lit] *adj.* **1** Completely clean; spotless: *immaculate* clothes. **2** Without sin or blemish.

a	add	**i**	it	**o͝o**	took	**oi**	oil
ā	ace	**ī**	ice	**o͞o**	pool	**ou**	pout
â	care	**o**	odd	**u**	up	**ng**	ring
ä	palm	**ō**	open	**û**	burn	**th**	thin
e	end	**ô**	order	**yo͞o**	fuse	**th**	this
ē	equal					**zh**	vision

ə = { a in *above* e in *sicken* i in *possible*; o in *melon* u in *circus* }

Immaculate Conception In the Roman Catholic Church, the doctrine that the Virgin Mary was, from the moment of conception, free from original sin.
im·ma·te·ri·al [im′ə·tir′ē·əl] *adj.* 1 Of no importance. 2 Not made of material substance.
im·ma·ture [im′ə·chŏŏr′ *or* im′ə·t(y)ŏŏr′] *adj.* Not fully grown, ripened, or developed. **—im′ma·ture′·ly** *adv.* **—im′ma·tur′i·ty** *n.*
im·meas·ur·a·ble [i·mezh′ər·ə·bəl] *adj.* Not capable of being measured; very great. **—im·meas′ur·a·bly** *adv.*
im·me·di·a·cy [i·mē′dē·ə·sē] *n., pl.* **im·me·di·a·cies** The condition or quality of being immediate.
im·me·di·ate [i·mē′dē·it] *adj.* 1 Done or happening without delay; at once. 2 Near, in time or space: the *immediate* future; my *immediate* neighborhood. 3 Closest: your *immediate* family. 4 Direct: in *immediate* contact.
im·me·di·ate·ly [i·mē′dē·it·lē] *adv.* 1 Without delay; instantly: Come home *immediately.* 2 In close relation; with nothing between: *Immediately* beyond our yard is a parking lot.
im·me·mo·ri·al [im′ə·môr′ē·əl] *adj.* Reaching back beyond everybody's memory; very old. **—im′me·mo′ri·al·ly** *adv.*
im·mense [i·mens′] *adj.* Very large; huge: an *immense* ship. **—im·mense′ly** *adv.*
im·men·si·ty [i·men′sə·tē] *n.* 1 The condition of being immense; hugeness; vastness. 2 Boundless space; infinity.
im·merse [i·mûrs′] *v.* **im·mersed, im·mers·ing** 1 To dip into liquid so as to cover completely. 2 To involve deeply: to be *immersed* in a book. 3 To baptize by dipping the entire body under water. **—im·mer·sion** [i·mûr′shən *or* i·mûr′zhən] *n.*
im·mi·grant [im′ə·grənt] *n.* A person who comes into a country or region where he or she was not born, in order to live there.
im·mi·grate [im′ə·grāt′] *v.* **im·mi·grat·ed, im·mi·grat·ing** To come into a country or region where one was not born, in order to live there. **—im′mi·gra′·tion** *n.*
im·mi·nent [im′ə·nənt] *adj.* Likely to happen soon; impending: to be in *imminent* danger. **—im′mi·nence** *n.* **—im′mi·nent·ly** *adv.* ◆ See EMINENT.
im·mo·bile [i·mō′bəl] *adj.* 1 Not movable; fixed tightly. 2 Not moving; motionless.
im·mo·bi·lize [i·mō′bə·līz′] *v.* **im·mo·bi·lized, im·mo·bi·liz·ing** To make immobile.
im·mod·er·ate [i·mod′ər·it] *adj.* More than is reasonable or proper; too much.
im·mod·est [i·mod′ist] *adj.* 1 Not modest; indecent. 2 Not humble; bold. **—im·mod′est·ly** *adv.*
im·mod·est·y [i·mod′is·tē] *n.* 1 A lack of modesty or decency. 2 A lack of humility.
im·mor·al [i·môr′əl] *adj.* 1 Morally bad; wicked. 2 Indecent; lewd. **—im·mor·al·i·ty** [im′ə·ral′ə·tē] *n.* **—im·mor′al·ly** *adv.*
im·mor·tal [i·môr′təl] 1 *adj.* Living, lasting, or remembered forever: a poet's *immortal* words; *immortal* gods. 2 *n.* A person who lives forever. 3 *n.* A person worthy of being remembered forever. **—im·mor′tal·ly** *adv.*
im·mor·tal·i·ty [im′ôr·tal′ə·tē] *n.* Life or fame lasting forever.
im·mor·tal·ize [i·môr′təl·īz′] *v.* **im·mor·tal·ized, im·mor·tal·iz·ing** To give eternal life or fame to; make immortal.
im·mov·a·ble [i·mōō′və·bəl] *adj.* 1 Not movable; fixed tightly. 2 Unchangeable; steadfast. **—im·mov′a·bly** *adv.*
im·mune [i·myōōn′] *adj.* 1 Protected against a disease, as by inoculation; *immune* to measles. 2 Not to be affected by; protected from: *immune* to corruption.
im·mu·ni·ty [i·myōō′nə·tē] *n., pl.* **im·mu·ni·ties** 1 The condition of being able to resist a disease, especially as a result of being inoculated or vaccinated: *immunity* to measles. 2 Exemption, as from rules or duties: diplomatic *immunity* from parking tickets.
im·mu·nize [im′yə·nīz′] *v.* **im·mu·nized, im·mu·niz·ing** To make immune, especially against a disease. **—im′mu·ni·za′tion** *n.*
im·mu·nol·o·gy [im′yə·nol′ə·jē] *n.* In medicine, the study of the body's immunity to diseases. **—im′mu·nol′o·gist** *n.*
im·mure [i·myŏŏr′] *v.* **im·mured, im·mur·ing** To enclose within walls; imprison; confine.
im·mu·ta·ble [i·myōō′tə·bəl] *adj.* That cannot change or be changed: the *immutable* laws of nature. **—im·mu′ta·bly** *adv.*
imp [imp] *n.* 1 A young or minor demon; evil spirit. 2 A mischievous child.
imp. 1 imperative. 2 imperfect. 3 imperial. 4 import. 5 important. 6 imported.
im·pact [im′pakt] *n.* A striking together; collision: the *impact* of clashing cymbals.
im·pact·ed [im·pak′tid] *adj.* Closely wedged in: used especially to describe a tooth confined between the jawbone and another tooth.
im·pair [im·pâr′] *v.* To make worse; damage; injure: Reading in dim light can *impair* vision. **—im·pair′·ment** *n.*
im·pal·a [im·pä′lə *or* im·pal′ə] *n.* A red African antelope that has large, curved horns and is known for its ability to leap.

Impala

im·pale [im·pāl′] *v.* **im·paled, im·pal·ing** 1 To pierce with or as if with something sharp and pointed. 2 To torture or put to death by thrusting a sharp stake through the body.
im·pal·pa·ble [im·pal′·pə·bəl] *adj.* 1 Not capable of being felt by the sense of touch, as a shadow. 2 Not marked enough to be grasped: *impalpable* differences. **—im·pal′pa·bly** *adv.*
im·pan·el [im·pan′əl] *v.* **im·pan·eled** or **im·pan·elled, im·pan·el·ing** or **im·pan·el·ling** 1 To add to a list, as for jury duty. 2 To select (a jury) from such a list.
im·part [im·pärt′] *v.* 1 To make known; disclose: to *impart* a secret. 2 To give a degree or measure of; give: Flowers *impart* freshness to a room.
im·par·tial [im·pär′shəl] *adj.* Not favoring one thing or person; unbiased: a jury's *impartial* verdict. **—im·par·ti·al·i·ty** [im′pär·shē·al′ə·tē] *n.* **—im·par′tial·ly** *adv.*
im·pass·a·ble [im·pas′ə·bəl] *adj.* That cannot be passed over or traveled through: *impassable* jungle. **—im·pass′a·bly** *adv.*
im·passe [im′pas *or* im·pas′] *n.* A position or situation from which there is no way out; deadlock.

im·pas·sioned [im·pash′ənd] *adj.* Filled with strong feeling; fervent: an *impassioned* plea.
im·pas·sive [im·pas′iv] *adj.* Not affected by emotion; showing no feeling: The opposition remained *impassive* but I was sympathetic. **—im·pas′sive·ly** *adv.*
im·pa·tience [im·pā′shəns] *n.* The quality or condition of being impatient.
im·pa·tient [im·pā′shənt] *adj.* 1 Lacking patience; easily annoyed, as at delay or discomfort. 2 Caused by or showing a lack of patience: an *impatient* sigh. 3 Very eager: *impatient* for success. **—im·pa′tient·ly** *adv.*
im·peach [im·pēch′] *v.* 1 To challenge or bring discredit upon: to *impeach* someone's honor. 2 To accuse of doing wrong. 3 To formally charge (a public official) with wrongdoing in office: to *impeach* a governor for bribery. **—im·peach′ment** *n.*
im·pec·ca·ble [im·pek′ə·bəl] *adj.* Free from fault or flaw. **—im·pec′ca·bly** *adv.*
im·pe·cu·ni·ous [im′pə·kyo͞o′nē·əs] *adj.* Having no money; poor; penniless.
im·pede [im·pēd′] *v.* **im·ped·ed, im·ped·ing** To put obstacles in the way of; obstruct: Snowstorms *impeded* the explorers' march.
im·ped·i·ment [im·ped′ə·mənt] *n.* 1 A hindrance; obstacle. 2 A physical defect, especially one that makes normal speech difficult.
im·ped·i·men·ta [im·ped′ə·men′tə] *n.pl.* Objects such as bulky baggage, equipment, or the like, that slow down movement or progress, especially of an army.
im·pel [im·pel′] *v.* **im·pelled, im·pel·ling** 1 To force or drive to an action; urge on: Pride *impelled* us to refuse the gift. 2 To push or drive forward; propel.
im·pend [im·pend′] *v.* To be about to occur: Disaster *impended,* but we did not know it.
im·pend·ing [im·pen′ding] *adj.* Likely to happen soon; imminent.
im·pen·e·tra·ble [im·pen′ə·trə·bəl] *adj.* 1 Not capable of being pierced, seen through, or entered: an *impenetrable* jungle. 2 Not capable of being understood: an *impenetrable* mystery.
im·pen·i·tent [im·pen′ə·tənt] *adj.* Not sorry, as for doing wrong. **—im·pen′i·tence** *n.* **—im·pen′i·tent·ly** *adv.*
imper. imperative.
im·per·a·tive [im·per′ə·tiv] 1 *adj.* Urgently necessary; unavoidable: Speed is *imperative.* 2 *n.* Something that is imperative, as a command. 3 *adj.* In grammar, of, having to do with, or being the mood of a verb that expresses a command, request, or plea. In "Go at once!" *go* is in the imperative mood. 4 *n.* In grammar, the imperative mood or a verb form in this mood.
im·per·cep·ti·ble [im′pər·sep′tə·bəl] *adj.* Too small or slight to be noticed: an *imperceptible* movement. **—im′per·cep′ti·bly** *adv.*
imperf. imperfect.
im·per·fect [im·pûr′fikt] *adj.* 1 Having a fault or faults; not perfect. 2 Incomplete or inadequate: an *imperfect* grasp of a situation. 3 In grammar, designating a tense that indicates a state or action, usually past, as continuing or uncompleted, as *was speaking* in "The teacher was speaking when I came in." **—im·per′fect·ly** *adv.*
im·per·fec·tion [im′pər·fek′shən] *n.* 1 An imperfect condition. 2 A defect; flaw.
im·pe·ri·al [im·pir′ē·əl] 1 *adj.* Of or having to do with an empire, an emperor, or an empress. 2 *adj.* Superior, as in size or quality; magnificent. 3 *n.* A small pointed beard just under the lower lip. **—im·pe′ri·al·ly** *adv.*
im·pe·ri·al·ism [im·pir′ē·əl·iz′əm] *n.* 1 The policy of increasing the power or dominion of a nation, as by conquering other nations and exerting influence in political and economic areas. 2 An imperial form of government. **—im·pe′ri·al·ist** *n., adj.* **—im·pe′ri·al·is′tic** *adj.*
im·per·il [im·per′il] *v.* **im·per·iled** or **im·per·illed, im·per·il·ing** or **im·per·il·ling** To place in peril; put in danger.
im·pe·ri·ous [im·pir′ē·əs] *adj.* 1 Proud and haughty; domineering; arrogant. 2 Urgent; imperative. **—im·pe′ri·ous·ly** *adv.*
im·per·ish·a·ble [im·per′ish·ə·bəl] *adj.* Not liable to decay, perish, or pass away.
im·per·ma·nent [im·pûr′mə·nənt] *adj.* Not permanent or lasting. **—im·per′ma·nence** *n.* **—im·per′·ma·nen·cy** *n.*
im·per·me·a·ble [im·pûr′mē·ə·bəl] *adj.* 1 Not allowing anything to pass through or into. 2 Impervious to liquids or moisture.
im·per·mis·si·ble [im′pər·mis′ə·bəl] *adj.* Unable to be permitted or allowed: Her rudeness is *impermissible.* **—im·per·mis′si·bly** *adv.*
im·per·son·al [im·pûr′sən·əl] *adj.* 1 Not being a person: the *impersonal* forces of nature. 2 Without reference to a particular person or persons: an *impersonal* observation. 3 In grammar, designating a verb having no specific subject. In "It will rain tonight," the verb *rain* is an impersonal verb. **—im·per′son·al·ly** *adv.*
im·per·son·ate [im·pûr′sən·āt′] *v.* **im·per·son·at·ed, im·per·son·at·ing** 1 To play the part of: The entire chorus *impersonates* pirates. 2 To adopt or mimic the appearance or mannerisms of: The child wore a uniform and badge to *impersonate* a police officer. **—im·per′son·a′tion** *n.*
im·per·son·a·tor [im·pûr′sən·ā′tər] *n.* 1 A person who pretends to be someone else. 2 An entertainer who imitates famous people.
im·per·ti·nence [im·pûr′tə·nəns] *n.* Deliberate disrespect; insolence; impudence.
im·per·ti·nent [im·pûr′tə·nənt] *adj.* Deliberately disrespectful; insolent; impudent: The *impertinent* child continued to make rude remarks.
im·per·turb·a·ble [im′pər·tûr′bə·bəl] *adj.* Almost never upset or excited; calm. **—im′per·turb′a·bly** *adv.*
im·per·vi·ous [im·pûr′vē·əs] *adj.* 1 Permitting no passage through or into: a hat *impervious* to rain. 2 Unreceptive or indifferent: to be *impervious* to reason. **—im·per′vi·ous·ness** *n.*
im·pe·ti·go [im′pə·tī′gō] *n.* A contagious skin disease marked by pimples filled with pus.
im·pet·u·os·i·ty [im·pech′o͞o·os′ə·tē] *n., pl.* **im·pet·u·**

I

a	add	**i**	it	**o͝o**	took	**oi**	oil
ā	ace	**ī**	ice	**o͞o**	pool	**ou**	pout
â	care	**o**	odd	**u**	up	**ng**	ring
ä	palm	**ō**	open	**û**	burn	**th**	thin
e	end	**ô**	order	**yo͞o**	fuse	**t͟h**	this
ē	equal					**zh**	vision

ə = a in *above* e in *sicken* i in *possible* o in *melon* u in *circus*

os·i·ties 1 The quality of being impetuous. 2 An impetuous act.

im·pet·u·ous [im·pech′ōō·əs] *adj.* 1 Acting on impulse and without thought; hasty; rash. 2 Moving with violent force: an *impetuous* storm. **—im·pet′u·ous·ly** *adv.*

im·pe·tus [im′pə·təs] *n.* 1 The force with which an object moves; momentum. 2 Any force that leads to action: Good grades can serve as an *impetus* to learning.

im·pi·e·ty [im·pī′ə·tē] *n., pl.* **im·pi·e·ties** 1 Lack of respect, especially for God or sacred things. 2 An impious act.

im·pinge [im·pinj′] *v.* **im·pinged, im·ping·ing** 1 To strike or collide: a beam of light *impinging* on the retina of the eye. 2 To intrude upon; encroach; infringe: to *impinge* on a teacher's authority.

im·pi·ous [im′pē·əs *or* im·pī′əs] *adj.* Lacking respect or reverence, as for God. **—im′pi·ous·ly** *adv.*

imp·ish [imp′ish] *adj.* Like an imp; full of mischief: an *impish* grin. **—imp′ish·ly** *adv.* **—imp′ish·ness** *n.*

im·pla·ca·ble [im·plā′kə·bəl *or* im·plak′ə·bəl] *adj.* Not capable of being pacified or soothed: *implacable* foes. **—im·pla′ca·bly** *adv.*

im·plant [*v.* im·plant′, *n.* im′plant′] 1 *v.* To plant firmly, as seeds in the ground; embed. 2 *v.* To fix in the mind: to *implant* new ideas. 3 *v.* To insert on or into the body, as a graft of living tissue, a medical device, or an artificial part. 4 *n.* Anything implanted. **—im′plant·a′tion** *n.*

im·plau·si·ble [im·plô′zə·bəl] *adj.* Not plausible; hard to believe: an *implausible* excuse.

im·ple·ment [*n.* im′plə·mənt, *v.* im′plə·ment′] 1 *n.* A thing used in work; utensil; tool. 2 *v.* To furnish with implements. 3 *v.* To put into effect; carry out; fulfill: to *implement* a tax reform law. **—im′ple·men·ta′tion** *n.*

im·pli·cate [im′plə·kāt′] *v.* **im·pli·cat·ed, im·pli·cat·ing** To show to be involved or connected, as in a plot or a crime: to be *implicated* in a robbery.

im·pli·ca·tion [im′plə·kā′shən] *n.* 1 The act of implicating. 2 The condition of being implicated. 3 The act of implying or suggesting. 4 Something that is implied: The *implication* was that I came late on purpose.

im·plic·it [im·plis′it] *adj.* 1 Absolute; complete: *implicit* confidence. 2 Implied, although not expressed: an *implicit* agreement. **—im·plic′it·ly** *adv.*

im·plode [im·plōd′] *v.* **im·plod·ed, im·plod·ing** To burst inward or undergo destructive compression. **—im·plo·sion** [im·plō′zhən] *n.*

im·plore [im·plôr′] *v.* **im·plored, im·plor·ing** 1 To beg; entreat; beseech: The prisoners *implored* their captors to free them. 2 To beg for urgently: I *implore* your mercy.

im·ply [im·plī′] *v.* **im·plied, im·ply·ing** To hint at or suggest without actually stating: Your silence *implied* approval. ◆ See INFER.

im·po·lite [im′pə·līt′] *adj.* Not polite; discourteous; rude. **—im′po·lite′ly** *adv.* **—im′po·lite′ness** *n.*

im·pol·i·tic [im·pol′ə·tik] *adj.* Not wise, prudent, or expedient: It is *impolitic* to offend one's employer.

im·pon·der·a·ble [im·pon′dər·ə·bəl] 1 *adj.* That cannot be estimated, evaluated, or weighed precisely. 2 *n.* Anything that is imponderable. **—im·pon′der·a·bly** *adv.*

im·port [*v.* im·pôrt′, *n.* im′pôrt′] 1 *v.* To bring into a country from abroad: The U.S. *imports* silk from Japan. 2 *n.* Something brought in from another country. 3 *n.* A bringing in from abroad; importation. 4 *v.* To have as its meaning: What did that remark *import*? 5 *n.* Meaning; significance. 6 *n.* Importance: a matter of no *import*.

im·por·tance [im·pôr′təns] *n.* A being important; significance; consequence.

im·por·tant [im·pôr′tənt] *adj.* 1 Having much significance, value, or influence: an *important* occasion. 2 Deserving special attention or notice: an *important* project. 3 Having power, authority, prestige, or high social rank: an *important* executive. 4 Giving the impression of importance; pretentious; pompous.

im·por·ta·tion [im′pôr·tā′shən] *n.* 1 The act of importing goods. 2 The goods imported.

im·port·er [im·pôr′tər] *n.* A person or company in the business of importing merchandise.

im·por·tu·nate [im·pôr′chə·nit] *adj.* 1 Asking or demanding again and again: an *importunate* beggar. 2 Made again and again, as a request.

im·por·tune [im′pôr·t(y)ōōn′ *or* im·pôr′chən] *v.* **im·por·tuned, im·por·tun·ing** To request or urge again and again.

im·por·tu·ni·ty [im′pôr·t(y)ōō′nə·tē] *n., pl.* **im·por·tu·ni·ties** An urging or requesting over and over again.

im·pose [im·pōz′] *v.* **im·posed, im·pos·ing** 1 To levy or exact: to *impose* taxes. 2 To inflict or enforce by influence or force: to *impose* one's wishes on others. 3 To take advantage; make unfair use: to *impose* on a friend by asking for too many favors. 4 To palm off as genuine.

im·pos·ing [im·pō′zing] *adj.* Impressive, as in appearance, manner, or size.

im·po·si·tion [im′pə·zish′ən] *n.* 1 A taking advantage of someone, as by asking for too great a favor. 2 The act of imposing or imposing on. 3 Something imposed, as a tax or punishment.

im·pos·si·bil·i·ty [im·pos′ə·bil′ə·tē] *n., pl.* **im·pos·si·bil·i·ties** 1 The condition of being impossible. 2 Something impossible.

im·pos·si·ble [im·pos′ə·bəl] *adj.* 1 Not capable of being, being done, or taking place; not possible: It is *impossible* to be in two places at the same time. 2 Not to be endured; intolerable: an *impossible* situation. **—im·pos′si·bly** *adv.*

im·post [im′pōst′] *n.* A tax, especially a tax on things imported into a country.

im·pos·tor [im·pos′tər] *n.* A person who deceives, especially one who pretends to be someone else.

im·pos·ture [im·pos′chər] *n.* Deception, especially the act of pretending to be someone else.

im·po·tent [im′pə·tənt] *adj.* Lacking power or strength; helpless; weak. **—im′po·tence** *n.*

im·pound [im·pound′] *v.* 1 To shut up in a pound, as a stray dog. 2 To seize and place in the custody of a court: to *impound* a company's files pending an investigation.

im·pov·er·ish [im·pov′ər·ish] *v.* 1 To make poor: Business losses *impoverished* me. 2 To take away the richness or strength of; make infertile, as the soil. **—im·pov′er·ish·ment** *n.*

im·prac·ti·ca·ble [im·prak′ti·kə·bəl] *adj.* 1 Not capable of being carried out: *impracticable* schemes. 2 Not suitable for use. **—im·prac′ti·ca·bil′i·ty** *n.*

im·prac·ti·cal [im·prak′ti·kəl] *adj.* Not practical; not useful or sensible.

im·pre·ca·tion [im′prə·kā′shən] *n.* 1 The act of cursing. 2 A curse.

im·pre·cise [im′pri·sīs′] *adj.* Not precise or definite; unclear; vague. **—im′pre·cise′ly** *adv.*

im·preg·na·ble [im·preg′nə·bəl] *adj.* Not capable of being conquered or overcome; unassailable: an *impregnable* defense.

im·preg·nate [im·preg′nāt′] *v.* **im·preg·nat·ed, im·preg·nat·ing** 1 To make pregnant or fertile. 2 To saturate or fill: Pickles are *impregnated* with brine. **—im′preg·na′tion** *n.*

im·pre·sa·ri·o [im′prə·sä′rē·ō] *n., pl.* **im·pre·sa·ri·os** A person who manages a performer or performance, especially one who directs an opera or ballet company.

im·press[1] [*v.* im·pres′, *n.* im′pres] 1 *v.* To affect the mind or feelings of: Your sincerity *impressed* me. 2 *n.* An effect on the mind or feelings; impression. 3 *v.* To fix firmly in the mind, as ideas or beliefs: to *impress* a fact on one's memory. 4 *v.* To make (a mark) by pressure; stamp: to *impress* the title in gold on the spine of a book. 5 *n.* A mark made by pressing or stamping. 6 *n.* Distinctive character or mark: The author's *impress* shows in every line of this book.

im·press[2] [im·pres′] *v.* 1 To compel to enter public service: to *impress* citizens into the navy. 2 To seize (property) for public use.

im·pres·sion [im·presh′ən] *n.* 1 An effect on the mind, senses, or feelings. 2 A feeling, notion, or idea: I got the *impression* that you were displeased. 3 Any mark made by pressing: the *impression* of a hand. 4 The act of impressing.

im·pres·sion·a·ble [im·presh′ən·ə·bəl] *adj.* Quickly and easily influenced; sensitive: an *impressionable* young student.

im·pres·sion·ism or **Im·pres·sion·ism** [im·presh′·ən·iz′əm] *n.* 1 A style of painting popular in the late 19th century that depicts its subject matter by using small strokes of paint in order to simulate real reflected light. 2 A musical style of the same period in which impressions and moods are created by rich harmonies and varied rhythms. **—im·pres′sion·ist** *n.* **—im·pres′sion·is′tic** *adj.*

Impressionism

im·pres·sive [im·pres′iv] *adj.* Producing a strong impression of admiration or awe: an *impressive* conductor; an *impressive* accomplishment. **—im·pres′sive·ly** *adv.*

im·pri·ma·tur [im′prə·mä′tər *or* im·prim′ə·to͝or] *n.* 1 Official permission to publish something, especially under conditions of censorship. 2 Any authoritative approval.

im·print [*v.* im·print′, *n.* im′print′] 1 *v.* To make (a mark, figure, or the like) by pressure. 2 *n.* A mark made by printing, stamping, or pressing: the *imprint* of a boot in the snow. 3 *v.* To fix firmly or impress, as in the mind: The final scene in the play is *imprinted* in my memory. 4 *n.* An effect or influence: the *imprint* of suffering. 5 *n.* A publisher's or printer's name, place of business, and other information, on the title page of a book.

im·pris·on [im·priz′(ə)n] *v.* 1 To put into prison. 2 To shut in closely; confine. **—im·pris′on·ment** *n.*

im·prob·a·ble [im·prob′ə·bəl] *adj.* Not probable; not likely to be true or to happen: an *improbable* excuse. **—im′prob·a·bil′i·ty** *n.* **—im·prob′a·bly** *adv.*

im·promp·tu [im·promp′t(y)o͞o] 1 *adj.* Not prepared in advance; offhand: *impromptu* remarks. 2 *adv.* Without preparation: to speak *impromptu.* 3 *n.* Anything produced on the impulse of the moment.

im·prop·er [im·prop′ər] *adj.* 1 Not in accord with accepted standards of behavior or good taste: It is *improper* to shout on a bus. 2 Incorrect: an *improper* address. **—im·prop′er·ly** *adv.*

improper fraction A fraction in which the numerator is larger than or equal to the denominator, as 4/3 or 5/5.

im·pro·pri·e·ty [im′prə·prī′ə·tē] *n., pl.* **im·pro·pri·e·ties** 1 The quality of being improper. 2 Something improper, as an exhibition of bad taste. 3 An error in speech or writing.

im·prove [im·pro͞ov′] *v.* **im·proved, im·prov·ing** 1 To make or become better, as in condition, quality, or value. 2 To use to good purpose: to *improve* one's leisure time.

im·prove·ment [im·pro͞ov′mənt] *n.* 1 The act of making better. 2 A becoming better. 3 Something that increases value or efficiency. 4 A person or thing superior to another: This report is an *improvement* over the first one you wrote.

im·prov·i·dent [im·prov′ə·dənt] *adj.* Not planning for the future; lacking foresight or thrift. **—im·prov′i·dence** *n.*

im·pro·vi·sa·tion [im·prov′ə·zā′shən] *n.* 1 The act of improvising. 2 Something improvised.

im·pro·vise [im′prə·vīz′] *v.* **im·pro·vised, im·pro·vis·ing** 1 To make up (music, verse, or a speech) at the time of performance and without preparation. 2 To make offhand from whatever material is available: to *improvise* a shelter from old boards.

An improvised bench

im·pru·dent [im·pro͞od′·(ə)nt] *adj.* Not prudent; lacking foresight; unwise. **—im·pru′dence** *n.* **—im·pru′dent·ly** *adv.*

im·pu·dence [im′pyə·dəns] *n.* Offensive boldness; lack of shame; rudeness.

im·pu·dent [im′pyə·dənt] *adj.* Offensively bold; rude; insolent. **—im′pu·dent·ly** *adv.*

im·pugn [im·pyo͞on′] *v.* To attack with criticism; call into question: Do you *impugn* my honesty?

im·pulse [im′puls] *n.* 1 A sudden desire or feeling which makes one want to act: an *impulse* of pity. 2 A driving force; push; thrust: the *impulse* of a strong wind. 3 The transference of a stimulus through a nerve fiber. 4 In radio and electricity, a pulse.

a	add	**i**	it	**o͝o**	took	**oi**	oil
ā	ace	**ī**	ice	**o͞o**	pool	**ou**	pout
â	care	**o**	odd	**u**	up	**ng**	ring
ä	palm	**ō**	open	**û**	burn	**th**	thin
e	end	**ô**	order	**yo͞o**	fuse	**t̶h̶**	this
ē	equal					**zh**	vision

ə = { a in *above* e in *sicken* i in *possible* / o in *melon* u in *circus* }

im·pul·sive [im·pul′siv] *adj.* 1 Acting suddenly and without careful thought: The *impulsive* shopper bought six new shirts. 2 Prompted by impulse: an *impulsive* act. 3 Having the power to impel or drive. **—im·pul′sive·ly** *adv.* **—im·pul′sive·ness** *n.*

im·pu·ni·ty [im·pyōō′nə·tē] *n.* Freedom from punishment or harmful result: You cannot neglect school work with *impunity.*

im·pure [im·pyŏŏr′] *adj.* 1 Not pure or clean. 2 Containing some foreign or less valuable substance; adulterated: *impure* copper. 3 Immoral; immodest; sinful.

im·pu·ri·ty [im·pyŏŏr′ə·tē] *n., pl.* **im·pu·ri·ties** 1 The condition of being impure. 2 Something that is impure or makes impure: *impurities* in the air.

im·pu·ta·tion [im′pyōō·tā′shən] *n.* 1 The charging of a wrongdoing or fault to someone; accusation. 2 Something imputed; slur.

im·pute [im·pyōōt′] *v.* **im·put·ed, im·put·ing** To lay the blame or responsibility for; blame: to *impute* the failure to someone.

in [in] 1 *adv.* From the outside to the inside: Come *in.* 2 *prep.* Into: Get *in* the car. 3 *adv.* At home, indoors, or inside a place: On rainy weekends we stay *in.* 4 *adj.* Being within or leading toward the inside: the *in* door. 5 *prep.* Held by or found within: a child *in* my arms. 6 *prep.* Surrounded by: buried *in* the mud. 7 *prep.* Within the range or limits of: *in* my hearing; *in* the city. 8 *prep.* Belonging to: *in* the navy. 9 *adv.* In or into some activity or place: to join *in*; to move *in.* 10 *n.* (*pl.*) The group in public office or in power. 11 *adj.* Having power or status: the *in* group. 12 *n. informal* A position of favor or influence: to have an *in* with the boss. 13 *prep. U.S.* At or before the end of: I'll come *in* a minute. 14 *prep.* During: *in* the evening. 15 *prep.* Wearing: an officer *in* a hat. 16 *prep.* Experiencing or showing the effects of: *in* doubt; *in* tears. 17 *prep.* Arranged or proceeding so as to form: *in* a row; to go *in* circles. 18 *prep.* Engaged at: *in* business. 19 *prep.* For the purpose of: to run *in* pursuit. 20 *prep.* By means of: to draw *in* crayon. 21 *prep.* According to: *in* my opinion. 22 *prep.* Regarding: I have faith *in* your ability. **—in for** *informal* Certain to experience: You're *in for* trouble. **—ins and outs** All the details and particulars. **—in that** Because.

in-[1] A prefix meaning: 1 In, as in *inhabit.* 2 Into, as in *inflammable.* 3 Within, as in *indoors.* 4 Toward, as in *inshore.* 5 On, as in *inscribe.* ◆ See EN-.

in-[2] A prefix meaning: Not, as in *insane.* ◆ See UN-.

in. inch(es).

In The symbol for the element indium.

IN Postal Service abbreviation of Indiana.

in·a·bil·i·ty [in′ə·bil′ə·tē] *n.* The condition of being unable; lack of means or power.

in·ac·ces·si·ble [in′ak·ses′ə·bəl] *adj.* Not possible or not easy to reach or approach.

in·ac·cu·ra·cy [in·ak′yər·ə·sē] *n., pl.* **in·ac·cu·ra·cies** 1 The condition of being inaccurate. 2 An error.

in·ac·cu·rate [in·ak′yər·it] *adj.* Not accurate; incorrect. **—in·ac′cu·rate·ly** *adv.*

in·ac·tion [in·ak′shən] *n.* Lack of action.

in·ac·tive [in·ak′tiv] *adj.* Not active or in use; idle; inert. **—in·ac′tive·ly** *adv.*

in·ac·tiv·i·ty [in′ak·tiv′ə·tē] *n.* Absence of activity or movement; inertia.

in·ad·e·qua·cy [in·ad′ə·kwə·sē] *n., pl.* **in·ad·e·qua·cies** 1 A being inadequate; insufficiency. 2 A defect.

in·ad·e·quate [in·ad′ə·kwit] *adj.* Less than is needed or required; not adequate. **—in·ad′e·quate·ly** *adv.*

in·ad·mis·si·ble [in′əd·mis′ə·bəl] *adj.* Not to be considered, approved, or allowed; not admissible: Such evidence is *inadmissible* in a court of law.

in·ad·ver·tent [in′əd·vûr′tənt] *adj.* Unintentional: an *inadvertent* snub. **—in·ad·ver′tence** *n.* **—in′ad·ver′tent·ly** *adv.*

in·ad·vis·a·ble [in′əd·vī′zə·bəl] *adj.* Not advisable; unwise. **—in′ad·vis′a·bly** *adv.*

in·al·ien·a·ble [in·āl′yən·ə·bəl] *adj.* That cannot be taken away or transferred: the *inalienable* rights of a citizen. **—in·al′ien·a·bly** *adv.*

in·ane [in·ān′] *adj.* Senseless; silly: an *inane* remark. **—in·ane′ly** *adv.*

in·an·i·mate [in·an′ə·mit] *adj.* 1 Lacking life; lifeless: A chair is an *inanimate* object. 2 Without spirit; dull: *inanimate* talk.

in·an·i·ty [in·an′ə·tē] *n., pl.* **in·an·i·ties** 1 Foolishness; silliness. 2 Something foolish, as a remark or action. 3 Emptiness.

in·ap·pli·ca·ble [in·ap′li·kə·bəl] *adj.* Not suitable or applicable; irrelevant.

in·ap·pre·cia·ble [in′ə·prē′shə·bəl] *adj.* Too small or slight to be noticed; negligible. **—in′ap·pre′cia·bly** *adv.*

in·ap·pro·pri·ate [in′ə·prō′prē·it] *adj.* Not right, proper, or suitable.

in·apt [in·apt′] *adj.* 1 Not suitable or to the point: an *inapt* remark. 2 Clumsy or lacking skill. **—in·apt′ly** *adv.* **—in·apt′ness** *n.*

in·ap·ti·tude [in·ap′tə·t(y)ōōd′] *n.* 1 Lack of skill. 2 Lack of fitness or suitability.

in·ar·tic·u·late [in′är·tik′yə·lit] *adj.* 1 Uttered but not in distinct sounds of spoken language: an *inarticulate* moan. 2 Not able to speak; mute. 3 Not able to express oneself fully or clearly. 4 Not segmented or jointed, as certain worms. **—in′ar·tic′u·late·ly** *adv.*

in·ar·tis·tic [in′är·tis′tik] *adj.* Not artistic, as in skill, taste, or execution. **—in′ar·tis′ti·cal·ly** *adv.*

in·as·much as [in′əz·much′] 1 Seeing that; since; because: We left early *inasmuch as* we had to be home for dinner. 2 In so far as; as much as: *Inasmuch as* the children are able, let them help.

in·at·ten·tion [in′ə·ten′shən] *n.* Lack of attention; carelessness.

in·at·ten·tive [in′ə·ten′tiv] *adj.* Not paying attention. **—in′at·ten′tive·ly** *adv.*

in·au·di·ble [in·ô′də·bəl] *adj.* Incapable of being heard. **—in·au′di·bly** *adv.*

in·au·gu·ral [in·ô′gyər·əl] 1 *adj.* Of or having to do with an inauguration. 2 *n.* An inaugural address, especially by a president.

in·au·gu·rate [in·ô′gyə·rāt′] *v.* **in·au·gu·rat·ed, in·au·gu·rat·ing** 1 To install in an office with a formal ceremony: to *inaugurate* a president. 2 To commence or begin: to *inaugurate* important changes. 3 To celebrate the public opening or first use of: to *inaugurate* a bridge.

in·au·gu·ra·tion [in·ô′gyə·rā′shən] *n.* 1 A ceremony installing a person in an office: a president's *inauguration.* 2 The act of inaugurating.

in·aus·pi·cious [in′ô·spish′əs] *adj.* Not favorable or lucky. **—in′aus·pi′cious·ly** *adv.*

in-be·tween [in′bi·twēn′] *adj.* Being or coming between: My father is at an *in-between* age, neither young nor old.

in·board [in′bôrd′] **1** *adj.* In ships and boats, within the hull. **2** *adj.* In aircraft, near the fuselage. **3** *adv.* Within the hull, as of a ship: to load freight *inboard.*

in·born [in′bôrn′] *adj.* That seems to have existed from birth; natural: an *inborn* trait.

in·bound [in′bound′] *adj.* Coming in; bound for home: an *inbound* airplane.

in·bred [in′bred′] **1** Past tense and past participle of INBREED. **2** *adj.* Inborn. **3** *adj.* Produced by inbreeding.

in·breed [in′brēd′] *v.* **in·bred, in·breed·ing** To breed (new animals) by mating animals that are closely related.

inc. **1** income. **2** incomplete. **3** (*often written* **Inc.**) incorporated. **4** increase.

In·ca [ing′kə] *n., pl.* **In·ca** or **In·cas** A member of a very advanced group of Indian tribes which ruled Peru at the time of the Spanish conquest. —**In′·can** *adj., n.*

in·cal·cu·la·ble [in·kal′kyə·lə·bəl] *adj.* **1** Too numerous or great to be calculated. **2** That cannot be predicted; uncertain. —**in·cal′cu·la·bly** *adv.*

in·can·des·cent [in′kən·des′ənt] *adj.* **1** Hot enough to give off light. **2** Very bright; brilliant. —**in′can·des′cence** *n.*

incandescent lamp A type of lamp in which an electric current heats a small wire or filament until it gives off light.

Incandescent lamp

in·can·ta·tion [in′kan·tā′shən] *n.* **1** The uttering of words or syllables supposed to produce magical results. **2** Such words or syllables.

in·ca·pa·ble [in·kā′pə·bəl] *adj.* Lacking the necessary ability, skill, or capacity: an *incapable* driver. —**incapable of** Not open or susceptible to: a problem *incapable of* solution.

in·ca·pac·i·tate [in′kə·pas′ə·tāt′] *v.* **in·ca·pac·i·tat·ed, in·ca·pac·i·tat·ing** To make unfit, especially for normal physical activity; disable: *incapacitated* with a broken back.

in·ca·pac·i·ty [in′kə·pas′ə·tē] *n., pl.* **in·ca·pac·i·ties** A lack of ability, power, or fitness.

in·cap·su·late [in·kap′sə·lāt′] *v.* **in·cap·su·lat·ed, in·cap·su·lat·ing** Another spelling of ENCAPSULATE.

in·car·cer·ate [in·kär′sə·rāt′] *v.* **in·car·cer·at·ed, in·car·cer·at·ing** To put in prison; imprison. —**in·car′·cer·a′tion** *n.*

in·car·nate [*adj.* in·kär′nit *or* in·kär′nāt′, *v.* in·kär′·nāt′] *adj., v.* **in·car·nat·ed, in·car·nat·ing** **1** *adj.* Having a body, especially a human body: a god *incarnate.* **2** *adj.* Appearing or being represented in some recognizable form or shape: The tyrant is cruelty *incarnate.* **3** *v.* To represent in some concrete form or shape: to *incarnate* one's hopes in a picture. **4** *v.* To be a type or example of; typify: Joan of Arc *incarnated* saintly courage.

in·car·na·tion [in′kär·nā′shən] *n.* **1** A taking on of human form. **2** (*written* **Incarnation**) The taking on of a human form by Jesus. **3** A person or thing that is an example or symbol of some quality or idea: Hitler was an *incarnation* of evil tyranny.

in·case [in·kās′] *v.* **in·cased, in·cas·ing** Another spelling of ENCASE.

in·cau·tious [in·kô′shəs] *adj.* Not cautious; reckless; heedless; careless. —**in·cau′tious·ly** *adv.* —**in·cau′tious·ness** *n.*

in·cen·di·ar·y [in·sen′dē·er′ē] *adj., n., pl.* **in·cen·di·ar·ies** **1** *adj.* Of or having to do with the malicious burning of property. **2** *n.* A person who maliciously sets fire to property. **3** *adj.* Causing or producing fire: an *incendiary* bomb. **4** *adj.* Stirring up trouble, rebellion, or the like: an *incendiary* speech.

in·cense[1] [in′sens′] *n.* **1** A substance that gives off a fragrant odor when burned. **2** The odor or smoke produced in burning it. **3** Any pleasing odor: the *incense* of lilacs.

in·cense[2] [in·sens′] *v.* **in·censed, in·cens·ing** To make angry; enrage: We were *incensed* at having to wait in line for two hours.

in·cen·tive [in·sen′tiv] *n.* Something that makes a person want to work or put forth effort: an *incentive* to study.

in·cep·tion [in·sep′shən] *n.* A beginning; start; origin: the *inception* of a new business.

in·ces·sant [in·ses′ənt] *adj.* Not ceasing; continuing without letup: *incessant* noise. —**in·ces′sant·ly** *adv.*

in·cest [in′sest′] *n.* Sexual intercourse between persons so closely related that marriage between them is forbidden by law.

in·ces·tu·ous [in·ses′chōō·əs] *adj.* **1** Having to do with or involving incest. **2** Having committed incest. —**in·ces′tu·ous·ly** *adv.*

inch [inch] **1** *n.* A measure of length equal to 1/12 of a foot. **2** *n.* A very small bit or amount: Neither runner could gain an *inch* on the other. **3** *v.* To move a very short distance at a time: The worm *inched* along the leaf. —**by inches** or **inch by inch** Very slowly; bit by bit. —**every inch** In every way; completely: *every inch* a champion. —**within an inch of** Exceedingly close to: *within an inch* of death. ◆ *Inch* comes from a Latin word meaning *inch, ounce,* or *the twelfth part*—in other words, a basic unit of measurement. It goes back to the Latin *unus,* which means one.

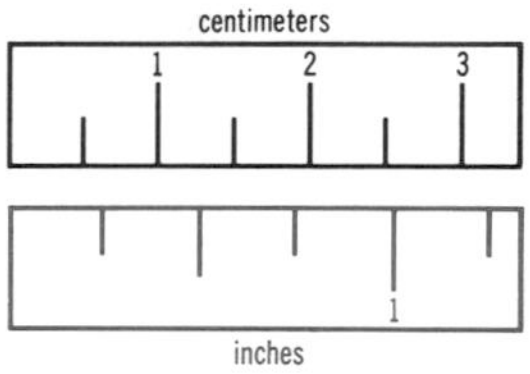

in·cho·ate [in·kō′it] *adj.* In the first stages; not yet fully developed or realized: *inchoate* theories about space.

inch·worm [inch′wûrm′] *n.* A worm, the larva of a moth, that moves by bringing its rear end forward and arching its back up in the middle, then moving its front end forward.

in·ci·dence [in′sə·dəns] *n.* **1** The rate or degree of occurrence or effect: a high *incidence* of crime. **2** The striking of a surface, as by a body or by radiation.

in·ci·dent [in′sə·dənt] **1** *n.* An event, often one of little importance. **2** *adj.* Naturally or usually

a	add	**i**	it	**o͝o**	took	**oi**	oil
ā	ace	**ī**	ice	**ōō**	pool	**ou**	pout
â	care	**o**	odd	**u**	up	**ng**	ring
ä	palm	**ō**	open	**û**	burn	**th**	thin
e	end	**ô**	order	**yōō**	fuse	**t͟h**	this
ē	equal					**zh**	vision

ə = {a in *above* e in *sicken* i in *possible*; o in *melon* u in *circus*}

belonging or having to do with: the dangers *incident* to flying.

in·ci·den·tal [in′sə·den′təl] 1 *adj.* Happening by chance or in the course of something else: an *incidental* remark. 2 *adj.* Naturally or usually belonging or having to do with: problems *incidental* to adolescence. 3 *n.* (*pl.*) Minor items or costs.

in·ci·den·tal·ly [in′sə·den′təl·ē] *adv.* 1 As a secondary, casual, or chance occurrence along with something else: The book *incidentally* contains some historical data. 2 By the way: *Incidentally,* where were you last night?

in·cin·er·ate [in·sin′ə·rāt′] *v.* **in·cin·er·at·ed, in·cin·er·at·ing** To burn to ashes. **—in·cin′er·a′tion** *n.*

in·cin·er·a·tor [in·sin′ə·rā′tər] *n.* A furnace for burning rubbish or waste.

in·cip·i·ent [in·sip′ē·ənt] *adj.* Just beginning; not fully developed: an *incipient* sore throat.

in·cise [in·sīz′] *v.* **in·cised, in·cis·ing** 1 To cut into with a sharp instrument. 2 To make by cutting; engrave: to *incise* a design.

in·ci·sion [in·sizh′ən] *n.* 1 A cut or gash, especially one made in surgery. 2 The act of incising.

in·ci·sive [in·sī′siv] *adj.* Sharp; keen; penetrating: *incisive* wit. **—in·ci′sive·ly** *adv.* **—in·ci′sive·ness** *n.*

in·ci·sor [in·sī′zər] *n.* A front tooth with a sharp edge for cutting. Humans have eight incisors, the front four upper and lower teeth.

in·cite [in·sīt′] *v.* **in·cit·ed, in·cit·ing** To stir up; rouse to action.

in·cite·ment [in·sīt′mənt] *n.* 1 The act of inciting or stirring up; rousing to action. 2 Something that incites or stirs up.

in·ci·vil·i·ty [in′sə·vil′ə·tē] *n., pl.* **in·ci·vil·i·ties** 1 Rudeness. 2 A rude act or remark.

incl. including.

in·clem·en·cy [in·klem′ən·sē] *n., pl.* **in·clem·en·cies** Severity; cruelty; harshness.

in·clem·ent [in·klem′ənt] *adj.* 1 Stormy; bad: said about the weather. 2 Without mercy; harsh. **—in·clem′ent·ly** *adv.*

in·cli·na·tion [in′klə·nā′shən] *n.* 1 A personal liking or preference: an *inclination* for study. 2 A tendency: the *inclination* of prices to rise. 3 A slant or slope: the *inclination* of a roof. 4 A bending or bowing: a slight *inclination* of the head.

in·cline [*v.* in·klīn′, *n.* in′klīn′ *or* in·klīn′] *v.* **in·clined, in·clin·ing,** *n.* 1 *v.* To lean; slant; slope: The land *inclined* gently to the sea. 2 *n.* A sloping surface; slope: a steep *incline.* 3 *v.* To bend or bow: to *incline* the head. 4 *v.* To have a preference or tendency: The children *incline* to talk a great deal.

in·clined [in·klīnd′] *adj.* 1 Having a preference or tendency. 2 Slanting or sloped.

inclined plane A plane surface, as a plank or track, set at an oblique angle with the horizontal plane. It is used for raising heavy objects.

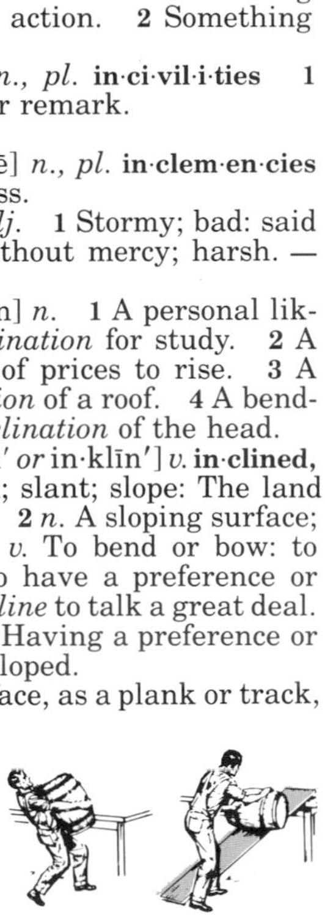

It is much harder to lift the barrel than to roll it up an inclined plane.

in·cli·nom·e·ter [in′klə·nom′i·tər] *n.* 1 An instrument for measuring the angle that the magnetic field of the earth makes with any specific point on the horizon. 2 An instrument for showing how much a ship or aircraft is inclined away from the horizon. 3 Any of various instruments for measuring angles of inclination.

in·close [in·klōz′] *v.* Another spelling of ENCLOSE.

in·clo·sure [in·klō′zhər] *n.* Another spelling of ENCLOSURE.

in·clude [in·klo͞od′] *v.* **in·clud·ed, in·clud·ing** 1 To put, shut up, or enclose: *Include* your address. 2 To hold or contain as a part or parts: The area *includes* many lakes. 3 To put into a group, total, or reckoning. ◆ When precisely used, *include* precedes an incomplete rather than a complete list: The southern states *include* Alabama and Georgia.

in·clu·sion [in·klo͞o′zhən] *n.* 1 The act of including. 2 The condition of being included. 3 Something included.

in·clu·sive [in·klo͞o′siv] *adj.* Including, especially including the limits specified or mentioned: Lincoln was president from 1861 to 1865 *inclusive,* a period of five years. **—in·clu′sive·ly** *adv.*

incog. incognito.

in·cog·ni·to [in·kog′nə·tō *or* in′kog·nē′tō] *adv., adj., n., pl.* **in·cog·ni·tos** 1 *adv., adj.* Under an assumed name or identity; in disguise: to travel *incognito;* to be *incognito.* 2 *n.* The condition of being incognito. 3 *n.* A person who is incognito. 4 *n.* An assumed name.

in·co·her·ent [in′kō·hir′ənt] *adj.* 1 Not clear; confused; disjointed: *incoherent* talk. 2 Not sticking together; loose: an *incoherent* mass. **—in′co·her′ence** *n.* **—in′co·her′ent·ly** *adv.*

in·com·bus·ti·ble [in′kəm·bus′tə·bəl] 1 *adj.* Not capable of being burned; fireproof. 2 *n.* A substance that cannot burn: Asbestos is an *incombustible.* **—in′com·bus′ti·bil′i·ty** *n.*

in·come [in′kum′] *n.* Money received by a person in return for labor, services, investment, or rental of property.

income tax A yearly tax on a person's income.

in·com·ing [in′kum′ing] 1 *adj.* Coming in or about to come in: *incoming* ships. 2 *n.* Entrance or arrival: the *incoming* of the tide.

in·com·men·su·rate [in′kə·men′shər·it] *adj.* 1 Not matched or on a par: a salary *incommensurate* with the job. 2 Not having a common measure or standard of comparison: Inches and ounces are *incommensurate.*

in·com·mode [in′kə·mōd′] *v.* **in·com·mod·ed, in·com·mod·ing** To bother or disturb.

in·com·mu·ni·ca·ble [in′kə·myo͞o′ni·kə·bəl] *adj.* That can't be communicated or passed on: an *incommunicable* disease; *incommunicable* secrets.

in·com·mu·ni·ca·do [in′kə·myo͞o′nə·kä′dō] *adv., adj.* Shut off from communication with anyone: The suspect was arrested and held *incommunicado.*

in·com·pa·ra·ble [in·kom′pər·ə·bəl] *adj.* 1 That can't be equaled or surpassed; matchless: Homer was an *incomparable* poet. 2 That can't be compared. **—in·com′pa·ra·bly** *adv.*

in·com·pat·i·ble [in′kəm·pat′ə·bəl] *adj.* 1 Not able to agree or get along well together: an *incompatible* couple. 2 Not able to exist together or be combined logically or harmoniously: *incompatible* colors. **—in·com·pat·i·bil·i·ty** [in′kəm·pat′ə·bil′ə·tē] *n.*

in·com·pe·tent [in·kom′pə·tənt] 1 *adj.* Lacking ability or skill; not competent. 2 *adj.* Not legally qualified: an *incompetent* witness. 3 *n.* A person who is incompetent. **—in·com′pe·tence** *n.* **—in·com′pe·tent·ly** *adv.*

in·com·plete [in′kəm·plēt′] *adj.* Not complete; un-

finished or imperfect: an *incomplete* song; *incomplete* growth. **—in'com·plete'ly** *adv.*
in·com·pre·hen·si·ble [in'kom·pri·hen'sə·bəl] *adj.* Incapable of being understood. **—in'com·pre·hen'·si·bly** *adv.*
in·com·pre·hen·sion [in'kom·pri·hen'shən] *n.* Failure to understand; lack of comprehension.
in·com·press·i·ble [in'kəm·pres'ə·bəl] *adj.* That cannot be compressed.
in·con·ceiv·a·ble [in'kən·sē'və·bəl] *adj.* Impossible to imagine or believe; unthinkable. **—in'con·ceiv'·a·bly** *adv.*
in·con·clu·sive [in'kən·klōō'siv] *adj.* Not leading to a conclusion or result: *inconclusive* evidence. **—in'·con·clu'sive·ly** *adv.* **—in'con·clu'sive·ness** *n.*
in·con·gru·i·ty [in'kən·grōō'ə·tē] *n., pl.* **in·con·gru·i·ties** 1 The condition of being incongruous. 2 Something incongruous.
in·con·gru·ous [in·kong'grōō·əs] *adj.* 1 Not suitable or appropriate: A tugboat is *incongruous* among sleek yachts. 2 Not consistent or harmonious. **—in·con'gru·ous·ly** *adv.*
in·con·se·quence [in·kon'sə·kwens'] *n.* The state or quality of being inconsequential.
in·con·se·quen·tial [in·kon'sə·kwen'shəl] *adj.* 1 Unimportant; minor. 2 Not following logically; irrelevant. **—in·con'se·quen'tial·ly** *adv.*
in·con·sid·er·a·ble [in'kən·sid'ər·ə·bəl] *adj.* Not worth considering; insignificant.
in·con·sid·er·ate [in'kən·sid'ər·it] *adj.* Lacking concern for the rights and feelings of others.
in·con·sis·ten·cy [in'kən·sis'tən·sē] *n., pl.* **in·con·sis·ten·cies** 1 The condition of being inconsistent. 2 Something that is inconsistent.
in·con·sis·tent [in'kən·sis'tənt] *adj.* 1 Not in agreement or harmony; contrary: Your words are *inconsistent* with your actions. 2 Not always the same in behavior or thought; changeable: an *inconsistent* person. **—in'con·sis'tent·ly** *adv.*
in·con·sol·a·ble [in'kən·sō'lə·bəl] *adj.* Not to be comforted or cheered; broken-hearted. **—in'con·sol'a·bly** *adv.*
in·con·spic·u·ous [in'kən·spik'yōō·əs] *adj.* Not very noticeable; not attracting attention. **—in'con·spic'·u·ous·ly** *adv.*
in·con·stan·cy [in·kon'stən·sē] *n.* Fickleness.
in·con·stant [in·kon'stənt] *adj.* Changeable; fickle: an *inconstant* friend.
in·con·test·a·ble [in'kən·tes'tə·bəl] *adj.* That cannot be disputed or questioned. **—in'con·test'a·bly** *adv.*
in·con·ti·nent [in·kon'tə·nənt] *adj.* Having no self-control or restraint: an *incontinent* eater. **—in·con'·ti·nence** *n.*
in·con·tro·vert·i·ble [in'kon·trə·vûr'tə·bəl] *adj.* Undeniable. **—in'con·tro·vert'i·bly** *adv.*
in·con·ven·ience [in'kən·vēn'yəns] *n., v.* **in·con·ven·ienced, in·con·ven·ienc·ing** 1 *n.* Trouble or bother: the *inconvenience* of a traffic jam. 2 *n.* Something that is inconvenient; trouble or bother. 3 *v.* To trouble or bother.
in·con·ven·ient [in'kən·vēn'yənt] *adj.* Troublesome or bothersome: to make a call at an *inconvenient* time. **—in'con·ven'ient·ly** *adv.*
in·cor·po·rate [in·kôr'pə·rāt'] *v.* **in·cor·po·rat·ed, in·cor·po·rat·ing** 1 To take in or include as a part of something else: The scientist *incorporated* the latest laboratory findings in a report. 2 To form into or become a corporation. 3 To combine or merge into something larger, as an organization or plan: All the small groups were *incorporated* into one large fellowship. **—in·cor'po·ra'tion** *n.*
in·cor·po·re·al [in'kôr·pôr'ē·əl] *adj.* Not consisting of or made of matter; spiritual.
in·cor·rect [in'kə·rekt'] *adj.* Not correct, proper, true, or suitable: an *incorrect* answer; *incorrect* behavior. **—in'cor·rect'ly** *adv.*
in·cor·ri·gi·ble [in·kôr'ə·jə·bəl] 1 *adj.* That cannot be corrected, improved, or reformed: an *incorrigible* thief. 2 *n.* An incorrigible person.
in·cor·rupt·i·ble [in'kə·rup'tə·bəl] *adj.* 1 That cannot be bribed; steadfastly honest: an *incorruptible* judge. 2 That cannot decay: It is built of hard, *incorruptible* stone.
in·crease [*v.* in·krēs', *n.* in'krēs'] *v.* **in·creased, in·creas·ing,** *n.* 1 *v.* To make or become greater or larger: *Increase* the number of exercises you do; The population *increases* daily. 2 *n.* A growing or becoming greater, as in size or amount. 3 *n.* The amount added by an increase. **—on the increase** Increasing; growing.
in·creas·ing·ly [in·krēs'ing·lē] *adv.* To an increasing degree; more and more.
in·cred·i·ble [in·kred'ə·bəl] *adj.* So strange, unusual, or extraordinary as to be unbelievable: an *incredible* tale. **—in·cred'i·bly** *adv.*
in·cre·du·li·ty [in'krə·d(y)ōō'lə·tē] *n.* Doubt; disbelief.
in·cred·u·lous [in·krej'ə·ləs] *adj.* Feeling, having, or showing doubt or disbelief: an *incredulous* person; an *incredulous* look. **—in·cred'u·lous·ly** *adv.*
in·cre·ment [in'krə·mənt] *n.* 1 An increase or addition: an *increment* in one's salary. 2 The amount by which a quantity increases: an *increment* of $40.
in·crim·i·nate [in·krim'ə·nāt'] *v.* **in·crim·i·nat·ed, in·crim·i·nat·ing** To declare or show to be guilty: Fingerprints at the scene of a crime can *incriminate* a suspect. **—in·crim'i·na'tion** *n.*
in·crust [in·krust'] *v.* Another spelling of ENCRUST.
in·cu·bate [in(g)'kyə·bāt'] *v.* **in·cu·bat·ed, in·cu·bat·ing** 1 To hatch (eggs) by sitting on them. 2 To hatch (eggs) in an incubator. 3 To grow or develop gradually, as a plan or idea. **—in'cu·ba'tion** *n.*
in·cu·ba·tor [in(g)'kyə·bā'tər] *n.* 1 A container in which eggs are hatched artificially. It is kept at a warm temperature. 2 A container for keeping warm a prematurely born baby.

Incubator

in·cu·bus [in(g)'kyə·bəs] *n., pl.* **in·cu·bus·es** or **in·cu·bi** [in(g)'kyə·bī] 1 A nightmare. 2 Anything that tends to oppress or discourage.

a	add	**i**	it	**o͝o**	took	**oi**	oil
ā	ace	**ī**	ice	**ōō**	pool	**ou**	pout
â	care	**o**	odd	**u**	up	**ng**	ring
ä	palm	**ō**	open	**û**	burn	**th**	thin
e	end	**ô**	order	**yōō**	fuse	**th**	this
ē	equal					**zh**	vision

ə = a in *above* e in *sicken* i in *possible* o in *melon* u in *circus*

I

in·cu·des [in·kyōō′dēz] Plural of INCUS.
in·cul·cate [in·kul′kāt′ *or* in′kul·kāt′] *v.* **in·cul·cat·ed, in·cul·cat·ing** To teach or impress upon the mind by frequent and forceful repetition: The army *inculcates* obedience in new soldiers. —**in′·cul·ca′tion** *n.*
in·cum·ben·cy [in·kum′bən·sē] *n., pl.* **in·cum·ben·cies** 1 The term served in office by an incumbent. 2 The act or fact of holding office and carrying out its responsibilities.
in·cum·bent [in·kum′bənt] 1 *n.* A person who holds an office or performs official duties. 2 *adj.* That is an incumbent: A candidate running for reelection is an *incumbent* candidate. 3 *adj.* Resting as a duty or moral obligation: It is *incumbent* on all to vote.
in·cum·brance [in·kum′brəns] *n.* Another spelling of ENCUMBRANCE.
in·cur [in·kûr′] *v.* **in·curred, in·cur·ring** To bring (something unpleasant) on oneself: to *incur* debts; to *incur* a penalty.
in·cur·a·ble [in·kyŏŏr′ə·bəl] 1 *adj.* Not curable. 2 *n.* A person who has an incurable disease. —**in·cur′a·bly** *adv.*
in·cur·sion [in·kûr′zhən] *n.* An invasion or raid, especially a sudden and brief one: an *incursion* into enemy territory.
in·cus [ing′kəs] *n., pl.* **in·cu·des** [in·kyōō′dēz] One of the three tiny bones in the middle ear; anvil.
Ind. 1 India. 2 Indian. 3 Indiana.
in·debt·ed [in·det′id] *adj.* 1 Owing money. 2 Owing gratitude or thanks, as for a benefit or favor: We are *indebted* for your hospitality.
in·debt·ed·ness [in·det′id·nis] *n.* 1 The condition of being indebted. 2 That which is owed: The insurance will take care of their *indebtedness.*
in·de·cen·cy [in·dē′sən·sē] *n., pl.* **in·de·cen·cies** 1 The condition of being indecent. 2 Something indecent, as an action or remark.
in·de·cent [in·dē′sənt] *adj.* 1 Not decent or proper: *indecent* pride. 2 Not moral or modest; obscene: *indecent* behavior. —**in·de′cent·ly** *adv.*
in·de·ci·sion [in′di·sizh′ən] *n.* Inability to make a decision; vacillation.
in·de·ci·sive [in′di·sī′siv] *adj.* 1 Not able to decide; hesitant or wavering. 2 Not bringing about a definite conclusion or solution: an *indecisive* fight. —**in′de·ci′sive·ly** *adv.*
in·dec·o·rous [in·dek′ər·əs] *adj.* Not fitting, proper, or in good taste.
in·deed [in·dēd′] 1 *adv.* In fact; truly: I am *indeed* sorry. 2 *interj.* A word used to express surprise, disbelief, irony, sarcasm, or anger.
indef. indefinite.
in·de·fat·i·ga·ble [in′də·fat′ə·gə·bəl] *adj.* Never tired or lacking energy. —**in′de·fat′i·ga·bly** *adv.*
in·de·fen·si·ble [in′di·fen′sə·bəl] *adj.* 1 That cannot be defended from attack: an *indefensible* outpost. 2 That cannot be justified or excused: an *indefensible* mistake. 3 That cannot be proved or supported: an *indefensible* theory. —**in′de·fen′si·bly** *adv.*
in·de·fin·a·ble [in′di·fī′nə·bəl] *adj.* That cannot be defined or described: an *indefinable* feeling of joy. —**in′de·fin′a·bly** *adv.*
in·def·i·nite [in·def′ə·nit] *adj.* 1 Not definite or precise; vague: an *indefinite* answer. 2 Not precisely known, determined, measured, or limited: an *indefinite* amount of money. —**in·def′i·nite·ly** *adv.* —**in·def′i·nite·ness** *n.*
indefinite article The word *a* or the word *an.*
indefinite pronoun A pronoun, as *one, any,* or *few,* that does not identify or limit the person, persons, thing, or things to which it refers.
in·de·his·cent [in′di·his′ənt] *adj.* Not opening at maturity to release seeds or pollen: *indehiscent* fruit.
in·del·i·ble [in·del′ə·bəl] *adj.* 1 That cannot be erased or blotted out: *indelible* memories. 2 Capable of making marks that are hard to get out: *indelible* pencils. —**in·del′i·bly** *adv.*
in·del·i·ca·cy [in·del′ə·kə·sē] *n., pl.* **in·del·i·ca·cies** 1 The quality of being indelicate. 2 Something that is indelicate.
in·del·i·cate [in·del′ə·kit] *adj.* 1 Not proper or decent: an *indelicate* remark. 2 Crude; coarse,
in·dem·ni·fy [in·dem′nə·fī] *v.* **in·dem·ni·fied, in·dem·ni·fy·ing** 1 To repay or compensate for loss, injury, or damage: The insurance company *indemnified* the driver for damage to the car. 2 To protect, as against future loss, injury, or damage; insure. —**in·dem′ni·fi·ca′tion** *n.*
in·dem·ni·ty [in·dem′nə·tē] *n., pl.* **in·dem·ni·ties** 1 Payment to cover loss, injury, or damage. 2 Insurance against loss or damage.
in·dent[1] [in·dent′] *v.* 1 To set in from the margin, as the first line of a paragraph. 2 To cut notches like teeth into the edge of: a shore *indented* with inlets. 3 To form a notch or bay.
in·dent[2] [in·dent′] *v.* To press or push in so as to make a dent; dent.
in·den·ta·tion [in′den·tā′shən] *n.* 1 A notch or recess. 2 The act of indenting. 3 A dent.
in·den·ture [in·den′chər] *n., v.* **in·den·tured, in·den·tur·ing** 1 *n.* A written contract or agreement, especially a contract in which a person agrees to work for another for a certain period of time. 2 *v.* To bind by an indenture.
in·de·pen·dence [in′di·pen′dəns] *n.* The condition of being independent; freedom.
Independence Day In the U.S., July 4, a holiday commemorating the adoption of the Declaration of Independence on July 4, 1776.
in·de·pen·dent [in′di·pen′dənt] 1 *adj.* Not subject to the authority of another; free: an *independent* country. 2 *adj.* Not affected, influenced, or guided by others: an *independent* voter. 3 *n.* A person who is independent, especially an independent voter. 4 *adj.* Not dependent on someone else for financial help; self-supporting. 5 *adj.* Big enough to live on without other support: an *independent* income. 6 *adj.* Not part of some larger group or system: an *independent* company. —**in′de·pen′dent·ly** *adv.*
independent clause A group of words containing a subject and predicate that expresses a complete thought and is capable of standing alone as a sentence. In the sentence "When it is snowing, I like to sit by the fire," *I like to sit by the fire* is an independent clause.
in-depth [in′depth′] *adj.* Going into great detail: an *in-depth* study of crime shows on TV.
in·de·scrib·a·ble [in′di·skrī′bə·bəl] *adj.* Not capable of being described: the *indescribable* horror of war. —**in′de·scrib′a·bly** *adv.*
in·de·struc·ti·ble [in′di·struk′tə·bəl] *adj.* Not capable of being destroyed. —**in′de·struc′ti·bil′i·ty** *n.* —**in′de·struc′ti·bly** *adv.*
in·de·ter·mi·na·ble [in′di·tûr′mə·nə·bəl] *adj.* Not capable of being determined, fixed, or decided: of

an *indeterminable* age. **—in'de·ter'mi·na·bly** *adv.*

in·de·ter·mi·nate [in'di·tûr'mə·nit] *adj.* 1 Not definite. 2 Not clear; vague. 3 Not settled.

in·dex [in'deks] *n., pl.* **in·dex·es** or **in·di·ces,** *v.* 1 *n.* A list in alphabetical order of topics, names, or subjects, at the end of a book, showing on which page or pages each appears. 2 *v.* To put (a topic or name) in an index. 3 *v.* To supply (a book) with an index. 4 *n.* Anything that serves to indicate or show something: One *index* of skill is speed. 5 *n.* An index finger. 6 *n.* Something that points, as the needle on a dial.

index finger The finger next to the thumb; forefinger.

India ink A thick, black ink used in printing signs, drawing, and lettering.

In·di·an [in'dē·ən] 1 *n.* A member of any of the races of people inhabiting North and South America when European explorers came to the New World. 2 *n.* Any of the languages of these people. 3 *adj.* Of or having to do with these people or any of their languages. 4 *adj.* Of or from India. 5 *n.* A person born in or a citizen of India.

Indian club A bottle-shaped wooden club used in gymnastic exercises, usually in pairs.

Indian corn Another name for CORN (def. 1).

Indian pipe A wild plant of a waxy whiteness, having a single flower, no leaves, and a scaly stem. It lives on dead or decaying organic matter.

Indian summer A period of mild warm weather in the fall, usually after the first frost.

India paper A thin but opaque paper used for very long books.

India rubber Rubber (def. 1).

indic. indicative.

in·di·cate [in'də·kāt'] *v.* **in·di·cat·ed, in·di·cat·ing** 1 To point out; show: to *indicate* the right page or road. 2 To be or give a sign of; signify: The red spots *indicate* measles.

in·di·ca·tion [in'də·kā'shən] *n.* 1 The act of indicating. 2 Something that indicates; sign.

in·dic·a·tive [in·dik'ə·tiv] 1 *adj.* Suggestive of or pointing out: The violinist's playing is *indicative* of a great musical talent. 2 *adj.* In grammar, of, having to do with, or being the mood of a verb in which an act or condition is stated or questioned as an actual fact. In "They went to the beach" and "Did you throw the ball?" the verbs *went* and *throw* are in the indicative mood. 3 *n.* In grammar, the indicative mood or a verb form in this mood.

in·di·ca·tor [in'də·kā'tər] *n.* A person or thing that indicates or points out.

in·di·ces [in'də·sēz] A plural of INDEX.

in·dict [in·dīt'] *v.* 1 To charge with a crime or offense; accuse. 2 To bring an indictment against: The grand jury *indicted* the company treasurer for fraud. ◆ *Indict* comes from an old French word, *enditer,* meaning *to make known.* The English spelling was influenced by the Latin form, *indictare.*

in·dict·ment [in·dīt'mənt] *n.* 1 The act of indicting. 2 The condition of being indicted. 3 A formal, written charge delivered by a grand jury, accusing someone of a crime for which the person should be tried in court.

in·dif·fer·ence [in·dif'rəns *or* in·dif'ər·əns] *n.* 1 Lack of interest; unconcern. 2 Unimportance: This is a matter of *indifference* to me.

in·dif·fer·ent [in·dif'rənt *or* in·dif'ər·ənt] *adj.* 1 Not caring; unconcerned: *indifferent* about which movie to see. 2 Not good nor bad; so-so: an *indifferent* singer. 3 Not important or vital: an *indifferent* matter. 4 Impartial; unbiased: an *indifferent* witness. **—in·dif'fer·ent·ly** *adv.*

in·dig·e·nous [in·dij'ə·nəs] *adj.* Native to the place where found; not brought in or exotic: The eucalyptus is *indigenous* to Australia.

in·di·gent [in'də·jənt] *adj.* Needy; poor. **—in'di·gence** *n.*

in·di·gest·i·ble [in'də·jes'tə·bəl] *adj.* Hard or impossible to digest.

in·di·ges·tion [in'də·jes'chən] *n.* 1 The inability to digest food or a difficulty in digesting food. 2 The discomfort that accompanies such inability or difficulty.

in·dig·nant [in·dig'nənt] *adj.* Angry because of something that is not right, just, or fair. **—in·dig'·nant·ly** *adv.*

in·dig·na·tion [in'dig·nā'shən] *n.* Anger aroused by something that is not right, just, or fair: to feel *indignation* at cruelty.

in·dig·ni·ty [in·dig'nə·tē] *n., pl.* **in·dig·ni·ties** Something that humiliates one or injures one's self-respect.

in·di·go [in'də·gō] *n., pl.* **in·di·gos** or **in·di·goes,** *adj.* 1 *n.* A blue dye obtained from certain plants related to the pea, or made artificially. 2 *n., adj.* Deep violet blue.

in·di·rect [in'də·rekt'] *adj.* 1 Not following a direct path or line; roundabout: an *indirect* route. 2 Not directly connected with or resulting from something else: *indirect* benefits. 3 Not frank or straightforward: an *indirect* answer. **—in'di·rect'·ly** *adv.*

indirect object A word or words designating the person or thing indirectly affected by the action of a verb, as *him* in "Give him the book" or *idea* in "Give the idea some thought."

indirect tax A tax made part of the original price of goods and thus passed on indirectly to the consumer.

in·dis·creet [in'dis·krēt'] *adj.* Not careful, wise, or prudent. **—in'dis·creet'ly** *adv.*

in·dis·cre·tion [in'dis·kresh'ən] *n.* 1 The condition of being indiscreet. 2 Something indiscreet, as an act or remark.

in·dis·crim·i·nate [in'dis·krim'ə·nit] *adj.* 1 Not seeing differences; showing no discrimination: an *indiscriminate* love of art, praising both the good and bad alike. 2 Confused; jumbled: an *indiscriminate* collection. **—in'dis·crim'i·nate·ly** *adv.*

in·dis·pen·sa·ble [in'dis·pen'sə·bəl] *adj.* Absolutely necessary; essential.

in·dis·posed [in'dis·pōzd'] *adj.* 1 Mildly ill; unwell. 2 Not willing: *indisposed* to act.

in·dis·po·si·tion [in'dis·pə·zish'ən] *n.* 1 A slight illness. 2 Unwillingness.

a	add	**i**	it	**o͝o**	took	**oi**	oil		
ā	ace	**ī**	ice	**o͞o**	pool	**ou**	pout		
â	care	**o**	odd	**u**	up	**ng**	ring		
ä	palm	**ō**	open	**û**	burn	**th**	thin		
e	end	**ô**	order	**yo͞o**	fuse	**t͟h**	this		
ē	equal					**zh**	vision		

ə = {a in *above* e in *sicken* i in *possible* / o in *melon* u in *circus*}

in·dis·put·a·ble [in′dis·pyōō′tə·bəl] *adj.* Incapable of being disputed; unquestionable. **—in′dis·put′a·bly** *adv.*

in·dis·sol·u·ble [in′di·sol′yə·bəl] *adj.* Incapable of being dissolved, separated into its parts, or destroyed: an *indissoluble* vow; a large, *indissoluble* mass.

in·dis·tinct [in′dis·tingkt′] *adj.* Not clear or distinct; vague, dim, or faint: an *indistinct* picture. **—in′dis·tinct′ly** *adv.* **—in′dis·tinct′ness** *n.*

in·dis·tin·guish·a·ble [in′di·sting′gwish·ə·bəl] *adj.* Incapable of being clearly seen, perceived, or known as separate or different: Colors are *indistinguishable* in a very dim light.

in·dite [in·dīt′] *v.* **in·dit·ed, in·dit·ing** To write; compose: seldom used today.

in·di·um [in′dē·əm] *n.* A soft, silvery metallic element used in transistors and in various alloys.

in·di·vid·u·al [in·də·vij′ōō·əl] **1** *adj.* Single: each *individual* person or thing. **2** *n.* A single human being, animal, or thing. **3** *n.* A person: an amusing *individual.* **4** *adj.* Of or meant for a single person, animal, or thing: *individual* rooms. **5** *adj.* Characteristic of a certain person, animal, or thing; unique; special: Mark Twain's *individual* sense of humor.

in·di·vid·u·al·ism [in′də·vij′ōō·əl·iz′əm] *n.* **1** A theory that lays stress on individual rights and independence of action, declaring these things to be as important as the community or nation. **2** Complete interest in oneself, without regard for others.

in·di·vid·u·al·ist [in′də·vij′ōō·ə·list] *n.* **1** A person who acts and thinks as he or she sees fit without the control or influence of others. **2** A person who upholds the theory of individualism.

in·di·vid·u·al·is·tic [in′də·vij′ōō·ə·lis′tik] *adj.* **1** Of or pertaining to individualism or individualists. **2** Different or special; distinctive: an *individualistic* style of singing.

in·di·vid·u·al·i·ty [in′də·vij′ōō·al′ə·tē] *n.* **1** A quality or trait that makes a person or thing different from all others. **2** The condition of being special or different.

in·di·vid·u·al·ly [in′də·vij′ōō·əl·ē] *adv.* **1** One at a time; as individuals: The principal spoke to each member of the club *individually.* **2** One from another: to differ *individually.*

in·di·vis·i·ble [in′də·viz′ə·bəl] *adj.* **1** Incapable of being divided. **2** Incapable of being divided without leaving a remainder: 9 is *indivisible* by 5. **—in′di·vis′i·bly** *adv.*

in·doc·tri·nate [in·dok′trə·nāt′] *v.* **in·doc·tri·nat·ed, in·doc·tri·nat·ing** To teach (a person or persons) certain doctrines, principles, or beliefs. **—in·doc′tri·na′tion** *n.*

In·do-Eu·ro·pe·an [in′dō·yŏŏr′ə·pē′ən] **1** *n.* A family of languages spoken in most European countries, in North and South America, and in parts of Asia. **2** *adj.* Of or having to do with this family of languages.

in·do·lent [in′də·lənt] *adj.* Habitually lazy. **—in′do·lence** *n.* **—in′do·lent·ly** *adv.*

in·dom·i·ta·ble [in·dom′i·tə·bəl] *adj.* Not easily defeated or overcome; persevering: an *indomitable* leader. **—in·dom′i·ta·bly** *adv.*

In·do·ne·sian [in′də·nē′zhən] **1** *adj.* Of or from Indonesia. **2** *n.* A person born in or a citizen of Indonesia. **3** *n.* The language of Indonesia.

in·door [in′dôr′] *adj.* That is, belongs, or takes place indoors: *indoor* equipment; *indoor* work.

in·doors [in′dôrz′] *adv.* Into or inside a house or other building: to play or go *indoors.*

in·dorse [in·dôrs′] *v.* **in·dorsed, in·dors·ing** Another spelling of ENDORSE. **—in·dorse′ment** *n.* **—in·dors′er** *n.*

in·du·bi·ta·ble [in·d(y)ōō′bə·tə·bəl] *adj.* Not to be doubted; unquestionable. **—in·du′bi·ta·bly** *adv.*

in·duce [in·d(y)ōōs′] *v.* **in·duced, in·duc·ing** **1** To influence (someone) to do something; persuade: They *induced* me to accept the challenge. **2** To cause; produce: The illness was *induced* by damp weather. **3** To reach (a conclusion, principle, or the like) by observing particular facts or examples. **4** To produce by electric or magnetic induction: to *induce* an electric current.

in·duce·ment [in·d(y)ōōs′mənt] *n.* **1** The act of inducing. **2** Something that induces or persuades; incentive: The reward was an *inducement* to return the lost diamond ring.

in·duct [in·dukt′] *v.* **1** To bring into military service: to *induct* a draftee. **2** To install formally, as in an office or society: to *induct* a new governor.

in·duc·tance [in·duk′təns] *n.* The ability of an electric circuit to produce induction.

in·duc·tee [in·duk′tē′] *n.* A person just inducted or being inducted, especially into the armed forces.

in·duc·tion [in·duk′shən] *n.* **1** The act of inducting. **2** The condition of being inducted. **3** The process of arriving at a general principle or conclusion by observing a number of particular facts or examples. **4** The creation of a magnetic or electric field by the nearness of another magnetic or electric field. **5** The creation of an electric field by a moving magnetic field, or of a magnetic field by a moving electric field.

induction coil An electrical apparatus, often used in automobile engines, that transforms an interrupted, low-voltage direct current into high-voltage alternating current.

in·duc·tive [in·duk′tiv] *adj.* **1** Of, having to do with, or resulting from induction: *inductive* reasoning. **2** Produced by or causing electrical or magnetic induction. **—in·duc′tive·ly** *adv.*

in·due [in·dōō′] *v.* Another spelling of ENDUE.

in·dulge [in·dulj′] *v.* **in·dulged, in·dulg·ing** **1** To yield to or give free rein to (a pleasure or desire): to *indulge* a love of ice cream. **2** To permit oneself to take pleasure in something: to *indulge* in daydreaming. **3** To give in to the desires or whims of: to *indulge* a sick child.

in·dul·gence [in·dul′jəns] *n.* **1** The act of indulging in something. **2** That which is indulged in: Expensive cars were their great *indulgence.* **3** The condition of being indulgent. **4** Something granted as a favor, such as extra time allowed for payment of a debt. **5** In the Roman Catholic Church, a freeing from the punishment still due in purgatory for a sin after it has been forgiven through the sacrament of penance.

in·dul·gent [in·dul′jənt] *adj.* Very kind and lenient; not strict or critical: an *indulgent* parent. **—in·dul′gent·ly** *adv.*

in·dus·tri·al [in·dus′trē·əl] *adj.* **1** Of, engaged in, or having to do with industry: an *industrial* product; *industrial* workers. **2** Of or having to do with the people working in industries. **3** Having many industries: an *industrial* area. **—in·dus′tri·al·ly** *adv.*

in·dus·tri·al·ist [in·dus′trē·əl·ist] *n.* A person who owns or manages an industry.

in·dus·tri·al·ize [in·dus′trē·əl·īz′] *v.* **in·dus·tri·al·ized, in·dus·tri·al·iz·ing** To make or become industrial: to *industrialize* a town. —**in·dus·tri·al·i·za·tion** [in·dus′trē·əl·ī·zā′shən] *n.*

Industrial Revolution The great social and economic change, beginning in the 18th century in England and later spreading to the United States and Europe, that resulted from the replacement of hand tools by power-driven machinery.

in·dus·tri·ous [in·dus′trē·əs] *adj.* Working hard and diligently. —**in·dus′tri·ous·ly** *n.*

in·dus·try [in′dəs·trē] *n., pl.* **in·dus·tries** 1 Any branch of manufacturing or business. 2 Manufacturing and business activity as a whole. 3 Hard, diligent work or effort: to live by one's own *industry.*

-ine A suffix meaning: Of, like, or related to, as in *equine.*

in·e·bri·ate [*v.* in·ē′brē·āt′, *n.* in·ē′brē·it] *v.* **in·e·bri·at·ed, in·e·bri·at·ing,** *n.* 1 *v.* To make drunk; intoxicate. 2 *n.* A drunkard.

in·e·bri·at·ed [in·ē′brē·a′tid] *adj.* Affected by alcohol; intoxicated; drunk.

in·ed·i·ble [in·ed′ə·bəl] *adj.* Unfit to eat.

in·ef·fa·ble [in·ef′ə·bəl] *adj.* Too great to be described or expressed: *ineffable* joy.

in·ef·fec·tive [in′i·fek′tiv] *adj.* 1 Not producing the effect expected or wanted; not effective: an *ineffective* medicine. 2 Not competent; incapable: an *ineffective* manager. —**in′ef·fec′tive·ly** *adv.*

in·ef·fec·tu·al [in′i·fek′cho͞o·əl] *adj.* Not effective; useless. —**in′ef·fec′tu·al·ly** *adv.*

in·ef·fi·cien·cy [in′i·fish′ən·sē] *n.* The condition or quality of being inefficient.

in·ef·fi·cient [in′i·fish′ənt] *adj.* 1 Lacking ability or skill; incompetent: an *inefficient* secretary. 2 Not able to do something without waste, as of energy or time: an *inefficient* engine. —**in′ef·fi′cient·ly** *adv.*

in·e·las·tic [in′i·las′tik] *adj.* Not elastic or adaptable; inflexible.

in·el·e·gant [in·el′ə·gənt] *adj.* 1 Not having elegance; plain: an *inelegant* meal. 2 Coarse; crude: *inelegant* manners or speech.

in·el·i·gi·ble [in·el′ə·jə·bəl] *adj.* Not eligible, suitable, or qualified: to be *ineligible* to vote. —**in·el·i·gi·bil·i·ty** [in·el′ə·jə·bil′ə·tē] *n.* —**in·el′i·gi·bly** *adv.*

in·ept [in·ept′] *adj.* 1 Not suitable or appropriate: an *inept* compliment. 2 Clumsy; awkward: an *inept* worker. —**in·ept′ly** *adv.*

in·ept·i·tude [i·nep′tə·to͞od *or* i·nep′tə·tyo͞od] *n.* 1 The state of being inept; awkwardness; bungling. 2 Something that is inept, as behavior or a comment.

in·e·qual·i·ty [in′i·kwol′ə·tē] *n., pl.* **in·e·qual·i·ties** 1 The condition of being unequal, as in size, position, or quantity. 2 The condition of being unequal, as in social position, opportunity, or justice: the *inequalities* that exist between the rich and the poor. 3 In mathematics, a statement that two numbers are not equal or that one number is greater or less than another.

inequality sign Any of various mathematical signs that indicate that numbers or quantities are not equal. ≠ means "is not equal to," ($a \neq b$), > means "is greater than," ($a > b$), < means "is smaller than," ($a < b$), ≧ means "is greater than or equal to," ($a \geqq b$), ≦ means "is smaller than or equal to," ($a \leqq b$).

in·eq·ui·ta·ble [in·ek′wə·tə·bəl] *adj.* Unfair; unjust.

in·eq·ui·ty [in·ek′wə·tē] *n., pl.* **in·eq·ui·ties** 1 Lack of equity or fairness; injustice. 2 An unfair action or situation.

in·e·rad·i·ca·ble [in′i·rad′ə·kə·bəl] *adj.* Impossible to remove or root out. —**in′e·rad′i·ca·bly** *adv.*

in·ert [in·ûrt′] *adj.* 1 Lacking the power to move or act: *inert* material. 2 Slow to move or act; sluggish. 3 Unable or unlikely to unite with another chemical element or substance: Helium and neon are *inert* gases. —**in·ert′ly** *adv.*

in·er·tia [in·ûr′shə] *n.* 1 The continuance of a body or mass in its particular state of rest or motion unless acted upon by some force. 2 A not wanting to act, move, or change.

in·es·cap·a·ble [in′ə·skā′pə·bəl] *adj.* Impossible to escape or avoid: an *inescapable* fate. —**in′es·cap′a·bly** *adv.*

in·es·ti·ma·ble [in·es′tə·mə·bəl] *adj.* Too great or valuable to be counted or measured.

in·ev·i·ta·ble [in·ev′ə·tə·bəl] *adj.* Unavoidable; certain. —**in·ev′i·ta·bly** *adv.*

in·ex·act [in′ig·zakt′] *adj.* Not exact; not completely accurate or true.

in·ex·cus·a·ble [in′ik·skyo͞o′zə·bəl] *adj.* Impossible to excuse or justify: *inexcusable* behavior. —**in′ex·cus′a·bly** *adv.*

in·ex·haust·i·ble [in′ig·zôs′tə·bəl] *adj.* 1 Incapable of being used up; unending: an almost *inexhaustible* supply of food. 2 Never getting tired; tireless: an *inexhaustible* speaker.

in·ex·o·ra·ble [in·ek′sər·ə·bəl] *adj.* Inflexible; relentless: the *inexorable* coming of winter. —**in·ex′o·ra·bly** *adv.*

in·ex·pe·di·ent [in′ik·spē′dē·ənt] *adj.* Not wise, suitable, or advisable. —**in′ex·pe′di·ent·ly** *adv.*

in·ex·pen·sive [in′ik·spen′siv] *adj.* Not expensive; costing little. —**in′ex·pen′sive·ly** *adv.*

in·ex·pe·ri·ence [in′ik·spir′ē·əns] *n.* Lack of experience or of the skill and knowledge gained from experience.

in·ex·pe·ri·enced [in′ik·spir′ē·ənst] *adj.* Lacking experience or the skill and knowledge gained from experience.

in·ex·pert [in·ek′spûrt] *adj.* Not expert.

in·ex·pli·ca·ble [in·eks′pli·kə·bəl *or* in′iks·plik′ə·bəl] *adj.* Impossible to explain.

in·ex·press·i·ble [in′ik·spres′ə·bəl] *adj.* Impossible to express or put into words.

in·ex·pres·sive [in′ik·spres′iv] *adj.* Not expressive; showing little or no meaning or feeling. —**in′ex·pres′sive·ness** *n.*

in·ex·tin·guish·a·ble [in′ik·sting′gwish·ə·bəl] *adj.* Incapable of being put out or extinguished.

in·ex·tri·ca·ble [in·eks′tri·kə·bəl] *adj.* 1 Impossible to get out of: an *inextricable* situation. 2 Impossible to solve or make clear: an *inextricable* problem. 3 Impossible to undo or disentangle, as a knot.

a	add	**i**	it	**o͝o**	took	**oi**	oil
ā	ace	**ī**	ice	**o͞o**	pool	**ou**	pout
â	care	**o**	odd	**u**	up	**ng**	ring
ä	palm	**ō**	open	**û**	burn	**th**	thin
e	end	**ô**	order	**yo͞o**	fuse	**th**	this
ē	equal					**zh**	vision

ə = a in *above*, e in *sicken*, i in *possible*, o in *melon*, u in *circus*

I

in·fal·li·ble [in·fal′ə·bəl] *adj.* 1 Free from error: an *infallible* judgment. 2 Not liable to fail or disappoint; sure: an *infallible* remedy. **—in·fal·li·bil·i·ty** [in·fal′ə·bil′ə·tē] *n.* **—in·fal′li·bly** *adv.*

in·fa·mous [in′fə·məs] *adj.* 1 Having a notoriously bad reputation: an *infamous* liar. 2 Shamefully wicked or evil: an *infamous* act.

in·fa·my [in′fə·mē] *n., pl.* **in·fa·mies** 1 A notoriously bad reputation; public disgrace: a name that will live in *infamy.* 2 Extreme wickedness. 3 A shamefully wicked act.

in·fan·cy [in′fən·sē] *n., pl.* **in·fan·cies** 1 The condition or time of being an infant; babyhood. 2 The earliest stage of anything.

in·fant [in′fənt] 1 *n.* A child in the earliest stages of life; baby. 2 *adj.* Of, like, or for an infant or infancy. 3 *adj.* Just beginning to exist or develop: an *infant* country.

Infant

in·fan·ti·cide [in·fan′tə·sīd′] *n.* 1 The killing of an infant. 2 A person who kills an infant.

in·fan·tile [in′fən·tīl′] *adj.* 1 Of or having to do with infants or infancy. 2 Babyish; childish: an *infantile* remark. 3 Being in the earliest stage of its development: an *infantile* river.

infantile paralysis Another name for POLIOMYELITIS.

in·fan·try [in′fən·trē] *n., pl.* **in·fan·tries** Soldiers, or a branch of the army, trained and equipped to fight on foot. ◆ *Infantry* comes from a Latin word meaning *boy, page,* or *foot soldier,* and goes back to the Latin *infans, infantis,* meaning *child.*

Infantry

in·fan·try·man [in′fən·trē·mən] *n., pl.* **in·fan·try·men** [in′fən·trē·mən] An infantry soldier.

in·fat·u·ate [in·fach′o͞o·āt′] *v.* **in·fat·u·at·ed, in·fat·u·at·ing** 1 To inspire with a foolish or exaggerated love or passion. 2 To cause to behave foolishly. **—in·fat′u·a′tion** *n.*

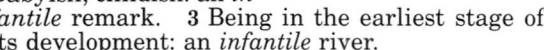

in·fect [in·fekt′] *v.* 1 To make ill or diseased by the introduction of a germ or virus: Dirt *infected* the cut on my knee; Don't *infect* everyone with your cold. 2 To have an influence on: The leader's courage *infected* us.

in·fec·tion [in·fek′shən] *n.* 1 The act of infecting. 2 The condition of being infected. 3 Something that infects. 4 A disease or other harmful condition caused by an invasion of germs.

in·fec·tious [in·fek′shəs] *adj.* 1 Spread by infection: an *infectious* disease. 2 Producing infection: an *infectious* germ. 3 Likely to spread easily: *infectious* laughter. **—in·fec′tious·ly** *adv.* **—in·fec′tious·ness** *n.*

infectious mon·o·nu·cle·o·sis [mon′ə·no͞o′klē·ō′sis *or* mon′ə·nyo͞o′klē·ō′sis] A contagious, probably viral disease common among teenagers and young adults. It is marked by fever, sore throat, tiredness, and swollen lymph nodes, and the presence in the blood of an abnormally high number of white corpuscles with single nuclei.

in·fe·lic·i·tous [in′fə·lis′ə·təs] *adj.* 1 Not fitting or proper; inappropriate: an *infelicitious* answer. 2 Causing misery or unhappiness: an *infelicitious* accident.

in·fe·lic·i·ty [in′fə·lis′ə·tē] *n., pl.* **in·fe·lic·i·ties** 1 The condition or quality of being infelicitous. 2 Something infelicitous.

in·fer [in·fûr′] *v.* **in·ferred, in·fer·ring** 1 To come to by reasoning: From your smile I *infer* that you are amused. 2 To lead to as a conclusion; imply: Smoke *infers* something burning. 3 To indicate without saying outright; imply. ◆ Both *infer* and *imply* are common in this sense, but *imply* has far better standing.

in·fer·ence [in′fər·əns] *n.* 1 The act of inferring. 2 Something inferred; conclusion.

in·fe·ri·or [in·fir′ē·ər] 1 *adj.* Not so good, as in quality, worth, or usefulness: an *inferior* car. 2 *adj.* Lower in rank, position, or importance: In diplomacy, a minister is *inferior* to an ambassador. 3 *n.* A person or thing that is inferior in some way.

in·fe·ri·or·i·ty [in·fir′ē·ôr′ə·tē] *n.* The quality or condition of being inferior.

inferiority complex A strong feeling of being inferior to other people.

in·fer·nal [in·fûr′nəl] *adj.* 1 Of or having to do with Hell: the *infernal* regions. 2 Horrible; terrible: *infernal* cruelty.

in·fer·no [in·fûr′nō] *n., pl.* **in·fer·nos** 1 Hell. 2 A place like hell, full of fire or great heat: The furnace was a roaring *inferno.*

in·fer·tile [in·fûr′til] *adj.* Not fertile or productive: *infertile* fields. **—in′fer·til′i·ty** *n.*

in·fest [in·fest′] *v.* To overrun or occupy in large numbers so as to be annoying or dangerous: The swamp was *infested* with mosquitoes. **—in′fes·ta′·tion** *n.*

in·fi·del [in′fə·dəl] 1 *n.* A person who has no religious beliefs. 2 *n.* Among Christians, a person who is not a Christian. 3 *n.* Among Muslims, a person who is not a Muslim. 4 *adj.* Rejecting all religions, especially rejecting Christianity or Islam: an *infidel* writer.

in·fi·del·i·ty [in′fə·del′ə·tē] *n., pl.* **in·fi·del·i·ties** 1 Unfaithfulness, as to a person, promise, or obligation; especially, unfaithfulness to one's husband or wife. 2 A disloyal act. 3 Lack of belief in religion or in a particular religion.

in·field [in′fēld′] *n.* 1 The part of a baseball field defended by the infielders. 2 The infielders as a group.

infield·er [in′fēld′ər] *n.* In baseball, the first baseman, second baseman, shortstop, or third baseman.

in·fil·trate [in·fil′trāt′ *or* in′fil·trāt′] *v.* **in·fil·trat·ed, in·fil·trat·ing** To pass through or enter into (as a substance, an organization, or an area) by or as if by filtering: Enemy spies were able to *infiltrate* our troops. **—in′fil·tra′tion** *n.*

infin. infintive.

in·fi·nite [in′fə·nit] 1 *adj.* Having no limits; endless or boundless. 2 *adj.* Very great: *infinite* patience. 3 *n.* Something infinite. **—in′fi·nite·ly** *adv.*

in·fin·i·tes·i·mal [in′fin·ə·tes′ə·məl] *adj.* So small or insignificant as to be close to nothing. **—in′fin·i·tes′i·mal·ly** *adv.*

in·fin·i·tive [in·fin′ə·tiv] *n.* A verb form that has no person or number and is often preceded by *to*. It is used in verb phases (Make him *go*), as a noun (*To go* to Europe was her great desire), and as a modifier (We study *to learn*).

in·fin·i·tude [in·fin′ə·t(y)o͞od′] *n.* 1 The quality of being infinite. 2 An unlimited quantity.

in·fin·i·ty [in·fin′ə·tē] *n., pl.* **in·fin·i·ties** 1 The condition or quality of being infinite. 2 Something considered infinite, as space or time. 3 A distance, extent, or number greater than any definite equivalent.

in·firm [in·fûrm′] *adj.* 1 Feeble or weak, as from old age or illness. 2 Not resolute.

in·fir·ma·ry [in·fûr′mə·rē] *n., pl.* **in·fir·ma·ries** A place for treating the sick, as in a school or factory.

in·fir·mi·ty [in·fûr′mə·tē] *n., pl.* **in·fir·mi·ties** Any weakness or illness: The patients tried to walk despite their *infirmities*.

in·fix [in·fiks′] *v.* 1 To set or fix firmly. 2 To impress upon the mind; instill.

in·flame [in·flām′] *v.* **in·flamed, in·flam·ing** 1 To make or become excited or angry: to *inflame* a crowd. 2 To increase (anger or hatred). 3 To make or become hot, swollen, or sore: Tight shoes can *inflame* toes.

in·flam·ma·ble [in·flam′ə·bəl] *adj.* 1 Capable of easily catching fire; flammable. 2 Easily excited or aroused.

in·flam·ma·tion [in′flə·mā′shən] *n.* 1 The act of inflaming. 2 An inflamed condition. 3 A red and painful swelling caused by infection or irritation.

in·flam·ma·to·ry [in·flam′ə·tôr′ē] *adj.* 1 Tending or meant to arouse anger or violence: an *inflammatory* speech. 2 Of, having to do with, or causing an inflammation.

in·flat·a·ble [in·flā′tə·bəl] *adj.* Capable of being inflated: an *inflatable* mattress.

in·flate [in·flāt′] *v.* **in·flat·ed, in·flat·ing** 1 *v.* To swell or puff out by filling with air or gas: to *inflate* a tire. 2 *v.* To puff up, as with pride or importance: The teacher's praise *inflated* the child's ego. 3 *v.* To increase (prices or the like) a great deal.

Inflating a tire

in·fla·tion [in·flā′shən] *n.* 1 The act of inflating. 2 An inflated condition. 3 A rise in price levels resulting from an increase in the amount of money or credit relative to available goods.

in·fla·tion·ar·y [in·flā′shə·ner′ē] *adj.* Of, related to, causing, or caused by inflation.

in·flect [in·flekt′] *v.* 1 To vary the tone or pitch of (the voice). 2 In grammar, to change the form of (a word) by inflection. 3 To bend or curve.

in·flec·tion [in·flek′shən] *n.* 1 A change in the tone, pitch, or loudness of the voice. 2 In grammar, the changes made in a word in order to show distinctions, as of case, number, gender, tense, or degree. The adjective *cold* is changed by inflection to *colder* or *coldest*, depending on the degree of comparison required. 3 An angle, bend, or curve.

in·flec·tion·al [in·flek′shən·əl] *adj.* Of, having to do with, or characterized by grammatical inflection.

in·flex·i·ble [in·flek′sə·bəl] *adj.* That cannot be bent, altered, or changed; rigid; unyielding: *inflexible* metal; an *inflexible* mind. —**in·flex·i·bil·i·ty** [in·flek′·sə·bil′ə·tē] *n.* —**in·flex′i·bly** *adv.*

in·flict [in·flikt′] *v.* 1 To strike; give; deal: to *inflict* a blow. 2 To impose: to *inflict* a heavy tax. —**in·flic′tion** *n.*

in·flow [in′flō′] *n.* 1 The act of flowing in or into. 2 Something that flows in.

in·flu·ence [in′flo͞o·əns] *n., v.* **in·flu·enced, in·flu·enc·ing** 1 *n.* The power of a person or thing to have an effect on others: The moon has a strong *influence* on the tides. 2 *n.* Such a power working without any direct force: Use your *influence* to get them to help. 3 *n.* A person or thing having this power. 4 *v.* To alter the nature, thoughts, or behavior of: The teacher *influenced* the students to read some good novels.

in·flu·en·tial [in′flo͞o·en′shəl] *adj.* Having or using influence.

in·flu·en·za [in′flo͞o·en′zə] *n.* A contagious virus disease causing inflammation of the nose, throat, and bronchial tubes, or of the intestines, and accompanied by fever, weakness, and discomfort.

in·flux [in′fluks′] *n.* A continuous flowing or coming in, as of people or things: an *influx* of gas; an *influx* of new students.

in·fold [in·fōld′] *v.* Another spelling of ENFOLD.

in·form [in·fôrm′] *v.* 1 To let know; tell; notify: *Inform* the boss that we are here. 2 To give secret or incriminating evidence: The criminal *informed* on the rest of the gang.

in·for·mal [in·fôr′məl] *adj.* 1 Not bound by a set form or rule; relaxed, casual, or friendly: *informal* manners; an *informal* agreement. 2 Not requiring formal dress: an *informal* dance. 3 Proper for daily conversation or familiar writing but not for formal speaking or writing. —**in·for′mal·ly** *adv.*

in·for·mal·i·ty [in′fôr·mal′ə·tē] *n., pl.* **in·for·mal·i·ties** 1 Informal nature or quality: the *informality* of the gathering. 2 An informal act or proceeding.

in·form·ant [in·fôr′mənt] *n.* A person who gives information about something to another.

in·for·ma·tion [in′fər·mā′shən] *n.* 1 The act of informing or an informed condition: a handbook for the *information* of students. 2 Facts about a subject or subjects: Textbooks and newspapers are sources of *information*.

in·form·a·tive [in·fôr′mə·tiv] *adj.* Giving information or knowledge: an *informative* book.

in·formed [in·fôrmd′] *adj.* 1 Having, showing, or using information: an *informed* reader of science magazines. 2 Arising from the possession of information: an *informed* opinion.

in·form·er [in·fôr′mər] *n.* A person who gives information against someone who has broken a rule or law; tattletale.

in·frac·tion [in·frak′shən] *n.* An act or instance of

a	add	**i**	it	**o͝o**	took	**oi**	oil
ā	ace	**ī**	ice	**o͞o**	pool	**ou**	pout
â	care	**o**	odd	**u**	up	**ng**	ring
ä	palm	**ō**	open	**û**	burn	**th**	thin
e	end	**ô**	order	**yo͞o**	fuse	**th̶**	this
ē	equal					**zh**	vision

ə = a in *above*, e in *sicken*, i in *possible*, o in *melon*, u in *circus*

breaking a rule or law; violation: The contractor was found guilty of a minor *infraction* of the town's building code.

in·fra·red [in′frə·red′] *adj.* Describing invisible electromagnetic waves that are longer than those of red light and shorter than radio waves.

in·fra·son·ic [in′frə·son′ik] *adj.* 1 Using or making sound waves of such low frequency that they cannot be heard. 2 Another word for SUBSONIC.

in·fre·quen·cy [in·frē′kwən·sē] *n.* A being infrequent; rarity: The *infrequency* of your visits upsets us.

in·fre·quent [in·frē′kwənt] *adj.* Not coming or happening often; not common; rare: an *infrequent* visitor. **—in·fre′quent·ly** *adv.*

in·fringe [in·frinj′] *v.* **in·fringed, in·fring·ing** 1 To break; violate: to *infringe* a law. 2 To trespass; encroach: to *infringe* on someone's rights. **—in·fringe′ment** *n.*

in·fu·ri·ate [in·fyŏŏr′ē·āt′] *v.* **in·fu·ri·at·ed, in·fu·ri·at·ing** To make furious or extremely angry; enrage.

in·fuse [in·fyōōz′] *v.* **in·fused, in·fus·ing** 1 To pour in; instill: The coach *infused* the will to win into the team. 2 To inspire: The coach *infused* them with determination. 3 To soak; steep, as tea leaves.

in·fu·sion [in·fyōō′zhən] *n.* 1 The act of infusing. 2 A solution resulting from infusing, as tea.

-ing[1] A suffix meaning: 1 The act or practice of, as in *writing.* 2 Something made or created by, as a *painting.* 3 Something used to make or do, as *flooring* or *lining.*

-ing[2] A suffix used to form the present participle of verbs: *talking; eating.*

in·gen·ious [in·jēn′yəs] *adj.* 1 Skillful or clever: an *ingenious* architect. 2 Worked out, made, or done in a clever way: an *ingenious* solution. **—in·gen′·ious·ly** *adv.* ◆ Don't confuse *ingenious* with INGENUOUS.

in·ge·nue or **in·gé·nue** [an′zhə·nōō′] *n.* 1 The role of a young woman or girl in a play or film. 2 An actress who plays such a part. 3 Any ingenuous young woman or girl.

in·ge·nu·i·ty [in′jə·n(y)ōō′ə·tē] *n.* Skill or cleverness, as shown in inventing or solving things: a detective's *ingenuity.*

in·gen·u·ous [in·jen′yōō·əs] *adj.* Showing artless innocence, trust, or sincerity; simple or frank: an *ingenuous* person. **—in·gen′u·ous·ly** *adv.* **—in·gen′·u·ous·ness** *n.*

in·gest [in·jest′] *v.* To take or put (food or drink) into the body. **—in·ges′tion** *n.*

in·gle·nook [ing′gəl·nŏŏk′] *n. British* A corner by the fire.

in·glo·ri·ous [in·glôr′ē·əs] *adj.* 1 Not bringing glory or honor; shameful; disgraceful: an *inglorious* war. 2 Not famous; unknown; humble: rarely used today.

Inglenook

in·got [ing′gət] *n.* A mass of metal cast into the shape of a bar or block.

in·graft [in·graft′] *v.* Another spelling of ENGRAFT.

in·grain [in·grān′] *v.* To fix firmly and deeply on the mind or character.

in·grained [in·grānd′] *adj.* Deep-seated; fixed.

in·grate [in′grāt′] *n.* An ungrateful person.

in·gra·ti·ate [in·grā′shē·āt′] *v.* **in·gra·ti·at·ed, in·gra·ti·at·ing** To bring (oneself) into someone's favor by trying to please: to *ingratiate* oneself with one's employer.

in·grat·i·tude [in·grat′ə·t(y)ōōd′] *n.* Lack of gratitude or appreciation.

in·gre·di·ent [in·grē′dē·ənt] *n.* 1 Something put into a mixture as a part of it: the *ingredients* of a cake. 2 A part in the makeup of anything: the *ingredients* of success.

in·gress [in′gres] *n.* 1 The act of going in or the right to go in: Reporters demanded *ingress.* 2 A place for going in; entrance.

in·grown [in′grōn′] *adj.* Grown into the flesh: an *ingrown* toenail.

in·hab·it [in·hab′it] *v.* 1 To live in as a place of residence; occupy: Deer *inhabit* the forest. 2 To be present in.

in·hab·it·a·ble [in·hab′it·ə·bəl] *adj.* Suitable for being lived in.

in·hab·i·tant [in·hab′ə·tənt] *n.* A person or animal that lives in a particular place; resident: an *inhabitant* of the city.

in·hal·ant [in·hā′lənt] 1 *n.* A medicine used by inhaling its vapor. 2 *adj.* Intended or used for inhaling.

in·ha·la·tion [in′hə·lā′shən] *n.* The act of or an instance of inhaling.

in·ha·la·tor [in′hə·lā′tər] *n.* A device used to administer medicated vapors.

in·hale [in·hāl′] *v.* **in·haled, in·hal·ing** To draw (air, smoke, a scent, or vapor) into the lungs; breathe in: to *inhale* fumes.

in·hal·er [in·hā′lər] *n.* 1 A person who inhales. 2 An inhalator.

in·har·mo·ni·ous [in′här·mō′nē·əs] *adj.* Lacking harmony; conflicting or clashing: *inharmonious* opinions; *inharmonious* sounds.

in·her·ent [in·hir′ənt *or* in·her′ənt] *adj.* Being in something as a built-in quality or element: the *inherent* strength of steel. **—in·her′ent·ly** *adv.*

in·her·it [in·her′it] *v.* 1 To get from someone after he or she dies, by will or law: to *inherit* an estate. 2 To get from a parent or ancestor as a characteristic: to *inherit* red hair. 3 To get from someone who has gone before: to *inherit* a problem.

in·her·i·tance [in·her′ə·təns] *n.* 1 The act, fact, or right of inheriting: to be wealthy by *inheritance.* 2 Something inherited, as money.

inheritance tax A tax a person is required to pay on inherited property.

in·her·i·tor [in·her′ə·tər] *n.* Someone who inherits something; heir.

in·hib·it [in·hib′it] *v.* To hold back, check, or restrain (as an act or impulse): My words were *inhibited* by shyness.

in·hi·bi·tion [in′(h)i·bish′ən] *n.* 1 The act of inhibiting. 2 An inhibited condition. A belief, feeling, fear, or other force within that keeps a person from acting or thinking freely.

in·hos·pi·ta·ble [in·hos′pi·tə·bəl *or* in′hos·pit′ə·bəl] *adj.* 1 Not kind and generous toward guests; not hospitable. 2 Providing no shelter or comfort: an *inhospitable* climate. **—in·hos′pi·ta·bly** or **in′hos·pit′a·bly** *adv.*

in·hu·man [in·(h)yōō′mən] *adj.* 1 Cruel, brutal, or monstrous: *inhuman* treatment. 2 Not human in nature or form. **—in·hu′man·ly** *adv.*

in·hu·man·i·ty [in′(h)yo͞o·man′ə·tē] *n., pl.* **in·hu·man·i·ties** 1 Extreme cruelty. 2 A cruel action or word.

in·im·i·cal [in·im′i·kəl] *adj.* 1 Unfavorable; opposed: Rust is *inimical* to machines. 2 Not friendly: an *inimical* nation.

in·im·i·ta·ble [in·im′ə·tə·bəl] *adj.* That cannot be copied or imitated; matchless: the dancer's *inimitable* grace. —**in·im′i·ta·bly** *adv.*

in·iq·ui·tous [in·ik′wə·təs] *adj.* Extremely wicked or unjust; sinful: an *iniquitous* act.

in·iq·ui·ty [in·ik′wə·tē] *n., pl.* **in·iq·ui·ties** 1 Great evil or injustice; wickedness. 2 An evil or unjust action; sin.

in·i·tial [in·ish′əl] *adj., n., v.* **in·i·tialed** or **in·i·tialled, in·i·tial·ing** or **in·i·tial·ling** 1 *adj.* Of or coming at the beginning; earliest; first: an *initial* attempt. 2 *n.* (*often pl.*) The first letter of a name or word. 3 *v.* To mark or sign with one's initials: The teacher *initialed* the note.

in·i·tial·ly [in·ish′əl·ē] *adv.* At the beginning; at first.

Initial Teaching Alphabet An alphabet of 43 characters representing the sounds of English, for use in teaching beginners to read.

in·i·ti·ate [*v.* in·ish′ē·āt′, *n,* i·nish′ē·it] *v.* **in·i·ti·at·ed, in·i·ti·at·ing,** *n.* 1 *v.* To set up or set going; start; begin: to *initiate* changes. 2 *v.* To make (someone) a member of a club or society, usually by putting the person through special ceremonies or tests. 3 *n.* A person who has recently been admitted to a club or society. 4 *v.* To instruct or introduce: We *initiated* the children into the art of cooking. —**in·i′ti·a·tor** *n.*

in·i·ti·a·tion [in·ish′ē·ā′shən] *n.* 1 An initiating or being initiated. 2 A ceremony or test a person must go through before becoming a member of a club or society.

in·i·ti·a·tive [in·ish′(ē·)ə·tiv] *n.* 1 The first step in starting or doing something: to take the *initiative.* 2 The power, ability, or right to take the first step: to have the *initiative.* 3 The right or procedure by which citizens may introduce bills in a legislature by petition.

in·ject [in·jekt′] *v.* 1 To drive or shoot in, especially to force (a fluid) into the body with a hypodermic needle or syringe: to *inject* an antitoxin. 2 To treat with injections: to *inject* a dog with serum. 3 To put or throw in (as a comment, suggestion, or quality): to *inject* humor into a play.

in·jec·tion [in·jek′shən] *n.* 1 The act of injecting. 2 The substance injected, especially a liquid solution of medicine.

in·ju·di·cious [in′jo͞o·dish′əs] *adj.* Not showing good judgment; thoughtless; unwise: an *injudicious* remark. —**in′ju·di′cious·ly** *adv.*

in·junc·tion [in·jungk′shən] *n.* 1 An order, direction, or command. 2 An order issued by a court of law forbidding or requiring someone to do something.

in·jure [in′jər] *v.* **in·jured, in·jur·ing** To hurt, harm, or damage: to *injure* one's arm; Gossip *injures* one's reputation.

in·ju·ri·ous [in·jo͝or′ē·əs] *adj.* Causing hurt or damage; harmful: *injurious* insects.

in·ju·ry [in′jər·ē] *n., pl.* **in·ju·ries** Hurt, harm, or damage done to someone or something: a head *injury*; an *injury* to one's pride.

in·jus·tice [in·jus′tis] *n.* 1 Lack of justice, fairness, or equal treatment: the *injustice* of an innocent person's being punished. 2 An unjust action; wrong: to do an *injustice.*

ink [ingk] 1 *n.* A black or colored liquid substance, used for writing, drawing, and printing. 2 *v.* To put ink on or over: to *ink* out a word. 3 *n.* The dark liquid that octopuses, squids, and cuttlefish shoot out into the water to hide themselves. —**ink′·i·ness** *n.*

ink·horn [ingk′horn′] 1 *n.* A small container, usually made of horn, formerly used to hold ink. 2 *adj.* Showily learned; pedantic: an *inkhorn* vocabulary.

ink·ling [ingk′ling] *n.* A slight suggestion or hint: to give an *inkling* of one's plans.

ink·stand [ingk′stand′] *n.* 1 A rack for holding pens and ink. 2 A container for ink.

ink·well [ingk′wel′] *n.* A container for ink, sometimes set into the surface of a desk.

Inkwells

ink·y [ing′kē] *adj.* **ink·i·er, ink·i·est** 1 Dark as black ink: the *inky* night. 2 Covered or stained with ink.

in·laid [in′lād′ *or* in·lād′] 1 Past tense and past participle of INLAY. 2 *adj.* Set into and even with the surface of something to form a design: a box with *inlaid* ivory. 3 *adj.* Decorated with pieces of contrasting material set evenly into the surface of something: an *inlaid* wall panel.

in·land [*adj.* in′lənd, *n., adv.* in′lənd *or* in′land′] 1 *adj.* Not near the coast or the borders of a country; of or in the interior: *inland* population; an *inland* state. 2 *n.* The inner part of a country; the interior. 3 *adv.* In or towards an interior region: We live *inland*; They traveled *inland.*

in-law [in′lô′] *n. informal* A relative by marriage instead of by blood.

in·lay [*v.* in·lā′ *or* in′lā′, *n.* in′lā′] *v.* **in·laid, in·lay·ing,** *n.* 1 *v.* To set into a surface so as to form a decoration or design: to *inlay* dark wood in light wood. 2 *v.* To decorate by inserting such designs: to *inlay* a wooden cabinet with tortoise shell. 3 *n.* Material or a design that has been inlaid: The antique chest was decorated with an ivory *inlay.* 4 *n.* A filling, as of gold, made to fit a cavity in a tooth and cemented into it.

Inlay

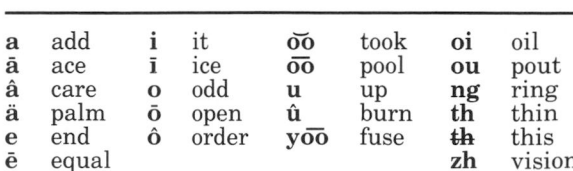

a	add	**i**	it	**o͝o**	took	**oi**	oil		
ā	ace	**ī**	ice	**o͞o**	pool	**ou**	pout		
â	care	**o**	odd	**u**	up	**ng**	ring		
ä	palm	**ō**	open	**û**	burn	**th**	thin		
e	end	**ô**	order	**yo͞o**	fuse	**th̶**	this		
ē	equal					**zh**	vision		

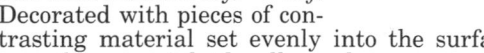

ə = a in *above* e in *sicken* i in *possible* o in *melon* u in *circus*

in·let [in′let′ *or* in′lət] *n.* 1 A narrow strip of water leading into the land from a larger body of water. 2 An entrance or opening.

Inlets

in·mate [in′māt′] *n.* 1 A person confined in a prison, asylum, or other such institution. 2 An inhabitant or resident.

in me·mo·ri·am [in′mə·môr′ē·əm] In memory or remembrance of: often engraved on gravestones. ◆ *In memoriam* is a Latin phrase.

in·most [in′mōst′] *adj.* Farthest in, deepest, or most secret: the *inmost* layer.

inn [in] *n.* A restaurant or hotel, usually located by a road and serving travelers.

in·nate [i·nāt′ *or* in′āt′] *adj.* Natural; inborn; inherent: *innate* ability. **—in·nate′ly** *adv.*

in·ner [in′ər] *adj.* 1 Farther inside; interior: the *inner* halls. 2 Of the mind or spirit: an *inner* life. 3 Private; intimate; secret: *inner* feelings.

inner ear In human beings, a place in the bone of the ear that contains organs that function in hearing and balance. See picture at EAR.

in·ner·most [in′ər·mōst′] *adj.* Farthest within; inmost.

inner tube A rubber tube used within some types of tires to hold air.

in·ning [in′ing] *n.* 1 A division of a baseball game during which each team has a turn at bat until it makes three outs. A regular baseball game has nine innings. 2 (*often pl.*) A chance for action, as by a person or party: Now the Democrats have their *innings*.

inn·keep·er [in′kē′pər] *n.* A person who owns or operates an inn.

in·no·cence [in′ə·səns] *n.* 1 Freedom from sin, guilt, or blame. 2 Natural simplicity; purity: a baby's *innocence*.

in·no·cent [in′ə·sənt] 1 *adj.* Free from sin, blame, or evil; guiltless: The suspect was *innocent* of the crime. 2 *adj.* Showing a lack of worldly wisdom; simple; naive: an *innocent* child. 3 *n.* An innocent person. 4 *adj.* Having no bad or evil effect or intention; harmless: an *innocent* pastime. **—in′no·cent·ly** *adv.*

in·noc·u·ous [i·nok′yo͞o·əs] *adj.* Not causing injury or harm; harmless: an *innocuous* snake; an *innocuous* remark. **—in·noc′u·ous·ly** *adv.*

in·no·va·tion [in′ə·vā′shən] *n.* 1 A change in the usual way of doing things: to make *innovations.* 2 Something newly introduced: Television was an *innovation* in 1945.

in·no·va·tor [in′ə·vā′tər] *n.* A person who introduces new ideas, methods, or devices.

in·nu·en·do [in′yo͞o·en′dō] *n., pl.* **in·nu·en·does** A sly hint, usually one that hurts somebody's reputation: to accuse by *innuendoes*.

in·nu·mer·a·ble [i·n(y)o͞o′mər·ə·bəl] *adj.* Too many to be counted; countless.

in·oc·u·late [in·ok′yə·lāt′] *v.* **in·oc·u·lat·ed, in·oc·u·lat·ing** 1 To give a mild and harmless form of a disease to (a person or animal) by injecting vaccines, serums, or other prepared substances into the body. This builds up immunity that prevents a serious attack of the disease later. 2 To put ideas or opinions into the mind of.

in·oc·u·la·tion [in·ok′yə·lā′shən] *n.* 1 The act or process of inoculating. 2 The injection of a vaccine to provide immunity to a disease.

in·of·fen·sive [in′ə·fen′siv] *adj.* Giving no offense; not annoying; harmless. **—in′of·fen′sive·ly** *adv.*

in·op·er·a·tive [in·op′ər·ə·tiv] *adj.* Not in force, effect, or operation: an *inoperative* mine.

in·op·por·tune [in·op′ər·t(y)o͞on′] *adj.* Not coming at a good or a convenient time: an *inopportune* request. **—in·op′por·tune′ly** *adv.* **—in·op′por·tune′·ness** *n.*

in·or·di·nate [in·ôr′də·nit] *adj.* Too great; excessive: an *inordinate* fondness for sweets. **—in·or′di·nate·ly** *adv.*

in·or·gan·ic [in′ôr·gan′ik] *adj.* 1 Lacking the organized physical structure of animal or vegetable life; not alive. Minerals are inorganic. 2 Not made by or derived from plants or animals: *inorganic* fertilizers. **—in′or·gan′i·cal·ly** *adv.*

in·o·si·tol [in·ō′sə·tol′] *n.* Any of a small group of alcohols, one of which is a member of the vitamin B complex and is present in many plant and animal tissues.

in·put [in′po͝ot′] *n., v.* **in·put·ted** or **in·put, in·put·ting** 1 *n.* Something that is put in, as electric current or other power put into a machine, or food taken into the body. 2 *n.* A point where something is put into a system. 3 *n.* Information entered into a computer in a specific order for processing. 4 *v.* To enter information into a computer in a specific order for processing. ◆ *Input* is useful as a computer term but is now overworked informally to mean "opinion," "comment," or "active role."

in·quest [in′kwest′] *n.* A legal investigation, especially one held before a jury, as that conducted by a coroner to determine the cause of a death.

in·quire [in·kwīr′] *v.* **in·quired, in·quir·ing** 1 To make an investigation or search: to *inquire* into the causes of heart disease. 2 To seek information or knowledge about: The traveler *inquired* the way. **—in·quir′er** *n.* **—in·quir′ing·ly** *adv.*

in·quir·y [in·kwīr′ē *or* in′kwər·ē] *n., pl.* **in·quir·ies** 1 An investigation, especially of some public matter. 2 A question: to reply to *inquiries.*

in·qui·si·tion [in′kwə·zish′ən] *n.* 1 (*written* **Inquisition**) A court set up by the Roman Catholic Church during the 13th century for the discovery and punishment of heretics. 2 An official investigation or inquiry, often judicial; inquest. 3 A thorough, searching investigation.

in·quis·i·tive [in·kwiz′ə·tiv] *adj.* 1 Full of questions; eager for knowledge; curious. 2 Too curious; prying. **—in·quis′i·tive·ly** *adv.* **—in·quis′i·tive·ness** *n.*

in·quis·i·tor [in·kwiz′ə·tər] *n.* A person who makes an official investigation.

in·road [in′rōd′] *n.* 1 (*usually pl.*) A destructive invasion or encroachment: Overwork and strain made *inroads* on the director's health. 2 A raid.

ins. inches.

in·sane [in·sān′] *adj.* 1 Suffering from or characteristic of someone suffering from insanity; not sane; crazy: an *insane* person. 2 For insane people: an *insane* asylum. 3 Mad; wild: *insane* schemes. **—in·sane′ly** *adv.*

in·san·i·tar·y [in·san′ə·ter′ē] *adj.* Not sanitary or hygienic; unhealthful.

in·san·i·ty [in·san′ə·tē] *n., pl.* **in·san·i·ties** 1 A condition characterized by a severe disorder or derangement of the mind. 2 Such a condition considered in relation to legal capacity or responsibility. 3 Extreme foolishness; folly.

in·sa·tia·ble [in·sā′shə·bəl] *adj.* Not able to be satisfied; never getting enough; greedy: an *insatiable* appetite. **—in·sa'tia·bly** *adv.*

in·scribe [in·skrīb'] *v.* **in·scribed, in·scrib·ing** 1 To write, mark, or engrave: to *inscribe* a monument with the names of donors. 2 To put (a name) on an official list or roll. 3 To establish firmly, as in the mind or memory. **—in·scrib'er** *n.*

in·scrip·tion [in·skrip'shən] *n.* 1 Something, as words or letters, that is inscribed: an *inscription* on an ancient vase. 2 The act of inscribing. 3 A written dedication, as of a book.

in·scru·ta·ble [in·skro͞o'tə·bəl] *adj.* Incapable of being understood; mysterious; puzzling: an *inscrutable* smile. **—in·scru'ta·bil'i·ty** *n.* **—in·scru'ta·bly** *adv.*

in·sect [in'sekt] *n.* Any of a large class of small animals with a head, thorax, and abdomen, six legs, and usually two pairs of wings. Bees, beetles, flies, and mosquitoes are true insects. Small animals such as spiders are often loosely called insects. ◆ *Insect* goes back to a Latin word meaning *to notch* or *cut into*, because the bodies of insects are divided or "cut" into three segments.

Insects

in·sec·ti·cide [in·sek'tə·sīd'] *n.* A poisonous substance for killing insects.

in·sec·ti·vore [in·sek'tə·vôr'] *n.* An insectivorous animal or plant.

in·sec·tiv·o·rous [in'sek·tiv'ər·əs] *adj.* Feeding on insects: *insectivorous* plants.

in·se·cure [in'sə·kyo͝or'] *adj.* 1 Apt to break, fall, or fail; not safe: an *insecure* bolt. 2 Not confident; anxious; uncertain: to feel *insecure.* **—in'se·cure'·ly** *adv.*

in·se·cu·ri·ty [in'sə·kyo͝or'ə·tē] *n., pl.* **in·se·cu·ri·ties** 1 Lack of safety; dangerous condition. 2 A condition of worry, anxiety, and uncertainty. 3 Something that is insecure.

in·sem·i·nate [in·sem'ə·nāt'] *v.* **in·sem·i·nat·ed, in·sem·i·nat·ing** 1 To inject semen into the vagina of. 2 To fix ideas firmly in. **—in·sem'i·na'tion** *n.*

in·sen·sate [in·sen'sāt'] *adj.* 1 Not able to feel; not alive: *insensate* stone. 2 Showing no mercy, pity, or sympathy; hard. 3 Without reason; senseless; stupid: *insensate* rage. **—in·sen'sate·ly** *adv.*

in·sen·si·ble [in·sen'sə·bəl] *adj.* 1 Unconscious: He lay *insensible* on the floor. 2 Unable to feel, perceive, or notice: *insensible* to pain; *insensible* to the troubles of others. 3 Not aware; not realizing: *insensible* of the risk. 4 So slight or gradual as to be hardly noticed: Daylight diminished by *insensible* stages. **—in·sen'si·bil'i·ty** *n.* **—in·sen'si·bly** *adv.*

in·sen·si·tive [in·sen'sə·tiv] *adj.* Not feeling, noticing, or responding; not sensitive: an *insensitive* person. **—in·sen'si·tive·ly** *adv.* **—in·sen'si·tive·ness** *n.* **—in·sen·si·tiv·i·ty** [in·sen'sə·tiv'i·tē] *n.*

in·sep·a·ra·ble [in·sep'ər·ə·bəl] *adj.* Incapable of being separated: *inseparable* companions. **—in·sep'a·ra·bly** *adv.*

in·sert [*v.* in·sûrt', *n.* in'sûrt'] 1 *v.* To put or place in something: to *insert* a key in a lock. 2 *n.* Something inserted, as pages of illustrations in a book.

in·ser·tion [in·sûr'shən] *n.* 1 The action of inserting. 2 Something inserted, as lace or embroidery sewn into cloth.

in·set [*v.* in·set', *n.* in'set'] *v.* **in·set, in·set·ting,** *n.* 1 *v.* To set in; insert. 2 *n.* Something inserted, as material in a garment.

in·shore [in'shôr'] *adj., adv.* Near or toward the shore: *inshore* fishing; to drift *inshore.*

in·side [*n., adj.* in'sīd' *or* in'sīd', *adv., prep.* in'sīd'] 1 *n.* The part, space, or surface that lies within; interior: the *inside* of a house. 2 *adv.* In or into the interior; within: Come *inside.* 3 *prep.* In or within: Put it *inside* the drawer. 4 *adj.* Found within; inner; internal: an *inside* part. 5 *n.* (*pl.*) *informal* The inner parts or organs of the body. 6 *adj.* Known only by a few; private; secret: *inside* information. 7 *adj.* Used or working indoors: *inside* clothing. **—inside out** So that the inside part is on the outside: I turned my pockets *inside out.*

in·sid·er [in'sī'dər] *n.* Someone who has special information or influence.

in·sid·i·ous [in·sid'ē·əs] *adj.* 1 Slyly treacherous, evil, or deceitful: an *insidious* plan to win. 2 Working in a hidden but dangerous way: an *insidious* disease. **—in·sid'i·ous·ly** *adv.*

in·sight [in'sīt'] *n.* The ability to see into the heart or inner nature of something or someone.

in·sight·ful [in·sīt'fəl] *adj.* Having or showing keen insight or understanding: an *insightful* report on crime.

in·sig·ni·a [in·sig'nē·ə] *n.pl.* Badges or emblems used as special marks of membership, office, or honor: the various royal *insignia.* ◆ *Insignia* was originally the plural of *insigne* in English as it had been in Latin. Now it is often used in the singular, with *insignias* as its accepted plural form: a display of *insignias.*

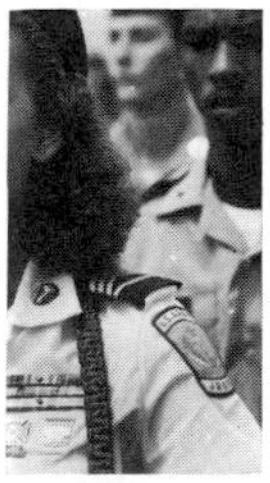
Insignia

in·sig·nif·i·cance [in'sig·nif'ə·kəns] *n.* Lack of importance, meaning, size, or worth.

in·sig·nif·i·cant [in'sig·nif'ə·kənt] *adj.* Lacking importance, meaning, size, or worth; trifling; trivial. **—in'sig·nif'i·cant·ly** *adv.*

in·sin·cere [in'sin·sir'] *adj.* Not expressing true feelings; not sincere or genuine. **—in'sin·cere'ly** *adv.*

in·sin·cer·i·ty [in'sin·ser'ə·tē] *n., pl.* **in·sin·cer·i·ties** 1 Lack of sincerity or honesty. 2 Something insincere.

in·sin·u·ate [in·sin'yo͞o·āt'] *v.* **in·sin·u·at·ed, in·sin·u·at·ing** 1 To suggest slyly without saying; hint: They *insinuated* that the idea was ridiculous. 2 To get or bring in gradually by indirect and subtle means: to *insinuate* oneself into someone's favor.

a	add	**i**	it	**o͝o**	took	**oi**	oil
ā	ace	**ī**	ice	**o͞o**	pool	**ou**	pout
â	care	**o**	odd	**u**	up	**ng**	ring
ä	palm	**ō**	open	**û**	burn	**th**	thin
e	end	**ô**	order	**yo͞o**	fuse	**th**	this
ē	equal					**zh**	vision

ə = a in *above* e in *sicken* i in *possible* o in *melon* u in *circus*

in·sin·u·a·tion [in·sin′yo͞o·ā′shən] *n.* 1 A sly hint; innuendo. 2 The act of insinuating.
in·sip·id [in·sip′id] *adj.* 1 Lacking flavor or taste; flat: *insipid* food. 2 Not lively or interesting; dull: an *insipid* speech.
in·sist [in·sist′] *v.* 1 To demand with determination: I *insist* that you do it. 2 To stand up strongly for a belief or opinion: I *insisted* that I was right.
in·sis·tent [in·sis′tənt] *adj.* 1 Insisting or persistent: *insistent* demands. 2 Demanding or holding the attention: an *insistent* rhythm. **—in·sis′tence** *n.* **—in·sis′tent·ly** *adv.*
in·snare [in·snâr′] *v.* **in·snared, in·snar·ing** Another spelling of ENSNARE.
in·so·far as [in′sō·fâr′] To such a degree that: *Insofar as* I know, Mother will be home at six.
in·sole [in′sōl′] *n.* 1 The fixed inner sole of a shoe. 2 An extra inside sole, as one put in to make a shoe fit better.
in·so·lent [in′sə·lənt] *adj.* Deliberately rude; insulting; sneering: an *insolent* manner. **—in′so·lence** *n.* **—in′so·lent·ly** *adv.*
in·sol·u·ble [in·sol′yə·bəl] *adj.* 1 Incapable of being dissolved: an *insoluble* salt. 2 Incapable of being solved: an *insoluble* problem. **—in·sol′u·bly** *adv.*
in·sol·vent [in·sol′vənt] *adj.* Unable to pay one's debts; bankrupt. **—in·sol′ven·cy** *n.*
in·som·ni·a [in·som′nē·ə] *n.* Difficulty in sleeping; sleeplessness.
in·so·much [in′sō·much′] *adv.* 1 To such a degree; so much: The brake is worn *insomuch* that it is unsafe. **—insomuch as** Because; seeing that: *Insomuch as* we were busy, we decided to postpone the meeting.
in·spect [in·spekt′] *v.* 1 To look at or examine carefully: to *inspect* a car for defects. 2 To review officially: to *inspect* troops.
in·spec·tion [in·spek′shən] *n.* 1 Careful or critical examination of something. 2 An official examination or review, as of troops.
in·spec·tor [in·spek′tər] *n.* 1 A person who inspects, especially in an official capacity: a meat *inspector.* 2 A police officer usually ranking next below the superintendent.
in·spi·ra·tion [in′spə·rā′shən] *n.* 1 A good idea or impulse that comes to someone, usually suddenly: to have an *inspiration.* 2 The power to inspire: the *inspiration* of the speaker's words. 3 An inspired condition: to lose one's *inspiration.* 4 A person or thing that inspires: Your example is an *inspiration.* 5 The action of drawing in the breath. **—in′spi·ra′tion·al** *adj.*
in·spire [in·spīr′] *n.* **in·spired, in·spir·ing** 1 To fill with a certain thought, feeling, or desire to do something: The teacher *inspired* us to work harder. 2 To arouse (a feeling or idea) in someone: The thought inspired *fear* in them. 3 To direct or guide, as if by some divine influence: The authors of the Bible wrote as if they were *inspired.* 4 To inhale.
in·spir·it [in·spir′it] *v.* To fill with new spirit, life, or courage; cheer.
in·sta·bil·i·ty [in′stə·bil′ə·tē] *n.* Lack of stability, firmness, or steadiness.
in·stall [in·stôl′] *v.* 1 To fix in position and adjust for service or use: to *install* an air conditioner. 2 To establish in a place; settle: The cat *installed* itself in the new chair. 3 To place officially in office with a ceremony: to *install* a new mayor.
in·stal·la·tion [in′stə·lā′shən] *n.* 1 The act of installing. 2 A mechanical device or system fixed in place for use. 3 A large, fixed military base, fort, or the like.
in·stall·ment[1] or **in·stal·ment**[1] [in·stôl′mənt] *n.* 1 One of several payments made on a debt at definite times until the whole debt is paid. 2 *adj. use: installment* buying. 3 One of several parts presented at different times, as one chapter of a serial in a newspaper.
in·stall·ment[2] or **in·stal·ment**[2] [in·stôl′mənt] *n.* The act of installing, or an installed condition.
installment plan or **instalment plan** An agreement with a dealer to pay for goods or services in regular installments.
in·stance [in·stəns′] *n.* A particular case or occasion: In that *instance* I was wrong. **—for instance** As an illustration; for example.
in·stant [in′stənt] 1 *n.* A very short time; moment. 2 *adj.* Without delay; immediate: *instant* recognition. 3 *adj.* Demanding quick attention; urgent: an *instant* need. 4 *adj.* Prepared quickly, as by adding water or milk: *instant* coffee. 5 *n.* A specific point in time: at the same *instant.* 6 *adj.* Of the present month: the 13th *instant*: seldom used today.
in·stan·ta·ne·ous [in′stən·tā′nē·əs] *adj.* Happening, done, or over in an instant: an *instantaneous* reaction; Death was *instantaneous.* **—in′stan·ta′ne·ous·ly** *adv.*
in·stant·ly [in′stənt·lē] *adv.* Immediately.
in·stead [in·sted′] *adv.* In the place of someone or something else. **—instead of** Rather than; in place of.
in·step [in′step′] *n.* 1 The arched upper part of the human foot, extending from the toes to the ankle. 2 The part of a shoe or stocking covering this.
in·sti·gate [in′stə·gāt′] *v.* **in·sti·gat·ed, in·sti·gat·ing** 1 To spur or urge on to some action. 2 To bring about by stirring up: to *instigate* treason. **—in′sti·ga′tion** *n.* **—in′sti·ga′tor** *n.*
in·still or **in·stil** [in·stil′] *v.* **in·stilled, in·still·ing** 1 To introduce gradually, as by teaching: to *instill* courage in one's child. 2 To pour in drop by drop: to *instill* a few drops of oil into a sauce.
in·stinct [*n.* in′stingkt, *adj.* in·stingkt′] 1 *n.* A natural tendency or impulse that causes animals to act in characteristic ways: Bees make honey by *instinct.* 2 *n.* A natural talent, skill, or ability; knack: to have an *instinct* for knowing what to do. 3 *adj.* Filled; abounding: a heart *instinct* with good will.
in·stinc·tive [in·stingk′tiv] *adj.* Of, having to do with, or coming from instinct: an *instinctive* reaction. **—in·stinc′tive·ly** *adv.*
in·sti·tute [in′stə·t(y)o͞ot′] *v.* **in·sti·tut·ed, in·sti·tut·ing,** *n.* 1 *v.* To set up or establish; found: The county *instituted* an annual fair. 2 *v.* To set going; start: to *institute* an investigation. 3 *n.* An organization, school, or society devoted to a special study or cause: an art *institute.*
in·sti·tu·tion [in′stə·t(y)o͞o′shən] *n.* 1 An established organization with a special purpose. Schools, banks, hospitals, and prisons are institutions. 2 An established principle, practice, law, or custom: Freedom of the press is a democratic *institution.* 3 An establishing or starting. **—in′sti·tu′tion·al** *adj.*
in·sti·tu·tion·al·ize [in′stə·to͞o′shən·ə·līz′] *v.* **in·sti·tu·tion·al·ized, in·sti·tu·tion·al·iz·ing** 1 To place (a person) in an institution, especially for treatment of

an illness. 2 To regard as, make into, or give the nature of an institution to: to *institutionalize* gambling.

in·struct [in·strukt′] *v.* 1 To teach or train. 2 To order, direct, or command: We were *instructed* to wait. 3 To give information to; inform: They *instructed* the prisoners of their legal rights.

in·struc·tion [in·struk′shən] *n.* 1 The act of instructing or teaching. 2 Something that trains or gives knowledge, as a lesson. 3 (*pl.*) Directions or orders: to follow *instructions.*

in·struc·tive [in·struk′tiv] *adj.* Giving knowledge or information: an *instructive* speech.

in·struc·tor [in·struk′tər] *n.* 1 A teacher. 2 A teacher in an American college who ranks below all of the professors.

in·stru·ment [in′strə·mənt] *n.* 1 A tool or implement, especially one used for work requiring great accuracy: a surgical *instrument.* 2 A person or thing used to accomplish a purpose; means: to use one's friends as *instruments* in gaining power. 3 A device or system for measuring, recording, or controlling, as one found in a car or airplane. 4 *adj. use*: an *instrument* panel. 5 A device for producing musical sounds, as a piano or trumpet. 6 A legal document, as a will.

in·stru·men·tal [in′strə·ment′əl] *adj.* 1 Serving as a means; helpful; useful: The senator was *instrumental* in getting the law passed. 2 Of, composed for, or performed on musical instruments: an *instrumental* concert.

in·stru·men·tal·ist [in′strə·ment′əl·ist] *n.* A person who performs on a musical instrument.

in·stru·men·tal·i·ty [in′strə·men·tal′ə·tē] *n., pl.* **in·stru·men·tal·i·ties** Means, agency, or assistance: to get a job through the *instrumentality* of one's relatives.

in·sub·or·di·nate [in′sə·bôr′də·nit] *adj.* Refusing to submit to authority; disobedient.

in·sub·or·di·na·tion [in′sə·bôr′də·nā′shən] *n.* Refusal to obey or submit; disobedience.

in·sub·stan·tial [in′səb·stan′shəl] *adj.* 1 Not real; imaginary: A daydream is *insubstantial.* 2 Not firm or solid; flimsy or fragile.

in·suf·fer·a·ble [in·suf′ər·ə·bəl] *adj.* That cannot be put up with; unbearable; intolerable: *insufferable* rudeness. **—in·suf′fer·a·bly** *adv.*

in·suf·fi·cien·cy [in′sə·fish′ən·sē] *n., pl.* **in·suf·fi·cien·cies** A lack of enough of something; deficiency: an *insufficiency* of air.

in·suf·fi·cient [in′sə·fish′ənt] *adj.* Not enough; not adequate. **—in′suf·fi′cient·ly** *adv.*

in·su·lar [in′s(y)ə·lər] *adj.* 1 Of, located on, or forming an island. 2 Of or like people living on an island; isolated. 3 Not broad-minded or liberal; narrow: *insular* attitudes. **—in·su·lar·i·ty** [in′·s(y)ə·lar′ə·tē] *n.*

in·su·late [in′sə·lāt′] *v.* **in·su·lat·ed, in·su·lat·ing** 1 To surround with material that keeps electricity, heat, or sound from leaking out or in: to *insulate* a wire with plastic. 2 To set apart from someone or something: They *insulated* the offender from society.

in·su·la·tion [in′sə·lā′shən] *n.* 1 Material used for insulating. 2 The act of insulating. 3 An insulated condition.

in·su·la·tor [in′sə·lā′tər] *n.* Something that insulates, especially a material, as glass, that does not conduct electricity.

in·su·lin [in′sə·lin] *n.* 1 A hormone produced in the pancreas which enables the body to break down sugar and use it. 2 A preparation of this hormone obtained from animals and taken by people suffering from diabetes.

in·sult [*v.* in·sult′, *n.* in′sult] 1 *v.* To treat with scorn and contempt, as by saying or doing something rude: The host *insulted* us by making fun of our gift. 2 *n.* A rude action or remark: a deliberate *insult.*

in·su·per·a·ble [in·s(y)ōō′pər·ə·bəl] *adj.* Not capable of being overcome: *insuperable* obstacles. **—in·su′·per·a·bly** *adv.*

in·sup·port·a·ble [in′sə·pôr′tə·bəl] *adj.* Not bearable or to be put up with; intolerable: *insupportable* insolence.

in·sur·a·ble [in·shŏŏr′ə·bəl] *adj.* Eligible for insurance; fit to be insured: A car that fails inspection is not *insurable.*

in·sur·ance [in·shŏŏr′əns] *n.* 1 Protection against damage, injury, or loss. This protection is provided by a contract, or **insurance policy,** which guarantees that if regular payments are made, money up to a specific amount will be paid in the event of death, accident, fire, or some other special cause of loss. 2 The business of providing such protection. 3 The amount regularly paid for insurance; premium: My automobile *insurance* is $200 a year. 4 The amount for which anything is insured: She has $25,000 *insurance* on her life.

in·sure [in·shŏŏr′] *v.* **in·sured, in·sur·ing** 1 To buy, give, or get insurance on: The insurance company won't *insure* our house against hurricanes; Pianists can *insure* their hands. 2 To make certain; guarantee: To *insure* good results, follow directions. 3 To make safe; guard or protect: This checking *insures* us against error. 4 Another spelling of ENSURE.

in·sured [in·shŏŏrd′] *n.* A person whose life, health, or personal possessions are insured against loss.

in·sur·gent [in·sûr′jənt] 1 *adj.* Rising in revolt against authority. 2 *n.* A rebel.

in·sur·mount·a·ble [in′sər·moun′tə·bəl] *adj.* Incapable of being overcome: an *insurmountable* difficulty.

in·sur·rec·tion [in′sə·rek′shən] *n.* A rebellion or uprising: to put down an *insurrection.* **—in′sur·rec′·tion·ist** *n.*

int. interest.

in·tact [in·takt′] *adj.* Whole or entire, with no part taken away or damaged: The heirs kept the family farm *intact.*

in·take [in′tāk′] *n.* 1 The act of taking in: a sudden *intake* of breath. 2 A thing or amount taken in: our *intake* of liquids. 3 The place where water, air, or gas goes into a pipe or channel. 4 The amount of energy or power taken into a machine.

in·tan·gi·ble [in·tan′jə·bəl] 1 *adj.* Not capable of being touched; not material: Darkness is *intan-*

a	add	**i**	it	**ŏŏ**	took	**oi**	oil
ā	ace	**ī**	ice	**ōō**	pool	**ou**	pout
â	care	**o**	odd	**u**	up	**ng**	ring
ä	palm	**ō**	open	**û**	burn	**th**	thin
e	end	**ô**	order	**yōō**	fuse	**t͟h**	this
ē	equal					**zh**	vision

ə = a in *above*, e in *sicken*, i in *possible*, o in *melon*, u in *circus*

I

gible. **2** *adj.* Not definite; vague: an *intangible* fear. **3** *n.* Something intangible.

in·te·ger [in′tə·jər] *n.* A positive or negative whole number or zero. 3, 130, and −18 are integers; 1/2 and 4 1/4 are not integers.

in·te·gral [in′tə·grəl] *adj.* **1** Necessary if a whole thing is to be complete; essential: Legs are *integral* parts of a table. **2** Whole or entire; complete. **3** Having to do with an integer.

in·te·grate [in′tə·grāt′] *v.* **in·te·grat·ed, in·te·grat·ing** **1** To fit or bring together into a whole: The author *integrated* the various episodes into a narrative. **2** *U.S.* To make the use or occupancy of (a school, park, neighborhood, or other facility) available to persons of all races. **3** To make complete. **—in′te·gra′tion** *n.*

integrated circuit A very small electronic circuit containing microscopic transistors and other semiconductor devices, made from a single chip of material, as silicon.

in·te·gra·tion·ist [in′tə·grā′shə·nist] *n.* A person who advocates or practices racial integration.

in·teg·ri·ty [in·teg′rə·tē] *n.* **1** Great sincerity, honesty, and virtue; strength of character. **2** The condition of being whole and entire; completeness: the lost *integrity* of Austria-Hungary.

in·teg·u·ment [in·teg′yə·mənt] *n.* An outer covering, as a skin, shell, husk, or rind.

in·tel·lect [in′tə·lekt] *n.* **1** The power of the mind to understand, think, and know; reason: the human *intellect.* **2** Mental power; great intelligence: to show signs of *intellect.* **3** A highly intelligent person.

in·tel·lec·tu·al [in′tə·lek′cho͞o·əl] **1** *adj.* Of or having to do with the intellect; mental: *intellectual* ability. **2** *adj.* Requiring use of the intellect: *intellectual* work. **3** *adj.* Having or showing intellect: an *intellectual* author. **4** *n.* An intellectual person, especially a person who is devoted to and trained in subjects such as the arts and literature. **—in′tel·lec′tu·al·ly** *adv.*

in·tel·li·gence [in·tel′ə·jəns] *n.* **1** The ability to understand and learn or to work out problems requiring thought. **2** *adj. use*: an *intelligence* test. **3** News; secret information: *intelligence* obtained by a spy. **4** The collecting of secret information or the agency that collects it: The agent works for enemy *intelligence.* ◆ *Intelligence* comes from Latin roots meaning *to choose between.*

intelligence quotient A number meant to show the level of a person's mental development; the IQ. To obtain this number, the mental age, as determined by standard tests, is multiplied by 100 and then divided by the real age.

intelligence test Any of various standard tests used to determine a person's level of mental development as measured in relation to that of others.

in·tel·li·gent [in·tel′ə·jənt] *adj.* Having or showing intelligence; smart; bright. **—in·tel′li·gent·ly** *adv.*

in·tel·li·gent·si·a [in·tel′ə·jent′sē·ə] *n.pl.* Intellectual or educated people considered as a group.

in·tel·li·gi·ble [in·tel′ə·jə·bəl] *adj.* Capable of being understood; clear. **—in·tel′li·gi·bly** *adv.*

in·tem·per·ance [in·tem′pər·əns] *n.* A failure to use self-control or restraint, especially in drinking alcoholic liquor.

in·tem·per·ate [in·tem′pər·it] *adj.* **1** Lacking restraint; too strong: *intemperate* words. **2** Using too much alcoholic liquor. **3** Not mild; severe, as a climate or the weather. **—in·tem′per·ate·ly** *adv.*

in·tend [in·tend′] *v.* **1** To have as a purpose; plan. **2** To make or set aside for a purpose; mean; design: The present was *intended* for you.

in·tend·ed [in·ten′did] **1** *adj.* Thought out beforehand; intentional: *intended* rudeness. **2** *adj. informal* Future: her *intended* husband. **3** *n. informal* The person one plans to marry.

in·tense [in·tens′] *adj.* **1** Very strong, great, or deep: *intense* cold. **2** Full of strong emotion or deep feelings: an *intense* look. **3** Done with effort and concentration; hard. **—in·tense′ly** *adv.*

in·ten·si·fi·er [in·ten′sə·fī′ər] *n.* Another name for INTENSIVE (def. 3).

in·ten·si·fy [in·ten′sə·fī] *v.* **in·ten·si·fied, in·ten·si·fy·ing** To make or become intense or more intense: Moving *intensified* the pain. **—in·ten′si·fi·ca′tion** *n.*

in·ten·si·ty [in·ten′sə·tē] *n., pl.* **in·ten·si·ties** **1** The quality of being intense; extreme force or strength: the *intensity* of the sunlight. **2** Degree of strength: a pain of low *intensity.* **3** The amount of force or energy, as of light, sound, heat, or radiation, for each unit of volume, area, or mass.

in·ten·sive [in·ten′siv] **1** *adj.* Done with energy and concentration; thorough and complete: an *intensive* effort. **2** *adj.* Adding emphasis or force: said about a word: an *intensive* pronoun. **3** *n.* A word, phrase, particle, or prefix that adds emphasis or force. *Herself* in "She herself did it" is an intensive. **—in·ten′sive·ly** *adv.*

in·tent [in·tent′] **1** *n.* Purpose, aim, or intention: with *intent* to steal. **2** *adj.* Directing all one's efforts or attention: *intent* upon a problem. **3** *adj.* Firmly directed or fixed; earnest: an *intent* gaze. **4** *n.* Meaning: the *intent* of a remark. **—to** (or **for**) **all intents and purposes** In almost every respect; practically. **—in·tent′ly** *adv.*

in·ten·tion [in·ten′shən] *n.* Plan, purpose, or intent: I have no *intention* of waiting.

in·ten·tion·al [in·ten′shən·əl] *adj.* Done on purpose; deliberate; intended. **—in·ten′tion·al·ly** *adv.*

in·ter [in·tûr′] *v.* **in·terred, in·ter·ring** To place in a grave or tomb; bury.

inter- A prefix meaning: **1** With or on one another, as in *intermingle* or *interdependent.* **2** Between or among, as in *intercollegiate.*

in·ter·act [in′tər·akt′] *v.* To act on each other: a study of the way students *interact* in school. **—in′·ter·ac′tion** *n.*

in·ter·ac·tive [in′tər·ak′tiv] Allowing dialogue, responses, or an exchange of information, as between a teacher and student or a computer program and its user: *interactive* learning.

in·ter·breed [in′tər·brēd′] *v.* **in·ter·bred, in·ter·breed·ing** To breed together (different species or varieties of animals or plants).

in·ter·ca·late [in·tûr′kə·lāt′] *v.* **in·ter·ca·lat·ed, in·ter·ca·lat·ing** To insert (as a day or month) in a calendar. **—in·ter′ca·la′tion** *n.*

in·ter·cede [in′tər·sēd′] *v.* **in·ter·ced·ed, in·ter·ced·ing** **1** To speak or plead on behalf of another. **2** To come between persons or sides that disagree, in an effort to reconcile them.

in·ter·cept [in′tər·sept′] *v.* **1** To seize or stop on the way to a destination: to *intercept* a message. **2** To meet and block the passage of: to *intercept* enemy aircraft. **3** In mathematics, to mark off or bound, as by two points. **—in′ter·cep′tion** *n.*

in·ter·cep·tor [in′tər·sep′tər] *n.* A person or thing that intercepts, especially a fighter plane.

in·ter·ces·sion [in′tər·sesh′ən] *n.* **1** The act of interceding: Through your *intercession* we were saved. **2** Prayer on behalf of others.

in·ter·ces·sor [in′tər·ses′ər] *n.* Someone who intercedes.

in·ter·change [*v.* in′tər·chānj′, *n.* in′tər·chānj′] *v.* **in·ter·changed, in·ter·chang·ing,** *n.* **1** *v.* To change or substitute one for another: You can *interchange* the first and last letters of "are" and get "era." **2** *v.* To give and receive in return; exchange: to *interchange* gifts. **3** *n.* The act of interchanging; exchange: an *interchange* of ideas. **4** *n.* An intersection of two highways designed so that cars can change roads without crossing other traffic.

Interchange

in·ter·change·a·ble [in′tər·chān′jə·bəl] *adj.* Capable of being put in place of one another: *interchangeable* parts. **—in′ter·change′a·bly** *adv.*

in·ter·col·le·giate [in′tər·kə·lē′jit] *adj.* Between colleges: *intercollegiate* sports.

in·ter·com [in′tər·kom′] *n. informal* A telephone or radio system for communicating within a limited space, as between offices or in a plane.

in·ter·com·mu·ni·cate [in′tər·kə·myo͞o′nə·kāt′] *v.* **in·ter·com·mu·ni·cat·ed, in·ter·com·mu·ni·cat·ing** To communicate one with the other, as by a telephone or radio system.

in·ter·com·mu·ni·ca·tion [in′tər·kə·myo͞o′nə·kā′·shən] *n.* Communication with one another, as by means of a telephone or radio system.

in·ter·con·nect [in′tər·kə·nekt′] *v.* To connect or become connected one with the other; link or be linked together. **—in′ter·con·nec′tion** *n.*

in·ter·con·ti·nen·tal [in′tər·kon′tə·nen′təl] *adj.* Between or able to travel between continents: an *intercontinental* missile.

in·ter·course [in′tər·kôrs′] *n.* **1** Dealings or relations between individuals or nations. **2** Sexual relations.

in·ter·de·nom·i·na·tion·al [in′tər·di·nom′ə·nā′·shən·əl] *adj.* Shared by or involving different religious denominations or sects: an *interdenominational* conference.

in·ter·de·pen·dent [in′tər·di·pen′dənt] *adj.* Dependent on one another. **—in′ter·de·pend′ence** *n.*

in·ter·dict [*v.* in′tər·dikt′, *n.* in′tər·dikt′] **1** *v.* To prohibit or forbid by authority. **2** *v.* In the Roman Catholic Church, to forbid (a person or group) to take part in certain sacraments and services. **3** *n.* A ban, especially one forbidding holy sacraments and services. **—in′ter·dic′tion** *n.*

in·ter·est [in′tər·ist *or* in′trist] **1** *n.* A desire to learn, know, have, do, see, or join in something: to have an *interest* in music. **2** *v.* To stir up or hold the curiosity, attention, or concern of: The play *interested* us. **3** *n.* The power to stir up attention: That subject has *interest* for me. **4** *n.* Something that stirs up attention: Baseball is my chief *interest.* **5** *n.* Attention: Does the story hold your *interest*? **6** *n.* What helps or profits someone; advantage; benefit: to consider one's own *interest.* **7** *v.* To cause to care about or join in; involve or concern: I tried to *interest* them in the club project. **8** *n.* A share or part, as in a business or estate: to own an *interest* in a company. **9** *n.* Something in which someone has a share, as a business. **10** *n.* (*usually pl.*) A group of persons involved in a certain business or cause: the dairy *interests.* **11** *n.* The money paid, as by a bank or borrower, for the use of money: to get 5 1/4% *interest* on a savings account. **—in the interest of** For the sake or purpose of: *In the interest of* safety, cross only at the corners.

in·ter·est·ed [in′tə·res′tid *or* in′tri·stid] *adj.* **1** Taking or showing an interest in: *interested* in science fiction. **2** Owning an interest or share. **3** Having a personal concern or bias: an *interested* witness in a murder trial.

in·ter·est·ing [in′tər·is·ting *or* in′tris·ting] *adj.* Stirring up or holding the interest or attention. **—in′·ter·est·ing·ly** *adv.*

in·ter·face [in′tər·fās′] *n., v.* **in·ter·faced, in·ter·fac·ing** **1** *n.* A device that connects one part of a computer system to another. **2** *v.* To connect one part of a computer system to another by means of such a device.

in·ter·fere [in′tər·fir′] *v.* **in·ter·fered, in·ter·fer·ing** **1** To meddle or intervene in other people's business: Don't *interfere* in their quarrel. **2** To get in the way; be an obstacle: The radio *interferes* with my studying.

in·ter·fer·ence [in′tər·fir′əns] *n.* **1** The act of interfering. **2** Something that interferes. **3** In sports, the act of hindering an opponent's play. Some ways are against the rules; others are allowable. **4** A disturbance in the reception of radio or television signals.

in·ter·fer·on [in′tər·fir′on′] *n.* A protein produced by cells invaded by an infectious virus to halt the growth of that virus.

in·ter·fold [in′tər·fōld′] *v.* To fold together or one within another.

in·ter·fuse [in′tər·fyo͞oz′] *v.* **in·ter·fused, in·ter·fus·ing** To mix; combine; blend.

in·ter·gal·ac·tic [in′tər·gal·ak′tik] *adj.* Between or among galaxies.

in·ter·im [in′tər·im] **1** *n.* A temporary period between times or events: in the *interim.* **2** *adj.* Temporary: an *interim* appointment.

in·te·ri·or [in·tir′ē·ər] **1** *n.* Inside part: the *interior* of a house. **2** *adj.* Of, situated on, or done on the inside; internal; inner: *interior* decorating. **3** *n.* The part of a country back from a border or coastline. **4** *adj.* Inland: an *interior* region. **5** *n.* The internal or domestic affairs of a country. The U.S. Department of the Interior has charge of mining, forestry, national parks, and public lands.

interior decoration The art or profession of decorating and furnishing rooms, offices, and homes to provide style, attractiveness, and comfort.

interior decorator A person whose job is interior decoration.

interj. interjection.

in·ter·ject [in′tər·jekt′] *v.* To throw in abruptly; insert: to *interject* a comment.

a	add	**i**	it	**o͝o**	took	**oi**	oil		
ā	ace	**ī**	ice	**o͞o**	pool	**ou**	pout		
â	care	**o**	odd	**u**	up	**ng**	ring		
ä	palm	**ō**	open	**û**	burn	**th**	thin		
e	end	**ô**	order	**yo͞o**	fuse	**th**	this		
ē	equal					**zh**	vision		

ə = a in *above*, e in *sicken*, i in *possible*, o in *melon*, u in *circus*

in·ter·jec·tion [in'tər·jek'shən] *n.* 1 In grammar, a word that expresses emotion and stands alone grammatically. "Ouch!" is an interjection. 2 The act of interjecting. 3 Something interjected.

in·ter·lace [in'tər·lās'] *v.* **in·ter·laced, in·ter·lac·ing** 1 To join (threads, strips, or other parts) by passing them over and under one another: to *interlace* rushes to make a mat. 2 To cross one another as if woven together: The vines *interlaced.*

Interlaced fingers

in·ter·lard [in'tər·lärd'] *v.* To give variety to by adding something different here and there: to *interlard* a lecture with jokes.

in·ter·line[1] [in'tər·līn'] *v.* **in·ter·lined, in·ter·lin·ing** To write between the lines of (a book, manuscript, or other written material).

in·ter·line[2] [in'tər·līn'] *v.* **in·ter·lined, in·ter·lin·ing** To put in an extra lining under the regular lining of (a garment).

in·ter·lin·ing [in'tər·lī'ning] *n.* An extra lining beneath the usual lining of a garment.

in·ter·lock [in'tər·lok'] *v.* To join or lock together firmly: Our hands *interlocked.*

in·ter·lo·per [in'tər·lō'pər] *n.* Someone who meddles in other people's business; intruder.

in·ter·lude [in'tər·lo͞od'] *n.* 1 A short interval of time that interrupts something: an *interlude* of calm in the storm. 2 A short, often funny, performance presented between the acts of a play. 3 A brief piece of music such as is played between stanzas of a song or acts of a play.

in·ter·mar·riage [in'tər·mar'ij] *n.* Marriage between members of different families, religions, or races.

in·ter·mar·ry [in'tər·mar'ē] *v.* **in·ter·mar·ried, in·ter·mar·ry·ing** 1 To marry someone of a different religion, race, or class. 2 To become connected through marriage: The two royal families *intermarried.*

in·ter·me·di·ar·y [in'tər·mē'dē·er'ē] *n., pl.* **in·ter·me·di·ar·ies,** *adj.* 1 *n.* Someone who goes between persons or sides in trying to settle something; go-between: an *intermediary* in a dispute. 2 *adj.* Acting as a go-between: an *intermediary* agent. 3 *adj.* Intermediate.

in·ter·me·di·ate [in'tər·mē'dē·it] 1 *adj.* Being or coming between two things, levels, stages, or events; in the middle: an *intermediate* course of study. 2 *n.* Something intermediate.

intermediate school 1 In some areas of the United States, a school including grades 4 to 6. 2 Another name for JUNIOR HIGH SCHOOL.

in·ter·ment [in·tûr'mənt] *n.* A burial.

in·ter·mez·zo [in'tər·mct'sō] *n., pl.* **in·ter·mez·zos** or **in·ter·mez·zi** [in'tər·met'sē] A short musical composition performed between the main parts of a long work.

in·ter·mi·na·ble [in·tûr'mə·nə·bəl] *adj.* Never ending or seeming never to end: an *interminable* wait. **—in·ter'mi·na·bly** *adv.*

in·ter·min·gle [in'tər·ming'gəl] *v.* **in·ter·min·gled, in·ter·min·gling** To mix or mingle together; mingle with one another.

in·ter·mis·sion [in'tər·mish'ən] *n.* A pause for a time between periods of activity; recess: an *intermission* between acts of a play.

in·ter·mit·tent [in'tər·mit'ənt] *adj.* Stopping and starting or coming and going from time to time: *intermittent* activity; an *intermittent* fever. **—in'·ter·mit'tent·ly** *adv.*

in·ter·mix [in'tər·miks'] *v.* To mix together.

in·ter·mix·ture [in'tər·miks'chər] *n.* 1 The act of intermixing. 2 A mixture.

in·tern [*n.* in'tûrn, *v.* in·tûrn'] 1 *n.* A graduate of medical school who lives in a hospital and assists in treating patients, to get practical experience under supervision. 2 *v.* To serve as an intern. 3 *v.* To confine in or keep from leaving a country or place during a war: to *intern* a warship or an enemy alien.

in·ter·nal [in·tûr'nəl] *adj.* 1 Of, on, or having to do with the inside; inner: *internal* medicine. 2 Having to do with the domestic affairs of a country: *internal* revenue. **—in·ter'nal·ly** *adv.*

in·ter·nal-com·bus·tion engine [in·tûr'nəl·kəm·bus'chən] An engine in which a mixture of fuel and air is exploded inside the cylinders to drive the pistons. It is the engine used in automobiles.

in·ter·na·tion·al [in'tər·nash'ən·əl] *adj.* 1 For or existing between or among nations: *international* trade agreements. 2 Having to do with the relations between nations: an *international* peace plan. **—in'ter·na'tion·al·ly** *adv.*

International Date Line An imaginary line approximately along the 180th meridian where, by international agreement, each calendar day begins. When it is Monday just east of the line, it is Tuesday just west of it.

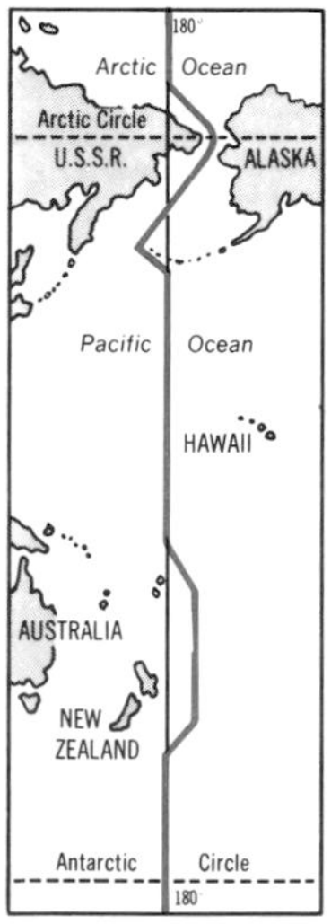

International Date Line

in·ter·na·tion·al·ism [in'tər·nash'ən·əl·iz'əm] *n.* A political and economic doctrine or policy of cooperation among nations for their mutual good.

in·ter·na·tion·al·ize [in'tər·nash'·ən·əl·īz'] *v.* **in·ter·na·tion·al·ized, in·ter·na·tion·al·iz·ing** To place under the control of several different nations: The Suez Canal was *internationalized* by an agreement in 1888.

in·terne [in'tûrn] *n.* Another spelling of INTERN.

in·ter·ne·cine [in'tər·nē'sin *or* in'·tər·nē'sīn'] *adj.* Very destructive, especially to both sides in a conflict; bloody: *internecine* warfare.

in·tern·ee [in'tûr·nē'] *n.* A person confined or detained, especially as an alien during a war.

in·tern·ment [in·tûrn'mənt] *n.* 1 The act of confining or holding: the *internment* of warships by a neutral country. 2 A being interned.

in·tern·ship [in'tûrn·ship'] *n.* A period of training while working, especially that of a recent graduate of a medical school serving in a hospital or clinic.

in·ter·plan·e·tar·y [in'tər·plan'ə·ter'ē] *adj.* Between or among planets: *interplanetary* space.

in·ter·play [in'tər·plā'] *n.* Action or influence of persons or things on each other.

in·ter·po·late [in·tûr'pə·lāt'] *v.* **in·ter·po·la·ted, in·ter·po·lat·ing** To insert (material) into a text or discourse, often with the aim of distorting its meaning: to *interpolate* incorrect statistics in a financial report. **—in·ter'po·la'tion** *n.*

in·ter·pose [in′tər·pōz′] *v.* **in·ter·posed, in·ter·pos·ing** **1** To put between: to *interpose* a line of police. **2** To come between, as if to settle an argument; intervene. **3** To put in or introduce (a question or comment) in a conversation or speech. **—in′ter·po·si′tion** *n.*

in·ter·pret [in·tûr′prit] *v.* **1** To explain or make clear: to *interpret* a story. **2** To judge in a personal way: I *interpret* your inquiry as a sign of interest. **3** To give or put forth one's own impression or understanding of: to *interpret* a piece of music. **4** To translate aloud: to *interpret* for the U.N.

in·ter·pre·ta·tion [in·tûr′prə·tā′shən] *n.* The act, process, or result of interpreting: The actor gave a fine *interpretation* of the role.

in·ter·pre·ta·tive [in·tûr′prə·tā′tiv] *adj.* Of or having to do with interpretation; explanatory.

in·ter·pret·er [in·tûr′prit·ər] *n.* A person who interprets or translates.

in·ter·pre·tive [in·tûr′prə·tiv] *adj.* Interpretative.

in·ter·ra·cial [in′tər·rā′shəl] *adj.* Of, for, or among people of different races: an *interracial* gathering; *interracial* misunderstanding.

in·ter·reg·num [in′tər·reg′nəm] *n., pl.* **in·ter·reg·nums** or **in·ter·reg·na** [in′tər·reg′nə] **1** The time between the end of a monarch's rule and the beginning of the next monarch's. **2** A pause.

in·ter·re·lat·ed [in′tər·ri·lā′tid] *adj.* Having a connection or relation to each other: *interrelated* problems.

in·ter·re·la·tion [in′tər·ri·lā′shən] *n.* The relation of one person or thing to another: the *interrelation* of family and friends.

in·ter·ro·gate [in·ter′ə·gāt′] *v.* **in·ter·ro·gat·ed, in·ter·ro·gat·ing** To question, usually in a formal examination: to *interrogate* a prisoner. **—in·ter′ro·ga′·tion** *n.*

interrogation mark or **interrogation point** Alternative names of QUESTION MARK.

in·ter·rog·a·tive [in′tə·rog′ə·tiv] **1** *adj.* Asking a question: an *interrogative* sentence. **2** *adj.* Used to ask a question: an *interrogative* pronoun. **3** *n.* A word used to ask a question.

in·ter·ro·ga·tor [in·ter′ə·gā′tər] *n.* A person who asks questions; examiner.

in·ter·rog·a·to·ry [in′tə·rog′ə·tôr′ē] *adj.* Asking or suggesting a question.

in·ter·rupt [in′tə·rupt′] *v.* **1** To cause (something or someone) to stop by breaking in: to *interrupt* a broadcast; Don't *interrupt* me. **2** To interfere or get in the way of: The wall *interrupts* the view. **3** To break the course or continuity of.

in·ter·rup·tion [in′tə·rup′shən] *n.* **1** The act of interrupting. **2** A being interrupted: I spoke without any *interruption.* **3** Something that interrupts.

in·ter·scho·las·tic [in′tər·skə·las′tik] *adj.* Between or among schools: an *interscholastic* game.

in·ter·sect [in′tər·sekt′] *v.* **1** To divide by cutting across or passing through: No streets *intersect* the elevated highway. **2** To cross each other: Lines on graph paper *intersect.*

in·ter·sec·tion [in′tər·sek′shən] *n.* **1** A crossing, especially a place where streets cross. **2** An intersecting.

in·ter·sperse [in′tər·spûrs′] *v.* **in·ter·spersed, in·ter·spers·ing** **1** To put here and there among other things: to *intersperse* FBI agents in the crowd. **2** To change or vary by putting in things here and there: red *interspersed* with gray.

in·ter·state [in′tər·stāt′] *adj.* Between, among, or having to do with different states of the U.S.

in·ter·stel·lar [in′tər·stel′ər] *adj.* Between or among the stars.

in·ter·stice [in·tûr′stis] *n., pl.* **in·ter·sti·ces** [in·tûr′·stə·sēz] A small opening; narrow space; chink: Moss filled *interstices* between logs. **—in·ter·sti·tial** [in′tər·stish′əl] *adj.*

in·ter·twine [in′tər·twīn′] *v.* **in·ter·twined, in·ter·twin·ing** To unite by twining or twisting together.

in·ter·ur·ban [in′tər·ûr′bən] *adj.* Between or among cities: an *interurban* railroad.

in·ter·val [in′tər·vəl] *n.* **1** The time between two events: the *interval* between school terms. **2** The distance or space between two objects or points: an *interval* of 20 feet. **3** In music, the difference in pitch between two tones. **—at intervals** **1** From time to time. **2** With spaces between.

in·ter·vene [in′tər·vēn′] *v.* **in·ter·vened, in·ter·ven·ing** **1** To come in to change a situation: to *intervene* to prevent a fight. **2** To come or be between two places or times.

in·ter·ven·tion [in′tər·ven′shən] *n.* **1** The act of intervening. **2** Interference in the affairs of one country by another: armed *intervention.*

in·ter·ven·tion·ism [in′tər·ven′shə·niz′əm] *n.* The policy of intervening or interfering in the political and economic affairs of one country by another.

in·ter·view [in′tər·vyo͞o′] **1** *n.* A meeting of two or more people arranged for a special purpose: an *interview* with a new student. **2** *n.* A meeting in which one or more reporters seek information for publication from another person. **3** *v.* To have an interview with: to *interview* a job applicant. **—in′·ter·view′er** *n.*

in·ter·weave [in′tər·wēv′] *v.* **in·ter·wove** or **in·ter·weaved, in·ter·wov·en, in·ter·weav·ing** **1** To weave together: to *interweave* fibers. **2** To connect closely; blend.

in·tes·tate [in·tes′tāt′ *or* in·tes′tit] *adj.* Not having made a will before death.

in·tes·ti·nal [in·tes′tə·nəl] *adj.* Of, in, or affecting the intestine: *intestinal* pain.

in·tes·tine [in·tes′tin] *n.* (*often pl.*) A long, coiled tube extending from the stomach to the anus and helping to digest food and eliminate waste matter from the body. It has two parts, the **small intestine** and the **large intestine.**

in·ti·ma·cy [in′tə·mə·sē] *n., pl.* **in·ti·ma·cies** An intimate condition or close relationship.

in·ti·mate[1] [in′tə·mit] **1** *adj.* Very close or friendly; familiar: an *intimate* companion. **2** *n.* A close friend. **3** *adj.* Deeply personal; private: *intimate* thoughts. **4**

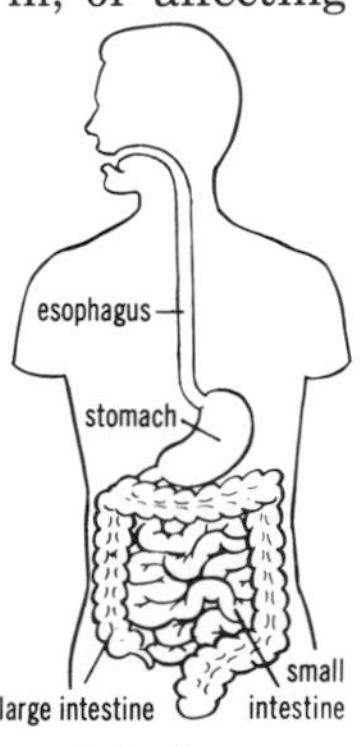

Intestines

a	add	**i**	it	**o͝o**	took	**oi**	oil
ā	ace	**ī**	ice	**o͞o**	pool	**ou**	pout
â	care	**o**	odd	**u**	up	**ng**	ring
ä	palm	**ō**	open	**û**	burn	**th**	thin
e	end	**ô**	order	**yo͞o**	fuse	**th**	this
ē	equal					**zh**	vision

ə = a in *above*, e in *sicken*, i in *possible*, o in *melon*, u in *circus*

adj. Resulting from firsthand knowledge or familiarity: *intimate* knowledge of the crime. **—in′·ti·mate·ly** *adv.*

in·ti·mate[2] [in′tə·māt′] *v.* **in·ti·mat·ed, in·ti·mat·ing** To hint; suggest; imply. **—in′ti·ma′tion** *n.*

in·tim·i·date [in·tim′ə·dāt′] *v.* **in·tim·i·dat·ed, in·tim·i·dat·ing** 1 To make timid; frighten: The bully *intimidated* us. 2 To frighten into doing or not doing something: to *intimidate* a witness. **—in·tim′·i·da′tion** *n.*

intl. international.

in·to [in′tōō] *prep.* 1 To or toward the inside of: to go *into* the forest; Cut *into* the melon. 2 To the form or state of: to change water *into* steam. 3 Dividing: Two *into* six is three. 4 *informal* Practicing, interested in, or absorbed in: My brother is *into* jogging.

in·tol·er·a·ble [in·tol′ər·ə·bəl] *adj.* 1 Too hard or painful to be endured. 2 More than one can be expected to put up with: *intolerable* noise.

in·tol·er·ance [in·tol′ər·əns] *n.* 1 Unwillingness to let others live, think, believe, or worship as they choose. 2 An inability to bear or stand; excessive sensitivity: an *intolerance* to penicillin.

in·tol·er·ant [in·tol′ər·ənt] *adj.* Unwilling to accept the right of others to live or worship as they choose. **—intolerant of** Not able or willing to endure. **—in·tol′er·ant·ly** *adv.*

in·to·na·tion [in′tō·nā′shən] *n.* 1 A reciting or chanting, as of a prayer. 2 The pattern the voice follows in rising and falling in pitch during speech: an American *intonation.*

in·tone [in·tōn′] *v.* **in·toned, in·ton·ing** To say or recite in a singing tone; chant: to *intone* a prayer.

in·tox·i·cant [in·tok′sə·kənt] *n.* Something that intoxicates, as an alcoholic drink.

in·tox·i·cate [in·tok′sə·kāt′] *v.* **in·tox·i·cat·ed, in·tox·i·cat·ing** 1 To make drunk. 2 To make very excited or elated.

in·tox·i·cat·ed [in·tok′sə·kā′tid] *adj.* 1 Drunk. 2 Very excited or elated.

in·tox·i·ca·tion [in·tok′sə·kā′shən] *n.* 1 Drunkenness. 2 Wild excitement or joy. 3 In medicine, a poisoned condition.

intr. intransitive.

intra- A prefix meaning: Within or inside of, as in *intramuscular.*

in·trac·ta·ble [in·trak′tə·bəl] *adj.* Not easily controlled; stubborn: an *intractable* horse.

in·tra·mu·ral [in′trə·myōō′rəl] *adj.* Happening between or among members of the same school or organization: *intramural* football.

in·tra·mus·cu·lar [in′trə·mus′kyə·lər] *adj.* Located within or injected into a muscle or muscle tissue.

in·tran·si·gent [in·tran′sə·jənt] 1 *adj.* Unwilling to compromise; refusing to give in. 2 *n.* A person who is intransigent. **—in·tran′si·gence** *n.* **—in·tran′·si·gent·ly** *adv.*

in·tran·si·tive [in·tran′sə·tiv] *adj.* Not taking or containing a direct object. In the sentence "She ran fast," *ran* is an intransitive verb and *ran fast* is an intransitive construction. **—in·tran′si·tive·ly** *adv.*

in·tra·ve·nous [in′trə·vē′nəs] *adj.* Into or within a vein: *intravenous* injections.

in·treat [in·trēt′] *v.* Another spelling of ENTREAT.

in·trench [in·trench′] *v.* Another spelling of ENTRENCH.

in·trep·id [in·trep′id] *adj.* Very brave; courageous; fearless. **—in·tre·pid·i·ty** [in′trə·pid′ə·tē] *n.*

in·tri·ca·cy [in′tri·kə·sē] *n., pl.* **in·tri·ca·cies** 1 The condition of being intricate. 2 Something intricate: the *intricacies* of the law.

in·tri·cate [in′tri·kit] *adj.* 1 Complicated or involved: *intricate* machinery. 2 Requiring close attention to follow or understand: an *intricate* problem. **—in′·tri·cate·ly** *adv.*

An intricate maze

in·trigue [*n.* in·trēg′ *or* in′trēg, *v.* in·trēg′] *n., v.* **in·trigued, in·tri·guing** 1 *n.* Sly, secret scheming or plotting. 2 *n.* A secret, crafty plot or scheme. 3 *v.* To plot or carry out an intrigue: to *intrigue* against the government. 4 *n.* A secret love affair. 5 *v.* To arouse the interest or curiosity of; fascinate.

in·trigu·ing [in·trēg′ing] *adj.* Arousing interest or curiosity; fascinating: The movie has an *intriguing* plot. **—in·trigu′ing·ly** *adv.*

in·trin·sic [in·trin′sik] *adj.* Belonging to the basic or real nature of a thing; essential: the *intrinsic* value of a diamond. **—in·trin′si·cal·ly** *adv.*

intro. introduction.

intro- A prefix meaning: Into or within, as in *introvert.*

in·tro·duce [in′trə·d(y)ōōs′] *v.* **in·tro·duced, in·tro·duc·ing** 1 To make acquainted; present: Let me *introduce* you to my parents. 2 To turn the attention of (someone) to a thing for the first time: The film *introduced* us to the world of science. 3 To bring into use or notice first: to *introduce* a new patent medicine. 4 To begin: to *introduce* a noun clause with the conjunction *that.* 5 To bring in as something added: The rabbit was *introduced* into Australia. 6 To put forward; propose: to *introduce* a resolution. 7 To put in; insert: to *introduce* a feeding tube into a patient's nostril.

in·tro·duc·tion [in′trə·duk′shən] *n.* 1 The act of introducing: the *introduction* of a new product. 2 A being introduced: My *introduction* to the piano was a turning point in my life. 3 Something that is introduced: The potato plant was an introduction from South America. 4 The opening part, as of a book or speech, which serves to lead up to what follows.

in·tro·duc·to·ry [in′trə·duk′tər·ē] *adj.* Serving as an introduction: *introductory* remarks.

in·tro·spec·tion [in′trə·spek′shən] *n.* The examining of one's own thoughts and emotions.

in·tro·spec·tive [in′trə·spek′tiv] *adj.* Having to do with or tending toward introspection.

in·tro·vert [in′trə·vûrt′] *n.* A person whose main interest is directed inward toward thoughts and feelings rather than toward the world outside. **—in′tro·vert′ed** *adj.*

in·trude [in·trōōd′] *v.* **in·trud·ed, in·trud·ing** 1 To come in without being invited or wanted: I hope I am not *intruding.* 2 To thrust or force in. **—in·trud′er** *n.*

in·tru·sion [in·trōō′zhən] *n.* The act of intruding: an unwelcome *intrusion.*

in·tru·sive [in·trōō′siv] *adj.* Coming or thrusting in without being wanted; intruding. **—in·tru′sive·ly** *adv.* **—in·tru′sive·ness** *n.*

in·trust [in·trust′] *v.* Another spelling of ENTRUST.

in·tu·i·tion [in′t(y)o͞o·ish′ən] *n.* 1 Direct knowledge or awareness that is based not on conscious reasoning but on an inner feeling: My *intuition* told me they would come back. 2 Something known in this way.

in·tu·i·tive [in·t(y)o͞o′ə·tiv] *adj.* 1 Knowing or working by intuition. 2 Known by intuition: *intuitive* knowledge. **—in·tu′i·tive·ly** *adv.*

I·nu·it [in′o͞o·it′ *or* in′yo͞o·it′] *n.* 1 A member of a people living along the Arctic coasts of North America. 2 The language of these people. Compare ESKIMO.

in·un·date [in′un·dāt′] *v.* **in·un·dat·ed, in·un·dat·ing** To cover by overflowing; flood.

in·un·da·tion [in′un·dā′shən] *n.* A flooding.

in·ure [in·yo͝or′] *v.* **in·ured, in·ur·ing** To make accustomed; harden: Living in a city *inures* one to street noises.

in·vade [in·vād′] *v.* **in·vad·ed, in·vad·ing** 1 To enter by force with the purpose of conquering: Hitler's armies *invaded* Poland. 2 To get inside and spread throughout: Germs *invaded* the patient's bloodstream. 3 To rush or swarm into; overrun. 4 To intrude or trespass upon: to *invade* someone's privacy. **—in·vad′er** *n.*

in·va·lid[1] [in′və·lid] 1 *n.* A sickly person who cannot live an active life the way a healthy person can: The disease confined the formerly healthy musician to a wheelchair as an *invalid.* 2 *adj.* Of or for an invalid. 3 *v.* To make an invalid. 4 *adj.* Weak and sickly: an *invalid* neighbor. 5 *v.* To release from active military duty because of ill health.

in·val·id[2] [in·val′id] *adj.* Not valid; not true or sound; worthless: an *invalid* conclusion.

in·val·i·date [in·val′ə·dāt′] *v.* **in·val·i·dat·ed, in·val·i·dat·ing** To make worthless or invalid: The erasure *invalidated* the check.

in·va·lid·i·ty [in′və·lid′ə·tē] *n.* The condition or quality of being not valid; worthlessness.

in·val·u·a·ble [in·val′y(o͞o·)ə·bəl] *adj.* Worth more than can be estimated; priceless. **—in·val′u·a·bly** *adv.*

in·var·i·a·ble [in·vâr′ē·ə·bəl] *adj.* Not changing or able to change; constant: an *invariable* fact. **—in·var′i·a·bly** *adv.*

in·va·sion [in·vā′zhən] *n.* 1 The act of invading: The armed *invasion* started a war. 2 An attack or spreading out of something harmful: an *invasion* of Japanese beetles. 3 An intruding.

in·vec·tive [in·vek′tiv] *n.* A harsh and ruthless attack in words; violent denunciation.

in·veigh [in·vā′] *v.* To make a harsh or bitter attack in words: to *inveigh* against high taxes.

in·vei·gle [in·vē′gəl *or* in·vā′gəl] *v.* **in·vei·gled, in·vei·gling** To coax or entice by flattery or trickery: I was *inveigled* into a loan of $10.

in·vent [in·vent′] *v.* 1 To think out or bring into being for the first time: The Wright brothers *invented* the airplane. 2 To think up as a matter of convenience: to *invent* a reason.

in·ven·tion [in·ven′shən] *n.* 1 Something invented: to patent an *invention.* 2 The act of inventing: the *invention* of a new synthetic fiber. 3 The power of inventing: The poet's *invention* was picturesque. 4 A false, made-up story: Their excuse was a mere *invention.*

in·ven·tive [in·ven′tiv] *adj.* 1 Skillful at inventing; original: an *inventive* mind. 2 Showing invention: an *inventive* novel.

in·ven·tor [in·ven′tər] *n.* A person who invents.

in·ven·to·ry [in′vən·tôr′ē] *n., pl.* **in·ven·to·ries,** *v.* **in·ven·to·ried, in·ven·to·ry·ing** 1 *n.* A complete list and valuation of goods: Some stores take *inventory* every summer. 2 *n.* The making of such a list: closed for *inventory.* 3 *n.* The available stock of goods: The sale reduced the store's *inventory.* 4 *v.* To make a detailed list or inventory of: The clerks stayed late to *inventory* the stock.

in·verse [in·vûrs′ *or* in′vûrs] 1 *adj.* Opposite or reversed in order, direction, or effect. 2 *n.* The direct opposite; reverse: Addition is the *inverse* of subtraction. **—in·verse′ly** *adv.*

in·ver·sion [in·vûr′zhən] *n.* 1 Something inverted. 2 The act of inverting: the *inversion* of subject and verb, as "Am I" for "I am." 3 A being inverted.

in·vert [in·vûrt′] *v.* 1 To turn upside down. 2 To reverse the order of.

in·ver·te·brate [in·vûr′tə·brit *or* in·vûr′tə·brāt′] 1 *n.* An animal without a backbone. Worms and insects are invertebrates. 2 *adj.* Of or having to do with an invertebrate.

in·vest [in·vest′] *v.* 1 To put (money) to use in order to make a profit: Buying a business, a property, or stocks are ways of *investing.* 2 To use or spend with the hope of getting some later advantage or profit: to *invest* time and effort on one's education. 3 To give power, authority, or rank to: Police are *invested* with the authority to make arrests. 4 To give a particular quality to; endow: The cobwebs *invested* the room with a gloomy air. 5 To clothe or cover. **—in·vest′or** *n.*

in·ves·ti·gate [in·ves′tə·gāt′] *v.* **in·ves·ti·gat·ed, in·ves·ti·gat·ing** To look into thoroughly in order to find out the facts or details: to *investigate* an alleged robbery. **—in·ves′ti·ga′tor** *n.*

in·ves·ti·ga·tion [in·ves′tə·gā′shən] *n.* A thorough search or inquiry; examination to find out facts or details.

in·ves·ti·ga·tor [in·ves′tə·ga′tər] *n.* 1 A person who investigates. 2 A person whose job it is to conduct investigations, especially a detective.

in·ves·ti·ture [in·ves′tə·chər] *n.* The process or formal ceremony of investing a person with an office, rank, or power.

in·vest·ment [in·vest′mənt] *n.* 1 The investing of something, as money or time, in order to get a profit or advantage. 2 Invested money. 3 Something in which money is invested: a good *investment.*

in·vet·er·ate [in·vet′ər·it] *adj.* 1 Firmly established by long use; deep-rooted: an *inverterate* custom. 2 Fixed in a particular habit or opinion; confirmed: an *inveterate* collector. **—in·vet′er·ate·ly** *adv.*

in·vid·i·ous [in·vid′ē·əs] *adj.* Likely to create ill will or resentment by unfairness: an *invidious* comparison of abilities. **—in·vid′i·ous·ly** *adv.*

a	add	**i**	it	**o͝o**	took	**oi**	oil
ā	ace	**ī**	ice	**o͞o**	pool	**ou**	pout
â	care	**o**	odd	**u**	up	**ng**	ring
ä	palm	**ō**	open	**û**	burn	**th**	thin
e	end	**ô**	order	**yo͞o**	fuse	**th**	this
ē	equal					**zh**	vision

ə = { a in *above* e in *sicken* i in *possible* o in *melon* u in *circus* }

in·vig·or·ate [in·vig′ər·āt′] *v.* **in·vig·or·at·ed, in·vig·or·at·ing** To give vigor and energy to: Walking in the fresh air *invigorates* me. **—in·vig′or·a′tion** *n.*

in·vin·ci·ble [in·vin′sə·bəl] *adj.* Not to be overcome or conquered: an *invincible* warrior. **—in·vin′ci·bil′·i·ty** *n.* **—in·vin′ci·bly** *adv.*

in·vi·o·la·ble [in·vī′ə·lə·bəl] *adj.* Not to be violated or profaned: an *inviolable* pledge; an *inviolable* shrine. **—in·vi′o·la·bil′i·ty** *n.*

in·vi·o·late [in·vī′ə·lit] *adj.* Not violated; not profaned or broken; intact.

in·vis·i·ble [in·viz′ə·bəl] *adj.* Not visible; not capable of being seen: Air is *invisible*; The image on film is *invisible* until developed. **—in·vis′i·bil′i·ty** *n.* **—in·vis′i·bly** *adv.*

in·vi·ta·tion [in′və·tā′shən] *n.* **1** An asking of someone to come to a place or do something: a formal *invitation.* **2** The act of inviting.

in·vite [in·vīt′] *v.* **in·vit·ed, in·vit·ing** **1** To ask (someone) courteously to come to a place or perform some action: We *invited* 20 friends to the party. **2** To make a polite request for: to *invite* suggestions. **3** To make more likely; tend to bring forth: Speeding *invites* accidents. **4** To tempt; entice.

in·vit·ing [in·vī′ting] *adj.* Tempting; enticing: The big, soft bed looked *inviting* to the tired traveler. **—in·vit′ing·ly** *adv.*

in vi·tro [in vē′trō] Growing or being observed outside the living body in an artificial medium, as in a test tube or laboratory dish. ◆ *In vitro* is a Latin phrase meaning "in or within glass."

in vi·vo [in vē′vō] Growing or being observed within a living organism.

in·vo·ca·tion [in′və·kā′shən] *n.* **1** An appeal or prayer, as for help or inspiration, to God or gods. **2** The words used to call up evil spirits.

in·voice [in′vois] *n., v.* **in·voiced, in·voic·ing** **1** *n.* A list sent to a customer describing the items shipped and including prices and delivery charges. **2** *v.* To list on an invoice.

in·voke [in·vōk′] *v.* **in·voked, in·vok·ing** **1** To call upon for help or protection, as in a prayer: to *invoke* the gods. **2** To ask or appeal for: to *invoke* revenge. **3** To call into operation; apply: to *invoke* the power of the court. **4** To call up by magic: to *invoke* spirits.

in·vol·un·tar·y [in′vol′ən·ter′ē] *adj.* **1** Not subject to conscious control: Breathing and sneezing are *involuntary* actions. **2** Not done intentionally; accidental. **—in·vol′un·tar′i·ly** *adv.*

in·volve [in·volv′] *v.* **in·volved, in·volv·ing** **1** To include as a necessary part; have to do with: The job *involves* hard work; Biology *involves* all living things. **2** To associate; implicate: Their abrupt departure *involved* them in the scandal. **3** To absorb; engross: *involved* in making a model. **—in·volve′ment** *n.*

in·volved [in·volvd′] *adj.* Complicated; intricate: directions too *involved* to follow.

in·vul·ner·a·ble [in·vul′nər·ə·bəl] *adj.* Not capable of being wounded or overcome by attack; impregnable: an *invulnerable* fortress. **—in·vul′ner·a·bly** *adv.*

in·ward [in′wərd] **1** *adv., adj.* Toward the inside: to push the door *inward*; an *inward* thrust. **2** *adj.* Inner; interior: an *inward* part of an animal. **3** *adj., adv.* Of or toward one's inner self: *inward* thoughts.

in·ward·ly [in′wərd·lē] *adv.* **1** In or toward the inside or interior. **2** Secretly; to oneself.

i·o·dide [ī′ə·dīd′] *n.* A compound composed of iodine and another element or a radical.

i·o·dine [ī′ə·dīn′ *or* ī′ə·din] *n.* **1** A nonmetallic element of the halogen group consisting of lustrous blackish crystals that sublime on heating. It occurs in sea water and in seaweed. Traces are essential in the diet. **2** Iodine in alcohol, used to kill germs.

i·o·dize [ī′ə·dīz′] *v.* **i·o·dized, i·o·diz·ing** To treat with iodine or an iodide.

i·on [ī′ən] *n.* An atom or group of atoms having a positive or negative electric charge due to a gain or loss of electrons.

-ion A suffix meaning: **1** The act or process of, as in *union.* **2** The result of, as in *invention.* **3** The condition of being, as in *relation.*

i·on·ic [ī·on′ik] *adj.* Containing or having to do with ions.

I·on·ic [ī·on′ik] *adj.* Of or indicating a style of Greek architecture marked by columns having scroll-like decorations carved at the top.

ionic bond A bond between ions formed when electrons are transferred from one kind of atom to another kind.

i·on·ize [ī′ən·īz′] *v.* **i·on·ized, i·on·iz·ing** To make or be made, fully or in part, into ions. **—i′on·i·za′·tion** *n.*

i·on·o·sphere [ī·on′ə·sfir′] *n.* Several layers of the earth's atmosphere where radiation from the sun and outer space has ionized the air.

i·o·ta [ī·ō′tə] *n.* **1** The ninth letter of the Greek alphabet. **2** A very small amount.

IOU or **I.O.U.** A note having on it these letters (meaning *I owe you*), to acknowledge a debt.

IQ or **I.Q.** intelligence quotient.

ir- A form of the prefix IN- meaning *not*, used before words beginning with *r*, as in *irresponsible.*

Ir The symbol for the element iridium.

Ir. Irish.

IRA **1** Individual Retirement Account. **2** (*often written* **I.R.A.**) Irish Republican Army.

I·ra·ni·an [i·rā′nē·ən] **1** *adj.* Of or from Iran. **2** *n.* A person born in or a citizen of Iran. **3** *n.* The language of Iran.

I·ra·qi [i·rak′ē *or* ē′rä′kē] **1** *adj.* Of or from Iraq. **2** *n.* A person born in or a citizen of Iraq. **3** *n.* The language of Iraq.

i·ras·ci·ble [i·ras′ə·bəl] *adj.* Quickly angered; irritable.

i·rate [ī′rāt *or* ī·rāt′] *adj.* **1** Angry. **2** Characterized or caused by anger: *irate* words.

IRBM or **I.R.B.M.** Intermediate range ballistic missile.

ire [īr] *n.* Intense anger, especially when it is openly displayed; wrath.

Ire. Ireland.

ire·ful [īr′fəl] *adj.* Feeling or showing ire; furiously angry. **—ire′ful·ly** *adv.*

i·ren·ic [ī·ren′ik *or* ī·rē′nik] *adj.* Promoting or tending to promote peace or conciliation; peaceful; pacific; conciliatory.

i·ren·i·cal [ī·ren′i·kəl *or* ī·rē′ni·kəl] *adj.* Irenic. **—i·ren·i·cal·ly** *adv.*

ir·i·des·cent [ir′ə·des′ənt] *adj.* Showing the colors of the rainbow in changing patterns, as mother-of-pearl and some gems. **—ir′i·des′cence** *n.* **—ir′i·des′cent·ly** *adv.*

i·rid·i·um [i·rid′ē·əm] *n.* A silver-white metallic element resistant to corrosion, found native along with platinum.

i·ris [ī′ris] *n.* 1 The colored part of the eye that encircles the pupil. 2 A plant with long, sword-shaped leaves and colorful flowers. 3 The flower. 4 The rainbow.

Iris

I·rish [ī′rish] 1 *adj.* Of or from Ireland. 2 *n.* (**the Irish**) The people of Ireland. 3 *n.* The dialect of English spoken in Ireland. 4 *n.* Irish Gaelic. ◆ Historically, the Irish spoke a Celtic language called *Gaelic,* related to the old language of Scotland. A modern version of Gaelic is still spoken, but English is now more widespread.

Irish Gaelic The Celtic language of the Irish, especially as spoken since the 16th century.

I·rish·man [ī′rish·mən] *n., pl.* **I·rish·men** [ī′rish·mən] A person born in or a citizen of Ireland or Northern Ireland.

Irish potato The common white potato.

Irish setter A breed of bird dog with a long, shiny red coat.

Irish terrier A breed of short-haired terrier of medium size, having a wiry red coat.

Irish wolfhound An old breed of very large dog having a rough, usually grayish coat.

I·rish·wom·an [ī′rish·wo͝om′ən] *n., pl.,* **I·rish·wom·en** [ī′rish·wim′in] A woman born in or a citizen of Ireland or Northern Ireland.

irk [ûrk′] *v.* To annoy or irritate; vex.

irk·some [ûrk′səm] *adj.* Tiresome; tedious: an *irksome* job. **—irk′some·ly** *adv.* **—irk′some·ness** *n.*

i·ron [ī′ərn] 1 *n.* A very abundant metallic element which has had important technological uses ever since prehistoric times and which in combined form is an essential component in plant and animal life. 2 *n.* Something made of iron. 3 *adj. use: iron* doors. 4 *adj.* Like iron; firm; strong: an *iron* constitution. 5 *n.* Something firm or unyielding, like iron: a will of *iron.* 6 *n.* (*pl.*) Iron chains or shackles. 7 *n.* A device, usually of iron, with a handle and smooth bottom that is heated and used to press clothes. 8 *v.* To press with an iron. **—iron out** To clear up or smooth over.

Iron Age A period in humanity's early history, after the Stone Age and the Bronze Age, when weapons and tools were made of iron.

i·ron·clad [ī′ərn·klad′] 1 *adj.* Covered with iron or armor. 2 *n.* An armored warship. 3 *adj.* Very firm; strict: an *ironclad* rule.

iron curtain 1 A barrier, as of censorship or secrecy, that isolates a country from others. 2 (*written* **Iron Curtain**) After World War II, such a barrier setting apart the Soviet Union and its satellite countries from the rest of Europe and the United States.

iron hand Strict or despotic control.

i·ron·ic [ī·ron′ik] *adj.* 1 Of, related to, expressing, or full of irony: an *ironic* comment. 2 Odd because so unexpected: It was *ironic* that the minute we gave up the search, we found the missing clue. **—i·ron′i·cal·ly** *adv.*

i·ron·i·cal [ī·ron′i·kəl] *adj.* Ironic.

ironing board A padded board, often with folding legs, on which to iron clothing.

iron lung A large machine for giving artificial respiration over long periods, as to a polio patient with lungs affected.

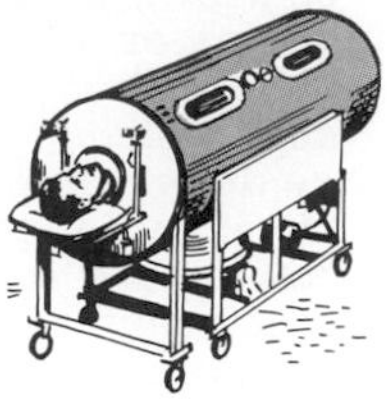
Iron lung

i·ron·mong·er [ī′ərn·mung′gər] *n. chiefly British* A dealer in hardware and other metal goods.

iron pyrites Another name for PYRITE (def. 1).

i·ron·stone [ī′ərn·stōn′] *n.* 1 A type of plain white pottery made into dishes. 2 Any of several kinds of rock that are rich in iron.

i·ron·ware [ī′ərn·wâr′] *n.* Utensils and articles made of iron, especially pots and pans.

i·ron·wood [ī′ərn·wo͝od′] *n.* 1 Any of various trees having very hard wood. 2 This wood.

i·ron·work [ī′ərn·wûrk′] *n.* Work in iron, such as window gratings, fences, and rails.

i·ron·works [ī′ərn·wûrks′] *n.pl.* (*usually used with a singular verb*) A factory or shop where iron is smelted or heavy iron goods are manufactured.

i·ro·ny [ī′rə·nē] *n., pl.* **i·ro·nies** 1 A way of implying the opposite of what the words expressed literally mean, often in an effort to be humorous or sarcastic, as when one says "Thanks" after being insulted. 2 A fact, result, or happening that seems the opposite of what one would naturally expect: the *irony* of being at sea without any water to drink.

Ir·o·quoi·an [ir′ə·kwoi′ən] *n.* A family of North American Indian languages spoken by the Iroquois.

Ir·o·quois [ir′ə·kwoi′ *or* ir′ə·kwoiz′] *n., pl.* **Ir·o·quois** 1 A group of North American Indian tribes once living in the NE U.S. They are often called the Five Nations. 2 A member of any of these tribes.

ir·ra·di·ate [i·rā′dē·āt′] *v.* **ir·ra·di·at·ed, ir·ra·di·at·ing** 1 To light up; illuminate: The moon *irradiated* the sky. 2 To make or be radiant. 3 To send forth like rays of light: to *irradiate* happiness. 4 To treat with or subject to radiation, especially X rays or ultraviolet light. **—ir·ra′di·a′tion** *n.*

ir·ra·tion·al [i·rash′ən·əl] *adj.* 1 Not able to reason or understand. 2 Not rational; not reasonable; senseless; illogical: an *irrational* fear of water. **—ir·ra′tion·al·ly** *adv.*

ir·ra·tion·al·i·ty [i·rash′ə·nal′ə·tē] *n.* 1 The condition or quality of being irrational. 2 Something irrational, as an action or thought.

irrational number A number which cannot be exactly expressed as a whole number or as the quotient of two whole numbers. $\sqrt{3}$ and π are irrational numbers.

ir·re·claim·a·ble [ir′i·klā′mə·bəl] *adj.* Not capable of being reclaimed: an *irreclaimable* swamp; an *irreclaimable* criminal.

a	add	**i**	it	**o͝o**	took	**oi**	oil
ā	ace	**ī**	ice	**o͞o**	pool	**ou**	pout
â	care	**o**	odd	**u**	up	**ng**	ring
ä	palm	**ō**	open	**û**	burn	**th**	thin
e	end	**ô**	order	**yo͞o**	fuse	**t͟h**	this
ē	equal					**zh**	vision

ə = a in *above* e in *sicken* i in *possible* o in *melon* u in *circus*

ir·rec·on·cil·a·ble [i·rek′ən·sī′lə·bəl] *adj.* Not able or willing to be reconciled: *irreconcilable* rivals.

ir·re·cov·er·a·ble [ir′i·kuv′ər·ə·bəl] *adj.* Not capable of being recovered or regained: the *irrecoverable* past.

ir·re·deem·a·ble [ir′i·dē′mə·bəl] *adj.* 1 Not capable of being recovered or exchanged: Postmarked stamps are *irredeemable.* 2 Beyond redeeming; past help: an *irredeemable* situation.

ir·re·duc·i·ble [ir′i·d(y)ōō′sə·bəl] *adj.* Not capable of being reduced or made simpler.

ir·ref·u·ta·ble [i·ref′yə·tə·bəl *or* ir′i·fyōō′tə·bəl] *adj.* Not capable of being disproved: *irrefutable* evidence

irreg. 1 irregular. 2 irregularity. 3 irregularly.

ir·reg·u·lar [i·reg′yə·lər] *adj.* 1 Not in accord with customary standards, established patterns, or traditional rules: *irregular* behavior. 2 Not even or symmetrical: an *irregular* coastline. 3 In grammar, not inflected in a standard way. **—ir·reg′u·lar·ly** *adv.*

ir·reg·u·lar·i·ty [i·reg′yə·lar′ə·tē] *n., pl.* **ir·reg·u·lar·i·ties** 1 The condition of being irregular. 2 Something irregular or improper.

ir·rel·e·vant [i·rel′ə·vənt] *adj.* Not related to the subject or topic; not applicable or pertinent: an *irrelevant* objection. **—ir·rel′e·vance** *n.* **—ir·rel′e·vant·ly** *adv.*

ir·re·lig·ious [ir′i·lij′əs] *adj.* 1 Indifferent to religion; not practicing religion. 2 Not in conformity with religious beliefs; blasphemous.

ir·re·me·di·a·ble [ir′i·mē′dē·ə·bəl] *adj.* Not capable of being remedied or corrected.

ir·rep·a·ra·ble [i·rep′ər·ə·bəl] *adj.* Not capable of being repaired, fixed, or set right: *irreparable* harm. **—ir·rep′a·ra·bly** *adv.*

ir·re·place·a·ble [ir′i·plā′sə·bəl] *adj.* Not capable of being replaced; having no substitute: an *irreplaceable* antique chair.

ir·re·pres·si·ble [ir′i·pres′ə·bəl] *adj.* Not capable of being controlled or held back: *irrepressible* humor. **—ir′re·pres′si·bly** *adv.*

ir·re·proach·a·ble [ir′i·prō′chə·bəl] *adj.* Not capable of being blamed or found fault with; blameless: *irreproachable* behavior.

ir·re·sis·ti·ble [ir′i·zis′tə·bəl] *adj.* Incapable of being resisted or opposed: an *irresistible* smile. **—ir′re·sis′ti·bly** *adv.*

ir·res·o·lute [i·rez′ə·lōōt′] *adj.* Not firm or resolute in acting or in making up one's mind.

ir·res·o·lu·tion [i·rez′ə·lōō′shən] *n.* A lack of firmness or resolution in acting or in making up one's mind; hesitation.

ir·re·spec·tive [ir′i·spek′tiv] *adj.* Regardless: Anyone can join, *irrespective* of age.

ir·re·spon·si·ble [ir′i·spon′sə·bəl] *adj.* Not responsible or reliable; having no sense of duty. **—ir′re·spon′si·bil′i·ty** *n.* **—ir′re·spon′si·bly** *adv.*

ir·re·triev·a·ble [ir′i·trē′və·bəl] *adj.* That cannot be recovered or repaired: an *irretrievable* loss. **—ir′re·triev′a·bly** *adv.*

ir·rev·er·ent [i·rev′ər·ənt] *adj.* Having or showing a lack of awe, reverence, or respect: an *irreverent* attitude toward authority. **—ir·rev′er·ence** *n.* **—ir·rev′er·ent·ly** *adv.*

ir·re·vers·i·ble [ir′i·vûr′sə·bəl] *adj.* Incapable of being reversed, changed, or undone: an *irreversible* decision. **—ir′re·vers′i·bly** *adv.*

ir·rev·o·ca·ble [i·rev′ə·kə·bəl] *adj.* Incapable of being brought back, undone, or altered: an *irrevocable* decision; the *irrevocable* past. **—ir·rev′o·ca·bly** *adv.*

ir·ri·gate [ir′ə·gāt′] *v.* **ir·ri·gat·ed, ir·ri·gat·ing** 1 To furnish (land) with water, by using pipes, ditches, or canals: The fruit growers of the West *irrigate* their crops. 2 To wash out, by applying a stream of water or other liquid: to *irrigate* a wound; to *irrigate* the nasal passages. **—ir′ri·ga′tion** *n.*

Irrigation system

ir·ri·ta·bil·i·ty [ir′ə·tə·bil′ə·tē] *n.* 1 The condition of being irritable. 2 The capacity of a plant or animal to respond to an external or internal stimulus.

ir·ri·ta·ble [ir′ə·tə·bəl] *adj.* 1 Easily annoyed or angered; snappish. 2 Very sensitive or sore. **—ir′ri·ta·bly** *adv.*

ir·ri·tant [ir′ə·tənt] 1 *adj.* Causing irritation: an *irritant* gas. 2 *n.* Something that irritates.

ir·ri·tate [ir′ə·tāt′] *v.* **ir·ri·tat·ed, ir·ri·tat·ing** 1 To annoy; bother: The constant ringing of the phone *irritated* me. 2 To make sore or inflamed: The rough wool *irritates* my skin. **—ir′ri·tat′ing·ly** *adv.*

ir·ri·ta·tion [ir′ə·tā′shən] *n.* 1 The act of irritating. 2 The condition of being irritated: their *irritation* with the constant noise. 3 Something that causes annoyance. 4 Inflammation or soreness of a part of the body: an eye *irritation.* **—ir′ri·ta′tor** *n.*

ir·rup·tion [i·rup′shən] *n.* A breaking or rushing in with great force: an *irruption* of water through the broken dike.

IRS or **I.R.S.** Internal Revenue Service.

is [iz] A form of the verb BE. It indicates the present time and is used with "he," "she," or "it," or with singular nouns: She *is* a lawyer. One package *is* arriving today. **—as is** Just as it is; with no change.

is. island(s).

I.S. intermediate school.

I·saac [ī′zək] *n.* In the Bible, the father of Jacob and Esau, and the son of Abraham and Sarah.

I·sa·iah [ī·zā′ə] *n.* 1 A Hebrew prophet who lived during the eighth century B.C. 2 A book of the Old Testament, containing his teachings.

ISBN International Standard Book Number.

is·chi·um [is′kē·əm] *n., pl.* **is·chi·a** [is′kē·ə] The lowest of the three principal bones that form each side of the human pelvis.

-ise *suffix* Alternate spelling of -IZE, used chiefly in Great Britain.

-ish A suffix meaning: 1 Of or belonging to, as in a *Polish* church. 2 Like, as in *childish.* 3 Somewhat; rather, as in *bluish.* 4 Fond of or inclined to, as in *bookish.*

Ish·mael [ish′mē·əl] *n.* 1 In the Bible, the son of Abraham and his maidservant. He was banished to the desert. 2 Any outcast from society.

i·sin·glass [ī′zing·glas′] *n.* 1 A type of gelatin made from fish bladders, used in jelly or glue. 2 Another name for MICA.

I·sis [ī′sis] *n.* In Egyptian myths, the goddess of fertility.

isl. island(s).

Is·lam [is·läm′ *or* is′ləm] *n.* 1 The religion of the Muslims, founded by Muhammad and in which there is only one God, called Allah. 2 All Muslims as a group. 3 The countries of the world where Islam is the chief religion.

Is·lam·ic [is·lam′ik *or* is·läm′ik] *adj.* Muslim.

is·land [ī′lənd] *n.* 1 A body of land entirely surrounded by water. The major continents of the world, however, are not usually considered islands. 2 Any place set apart from its surroundings: The park was an *island* of quiet in the city. ◆ *Island* comes from the Old English word *igland.* The *s* was added in the 15th century because of a mistaken association with *isle. Isle* actually has nothing to do with the Old English word; it came into English from Old French and goes back to the Latin *insula.*

is·land·er [ī′lən·dər] *n.* A person who comes from or lives on an island.

island of Lan·ger·hans [läng′ər·häns′] Any of the small masses of endocrine cells in the pancreas that produce insulin.

isle [īl] *n.* An island, especially a small one. ◆ See ISLAND.

is·let [ī′lit] *n.* A very small island.

islet of Langerhans Another name for ISLAND OF LANGERHANS.

ism [iz′əm] *n. informal* A special theory, doctrine, or system.

-ism A suffix meaning: 1 A system, practice, or belief, as in *socialism.* 2 The act or result of, as in *baptism.* 3 The quality or behavior of, as in *patriotism.* 4 The condition of being, as in *skepticism.* 5 An example of, as in *colloquialism.*

is·n't [iz′ənt] Is not.

i·so·bar [ī′sə·bär′] *n.* A line on a map connecting points having equal barometric pressures.

i·so·late [ī′sə·lāt′] *v.* **i·so·lat·ed, i·so·lat·ing** To place apart or alone; separate from others: Their unfriendliness *isolated* them from the neighbors. ◆ The verb *isolate* was formed from the adjective *isolated,* which goes back to the Latin word *insula,* meaning *island.*

i·so·la·tion [ī′sə·lā′shən] 1 *n.* The act of isolating: the *isolation* of a hepatitis patient. 2 *n.* The state of being isolated: a troublesome prisoner in *isolation.* 3 *adj. use*: the *isolation* wing of a hospital.

i·so·la·tion·ism [ī′sə·lā′shən·iz′əm] *n.* A belief that a country should keep apart from other nations and not take part in international alliances or affairs. **—i′so·la′tion·ist** *n.*

i·so·mer [ī′sə·mər] *n.* Any of a group of chemical compounds that are made up of the same elements in the same proportions but with different arrangements of their atoms.

i·so·met·ric [ī′sə·met′rik] *adj.* Of, relating to, or based on muscular contractions in which a muscle is tensed in opposition to another muscle or to an immovable object.

i·so·met·rics [ī′sə·met′riks] *n.* Exercises using isometric contractions to improve muscle tone. ◆ See -ICS.

i·sos·ce·les [ī·sos′ə·lēz′] *adj.* Indicating a triangle having two of its sides equal.

i·so·term [ī′sə·thûrm′] *n.* A line on a weather map drawn so that all points on the line have the same average temperature.

i·so·tope [ī′sə·tōp′] *n.* Any of two or more forms of an element that have the same atomic number and chemical properties but which have different atomic weights.

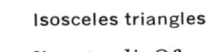

Isosceles triangles

Isr. 1 Israel. 2 Israeli.

Is·rae·li [iz·rā′lē] *adj., n., pl.* **Is·rae·lis** 1 *adj.* Of or from modern Israel. 2 *n.* A person born in or a citizen of modern Israel.

Is·ra·el·ite [iz′rē·əl·īt′] *n.* Any of the people of ancient Israel or their descendants; Hebrew or Jew.

is·su·ance [ish′ōō·əns] *n.* The act of issuing.

is·sue [ish′ōō] *n., v.* **is·sued, is·su·ing** 1 *n.* A sending out or supplying: an emergency *issue* of food. 2 *n.* Something supplied, distributed, or sent out, as a magazine or stamps. 3 *v.* To give out; distribute: The army *issued* new rifles. 4 *v.* To send forth or out; publish: The book was first *issued* in England. 5 *n.* A going out; outflow: an *issue* of hot water from the faucet. 6 *v.* To come forth; flow out: Blood *issued* from the cut. 7 *n.* The outcome; result: The *issue* of the game was in doubt. 8 *v.* To come as a result or consequence: What *issued* from your efforts? 9 *n.* A topic or problem under discussion: the *issues* of the meeting. 10 *n.* Offspring; a child or children: The couple died without *issue.* **—at issue** To be resolved; under discussion. **—take issue** To disagree.

I

-ist A suffix meaning: 1 A person who makes or does, as in *tourist.* 2 A person whose work or job is, as in *pharmacist.* 3 A person who knows about, performs on, or is skilled in, as in *pianist.* 4 A person who believes in or advocates, as in *communist.*

isth·mus [is′məs] *n.* A narrow strip of land, with water on each side, that connects two larger masses of land.

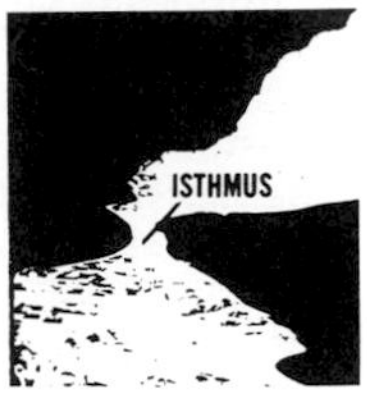

it [it] 1 *pron.* The animal, thing, happening, place, or idea being talked about: The child took a cookie and bit *it* in two; I don't believe *it.* 2 *pron.* The apparent subject of a verb when the real subject follows: *It* was decided that we should go. 3 *pron.* The subject of an impersonal verb: *It* rained last night. 4 *pron.* An object having no definite meaning, used with certain verbs: We brazened *it* out. 5 *n.* The person in certain children's games who must catch or find another.

It. 1 Italian. 2 Italy.

ital. 1 italic. 2 (*often written* **itals.**) italics.

Ital. 1 Italian. 2 Italy.

I·tal·ian [i·tal′yən] 1 *adj.* Of or from Italy. 2 *n.* A person born in or a citizen of Italy. 3 *n.* The language of Italy.

i·tal·ic [i·tal′ik *or* ī·tal′ik] 1 *n.* (*usually pl.*) A kind of printing type in which the letters slant to the right. It is used to stress or call attention to words. *These words are printed in italics.* 2 *adj.* Describing or printed in this type.

i·tal·i·cize [i·tal′ə·sīz′ *or* ī·tal′ə·sīz′] *v.* **i·tal·i·cized, i·tal·i·ciz·ing** 1 To print in italics. 2 To underline (something written) to show that it should be printed in italics.

a	add	**i**	it	**ŏŏ**	took	**oi**	oil
ā	ace	**ī**	ice	**ōō**	pool	**ou**	pout
â	care	**o**	odd	**u**	up	**ng**	ring
ä	palm	**ō**	open	**û**	burn	**th**	thin
e	end	**ô**	order	**yōō**	fuse	**th**	this
ē	equal					**zh**	vision

ə = a in *above*, e in *sicken*, i in *possible*, o in *melon*, u in *circus*

itch [ich] 1 *v.* To have a tickling feeling on the skin that makes one want to scratch. 2 *n.* Such a tickling feeling. 3 *n.* A skin disease that causes this feeling. 4 *v.* To have a restless desire: I'm *itching* to travel. 5 *n.* A restless desire.

itch·y [ich'ē] *adj.* **itch·i·er, itch·i·est** 1 Affected by or causing an itch: an *itchy* leg; an *itchy* bandage. 2 Impatient; restless. **—itch'i·ness** *n.*

-ite A suffix meaning: 1 A person of or from, as in *Israelite.* 2 A person who believes in, follows, or is involved with, as in *socialite.*

i·tem [ī'təm] *n.* 1 Any one thing in a group. 2 A single piece of news or information.

i·tem·ize [ī'təm·īz'] *v.* **i·tem·ized, i·tem·iz·ing** To list each item of: Please *itemize* the bill.

it·er·ate [it'ə·rāt'] *v.* **it·er·at·ed, it·er·at·ing** To state or utter again; repeat.

i·tin·er·ant [ī·tin'ər·ənt] 1 *adj.* Going from place to place; traveling: an *itinerant* farm worker. 2 *n.* A person who travels from place to place, especially one who moves from job to job.

i·tin·er·ar·y [ī·tin'ə·rer'ē] *n., pl.* **i·tin·er·ar·ies** 1 The plan or route of a journey. 2 A detailed record of a journey.

-itis A suffix meaning: 1 Inflammation of, as in *appendicitis.* 2 *informal* Too much use of or concern with, as in *telephonitis.*

it'll [it'(ə)l] 1 It will. 2 It shall.

its [its] *pron.* The possessive form of *it*: The dog had *its* dinner.

it's [its] 1 It is: *It's* a beautiful day. 2 It has: *It's* been a beautiful day. ◆ Many people confuse this contraction with the possessive pronoun ITS.

it·self [it·self'] *pron.* Its own self. *Itself* is used: 1 As the object of a verb or preposition, referring, in both cases, back to the subject: The dog hurt *itself*; The motor started by *itself.* 2 To give emphasis to a noun: This drawing is simplicity *itself.* 3 To describe a normal or usual condition: The house isn't *itself* with the children gone.

-ity A suffix meaning: The condition or quality of being, as in *stability.*

IU or **I.U.** international unit.

IV or **I.V.** intravenous.

I've [īv] I have.

-ive A suffix meaning: 1 Likely to; tending to, as in *descriptive.* 2 Having the nature, character, or quality of, as in *instinctive.*

i·vied [ī'vēd] *adj.* Covered or overgrown with ivy: an *ivied* cottage.

i·vo·ry [ī'vər·ē] *n., pl.* **i·vo·ries,** *adj.* 1 *n.* The hard, smooth, white substance of which the tusks of elephants and walruses are composed. 2 *adj. use*: an *ivory* box. 3 *n.* Any hard, white substance like ivory. 4 *n.* (*pl.*) *slang* The keys of a piano. 5 *adj., n.* Creamy white.

ivory nut The hard, ivorylike seed of a South American palm, often carved into figurines or buttons.

ivory tower *n.* A place in which to escape from everyday realities and practical concerns.

i·vy [ī'vē] *n., pl.* **i·vies** 1 A climbing vine with shiny, evergreen leaves. 2 Any of the various other plants like this.

Ivy

Ivy League 1 A group of older colleges and universities in the NE United States having a reputation for high academic achievement and social prestige. 2 *adj. use*: an *Ivy League* football team; *Ivy League* clothes.

Ivy Lea·guer [lē'gər] 1 A student attending an Ivy League college. 2 A graduate of an Ivy League college.

IWW or **I.W.W.** International Workers of the World.

-ize A suffix meaning: 1 To cause to be, as in *legalize.* 2 To make or become, as in *stabilize.* 3 To make or change into, as in *crystallize.* 4 To subject to the action of; affect with, as in *oxidize.*

Jj

J is the tenth letter of the alphabet. Its history until the Middle Ages is identical with that of the letter *I*. The sign that became *J* originated among Semitic people in the Near East, in the region of Palestine and Syria, probably in the middle of the second millennium B.C. Little is known about the sign until around 1000 B.C., when the Phoenicians began using it. They named it *yodh* and used it for a *y*-like sound.

When the Greeks adopted the Phoenician alphabet around the ninth century B.C., they had no use for the sign because the consonant *y* sound had disappeared from the Greek language long before. The Greeks, therefore, used the sign for the vowel *i*. They renamed it *iota* and simplified its shape.

As early as the eighth century B.C., the Etruscans adopted the Greek alphabet. It is from the Etruscans that the Romans took the sign for *I*. The Romans used the sign for the sounds of long and short *i* and of consonantal *y*.

The differentiation of *I* and *J* may be credited to the scribes of the Middle Ages. It became their custom, while preparing manuscripts, to lengthen the *I* and end it with a curve to the left whenever it appeared in a prominent position. Such positions might be an initial letter or before another *I*. Both signs stood for *i* sounds. In prominent positions, however, *I* often took on the sound of the consonant *y* (as in *yacht*). Eventually, beginning around the fourteenth century, the lengthened form of the letter became identified with the consonant sound, and the shorter form became identified with the vowel sound. The distinction was not made in England until 1630. The use of the sign for the soft *g* sound (as in *gem* or *judge*) resulted from French influence. The *majuscule,* or capital letter, *J* is undotted.

The *minuscule,* or small letter, *j* is also a late innovation. Its form is that of the lengthened *i* with the dot retained.

Early Phoenician (late 2nd millennium B.C.)
Phoenician (8th century B.C.)
Early Greek (9th-7th centuries B.C.)
Western Greek (6th century B.C.)
Classical Greek (403 B.C. onward)
Early Etruscan (8th century B.C.)
Monumental Latin (4th century B.C.)
Classical Latin
Roman uncial (4th-8th centuries)
Black-letter majuscule (15th century)
Black-letter minuscule (15th century)

J

j or **J** [jā] *n., pl.* **j's** or **J's** The tenth letter of the English alphabet.
J joule.
J. 1 journal. 2 judge. 3 justice.
JA 1 joint account. 2 (*often written* **J.A.**) Judge Advocate.
jab [jab] *n., v.* **jabbed, jab·bing** 1 *n.* A sharp poke or nudge. 2 *v.* To poke or nudge sharply. 3 *n.* A rapid punch. 4 *v.* To punch or strike with short, quick blows.
jab·ber [jab′ər] 1 *v.* To speak rapidly without making sense; chatter. 2 *n.* Rapid, senseless talk; chatter. **—jab′ber·er** *n.*
ja·bot [zha·bō′] *n., pl.* **ja·bots** [zha·bōz′] A ruffle or frill falling from the neckline of a blouse, dress, or shirt.
jac·a·ran·da [jak′ə·ran′də] *n.* An American tropical tree with clusters of bluish-violet flowers.
jack [jak] 1 *n.* A device or tool using a screw or lever to raise a heavy weight a short distance, as part of a car when a tire must be changed. 2 *v.* To lift with a jack. 3 *n.* A boy or man; fellow: seldom used today. 4 *n.* The male of certain animals. 5 *n.* A jackass. 6 *n.* A playing card bearing the face of a young man. It usually ranks just below the queen. 7 *n.* One of a set of stones or small metal pieces used in a children's game. 8 *n.* (*pl., used with a singular verb*) The game played with these pieces. 9 *n.* A small flag flown from a ship as a signal or an indication of nationality. 10 *n. slang* Money. **—jack up** 1 To raise with or as if with a jack: to *jack up* a car. 2 To raise (as the level of prices or fees).

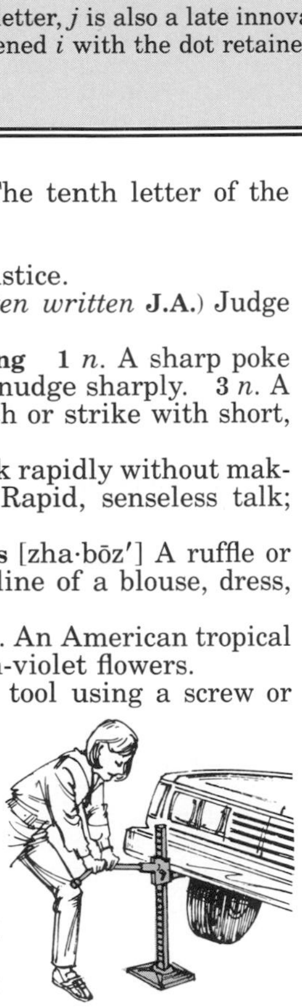

Jack

jack·al [jak′əl] *n.* 1 A doglike mammal of Asia and Africa which feeds on small animals and decaying carcasses. 2 A person who helps another do base deeds; accomplice. 3 A person who does lowly work for another.
jack·a·napes [jak′ə·nāps′] *n.* An impudent or mischievous person; rascal.
jack·ass [jak′as′] *n.* 1 A male ass; donkey. 2 A stupid person; fool.
jack·boot [jak′bo͞ot′] *n.* A strong, heavy boot reaching above the knee.
jack·daw [jak′dô′] *n.* A glossy, black, crowlike bird of Europe, sometimes tamed as a pet.

a	add	**i**	it	**o͝o**	took	**oi**	oil
ā	ace	**ī**	ice	**o͞o**	pool	**ou**	pout
â	care	**o**	odd	**u**	up	**ng**	ring
ä	palm	**ō**	open	**û**	burn	**th**	thin
e	end	**ô**	order	**yo͞o**	fuse	**t̶h̶**	this
ē	equal					**zh**	vision

ə = {a in *above* e in *sicken* i in *possible* / o in *melon* u in *circus*}

jack·et [jak′it] **1** *n.* A short coat. **2** *n.* A wrapper or outer covering, as a removable paper covering for a book or the skin of a cooked potato. **3** *v.* To enfold or protect with a jacket.

Jack Frost Frosty, wintry weather, thought of as a person.

jack·ham·mer [jak′ham′ər] *n.* A noisy pneumatic machine, usually operated by hand, for drilling rock and hard surfaces.

jack-in-the-box [jak′in·thə·boks′] *n.* A child's toy, consisting of a box with a figure that springs up when the lid is unfastened.

Jack-in-the-box

jack-in-the-pul·pit [jak′in·thə·po͝ol′pit] *n.* A woodland plant having a flower stalk partly covered by a green or purplish hood.

jack·knife [jak′nīf′] *n., pl.* **jack·knives** [jak′nīvz′], *v.* **jack·knifed, jack·knif·ing** **1** *n.* A large knife with folding blades, carried in the pocket. **2** *n.* A dive in which the diver bends over and touches the ankles with the hands while in the air, then straightens out and enters the water head first. **3** *v.* To double up like a jackknife.

jack-of-all-trades [jak′əv·ôl′trādz′] *n., pl.* **jacks-of-all-trades** A person who is able to do many kinds of work.

jack-o'-lan·tern [jak′ə·lan′tərn] *n.* A lantern made of a hollowed pumpkin carved into a face.

jack·pot [jak′pot′] *n.* The big prize in a contest or game of chance.

jack rabbit A large American hare with very long ears and long hind legs.

Jack rabbit

jack·screw [jak′skro͞o′] *n.* A type of jack for raising heavy weights, operated by means of a screw.

jack·stone [jak′stōn′] *n.* **1** A jack (def. 7). **2** (*pl., used with a singular verb*) The game of jacks.

jack·straw [jak′strô′] *n.* **1** One of a set of thin rods used in a game. They must be picked out of a heap one at a time without moving any of the others. **2** (*pl., used with a singular verb*) The game itself.

Ja·cob [jā′kəb] *n.* In the Bible, a son of Isaac and father of the founders of the twelve Hebrew tribes.

jac·quard or **Jac·quard** [jak′ärd *or* jə·kärd′] *n.* A fabric woven in elaborate, figured patterns on a special loom.

jade[1] [jād] **1** *n.* A hard, usually green mineral used as a gem. **2** *adj., n.* Pale to dark green.

jade[2] [jād] *v.* **jad·ed, jad·ing,** *n.* **1** *v.* To make or become weary, as through hard or boring work; tire. **2** *n.* An old or useless horse. **3** *n.* A coarse or bad-tempered woman; hussy.

jad·ed [jā′did] *adj.* **1** Tired, as from hard or boring work. **2** Dulled, as by overindulgence.

jag [jag] *n., v.* **jagged, jag·ging** **1** *n.* A sharp projecting point or protuberance, as on an edge or surface. **2** *v.* To cut jags in; notch.

jagged [jag′id] *adj.* Having sharp points or notches.

jag·uar [jag′wär] *n.* A large, spotted cat resembling a leopard, found in Central and South America. ◆ *Jaguar* comes from a Portuguese word derived from a South American Indian word.

Jaguar

jai a·lai [hī′lī′ *or* hī′ə·lī] A game popular in Spain and in Latin America in which a ball is flung against a wall and caught with a long, curved wicker basket strapped to the player's arm.

jail [jāl] **1** *n.* A place for confining persons guilty of minor offenses or those awaiting trial. **2** *v.* To put or hold in jail. ◆ Contrast the words *jail* and *prison.* A jail is a local building used to hold people awaiting trial or serving a short sentence. *Prison* usually refers to the place where a convicted criminal serves out a sentence.

jail·bird [jāl′bûrd′] *n. informal* A person who is serving or has served a term in prison or jail.

jail·er or **jail·or** [jā′lər] *n.* The officer in charge of a jail or of the prisoners in it.

ja·lop·y [jə·lop′ē] *n., pl.* **ja·lop·ies** *U.S. informal* An old automobile in bad shape.

jal·ou·sie [jal′o͞o·sē] *n.* A screen or shutter consisting of overlapping horizontal slats that can be tilted to keep out sun and rain while admitting light and air.

jam[1] [jam] *v.* **jammed, jam·ming,** *n.* **1** *v.* To press or squeeze into a tight space: to *jam* things into a box. **2** *v.* To block up, as by crowding: People *jammed* the halls. **3** *n.* A number of people or things crowded together: a traffic *jam.* **4** *v.* To make or become wedged or stuck, as a machine, door, or part. **5** *v.* To interfere with (radio signals) by broadcasting on the same frequency. **6** *v.* To injure by force or pressure: My foot was *jammed* in the door. **7** *v.* To push with force: to *jam* on the brakes. **8** *n. informal* An embarrassing or dangerous situation; predicament: Cheating on their finals got the students into a real *jam.* **9** *v.* In jazz, to play in a jam session.

jam[2] [jam] *n.* A preserve of fruit boiled with sugar until the mixture is thick.

Ja·mai·can [jə·mā′kən] **1** *adj.* Of or from Jamaica. **2** *n.* A person born in or a citizen of Jamaica.

jamb [jam] *n.* A side post or side of a doorway or window.

jam·bo·ree [jam′bə·rē′] *n.* **1** *informal* A loud, lively party. **2** A large assembly of Boy Scouts.

jam session A performance by a group of jazz musicians who improvise together.

Jan. January.

Jane Doe The name used for a woman involved in a legal proceeding whose real name is not known.

jan·gle [jang′gəl] *n., v.* **jan·gled, jan·gling** **1** *n.* A harsh, unmusical sound. **2** *v.* To make or cause to make harsh, unmusical sounds. **3** *n.* A quarrel; wrangling. **4** *v.* To quarrel.

jan·i·tor [jan′i·tər] *n.* A person hired to clean and take care of a building.

Jan·u·ar·y [jan′yŏŏ·er′ē] *n., pl.* **Jan·u·ar·ies** The first month of the year, having 31 days.

Ja·nus [jā′nəs] *n.* In Roman myths, the god of gates and doors, who watched over beginnings and endings. He is pictured as having two faces looking in opposite directions.

Head of Janus

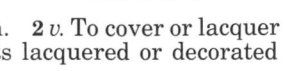

Jap. 1 Japan. 2 Japanese.

ja·pan [jə·pan′] *n., v.* **ja·panned, ja·pan·ning** 1 *n.* A hard black varnish originally made in Japan. 2 *v.* To cover or lacquer with japan. 3 *n.* Objects lacquered or decorated in the Japanese manner.

Jap·a·nese [jap′ə·nēz′] 1 *adj.* Of or from Japan. 2 *n.* A person born in or a citizen of Japan. 3 *n.* (**the Japanese**) The people of Japan. 4 *n.* The language of Japan.

Japanese beetle A beetle that destroys crops, introduced into the U.S. from Japan.

Japanese beetle

ja·pon·i·ca [jə·pon′i·kə] *n.* 1 A shrub native to Japan and grown for its bright red blossoms. 2 Another name for CAMELLIA.

jar[1] [jär] *n., v.* **jarred, jar·ring** 1 *n.* A shaking, as from a sudden shock. 2 *v.* To cause to tremble or shake; jolt. 3 *v.* To strike with unpleasant or painful effect: The speaker's shrill voice *jars* on my nerves. 4 *n.* A harsh, grating sound. 5 *v.* To clash; conflict: The rumors *jarred* with the facts.

jar[2] [jär] *n.* 1 A deep earthenware or glass container with a wide opening at the top. 2 The quantity a jar contains.

jar·gon [jär′gən] *n.* 1 Confused speech which cannot be understood; gibberish. 2 A mixture of two or more languages. 3 The special words or terms used by the members of a particular profession or class: legal *jargon.*

jas·mine [jas′min *or* jaz′min] *n.* A shrub with fragrant white, yellow, or red flowers.

Ja·son [jā′sən] *n.* In Greek myths, the leader of the Argonauts in their search for the Golden Fleece.

jas·per [jas′pər] *n.* A variety of quartz, usually red, brown, or yellow in color.

jaun·dice [jôn′dis] *n., v.* **jaun·diced, jaun·dic·ing** 1 *n.* A diseased condition of the liver in which there is a yellowness of the skin and the whites of the eyes caused by bile in the bloodstream. 2 *v.* To affect with jaundice. 3 *n.* A state of mind caused by prejudice, envy, or gloom. 4 *v.* To affect the judgment of by prejudice or envy.

jaun·diced [jôn′dist *or* jän′dist] *adj.* 1 Ill with jaundice. 2 Prejudiced or distorted, as by envy, resentment, or hostility: a *jaundiced* view of the world.

jaunt [jônt] 1 *n.* A short journey for pleasure. 2 *v.* To make such a journey.

jaunt·y [jôn′tē] *adj.* **jaunt·i·er, jaunt·i·est** 1 Having a lively or self-confident air or manner. 2 Dashing; perky: a *jaunty* hat. —**jaunt′i·ly** *adv.* —**jaunt′i·ness** *n.*

ja·va [jä′və *or* jav′ə] *n. informal* Coffee that has been brewed.

Java man A forerunner of modern humans. Fossil bones of Java man were found in central Java.

jave·lin [jav′(ə·)lin] *n.* A light spear once used as a weapon, but now thrown for distance in athletic contests.

Throwing a javelin

jaw [jô] 1 *n.* Either of the two bony parts of the skull in which the teeth grow; the framework of the mouth. 2 *n.* A jawbone. 3 *n.* The mouth, including the jaws and teeth. 4 *n.* (*often plural*) Anything resembling the mouth and its actions, as the gripping parts of a vise or the narrow opening of a canyon. 5 *v. slang* To talk or gossip, especially in a dull, long-winded way.

jaw·bone [jô′bōn′] *n., v.* **jaw·boned, jaw·bon·ing** 1 One of the bones forming the framework of the mouth, especially the lower jaw. 2 *v. informal* To try to sway by strong argument, especially to persuade to agree willingly to official policy.

jaw·break·er [jô′brā′kər] *n.* 1 A type of very hard candy. 2 *informal* A word that is difficult to pronounce.

jay [jā] *n.* A noisy bird related to the crow but highly colored, as the blue jay.

jay·walk [jā′wôk′] *v. informal* To walk across a street carelessly and in violation of traffic rules or signals. —**jay′walk′er** *n.*

jazz [jaz] 1 *n.* A kind of popular music that originated with Blacks in the southern U.S. It uses strongly syncopated rhythms and has a characteristic style of melody and harmony. 2 *adj. use*: a *jazz* band; *jazz* musicians. 3 *v.* To play or arrange (music) in the style of jazz. 4 *v.* To play jazz. 5 *n.* Empty, exaggerated, insincere, or nonsensical talk or actions. 6 *v.* To talk to or act in an empty, exaggerated, insincere, or nonsensical way. 7 *n.* Various similar but unspecified things: to discuss art, music, and that *jazz.* —**jazz up** To improve, as by making more interesting or lively.

jazz-rock [jaz′rok′] *n.* In popular music, a mixture of jazz and rock.

JCS or **J.C.S.** Joint Chiefs of Staff.

jct. junction.

JD or **J.D.** 1 Justice Department. 2 juvenile delinquent.

Je or **Je.** June.

jeal·ous [jel′əs] *adj.* 1 Fearful of losing someone's love to a rival. 2 Caused by this fear: *jealous* actions. 3 Begrudging someone what he or she has; envious. 4 Careful in protecting; watchful: to be *jealous* of one's reputation. 5 Demanding absolute loyalty, faithfulness, or worship: a *jealous* God. —**jeal′ous·ly** *adv.*

jeal·ous·y [jel′ə·sē] *n., pl.* **jeal·ous·ies** The condition or quality of being jealous.

jean [jēn] *n.* 1 A strong cotton cloth used in making workclothes. 2 (*pl.*) Trousers or overalls made of this material or of denim.

a	add	**i**	it	**ŏŏ**	took	**oi**	oil
ā	ace	**ī**	ice	**ōō**	pool	**ou**	pout
â	care	**o**	odd	**u**	up	**ng**	ring
ä	palm	**ō**	open	**û**	burn	**th**	thin
e	end	**ô**	order	**yōō**	fuse	**t̶h̶**	this
ē	equal					**zh**	vision

ə = a in *above* e in *sicken* i in *possible* o in *melon* u in *circus*

J

jeep [jēp] *n.* A small, sturdy automobile first used by the U.S. Army.

Jeep

jeer [jir] **1** *v.* To make fun of with insulting words; ridicule; mock. **2** *n.* A bitter and sarcastic remark.

Je·ho·vah [ji·hō′və] *n.* In the Old Testament, one of the names for God.

Jehovah's Witnesses A Christian sect founded in the late 1800's in the United States. Its members practice personal evangelism and distribute literature describing the beliefs of the sect.

je·june [ji·jo͞on′] *adj.* **1** Dull and lifeless. **2** Immature; juvenile, **—je·june′ly** *adv.*

je·jun·um [ji·jo͞o′nəm] *n., pl.* **je·ju·na** [ji·jo͞o′nə] The section of the small intestine extending from the duodenum to the ileum.

Jek·yll and Hyde [jek′əl·ən·hīd′ *or* jē′kəl·ən·hīd′] A person with a two-sided nature that changes back and forth from good to evil, from agreeable to disagreeable. ◆ *Jekyll* and *Hyde* are the names given a single character in the story *The Strange Case of Dr. Jekyll and Mr. Hyde* by Robert Louis Stevenson.

jell [jel] *v.* **1** To thicken and turn to jelly. **2** *informal* To assume or cause to assume definite form: Our vacation plans have finally *jelled.*

jel·lied [jel′ēd] *adj.* **1** Made into a jelly or jellylike substance, as by chilling: a *jellied* consommé. **2** Covered with a jellylike substance.

jel·ly [jel′ē] *n., pl.* **jel·lies,** *v.* **jel·lied, jel·ly·ing** **1** *n.* A thick, sticky substance that quivers when shaken but will not flow, as a spread made from fruit juice boiled with sugar. **2** *v.* To make into or become jelly. **3** *n.* Any substance like jelly.

jel·ly·bean [jel′ē·bēn′] *n.* A bean-shaped candy with a hard covering and a gummy center.

jel·ly·fish [jel′ē·fish′] *n., pl.* **jel·ly·fish** or **jel·ly·fish·es** A sea animal with a jellylike, umbrella-shaped body and long trailing tentacles that capture and poison its prey.

Jellyfish

jen·net [jen′it] *n.* A small Spanish horse.

jen·ny [jen′ē] *n., pl.* **jen·nies** **1** A machine for spinning yarn. **2** The female of some birds and animals: a *jenny* wren.

jeop·ar·dize [jep′ər·dīz′] *v.* **jeop·ar·dized, jeop·ar·diz·ing** To put in danger; place in jeopardy.

jeop·ar·dy [jep′ər·dē] *n.* Danger of death, loss, or injury; peril.

jer·bo·a [jər·bō′ə] *n.* A small rodent of Asia and North Africa, having very long hind legs that enable it to move by great leaps.

Jer·e·mi·ah [jer′ə·mī′ə] *n.* **1** A Hebrew prophet who lived during the seventh century B.C. **2** A book of the Old Testament containing his prophecies.

jerk[1] [jûrk] **1** *n.* A sudden, sharp pull or twist: a *jerk* of the wrist. **2** *v.* To give a sharp, sudden pull or twist to; pull or tug at: to *jerk* a rope. **3** *n.* An involuntary tightening of a muscle; twitch. **4** *n.* A sudden, sharp movement: I turned with a *jerk.* **5** *v.* To move suddenly or unevenly: to *jerk* one's head. **6** *n. slang* A silly or stupid person.

jerk[2] [jûrk] *v.* To cure (meat, especially beef) by cutting into strips and drying.

jer·kin [jûr′kin] *n.* A tight jacket or vest, usually sleeveless, popular in the 16th and 17th centuries.

Jerkin

jerk·y[1] [jûr′kē] *adj.* **jerk·i·er, jerk·i·est** Moving with sudden starts and stops: a *jerky* train. **—jerk′·i·ly** *adv.* **—jerk′i·ness** *n.*

jerk·y[2] [jûr′kē] *n.* Meat, especially beef, that has been cut into strips and dried in the sun.

jer·ry-built [jer′ē·bilt′] *adj.* **1** Flimsily and hastily constructed, usually of poor materials: a *jerry-built* house. **2** Put together or developed in a hasty or careless way: a *jerry-built* project.

jer·sey [jûr′zē] *n., pl.* **jer·seys** **1** A cloth knitted by machine. **2** A knitted shirt or sweater pulled on over the head. **3** (*written* **Jersey**) One of a breed of small cattle giving rich milk.

jes·sa·mine [jes′ə·min] *n.* Another name for JASMINE.

jest [jest] **1** *n.* Something said or done to provoke laughter; joke. **2** *n.* An object of laughter; laughingstock. **3** *v.* To tell jokes. **4** *v.* To speak or act in a playful way.

jest·er [jes′tər] *n.* A person who jests; especially, in former times, a clown whose job was to amuse a monarch.

Jes·u·it [jezh′o͞o·it *or* jez′yo͞o·it] *n.* A member of the Society of Jesus, a Roman Catholic religious order founded in 1534.

Je·sus [jē′zəs] *n.* The person whose life, teachings, and death are the basis of the Christian religion. He is also called **Jesus Christ.**

jet[1] [jet] **1** *n.* A hard, black mineral used for jewelry, buttons, and other objects. **2** *adj. use: jet* buttons. **3** *adj., n.* Deep, glossy black.

jet[2] [jet] *n., v.* **jet·ted, jet·ting** **1** *n.* A gush or spurt of gas or liquid from a small opening. **2** *v.* To shoot out in a jet or jets. **3** *n.* A nozzle or spout. **4** *n.* A jet-propelled aircraft. **5** *v.* To fly in a jet airplane.

jet-black [jet′blak′] *adj.* Deep, glossy black, like jet.

jet engine An engine that draws in air, mixes it with fuel, and ignites the mixture, producing a blast of hot gases to the rear and creating a strong forward thrust by reaction.

jet lag The various psychological and physical disturbances brought on by traveling through several time zones in a jet airplane.

jet plane A jet-propelled aircraft.

jet-pro·pelled [jet′prə·peld′] *adj.* Driven by jet propulsion.

jet propulsion Propulsion, as of an airplane, by means of jets or jet engines.

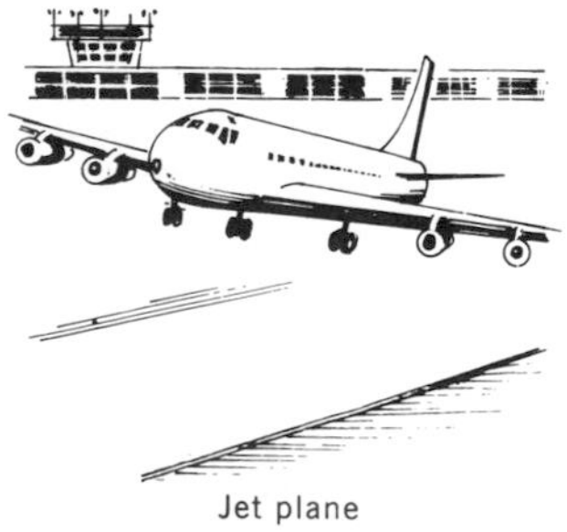
Jet plane

jet·sam [jet′səm] *n.* **1** Goods thrown into the sea to lighten a ship in danger of sinking. **2** Such goods washed ashore.

jet set An international group of fashionable people who travel by jet plane from one expensive resort to another.

jet setter A member of the jet set.

jet stream 1 A current of winds blowing from the west at speeds often above 250 miles an hour, usually 30,000 to 45,000 feet up. 2 The blast of gases from a jet engine.

jet·ti·son [jet′ə·sən] *v.* 1 To throw (cargo or goods) overboard to lighten in an emergency: As the ship took on water, the sailors *jettisoned* the cargo. 2 To throw away; discard as useless.

jet·ty [jet′ē] *n., pl.* **jet·ties** 1 A structure of stone or piles extending into a body of water to divert a current or protect a harbor. 2 A wharf or pier.

Jetty

Jew [jo͞o] *n.* 1 A member of the Hebrew people; Israelite. 2 A person who believes in and practices Judaism.

jew·el [jo͞o′əl] *n., v.* **jew·eled** or **jew·elled, jew·el·ing** or **jew·el·ling** 1 *n.* A precious stone; gem. 2 *n.* Anything of rare excellence or value. 3 *v.* To set or adorn with jewels or something like a jewel: The grass was *jeweled* with dew. 4 *n.* A bit of ruby or other hard mineral used as a bearing, as in a watch.

jew·el·er [jo͞o′əl·ər] *n.* A person who sells or makes jewelry.

jew·el·ry [jo͞o′əl·rē] *n.* Personal ornaments, as rings and bracelets, often made from precious metals and with precious stones.

Jew·ish [jo͞o′ish] *adj.* Of or having to do with the Jews, their religion, or their customs. **—Jew′ish·ness** *n.*

Jew·ry [jo͞o′rē] *n.* The Jewish people.

jew's-harp or **jews'-harp** [jo͞oz′härp′] *n.* A small metal musical instrument that is held between the teeth and played by striking a bent piece of metal with the finger.

Jez·e·bel [jez′ə·bəl] *n.* 1 In the Bible, a very wicked woman, the wife of King Ahab. 2 Any bold or wicked woman.

JFK or **J.F.K.** John Fitzgerald Kennedy International Airport.

JHS or **J.H.S.** junior high school.

jib [jib] *n.* A triangular sail set forward of the foremast.

jibe[1] [jīb] *v.* **jibed, jib·ing** 1 To swing to the other side of a boat sailing before the wind: said about a sail. 2 To cause (a sail) to shift in this way, on purpose.

jibe[2] [jīb] *v.* **jibed, jib·ing** Another spelling of GIBE.

jibe[3] [jīb] *v.* **jibed, jib·ing** *informal* To agree: Their stories appeared to *jibe.*

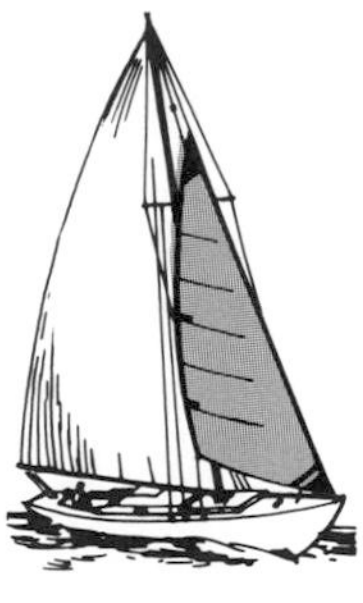
Jib

jif·fy [jif′ē] *n., pl.* **jif·fies** *informal* An instant: I'll be with you in a *jiffy.*

jig [jig] *n., v.* **jigged, jig·ging** 1 *n.* A gay, lively dance, or the music for such a dance. 2 *v.* To dance a jig. 3 *n.* A device for guiding a tool. 4 *n.* A fishhook that wiggles in the water to attract fish.

jig·ger [jig′ər] *n.* 1 A small container used to measure liquor when mixing drinks. 2 The amount of liquor contained in a jigger.

jig·gle [jig′əl] *v.* **jig·gled, jig·gling,** *n.* 1 *v.* To vibrate with short, quick jerks. 2 *n.* A jerky, unsteady movement.

jig·saw [jig′sô′] *n.* A saw with a slim blade set vertically in a frame and moved up and down, used for cutting curved or irregular lines.

jigsaw puzzle A puzzle consisting of a picture mounted on cardboard or wood and then cut into irregularly shaped pieces to be fitted together again.

jilt [jilt] *v.* To cast off or discard, as a lover or sweetheart.

Jim Crow or **jim crow** [jim′krō′] *informal* The policy of segregating and discriminating against black people. **—Jim′-Crow′ism** or **jim′-crow′ism** *n.* **—Jim′-Crow′** or **jim′-crow′** *adj.* ◆ *Jim Crow* was the name of a black character in a song from a 19th-century minstrel show.

jim·my [jim′ē] *n., pl.* **jim·mies,** *v.* **jim·mied, jim·my·ing** 1 *n.* A burglar's crowbar. 2 *v.* To break or pry open, as with a jimmy.

jim·son·weed [jim′sən·wēd′] *n.* A tall, very poisonous weed having a rank odor and large, funnel-shaped flowers.

jin·gle [jing′gəl] *n., v.* **jin·gled, jin·gling** 1 *n.* A tinkling, clinking, or rapid ringing. 2 *v.* To make or cause to make light, ringing or tinkling sounds: to *jingle* coins. 3 *n.* A catchy song or poem, especially for advertising purposes.

jin·go [jing′gō] *n., pl.* **jin·goes,** *adj.* 1 *n.* A person characterized by jingoism. 2 *adj.* Of or having to do with a jingo. 3 *adj.* Of or having to do with jingoism.

jin·go·ism [jing′gō·iz′əm] *n.* National chauvinism characterized by or advocating a militant foreign policy; excessive, bellicose patriotism. **—jin′go·is′·tic** *adj.*

jin·ni [jin′ē *or* ji·nē′] *n., pl.* **jinn** [jin] Another spelling of GENIE.

jin·rik·sha or **jin·rik·i·sha** [jin·rik′shə *or* jin·rik′·shô] *n.* A small two-wheeled carriage pulled by one or two people, used in parts of the Orient.

jinx [jingks] *informal* 1 *n.* A person or thing supposed to bring bad luck. 2 *v.* To bring bad luck to.

jit·ney [jit′nē] *n., pl.* **jit·neys** *informal* A small bus or car that follows a regular route and carries passengers for a small fare.

jit·ter [jit′ər] *informal* 1 *v.* To be restless or nervous; fidget. 2 *n.* (*pl.*) A state of nervousness or fear: a case of the *jitters.* **—jit′ter·y** *adj.*

jit·ter·bug [jit′ər·bug′] *n., v.* **jit·ter·bugged, jit·ter·bug·ging** *informal* 1 *n.* A very fast energetic dance of the 1940's done to jazz or swing music. 2 *v.* To dance the jitterbug. 3 *n.* A person who dances the jitterbug.

jit·ter·y [jit′ər·ē] *adj.* Nervous; fearful.

jiu·jit·su [jo͞o·jit′so͞o] *n.* Another spelling of JUJITSU.

a	add	**i**	it	**o͝o**	took	**oi**	oil
ā	ace	**ī**	ice	**o͞o**	pool	**ou**	pout
â	care	**o**	odd	**u**	up	**ng**	ring
ä	palm	**ō**	open	**û**	burn	**th**	thin
e	end	**ô**	order	**yo͞o**	fuse	**th**	this
ē	equal					**zh**	vision

ə = a in *above*, e in *sicken*, i in *possible*, o in *melon*, u in *circus*

jive [jīv] *n., v.* **jived, jiv·ing** *slang* 1 *n.* Jazz or swing music. 2 *v.* To play jive. 3 *n.* The special words used by jazz and swing musicians or their fans. 4 *n.* Silly or deceptive talk. 5 *v.* To talk nonsense. 6 *v.* To deceive.

job [job] *n., v.* **jobbed, job·bing,** *adj.* 1 *n.* Anything that is to be done; piece of work; task. 2 *v.* To perform work that is undertaken and paid for by the job; do piecework. 3 *adj.* Of or doing work that is undertaken and paid for by the job: a *job* printer. 4 *n.* A position or situation of employment. 5 *v.* To buy (merchandise) from manufacturers and sell to retailers.

Job [jōb] *n.* 1 In the Bible, a patient man who despite much suffering kept his faith in God. 2 A book of the Old Testament concerning him.

job·ber [job′ər] *n.* A person who buys in quantity from a manufacturer and sells to retail dealers.

job·less [job′lis] *adj.* 1 Having no job or work; unemployed. 2 Of or having to do with persons who are unemployed. **—job′less·ness** *n.*

Jo·cas·ta [jō·kas′tə] *n.* In Greek myths, a queen who, without knowing who he was, married her son Oedipus and killed herself when she discovered the truth.

jock [jok] *n.* 1 *slang* An athlete, especially one who is in college. 2 A jockstrap.

jock·ey [jok′ē] *n., pl.* **jock·eys,** *v.* 1 *n.* A person employed to ride horses in races. 2 *v.* To ride as a jockey. 3 *v.* To manipulate or trick: to *jockey* someone into a bad position. 4 *v.* To maneuver in a tricky or skillful way.

Jockey

jock·strap or **jock strap** [jok′strap′] *n.* An elastic supporter for the male genitals, worn during athletics or strenuous activities.

jo·cose [jō·kōs′] *adj.* Merry; humorous; joking: a *jocose* manner. **—jo·cose′ly** *adv.*

jo·cos·i·ty [jō·kos′ə·tē] *n. pl.* **jo·cos·i·ties** 1 The condition or quality of being jocose. 2 A jocose action or remark; joke; jest.

joc·u·lar [jok′yə·lər] *adj.* 1 Making jokes; given to joking. 2 Intended as a joke. **—joc·u·lar·i·ty** [jok′·yə·lâr′ə·tē] *n.* **—joc′u·lar·ly** *adv.*

jo·cund [jok′ənd *or* jō′kənd] *adj.* Cheerful; gay; jovial: seldom used today.

jodh·purs [jod′pərz] *n.pl.* Riding breeches that fit tightly from ankle to knee and loosely from the knee upward.

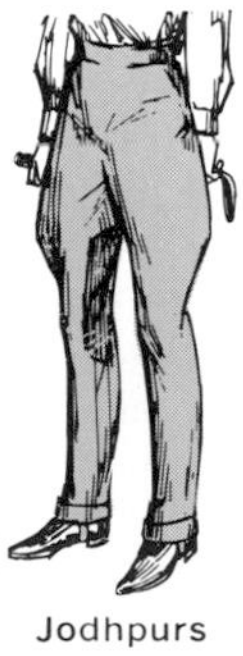
Jodhpurs

jo·ey [jō′ē] *n., pl.* **jo·eys** A very young animal, especially a young kangaroo. ◆ *Joey* is a native Australian word.

jog [jog] *v.* **jogged, jog·ging,** *n.* 1 *v.* To push or shake lightly, as though to get the attention of; nudge. 2 *n.* A nudge. 3 *v.* To urge on; stimulate: to *jog* one's memory. 4 *n.* An urging or stimulation. 5 *v.* To move slowly or monotonously: to *jog* along. 6 *v.* To run at a slow, leisurely pace. 7 *n.* A horse's slow gait. 8 *v.* To go or cause to go at a jog: We *jogged* back to the stable.

jog·ger [jog′ər] *n.* A person who jogs, especially as a form of exercise.

jog·gle [jog′əl] *v.* **jog·gled, jog·gling,** *n.* 1 *v.* To shake slightly; jog. 2 *n.* A mild jolt.

John [jon] *n.* 1 In the Bible, one of the twelve Apostles of Jesus. 2 The Fourth Gospel or any of three other books of the New Testament ascribed to him.

John Bull [bo͝ol] 1 The English people. 2 A typical Englishman.

John Doe [dō] 1 The name used for a man involved in a legal proceeding whose real name is not known. 2 The average man; any man.

John Han·cock [han′kok] *U.S. informal* A signature: Put your *John Hancock* on the deed.

John Hen·ry [hen′rē] *informal* A signature.

john·ny·cake [jon′ē·kāk′] *n.* A flat cornmeal cake baked on a griddle.

John·ny-jump-up [jon′ē·jump′up′] *n.* 1 Any of several American violets. 2 A variety of pansy.

John·ny Reb [jon′ē reb′] A Confederate soldier.

join [join] 1 *v.* To connect or combine; make or become one or as one; unite: to *join* two wires. 2 *n.* A point where things connect; joint. 3 *v.* To become a member of (as a group or club): to *join* the navy. 4 *v.* To keep company with: *Join* us for supper. 5 *v.* To take part: Come *join* in the fun. 6 *v.* To return to or meet: *Join* us here later. **—join battle** To start to fight.

join·er [joi′nər] *n.* 1 A person or thing that joins. 2 A carpenter who finishes woodwork.

join·er·y [joi′nə·rē] *n.* 1 The trade or skill of a joiner. 2 Articles of woodwork made by a joiner.

joint [joint] 1 *n.* The place, point, line, or surface where two things are joined. 2 *v.* To fasten by means of a joint. 3 *n.* A point in an animal's body where two or more parts or bones are joined, usually in a way that allows them to move. 4 *n.* A large cut of meat that contains a bone. 5 *v.* To divide into joints or cut apart at the joints. 6 *adj.* Done, owned, or shared by two or more persons: a *joint* effort. 7 *adj.* Sharing with another or others: *joint* owners. 8 *n. informal* A dingy or disreputable place, often a cheap bar. **—out of joint** Out of position at a joint, as a bone; dislocated.

Joint Chiefs of Staff The board of top military advisors to the President of the United States, made up of the commanding officers of the Army, Air Force, and Navy, and sometimes the Marine Corps.

joint·ed [join′tid] *adj.* Having a joint or joints.

joint·ly [joint′lē] *adv.* In common; together: a house owned *jointly* by two families.

joist [joist] *n.* A horizontal beam of a floor.

joke [jōk] *n., v.* **joked, jok·ing** 1 *n.* Something said or done for the purpose of creating laughter or amusement; jest. 2 *v.* To make jokes; jest. 3 *n.* Something humorous.

Joists

jok·er [jō′kər] *n.* 1 A person who jokes. 2 An extra playing card, used in some games. 3 A hidden difficulty, as a clause of a legislative bill that weakens its effectiveness.

jol·ly [jol′ē] *adj.* **jol·li·er, jol·li·est** 1 Full of life and merriment; jovial. 2 Arousing gaiety; festive; merry. **—jol·li·ty** [jol′ə·tē] *n.*

Jolly Roger [roj′ər] The pirate flag bearing a skull and crossbones.

Jolly Roger

jolt [jōlt] 1 *n.* A sudden shock. 2 *v.* To shake roughly: The bump *jolted* us. 3 *v.* To move with jerks: The bus *jolted* along.

Jo·nah [jō′nə] *n.* 1 In the Bible, a Hebrew prophet who was thrown overboard, swallowed by a great fish, and cast up on shore alive three days later. 2 A book of the Old Testament concerning him. 3 (*written* **jonah**) A person whose presence is thought to bring ill fortune.

Jon·a·than [jon′ə·thən] *n.* In the Bible, the son of Saul and close friend of David.

jon·quil [jon′kwil *or* jong′kwil] *n.* A type of narcissus related to the daffodil, having fragrant white or yellow flowers.

Jor·da·ni·an [jôr·dā′nē·ən] 1 *adj.* Of or from Jordan. 2 *n.* A person born in or a citizen of Jordan.

Jo·seph [jō′zəf] *n.* 1 In the New Testament, husband of Mary, the mother of Jesus. 2 In the Old Testament, the favorite son of Jacob, sold into slavery in Egypt by his brothers.

josh [josh] *v. slang* To make good-humored fun of (someone).

Josh·u·a [josh′ōō·ə] *n.* 1 In the Bible, an Israelite leader and successor to Moses. 2 A book of the Old Testament relating his story.

joss [jos] *n.* A representation of a Chinese god; Chinese idol or cult image.

joss house A Chinese temple or shrine.

jos·tle [jos′(ə)l] *v.* **jos·tled, jos·tling,** *n.* 1 *v.* To push or crowd against; elbow; shove; bump. 2 *n.* A hard shove or bump.

jot [jot] *v.* **jot·ted, jot·ting,** *n.* 1 *v.* To make a hasty and brief note of. 2 *n.* The least bit; iota.

joule [jōōl] *n.* In the meter-kilogram-second system of units, the unit of work or energy that is equal to the work done by a force of one newton acting through a distance of one meter. It is equivalent to 10,000,000 ergs.

jounce [jouns] *n., v.* **jounced, jounc·ing** 1 *n.* A shake; bump. 2 *v.* To shake or move roughly up and down; bounce; jolt: The wagon *jounced* along.

jounc·y [joun′sē] *adj.* **jounc·i·er, jounc·i·est** Characterized by a jouncing motion; bumpy: a *jouncy* ride.

jour·nal [jûr′nəl] *n.* 1 A daily record or account, as of events, business transactions, or thoughts. 2 A newspaper, magazine, or other periodical. 3 The part of a shaft or axle that turns in or against a bearing.

jour·nal·ese [jûr′nəl·ēz′] *n.* A style of writing, often slick and sensational, thought to be characteristic of newspapers and magazines.

jour·nal·ism [jûr′nəl·iz′əm] *n.* 1 The occupation of writing, editing, or managing a newspaper or other periodical. 2 Writing intended for publication in a newspaper or periodical.

jour·nal·ist [jûr′nəl·ist] *n.* A person whose occupation is journalism.

jour·nal·is·tic [jûr′nəl·is′tik] *adj.* Of or having to do with journalism or journalists.

jour·nal·ize [jûr′nəl·īz′] *v.* **jour·nal·ized, jour·nal·iz·ing** 1 To record in a journal. 2 To keep a financial or personal journal.

jour·ney [jûr′nē] 1 *n.* Travel from one place to another; trip. 2 *n.* The distance traveled. 3 *v.* To make a trip; travel.

jour·ney·man [jûr′nē·mən] *n., pl.* **jour·ney·men** [jûr′·nē·mən] A worker who has completed an apprenticeship in a skilled trade or craft.

joust [joust *or* just] 1 *n.* A formal combat between two mounted knights armed with lances; tilt. 2 *v.* To take part in a joust.

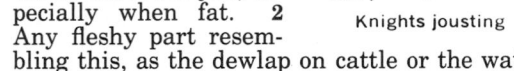

Knights jousting

Jove [jōv] *n.* In Roman myths, the god Jupiter. **—Jov·i·an** [jō′vē·ən] *adj.*

jo·vi·al [jō′vē·əl] *adj.* Possessing or showing good nature; jolly; happy. **—jo·vi·al·i·ty** [jō′vē·al′ə·tē] *n.* **—jo′vi·al·ly** *adv.*

jowl[1] [joul] *n.* 1 The flesh under the lower jaw, especially when fat. 2 Any fleshy part resembling this, as the dewlap on cattle or the wattles on some birds.

jowl[2] [joul] *n.* 1 The cheek. 2 The jaw, especially the lower jaw.

joy [joi] *n.* 1 A strong feeling of happiness, contentment, or satisfaction. 2 Something that causes this feeling.

joy·ful [joi′fəl] *adj.* 1 Full of joy. 2 Showing or causing joy. **—joy′·ful·ly** *adv.*

joy·less [joi′lis] *adj.* Lacking in joy; dreary; sad.

joy·ous [joi′əs] *adj.* Joyful. **—joy′·ous·ly** *adv.*

joy·stick [joi′stik] *n.* 1 A control lever on an airplane. 2 A similar device connected to a computer terminal, used to move the cursor or part of the display.

JP or **J.P.** justice of the peace.

jr. or **Jr.** junior.

ju·bi·lant [jōō′bə·lənt] *adj.* Expressing great joy; joyful; exultant. **—ju′bi·lant·ly** *adv.*

ju·bi·la·tion [jōō′bə·lā′shən] *n.* Rejoicing; gladness.

ju·bi·lee [jōō′bə·lē′] *n.* 1 An anniversary celebration, especially for a twenty-fifth, fiftieth, or seventy-fifth anniversary. 2 A time of festivity or rejoicing. ◆ In Jewish history, a *jubilee* was a year during which Hebrew slaves were to be freed and the land left uncultivated. The word comes from a Hebrew word for a *ram's horn* or *trumpet* with which the beginning of a jubilee was announced.

Ju·dah [jōō′də] *n.* 1 In the Bible, the fourth son of Jacob and Leah. 2 The tribe of Israel descended from him. 3 The kingdom made up of the tribes of Judah and Benjamin.

Ju·da·ic [jōō·dā′ik] *adj.* Of or having to do with the Jews.

a	add	**i**	it	**ŏŏ**	took	**oi**	oil
ā	ace	**ī**	ice	**ōō**	pool	**ou**	pout
â	care	**o**	odd	**u**	up	**ng**	ring
ä	palm	**ō**	open	**û**	burn	**th**	thin
e	end	**ô**	order	**yōō**	fuse	**th**	this
ē	equal					**zh**	vision

ə = a in *above* e in *sicken* i in *possible* o in *melon* u in *circus*

Ju·da·ism [jōō′dē·iz′əm] *n.* The religion of the Jews, taught by Moses and the Hebrew prophets.

Ju·das [jōō′dəs] 1 In the Bible, the disciple who betrayed Jesus. 2 (*sometimes written* **judas**) A person who betrays another; traitor.

Judas Is·car·i·ot [is·kar′ē·ət] Judas (def. 1).

Judas tree Any of a group of trees and shrubs having bright, showy, sometimes red, flowers. ◆ The *Judas tree* is so named from the belief that Judas Iscariot hanged himself from such a tree.

Ju·de·o-Chris·tian [jōō·dā′ō·kris′chən] *adj.* Based on or rooted in both Judaism and Christianity.

judge [juj] *n., v.* **judged, judg·ing** 1 *n.* An official who administers justice by hearing and deciding cases in a court of law. 2 *v.* To hear and decide the merits of (a case) or the guilt of (a person); try. 3 *n.* A person appointed to make decisions, as in a contest. 4 *v.* To decide officially, as a contest. 5 *v.* To form a judgment or opinion about (something): Don't *judge* people without sympathy; to *judge* wisely. 6 *n.* A person having expert knowledge: a good *judge* of art. 7 *v.* To act as a judge. 8 *v.* To consider; suppose: How old do you *judge* that painting to be?

Judg·es [juj′iz] *n.pl.* A book in the Old Testament containing a history of the Jews from the death of Joshua to the beginning of the monarchy.

judge·ship [juj′ship′] *n.* The office, functions, or period in office of a judge.

judg·ment or **judge·ment** [juj′mənt] *n.* 1 The act of judging. 2 The ability to decide wisely. 3 The result of judging, especially the decision or sentence of a court. 4 Blame or condemnation: to pass *judgment.* 5 A disaster or misfortune thought to come as punishment from God.

Judgment Day 1 In some religions, the day on which God makes final judgment of human beings. 2 (written **judgment day**) Any day of final judgment or reckoning.

ju·di·cial [jōō·dish′əl] *adj.* 1 Of or having to do with the administration of justice: *judicial* procedure. 2 Of or having to do with judges or courts of law: *judicial* duties. 3 Capable of forming fair and impartial judgments: a *judicial* mind. —**ju·di′·cial·ly** *adj.*

ju·di·ci·ar·y [jōō·dish′ē·er′ē *or* jōō·dish′ə·rē] *n., pl.* **ju·di·ci·ar·ies,** *adj.* 1 *n.* The branch of government that interprets and applies the law. 2 *n.* The system of courts of law. 3 *n.* Judges collectively. 4 *adj.* Of or having to do with courts, judges, and their judgments: a *judiciary* committee.

ju·di·cious [jōō·dish′əs] *adj.* Having, showing, or using good judgment; wise. —**ju·di′cious·ly** *adv.*

Ju·dith [jōō′dith] *n.* In the Bible, a Jewish widow who saved her countrymen by charming, tricking, and killing an Assyrian general.

ju·do [jōō′dō] *n.* A method of defending oneself against physical attack, developed from jujitsu. ◆ *Judo* comes from two Japanese words meaning *gentle art* or *soft way.*

jug [jug] *n., v.* **jugged, jug·ging** 1 *n.* A glass or earthenware container for liquids, having a narrow neck and a handle. 2 *n.* A pitcher or similar container. 3 *v.* To put into a jug. 4 *v.* To cook in a jug: to *jug* a hare.

jug band An informal band in which the players use makeshift instruments such as washboards, jugs, and metal tubs.

jug·ger·naut [jug′ər·nôt′] *n.* A slow and irresistible force or object that destroys everything in its path.

jug·gle [jug′əl] *v.* **jug·gled, jug·gling** 1 To keep a number of objects continuously moving in the air by skillful tossing and catching. 2 To perform as a juggler. 3 To manipulate in a dishonest way: to *juggle* financial accounts.

Juggler

jug·gler [jug′lər] *n.* 1 A person who provides entertainment by juggling. 2 A dishonest, conniving person; cheat.

jug·u·lar [jug′yə·lər] 1 *adj.* Of or having to do with the throat, neck, or a jugular vein. 2 *n.* The jugular vein. —**go for the jugular** To attack someone in a very vulnerable, sensitive area.

jugular vein One of the two large veins in the neck that return blood from the brain and head to the heart.

juice [jōōs] *n.* 1 The liquid part of vegetable or animal matter: grapefruit *juice;* meat *juice.* 2 (*often pl.*) Body fluids: digestive *juices.* 3 *U.S. slang* Electricity. —**juice up** *informal* To add to, as interest, attractiveness, speed, or energy.

juic·er [jōō′sər] *n.* An electrical or hand-operated appliance for squeezing juice from fruits and vegetables.

juic·y [jōō′sē] *adj.* **juic·i·er, juic·i·est** 1 Full of juice; moist. 2 Interesting; colorful; spicy: a *juicy* tale. —**juic′i·ness** *n.*

ju·jit·su [jōō·jit′sōō] *n.* A Japanese system of hand-to-hand fighting or wrestling in which an opponent's strength is used to his or her own disadvantage.

ju·jube [jōō′jōōb′ *or* jōō′jōō·bē′] *n.* A fruit-flavored, usually chewy candy.

juke box [jōōk] An automatic phonograph that allows records to be selected for playing after one or more coins are deposited.

Jul. July.

Jul·ian calendar [jōōl′yən] The calendar prescribed by Julius Caesar in 46 B.C. It was replaced by the Gregorian calendar.

ju·li·enne [jōō·lē·en′] 1 *adj.* Cut into long, fine strips: *julienne* vegetables. 2 *n.* A clear soup that contains julienne vegetables.

Ju·li·et [jōō′lē·et *or* jōōl′yit] *n.* In Shakespeare's *Romeo and Juliet,* the heroine.

Ju·ly [jōō·lī′ *or* jōō·lī′] *n.* The seventh month of the year, having 31 days.

jum·ble [jum′bəl] *n., v.* **jum·bled, jum·bling** 1 *n.* A confused mixture or collection. 2 *v.* To throw together in a confused mass; mix up. 3 *v.* To mix up in the mind; muddle.

jum·bo [jum′bō] *n., pl.* **jum·bos** 1 *n.* A very large person, animal, or thing. 2 *adj.* Very large; extra large: a *jumbo* ice cream cone.

jump [jump] 1 *v.* To spring from the ground, floor, or other surface by bending and quickly straightening the legs: to *jump* up and touch the ceiling. 2 *v.* To move in this way; bounce: to *jump* into bed. 3 *v.* To pass over or across (an object or obstacle) in this way: to *jump* a fence. 4 *n.* Something that is jumped over, as a fence or hurdle. 5 *v.* To cause to leap over an obstacle: to *jump* a horse. 6 *n.* The action of jumping; leap. 7 *n.* The height or distance covered by jumping: a six-foot *jump.* **8** *n.* A sporting contest in jumping: the high *jump.* **9** *v.* To move suddenly or jerkily, as though startled or surprised: When the floor creaked, I *jumped.* **10** *n.* A startled movement. **11** *v.* To increase or cause to increase suddenly: The temperature *jumped* sharply. **12** *n.* A sudden increase. **13** *v.* To make a sudden shift, as in thought or conversation: to *jump* from one topic to another. **14** *v. informal* To attack (a person or group) by surprise; ambush. **—jump at** To accept with haste: to *jump at* the chance. **—jump the gun** *slang* To begin before the correct time.

jump ball In basketball, a way for the referee to start play or decide possession of the ball by throwing it up between two opposing players who then jump and try to hit it to a teammate.

jump·er[1] [jum'pər] *n.* A person, animal, or thing that jumps.

jum·per[2] [jum'pər] *n.* **1** A sleeveless dress, usually worn over a blouse or sweater. **2** A loose jacket or smock worn over other clothes.

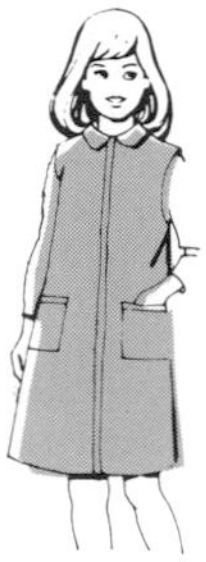
Jumper

jumping bean The seed of any of various Mexican shrubs that jumps or rolls about because of the activity of a moth larva that lives inside the seed.

jumping jack A toy figure of a person, whose jointed limbs are moved by strings.

jump shot In basketball, a shot in which a player jumps and releases the ball toward the basket at the height of the jump.

jump·suit [jump'sŏŏt'] *n.* **1** A garment like a coverall, worn by parachutists. **2** A similar garment for casual or sports wear.

jump·y [jum'pē] *adj.* **jump·i·er, jump·i·est** **1** Moving with jumps; jerky. **2** Nervous; uneasy.

jun. or **Jun.** junior.

Jun. June.

junc. junction.

jun·co [jung'kō] *n., pl.* **jun·cos** or **jun·coes** A small North American finch, commonly seen in flocks during the winter; snowbird.

junc·tion [jungk'shən] *n.* **1** A point where things meet or join. **2** The act of joining. **3** The condition of being joined.

junc·ture [jungk'chər] *n.* **1** A joint or union. **2** A particular, often critical, point in time or circumstances, especially in the phrase **at this juncture,** at this moment, or at this particular turn of events.

June [jōōn] *n.* The sixth month of the year, having 30 days.

June bug A large brown or greenish beetle that begins to fly early in June.

jun·gle [jung'gəl] *n.* **1** A dense, tropical forest, usually filled with wild animals. **2** Anything that seems like such a forest: the *jungle* of a city slum.

jun·ior [jōōn'yər] **1** *adj.* Younger, lower in rank, or having served for a shorter time: a *junior* member of a law firm. **2** *n.* The one who is younger or lower in rank. **3** *n.* The younger: written after the name of a son whose father has the same name, and usually abbreviated: John Sneed, *Jr.* **4** *adj.* Indicating the next to last year of high school or college. **5** *n.* A student in the next to last year of high school or college.

junior college A school offering a two-year program equivalent to that of the first two years in a four-year college.

junior high school In the U.S., a school coming between elementary and high school, and usually covering grades 7, 8, and 9.

ju·ni·per [jōō'nə·pər] *n.* An evergreen shrub or tree with dark blue berries.

junk[1] [jungk] **1** *n.* Worthless or worn-out things; trash; rubbish. **2** *v. informal* To discard as worthless: Let's *junk* this old sofa.

junk[2] [jungk] *n.* A large Chinese ship with lugsails, high stern, and flat bottom.

Junk

jun·ket [jung'kit] **1** *n.* Curdled, sweetened, and flavored milk, sometimes served as a dessert. **2** *n.* A feast, picnic, or banquet. **3** *n.* A pleasure trip, often at public expense. **4** *v.* To go on a pleasure trip.

junk food Various types of food sold in fast-food restaurants or packaged as snacks, often of poor nutritional quality.

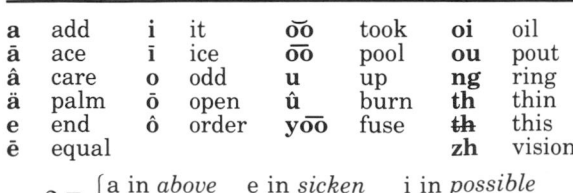

junk·ie or **junk·y** [jung'kē] *n. slang* **1** A narcotics addict, especially one addicted to heroin. **2** A person having a great enthusiasm, taste, or love for something: a TV *junkie.*

junk mail Third-class mail, such as circulars or advertisements, sent in great quantities to people who have not requested it.

junk·man [jungk'man'] *n., pl.* **junk·men** [jungk'·men'] A dealer in junk that has resale value.

junk·yard [jungk'yärd'] *n.* A yard or area used to store junk, especially for resale.

Ju·no [jōō'nō] *n.* In Roman myths, the wife of Jupiter and the goddess of marriage. She was called Hera by the Greeks.

jun·ta [jun'tə *or* hŏŏn'tə] *n.* **1** A group or council that runs a government, especially a small group that has seized power by force. **2** A group involved in political plotting.

jun·to [jun'tō] *n., pl.* **jun·tos** A small, usually secret group of persons joined for a particular purpose, often political.

Ju·pi·ter [jōō'pə·tər] *n.* **1** In Roman myths, the god ruling over all other gods and all men. He was called Zeus by the Greeks. **2** The largest planet in the solar system, fifth in distance from the sun.

Ju·ras·sic [jōō·ras'ik] **1** *n.* The second geological period of the Mesozoic era, during which many dinosaurs and the first birds appeared. **2** *adj.* Of the Jurassic.

a	add	**i**	it	**ŏŏ**	took	**oi**	oil		
ā	ace	**ī**	ice	**ōō**	pool	**ou**	pout		
â	care	**o**	odd	**u**	up	**ng**	ring		
ä	palm	**ō**	open	**û**	burn	**th**	thin		
e	end	**ô**	order	**yōō**	fuse	**th**	this		
ē	equal					**zh**	vision		

ə = a in *above*, e in *sicken*, i in *possible*, o in *melon*, u in *circus*

ju·ris·dic·tion [jŏŏr′is·dik′shən] *n.* 1 The legal right to exercise official authority. 2 The area or the affairs over which such authority may be exercised. 3 The power of those in authority.
ju·ris·pru·dence [jŏŏr′is·prōōd′əns] *n.* 1 The science of law. 2 A system of laws.
ju·rist [jŏŏr′ist] *n.* A person trained and skilled in the science of law.
ju·ror [jŏŏr′ər] *n.* A member of a jury.
ju·ry [jŏŏr′ē] *n., pl.* **ju·ries** 1 A qualified group of people sworn to give a true verdict after hearing the evidence in a trial in a court of law. It is sometimes called a **trial jury** to distinguish it from a **grand jury,** which decides whether or not a person should be brought to trial. 2 A group chosen to select a winner in a competition.
just[1] [just] 1 *adj.* Fair and impartial, as in dealing with people or making decisions: a *just* teacher. 2 *adj.* True; accurate: a *just* picture of world events. 3 *adj.* Well deserved; fairly earned: a *just* reward. 4 *adj.* Felt with good reason: *just* indignation. 5 *adv.* Not long ago; very recently: They *just* left; You *just* missed the train. 6 *adv.* Only; merely: I'm *just* sleepy. 7 *adv. informal* Really; very: Your party was *just* great. **—just′ly** *adv.*
just[2] [just] *n., v.* Another spelling of JOUST.
jus·tice [jus′tis] *n.* 1 The condition or quality of being just; fairness and impartiality according to the principles of right and wrong: *Justice* demands that the guilty be punished; There is *justice* in your plea for equal treatment. 2 What is due or deserved: to receive *justice* in court. 3 The administration of law. 4 A judge, especially one of high rank. **—do justice** 1 To act or treat fairly. 2 To show appreciation for.
justice of the peace A local judge able to try minor offenses, send cases to higher courts, and perform marriages.
jus·ti·fi·a·ble [jus′tə·fī′ə·bəl] *adj.* Capable of being shown to be just or proper: *justifiable* pride in one's work. **—jus′ti·fi′a·bly** *adv.*
jus·ti·fi·ca·tion [jus′tə·fə·kā′shən] *n.* 1 The act of justifying. 2 The fact of being justified. 3 An acceptable excuse or defense: Ignorance of the law is not a *justification* for breaking it.
jus·ti·fy [jus′tə·fī′] *v.* **jus·ti·fied, jus·ti·fy·ing** 1 To show to be just, right, or reasonable: Your achievements *justified* my confidence in you. 2 To provide good reason for: Bad conduct *justified* the employee's dismissal.
jus·tle [jus′(ə)l] *v.* **jus·tled, jus·tling,** *n.* Another spelling of JOSTLE.
jut [jut] *v.* **jut·ted, jut·ting** To extend outward; project: The shelf *juts* out too far.
jute [jōōt] *n.* 1 A tall plant that grows in Asia. 2 The tough fiber from the bark of this plant, used for making burlap and cord.
Jute [jōōt] *n.* A member of a Germanic tribe that invaded Britain in the fifth century.
ju·ve·nile [jōō′və·nəl *or* jōō′və·nīl′] 1 *adj.* Young, youthful, or immature. 2 *adj.* Of, like, or for young persons. 3 *n.* A young person; youth. 4 *n.* A book for children. 5 *n.* An actor who plays youthful roles.
juvenile court A law court that deals with cases involving children and adolescents below a certain age, usually 18 years.
juvenile delinquency The illegal or destructive behavior of juvenile delinquents.
juvenile delinquent A person who has broken the law or behaved destructively, but is too young to be punished as an adult criminal.
jux·ta·pose [juks′tə·pōz′] *v.* **jux·ta·posed, jux·ta·pos·ing** To place close together or side by side. **—jux·ta·po·si·tion** [juks′tə·pə·zish′ən] *n.*
JV or **J.V.** junior varsity.

Kk

K is the eleventh letter of the alphabet. The sign for it originated among Semitic people in the Near East, in the region of Palestine and Syria, probably in the middle of the second millennium B.C. Little is known about the sign until around 1000 B.C., when the Phoenicians began using it. The Phoenicians named the sign *kaph* and used it for the sound of the consonant *k*.

When the Greeks adopted the Phoenician alphabet around the ninth century B.C., they called it *kappa*. The Greeks reversed the direction of the sign and made it symmetrical. They used both *K* and *Q* for the sound of the consonant *k* (see *Q*).

As early as the eighth century B.C., the Etruscans adopted the Greek alphabet. They used three signs for the *k* sound: *C* was used when the *k* sound came before *E* or *I; K* was used when the *k* sound came before *A;* and *Q* was used when the *k* sound came before *U*. The Etruscans had no *o* sound. The Romans took all three signs from the Etruscans, along with the Etruscan way of using them. In time, however, the Romans all but dropped the *K* sign, keeping it only in a few official words such as *Kalendae,* which meant "the first day of the month."

K was used only rarely in English before the Norman Conquest (1066). The Normans, however, introduced many French words using *C* with the soft sound of *s* before *E* or *I*. For clarity, *K* came to be used for such native English words as *cēne* (now *keen*) and *cynn* (now *kin*). The French words retained the *C* in their spelling.

The *minuscule,* or small letter, *k* is a slightly altered version of the capital letter. A forerunner of it appeared in the Roman *uncial* handwriting of the fourth to the eighth centuries. It remained relatively undeveloped for many years, but when it did appear, in the black-letter script of the fifteenth century, its shape was quite elaborate.

Early Phoenician (late 2nd millennium B.C.)
Phoenician (8th century B.C.)
Early Greek (9th-7th centuries B.C.)
Eastern Greek (6th century B.C.)
Western Greek (6th century B.C.)
Classical Greek (403 B.C. onward)
Early Etruscan (8th century B.C.)
Monumental Latin (4th century B.C.)
Classical Latin
Uncial
Black-letter minuscule (15th century)

k or **K** [kā] *n., pl.* **k's** or **K's** The 11th letter of the English alphabet.
k or **k.** 1 karat(s). 2 kilogram(s).
K The symbol for the element potassium.
K Kelvin.
Kaa·ba [kä'bə *or* kä'ə·bə] *n.* A shrine at Mecca that is sacred to Muslims and toward which they face while praying.
ka·bob [kə·bob'] *n.* Another name for SHISH KEBAB.
Ka·bu·ki [kä·bo͞o'kē *or* kə·bo͞o'kē] *n.* A kind of Japanese drama dating from the 16th century in which actors wear elaborate costumes and act, dance, and sing in a very stylized manner.
kaf·tan [kaf'tən *or* kaf'tän] *n.* Another spelling of CAFTAN.
kai·ak [kī'ak] *n.* Another spelling of KAYAK.
kai·ser [kī'zər] *n.* An emperor, especially an emperor of Austria or Germany before 1918.
kale [kāl] *n.* A cabbage with loose, curled leaves that do not form a head.
ka·lei·do·scope [kə·lī'də·skōp'] *n.* **1** A tubelike device containing loose bits of colored glass and a set of mirrors. When it is held to the eye and turned, the bits of glass move and are reflected in constantly changing patterns. **2** Any changing pattern, view, or scene.
ka·lei·do·scop·ic [kə·lī'də·skop'ik] *adj.* Of or like a kaleidoscope; always changing.
ka·mi·ka·ze [kä'mi·kä'zē] *n.* In World War II, any of a group of Japanese pilots who made suicidal dives into ships and other large targets in order to blow them up.
Kan. Kansas.
kan·ga·roo [kang'gə·ro͞o'] *n., pl.* **kan·ga·roos** or **kan·ga·roo** An Australian animal that has short, weak forelegs, strong hind legs used for leaping, and a long, thick tail. The female has a pouch in which to carry the young. ◆ *Kangaroo* comes from a native Australian language.

Kangaroo

kangaroo rat Any of several rodents of the SW United States and Mexico that have long hind legs used for jumping.
Kans. Kansas.
ka·o·lin [kā'ə·lin] *n.* A fine, white clay, widely used to make porcelain.
ka·pok [kā'pok'] *n.* A silky fiber that covers the

a	add	**i**	it	**o͝o**	took	**oi**	oil
ā	ace	**ī**	ice	**o͞o**	pool	**ou**	pout
â	care	**o**	odd	**u**	up	**ng**	ring
ä	palm	**ō**	open	**û**	burn	**th**	thin
e	end	**ô**	order	**yo͞o**	fuse	**th**	this
ē	equal					**zh**	vision

ə = {a in *above* e in *sicken* i in *possible* / o in *melon* u in *circus*}

seeds of a tropical tree, used especially as a filling for mattresses and life preservers and as insulation.

kap·pa [kap′ə] *n.* The tenth letter of the Greek alphabet.

kar·a·kul [kar′ə·kəl] *n.* Another spelling of CARACUL.

kar·at [kar′ət] *n.* The 24th part by weight of pure gold in an alloy. Pure gold has 24 karats.

ka·ra·te [ka·rä′tē] *n.* A Japanese method of self-defense in which the hands, feet, elbows, and knees are used to strike blows at sensitive parts of an opponent's body.

kar·ma [kär′mə] *n.* **1** In Buddhism and Hinduism, the idea that one's conduct in this life decides one's fate in the next life. **2** Fate; destiny.

ka·sha [kä′shə] *n.* Crushed buckwheat grain that is cooked into a kind of mush.

Kashmir goat A goat of India and Tibet prized for its soft undercoat which is spun into cashmere.

ka·ty·did [kā′tē·did′] *n.* A green insect that looks like a grasshopper. The male makes a shrill sound by rubbing its wings together.

kay·ak [kī′ak] *n.* An Eskimo canoe made of a light frame fully enclosed by skins, with an opening for the user.

Kayak

kc or **kc.** kilocycle(s).

ke·a [kē·ə] *n.* A large green parrot of New Zealand.

ke·bab or **ke·bob** [kə·bob′] *n.* Other spellings of KABOB.

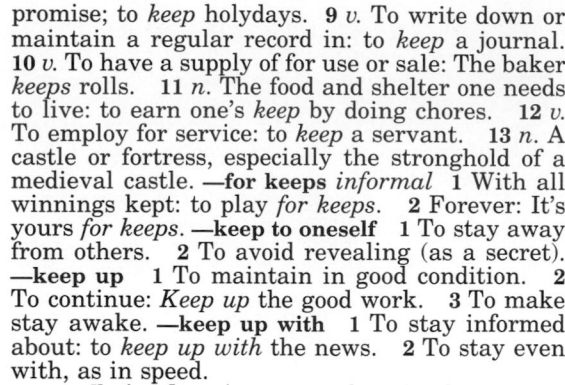

keel [kēl] *n.* **1** The main structural timber or steel bar running along the center of a ship's bottom. **2** Any part or object that resembles or functions like a keel. **—keel over 1** To turn upside down. **2** To fall, as in a swoon. **—on an even keel** In equilibrium; steady.

keel·boat [kēl′bōt′] *n.* A shallow freight boat with no sails, propelled by poles or oars.

keel·haul [kēl′hôl′] *v.* **1** To haul under the keel of a ship from one side to the other or from bow to stern as punishment. **2** To rebuke or chastise; scold soundly.

keel·son [kēl′sən] *n.* A beam fastened along the top of the keel of a ship to stiffen it.

keen[1] [kēn] *adj.* **1** Able to cut easily; very sharp: a *keen* knife. **2** Acute or sensitive, as in vision or mental perception: a *keen* mind; *keen* hearing. **3** Eager; enthusiastic; intense: a *keen* interest; My friend is *keen* about meeting you. **4** Piercing or cutting in force; sharp: a *keen* wind. **5** *slang* Fine; excellent: We had a really *keen* time. **—keen′ly** *adv.* **—keen′ness** *n.*

keen[2] [kēn] **1** *n.* A loud, wailing sound to mourn the dead. **2** *v.* To mourn by wailing loudly.

keep [kēp] *v.* **kept, keep·ing,** *n.* **1** *v.* To retain possession or control of; hold, hold back, or hold on to: to *keep* a secret; to *keep* one's earnings. **2** *v.* To prevent or restrain: The rope *kept* the climber from falling down the mountain. **3** *v.* To save; reserve: to *keep* a piece of cake for later. **4** *v.* To take care of; tend: to *keep* the flock. **5** *v.* To stay or cause to stay in good condition, as food. **6** *v.* To remain; stay: *Keep* away. **7** *v.* To continue or maintain: *Keep* the game going; *Keep* dancing. **8** *v.* To be faithful to, observe, or fulfill: to *keep* a promise; to *keep* holydays. **9** *v.* To write down or maintain a regular record in: to *keep* a journal. **10** *v.* To have a supply of for use or sale: The baker *keeps* rolls. **11** *n.* The food and shelter one needs to live: to earn one's *keep* by doing chores. **12** *v.* To employ for service: to *keep* a servant. **13** *n.* A castle or fortress, especially the stronghold of a medieval castle. **—for keeps** *informal* **1** With all winnings kept: to play *for keeps.* **2** Forever: It's yours *for keeps.* **—keep to oneself 1** To stay away from others. **2** To avoid revealing (as a secret). **—keep up 1** To maintain in good condition. **2** To continue: *Keep up* the good work. **3** To make stay awake. **—keep up with 1** To stay informed about: to *keep up with* the news. **2** To stay even with, as in speed.

keep·er [kē′pər] *n.* A person who guards or takes care of people, animals, or things; attendant, guardian, overseer, or warden.

keep·ing [kē′ping] *n.* **1** Charge; custody: to be in a doctor's *keeping.* **2** Observing or maintaining: the *keeping* of a holiday. **3** Agreement; conformity: conduct in *keeping* with the rules.

keep·sake [kēp′sāk′] *n.* Something kept as a remembrance of the person who gave it.

keg [keg] *n.* A small barrel, usually one that holds up to 10 gallons.

kelp [kelp] *n.* **1** A coarse, brown seaweed. **2** Its ash, a source of iodine.

Kel·vin [kel′vin] *adj.* Of or having to do with the Kelvin scale.

Kelvin scale A temperature scale that places zero at absolute zero and uses degrees of the same size as the centigrade scale.

ken [ken] *v.* **kenned, ken·ning,** *n.* **1** *v.* To know: used chiefly in Scotland. **2** *n.* Range of sight or knowledge: It's beyond my *ken.*

Ken. Kentucky.

ken·nel [ken′əl] *n., v.* **ken·neled** or **ken·nelled, ken·nel·ing** or **ken·nel·ling 1** *n.* A house for a dog or a pack of dogs. **2** *n.* (*often pl.*) A place where dogs are bred and housed. **3** *v.* To place or keep in a kennel.

Ken·yan [ken′yən *or* kēn′yən] **1** *adj.* Of or from Kenya. **2** *n.* A person born in or a citizen of Kenya.

kept [kept] Past tense and past participle of KEEP.

ker·a·tin [ker′ə·tin] *n.* The tough protein substance that forms the basis of such structures as hair, nails, hoofs, horns, bills, and claws.

ker·chief [kûr′chif] *n.* **1** A piece of fabric, usually square, worn over the head or around the neck. **2** A handkerchief.

ker·nel [kûr′nəl] *n.* **1** A seed or grain, as of wheat or corn. **2** The soft, often edible part inside a nut or fruit pit. **3** The central part, as of a plan or theory; nucleus; gist.

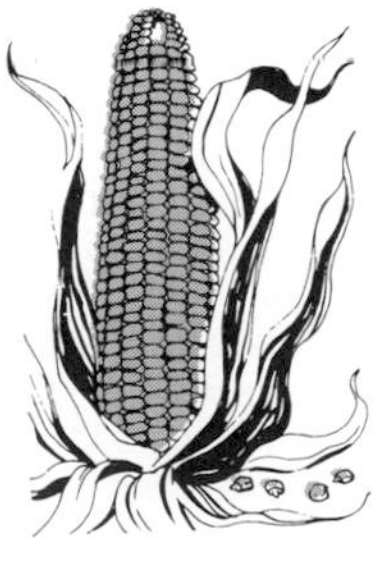
Kernels of corn

ker·o·sene [ker′ə·sēn′] *n.* A thin oil made from petroleum, used as fuel in lamps and stoves.

ketch [kech] *n.* A vessel with a tall mast forward and a shorter one aft.

ketch·up [kech′əp] *n.* A thick red sauce made with tomatoes and spices.

ket·tle [ket′(ə)l] *n.* **1** A metal vessel for boiling or stewing. **2** A teakettle. **—kettle of fish** A difficult or awkward situation.

ket·tle·drum [ket′(ə)l·drum′] *n.* A large drum consisting of a metal hemisphere with a head that adjusts to pitch.

Kettledrums

key[1] [kē] *n., pl.* **keys,** *v.* **keyed, key·ing,** *adj.* **1** *n.* A small metal instrument for moving the bolt or tumblers of a lock, as in locking or unlocking a door, drawer, or padlock. **2** *n.* A wedge or pin to lock parts together. **3** *n.* An instrument like a key in form or function, as the winding mechanism on a clock. **4** *n.* Anything that opens, explains, identifies, or solves something, as a set of answers to problems or a translation of a book in a foreign language. **5** *v.* To prepare or provide with such a key. **6** *n.* A person, place, or thing that controls or is important to something else: Hard work is one of the *keys* to success. **7** *adj.* Controlling or important: a *key* figure in the conspiracy. **8** *n.* One of the parts pressed down with the fingers, as used in playing a piano or using a typewriter. **9** *n.* In music, a system of tones, chiefly of a major or minor scale, in which a particular tone predominates and after which the system is named. **10** *v.* To regulate the pitch or tone of. **11** *v.* To harmonize or fit: decor *keyed* to the room. **12** *n.* A style, tone, or manner: a play written in a somber *key.* **—key up** To cause excitement, nervousness, or expectancy in.

key[2] [kē] *n., pl.* **keys** A low island, especially one of coral, along a coast: the Florida *Keys.*

key·board [kē′bôrd′] **1** *n.* A row or rows of keys, as on a piano, typewriter, or computer. **2** *v.* To use a computer keyboard.

key·hole [kē′hōl′] *n.* A hole for a key, as in a lock or door.

key·note [kē′nōt′] **1** *n.* The note that a musical key is named after and based upon. **2** *n.* The basic idea or principle, as of a speech, philosophy, or policy. **3** *v.* To give or set the keynote of. **4** *v.* To give the keynote address at. **—key′not·er** *n.*

keynote address or **keynote speech** A speech, as at a political convention, that presents the issues and policies under consideration.

key·punch [kē′punch′] **1** *n.* A machine operated by a keyboard that punches holes in cards. It is used in data processing. **2** *v.* To operate a keypunch.

key signature In music, the sharps or flats written to the right of the clef to establish the key.

key·stone [kē′stōn′] *n.* **1** The middle stone at the top of an arch, serving to lock the other stones in place. **2** A basic or fundamental part, as of a science.

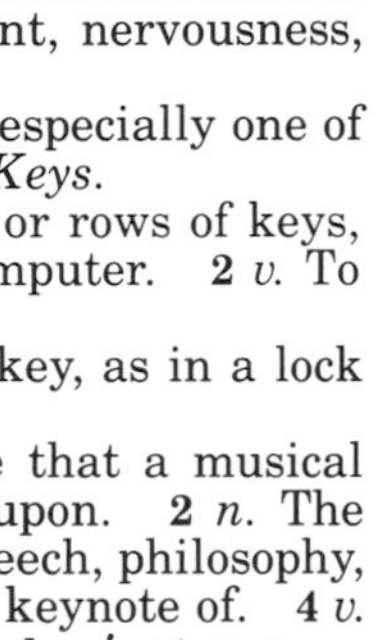

kg or **kg.** kilogram(s).

khak·i [kak′ē] *n., pl.* **khak·is,** *adj.* **1** *n., adj.* Yellowish brown. **2** *n.* A strong cotton cloth of this color. **3** *n.* (*pl.*) A uniform made of khaki. ◆ *Khaki,* which describes an earthy color, comes from a Persian word meaning *dust.*

khan [kän] *n.* **1** A title once used by Mongol rulers. **2** A title for a ruler or high-ranking official in central Asia, Afghanistan, and Iran.

khe·dive [kə·dēv′] *n.* A title used by the Turkish viceroys of Egypt from 1867 to World War I.

kib·butz [ki·bo͝ots′] *n., pl.* **kib·but·zim** [ki·bo͝ot′sēm] In modern Israel, a collective farm or settlement.

kib·itz [kib′its] *v. informal* To act as a kibitzer.

kib·itz·er [kib′it·sər] *n. informal* A person who observes and offers unwanted comments or advice, as at a card game.

kick [kik] **1** *v.* To strike forcefully with the foot: Will the mule *kick* me? **2** *v.* To strike out with the foot or feet: This horse *kicks.* **3** *n.* A blow with the foot. **4** *v.* To cause to move by striking with the foot: to *kick* a ball. **5** *v.* To snap back suddenly, as a gun does when fired. **6** *n.* A sudden recoil, as of a gun when fired. **7** *v. informal* To complain or object. **8** *n. informal* A complaint or objection. **9** *n.* The act of kicking. **10** *n. slang* An excited sensation; thrill: They went to the carnival for *kicks.* **—kick around 1** To treat harshly or cruelly. **2** To consider or discuss: to *kick around* two plans of action. **—kick back** To pay a kickback. **—kick off 1** In football, to make a kickoff. **2** *informal* To begin; start. **—kick out** *slang* To dismiss or put out forcibly. **—kick′er** *n.*

kick·back [kik′bak′] *n.* **1** A springing back; recoil. **2** *slang* A payment made, as by secret arrangement or under coercion, to someone who controls or influences the income of the person making the payment.

kick·off [kik′ôf′] *n.* **1** In football and soccer, the kick that puts the ball into play. **2** *informal* An opening or beginning.

kick·y [kik′ē] *adj.* **kick·i·er, kick·i·est** *slang* Exciting or appealing: a *kicky* horror film; *kicky* clothes.

kid [kid] *n., v.* **kid·ded, kid·ding** **1** *n.* A young goat. **2** *n.* The leather made from its skin. **3** *adj. use*: *kid* gloves. **4** *n. informal* A child. **5** *v. slang* To make fun of; tease.

kid·nap [kid′nap′] *v.* **kid·napped** or **kid·naped, kid·napp·ing** or **kid·nap·ing** To carry off, as by force or fraud, usually so as to demand a ransom. **—kid′·nap·er** or **kid′nap·per** *n.*

kid·ney [kid′nē] *n., pl.* **kid·neys** **1** Either of a pair of organs close to the spinal cord, that separate excess water and waste products from the blood and pass them out as urine. **2** The kidneys of certain animals, used as food. **3** Temperament, nature, or kind: a scientist of Mme. Curie's *kidney.*

kidney bean **1** A reddish bean, shaped like a kidney, served as a vegetable. **2** The plant producing this bean.

kid·skin [kid′skin′] *n.* Kid (def. 2).

kill [kil] **1** *v.* To cause the death of or put an end to life. **2** *v.* To slaughter for food. **3** *n.* The act of killing. **4** *n.* The animal or animals killed as prey or in a hunt. **5** *v.* To bring to an end; destroy; ruin. **6** *v.* To spoil the effect of. **7** *v.* To veto or defeat (legislation). **8** *v.* To pass (time) aimlessly. **9** *v. slang* To overwhelm, as with laughter or pain.

kill·deer [kil′dir′] *n., pl.* **kill·deers** or **kill·deer** A

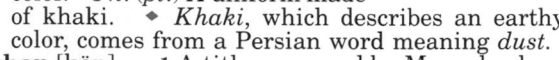

a	add	**i**	it	**o͝o**	took	**oi**	oil
ā	ace	**ī**	ice	**o͞o**	pool	**ou**	pout
â	care	**o**	odd	**u**	up	**ng**	ring
ä	palm	**ō**	open	**û**	burn	**th**	thin
e	end	**ô**	order	**yo͞o**	fuse	**t͟h**	this
ē	equal					**zh**	vision

ə = a in *above* e in *sicken* i in *possible* o in *melon* u in *circus*

K

North American wading bird related to the plover, having a loud cry.

kill·er [kil′ər] *n.* 1 A person or thing that kills. 2 The killer whale.

killer bee A hybrid bee that developed in Brazil in the 1960's and spread to the southern U.S. by the late 1980's. If disturbed, swarms of killer bees may attack and kill animals and even humans.

killer whale A black and white whale that preys on large fish, seals, penguins, and at times, other whales.

kill·ing [kil′ing] 1 *n.* The act of a person or thing that kills; murder; slaughter. 2 *adj.* Tending to kill; fatal. 3 *adj.* Very destructive: a *killing* drought. 4 *adj.* Very tiring; exhausting: a *killing* work schedule. 5 *n. informal* A sudden, great profit: A *killing* in the stock market.

kill·joy [kil′joi′] *n.* A person who spoils other people's fun or pleasure.

kiln [kil(n)] *n.* An oven or furnace for baking, burning, or drying bricks, pottery, lime, etc.

kil·o [kil′ō *or* kē′lō] *n., pl.* **kil·os** 1 A kilogram. 2 A kilometer.

kilo- A combining form meaning: One thousand, as in *kilometer.*

kil·o·cy·cle [kil′ə·sī′kəl] *n.* In physics, 1,000 cycles, especially 1,000 cycles per second.

kil·o·gram [kil′ə·gram′] *n.* In the metric system, a unit of mass or weight equal to 1,000 grams or about 2.2 pounds.

kil·o·hertz [kil′ō·hûrts′] *n.* A unit of frequency equal to 1,000 hertz or 1,000 cycles per second.

kil·o·li·ter [kil′ə·lē′tər] *n.* In the metric system, a unit of volume equal to 1,000 liters.

kil·o·me·ter [kil′ə·mē′tər *or* ki·lom′ə·tər] *n.* In the metric system, a unit of length equal to 1,000 meters or about 5/8 of a mile.

kil·o·ton [kil′ə·tun′] *n.* 1 In the metric system, a unit of weight equal to 1,000 tons. 2 A unit of explosive force equal to that of 1,000 tons of TNT.

kil·o·watt [kil′ə·wot′] *n.* A unit of power equal to 1,000 watts.

kil·o·watt-hour [kil′ə·wot′our′] *n.* The work done or the energy delivered by one kilowatt acting for one hour. Electric power is usually sold by the kilowatt-hour.

kilt [kilt] *n.* A short pleated skirt, often plaid, originally worn by men in the Scottish Highlands.

kil·ter [kil′tər] *n. informal* Proper working order, especially in the phrase **out of kilter:** My old car is *out of kilter.*

ki·mo·no [kə·mō′nə] *n., pl.* **ki·mo·nos** 1 A loose robe worn as an outer garment in Japan. 2 A robe or dressing gown resembling this.

Kimono

kin [kin] 1 *n.* Relatives; family. 2 *adj.* Related: A dog is *kin* to a wolf. **—next of kin** The nearest relative or relatives.

kind¹ [kīnd] *n.* 1 Sort; type; variety: an ancient *kind* of javelin. 2 A natural grouping or class; species. **—in kind** 1 With goods rather than money: to pay taxes *in kind.* 2 With the same sort of thing: to return an insult *in kind.* **—kind of** *informal* Somewhat. **—of a kind** Belonging to the same kind or sort. ◆ *Kind of* (or *sort of*), when used before a singular noun, as in *this kind of book*, is generally accepted in formal speaking and writing. *Kind of*, when used after *these* and before a plural noun, as in *these kind of books*, is not accepted in formal English, the correct form being *these kinds of books* followed by a plural verb. The expressions *kind of a* and *sort of a* are informal: It was that *kind of a* day. In formal writing, omit the *a.*

kind² [kīnd] *adj.* 1 Willing to help; gentle; friendly; sympathetic: Six *kind* people offered to help. 2 Coming from or showing goodness, sympathy, or friendliness: It was *kind* of you to meet me.

kin·der·gar·ten [kin′dər·gär′tən] *n.* A school or class for young children, usually from the ages of four to six, which develops basic skills and serves as a preparation for regular school work. ◆ *Kindergarten* comes directly from German, where it means *children's garden.*

kin·der·gart·ner [kin′dər·gärt′nər] *n.* 1 A child who is attending or is of an age to attend kindergarten. 2 A teacher at a kindergarten.

kind·heart·ed [kīnd′här′tid] *adj.* Kind and sympathetic.

kin·dle [kin′dəl] *v.* **kin·dled, kin·dling** 1 To set fire to; light: They *kindled* the paper with a match. 2 To catch fire; start to burn: The wet paper did not *kindle.* 3 To excite or arouse: The brutal deed *kindled* our rage. 4 To brighten or glow: a face *kindled* with eager curiosity.

kind·li·ness [kīnd′lē·nis] *n.* 1 The condition of quality of being kind. 2 A kindly act.

kin·dling [kind′ling] *n.* Small pieces of dry material, as wood or twigs, for starting a fire.

kind·ly [kīnd′lē] *adj.* **kind·li·er, kind·li·est,** *adv.* 1 *adj.* Kind; sympathetic. 2 *adv.* In a kind or sympathetic way. 3 *adj.* Pleasant or favorable: a *kindly* wind. 4 *adv.* So as to please or oblige: *Kindly* leave.

kind·ness [kīnd′nis] *n.* 1 The condition of being kind. 2 A kind act or service.

kin·dred [kin′drid] 1 *n.* A person's relatives by blood. 2 *adj.* Belonging to the same family. 3 *n.* A family, clan, or other group related by blood. 4 *adj.* Having a similar nature. 5 *n.* Kinship.

kine [kīn] *n.pl.* Cattle: seldom used today.

kin·e·mat·ics [kin′ə·mat′iks] *n.* The study of motion and moving bodies, considered separately from the masses and forces involved. ◆ See ICS.

kin·e·scope [kin′ə·skōp′] *n., v.* **kin·e·scoped, kin·e·scop·ing** 1 *n.* A picture tube in a television set. 2 *n.* A film recording of a television program. 3 *v.* To make a kinescope of (a television program).

ki·net·ic [ki·net′ik] *adj.* Of or having to do with motion.

kinetic art A type of sculpture or assemblage made up of parts that can be set in motion, as by a motor or air current.

kinetic energy Energy that an object has because it is in motion.

kin·folk [kin′fōk′] *n.pl.* Family; kin; relations.

kin·folks [kin′fōks′] *n.pl.* Kinfolk.

king [king] *n.* 1 A male ruler of a country, especially one whose position is inherited. 2 A person, animal, or thing that holds a chief position, as in some field or class. 3 A playing card marked with a picture of a king. 4 In chess, the principal piece. 5 A piece in checkers that has reached the opponent's end of the board.

King Arthur See ARTHUR.

king·bird [king′bûrd′] *n.* A flycatcher of North America that eats insects and attacks larger birds, as crows and hawks.
king·bolt [king′bōlt′] *n.* A vertical bolt used for such purposes as connecting the body of a wagon or other vehicle to the front axle of the vehicle.
king crab 1 Any of several varieties of large edible crabs found in the waters of the northern Pacific. 2 Another name for HORSESHOE CRAB.
king·dom [king′dəm] *n.* 1 A country ruled by a king or queen. 2 An area or sphere where someone or something is dominant: the *kingdom* of the sea. 3 A primary division in the natural world: the animal, vegetable, and mineral *kingdoms.*
king·fish·er [king′fish′ər] *n.* A brightly-colored bird with a short tail and strong bill, that usually feeds on fish.

Kingfisher

King James Version Another name for AUTHORIZED VERSION.
king·ly [king′lē] *adj.* **king·li·er, king·li·est** Of, having to do with, or fit for a king; regal; royal.
king·pin [king′pin′] *n.* 1 In bowling, the pin at the front or head of the triangular group to be knocked down with the ball. 2 A kingbolt. 3 The head person of a group or organization: the *kingpin* of gambling.
Kings [kingz] *n.* 1 Either of two books of the Old Testament that give the history of the Hebrew kings after David. 2 Any of four books in the Roman Catholic Bible corresponding to I and II Samuel and the two above.
king salmon A large salmon found widely in the northern Pacific and prized as a food fish.
King's English Standard, correct English, especially as it is spoken, written, and used in Great Britain.
king·ship [king′ship′] *n.* 1 The office or power of a king. 2 Government by a king; monarchy.
king-size [king′sīz′] *adj. informal* Extra large or long: a *king-size* package.
king snake Any of various bright-colored, nonpoisonous snakes of the central and southern United States that feed on other snakes and rodents.
kink [kingk] 1 *n.* A sharp bend, twist, or curl, as in a hair or wire. 2 *v.* To form a kink or kinks. 3 *n.* A painful muscular cramp; crick. 4 *n.* A queer idea; odd notion. 5 *n.* A difficulty or flaw, as in a plan or procedure.
kin·ka·jou [king′kə·jōō′] *n.* A small, slender animal of tropical America that has a long tail and soft, yellowish brown fur.

Kinkajou

kink·y [kingk′ē] *adj.* **kink·i·er, kink·i·est** 1 Full of kinks. 2 Peculiar; offbeat. —**kink′i·ness** *n.*
kins·folk [kinz′fōk′] *n.pl.* Another word for KINFOLK.
kin·ship [kin′ship′] *n.* Relationship, especially by blood.
kins·man [kinz′mən] *n., pl.* **kins·men** [kinz′mən] A relative, especially a male relative.
kins·wom·an [kinz′wŏŏm′ən] *n., pl.* **kins·wom·en** [kinz′wim′in] A female relative, as an aunt.
ki·osk [kē′osk′] *n.* 1 A small structure with one or more open sides, used especially as a newsstand, booth, or bandstand. 2 In Turkey, an open pavilion used as a shady resting place.

Kiosk

Ki·o·wa [kī′ə·wô *or* kī′ə·wä *or* kī′ə·wā] *n., pl.* **Ki·o·wa** or **Ki·o·was** 1 A tribe of North American Plains Indians now living in Oklahoma. 2 A member of this tribe. 3 The language of this tribe.
kip·per [kip′ər] 1 *v.* To split and salt (a fish), and then dry or smoke it. 2 *n.* A fish that is kippered, especially a herring.
kirk [kûrk] *n.* A church: a Scottish word.
kir·tle [kûr′t(ə)l] *n.* 1 A skirt or petticoat. 2 A man's tunic. ◆ This word is seldom used today.
kis·met [kiz′met′] *n.* Destiny; fate.
kiss [kis] 1 *v.* To touch with the lips as a token of love, respect, or greeting. 2 *n.* The act of kissing. 3 *v.* To touch lightly: The marbles just *kissed.* 4 *n.* A light or gentle touch. 5 *n.* A small candy.
kit [kit] *n.* 1 A collection of tools or equipment for some special purpose: a repair *kit.* 2 A box or bag for equipment or gear. 3 A packaged set of parts from which an article may be assembled: a furniture *kit.* 4 A collection of articles carried for a person's own use: a soldier's *kit.*
kitch·en [kich′ən] *n.* A room where food is prepared and cooked.
kitchen cabinet 1 A cabinet, as for storage of food and utensils, in a kitchen. 2 An unofficial group of advisers to a government leader, as a president of the U.S.
kitch·en·ette [kich′ən·et′] *n.* A small kitchen or area used as a kitchen.
kitchen police 1 In the armed services, enlisted persons assigned to work in the kitchen. 2 The work performed by kitchen police.
kitch·en·ware [kich′ən·wâr′] *n.* Kitchen utensils, as pots or pans.
kite [kīt] *n.* 1 A light frame, as of wood, covered with paper or cloth, designed to be flown in the wind on a long string. 2 A hawk with long pointed wings and a forked tail.
kith [kith] *n.* Friends, now used only in the phrase **kith and kin,** friends and relatives.
kit·ten [kit′(ə)n] *n.* A young cat.
kit·ty[1] [kit′ē] *n., pl.* **kit·ties** A cat or kitten: often used as a pet name for a cat.
kit·ty[2] [kit′ē] *n., pl.* **kit·ties** A sum of money collected from a group of persons for a specific use; pool.
kit·ty-cor·ner [kit′ē·kôr′nər] *adj., adv.* Another word for CATERCORNER.
kit·ty-cor·nered [kit′ē·kôr′nərd] *adj., adv.* Another word for CATERCORNER.

a	add	**i**	it	**ŏŏ**	took	**oi**	oil
ā	ace	**ī**	ice	**ōō**	pool	**ou**	pout
â	care	**o**	odd	**u**	up	**ng**	ring
ä	palm	**ō**	open	**û**	burn	**th**	thin
e	end	**ô**	order	**yōō**	fuse	**th̶**	this
ē	equal					**zh**	vision

ə = a in *above* e in *sicken* i in *possible* o in *melon* u in *circus*

K

ki·wi [kē′wē] *n., pl.* **ki·wis** 1 A bird of New Zealand that cannot fly. It has a rounded body, soft, furlike feathers, and a long bill. 2 The sweet, edible fruit of an Asian vine, having a fuzzy brown rind.

KJV King James Version (Bible).

KKK or **K.K.K.** Ku Klux Klan.

kl or **kl.** kiloliter(s).

klep·to·ma·ni·a [klep′tə·mā′nē·ə] *n.* An abnormal urge in some persons to steal, especially things they have little need for. —**klep′to·ma′ni·ac** *n.*

klieg light [klēg] A very bright arc light used in filming movies.

klutz [kluts] *n. slang* A clumsy, inept, or bungling person. —**klutz′i·ness** *n.* —**klutz′y** *adj.* ◆ *Klutz* is a Yiddish word based on the German word *klotz,* which means *wooden block.*

km or **km.** kilometer(s).

knack [nak] *n.* Ability or skill; talent: to have the *knack* of saying the right thing at the right time.

knap·sack [nap′sak′] *n.* A large bag for supplies, worn strapped to the back.

Knapsack

knave [nāv] *n.* 1 A sly, dishonest person; rogue. 2 The jack, a playing card. —**knav′ish** *adj.*

knav·er·y [nā′vər·ē] *n., pl.* **knav·er·ies** 1 The behavior of a knave. 2 An act of trickery.

knead [nēd] *v.* 1 To mix and work (as dough or clay) into a mass by pressing or squeezing. 2 To work upon by pressing or squeezing with the hands; massage: to *knead* a sprained muscle. 3 To make by or as if by kneading.

knee [nē] *n.* 1 The joint between the upper and lower bones of the leg. 2 The area around this joint. 3 Anything shaped like a bent knee. 4 The part of a garment that covers the knee.

knee·cap [nē′kap′] *n.* The flat, movable bone in the front of the knee.

knee-deep [nē′dēp′] *adj.* 1 So deep or high as to come to the knees: The stream was *knee-deep.* 2 Sunk to the knees: *knee-deep* in mud. 3 Deeply absorbed or involved: *knee-deep* in homework.

knee-high [nē′hī′] 1 *adj.* Reaching up to the knees. 2 *n.* A stocking that covers the leg to the knee.

knee-jerk [nē′jûrk′] *adj.* 1 Mechanical; automatic: Running away is a *knee-jerk* reaction to danger. 2 Reacting in an automatic and predictable way: a *knee-jerk* optimist.

knee jerk A reflex in which a sharp blow to the tendon below the kneecap causes a forward kick of the lower leg.

kneel [nēl] *v.* **knelt** or **kneeled, kneel·ing** To sink down or rest on one or both knees: They *knelt* to pray.

knee·pad [nē′pad′] *n.* In certain sports, as football and hockey, a pad worn to protect the knee.

knee·pan [nē′pan′] *n.* The kneecap.

knell [nel] 1 *n.* The sound of a bell slowly ringing, as at a funeral. 2 *v.* To ring a bell slowly and solemnly. 3 *v.* To announce, summon, or warn by or as if by a bell. 4 *n.* A warning of the passing or end of something: Electric lights sounded the *knell* of gas lamps.

knelt [nelt] A past tense and past participle of KNEEL.

knew [n(y)o͞o] Past tense of KNOW.

knick·er·bock·ers [nik′ər·bok′ərz] *n. pl.* Loosefitting, short trousers, gathered in below the knee.

Knickerbockers

knick·ers [nik′ərz] *n.pl.* Knickerbockers.

knick·knack [nik′nak′] *n.* A small ornament or article of trifling value.

knife [nīf] *n., pl.* **knives** [nīvz], *v.* **knifed, knif·ing** 1 *n.* A cutting tool having a sharp, often pointed blade set in a handle. 2 *v.* To stab or cut with a knife. 3 *n.* A cutting blade in a machine.

knight [nīt] 1 *n.* In the Middle Ages, a man having the rank and duties of a mounted officer, usually after service as a page and squire. 2 *n.* In the British Commonwealth, a man given an honorary rank and the title "Sir" before his name in recognition of his merits or service. 3 *v.* To make into a knight. 4 *n.* A chess piece having a horse's head.

knight-er·rant [nīt′er′ənt] *n., pl.* **knights-er·rant** In the Middle Ages, a knight who traveled in search of adventure.

knight-er·rant·ry [nīt′er′ən·trē] *n., pl.* **knight-er·rant·ries** 1 The conduct and customs of the knights-errant. 2 Action that is brave and romantic but impractical.

knight·hood [nīt′ho͝od′] *n.* 1 The character, rank, or profession of a knight. 2 Knights as a group. 3 The customs and conduct of knights.

knight·ly [nīt′lē] 1 *adj.* Of, having to do with, or befitting a knight. 2 *adv.* In a manner befitting a knight. —**knight′li·ness** *n.*

knit [nit] *v.* **knit·ted** or **knit, knit·ting** 1 To make (cloth or clothing) by interlocking loops of yarn or thread with special needles. 2 To fasten or unite closely and firmly: The broken bone *knit* well. 3 To draw (the brows) together. —**knit′ter** *n.*

knit·ting [nit′ing] *n.* 1 The act of a person or machine that knits. 2 Knitted work.

knitting needle A long, thin rod, sometimes curved, as or bone, metal, or plastic, used for hand knitting.

knit·wear [nit′wâr′] *n.* Garments made of knitted fabric.

knives [nīvz] Plural of KNIFE.

knob [nob] *n.* 1 A rounded handle, as on a door or radio. 2 A rounded, projecting part: the *knobs* on a tree trunk. 3 A rounded hill.

knob·by [nob′ē] *adj.* **knob·bi·er, knob·bi·est** 1 Full of knobs: a *knobby* tree trunk. 2 Shaped like a knob: *knobby* knees.

knock [nok] 1 *v.* To strike with a sharp blow; hit: to *knock* someone on the head. 2 *v.* To strike so as to make fall: The ball *knocked* the bowling pins down. 3 *v.* To strike together: They *knocked* heads. 4 *v.* To make by striking: to *knock* a hole in a wall. 5 *v.* To make a sharp noise, as of rapping, rattling, clanking, or pounding: the sound of a car *knocking*; to *knock* on a door. 6 *n.* A sharp blow or rap, or the sound accompanying it. 7 *v. informal* To find fault with; be critical of. —**knock about** (or **around**) *informal* 1 To wander around. 2 To treat roughly or brutally. —**knock down** 1 To take apart for shipping or storage. 2 At auctions, to sell to the highest bidder. —**knock off** *informal* 1 To stop (doing something). 2 To deduct. 3 To finish; accomplish. 4 *slang* To kill. 5 *slang* To rob; hold up. 6 To copy, as a stylish garment. **—knock out** 1 To defeat by a knockout in boxing. 2 To make unconscious. 3 *informal* To make very tired; exhaust.

knock·a·bout [nok′ə·bout′] 1 *n.* A small, one-masted sailboat having a mainsail and jib, but no bowsprit or topmast. 2 *adj.* Intended for rough or everyday use: a *knockabout* hat. 3 *adj.* Noisy: boisterous: a *knockabout* vaudeville show.

knock·er [nok′ər] *n.* 1 A person or thing that knocks. 2 Something, as a ring or knob, that is hinged to a door and used in knocking.

Knocker

knock-kneed [nok′·nēd′] *adj.* Having legs that curve inward at the knees.

knock·off [nok′ôf′] *n. informal* A copy, as of a stylish garment, made to sell for less than the original.

knock·out [nok′out′] 1 *n.* In boxing, the knocking of a fighter to the floor with a blow that makes the fighter unconscious or so hurt that it is impossible to stand up before the referee counts to ten. 2 *n.* The blow that knocks out a fighter. 3 *adj.* Forcible enough to cause a knockout; overpowering; stunning.

knoll [nōl] *n.* A small round hill; mound.

knot [not] *n., v.* **knot·ted, knot·ting** 1 *n.* A fastening made by the tying or looping together of one or more ropes, cords, or the like. There are many types of knots. 2 *n.* A lump or tangle like a knot. 3 *n.* An ornamental bow, as of silk, lace, or braid. 4 *v.* To tie in or form a knot. 5 *v.* To fasten with a knot. 6 *v.* To become knotted or tangled. 7 *n.* A group or cluster, as of people or things. 8 *n.* A bond or union: the marriage *knot.* 9 *n.* A difficulty; problem. 10 *n.* A hard, gnarled lump on the trunk of a tree where a branch grows out. 11 *n.* A cross section of such a lump in a piece of sawed number. 12 *n.* A speed equal to one nautical mile (6,076.1 feet) per hour.

knot·hole [not′hōl′] *n.* A hole in a board where a knot has fallen out.

knot·ty [not′ē] *adj.* **knot·ti·er, knot·ti·est** 1 Full of knots: a *knotty* board; *knotty* rope. 2 Difficult or complex: a *knotty* puzzle.

know [nō] *v.* **knew, known, know·ing** 1 To be certain of or have the facts about: I *know* that the sun will rise tomorrow; Do you *know* the answer? 2 To have knowledge, understanding, or command of: to *know* the facts. 3 To be acquainted or familiar with: Do you *know* my cousin?; to *know* a song. 4 To be able to identify; recognize: I'll *know* it if I see it. 5 To be aware of; understand or realize: Do you *know* what you're saying? 6 To distinguish between: to *know* right from wrong. **—in the know** Having information known only to a few.

know-how [nō′hou′] *n. informal* Knowledge or skill: engineering *know-how*; American *know-how.*

know·ing [nō′ing] *adj.* 1 Having knowledge or information; informed. 2 Showing secret or sly knowledge: a *knowing* smile. 3 Shrewd or alert. **—know′ing·ly** *adv.*

knowl·edge [nol′ij] *n.* 1 The fact or condition of knowing or being aware: *Knowledge* of the instructions is important. 2 What a person knows: to have a good *knowledge* of physics. 3 All that is or may be known by people. **—to (one's) knowledge** or **to the best of (one's) knowledge** As far as one knows or is aware.

knowl·edge·a·ble [nol′ə·jə·bəl] *adj.* Having considerable knowledge or information: to be *knowledgeable* about music. **—knowl′edge·a·bly** *adv.*

known [nōn] Past participle of KNOW.

knuck·le [nuk′əl] *n., v.* **knuck·led, knuck·ling** 1 *n.* One of the joints of the fingers, especially one connecting a finger to the hand. 2 *n.* The knee or hock joint of a pig, calf, or other animal, the flesh of which is used as food. 3 *v.* To rub, press, or hit with the knuckles. **—knuckle down** To apply oneself seriously. **—knuckle under** To give in; submit.

ko·a·la [kō·ä′lə] *n.* A small, bearlike animal of Australia that lives in trees.

Koala

kohl·ra·bi [kōl·rä′bē *or* kōl′rä′bē] *n., pl.* **kohl·ra·bies** A kind of cabbage with an edible, turnip-shaped stem.

ko·la [kō′lə] *n.* 1 An African tree bearing nuts used in flavoring soft drinks. 2 The nut of this tree.

koo·doo [kōō′dōō] *n., pl.* **koo·doos** Another spelling of KUDU.

kook·a·bur·ra [kŏŏk′ə·bûr′ə] *n.* A bird of Australia whose cry is like loud laughter.

ko·peck or **ko·pek** [kō′pek] *n.* A Russian coin equal to one hundredth of a ruble.

Ko·ran [kō·rän′] *n.* The sacred book of Islam.

Ko·re·an [kô·rē′ən *or* kō·rē′ən] 1 *adj.* Of or from North or South Korea. 2 *n.* A person born in or a citizen of North or South Korea.

ko·sher [kō′shər] *adj.* Clean or proper, according to Jewish religious laws: *kosher* food.

kow·tow [kou′tou′] *v.* 1 To kneel and touch the ground with the forehead as a sign of respect or obedience. 2 To be slavish or submissive, as in seeking favor.

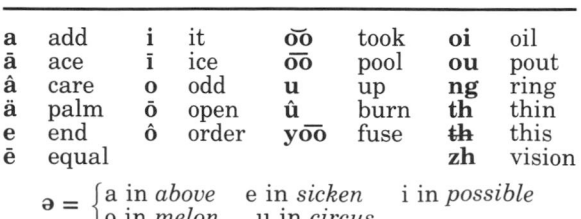

Men kowtowing

KP or **K.P.** kitchen police.

Kr The symbol for the element krypton.

kraal [kräl] *n.* 1 In southern Africa, a native village or group of huts, usually enclosed by a stockade. 2 In southern Africa, a pen for livestock.

Krem·lin [krem′lin] *n.* A large fortress in the central part of Moscow, that houses the government offices of the Soviet Union.

K

a	add	**i**	it	**ŏŏ**	took	**oi**	oil
ā	ace	**ī**	ice	**ōō**	pool	**ou**	pout
â	care	**o**	odd	**u**	up	**ng**	ring
ä	palm	**ō**	open	**û**	burn	**th**	thin
e	end	**ô**	order	**yōō**	fuse	**t̶h̶**	this
ē	equal					**zh**	vision

ə = {a in *above* e in *sicken* i in *possible* / o in *melon* u in *circus*}

Kriss Krin·gle [kris′ kring′gəl] Santa Claus.

kryp·ton [krip′ton′] *n.* A rare, colorless, gaseous element found in very small amounts in the atmosphere, inert chemically except for a few compounds formed with fluorine.

KS Postal Service abbreviation of Kansas.

ku·dos [k(y)ōō′dōz′ *or* k(y)ōō′dos′] *n.* (*used with singular verb*) Fame or great praise gained by some achievement.

ku·du [kōō′dōō] *n., pl.* **ku·du** or **ku·dus** A large, striped antelope of Africa with long, spiraled horns.

Ku Klux Klan [kōō′kluks′klan′] **1** A secret organization founded in the southern U.S. after the Civil War that advocated white supremacy. **2** A society inspired by the original Klan, founded in 1915 and active in various parts of the U.S.

kum·quat [kum′kwot′] *n.* A sour, tangy citrus fruit resembling a small orange, used mainly for preserves.

kung fu [kung′fōō′ *or* gung′fōō′] A Chinese system of self-defense similar to karate.

Ku·wai·ti [kə·wā′tē] **1** *adj.* Of or from Kuwait. **2** *n.* A person born in or a citizen of Kuwait.

kvetch [kvech] **1** *v.* To complain or find fault endlessly. **2** *n.* A person who constantly whines or complains. ◆ *Kvetch* is a Yiddish word.

kw, KW, or **k.w.** kilowatt(s).

Kwan·za or **Kwan·zaa** [kwän′zə] An African-American holiday based on traditional African harvest festivals, celebrating various aspects of black culture during the week beginning December 26th. ◆ The word *kwanza* comes from a Swahili phrase meaning "first fruits."

kwh, kWh, k.w.h., or **K.W.H.** kilowatt-hour(s).

Ky. Kentucky.

KY Postal Service Abbreviation of Kentucky.

ky·mo·graph [kī′mə·graf′] *n.* A machine that measures and makes a record of changes in the pressure of a fluid, as blood.

L is the twelfth letter of the alphabet. The sign for it originated among Semitic people in the Near East, in the region of Palestine and Syria, probably in the middle of the second millennium B.C. Little is known about the sign until around 1000 B.C., when the Phoenicians began using it. They named it *lamedh* and used it for the consonant *l* sound that we still use it for today.

When the Greeks adopted the Phoenician sign around the ninth century B.C., they called it *lambda* and varied its shape, settling in classical times upon the upside-down V shape that *lambda* still has in modern Greek. *Lambda,* too, stood for the *l* sound.

As early as the eighth century B.C., the Etruscans adopted the Greek alphabet, using a variant of the early Greek form for the letter *L*. It is from the Etruscans that the Romans took the letter, using it, as earlier people had, for the consonant *l* sound.

Around the time of the Caesars, the Romans made the shape of the letter more graceful. It was then that the oblique stroke became horizontal. The model of the letter found on the base of Trajan's column, erected in Rome in 114, is considered a masterpiece of letter design. A Trajan-style *majuscule,* or capital letter, *L* opens this essay.

The *minuscule,* or small letter, *l* developed, between the third and the ninth centuries, in the handwriting that scribes used for copying books. Contributing to its shape were the Roman *uncials* of the fourth to the eighth centuries and the *half uncials* of the fifth to ninth centuries. The most direct parent to our present-day lowercase *l,* however, is found in the script that evolved under the encouragement of Charlemagne (742-814). This letter was one of those known as the *Caroline minuscules,* a script that became the principal handwriting system used on the medieval manuscripts of the ninth and tenth centuries.

Ll

Early Phoenician (late 2nd millennium B.C.)

Phoenician (8th century B.C.)

Early Greek (9th-7th centuries B.C.)

Western Greek (6th century B.C.)

Classical Greek (403 B.C. onward)

Early Etruscan (8th century B.C.)

Monumental Latin (4th century B.C.)

Classical Latin

Uncial

Half uncial

Caroline minuscule

l or **L** [el] *n., pl.* **l's** or **L's** 1 The 12th letter of the English alphabet. 2 (*written* **L**) The Roman numeral for 50.

l or **l.** liter(s).

l. or **L.** 1 left. 2 length.

L 1 Latin. 2 (*often written* **£**) pound sterling.

la [lä] *n.* In music, a syllable used to represent the sixth tone of a major scale or the first tone of a minor scale, or in a fixed system, the tone A.

La The symbol for the element lanthanum.

La. Louisiana.

LA Postal Service abbreviation of Louisiana.

L.A. Los Angeles.

lab [lab] *n. U.S. informal* Laboratory.

la·bel [lā′bəl] *n., v.* **la·beled** or **la·belled, la·bel·ing** or **la·bel·ling** 1 *n.* Something, as a slip of paper or strip of cloth, fastened to an object to tell what it is, who made it, whom it belongs to, or where it is going. 2 *v.* To fasten a label to: to *label* a jar or box. 3 *v.* To classify as; call: to be *labeled* a beginner.

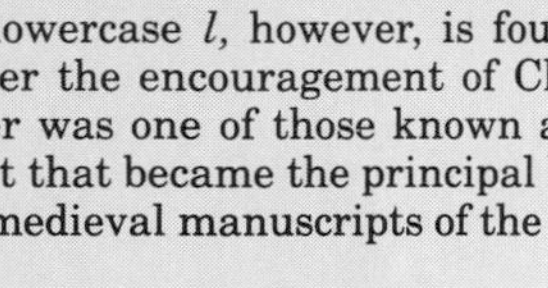

Labels

la·bi·al [lā′bē·əl] 1 *adj.* Of or having to do with the lips. 2 *adj.* Formed by the lips, as the sounds for the letters *p, b,* and *m.* 3 *n.* A sound formed by the lips.

la·bor [lā′bər] 1 *n.* Work, especially hard work: manual *labor.* 2 *v.* To work hard: to *labor* in the fields. 3 *n.* A piece of work; task. 4 *n.* Working people as a group: Unions represent *labor.* 5 *v.* To move slowly and with difficulty. 6 *n.* The process of giving birth to a child.

lab·o·ra·to·ry [lab′rə·tôr′ē] *n., pl.* **lab·o·ra·to·ries** A building or room equipped for doing scientific work or experiments.

Labor Day The first Monday in September, in the U.S. and Canada a legal holiday in honor of working people.

la·bored [lā′bərd] *adj.* Done with effort, not with ease; forced: *labored* breathing.

la·bor·er [lā′bər·ər] *n.* A person who does physical or manual work, especially work that calls for strength rather than skill.

la·bo·ri·ous [lə·bôr′ē·əs] *adj.* 1 Requiring great effort; hard: a *laborious* task. 2 Hardworking; diligent. **—la·bo′ri·ous·ly** *adv.*

la·bor·sav·ing [lā′bər·sā′ving] *adj.* Designed to lessen or eliminate human, especially manual, labor: a *laborsaving* device.

a add	**i** it	**o͝o** took	**oi** oil
ā ace	**ī** ice	**o͞o** pool	**ou** pout
â care	**o** odd	**u** up	**ng** ring
ä palm	**ō** open	**û** burn	**th** thin
e end	**ô** order	**yo͞o** fuse	**th** this
ē equal			**zh** vision

ə = {a in *above* e in *sicken* i in *possible*; o in *melon* u in *circus*}

labor union An association of workers organized to improve working conditions and to protect the interests of members.

la·bur·num [lə·bûr′nəm] *n.* A small tree with yellow flowers that hang in clusters.

lab·y·rinth [lab′ə·rinth] *n.* An arrangement of winding passages or paths designed to confuse anyone trying to find a way through; maze. ◆ This word comes from the name of the maze in Greek myths which Daedalus made to confine the Minotaur.

Labyrinth

lab·y·rin·thi·an [lab′ə·rin′thē·ən] *adj.* Labyrinthine.

lab·y·rin·thine [lab′ə·rin′thin] *adj.* Like a labyrinth; highly complicated; intricate.

lac [lak] *n.* A gummy brown substance, given off by an insect of southern Asia and used in making shellac.

lace [lās] *n., v.* **laced, lac·ing** 1 *n.* A delicate network of threads of linen, silk, or other material, worked into a pattern. 2 *adj. use*: a *lace* curtain. 3 *v.* To trim with lace. 4 *n.* A cord or string passed through holes or over hooks to pull and hold together the edges of a shoe or garment. 5 *v.* To fasten with a lace or laces: to *lace* up ice skates. 6 *v.* To twist together; intertwine: They *laced* arms.

lac·er·ate [las′ər·āt′] *v.* **lac·er·at·ed, lac·er·at·ing** 1 To tear in a ragged way so as to wound: The hiker's legs had been *lacerated* by briars. 2 To hurt painfully: to *lacerate* someone's feelings.

lac·er·a·tion [las′ər·ā′shən] *n.* 1 The act of lacerating. 2 A ragged wound made by tearing.

lace·wing [lās′wing′] *n.* Any of various green or brown insects with long antennae and four wings whose patterns resemble lace.

lach·ry·mal [lak′rə·məl] *adj.* Of, having to do with, or producing tears: *lachrymal* glands.

lach·ry·mose [lak′rə·mōs′] *adj.* 1 Shedding tears or likely to do so: *lachrymose* children. 2 Causing tears: a *lachrymose* tale. **—lach′ry·mose′ly** *adv.*

lack [lak] 1 *n.* A deficiency or complete absence of something needed or desired. 2 *v.* To be without or have too little: to *lack* talent. 3 *v.* To be short by: I *lack* $5 of the required amount. 4 *v.* To be absent or insufficient: Vitamins were *lacking* in the child's diet. 5 *n.* A thing needed; need.

lack·a·dai·si·cal [lak′ə·dā′zi·kəl] *adj.* Without interest, energy, or concern; listless.

lack·ey [lak′ē] *n., pl.* **lack·eys** 1 A male servant in a uniform; footman. 2 Anyone who takes orders from another as a servant does.

lack·lus·ter [lak′lus′tər] *adj.* Lacking brightness; dim; dull.

la·con·ic [lə·kon′ik] *adj.* Using no unnecessary words; brief and concise: a *laconic* answer.

lac·quer [lak′ər] 1 *n.* A varnish made by dissolving shellac or various resins in alcohol. 2 *n.* A natural varnish obtained from an oriental tree. 3 *v.* To coat with lacquer. 4 *n.* Wooden articles coated with lacquer.

la·crosse [lə·krôs′] *n.* A ball game played with long, racketlike implements by two teams of ten players each. The object is to advance the ball down the field and into the opponent's goal.

lac·tase [lak′tās′] *n.* An enzyme that occurs in yeast and in the intestinal juices of mammals, and breaks down lactose into two other sugars.

lac·ta·tion [lak·tā′shən] *n.* 1 The forming and secreting of milk by mammals. 2 The period during which milk is produced.

lac·te·al [lak′tē·əl] *adj.* Of or like milk.

lac·tic [lak′tik] *adj.* Of, having to do with, or derived from milk.

lactic acid An acid present in sour milk.

lac·tose [lak′tōs′] *n.* A white, odorless sugar present in milk.

la·cu·na [lə·kyo͞o′nə] *n., pl.* **la·cu·nae** [lə·kyo͞o′nē] or **la·cu·nas** 1 An empty space or missing part; gap. 2 A small hollow or sunken place in the structure of a person, animal, or plant.

lac·y [lā′sē] *adj.* **lac·i·er, lac·i·est** Made of or resembling lace: a *lacy* collar.

lad [lad] *n.* A boy or youth.

lad·der [lad′ər] *n.* 1 A device for climbing up or down, usually consisting of two side pieces connected by crosspieces placed at regular intervals to serve as steps. 2 A means by which one can move upward: at the bottom of the social *ladder.*

lad·die [lad′ē] *n.* A young boy.

lade [lād] *v.* **lad·ed, lad·ed** or **lad·en, lad·ing** 1 To load. 2 To dip or ladle (a liquid).

lad·en [lād′(ə)n] 1 Alternative past participle of LADE. 2 *adj.* Weighed down; loaded; burdened.

lad·ing [lā′ding] *n.* A load or cargo, often used in the term **bill of lading,** a receipt listing goods received for transportation.

la·dle [lād′(ə)l] *n., v.* **la·dled, la·dling** 1 *n.* A cup-shaped spoon with a long handle for dipping out or serving liquids. 2 *v.* To dip out and pour with a ladle: *Ladle* out the soup.

Ladle

la·dy [lā′dē] *n., pl.* **la·dies** 1 A woman who has good manners, good character, and refinement. 2 A woman having the rights and powers of a lord; mistress. 3 (*written* **Lady**) In Great Britain, a title used with the last or first name of certain women of high rank, as countesses, the wives of knights, or the daughters of dukes. 4 A man's wife or sweetheart. 5 A term of reference or address for any woman. **—Our Lady** The Virgin Mary.

la·dy·bird [lā′dē·bûrd′] *n.* Another name for LADYBUG.

la·dy·bug [lā′dē·bug′] *n.* A small, brightly colored beetle, usually red spotted with black.

Ladybug

la·dy·fin·ger [lā′dē·fing′gər] *n.* A small sponge cake shaped like a finger.

lady in waiting A lady appointed to serve or wait upon a queen or princess.

la·dy·like [lā′dē·līk′] *adj.* Like or suitable to a lady.

la·dy·ship [lā′dē·ship′] *n.* 1 The rank or position of a lady. 2 (*written* **Ladyship**) The form of address used in speaking to or of a woman having the title of Lady: Yes, your *Ladyship;* her *Ladyship's* garden.

lady's-slip·per [lā′dēz·slip′ər] *n.* A kind of wild orchid, having a flower that resembles a slipper.

lag [lag] *v.* **lagged, lag·ging,** *n.* 1 *v.* To move slowly; stay or fall behind: to *lag* behind. 2 *n.* The condition or act of falling behind. 3 *n.* The amount by which or time during which there is a falling behind or delay: a *lag* between the idea and the accomplishment.

la·ger [lä′gər] *n.* A beer that is permitted to age, in storage, for from six weeks to six months before being sold.

lag·gard [lag′ərd] 1 *n.* A person who lags; loiterer. 2 *adj.* Falling behind; slow.

la·goon [lə·go͞on′] *n.* 1 A body of shallow water, as a pond or inlet, usually connecting with a river, a larger lake, or the sea. 2 The water enclosed by a ring-shaped coral island.

laid [lād] Past tense and past participle of LAY[1]: I *laid* the board down on the ground; I had *laid* the book on the table.

laid-back [lād′bak′] *adj. informal* Relaxed in character or behavior; easygoing; not tense: a *laid-back* way of teaching.

lain [lān] Past participle of LIE[1]: I had just *lain* on the bed when the phone rang.

lair [lâr] *n.* The den of a wild animal.

laird [lârd] *n.* The Scottish word for the owner of a landed estate.

lais·sez faire [les′ā·fâr′] The doctrine that government should exercise as little control as possible in economic affairs.

la·i·ty [lā′ə·tē] *n.* 1 The people who are members of a church but are not members of its clergy. 2 All of those outside a specific profession or occupation.

La·ius [lā′yəs] *n.* In Greek myths, a king of Thebes who was killed by his son Oedipus.

lake [lāk] *n.* 1 A body of fresh or salt water enclosed by land. 2 A large pool of any liquid.

lake dweller One of the prehistoric peoples who lived in dwellings built over water and resting on supports.

lake trout A trout that is an important source of food found in the freshwater lakes of North America.

lam[1] [lam] *v.* **lammed, lam·ming** *slang* To beat soundly; strike; thrash.

lam[2] [lam] *v.* **lammed, lam·ming,** *n. slang* 1 *v.* To flee hastily or suddenly; escape, especially from prison or the police. 2 *n.* A hasty or sudden flight, especially from prison or the police: on the *lam.*

la·ma [lä′mə] *n.* A Buddhist priest or monk in Tibet or Mongolia.

la·ma·ser·y [lä′mə·ser′ē] *n., pl.* **la·ma·ser·ies** A Buddhist monastery in Tibet or Mongolia.

lamb [lam] 1 *n.* A young sheep. 2 *v.* To give birth to a lamb. 3 *n.* The meat of a lamb used as food. 4 *n.* Any gentle or innocent person.

lam·baste [lam·bāst′] *v.* **lam·bast·ed, lam·bast·ing** *slang* 1 To beat or thrash. 2 To lash with harsh words; scold severely.

lamb·da [lam′də] *n.* The 11th letter of the Greek alphabet.

lam·bent [lam′bənt] *adj.* 1 Playing over a surface with a flickering movement, as a flame. 2 Softly radiant. 3 Playfully brilliant, as wit.

lamb·kin [lam′kin] *n.* A little lamb.

lamb·skin [lam′skin′] *n.* 1 The skin of a lamb, especially when it is used as a garment with the wool left on the hide. 2 Leather prepared from the skin of a lamb.

lame [lām] *adj.* **lam·er, lam·est,** *v.* **lamed, lam·ing** 1 *adj.* Crippled or disabled, especially in a leg or foot. 2 *v.* To make lame; cripple. 3 *adj.* Sore; stiff; painful: a *lame* back. 4 *adj.* Weak and not effective: a *lame* attempt at humor. **—lame′ly** *adv.* **—lame′ness** *n.*

la·mé [la·mā′] *n.* A cloth woven of flat gold or silver thread mixed with silk or other fiber.

lame·brain [lām′brān′] *n. slang* A stupid person. —**lame·brained** [lām′brānd′] *adj.*

lame-duck [lām′duk′] *adj.* Of, having to do with, or being a lame duck: a *lame-duck* senator; the *lame-duck* Congress.

lame duck 1 An elected government official or group that completes a term of office after being defeated in an attempt to be reelected. 2 A person who is helpless or not effective; weakling.

la·ment [lə·ment′] 1 *v.* To feel or express great sorrow over: to *lament* a death. 2 *v.* To mourn. 3 *n.* An expression of grief or remorse, as wailing, words, or a song expressing sorrow.

lam·en·ta·ble [lam′ən·tə·bəl *or* lə·ment′ə·bəl] *adj.* Bad or unfortunate enough to inspire regret or pity: a *lamentable* failure. **—lam′en·ta·bly** *adv.*

lam·en·ta·tion [lam′ən·tā′shən] *n.* 1 The act of lamenting. 2 A lament; wail; moan.

lam·i·na [lam′ə·nə] *n., pl.* **lam·i·nae** [lam′ə·nē] or **lam·i·nas** 1 A thin layer, sheet, or plate. 2 The wide part of a plant leaf.

lam·i·nate [lam′ə·nāt′] *v.* **lam·i·nat·ed, lam·i·nat·ing** 1 To beat, roll, or press into thin layers. 2 To form by uniting separate layers. 3 To cover with thin layers. **—lam′i·na′tion** *n.*

lamp [lamp] *n.* A device for producing light, as a holder or stand with a socket for an electric light bulb, or a vessel in which oil is burned through a wick.

Lamp

lamp·black [lamp′blak′] *n.* A fine black soot of almost pure carbon, obtained by burning oil, tar, or gas, used in ink and paints.

lamp·light·er [lamp′lī′tər] *n.* A person or device that lights street lamps.

lam·poon [lam·po͞on′] 1 *n.* A written attack on an individual, using humor to make fun of the person. 2 *v.* To attack or ridicule in a lampoon.

lamp·post [lamp′pōst′] *n.* A post on which a street lamp is mounted.

lam·prey [lam′prē] *n., pl.* **lam·preys** A water animal

a	add	**i**	it	**o͝o**	took	**oi**	oil
ā	ace	**ī**	ice	**o͞o**	pool	**ou**	pout
â	care	**o**	odd	**u**	up	**ng**	ring
ä	palm	**ō**	open	**û**	burn	**th**	thin
e	end	**ô**	order	**yo͞o**	fuse	**th̶**	this
ē	equal					**zh**	vision

ə = a in *above*, e in *sicken*, i in *possible*, o in *melon*, u in *circus*

L

resembling an eel and having a round, sucking mouth lined with sharp teeth.

lance [lans] *n., v.* **lanced, lanc·ing** 1 *n.* A weapon with a long shaft and a sharp metal head. 2 *v.* To pierce with a lance. 3 *n.* A soldier armed with a lance. 4 *n.* A slender, sharp instrument resembling a lance, as a whaler's spear or a surgeon's lancet. 5 *v.* To cut open with a lancet: to *lance* an abscess.

Lance

lance corporal A member of the U.S. Marine Corps who ranks above a private first class and below a corporal.

Lan·ce·lot [lan′sə·lot′] *n.* In English legend, the bravest knight at King Arthur's court.

lanc·er [lan′sər] *n.* A soldier on horseback armed with a lance.

lan·cet [lan′sit] *n.* A small knife with two sharp edges, used by doctors, as to open boils.

lance·wood [lans′wo͝od′] *n.* 1 The hard but elastic wood of any of a group of tropical American trees. 2 A tree that has such wood.

land [land] 1 *n.* The solid, exposed surface of the earth. 2 *n.* A country or region. 3 *n.* Ground considered with reference to its uses, location, or value: pasture *land*; The family's wealth is in *land.* 4 *v.* To move from a ship to the shore: to *land* cargo; The passengers *landed.* 5 *v.* To touch at a port; come to shore, as a ship. 6 *v.* To bring or come to rest on a surface, as after a flight, jump, or fall: to *land* a plane; The acrobat *landed* feet first. 7 *v.* To arrive or cause to arrive: to *land* in jail; to *land* a punch. 8 *v.* To pull (a fish) out of the water; catch: to *land* a trout. 9 *v. informal* To obtain; win: to *land* a good job.

lan·dau [lan′dô′ *or* lan′dou′] *n.* 1 A four-wheeled carriage having facing passenger seats covered by a folding top that can be lowered, and with a raised outside seat for the driver. 2 An early automobile with a collapsible top over the rear passenger section.

land·ed [lan′did] *adj.* 1 Owning land: *landed* gentry. 2 Consisting of land: *landed* property.

land·er [lan′dər] *n.* A device or mechanism used in landing, especially a vehicle for conveying astronauts or scientific equipment from an orbiting craft to a landing on a planet in outer space.

land·fall [land′fôl′] *n.* 1 The act of sighting or reaching land in a voyage or flight. 2 The land thus sighted or reached.

land·fill [land′fil′] *n.* 1 The practice of disposing of trash, garbage, sewage, or other waste by burying it between layers of earth. 2 An area of land built up as a result of that practice.

land·form [land′fôrm′] *n.* Any of the earth's surface features, such as mountains, plateaus, and valleys, that are produced by nature.

land grant A gift of public land made by a government, especially for the construction or operation of a college, railroad, or highway. **—land-grant** *adj.*

land·hold·er [land′hōl′dər] *n.* An owner or occupant of land.

land·ing [lan′ding] *n.* 1 The act of going or putting on shore from a ship. 2 The place where a ship lands; wharf; pier. 3 The act of bringing or coming down after a flight, jump, or fall. 4 A platform at the head of a staircase or between flights of stairs.

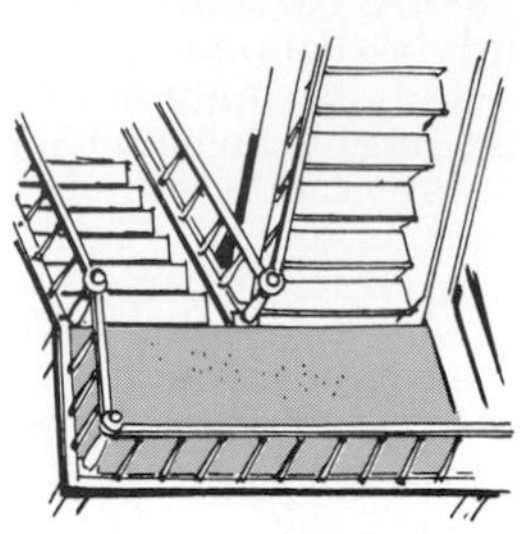
Landing

landing craft A flat-bottom naval vessel used to convey military personnel and equipment from a troopship to or near the shore of a destination.

landing field A level strip of land prepared so that planes may land on it and take off from it.

landing gear The under part of an airplane upon which the craft moves and rests for support when on the ground or water.

landing strip A narrow landing field, especially one in a remote area or one built in a war zone for use by military aircraft.

land·la·dy [land′lā′dē] *n., pl.* **land·la·dies** 1 A woman who owns and rents out buildings, apartments, or land. 2 A woman who keeps an inn, boarding house, or rooming house.

land·less [land′lis] *adj.* Having or owning no land.

land·locked [land′lokt′] *adj.* 1 Entirely or nearly shut in by land. 2 Confined to fresh water shut off from the sea: *landlocked* salmon.

land·lord [land′lôrd′] *n.* 1 A person who owns and rents out buildings, apartments, or land. 2 A person who keeps an inn, boarding house, or rooming house.

land·lub·ber [land′lub′ər] *n.* A sailor's term for someone new to sailing and clumsy on ships.

land·mark [land′märk′] *n.* 1 A fixed object marking the boundary of a piece of land. 2 A familiar or outstanding object in a landscape which may serve as a guide to aircraft, ships, or travelers. 3 A fact or event marking an important change or a new advance: The discovery of penicillin was a medical *landmark.*

land·mass [land′mas′] *n.* A large area of land.

land mine A hidden explosive buried in shallow earth and designed to go off when it is neared or passed over by troops.

land·own·er [land′ō′nər] *n.* A person who owns land.

land-poor [land′po͝or′] *adj.* Owning much land but getting insufficient income from it to cover the expense of taxes and maintenance.

land·scape [land′skāp′] *n., v.* **land·scaped, land·scap·ing** 1 *n.* A stretch of natural scenery on land as seen from a single point. 2 *n.* A picture representing such scenery. 3 *v.* To change or improve the appearance of (a piece of land) by adding or arranging trees, flowers, and bushes. ◆ The word *landscape* comes from Dutch.

landscape architect An architect who plans the arrangement of buildings, roads, and other useful structures of an area so as to make them attractive in relation to the natural scenery.

landscape gardener A person who plans the arrangement of trees, shrubs, and other plants around a building or within a park or other area.

land·slide [land′slīd′] *n.* 1 The slipping down of a mass of loose soil or rock on a mountainside or other steep slope. **2** The mass that slips down. **3** A great majority of votes for one party or candidate in an election.

lands·man [landz′mən] *n., pl.* **lands·men** [landz′·mən] **1** A person who lives or works on land and is unfamiliar with the life of a seaman. **2** One's fellow countryman.

land·ward [land′wərd] **1** *adv.* Toward the land. **2** *adj.* Being, facing, or moving toward land.

land·wards [land′wərdz] *adv.* Toward the land.

lane [lān] *n.* **1** A narrow path or road, as one between fences, walls, or hedges: a country *lane.* **2** A wooden pathway down which bowling balls are rolled. **3** Any narrow way or passage: a *lane* through a crowd of people. **4** A marked division of a road, to be used by vehicles going in the same direction. **5** A set route followed by ships at sea or airplanes in the sky. **6** On a racetrack, any of several parallel courses in which the contestants must stay while racing.

lan·guage [lang′gwij] *n.* **1** The sounds spoken and heard or the symbols written and read by human beings to express emotions and ideas or to record facts. **2** The words which a certain nation or group uses in speaking and writing: the French *language.* **3** The study of a language or of languages. **4** Any means of expressing ideas or emotions: sign *language.* **5** The special words used in a certain field: scientific *language.* **6** A particular style or manner of expression: Milton's *language*; strong *language.* **7** Any set of instructions that can be changed to machine language for a computer to process. **8** Machine language.

lan·guid [lang′gwid] *adj.* Lacking energy or spirit; listless; weak. **—lan′guid·ly** *adv.*

lan·guish [lang′gwish] *v.* **1** To become weak or feeble. **2** To droop from restless longing; pine or suffer: to *languish* in a depressing hospital ward. **3** To put on a sad, tender, or weary look in order to gain sympathy.

lan·guor [lang′gər] *n.* **1** A weak, tired, or listless condition. **2** A tender or dreamy mood. **3** Inactivity or stillness. **—lan′guor·ous** *adj.*

lank [langk] *adj.* **1** Very lean: a *lank* child. **2** Long and straight; not curly: *lank* hair.

lank·y [lang′kē] *adj.* **lank·i·er, lank·i·est** Ungracefully tall and thin. **—lank′i·ness** *n.*

lan·o·lin [lan′ə·lin] *n.* A fatty substance taken from wool and used in the making of ointments, cosmetics, and soap.

lan·tern [lan′tərn] *n.* A case to hold and protect a light, having sides of glass, paper, or other material, through which the light can be seen.

Lantern

lan·tha·num [lan′thə·nəm] *n.* A metallic element occurring in rare earths. See RARE-EARTH ELEMENT.

lan·yard [lan′yərd] *n.* **1** A short rope used on a ship to fasten things. **2** A cord worn around the neck. A sailor may attach a knife to it. **3** A cord used in firing certain cannons.

La·o·tian [lā·ō′shən] **1** *adj.* Of or from Laos. **2** *n.* A person born in or a citizen of Laos.

lap[1] [lap] *n.* **1** The front part from waist to knees of a person sitting down. **2** The part of the clothing covering the lap, as the front of a skirt. **3** An environment that holds or protects: in the *lap* of luxury.

lap[2] [lap] *v.* **lapped, lap·ping,** *n.* **1** *v.* To wrap, fold, or wind: to *lap* a bandage around the leg. **2** *v.* To lay (one thing) so that it partly covers something else: to *lap* each shingle over another in repairing a roof. **3** *v.* To lie partly over (another or each other); overlap. **4** *v.* To extend over, into, or beyond something else. **5** *n.* The amount by which one thing overlaps another, or the overlapping part. **6** *n.* One of several trips made around a race track.

lap[3] [lap] *v.* **lapped, lap·ping,** *n.* **1** *v.* To drink as an animal does by licking up with the tongue. **2** *v.* To wash with a licking sound, as waves. **3** *n.* The act or sound of lapping.

lap dog A dog small enough to hold on the lap.

la·pel [lə·pel′] *n.* Either part of the front of a coat that is folded back below the collar.

lap·i·dar·y [lap′ə·der′ē] *n., pl.* **lap·i·dar·ies** A person whose work or hobby is to cut, engrave, or polish precious stones.

lap·is laz·u·li [lap′is laz′yo͝o·lī] **1** A deep blue mineral sometimes used as a semiprecious stone. **2** Deep blue; sky blue.

Lap·land·er [lap′lan′dər] *n.* Lapp (def. 1).

Lapp [lap] *n.* **1** A member of a wandering people living in Lapland. **2** Their language.

lap robe A heavy blanket used to cover the lap and legs of a person seated outdoors or riding in an open vehicle.

lapse [laps] *n., v.* **lapsed, laps·ing** **1** *n.* A minor, momentary slip or mistake: a *lapse* of judgment. **2** *n.* A slip or fall, as from a better to a worse condition: a *lapse* into despair. **3** *v.* To fall away from good behavior: to *lapse* into bad habits. **4** *v.* To pass gradually; slip: to *lapse* into a coma. **5** *n.* A gradual passing away: a *lapse* of time. **6** *n.* The ending of a right or benefit, through failure to fill certain conditions: the *lapse* of an insurance policy. **7** *v.* To become void; end: To let one's membership *lapse.*

lap·wing [lap′wing′] *n.* A bird of Europe and Asia noted for its awkward way of flying and its shrill cry.

Lapwing

lar·board [lär′bərd] **1** *adj.* Being on or toward the left side of a ship as one faces forward. **2** *n.* The left side of a ship; port.

lar·ce·ny [lär′sə·nē] *n., pl.* **lar·ce·nies** The unlawful taking of another's goods; theft. **—lar′ce·nous** *adj.*

larch [lärch] *n.* **1** A tree bearing cones and having needlelike leaves that drop off in the autumn. **2** The strong wood of this tree.

L

a	add	**i**	it	**o͝o**	took	**oi**	oil
ā	ace	**ī**	ice	**o͞o**	pool	**ou**	pout
â	care	**o**	odd	**u**	up	**ng**	ring
ä	palm	**ō**	open	**û**	burn	**th**	thin
e	end	**ô**	order	**yo͞o**	fuse	**t͟h**	this
ē	equal					**zh**	vision

ə = { a in *above* e in *sicken* i in *possible* / o in *melon* u in *circus* }

lard [lärd] **1** *n.* The fat of a hog after being melted and made clear. **2** *v.* To cover or smear with lard. **3** *v.* To insert strips of bacon or fat in (meat) before cooking. **4** *v.* To fill or enrich with: to *lard* a speech with quotations.

lar·der [lär′dər] *n.* **1** A place where food is stored; pantry. **2** A stock or supply of food.

lar·don [lär′don′] *n.* A lardoon.

lar·doon [lär·do͞on′] *n.* A strip, as of fat or salt pork, used to lard meat.

lar·es and pe·na·tes [lâr′ēz and pə·nā′tēz] The valued household possessions of a family. ◆ This expression comes from the names of ancient Roman household gods called Lares and Penates.

large [lärj] *adj.* **larg·er, larg·est** **1** Big, as in size, amount, or extent: a *large* refrigerator. **2** Bigger than usual or than the average: Give me the *large* size. **—at large** **1** Free; loose: A wild animal is *at large.* **2** Elected from the whole area, not from a particular district: a representative *at large.* **3** In general: the people *at large.*

large calorie Another name for CALORIE (def. 2).

large-heart·ed [lärj′här′tid] *adj.* Generous; liberal. **—large′heart′ed·ness** *n.*

large intestine The short, thick, lower part of the intestine, leading from the small intestine to the anus.

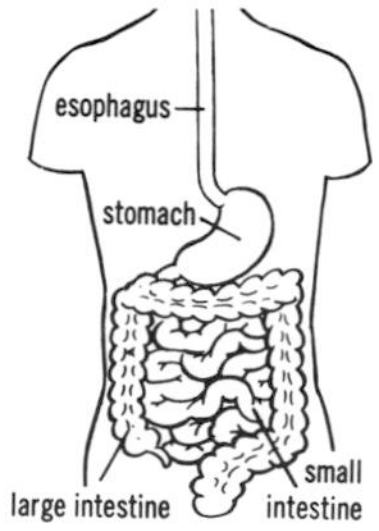

large·ly [lärj′lē] *adv.* To a great extent; chiefly: Her success was *largely* due to hard work.

large-scale [lärj′skāl′] *adj.* **1** Having great range or scope: *large-scale* plans. **2** Over a large area; widespread; extensive: a *large-scale* epidemic. **3** Drawn on a scale that shows much detail: a *large-scale* map.

lar·gess or **lar·gesse** [lär·jes′ *or* lär′jis] *n.* **1** Generous giving. **2** A generous gift.

lar·ghet·to [lär·get′ō] *adj., adv., n., pl.* **lar·ghet·tos** **1** *adj.* In music, moderately slow. **2** *adv.* Moderately slowly. **3** *n.* A moderately slow musical movement or passage.

lar·go [lär′gō] *n., pl.* **lar·goes,** *adj., adv.* **1** *n.* A slow movement or passage in music. **2** *adj.* Slow. **3** *adv.* In a slow tempo.

lar·i·at [lar′ē·ət] *n.* **1** A lasso. **2** A rope used to tie grazing animals to a stake.

lark[1] [lärk] *n.* **1** Any of various small European songbirds, especially the skylark. **2** A similar bird, as the meadowlark of North America.

lark[2] [lärk] **1** *n.* A carefree adventure; good time. **2** *v.* To have fun or play pranks; frolic.

lark·spur [lärk′spûr′] *n.* A tall plant with loose clusters of flowers that resemble a bird's foot in shape.

lar·rup [lar′əp] *v. informal* To beat; thrash.

lar·va [lär′və] *n., pl.* **lar·vae** [lär′vē] or **lar·vas** An insect in its early stage as a caterpillar, grub, or maggot, between hatching from an egg and becoming a pupa: *Larvae* of moths are caterpillars.

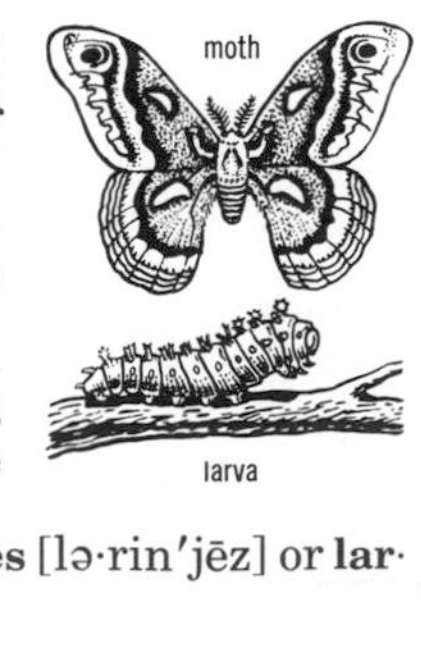

lar·val [lär′vəl] *adj.* **1** Of or having to do with larvae. **2** In the stage of a larva.

lar·yn·gi·tis [lar′ən·jī′tis] *n.* Inflammation of the larynx, as during a cold, when the voice becomes faint or hoarse.

lar·ynx [lar′ingks] *n., pl.* **la·ryn·ges** [lə·rin′jēz] or **lar·ynx·es** The upper part of the windpipe, containing the vocal cords.

la·sa·gna or **la·sa·gne** [lə·zän′yə] *n.* **1** A dish consisting of boiled noodles baked with layers of ground meat, tomatoes, and cheese. **2** The wide, flat noodles of such a dish.

las·civ·i·ous [lə·siv′ē·əs] *adj.* Having or causing lust; lewd. **—las·civ′i·ous·ly** *adv.*

la·ser [lā′zər] *n.* A device that produces an intense beam of light whose waves are parallel, of the same wavelength, and exactly in step.

lash[1] [lash] **1** *n.* A whip, especially the flexible cord or its tip. **2** *v.* To strike, punish, or command with or as if with a lash; whip; flog. **3** *n.* A single stroke with a whip: to receive 20 *lashes.* **4** *v.* To move back and forth in a whiplike manner: The dog *lashed* its tail in excitement. **5** *v.* To beat or dash against violently: The waves *lashed* the rocks. **6** *v.* To scold in speech or writing: A newspaper editorial *lashed* the governor. **7** *v.* To stir or arouse. **8** *n.* An eyelash.

lash[2] [lash] *v.* To bind or tie, especially with rope or cord: to *lash* a bicycle to the top of a car.

lass [las] *n.* A young woman; girl.

las·sie [las′ē] *n.* A young or small girl.

las·si·tude [las′ə·t(y)o͞od′] *n.* **1** A feeling of weariness; lack of energy; fatigue. **2** A feeling of indolent indifference; languor.

las·so [las′ō] *n., pl.* **las·sos** or **las·soes** **1** *n.* A long rope having a loop with a slipknot at one end, used for catching horses and cattle. **2** *v.* To catch with or as if with a lasso.

last[1] [last] **1** *adj.* Coming after all others; being at the end; final: the *last* page of a book. **2** *adv.* After all others in time or order: to be served *last.* **3** *n.* A person or thing that is last: I was the *last* to arrive. **4** *adj.* Nearest before the present time: *last* month. **5** *adv.* At the time nearest to the present: The keys were *last* seen on the table. **6** *adj.* Being the only one remaining: my *last* dollar. **7** *adj.* Least suitable or likely. **8** *adv.* In conclusion; finally. **9** *n.* The final part or portion; the end. **—at last** Finally.

last[2] [last] *v.* **1** To continue; go on: How long does the movie *last*? **2** To remain in good condition. **3** To hold out: Our food *lasted* a week.

last[3] [last] **1** *n.* A wood or metal model of a human foot on which to make or repair a shoe or boot. **2** *v.* To fit to or form on a last.

last-ditch [last′dich′] *adj.* Done in a final great effort to prevent a misfortune that threatens: a *last-ditch* defense of the city.

last·ing [las′ting] *adj.* Continuing for a long time; durable: a *lasting* friendship.

Last Judgment Another term for JUDGMENT DAY.

last·ly [last′lē] *adv.* In the last place; in conclusion; finally.

last straw The last in a series of annoyances or injuries that drives the person who has suffered them to the point of taking remedial action.

Last Supper The last meal Jesus had with his disciples, on the night before his Crucifixion.

last word **1** The final word or words spoken, especially in an argument or dispute. **2** Something that decides a matter on which there has been lack of agreement. **3** The right or power to make a final judgment. **4** *informal* The finest or most modern item of its kind.

lat. latitude.

Lat. Latin.

latch [lach] **1** *n.* A movable bar of metal or wood that slides or drops into a notch to fasten a window, door, or gate. **2** *v.* To fasten by means of a latch; close. **—latch on to** *slang* **1** To get; obtain. **2** To attach oneself to.

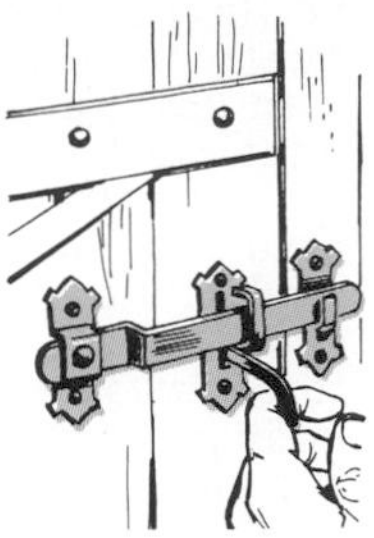

Latch

latch·key [lach′kē′] *n.* A key for unfastening a latch, especially on an outside or front door.

latchkey child A young child who spends part of each day at home without parental supervision.

latch·string [lach′string′] *n.* A string on a latch that is passed through a hole in a door so that the latch can be unfastened from the outside.

late [lāt] *adj.* **lat·er** or **lat·ter, lat·est** or **last,** *adv.* **1** *adj.* Appearing or coming after the expected time; tardy. **2** *adv.* After the expected time; tardily. **3** *adj.* Occurring at an unusually advanced time: a *late* departure. **4** *adv.* At or until an advanced time (as of the day or year): to sleep *late.* **5** *adj.* Toward the end or close, as of a period or season: in *late* spring. **6** *adj.* Recent or fairly recent: the *late* elections. **7** *adj.* Having died recently: my *late* uncle. **8** *adj.* Having left office a short time ago: our *late* mayor. **—of late** Recently. **—late′ness** *n.* ◆ The two comparative forms of *late* are often confused. *Later* (like *sooner*) refers to time; *latter* is the second of two, the opposite of FORMER.

late·com·er [lāt′kum′ər] *n.* A person who arrives later than expected.

la·teen sail [lə·tēn′] A triangular sail held by a slanting yard and usually a boom.

Lateen sails

Late Greek The Greek language in use from about A.D. 300 to 600.

Late Latin The Latin language in use from about A.D. 200 to 700.

late·ly [lāt′lē] *adv.* Not long ago; recently.

la·tent [lā′tənt] *adj.* Hidden or not active, but present: *latent* musical ability.

lat·er·al [lat′ər·əl] **1** *adj.* Of, situated at, coming from, or directed toward the side. **2** *n.* In football, a pass of the ball directed sideways rather than forward toward the opponents' goal. **3** *v.* To throw such a pass in football. **—lat′er·al·ly** *adv.*

la·tex [lā′teks] *n.* The sticky, milky juice secreted by various plants, especially the rubber tree, used to make rubber, gutta-percha, and chicle.

lath [lath] **1** *n.* One of the thin strips of wood used as a base, as for plaster or tile. **2** *n.* Sheet metal with holes in it, used in place of wooden laths. **3** *v.* To cover or line with laths.

lathe [lā*th*] *n.* A machine that holds and turns an article against a cutting tool so as to shape it.

lath·er [la*th*′ər] **1** *n.* The suds or foam formed by soap or detergents moistened with water. **2** *v.* To spread over with lather. **3** *n.* The froth formed in sweating, as on a racehorse. **4** *v.* To become covered with or form lather. **—in a lather** *U.S. slang* Very excited or upset.

Lat·in [lat′(ə)n] **1** *n.* The language of ancient Rome. **2** *adj.* Having to do with ancient Rome, its language, or its people. **3** *adj.* Of or having to do with the people or countries, such as France, Italy, and Spain, whose language and culture are derived from ancient Rome. **4** *n.* A person whose language is derived from Latin, as a Spaniard.

Lat·in-A·mer·i·can [lat′(ə)n·ə·mer′ə·kən] *adj.* Of, from, or in Latin America.

Latin American A person born or living in Latin America.

Latin cross A cross consisting of a long vertical part intersected near its top by a shorter horizontal part.

La·ti·no [la·tē′nō] *n.* A person living in the United States who was born in Latin America, or whose parents or ancestors were Latin Americans or residents of other Spanish-speaking countries.

lat·i·tude [lat′ə·t(y)o͞od′] *n.* **1** Distance north or south of the equator, measured as an angle at the earth's center and expressed in degrees. **2** A particular region north or south of the equator. **3** Freedom from narrow restrictions or limitations: *latitude* to choose for oneself. **—lat′i·tu′di·nal** *adj.*

Parallels of latitude

la·trine [lə·trēn′] *n.* A toilet or something that serves as a toilet, especially in a military base or camp.

lat·ter [lat′ər] **1** *adj.* Later or nearer to the end: the *latter* part of the artist's life. **2** *adj.* Being the second of two things referred to. **3** *n. use:* The second of two things referred to: I prefer the *latter* to the former.

Lat·ter-day Saint A member of the Church of Jesus Christ of Latter-day Saints; Mormon.

lat·ter·ly [lat′ər·lē] *adv.* Recently; lately.

lat·tice [lat′is] *n., v.* **lat·ticed, lat·tic·ing** **1** *n.* A structure made of strips of metal, wood, or other material, crossed or interlaced to form regularly spaced openings. **2** *v.* To form into or cover with a lattice.

Lattice fence

lat·tice·work [lat′is·wûrk′] *n.* Openwork made of or like a lattice.

Lat·vi·an [lat′vē·ən] **1** *adj.* Of or from Latvia. **2** *n.* A person born or living in Latvia. **3** *n.* The language of Latvia.

laud [lôd] **1** *v.* To praise highly. **2** *n.* A hymn of praise or honor.

a	add	**i**	it	**o͝o**	took	**oi**	oil
ā	ace	**ī**	ice	**o͞o**	pool	**ou**	pout
â	care	**o**	odd	**u**	up	**ng**	ring
ä	palm	**ō**	open	**û**	burn	**th**	thin
e	end	**ô**	order	**yo͞o**	fuse	***th***	this
ē	equal					**zh**	vision

ə = a in *above* e in *sicken* i in *possible* o in *melon* u in *circus*

laud·a·ble [lô′də·bəl] *adj.* Deserving praise or approval; praiseworthy. **—laud′a·bly** *adv.*

lau·da·num [lô′də·nəm] *n.* A solution of opium in alcohol, used in former times as a medicine.

laud·a·to·ry [lô′də·tôr′ē] *adj.* Expressing praise and approval: a *laudatory* review of a play.

laugh [laf] **1** *v.* To make the sounds and those movements of the mouth, eyes, and face, that show joy, amusement, happiness, or, sometimes, scorn. **2** *n.* An act or sound of laughing. **3** *v.* To bring to a certain condition by laughing: I *laughed* myself sick. **—have the last laugh** To succeed or win after seeming to fail or lose. **—laugh at 1** To express amusement. **2** To ridicule; mock.

laugh·a·ble [laf′ə·bəl] *adj.* Causing or likely to cause laughter; ridiculous; funny.

laughing gas Another term for NITROUS OXIDE.

laugh·ing·stock [laf′ing·stok′] *n.* A person or thing that is the object of ridicule.

laugh·ter [laf′tər] *n.* The characteristic sound, facial expression, or action of laughing.

launch[1] [lônch] *v.* **1** To move or push (as a boat) into the water, especially for the first time. **2** To start; open: to *launch* a campaign. **3** To hurl; fling: to *launch* a rocket.

launch[2] [lônch] *n.* **1** A large, open motorboat, as one used for pleasure or as a patrol boat. **2** In former times, the largest boat carried by a ship.

launch pad or **launching pad** A platform from which a rocket, missile, or spacecraft is launched.

laun·der [lôn′dər] *v.* **1** To wash, or wash and iron (clothing, linens, and the like). **2** To conceal the true source of (money gotten unlawfully) by routing it through a third person, organization, or institution, such as a foreign bank.

laun·der·er [lôn′dər·ər] *n.* A person paid to launder clothes and linens.

laun·dress [lôn′dris] *n.* A woman who is paid to launder clothes and linens.

laun·dro·mat [lôn′drə·mat′] *n. U.S.* A place where customers bring laundry to be washed and dried in automatic machines operated by coins. ◆ The word *laundromat* was taken from a trademark, *Laundromat.*

laun·dry [lôn′drē] *n., pl.* **laun·dries 1** A room in a home, or a place of business, where clothes are washed and ironed. **2** Articles to be laundered or that have just been laundered.

laun·dry·man [lôn′drē·mən] *n., pl.* **laun·dry·men** [lôn′drē·mən] A person who works in a commercial laundry.

laun·dry·wom·an [lôn′drē·wo͝om′ən] *n., pl.* **laun·dry·wom·en** [lôn′drē·wim′in] A woman who works in a commercial laundry.

lau·re·ate [lô′rē·it] **1** *adj.* Singled out for special honor. **2** *adj.* Crowned or decked with laurel as a mark of honor. **3** *n.* A poet laureate.

lau·rel [lôr′əl] *n.* **1** An evergreen shrub of southern Europe with fragrant lance-shaped leaves, used by the ancients to make wreaths for heroes. **2** Any of various trees or shrubs resembling the laurel. **3** (*pl.*) Honor; fame. **—rest on one's laurels** To be content with what one has already achieved or accomplished.

la·va [lä′və *or* lav′ə] *n.* **1** Molten rock that flows from an active volcano. **2** Solid rock formed when this substance cools.

lav·a·to·ry [lav′ə·tôr′ē] *n., pl.* **lav·a·to·ries 1** A room with a basin or sink for washing, and usually with a toilet. **2** A basin or small sink, used for washing the hands and face. **3** Another word for TOILET.

lave [lāv] *v.* **laved, lav·ing** To wash or bathe: used mostly in poems.

lav·en·der [lav′ən·dər] **1** *n.* A plant related to mint, cultivated for its flowers and aromatic oils. **2** *n.* The dried flowers and leaves of this plant, used to scent linen and clothing. **3** *n., adj.* Pale, reddish violet.

lav·ish [lav′ish] **1** *adj.* Generous or too generous: to be *lavish* with gifts. **2** *adj.* Provided or used up in great abundance: I received a *lavish* helping of turkey. **3** *v.* To give freely; squander. **—lav′ish·ly** *adv.*

law [lô] *n.* **1** A rule of action or conduct set down by custom or authority and followed by a nation or group of people. **2** A system or body of such rules: civil *law.* **3** The condition of society when such rules are observed: *law* and order. **4** All such rules relating to a specified subject or area: criminal *law.* **5** The system, as a court or its magistrates, which enforces such rules. **6** The profession of a lawyer or judge. **7** A scientific statement of what always happens in the natural world under certain conditions. **8** Any generally accepted rule: the *laws* of golf.

law-a·bid·ing [lô′ə·bī′ding] *adj.* Obedient to the law: a *law-abiding* citizen.

law·break·er [lô′brā′kər] *n.* A person who violates the law. **—law′break′ing** *n., adj.*

law·ful [lô′fəl] *adj.* **1** Permitted or not forbidden by law. **2** Recognized by the law: a *lawful* debt. **—law′ful·ly** *adv.*

law·giv·er [lô′giv′ər] *n.* A person who makes or sets up a law or system of laws.

law·less [lô′lis] *adj.* **1** Refusing to obey or pay attention to the law: a *lawless* gang of thieves. **2** Difficult to keep orderly; unruly. **3** Having no laws: a *lawless* town of the old West. **—law′less·ly** *adv.* **—law′less·ness** *n.*

law·mak·er [lô′mā′kər] *n.* A person who makes or helps make laws, especially a legislator. **—law′·mak′ing** *n., adj.*

lawn[1] [lôn] *n.* A piece of ground covered with grass that is kept short by mowing.

lawn[2] [lôn] *n.* A fine, thin linen or cotton fabric, used for handkerchiefs and other items.

lawn bowling Another term for BOWLS.

lawn mower A machine operated by a motor or pushed with the hands, used to cut grass.

Lawn mower

lawn tennis Another name for TENNIS.

law·ren·ci·um [lô·ren′sē·əm] *n.* An artificially made metallic element with a radioactive half-life of less than one minute.

law·suit [lô′so͞ot′] *n.* Some legal matter, as a claim, brought to a court of law for settlement.

law·yer [lô′yər] *n.* A member of the legal profession, especially one qualified to advise clients about laws and act for them in court.

lax [laks] *adj.* **1** Not strict or forceful; weak: a *lax* official; *lax* conduct. **2** Not precise or exact; vague: a *lax* interpretation of the law. **3** Not taut or firm; slack. **—lax′ness** *n.*

lax·a·tive [lak′sə·tiv] **1** *n.* A medicine taken to empty the bowels. **2** *adj.* Causing the bowels to move.

lax·i·ty [lak′sə·tē] *n., pl.* **lax·i·ties** The condition or quality of being lax.

lay[1] [lā] *v.* **laid, lay·ing,** *n.* 1 *v.* To place in a horizontal or reclining position: to lay a sleeping child down. 2 *v.* To put or place, especially in a specified position or order: to *lay* a rug on the floor; to *lay* bricks. 3 *v.* To produce (an egg or eggs) as a hen or fish does. 4 *v.* To think out; devise: to *lay* plans. 5 *v.* To place: to *lay* great importance on education. 6 *v.* To set forth; present: to *lay* a claim before a court. 7 *v.* To knock down; level: to *lay* someone low in a fight. 8 *v.* To cause to settle: to *lay* the dust. 9 *v.* To make ineffective; quiet down: to *lay* a ghost. 10 *v.* To set, place, or locate: to *lay* the scene of a play in Italy. 11 *v.* To offer as a wager; bet. 12 *n.* The manner in which something lies or is situated: the *lay* of the land. **—lay aside** To save for future use. **—lay away** To store up; save. **—lay by** To save; reserve, as money. **—lay down** 1 To give up; sacrifice: to *lay down* one's life. 2 To state firmly: to *lay down* the rules. **—lay in** To get and store: to *lay in* a supply of food. **—lay into** *informal* To attack with blows or words. **—lay off** 1 *U.S.* To dismiss from a job. 2 To mark out; plan. **—lay open** 1 To cut deeply; gash: The knife *laid open* the fish. 2 To leave exposed, as to attack or blame. **—lay out** 1 To set out or arrange for use or inspection. 2 To arrange according to a plan. 3 To spend or supply: to *lay out* the room rent. 4 To prepare (a corpse) for burial. **—lay up** 1 To save or store away. 2 To confine, as by illness or injury: Pneumonia *laid* me *up* for six weeks. ◆ The verbs *lay* and *lie* should always be distinguished in formal writing. *Lay* takes an object: The student *is laying the book* on the table. *Lie,* meaning *to recline* or *be located,* does not take an object: The book *will lie* there until someone picks it up. The past tense of *lie* is *lay*: I *lay* there all last night. The past tense of *lay* is *laid*: I *laid* it on the table.

lay[2] [lā] *adj.* 1 Of or having to do with people other than the clergy. 2 Not belonging to or coming from a particular profession: a *lay* opinion.

lay[3] [lā] Past tense of LIE[1].

lay[4] [lā] *n.* 1 A song, ballad, or poem that tells a story. 2 A melody or song.

lay·er [lā′ər] 1 *n.* A single thickness, coating, or covering: a *layer* of cloth. 2 *v.* To form a layer or layers. 3 *n.* A person or thing that lays: These hens are good *layers.*

A piece of three-layer cake

lay·ette [lā·et′] *n.* The supply of clothing and bedding provided for a newborn infant.

lay·man [lā′mən] *n., pl.* **lay·men** [lā′mən] A person who is a member of the laity.

lay·off [lā′ôf′] *n.* 1 The act of dismissing from a job. 2 A period during which a person is out of work. **—lay off** *slang* To stop; cease: Tell them to *lay off* giving us orders.

lay·out [lā′out′] *n.* 1 The act of laying out or planning. 2 A planned arrangement; design: a *layout* of the new playground. 3 The thing that is arranged or designed.

lay·o·ver [lā′ō′vər] *n.* A short stop or interruption in a journey; stopover.

lay·per·son [lā′pûr′sən] *n.* A layman or a laywoman.

lay-up [lā′ŭp′] *n.* In basketball, a shot made close to the basket, usually from a jumping position and with the backboard as a rebounding surface.

lay·wom·an [lā′wŏŏm′ən] *n., pl.* **lay·wom·en** [lā′·wim′in] A woman who is a member of the laity.

Laz·a·rus [laz′ə·rəs] *n.* In the Bible: 1 The brother of Martha and Mary, raised from the dead by Jesus. 2 A sick beggar in the parable of the rich man and the poor man.

laze [lāz] *v.* **lazed, laz·ing** 1 To be idle or lazy; loaf. 2 To spend (time) in being idle: She *lazed* the summer away at the beach.

la·zy [lā′zē] *adj.* **laz·i·er, laz·i·est** 1 Unwilling to work or to keep busy; indolent. 2 Moving or acting slowly; sluggish. **—la′zi·ly** *adv.* **—la′zi·ness** *n.*

lb. 1 pound. 2 (*often written* **lbs.**) pounds.

lc or **l.c.** lower case (letters).

LC landing craft.

L.C. Library of Congress.

l.c.d. or **L.C.D.** least common denominator.

lea [lē] *n.* A meadow: used mostly in poems.

leach [lēch] *v.* 1 To make water or other liquid run or filter through (something) in order to remove certain materials: to *leach* ore. 2 To remove or be removed by such a filtering action: to *leach* alkali out of ashes.

lead[1] [lēd] *v.* **led, lead·ing,** *n.* 1 *v.* To guide or conduct: We *led* the child by the hand; This path *led* us to the hut. 2 *v.* To be in command or control of; direct: to *lead* a discussion. 3 *n.* Guidance; example: Follow my *lead.* 4 *v.* To be first among; be at the head of: She *led* the class with a 98 percent average. 5 *v.* To be first or in advance: Our runners *led* all the way. 6 *n.* Position in advance or at the head. 7 *n.* The amount or distance by which one is ahead: a *lead* of three runs. 8 *n.* The opening part of a news story or magazine article, as the first paragraph. 9 *adj. use*: a *lead* article. 10 *n.* The principal role, as in a play or motion picture. 11 *v.* To begin or start: The fighter *led* with a wild swing. 12 *n.* In games or sports, the first play or the right to play first. 13 *v.* To influence the ideas or actions of: The teacher's encouragement *led* me to work harder. 14 *v.* To result in: Good work can *lead* to a raise in pay. 15 *v.* To go or extend: These wires *lead* to the barn. 16 *v.* To experience or cause to experience: to *lead* a merry life. 17 *n.* A clue: Give me a *lead.* **—lead off** 1 To begin; open: She *led off* her remarks with an apology. 2 To be the first batter in an inning of a baseball game. **—lead on** To attract or lure (a person) into a course of action, especially into an unfavorable one. **—lead the way** 1 To go first; guide on a path or course. 2 To set a course or example for others. **—lead up to** 1 To precede and prepare the way for: Local competitions *lead up to* the national championship game. 2 To approach (a subject) indirectly or methodically: Her

L

a	add	**i**	it	**ŏŏ**	took	**oi**	oil
ā	ace	**ī**	ice	**ōō**	pool	**ou**	pout
â	care	**o**	odd	**u**	up	**ng**	ring
ä	palm	**ō**	open	**û**	burn	**th**	thin
e	end	**ô**	order	**yōō**	fuse	**th̶**	this
ē	equal					**zh**	vision

ə = { a in *above* e in *sicken* i in *possible*
  o in *melon* u in *circus* }

opening remark *led up to* the most important topic.

lead² [led] 1 *n.* A soft, heavy, dull gray, metallic element, used to make pipes, printing type, and other objects. 2 *adj. use:* a *lead* pipe. 3 *n.* Any object made of lead, especially a weight at the end of a line used to measure the depth of water. 4 *v.* To cover, join, fasten, or make heavier with lead: to *lead* stained glass windows. 5 *n.* Thin rods or sticks of graphite, used in pencils. 6 *n.* Bullets or shot.

lead·ed [led′id] *adj.* Containing a chemical compound of lead: The car runs on *leaded* gasoline.

lead·en [led′(ə)n] *adj.* 1 Dull gray. 2 Made of lead. 3 Heavy or feeling heavy: *leaden* legs. 4 Dark and gloomy: a *leaden* spirit.

lead·er [lē′dər] *n.* A person or thing that leads, as by going ahead or guiding.

lead·er·ship [lē′dər·ship′] *n.* 1 The condition of being a leader. 2 The ability to lead. 3 Control or guidance: The scouts had excellent *leadership.* 4 A group of leaders.

lead·ing [lē′ding] *adj.* 1 Located or going at the front; first: the *leading* car in the parade. 2 Most important; chief; principal: the town's *leading* citizen. 3 Guiding; controlling.

lead·off [lēd′ôf′] 1 *n.* The first in a series, as of actions or moves. 2 *n.* A person who leads off. 3 *adj.* In baseball, of, designating, or made by the first batter in a lineup or in an inning.

leaf [lēf] *n., pl.* **leaves** [lēvz], *v.* 1 *n.* One of the flat, thin, usually green parts of a plant or tree growing from a stem or root. 2 *n.* A petal: the pressed *leaves* of a rose. 3 *v.* To grow or produce leaves. 4 *n.* One of the sheets of paper, as in a book or magazine, each side being a single page. 5 *v.* To turn over or glance at the pages of (as a book): to *leaf* through a magazine. 6 *n.* Metal in a very thin sheet: gold *leaf.* 7 *n.* A flat, movable piece attached or fitted to a table to make it larger. —**turn over a new leaf** To make a fresh start so as to correct one's past conduct or record of failure.

Leaves

leaf·age [lēf′ij] *n.* Foliage.

leaf·hop·per [lēf′hop′ər] *n.* A leaping insect that sucks the juices of plants.

leaf·less [lēf′lis] *adj.* Having no leaves.

leaf·let [lēf′lit] *n.* 1 A small leaf or leaflike part. 2 A small, printed sheet of paper, usually folded: to slip a *leaflet* under a door.

leaf·stalk [lēf′stôk′] *n.* Another word for PETIOLE.

leaf·y [lē′fē] *adj.* **leaf·i·er, leaf·i·est** 1 Bearing or covered with many leaves: Lettuce is a *leafy* vegetable. 2 Like a leaf.

league¹ [lēg] *n., v.* **leagued, lea·guing** 1 *n.* A number of persons, groups, or countries, united for some common purpose. 2 *n.* A group of athletic teams that compete mostly among themselves. 3 *v.* To form or unite in league. —**in league** Working or acting closely together.

league² [lēg] *n.* An old measure of length, usually equal to about three miles.

League of Nations A group of nations established in 1920 to preserve world peace. In 1946 it was replaced by the United Nations.

lea·guer [lē′gər] *n.* A person belonging to a league.

Le·ah [lē′ə] *n* In the Bible, the first wife of Jacob and the older sister of Rachel.

leak [lēk] 1 *n.* An opening, as a crack or hole, that accidentally lets something in or out: a *leak* in a gas tank. 2 *v.* To let something, as a liquid or gas, accidentally get in or out through a hole or crack: The rowboat *leaked* badly. 3 *v.* To pass or let pass through a hole or crack: Air *leaked* out of the balloon; Your car is *leaking* oil. 4 *n.* Any way by which something is accidentally allowed to escape or become known: a *leak* in our secret files. 5 *v.* To become known despite efforts at secrecy: The plans *leaked* out. 6 *n.* The act of leaking; leakage: a slow *leak.*

leak·age [lē′kij] *n.* 1 The act of leaking. 2 That which leaks. 3 The amount leaked.

leak·y [lē′kē] *adj.* **leak·i·er, leak·i·est** Having a leak: a *leaky* roof. —**leak′i·ness** *n.*

lean¹ [lēn] *v.* **leaned** or **leant, lean·ing** 1 To rest or incline for support: I *leaned* against the tree; I *leaned* the hoe on the wall. 2 To bend or slant from an upright position: The trees *leaned* in the wind. 3 To rely or depend on, as for help, comfort, or advice: to *lean* on a friend in times of trouble. 4 To favor or prefer: The teacher *leans* toward strictness in the classroom.

lean² [lēn] 1 *adj.* Having little fat or none: *lean* meat; a *lean* person. 2 *n.* Meat or flesh having little or no fat. 3 *adj.* Not plentiful; meager: a *lean* crop of corn. —**lean over backward** To make every possible concession for the benefit of another as a means of demonstrating fairness or good will. —**lean′ness** *n.*

lean·ing [lē′ning] *n.* An inclination or tendency.

leant [lent] Alternative past tense and past participle of LEAN¹.

lean-to [lēn′to͞o′] *n., pl.* **lean-tos** 1 A rough shelter, sloping to the ground at one end. 2 A low building built against one wall of a taller one, from which its roof slopes out and down.

leap [lēp] *v.* **leaped** or **leapt, leap·ing,** *n.* 1 *v.* To rise by a sudden thrust of the legs; jump or spring: The dog *leaped* up from the ground. 2 *v.* To jump over: to *leap* a fence. 3 *v.* To cause to jump: to *leap* a horse. 4 *n.* The act of leaping; jump. 5 *n.* The space covered by leaping: a long *leap.*

leap·frog [lēp′frog′] *n., v.* **leap·frogged, leap·frog·ging** 1 *n.* A game in which each player puts hands on the back of another player, who is bending over, and leaps over the other player in a straddlng position. 2 *v.* To leap over (another player) in such a game. 3 *v.* To advance or progress by skipping over or bypassing (one or more steps or stages in a course).

leapt [lept *or* lēpt] Alternative past tense and past participle of LEAP.

leap year A year of 366 days, the extra day being the 29th of February. If a year can be divided by 4 and have no remainder (as 1988 ÷ 4 = *exactly* 497), it is a leap year. But if it completes a century, it must be exactly divisible by 400 (as the years 1600 and 2000).

Lear [lir] *n.* A legendary king of Britain and main character in Shakespeare's tragedy *King Lear.*

learn [lûrn] *v.* **learned** or **learnt, learn·ing** 1 To get knowledge of or skill in: The child *learned* reading at an early age; to *learn* to swim. 2 To gain knowledge or skill: The student *learns* easily. 3 To find out; come to know or realize: We *learned* that the train was late. 4 To memorize: to *learn* poems. 5 To get by example or experience: to *learn* good habits. **—learn'er** *n.* ◆ See TEACH.

learn·ed [lûr'nid] *adj.* Full of or characterized by much learning or knowledge; erudite: a *learned* teacher; a *learned* profession.

learn·ing [lûr'ning] *n.* 1 The process of getting knowledge or skill. 2 Knowledge gotten by study or instruction.

learnt [lûrnt] Alternative past tense and past participle of LEARN: I *learnt* how to spell.

lease [lēs] *n., v.* **leased, leas·ing** 1 *n.* A contract in which an owner agrees to let someone else live in or use property for a certain time in return for money paid as rent. 2 *v.* To rent or use by means of a lease: We *leased* the garage for a year. **—a new lease on life** An extension or renewal of life that promises better things.

leash [lēsh] 1 *n.* Something, as a cord, rope, or chain, by which a dog or other animal is led or held. 2 *v.* To hold or control with a leash: to *leash* a dog. 3 *v.* To control or hold back: Learn to *leash* your emotions in public.

Leash

least [lēst] 1 A superlative of LITTLE. 2 *adj.* Smallest, as in size, amount, value, or importance: The *least* piece of pie is better than none. 3 *n.* Some person or thing that is the smallest, slightest, or most unimportant. 4 *adv.* In the smallest degree or amount: I was *least* tired of all the players. **—at least** 1 At the lowest possible estimate. 2 At any rate: *At least* we now know the truth. **—in the least** At all; to any degree: I don't care *in the least.* **—least of all** Especially not: I do not like loud music, *least of all* in a subway.

least common denominator The least common multiple of the denominators of a set of fractions. 24 is the least common denominator of 3/4, 1/8, and 1/12.

least common multiple The smallest counting number that is evenly divisible by each member of a set of counting numbers. The least common multiple of 2, 3, 4, and 6 is 12.

least·wise [lēst'wīz'] *adv. informal* At least; at any rate: *Leastwise* we'll know next time.

leath·er [leth'ər] 1 *n.* Animal skin or hide, usually with the hair or fur removed, and made ready for many uses by cleaning and tanning. 2 *adj. use: leather* gloves; a *leather* strap. 3 *v.* To cover or furnish with leather. 4 *v.* To beat with a strap.

Leath·er·ette [leth'ə·ret'] *n.* A plastic or cloth material made to resemble leather: a trademark.

leath·ern [leth'ərn] *adj.* Made of leather.

leath·er·neck [leth'ər·nek'] *n. slang* A member of the Marine Corps.

leath·er·y [leth'ər·ē] *adj.* Like leather in appearance to toughness: *leathery* hands.

leave[1] [lēv] *v.* **left, leav·ing** 1 To go or depart from: We *left* our friends on the corner. 2 To go away: We *left* late. 3 To end one's connection with: I *left* the firm. 4 To abandon; desert: to *leave* one's family. 5 To allow to be or remain: I *left* my bicycle on the porch. 6 To have or cause as a result: Oil *leaves* stains. 7 To give to another to do, decide, or solve: *Leave* your problem to me. 8 To have remaining after one's death: The doctor *left* three children. 9 To give in a will at one's death: The tycoon *left* a large fortune. 10 In arithmetic, to have as a difference: 12 minus 8 *leaves* 4. **—leave alone** To refrain from annoying or interfering with. **—leave off** 1 To stop; cease. 2 To stop using. **—leave out** 1 To take out or omit. 2 To decide not to include. ◆ *Leave* and *let* do not have the same meaning. *Leave* (def. 5) means *to permit to remain:* I *left* my hat in the closet. *Let* means simply *to permit: Let* me speak (Permit me to speak).

leave[2] [lēv] *n.* 1 Permission: Give them *leave* to buy what they need. 2 Permission to be absent, as from one's job or the armed forces, often called **leave of absence.** 3 The length of time for which such permission is given: a three-month *leave.* 4 Departure, especially in the expression **take one's leave,** to say good-by and depart.

leave[3] [lēv] *v.* **leaved, leav·ing** To put forth leaves; leaf.

leav·en [lev'ən] 1 *n.* A substance, as yeast, that when added to dough or batter helps it to rise and become light and fluffy. 2 *v.* To make rise by using leaven. 3 *n.* Anything that lightens, improves, or otherwise changes the character of something else: Wit is a *leaven* to a dull speech. 4 *v.* To lighten, improve, or otherwise change the character of.

leav·en·ing [lev'ə·ning] *n.* Leaven.

leave-tak·ing [lēv'tā'king] *n.* The act of saying good-by; farewell.

leav·ings [lē'vingz] *n.pl.* The leftover parts of anything, such as those that have not been used or eaten.

Leb·a·nese [leb'ə·nēz'] *adj., n., pl.* **Leb·a·nese** 1 *adj.* Of or from Lebanon. 2 *n.* A person born in or a citizen of Lebanon.

lech·er [lech'ər] *n.* A person who engages in lechery.

lech·er·ous [lech'ər·əs] *adj.* Inclined to or marked by lechery. **—lech'er·ous·ly** *adv.* **—lech'er·ous·ness** *n.*

lech·er·y [lech'ər·ē] *n.* Excessive indulgence in sexual activity.

lec·i·thin [les'ə·thən] *n.* 1 Any of a group of fatty substances in animal and plant tissues. 2 A form of such substances obtained from egg yolks, corn, and soybeans, and used in the preparation of food products and in the making of medicines, cosmetics, candles, and inks.

a	add	**i**	it	**o͝o**	took	**oi**	oil
ā	ace	**ī**	ice	**o͞o**	pool	**ou**	pout
â	care	**o**	odd	**u**	up	**ng**	ring
ä	palm	**ō**	open	**û**	burn	**th**	thin
e	end	**ô**	order	**yo͞o**	fuse	**th**	this
ē	equal					**zh**	vision

ə = a in *above* e in *sicken* i in *possible* o in *melon* u in *circus*

lec·tern [lek′tərn] *n.* A stand having an inclined top on which a speaker may put books or papers to read from.

Lectern

lec·ture [lek′chər] *n., v.* **lec·tured, lec·tur·ing** 1 *n.* A speech on a particular subject, usually given to instruct or inform. 2 *v.* To give a lecture or teach by lectures. 3 *n.* A long or severe scolding. 4 *v.* To scold. **—lec′tur·er** *n.*

led [led] Past tense and past participle of LEAD[1]: I *led* the dog home.

LED An electronic device that gives off light when a current passes through it in the correct direction. It is used to show numbers, as on digital clocks, watches, and calculators. ◆ *LED* stands for *L(ight)-E(mitting) D(iode).*

Le·da [lē′də] *n.* In Greek mythology, a noblewoman of Sparta who was the mother of two immortals, Helen and Pollux, and of two mortals, Castor and Clytemnestra.

ledge [lej] *n.* 1 A narrow, shelflike piece of land or rock jutting out from the side of a mountain or cliff. 2 A shelf, sill, or other surface jutting out from a wall or window.

led·ger [lej′ər] *n.* A book in which a business keeps a record of money spent and received.

ledger line A short line used to locate notes above or below a musical staff.

lee [lē] 1 *n.* Shelter or protection, especially from the wind. 2 *n.* A place or side, usually of a ship, that is sheltered from the wind: the *lee* of the rock. 3 *adj. use*: the *lee* side of the ship.

leech [lēch] *n.* 1 A worm that lives in the water and sucks the blood of animals and humans. 2 A person who sticks close to another person in order to gain something. ◆ *Leeches* were formerly used by physicians to draw the blood of patients in the treatment of certain diseases. In fact the Old English word for this worm originally meant *physician.*

leek [lēk] *n.* A vegetable similar to an onion but having a smaller bulb and milder taste.

leer [lir] 1 *n.* A sly, knowing look or glance, usually made out of the corner of the eye. 2 *v.* To look with a leer: The stranger *leered* at us.

leer·y [lir′ē] *adj.* **leer·i·er, leer·i·est** *informal* Suspicious; doubtful; wary: We were *leery* of the unfamiliar route.

lees [lēz] *n.pl.* Sediment, as that formed in wine during fermentation and aging; dregs.

lee shore A shore toward which the wind is blowing and toward which a ship may be driven in a storm.

lee·ward [lē′wərd *or* lo͞o′ərd] 1 *adj.* In the direction toward which the wind is blowing. 2 *n.* The leeward side or direction. 3 *adj., adv.* On or toward the side sheltered from the wind.

lee·way [lē′wā′] *n.* 1 Something extra, as space, time, or money, to be used if needed: The high ceilings gave us *leeway* to move the ladders. 2 The drifting of a ship or plane to the side.

left[1] [left] 1 *adj.* On, to, or indicating the side of the body that is toward the north when one faces east: a *left* arm; a *left* shoe. 2 *adv.* To or toward the left hand or side: Turn *left.* 3 *n.* The left side, direction, or hand. 4 *adj.* Nearer to the left side: Go through the *left* door. 5 *adj.* Liberal or radical in political views. 6 *n.* A group or party having liberal or radical political views.

left[2] [left] Past tense and past participle of LEAVE[1].

left field 1 In baseball, the part of the outfield lying to the batter's left as viewed from home plate. 2 The position of the player who defends that area. **—out in left field** *informal* Improbable, unreasonable, or incorrect.

left fielder The baseball player stationed in left field to defend it when the opposing team is at bat.

left-hand [left′hand′] *adj.* 1 Of, for, or on the left side or the left hand: a *left-hand* glove. 2 Left-handed: a *left-hand* pitcher.

left-hand·ed [left′han′did] 1 *adj.* Using the left hand more easily and more often than the right. 2 *adj.* Done with or meant to be used by the left hand: a *left-handed* pitch; a *left-handed* golf club. 3 *adj.* Turning from right to left. 4 *adv.* With the left hand. 5 *adj.* Insincere or doubtful: a *left-handed* compliment.

left-hand·er [left′han′dər] *n.* A left-handed person, especially a baseball pitcher.

left·ist [lef′tist] 1 *n.* A person having liberal or radical political views. 2 *adj.* Of or marked by liberal or radical political views. **—left′ism** *n.*

left·o·ver [left′ō′vər] *n.* 1 (*usually pl.*) An unused part, especially food that has not been eaten. 2 *adj. use: leftover* potatoes.

left-wing [left′wing′] *adj.* Of or having to do with liberal or radical political views.

left wing A group or party having liberal or radical political views, or a portion of a political party holding such views.

left-wing·er [left′wing′ər] *n.* A leftist.

left·y [lef′tē] *adj., n., pl.* **left·ies,** *adv. informal* 1 *adj.* Left-handed. 2 *n.* A person who is left-handed. 3 *adv.* With the left hand or in a left-handed way. 4 *n.* A leftist.

leg [leg] *n., v.* **legged, leg·ging** 1 *n.* One of the limbs of animals and humans that serve as supports in standing and walking. 2 *n.* The part of an article of clothing meant to cover a leg. 3 *n.* Anything like a leg in shape or use: a table *leg.* 4 *n.* A section or part, as of a journey. 5 *n.* Either of the sides of a triangle as distinguished from its base or hypotenuse. 6 *v. informal* To walk or run: Let's *leg* it from here. **—on one's last legs** Nearly worn out or dead. **—pull one's leg** *informal* To fool or tease a person.

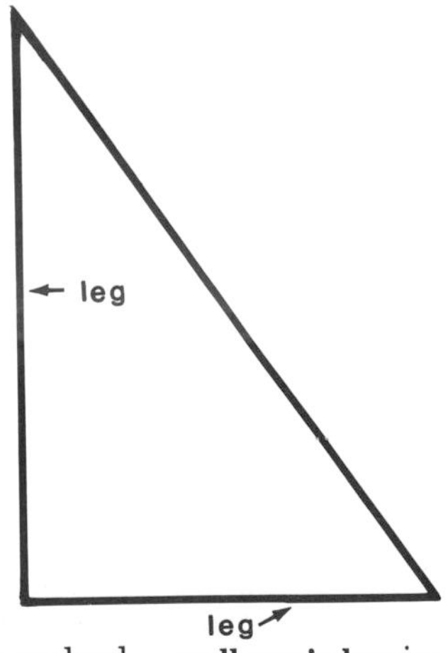

leg·a·cy [leg′ə·sē] *n., pl.* **leg·a·cies** 1 Something, as money or property, that has been left to one by a will; bequest. 2 Something inherited.

le·gal [lē′gəl] *adj.* 1 Of or having to do with law: *legal* papers. 2 Permitted by or based on law. 3

Of, for, or characteristic of lawyers: a *legal* mind. **—le′gal·ly** *adv.*

legal age The age, usually 21 years, when a person becomes qualified to take on the rights and responsibilities of an adult as defined by law.

le·gal·i·ty [li·gal′ə·tē] *n.* The condition of being lawful.

le·gal·ize [lē′gəl·īz′] *v.* **le·gal·ized, le·gal·iz·ing** To make legal.

legal tender Money that may be legally offered to pay a debt and which a creditor must accept.

leg·ate [leg′it] *n.* A person who officially represents a government or ruler, especially a person who represents the Pope.

leg·a·tee [leg′ə·tē′] *n.* A person who inherits money or property in a will.

le·ga·tion [li·gā′shən] *n.* **1** The residence or offices of an official who represents a government in a foreign country and has a lower rank than an ambassador. **2** The official and staff.

le·ga·to [li·gä′tō] *adj., adv., n., pl.* **le·ga·tos** **1** *adj.* In music, smooth and flowing. **2** *adv.* In a smooth and flowing manner. **3** *n.* A legato passage or movement.

leg·end [lej′ənd] *n.* **1** A story that has come down from earlier times and is often thought by many people to be partly true. **2** A group of such stories. **3** The writing on a coin, monument, or banner. **4** A short explanation or title accompanying a picture, map, or chart.

leg·en·dar·y [lej′ən·der′ē] *adj.* **1** Of, having to do with, or like a legend. **2** Famous in or as in a legend: a *legendary* palace.

leg·er·de·main [lej′ər·də·mān′] *n.* **1** Tricks of magic or sleight of hand. **2** Trickery; deception. ◆ *Legerdemain* comes from the French words *léger de main,* meaning *light of hand.*

leg·ged [leg′id *or* legd] *adj.* Having a certain number or kind of legs: often used in combination, as in *four-legged.*

leg·ging [leg′ing] *n.* (*usually pl.*) A covering for the leg, usually reaching from the ankle to the knee.

leg·gy [leg′ē] *adj.* **leg·gi·er, leg·gi·est** **1** Having legs that are too long and awkward. **2** Having legs that are long and attractive. **3** Characterized by long, spindly stems, as certain plants.

leg·horn [leg′hôrn′] *n.* **1** (*sometimes written* **Leghorn**) A breed of small domestic chicken. **2** A fine, braided straw made from Italian wheat. **3** A hat of such straw.

leg·i·ble [lej′ə·bəl] *adj.* Easy to read: *legible* handwriting. **—leg′i·bil′i·ty** *n.* **—leg′i·bly** *adv.*

le·gion [lē′jən] *n.* **1** In ancient Rome, a large military unit of foot soldiers and cavalry, numbering up to 6,000 people. **2** Any large military force; army. **3** A great number; multitude.

le·gion·ar·y [lē′jən·er′ē] *adj., n., pl.* **le·gion·ar·ies** **1** *adj.* Of or making up a legion. **2** *n.* A member of a legion.

le·gion·naire [le′jə·nâr′] *n.* A member of a legion.

leg·is·late [lej′is·lāt′] *v.* **leg·is·lat·ed, leg·is·lat·ing** **1** To make laws. **2** To create or change by passing laws: to *legislate* new taxes.

leg·is·la·tion [lej′is·lā′shən] *n.* **1** The act of making laws. **2** The laws made.

leg·is·la·tive [lej′is·lā′tiv] *adj.* **1** Of or having to do with laws or with making laws: *legislative* duties. **2** Having the power to make laws: the *legislative* branch of government. **3** Of or having to do with a legislature.

leg·is·la·tor [lej′is·lā′tər] *n.* A member of a lawmaking body, as a member of Congress.

leg·is·la·ture [lej′is·lā′chər] *n.* A group of persons who make the laws of a nation or state.

le·git·i·ma·cy [lə·jit′ə·mə·sē] *n.* The condition of being legitimate.

le·git·i·mate [lə·jit′ə·mit] *adj.* **1** Permitted or approved by law; lawful: You have a *legitimate* right to sue. **2** Logical; reasonable; justified: a *legitimate* fear. **3** Genuine; real; authentic: a *legitimate* cause for complaint. **4** Born of parents who are married to each other. **5** Having to do with plays put on by professionals as distinguished from other forms of entertainment, such as burlesque and vaudeville: the *legitimate* theater.

le·git·i·mize [li·jit′ə·mīz′] *v.* **le·git·i·mized, le·git·i·miz·ing** To make legitimate.

leg·ume [leg′yo͞om′ *or* lə·gyo͞om′] *n.* **1** The edible fruit or seed of various plants that bear pods, as the bean, pea, or lentil. **2** A pod containing such seeds, or the plant itself.

le·gu·mi·nous [lə·gyo͞o′mə·nəs] *adj.* **1** Of or belonging to various plants having legumes, as the bean or pea. **2** Of or bearing legumes.

lei [lā *or* lā′ē] *n., pl.* **leis** In Hawaii, a garland of flowers and leaves, often worn around the neck.

Lei

lei·sure [lē′zhər *or* lezh′ər] **1** *n.* Time free from work, study, or any duties: a day of *leisure.* **2** *adj.* Free from work or duties: *leisure* hours. **—at one's leisure** Whenever one has the time or the chance: Call me *at your leisure.*

lei·sure·ly [lē′zhər·lē *or* lezh′ər·lē] **1** *adj.* Relaxed and unhurried: a *leisurely* stroll. **2** *adv.* In a slow, relaxed manner.

LEM [lem] *n.* A lunar excursion module.

lem·ming [lem′ing] *n.* Any of several small ratlike animals living in arctic regions and having a short tail and furry feet. Lemmings are noted for migrating in vast numbers and often throwing themselves into the sea to drown.

lem·on [lem′ən] **1** *n.* An oval-shaped citrus fruit, having a juicy, sour pulp and a yellow skin, used to flavor foods and in perfumes. **2** *n.* The tree bearing this fruit. **3** *n., adj.* Pale or bright yellow. **4** *n. slang* A failure; disappointment.

lem·on·ade [lem′ən·ād′] *n.* A drink made of lemon juice, sugar, and water.

a	add	**i**	it	**o͝o**	took	**oi**	oil
ā	ace	**ī**	ice	**o͞o**	pool	**ou**	pout
â	care	**o**	odd	**u**	up	**ng**	ring
ä	palm	**ō**	open	**û**	burn	**th**	thin
e	end	**ô**	order	**yo͞o**	fuse	**th**	this
ē	equal					**zh**	vision

ə = {a in *above* e in *sicken* i in *possible* / o in *melon* u in *circus*}

le·mur [lē′mər] *n.* A small animal that lives in trees and is related to the monkey. It is found chiefly in Madagascar.

Ring-tailed lemur

lend [lend] *v.* **lent, lend·ing** 1 To permit the use of with the understanding that the thing, or its equivalent, will be returned: to *lend* a book; to *lend* a cup of flour. 2 To permit the use of (money) to be returned later, sometimes with interest. 3 To give; add; contribute: Fog *lent* an air of mystery to the scene. **—lend′er** *n.*

lending library Another term for CIRCULATING LIBRARY.

length [leng(k)th] *n.* 1 The longest part or side of something rather than its width or thickness: the *length* of a car. 2 The measure of something from end to end: The *length* is just 25 feet. 3 The condition of being long. 4 The size, extent, or period covered from beginning to end: the *length* of a book; a short *length* of time. 5 A piece of something, usually of a standard size: a *length* of pipe. **—at length** 1 After a while; finally. 2 Without leaving anything out; fully. **—go to great lengths** or **go to any length** To do all that is possible: They *went to great lengths* to entertain their friends.

length·en [leng(k)′thən] *v.* To make or grow longer: The tailor *lengthened* the pants.

length·ways [leng(k)th′wāz′] *adv.* Lengthwise.

length·wise [leng(k)th′wīz′] *adj., adv.* In the direction of the length: a *lengthwise* path across the field; to swim the pool *lengthwise.*

length·y [leng(k)′thē] *adj.* **length·i·er, length·i·est** Unusually long; too long: a *lengthy* voyage by ship. **—length′i·ly** *adv.*

le·ni·ence [lē′nē·əns *or* lēn′yəns] *n.* Leniency.

le·ni·en·cy [lē′nē·ən·sē *or* lēn′yən·sē] *n.* The quality of being lenient; gentleness; mercy: the *leniency* of the judge's sentence.

le·ni·ent [lē′nē·ənt *or* lēn′yənt] *adj.* Gentle or merciful; not stern or severe; mild: a *lenient* punishment. **—le′ni·ent·ly** *adv.*

len·i·tive [len′ə·tiv] 1 *adj.* Tending to alleviate or capable of alleviating pain or discomfort; soothing. 2 *n.* Something lenitive, as a medicine or application.

len·i·ty [len′ə·tē] *n.* Leniency; mercifulness.

lens [lenz] *n.* 1 A piece of glass or other transparent material having one surface or two opposite surfaces curved in such a way that light rays passing through it are bent apart or together. Lenses are used to magnify things and to bring images into focus. 2 A transparent part of the eye located behind the iris and serving to focus an image on the retina.

lent [lent] Past tense and past participle of LEND: I *lent* you the book three weeks ago.

Lent [lent] *n.* The 40 days (not including Sundays) from Ash Wednesday to Easter. Lent is a Christian season of fasting and self-denial.

Lent·en [len′tən] *adj.* (*sometimes written* **lenten**) Of, occurring in, or suitable for Lent.

len·til [len′təl] *n.* 1 A plant having large pods that contain flat, edible, pealike seeds. 2 The seed of this plant.

len·to [len′tō] *adj., adv., n., pl.* **len·tos** 1 *adj.* In music, slow. 2 *adv.* In a slow manner. 3 *n.* A lento passsage or movement.

Leo [lē′ō] *n.* 1 A large constellation in the Northern Hemisphere, near Cancer. 2 The fifth sign of the zodiac. 3 A person born under this sign. ◆ The shape of this constellation suggests that of a lion. It is called Leo because that is the Latin word for *lion.*

le·o·nine [lē′ə·nīn′] *adj.* Of or like a lion.

leop·ard [lep′ərd] *n.* A ferocious animal of the cat family, found in Asia and Africa and having a brownish yellow coat with black spots.

Leopard

le·o·tard [le′ə·tärd′] *n.* 1 (*sometimes written* **leotards**) A close-fitting one-piece garment, usually extending from the neck to the wrists and ankles, worn by ballet dancers and acrobats. 2 (*written* **leotards**) Tights.

lep·er [lep′ər] *n.* A person who has leprosy.

lep·re·chaun [lep′rə·kôn′] *n.* In Irish folk stories, a tiny elf, often a cobbler, who was supposed to tell where the treasure was, if caught.

lep·ro·sy [lep′rə·sē] *n.* A mildly contagious disease marked by sores and scales on the skin and a gradual rotting away of parts of the body.

lep·rous [lep′rəs] *adj.* 1 Having leprosy. 2 Of, caused by, or like leprosy: a *leprous* sore.

lese ma·jes·ty [lēz′ maj′is·tē] A crime against a ruler or against the ruler's authority.

le·sion [lē′zhən] *n.* A harmful change to an organ or tissue of the body, as an injury.

less [les] 1 A comparative of LITTLE. 2 *adj.* Not as much or as great in size, amount, value, or importance: *less* candy; *less* speed. 3 *n.* Something smaller or less important or valuable: There is *less* left than I had thought. 4 *adv.* To a smaller or not so great degree, amount, or extent: *less* loudly. 5 *prep.* Minus: 8 *less* 5 is 3. ◆ *Less* and *fewer* are both used to compare unequal things. *Less* is usually used for things that cannot be counted or measured separately: There was *less* rain this year than last year. *Fewer* is used for things that can be counted or measured in separate units: *fewer* people. Thus we speak of *less* time but *fewer* hours.

-less A suffix meaning: 1 Not having; without, as in *jobless* or *harmless.* 2 Not able to do or not capable of being, as in *restless* or *countless.*

les·see [les·ē′] *n.* A person who has a lease to rent or use property; tenant.

less·en [les′(ə)n] *v.* To make or become less: The rain *lessened* during the night. ◆ See LESSON.

less·er [les′ər] *adj.* Not as large, great, or important: The *lesser* crime of the two.

lesser panda A panda (def. 1).

les·son [les′(ə)n] *n.* 1 A regular part of a course of study; period of instruction: a history *lesson;* a driving *lesson.* 2 Something to be studied or learned, as by a student; assignment. 3 An action or experience from which something can be learned: Let that be a *lesson* to you! 4 A portion of the Bible meant to be read at a religious service. ◆ *Lesson* and *lessen,* although pronounced alike, are not related in meaning. *Lessen* is a verb meaning *to make less*: Stiff competition *lessened* our chances of winning. *Lesson* is a noun meaning *something to be learned*: a *lesson* in cooking.

less·or [les′ôr] *n.* A person who gives another person a lease to rent property; landlord.

lest [lest] *conj.* **1** For fear that: We hid *lest* they should see us. **2** That: used after expressions of fear or anxiety: We worried *lest* it should rain.

let¹ [let] *v.* **let, let·ting** **1** To allow or permit: We *let* them borrow the car. **2** To permit to pass, come, or go: *Let* me by. **3** To cause; make: *Let* me know when you arrive. **4** To cause to flow: to *let* blood. **5** To rent or be rented: We *let* our cottage for the summer; rooms to *let.* ◆ *Let* may also be used with other verbs in order to give a command, as in *Let us go,* to express willingness or assent, as in *Let it rain,* or to assume or suppose, as in *Let X equal the sum of two numbers.* **—let alone** **1** To leave undisturbed. **2** *informal* Not to mention; and surely not: I can't even float, *let alone* swim. **—let be** To refrain from disturbing or tampering with: *Let* the camera *be.* **—let down** **1** To lower. **2** To disappoint: You *let* me *down.* **—let loose** To set free; release. **—let off** **1** To let go; release. **2** To dismiss or excuse, as from a punishment or from work. **—let on** *informal* **1** To pretend: *Let on* you don't know. **2** To make known; reveal: Don't *let on* that I told you. **—let out** **1** To give forth: to *let out* a yell. **2** To set free; release. **3** To unfasten so as to make wider or longer: to *let out* a hem. **—let up** To grow or cause to grow less: The noise *let up* a bit. ◆ See LEAVE.

let² [let] *n.* **1** An obstacle, often used in the phrase **without let or hindrance,** without anything to hinder, prevent, or stand in the way. **2** In tennis and other net games, a stroke that must be repeated because of interference with the ball's flight.

-let A suffix meaning: **1** Small; little, as in *booklet.* **2** A band or ornament for, as in *anklet.*

let·down [let′doun′] *n.* **1** A decrease or slackening, as of energy or speed. **2** *informal* Disappointment; discouragement; disillusionment: The story's end was a *letdown.*

le·thal [lē′thəl] *adj.* Causing death; deadly.

le·thar·gic [li·thär′jik] *adj.* **1** Drowsy, listless, and dull: Fever made me *lethargic.* **2** Causing lethargy: a *lethargic* climate.

leth·ar·gy [leth′ər·jē] *n.* The condition of feeling tired, dull, and listless.

Le·the [lē′thē] *n.* In Greek myths, a river in Hades whose waters, when drunk, made a person forget the past.

let's [lets] Let us.

let·ter [let′ər] **1** *n.* A sign or mark used in writing or printing to represent a speech sound; character in an alphabet. **2** *v.* To form letters, as by hand: The sign painter *letters* very well. **3** *v.* To make or mark with letters: to *letter* a name. **4** *n.* A written or printed message, usually sent by mail. **5** *n.* (*pl.*) Literature in general: a person of *letters.* **6** *n.* An emblem in the form of the first letter of the name of a school or college, given as an award for achievement in athletics or other activities. **7** *n.* The absolute and exact meaning of something as opposed to the general interpretation: the *letter* of the law. **—to the letter** Precisely as written or directed: Follow my instructions *to the letter.*

letter carrier A mail carrier; mailman.

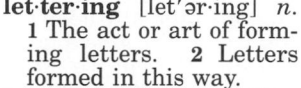

let·ter·head [let′ər·hed′] *n.* **1** The name and usually the address of a person or business printed at the top of a sheet of stationery. **2** A sheet of paper with such a heading.

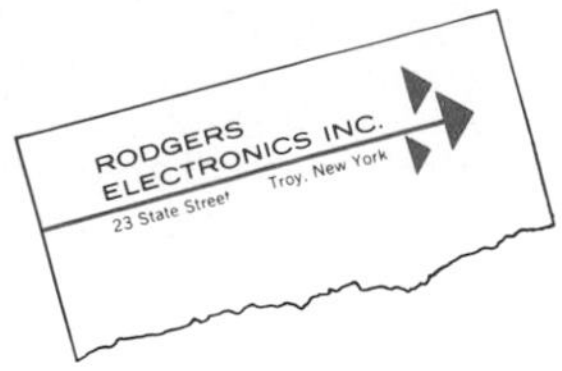

Letterhead

let·ter·ing [let′ər·ing] *n.* **1** The act or art of forming letters. **2** Letters formed in this way.

let·ter-per·fect [let′ər·pûr′fikt] *adj.* Correct in every detail: a *letter-perfect* recitation.

let·tuce [let′is] *n.* A plant having crisp, green, edible leaves, used in salads.

let·up [let′up′] *n.* *informal* A pausing, relaxing, or brief stopping of some activity or effort.

leu·co·cyte [lo͞o′kə·sīt′] *n.* A leukocyte.

leu·ke·mi·a [lo͞o·kē′mē·ə] *n.* A disease of the blood in which there is a very great increase in the number of leucocytes formed.

leu·ko·cyte [lo͞o′kə·sīt′] *n.* Any of various cells in the blood which do not contain hemoglobin. Some leukocytes, which resemble amebas, engulf and destroy bacteria and other foreign particles in the blood.

Le·van·tine [ləv′ən·tīn′ *or* ləv′ən·tēn′] **1** *n.* A person born in or living in the Levant. **2** *adj.* Of or relating to the Levant.

lev·ee¹ [lev′ē] *n.* **1** A bank built along the shore of a river to keep it from flooding. **2** A landing place for boats on a river.

lev·ee² [lev′ē *or* lə·vē′] *n.* An official morning reception held in former times by a monarch or other person of high rank.

lev·el [lev′əl] *adj., n., v.* **lev·eled** or **lev·elled, lev·el·ing** or **lev·el·ling** **1** *adj.* Having a flat surface, with each part at the same height: a *level* board. **2** *adj.* Equal in height; even: Make this pile of bricks *level* with that one. **3** *n.* Height; depth: The snowfall reached a *level* of 10 feet. **4** *n.* A position that is at the same height: The bookcase is on a *level* with the desk. **5** *v.* To give an even, horizontal, or level surface to: *Level* the board. **6** *adj.* Being parallel to the horizon; horizontal: *level* flight. **7** *n.* An instrument, as a glass tube of liquid containing an air bubble, used to see if a surface is level. **8** *n.* A flat expanse, as of land. **9** *n.* A degree or stage: a high reading *level.* **10**

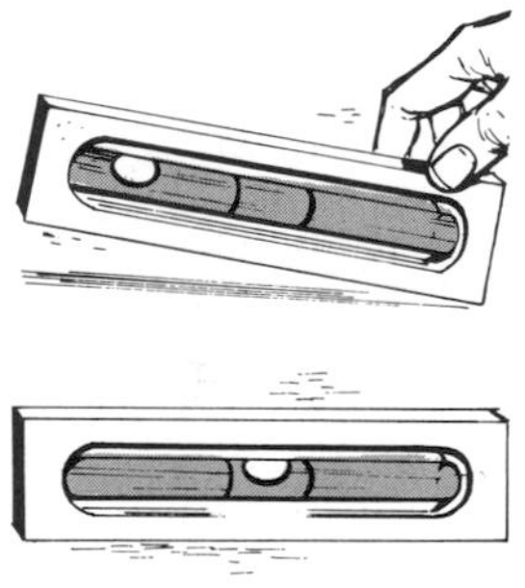
Level

a add	**i** it	**o͝o** took	**oi** oil
ā ace	**ī** ice	**o͞o** pool	**ou** pout
â care	**o** odd	**u** up	**ng** ring
ä palm	**ō** open	**û** burn	**th** thin
e end	**ô** order	**yo͞o** fuse	**t͟h** this
ē equal			**zh** vision

ə = {a in *above* e in *sicken* i in *possible*; o in *melon* u in *circus*}

v. To bring to a common state or condition: The ruling *leveled* all social classes. **11** *adj.* Not excited; calm; sensible: a *level* head. **12** *v.* To destroy or knock down: The bulldozer *leveled* the entire block; to *level* an opponent. **13** *v.* To aim or direct: to *level* a gun at someone. **—level best** A person's very best; utmost. **—level off** **1** To move or fly horizontally after gaining or losing altitude: The plane *leveled off* at 15,000 feet. **2** To give a level, even surface to. **—level with** *informal* To speak openly and truthfully: *Level with* me about my chance of being promoted. **—on the level** *informal* Fair and honest. **—lev′el·er** *n.* **—lev′el·ness** *n.*

lev·el·head·ed [lev′əl·hed′id] *adj.* **1** Not easily excited; calm. **2** Sensible; reasonable.

lev·er [lev′ər *or* lē′vər] **1** *n.* A mechanical device for lifting or prying up heavy objects. It consists of a straight bar that rests on a fixed support called a fulcrum. When force is applied at one end of the bar, the weight at the other end is moved or lifted. **2** *n.* Any bar used to turn, move, or control something: Pull that *lever* and the machinery will stop. **3** *v.* To move or pry with or as if with a lever.

Lever

lev·er·age [lev′ər·ij *or* lē′vər·ij] *n.* **1** The use of a lever. **2** The advantage or extra force gained by using a lever. **3** *n.* The use of borrowed funds to finance investments or business operations. **4** *v.* To make use of leverage: A corporation that is heavily in debt is highly *leveraged.*

leveraged buyout The purchase of a corporation through loans secured by the company's assets.

Le·vi [lē′vī] *n.* In the Bible, a son of Jacob.

le·vi·a·than [lə·vī′ə·thən] *n.* **1** A gigantic water beast mentioned in the Bible. **2** Any enormous creature or thing, as a whale or large ship.

Le·vite [lē′vīt′] *n.* In the Bible, one of the tribe of Levi. The Levites were chosen to assist the priests in the Jewish temple.

Le·vit·i·cus [li·vit′ə·kəs] *n.* The third book of the Old Testament, dealing with the laws of Jewish religious observance.

lev·i·ty [lev′ə·tē] *n., pl.* **lev·i·ties** Joking and gaiety, especially at the wrong time or in the wrong place.

lev·y [lev′ē] *v.* **lev·ied, lev·y·ing,** *n., pl.* **lev·ies** **1** *v.* To demand and collect by law: to *levy* a tax or a fine. **2** *v.* To draft for military service: to *levy* troops. **3** *v.* To prepare for or wage (war). **4** *n.* The act of levying. **5** *n.* Something that is levied.

lewd [lo͞od] *adj.* Vulgar and obscene; indecent.

lex·i·cal [lek′si·kəl] *adj.* **1** Of or having to do with the words or morphemes in a language as contrasted with its grammar and syntax. **2** Of or having to do with lexicography or a lexicon.

lex·i·cog·ra·phy [lek′sə·kog′rə·fē] *n.* The act or profession of writing dictionaries. **—lex′i·cog′ra·pher** *n.*

lex·i·con [lek′sə·kon′] *n.* **1** A dictionary, especially of Latin, Greek, or Hebrew. **2** A list of words used in or having to do with a particular subject.

Ley·den jar [līd′ən] An early type of electrical capacitor consisting of a glass jar lined inside and out with tinfoil, the inner foil connected to a metal conducting rod that extends from the inside of the jar through an insulated stopper. ◆ The jar bears the name of the Netherlands city where it was developed.

Li The symbol for the element lithium.

li·a·bil·i·ty [lī′ə·bil′ə·tē] *n., pl.* **li·a·bil·i·ties** **1** The condition of being liable. **2** (*pl.*) The money a person or business owes; debts. **3** A hindrance or drawback; disadvantage.

li·a·ble [lī′ə·bəl] *adj.* **1** Subject or susceptible, as to illness or injury: cuts *liable* to infection. **2** Likely; apt: It's *liable* to rain. **3** Legally responsible: They are *liable* for the damage done.

li·ai·son [lē′ə·zon′ *or* lē·ā′zon′] *n.* Contacts and communication between units or groups, as of an army or government, to secure better cooperation.

li·ar [lī′ər] *n.* A person who lies.

li·ba·tion [lī·bā′shən] *n.* **1** The act of pouring out a liquid, as wine, in honor of a god. **2** The liquid poured out.

li·bel [lī′bəl] *n., v.* **li·beled** or **li·belled, li·bel·ing** or **li·bel·ling** **1** *n.* A written statement or a picture, especially if published, that damages a person's reputation or dignity. **2** *n.* The act or crime of making or publishing such a statement or picture. **3** *v.* To make or publish a libel against. **—li′bel·er** *n.* **—li′bel·ous** *adj.*

lib·er·al [lib′ər·əl *or* lib′rəl] **1** *adj.* Very generous: a *liberal* gift to the museum. **2** *adj.* Abundant; ample: We freeze a *liberal* supply of vegetables every summer. **3** *adj.* Not narrow-minded or prejudiced; tolerant; broad. **4** *adj.* Based on the liberal arts: a *liberal* education. **5** *adj.* Favoring progress, reform, and the use of governmental power to achieve social or political goals. **6** *n.* A person who is liberal or has liberal political views. **—lib′er·al·ly** *adv.* **—lib′er·al·ness** *n.*

liberal arts A group of college courses, as literature, philosophy, history, and languages, giving a broad, general education rather than a scientific or technical one.

lib·er·al·ism [lib′ər·əl·iz′əm] *n.* **1** The condition of being liberal. **2** Liberal beliefs or actions, especially in politics and religion.

lib·er·al·i·ty [lib′ə·ral′ə·tē] *n., pl.* **lib·er·al·i·ties** **1** Generosity in giving. **2** Tolerance and understanding; broad-mindedness.

lib·er·al·ize [lib′ər·əl·īz′] *v.* **lib·er·al·ized, lib·er·al·iz·ing** To make or become more liberal. **—lib′er·al·i·za′tion** *n.*

lib·er·ate [lib′ə·rāt′] *v.* **lib·er·at·ed, lib·er·at·ing** To set free; release: to *liberate* a conquered country; to *liberate* hydrogen. **—lib′er·a′tion** *n.* **—lib′er·a′tor** *n.*

Li·be·ri·an [lī·bir′ē·ən] **1** *adj.* Of or from Liberia. **2** *n.* A person born in or a citizen of Liberia.

lib·er·tar·i·an [lib′ər·târ′ē·ən] *n.* A person who believes strongly in personal liberty, including freedom of action and thought. **—lib′er·tar′i·an·ism** *n.*

lib·er·tine [lib′ər·tēn′] *n.* A person who lives an immoral life without restraint.

lib·er·ty [lib′ər·tē] *n., pl.* **lib·er·ties** **1** Freedom from any arbitrary control by others. **2** Freedom to think or act as one wishes, regarded as a very important human right. **3** Permission to be in and make use of a particular place: Our class was given *liberty* of the entire beach. **4** In the Navy, permission to be absent from one's ship or one's place of duty. **—at liberty** **1** Free to do something. **2** Not busy: The doctor wants to see you when she is *at liberty.* **—take liberties** To behave with too much boldness, friendliness, or familiarity.

Liberty Bell The bell in Independence Hall, Philadelphia, that was rung on July 8, 1776, to mark the signing of the Declaration of Independence.

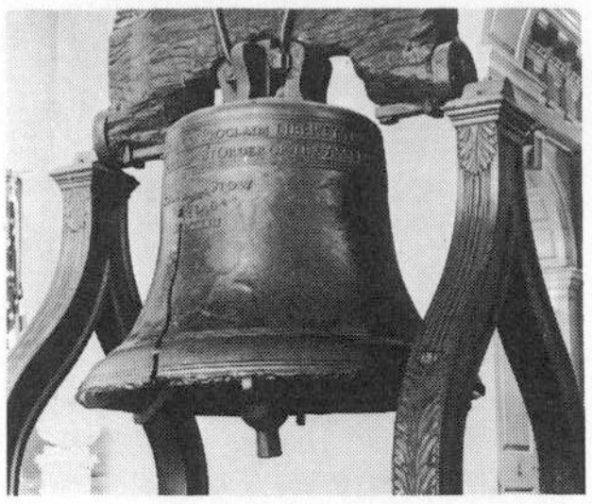
Liberty Bell

Li·bra [lī′brə *or* lē′brə] *n.* **1** A constellation in the Southern Hemisphere near Virgo and Scorpio. **2** The seventh sign of the zodiac. **3** A person born under this sign. ◆ Libra is named for the Latin word for *balance,* or *pair of scales,* whose appearance this constellation suggests.

li·brar·i·an [lī·brâr′ē·ən] *n.* A person in charge of a library or trained in library work. **—li·brar′i·an·ship** *n.*

li·brar·y [lī′brer′ē *or* lī′brə·rē] *n., pl.* **li·brar·ies** **1** A collection of books, magazines, newspapers, and other materials, especially when arranged and catalogued for public use. **2** A building, room, or other place in which such a collection is kept.

library card A card, issued by a library, that permits the holder to borrow its books and other materials.

library service or **library science** The study of libraries and their management.

li·bret·tist [li·bret′ist] *n.* A person who writes a libretto or librettos.

li·bret·to [li·bret′ō] *n., pl.* **li·bret·tos** or **li·bret·ti** [li·bret′ē] **1** The words of an opera or other big vocal work. **2** A book or pamphlet containing these words.

Lib·y·an [lib′ē·ən] **1** *adj.* Of or from Libya. **2** *n.* A person born in or a citizen of Libya.

lice [līs] Plural of LOUSE.

li·cense [lī′səns] *n., v.* **li·censed, li·cens·ing** **1** *n.* Legal permission to do, be, or own something. **2** *n.* A document, tag, or plate showing such permission: our car's *license.* **3** *v.* To issue a license to or for: to *license* a dog. **4** *n.* Too much freedom or laxity in conduct. **5** *n.* Freedom to disregard usual rules so as to get special effects: poetic *license.*

li·cen·see [lī′sən·sē′] *n.* A person who has been granted a license.

license plate A metal plate, as for an automobile, that bears the number of a license granted to the owner.

li·cen·tious [lī·sen′shəs] *adj.* Not held back by rules of morality or decency; immoral; lewd. **—li·cen′tious·ly** *adv.* **—li·cen′tious·ness** *n.*

li·chee [lē′chē] *n.* Another word for LITCHI.

li·chen [lī′kən] *n.* A mosslike plant, made up of a fungus and an alga, which grows in patches on rocks and trees.

Lichen

lick [lik] **1** *v.* To pass the tongue over the surface of: Be sure to *lick* each stamp. **2** *v.* To move or pass over or about: The flames *licked* the coals. **3** *n.* The act of licking: My dog gave me a *lick* on my face. **4** *n. informal* A quick or careless action or effort. **5** *n. informal* A bit or small amount: We did every *lick* of work on it ourselves. **6** *v. informal* To defeat or thrash: We *licked* them easily. **7** *n. informal* A sharp blow or hit. **8** *n.* A salt lick.

lick·e·ty-split [lik′ə·te·split′] *adv. informal* With great speed.

lic·o·rice [lik′ə·ris *or* lik′rish] *n.* **1** A plant that grows in central and southern Europe. **2** Its root, used in medicine or to flavor things. **3** A candy flavored with licorice. ◆ *Licorice* comes from two Greek words meaning *sweet root.*

lid [lid] *n.* **1** A hinged or removable cover, as for a box or pot. **2** An eyelid. **3** *slang* A hat.

lie[1] [lī] *v.* **lay, lain, ly·ing** **1** To be in a flat, horizontal position: The tree *lay* on the ground. **2** To put oneself in a horizontal position: I *lay* down on the bed. **3** To be buried: Juliet *lay* in her tomb. **4** To be or remain in some particular condition: The seeds *lay* dormant all winter. **5** To exist: Our strength *lies* in our numbers. **6** To be in a certain location; be situated: New York *lies* northeast of Philadelphia. **7** To continue or extend: The future *lies* before us. **—lie down on the job** To do less than one should; shirk. **—lie in wait** To keep watch for someone while in a hidden position; be in ambush. **—lie low** To conceal oneself or one's plans. ◆ See LAY.

lie[2] [lī] *n., v.* **lied, ly·ing** **1** *n.* Something said or written that is not true and is meant to deceive; falsehood. **2** *v.* To tell or write a lie; deceive on purpose. **3** *v.* To give a wrong impression; be inaccurate: Figures don't *lie.* **—give the lie to** **1** To show or prove the falseness of: The mayor's speech *gave the lie to* rumors that she would not run again. **2** To accuse (someone) of lying.

lie detector An apparatus that registers small changes in a person's pulse rate, breathing, perspiration, and the like, which are often telltale signs of lying in response to an embarrassing question.

lief [lēf] *adv.* Willingly; gladly, now used only in the phrase **would as lief**: The bully *would as lief* knock you down as look at you.

liege [lēj] **1** *n.* In the Middle Ages, a lord or ruler to whom feudal service or allegiance was due. **2** *n.* A vassal or subject who owed such service. **3** *adj.* Entitled to receive feudal allegiance: a *liege* lord. **4** *adj.* Owing feudal allegiance: a *liege* vassal.

liege·man [lēj′mən] *n., pl.* **liege·men** [lēj′mən] **1** A feudal vassal. **2** A loyal follower or subject.

lien [lēn] *n.* The legal right of one party to claim and hold or sell the property of a second party who is the first party's debtor.

a	add	**i**	it	**o͝o**	took	**oi**	oil
ā	ace	**ī**	ice	**o͞o**	pool	**ou**	pout
â	care	**o**	odd	**u**	up	**ng**	ring
ä	palm	**ō**	open	**û**	burn	**th**	thin
e	end	**ô**	order	**yo͞o**	fuse	**t͟h**	this
ē	equal					**zh**	vision

ə = {a in *above* e in *sicken* i in *possible* / o in *melon* u in *circus*}

L

lieu [lo͞o] *n.* Place; stead, now used only in the phrase **in lieu of:** I will send a note *in lieu of* calling.

lieut. or **Lieut.** lieutenant.

lieu·ten·an·cy [lo͞o·ten′ən·sē′] *n., pl.* **lieu·ten·an·cies** The position, rank, or term of service of a lieutenant.

lieu·ten·ant [lo͞o·ten′ənt] *n.* 1 A military rank. In the U.S. Army, either of two commissioned officers, a **first lieutenant** ranking next below a captain, or a **second lieutenant** ranking next below a first lieutenant. 2 A naval rank. In the U.S. Navy, either of two commissioned officers, a **lieutenant** ranking next below a lieutenant commander, or a **lieutenant junior grade** ranking next above an ensign. 3 A person able to perform the duties of a superior, either in the latter's absence or under the superior's direction. ◆ *Lieutenant* comes from the French words *lieu* and *tenant,* which mean *holding the place* (of a superior).

lieutenant colonel A military rank. In the U.S. Army, Air Force, and Marine Corps, an officer ranking next above a major and next below a colonel.

lieutenant commander A naval rank. In the U.S. Navy and Coast Guard, an officer ranking next above a lieutenant and next below a commander.

lieutenant general A military rank. In the U.S. Army, Air Force, and Marine Corps, an officer ranking next above a major general and next below a general.

lieutenant governor An elected official who performs the duties of a governor of a state during the governor's absence or who replaces the governor in case of death or resignation.

lieutenant junior grade *pl.* **lieutenants junior grade** In the U.S. Navy or Coast Guard, a commissioned officer who ranks above an ensign and below a lieutenant.

life [līf] *n., pl.* **lives** [līvz] 1 The form of existence marked by growth, metabolism, reproduction, and adaptation to the environment. Life is what makes people, plants, and animals different from such things as rocks or other inorganic matter or from dead organisms. 2 A living being; person: to save a *life.* 3 Living organisms as a group: *life* on Mars. 4 The period of a person's existence: a long, happy *life.* 5 The period of time during which something continues to work or be useful: the *life* of an engine. 6 The way or manner in which a person or group lives: city *life.* 7 Energy; vitality; spirit: to be full of *life.* 8 An account of the events of a person's lifetime; biography. **—as large as life** Of the same size or dimension as something in real life; life-size. **—bring to life** 1 To cause to regain consciousness. 2 To give vitality to; make seem real; animate. **—come to life** 1 To regain consciousness. 2 To gain vitality; become animated. **—for dear life** or **for one's life** At the utmost; urgently; desperately. **—for the life of (one)** Even with the greatest effort: She couldn't recall it *for the life of* her. **—not on your life** Emphatically not. **—take a life** To kill. **—to the life** With an exact or very close resemblance.

life-and-death [līf′ən·deth′] *adj.* 1 Affecting or culminating in life or death. 2 Having the greatest importance, as if involving life or death.

life belt A life preserver in the form of a belt.

life·blood [līf′blud′] *n.* 1 The blood necessary to life. 2 Any source of strength, vigor, or power.

life·boat [līf′bōt′] *n.* A boat equipped for saving lives at sea or along a shore, especially such a boat carried aboard a ship.

Lifeboat

life buoy A life preserver, often in the form of a ring.

life cycle The entire series of biological processes and stages through which an organism passes from egg to adult: the *life cycle* of a butterfly.

life expectancy The number of years an individual or class of individuals is expected to live, as determined by statistics.

life·guard [līf′gärd′] *n.* An expert swimmer employed at a beach or pool to protect the safety of bathers.

life insurance Insurance on the life of an individual who pays regular payments or premiums during his or her lifetime. At the person's death, a sum of money is given to the person's beneficiary.

life jacket A life preserver in the form of a jacket without sleeves.

life·less [līf′lis] *adj.* 1 Having lost life; dead. 2 Not ever having had life: A toy bear is *lifeless.* 3 Lacking vitality; dull: a *lifeless* book. **—life′less·ly** *adv.* **—life′less·ness** *n.*

life·like [līf′līk′] *adj.* 1 Looking like a person or thing that is or was alive: a *lifelike* picture. 2 Accurately representing actual events or circumstances: a *lifelike* movie.

life·line [līf′līn′] *n.* 1 A rope used to lower or raise an underwater diver. 2 Any rope giving support or aid, as to bathers in surf. 3 Any land, air, or sea route used for transporting supplies necessary for life.

life·long [līf′lông′] *adj.* Lasting or continuing throughout one's life: a *lifelong* friendship.

life preserver Any of various devices, often in the form of a belt, jacket, or ring, used to keep afloat a person who is in danger of drowning.

Life preserver

life raft A raft or lifeboat used in emergencies, as by people forced to abandon a sinking ship.

life·sav·er [līf′sā′vər] *n.* 1 A person who saves a life, especially by keeping another from drowning. 2 A person or thing that provides great aid in an emergency. 3 A ring-shaped life preserver that encircles the body.

life·sav·ing [līf′sāv′ing] *n.* 1 The act of saving a life. 2 Any of various methods used to save the lives of those who are drowning or have been injured in some way. 3 *adj. use: lifesaving* equipment.

life science Any of the branches of learning that study human or animal life, especially from a medical or biological point of view.

life sentence A punishment consisting of spending the remainder of one's life in prison, upon being found guilty of certain serious crimes.

life-size [līf′sīz′] *adj.* Having the same size as the thing or person represented or portrayed: a *life-size* replica of a dinosaur.

life-sized [līf′sīzd′] *adj.* Life-size.

life span 1 The period during which a living thing remains alive. 2 The average length of life of a person or animal, or the period during which a nonliving thing remains serviceable.

life-style [līf′stīl′] *n.* The way in which a person or group lives, determined by attitudes, beliefs, standards, ideals, and other values, and shown especially in one's home environment, manner of dress, and forms of recreation.

life-sup·port system [līf′sə·pôrt′] **1** A system that provides things necessary for human life, such as oxygen, food, and water, to persons in outer space. **2** Any of a group of mechanical devices used in a hospital or sanitarium to maintain or prolong the life of a sick person.

life·time [līf′tīm′] *n.* **1** The period of time during which a person, animal, or plant has life. **2** The period of time during which something lasts.

life·work [līf′wûrk′] *n.* **1** The chief things produced by a person during his or her lifetime: These few paintings are the artist's entire *lifework.* **2** The work that a person does during his or her life.

lift [lift] **1** *v.* To take hold of and raise to a higher position: *Lift* the table. **2** *v.* To bring to a higher or better condition: The coach's talk *lifted* the team's spirits. **3** *v.* To rise or ascend: My brows *lifted* in surprise. **4** *v.* To go or move away: The fog *lifted.* **5** *v.* To cancel, end, or revoke: to *lift* a curfew. **6** *n.* The act of lifting or raising. **7** *n.* An amount lifted; load. **8** *n.* The height or distance to which something is lifted. **9** *n.* Assistance; aid: Please give me a *lift* with this trunk. **10** *n.* A feeling of happiness or well-being: The good news gave us a *lift.* **11** *n.* A ride given a traveler to help him or her along the way. **12** *v. informal* To steal. **13** *n.* The British word for an elevator. **—lift′er** *n.*

lift-off [lift′ôf′] *n.* The vertical movement of a rocket or spacecraft at the time it leaves its launching site.

lig·a·ment [lig′ə·mənt] *n.* A band of firm, strong tissue that connects bones or helps to support an organ of the body.

li·gate [lī′gāt′] *v.* **li·gat·ed, li·gat·ing** To tie up or bind with a ligature.

lig·a·ture [lig′ə·chŏŏr′ *or* lig′ə·chər] *n.* **1** A band or strip, used to tie or bind something. **2** In surgery, a thread or wire tied around a blood vessel to prevent bleeding. **3** In printing and writing, a character made up of two or more connected letters, as *æ, fi, ffi.*

light[1] [līt] *n., v.* **light·ed** or **lit, light·ing,** *adj.* **1** *n.* A form of energy that stimulates the eyes and makes it possible to see things. **2** *n.* Brightness: A lot of *light* comes in this window. **3** *v.* To make or become light or bright. **4** *v.* To cause to give off light: *Light* the bulb on the cellar stairs. **5** *n.* A source of light or brightness, as an electric light bulb or candle. **6** *adj.* Full of light; not dark; bright: a *light* room. **7** *n.* Daylight or dawn. **8** *n.* Something that admits light, as a window or skylight. **9** *v.* To guide or conduct with light: The flashlight *lit* my way home. **10** *adj.* Pale: a *light* blue scarf. **11** *v.* To cause or start to burn: *Light* the kindling in the fireplace; It *lights* quickly. **12** *n.* Something that ignites or sets fire to something else: a *light* for a stove. **13** *n.* A lively or intense expression on the face or in the eyes. **14** *v.* To make or become radiant or cheerful: A smile *lit* my face; Their eyes *lit* up with joy. **15** *n.* Knowledge or understanding: Get all the *light* you can on this subject. **16** *n.* Public attention or knowledge: to bring new facts to *light.* **17** *n.* The way in which something impresses or appears to one: to see things in a new *light.* **18** *n.* An outstanding or famous person: a lesser *light.* **—bring to light** To expose or reveal: The trial *brought to light* enough evidence to clear the defendant. **—in the light of** In view of; considering: *In the light of* what we have heard about your past job performance, we would like to offer you the job. **—see the light** **1** To come into being; be born. **2** To be brought to the attention of the public. **3** To get knowledge or understanding. **—shed light on** or **throw light on** To explain or make clear.

light[2] [līt] *adj., v.* **light·ed** or **lit, light·ing** **1** *adj.* Having little weight, especially in relation to size or bulk: a *light* cotton cloth; a *light* plane. **2** *adj.* Not heavy; easily carried or done: a *light* package; *light* work. **3** *adj.* Intended as entertainment: *light* reading. **4** *adj.* Not great, as in amount or force: a *light* rain. **5** *adj.* Cheerful; gay: a *light* laugh. **6** *adj.* Not clumsy; graceful: to be *light* on one's feet. **7** *adj.* Dizzy; giddy: a *light* head. **8** *adj.* Gentle: a *light* tap on the door. **9** *adj.* Not coarse or heavy, as in texture or feel: *light* biscuits. **10** *adj.* Not rich or heavy: a *light* meal; a *light* wine. **11** *adj.* Not carrying huge or heavy weapons or armor: a *light* tank. **12** *v.* To come down and settle, as after flight. **13** *v.* To happen or come, as by chance: We *lighted* upon the best bargains in town. **14** *v.* To fall; strike: The heavy branch *lighted* on the roof. **15** *v.* To get down, as from a horse; dismount. **—light into** *informal* To attack: We *lit into* the speaker with our arguments. **—light out** *informal* To leave or go in haste. **—make light of** To consider or treat as unimportant, silly, or trivial: To *make light* of someone's troubles.

light bulb Another term for INCANDESCENT LAMP.

light·en[1] [līt′(ə)n] *v.* **1** To make or become light or bright. **2** To give off or display lightning flashes: The sky *lightened* in the west.

light·en[2] [līt′(ə)n] *v.* **1** To make or become less heavy: *Lighten* your luggage. **2** To make or become less troublesome or severe: The judge *lightened* the sentence. **3** To make or become more cheerful; gladden: to *lighten* one's spirits.

light·er[1] [līt′ər] *n.* A person or thing that lights, especially a device to light cigarettes.

light·er[2] [līt′ər] *n.* A bargelike vessel used in loading or unloading ships.

light·face [līt′fās′] *n.* A printing type in which the lines of the characters are thin and the impression is not heavy.

light-foot·ed [līt′fŏŏt′id] *adj.* Stepping or running lightly and gracefully. **—light′-foot′ed·ly** *adv.*

light-head·ed [līt′hed′id] *adj.* **1** Silly and giddy in manner or behavior. **2** Slightly faint of dizzy.

a	add	**i**	it	**ŏŏ**	took	**oi**	oil
ā	ace	**ī**	ice	**ōō**	pool	**ou**	pout
â	care	**o**	odd	**u**	up	**ng**	ring
ä	palm	**ō**	open	**û**	burn	**th**	thin
e	end	**ô**	order	**yōō**	fuse	**th**	this
ē	equal					**zh**	vision

ə = a in *above* e in *sicken* i in *possible* o in *melon* u in *circus*

L

light·heart·ed [līt′här′tid] *adj.* Free from care or trouble; happy. **—light′heart′ed·ly** *adv.*

light heavyweight A boxer of a class whose weight must be no less than 161 pounds and no more than 175.

light·house [līt′hous′] *n.* A tower equipped with a powerful light and used to guide ships or warn them of rocks or similar dangers.

Lighthouse

light·ing [lī′ting] *n.* **1** The act or result of providing artificial light. **2** A device or an arrangement that provides such light. **3** The act of causing to burn; igniting.

light·ly [līt′lē] *adv.* **1** With little weight or pressure; softly; gently: I pushed the swing *lightly.* **2** In a small amount or degree; moderately: I was *lightly* dressed. **3** With a swift, light step or motion: to skim *lightly* over the water. **4** In a carefree manner: to laugh *lightly.* **5** Without seriousness; frivolously. **6** In a slighting or almost insulting manner: to speak *lightly* of someone.

light meter An instrument that indicates how much light is entering it, used by photographers to determine correct exposure for films.

light-mind·ed [līt′mīn′did] *adj.* Lacking a serious attitude or purpose; frivolous. **—light′-mind′ed·ly** *adv.* **—light′-mind′ed·ness** *n.*

light·ness[1] [līt′nis] *n.* **1** The condition of being bright or illuminated: the *lightness* of a room. **2** Paleness of color: the *lightness* of the sky.

light·ness[2] [līt′nis] *n.* **1** The condition of having little weight, especially in relation to size or bulk: The *lightness* of this car is a drawback. **2** Ease of motion; agility; grace: the *lightness* of the dancer. **3** Freedom from sorrow or care. **4** Lack of seriousness; levity.

light·ning [līt′ning] *n.* A sudden flash of light caused by a discharge of electricity between two clouds or between a cloud and the earth.

lightning bug Another word for FIREFLY.

lightning rod A pointed metal rod that protects a building by conducting lightning from above it into the ground.

light opera Another term for OPERETTA.

light·ship [līt′ship′] *n.* A vessel equipped with a bright light and signals, and moored in dangerous waters as a guide to ships.

light·some [līt′səm] *adj.* **1** Cheerful and gay; carefree. **2** Easy and graceful in movement. **3** Not serious; frivolous; flighty.

light·weight [līt′wāt′] **1** *n.* A person or animal of much less than average weight. **2** *adj.* Of less than average or required weight. **3** *n.* A boxer weighing between 127 and 135 pounds. **4** *n. informal* A person who is not equal in intelligence or skill to others in a certain group or category: Roger is the *lightweight* on our debate team. **5** *adj.* Lacking seriousness of purpose or content: a *lightweight* movie.

light-year [līt′yir′] *n.* The distance traveled by light in one year, about six trillion miles.

lig·nite [lig′nīt′] *n.* A soft, brownish coal, still showing the structure of wood.

lik·a·ble [lī′kə·bəl] *adj.* Easy to like; pleasant; cheerful; affable. **—lik′a·ble·ness** *n.*

like[1] [līk] **1** *prep.* Having a close resemblance to; similar to: The twins are *like* one another. **2** *prep.* In the same way or manner of: to swim *like* a fish. **3** *prep.* Typical or characteristic of: How *like* you to say that. **4** *adj.* Similar: a *like* answer to mine. **5** *adj.* Equal or nearly equal: Both pitchers held a *like* quantity of water. **6** *n.* A person or thing of equal value, importance, or size: We shall not see their *like* again. **7** *prep.* Likely to result in: It looks *like* rain. **8** *prep.* In need of; desirous of: I feel *like* resting. **9** *conj. informal* The same as; as: It turned out *like* you said. **10** *conj. informal* As if: It looks *like* it's going to rain. **11** *adv. informal* Probably: *Like* enough I'll go. **—and the like** And other similar things or qualities: The coach talked of good manners, sportsmanship, *and the like.* **—like anything** or **like mad** or **like crazy** *slang* With great force, speed, or energy. ◆ *Like* is not used as a conjunction in place of *as* or *as if* in formal speech. "The machine works *like* it should" is incorrect. "The machine works *as* it should" is correct. "You talk *like* you were an expert" is incorrect. "You talk *as* if you were an expert" is correct. *Like* is used as a preposition when no verb is expressed: You look *like* your cousin; The player bats *like* a champ. *Like* is also acceptable in place of *as if* when followed by a short expression containing no verb: It looks *like* new.

like[2] [līk] *v.* **liked, lik·ing,** *n.* **1** *v.* To take pleasure in; enjoy: I *like* swimming. **2** *v.* To feel affection for: I *like* you. **3** *v.* To wish or desire; prefer: Do as you *like.* **4** *n.* (*usually pl.*) Those things one enjoys or prefers, especially in the phrase **likes and dislikes.**

-like A suffix meaning: **1** Resembling or similar to, as in *ironlike.* **2** Characteristic of; proper to or for, as in *childlike.* ◆ Compound words formed with *-like* are usually written as one word, except those that would bring three *l*'s together, which are hyphenated, as in *shell-like.*

like·a·ble [lī′kə·bəl] *adj.* Likable.

like·li·hood [līk′lē·ho͝od′] *n.* The possibility or probability that something will happen: Is there any *likelihood* that they will arrive early?

like·ly [līk′lē] *adj.* **like·li·er, like·li·est,** *adv.* **1** *adj.* Having or showing a tendency or possibility to do or be; apt: They are *likely* to go. **2** *adv.* Probably: I will *likely* go shopping. **3** *adj.* Probably about to happen: Your promotion seems *likely.* **4** *adj.* Probably true; believable: a *likely* story. **5** *adj.* Suitable; appropriate: a *likely* spot for a picnic. **6** *adj.* Able to please or be successful; promising: a *likely* candidate.

like-mind·ed [līk′mīn′did] *adj.* Of the same opinion, outlook, or purpose. **—like′-mind′ed·ly** *adv.* **—like′-mind′ed·ness** *n.*

lik·en [lī′kən] *v.* To represent as alike or similar; compare.

like·ness [līk′nis] *n.* **1** The condition or fact of being alike or similar: There is a real *likeness* between the two dogs. **2** An image, as a painting or photograph, of a person or thing. **3** Form; guise: to appear in the *likeness* of a clown.

like·wise [līk′wīz′] *adv.* **1** In like manner; the same: The others recited well; now you do *likewise.* **2** In addition; besides: The teacher coaches football and *likewise* track. ◆ *Likewise* was formed by combining *like* with *wise,* an old word meaning *manner* or *way of doing.*

lik·ing [lī′king] *n.* **1** A feeling of affection; fondness: to have a *liking* for someone. **2** Preference: to have a *liking* for classical music.

li·lac [lī′lak′ *or* lī′lək] **1** *n.* A large shrub having clusters of numerous tiny, fragrant flowers, usually purple or white in color. **2** *n., adj.* Light purple. ◆ *Lilac* comes from an Arabic word derived from a Persian word meaning *bluish.*

Lil·li·put [lil′ə·put′] *n.* An island in Swift's *Gulliver's Travels,* on which the inhabitants are six inches tall.

lil·li·pu·tian [lil′ə·pyōō′shən] *adj.* **1** (*usually written* **Lilliputian**) Of or relating to Lilliput or its people. **2** Tiny, miniature.

lilt [lilt] **1** *n.* A lively or rhythmical way of speaking or singing: to have a *lilt* in one's voice. **2** *n.* A cheerful tune. **3** *v.* To speak, sing, or move in a cheerful, rhythmic way.

lil·y [lil′ē] *n., pl.* **lil·ies,** *adj.* **1** *n.* A wild or cultivated plant growing from a bulb and having showy white or colored flowers. **2** *n.* Any flower like the lily, as the water lily. **3** *adj.* Like a lily, as in beauty or whiteness.

lily of the valley *pl.* **lilies of the valley** A plant having two large green leaves and small, fragrant white flowers arranged along a stem.

li·ma bean [lī′mə] **1** A large, flat, edible bean. **2** The plant producing this bean.

limb [lim] *n.* **1** An arm, leg, or wing. **2** A large branch, as of a tree.

lim·ber [lim′bər] **1** *adj.* Flexible; pliant: a *limber* twig. **2** *adj.* Agile or supple: a *limber* body. **3** *v.* To make or become limber: Exercise *limbers* up the body. **—lim′ber·ness** *n.*

lim·bo [lim′bō] *n., pl.* **lim·bos** **1** (*often written* **Limbo**) In some Christian belief, a region on the edge of hell for the souls of unbaptized infants and those of the righteous who died before the coming of Christ. **2** A place or condition for unwanted or forgotten people or things.

Lim·burg·er [lim′bûr′gər] *n.* A soft, white cheese with a strong odor.

lime[1] [līm] *n., v.* **limed, lim·ing** **1** *n.* A white material made by heating limestone, chalk, or seashells to a high temperature. It is used in making mortar, cement, and fertilizer. **2** *v.* To treat, mix, or spread with lime.

lime[2] [līm] *n.* **1** A small, green, citrus fruit whose sour juice is used for flavoring and in drinks. **2** The tree on which it grows.

lime[3] [līm] *n.* A type of linden tree.

lime·light [līm′līt′] *n.* **1** A bright light used on the stage as a spotlight. **2** Public attention or notice: The author's new book was in the *limelight.*

lim·er·ick [lim′rik *or* lim′ər·ik] *n.* A humorous, five-line poem.

lime·stone [līm′stōn′] *n.* A type of rock, as marble, that contains mainly calcium carbonate.

lime·wa·ter [līm′wô′tər] *n.* A solution of lime and water, used in medicine.

lim·it [lim′it] **1** *n.* The furthest or utmost point beyond which something does not or cannot go. **2** *n.* (*usually pl.*) The bounds of a certain area: the city *limits.* **3** *n.* The largest permissible quantity or amount. **4** *v.* To set a limit to; restrict.

lim·i·ta·tion [lim′ə·tā′shən] *n.* **1** A limiting or being limited. **2** Something that limits, especially a shortcoming.

lim·it·ed [lim′it·id] **1** *adj.* Confined within a limit or limits; restricted: *limited* space. **2** *adj.* Making few stops and carrying a limited number of people. **3** *n.* A train that makes few stops and carries a limited number of people. **4** *adj.* Of or relating to a business establishment in which the liability of each stockholder or partner for the company's indebtedness is no greater than the actual investment of that person.

lim·it·less [lim′it·lis] *adj.* Boundless.

limn [lim] *v.* **1** To draw or paint. **2** To describe in words.

lim·ou·sine [lim′ə·zēn′] *n.* A large, closed automobile often having a glass partition between the driver in front and the passengers in back.

limp[1] [limp] **1** *v.* To walk with a halting or irregular step, as with an injured leg or foot. **2** *n.* Such a walk or step.

limp[2] [limp] *adj.* **1** Lacking stiffness; flabby. **2** Lacking strength; weak. **—limp′ly** *adv.*

lim·pet [lim′pit] *n.* A small shellfish that clings fast to rocks and timbers.

lim·pid [lim′pid] *adj.* Clear; transparent. **—lim·pid′·i·ty** *n.* **—lim′pid·ly** *adv.*

lim·y [lī′mē] *adj.* **lim·i·er lim·i·est** Of or containing lime.

lin·age or **line·age** [lī′nij] The number of printed or written lines in an article, advertisement, or other published matter.

linch·pin [linch′pin′] *n.* **1** A metal pin inserted crosswise through the end of a shaft to secure a part of a mechanism, such as a wheel or an axle. **2** Something that holds together the details of a plan or undertaking; keystone.

lin·den [lin′dən] *n.* Any of a number of trees having soft, white wood, heart-shaped leaves, and fragrant, cream-colored flowers.

line[1] [līn] *n., v.* **lined, lin·ing** **1** *n.* A slender, continuous mark, as that drawn by a pen. **2** *n.* A crease, as in the skin. **3** *v.* To mark or cover with lines: to *line* paper; Water *lined* the rocks. **4** *n.* Something that is shaped like a line, as a rope or string: a fishing *line.* **5** *n.* A pipe or a system of pipes: a gas *line.* **6** *n.* A wire, or system of wires, used to carry electric power or telephone messages. **7** *n.* A row: a *line* of people. **8** *v.* To form a row or line along: Statues *lined* the walk. **9** *n.* A succession of related people or things: a family *line.* **10** *n.* An arrangement, as of soldiers, troops, or weapons, aligned abreast, or nearly so: the front *line.* **11** *n.* In football, the linemen, collectively. **12** *n.* A boundary or border: the state *line.* **13** *n.* A transportation company having an established route or routes: a bus *line.* **14** *n.* One of these routes: the main *line.* **15** *n.* A path; course: the *line* of fire. **16** *n.* A course of action or thought: the Communist *line.* **17** *n.* (*often pl.*) A general plan or concept: a work on modern *lines.* **18** *n.* A short letter; note: Drop me a *line.* **19** *n.* (*pl.*) The words of an actor's or performer's part. **20** *n.* A verse in poetry. **21** *n.* All the words in one row

a	add	**i**	it	**ŏŏ**	took	**oi**	oil
ā	ace	**ī**	ice	**ōō**	pool	**ou**	pout
â	care	**o**	odd	**u**	up	**ng**	ring
ä	palm	**ō**	open	**û**	burn	**th**	thin
e	end	**ô**	order	**yōō**	fuse	**t͟h**	this
ē	equal					**zh**	vision

ə = {a in *above*, e in *sicken*, i in *possible*, o in *melon*, u in *circus*}

L

in one column of printed material: Read the next *line.* **22** *n.* In mathematics, a straight path that extends forever in both directions with no endpoints. **23** *n.* A straight line: to be in a *line* with each other. **24** *n.* The equator: The ship crossed the *line.* **25** *n.* A business; occupation: My *line* is insurance. **26** *n.* A make or brand of goods: a famous *line* of women's clothing. **27** *v.* In baseball, to hit hard and on a more or less flat course, as a ball: to *line* a ball to center field. **—all along the line** At every point; everywhere. **—draw the line** (at *or* on) To set a limit: to *draw the line* at cheating. **—get a line on** *U.S. informal* To get information about. **—hold the line** To remain firm in opposition to something; be unyielding. **—in line 1** Forming a line or row. **2** In agreement; conforming. **—in line for** In a position to receive something by right of succession or merit; next in order: *in line* for a better job. **—into line 1** Into a line or row. **2** Into conformity with something. **—line out** In baseball, to hit a line drive that is caught by a fielder before it bounces. **—line up** To form or bring into a line or row. **—on a line** In alignment or agreement; even. **—on the line** In a position to be won or lost; at stake: The scientist put his reputation *on the line.* **—out of line 1** Not in a line or row. **2** Not conforming. **—read between the lines** To find a hidden meaning.

line² [līn] *v.* **lined, lin·ing 1** To put a covering or layer on the inner surface of: to *line* a jacket with wool. **2** To serve as a lining of.

lin·e·age [lin'ē·ij] *n.* **1** Line of descent; ancestry. **2** A family or stock.

lin·e·al [lin'ē·əl] *adj.* **1** In the direct line of descent. **2** Linear. **—lin'e·al·ly** *adv.*

lin·e·a·ment [lin'ē·ə·mənt] *n.* A feature or contour of the face.

lin·e·ar [lin'ē·ər] *adj.* **1** Of or having to do with a line or lines. **2** Of , having to do with, or involving a linear equation. **3** Consisting of or characterized by the use of lines: *linear* art. **4** Being long with nearly parallel sides: a *linear* leaf.

linear equation An algebraic equation in which variables are used as factors no more than once in each term. $2x + 4y = 30$ is a linear equation. The graph of a linear equation is a straight line.

linear measure 1 Measurement of length. **2** A system for the measurement of length. **3** A unit in such a system, such as a foot or meter.

line·back·er [līn'bak'·ər] *n.* In football, any of a group of defensive players normally positioned between their team's linemen and defensive backs.

line drive In baseball, a sharply hit ball that travels in a nearly straight line close to the ground.

line·man [līn'mən] *n., pl.* **line·men** [līn'mən] **1** A person who installs or repairs telephone or electric power lines. **2** In football, a player on the forward line; a center, guard, tackle, or end.

lin·en [lin'ən] **1** *n.* Thread or cloth made of flax fibers. **2** *adj.* Made of linen. **3** *n.* Articles made or formerly made of linen: table *linen.*

line of credit The maximum amount of goods, services, or money that a seller or lender extends to a customer who is not making immediate or quick payment in return.

line of force A line that shows the direction of a force in a magnetic or other field.

line of scrimmage See SCRIMMAGE.

lin·er¹ [lī'nər] *n.* **1** A ship or airplane operated by a transportation line. **2** A line drive.

lin·er² [lī'nər] *n.* **1** A person who lines. **2** Something used as a lining or backing. **3** A protective jacket for a phonograph record.

line segment Two points on a line and all the points between them.

lines·man [līnz'mən] *n., pl.* **lines·men** [līnz'mən] **1** A lineman who works on power lines or telephone lines. **2** In football, the official who marks the distance gained or lost on each play.

line·up or **line-up** [līn'up'] *n.* **1** A list of starting players on a team for a game. **2** These players. **3** A row of possible criminal suspects displayed for purposes of identification.

-ling A suffix meaning: **1** A person or thing belonging to or connected with someone, as in *hireling.* **2** A person having a specific rank or quality, as in *underling.* **3** A person or animal that is young or small, as in *nursling* or *duckling.*

lin·ger [ling'gər] *v.* To stay on as if unwilling to go; loiter: The twilight *lingered.*

lin·ge·rie [län'zhə·rē *or* län'zhə·rā'] *n.* Women's underwear.

lin·go [ling'gō] *n., pl.* **lin·goes** A language or talk that seems outlandish or is not understood: jazz *lingo*; a foreign *lingo.* ◆ This word is used in humor or contempt.

lin·gual [ling'gwəl] *adj.* **1** Of or resembling the tongue. **2** Sounded mainly with the tongue, for example, the letters *n* and *t.* **3** Linguistic. **—lin'·gual·ly** *adv.*

lin·gui·ne or **lin·gui·ni** [ling·gwē'nē] *n.* Pasta formed into long, narrow, flat strips.

lin·guist [ling'gwist] *n.* **1** A person who speaks several languages. **2** An expert or student in linguistics.

lin·guis·tic [ling·gwis'tik] *adj.* Of or having to do with language or linguistics.

lin·guis·tics [ling·gwis'tiks] *n.* The scientific study of language. ◆ See -ICS.

lin·i·ment [lin'ə·mənt] *n.* A liquid rubbed on the skin to relieve sprains and stiffness.

lin·ing [lī'ning] *n.* A covering of an inner surface: the *lining* of a jacket.

Lining

link [lingk] **1** *n.* One of the rings or loops of a chain. **2** *n.* A single part or element of any chain or series. **3** *n.* Something that joins or connects: a *link* with another world. **4** *v.* To join or connect; unite: to *link* arms. **5** *n.* A sausage in a string of sausages.

link·age [ling'kij] *n.* **1** The act of linking. **2** The condition of being linked. **3** A system of links.

linking verb A verb that connects the subject of a sentence to a noun, pronoun, or adjective that refers to the subject. *Is* and *feel* are linking verbs in "She is our new mayor" and "I feel happy."

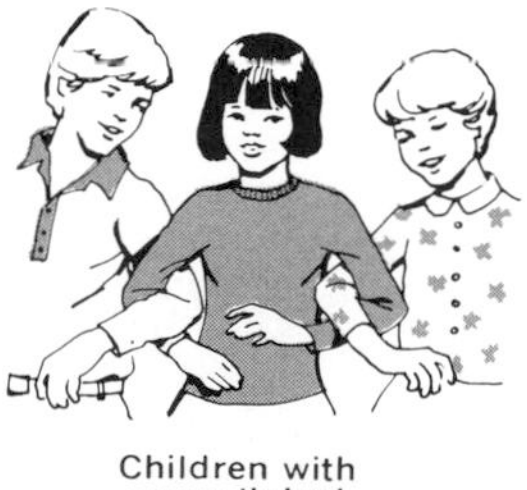

Children with arms linked

links [lingks] *n.pl.* A golf course.

lin·net [lin'it] *n.* A small songbird of Europe, Asia, and Africa, often caged.

li·no·le·um [li·nō′lē·əm] *n.* A floor covering made by pressing a mixture of ground cork and linseed oil on canvas or burlap.
Li·no·type [lī′nə·tīp′] *n.* A machine for setting type, operated from a keyboard and producing each line in the form of a single metal slug: a trademark.
lin·seed [lin′sēd′] *n.* Flaxseed.
linseed oil A yellowish oil obtained from flaxseed, used in paints, printing inks, and linoleum.
lin·sey-wool·sey [lin′zē·wo͝ol′zē] *n.* A coarse cloth woven of linen and wool or cotton and wool.
lint [lint] *n.* **1** A soft material made by scraping linen, used to dress wounds. **2** Bits of thread and fluff from yarn or fabric.
lin·tel [lin′təl] *n.* The horizontal part above the opening of a door or window, supporting the wall above it.

Lintel

li·on [lī′ən] *n.* **1** A large, tawny, powerful animal related to the cat, found in Africa and SW Asia. The adult male lion has a shaggy mane. **2** A person of noble courage and great strength. **3** A celebrity.
li·on·ess [lī′ən·is] *n.* A female lion.
li·on·heart·ed [lī′ən·här′·tid] *adj.* Having great courage. **—li′on·heart′·ed·ness** *n.*

Lion

li·on·ize [lī′ə·nīz′] *v.* **li·on·ized, li·on·iz·ing** To regard or treat as famous; shower with attention and respect.
lip [lip] **1** *n.* One of the two folds of flesh that border the mouth. **2** *n.* Any rim or edge, as of an opening, cavity, or container: the *lip* of a cup. **3** *adj.* Merely spoken; insincere, as in **lip service,** devotion or regard expressed in words but not really felt or acted upon. **4** *n.* One of the protruding parts formed by the division of the corolla or calyx of certain plants, such as the orchid or snapdragon. **5** *n. slang* Impudent or disrespectful replies; back talk. **—button one's lip** *slang* To stop talking. **—keep a stiff upper lip** To be brave in a time of trouble.
lip·ase [lip′ās′ *or* lī′pās′] *n.* A digestive enzyme that breaks down fats.
lip reading The act or skill of finding out what someone is saying by watching the movement of the person's lips, used especially by the deaf.
lip·stick [lip′stik′] *n.* A stick of waxy cosmetic, usually in a tube, used to color the lips.
liq·ue·fac·tion [lik′wə·fak′shən] *n.* **1** The process of becoming liquid. **2** The condition of being liquid.
liq·ue·fy [lik′wə·fī′] *v.* **liq·ue·fied, liq·ue·fy·ing** To make or become liquid.
li·queur [li·kûr′] *n.* A strong, sweet, flavored alcoholic liquor: cherry *liqueur.*
liq·uid [lik′wid] **1** *n.* A substance that flows more or less freely and may be poured from its container, as water or oil; fluid that is not a gas. **2** *adj.* Able to flow. **3** *adj.* Graceful and flowing. **4** *adj.* Sweet and clear. **5** *adj.* Readily converted into cash: *liquid* assets.
liquid air Air changed into a liquid by great compression and cooling.
liq·ui·date [lik′wə·dāt′] *v.* **liq·ui·dat·ed, liq·ui·dat·ing** **1** To settle, as debts. **2** To settle accounts and finish up the operation of. **3** To put to death; kill or have killed: The dictator *liquidated* his rivals. **—liq′ui·da′tion** *n.*
li·quid·i·ty [li·kwid′ə·tē] *n.* The condition or quality of being liquid.
liquid measure A unit or system of units for measuring liquids.
liquid oxygen Oxygen in liquid form, used to burn with fuels in rocket engines, produced by compressing gaseous oxygen and then cooling it.
liq·uor [lik′ər] *n.* **1** An alcoholic drink, especially a distilled spirit, as whisky or rum. **2** Any liquid, as broth or juice.
li·ra [lir′ə] *n., pl.* **li·re** [lir′ā] or **li·ras** The basic unit of money in Italy.
lisle [līl] *n.* **1** A fine twisted cotton thread or a fabric made from it. **2** *adj. use: lisle* socks.
lisp [lisp] **1** *n.* A speech defect in which the sounds of *s* and *z* are pronounced like *th* and *t͟h,* as "yeth" for "yes" and "eat͟hy" for "easy." **2** *v.* To say or speak with a lisp.
lis·some or **lis·som** [lis′əm] *adj.* Lithe.
list[1] [list] **1** *n.* An itemized series, as of names or words, usually set down in a certain order. **2** *v.* To make a list of or enter in a list.
list[2] [list] **1** *v.* To lean or tilt to one side: said about a ship. **2** *n.* Such a lean or tilt.
list[3] [list] *v.* To listen or listen to: used mostly in poems.
lis·ten [lis′(ə)n] *v.* To pay attention so as to hear or understand what is heard: to *listen* to a song. **—listen in** **1** To listen to a radio program: There were millions of people *listening in* and the performers were extremely nervous. **2** To eavesdrop. **—lis′ten·er** *n.*

Listing ship

list·ing [lis′ting] *n.* **1** The act of making or including in a list or itemized series. **2** An entry in such a list. **3** A list.
list·less [list′lis] *adj.* Lacking energy or interest in anything. **—list′less·ly** *adv.* **—list′less·ness** *n.*
list price The price of something, as stated in a published or advertised listing, before any reduction is made through discounts.
lists [lists] *n.pl.* The field where knights fought in medieval tournaments. **—enter the lists** To engage in a contest or controversy.
lit[1] [lit] An alternate past tense and past participle of LIGHT[1]: I *lit* the lamp.
lit[2] [lit] An alternate past tense and past participle of LIGHT[2]: The bird *lit* on a rock.
lit. **1** liter(s). **2** literally. **3** literary. **4** literature.

a	add	**i**	it	**o͝o**	took	**oi**	oil
ā	ace	**ī**	ice	**o͞o**	pool	**ou**	pout
â	care	**o**	odd	**u**	up	**ng**	ring
ä	palm	**ō**	open	**û**	burn	**th**	thin
e	end	**ô**	order	**yo͞o**	fuse	**t͟h**	this
ē	equal					**zh**	vision

ə = { a in *above* e in *sicken* i in *possible* / o in *melon* u in *circus* }

lit·a·ny [lit′ə·nē] *n., pl.* **lit·a·nies** A prayer consisting of a series of supplications by the minister with responses by the people.

li·tchi [lē′chē] *n., pl.* **li·tchis** [lē′chēz] **1** The edible fruit of a Chinese tree, consisting of soft, juicy pulp enclosed in a thin shell. Also written **litchi nut. 2** The tree bearing this fruit.

li·ter [lē′tər] *n.* In the metric system, a measure of volume equal to that of one kilogram of water at 4°C, or of 1.0567 quarts liquid measure.

lit·er·a·cy [lit′ər·ə·sē] *n.* The ability to read and write.

lit·er·al [lit′ər·əl] *adj.* **1** Following the exact words and order of an original: a *literal* translation. **2** Based on or following exactly what is said: a *literal* meaning; a *literal* mind. **3** Straightforward; unembellished: the *literal* truth. **—lit′er·al·ly** *adv.*

lit·er·ar·y [lit′ə·rer′ē] *adj.* **1** Having to do with literature. **2** Knowing or devoted to literature. **3** Having literature as a profession.

lit·er·ate [lit′ə·rit] **1** *adj.* Able to read and write. **2** *n.* An educated person.

lit·er·a·ture [lit′ər·ə·chər] *n.* **1** Written works collectively, especially those showing imagination and artistic skill. **2** The writings on a particular subject: medical *literature.* **3** Writing as a profession. **4** *informal* Any printed matter for advertising or publicity: campaign *literature.*

lith. 1 lithograph. **2** lithography.

Lith. 1 Lithuania. **2** Lithuanian.

lithe [lī*th*] *adj.* Supple; limber: *lithe* as a cat.

lith·i·um [lith′ē·əm] *n.* A soft, very reactive metallic element, the lightest of all metals, having numerous uses in industry and medicine.

lith·o·graph [lith′ə·graf′] **1** *n.* A print that is made by lithography. **2** *v.* To produce or reproduce by lithography.

li·thog·ra·phy [li·thog′rə·fē] *n.* The act or process of producing printed matter from a flat stone or a metal plate on which a drawing or design has been made. **—li·thog′ra·pher** *n.*

lith·o·sphere [lith′ə·sfir′] *n.* The solid crust of the earth.

Lith·u·a·ni·an [lith′o͞o·ā′nē·ən] **1** *adj.* Of or from Lithuania. **2** *n.* A person born in or living in Lithuania. **3** *n.* The language of Lithuania.

lit·i·gant [lit′ə·gənt] *n.* A person taking part in a lawsuit.

lit·i·gate [lit′i·gāt′] *v.* **lit·i·gat·ed, lit·i·gat·ing 1** To make (something) the subject of a lawsuit. **2** To bring or carry on a lawsuit. **—lit′i·ga′tor** *n.*

lit·i·ga·tion [lit′ə·gā′shən] *n.* **1** The bringing or carrying on of a lawsuit. **2** A lawsuit.

lit·mus [lit′məs] *n.* A dyestuff made from certain lichens. It is turned red by acids and blue by alkalis.

litmus paper Paper dyed with litmus, used to test solutions for acidity or alkalinity.

li·tre [lē′tər] *n. British* A spelling of LITER.

lit·ter [lit′ər] **1** *n.* Scraps or other things strewn about; clutter. **2** *v.* To make untidy or unsightly with litter: to *litter* the sidewalk with trash. **3** *n.* The young brought forth at one birth by a mammal normally having several offspring at a time. **4** *v.* To give birth to (young). **5** *v.* To have a litter. **6** *n.* Something, as straw or hay, spread as bedding for animals. **7** *n.* A stretcher for carrying sick or wounded persons. **8** *n.* A vehicle consisting of a couch on two poles carried by people or animals.

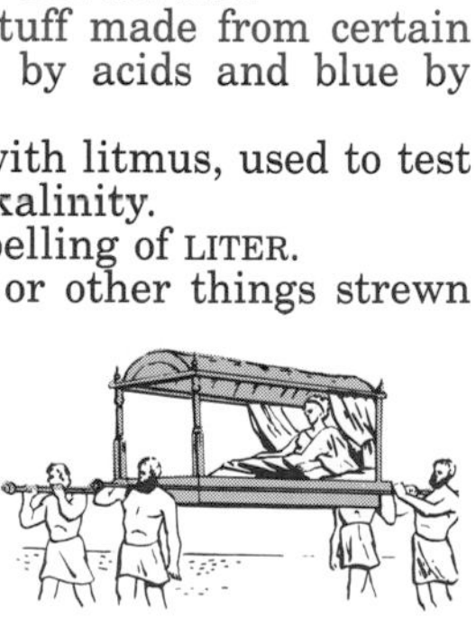
Litter

lit·ter·bag [lit′ər·bag′] *n.* A bag used temporarily to dispose of trash, as in an automobile.

lit·ter·bug [lit′ər·bug′] *n. slang* A person who makes public areas unsightly by leaving discarded things in them.

lit·tle [lit′(ə)l] *adj.* **lit·tler** or for defs. 3 and 6 **less** or **less·er, lit·tlest** or for defs. 3 and 6 **least,** *n., adv.* **less, least 1** *adj.* Not big; small: a *little* dog. **2** *n.* A small amount: Give me a *little.* **3** *adj., adv.* Not much: *little* power; He sleeps *little.* **4** *n.* A very small amount: *Little* can be done. **5** *adv.* Not at all: She *little* suspects what happened. **6** *adj.* Short or brief: in a *little* time. **7** *n.* A short time or distance: We walked a *little.* **8** *adj.* Trivial: *little* details. **8** *adj.* Petty or mean: a *little* mind. **—little by little** Gradually. **—make little of** To treat or regard as of no importance. **—not a little** Quite a bit; much: *not a little* influence. **—think little of** To regard as unimportant or worthless. **—lit′tle·ness** *n.*

Little Bear The constellation Ursa Minor.

Little Dipper A group of stars in Ursa Minor having an outline resembling a dipper (def. 2).

little finger The smallest finger of each hand, located farthest from the thumb.

Little League An international program of baseball for teams whose players are not over the age of twelve.

little slam Slam[3].

little theater 1 A small theater company that regularly produces works either experimental or otherwise unsuited to large commercial theaters. **2** A theater for actors and others who are not professionals.

little toe The smallest and outermost toe of each foot.

li·tur·gic [li·tûr′jik] *adj.* Liturgical.

li·tur·gi·cal [li·tûr′ji·kəl] *adj.* Of or relating to liturgy. **—li·tur′gi·cal·ly** *adv.*

lit·ur·gy [lit′ər·jē] *n., pl.* **lit·ur·gies** In various religions, the form of public worship.

liv·a·ble [liv′ə·bəl] *adj.* **1** Fit or pleasing to live in. **2** Tolerable: *livable* conditions.

live[1] [liv] *v.* **lived, liv·ing 1** To be alive. **2** To remain alive: while I *live.* **3** To pass life in a certain way: to *live* in peace. **4** To enjoy a varied or satisfying life. **5** To reside: We *live* in Maine. **6** To maintain life; feed: Squirrels *live* on nuts, seeds, and berries. **7** To maintain or support oneself: to *live* on one's income. **8** To continue: The custom *lives* on. **9** To put into practice in one's life: to *live* one's beliefs. **—live down** To behave so as to erase the memory of, as a crime or mistake. **—live in** To reside in the home where one is employed. **—live it up** *informal* To indulge oneself freely in pleasure and luxuries. **—live up to** To satisfy or fulfill: The novel fully *lived up to* my expectations. **—live with** To bear with; tolerate or endure.

live[2] [līv] *adj.* **1** Having life; alive. **2** Energetic; dynamic: a *live* personality. **3** Of present interest and importance: a *live* issue. **4** Burning or glowing: a *live* coal. **5** Charged with electricity: a *live* wire. **6** Capable of being exploded: a *live* firecracker. **7** Actually being performed as it is being broadcast: a *live* show.

live·a·ble [liv′ə·bəl] *adj.* A spelling of LIVABLE.

live·li·hood [līv′lē·hŏŏd′] *n.* The means by which one supports one's life: How do you earn your *livelihood?*
live·long [liv′lông′] *adj.* Whole; entire: the *livelong* day.
live·ly [līv′lē] *adj.* **live·li·er, live·li·est,** *adv.* 1 *adj.* Full of life; spirited: a *lively* song; a *lively* dancer. 2 *adj.* Full of activity or excitement: a *lively* season. 3 *adj.* Bright; cheerful: *lively* colors. 4 *adj.* Full of bounce: a *lively* ball. 5 *adv.* Briskly: Step *lively.* **—live′li·ness** *n.*
liv·en [lī′vən] *v.* To make or become lively.
live oak Any of several evergreen oak trees of the southern United States or western North America.
liv·er[1] [liv′ər] *n.* 1 A large gland in humans and other vertebrates that produces bile and regulates digestive processes. 2 Food prepared from or consisting of animal liver.

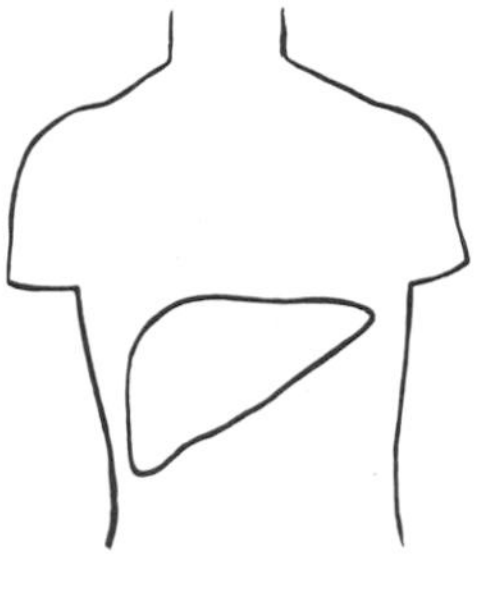
Liver

liv·er[2] [liv′ər] *n.* 1 A person who lives in a certain manner: a quiet *liver.* 2 A dweller.
liv·er·ied [liv′ər·ēd] *adj.* Dressed in livery.
liv·er·wort [liv′ər·wûrt′] *n.* 1 A small, mosslike plant found in shady places. 2 A hepatica.
liv·er·wurst [liv′ər·wûrst′] *n.* A sausage made mainly of chopped liver, often mixed with pork.
liv·er·y [liv′ər·ē] *n., pl.* **liv·er·ies** 1 The uniform worn by servants. 2 The stabling and care of horses for pay.
livery stable A stable where horses and vehicles are cared for or kept for hire.
lives [līvz] Plural of LIFE.
live·stock [līv′stok′] *n.* Domestic farm animals, as horses, cattle, sheep, and pigs.
live wire 1 A wire carrying an electric current. 2 *informal* A person who is very active, spirited, or aggressive.
liv·id [liv′id] *adj.* 1 Purplish, bluish, or ashen, as from a bruise or anger. 2 *informal* Extremely angry. **—liv′id·ly** *adv.* **—liv′id·ness** *n.*
liv·ing [liv′ing] 1 *adj.* Not dead; alive. 2 *n.* A being alive. 3 *n. use:* Those who are or were alive: The *living* rebuilt the town. 4 *adj.* Still existing or used: within *living* memory. 5 *n.* Manner or conduct of life: virtuous *living.* 6 *adj.* Of or having to do with everyday life: *living* conditions. 7 *n.* A livelihood. 8 *adj.* Used or intended for a livelihood: a *living* wage. 9 *adj.* Likelife: You are the *living* image of your cousin.
living room A room in a house for talking, reading, entertainment, and general use.
living standard Another term for STANDARD OF LIVING.
living wage A salary large enough to provide the necessities of life but few if any luxuries.
living will A will (def. 7) that states a person's wish not to have life prolonged by artificial medical means if the person becomes so ill or disabled that recovery is impossible.
liz·ard [liz′ərd] *n.* Any of certain reptiles, most of them small, with slender, scaly bodies, long tails, and four legs.
lla·ma [lä′mə] *n.* A South American beast of burden, like a small camel with no hump.

Llama

lla·no [lä′nō] *n., pl.* **lla·nos** A flat, treeless plain of Spanish America.
LM lunar module.
lo [lō] *interj.* See! behold!: seldom used today.
load [lōd] 1 *n.* What a person or thing is carrying; burden. 2 *n.* The quantity usually carried at one time, taken as a unit: to deliver a *load* of gravel. 3 *v.* To put in or on something for carrying: to *load* furniture on a truck. 4 *v.* To put a load in or on: to *load* a ship, aircraft, or other conveyance. 5 *v.* To take on a load: The ship was *loading* at the pier. 6 *v.* To burden or overburden: The president is *loaded* with many responsibilities. 7 *v.* To supply abundantly or excessively: They *loaded* the winner with honors. 8 *n.* The charge or ammunition, as for a firearm or shell. 9 *v.* To fill with something necessary for working: to *load* a pistol with cartridges or a camera with film. 10 *n.* The electricity supplied by a generator. 11 *n.* (*pl.*) *informal* Lots: *loads* of fun. **—load′er** *n.*
load·ed [lō′did] *adj.* 1 Bearing or having a load. 2 Unfair because prejudiced or intended to embarrass or entrap: a *loaded* question. 3 *slang* Drunk. 4 *slang* Wealthy.
load·star [lōd′stär′] *n.* Another spelling of LODESTAR.
load·stone [lōd′stōn′] *n.* Another spelling of LODESTONE.
loaf[1] [lōf] *n., pl.* **loaves** 1 A shaped portion of bread baked in a single piece. 2 Any shaped mass of food: a meat *loaf;* a sugar *loaf.*
loaf[2] [lōf] *v.* To do nothing; idle.
loaf·er [lōf′ər] *n.* 1 An idler. 2 An informal shoe like a moccasin but with a sole and heel.
loam [lōm] *n.* Rich soil made up of sand, clay, and much humus. **—loam′y** *adj.*
loan [lōn] 1 *n.* The act of lending: a *loan* of a book. 2 *n.* Something lent, especially a sum of money. 3 *v. U.S.* To lend. ◆ *Loan,* as a verb, is not accepted by the British but is standard in the U.S., especially in business English.
loan shark *informal* A person whose occupation is lending money at illegally high rates of interest; usurer.
loath [lōth] *adj.* Unwilling: I'm *loath* to go.
loathe [lō*th*] *v.* **loathed, loath·ing** To detest; abhor: to *loathe* hot weather.
loath·ing [lō′*th*ing] *n.* Extreme dislike or disgust: a *loathing* for greasy food.

a	add	**i**	it	**ŏŏ**	took	**oi**	oil
ā	ace	**ī**	ice	**ōō**	pool	**ou**	pout
â	care	**o**	odd	**u**	up	**ng**	ring
ä	palm	**ō**	open	**û**	burn	**th**	thin
e	end	**ô**	order	**yōō**	fuse	***th***	this
ē	equal					**zh**	vision

ə = a in *above* e in *sicken* i in *possible* o in *melon* u in *circus*

L

loath·some [lōth'səm] *adj.* Detestable; repulsive; abhorrent. **—loath'some·ness** *n.*

loaves [lōvz] Plural of LOAF[1].

lob [lob] *v.* **lobbed, lob·bing,** *n.* **1** *v.* To hit (a ball) in a high, arching curve, as in tennis. **2** *n.* A ball hit in a high, arching curve, as in tennis. **3** *v.* To throw or toss (a ball) slowly.

lo·bar [lō'bər *or* lō'bär'] *adj.* **1** Of or having to do with a lobe. **2** Affecting one or more lobes of the lung: *lobar* pneumonia.

lob·by [lob'ē] *n., pl.* **lob·bies,** *v.* **lob·bied, lob·by·ing** **1** *n.* An entrance hall, vestibule, or public lounge. **2** *v. U.S.* To try to influence legislators in favor of some special interest. **3** *v. U.S.* To work for or against (a bill) by lobbying. **4** *n. U.S.* A group that lobbies: a farmers' *lobby.*

lob·by·ist [lob'ē·ist] *n.* A person who lobbies.

lobe [lōb] *n.* A curved or rounded projecting part, as of a leaf or an organ of the body: an ear *lobe;* a *lobe* of the lung.

lobed [lōbd] *adj.* Having a lobe or lobes.

lo·be·li·a [lō·bē'lē·ə *or* lō·bēl'yə] *n.* A plant with flower clusters in any of several colors.

lob·lol·ly pine [lob'lol'ē] **1** A pine tree of the southern U.S. with long needles and heavy bark. **2** Its coarse wood.

lob·ster [lob'stər] *n.* **1** A large crustacean with a pair of pincers in front, and four pairs of legs behind them. **2** Its flesh, eaten as food.

Lobster

lobster pot A cagelike trap to catch lobsters.

lo·cal [lō'kəl] **1** *adj.* Of or having to do with a neighborhood, region, or relatively small area: the *local* people. **2** *adj.* Affecting only a certain part of the body: a *local* anesthetic. **3** *adj.* Stopping at all or almost all stations along its run. **4** *n.* A means of public transportation, as a train or bus, that does this. **5** *n.* A branch or chapter of an organization, as a trade union.

lo·cale [lō·kal'] *n.* The setting of an event or dramatic action; scene.

lo·cal·ism [lō'kəl·iz'əm] *n.* A local custom, as a word or expression, not used elsewhere.

lo·cal·i·ty [lō·kal'ə·tē] *n., pl.* **lo·cal·i·ties** A certain place, area, region, or the like.

lo·cal·ize [lō'kəl·īz'] *v.* **lo·cal·ized, lo·cal·iz·ing** To make or keep local; limit to a particular place: to keep a forest fire *localized.*

lo·cal·ly [lō'kə·lē] *adv.* **1** In a local area. **2** In only a few places; not everywhere.

lo·cate [lō'kāt'] *v.* **lo·cat·ed, lo·cat·ing** **1** To place; situate: The phone is *located* here. **2** *U.S. informal* To settle: to *locate* in Boston. **3** To discover the position of; find: to *locate* a missing person. **4** To show or indicate the position of.

lo·ca·tion [lō·kā'shən] *n.* **1** A place or site: a good *location* for a camp. **2** The act of locating: The *location* of the stolen jewels took a month. **3** The state of being located.

loch [lok] *n.* A Scottish word for: **1** A lake. **2** A bay or arm of the sea.

lo·ci [lō'sī] Plural of LOCUS.

lock[1] [lok] **1** *n.* A device for fastening something, as a door or safe. It is usually opened only by a key with a special shape. **2** *v.* To fasten with a lock. **3** *v.* To become locked. **4** *v.* To shut in or out; keep: to *lock* money in a safe; A barge was *locked* in the ice; I was *locked* out of the house. **5** *n.* Anything that fastens, secures, or holds something else in place. **6** *v.* To join, link, or jam: to *lock* bumpers. **7** *n.* An enclosed section of a canal in which ships can be raised or lowered by letting water in or out. **8** *n.* The mechanism that fires the charge of a gun. **—lock out** To keep (employees) from work by means of a lockout. **—lock, stock, and barrel** Affecting all parts; completely. **—lock up** **1** To secure from entry by means of a lock or locks. **2** To imprison (a person) following an arrest.

lock[2] [lok] *n.* **1** A curl or strand of hair. **2** A small tuft, as one of cotton or wool.

lock·er [lok'ər] *n.* **1** A closet or cabinet, often metal, and fastened by a lock: a gym *locker.* **2** A refrigerated cabinet or compartment for storing frozen food.

locker room A room with lockers for storing clothing and other belongings, especially those of athletes when they dress for a sports event.

lock·et [lok'it] *n.* A small case for a picture or keepsake, worn on a chain around the neck.

lock·jaw [lok'jô'] *n.* A form of tetanus causing rigid locking of the jaws.

lock·out [lok'out'] *n.* The closing of a business by an employer in order to make employees agree to certain terms.

lock·smith [lok'smith'] *n.* A person who makes and repairs locks and keys.

lock·up [lok'up'] *n.* A jail or prison cell.

lo·co·mo·tion [lō'kə·mō'shən] *n.* The act or power of moving from one place to another.

lo·co·mo·tive [lō'kə·mō'tiv] **1** *n.* An engine that moves by its own power, used to pull trains on a railroad. **2** *adj.* Of, capable of, or used in moving by its own power.

lo·co·weed [lō'kō·wēd'] *n.* Any of several plants of the western United States that cause chronic poisoning in horses, cattle, and sheep.

lo·cus [lō'kəs] *n., pl.* **lo·ci** [lō'sī] **1** A place; locality; area. **2** In mathematics, the set of all the points that satisfy a given set of conditions. A circle is the locus of all the points in a plane that are at a certain distance from a given point.

lo·cust [lō'kəst] *n.* **1** An insect like a grasshopper that often moves in swarms and destroys crops. **2** A cicada. **3** A tree having compound leaves made up of leaflets, and clusters of fragrant, white flowers.

lo·cu·tion [lō·kyōō'shən] *n.* **1** A particular word or expression, especially one that reflects a characteristic style of speech or writing. **2** The style of expression of a speaker or writer.

lode [lōd] *n.* A vein of ore of a metal.

lode·star [lōd'stär'] *n.* A guiding star, especially the North Star.

lode·stone [lōd'stōn'] *n.* A naturally magnetized piece of magnetite, an iron ore.

lodge [loj] *n., v.* **lodged, lodg·ing** **1** *n.* A small dwelling, as a house or cabin, where a person may stay, as for a vacation. **2** *n.* An inn or hotel. **3** *v.* To house for a time: to *lodge* a guest. **4** *v.* To live temporarily, especially as a paying guest. **5** *n.* The shelter or den of a beaver, otter, or certain other animals. **6** *n.* A local branch of any of certain societies: a Masonic *lodge.* **7** *n.* Its meeting place. **8** *v.* To place or implant firmly: to *lodge* a stake in the ground. **9** *v.* To become fixed or embedded: The idea had *lodged* in my mind. **10** *v.* To submit or enter formally: to *lodge* a complaint with the police.

lodge·ment [loj′mənt] *n.* A spelling of LODGMENT.

lodg·er [loj′ər] *n.* A person who lives in one or more rented rooms in someone else's house.

lodg·ing [loj′ing] *n.* **1** A temporary place to live. **2** (*pl.*) Living quarters consisting of a rented room or rooms in someone else's house.

lodg·ment [loj′mənt] *n.* **1** The act of lodging. **2** The condition of being lodged. **3** Something lodged or deposited: a *lodgment* of driftwood on a shoal.

lo·ess [lō′is] *n.* A yellowish loam deposited by wind in some places.

loft [lôft] **1** *n.* An attic or other space just under a roof. **2** *n.* An upper story of a warehouse, storehouse, or factory. **3** *n.* An upper section or gallery, as one in a church or theater. **4** *v.* To hit or send high up: to *loft* a ball over the trees.

loft·y [lôf′tē] *adj.* **loft·i·er, loft·i·est** **1** Very high. **2** Exalted: *lofty* poetry. **3** Proud; arrogant. **—loft′i·ly** *adv.* **—loft′i·ness** *n.*

log^1 [lôg *or* log] *n., v.* **logged, log·ging** **1** *n.* Part of the trunk or a limb of a felled tree, stripped of branches. **2** *adj. use*: a *log* cabin. **3** *v.* To cut the timber on (land). **4** *v.* To cut (trees) into logs. **5** *n.* A daily record of a ship's voyage. **6** *n.* Any record of operation or progress: the *log* of an airplane flight. **7** *n.* A device used to measure a ship's speed through the water. **—log′ger** *n.*

log^2 [lôg *or* log] *n.* A logarithm.

lo·gan·ber·ry [lō′gən·ber′ē] *n., pl.* **lo·gan·ber·ries** **1** A prickly plant related to the red raspberry and the blackberry. **2** Its edible, purple berry.

log·a·rithm [lôg′ə·rith·əm *or* log′ə·rith·əm] *n.* The exponent that must be applied to a fixed number, usually 10, in order to make some other number. $100 = 10^2$, so $\log 100 = 2$. $125 = 10^{2.09691}$, so $\log 125 = 2.09691$. Using logarithms simplifies calculation since $\log a + \log b = \log ab$, and $\log a - \log b = \log a/b$. ◆ *Logarithm* comes from two Greek words, one meaning *word* or *ratio* and the other meaning *number.*

log·a·rith·mic [lôg′ə·rith′mik *or* log′ə·rith′mik] *adj.* Of or having to do with a logarithm.

log·book [lôg′bŏŏk′ *or* log′bŏŏk′] *n.* The book in which a record, as of a voyage, is entered.

loge [lōzh] *n.* **1** A box in a theater. **2** The front section of the mezzanine of a theater.

log·ger [lô′gər *or* log′ər] *n.* **1** A person whose occupation is logging; lumberjack. **2** A machine for loading or hauling logs.

log·ger·head [lôg′ər·hed′ *or* log′ər·hed′] *n.* **1** A large sea turtle found in tropical Atlantic waters. **2** A stupid person; blockhead. **—at loggerheads** Quarreling.

log·gi·a [loj′(ē·)ə] *n.* A roofed gallery or arcade open to air on one or more sides.

log·ging [lôg′ing *or* log′ing] *n.* The business or job of felling timber and getting the logs out of the woods.

log·ic [loj′ik] *n.* **1** The science of reasoning and of proving. **2** The proper rules of reasoning. **3** Sound reasoning. **4** A way or method of reasoning: poor *logic.*

log·i·cal [loj′ə·kəl] *adj.* **1** Of or based on logic: a *logical* argument. **2** Using clear reasoning: a *logical* writer. **3** Reasonably to be expected: The *logical* response was to offer our help. **—log′i·cal·ly** *adv.*

lo·gi·cian [lō·jish′ən] *n.* A person skilled in logic.

lo·gis·tic [lō·jis′tik] *adj.* Of or dealing with logistics. **—lo·gis′ti·cal** *adj.* **—lo·gis′ti·cal·ly** *adv.*

lo·gis·tics [lō·jis′tiks] *n.* **1** The branch of military science that deals with the acquiring and handling of troops and equipment for a military operation, including the details of supplying, maintaining, replacing, and moving them. **2** The handling of details for any operation. ◆ See -ICS.

log·jam [lôg′jam′] *n.* **1** A pile of logs that become jammed in a waterway and are unable to move. **2** Any obstacle that prevents progress in transacting business.

LO·GO [lō′gō] *n.* A computer programming language designed for schoolchildren.

log·roll·ing [lôg′rōl′ing *or* log′rōl′ing] *n. U.S.* **1** A contest in which two people balance on a floating log and roll it until one falls off. **2** The trading of votes and influence between politicians.

lo·gy [lō′gē] *adj.* **lo·gi·er, lo·gi·est** *U.S.* Dull; lethargic: Hot weather makes me *logy.*

-logy A suffix meaning: **1** The study or science of, as in *biology.* **2** A form of written or spoken expression, as in *phraseology.* **3** A group or collection, as in *trilogy.*

loin [loin] *n.* **1** (*usually pl.*) The part of the back on each side of the backbone between the lower ribs and the hipbone. **2** Such a section of meat, with the flank removed: a *loin* of beef.

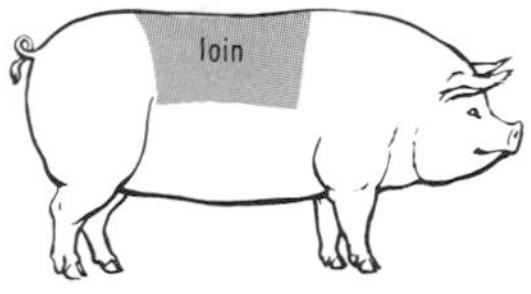

loin·cloth [loin′klôth′] *n.* A piece of cloth worn around the hips and between the legs.

loi·ter [loi′tər] *v.* **1** To linger or dawdle. **2** To pass idly: to *loiter* time away. **—loi′ter·er** *n.*

Lo·ki [lō′kē] *n.* In Norse myths, the god of mischief and destruction.

loll [lol] *v.* **1** To lounge: to *loll* around the house. **2** To hang loosely; droop. **3** To allow to droop: The dog *lolled* out its tongue.

lol·li·pop or **lol·ly·pop** [lol′ē·pop′] *n.* A lump or piece of candy on the end of a stick.

London broil Flank steak, broiled and sliced across the grain in thin strips.

lone [lōn] *adj.* Single; alone: a *lone* bird.

lone·ly [lōn′lē] *adj.* **lone·li·er, lone·li·est** **1** Feeling alone and longing for the presence of friends. **2** Without others nearby; solitary. **3** Deserted; desolate. **—lone′li·ness** *n.*

lon·er [lō′nər] *n. informal* A person who avoids the company of others.

lone·some [lōn′səm] *adj.* **1** Feeling lonely. **2** Causing or expressing loneliness.

a add	**i** it	**ŏŏ** took	**oi** oil
ā ace	**ī** ice	**ōō** pool	**ou** pout
â care	**o** odd	**u** up	**ng** ring
ä palm	**ō** open	**û** burn	**th** thin
e end	**ô** order	**yōō** fuse	**th** this
ē equal			**zh** vision

ə = a in *above* e in *sicken* i in *possible* o in *melon* u in *circus*

lone wolf *informal* A loner.
long[1] [lông] 1 *adj.* Extending quite far between ends, in space or time: a *long* tunnel. 2 *adj.* Having a specified extent or duration: ten miles *long*; three days *long*. 3 *adv.* For a long time: an improvement *long* needed. 4 *adv.* At a time far from another time indicated: *long* ago; *long* since. 5 *n.* A long time: The storm will not last for *long*. 6 *adv.* Throughout the whole duration of: It rained all day *long*. 7 *adj.* Taking rather a long time to sound, as the vowel sounds in *ace* [ās], *ice* [īs], and *hope* [hōp]. **—as long as** or **so long as** 1 For or during the time that. 2 Seeing that; since. 3 Provided; if: *As long as* they come, I'll be happy. **—before long** Soon. **—no longer** Not now, as before; not any more. **—so long** Good-bye.
long[2] [lông] *v.* To want greatly; yearn.
long. longitude.
long·boat [lông′bōt′] *n.* The longest boat carried by a sailing ship.
long·bow [lông′bō′] *n.* A large bow for shooting arrows, formerly used as a weapon.
long-dis·tance [lông′dis′təns] *adj.* 1 Connecting distant points: a *long-distance* telephone call. 2 Covering a rather long distance: a *long-distance* runner.
long division In arithmetic, the division of one number by another, specifically by one having more than one digit, in which each step is written down rather than merely calculated in the mind.
lon·gev·i·ty [lon·jev′ə·tē] *n.* Long life.
long face A facial expression of displeasure or sadness.
long·hair [lông′hâr′] *n. informal* 1 A person much interested in the arts, especially classical or serious contemporary music. 2 A person having mostly intellectual interests. 3 A person who has long hair, especially a hippie.
long·hand [lông′hand′] *n.* Writing in which the letters of each word are joined.
long·horn [lông′hôrn′] *n.* One of a former breed of beef cattle with long horns.

Longhorn

long·ing [lông′ing] *n.* Great desire; yearning: a *longing* for peace. **—long′ing·ly** *adv.*
lon·gi·tude [lon′jə·t(y)ōōd′] *n.* Distance east or west of the prime meridian, running through Greenwich, England, measured as an angle at the earth's axis and expressed in degrees or units of time.

Lines of longitude

lon·gi·tu·di·nal [lon′jə·t(y)ōō′də·nəl] *adj.* 1 Of or having to do with longitude or length. 2 Running lengthwise: *longitudinal* bars.
long jump In athletics, a contest to see who can jump the farthest rather than the highest.
long-lived [lông′līvd′ *or* lông′livd′] *adj.* Living or lasting for a long time.
long-play·ing [lông′plā′ing] *adj.* Having small grooves and played at a speed of 33 1/3 revolutions per minute: said about a phonograph record.
long-range [lông′rānj′] *adj.* 1 Designed to shoot or travel over a long distance: a *long-range* missile. 2 Covering a long span of time, usually partly in the future: *long-range* plans.
long·shore·man [lông′shôr′mən] *n., pl.* **long·shore·men** [lông′shôr′mən] A person who loads and unloads ships; stevedore.
long shot 1 A contestant whose chance of winning is considered to be very small. 2 An undertaking that involves great risk but also the possibility of great gain if successful.
long-stand·ing [lông′stan′ding] *adj.* Existing for a long time; enduring.
long-suf·fer·ing [lông′suf′ər·ing] *adj.* Quietly enduring pain or misfortune for a long time.
long-term [lông′tûrm′] *adj.* 1 Extending over a long period. 2 In finance, coming due (as payment) after a long period: a *long-term* loan.
long·time [lông′tīm′] *adj.* Long-standing.
long-wind·ed [lông′win′did] *adj.* Long and tiresome in speech or writing.
look [lŏŏk] 1 *v.* To turn or direct the eyes to see or try to see something. 2 *v.* To keep the eyes fixed on: to *look* someone in the face. 3 *n.* The act of looking: a *look* at a picture. 4 *v.* To face in a certain direction: The house *looks* on the park. 5 *v.* To turn one's attention; consider: *Look* at the applicant's record. 6 *v.* To search: *Look* for the ball. 7 *v.* To seem: It *looks* safe. 8 *n.* An aspect or expression: a saintly *look*. 9 *n.* (*often pl.*) *informal* General appearance: I like the *looks* of this place. 10 *n.* (*pl.*) *informal* Personal appearance: good *looks*. **—look after** To take care of. **—look back** To think about the past; recall. **—look down on** To despise. **—look for** To expect. **—look forward to** To anticipate with pleasure. **—look in on** To visit briefly. **—look into** To examine or inquire about. **—look on** 1 To be a spectator. 2 To regard: I *look on* this novel as a great work. **—look out** To be careful; watch out. **—look out for** 1 To be on guard against. 2 To protect or support. **—look over** To inspect. **—look to** To regard (a person) as a source of something needed. **—look up** 1 To search for and find, as in a dictionary or file. 2 *informal* To locate and pay a visit to: to *look up* an old friend. 3 *informal* To become better. **—look up to** To have great respect for.
look·er-on [lŏŏk′ər·on′] *n., pl.* **look·ers-on** A person watching but not taking part.
looking glass A glass mirror.
look·out [lŏŏk′out′] *n.* 1 A close watch: Be on the *lookout* for their arrival. 2 The place where such a watch is kept. 3 A watchman; sentry.
loom[1] [lōōm] *n.* A machine on which thread or yarn is woven into cloth.
loom[2] [lōōm] *v.* To appear indistinctly but seeming large or ominous: The mountains *loomed* up in the distance; Trouble *looms* ahead.

An Indian hand loom

loon[1] [lōōn] *n.* A web-footed diving bird resembling a duck, but with a pointed bill and a weird, laughing cry.
loon[2] [lōōn] *n.* A stupid or crazy person.

loon·y [lōō'nē] *adj.* **loon·i·er, loon·i·est** *slang* Insane; crazy.

loop [lōōp] 1 *n.* The shape of a curved line that crosses back over itself, as in a written *h.* 2 *v.* To make a loop or loops: The gull *looped* through the sky. 3 *n.* Something having the shape of a loop: a *loop* of string. 4 *v.* To form a loop in or of: to *loop* a cord. 5 *n.* A round or oval opening: The horse caught its leg in a *loop* of the rope. 6 *v.* To fasten or encircle with a loop: to *loop* a halter around a post. 7 *n.* In a computer program, the repetition of a set of instructions until certain specified conditions are satisfied.

loop·hole [lōōp'hōl'] *n.* 1 A small hole or slit in a wall, to look or shoot through. 2 A means of getting out of the intended meaning of a law or agreement: The lawyer found a *loophole* and was able to avoid paying the tax.

loose [lōōs] *adj.* **loos·er, loos·est,** *v.* **loosed, loos·ing,** *adv.* 1 *adj.* Not fastened or confined: *loose* hair. 2 *v.* To release: to *loose* an arrow. 3 *adj.* Not drawn tight; slack: a *loose* knot. 4 *adj.* Not firmly fitted, embedded, or packed: a *loose* window; a *loose* tooth. 5 *v.* To make less tight; loosen: to *loose* a knot. 6 *adj.* Not bound or fastened together: *loose* sheets of paper. 7 *adj.* Not in a package or container: *loose* salt. 8 *adv.* In a loose manner: to hang *loose.* 9 *adj.* Immoral: *loose* living. 10 *adj.* Not precise: a *loose* translation. **—at loose ends** In a confused state. **—break loose** To become free. **—cast loose** To untie, as a boat from a dock. **—let loose** 1 To set free. 2 To release one's hold. 3 To express anger by means of speech. **—on the loose** *informal* Free of confinement or ties. **—set loose** or **turn loose** To set free. **—loose'ly** *adv.* **—loose'ness** *n.* ◆ The verbs *loose* [lōōs] and *lose* [lōōz] both mean to part with. To *loose* is to release intentionally: You can *loose* your dog for a run in the woods by taking off its leash. To *lose* is to mislay or be unable to find: If your dog runs too far away, you may *lose* your pet. *Loose* is more commonly used as an adjective: a *loose* hinge. *Lose* is always a verb.

loose-jointed [lōōs'join'tid] *adj.* 1 Having joints not closely fitted. 2 Free or limber in bodily movement.

loose-leaf [lōōs'lēf'] *adj.* Designed so that pages can be easily inserted or removed.

loos·en [lōō'sən] *v.* To make or become loose or looser: to *loosen* a belt.

loot [lōōt] 1 *n.* Spoils; booty. 2 *v.* To rob; plunder. **—loot'er** *n.*

lop[1] [lop] *v.* **lopped, lop·ping** 1 To cut off: to *lop* off the sleeves at the elbows. 2 To cut or trim the branches from: to *lop* a tree.

lop[2] [lop] *v.* **lopped, lop·ping,** *adj.* 1 *v.* To droop or flop. 2 *adj.* Drooping: *lop* ears.

lope [lōp] *v.* **loped, lop·ing,** *n.* 1 *v.* To run with a steady swinging stride or gallop. 2 *n.* Such a stride or gallop.

lop·sid·ed [lop'sī'did] *adj.* Heavier, larger, or sagging on one side. **—lop'sid'ed·ly** *adv.* **lop'sid'ed·ness** *n.*

lo·qua·cious [lō·kwā'shəs] *adj.* Talkative.

lo·quac·i·ty [lō·kwas'ə·tē] *n.* A tendency to talk a great deal.

lo·ran [lôr'an] *n.* An electronic device that uses signals from two radio stations to enable a navigator to determine the exact location of a ship or airplane.

lord [lôrd] 1 *n.* A ruler or master. 2 *n.* A member of the House of Lords. 3 *n.* A feudal landlord. 4 *v.* To rule as or like a lord, especially in the expression **lord it over,** to treat in a domineering or arrogant way.

Lord [lôrd] *n.* 1 God. 2 Jesus. 3 A title used in Great Britain in speaking to or of a nobleman who is a baron or higher. 4 (*pl.*) The House of Lords.

lord·ly [lôrd'lē] *adj.* **lord·li·er, lord·li·est** 1 Suitable for a lord; splendid. 2 Arrogant; haughty: *lordly* airs.

lord·ship [lôrd'ship'] *n.* 1 The power of authority of a lord. 2 (*often written* **Lordship**) The title used in speaking of or addressing a lord when the person's name is not used: your *Lordship.*

Lord's Prayer The prayer beginning "Our Father," taught by Christ to his disciples.

Lord's Supper 1 The Last Supper. 2 Holy Communion.

lore [lôr] *n.* 1 Facts or stories about a subject: Scottish *lore;* bird *lore.* 2 Knowledge or learning.

lor·gnette [lôr·nyet'] *n.* A pair of eyeglasses or opera glasses with a handle.

Lorgnette

lorn [lôrn] *adj.* Forlorn: seldom used today.

lor·ry [lôr'ē] *n., pl.* **lor·ries** 1 A low wagon without sides, drawn by a horse. 2 *British* A truck.

lose [lōōz] *v.* **lost, los·ing** 1 To be unable to find or discover; mislay. 2 To fail to keep, control, or maintain: to *lose* one's balance. 3 To be deprived of, as by accident, death, or change: I *lost* my best friend when we moved. 4 To be defeated or fail to win: We *lost;* to *lose* a game. 5 To fail to use; waste: to *lose* a chance. 6 To fail to see or hear; miss: I *lost* what he was saying. 7 To bring to death or destruction: The ship was *lost.* 8 To cause to lose: One fumble *lost* the game. 9 To gain or win less than is risked, spent, or given up, as in business. 10 To wander from so as to be unable to find: The lamb *lost* its way. **—lose oneself** 1 To let oneself stray and not know where one is. 2 To become engrossed: to *lose oneself* in thought. **—lose out** To be defeated or deprived. **—lose out on** To be deprived of; miss. **—los'er** *n.* ◆ See LOOSE.

los·ing [lōō'zing] *adj.* That cannot or does not win: a *losing* venture; a *losing* team.

loss [lôs] *n.* 1 The act of losing. 2 The state of being lost. 3 A person, thing, number, or amount that is lost. 4 The harm or cost caused by losing someone or something. **—at a loss** In a state of confusion.

lost [lôst] 1 The past tense and past participle of LOSE. 2 *adj.* Missing: a *lost* shoe. 3 *adj.* No

a	add	**i**	it	**ŏŏ**	took	**oi**	oil
ā	ace	**ī**	ice	**ōō**	pool	**ou**	pout
â	care	**o**	odd	**u**	up	**ng**	ring
ä	palm	**ō**	open	**û**	burn	**th**	thin
e	end	**ô**	order	**yōō**	fuse	**th̸**	this
ē	equal					**zh**	vision

ə = {a in *above* e in *sicken* i in *possible* / o in *melon* u in *circus*}

longer held or possessed: *lost* athletic skills. **4** *adj.* Having gone astray: a *lost* child. **5** *adj.* Not won: a *lost* fight. **6** *adj.* Confused or helpless. **7** *adj.* Wasted: a *lost* chance. **8** *adj.* Ruined or destroyed. **9** *adj.* No longer known: *lost* arts. **—be lost in** To be engrossed in.

lot [lot] *n.* **1** A small object chosen at random from a group of similar objects to determine something by chance: to draw *lots.* **2** The use of such objects as a way to determine something: The winner was chosen by *lot.* **3** A choice or decision made in this way: The *lot* fell to our team to begin the game. **4** A share or portion received by lot. **5** A person's portion in life, ascribed to chance or fate: A soldier's *lot* is a hard one. **6** A number of things or persons considered as a single group or unit: the best of the *lot.* **7** A small plot of land: a vacant *lot.* **8** (*often pl.*) *informal* A great deal: *lots* of money; a *lot* of trouble. ◆ *A lot* and *lots* are acceptable in informal writing and in speech, but in formal writing they should be avoided, as by using *a great many* or *a great deal* instead. ◆ *A lot* is often misspelled as one word: *alot.*

Lot [lot] *n.* In the Bible, a nephew of Abraham. His wife, disobeying a warning, was turned into a pillar of salt when she looked back on burning Sodom from which they were fleeing.

loth [lōth] *adj.* Another spelling of LOATH.

lo·tion [lō′shən] *n.* A liquid containing medicine, for cleaning, soothing, or healing the skin or eyes.

lot·ter·y [lot′ər·ē] *n., pl.* **lot·ter·ies** A game of chance in which numbered tickets are sold, winning numbers are drawn by lot, and prizes are awarded to the holders of the winning numbers.

lo·tus [lō′təs] *n.* **1** A water lily of Asia and Egypt. **2** A plant related to the pea, with red, pink, or white flowers. **3** A tree whose fruit was thought by the ancient Greeks to cause dreaminess.

loud [loud] **1** *adj.* Strong or intense in sound; not soft or quiet: *loud* thunder. **2** *adj.* Noisy: a *loud* party. **3** *adj.* Insistent and clamorous: *loud* demands. **4** *adv.* In a loud manner. **5** *adj. informal* Crude; vulgar: a *loud* person. **6** *adj. informal* Too showy; flashy: a *loud* tie. **—loud′ly** *adv.* **—loud′·ness** *n.*

loud·mouth [loud′mouth′] *n. informal* A person who speaks loudly and offensively.

loud·speak·er [loud′spē′kər] *n.* A device that changes a varying electric current into sound loud enough to be heard throughout a room or area.

lou·is d'or [lo͞o′ē dôr′] **1** An old French coin worth about four dollars. **2** A later French coin, no longer used, worth 20 francs.

lounge [lounj] *v.* **lounged, loung·ing,** *n.* **1** *v.* To recline or lean in a relaxed way. **2** *v.* To pass time in a lazy manner; loaf. **3** *n.* A room, as one in a hotel or theater, containing comfortable furniture where people can relax. **4** *n.* A sofa.

lour [lou′ər] *v., n.* Another spelling of LOWER¹.

louse [lous] *n., pl.* **lice** [līs] **1** A small, wingless insect that infests the skin or hair of humans and other animals. It lives by sucking their blood. **2** Any similar insect living on plants. **3** *slang* A mean or contemptible person.

lous·y [lou′zē] *adj.* **lous·i·er, lous·i·est** **1** Infested or covered with lice. **2** *slang* Unpleasant or worthless: a *lousy* play. **3** *slang* Very well supplied: *lousy* with money.

lout [lout] *n.* An awkward, stupid person. **—lout′ish** *adj.*

lou·ver [lo͞o′vər] *n.* **1** One of a series of overlapping slats in a window or opening, sloped downward to shed rain while still admitting light and air. **2** A window provided with louvers.

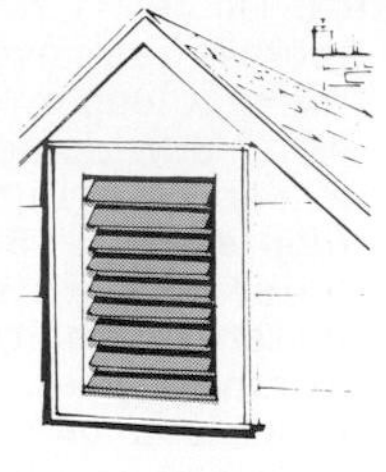
Louver

Lou·vre [lo͞o′vr(ə)] *n.* A famous art museum in Paris, built as a palace for French kings.

lov·a·ble or **love·a·ble** [luv′ə·bəl] *adj.* Worthy of affection or love; charming; dear. **—lov′a·bly** *adv.*

love [luv] *n., v.* **loved, lov·ing** **1** *n.* A deep, passionate affection, as for a sweetheart. **2** *v.* To be in love with. **3** *v.* To have a deep devotion for: to *love* one's parents. **4** *n.* A very great interest in or enjoyment of something: a *love* of the theater. **5** *v.* To enjoy very much: She *loves* the out-of-doors. **6** *n.* A person or thing that is loved: You are the only *love* of my life; Her *love* is science. **7** *n.* In tennis, a score of nothing. **—fall in love** To begin to feel love for someone or something. **—for the love of** For the sake of. **—in love** Experiencing love for someone or something.

love affair **1** An amorous relationship between lovers. **2** An ardent enthusiasm.

love·bird [luv′bûrd′] *n.* One of several kinds of small parrots kept in cages. They like to nestle up against their mates.

love·less [luv′lis] *adj.* Receiving no love; unloved.

love·lorn [luv′lôrn′] *adj.* Longing hopelessly for love; abandoned by the person one loves.

love·ly [luv′lē] *adj.* **love·li·er, love·li·est** **1** Having qualities that make people love one: a *lovely* child. **2** Beautiful: a *lovely* rose. **3** *informal* Enjoyable; pleasant: to have a *lovely* time. **—love′li·ness** *n.*

lov·er [luv′ər] *n.* **1** A person who is in love. **2** A person who is very fond of something: a *lover* of animals.

love seat An upholstered chair or sofa that seats two persons.

love·sick [luv′sik′] *adj.* So strongly affected by love as not to be one's usual self.

lov·ing [luv′ing] **1** Present participle of LOVE. **2** *adj.* Experiencing or showing love: a *loving* parent; *loving* words. **—lov′ing·ly** *adv.*

loving cup A large ornamental cup, usually of silver, given as a trophy, especially to the winner of a competition.

low¹ [lō] **1** *v.* To make the hollow, mournful sound of a cow; moo. **2** *n.* This sound.

low² [lō] **1** *adj.* Not high or tall: a *low* hill; a *low* tree. **2** *adj.* Lying or situated below the usual height: a *low* marsh; a *low* table. **3** *adj.* Close to the ground: *low* clouds. **4** *adj.* Fitted so as to show part of the wearer's chest and back: a *low* neckline. **5** *n.* Something low, as position, level, or degree: The stock market reached a new *low* this week. **6** *adv.* In or to a low level, position, or degree: to bow *low.* **7** *adj.* Not good in quality: a *low* grade of meat. **8** *adj.* Inexpensive; economical: a *low* price. **9** *adj.* Poor or humble, as in position or rank: of *low* birth. **10** *adj.* Unfavorable; poor: to have a *low* opinion of oneself. **11** *adj.* Not refined; vulgar: *low* companions. **12** *adj.* Not high or shrill in pitch: the *low* notes of a cello. **13** *adj.* Not loud; faint: a *low* moan. **14** *adv.* Softly: Please speak *low.* **15** *adj.* Depressed; sad: I was feeling *low* after arguing with my friend. **16** *adj.*

Without much strength; weak: The fire is *low.* **17** *adj.* Having a small supply of: to be *low* on groceries. **18** *n.* An arrangement of gears, as in an automobile, that gives the greatest power but the slowest speed. **19** *n.* In meteorology, an area of low atmospheric pressure. **—lay low** To strike down; defeat. **—lie low** *informal* To remain in hiding: Thieves *lie low* after they have committed a robbery. **—low′ness** *n.*

low·born [lō′bôrn′] *adj.* Having parents of low social rank.

low·boy [lō′boi′] *n.* A low chest of drawers having short legs.

low·brow [lō′brou′] *informal* **1** *n.* A person who does not have refined or cultured tastes in art, music, or literature. **2** *adj.* Of or suited to such a person: *lowbrow* amusements.

low·down [lō′doun′] *n. slang* The truth, especially the secret facts; inside information; dope: to get the *lowdown* on a dishonest politician.

low-down [lō′doun′] *adj. slang* Mean or contemptible: a *low-down* trick.

low·er[1] [lou′ər] **1** *v.* To look angry; scowl. **2** *n.* A frown or scowl. **3** *v.* To appear dark and threatening, as the sky before a storm.

low·er[2] [lō′ər] **1** Comparative of LOW: Their grades are *lower* than mine. **2** *adj.* Situated below something else: the *lower* jaw. **3** *v.* To let down or pull down: to *lower* a lifeboat. **4** *adj.* Having less importance; inferior in rank: the *lower* house of a legislature. **5** *v.* To make or become less, as in amount, quality, or pitch: The owner *lowered* the price; The volume *lowered.* **6** *v.* To weaken: Lack of sleep *lowers* the body's resistance.

low·er·case [lō′ər·kās′] *n., adj., v.* **low·er·cased, low·er·cas·ing** **1** *n.* (*also written* **lower case**) Small letters, as distinguished from capital letters. **2** *adj.* Of, having to do with, or being in the lower case. **3** *v.* To set or print in lowercase letters. ◆ See UPPERCASE.

low·er-class [lō′ər·klas′] *adj.* **1** Of or having to do with the lower class. **2** Inferior or low in rank: a *lower-class* specimen of its kind.

lower class The part of a society, including the laboring class, that occupies an inferior social and economic position.

lower house In a legislature of two branches, usually the branch with the greater number of members, who are elected by and represent rather small, or local, areas. The House of Representatives of the United States is an example of such a branch.

low·er·most [lō′ər·mōst′] *adj.* Lowest.

low frequency Any radio-wave frequency between 30 and 300 kilohertz.

Low German Any of several German dialects of northern Germany.

low-keyed [lō′kēd′] *adj.* Quiet or easygoing; not tense or hurried.

low·land [lō′lənd] *n.* (*usually pl.*) Land lying lower than the country around it.

Low·land·er [lō′lən·dər] *n.* A person born or living in the Scottish Lowlands.

low·ly [lō′lē] *adj.* **low·li·er, low·li·est** **1** *adj.* Humble or low, as in rank or position: a *lowly* freshman. **2** *adj.* Humble; meek: a *lowly* request. **3** *adv.* Modestly; humbly. **—low′li·ness** *n.*

low-pitched [lō′picht′] *adj.* **1** Low in tone. **2** Moderate in slope: *low-pitched* roof.

low-pressure [lō′presh′ər] *adj.* **1** Exerting, having, or operating under little pressure. **2** Easygoing; low-keyed.

low profile Behavior intended to attract little attention; inconspicuousness.

low relief Another term for BAS-RELIEF.

low-spir·it·ed [lō′spir′it·id] *adj.* Sad and unhappy; depressed: to feel *low-spirited.*

low tide **1** The outgoing tide at its lowest point. **2** The time when this happens.

low water **1** The lowest level of water in a river, lake, or other body. **2** Low tide.

lox[1] [loks] *n.* Liquid oxygen.

lox[2] [loks] *n.* Salty smoked salmon. ◆ *Lox* comes from a Yiddish word derived from a German word for *salmon.*

loy·al [loi′əl] *adj.* **1** Faithful to one's country: a *loyal* citizen. **2** Constant and faithful to one's family, friends, or obligations: a *loyal* companion **—loy′al·ly** *adv.*

loy·al·ist [loi′əl·ist] *n.* A person who remains loyal to a certain government or political party during a revolution or other uprising.

loy·al·ty [loi′əl·tē] *n., pl.* **loy·al·ties** The condition or fact of being loyal.

loz·enge [loz′inj] *n.* **1** A small tablet of candy or a medicated cough drop, formerly made in the shape of a diamond. **2** A figure in the shape of a diamond.

LP [el′pē′] *n., pl.* **LP's** A long-playing phonograph record: a trademark.

LPN or **L.P.N.** licensed practical nurse.

Lr The symbol for the element lawrencium.

LSD A powerful drug capable of producing hallucinations and other mental disorders. ◆ *LSD* is an abbreviation of the drug's chemical name, lysergic acid diethylamide.

Lt. lieutenant.

Lt. Col. lieutenant colonel.

Lt. Comdr. lieutenant commander.

ltd or **Ltd.** limited.

Lt. Gen. lieutenant general.

Lt. Gov. lieutenant governor.

Lu The symbol for the element lutetium.

lu·au [lo͞o·ou′ *or* lo͞o′ou′] *n.* An elaborate meal of Hawaiian food.

lub·ber [lub′ər] *n.* **1** An awkward, clumsy fellow. **2** A clumsy, inexperienced sailor on a ship.

lu·bri·cant [lo͞o′brə·kənt] *n.* A substance, as oil or grease, used to coat moving parts of a machine so that they will slide smoothly against each other and not wear out so quickly.

lu·bri·cate [lo͞o′brə·kāt′] *v.* **lu·bri·cat·ed, lu·bri·cat·ing** To apply a lubricant to: to *lubricate* engine parts. **—lu′bri·ca′tion** *n.*

lu·cent [lo͞o′sənt] *adj.* **1** Giving off radiance; bright. **2** Clear; transparent.

lu·cid [lo͞o′sid] *adj.* **1** Easily understood; clear; plain: a *lucid* explanation. **2** Thinking clearly;

a	add	**i**	it	**o͝o**	took	**oi**	oil		
ā	ace	**ī**	ice	**o͞o**	pool	**ou**	pout		
â	care	**o**	odd	**u**	up	**ng**	ring		
ä	palm	**ō**	open	**û**	burn	**th**	thin		
e	end	**ô**	order	**yo͞o**	fuse	**th**	this		
ē	equal					**zh**	vision		

ə = a in *above*, e in *sicken*, i in *possible*, o in *melon*, u in *circus*

L

mentally sound: a *lucid* mind. **3** Clear; transparent, as water. **4** Shining; bright: used in poems. **—lu·cid′i·ty** *n.* **—lu′cid·ly** *adv.*

Lu·ci·fer [lo͞o′sə·fər] *n.* The archangel who led the revolt of the angels and was thrown from Heaven; Satan; the Devil.

Lu·cite [lo͞o′sīt′] *n.* A transparent resin or plastic: a trademark.

luck [luk] *n.* **1** Good fortune; success: I had *luck* in finding a good job. **2** Something that happens by chance; fortune: Their team always seems to have good *luck* in the finals. **—in luck** Successful; lucky. **—out of luck** Unlucky.

luck·i·ly [luk′ə·lē] *adv.* By good fortune; fortunately: *Luckily* we got there on time.

luck·less [luk′lis] *adj.* Having bad luck. **—luck′less·ly** *adv.*

luck·y [luk′ē] *adj.* **luck·i·er, luck·i·est** **1** Having good luck: to be *lucky* at games. **2** Resulting in good fortune: to make a *lucky* move in checkers; a *lucky* day. **3** Believed to bring good fortune: a *lucky* penny. **—luck′i·ness** *n.*

lu·cra·tive [lo͞o′krə·tiv] *adj.* Bringing in a great deal of money; profitable: a *lucrative* business.

lu·cre [lo͞o′kər] *n.* Money or wealth, usually used in the phrase **filthy lucre.**

lu·di·crous [lo͞o′də·krəs] *adj.* Causing laughter, scorn, or ridicule; ridiculous; absurd: His antics were *ludicrous.* **—lud′i·crous·ly** *adv.*

Ludicrous antics

luff [luf] **1** *n.* The turning of a ship closer to the wind. **2** *n.* The foremost edge of a fore-and-aft sail. **3** *v.* To bring the head of a sailing vessel toward or into the wind.

lug[1] [lug] *n.* An earlike part that sticks out, used for holding or supporting something.

lug[2] [lug] *v.* **lugged, lug·ging** To carry or pull with effort: to *lug* large rocks.

luge [lo͞ozh] *n.* A small racing sled on which the rider lies face upward.

lug·gage [lug′ij] *n.* Suitcases, bags, and trunks used in traveling; baggage.

lug·ger [lug′ər] *n.* A boat having lugsails. It may have one, two, or three masts.

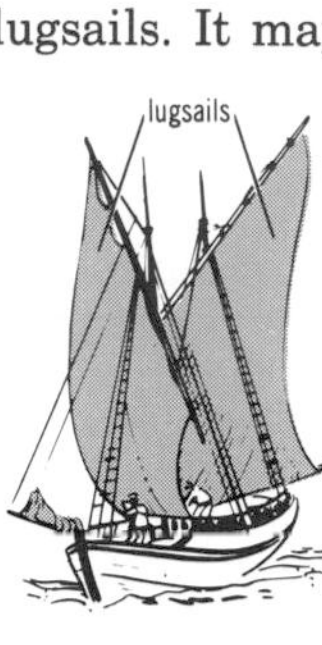

Lugger

lug·sail [lug′sāl′ *or* lug′səl] *n.* A four-cornered sail having no boom. It is hung from a yard that slants across the mast.

lu·gu·bri·ous [lo͞o·go͞o′brē·əs] *adj.* Sad, mournful, or pretending sadness: Hounds often have *lugubrious* faces. **—lu·gu′bri·ous·ly** *adv.*

lug·worm [lug′wûrm′] *n.* Any of a group of marine worms, often used as bait in fishing.

Luke [lo͝ok] *n.* **1** An early Christian and saint who was a physician and a companion of St. Paul. **2** The third book of the New Testament, which he is believed to have written.

luke·warm [lo͞ok′wôrm′] *adj.* **1** Barely warm; tepid: *lukewarm* soup. **2** Lacking in warmth or enthusiasm: a *lukewarm* greeting.

lull [lul] **1** *v.* To quiet or put to sleep by soothing sounds or motions. **2** *v.* To make or become quiet or calm: to *lull* someone's distrust; The wind *lulled.* **3** *n.* A time of calm or quiet during a period of noise or activity: a *lull* in business.

lull·a·by [lul′ə·bī] *n., pl.* **lull·a·bies** **1** A song to soothe a baby to sleep. **2** A piece of instrumental music that sounds like a lullaby.

lum·ba·go [lum·bā′gō] *n.* A form of rheumatism that affects the lower part of the back.

lum·bar [lum′bər] *adj.* Of or near the lower part of the back: a *lumbar* nerve.

lum·ber[1] [lum′bər] **1** *n.* Timber that has been sawed into boards, planks, and beams. **2** *v.* To cut down and saw (timber) for marketing. **3** *n.* *British* Household articles and furniture no longer used and usually stored away.

lum·ber[2] [lum′bər] *v.* **1** To move along clumsily and heavily. **2** To move with a rumbling noise, as a heavy truck.

lum·ber·ing [lum′bər·ing] *n.* The business of cutting down timber and sawing it into lumber for the market.

lum·ber·jack [lum′bər·jak′] *n.* A person whose work it is to saw down trees and transport them to the sawmill.

lum·ber·man [lum′bər·mən] *n., pl.* **lum·ber·men** [lum′bər·mən] **1** A lumberjack. **2** A person who is in the business of lumbering.

lum·ber·yard [lum′bər·yärd′] *n.* A place where lumber and other building materials are displayed and sold.

lu·men [lo͞o′mən] *n., pl.* **lu·mi·na** [lo͞o′mə·nə] **1** The space inside a tubular bodily structure as a vein, artery, or intestine. **2** A unit for measuring the rate at which light flows from a source, equal to the light received by a surface with an area of one square unit having all its points one unit of distance from a source rated at one candela.

lu·mi·nar·y [lo͞o′mə·ner′ē] *n., pl.* **lu·mi·nar·ies** **1** A body that gives out light, as a star. **2** A person who has achieved great fame.

lu·mi·nes·cent [lo͞o′mə·nes′ənt] *adj.* Giving out light at a temperature below that of incandescence. Fluorescent lights and fireflies are luminescent because they give off light, though cool to the touch. **—lu′mi·nes′cence** *n.*

lu·mi·nos·i·ty [lo͞o′mə·nos′ə·tē] *n., pl.* **lu·mi·nos·i·ties** **1** The quality of being luminous. **2** Something luminous.

lu·mi·nous [lo͞o′mə·nəs] *adj.* **1** Full of light; glowing: *luminous* with moonlight. **2** Giving off light: *luminous* insects. **3** Easily understood: a *luminous* remark. **—lu′mi·nous·ly** *adv.*

lum·mox [lum′əks] *n.* A clumsy, boorish person.

lump [lump] **1** *n.* A shapeless mass, especially a small one: a *lump* of dough. **2** *n.* A swelling on the body: The *lump* on the child's head was caused by a fall. **3** *v.* To form lumps in or on. **4** *v.* To put in one mass or group: to *lump* all the facts together. **5** *v. slang* To put up with; bear: You can like it or *lump* it. **—lump sum** A full or single amount of money paid at one time.

lump·ish [lump′ish] *adj.* **1** Like a lump; thick and shapeless. **2** Clumsy and stupid.

lump·y [lum′pē] *adj.* **lump·i·er, lump·i·est** **1** Full of lumps. **2** Covered with or having lumps: a *lumpy* bed. **—lump′i·ness** *n.*

Lu·na [lo͞o′nə] *n.* In Roman myths, the goddess of the moon.

lu·na·cy [lo͞o′nə·sē] *n., pl.* **lu·na·cies** **1** Unwise or reckless conduct: It is *lunacy* to drive so fast. **2** Mental illness; insanity.

luna moth A large pale-green moth with taillike extensions on the rear wings.
lu·nar [lo͞o′nər] *adj.* **1** Of or having to do with the moon: A *lunar* eclipse is caused by the moon's passing through the earth's shadow. **2** Round or crescent-shaped like the moon.
lunar eclipse An eclipse (def. 2).
lunar excursion module A spacecraft for carrying astronauts from a craft that is orbiting the moon to the moon's surface and then back to the orbiting craft. Also written **lunar module.**
lunar month The time it takes for the moon to go once around the earth, equal to 29.53 days.
lunar year A unit of time equal to 12 lunar months.
lu·na·tic [lo͞o′nə·tik] **1** *adj.* Wildly foolish; senseless. **2** *adj.* Mentally ill; insane. **3** *adj.* For or having to do with mentally ill persons. **4** *n.* A mentally ill person. ◆ *Lunatic* comes from *luna,* the Latin word for *moon.* People used to believe that insanity increased and decreased with the phases of the moon.
lunch [lunch] **1** *n.* A light meal, especially the noonday meal. **2** *n.* The food provided for such a meal. **3** *v.* To eat lunch.
lunch·eon [lun′chən] *n.* A noonday meal, especially a formal one.
lunch·eon·ette [lun′chə·net′] *n.* A small restaurant that serves light meals.
lunch·room [lunch′ro͞om′] *n.* A place in a school or other building where lunch is served.
lung [lung] *n.* Either of the two saclike organs of breathing found in the chest of humans and other vertebrate animals that breathe air. The lungs bring oxygen to and remove carbon dioxide from the blood.

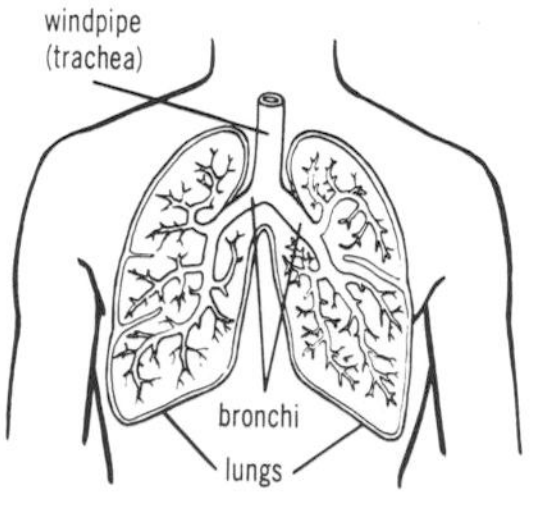

lunge [lunj] *n., v.* **lunged, lung·ing** **1** *n.* A quick movement or plunge forward, as a thrust with a sword. **2** *v.* To make a lunge.
lung·fish [lung′fish′] *n., pl.* **lung·fish** or **lung·fish·es** A fish capable of breathing both by means of gills and by a bladder resembling a lung.
lu·pine or **lu·pin** [lo͞o′pin] *n.* A plant related to the pea, having long spikes of flowers and bean-shaped seeds in flat pods.
lurch[1] [lûrch] **1** *v.* To roll or pitch suddenly to one side, as from loss of balance: to *lurch* across a tilting deck. **2** *n.* A rolling or pitching motion.
lurch[2] [lûrch] *n.* An embarrassing or difficult position or situation, now used only in the phrase **leave in the lurch,** to abandon (someone) having difficulties and needing help.
lure [lo͝or] *n., v.* **lured, lur·ing** **1** *n.* Anything that invites or attracts, as by offering pleasure or gain: the *lure* of a big city. **2** *v.* To attract or entice, especially into danger: to *lure* birds into traps. **3** *n.* Artificial bait made of feathers, wood, or other material, used in catching fish.

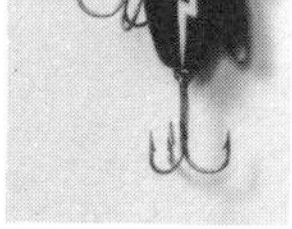
Lure

lu·rid [lo͝or′id] *adj.* **1** Causing horror or fear; shocking: a *lurid* crime. **2** Lighted up or glowing with a yellowish red glare, especially as seen through smoke or darkness: a *lurid* explosion.
lurk [lûrk] *v.* **1** To lie hidden; stay out of sight. **2** To creep along stealthily; slink.
lus·cious [lush′əs] *adj.* **1** Very good to taste and smell; delicious: a *luscious,* ripe pear. **2** Pleasing to any sense or to the mind: a *luscious* red rose. **—lus′cious·ly** *adv.*
lush [lush] *adj.* **1** Full of a healthy growth, as of trees or plants: *lush* jungles. **2** Growing with vigor: *lush* grass. **3** Elaborate or ornate: *lush* prose. **4** Delicious; savory: *lush* fruit. **5** Appealing to the eyes, ears, or other senses: a *lush* sound. **6** Prosperous: a *lush* business.
lust [lust] **1** *n.* A strong desire or craving: a *lust* for money. **2** *n.* A strong sexual appetite. **3** *v.* To have a strong desire or craving: to *lust* after power. **—lust′ful** *adj.*
lus·ter or **lus·tre** [lus′tər] *n.* **1** Soft, reflected light playing over a surface; sheen: the *luster* of polished wood. **2** Brightness; radiance: The lights had lost their *luster.* **3** Brilliance or glory, as of achievement or beauty. **4** A glossy, often iridescent finish baked on the surface of certain kinds of pottery.
lus·trous [lus′trəs] *adj.* Having a luster or gleam; glossy; shiny: a cat's *lustrous* fur.
lust·y [lus′tē] *adj.* **lust·i·er, lust·i·est** **1** Full of health and vigor; robust: a *lusty* infant. **2** Hearty; strong; powerful: a *lusty* appetite. **—lust′i·ly** *adv.* **—lust′i·ness** *n.*
lute [lo͞ot] *n.* An old stringed instrument somewhat like a guitar. It is played by plucking with the fingers.

Lute

Lu·ther·an [lo͞o′thər·ən] **1** *n.* A member of the Protestant church that was founded by Martin Luther in Germany in the 16th century. **2** *adj.* Of or having to do with Martin Luther, Lutherans, or with their church or doctrines.
lux·u·ri·ant [lug·zho͝or′ē·ənt] *adj.* **1** Growing thickly and abundantly; lush: *luxuriant* plants. **2** Very rich, fancy, or elaborate, as in decorations, furnishings, or ornaments. **—lux·u′ri·ance** *n.* **—lux·u′ri·ant·ly** *adv.*
lux·u·ri·ate [lug·zho͝or′ē·āt′] *v.* **lux·u·ri·at·ed, lux·u·ri·a·ting** **1** To take great pleasure; enjoy oneself fully: to *luxuriate* in a soft bed. **2** To live in luxury. **3** To grow thickly and abundantly as plants.
lux·u·ri·ous [lug·zho͝or′ē·əs] *adj.* **1** Characterized by luxury: a *luxurious* palace. **2** Loving luxury. **—lux·u′ri·ous·ly** *adv.* **—lux·u′ri·ous·ness** *n.*

a	add	**i**	it	**o͝o**	took	**oi**	oil
ā	ace	**ī**	ice	**o͞o**	pool	**ou**	pout
â	care	**o**	odd	**u**	up	**ng**	ring
ä	palm	**ō**	open	**û**	burn	**th**	thin
e	end	**ô**	order	**yo͞o**	fuse	**t͟h**	this
ē	equal					**zh**	vision

ə = {a in *above* e in *sicken* i in *possible* / o in *melon* u in *circus*}

lux·u·ry [luk′shər·ē] *n., pl.* **lux·u·ries** 1 Anything costly that gives comfort or pleasure, but is not necessary to life or health: A diamond ring is a *luxury.* 2 A way of life in which one has great ease and comfort: to live in *luxury.* 3 Any pleasure.

-ly[1] A suffix meaning: 1 Like or suited to, as in *brotherly.* 2 Toward or from a certain direction, as in *northerly.* 3 Happening at regular intervals of time, as in *daily.* 4 Of or having to do with, as in *earthly.*

-ly[2] A suffix meaning: 1 In a certain manner, as in *carefully.* 2 To a certain degree or extent, as in *highly.* 3 In certain respects or ways, as in *mentally.* 4 At or in a certain order or time, as in *recently* or in *fourthly.*

ly·cée [lē·sā′] *n.* In France, a secondary school financed by the government, that prepares its students for a university.

ly·ce·um [lī·sē′əm] *n.* 1 An organization that gives lectures, concerts, and other events, for the public. 2 A hall where such lectures and concerts are held.

lye [lī] *n.* A strong, alkaline solution, now usually sodium hydroxide, used for several purposes, including making soap and refining oil.

ly·ing[1] [lī′ing] Present participle of LIE[1]: The dog is *lying* in the shade.

ly·ing[2] [lī′ing] 1 Present participle of LIE[2]: Are you *lying* about your absence from class? 2 *n.* The act of telling lies. 3 *adj.* Telling lies; untruthful: a *lying* witness.

lymph [limf] *n.* A watery, yellowish liquid containing lymphocytes and similar to blood plasma.

lym·phat·ic [lim·fat′ik] *adj.* 1 Containing or carrying lymph: the *lymphatic* vessels. 2 Lacking energy; listless: a *lymphatic* boy.

lymph node or **lymph gland** Any of numerous glandlike bodies found along the lymphatic vessels. Lymph nodes produce lymphocytes and filter out harmful matter from lymph.

lym·pho·cyte [lim′fə·sīt′] *n.* A type of white blood cell produced in the lymph nodes.

lym·phoid [lim′foid′] *adj.* Of, having to do with, or like lymph or the tissue of lymphatic vessels.

lynch [linch] *v.* To kill (an accused person) by mob action, as by hanging, without legal sanction.

lynx [lingks] *n., pl.* **lynx** or **lynx·es** A wildcat of North America, having a short tail, tufted ears, and rather long legs.

Lynx

lynx-eyed [lingks′īd′] *adj.* Having very good sight.

ly·on·naise [lī′ə·nāz′] *adj.* Cooked with finely chopped onions: *lyonnaise* potatoes.

Ly·ra [lī′rə] *n.* A constellation containing the star Vega.

lyre [līr] *n.* An ancient stringed instrument like a harp. It was used by the ancient Greeks to accompany singing or poetry.

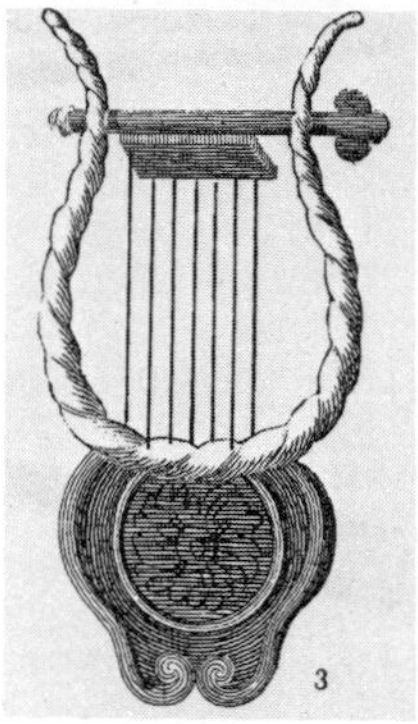
Lyre

lyre·bird [līr′bûrd′] *n.* A large bird of Australia, the male of which spreads its long tail feathers into the shape of a lyre.

lyr·ic [lir′ik] 1 *n.* A poem expressing the writer's personal feelings or thoughts, as a poem about love or grief. 2 *adj.* Of or having to do with such poems. 3 *adj.* Describing a singing voice that is light, graceful, and melodic: a *lyric* soprano. 4 *n.* (*pl.*) The words of a popular song. 5 *adj.* Meant to be sung; like a song.

lyr·i·cal [lir′ə·kəl] *adj.* 1 Lyric. 2 Full of emotion, excitement, or enthusiasm: a *lyrical* account of a vacation. **—lyr′i·cal·ly** *adv.*

lyr·i·cist [lir′ə·sist] *n.* A person who writes song lyrics.

ly·sin [lī′sin] *n.* Any of a class of substances that are formed in the body and which have the power to destroy blood cells and bacteria.

M is the thirteenth letter of the alphabet. The sign for it originated among Semitic people in the Near East, in the region of Palestine and Syria, probably in the middle of the second millennium B.C. Little is known about the sign until around 1000 B.C., when the Phoenicians began using it. They named it *mem* and used it for the sound of the consonant *m*.

When the Greeks adopted the Phoenician sign around the ninth century B.C., they called it *mu*. They made the "legs" of the letter of even length and used the sign for the *m* sound.

As early as the eighth century B.C., the Etruscans adopted the Greek alphabet, using an irregular *M* form similar to that of earlier Greek *M* forms. It is from the Etruscans that the Romans took the letter, using it, too, for the *m* sound. Around the time of the Caesars, the Romans made the shape of the letter more graceful. The model of the letter found on the base of Trajan's column, erected in Rome in 114, is considered a masterpiece of letter design. A Trajan-style *majuscule,* or capital letter, *M* opens this essay.

The *minuscule,* or small letter, *m* developed gradually, between the third and ninth centuries, in the handwriting that scribes used for copying books. Contributing to its shape were the Roman *uncials* of the fourth to the eighth centuries and the *half uncials* of the fifth to the ninth centuries. The true ancestor of the lowercase *m,* however, can be found in the script that evolved under the encouragement of Charlemagne (742-814). This letter was one of those known as the *Caroline minuscules,* which became the principal handwriting system used on the medieval manuscripts of the ninth and tenth centuries.

In all its forms, the lowercase *m* is essentially a smaller version of the capital letter. From the Middle Ages until the seventeenth century, however, it was often omitted from manuscripts. A stroke was put over the preceding letter instead. Thus, *punctum* became *punctū*.

Mm

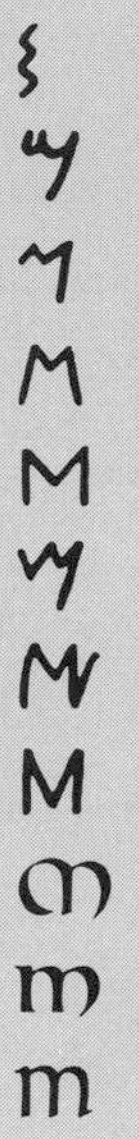

Early Phoenician (late 2nd millennium B.C.)
Phoenician (8th century B.C.)
Early Greek (9th-7th centuries B.C.)
Western Greek (6th century B.C.)
Classical Greek (403 B.C. onward)
Early Etruscan (8th century B.C.)
Monumental Latin (4th century B.C.)
Classical Latin
Uncial
Half uncial
Caroline minuscule

m or **M** [em] *n., pl.* **m's** or **M's** 1 The 13th letter of the English alphabet. 2 (*written* **M**) The Roman numeral for 1,000.

m. 1 meridian. 2 meter(s). 3 mile(s). 4 minute(s). 5 month.

M. 1 Majesty. 2 Master. 3 Monday. 4 Monsieur.

ma [mä] *n. informal* Mama. ◆ See MAMA.

MA Postal Service abbreviation of Massachusetts.

M.A. Master of Arts.

ma'am [mam, mäm, *or* məm] *n.* Madam. ◆ See MADAM.

ma·ca·bre [mə·kä′brə *or* mə·kä′bər] *adj.* 1 Suggesting or having to do with death. 2 Horrifying; gruesome: *macabre* paintings of war.

mac·ad·am [mə·kad′əm] *n.* 1 Small, broken stones used to cover a road. 2 A road made from such stones.

mac·a·da·mi·a nut [mak′ə·dā′mē·ə] An edible nut somewhat like a hazelnut produced by an Australian tree that is widely cultivated in Hawaii.

mac·ad·am·ize [mə·kad′ə·mīz′] *v.* **mac·ad·am·ized, mac·ad·am·iz·ing** To surface or cover a road with macadam, and often with a binder of tar or cement.

ma·caque [mə·käk′] *n.* Any of several monkeys found chiefly in Asia, Africa, and the East Indies, especially the rhesus monkey.

mac·a·ro·ni [mak′ə·rō′nē] *n.* A dried flour paste in tubular shape that is boiled and eaten.

mac·a·roon [mak′ə·ro͞on′] *n.* A small cookie made chiefly of egg whites, sugar, and almonds or coconut.

ma·caw [mə·kô′] *n.* Any of various large parrots of South and Central America, having a long tail, harsh voice, and brilliant plumage.

Macaw

Mac·beth [mək·beth′] *n.* 1 A play by Shakespeare. 2 The Scottish general in it who murdered the king and took the throne.

mace[1] [mās] *n.* 1 A heavy, medieval, clublike weapon, usually with a spiked metal head. 2 An ornamental staff carried before or by an official to symbolize power or authority.

mace[2] [mās] *n.* A fragrant spice made from the covering of the nutmeg seed.

a	add	**i**	it	**o͝o**	took	**oi**	oil
ā	ace	**ī**	ice	**o͞o**	pool	**ou**	pout
â	care	**o**	odd	**u**	up	**ng**	ring
ä	palm	**ō**	open	**û**	burn	**th**	thin
e	end	**ô**	order	**yo͞o**	fuse	**th̶**	this
ē	equal					**zh**	vision

ə = { a in *above* e in *sicken* i in *possible* o in *melon* u in *circus*

Mace [mās] *n.* A chemical mixture, made to be sprayed, used like tear gas to irritate the eyes and cause nausea, dizziness, and immobilization: a trademark.

mac·er·ate [mas′ə·rāt′] *v.* **mac·er·at·ed, mac·er·at·ing** **1** To soften or separate into parts by or as if by soaking. **2** To cause to grow thin or waste away. **—mac′er·a′tion** *n.*

ma·chet·e [mə·shet′ē *or* mə·shet′] *n.* A heavy knife used as a tool and as a weapon, especially in South America and the West Indies.

Mach·i·a·vel·li·an [mak′ē·ə·vel′ē·ən] *adj.* Having to do with or resembling the theories of Niccolò Machiavelli.

mach·i·na·tion [mak′ə·nā′shən] *n.* (*usually pl.*) A secret scheming and working for a purpose, usually an evil or improper one.

ma·chine [mə·shēn′] *n., v.* **ma·chined, ma·chin·ing** **1** *n.* An arrangement of parts that transmits energy so as to produce a desired result. **2** *v.* To make, shape, mill, or construct, by means of a machine. **3** *n.* An airplane, automobile, or other mechanical vehicle. **4** *n.* Any of various simple devices by which small amounts of energy can be made to exert a maximum force. **5** *n.* A person whose actions are machinelike, showing no evidence of thought or will. **6** *n.* The people who control a political party.

ma·chine-gun [mə·shēn′gun′] *v.* **ma·chine-gunned, ma·chine-gun·ning** To shoot at or kill with a machine gun.

machine gun An automatic gun that fires many bullets rapidly and continuously.

Machine gun

machine language A language used directly by a computer without any need for translation into another language.

ma·chin·er·y [mə·shēn′(ə·)rē] *n.* **1** A collection of machines: a shop filled with *machinery.* **2** The parts of a machine: the *machinery* of a watch. **3** The principles or processes by which something works: the *machinery* of the law.

machine shop A shop where metals or other materials are cut, shaped, or finished.

machine tool A power-driven tool, partly or fully automatic, for cutting or shaping.

ma·chin·ist [mə·shē′nist] *n.* **1** A person who is skilled in the operation of machine tools. **2** A person who is skilled in the construction, operation, or repair of machinery.

ma·chis·mo [mä·chēz′mō] *n.* A strong or exaggerated pride in being male, characterized by aggressive masculine behavior.

Mach·me·ter [mäk′mē′tər] *n.* An instrument in an aircraft that indicates the ratio of the speed of the aircraft to the speed of sound in the surrounding atmosphere.

Mach number [mäk] The ratio of the speed of an object traveling in a fluid, as air, to the speed of sound in that fluid.

ma·cho [mä′chō] *adj., n., pl.* **ma·chos** **1** *adj.* Masculine in an exaggerated and aggressive way. **2** *n.* Machismo. **3** *n.* A person who shows an aggressive, exaggerated kind of masculinity.

mack·er·el [mak′ər·əl] *n., pl.* **mack·er·el** or **mack·er·els** A fish of the Atlantic Ocean, used for food.

mackerel sky Small, fleecy, white clouds in rows like the markings on a mackerel's back.

mack·i·naw [nak′ə·nô′] *n.* A heavy, short, woolen coat, usually with a plaid pattern.

Mackinaw

mack·in·tosh [mak′ən·tosh′] *n.* A waterproof coat or cloak; raincoat. ◆ The word *mackintosh* was named after Charles *Macintosh,* a Scottish chemist who invented the cloth.

mac·ra·me [mak′rə·mā′] *n.* A coarse lace or trimming made by knotting threads or cords, usually in a geometric pattern.

mac·ro·bi·ot·ic [mak′rō·bī·ot′ik] *adj.* Of or having to do with a special diet, as one made up principally of whole grains and vegetables, that is supposed to promote health and long life.

mac·ro·cosm [mak′rə·koz′əm] *n.* The whole universe.

ma·cron [mā′kron′] *n.* A straight line (¯) placed over a vowel to show that it is pronounced in a certain way, as *ā* in *made.*

mad [mad] *adj.* **mad·der, mad·dest** **1** Suffering from or showing severe mental disorder; insane: A *mad* person may be committed to an asylum. **2** Uncontrollably excited by strong feeling; wildly emotional: to be *mad* with jealousy. **3** *informal* Angry: I was so *mad* at him that we fought. **4** Foolish; rash: It was a *mad* idea. **5** Confused; disorderly: We'd thrown everything into a *mad* jumble. **6** *informal* Very enthusiastic or fond: to be *mad* about singing folk songs. **7** *informal* Very gay or funny; hilarious: a *mad* time. **8** Having rabies: a *mad* dog.

Mad·a·gas·can [mad′ə·gas′kən] **1** *adj.* Of or from Madagascar. **2** *n.* A person born in or a citizen of Madagascar.

mad·am [mad′əm] *n., pl.* **mes·dames** [mā·däm′] **1** A title of courtesy, used alone in speaking or writing to a woman. **2** A title of courtesy, used before a woman's surname or before a word that indicates rank or office: *Madam* President. ◆ *Madam* is the English spelling of the French *madame,* although the French spelling is itself often used in English. *Madame* in French literally means *my lady,* going back to the Latin words *mea,* meaning *my,* and *domina, a mistress of a household.*

ma·dame [mə·dam′ *or* mä·däm′] *n., pl.* **mes·dames** [mā·däm′] The French title of courtesy for a married woman, equivalent to *Mrs.* ◆ See MADAM.

mad·cap [mad′kap′] **1** *adj.* Wild; rash: a *madcap* adventure. **2** *n.* A person who acts wildly or rashly.

mad·den [mad′(ə)n] *v.* To make or become mad; infuriate: Their inconsiderate actions *maddened* me.

mad·den·ing [mad′ən·ing] *adj.* Causing anger or frustrated resentment; infuriating. **—mad′den·ing·ly** *adv.*

mad·der [mad′ər] *n.* **1** A plant of Asia and Europe having yellow flowers and a fleshy red root. **2** A red dye made from the root of the madder. **3** Any of several similar plants.

mad·ding [mad′ing] *adj.* **1** An old-fashioned word for MADDENING. **2** Behaving as if mad.

made [mād] Past tense and past participle of MAKE.

mad·e·moi·selle [mad′ə·mə·zel′] *n., pl.* **mad·e·moi·selles** or **mes·de·moi·selles** [mād′mwä·zel′] The French title of courtesy equivalent to *Miss.*

made-up [mād′up′] *adj.* 1 Not real; invented; false: a *made-up* name. 2 Changed or made more attractive by cosmetics or makeup: the mime's carefully *made-up* face.

mad·house [mad′hous′] *n.* 1 A hospital for the mentally ill; insane asylum. 2 A place of disorder and uproar: The gym was a *madhouse.*

Madison Avenue 1 An avenue in New York City considered as the center of the American advertising industry. 2 The American advertising industry in general.

mad·ly [mad′lē] *adv.* In a mad manner; insanely; angrily; rashly.

mad·man [mad′man′] *n., pl.* **mad·men** [mad′men′] A person who is mad; maniac.

mad·ness [mad′nis] *n.* 1 Insanity. 2 Great anger or fury. 3 Extreme foolishness; folly.

Ma·don·na [mə·don′ə] *n.* 1 The Virgin Mary. 2 A painting or statue of the Virgin Mary.

ma·dras [mə·dras′ *or* mad′rəs] *n.* A cotton cloth in woven checked, plaid, or striped patterns. ◆ *Madras* was named after *Madras,* a city and province of southern India, where it was originally made.

mad·ri·gal [mad′rə·gəl] *n.* 1 An unaccompanied song, with parts for several voices. 2 A short poem, usually about love or rural life, that is suitable for such a song.

mael·strom [māl′strəm] *n.* 1 (*written* **Maelstrom**) A violent and dangerous whirlpool off the NW coast of Norway. 2 Any whirlpool. 3 A dangerous and irresistible force that resembles a maelstrom in its action: the destructive *maelstrom* of hatred.

maes·tro [mīs′trō] *n.* A master in any art, especially an important conductor, composer, or performer of music.

Ma·fi·a [mä′fē·ə] *n.* 1 A secret criminal organization in Sicily. 2 An alleged secret organization of criminals said to be active in the United States and other countries. 3 (*often written* **mafia**) *slang* A powerful and ruthless group of people.

Ma·fi·o·so [mä′fē·ō′sō] *n., pl.* **Ma·fi·o·si** [mä′fē·ō′sē] A member of the Mafia.

mag·a·zine [mag′ə·zēn′ *or* mag′ə·zēn′] *n.* 1 A publication that appears at regular intervals, containing articles, stories, and other features by various writers. 2 A storage place, especially for military supplies. 3 A building for storing explosives, or a room in a ship or a fort for such a purpose. 4 A container, as one in a rifle or pistol, that holds cartridges and feeds them into the chamber. 5 The enclosed space in a camera that holds the film.

ma·gen·ta [mə·jen′tə] *n., adj.* Purplish rose or purplish red.

mag·got [mag′ət] *n.* The legless larva of an insect, as the housefly, usually found in decaying matter.

Ma·gi [mā′jī] *n.pl.* In the Bible, the three wise men who came with gifts for the baby Jesus.

mag·ic [maj′ik] *n.* 1 The use of such things as formulas, charms, or rites to gain supposed supernatural power. 2 *adj. use*: a *magic* charm. 3 Any unusual or powerful influence or effect: the *magic* of the moonlight. 4 Tricks performed by a magician; sleight of hand. ◆ *Magic, witchcraft,* and *voodoo* all have to do with matters that are apparently supernatural. *Magic* is the common term and includes tricks such as pulling rabbits out of hats as well as magic used for evil purposes. *Witchcraft* is magic used for personal or evil motives. *Voodoo* was initially a religion that originated in Africa. It involves a belief in evil magic and the use of charms and fetishes.

mag·i·cal [maj′i·kəl] *adj.* Of, having to do with, or produced by magic. —**mag′i·cal·ly** *adv.*

ma·gi·cian [mə·jish′ən] *n.* A person who performs magic, especially an entertainer specializing in magic tricks.

magic lantern An old-fashioned term for SLIDE PROJECTOR.

mag·is·te·ri·al [maj′is·tir′ē·əl] *adj.* 1 Of or having to do with a magistrate: *magisterial* duties. 2 Dictatorial; pompous; authoritative: a *magisterial* manner of speaking.

mag·is·tra·cy [maj′is·trə·sē] *n., pl.* **mag·is·tra·cies** 1 The office, duties, or term of a magistrate. 2 Magistrates as a group.

mag·is·trate [maj′is·trāt′ *or* maj′is·trit] *n.* 1 A high public official having many executive or legal powers, as the president of a nation. 2 A minor judge, as a justice of the peace.

mag·lev [mag′lev′] *n.* A high-speed railroad train that floats along its tracks on a magnetic field.

mag·ma [mag′mə] *n., pl.* **mag·ma·ta** [mag′mə·tə] The hot, partly liquid mass of rock material within the earth from which igneous rocks are formed.

Mag·na Char·ta or **Mag·na Car·ta** [mag′nə kär′·tə] 1 The document that guaranteed certain liberties to the English people which the barons of England forced King John to sign in 1215. 2 Any document that secures liberty and rights.

mag·na cum lau·de [mäg′nä ko͝om lou′də *or* mag′·nə ko͝om lôd′ē] With great praise or high honor. ◆ This is a Latin phrase used to indicate that a person is graduating with an excellent record from a college or university.

mag·na·nim·i·ty [mag′nə·nim′ə·tē] *n., pl.* **mag·na·nim·i·ties** 1 The quality of being magnanimous. 2 A magnanimous act.

mag·nan·i·mous [mag·nan′ə·məs] *adj.* Showing generosity in forgiving insults or injuries; not given to resentment. —**mag·nan′i·mous·ly** *adv.*

mag·nate [mag′nāt′] *n.* A person of rank or importance: an industrial *magnate.*

mag·ne·sia [mag·nē′zhə *or* mag·nē′shə] *n.* A white, powdery magnesium compound, used in making firebrick and as a laxative.

mag·ne·si·um [mag·nē′zē·əm *or* mag·ne′zhəm] *n.* An abundant, very reactive, silvery white metallic element never found free in nature, used in technology and essential in biological systems.

mag·net [mag′nit] *n.* An object that creates a magnetic field around itself and so is able to attract iron or steel.

a	add	**i**	it	**o͝o**	took	**oi**	oil
ā	ace	**ī**	ice	**o͞o**	pool	**ou**	pout
â	care	**o**	odd	**u**	up	**ng**	ring
ä	palm	**ō**	open	**û**	burn	**th**	thin
e	end	**ô**	order	**yo͞o**	fuse	**t͟h**	this
ē	equal					**zh**	vision

ə = {a in *above*, e in *sicken*, i in *possible*, o in *melon*, u in *circus*}

M

mag·net·ic [mag·net′ik] *adj.* 1 Capable of being attracted by a magnet: a *magnetic* metal. 2 Acting as a magnet: *magnetic* scissors. 3 Capable of being magnetized, as iron. 4 Of, related to, or operating by magnetism. 5 Exercising a strong attraction or personal power: The politician has a *magnetic* personality.

magnetic field A region surrounding a magnet, an electromagnet, or a moving electric charge, in which magnetism may be detected.

magnetic flux The lines of force in a magnetic field.

magnetic needle A magnet in the form of a slender bar which, when able to move freely, points its poles toward the magnetic poles of the earth, roughly indicating north and south.

magnetic north The direction toward which the north-seeking end of a compass needle points, indicating the northern point of the earth's magnetic field rather than true north.

magnetic pole 1 One of the points of a magnet or electromagnet where the magnetic field is strongest. 2 One of the points where the earth's magnetic field is strongest, close to but not at the geographical North and South Poles.

magnetic tape A plastic or paper tape coated with magnetic particles, used in recording sound, television programs, and computer data.

mag·net·ism [mag′nə·tiz′əm] *n.* 1 An effect seen in the attraction of iron by a magnet and in the ability of magnetic poles to attract and repel each other. This effect occurs in connection with moving electricity. 2 The science that deals with such effects. 3 The personal quality that attracts or influences: The star's *magnetism* was the reason for the movie's success.

mag·net·ite [mag′nə·tīt′] *n.* A heavy, strongly magnetic mineral, an important iron ore.

mag·net·ize [mag′nə·tīz′] *v.* **mag·net·ized, mag·net·iz·ing** 1 To make into a magnet: to *magnetize* a steel bar. 2 To attract by strong, personal influence; captivate.

mag·ne·to [mag·nē′tō] *n., pl.* **mag·ne·tos** A type of electrical generator with permanent magnets, often used to produce the electrical spark in certain internal-combustion engines.

mag·ne·to·sphere [mag·nē′tō·sfir′] *n.* 1 A region of the earth's upper atmosphere in which the earth's magnetic field is so strong that charged particles are trapped in it. 2 A similar region surrounding other heavenly bodies.

magnet school A public school that offers a specialized or enriched program in order to attract students from a wide area of the community.

magni- A prefix meaning: Great or large, as in *magnification.*

mag·ni·fi·ca·tion [mag′nə·fə·kā′shən] *n.* 1 The act or process of magnifying. 2 The condition of being magnified. 3 The amount or degree of magnifying. 4 Something that has been magnified.

mag·nif·i·cence [mag·nif′ə·səns] *n.* Impressive splendor, beauty, or grandeur.

mag·nif·i·cent [mag·nif′ə·sənt] *adj.* 1 Grand and stately; splendid: a *magnificent* house. 2 Exalted; superb: a *magnificent* poem.

mag·ni·fy [mag′nə·fī′] *v.* **mag·ni·fied, mag·ni·fy·ing** 1 To make (something) look larger than its actual or normal size: Telescopes *magnify* images of stars. 2 To cause to seem greater or more important; exaggerate: He *magnifies* his difficulties. **—mag′ni·fi′er** *n.*

magnifying glass A lens or system of lenses that makes objects seen through it look larger.

Magnifying glass

mag·nil·o·quent [mag·nil′ə·kwənt] *adj.* Speaking or spoken in a pompous, showy way: a *magniloquent* speech. **—mag·nil′o·quence** *n.*

mag·ni·tude [mag′nə·t(y)o͞od′] *n.* 1 Size or extent: an art collection of great *magnitude.* 2 Greatness or importance: a problem of no *magnitude.* 3 A number indicating the relative brightness of a star. A star with a magnitude of 6 can barely be seen; a star with a magnitude of 1 is a hundred times brighter.

mag·no·li·a [mag·nō′lē·ə *or* mag·nōl′yə] *n.* An ornamental flowering shrub or tree with large, fragrant, white, pink, purple, or yellow flowers.

mag·pie [mag′pī] *n.* 1 Any of various large, noisy birds, having a long tapering tail and black and white plumage. 2 A person who talks a lot.

ma·guey [ma·gā′ *or* mag′wā] *n., pl.* **ma·gueys** 1 Any of several plants of Mexico and tropical America having large, stiff, fleshy leaves from which rope is made. 2 The rope or fiber from this plant.

Mag·yar [mag′yär] 1 *n.* A member of the main group of the population of Hungary. 2 *n.* The Hungarian language of these people. 3 *adj.* Of or having to do with the Magyars or their language.

ma·ha·ra·ja or **ma·ha·ra·jah** [mä′hə·rä′jə] *n.* A title of certain princes of India, particularly one ruling an Indian state.

ma·ha·ra·ni or **ma·ha·ra·nee** [mä′hə·rä′nē] *n.* 1 The wife of a maharaja. 2 An Indian princess.

ma·hat·ma [mə·hat′mə *or* mə·hät′mə] *n.* In some Asian religions, a holy person who has special knowledge and power.

Ma·hi·can [mə·hē′kən] *n., pl.* **Ma·hi·can** or **Ma·hi·cans** 1 A tribe of North American Indians once living in the upper Hudson River valley. 2 A member of this tribe. 3 The language of this tribe.

mah-jongg or **mah·jong** [mä′zhong′] *n.* A game of Chinese origin, usually played by four persons with 144 tiles.

ma·hog·a·ny [mə·hog′ə·nē] *n., pl.* **ma·hog·a·nies** 1 Any of various tropical trees yielding reddish brown hardwood, used for furniture. 2 The wood itself. 3 *adj., n.* Reddish brown.

ma·hout [mə·hout′] *n.* A person who keeps and drives an elephant.

maid [mād] *n.* 1 A young, unmarried woman or girl; maiden. 2 A female servant.

maid·en [mād′(ə)n] 1 *n.* An unmarried woman, especially if young. 2 *adj. use: maiden* modesty. 3 *adj.* Unmarried: a *maiden* aunt. 4 *adj.* Of or having to do with the first use, trial, or experience: a ship's *maiden* voyage.

maid·en·hair [mād′(ə)n·hâr′] *n.* A very delicate and graceful fern with a thin black stem, common in damp, rocky woods.

maid·en·hood [mād′(ə)n·ho͝od′] *n.* The state or time of being a maiden.

maid·en·ly [mād′(ə)n·lē] *adj.* Of, having to do with, or suiting a maiden.

maiden name A woman's last name before she is married.

maid-in-wait·ing [mād′ən·wāt′ing] *n., pl.* **maids-in-waiting** [mādz′ən·wāt′ing] An unmarried woman or girl, usually a noblewoman, who attends a queen or princess.
maid of honor 1 The chief unmarried woman attendant of a bride at a wedding. 2 An unmarried woman, usually of noble birth, attending an empress, queen, or princess.
maid·ser·vant [mād′sûr′vənt] *n.* A female servant.
mail[1] [māl] 1 *n.* Letters or parcels sent or received through a governmental postal system. 2 *n.* The postal system itself. 3 *n.* Postal matter collected or delivered at a certain time: the morning *mail.* 4 *adj. use*: a *mail* truck. 5 *v.* To send by mail; put into the mail.
mail[2] [māl] *n.* Flexible armor made of linking rings or overlapping scales.
mail·a·ble [mā′lə·bəl] *adj.* Adapted or legally acceptable for mailing.

Mail armor

mail·box [māl′boks′] *n.* 1 A box in which mail is deposited for collection. 2 A private box for arriving mail.
mail carrier A person who carries and delivers mail.
Mail·gram [māl′gram′] A message sent by telegraph to a local post office and then delivered with regular mail: a trademark.
mail·man [māl′man′] *n., pl.* **mail·men** [māl′men′] A mail carrier.
mail order An order sent by mail for goods to be shipped to the buyer.
maim [mām] *v.* To take away a part of the body or the use of it; cripple: The automobile accident *maimed* the driver.
main [mān] 1 *adj.* First or chief, as in size, rank, or importance; principal; leading: the *main* building; the *main* event. 2 *n.* A principal pipe in a system, as one for conveying gas or water. 3 *n.* The open sea: used mostly in poems. **—by main force** or **by main strength** By full effort or exertion. **—in the main** For the most part; on the whole; chiefly; principally. **—with might and main** With utmost effort.
main clause Another term for INDEPENDENT CLAUSE.
main·frame [mān′frām′] *n.* 1 The main part (or central processing unit) of a large computer. 2 A large central computer to which a number of data terminals can be connected.
main·land [mān′land′ *or* mān′lənd] *n.* The main part of a continent, as distinguished from an island or peninsula.
main·ly [mān′lē] *adv.* For the most part; chiefly; principally.
main·mast [mān′məst *or* mān′mast′] *n.* The principal mast of a vessel, usually the second mast from the bow.
main·sail [mān′səl *or* mān′sāl′] *n.* The principal sail on a mainmast.
main·spring [mān′spring′] *n.* 1 The principal spring of a mechanism, as a watch. 2 The chief cause: the *mainspring* of conflict.
main·stay [mān′stā′] *n.* 1 The rope leading forward from the mainmast, used to steady the mast. 2 A chief support: the *mainstay* of a family.
main·stream [mān′strēm′] *n.* The prevailing or dominant course, direction, or trend: Her work is outside the *mainstream* of modern art.
main·tain [mān·tān′] *v.* 1 To carry on or continue: to *maintain* a constant speed. 2 To preserve or keep: to *maintain* an open mind. 3 To keep in proper condition: to *maintain* roads. 4 To supply with means of support; provide for: to *maintain* a family. 5 To state or declare; insist: They *maintain* that their opinion is right. 6 To hold or defend, as a military position.
main·tain·er [mān·tān′ər] *n.* A worker hired to keep a place, as a building, in good condition.
main·te·nance [mān′tə·nəns] *n.* 1 The act of maintaining. 2 A being maintained; support: to provide for *maintenance.* 3 Means of support.
main·top [mān′top′] *n.* A platform on a ship's mainmast.
maize [māz] *n.* Corn, the plant or its seeds; Indian corn.
Maj. major.
ma·jes·tic [mə·jes′tik] *adj.* Having or showing majesty; stately; royal: a *majestic* manner. **—ma·jes′·ti·cal·ly** *adv.*
maj·es·ty [maj′is·tē] *n., pl.* **maj·es·ties** 1 Great dignity, beauty, and grandeur: the *majesty* of the sea. 2 Supreme authority: the *majesty* of the law. 3 (*written* **Majesty**) A title or form of address for a monarch.
Maj. Gen. major general.
ma·jor [mā′jər] 1 *adj.* Greater, as in quantity, number, or extent: The *major* part of my work is done. 2 *adj.* Having great importance, quality, or rank: She's a *major* writer. 3 *adj.* Indicating or based on a musical scale that has semitones between the third and fourth and seventh and eighth tones and whole tones between all the others. 4 *adj.* Indicating a chord that could be formed from the first, third, and fifth or fifth, seventh, and second tones of a major scale. 5 *n.* A military rank. In the U.S. Army, a major is an officer ranking next above a captain and next below a lieutenant colonel. 6 *n.* The subject or field of study a student selects as the chief one: My *major* is French. 7 *n.* The student: Sue is a physics *major.* 8 *v.* To study a subject as a major.
ma·jor-do·mo [mā′jər·dō′mō] *n., pl.* **ma·jor-do·mos** The chief steward or butler, especially of a royal or noble household.
ma·jor·ette [mā′jə·ret′] *n.* Another name for DRUM MAJORETTE.
major general A military rank. In the U.S. Army, a major general is an officer ranking next above a brigadier general and next below a lieutenant general.
ma·jor·i·ty [mə·jôr′ə·tē] *n., pl.* **ma·jor·i·ties** 1 More than half of a given number or group; the greater part: The *majority* of students voted for her. 2 The number of votes for a person or measure in

a	add	**i**	it	**o͝o**	took	**oi**	oil
ā	ace	**ī**	ice	**o͞o**	pool	**ou**	pout
â	care	**o**	odd	**u**	up	**ng**	ring
ä	palm	**ō**	open	**û**	burn	**th**	thin
e	end	**ô**	order	**yo͞o**	fuse	**t͟h**	this
ē	equal					**zh**	vision

ə = a in *above* e in *sicken* i in *possible* o in *melon* u in *circus*

M

excess of the sum of the votes for others: When a vote comes out 60, 40, and 10, the winner has a *majority* of 10 or a plurality of 20. **3** The legal age at which a person assumes adult rights and responsibilities.

major league **1** One of the two principal groups of professional baseball teams in the U.S. **2** A league of the principal teams in another professional sport.

major scale A musical scale having eight tones, with whole steps between all the tones except the third to fourth and seventh to eighth, both of which are separated by half steps.

ma·jus·cule [maj′əs·kyōōl′ *or* mə·jus′kyōōl′] *n.* A large letter, as a capital or uncial.

make [māk] *v.* **made, mak·ing,** *n.* **1** *v.* To form, produce, or bring into existence, as by putting parts together or shaping: to *make* a car; to *make* a new dress. **2** *n.* Type or brand: What *make* of car is that? **3** *n.* The manner or style in which something is made: Is the *make* becoming to me? **4** *v.* To bring about; cause: to *make* trouble; to *make* a sound. **5** *v.* To cause to be: The wind *makes* us cold. **6** *v.* To appoint: The class *made* me president. **7** *v.* To form in the mind: Let's *make* plans. **8** *v.* To understand: What do you *make* of this story? **9** *v.* To utter: to *make* an announcement. **10** *v.* To engage in: to *make* war. **11** *v.* To get, earn, or acquire: to *make* a fortune. **12** *v.* To act so as to gain: to *make* new friends. **13** *v.* To add up or amount to: Four quarts *make* a gallon. **14** *v.* To bring the total to: This *makes* three days of continuous rain. **15** *v.* To draw up, enact, or establish: to *make* a will; to *make* a treaty. **16** *v.* To prepare for use: to *make* a bed. **17** *v.* To force; compel: Then a detour sign *made* us turn off. **18** *v.* To be the essential part of: Fresh fruit *makes* a nourishing snack. **19** *v.* To provide: *Make* a place in the line for us. **20** *v.* To become through development: You will *make* a good golfer. **21** *v.* To cause the success of: Her last book *made* her. **22** *v.* To perform; do: to *make* a gesture. **23** *v.* To act or behave in a certain manner: to *make* merry. **24** *v.* To travel at the rate of: to *make* 60 miles an hour. **25** *v.* To arrive at; reach: We'll *make* Wichita by noon. **26** *v.* To arrive in time for: We barely *made* our train. **27** *v. informal* To win a place on: to *make* the track team. **28** *v. informal* To attain the rank or position of: to *make* colonel in the army. **—make after** To pursue; follow. **—make away with** **1** To carry off; steal. **2** To kill. **3** To get rid of. **—make believe** To pretend. **—make for** **1** To go toward: Let's *make for* the city. **2** To bring about: Automobile seat belts *make for* safer driving. **—make good** **1** To succeed. **2** To carry out: to *make good* a threat. **3** To compensate for: Will your insurance company *make good* your losses in the robbery? **—make it** *informal* To succeed in doing something. **—make off with** To steal. **—make out** **1** To see: I can't quite *make out* the road ahead. **2** To understand. **3** To succeed: How are you *making out* in school? **4** To fill out, as a paper with blanks. **5** To portray or represent as being: The story *made* us *out* to be brave. **—make over** **1** To put into a changed form: to *make over* a suit. **2** To transfer title or possession of: to *make over* an estate. **—make time** To travel with speed. **—make up** **1** To compound, as a prescription. **2** To be the parts of: What *makes up* this soup? **3** To settle differences and be friendly again. **4** To invent: to *make up* an answer. **5** To supply the lack in: Will you *make up* the money we need? **6** To compensate: How can you *make up* for all the wrong you did? **7** To settle; decide: to *make up* one's mind. **8** To arrange lines of type or illustrations, as for a book. **9** To put cosmetics on. **—make up to** *informal* To make a show of friendliness and affection toward; flatter. **—mak′er** *n.*

make-be·lieve [māk′bi·lēv′] **1** *n.* Something not true or real; sham; pretense. **2** *adj.* Pretended; unreal: a *make-believe* zoo with toy animals.

make·shift [māk′shift′] *n.* **1** A temporary substitute. **2** *adj. use*: a *makeshift* table.

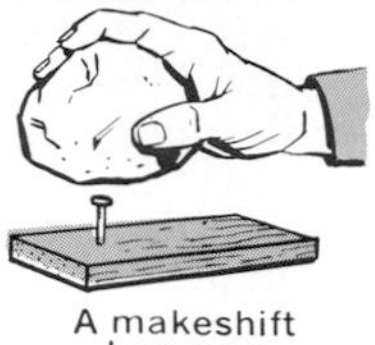
A makeshift hammer

make·up or **make-up** [māk′up′] *n.* **1** The arrangement or combination of parts of anything: the *makeup* of a chemical compound. **2** The powder, paint, wigs, and pads used by an actor portraying a character. **3** Cosmetics. **4** The physical or mental characteristics of a person: a slim *makeup*; a cheerful *makeup*. **5** The arrangement of type and illustrations in a magazine, newspaper, or other printed work. **6** A test given to a student who has missed a previous one.

mal·a·chite [mal′ə·kīt′] *n.* A brittle, green mineral, often used to make ornamental articles.

mal·ad·just·ed [mal′ə·jus′tid] *adj.* Badly adjusted, especially badly suited to or in conflict with the persons, things, and conditions that surround one in life. **—mal′ad·just′ment** *n.*

mal·a·droit [mal′ə·droit′] *adj.* Lacking skill; clumsy; awkward. **—mal′a·droit′ly** *adv.* **—mal′a·droit′ness** *n.*

mal·a·dy [mal′ə·dē] *n., pl.* **mal·a·dies** A disease, sickness, or illness.

mal·a·mute or **mal·e·mute** [mal′ə·myōōt′] *n.* A breed of sled dog from northern North America.

mal·a·prop·ism [mal′ə·prop·iz′əm] *n.* **1** The humorous misuse of a word, usually unintentional. **2** An example of malapropism, as "You could have knocked me over with a fender" (feather). ◆ The word *malapropism* comes from Mrs. *Malaprop,* a character noted for the misuse of words in *The Rivals,* a play by Richard Brinsley Sheridan.

ma·lar·i·a [mə·lâr′ē·ə] *n.* A disease spread by the bite of an infected anopheles mosquito and marked by recurrent attacks of chills, fever, and sweating. **—ma·lar′i·al** *adj.* ◆ *Malaria* comes from the Italian *mala aria,* meaning *bad air.* Later it came to mean the disease which was supposed to be caused by foul air coming from swamps.

ma·lar·key [mə·lär′kē] *n. slang* Meaningless or insincere talk.

Ma·lay [mā′lā′ *or* mə·lā′] **1** *n.* One of a people living on the Malay Peninsula and adjacent areas. **2** *n.* Their language. **3** *adj.* Of or having to do with the Malays. **—Ma·lay·an** [mə·lā′ən] *adj., n.*

Ma·lay·sian [mə·lā′zhən] **1** *adj.* Of or from Malaysia. **2** *n.* A person born in or a citizen of Malaysia.

mal·con·tent [mal′kən·tent′] **1** *adj.* Discontented or dissatisfied; rebellious. **2** *n.* A person who is malcontent; rebel.

mal de mer [mal′də·mâr′] Seasickness.

Mal·div·i·an [mal·div′ē·ən] **1** *adj.* Of or from the Maldives. **2** *n.* A person born in or a citizen of the Maldives.

male [māl] **1** *adj.* Of the sex that can fertilize eggs or, in plants, produce pollen. **2** *n.* A person, animal, or plant of this sex. **3** *adj.* Of or having to do with this sex: *male* characteristics.

mal·e·dic·tion [mal'ə·dik'shən] *n.* A calling for evil or injury to happen to another person.

mal·e·fac·tor [mal'ə·fak'tər] *n.* **1** A person who commits a crime. **2** A person who does evil.

ma·lev·o·lent [mə·lev'ə·lənt] *adj.* Wishing evil to others; malicious. **—ma·lev'o·lence** *n.* **—ma·lev'o·lent·ly** *adv.*

mal·fea·sance [mal·fē'zəns] *n.* A wrong or dishonest act, especially by a public official.

mal·for·ma·tion [mal'fôr·mā'shən] *n.* A wrong or defective formation, especially of some part of the body.

mal·formed [mal·fôrmd'] *adj.* Badly formed.

mal·func·tion [mal·fungk'shən] **1** *v.* To fail to work properly. **2** *n.* A failure to work properly.

Ma·li·an [mä'lē·ən] **1** *adj.* Of or from Mali. **2** *n.* A person born in or a citizen of Mali.

mal·ice [mal'is] *n.* An intention or desire to hurt or injure someone; ill will; spite.

ma·li·cious [mə·lish'əs] *adj.* Showing or having malice; spiteful. **—ma·li'cious·ly** *adv.*

ma·lign [mə·līn'] **1** *v.* To speak evil of; slander. **2** *adj.* Evil; malicious. **3** *adj.* Harmful; injurious. **—ma·lign'er** *n.*

ma·lig·nan·cy [mə·lig'nən·sē] *n., pl.* **ma·lig·nan·cies** **1** The condition of being malignant. **2** A very bad tumor, often fatal.

ma·lig·nant [mə·lig'nənt] *adj.* **1** Tending to do great harm; evil; injurious: *malignant* forces. **2** Very harmful physically, as a disease that grows progressively worse. **—ma·lig'nant·ly** *adv.*

ma·lig·ni·ty [mə·lig'nə·tē] *n., pl.* **ma·lig·ni·ties** **1** Intense ill will; malice. **2** Harmfulness; injuriousness.

ma·lin·ger [mə·ling'gər] *v.* To pretend sickness so as to avoid work or duty. **—ma·lin'ger·er** *n.*

mall [môl] *n.* **1** A promenade or walk, usually public and often shaded. **2** An area with many stores that is closed to vehicles. **3** A shopping center. **4** A strip of grass or concrete dividing a road or highway.

mal·lard [mal'ərd] *n., pl.* **mal·lard** or **mal·lards** A common wild duck having brownish plumage and, in the male, a bright green head.

mal·le·a·ble [mal'ē·ə·bəl] *adj.* **1** Capable of being hammered or rolled out without breaking: Gold is *malleable.* **2** Easily adapted or influenced: a *malleable* personality. **—mal'le·a·bil'i·ty** *n.*

mal·let [mal'it] *n.* **1** A hammer, usually with a wooden head. **2** A long-handled wooden hammer, used in croquet and in polo.

Mallet

mal·le·us [mal'ē·əs] *n., pl.* **mal·le·i** [mal'ē·ī'] The largest, outermost of the three small bones in the middle ear; hammer.

mal·low [mal'ō] *n.* A type of herb having rounded leaves and pale pink, purplish, or white flowers.

malm·sey [mäm'zē] *n., pl.* **malm·seys** A strong, sweet, white wine.

mal·nour·ished [mal·nûr'isht] *adj.* Suffering from malnutrition; not having had the proper food or nourishment.

mal·nu·tri·tion [mal'n(y)o͞o·trish'ən] *n.* A harmful condition of the body caused by lack of enough or proper food or nourishment.

mal·oc·clu·sion [mal'ə·klo͞o'zhən] *n.* An abnormal condition in which the teeth of the upper and lower jaws do not meet properly.

mal·o·dor·ous [mal·ō'də·rəs] *adj.* Having an unpleasant odor; smelling bad. **—mal·o'dor·ous·ly** *adv.* **—mal·o'dor·ous·ness** *n.*

mal·prac·tice [mal·prak'tis] *n.* **1** In medicine, harmful treatment or neglect of a patient. **2** Improper conduct in any profession.

malt [môlt] **1** *n.* Grain, usually barley, that is soaked in water, allowed to sprout, and then dried in a kiln, used to make beer, ale, or whisky. **2** *v.* To cause (grain) to become malt. **3** *v.* To mix with malt: a *malted* milk.

Mal·tese [môl·tēz'] **1** *adj.* Of or from Malta. **2** *n.* A person born in or a citizen of Malta. **3** *n.* The language of Malta.

Maltese cat A cat with long, silky, bluish gray fur.

Maltese cross An eight-pointed cross.

Maltese cross

malt liquor An alcoholic beverage, as beer or ale, that is fermented from malt.

malt·ose [môl'tōs'] *n.* A white crystalline sugar formed by the action of an enzyme on starch.

mal·treat [mal·trēt'] *v.* To treat badly, roughly, or unkindly; abuse. **—mal·treat'ment** *n.*

ma·ma or **mam·ma** [mä'mə *or* mə·mä'] *n.* Mother: used especially by or in talking to children. ◆ *Mama* is a baby's word for mother. It is a repetition of the sound [mä].

mam·ba [mäm'bə] *n.* Any of several large African venomous snakes.

mam·bo [mäm'bō] *n., pl.* **mam·bos,** *v.* **mam·boed, mam·bo·ing** **1** *n.* A Latin American dance that is somewhat like the rumba. **2** *n.* The music for this dance. **3** *v.* To dance this dance.

mam·mal [mam'əl] *n.* Any of the vertebrate animals the females of which produce milk for their young. People, cows, cats, mice, and whales are mammals.

mam·ma·li·an [ma·mā'lē·ən *or* ma·māl'yən] *adj.* Of or having to do with mammals.

mam·ma·ry [mam'ər·ē] *adj.* Of or having to do with the breast.

mammary gland A milk-secreting gland, such as a breast or udder, found in female mammals.

mam·mo·gram [mam'ə·gram'] *n.* An X-ray photograph of the breasts.

mam·mog·ra·phy [mə·mog'rə·fē] *n.* The technique of medically examining the breasts by X ray.

mam·mon [mam'ən] *n.* Wealth thought of as an evil influence and a bad thing to strive for.

a	add	**i**	it	**o͝o**	took	**oi**	oil
ā	ace	**ī**	ice	**o͞o**	pool	**ou**	pout
â	care	**o**	odd	**u**	up	**ng**	ring
ä	palm	**ō**	open	**û**	burn	**th**	thin
e	end	**ô**	order	**yo͞o**	fuse	**th̸**	this
ē	equal					**zh**	vision

ə = a in *above* e in *sicken* i in *possible* / o in *melon* u in *circus*

M

mam·moth [mam′əth] 1 *n.* A large, now extinct animal related to the elephant. It had long tusks that curved upward and a hairy skin. 2 *adj.* Huge; colossal.

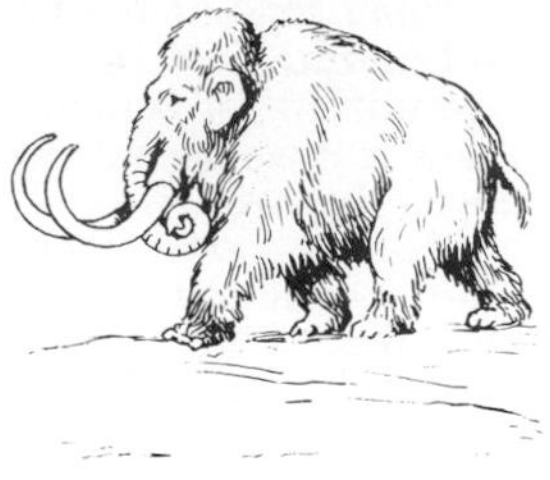
Mammoth

mam·my [mam′ē] *n., pl.* **mam·mies** 1 Mother. 2 A black woman hired to care for white children, especially formerly in the southern U.S.

man [man] *n., pl.* **men** [men], *v.* **manned, man·ning** 1 *n.* An adult male human being. 2 *v.* To supply with people, as for work or defense: to *man* a fort. 3 *n.* Any person: All *men* should be free. 4 *n.* Human beings in general; the human race: *man's* efforts toward conquering disease. 5 *n.* A male employee, servant, or follower: the supevisor and his *men.* 6 *n.* A husband: *man* and wife. 7 *n.* A piece used in certain games, as chess or checkers. 8 *v.* To take a place on, at, or in, as for work or defense. **—as one man** Unanimously. **—to a man** Unanimously.

Man. Manitoba.

man·a·cle [man′ə·kəl] *n., v.* **man·a·cled, man·a·cling** 1 *n.* A handcuff. 2 *v.* To put handcuffs on. 3 *v.* To restrain or hamper.

man·age [man′ij] *v.* **man·aged, man·ag·ing** 1 To direct or control; have charge of: to *manage* a hotel. 2 To accomplish somehow; contrive. 3 To cause to do what one wants: to *manage* a crowd. 4 To use; handle: to *manage* a power saw. 5 To make out; get by.

man·age·a·ble [man′ij·ə·bəl] *adj.* Capable of being managed, controlled, or directed.

man·age·ment [man′ij·mənt] *n.* 1 The act or practice of managing. 2 The person or persons who manage something, as a business or institution. 3 People who manage business, as a group.

man·ag·er [man′ij·ər] *n.* A person who manages a business, institution, or enterprise.

man·a·ge·ri·al [man′ə·jir′ē·əl] *adj.* Of or having to do with a manager or management.

ma·ña·na [mä·nyä′nä] 1 *adv.* Tomorrow. 2 *adv.* At some time in the future. 3 *n.* Tomorrow or a future day. ◆ *Mañana* is a Spanish word meaning *tomorrow.*

man-at-arms [man′ət·ärmz′] *n., pl.* **men-at-arms** [men′ət·ärmz′] A soldier, especially a heavily armed soldier of medieval times who rode horseback.

man·a·tee [man′ə·tē′] *n.* A mammal that lives off Florida and in the Gulf of Mexico. It has flippers, a broad flat tail, and eats only plants.

Manatee

Man·chu [man·cho͞o′ *or* man′cho͞o] *n.* 1 A member of a people from Manchuria that conquered China. They ruled it from 1644 to 1912. 2 The language of this people.

man·da·rin [man′də·rin] *n.* 1 A member of any of nine grades of public officials who served the emperors of China until 1912. 2 (*written* **Mandarin**) The most widespread dialect of the Chinese language. 3 A tangerine.

man·date [man′dāt′] *n.* 1 A formal, usually written command from someone in authority. 2 In politics, the wishes of the voters, regarded as an order, as expressed in an election.

man·da·to·ry [man′də·tôr′ē] *adj.* Demanded or required by custom, duty, or someone in authority.

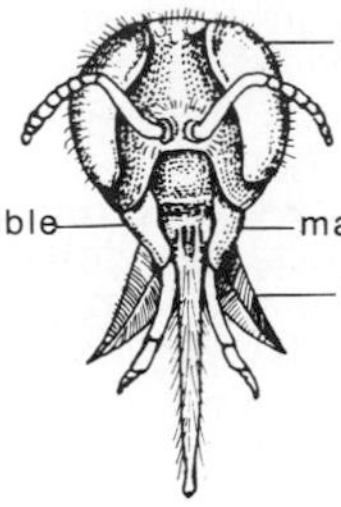

Mandible of an insect

man·di·ble [man′də·bəl] *n.* 1 The lower jawbone. 2 Either the upper or lower part of a bird's beak or an insect's jaws.

man·do·lin [man′də·lin *or* man′də·lin′] *n.* A musical instrument with a pear-shaped body and eight to twelve metal strings.

Mandolin

man·drake [man′drāk′] *n.* A plant related to belladonna, having roots sometimes resembling the human form.

man·drel or **man·dril** [man′·drəl] *n.* 1 A spindle or shaft, usually tapered, used to support material that is being shaped or worked on a lathe. 2 A metal bar or rod that is used as a core around which material such as metal or glass may be cast, molded, or otherwise shaped.

man·drill [man′dril] *n.* A powerful baboon of West Africa, having strong teeth and bright scarlet and blue patches on the face and rump.

mane [mān] *n.* The long hair growing on and about the neck of some animals, as the horse and lion.

ma·neu·ver [mə·n(y)o͞o′vər] 1 *n.* A planned movement or action, as of troops or warships. 2 *v.* To put (as troops or warships) through a maneuver or maneuvers. 3 *n.* Any skillful move or action. 4 *v.* To use planned moves skillfully. 5 *v.* To force or trick by skillful moves.

man Friday A reliable male employee, especially one who performs many different duties.

man·ful [man′fəl] *adj.* Brave and resolute; manly. **—man′ful·ly** *adv.*

man·ga·nese [mang′gə·nēz′ *or* mang′gə·nēs′] *n.* A hard, brittle, reactive metallic element resembling iron, used in various alloys and biologically important as a constituent of various enzymes.

mange [mānj] *n.* A skin disease of animals marked by itching and loss of hair.

man·ger [mān′jər] *n.* A trough or box for feeding horses or cattle.

man·gle[1] [mang′gəl] *v.* **man·gled, man·gling** 1 To tear or disfigure, as by cutting, bruising, or crushing: Our dog *mangled* a cat in a fight. 2 To mar or ruin; spoil; botch: to *mangle* one's part in a play.

man·gle[2] [mang′gəl] *n., v.* **man·gled, man·gling** 1 *n.* A machine for smoothing and pressing fabrics by passing them between rollers. 2 *v.* To smooth with a mangle: to *mangle* sheets.

man·go [mang′gō] *n., pl.* **man·goes** or **man·gos** 1 A

juicy tropical fruit having a slightly acid taste. 2 The tree it grows on.
man·grove [mang′grōv′] *n.* An evergreen tree or shrub of warm, marshy regions, having thick, leathery leaves and branches that take root and form a dense tangle of new growths.
man·gy [mān′jē] *adj.* **man·gi·er, man·gi·est** 1 Having mange: a *mangy* animal. 2 Dirty; shabby: a *mangy* blanket. **—man′gi·ness** *n.*
man·han·dle [man′han′dəl] *v.* **man·han·dled, man·han·dling** To handle with rough force.
man·hole [man′hōl′] *n.* A usually circular and covered opening by which a person may enter a sewer or boiler.

Manhole

man·hood [man′ho͝od′] *n.* 1 The condition or the time of being a man. 2 Manly qualities. 3 Men as a group.
man-hour [man′our′] *n.* An industrial unit of measurement, representing the amount of work one person can do in one hour.
man·hunt [man′hunt′] *n.* An organized, thorough, often extensive search for a person, especially for a criminal.
ma·ni·a [mā′nē·ə *or* mān′yə] *n.* 1 A mental disorder marked by excessive excitement, sometimes violence, and often swift changes of mood. 2 An exaggerated interest, desire, or enthusiasm: My cousin has a *mania* for parties.
ma·ni·ac [mā′nē·ak′] 1 *n.* A person who is violently insane; madman. 2 *adj.* Maniacal.
ma·ni·a·cal [mə·nī′ə·kəl] *adj.* 1 Violently insane; mad. 2 Suggesting madness or insanity: a *maniacal* laugh. **—ma·ni′a·cal·ly** *adv.*
man·ic [man′ik] *adj.* Having to do with, like, or affected by mania.
man·ic-de·pres·sive [man′ik·di·pres′iv] 1 *adj.* Having to do with a mental illness in which periods of depression alternate with periods of excitement. 2 *n.* A person suffering from this illness.
ma·ni·cot·ti [man′i·kot′ē] *n., pl.* **ma·ni·cot·ti** Pasta shaped like tubes, usually stuffed with cheese or a meat mixture and served with tomato sauce.
man·i·cure [man′ə·kyo͝or′] *n., v.* **man·i·cured, man·i·cur·ing** 1 *n.* The cosmetic care of the hands and fingernails. 2 *v.* To take care of (the hands and fingernails). **—man′i·cur′ist** *n.*
man·i·fest [man′ə·fest′] 1 *adj.* Easy to see or understand; evident: a *manifest* error. 2 *v.* To make apparent; reveal; show: to *manifest* a desire. 3 *n.* A list, as of cargo or passengers, for a ship or airplane.
man·i·fes·ta·tion [man′ə·fes·tā′shən] *n.* 1 The act of manifesting. 2 Something that manifests: Tears are a *manifestation* of sorrow.
man·i·fes·to [man′ə·fes′tō] *n., pl.* **man·i·fes·toes** or **man·i·fes·tos** An official statement or explanation, as of principles, plans, or motives, usually by a government or political group.
man·i·fold [man′ə·fōld′] 1 *adj.* Having many forms, kinds, or types; varied: *manifold* tasks. 2 *adj.* Having many parts or features: the *manifold* themes in a novel. 3 *v.* To make more than one copy of, as with carbon paper. 4 *n.* A copy made in this way. 5 *n.* A pipe having several openings, so as to connect it with other pipes.
man·i·kin [man′ə·kin] *n.* 1 A model of the human body used for demonstrating anatomy. 2 A little man; dwarf. 3 Another spelling of MANNEQUIN.

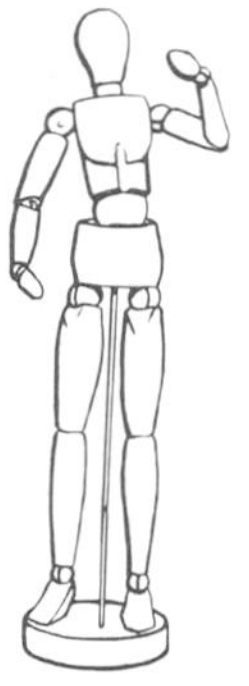
Manikin

Manila hemp The tough, inner fiber of a plant related to the banana, much used in making ropes and cords.
Manila paper A heavy, brown paper made from Manila hemp and similar plant fibers. It is used for making items such as wrapping paper and envelopes.
man·i·oc [man′ē·ok] *n.* Another name for CASSAVA, a tropical plant.
ma·nip·u·late [mə·nip′yə·lāt′] *v.* **ma·nip·u·lat·ed, ma·nip·u·lat·ing** 1 To operate or work with the hands; handle: to *manipulate* a truck in traffic. 2 To manage, control, or influence in a shrewd or dishonest way: to *manipulate* people for one's own benefit. 3 To alter or change, usually for dishonest reasons: to *manipulate* figures. **—ma·nip′u·la′·tor** *n.* ◆ *Manipulate* was formed from *manipulation,* which came into English first, based on the Latin word *manus,* meaning *hand.*
ma·nip·u·la·tion [mə·nip′yə·lā′shən] *n.* 1 The act of manipulating. 2 The condition of being manipulated. 3 An instance or example of manipulating: a dishonest *manipulation* of the figures.
man·kind *n.* 1 [man′kīnd′ *or* man′kīnd′] The whole human race; every human being. 2 [man′kīnd] Men as a group, as distinguished from women.
man·ly [man′lē] *adj.* **man·li·er, man·li·est** 1 Having the qualities considered appropriate to a man. 2 Having to do with or appropriate for a man: a *manly* voice. **—man′li·ness** *n.*
man-made [man′mād′] *adj.* Produced by humans rather than by nature.
man·na [man′ə] *n.* 1 In the Bible, the food miraculously given to the Israelites in the wilderness as they fled from Egypt. 2 Any unexpected help or gift.
man·ne·quin [man′ə·kin] *n.* 1 A life-sized model of a complete or partial human figure used for cutting, fitting, or displaying garments. 2 A person who models clothing; model.
man·ner [man′ər] *n.* 1 A way of doing, being done, or occurring: Fold it in this *manner.* 2 A way of behaving: a cheerful *manner.* 3 (*pl.*) Behavior judged by rules of politeness: good *manners.* 4 (*pl.*) Polite behavior: These children have no *manners.* 5 (*pl.*) Social customs. 6 Kind; sort: What *manner* of creature is this?
man·nered [man′ərd] *adj.* 1 Having (a certain kind of) manner or manners: often used in com-

a	add	**i**	it	**o͝o**	took	**oi**	oil
ā	ace	**ī**	ice	**o͞o**	pool	**ou**	pout
â	care	**o**	odd	**u**	up	**ng**	ring
ä	palm	**ō**	open	**û**	burn	**th**	thin
e	end	**ô**	order	**yo͞o**	fuse	**th̶**	this
ē	equal					**zh**	vision

ə = {a in *above* e in *sicken* i in *possible*
o in *melon* u in *circus*}

M

bination, as in *mild-mannered.* **2** Having mannerisms in writing or speaking.

man·ner·ism [man′ər·iz′əm] *n.* **1** An excessive or artificial use of a special manner or style: The author's writing has many *mannerisms.* **2** A personal habit, as of speech or behavior.

man·ner·ly [man′ər·lē] **1** *adj.* Having good manners; polite. **2** *adv.* With good manners; politely.

man·nish [man′ish] *adj.* Resembling, characteristic of, or suitable to a man; masculine: a *mannish* walk.

ma·noeu·ver [mə·n(y)ōō′vər] *n., v.* Another spelling of MANEUVER.

man-of-war [man′ə(v)·wôr′] *n., pl.* **men-of-war** [men′ə(v)·wôr′] An armed ship of any recognized navy; warship.

ma·nom·e·ter [mə·nom′ə·tər] *n.* An instrument used to measure the pressure of a fluid.

man·or [man′ər] *n.* **1** In Europe of the Middle Ages, an estate which belonged to a lord and was partly divided among peasants who paid for the use of the land in money, goods, or labor. **2** The house found on a manor; mansion.

ma·no·ri·al [mə·nôr′ē·əl] *adj.* Of, like, or having to do with a manor.

man·pow·er [man′pou′ər] *n.* **1** The power or energy supplied by human physical work. **2** The total number of people working or available for work or service, as in industry or the armed forces.

man·sard [man′särd′] *n.* **1** A four-sided roof having two different slopes on each of the four sides. **2** *adj. use*: a *mansard* roof.

Mansard roof

manse [mans] *n.* A clergyman's house; parsonage.

man·ser·vant [man′sûr′·vənt] *n., pl.* **men·ser·vants** [men′sûr′vənts] An adult male servant.

man·sion [man′shən] *n.* A large and impressive house, as of a wealthy person or family.

man·slaugh·ter [man′slô′tər] *n.* The killing of a human being unlawfully but without malice, as in an automobile accident.

man·ta or **man·ta ray** [man′tə] *n.* A large ocean fish having a flat body and winglike fins; devilfish (def. 1).

man·tel [man′təl] *n.* **1** The shelf above a fireplace. **2** The material, as wood, brick, or stone, that surrounds and decorates a fireplace.

man·tel·piece [man′təl·pēs′] *n.* Another name for MANTEL.

man·til·la [man·tē′(y)ə *or* man·til′ə] *n.* A large, lacy scarf or shawl usually worn over the shoulders and head by women, especially in Spain and Latin America.

Praying mantis

man·tis [man′tis] *n.* An insect with a long body and swiveling head, that folds its forelegs as if in prayer. It feeds on other insects.

man·tis·sa [man·tis′ə] *n.* The part of a common logarithm that is a decimal. For example, if 2.345 is a logarithm, .345 is the mantissa.

man·tle [man′təl] *n., v.* **man·tled, man·tling** **1** *n.* A loose and usually sleeveless garment worn over other garments; cloak. **2** *n.* Anything that clothes, covers, or conceals: a *mantle* of ice. **3** *v.* To cover with or as if with a mantle; conceal. **4** *n.* A cylindrical device made of a special, screenlike material that glows when a gas flame is lit inside of it. **5** *v.* To blush.

man·u·al [man′yōō·əl] **1** *adj.* Of or having to do with the hands. **2** *adj.* Done, operated, or used by the hands: *manual* work. **3** *n.* A small guidebook, reference book, or book of instructions; handbook. **—man′u·al·ly** *adv.*

manual alphabet An alphabet used by the deaf, in which different finger positions indicate different letters of the alphabet.

manual training In U.S. schools, practical training in work that involves the hands, as carpentry or metalworking.

man·u·fac·ture [man′yə·fak′chər] *v.* **man·u·fac·tured, man·u·fac·tur·ing,** *n.* **1** *v.* To make (a product), especially on a large scale and with machinery: to *manufacture* toys. **2** *v.* To make as if by manufacturing: A hive of bees *manufactures* honey. **3** *n.* The act of manufacturing. **4** *n.* Something that is manufactured. **5** *v.* To make up; invent: to *manufacture* a story. **—man′u·fac′·tur·er** *n.*

ma·nure [mə·n(y)ŏŏr′] *n., v.* **ma·nured, ma·nur·ing** **1** *n.* Any substance used to fertilize soils, as dung. **2** *v.* To apply manure to.

man·u·script [man′yə·skript′] *n.* Something, as a book, article, or document, written by hand or with a typewriter: The writer sent the finished *manuscript* to a publisher.

Manx [mangks] **1** *adj.* Of or having to do with the Isle of Man, or its people, customs, or language. **2** *n.* The Celtic language that was spoken on the Isle of Man, now virtually extinct. **3** *n.* (**the Manx**) The people born on or living on the Isle of Man.

Manx cat A breed of domestic cat with short hair and no visible tail.

man·y [men′ē] *adj.* **more, most,** *n., pron.* **1** *adj.* Adding up to a large number; numerous: There are *many* children in the school. **2** *n., pron.* A large number: *Many* applied for the job. **3** *n.* The majority of people; masses: The song was popular with the *many.* **—a good many** (*used with plural verb*) A rather large number: *A good many* of our high school students go on to college.

Mao·ism [mou′iz·əm] *n.* The political ideas and practices of Mao Zedong and his followers. **—Mao′·ist** *n., adj.*

Mao·ri [mou′rē *or* mä′ō·rē] *n., pl.* **Mao·ris** **1** One of an aboriginal people of New Zealand. **2** The language of these people.

map [map] *n., v.* **mapped, map·ping** **1** *n.* A drawing or representation, usually on a flat surface, of any region, as of a country or city. **2** *n.* A representation of the sky, showing the location of the stars, planets, and other bodies. **3** *v.* To make a map of. **4** *v.* To plan in detail: We *mapped* out our vacation.

ma·ple [mā′pəl] *n.* **1** Any of various trees of north temperate regions, having hard wood used for flooring and furniture. One variety yields sugar. **2** The light-colored wood of any of these trees. **3** The flavor of the sap of the maple that yields sugar.

maple sugar A sugar made by evaporating maple syrup.

maple syrup The sap of the sugar maple after it has been boiled down and refined.

mar [mär] *v.* **marred, mar·ring** To do harm or injury to; hurt the appearance of; damage: to *mar* furniture.

Mar. March.

mar·a·bou [mar′ə·bo͞o′] *n.* **1** A large African stork with soft, fluffy feathers. **2** The down of this bird, used for trimming hats and other clothing.

ma·ra·ca [mə·rä′kə] *n.* A musical instrument made of a gourd or gourd-shaped rattle with pebbles in it.

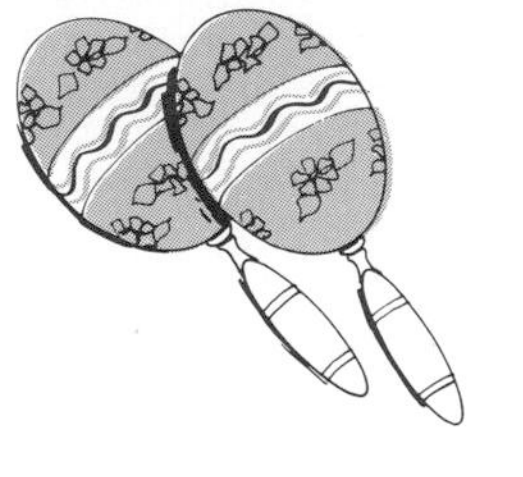
Maracas

mar·a·schi·no cherry [mar′ə·skē′nō *or* mar′ə·shē′nō] A cherry preserved in a sweet syrup and used in drinks, salads, and desserts.

mar·a·thon [mar′ə·thon′] **1** A foot race of 26 miles, 385 yards, a feature of the Olympic Games: so called from a messenger's run from Marathon to Athens to announce a victory over the Persians. **2** Any contest of endurance.

ma·raud [mə·rôd′] *v.* To roam or raid in search of plunder: Pirates *marauded* cities on the coast. —**ma·raud′er** *n.*

mar·ble [mär′bəl] *n., adj., v.* **mar·bled, mar·bling** **1** *n.* A hard, partly crystallized limestone occurring in many colors, used especially in building. **2** *adj. use*: a *marble* statue. **3** *adj.* Like marble, as in coldness, hardness, and lack of feeling. **4** *n.* A small ball, as of glass or stone. **5** *n.* (*pl.*) A children's game played with these small balls. **6** *v.* To color or streak in imitation of marble, as the edges of a book.

mar·cel [mär·sel′] *v.* **mar·celled, mar·cel·ling,** *n.* **1** *v.* To arrange the hair in even, continuous waves with a special machine. **2** *n.* This hair style.

march[1] [märch] **1** *v.* To walk with even, rhythmic steps, as a soldier. **2** *n.* A marching, as of soldiers. **3** *n.* The distance passed over in marching. **4** *v.* To walk in a solemn or dignified way, as in a ceremony. **5** *v.* To cause to march. **6** *n.* A musical composition with a strong, steady beat to march to. **7** *v.* To advance or progress steadily: Science *marches* on. **8** *n.* Onward progress. —**steal a march on** To win an advantage over, especially secretly or slyly. —**march′er** *n.*

march[2] [märch] *n.* A region lying along a boundary line; border; frontier.

March [märch] *n.* The third month of the year, having 31 days.

mar·chion·ess [mär′shən·is] *n.* **1** The wife or widow of a marquis. **2** A woman with a rank equal to that of a marquis.

Mar·di gras [mär′dē grä′] The Tuesday before Ash Wednesday, the first day of Lent. It is celebrated as a carnival in some cities.

mare [mâr] *n.* The female of the horse and other animals like it, as the donkey.

ma·re [mä′rā] *n., pl.* **ma·ri·a** [mä′rē·ə] Any of several dark low areas on the surface of the moon or Mars.

mar·ga·rine [mär′jə·rin] *n.* A substitute for butter, made of vegetable oils and other ingredients.

mar·gin [mär′jin] *n.* **1** The blank part of a page around the written or printed text. **2** An edge or border. **3** An extra amount or allowance of something, beyond what is needed: to win by a safe *margin.*

mar·gi·nal [mär′jə·nəl] *adj.* **1** Of, having to do with, or near a margin. **2** Written or printed on a margin. **3** At the point beyond which something stops being worth using or doing.

mar·gi·na·li·a [mär·jə·nal′yə] *n.pl.* Notes in the margin of a book.

mar·gue·rite [mär′gə·rēt′] *n.* Any of several flowers, especially a kind of daisy.

mar·i·gold [mar′ə·gōld′] *n.* A plant with golden yellow flowers that have a pungent smell.

mar·i·jua·na or **ma·ri·hua·na** [mar′ə·wä′nə] *n.* The dried leaves and flower tops of the hemp plant, which contain a narcotic.

ma·rim·ba [mə·rim′bə] *n.* A kind of xylophone that has resonating tubes beneath tuned wooden bars.

Marimba

ma·ri·na [mə·rē′nə] *n.* A place where small boats and yachts can dock and get supplies.

mar·i·nade [mar′ə·nād′] *n.* A liquid mixture, usually including vinegar, oil, spices, and other ingredients, in which foods, especially meat and fish, are soaked before cooking, to improve their flavor.

M

mar·i·nar·a [mär′ə·när′ə *or* mar′ə·nar′ə] *adj.* Being or served with a sauce of tomatoes flavored with garlic, onions, and spices.

mar·i·nate [mar′ə·nāt′] *v.* **mar·i·nat·ed, mar·i·nat·ing** To soak (as meat or fish) in brine, spiced vinegar and oil, wine, or the like.

ma·rine [mə·rēn′] **1** *adj.* Of, having to do with, formed by, or found in the sea: *marine* fish; *marine* salt. **2** *adj.* Having to do with shipping or sailing; maritime: *marine* laws. **3** *adj.* Used at sea: a *marine* compass. **4** *n.* (*sometimes written* **Marine**) A member of the Marine Corps.

Marine Corps A service within the U.S. Navy department having several sections, including combat troops and air forces.

mar·i·ner [mar′ə·nər] *n.* A sailor; seaman.

mar·i·o·nette [mar′ē·ə·net′] *n.* A jointed figure or doll made to move by pulling strings, used in shows on small stages; puppet.

Marionette

a	add	**i**	it	**o͝o**	took	**oi**	oil
ā	ace	**ī**	ice	**o͞o**	pool	**ou**	pout
â	care	**o**	odd	**u**	up	**ng**	ring
ä	palm	**ō**	open	**û**	burn	**th**	thin
e	end	**ô**	order	**yo͞o**	fuse	**t̶h̶**	this
ē	equal					**zh**	vision

ə = {a in *above* e in *sicken* i in *possible* / o in *melon* u in *circus*}

mar·i·tal [mar′ə·təl] *adj.* Of or having to do with marriage or the married state.
mar·i·time [mar′ə·tīm′] *adj.* 1 Located on or near the sea. 2 Of or having to do with the sea, as its shipping, trade, and laws.
mar·jo·ram [mär′jər·əm] *n.* An herb related to mint, used as a seasoning in cooking.
mark[1] [märk] 1 *n.* Something, as a line, spot, or stain, visible on a surface. 2 *v.* To make a mark or marks on: to *mark* the walls with chalk. 3 *n.* A symbol, seal, or label; trademark. 4 *v.* To write or draw: He *marks* his initials on all his books. 5 *n.* A sign made by a person who cannot write his or her name. 6 *n.* A grade; rating: She got high *marks* in school. 7 *v.* To give a grade or rating to. 8 *n.* A written or printed symbol: a punctuation *mark.* 9 *n.* A sign that shows a quality or trait: Shaking hands is a *mark* of courtesy. 10 *v.* To set apart; distinguish: a year *marked* by great events. 11 *n.* A target: The arrow split the thin sapling chosen as a *mark.* 12 *n.* Something, as a line or point, that shows position: The flood reached this *mark.* 13 *v.* To show by making a mark or marks: *Mark* all the rivers in New York on this map. 14 *n.* An object, point, or sign that serves to guide or indicate. 15 *v.* To make known or clear: The horse's strong build *marks* it as a good worker. 16 *n.* Notice; attention: This play is worthy of *mark.* 17 *v.* To pay attention to: *Mark* my warning! 18 *n.* A standard of quality or performance: Their behavior in school was below the *mark.* 19 *n.* Influence: Shakespeare left his *mark* on the English language. 20 *n.* Fame; distinction: an artist of *mark.* 21 *n.* The starting line of a race or contest. **—hit the mark** 1 To be accurate. 2 To reach one's goal; be successful. **—make one's mark** To achieve fame and success. **—mark down** 1 To note in writing. 2 To put a lower price on, as for a sale. **—mark off** or **mark out** To mark the boundaries of, as by drawing lines. **—mark time** 1 To keep time by moving the feet as in marching, but without going forward. 2 To pass time without making any progress. **—mark up** 1 To make marks on. 2 To raise the price of. **—miss the mark** 1 To fail in something. 2 To be incorrect.
mark[2] [märk] *n.* The basic unit of money in East Germany and West Germany.
Mark [märk] *n.* 1 A Christian evangelist and saint who wrote the second Gospel. 2 The second Gospel of the New Testament.
mark·down [märk′doun′] *n.* 1 A reduction in price: a *markdown* from $79.95 to $63.95. 2 The amount of such a reduction: The *markdown* on my coat was $27.50.
marked [märkt] *adj.* 1 Very obvious; evident: with *marked* disgust. 2 Singled out as an object, as of suspicion or vengeance: a *marked* person. 3 Having a mark or marks. **—mark·ed·ly** [mär′kid·lē] *adv.*
mark·er [mär′kər] *n.* 1 Something that marks, as a bookmark, a milestone, or a gravestone. 2 A person who marks, as one who gives grades; scorekeeper.
mar·ket [mär′kit] 1 *n.* A coming together of people for buying and selling. 2 *n.* The people who come together in this way. 3 *n.* A place where many kinds of goods are sold, especially a space outdoors or a building with stalls. 4 *n.* A store where food is sold. 5 *v.* To buy groceries, meat, and other supplies in a market. 6 *n.* A country or region where one can buy or sell: the Canadian *market.* 7 *n.* A special group of people who are buyers: the college *market.* 8 *n.* A demand: There is no *market* for heavy woolens in the summer. 9 *v.* To sell: Farmers *market* their crops. **—be in the market for** To want or seek to buy. **—put on the market** To offer for sale.
mar·ket·a·ble [mär′kit·ə·bəl] *adj.* 1 Fit to be put on sale in a market. 2 In demand by buyers. **—mar·ket·a·bil·i·ty** [mär′kit·ə·bil′ə·tē] *n.*
mar·ket·place *n.* [mär′kit·plās′] A place where goods are bought and sold, especially an open space or a hall with stalls and counters.
mark·ing [mär′king] *n.* 1 A mark. 2 (*often pl.*) The color pattern of a bird's feathers or an animal's fur.
marks·man [märks′mən] *n., pl.* **marks·men** [märks′·mən] A person who is good at hitting a target, as with a weapon. **—marks′man·ship** *n.*
mark·up [märk′up′] *n.* 1 An increase in price. 2 The amount a business adds to the cost of an item to determine a selling price.
marl [märl] *n.* Crumbly soil containing clay and calcium carbonate, used as fertilizer.
mar·lin [mär′lin] *n.* Any of several large game fishes of the Atlantic and Pacific Oceans, related to the sailfish.

Marlin

mar·line [mär′lin] *n.* A small rope of two loosely twisted strands, used chiefly by sailors for winding around ends of ropes.
mar·line·spike or **mar·lin·spike** [mär′lin·spīk′] *n.* A sharp-pointed iron tool used for separating strands of rope or wire, as in splicing.
mar·ma·lade [mär′mə·lād′] *n.* A jam, usually of citrus fruits, with pieces of peel in it.
mar·mo·set [mär′mə·zet′] *n.* A small monkey of South and Central America, with soft, woolly hair and a long tail.
mar·mot [mär′mət] *n.* Any of various rodents, as the woodchuck.
ma·roon[1] [mə·ro͞on′] *v.* 1 To put ashore and leave on a barren island or coast. 2 To desert or leave helpless.
ma·roon[2] [mə·ro͞on′] *n., adj.* Dull, dark red.
mar·quee [mär·kē′] *n.* A canopy, usually made of metal, projecting over the entrance, as of a theater or hotel.

Marquee

mar·quess [mär′kwis] *n.* *British* Another spelling of MARQUIS.
mar·quis [mär′kwis *or* mär·kē′] *n.* The title of a nobleman next in rank below a duke.
mar·quise [mär·kēz′] *n.* 1 The wife or widow of a marquis. 2 A woman with the rank of a marquis.
mar·qui·sette [mär′ki·zet′ *or* mär′kwi·zet′] *n.* A loosely woven fabric, as of cotton, silk, or nylon.
mar·riage [mar′ij] *n.* 1 The act of marrying. 2 The ceremony of marrying, especially a formal wedding with its attendant festivities. 3 The con-

dition of being married; wedlock. 4 Any close union: The play was a completely successful *marriage* of poetry and prose.

mar·riage·a·ble [mar′ij·ə·bəl] *adj.* Fitted or suitable for marriage: of *marriageable* age.

mar·ried [mar′ēd] *adj.* 1 Having a husband or wife. 2 United by marriage: a *married* couple. 3 Of or having to do with marriage or married persons.

mar·row [mar′ō] *n.* 1 A soft, spongy substance contained in the hollow interiors of many bones. 2 The main substance or essence; pith: the *marrow* of a story.

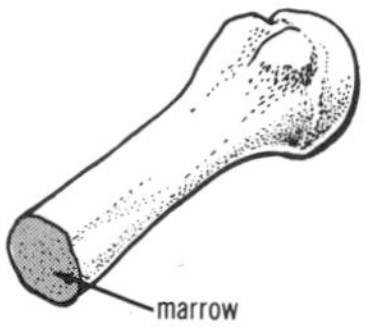

mar·row·bone [mar′ō·bōn′] *n.* A bone that contains edible marrow, used in cooking soups and stews.

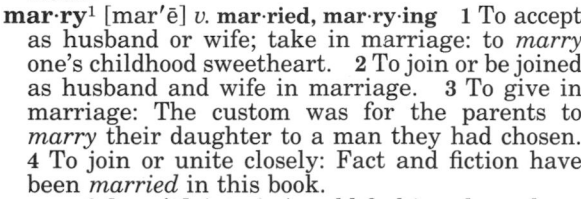

mar·ry[1] [mar′ē] *v.* **mar·ried, mar·ry·ing** 1 To accept as husband or wife; take in marriage: to *marry* one's childhood sweetheart. 2 To join or be joined as husband and wife in marriage. 3 To give in marriage: The custom was for the parents to *marry* their daughter to a man they had chosen. 4 To join or unite closely: Fact and fiction have been *married* in this book.

mar·ry[2] [mar′ē] *interj.* An old-fashioned word expressing surprise, emphasis, or agreement.

Mars [märz] *n.* 1 In Roman myths, the god of war. His Greek name was Ares. 2 A planet of the solar system, seventh largest in size, and fourth in distance from the sun.

Mar·seil·laise [mär′sə·lāz′ *or* mär′sā·yez′] *n.* The national anthem of France.

marsh [märsh] *n.* An area of low, wet land; swamp; bog. **—marsh′y** *adj.*

mar·shal [mär′shəl] *n., v.* **mar·shaled** or **mar·shalled, mar·shal·ing** or **mar·shal·ling** 1 *n.* In some foreign countries, a military officer of very high rank. 2 *n.* An officer of the federal courts, having duties like those of a sheriff. 3 *n.* In some cities, the chief of the police or fire department. 4 *n.* An officer who organizes and is in charge of parades and other ceremonies. 5 *v.* To lead or usher. 6 *v.* To arrange or draw up, as troops for battle. 7 *v.* To arrange in order, as facts or thoughts. ◆ A *marshal* did not always refer to someone so high up in the world. The word comes from two old German words meaning *horse servant,* and actually once meant a person in charge of stables.

marsh gas Methane, a gas found in marshes.

marsh·mal·low [märsh′mel′ō] *n.* A white, spongy candy made from the root of the marsh mallow or from starch, gelatin, sugar, and other ingredients, coated with powdered sugar.

marsh mallow A tall plant with pink flowers and a root used to make candy.

marsh marigold A plant found in damp places in North America, bearing bright yellow flowers that resemble the buttercup.

marsh·y [mär′shē] *adj.* **marsh·i·er, marsh·i·est** 1 Being or resembling a marsh. 2 Having to do with or found in a marsh.

mar·su·pi·al [mär·so͞o′pē·əl] 1 *n.* Any of various animals, the females of which carry their undeveloped young in a pouch. The opossum, the wombat, and the kangaroo are marsupials. 2 *adj.* Of or pertaining to marsupials.

mart [märt] *n.* A place where goods are bought and sold; market.

mar·ten [mär′tən] *n., pl.* **mar·ten** or **mar·tens** 1 An animal like a weasel. 2 Its valuable, dark brown fur.

Marten

Mar·tha [mär′thə] *n.* In the Bible, the sister of Lazarus and Mary.

mar·tial [mär′shəl] *adj.* 1 Of or having to do with war or military life. 2 Liking or experienced in war; warlike. **—mar′tial·ly** *adv.* ◆ *Martial* comes from *Mars,* the Roman god of war.

martial art Any of several Oriental methods of self-defense or combat, including judo, karate, and jiujitsu.

martial law Temporary rule by the military instead of by civilian authorities, as during a war or crisis.

Mar·tian [mär′shən] 1 *adj.* Of or having to do with the planet Mars. 2 *n.* One of the supposed inhabitants of Mars.

mar·tin [mär′tən] *n.* A bird related to the swallow, especially a North American species having a bluish black body and a square or forked tail.

mar·ti·net [mär′tə·net′] *n.* A person who always enforces rules strictly and exactly, as some army officers.

mar·tin·gale [mär′tən·gāl′] *n.* A strap forming part of a horse's harness that runs from under the animal's belly to the head, used mainly to prevent the horse from throwing its head back.

mar·ti·ni [mär·tē′nē] *n., pl.* **mar·ti·nis** A cocktail made of gin or vodka and dry vermouth.

mar·tyr [mär′tər] 1 *n.* A person who accepts death or torture rather than give up his or her religion or beliefs. 2 *n.* A person who suffers a great deal. 3 *v.* To torture, persecute, or kill (a person) for not giving up beliefs or religion.

mar·tyr·dom [mär′tər·dəm] *n.* 1 The sufferings of a martyr. 2 Long, terrible suffering.

mar·vel [mär′vəl] *v.* **mar·veled** or **mar·velled, mar·vel·ing** or **mar·vel·ling,** *n.* 1 *v.* To be astonished or awestruck; wonder. 2 *n.* Something that excites wonder.

mar·vel·ous or **mar·vel·lous** [mär′vəl·əs] *adj.* 1 Causing astonishment and wonder; amazing. 2 *informal* Very good; excellent. **—mar′vel·ous·ly** or **mar′vel·lous·ly** *adv.*

Marx·ism [märk′siz′əm] *n.* The political, economic, and social theories and policies of Karl Marx and Friedrich Engels that formed the basis for modern socialism and communism. **—Marx′ist** *n., adj.*

Mar·y [mâr′ē] *n.* 1 In the Bible, the mother of Jesus, often called the Virgin Mary. 2 In the Bible, the sister of Lazarus and Martha.

a	add	**i**	it	**o͝o**	took	**oi**	oil		
ā	ace	**ī**	ice	**o͞o**	pool	**ou**	pout		
â	care	**o**	odd	**u**	up	**ng**	ring		
ä	palm	**ō**	open	**û**	burn	**th**	thin		
e	end	**ô**	order	**yo͞o**	fuse	**t̶h̶**	this		
ē	equal					**zh**	vision		

ə = {a in *above* e in *sicken* i in *possible*
o in *melon* u in *circus*

Mary Mag·da·lene [mag'də·lin *or* mag'də·lēn'] In the Bible, a repentant sinner whom Jesus forgave.

mar·zi·pan [mär'zə·pan' *or* märt'sə·pan'] *n.* A confection made with ground almonds, sugar, and egg white.

masc. masculine.

mas·car·a [mas·kar'ə] *n.* A cosmetic used to color the eyelashes and eyebrows.

mas·cot [mas'kot] *n.* A person, animal, or thing thought to bring good luck by its presence.

mas·cu·line [mas'kyə·lin] *adj.* **1** Of or having to do with the male sex. **2** Of, related to, like, or fit for males. **3** In grammar, of the gender to which words denoting males belong: *He, duke,* and *colt* are in the *masculine* gender. **—mas·cu·lin·i·ty** [mas'·kyə·lin'ə·tē] *n.*

ma·ser [mā'zər] *n.* A device that generates and amplifies microwaves.

mash [mash] **1** *n.* A soft, pulpy mixture or mass. **2** *v.* To crush into a mash. **3** *n.* A mixture of meal or bran and water fed to horses and cattle. **4** *n.* Crushed grain or malt steeped in hot water and used in making beer.

MASH or **M.A.S.H.** Mobile Army Surgical Hospital.

mask [mask] **1** *n.* A covering used to hide or protect all or part of the face: a fencing *mask.* **2** *n.* A copy of a person's face, usually of plaster. **3** *v.* To put on a mask: We *mask* ourselves on Halloween. **4** *n.* Something that hides or conceals: a *mask* of kindness. **5** *v.* To hide or conceal; disguise: to *mask* anger with a grin.

Mask

mas·o·chism [mas'ə·kiz'əm *or* maz'ə·kiz'əm] *n.* An abnormal condition characterized by the derivation of pleasure in being abused, hurt, dominated, or humiliated. **—mas'o·chist** *n.*

ma·son [mā'sən] *n.* A person who is skilled in building with stone, brick, concrete, or other materials.

Ma·son [mā'sən] *n.* A Freemason.

ma·son·ic [mə·son'ik] *adj.* **1** Of or having to do with masons or masonry. **2** (*usually written* **Masonic**) Of or related to the Freemasons.

Mason jar A jar with a wide mouth and a special cover, used mainly in home canning.

ma·son·ry [mā'sən·rē] *n., pl.* **ma·son·ries** **1** The art or work of a mason. **2** A structure, as one of stone or brick, built by a mason.

masque [mask] *n.* **1** An entertainment with music, costumes, and dancing, popular in the 16th and 17th centuries. **2** A masquerade (def. 1).

mas·quer·ade [mas'kə·rād'] *n., v.* **mas·quer·ad·ed, mas·quer·ad·ing** **1** *n.* A party at which the guests wear masks and fancy costumes. **2** *n.* A costume or disguise for such a party. **3** *v.* To take part in a masquerade. **4** *n.* A false show; pretense: a *masquerade* of wealth. **5** *v.* To disguise oneself; pose: The children *masqueraded* as clowns. **—mas'·quer·ad'er** *n.*

mass [mas] **1** *n.* A body of matter with no definite shape or size: a *mass* of clay. **2** *n.* A large number or amount; great quantity: a *mass* of evidence. **3** *v.* To form into a mass. **4** *n.* The main or greater part: the *mass* of voters. **5** *adj.* Of or having to do with a large number of persons or things: *mass* education; This news magazine has a *mass* circulation. **6** *adj.* On a large scale: *mass* production of cars. **7** *n.* Great size; volume; bulk: the *mass* of a huge mountain. **8** *n.* The amount of matter in a body as measured by its resistance to change of motion or by the gravitational force it exerts. **—in the mass** As a whole. **—the masses** Ordinary people as a group.

Mass [mas] *n.* (*sometimes written* **mass**) **1** In the Roman Catholic and some Protestant churches, the service that celebrates the Eucharist. **2** Music written for some parts of this service.

Mass. Massachusetts.

mas·sa·cre [mas'ə·kər] *n., v.* **mas·sa·cred, mas·sa·cring** **1** *n.* A brutal, pitiless killing of a large number of people or animals. **2** *v.* To kill or slaughter in large numbers.

mas·sage [mə·säzh'] *n., v.* **mas·saged, mas·sag·ing** **1** *n.* A rubbing or kneading of parts of the body, as to stimulate circulation or relax muscles. **2** *v.* To give a massage to.

mass-en·er·gy equivalence [mas'en'ər·jē] The principle in physics that, given the appropriate conditions, a certain quantity of mass is convertible into a certain quantity of energy and vice versa. The principle is often expressed by the equation $E = mc^2$, where E is energy, m is mass, and c is the speed of light.

mas·seur [mə·sûr'] *n.* A man who gives massages as a profession.

mas·seuse [mə·so͞os' *or* mə·so͞oz'] *n.* A woman who gives massages as a profession.

mas·sive [mas'iv] *adj.* Large, heavy, or bulky: a *massive* wall. **—mas'sive·ness** *n.*

mass media Radio, television, newspapers, and magazines, movies, and other forms of communication that reach a large public.

mass number The total number of neutrons and protons present in the nucleus of an atom.

mass-pro·duce [mas'prə·d(y)o͞os'] *v.* **mass-pro·duced, mass-pro·duc·ing** To produce in large quantities, especially by using machinery. **—mass production**

mast [mast] *n.* A long pole set upright in a sailing ship to hold up the sails or yards. **—sail before the mast** To serve as a common sailor.

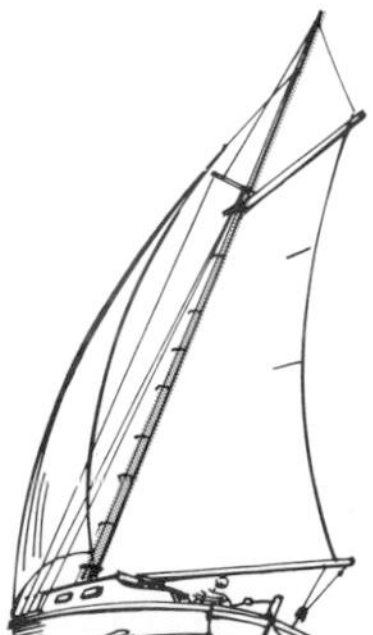
Mast

mas·tec·to·my [mas·tek'tə·mē] *n., pl.* **mas·tec·to·mies** The surgical removal of a breast.

mas·ter [mas'tər] **1** *n.* A person who has control or authority, as over workers, a household, or a ship. **2** *v.* To bring under control; defeat: to *master* one's shyness. **3** *n.* A person who is especially gifted or skilled: a *master* of the violin. **4** *adj. use*: a *master* chef. **5** *v.* To become an expert in: to *master* Greek. **6** *n. British* A male teacher. **7** *adj.* Principal; main; controlling: a *master* switch; a *master* copy. **8** *n.* The title of respect given to a young boy: *Master* Edward Smith. **9** *n.* A person who has received an academic degree more advanced than a bachelor's, but less advanced than a doctor's, such as a **Master of Arts** or a **Master of Science.**

mas·ter·ful [mas'tər·fəl] *adj.* **1** Like a master; pos-

itive or domineering. **2** Having or showing great skill. **—mas′ter·ful·ly** *adv.*
master key A key that can open several locks.
mas·ter·ly [mas′tər·lē] *adj.* Characteristic of or from a master: a *masterly* performance.
mas·ter·mind [mas′tər·mīnd′] **1** *n.* A person who plans or supervises a project or activity, usually in a clever or skillful way. **2** *v.* To plan or supervise a project or activity.
master of ceremonies A person who presides over an event, as a performance or a dinner, and introduces the performers or speakers.
mas·ter·piece [mas′tər·pēs′] *n.* **1** Something of outstanding excellence; great achievement. **2** The greatest thing done by its creator: The sculpture was Nevelson's *masterpiece.*
master sergeant A military rank. In the U.S. Army and Marines, the second highest noncommissioned officer; in the U.S. Air Force, the third highest noncommissioned officer.
mas·ter·y [mas′tər·ē] *n.* **1** The state of being master; control: The diver tried to gain *mastery* over the new apparatus. **2** Great knowledge or skill: a *mastery* of languages. **3** Victory, as in a contest.
mast·head [mast′hed′] *n.* **1** The top of a mast. **2** The part of a newspaper or magazine that gives the names of the editors, staff, and owners, and tells where it is published.
mas·tic [mas′tik] *n.* A gummy resin obtained from certain evergreen trees of the Mediterranean that are related to the cashew. It is used in varnishes and chewing gum, and sometimes as a flavoring agent.
mas·ti·cate [mas′tə·kāt′] *v.* **mas·ti·cat·ed, mas·ti·cat·ing** To chew. **—mas′ti·ca′tion** *n.*
mas·tiff [mas′tif] *n.* A breed of large hunting dog with strong jaws and drooping ears.

Mastiff

mas·to·don [mas′tə·don′] *n.* A large, extinct mammal much like the elephant but having differently shaped molar teeth.
mas·toid [mas′toid′] *n.* A small, conelike projection of the bone just behind the human ear.
mat[1] [mat] *n., v.* **mat·ted, mat·ting** **1** *n.* A rough, flat piece of material made of hemp, straw, rope, or other material, and used to cover floors, to wipe one's feet on, or to sit or lie on. **2** *n.* A thick pad placed on the floor for protection in gymnastic sports. **3** *n.* A small, flat piece of material, as lace or straw, used to protect or be an ornament for a table. **4** *v.* To cover with or as if with a mat. **5** *n.* A tangled mass, as of hair. **6** *v.* To make or become knotted or tangled.
mat[2] [mat] *n.* A piece of material, as cardboard, serving as the frame or border of a picture.
mat·a·dor [mat′ə·dôr′] *n.* In bullfighting, the person who kills the bull with a sword.
match[1] [mach] *n.* **1** A small, thin piece of wood or cardboard tipped with a substance that catches fire quickly when rubbed against a chemically treated or rough surface. **2** A wick or cord formerly used for firing cannon.
match[2] [mach] **1** *n.* A person or thing that is like or equal to another: She met her *match* when she played the former champion. **2** *v.* To be like or in agreement with: Your smile *matches* the spring day. **3** *n.* Either of two persons or things that go with each other: This hat is a good *match* for my coat. **4** *n.* A suitable or fit pair: The hat and coat are a good *match.* **5** *v.* To be alike or go with: The colors of the hat and coat *match.* **6** *v.* To make or select as equals or as fit to go together: to *match* a hat and coat. **7** *n.* A game or contest: a boxing *match.* **8** *v.* To set against one another in a game or contest: to *match* two boxers. **9** *v.* To equal, as in a contest. **10** *v.* To test or oppose: They *matched* wits in a guessing game. **11** *n.* A marriage or an agreement to marry: a *match* between a computer programmer and a cellist. **12** *n.* A possible marriage partner: My best friend would be a good *match* for your cousin. **13** *v.* To marry.
match·book [mach′bo͝ok′] *n.* A small cardboard folder containing paper matches.
match·box [mach′boks′] *n.* A usually small box for holding matches.
match·less [mach′lis] *adj.* Having no match or equal; incomparable.
match·lock [mach′lok′] *n.* Formerly, a type of musket in which the gunpowder was lit by a slow-burning wick or cord.
match·mak·er [mach′mā′kər] *n.* **1** A person who arranges or attempts to arrange marriages. **2** A person who arranges sports competitions, especially boxing or wrestling matches.
mate[1] [māt] *n., v.* **mat·ed, mat·ing** **1** *n.* One of a pair: a robin and its *mate*; a shoe and its *mate.* **2** *v.* To join or match closely together; pair. **3** *n.* A husband or wife. **4** *v.* To marry. **5** *v.* To join or be joined for breeding, as animals. **6** *n.* A companion; comrade. **7** *n.* An officer of a merchant ship ranking next below the captain. **8** *n.* A petty officer in the navy.
mate[2] [māt] *n., v.* **mat·ed, mat·ing** Another word for CHECKMATE.
ma·té [mä′tā *or* mat′ā] *n.* A plant related to the holly. It grows in South America and its leaves are used to make a beverage like tea.
ma·te·ri·al [mə·tir′ē·əl] **1** *n.* The stuff or substance of which a thing is made. **2** *adj.* Of or having to do with matter: the *material* universe. **3** *n.* Cloth or fabric. **4** *adj.* Of or having to do with the body or its needs: *material* well-being. **5** *adj.* Of or having to do with physical or worldly rather than spiritual things. **6** *adj.* Important or pertinent: There are *material* differences between cats and dogs.
ma·te·ri·al·ism [mə·tir′ē·əl·iz′əm] *n.* **1** Too much regard for the material or physical side of life, rather than for the mind or the spirit. **2** The philosophical idea that nothing exists except matter and everything can be explained in terms of

a	add	**i**	it	**o͝o**	took	**oi**	oil
ā	ace	**ī**	ice	**o͞o**	pool	**ou**	pout
â	care	**o**	odd	**u**	up	**ng**	ring
ä	palm	**ō**	open	**û**	burn	**th**	thin
e	end	**ô**	order	**yo͞o**	fuse	**t͟h**	this
ē	equal					**zh**	vision

ə = a in *above* e in *sicken* i in *possible* / o in *melon* u in *circus*

physical laws. **—ma·te′ri·al·ist** *n.* **—ma·te′ri·al·is′tic** *adj.*

ma·te·ri·al·ize [mə·tir′ē·əl·īz′] *v.* **ma·te·ri·al·ized, ma·te·ri·al·iz·ing** **1** To make or become material or actual; to be carried out: My plans for a vacation did not *materialize.* **2** To take on visible form; appear: The mountain top *materialized* from behind the clouds. **3** To appear or cause to appear, as a spirit. **—ma·te′ri·al·i·za′tion** *n.* **—ma·te′ri·al·iz′er** *n.*

ma·te·ri·al·ly [mə·tir′ē·əl·ē] *adv.* **1** In an important way or to a large degree: It did not affect us *materially.* **2** With regard to what is physical or material.

ma·té·ri·el or **ma·te·ri·el** [mə·tir′ē·el′] *n.* The equipment and supplies of an army.

ma·ter·nal [mə·tûr′nəl] *adj.* **1** Of or having to do with a mother; motherly. **2** Related through or inherited from one's mother: *maternal* grandparents. **—ma·ter′nal·ly** *adv.* ◆ *Maternal* and *matrimony* both are based on the Latin word *mater,* meaning *a mother.*

ma·ter·ni·ty [mə·tûr′nə·tē] *n.* **1** The state of being a mother; motherhood. **2** *adj.* Of, having to do with, or for pregnancy or childbirth: *maternity* clothes; a *maternity* ward.

math [math] *n. informal* Mathematics. ◆ *Math* is a shortened or "clipped" form of *mathematics.*

math·e·mat·i·cal [math′ə·mat′i·kəl] *adj.* **1** Of, related to, or like mathematics. **2** Very exact or precise. **—math′e·mat′i·cal·ly** *adv.*

math·e·ma·ti·cian [math′ə·mə·tish′ən] *n.* A person who is an expert in mathematics.

math·e·mat·ics [math′ə·mat′iks] *n.* The science that deals with size, position, form, and magnitude, in terms of numbers and symbols that stand for numbers, using operations that are derived in a logical and consistent way. Arithmetic, algebra, geometry, and calculus are branches of mathematics. ◆ See -ICS.

mat·i·nee or **mat·i·née** [mat′ə·nā′] *n.* A performance, as of a play, movie, or concert, held in the daytime, usually in the afternoon.

mat·ins [mat′inz] *n.pl.* The prayers that are said in the Roman Catholic Church at midnight or dawn and in the Church of England in the morning.

ma·tri·arch [mā′trē·ärk′] *n.* A woman who is the ruler or head, as of her family, tribe, or community. **—ma′tri·ar′chal** *adj.*

ma·tri·ar·chy [mā′trē·är′kē] *n., pl.* **ma·tri·ar·chies** **1** A social structure, as a family, tribe, or community, ruled by a matriarch. **2** A social system in which descent and inheritance are traced through the maternal line.

mat·ri·cide [mat′ri·sīd′] *n.* **1** The act of killing one's mother. **2** A person who kills his or her mother.

ma·tric·u·late [mə·trik′yə·lāt′] *v.* **ma·tric·u·lat·ed, ma·tric·u·lat·ing** To enroll as a student, especially in a college or university. **—ma·tric′u·la′tion** *n.*

mat·ri·mo·ni·al [mat′rə·mō′nē·əl] *adj.* Of or having to do with marriage.

mat·ri·mo·ny [mat′rə·mō′nē] *n., pl.* **mat·ri·mo·nies** **1** A being married; marriage. **2** The act or ceremony of marriage. ◆ See MATERNAL.

ma·trix [mā′triks] *n., pl.* **ma·trix·es** or **ma·tri·ces** [mā′trə·sēz] A place in which anything originates, develops, takes shape, or is contained. A mold for casting is a matrix.

ma·tron [mā′trən] *n.* **1** A married woman or widow, especially one no longer young. **2** A woman in charge of others, as at an institution.

ma·tron·ly [mā′trən·lē] *adj.* Of, like, or suitable for a matron.

matron of honor *pl.* **matrons of honor** The chief married woman attendant of a bride at a wedding.

matte [mat] **1** *adj.* Having no shine, gloss, or luster; dull. **2** *n.* A dull finish, as on paper.

mat·ted [mat′id] *adj.* **1** Covered with or made from a mat or matting. **2** Tangled or twisted.

mat·ter [mat′ər] **1** *n.* The substance of anything, especially of materially existing things. **2** *n.* Anything physically existing and occupying space, as solids, liquids, or gases. **3** *n.* A specific kind or form of material: organic *matter.* **4** *n.* A subject, event, or situation about which there is concern, feeling, or discussion. **5** *n.* Importance: It's of no *matter.* **6** *v.* To be of concern or importance; signify: It *matters* little. **7** *n.* An unpleasant or unfortunate condition; trouble: What's the *matter* with you? **8** *n.* The ideas, facts, or meaning, as of a book or speech, apart from the style. **9** *n.* Anything sent or to be sent by mail: third-class *matter.* **10** *n.* An amount, quantity, or extent: a *matter* of a few dollars. **11** *n.* Pus. **—as a matter of fact** In truth; really. **—for that matter** As far as that goes. **—no matter** **1** It isn't important; never mind. **2** In spite of.

mat·ter-of-fact [mat′ər·əv·fakt′] *adj.* Closely sticking to facts; not emotional or imaginative.

Mat·thew [math′yo͞o] *n.* **1** In the Bible, one of the twelve apostles of Jesus, and a saint. **2** The first book of the New Testament, written by him.

mat·ting [mat′ing] *n.* A fabric of fiber, straw, or other material, used as a floor covering.

mat·tock [mat′ək] *n.* A garden tool, somewhat like a pickax, used for cutting roots, breaking up soil, and other chores.

Mattock

mat·tress [mat′rəs] *n.* A large pad made of a strong fabric and filled with cotton, foam rubber, or springs, used on a bed.

mat·u·ra·tion [mach′o͞o·rā′shən] *n.* **1** The act or process of becoming mature. **2** The act or process of discharging pus; suppuration.

ma·ture [mə·t(y)o͝or′ *or* mə·cho͝or′] *adj., v.* **ma·tured, ma·tur·ing** **1** *adj.* Completely developed, grown, or ripened, as plants, fruit, or animals. **2** *v.* To make or become ripe or completely developed. **3** *adj.* Highly developed or advanced in intelligence: a *mature* thinker. **4** *adj.* Fully worked out or perfected: a *mature* scheme. **5** *v.* To perfect or complete. **6** *adj.* Having reached its time limit; due and payable: a *mature* bond. **7** *v.* To become due, as a note or a bond.

ma·tur·i·ty [mə·t(y)o͝or′ə·tē *or* mə·cho͝or′ə·tē] *n.* **1** The condition of being mature or fully developed. **2** The time at which something, as a note or bill, becomes due.

mat·zo [mät′sə] *n., pl.* **mat·zos** A flat piece of unleavened bread eaten during Passover.

maud·lin [môd′lin] *adj.* Tearfully emotional or too sentimental.

maul [môl] 1 *n.* A heavy mallet. 2 *v.* To beat and bruise. 3 *v.* To handle roughly.

maun·der [môn′dər] *v.* 1 To talk aimlessly; ramble. 2 To wander idly or in confusion.

Maun·dy Thursday [môn′dē] The Thursday before Easter, commemorating the Last Supper.

Mau·ri·ta·ni·an [môr′ə·tā′nē·ən] 1 *adj.* Of or from Mauritania. 2 *n.* A person born in or a citizen of Mauritania.

Mau·ri·ti·an [mô·rish′ən] 1 *adj.* Of or from Mauritius. 2 *n.* A person born in or a citizen of Mauritius.

mau·so·le·um [mô′sə·lē′əm] *n.* A large tomb.

mauve [mōv] *n., adj.* Purplish rose.

ma·ven or **ma·vin** or **may·vin** [mā′vən] *n. informal* A person who is especially interested in or knowledgeable about a subject: a movie *maven.*

mav·er·ick [mav′ər·ik] *n.* 1 An animal, especially a lost calf, that has not been branded by its owner. 2 *informal* A person who thinks and acts independently. ◆ Samuel *Maverick* was a Texan of the 1800's who did not brand his cattle.

ma·vis [mā′vəs] *n., pl.* **ma·vis·es** Another name for SONG THRUSH.

maw [mô] *n.* 1 The jaws, mouth, or gullet of some animals, as the lion. 2 The craw of a bird. 3 The stomach.

mawk·ish [mô′kish] *adj.* 1 Full of sickening sentimentality or false emotion. 2 Nauseating or insipid in taste. **—mawk′ish·ness** *n.*

max. maximum.

max·i [mak′sē] *n., pl.* **max·is** A long dress, skirt, or coat that extends to the ankles.

max·il·la [mak·sil′ə] *n., pl.* **max·il·lae** [mak·sil′ē] 1 The upper jawbone. 2 One of the two pairs of appendages behind the mandibles in insects, crustaceans, and related arthropods. **—max′il·lar′y** *adj.*

max·im [mak′sim] *n.* A brief statement of a rule of conduct or a general principle.

max·i·mize [mak′sə·mīz′] *v.* **max·i·mized, max·i·miz·ing** To increase to a maximum; make as large or great as possible.

max·i·mum [mak′sə·məm] *n., pl.* **max·i·mums** or **max·i·ma** [mak′sə·mə] 1 *n.* The greatest possible quantity, number, or degree: Two hundred pounds was the *maximum* the horse could carry. 2 *n.* The greatest quantity, number, or degree reached or recorded. 3 *adj.* Greatest; highest possible: The *maximum* grade is 100.

may [mā] *v. Present tense for all subjects* **may,** *past tense* **might** *May* is a helping verb having the following senses: 1 To have permission or be allowed to: *May* I go? 2 To be able to as a consequence: They stayed that we *might* go. 3 To be possible: It *may* snow. *May* is also used to express: Desire, prayer, or wish, as in "*May* you always be happy." ◆ In formal written English, *may,* not *can,* is preferred in the sense of asking for permission. See CAN[1] (def. 4).

May [mā] *n.* The fifth month of the year, having 31 days.

Ma·ya [mä′yə] *n.* 1 A member of a tribe of Indians of southern Mexico and parts of Central America who had an advanced civilization before they were conquered by the Spanish in the 16th century. 2 Their language. **—Ma′yan** *n., adj.*

may·be [mā′bē] *adv.* Perhaps; possibly. ◆ Do not confuse the verb phrase *may be* with the adverb *maybe*: The defendant's alibi *may be* the truth, but *maybe* it's not.

May·day [mā′dā′] *n.* An international radiotelephone signal word used as a distress call by airplanes and ships. ◆ The word *Mayday* comes from the French *m'aider,* meaning *help me.*

May Day The first day of May, celebrated by such festivities as crowning a May queen and dancing around a Maypole. In some countries it is a holiday in honor of laboring people.

may·flow·er [mā′flou′ər] *n.* Any of several plants that blossom in the spring, especially the arbutus.

May·flow·er [mā′flou′ər] *n.* The ship on which the Pilgrims came to America in 1620.

may·fly [mā′flī′] *n., pl.* **may·flies** An insect with two pairs of delicate, membranous wings, noted for living only a day or two as an adult.

may·hem [mā′hem] *n.* The crime of hurting someone very badly, so that the person is crippled or maimed.

mayn't [mā′ənt] May not.

may·on·naise [mā′ə·nāz′ *or* mā′ə·nāz′] *n.* A creamy dressing, as for salads, made with egg yolk, oil, lemon juice or vinegar, and seasonings.

may·or [mā′ər] *n.* The chief governing official of a city or town.

may·or·al·ty [mā′ər·əl·tē] *n., pl.* **may·or·al·ties** The position or term of office of a mayor.

May·pole [mā′pōl′] *n.* (*often written* **maypole**) A pole decorated with flowers and streamers around which people dance on May Day.

mayst [māst] *v.* A form of the verb MAY, used with *thou*: seldom used today.

maze [māz] *n.* 1 A complicated network of paths or passages in which it is hard to find one's way. 2 A state of bewilderment or confusion.

Maze

ma·zur·ka or **ma·zour·ka** [mə·zûr′kə] *n.* 1 A lively Polish dance. 2 Music for this dance.

maz·y [mā′zē] *adj.* **maz·i·er, maz·i·est** Like a maze; complicated, confusing, or convoluted.

M.B.A. Master of Business Administration.

m.c. or **M.C.** master of ceremonies.

Md The symbol for the element mendelevium.

Md. Maryland.

MD Postal Service abbreviation of Maryland.

M.D. Doctor of Medicine, used after a doctor's name: Carol Davies, *M.D.*

me [mē] *pron.* The form of *I* that serves as the object of verbs and prepositions: Take *me* with you; Talk to *me.* ◆ Nowadays many people would regard "It is I," in answer to the question "Who's there?"

a	add	**i**	it	**o͝o**	took	**oi**	oil
ā	ace	**ī**	ice	**o͞o**	pool	**ou**	pout
â	care	**o**	odd	**u**	up	**ng**	ring
ä	palm	**ō**	open	**û**	burn	**th**	thin
e	end	**ô**	order	**yo͞o**	fuse	**th**	this
ē	equal					**zh**	vision

ə = {a in *above*, e in *sicken*, i in *possible*, o in *melon*, u in *circus*}

as a little stuffy. Although in formal speech and writing *It is I* (or *It is we,* and so forth) is the preferred form, *It's me* (or *It's us,* and so forth) is now acceptable in informal conversation.

Me. Maine.

ME Postal Service abbreviation of Maine.

mead[1] [mēd] *n.* An alcoholic drink made of fermented honey, water, and spices.

mead[2] [mēd] *n.* A meadow: used mostly in poems.

mead·ow [med'ō] *n.* A tract of land where grass is grown for hay or for grazing.

mead·ow·lark [med'ō·lärk'] *n.* Any of various songbirds of North America, usually having black markings on a yellow breast.

mea·ger or **mea·gre** [mē'gər] *adj.* **1** Lacking in quality or quantity; not adequate; inferior. **2** Thin; lean: a *meager* frame.

meal[1] [mēl] *n.* **1** The edible seeds of any grain, coarsely ground: a sack of *meal.* **2** Any powdery material produced by grinding.

meal[2] [mēl] *n.* **1** The food served or eaten at certain times during the day. **2** The time or occasion of eating.

meal·time [mēl'tīm'] *n.* The time at which one usually has a meal.

meal·y [mē'lē] *adj.* **meal·i·er, meal·i·est** **1** Like meal; dry; powdery. **2** Made of, containing, or covered with meal. **3** Pale or anemic.

meal·y·mouthed [mē'lē·mouthd' *or* mē·lē·moutht'] *adj.* Talking in a vague, evasive manner because of an unwillingness to speak one's thoughts or take a stand.

mean[1] [mēn] *v.* **meant, mean·ing** **1** To have in mind as a purpose; intend: I *mean* to visit my friends. **2** To intend for some purpose: Was that remark *meant* for me? **3** To intend to express or convey: That's not what I *mean.* **4** To have as the sense; signify; denote: Dictionaries tell what words *mean.* **5** To be of a specified importance: Her work *means* everything to her. **—mean well** To intend to do good.

mean[2] [mēn] *adj.* **1** Poor or inferior in grade or quality: *mean* garments. **2** Humble in rank; lowly: a person of *mean* birth. **3** Poor in appearance; shabby: a *mean* house. **4** Not noble in mind or character; base: It's *mean* to lie. **5** Having the qualities of a miser; stingy: to be *mean* with money. **6** *informal* Selfish or nasty: a *mean* child. **7** *informal* Vicious; ill-tempered: a *mean* old dog. **—mean'ly** *adv.*

mean[3] [mēn] **1** *n.* The middle point or state between two extremes: The *mean* between stinginess and being a spendthrift is moderation. **2** *adj.* Coming halfway between two limits or extremes; average: The *mean* rainfall is the average rainfall over a certain period of time. **3** *n.* A number that is considered to be typical and representative of a whole set of numbers; average. **4** *n.* (*pl.*) A way in which something is accomplished or brought about: Travel is a *means* of enjoyment. **5** *n.* (*pl.*) Money, property, or other wealth: a person of *means.* **—by all means** Of course; certainly. **—by any means** In any way possible. **—by means of** With the help of; by using. **—by no means** Most certainly not.

me·an·der [mē·an'dər] **1** *v.* To wind and turn in a course, as a river. **2** *n.* A winding or rambling course or movement. **3** *v.* To wander aimlessly, without purpose.

mean·ing [mē'ning] **1** *n.* Something meant or to be understood; significance: the *meaning* of a word. **2** *adj.* Showing or having meaning; expressive: a *meaning* glance.

mean·ing·ful [mē'ning·fəl] *adj.* Having or full of meaning. **—mean'ing·ful·ly** *adv.*

mean·ing·less [mē'ning·lis] *adj.* Having no meaning or importance; senseless. **—mean'ing·less·ly** *adv.*

mean·ness [mēn'nis] *n.* **1** The condition of being mean. **2** A mean act.

meant [ment] Past tense and past participle of MEAN[1].

mean·time [mēn'tīm'] **1** *n.* The time between. **2** *adv.* In or during the time between. **3** *adv.* At the same time.

mean·while [mēn'(h)wīl'] *n., adv.* Meantime.

mea·sles [mē'zəlz] *n.pl.* (*used with singular verb*) A contagious virus disease marked by fever and an outbreak of small red spots on the skin, particularly common among children.

meas·ly [mēz'lē] *adj.* **meas·li·er, meas·li·est** **1** *slang* Worth so little as to be contemptible; skimpy; meager. **2** Having or resembling measles.

meas·ur·a·ble [mezh'ər·ə·bəl] *adj.* Capable of being measured. **—meas'ur·a·bly** *adv.*

meas·ure [mezh'ər] *n., v.* **meas·ured, meas·ur·ing** **1** *n.* A unit or standard, as a foot, ounce, pint, or minute, used for comparison. **2** *n.* A ruler, scale, or other device for using standard units. **3** *v.* To find out, in standard units, the extent, contents, weight, time, or degree of: *Measure* the wire in yards. **4** *n.* The extent, weight, or time, found in this way. **5** *v.* To set apart, mark off, or allot, by or as if by measuring: *Measure* off two pints of milk. **6** *v.* To have a certain measurement: The table *measures* two feet by four feet. **7** *v.* To serve as an instrument for measuring: Thermometers *measure* temperature. **8** *n.* A system of measurement: liquid *measure.* **9** *v.* To make or take measurements. **10** *n.* A standard or criterion, as of comparison or judgment: Are grades a true *measure* of intelligence? **11** *v.* To find out or estimate by a standard or criterion: The hare's running speed was *measured* against the tortoise's. **12** *n.* A fixed limit or bound: talkative beyond all *measure.* **13** *n.* A certain amount or degree: The students had a *measure* of freedom in choosing their courses. **14** *n.* (*pl.*) Actions or steps: We have taken *measures* to send out all checks by the 15th of the month. **15** *n.* A bill or law. **16** *n.* The portion of music between two bar lines; bar. **17** *n.* Rhythm or meter, as in poetry or music. **—beyond measure** More than can be measured. **—for good measure** As something added or extra. **—measure up to** To meet or satisfy, as expectations.

Four measures of music

meas·ured [mezh'ərd] *adj.* **1** Set or determined by some standard: the *measured* form of classical architecture. **2** Slow and stately; rhythmical: a *measured* step. **3** Carefully thought out: *measured* speech.

meas·ure·less [mezh'ər·lis] *adj.* Too big to be measured; very great; immense.

meas·ure·ment [mezh'ər·mənt] *n.* **1** The act of measuring anything. **2** The size, quantity, or amount, found by measuring. **3** A system of measures: linear *measurement.*

measuring worm The larva of certain moths. It moves by advancing its rear end, humping up in the middle, then advancing its front end.

meat [mēt] *n.* 1 The flesh of animals used as food, especially the flesh of mammals, as the cow or pig, and not of fish or fowl. 2 The part of anything that can be eaten: the *meat* of a coconut. 3 Anything used as food, now used mainly in the phrase **meat and drink.** 4 The main idea; gist: the *meat* of the story.

meat·y [mē′tē] *adj.* **meat·i·er, meat·i·est** 1 Of, having to do with, or like meat. 2 Full of meat. 3 Full of meaning; significant.

me·chan·ic [mə·kan′ik] *n.* A person who is skilled in the making, operating, or repairing of tools or machinery.

me·chan·i·cal [mə·kan′i·kəl] *adj.* 1 Of or having to do with a machine or machinery. 2 Operated or produced by a machine. 3 Having to do with the science of mechanics. 4 Made or done as if by a machine; automatic: a *mechanical* speech. —**me·chan′i·cal·ly** *adv.*

mechanical advantage A number equal to the force a machine applies to its load divided by the force supplied to the machine.

mechanical drawing A drawing, usually of mechanical parts or objects, done with the aid of compasses, squares, and other instruments.

me·chan·ics [mə·kan′iks] *n.* The branch of physics that deals with motion and with the action of forces on bodies. ◆ See -ICS.

mech·a·nism [mek′ə·niz′əm] *n.* 1 The parts or the arrangement of parts of a machine. 2 Something like a machine in the working of its parts: the *mechanism* of government.

mech·a·nize [mek′ə·nīz′] *v.* **mech·a·nized, mech·a·niz·ing** 1 To make mechanical. 2 To convert, as an industry, to machine production. 3 To equip, as an army, with tanks, trucks, and other materials.

med. 1 medical. 2 medicine. 3 medieval. 4 medium.

med·al [med′(ə)l] *n.* 1 A small piece of metal with an image or writing on it, given as an award for an outstanding act or service. 2 Such a piece of metal bearing a religious image or inscription.

Medals

med·al·ist [med′ə·list] *n.* 1 A person who designs, engraves, or makes medals. 2 A person who has been awarded a medal.

me·dal·lion [mə·dal′yən] *n.* 1 A large medal. 2 A round or oval design or ornament that looks like a large medal.

med·dle [med′(ə)l] *v.* **med·dled, med·dling** To interfere or tamper carelessly. —**med′dler** *n.*

med·dle·some [med′(ə)l·səm] *adj.* Tending to meddle; interfering.

Mede [mēd] *n.* A person born in or a citizen of ancient Media.

Me·de·a [mə·dē′ə] *n.* In Greek myths, the woman who helped Jason obtain the Golden Fleece.

me·di·a [mē′dē·ə] A plural of MEDIUM.

me·di·ae·val [mē′dē·ē′vəl] *adj.* Another spelling of MEDIEVAL.

me·di·al [mē′dē·əl] *adj.* 1 Of, having to do with, located, or happening in the middle. 2 Average or mean.

me·di·an [mē′dē·ən] 1 *adj.* In the middle; medial. 2 *n.* The middle number in a series, as 5 in 1, 2, 5, 6, 9. 3 *n.* A median strip.

median strip A paved or planted strip separating opposing traffic on a highway.

me·di·ate [*v.* mē′dē·āt′, *adj.* mē′dē·it] *v.* **me·di·at·ed, me·di·at·ing,** *adj.* 1 *v.* To settle, as a quarrel, by acting as a peacemaker or a go-between. 2 *v.* To act between disputing parties as a peacemaker. 3 *v.* To bring about (as a settlement) by acting as a go-between. 4 *adj.* Acting as a go-between; indirect. —**me′di·a′tion** *n.* —**me′di·a′tor** *n.*

med·ic [med′ik] *n. informal* 1 A medical doctor or intern. 2 A soldier or sailor trained in medical work.

Med·i·caid or **med·i·caid** [med′i·kād′] *n. U.S.* A program of health insurance for low-income people, financed jointly by the federal and state governments.

med·i·cal [med′i·kəl] *adj.* Of or having to do with medicine. —**med′i·cal·ly** *adv.*

med·i·ca·ment [med′ə·kə·mənt *or* mə·dik′ə·mənt] *n.* A medicine.

Med·i·care or **med·i·care** [med′i·kâr′] *n. U.S.* A program of health insurance for the aged, sponsored by the federal government.

med·i·cate [med′ə·kāt′] *v.* **med·i·cat·ed, med·i·cat·ing** 1 To treat medically. 2 To put medicine on or in.

med·i·ca·tion [med′ə·kā′shən] *n.* 1 The act or process of medicating. 2 A medicine.

me·dic·i·nal [mə·dis′ə·nəl] *adj.* Being or acting as a medicine; healing; curative.

med·i·cine [med′ə·sən] *n.* 1 Any substance used in treating disease, in healing, or in relieving pain. 2 The science of restoring and preserving health and of preventing and treating disease. 3 The profession of medicine. 4 Among American Indians, any object or ceremony supposed to have magic power or curative effects.

medicine ball A large, heavy, stuffed, leather-covered ball used for exercising.

medicine man Among North American Indians, a person believed to have magic powers of healing or of keeping away evil spirits.

me·di·e·val [mē′dē·ē′vəl *or* med′ē·ē′vəl] *adj.* Of, relating to, or belonging to the Middle Ages.

Medieval Latin The Latin language as used from about 700 to 1500.

me·di·o·cre [mē′dē·ō′kər] *adj.* Of only average quality; neither good nor bad; ordinary.

me·di·oc·ri·ty [mē′dē·ok′rə·tē] *n., pl.* **me·di·oc·ri·ties** 1 The condition of being mediocre or ordinary. 2 Mediocre ability or performance. 3 A mediocre person.

med·i·tate [med′ə·tāt′] *v.* **med·i·tat·ed, med·i·tat·ing** 1 To think quietly and deeply over a period of time; muse. 2 To think about doing; plan: to *meditate* mischief.

a	add	**i**	it	**o͝o**	took	**oi**	oil
ā	ace	**ī**	ice	**o͞o**	pool	**ou**	pout
â	care	**o**	odd	**u**	up	**ng**	ring
ä	palm	**ō**	open	**û**	burn	**th**	thin
e	end	**ô**	order	**yo͞o**	fuse	**th̶**	this
ē	equal					**zh**	vision

ə = a in *above* e in *sicken* i in *possible* o in *melon* u in *circus*

med·i·ta·tion [med′ə·tā′shən] *n.* 1 The act or process of meditating; contemplation; reflection. 2 A discourse based on religious or philosophical reflections.

med·i·ta·tive [med′ə·tā′tiv] *adj.* Given to or characterized by meditation; contemplative; reflective; pensive.

me·di·um [mē′dē·əm] *n., pl.* **me·di·ums** or **me·di·a** [mē′dē·ə], *adj.* 1 *n.* A degree or condition between two extremes. 2 *adj.* Between two extremes, as in quantity, quality, size, or degree; middle: a dog of *medium* size. 3 *n.* A substance, as water, that an organism lives in. 4 *n.* A substance through which a force may act or an effect be produced. Air is a medium of sound. 5 *n.* A means or instrument by which something is made, done, accomplished, or transferred: Money is a *medium* of exchange. 6 *n., pl.* **mediums** A person through whom the dead are believed to speak, as at a seance. 7 *n.* The material with which an artist works. 8 *n.* Any of the techniques or means of expression used by an artist. 9 *n., pl.* **media** Any of the channels of mass communication: Television and motion pictures are more popular *media* than magazines.

med·ley [med′lē] *n., pl.* **med·leys** 1 A mixture of unlike or unrelated things; jumble. 2 A series of songs or tunes arranged to be played as a single piece.

me·dul·la [mə·dul′ə] *n.* 1 The soft, inner portion of an organ or part, as of the adrenal gland or spinal cord. 2 The pith of a plant.

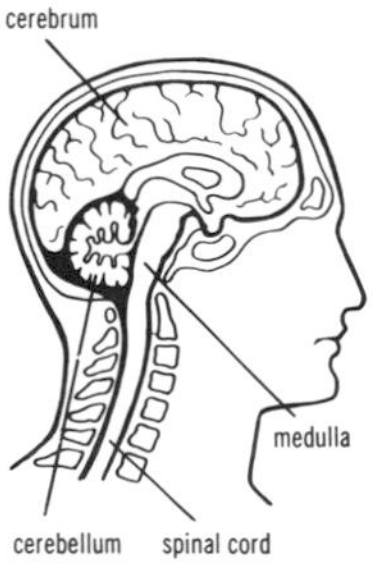

medulla ob·lon·ga·ta [ob′lông·gä′tə] The lowest part of the brain, topping the spinal chord. It controls circulation, breathing, and other body functions.

Me·du·sa [mə·d(y)ōō′sə] *n.* In Greek myths, one of the Gorgons, killed by Perseus.

meek [mēk] *adj.* 1 Having a patient, gentle disposition; mild. 2 Lacking spirit or courage; submissive. **—meek′·ly** *adv.* **—meek′ness** *n.*

meer·schaum [mir′shəm] *n.* 1 A soft, lightweight, white, claylike mineral. 2 A pipe for smoking, made of this mineral. ◆ *Meerschaum,* which resembles froth or foam in color, comes from two German words meaning *sea foam.*

meet[1] [mēt] *v.* **met, meet·ing,** *n.* 1 *v.* To come upon; come face to face with: He happened to *meet* a friend. 2 *v.* To become acquainted with: Have you *met* Jane? 3 *v.* To be introduced or become acquainted: We've already *met.* 4 *v.* To keep an appointment with: I'll *meet* you there. 5 *v.* To be waiting for on arrival: She *met* my plane. 6 *v.* To come together and join or merge: where two streams *meet.* 7 *v.* To come into contact with: where the path *meets* the road. 8 *v.* To assemble: How often does the club *meet*? 9 *n.* A meeting, as for a sports event: a track *meet.* 10 *v.* To experience; undergo: to *meet* difficulties. 11 *v.* To deal or cope with: The salesperson *met* and overcame our objections. 12 *v.* To satisfy or fulfill, as requirements or a need. 13 *v.* To pay (as a bill or debt). **—meet with** 1 To come upon; encounter. 2 To experience: to *meet with* hardships.

meet[2] [mēt] *adj.* Suitable; proper.

meet·ing [mē′ting] *n.* 1 A coming together. 2 A gathering of persons, as for religious worship or some other common purpose; assembly.

meeting house A building used for public worship, especially for Quaker meetings.

mega- or **meg-** A combining form meaning: 1 Large; great, as in *megaphone.* 2 One million; one million times (a specified unit), as in *megahertz.*

meg·a·cy·cle [meg′ə·sī′kəl] *n.* One million cycles, especially one million cycles per second.

meg·a·hertz [meg′ə·hûrts′] *n.* A unit of frequency equal to one million hertz or one million cycles per second.

meg·a·lith [meg′ə·lith′] *n.* A huge stone used in the construction of prehistoric monuments. **—meg′a·lith′ic** *adj.*

meg·a·lo·ma·ni·a [meg′ə·lə·mā′nē·ə] *n.* A mental disorder characterized by a false and exaggerated sense of one's own importance, power, or wealth. **—meg′a·lo·ma′ni·ac** *n.*

meg·a·lop·o·lis [meg′ə·lop′ə·lis] *n.* An extensive, highly populated region, usually made up of several cities and their suburbs and considered to be a single urban unit.

meg·a·phone [meg′ə·fōn′] *n.* A funnel-shaped tube which one talks or yells through to make the voice sound loud and go far. ◆ See OMEGA.

Megaphone

meg·a·struc·ture [meg′ə·struk′·chər] *n.* A very large, tall building or group of buildings.

meg·a·ton [meg′ə·tun′] *n.* A unit used mainly to measure the force of a nuclear explosion. One megaton equals the explosive force of one million tons of TNT.

meg·a·watt [meg′ə·wot′] *n.* A unit of power equal to one million watts.

me·gil·lah or **me·gil·la** [mə·gil′ə] *n. slang* 1 A long, involved story. 2 A complicated matter.

mei·o·sis [mī·ō′sis] *n.* A form of cell division in which the chromosomes of reproductive cells are reduced by half.

mel·an·cho·li·a [mel′ən·kō′lē·ə] *n.* A mental disorder characterized by feelings of depression, self-criticism, and anxiety, often accompanied by physical complaints like loss of appetite and sleeplessness.

mel·an·chol·ic [mel′ən·kol′ik] *adj.* 1 Of, having to do with, or subject to melancholy. 2 Of, having to do with, or suffering from melancholia.

mel·an·chol·y [mel′ən·kol′ē] 1 *adj.* Very gloomy; sad; dejected. 2 *n.* Low spirits; depression; sadness. 3 *adj.* Causing or suggesting sadness: the *melancholy* sound of a cello.

Mel·a·ne·sian [mel′ə·nē′zhən] 1 *adj.* Of or from Melanesia. 2 *n.* A person born or living in Melanesia. 3 *n.* Any of the languages of Melanesia.

mé·lange [mā·länzh′] *n.* A mixture, often of things that do not ordinarily go together.

mel·a·nin [mel′ə·nin] *n.* A dark pigment found in animals, as in the skin and hair.

Mel·ba toast [mel′bə] Toast in very thin, crisp slices.

meld[1] [meld] 1 *v.* In certain card games, to declare or show (a card or combination of cards) in order to score. 2 *n.* The act of melding. 3 *n.* The card or cards melded.

meld[2] *v.* To blend or merge.

me·lee [mā′lā′ *or* mā·lā′] *n.* A confused, hand-to-hand fight in which many people are involved.

mel·lif·lu·ous [mə·lif′lo͞o·əs] *adj.* Flowing in a sweet, smooth way: *mellifluous* speech.

mel·low [mel′ō] 1 *adj.* Soft, sweet, and full of flavor; ripe, as fruit. 2 *adj.* Soft and pleasant to the taste; well aged: *mellow* cheese. 3 *adj.* Rich and soft in quality, as colors or sounds. 4 *adj.* Made gentle and sympathetic by age or experience. 5 *v.* To make or become mellow: Age *mellowed* the memory. **—mel′low·ness** *n.*

me·lod·ic [mə·lod′ik] *adj.* 1 Having to do with or containing melody. 2 Melodious.

me·lo·di·ous [mə·lō′dē·əs] *adj.* 1 Producing melody or full of melody; tuneful. 2 Pleasant to hear; musical. **—me·lo′di·ous·ly** *adv.*

mel·o·dra·ma [mel′ə·drä′mə] *n.* 1 A play using exaggeration or shocking events to stir up the feelings. It is often too full of violence, emotion, or sentimentality to be true to life. 2 Action or language suiting such a play.

mel·o·dra·mat·ic [mel′ə·drə·mat′ik] *adj.* Of, suitable to, or like melodrama, as in being too dramatic, too emotional, or violent. **—mel′o·dra·mat′·i·cal·ly** *adv.*

mel·o·dy [mel′ə·dē] *n., pl.* **mel·o·dies** 1 A rhythmically organized succession of musical tones in a single part or voice; tune. 2 The leading part or voice in a harmonic composition. 3 Any pleasant series or succession of sounds.

mel·on [mel′ən] *n.* A large, juicy fruit growing on vines, as the watermelon or cantaloupe.

melt [melt] *v.* 1 To change from a solid to a liquid condition by heat: The candle wax *melted*; to *melt* ice. 2 To fill with warm, tender feelings; soften: Sympathy *melted* my hard heart. 3 To dissolve, as in water: food so tender it seems to *melt* in the mouth. 4 To fade away or disappear: The fog *melted* away. 5 To blend little by little; merge: red *melting* into gold in a sunset.

melting point The temperature at which a given solid becomes liquid.

melting pot 1 A container in which a substance, as a metal, is melted; crucible. 2 A place where people of different races or cultures live together and become assimilated.

mem·ber [mem′bər] *n.* 1 A person who belongs to a group, as a family, club, or legislature. 2 A part of the body, especially an arm or leg. 3 An element of a set or of any whole thing.

mem·ber·ship [mem′bər·ship′] *n.* 1 The condition of being a member. 2 All of the members of some group. 3 The total number of members.

mem·brane [mem′brān′] *n.* A thin, flexible layer of tissue that covers or lines certain organs or parts of plants and animals. **—mem·bra·nous** [mem′brə·nəs] *adj.*

me·men·to [mə·men′tō] *n., pl.* **me·men·tos** or **me·men·toes** Anything kept or given as a reminder of the past; souvenir.

mem·o [mem′ō] *n., pl.* **mem·os** *informal* A memorandum.

mem·oir [mem′wär] *n.* 1 (*usually pl.*) The story of a person's own life and experiences. 2 An account of a person written by someone else, usually someone who knew the person. 3 (*often pl.*) A written account or report based on what the writer has experienced, observed, or learned.

mem·o·ra·bil·i·a [mem′ə·rə·bil′ē·ə *or* mem′ə·rə·bil′·yə] *n.pl.* 1 Things worth remembering or keeping. 2 A written record of such things.

mem·o·ra·ble [mem′ər·ə·bəl] *adj.* Worth remembering; hard to forget. **—mem′o·ra·bly** *adv.*

mem·o·ran·dum [mem′ə·ran′dəm] *n., pl.* **mem·o·ran·dums** or **mem·o·ran·da** [mem′ə·ran′də] 1 A brief note of something to be remembered. 2 An informal letter, usually sent between departments in an office.

me·mo·ri·al [mə·môr′ē·əl] 1 *adj.* Devoted to the memory of a person or event: a *memorial* library. 2 *n.* Something designed to remind people of a person or event, as a monument, a speech, or a ceremony. 3 *n.* A written statement of facts directed to the attention of a governing body or an executive, often accompanied by a petition.

Memorial Day *U.S.* A day for honoring the dead of American wars. It was formerly celebrated on May 30, but it is now observed as a legal holiday on the last Monday in May in most states.

me·mo·ri·al·ize [mə·môr′ē·ə·līz′] *v.* **me·mor·i·a·lized, me·mor·i·a·liz·ing** 1 To commemorate, as with a memorial. 2 To direct a memorial to; petition.

mem·o·rize [mem′ə·rīz′] *v.* **mem·o·rized, mem·o·riz·ing** To commit to memory; learn by heart. **—mem·o·ri·za·tion** [mem′ə·rə·zā′shən] *n.*

mem·o·ry [mem′ər·ē] *n., pl.* **mem·o·ries** 1 The mental act of or capacity for remembering: a good *memory* for names. 2 The total of what a person remembers: to commit a poem to *memory.* 3 Something remembered: *memories* of childhood. 4 The period of time covered by the ability to remember: beyond the *memory* of recorded time. 5 The part of a computer where data is stored; data storage. 6 The capacity a computer has for storing data. **—in memory of** As a reminder of or memorial to.

men [men] Plural of MAN.

men·ace [men′is] *v.* **men·aced, men·ac·ing,** *n.* 1 *v.* To threaten with evil or harm: a beach *menaced* by a hurricane. 2 *n.* A threat. 3 *n. informal* A troublesome person; pest.

me·nag·er·ie [mə·naj′ər·ē] *n.* 1 A collection of caged wild animals kept for exhibition. 2 The enclosure in which they are kept.

mend [mend] 1 *v.* To repair: to *mend* a broken toy. 2 *n.* A mended place, as in a garment. 3 *v.* To correct faults in; improve. 4 *v.* To get or make better, as in health. **—on the mend** Getting well. **—mend′er** *n.*

men·da·cious [men·dā′shəs] *adj.* 1 Lying or likely to tell lies. 2 Not true; false.

men·dac·i·ty [men·das′ə·tē] *n., pl.* **men·dac·i·ties** 1 The tendency to tell lies. 2 A lie.

men·de·le·vi·um [men′də·le′vē·əm] *n.* A radioactive metallic element known only from minute amounts that have been made artificially.

men·di·cant [men′də·kənt] 1 *adj.* Depending on charity for a living; begging: a *mendicant* friar. 2 *n.* A beggar. 3 *n.* A begging friar.

a	add	**i**	it	**o͝o**	took	**oi**	oil
ā	ace	**ī**	ice	**o͞o**	pool	**ou**	pout
â	care	**o**	odd	**u**	up	**ng**	ring
ä	palm	**ō**	open	**û**	burn	**th**	thin
e	end	**ô**	order	**yo͞o**	fuse	**t͟h**	this
ē	equal					**zh**	vision

ə = a in *above* e in *sicken* i in *possible* o in *melon* u in *circus*

M

Men·e·la·us [men'ə·lā'əs] *n.* In Greek myths, the king of Sparta who fought for the return of his abducted wife, Helen.

men·folk [men'fōk'] *n.pl. informal* 1 Men as a group. 2 The male members of a family or community.

men·folks [men'fōks'] *n.pl. informal* Menfolk.

men·ha·den [men·hād'(ə)n] *n.* A fish related to the herring, common off the Atlantic coast. It is used as a source of oil and as fertilizer.

me·ni·al [mē'nē·əl *or* mēn'yəl] 1 *adj.* Having to do with or appropriate to servants: a *menial* job. 2 *n.* A servant. **—me'ni·al·ly** *adv.*

me·nin·ges [mə·nin'jēz] *n.pl.* The membranes that enclose the brain and spinal cord. ◆ The singular form of this word, less frequently used than the plural, is *meninx*.

men·in·gi·tis [men'ən·jī'tis] *n.* A serious disease in which the membranes covering the brain or spinal cord become inflamed, usually by infection.

me·ninx [mē'ningks] The singular of MENINGES.

me·nis·cus [mə·nis'kəs] *n., pl.* **me·nis·ci** [mə·nis'ī] or **me·nis·cus·es** 1 A crescent-shaped object. 2 The curved surface of a column of liquid in a container. The meniscus is concave if the liquid wets the walls of the container and convex if it does not. 3 A lens that is concave on one side and convex on the other.

Men·non·ite [men'ən·īt'] *n.* A member of a Christian sect that is opposed to taking oaths, holding public office, and military service.

Me·nom·i·nee [mə·nom'ə·nē] *n., pl.* **Me·nom·i·nee** or **Me·nom·i·nees** 1 A tribe of North American Indians living in Wisconsin. 2 A member of this tribe. 3 The language of this tribe.

men·o·pause [men'ə·pôz'] *n.* The time of a woman's life when menstruation ceases permanently.

Me·no·rah [mə·nôr'ə] *n.* In Judaism, a candelabrum used during religious ceremonies.

men·ses [men'sēz] *n.pl.* Another word for MENSTRUATION.

men·stru·al [men'strōō·əl] *adj.* Of or having to do with menstruation.

men·stru·ate [men'strōō·āt'] *v.* **men·stru·at·ed, men·stru·at·ing** To have a discharge of blood from the uterus about every 28 days. This is a normal occurrence in women from puberty until some time in middle age.

men·stru·a·tion [men'strōō·ā'shən] *n.* The process of menstruating.

men·sur·a·ble [men'sər·ə·bəl *or* men'shər·ə·bəl] *adj.* Capable of being measured. **—men·sur·a·bil·i·ty** [men'sər·ə·bil'ə·tē *or* men'shər·ə·bil'ə·tē] *n.*

men·sur·al [men'sər·əl *or* men'shər·əl] *adj.* Of or having to do with measure.

men·su·ra·tion [men'sə·rā'shən] *n.* The act or process of measuring.

mens·wear [menz'wâr'] *n.* Clothing, including haberdashery, for men.

-ment A suffix meaning: 1 The act of, as in *development*. 2 The result of, as in *achievement*. 3 A means of or thing that, as in *punishment*. 4 The condition of being, as in *astonishment*.

men·tal [men'təl] *adj.* 1 Of or having to do with the mind: *mental* ability; *mental* illness. 2 Done by or in the mind: *mental* arithmetic. 3 Having a sick or disordered mind: a *mental* patient. 4 For the care of people with sick or disordered minds: a *mental* hospital.

mental age A level of mental development equal to that of the average child of a given age: She is only nine but her *mental age* is twelve.

men·tal·i·ty [men·tal'ə·tē] *n., pl.* **men·tal·i·ties** Mental capacity or power; intelligence.

men·tal·ly [men'tə·lē] *adv.* In or with the mind: *mentally* retarded; to add *mentally*.

mental deficiency A condition in which the intellect fails to develop normally, resulting in deficiencies that range from learning difficulties to an inability to perform necessary functions of everyday life.

men·thol [men'thôl] *n.* A white crystalline substance obtained from peppermint oil. It has a cooling taste and is used in medicine and perfume.

men·tion [men'shən] 1 *v.* To refer to briefly or name in passing. 2 *n.* A brief remark or statement about or a reference to something. **—make mention of** To refer to; mention.

men·tor [men'tər] *n.* A wise, devoted adviser.

men·u [men'yōō] *n.* 1 A list of the foods provided for a meal. 2 The foods provided. 3 On a computer screen, a list showing the different things that the person using the program may do.

me·ow [mē·ou'] 1 *n.* The crying sound made by a cat. 2 *v.* To make this sound.

Meph·i·stoph·e·les [mef'is·tof'ə·lēz'] *n.* In the legend of Faust, the devil to whom Faust sold his soul.

mer·can·tile [mûr'kən·tēl' *or* mûr'kən·tīl'] *adj.* Having to do with merchants or commerce.

mer·can·til·ism [mûr'kən·tē·liz'əm] *n.* An economic system developed in Europe during the decline of feudalism that sought to strengthen a nation's power through strict government control of the nation's economy. It stressed the importance of making profit from foreign trade, the acquisition of colonies and foreign trading monopolies, and the accumulation of wealth in the form of gold and silver.

Mer·ca·tor projection [mər·kā'tər] A form of map projection in which the meridians are parallel and equally spaced and the lines of latitude, which intersect the meridians at right angles, are parallel but spaced farther apart from each other as their distance from the equator increases.

Mercator projection

mer·ce·nar·y [mûr'sə·ner'ē] *adj., n., pl.* **mer·ce·nar·ies** 1 *adj.* Influenced only by the desire for money or reward; greedy: The family showed a *mercenary* concern about their rich relative's health. 2 *n.* A soldier who serves for pay in the army of a foreign government.

mer·cer·ize [mûr'sə·rīz'] *v.* **mer·cer·ized, mer·cer·iz·ing** To treat (cotton fiber or fabrics) with a chemical that makes the fibers stronger, glossy, and better able to take dyes.

mer·chan·dise [*n.* mûr'chən·dīz' *or* mûr'chən·dīs', *v.* mûr'chən·dīz'] *n., v.* **mer·chan·dised, mer·chan·dis·ing** 1 *n.* Goods bought and sold for profit. 2

v. To buy and sell for profit. **3** *v.* To promote the sale of (goods).
mer·chant [mûr′chənt] **1** *n.* A person who buys and sells things for profit; trader. **2** *adj.* Of, having to do with, or used in trade; commercial: *merchant* ships. **3** *n.* A storekeeper.
mer·chant·man [mûr′chənt·mən] *n., pl.* **mer·chant·men** [mûr′chənt·mən] A ship used in trade.
merchant marine Those ships and sailors of a nation that are engaged in trade, not defense.
mer·ci·ful [mûr′sə·fəl] *adj.* Full of or showing mercy; kind. **—mer′ci·ful·ly** *adv.*
mer·ci·less [mûr′sə·lis] *adj.* Having or showing no mercy. **—mer′ci·less·ly** *adv.*
mer·cu·ri·al [mər·kyŏŏr′ē·əl] *adj.* **1** Lively; clever; changeable. **2** Of, having to do with, containing, or caused by the element mercury.
Mer·cu·ro·chrome [mər·kyŏŏr′ə·krōm′] *n.* A red antiseptic liquid: a trademark.
mer·cu·ry [mûr′kyə·rē] *n., pl.* **mer·cu·ries** **1** A heavy, toxic, silver-white metallic element that is liquid and volatile at ordinary temperatures; quicksilver. Pure mercury is used in thermometers and barometers, and its compounds have many safe uses in dentistry, medicine, and industry. **2** (*written* **Mercury**) In Roman myths, the messenger of the gods and the god of commerce, eloquence, and skill. ◆ See the picture at HERMES, his Greek name. **3** (*written* **Mercury**) A planet of the solar system, the smallest one and the one nearest to the sun.
mer·cy [mûr′sē] *n., pl.* **mer·cies** **1** Kind treatment or mildness where severity is expected or deserved. **2** The power to show kindness or pity: Because my book report was late, I threw myself on the teacher's *mercy.* **3** A thing to be thankful for: It's a *mercy* I got here in time. **—at the mercy of** Completely in the power of.
mere[1] [mir] *adj.* **mer·est** Being nothing more or less than; being nothing but: a *mere* trifle.
mere[2] [mir] *n.* A lake, pond, or marsh: seldom used today.
mere·ly [mir′lē] *adv.* Nothing more than; only.
mer·e·tri·cious [mer′ə·trish′əs] *adj.* Showy and meant to attract but really false or cheap. **—mer′·e·tri′cious·ly** *adv.* **—mer′e·tri′cious·ness** *n.*
mer·gan·ser [mər·gan′sər] *n., pl.* **mer·gan·ser** or **mer·gan·sers** A diving duck with a long, slender bill and usually a crest.
merge [mûrj] *v.* **merged, merg·ing** To combine or be combined so as to lose separate identity: The two lanes of traffic *merged,* becoming one.
merg·er [mûr′jər] *n.* The act of merging, as the combining of separate companies into one.
me·rid·i·an [mə·rid′ē·ən] *n.* **1** Any imaginary semicircle drawn on the earth's surface from the North to the South Pole. Meridians are used in measuring longitude. **2** The highest point that the sun or a star seems to climb to. **3** The highest point of anything, as of a life.

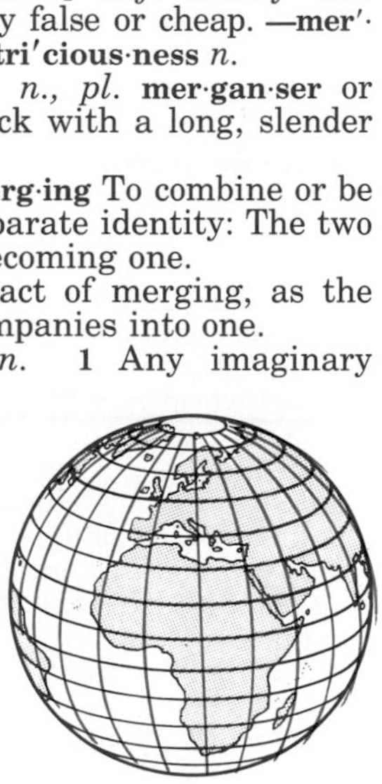
Meridians

me·ringue [mə·rang′] *n.* The stiffly beaten whites of eggs, blended with sugar, usually baked on top of a pie filling or as a small cake or shell.
me·ri·no [mə·rē′nō] *n., pl.* **me·ri·nos** **1** A breed of sheep with fine, silky wool. The male has heavy, curled horns. **2** The wool of this sheep. **3** A fine, soft, woolen fabric originally made of this wool. **4** A fine yarn.

Merino

mer·it [mer′it] **1** *n.* Worth or value; high quality; excellence: an idea with *merit;* That scheme has little *merit.* **2** *n.* (*pl.*) The actual rights or wrongs of a matter: Consider the case on its *merits.* **3** *v.* To be entitled to; deserve: Parents *merit* respect.
mer·i·toc·ra·cy [mer′i·tok′rə·sē] *n., pl.* **mer·i·toc·ra·cies** **1** A system, as in education or employment, that allows people to move ahead on the basis of their intelligence, talent, and achievement. **2** Leadership by such people.
mer·i·to·ri·ous [mer′ə·tôr′ē·əs] *adj.* Having merit, worthy; commendable.
Mer·lin [mûr′lin] *n.* In English legend, a magician and prophet at King Arthur's court.
mer·maid [mûr′mād′] *n.* A legendary sea creature having the head and upper body of a woman and the tail of a fish.
mer·man [mûr′man′] *n., pl.* **mer·men** [mûr′men′] A legendary sea creature having the head and upper body of a man and the tail of a fish.
mer·ri·ment [mer′i·mənt] *n.* Laughter; fun.
mer·ry [mer′ē] *adj.* **mer·ri·er, mer·ri·est** Full of fun and laughter; joyous; gay; zestful: a *merry* dance. **—mer′ri·ly** *adv.*
mer·ry-an·drew [mer′ē·an′drōō] *n.* A clown.
mer·ry-go-round [mer′ē·gō·round′] *n.* **1** A revolving platform fitted with wooden horses, and seats on which people, especially children, ride for amusement. **2** A rapid going around or whirl, as of social events.
mer·ry·mak·ing [mer′ē·mā′king] **1** *n.* Fun and gaiety; laughter and joking. **2** *adj.* Festive and gay. **3** *n.* A merry time. **—mer′·ry·mak′er** *n.*
me·sa [mā′sə] *n.* A hill or small plateau with a flat top and steep sides, common in the SW U.S. ◆ *Mesa* comes directly from Spanish and goes back to the Latin word *mensa,* meaning *table.*

Mesa

a	add	**i**	it	**ŏŏ**	took	**oi**	oil
ā	ace	**ī**	ice	**ōō**	pool	**ou**	pout
â	care	**o**	odd	**u**	up	**ng**	ring
ä	palm	**ō**	open	**û**	burn	**th**	thin
e	end	**ô**	order	**yōō**	fuse	**th**	this
ē	equal					**zh**	vision

ə = a in *above* e in *sicken* i in *possible*
o in *melon* u in *circus*

M

mes·cal [mes·kal′] *n.* A cactus of northern Mexico and the sw U.S., having rounded, buttonlike growths that are the source of mescaline.

mes·ca·line [mes′kə·lən *or* mes′kə·lēn′] *n.* A drug found in mescal that produces hallucinations.

mes·dames [mā·däm′] **1** Plural of MADAM. **2** Plural of MADAME.

mes·de·moi·selles [mād′mwä·zel′ *or* mā′də·mə·zel′] A plural of MADEMOISELLE.

mesh [mesh] **1** *n.* One of the open spaces between the cords of a net or the wires of a screen. **2** *n.* (*pl.*) The cords or wires that make up a network. **3** *v.* To trap or ensnare, as in a net. **4** *v.* To fit into place, as the teeth of interlocking gears. **—in mesh** In gear.

mes·mer·ism [mez′mə·riz′əm] *n.* Hypnotism.

mes·mer·ize [mez′mə·rīz′] *v.* **mes·mer·ized, mes·mer·iz·ing** To hypnotize.

mes·on [mez′on *or* mes′on] *n.* Any of a class of short-lived atomic particles having a mass between those of the electron and the proton.

mes·o·sphere [mez′ə·sfir′ *or* mes′ə·sfir′] *n.* The layer of the earth's atmosphere just above the stratosphere, extending to about 50 miles above the surface of the earth.

Mes·o·zo·ic [mez′ə·zō′ik *or* mes′ə·zō′ik] **1** *n.* The third geological era, between the Paleozoic and the Cenozoic. During the Mesozoic the Americas separated from Europe and Africa and reptiles were dominant forms of life. **2** *adj.* Of the Mesozoic.

mes·quite [mes·kēt′] *n.* A spiny shrub or small tree found in the sw U.S., Mexico, and Central America. Its pods are fed to cattle.

mess [mes] **1** *n.* A state of disorder, especially a condition of dirty or untidy confusion: The place was in a *mess* after the party. **2** *n.* An unpleasant or confused mixture; jumble; muddle: a *mess* of clothes piled in the corner; to make a *mess* of the homework. **3** *v.* To make a mess of: Don't *mess* up my hair. **4** *v.* To busy oneself; putter: Stop *messing* with those papers. **5** *n.* A number of persons who regularly take their meals together, as in the army. **6** *n.* A meal taken by them, or the place where the meal is served. **7** *n.* A portion, as of food. **8** *n.* A serving of soft, partly liquid food.

mes·sage [mes′ij] *n.* **1** Advice, news, instructions, or other communication sent to another person. **2** A lesson or idea, as one contained in a speech or story.

mes·sen·ger [mes′ən·jər] *n.* A person sent with a message or on an errand.

Mes·si·ah [mə·sī′ə] *n.* **1** In the Jewish religion, the awaited deliverer of the Jewish people promised by God. **2** In the Christian religion, Jesus. **3** (*written* **messiah**) An expected liberator of a country or people.

Mes·si·an·ic [mes′ē·an′ik] *adj.* **1** Of or having to do with the Messiah. **2** (*written* **messianic**) Of or having to do with a messiah.

mes·sieurs [mes′ərz] Plural of MONSIEUR.

mess kit A complete kit of utensils and containers for eating, used chiefly by soldiers and campers.

Messrs. [mes′ərz] An abbreviation used as the plural of MR. ◆ *Messrs.* is an abbreviation of the French word *messieurs,* plural of *monsieur.*

mess·y [mes′ē] *adj.* **mess·i·er, mess·i·est** **1** Dirty, sloppy, or disorderly. **2** Difficult or unpleasant. **—mess′i·ly** *adv.* **—mess′i·ness** *n.*

mes·ti·zo [me·stē′zō] *n., pl.* **mes·ti·zos** or **mes·ti·zoes** A person of mixed ancestry, especially a person of European and American Indian ancestry.

met [met] Past tense and past participle of MEET[1].

me·tab·o·lism [mə·tab′ə·liz′əm] *n.* All of the processes by which a plant or animal converts materials taken from its environment into the energy required to maintain itself, grow, and carry on all vital activities. **—met·a·bol·ic** [met′ə·bol′ik] *adj.*

met·a·car·pal [met′ə·kär′pəl] **1** *adj.* Of or having to do with the metacarpus. **2** A metacarpal bone.

met·a·car·pus [met′ə·kär′pəs] *n., pl.* **met·a·car·pi** [met′ə·kär′pī] **1** The part of a hand between the fingers and the wrist, containing five bones. **2** A similar section of an animal's forefoot.

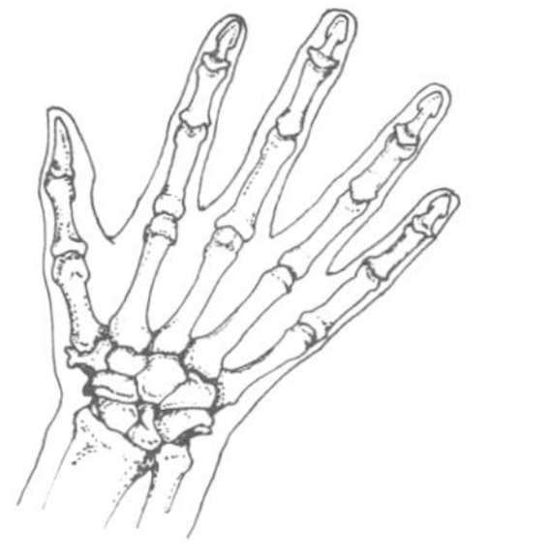

Metacarpus

met·al [met′(ə)l] *n.* Any of the class of usually gray or white lustrous elements that lose electrons and become positive ions that form bases in chemical reactions with nonmetals. Metals like iron, silver, gold, and copper are familiar as malleable, fusible solids that are good conductors of heat and electricity. But other metals are so reactive chemically that they ordinarily exist only in compounds that lack the physical properties of typical metals.

me·tal·lic [mə·tal′ik] *adj.* **1** Of or having to do with metal. **2** Like or suggesting metal: a sharp, *metallic* noise.

met·al·loid [met′ə·loid′] **1** *n.* An element that has both metallic and nonmetallic properties, as bismuth or arsenic. **2** *adj.* Of, having to do with, or being a metalloid. **3** *adj.* Resembling a metal.

met·al·lur·gy [met′ə·lûr′jē] *n.* The science of removing metals from their ores, refining them, and using them, as in alloys. **—met′al·lur′gist** *n.*

met·al·work [met′əl·wûrk′] *n.* **1** Objects made of metal. **2** The act or process of making things from metal.

met·a·mor·phic [met′ə·môr′fik] *adj.* Of or resulting from a change in form or structure.

met·a·mor·phism [met′ə·môr′fiz′əm] *n.* A change in the structure, texture, or composition of rock produced by natural forces, as pressure, heat, and water.

met·a·mor·phose [met′ə·môr′fōz′] *v.* **met·a·mor·phosed, met·a·mor·phos·ing** To change or be changed from one form or structure into another: A silkworm *metamorphoses* into a moth.

met·a·mor·pho·sis [met′ə·môr′fə·sis] *n., pl.* **met·a·mor·pho·ses** [met′ə·môr′fə·sēz] **1** A change from one form, shape, or substance into another, as the development of a tadpole into a frog. **2** A complete change, as in someone's character: the *metamorphosis* of a shy child into an outgoing teenager.

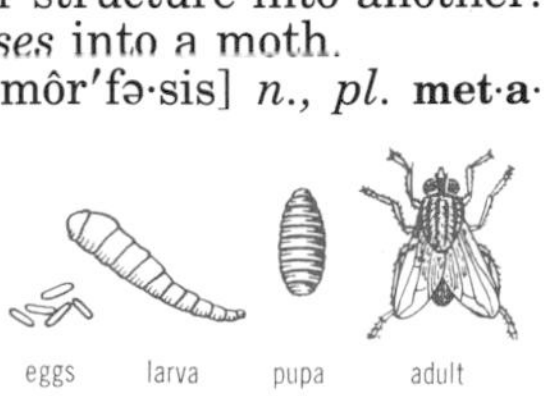

Metamorphosis of a fly

met·a·phor [met′ə·fôr′] *n.* A figure of speech which suggests, without saying so, that one thing is like another. It applies a word or phrase to something to which it does not actually or ordinarily apply, as in "The room was a *beehive* of activity."

met·a·phor·i·cal [met′ə·fôr′i·kəl] *adj.* Of or using a metaphor. **—met′a·phor′i·cal·ly** *adv.*

met·a·phys·i·cal [met′ə·fiz′i·kəl] *adj.* **1** Of or having to do with metaphysics. **2** Highly abstract and often difficult to understand.

met·a·phy·si·cian [met′ə·fi·zish′ən] *n.* A philosopher skilled in metaphysics.

met·a·phys·ics [met′ə·fiz′iks] *n.* The branch of philosophy that investigates reality, being, and knowledge. ◆ See -ICS.

me·tas·ta·sis [mə·tas′tə·sis] *n., pl.* **me·tas·ta·ses** [mə·tas′tə·sēz′] The spread of a disease, as cancer, from one part of the body to another.

me·tas·ta·size [mə·tas′tə·sīz′] *v.* **me·tas·ta·sized, me·tas·ta·siz·ing** To spread from one part of the body to another, as cancer and certain other diseases.

met·a·tar·sal [met′ə·tär′səl] **1** *adj.* Of or having to do with the metatarsus. **2** *n.* One of the bones of the metatarsus.

met·a·tar·sus [met′ə·tär′səs] *n., pl.* **met·a·tar·si** [met′ə·tär′sī] **1** The part of a human foot that contains the five bones between the toes and the ankle. **2** A similar part of a bird's foot or of a four-legged animal's hind foot.

met·a·zo·an [met′ə·zō′ən] **1** *n.* An animal having a body made up of cells differentiated into tissues and organs. **2** *adj.* Of or having to do with such an animal.

mete [mēt] *v.* **met·ed, met·ing** To give according to measure or one's judgment: to *mete* out five dollars per person; to *mete* out justice.

me·te·or [mē′tē·ər] *n.* A small fragment of matter from outer space that is heated white-hot by friction with the earth's atmosphere and appears briefly as a streak of light; shooting star.

me·te·or·ic [mē·tē·ôr′ik] *adj.* **1** Of or made up of meteors. **2** Brilliant, rapid, and dazzling, like a meteor: a *meteoric* career.

me·te·or·ite [mē′tē·ə·rīt′] *n.* A part of a meteor that is not burned up and strikes the earth as a lump of stone or metal.

me·te·or·oid [mē′tē·ə·roid′] *n.* One of the pieces of matter in outer space that form meteors upon entering the earth's atmosphere.

me·te·or·o·log·i·cal [mē′tē·ôr′ə·loj′i·kəl] *adj.* Of or having to do with the atmosphere, winds, and weather, or with meteorology.

me·te·or·ol·o·gy [mē′tē·ə·rol′ə·jē] *n.* The science that studies the atmosphere, winds, and weather. **—me′te·or·ol′o·gist** *n.*

me·ter[1] [mē′tər] *n.* **1** The measured rhythm used in poetry, a pattern of accented and unaccented syllables. **2** The pattern of beats and accents in a measure of music.

me·ter[2] [mē′tər] *n.* In the metric system, the standard unit of length, equal to 39.37 inches.

me·ter[3] [mē′tər] *n.* An instrument used to measure and often record a quantity or an amount used: a gas *meter.*

-meter A combining form meaning: A device for measuring, as in *speedometer.*

me·ter-kil·o·gram-sec·ond [mē′tər·kil′ə·gram′sek′·ənd] *adj.* Of, having to do with, or being a system of measurement that uses the meter as the unit of length, the kilogram as the unit of mass, and the second as the unit of time.

meth·a·done [meth′ə·dōn′] *n.* A drug used as a painkiller and in treating heroin addiction.

meth·ane [meth′ān′] *n.* A colorless, odorless gas that burns easily and is a main part of the gas used for cooking. It is formed by decaying plants and found in coal mines and oil wells, among other places.

meth·a·nol [meth′ə·nôl′] *n.* Methyl alcohol.

me·thinks [mē·thingks′] *v.* **me·thought** It seems to me: seldom used today.

meth·od [meth′əd] *n.* **1** A way of doing or accomplishing something: the offset *method* of printing. **2** System, order, or regularity: To study without *method* is a waste of time.

me·thod·i·cal [mə·thod′i·kəl] *adj.* Using or showing the use of a strict, orderly system: a *methodical* search. **—me·thod′i·cal·ly** *adv.*

Meth·od·ism [meth′əd·iz′əm] *n.* The doctrines, practice, and way of worship of the Methodists.

Meth·od·ist [meth′əd·ist] **1** *n.* A member of a Christian church that grew out of the religious movement started by John Wesley. **2** *adj.* Of or having to do with Methodists or their church.

meth·od·ol·o·gy [meth′ə·dol′ə·jē] *n., pl.* **meth·od·ol·o·gies** A system of principles and procedures, as those used in a science. **—meth·od·o·log·i·cal** [meth′ə·də·loj′i·kəl] *adj.* **—meth·od·ol·o·gist** [meth′ə·dol′ə·jist] *n.*

me·thought [mē·thôt′] Past tense of METHINKS.

Me·thu·se·lah [mə·th(y)ōō′zə·lə] *n.* **1** In the Bible, a man who was said to have lived for 969 years. **2** Any very old person.

meth·yl alcohol [meth′əl] A highly poisonous form of alcohol; wood alcohol.

me·tic·u·lous [mə·tik′yə·ləs] *adj.* Extremely careful or too careful about minor details. **—me·tic′u·lous·ly** *adv.* **—me·tic′u·lous·ness** *n.*

me·tre [mē′tər] *n.* The British spelling of METER[1] and METER[2].

met·ric [met′rik] *adj.* **1** Of, in, having to do with, or using the metric system. **2** Metrical. ◆ *Metric* comes from the French *métrique,* which was formed by combining *mètre,* meaning *meter,* with the suffix *-ique.*

met·ri·cal [met′ri·kəl] *adj.* **1** Of, arranged in, or using meter: Blank verse is written in *metrical* feet; *metrical* music. **2** Of, having to do with, or used in measurement.

met·ri·cate [met′ri·kāt′] *v.* **met·ri·cat·ed, met·ri·cat·ing** *British* To metricize. **—met′ri·ca′tion** *n.*

met·ri·cize [met′ri·sīz′] *v.* **met·ri·cized, met·ri·ciz·ing** To change to or express in the metric system.

metric system A system of weights and measures in which all units are formed by multiplying or dividing a standard unit by 10, 100, 1000, and so forth. The standard unit of length in the metric system is the meter. The liter is the unit of volume, and the gram is commonly used to measure weight or mass.

metric ton In the metric system, a measure of mass

a	add	**i**	it	**ŏŏ**	took	**oi**	oil		
ā	ace	**ī**	ice	**ōō**	pool	**ou**	pout		
â	care	**o**	odd	**u**	up	**ng**	ring		
ä	palm	**ō**	open	**û**	burn	**th**	thin		
e	end	**ô**	order	**yōō**	fuse	**th̶**	this		
ē	equal					**zh**	vision		

ə = a in *above* e in *sicken* i in *possible* o in *melon* u in *circus*

equaling 1000 kilograms, having a weight equivalent to 2204.62 pounds avoirdupois.

met·ro [me′trō] *adj.* Of, having to do with, or being an area comprising a large city and its suburbs; metropolitan.

met·ro·nome [met′rə·nōm′] *n.* An instrument that makes clicks at an even but adjustable rate, used to set a tempo in practicing music.

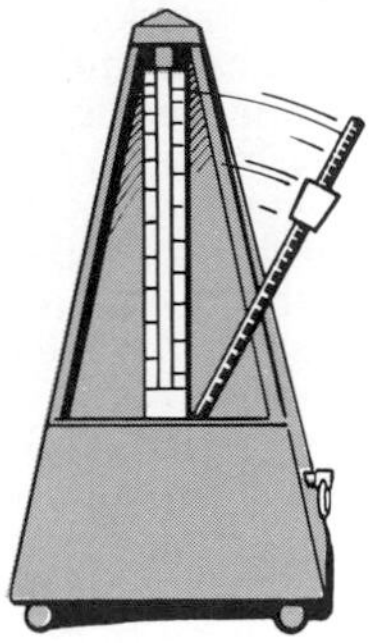
Metronome

me·trop·o·lis [mə·trop′ə·lis] *n.* **1** The largest or most important city of a country, state, or area. **2** Any large city or center of activity.

met·ro·pol·i·tan [met′rə·pol′ə·tən] **1** *adj.* Of, having to do with, or making up a large city or metropolis: the *metropolitan* area. **2** *n.* A person who lives in a large city or who has characteristics associated with city people. **3** *n.* In various churches, an archbishop.

-metry A combining form meaning: The science or way of measuring, as in *optometry.*

met·tle [met′(ə)l] *n.* Spirit, courage, or resolution: to test a person's *mettle.* **—on one's mettle** Ready to do the best one can.

met·tle·some [met′l·səm] *adj.* Full of mettle; spirited; courageous.

MeV or **Mev** A million electron volts.

mew[1] [myōō] *n.* A sea gull.

mew[2] [myōō] **1** *n.* A cage in which hawks are kept when they are shedding their feathers. **2** *v.* To confine in or as if in a cage.

mew[3] [myōō] **1** *n.* The crying sound typical of a cat. **2** *v.* To make the crying sound of a cat.

mewl [myōōl] **1** *v.* To whimper or cry feebly, as a baby does. **2** *n.* A whimper or feeble cry.

mews [myōōz] *n.pl.* (*used with singular or plural verb*) A narrow residential street, often lined with houses converted from old stables.

Mex. 1 Mexican. Mexico.

Mex·i·can [mek′sə·kən] **1** *adj.* Of or from Mexico. **2** *n.* A person born in or a citizen of Mexico.

Mexican jumping bean Another name for JUMPING BEAN.

Mexican War The war between the U.S. and Mexico from 1846 to 1848.

me·zu·zah or **me·zu·za** [mə·zōōz′ə] *n.* A parchment inscribed with Biblical passages and a Hebrew word for God, rolled inside a small container and attached to a door frame of the home by some Jewish families.

mez·za·nine [mez′ə·nēn′] *n.* **1** A story in a building between two main floors, usually just above the ground floor and sometimes extending over it like a balcony. **2** In a theater, the first balcony or the front rows of the balcony.

mez·zo [met′sō] *adj.* Half; medium; moderate.

mez·zo-so·pran·o [met′sō·sə·pran′ō] *n., pl.* **mez·zo-so·pran·os** **1** A female singing voice of a quality and range between soprano and contralto. **2** A singer having such a voice.

mg or **mg.** milligram.

Mg The symbol for the element magnesium.

mgr. manager.

Mgr. 1 Monseigneur. **2** Monsignor. **3** Manager.

mi [mē] *n.* In music, a syllable used to represent the third tone of a major scale or the fifth tone of a minor scale, or, in a fixed system, the tone E.

mi. **1** mile(s). **2** mill(s) (monetary unit).

MI Postal Service abbreviation of Michigan.

mi·aou or **mi·aow** [mē·ou′] *n., v.* Other spellings of MEOW.

mi·as·ma [mī·az′mə] *n.* A heavy vapor rising from the earth, especially from decaying matter in swamps, formerly thought to cause disease.

mi·ca [mī′kə] *n.* A shiny mineral that is easily split into thin, flexible, partly transparent layers.

Mi·cah [mī′kə] *n.* **1** In the Bible, a Hebrew prophet of the eighth century B.C. **2** A book of the Old Testament.

mice [mīs] Plural of MOUSE.

Mich. Michigan.

Mi·chael [mī′kəl] *n.* One of the archangels.

Mich·ael·mas [mik′əl·məs] *n.* September 29, a church feast honoring the archangel Michael.

Mic·mac [mik′mak′] *n., pl.* **Mic·mac** or **Mic·macs** **1** A tribe of North American Indians of eastern Canada. **2** A member of this tribe. **3** The language of this tribe.

mi·cra [mī′krə] A plural of MICRON.

micro- or **micr-** A combining form meaning: **1** Very small, as in *microorganism.* **2** Enlarging or amplifying, as in *microscope.* **3** One millionth part of (a specific unit), as in *microgram.*

mi·crobe [mī′krōb′] *n.* An organism too tiny to be seen except with a microscope, especially one of the bacteria that cause disease; germ.

mi·cro·bi·ol·o·gy [mī′krō·bī·ol′ə·jē] *n.* The branch of biology concerned with the study of microorganisms. **—mi′cro·bi·ol′o·gist** *n.*

mi·cro·coc·cus [mī′krō·kok′əs] *n., pl.* **mi·cro·coc·ci** [mī′krō·kok′sī] Any of a group of bacteria that are shaped like spheres and occur in irregular groups.

mi·cro·com·put·er [mī′krō·kəm·pyōō′tər] *n.* A very small, relatively inexpensive computer having at least one microprocessor as its central processing unit.

mi·cro·cop·y [mī′krō·kop′ē] *n., pl.* **mi·cro·cop·ies** A photographic copy of printed or pictorial matter greatly reduced in size.

mi·cro·cosm [mī′krə·koz′əm] *n.* **1** A little world. **2** Something regarded as a miniature representation of a much larger place or activity; likeness on a small scale: A beehive is a *microcosm* of modern industrial society.

mi·cro·fiche [mi′krō·fēsh′] *n.* A sheet of microfilm, usually 4 × 6 inches, on which many pages, as of printed matter, can be recorded and stored.

Microfiche

mi·cro·film [mī′krə·film′] **1** *n.* Film used to take tiny photographs of printed matter, as papers, records, or books, for storage in small space. **2** *v.* To photograph on microfilm: The company will *microfilm* all personnel records.

mi·cro·gram [mī′krə·gram′] *n.* In the metric system, a unit of mass or weight equal to one millionth of a gram.

mi·crom·e·ter[1] [mī·krom′ə·tər] *n.* 1 A caliper used to make very precise measurements. 2 An instrument used with a microscope or telescope to measure very small distances. ◆ See OMEGA.

Micrometer caliper

mi·cro·me·ter[2] [mī′krō·mē′tər] *n.* In the metric system, a unit of length equal to one millionth of a meter.
mi·cron [mī′kron′] *n., pl.* **mi·crons** or **mi·cra** [mī′krə] A micrometer[2].
Mi·cro·ne·sian [mī′krə·nē′zhən] 1 *adj.* Of or from Micronesia. 2 *n.* A person born or living in Micronesia. 3 *n.* Any of the languages of Micronesia.
mi·cro·nu·cle·us [mī′krō·n(y)o͞o′klē·əs] *n., pl.* **mi·cro·nu·cle·i** [mī′krō·n(y)o͞o′klē·ī] or **mi·cro·nu·cle·us·es** The smaller of the two nuclei in certain protozoans.
mi·cro·or·gan·ism [mī′krō·ôr′gən·iz′əm] *n.* An organism so small that it can be seen only through a microscope, especially one of the bacteria, a protozoan, or a virus.
mi·cro·phone [mī′krə·fōn′] *n.* A device that converts sound waves into alternating electric currents, used for broadcasting and amplifying sound, as speech or music.
mi·cro·proc·es·sor [mī′krō·pros′es·ər] *n.* A miniaturized integrated circuit, usually contained on a single chip, that is capable of performing all the functions of a central processing unit.
mi·cro·scope [mī′krə·skōp′] *n.* An instrument usually consisting of a combination of lenses, used to magnify objects too small to be seen or clearly observed by the naked eye.

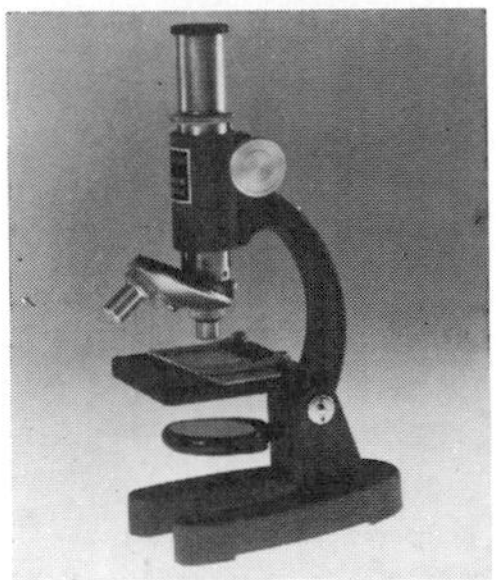
Microscope

mi·cro·scop·ic [mī′krə·skop′ik] *adj.* 1 So small as to be visible only under a microscope. 2 Very small; minute. 3 Of, like, having to do with, or performed with a microscope: a *microscopic* examination. 4 Showing very close observation or attention to details: a *microscopic* search. **—mi′cro·scop′i·cal·ly** *adv.*
mi·cros·co·py [mī·kros′kə·pē] *n.* 1 The use of a microscope. 2 An investigation by use of a microscope. **—mi·cros′co·pist** *n.*
mi·cro·wave [mī′krə·wāv′] *n.* An electromagnetic wave having a frequency between about 1,000 and 30,000 megahertz.
microwave oven An oven that makes possible the rapid cooking of food by heat produced within the food when penetrated by microwaves.
mid[1] [mid] *adj.* Middle.
mid[2] or **'mid** [mid] *prep.* Amid; among: used mostly in poems.
mid- A prefix meaning: 1 The middle or the middle part of, as in *midwinter.* 2 Being in, at, or near the middle or center, as in *midpoint.*
mid·air [mid′âr′] *n.* A point or region in the air not very near the ground: the thrill of balloonists floating in *midair.*
Mi·das [mī′dəs] *n.* In Greek legend, a king whose magic touch would turn anything to gold.
mid·brain [mid′brān′] *n.* 1 The middle portion of the brain of the embryo of a human being or other vertebrate. 2 The part of the adult brain that develops from that portion.
mid·day [mid′dā′] *n.* 1 The middle of the day; noon. 2 *adj. use:* a *midday* snack.
mid·dle [mid′(ə)l] 1 *n.* The part, point, position, or area in the center, equally distant from the ends, sides, or edges: the *middle* of the night; in the *middle* of a group; I want to sit in the *middle.* 2 *adj.* Being in, at, or near the middle: a *middle* position. 3 *adj.* Coming halfway between others; in between: the *middle* child in a family. 4 *n.* The waist.
middle age The period of a person's life extending from about the age of 40 to about the age of 65.
mid·dle-aged [mid′(ə)l·ājd′] *adj.* Being no longer young but not yet old: said about people.
Middle Ages The period in European history between the downfall of Rome and the Renaissance, extending from 476 to about 1450.
Middle America The U.S. middle class, especially that part of it which is conservative in beliefs and values.
middle C A musical tone whose pitch is indicated by a note on the first ledger line below the treble clef and the first ledger line above the bass clef.
mid·dle-class [mid′(ə)l·klas′] *adj.* Of, having to do with, or characteristic of the middle class: a political candidate wooing *middle-class* voters.
middle class The part of a society in a social or economic position between the laboring class and the very wealthy or the nobility.
middle ear A small cavity between the eardrum and the inner ear where three small bones pass sound waves along to the inner ear; tympanum.
Middle Eastern Of or from the Middle East. — **Middle Easterner**
Middle English The English language as it existed from about 1100 to 1500.
mid·dle·man [mid′(ə)l·man′] *n., pl.* **mid·dle·men** [mid′(ə)l·men′] 1 A go-between or agent. 2 A person who buys in large quantities from producers and sells to retailers or consumers.
middle name The name between one's first name and the name of one's family.
mid·dle-of-the-road [mid′(ə)l·əv·t͟hə·rōd′] *adj.* Having or favoring a moderate position or policy rather than an extreme one: a *middle-of-the-road* politician, whose philosophy is midway between liberal and conservative.
middle school A school whose level usually extends from grades 5 through 8.
mid·dle·weight [mid′(ə)l·wāt′] *n.* 1 A person or animal of average weight. 2 A boxer weighing between 147 and 160 pounds.

a	add	**i**	it	**o͝o**	took	**oi**	oil
ā	ace	**ī**	ice	**o͞o**	pool	**ou**	pout
â	care	**o**	odd	**u**	up	**ng**	ring
ä	palm	**ō**	open	**û**	burn	**th**	thin
e	end	**ô**	order	**yo͞o**	fuse	**t͟h**	this
ē	equal					**zh**	vision

ə = {a in *above*, e in *sicken*, i in *possible*, o in *melon*, u in *circus*}

M

Middle Western Of or from the Middle West.

mid·dling [mid′ling] 1 *adj.* Of middle or average size, quality, or condition; ordinary. 2 *n.* (*pl.*) Various products of medium size, quality, or condition. 3 *n.* (*pl.*) The coarser part of ground grain.

mid·dy [mid′ē] *n., pl.* **mid·dies** 1 A loose blouse (also called a **middy blouse**) with a large collar that is square in back. 2 *informal* A midshipman.

Middy

mid·field [mid′fēld′] *n.* The middle of a playing field, especially the middle area of a soccer field.

mid·field·er [mid′fēl′·dər] *n.* In soccer, a player assigned to the midfield.

Mid·east·ern [mid′ēs′·tərn] *adj.* Middle Eastern.

midge [mij] *n.* A gnat or small fly.

midg·et [mij′it] *n.* 1 A person of much less than normal size but with normal physical proportions. 2 Anything very small of its kind.

mid·land [mid′lənd] 1 *n.* The central or inland part of a country or region; interior. 2 *adj.* Of or in an inland or interior region.

mid·most [mid′mōst′] *adj.* Situated exactly or most nearly in the middle.

mid·night [mid′nīt′] 1 *n.* The middle of the night; twelve o'clock at night. 2 *adj. use*: a *midnight* snack. 3 *adj.* As dark as midnight.

midnight sun The sun when visible at midnight in summer in the Arctic or Antarctic.

mid·point [mid′point′] *n.* A point halfway between the ends, as of a line segment.

mid·rib [mid′rib′] *n.* The central vein of a leaf.

mid·riff [mid′rif] *n.* 1 The part of the body between the chest and the abdomen. 2 The diaphragm.

mid·sec·tion [mid′sek′shən] *n.* 1 The middle section or part of a thing. 2 The midriff (def. 1).

mid·ship [mid′ship′] *adj.* Of, having to do with, or in the middle of a ship.

mid·ship·man [mid′ship′mən] *n., pl.* **mid·ship·men** [mid′ship′mən] 1 In the U.S. Navy, a student at the U.S. Naval Academy. 2 In the British Navy, an officer ranking between a naval cadet and the lowest commissioned officer.

mid·ships [mid′ships′] *adv.* Another word for AMIDSHIPS.

midst [midst] 1 *n.* The central or inner part; middle. 2 *prep.* Amid. —**in the midst of** 1 Surrounded by or occupied with. 2 During.

mid·stream [mid′strēm′] *n.* 1 The middle of a stream. 2 The middle of a course of time or action: The mayor changed his policies in *midstream.*

mid·sum·mer [mid′sum′ər] *n.* 1 The middle of summer. 2 The summer solstice, around June 21.

mid·term [mid′tûrm′] 1 *n.* The middle of a term, as a school term or term of political office. 2 *n.* An examination given at the middle of a school term. 3 *adj.* Of, having to do with, or occurring at midterm.

mid·town [mid′toun′] 1 *n.* The central part of a town or a city, especially the part midway between the downtown and uptown areas. 2 *adj.* Of or situated in such a part.

mid·way [mid′wā′] 1 *adj., adv.* In, to, or at the middle; halfway. 2 *n. U.S.* The amusement area at a fair or exposition.

mid·week [mid′wēk′] 1 *n.* The middle of a week. 2 *adj.* In the middle of a week. —**mid′week′ly** *adv.*

Mid·west·ern [mid′wes′tərn] *adj.* Middle Western.

Mid·west·ern·er [mid′wes′tə(r)·nər] *n.* A person born or living in the Middle West.

mid·wife [mid′wīf′] *n., pl.* **mid·wives** [mid′wīvz′] A person whose occupation is assisting women in childbirth.

mid·win·ter [mid′win′tər] *n.* 1 The middle of winter. 2 The winter solstice, around Dec. 22.

mid·year [mid′yir′] 1 *n.* The middle of a calendar year or school year. 2 *adj.* Of or occurring in the middle of a calendar or school year. 3 *n.* A school examination given at midyear. —**mid′year′ly** *adv.*

mien [mēn] *n.* A person's air, manner, facial expression, or bearing.

miff [mif] *v.* To offend; annoy.

might[1] [mīt] *n.* Great power; force; strength.

might[2] [mīt] Past tense of MAY.

might·i·ly [mī′tə·lē] *adv.* 1 With might, force, energy, or effort: to strive *mightily.* 2 Greatly; extremely: I was *mightily* relieved.

might·y [mī′tē] *adj.* **might·i·er, might·i·est,** *adv.* 1 *adj.* Extremely strong; powerful. 2 *adj.* Very great, as in size, influence, or force: a *mighty* gale. 3 *adv. informal* Extremely; very: a *mighty* fine person. —**might′i·ness** *n.*

mi·gnon·ette [min′yən·et′] *n.* A plant having small, very fragrant, yellowish green flowers.

mi·graine [mī′grān′] *n.* A very bad kind of headache, usually in one side of the head, and often accompanied by nausea.

mi·grant [mī′grənt] 1 *n.* A person, animal, or bird that migrates. 2 *adj.* Moving regularly from place to place: *migrant* workers.

mi·grate [mī′grāt′] *v.* **mi·grat·ed, mi·grat·ing** 1 To move from one country or region to settle in another. 2 To move from one region or climate to another at the change of season. —**mi·gra′tion** *n.*

mi·gra·to·ry [mī′grə·tôr′ē] *adj.* Migrating or moving regularly from place to place.

mi·ka·do [mi·kä′dō] *n., pl.* **mi·ka·dos** An emperor of Japan.

mike [mīk] *n., v.* **miked, mik·ing** *informal* 1 *n.* A microphone. 2 *v.* To amplify or provide with amplification: to *mike* a show; to *mike* an auditorium.

mil [mil] *n.* A unit of length equal to one thousandth of an inch, used especially to measure the diameter of a wire.

mi·la·dy [mi·lā′dē] *n., pl.* **mi·la·dies** A title of respect for an English woman of high social rank.

milch [milch] *adj.* Giving milk, as a cow.

mild [mīld] *adj.* 1 Kind and gentle: a meek and *mild* person. 2 Gentle or moderate; not rough or severe: a *mild* rebuke; *mild* weather. 3 Not strong, sharp, or bitter, as in taste: *mild* cheese. —**mild′ly** *adv.* —**mild′ness** *n.*

mil·dew [mil′d(y)o͞o′] 1 *n.* A whitish or discolored coating deposited by a fungus on plants, damp cloth or paper, and other surfaces. 2 *n.* The fungus itself. 3 *v.* To coat or become coated with mildew. ◆ Today *mildew* brings to mind an unpleasant, musty odor. But the Old English form of the word referred to the sweet-tasting *honeydew,* whose whitish color served to link it with the whitish coating now called *mildew.*

mile [mīl] *n.* A measure of distance equal to 5,280

feet. A nautical mile, air mile, or geographical mile is about 6,076 feet. ◆ *Mile* goes back to the Latin word for *thousand,* as the mile in ancient Rome was a thousand paces.

mile·age or **mil·age** [mī′lij] *n.* 1 The number of miles traveled or to be traveled: Did you record the *mileage* from Philadelphia to New York? 2 The approximate number of miles a vehicle can travel on a gallon of fuel. 3 *U.S.* An allowance of money given for traveling, usually figured at a fixed amount per mile. 4 *informal* Effective use or wear: getting more *mileage* out of an old suit.

mile·post [mīl′pōst′] *n.* A signpost giving the distance in miles to a stated point.

mile·stone [mīl′stōn′] *n.* 1 A stone, post, or pillar set up to indicate the distance in miles to a stated point. 2 An important event or a turning point, as in a lifetime or career.

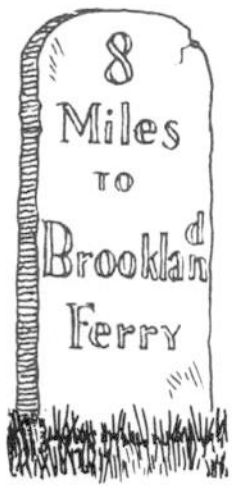

An old milestone

mi·lieu [mil·yo͞o′ *or* mēl·yo͞o′] *n.* An environment; setting; surroundings: the scholarly *milieu* of a professor.

mil·i·tant [mil′ə·tənt] *adj.* Taking or ready to take aggressive action, as on behalf of beliefs or rights; fighting or ready to fight. **—mil′i·tan·cy** *n.* **—mil′·i·tant·ly** *adv.*

mil·i·ta·rism [mil′ə·tə·riz′əm] *n.* 1 A national policy favoring the maintenance of a powerful military force and constant preparation for war. 2 Emphasis on military ideals. **—mil′i·ta·rist** *n.* **—mil′i·ta·ris′tic** *adj.*

mil·i·ta·rize [mil′ə·tə·rīz′] *v.* **mil·i·ta·rized, mil·i·ta·riz·ing** 1 To prepare or equip for war: to *militarize* a nation by strengthening its armies. 2 To make military in nature. 3 To fill with warlike fervor. **—mil·i·ta·ri·za·tion** [mil′ə·tə·rə·zā′shən] *n.*

mil·i·tar·y [mil′ə·ter′ē] 1 *adj.* Of or having to do with the army, the armed forces, or warfare: *military* uniforms; a *military* objective. 2 *adj.* Of, suitable to, or done by soldiers: a *military* bearing; *military* maneuvers. 3 *n.* The armed forces of a nation, or sometimes a group of officers who are leaders in the armed forces: The *military* took over control of the government. **—mil′i·tar′i·ly** *adv.*

military police Members of the armed forces who perform police duties.

mil·i·tate [mil′ə·tāt′] *v.* **mil·i·tat·ed, mil·i·tat·ing** To have influence or effect; work: The evidence *militated* against the defendant.

mi·li·tia [mə·lish′ə] *n.* A body of citizens given military training outside the regular armed forces and called up in emergencies. **—mi·li′tia·man** *n.*

milk [milk] 1 *n.* A white liquid secreted by female mammals for nourishing their young, especially cow's milk drunk or used by human beings. 2 *v.* To draw milk from: to *milk* a cow or goat. 3 *v.* To draw everything useful or valuable from, as if by milking: to *milk* someone of information. 4 *n.* Any milklike liquid or juice, as the liquid contained in a coconut.

milk·maid [milk′mād′] *n.* A woman who milks cows.

milk·man [milk′man′] *n., pl.* **milk·men** [milk′men′] A person who sells or delivers milk.

milk of magnesia A white, powdery magnesium compound suspended in water, used as a laxative or to counteract stomach acidity.

milk shake A drink made of chilled, flavored milk, and often ice cream, mixed thoroughly.

milk·sop [milk′sop′] *n.* A weak, timid person.

milk sugar Another word for LACTOSE.

milk tooth One of the temporary first teeth of a child or other mammal.

milk·weed [milk′wēd′] *n.* Any of various plants having stems filled with a milky juice.

milk·y [mil′kē] *adj.* **milk·i·er, milk·i·est** 1 Like milk, as in whiteness: *milky* glass. 2 Of or containing milk. **—milk′i·ness** *n.*

Milky Way A band of soft light seen across the sky at night, made up of stars and nebulae too far away for the eye to see them separately.

mill[1] [mil] 1 *n.* A machine or device for grinding or crushing, as corn or coffee. 2 *n.* A place, as a building or establishment, in which grain is ground into meal or flour. 3 *n.* Any of various machines that prepare materials or perform a continuous operation: often used in combination, as in saw*mill* or wind*mill.* 4 *n.* A factory equipped with machinery: a steel *mill.* 5 *v.* To grind, make, shape, or prepare in or with a mill. 6 *v.* To raise, indent, or ridge the edge of (as a coin). 7 *v.* To move or circle about without order or method: The audience was *milling* about in the lobby. **—run of the mill** Commonplace; ordinary. **—through the mill** Through a difficult or demanding experience or course of action.

mill[2] [mil] *n.* In the U.S., one tenth of a cent, not a coin but a unit used in figuring.

mill·dam [mil′dam′] *n.* A dam built across a stream to raise the water level so that the overflow produces power to run a mill.

mil·len·ni·um [mi·len′ē·əm] *n., pl.* **mil·len·ni·a** [mi·len′ē·ə] or **mil·len·ni·ums** 1 A period of a thousand years. 2 According to the New Testament, the thousand years during which Christ is to rule the world. 3 Any period in which life seems ideally peaceful and happy. **—mil·len′ni·al** *adj.*

mill·er [mil′ər] *n.* 1 A person who operates or works in a flour mill. 2 A moth whose wings seem to have been dusted with flour.

mil·let [mil′it] *n.* 1 A grass grown in the U.S. for use as hay. 2 The seeds of this grass used as food in Asia and Europe.

milli- A combining form meaning: One thousandth of, as in *millimeter.*

mil·li·bar [mil′ə·bär′] *n.* A unit of pressure used mostly for measurements of the atmosphere, equal to 1000 dynes per square centimeter.

mil·li·gram [mil′ə·gram′] *n.* In the metric system, a unit of mass or weight equal to one thousandth of a gram, or about .0154 grain.

mil·li·li·ter [mil′ə·lē′tər] *n.* In the metric system, a unit of capacity equal to one thousandth of a liter, or about .034 fluid ounce.

mil·li·me·ter [mil′ə·mē′tər] *n.* In the metric system, a unit a length equal to one thousandth of a meter, or about .03937 inch.

a	add	**i**	it	**o͝o**	took	**oi**	oil		
ā	ace	**ī**	ice	**o͞o**	pool	**ou**	pout		
â	care	**o**	odd	**u**	up	**ng**	ring		
ä	palm	**ō**	open	**û**	burn	**th**	thin		
e	end	**ô**	order	**yo͞o**	fuse	**t̶h̶**	this		
ē	equal					**zh**	vision		

ə = { a in *above* e in *sicken* i in *possible* / o in *melon* u in *circus* }

mil·li·ner [mil′ə·nər] *n.* A person who designs, makes, trims, or sells women's hats.
mil·li·ner·y [mil′ə·ner′ē] *n.* 1 Women's hats. 2 The business or occupation of a milliner.
mill·ing [mil′ing] *n.* 1 The act or process of grinding, as the grinding of grain in a mill to produce flour or meal. 2 The process of cutting, shaping, or finishing metal in a mill. 3 The ridges out along the edges of coins.
mil·lion or **1,000,000** [mil′yən] *n., adj.* A thousand thousands.
mil·lion·aire [mil′yən·âr′] *n.* 1 A person whose wealth is valued at a million or more dollars, pounds, or other monetary units. 2 A very rich person.
mil·lionth [mil′yənth] 1 *adj.* Next after the 999,999th. 2 *n.* The millionth one. 3 *adj.* Being one of a million equal parts. 4 *n.* A millionth part.
mil·li·pede or **mil·le·pede** [mil′ə·pēd′] *n.* Any of a group of crawling animals with wormlike bodies composed of many segments, most of which have two pairs of legs.
mill·pond [mil′pond′] *n.* A pond formed by a milldam, used to provide power for operating a mill.
mill·race [mil′rās′] *n.* 1 The current of water that turns or drives a mill wheel. 2 The channel through which such a current runs.
mill·stone [mil′stōn′] *n.* 1 One of a pair of heavy, flat, round stones used for grinding grain. 2 A heavy burden, as one that weighs on a person. ◆ *Mill* and *stone* were combined to form the compound word *millstone.*

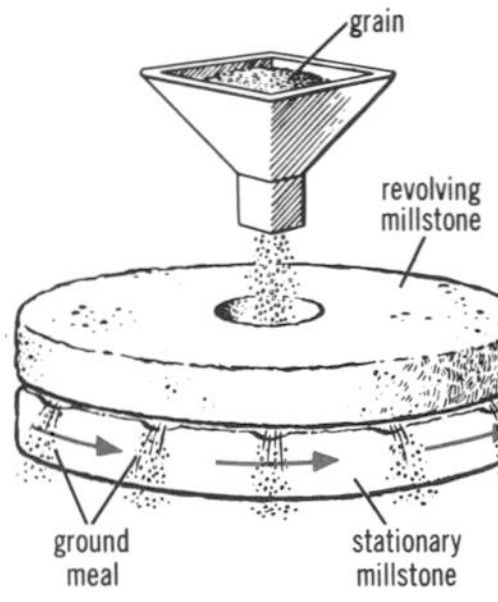

mill·stream [mil′strēm′] *n.* 1 A stream whose water operates a mill. 2 The water of a millrace.
mill wheel A water wheel that furnishes the power to operate a mill.
mi·lord [mi·lôrd′] *n.* A title of respect for an English man of the nobility or of high social rank.
mil·que·toast [milk′tōst′] *n.* A person who is timid or meek. ◆ This word comes from the name of the leading character, Casper *Milquetoast,* of a comic strip, *The Timid Soul,* created by the American cartoonist H.T. Webster.
milt [milt] *n.* 1 The sperm of fish and the milky secretion containing the sperm. 2 The reproductive glands of a male fish when filled with this secretion.
mime [mīm] *n., v.* **mimed, mim·ing** 1 *n.* An actor who does mimicry or pantomime. 2 *v.* To perform as a mime, usually without words.
mim·e·o·graph [mim′ē·ə·graf′] 1 *n.* A machine that prints copies from a usually typewritten stencil. 2 *v.* To print (copies) with this machine.
mim·ic [mim′ik] *v.* **mim·icked, mim·ick·ing,** *n., adj.* 1 *v.* To imitate the speech or actions of, usually in order to make fun of someone. 2 *n.* A person who mimics, especially one skillful at it. 3 *v.* To copy closely; ape. 4 *adj.* Of mimicry; imitative: *mimic* gestures. 5 *adj.* Simulated; mock: a *mimic* battle. 6 *v.* To have or assume the appearance of: Some insects *mimic* twigs.
mim·ic·ry [mim′ik·rē] *n., pl.* **mim·ic·ries** 1 The act, practice, or art of mimicking. 2 The resemblance of a living thing to its surroundings or to another living thing for the purpose of concealment or protection.
mi·mo·sa [mi·mō′sə] *n.* A plant or tree of warm regions having feathery leaves and clusters of small yellow, pink, or white flowers.
min. 1 minimum. 2 mining. 3 minister. 4 minute(s).
min·a·ret [min′ə·ret′] *n.* A tower on a mosque from which a crier summons the people to prayer.

Minarets

mince [mins] *v.* **minced, minc·ing** 1 To cut or chop (food) into small bits. 2 To lessen the force or strength of (as language or ideas): He didn't *mince* words. 3 To say or express with affected elegance or daintiness. 4 To walk with dainty steps.
mince·meat [mins′mēt′] *n.* A mixture of chopped apples, raisins, spices, and other ingredients, used as a pie filling.
minc·ing [min′sing] *adj.* Affectedly dainty or elegant: a *mincing* walk. **—minc′ing·ly** *adv.*
mind [mīnd] 1 *n.* All of the processes by which a person thinks, feels, remembers, or imagines, consciously or unconsciously. 2 *n.* Capability for thought or reasoning; intelligence: a good *mind.* 3 *n.* Way of thinking: a logical *mind.* 4 *n.* A person's opinions, ideas, or plans: to change one's *mind.* 5 *n.* Memory; recall: Within the *mind* of civilization, such technological advances have never happened. 6 *n.* Sanity; reason: to lose one's *mind.* 7 *n.* Attention: Put your *mind* on the test. 8 *v.* To pay attention to: *Mind* what the instructor says. 9 *v.* To be careful about: *Mind* your appearance. 10 *v.* To obey: *Mind* the teacher. 11 *v.* To look after; tend: *Mind* the bonfire. 12 *v.* To object to: to *mind* the heat. **—a piece of one's mind** A severe scolding. **—bear in mind** or **keep in mind** To be sure to remember. **—be of one mind** To agree. **—have a mind to** To be tempted to: I *have a* good *mind to* leave without saying good-bye. **—have in mind** To be thinking about. **—make up one's mind** To decide. **—never mind** Give no further thought to; disregard. **—on one's mind** In one's thoughts or concern. **—out of one's mind** 1 Insane; mad. 2 Frantic. **—to one's mind** In one's opinion: *To my mind*, leaving is a mistake.
mind-blowing [mīnd′blō′ing] *adj. slang* 1 Producing hallucinations; hallucinogenic. 2 Overwhelming to the mind or emotions; astounding.
mind-bog·gling [mīnd′bog′ling] *adj. informal* So amazing, alarming, or perplexing as to overwhelm: The number of problems to be solved was *mind-boggling.*
mind·ed [mīn′did] *adj.* 1 Having a specified kind of mind: used in combination: evil-*minded.* 2 Disposed: I was *minded* to argue.
mind·ful [mīnd′fəl] *adj.* Keeping in mind; aware: Be *mindful* of the needs of other people.
mind·less [mīnd′lis] *adj.* 1 Having little or no intelligence. 2 Heedless; thoughtless.

mind's eye The imagination.

mine[1] [mīn] *pron.* 1 The one or ones that belong to or have to do with me: That ball is *mine.* 2 My: *mine* eyes: seldom used today.

mine[2] [mīn] *n., v.* **mined, min·ing** 1 *n.* A large hole or deep tunnel made for removing minerals from the earth. 2 *v.* To dig from a mine: to *mine* coal. 3 *v.* To dig for minerals; work in a mine. 4 *v.* To dig a mine or mines in: to *mine* the earth. 5 *n.* An abundant source: a *mine* of ideas. 6 *n.* A hidden explosive set to go off when an enemy (as a ship, tank, or soldier) comes near it. 7 *v.* To hide such explosives in or under: to *mine* a field.

mine·field [mīn'fēld'] *n.* An area of land or water in which explosive mines have been placed.

mine·lay·er [mīn'lā'ər] *n.* A ship for laying explosive mines under water.

min·er [mīn'ər] *n.* A person who works digging minerals from the earth.

min·er·al [min'ər·əl] 1 *n.* A natural substance that is not a plant or animal and has a fairly definite physical and chemical makeup, as quartz, coal, or diamond. 2 *adj.* Like, being, or containing a mineral or minerals.

min·er·al·o·gy [min'ə·ral'ə·jē *or* min'ə·rol'ə·jē] *n.* The scientific study of minerals. **—min'er·al'o·gist** *n.*

mineral oil An oil refined from petroleum, often used as a laxative.

mineral water Any water that contains, either artificially or naturally, mineral salts or gases.

Mi·ner·va [mi·nûr'və] *n.* In Roman myths, the goddess of wisdom, invention, and handicraft. Her Greek name was Athena.

min·e·stro·ne [min'ə·strō'nē] *n.* A thick vegetable soup containing macaroni or other pasta.

mine·sweep·er [mīn'swē·pər] *n.* A ship built for clearing areas of water of enemy mines by removing or destroying them or disarming them.

Ming [ming] 1 *n.* A Chinese dynasty extending from 1368 to 1644, characterized by scholarly and artistic achievements. 2 *adj.* Of or having to do with that dynasty.

min·gle [ming'gəl] *v.* **min·gled, min·gling** 1 To bring or come together; mix or join: to *mingle* different ingredients. 2 To associate or mix: to *mingle* with a group or crowd.

min·i [min'ē] *n. informal* 1 Something smaller than other things like it. 2 A miniskirt.

min·i·a·ture [min'(ē·)ə·chər] 1 *n.* Something made or represented on a small scale. 2 *n.* A tiny painting, most often a portrait. 3 *adj.* Very small; tiny.

min·i·a·tur·ize [min'(ē·)ə·chər·iz'] *v.* **min·i·a·tur·ized, min·i·a·tur·iz·ing** To make in an unusually small size, as a radio or machine.

min·i·com·put·er [min'ē·kəm·pyōō'tər] *n.* A relatively inexpensive computer, similar to a microcomputer but with more memory and greater capability.

min·im [min'əm] *n.* 1 A unit of liquid measure equal to one-sixteenth of a fluid dram. 2 Another word for HALF NOTE. 3 Something extremely small.

min·i·mal [min'ə·məl] *adj.* Smallest or least possible in size, amount, or degree. **—min'i·mal·ly** *adv.*

min·i·mal·ism [min'ə·məl·iz'əm] *n.* In the arts, a movement or technique in which only the simplest forms are used. **—min·i·mal·ist** *adj., n.*

min·i·mize [min'ə·mīz'] *v.* **min·i·mized, min·i·miz·ing** 1 To reduce to the smallest possible amount or degree: to *minimize* a danger. 2 To make as little of as possible: to *minimize* the importance of something.

min·i·mum [min'ə·məm] *n., pl.* **min·i·mums** or **min·i·ma** [min'ə·mə] 1 The least amount possible or allowed. 2 The lowest point or smallest amount reached. 3 *adj. use*: a *minimum* wage.

minimum wage The lowest wage that may be paid, according to law or contract.

min·ing [mī'ning] *n.* 1 The extracting, as of coal or ore, from a mine or mines. 2 The laying of an explosive mine or mines.

min·ion [min'yən] *n.* A servant or follower, especially one who is slavish.

min·i·se·ries [min'ē·sir'ēz] *n., pl.* **min·i·se·ries** A TV drama presented in a number of episodes, usually broadcast on consecutive nights.

min·i·skirt [min'ē·skûrt'] *n.* A skirt that ends several inches above the knee.

min·is·ter [min'is·tər] 1 *n.* A clergyman, especially a Protestant clergyman who is pastor of a church. 2 *v.* To give help or attention: to *minister* to a sick person. 3 *n.* The head of a department of a government: the *Minister* of Finance. 4 *n.* A diplomat who is a government representative in a foreign country. **—min·is·te·ri·al** [min'is·tir'ē·əl] *adj.*

min·is·trant [min'is·trənt] 1 *adj.* Ministering. 2 *n.* A person who ministers.

min·is·tra·tion [min'is·trā'shən] *n.* (*usually pl.*) Help or aid given to others.

min·is·try [min'is·trē] *n., pl.* **min·is·tries** 1 The profession, duties, or service of a clergyman. 2 The clergy. 3 A body of government ministers. 4 A department of government headed by a minister. 5 The act of ministering.

mink [mingk] *n.* 1 An animal like, but slightly larger than, a weasel, found in North America. 2 The valuable brown fur of this animal.

Mink

Minn. Minnesota.

min·now [min'ō] *n.* 1 A small, freshwater fish related to the carp, common in North America and much used for bait. 2 Any small fish.

Mi·no·an [mi·nō'ən] *adj.* Of or having to do with the civilization and culture of Crete from about 3000 to 1100 B.C.

mi·nor [mī'nər] 1 *adj.* Smaller; lesser: Compared to Jupiter, Earth is a *minor* planet. 2 *adj.* Not important: a *minor* problem. 3 *n.* A person below the legal age for adult rights and responsibilities. 4 *n.* A subject or field of study second in importance to a major. 5 *v.* To spend time and study with a minor: to *minor* in physics. 6 *adj.* Indicating or based on a musical scale that has a

a	add	**i**	it	**o͝o**	took	**oi**	oil
ā	ace	**ī**	ice	**o͞o**	pool	**ou**	pout
â	care	**o**	odd	**u**	up	**ng**	ring
ä	palm	**ō**	open	**û**	burn	**th**	thin
e	end	**ô**	order	**yo͞o**	fuse	**th̶**	this
ē	equal					**zh**	vision

ə = a in *above*, e in *sicken*, i in *possible*, o in *melon*, u in *circus*

semitone between its second and third tones and whole tones between the first and second, third and fourth, and fourth and fifth, the remaining tones varying with the direction of the melody. **7** *adj.* Indicating a chord that could be formed from the first, third, and fifth tones of a minor scale.

mi·nor·i·ty [mə·nôr′ə·tē] *n., pl.* **mi·nor·i·ties** **1** The smaller in number of two parts or parties. **2** A group of people different in some way from the larger group of which it is a part. **3** The condition or time of being a minor.

minor league A professional sports league other than a major league.

mi·nor-league [mī′nər·lēg′] *adj.* Of, having to do with, or belonging to a minor league.

Mi·nos [mī′nəs] *n.* In Greek myths, a king of Crete.

Min·o·taur [min′ə·tôr′] *n.* In Greek myths, a monster with a man's body and a bull's head. It was kept in a labyrinth at Crete where it ate human captives until slain by Theseus.

min·strel [min′strəl] *n.* **1** In the Middle Ages, a wandering musician, poet, and entertainer. **2** A performer in a minstrel show.

minstrel show A stage show including songs, jokes, and dances, put on by actors disguised as Blacks, popular in the 19th century.

min·strel·sy [min′strəl·sē] *n., pl.* **min·strel·sies** **1** The art or occupation of a minstrel. **2** A collection of ballads or lyrics. **2** A troupe of minstrels.

mint[1] [mint] *n.* **1** Any of several sweet-smelling plants whose leaves are used for flavoring, especially peppermint and spearmint. **2** A candy flavored with mint. **—mint′y** *adj.*

mint[2] [mint] **1** *n.* A place where coins are lawfully made. **2** *v.* To make (coins). **3** *n.* A large amount. **4** *adj.* In original condition; brand-new.

mint·age [min′tij] *n.* **1** The act or process of making coins. **2** The money produced by a mint. **3** The cost of making coins. **4** An impression made on a coin.

min·u·end [min′yōō·end′] *n.* A number from which another number is to be subtracted. In 10 − 4 = 6, 10 is the *minuend.*

min·u·et [min′yōō·et′] *n.* **1** A stately dance popular in the 18th century. **2** A piece of music for, or in the rhythm of this dance.

mi·nus [mī′nəs] **1** *prep.* Made less by; less: ten *minus* five. **2** *n.* A minus sign. **3** *adj.* Less than zero; negative: a *minus* score. **4** *prep. informal* Lacking; without: *minus* two teeth.

min·us·cule [min′əs·kyōōl′ *or* mi·nus′kyōōl′] **1** *n.* A small script developed from uncial and used in medieval manuscript. **2** *n.* A letter written in this script. **3** *n.* A lowercase letter. **4** *adj.* Very small; tiny.

minus sign A sign (−) indicating subtraction or a negative quantity: 6 − 2 = 4.

min·ute[1] [min′it] *n.* **1** The 60th part of an hour; 60 seconds. **2** A very brief time; moment. **3** A specific instant of time: Do it this *minute*! **4** The 60th part of a degree of an arc or angle. **5** (*pl.*) An official record of the events and discussions of a particular meeting.

mi·nute[2] [mī·n(y)ōōt′] *adj.* **1** Tiny. **2** Very careful and precise in small details: a *minute* examination. **—mi·nute′ly** *adv.* **—mi·nute′ness** *n.*

min·ute·man [min′it·man′] *n., pl.* **min·ute·men** [min′it·men′] During the Revolutionary War, one of the armed citizens who pledged to be ready to fight the British at a minute's notice.

mi·nu·ti·ae [mi·n(y)ōō′shē·ē] *n.pl.* Very small or trivial details.

minx [mingks] *n.* A bold or flirtatious person.

Mi·o·cene [mī′ə·sēn′] **1** *n.* The fourth geological epoch of the Tertiary period of the Cenozoic era. During the Miocene whales, dogs, and grazing animals appeared. **2** *adj.* Of the Miocene.

mir·a·cle [mir′ə·kəl] *n.* **1** A happy or wondrous event that cannot be explained by any known natural or scientific law. **2** Any wonderful thing or person: a *miracle* of foresight.

miracle play In the Middle Ages, a religious drama based on episodes from the life of a saint or martyr who performed a miracle or miracles.

mi·rac·u·lous [mi·rak′yə·ləs] *adj.* **1** Seeming to be contrary to natural law. **2** Amazing or wondrous. **—mi·rac′u·lous·ly** *adv.*

mi·rage [mi·räzh′] *n.* An optical illusion, as of a lake and palm trees in a desert or an upside-down ship at sea, appearing quite close, but actually being images of distant objects reflected by the atmosphere.

mire [mīr] *n., v.* **mired, mir·ing** **1** *n.* Swampy ground or deep mud. **2** *v.* To sink or stick in mire. **3** *v.* To soil or smear with mud.

mir·ror [mir′ər] **1** *n.* A smooth surface that reflects light, especially a surface of glass backed with a coating of metal. **2** *v.* To reflect or show an image of: The pond *mirrored* the trees on the bank. **3** *n.* Something that reflects or pictures truly: The book is a *mirror* of modern times.

mirth [mûrth] *n.* Spirited fun and gaiety.

mirth·ful [mûrth′fəl] *adj.* Full of mirth; laughing; merry. **—mirth′ful·ly** *adv.*

mirth·less [mûrth′lis] *adj.* Joyless; sad. **—mirth′·less·ly** *adv.*

MIRV [mûrv] *n.* A guided missile having several warheads, each capable of being aimed at different targets. ◆ MIRV is an acronym formed from *M*ultiple *I*ndependently targeted *R*eentry *V*ehicle.

mis- A prefix meaning: **1** Bad or wrong, as in *misbehavior.* **2** Badly or wrongly, as in *miscount.*

mis·ad·ven·ture [mis′əd·ven′chər] *n.* An unlucky happening or accident; bit of bad luck.

mis·an·thrope [mis′ən·thrōp′] *n.* A person who hates or distrusts other people.

mis·an·thro·py [mis·an′thrə·pē] *n.* The hatred or distrust of other people. **—mis·an·throp·ic** [mis′ən·throp′ik] *adj.*

mis·ap·ply [mis′ə·plī′] *v.* **mis·ap·plied, mis·ap·ply·ing** To use or apply wrongly. **—mis·ap·pli·ca·tion** [mis′·ap·lə·kā′shən] *n.*

mis·ap·pre·hend [mis′ap·ri·hend′] *v.* To misunderstand. **—mis′ap·pre·hen′sion** *n.*

mis·ap·pro·pri·ate [mis·ə·prō′prē·āt′] *v.* **mis·ap·pro·pri·at·ed, mis·ap·pro·pri·at·ing** To use or take improperly or dishonestly: The politician was accused of *misappropriating* public funds. **—mis′ap·pro′pri·a′tion** *n.*

mis·be·got·ten [mis′bi·got′(ə)n] *adj.* **1** Unlawfully conceived; illegitimate. **2** Wretched; contemptible.

mis·be·have [mis′bi·hāv′] *v.* **mis·be·haved, mis·be·hav·ing** To behave badly.

mis·be·hav·ior [mis′bi·hāv′yər] *n.* Bad or improper conduct.

mis·be·lief [mis′bi·lēf′] *n.* A belief that is false or in error.

misc. miscellaneous.

mis·cal·cu·late [mis·kal′kyə·lāt′] *v.* **mis·cal·cu·lat·**

ed, mis·cal·cu·lat·ing To calculate or plan incorrectly. **—mis′cal·cu·la′tion** *n.*
mis·call [mis·kôl′] *v.* To call by a wrong name.
mis·car·riage [mis·kar′ij] *n.* 1 The birth of a baby before it is well enough developed to live. 2 Failure to reach a proper conclusion or destination: a *miscarriage* of justice.
mis·car·ry [mis·kar′ē] *v.* **mis·car·ried, mis·car·ry·ing** 1 To reach a wrong conclusion or destination: The plan *miscarried*; The freight has *miscarried.* 2 To have a miscarriage.
mis·cast [mis·kast′] *v.* **mis·cast, mis·cast·ing** To cast badly: to *miscast* a performer; to *miscast* a play.
mis·cel·la·ne·ous [mis′ə·lā′nē·əs] *adj.* 1 Composed of many different things or elements: a *miscellaneous* mixture. 2 Various: *miscellaneous* details. **—mis′cel·la′ne·ous·ly** *adv.*
mis·cel·la·ny [mis′ə·lā′nē] *n., pl.* **mis·cel·la·nies** A miscellaneous collection, especially of written things in a single book.
mis·chance [mis·chans′] *n.* Bad luck or a mishap.
mis·chief [mis′chif] *n.* 1 Thoughtless conduct that may cause harm: Don't get into *mischief* with matches. 2 Harm, trouble, or injury: High winds can cause great *mischief.* 3 Teasing or pranks. 4 A person or animal that teases or does harm in play.
mis·chie·vous [mis′chi·vəs] *adj.* 1 Inclined to or full of mischief: a *mischievous* child. 2 Slightly troubling or annoying: a *mischievous* act. 3 Causing or tending to cause harm or injury: a *mischievous* rumor. **—mis′chie·vous·ly** *adv.* **—mis′·chie·vous·ness** *n.*
mis·con·ceive [mis′kən·sēv′] *v.* **mis·con·ceived, mis·con·ceiv·ing** To understand wrongly; misunderstand.
mis·con·cep·tion [mis′kən·sep′shən] *n.* Something false or mistaken, as a notion, idea, or concept.
mis·con·duct [*n.* mis·kon′dukt, *v.* mis′kən·dukt′] 1 *n.* Improper or immoral behavior. 2 *v.* To behave (oneself) improperly. 3 *n.* Mismanagement. 4 *v.* To manage badly or wrongly.
mis·con·struc·tion [mis′kən·struk′shən] *n.* 1 The act of misconstruing. 2 A wrong interpretation or understanding of something.
mis·con·strue [mis′kən·stro͞o′] *v.* **mis·con·strued, mis·con·stru·ing** To interpret wrongly; misunderstand: to *misconstrue* a signal.
mis·count [mis·kount′] 1 *v.* To count incorrectly. 2 *n.* An incorrect count.
mis·cre·ant [mis′krē·ənt] 1 *n.* An evildoer; villain. 2 *adj.* Doing evil; wicked.
mis·deal [mis·dēl′] *v.* **mis·dealt, mis·deal·ing,** *n.* 1 *v.* To deal (cards) incorrectly. 2 *n.* An incorrect deal of cards.
mis·deed [mis·dēd′] *n.* A wrong or evil act.
mis·de·mean·or [mis′di·mē′nər] *n.* Any legal offense less serious than a felony, as disorderly conduct or littering a public place.
mis·di·rect [mis′di·rekt′] *v.* To direct or guide wrongly: to *misdirect* a person.
mis·do·ing [mis·do͞o′ing] *n.* A misdeed.
mi·ser [mī′zər] *n.* A greedy, stingy person who hoards money simply because of a love of money.
mis·er·a·ble [miz′ər·ə·bəl] *adj.* 1 In misery; very unhappy or wretched. 2 Causing misery or great discomfort: a *miserable* toothache. 3 Very poor; awful: a *miserable* play. **—mis′er·a·bly** *adv.*
mi·ser·ly [mī′zər·lē] *adj.* Like a miser; greedy and stingy. **—mi′ser·li·ness** *n.*
mis·er·y [miz′ər·ē] *n., pl.* **mis·er·ies** 1 A condition of great wretchedness or suffering. 2 A cause or source of such suffering.
mis·fire [*v.* mis·fīr′, *n.* mis′fīr′] *v.* **mis·fired, mis·fir·ing,** *n.* 1 *v.* To fail to fire, ignite, or explode at the right time, as a gun or an engine. 2 *n.* A misfiring. 3 *v.* To go wrong; fail: The plan *misfired.*
mis·fit [*v.* mis·fit′, *n.* mis′fit′] *v.* **mis·fit·ted, mis·fit·ting** *n.* 1 *v.* To fail to fit or make fit. 2 *n.* Something that fits badly. 3 *n.* A person who gets on badly with other people or in a given situation.
mis·for·tune [mis·fôr′chən] *n.* 1 Ill fortune; bad luck. 2 A mishap or calamity.
mis·giv·ing [mis·giv′ing] *n.* (*often pl.*) A feeling of doubt, distrust, or worry.
mis·gov·ern [mis·guv′ərn] *v.* To govern or administer badly. **—mis·gov′ern·ment** *n.*
mis·guid·ed [mis·gī′did] *adj.* Led by or resulting from bad advice or wrong ideas: a *misguided* person; a *misguided* effort.
mis·han·dle [mis·han′dəl] *v.* **mis·han·dled, mis·han·dling** To handle, treat, or manage badly.
mis·hap [mis′hap] *n.* An unfortunate accident.
mish·mash [mish′mash′] *n.* A mixture of parts that do not make a clear or coherent whole; jumble; hodgepodge.
mis·in·form [mis′in·fôrm′] *v.* To give wrong or false information to. **—mis′in·for·ma′tion** *n.*
mis·in·ter·pret [mis′in·tûr′prit] *v.* To interpret or understand incorrectly. **—mis′in·ter′pre·ta′tion** *n.*
mis·judge [mis·juj′] *v.* **mis·judged, mis·judg·ing** To judge wrongly or unfairly.
mis·lay [mis·lā′] *v.* **mis·laid, mis·lay·ing** 1 To put in a place not remembered later: to *mislay* a book. 2 To place or put down incorrectly: to *mislay* tiles.
mis·lead [mis·lēd′] *v.* **mis·led, mis·lead·ing** 1 To guide or lead in the wrong direction. 2 To lead into wrongdoing: Poor judgment *misled* us into the situation. 3 To lead into an error or wrong judgment: The small print in the ad *misled* me as to the price. ◆ See DECEIVE.
mis·lead·ing [mis·lē′ding] *adj.* Tending to mislead or deceive. **—mis·lead′ing·ly** *adv.*
mis·man·age [mis·man′ij] *v.* **mis·man·aged, mis·man·ag·ing** To manage badly or improperly. **—mis·man′age·ment** *n.*
mis·match [mis·mach′] 1 *v.* To join (two or more persons or things) in an incompatible arrangement; match incorrectly or unsuitably. 2 *n.* The result of such joining; incorrect or unsuitable match.
mis·name [mis·nām′] *v.* **mis·named, mis·nam·ing** To give a wrong name to.
mis·no·mer [mis·nō′mər] *n.* 1 An incorrect name: "Insect" is a *misnomer* for a spider, which is really an arachnid. 2 The act of misnaming.
mi·sog·y·ny [mi·soj′ə·nē] *n.* Hatred of women. **—mi·sog′y·nist** *n.*

a	add	**i**	it	**o͝o**	took	**oi**	oil
ā	ace	**ī**	ice	**o͞o**	pool	**ou**	pout
â	care	**o**	odd	**u**	up	**ng**	ring
ä	palm	**ō**	open	**û**	burn	**th**	thin
e	end	**ô**	order	**yo͞o**	fuse	**t͟h**	this
ē	equal					**zh**	vision

ə = {a in *above* e in *sicken* i in *possible* / o in *melon* u in *circus*}

M

mis·place [mis·plās′] *v.* **mis·placed, mis·plac·ing** 1 To put in a wrong place. 2 To put aside and forget where; mislay. 3 To give or place (as love or faith) wrongly or unwisely.

mis·play [mis·plā′] 1 *v.* In games and sports, to play wrongly or badly. 2 *n.* A bad play or move.

mis·print [*n.* mis′print′, *v.* mis·print′] 1 *n.* An error in printing. 2 *v.* To print incorrectly.

mis·pro·nounce [mis′prə·nouns′] *v.* **mis·pro·nounced, mis·pro·nounc·ing** To pronounce incorrectly.

mis·pro·nun·ci·a·tion [mis′prə·nun′sē·ā′shən] *n.* An incorrect pronunciation.

mis·quote [mis·kwōt′] *v.* **mis·quot·ed, mis·quot·ing** To quote incorrectly. **—mis′quo·ta′tion** *n.*

mis·read [mis·rēd′] *v.* **mis·read, mis·read·ing** To read incorrectly or with a wrong meaning.

mis·rep·re·sent [mis′rep·ri·zent′] *v.* 1 To give a false or misleading idea of: to *misrepresent* facts. 2 To serve as an unsatisfactory or improper representative of: This painting *misrepresents* the quality of the artist's work. **—mis′rep·re·sen·ta′tion** *n.*

mis·rule [mis·rōōl′] *v.* **mis·ruled, mis·rul·ing,** *n.* 1 *v.* To rule unwisely or unjustly. 2 *n.* Bad or unjust rule or government. 3 *n.* Disorder or confusion, as from lawlessness.

miss [mis] 1 *v.* To fail to hit, strike, reach, or land upon (an object): to *miss* a target; to swing and *miss.* 2 *n.* Such a failure. 3 *v.* To fail to meet or catch: to *miss* a train. 4 *v.* To fail to see, hear, notice, or understand: I *missed* that remark; You *missed* the point. 5 *v.* To fail to attend, keep, or perform: to *miss* an appointment. 6 *v.* To overlook or not take advantage of: to *miss* a chance. 7 *v.* To discover the absence of: to *miss* one's watch. 8 *v.* To be sad about the absence of: to *miss* a pet. 9 *v.* To escape; avoid: He barely *missed* falling.

Miss [mis] *n.* 1 A title for an unmarried girl or woman. 2 (*written* **miss**) A young, unmarried girl.

Miss. Mississippi.

mis·sal [mis′əl] *n.* A book containing all the prayers and responses for celebrating Mass.

mis·shap·en [mis·shā′pən] *adj.* Deformed.

mis·sile [mis′əl] *n.* An object, especially a weapon, intended to be thrown or shot, as a bullet, arrow, stone, or guided missile. ◆ *Missile* comes from the Latin word *missus,* meaning *sent.*

mis·sing [mis′ing] *adj.* Absent or lost: I need the *missing* book; *missing* persons.

mis·sion [mish′ən] *n.* 1 The task, business, or duty that a person or group is sent forth to do. 2 A group of people sent out to perform some task. 3 A group of persons sent to represent their government in a foreign country. 4 A group of missionaries, the work they do, or their living and working quarters. 5 One's chief purpose or task in life; calling.

Mission

mis·sion·ar·y [mish′ən·er′ē] 1 *n.* A person sent out to convert people to a certain religion. 2 *adj.* Of or having to do with religious missions or missionaries.

mis·sive [mis′iv] *n.* A written message.

mis·spell [mis·spel′] *v.* **mis·spelled** or **mis·spelt, mis·spell·ing** To spell incorrectly.

mis·spend [mis·spend′] *v.* **mis·spent** [mis·spent′], **mis·spend·ing** To spend or use foolishly or wastefully, as time.

mis·state [mis·stāt′] *v.* **mis·stat·ed, mis·stat·ing** To state wrongly or falsely. **—mis·state′ment** *n.*

mis·step [mis·step′] *n.* 1 A false step; stumble. 2 An error or blunder, as in conduct.

mist [mist] 1 *n.* A cloud of fine droplets of water. 2 *v.* To rain in fine droplets: It's *misting* out. 3 *v.* To make or become misty. 4 *n.* A film or haze that blurs the vision: a *mist* of tears. 5 *n.* Something that clouds, as the mind, memory, or thoughts: the *mists* of time.

mis·take [mis·tāk′] *n., v.* **mis·took, mis·tak·en, mis·tak·ing** 1 *n.* An error or blunder. 2 *v.* To take to be another: to *mistake* a math book for an English book. 3 *v.* To misunderstand; misinterpret: to *mistake* someone's purpose.

mis·tak·en [mis·tā′kən] 1 Past participle of MISTAKE. 2 *adj.* Wrong: a *mistaken* notion. **—mis·tak′·en·ly** *adv.*

Mis·ter [mis′tər] *n.* 1 A title for a man: used before his name or position and abbreviated to **Mr.** in writing. 2 (*written* **mister**) *informal* Sir: used without the name.

mis·tle·toe [mis′əl·tō′] *n.* A small evergreen plant that grows as a parasite on certain trees. It bears white, waxy berries and is often used as a Christmas decoration.

mis·took [mis·tŏŏk′] Past tense of MISTAKE.

mis·treat [mis·trēt′] *v.* To treat badly or improperly. **—mis·treat′ment** *n.*

mis·tress [mis′tris] *n.* 1 A woman in a position of authority or control: Cleopatra was soon *mistress* of Egypt. 2 (*sometimes written* **Mistress**) Anything considered feminine that has rule or power over something else: England was *mistress* of the seas. 3 A woman who lives intimately for a period of time with a man who is not her husband. 4 (*written* **Mistress**) A former title for any woman.

mistress of ceremonies A woman who presides over an event, as a performance or dinner, and introduces performers or speakers.

mis·tri·al [mis·trī′əl] *n.* 1 A trial that is set aside because of a legal defect or error. 2 A trial in which the jury cannot reach a verdict.

mis·trust [mis·trust′] 1 *v.* To regard with suspicion or doubt. 2 *n.* Lack of trust.

mis·trust·ful [mis·trust′fəl] *adj.* Having mistrust; suspicious. **—mis·trust′ful·ly** *adv.*

mist·y [mis′tē] *adj.* **mist·i·er, mist·i·est** 1 Of or like mist: a *misty* haze. 2 Covered with or obscured by mist: a *misty* glass; a *misty* landscape. 3 Not clear; vague: *misty* ideas or concepts. **—mist′i·ness** *n.*

mis·un·der·stand [mis′un·dər·stand′] *v.* **mis·un·der·stood, mis·un·der·stand·ing** To understand incorrectly.

mis·un·der·stand·ing [mis′un·dər·stan′ding] *n.* 1 A failure to understand someone or something correctly. 2 A disagreement or quarrel.

mis·use [*v.* mis·yōōz′, *n.* mis·yōōs′] *v.* **mis·used, mis·us·ing,** *n.* 1 *v.* To use or apply wrongly or improperly. 2 *n.* An incorrect use or usage: a *misuse* of a noun. 3 *v.* To mistreat.

mite[1] [mīt] *n.* 1 Something very small; tiny bit. 2 A very small coin or sum of money.

mite[2] [mīt] *n.* Any of a number of small, spiderlike animals, such as chiggers, mainly living on plants or other animals or in certain foods.

mi·ter [mī′tər] **1** *n.* A tall headdress worn by a pope, bishop, or abbot. **2** *n.* A joint made of two pieces of material whose ends have been beveled at equal angles, as at the corner of a picture frame. **3** *v.* To join with such a joint.

Miter

mit·i·gate [mit′ə·gāt′] *v.* **mit·i·gat·ed, mit·i·gat·ing** To make or become milder or less severe: to *mitigate* pain. **—mit′i·ga′tion** *n.*

mi·to·sis [mī·tō′səs] *n.* The phases in the division of the chromosomes in the nucleus of a cell resulting in the production of two sets of chromosomes identical with the original set. Mitosis precedes the division of the entire cell into two identical cells.

mi·tre [mī′tər] *n., v.* **mi·tred** [mī′tərd], **mi·tring** [mī′·tər·ing] Another spelling of MITER.

mitt [mit] *n.* **1** In baseball, a covering something like a mitten to protect the hand in catching the ball: a catcher's *mitt.* **2** A glove sometimes extending to or above the elbow but without fully covering the fingers. **3** A mitten. **4** *slang* (*usually pl.*) A hand. **5** *slang* A boxing glove.

Mitt

mit·ten [mit′ən] *n.* A glove encasing four fingers together and the thumb separately.

mix [miks] *v.* **mixed** or **mixt, mix·ing,** *n.* **1** *v.* To combine or add so as to blend: to *mix* fuel with air; Oil and water won't *mix; Mix* in two eggs. **2** *v.* To make by mixing: to *mix* a milk shake. **3** *n.* A mixture, especially one containing the ingredients for something except for certain liquids: a biscuit *mix.* **4** *v.* To combine or join: to *mix* age and wisdom. **5** *v.* To get along or associate: to *mix* with strangers. **—mix up 1** To confuse. **2** To involve or implicate.

mixed [mikst] *adj.* **1** Composed of different elements, qualities, or types: a *mixed* basket of fruit. **2** Made up of or involving people of both sexes: a *mixed* chorus. **3** Confused: We got our signals *mixed.*

mixed grill A dish of broiled or grilled meat, usually served with vegetables.

mixed metaphor Two or more metaphors, within a single sentence, that are not suited to one another and thus create a ridiculous or incongruous effect, as "Ronald smelled a rat, and vowed to nip it in the bud."

mixed number A number made up of a whole number and a fraction or a whole number and a decimal, as 3.28 or 5 3/4.

A hand mixer

mix·er [mik′sər] *n.* **1** A person or thing that mixes. **2** *informal* A person who gets along well socially with others.

mix·ture [miks′chər] *n.* **1** The act of mixing. **2** The result of mixing. **3** A combination of things mixed or blended together.

mix-up [miks′up′] *n.* **1** A muddle; confusion. **2** *informal* A fight or melee.

miz·zen [miz′(ə)n] *n.* **1** A principal sail set on the mizzenmast. **2** A mizzenmast.

miz·zen·mast [miz′(ə)n·mast′ *or* miz′(ə)n·məst] *n.* In a ship with three or more masts, the third mast from the bow.

mks, m.k.s., MKS, or **M.K.S.** meter-kilogram-second(s).

mkt. market.

ml or **ml.** milliliter(s).

Mlle. Mademoiselle.

Mlles. Mesdemoiselles.

mm or **mm.** millimeter(s).

MM Messieurs.

Mme. Madame.

Mmes. Mesdames.

Mn The symbol for the element manganese.

MN Postal Service abbreviation of Minnesota.

mne·mon·ic [ni·mon′ik] **1** *adj.* Of or relating to the memory. **2** *adj.* Serving or designed to help the memory. **3** *n.* Something, as a rhyme, formula, phrase, or code, used to help the memory. **—mne·mon′i·cal·ly** *adv.*

mo. month.

Mo The symbol for the element molybdenum.

Mo. Missouri.

MO Postal Service abbreviation of Missouri.

mo·a [mō′ə] *n.* An extinct, tall, ostrichlike bird that lived in New Zealand.

moan [mōn] **1** *n.* A low, sustained, mournful sound, as from grief or pain. **2** *n.* Any similar sound: the *moan* of the wind. **3** *v.* To produce a moan or moans. **4** *v.* To lament; mourn: to *moan* for the dead. **5** *v.* To complain; whine. **6** *v.* To speak or say with moans.

moat [mōt] *n.* A ditch, usually full of water, around a castle, fortress, or other structure, used as a defense against attackers.

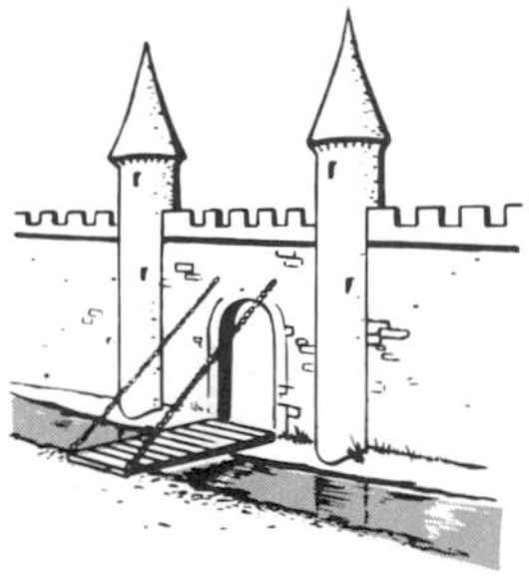
Moat

mob [mob] *n., v.* **mobbed, mob·bing 1** *n.* A large or disorderly crowd. **2** *v.* To crowd around or attack in or as if in a mob: to *mob* a jail; to *mob* a bargain counter. **3** *n.* The ordinary mass of people: used to show contempt. **4** *n. informal* A gang of criminals. ◆ *Mob* comes from the Latin *mob(ile vulgus)* meaning *a movable,* or *excitable, crowd.*

mo·bile [*adj.* mō′bəl *or* mō′bēl, *n.* mō′bēl] **1** *adj.* Easily transported or movable: a *mobile* hospital; *mobile* troops. **2** *adj.* Changing quickly, as in response to feelings or situations: a *mobile* face. **3** *adj.* Characterized by or permitting movement from one class or level in society to another: an

a	add	**i**	it	**o͝o**	took	**oi**	oil
ā	ace	**ī**	ice	**o͞o**	pool	**ou**	pout
â	care	**o**	odd	**u**	up	**ng**	ring
ä	palm	**ō**	open	**û**	burn	**th**	thin
e	end	**ô**	order	**yo͞o**	fuse	**t̶h̶**	this
ē	equal					**zh**	vision

ə = {a in *above* e in *sicken* i in *possible* / o in *melon* u in *circus*}

M

upwardly *mobile* member of the middle class. **4** *n.* A sculpture made of movable parts hung from or balanced on rods or wires, so as to move with slight air currents. **—mo·bil·i·ty** [mō·bil′ə·tē] *n.*

mo·bi·lize [mō′bə·līz′] *v.* **mo·bi·lized, mo·bi·liz·ing** **1** To prepare for war: The nation *mobilized.* **2** To assemble and organize for use: to *mobilize* resources. **—mo′bi·li·za′tion** *n.*

Mö·bi·us strip [mû′bē·əs] A one-sided surface formed from a rectangular strip by holding one end of the strip in place, turning the opposite end 180°, and attaching that end to the first.

mob·ster [mob′stər] *n. slang* A member of a criminal gang; gangster.

moc·ca·sin [mok′ə·sin] *n.* **1** A shoe or slipper with soft soles and no heels, formerly worn by North American Indians. **2** A shoe or slipper resembling it. **3** The water moccasin, a snake. ◆ *Moccasin* comes from an Algonquian Indian word.

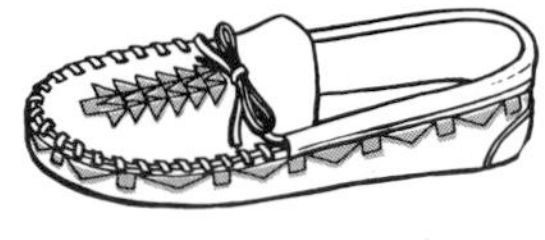
Moccasin

moccasin flower Another name for LADY'S SLIPPER.

mo·cha [mō′kə] *n.* A choice coffee originally from Arabia.

mock [mok] **1** *v.* To ridicule or deride. **2** *v.* To mimic or imitate. **3** *v.* To express or treat with contempt. **4** *n.* An act of mocking. **5** *n.* A person or thing that is mocked. **6** *adj.* Not real but made to look so: *mock* anger. **—mock′er** *n.*

mock·er·y [mok′ər·ē] *n., pl.* **mock·er·ies** **1** A mocking; ridicule. **2** A mocking speech or act. **3** A person or thing that is mocked or deserves to be mocked. **4** A ridiculously poor imitation: a *mockery* of a trial. **5** Something very poor and disappointing.

mock·ing·bird [mok′ing·bûrd′] *n.* A bird of the southern U.S. that mimics other bird calls.

mock-up [mok′up′] *n.* A full-scale model, as of a spacecraft or building interior, used for study, demonstration, or testing.

mod [mod] *adj. informal* Modern; up-to-date, especially in a flamboyant or unconventional way.

mo·dal [mōd′əl] *adj.* Of or relating to a mode or modes.

modal auxiliary Any one of a group of English verbs used with other verbs to indicate tense or mood. Examples are *can, may, shall, will, should, would, must,* and *ought.*

mode [mōd] *n.* **1** A way; method: a *mode* of living. **2** Prevailing or current style or fashion, as in dress. **3** A mood, as of a verb.

mod·el [mod′əl] *n., v.* **mod·eled** or **mod·elled, mod·el·ing** or **mod·el·ling** **1** *n.* A miniature copy or replica of an object: a *model* of a building. **2** *adj. use*: a *model* automobile. **3** *n.* A representation of something that is to be copied later in a more lasting material: a wax *model* of a statue. **4** *v.* To make a model of (as an object or figure): to *model* a head. **5** *v.* To make (a material) into a model: He *modeled* the clay into a small statue. **6** *n.* A person or thing that is worth imitating: a *model* of good taste. **7** *adj. use*: a *model* student. **8** *v.* To plan or form after a model: a table *modeled* on an antique; *Model* yourself on someone who has made a name in your field. **9** *n.* A particular style, plan, or design: a new *model* of boat. **10** *n.* Someone who poses for a painter, sculptor, or photographer. **11** *v.* To pose for an artist or photographer. **12** *n.* A person hired to wear and display clothing. **13** *v.* To wear and display (clothing). **—mod′el·er** or **mod′el·ler** *n.*

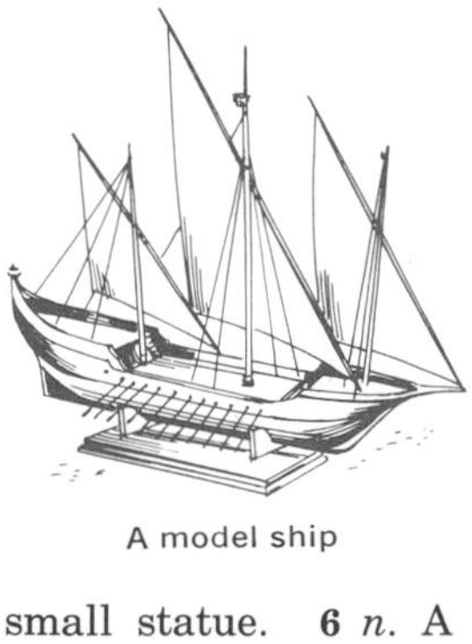
A model ship

mo·dem [mō′dəm] *n.* An electronic device that makes it possible for computers to send or receive data over telephone lines or other lines of communication.

mod·er·ate [*adj., n.* mod′ər·it, *v.* mod′ə·rāt′] *adj., n., v.* **mod·er·at·ed, mod·er·at·ing** **1** *adj.* Not extreme or excessive: There will be a *moderate* delay; These are *moderate* prices. **2** *adj.* Not extreme or radical in beliefs or actions: to be a *moderate* spender; They have *moderate* political views. **3** *n.* A person who has moderate ideas or opinions, especially in politics or religion. **4** *adj.* Not exceptional; average: a *moderate* intelligence. **5** *v.* To make or become moderate or more moderate: You must *moderate* some of your more extreme opinions. **6** *v.* To be a moderator. **7** *v.* To preside over as a moderator: to *moderate* a debate. **—mod′·er·ate·ly** *adv.*

mod·er·a·tion [mod′ə·rā′shən] *n.* **1** The condition or quality of being moderate. **2** The act of moderating.

mod·e·ra·to [mod′ə·rä′tō] *adj., adv., n., pl.* **mod·e·ra·tos** **1** *adj., adv.* In music, in or at a moderate tempo. **2** *n.* A musical composition or a section of one in a moderate tempo.

mod·er·a·tor [mod′ə·rā′tər] *n.* **1** A person who moderates, as the presiding officer of a meeting or debate. **2** A substance, such as graphite, used in a nuclear reactor to slow the speed of neutrons.

mod·ern [mod′ərn] **1** *adj.* Of or having to do with present or recent time. **2** *adj.* Not old-fashioned; up-to-date. **3** *n.* A modern person.

Modern English The English language since about 1500.

mod·ern·ism [mod′ər·niz′əm] *n.* **1** Something, as an idea, practice, convention, or usage, that is peculiar to modern times. **2** The theories and practices of modern art. **—mod′ern·ist** *adj., n.*

mod·ern·is·tic [mod′ər·nis′tik] *adj.* **1** Of or derived from modernism. **2** Modern.

mod·ern·ize [mod′ərn·īz′] *v.* **mod·ern·ized, mod·ern·iz·ing** To make or become modern or more modern. **—mod′ern·i·za′tion** *n.*

mod·est [mod′ist] *adj.* **1** Not boastful; humble: a *modest* hero. **2** Quietly decent and proper, as in behavior, manner, or speech: a *modest* person. **3** Not elaborate, showy, or gaudy: a *modest* meal. **4** Not excessive or extreme; moderate: a *modest* price. **5** Bashful; shy. **—mod′est·ly** *adv.*

mod·es·ty [mod′is·tē] *n.* The condition or quality of being modest.

mod·i·cum [mod′ə·kəm] *n.* A moderate or small amount: a *modicum* of bother.

mod·i·fi·ca·tion [mod′ə·fə·kā′shən] *n.* **1** The act of modifying. **2** The condition of being modified. **3** A qualification or mild change: The plan needs *modification.* **4** Something made by modifying: a *modification* of an old model.

mod·i·fi·er [mod′ə·fī′ər] *n.* **1** A person or thing that modifies. 2 A word or group of words that describes or limits the meaning of another word or group of words, as an adjective or adverb.

mod·i·fy [mod′ə·fī] *v.* **mod·i·fied, mod·i·fy·ing** 1 To change moderately. 2 To make less extreme or severe; moderate: to *modify* one's views. 3 To describe or limit the meaning of: Adjectives *modify* nouns.

mod·ish [mō′dish] *adj.* Fashionable; stylish. —**mod′·ish·ly** *adv.* —**mod′ish·ness** *n.*

mod·u·late [moj′ŏŏ·lāt′] *v.* **mod·u·lat·ed, mod·u·lat·ing** 1 To vary the tone, inflection, pitch, or volume of: to *modulate* one's voice. 2 To regulate or adjust; modify: to *modulate* air pressure. 3 To change some characteristic of (a radio wave) in a way that corresponds with a sound or other signal transmitted. 4 In music, to go from one key to another.

mod·u·la·tion [moj′ŏŏ·lā′shən] *n.* 1 The act of modulating. 2 The condition of being modulated. 3 In music, a change from one key to another.

mod·ule [moj′ōōl *or* mod′yōōl] *n.* 1 A standard or unit of measurement. 2 One of a group of standardized units that are combined in construction. 3 Any of a group of assemblies of electronic components, individually packaged, that are combined in a complex system. 4 A self-contained unit of a spacecraft designed for a specific function or task. —**mod′u·lar** *adj.*

Mo·gul [mō′gul] *n.* 1 A Mongol, especially one of the Mongolian conquerors of India or a descendant of one of them. 2 (*written* **mogul**) A very important person.

mo·hair [mō′hâr′] *n.* 1 The hair of the Angora goat. 2 A cloth made of mohair, usually in combination with other materials, as with cotton or wool.

Mo·ham·me·dan [mō·ham′ə·dən] *n., adj.* Another spelling of MUHAMMADAN.

Mo·ham·me·dan·ism [mō·ham′ə·dən·iz′əm] *n.* Another spelling of MUHAMMADANISM.

Mo·hawk [mō′hôk′] *n., pl.* **Mo·hawk** or **Mo·hawks** 1 A tribe of North American Indians once living in central New York State. 2 A member of this tribe. 3 The language of this tribe.

Mo·he·gan [mō·hē′gən] *n., pl.* **Mo·he·gan** or **Mo·he·gans** 1 A tribe of North American Indians once living in Connecticut. 2 A member of this tribe. 3 The language of this tribe.

Mo·hi·can [mō·hē′kən] *n., pl.* **Mo·hi·can** or **Mo·hi·cans** Another spelling of MAHICAN.

Mohs scale [mōz] A scale of hardness for minerals, based on their ability to scratch or be scratched by any of a set of standard minerals.

moi·dore [moi′dôr′] *n.* An old Portuguese coin.

moi·e·ty [moi′ə·tē] *n., pl.* **moi·e·ties** 1 A half. 2 Any portion, part, or share.

moist [moist] *adj.* Slightly wet or damp. —**moist′·ness** *n.*

mois·ten [mois′ən] *v.* To make or become moist.

mois·ture [mois′chər] *n.* Water or other liquid in very small drops causing dampness in the air or through or on the surface of something.

mois·tur·ize [mois′chə·rīz′] *v.* **mois·tur·ized, mois·tur·iz·ing** To supply or restore moisture to.

mo·lar [mō′lər] *n.* A tooth with a broad crown, adapted for grinding. An adult person has three on each side at the back of each jaw.

mo·las·ses [mə·las′iz] *n.* A sweet, dark-colored syrup obtained in making sugar, especially from sugar cane.

mold[1] [mōld] 1 *n.* A hollow form that gives a particular shape to something in a soft or fluid condition. 2 *v.* To shape or form in a mold. 3 *n.* Something shaped or made in a mold: a *mold* of wax. 4 *n.* The shape or pattern formed by a mold. 5 *v.* To shape, form, or direct: Newspapers often *mold* public opinion. 6 *n.* A special or distinctive nature, character, or type: an aristocratic *mold.*

Molds

mold[2] [mōld] 1 *n.* A furry fungous growth found on a surface of decaying food or other decaying organic matter. 2 *v.* To become moldy.

mold[3] [mōld] *n.* Soft earth that is good for plants because it is rich in decaying organic matter.

mold·er [mōl′dər] *v.* To decay gradually and turn to dust; crumble.

mold·ing [mōl′ding] *n.* 1 The act of molding or shaping. 2 Something that is molded. 3 A decorative strip of wood or other material fastened around something, as a wall, door frame, or window.

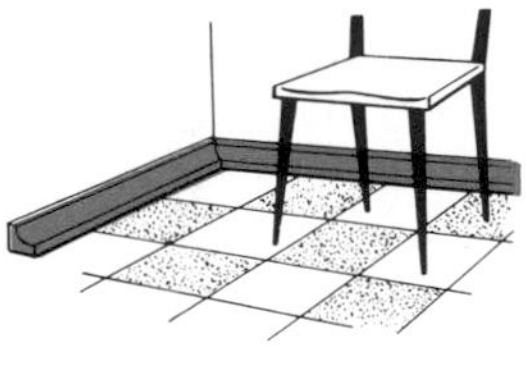

Baseboard molding

mold·y [mōl′dē] *adj.* **mold·i·er, mold·i·est** 1 Of, covered with, or containing mold: *moldy* cake. 2 Musty; stale: a *moldy* room. —**mold′i·ness** *n.*

mole[1] [mōl] *n.* A small, often dark and hairy spot on the skin.

mole[2] [mōl] *n.* 1 A small mammal that lives in underground burrows. It has tiny, weak eyes, soft fur, and forefeet adapted for digging. 2 A spy who works secretly within the government of a rival country.

Mole

mole[3] [mōl] *n.* A massive, usually stone barricade in the sea, serving as a breakwater or pier.

mole[4] [mōl] *n.* Another name for GRAM MOLECULE.

mo·lec·u·lar [mə·lek′yə·lər] *adj.* Of, produced by, or having to do with molecules.

molecular weight The sum of the atomic weights of the atoms forming a molecule.

mol·e·cule [mol′ə·kyōōl′] *n.* The smallest part of an element or compound that can exist separately without loss of its chemical properties: A *molecule* of water is made up of two atoms of hydrogen and one of oxygen. 2 A very small particle.

a	add	**i**	it	**ŏŏ**	took	**oi**	oil
ā	ace	**ī**	ice	**ōō**	pool	**ou**	pout
â	care	**o**	odd	**u**	up	**ng**	ring
ä	palm	**ō**	open	**û**	burn	**th**	thin
e	end	**ô**	order	**yōō**	fuse	**th̶**	this
ē	equal					**zh**	vision

ə = a in *above*, e in *sicken*, i in *possible*, o in *melon*, u in *circus*

M

mole·hill [mōl′hil′] *n.* 1 A small mound of earth raised by a burrowing mole. 2 Something trivial, especially in the expression **make a mountain out of a molehill,** to make a fuss over nothing.
mo·lest [mə·lest′] *v.* To interfere with in a bad or wrong way; harm or bother. **—mo′les·ta′tion** *n.*
mol·lie or **mol·ly** [mol′ē] *n., pl.* **mol·lies** Any of a group of brightly colored tropical and subtropical fish.
mol·li·fy [mol′ə·fī′] *v.* **mol·li·fied, mol·li·fy·ing** To soothe or soften: to *mollify* someone's anger.
mol·lusk [mol′əsk] *n.* Any of a large group of animals having soft bodies that are not divided into segments, usually protected by a hard shell, as snails, oysters, and clams.
mol·ly·cod·dle [mol′ē·kod′(ə)l] *n., v.* **mol·ly·cod·dled, mol·ly·cod·dling** 1 *n.* A pampered person; sissy. 2 *v.* To pamper; coddle. ◆ *Mollycoddle* comes from *Molly,* a girl's name, plus *coddle.*
Mo·loch [mol′ək *or* mō′lok′] *n.* In the Old Testament, a god to whom children were sacrificed.
molt [mōlt] *v.* To shed (as feathers, horns, or skin) in preparation for a new growth, as do certain animals such as snakes or birds.
mol·ten [mōl′tən] *adj.* 1 Made liquid, as by great heat: *molten* metal. 2 Made by melting and casting in a mold: a *molten* statue.
mo·lyb·de·num [mə·lib′də·nəm] *n.* A silvery white, very hard metallic element, important as an alloying element in steel and in small amounts playing an essential part in plants and animals.
mom [mom] *n. informal* Mother.
mo·ment [mō′mənt] *n.* 1 A very short period of time; instant. 2 A particular point in time, often the present time: The phone is busy at the *moment.* 3 Importance: matters of great *moment.*
mo·men·tar·i·ly [mō′mən·ter′ə·lē] *adj.* 1 For a moment: We saw the sun *momentarily.* 2 At any moment: Their call was expected *momentarily.* 3 Moment by moment: Our anticipation grew *momentarily.*
mo·men·tar·y [mō′mən·ter′ē] *adj.* Lasting for a moment.
mo·men·tous [mō·men′təs] *adj.* Very important: a *momentous* event.
mo·men·tum [mō·men′təm] *n.* 1 The amount of force that can be exerted by a moving body, equal to its mass multiplied by its speed. 2 Force, speed, or impetus, usually growing in strength or intensity: The children's excitement gained *momentum* as Christmas approached.
Mon. Monday.
Mon·a·can [mon′ə·kən *or* mə·nä′kən] 1 *adj.* Of or from Monaco. 2 *n.* A person born in or a citizen of Monaco.
Mo·na Li·sa [mō′nə lē′zə] A portrait by Leonardo da Vinci of a Neapolitan woman. The painting is famous for the mysterious expression, often regarded as a smile, on the woman's face.

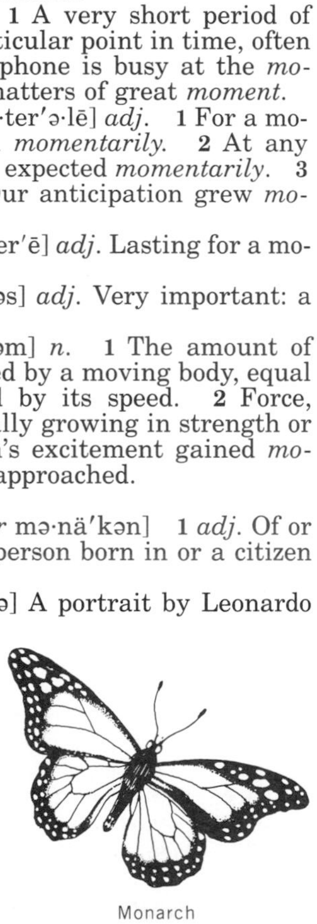
Monarch

mon·arch [mon′ərk] *n.* 1 A ruler, as a king or queen. 2 A large orange and black North American butterfly.
mo·nar·chi·cal [mə·när′ki·kəl] *adj.* 1 Of, having to do with, or like a monarch or monarchy. 2 Governed by a monarch. 3 Favoring monarchy.
mon·ar·chism [mon′ər·kiz′əm] *n.* 1 The principles of monarchy. 2 Belief in or advocacy of monarchy. **—mon′ar·chist** *n.*
mon·ar·chy [mon′ər·kē] *n., pl.* **mon·ar·chies** 1 Government by a monarch. 2 A government or country ruled by a monarch.
mon·as·ter·y [mon′əs·ter′ē] *n., pl.* **mon·as·ter·ies** A place where monks live in seclusion.
mo·nas·tic [mə·nas′tik] *adj.* Of, having to do with, or like monasteries, monks, or the religious life as practiced in a monastery.
mon·au·ral [mon·ôr′əl] *adj.* 1 Of, having to do with, or for the reception of sound by one ear only. 2 Another word for MONOPHONIC (def. 2).
Mon·day [mun′dē *or* mun′dā] *n.* The second day of the week.
Mon·e·gasque [mon′ə·gask′] 1 *adj.* Of or from Monaco. 2 *n.* A person born in or a citizen of Monaco.
mon·e·tar·y [mon′ə·ter′ē] *adj.* Of or in money: The dollar is the *monetary* unit of the U.S.; to receive a *monetary* reward.
mon·ey [mun′ē] *n., pl.* **mon·eys** or **mon·ies** 1 Coins and paper currency issued by a government to be used in paying debts and obligations. 2 Anything used in this way. 3 Wealth; riches: a person of *money.* ◆ See CURRENCY.
mon·eyed [mun′ēd] *adj.* 1 Having much money; wealthy. 2 Made up of, coming from, or representing money or wealth: *moneyed* interests.
money order An order for the payment of a specified sum of money, issued at one bank or post office and payable at another.
Mon·gol [mong′gəl] 1 *n.* A native of Mongolia. 2 *n.* The language of Mongolia. 3 *n.* A Mongoloid person. 4 *adj.* Mongolian.
Mon·go·li·an [mong·gō′lē·ən] 1 *adj.* Of or from Mongolia. 2 *n.* A person born in or a citizen of Mongolia. 3 *n.* The language of Mongolia. 4 *n.* Any person belonging to the Mongoloid division of mankind. 5 *adj.* (written **mongolian**) Of or having mongolism.
mon·gol·ism [mon′gə·liz′əm] *n.* A congenital disorder characterized by mental deficiency and various physical abnormalities including a broad, flattened skull. **—mon′go·loid** *adj.*
Mon·go·loid [mong′gə·loid] *adj.* 1 Of, having to do with, or belonging to a major ethnic division of human beings, characterized by such features as a yellowish skin, eyes that appear slanted, straight hair, and high cheekbones. Chinese, Japanese, and Eskimos are Mongoloid people. 2 (written **mongoloid**) Of or having mongolism.
mon·goose [mong′gōōs′] *n., pl.* **mon·goos·es** A small animal of Asia and Africa. It resembles the ferret and preys on snakes and rats.

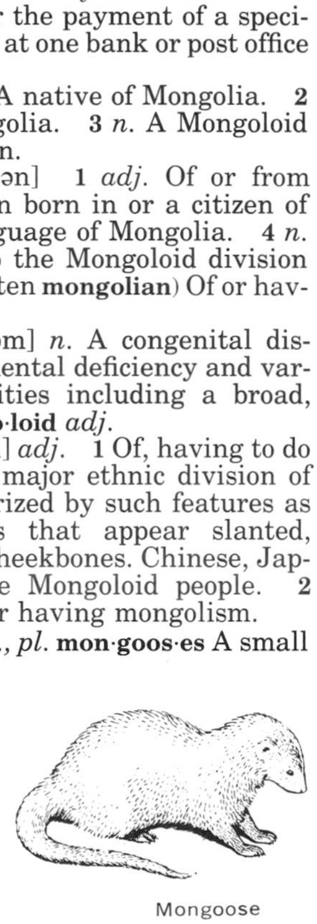
Mongoose

mon·grel [mung′grəl *or* mong′grəl] *n.* A dog or any animal or plant of mixed breed.
mon·ied [mun′ēd] *adj.* Another spelling of MONEYED.
mon·ies [mun′ēz] A plural of MONEY.
mon·i·tor [mon′ə·tər] 1 *n.* A pupil chosen to assist a teacher, as in administrative tasks or maintain-

ing order. **2** *n.* A person or thing that warns or reminds. **3** *n.* A device that allows the operation or activity of a thing or person to be observed constantly. **4** *v.* To observe with or as if with a monitor: to *monitor* a broadcast. **5** *n.* The screen that displays information stored in a computer.

mon·i·to·ry [mon′ə·tôr′ē] *adj.* Giving a warning; admonitory.

monk [mungk] *n.* A man who is a member of a religious order and lives usually in a monastery under a rule and vow of poverty, chastity, and obedience.

mon·key [mung′kē] *n., pl.* **mon·keys,** *v.* **1** *n.* Any of a large group of animals resembling the ape, but smaller and more agile and having long tails by which many of them can hang. **2** *n.* A mischievous child. **3** *v. informal* To play or trifle; meddle: Don't *monkey* with matches.

monkey wrench A wrench having an adjustable jaw for grasping things, as nuts and bolts, of various sizes.

Monkey wrench

monk·ish [mung′kish] *adj.* Of or like a monk or monks.

monks·hood [mungks′ho͝od′] *n.* A poisonous plant having hood-shaped flowers; aconite.

mon·o [mon′ō] *n. informal* Infectious mononucleosis.

mon·o·chro·mat·ic [mon′ə·krō·mat′ik] *adj.* **1** Of or having one color. **2** Consisting of or producing light of only one wavelength or of a very small range of wavelengths.

mon·o·chrome [mon′ə·krōm′] *n.* A painting, drawing, or photograph having shades of one color.

mon·o·cle [mon′ə·kəl] *n.* An eyeglass for one eye.

Monocle

mon·o·cot·y·le·don [mon′ə·kot′ə·lēd′(ə)n] *n.* A plant whose seeds contain but one cotyledon, as grasses and palms.

mo·noc·u·lar [mə·nok′yə·lər] *adj.* **1** Having only one eye. **2** Of, having to do with, or suitable for the use of only one eye.

mo·nog·a·my [mə·nog′ə·mē] *n.* The condition or practice of having only one husband or wife at a time. **—mo·nog′a·mist** *n.* **—mo·nog′a·mous** *adj.*

mon·o·gram [mon′ə·gram′] *n., v.* **mon·o·grammed, mon·o·gram·ming** **1** *n.* A design made from the initials of a name. **2** *v.* To provide with a monogram.

A monogram

mon·o·graph [mon′ə·graf′] *n.* A book, pamphlet, or long article on a single subject.

mon·o·lith [mon′ə·lith′] *n.* A single block of stone, usually very large, or a statue, column, or other sculpted piece made of such a block.

mon·o·lith·ic [mon′ə·lith′ik] *adj.* **1** Of, having to do with, or like a monolith. **2** Having a massive, uniform structure; unvarying.

mo·nol·o·gist [mə·nol′ə·jəst] *n.* An actor who performs monologues.

mon·o·logue [mon′ə·lôg′] *n.* **1** A long speech by one person, especially one that interrupts conversation. **2** A dramatic work for one actor. **3** Something, as a poem or part of a play, performed by one actor.

mon·o·ma·ni·a [mon′ə·mā′nē·ə] *n.* **1** A mental disorder in which a person, otherwise rational, is obsessed with one idea or subject. **2** An extreme and irrational interest in one thing. **—mon·o·ma·ni·ac** [mon′ə·mā′nē·ak′] *n.* **—mon·o·ma·ni·a·cal** [mon′ə·mə·nī′ə·kəl] *adj.*

mo·no·mi·al [mō·nō′mē·əl] **1** *adj.* Being a single algebraic term. **2** *adj.* Consisting of a single word or term. **3** *n.* A monomial expression or name.

mon·o·nu·cle·o·sis [mon′ə·n(y)o͞o′klē·ō′sis] *n.* **1** Another name for INFECTIOUS MONONUCLEOSIS. **2** The presence in the bloodstream of an abnormal number of leukocytes with single nuclei.

mon·o·phon·ic [mon′ə·fon′ik] *adj.* **1** Consisting of a single melodic line with little or no accompaniment. **2** That uses or involves a single channel to record, transmit, or reproduce sound. **—mon′o·pho′ni·cal·ly** *adv.*

mon·o·plane [mon′ə·plān′] *n.* An airplane having a single pair of wings, one wing on each side of the airplane.

mo·nop·o·list [mə·nop′ə·list] *n.* A person who monopolizes or has a monopoly. **—mo·nop′o·lis′tic** *adj.*

mo·nop·o·lize [mə·nop′ə·līz′] *v.* **mo·nop·o·lized, mo·nop·o·liz·ing** **1** To get or have a monopoly of. **2** To possess, use, or control all of: Ballet lessons *monopolize* the dancer's time.

mo·nop·o·ly [mə·nop′ə·lē] *n., pl.* **mo·nop·o·lies** **1** Exclusive control of a product or service in a certain area by a single person or group, with a resulting power over prices and competition. **2** Such control granted and supervised by a government. **3** A company, group, or person that holds a monopoly. **4** A product or service controlled by a monopoly. **5** Exclusive possession or control.

M

mon·o·rail [mon′ō·rāl′] *n.* **1** A railway whose cars run on or are suspended from a single track or rail. **2** This track or rail.

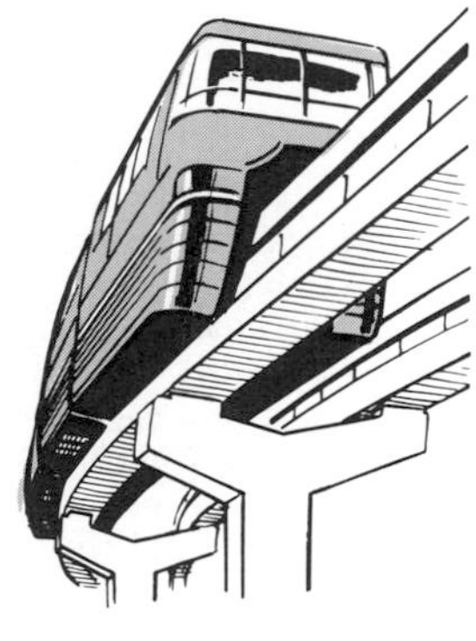
A monorail train

mon·o·so·di·um glu·ta·mate [mon′ə·sō′dē·əm glo͞o′tə·māt′] A white crystalline salt used in cooking.

mon·o·syl·lab·ic [mon′ə·si·lab′ik] *adj.* **1** Having only one syllable. **2** Using or composed of monosyllables: a *monosyllabic* answer.

mon·o·syl·la·ble [mon′ə·sil′ə·bəl] *n.* A word of one syllable.

mon·o·the·ism [mon′ə·thē·iz′əm] *n.* The doctrine or belief that there is but one God.

mon·o·tone [mon′ə·tōn′] *n.* **1** A succession of syl-

a	add	**i**	it	**o͝o**	took	**oi**	oil
ā	ace	**ī**	ice	**o͞o**	pool	**ou**	pout
â	care	**o**	odd	**u**	up	**ng**	ring
ä	palm	**ō**	open	**û**	burn	**th**	thin
e	end	**ô**	order	**yo͞o**	fuse	**th**	this
ē	equal					**zh**	vision

ə = {a in *above* e in *sicken* i in *possible*
o in *melon* u in *circus*

lables or words uttered in a single tone. 2 Boring sameness, as of color.
mo·not·o·nous [mə·not′ə·nəs] *adj.* 1 Not changing in pitch or tone: *monotonous* talk. 2 Boring because of lack of variety or change: a *monotonous* task. **—mo·not′o·nous·ly** *adv.*
mo·not·o·ny [mə·not′ə·nē] *n.* The condition or quality of being monotonous; sameness.
mon·ox·ide [mon·ok′sīd′] *n.* An oxide containing a single atom of oxygen in each molecule.
Monroe Doctrine President Monroe's statement, in his message to Congress in 1823, that any attempt by a European nation to interfere or acquire territory in the Western Hemisphere would be regarded as an unfriendly act by the U.S.
Mon·sei·gneur [mōn·sen·yûr′] *n., pl.* **Mes·sei·gneurs** [mā·sen·yûr′] 1 An honorary French title conferred on certain persons of the nobility or on high-ranking clergymen. 2 (*often written* **monseigneur**) A person who has this title.
mon·sieur [mə·syûr′] *n., pl.* **mes·sieurs** [mes′ərz] The French title of courtesy for a man, equivalent to *Mr.*
Mon·si·gnor [mon·sēn′yər] *n.* 1 In the Roman Catholic Church, a title of honor of certain priests. 2 A priest having this title.
mon·soon [mon·so͞on′] *n.* 1 A seasonal wind of southern Asia and the Indian Ocean, blowing from the northeast in winter and from the southwest in summer. 2 The rainy season in India and adjacent countries, extending from June to September.
mon·ster [mon′stər] *n.* 1 A plant or animal that is abnormal in form or structure, as a calf with two heads. 2 Any of various mythical, often terrifying beasts, as dragons or griffins. 3 A person who is very cruel, evil, or ugly. 4 An extremely large person, animal, or thing.
mon·stros·i·ty [mon·stros′ə·tē] *n., pl.* **mon·stros·i·ties** 1 The condition or quality of being monstrous. 2 A monster.
mon·strous [mon′strəs] *adj.* 1 Differing greatly from the natural or normal, as in form, looks, or character. 2 Horrible; atrocious: *monstrous* deeds. 3 Completely or strikingly wrong; absurd: a *monstrous* error. 4 Huge; enormous.
Mont. Montana.
mon·tage [mon·täzh′] *n.* 1 A single picture made from different pictures or parts of them, combined or superimposed on one another. 2 The art or technique of making such pictures. 3 In motion pictures, a sequence of images or short scenes juxtaposed or superimposed on one another. 4 The technique of film editing that produces such a sequence.
month [munth] *n.* 1 Any of the 12 parts into which a year is divided according to the Gregorian calendar. 2 A period of 30 days or of 4 weeks. 3 The time the moon takes to revolve completely around the earth, about 29 1/2 days.
month·ly [munth′lē] *adv., adj., n., pl.* **month·lies** 1 *adv.* Once a month; every month. 2 *adj.* Of or having to do with a month. 3 *adj.* Happening monthly. 4 *adj.* Lasting for a month. 5 *n.* A magazine that appears monthly.
mon·u·ment [mon′yə·ment] *n.* 1 A thing built in memory of a person or event. 2 A work, as of art, literature, or scholarship, thought to have lasting value: This work in chemistry is a *monument* of science.
mon·u·men·tal [mon′yə·men′təl] *adj.* 1 Of, like, being, or found on a monument: *monumental* script. 2 Impressive or important; great; grand: *monumental* art. 3 Huge; enormous: a *monumental* fraud. **—mon′u·men′tal·ly** *adv.*
moo [mo͞o] *n., pl.* **moos,** *v.* **mooed, moo·ing** 1 *n.* The sound made by a cow. 2 *v.* To make this sound.
mood[1] [mo͞od] *n.* A state of mind or emotion.
mood[2] [mo͞od] *n.* In grammar, the form of a verb used to express a speaker's attitude toward what is being said. In English there are three moods, the indicative, the subjunctive, and the imperative.
mood·y [mo͞o′dē] *adj.* **mood·i·er, mood·i·est** 1 Often falling into sad, gloomy moods. 2 Showing or expressing such moods: a *moody* reply. **—mood′i·ly** *adv.* **—mood′i·ness** *n.*
moon [mo͞on] 1 *n.* A large natural satellite of the earth that often shines at night by reflecting sunlight. ◆ Adj., *lunar.* 2 *n.* Any satellite, especially a natural one. 3 *n.* Something suggesting the visible shape of the moon. 4 *n.* Moonlight. 5 *v.* To behave or move about as though dazed. 6 *n.* A month.
moon·beam [mo͞on′bēm′] *n.* A ray of moonlight.
moon·light [mo͞on′līt′] *n.* 1 Light from the moon. 2 *adj. use*: a *moonlight* excursion.
moon·lit [mo͞on′lit′] *adj.* Lighted by the moon.
moon·scape [mo͞on′skāp′] *n.* A picture or other representation of the surface of the moon.
moon·shine [mo͞on′shīn′] *n.* 1 *informal* Smuggled or illegally distilled liquor. 2 Moonlight. 3 Empty, foolish talk or ideas; nonsense.
moon·stone [mo͞on′stōn′] *n.* A milky white, lustrous mineral, often used as a gemstone.
moon·struck [mo͞on′struk′] *adj.* Crazed; dazed.
moor[1] [mo͝or] *n.* 1 *British* An area of open country. 2 Marshy wasteland.
moor[2] [mo͝or] *v.* To secure or fasten with cables, ropes, or anchors, as a ship.
Moor [mo͝or] *n.* One of a Muslim people of NW Africa who conquered Spain in the 8th century and lived there until they were driven out in the late 15th century. **—Moor′ish** *adj.*
moor·ing [mo͝or′ing] *n.* 1 A place where a thing is moored. 2 (*often pl.*) The line, cable, or anchor that holds something in place: Our boat had slipped its *moorings* during the night.
moose [mo͞os] *n., pl.* **moose** A large mammal related to the deer, found in North America. ◆ *Moose* comes from an Algonquian Indian word meaning *he strips off,* because the animal eats bark from trees.

Moose

moot [mo͞ot] 1 *adj.* Open to argument; debatable: a *moot* point. 2 *v.* To debate. 3 *v.* To bring up for discussion.
mop [mop] *n., v.* **mopped, mop·ping** 1 *n.* A handle with rags, yarn, or a sponge attached to the end for cleaning floors. 2 *v.* To clean with or as if with a mop. 3 *n.* Something that suggests a mop, as thick, matted hair. **—mop up** 1 In war, to clear (a captured area) of remaining enemy resistance. 2 *informal* To complete, as a job or task.

mope [mōp] *v.* **moped, mop·ing,** *n.* 1 *v.* To be gloomy and depressed; sulk. 2 *v.* To move or pass time without purpose; dawdle. 3 *n.* A person who mopes.

mo·ped [mō′ped′] *n.* A vehicle like a heavy bicycle operated by pedaling or by use of an attached small motor.

mop·pet [mop′it] *n.* A young child.

Mor. 1 Moroccan. 2 Morocco.

mo·raine [mə·rān′] *n.* A mass of rocks, gravel, or other material carried and deposited by a glacier.

mor·al [môr′əl] 1 *adj.* Good or virtuous in behavior or character: a thoughtful, *moral* person. 2 *adj.* Having to do with standards of right and wrong: a *moral* problem. 3 *adj.* Able to distinguish between right and wrong: A wolf is not a *moral* being. 4 *n.* (*pl.*) Behavior or habits in respect to right and wrong: to have poor *morals.* 5 *adj.* Teaching standards of right and wrong: a *moral* tale. 6 *n.* The lesson contained in a fable or story. 7 *adj.* Mental or spiritual but not physical or concrete: *moral* support; a *moral* victory. 8 *adj.* Highly probable but not certain; virtual: a *moral* certainty. **—mor′al·ly** *adv.*

mor·ale [mə·ral′] *n.* State of mind, especially in terms of confidence, courage, or hope. ◆ *Morale* (a noun) refers to mood or spirit; MORAL (chiefly an adjective) to good behavior or character.

mor·al·ist [môr′əl·ist] *n.* 1 A person who leads a moral life. 2 A person who moralizes.

mor·al·is·tic [môr′ə·lis′tik] *adj.* 1 Of or concerned with morals or morality. 2 Advocating strict moral standards, especially in a self-righteous way.

mo·ral·i·ty [mə·ral′ə·tē] *n., pl.* **mo·ral·i·ties** 1 The quality of an action, in terms of good and evil. 2 A system of standards or rules of conduct. 3 Virtuous conduct.

mor·al·ize [môr′əl·īz′] *v.* **mor·al·ized, mor·al·iz·ing** 1 To discuss morals. 2 To draw a moral from. 3 To improve the morals of.

mo·rass [mə·ras′] *n.* A stretch of soft, wet ground; marsh; bog.

mor·a·to·ri·um [môr′ə·tôr′ē·əm] *n.* 1 A legal authorization to delay payments on a debt. 2 The period for which the delay is granted.

mo·ray [môr′ā] *n.* Any of numerous eels of tropical marine waters that have teeth sharp enough to inflict a savage bite.

mor·bid [môr′bid] *adj.* 1 Having or showing an abnormal interest in gruesome or unwholesome matters. 2 Grisly; gruesome: a *morbid* fantasy. 3 Caused by or affected with disease: a *morbid* growth. **—mor′bid·ly** *adv.* **—mor′bid·ness** *n.*

mor·bid·i·ty [môr·bid′ə·tē] *n.* 1 The condition of being morbid. 2 The rate of occurrence of disease in a given place.

mor·dant [môr′dənt] 1 *adj.* Biting; sarcastic: a *mordant* wit. 2 *n.* A substance that makes color fast in dyeing. **—mor′dant·ly** *adv.*

more [môr] 1 Comparative of MUCH, MANY. 2 *adj.* Greater in number, degree, or amount: I have *more* books than you. 3 *adj.* Additional; extra: We have to buy *more* books today. 4 *n.* A larger or additional portion, number, or amount: *More* of the books are now available. 5 *adv.* In or to a greater extent or degree: The class reads *more* now. ◆ *More* may be used to form the comparative of some adjectives and adverbs: *more* sensible; *more* quickly. 6 *adv.* In addition; further; again: Read it once *more.* 7 *n.* Something that exceeds or excels something else: *more* than enough. **—more or less** 1 Somewhat. 2 Approximately.

more·o·ver [môr·ō′vər] *adv.* Also; besides.

mo·res [môr′āz] *n.pl.* 1 Customs and traditions that over many years of observance develop the force of law as a standard of behavior for a particular group or society. 2 Behavioral conventions and attitudes; manners; habits; ways: the *mores* of a small town contrasted with the *mores* of a big city.

morgue [môrg] *n.* 1 A place where the bodies of unknown dead persons and of those dead of violence or unknown causes are kept to be examined or identified. 2 In a newspaper, a reference library and its books, files, and other materials.

mor·i·bund [môr′ə·bund′] *adj.* Near death; dying.

Mor·mon [môr′mən] *n.* A member of the Church of Jesus Christ of Latter-day Saints, founded in the U.S. by Joseph Smith in 1830.

morn [môrn] *n.* Morning: used mostly in poems.

morn·ing [môr′ning] *n.* 1 The early part of the day, from midnight to noon, or from sunrise to noon. 2 *adj. use: morning* exercises.

morning glory A climbing plant with funnel-shaped flowers of various colors. The flowers usually open in the morning and close in the afternoon.

Morning glory

morning star A planet, usually Venus, that appears in the eastern sky before sunrise.

Mo·roc·can [mə·rok′ən] 1 *adj.* Of or from Morocco. 2 *n.* A person born in or a citizen of Morocco.

mo·ron [môr′on] *n.* 1 An adult having a mental ability equal to that of a normal 12-year-old child. 2 A stupid or very foolish person.

mo·rose [mə·rōs′] *adj.* Gloomy or sullen: a *morose* person. **—mo·rose′ly** *adv.* **—mo·rose′ness** *n.*

mor·pheme [môr′fēm′] *n.* The smallest unit of meaning in speech. It may be a whole word, as *car,* or part of a word, as *car* and *s* in *cars.*

Mor·phe·us [môr′fē·əs *or* môr′fyo͞os] *n.* In Greek myths, the god of dreams.

mor·phine [môr′fēn′] *n.* A bitter, crystalline substance extracted from opium, used in medicine to cause sleep or lessen pain.

mor·pho·log·ic [môr′fə·loj′ik] *adj.* Morphological.

mor·pho·log·i·cal [môr′fə·loj′ə·kəl] *adj.* Of or having to do with morphology. **—mor′pho·log′i·cal·ly** *adv.*

mor·phol·o·gy [môr·fol′ə·jē] *n.* 1 A branch of bi-

a	add	**i**	it	**o͝o**	took	**oi**	oil
ā	ace	**ī**	ice	**o͞o**	pool	**ou**	pout
â	care	**o**	odd	**u**	up	**ng**	ring
ä	palm	**ō**	open	**û**	burn	**th**	thin
e	end	**ô**	order	**yo͞o**	fuse	**t̶h̶**	this
ē	equal					**zh**	vision

ə = { a in *above* e in *sicken* i in *possible* / o in *melon* u in *circus* }

ology that deals with the form and structure of plants and animals. **2** The form and structure of an organism. **3** The branch of linguistics that studies patterns of word formation in a language, including derivation and inflection.

mor·ris dance [môr′is] An old English dance, usually performed on May Day, in which the performers wear costumes and bells.

mor·row [môr′ō] *n.* **1** The following day. **2** Morning. ◆ This word is seldom used today.

Morse code A system of dots and dashes or short and long sounds that represent letters and numerals, used in telegraphy.

mor·sel [môr′səl] *n.* **1** A small piece or bite of food. **2** A small piece or bit: a choice *morsel* of gossip.

mor·tal [môr′təl] **1** *adj.* Certain to die eventually. **2** *n.* A human being. **3** *adj.* Of or natural to human beings as imperfect creatures; human. **4** *adj.* Of or related to death. **5** *adj.* Causing physical or spiritual death: a *mortal* blow; *mortal* sin. **6** *adj.* Lasting or remaining until death: *mortal* combat; *mortal* enemies. **7** *adj. informal* Very great: *mortal* terror.

mor·tal·i·ty [môr·tal′ə·tē] *n., pl.* **mor·tal·i·ties** **1** The condition or quality of being mortal. **2** The death of many people. **3** The number of deaths in proportion to the population; death rate.

mor·tal·ly [môr′tə·lē] *adv.* **1** Fatally: *mortally* hurt. **2** Extremely: *mortally* offended.

mor·tar[1] [môr′tər] *n.* A bowl in which materials are crushed with a pestle.

Mortar and pestle

mor·tar[2] [môr′tər] *n.* A mixture of lime or cement with sand and water, used in building, as to keep bricks together or to plaster walls.

mor·tar[3] [môr′tər] *n.* A short cannon, loaded through the muzzle and fired at a high angle.

mor·tar·board [môr′tər·bôrd′] *n.* **1** A square board, often with a handle, for holding mortar. **2** A cap with a flat, stiff, square top, worn in some school or college ceremonies, as at graduation.

mort·gage [môr′gij] *n., v.* **mort·gaged, mort·gag·ing** **1** *n.* A claim on property, given as security for a loan. **2** *n.* The contract that establishes such a claim. **3** *v.* To give a claim on (property) as security for a loan. **4** *v.* To risk; hazard: to *mortgage* one's future.

mort·ga·gee [môr′gi·jē′] *n.* The lender to whom a mortgage is given.

mort·ga·gor [môr′gi·jər] *n.* A borrower who mortgages property as security for a loan.

mor·tice [môr′tis] *n., v.* **mor·ticed, mor·tic·ing** Another spelling of MORTISE.

mor·ti·cian [môr·tish′ən] *n. U.S.* A funeral director; undertaker.

mor·ti·fi·ca·tion [môr′tə·fə·kā′shən] *n.* **1** A feeling of loss of self-respect or pride; humiliation. **2** An act or situation that causes this. **3** The use of strict disciplines, as fasting, to subdue one's appetites and strengthen one's will. **4** The death of one part of a living body, as by gangrene.

mor·ti·fy [môr′tə·fī′] *v.* **mor·ti·fied, mor·ti·fy·ing** **1** To deprive of self-respect or pride; humiliate. **2** To subject (as one's body or desires) to severe discipline. **3** To make or become dead or decayed, as with gangrene.

mor·tise [môr′tis] *n., v.* **mor·tised, mor·tis·ing** **1** *n.* A hole cut in a piece of wood, stone, or other material, to fit a tenon of another piece and form a joint. **2** *v.* To join by a mortise.

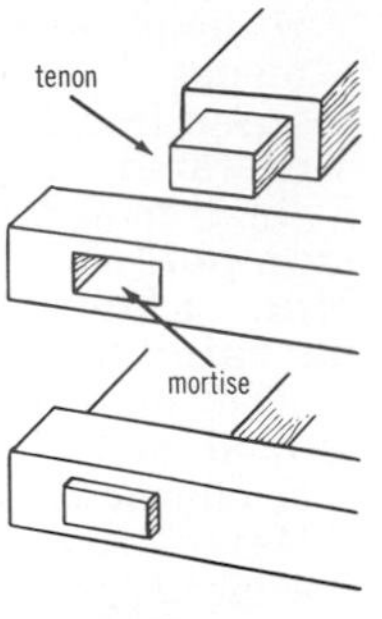

mor·tu·ar·y [môr′cho͞o·er′ē] *n., pl.* **mor·tu·ar·ies** A place for keeping corpses before burial.

mos. months.

mo·sa·ic [mō·zā′ik] *n.* **1** A picture or design made from bits of colored stone or glass. **2** A picture or design that is like a mosaic. **3** *adj. use: mosaic* tiles; *mosaic* tables. **4** The art or craft of constructing or building mosaics.

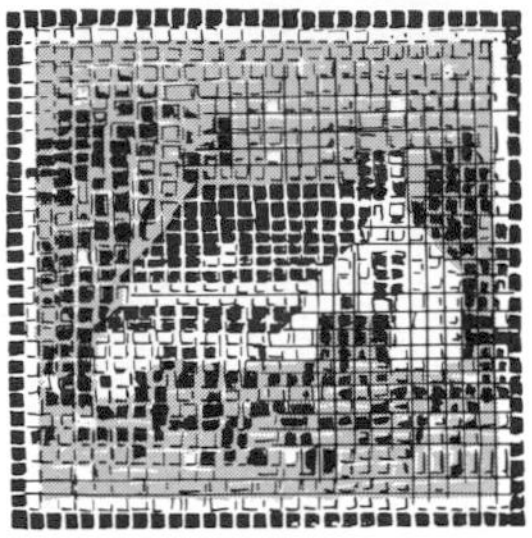
A mosaic

Mo·sa·ic [mō·zā′ik] *adj.* Of or having to do with Moses or the laws and writings ascribed to him.

Mo·ses [mō′zis] *n.* In the Old Testament, a man who led the Israelites from bondage in Egypt, received the Ten Commandments from God, and made laws for the people.

Mos·lem [moz′ləm *or* mos′ləm] *n., adj.* Another spelling of MUSLIM.

mosque [mosk] *n.* A Muslim temple of worship.

mos·qui·to [məs·kē′tō] *n., pl.* **mos·qui·toes** or **mos·qui·tos** A small flying insect with two wings, the female of which bites and sucks blood from people or animals. Some kinds spread malaria, yellow fever, or other diseases.

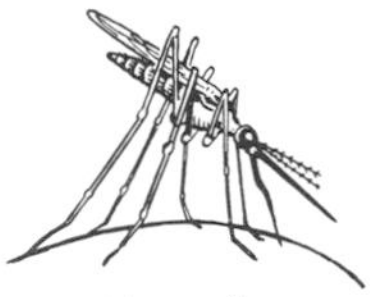
Mosquito

mosquito net A closely woven net or screen used to keep out mosquitoes.

moss [môs] *n.* A tiny, delicate, flowerless plant that grows in clumps on trees and rocks.

moss·y [môs′ē] *adj.* **moss·i·er, moss·i·est** Like or covered with moss.

most [mōst] **1** Superlative of MANY, MUCH. **2** *adj.* Being the greatest in number: *Most* dogs bark. **3** *n.* The greatest number: *Most* of the children are here. **4** *adj.* Being the greatest in amount or degree: to have the *most* power. **5** *n.* The greatest amount, quantity, or degree: *Most* of the air is out of the tire. **6** *adv.* In or to the greatest or highest degree, quantity, or extent: But who suffered *most*? ◆ *Most* may be used to form the superlative of some adjectives and adverbs: *most* sensible; *most* quickly. **7** *adv.* Very: a *most* pleasing gift. **8** *adv. informal* Almost: It grows *most* anywhere. **—at (the) most** At the maximum. **—for the most part** Generally or usually. **—make the most of** To get the maximum advantage from.

-most A suffix meaning: In or to the greatest extent or degree, as in *outmost.*

most·ly [mōst′lē] *adv.* Principally; chiefly.

mote [mōt] *n.* A tiny particle, as of dust.

mo·tel [mō·tel′] *n. U.S.* A hotel designed to accommodate motorists. ◆ *Motel* was formed by combining *mo(tor)* and *(ho)tel.*

moth [môth] *n., pl.* **moths** [mô~~th~~z *or* môths] An insect like a butterfly, but with smaller wings and duller coloring, active mainly at night. The larvae of one variety feed on such materials as wool and fur.

Moth

moth·ball [môth′bôl′] *n.* A round pellet whose odor drives moths away from stored items, as clothing and blankets.
moth-eat·en [môth′ēt′(ə)n] *adj.* **1** Damaged by moth larvae, as clothing. **2** Worn out or old-fashioned: a *moth-eaten* joke.
moth·er[1] [mu~~th~~′ər] **1** *n.* The female parent of a child. **2** *adj. use*: a *mother* cat. **3** *adj.* Of, like, or from a mother: *mother* love. **4** *v.* To take care of or protect as a mother does. **5** *adj.* Native: one's *mother* tongue. **6** *adj.* Having a relation like that of a mother: the *mother* church. **7** *n.* The source or cause of something: Repetition is the *mother* of memory. **8** *n.* (*written* **Mother**) A mother superior.
moth·er[2] [mu~~th~~′ər] *n.* A slimy film formed of the bacteria that make vinegar.
Mother Goose The fictitious name given to the author of a collection of popular nursery rhymes first published in the 18th century.
moth·er·hood [mu~~th~~′ər·hŏŏd′] *n.* **1** The condition of being a mother. **2** The character or qualities of a mother. **3** Mothers as a group.
moth·er-in-law [mu~~th~~′ər·in·lô′] *n., pl.* **moth·ers-in-law** The mother of one's spouse.
moth·er·land [mu~~th~~′ər·land′] *n.* One's own or one's ancestors' native country.
moth·er·ly [mu~~th~~′ər·lē] *adj.* Of or like a mother; protective; warm: *motherly* care.
moth·er-of-pearl [mu~~th~~′ər·əv·pûrl′] *n.* The pearly, lustrous inside layer of certain seashells, used to make buttons and other ornaments.
Mother's Day The second Sunday in May, celebrated annually in the U.S. as a tribute to mothers.
mother superior A nun who heads a religious community of women, as a convent.
mother tongue **1** A person's native language. **2** A language from which one or more other languages were formed.
mo·tif [mō·tēf′] *n.* **1** A main idea or central theme in a work of art or literature. **2** A distinct design in a decoration. **3** A short and easily recognizable melodic fragment in a musical composition.
mo·tile [mōt′əl] *adj.* Moving or able to move spontaneously. **—mo·til′i·ty** *n.*
mo·tion [mō′shən] **1** *n.* Any change in position or location; movement. **2** *n.* An expressive movement of some part of the body; gesture. **3** *v.* To signal by a gesture. **4** *n.* A proposal to be discussed and voted on, as by an assembly.
mo·tion·less [mō′shən·lis] *adj.* Not moving.
mo·tion-pic·ture [mō′shən·pik′chər] *adj.* Of or having to do with a motion picture or with motion pictures.
motion picture **1** A series of pictures flashed on a screen in rapid succession, creating the illusion that things in them are moving. **2** A story told by the use of such pictures; film.
motion sickness Sickness, characterized by symptoms such as dizziness or nausea, experienced as a result of motion during travel, as by automobile, airplane, or ship.
mo·ti·vate [mō′tə·vāt′] *v.* **mo·ti·vat·ed, mo·ti·vat·ing** To provide with a motive.
mo·ti·va·tion [mō′tə·vā′shən] *n.* **1** The act of motivating. **2** A motive; incentive.
mo·tive [mō′tiv] **1** *n.* A reason or cause that makes a person act. **2** *n.* A motif. **3** *adj.* Of or having to do with motion. ◆ See REASON.
mot·ley [mot′lē] **1** *adj.* Having a mixture of colors. **2** *n.* A motley fabric or garment, as that of a jester. **3** *adj.* Containing very different and often clashing elements: a *motley* group of children.
mo·tor [mō′tər] **1** *n.* A machine that transforms electrical energy into mechanical energy, as in a vacuum cleaner. **2** *n.* An internal-combustion engine, as in a tractor. **3** *adj.* Having or driven by a motor: a *motor* scooter. **4** *adj.* Of, for, or having to do with a motor: *motor* power. **5** *v.* To travel by automobile. **6** *adj.* Of, for, or by a motor vehicle: a *motor* trip. **7** *adj.* Having to do with movements of the muscles.
mo·tor·bike [mō′tər·bīk′] *n.* **1** A bicycle propelled by a small motor. **2** A small, light motorcycle.
mo·tor·boat [mō′tər·bōt′] *n.* A boat powered by a motor.
mo·tor·cade [mō′tər·kād′] *n.* A procession of motor vehicles.
mo·tor·car [mō′tər·kär′] *n.* An automobile.
mo·tor·cy·cle [mō′tər·sī′kəl] *n.* A vehicle like a large, heavy bicycle powered by a gasoline engine.

Motorcycle

mo·tor·ist [mō′tər·ist] *n.* A person who drives or travels by automobile.
mo·tor·ize [mō′tə·rīz′] *v.* **mo·tor·ized, mo·tor·iz·ing** **1** To provide with a motor. **2** To furnish with motor-driven vehicles. **—mo′tor·i·za′tion** *n.*
mo·tor·man [mō′tər·mən] *n., pl.* **mo·tor·men** [mō′tər·mən] A person who operates an electric streetcar or subway train.
motor scooter A small, two-wheeled vehicle somewhat like a child's scooter but equipped with a seat for a driver and propelled by a motor.
motor vehicle Any vehicle powered by a motor and designed for travel on streets and highways, as an automobile, bus, or truck.
mot·tle [mot′(ə)l] *v.* **mot·tled, mot·tling,** *n.* **1** *v.* To mark with spots of different colors; blotch. **2** *n.* A spotted or blotched appearance or design.
mot·to [mot′ō] *n., pl.* **mot·toes** or **mot·tos** **1** A word or short saying expressing a rule of conduct or action. **2** A word or phrase that expresses a prin-

a	add	**i**	it	**ŏŏ**	took	**oi**	oil
ā	ace	**ī**	ice	**ōō**	pool	**ou**	pout
â	care	**o**	odd	**u**	up	**ng**	ring
ä	palm	**ō**	open	**û**	burn	**th**	thin
e	end	**ô**	order	**yōō**	fuse	**~~th~~**	this
ē	equal					**zh**	vision

ə = a in *above*, e in *sicken*, i in *possible*, o in *melon*, u in *circus*

ciple or slogan, inscribed on a seal, coin, or other object.
mould [mōld] *n., v.* Another spelling of MOLD.
mould·er [mōld′ər] *v.* Another spelling of MOLDER.
mould·ing [mōld′ing] *n.* Another spelling of MOLDING.
mould·y [mōld′ē] *adj.* **mould·i·er, mould·i·est** Another spelling of MOLDY.
moult [mōlt] *n., v.* Another spelling of MOLT.
mound [mound] 1 *n.* A small hill or pile, as of earth, debris, or rocks. 2 *v.* To heap up or enclose in a mound. 3 *n.* The slightly raised ground from which a baseball pitcher pitches.
mount[1] [mount] 1 *v.* To climb (as a slope or stairs). 2 *v.* To get up on (as a horse or camel). 3 *n.* A horse or other animal used for riding. 4 *v.* To furnish with such a mount. 5 *v.* To set or fix, as in a frame, support, or setting, as for display. 6 *n.* A support or setting for something. 7 *v.* To increase, as in amount or degree. 8 *v.* To prepare and begin (as an attack). 9 *v.* To be equipped with (weapons): a plane *mounting* eight rockets.
mount[2] [mount] *n.* A mountain or hill: used mostly in poems or as part of a name: *Mount* Olympus.
moun·tain [moun′tən] *n.* 1 A mass of land, higher than a hill, rising far above its surroundings. 2 *adj. use: mountain* greenery. 3 A pile; heap: a *mountain* of work.
mountain chain A series of mountains that are connected.
moun·tain·eer [moun′tən·ir′] 1 *n.* A person who lives in a mountainous area. 2 *n.* A mountain climber. 3 *v.* To climb mountains.
mountain goat A goatlike antelope of the Rocky Mountains, with white hair and black horns.
mountain laurel An evergreen shrub of the eastern U.S., with pink or white flowers.
mountain lion Another name for COUGAR.
moun·tain·ous [moun′tən·əs] *adj.* 1 Full of mountains. 2 Huge; gigantic.
mountain range A group or row of mountains.
mountain standard time (*sometimes written* **Mountain Standard Time**) The standard time observed in the time zone that includes the Rocky Mountains. It is seven hours earlier than Greenwich time.

Mountain goat

moun·te·bank [moun′tə·bangk′] *n.* 1 A person who draws a crowd by tricks and jokes and sells quack remedies. 2 Any cheap swindler.
Moun·tie [moun′tē] *n. informal* A member of the Royal Canadian Mounted Police.
mount·ing [moun′ting] *n.* A frame or support.
mourn [môrn] *v.* To be sad or show sorrow over (as over someone dead or a loss). **—mourn′er** *n.*
mourn·ful [môrn′fəl] *adj.* Showing or causing grief; sorrowful. **—mourn′ful·ly** *adv.*
mourn·ing [môr′ning] *n.* 1 A sorrowing; grieving. 2 An expression of sorrow for the dead, such as the wearing of black. 3 Black clothes or other symbols of sorrow.
mourning dove A dove of North America that has a mournful call.
mouse [*n.* mous, *v.* mouz] *n., pl.* **mice** [mīs], *v.* **moused, mous·ing** 1 *n.* A small rodent with a long tail, often found in fields and houses. 2 *v.* To hunt or catch mice. 3 *v.* To prowl, as a cat does. 4 *n. U.S. informal* A timid person. 5 *n.* A small device used to give instructions to a computer without the use of a keyboard.
mous·er [mou′zər] *n.* An animal that catches mice.
mouse·trap [mous′trap′] *n.* A trap for mice.
mousse [mo͞os] *n.* 1 A chilled dessert usually combining cream and gelatin with other ingredients. 2 A whipped hair dressing.
mous·tache [mus′tash′ *or* məs·tash′] *n.* Another spelling of MUSTACHE.
mous·y [mou′sē] *adj.* **mous·i·er, mous·i·est** Shy, timid, and drab.
mouth [*n.* mouth, *v.* mouth] *n., pl.* **mouths** [mouthz], *v.* 1 *n.* The opening at which food is taken into the body and through which sounds are uttered. 2 *n.* The space between the lips and the throat, containing the tongue and teeth. 3 *v.* To take in, hold, or rub with the mouth. 4 *v.* To form with the mouth, as words or letters. 5 *v.* To speak in an insincere or affected way: to *mouth* a greeting. 6 *n.* Something like a mouth in shape or function, as the part of a stream where its waters enter a larger body of water. **—down at** (or **in**) **the mouth** *informal* Unhappy; dejected.
mouth·ful [mouth′fo͝ol′] *n., pl.* **mouth·fuls** 1 As much as can be held in the mouth. 2 As much as is usually taken or put in the mouth at one time. 3 A small quantity.
mouth organ Another name for HARMONICA.
mouth·piece [mouth′pēs′] *n.* 1 The part put in or near the mouth, as of a trumpet or a telephone. 2 A person used by another or others to express views or beliefs; spokesperson.
mouth·wash [mouth′wäsh′ *or* mouth′wôsh′] *n.* A liquid preparation used to cleanse the mouth and teeth or to freshen the breath.
mov·a·ble [mo͞o′və·bəl] *adj.* Capable of being moved; not fixed: *movable* furniture.
move [mo͞ov] *v.* **moved, mov·ing,** *n.* 1 *v.* To change position or place: Don't *move* yet. 2 *v.* To change the position or place of: *Move* the bed to the window. 3 *v.* To change one's residence. 4 *n.* An act of moving; change, as in position or residence; movement. 5 *v.* To make act or operate: A breeze *moved* the branches. 6 *v.* To begin to take action; act: to *move* on the matter. 7 *n.* An act toward some purpose or goal; step: a clever *move.* 8 *v.* To progress; advance: The play *moves* quickly. 9 *v. informal* To depart; go: to *move* on. 10 *v.* To change (as a chess piece or checker) from one position to another. 11 *n.* A turn to play in a game such as chess, or the play made. 12 *v.* To cause; influence: What *moved* you to change your mind? 13 *v.* To affect the emotions of; touch: The story *moved* us to tears. 14 *v.* To make a suggestion or proposal, as at a meeting: to *move* to adjourn. **—on the move** *informal* 1 Moving about constantly. 2 Progressing.
move·a·ble [mo͞o′və·bəl] *adj.* Another spelling of MOVABLE.
move·ment [mo͞ov′mənt] *n.* 1 The act of moving; motion: the *movement* of the waves. 2 A particular manner of moving: a dance *movement.* 3 A series, as of actions or efforts, directed toward some end: a peace *movement.* 4 An arrangement of moving parts, as of a clock. 5 A rhythm or

tempo. 6 One of the sections of a sonata, symphony, or other long musical piece. 7 An emptying of the bowels.

mov·er [mo͞o′vər] *n.* A person or thing that moves, especially one whose job is moving household goods from one place to another.

mov·ie [mo͞o′vē] *n. informal* 1 A motion picture. 2 A motion picture theater.

mov·ing [mo͞ov′ing] *adj.* 1 In motion or capable of movement. 2 Causing movement or change. 3 Affecting the feelings; touching: a *moving* appeal for peace.

moving picture A motion picture.

mow[1] [mou] *n.* 1 Stored hay or grain. 2 The place where hay or grain is stored.

mow[2] [mō] *v.* **mowed, mowed** or **mown** [mōn], **mow·ing** 1 To cut down (grass or grain), as with a scythe. 2 To cut the grass or grain of: to *mow* the lawn. 3 *informal* To knock down or kill: to *mow* the enemy down. **—mow′er** *n.*

Mo·zam·bi·can [mō′zəm·bē′kən] 1 *adj.* Of or from Mozambique. 2 *n.* A person born in or a citizen of Mozambique.

moz·za·rel·la [mot′sə·rel′ə] *n.* A mild-flavored white cheese with a semisoft, rubbery texture.

MP military police.

M.P. Member of Parliament.

mpg or **m.p.g.** miles per gallon.

mph or **m.p.h.** miles per hour.

Mr. Mister: a title used before a man's name.

Mrs. [mis′iz] A title of a married woman: used before her name.

ms, ms., or **MS.** 1 manuscript. 2 (*written* **mss, mss.,** or **MSS.**) manuscripts.

Ms. or **Ms** [miz *or* em′es′] A title for a girl or woman, married or single, like Mr. for a man.

MS Postal Service abbreviation of Mississippi.

M.S. Master of Science.

M.Sc. Master of Science.

MSG monosodium glutamate.

Msgr. 1 Monseigneur. 2 Monsignor.

m.sgt. or **M.Sgt.** master sergeant.

MST or **M.S.T.** mountain standard time.

mt. 1 mount. 2 mountain. 3 (*written* **mts.**) mounts. 4 (*written* **mts.**) mountains.

Mt. Mount: used before proper names: *Mt.* McKinley.

MT Postal Service abbreviation of Montana.

mu [m(y)o͞o] *n.* The 12th letter of the Greek alphabet.

much [much] *adj.* **more, most,** *n., adv.* 1 *adj.* Great, as in amount or extent: *much* noise. 2 *n.* A great amount or extent: *Much* of the story is well written. 3 *adv.* To a great degree; greatly: *much* obliged. 4 *n.* A remarkable or important thing: It isn't *much.* 5 *adv.* Nearly or almost: I feel *much* the same as you.

mu·ci·lage [myo͞o′sə·lij] *n.* A sticky substance, used to glue things together.

muck [muk] *n.* 1 Moist animal manure. 2 Rich, dark brown soil with decaying vegetable matter, as leaves, in it. 3 Mud or filth.

muck·rake [muk′rāk′] *v.* **muck·raked, muck·rak·ing** To search out and make public graft or misconduct in politics or business. **—muck′rak′er** *n.*

mu·cous [myo͞o′kəs] *adj.* 1 Giving off mucus. 2 Of or like mucus; slimy.

mucous membrane The thin, moist lining of the nose, throat, and other cavities that open to the outside.

mu·cus [myo͞o′kəs] *n.* A thick, slimy secretion that keeps mucous membranes moist.

mud [mud] *n.* Soft and sticky wet earth.

mud·dle [mud′(ə)l] *v.* **mud·dled, mud·dling,** *n.* 1 *v.* To confuse or mix up: to *muddle* the message. 2 *v.* To think or act in a confused manner. 3 *n.* A condition of confusion; mix-up.

mud·dle·head·ed [mud′(ə)l·hed′id] *adj.* 1 Mentally confused. 2 Inept, stupid, or blundering.

mud·dy [mud′ē] *adj.* **mud·di·er, mud·di·est,** *v.* **mud·died, mud·dy·ing** 1 *adj.* Soiled by or full of mud: *muddy* shoes. 2 *adj.* Not clear; dirty: *muddy* water. 3 *adj.* Vague; mixed up: *muddy* ideas. 4 *v.* To make or become muddy.

mud puppy Any of several North American aquatic salamanders having external clusters of reddish gills.

mud·sling·er [mud′sling′ər] *n.* A person who makes malicious personal charges against an opponent, especially in a political campaign.

mu·ez·zin [m(y)o͞o·ez′in] *n.* A public crier in Muslim countries who calls the people to prayer.

muff [muf] 1 *n.* A tubelike covering, often of fur, open at both ends, for warming the hands. 2 *n.* A clumsy action, especially dropping a ball one should have caught. 3 *v.* To perform (some act) clumsily, especially to fail to catch (a ball).

Muff

muf·fin [muf′in] *n.* A bread that is shaped like a cupcake and is usually eaten hot.

muf·fle [muf′əl] *v.* **muf·fled, muf·fling,** *n.* 1 *v.* To wrap up in order to hide or keep warm. 2 *v.* To deaden the sound of by, or as if by, wrapping: to *muffle* a cry. 3 *n.* Something used for muffling. 4 *v.* To deaden (a sound).

muf·fler [muf′lər] *n.* 1 A device used to reduce noise, as from the exhaust of an engine. 2 A heavy scarf worn around the neck.

muf·ti [muf′tē] *n.* Ordinary civilian clothes worn by someone who usually wears a uniform.

mug[1] [mug] *n.* 1 A large drinking cup usually with a handle. 2 As much as will fill a mug.

mug[2] [mug] *v.* **mugged, mug·ging,** *n. slang* 1 *v.* To assault and rob. 2 *n.* The face, especially the mouth.

mug·gy [mug′ē] *adj.* **mug·gi·er, mug·gi·est** Warm, humid, and close: *muggy* weather.

Mug

a	add	**i**	it	**o͝o**	took	**oi**	oil		
ā	ace	**ī**	ice	**o͞o**	pool	**ou**	pout		
â	care	**o**	odd	**u**	up	**ng**	ring		
ä	palm	**ō**	open	**û**	burn	**th**	thin		
e	end	**ô**	order	**yo͞o**	fuse	**t͟h**	this		
ē	equal					**zh**	vision		

ə = { a in *above* e in *sicken* i in *possible* / o in *melon* u in *circus* }

M

mug·wump [mug′wump′] *n.* A person who is independent, especially in politics.
Mu·ham·mad·an [mo͞o·ham′ə·dən] **1** *n.* A Muslim. **2** *adj.* Of or having to do with Muhammad or Islam.
Mu·ham·mad·an·ism [mo͞o·ham′ə·dən·iz′əm] *n.* Another name for ISLAM.
mu·lat·to [mə·lat′ō *or* myo͞o·lat′ō] *n., pl.* **mu·lat·toes** A person with one white and one black parent.
mul·ber·ry [mul′ber′ē] *n., pl.* **mul·ber·ries,** *adj.* **1** *n.* Any of various trees bearing a juicy, edible fruit resembling the blackberry. Silkworms feed on the leaves of some mulberries. **2** *n.* The purplish red, berrylike fruit of this tree. **3** *adj., n.* Purplish red.
mulch [mulch] **1** *n.* Any loose material, as straw or leaves, spread on the ground around plants to protect their roots from drying out or freezing. **2** *v.* To cover with mulch.
mulct [mulkt] **1** *v.* To cheat or swindle: The rascal *mulcted* me of $30. **2** *v.* To punish with a fine. **3** *n.* A fine or penalty.
mule[1] [myo͞ol] *n.* **1** The offspring of a donkey and a horse. **2** *informal* A stubborn person. **3** A machine that spins fibers into yarn and winds it on spindles.
mule[2] [myo͞ol] *n.* A lounging slipper with no back.
mu·le·teer [myo͞o′lə·tir′] *n.* A mule driver.
mul·ish [myo͞o′lish] *adj.* Like a mule; stubborn.
mull[1] [mul] *v.* To think at length; ponder: to *mull* over the problem.
mull[2] [mul] *v.* To heat and spice, as wine.
mul·lah [mul′ə *or* mo͝ol′ə] *n.* A Muslim religious teacher or leader.
mul·lein or **mul·len** [mul′ən] *n.* A tall, weedy herb with coarse, woolly leaves and spikes of yellow, red, purple, or white flowers.
mul·let [mul′it] *n., pl.* **mul·let** or **mul·lets** A fish with a reddish or silvery color, living in either fresh or salt water.
multi- A combining form meaning: **1** Having many or much, as in *multifaceted.* **2** Many times over, as in *multimillionaire.*
mul·ti·fac·et·ed [mul′ti·fas′i·tid] *adj.* **1** Having many facets: a *multifaceted* gem. **2** Having several aspects, sides, or phases: a *multifaceted* problem; a *multifaceted* talent.
mul·ti·far·i·ous [mul′tə·fâr′ē·əs] *adj.* Having many forms or much variety.
mul·ti·form [mul′ti·fôrm′] *adj.* Having many forms, shapes, or appearances.
mul·ti·lat·er·al [mul′ti·lat′ər·əl] *adj.* **1** Having many sides. **2** Involving more than two nations: a *multilateral* agreement.
mul·ti·me·di·a [mul′ti·mē′dē·ə] *n., adj.* Of, having to do with, or involving several media of expression, communication, or entertainment: the *multimedia* promotion of a new product.
mul·ti·mil·lion·aire [mul′ti·mil′yən·âr′] *n.* A person who has a fortune of many millions.
mul·ti·na·tion·al [mul′ti·nash′ə·nəl] **1** *adj.* Of, having to do with, or involving more than two nations or nationalities. **2** *n.* A large business organization with operations or investments in more than two countries. **3** *adj.* Of, having to do with, or involving such an organization.
mul·ti·ple [mul′tə·pəl] **1** *adj.* Of, like, or having more than one part or element. **2** *n.* A number which has a given number as one of its factors: 64 is a *multiple* of 16.
multiple sclerosis A disease of the central nervous system, characterized by hardening of tissue in the brain and spinal cord and leading to partial or complete paralysis.
mul·ti·pli·cand [mul′tə·plə·kand′] *n.* A number multiplied or to be multiplied by another.
mul·ti·pli·ca·tion [mul′tə·plə·kā′shən] *n.* **1** The act of increasing in number or degree. **2** The state of being increased in number or degree. **3** The process of adding one or more of the same number together, that is, finding the sum of $n_1 + n_2 + n_3 \ldots + n_x$, where n is any number and x tells how many n's there are. $5 \times 2 = 2 + 2 + 2 + 2 + 2 = 10.$
multiplication sign The symbol (×) placed between two numbers to show that the first number is to be multiplied by the second, as $4 \times 2 = 8$.
mul·ti·plic·i·ty [mul′tə·plis′ə·tē] *n., pl.* **mul·ti·plic·i·ties** A large number or variety.
mul·ti·pli·er [mul′tə·plī′ər] *n.* **1** A person or thing that multiplies. **2** The number by which another number is multiplied.
mul·ti·ply [mul′tə·plī] *v.* **mul·ti·plied, mul·ti·ply·ing** **1** To make or become more in number or degree; increase: The company's holdings *multiplied.* **2** To add (a whole number) a specified number of times: 2 *multiplied* by 3 is 6 because 2 + 2 + 2 = 6; To *multiply* numbers represented by fractions, *multiply* their numerators and *multiply* their denominators. **3** To apply multiplication to: to *multiply* 2 by 5.
mul·ti·tude [mul′tə·t(y)o͞od′] *n.* A great number of persons or things; crowd; throng.
mul·ti·tu·di·nous [mul′tə·t(y)o͞o′də·nəs] *adj.* In great numbers; very many: *multitudinous* stars.
mum [mum] *adj.* Silent: The group kept *mum* about their activities. **—mum's the word** Keep silent.
mum·ble [mum′bəl] *v.* **mum·bled, mum·bling** To speak in a low, unclear way, as with lips nearly closed: We *mumbled* our thanks. **—mum′bler** *n.*
mum·mer [mum′ər] *n.* **1** A person who acts or frolics in a mask or costume. **2** An actor.
mum·mer·y [mum′ər·ē] *n., pl.* **mum·mer·ies** **1** A performance by mummers. **2** A ridiculous, pretentious, or hypocritical ritual.
mum·mi·fy [mum′ə·fī′] *v.* **mum·mi·fied, mum·mi·fy·ing** **1** To make a mummy of. **2** To dry up or shrivel up. **—mum′mi·fi·ca′tion** *n.*
mum·my [mum′ē] *n., pl.* **mum·mies** A dead body, wrapped in cloth and preserved from decay by certain chemical preparations, as was done by the ancient Egyptians. ◆ *Mummy* comes from an Arabic word derived from the Persian word for *wax,* which was used in embalming.

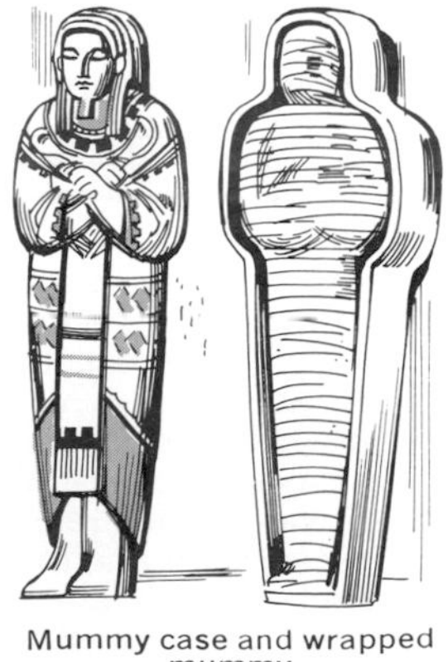
Mummy case and wrapped mummy

mumps [mumps] *n.pl.* (*used with a singular verb*) A contagious virus disease that causes inflammation and swelling of certain glands, particularly below the ear.
munch [munch] *v.* To chew with a crunching noise: to *munch* popcorn. **—munch′er** *n.*
mun·dane [mun·dān′ *or* mun′dān′] *adj.* **1** Practi-

cal or ordinary: the *mundane* problems of cooking a meal. **2** Of the world; earthly.

mu·nic·i·pal [myo͞o·nis′ə·pəl] *adj.* Of or having to do with a town or city or its local government: *municipal* parks. **—mu·nic′i·pal·ly** *adv.*

mu·nic·i·pal·i·ty [myo͞o·nis′ə·pal′ə·tē] *n., pl.* **mu·nic·i·pal·i·ties** A town or city with the power of self-government in local affairs.

mu·nif·i·cent [myo͞o·nif′ə·sənt] *adj.* Very generous; liberal. **—mu·nif′i·cence** *n.* **—mu·nif′i·cent·ly** *adv.*

mu·ni·tion [myo͞o·nish′ən] **1** *n.* (*usually pl.*) Materials and supplies for war, as ammunition and guns. **2** *v.* To supply with munitions.

mu·ral [myo͝or′əl] *n.* A painting done on a wall.

mur·der [mûr′dər] **1** *n.* The unlawful and intentional killing of one person by another. **2** *v.* To kill (someone) unlawfully and intentionally. **3** *v.* To spoil or ruin, as by a bad performance or improper pronunciation.

mur·der·er [mûr′dər·ər] *n.* A person who is guilty of committing murder.

mur·der·ous [mûr′dər·əs] *adj.* **1** Of, like, or involving murder: a *murderous* plot. **2** Capable of murdering or likely to murder: a *murderous* fiend. **—mur′der·ous·ly** *adv.*

murk [mûrk] *n.* Darkness; gloom.

murk·y [mûr′kē] *adj.* **murk·i·er, murk·i·est** Dark, gloomy, or obscure: the *murky* depths.

mur·mur [mûr′mər] **1** *n.* A low, unclear, steady sound, as of many voices or a quiet brook. **2** *v.* To make a low, unclear, steady sound. **3** *n.* A mumbled complaint. **4** *v.* To complain, utter, or speak in a murmur. ◆ The sound [mûr] suggests the low, muffled sound of an actual murmur. The sound was simply repeated to form the word.

Mur·phy's Law [mûr′fēz] The humorous scientific theory which states that if it is possible for something to go wrong, it will go wrong.

mur·rain [mûr′in] *n.* Any of several contagious diseases that attack cattle.

mus·ca·tel [mus′kə·tel′] *n.* A sweet wine.

mus·cle [mus′əl] *n.* **1** One of the bundles of fibrous tissue in the body that, by contraction and stretching, produce the body's voluntary and involuntary movements. **2** An organ or structure made up of this tissue: leg *muscles.* **3** Muscular strength; brawn. ◆ *Muscle* comes from a Latin word that means *a little mouse,* because a bunched muscle can look like a little mouse.

mus·cle·bound [mus′əl·bound′] *adj.* Having some muscles that are enlarged and not as elastic as they should be, often as a result of excessive or incorrectly performed exercise.

mus·cu·lar [mus′kyə·lər] *adj.* **1** Of, using, or made of muscle: *muscular* tissue; *muscular* activity. **2** Having strong, well-developed muscles; powerful.

muscular dys·tro·phy [dis′trə·fē] A disease marked by progressive deterioration and wasting away of the muscles.

mus·cu·la·ture [mus′kyə·lə·chər] *n.* The system of muscles in all or part of the animal body.

muse [myo͞oz] *v.* **mused, mus·ing** To ponder or contemplate thoughtfully.

Muse [myo͞oz] *n.* **1** In Greek myths, any of the nine goddesses of the arts and sciences. **2** (*often written* **muse**) A spirit or power thought to inspire poets, artists, and other creative people.

mu·se·um [myo͞o·zē′əm] *n.* A place for keeping and exhibiting works of nature and art, scientific objects, curiosities, and other items.

mush[1] [mush] *n.* **1** A porridge made with cornmeal. **2** Anything soft, thick, and pulpy.

mush[2] [mush] *v.* To travel, especially over snow with a dog team.

mush·room [mush′ro͞om′] **1** *n.* A fungus, shaped like an umbrella or a cone, that grows very quickly. Some kinds, often called toadstools, are poisonous. **2** *adj.* Of, like, or shaped like a mushroom. **3** *v.* To grow or spread out quickly.

Mushroom

mush·y [mush′ē] *adj.* **mush·i·er, mush·i·est** **1** Soft; spongy: *mushy* ground. **2** *informal* Too sentimental or emotional: a *mushy* love letter.

mu·sic [myo͞o′zik] *n.* **1** The art of combining sounds, usually of voices or instruments, into patterns that are organized and expressive. **2** A composition consisting of such patterns. **3** The notation in which music is written: to read *music.* **4** Any pleasing series of sounds. **—face the music** To accept the consequences of one's actions.

mu·si·cal [myo͞o′zi·kəl] **1** *adj.* Of, related to, or used to make music. **2** *adj.* Fond of or skilled in music: a *musical* society. **3** *adj.* Like music; melodious; harmonious: a *musical* voice. **4** *adj.* Set to, accompanied by, or containing music. **5** *n.* A musical comedy. **—mu′si·cal·ly** *adv.*

musical comedy A show with music, songs, and dances, often based on a slight plot.

mu·si·cale [myo͞o′zə·kal′] *n.* A private concert or recital, as in a home.

music box A box fitted with a mechanism that plays a tune when activated, as by clockwork.

music hall An auditorium or theater for musical performances.

mu·si·cian [myo͞o·zish′ən] *n.* A person who is skilled in music, especially a professional composer or performer of music. **—mu·si′cian·ship′** *n.*

mu·si·col·o·gy [myo͞o′zə·kol′ə·jē] *n., pl.* **mu·si·col·o·gies** The science and historical study of the forms, theory, and methods of music. **—mu′si·col′o·gist** *n.*

musk [musk] *n.* **1** A substance with a strong scent, used in perfumes, obtained from a male musk deer. **2** Any similar substance from some other animals, as the civet or the muskrat. **3** This scent. **—musk′y** *adj.*

musk deer A small deer without horns, of central Asia. The male secretes musk.

mus·kel·lunge [mus′kə·lunj′] *n., pl.* **mus·kel·lunge** or **mus·kel·lunges** A large, North American, freshwater fish, a kind of pike.

a	add	**i**	it	**o͝o**	took	**oi**	oil
ā	ace	**ī**	ice	**o͞o**	pool	**ou**	pout
â	care	**o**	odd	**u**	up	**ng**	ring
ä	palm	**ō**	open	**û**	burn	**th**	thin
e	end	**ô**	order	**yo͞o**	fuse	**th̶**	this
ē	equal					**zh**	vision

ə = { a in *above* e in *sicken* i in *possible* / o in *melon* u in *circus* }

mus·ket [mus'kit] *n.* An old type of firearm, now replaced by the rifle.

mus·ket·eer [mus'kə·tir'] *n.* In former times, a soldier armed with a musket.

mus·ket·ry [mus'kit·rē] *n.* 1 Muskets or musket fire. 2 The art of firing small arms.

musk·mel·on [musk'mel'ən] *n.* 1 Any of several varieties of melon with sweet, juicy meat and tough rind, as the cantaloupe. 2 The plant bearing this melon.

Musket

musk ox *pl.* **musk oxen** An arctic animal with a musky smell, shaggy hair, and curved horns, resembling both the sheep and the ox.

Musk ox

musk·rat [musk'rat'] *n., pl.* **musk·rats** or **musk·rat** 1 A rodent with glossy, brown fur and a musky odor that lives in the marshes and ponds of North America. 2 Its fur. ◆ The word *muskrat* was formed because the original Algonquian Indian name for this animal, *musquash,* was confusing to English-speaking people. The animal does have a musky odor and does resemble a rat.

musk·y [mus'kē] *adj.* **musk·i·er, musk·i·est** Having or resembling the smell of musk. —**musk'i·ness** *n.*

Mus·lim [muz'ləm *or* mo͝oz'ləm *or* mo͞os'ləm] 1 *n.* A believer in Islam. 2 *adj.* Of or having to do with Islam or its followers.

mus·lin [muz'lin] *n.* A strong cotton cloth, often used for sheets or curtains.

muss [mus] *informal* 1 *n.* A state of disorder; mess. 2 *v.* To make messy; rumple.

mus·sel [mus'əl] *n.* A shellfish like a small clam with a shell of two hinged parts.

Mus·sul·man [mus'əl·mən] *n., pl.* **Mus·sul·mans** or **Mus·sul·men** [mus'əl·mən] A Muslim.

muss·y [mus'ē] *adj.* **muss·i·er, muss·i·est** *U.S. informal* Rumpled; messy.

must [must] *v.* A helping verb used to express: 1 Necessity or obligation: *Must* you go? I *must.* 2 Probability: He *must* have been tired. 3 Certainty or conviction: Day *must* follow night. ◆ *Must* has only this one form, used for all tenses and persons.

mus·tache [mus'tash' *or* məs·tash'] *n.* 1 The hair on a man's upper lip, especially when cultivated or groomed. 2 The hair or bristles growing near an animal's mouth.

mus·ta·chio [məs·tä'shō] *n., pl.* **mus·ta·chios** A mustache, especially a large mustache.

mus·tang [mus'tang] *n.* A small wild horse of the SW plains of the U.S., descended from Spanish horses that ran away.

Mustang

mus·tard [mus'tərd] *n.* 1 A plant with yellow flowers and small seed pods. 2 A sharp, brownish yellow seasoning made by grinding the seeds of this plant into a powder or paste.

mus·ter [mus'tər] 1 *v.* To call or bring together; assemble. 2 *n.* A gathering or assembling, as of troops for inspection. 3 *n.* The persons or things assembled together. 4 *v.* To gather or collect: to *muster* up courage. 5 *n.* A list of officers and enlisted personnel in a military unit. —**muster out** To discharge from military service. —**pass muster** To pass an inspection.

must·n't [mus'ənt] Must not.

must·y [mus'tē] *adj.* **must·i·er, must·i·est** 1 Having a moldy odor or taste. 2 Stale or old: *musty* humor. —**must'i·ness** *n.*

mu·ta·ble [myo͞o'tə·bəl] *adj.* 1 Frequently changing; inconstant. 2 Capable of or subject to change. —**mu·ta·bil·i·ty** [myo͞o'tə·bil'ə·tē] *n.*

mu·tant [myo͞o'tənt] *n.* 1 A new variety of plant or animal differing from its parents as a result of mutation. 2 A person or thing that changes or is capable of change.

mu·tate [myo͞o'tāt'] *v.* **mu·tat·ed, mu·tat·ing** To undergo or cause to undergo mutation.

mu·ta·tion [myo͞o·tā'shən] *n.* 1 A change or variation. 2 A sudden variation by which an organism differs from its parents in one or more characteristics that can be inherited.

mute [myo͞ot] *adj., n., v.* **mut·ed, mut·ing** 1 *adj.* Lacking the power of speech. 2 *n.* A mute person, especially a deaf-mute. 3 *adj.* Not making noise or speaking; silent. 4 *adj.* Not pronounced; silent, as the *e* in *gone.* 5 *n.* A device used to muffle the tone of a musical instrument. 6 *v.* To make softer in sound. —**mute'ly** *adv.* —**mute'ness** *n.*

mu·ti·late [myo͞o'tə·lāt'] *v.* **mu·ti·lat·ed, mu·ti·lat·ing** 1 To cut off or destroy a leg or other vital part of. 2 To damage, disfigure, or spoil, as by cutting out parts: to *multilate* a painting. —**mu'ti·la'tion** *n.*

mu·ti·neer [myo͞o'tə·nir'] *n.* A person who takes part in a mutiny.

mu·ti·nous [myo͞o'tə·nəs] *adj.* Stirring up or involved in a mutiny; rebellious.

mu·ti·ny [myo͞o'tə·nē] *n., pl.* **mu·ti·nies,** *v.* **mu·ti·nied, mu·ti·ny·ing** 1 *n.* A rebellion against authority, as by a group of soldiers or sailors against their commanders. 2 *v.* To take part in a mutiny; rebel.

mutt [mut] *n. slang* 1 A dog, especially a mongrel. 2 A stupid person; muttonhead.

mut·ter [mut'ər] 1 *v.* To speak in a low tone with half-closed lips. 2 *n.* A low, unclear utterance or tone. 3 *v.* To complain; grumble.

mut·ton [mut'(ə)n] *n.* The flesh of sheep, especially an adult sheep, used as food.

mut·ton·chops [mut'(ə)n·chops'] *n.pl.* Side whiskers that are shaped like chops of mutton, narrow at the top and broad and round at the bottom.

mut·ton·head [mut'(ə)n·hed'] *n. slang* A stupid person; dolt.

mu·tu·al [myo͞o'cho͞o·əl] *adj.* 1 Directed toward and received by each of two or more, as persons or groups: *mutual* dislike. 2 Having the same attitude toward or relationship with each other or others: *mutual* friends. 3 Held in common: *mutual* interests. —**mu'tu·al·ly** *adv.*

mutual fund An investment company that freely sells and buys its shares to the public, and invests the money of its shareholders in securities of other companies.

muz·zle [muz′(ə)l] *n., v.* **muz·zled, muz·zling** 1 *n.* The snout of an animal, as a dog or horse. 2 *n.* A guard for a snout that prevents an animal from biting. 3 *v.* To fasten a muzzle to the snout of. 4 *v.* To prevent from speaking or giving an opinion. 5 *n.* The front end of a firearm.

Muzzle

MVP most valuable player.

my [mī] 1 *pron.* Of, belonging to, done by, or having to do with me: the possessive form of *I*: *my* book; *my* work. 2 *interj.* A word used to show surprise or dismay: Oh *my*! What a shame!

my·ce·li·um [mī·sē′lē·əm] *n., pl.* **my·ce·li·a** [mī·sē′lē·ə] The mass of threadlike structures that form the main body of a fungus.

my·col·o·gy [mī·kol′ə·jē] *n.* The branch of botany that deals with fungi.

my·e·lin [mī′ə·lin] *n.* A white, fatty substance that serves as a casing for some nerve fibers.

my·na or **my·nah** [mī′nə] *n.* An Asian bird related to the starling, often taught to speak.

my·o·pi·a [mī·ō′pē·ə] *n.* 1 A visual defect in which distant objects are not seen clearly; nearsightedness. 2 Lack of discernment, openmindedness, or foresight.

my·op·ic [mī·op′ik] *adj.* 1 Of, having to do with, or affected by myopia; nearsighted. 2 Lacking discernment, openmindedness, or foresight.

myr·i·ad [mir′ē·əd] *n.* 1 Ten thousand. 2 A vast indefinite number.

myr·mi·don [mûr′mə·don′] *n.* 1 A faithful follower, especially one who follows orders without question. 2 (*written* **Myrmidon**) In Greek myths, any of the warriors who fought under their king, Achilles, in the Trojan War.

myrrh [mûr] *n.* A fragrant gum resin obtained from certain small trees of Arabia and Africa, used in perfumes and incense.

myr·tle [mûr′təl] *n.* 1 An evergreen shrub of southern Europe, with white or rose-colored flowers and black berries. 2 Any of several evergreen plants, as the periwinkle.

my·self [mī·self′] *pron.* 1 The one that I really am; my very own self. ◆ *Myself* in this sense is used to refer back to the subject *I* or to make the *I* more emphatic: I cut *myself*; I saw him *myself*. 2 My normal, healthy, usual, or proper condition: I was *myself* in no time at all. ◆ Do not use *myself* as a replacement for the subject pronoun *I* or the object *me*: Mr. Davis and I [not *myself*] will attend the conference; The mayor asked Mr. Davis and *me* [not *myself*] to represent the city.

mys·te·ri·ous [mis·tir′ē·əs] *adj.* 1 Of, having to do with, consisting of, or suggesting mystery. 2 Impossible or difficult to explain or understand. —**mys·te′ri·ous·ly** *adv.*

mys·ter·y [mis′tər·ē] *n., pl.* **mys·ter·ies** 1 Something that is not known, understood, or explained. 2 Anything, as an action or affair, that arouses curiosity because it is not understood or explained. 3 Something, as a story or play, about such an action or affair. 4 A quality of secrecy or obscurity. 5 A mystery play.

mystery play A medieval religious drama based on the Bible, especially one dealing with events in Christ's life.

mys·tic [mis′tik] 1 *n.* A person who believes that knowledge of God and spiritual truth is best obtained through devotion and contemplation rather than by reason. 2 *adj.* Of or related to mystics or mysticism. 3 *adj.* Mysterious; uncanny: *mystic* abilities.

mys·ti·cal [mis′ti·kəl] *adj.* 1 Of or having a quality or meaning that is spiritual and beyond human reason. 2 Of or related to mystics or mysticism. 3 Mysterious or secret. —**mys′ti·cal·ly** *adv.*

mys·ti·cism [mis′tə·siz′əm] *n.* 1 The beliefs and practices of mystics; the search for God and truth through contemplation and love, with no use of reason. 2 Vague or confused thinking.

mys·ti·fi·ca·tion [mis′tə·fi·kā′shən] *n.* 1 The act of mystifying. 2 The condition of being mystified. 3 Something mystifying.

mys·ti·fy [mis′tə·fī] *v.* **mys·ti·fied, mys·ti·fy·ing** 1 To puzzle or baffle; bewilder. 2 To make obscure or mysterious; complicate.

myth [mith] *n.* 1 A traditional story, usually about such creatures as gods and heroes, often offering an explanation of something in nature or of past events. 2 Anything made-up, as a story, person, or event.

myth·i·cal [mith′ə·kəl] *adj.* 1 Of, like, in, or having to do with a myth or myths. 2 Imaginary; made-up. —**myth′i·cal·ly** *adv.*

myth·o·log·i·cal [mith′ə·loj′i·kəl] *adj.* Of or having to do with mythology. —**myth′o·log′i·cal·ly** *adv.*

my·thol·o·gy [mi·thol′ə·jē] *n., pl.* **my·thol·o·gies** 1 A group or collection of myths, especially of a particular people. 2 The study of myths.

M

a	add	**i**	it	**o͝o**	took	**oi**	oil
ā	ace	**ī**	ice	**o͞o**	pool	**ou**	pout
â	care	**o**	odd	**u**	up	**ng**	ring
ä	palm	**ō**	open	**û**	burn	**th**	thin
e	end	**ô**	order	**yo͞o**	fuse	**th̶**	this
ē	equal					**zh**	vision

ə = {a in *above* e in *sicken* i in *possible*; o in *melon* u in *circus*}

Nn

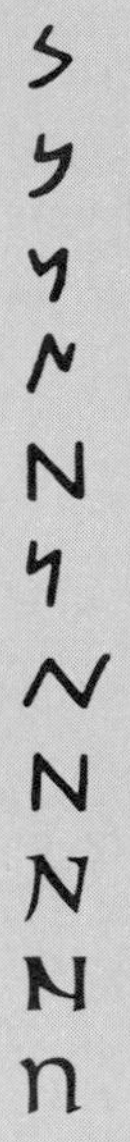

- Early Phoenician (late 2nd millennium B.C.)
- Phoenician (8th century B.C.)
- Early Greek (9th-7th centuries B.C.)
- Western Greek (6th century B.C.)
- Classical Greek (403 B.C. onward)
- Early Etruscan (8th century B.C.)
- Monumental Latin (4th century B.C.)
- Classical Latin
- Uncial
- Half uncial
- Caroline minuscule

N is the fourteenth letter of the alphabet. The sign for it originated among Semitic people in the Near East, in the region of Palestine and Syria, probably in the middle of the second millennium B.C. Little is known about the sign until around 1000 B.C., when the Phoenicians began using it. The Phoenicians named the sign *nun* and used it for the sound of the consonant *n*.

When the Greeks adopted the Phoenician sign around the ninth century B.C., they called it *nu*. Like the Phoenicians, the Greeks used the sign for the sound of *n*. Later, the Greeks reversed the direction in which they wrote the letter, starting it at the line and ending above the line.

As early as the eighth century B.C., the Etruscans adopted the Greek alphabet. It is from the Etruscans that the Romans took the sign for *N*, using it for the consonant *n* sound. Around the time of the Caesars, the Romans made the shape of the letter more graceful. The model of the letter found on the base of Trajan's column, erected in Rome in 114, is considered a masterpiece of letter design. A Trajan-style *majuscule,* or capital letter, *N* opens this essay.

The *minuscule,* or small letter, *n* developed gradually, between the third and the ninth centuries, in the handwriting that scribes used for copying books. Its development, in general, was a little slower than that of the minuscule *m*. Contributing to its shape were the Roman *uncials* of the fourth to the eighth centuries and the *half uncials* of the fifth to the ninth centuries. The true ancestor of the lowercase *n*, however, is found in the *Caroline minuscules,* the script that evolved under the encouragement of Charlemagne (742-814). This script became the principal handwriting system used on the medieval manuscripts of the ninth and tenth centuries. In all its forms, the lowercase *n* was essentially a smaller version of the capital letter, except that it was made without lifting the pen from the paper.

n or **N** [en] *n., pl.* **n's** or **N's** 1 The 14th letter of the English alphabet. 2 In mathematics, an indefinite number or quantity.

n or **n., N** or **N.** 1 north. 2 northern.

n. 1 name. 2 noon. 3 noun. 4 number.

N The symbol for the element nitrogen.

N. Navy.

Na The symbol for the element sodium. ◆ The Latin word for sodium is *natrium.*

N.A. North America.

NAACP or **N.A.A.C.P.** National Association for the Advancement of Colored People.

nab [nab] *v.* **nabbed, nab·bing** *informal* 1 To catch or arrest: They *nabbed* the thief at the airport. 2 To take or grab suddenly; snatch.

na·bob [nā′bob′] *n.* 1 A rich, important person. 2 A European who has made a fortune in India. 3 A governor in provincial India under the Moguls.

na·celle [nə·sel′] *n.* A protective enclosure on the fuselage of an aircraft. It is used to house the engine, cargo, and sometimes crew members.

na·cre [nā′kər] *n.* Another word for MOTHER-OF-PEARL.

na·cre·ous [nā′krē·əs] *adj.* Of or like mother-of-pearl; pearly.

na·dir [nā′dər] *n.* 1 The point in the sky directly opposite the zenith. It is on the other side of the earth, straight below the observer. 2 The lowest possible point: the *nadir* of despair.

nag[1] [nag] *n.* Any horse, especially an old, broken-down, or worthless one.

nag[2] [nag] *v.* **nagged, nag·ging** To bother, as with urging or complaints; scold; pester: My parents often *nag* me to clean up my room. **—nag′ger** *n.*

Na·hua·tl [nä′wät′(ə)l] *n.* 1 A group of Indian tribes of central Mexico and parts of Central America that includes the Aztecs. 2 A member of any of these tribes. 3 The language of these tribes.

Na·hum [nā′əm *or* nā′həm] *n.* 1 A Hebrew prophet who lived during the seventh century B.C. 2 A book of the Old Testament concerning him.

nai·ad [nā′ad *or* nī′ad] *n., pl.* **nai·ads** or **nai·ad·es** [nā′ə·dēz *or* nī′ə·dēz] In Greek and Roman myths, one of the nymphs that lived in and guarded bodies of water, as fountains and rivers.

nail [nāl] 1 *n.* A slender, pointed piece of metal, usually with a head at the top end, to be driven into or through pieces of wood or other material, to fasten them together. 2 *v.* To fasten in place by a nail or nails. 3 *n.* A thin, horny substance that grows at the ends of the fingers and toes. 4 *v. informal* To catch: to *nail* someone in a lie. **—hit the nail on the head** To be exactly right.

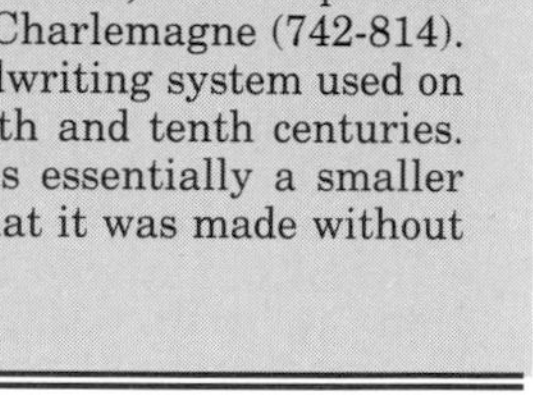

Nails

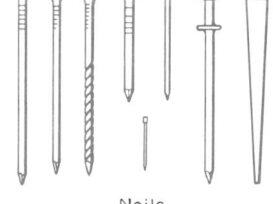

nain·sook [nān′so͝ok′] *n.* A soft, lightweight cotton cloth.

na·ive or **na·ïve** [nä·ēv′] *adj.* 1 Simple and unaffected; childlike. 2 Foolish or inexperienced. 3

Not carefully thought out: a *naive* idea. **—na·ive′·ly** *adv.* ◆ See NATIVE.

na·ive·té or **na·ïve·té** [nä·ēv′tā′] *n.* 1 Childlike innocence or inexperience. 2 A naive remark or act.

na·ked [nā′kid] *adj.* 1 Not wearing any clothes; nude. 2 Not covered; stripped bare: a *naked* tree. 3 Not protected; exposed: the *naked* mountain top. 4 Having nothing added; stark; plain: *naked* truth. **—na′ked·ly** *adv.* **—na′ked·ness** *n.*

naked eye The human eye, not helped by glasses, microscope, telescope, or other instrument.

nam·by-pam·by [nam′bē·pam′bē] *adj., n., pl.* **nam·by-pam·bies** 1 *adj.* Weakly sentimental; insipid. 2 *n.* A namby-pamby person.

name [nām] *n., v.* **named, nam·ing** 1 *n.* A word or group of words by which a person, animal, place, or thing is known or spoken of. 2 *v.* To give a name to: to *name* a cat. 3 *v.* To speak or write the name of; mention: *Name* five stars. 4 *n.* A reputation: to have a bad *name.* 5 *n.* An insulting word or phrase: They called the child *names.* 6 *v.* To designate for a particular job or office; appoint: The assistant director was *named* project head. **—in the name of** 1 For the sake of: *in the name of* peace. 2 By the authority of: *in the name of* Congress. **—make a name for oneself** To become famous. **—to one's name** In one's possession: I haven't got a cent *to my name.*

name·a·ble or **nam·a·ble** [nā′mə·bəl] *adj.* 1 Capable of being named. 2 Worthy of being named.

name·less [nām′lis] *adj.* 1 Having no name. 2 Not known by name; anonymous: a *nameless* crowd. 3 Not fit or able to be spoken of; unmentionable: *nameless* terror; *nameless* crimes. 4 Not mentioned by name.

name·ly [nām′lē] *adv.* That is to say; to wit: Two metals, *namely* copper and gold, are used.

name·sake [nām′sāk′] *n.* A person given or having the same name as another person.

nan·keen or **nan·kin** [nan·kēn′] *n.* A buff-colored, Chinese cotton fabric.

nan·ny [nan′ē] *n., pl.* **nan·nies** A child's nurse; nursemaid.

nanny goat A female goat.

nap[1] [nap] *n., v.* **napped, nap·ping** 1 *n.* A short sleep. 2 *v.* To sleep for a short time; doze. 3 *v.* To be unprepared or off guard: to be caught *napping.*

nap[2] [nap] *n.* The short fibers forming a fuzzy surface, as on flannel or velvet.

na·palm [nā′päm′] 1 *n.* Gasoline and chemicals mixed together to form a flammable jelly that is used in incendiary bombs and flamethrowers. 2 *v.* To attack with weapons that use napalm.

nape [nāp] *n.* The back part of the neck.

na·per·y [nā′pər·ē] *n.* Linens used for the table, especially tablecloths and napkins.

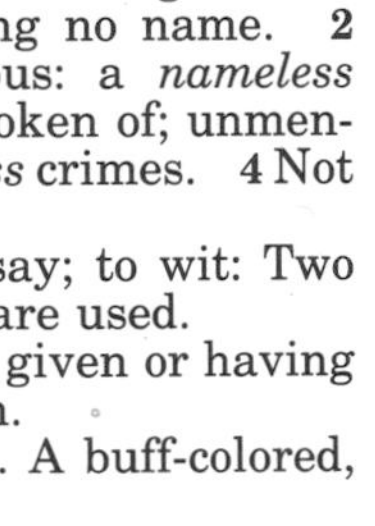

Nape

naph·tha [naf′thə *or* nap′thə] *n.* An oily substance distilled from petroleum, used as a fuel, solvent, and cleaning fluid.

naph·tha·lene [naf′thə·lēn′ *or* nap′thə·lēn′] *n.* A white crystalline hydrocarbon prepared from coal tar or petroleum, used as a moth repellent and in dyes.

nap·kin [nap′kin] *n.* 1 A small cloth or paper used at meals to protect clothing and to wipe the hands and mouth. 2 A small towel or piece of cloth.

na·po·le·on [nə·pō′lē·ən] *n.* A pastry consisting of crisp, flaky layers of dough with a custard or cream filling between the layers.

Na·po·le·on·ic [nə·pō′lē·on′ik] *adj.* Of or having to do with Napoleon Bonaparte.

nar·cis·sism [när′sə·siz′əm] *n.* An excessive admiration or love of oneself.

nar·cis·sus [när·sis′əs] *n., pl.* **nar·cis·sus·es** or **nar·cis·si** [när·sis′ī] 1 A spring plant that grows from a bulb and bears white or yellow flowers. Daffodils and jonquils are species of narcissus. 2 (*written* **Narcissus**) In Greek myths, a youth who was made to fall in love with his own reflection in water and who pined for it until he died and was turned into a narcissus.

Narcissus

nar·cot·ic [när·kot′ik] 1 *n.* A drug, as morphine, that produces sleep and dulls pain when taken in small doses but may be poisonous in large doses. 2 *adj.* Of, like, or having the effects of a narcotic.

nar·rate [na·rāt′ *or* nar′āt′] *v.* **nar·rat·ed, nar·rat·ing** 1 To tell or relate, as a story. 2 To talk along with in order to explain: to *narrate* a film.

nar·ra·tion [na·rā′shən] *n.* 1 A telling, as of a story or event. 2 A talk given to explain something, as a film.

nar·ra·tive [nar′ə·tiv] 1 *n.* An account, story, or tale. 2 *n.* The act of narrating; narration. 3 *adj.* Telling a story: a *narrative* poem.

nar·rat·or [na·rāt′ər *or* nar′ā·tər] *n.* 1 A person who tells a story. 2 A person who talks along with a presentation, as a film or television program, and explains it or comments on it.

nar·row [nar′ō] 1 *adj.* Having little width or less than a standard or expected width; not broad: a *narrow* bridge; *narrow* ribbon. 2 *v.* To make or become less wide: The brook *narrows* to a trickle. 3 *n.* (*usually pl.*) A narrow part, as of a strait. 4 *adj.* Limited in breadth, as of vision or tolerance: *narrow* views. 5 *adj.* Limited or small: a family of *narrow* means. 6 *adj.* Nearly unsuccessful or disastrous; close: a *narrow* escape. **—nar′row·ly** *adv.* **—nar′row·ness** *n.*

nar·row-mind·ed [nar′ō·mīn′did] *adj.* Having narrow ideas; not liberal; bigoted.

a	add	**i**	it	**o͝o**	took	**oi**	oil
ā	ace	**ī**	ice	**o͞o**	pool	**ou**	pout
â	care	**o**	odd	**u**	up	**ng**	ring
ä	palm	**ō**	open	**û**	burn	**th**	thin
e	end	**ô**	order	**yo͞o**	fuse	**th̶**	this
ē	equal					**zh**	vision

ə = a in *above*, e in *sicken*, i in *possible*, o in *melon*, u in *circus*

N

nar·whal [när′(h)wəl] *n.* A small whale of arctic waters. The male has a long, spiral tusk.

Narwhal

nar·y [nâr′ē] *adj. informal* Not one: There was *nary* a person out that stormy night.
NASA National Aeronautics and Space Administration.
na·sal [nā′zəl] **1** *adj.* Of or having to do with the nose: *nasal* congestion. **2** *adj.* Produced with the voice passing through the nose, as [m], [n], or [ng]. **3** *n.* A nasal sound.
nas·cent [nā′sənt] *adj.* Beginning to exist or grow; coming into being.
na·stur·tium [nə·stûr′shəm] *n.* A garden plant with a strong odor and funnel-shaped flowers of red, orange, or yellow. ◆ *Nasturtium* comes from a Latin phrase *nasus tortus,* meaning *twisted nose,* describing how the flower's sharp odor makes a person's nose draw up.
nas·ty [nas′tē] *adj.* **nas·ti·er, nas·ti·est** **1** Disgusting to smell or taste. **2** Filthy. **3** Indecent; foul: *nasty* language. **4** Bad, ugly, or painful: a *nasty* cut. **5** Mean or vicious: a *nasty* temper. **—nas′ti·ly** *adv.* **—nas′ti·ness** *n.*
na·tal [nā′təl] *adj.* Of or having to do with one's birth; dating from birth. ◆ See NATIVE.
na·tion [nā′shən] *n.* **1** A group of people who live in a particular area, have a distinctive way of life, and are organized under a central government. They usually speak the same language. **2** A tribe or federation: the Iroquois *nation.* ◆ See NATIVE.
na·tion·al [nash′ən·əl] **1** *adj.* Of, belonging to, or having to do with a nation as a whole: a *national* law; a *national* crisis. **2** *n.* A citizen of a nation. **—na′tion·al·ly** *adv.*
National Guard A military force of a state, paid for in part by the U.S. government and subject to federal service in times of emergency.
na·tion·al·ism [nash′ən·əl·iz′əm] *n.* **1** Patriotic feelings for one's own nation. **2** A desire or movement for independence as a nation. **—na′tion·al·ist** *n.* **—na′tion·al·is′tic** *adj.* **—na′tion·al·is′ti·cal·ly** *adv.*
na·tion·al·i·ty [nash′ən·al′ə·tē] *n., pl.* **na·tion·al·i·ties** **1** A group of people who form a nation. **2** The condition of belonging to a particular nation, as by birth or naturalization. **3** The condition of existing as a nation.
na·tion·al·ize [nash′ən·əl·īz′] *v.* **na·tion·al·ized, na·tion·al·iz·ing** **1** To place (the industries and resources of a nation) under the control or ownership of the state. **2** To make national, as in character or scope. **—na·tion·al·i·za·tion** [nash′ən·əl·ə·zā′shən] *n.*
national park Land that is set aside and maintained by the federal government for recreational use by the public.
National Socialism The principles of Nazism.
na·tion·wide [nā′shən·wīd′] *adj.* Extending throughout or across a nation.
na·tive [nā′tiv] **1** *adj.* Born, grown, or living naturally in a particular area. **2** *n.* A person, plant, or animal native to an area. **3** *n.* One of the original inhabitants of a place; aborigine. **4** *adj.* Related or belonging to a person by birth or place of birth: one's *native* language. **5** *adj.* Not learned; inborn: *native* charm. **6** *adj.* Found in a pure state in nature: *native* gold. ◆ *Native* and *naive* come from two different French words that were both derived from one Latin word, *nativus,* meaning *natural* or *inborn. Nativus* is based on the Latin word *nasci,* meaning *to be born,* from which such words as *nation* and *natal* are also derived.
Native American **1** One of or a descendant of the peoples living in the Western Hemisphere before the first Europeans came. **2** An American Indian.
na·tive-born [nā′tiv·bôrn′] *adj.* Born in the area or country stated: a *native-born* Mexican.
na·tiv·i·ty [nə·tiv′ə·tē] *n., pl.* **na·tiv·i·ties** Birth. **—the Nativity** **1** The birth of Jesus. **2** Christmas Day.
natl. national.
NATO [nā′tō] North Atlantic Treaty Organization.
nat·ty [nat′ē] *adj.* **nat·ti·er, nat·ti·est** Smart in looks or dress; neat. **—nat′ti·ly** *adv.* **—nat′ti·ness** *n.*
nat·u·ral [nach′ər·əl] **1** *adj.* Produced by or existing in nature; not artificial: a *natural* bridge. **2** *adj.* Having to do with the study of nature: *natural* sciences. **3** *adj.* Inborn; native: *natural* talent. **4** *adj.* Being so by nature: a *natural* athlete. **5** *adj.* Happening in a normal or expected way: a *natural* death. **6** *adj.* Resembling nature closely; lifelike: a *natural* pose. **7** *adj.* Not forced or affected: *natural* behavior. **8** *adj.* Felt by instinct to be just: *natural* rights. **9** *adj.* In music, not sharp or flat, as a note. **10** *n.* A natural note. **11** *n.* A sign (♮) used to cancel sharps and flats. **12** *n. U.S. informal* A person or thing that is well suited for some job or purpose. **—nat′u·ral·ness** *n.*
natural gas A colorless, odorless combustible mixture of hydrocarbons that consists principally of methane. It occurs naturally with petroleum deposits and is used for fuel.
natural history The study of nature, especially as related to the earth and living things.
nat·u·ral·ist [nach′ər·əl·ist] *n.* A person who is trained in natural history.
nat·u·ral·is·tic [nach′ər·ə·lis′tik] *adj.* Of, resembling, or in accordance with nature. **—nat′u·ral·is′ti·cal·ly** *adv.*
nat·u·ral·ize [nach′ər·əl·īz′] *v.* **nat·u·ral·ized, nat·u·ral·iz·ing** **1** To make into or accept as a citizen: to *naturalize* an immigrant. **2** To adopt into common use, as a foreign word or custom. **3** To adapt to a country or place, as a foreign plant or animal. **—nat·u·ral·i·za·tion** [nach′ər·əl·ə·zā′shən] *n.*
nat·u·ral·ly [nach′ər·əl·ē] *adv.* **1** In a natural, normal, or usual manner. **2** By nature: Deltas form *naturally.* **3** Of course; certainly.
natural number A positive integer, as 1 or 2.
natural resource (*often pl.*) A source of raw material, power, or wealth provided by nature, as forests, minerals, and water supply.
natural science **1** Any science that deals with the physical world, such as biology, chemistry, or physics. **2** All such sciences together.
natural selection The theory that animals and plants best able to adapt to a specific environment tend to survive and that successive generations show an increasing adaptation to that environment.
na·ture [nā′chər] *n.* **1** The overall pattern or system of objects, forces, and events in the universe: laws of *nature.* **2** The physical world, especially when unaltered by human beings: a walk in the forest to study *nature.* **3** The basic qualities and

character of a thing or person: the *nature* of war; her daring *nature.* 4 The natural tendencies directing conduct: Such behavior is against *nature.* 5 Sort; kind; variety: nothing of that *nature.*

naught [nôt] *n.* 1 Nothing. 2 The numeral 0; zero.

naugh·ty [nô′tē] *adj.* **naugh·ti·er, naugh·ti·est** 1 Badly behaved; mischievous; disobedient: a *naughty* child. 2 A little improper: a *naughty* word. **—naugh′ti·ly** *adv.* **—naugh′ti·ness** *n.*

Na·u·ru·an [nä·o͞o′ro͞o·ən] 1 *adj.* Of or from Nauru. 2 *n.* A person born in or a citizen of Nauru.

nau·se·a [nô′zē·ə *or* nô′zhə] *n.* 1 A sick feeling that comes along with an urge to vomit. 2 Disgust or loathing. ◆ *Nausea* comes originally from a Greek word meaning *seasickness.*

nau·se·ate [nô′zē·āt′ *or* nô′sē·āt′] *v.* **nau·se·at·ed, nau·se·at·ing** To feel or cause to feel nausea or disgust.

nau·seous [nô′shəs *or* nô′zē·əs] *adj.* Causing nausea; sickening: *nauseous* fumes. **—nau′seous·ly** *adv.* **—nau′seous·ness** *n.* ◆ Many people mistakenly use *nauseous* as a substitute for *nauseated.* But *nauseous* strictly means "causing sickness," not "being sick."

nau·ti·cal [nô′ti·kəl] *adj.* Of or having to do with ships, sailors, or the sea. **—nau′ti·cal·ly** *adv.*

nautical mile A measure of distance equal to about 6,076 feet.

nau·ti·lus [nô′tə·ləs] *n.* 1 A small sea animal that lives in the largest and outermost chamber of a spiral shell having many chambers. 2 An eight-armed sea creature related to the octopus, the female of which has a thin, delicate shell.

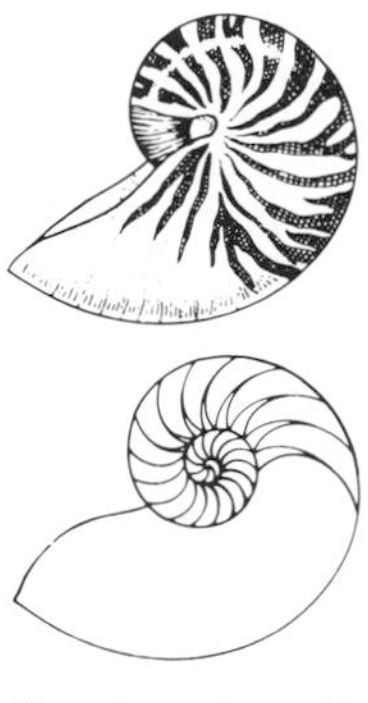

Chambered nautilus and cross section of its shell

Nav·a·ho [näv′ə·hō′ *or* nav′ə·hō′] *n., pl.* **Nav·a·ho** or **Nav·a·hos** or **Nav·a·hoes** 1 The largest tribe of North American Indians, now living in Arizona, New Mexico, and Utah. 2 A member of this tribe. 3 The language of this tribe.

Nav·a·jo [näv′ə·hō′ *or* nav′ə·hō′] *n., pl.* **Nav·a·jo** or **Nav·a·jos** or **Nav·a·joes** Another spelling of NAVAHO.

na·val [nā′vəl] *adj.* Of, for, done by, or having a navy: *naval* officers; a *naval* base.

nave [nāv] *n.* The main part of a church, located between the side aisles.

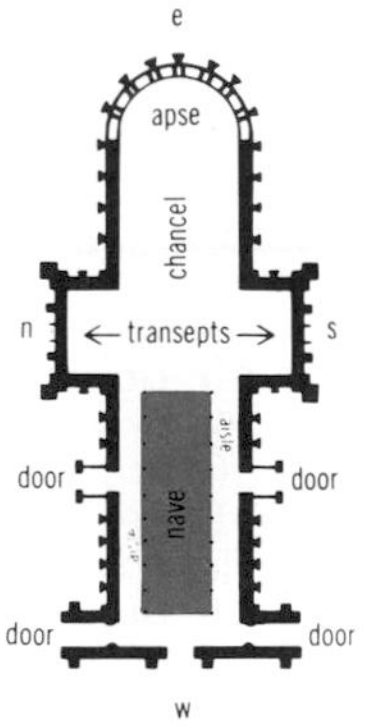

na·vel [nā′vəl] *n.* 1 The scar at the center of the abdomen where the umbilical cord was attached. 2 A central part or point.

navel orange An orange without seeds that has a navel-like depression at one end.

nav·i·ga·ble [nav′ə·gə·bəl] *adj.* 1 Deep and wide enough for ships to sail on: a *navigable* river. 2 Capable of being steered, as a dirigible. **—nav·i·ga·bil·i·ty** [nav′ə·gə·bil′ə·tē] *n.*

nav·i·gate [nav′ə·gāt′] *v.* **nav·i·gat·ed, nav·i·gat·ing** 1 To travel or travel on, through, or over, as by boat. 2 To chart or control the course and position of, as a ship or aircraft.

nav·i·ga·tion [nav′ə·gā′shən] *n.* 1 The act or practice of navigating. 2 The art of charting the position and course of a ship or aircraft.

nav·i·ga·tor [nav′ə·gā′tər] *n.* 1 A person who navigates. 2 A person trained in charting the position and course of a ship or aircraft.

na·vy [nā′vē] *n., pl.* **na·vies** 1 (*often written* **Navy**) The entire military sea force of a country, including its ships, personnel, and the government department in charge. 2 Navy blue. 3 A fleet of ships: seldom used today.

navy bean Any of several small, white varieties in the kidney bean family, used especially for baked beans and soups. ◆ The navy bean is so named because of its use by the U.S. Navy.

navy blue A very dark blue.

nay [nā] 1 *adv.* No: seldom used today. 2 *adv.* No, rather; not only that, but also: The store owner is somewhat odd, *nay,* insane. 3 *n.* A negative vote. 4 *n.* A denial or refusal.

Naz·a·rene [naz′ə·rēn′] *n.* A person born or living in Nazareth. **—the Nazarene** Jesus.

Na·zi [nä′tsē] *n.* A member of the fascist political party that controlled Germany from 1933 to 1945 under Adolf Hitler. **—Naz′ism** or **Na′zi·ism** *n.*

n.b. or **N.B.** Take notice; observe carefully. ◆ *n.b.* is an abbreviation of the Latin phrase *nota bene,* meaning *note well.*

Nb The symbol for the element niobium.

N.B. New Brunswick.

NBA or **N.B.A.** 1 National Basketball Association. 2 National Boxing Association.

NBC National Broadcasting Corporation.

Nbe north by east.

Nbw north by west.

NC Postal Service abbreviation of North Carolina.

N.C. North Carolina.

NCAA National Collegiate Athletic Association.

NCO or **N.C.O.** noncommissioned officer.

Nd The symbol for the element neodymium.

ND Postal Service abbreviation of North Dakota.

N.D. North Dakota.

ne or **n.e., NE** or **N.E.** 1 northeast. 2 northeastern.

Ne The symbol for the element neon.

NE Postal Service abbreviation of Nebraska.

N.E. New England.

NEA or **N.E.A.** National Education Association.

Ne·an·der·thal man [nē·an′dər·täl′ *or* nē·an′dər·thôl′] An extinct species of human being that lived in caves and used stone tools.

Ne·a·pol·i·tan [nē′ə·pol′ə·tən] 1 *adj.* Of or coming from Naples. 2 *n.* A person born or living in Naples.

neap tide [nēp] The tide soon after the first and third quarters of the moon, when the difference between high tide and low tide is very slight.

a	add	**i**	it	**o͝o**	took	**oi**	oil		
ā	ace	**ī**	ice	**o͞o**	pool	**ou**	pout		
â	care	**o**	odd	**u**	up	**ng**	ring		
ä	palm	**ō**	open	**û**	burn	**th**	thin		
e	end	**ô**	order	**yo͞o**	fuse	**t͟h**	this		
ē	equal					**zh**	vision		

ə = a in *above* e in *sicken* i in *possible* o in *melon* u in *circus*

near [nir] **1** *adv., adj.* Not distant in place, time, or degree; close: He came *near*; The town is *near.* **2** *prep.* Close by or to. **3** *v.* To come near; approach: My arrow *neared* the target. **4** *adv. informal* Nearly; almost: *near* perfect weather. **5** *adj.* Barely escaped or avoided; close: a *near* tragedy. **6** *adj.* Close in relationship or affection: a *near* and dear person. **7** *adj.* Saving distance or time; short: 20 miles by the *nearest* route. **8** *adj.* Stingy; cheap. **—near'ness** *n.* ◆ In Old English *near* was the comparative of *nēah,* meaning *nigh* or *close.* Now, however, *near* has taken the place of *nigh,* and *nearer* has become the comparative form.

near·by [*adj.* nir'bī', *adv.* nir'bī'] *adj., adv.* Close by; near: a *nearby* hut; to fly *nearby.*

Near Eastern Of or from the Near East.

near·ly [nir'lē] *adv.* **1** Almost; practically; approximately: It is *nearly* bedtime. **2** Closely.

near·sight·ed [nir'sī'tid] *adj.* Able to see clearly at short distances only. **—near'sight'ed·ly** *adv.* **—near'sight'ed·ness** *n.*

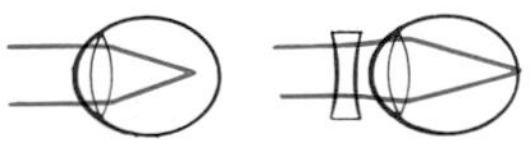
The focus of light rays entering a nearsighted eye is in front of the retina. A concave lens corrects this.

neat [nēt] *adj.* **1** Orderly, tidy, and clean: a *neat* house; Cats are *neat* animals. **2** Precise: *neat* work. **3** Not mixed or diluted, as liquor. **4** *slang* Cleverly done: a *neat* trick. **—neat'ly** *adv.* **—neat'ness** *n.*

neath or **'neath** [nēth] *prep.* Beneath; under: used mostly in poems.

Neb. Nebraska.

NEbE northeast by east.

NEbN northeast by north.

Nebr. Nebraska.

neb·u·la [neb'yŏŏ·lə] *n., pl.* **neb·u·las** or **neb·u·lae** [neb'yŏŏ·lē] **1** A shining or dark celestial mass consisting of a cloud of gases and cosmic dust, sometimes enveloping one or more stars. **2** A very distant system of stars; galaxy.

neb·u·lous [neb'yŏŏ·ləs] *adj.* **1** Vague or unclear: a *nebulous* feeling. **2** Of, having to do with, or like a nebula. **3** Cloudlike; misty. **—neb'u·lous·ly** *adv.* **—neb'u·lous·ness** *n.*

nec·es·sar·i·ly [nes'ə·ser'ə·lē] *adv.* By necessity; inevitably: The majority is not *necessarily* right.

nec·es·sar·y [nes'ə·ser'ē] *adj., n., pl.* **nec·es·sar·ies** **1** *adj.* Not to be done without; essential: Your help is *necessary.* **2** *n.* (*often pl.*) Something that cannot be done without, as food. **3** *adj.* Bound to happen; inevitable: Heat is a *necessary* result of friction.

ne·ces·si·tate [nə·ses'ə·tāt'] *v.* **ne·ces·si·tat·ed, ne·ces·si·tat·ing** To make necessary; force: The rain *necessitated* a delay.

ne·ces·si·ty [nə·ses'ə·tē] *n., pl.* **ne·ces·si·ties** **1** (*often pl.*) Something that cannot be done without, such as food: They could barely afford *necessities.* **2** Extreme need: Wake me in case of *necessity.* **3** A need or force that compels: *Necessity* made us learn to cook. **4** Great poverty: to live in *necessity.* **—of necessity** With no possibility of being otherwise.

neck [nek] *n.* **1** The part of an animal that connects the head with the trunk. **2** The part of a garment that comes nearest to or touches the neck. **3** Something thought to resemble a neck, as the narrow part of a violin or bottle, or a narrow piece of land between two bodies of water. **—neck and neck** Abreast or even, as in a race. **—stick one's neck out** *informal* To expose oneself, as to trouble, failure, or ridicule, by taking a risk.

neck·er·chief [nek'ər·chif] *n.* A kerchief worn around the neck.

neck·lace [nek'lis] *n.* An ornament, as a string of beads or gems, worn around the neck.

Neckerchief

neck·line [nek'līn'] *n.* The line or shape formed by the neck of a garment.

neck·tie [nek'tī'] *n.* A narrow strip of cloth worn around the neck under a collar and tied in front.

neck·wear [nek'wâr'] *n.* Articles of clothing, such as ties and scarves, worn around the neck: an exclusive men's clothing store specializing in *neckwear.*

nec·ro·man·cy [nek'rə·man'sē] *n.* **1** The telling of the future by supposedly consulting the dead. **2** Magic; witchcraft. **—nec'ro·man'cer** *n.*

nec·tar [nek'tər] *n.* **1** In Greek myths, the drink of the gods. **2** A delicious or satisfying drink. **3** A sweet liquid found in flowers, collected by bees to make honey.

nec·tar·ine [nek'tə·rēn'] *n.* A type of peach having a smooth skin and a firm pulp.

née or **nee** [nā] *adj.* Born with the name of: used to indicate the maiden name of a married woman: Mrs. Mary Lincoln, *née* Todd. ◆ *Née* comes directly from the French, in which it is the feminine form of *né,* meaning *born.*

need [nēd] **1** *v.* To require; find necessary: Everyone *needs* food. **2** *n.* A lack of something required or wanted: a *need* for nurses. **3** *n.* The thing wanted or required but lacking: Our great *need* was money. **4** *n.* A condition of requiring help: a friend in *need.* **5** *n.* Poverty: My neighbor is in great *need.* **6** *v.* To have to; ought to: They *need* to study more. **7** *n.* Obligation; necessity: Is there any *need* to hurry? **—if need be** If necessary. ◆ *Need* is sometimes used in negative statements and in questions as an unchanging helping verb: He *need* not go; *Need* he come?

need·ful [nēd'fəl] *adj.* Needed; necessary. **—need'·ful·ly** *adv.* **—need'ful·ness** *n.*

nee·dle [nēd'(ə)l] *n., v.* **nee·dled, nee·dling** **1** *n.* A small, thin, steel rod with a hole in one end, used to carry thread through cloth in sewing. **2** *n.* The thin, hollow tube at the end of a hypodermic syringe. **3** *n.* A pointer, as in a gauge or compass. **4** *n.* A short rod, often tipped with a hard material, as diamond, used to pick up vibrations from a phonograph record. **5** *n.* A slender rod used in knitting. **6** *n.* Something that suggests the shape of a needle, as a leaf of a pine or an obelisk. **7** *v. informal* To tease or heckle.

nee·dle·point [nēd'(ə)l·point'] *n.* Embroidery worked with yarn in even stitches on a netlike canvas.

need·less [nēd'lis] *adj.* Not needed or necessary; useless. **—need'less·ly** *adv.* **—need'less·ness** *n.*

nee·dle·work [nēd'(ə)l·wûrk'] *n.* Work done using a needle, as embroidery or sewing.

need·n't [nēd'(ə)nt] Need not.

needs [nēdz] *adv.* Necessarily: seldom used today: A person must *needs* be a good manager to run a household or an office.

need·y [nē′dē] *adj.* **need·i·er, need·i·est** In need or want; very poor. **—need′i·ness** *n.*

ne′er [nâr] *adv.* Never: used mostly in poems.

ne′er-do-well [nâr′do͞o·wel′] *n.* A worthless, good-for-nothing person.

ne·far·i·ous [ni·fâr′ē·əs] *adj.* Extremely wicked; evil. **—ne·far′i·ous·ly** *adv.* **—ne·far′i·ous·ness** *n.*

neg. negative.

ne·gate [ni·gāt′] *v.* **ne·gat·ed, ne·gat·ing** 1 To cancel the effect of; abolish; nullify. 2 To deny or contradict.

ne·ga·tion [ni·gā′shən] *n.* 1 The act of denying. 2 The absence or reverse of something: Silence is the *negation* of sound.

neg·a·tive [neg′ə·tiv] *adj., n., v.* **neg·a·tived, neg·a·tiv·ing** 1 *adj.* Expressing refusal, denial, or opposition: a *negative* answer. 2 *n.* A negative word or expression: *No* is a *negative.* 3 *adj.* Contrary or resisting; not helpful: a *negative* attitude. 4 *v.* To negate or veto. 5 *n.* The group that argues against a point, as in a debate. 6 *adj.* Opposite from positive; minus: a *negative* number. 7 *adj.* Indicating or having the kind of electricity that repels electrons and attracts protons. 8 *adj.* Indicating that something looked for or tested for is not there or does not happen: *negative* results. 9 *adj.* In photography, having the light and dark areas reversed. 10 *n.* A negative picture or film. **—double negative** A sentence or phrase that uses two negatives, as "He hasn't got none." ◆ In Old English the double negative was standard English, but in modern English it is unacceptable. Such statements as *I am not unhappy,* however, are standard and have the effect of weak affirmatives. **—in the negative** In a manner indicating refusal or denial. **—neg′a·tive·ly** *adv.* **—neg′a·tive·ness** *n.*

negative positive

neg·lect [ni·glekt′] 1 *v.* To fail to care for or attend to: to *neglect* a child. 2 *v.* To omit or fail to do: I *neglected* to mail these letters. 3 *v.* To pay no attention to; ignore: They *neglected* his advice. 4 *n.* The act of neglecting. 5 *n.* A neglected condition; want of attention or care. **—neg·lect′er** *n.*

neg·lect·ful [ni·glekt′fəl] *adj.* Heedless; careless.

neg·li·gee or **neg·li·gée** [neg′li·zhā′ *or* neg′li·zhā′] *n.* A loose dressing gown worn by women.

neg·li·gent [neg′lə·jənt] *adj.* 1 Failing to do what one should; showing neglect. 2 Failing to use proper caution; reckless. **—neg′li·gence** *n.* **—neg′li·gent·ly** *adv.*

neg·li·gi·ble [neg′lə·jə·bəl] *adj.* Not worth considering; too small to bother with.

ne·go·ti·a·ble [ni·gō′shē·ə·bəl *or* ni·gō′shə·bəl] *adj.* Capable of being sold or transferred to another person: a *negotiable* check.

ne·go·ti·ate [ni·gō′shē·āt′] *v.* **ne·go·ti·at·ed, ne·go·ti·at·ing** 1 To bargain and talk with others in hope of reaching an agreement. 2 To arrange by negotiating: to *negotiate* a treaty. 3 To sell or transfer ownership of, as a bond. 4 *informal* To manage to climb, cross, or scale: to *negotiate* a steep hill. **—ne·go′ti·a′tion** *n.* **—ne·go′ti·a′tor** *n.*

Ne·gro [nē′grō] *adj., n., pl.* **Ne·groes** 1 *n.* A member of a people of African origin; Black. 2 *n.* A person with any Negro ancestors. 3 *adj.* Of or having to do with Negroes.

Ne·groid [nē′groid′] *adj.* Having to do with, like, or characteristic of Negroes.

neigh [nā] 1 *v.* To make the cry of a horse. 2 *n.* The cry made by a horse.

neigh·bor [nā′bər] 1 *n.* A person or thing that is near another. 2 *n.* A person living near another. 3 *v.* To be near to; border on: Their land *neighbors* mine. 4 *n.* A fellow human being.

neigh·bor·hood [nā′bər·ho͝od′] *n.* 1 A small area or section of a city or town, often having a distinctive quality or character. 2 The people living in such a section. **—in the neighborhood of** 1 Near; close to. 2 *informal* About; approximately.

neigh·bor·ing [nā′bər·ing] *adj.* Located or living nearby; adjacent.

neigh·bor·ly [nā′bər·lē] *adj.* Being or like a good or pleasant neighbor; friendly; considerate. **—neigh′·bor·li·ness** *n.*

nei·ther [nē′t͟hər *or* nī′t͟hər] 1 *adj., pron.* Not one nor the other; not either: *Neither* plan is any good; *Neither* will do. 2 *conj.* Not either; not: *neither* rain nor snow. 3 *conj.* Nor yet: They can't read; *neither* can they write. ◆ *Neither* should be followed by *nor,* not *or*: He can *neither* read *nor* write. ◆ See EITHER.

nem·a·tode [nem′ə·tōd′] *n.* Another word for ROUNDWORM.

nem·e·sis [nem′ə·sis] *n., pl.* **nem·e·ses** [nem′ə·sēz] 1 A person or thing that is the cause of just punishment. 2 Just punishment or vengeance. 3 A problem or opponent that one cannot overcome or master: Arithmetic is my *nemesis.*

neo- A prefix meaning: 1 New, most recent, as in *Neophyte.* 2 In a new form, as in *neoliberals.*

ne·o·dym·i·um [nē′ō·dim′ē·əm] *n.* A metallic element found in rare earths. ◆ See RARE-EARTH ELEMENT.

Ne·o·lith·ic [nē′ə·lith′ik] *adj.* Of or having to do with the late Stone Age, when people were making and using polished stone weapons and tools.

ne·ol·o·gism [nē·ol′ə·jiz′əm] *n.* A new word or phrase or a new meaning for an existing one.

ne·on [nē′on] *n.* A colorless, odorless gaseous element that does not combine easily with other elements, and occurs in small amounts in air.

neon sign A sign or display in which glass tubes filled with neon or other gases are bent into designs and shapes, often of letters, and made to glow in colors by passing electricity through them.

ne·o·phyte [nē′ə·fīt′] *n.* 1 A person who is newly converted to a religion or has recently joined a religious order; proselyte or novice. 2 Any beginner or novice; tyro; apprentice.

Ne·pa·lese [nep′ə·lēz′] *adj., n., pl.* **Ne·pa·lese** 1 *adj.* Of or from Nepal. 2 *n.* A person born in or a citizen of Nepal.

neph·ew [nef′yo͞o] *n.* A son of one's brother or sister, or of one's brother-in-law or sister-in-law.

a	add	**i**	it	**o͝o**	took	**oi**	oil
ā	ace	**ī**	ice	**o͞o**	pool	**ou**	pout
â	care	**o**	odd	**u**	up	**ng**	ring
ä	palm	**ō**	open	**û**	burn	**th**	thin
e	end	**ô**	order	**yo͞o**	fuse	**t͟h**	this
ē	equal					**zh**	vision

ə = { a in *above* e in *sicken* i in *possible* / o in *melon* u in *circus* }

ne·phri·tis [ni·frī'tis] *n.* Inflammation of the kidneys.

ne·phro·sis [ni·frō'səs] *n.* A noninflammatory kidney disease characterized by degeneration of the renal tubules.

nep·o·tism [nep'ə·tiz'əm] *n.* The practice of giving jobs or special favors to relatives, especially when done by government officials.

Nep·tune [nep't(y)ōōn'] *n.* **1** In Roman myths, the god of the sea. His Greek name was Poseidon. **2** A planet of the solar system, fourth largest in size and eighth in distance from the sun.

Neptune

nep·tu·ni·um [nep·t(y)ōō'·nē·əm] *n.* A radioactive metallic element present in traces in uranium ores and produced as a by-product of plutonium production in nuclear reactors.

Ne·re·id [nir'ē·id] *n., pl.* **Ne·re·i·des** [ni·rē'ə·dēz] or **Ne·re·ids** In Greek myths, one of the 50 sea nymphs who attended the god Poseidon.

nerve [nûrv] *n., v.* **nerved, nerv·ing** **1** *n.* Any of the fibers or bundles of fibers that carry impulses between the brain or spinal cord and all parts of the body. **2** *n.* Courage: to lose one's *nerve.* **3** *n. informal* Offensive boldness; impudence: You have some *nerve* to say that. **4** *v.* To make strong or courageous: He *nerved* himself to take the test. **5** *n.* (*usually pl.*) Self-control: cool *nerves.* **6** *n.* (*usually pl.*) A feeling of being very upset: a bad case of *nerves.* **7** *n.* A vein in a leaf. **—get on one's nerves** *informal* To annoy or upset. **—strain every nerve** To try with all of one's strength.

nerve cell Another name for NEURON.

nerve fiber Any of the threadlike axons and dendrites that make up a nerve cell.

nerve·less [nûrv'lis] *adj.* **1** Lacking strength; feeble; slack: a *nerveless* arm. **2** Having no nerves, as the hair or nails. **—nerve'less·ly** *adv.* **—nerve'·less·ness** *n.*

nerve-rack·ing or **nerve-wracking** [nûrv'rak'·ing] *adj.* Extremely irritating, annoying, or trying: a *nerve-racking* ordeal.

ner·vous [nûr'vəs] *adj.* **1** Showing unusual or abnormal restlessness, anxiety, or tension. **2** Fearful; timid. **3** Energetic or forceful: a *nervous* style of writing. **4** Of or having to do with nerves: a *nervous* disorder. **—ner'vous·ly** *adv.* **—ner'vous·ness** *n.*

nervous breakdown A severely impairing mental disorder or emotional disturbance.

nervous system In vertebrates, the network of neurons and nerve fibers, with the brain and spinal cord as centers, by which impulses are carried throughout the body.

nerv·y [nûr'vē] *adj.* **nerv·i·er, nerv·i·est** **1** *informal* Insolently bold; rude; impudent: a *nervy* remark. **2** Having or showing strength or courage: a *nervy* climb. **—nerv'i·ness** *n.*

-ness A suffix meaning: **1** The condition or quality of being, as in *darkness.* **2** An instance of being, as in *kindness.*

nest [nest] **1** *n.* A structure built by a bird for laying its eggs and raising its young. **2** *n.* A place in which insects, mice, squirrels, and other animals live and raise their young. **3** *v.* To build or occupy a nest: Rats *nested* in the cellar. **4** *n.* The group of birds, animals, or insects that live in a nest. **5** *n.* A snug or cozy place. **6** *n.* A place full of something bad or dangerous: a *nest* of pirates. **7** *n.* A set of similar objects of different sizes, made to fit into one another: a *nest* of mixing bowls.

nest egg A sum of money saved up for the future.

nes·tle [nes'əl] *v.* **nes·tled, nes·tling** **1** To lie closely or snugly; cuddle: The kittens *nestled* together. **2** To place or press snugly or with affection: They *nestled* the frightened children on their shoulders. **3** To settle down in comfort: to *nestle* among pillows. **4** To lie sheltered or partly hidden: The hut *nestled* in a shady valley.

nest·ling [nes(t)'ling] *n.* A bird too young to leave the nest.

net[1] [net] *n., v.* **net·ted, net·ting** **1** *n.* A fabric, as one made of thread, cord, or rope, knotted or woven together in an open pattern. **2** *v.* To make into a net. **3** *n.* An object made from fabric that is netted: a fish *net*; a tennis *net.* **4** *v.* To catch in or as in a net. **5** *n.* A delicate, meshed, lacelike fabric. **6** *v.* To cover or shelter with a net. **7** *n.* Anything that traps: a *net* of falsehoods.

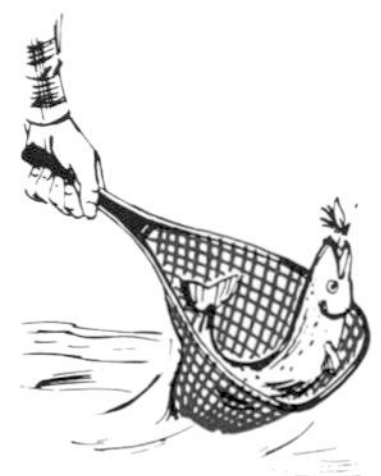
Net

net[2] [net] *adj., n., v.* **net·ted, net·ting** **1** *adj.* Remaining after all necessary subtractions have been made, as of losses, taxes, expenses, or weight of container. **2** *n.* Something net, as profit or weight. **3** *v.* To earn or produce as a net amount.

NET National Educational Television.

Neth. Netherlands.

neth·er [neth'ər] *adj.* Located beneath or below.

Neth·er·land·er [neth'ər·lan'dər] *n.* A person born in or a citizen of the Netherlands.

neth·er·most [neth'ər·mōst'] *adj.* Lowest.

net·ting [net'ing] *n.* A fabric or material having large open spaces in it; net.

net·tle [net'(ə)l] *n., v.* **net·tled, net·tling** **1** *n.* A plant with hairline needles that sting when touched. **2** *v.* To annoy or irritate: The passengers were *nettled* by the delay.

net·work [net'wûrk'] *n.* **1** Netting. **2** Any system having parts that cross or are connected somewhat like the cords of a net. **3** A chain of radio or television broadcasting stations. **4** A group of computers or other electronic devices connected by communication lines. ◆ *Network,* formed by combining *net* and *work*, originally referred only to actual netting, but now is more commonly used of things that crisscross and connect in many places, like netting: a *network* of roads; a radio *network.*

net·work·ing [net′wûrk′ing] *n.* Getting assistance from a group of others to do or get something, especially to advance in business.
neu·ral [n(y)o͝or′əl] *adj.* Of or having to do with a nerve, neuron, or the nervous system.
neu·ral·gi·a [n(y)o͝o·ral′jə] *n.* A sharp pain along the course of a nerve. **—neu·ral′gic** *adj.*
neu·ri·tis [n(y)o͝o·rī′tis] *n.* Inflammation of a nerve.
neu·rol·o·gy [n(y)o͝o·rol′ə·jē] *n.* The branch of medicine that deals with the nervous system and its disorders. **—neu·rol′o·gist** *n.*
neu·ron [n(y)o͝or′on] *n.* The basic cell unit of nerves, having a nucleus and many nerve fibers.
neu·ro·sis [n(y)o͝o·rō′sis] *n., pl.* **neu·ro·ses** [n(y)o͝o·rō′·sēz] A mental or emotional disturbance marked by such emotions as unusual anxiety, depression, or fear, usually not very serious.
neu·rot·ic [n(y)o͝o·rot′ik] 1 *adj.* Of, resulting from, or suffering from a neurosis. 2 *n.* A neurotic person. **—neu·rot′ic·al·ly** *adv.*
neut. neuter.
neu·ter [n(y)o͞o′tər] 1 *adj.* Neither masculine nor feminine, as a noun or pronoun. 2 *n.* A neuter word. 3 *n.* The neuter gender: The pronoun *it* is in the *neuter.* 4 *adj.* Having no sex or having neither sex developed: Worker bees are *neuter.* 5 *n.* A neuter plant or animal.
neu·tral [n(y)o͞o′trəl] 1 *adj.* Not interfering or taking sides, as in a dispute, contest, or war. 2 *adj.* Belonging to none of the opposing sides: *neutral* territory. 3 *adj.* Belonging to neither one category nor the other; in the middle. 4 *adj.* Neither acid nor alkaline. 5 *adj.* Having neither a positive nor negative electric charge. 6 *adj.* Not strongly defined; middling: a *neutral* color. 7 *n.* A neutral person or thing. 8 *n.* The position of gearwheels in which the teeth are not meshed.
neu·tral·ism [n(y)o͞o′trəl·iz′əm] *n.* The policy of staying neutral, especially of a nation that does not ally itself with other warring nations.
neu·tral·i·ty [n(y)o͞o·tral′ə·tē] *n.* A neutral condition, attitude, or policy, especially of a nation in time of war.
neu·tral·ize [n(y)o͞o′trəl·īz′] *v.* **neu·tral·ized, neu·tral·iz·ing** 1 To declare (as a nation or area) neutral in time of war. 2 To offset or make ineffective by an opposite force: Vinegar *neutralizes* an alkali. **—neu·tral·i·za·tion** [n(y)o͞o′trəl·ə·zā′shən] *n.* **—neu′·tral·iz′er** *n.*
neutral vowel Another expression for SCHWA.
neu·tri·no [n(y)o͞o·trē′nō] *n., pl.* **neu·tri·nos** An atomic particle that is stable, electrically neutral, has a mass near zero, and rarely interacts with other matter.
neu·tron [n(y)o͞o′tron′] *n.* A particle found in the nucleus of most atoms, having no electrical charge and a mass about equal to that of a proton.
Nev. Nevada.
nev·er [nev′ər] *adv.* 1 Not at any time; not ever. 2 Not at all; certainly not: *Never* fear.
nev·er·more [nev′ər·môr′] *adv.* Never again.
nev·er·the·less [nev′ər·thə·les′] 1 *adv.* In any case; anyhow: It rained, but we went *nevertheless.* 2 *conj.* But; however: It was cold; *nevertheless* the game was played.
new [n(y)o͞o] 1 *adj.* Recently made, grown, or constructed: *new* leaves. 2 *adj.* Found, invented, or arrived at for the first time: a *new* theory. 3 *adj.* Having been in a place, condition, or relationship for only a short time: a *new* partner. 4 *adj.* Not used or worn: a *new* piano. 5 *adj.* Changed for the better; renewed: *new* courage. 6 *adj.* Not trained or experienced: *new* at a job. 7 *adj.* Following an earlier one; beginning over: a *new* moon. 8 *adj.* Additional; further: a *new* supply. 9 *adv.* Newly; recently: used only in combination, as in *newborn* lamb. **—new′ness** *n.*
new·born [n(y)o͞o′bôrn′] *adj.* 1 Just lately born. 2 Born again; renewed: *newborn* hope.
new·com·er [n(y)o͞o′kum′ər] *n.* A person who has recently arrived.
New Deal The political, economic, and social policies and measures advocated by President Franklin D. Roosevelt.
new·el [n(y)o͞o′əl] *n.* The post that supports an end of the handrail of a staircase.

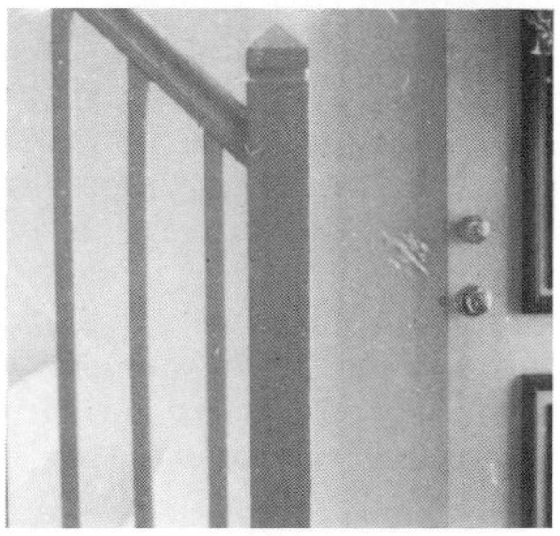
Newel

New Eng·land·er [ing′glən·dər] A person born or living in New England.
new·fan·gled [n(y)o͞o′·fang′gəld] *adj.* 1 Of the latest style; modern. 2 Fond of novelty.
Newfoundland standard time (*sometimes written* **Newfoundland Standard Time**) The standard time observed in the province of Newfoundland. It is three and a half hours earlier than Greenwich time.
new·ly [n(y)o͞o′lē] *adv.* Very recently; lately: a *newly* bought radio.
new·ly·wed [n(y)o͞o′lē·wed′] *n.* A recently married person.
new math A method of teaching basic mathematics that stresses set theory and fundamental understanding of concepts.
new moon The phase of the moon when it is invisible or is seen as a small, thin crescent.
new penny *pl.* **new pence** A British unit of money equal to 1/100 pound.
news [n(y)o͞oz] *n.pl.* (*used with singular verb*) 1 Information about events that have just taken place, as reported regularly in a newspaper or on the radio or television. 2 Any new information.
news·cast [n(y)o͞oz′kast′] *n.* A radio or television broadcast of news. ◆ *Newscast* comes from combining *news* (*broad*)*cast.* **—news′cast′er** *n.*
news·deal·er [n(y)o͞oz′dē′lər] *n.* A person who sells newspapers and magazines.
news·let·ter [n(y)o͞oz′let′ər] *n.* A printed letter or report for circulation to a special group, often sent regularly, and containing news and advice.
news·man [n(y)o͞oz′man′] *n., pl.* **news·men** [n(y)o͞oz′·men′] A person whose job is gathering, reporting,

a	add	**i**	it	**o͝o**	took	**oi**	oil
ā	ace	**ī**	ice	**o͞o**	pool	**ou**	pout
â	care	**o**	odd	**u**	up	**ng**	ring
ä	palm	**ō**	open	**û**	burn	**th**	thin
e	end	**ô**	order	**yo͞o**	fuse	**th**	this
ē	equal					**zh**	vision

ə = a in *above*, e in *sicken*, i in *possible*, o in *melon*, u in *circus*

or commenting on news, as for a newspaper or a radio or television station.

news·pa·per [n(y)ōōz′pā′pər] *n.* A publication, usually put out daily or weekly, containing news, editorials, advertisements, and other items.

news·pa·per·man [n(y)ōōz′pā′pər·man′] *n., pl.* **news·pa·per·men** [n(y)ōōz′pā′pər·men′] **1** A writer for or an editor of a newspaper. **2** A person who owns or manages a newspaper.

news·pa·per·wom·an [n(y)ōōz′pā′pər·wŏŏm′ən] *n., pl.* **news·pa·per·wom·en** [n(y)ōōz′pā′pər·wim′in] **1** A woman who writes for or edits a newspaper. **2** A woman who owns or manages a newspaper.

news·print [n(y)ōōz′print′] *n.* The thin, inexpensive paper on which newspapers are usually printed.

news·reel [n(y)ōōz′rēl′] *n.* A news report in the form of a motion picture.

news·stand [n(y)ōōz′stand′] *n. U.S.* A stand at which newspapers and magazines are sold.

news·wom·an [n(y)ōōz′wŏŏm′ən] *n., pl.* **news·wom·en** [n(y)ōōz′wim′in] A woman whose job is gathering, reporting, or commenting on news, as for a newspaper or a radio or television station.

news·wor·thy [n(y)ōōz′wûr′thē] *adj.* Having enough importance or interest for the public to be printed in a newspaper.

news·y [n(y)ōō′zē] *adj.* **news·i·er, news·i·est** *informal* Full of news.

newt [n(y)ōōt] *n.* A small salamander that lives both on land and in the water.

Newt

New Testament The part of the Bible containing the life and teaching of Jesus as told by his followers, and their acts and teachings.

new·ton [n(y)ōōt′(ə)n] *n.* In the mks system, a unit of force equal to the force necessary to accelerate a mass of one kilogram one meter per second per second.

New Year or **New Year's Day** January 1, the first day of the year.

New Zea·land·er [zē′lən·dər] A person born in or a citizen of New Zealand.

next [nekst] **1** *adj.* Following immediately, as in time, order, or position. **2** *adv.* In the nearest place or time: My brother sits *next* to me; The teacher called on me *next.* **3** *adj.* Adjoining or nearest in space: the *next* town. **4** *prep.* Nearest to: *next* his heart. **5** *adv.* On the nearest following occasion: when *next* we see them. **—next door 1** The next house, building, or apartment. **2** In, at, or to the next building. **—next to 1** Close to; beside: Park your car *next to* mine. **2** Nearly or almost; practically: I bought the old bicycle for *next to* nothing.

Nez Percé [nez′ pûrs′ *or* nā·per·sā′] *pl.* **Nez Percé** [nez′ pûrs′ *or* nā·per·sā′] or **Nez Per·ces** [nez′pûr′·siz] **1** A tribe of North American Indians once living in Idaho, Oregon, and Washington. **2** A member of this tribe. **3** The language of this tribe. ◆ *Nez Percé* comes from the French words meaning *pierced nose.*

NFL or **N.F.L.** National Football League.

Nfld. Newfoundland.

n.g. or **N.G.** no good.

N.G. **1** National Guard. **2** New Guinea.

NH Postal Service abbreviation of New Hampshre.

N.H. New Hampshire.

NHL or **N.H.L.** National Hockey League.

Ni The symbol for the element nickel.

N.I. Northern Ireland.

ni·a·cin [nī′ə·sin] *n.* A member of the vitamin B complex, found in such foods as meat, eggs, milk, and wheat germ. Lack of it causes pellagra.

Ni·ag·a·ra [nī·ag′(ə·)ra] *n.* A torrent; flood.

nib [nib] *n.* **1** The point of a pen. **2** The pointed part of anything; tip. **3** The beak of a bird.

nib·ble [nib′əl] *v.* **nib·bled, nib·bling,** *n.* **1** *v.* To eat or bite in a quick, gentle way: to *nibble* lettuce. **2** *n.* The act of nibbling. **3** *n.* A small bit of food; small bite.

Nic·a·ra·guan [nik′ə·rä′gwən] **1** *adj.* Of or from Nicaragua. **2** *n.* A person born in or a citizen of Nicaragua.

nice [nīs] *adj.* **nic·er, nic·est** **1** Pleasing or suitable; agreeable: *nice* manners. **2** Friendly or kind: *nice* neighbors. **3** Precise or needing exactness; fine: a *nice* distinction; a *nice* fit. **—nice and** Very; pleasantly: The soup was *nice and* hot; The moon was *nice and* bright. **—nice′ly** *adv.* ◆ *Nice,* which refers to something attractive or pleasant, originally meant *ignorant, foolish,* or *stupid.* Later, *nice* meant *precise* or *accurate,* and it still does, although it is now more often used loosely to indicate general approval: *nice* people; *nice* weather.

ni·ce·ty [nī′sə·tē] *n., pl.* **ni·ce·ties** **1** A fine or delicate point; detail: the *niceties* of grammar. **2** A delicacy or refinement: *niceties* of living. **3** Great refinement or delicacy, as of taste; fussiness. **4** Exactness; precision or accuracy. **—to a nicety** Exactly right: cooked *to a nicety.*

niche [nich] *n., v.* **niched, nich·ing** **1** *n.* A recess or hollow in a wall, as for a statue. **2** *n.* A position or situation that is suitable. **3** *v.* To place in a niche.

Niche

Nich·o·las [nik′ə·ləs] *n.* **1** A fourth-century Christian bishop, patron saint of Russia, of seamen, and of children. **2** Santa Claus.

nick [nik] **1** *n.* A slight cut, notch, or dent in a surface or edge. **2** *v.* To make a nick on or in. **3** *v.* To barely make contact with; graze: The ball *nicked* the pitcher's ear. **—in the nick of time** Barely soon enough; just in time.

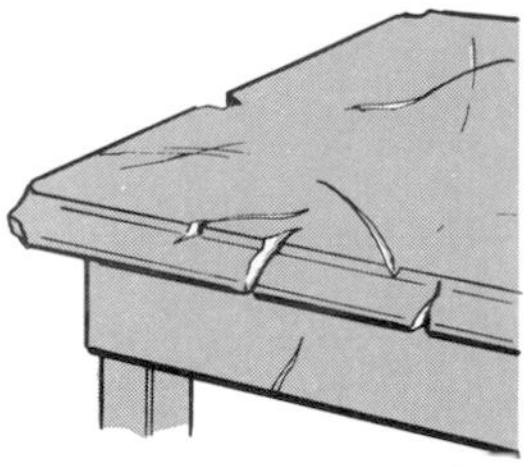
A badly nicked table

nick·el [nik′əl] *n.* **1** A hard metallic element, having the color of silver and used in making alloys and in electroplating metals. **2** A five-cent coin of the U.S. and Canada.

nickel silver Any of various silver-white alloys of nickel, copper, and zinc.

nick·nack [nik′nak′] *n.* Another spelling of KNICKKNACK.

nick·name [nik′nām′] *n., v.* **nick·named, nick·nam·ing** **1** *n.* A familiar or shortened form of a proper name, as *Liz* for *Elizabeth.* **2** *n.* A descriptive name, as *Honest Abe.* **3** *v.* To give a nickname to.

nic·o·tine [nik′ə·tēn′] *n.* A bitter, oily, poisonous compound obtained from dried tobacco leaves.
nic·o·tin·ic acid [nik′ə·tin′ik] Another name for NIACIN.
niece [nēs] *n.* A daughter of one's brother or sister, or of one's brother-in-law or sister-in-law.
nif·ty [nif′tē] *adj.* **nif·ti·er, nif·ti·est** *slang* Stylish; pleasing; attractive.
Ni·ge·ri·an [nī·jir′ē·ən] 1 *adj.* Of or from Nigeria. 2 *n.* A person born in or a citizen of Nigeria.
nig·gard [nig′ərd] 1 *n.* A stingy person; miser. 2 *adj.* Stingy; miserly.
nig·gard·ly [nig′ərd·lē] 1 *adj.* Very stingy. 2 *adj.* Small or scanty: a *niggardly* piece of cake. 3 *adv.* In a stingy way. **—nig′gard·li·ness** *n.*
nigh [nī] 1 *prep.* Near: *nigh* home. 2 *adv.* Near: as summer draws *nigh.* 3 *adv.* Nearly; almost: *nigh* a year. 4 *adj.* Close; near.
night [nīt] *n.* 1 The period from sunset to sunrise, especially when it is dark. 2 *adj. use: night* clothes. 3 Darkness; the dark. 4 A condition of darkness, misery, or ignorance.
night blindness The condition of not being able to see normally in a dim light. It is often caused by a deficiency of vitamin A.
night·cap [nīt′kap′] *n.* 1 A cap worn in bed at night. 2 A relaxing drink taken at bedtime.
night·clothes [nīt′klō(t͟h)z′] *n.pl.* Clothes, such as nightgowns or pajamas, designed to be worn in bed.
night·club [nīt′klub′] *n.* A restaurant open until late at night and providing music, dancing, and other entertainment.
night crawl·er [krô′lər] A large earthworm that comes to the surface of the ground at night. It is often used as fishing bait.
night·fall [nīt′fôl′] *n.* The close of day.
night·gown [nīt′goun′] *n.* A loose garment worn in bed.
night·hawk [nīt′hôk′] *n.* 1 Any of several birds with long wings, related to the whippoorwill, that fly mostly at night. 2 A night owl.

Nighthawk

night·in·gale [nīt′ən·gāl′] *n.* A small, reddish brown, European bird. The male, who sings until late at night, is noted for its song.
night·light [nīt′līt′] *n.* A dim light kept burning all night, as at a bedside.
night·ly [nīt′lē] 1 *adj.* Done at or happening each night: a *nightly* task. 2 *adv.* Every night or at night: The film is shown *nightly.*
night·mare [nīt′mâr′] *n.* A horrible and frightening dream. 2 Any horrible or frightening experience: the *nightmare* of war.
night owl A person who likes to stay up late at night.
night·shade [nīt′·shād′] *n.* Any of several plants related to the potato and tomato and bearing black or red berries. Some are poisonous, especially the **deadly nightshade** or belladonna.

Nightshade

night·shirt [nīt′shûrt′] *n.* A long, loose garment worn in bed.
night·stand [nīt′stand′] *n.* A night table.
night·stick [nīt′stik′] *n.* Another word for BILLY.
night table A small table or stand at the side of a bed.
night·time [nīt′tīm′] *n.* The time from sunset to sunrise, or from dark to dawn.
ni·hil·ism [nī′ə·liz′əm] *n.* Rejection of all beliefs, institutions, and values. **—ni′hil·ist** *n.* **—ni′hil·is′·tic** *adj.*
nil [nil] *n.* Nothing: The profits are *nil.*
nim·ble [nim′bəl] *adj.* **nim·bler, nim·blest** 1 Light and quick in movement; lively: a *nimble* dancer. 2 Quick in grasping or understanding; keen: a *nimble* mind. **—nim′ble·ness** *n.* **—nim′bly** *adv.*
nim·bo·stra·tus [nim′bō·strā′təs *or* nim′bō·strat′əs] *n.* A type of cloud that is low, dark, and layerlike, and that usually brings precipitation.
nim·bus [nim′bəs] *n., pl.* **nim·bus·es** or **nim·bi** [nim′·bī] 1 A halo, as shown behind the head of a holy person in a painting. 2 Any atmosphere of glory or fame about a person or thing. 3 A rain or snow cloud.

Nimbus

Nim·rod [nim′rod′] *n.* 1 In the Bible, a great hunter, the grandson of Noah. 2 Any hunter.
nin·com·poop [nin′kəm·po͞op′] *n.* An idiot or fool; stupid person.
nine or **9** [nīn] *n., adj.* One more than eight.
nine·pins [nīn′pinz′] *n.pl.* (*often used with singular verb*) A bowling game somewhat like tenpins, using nine large wooden pins.
nine·teen or **19** [nīn′tēn′] *n., adj.* One more than eighteen.
nine·teenth or **19th** [nīn′tēnth′] 1 *adj.* Next after the eighteenth. 2 *n.* The nineteenth one. 3 *adj.* Being one of nineteen equal parts. 4 *n.* A nineteenth part.
nine·ti·eth or **90th** [nīn′tē·ith] 1 *adj.* Tenth in order after the eightieth. 2 *n.* The ninetieth one. 3 *adj.* Being one of ninety equal parts. 4 *n.* A ninetieth part.
nine·ty or **90** [nīn′tē] *n., pl.* **nine·ties** or **90's,** *adj.* 1 *n., adj.* Ten more than eighty. 2 *n.* (*pl.*) The years between the age of 90 and 100.
nin·ny [nin′ē] *n., pl.* **nin·nies** A fool; dunce.
ninth or **9th** [nīnth] 1 *adj.* Next after the eighth. 2 *n.* The ninth one. 3 *adj.* Being one of nine equal parts. 4 *n.* A ninth part.
Ni·o·be [nī′ə·bē] *n.* In Greek myths, a weeping mother whose great pride in her children had led

N

a	add	**i**	it	**o͝o**	took	**oi**	oil		
ā	ace	**ī**	ice	**o͞o**	pool	**ou**	pout		
â	care	**o**	odd	**u**	up	**ng**	ring		
ä	palm	**ō**	open	**û**	burn	**th**	thin		
e	end	**ô**	order	**yo͞o**	fuse	**t͟h**	this		
ē	equal					**zh**	vision		

ə = { a in *above* e in *sicken* i in *possible* / o in *melon* u in *circus* }

the gods to kill them. Zeus turned her to stone, from which her tears continued to flow.

ni·o·bi·um [nī·ō′bē·əm] *n.* A soft, white metallic element resembling tantalum and used chiefly in alloys.

nip[1] [nip] *v.* **nipped, nip·ping,** *n.* **1** *v.* To pinch or bite sharply with the fingers, the teeth, or with claws, as a crab. **2** *n.* A sudden, sharp pinch or bite. **3** *v.* To remove by pinching or clipping: to *nip* off dead blossoms from a plant. **4** *v.* To injure or pain as by cold: A sharp wind *nipped* our ears; The frost *nipped* our plants. **5** *n.* Severe cold or frost: the *nip* of winter. **—nip and tuck** Very close, even, or uncertain. **—nip in the bud** To stop at the very beginning or outset.

nip[2] [nip] *n.* A small drink or sip of liquor.

nip·per [nip′ər] *n.* **1** A person or thing that nips. **2** The claw of a crab or lobster. **3** (*pl.*) Any of various tools used for nipping or grasping, as pliers or pincers.

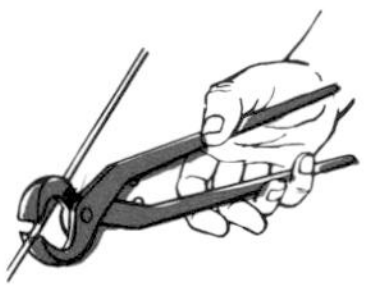
Nippers

nip·ple [nip′əl] *n.* **1** The pointed projection on the breast or udder of a mammal through which the milk passes to the baby or young animal. **2** A rubber or plastic mouthpiece through which a baby sucks liquid from a bottle.

nip·py [nip′ē] *adj.* **nip·pi·er, nip·pi·est** Biting and sharp, as cold weather.

N. Ire. Northern Ireland.

nir·va·na [nir·vä′nə] *n.* **1** In Buddhism, a state of complete bliss that is free from all passion, desire, or suffering. **2** Any completely happy condition.

Ni·sei [nē′sā] *n., pl.* **Nisei** or **Niseis** A native-born American whose parents were Japanese immigrants.

nit [nit] *n.* **1** The egg of a louse or other parasitic insect. **2** A young louse.

ni·ter [nī′tər] *n.* Either of two minerals containing nitrates, once much used in manufacturing fertilizer and explosives.

nit·pick [nit′pik′] *v.* To look for or criticize unimportant details; fuss. **—nit′pick′er** *n.*

nit-pick·ing [nit′pik′ing] *n.* Criticism of unimportant details.

ni·trate [nī′trāt′] *n.* Any of a large group of chemical compounds derived from nitric acid, especially its salts.

ni·tric [nī′trik] *adj* Of, containing, or derived from nitrogen.

nitric acid A strong, colorless liquid containing nitrogen, that fumes in air and eats into cloth, flesh, and most metals.

ni·tro·gen [nī′trə·jən] *n.* An odorless, colorless, gaseous element that makes up nearly four-fifths of the earth's atmosphere. It forms many useful compounds and is a necessary element in all living things.

nitrogen cycle The series of chemical changes by which nitrogen from the atmosphere is made available to and used by living things and released again.

ni·tro·gen-fix·ing bacteria [nī′trə·jən·fik′sing] Any of the bacteria in the soil that take nitrogen from the air and make it into compounds that can be used by living things.

ni·trog·e·nous [nī·troj′ə·nəs] *adj.* Having to do with or containing nitrogen.

ni·tro·glyc·er·in or **ni·tro·glyc·er·ine** [nī′trō·glis′·ər·in] *n.* A thick, oily, highly explosive liquid, used in medicine and in making dynamite.

ni·trous [nī′trəs] *adj.* Of, containing, or derived from nitrogen.

nitrous acid An unstable compound of nitrogen, hydrogen, and oxygen, occurring only in solution or in the form of its salts.

nitrous oxide A gas sometimes used as an anesthetic, especially by dentists.

nit·wit [nit′wit′] *n.* A silly or stupid person.

nix [niks] *slang* **1** *n.* Nothing. **2** *adv.* No. **3** *interj.* Don't do that! Stop! **4** *v.* To give a negative reply to; reject: to *nix* the plan for a meeting.

NJ Postal Service abbreviation of New Jersey.

N.J. New Jersey.

NLRB or **N.L.R.B.** National Labor Relations Board.

NM Postal Service abbreviation of New Mexico.

N. Mex. New Mexico.

NNE north-northeast.

NNW north-northwest.

no or **no., No** or **No.** **1** north. **2** northern. **3** number.

no [nō] *adv., adj., n., pl.* **noes** **1** *adv.* A word used to show that one disagrees, denies, or doesn't want something: Don't you like this hat? *No.*; are you feeling ill? *No.* **2** *n.* A negative reply: They just won't take *no* for an answer. **3** *n.* A negative vote or voter: The *noes* have it. **4** *adj.* Not any: *No* seats are left. **5** *adv.* Not at all: I can wait *no* longer. ◆ Do not use *no* with another negative, as in "I don't have no gum." Use either "I *have no* gum" or "I *don't* have *any* gum."

No The symbol for the element nobelium.

No·ah [nō′ə] *n.* In the Bible, a good man who, at God's command, built an ark that saved him, his family, and two of every kind of animal from the Flood.

no·be·li·um [nō·bē′lē·əm] *n.* A human-made radioactive metallic element with a half-life of about three minutes for its most stable isotope.

No·bel prize [nō·bel′] One of the six prizes awarded each year for great work in physics, chemistry, literature, physiology or medicine, economics, and the advancement of world peace.

no·bil·i·ty [nō·bil′ə·tē] *n., pl.* **no·bil·i·ties** **1** In certain countries, a group of people who have hereditary titles and rank, as kings, queens, duchesses, dukes, countesses, and earls. **2** The condition or quality of being noble.

no·ble [nō′bəl] *adj.* **nob·ler, nob·lest,** *n.* **1** *adj.* Having or showing outstandingly good or moral qualities: a *noble* human being. **2** *adj.* Of or having a high rank or title; aristocratic. **3** *n.* A member of the nobility. **4** *adj.* Impressive and handsome: a *noble* face. **—no′ble·ness** *n.* **—no′bly** *adv.*

no·ble·man [nō′bəl·mən] *n., pl.* **no·ble·men** [nō′bəl·mən] A person of noble rank.

no·ble·wom·an [nō′bəl·wo͝om′ən] *n., pl.* **no·ble·wom·en** [nō′bəl·wim′in] A woman of noble rank.

no·bod·y [nō′bod′ē] *pron., n., pl.* **no·bod·ies** **1** *pron.* Not anybody; no one at all. **2** *n.* A person of no importance or influence.

noc·tur·nal [nok·tûr′nəl] *adj.* **1** Of or happening at night: *nocturnal* noises. **2** Active or blooming at night, as certain animals or plants. **—noc·tur′·nal·ly** *adv.*

noc·turne [nok′tûrn′] *n.* In music, a dreamy or melancholy composition, often for the piano.

nod [nod] *n., v.* **nod·ded, nod·ding** **1** *v.* To lower the head forward briefly, as in agreement or greeting.

2 *v.* To let the head fall forward, as when sleepy. **3** *n.* The act of nodding the head. **4** *v.* To sway or bend at the top or upper part.

node [nōd] *n.* A swelling or knob of tissue: a lymph *node.* **2** A knot or joint on the stem of a plant from which leaves grow. **—no'dal** *adj.*

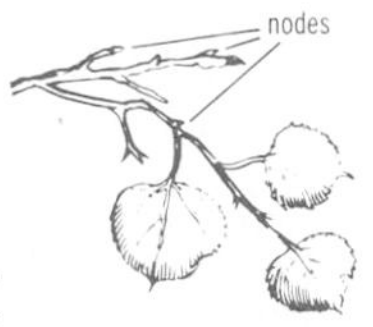

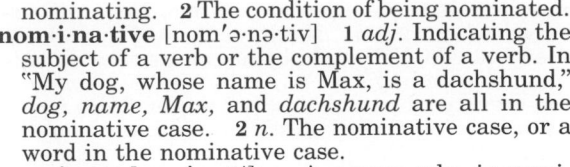

nod·ule [noj'o͞ol *or* nod'yo͞ol] *n.* A small growth or lump in or on an animal or plant.

No·el or **No·ël** [nō·əl'] *n.* **1** Christmas. **2** (*often written* **noel** or **noël**) A Christmas carol.

nog·gin [nog'in] *n.* **1** *informal* A person's head. **2** A small mug or cup. **3** A small drink equal to one-fourth of a pint.

noise [noiz] *n., v.* **noised, nois·ing** **1** *n.* A loud, confused, disturbing sound. **2** *n.* A sound of any kind. **3** *n.* In electronics, anything that interferes with a signal in an unpredictable way; static. **4** *v.* To spread, report, or rumor: It was *noised* about that the mayor was going to run again.

noise·less [noiz'lis] *adj.* Causing or making little or no noise; quiet; silent: a *noiseless* air conditioner. **—noise'less·ly** *adv.* **—noise'less·ness** *n.*

noise·mak·er [noiz'mā'kər] *n.* Something used to make noise, as at parties and other gatherings, as a horn or rattle.

Noisemakers

noi·some [noi'səm] *adj.* **1** Foul or disgusting, especially in smell; stinking: a *noisome* sewer. **2** Harmful; injurious.

nois·y [noi'zē] *adj.* **nois·i·er, nois·i·est** **1** Making a loud noise: a *noisy* dog; a *noisy* truck. **2** Full of noise: a *noisy* street. **3** Accompanied by noise: a *noisy* argument. **—nois'i·ly** *adv.* **—nois'i·ness** *n.*

no·mad [nō'mad] *n.* **1** A member of a people moving constantly from place to place to find food and pasture. **2** *adj. use: nomad* tribes. **3** A person who wanders aimlessly from place to place.

no·mad·ic [nō·mad'ik] *adj.* **1** Moving from place to place in search of food or pasture: *nomadic* herdsmen. **2** Wandering; roaming. **—no·mad'i·cal·ly** *adv.*

no-man's-land [nō'manz'land'] *n.* **1** The land that separates opposing armies and is controlled by neither side. **2** An unowned, unclaimed, or uninhabited tract of land. **3** A place or state that is uncertain, ambiguous, or indefinite.

nom de plume [nom' də plo͞om'] A name used by a writer in place of his or her real name.

no·men·cla·ture [nō'mən·klā'chər] *n.* The system of names used to describe the various elements in a particular science or art: the *nomenclature* of zoology.

nom·i·nal [nom'ə·nəl] *adj.* **1** Existing in name only; not actual or real: a *nominal* peace. **2** Small or trifling: a *nominal* sum. **—nom'i·nal·ly** *adv.*

nom·i·nate [nom'ə·nāt'] *v.* **nom·i·nat·ed, nom·i·nat·ing** **1** To name as a candidate for an elective office: We *nominated* the leading student for class president. **2** To appoint, as to some office, duty, or honor: We *nominated* our best friend to be head of the library committee.

nom·i·na·tion [nom'ə·nā'shən] *n.* **1** The act of nominating. **2** The condition of being nominated.

nom·i·na·tive [nom'ə·nə·tiv] **1** *adj.* Indicating the subject of a verb or the complement of a verb. In "My dog, whose name is Max, is a dachshund," *dog, name, Max,* and *dachshund* are all in the nominative case. **2** *n.* The nominative case, or a word in the nominative case.

nom·i·nee [nom'ə·nē'] *n.* A person who is nominated, as for some elective office, duty, or other post.

non- A prefix meaning: Not, as in *nonaggression.* If *non-* is combined with a capitalized word, it is hyphenated, as in *non-American.* Otherwise, no hyphen is used.

non·ag·gres·sion [non'ə·gresh'ən] *n.* A holding back from aggression or attack.

non·a·gon [non'ə·gon'] *n.* A closed plane figure bounded by nine straight lines that form nine interior angles.

non·al·co·hol·ic [non'al·kə·hôl'ik] *adj.* With no alcohol in it, as a drink.

nonce [nons] *n.* The present time or occasion: now mostly used in the phrase **for the nonce,** for the time being; for the present.

nonce word A word coined for a particular use or occasion.

non·cha·lant [non'shə·länt'] *adj.* Showing a jaunty coolness; not excited or concerned: She accepted the prize with a *nonchalant* air. **—non'cha·lance'** *n.* **—non'cha·lant'ly** *adv.*

non·com·bat·ant [non'kəm·bat'ənt *or* non'kom'bə·tənt] *n.* **1** A member of the armed forces whose duties do not involve fighting, as a medical officer or chaplain. **2** A civilian in wartime.

non·com·mis·sioned officer [non'kə·mish'ənd] In the U.S. armed services, an enlisted person who ranks above a private but has no commission. Corporals and sergeants are noncommissioned officers.

non·com·mit·tal [non'kə·mit'(ə)l] *adj.* Not binding one to an opinion, attitude, or plan of action: "Maybe" is a *noncommittal* answer.

non·com·pli·ance [non'kəm·plī'əns] *n.* A refusal or failure to comply, as with a request, demand, or regulation.

non·con·duc·tor [non'kən·duk'tər] *n.* A substance that does not easily conduct certain forms of energy, as heat, sound, and electricity. Glass and rubber are nonconductors of electricity.

non·con·form·ist [non'kən·fôr'mist] *n.* **1** A person who does not conform to generally accepted beliefs and customs. **2** (*often written* **Nonconformist**) A person who does not belong to an established church, especially a British Protestant who does not belong to the Church of England. **—non'con·form'i·ty** *n.*

non·de·script [non'də·skript] *adj.* Not distinctive and thus difficult to describe.

a	add	**i**	it	**o͝o**	took	**oi**	oil
ā	ace	**ī**	ice	**o͞o**	pool	**ou**	pout
â	care	**o**	odd	**u**	up	**ng**	ring
ä	palm	**ō**	open	**û**	burn	**th**	thin
e	end	**ô**	order	**yo͞o**	fuse	**t̶h̶**	this
ē	equal					**zh**	vision

ə = {a in *above* e in *sicken* i in *possible* / o in *melon* u in *circus*}

N

none [nun] 1 *pron.* Not one; no one: *None* will arrive today. 2 *pron.* Not any: *None* of the cake is left. 3 *adv.* Not at all; by no means: The class is *none* too willing.

non·en·ti·ty [non·en′tə·tē] *n., pl.* **non·en·ti·ties** A person or thing that is of little or no importance or interest; a nothing.

non·es·sen·tial [non′ə·sen′shəl] 1 *adj.* Not essential; not really needed. 2 *n.* A person or thing that is nonessential.

none·the·less or **none the less** [nun′thə·les′] *adv.* In spite of everything; nevertheless.

non·ex·is·tent [non′ig·zis′tənt] *adj.* Not existing; not real or actual: to boast about *nonexistent* wealth. **—non′ex·is′tence** *n.*

non·fat [non′fat′] *adj.* 1 Having no fat solids. 2 Having the normal fat content removed: *nonfat* chocolate milk.

non·fic·tion [non′fik′shən] *n.* Writing that does not tell a story of made-up people or events. Books on such subjects as science and history are nonfiction. **—non′fic′tion·al** *adj.*

non·flam·ma·ble [non·flam′ə·bəl] *adj.* Not flammable; not likely to catch fire easily and burn quickly.

non·met·al [non·met′(ə)l] *n.* Any of the chemical elements that lack the characteristics of metals. Nonmetals usually gain electrons and form negative ions in chemical reactions and are poor conductors of heat and electricity in a solid state.

non·me·tal·lic [non′mə·tal′ik] *adj.* Not metal; not having the properties of a metal. Carbon, oxygen, and nitrogen are nonmetallic elements.

no-no [nō′nō′] *n., pl.* **no-no's** or **no-nos** *slang* Something that is forbidden or not acceptable.

non·pa·reil [non′pə·rel′] 1 *adj.* Having no equal; matchless. 2 *n.* A person or thing that has no equal; model of excellence.

non·par·ti·san [non·pär′tə·zən] *adj.* Not strongly supporting a person, cause, or party, especially not one political party.

non·pay·ment [non·pā′mənt] *n.* A failure to pay money that is owed.

non·plus [non·plus′ *or* non′plus] *v.* **non·plused** or **non·plussed, non·plus·ing** or **non·plus·sing** To place in a state of bewilderment or confusion: We were *nonplused* at the news.

non·poi·son·ous [non·poi′zən·əs] *adj.* Not poisonous; harmless: a *nonpoisonous* snake.

non·pro·duc·tive [non′prə·duk′tiv] *adj.* 1 Not producing that which is wanted or needed: a *nonproductive* farm. 2 Not directly producing goods: Office workers are *nonproductive* labor. **—non′pro·duc′tive·ly** *adv.* **—non′pro·duc′tive·ness** *n.*

non·prof·it [non·prof′it] *adj.* Not organized or run to make money: a *nonprofit* organization.

non·res·i·dent [non·rez′ə·dənt] 1 *adj.* Not living in the place where one works, owns property, or goes to school. 2 *n.* A person who is nonresident.

non·re·stric·tive [non′ri·strik′tiv] *adj.* In grammar, describing a word or group of words, usually an adjective clause set off by commas, that can be omitted from a sentence without changing its essential meaning, as *which is for sale* in *Our house, which is for sale, needs repairs.*

non·sec·tar·i·an [non′sek·târ′ē·ən] *adj.* Not connected with or run by a particular religious sect.

non·sense [non′sens′] *n.* Words or actions that are meaningless or silly; foolishness: Let's stop the *nonsense.*

non·sen·si·cal [non·sen′si·kəl] *adj.* Making no sense; foolish.

non·stan·dard [non·stan′dərd] *adj.* 1 Of a quality below the acceptable standard. 2 Not conforming to a level of language usage considered acceptable by educated speakers and writers: "I write good" is *nonstandard* English.

non·stop [non′stop′] *adj., adv.* Without making a stop: a *nonstop* train; to fly *nonstop.*

non·un·ion [non·yōōn′yən] *adj.* 1 Not belonging to a trade union: a *nonunion* plumber. 2 Not hiring union workers: a *nonunion* shop. 3 Not produced by union labor.

non·vi·o·lence [non·vī′ə·ləns] *n.* The principle or practice of not using violence of any kind to achieve a desired goal. **—non·vi′o·lent** *adj.* **—non·vi′o·lent·ly** *adv.*

noo·dle[1] [nōōd′(ə)l] *n.* A thin strip of dried dough, often made with eggs. ◆ *Noodle* comes from the German word *nudel.*

noodle[2] [nōōd′(ə)l] *n.* 1 A weak-minded or foolish person. 2 *slang* The head.

nook [nŏŏk] *n.* 1 A corner or alcove set off from the main part of a room: a chimney *nook.* 2 Any cozy, sheltered place: a shady *nook.*

noon [nōōn] *n.* Twelve o'clock in the daytime; midday.

noon·day [nōōn′dā′] *adj.* Of or happening at noon: the *noonday* meal.

no one No person; nobody.

noon·tide [nōōn′tīd′] *n.* Noon; midday.

noon·time [nōōn′tīm′] *n.* Noon; midday.

noose [nōōs] *n.* 1 A loop, as of rope, with a slipknot that binds more closely as it is pulled. 2 Anything that traps or binds.

Noose

nor [nôr] *conj.* And not; likewise not. ◆ *Nor* is usually paired with a negative word that precedes it, as *neither, not, no,* or *never*: The child is neither fat *nor* thin; He has not offered us any of his candy, *nor* will he; I have never seen a dragon, *nor* do I expect to see one.

Nor. 1 Norman. 2 North. 3 Norway. 4 Norwegian.

Nor·dic [nôr′dik] 1 *adj.* Describing or belonging to a type of tall, blond, usually blue-eyed people chiefly from northern Europe. Norwegians are Nordic people. 2 *n.* A Nordic person.

norm [nôrm] *n.* A pattern, standard, or model considered typical or average: She is above the *norm* in achievement for her grade.

nor·mal [nôr′məl] 1 *adj.* Agreeing with the usual standard; average; regular: *normal* tides; *normal* eyesight; a *normal* way of acting. 2 *adj.* Not ill or defective in body or mind: a *normal* baby. 3 *n.* Something typical or average, as an amount or degree: a temperature above *normal.* **—nor′mal·cy** *n.* **—nor·mal·i·ty** [nôr·mal′ə·tē] *n.*

nor·mal·ize [nôr′mə·līz′] *v.* **nor·mal·ized, nor·mal·iz·ing** To make normal: *normalized* diplomatic relations by ending the embargo.

nor·mal·ly [nôr′mə·lē] *adv.* 1 In a normal way. 2 As a rule; usually: *Normally* we eat early.

normal school A school that prepares high-school graduates to become teachers.

Nor·man [nôr′mən] 1 *n.* A person born or living in Normandy. 2 *n.* One of the people of mixed Scandinavian and French descent who conquered

England in 1066. **3** *adj.* Of or having to do with Normandy or the Normans.

Norman Conquest The conquest of England in 1066 by the Normans under the leadership of William the Conqueror.

Norman French **1** The French language of Normandy during the Middle Ages. **2** The modern French dialect of Normandy.

Norn [nôrn] *n.* In Scandinavian myths, one of the three goddesses of fate.

Norse [nôrs] **1** *adj.* Of or from Scandinavia. **2** *n.* **(the Norse)** The people of Scandinavia. **3** *n.* The language of Scandinavia, especially Norwegian. **4** *n.* The language of ancient Scandinavia.

Norse·man [nôrs'mən] *n., pl.* **Norse·men** [nôrs'mən] A Scandinavian of ancient times.

north [nôrth] **1** *n.* The direction to the left of a person facing east and one of the four cardinal points of the compass. If you face the sun at sunrise, the north is to your left. **2** *adj.* To, toward, or in the north; northern. **3** *adj.* Coming from the north: the *north* wind. **4** *adv.* In or toward the north; northward. **—north of** Farther north than: Vermont is *north of* Massachusetts. **—the North** **1** In the U.S., the states north of Maryland, the Ohio River, and Missouri. **2** (*often written* **the north**) The parts of the world that are farthest north; the arctic regions.

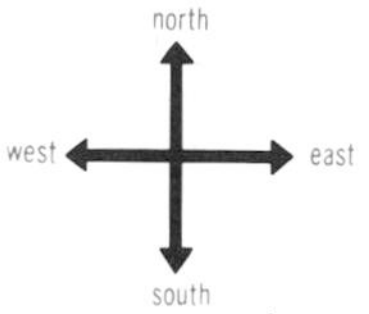

North American **1** Of or from North America. **2** A person born or living in North America.

north·bound [nôrth'bound'] *adj.* Going north.

north by east The direction or compass point midway between north and north-northeast; 11 degrees 15 minutes east of due north.

north by west The direction or compass point midway between north and north-northwest; 11 degrees 15 minutes west of due north.

north·east [nôrth'ēst'] **1** *n.* The direction or compass point midway between north and east; 45 degrees east of due north. **2** *n.* Any region lying in or toward this direction. **3** *adj.* To, toward, or in the northeast; northeastern. **4** *adj.* Coming from the northeast: a *northeast* breeze. **5** *adv.* In or toward the northeast. **—northeast of** Farther northeast than: Boston is *northeast of* New York.

northeast by east The direction or compass point midway between northeast and east-northeast; 11 degrees 15 minutes east of northeast.

northeast by north The direction or compass point midway between northeast and north-northeast; 11 degrees 15 minutes north of northeast.

north·east·er [nôrth'ēs'tər] *n.* A gale or storm from the northeast.

north·east·er·ly [nôrth'ēs'tər·lē] *adj., adv.* **1** To, toward, or in the northeast. **2** From the northeast.

north·east·ern [nôrth'ēs'tərn] *adj.* **1** To, toward, or in the northeast: *northeastern* New Jersey. **2** Coming from the northeast: a *northeastern* wind.

north·er·ly [nôr'thər·lē] *adj., adv.* **1** To, toward, or in the north. **2** From the north.

north·ern [nôr'thərn] *adj.* **1** To, toward, or in the north. **2** Coming from the north: a *northern* mass of cold, dry air.

north·ern·er [nôr'thər·nər] *n.* **1** A person born or living in the north. **2** (*sometimes written* **Northerner**) A person born or living in the North.

northern lights Another name for AURORA BOREALIS.

north·ern·most [nôr'thərn·mōst'] *adj.* Farthest north: the *northernmost* point in Europe.

North·man [nôrth'mən] *n., pl.* **North·men** [nôrth'·mən] One of a fair, tall people of ancient Scandinavia, especially a viking.

north-north·east [nôrth'nôrth'ēst'] **1** *n.* The direction or compass point midway between north and northeast; 22 degrees 30 minutes east of due north. **2** *adj.* To, toward, or in the north-northeast. **3** *adv.* In or toward the north-northeast.

north-north·west [nôrth'nôrth'west'] **1** *n.* The direction or compass point midway between north and northwest; 22 degrees 30 minutes west of due north. **2** *adj.* To, toward, or in the north-northwest. **3** *adv.* In or toward the north-northwest.

North Star A bright star that is almost directly above the North Pole; Polaris.

north·ward [nôrth'wərd] **1** *adj., adv.* To, toward, or in the north. **2** *n.* A northward direction or location.

north·wards [nôrth'wərdz] *adv.* Northward.

north·west [nôrth'west'] **1** *n.* The direction or compass point midway between north and west; 45 degrees west of due north. **2** *n.* Any region lying in or toward this direction. **3** *adj.* To, toward, or in the northwest; northwestern. **4** *adj.* Coming from the northwest. **5** *adv.* In or toward the northwest. **—northwest of** Farther northwest than: Detroit is *northwest of* Cleveland.

northwest by north The direction or compass point midway between northwest and north-northwest; 11 degrees 15 minutes north of northwest.

northwest by west The direction or compass point midway between northwest and west-northwest; 11 degrees 15 minutes west of northwest.

north·west·er [nôrth'wes'tər] *n.* A gale or storm from the northwest.

north·west·er·ly [nôrth'wes'tər·lē] *adj., adv.* **1** To, toward, or in the northwest. **2** From the northwest.

north·west·ern [nôrth'wes'tərn] *adj.* **1** To, toward, or in the northwest. **2** Coming from the northwest.

Nor·we·gian [nôr·wē'jən] **1** *adj.* Of or from Norway. **2** *n.* A person born in or a citizen of Norway. **3** *n.* The language of Norway.

nose [nōz] *n., v.* **nosed, nos·ing** **1** *n.* The projecting part in the middle of the face that contains two air passages for breathing and the organ of smell. ◆ Adj., *nasal.* **2** *n.* The sense of smell; power of smelling: This hunting dog has a good *nose.* **3** *v.* To sniff or smell. **4** *v.* To touch or rub with the nose; nuzzle. **5** *n.* Something that looks like a nose because of its shape or position, as the forward part of an aircraft or a boat. **6** *v.* To move forward cautiously with the front end foremost:

a	add	**i**	it	**o͝o**	took	**oi**	oil
ā	ace	**ī**	ice	**o͞o**	pool	**ou**	pout
â	care	**o**	odd	**u**	up	**ng**	ring
ä	palm	**ō**	open	**û**	burn	**th**	thin
e	end	**ô**	order	**yo͞o**	fuse	**th**	this
ē	equal					**zh**	vision

ə = { a in *above* e in *sicken* i in *possible* / o in *melon* u in *circus* }

The bus *nosed* its way through traffic. **7** *n.* The ability to find or recognize: a *nose* for news. **8** *v.* To meddle; pry; snoop: That reporter can *nose* out a scandal anywhere. **—by a nose** By a very little: to win a race *by a nose.* **—look down one's nose at** To consider beneath one; feel contempt or scorn for. **—pay through the nose** *slang* To pay much too high a price for something. **—turn up one's nose at** To show dislike for; disdain. **—under one's nose** Clearly visible; in plain sight.

nose·bleed [nōz′blēd′] *n.* Bleeding from the nose.

nose cone The cone-shaped front section of a spacecraft, where cargo or people are carried.

nose-dive [nōz′dīv′] *v.* **nose-dived, nose-div·ing** To take a nose dive; plunge downward.

nose dive **1** A steep, downward plunge of an aircraft, nose end first. **2** Any steep fall.

nose·gay [nōz′gā′] *n.* A small bunch of flowers.

nos·ey [nō′zē] *adj.* **nos·i·er, nos·iest** Nosy.

nos·tal·gi·a [nos·tal′jə] *n.* A longing for some pleasant place, happening, or condition that is past or far away: *nostalgia* for one's childhood.

nos·tal·gic [nos·tal′jik] *adj.* Having, showing, or coming from nostalgia: a *nostalgic* mood. **—nos·tal′gi·cal·ly** *adv.*

nos·tril [nos′tril] *n.* Either of the two openings in the nose for letting in air and smells. ◆ *Nostril* comes from two Old English words meaning *nose hole.*

nos·trum [nos′trəm] *n.* **1** A mixture of secret ingredients offered as a cure for bodily ills; quack medicine. **2** A favorite remedy or plan for solving some problem or correcting an evil.

nos·y [nō′zē] *adj.* **nos·i·er, nos·i·est** *informal* Prying and snooping into other people's affairs.

not [not] *adv.* In no way or to no extent or degree: I will *not* go; She is *not* a history major.

no·ta·ble [nō′tə·bəl] **1** *adj.* Worthy of note; remarkable; famous: a *notable* poet. **2** *n.* A person who is notable. **—no′ta·bly** *adv.*

no·ta·rize [nō′tə·rīz′] *v.* **no·ta·rized, no·ta·riz·ing** To witness or authenticate as a notary.

no·ta·ry [nō′tə·rē] *n., pl.* **no·ta·ries** A public official authorized to witness the signing of contracts or other documents and to certify that a person swears that something is true. Also **notary public.**

no·ta·tion [nō·tā′shən] *n.* **1** A set of symbols or abbreviations used to represent things, as numbers, quantities, words, or notes: algebraic *notation*; musical *notation.* **2** A brief note made to help a person remember something. **3** The act of making such a note.

notch [noch] **1** *n.* A V-shaped cut made in an edge or curve. **2** *v.* To cut a notch or notches in. **3** *n.* A narrow pass between mountains. **4** *n.* *informal* A degree; level: As an athlete, she is a *notch* above her classmates.

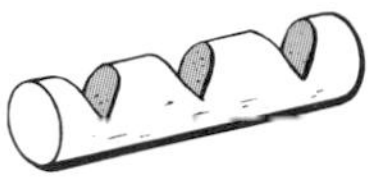

Notches

note [nōt] *n., v.* **not·ed, not·ing** **1** *n.* A brief record or jotting down of a word, sentence, fact, or other piece of information that one wishes to remember: to make *notes* on a lecture. **2** *v.* To record or set down in writing: *Note* the date of his birthday. **3** *n.* Close attention; heed: What the officer said is worthy of *note.* **4** *v.* To pay careful attention to: *Note* how I do this. **5** *v.* To become aware of; observe: I *noted* the student's absence. **6** *v.* To mention. **7** *n.* A written comment, as at the bottom of a page or at the back of a book, explaining or adding more information to something: Shakespeare's plays have many *notes* to help the student. **8** *n.* A short letter. **9** *n.* A formal or official letter from one country or government to another. **10** *n.* In music, a symbol whose position on a staff indicates the pitch of the tone and whose form indicates its length. **11** *n.* Any more or less musical sound: the *notes* of a bird. **12** *n.* Any of the keys on a piano or other instrument. **13** *n.* A sign or quality: a *note* of winter in the air. **14** *n.* A piece of paper money issued by a government or a bank. **15** *n.* A written agreement to pay a sum of money at a certain time. **16** *n.* Importance; fame: a scientist of great *note.* **—compare notes** To exchange ideas about something.

note·book [nōt′bŏŏk′] *n.* A book in which one may write notes on things one wants to remember.

not·ed [nō′tid] **1** Past participle of NOTE. **2** *adj.* Well-known; famous: a *noted* author.

note·wor·thy [nōt′wûr′thē] *adj.* Deserving of attention; remarkable; important.

noth·ing [nuth′ing] **1** *n.* Not anything; not something: *Nothing* interesting happened today. **2** *n.* A person or thing that is of little or no importance. **3** *adv.* Not at all; to no degree: *Nothing* daunted, I jumped on the horse and rode away. **—for nothing** **1** Without charge; free. **2** To no avail; in vain: All our hard work was *for nothing.* **3** For no reason; without cause.

noth·ing·ness [nuth′ing·nis] *n.* **1** The condition of being nothing; nonexistence: At noon, the mist faded into *nothingness.* **2** Complete worthlessness or uselessness.

no·tice [nō′tis] *n., v.* **no·ticed, no·tic·ing** **1** *n.* Observation; attention; heed: Bring this book to the librarian's *notice.* **2** *v.* To pay attention to; observe; see: Did you *notice* their leaving? **3** *n.* Announcement; warning; information: *notice* of an approaching storm. **4** *n.* A written or printed announcement: a wedding *notice* in the paper. **5** *n.* A formal announcement that one is leaving, as a job or a rented place: Landlords like 30 days' *notice.* **6** *n.* A short critical article or review: Did the book get good *notices*? **7** *v.* To refer to; mention, as in a speech or article. **8** *n.* Polite or respectful treatment.

no·tice·a·ble [nō′tis·ə·bəl] *adj.* **1** Attracting one's attention; easily seen: a *noticeable* difference. **2** Worthy of notice: The dancers were *noticeable* for their grace. **—no′tice·a·bly** *adv.*

no·ti·fi·ca·tion [nō′tə·fə·kā′shən] *n.* **1** The act of notifying or giving notice. **2** The notice given: We received *notification* of a sale.

no·ti·fy [nō′tə·fī] *v.* **no·ti·fied, no·ti·fy·ing** To give notice to; inform: The teacher *notified* us that we had passed the test.

no·tion [nō′shən] *n.* **1** A general idea or impression: I have a *notion* that he'll go. **2** An opinion or belief: to have the *notion* that cold baths are healthful. **3** A whim, inclination, or fancy: I took a *notion* to stand on my head. **4** (*pl.*) Small articles for sale, as ribbons, thread, and pins.

no·to·chord [nō′tə·kôrd′] *n.* A tough, flexible rod of supporting tissue that runs along the back of certain primitive animals and of the embryos of higher vertebrate animals.

no·to·ri·e·ty [nō′tə·rī′ə·tē] *n., pl.* **no·to·ri·e·ties** The condition of being widely known or notorious, usually in an unfavorable sense.

no·to·ri·ous [nō·tôr′ē·əs] *adj.* Widely known, especially for bad reasons: a *notorious* thief. **—no·to'·ri·ous·ly** *adv.* **—no·to'ri·ous·ness** *n.* ◆ *Notorious* and *famous* are not synonyms. *Notorious* means not just "famous" but "famous for something bad."

not·with·stand·ing [not'with·stan'ding] **1** *adv.* All the same; nevertheless: Although the exam was difficult, I passed *notwithstanding.* **2** *prep.* In spite of: *Notwithstanding* the weather, they insist on leaving. **3** *conj.* Although: They had to push on, *notwithstanding* they were exhausted.

nou·gat [no͞o'gət] *n.* A candy made of chopped nuts and other ingredients mixed with a sugar paste.

nought [nôt] *n.* **1** Nothing; naught: My efforts came to *nought.* **2** The character 0; zero.

noun [noun] *n.* **1** A word used as the name of a person, thing, place, action, quality, condition, or class, as *John, bat, Ohio, attack, kindness, illness,* and *plants.* Nouns commonly function as subjects of verbs, complements, and objects of verbs or prepositions. **2** *adj. use:* a *noun* clause.

nour·ish [nûr'ish] **1** *v.* To keep alive and healthy or help to grow with food. **2** *adj. use: nourishing* food. **3** *v.* To keep up; maintain: to *nourish* feelings of contentment.

nour·ish·ment [nûr'ish·mənt] *n.* **1** The act of nourishing. **2** Something that nourishes; food: Fish has a great deal of *nourishment.* **3** The condition of being nourished.

Nov. November.

no·va [nō'və] *n., pl.* **nov·as** or **nov·ae** [nō'vē] A star that suddenly flares up, shines, and then fades away after a few weeks or months.

nov·el [nov'əl] **1** *n.* A long piece of fiction, usually of book length. Novels tell a story of imaginary people, their feelings, thoughts, and adventures. **2** *adj.* New, strange, or unusual: Using the elbows is a *novel* way to play the piano.

nov·el·ette [nov'əl·et'] *n.* A short novel.

nov·el·ist [nov'əl·ist] *n.* A person who writes novels.

nov·el·ty [nov'əl·tē] *n., pl.* **nov·el·ties** **1** Something new or different: It was a *novelty* to sleep late. **2** The quality of being new and unusual; newness: the *novelty* of sending rockets into space. **3** (*usually pl.*) Any small, inexpensive article, as a toy or piece of jewelry.

No·vem·ber [nō·vem'bər] *n.* The 11th month of the year, having 30 days.

no·ve·na [nō·vē'nə] *n.* A Roman Catholic devotion consisting of a series of prayers recited on nine consecutive days.

nov·ice [nov'is] *n.* **1** A beginner or inexperienced person. **2** A person taken into a religious order on trial before being allowed to become a monk or nun.

no·vi·ti·ate or **no·vi·ci·ate** [nō·vish'ē·it] *n.* **1** The condition or period of being a novice, especially in a religious order. **2** The quarters occupied by novices, as in a monastery.

No·vo·cain [nō'və·kān'] *n.* A drug that deadens sensation, used in medicine and dentistry as a local anesthetic: a trademark.

now [nou] **1** *adv.* At once; immediately: Please do it *now.* **2** *adv.* At or during the present time: *Now* the mail carrier is coming up the walk. **3** *n.* The present time: Until *now,* the team hadn't won a game. **4** *adv.* Under such circumstances; with things being what they are: *Now* we'll never get home. **5** *conj.* Seeing that; since: *Now* that you have finished your homework, do you want to go to the movies? **6** *adv.* Sometimes: *now* this, *now* that. **7** *interj. Now* is often used to make a command or request stronger: Come, *now,* you'd better hurry; *Now, now,* don't think about it. **—just now** **1** In the immediate past: The newscaster said so *just now.* **2** In the immediate future: The whole class is going *just now.* **—now and again** or **now and then** From time to time; once in a while.

NOW [nou] National Organizaton for Women.

now·a·days [nou'ə·dāz'] *adv.* In the present time or age: *Nowadays* people live longer.

no·way [nō'wā'] *adv.* In no way, manner, or degree; not at all.

no·ways [nō'wāz'] *adv.* Noway.

no·where [nō'(h)wâr'] **1** *adv.* In or to no place; not anywhere: I can find my boots *nowhere.* **2** *n.* No place: We were miles from *nowhere.*

no·wise [nō'wīz'] *adv.* In no manner; not at all: The play was *nowise* a success.

nox·ious [nok'shəs] *adj.* Harmful to health or morals: *noxious* slums; *noxious* smells.

noz·zle [noz'əl] *n.* A spout or small opening, as at the end of a hose or pipe.

Nozzle

Np The symbol for the element neptunium.

N.S. Nova Scotia.

N.T. New Testament.

nth [enth] *adj.* Extremely or indefinitely large or small, especially in the phrase **to the nth degree,** to the most extreme degree.

nt. wt. net weight.

nu [n(y)o͞o] *n.* The 13th letter of the Greek alphabet.

nu·ance [no͞o·äns'] *n.* A very slight variation, as of color, tone, or meaning: There are many *nuances* of meaning in these poems.

nub [nub] *n.* **1** A knob or swelling. **2** *informal* The point, core, or gist of anything: the *nub* of a joke.

nub·bin [nub'in] *n.* A small or imperfect ear of corn. **2** Any small or imperfect thing.

nub·by [nub'ē] *adj.* **nub·bi·er, nub·bi·est** Having nubs; lumpy: a *nubby* texture; a *nubby* material.

nu·bile [n(y)o͞o'bəl *or* n(y)o͞o'bīl'] *adj.* Of marriageable age. **—nu·bil·i·ty** [n(y)o͞o·bil'ə·tē] *n.*

nu·cle·ar [n(y)o͞o'klē·ər] *adj.* **1** Of, having to do with, or like a nucleus or nuclei. Of, having to do with, or using atomic energy.

nuclear energy Another name for ATOMIC ENERGY.

nuclear family A family unit made up of only a mother and father and their children.

nuclear fission The splitting that takes place when the nucleus of a heavy atom absorbs a neutron. The split forms nuclei of lighter atoms and releases great energy. The rate of fission may increase rapidly, as in a bomb, or be controlled to provide power for practical use.

a	add	**i**	it	**o͝o**	took	**oi**	oil
ā	ace	**ī**	ice	**o͞o**	pool	**ou**	pout
â	care	**o**	odd	**u**	up	**ng**	ring
ä	palm	**ō**	open	**û**	burn	**th**	thin
e	end	**ô**	order	**yo͞o**	fuse	**t͟h**	this
ē	equal					**zh**	vision

ə = a in *above*, e in *sicken*, i in *possible*, o in *melon*, u in *circus*

N

nuclear fusion Any process for joining the nuclei from atoms of light elements, thereby forming atomic nuclei of heavier elements and releasing enormous nuclear energy.

nuclear physics The branch of physics that deals with the structure, properties, and behavior of atomic nuclei.

nuclear reactor Another name for REACTOR (def. 2).

nu·cle·ic acid [n(y)o͞o·klē′ik] Any of the large, chainlike, acid molecules found in the nuclei of cells, especially ribonucleic acid and deoxyribonucleic acid.

nu·cle·o·lus [n(y)o͞o·klē′ə·ləs] *n., pl.* **nu·cle·o·li** [n(y)o͞o·klē′ə·lī′] A small, usually spherical body found in the nucleus of a cell.

nu·cle·on [n(y)o͞o′klē·on] *n.* Any particle found in the nucleus of an atom, as the proton, neutron, and meson.

nu·cle·us [n(y)o͞o′klē·əs] *n., pl.* **nu·cle·i** [n(y)o͞o′klē·ī] or **nu·cle·us·es** 1 The small central mass embedded in the cytoplasm of most plant and animal cells. It is surrounded by a membrane and contains the chromatin or chromosomes, and other structures essential to the cell's growth, reproduction, and other functions. 2 The central core of an atom, carrying a positive electric charge and around which the negatively charged electrons revolve. 3 Any central point or part around which other things are gathered: Four novels form the *nucleus* of the semester's work.

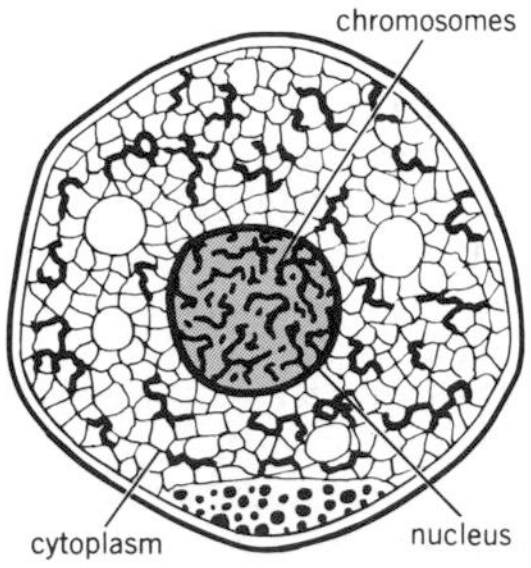

nude [n(y)o͞od] 1 *adj.* Wearing no clothing or covering; naked; bare. 2 *n.* A nude figure of a person, especially as represented in art, as in a painting or sculpture. **—nu′di·ty** *n.*

nudge [nuj] *v.* **nudged, nudg·ing,** *n.* 1 *v.* To touch or push gently, as with the elbow so as to attract attention. 2 *n.* A gentle push, as with the elbow.

nug·get [nug′it] *n.* 1 A lump, especially of gold in its natural state. 2 Any valuable bit or piece: *nuggets* of information.

nui·sance [n(y)o͞o′səns] *n.* Anything, as a person, thing, or condition, that annoys, bothers, or irritates.

null [nul] *adj.* 1 Having no legal force or effect. 2 Having no value; useless. **—null and void** Without legal force or effect: This contract is *null and void.*

nul·li·fy [nul′ə·fī] *v.* **nul·li·fied, nul·li·fy·ing** 1 To make useless; bring to nothing: During the day, the light of the sun *nullifies* that of the stars. 2 To take away the legal force or effect of; annul: to *nullify* a will. **—nul′li·fi·ca′tion** *n.*

numb [num] 1 *adj.* Having no sensation or feeling: fingers *numb* with cold; to be *numb* with fear. 2 *v.* To make numb: The blow *numbed* my jaw and cheek. **—numb′ly** *adv.* **—numb′ness** *n.*

num·ber [num′bər] 1 *n.* An element of arithmetic on which operations such as addition and multiplication are performed and which tells how many elements there are in a set; cardinal number. 2 *v.* To count; make a total of: I *number* the stamps in my collection at 2,000. 3 *n.* A quantity or amount of things or persons; sum or total: The *number* of players on a baseball team is nine. 4 *v.* To amount to; total: Our club *numbers* 20 members. 5 *n.* (*usually pl.*) A rather large group of persons or things: *Numbers* of library books are lost each year. 6 *n.* A number given to a person or piece of merchandise for identification: All cars have serial *numbers.* 7 *v.* To give or assign a number to: to *number* the pages of a long letter. 8 *n.* One of a series of things: the July *number* of a magazine; The pianist's last *number* on the program was very short. 9 *v.* To include as one of a collection or group: She *numbers* dancing among her talents. 10 *v.* To set or limit the number of: The crew's days on this job are *numbered.* 11 *n.* In grammar, the form of a word that indicates whether the word is singular or plural. **—any number of** A good many; quite a lot of. **—beyond number** or **without number** Of or to a number too large to be counted. **—num′ber·er** *n.* ◆ A *number* is the idea or concept; a *numeral* is a symbol used to express a *number.* Forty, 40, and XL are all *numerals* for the same *number.*

num·ber·less [num′bər·lis] *adj.* Very numerous; countless: *numberless* flakes of snow.

number line A line considered to represent the set of real numbers, often labeled with numerals at regular intervals.

Num·bers [num′bərz] *n.pl.* (*used with singular verb*) The fourth book of the Old Testament.

numb·skull [num′skul′] *n.* Another spelling of NUMSKULL.

nu·mer·a·ble [n(y)o͞o′mər·ə·bəl] *adj.* Capable of being counted.

nu·mer·al [n(y)o͞o′mər·əl] *n.* 1 A symbol, letter, or word used alone or with others to express a number. Arabic numerals 24 and 190 show the same numbers as the Roman numerals XXIV and CXC. 2 (*pl.*) Figures of cloth showing the year a student will graduate, awarded for playing on a class team in a sport. ◆ See NUMBER.

nu·mer·a·tion [n(y)o͞o′mə·rā′shən] *n.* The act, process, or system of reading or naming numbers.

nu·mer·a·tor [n(y)o͞o′mə·rā′tər] *n.* In a fraction, the number that is to be divided by another number; dividend.

nu·mer·i·cal [n(y)o͞o·mer′i·kəl] *adj.* 1 Of or having to do with numbers: a *numerical* advantage. 2 By numbers: to put in *numerical* order. 3 Expressed in numerals. **—nu·mer′i·cal·ly** *adv.*

nu·mer·ous [n(y)o͞o′mə·rəs] *adj.* 1 Very many: *numerous* mistakes. 2 Consisting of a great number of persons or things.

nu·mis·mat·ics [n(y)o͞o′miz·mat′·iks] *n.* The study or collecting of coins and medals. **—nu·mis·ma·tist** [n(y)o͞o·miz′mə·tist] *n.* ◆ See -ICS.

The blue numeral is the numerator.

num·skull [num′skul′] *n.* A very stupid person.

nun [nun] *n.* A woman who has taken religious vows, belongs to a religious order, and commonly lives in a convent. Many nuns serve as teachers or nurses, or do charitable work.

nun·ci·o [nun′shē·ō *or* nun′sē·ō] *n., pl.* **nun·ci·os** An ambassador whom the Pope sends to represent him in other countries.

hardhearted; unfeeling: an *obdurate* decision. **2** Stubborn: an *obdurate* denial. **—ob′du·rate·ly** *adv.* **—ob′du·rate·ness** *n.*

o·be·di·ence [ō·bē′dē·əns] *n.* The act, habit, or condition of obeying; compliance, as with rules, regulations, or laws.

o·be·di·ent [ō·bē′dē·ənt] *adj.* Willing or tending to obey; complying, as with rules, regulations or laws. **—o·be′di·ent·ly** *adv.*

o·bei·sance [ō·bā′səns *or* ō·bē′səns] *n.* **1** An act of courtesy or reverence, as bowing or a bending of the knee. **2** Homage; respect: As ruler, the monarch demanded *obeisance* from all.

ob·e·lisk [ob′ə·lisk] *n.* A square shaft of stone that tapers to a top shaped like a pyramid.

Obelisk

O·ber·on [ō′bə·ron′] *n.* In medieval legends, the king of the fairies, husband of Titania.

o·bese [ō·bēs′] *adj.* Very fat; exceedingly stout. **—o·bes·i·ty** [ō·bē′sə·tē *or* ō·bes′ə·tē] *n.*

o·bey [ō·bā′] *v.* **1** To follow the commands or requests of: to *obey* one's superiors. **2** To comply with: to *obey* the law. **3** To be guided or controlled by: to *obey* one's impulses. **4** To behave in an obedient manner.

o·bi [ō′bē] *n.* A wide sash worn with a Japanese kimono.

o·bit·u·ar·y [ō·bich′o͞o·er′ē] *n., pl.* **o·bit·u·ar·ies,** *adj.* **1** *n.* Published notice of a person's death, often including a brief biography. **2** *adj.* Of or recording a death: an *obituary* column in a newspaper.

obj. object.

ob·ject [*n.* ob′jikt *or* ob′jekt, *v.* əb·jekt′] **1** *n.* Anything that is or may be seen or touched. **2** *n.* The purpose of an action: What was your *object* in coming here? **3** *n.* A person or thing toward which some action, thought, or feeling is directed: the *object* of one's love. **4** *n.* In grammar, a word or group of words that receives the action of a verb or follows a preposition which relates it to another word. In "Put some cream in your coffee," *cream* is the object of *put* and *coffee* the object of *in.* **5** *v.* To be opposed: My parents *object* to our trip. **6** *v.* To offer as a reason for opposition: We wanted to go to a movie, but our parents *objected* that it was too late to go. **—ob·jec′tor** *n.*

ob·jec·tion [əb·jek′shən] *n.* **1** A statement or feeling of disagreement or opposition. **2** The cause or reason for such disagreement: The *objection* to our plan was that it was too difficult.

ob·jec·tion·a·ble [əb·jek′shən·ə·bəl] *adj.* Deserving or causing disapproval; offensive.

ob·jec·tive [əb·jek′tiv] **1** *adj.* Free from personal feelings or opinions; detached: A jury must be *objective.* **2** *adj.* Having to do with what is external and real rather than what is in the mind. **3** *n.* A goal or end: My *objective* is to attend college. **4** *adj.* In grammar, indicating the object of a verb or preposition. In "I want a book for my brother," both *book* and *brother* are in the objective case. **5** *n.* The objective case. **—ob·jec′tive·ly** *adv.* **—ob·jec′tive·ness** *n.*

objective complement A noun, adjective, or pronoun used as a complement to a verb to qualify the object of the verb and complete the meaning of the sentence. In "They elected Mary chairwoman," *chairwoman* is an objective complement.

ob·jec·tiv·i·ty [ob′jek·tiv′ə·tē] *n.* A being objective: *Objectivity* must be a jury's goal.

object lesson A practical example or illustration of some principle, truth, or theory.

ob·jet d'art [ōb·zhā·där′] *pl.* **ob·jets d'art** [ōb·zhā·där′] An object, such as a bowl or vase, valued for its artistic merit.

ob·la·tion [ob·lā′shən] *n.* **1** The act of offering worship or sacrifice to God or a god. **2** The thing that is offered, especially the bread and wine of Holy Communion.

ob·li·gate [ob′lə·gāt′] *v.* **ob·li·gat·ed, ob·li·gat·ing** To bind or compel, as by contract, law, or conscience: We are *obligated* to pay taxes.

ob·li·ga·tion [ob′lə·gā′shən] *n.* **1** A duty required by law, a promise, or one's conscience: the *obligation* to pay taxes. **2** A debt of gratitude for a service or favor. **3** A debt: The company is paying off its *obligations.*

ob·lig·a·to·ry [ə·blig′ə·tôr′ē *or* ob′lə·gə·tôr′ē] *adj.* Binding, as by law or conscience; required: Classroom attendance is *obligatory.*

o·blige [ə·blīj′] *v.* **o·bliged, o·blig·ing** **1** To place under obligation, as for a service or a favor: I am *obliged* to you for the work you have done. **2** To compel; bind; force: The traffic laws *oblige* us to drive carefully. **3** To do a favor or service for: Will you *oblige* me by closing the window?

o·blig·ing [ə·blī′jing] *adj.* Inclined to do favors; good-natured; kind. **—o·blig′ing·ly** *adv.*

ob·lique [ə·blēk′] *adj.* **1** Neither level nor straight up and down; slanting. **2** Not direct or straightforward: an *oblique* answer. **—ob·lique′ly** *adv.*

oblique angle An angle that is not a right angle.

ob·lit·er·ate [ə·blit′ə·rāt′] *v.* **ob·lit·er·at·ed, ob·lit·er·at·ing** **1** To destroy completely; leave no trace of: A bomb had *obliterated* the chapel. **2** To blot or wipe out; erase, as writing. **—ob·lit′er·a′tion** *n.*

O

ob·liv·i·on [ə·bliv′ē·ən] *n.* **1** The state or fact of being completely forgotten: The reason for their argument soon faded into *oblivion.* **2** The fact of forgetting; forgetfulness.

ob·liv·i·ous [ə·bliv′ē·əs] *adj.* **1** Not conscious or aware: He was *oblivious* to his surroundings. **2** Causing forgetfulness: *oblivious* sleep.

ob·long [ob′lông′] **1** *adj.* Longer in one dimension than in another: A football field is *oblong.* **2** *n.* Something oblong, as a figure or object.

Oblongs

ob·lo·quy [ob′lə·kwē] *n., pl.* **ob·lo·quies** **1** Abusive and critical language, especially when directed against a person by the public. **2** Disgrace; shame.

ob·nox·ious [əb·nok′shəs] *adj.* Very disagreeable or unpleasant; objectionable; hateful; offensive. **—ob·nox′ious·ly** *adv.* **—ob·nox′ious·ness** *n.*

a	add	**i**	it	**o͝o**	took	**oi**	oil
ā	ace	**ī**	ice	**o͞o**	pool	**ou**	pout
â	care	**o**	odd	**u**	up	**ng**	ring
ä	palm	**ō**	open	**û**	burn	**th**	thin
e	end	**ô**	order	**yo͞o**	fuse	**th̶**	this
ē	equal					**zh**	vision

ə = {a in *above* e in *sicken* i in *possible*
o in *melon* u in *circus*

o·boe [ō'bō] *n.* A high-pitched woodwind instrument that has a conical body and a double reed. ◆ *Oboe* comes from the French *hautbois,* meaning *high wood.* It was originally written *hautbois* in English too, and was pronounced [hō'boi *or* ō'·boi], but the spelling and pronunciation now used come from the Italian word for the instrument.

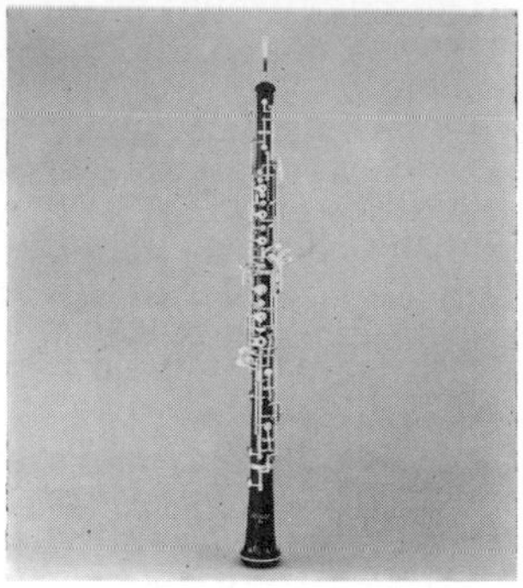

ob·scene [əb·sēn' *or* ob·sēn'] *adj.* **1** Offensive to accepted standards of morality or decency; indecent; immodest. **2** Repulsive; disgusting; abominable. **—ob·scene'ly** *adv.*

ob·scen·i·ty [əb·sen'ə·tē *or* əb·sē'nə·tē] *n., pl.* **ob·scen·i·ties** **1** The quality or condition of being obscene: the *obscenity* of a nuclear holocaust. **2** Obscene action or speech.

ob·scure [əb·skyŏŏr'] *adj.* **ob·scur·er, ob·scur·est,** *v.* **ob·scured, ob·scur·ing** **1** *adj.* Not clear to the mind; hard to understand: an *obscure* statement. **2** *adj.* Not clear to the senses: an *obscure* figure; an *obscure,* muffled sound. **3** *v.* To make vague or hard to understand: The difficult vocabulary *obscured* the meaning of the story. **4** *v.* To make dim or indistinct: Fog *obscured* the mountains. **5** *adj.* Not easily found; hidden: an *obscure* country path. **6** *adj.* Without fame: an *obscure* artist. **7** *adj.* Having little or no light; dark: *obscure* cellar stairs. **—ob·scure'ly** *adv.* **—ob·scure'ness** *n.*

ob·scu·ri·ty [əb·skyŏŏr'ə·tē] *n., pl.* **ob·scu·ri·ties** The condition or quality of being obscure.

ob·se·qui·ous [əb·sē'kwē·əs] *adj.* Too ready to please, praise, or obey; fawning; flattering; servile. **—ob·se'qui·ous·ly** *adv.* **—ob·se'qui·ous·ness** *n.*

ob·se·quy [ob'sə·kwē] *n., pl.* **ob·se·quies** Funeral rite; burial service.

ob·serv·a·ble [əb·zûr'və·bəl] *adj.* **1** Capable of being observed; noticeable: an *observable* change. **2** Requiring observance: an *observable* religious holiday. **—ob·serv'a·bly** *adv.*

ob·ser·vance [əb·zûr'vəns] *n.* **1** The act of observing, as a command, law, or holiday. **2** A customary ceremony, act, or rite: the *observance* of an anniversary.

ob·ser·vant [əb·zûr'vənt] *adj.* **1** Quick to observe or notice; alert. **2** Strict or careful in observing, as a custom, law, or holiday. **—ob·serv'ant·ly** *adv.*

ob·ser·va·tion [ob'zər·vā'shən] *n.* **1** The act, ability, or habit of observing. **2** The fact of being observed: We wanted to avoid *observation.* **3** The act of observing scientifically and making notes on what is observed: astronomical *observations.* **4** A comment or incidental remark: a reporter's critical *observations.* **—ob'ser·va'tion·al** *adj.*

ob·ser·va·to·ry [əb·zûr'və·tôr'ē] *n., pl.* **ob·ser·va·to·ries** A building equipped with telescopes or other instruments for studying the stars, weather conditions, or other natural phenomena.

ob·serve [əb·zûrv'] *v.* **ob·served, ob·serv·ing** **1** To see or notice: I *observed* you when you came in. **2** To watch attentively: to *observe* the patients. **3** To make careful examination of, especially for scientific purposes: to *observe* the cells of a plant under a microscope. **4** To comment or remark: I *observed* that it was a very warm day. **5** To follow or comply with: to *observe* the law. **6** To celebrate in the proper way, as a holiday. **—ob·serv'er** *n.*

ob·sess [əb·ses'] *v.* To fill or trouble the mind of excessively; haunt: Worries about falling grain prices *obsessed* the farmer all summer.

ob·ses·sion [əb·sesh'ən] *n.* **1** A thought, feeling, or idea that fills the mind and cannot be driven out. **2** The condition of being obsessed by such a thought or feeling.

ob·ses·sive [əb·ses'iv] *adj.* Of, having to do with, like, or causing an obsession.

ob·sid·i·an [əb·sid'ē·ən] *n.* A hard, glassy rock, usually black, formed by the cooling of hot lava.

ob·so·les·cent [ob'sə·les'ənt] *adj.* Passing out of use or fashion. **—ob'so·les'cence** *n.*

ob·so·lete [ob'sə·lēt' *or* ob'sə·lēt'] *adj.* **1** Old; out-of-date: an *obsolete* automobile. **2** No longer used or practiced: an *obsolete* word.

ob·sta·cle [ob'stə·kəl] *n.* Something that stands in the way or interferes; hindrance; obstruction: Lack of education is an *obstacle* to success.

ob·stet·ric [ob·stet'rik] *adj.* Of or having to do with obstetrics.

ob·stet·ri·cal [ob·stet'ri·kəl] *adj.* Obstetric.

ob·ste·tri·cian [ob'stə·trish'ən] *n.* A doctor who specializes in obstetrics.

ob·stet·rics [əb·stet'riks] *n.* The branch of medicine that deals with the care and treatment of women in the time leading up to, during, and just after the birth of a child. ◆ See -ICS.

ob·sti·na·cy [ob'stə·nə·sē] *n., pl.* **ob·sti·na·cies** **1** A being obstinate; stubbornness. **2** Something obstinate, as an act or feeling.

ob·sti·nate [ob'stə·nit] *adj.* **1** Stubbornly holding to one's opinions or purposes; unyielding: The senior officers are so *obstinate* that they will never change the ruling. **2** Hard to overcome, control, or cure: an *obstinate* habit. **—ob'sti·nate·ly** *adv.* ◆ *Obstinate* and *stubborn* both mean fixed and unchanging in opinion or action. A person who is *obstinate* seems unreasonably determined not to change opinions, whereas a *stubborn* person may stick to a course for good reasons: a *stubborn* refusal to give up; They *obstinately* defied the law.

ob·strep·er·ous [əb·strep'ər·əs] *adj.* Unruly or noisy: *Obstreperous* children are hard to teach. **—ob·strep'er·ous·ly** *adv.* **—ob·strep'er·ous·ness** *n.*

ob·struct [əb·strukt'] *v.* **1** To stop or retard movement through; block; clog: The water pipes are *obstructed* by rust. **2** To hinder: to *obstruct* the work on the new bridge. **3** To cut off or be in the way of: Tall buildings *obstruct* the view. **—ob·struc′·tive** *adj.*

ob·struc·tion [əb·struk′shən] *n.* **1** Something that obstructs; obstacle; hindrance: Some *obstruction* was blocking the drain. **2** The act of obstructing. **3** The condition of being obstructed: the *obstruction* of a blood vessel.

ob·struc·tion·ism [əb·struk′shən·iz′əm] *n.* The act or process of obstructing the progress of work or business, especially in a legislative body or meeting. **—ob·struc′tion·ist** *n.*

ob·tain [əb·tān′] *v.* **1** To gain possession of, especially by effort; get; acquire: I *obtained* a good knowledge of French in Europe. **2** To be in effect: Old customs still *obtain* here.

ob·tain·a·ble [əb·tān′ə·bəl] *adj.* Capable of being obtained.

ob·trude [əb·trōōd′] *v.* **ob·trud·ed, obtrud·ing** **1** To force upon another without request: to *obtrude* an unwanted opinion. **2** To intrude oneself: to *obtrude* upon another's happiness. **3** To push forward or out.

ob·tru·sion [əb·trōō′zhən] *n.* **1** The act or an example of obtruding. **2** Something that obtrudes.

ob·tru·sive [əb·trōō′siv] *adj.* Having a tendency to obtrude or push oneself forward. **—ob·tru′sive·ly** *adv.* **—ob·tru′sive·ness** *n.*

ob·tuse [əb·t(y)ōōs′] *adj.* **1** Slow to understand; dull; stupid: The new employee was too *obtuse* to follow instructions. **2** Not having a sharp edge or point; blunt. **—ob·tuse′ly** *adv.* **—ob·tuse′ness** *n.*

obtuse angle An angle greater than a right angle and less than 180°.

ob·verse [ob′vûrs] *n.* The front or principal side of anything, especially the side of a coin that has the main design on it. **—ob·verse′ly** *adv.*

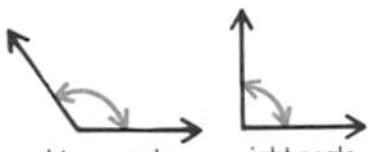
obtuse angle right angle

ob·vi·ate [ob′vē·āt′] *v.* **ob·vi·at·ed, ob·vi·at·ing** To anticipate and prevent; provide for in advance: to *obviate* risks; to *obviate* difficulties.

ob·vi·ous [ob′vē·əs] *adj.* Easily perceived; clear; visible: an *obvious* error. **—ob′vi·ous·ly** *adv.* **—ob′vi·ous·ness** *n.*

oc·a·ri·na [ok′ə·rē′nə] *n.* A small musical instrument in the shape of a sweet potato, with a mouthpiece and finger holes. ◆ *Ocarina* comes from the Italian word for *little goose,* because its shape suggested a goose ready for cooking.

Ocarina

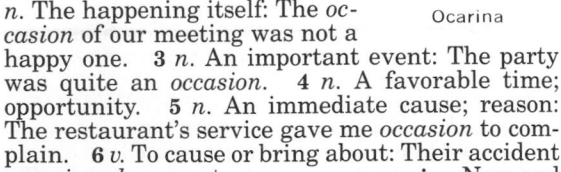

oc·ca·sion [ə·kā′zhən] **1** *n.* The particular time of a happening: I met them on one *occasion.* **2** *n.* The happening itself: The *occasion* of our meeting was not a happy one. **3** *n.* An important event: The party was quite an *occasion.* **4** *n.* A favorable time; opportunity. **5** *n.* An immediate cause; reason: The restaurant's service gave me *occasion* to complain. **6** *v.* To cause or bring about: Their accident *occasioned* us great worry. **—on occasion** Now and then.

oc·ca·sion·al [ə·kā′zhən·əl] *adj.* **1** Occurring now and then: an *occasional* visit. **2** Made, intended, or suitable for a special occasion: *occasional* verse.

oc·ca·sion·al·ly [ə·kā′zhən·əl·ē] *adv.* Now and then; sometimes: We see them *occasionally.*

Oc·ci·dent [ok′sə·dənt] *n.* (*sometimes written* **occident**) The countries west of Asia, especially those of Europe and the Americas; the West.

Oc·ci·den·tal [ok′sə·den′təl] **1** *adj.* (*sometimes written* **occidental**) Of or from the Occident. **2** *n.* A person born or living in the Occident. **3** *adj.* (*sometimes written* **occidental**) Of or having to do with an Occidental.

oc·cip·i·tal bone [ok·sip′ə·təl] The bone that forms the lower back part of the skull.

oc·ci·put [ok′sə·put] *n., pl.* **oc·cip·i·ta** [ok·sip′ə·tə] The lower back part of the skull.

oc·clude [ə·klōōd′] *v.* **oc·clud·ed, oc·clud·ing** **1** To shut up or close, as pores or openings. **2** To shut in, out, or off. **3** To meet with the cusps fitting closely: Your upper and lower teeth *occlude* properly. **4** To take up (gases or liquids); absorb or adsorb. **—oc·clu·sion** [ə·klōō′zhən] *n.*

oc·cult [ə·kult′ *or* ok′ult] *adj.* **1** Of or having to do with various magical or mysterious arts and practices, as astrology and spiritualism. **2** Beyond human understanding; mysterious.

oc·cult·ism [ə·kul′tiz′əm *or* ok′əl·tiz′əm] *n.* A belief in or study of occult arts, practices, or powers.

oc·cu·pan·cy [ok′yə·pən·sē] *n., pl.* **oc·cu·pan·cies** **1** The act of occupying. **2** The condition of being occupied. **3** The period of time during which a person is an occupant.

oc·cu·pant [ok′yə·pənt] *n.* A person who occupies something, as a house, lands, or a position.

oc·cu·pa·tion [ok′yə·pā′shən] *n.* **1** Any activity in which a person is engaged, especially the regular work by which the person earns a living. **2** The act of occupying. **3** The taking and holding of land by a military force. ◆ *Occupation, vocation,* and *business* all refer to one's work. An *occupation* is what one does for a living or how one spends most of one's time. A *vocation* has more to do with one's abilities and desires: She is an office worker by *occupation,* but her real *vocation* is acting. One's *business* refers to the field in which one makes a living: He is in the insurance *business.*

oc·cu·pa·tion·al [ok′yə·pā′shə·nəl] *adj.* Of or having to do with one's occupation: the *occupational* risks of a miner.

oc·cu·py [ok′yə·pī′] *v.* **oc·cu·pied, oc·cu·py·ing** **1** To take and hold possession of, as by conquest. **2** To fill or take up: The estate *occupies* ten acres. **3** To live in; inhabit: We *occupy* this house. **4** To hold; fill: to *occupy* a minor government position. **5** To busy or engage; employ: to *occupy* oneself with unimportant matters. **—oc′cu·pi′er** *n.*

oc·cur [ə·kûr′] *v.* **oc·curred, oc·cur·ring** **1** To happen or take place. **2** To be found; appear: Meteors *occur* frequently in August. **3** To suggest itself; come to mind.

oc·cur·rence [ə·kûr′əns] *n.* **1** The act or fact of occurring: In this weather, the *occurrence* of a

a	add	**i**	it	**o͝o**	took	**oi**	oil
ā	ace	**ī**	ice	**o͞o**	pool	**ou**	pout
â	care	**o**	odd	**u**	up	**ng**	ring
ä	palm	**ō**	open	**û**	burn	**th**	thin
e	end	**ô**	order	**yo͞o**	fuse	**th**	this
ē	equal					**zh**	vision

ə = a in *above* e in *sicken* i in *possible* o in *melon* u in *circus*

O

tornado is possible. 2 Something that occurs; event; incident: an unusual *occurrence.*

o·cean [ō′shən] *n.* 1 The great body of salt water that covers about 70 percent of the earth's surface. 2 (*often written* **Ocean**) Any one of its divisions having a distinct basin, as the Atlantic, Pacific, Indian, and Arctic.

O·ce·an·i·an [ō′shē·an′ē·ən] 1 *adj.* Of or from Oceania. 2 *n.* A person born or living in Oceania.

o·ce·an·ic [ō′shē·an′ik] *adj.* 1 Of, living in, or produced by the ocean, especially the open sea rather than coastal waters. 2 Like an ocean; vast.

o·ce·an·og·ra·phy [ō′shē·ən·og′rə·fē *or* ō′shən·og′·rə·fē] *n.* The science that studies the oceans, including their physical features, their chemistry, and the life in them. **—o′ce·an·og′ra·pher** *n.* **—o·cean·o·graph·ic** [ō′shə·nə·graf′ik] *adj.*

o·ce·lot [ō′sə·lət *or* os′ə·lot] *n.* A wildcat of Central and South America, having a spotted, yellowish coat.

Ocelot

o·cher or **o·chre** [ō′kər] 1 *n.* An earthy material containing iron. It varies in color from light yellow to deep orange or red and is used as a pigment. 2 *n., adj.* Dark yellow.

o'clock [ə·klok′] Of or according to the clock: six *o'clock* in the evening.

OCS Officer Candidate School.

Oct. October.

oc·ta·gon [ok′tə·gon′] *n.* A closed plane figure bounded by eight straight lines that form eight interior angles.

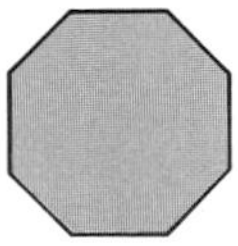
Octagon

oc·tag·o·nal [ok·tag′ə·nəl] *adj.* Having eight angles and eight sides. **—oc·tag′·o·nal·ly** *adv.*

oc·tane [ok′tān′] *n.* A liquid hydrocarbon found in petroleum and chemically related to methane.

octane number A number that indicates the rating of a given gasoline in terms of its resistance to engine knocking; the higher the number, the greater the resistance to knocking.

oc·tave [ok′tiv *or* ok′tāv′] *n.* 1 The shortest distance between two musical tones that have the same name. The higher tone has twice the frequency of vibration of the lower tone. 2 A tone at this distance above or below any other, considered in relation to that other. 3 Two tones at this distance, sounded together. 4 The series of tones within this distance. 5 Any group or series of eight.

oc·ta·vo [ok·tā′vō] *n., pl.* **oc·ta·vos** 1 The size of a page, usually 6 × 9 1/2 inches, made from printer's sheets folded and cut into eight leaves. 2 A book made up of pages of this size. 3 *adj. use: octavo* pages.

oc·tet [ok·tet′] *n.* 1 In music, a composition for eight voices or instruments. 2 A group of eight singers or musicians. 3 Any group of eight.

Oc·to·ber [ok·tō′bər] *n.* The tenth month of the year, having 31 days. ◆ In the Roman calendar, *October* was the eighth month.

oc·to·ge·nar·i·an [ok′tə·jə·nâr′ē·ən] 1 *adj.* Between 80 and 90 years of age. 2 *n.* A person between 80 and 90 years of age.

oc·to·pus [ok′tə·pəs] *n., pl.* **oc·to·pus·es** or **oc·to·pi** [ok′tə·pī] 1 A soft-bodied sea animal related to the squid, having a large oval head, prominent eyes, and eight long arms each having two rows of suckers. 2 Anything like an octopus, as a powerful organization that is far-reaching and possibly dangerous.

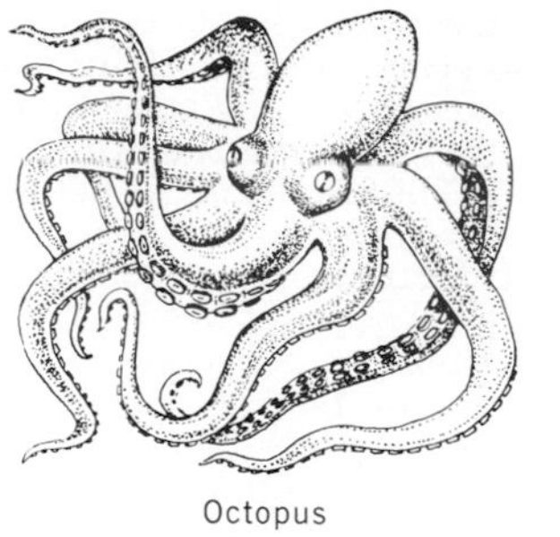
Octopus

oc·u·lar [ok′yə·lər] *adj.* 1 Of, having to do with, or like the eye: an *ocular* weakness. 2 Of or having to do with something that has been seen: *ocular* proof.

oc·u·list [ok′yə·list] *n.* 1 An optometrist. 2 An opthalmologist.

OD overdose.

odd [od] *adj.* 1 Strange or unusual; peculiar; queer: an *odd* look on one's face. 2 Not part of a routine; casual: *odd* jobs. 3 Being part of something incomplete, as a pair or set: an *odd* sock. 4 Leaving a remainder when divided by two; not even: Five is an *odd* number. 5 Having an odd number: The *odd* addresses are on the north side of the street. 6 And a little extra; a few more: I have seventy-*odd* dollars in the bank. **—odd′ness** *n.*

odd·i·ty [od′ə·tē] *n., pl.* **odd·i·ties** 1 A person or thing that is odd or peculiar. 2 The condition of being odd; strangeness; queerness.

odd·ly [od′lē] *adv.* Strangely; queerly.

odds [odz] *n.pl.* (*sometimes used with singular verb*) 1 An advantage given to a weaker opponent: The visitors gave the home team *odds* in the playoffs. 2 In betting, the ratio of the amount that can be won to the amount bet: The *odds* are three to one. 3 A chance or probability: *Odds* are that it won't rain. 4 Advantage; benefit, especially in a contest: The *odds* are in his favor. **—at odds** In disagreement. **—odds and ends** A number of different things left over: *odds and ends* from today's lunch.

ode [ōd] *n.* A poem that deals with a dignified theme in a lofty, exalted style.

O·din [ō′din] *n.* In Norse myths, the supreme god. He was the god of war, art, and wisdom.

o·di·ous [ō′dē·əs] *adj.* Arousing hate or disgust; offensive; detestable: *odious* crimes. **—o′di·ous·ly** *adv.* **—o′di·ous·ness** *n.*

o·di·um [ō′dē·əm] *n.* 1 Extreme dislike or hatred, especially widespread hatred. 2 Disgrace or shame: the *odium* of being a criminal.

o·dom·e·ter [ō·dom′ə·tər] *n.* A device for measuring the distance traveled by a vehicle.

o·dor [ō′dər] *n.* 1 A smell or scent, whether pleasing or not. 2 Regard or reputation: The senator is in bad *odor* since the scandal.

o·dor·if·er·ous [ō′də·rif′ər·əs] *adj.* Having or giving off an odor, especially a pleasant odor.

o·dor·less [ō′dər·lis] *adj.* Having no odor.

o·dor·ous [ō′dər·əs] *adj.* Having or giving off an odor, especially a fragrant odor. **—o′dor·ous·ly** *adv.* **—o′dor·ous·ness** *n.*

O·dys·seus [ō·dis′yōōs *or* ō·dis′ē·əs] *n.* In Greek legends, one of the leaders in the Greek war against Troy and the hero of Homer's *Odyssey.* His Latin name is Ulysses.

Od·ys·sey [od′ə·sē] *n.* 1 An ancient Greek poem by Homer, describing the wanderings of Odysseus after the fall of Troy. 2 (*written* **odyssey,** *pl.* **od·ys·seys**) A long, adventurous journey.

O.E.D. Oxford English Dictionary.

Oed·i·pus [ed′ə·pəs *or* ē′də·pəs] *n.* In Greek legend, a king who, without knowing who they were, killed his father and married his mother.

o'er [ôr] *prep., adv.* Over: used mostly in poems.

of [uv, ov, *or* əv] *prep.* 1 Coming from: Saint Francis *of* Assisi. 2 Connected with: Is this group *of* your party? 3 Located at: the Colossus *of* Rhodes. 4 Away from: We're within six miles *of* home. 5 Specified as; named: the city *of* Newark. 6 Having as a quality: a person *of* strength. 7 In reference to: sharp *of* tongue. 8 About; concerning: Don't speak *of* it. 9 Owing to: I'm tired *of* your complaints. 10 Possessing: a person *of* great wealth. 11 Belonging to: the lid *of* a box. 12 Made with or from: a ship *of* steel. 13 Containing: a glass *of* water. 14 Taken from: six *of* the seven students; most *of* my time. 15 So as to be without: relieved *of* trouble. 16 Created by: the plays *of* Shakespeare. 17 Directed toward: a love *of* music. 18 During: *of* recent years. 19 Devoted to: a program *of* folk music. 20 Before; until: used in telling time: It's ten minutes *of* ten. ◆ Because the verb *have* sounds like *of,* many people mistakenly write *of* in verb phrases like *could have* or *might have.*

off [ôf *or* of] 1 Away from: The pencil rolled *off* the desk; The plane rose *off* the runway. 2 *adv.* Away, as in space or time: The dog trotted *off*; The holiday is a week *off.* 3 *prep.* Not on; not in: *off* the street; *off* duty; *off* balance; *off* key. 4 *adv.* So as to make or become smaller or fewer: to wear *off*; die *off.* 5 *adv.* Away from the usual position or contact: Peel *off* the rind; Take your coat *off.* 6 *adj.* Not in the usual position; not attached: My coat button is *off.* 7 *adv.* So as not to work or happen: Turn the radio *off.* 8 *adj.* Not working or happening: The gas is *off.* 9 *prep.* Less than; below: ten cents *off* the regular price. 10 *adj.* Not up to a standard; not busy: an *off* season for business. 11 *adv.* So as to be below standard: The business dropped *off.* 12 *prep.* Below standard in: to be *off* one's golf game. 13 *adj.* Free from work or duty: my day *off.* 14 *adj.* Not likely; remote: an *off* chance. 15 *adj.* Provided for; situated: to be well *off.* 16 *adj.* Not correct; wrong. 17 *adj.* On the right: said of one of a team of horses. 18 *prep.* On or from: living *off* nuts and berries. 19 *prep. informal* No longer doing: to be *off* rich desserts. 20 *interj.* Go away! **—be off** To leave; depart. **—off and on** Now and then; occasionally. **—off with** Take off; remove: *Off with* your head! ◆ The *of* in sentences such as *I fell off of the horse* should be left out.

of·fal [ô′fəl] *n.* 1 The waste parts of a butchered animal. 2 Rubbish or refuse of any kind.

off·beat [ôf′bēt′] 1 *n.* In a musical measure, a beat that is not accented. 2 *adj. informal* Out of the ordinary; not of the usual kind; unconventional; different: an *offbeat* book.

off-col·or [ôf′kul′ər] *adj.* 1 Not having the usual color: an *offcolor* ruby. 2 Not in good taste; improper: an *offcolor* joke.

of·fence [ə·fens′] *n. British* A spelling of OFFENSE.

of·fend [ə·fend′] *v.* 1 To give offense to; displease; anger: Your hasty refusal *offended* me. 2 To be disagreeable or unpleasant to: The bright colors in the room *offended* my eyes. 3 To commit an offense, crime, or sin. **—of·fend′er** *n.*

of·fense [ə·fens′] *n.* 1 Any violation, as of a rule, duty, or law. 2 The act of offending: I meant no *offense.* 3 A being offended: I felt *offense* at the unkind words. 4 Something that offends or causes displeasure: The noise was an *offense* to the ears. 5 [*also* ô′fens] The act of attacking: an *offense* against the enemy. 6 [*also* ô′fens] In such games as football and hockey, the team possessing the ball or puck. **—give offense** To offend or cause anger or resentment. **—take offense** To be offended; feel angry or hurt.

of·fen·sive [ə·fen′siv] 1 *adj.* Unpleasant or disagreeable: an *offensive* odor; an *offensive* remark. 2 *adj.* Of or having to do with attack: Today our troops began an *offensive* operation. 3 *n.* An attack or an arrangement of forces for attacking. **—of·fen′sive·ly** *adv.* **—of·fen′sive·ness** *n.*

of·fer [ô′fər] 1 *v.* To present for taking if wanted; volunteer: to *offer* a loan. 2 *v.* To suggest or propose: to *offer* a plan of action. 3 *v.* To present solemnly, as in worship: to *offer* up a prayer. 4 *v.* To show readiness or willingness: I *offered* to go with him. 5 *v.* To attempt or try: Their team *offered* only minor resistance. 6 *v.* To suggest as payment; bid: I *offered* three dollars for the vase. 7 *n.* The act of offering: an *offer* of money.

of·fer·ing [ô′fər·ing] *n.* 1 The act of making an offer. 2 The thing that is offered, as a contribution or gift.

of·fer·to·ry [ô′fər·tôr′ē] *n., pl.* **of·fer·to·ries** 1 A part of a church service during which money is collected from the congregation. 2 The prayers said or the music played or sung during this part of the church service.

off·hand [ôf′hand′] 1 *adv.* Without preparation or thought: I could not remember the name of the movie *offhand.* 2 *adj.* Done, said, or made casually; informal: The comedian made some *offhand* remarks.

off·hand·ed [ôf′han′did] *adj.* Offhand. **—off′hand′·ed·ly** *adv.* **—off′hand′ed·ness** *n.*

of·fice [ôf′is] *n.* 1 A place in which a business or profession is carried on: a doctor's *office*; an accounting *office.* 2 The people who work as a group in an office. 3 Any position, especially a public position of authority: the *office* of president. 4 The duties or responsibilities a person has in a particular position. 5 (*usually pl.*) Any act or service done for another: The trip was arranged through their kind *offices.* 6 A religious ceremony or service.

of·fice·hold·er [ôf′is·hōl′dər] *n.* A person who holds an office under a government.

of·fi·cer [ôf′ə·sər] *n.* 1 In the armed forces, a person who has the rank to command others. 2 A person who holds an office or post, as in a corporation,

O

a	add	**i**	it	**o͝o**	took	**oi**	oil
ā	ace	**ī**	ice	**o͞o**	pool	**ou**	pout
â	care	**o**	odd	**u**	up	**ng**	ring
ä	palm	**ō**	open	**û**	burn	**th**	thin
e	end	**ô**	order	**yo͞o**	fuse	**th̶**	this
ē	equal					**zh**	vision

ə = {a in *above* e in *sicken* i in *possible* / o in *melon* u in *circus*}

government, or club. **3** A member of the police force. **4** The captain of a merchant or passenger ship or any of the chief assistants.

of·fi·cial [ə·fish′əl] **1** *n.* A person who holds an office or position, as in the government or a business. **2** *adj.* Of or having to do with a position of authority: an *official* act. **3** *adj.* Coming from or supported by authority; authorized: an *official* request. **4** *adj.* Authorized to carry out some special duty: the *official* timekeeper. **5** *adj.* Appropriate for an official; formal or ceremonial: *official* robes. **—of·fi′cial·ly** *adv.*

of·fi·cial·dom [ə·fish′əl·dəm] *n.* Officials as a group or class.

of·fi·ci·ate [ə·fish′ē·āt′] *v.* **of·fi·ci·at·ed, of·fi·ci·at·ing** **1** To conduct a service, as a priest or minister: to *officiate* at a wedding. **2** To perform the functions of any office or position: to *officiate* as referee at a boxing match.

of·fi·cious [ə·fish′əs] *adj.* Too forward in offering service or advice; meddlesome. **—of·fi′cious·ly** *adv.* **—of·fi′cious·ness** *n.*

off·ing [ôf′ing] *n.* **1** That part of the sea which is distant but visible from the shore. **2** A position some distance from the shore. **—in the offing** **1** In sight and not very distant. **2** Ready or soon to happen: Big things are *in the offing.*

off·ish [ôf′ish] *adj.* Distant in manner; aloof.

off-line [ôf′līn′] *adj.* Not connected to the central processing unit of a computer.

off·set [*v.* ôf′set′, *n.* ôf′set′] *v.* **off·set, off·set·ting,** *n.* **1** *v.* To make up for; compensate for: to *offset* a defeat by a victory. **2** *n.* Something that compensates for or balances. **3** *n.* An offshoot. **4** *n.* A method of printing in which the inked impression is transferred to a rubber-covered cylinder and from that to the paper.

offset printing Offset (def. 4).

off·shoot [ôf′sho͞ot′] *n.* **1** A shoot or branch from the main stem of a plant. **2** Anything that comes from or branches off from a principal source.

off·shore [ôf′shôr′] **1** *adj.* Moving or located away from the shore: an *offshore* breeze. **2** *adv.* At a distance from the shore: The boat is anchored *offshore.* **3** *adv.* From or away from the shore.

off·side [ôf′sīd′] **1** *adj.* In football, being illegally ahead of the ball. **2** *adj.* In hockey, being illegally ahead of the puck. **3** *adv.* In or to an offside position.

off·spring [ôf′spring′] *n., pl.* **off·spring** or **off·springs** Something that is descended from a person, animal, or plant; progeny; young.

off·stage [ôf′stāj′] **1** *adj.* In or from the part of the stage that an audience cannot see. **2** *adv.* Away from the stage or the part of the stage that an audience sees.

oft [ôft] *adv.* Often: used mostly in poems.

oft·en [ôf′ən] *adv.* Frequently or repeatedly; many times: We go there *often.*

oft·en·times [ôf′ən·tīmz′] *adv.* Often: seldom used today.

oft·times [ôf′tīmz′] *adv.* Often: seldom used today.

o·gle [ō′gəl *or* og′əl] *v.* **o·gled, o·gling,** *n.* **1** *v.* To look or stare at with admiration. **2** *n.* An ogling look or glance. **—o′gler** *n.*

o·gre [ō′gər] *n.* **1** In fairy tales, a giant or monster that eats people. **2** A brutal person.

oh [ō] *interj.* A word expressing surprise or sudden emotion: *Oh*! How could you!

OH Postal Service abbreviation of Ohio.

ohm [ōm] *n.* A unit of electrical resistance, equal to the resistance of a conductor across which one volt is developed when a current of one ampere flows through it. ◆ *Ohm* comes from Georg Simon *Ohm,* a German physicist who studied electric current.

-oid A suffix meaning: Shaped like or resembling, as in *ovoid.*

oil [oil] **1** *n.* Any of various fatty or greasy liquids that are obtained from plants, animals, or minerals. Oils will dissolve in alcohol but not in water, are sometimes volatile, and usually burn easily. Mineral oils are used mainly for fuel and to lubricate machinery. Vegetable and animal oils have many uses, as in cooking, soaps, and perfumes. **2** *adj. use*: an *oil* slick; an *oil* burner. **3** *n.* Petroleum. **4** *n.* An oil color. **5** *n.* An oil painting. **6** *v.* To smear or lubricate with oil.

oil burner A furnace or heating unit that operates on oil fuel.

oil·can [oil′kan′] *n.* A can with a spout, used for applying oil to machinery.

oil·cloth [oil′klôth′] *n.* A cloth made waterproof by a coating of oil or paint, used as a covering, as for tables and shelves.

oil color A paint made of pigment ground in linseed or other oil, used chiefly by artists.

oil·er [oi′lər] *n.* **1** A person or thing that oils, especially a person who oils engines or machinery. **2** A ship that carries oil as its cargo; tanker.

oil paint Another term for OIL COLOR.

oil painting **1** A painting done in oil colors. **2** The art of painting in oil colors.

oil·skin [oil′skin′] *n.* **1** Cloth made waterproof with oil. **2** A garment of such cloth.

oil well A well that is dug or drilled to obtain petroleum.

oil·y [oi′lē] *adj.* **oil·i·er, oil·i·est** **1** Of or like oil. **2** Full of, smeared with, or soaked with oil: *oily* rags; *oily* salad dressing. **3** Too smooth or unctuous, as in behavior or speech. **—oil′i·ness** *n.*

oint·ment [oint′mənt] *n.* A preparation, usually oily, used as a medicine for the skin.

O·jib·wa [ō·jib′wā *or* ō·jib′wə] *n., pl.* **O·jib·wa** or **Ojib·was** **1** A tribe of North American Indians once living on the shores of Lake Superior in the U.S. and Canada. **2** A member of this tribe. **3** The language of this tribe.

O·jib·way [ō·jib′wā] *n., pl.* **O·jib·way** or **O·jib·ways** Another spelling of OJIBWA.

OK or **O.K.** *adj., adv., interj., n., v.* **OK'd** or **O.K.'d, OK'ing** or **O.K.'ing** **1** *adj., adv., interj.* [ō′kā′] All correct; all right. **2** *n.* [ō′kā′] Approval; agreement. **3** *v.* [ō·kā′] To approve; agree. ◆ Though *OK* is the most common way to spell this word, *O.K.* and *okay* are also correct.

Okapi

o·ka·pi [ō·kä′pē] *n.* An African mammal related to the giraffe, but smaller and with a shorter neck.

o·kay Another spelling of OK.

Okla. Oklahoma.

o·kra [ō′krə] *n.* The sticky green pods of an annual plant, used in soups and as a vegetable. ◆ *Okra* comes from a West African language.

old [ōld] *adj.* **old·er** or **eld·er, old·est** or **eld·est,** *n.* 1 *adj.* Living or existing for a long time: an *old* woman; *old* cities. 2 *n. use* Old people: The *old* are easily tired. 3 *adj.* Showing the characteristics of an aged person: When you are tired, you look *old.* 4 *adj.* Of age; in existence: The building is two years *old.* 5 *n.* Past time: days of *old.* 6 *adj.* Belonging to the past: *old* superstitions. 7 *adj.* Worn with age or use: an *old* suit of clothes. 8 *adj.* Known or familiar for a long time: an *old* friend. 9 *adj.* Of former times: my father's *old* high school. 10 *adj.* Skilled through long experience: an *old* hand at politics. 11 *adj.* (*usually written* **Old**) Indicating the earlier or earliest of two or more things: the *Old* Testament. 12 *adj. informal* Good; dear: *old* buddy of mine. **—old'ness** *n.* ◆ *Old, aged* [ā'jid], and *elderly* all refer to persons who have lived a long time, but *old* may refer also to things not alive: an *old* house. An *aged* person is very *old,* and often feeble. *Elderly* suggests someone who is approaching *old* age but is still fairly vigorous. The word is sometimes used as a pleasant substitute (or *euphemism*) for *old.*

old country The native country of an immigrant, especially a European country.

old·en [ōl'dən] *adj.* Old; ancient: used mostly in poems: *olden* times.

Old English The language of England from about 450 to 1050; Anglo-Saxon.

Old English sheepdog One of a breed of medium-sized dogs having a long, shaggy coat that is gray or bluish gray with white markings.

Old English sheepdog

old-fash·ioned [ōld'·fash'ənd] *adj.* 1 Out of fashion; out-of-date; antiquated: *old-fashioned* furniture. 2 Of or having to do with former times: *old-fashioned* ideas. 3 Attached to or favoring old customs, ways, or behavior: an *old-fashioned* parent.

Old French The French language from about the 9th to the 16th century.

Old Glory The flag of the U.S.

old hand A veteran (def. 2).

Old High German The High German language before the beginning of the 12th century.

old·ish [ōl'dish] *adj.* Somewhat old.

old maid 1 An older woman who has never married. 2 A simple game involving the matching of pairs of cards.

Old Norse The Germanic language of Scandinavia before the middle of the 14th century.

old·ster [ôld'stər] *n. informal* An old or elderly person.

Old Testament The first of the two main divisions of the Bible, dealing with the history of the Hebrews, the laws of Moses, and the writings of the prophets.

old-time [ōld'tīm'] *adj.* Of, having to do with, or like a former time.

old-tim·er [ōld'tī'mər] *n. informal* A person who has been a member or resident for a long time.

old-world [ōld'wûrld'] *adj.* 1 (*often written* **Old-World**) Of or having to do with the Old World: *old-world* customs. 2 Ancient; antique.

o·le·an·der [ō'lē·an'dər] *n.* An evergreen shrub with poisonous leaves and clusters of white, pink, or red flowers.

o·le·o·mar·ga·rine [ō'lē·ō·mär'jə·rin] *n.* An early substitute for butter, similar to margarine but with more animal fat.

ol·fac·to·ry [ol·fak'tər·ē] *adj.* Of or having to do with the sense of smell: *olfactory* nerves.

olig- or **oligo-** A combining form meaning: Few, as in *oligarchy.*

ol·i·garch [ol'ə·gärk'] *n.* A ruler in an oligarchy.

ol·i·gar·chic [ol'ə·gär'kik] *adj.* Of, having to do with, or governed by an oligarchy.

ol·i·gar·chy [ol'ə·gär'kē] *n., pl.* **ol·i·gar·chies** 1 A form of government in which the ruling power is held by a few persons. 2 A state or country governed in this way. 3 The few persons who rule.

O·li·go·cene [ol'ə·gō·sēn' *or* ōl'ə·gō·sēn'] 1 *n.* The third geological epoch of the Tertiary period of the Cenozoic era. During the Oligocene, primitive apes appeared. 2 *adj.* Of the Oligocene.

ol·ive [ol'iv] 1 *n.* A small, oily fruit eaten green or ripe as a relish. 2 *n.* The evergreen tree that produces this fruit. 3 *n., adj.* Dull yellowish green or brown. 4 *adj.* Tinged with this color: an *olive* complexion.

olive branch 1 A branch of the olive tree considered as a symbol of peace. 2 Anything offered as a symbol of peace.

olive drab 1 Dull brownish green. 2 A fabric having this color, often used for military uniforms.

olive oil A yellow oil pressed from olives, used in preparing salads and in cooking, in making soap, and as an emollient.

O·lym·pi·ad [ō·lim'pē·ad'] *n.* 1 A holding of the modern Olympic games. 2 A period of four years between celebrations of the Olympic games, used by the ancient Greeks as a unit of time.

O·lym·pi·an [ō·lim'pē·ən] 1 *adj.* Of or having to do with Mount Olympus or with Olympia. 2 *n.* Any of the twelve chief gods who dwelt on Mount Olympus. 3 *adj.* Godlike in manner; majestic. 4 *n.* A contestant in the Olympic games.

O·lym·pic games [ō·lim'pik] 1 In ancient Greece, athletic games, races, and contests in poetry held every four years at the plain of Olympia as a festival in honor of Zeus. 2 A modern international athletic competition held every four years in a different country. Also **the Olympics.**

O·ma·ni [ō·mä'nē] 1 *adj.* Of or from Oman. 2 *n.* A person born in or a citizen of Oman.

om·buds·man [om'budz'mən] *n., pl.* **om·buds·men** [om'budz'mən] In some countries, a government official who looks into complaints that citizens make about governmental officials or agencies.

a	add	**i**	it	**o͝o**	took	**oi**	oil
ā	ace	**ī**	ice	**o͞o**	pool	**ou**	pout
â	care	**o**	odd	**u**	up	**ng**	ring
ä	palm	**ō**	open	**û**	burn	**th**	thin
e	end	**ô**	order	**yo͞o**	fuse	**t̶h̶**	this
ē	equal					**zh**	vision

ə = {a in *above* e in *sicken* i in *possible* / o in *melon* u in *circus*}

having shiny evergreen leaves and fragrant white flowers. **3** *n., adj.* Reddish yellow. ◆ *Orange* comes originally from a Persian word.

or·ange·ade [ôr′inj·ād′ *or* or′inj·ād′] *n.* A drink made of orange juice, sugar, and water.

orange blossom The white, fragrant blossom of the orange tree, often carried by brides.

orange pe·koe [pē′kō′] A very fine black tea of India, Sri Lanka, and Java.

o·rang-ou·tang [ō·rang′ə·tang′ *or* ō·rang′o͞o·tang′] *n.* Another word for ORANGUTAN.

o·rang·u·tan [ō·rang′ə·tan′ *or* ō·rang′o͞o·tan′] *n.* A large ape having brownish red hair and extremely long arms, found in Borneo and Sumatra. ◆ *Orangutan* comes from two Malay words meaning *forest man.*

Orangutan

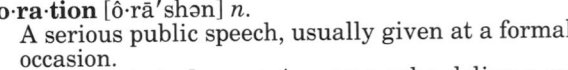

o·rate [ôr′āt *or* ô·rāt′] *v.* **o·rat·ed, o·rat·ing** To speak in a pompous manner.

o·ra·tion [ô·rā′shən] *n.* A serious public speech, usually given at a formal occasion.

or·a·tor [ôr′ə·tər] *n.* **1** A person who delivers an oration. **2** Any good public speaker.

or·a·tor·i·cal [ôr′ə·tôr′i·kəl] *adj.* Of, like, or having to do with an orator or oratory.

or·a·to·ri·o [ôr′ə·tôr′ē·ō] *n., pl.* **or·a·to·ri·os** A large musical composition for solo voices, chorus, and orchestra, usually dramatizing a sacred story but without scenery or acting.

or·a·to·ry[1] [ôr′ə·tôr′ē] *n.* The art of speaking before an audience.

or·a·to·ry[2] [ôr′ə·tôr′ē] *n., pl.* **or·a·to·ries** A place for prayer, as a private chapel.

orb [ôrb] *n.* **1** A sphere or globe. **2** A heavenly body, as the sun or a planet. **3** The eye: used mostly in poems.

or·bit [ôr′bit] **1** *n.* The path taken by a celestial body or artificial satellite as it moves around its center of attraction. Orbits are usually in the form of ellipses. **2** *n.* The probable position of an electron in relation to its atomic nucleus. **3** *v.* To move or cause to move in or as if in an orbit.

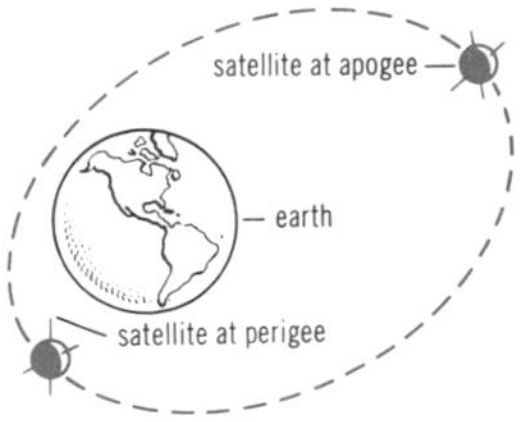

Orbit of a satellite

or·bi·tal [ôr′bit·əl] *adj.* Of, related to, or moving in an orbit: an *orbital* electron.

orch. orchestra.

or·chard [ôr′chərd] *n.* **1** A large group of trees, planted and cultivated for their products. **2** The ground on which these trees grow.

or·ches·tra [ôr′kəs·trə] *n.* **1** A group of musicians playing together, especially a large group including such performers as violinists and cellists. **2** The instruments such musicians play. **3** In a theater, the place just in front of the stage where the musicians sit. **4** The seats and seating area on the main floor of a theater. **—or·ches·tral** [ôr·kes′trəl] *adj.* **—or·ches′tral·ly** *adv.*

or·ches·trate [ôr′kəs·trāt′] *v.* **or·ches·trat·ed, or·ches·trat·ing** To arrange (music) for an orchestra. **—or′ches·tra′tion** *n.* **—or′ches·tra′tor** *n.*

or·chid [ôr′kid] **1** *n.* Any of a large number of plants bearing often beautiful and irregular flowers, usually having three petals of which one is large and shaped differently from the others. **2** *n., adj.* Pale, rosy purple.

Orchid

or·dain [ôr·dān′] *v.* **1** To order; decree: The monarch *ordained* a great council. **2** To arrange to happen; predestine: said of God or fate: Fate *ordained* that Molly Pitcher should be famous. **3** To make (someone) a minister or priest.

or·deal [ôr·dēl′, ôr·dē′əl, *or* ôr′dēl′] *n.* **1** A very difficult or trying experience. **2** A former method of trying a person for a crime. The accused was put through some painful physical tests which were not supposed to harm the person if he or she were innocent.

or·der [ôr′dər] **1** *n.* A condition in which everything is in its proper or logical place: This messy room must be put in *order.* **2** *n.* A special or particular arrangement or placement of things one after the other: List the pupils in *order* of age. **3** *v.* To put in a proper or particular condition or arrangement: You must *order* your life. **4** *n.* The customary or set method, form, or procedure for doing something: the *order* of conducting a meeting. **5** *n.* An existing state; condition: This machine is not in working *order.* **6** *n.* A social condition of peace and harmony: to restore *order* after a riot. **7** *n.* A command or direction to do something: Here are your *orders.* **8** *v.* To give a command or direction to: I *order* you to stay. **9** *v.* To demand or ask for: The teacher *ordered* more homework from us all. **10** *n.* A demand or request, usually written, to buy, sell, or supply something: an *order* for groceries. **11** *n.* That which is bought or received. **12** *v.* To give an order for: to *order* a new suit. **13** *n.* (*often written* **Order**) A body of persons united by some common bond or purpose: the Masonic *Order.* **14** *n.* A monastic or religious body: an *order* of monks. **15** *n.* (*often written* **Order**) A group of persons honored in some way, or the ribbon, medal, or other insignia they are entitled to wear: The *Order* of the Garter is the highest *order* of knighthood in Great Britain. **16** *n.* (*usually pl.*) Any of the various ranks or grades of the Christian ministry: Is he in *orders*? **17** *n.* In biology, a grouping of related animals or plants ranking below the class and above the family. **18** *n.* A kind or degree: She has talent of a high *order.* **19** *n.* A style of ancient architecture, usually known by the style or character of its columns: Doric, Ionic, and Corinthian are the main *orders* of ancient buildings. **—by order** In accordance with an order given by someone in authority. **—call to order** To ask for quiet so as to begin work or a meeting. **—in order 1** In accordance with the rules. **2** In a proper or working condition. **3** Neat; tidy. **—in order that** So that; to the end that. **—in order to** For the purpose of. **—in short order** Quickly; without delay. **—on order** Requested or ordered but not yet received: a library book *on order*. **—on the order of** Similar to; like. **—order about** or **order around** To command to do this or that or go here or there. **—out of order** 1 Not working; broken. 2 Not according to rules or proper procedure. 3 Not in its proper place, arrangement, or sequence. 4 Not suitable or proper. **—take orders** 1 To obey. 2 To become a minister or priest. **—to order** According to the wishes or specifications of the buyer.

ordered pair In mathematics, a pair of numbers, such as (3, 5), arranged in order so that there is a first number and a second number.

or·der·ly [ôr′dər·lē] *adj., n., pl.* **or·der·lies** 1 *adj.* Neat and tidy: an *orderly* kitchen. 2 *adj.* Peaceful and well-behaved: an *orderly* assembly. 3 *adj.* Characterized by or liking order or method: to have an *orderly* mind. 4 *n.* A soldier who performs various services for an officer. 5 *n.* A worker in a hospital who helps the doctors and nurses. **—or′der·li·ness** *n.*

Order of the Garter The highest order of knighthood in Great Britain.

or·di·nal [ôr′də·nəl] 1 *adj.* Of or indicating relative order in a series: an *ordinal* rank of third in the family. 2 *n.* An ordinal number.

ordinal number A number that shows place or order in a series: Second, third, and fifth are *ordinal numbers*; two, three, and five are the corresponding cardinal numbers.

or·di·nance [ôr′də·nəns] *n.* An order, law, or decree, especially one made by a city government: an *ordinance* against littering in the park.

or·di·nar·i·ly [ôr′də·ner′ə·lē *or* ôr′də·nâr′ə·lē] *adv.* Commonly; usually; normally.

or·di·nar·y [ôr′də·ner′ē] *adj.* 1 Of common or everyday occurrence; usual: an *ordinary* problem. 2 Average in quality or ability; not special: an *ordinary* play. 3 Normal; regular: The *ordinary* tuition is very high. **—out of the ordinary** Not common or usual; very special. **—or′di·nar′i·ness** *n.*

or·di·nate [ôr′də·nit] *n.* On a graph, the distance of a point from the horizontal axis.

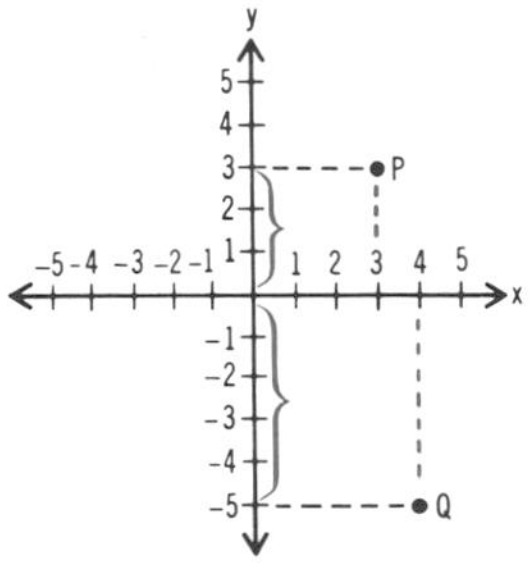

The ordinate of *P* is 3. The ordinate of *Q* is –5.

or·di·na·tion [ôr′də·nā′·shən] *n.* 1 The act or ceremony of ordaining a minister or priest. 2 The condition of being ordained.

ord·nance [ôrd′nəns] *n.* 1 Military equipment, as weapons and ammunition. 2 Cannon or artillery.

Or·do·vi·cian [ôr′də·vish′·ən] 1 *n.* The second geological period of the Paleozoic era. Rocks of this period yield fossils of the first fish. 2 *adj.* Of the Ordovician.

ore [ôr *or* ōr] *n.* A natural substance, as a rock or mineral, that contains a valuable metal or other substance: gold *ore*; sulfur *ore*.

Ore. Oregon.

Oreg. Oregon.

o·reg·a·no [ə·reg′ə·nō′] *n.* Any of several plants of the mint family, the leaves of which are used as a seasoning in cooking.

O·res·tes [ə·res′tēz] *n.* In Greek legend, the son of Agamemnon who, with his sister Electra, avenges the murder of his father by killing his mother Clytemnestra.

org. 1 organic. 2 organization. 3 organized.

or·gan [ôr′gən] *n.* 1 A musical instrument consisting of a collection of pipes that are made to sound when, by pressing down a key or pedal, compressed air is sent through them. 2 Any musical instrument similar to this in sound or in some aspect of its mechanism. 3 Any part of a plant or animal that performs some definite function: The heart is a body *organ*; The stamen is a plant *organ*. 4 A newspaper or magazine. 5 An agency for or a means of getting something done: Congress is an *organ* of government.

Organ

or·gan·dy or **or·gan·die** [ôr′gən·dē] *n., pl.* **or·gan·dies** A thin, crisp, cotton cloth, used mainly for clothing, as dresses, collars, and cuffs.

organ grinder A street musician who plays a small, portable hand organ.

or·gan·ic [ôr·gan′ik] *adj.* 1 Of, having, or related to bodily organs. 2 Affecting or altering the shape of an organ or part: *organic* disease. 3 Of, like, or produced by animals or plants: an *organic* substance. 4 Grown without chemical fertilizers: *organic* vegetables. 5 Of or related to compounds containing carbon. 6 Having parts that are arranged according to a system. 7 Fundamental. **—or·gan′i·cal·ly** *adv.*

organic chemistry The branch of chemistry that studies compounds of carbon.

or·gan·ism [ôr′gən·iz′əm] *n.* 1 An animal or plant considered as a structure of interdependent organs or parts. 2 Any structure or thing made up of many smaller, interdependent parts: A city is a social *organism*.

or·gan·ist [ôr′gən·ist] *n.* A person who plays an organ.

or·gan·i·za·tion [ôr′gən·ə·zā′shən] *n.* 1 The act of organizing. 2 The condition of being organized. 3 The manner in which something is organized: the complicated *organization* of an ant hill. 4 A number of people systematically united for some special work or purpose.

or·gan·ize [ôr′gən·īz′] *v.* **or·gan·ized, or·gan·iz·ing** 1 To form or be formed as a whole: to *organize* a club. 2 To come or bring together for some special work or purpose: to *organize* workers into a union. 3 To arrange or put in good order: to *organize* one's

a	add	**i**	it	**o͝o**	took	**oi**	oil
ā	ace	**ī**	ice	**o͞o**	pool	**ou**	pout
â	care	**o**	odd	**u**	up	**ng**	ring
ä	palm	**ō**	open	**û**	burn	**th**	thin
e	end	**ô**	order	**yo͞o**	fuse	**th**	this
ē	equal					**zh**	vision

ə = a in *above*, e in *sicken*, i in *possible*, o in *melon*, u in *circus*

O

of Argentina and Uruguay, extending from the Atlantic Ocean to the Andes Mountains.

pam·per [pam′pər] *v.* To give in to all the wishes of; treat indulgently; coddle.

pam·phlet [pam′flit] *n.* A booklet with a paper cover, often on a topic of current interest.

pam·phlet·eer [pam′flə·tir′] **1** *n.* A person who writes pamphlets. **2** *v.* To write and publish pamphlets.

pan[1] [pan] *n., v.* **panned, pan·ning** **1** *n.* A wide, shallow container, usually of metal, used to hold liquids or in cooking. **2** *n.* A container similar to this, as the one used in washing gold out of the earth or gravel. **3** *v.* To wash (earth or gravel) in a pan in search of gold. **4** *v.* To separate (gold) from earth or gravel in such a way. **5** *n.* A cup in the lock of an old gun that holds a little powder to set off the charge. **6** *v. informal* To criticize severely. **—pan out** To turn out: How did your plans *pan out*?

pan[2] *v.* **panned, pan·ning,** *n.* **1** *v.* To turn (a movie or television camera) on a pivot so as to follow a moving object or scan a wide area. **2** *n.* An act of panning a camera or the resulting shot.

Pan [pan] *n.* In Greek myths, a god of forests, flocks, and shepherds, having the horns and hoofs of a goat.

Pan. Panama.

pan·a·ce·a [pan′ə·sē′ə] *n.* A remedy for all diseases or ills; cure-all.

Pan-Af·ri·can·ism [pan′af′rə·kə·niz′əm] *n.* A movement to unite the African nations politically.

panama hat A hat woven from the leaves of a tree that grows in Central and South America.

Pan·a·ma·ni·an [pan′ə·mā′nē·ən] **1** *adj.* Of or from Panama. **2** *n.* A person born in or a citizen of Panama.

Pan-A·mer·i·can [pan′ə·mer′ə·kən] *adj.* Including or having to do with North and South America or all Americans.

pan-broil [pan′broil′] *v.* To cook in a frying pan over direct heat using little or no fat.

pan·cake [pan′kāk′] *n.* A thin, flat cake made of batter fried in a pan or on a griddle.

pan·chro·mat·ic [pan′krō·mat′ik] *adj.* Sensitive to all colors of light: *panchromatic* film.

pan·cre·as [pan′krē·əs] *n.* A large gland behind the lower part of the stomach that discharges digestive juices into the intestine and insulin into the blood.

pan·cre·at·ic [pan′krē·at′ik] *adj.* Of, from, or having to do with the pancreas.

pan·da [pan′də] *n.* **1** A small racoonlike animal of the Himalayas with reddish brown fur and a long ringed tail. **2** A related bearlike animal of Tibet and China, having a black and white coat and dark rings around the eyes.

Giant panda

pan·de·mo·ni·um [pan′də·mō′nē·əm] *n.* **1** A place of disorder and uproar. **2** Great disorder and uproar.

pan·der [pan′dər] **1** *n.* A person who exploits the base desires and weaknesses of others. **2** *v.* To act as a pander. **—pan′der·er** *n.*

Pan·do·ra [pan·dôr′ə] *n.* In Greek myths, a woman who let all human ills into the world when she opened a box which had been given to her by Zeus and which he had commanded her not to open.

pane [pān] *n.* A single sheet of glass set in a frame, as of a window or door.

pan·e·gyr·ic [pan′ə·jir′ik] *n.* **1** Formal public praise of someone or something, either spoken or written. **2** Extravagant praise.

pan·el [pan′əl] *n., v.* **pan·eled** or **pan·elled, pan·el·ing** or **pan·el·ling** **1** *n.* An oblong or square part, as of a wall, ceiling, or door, that is set off from the rest of the surface, as by being raised above the general level or by being of a different material. **2** *v.* To fit or provide with a panel or panels. **3** *n.* A piece of fabric sewn lengthwise into a skirt or the skirt of a dress. **4** *n.* A picture very long for its width. **5** *n.* A group of persons from which a jury is selected. **6** *n.* A jury. **7** *n.* A group of persons chosen to hold a discussion, judge a contest, or otherwise act together. **8** *n.* A board or mount holding dials and controls, as for an automobile, airplane, or engine room.

panel discussion A discussion, held in front of an audience, of a special subject by a selected group of people.

pan·el·ing [pan′əl·ing] *n.* **1** Wood used to make panels. **2** A group of connected panels, as on a wall.

pan·el·ist [pan′əl·ist] *n.* A person serving on a panel, especially in a panel discussion.

panel truck A small enclosed truck used for carrying small loads and for making deliveries.

pang [pang] *n.* A sudden, sharp pain or twinge: *pangs* of conscience; *pangs* of illness.

pan·go·lin [pan·gō′lin] *n.* A mammal of Asia and Africa that is covered with scales and has sharp claws and a long tongue with which it catches and eats ants.

pan·gram [pan′gram′] *n.* A short sentence that contains all the letters of the alphabet. *Now the brave grizzled fox jumps quickly* is a pangram.

pan·han·dle [pan′han′dəl] *n.,v.* **pan·han·dled, pan·han·dling** **1** *n.* The handle of a pan or pot. **2** A narrow strip of land that resembles the handle of a pan because it is attached to a wider area: *the Florida Panhandle.* **3** *v. slang* To beg for money in a public place. **—pan′han′dler** *n.*

pan·ic [pan′ik] *n., v.* **pan·icked, pan·ick·ing** **1** *n.* Sudden, overwhelming fear, often affecting many people at once: The blast caused great *panic.* **2** *v.* To affect or become affected with panic.

pan·ick·y [pan′ik·ē] *adj.* **1** Like, caused by, or showing panic. **2** Likely or tending to panic; fearful.

pan·ic-strick·en [pan′ik·strik′ən] *adj.* Helpless or weak because of a feeling of panic.

pan·nier [pan′yər] *n.* One of a pair of baskets hung across the back of an animal, used for carrying burdens.

pan·o·plied [pan′ə·plēd] *adj.* Having or wearing a panoply.

pan·o·ply [pan′ə·plē] *n., pl.* **pan·o·plies** **1** A full set of armor and weapons. **2** Any complete covering that protects or is decorative.

pan·o·ram·a [pan′ə·ram′ə] *n.* **1** A clear view in all directions, as from a mountain. **2** A wide picture which, by being unrolled a little at a time, passes slowly before the viewer. **3** A complete view or treatment of a subject or of passing events or sights: This book gives an excellent *panorama* of the development of space travel.

pan·o·ram·ic [pan'ə·ram'ik] *adj.* Of, like, or having to do with a panorama or panoramas.
pan·pipe [pan'pīp'] *n.* (*often pl.*) A primitive, flute-like musical instrument made of a graduated series of hollow reeds or wooden tubes bound together.
pan·sy [pan'zē] *n., pl.* **pan·sies** A common garden flower that grows in a variety of colors. ◆ *Pansy*, known as the flower of thought or remembrance, comes from the French word *pensée*, meaning *a thought.*
pant [pant] **1** *v.* To breath quickly and jerkily. **2** *n.* A short, gasping breath. **3** *v.* To say while panting: "Hurry," he *panted.* **4** *v.* To make noisy puffs, as of smoke or steam. **5** *n.* A noisy puff, as of steam. **6** *v.* To desire strongly; long: to *pant* after power.
pan·ta·lets or **pan·ta·lettes** [pan'tə·lets'] *n.pl.* Long, ruffled or embroidered underpants showing below the skirt, worn in the 19th century.
pan·ta·loon [pan'tə·lo͞on'] *n.* **1** (*pl.*) Trousers, especially tight-fitting ones with straps that fit under the instep, worn in former times. **2** (*written* **Pantaloon**) In pantomimes, an absurd old person on whom the clown plays tricks.
pant·dress [pant'dres'] *n.* **1** A dress with a full skirt that is divided to form pants or shorts. **2** A dress worn over shorts.
pan·the·ism [pan'thē·iz'əm] *n.* **1** The belief that everything in the universe is a part of God. **2** Belief in many or all gods. —**pan'the·ist** *n.*
pan·the·on [pan'thē·on] *n.* **1** All the gods of a people: the Greek *pantheon.* **2** (*written* **Pantheon**) A circular temple with a dome, dedicated to all the gods, built in Rome in 27 B.C.
pan·ther [pan'thər] *n.* **1** A leopard, especially the black leopard of southern Asia. **2** The cougar or mountain lion. **3** The jaguar.

Panther

pant·ies [pan'tēz] *n.pl.* A pair of underpants.
pan·to·mime [pan'tə·mīm'] *n., v.* **pan·to·mimed, pan·to·mim·ing** **1** *n.* A play in which the actors express their meaning without speaking. **2** *n.* Gestures without speech. **3** *v.* To express or act out in gestures alone.
pan·to·then·ic acid [pan'tə·then'ik] A member of the vitamin B complex that is widely distributed in plants and animals and plays a part in the metabolism of fats and carbohydrates.
pan·try [pan'trē] *n., pl.* **pan·tries** A small room or closet adjacent to a kitchen where such things as food and kitchen supplies are stored.
pants [pants] *n.pl.* **1** Trousers. **2** Underpants. ◆ The word *pants* is short for *pantaloons.*
pant·suit or **pants suit** [pant'so͞ot'] *n.* An outfit for girls or women consisting of a jacket and matching slacks.
pan·ty hose [pan'tē] A one-piece undergarment for women consisting of a pair of underpants with stockings attached.
pap [pap] *n.* Soft food for babies or invalids.
pa·pa [pä'pə *or* pə·pä'] *n.* Father: used especially by or in talking to children.
pa·pa·cy [pā'pə·sē] *n., pl.* **pa·pa·cies** **1** The office or power of a Pope. **2** The time of a Pope's reign. **3** The succession of Popes. **4** (*written* **Papacy**) The government of the Roman Catholic Church.
pa·pal [pā'pəl] *adj.* Of or having to do with a Pope, the papacy, or the Roman Catholic Church: a *papal* letter; a *papal* decree.
pa·paw [pə·pô' *or* pô'pô'] *n.* **1** A tree or shrub of North America having fleshy, edible fruit. **2** The fruit of this tree.
pa·pa·ya [pə·pä'yə] *n.* **1** An edible, yellow, melonlike fruit that grows in tropical America. **2** The tree that bears this fruit.
pa·per [pā'pər] **1** *n.* A material made mainly of wood pulp and rags, formed in thin sheets and used for several purposes, including writing, printing, wrapping things, and covering walls. **2** *n.* A sheet of this material. **3** *adj. use: paper* money; *paper* towels. **4** *n.* An essay, report, or other written or printed matter. **5** *n.* (*pl.*) A collection, as of letters or diaries, usually by one person: the Jefferson *papers.* **6** *n.* A newspaper. **7** *n.* (*pl.*) Important or official documents, as personal identification or contracts. **8** *n.* A written or printed promise to pay money; note. **9** *adj. use: paper* profits. **10** *n.* Wallpaper. **11** *v.* To cover or finish with wallpaper. **12** *n.* A wrapper used to hold small articles for sale: a *paper* of pins. **—on paper** **1** In written or printed form. **2** In theory, but not necessarily in fact: The plan looks good *on paper*, but it isn't practical. —**pa'per·er** *n.* ◆ *Paper* comes from the Latin word *papyrus*, which also gives us our word *papyrus.* In old French, Latin *papyrus* became *papier*, which is the basis of our English word *paper.*
pa·per·back [pā'pər·bak'] *n.* A book bound with a paper cover.
pa·per·boy [pā'pər·boi'] *n.* A person who sells or delivers newspapers, especially to customers' homes.
paper clip A small curved piece of wire or plastic made to hold sheets of paper together.
pa·per·hang·er [pā'pər·hang'ər] *n.* A person whose business is to cover walls with wallpaper.
pa·per-train [pā'pər·trān'] *v.* To teach (a dog or other pet) to urinate or move the bowels on paper set aside in the home.
pa·per·weight [pā'pər·wāt'] *n.* A small, heavy object placed on loose papers to prevent them from falling or blowing away.
pa·per·work [pā'pər·wûrk'] *n.* Work that involves the filling out and handling of letters, forms, and reports.
pa·pier-mâ·ché [pā'pər·mə·shā'] **1** *n.* Paper pulp mixed with oil, glue, or resin, which can be molded when wet and becomes hard and tough when dry. **2** *adj. use*: a *papier-mâché* doll.
pa·pil·la [pə·pil'ə] *n. pl.* **pa·pil·lae** [pə·pil'ē] or **pa·**

a	add	**i**	it	**o͝o**	took	**oi**	oil		
ā	ace	**ī**	ice	**o͞o**	pool	**ou**	pout		
â	care	**o**	odd	**u**	up	**ng**	ring		
ä	palm	**ō**	open	**û**	burn	**th**	thin		
e	end	**ô**	order	**yo͞o**	fuse	**t͟h**	this		
ē	equal					**zh**	vision		

ə = a in *above*, e in *sicken*, i in *possible*, o in *melon*, u in *circus*

P

pil·las A small, nipplelike projection, as on the tongue or at the root of a hair.

pa·poose or **pap·poose** [pa·po͞os'] *n.* A North American Indian baby or small child.

pa·pri·ka [pa·prē'kə *or* pap'rə·kə] *n.* A spice made from a mild variety of red pepper.

pa·py·rus [pə·pī'rəs] *n., pl.* **pa·py·ri** [pə·pī'rī] or **pa·py·rus·es** **1** A tall rushlike water plant native in Israel, Jordan, Syria, and Ethiopia and once common in Egypt. **2** A kind of paper used by the Egyptians, Greeks, and Romans made from the pith of the plant. **3** A manuscript written on this. ◆ See PAPER.

par [pär] **1** *n.* An accepted standard of comparison: This year's work is on a *par* with last year's. **2** *n.* A normal or average amount, quality, condition, or degree: Production is not up to *par.* **3** *adj.* Normal or average; ordinary. **4** *n.* In golf, a standard number of strokes in which a hole or course should be completed. **5** *n.* The value that is printed on the face of a stock, bond, or other security. **6** *adj. use: par* value.

par. **1** paragraph. **2** parallel.

Par. Paraguay.

par·a [par'ə] *n. informal* **1** A paraprofessional. **2** A paralegal.

par·a·ble [par'ə·bəl] *n.* A short tale teaching a moral or religious lesson by comparison with natural or familiar things.

pa·rab·o·la [pə·rab'ə·lə] *n.* The curve formed by the set of all the points that are equally distant from a fixed line and a fixed point; path of a thrown ball if there is no wind.

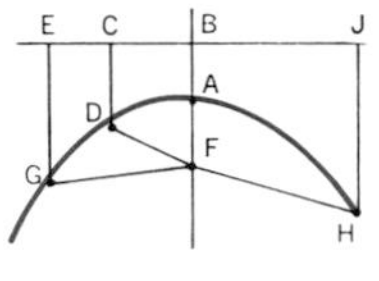

Parabola
Distance *AB* = *AF*, *EG* = *GF*, *CD* = *DF*, *JH* = *HF*

par·a·chute [par'ə·sho͞ot'] *n., v.* **par·a·chut·ed, par·a·chut·ing** **1** *n.* A large, expanding, umbrella-shaped device that retards the speed, especially in falling, of an object or person to which it is attached. Parachutes are used in making a descent from an airplane, in dropping supplies from an airplane, or in slowing down an airplane when it lands. **2** *v.* To descend or cause to descend with a parachute.

par·a·chut·ist [par'ə·sho͞ot'ist] *n.* A person who parachutes, as for sport or in battle: Skydivers and paratroopers are *parachutists.*

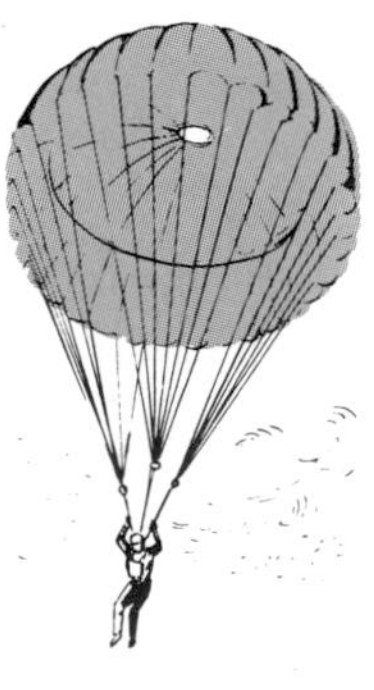
Parachute

pa·rade [pə·rād'] *n., v.* **pa·rad·ed, pa·rad·ing** **1** *n.* A procession or march for ceremony or display. **2** *v.* To march formally or with display. **3** *n.* A gathering or marching of troops for display or official inspection. **4** *n.* The place where military parades are held. **5** *v.* To cause to march or gather for military display or inspection: to *parade* troops. **6** *n.* A promenade or public walk. **7** *n.* A group of people promenading. **8** *v.* To walk in public in order to show oneself; promenade. **9** *n.* Vain show or display. **10** *v.* To display or show off; flaunt: to *parade* one's accomplishments.

par·a·digm [par'ə·dīm'] *n.* **1** A pattern or example to be used as a model. **2** A list of all the inflected forms of a word used as a pattern for similar words.

par·a·dise [par'ə·dīs'] *n.* **1** Heaven. **2** Any place or condition of great beauty or delight. **3** (*written* **Paradise**) Eden.

par·a·dox [par'ə·doks'] *n.* **1** A statement that seems contradictory, but may in fact be true, as "Stone walls do not a prison make, nor iron bars a cage." **2** A statement that contradicts itself, or is false or absurd, as "Everything I say is a lie." **3** A person or thing that seems to act in a contradictory way.

par·a·dox·i·cal [par'ə·doks'i·kəl] *adj.* Of, like, or having to do with a paradox.

par·af·fin [par'ə·fin] **1** *n.* A white, waxy mixture of substances obtained chiefly from petroleum. Its uses include making candles and sealing jelly or preserves. **2** *v.* To treat with paraffin.

par·a·gon [par'ə·gon'] *n.* A model or pattern of excellence: a *paragon* of scholarship.

par·a·graph [par'ə·graf'] **1** *n.* A distinct, separate part or section of something written, generally beginning on a new line and indented from the margin. **2** *v.* To arrange in or into paragraphs. **3** *n.* A short article or item, as in a newspaper. **4** *v.* To write paragraphs about. **5** *n.* A sign (¶) used to indicate a new paragraph or as a reference to a paragraph.

Par·a·guay·an [par'ə·gwā'ən *or* par'ə·gwī'ən] **1** *adj.* Of or from Paraguay. **2** *n.* A person born in or a citizen of Paraguay.

par·a·keet [par'ə·kēt'] *n.* Any of various small parrots with long tails, kept as pets.

par·a·le·gal [par'ə·lē'gəl] **1** *n.* A person who is trained to assist lawyers in preparing legal work. **2** *adj.* Of or being a person trained to assist lawyers.

par·al·lax [par'ə·laks'] *n.* An apparent change in the position of an object caused by a change in the position of the observer. Parallax is used in astronomy for determining distances.

par·al·lel [par'ə·lel] *adj., n., v.* **par·al·leled** or **par·al·lelled, par·al·lel·ing** or **par·al·lel·ling** **1** *adj.* Never having a point in common, no matter how far extended, as two lines or two flat surfaces: The floor is *parallel* to the ceiling. **2** *n.* An object or surface that is always an equal distance from another. **3** *n.* A parallel line or surface. **4** *v.* To be parallel to: The railroad track *parallels* the road. **5** *adj.* Very much alike; closely similar: stories with *parallel* plots. **6** *n.* A comparison: to draw a *parallel* between two things. **7** *v.* To be, find, or provide the equal of: Can you *parallel* that? **8** *n.* Something that is similar to or like something else; match. **9** *v.* To compare; liken. **10** *n.* One of the imaginary circles around the earth parallel to the equator and connecting all the points having a particular latitude. **11** *n.* In an electric circuit, a connection of devices so made that each can be removed without stopping the current to or from any of the others.

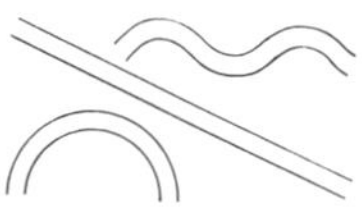
Sets of parallels

parallel bars A piece of gymnastic equipment having two horizontal poles set parallel to each other at adjustable heights above the floor.

par·al·lel·e·pi·ped [par'ə·lel'ə·pī'pid] *n.* A solid form with six sides that are all parallelograms.

par·al·lel·ism [par'ə·lel·iz'əm] *n.* **1** The quality or condition of being parallel. **2** Close resemblance or similarity.

par·al·lel·o·gram [par′ə·lel′ə·gram′] *n.* A four-sided plane figure having all of its opposite sides parallel.

pa·ral·y·sis [pə·ral′ə·sis] *n., pl.* **pa·ral·y·ses** [pə·ral′·ə·sēz′] **1** The loss or lessening of the power of movement or of feeling in any part of the body. **2** A stopping or crippling of normal activities: Snow caused *paralysis* of travel.

par·a·lyt·ic [par′ə·lit′ik] **1** *adj.* Of, having, or causing paralysis. **2** *n.* A person with paralysis.

par·a·lyze [par′ə·līz′] *v.* **par·a·lyzed, par·a·lyz·ing** **1** To bring about paralysis in. **2** To make powerless, helpless, or inactive: The strike *paralyzed* the industry.

par·a·me·ci·um [par′ə·mē′shē·əm *or* par′ə·mē′sē·əm] *n., pl.* **par·a·me·ci·a** [par′ə·mē′shē·ə *or* par′ə·mē′sē·ə] or **par·a·me·ci·ums** A tiny slipper-shaped, one-celled animal covered with fine hairs, or cilia, by which it swims about.

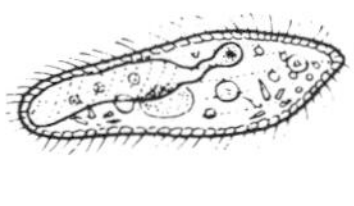
A paramecium

par·a·med·ic [par′ə·med′ik] *n.* A person who is trained to assist a doctor or to give first aid or emergency treatment, as from an ambulance.

pa·ram·e·ter [pə·ram′ə·tər] *n.* **1** A number whose value determines or restricts the form of a mathematical expression or the physical phenomenon the expression describes. **2** A property or characteristic. **3** *informal* A limit or boundary.

par·a·mount [par′ə·mount′] *adj.* Superior to all others; chief in importance or rank.

par·a·mour [par′ə·mo͝or′] *n.* A lover, especially a lover of someone who is married to another.

par·a·noi·a [par′ə·noi′ə] *n.* A mental disorder in which a person often imagines persecution by others or imagines being a more important person than he or she actually is.

par·a·noid [par′ə·noid′] **1** *adj.* Resembling or suggestive of paranoia. **2** *n.* A person having paranoia or showing some of its symptoms.

par·a·pet [par′ə·pit *or* par′ə·pet] *n.* **1** A low wall around the edge of a structure, as a roof or terrace. **2** A low wall built by soldiers as a defense.

par·a·pher·na·li·a [par′ə·fər·nāl′yə] *n.pl.* **1** Personal possessions. **2** (*often used with a singular verb*) A group of things, especially as used in some activity; equipment.

par·a·phrase [par′ə·frāz′] *n., v.* **par·a·phrased, par·a·phras·ing** **1** *n.* A statement expressed in other words of the meaning of something, as a passage or work. **2** *v.* To express in other words the meaning of something, as a passage or work.

par·a·ple·gic [par′ə·plē′jik] **1** *n.* A person who has lost the use of the lower part of the body, usually because of an injury to or disease of the spine. **2** *adj.* Of, for, or being a paraplegic.

par·a·pro·fes·sion·al [par′ə·prə·fesh′ən·əl] *n.* A person trained to assist a teacher, lawyer, doctor, or other professional.

par·a·quat [par′ə·kwot′] *n.* A poisonous chemical that is used to kill weeds and other unwanted plants.

par·a·site [par′ə·sīt′] *n.* **1** A plant or animal that lives in or on another and gets its food and often shelter from the other, as a flea or tapeworm. **2** A person who lives at the expense of another without making proper return.

par·a·sit·ic [par′ə·sit′ik] *adj.* Of, like, or caused by a parasite or parasites.

par·a·sol [par′ə·sôl′] *n.* A small, light umbrella carried to protect someone from the sun.

par·a·thy·roid gland [par′ə·thī′roid] One of several, usually four, small bean-shaped glands arranged in pairs behind the thyroid gland. They control the amount of calcium in the blood.

par·a·troop·er [par′ə·tro͞o′pər] *n.* A soldier trained to parachute into battle from an airplane.

par·a·troops [par′ə·tro͞ops′] *n.pl.* Troops trained to parachute into battle.

par·boil [pär′boil′] *v.* To cook partially by boiling, as in preparation for roasting.

par·cel [pär′səl] *n., v.* **par·celed** or **par·celled, par·cel·ing** or **par·cel·ling** **1** *n.* Something that is wrapped up; package. **2** *n.* A distinct portion of land: We sold that rocky *parcel* near the river. **3** *v.* To divide or give in parts or shares: to *parcel* out food.

parcel post A mail service for the carrying and delivering of parcels.

parch [pärch] *v.* **1** To make or become dry with heat; shrivel. **2** To make or become thirsty.

parch·ment [pärch′mənt] *n.* **1** The skin of sheep, goats, and other animals, prepared to be written or painted on. **2** A manuscript written on parchment. **3** Paper that looks like parchment, as that used in stationery and lamp shades.

par·don [pär′dən] **1** *v.* To forgive: *Pardon* me for being late. **2** *n.* The act of forgiving; forgiveness: I beg your *pardon.* **3** *v.* To excuse or free from further punishment: The convict was *pardoned.* **4** *n.* The decision or the legal order that frees a person from punishment.

par·don·a·ble [pär′dən·ə·bəl] *adj.* Capable of being pardoned: a *pardonable* offense.

pare [pâr] *v.* **pared, par·ing** **1** To remove the outer layer or skin of (a fruit or vegetable). **2** To make less or smaller, little by little: to *pare* costs.

Paring an apple

par·e·gor·ic [par′ə·gôr′ik] *n.* A solution of camphor and a small amount of opium in alcohol, used to relieve pain, coughing, and other symptoms.

par·ent [pâr′ənt] **1** *n.* A father or mother. **2** *n.* Any plant or animal that produces offspring. **3** *n.* A source or cause: Good work can be the *parent* of pride. **4** *v.* To act as a parent to.

par·ent·age [pâr′ən·tij] *n.* Descent from parents; lineage; origin.

pa·ren·tal [pə·ren′təl] *adj.* Of, having to do with, or like a parent. **—pa·ren′tal·ly** *adv.*

pa·ren·the·sis [pə·ren′thə·sis] *n., pl.* **pa·ren·the·ses** [pə·ren′thə·sēz] **1** Something, as a word or phrase, added to an already complete sentence but set off from it, as *thank heaven* in "He went (thank

a	add	**i**	it	**o͝o**	took	**oi**	oil
ā	ace	**ī**	ice	**o͞o**	pool	**ou**	pout
â	care	**o**	odd	**u**	up	**ng**	ring
ä	palm	**ō**	open	**û**	burn	**th**	thin
e	end	**ô**	order	**yo͞o**	fuse	**t͟h**	this
ē	equal					**zh**	vision

ə = {a in *above* e in *sicken* i in *possible* / o in *melon* u in *circus*}

P

heaven) home." **2** Either or both of the curved lines ( ) used to enclose such a word or phrase.

par·en·thet·ic [par′ən·thet′ik] *adj.* Parenthetical.

par·en·thet·i·cal [par′ən·thet′i·kəl] *adj.* **1** Put in as a parenthesis: a *parenthetical* remark. **2** Enclosed in a parenthesis. **3** Using many parentheses. **—par′en·thet′i·cal·ly** *adv.*

par·ent·hood [pâr′ənt·hŏŏd′] *n.* The condition of being a parent.

par·ent·ing [pâr′ən·ting] *n.* The art and skill of being an effective parent.

par·fait [pär·fā′] *n.* A frozen dessert made with such ingredients as eggs, sugar, whipped cream, and flavoring.

pa·ri·ah [pə·rī′ə] *n.* A person with whom others do not associate; outcast.

par·ing [pâr′ing] *n.* (*often pl.*) Something that has been pared off, as skin or rind.

paring knife A small knife with a short blade, used for paring.

Par·is [par′is] *n.* In Greek myths, a Trojan prince who kidnapped Helen, the queen of Sparta, thus causing the Trojan War.

par·ish [par′ish] *n.* **1** In certain religious groups, a district, usually part of a diocese, having its own church and clergy. **2** All the people who worship at one church. **3** A district in Louisiana corresponding to a county.

pa·rish·ion·er [pə·rish′ən·ər] *n.* A member of a parish.

Pa·ri·sian [pə·rē′zhən] **1** *adj.* Of or from Paris, France. **2** *n.* A person born in or a citizen of Paris.

par·i·ty [par′ə·tē] *n.* Equality, as of condition, rank, or value.

park [pärk] **1** *n.* A piece of land for public use, having trees, grass, benches, walks, and playgrounds. **2** *n.* An area set aside for public use by a national or state government because of some unique property, as its beauty or wildlife. **3** *n.* The grounds of a country estate. **4** *v.* To leave (an automobile or other vehicle) standing somewhere for a time. **5** *v.* To drive (as an automobile) into a place where it may be left.

par·ka [pär′kə] *n.* A fur or cloth jacket or coat with a hood.

Parka

parking lot An area set aside for parking motor vehicles.

parking meter A timer, usually mounted on a pole, into which people put coins for the right to use a parking space for a particular period of time.

parking orbit An orbit temporarily maintained by an artificial satellite or a space vehicle.

park·way [pärk′wā′] *n.* A wide street or road whose edges are planted with grass and trees.

par·lance [pär′ləns] *n.* Manner of speech; language: legal *parlance.*

par·lay [pär′lā *or* pär′lē] **1** *v.* To bet (money and winnings from one bet) on one or more following contests or races. **2** *n.* A bet or series of bets made by taking the original wager and winnings and placing it on one or more following contests. **3** *v.* To use or increase successfully: She *parlayed* a bit part into a starring role.

par·ley [pär′lē] *n., pl.* **par·leys,** *v.* **1** *n.* A conference, as with an enemy; discussion of terms. **2** *v.* To hold such a conference.

par·lia·ment [pär′lə·mənt] *n.* **1** An assembly whose function is making the laws of a country. **2** (*written* **Parliament**) The legislature of Great Britain, or of any of the self-governing members of the Commonwealth.

par·lia·men·tar·i·an [pär′lə·men·târ′ē·ən] *n.* An expert in the rules governing the procedure of legislatures and other deliberative bodies.

par·lia·men·ta·ry [pär′lə·men′tər·ē] *adj.* **1** Of, having to do with, or done by a parliament. **2** According to the rules of a parliament: *parliamentary* procedure. **3** Governed by or having a parliament.

par·lor [pär′lər] *n.* **1** A room for receiving visitors or entertaining guests. **2** A place where a certain kind of business is conducted: a *beauty* parlor.

parlor car A railroad car offering greater comfort and service than an ordinary passenger car.

par·lous [pär′ləs] *adj.* Dangerous or exciting; perilous: seldom used today.

Par·me·san cheese [pär′mə·zän′] A hard, pale yellow, dry Italian cheese that is usually grated and used on spaghetti, soups, and other dishes.

pa·ro·chi·al [pə·rō′kē·əl] *adj.* **1** Belonging to, supported by, or limited to a church parish. **2** Limited in scope; narrow: *parochial* ideas. **—pa·ro′chi·al·ism** *n.*

parochial school A school that is run and maintained by a church or other religious organization.

par·o·dy [par′ə·dē] *n., pl.* **par·o·dies,** *v.* **par·o·died, par·o·dy·ing** **1** *n.* A humorous imitation of a serious literary or musical work. **2** *v.* To make or perform a parody of.

pa·role [pə·rōl′] *n., v.* **pa·roled, pa·rol·ing** **1** *n.* The release of a prisoner from part of the sentence on the conditions that the prisoner observe certain rules and behave well. **2** *v.* To release (a prisoner) on these conditions. **3** *n.* A pledge by a prisoner of war to abide by certain conditions in return for release or for special privileges.

Parquet

par·ox·ysm [par′ək·siz′əm] *n.* A sudden and violent outburst; fit: a *paroxysm* of tears.

par·quet [pär·kā′] *n.* **1** Flooring of parquetry. **2** The main floor of a theater; orchestra.

par·quet·ry [pär′kit·rē] *n.* Pieces of wood fitted into a pattern, used mainly for floors.

par·ra·keet [par′ə·kēt′] *n.* Another spelling of PARAKEET.

par·ri·cide [par′ə·sīd′] *n.* **1** The killing of a parent. **2** A person who has killed a parent.

par·rot [par′ət] **1** *n.* Any of various brightly colored birds with hooked bills, some of which can imitate human speech. **2** *v.* To imitate or repeat without understanding. **3** *n.* A person who parrots.

Parrot

par·ry [par′ē] *v.* **par·ried, par·ry·ing,** *n., pl.* **par·ries** **1** *v.* To ward off, as a blow or a thrust from a sword. **2** *v.* To avoid or evade, as a question. **3**

n. The movement or act of parrying, as a blow.

parse [pärs] *v.* **parsed, pars·ing** **1** To separate (a sentence) into the parts that make it up, explaining the form, function, and relationship of each of them. **2** To describe (a word) in a sentence, telling its part of speech, its function, and its relationship to the other words.

Par·si or **Par·see** [pär′sē] *n.* A member of a religious sect in India, descended from Persians who fled there in the 8th century.

par·si·mo·ni·ous [pär′sə·mō′nē·əs] *adj.* Too thrifty; stingy. —**par′si·mo′ni·ous·ly** *adv.*

par·si·mo·ny [pär′sə·mō′nē] *n.* Too much thriftiness; stinginess.

pars·ley [pärs′lē] *n.* A common herb cultivated for its leaves which are used to flavor and decorate foods.

pars·nip [pärs′nip] *n.* An herb with a large carrotlike root that can be eaten.

par·son [pär′sən] *n.* A clergyman; minister.

par·son·age [pär′sən·ij] *n.* The house that a church provides for its parson.

part [pärt] **1** *n.* A portion or piece of a whole, often one of a group of equal pieces. **2** *v.* To divide or break into parts. **3** *n.* Any of the separate things that make up a working whole, as in a machine: radio *parts.* **4** *n.* A portion, as an organ or limb, of a plant or animal. **5** *n.* A share, as of work or obligation: to do one's *part.* **6** *adj.* Being incomplete; not whole: a *part* owner. **7** *adv.* Partly: The idea is *part* mine. **8** *n.* A side, as in a disagreement or dispute. **9** *n.* The role or lines given to an actor, as in a play. **10** *n.* The music intended for a voice or instrument or a particular group of voices or instruments in a composition: the flute *part.* **11** *n.* A line on the scalp made by combing the hair in opposite directions. **12** *v.* To divide (the hair) by combing in different directions. **13** *v.* To break off, as a relationship: to *part* company. **14** *v.* To separate: to *part* the two fighters; They *parted* at noon. **15** *n.* (*usually pl.*) A gift of mind or character: a creator of *parts.* **16** *n.* (*usually pl.*) A region or territory: foreign *parts.* —**for one's part** As far as one is concerned. —**for the most part** To the greatest extent; generally. —**in part** Partly; not wholly. —**part and parcel** An essential or very important part. —**part with** To give up. —**take part** To join in or share; participate.

part. **1** participle. **2** particular.

par·take [pär·tāk′] *v.* **par·took, par·tak·en, par·tak·ing** **1** To take part or have a share: All her friends *partook* in her good fortune. **2** To receive or take a portion or share: They *partook* of the evening meal. **3** To have something of the quality: answers that *partake* of rudeness. —**par·tak′er** *n.*

par·the·no·gen·e·sis [pär′thə·nō·jen′ə·sis] *n.* Reproduction in which a new organism develops from an egg cell that has not been fertilized.

Par·the·non [pär′thə·non′] *n.* A famous Greek temple on the Acropolis of Athens.

The Parthenon

par·tial [pär′shəl] *adj.* **1** Involving or made up of only a part. **2** Favoring one side; prejudiced; biased. **3** Having a special liking: I'm *partial* to ice cream. —**par′tial·ly** *adv.*

par·ti·al·i·ty [pär′shē·al′ə·tē] *n., pl.* **par·ti·al·i·ties** **1** The condition or quality of being partial. **2** A special fondness.

par·tic·i·pant [pär·tis′ə·pənt] *n.* A person who participates or takes part.

par·tic·i·pate [pär·tis′ə·pāt′] *v.* **par·tic·i·pat·ed, par·tic·i·pat·ing** To take part or have a share with others: We all *participated* in the school bazaar. —**par·tic′i·pa′tion** *n.*

par·ti·cip·i·al [pär′tə·sip′ē·əl] **1** *adj.* Having the form or use of a participle. **2** *adj.* Like or based on a participle. **3** *n.* A participle.

par·ti·ci·ple [pär′tə·sip′əl] *n.* Either of two verb forms, the past participle (usually ending in *-ed* or *-en*) and the present participle (ending in *-ing*). Participles are used with auxiliary verbs to form certain tenses and can also function as adjectives and sometimes as nouns.

par·ti·cle [pär′ti·kəl] *n.* **1** A very small part, piece, or amount; speck. **2** One of the smallest bits of matter, as an atom. **3** An elementary particle. **4** A short word, as an article, preposition, or conjunction. **5** A prefix or suffix.

particle accelerator A machine that raises the speeds of atomic particles to very high values.

particle board A board made up of small pieces of wood bonded together with strong glue or resin.

par·ti-col·ored [pär′tē·kul′ərd] *adj.* Differently colored in different parts.

par·tic·u·lar [pər·tik′yə·lər] **1** *adj.* Having to do with one certain person, thing, time, or place; specific: Building airplane models is my *particular* hobby. **2** *adj.* Apart from others: Each student must choose a *particular* subject for a term paper. **3** *adj.* Especially noteworthy; special: The lecture you missed was of *particular* importance. **4** *adj.* Careful; fastidious: *particular* about the way he dresses. **5** *n.* An item; detail: Give me the *particulars.* —**in particular** Particularly; especially: We did nothing *in particular* last night.

par·tic·u·lar·i·ty [pər·tik′yə·lar′ə·tē] *n., pl.* **par·tic·u·lar·i·ties** **1** Exactness in attention to details. **2** A special trait or characteristic. **3** A circumstance or detail; particular.

par·tic·u·lar·ize [pər·tik′yə·lə·rīz′] *v.* **par·tic·u·lar·ized, par·tic·u·lar·iz·ing** **1** To speak of or treat in detail. **2** To be specific. —**par·tic′u·lar·i·za′tion** *n.*

par·tic·u·lar·ly [pər·tik′yə·lər·lē] *adv.* **1** In a particular way: to emphasize one point *particularly;* to study a blueprint *particularly.* **2** More than usually: a *particularly* good meal.

part·ing [pär′ting] **1** *n.* The act of separating. **2** *n.* The condition of being separated. **3** *adj.* Separating; dividing. **4** *n.* A taking leave; departure. **5** *adj.* Given, done, or said at parting: a *parting* glance. **6** *adj.* Of or having to do with a departure. **7** *adj.* Departing; going.

parting shot A sharp remark or aggressive action made by a person who is in the act of leaving.

a	add	**i**	it	**o͝o**	took	**oi**	oil
ā	ace	**ī**	ice	**o͞o**	pool	**ou**	pout
â	care	**o**	odd	**u**	up	**ng**	ring
ä	palm	**ō**	open	**û**	burn	**th**	thin
e	end	**ô**	order	**yo͞o**	fuse	**t̶h̶**	this
ē	equal					**zh**	vision

ə = { a in *above* e in *sicken* i in *possible* / o in *melon* u in *circus* }

P

do with punishment: a *penal* colony; a *penal* offense; a *penal* code.

pe·nal·ize [pē′nəl·īz′ *or* pen′əl·īz′] *v.* **pe·nal·ized, pe·nal·iz·ing** 1 To punish by putting on a penalty: to *penalize* a player for breaking rules. 2 To provide a penalty for: Lateness is *penalized* by making offenders stay after school.

pen·al·ty [pen′əl·tē] *n., pl.* **pen·al·ties** 1 The legal punishment for having broken a law: a *penalty* of up to 3 months in jail for driving offenses. 2 In sports, a disadvantage put on one side or player for fouling or breaking the rules. 3 Any unpleasant consequence or result: Lack of privacy is one of the *penalties* of fame.

penalty box The place next to an ice-hockey rink to which players go when they have been penalized for breaking a rule.

pen·ance [pen′əns] *n.* A punishment that a person accepts and endures, or an action that a person performs, to show regret for committing sins or faults and a desire to be forgiven.

pence [pens] Plural of PENNY (def. 2).

pen·chant [pen′chənt] *n.* A strong liking or inclination: to have a *penchant* for modern art.

pen·cil [pen′səl] *n., v.* **pen·ciled** or **pen·cilled, pen·cil·ing** or **pen·cil·ling** 1 *n.* An implement having a stick of graphite, colored chalk, or the like, encased in wood or metal, used for writing, drawing, or marking. 2 *v.* To write or mark with a pencil.

pen·dant or **pen·dent** [pen′dənt] *n.* Anything that hangs from something else, especially an ornament, as a jewel on a chain.

pen·dent or **pen·dant** [pen′dənt] *adj.* 1 Hanging downward: *pendent* limbs of trees. 2 Projecting; overhanging: a *pendent* rock. 3 Pending.

pend·ing [pen′ding] 1 *adj.* Not yet decided or settled: a case that is *pending.* 2 *prep.* While awaiting; until: *pending* the verdict. 3 *prep.* During: Rationing will continue, *pending* the shortage. 4 *adj.* Ready to happen; threatening: *pending* evils.

pen·du·lous [pen′jŏŏ·ləs] *adj.* 1 Hanging, especially so as to swing freely: a *pendulous* branch, heavy with fruit. 2 Wavering; undecided. —**pen′·du·lous·ly** *adv.* —**pen′du·lous·ness** *n.*

pen·du·lum [pen′jŏŏ·ləm *or* pen′də·ləm] *n.* A weight hung from a support and allowed to swing back and forth. Since the time required for one complete swing is constant, pendulums can be used to regulate clocks.

Pendulum

Pe·nel·o·pe [pə·nel′ə·pē] *n.* In the *Odyssey* by Homer, the faithful wife of Odysseus.

pen·e·tra·ble [pen′ə·trə·bəl] *adj.* That can be penetrated: *penetrable* defenses. —**pen·e·tra·bil·i·ty** [pen′ə·trə·bil′ə·tē] *n.*

pen·e·trate [pen′ə·trāt′] *v.* **pen·e·trat·ed, pen·e·trat·ing** 1 To enter into or through; pierce: The arrow *penetrated* the target. 2 To see through: We could not *penetrate* the darkness. 3 To come to know or understand: to *penetrate* a theory. 4 To affect or move deeply: The music *penetrated* his whole being. ◆ *Penetrate* and *permeate* both carry the idea of entering into. Something that *penetrates* moves in a particular direction into or through something else. Whatever *permeates*, however, simply spreads out in all directions, intermixing with another element. A bullet *penetrates* a wall, and the odor of smoke *permeates* the air.

pen·e·trat·ing [pen′ə·trā′ting] *adj.* Able to penetrate, as by being sharp, keen, or piercing: a *penetrating* chill; a *penetrating* mind.

pen·e·tra·tion [pen′ə·trā′shən] *n.* 1 The act of penetrating. 2 Keen mental ability or insight. 3 The depth to which a thing penetrates.

pen·guin [pen(g)′gwin] *n.* A black and white swimming bird of Antarctic regions with flipperlike wings, webbed feet, and very short legs on which it stands erect.

Penguin

pen·i·cil·lin [pen′ə·sil′in] *n.* A powerful antibiotic obtained from the mold penicillium.

pen·i·cil·li·um [pen′ə·sil′ē·əm] *n., pl.* **pen·i·cil·li·ums** or **pen·i·cil·li·a** [pen′ə·sil′ē·ə] Any of various blue or green molds growing on decaying fruit, ripening cheese, and other foods. One of these molds is the source of penicillin.

pen·in·su·la [pə·nin′s(y)ə·lə] *n.* A piece of land nearly surrounded by water and joined to a larger land mass. Italy and Florida are peninsulas. —**pen·in′su·lar** *adj.*

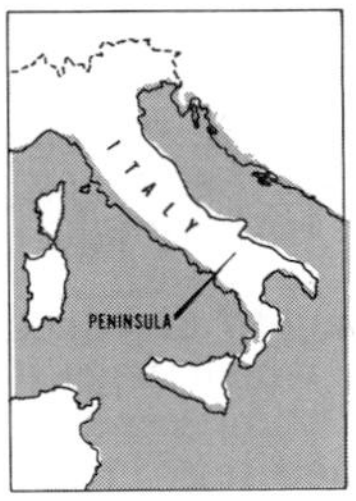

pe·nis [pē′nis] *n., pl.* **pe·nis·es** or **pe·nes** [pē′nēz′] A male animal's sex organ and, in most male mammals, the organ used for urination.

pen·i·tence [pen′ə·təns] *n.* Sincere sorrow for one's sins or wrongful acts; repentance.

pen·i·tent [pen′ə·tənt] 1 *adj.* Sorry for one's sins or faults; contrite. 2 *n.* A person who is sorry for having sinned or committed faults. —**pen′i·tent·ly** *adv.*

pen·i·ten·tial [pən′ə·ten′shəl] *adj.* Of, having to do with, or expressing penitence or penance.

pen·i·ten·tia·ry [pen′ə·ten′shər·ē] *n., pl.* **pen·i·ten·tia·ries,** *adj.* 1 *n.* A prison, especially one run by a state or federal government. 2 *adj.* That is punishable by imprisonment: said about a crime. 3 *adj.* Used for punishment or discipline. 4 *adj.* Of or having to do with penance.

pen·knife [pen′nīf′] *n., pl.* **pen·knives** [pen′nīvz′] A small pocketknife.

pen·man [pen′mən] *n., pl.* **pen·men** [pen′mən] 1 A person who has a fine handwriting. 2 A person who writes or copies. 3 An author.

pen·man·ship [pen′mən·ship′] *n.* 1 The style or quality of handwriting. 2 The art of writing.

Penn. Pennsylvania.

Penna. Pennsylvania.

pen name A made-up name with which an author signs work: The *pen name* of Mary Ann Evans was George Eliot.

pen·nant [pen′ənt] *n.* 1 A long, narrow, often triangular flag, as one used for a school emblem or on a ship for signaling. 2 A flag that symbolizes championship, especially in a professional baseball league.

pen·ni·less [pen′i·lis] *adj.* Extremely poor.

pen·non [pen′ən] *n.* **1** A small flag ending in a point or points, once carried by knights on their lances. **2** Any banner or flag. **3** A wing.

Pennsylvania Dutch **1** People of German descent whose ancestors settled in Pennsylvania. **2** The kind of German dialect that they speak. ◆ See DUTCHMAN.

pen·ny [pen′ē] *n., pl.* **pen·nies,** for def. 2 **pence** [pens] **1** A U.S. or Canadian coin worth one cent. **2** A British coin worth 1/100 of a pound or, before 1971, 1/240 of a pound. **3** Money in general. **—a pretty penny** *informal* Quite a lot of money.

pen·ny·weight [pen′ē·wāt′] *n.* In troy weight, a unit equal to 1/20 of an ounce or 24 grains.

pen·ny-wise [pen′ē·wīz′] *adj.* Very careful about saving small sums of money. **—penny-wise and pound-foolish** Careful and thrifty in small matters but wasteful in large ones.

pen·ny·worth [pen′ē·wûrth′] *n.* **1** As much as a penny will buy. **2** An insignificant amount. **3** A bargain.

pe·nol·o·gy [pē·nol′ə·jē] *n.* The study of managing prisons and prisoners. **—pe·no·log·i·cal** [pē′nə·loj′ə·kəl] *adj.* **—pe·nol′o·gist** *n.*

pen pal A person one writes to and receives letters from, often a person one has never met.

pen·sion¹ [pen′shən] **1** *n.* An allowance regularly paid to a person who has retired from work after long service or because of injury. A pension is sometimes paid to a pensioner's family after the person's death. **2** *v.* To grant a pension to.

pen·sion² [pän·syōn′] *n.* A small European hotel or boarding house.

pen·sion·er [pen′shən·ər] *n.* A person who receives a pension.

pen·sive [pen′siv] *adj.* Quietly and seriously thoughtful, often with a touch of sadness: a *pensive* person or mood. **—pen′sive·ly** *adv.*

pent [pent] **1** A past tense and past participle of PEN¹. **2** *adj.* Penned up or in; closely confined.

penta- A combining form meaning: Five, as in *pentameter.*

pen·ta·gon [pen′tə·gon′] *n.* A closed figure having five straight sides and five angles. ◆ *Pentagon* comes from Greek words meaning *five angles.*

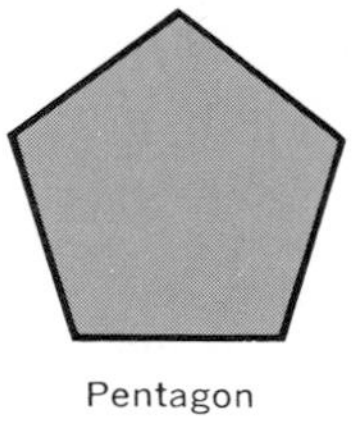

Pentagon

Pentagon, the **1** The five-sided building in Arlington, Virginia, in which the U.S. Department of Defense is located. **2** The U.S. Department of Defense.

pen·tag·o·nal [pen·tag′ə·nəl] *adj.* Having the five sides and five angles of a pentagon: *pentagonal* tiles.

pen·tam·e·ter [pen·tam′ə·tər] *n.* A line of verse made up of five rhythmic feet, as: "A bŏok/ ŏf vĕr/ sĕs ūn/ dĕrnēath/ thĕ bōugh."

Pen·ta·teuch [pen′tə·t(y)o͞ok′] *n.* The first five books of the Old Testament.

pen·tath·lon [pen·tath′lən] *n.* An athletic contest made up of five separate events. Each contestant must participate in all events.

Pen·te·cost [pen′tə·kôst′] *n.* **1** A Christian festival coming on the seventh Sunday after Easter and commemorating the descent of the Holy Ghost upon the apostles. It is also called Whitsunday. **2** A Jewish festival coming 50 days after Passover; Shabuoth.

pent·house [pent′hous′] *n.* An apartment, house, or other structure built on the roof of a building.

pent-up [pent′up′] *adj.* Held back; kept in; restrained: *pent-up* emotions.

pe·nult [pē′nult′] *n.* The next to the last syllable of a word.

pe·nul·ti·mate [pə·nul′tə·mit] **1** *adj.* Next to the last: the *penultimate* syllable of a word. **2** The one that is next to the last.

pe·num·bra [pi·num′brə] *n., pl.* **pe·num·bras** or **pe·num·brae** [pi·num′brē] That part of a shadow which is not completely dark, as the outer, partial shadow in an eclipse.

pe·nu·ri·ous [pə·n(y)o͝or′ē·əs] *adj.* Extremely stingy with money. **—pe·nu′ri·ous·ly** *adv.*

pen·u·ry [pen′yə·rē] *n.* Extreme poverty; want.

pe·on [pē′ən *or* pē′on] *n.* In Latin America, an unskilled laborer who gets very low wages. A peon used to be a debtor who was forced to serve until the debt had been worked off.

pe·on·age [pē′ən·ij] *n.* **1** The condition of being a peon. **2** The system by which debtors are forced to serve in order to work off debt.

pe·o·ny [pē′ə·nē] *n., pl.* **pe·o·nies** **1** A garden plant with showy, often double flowers ranging from white to red. **2** The flower.

peo·ple [pē′pəl] *n., pl.* **peo·ple,** for def. 2 **peo·ples,** *v.* **peo·pled, peo·pling** **1** *n.* Men, women, and children; human beings. **2** *n.* All of the persons making up a nation, race, religion, or cultural group: the Russian *people*; the *peoples* of the earth. **3** *n.* The persons of a given group, place, or class: rich *people*; the *people* of Ohio. **4** *v.* To fill with people or inhabitants; populate: to *people* other planets. **5** *n.* Ordinary persons as distinguished from a class which enjoys special privilege: government by the *people.* **6** *n.* A person's family or relatives: his wife's *people.*

pep [pep] *n., v.* **pepped, pep·ping** *informal* **1** *n.* Energy and high spirits. **2** *v.* To fill with energy or vigor: A nap *pepped* me up.

pep·per [pep′ər] **1** *n.* A seasoning that tastes hot, prepared from the dried immature berries of a tropical plant. Black pepper is ground from the entire berries, white pepper after the outer coats are removed. **2** *n.* The tropical plant itself. **3** *v.* To season with pepper or something like it. **4** *v.* To sprinkle or shower with small objects: to *pepper* a target with bullets. **5** *n.* Red pepper; cayenne. **6** *n.* Any of several garden plants with a large, hollow, sweet or hot fruit. **7** *n.* The green or red fruit of these plants, eaten as a vegetable, as in salads and relishes.

pep·per·corn [pep′ər·kôrn′] *n.* A berry of the pepper plant to be ground into black pepper.

pepper mill A utensil that grinds peppercorns.

pep·per·mint [pep′ər·mint′] *n.* **1** A fragrant herb related to the mint, yielding an oil that tastes

a	add	**i**	it	**o͝o**	took	**oi**	oil
ā	ace	**ī**	ice	**o͞o**	pool	**ou**	pout
â	care	**o**	odd	**u**	up	**ng**	ring
ä	palm	**ō**	open	**û**	burn	**th**	thin
e	end	**ô**	order	**yo͞o**	fuse	**th̶**	this
ē	equal					**zh**	vision

ə = {a in *above* e in *sicken* i in *possible*; o in *melon* u in *circus*}

P

sweet. **2** The oil itself, used as a flavoring. **3** Candy flavored with the oil.

pep·per·y [pep′ər·ē] *adj.* **1** Like or flavored with pepper; hot: a *peppery* dish. **2** Sharp and stinging: *peppery* language. **3** Quick-tempered.

pep·py [pep′ē] *adj.* **pep·pi·er, pep·pi·est** *informal* Full of pep and enthusiasm; energetic.

pep·sin [pep′sin] *n.* **1** An enzyme secreted in the stomach. It acts to break down the proteins in food. **2** A medicine prepared from this substance, used to aid digestion.

pep talk A short speech given to raise a person's or group's enthusiasm and morale.

pep·tic [pep′tik] *adj.* **1** Of or having to do with digestion. **2** Of, caused by, or relating to pepsin or to other digestive juices: a *peptic* ulcer.

per [pûr] *prep.* **1** By means of; by; through: *per* bearer. **2** To or for each: 25 cents *per* yard. **3** By the; every: 70 feet *per* second.

per·ad·ven·ture [pûr′əd·ven′chər] *adv.* It may be; perhaps: seldom used today.

per·am·bu·late [pə·ram′byə·lāt′] *v.* **per·am·bu·lat·ed, per·am·bu·lat·ing** **1** To walk through or around, so as to inspect: to *perambulate* the halls. **2** To walk about; stroll. **—per·am′bu·la′tion** *n.*

per·am·bu·la·tor [pə·ram′byə·lā′tər] *n. British* A baby carriage.

per an·num [pûr an′əm] By or for the year: a salary of $30,000 *per annum.*

per·cale [pər·kāl′] *n.* A strong, soft cotton cloth, used in making sheets and pillowcases.

per cap·i·ta [pûr kap′ə·tə] For each person: Taxes are based on *per capita* income. ◆ *Per capita* in Latin means literally *by heads.*

per·ceive [pər·sēv′] *v.* **per·ceived, per·ceiv·ing** **1** To become aware of by means of one of the senses; see, hear, feel, smell, or taste. **2** To come to understand. **3** To observe; notice.

per·cent or **per cent** [pər·sent′] *n.* Parts in each hundred; hundredths: 12 *percent* or 12% = 12/100 or .12.

per·cent·age [pər·sen′tij] *n.* **1** Proportion in a hundred parts; rate per hundred. **2** A proportion or part considered in relation to the whole: What *percentage* of the profit will be mine?

per·cen·tile [pər·sen′tīl′ *or* pər·sen′til] *n.* Any point on a scale of 100 formed by arranging a set of numbers under study in sequence and dividing them into 100 groups of equal size: The ninety-fifth *percentile* is sixth from the top.

per·cep·ti·ble [pər·sep′tə·bəl] *adj.* That can be noticed; observable: a *perceptible* movement of the head. **—per·cep′ti·bly** *adv.*

per·cep·tion [pər·sep′shən] *n.* **1** The act or power of perceiving through a sense or the senses: a keen *perception* of sound. **2** Knowledge obtained by perceiving; understanding.

per·cep·tive [pər·sep′tiv] *adj.* Capable of a quick, ready understanding: a *perceptive* mind.

perch¹ [pûrch] **1** *n.* Something, as a pole, branch, or bar, used as a roost for birds. **2** *n.* Any place for sitting or standing, especially if high. **3** *v.* To sit or place on or as on a perch: to *perch* oneself on a ladder; The canary *perched* on my finger. **4** *n.* A measure of length equal to 5 1/2 yards.

perch² [pûrch] *n., pl.* **perch** or **perch·es** Any of several freshwater fishes used as food.

per·chance [pər·chans′] *adv.* Possibly; perhaps: used mostly in poems.

per·co·late [pûr′kə·lāt′] *v.* **per·co·lat·ed, per·co·lat·ing** **1** To cause a liquid to pass through many tiny openings; filter. **2** To ooze or seep through a porous substance. **3** To prepare or be prepared in a percolator.

per·co·la·tor [pûr′kə·lā′tər] *n.* A type of coffeepot in which boiling water keeps rising in a tube and then filters down through ground coffee to the bottom.

per·cus·sion [pər·kush′ən] *n.* **1** The sharp striking of one body against another. **2** The vibration, sound, or shock produced by the striking of one body against another.

percussion cap A thin metal cap containing a small amount of a sensitive explosive that explodes when the cap is struck, usually to set off a larger charge.

percussion instrument A musical instrument whose tone is produced by striking or hitting, as a cymbal or drum.

per di·em [pər dē′əm] **1** By the day. **2** An allowance for daily expenses. ◆ *Per diem* is a Latin phrase.

per·di·tion [pər·dish′ən] *n.* **1** Everlasting damnation; loss of one's soul. **2** Hell.

per·e·gri·nate [per′ə·gri·nāt′] *v.* **per·e·gri·nat·ed, per·e·gri·nat·ing** **1** To travel from place to place. **2** To travel through or along.

per·e·gri·na·tion [per′ə·grə·nā′shən] *n.* A journey; traveling.

per·e·grine falcon [per′ə·grin] A type of hawk used in falconry.

per·emp·to·ry [pə·remp′tər·ē] *adj.* **1** Not open to argument or refusal: a *peremptory* order. **2** Urgent; final: a *peremptory* writ from a court. **3** Imperious; arrogant: a *peremptory* manner. **—per·emp′tor·i·ly** *adv.*

per·en·ni·al [pə·ren′ē·əl] **1** *adj.* Continuing all year or through many years. **2** *adj.* Everlasting; perpetual: a *perennial* favorite. **3** *adj.* Lasting and growing for more than two years: a *perennial* plant. **4** *n.* A plant that lives for more than two years. **—per·en′ni·al·ly** *adv.*

per·fect [*adj.* pûr′fikt, *v.* pər·fekt′] **1** *adj.* Without defects or faults; excellent: a *perfect* set of teeth. **2** *adj.* Complete in all its parts: a *perfect* set of dishes. **3** *v.* To finish or improve; make perfect: to *perfect* a new method of teaching reading. **4** *adj.* Accurate; exact: a *perfect* translation. **5** *adj.* Total; utter: a *perfect* fool. **6** *adj.* Completely effective; ideal: a *perfect* answer. **7** *adj.* In grammar, denoting the tense of a verb that expresses an action completed in the past or before a time indicated. ◆ Avoid the weaker informal use of *perfect* to mean merely *very good.*

per·fec·ta [pər·fek′tə] *n.* A kind of bet that is won by picking the first and second place finishers in a race or contest.

per·fect·i·ble [pər·fek′tə·bəl] *adj.* Capable of being perfect or arriving at perfection. **—per·fect′i·bil′i·ty** *n.*

per·fec·tion [pər·fek′shən] *n.* **1** The condition of being perfect. **2** The act of perfecting: the *perfection* of a new invention. **3** A person or thing that is ideal or excellent: As a swimmer, she is *perfection.* **—to perfection** Exactly; perfectly.

per·fec·tion·ist [pər·fek′shən·ist] *n.* A person who demands of everyone and everything an exceedingly high degree of excellence.

per·fect·ly [pûr′fikt·lē] *adv.* **1** In a perfect manner. **2** Completely; altogether: *perfectly* true.

perfect number A positive integer that is equal to the sum of its factors including 1 but not including the number itself. For example, 28 is a perfect number because 1 + 2 + 4 + 7 + 14 = 28.

per·fid·i·ous [pər·fid′ē·əs] *adj.* Treacherous; unfaithful: a *perfidious* attack on a friend. **—per·fid′·i·ous·ly** *adv.*

per·fi·dy [pûr′fə·dē] *n., pl.* **per·fi·dies** The act of breaking faith; treachery.

per·fo·rate [pûr′fə·rāt′] *v.* **per·fo·rat·ed, per·fo·rat·ing** 1 To make a hole or holes through, as by punching or drilling. 2 To pierce with holes in rows, as sheets of postage stamps.

per·fo·ra·tion [pûr′fə·rā′shən] *n.* 1 A hole drilled in or punched through something. 2 The act of perforating. 3 The condition of being perforated.

Perforations allow the coupon to be torn out neatly.

per·force [pər·fôrs′] *adv.* By or of necessity.

per·form [pər·fôrm′] *v.* 1 To do; accomplish: to *perform* surgery. 2 To fulfill or discharge, as a duty. 3 To give an exhibition of artistic skill, as by acting, singing, or playing a musical intrument. 4 To operate or function: The machine *performed* well.

per·form·ance [pər·fôr′məns] *n.* 1 The act of performing or doing: A firefighter was burned in the *performance* of duty. 2 A presentation before an audience, as of a concert, play, or opera. 3 An action performed; deed; feat. 4 The manner of operating or functioning: Repairs improved the car's *performance.*

per·form·er [pər·fôr′mər] *n.* A person who performs, especially an actor, musician, or other artist.

per·fume [*n.* pûr′fyo͞om; *v.* pər·fyo͞om′] *n., v.* **per·fumed, per·fum·ing** 1 *n.* A fragrant liquid used to scent things, as the body or clothing. 2 *n.* A pleasant odor, as from flowers. 3 *v.* To fill or scent with a fragrant odor: Flowers *perfumed* the room; to *perfume* a handkerchief.

per·fum·er·y [pər·fyo͞o′mər·ē] *n., pl.* **per·fum·er·ies** 1 The art or business of preparing perfumes. 2 A perfume or perfumes.

per·func·to·ry [pər·fungk′tər·ē] *adj.* 1 Done mechanically and merely for the sake of getting through: a *perfunctory* piece of work. 2 Careless or indifferent: a *perfunctory* student; a *perfunctory* glance. **—per·func′to·ri·ly** *adv.*

per·haps [pər·haps′] *adv.* Maybe; possibly.

per·i·car·di·um [per′ə·kär′dē·əm] *n.* The membrane that surrounds the heart.

per·i·gee [per′ə·jē] *n.* The point in the orbit of a satellite at which it is closest to the earth. ◆ See APHELION.

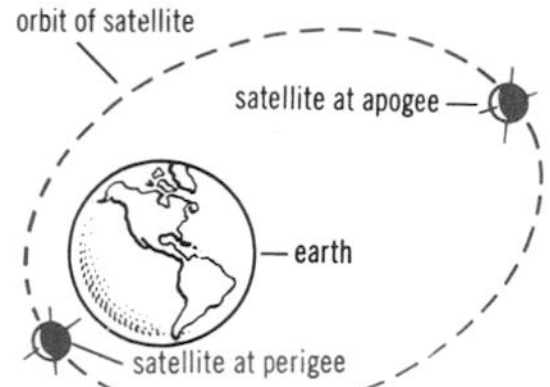

per·i·he·li·on [per′ə·hē′lē·ən] *n.* The point in the orbit of a planet or comet where it is nearest to the sun. ◆ See APHELION.

per·il [per′əl] *n., v.* **per·iled** or **per·illed, per·il·ing** or **per·il·ling** 1 *n.* Exposure to the chance of injury, loss, or destruction; danger; risk. 2 *v.* To expose to danger; imperil: to *peril* a boat in a storm.

per·il·ous [per′əl·əs] *adj.* Full of peril; risky; dangerous. **—per′il·ous·ly** *adv.* **—per′il·ous·ness** *n.*

pe·rim·e·ter [pə·rim′ə·tər] *n.* The outer boundary or the length of the outer boundary of any plane figure.

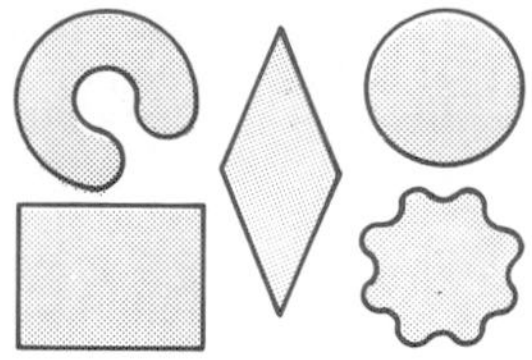

The perimeters of the figures are outlined in brown.

pe·ri·od [pir′ē·əd] *n.* 1 A portion of time with a definite beginning and end marked by events that repeat themselves again and again. 2 A time of indefinite length having some specified quality or circumstance. 3 A set portion of time: a lunch *period.* 4 A completion or end. 5 A dot (.) used as a mark of punctuation at the close of a declarative sentence and after abbreviations.

pe·ri·od·ic [pir′ē·od′ik] *adj.* 1 Recurring at regular intervals: *periodic* dental checkups. 2 Happening every now and then; intermittent: *periodic* trips to Europe. 3 Having several clauses and constructed so that its meaning is not completed until the end: a *periodic* sentence.

pe·ri·od·i·cal [pir′ē·od′i·kəl] 1 *n.* A publication that appears weekly, monthly, or at longer intervals. Magazines are periodicals. 2 *adj.* Published weekly, monthly, or at larger intervals. 3 *adj.* Periodic. **—pe′ri·od′i·cal·ly** *adv.*

periodic law A law of chemistry that states that when all elements are arranged in order of their atomic numbers, there is a regular variation in their properties.

periodic table A table in which all the chemical elements are arranged in order according to their atomic numbers and in groups according to the similarity of their properties.

per·i·pa·tet·ic [per′i·pə·tet′ik] *adj.* Walking about from place to place; traveling a great deal: a *peripatetic* newspaper reporter.

pe·riph·er·al [pə·rif′ər·əl] 1 *adj.* Of, having to do with, or forming the outer part or boundary of something. 2 *n.* A device connected to and working in conjunction with a computer, as a terminal or printer. **—pe·riph′er·al·ly** *adv.*

pe·riph·er·y [pə·rif′ər·ē] *n., pl.* **pe·riph·er·ies** 1 The outside or outer surface of something. 2 The line bounding a curved figure, especially a circle. 3 A surrounding region or area.

per·i·scope [per′ə·skōp′] *n.* A tube with mirrors and lenses so arranged in it that an observer can see over an obstruction. Periscopes allow people in submerged submarines to see objects on the surface.

per·ish [per′ish] *v.* To be completely destroyed; die: The crew *perished* in the plane crash.

per·ish·a·ble [per′ish·ə·bəl] 1 *adj.* Likely to decay or wither quickly: *perishable* crops. 2 *n.* (*usually*

a	add	**i**	it	**o͝o**	took	**oi**	oil		
ā	ace	**ī**	ice	**o͞o**	pool	**ou**	pout		
â	care	**o**	odd	**u**	up	**ng**	ring		
ä	palm	**ō**	open	**û**	burn	**th**	thin		
e	end	**ô**	order	**yo͞o**	fuse	**t̶h̶**	this		
ē	equal					**zh**	vision		

ə = {a in *above* e in *sicken* i in *possible*; o in *melon* u in *circus*}

pl.) Something likely to spoil or decay, as food.

per·i·stal·sis [per′ə·stal′sis *or* per′ə·stäl′sis] *n.* The waves of successive contractions in an organ, such as the intestines, that force the contents to move through, usually in one direction. **—per·i·stal·tic** [per′ə·stal′tik *or* per′ə·stäl′tik] *adj.*

per·i·to·ne·um [per′ə·tə·nē′əm] *n., pl.* **per·i·to·ne·ums** or **per·i·to·ne·a** [per′ə·tə·nē′ə] The transparent membrane that lines the inside of the abdomen and covers the organs in the abdomen. **—per·i·to·ne·al** [per′ə·tə·nē′əl] *adj.*

per·i·to·ni·tis [per′ə·tə·nī′tis] *n.* Inflammation of the peritoneum.

per·i·wig [per′ə·wig′] *n.* A wig or peruke.

per·i·win·kle[1] [per′ə·wing′kəl] *n.* A small sea snail with a coiled shell. It is eaten as a delicacy.

per·i·win·kle[2] [per′ə·wing′kəl] *n.* A plant having shiny evergreen leaves and white or blue flowers.

per·jure [pûr′jər] *v.* **per·jured, per·jur·ing** To make (oneself) guilty of perjury. **—per′jur·er** *n.*

per·ju·ry [pûr′jə·rē] *n., pl.* **per·ju·ries** 1 A false statement made deliberately while under oath, as in a court of law. 2 The act of making such a false statement.

perk [pûrk] *v.* 1 To raise quickly and smartly: The donkey *perked* up its long ears. 2 To make trim and smart in appearance: For the party, the whole family was *perked* out in new clothes. **—perk up** To become gay and lively; recover one's spirits.

perk·y [pûr′kē] *adj.* **perk·i·er, perk·i·est** Pert and lively: a *perky* kitten.

per·lite [pûr′līt′] *n.* A kind of volcanic glass, used in a fluffy, expanded form as a component of concrete and plaster and in insulation.

per·ma·frost [pûr′mə·frôst′] *n.* A permanently frozen layer of ground found in the cold regions of the earth.

per·ma·nence [pûr′mə·nəns] *n.* The condition or quality of being permanent or lasting.

per·ma·nen·cy [pûr′mə·nən·sē] *n., pl.* **per·ma·nen·cies** 1 Permanence. 2 Something permanent.

per·ma·nent [pûr′mən·ənt] *adj.* Continuing or intended to continue without change; lasting; enduring; durable: a *permanent* dye. **—per′ma·nent·ly** *adv.*

per·ma·nent-press [pûr′mən·ənt·pres′] *adj.* Treated so that the fabric can be worn after washing with little or no ironing needed.

permanent wave An artificial wave or curl chemically set in the hair and lasting for several months.

per·me·able [pûr′mē·ə·bəl] *adj.* Capable of being permeated, especially permitting fluids to pass through: Cotton cloth is *permeable* by water. **—per′me·a·bil′i·ty** *n.*

per·me·ate [pûr′mē·āt′] *v.* **per·me·at·ed, per·me·at·ing** 1 To spread itself or spread through: A spirit of fun *permeated* the group. 2 To pass through the openings or pores of. **—per′me·a′tion** *n.* ◆ See PENETRATE.

Per·mi·an [pûr′mē·ən] 1 *n.* The final geological period of the Paleozoic era, during which the continents were probably linked, ferns grew worldwide, and reptiles were abundant. 2 *adj.* Of the Permian.

per·mis·si·ble [pər·mis′ə·bəl] *adj.* That can be permitted; allowable. **—per·mis′si·bly** *adv.*

per·mis·sion [pər·mish′ən] *n.* The act of permitting; authorization; leave: Do you have *permission* to go home early?

per·mis·sive [pər·mis′iv] *adj.* 1 Granting permission; allowing. 2 Permitted. 3 Not strict in discipline; lenient: *permissive* parents.

per·mit [*v.* pər·mit′; *n.* pûr′mit] *v.* **per·mit·ted, per·mit·ting,** *n.* 1 *v.* To allow; let: *Permit* me to help; Parking is not *permitted.* 2 *v.* To furnish an opportunity: If time *permits,* I'll come to see you. 3 *n.* An official document or card giving permission; license: a driving *permit.* ◆ See TRANSMIT.

per·mu·ta·tion [pûr′myo͞o·tā′shən] *n.* 1 A complete change in character. 2 Any ordered arrangement of the members of a set: xyz, xzy, zyx, yxz, and yzx are *permutations* of the set containing x, y, and z. 3 The act of changing the order of the members of a set.

per·ni·cious [pər·nish′əs] *adj.* 1 Highly injurious; very harmful: a climate *pernicious* to health. 2 Killing; deadly. **—per·ni′cious·ly** *adv.*

per·nick·e·ty [pər·nik′ə·tē] *adj.* Persnickety.

per·o·ra·tion [per′ə·rā′shən] *n.* The conclusion of a speech, which sums up and urges the points made.

per·ox·ide [pə·rok′sīd′] *n.* An oxide in which two atoms of oxygen occupy the place usually taken by one.

per·pen·dic·u·lar [pûr′pən·dik′yə·lər] 1 *adj.* Straight up and down; vertical: the canyon's *perpendicular* walls. 2 *adj.* Forming a right angle with another line or plane: The shelf is *perpendicular* to the wall. 3 *n.* A line or plane at right angles to another.

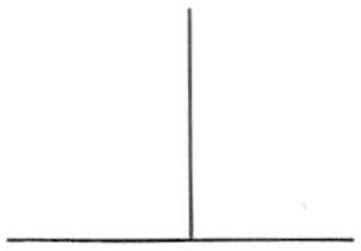

Perpendicular

per·pe·trate [pûr′pə·trāt′] *v.* **per·pe·trat·ed, per·pe·trat·ing** To do, perform, or commit (a crime or other evil). **—per′pe·tra′tion** *n.* **—per′pe·tra′tor** *n.*

per·pet·u·al [pûr·pech′o͞o·əl] *adj.* 1 Continuing indefinitely; eternal. 2 Incessant; constant: a *perpetual* bother. **—per·pet′u·al·ly** *adv.*

per·pet·u·ate [pər·pech′o͞o·āt′] *v.* **per·pet·u·at·ed, per·pet·u·at·ing** To cause to last or to be remembered for a very long time: The Bunker Hill monument *perpetuates* the memory of a battle of the American Revolution. **—per·pet′u·a′tion** *n.*

per·pe·tu·i·ty [pûr′pə·t(y)o͞o′ə·tē] *n.* 1 The state of being perpetual. 2 Unlimited time; eternity. **—in perpetuity** Forever.

per·plex [pər·pleks′] *v.* To cause to hesitate or doubt; confuse; bewilder; puzzle.

per·plex·i·ty [pər·plek′sə·tē] *n., pl.* **per·plex·i·ties** 1 A perplexed condition; doubt; confusion. 2 Something that perplexes.

per·qui·site [pûr′kwə·zit] *n.* Any profit from employment in addition to salary, as a tip.

Pers. 1 Persia. 2 Persian.

per se [pûr sā′] In or of itself; as such: A brick is not a weapon *per se*, but it can be used as one. ◆ *Per se* is a Latin phrase.

per·se·cute [pûr′sə·kyo͞ot′] *v.* **per·se·cut·ed, per·se·cut·ing** 1 To keep after so as to attack or injure. 2 To mistreat or oppress because of religion, race, or beliefs. 3 To harass; annoy constantly. **—per′se·cu′tion** *n.* **—per′se·cu′tor** *n.* ◆ *Persecute* and *prosecute* both come from Latin roots meaning *to follow* or *pursue*, but each is combined with a different prefix. *Per-* means *thoroughly*, and a person who *persecutes* does pursue relentlessly and cruelly. *Pro-* means *forward*, and a person who *prosecutes* does carry forward a legal action to its completion.

Per·seph·o·ne [pər·sef′ə·nē] *n.* The Greek name for PROSERPINE.
Per·seus [pûr′syo͞os′] *n.* 1 In Greek myths, the slayer of Medusa and rescuer of Andromeda from a sea monster. 2 A northern constellation.
per·se·ver·ance [pûr′sə·vir′əns] *n.* The act or habit of persevering; persistence.
per·se·vere [pûr′sə·vir′] *v.* **per·se·vered, per·se·ver·ing** To continue to try to do something in spite of difficulties: The tortoise *persevered* in the race, even though the hare was swifter.
Per·sian [pûr′zhən] 1 *adj.* Of or from Persia. 2 *n.* A person born in or a citizen of Iran. 3 *n.* A person who was born or lived in ancient Persia. 4 *n.* The language of Iran. 5 *n.* The language of ancient Persia.
Persian cat A breed of cat with a round head and long, silky fur.

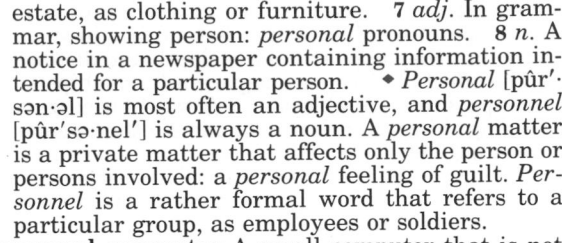

Persian lamb The tightly curled black or gray fur from a young caracul lamb.
per·si·flage [pûr′sə·fläzh′] *n.* A light, playful style of writing or speaking; gentle teasing.
per·sim·mon [pər·sim′·ən] *n.* 1 A North American tree that bears reddish, plumlike fruit. 2 This fruit, which puckers the mouth when green but is sweet to eat when ripe.
per·sist [pər·sist′] *v.* 1 To continue firmly or stubbornly in spite of opposition, warning, or difficulty: to *persist* in breaking a rule. 2 To be insistent, as in saying something or asking a question. 3 To continue to exist; endure: My plants die, but the weeds *persist.*
per·sis·tence [pər·sis′təns] *n.* 1 The act of persisting; perseverance. 2 Continuing occurrence or existence: The *persistence* of fever was worrisome.
per·sis·ten·cy [pər·sis′tən·sē] *n.* Persistence.
per·sis·tent [pər·sis′tənt] *adj.* 1 Persevering or undaunted: a *persistent* salesman. 2 Enduring; continuing: a *persistent* cough. **—per·sis′tent·ly** *adv.*
per·snick·e·ty [pər·snik′i·tē] *adj. informal* Very fussy about small details; picky.
per·son [pûr′sən] *n.* 1 A human being; individual. 2 The body of a human being: Keep some identification on your *person* at all times. 3 In grammar, a form of a pronoun or verb distinguishing the speaker (**first person**), the person or thing spoken to (**second person**), and the person or thing spoken of (**third person**). **—in person** 1 Physically present; live. 2 Acting for oneself.
per·son·a·ble [pûr′sən·ə·bəl] *adj.* Good-looking; handsome; attractive: a *personable* staff.
per·son·age [pûr′sən·ij] *n.* 1 A person of importance or rank. 2 A person; individual. 3 A character in a book or drama.
per·son·al [pûr′sən·əl] 1 *adj.* Of or having to do with a particular person or persons: a *personal* matter. 2 *adj.* Having to do with the body or physical appearance: *personal* cleanliness. 3 *adj.* Private: *personal* mail. 4 *adj.* Referring to a particular person, especially in a critical or offensive way: *personal* remarks. 5 *adj.* Done in person: a *personal* visit. 6 *adj.* Having to do with private property that can be moved and is not part of real estate, as clothing or furniture. 7 *adj.* In grammar, showing person: *personal* pronouns. 8 *n.* A notice in a newspaper containing information intended for a particular person. ◆ *Personal* [pûr′·sən·əl] is most often an adjective, and *personnel* [pûr′sə·nel′] is always a noun. A *personal* matter is a private matter that affects only the person or persons involved: a *personal* feeling of guilt. *Personnel* is a rather formal word that refers to a particular group, as employees or soldiers.
personal computer A small computer that is not connected to a larger central computer and is meant to be used on its own by one person.
per·son·al·i·ty [pûr′sən·al′ə·tē] *n., pl.* **per·son·al·i·ties** 1 The qualities or characteristics that make one person different from every other person. 2 Attractive personal qualities, as charm, friendliness, and enthusiasm. 3 The condition or fact of being a person and not a thing or idea. 4 A person, especially one of outstanding qualities. 5 (*often pl.*) A personal or slighting remark: Avoid *personalities* in a debate.
per·son·al·ize [pûr′sə·nə·līz′] *v.* **per·son·al·ized, per·son·al·iz·ing** 1 To make personal or individual: He *personalized* his comments to each student. 2 To mark with name, initials, or other identification.
per·son·al·ly [pûr′sən·əl·ē] *adv.* 1 In person, not through an agent. 2 As though intended for or directed toward oneself: Don't take those remarks *personally.* 3 As regards one's own opinions or tastes: *Personally,* I enjoy the movies. 4 With regard to a person as an individual: I like her *personally,* but I disagree with her politically.
personal pronoun In grammar, a pronoun that indicates person. *I, me, we,* and *us* indicate the person speaking. *You* indicates the person spoken to. *He, him, she, her, it, they,* and *them* indicate the person or thing spoken about.
per·so·na non gra·ta [pər·sō′nə non grä′tə *or* pər·son′ə non grat′ə] A person who is not welcome or acceptable. ◆ *Persona non grata,* which usually refers to a diplomat declared unacceptable to a foreign government, is a Latin expression.
per·son·i·fi·ca·tion [pər·son′ə·fə·kā′shən] *n.* 1 A figure of speech in which inanimate objects or qualities are spoken of as having human characteristics, as in the saying "Necessity is the mother of invention." 2 A person or being who is made to represent an abstraction: Uncle Sam is a *personification* of the U.S. government. 3 A person or thing that typifies a quality; embodiment.
per·son·i·fy [pər·son′ə·fī′] *v.* **per·son·i·fied, per·son·i·fy·ing** 1 To think of or represent as having life or human qualities. 2 To be a representation or embodiment of.
per·son·nel [pûr′sə·nel′] *n.* The persons employed in a business, engaged in military service, or forming some other group. ◆ See PERSONAL.

a	add	**i**	it	**o͝o**	took	**oi**	oil		
ā	ace	**ī**	ice	**o͞o**	pool	**ou**	pout		
â	care	**o**	odd	**u**	up	**ng**	ring		
ä	palm	**ō**	open	**û**	burn	**th**	thin		
e	end	**ô**	order	**yo͞o**	fuse	**t͟h**	this		
ē	equal					**zh**	vision		

ə = a in *above* e in *sicken* i in *possible* / o in *melon* u in *circus*

phase [fāz] *n., v.* **phased, phas·ing** 1 *n.* A stage in the changing apparent shape of the moon or of a planet. 2 *n.* A single stage in any development or cycle. 3 *n.* A view or aspect of something: We covered that *phase* of the report today. 4 *n.* A step or part of a series. 5 *v.* To plan or conduct in stages. **—phase in** To introduce in stages: to *phase in* a tax increase. **—phase out** To eliminate or end in stages: to *phase out* an obsolete machine.

phase·out [fāz′out′] *n.* A gradual ending of operations.

Ph.D. Doctor of Philosophy.

pheas·ant [fez′ənt] *n.* A long-tailed bird noted for the brilliant feathers of the male, often hunted for sport.

Pheasant

phe·nix [fē′niks] *n.* Another spelling of PHOENIX.

phe·nol [fē′nōl] *n.* A poisonous crystalline compound with a sharp odor, present in coal tar; carbolic acid. It is used in making plastics and as a disinfectant.

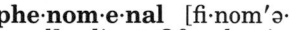

phe·nom·e·nal [fi·nom′ə·nəl] *adj.* 1 Of or having to do with phenomena. 2 Extraordinary or marvelous. **—phe·nom′e·nal·ly** *adv.*

phe·nom·e·non [fi·nom′ə·non′] *n., pl.* **phe·nom·e·na** [fi·nom′ə·nə] or **phe·nom·e·nons** 1 Any event, occurrence, or condition that can be seen, experienced, and described scientifically. 2 Any rare or unusual person or thing.

pher·o·mone [fer′ə·mōn′] *n.* A chemical substance, such as a scent, that one animal produces to affect or attract other animals of the same species.

phi [fī] *n.* The 21st letter of the Greek alphabet.

phi·al [fī′əl] *n.* Another spelling of VIAL.

phil·an·throp·ic [fil′ən·throp′ik] *adj.* 1 Of, having to do with, or displaying philanthropy. 2 Charitable; benevolent.

phil·an·throp·i·cal [fil′ən·throp′ə·kəl] *adj.* Philanthropic. **—phil′an·throp′i·cal·ly** *adv.*

phi·lan·thro·pist [fi·lan′thrə·pist] *n.* A person who devotes time and money to helping others.

phi·lan·thro·py [fi·lan′thrə·pē] *n., pl.* **phi·lan·thro·pies** 1 Love of human beings, especially as shown in the desire and effort to lessen the misery of others and in the giving of money for worthwhile causes. 2 A charitable act or gift.

phil·a·tel·ic [fil′ə·tel′ik] *adj.* Of or having to do with philately or philatelists.

phi·lat·e·ly [fi·lat′ə·lē] *n.* The hobby of studying and collecting postage stamps, stamped envelopes, and related items. **—phi·lat′e·list** *n.*

phil·har·mon·ic [fil′här·mon′ik] 1 *adj.* Loving or devoted to music: a *philharmonic* society. 2 *n.* (*often written* **Philharmonic**) A philharmonic society or the symphony orchestra it may support.

Phil·ip·pine [fil′ə·pēn′] *adj.* Of or from the Philippines.

Phi·lis·tine [fil′əs·tēn′ *or* fi·lis′tin] 1 *n.* One of an ancient, warlike people from coastal Palestine who were early foes of the Israelites. 2 *adj.* Of or having to do with the ancient Philistines. 3 *n.* (*often written* **philistine**) A person with commonplace tastes and ideas who has no interest in the arts or learning.

phil·o·den·dron [fil′ə·den′drən] *n.* A popular house plant having glossy, evergreen leaves.

phi·lol·o·gy [fi·lol′ə·jē] *n.* 1 The study of literary texts in order to determine their original form and meaning. 2 An older word for LINGUISTICS. **—phi·lol′o·gist** *n.*

phi·los·o·pher [fi·los′ə·fər] *n.* 1 A student of philosophy. 2 A person who originates a system of philosophy. 3 A person who lives and reasons according to such a system. 4 A wise and patient person.

phil·o·soph·ic [fil′ə·sof′ik] *adj.* 1 Having to do with philosophy. 2 Calm and reasonable: a *philosophic* point of view.

phil·o·soph·i·cal [fil′ə·sof′ə·kəl] *adj.* Philosophic. **—phil′o·soph′i·cal·ly** *adv.*

phi·los·o·phize [fi·los′ə·fīz′] *v.* **phi·los·o·phized, phi·los·o·phiz·ing** To reason like a philosopher and try to explain things: to *philosophize* about the meaning of life and death.

phi·los·o·phy [fi·los′ə·fē] *n., pl.* **phi·los·o·phies** 1 A system of thought that concerns itself with truth and wisdom. Among other things, philosophy attempts to study and explain the meanings of life and death, of faith, and of religion, the differences between right and wrong, and the purposes and principles of art and beauty. 2 The basic principles or truths of any system: the *philosophy* of education. 3 Wisdom, strength, and calmness of mind in dealing with the experiences and misfortunes of life.

phil·ter or **phil·tre** [fil′tər] *n.* A magic drink supposed to make one fall in love.

phlegm [flem] *n.* 1 The stringy mucus discharged from the nose and throat, as during a cold. 2 Indifference; coldness; apathy.

phleg·mat·ic [fleg·mat′ik] *adj.* Not easily moved or excited; calm; indifferent.

phlo·em [flō′em] *n.* The plant tissue that conducts the sap to all parts of a tree or plant.

phlox [floks] *n.* A plant with clusters of small, fragrant, variously colored flowers.

pho·bi·a [fō′bē·ə] *n.* 1 An unreasonable and persistent fear of a particular thing: a *phobia* about heights. 2 Any strong dislike.

phoe·be [fē′bē] *n.* A grayish brown, American flycatcher with a crested head.

Phoe·bus [fē′bəs] *n.* 1 In Greek myths, a sun god; Apollo. 2 The sun: used mostly in poems.

Phoe·ni·cian [fə·nish′ən *or* fə·nē′shən] 1 *adj.* Of or from Phoenicia. 2 *n.* A person who was born or lived in Phoenicia. 3 *n.* The language of Phoenicia.

phoe·nix [fē′niks] *n.* In Egyptian myths, a beautiful bird said to live for 500 or 600 years before burning itself to ashes on an altar, only to rise again young and beautiful to live through another cycle.

phon- or **phono-** A combining form meaning: Sound; voice; speech, as in *phonograph*.

phone [fōn] *n., v.* **phoned, phon·ing** *informal* 1 *n.* A telephone. 2 *v.* To telephone. ◆ *Phone* is the shortened form of *telephone*.

-phone A combining form meaning: Sound; voice, as in *headphone*.

phone-in [fō′nin′] *n.* A radio program that receives and broadcasts telephone calls from listeners.

pho·neme [fō′nēm′] *n.* One of a set of the smallest units of sound serving to distinguish one word from another. The words *pin* and *tin* are distinguished by the phonemes *p* and *t*.

pho·nem·ic [fə·nē′mik] *adj.* Having to do with or indicating a phoneme or phonemes.

pho·net·ic [fə·net′ik] *adj.* 1 Of or having to do with phonetics. 2 Representing sounds as actually spoken: A *phonetic* spelling of "loved" is [luvd]. **—pho·net′i·cal·ly** *adv.*

pho·net·ics [fə·net′iks] *n.* 1 The study of speech sounds and the ways in which they are produced by the organs of speech. 2 The system of sounds of any language: the *phonetics* of English. ◆ See -ICS.

phon·ic [fon′ik] *adj.* Having to do with sound, especially spoken sound.

phon·ics [fon′iks] *n.* 1 Phonetics. 2 The use of simple phonetic spellings to teach reading and pronunciation. ◆ See -ICS.

pho·no·graph [fō′nə·graf′] *n.* A device that reproduces sound from the ridges and bends in the grooves of a record.

pho·no·graph·ic [fō′nə·graf′ik] *adj.* Of, related to, like, or produced by a phonograph.

pho·ny [fō′nē] *adj.* **pho·ni·er, pho·ni·est,** *n., pl.* **pho·nies** *slang* 1 *adj.* Not genuine; false; fake: *phony* money. 2 *n.* A person or thing that is a false imitation of a real thing: The fireplace was a *phony.*

phos·phate [fos′fāt′] *n.* 1 A salt of an acid containing phosphorus, especially one used as a fertilizer. 2 A soft drink made from syrup, carbonated water, and a little phosphoric acid.

phos·phor [fos′fər] *n.* A phosphorescent substance.

phos·phor·es·cent [fos′fə·res′ənt] *adj.* Giving off light without heat: *phosphorescent* insects. **—phos′·phor·es′cence** *n.*

phos·phor·ic [fos·fôr′ik] *adj.* Of or containing phosphorus, especially in its higher valence.

phos·phor·ous [fos′fər·əs] *adj.* Of or containing phosphorus, especially in its lower valence.

phos·phor·us [fos′fər·əs] *n.* A nonmetallic element that forms many compounds essential to life but in the elemental state is ordinarily a yellow or white waxy solid that is exceedingly poisonous and ignites spontaneously in air.

phot- or **photo-** A combining form meaning: 1 Light, as in *photon.* 2 Photograph or photographic, as in *photoengraving.*

pho·to [fō′tō] *n., pl.* **pho·tos** *informal* A photograph.

pho·to·cop·i·er [fō′tō·kop′ē·ər] *n.* A machine used to make photocopies.

pho·to·cop·y [fō′tō·kop′e] *v.* **pho·to·cop·ied, pho·to·cop·y·ing,** *n., pl.* **pho·to·cop·ies** 1 *v.* To make one or more copies of (written or printed matter) by a photographic process, usually in a fast-working machine. 2 A copy made in this way.

pho·to·e·lec·tric cell [fō′tō·ə·lek′trik] A device whose electrical resistance changes in response to the amount of light striking it, used to trigger mechanisms, such as burglar alarms and elevator doors.

pho·to·en·grav·ing [fō′tō·in·grā′ving] *n.* 1 A process for printing illustrations in which a photographic image of the subject is transferred onto a metal plate and then etched. 2 A plate or print made by photoengraving.

pho·to·gen·ic [fō′tō·jen′ik] *adj.* Having qualities that photograph well: a *photogenic* face.

pho·to·graph [fō′tə·graf′] 1 *v.* To take a picture or a picture of with a camera. 2 *n.* A picture made with a camera. 3 *v.* To appear in a photograph: Our garden *photographs* beautifully.

pho·tog·ra·pher [fə·tog′rə·fər] *n.* A person who takes pictures or makes a business of photography.

pho·to·graph·ic [fō′tə·graf′ik] *adj.* 1 Of, having to do with, used in, or produced by photography. 2 Like a photograph, as in accuracy: a *photographic* painting. **—pho′to·graph′i·cal·ly** *adv.*

pho·tog·ra·phy [fə·tog′rə·fē] *n.* 1 The process or art of forming and preserving an image by using the chemical action of light on a sensitive film in a camera. 2 The art or business of producing and printing photographs.

pho·ton [fō′ton] *n.* The smallest possible unit of light, resembling in some ways a particle; quantum of light.

pho·to·scan [fō′tō·skan′] *v.* **pho·to·scanned, pho·to·scan·ning,** *n.* 1 *v.* To take a photograph of rays emitted by (body tissues) after the tissues have been injected with a radioactive substance. 2 *n.* A photograph taken in this manner.

pho·to·sen·si·tive [fō′tō·sen′sə·tiv] *adj.* Capable of changing physically or chemically as a result of the action of light or other rays.

pho·to·sphere [fō′tə·sfir′] *n.* The shining surface of the sun.

Pho·to·stat [fō′tə·stat′] 1 *n.* A device used to make photocopies quickly: a trademark. 2 *n.* A copy made using a Photostat. 3 *v.* To make a copy of with a Photostat.

pho·to·syn·the·sis [fō′tō·sin′thə·sis] *n.* The process by which plants, in the presence of chlorophyll, and using energy from the sun, form carbohydrates from carbon dioxide and water.

phrase [frāz] *n., v.* **phrased, phras·ing** 1 *n.* In grammar, a sequence of two or more words, used as a single part of speech, that does not contain a subject and predicate: "In the sky" is a *phrase.* 2 *n.* A brief, catchy expression: to turn a *phrase.* 3 *v.* To express in a particular way: The debater *phrased* the argument carefully. 4 *n.* In music, a small unit containing smaller, often rhythmical units within it, which is itself employed in larger structural units. 5 *v.* To group into, or as into, spoken or musical phrases.

phra·se·ol·o·gy [frā′zē·ol′ə·jē] *n., pl.* **phra·se·ol·o·gies** The choice of words and phrases in expressing ideas: medical *phraseology.*

phre·nol·o·gy [fri·nol′ə·jē] *n.* A supposed science of interpreting what the bumps on a person's skull indicate about the person's intelligence, disposition, and character.

phthi·sis [thī′sis] *n.* Tuberculosis of the lungs: seldom used today.

phy·lum [fī′ləm] *n., pl.* **phy·la** [fī′lə] In the classification of animals and, sometimes, plants, a very large grouping comprising classes that have basic features in common.

phys·ic [fiz′ik] *n., v.* **phys·icked, phys·ick·ing** 1 *n.*

a	add	**i**	it	**o͝o**	took	**oi**	oil
ā	ace	**ī**	ice	**o͞o**	pool	**ou**	pout
â	care	**o**	odd	**u**	up	**ng**	ring
ä	palm	**ō**	open	**û**	burn	**th**	thin
e	end	**ô**	order	**yo͞o**	fuse	**th**	this
ē	equal					**zh**	vision

ə = a in *above*, e in *sicken*, i in *possible*, o in *melon*, u in *circus*

piece of eight The silver dollar used in the Spanish and British colonies in America during the Revolutionary War.
piece·work [pēs′wûrk′] *n.* Work done and paid for by the piece or by the amount done, not by the time spent. **—piece′work′er** *n.*
pied [pīd] *adj.* Having two or more colors in patches; mottled; dappled; piebald.
Pied Piper In German legends, a piper who charmed away all the children of the town of Hamelin when refused payment for ridding the town of rats.
pier [pir] *n.* **1** A structure built on pillars and extending out over water, used as a landing place that provides access to ships. **2** A massive support, as for the arch of a bridge. **3** A solid portion of a wall between openings, as between windows.

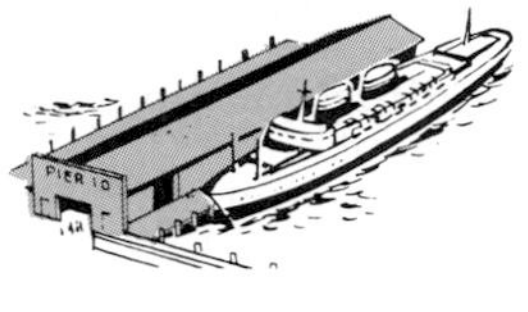

Pier

pierce [pirs] *v.* **pierced, pierc·ing** **1** To pass into or through, as something sharp does; penetrate: The needle *pierced* the cloth. **2** To go through like a knife; affect sharply or deeply: The bitter cold *pierced* us to the bone. **3** To make a hole in, into, or through. **4** To force a way into or through: to *pierce* the wilderness. **5** To solve or understand: to *pierce* a mystery.
pierc·ing [pir′sing] *adj.* **1** Loud or shrill: the soprano's *piercing* upper register. **2** Bitterly cold: a *piercing* wind. **3** Penetrating; intense: a *piercing* glance. **4** Sarcastic; cutting: a *piercing* wit.
pi·e·tà [pē′ā·tä′] *n.* A sculpture or painting of the Virgin Mary holding the dead body of Christ.
pi·e·ty [pī′ə·tē] *n., pl.* **pi·e·ties** **1** Reverence, strictness, and devotion in practicing one's religion. **2** Honor and obedience, as due to parents or superiors. **3** Something pious, as an act or wish.
pi·e·zo·e·lec·tric·i·ty [pī·ē′zō·i·lek′tris′ə·tē] *n.* **1** Electricity produced by pressure applied to certain crystals or ceramics. **2** Mechanical effects produced when electricity is applied to such substances. **—pi·e·zo·e·lec·tric** [pī·ē′zō·i·lek′trik] *adj.*
pig [pig] *n.* **1** An animal having a short, thick body, cloven hooves, a long snout, and a thick, bristly skin; swine; hog. **2** Its meat; pork. **3** *informal* A person with a hog's bad features; greedy, selfish, or dirty person. **4** A rough or crude casting of metal, especially iron.
pi·geon [pij′ən] *n.* **1** A bird with short legs, a small head, and a sturdy body; dove. **2** *slang* A person who is easy to fool or cheat.
pi·geon·hole [pij′ən·hōl′] *n., v.* **pi·geon·holed, pi·geon·hol·ing** **1** *n.* A hole for pigeons to nest in, especially one of a number of such holes. **2** *n.* A small compartment, as in a desk, for filing papers. **3** *v.* To place in a pigeonhole; file. **4** *v.* To lay aside or file away and ignore: to *pigeonhole* a request. **5** *v.* To arrange in classes or groups; classify.

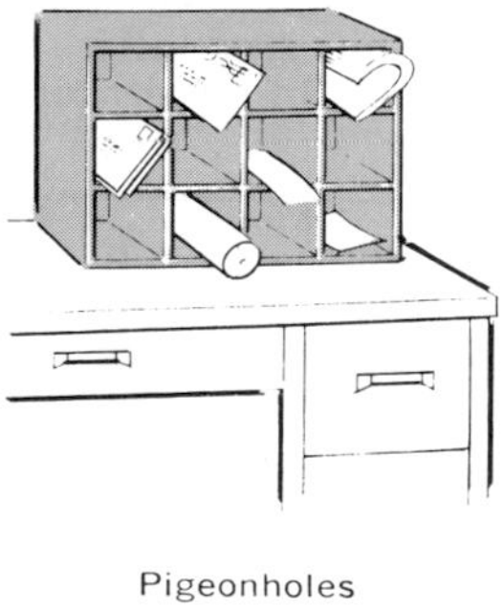
Pigeonholes

pi·geon-toed [pij′ən·tōd′] *adj.* Having the toes or feet turned inward.
pig·gish [pig′ish] *adj.* Behaving like a pig; greedy or dirty.
pig·gy·back [pig′ē·bak′] *adv., adj.* **1** On the back or shoulders: to ride *piggyback.* **2** Of or by a method of transportation in which loaded truck trailers are shipped on railway flatcars.

Piggyback ride

piggy bank A coin bank, often in the shape of a pig, with a slot for inserting coins.
pig·head·ed [pig′hed′·id] *adj.* Stubborn.
pig iron Crude iron as it comes from a blast furnace, usually cast in oblong molds.
pig·ment [pig′mənt] *n.* Coloring matter, such as one of the powdered substances mixed with a liquid to give paint its color, or a natural substance that colors living cells or tissues, as the chlorophyll that makes leaves green.
pig·men·ta·tion [pig′mən·tā′shən] *n.* The coloring that pigments give to a person or thing.
Pig·my [pig′mē] *n., pl.* **Pig·mies** (*sometimes written* **pigmy**) Another spelling of PYGMY.
pig·pen [pig′pen′] *n.* **1** A pen for pigs. **2** Any filthy place.
pig·skin [pig′skin′] *n.* **1** The skin of a pig or leather made from it. **2** Something made of this skin, as a saddle. **3** *informal* A football.
pig·sty [pig′stī′] *n., pl.* **pig·sties** A pigpen.
pig·tail [pig′tāl′] *n.* A braid or plait of hair hanging down from the back of the head.
pi·ka [pī′kə *or* pē′kə] *n.* A small mammal related to rabbits and hares, having ears that are shorter and rounder than a rabbit's.
pike[1] [pīk] *n.* A long pole with a metal spearhead, used by foot soldiers in medieval times.
pike[2] [pīk] *n.* An edible freshwater fish with a slender body, a long snout, and spiny fins.
pike[3] [pīk] *n.* A turnpike.
pike[4] [pīk] *n.* A sharp point or spike, such as the tip of a spear.
pik·er [pī′kər] *n. slang* A person who is stingy, petty, or overcautious.
pike·staff [pīk′staf′] *n., pl.* **pike·staves** [pīk′stāvz′] The wooden handle of a pike.
pi·laf or **pi·laff** [pi·läf′ *or* pē·läf′] *n.* Rice cooked in a seasoned broth, often served with meat or vegetables.
pi·las·ter [pi·las′tər] *n.* A rectangular column that is part of a wall and projects out a bit from it.

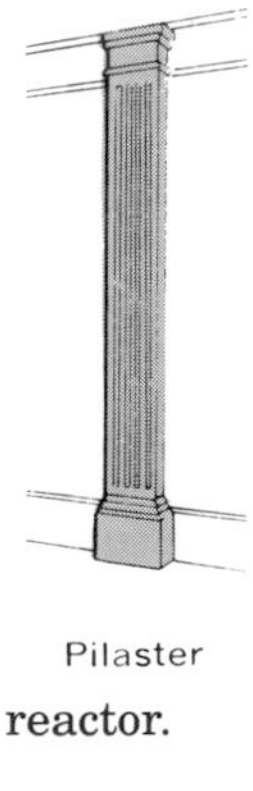
Pilaster

pile[1] [pīl] *n., v.* **piled, pil·ing** **1** *n.* A number of things stacked up. **2** *n.* A heap; mound: a *pile* of sand. **3** *v.* To make a pile of: to *pile* up papers or hay. **4** *v.* To accumulate in or as if in a pile: The sand *piled* against the side of the cabin; The work *piled* up. **5** *v.* To cover or heap with a large amount: to *pile* a plate with food. **6** *n. informal* A large amount: a *pile* of money. **7** *v.* To move in a confused mass; crowd: They *piled* onto the bus. **8** *n.* A massive building or group of buildings. **9** *n.* A funeral pyre. **10** *n.* In physics, a reactor.

pile[2] [pīl] *n.* A heavy beam of wood or steel or a concrete pillar driven into the earth to form a foundation for a building, bridge, or other structure.

pile[3] [pīl] *n.* 1 A mass of cut or uncut loops forming the surface of a rug or of a fabric such as velvet or corduroy. 2 Soft, fine hair.

pile driver A machine used for hammering piles into the ground.

piles [pīlz] *n.pl.* Another word for HEMORRHOIDS.

pil·fer [pil′fər] *v.* To steal by taking a little at a time: to *pilfer* candy.

pil·grim [pil′grim] *n.* 1 A person who journeys to some sacred place for religious reasons. 2 Any wanderer or traveler. 3 (*written* **Pilgrim**) One of the English Puritans who established a colony at Plymouth, Massachusetts, in 1620.

pil·grim·age [pil′grə·mij] *n.* 1 A journey to a place that is held in reverence or honor. 2 Any long or difficult journey.

pill [pil] *n.* A small ball or pellet containing medicine, that can be swallowed whole. ◆ *Pill* comes from the Latin word *pilula*, meaning a *little ball* or *globule*.

pil·lage [pil′ij] *v.* **pil·laged, pil·lag·ing,** *n.* 1 *v.* To rob openly and destructively, as in war; plunder. 2 *n.* The act of robbing in this way. 3 *n.* Goods stolen in this way; plunder; loot.

pil·lar [pil′ər] *n.* 1 A slender, firm, upright structure of stone, wood, or other material, as one supporting a roof or standing as a monument; column or shaft. 2 Anything resembling a pillar: a *pillar* of dust. 3 A leading member and main support: The head of the school board is a *pillar* of the community. **—from pillar to post** From one predicament to another.

pill·box [pil′boks′] *n.* 1 A small box to hold pills. 2 A small cylindrical hat without a brim, worn by women. 3 A low concrete structure for machine guns or other weapons.

pil·lion [pil′yən] *n.* A seat behind the saddle of a horse or motorcycle for a second rider.

pil·lo·ry [pil′ə·rē] *n., pl.* **pil·lo·ries,** *v.* **pil·lo·ried, pil·lo·ry·ing** 1 *n.* A wooden frame having holes cut in it through which a person's head and hands were put and fastened as a form of public punishment. 2 *v.* To put in a pillory. 3 *v.* To hold up to public scorn or ridicule.

pil·low [pil′ō] 1 *n.* A bag or case filled with a soft material, as feathers or foam rubber, on which to rest one's head. 2 *v.* To rest on or as if on a pillow. 3 *v.* To act as a pillow for: A jacket *pillowed* the child's head.

pil·low·case [pil′ō·kās′] *n.* A cloth covering which is slipped over a pillow.

pi·lot [pī′lət] 1 *n.* The person who operates or guides an aircraft during flight. 2 *n.* A person licensed to direct ships in and out of ports or through dangerous waters. 3 *n.* A helmsman. 4 *n.* Any guide. 5 *v.* To act or serve as the pilot of; steer; guide. 6 *v.* To guide, conduct, or steer, as past obstacles: Senator Dunn *piloted* the bill through the Senate.

pilot fish A small ocean fish, often found swimming alongside sharks.

pi·lot·house [pī′lət·hous′] *n., pl.* **pi·lot·hou·ses** [pī′·lət·hou′zəz] An enclosed structure on the deck of a ship, housing the equipment for steering and navigating.

pilot light 1 A small flame that is kept burning to ignite a gas burner when it is turned on. 2 A small light that shows that an electrical appliance is turned on.

pi·men·to [pi·men′tō] *n., pl.* **pi·men·tos** 1 Pimiento. 2 Another word for ALLSPICE.

pi·mien·to [pi·myen′tō] *n., pl.* **pi·mien·tos** A sweet pepper plant or its ripe fruit, used as a relish and a filling for olives.

pim·per·nel [pim′pər·nel] *n.* A plant related to the primrose, usually having red flowers.

pim·ple [pim′pəl] *n.* A small swelling of the skin, usually reddish and sore at the base.

pin [pin] *n., v.* **pinned, pin·ning** 1 *n.* A short, stiff piece of wire with a sharp point and a round, usually flattened, head, used for fastening things together. 2 *n.* Anything like a pin in form or use, as a hairpin. 3 *n.* An ornament, as a brooch or badge, mounted on a pin: a club *pin.* 4 *n.* A wooden or metal peg or bar used to hang things on, fasten things together, or hold things in place. 5 *v.* To fasten with or as if with a pin or pins. 6 *v.* To hold firmly in one place: The tacks *pinned* the map to the wall. 7 *n.* In bowling, one of the bottle-shaped pieces to be knocked down. **—on pins and needles** Uneasy or anxious; nervous. **—pin on** *U.S. slang* To accuse of or blame for: They *pinned* the crime *on* the thief. **—pin (someone) down** To force (someone) to give a definite answer or make a definite decision.

pin·a·fore [pin′ə·fôr′] *n.* A sleeveless, apronlike garment, worn as a dress or protective smock by girls and women.

pi·ña·ta [pēn·yä′tə *or* pin·yä′tə] *n.* A decorated, candy-filled container that is hung from the ceiling at traditional Latin American celebrations. Blindfolded children try to break open the piñata with a stick.

pince-nez [pans′nā′] *n., pl.* **pince-nez** [pans′nā(z)′] Eyeglasses that are held on the bridge of the nose by a clip.

pin·cers [pin′sərz] *n.pl.* (*sometimes used with singular verb*) 1 An instrument having two handles and a pair of jaws working on a pivot, used for holding objects. 2 The claw of a lobster, crab, or similar animal.

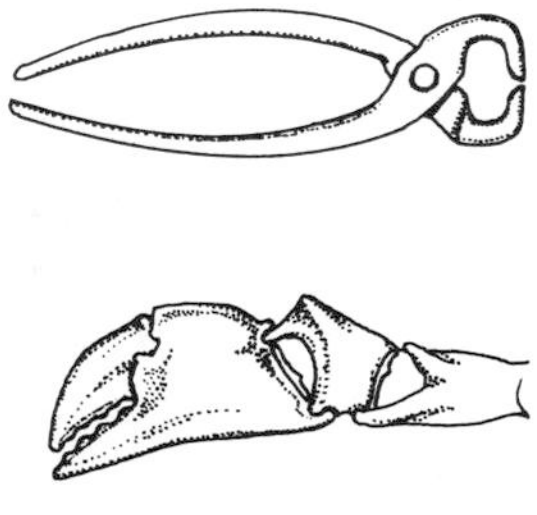

Pincers

pinch [pinch] 1 *v.* To squeeze between two edges or surfaces, as between a finger and thumb. 2 *n.* The act of pinching; squeeze: a *pinch* on the cheek. 3 *n.* As much of a substance as can be taken between the finger and thumb: a *pinch* of salt. 4 *v.* To

a	add	**i**	it	**o͝o**	took	**oi**	oil
ā	ace	**ī**	ice	**o͞o**	pool	**ou**	pout
â	care	**o**	odd	**u**	up	**ng**	ring
ä	palm	**ō**	open	**û**	burn	**th**	thin
e	end	**ô**	order	**yo͞o**	fuse	**t̶h̶**	this
ē	equal					**zh**	vision

ə = {a in *above*   e in *sicken*   i in *possible*
    {o in *melon*   u in *circus*

squeeze or press upon painfully. **5** *n.* Painful pressure of any kind: the *pinch* of stiff shoes. **6** *v.* To make thin, shriveled, or wrinkled, as from cold or hunger. **7** *n.* An emergency or a time of sudden need. **8** *v.* To be economical or stingy, as with money. **9** *v. slang* To steal. **10** *n. slang* A theft. **11** *v. slang* To arrest or capture. **12** *n. slang* An arrest.

pinch·ers [pin'chərz] *n.pl.* Pincers.

pinch-hit [pinch'hit'] *v.* **pinch-hit, pinch-hit·ting** **1** In baseball, to bat for someone else. **2** *U.S. informal* To substitute for someone else in an emergency. **—pinch hitter**

pin·cush·ion [pin'ko͝osh'ən] *n.* A small cushion into which pins are stuck when not being used.

pine[1] [pīn] *n.* **1** Any of a number of trees bearing cones and needle-shaped evergreen leaves in clusters. **2** The wood of any of these trees.

pine[2] [pīn] *v.* **pined, pin·ing** **1** To grow thin or weak, as with longing or grief: The imprisoned captive *pined* away. **2** To have great desire or longing: to *pine* for one's homeland.

pin·e·al body [pin'ē·əl] A small structure found in the brain that helps regulate certain biological functions in some vertebrates.

pine·ap·ple [pīn'ap'əl] *n.* **1** A large, juicy, tropical fruit resembling a pine cone. **2** The plant it grows on, having spiny, curved leaves.

pine needle The leaf of a pine.

pin·ey [pī'nē] *adj.* **pin·i·er, pin·i·est** Another spelling of PINY.

pin·feath·er [pin'feth'ər] *n.* An undeveloped feather, like a short stub.

Ping-Pong [ping'pông' *or* ping'pong'] *n.* Another word named for TABLE TENNIS: a trademark.

pin·hole [pin'hōl'] *n.* A tiny puncture made by or as if by a pin.

pin·ion[1] [pin'yən] **1** *n.* The outer part or segment of a bird's wing. **2** *n.* A wing. **3** *n.* A feather; quill. **4** *v.* To prevent (a bird) from flying by cutting off a pinion or binding the wings. **5** *v.* To cut or bind (the wings). **6** *v.* To bind or hold the arms of (someone) to make the person helpless. **7** *v.* To bind or hold (the arms).

pin·ion[2] [pin'yən] *n.* A small cogwheel driving or driven by a larger cogwheel.

pink[1] [pingk] **1** *n., adj.* Pale red. **2** *n.* Any of several garden plants having fragrant, often pink, flowers. **—in the pink** *informal* In excellent health. **—pink'ish** *adj.*

pink[2] [pingk] *v.* **1** To cut the edges of (cloth) with a scalloped pattern made by scissors called **pinking shears,** as to prevent raveling. **2** To decorate with a pattern of holes, as leather. **3** To prick or stab with a pointed weapon.

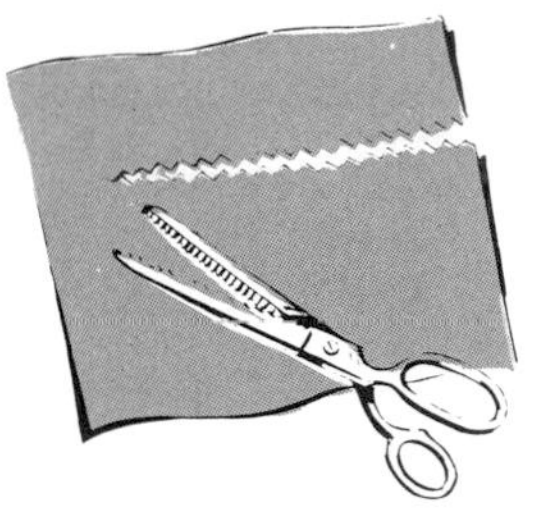

Pinked cloth

pink·eye [pingk'ī'] *n.* A contagious disease in which the eyeball becomes pinkish or red.

pink·ie or **pink·y** [ping'kē] *n., pl.* **pink·ies** The smallest finger, the one farthest from the thumb.

pin money A small sum of money, as an allowance, used for minor, personal expenses.

pin·nace [pin'is] *n.* **1** Any small boat on a ship. **2** A small sailing ship.

pin·na·cle [pin'ə·kəl] *n., v.* **pin·na·cled, pin·na·cling** **1** *n.* A tapering turret or spire, as one rising over a roof. **2** *v.* To provide or top with a pinnacle. **3** *n.* A high peak; summit, as of a mountain. **4** *n.* The highest point: the *pinnacle* of success. **5** *v.* To place on or as if on a pinnacle.

pin·nate [pin'āt'] *adj.* Like a feather, especially having similar parts arranged on each side of a stem or stalk: a *pinnate* leaf.

pi·noch·le [pē'nuk·əl] *n.* A card game played with a deck of 48 cards having two of every nine, ten, jack, queen, king, and ace.

pi·ñon [pin'yən *or* pin'yōn'] *n., pl.* **pi·ñons** or **pi·ño·nes** [pin·yō'nēz] **1** A low pine tree of western North America. **2** The edible seed of this tree.

pin·point [pin'point'] **1** *n.* The point of a pin. **2** *n.* Something that is very small. **3** *v.* To locate or define precisely: to *pinpoint* a target.

pint [pīnt] *n.* **1** A measure of volume for liquids or dry things, equal to half a quart. **2** A container having the capacity of a pint.

pin·to [pin'tō] *adj., n., pl.* **pin·tos** **1** *adj.* Having spots, usually of two or more colors. **2** *n.* A pinto horse or pony.

pin·wheel [pin'(h)wēl'] *n.* **1** A toy consisting of a stick to which is attached a small wheel with blades that spin in the wind. **2** A firework that revolves and throws off colored sparks.

Pinwheel

pin·worm [pin'wûrm'] *n.* A small parasitic worm that lives in the lower part of the human intestinal tract.

pin·y [pī'nē] *adj.* **pin·i·er, pin·i·est** **1** Covered with or full of pine trees: a *piny* hillside. **2** Resembling pine, especially in scent: a *piny* bath oil.

Pin·yin or **pin·yin** [pin'yin'] *n.* A system used to represent Chinese speech sounds with letters of the Roman alphabet.

pi·o·neer [pī'ə·nir'] **1** *n.* One of the first explorers, settlers, or colonists of a new country or region. **2** *n.* Someone who leads the way, as in developing a new field. **3** *v.* To lead the way, as into new territory: Copernicus *pioneered* in modern astronomy. **4** *v.* To be a pioneer of: to *pioneer* a new technique of surgery.

pi·ous [pī'əs] *adj.* Religious; devout; reverent.

pip[1] [pip] *n.* **1** A small fruit seed, as of an apple or orange. **2** *slang* A person or thing that is outstanding or admirable in some way.

pip[2] [pip] *n.* A contagious disease of fowls.

pip[3] [pip] *n.* Any of the marks or spots on playing cards, dominoes, dice, or other game pieces.

pip[4] [pip] *v.* **pipped, pip·ping** To break through (an eggshell) in hatching.

pipe [pīp] *n., v.* **piped, pip·ing** **1** *n.* A long tube, as of metal, wood, or concrete, for conveying such materials as gas, steam, and liquids from one place to another. **2** *v.* To convey by pipes: to *pipe* oil into a tank. **3** *v.* To provide with pipes. **4** *n.* A hollow stem with a small bowl at one end, as for smoking tobacco. **5** *n.* A tube, as of reed, wood, or metal, that produces musical notes when air is blown through it. **6** *n.* (*pl.*) The bagpipe. **7** *v.* To play on a pipe or bagpipe: to *pipe* a tune. **8** *v.* To speak or sing in a shrill, high-pitched tone. **9** *n.* A bird's note or call. **—pipe down** *slang* To become silent; stop talking or making noise.

pipe·line [pīp′līn′] *n.* A line of pipes for conveying water, oil, gas, and other materials.

pip·er [pī′pər] *n.* A person who plays on a pipe or pipes, especially on a bagpipe.

pi·pette [pī·pet′] *n.* A small tube for taking up measured quantities of a liquid.

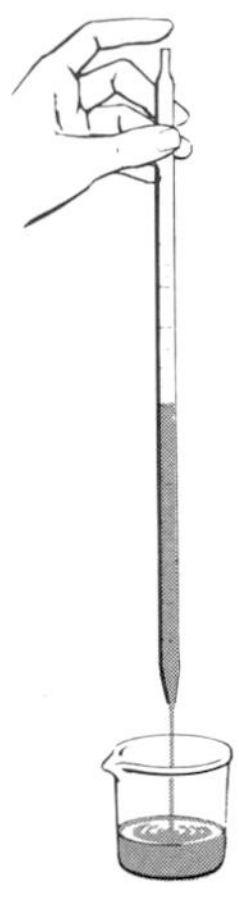
Pipette

pip·ing [pī′ping] **1** *n.* Music made by playing pipes. **2** *n.* A shrill sound. **3** *adj.* Shrill or high-pitched: *piping* voices. **4** *n.* A system of pipes, as for drainage. **5** *n.* A narrow strip of folded cloth, used for trimming edges or seams. **—piping hot** So hot as to sizzle.

pip·it [pip′it] *n.* A small brown songbird.

pip·pin [pip′in] *n.* Any of several varieties of apple.

pi·quant [pē′kənt *or* pē·känt′] *adj.* **1** Having an agreeably sharp or spicy taste: a *piquant* relish. **2** Lively and interesting or charming: a *piquant* manner. **—pi·quan·cy** [pē′kən·sē] *n.*

pique [pēk] *n., v.* **piqued, pi·quing** **1** *n.* A feeling of anger or resentment coming from wounded pride. **2** *v.* To arouse a hurt and angry or resentful feeling in: The rude remarks *piqued* the guests. **3** *v.* To stimulate; arouse: to *pique* one's curiosity.

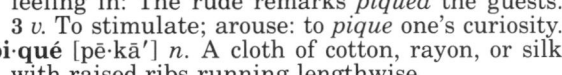

pi·qué [pē·kā′] *n.* A cloth of cotton, rayon, or silk with raised ribs running lengthwise.

pi·ra·cy [pī′rə·sē] *n., pl.* **pi·ra·cies** **1** The robbing of ships on the high seas. **2** The stealing of another's creation, as a literary work or invention.

pi·ra·nha [pi·rä′nyə] *n.* A small, fierce, freshwater fish of tropical South America, with powerful jaws and sharp teeth. In schools they will attack people and large animals.

pi·rate [pī′rit] *n., v.* **pi·rat·ed, pi·rat·ing** **1** *n.* A person guilty of piracy, especially a leader or member of a band that sails the high seas robbing ships. **2** *v.* To make copies of a movie, record album, computer program, or the like, and sell or use them illegally.

pi·rogue [pē′rōg′] *n.* A dugout or other canoe.

pir·ou·ette [pir′o͞o·et′] *n., v.* **pir·ou·et·ted, pir·ou·et·ting** **1** *n.* In dancing, a rapid whirling on the toes or ball of one foot. **2** *v.* To make a pirouette.

Pis·ces [pī′sēz *or* pis′ēz] *n.* **1** A constellation in the northern sky, thought to look like a pair of fish. **2** The twelfth sign of the zodiac. **3** A person born under this sign.

pis·ta·chi·o [pis·tä′shē·ō *or* pis·tash′ē·ō] *n., pl.* **pis·ta·chi·os,** *adj.* **1** *n.* An edible green nut. **2** *n.* The small tree it grows on, native to western Asia and the Levant. **3** *n.* The flavor of the nut, or a food flavored with it, as ice cream. **4** *n., adj.* Light, yellowish green.

pis·til [pis′təl] *n.* The seed-bearing organ of flowering plants, composed of the ovary, the stigma, and usually the style.

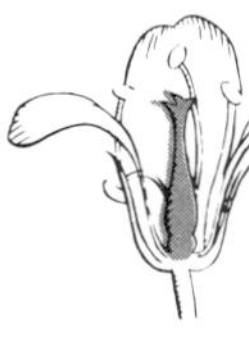
Pistil

pis·tol [pis′təl] *n.* A small gun made to be held and fired in one hand.

pis·ton [pis′tən] *n.* A disk or cylinder fitted closely in a tube or hollow cylinder and moved back and forth by pressure of gas or steam, as in an engine, or by a rod, as in a pump.

piston ring An adjustable metal ring fitting around the rim of a piston to make a tight fit between the piston and cylinder wall.

piston rod A rod that transmits motion to or from a piston.

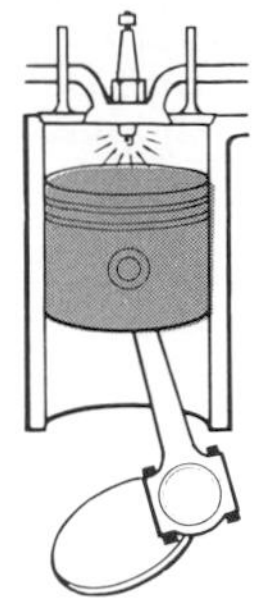
Piston rod

pit[1] [pit] *n., v.* **pit·ted, pit·ting** **1** *n.* A hole or cavity in the ground, either natural or dug: the *pit* of a mine. **2** *n.* Any cavity, depression, or scar in or on the body: the *pit* of the stomach. **3** *v.* To mark or become marked, as with pits, dents, or scars: a face *pitted* with pockmarks. **4** *n.* A hole dug in the ground and camouflaged, to trap wild animals. **5** *n.* An enclosed place where animals are made to fight each other. **6** *v.* To put to fight or compete against: to *pit* one's cunning against the cunning of an animal. **7** *n.* A sunken area in front of the stage of a theater, where the musicians sit.

pit[2] [pit] *n., v.* **pit·ted, pit·ting** **1** *n.* The hard stone in certain fruits, as peaches or cherries. **2** *v.* To remove the pit or pits from. ◆ *Pit* comes directly from Dutch and goes back to an older Dutch word meaning *pith* or *kernel.*

pi·ta [pē′tə] *n.* An eastern Mediterranean bread baked in disks that can be split open for making sandwiches.

pitch[1] [pich] **1** *v.* To throw, toss, or hurl: to *pitch* hay. **2** *v.* In baseball, to throw (the ball) to the batter. **3** *n.* The act or manner of pitching: a wild *pitch.* **4** *n.* Something pitched, as a ball: The batter swung at the *pitch.* **5** *v.* To erect or set up: to *pitch* a tent; to *pitch* camp. **6** *v.* To set the level, angle, or degree of: to *pitch* a roof at 45 degrees. **7** *v.* To slope downward: The hill *pitched* steeply at the top. **8** *n.* The amount or degree of slope: the *pitch* of a roof. **9** *v.* To fall or plunge forward or headlong. **10** *v.* To rise and fall alternately at the bow and stern: The ship *pitched* and rolled in the gale. **11** *n.* A particular point, degree, or level: The game was played at a high *pitch* of excitement. **12** *n.* The level of a sound's highness or lowness. The pitch of notes depends on their vibration rates. **13** *v.* To set at a certain pitch or in a certain key: *Pitch* the song lower. **14** *n. slang* Talk calculated to persuade: a salesman's *pitch.* **—pitch in** *informal* To start working energetically. **—pitch into** To attack.

pitch[2] [pich] *n.* **1** A thick, sticky, black substance obtained from boiling down tar or other materials, and used to pave roads and cover roofs. **2** The sticky sap of certain pines. **—pitch′y** *adj.*

pitch-black [pich′blak′] *adj.* Extremely black.

pitch·blende [pich′blend′] *n.* A blackish or brown material that is an important ore of radium and uranium.

a	add	**i**	it	**o͝o**	took	**oi**	oil
ā	ace	**ī**	ice	**o͞o**	pool	**ou**	pout
â	care	**o**	odd	**u**	up	**ng**	ring
ä	palm	**ō**	open	**û**	burn	**th**	thin
e	end	**ô**	order	**yo͞o**	fuse	**th**	this
ē	equal					**zh**	vision

ə = a in *above* e in *sicken* i in *possible* o in *melon* u in *circus*

P

pitch-dark [pich′därk′] *adj.* Extremely dark.
pitch·er[1] [pich′ər] *n.* 1 A container with a handle and either a lip or spout, used for holding and pouring liquids. 2 As much as a pitcher will hold. **—pitch′er·ful′** *n.*
pitch·er[2] [pich′ər] *n.* 1 A person who pitches. 2 In baseball, the player who throws the ball that the batter is to hit.
pitcher plant A plant having pitcherlike leaves filled with liquid in which insects are trapped and digested.
pitch·fork [pich′fôrk′] *n.* A large fork with a long handle, used to lift and throw hay.
pitch·out [pich′out′] *n.* 1 A baseball pitch deliberately thrown high and wide to make it easier for the catcher to throw out a base runner. 2 A lateral pass in football, made behind the line of scrimmage between two backs.
pitch pipe A small pipe that sounds a particular tone when blown, used to find a certain pitch for singers or instrumental players.
pit·e·ous [pit′ē·əs] *adj.* Arousing or deserving pity: a *piteous* wail. **—pit′e·ous·ly** *adv.* **—pit′e·ous·ness** *n.*
pit·fall [pit′fôl′] *n.* 1 A camouflaged pit used to trap wild animals. 2 Any hidden danger.
pith [pith] *n.* 1 The mass of soft, spongy tissue that fills the center of the stems and branches of certain plants. 2 Any similar soft substance, as in a feather or hair. 3 The essential part; gist: the *pith* of my argument.
pith·e·can·thro·pus [pith′ə·kan′thrə·pəs] *n., pl.* **pith·e·can·thro·pi** [pith′ə·kan′thrə·pī′] An extinct race of hominids known from fossil remains found in Java.
pith helmet A hard, light hat made of dried pith, worn in the tropics.
pith·y [pith′ē] *adj.* **pith·i·er, pith·i·est** 1 Of, like, or filled with pith. 2 Brief and forceful: a *pithy* remark. **—pith′i·ly** *adv.*
pit·i·a·ble [pit′ē·ə·bəl] *adj.* Arousing or deserving pity or contempt. **—pit′i·a·bly** *adv.*
pit·i·ful [pit′i·fəl] *adj.* 1 Arousing pity or compassion. 2 Arousing a feeling of scorn or contempt. **—pit′i·ful·ly** *adv.*
pit·i·less [pit′i·lis] *adj.* Without pity; cruel; ruthless. **—pit′i·less·ly** *adv.*
pit·tance [pit′əns] *n.* 1 A small allowance of money. 2 Any meager amount or share.
pit·ter-pat·ter [pit′ər·pat′ər] *n.* A quick, light, tapping sound: the *pitter-patter* of rain on the window.
pi·tu·i·tar·y [pi·t(y)o͞o′ə·ter′ē] 1 *adj.* Of or having to do with the pituitary gland. 2 *n.* The pituitary gland.
pituitary gland A small, oval endocrine gland at the base of the brain. It secretes hormones that influence growth and most basic body functions.
pit viper Any of several venomous snakes, such as the rattlesnake, copperhead, and bushmaster, with a small heat-sensitive pit on each side of the head and hollow fangs.
pit·y [pit′ē] *n., pl.* **pit·ies,** *v.* **pit·ied, pit·y·ing** 1 *n.* A feeling of keen regret or sorrow for the misfortunes or sufferings of others; sympathy. 2 *v.* To feel pity for: *Pity* the poor, lost child. 3 *n.* A reason for regret or sorrow: What a *pity* that you missed the picnic! **—have pity on** or **take pity on** To show pity for.
Pi·ute [pī′·yo͞ot′ *or* pī·yo͞ot′] *n., pl.* **Pi·ute** or **Pi·utes** Another spelling of PAIUTE.
piv·ot [piv′ət] 1 *n.* Something, as a pin or short shaft, on which a part turns: The needle of a compass rests on a *pivot.* 2 *v.* To place on or provide with a pivot. 3 *v.* To turn on or as if on a pivot: The player *pivoted* before throwing the basketball. 4 *n.* A turning or pivoting movement: to make a *pivot.* 5 *n.* A person or thing upon which something hinges or depends: The coded telegram was the *pivot* of our plan.

The pivot allows the compass needle to revolve freely.

piv·ot·al [piv′ət·(ə)l] *adj.* 1 Of, having to do with, or acting as a pivot. 2 Very important; crucial: a *pivotal* decision.
pix·ie or **pix·y** [pik′sē] *n., pl.* **pix·ies** A fairy or elf.
piz·za [pēt′sə] *n.* A baked Italian food consisting of a crust overlaid with a mixture of cheese, tomatoes, spices, and other ingredients.
piz·ze·ri·a [pēt′sə·rē′ə] *n.* A place where pizzas are prepared, sold, and eaten.
piz·zi·ca·to [pit′si·kä′tō] *adj., adv.* Played by plucking the strings instead of by using a bow.
pk. 1 pack. 2 peak. 3 peck.
pkg. package.
pkgs. packages.
pks. 1 packs. 2 peaks. 3 pecks.
pkwy. or **Pkwy.** parkway.
pl. 1 place. 2 plate. 3 plural.
pla·ca·ble [plak′ə·bəl *or* plā′kə·bəl] *adj.* Capable of being calmed or pacified; forgiving.
plac·ard [plak′ärd] 1 *n.* A poster publicly displayed. 2 *v.* To post placards on or in.
pla·cate [plā′kāt′ *or* plak′āt′] *v.* **pla·cat·ed, pla·cat·ing** To calm the anger of; pacify.
place [plās] *n., v.* **placed, plac·ing** 1 *n.* A space or area occupied by or proper for a certain person or thing: Put each record in its proper *place.* 2 *n.* A city, town, or other locality. 3 *n.* An open area, short street, or city square. 4 *n.* A house or dwelling: our *place* at the shore. 5 *n.* Any building or area used for a special purpose: a *place* of business; an eating *place.* 6 *n.* A particular point or part: a soiled *place* on the tablecloth; a card to mark your *place* in a book. 7 *v.* To put in a particular place or position: *Place* your hands on the table. 8 *v.* To direct or rest with confidence: to *place* trust in a leader. 9 *n.* Order, position, or rank in relation to others: to finish in first *place.* 10 *v.* To finish, as a race or contest, in a certain position: Our team *placed* fifth. 11 *n.* In mathematics, the position of a symbol in an Arabic numeral. In 148, 1 is in the hundreds place and is therefore equal to 100. 12 *n.* Social class, rank, or station: one's *place* in society. 13 *n.* A situation, position, or job: In his *place,* I'd have acted differently; No one can take your *place*; a *place* in a firm. 14 *n.* Right or duty: It isn't our *place* to decide the issue. 15 *n.* The right or proper position, location, or time: This is no *place* for laughter. 16 *v.* To think of in relation to a place, time, or set of circumstances; identify: I've seen your face before, but I can't *place* you. **—give place** 1 To make room. 2 To give in or surrender. **—go places** *slang* To advance toward or achieve success. **—in place** 1 In its

natural or proper place. **2** Right or suitable. **—in place of** Instead of. **—out of place** **1** Not in its right or proper place. **2** Not suitable; inappropriate. **—take place** To happen; occur. ◆ *Place, piazza,* and *plaza* all go back to the Latin word *platea*, meaning *a wide street*, but they came into English by way of French, Italian, and Spanish, respectively. *Place* has many other meanings, but it is often used in names to mean an open area, square, or small street: Park *Place*. *Piazza* is usually used of such open areas in Italy, where they abound. Elsewhere, *plaza* is preferred: Rockefeller *Plaza*.

pla·ce·bo [plə·sē'bō] *n., pl.* **pla·ce·bos** or **pla·ce·boes** A substance designed to look like medicine, but having no medicinal value, given to soothe a patient or as part of a test of effectiveness of a real drug. ◆ *Placebo* comes from a Latin word meaning *I will please*.

place-kick [plās'kik'] *v.* To kick (a football) that has been propped up on the ground.

place kick In football, a kick in which the ball is first propped up on the ground.

place·ment [plās'mənt] *n.* **1** The act or an instance of placing. **2** A place kick. **3** The placing of people in jobs, schools, or other situations.

pla·cen·ta [plə·sen'tə] *n.* In women and most female mammals, a broad, flat, spongy organ by which a fetus in the uterus is nourished and its wastes are removed.

plac·er [plas'ər] *n.* A deposit, as one of sand or gravel, containing gold or other valuable minerals in particles large enough to be washed out.

plac·id [plas'id] *adj.* Calm; peaceful. **—pla·cid·i·ty** [plə·sid'ə·tē] *n.* **—plac'id·ly** *adv.*

plack·et [plak'it] *n.* An opening in a garment, as a skirt, that makes the garment easy to put on. It is usually closed by a zipper.

pla·gia·rism [plā'jə·riz'əm] *n.* The act of plagiarizing. **—pla'gia·rist** *n.*

pla·gia·rize [plā'jə·rīz'] *v.* **pla·gia·rized, pla·gia·riz·ing** To steal and pass off as one's own (the writings, ideas, or other creative work of someone else).

plague [plāg] *n., v.* **plagued, pla·guing** **1** *n.* A very contagious, often fatal, disease that spreads rapidly over a large area, as the bubonic plague. **2** *n.* Anything troublesome or distressing. **3** *v.* To trouble, torment, or annoy: to *plague* someone with silly questions.

plaice [plās] *n., pl.* **plaice** or **plaic·es** A large, edible flatfish, related to the flounder.

plaid [plad] **1** *n.* A cloth having horizontal and vertical stripes of various widths and colors crossing each other to form distinctive patterns. **2** *n.* A long, woolen scarf having this pattern, worn in the Scottish Highlands as a cloak over one shoulder. **3** *adj.* Having this pattern. ◆ *Plaid* comes from a Scottish Gaelic word meaning *a blanket*.

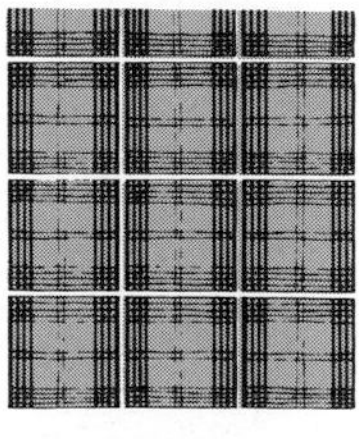

Plaid

plain [plān] **1** *adj.* Not obstructed; open; clear: in *plain* sight. **2** *adj.* Easy to understand; clear; obvious: a *plain* statement. **3** *adj.* Not complicated; simple. **4** *adj.* Straightforward; frank: *plain* speaking. **5** *adv.* In a plain manner. **6** *adj.* Not highly educated or sophisticated; ordinary: *plain* folks. **7** *adj.* Not rich, luxurious, or fancy: *plain* food. **8** *adj.* Not decorated or figured: *plain* cloth. **9** *adj.* Not pretty or handsome. **10** *n.* An expanse of almost level, nearly treeless land; prairie. **11** *adj.* Level. **—plain'ly** *adv.* **—plain'ness** *n.*

plain·clothes·man [plān'klō(th)z'mən] *n., pl.* **plain·clothes·men** [plān'klō(th)z'mən] A police officer who wears civilian clothes while on duty.

Plains Indians Any of the North American Indian tribes once living and hunting buffalo on the Great Plains.

plain·song [plān'sông'] *n.* Music from medieval times, sung in unison without accompanying instruments.

plain-spo·ken [plān'spō'kən] *adj.* Frank.

plaint [plānt] *n.* A lament or complaint.

plain·tiff [plān'tif] *n.* The person who brings a lawsuit against another called the defendant.

plain·tive [plān'tiv] *adj.* Expressing sadness; mournful; melancholy. **—plain'tive·ly** *adv.*

plait [plat *or* plāt] **1** *n.* A braid, as of hair. **2** *v.* To braid. **3** *n.* A pleat. **4** *v.* To pleat.

plan [plan] *n., v.* **planned, plan·ning** **1** *n.* A scheme, method, or design for attaining some object or goal. **2** *v.* To form a scheme or method for doing or achieving (something): to *plan* an investigation. **3** *v.* To intend: I *plan* to leave at noon. **4** *n.* (*pl.*) Intentions or arrangements worked out in advance: holiday *plans*. **5** *v.* To make plans. **6** *n.* A drawing showing how the parts or sections of something are arranged: the *plan* of a building. **7** *v.* To make a design or drawing of: to *plan* a seating arrangement.

pla·nar·i·an [plə·nâr'ē·ən] *n.* A small, broad-headed flatworm that lives in fresh water.

plane[1] [plān] **1** *n.* In mathematics, a surface that includes all the points of a line that connects any two points in it. **2** *adj.* Level; flat. **3** *n.* Any flat surface. **4** *adj.* Dealing only with flat surfaces: *plane* geometry. **5** *n.* A level or stage of existence or development: to talk on an intellectual *plane*. **6** *n.* An airplane.

plane[2] [plān] *n., v.* **planed, plan·ing** **1** *n.* A tool used for smoothing boards or other surfaces of wood. **2** *v.* To make smooth or even with a plane. **3** *v.* To remove with or as if with a plane.

Plane

plane[3] [plān] *n.* A plane tree.

plane geometry A branch of geometry that deals with plane figures.

plan·er [plā'nər] *n.* Someone or something that planes, especially a power tool for planing wood or metal surfaces.

P

a	add	i	it	o͝o	took	oi	oil
ā	ace	ī	ice	o͞o	pool	ou	pout
â	care	o	odd	u	up	ng	ring
ä	palm	ō	open	û	burn	th	thin
e	end	ô	order	yo͞o	fuse	th	this
ē	equal					zh	vision

ə = { a in *above* e in *sicken* i in *possible* / o in *melon* u in *circus* }

plan·et [plan′it] *n.* Any of the relatively large, nonglowing bodies that move in orbits around the sun or another star. The known planets are Mercury, Venus, Earth, Mars, Jupiter, Saturn, Uranus, Neptune, and Pluto.

plan·e·tar·i·um [plan′ə·târ′ē·əm] *n., pl.* **plan·e·tar·i·ums** or **plan·e·tar·i·a** [plan′ə·târ′ē·ə] **1** A room or building having an apparatus that shows on a domed ceiling the stars and other celestial bodies as they appear or appeared at any time and from any place on earth. **2** Such an apparatus.

plan·e·tar·y [plan′ə·ter′ē] *adj.* Of or having to do with a planet or planets.

plan·et·oid [plan′ə·toid′] *n.* Another name for ASTEROID.

plan·e·tol·o·gy [plan′ə·tol′ə·jē] *n.* The study of the planets, moons, comets, and other condensed matter of the solar system. **—plan′e·tol′o·gist** *n.*

plane tree Any of various large, spreading trees with broad leaves, as the sycamore.

plank [plangk] **1** *n.* A broad piece of sawed timber, thicker than a board. **2** *v.* To cover with planks: to *plank* a floor. **3** *v.* To broil or bake and serve on a board or plank: to *plank* fish. **4** *n.* One of the principles, ideals, or aims stated in a political platform. **—plank down** *informal* **1** To put down with force or emphasis. **2** To pay. **—walk the plank** To walk off a plank projecting from the side of a ship and die by drowning.

plank·ton [plangk′tən] *n.* Marine and freshwater plants and animals that cannot swim but only float or drift in the water. They range in size from microorganisms to jellyfish.

plan·ner [plan′ər] *n.* A person who plans.

plant [plant] **1** *n.* A living organism that is not an animal. A plant lacks a nervous system and cannot move from place to place by itself. Plants containing chlorophyll are able to make their own food by photosynthesis. Vegetables, herbs, trees, fungi, and algae all are plants. **2** *n.* One of the smaller forms of vegetable life, as distinguished from shrubs and trees: a potted *plant.* **3** *v.* To set in the ground to grow: to *plant* seeds. **4** *v.* To furnish with plants or seed: to *plant* a field. **5** *v.* To deposit (fish or spawn) in a body of water. **6** *v.* To set or fix firmly: The climber *planted* the pick in the ground. **7** *v.* To introduce into the mind; instill: to *plant* an idea. **8** *v.* To found; establish. **9** *n.* The machinery, appliances, equipment, and, often, the buildings and grounds used in operating a business or institution. **10** *n.* A factory.

plan·tain¹ [plan′tin] *n.* A common weed with large leaves and long spikes of tiny flowers.

plan·tain² [plan′tin] *n.* **1** A tropical herb sometimes growing to a height of 30 feet. **2** Its bananalike fruit, edible when cooked.

plan·ta·tion [plan·tā′shən] *n.* **1** A farm or estate of many acres having a crop of cotton, tobacco, rice, or other products, planted and tended by laborers who live there. **2** A grove of plants or trees grown to provide a certain product: a rubber *plantation.* **3** A colony, as of new settlers in a country.

plant·er [plan′tər] *n.* **1** A person or an implement that plants. **2** An owner of a plantation. **3** An early settler. **4** An attractive container in which plants are grown for decoration.

plaque [plak] *n.* **1** A flat piece, as one of metal, wood, porcelain, or ivory, having designs or lettering on one side. Plaques may be hung up as ornaments and used as memorial tablets. **2** A film on tooth surfaces that hardens and attracts decay-causing bacteria. **3** Material that collects on the inner walls of blood vessels.

plash [plash] **1** *v.* To splash. **2** *n.* A splash.

plas·ma [plaz′mə] *n.* The liquid part of blood, without the blood corpuscles.

plas·ter [plas′tər] **1** *n.* A mixture of lime, sand, and water for coating walls, ceilings, and partitions. It hardens as it dries. **2** *v.* To cover with or as if with plaster: to *plaster* a ceiling; clothes *plastered* with mud. **3** *v.* To apply like plaster: to *plaster* posters on a fence. **4** *n.* A sticky substance spread on cloth and applied to some part of the body for healing: a mustard *plaster.* **5** *v.* To lay flat: to *plaster* down a cowlick. **6** *n.* Plaster of Paris. **—plas′ter·er** *n.*

plas·ter·board [plas′tər·bôrd′] *n.* A building material made of layers of paper or board bonded with plaster.

plaster of Paris Powdered gypsum mixed with water to form a paste used for making casts, molds, bandages, and ornamental objects.

plas·tic [plas′tik] **1** *adj.* Capable of being molded: Clay and wax are *plastic.* **2** *n.* Any of a class of various materials chemically made and capable of being molded, cast, woven, or formed into many products. Cellophane is a plastic. **3** *adj.* Made of plastic: a *plastic* toy. **4** *adj.* Giving form or shape to matter: *plastic* art.

plas·tic·i·ty [plas·tis′ə·tē] *n.* The quality or condition of being plastic or easily molded.

plas·ti·cize [plas′tə·sīz′] *v.* **plas·ti·cized, plas·ti·ciz·ing** To make or become plastic.

plastic surgery Surgery in which lost, wounded, or deformed parts of the body are restored or repaired, as by grafts of skin or bone.

plat¹ [plat] *n.* **1** A small plot of ground. **2** A map or plan, especially one of a town or proposed town.

plat² [plat] *n., v.* **plat·ted, plat·ting** Another spelling of PLAIT.

plate [plāt] *n., v.* **plat·ed, plat·ing** **1** *n.* A shallow dish used to hold food at the table. **2** *n.* The food served on a plate. **3** *n.* An individual meal: a benefit dinner at $100 a *plate.* **4** *n.* A dish like a table plate used in taking up collections. **5** *n.* A thin, flat piece or a sheet of metal, glass, or other material. **6** *v.* To cover with metal plates for protection: to *plate* the side of a ship. **7** *v.* To coat with a thin layer, as one of gold or silver. **8** *n.* Household articles, as serving dishes or utensils, made of or coated with gold or silver. **9** *n.* A piece of flat metal bearing a design or inscription, especially one that is engraved or embossed. **10** *n.* A reproduction made from a plate of this kind. **11** *n.* A full-page book illustration printed on special paper. **12** *n.* A metal reproduction of a page of type, for printing. **13** *n.* A sheet, as one of glass or metal, that is coated with a material sensitive to light, used for taking photographs. **14** *n.* A set of false teeth. **15** *n.* In baseball, home base. **16** A large, independently moving section of the crust of the earth. **—plate′ful′** *n.*

pla·teau [pla·tō′] *n.* **1** A broad stretch of high, level land; high plain. **2** A time when change or progress stops temporarily: a *plateau* in the city's growth.

plate glass Glass in clear, thick sheets, suitable for such items as mirrors and display windows.

plate·let [plāt′lit] *n.* One of the tiny circular or oval bodies present in blood and necessary for the clotting of blood.

plate tec·ton·ics [tek·ton′iks] A theory in geology that the earth's crust is divided into sections, called plates, that move and shift. ◆ See -ICS.

plat·form [plat′fôrm′] *n.* **1** A raised flat surface or floor: a *platform* for a speaker; a *platform* by the track in a station. **2** A set or statement of principles, ideals, or aims put forth by a political party or other group.

platform tennis A game resembling tennis, played with wooden rackets and a rubber ball on a wooden platform enclosed by a fence.

plat·ing [plā′ting] *n.* **1** A layer or coating of metal: silver *plating.* **2** A coating of metal plates, as of armor.

plat·i·num [plat′ə·nəm] *n.* A heavy, gray, metallic element that does not tarnish, is very resistant to chemicals, and can be easily worked into many shapes. It is used in industry and science, and in making jewelry.

plat·i·tude [plat′ə·t(y)o͞od′] *n.* A flat, dull, or commonplace statement, such as "You get what you pay for."

plat·i·tu·di·nous [plat′ə·t(y)o͞od′ən·əs] *adj.* **1** Characterized by or using platitudes: a *platitudinous* speech. **2** Commonplace; trite.

Pla·ton·ic [plə·ton′ik] *adj.* **1** Of, having to do with, or like Plato or his philosophy. **2** (*usually written* **platonic**) Friendly but without passion: *platonic* love.

pla·toon [plə·to͞on′] *n.* **1** A subdivision of a company, troop, or other military unit, commanded by a lieutenant. **2** Any similar group.

plat·ter [plat′ər] *n.* A shallow, oblong dish on which food is served.

plat·y [plat′ē] *n., pl.* **plat·ys** or **plat·ies** A small, brilliantly colored tropical freshwater fish, often kept in home aquariums.

plat·y·pus [plat′ə·pəs] *n., pl.* **plat·y·pus·es** or **plat·y·pi** [plat′ə·pī] A small, egg-laying water mammal of Australia, having a ducklike bill, webbed feet, and a broad, flat tail.

Platypus

plau·dit [plô′dit] *n.* (*usually pl.*) An expression of approval or praise, as by cheering or applauding.

plau·si·ble [plô′zə·bəl] *adj.* Seeming reasonable on the surface and appearing worthy to be believed or trusted, yet possibly deceiving: a *plausible* story; a *plausible* liar. **—plau·si·bil·i·ty** [plô′zə·bil′·ə·tē] *n.* **—plau′si·bly** *adv.*

play [plā] **1** *v.* To have fun; amuse oneself: to *play* on the beach. **2** *n.* Some act or recreation done for fun and amusement: an hour for *play.* **3** *v.* To pretend: Let's *play* that we're astronauts. **4** *v.* To do or perform for fun: to *play* a trick. **5** *n.* Fun; jest: to say something in *play.* **6** *v.* To engage in (as a sport or game): to *play* tennis. **7** *v.* To oppose in a game or contest: We *played* their best team. **8** *n.* The act of playing: *Play* will continue later. **9** *n.* A move, manuever, or turn in a game: a winning *play*; It's your *play.* **10** *n.* Proper use or motion according to the rules of a game: When a spectator touched it, the ball became out of *play.* **11** *v.* To bet on: to *play* the horses. **12** *n.* Gambling: to lose at *play.* **13** *v.* To act or behave carelessly, lightly, or insincerely; trifle: to *play* with another's affections. **14** *v.* To act or behave: *Play* fair. **15** *n.* Manner of acting toward or dealing with others: fair *play.* **16** *n.* A story or drama written to be acted, as on a stage or on television. **17** *v.* To act the part of: to *play* a witch. **18** *v.* To perform or be performed: to *play* a part; What is *playing* at that theater? **19** *v.* In music, to perform or perform on: to *play* a piano sonata; to *play* the piano. **20** *v.* To give forth sound or music: The radio is *playing.* **21** *v.* To move or cause to move quickly, continuously, or irregularly: Shadows were *playing* over the path; The usher *played* a flashlight over the rows of seats. **22** *n.* Light, quick, or easy movement: the *play* of moonbeams. **23** *n.* Freedom or looseness, as of movement or activity: The storyteller gave his imagination full *play*; That control stick has too much *play* in it. **24** *n.* Active operation: She brought all her skill into *play.* **25** *v.* To bring about; cause: to *play* havoc. **—a play on words** A pun. **—play along** To cooperate or pretend to cooperate with a scheme or idea. **—play back** To replay (a newly made tape or recording). **—play down** To treat as being of little importance. **—played out** **1** Exhausted. **2** Finished. **—play into someone's hands** To act or respond in a way that gives someone else an advantage over one. **—play off** **1** To oppose one against another, as in a rivalry. **2** To decide (a tie) by playing one more game. **—play on** or **play upon** To take unfair advantage of (another's feelings or hopes) in order to get something: to *play on* one's sympathy. **—play out** To let out (a rope) little by little. **—play up** *informal* To emphasize. **—play up to** *informal* To try to win the favor of by flattery.

pla·ya [plī′ə] *n.* A flat area at the bottom of a desert basin, at times covered with water.

play·back [plā′bak′] *n.* The act of replaying a recorded sound or picture, often just after recording.

play·bill [plā′bil′] *n.* **1** A bill or poster advertising a play. **2** A program of a play.

play·boy [plā′boi′] *n.* A wealthy man who spends his life pursuing pleasure.

play·er [plā′ər] *n.* **1** A person who takes part in a game. **2** A person who plays a musical instrument: a horn *player.* **3** An actor or actress.

player piano A piano that is played by mechanical means.

play·fel·low [plā′fel′ō] *n.* A playmate.

play·ful [plā′fəl] *adj.* **1** Full of high spirits; fond of playing; frolicsome: a *playful* puppy. **2** Humorous; joking: a *playful* challenge. **—play′ful·ly** *adv.* **—play′ful·ness** *n.*

play·girl [plā′gûrl′] *n.* A woman who spends her life pursuing pleasure.

play·ground [plā′ground′] *n.* An area, often next to a school, for children to play in.

a	add	**i**	it	**o͝o**	took	**oi**	oil		
ā	ace	**ī**	ice	**o͞o**	pool	**ou**	pout		
â	care	**o**	odd	**u**	up	**ng**	ring		
ä	palm	**ō**	open	**û**	burn	**th**	thin		
e	end	**ô**	order	**yo͞o**	fuse	**t͟h**	this		
ē	equal					**zh**	vision		

ə = { a in *above* e in *sicken* i in *possible* / o in *melon* u in *circus* }

P

play·house [plā′hous′] *n.* **1** A theater. **2** A small house for children to play with or in.
playing card One card of a pack used in playing various games. A pack usually consists of 52 cards divided into four suits (spades, hearts, diamonds, and clubs) of 13 cards each.

Playing cards

play·mate [plā′māt′] *n.* A companion in play.
play-off [plā′ôf′] *n.* **1** An additional game or contest played in order to break a tie. **2** A final contest or series to determine a champion or those who will play in a championship game or series.
play·pen [plā′pen′] *n.* An enclosed, portable structure for a baby to play in.
play·room [plā′ro͞om′ *or* plā′ro͝om′] *n.* A room designed or set aside for children to play in.
play·thing [plā′thing′] *n.* A toy.
play·wright [plā′rīt′] *n.* A writer of plays.
pla·za [plä′zə *or* plaz′ə] *n.* An open square or marketplace in a town or city. ◆ See PLACE.
plea [plē] *n.* **1** An appeal or request: a *plea* for aid. **2** An excuse: His *plea* was that he didn't hear the bell. **3** In law, a statement made by or for a defendant concerning the charge: The lawyer made a *plea* of not guilty.
plead [plēd] *v.* **plead·ed** or **pled, plead·ing** **1** To ask earnestly; beg: to *plead* for help. **2** To argue in a court of law: to *plead* a case. **3** To make a plea of: to *plead* guilty. **4** To give as an excuse or defense: to *plead* insanity.
pleas·ant [plez′ənt] *adj.* **1** Giving pleasure; pleasing. **2** Agreeable or friendly, as in manner or appearance: a *pleasant* receptionist. **—pleas′ant·ly** *adv.* **—pleas′ant·ness** *n.*
pleas·an·try [plez′ən·trē] *n., pl.* **pleas·an·tries** A good-natured remark or joke.
please [plēz] *v.* **pleased, pleas·ing** **1** To give pleasure to or satisfy: Your work *pleases* me; A good book always *pleases.* **2** To be so kind as to: usually used when requesting something: *Please* pass the bread. **3** To wish, desire, or prefer: Go where you *please.* **4** To be the will or wish of: May it *please* your Honor.
pleas·ing [plē′zing] *adj.* Pleasant; agreeable.
pleas·ur·a·ble [plezh′ər·ə·bəl] *adj.* Pleasant.
pleas·ure [plezh′ər] *n.* **1** A feeling of enjoyment, delight, or satisfaction: Dancing gives me *pleasure.* **2** A thing that pleases; source of enjoyment: Reading was their main *pleasure.* **3** Amusement or gratification: to seek *pleasure.* **4** Preference or choice: What is your *pleasure*?
pleat [plēt] **1** *n.* A flat fold of cloth doubled on itself and pressed or sewn in place. **2** *v.* To make pleats in; arrange in pleats: to *pleat* a skirt.

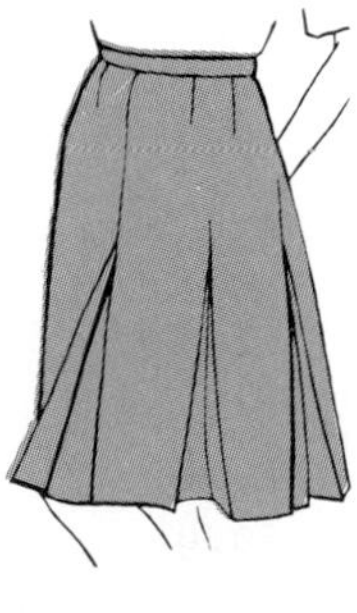
Pleated skirt

plebe [plēb] *n.* A freshman at the U.S. Military Academy or the U.S. Naval Academy.
ple·be·ian [pli·bē′ən] **1** *n.* One of the common people, especially of ancient Rome. **2** *n.* A person who is common or vulgar. **3** *adj.* Of, resembling, or having to do with plebeians.
pleb·i·scite [pleb′ə·sīt′] *n.* A vote by all the voters of a state or nation concerning some important question, as a change in a constitution.
plec·trum [plek′trəm] *n., pl.* **plec·trums** or **plec·tra** [plek′trə] A small object used for plucking the strings of a musical instrument, as a guitar or mandolin.
pled [pled] Alternative past tense and past participle of PLEAD.
pledge [plej] *n., v.* **pledged, pledg·ing** **1** *n.* A formal or solemn promise: a *pledge* of loyalty. **2** *v.* To bind by a solemn promise. **3** *v.* To promise to give: to *pledge* money for the new library. **4** *n.* Something that is pledged in this way: a *pledge* of $100.00. **5** *n.* Something given or held as security for a debt. **6** *v.* To give or offer as security for a debt; pawn. **7** *n.* The condition of being held as security for a debt: The guitar is in *pledge.* **8** *n.* The drinking of a toast to one's health. **9** *v.* To drink a toast to: We *pledged* the couple's health.
Plei·a·des [plē′ə·dēz′] *n.pl.* **1** A cluster of stars, including six which are visible to the naked eye. **2** In Greek myths, the seven daughters of Atlas, set among the stars by Zeus.
Pleis·to·cene [plīs′tə·sēn′] **1** *n.* The earlier of the two geological epochs of the Quaternary period of the Cenozoic era. During the Pleistocene, glaciers advanced and retreated in the Northern Hemisphere. The human species appeared but many other mammals became extinct. **2** *adj.* Of the Pleistocene.
ple·na·ry [plē′nə·rē *or* plen′ə·rē] *adj.* **1** Full in all respects; complete; entire. **2** Attended by everyone who has a right to be there.
plen·i·po·ten·ti·ar·y [plen′i·pə·ten′shē·er′ē] *n., pl.* **plen·i·po·ten·ti·ar·ies,** *adj.* **1** *n.* A person having full power to represent a government, as an ambassador. **2** *adj.* Having or giving full power.
plen·i·tude [plen′ə·t(y)o͞od′] *n.* The condition of being full or abundant; fullness.
plen·te·ous [plen′tē·əs] *adj.* Plentiful.
plen·ti·ful [plen′ti·fəl] *adj.* **1** Existing in great quantity; more than enough. **2** Giving or containing plenty. **—plen′ti·ful·ly** *adv.*
plen·ty [plen′tē] *n.* As much as could be needed; an abundance: I have *plenty* of food.
ple·si·o·saur [plē′sē·ə·sôr′] *n.* A large, extinct saltwater reptile with a long neck and four limbs shaped like paddles.
pleth·o·ra [pleth′ər·ə] *n.* Too great an amount; excess; superfluity.
pleu·ra [plo͝or′ə] *n., pl.* **pleu·rae** [plo͝or′ē] Either of the two membranous sacs that enclose the lungs and line the chest cavity.
pleu·ri·sy [plo͝or′ə·sē] *n.* Inflammation of the membrane that covers the lungs and lines the chest cavity. It causes painful breathing, fever, and a cough.
Plex·i·glas [plek′si·glas′] *n.* A strong, transparent plastic: a trademark.
plex·us [plek′səs] *n., pl.* **plex·us·es** or **plex·us** A network of cordlike structures, as blood vessels or nerves.
pli·a·ble [plī′ə·bəl] *adj.* **1** Easily bent, twisted, or molded. **2** Easily persuaded or controlled. **—pli·a·bil·i·ty** [plī′ə·bil′ə·tē] *n.*
pli·an·cy [plī′ən·sē] *n.* The condition or quality of being pliant; pliability.
pli·ant [plī′ənt] *adj.* **1** Easy to bend, twist, or mold. **2** Easy to influence; compliant.

pli·ers [plī′ərz] *n.pl.* Small pincers for bending, holding, or cutting things.

plight¹ [plīt] *n.* A condition or situation, usually bad.

plight² [plīt] *v.* To promise solemnly; pledge. **—plight one's troth** To promise to marry.

plinth [plinth] *n.* The slab, block, or stone on which a column, pedestal, or statue rests.

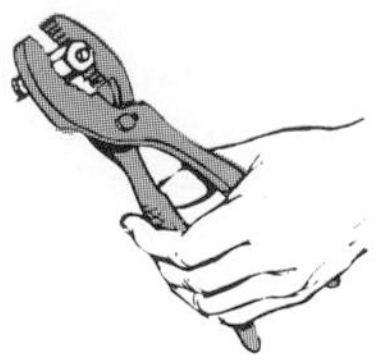

Pliers

Pli·o·cene [plī′ə·sēn′] **1** *n.* The fifth and final geological epoch of the Tertiary period of the Cenozoic era. During the Pliocene many modern plants and animals appeared and climates became cooler and drier. **2** *adj.* Of the Pliocene.

PLO or **P.L.O.** Palestine Liberation Organization.

plod [plod] *v.* **plod·ded, plod·ding** **1** To walk heavily or with great effort; trudge. **2** To work in a dull, laborious way; drudge. **—plod′der** *n.*

plop [plop] *v.* **plopped, plop·ping,** *n., adv.* **1** *v.* To drop or fall heavily, causing a sound like something falling into water. **2** *n.* The sound or act of plopping. **3** *adv.* With the sound of something hitting water: The soap fell *plop* into the tub.

plot [plot] *n., v.* **plot·ted, plot·ting** **1** *n.* A small piece of ground: a *plot* for vegetables. **2** *n.* A chart, diagram, or map. **3** *v.* To make a map, chart, or plan of, as a ship's course. **4** *n.* A secret plan to do some usually evil or unlawful thing. **5** *v.* To plan in secret; scheme: to *plot* someone's downfall. **6** *n.* The basic story or course of events, as in a play or novel. **—plot′ter** *n.*

plough [plou] *n., v.* Another spelling of PLOW.

plov·er [pluv′ər *or* plō′vər] *n.* A bird that lives on the shore, having long pointed wings and a short tail.

plow [plou] **1** *n.* A large tool used for breaking up or turning over the soil in preparation for planting. **2** *n.* Something that operates like this, as a machine for moving snow. **3** *v.* To break up and turn over the soil of with a plow; furrow: to *plow* a field. **4** *v.* To use a plow. **5** *v.* To move as a plow; force a passage: We *plowed* through the crowded lobby. **—plow back** To reinvest (profit or earnings) in a business.

Plow

plow·man [plou′mən] *n., pl.* **plow·men** [plou′mən] **1** A person who uses a plow. **2** A farmer.

plow·share [plou′shâr′] *n.* The blade or part of a plow that cuts a furrow in the soil.

ploy [ploi] *n.* A tricky action or strategy designed to promote one's interest or gain an advantage over an opponent; scheme; device.

pluck [pluk] **1** *v.* To pull off or out; pick: to *pluck* a flower. **2** *v.* To pull with force; snatch; drag: to *pluck* a sword from its sheath. **3** *v.* To pull the feathers from: to *pluck* a chicken. **4** *v.* To quickly pull and release (the strings of a musical instrument). **5** *n.* A quick or sudden pull. **6** *n.* Courage or nerve. **—pluck up** To rouse or summon, as one's courage.

pluck·y [pluk′ē] *adj.* **pluck·i·er, pluck·i·est** Brave; courageous. **—pluck′i·ly** *adv.*

plug [plug] *n., v.* **plugged, plug·ging** **1** *n.* A piece of rubber, cork, or other material, used to stop a hole. **2** *v.* To stop or close; put a plug into. **3** *n.* A device with two prongs at the end of an electric cord, used to connect a lamp, radio, or appliance to a power line or circuit. **4** *n.* A fireplug. **5** *n.* A flat cake of pressed tobacco for chewing. **6** *n. informal* An old, worn-out horse. **7** *n. slang* A favorable mention or piece of publicity. **8** *v. slang* To mention favorably; publicize. **9** *v. informal* To work doggedly; plod. **10** *v. slang* To shoot a bullet into. **—plug in** To connect (as a lamp or radio) by inserting the plug in an outlet.

plum [plum] **1** *n.* A fruit having a smooth skin, juicy pulp, and a smooth pit. **2** *n.* A tree that bears this fruit. **3** *n.* A raisin, especially as used in cooking. **4** *n., adj.* Dark, reddish purple. **5** *n.* Something desirable or greatly prized: Her appointment as college president is a *plum.*

plum·age [plo͞o′mij] *n.* The feathers of a bird.

plumb [plum] **1** *n.* A weight hung on the end of a cord, used to see if a wall is vertical or to test the depth of water. **2** *v.* To test, as for depth or position, with a plumb. **3** *v.* To investigate fully; get to the bottom of: to *plumb* a mystery. **4** *adj.* Exactly vertical: a *plumb* post. **5** *adv.* Straight down or straight up and down; vertically: The apple fell *plumb* to earth. **6** *adv. informal* Completely; entirely: That's *plumb* stupid. **—out of plumb** or **off plumb** Not truly vertical.

plumb bob The weight hung on a plumb line.

plumb·er [plum′ər] *n.* A person whose business is installing or repairing plumbing.

plumb·ing [plum′ing] *n.* **1** The system of pipes and fixtures through which water or gas flows in a building. **2** The work or technique of installing and repairing such systems.

plumb line A cord with a weight attached to one end, used to establish a true vertical line.

plume [plo͞om] *n., v.* **plumed, plum·ing** **1** *n.* A feather, especially if long and ornamental. **2** *n.* A large feather or group of feathers used as an ornament, as on a helmet or hat. **3** *v.* To decorate, dress, or furnish with plumes. **4** *v.* To smooth (itself or its feathers), as a bird. **5** *v.* To congratulate or take pride in (oneself): The winners *plumed* themselves on their cleverness.

plum·met [plum′it] **1** *n.* A plumb. **2** *v.* To fall straight down; plunge.

plump¹ [plump] **1** *adj.* Slightly fat or rounded. **2** *v.* To make or become plump. **—plump′ness** *n.*

plump² [plump] **1** *v.* To fall or let fall suddenly or heavily: The big dog *plumped* before the fire; He *plumped* the box of groceries on the kitchen table. **2** *n.* The action or sound of plumping or falling: The book hit the floor with a *plump.* **3** *adv.* Sud-

a	add	**i**	it	**o͝o**	took	**oi**	oil		
ā	ace	**ī**	ice	**o͞o**	pool	**ou**	pout		
â	care	**o**	odd	**u**	up	**ng**	ring		
ä	palm	**ō**	open	**û**	burn	**th**	thin		
e	end	**ô**	order	**yo͞o**	fuse	**th**	this		
ē	equal					**zh**	vision		

ə = {a in *above* e in *sicken* i in *possible* / o in *melon* u in *circus*}

P

denly or heavily: to fall *plump* on the bed. 4 *adj.* Direct; blunt: a *plump* refusal. **—plump for** To give full support to: to *plump for* a candidate.

plum pudding A boiled pudding made with flour, suet, raisins, currants, spices, and other ingredients.

plun·der [plun′dər] 1 *v.* To rob of goods or property by force; loot: The enemy *plundered* the village. 2 *n.* Goods taken by force. 3 *n.* The act of plundering. **—plun′der·er** *n.*

plunge [plunj] *v.* **plunged, plung·ing,** *n.* 1 *v.* To thrust or force suddenly: I *plunged* my hand into the bag; to *plunge* one's friends into despair. 2 *v.* To jump, dive, or fall, as into water or a chasm. 3 *n.* A jump, dive, or fall, especially into water. 4 *v.* To move suddenly or with a rush: to *plunge* into action. 5 *v.* To toss violently, as a ship or aircraft. 6 *v. informal* To gamble wildly. 7 *n. informal* A gamble or bet. 8 *n.* A short swim.

plung·er [plun′jər] *n.* 1 A person who plunges. 2 A device or machine that works with an up-and-down motion, as a piston.

plunk [plungk] 1 *v.* To fall or let fall heavily: The ball *plunked* into the lake; The customer *plunked* the money on the table. 2 *v.* To pluck, as the strings of a musical instrument. 3 *v.* To make a sound like a plucked string. 4 *n.* The act of plunking. 5 *n.* The sound made by plunking.

plu·per·fect [plo͞o·pûr′fikt] 1 *n.* Another name for PAST PERFECT. 2 *adj.* Of or in the past perfect tense.

plu·ral [plo͝or′əl] 1 *adj.* Being or indicating more than one: a *plural* noun. 2 *n.* The form that a word takes when it indicates more than one: "Children" is the *plural* of "child." ◆ The plurals of most nouns are formed by adding *s* to the singular: girl-girl*s*; pocket-pocket*s*; tire-tire*s*. Nouns that end in *y* following a consonant or *qu* become plural by changing the *y* to *i* and adding *es*: cry-cr*ies*; soliloquy-soliloqu*ies*. Nouns ending in *ss, sh, ch, s, x,* and *zz* usually form their plurals by adding *es*: class-class*es*; dish-dish*es*; crutch-crutch*es*; gas-gas*es*; box-box*es*; buzz-buzz*es*. Many plurals, such as *men, moose, crises,* and *data*, are formed irregularly.

plu·ral·i·ty [plo͝o·ral′ə·tē] *n., pl.* **plu·ral·i·ties** 1 The number of votes by which the winner of an election defeats the nearest rival. 2 The greater portion or number. 3 A large number, as of persons or things; multitude. 4 The condition of being plural.

plu·ral·ize [plo͝or′ə·līz′] *v.* **plu·ral·ized, plu·ral·iz·ing** To make or become plural.

plus [plus] *prep., n., pl.* **plus·es** or **plus·ses,** *adj.* 1 *prep.* Added to: Three *plus* two equals five. 2 *prep.* Increased by: salary *plus* commission. 3 *n.* A plus sign. 4 *adj.* Indicating addition. 5 *adj.* Extra; additional: There were many *plus* values. 6 *n.* An additional or favorable quality or factor: Her good record is a *plus* in her bid for reelection. 7 *adj.* Greater than zero; positive. 8 *adj.* And a little more: a grade of B *plus*.

plush [plush] 1 *n.* A cloth something like velvet but having a deeper pile. 2 *adj.* Having to do with, like, or made of plush. 3 *adj. informal* Characterized by or indicating wealth or luxury: a *plush* hotel.

plus sign A symbol (+) indicating addition or a positive quantity.

Plu·to [plo͞o′tō] *n.* 1 In Greek and Roman myths, the god of the dead. 2 A small planet of the solar system that is ninth in distance from the sun.

plu·toc·ra·cy [plo͞o·tok′rə·sē] *n., pl.* **plu·toc·ra·cies** 1 Government by wealthy people. 2 A governing class of wealthy people.

plu·to·crat [plo͞o′tə·krat′] *n.* 1 A member of a class or group that has power and influence because of its wealth. 2 Any wealthy person.

plu·to·crat·ic [plo͞o′tə·krat′ik] *adj.* Of or having to do with plutocrats or a plutocracy.

plu·to·ni·um [plo͞o·tō′nē·əm] *n.* A spontaneously fissionable, chemically reactive, toxic radioactive metallic element present in minute traces in uranium ores and produced in quantity in nuclear reactors.

ply[1] [plī] *n., pl.* **plies** 1 A layer or thickness, as of cloth or wood. 2 A strand, as one of rope, yarn, or thread: three-*ply* yarn.

ply[2] [plī] *v.* **plied, ply·ing** 1 To use, as in working or fighting: to *ply* an axe. 2 To work at; be engaged in: to *ply* a trade. 3 To supply with or offer repeatedly to: to *ply* a person with food. 4 To address (a person) over and over again, as with questions or demands. 5 To make regular trips: Delivery trucks *ply* between New York and its suburbs.

ply·wood [plī′wo͝od′] *n.* A kind of board made of thin layers of wood glued together.

p.m. 1 post meridiem. 2 postmortem.

Pm The symbol for the element promethium.

P.M. 1 post meridiem. 2 prime minister. 3 postmaster.

pneu·mat·ic [n(y)o͞o·mat′ik] *adj.* 1 Operated by compressed air: a *pneumatic* drill. 2 Filled with compressed air: a *pneumatic* tire. 3 Having to do with air or other gases.

pneu·mat·ics [n(y)o͞o·mat′iks] *n.* The branch of physics that deals with the mechanical properties of air and other gases. ◆ See -ICS.

pneu·mo·nia [n(y)o͞o·mōn′yə] *n.* A disease caused by bacterial or virus infection and marked by inflammation of one or both lungs.

Po The symbol for the element polonium.

P.O. post office.

poach[1] [pōch] *v.* To cook in simmering water, milk, or other liquid, as eggs or fish.

poach[2] [pōch] *v.* 1 To trespass on another's property, especially to hunt or fish. 2 To hunt or fish unlawfully. **—poach′er** *n.*

pock [pok] *n.* 1 An eruption of the skin caused by smallpox or a similar disease. 2 A pockmark.

pock·et [pok′it] 1 *n.* A small pouch sewn into a garment, for carrying money or small objects. 2 *v.* To put into a pocket: The musician *pocketed* the harmonica. 3 *adj.* Having to do with, for, or carried in a pocket: a *pocket* watch. 4 *adj.* Small: a *pocket* book. 5 *n.* A hole or container for something to go into: the *pockets* of a pool table. 6 *v.* To enclose; shut in; hem in. 7 *v.* To take for one's own, especially dishonestly: to *pocket* company funds. 8 *v.* To accept without anger or reply, as an insult. 9 *v.* To conceal or suppress: to *pocket* one's pride. 10 *n.* A sudden downward air current; air pocket.

pock·et·book [pok′it·bo͝ok′] *n.* 1 A small case for carrying money and papers in the pocket; wallet. 2 A purse or handbag.

pock·et·ful [pok′it·fo͝ol′] *n., pl.* **pock·et·fuls** As much as a pocket will hold.

pock·et·knife [pok′it·nīf′] *n., pl.* **pock·et·knives** A small knife having one or more blades that fold into the handle.

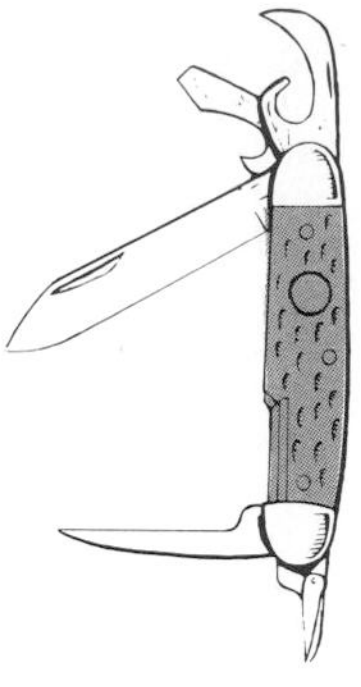
Pocketknife

pocket veto *U.S.* A method by which the President or a governor can kill without vetoing a bill sent for signature late in a legislative session. The executive keeps it, unsigned, until the session ends.
pock·mark [pok′märk′] *n.* A pit or scar left on the skin by smallpox or a similar disease.
pod [pod] *n., v.* **pod·ded, pod·ding** 1 *n.* The shell or case in which peas, beans, and certain other plants have their seeds enclosed. 2 *v.* To fill out like a pod. 3 *v.* To grow pods.
po·di·a·try [pə·dī′ə·trē] *n.* The care and treatment of the feet and of foot ailments and injuries. —**po·di′a·trist** *n.*
po·di·um [pō′dē·əm] *n., pl.* **po·di·ums** or **po·di·a** [pō′·dē·ə] A small platform on which the conductor of an orchestra stands.
po·em [pō′əm] *n.* A composition in verse and often also in rhyme. The language is used in a very imaginative way to express intense thoughts and feelings and vivid images.
po·e·sy [pō′ə·sē *or* pō′ə·zē] *n.* Poetry.
po·et [pō′it] *n.* A person who writes poetry.
po·et·ic [pō·et′ik] *adj.* 1 Of, like, relating to, or suitable for poetry or poets. 2 Imaginatively beautiful. —**po·et′i·cal·ly** *adv.*
po·et·i·cal [pō·et′i·kəl] *adj.* Poetic.
poetic justice Punishment or reward that is particularly appropriate for the evil or good one has done.
poet laureate *pl.* **poets laureate** In Great Britain, a poet appointed for life by the king or queen to be official poet of the kingdom.
po·et·ry [pō′ə·trē] *n.* 1 The art of writing poems. 2 Poems collectively. 3 The quality or feeling in a poem or in something poetic.
po·go stick [pō′gō] A pole with a spring and footrests on which a person can stand and jump along the ground.
po·grom [pə·grom′ *or* pō′grəm] *n.* An organized massacre of or attack upon a minority group, especially Jews.
poi [poi] *n.* A Hawaiian food made from cooked, fermented taro root that has been pounded into a paste.
poign·an·cy [poin′yən·sē] *n.* The quality of being poignant.
poign·ant [poin′yənt] *adj.* 1 Keenly felt; painfully affecting: *poignant* grief. 2 Affecting the feelings; touching; moving: a *poignant* scene in a play. 3 Cutting through to the truth; sharp and penetrating: *poignant* criticism; a *poignant* description of life in the slums. —**poign′ant·ly** *adv.*
poin·set·ti·a [poin·set′(ē·)ə] *n.* A tropical American plant having small yellow flowers and red leaves that resemble petals.
point [point] 1 *n.* The sharp or tapered end of something: the *point* of a needle; the *point* of the chin. 2 *v.* To shape or sharpen to a point: to *point* a pencil. 3 *n.* In printing or writing, a dot: a decimal *point.* 4 *n.* A punctuation mark, especially a period. 5 *v.* To mark, as with punctuation or decimal points: to *point* a sentence; to *point* off a decimal fraction. 6 *n.* A particular spot or place; location. 7 *n.* In mathematics, an exact location in space, as the place where two lines cross. 8 *n.* One of the 32 equally spaced divisions shown on a compass card. 9 *v.* To direct or aim, as a finger or weapon. 10 *v.* To indicate or direct attention to: to *point* the way; to *point* out errors. 11 *v.* To call attention or indicate direction with or as if with the finger: to *point* at a map; to *point* up the road. 12 *v.* To show the location of game by standing and aiming the body, as a hunting dog. 13 *v.* To be headed or directed: The car *pointed* east; The indicator *points* to 100. 14 *n.* A particular moment or time: At that *point,* we went home. 15 *n.* A particular degree or condition reached: the *point* of exhaustion; the boiling *point.* 16 *n.* A narrow piece of land extending into water; cape. 17 *n.* Purpose or advantage: What is the *point* of that? 18 *n.* A unit, as used for measuring, counting, or scoring: A touchdown equals six *points.* 19 *n.* The main idea; gist: the *point* of a joke. 20 *n.* A prominent feature, quality, or attribute: The book's good *points* are its colorful language and exciting plot. 21 *v.* To give force or emphasis to: to *point* up the logic of an argument. 22 *n.* A single item; detail: to explain something *point* by *point.* —**at the point of** Very near to. —**beside the point** Off the subject; immaterial. —**in point** Related to the matter at hand; pertinent. —**make a point of** To treat as very important. —**on the point of** Almost in the act or condition of. —**point out** To draw attention to; indicate. —**stretch a point** To make an exception. —**to the point** Related to the matter at hand: The answer was short and *to the point.*
point-blank [point′blangk′] 1 *adj.* Aimed directly at a target without allowing for the effect of gravity, as a pistol. 2 *adj.* Close enough to allow this kind of aim: *point-blank* range. 3 *adv.* In a straight line or from close range. 4 *adj.* Direct; plain: a *point-blank* refusal. 5 *adv.* Directly; plainly: to refuse *point-blank.*
point·ed [poin′tid] *adj.* 1 Having a point or points. 2 Sharp and cutting, as a remark. 3 Clearly noticeable; emphatic. 4 Directed or aimed, as at a person. —**point′ed·ly** *adv.*
point·er [poin′tər] *n.* 1 A hand, finger, or other indicator, as on a clock or meter. 2 A slender rod used to point out things, as on maps or charts. 3 A smooth-haired dog trained to scent and point out game. 4 *informal* A useful bit of information; hint; tip.

Typical pointer

a	add	**i**	it	**o͝o**	took	**oi**	oil
ā	ace	**ī**	ice	**o͞o**	pool	**ou**	pout
â	care	**o**	odd	**u**	up	**ng**	ring
ä	palm	**ō**	open	**û**	burn	**th**	thin
e	end	**ô**	order	**yo͞o**	fuse	**th**	this
ē	equal					**zh**	vision

ə = {a in *above* e in *sicken* i in *possible*; o in *melon* u in *circus*}

P

point·less [point′lis] *adj.* 1 Not pointed; blunt. 2 Having no meaning or purpose. 3 Having no effect. —**point′less·ly** *adv.*
point of view *pl.* **points of view** 1 The position from which a person looks at or considers something, as an object or situation: an unusual *point of view.* 2 An attitude or viewpoint.
poise [poiz] *v.* **poised, pois·ing,** *n.* 1 *v.* To balance or hold in balance: The cat *poised* itself on its hind legs. 2 *n.* Balance or equilibrium. 3 *n.* Ease of manner; self-possession.
poi·son [poi′zən] 1 *n.* A substance whose chemical action is harmful or deadly to a living thing that absorbs or eats it, even in small amounts. 2 *v.* To give or apply poison to; kill or harm with poison. 3 *v.* To put poison into or on: to *poison* a well. 4 *n.* Anything that harms or destroys. 5 *v.* To affect in a bad way; corrupt.
poison ivy A climbing plant having glossy leaves growing in groups of three. It gives most people a severe skin rash if they touch it.
poison oak A plant related to poison ivy.
poi·son·ous [poi′zən·əs] *adj.* Being, containing, or having the effect of a poison.
poison sumac A shrub related to poison ivy, causing a similar rash.
poke[1] [pōk] *v.* **poked, pok·ing,** *n.* 1 *v.* To push or jab, as with the elbow: to *poke* someone in the ribs. 2 *n.* A push or jab, as with the elbow. 3 *v.* To make by jabbing or thrusting: to *poke* a hole. 4 *v.* To thrust or push in, out, or through: to *poke* one's hand through a hole. 5 *v.* To pry; meddle: to *poke* into someone's business. 6 *v.* To search through: to *poke* around the cellar. 7 *v.* To move about in a slow or sluggish way. 8 *n.* A lazy or slow person. 9 *v. slang* To hit with the fist; punch. 10 *n. slang* A punch. 11 *n.* A bonnet with a brim wide in front. —**poke fun at** To mock; ridicule.

Poison sumac

poke[2] [pōk] *n.* A small bag or sack: now used only in certain regions.
pok·er[1] [pō′kər] *n.* 1 A metal rod for stirring up a fire. 2 A person or thing that pokes.
pok·er[2] [pō′kər] *n.* Any of several card games in which each player bets that his or her hand is better than those of the other players.
pok·y or **pok·ey** [pō′kē] *adj.* **pok·i·er, pok·i·est** 1 Not brisk; dull; slow. 2 Cramped and stuffy. 3 Shabby or dowdy.
pol. 1 political. 2 politics.
Pol. 1 Poland. 2 Polish.
po·lar [pō′lər] *adj.* 1 Of or having to do with a pole or poles. 2 Having to do with, coming from, or found near the North or South Pole. 3 Directly opposite in action or character.
polar bear A large bear with white fur, found in the arctic regions.

Polar bear

Po·lar·is [pō·lar′is] *n.* The North Star.
po·lar·i·ty [pō·lar′ə·tē] *n., pl.* **po·lar·i·ties** The condition of having poles with opposite properties at the ends of an axis, as in a magnet.
po·lar·ize [pō′lə·rīz′] *v.* **po·lar·ized, po·lar·iz·ing** To become or make polar; give polarity to. —**po′lar·i·za′tion** *n.*
Po·lar·oid [pō′lə·roid′] *n.* 1 A transparent plastic material that polarizes light and reduces glare: a trademark. 2 A camera that develops the picture it shoots, producing a finished print in seconds. Also called **Polaroid Land Camera** and **Polaroid camera**: a trademark.
pol·der [pōl′dər] *n.* A low area of land that has been protected by dikes and emptied of water, as in the Netherlands.
pole[1] [pōl] *n., v.* **poled, pol·ing** 1 *n.* A long, thin, wooden or metal rod, usually rounded. 2 *v.* To push along with a pole, as a boat.
pole[2] [pōl] *n.* 1 Either end of the axis of a sphere. 2 Either end of the earth's axis; the North Pole or the South Pole. 3 A point of maximum strengh in a magnetic or electric field.
Pole [pōl] *n.* A person born in or a citizen of Poland.
pole·cat [pōl′kat′] *n.* 1 A European animal related to a weasel, known for its foul odor when annoyed or frightened. 2 *U.S.* A skunk.
po·lem·ic [pə·lem′ik] 1 *adj.* Of or having to do with dispute or argument. 2 *n.* An argument, especially about political or religious beliefs.
pole·star [pōl′stär′] *n.* 1 The North Star; Polaris. 2 Something that guides or governs.
pole vault A jump over a high, horizontal bar, made with the aid of a long pole.

Pole vault

po·lice [pə·lēs′] *n., v.* **po·liced, po·lic·ing** 1 *n.* An official force organized to maintain order, prevent and detect crime, and enforce laws. 2 *adj. use*: a *police* car; a *police* station. 3 *n.* (*used with pl. verb*) The members of such a force. 4 *v.* To protect or maintain law and order in, as a city. 5 *n. U.S.* The cleaning of an army camp, or those assigned to clean it. 6 *v. U.S.* To clean, as an army camp.
police dog 1 Any dog trained to assist in police work. 2 Another name for GERMAN SHEPHERD.
po·lice·man [pə·lēs′mən] *n., pl.* **po·lice·men** [pə·lēs′·mən] A member of a police force.
police officer A member of a police force.
police state A country in which the government closely watches and controls the activities of the citizens, especially through a secret police force.
po·lice·wom·an [pə·lēs′wŏŏm′ən] *n., pl.* **po·lice·wom·en** [pə·lēs′wim′in] A woman who is a police officer.

pol·i·cy[1] [pol′ə·sē] *n., pl.* **pol·i·cies** A plan or method of action or conduct: a nation's foreign *policy;* Honesty is the best *policy.*

pol·i·cy[2] [pol′ə·sē] *n., pl.* **pol·i·cies** A written contract by which an insurance company insures someone, as against loss by accident or theft.

po·li·o [pō′lē·ō] *n. informal* Poliomyelitis.

po·li·o·my·e·li·tis [pō′lē·ō·mī′ə·lī′tis] *n.* An acute, infectious virus disease most common in children and young adults, marked by inflammation of the spinal cord, and often followed by paralysis; infantile paralysis.

pol·ish [pol′ish] **1** *n.* Smoothness and glossiness of a surface. **2** *n.* Something rubbed on a surface to make it smooth and shiny. **3** *v.* To make or become smooth and shiny, as by rubbing: to *polish* furniture. **4** *v.* To make more nearly perfect: to *polish* a story. **5** *n.* Elegance or refinement, as of manner or style. **—polish off** To finish quickly and completely. **—pol′ish·er** *n.*

Po·lish [pō′lish] **1** *adj.* Of or from Poland. **2** *n.* **(the Polish)** The people of Poland. **3** *n.* The language of Poland.

po·lit·bu·ro [pol′it·byo͝or′ō] *n.* A committee that decides on policies for a Communist party.

po·lite [pə·līt′] *adj.* **po·lit·er, po·lit·est** **1** Showing consideration for others; mannerly: It would be *polite* to ask them to join us. **2** Refined; cultured: *polite* society. **—po·lite′ly** *adv.* **—po·lite′ness** *n.*

pol·i·tic [pol′ə·tik] *adj.* **1** Skillful, ingenious, or shrewd; crafty: a *politic* statesman. **2** Planned to fit the situation; prudent; expedient: a *politic* remark. **3** Political.

po·lit·i·cal [pə·lit′i·kəl] *adj.* **1** Of, having to do with, or involved in government or politics. **2** Of or about politicians. **—po·lit′i·cal·ly** *adv.*

political science The study of the principles of government.

pol·i·ti·cian [pol′ə·tish′ən] *n.* **1** A person who takes part in or is skillful at politics. **2** A person who takes part in politics for selfish reasons.

pol·i·tics [pol′ə·tiks] *n.* **1** The science or technique of government; political science. **2** The affairs and activities of those who control or seek to control a government. **3** Political principles, as of a party or individual. **4** The occupation or life of a politician: to succeed in *politics.* ◆ See -ICS.

pol·i·ty [pol′ə·tē] *n., pl.* **pol·i·ties** **1** The form or system of a government. **2** A community under some definite government.

pol·ka [pō(l)′kə] *n.* **1** A kind of fast, lively dance. **2** Music for this dance, in duple time.

polka dot **1** One of a series of round dots forming a pattern. **2** The pattern so formed.

poll [pōl] **1** *n.* A collection of votes or opinions, as in an election or a public survey. **2** *n.* The total number of votes cast. **3** *n.* (*often pl.*) The place where votes are cast and counted. **4** *n.* A list of persons. **5** *v.* To register or record the votes or opinions of: to *poll* a jury. **6** *v.* To vote. **7** *v.* To receive (a certain number of votes). **8** *n.* The head. **9** *v.* To cut off the hair, horns, or top of: to *poll* cattle.

pol·len [pol′ən] *n.* A powder containing the male reproductive cells of plants, found on the stamens of flowers. When pollen is transfered to the pistil, it fertilizes the flower.

pol·li·nate [pol′ə·nāt′] *v.* **pol·li·nat·ed, pol·li·nat·ing** To carry pollen to: Bees and wind *pollinate* flowers. **—pol′li·na′tion** *n.*

pol·li·wog [pōl′ē·wog′] *n.* Another name for TADPOLE.

poll·ster [pōl′stər] *n.* A person who takes public surveys or analyzes them.

poll tax A fixed tax on each person, often used as a requirement for voting.

pol·lu·tant [pə·lo͞o′tənt] *n.* A substance, often a waste material like smoke or dust, that pollutes the environment.

pol·lute [pə·lo͞ot′] *v.* **pol·lut·ed, pol·lut·ing** To make unclean or impure; dirty; corrupt. **—pol·lu′tion** *n.*

pol·ly·wog [pol′ē·wog′] *n.* Another spelling for POLLIWOG.

po·lo [pō′lō] *n.* A game in which players mounted on horses try to drive a wooden ball into the opponents' goal with long-handled mallets.

Polo player

pol·o·naise [pol′ə·nāz′ *or* pō′lə·nāz′] *n.* **1** A stately, marchlike Polish dance. **2** Music for this dance, in three-quarter time.

po·lo·ni·um [pə·lō′nē·əm] *n.* An intensely radioactive metallic element occurring in minute traces in uranium ores and also made artificially.

pol·troon [pol·tro͞on′] **1** *n.* A base coward. **2** *adj.* Characterized by base cowardice, cowardly.

poly- A combining form meaning: More than one; several; many, as in *polygon.*

poly·chlo·ri·nat·ed bi·phe·nyl [pol′ē·klôr′ə·nā′tid bī·fen′(ə)l] See PCB.

pol·y·es·ter [pol′ē·es′tər] **1** *n.* Any of several strong, light, synthetic resins used in making textiles and plastics. **2** *adj.* Made of polyester: a *polyester* suit.

pol·y·eth·y·lene [pol′ē·eth′ə·lēn′] *n.* Any of several strong, lightweight plastics used for packaging and insulating.

po·lyg·a·my [pə·lig′ə·mē] *n.* The condition or practice of having more than one wife or husband at a time. **—po·lyg′a·mist** *n.* **—po·lyg′a·mous** *adj.*

pol·y·glot [pol′i·glot′] *adj.* **1** Expressed in or written in many languages: a *polyglot* sign. **2** Able to speak or write several languages.

pol·y·gon [pol′i·gon′] *n.* A closed plane figure bounded by three or more straight lines. **—po·lyg·on·al** [pə·lig′ə·nəl] *adj.*

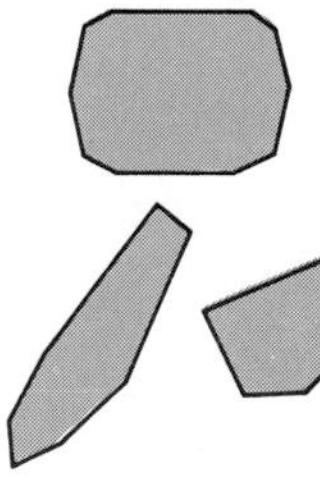
Polygons

pol·y·graph [pol′ē·graf′] *n.* An instrument that records body temperature, blood pressure, and other measures

a	add	**i**	it	**o͝o**	took	**oi**	oil
ā	ace	**ī**	ice	**o͞o**	pool	**ou**	pout
â	care	**o**	odd	**u**	up	**ng**	ring
ä	palm	**ō**	open	**û**	burn	**th**	thin
e	end	**ô**	order	**yo͞o**	fuse	***th***	this
ē	equal					**zh**	vision

ə = a in *above* e in *sicken* i in *possible* o in *melon* u in *circus*

of body functioning, often used to try to determine if a person is lying.

pol·y·he·dron [pol′i·hē′drən] *n., pl.* **pol·y·he·dra** [pol′i·hē′drə] or **pol·y·he·drons** A solid figure bounded by plane faces.

pol·y·mer [pol′i·mər] *n.* A substance, as some plastics, made by joining similar small molecules to form large ones.

Pol·y·ne·sian [pol′i·nē′zhən] 1 *adj.* Of or from Polynesia. 2 *n.* A person born or living in Polynesia. 3 *n.* Any of the languages of Polynesia, including Hawaiian, Maori, and Tahitian.

pol·y·no·mi·al [pol′i·nō′mē·əl] 1 *adj.* Of or consisting of many names or terms. 2 *n.* A mathematical expression, as $3a - 12b + \sqrt{c}$, that contains two or more terms. 3 *n.* A scientific name that has more than two parts.

pol·yp [pol′ip] *n.* A water animal shaped like a tube, having a mouth surrounded by tentacles at one end, often found growing in large colonies.

pol·y·phon·ic [pol′i·fon′ik] *adj.* Having two or more melodies to be played or sung together.

po·lyph·o·ny [pə·lif′ə·nē] *n.* Music that has two or more separate harmonious melodic voices.

pol·y·syl·lab·ic [pol′i·si·lab′ik] *adj.* Having more than three syllables, as the words *multifarious* and *plenipotentiary.*

pol·y·tech·nic [pol′i·tek′nik] 1 *adj.* Having to do with or teaching many technical or scientific subjects. 2 *n.* A polytechnic school.

pol·y·the·ism [pol′i·thē·iz′əm] *n.* The belief in and worship of more than one god. **—pol′y·the′ist** *n., adj.*

pol·y·un·sat·u·rat·ed [pol′ē·un·sach′ə·rā′təd] *adj.* Of, having to do with, or being a fat or oil whose molecules have at least two double or triple bonds between carbon atoms.

pol·y·ur·e·thane [pol′ē·yŏŏr′ə·thān′] *n.* Any of several plastic resins used in making adhesives, protective coatings, and insulation.

po·made [pə·mād′] *n.* A perfumed hair dressing or an ointment for the scalp.

po·man·der [pō′man·dər *or* pō·man′dər] *n.* 1 A mixture of aromatic substances, often shaped like a ball, that was worn or carried in former times as a guard against infection. 2 A bag, box, or other container for holding pomander.

pome [pōm] *n.* A type of fruit, such as an apple or pear, having seeds in the center and a fleshy, edible outer part.

pome·gran·ate [pom′gran′it *or* pum′gran′it] *n.* 1 A tropical fruit about the size of an orange, having a pleasantly acid pulp and many seeds. 2 The tree on which this fruit grows.

Pom·er·a·ni·an [pom′ə·rā′nē·ən] *n.* A small dog with long silky hair and a bushy, upturned tail.

pom·mel [pum′əl *or* pom′əl] *n., v.* **pom·meled** or **pom·melled, pom·mel·ing** or **pom·mel·ling** 1 *n.* A knob, as on the hilt of a sword. 2 *v.* Another spelling of PUMMEL. 3 *n.* A knob that sticks up at the front of a saddle.

pomp [pomp] *n.* Magnificent, stately display; splendor: the *pomp* of a state funeral.

pom·pa·dour [pom′pə·dôr′] *n.* A way of arranging the hair in which it is made to puff straight up from the forehead.

pom·pa·no [pom′pə·nō′] *n., pl.* **pom·pa·nos** An edible, flat-bodied, usually silver-colored fish of warm Atlantic waters.

pom·pom [pom′pom′] *n.* A pompon (def. 1).

pom·pon [pom′pon′] *n.* 1 A tuft or ball, as of wool, used to ornament clothing, especially hats. 2 A type of chrysanthemum or dahlia having compact, globe-shaped flowers.

Pompon

pom·pos·i·ty [pom·pos′ə·tē] *n.* The condition or quality of being pompous or pretentious.

pom·pous [pom′pəs] *adj.* 1 Too conscious and proud of one's dignity; self-important: a *pompous* executive. 2 High-flown or ornate: a *pompous* speech. **—pom′pous·ly** *adv.* **—pom′pous·ness** *n.*

pon·cho [pon′chō] *n., pl.* **pon·chos** 1 A South American cloak like a blanket with a hole in the middle for the head. 2 A similar waterproof garment used as a raincoat.

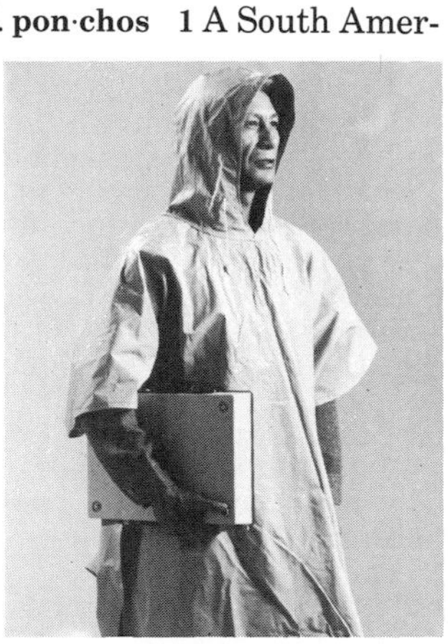

Poncho

pond [pond] *n.* A body of still water smaller than a lake.

pon·der [pon′dər] *v.* To consider carefully; puzzle over: to *ponder* a decision.

pon·der·ous [pon′dər·əs] *adj.* 1 Large, heavy, and often clumsy; lumbering: The elephant is a *ponderous* animal. 2 Dull; boring: a *ponderous* lecture. **—pon′der·ous·ly** *adv.*

pon·gee [pon·jē′] *n.* A thin natural silk having a knotty, rough weave.

pon·iard [pon′yərd] *n.* A dagger.

pon·tiff [pon′tif] *n.* 1 A bishop. 2 A pope.

pon·tif·i·cal [pon·tif′i·kəl] *adj.* Of or having to do with a pope or bishop.

pon·tif·i·cate [pon·tif′ə·kāt′] *v.* **pon·tif·i·cat·ed, pon·tif·i·cat·ing** 1 To perform the duties of a bishop. 2 To write or speak in a pompous or dogmatic way.

pon·toon [pon·tōōn′] *n.* 1 A flat-bottomed boat. 2 A float, often in the form of a flat-bottomed boat or a sealed metal tube, used in building a temporary floating bridge. 3 Either of the floats on the landing gear of a seaplane.

pontoon bridge A bridge supported on pontoons.

po·ny [pō′nē] *n., pl.* **po·nies** One of any of several breeds of very small horses.

pony express An early system for sending mail between Missouri and California by relays of horsemen.

po·ny·tail [pō′nē·tāl′] *n.* A hairstyle in which the hair is drawn back and gathered so that it hangs like a horse's tail.

pooch [pōōch] *n. slang* A dog.

poo·dle [pōōd′(ə)l] *n.* One of a breed of intelligent dogs with thick, usually curly hair.

pooh [pōō] *interj.* An exclamation used to show such

reactions as disbelief, annoyance, or disapproval.

pooh-pooh [po͞o′po͞o′] *v.* To dismiss or reject with disdain: to *pooh-pooh* a plan.

pool[1] [po͞ol] *n.* 1 A small body of still water. 2 A deep place in a stream. 3 A puddle: a *pool* of blood. 4 A swimming pool.

pool[2] [po͞ol] 1 *n.* A game whose object is to use a cue to make a ball hit others into the pockets of a special table. 2 *n.* A sum of money put together by a group of people for use in a common venture or as the stakes in a contest or race. 3 *n.* A number of persons or things used or available for use by a particular group: a *pool* of typists. 4 *v.* To combine (as money, things, or efforts) for common benefit.

poop[1] [po͞op] *n.* 1 The stern, or aft end, of a ship. 2 A short deck at the stern of a ship, raised above the main deck.

poop[2] [po͞op] *v.* To tire or exhaust.

poor [po͝or] *adj.* 1 Having too little money and property to live in comfort; needy. 2 Marked by poverty: a *poor* neighborhood. 3 Lacking in quantity or quality; not good: a *poor* crop; a *poor* job; *poor* soil. 4 Deserving pity; unhappy; wretched: The *poor* cat was in pain. 5 Lacking vigor; feeble; frail: in *poor* health. **—poor′ness** *n.*

poor·house [po͝or′hous′] *n.* A home for poor people, maintained by public funds.

poor·ly [po͝or′lē] *adv.* In a poor way; badly; unsatisfactorily.

pop[1] [pop] *n., v.* **popped, pop·ping** 1 *n.* A sharp, explosive noise. 2 *v.* To make a sharp, explosive sound. 3 *v.* To break open or explode or cause to break open or explode with such a sound: The balloon *popped*; to *pop* corn. 4 *v.* To move or put suddenly: to *pop* into a room; He *popped* his head through the door. 5 *v.* To bulge, as the eyes. 6 *v.* To hit a baseball high but not very far, so that it is easily caught: to *pop* out. 7 *n.* Sweetened and flavored carbonated water; soda.

pop[2] [pop] *n. slang* Father.

pop[3] [pop] *adj. informal* Popular: *pop* songs.

pop·corn [pop′kôrn′] *n.* 1 A kind of corn whose kernels pop open and puff up when heated. 2 The kernels after they have popped open.

pope [pōp] *n.* (*usually written* **Pope**) The bishop of Rome, head of the Roman Catholic Church.

pop fly In baseball, a short, high fly ball.

pop·gun [pop′gun′] *n.* A toy gun that shoots pellets such as corks with a popping sound.

pop·in·jay [pop′in·jā′] *n.* 1 A vain, silly chatterbox. 2 A parrot: seldom used today.

pop·lar [pop′lər] *n.* 1 A tree related to the willow, that grows rapidly and has light, soft wood. 2 The wood of this tree.

pop·lin [pop′lin] *n.* A strong ribbed cloth made of silk, cotton, rayon, or other fiber.

pop·o·ver [pop′ō′vər] *n.* A light muffin that puffs up and is hollow in the center.

pop·pet [pop′it] *n. British* A dainty little person or small child.

pop·py [pop′ē] *n., pl.* **pop·pies** 1 Any of various plants having showy red, yellow, or white flowers. One kind of poppy produces opium. 2 The flower of any of these plants.

pop·py·cock [pop′ē·kok′] *n.* Nonsense.

pop-top [pop′top′] *adj.* Opened by pulling a tab: a *pop-top* soda can.

pop·u·lace [pop′yə·lis] *n.* The common people of a community or an area.

pop·u·lar [pop′yə·lər] *adj.* 1 Liked by or suited to many people: a *popular* remedy for headaches. 2 Having many friends; well-liked. 3 Of, for, or by the people at large: *popular* government. 4 Suited to the means of most people: *popular* prices. **—pop′u·lar·ly** *adv.*

pop·u·lar·i·ty [pop′yə·lar′ə·tē] *n.* The quality or condition of being popular.

pop·u·lar·ize [pop′yə·lə·rīz′] *v.* **pop·u·lar·ized, pop·u·lar·iz·ing** To make popular: to *popularize* modern art. **—pop′u·lar·i·za′tion** *n.*

pop·u·late [pop′yə·lāt′] *v.* **pop·u·lat·ed, pop·u·lat·ing** 1 To provide with inhabitants: England *populated* parts of her colonies. 2 To inhabit: Many strange creatures *populate* the jungle.

pop·u·la·tion [pop′yə·lā′shən] *n.* 1 The total number of people living in a place, as a country or city. 2 The total number of people of a particular group: the Irish *population.* 3 The group of individuals from which a statistical sample is taken.

pop·u·lous [pop′yə·ləs] *adj.* Having many inhabitants; thickly settled.

por·ce·lain [pôrs′lin *or* pôr′sə·lin] *n.* A fine, hard, white earthenware, somewhat translucent, used for plates, dishes, cups, and the like; china.

porch [pôrch] *n.* 1 A covered structure at the entrance to a building. 2 A veranda, either open or closed, along one or more sides of a building.

por·cu·pine [pôr′kyə·pīn′] *n.* A large clumsy rodent covered with spines or quills that stand up when it is attacked.

Porcupine

pore[1] [pôr] *v.* **pored, por·ing** 1 To gaze steadily or intently. 2 To read or study with great care and attention: to *pore* over one's schoolwork.

pore[2] [pôr] *n.* A tiny opening, as in the skin or a leaf, serving as an outlet or inlet. Perspiration escapes through pores in the skin.

por·gy [pôr′gē] *n., pl.* **por·gy** or **por·gies** Any of various saltwater fishes used for food.

pork [pôrk] *n.* The flesh of a pig used for food. ◆ *Pork* goes back through French to the Latin word *porcus*, meaning a *pig.*

pork·er [pôr′kər] *n.* A pig or hog, especially one fattened for slaughter.

por·nog·ra·phy [pôr·nog′rə·fē] *n.* Writing or pictures meant to arouse people's sexual feelings.

po·ros·i·ty [pô·ros′ə·tē] *n.* The quality of being porous.

por·ous [pôr′əs] *adj.* Full of tiny openings that allow a substance, as air or water, to pass through.

por·phy·ry [pôr′fə·rē] *n., pl.* **por·phy·ries** A hard rock enclosing white or red crystals.

a	add	**i**	it	**o͝o**	took	**oi**	oil
ā	ace	**ī**	ice	**o͞o**	pool	**ou**	pout
â	care	**o**	odd	**u**	up	**ng**	ring
ä	palm	**ō**	open	**û**	burn	**th**	thin
e	end	**ô**	order	**yo͞o**	fuse	**t̶h̶**	this
ē	equal					**zh**	vision

ə = a in *above* e in *sicken* i in *possible* o in *melon* u in *circus*

P

por·poise [pôr′pəs] *n., pl.* **por·pois·es** or **por·poise** 1 A sea mammal like a small whale, mostly blackish, with a blunt snout, often seen in schools. 2 A dolphin.

Porpoise

por·ridge [pôr′ij] *n.* A soft food made by boiling oatmeal or some other grain in water, milk, or other liquid.
por·rin·ger [pôr′in·jər] *n.* A small shallow bowl used for food, as porridge or soup.
port[1] [pôrt] *n.* A city or place where ships arrive and depart; harbor.
port[2] [pôrt] *n.* A sweet, usually red wine.
port[3] [pôrt] *n.* 1 A small opening in the side of a ship; porthole. 2 A covering for a porthole. 3 An opening, as in an engine or valve, for the passage of air, gas, or a liquid.
port[4] [pôrt] 1 *n.* The left side of a ship or boat, facing the bow. 2 *adj. use*: the *port* side; the *port* guns. 3 *v.* To turn to the left, as a ship.
port[5] [pôrt] *n.* The way a person stands or moves; carriage; bearing: a graceful *port.*
port·a·ble [pôr′tə·bəl] *adj.* That can be easily carried or moved: a *portable* cot.
port·age [pôr′tij] *n.* 1 The carrying of boats and goods overland between two bodies of water. 2 The route over which this is done. 3 The charge for such transportation.
por·tal [pôr′təl] *n.* (*often pl.*) An entrance, door, or gate, especially an impressive one.
port·cul·lis [pôrt·kul′is] *n.* A grating made of strong bars that can be let down to close off the entrance of a fort or castle.

Portcullis

por·tend [pôr·tend′] *v.* To warn or be an omen of: Their silence *portends* refusal.
por·tent [pôr′tent′] *n.* A warning or sign of what is to come; omen.
por·ten·tous [pôr·ten′təs] *adj.* 1 Warning of things to come; ominous: *portentous* thunder. 2 Astonishing; extraordinary: *portentous* strength.
por·ter[1] [pôr′tər] *n.* A keeper of a door or gate; doorman.
por·ter[2] [pôr′tər] *n.* 1 A person hired to carry luggage, as in an airport or station. 2 *U.S.* An attendant on a train. 3 A person hired to sweep, clean, and do odd jobs.
por·ter[3] [pôr′tər] *n.* A dark, heavy ale.
por·ter·house [pôr′tər·hous′] *n.* A choice cut of beef, including part of the tenderloin.
port·fo·li·o [pôrt·fō′lē·ō] *n., pl.* **port·fo·li·os** 1 A portable case for holding things, as papers and drawings. 2 A list of the holdings of an investor, bank, or organization. 3 The office and duties of a cabinet member or a minister of state.
port·hole [pôrt′hōl′] *n.* 1 A small, windowlike opening in the side of a ship to admit air and light. 2 An opening in the side of a ship, wall, or fort for shooting through.
por·ti·co [pôr′ti·kō′] *n., pl.* **por·ti·coes** or **por·ti·cos** An open space or walk covered by a roof held up by columns.

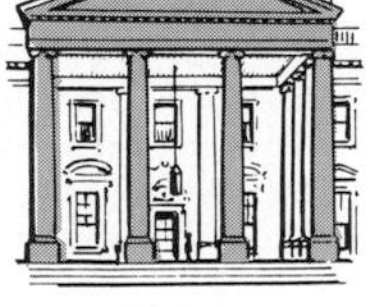
A portico

por·tière [pôr·tyâr′] *n.* A curtain that hangs at a doorway.
por·tion [pôr′shən] 1 *n.* A part or division of a whole. 2 *n.* A part or amount of something given or served to someone; share. 3 *v.* To divide into shares, often for distribution: The farm was *portioned* out between them.
port·land cement [pôrt′lənd] A kind of cement made by mixing clay with pulverized, heat-treated minerals of calcium and other elements. It hardens after being mixed with water.
port·ly [pôrt′lē] *adj.* **port·li·er, port·li·est** 1 Fat; stout. 2 Stately and dignified: a *portly* old general. **—port′li·ness** *n.*
port·man·teau [pôrt·man′tō] *n., pl.* **port·man·teaus** or **port·man·teaux** [pôrt·man′tōz] *British* A suitcase hinged at the back to form two separate compartments.
por·trait [pôr′trit *or* pôr′trāt′] *n.* 1 A drawing, painting, or photograph of a person, showing especially the face. 2 A vivid or imaginative description: Her new novel contains a wonderful *portrait* of the country and its people.
por·trait·ist [pôr′trā·tist] *n.* A person who makes portraits; portrait painter or photographer.
por·trai·ture [pôr′tri·chər] *n.* 1 The art or practice of making portraits. 2 A portrait.
por·tray [pôr·trā′] *v.* 1 To make a picture of, as in a drawing or painting. 2 To describe or depict in words. 2 To represent, as in a play: to *portray* Anne Frank.
por·tray·al [pôr·trā′əl] *n.* 1 The act or process of portraying. 2 A portrait.
Por·tu·guese [pôr′chə·gēz′] *adj., n., pl.* **Por·tu·guese** 1 *adj.* Of or from Portugal. 2 *n.* A person born or living in Portugal. 3 *n.* The language of Portugal.
Portuguese man-of-war A colony of sea animals having an inflated floating sac and long, stinging tentacles.
pose [pōz] *v.* **posed, pos·ing,** *n.* 1 *v.* To assume or hold a position, as for a portrait. 2 *v.* To cause to assume a position: The artist *posed* the model for the photograph. 3 *n.* A position of the body, especially one taken for a portrait. 4 *v.* To represent oneself: to *pose* as an expert. 5 *n.* A pretense or sham; affectation: The director's sternness is only a *pose.* 6 *v.* To present or put forward: to *pose* a question.

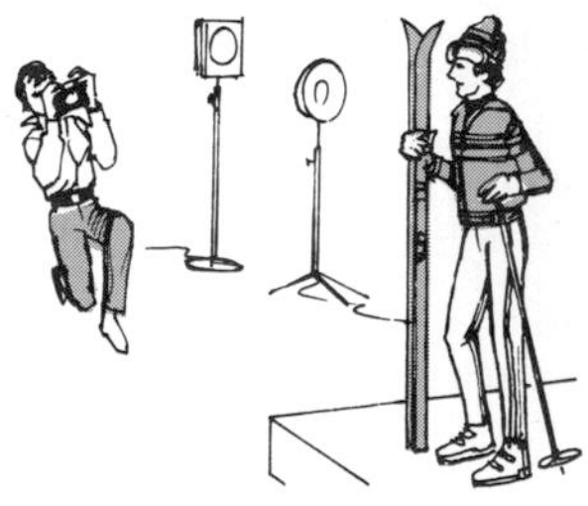
A model striking a pose

Po·sei·don [pə·sī′dən] *n.* In Greek myths, the god of the sea. His Roman name was Neptune.
pos·er[1] [pō′zər] *n.* A puzzling question or riddle.
pos·er[2] [pō′zər] *n.* A person who poses, as for an artist or photographer.
posh [posh] *adj. informal* Luxurious or elegant.
po·si·tion [pə·zish′ən] 1 *n.* The way in which a person or thing is placed: a standing *position*; an upside-down *position.* 2 *n.* The place occupied by a person or thing. 3 *n.* The correct or accustomed place: to be in *position.* 4 *v.* To put in a particular or accustomed place: to *position* a chair. 5 *n.* Condition or situation: an embarrassing *position.*

6 *n.* Social standing; rank, especially high rank. 7 *n.* An attitude or point of view; stand: What is your *position* on this question? 8 *n.* A job; post: She has a splendid *position* with an exporting firm.

pos·i·tive [poz′ə·tiv] 1 *adj.* Not allowing doubt, question, or denial: *positive* proof. 2 *adj.* Completely certain; convinced: I'm *positive* he's gone. 3 *adj.* Confident or too confident: a *positive* attitude. 4 *adj.* Complete; unqualified; definite: a *positive* failure. 5 *adj.* Helpful or useful: *positive* criticism. 6 *adj.* Being affirmative; saying "yes": a *positive* answer. 7 *adj.* Existing of or by itself; not relative or dependent on other things; real; absolute: a *positive* good. 8 *adj.* Greater than zero, as a number or quantity. 9 *adj.* Being or having the kind of electricity that attracts and is neutralized by electrons. 10 *adj.* Indicating the presence of a certain condition or disease: The result of the test for tuberculosis was *positive.* 11 *n.* Something that is positive or capable of being affirmed. 12 *adj.* In grammar, designating the simple form of an adjective or adverb, used when no comparison is being made. 13 *n.* In grammar, the positive degree of an adjective or adverb. 14 *n.* A photograph having the light and dark areas exactly as they were in the original subject; print. **—pos′i·tive·ly** *adv.*

pos·i·tron [poz′i·tron′] *n.* A subatomic particle with mass equal to that of an electron and an equal but positive charge.

pos·se [pos′ē] *n.* A force of people summoned by a sheriff to help in some official duty, as to stop a riot or make an arrest.

pos·sess [pə·zes′] *v.* 1 To have as property; own. 2 To have as a quality or feature: to *possess* a conscience. 3 To enter and control, sometimes as a demon or evil spirit: The idea *possessed* him.

pos·sessed [pə·zest′] *adj.* 1 Having as a quality; in possession: a musician *possessed* of a great talent. 2 Controlled or dominated by or as if by an evil spirit: shrieking like a *possessed* creature.

pos·ses·sion [pə·zesh′ən] *n.* 1 The fact or condition of possessing: to come into *possession* of a relative's fortune. 2 A being possessed, as by an idea or an evil spirit. 3 Something that is possessed. 4 A territory outside of, but controlled by, a country: Guam is a U.S. *possession.* 5 Self-control.

pos·ses·sive [pə·zes′iv] 1 *adj.* Of or related to possession or ownership. 2 *adj.* Having a strong desire for possessions. 3 *adj.* Having a desire or need to dominate or control someone: *possessive* parents. 4 *adj.* Of, having to do with, or being in the possessive case. 5 *n.* The possessive case, or a word in the possessive case. **—pos·ses′sive·ly** *adv.* **—pos·ses′sive·ness** *n.*

possessive adjective A pronoun that shows possession and is used before a noun, as *my* in "Here is my book."

possessive case The form of a noun or pronoun that shows possession. In "Here is my book, and there is Lauren's," *my* and *Lauren's* are in the possessive case.

possessive pronoun A pronoun that shows possession and is used in place of a noun phrase, as *yours* in "Here is my book, but where is yours?"

pos·ses·sor [pə·zes′ər] *n.* A person who possesses; owner.

pos·si·bil·i·ty [pos′ə·bil′ə·tē] *n., pl.* **pos·si·bil·i·ties** 1 The fact or condition of being possible: There is a *possibility* that our plans will be changed. 2 A thing that is possible: A change of plans is always a *possibility.*

pos·si·ble [pos′ə·bəl] *adj.* 1 Having a chance of happening; not contrary to fact or natural law: It is *possible* that you'll grow to over six feet. 2 Having some chance of happening; uncertain but not unlikely: It's *possible* that we'll arrive on time. 3 Capable of being done, acquired, made, or known: a *possible* purchase.

pos·si·bly [pos′ə·blē] *adv.* 1 Under any circumstances; for any reason: I can't *possibly* let the children go. 2 By any possible means: The horse can't *possibly* jump that far. 3 Maybe; perhaps: *Possibly* I can do it.

pos·sum [pos′əm] *n.* An informal name for OPOSSUM. **—play possum** To act as if dead, asleep, or ill.

post[1] [pōst] 1 *n.* An upright piece of timber or other material, usually used as a support. 2 *v.* To put up (as a poster or sign) in a public place. 3 *v.* To announce by or as if by a poster: to *post* a reward. 4 *v.* To put up signs forbidding trespassing on: to *post* your land during hunting season. 5 *v.* To enter on a list for public notice: to *post* a plane departure. 6 *v.* To fasten a poster or sign on or in.

Post

post[2] [pōst] 1 *n.* An assigned position or place of duty: a sentry's *post.* 2 *n.* A job, office, or position: The ambassador has a *post* with the new government. 3 *n.* A place where soldiers are stationed. 4 *n.* The soldiers stationed at such a place. 5 *v.* To assign a post to: We *posted* soldiers at each exit. 6 *v.* To give or put up: to *post* bond. 7 *n.* A trading post.

post[3] [pōst] 1 *n. chiefly British* Mail or a single delivery of mail: the morning *post.* 2 *v.* To mail: Please *post* these letters. 3 *n.* In former times, any of the stations furnishing relays of people and horses along certain fixed routes. 4 *v.* To inform: Their phone call *posted* us on the latest news. 5 *v.* To travel with speed; hurry.

post- A prefix meaning: 1 After or later in time; following, as in *postwar.* 2 After in position; behind, as in *postnasal.*

post·age [pōs′tij] *n.* The charge for sending mail.

postage meter A machine that stamps letters or packages with postage amounts and keeps track of the total postage.

postage stamp A small, printed, government label

a	add	**i**	it	**o͝o**	took	**oi**	oil
ā	ace	**ī**	ice	**o͞o**	pool	**ou**	pout
â	care	**o**	odd	**u**	up	**ng**	ring
ä	palm	**ō**	open	**û**	burn	**th**	thin
e	end	**ô**	order	**yo͞o**	fuse	**t͟h**	this
ē	equal					**zh**	vision

ə = { a in *above* e in *sicken* i in *possible* / o in *melon* u in *circus* }

that is put on mail as evidence that postage has been paid.

post·al [pōs′təl] *adj.* Of or having to do with the mails or with post offices.

postal card 1 A card with a stamp printed on it, issued by the government and used to send messages through the mail. 2 A postcard.

postal service The Post Office (def. 1).

post·card [pōst′kärd′] *n.* 1 Another name for POSTAL CARD. 2 A card, usually with a picture on the front side, that can be sent through the mails.

post chaise A closed, four-wheeled carriage for hire, formerly used for traveling.

post·date [pōst′dāt′] *v.* **post·dat·ed, post·dat·ing** 1 To write a date on that is later than the actual date: to *postdate* a check. 2 To come after in time: The Renaissance *postdates* the Middle Ages.

post·er [pōs′tər] *n.* A sign, printed notice, or advertisement posted in some public place.

Poster

pos·te·ri·or [pos·tir′ē·ər] *adj.* 1 Situated behind or toward the back part. 2 Coming after another in a series. 3 Coming after in time; later.

pos·ter·i·ty [pos·ter′ə·tē] *n.* 1 All the people of future times. 2 All of one person's descendants.

pos·tern [pōs′tərn] 1 *n.* A small back gate or door, especially in a fortification or castle. 2 *adj.* Situated at the back or side.

post exchange A store at a military base that sells goods and services to military employees and their families.

post·grad·u·ate [pōst′graj′o͞o·it *or* pōst′graj′o͞o·āt′] 1 *adj.* Of or having to do with studies pursued after receiving a diploma or degree. 2 *n.* A person who goes on with such studies.

post·haste [pōst′hāst′] *adv.* With great speed.

post·hu·mous [pos′cho͞o·məs] *adj.* 1 Born after the death of its father: a *posthumous* child. 2 Published after the author's death: a *posthumous* novel. 3 Coming after one's death: *posthumous* fame. **—post′hu·mous·ly** *adv.*

pos·til·ion or **pos·til·lion** [pōs·til′yən *or* pos·til′yən] *n.* A person who rides as a guide on one of the horses drawing a carriage.

post·im·pres·sion·ism [pōst′im·presh′ən·iz′əm] *n.* A period of painting that occurred in the late 19th and early 20th centuries in France. It shows a strong sense of line and structure. **—post′im·pres′·sion·ist** *adj., n.*

post·man [pōst′mən] *n., pl.* **post·men** [pōst′mən] A mail carrier.

post·mark [pōst′märk′] 1 *n.* A mark put on mail to cancel stamps and to give the date and place of mailing. 2 *v.* To stamp with a postmark.

post·mas·ter [post′mas′tər] *n.* An official who is in charge of a post office.

postmaster general *pl.* **postmasters general** An official who is in charge of the postal service of an entire country.

post me·ri·di·em [pōst′mə·rid′ē·əm] The part of the day from noon to midnight. ◆ *Post meridiem* is almost always used in its abbreviated form, *p.m.* It is a Latin expression meaning *after midday.*

post·mis·tress [pōst′mis′tris] *n.* An old title of a woman who was an official in charge of a post office.

post·mor·tem [pōst′môr′təm] 1 *adj.* Happening or performed after death. 2 *n.* A thorough examination of a human body made after death.

post·na·tal [pōst′nā′təl] *adj.* Happening after birth, especially soon after birth.

post office 1 (*often written* **Post Office**) The branch of a government responsible for carrying and delivering the mail. 2 Any local office that handles mail and sells stamps and other postal materials.

post·op·er·a·tive [pōst′op′ər·ə·tiv] *adj.* Happening soon after a surgical operation.

post·paid [pōst′pād′] *adj.* Having the postage paid for by the sender.

post·pone [pōst·pōn′] *v.* **post·poned, post·pon·ing** To put off to a future time; delay: We *postponed* our picnic. **—post·pone′ment** *n.*

post road In former times, a road built for carrying mail, and having stations at regular intervals to furnish fresh horses.

post·script [pōst′skript′] *n.* 1 Any message added to a letter below the writer's signature. 2 A part added to any written or printed work.

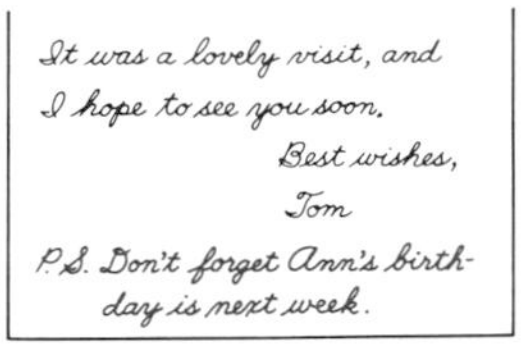
It was a lovely visit, and
I hope to see you soon.
Best wishes,
Tom
P.S. Don't forget Ann's birthday is next week.
Postscript

pos·tu·late [*v.* pos′chə·lāt′, *n.* pos′chə·lit] *v.* **pos·tu·lat·ed, pos·tu·lat·ing,** *n.* 1 *v.* To assume or claim the truth of; take for granted, as in reasoning or arguing: to *postulate* the roundness of the earth. 2 *n.* A fundamental truth or necessary condition claimed or held as a basis for argument or reasoning. 3 *v.* To claim, demand, or require.

pos·ture [pos′chər] *n., v.* **pos·tured, pos·tur·ing** 1 *n.* The way a person carries her or his body or a part of it: an erect *posture.* 2 *n.* A particular way of holding the body, as in posing for an artist. 3 *v.* To place in a specific position or pose. 4 *v.* To assume a certain bodily position, especially to pose for effect. 5 *v.* To assume an attitude. 6 *n.* An official postion or point of view, as of a nation or major political group: the bellicose *posture* of the junta.

post·war [pōst′wôr′] *adj.* After a war.

po·sy [pō′zē] *n., pl.* **po·sies** 1 A single flower or a bouquet. 2 A brief inscription or motto.

pot [pot] *n., v.* **pot·ted, pot·ting** 1 *n.* A usually round, deep container made of metal, glass, or earthenware and used for cooking, growing plants, or other household purposes. 2 *n.* Such a container and its contents: a *pot* of stew. 3 *n.* The amount a pot will hold: a *pot* of tea. 4 *v.* To put into a pot or pots: to *pot* plants. 5 *v.* To preserve in a pot. 6 *n.* A trap, as for lobsters or fish. 7 *n.* In certain card games, the amount of money bet or played for. 8 *n.* A fund of money contributed by a group of people and used by all of them. 9 *n. informal* A large sum of money. 10 *n. slang* Another name for MARIJUANA. **—go to pot** To become bad, as in character or quality.

po·ta·ble [pō′tə·bəl] 1 *adj.* Fit for drinking: *potable* water. 2 *n.* (*pl.*) Liquids that are fit for drinking.

pot·ash [pot′ash′] *n.* A white substance made from wood ashes, used as a fertilizer and in making glass, soap, and other products.

po·tas·si·um [pə·tas′ē·əm] *n.* A soft, silvery white

metallic element forming many compounds used in industry and medicine and having essential functions in living organisms.

po·ta·to [pə·tā′tō] *n., pl.* **po·ta·toes** 1 The thickened, underground stem or tuber of a cultivated plant. It is starchy and widely used as a vegetable. 2 The plant itself. 3 A sweet potato.

potato chip A very thin slice of potato fried crisp and salted.

pot·bel·lied [pot′bel′ēd] *adj.* 1 Having a large, bulging belly. 2 Having a rounded, bulging part that suggests a large belly: a *potbellied* wood stove.

pot·bel·ly [pot′bel′ē] *n., pl.* **pot·bel·lies** 1 A large, bulging belly. 2 A person with a large, bulging belly.

pot·boil·er [pot′boi′lər] *n.* A piece of writing or art done just to make money.

po·ten·cy [pōt′(ə)n·sē] *n.* The quality of being potent; power; force.

po·tent [pōt′(ə)nt] *adj.* 1 Physically powerful. 2 Having great authority: a *potent* ruler. 3 Able to convince or influence: a *potent* argument. 4 Strong in its physical or chemical effects: a *potent* drug or medicine.

po·ten·tate [pōt′(ə)n·tāt′] *n.* A person who has great power or authority; ruler.

po·ten·tial [pə·ten′chəl] 1 *adj.* Possible, but not yet actual: a *potential* danger; a *potential* customer. 2 *n.* Qualities that make the development of a talent, power, or skill possible or likely: a student with great *potential.* 3 *n.* The difference between two electric charges, or the difference between one charge and zero. —**po·ten′tial·ly** *adv.*

potential energy The energy that matter has because of its position or structure rather than motion.

po·ten·ti·al·i·ty [pə·ten′chē·al′ə·tē] *n., pl.* **po·ten·ti·al·i·ties** 1 Something capable of being developed. 2 Capacity for development or advancement.

poth·er [pot͟h′ər] 1 *n.* Fuss and commotion. 2 *v.* To worry; bother.

pot·hole [pot′hōl′] *n.* A large hole in a street or road or in the bed of a stream.

po·tion [pō′shən] *n.* A liquid that is supposed to have medicinal, poisonous, or magical qualities.

pot·latch [pot′lach′] *n.* A feast held by Indian tribes in NW North America in which the host gives away or destroys objects of value.

pot·luck [pot′luk′] *n.* Whatever food may have been prepared for the family and not especially for guests: Stay with us and take *potluck.*

pot·pie [pot′pī′] *n.* A dish of meat and vegetables covered with a crust and baked in the oven.

pot·pour·ri [pō·po͞o·rē′] *n.* 1 A mixture of dried flower petals and spices kept for its fragrance. 2 A medley of tunes or a miscellany of writings: a *potpourri* of opera tunes.

pot roast A piece of meat, usually beef, braised slowly in a covered pot.

pot·sherd [pot′shûrd′] *n.* A small piece of broken pottery.

pot·shot [pot′shot′] *n.* 1 A sure, easy shot, as one to kill game for food. 2 *informal* A critical remark tossed at an easy, tempting target.

pot·tage [pot′ij] *n.* A thick soup or stew.

pot·ter[1] [pot′ər] *n.* A person who makes pottery.

pot·ter[2] [pot′ər] *v. British* To putter.

potter's field A burial ground for poor or unknown people or, sometimes, for criminals.

potter's wheel A horizontal, rotating disk for holding clay that is being shaped by a potter.

Potter's wheel

pot·ter·y [pot′ər·ē] *n., pl.* **pot·ter·ies** 1 Things, as vases or pots, molded from clay and hardened by intense heat. 2 The art of making pottery. 3 The place where pottery is made.

pot·to [pot′ō] *n., pl.* **pot·tos** A small, tree-dwelling African primate with a round head, a pointed snout, and a stumpy tail.

pouch [pouch] 1 *n.* A small bag or sack. 2 *n.* The pocket of skin on the belly of certain animals, as the kangaroo and opossum, in which the animal's young are carried. 3 *n.* Any similar part, as in the cheeks of a squirrel or in the bill of a pelican. 4 *v.* To put or form into a pouch or into something like a pouch.

poul·tice [pōl′tis] *n.* A moist, usually hot mass of flour, mustard, or other substance, applied to a sore or inflamed part of the body.

poul·try [pōl′trē] *n.* Fowl kept for meat or eggs, as chickens, ducks, and turkeys.

pounce [pouns] *v.* **pounced, pounc·ing,** *n.* 1 *v.* To swoop down or spring, as in seizing prey: The hawk *pounced* on the chicken. 2 *n.* The act of pouncing; sudden swoop or spring.

pound[1] [pound] *n.* 1 A unit of weight in avoirdupois equal to 16 ounces. 2 A unit of weight in troy equal to 12 ounces. 3 The pound sterling. 4 The basic unit of money in several other countries, including Ireland, Egypt, and Israel.

pound[2] [pound] 1 *v.* To strike heavily and repeatedly; beat: to *pound* a nail into a board; to *pound* a friend on the back; to *pound* on a door; to *pound* on a typewriter. 2 *n.* A heavy blow, or the sound of a heavy blow. 3 *v.* To crush into a pulp or powder: to *pound* grain into meal. 4 *v.* To move with heavy, plodding steps: to *pound* down the stairs. 5 *v.* To beat or throb heavily: The frightened animal's heart *pounded.*

pound[3] [pound] *n.* A place for keeping stray animals, especially stray or unlicensed dogs.

pound-foolish [pound′fo͞o′lish] *adj.* Wasteful or unwise in dealing with large sums or important matters. See PENNY-WISE.

pound sterling The basic unit of British money, equal to 100 new pence: symbol £.

pour [pôr] 1 *v.* To flow or cause to flow in a continuous stream: to *pour* water into a pot; People *poured* out of the theater. 2 *v.* To rain heavily. 3 *v.* To tell or write about freely: to *pour* forth one's sorrows. 4 *v.* To act as a host by pouring tea, coffee, or other beverage. 5 *n.* Something poured, as rain.

pout [pout] 1 *v.* To thrust out the lips, especially when one is discontented or annoyed. 2 *n.* A

a	add	**i**	it	**o͝o**	took	**oi**	oil
ā	ace	**ī**	ice	**o͞o**	pool	**ou**	pout
â	care	**o**	odd	**u**	up	**ng**	ring
ä	palm	**ō**	open	**û**	burn	**th**	thin
e	end	**ô**	order	**yo͞o**	fuse	**t͟h**	this
ē	equal					**zh**	vision

ə = a in *above* e in *sicken* i in *possible* / o in *melon* u in *circus*

P

sulky expression made in this way. **3** *v.* To be gloomy or discontented; sulk. **—pout'er** *n.*

pout·er [pou'tər] *n.* A domestic pigeon that can inflate part of its crop so that the breast puffs out.

Pouter

pov·er·ty [pov'ər·tē] *n.* **1** The condition of being very poor. **2** A lack or small amount: a *poverty* of talent. **3** Poorness in quality: the *poverty* of the soil.

pov·er·ty-strick·en [pov'ər·tē·strik'ən] *adj.* Suffering from poverty; very poor.

POW or **P.O.W.** prisoner of war.

pow·der [pou'dər] **1** *n.* A dry mass of fine particles made by crushing or grinding a solid substance. **2** *n.* Any kind of powder prepared in this way, as talcum powder. **3** *v.* To reduce to powder; grind: *powdered* sugar. **4** *v.* To sprinkle or cover with or as if with powder. **5** *v.* To use powder as a cosmetic, especially on the face.

powder horn The hollow horn of an ox or cow, used in former times for holding gunpowder.

Powder horn

powder puff A soft pad used to apply powder to the skin.

pow·der·y [pou'dər·ē] *adj.* **1** Of or like powder. **2** Covered with or as if with powder; dusty. **3** Capable of being easily crushed into powder.

pow·er [pou'ər] **1** *n.* Ability or capacity to do something or to produce a certain effect: the *power* of speech; the *power* of a novel. **2** *n.* Physical strength or force: to have *power* in one's fists. **3** *n.* Legal authority or capability: the *power* of the Supreme Court. **4** *n.* Any person or thing that has control or influence over others: That country is a *power* in the world. **5** *n.* In physics, the rate at which work is done, measured in such units as watts or horsepower. **6** *n.* Any form of energy available for doing work, as electricity. **7** *adj. use*: a *power* saw. **8** *n.* The result of a number multiplied by itself a given number of times: The third *power* of 2 is 8. **9** *n.* Magnifying capacity, as of a lens. **10** *v.* To provide with power: This saw is *powered* by a gasoline engine. **—in power** In control: Hitler was *in power* for 12 years.

pow·er·boat [pou'ər·bōt'] *n.* Another word for MOTORBOAT.

pow·er·ful [pou'ər·fəl] *adj.* Having great power: a *powerful* army; a *powerful* country; a *powerful* play. **—pow'er·ful·ly** *adv.*

pow·er·house [pou'ər·hous'] *n.* **1** A station where electricity is generated. **2** *slang* A person or group of great force or energy.

pow·er·less [pou'ər·lis] *adj.* Without power: *powerless* to act. **—pow'er·less·ly** *adv.*

power of attorney **1** A written document that gives one person the legal authority to act for another, as in signing papers and handling business. **2** The legal authority given by such a document.

power pack A portable device that converts electric current from the supply to a voltage suitable for a particular piece of equipment.

power plant A factory, engine, or collection of machines that generates power, especially electric power.

power play **1** A situation in ice hockey in which one team has more players on the field than the other because of players in the penalty box. **2** A play, as in football or soccer, in which many of a team's players are concentrated in one part of the field. **3** A military, political, or diplomatic move in which power is used to gain an advantage over a weaker party.

power shovel A large, power-driven machine used for digging.

pow·wow [pou'wou'] **1** *n. informal* Any meeting or conference. **2** *v.* To hold a powwow. **3** *n.* A conference with or of North American Indians. ◆ *Powwow* comes from the Algonquian Indian word *pauwaw*, meaning *he dreams*. A *powwow* was originally an Indian medicine man or priest, who was supposed to have gotten magic powers from dreams.

pox [poks] *n.* A disease in which the skin breaks out in blisters, as in chicken pox.

pp very softly. ◆ *pp* is an abbreviation of the Italian *pianissimo*, a musical direction meaning *very soft* or *very softly*.

pp. 1 pages. 2 past participle.

p.p. 1 (*often written* **P.P.**) parcel post. 2 past participle. 3 postpaid.

ppd. 1 postpaid. 2 prepaid.

ppr. or **p.pr.** present participle.

pr. 1 pair. 2 present. 3 price. 4 pronoun.

Pr The symbol for the element praseodymium.

PR 1 Postal Service abbreviation of Puerto Rico. 2 Public Relations.

P.R. Puerto Rico.

prac·ti·ca·ble [prak'ti·kə·bəl] *adj.* **1** Capable of being put into practice; possible. **2** Capable of being used; usable. **—prac·ti·ca·bil·i·ty** [prak'ti·kə·bil'ə·tē] *n.* **—prac'ti·ca·bly** *adv.* ◆ See PRACTICAL.

prac·ti·cal [prak'ti·kəl] *adj.* **1** Having to do with actual practice, use, or action rather than ideas or theories: *practical* knowledge. **2** That can be put to use or account; useful: *practical* clothes for hiking. **3** Having or showing common sense; sensible; realistic: a *practical* person; a *practical* plan. **4** Gained from actual practice or experience: a good *practical* knowledge of how to set a bone. **5** Being so in effect though not in name; virtual: Although she is not the principal, she is the *practical* head of our school. **—prac·ti·cal·i·ty** [prak'ti·kal'ə·tē] *n. adv.* ◆ A particular scheme for making money may be *practicable* (that is, it may be possible) without being *practical* (that is, without being sensible, useful, or realistic). In the same way, a person can be *practical*, but one would never say a person was *practicable*.

practical joke A joke, prank, or trick played on someone.

prac·ti·cal·ly [prak'ti·k(ə·)lē] *adv.* **1** Almost, but not completely; nearly: He's *practically* as tall as his father. **2** In a practical way.

practical nurse A person who has some training and experience in caring for the sick, but who is not a graduate of a nursing school.

prac·tice [prak'tis] *v.* **prac·ticed, prac·tic·ing,** *n.* 1 *v.* To do over and over to gain greater skill: to *practice* batting. 2 *n.* An action done over and over to gain greater skill: Playing the violin takes *practice.* 3 *n.* The skill gained by such action: I'm out of *practice.* 4 *v.* To do, perform, or make use of regularly or habitually: to *practice* kindness. 5 *n.* A person's customary action; habit: It was my *practice* to save a little bit a week. 6 *n.* An established custom: It is the *practice* in our school to have a ten-minute break between classes. 7 *v.* To apply in action: *Practice* what you preach. 8 *v.* To work at (a profession or occupation): to *practice* law. 9 *n.* The following of a profession: the *practice* of medicine. 10 *n.* The business built up by a lawyer or doctor: Our doctor has a large *practice.* ◆ *Practice, drill,* and *exercise* all refer to some repeated action that is done to gain skill. *Practice* may refer to complicated skills as well as simple ones: acrobats *practicing* on the high trapeze. *Drill* is more routine. It usually has the aim of enabling one to do an action automatically, without thinking: The Spanish teacher *drilled* the class in verb forms. Physical *exercises* are done to stay healthy or vigorous; study *exercises,* however, are lessons that give one practice in solving problems.

prac·ticed or **prac·tised** [prak'tist] *adj.* Skilled; experienced; expert.

prac·tise [prak'tis] *v.* **prac·tised, prac·tis·ing,** *n.* Another spelling of PRACTICE.

prac·ti·tion·er [prak·tish'ən·ər] *n.* A person who practices something, as an art, profession, or craft.

prae·tor [prē'tər] *n.* A city magistrate of ancient Rome ranking below a consul.

prae·to·ri·an [pri·tôr'ē·ən] 1 *adj.* Of or having to do with a praetor. 2 *n.* A praetor. 3 *adj.* (*written* **Praetorian**) Of or having to do with the bodyguard of the Roman emperors. 4 *n.* (*written* **Praetorian**) A member of this guard.

prag·mat·ic [prag·mat'ik] *adj.* 1 Concerned with practical results rather than with theories or ideas. 2 Of or having to do with the philosophy of pragmatism.

prag·ma·tism [prag'mə·tiz'əm] *n.* 1 A philosophy holding that beliefs should be evaluated by their practical effects. 2 A practical approach to solving problems. **—prag'ma·tist** *n.*

prai·rie [prâr'ē] *n.* A large tract or area of more or less level, grassy land having few or no trees, especially the broad, grassy plain of central North America.

prairie chicken Either of two game birds inhabiting the plains or prairies of North America.

prairie dog A small rodent of the plains of North America that lives in large communities and is very destructive to vegetation.

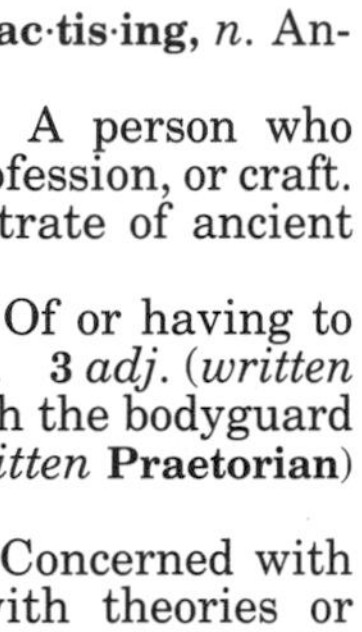

Prairie dog

prairie schooner A covered wagon used for travel by pioneers.

prairie wolf Another name for COYOTE.

praise [prāz] *n., v.* **praised, prais·ing** 1 *n.* An expression of approval or favor. 2 *v.* To express approval or favor of (someone or something): The boss *praised* the staff for a job well done. 3 *n.* Worship, as of a deity or idol. 4 *v.* To express adoration of: Let us *praise* God in song.

praise·wor·thy [prāz'wûr'~~th~~ē] *adj.* Worthy of praise.

pra·line [prä'lēn' *or* prā'lēn'] *n.* A candy made of nuts coated with boiled brown sugar or maple syrup.

pram [pram] *n. British* A baby carriage.

Pram

prance [prans] *v.* **pranced, pranc·ing,** *n.* 1 *v.* To bound or spring from the hind legs or move with high steps, as a horse. 2 *v.* To ride a horse that moves in such a way. 3 *v.* To walk or move in a lively, proud way; swagger. 4 *n.* The act of prancing; lively, high step. **—pranc'er** *n.*

prank [prangk] *n.* A mischievous, playful act or trick. **—prank'ish** *adj.*

pra·se·o·dym·i·um [prā'zē·ō·dim'ē·əm *or* prā'sē·ō·dim'ē·əm] *n.* A metallic element occurring in rare earths. ◆ See RARE-EARTH ELEMENT.

prate [prāt] *v.* **prat·ed, prat·ing** To talk foolishly and at length; chatter. **—prat'er** *n.*

prat·fall [prat'fôl'] *n.* A fall backwards on the buttocks.

prat·tle [prat'(ə)l] *v.* **prat·tled, prat·tling,** *n.* 1 *v.* To talk foolishly or like a child. 2 *n.* Foolish or childish talk. 3 *n.* The sound of childish speech, or a sound like it. **—prat'tler** *n.*

prawn [prôn] *n.* An edible shellfish related to the shrimp but larger.

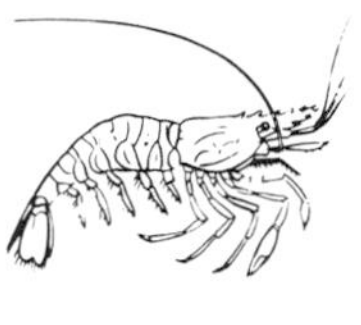

Prawn

pray [prā] *v.* 1 To address words or prayers to God, or to an idol or deity: They *prayed* for two hours. 2 To ask or beg by prayers or with great earnestness: The farmer *prayed* for rain. 3 To be so good as to; please: *Pray* be still awhile. 4 To get or bring about by praying.

prayer [prâr] *n.* 1 The act of praying. 2 An expression of worship, appeal, or thanks to God. 3 A set form of words used in praying. 4 Something prayed for. 5 Any earnest request.

prayer book A book of prayers.

prayer·ful [prâr'fəl] *adj.* 1 Inclined or given to praying. 2 Of or like a prayer. **—prayer'ful·ly** *adv.* **—prayer'ful·ness** *n.*

praying mantis See MANTIS.

pre- A prefix meaning: Before in time or order, as in *preschool.*

preach [prēch] *v.* 1 To deliver a sermon. 2 To urge or recommend strongly: to *preach* kindness. 3 To give advice, often in a boring or tiresome way.

a	add	**i**	it	**o͝o**	took	**oi**	oil
ā	ace	**ī**	ice	**o͞o**	pool	**ou**	pout
â	care	**o**	odd	**u**	up	**ng**	ring
ä	palm	**ō**	open	**û**	burn	**th**	thin
e	end	**ô**	order	**yo͞o**	fuse	**~~th~~**	this
ē	equal					**zh**	vision

ə = { a in *above* e in *sicken* i in *possible*; o in *melon* u in *circus* }

P

preach·er [prē′chər] *n.* A person who preaches, especially a clergyman.

preach·y [prē′chē] *adj.* **preach·i·er, preach·i·est** Tending to preach or moralize.

pre·am·ble [prē′am·bəl] *n.* An introductory statement, especially an introduction to a formal document explaining its purpose.

pre·amp [prē′amp′] *n.* An informal word for PREAMPLIFIER.

pre·am·pli·fi·er [prē·am′plə·fī′ər] *n.* A device, as in a radio or phonograph, that is used to increase the power of a weak signal before it reaches the main amplifier.

pre·ar·ranged [prē′ə·rānjd′] *adj.* Arranged ahead of time: a *prearranged* signal.

Pre·cam·bri·an [prē·kam′brē·ən] **1** *n.* The earliest geological era, extending from the formation of the oldest known rocks to the first appearance of life. **2** *adj.* Of the Precambrian.

pre·car·i·ous [pri·kâr′ē·əs] *adj.* **1** Risky; uncertain: a *precarious* way of earning a living. **2** Dangerous; hazardous: a *precarious* path up the mountain. **—pre·car′i·ous·ly** *adv.*

pre·cau·tion [pri·kô′shən] *n.* **1** Something done in order to avoid a possible danger or evil: As a *precaution,* we threw water on the campfire. **2** Any care taken ahead of time; caution in advance. **—pre·cau′tion·ar′y** *adj.*

pre·cede [pri·sēd′] *v.* **pre·ced·ed, pre·ced·ing** To be, go, or come before, as in order, place, rank, or time: Egypt *preceded* Greece in creating a great civilization.

prec·e·dence [pres′ə·dəns *or* pri·sēd′əns] *n.* **1** The act of preceding. **2** The right or condition of being ahead in place, time, or rank: Your business has *precedence* over mine.

prec·e·dent [*n.* pres′ə·dənt, *adj.* pri·sēd′(ə)nt] **1** *n.* Something, as an action, decision, or usage, that can be used as a guide for a later similar action, decision, etc. **2** *adj.* Going or coming before, as in time or place.

pre·ced·ing [pri·sē′ding] *adj.* That precedes; previous: the *preceding* chapter.

pre·cept [prē′sept′] *n.* A rule or direction to guide conduct or action.

pre·cep·tor [pri·sep′tər] *n.* A teacher.

pre·ces·sion [pri·sesh′ən] *n.* **1** The act of preceding. **2** A slow, circular movement of the axis of rotation of a spinning body.

pre·cinct [prē′singkt′] *n.* **1** An area, as of a city, town, or township, marked off as a district for voting or for police supervision. **2** (*often pl.*) A place or enclosure marked off by fixed limits: school *precincts.* **3** A boundary; limit.

pre·cious [presh′əs] **1** *adj.* Highly priced or prized; valuable: a *precious* gem. **2** *adj.* Beloved; cherished; dear: a *precious* child; a *precious* friendship. **3** *adj.* Too refined or delicate, as a style of writing. **4** *adj.* Very great: a *precious* scoundrel. **5** *adv.* Very: *precious* little chance of that. **—pre′cious·ly** *adv.*

prec·i·pice [pres′i·pis] *n.* A face of a cliff that is straight up and down or almost so.

pre·cip·i·tate [*v.* pri·sip′ə·tāt′, *adj., n.* pri·sip′ə·tit *or* pri·sip′ə·tāt′] *v.* **pre·cip·i·tat·ed, pre·cip·i·tat·ing,** *adj., n.* **1** *v.* To bring about quickly or suddenly: to *precipitate* a quarrel. **2** *v.* To hurl forcefully; throw as from a height. **3** *adj.* Moving or acting with or showing reckless speed; rash. **4** *v.* To separate (a substance) from a solution as a solid. **5** *n.* A substance separated as a solid from a solution. **6** *v.* To cause water vapor to condense and fall as dew, rain, or snow. **—pre·cip′i·tate·ly** *adv.*

pre·cip·i·ta·tion [pri·sip′ə·tā′shən] *n.* **1** The act or an instance of precipitating: the *precipitation* of a war between nations. **2** Reckless haste or hurry. **3** The depositing of rain or snow from the atmosphere on the earth; also, the amount of rain or snow so deposited. **4** The process of separating a substance from a solution as a solid. **5** The substance so separated.

pre·cip·i·tous [pri·sip′ə·təs] *adj.* **1** Like a precipice; very steep. **2** Hasty; rash; reckless. **—pre·cip′i·tous·ly** *adv.*

pre·cise [pri·sīs′] *adv.* **1** Strictly accurate; exact: the *precise* amount of money. **2** Careful or even fussy, as in observing rules or diction. **3** Particular; very: At that *precise* second, the bell sounded. **—pre·cise′ly** *adv.* **—pre·cise′ness** *n.*

pre·ci·sion [pri·sizh′ən] *n.* **1** The condition or quality of being precise; accuracy. **2** *adj. use: precision* instruments.

pre·clude [pri·klo͞od′] *v.* **pre·clud·ed, pre·clud·ing** To make impossible; prevent: Padded crates *preclude* damage in handling.

pre·co·cious [pri·kō′shəs] *adj.* Unusually mature or advanced for one's age: a *precocious* child. **—pre·co′cious·ly** *adv.* **—pre·coc·i·ty** [pri·kos′ə·tē] *n.*

pre-Co·lum·bi·an [prē′kə·lum′bē·ən] *adj.* Of or from the period in the Western Hemisphere before Columbus's arrival in 1492: *pre-Columbian* empires.

pre·con·ceived [prē′kən·sēvd′] *adj.* Formed in advance: a *preconceived* plan.

pre·con·cep·tion [prē′kən·sep′shən] *n.* **1** An idea formed in advance. **2** A prejudice; bias.

pre·con·cert·ed [prē′kən·sûr′tid] *adj.* Arranged or agreed upon ahead of time.

pre·cook [prē′ko͝ok′] *v.* To cook entirely or partly before the time when the food is cooked to be served.

pre·cur·sor [pri·kûr′sər] *n.* A person or thing that comes before and indicates what is to follow; forerunner.

The rebec was a precursor of the modern violin.

pre·date [prē·dāt′] *v.* **pre·dat·ed, pre·dat·ing** **1** To come before; antedate: Christmas Day *predates* New Year's Day by one week. **2** To mark with an earlier date than the actual date: She *predated* the check to make it look as if it were sent out on time.

pred·a·tor [pred′ə·tər] *n.* A predatory person or animal.

pred·a·to·ry [pred′ə·tôr′ē] *adj.* **1** Of, having to do with, or characterized by plundering or robbery. **2** Living by preying upon others: A hawk is a *predatory* bird.

pred·e·ces·sor [pred′ə·ses′ər] *n.* A person who goes or has gone before another in point of time, as a previous holder of a job or position.

pre·des·ti·na·tion [prē·des′tə·nā′shən] *n.* **1** The theory that God has determined everything that is to happen, including the damnation or salvation of every soul. **2** A person's destiny or fate.

pre·des·tine [prē·des′tin] *v.* **pre·des·tined, pre·des·tin·ing** To decide or determine in advance.

pre·de·ter·mine [prē′di·tûr′min] *v.* **pre·de·ter·**

mined, pre·de·ter·min·ing To determine beforehand; decide in advance: a *predetermined* orbit.
pre·dic·a·ment [pri·dik′ə·mənt] *n.* A situation that is trying, dangerous, or embarrassing: We had forgotten they were coming to dinner. What a *predicament*!
pred·i·cate [*n.* pred′i·kit, *v.* pred′i·kāt′] *n., v.* **pred·i·cat·ed, pred·i·cat·ing** 1 *n.* In grammar, the word or words in a sentence or clause that express something about the subject. A predicate consists of a verb with or without an object or complement and modifiers, as *ate their meal slowly* in "The diners ate their meal slowly." 2 *v.* To found or base (as an action or argument): The class rules were *predicated* on reason and fairness. 3 *v.* To prove or state as a quality or attribute: Does bravery *predicate* good character? 4 *v.* To declare; proclaim.
predicate adjective An adjective complement that follows a linking verb and modifies the subject of the verb, as *hot* in "The stove is hot."
predicate nominative A noun or pronoun complement that follows a linking verb and refers to the same person or thing as the subject of the verb, as *lawyer* in "She is a lawyer."
predicate noun A noun that is a predicate nominative.
pre·dict [pri·dikt′] *v.* To state beforehand; foretell: to *predict* the outcome of a game.
pre·dict·a·ble [pri·dik′tə·bəl] *adj.* Capable of being predicted.
pre·dic·tion [pri·dik′shən] *n.* 1 The act of predicting. 2 Something predicted; prophecy.
pre·di·lec·tion [prē′də·lek′shən *or* pred′ə·lek′shən] *n.* A preference or liking; partiality.
pre·dis·pose [prē′dis·pōz′] *v.* **pre·dis·posed, pre·dis·pos·ing** To give a tendency; incline: Exhaustion *predisposes* one to sickness. **—pre·dis·po·si·tion** [prē′dis·pə·zish′ən] *n.*
pre·dom·i·nant [pri·dom′ə·nənt] *adj.* Greater or superior in power, effect, or number: The *predominant* color of the rock is dark brown. **—pre·dom′i·nance** *n.* **—pre·dom′i·nant·ly** *adv.*
pre·dom·i·nate [pri·dom′ə·nāt′] *v.* **pre·dom·i·nat·ed, pre·dom·i·nat·ing** 1 To be greater, as in power, effect, or number: In this group, science majors *predominate.* 2 To be in control; prevail.
pre·em·i·nent [prē·em′ə·nənt] *adj.* Outstandingly superior; very fine; supreme. **—pre·em′i·nence** *n.* **—pre·em′i·nent·ly** *adv.*
pre·empt [prē·empt′] *v.* 1 To acquire for oneself before others can: to *preempt* the newest typewriter. 2 To occupy (public land) so as to get the right to purchase it.
preen [prēn] *v.* 1 To clean and arrange (as feathers) with the beak, as a bird. 2 To dress or tidy (oneself) carefully: The performers *preened* themselves before the mirror.
pre·ex·ist [prē′ig·zist′] *v.* To exist before.
pre·ex·is·tent [prē′ig·zis′tənt] *adj.* Existing before. **—pre′ex·is′tence** *n.*
pre·fab [prē′fab′] *n. informal* A building or other structure that is prefabricated.
pre·fab·ri·cate [prē·fab′rə·kāt′] *v.* **pre·fab·ri·cat·ed, pre·fab·ri·cat·ing** To manufacture in standard sections that can be rapidly set up and put together: to *prefabricate* a house.
pref·ace [pref′is] *n., v.* **pref·aced, pref·ac·ing** 1 *n.* A brief introduction, as to a book or speech. 2 *v.* To introduce or furnish with a preface.
pref·a·to·ry [pref′ə·tôr′ē] *adj.* Of, like, or serving as a preface; introductory.
pre·fect [prē′fekt′] *n.* 1 In ancient Rome, any of various civil and military officials. 2 Any high official or chief officer, as in France.
pre·fec·ture [prē′fek′chər] *n.* The office, jurisdiction, or district of a prefect.
pre·fer [pri·fûr′] *v.* **pre·ferred, pre·fer·ring** 1 To like better; value more: I *prefer* history to geography. 2 To bring forward, as charges, before a law court.
pref·er·a·ble [pref′ər·ə·bəl] *adj.* Fit to be preferred; more desirable. **—pre′fer·a·bly** *adv.*
pref·er·ence [pref′ər·əns] *n.* 1 The act of preferring: to show good judgment in one's *preferences.* 2 A person or thing preferred: My *preference* is cold weather. 3 The right or power to choose: to give a person a *preference.* 4 A favoring of one person or thing over another or others; partiality: Don't show *preference* when you assign jobs.
pref·er·en·tial [pref′ə·ren′shəl] *adj.* Showing preference or partiality: *preferential* treatment.
pre·fer·ment [pri·fûr′mənt] *n.* Advancement or promotion to something higher, as a rank, office, or position.
preferred stock A corporation's stock on which dividends must be paid before they are paid on common stock.
pre·fig·ure [prē·fig′yər] *v.* **pre·fig·ured, pre·fig·ur·ing** 1 To show in advance; be an indication of. 2 To picture to oneself beforehand.
pre·fix [*n.* prē′fiks′, *v.* prē·fiks′] 1 *n.* A syllable or syllables put at the beginning of a word or root to modify its meaning or make a new word. *Re* in "renew" is a prefix. 2 *v.* To put or attach before: to *prefix* a title to a person's name.
pre·flight [prē′flīt′] *adj.* Taking place before an airplane flight: a *preflight* briefing for pilots.
preg·nan·cy [preg′nən·sē] *n., pl.* **preg·nan·cies** The condition of being pregnant.
preg·nant [preg′nənt] *adj.* 1 Carrying an unborn child or unborn young in the womb; being with child or with young. 2 Having significance; full of meaning: a *pregnant* pause. 2 Full or filled: *pregnant* with meaning.
pre·hen·sile [prē·hen′sil] *adj.* Capable of holding or grasping: An opossum has a *prehensile* tail.
pre·his·tor·ic [prē′his·tôr′ik] *adj.* Of or belonging to the period before the start of written history: *prehistoric* reptiles. **—pre′his·tor′i·cal·ly** *adv.*
pre·his·tor·i·cal [prē′his·tôr′i·kəl] *adj.* Prehistoric.
pre·judge [prē·juj′] *v.* **pre·judged, pre·judg·ing** To judge beforehand or without proper knowledge.
prej·u·dice [prej′o͝o·dis] *n., v.* **prej·u·diced, prej·u·dic·ing** 1 *n.* An unfair opinion or judgment formed in advance of or without examination of the available facts: a *prejudice* against a new medicine. 2 *n.* Hatred of or dislike for a particular group, race, or religion. 3 *v.* To cause to have a prejudice;

a	add	**i**	it	**o͝o**	took	**oi**	oil
ā	ace	**ī**	ice	**o͞o**	pool	**ou**	pout
â	care	**o**	odd	**u**	up	**ng**	ring
ä	palm	**ō**	open	**û**	burn	**th**	thin
e	end	**ô**	order	**yo͞o**	fuse	**th**	this
ē	equal					**zh**	vision

ə = a in *above* e in *sicken* i in *possible* / o in *melon* u in *circus*

P

bias: That novel *prejudiced* me against adventure stories. **4** *n.* Injury or damage: The lawyer's manner operated to the *prejudice* of a strong case. **5** *v.* To cause harm or disadvantage to: A sliced drive *prejudiced* her chance of winning the match. ◆ *Prejudice* and *bias* both refer to feelings that make a fair judgment impossible. Some forms of *bias* are perfectly understandable. Few people would blame parents for being *biased* in favor of their own children. But other kinds of *bias*, such as hatred of other people because of their race or religion, are unreasonable and harmful. Such *biases* are forms of *prejudice*.

prej·u·di·cial [prej'ōō·dish'əl] *adj.* Causing prejudice; damaging.

prel·a·cy [prel'ə·sē] *n., pl.* **prel·a·cies** **1** The system of church government by prelates. **2** The position or office of a prelate. **3** Prelates as a group.

prel·ate [prel'it] *n.* A clergyman of high rank, as a bishop or archbishop.

pre·lim·i·nar·y [pri·lim'ə·ner'ē] *adj., n., pl.* **pre·lim·i·nar·ies** **1** *adj.* Coming before the main event, proceeding, or business; introductory. **2** *n.* Something preliminary, as an act or step: I cleared my throat as a *preliminary* to speaking.

prel·ude [prel'yōōd' *or* prā'lōōd'] *n., v.* **prel·ud·ed, prel·ud·ing** **1** *n.* Any introductory action or event. **2** *n.* An opening section or movement of a musical composition. **3** *n.* An instrumental composition of moderate length. **4** *v.* To introduce with a prelude. **5** *v.* To be a prelude to.

pre·ma·ture [prē'mə·chŏŏr' *or* prē'mə·t(y)ŏŏr'] *adj.* Before the natural or proper time; too early or soon. **—pre'ma·ture'ly** *adv.*

pre·med [prē'med'] *informal* **1** *adj.* Premedical. **2** *n.* A premedical student.

pre·med·i·cal [prē·med'i·kəl] *adj.* Of, having to do with, or preparing for the study of medicine.

pre·med·i·tat·ed [prē·med'ə·tā'tid] *adj.* Planned or thought about beforehand.

pre·med·i·ta·tion [prē·med'ə·tā'shən] *n.* The act of planning or thinking about beforehand.

pre·mi·er [*adj.* prē'mē·ər, *n.* pri·mir'] **1** *adj.* First in rank or position; principal. **2** *n.* The chief minister and often the chief executive of a government. **3** *adj.* First in occurrence; earliest.

pre·mière [pri·mir' *or* prə·myâr'] *n.* The first performance, as of a play or movie.

prem·ise [*n.* prem'is, *v.* prem'is *or* pri·mīz'] *n., v.* **pre·mised, pre·mis·ing** **1** *n.* A statement or belief that serves as a basis for an argument, conclusion, or theory: An early false *premise* was the belief that the earth is flat. **2** *v.* To state as a premise. **3** *n.* (*pl.*) An area of land with the buildings that are on it.

pre·mi·um [prē'mē·əm] *n.* **1** A prize or reward offered to help persuade someone to do or buy something. **2** An extra amount or bonus, as one paid in addition to a regular wage or price. **3** The amount paid for insurance, usually in installments. **4** High regard or value: to put a *premium* on truth. **—at a premium** **1** Valuable, usually because in great demand. **2** Above the usual price.

pre·mo·lar [prē·mō'lər] **1** *n.* One of the eight bicuspid, permanent teeth, two on each side of each jaw, located between the canine teeth and the molars. **2** *adj.* Of or being such a tooth or teeth.

pre·mo·ni·tion [prē'mə·nish'ən *or* prem'ə·nish'ən] *n.* A feeling or warning that something is going to happen, usually something bad.

pre·na·tal [prē·nāt'(ə)l] *adj.* Existing or occurring before birth.

pre·oc·cu·py [prē·ok'yə·pī] *v.* **pre·oc·cu·pied, pre·oc·cu·py·ing** **1** To interest or occupy fully: The work *preoccupied* the students for hours. **2** To take possession of first. **—pre·oc'cu·pa'tion** *n.*

pre·or·dain [prē'ôr·dān'] *v.* To determine or decide in advance what is going to happen.

prep. preposition.

pre·paid [prē'pād'] **1** Past tense and past participle of PREPAY. **2** *adj.* Paid for in advance.

prep·a·ra·tion [prep'ə·rā'shən] *n.* **1** The act or process of preparing. **2** A being prepared; readiness. **3** Something done so as to get ready. **4** Something made or prepared, as a medicine.

pre·par·a·to·ry [pri·par'ə·tôr'ē] *adj.* **1** Used or serving as preparation; helping to make ready: *preparatory* work. **2** Occupied in preparation: a *preparatory* scholar.

preparatory school A private school that prepares students for college admission.

pre·pare [pri·pâr'] *v.* **pre·pared, pre·par·ing** **1** To make ready, fit, or qualified: to *prepare* a class for a test. **2** To get ready: to *prepare* for a trip. **3** To provide with what is needed; outfit; equip: to *prepare* an expedition. **4** To put together; make: to *prepare* a meal.

pre·par·ed·ness [pri·pâr'id·nis *or* pri·pârd'nis] *n.* Readiness, especially readiness for war.

pre·pay [prē·pā'] *v.* **pre·paid, pre·pay·ing** To pay or pay for in advance. **—pre·pay'ment** *n.*

pre·pon·der·ant [pri·pon'dər·ənt] *adj.* Having greater force, weight, influence, or quantity: Weather rather than careful planning had the *preponderant* effect on our vacation. **—pre·pon'·der·ance** *n.*

pre·pon·der·ate [pri·pon'də·rāt'] *v.* **pre·pon·der·at·ed, pre·pon·der·at·ing** To be greater in force, weight, influence, or quantity: Apartment buildings *preponderate* over houses in the middle of big cities.

prep·o·si·tion [prep'ə·zish'ən] *n.* A word that is used to indicate the relation of its object, a noun or pronoun, to another word in a sentence. **—prep'·o·si'tion·al** *adj.* ◆ It was once said that a sentence should never end with a preposition, but good English sentences sometimes do. "What did you laugh at?" is perfectly acceptable English, while "At what did you laugh?" seems awkward and unnatural.

pre·pos·sess·ing [prē'pə·zes'ing] *adj.* Creating a favorable impression; pleasing; attractive.

pre·pos·ter·ous [pri·pos'tər·əs] *adj.* Contrary to nature, reason, or common sense; absurd; ridiculous. **—pre·pos'ter·ous·ly** *adv.*

prep·pie or **prep·py** [prep'ē] *informal* **1** *n.* A student at a preparatory school. **2** *n.* A young person who adopts the neatly dressed, well-behaved style of typical preparatory school students. **3** *adj.* Of or having to do with a preppie.

prep school [prep] An informal name for PREPARATORY SCHOOL.

pre·req·ui·site [prē·rek'wə·zit] **1** *adj.* Necessary to something that follows: Chemistry is a *prerequisite* course for medical training. **2** *n.* Something necessary to something else that follows, as a course that a student must pass before taking a more advanced course.

pre·rog·a·tive [pri·rog'ə·tiv] *n.* A right or privilege belonging to a particular person or class: The governor has the *prerogative* of a new house near the capital.

pres. 1 present. 2 (*often written* **Pres.**) president.

pres·age [*n.* pres′ij, *v.* pri·sāj′] *n., v.* **pre·saged, pre·sag·ing** 1 *n.* An indication or warning of something to come. 2 *v.* To give an indication or warning of: The words *presaged* trouble. 3 *n.* A feeling that something bad is going to happen. 4 *v.* To have a feeling or presentiment about.

pres·by·ter [prez′bə·tər] *n.* 1 In the early Christian church, an elder. 2 In certain churches, a priest. 3 In the Presbyterian church, a lay person or elder who is a church official.

Pres·by·te·ri·an [prez′bə·tir′ē·ən] 1 *n.* A member of a Protestant church that is governed by elders or presbyters. 2 *adj.* Of or having to do with Presbyterians or their church. **—Pres′by·te′ri·an·ism** *n.*

pres·by·ter·y [prez′bə·ter′ē] *n., pl.* **pres·by·ter·ies** 1 A Presbyterian church court made up of the ministers and presbyters of a district. 2 The district so represented. 3 That part of a church set apart for the clergy.

pre·school [prē′sko͞ol′] *adj.* Of or having to do with a child's life before school, usually between the ages of two and five.

pre·sci·ence [prē′shē·əns *or* presh′ē·əns] *n.* Correct knowledge of what will happen in the future.

pre·sci·ent [prē′shē·ənt *or* presh′ē·ənt] *adj.* Having knowledge of events before they take place; foreseeing.

pre·scribe [pri·skrīb′] *v.* **pre·scribed, pre·scrib·ing** 1 To set down (as a rule or direction) to be followed or obeyed; order. 2 To order the use of something, as a medicine or treatment.

pre·scrip·tion [pri·skrip′shən] *n.* 1 A physician's formula for preparing and ordering a medicine, usually with directions about its use. 2 The medicine itself. 3 A rule; direction; order.

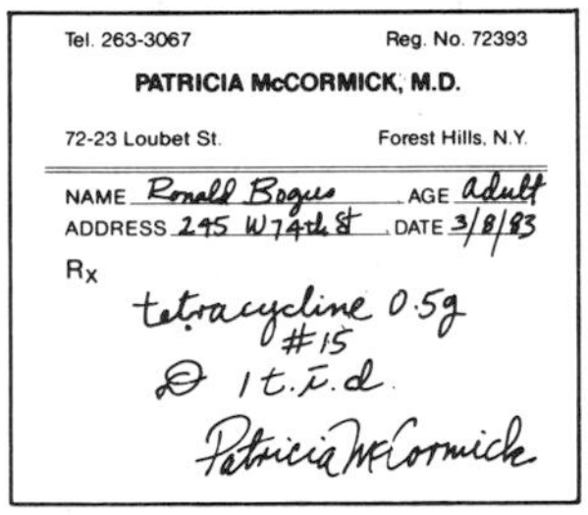
Tel. 263-3067 Reg. No. 72393
PATRICIA McCORMICK, M.D.
72-23 Loubet St. Forest Hills, N.Y.
NAME Ronald Bogus AGE Adult
ADDRESS 245 W 74th St DATE 3/8/83
Rx
tetracycline 0.5g
#15
1 t.i.d.
Patricia McCormick

Prescription

pre·scrip·tive [pri·skrip′tiv] *adj.* Laying down rules, directions, or orders.

pres·ence [prez′əns] *n.* 1 The fact or condition of being present: Her *presence* made me happy. 2 The area directly around a person or thing: Do not talk in his *presence*. 3 The bearing or appearance of a person: a dignified *presence*. 4 Something invisible that is felt to be near.

presence of mind Full control of one's thoughts and actions, especially in an emergency.

pres·ent[1] [prez′ənt] 1 *adj.* Now existing or going on; not past or future: the *present* time; their *present* work. 2 *n.* The time now going on; the current time: For the *present*, I am acting as class secretary. 3 *adj.* Being in view or at hand; not absent: Is the whole class *present*? 4 *adj.* Now being discussed or considered: the *present* problem. 5 *n.* In grammar, the present tense or a verb form in this tense. 6 *adj.* Of, having to do with, or being the present tense or a verb form in this tense. **—at present** Now.

pre·sent[2] [*v.* pri·zent′, *n.* prez′ənt] 1 *v.* To give as a gift: I *present* this watch to you. 2 *v.* To give a gift to: Our friends *presented* us with the silver box. 3 *n.* A gift. 4 *v.* To cause to be known; introduce: May I *present* my parents? 5 *v.* To exhibit or show; display: to *present* a good appearance; to *present* a play. 6 *v.* To suggest to the mind: Snow *presents* a problem.

pre·sent·a·ble [pri·zen′tə·bəl] *adj.* 1 Fit to be presented, especially in regard to personal appearance. 2 Capable of being presented or expressed: a story that is *presentable* either as a play or as a motion picture.

pres·en·ta·tion [prez′ən·tā′shən *or* prē′zən·tā′shən] *n.* 1 The act of presenting, giving, or introducing. 2 The thing that is presented, as a play or a gift.

pres·ent-day [prez′ənt·dā′] *adj.* Of the present time; current: *present-day* events.

pre·sen·ti·ment [pri·zen′tə·mənt] *n.* A feeling that something is about to happen; premonition.

pres·ent·ly [prez′ənt·lē] *adv.* 1 Shortly; soon: Sheila will be here *presently*. 2 Now: Where are you working *presently*?

pre·sent·ment [pri·zent′mənt] *n.* 1 The act of presenting or showing. 2 Something presented.

present participle A participle that expresses present action or state of being.

present perfect tense The tense used to express action or a state of being completed at the time of speaking.

present tense The tense used to express action or a state of being in the present. *Am* in "I am here" is in the present tense.

pres·er·va·tion [prez′ər·vā′shən] *n.* 1 The act of preserving. 2 A being preserved.

pre·ser·va·tive [pri·zûr′və·tiv] 1 *adj.* Having the power or ability to preserve. 2 *n.* Something that preserves, especially a substance added to food to prevent spoiling.

pre·serve [pri·zûrv′] *v.* **pre·served, pre·serv·ing,** *n.* 1 *v.* To keep from danger or harm; watch over; protect: May Heaven *preserve* you. 2 *v.* To keep unchanged; maintain; keep up: to *preserve* appearances. 3 *v.* To prepare (food) for future use, as by salting or pickling. 4 *n.*(*usually pl.*) Fruit that has been cooked, usually with sugar. 5 *v.* To keep from spoiling or decaying: to *preserve* a specimen in alcohol. 6 *n.* An area set apart for the protection of something, as wildlife or forests. 7 *n.* Such an area kept for limited hunting or fishing. **—pre·serv′er** *n.*

pre·side [pri·zīd′] *v.* **pre·sid·ed, pre·sid·ing** 1 To be in authority, as over a meeting; act as chairman or president. 2 To have direction or control: to *preside* over a government.

pres·i·den·cy [prez′ə·dən·sē] *n., pl.* **pres·i·den·cies** 1 The office or duties of a president. 2 The time in office of a president.

pres·i·dent [prez′ə·dənt] *n.* 1 A person chosen to direct or control an organized body, as a business

P

a	add	**i**	it	**o͝o**	took	**oi**	oil
ā	ace	**ī**	ice	**o͞o**	pool	**ou**	pout
â	care	**o**	odd	**u**	up	**ng**	ring
ä	palm	**ō**	open	**û**	burn	**th**	thin
e	end	**ô**	order	**yo͞o**	fuse	**t͟h**	this
ē	equal					**zh**	vision

ə = a in *above*, e in *sicken*, i in *possible*, o in *melon*, u in *circus*

efit. **2** *v.* To be of advantage or benefit to: Quarrels *profit* no one. **3** *v.* To get an advantage; benefit: We *profited* from the sale of our old car. **4** *n.* (*often pl.*) The amount of money gained in a business transaction after deducting all expenses.

prof·it·a·ble [prof′it·ə·bəl] *adj.* Bringing profit or gain. **—prof′it·a·bly** *adv.*

prof·i·teer [prof′ə·tir′] **1** *n.* A person who makes an unfair profit by charging high prices for badly needed goods. **2** *v.* To make such profits.

prof·li·ga·cy [prof′lə·gə·sē] *n.* **1** Wild or immoral behavior. **2** Extravagance in spending money.

prof·li·gate [prof′lə·git] **1** *adj.* Without virtue or morals; wicked. **2** *adj.* Spending money wildly. **3** *n.* A person who is profligate.

pro·found [prə·found′] *adj.* **1** Showing deep or penetrating intellect or knowledge. **2** Deep; complete: *profound* sleep. **3** Thorough; sweeping: *profound* changes. **4** Intensely felt: *profound* love. **—pro·found′ly** *adv.*

pro·fun·di·ty [prə·fun′də·tē] *n., pl.* **pro·fun·di·ties** **1** The condition or quality of being profound. **2** Something profound, as a statement or idea.

pro·fuse [prə·fyo͞os′] *adj.* **1** Giving lavishly; liberal: *profuse* in their thanks. **2** Overflowing; abundant: *profuse* tears. **—pro·fuse′ly** *adv.* **—pro·fuse′ness** *n.*

pro·fu·sion [prə·fyo͞o′zhən] *n.* A large or abundant supply: a *profusion* of ornaments.

pro·gen·i·tor [prō·jen′ə·tər] *n.* An ancestor.

prog·e·ny [proj′ə·nē] *n.* Children; descendants.

prog·no·sis [prog·nō′sis] *n., pl.* **prog·no·ses** [prog·nō′sēz′] **1** A prediction about the future course of a disease and the patient's chances of recovery. **2** Any prediction; forecast.

prog·nos·tic [prog·nos′tik] **1** *adj.* Predicting or foretelling. **2** *n.* A sign of some future occurrence; omen.

prog·nos·ti·cate [prog·nos′tə·kāt′] *v.* **prog·nos·ti·cat·ed, prog·nos·ti·cat·ing** To foretell or predict. **—prog·nos′ti·ca′tion** *n.*

pro·gram [prō′gram′] *n., v.* **pro·gramed** or **pro·grammed, pro·gram·ing** or **pro·gram·ming** **1** *n.* A performance, entertainment, or ceremony, especially a scheduled performance on radio or television. **2** *v.* To include in a program. **3** *n.* A printed announcement or schedule of events, especially one for a theatrical performance. **4** *n.* Any course or plan arranged in advance: I have a good *program* in school. **5** *n.* In computer technology, a set of instructions, as for performing an operation or solving a problem. **6** *n.* Such instructions put into language used with a computer. **7** *v.* To provide (a computer) with a program.

pro·gramme [prō′gram′] *n. British* Program.

pro·gram·mer or **pro·gram·er** [prō′gram′ər] *n.* A person who prepares programs for a computer.

prog·ress [*n.* prog′res, *v.* prə·gres′] **1** *n.* A moving forward in space. **2** *v.* To move forward. **3** *n.* A gradual development; improvement: the *progress* of civilization. **4** *v.* To advance; develop; improve: to *progress* in one's studies. **—in progress** Currently taking place; going on.

pro·gres·sion [prə·gresh′ən] *n.* **1** A progressing; advancement. **2** A series or sequence, as of actions: A *progression* of jobs led to my present position. **3** A sequence of numbers in which every number is related to the ones after and before it by the same rule, as 3, 8, 13, and 18.

pro·gres·sive [prə·gres′iv] **1** *adj.* Moving forward; advancing: *progressive* stages of development. **2** *adj.* Spreading from one part to others; increasing: *progressive* paralysis. **3** *adj.* Working for or desiring progress or reform, especially in politics, education, and religion. **4** *n.* A person who believes in progress or reform. **5** *adj.* In grammar, indicating action or a state of being in progress. **—pro·gres′sive·ly** *adv.*

pro·hib·it [prō·hib′it] *v.* **1** To forbid, especially by authority or law: to *prohibit* parking. **2** To prevent or hinder: Icy roads *prohibited* us from driving.

pro·hi·bi·tion [prō′ə·bish′ən] *n.* **1** The act of prohibiting. **2** A law forbidding anything, especially the making and selling of alcoholic liquors. **3** (*written* **Prohibition**) The years from 1920 to 1933, when federal law prohibited the making and selling of alcoholic liquors. **—pro′hi·bi′tion·ist** *n.*

pro·hib·i·tive [prō·hib′ə·tiv] *adj.* Prohibiting; tending to prevent: The *prohibitive* cost of mink coats keeps many people from buying them.

proj·ect [*n.* proj′ekt, *v.* prə·jekt′] **1** *n.* Something thought of in the mind, as a course of action; plan. **2** *v.* To propose or plan. **3** *n.* A problem, task, or piece of work, as one given to a student or a group of students. **4** *v.* To extend forward or out; jut: Bay windows *project* from houses. **5** *v.* To throw forward, as a missile. **6** *v.* To cause (an image or shadow) to be visible on a surface: to *project* a slide on a screen.

pro·jec·tile [prə·jek′təl] **1** *adj.* Projecting or thrusting forward. **2** *n.* An object thrown or to be thrown by force, especially one fired from a cannon, gun, or other weapon.

pro·jec·tion [prə·jek′shən] *n.* **1** A projecting. **2** Something that projects or juts out. **3** A representation of the earth, another celestial body, or a part of it on a flat surface. **4** An estimate of a future figure or outcome, based on present information and trends.

pro·jec·tion·ist [prə·jek′shə·nist] *n.* A person who runs a movie, slide, or video projector.

pro·jec·tor [prə·jek′tər] *n.* A device for projecting slides or movies onto a screen.

Projector

pro·le·tar·i·an [prō′lə·târ′ē·ən] **1** *adj.* Of or having to do with the proletariat, or working class. **2** *n.* A member of the proletariat.

pro·le·tar·i·at [prō′lə·târ′ē·ət] *n.* The working class, especially those people who do manual labor or industrial work.

pro·lif·er·ate [prō·lif′ə·rāt′] *v.* **pro·lif·er·at·ed, pro·lif·er·at·ing** To increase or reproduce rapidly. **—pro·lif′er·a′tion** *n.*

pro·lif·ic [prō·lif′ik] *adj.* **1** Producing offspring or fruit abundantly. **2** Producing a great deal: a *prolific* writer. **—pro·lif′i·cal·ly** *adv.*

pro·lix [prō′liks′] *adj.* Too wordy; too long and boring. **—pro·lix′i·ty** *n.* **—pro·lix′ly** *adv.*

pro·logue or **pro·log** [prō′lôg′] *n.* **1** An introduction, as a preface to a book or a speech by one of the actors to an audience before a play begins. **2** Any introductory act or event.

pro·long [prə·lông′] *v.* To make longer in time or space; continue; lengthen: to *prolong* a meal.

pro·lon·ga·tion [prō′lông·gā′shən] *n.* **1** The act of prolonging. **2** Something added; extension: a week's *prolongation* of summer school.

prom [prom] *n. U.S. informal* A formal dance or ball at a school or college.

prom·e·nade [prom′ə·nād′ *or* prom′ə·näd′] *n., v.* **prom·e·nad·ed, prom·e·nad·ing** **1** *n.* A walk for amusement or exercise; stroll. **2** *v.* To take a promenade. **3** *n.* A place for promenading, as a boardwalk or deck of a ship. **4** *n.* A march, as at the beginning of a ball.

Pro·me·theus [prə·mē′thyo͞os′ *or* prə·mē′thē·əs] *n.* In Greek myths, the Titan who stole fire from heaven and gave it to human beings. He was chained to a rock by Zeus as a punishment.

pro·me·thi·um [prə·mē′thē·əm] *n.* A synthetic radioactive metallic element having the same chemical and physical properties as the elements found in rare earths. ◆ See RARE-EARTH ELEMENT.

prom·i·nence [prom′ə·nəns] *n.* **1** A being prominent: The mayor's *prominence* in the political world was very great. **2** Something prominent. **3** One of the tongues of flame that shoot out from the sun's surface, seen during a total eclipse.

prom·i·nent [prom′ə·nənt] *adj.* **1** Jutting out; projecting: *prominent* teeth. **2** Well-known; eminent: *prominent* in the community. **3** Easily seen; conspicuous: The radio tower was a *prominent* feature on the prairie. **—prom′i·nent·ly** *adv.*

prom·is·cu·i·ty [prom′is·kyo͞o′ə·tē] *n.* The quality of being promiscuous.

pro·mis·cu·ous [prə·mis′kyo͞o·əs] *adj.* **1** Mixed together without order: a *promiscuous* pile of papers. **2** Lacking any thought, purpose, or plan: a *promiscuous* taste in television programs. **3** Having sexual relations without careful choice. **—pro·mis′cu·ous·ly** *adv.*

prom·ise [prom′is] *n., v.* **prom·ised, prom·is·ing** **1** *n.* A positive statement made by one person to another about performing (or not performing) a certain act. **2** *v.* To make a promise: to *promise* that goods will be delivered. **3** *v.* To make a promise of: The store *promised* delivery next week. **4** *n.* Something that gives hope or expectation of future excellence or success: to show *promise* as an athlete. **5** *v.* To give reason for expecting: Clouds *promise* rain.

Promised Land In the Bible, Canaan, the land promised to Abraham by God. **2** (*written* **promised land**) Any place of expected happiness.

prom·is·ing [prom′is·ing] *adj.* Giving promise of good results or success: a *promising* student.

prom·is·so·ry [prom′ə·sôr′ē] *adj.* Containing or suggesting a promise.

promissory note A written promise to pay a sum of money at a given time or on demand.

prom·on·to·ry [prom′ən·tôr′ē] *n., pl.* **prom·on·to·ries** A high point of land sticking out into the sea; headland.

pro·mote [prə·mōt′] *v.* **pro·mot·ed, pro·mot·ing** **1** To contribute to the progress, development, or growth of; work for: to *promote* good health. **2** To advance to a higher position, grade, or honor: The students were *promoted* from the third grade to the fourth. **3** To try to make popular, as by advertising.

pro·mot·er [prə·mō′tər] *n.* **1** A person or thing that promotes. **2** A person who tries to make a business successful, as by raising money for it, selling its products, and advertising.

pro·mo·tion [prə·mō′shən] *n.* **1** Advancement in rank or grade. **2** Encouragement; advancement: *promotion* of a good cause.

prompt [prompt] **1** *adj.* Ready; quick; on time; punctual: *prompt* to obey. **2** *adj.* Done quickly: *prompt* service. **3** *v.* To urge; stir up; incite: The insult *prompted* them to fight. **4** *v.* To suggest; inspire: Fog *prompts* gloom. **5** *v.* To act as a prompter to: to *prompt* an actor. **—prompt′ly** *adv.* **—prompt′ness** *n.*

prompt·er [promp′tər] *n.* In a theater, a person who reminds the actors of their lines when they forget them.

promp·ti·tude [promp′tə·t(y)o͞od′] *n.* Promptness; liveliness; readiness.

pro·mul·gate [prō·mul′gāt′ *or* prom′əl·gāt′] *v.* **pro·mul·gat·ed, pro·mul·gat·ing** To make known officially; put into effect by public announcement: to *promulgate* a new law. **—pro′mul·ga′tion** *n.*

pron. **1** pronoun. **2** pronunciation.

prone [prōn] *adj.* **1** Lying flat, especially with the face downward. **2** Given or inclined; disposed: He is *prone* to accidents. **—prone′ness** *n.*

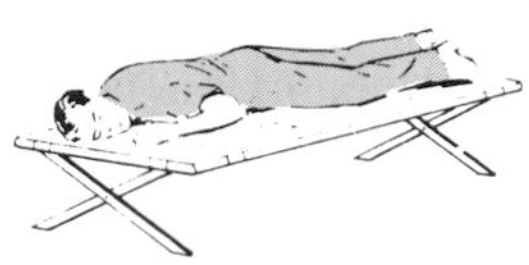

Prone position

prong [prông *or* prong] *n.* **1** A pointed end of an instrument, as the tine of a fork. **2** Any pointed part that projects, as on a deer's antler.

pronged [prôngd *or* prongd] *adj.* Having prongs.

prong·horn [prông′hôrn′ *or* prong′hôrn′] *n., pl.* **prong·horns** or **prong·horn** An animal like the antelope, found in western North America.

Pronghorn

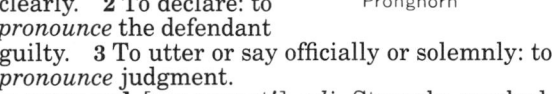

pro·noun [prō′noun′] *n.* A word that takes the place of a noun or nouns or of a noun equivalent.

pro·nounce [prə·nouns′] *v.* **pro·nounced, pro·nounc·ing** **1** To make the sound or sounds of: to *pronounce* a word clearly. **2** To declare: to *pronounce* the defendant guilty. **3** To utter or say officially or solemnly: to *pronounce* judgment.

pro·nounced [prə·nounst′] *adj.* Strongly marked; quite noticeable; decided: to talk with a *pronounced* lisp.

pro·nounce·ment [prə·nouns′mənt] *n.* A formal declaration or announcement.

pron·to [pron′tō] *adv. informal* Right away; quickly.

pro·nun·ci·a·tion [prə·nun′sē·ā′shən] *n.* The act or

a	add	**i**	it	**o͝o**	took	**oi**	oil
ā	ace	**ī**	ice	**o͞o**	pool	**ou**	pout
â	care	**o**	odd	**u**	up	**ng**	ring
ä	palm	**ō**	open	**û**	burn	**th**	thin
e	end	**ô**	order	**yo͞o**	fuse	**t͟h**	this
ē	equal					**zh**	vision

ə = { a in *above* e in *sicken* i in *possible* / o in *melon* u in *circus* }

P

folds or wrinkles: to *pucker* the lips. **2** *n.* A wrinkle or small fold.

puck·ish [puk′ish] *adj.* Having a mischievous, impish quality.

pud·ding [po͝od′ing] *n.* A sweetened and flavored dessert of soft food, usually made of such ingredients as milk, fruit, and eggs.

pud·dle [pud′(ə)l] *n., v.* **pud·dled, pud·dling** **1** *n.* A small pool of liquid, especially dirty water. **2** *v.* To make muddy or dirty. **3** *n.* A thick mixture of clay, sand, and water, used to seal cracks and make surfaces waterproof. **4** *v.* To mix (clay, sand, and water) so as to form such a mixture. **5** *v.* To convert (pig iron) into wrought iron by melting and stirring in the presence of oxidizing substances.

pudg·y [puj′ē] *adj.* **pudg·i·er, pudg·i·est** Short and fat; dumpy; chubby: a *pudgy* child. **—pudg′i·ness** *n.*

pueb·lo [pweb′lō] *n., pl.* **pueb·los** or **pueb·lo** **1** An adobe or stone building or group of buildings of the Indians of the SW U.S. **2** (*written* **Pueblo**) A member of one of the Indian tribes that live in such buildings. ◆ *Pueblo* comes directly from the Spanish word for *village,* which goes back to a Latin word meaning *people.*

Pueblo

pu·er·ile [pyo͞or′il] *adj.* Childish; immature; silly: a *puerile* remark.

Puer·to Ri·can [pwer′tō rē′kən *or* pôr′tə rē′kən] **1** Of or from Puerto Rico. **2** A person born or living in Puerto Rico.

puff [puf] **1** *n.* A sudden, short gust of breath, wind, smoke, or steam. **2** *v.* To breathe heavily; be out of breath: The runners were *puffing* after the race. **3** *v.* To blow in puffs, as the wind. **4** *v.* To send out puffs, as of steam or smoke, usually while moving or acting: The locomotive *puffed* across the plains. **5** *v.* To smoke (a cigar, cigarette, or pipe) with puffs. **6** *v.* To swell or cause to swell: The wet shirts *puffed* out in the wind; to *puff* out one's chest with pride. **7** *n.* A slight swelling. **8** *n.* A light, hollow piece of pastry, usually filled with custard or whipped cream. **9** *n.* A loose roll of hair, as in a hairdo. **10** *v.* To arrange something, as hair, in puffs. **11** *n.* A powder puff. **12** *n.* A quilted bed covering. **13** *n.* A notice or review praising a person or thing. **14** *v.* To praise or advertise highly or too highly.

puff·ball [puf′bôl′] *n.* A rounded fungus which, when ripe, bursts at a touch and sprays out a cloud of spores like brown powder.

puff·er [puf′ər] *n.* **1** A person or thing that puffs. **2** Any of several fish that can expand their bodies with water or air.

puf·fin [puf′in] *n.* A sea bird of northern regions, having a stubby, ducklike body, black and white plumage, and a thin, brightly colored, triangular bill.

Puffin

puff·y [puf′ē] *adj.* **puff·i·er, puff·i·est** **1** Swollen; bloated: *puffy* fingers. **2** Lightly rounded or filled, as with air: *puffy* sleeves. **3** Coming in puffs: *puffy* breathing. **4** Vain; showy: a *puffy* person. **—puff′i·ly** *adv.* **—puff′i·ness** *n.*

pug [pug] *n.* A type of dog having a short, square body, a tightly curled tail, and a flat, upturned nose.

Pug

pu·gi·lism [pyo͞o′jə·liz′əm] *n.* The activity or sport of boxing. **—pu′gi·list** *n.* **—pu′gi·lis′tic** *adj.*

pug·na·cious [pug·nā′·shəs] *adj.* Fond of fighting; quarrelsome. **—pug·na′cious·ly** *adv.*

pug·nac·i·ty [pug·nas′ə·tē] *n.* Fondness for fighting; inclination to fight.

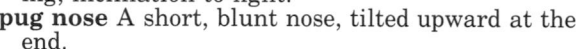

pug nose A short, blunt nose, tilted upward at the end.

puis·sance [pwis′əns *or* pyo͞o′ə·səns *or* pyo͞o·is′əns] *n.* Power; might; force. **—puis′sant** *adj.* **—puis′·sant·ly** *adv.*

puke [pyo͞ok] *v.* **puked, puk·ing,** *n. slang* **1** *v.* To vomit. **2** *n.* Vomit.

pul·chri·tude [pul′krə·t(y)o͞od′] *n.* Beauty, especially physical beauty; loveliness.

pule [pyo͞ol] *v.* **puled, pul·ing** To whimper as a small child does; whine.

pull [po͝ol] **1** *v.* To apply force to (a person or thing) so as to bring it closer to or in the direction of the person or thing exerting the force: to *pull* a fish out of water; to *pull* the curtains shut; to *pull* a wagon. **2** *n.* The act or an instance of pulling: The trainer gave a *pull* at the dog's leash. **3** *n.* The effort exerted in pulling: a hard *pull.* **4** *n.* Something used in pulling, as the handle on a dresser drawer. **5** *v.* To be capable of moving when pulled: This cart *pulls* easily. **6** *v.* To draw from a fixed place, often with a tool: to *pull* a cork out of a bottle; to *pull* a tooth. **7** *v.* To strain so as to cause injury: to *pull* a tendon. **8** *v.* To draw, rip, or tear apart: The baby *pulled* the magazine to pieces. **9** *v.* To move; go: We *pulled* over to the side of the road for our picnic. **10** *v.* To row: to *pull* for shore. **11** *v. slang* To do; carry out: to *pull* a practical joke. **12** *n. slang* Help or influence: to get a job through *pull.* **13** *v. slang* To draw out so as to use: to *pull* a knife. **—pull for** *informal* To hope or work for the success of: to *pull for* the home team. **—pull in** **1** To restrain. **2** *informal* To arrive. **—pull off** *informal* To succeed in doing. **—pull oneself together** To get back one's self-control. **—pull out** To leave; go away: We *pulled out* for the mountains at dawn. **—pull over** To stop one's vehicle at the roadside. **—pull through** *informal* To manage to get through a dangerous situation, illness, or other difficulty. **—pull up** **1** To come to a halt: The car *pulled up* at our doorstep. **2** To move ahead: *Pull up* to the gas pump. **3** To remove by or as if by the roots: to *pull up* weeds. **—pull up with** To come to a position even with. **—pull′er** *n.*

pull·back [po͝ol′bak′] *n.* A pulling back, especially a planned withdrawal of military troops from an area.

pull date A date that a company stamps on the container of a perishable item to show when it should be removed from sale.

pul·let [po͝ol′it] *n.* A young hen, especially in its first year.

pul·ley [pŏŏl'ē] *n., pl.* **pul·leys** A small wheel with a grooved rim over which is passed a rope or chain that moves freely with the turning of the wheel.

A pulley

Pull·man [pŏŏl'mən] *n.* A railroad car having small, private compartments that can be converted into sleeping quarters: a trademark. Also **Pullman car.**

pull·out [pŏŏl'out'] *n.* **1** A section, as of a magazine, that is meant to be pulled out or removed. **2** A withdrawal: a troop *pullout.*

pull·o·ver [pŏŏl'ō'vər] *n.* A garment that is put on by being drawn over the head, as certain sweaters or shirts.

pul·mo·na·ry [pŏŏl'mə·ner'ē *or* pul'mə·ner'ē] *adj.* Of, having to do with, or affecting the lungs: the *pulmonary* artery; *pulmonary* tuberculosis.

pulp [pulp] **1** *n.* The soft, usually edible part of certain fruits or vegetables. **2** *n.* A wet mixture of wood fibers or rags from which paper is manufactured. **3** *v.* To make into or become pulp. **4** *n.* The soft inner part of a tooth containing blood vessels and nerves.

pul·pit [pŏŏl'pit] *n.* **1** A raised platform or desk for a preacher in a church. **2** The work or profession of preaching.

Pulpit

pulp·wood [pulp'·wŏŏd'] *n.* The soft wood of certain trees, used in making paper.

pulp·y [pul'pē] *adj.* **pulp·i·er, pulp·i·est 1** Of or like pulp. **2** Soft and juicy.

pul·sar [pul'sär'] *n.* A celestial body that sends pulses of radio waves at rapid, regular intervals.

pul·sate [pul'sāt'] *v.* **pul·sat·ed, pul·sat·ing 1** To throb or beat rhythmically, as the pulse or heart does. **2** To vibrate; quiver. **—pul·sa'tion** *n.*

pulse¹ [puls] *n., v.* **pulsed, puls·ing 1** *n.* The rhythmical beating of the arteries resulting from the contractions of the heart, especially as felt in the artery at the wrist. **2** *n.* Any regular throbbing or beat. **3** *n.* A short burst, as of electricity, a radio wave, or light. Pulses are used in communications, radar, and computers. **4** *v.* To pulsate; throb.

pulse² [puls] *n.* **1** Plants such as peas and beans. **2** Their edible seeds.

pul·ver·ize [pul'və·rīz'] *v.* **pul·ver·ized, pul·ver·iz·ing 1** To make into powder or dust, as by crushing. **2** To become dust. **3** To demolish; destroy: The blast *pulverized* the wall.

pu·ma [pyōō'mə] *n.* Another name for COUGAR.

pum·ice [pum'is] *n.* Volcanic lava that has hardened on cooling into a spongy, very light rock. It is used, in solid or powdered form, for smoothing, polishing, or cleaning.

pum·mel [pum'əl] *v.* **pum·meled** or **pum·melled, pum·mel·ing** or **pum·mel·ling,** *n.* To beat with the fists.

pump¹ [pump] **1** *n.* A mechanical device for raising, circulating, or compressing liquids or gases by drawing or forcing them through pipes: a gasoline *pump*; a water *pump.* **2** *v.* To raise or move (something) with a pump: to *pump* water. **3** *v.* To inflate with air by means of a pump: to *pump* up an air mattress. **4** *v.* To remove something, as water, from: to *pump* a flooded ditch dry. **5** *v.* To move or force with a pumping action: The heart *pumps* blood. **6** *v.* To move up and down like a pump or pump handle: The candidate *pumped* my hand. **7** *v.* To get information from by asking many questions: to *pump* a witness. **8** *v.* To get something, as information, by such a method: We *pumped* the true story out of the witness.

pump² [pump] *n.* A low-cut shoe without laces or fastenings and having either a high or low heel.

pum·per·nick·el [pum'pər·nik'əl] *n.* A coarse, sour, dark bread made from unsifted rye.

pump·kin [pump'kin *or* pung'kin] *n.* A large, round, yellow-orange fruit that grows on a trailing vine. Its pulp is often used in a pie filling.

pun [pun] *n., v.* **punned, pun·ning 1** *n.* The humorous use of two or more words having the same or similar sounds, but different meanings, as in "When the bear lost its fur, it was all bare." **2** *v.* To make puns.

punch¹ [punch] **1** *v.* To strike sharply, especially with the fists. **2** *n.* A swift blow or poke; jab. **3** *v.* To herd (cattle).

punch² [punch] **1** *n.* A machine used to stamp and cut a design, especially on a piece of metal. **2** *v.* To cut, perforate, or make with a punch: to *punch* holes in metal; to *punch* a card.

punch³ [punch] *n.* A hot or cold drink made of various mixtures of beverages, such as fruit juices, soft drinks, alcoholic liquors, or milk.

Punch [punch] *n.* A quarrelsome, hook-nosed puppet who is the hero of a comic puppet show, **Punch and Judy.** He always fights with Judy, his wife. **—pleased as Punch** Very pleased; very happy.

Punch and Judy

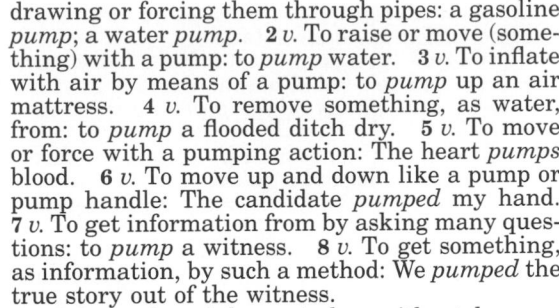

punch card A card in which holes are punched for use with data processing equipment.

pun·cheon¹ [pun'chən] *n.* A large barrel for liquor, holding from 72 to 120 gallons.

pun·cheon² [pun'chən] *n.* **1** A tool for piercing, stamping, or punching. **2** A piece of roughly finished timber with one flat side.

punching bag A stuffed or inflated bag hung so that it can be punched for exercise or boxing practice.

punch line The last line of a joke or funny story, carrying the humor or meaning.

punch·y [pun'chē] *adj.* **punch·i·er, punch·i·est** Dazed, groggy, or confused, as from having received too many head blows in boxing.

punc·til·i·o [pungk·til'ē·ō'] *n., pl.* **punc·til·i·os 1** A

a	add	**i**	it	**ŏŏ**	took	**oi**	oil
ā	ace	**ī**	ice	**ōō**	pool	**ou**	pout
â	care	**o**	odd	**u**	up	**ng**	ring
ä	palm	**ō**	open	**û**	burn	**th**	thin
e	end	**ô**	order	**yōō**	fuse	**t͟h**	this
ē	equal					**zh**	vision

ə = { a in *above* e in *sicken* i in *possible* / o in *melon* u in *circus* }

fine point of proper behavior or etiquette. 2 Careful attention to minor details.

punc·til·i·ous [pungk·til′ē·əs] *adj.* 1 Very careful or exact in one's social manners and behavior. 2 Careful and painstaking: *punctilious* scientific analysis.

punc·tu·al [pungk′cho͞o·əl] *adj.* Acting, finished, or arriving on time: to be *punctual* with homework. **—punc·tu·al·i·ty** [pungk′cho͞o·al′ə·tē] *n.* **—punc′tu·al·ly** *adv.*

punc·tu·ate [pungk′cho͞o·āt′] *v.* **punc·tu·at·ed, punc·tu·at·ing** 1 To divide or mark with punctuation marks: *Punctuate* this sentence. 2 To interrupt from time to time: The speech was *punctuated* with many stale jokes.

punc·tu·a·tion [pungk′cho͞o·ā′shən] *n.* 1 The use of punctuation marks to make clearer the meaning of written or printed matter. 2 Punctuation marks.

punctuation mark Any of the various marks used in printed or written matter to clarify the meaning, as the period, comma, question mark, semicolon, colon, exclamation mark, and dash.

punc·ture [pungk′chər] *v.* **punc·tured, punc·tur·ing,** *n.* 1 *v.* To pierce or become pierced with or as if with a sharp point: to *puncture* the skin with a needle; The tire *punctured* a mile from home. 2 *n.* A hole made by piercing with or as if with a sharp point. 3 *v.* To make useless; destroy: to *puncture* a person's self-respect.

pun·dit [pun′dit] *n.* A respected authority whose opinions are widely read or listened to.

pun·gen·cy [pun′jən·sē] *n.* The condition or quality of being pungent.

pun·gent [pun′jənt] *adj.* 1 Sharp or piercing to the taste or smell: *pungent* mustard. 2 Keen and sharp to the mind, often painfully so; biting: The comedian has a *pungent* sense of humor. **—pun′·gent·ly** *adv.*

pun·ish [pun′ish] *v.* 1 To cause to undergo a penalty, as pain, discomfort, or imprisonment, for a crime or wrongdoing. 2 To inflict a penalty for: to *punish* traffic violations. 3 To inflict punishment: A tyrant *punishes* for the least fault. 4 *informal* To cause discomfort or injury to: The hot sun *punished* us.

pun·ish·a·ble [pun′ish·ə·bəl] *adj.* Deserving of or liable to punishment.

pun·ish·ment [pun′ish·mənt] *n.* 1 The act of punishing. 2 The penalty given for a crime or wrongdoing: The student's *punishment* was to rewrite the report. 3 *informal* Rough handling, as in a boxing match.

pu·ni·tive [pyo͞o′nə·tiv] *adj.* Having to do with or inflicting punishment: *punitive* laws.

punk¹ [pungk] *n.* 1 A dry, often spongy substance that burns slowly, used to light firecrackers. 2 Decayed wood used as tinder to light fires.

punk² [pungk] *slang* 1 *n.* A hoodlum. 2 *n.* A young, inexperienced person. 3 *adj.* Worthless; poor: a *punk* story. 4 *adj.* Not in good health; unwell: I feel *punk.* 5 *n. slang* A person who adopts a style of rough and outlandish dress, hair style, and makeup. 6 *adj. slang* Of or in such a style of dress.

punk rock Rock music played in a hard, driving style, often with angry or deliberately offensive lyrics.

pun·ster [pun′stər] *n.* A person who enjoys making puns.

punt¹ [punt] 1 *n.* In football, a kick made by dropping the ball from the hands and kicking it before it touches the ground. 2 *v.* In football, to propel (the ball) with a punt. **—punt′er** *n.*

punt² [punt] 1 *n.* A flat-bottomed boat with square ends. 2 *v.* To propel (a boat) by pushing with a pole against the bottom of a lake, stream, or other body of water. **—punt′er** *n.*

Punt

pu·ny [pyo͞o′nē] *adj.* **pu·ni·er, pu·ni·est** Small and feeble; weak and insignificant: a *puny* kitten.

◆ *Puny* comes from an Old French word *puisne,* meaning *younger* or *junior,* and that is what it originally meant in English. The meanings of *small* and *weak* came later.

pup [pup] *n.* 1 A young dog; puppy. 2 A young seal or shark or any of the young of certain other animals.

pu·pa [pyo͞o′pə] *n., pl.* **pu·pas** or **pu·pae** [pyo͞o′pē] 1 The stage in the development of an insect between the larva and the adult. 2 An insect in this stage. **—pu′pal** *adj.*

pu·pate [pyo͞o′pāt′] *v.* **pu·pat·ed, pu·pat·ing** To become or pass through the stage of being a pupa. **—pu·pa′tion** *n.*

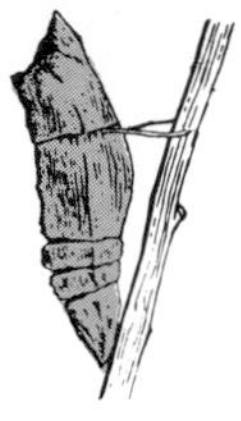
Pupa

pu·pil¹ [pyo͞o′pəl] *n.* The dark, central opening of the eye through which light is admitted to the retina. The pupil expands and contracts to let in more or less light.

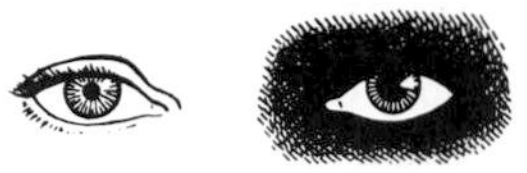
The pupil dilates in the dark.

pu·pil² [pyo͞o′pəl] *n.* A person of any age who is being instructed by a teacher; student.

pup·pet [pup′it] *n.* 1 A small figure of a person or animal, usually with a cloth body and a solid head, fitting over and moved by the hand. 2 A small figure or doll whose jointed limbs, head, and body are attached to and moved by wires or strings; marionette. 3 A person without much will power who is told what to do or say by others.

pup·pet·eer [pup′ə·tēr′] *n.* A person who operates puppets in a puppet show.

pup·pet·ry [pup′ə·trē] *n., pl.* **pup·pet·ries** The art of making and operating puppets.

puppet show A play acted with puppets.

pup·py [pup′ē] *n., pl.* **pup·pies** 1 A young dog; pup. 2 A conceited, silly young person.

pup tent A small tent, large enough for two adults, usually constructed by fastening two or more sections together.

pur·blind [pûr′blīnd′] *adj.* 1 Almost blind. 2 Slow to understand or see.

pur·chase [pûr′chəs] *v.* **pur·chased, pur·chas·ing,** *n.* 1 *v.* To get by paying money; buy: to *purchase* a suit. 2 *n.* Anything that is bought with money: We made many *purchases.* 3 *n.* The act of purchasing: the *purchase* of groceries. 4 *v.* To get as a result of great effort or sacrifice: The company's success was *purchased* by hard work. 5 *n.* A device, as a tackle or lever, that helps a person to lift or move something. 6 *v.* To use such a device to move or lift (heavy objects). 7 *n.* A firm grasp when moving heavy objects. **—pur′chas·er** *n.*

pur·dah [pûr′də] *n.* 1 A screen or curtain used in India to keep women from being seen by men or strangers. 2 The custom of secluding women in this way.

pure [pyŏŏr] *adj.* **pur·er, pur·est** 1 Not mixed with other substances: *pure* silk. 2 Free from germs or anything unhealthful: *pure* milk; *pure* air. 3 Morally clean; innocent; good: a *pure* life. 4 Nothing but; absolute; sheer: *pure* foolishness. 5 Directed toward or dealing with theory or research more than with practical uses or applications: *pure* science. **—pure′ness** *n.*

pure·bred [pyŏŏr′bred′] 1 *adj.* Having all ancestors for many generations of the same breed or kind: a *purebred* collie. 2 *n.* A purebred animal.

pu·rée [pyŏŏ·rā′] *n., v.* **pu·réed, pu·rée·ing** 1 *n.* A thick paste made by forcing food boiled to pulp through a sieve. 2 *n.* A thick soup made with such paste. 3 *v.* To make a purée of.

pure·ly [pyŏŏr′lē] *adv.* 1 Without anything harmful or strange: to speak a language *purely.* 2 Innocently; virtuously: to live *purely.* 3 Completely; totally: It is *purely* your decision. 4 Merely; simply: It was done *purely* for fun.

pur·ga·tive [pûr′gə·tiv] 1 *adj.* Cleansing; purifying: This medicine has a *purgative* effect. 2 *n.* A medicine that causes the bowels to move.

pur·ga·to·ri·al [pûr′gə·tôr′ē·əl] *adj.* 1 Serving to cleanse of sin. 2 Of or like purgatory.

pur·ga·to·ry [pûr′gə·tôr′ē] *n., pl.* **pur·ga·to·ries** 1 In Roman Catholic belief, a place where the souls of those who have committed minor sins are made fit for paradise by being punished for a time. 2 Any condition of misery or suffering.

purge [pûrj] *v.* **purged, purg·ing,** *n.* 1 *v.* To remove what is impure or harmful from; make clean. 2 *v.* To rid of guilt, sin, or defilement. 3 *v.* To cause (the bowels) to empty thoroughly by means of a medicine. 4 *n.* A medicine that empties the bowels; cathartic. 5 *v.* To rid of members considered undesirable or disloyal. 6 *n.* The act of purging.

pu·ri·fy [pyŏŏr′ə·fī′] *v.* **pu·ri·fied, pu·ri·fy·ing** To make or become pure or clean: Thunderstorms *purify* the air; The smoky air soon *purified.* **—pu′·ri·fi·ca′tion** *n.*

Pu·rim [pŏŏr′im] *n.* A Jewish festival celebrated in early spring. It commemorates Queen Esther's success in rescuing ancient Jews from a plot to massacre them.

pu·rine [pyŏŏr′ēn′] *n.* 1 A colorless, crystalline chemical base. 2 Any of several organic compounds that have similar molecular structures, such as caffeine.

pur·ist [pyŏŏr′ist] *n.* A person who is extremely particular or fussy about things, as correctness of language, matters of style, or the following of certain rules.

Pu·ri·tan [pyŏŏr′ə·tən] *n.* 1 One of a group of Protestants of England and the American colonies who, in the 16th and 17th centuries, wanted stricter moral laws and simpler services in the Church of England. 2 (*written* **puritan**) A person who leads a very strict moral or religious life.

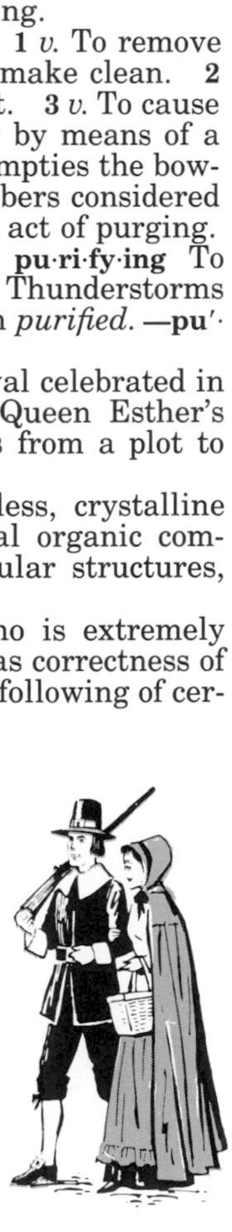
Puritans

pu·ri·tan·ic [pyŏŏr′ə·tan′ik] *adj.* Puritanical.

pu·ri·tan·i·cal [pyŏŏr′ə·tan′i·kəl] *adj.* 1 Strict in religion and morals. 2 (*sometimes written* **Puritanical**) Of or having to do with the Puritans.

pu·ri·tan·ism [pyŏŏr′ə·tən·iz′əm] *n.* 1 Strictness in moral and religious life. 2 (*sometimes written* **Puritanism**) The beliefs and practices of the Puritans.

pu·ri·ty [pyŏŏr′ə·tē] *n.* The quality or condition of being pure.

purl[1] [pûrl] *v.* In knitting, to make a stitch backward, usually so as to make a rib in the fabric.

purl[2] [pûrl] 1 *v.* To flow with a bubbling, murmuring sound, as a brook. 2 *v.* To flow in a swirling or circling motion. 3 *n.* The sound or movement of bubbling or swirling water.

pur·lieu [pûr′l(y)ōō] *n.* (*usually pl.*) The outlying parts or outskirts: the *purlieus* of a large town.

pur·loin [pər·loin′] *v.* To steal; filch.

pur·ple [pûr′pəl] *n., v.* **pur·pled, pur·pling** 1 *n.* A color that is a mixture of red and blue. 2 *adj.* Of or having this color. 3 *n.* Deep red robes formerly worn by monarchs and other persons of high rank. 4 *n.* Royal power or high rank, usually in the phrase **born to the purple.**

Purple Heart A decoration given to members of the U.S. armed services who have been wounded in action against an enemy.

pur·plish [pûr′plish] *adj.* Somewhat purple.

pur·port [*v.* pər·pôrt′, *n.* pûr′pôrt′] 1 *v.* To mean or intend: What does the speech *purport?* 2 *v.* To claim: The newspaper *purports* to give all the facts. 3 *n.* The meaning or substance of something: What is the *purport* of that remark?

pur·pose [pûr′pəs] *n., v.* **pur·posed, pur·pos·ing** 1 *n.* What one intends or wants to accomplish; plan; aim: What is the *purpose* of your visit? 2 *v.* To intend: aim: seldom used today. 3 *n.* Result or effect: It was all done to no *purpose.* 4 *n.* The reason for which a thing exists; use: What is the *purpose* of the cleats on baseball shoes? 5 *n.* Determination; resolve: She has always been a person of *purpose.* **—on purpose** Intentionally; deliberately: I'm afraid the records were lost *on purpose.* **—to good purpose** With a good result or effect. ◆ See REASON.

pur·pose·ful [pûr′pəs·fəl] *adj.* 1 Done or acting on purpose; intentional. 2 Full of purpose or determination. **—pur′pose·ful·ly** *adv.* **—pur′pose·ful·ness** *n.*

pur·pose·less [pûr′pəs·lis] *adj.* Having no definite purpose; aimless or meaningless.

pur·pose·ly [pûr′pəs·lē] *adv.* For a purpose; intentionally; on purpose.

purr [pûr] 1 *n.* A murmuring sound, such as a cat makes when pleased. 2 *v.* To make this sound.

purse [pûrs] *n., v.* **pursed, purs·ing** 1 *n.* A small bag or pouch for carrying money. 2 *n.* A larger bag used to hold money, cosmetics, and other small articles; handbag. 3 *n.* A sum of money, used as a gift or prize. 4 *v.* To draw into wrinkles; pucker, as the lips.

a	add	**i**	it	**ŏŏ**	took	**oi**	oil
ā	ace	**ī**	ice	**ōō**	pool	**ou**	pout
â	care	**o**	odd	**u**	up	**ng**	ring
ä	palm	**ō**	open	**û**	burn	**th**	thin
e	end	**ô**	order	**yōō**	fuse	**t͟h**	this
ē	equal					**zh**	vision

ə = a in *above*, e in *sicken*, i in *possible*, o in *melon*, u in *circus*

P

purs·er [pûr′sər] *n.* An officer on a ship who keeps financial accounts and acts as a cashier.
purs·lane [pûrs′lin *or* pûrs′lān′] *n.* A common garden plant with a reddish stem and leaves and small yellow flowers, sometimes used in salads.
pur·su·ance [pər·s(y)ōō′əns] *n.* The act of pursuing or carrying out, especially in the expression **in pursuance of**: *In pursuance of* the orders, the class remained seated.
pur·su·ant [pər·s(y)ōō′ənt] *adj.* Done in accordance with; following; carrying out. **—pursuant to** In accordance with; following.
pur·sue [pər·s(y)ōō′] *v.* **pur·sued, pur·su·ing** 1 To follow in an attempt to overtake or capture; chase: to *pursue* a speeding car. 2 To proceed with; keep on with: to *pursue* a career; to *pursue* a hobby; to *pursue* an interesting topic of conversation. 3 To try to get; seek to obtain: to *pursue* happiness. 4 To bother; annoy: Poor health *pursued* him all his life. **—pur·su′er** *n.*
pur·suit [pər·s(y)ōōt′] *n.* 1 The act of pursuing; chase. 2 Something that is regularly done or followed, as a profession, hobby, or sport.
pur·vey [pər·vā′] *v.* To furnish (supplies); provide: Dairies *purvey* milk, cheese, and butter. **—pur·vey′or** *n.*
pur·vey·ance [pər·vā′əns] *n.* 1 The act of purveying. 2 Something purveyed, as food supplies.
pus [pus] *n.* A thick, yellowish matter discharged from infected tissues, as wounds or boils. **—pus·sy** [pus′ē] *adj.*
push [pŏŏsh] 1 *v.* To exert force against (an object) in order to move it: to *push* a stalled car; You *push*, and I'll pull. 2 *n.* An act of pushing: She gave the sled a *push.* 3 *v.* To make (a passage) by force: The explorers *pushed* their way through the jungle. 4 *v.* To urge or force to do something: The new teacher didn't *push* the students to study. 5 *v.* To stick out or project: The point *pushed* far out into the sea. 6 *v.* To exert great effort: We all *pushed* for more pay. 7 *v.* To advocate or promote vigorously: to *push* a new product. 8 *n. informal* Great energy and determination; drive: This employee has no *push.* **—push around** To treat in a rough or belittling way.
push-but·ton [pŏŏsh′but′ən] *adj.* Controlled or operated by or as if by a push button.
push button A small button that is used to operate an electrical device.
push·cart [pŏŏsh′kärt′] *n.* A small cart that is pushed by hand, especially one from which goods are sold in the streets.
push·er [pŏŏsh′ər] *n.* 1 A person or thing that pushes. 2 *slang* A person who sells illegal drugs.
push·o·ver [pŏŏsh′ō′vər] *n. slang* 1 Anything that can be done with little or no effort. 2 A person who is easily taken advantage of or beaten.
push-up [pŏŏsh′up′] *n.* An exercise in which one lies face down on the floor and pushes one's body up with the arms until it is supported only on the hands and toes.
push·y [pŏŏsh′ē] *adj.* **push·i·er, push·i·est** Aggressive or bold in an annoying way; forward.
pu·sil·lan·i·mous [pyōō′sə·lan′ə·məs] *adj.* Not courageous; fainthearted; timid.
puss[1] [pŏŏs] *n. informal* A cat or kitten.
puss[2] [pŏŏs] *n. slang* 1 The face. 2 The mouth.
pus·sy [pŏŏs′ē] *n., pl.* **pus·sies** 1 A cat or kitten. 2 A silky catkin, as of a willow.
puss·y·foot [pŏŏs′ē·fŏŏt′] *v.* 1 To avoid taking a clear and definite position. 2 To move quietly and cautiously.
pussy willow A small American willow that has silky catkins in the early spring.

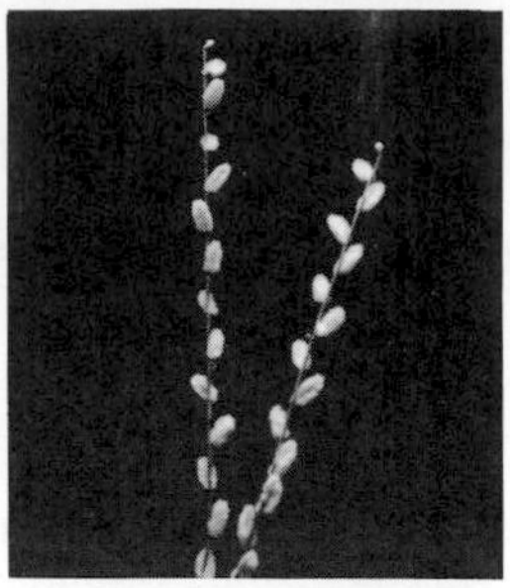
Pussy willows

pus·tule [pus′chōōl′] *n.* 1 A small bump on the skin that is filled with pus; pimple. 2 Any small swelling resembling a blister or pimple.
put [pŏŏt] *v.* **put, put·ting** 1 To set, lay, or place in a given spot or position: to *put* a saddle on a horse; to *put* knives and forks on the table. 2 To bring to a certain condition or action: The music *put* us in a better mood; They *put* us to work. 3 To express in words; state: Try to *put* your questions more clearly. 4 To assign or impose: to *put* a tax on leather goods; to *put* a high value on one's reputation. 5 To estimate: I *put* the time at about 5 o'clock. 6 To bring to bear; apply: *Put* your mind on your lesson. 7 To give or submit, as for debate or answering: to *put* a question to the class. 8 To move or go: The ship *put* out to sea. 9 To throw with a pushing movement of the arm and shoulder: He *put* the shot 10 meters. **—put about** To change the direction of (a ship or boat). **—put across** *slang* To cause to be understood or received favorably: This journalist is able to *put across* new ideas. **—put aside** 1 To save for later. 2 To discard. **—put away** 1 To save for later. 2 *informal* To eat or drink. 3 To give up; abandon. 4 *informal* To kill or have killed. 5 *informal* To put into an institution. **—put by** To save for future use: The employees *put by* part of their salary each week. **—put down** 1 To write down; record. 2 To repress; put an end to, as an uprising. 3 *informal* To criticize or belittle. **—put forth** To grow, as shoots or buds. **—put forward** To offer. **—put in** 1 To enter a harbor or place of shelter. 2 To spend, as time: to *put in* a Sunday afternoon playing tennis. **—put off** 1 To delay; postpone. 2 To get rid of or avoid, often by excuses: to *put off* a caller. **—put on** 1 To pretend. 2 To don, as clothing. 3 To present, as a play or entertainment. 4 To turn on, as a light. **—put out** 1 To extinguish, as a fire. 2 To cause to leave; eject. 3 To annoy or inconvenience. **—put over** *informal* To accomplish or perform successfully: to *put over* a song on the radio. **—put through** 1 To cause to undergo or do: to *put* a monkey *through* its tricks. 2 To accomplish successfully: to *put through* a long-distance phone call. **—put up** 1 To preserve or can (vegetables, fruit, or other foods). 2 To build; erect. 3 To supply, as money. 4 To provide with a place to live. 5 To offer: to *put up* a farm for sale. **—put upon** To take unfair advantage of. **—put up to** To urge on to some action: Who *put* you *up to* this silly plan? **—put up with** To endure; bear patiently.
put-down [pŏŏt′doun′] *n. slang* A remark made to criticize or belittle someone.
put-on [pŏŏt′on′] 1 *adj.* Pretended; not genuine: *put-on* friendliness. 2 *n. slang* A deliberate deception, done for amusement or to tease someone.
put·out [pŏŏt′out′] *n.* In baseball, a play that causes a member of the team at bat to be out.

pu·tre·fy [pyo͞o'trə·fī'] *v.* **pu·tre·fied, pu·tre·fying** To decay or cause to decay; rot; decompose. **—pu·tre·fac·tion** [pyo͞o'trə·fak'shən] *n.*

pu·trid [pyo͞o'trid] *adj.* 1 Decaying; rotten: *putrid* meat. 2 Produced by decay: a *putrid* odor.

putt [put] 1 *n.* In golf, a light stroke made to roll the ball into or near the hole. 2 *v.* To strike (the ball) with such a stroke.

put·tee [put'ē *or* pu·tē'] *n.* A protective covering for the lower part of the leg in the form of a leather gaiter or a strip of cloth wound spirally from the ankle to the knee.

put·ter[1] [put'ər] *n.* 1 In golf, a person who putts. 2 A golf club used in putting.

put·ter[2] [put'ər] *v.* To work or be busy without really accomplishing much: to *putter* all day.

putting green [put'ing] The smooth, grassy area that surrounds a hole on a golf course.

put·ty [put'ē] *n., pl.* **put·ties,** *v.* **put·tied, put·ty·ing** 1 *n.* A soft mixture of powdered chalk and linseed oil, used for filling cracks and holding panes of glass in windows. 2 *v.* To secure or fill with putty.

puz·zle [puz'əl] *n., v.* **puz·zled, puz·zling** 1 *v.* To confuse or perplex; mystify: The new instructions *puzzled* me. 2 *v.* To weigh in the mind; ponder: We *puzzled* for a long time on what to say. 3 *n.* Something that puzzles or baffles: It's a *puzzle* how the news got out. 4 *n.* Something, as a toy or word game, that tests one's mental skills or alertness: a picture *puzzle.* **—puzzle out** or **puzzle over** To think about or solve with much effort or study: to *puzzle out* a code; to *puzzle over* a hard decision. **—puz'zler** *n.*

puz·zle·ment [puz'əl·mənt] *n.* 1 The condition of being puzzled or confused. 2 Something that puzzles or confuses.

pvt. or **Pvt.** private (soldier).

pwt pennyweight.

PX Post Exchange.

Pyg·ma·lion [pig·māl'yən] *n.* In Greek and Roman legends, a sculptor of Cyprus who fell in love with a statue he had carved. It was brought to life for him by Aphrodite.

Pyg·my [pig'mē] *n., pl.* **Pyg·mies,** *adj.* 1 *n.* A member of a small Negroid people of central Africa who are not much more than four feet tall. 2 *adj.* Of or having to do with the Pygmies. 3 *n.* (*written* **pygmy**) A small or insignificant person or thing. 4 *adj.* (*written* **pygmy**) Small or dwarfed.

py·ja·mas [pə·jä'məz] *n.pl.* A British spelling of PAJAMAS.

py·lon [pī'lon'] *n.* 1 A high tower used to mark a course an airplane should fly or to carry high-tension wires. 2 A large gateway to an Egyptian temple or other large building.

py·lo·rus [pī·lôr'əs] *n., pl.* **py·lo·ri** [pī·lôr'ī'] The passage between the stomach and the small intestine.

py·or·rhe·a or **py·or·rhoe·a** [pī'ə·rē'ə] *n.* A disease in which the gums become inflamed, discharge pus, and shrink away from the teeth, which become loose.

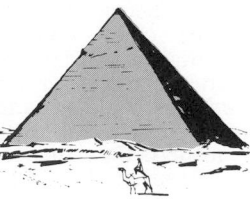

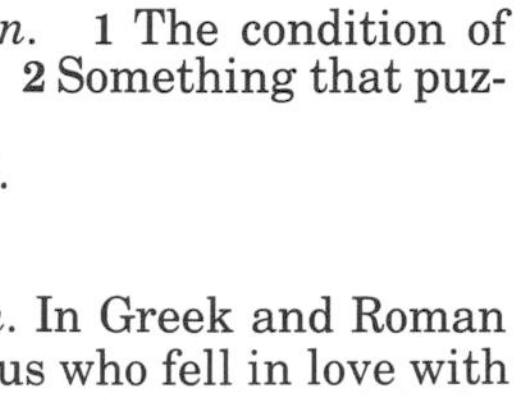
Egyptian pyramid

pyr·a·mid [pir'ə·mid] *n.* 1 A geometrical figure having a flat base of three or more sides. All sides of a pyramid are trangles that slope upward to meet in a point at the top. 2 Any of the huge structures shaped like a pyramid in which ancient Egyptian monarchs were buried.

py·ram·i·dal [pi·ram'ə·dəl] *adj.* Of, having to do with, or shaped like a pyramid.

pyre [pīr] *n.* A heap of wood used for burning a dead body, often as a religious ceremony.

py·re·thrum [pī·rē'thrəm] *n.* 1 A plant of the chrysanthemum family. 2 An insecticide made from the dried, powdered flowers of this plant.

Py·rex [pī'reks'] *n.* A type of glassware that does not break when heated, used to cook foods in the oven or on top of the stove: a trade-mark.

pyr·i·dox·ine [pir'ə·dok'sēn'] *n.* A vitamin belonging to the vitamin B complex and present in many cereals.

py·rite [pī'rīt'] *n.* A pale yellow mineral consisting of iron and sulfur. It resembles gold and is sometimes called fool's gold.

py·rites [pə·rīt'ēz *or* pī'rīts'] *n., pl.* **py·rites** Any of a group of metallic-looking minerals consisting of sulfides of various metals.

py·ro·ma·ni·a [pī'rə·mā'nē·ə] *n.* A mental disturbance in which a person has strong urges to set things on fire. **—py·ro·ma·ni·a·cal** [pī'rə·mə·nī'ə·kəl] *adj.*

py·ro·ma·ni·ac [pī'rə·mā'nē·ak'] *n.* A person afflicted with pyromania.

py·rom·e·ter [pī·rom'ə·tər] *n.* An instrument for measuring very high temperatures.

py·ro·tech·nic [pī'rə·tek'nik] *adj.* 1 Of or having to do with fireworks. 2 Brilliant or sensational like fireworks.

py·ro·tech·ni·cal [pī'rə·tek'ni·kəl] *adj.* Pyrotechnic.

py·ro·tech·nics [pī'rə·tek'niks] *n.pl.* 1 (*used with a singular verb*) The art of making or using fireworks. 2 A brilliant display of fireworks. 3 Any showy display, as of public speaking or skill in playing a musical instrument. ◆ See ICS.

Pyr·rhic victory [pir'ik] A victory won at such a great cost that it is almost a defeat: so called after **Pyr·rhus** [pir'əs], a king of Greece, whose victory over the Romans in 280 B.C. cost the lives of most of his soldiers.

Py·thag·o·re·an theorem [pə·thag'ə·rē'ən] A theorem in geometry stating that the square of the length of the side opposite the right angle of a right triangle is equal to the sum of the squares of the lengths of the other two sides.

Pyth·i·as [pith'ē·əs] *n.* See DAMON.

py·thon [pī'thon' *or* pī'·thən] *n.* A very large, nonpoisonous snake of warm regions, as Africa and Asia, that kills its prey by squeezing.

Python

a	add	**i**	it	**o͝o**	took	**oi**	oil
ā	ace	**ī**	ice	**o͞o**	pool	**ou**	pout
â	care	**o**	odd	**u**	up	**ng**	ring
ä	palm	**ō**	open	**û**	burn	**th**	thin
e	end	**ô**	order	**yo͞o**	fuse	**t͟h**	this
ē	equal					**zh**	vision

ə = {a in *above* e in *sicken* i in *possible* / o in *melon* u in *circus*}

Phoenician (8th century B.C.)

Early Greek (9th-7th centuries B.C.)

Eastern Greek (6th century B.C.)

Western Greek (6th century B.C.)

Early Etruscan (around 8th century B.C.)

Classical Etruscan (around 400 B.C.)

Monumental Latin (around 4th century B.C.)

Classical Latin

Uncial

Half uncial

Caroline minuscule

Q is the seventeenth letter of the alphabet. The sign for it originated among Semitic people in the Near East, in the region of Palestine and Syria, probably in the middle of the second millennium B.C. Little is known about the sign until around 1000 B.C., when the Phoenicians began using it. They named it *qoph* (or *koph*) and used it for a guttural sound pronounced farther back in the throat than was *kaph*—forerunner of the letter *K*.

When the Greeks adopted the Phoenician sign around the ninth century B.C., they had no use for the guttural sound. They used the sign, which they called *quoppa* (or *koppa*), to represent the *k* sound. Since this sound was already represented in Greek by *kappa,* the sign fell into disuse and was dropped entirely from the classical Greek alphabet.

As early as the eighth century B.C., the Etruscans adopted the Greek alphabet. They retained the *Q* sign, which they used, along with *C* and *K,* for the *k* sound. *Q* was used only before *U,* however, and this usage was continued when the Romans took the alphabet from the Etruscans. (For other ways of writing the *k* sound, see *C* and *K*.) The combination of *Q* with *U* holds to the present day in English, in which it generally has the sound of *kw.*

Around the time of the Caesars, the Romans made the shape of the letter more graceful. The model of the letter found on the base of Trajan's column, erected in Rome in 114, is considered a masterpiece of letter design. A Trajan-style *majuscule,* or capital letter, *Q* opens this essay.

The *minuscule,* or small letter, *q* developed gradually, between the third and ninth centuries, in the handwriting that scribes used for copying books. Contributing to its shape were the Roman *uncials* of the fourth to the eighth centuries, the *half uncials* of the fifth to the ninth centuries, and the *Caroline minuscules,* a script that evolved under the encouragement of Charlemagne (742-814).

q or **Q** [kyo͞o] *n., pl.* **q's** or **Q's** The 17th letter of the English alphabet.

q. 1 quart. 2 quarter. 3 quarterly. 4 quarto. 5 query. 6 question. 7 quire.

Q. 1 quarts. 2 Quebec. 3 Queen. 4 question.

qb. quarterback.

QC or **Q.C.** quartermaster corps.

Q.E.D. which was to be proved.

qlty. quality.

QM or **Q.M.** quartermaster.

qt. 1 quart. 2 (*usually written* **qts.**) quarts. 3 quantity.

q.t. [kyo͞o′tē′] *n. slang* Quiet, used especially in the phrase **on the q.t.**: They met a number of times *on the q.t.*

qty. quantity.

qu. 1 queen. 2 query. 3 question.

quack[1] [kwak] 1 *v.* To make a harsh, croaking cry, as a duck. 2 *n.* The sound made by a duck, or a similar croaking sound.

quack[2] [kwak] 1 *n.* Someone who pretends to have great knowledge, especially of medicine and healing; charlatan. 2 *adj. use*: a *quack* doctor. 3 *adj.* Of or related to quacks or quackery: a *quack* cure.

quack·er·y [kwak′ər·ē] *n., pl.* **quack·er·ies** The activities and practices of a quack.

quad[1] [kwod] *n.* An informal word for QUADRANGLE.

quad[2] [kwod] *n.* An informal word for QUADRUPLET.

quad·ran·gle [kwod′rang·gəl] *n.* 1 A square or oblong courtyard, or the buildings that surround such a courtyard. 2 A closed figure bounded by four straight lines; quadrilateral.

quad·rant [kwod′rənt] *n.* 1 One quarter of a circle; a sector or arc of 90°. 2 An instrument having a 90° scale, used to measure angles.

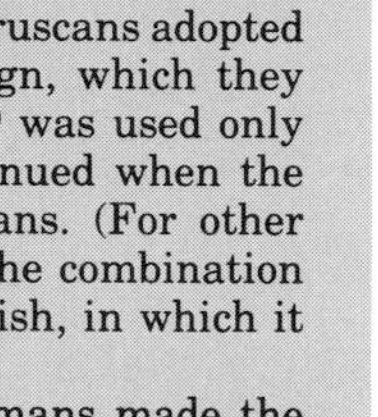

Quadrants

quad·ra·phon·ic [kwod′rə·fon′·ik] *adj.* Of or having to do with a sound-reproduction system that uses four channels to transmit sounds.

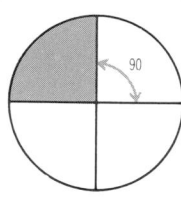

quad·rat·ic [kwod·rat′ik] *adj.* Indicating a mathematical expression or equation of the second degree: $x^2 + 3x - 2 = 16$ is a *quadratic* equation.

quad·ren·ni·al [kwod·ren′ē·əl] *adj.* 1 Happening every four years: the *quadrennial* election. 2 Lasting for four years. **—quad·ren′ni·al·ly** *adv.*

quad·ri·ceps [kwod′ri·seps′] *n.* The large muscle at the front of the thigh.

quad·ri·lat·er·al [kwod′rə·lat′ər·əl] 1 *n.* A closed figure bounded by four straight lines. 2 *adj.* Four-sided.

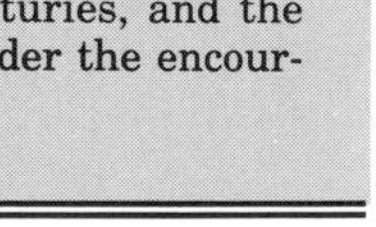

Quadrilaterals

qua·drille [kwə·dril′] *n.* 1 A square dance for four couples. 2 Music for this dance.

quad·ril·lion [kwo·dril′yən] *n.* 1 In the U.S., a thousand trillion, written as 10^{15} or 1 followed by 15 zeroes. 2 In Great Britain, a trillion trillion, written as 10^{24} or 1 followed by 24 zeroes.

quad·ru·ped [kwod′ro͞o·ped′] 1 *n.* A four-footed animal. 2 *adj.* Having four feet.

quad·ru·ple [kwod·ro͞o′pəl *or* kwod′ro͞o·pəl] *adj., v.*

quad·ru·pled, quad·ru·pling 1 *adj.* Being four times as large or four times as many. 2 *adj.* Being in four parts or made up of four persons or things: a *quadruple* alliance. 3 *v.* To multiply by four; increase by four times: The investors *quadrupled* their money; The distance *quadrupled.*

quad·ru·plet [kwod·ro͞o'plit *or* kwod'ro͞o·plit] *n.* 1 One of four children produced by one mother in a single birth. 2 One of a set or collection of four things.

quaff [kwof *or* kwaf] *v.* To drink in large amounts and with zest: to *quaff* a cool beverage.

quag·ga [kwag'ə *or* kwä'gə] *n.* An extinct African animal related to the zebra.

quag·mire [kwag'mīr'] *n.* 1 An area of deep, soft mud; bog. 2 A bad or trying situation.

qua·hog or **qua·haug** [kwô'hôg' *or* kwō'hog'] *n.* A hard-shelled, edible clam found along the Atlantic coast of North America.

quail[1] [kwāl] *v.* To shrink with fear; lose heart or courage.

quail[2] [kwāl] *n., pl.* **quail** or **quails** Any of several birds related to the partridge, often hunted for food.

Quail

quaint [kwānt] *adj.* Pleasantly odd or old-fashioned. —**quaint'·ly** *adv.* —**quaint'ness** *n.*

quake [kwāk] *v.* **quaked, quak·ing,** *n.* 1 *v.* To shake or tremble, often with great force: to *quake* with fear; The ground *quaked* from the blast. 2 *n.* A shaking or trembling. 3 *n.* An earthquake.

Quak·er [kwā'kər] 1 *n.* A member of the Society of Friends. 2 *adj.* Of or having to do with Quakers or the Society of Friends. ◆ *Quakers* got their name because their founder told them to tremble at the word of the Lord. —**Quak'er·ism** *n.*

qual·i·fi·ca·tion [kwol'ə·fə·kā'shən] *n.* 1 The act of qualifying. 2 The condition of being qualified. 3 (*sometimes pl.*) Abilities, qualities, and training that make a person fit for a particular profession or occupation. 4 Something that limits or restricts: We liked the play, but with certain *qualifications.*

qual·i·fied [kwol'ə·fīd'] *adj.* 1 Suitable or competent, as for a particular occupation: a *qualified* engineer. 2 Limited or restricted: an attitude of *qualified* hope.

qual·i·fi·er [kwol'ə·fī'ər] *n.* 1 A person or thing that qualifies. 2 A word, as an adjective or adverb, that modifies another word or words.

qual·i·fy [kwol'ə·fī'] *v.* **qual·i·fied, qual·i·fy·ing** 1 To be or cause to be suitable or fit, as for a job, office, or privilege: She *qualified* for the job; His knowledge *qualifies* him to speak. 2 To limit, restrict, or soften in some way: to *qualify* a remark; to *qualify* a penalty.

qual·i·ta·tive [kwol'ə·tā'tiv] *adj.* Of or having to do with quality. —**qual'i·ta'tive·ly** *adv.*

qualitative analysis A testing to see what chemical elements or components are present in a substance.

qual·i·ty [kwol'ə·tē] *n., pl.* **qual·i·ties** 1 That which makes something the way it is; distinctive feature or characteristic: Wetness is a *quality* of water. 2 The nature or character of something: The poem catches the *quality* of summer. 3 The degree of excellence or worth of something: a poor *quality* of cloth. 4 Excellence: Aim for *quality,* not quantity. 5 A personal characteristic or trait: Everyone has some good and some bad *qualities.* 6 The character of a sound apart from pitch and loudness; timbre. 7 High social rank: seldom used today: a person of *quality.*

qualm [kwäm] *n.* 1 A twinge of conscience; guilty feeling: to have *qualms* about cheating. 2 A touch of fear or anxiety: to have *qualms* about flying. 3 A slight feeling of sickness.

quan·da·ry [kwon'də·rē *or* kwon'drē] *n., pl.* **quan·da·ries** A condition of perplexity; dilemma; puzzle.

quan·ti·ta·tive [kwon'tə·tā'tiv] *adj.* 1 Of or related to quantity. 2 Capable of being measured: a *quantitative* change. —**quan'ti·ta'tive·ly** *adv.*

quantitative analysis A testing to determine the amount or proportion of each of the components that make up a substance or mixture.

quan·ti·ty [kwon'tə·tē] *n., pl.* **quan·ti·ties** 1 An amount or number: Buy equal *quantities* of flour and sugar. 2 (*often pl.*) A large amount or number: *quantities* of food; to order in *quantity.* 3 Something having length, size, or volume that can be measured and expressed in suitable units: Pressure is a *quantity.*

quan·tum [kwon'təm] *n., pl.* **quan·ta** [kwon'tə] A very small, indivisible quantity or unit of energy. For light or any other electromagnetic radiation, one quantum is equal to its frequency multiplied by a particular number that never changes. The energy contained in a moving atomic particle or in a field is also expressed as some multiple of one of its quanta.

quantum theory The theory that energy in its various forms exists as numbers of indivisible units, and that energy and mass are equivalent.

quar. 1 quarter. 2 quarterly.

quar·an·tine [kwôr'ən·tēn'] *n., v.* **quar·an·tined, quar·an·tin·ing** 1 *n.* The isolation for a certain period of time of a ship arriving in port to make sure that there is no infectious disease on board. 2 *n.* The keeping of persons or things that have been infected by or exposed to contagious diseases away from other people or things. 3 *n.* The place or length of time of such isolation. 4 *v.* To hold or confine in quarantine: to *quarantine* a child having whooping cough.

quark [kwärk *or* kwôrk] *n.* Any of a set of hypothetical particles believed by some scientists to be the constituents of protons, neutrons, and other subatomic particles.

quar·rel [kwôr'əl] *n., v.* **quar·reled** or **quar·relled, quar·rel·ing** or **quar·rel·ling** 1 *n.* An angry or violent dispute or argument; disagreement ending friendly relations. 2 *n.* The cause of a dispute. 3 *v.* To take part in a quarrel. 4 *v.* To find fault: to *quarrel* with someone's ideas.

a	add	**i**	it	**o͝o**	took	**oi**	oil		
ā	ace	**ī**	ice	**o͞o**	pool	**ou**	pout		
â	care	**o**	odd	**u**	up	**ng**	ring		
ä	palm	**ō**	open	**û**	burn	**th**	thin		
e	end	**ô**	order	**yo͞o**	fuse	**th̸**	this		
ē	equal					**zh**	vision		

ə = a in *above* e in *sicken* i in *possible* o in *melon* u in *circus*

quar·rel·some [kwôr′əl·səm] *adj.* Tending or liking to quarrel or find fault.

quar·ri·er [kwôr′ē·ər] *n.* A person whose work is digging in a stone quarry.

quar·ry[1] [kwôr′ē] *n., pl.* **quar·ries** 1 An animal being hunted by a human being or another animal. 2 Anything that is hunted or eagerly pursued.

quar·ry[2] [kwôr′ē] *n., pl.* **quar·ries,** *v.* **quar·ried, quar·ry·ing** 1 *n.* An excavation from which stone is taken for use in building. 2 *v.* To cut out or take from a quarry: to *quarry* marble.

quart [kwôrt] *n.* 1 A measure of liquid volume equal to 32 ounces, two pints, or 1/4 gallon. 2 A measure of volume for dry things, as grains or berries, equal to 1/8 peck. 3 A container that will hold one quart.

quar·ter [kwôr′tər] 1 *n.* One of four equal parts that make up a whole. 2 *v.* To divide or cut into four equal or almost equal parts: to *quarter* a loaf of bread. 3 *adj.* Being one of four equal or almost equal parts: a *quarter* share of the food. 4 *n.* A U.S. or Canadian coin worth 25 cents. 5 *n.* A period of 15 minutes, especially before or after an hour: It is *quarter* past two. 6 *n.* One of the four periods into which a year is divided, starting on the first day of the first, fourth, seventh, and tenth months. 7 *n.* The time it takes the moon to move one fourth the distance of its path around the earth, about seven days. 8 *n.* One of the four periods of a game, as a football game. 9 *n.* Any of the four legs or limbs of an animal, together with the adjacent parts. 10 *n.* One of the four main points of the compass. 11 *n.* A section of a city; district: the French *quarter.* 12 *n.* (*pl.*) A place to live in, or sometimes just to sleep in: They found *quarters* in an inn. 13 *v.* To provide with living or sleeping space: Soldiers were *quartered* in barracks. 14 *n.* Source or place of origin: There's no news from that *quarter.* 15 *n.* Mercy, as shown to a defeated enemy: No *quarter* will be asked or given. **—at close quarters** Close by; at close range.

quar·ter·back [kwôr′tər·bak′] *n.* In football, the player in the backfield who usually calls the signals and receives the ball from the center.

quar·ter·deck or **quar·ter-deck** [kwôr′tər·dek′] *n.* The rear part of a ship's upper deck, reserved for officers.

quarter horse A strong American horse bred for riding.

quar·ter·ly [kwôr′tər·lē] *adj., n., pl.* **quar·ter·lies,** *adv.* 1 *adj.* Happening at three-month intervals: *quarterly* payments. 2 *n.* Something, as a magazine, issued once every three months. 3 *adv.* Once every three months: to pay taxes *quarterly.*

quar·ter·mas·ter [kwôr′tər·mas′tər] *n.* 1 A military officer in charge of housing, clothing, and supplies for troops. 2 On a ship, a petty officer responsible for steering and signals.

quarter note A musical note that is one-fourth as long as a whole note.

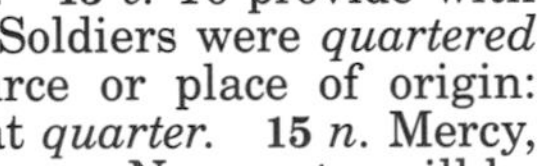
Quarter notes

quar·ter·staff [kwôr′tər·staf′] *n., pl.* **quar·ter·staves** [kwôr′tər·stāvz′] A long, stout pole with an iron tip, once used in England as a weapon.

quar·tet [kwôr·tet′] *n.* 1 A musical composition for four voices or instruments. 2 The people who perform such a composition. 3 A set of four similar things.

quar·to [kwôr′tō] *n., pl.* **quar·tos** 1 A page size equal to a quarter of a full sheet. 2 A book whose pages are of this size.

quartz [kwôrts] *n.* A hard, glasslike mineral composed mainly of silica, sometimes found in colored forms as amethyst, onyx, and other gems.

quartz·ite [kwôrt′sīt′] *n.* A type of hard rock formed of sandstone and quartz.

qua·sar [kwā′zär′] *n.* A very distant celestial object that emits radio waves and light whose spectrum indicates that it is moving at very high speeds away from the earth. ◆ *Quasar* is an acronym formed from *quasi-stellar radio source.*

quash[1] [kwosh] *v.* In law, to cancel or set aside, as an indictment or writ; annul.

quash[2] [kwosh] *v.* To put down or suppress with force: to *quash* a revolt.

qua·si [kwä′zē *or* kwā′zī] 1 *adj.* Resembling or like but not quite the same as: often used in combination with nouns, as in *quasi-illness.* 2 *adv.* Nearly; almost: often used in combination with adjectives, as in *quasi-comic.* ◆ *Quasi* comes from a Latin word meaning *as if* or *as if it were.*

Qua·ter·nar·y [kwot′ər·ner′ē] 1 *n.* The second geological period of the Cenozoic era, including the present. During the Quaternary the physical features and climates of the earth as we know them have developed and human beings have appeared. 2 *adj.* Of the Quaternary.

quat·rain [kwot′rān′] *n.* A verse stanza of four lines.

qua·ver [kwā′vər] 1 *v.* To tremble or shake in an uncertain way, as a voice. 2 *n.* A trembling, especially of the voice. 3 *v.* To say or sing in a nervous, shaky voice: to *quaver* a plea for mercy.

quay [kē] *n.* A wharf or artificial structure where a ship may dock and load or unload.

A quay

Que. Quebec.

quea·sy [kwē′zē] *adj.* **quea·si·er, quea·si·est** 1 Sick or causing sickness at the stomach. 2 Having an easily upset stomach. 3 Ill at ease; uncomfortable. 4 Easily upset; delicate; squeamish. **—quea′si·ly** *adv.* **—quea′si·ness** *n.*

que·bra·cho [kā·brä′chō] *n., pl.* **que·bra·chos** Any of several hardwood trees found in South America, especially in Chile.

Que·chu·a [kech′(ə·)wə] *n.* 1 A member of an Indian people of Peru whose ancestors formed the ruling class of the Inca Empire. 2 The language of this people, spoken in various parts of western South America. **—Que′chu·an** *adj.*

queen [kwēn] *n.* 1 The wife of a king, or a woman who rules a country in her own right. 2 A woman who is very important or famous: a movie *queen.* 3 In chess, the most powerful piece, capable of moving any number of squares in any straight or diagonal line. 4 Any of the four playing cards having a picture of a queen. 5 In a colony, as one of ants or bees, a fully developed female, usually the only one, that lays eggs.

Queen Anne's lace [anz] A wild carrot whose white flower resembles a piece of lace.

queen consort The wife of a reigning king.
queen·ly [kwēn′lē] *adj.* **queen·li·er, queen·li·est** 1 Of, having to do with, or like a queen. 2 Fit or suitable for a queen.
queen mother A king's widow who is the mother of a reigning king or queen.
queen-size [kwēn′sīz′] *adj.* Of, for, or being a bed that is about 60 inches wide by 80 inches long.
queer [kwir] 1 *adj.* Unusual or abnormal; odd; strange: a *queer* notion; a *queer* old person. 2 *adj.* Suspicious or questionable: *queer* actions. 3 *adj. slang* Counterfeit: *queer* money. 4 *adj.* Not well; queasy: I felt *queer* all day. 5 *v. slang* To spoil or ruin; botch. **—queer′ly** *adv.* **—queer′ness** *n.*
quell [kwel] *v.* 1 To put down or suppress by force: to *quell* a revolt. 2 To quiet or end, as pain or fear: My suspicions were *quelled.*
quench [kwench] *v.* 1 To put out (a fire) by throwing water on it. 2 To end or satisfy with water, as thirst. 3 To cool, as a hot metal, by thrusting into water or other liquid.
quer·u·lous [kwer′(y)ə·ləs] *adj.* 1 Tending to complain or find fault: a *querulous* person. 2 Showing or full of complaints; whining: a *querulous* remark. **—quer′u·lous·ly** *adv.*
que·ry [kwir′ē] *n., pl.* **que·ries,** *v.* **que·ried, que·ry·ing** 1 *n.* A question or inquiry. 2 *v.* To ask questions of or about: to *query* a witness; to *query* a loss of money. 3 *n.* A question mark. 4 *v.* To express doubt about: to *query* a statement.
ques. question.
quest [kwest] 1 *n.* A seeking or looking for something; search. 2 *v.* To seek or look for (something). 3 *n.* An expedition, as by a knight seeking adventure. **—quest′er** *n.*
ques·tion [kwes′chən] 1 *n.* Something that is asked in order to find out something; something that requires an answer. 2 *n.* The form of a sentence or clause that asks a question. 3 *v.* To ask a question or questions of: The principal *questioned* the pupil thoroughly. 4 *n.* A subject of inquiry or disagreement; matter of doubt; problem. 5 *v.* To have a doubt about or an objection to; dispute: to *question* a decision. 6 *n.* A matter under discussion: to vote on a *question.* 7 *n.* Doubt or uncertainty: There is no *question* about her talent. **—call in question** To raise objection to; challenge. **—in question** Under discussion or consideration. **—out of the question** Not to be considered; impossible. **—ques′tion·er** *n.*
ques·tion·a·ble [kwes′chən·ə·bəl] *adj.* 1 Of or showing doubtful, as character, honesty, or morality; suspicious: *questionable* behavior. 2 Likely to be questioned or doubted: a *questionable* conclusion. **—ques′tion·a·bly** *adv.*
question mark A punctuation mark (?) placed at the end of a written question.
ques·tion·naire [kwes′chən·âr′] *n.* A list of questions, usually printed, used to get information from a person or persons.
quet·zal [ket·säl′] *n.* A brightly colored bird, the male of which has very long tail feathers. It is found in Central America.

Quetzal

queue [kyōō] *n., v.* **queued, queu·ing** 1 *n.* A single braid of hair hanging from the back of the head; pigtail. 2 *n.* A line, as one of persons or cars, waiting for something. 3 *v. British* To form such a line: The movie fans *queued* up for tickets.
quib·ble [kwib′əl] *n., v.* **quib·bled, quib·bling** 1 *n.* The use of words in twisted senses or the making of minor objections to avoid the main points in an argument or discussion. 2 *v.* To make quibbles. **—quib′bler** *n.*
quiche [kēsh] *n.* An unsweetened egg custard mixed with cheese, bacon bits, or other ingredients and baked in a pie shell.
quick [kwik] 1 *adj.* Done or happening in a short time; swift; fast. 2 *adv.* Rapidly; fast: Please come *quick.* 3 *adj.* Swift to learn, understand, or perceive; alert: a *quick* mind; a *quick* ear. 4 *adj.* Easily excited or aroused: a *quick* temper. 5 *adj.* Able to move rapidly; speedy: *quick* fingers. 6 *n.* All living people, now only in the phrase **the quick and the dead.** 7 *n.* The delicate, tender flesh under a fingernail or toenail. 8 *n.* Deep, sensitive feelings: an insult that cuts to the *quick.* **—quick′·ly** *adv.* **—quick′ness** *n.*
quick·en [kwik′ən] *v.* 1 To go or cause to go faster: The pedestrians *quickened* their pace; The flow *quickened.* 2 To make sooner; hasten: Please *quicken* your departure. 3 To return to life or activity; revive: Spring *quickens* the countryside.
quick-freeze [kwik′frēz′] *v.* **quick-froze, quick-fro·zen, quick-freez·ing** To freeze (food) rapidly at low temperatures so as to store without loss of taste or nourishment.
quick·lime [kwik′līm′] *n.* A form of lime used to make mortar. It reacts strongly with water.
quick·sand [kwik′sand′] *n.* A deep bed of sand so filled and soaked with water that it swallows up a person, animal, or object that tries to rest or move upon it.
quick·sil·ver [kwik′sil′vər] *n.* The metal mercury in its liquid form.
quick·step [kwik′step′] *n.* A musical march with a fast tempo.
quick-tem·pered [kwik′tem′pərd] *adj.* Easily made angry.
quick time The normal pace of marching used in the U.S., with 120 thirty-inch steps a minute.
quick-wit·ted [kwik′wit′id] *adj.* Having a mind that works quickly; mentally alert.
quid[1] [kwid] *n.* A small piece of tobacco for chewing.
quid[2] [kwid] *n., pl.* **quid** *British slang* A pound sterling.
qui·es·cent [kwī·es′ənt] *adj.* In a state of rest; inactive; quiet. **—qui·es′cence** *n.*
qui·et [kwī′ət] 1 *adj.* Having or making little or no noise: a *quiet* room; a *quiet* machine. 2 *adj.* Not moving very much or at all; still; calm: a *quiet* pond. 3 *adj.* Free from stress, strain, or hurried activity: a *quiet* day in the park. 4 *adj.* Calm and restful; gentle; mild: a *quiet* manner. 5 *adj.* Not

a	add	**i**	it	**ŏŏ**	took	**oi**	oil
ā	ace	**ī**	ice	**ōō**	pool	**ou**	pout
â	care	**o**	odd	**u**	up	**ng**	ring
ä	palm	**ō**	open	**û**	burn	**th**	thin
e	end	**ô**	order	**yōō**	fuse	**th**	this
ē	equal					**zh**	vision

ə = a in *above* e in *sicken* i in *possible* / o in *melon* u in *circus*

Q

showy or overdone; modest; restrained: *quiet* decorations. **6** *v.* To make or become quiet: *Quiet* the animal down!; The sea *quieted* after the storm. **7** *n.* A state or condition of calm, repose, or silence: peace and *quiet*. **—qui′et·ly** *adv.* **—qui′et·ness** *n.*

qui·e·tude [kwī′ə·t(y)o͞od′] *n.* A state or condition of calm and repose; quiet; rest.

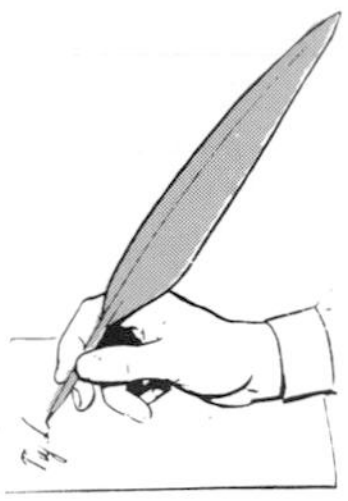
Quill pen

qui·e·tus [kwī·ē′təs] *n.* **1** A silencing or suppressing, as of a rumor. **2** A final settlement or payment, as of a debt. **3** Death, or something that causes death: seldom used today.

quill [kwil] *n.* **1** A large, strong feather from the wing or tail of a bird. **2** Something made from such a feather, especially an old-fashioned pen. **3** A large, sharp spine, as of a porcupine.

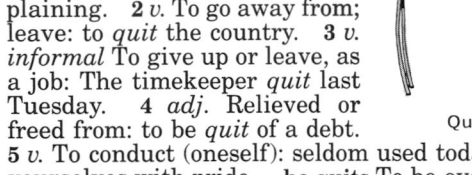

quilt [kwilt] **1** *n.* A covering for a bed made by stitching together two layers of cloth in patterns or crossing lines. Between these layers there is another layer of soft, warm material. **2** *v.* To make quilts: The sewing bee *quilted* all day. **3** *v.* To make of quilting, or stitch like a quilt, with a warm inner layer: to *quilt* a skirt.

quilt·ing [kwil′ting] *n.* **1** The act of making a quilt. **2** A material for or like a quilt.

quince [kwins] *n.* **1** A hard, acid, yellowish fruit that looks like an apple, used for jelly or preserves. **2** The tree that bears this fruit.

qui·nine [kwī′nīn′] *n.* A bitter, crystalline substance contained in the bark of the cinchona tree, used in making drugs to treat malaria. ◆ *Quinine* comes from a South American Indian word.

quinine water A soft drink of carbonated water flavored with quinine.

quin·sy [kwin′zē] *n.* A severe swelling and soreness of the tonsils and throat together with the formation of abscesses.

quint [kwint] *n.* An informal word for QUINTUPLET.

quin·tes·sence [kwin·tes′əns] *n.* **1** The most essential part of anything, usually in a very pure or concentrated form: The *quintessence* of poetry is rhythm. **2** A perfect or typical example **—quin·tes·sen·tial** [kwin′tə·sen′shəl] *adj.*

quin·tet or **quin·tette** [kwin·tet′] *n.* **1** A piece of music for five voices or instruments. **2** The five persons who perform such a piece of music. **3** A group of five persons or things.

quin·tup·le [kwin·tup′əl *or* kwin·t(y)o͞o′pəl] *adj., v.* **quin·tup·led, quin·tup·ling,** *n.* **1** *adj.* Five times as many or as great. **2** *v.* To make five times as many or as great. **3** *n.* A number or amount that is five times as many or as great. **4** *adj.* Having five parts.

quin·tu·plet [kwin·tup′lit *or* kwin·t(y)o͞o′plit *or* kwin′t(y)o͞o·plit] *n.* **1** One of five children born of the same mother at one birth. **2** One of a set of five things.

quip [kwip] *n., v.* **quipped, quip·ping** **1** *n.* A clever or witty, and sometimes sarcastic, remark; gibe. **2** *v.* To make a witty remark; jest.

qui·pu [kē′po͞o] *n.* An arrangement of knotted ropes used by the ancient Incas for calculating, keeping accounts, and maintaining records.

quire [kwīr] *n.* A group of 24 or 25 sheets of paper of the same size and kind; 1/20 of a ream.

quirk [kwûrk] *n.* **1** An odd habit or mannerism; peculiarity. **2** A quibble. **3** A sudden curve or twist, as in handwriting. **4** A clever retort.

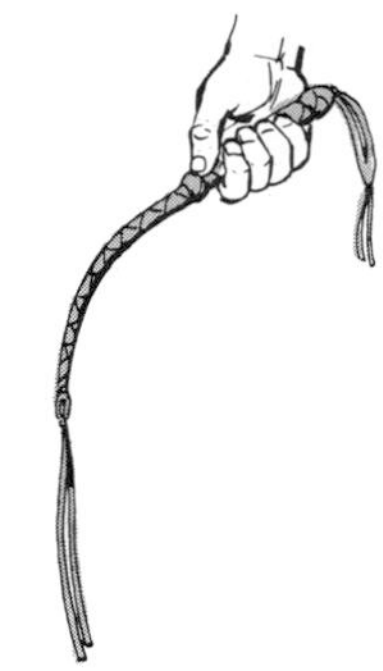
Quirt

quirt [kwûrt] *n.* A whip with a short handle and a braided rawhide lash, used by horseback riders.

quis·ling [kwiz′ling] *n.* A person who betrays his or her country to an enemy and is then given political power by the conquerors.

quit [kwit] *v.* **quit** or **quit·ted, quit·ting** **1** *v.* To cease from; stop: We *quit* work early; to *quit* complaining. **2** *v.* To go away from; leave: to *quit* the country. **3** *v.* *informal* To give up or leave, as a job: The timekeeper *quit* last Tuesday. **4** *adj.* Relieved or freed from: to be *quit* of a debt. **5** *v.* To conduct (oneself): seldom used today: *Quit* yourselves with pride. **—be quits** To be even (with another).

quit·claim [kwit′klām′] *n.* A legal agreement in which one gives up some claim, demand, or right.

quite [kwīt] *adv.* **1** To the full extent; completely; entirely: *quite* ready. **2** Really; truly: I am *quite* able to go. **3** *informal* To a great extent; very much; considerably: *quite* ill. ◆ The phrase *quite a* is used in many expressions to show a large but indefinite number, size, or quantity: *Quite a few* means *many*; *quite a while* means *a long while*. *Quite a* is also used informally to mean *a great* or *a wonderful*: It was *quite a* party.

quit·tance [kwit′(ə)ns] *n.* **1** Release, as from a debt or obligation. **2** A document certifying this; receipt. **3** Something given in return or revenge.

quit·ter [kwit′ər] *n.* A person who gives up without making a real effort.

quiv·er[1] [kwiv′ər] **1** *v.* To make a slight trembling motion; vibrate. **2** *n.* A trembling or shaking.

quiv·er[2] [kwiv′ər] *n.* A case or container for carrying arrows.

Quixote, Don See DON QUIXOTE.

quix·ot·ic [kwik·sot′ik] *adj.* Extremely romantic, chivalrous, or idealistic, but foolish and impractical at the same time. **—quix·ot′i·cal·ly** *adv.*

quiz [kwiz] *n., pl.* **quiz·zes,** *v.* **quizzed, quiz·zing** **1** *n.* The act of questioning, especially a short or informal test given to a student or students. **2** *v.* To examine by asking questions.

quiz show A radio or television program in which contestants answer questions to get prizes.

quiz·zi·cal [kwiz′i·kəl] *adj.* **1** Poking fun; mocking: a *quizzical* smirk. **2** Questioning; puzzled: a *quizzical* frown. **—quiz′zi·cal·ly** *adv.*

quoin [koin *or* kwoin] *n.* **1** An external corner or angle of a building. **2** A stone or group of stones forming such a corner.

quoit [kwoit] *n.* **1** A metal or rope ring made so that it may be thrown over a peg set in the ground. **2** (*pl.*) (*used with a singular verb*) A game whose object is the throwing of these rings over a peg.

Quoits

quon·dam [kwon′dəm] *adj.* Having been before; former: a *quondam* companion.

Quon·set hut [kwon′sit] A metal building in the form of half a cylinder resting lengthwise on the ground. It is made up of ready-made sections that may be put together easily: a trademark.

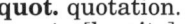

quo·rum [kwôr′əm] *n.* The smallest number of a group or assembly that must be present in order to make binding decisions or carry on business.

quot. quotation.

quo·ta [kwō′tə] *n.* A number or amount that is required from or given to a person or group: The factory produced its *quota* of cars.

quot·a·ble [kwō′tə·bəl] *adj.* **1** Worth quoting, as a wise or clever saying. **2** Suitable for quoting.

quo·ta·tion [kwō·tā′shən] *n.* **1** Something said or written by one person repeated exactly by another person. **2** The act of quoting. **3** A price, as of stocks or bonds.

quotation mark Either of the marks (“ and ”) or (‘ and ’) used at the beginning and end of a quoted passage.

quote [kwōt] *v.* **quot·ed, quot·ing** **1** To use the exact words of: to *quote* a book. **2** To use a quotation or quotations: This writer *quotes* too often from others. **3** To use (as a rule or legal decision) as an authority or illustration: The lawyer *quoted* an old Supreme Court case. **4** To state (a price): The dealer *quoted* $70 as the lowest price. **5** To give the price of: to *quote* a stock at $70 per share.

quoth [kwōth] *v.* Said; spoke: seldom used today except in poems.

quo·tient [kwō′shənt] *n.* The number that results if one number is divided by another. If 6 is divided by 3, 2 is the quotient. If 7 is divided by 3, 2 is the quotient and the remainder is 1.

Qur·'an or **Qur·an** [kŏŏ·rän′ *or* kŏŏ·ran′] *n.* Another spelling of KORAN.

q.v. which see.

a	add	**i**	it	**ŏŏ**	took	**oi**	oil
ā	ace	**ī**	ice	**ōō**	pool	**ou**	pout
â	care	**o**	odd	**u**	up	**ng**	ring
ä	palm	**ō**	open	**û**	burn	**th**	thin
e	end	**ô**	order	**yōō**	fuse	**th̶**	this
ē	equal					**zh**	vision

ə = {a in *above* e in *sicken* i in *possible* / o in *melon* u in *circus*}

Rr

R is the eighteenth letter of the alphabet. The sign for it originated among Semitic people in the Near East, in the region of Palestine and Syria, probably in the middle of the second millennium B.C. Little is known about the sign until around 1000 B.C., when the Phoenicians began using it. They named it *resh* and used it for the sound of the consonant *r*.

When the Greeks adopted the Phoenician sign around the ninth century B.C., they called it *rho* and changed its shape—from a triangular loop on a stem to a rounded one—and direction. Western Greeks added a small tail to the sign, a feature that was to reappear in later centuries.

As early as the eighth century B.C., the Etruscans adopted the Greek alphabet. It was from the Etruscans that the Romans took their alphabet. For the *R* sign, however, they reached back to the Western Greek form. Later the Romans lengthened the tail of the *R*, thus forming the letter we know today.

Pronunciation of the Roman letter was much as our own. This differed from the Greek pronunciation, which probably was unvoiced or whispered. When the Romans began borrowing Greek words into Latin, they noted this difference in pronunciation by spelling the Greek words with *RH*. Many English words beginning with *R* and borrowed from the Greek language retain this spelling. Some examples are *rhetoric* and *rheumatism*.

The *minuscule,* or small letter, *r* developed gradually, between the third and the ninth centuries, in the handwriting that scribes used for copying books. It underwent many changes. Contributing to its shape were the Roman *uncials* of the fourth to the eighth centuries, the *half uncials* of the fifth to the ninth centuries, and the *Caroline minuscules,* a script that evolved under the encouragement of Charlemagne (742-814). The Caroline minuscules became the principal handwriting system used on the medieval manuscripts of the ninth and tenth centuries.

Early Phoenician (late 2nd millennium B.C.)
Phoenician (8th century B.C.)
Early Greek (9th-7th centuries B.C.)
Western Greek (6th century B.C.)
Classical Greek (403 B.C. onward)
Early Etruscan (8th century B.C.)
Monumental Latin (4th century B.C.)
Classical Latin
Uncial
Half uncial
Caroline minuscule

r or **R** [är] *n., pl.* **r's** or **R's** The 18th letter of the English alphabet. **—the three R's** Reading, writing, and arithmetic.

r 1 roentgen. 2 (*often written* **R**) resistance (electricity). 3 (*often written* **R**) radius.

r. 1 right. 2 rod.

R. 1 rabbi. 2 Republican. 3 river. 4 road.

r.a. or **R.A.** rear admiral.

Ra The symbol for the element radium.

Ra [rä] *n.* The sun god of ancient Egypt.

rab·bi [rab′ī] *n., pl.* **rab·bis** or **rab·bies** A person learned in Jewish religious law who is trained and ordained to be the spiritual head of a Jewish community or a teacher of the religious law.

rab·bin·i·cal [rə·bin′i·kəl] *adj.* Of or having to do with rabbis or their writings or teachings.

rab·bit [rab′it] *n.* 1 A small animal with long ears, soft fur, and a short tail. Rabbits are smaller than hares, live in burrows, and move by jumping. 2 The fur of this animal.

Rabbit

rabbit ears An indoor television antenna made of two adjustable rods attached to a base in a V shape.

rab·ble [rab′əl] *n.* A noisy, disorderly crowd or mob. **—the rabble** The lowest class of people, often thought of as a rude, ignorant mob.

rab·ble-rous·er [rab′əl·rou′zər] *n.* A person who tries to arouse the passions or prejudices of the public; demagogue; agitator.

rab·id [rab′id] *adj.* 1 Having rabies; mad: a *rabid* dog. 2 Going to unreasonable extremes in showing or expressing an opinion or feeling: *rabid* supporters. 3 Furious; raging.

ra·bies [rā′bēz] *n.* A disease that affects the central nervous system of mammals; hydrophobia. It is fatal when not treated. A person may get it if bitten by a rabid animal, as a mad dog.

rac·coon [ra·ko͞on′] *n.* 1 A small animal with grayish brown fur and a bushy, striped tail. It lives chiefly in trees and is active at night. 2 Its fur. ◆ *Raccoon* comes from a North American Indian word meaning *he scratches with the hands.*

Raccoon

race[1] [rās] *n., v.* **raced, rac·ing** 1 *n.* A contest to decide the comparative speed of the contestants. 2 *v.* To take part in a contest of speed: Runners, swimmers, or sailboats may *race.* 3 *v.* To compete with or cause to compete in a race: The runners *raced* to the finish line; to *race* horses. 4 *v.* To run or move swiftly: She *raced* to the fire alarm box. 5 *v.* To run at a high speed with no load: to *race* a motor. 6 *n.* A swift current of water or its channel, as a millrace. 7 *n.* Any contest, as for office: a mayoralty *race.*

race[2] [rās] *n.* 1 One of the major divisions of human beings, whose members are regarded as having a common ancestry or origin and similar physical traits. 2 The condition of belonging to a certain

branch of humanity: to be proud of one's *race.* 3 A group or class of plants or animals having common characteristics: a *race* of sturdy wheat. 4 A group or kind of people: the *race* of engineers. 5 A clan, tribe, nation, or people.
race·course [rās′kôrs′] *n.* A course for racing; racetrack.
race·horse [rās′hôrs′] *n.* A horse bred and trained for racing.
ra·ceme [rā·sēm′] *n.* A flower cluster having its flowers, each growing on a short stalk, spaced along a stem, as in a lily of the valley.
rac·er [rā′sər] *n.* 1 A person, animal, or vehicle that races. 2 The blacksnake of the U.S.
race·track [rās′trak′] *n.* A track or course over which a race, such as a horse race, is run.

Racetrack

Ra·chel [rā′chəl] *n.* In the Bible, the second wife of Jacob, mother of Joseph and Benjamin.
ra·cial [rā′shəl] *adj.* Of or having to do with race, origins, or lineage. **—ra′cial·ly** *adv.*
ra·cism [rā′siz·əm] *n.* 1 Exaggeration of the racial differences between individuals. 2 Prejudice in favor of a particular race. **—ra′cist** *n.*
rack[1] [rak] 1 *n.* Something, as a frame or stand, that holds things, as for storage or display: a hat *rack*; a book *rack.* 2 *n.* A frame attached to a wagon, as one for carrying hay or straw. 3 *n.* An instrument of torture that stretches the arms and legs of victims. 4 *v.* To torture or torment, by or as if by putting on the rack: to be *racked* with pain. 5 *n.* A bar with teeth on one side that mesh with the teeth of a gearwheel. **—rack one's brains** To think as hard as possible.

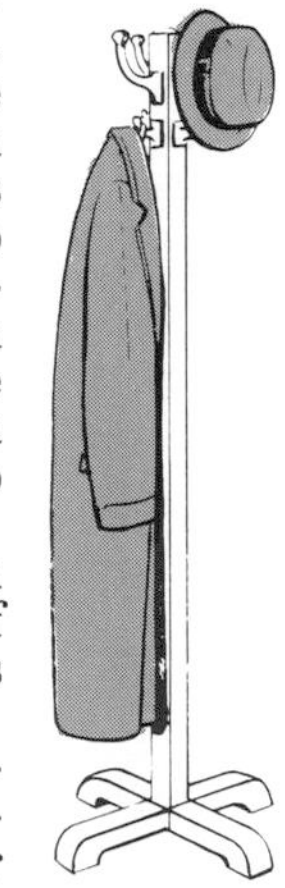
Clothes rack

rack[2] [rak] *n.* Destruction, especially in the phrase **rack and ruin**: Because of the owner's neglect, the business went to *rack and ruin.*
rack·et[1] [rak′it] *n.* 1 Loud noise, clatter, clamor, or commotion. 2 *informal* A dishonest method or scheme for getting something, as money or goods, often by the use of force.
rack·et[2] [rak′it] *n.* A light bat used in certain sports, as tennis or badminton, consisting of a handle attached to an oval frame strung with a network usually of catgut or nylon. ◆ *Racket* comes from an Arabic word meaning *palm of the hand.*
rack·et·eer [rak′ə·tir′] 1 *n.* A criminal who carries on some illegal business to get money, often by using threats, force, or bribery. 2 *v.* To get money by such methods.
ra·con·teur [rak′on·tûr′] *n.* A person who is good at telling stories.
ra·coon [ra·ko͞on′] *n.* Another spelling of RACCOON.
rac·quet [rak′it] *n.* Another spelling of RACKET[2].
rac·quet·ball [rak′it·bôl′] *n.* A game like handball but played with a short-handled racket.
rac·y [rā′sē] *adj.* **rac·i·er, rac·i·est** 1 Spirited or lively: a *racy* style of writing. 2 Slightly immodest or indecent: a *racy* story.
rad. 1 radical. 2 radio. 3 radius.
ra·dar [rā′där] *n.* A device for locating objects and determining their size and speed by sending out radio waves and observing how and from where they are reflected by the objects. ◆ *Radar* comes from *ra(dio) d(etection) a(nd) r(anging).*
ra·di·al [rā′dē·əl] *adj.* 1 Of, being, or like a ray or radius. 2 Extending outward in all directions from one center. **—ra′di·al·ly** *adv.*
radial tire An air-filled tire having the cords of its inner fabric placed at right angles to the center line of the tread.
ra·di·ance [rā′dē·əns] *n.* Shining brightness.
ra·di·ant [rā′dē·ənt] *adj.* 1 Very bright and shining; brilliant. 2 Beaming, as with joy, love, or energy: a *radiant* smile. 3 Giving off radiant energy. 4 Coming in rays from a central source: *radiant* heat. **—ra′di·ant·ly** *adv.*
radiant energy Energy that is transmitted in the form of waves, especially electromagnetic waves, as light or X rays.
ra·di·ate [*v.* rā′dē·āt′, *adj.* rā′dē·it] *v.* **ra·di·at·ed, ra·di·at·ing,** *adj.* 1 *v.* To send out rays or radiation 2 *v.* To send out in rays: The sun *radiates* heat. 3 *v.* To come out in rays: Light *radiates* from the sun. 4 *v.* To spread out from a center, as the spokes of a wheel. 5 *adj.* Having rays or radiating parts: The sunflower is a *radiate* flower. 6 *v.* To show as if shining in rays: to *radiate* joy.
ra·di·a·tion [rā′dē·ā′shən] *n.* 1 The sending out of radiant energy, as from radioactive substances. 2 The energy sent out.
radiation sickness Sickness caused by overexposure to radiation. Its effects can range from nausea and fatigue to loss of blood-forming capacity and death.
ra·di·a·tor [rā′dē·ā′tər] *n.* 1 A network of pipes through which is passed steam or hot water to provide heat, as for a room. 2 A set of pipes for cooling circulating water that carries heat away from an engine, as in automobiles.
rad·i·cal [rad′i·kəl] 1 *adj.* Of, coming from, or going to the root; fundamental: *radical* differences. 2 *adj.* In mathematics, indicating or having to do with a square root or cube root. 3 *adj.* Extreme; thoroughgoing: *radical* changes in behavior. 4 *n.* A person who favors rapid and widespread changes or reforms, especially in politics or government. 5 *adj.* Favoring or having to do with such rapid changes. 6 *n.* A group of atoms that acts as a unit in one or more compounds and that always appears in combination. **—rad′i·cal·ism** *n.* **—rad·i·cal·ly** [rad′ik·lē] *adv.*
radical sign A sign ($\sqrt{\ }$) that indicates a specified root of the number written under it. $\sqrt[3]{8}$ = the cube root of 8, that is, 2.

R

a	add	**i**	it	**o͝o**	took	**oi**	oil
ā	ace	**ī**	ice	**o͞o**	pool	**ou**	pout
â	care	**o**	odd	**u**	up	**ng**	ring
ä	palm	**ō**	open	**û**	burn	**th**	thin
e	end	**ô**	order	**yo͞o**	fuse	**t̶h̶**	this
ē	equal					**zh**	vision

ə = a in *above* e in *sicken* i in *possible* o in *melon* u in *circus*

rad·i·cand [rad'ə·kand'] *n.* The number written under a radical sign: 8 is the *radicand* of $\sqrt[3]{8}$.
rad·i·ces [rad'i·sēz'] A plural of RADIX.
ra·di·i [rā'dē·ī] Plural of RADIUS.
ra·di·o [rā'dē·ō] *n., pl.* **ra·di·os,** *v.* **ra·di·oed, ra·di·o·ing** 1 *n.* The devices and methods by which sounds or other signals are changed into variations of an electromagnetic wave that travels through space to a receiver where the signals are recovered. 2 *adj. use*: a *radio* beam; a *radio* broadcast. 3 *n.* A receiver, transmitter, or other radio apparatus. 4 *v.* To send (a message) or communicate with (someone) by radio. 5 *n.* The radio business or industry.
ra·di·o·ac·tive [rā'dē·ō·ak'tiv] *adj.* Containing a nucleus which is inherently unstable in some way and which decays toward a more stable configuration by emitting matter or energy.
ra·di·o·ac·tiv·i·ty [rā'dē·ō·ak·tiv'i·tē] *n.* 1 The condition or quality of being radioactive. 2 Any of the matter or energy emitted by the decay of a radioactive nucleus.
radio astronomy The study of celestial bodies by observing the radio waves they give off.
radio beam A beam of signals sent out by a radio beacon to guide ships and aircraft.
ra·di·o·car·bon [rā'dē·ō·kär'bən] *n.* Another name for CARBON 14.
radio frequency An electronmagnetic wave frequency in the range within which radio waves may be transmitted.
ra·di·o·gram [rā'dē·ō·gram'] *n.* A message sent by a wireless telegraph.
ra·di·o·graph [rā'dē·ō·graf'] 1 *n.* A picture made by X rays or some other form of radiation other than visible light. 2 *v.* To make a radiograph of.
ra·di·o·i·so·tope [rā'dē·ō·ī'sə·tōp'] *n.* A radioactive isotope of a chemical element.
ra·di·ol·o·gy [rā'dē·ol'ə·jē] *n.* 1 The scientific study of radiation and radioactive substances. 2 The use of X rays and other forms of radiation to diagnose and treat diseases. 3 The use of X rays or other radiation to study physical objects. **—ra'·di·ol'o·gist** *n.*
ra·di·om·e·ter [rā'dē·om'ə·tər] *n.* An instrument for measuring the strength of radiant energy, consisting of a glass globe containing a set of vanes blackened on one side that spin about the central axis on which they are suspended when they are exposed to light.
ra·di·os·co·py [rā'dē·os'kə·pē] *n.* The observation of objects opaque to light by another form of radiation.
ra·di·o·sonde [rā'dē·ō·sond'] *n.* A package of instruments carried aloft by a balloon, designed to gather information about the weather and radio it back to earth.
radio star A star that emits mostly radio waves.
ra·di·o·tel·e·phone [rā'dē·ō·tel'ə·fōn'] *n.* A telephone that transmits sound by radio waves.
radio telescope An instrument used to receive radio waves given off by celestial bodies.
ra·di·o·ther·a·py [rā'dē·ō·ther'ə·pē] *n.* The use of X rays or other radiation to treat disease.
radio wave An electromagnetic wave having a frequency between about 10 kilohertz and 300,000 megahertz.
rad·ish [rad'ish] *n.* 1 A small, crisp, sharp-tasting plant root, eaten raw. It has a red or white skin. 2 The plant yielding this root.
ra·di·um [rā'dē·əm] *n.* A strongly radioactive metallic element found in ores of uranium. Its salts are sometimes used in medicine.
ra·di·us [rā'dē·əs] *n., pl.* **ra·di·i** [rā'dē·ī'] or **ra·di·us·es** 1 A straight line from the center of a circle or sphere to the circumference or surface. 2 A circular area or boundary measured by the length of its radius: only two stores within a *radius* of 15 miles. 3 The thicker and shorter bone of the forearm.

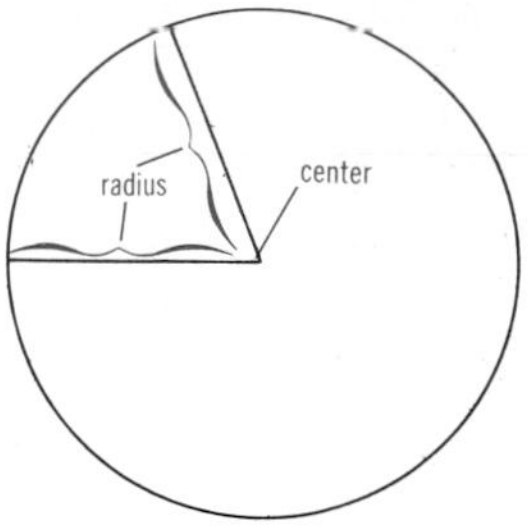

ra·dix [rā'diks] *n., pl.* **rad·i·ces** or **ra·dix·es** The base of a number system: The *radix* of the decimal system is 10.
ra·don [rā'don'] *n.* A heavy, radioactive, inert gaseous element consisting of several isotopes with short half-lives that originate as emanations from radium, thorium, and actinium.
rad·u·la [raj'ə·lə] *n., pl.* **rad·u·lae** [raj'ə·lē'] In most mollusks, a tooth-covered organ like a tongue that tears up food and carries it into the mouth.
RAF or **R.A.F.** Royal Air Force.
raf·fi·a [raf'ē·ə] *n.* Fiber from the leaves of a cultivated palm tree, used for baskets and other items.
raf·fle [raf'əl] *n., v.* **raf·fled, raf·fling** 1 *n.* A lottery in which many people buy tickets, each hoping to win the prize. 2 *v.* To offer as a prize in a raffle: to *raffle* off a turkey.
raft[1] [raft] *n.* A floating platform made of logs or planks fastened together.
raft[2] [raft] *n.* A large amount or collection.
raft·er [raf'tər] *n.* A sloping timber or beam giving form and support to a roof.

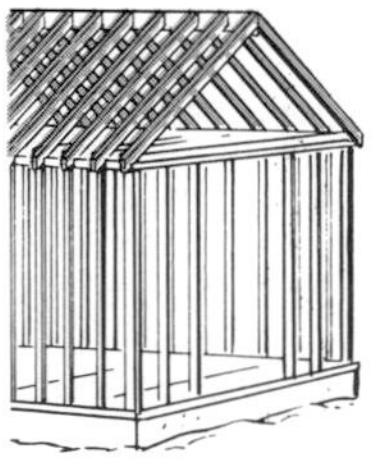
Rafters

rag[1] [rag] *n.* 1 A torn, worn-out, or discarded piece of cloth. 2 A small cloth, as one used for cleaning or polishing. 3 (*pl.*) Tattered or shabby clothes.
rag[2] [rag] *v.* **ragged, rag·ging** *slang* 1 To tease or bother. 2 To scold.
ra·ga [rä'gə] *n.* One of the traditional forms of Hindu music, characteristically consisting of a melodic theme and improvised variations.
rag·a·muf·fin [rag'ə·muf'in] *n.* A dirty, ragged person, especially a child.
rage [rāj] *n., v.* **raged, rag·ing** 1 *n.* Violent anger; fury; wrath: white-faced with *rage.* 2 *n.* A fit of violent anger: to fly into a *rage* at the insult. 3 *v.* To feel or show furious anger. 4 *v.* To move or proceed with great violence: The storm *raged.* 5 *n.* Any great violence, as of a storm. 6 *v.* To spread wildly and uncontrolled, as an epidemic. 7 *n.* A fad; fashion: Bulky sweaters were the *rage* last fall.
rag·ged [rag'id] *adj.* 1 Torn or worn into rags; tattered: *ragged* clothes. 2 Wearing tattered or shabby clothes: a *ragged* beggar. 3 Rough, shaggy, or uneven: a *ragged* haircut; *ragged* margins. 4 Jagged; rough: *ragged* rocks. **—rag'ged·ly** *adv.* **—rag'ged·ness** *n.*
rag·ing [rā'jing] *adj.* 1 Causing intense pain or distress: a *raging* toothache. 2 Caused or characterized by strong feelings; violent: a *raging* ar-

gument. **3** Unusually great; tremendous: a *raging* success.

rag·lan [rag′lən] **1** *n.* An overcoat or topcoat with sleeves that extend in one piece up to the neckline. **2** *adj. use: raglan* sleeves.

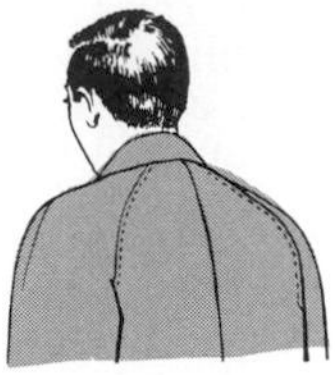

Raglan sleeves

ra·gout [ra·go͞o′] *n.* Meat and vegetables stewed with many herbs and spices.

rag·time [rag′tīm′] *n.* An early form of jazz using fast, syncopated rhythms.

rag·weed [rag′wēd′] *n.* A coarse, very common weed. Its pollen gives some people hay fever.

rah-rah [rä′rä′] *adj. slang* Energetically enthusiastic, as people at a college sports event.

raid [rād] **1** *n.* A sudden attack, as by a band of soldiers. **2** *n.* A sudden entering and seizing of what is found inside: The hungry children made a *raid* on the refrigerator. **3** *v.* To make a raid on. **4** *v.* To take part in a raid. **—raid′er** *n.*

rail[1] [rāl] *n.* **1** A bar, as one of wood or metal, held up by supports, as in a fence or at the side of a stairway. **2** Either of the parallel steel bars that form a track, as for a train. **3** A railroad: to ship goods by *rail.*

rail[2] [rāl] *v.* To complain in angry, bitter, or scornful words: to *rail* at one's enemies.

rail[3] [rāl] *n., pl.* **rail** or **rails** A bird with short wings and long legs, living in marshes.

rail·ing [rā′ling] *n.* **1** A fence or other barrier made up of one or more rails resting on supports. **2** Rails, or material to make rails.

rail·ler·y [rā′lər·ē] *n.* Good-natured teasing.

rail·road [rāl′rōd′] **1** *n.* A road having parallel steel rails that form a track for the wheels of trains to travel on. **2** *n.* A transportation system consisting of all the tracks and trains under one management, along with the stations, equipment, and employees. **3** *v.* To work on or for a railroad. **4** *v. U.S. informal* To rush or force very fast, without enough discussion: to *railroad* a bill through Congress.

rail·way [rāl′wā′] *n.* **1** A railroad. **2** Any tracks similar to those of a railroad.

rai·ment [rā′mənt] *n.* Wearing apparel; clothing: seldom used today.

rain [rān] **1** *n.* Condensed water vapor from the atmosphere, falling to earth in drops. **2** *n.* A fall of such drops; rainstorm or shower. **3** *v.* To fall from the clouds in drops: It is *raining.* **4** *n.* A fast, heavy fall of many similar things: a *rain* of arrows. **5** *v.* To fall like a heavy rain: Tears *rained* down their cheeks. **6** *v.* To send or pour like rain; shower.

rain·bow [rān′bō′] *n.* An arc of light exhibiting many colors: violet, indigo, blue, green, yellow, orange, and red. It appears in the atmosphere when sunlight passes through droplets of water, as mist, spray, or falling rain. ◆ *Rainbow* comes from the Old English word *regnboga,* which was a combination of the words for *rain* and *bow* (the bow of an archer).

rain·coat [rān′kōt′] *n.* A coat, usually waterproof, to be worn in rainy weather.

rain·drop [rān′drop′] *n.* A drop of rain.

rain·fall [rān′fôl′] *n.* **1** A shower. **2** The amount of water that falls as rain, hail, snow, or sleet in a given region within a certain length of time.

rain forest A dense tropical forest in a region that gets at least 100 inches of rain per year.

rain·storm [rān′stôrm′] *n.* A storm accompanied by rain.

rain·y [rā′nē] *adj.* **rain·i·er, rain·i·est** **1** Having much rain. **2** Bringing rain. **3** Made wet by rain: a *rainy* hike.

rainy day Some possible future time of need.

raise [rāz] *v.* **raised, rais·ing,** *n.* **1** *v.* To cause to move upward or to a higher level; lift: He *raised* his hand. **2** *v.* To set up or build; erect: to *raise* a monument. **3** *v.* To make greater, as in amount, size, value, or volume: to *raise* prices; Don't *raise* your voice. **4** *n.* An increase in amount. **5** *n.* An increase in pay. **6** *v.* To grow or breed: to *raise* corn; to *raise* horses. **7** *v. U.S.* To bring up; rear: to *raise* children. **8** *v.* To bring up for consideration: to *raise* a question. **9** *v.* To bring out; cause: The witty comment *raised* a laugh. **10** *v.* To stir up; make active; arouse. **11** *v.* To gather together; obtain or collect: to *raise* funds. **12** *v.* To end; lift: to *raise* a blockade. ◆ See RISE.

rai·sin [rā′zən] *n.* A sweet grape of a special sort dried in the sun or in an oven.

rai·son d'ê·tre [rā′zōn′de′tr(ə)] Reason or justification for being or existence.

ra·ja or **ra·jah** [rä′jə] *n.* **1** A Hindu prince or tribal chief in India. **2** A Malay ruler.

rake[1] [rāk] *n., v.* **raked, rak·ing** **1** *n.* A garden or farm tool consisting of a long handle with evenly spaced long teeth or prongs at the end. **2** *v.* To scrape together with or as if with a rake: to *rake* leaves. **3** *v.* To smooth, clean, or prepare with a rake: to *rake* soil or a lawn. **4** *v.* To search closely or carefully: to *rake* the stores for bargains. **5** *v.* To fire along the length of: Enemy guns *raked* the trenches.

Rake

rake[2] [rāk] *n.* A person who indulges too much in harmful pleasures, such as gambling or loose living.

rake[3] [rāk] *n., v.* **raked, rak·ing** **1** *n.* A slope, as of a ship's stern or mast. **2** *v.* To slant or cause to slant.

rake-off [rāk′ôf′] *n. informal* A commission, rebate, or percentage of the profits, especially when given or obtained as part of an illegal transaction.

rak·ish [rā′kish] *adj.* **1** Dashing; jaunty; smart: a cap worn at a *rakish* angle. **2** Having an appearance that suggests speed, as a boat.

ral·ly[1] [ral′ē] *n., pl.* **ral·lies,** *v.* **ral·lied, ral·ly·ing** **1**

a	add	**i**	it	**o͝o**	took	**oi**	oil
ā	ace	**ī**	ice	**o͞o**	pool	**ou**	pout
â	care	**o**	odd	**u**	up	**ng**	ring
ä	palm	**ō**	open	**û**	burn	**th**	thin
e	end	**ô**	order	**yo͞o**	fuse	**th̶**	this
ē	equal					**zh**	vision

ə = a in *above* e in *sicken* i in *possible* o in *melon* u in *circus*

R

n. A mass meeting or assembly of persons for some common purpose. **2** *v.* To bring or come together for united or efficient action: to *rally* fleeing troops. **3** *v.* To come to the support of: to *rally* to the cause of peace. **4** *v.* To regain strength; revive: The patient *rallied.* **5** *n.* The act of rallying.

ral·ly[2] [ral′ē] *v.* **ral·lied, ral·ly·ing** To make fun of good-humoredly; tease.

ram [ram] *n., v.* **rammed, ram·ming** **1** *n.* A male sheep. **2** *v.* To strike with force: The ship *rammed* into the pier. **3** *v.* To drive or force down or into something. **4** *n.* A machine that strikes powerful blows, as a battering ram.

RAM RANDOM-ACCESS MEMORY.

ram·ble [ram′bəl] *v.* **ram·bled, ram·bling,** *n.* **1** *v.* To walk or stroll freely and aimlessly; roam; wander. **2** *n.* An aimless, unhurried walk or hike. **3** *v.* To speak or write in a disorganized way, wandering from subject to subject. **4** *v.* To twist irregularly, as a vine or path.

ram·bler [ram′blər] *n.* **1** A person or thing that rambles. **2** A type of climbing rose.

ram·bling [ram′bling] *adj.* **1** Wandering aimlessly; roaming. **2** Following an irregular course; twisting; winding. **3** Going from subject to subject in an inconsistent discursive way: a long *rambling* speech. **4** Moving or extending irregularly: a *rambling* mansion with many additions.

ram·bunc·tious [ram·bungk′shəs] *adj. U.S. informal* Wild, unruly, and boisterous in behavior.

ram·i·fi·ca·tion [ram′ə·fə·kā′shən] *n.* **1** The act or process of branching. **2** A branch or branchlike part. **3** Something that develops like a small branch on a big one; outgrowth; result: the *ramifications* of the plan.

ram·i·fy [ram′ə·fī] *v.* **ram·i·fied, ram·i·fy·ing** To divide or spread out into or as if into branches.

ramp [ramp] *n.* **1** An inclined or sloping passageway or roadway connecting a higher and a lower level. **2** A movable stairway by which passengers enter or leave an airplane.

Ramp

ram·page [*n.* ram′pāj′, *v.* ram·pāj′] *n., v.* **ram·paged, ram·pag·ing** **1** *n.* A spree of violent, wild, or angry behavior or dashing about: The dog went on a *rampage.* **2** *v.* To go on a rampage.

ram·pant [ram′pənt] *adj.* **1** Spreading, growing, or acting without check or restraint; wild: Weeds ran *rampant* over the field. **2** Widespread. **3** Standing on one or both hind legs with both forelegs up: a lion *rampant* in a coat of arms.

ram·part [ram′pärt′] *n.* **1** A bank of earth, often with a parapet on top, surrounding a fort as a defense. **2** Any defense or bulwark.

ram·rod [ram′rod′] *n.* **1** A rod used to push down the charge in a gun loaded through the muzzle. **2** A rod for cleaning a weapon, as a rifle or gun.

ram·shack·le [ram′shak′əl] *adj.* Seeming about to fall apart; rickety: a *ramshackle* cabin.

ran [ran] Past tense of RUN.

ranch [ranch] **1** *n.* A large farm devoted to raising or grazing large herds of animals, as cattle or horses. **2** *n.* A large farm: a fruit *ranch.* **3** *v.* To manage or work on a ranch. **—ranch′er** *n.*

ran·cid [ran′sid] *adj.* Having the bad taste or smell of spoiled fat or oil: *rancid* butter.

ran·cor [rang′kər] *n.* Bitter resentment, great hatred, or deep spite. **—ran′cor·ous** *adj.*

rand [rand] *n.* The basic unit of money in the Republic of South Africa.

ran·dom [ran′dəm] *adj.* Not planned or organized; chance: a *random* selection. **—at random** Without plan, method, or aim; haphazardly.

ran·dom-ac·cess memory [ran′dəm·ak′ses] A computer memory whose contents can be accessed in any order a user desires.

ran·dom·ize [ran′dəm·īz′] *v.* **ran·dom·ized, ran·dom·iz·ing** To make random.

random sample A method of collecting data, as for an opinion poll, that gives each element (here, each person) equal probability of being selected.

rang [rang] Past tense of RING[1].

range [rānj] *n., v.* **ranged, rang·ing** **1** *n.* The extent or set of limits within which something can move, operate, vary, or be found: the *range* of a missile; the *range* of a voice. **2** *v.* To vary or lie within certain limits: Their ages *ranged* from four to six. **3** *n.* A set, selection, or variation within limits: a wide *range* of styles. **4** *n.* The difference between the highest and lowest number in a set of data. **5** *n.* A broad tract of land where animals roam and graze. **6** *v.* To roam over: Lions *range* the African plains. **7** *n.* A row, line, or series, as of mountains. **8** *v.* To place or arrange in order: to *range* pictures on a wall. **9** *v.* To place (oneself) in line: The Tories *ranged* themselves with the redcoats. **10** *n.* A place where one can practice shooting: a rifle *range.* **11** *n.* A large stove.

rang·er [rān′jər] *n.* **1** An official who patrols and protects a government forest or park. **2** A member of an armed patrol that protects a region. **3** A person or thing that ranges or roves.

rang·y [rān′jē] *adj.* **rang·i·er, rang·i·est** Having long, slender legs and a lean body.

rank[1] [rangk] **1** *n.* A grade in a fixed scale of authority or honor: the *rank* of major. **2** *n.* Relative standing or position: a school of the first *rank.* **3** *v.* To place in a certain order, class, or grade: Would you *rank* this artist among the great painters? **4** *v.* To hold a particular place or rank: A trip to Paris *ranks* high on my list. **5** *n.* High degree or position: a person of *rank.* **6** *v.* To have a high rank or the highest rank. **7** *v.* To outrank. **8** *n.* A line, as of soldiers, drawn up side by side. **9** *n.* (*pl.*) All the enlisted personnel in the armed forces. **10** *n.* (*pl.*) A social or professional class: the *ranks* of authors. **—rank and file** **1** The members of a group, as an army or union, who are not officers or leaders. **2** The common people.

rank[2] [rangk] *adj.* **1** Growing thickly and abundantly in a coarse way: *rank* weeds. **2** Strong and disagreeable to the taste or smell: a *rank* cigar. **3** Extreme or complete: said about something bad: *rank* injustice. **—rank′ly** *adv.*

ran·kle [rang′kəl] *v.* **ran·kled, ran·kling** To cause pain, anger, or bitterness.

ran·sack [ran′sak′] *v.* **1** To search through every part of: to *ransack* a desk for a letter. **2** To search for plunder: Armies *ransacked* the city.

ran·som [ran′səm] **1** *n.* The price demanded or paid for the release of a person held captive. **2** *v.* To cause to be set free by paying ransom for: to *ransom* a kidnaped person. **3** *n.* The freeing of a captive through payment of ransom.

rant [rant] 1 *v.* To speak loudly, wildly, or excitedly; rave. 2 *n.* Wild, extravagant talk.

rap[1] [rap] *v.* **rapped, rap·ping,** *n.* 1 *v.* To knock or strike sharply and quickly: to *rap* on wood. 2 *n.* A light, sharp knock or tap. 3 *v.* To utter in a sharp, forceful way: To *rap* out a command. 4 *v.* To discuss something frankly; talk freely. 5 *n.* A frank discussion; talk. 6 *n.* A type of popular music consisting of rhymed verses chanted to a strong beat. 7 *n. slang* The blame or punishment for misbehavior, mistake, or crime.

rap[2] [rap] *n.* The smallest amount or degree; tiny bit: doesn't care a *rap.*

ra·pa·cious [rə·pā'shəs] *adj.* 1 Ready to take by force whatever one wants: *rapacious* conquerors. 2 Grasping; greedy. 3 Living on prey, as hawks do; predatory. **—ra·pa'cious·ly** *adv.*

ra·pac·i·ty [rə·pas'ə·tē] *n.* The condition of being rapacious.

rape[1] [rāp] *n., v.* **raped, rap·ing** 1 *n.* A snatching and carrying off by force. 2 *n.* The crime of having sexual intercourse with a woman or girl against her will and by force. 3 *v.* To commit rape upon (a woman or girl).

rape[2] [rāp] *n.* A European plant whose leaves are used as food for cattle and whose seeds produce an oil.

rap·id [rap'id] 1 *adj.* Very quick, swift, or fast. 2 *n.* (*pl.*) A part of a river or stream where the current runs very fast because the bed slopes steeply. **—rap'id·ly** *adv.*

Rapids

rap·id-fire [rap'id·fīr'] *adj.* 1 Firing shots rapidly. 2 Marked by speed, one thing coming rapidly after another: *rapid-fire* questions.

ra·pid·i·ty [rə·pid'ə·tē] *n.* Swiftness; speed: the *rapidity* of the current.

ra·pi·er [rā'pē·ər] *n.* A long, narrow sword of light weight, used for thrusting.

rap·ine [rap'in] *n.* The taking of property by force, as in war; pillage; plunder.

rap·pel [rə·pəl'] *v.* **rap·peled** or **rap·pelled, rap·pel·ing** or **rap·pel·ling,** *n.* 1 *v.* To go down a cliff or other steep height on a rope passed under one thigh and over the opposite shoulder. 2 *n.* A descent by rappeling.

rap·port [ra·pôr'] *n.* A relationship of sympathy and mutual understanding: Good *rapport* with players is important for a coach.

rap·proche·ment [rä'prōsh·män'] *n.* 1 The establishment or a renewal of friendly relations, as between two countries. 2 A condition of friendly relations.

rap·scal·lion [rap·skal'yən] *n.* A rascal.

rapt [rapt] *adj.* 1 So taken up with one thing as not to know what else is going on: to read with *rapt* attention. 2 Carried away with emotion; enraptured.

rap·tor [rap'tər] *n.* A bird of prey.

rap·ture [rap'chər] *n.* Very great or complete pleasure or delight; ecstasy.

rap·tur·ous [rap'chər·əs] *adj.* Feeling, showing, or full of rapture. **—rap'tur·ous·ly** *adv.*

rare[1] [râr] *adj.* **rar·er, rar·est** 1 Seldom seen or found; unusual; uncommon. 2 Highly valued because scarce or not commonplace: a *rare* book; *rare* beauty. 3 Splendid. 4 Not dense; rarefied: *rare* air. **—rare'ly** *adv.* **—rare'ness** *n.*

rare[2] [râr] *adj.* **rar·er, rar·est** Not thoroughly cooked: *rare* meat. **—rare'ness** *n.*

rare·bit [râr'bit] *n.* Welsh rabbit.

rare earth Any of a group of clayey minerals composed mainly of oxides of the rare-earth elements. ◆ *Rare earth* at one time signified that these minerals were thought to be very uncommon, and the term has persisted even though they are now known to be fairly abundant in the earth's crust.

rare-earth element Any of a group of chemically similar metallic elements mostly occurring together as oxides in the rare earths and including cerium, dysprosium, erbium, europium, gadolinium, holmium, lanthanum, lutetium, neodymium, praseodymium, promethium, samarium, terbium, thulium, ytterbium, and sometimes yttrium and scandium. These elements are difficult to separate from each other and to obtain in the elemental state. Many of their compounds have a clear, bright, distinctive color, and many are slightly toxic. As elemental metals they are soft, silvery white, and ductile.

rar·e·fy [râr'ə·fī'] *v.* **rar·e·fied, rar·e·fy·ing** 1 To make or become rare or less dense, as air. 2 To make more refined or delicate.

rar·i·ty [râr'ə·tē] *n., pl.* **rar·i·ties** 1 The condition of being rare, uncommon, or infrequent. 2 Something rare or scarce: A $2 bill is a *rarity.* 3 Thinness, as of the air.

ras·cal [ras'kəl] *n.* 1 A mean, dishonest person; rogue; scoundrel. 2 A playfully mischievous child or animal. **—ras'cal·ly** *adj., adv.*

ras·cal·i·ty [ras·kal'ə·tē] *n., pl.* **ras·cal·i·ties** 1 The character or behavior of a rascal. 2 A dishonest or mischievous act.

rash[1] [rash] *adj.* Too bold, hasty, or imprudent; reckless. **—rash'ly** *adv.* **—rash'ness** *n.*

rash[2] [rash] *n.* A breaking out of the skin in reddish blotches: a *rash* from poison ivy.

rash·er [rash'ər] *n.* A thin slice of bacon.

rasp [rasp] 1 *v.* To make a rough, harsh, grating sound. 2 *v.* To say in a harsh, grating voice: to *rasp* out a threat. 3 *n.* A harsh, rough, or grating sound. 4 *v.* To scrape or grate with or as if with a file. 5 *v.* To irritate. 6 *n.* A rough file having sharp points rather than ridges on its cutting surfaces.

rasp·ber·ry [raz'ber'ē] *n., pl.* **rasp·ber·ries** 1 A small, round, red or black fruit full of seeds. 2 The prickly bush on which it grows. 3 *slang* A sound of derision, disgust, or contempt made by protruding the tongue through the lips and expelling air forcibly to vibrate the tongue.

rasp·y [ras'pē] *adj.* **rasp·i·er, rasp·i·est** 1 Rough or harsh: a *raspy* voice. 2 Easily upset or annoyed; irritable.

R

a	add	**i**	it	**o͝o**	took	**oi**	oil
ā	ace	**ī**	ice	**o͞o**	pool	**ou**	pout
â	care	**o**	odd	**u**	up	**ng**	ring
ä	palm	**ō**	open	**û**	burn	**th**	thin
e	end	**ô**	order	**yo͞o**	fuse	**t͟h**	this
ē	equal					**zh**	vision

ə = a in *above* e in *sicken* i in *possible* o in *melon* u in *circus*

rat [rat] *n., v.* **rat·ted, rat·ting** 1 *n.* A gnawing animal similar to a mouse, but larger. Rats are gray, brown, or black. 2 *v.* To hunt rats. 3 *n. slang* A sneaky, mean, contemptible person, as a traitor. 4 *v. slang* To inform or squeal: The thief *ratted* on the others involved in the crime. **—smell a rat** To suspect that something is wrong.

Rat

ra·tan [ra·tan′] *n.* Another spelling of RATTAN.
ratch·et [rach′it] *n.* 1 A wheel or bar with slanted notches on its edge that catch on a pawl, preventing reverse motion. 2 The pawl. 3 The entire mechanism.
rate[1] [rāt] *n., v.* **rat·ed, rat·ing** 1 *n.* Amount or degree measured in proportion to something else: a high *rate* of speed. 2 *n.* In mathematics, the ratio of the measures of two quantities. If you go 60 miles in 3 hours, the rate, or speed, is 20 miles an hour. 3 *n.* A price, charge, or payment per unit: a hotel's daily *rates*; a bank's interest *rate*. 4 *v.* To assign a value or grade to: to *rate* someone's work. 5 *n.* A rank or class: first *rate*. 6 *v.* To have a certain worth or rank: Her work *rates* high. 7 *v.* To consider: He is *rated* as a great artist. 8 *v. informal* To deserve: The stock clerk *rates* a promotion. **—at any rate** In any case; anyhow.
rate[2] [rāt] *v.* **rat·ed, rat·ing** To rebuke angrily; scold.
rath·er [rath′ər] 1 *adv.* With greater preference; more willingly: I would *rather* walk than ride. 2 *adv.* Instead of; more properly: You, *rather* than I, should go. 3 *adv.* More accurately: that evening, or, *rather,* late that night. 4 *adv.* On the contrary: The rain didn't hurt the crops; *rather,* it helped them. 5 *adv.* Somewhat: It's *rather* hot. 6 *interj. British* Yes indeed! **—had rather** Would prefer to or prefer that: I *had rather* not go.
rat·i·fy [rat′ə·fī] *v.* **rat·i·fied, rat·i·fy·ing** To give official approval to; make legal by approving; confirm: to *ratify* a treaty. **—rat·i·fi·ca·tion** [rat′ə·fə·kā′shən] *n.*
rat·ing [rā′ting] *n.* A grade, rank, or standing in relation to other people or things rated: a credit *rating*; a TV show's *rating*.
ra·tio [rā′shō *or* rā′shē·ō] *n., pl.* **ra·tios** The way in which one quantity is related to another; proportion. It is expressed as the quotient of the first divided by the second: In a group of 10 juniors and 5 seniors, the *ratio* of juniors to seniors is 2 to 1, or 2/1.
ra·ti·o·ci·nate [rash′ē·os′ə·nāt′] *v.* **ra·ti·o·ci·nat·ed, ra·ti·o·ci·nat·ing** To think logically; reason. **—ra′ti·o′ci·na′tion** *n.*
ra·tion [rash′ən *or* rā′shən] 1 *v.* To limit the amount of (something scarce) that a person can have or use: to *ration* meat in wartime. 2 *n.* A portion; share. 3 *n.* Food for one person for one day. 4 *v.* To issue rations to, as an army.
ra·tion·al [rash′ən·əl] *adj.* 1 Able to reason: A porpoise is a *rational* animal. 2 Based on or guided by reason: a *rational* argument. 3 Sane, sensible, or reasonable. **—ra·tion·al·i·ty** [rash′ən·al′ə·tē] *n.* **—ra′tion·al·ly** *adv.*
ra·tion·ale [rash′ə·nal′] *n.* A reason that justifies something; rational basis.
ra·tion·al·ism [rash′ən·əl·iz′əm] *n.* Belief in reason as the basis for knowledge, action, or faith.
ra·tion·al·ize [rash′ən·əl·īz′] *v.* **ra·tion·al·ized, ra·tion·al·iz·ing** To explain (as behavior) in a way that is false but seems reasonable, often done unconsciously to protect one's pride: to *rationalize* fear as caution. **—ra·tion·al·i·za·tion** [rash′ən·əl·ə·zā′·shən] *n.*
rational number A number which is an integer or the quotient of two integers.
rat·line or **rat·lin** [rat′lin] *n.* One of the small ropes fastened across the shrouds of a ship, serving as the steps of a rope ladder.

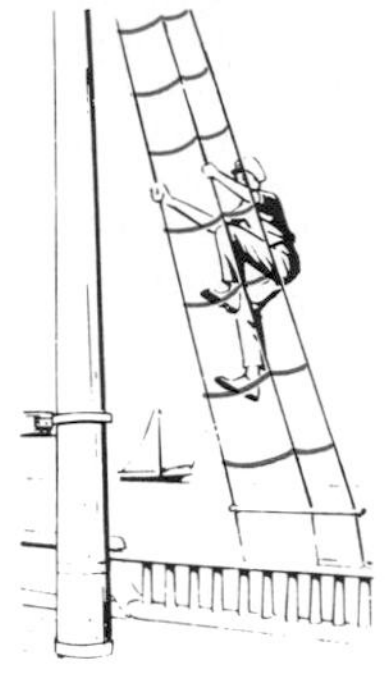

Ratlines

rat race *slang* An activity or routine that is hectic, competitive, and exhausting.
rat·tan [ra·tan′] *n.* 1 The long, tough, flexible stem of various palm trees, used in making wickerwork, light furniture, and other items. 2 The tree itself. 3 A cane or switch of rattan.
rat·tle [rat′(ə)l] *v.* **rat·tled, rat·tling,** *n.* 1 *v.* To make or cause to make a rapid series of quick, sharp noises: The windows *rattled*; to *rattle* keys. 2 *n.* A rapid series of quick, sharp sounds. 3 *n.* A toy or implement made to produce a rattling noise. 4 *n.* Any of the horny rings in the tail of a rattlesnake. 5 *v.* To move with a rattling noise: The carriage *rattled* along. 6 *v.* To talk rapidly and aimlessly; chatter. 7 *v.* To utter rapidly: to *rattle* off an answer. 8 *v. informal* To confuse or upset: to *rattle* a performer by heckling.
rat·tler [rat′lər] *n.* A rattlesnake.
rat·tle·snake [rat′(ə)l·snāk′] *n.* A poisonous American snake with a tail ending in a series of horny joints that rattle when shaken.

Rattlesnake

rat·tle·trap [rat′(ə)l·trap′] *n.* Something that is rickety and rattling, especially an old car or other vehicle.
rau·cous [rô′kəs] *adj.* Rough in sound; hoarse; harsh: a *raucous* voice. **—rau′cous·ly** *adv.*
rav·age [rav′ij] *v.* **rav·aged, rav·ag·ing,** *n.* 1 *v.* To hurt or damage severely; destroy. 2 *n.* Destructive action or result: the *ravages* of the hurricane.
rave [rāv] *v.* **raved, rav·ing,** *n.* 1 *v.* To talk in a wild, confused way. 2 *v.* To howl and rage, as the wind does. 3 *v.* To speak with great or too great praise: They *raved* about the play. 4 *n. informal* A highly favorable comment. 5 *adj. use: rave* reviews of the new Italian film. 6 *n.* The act of raving.
rav·el [rav′əl] *v.* **rav·eled** or **rav·elled, rav·el·ing** or **rav·el·ling** 1 To separate into loose threads or fibers: This sweater has begun to *ravel.* 2 To separate the threads of; unravel.
ra·ven [rā′vən] 1 *n.* A large, glossy, black crow with shaggy throat feathers and a powerful beak. 2 *adj.* Black and shining: *raven* hair.
rav·en·ing [rav′ən·ing] *adj.* Greedy; rapacious.
rav·en·ous [rav′ən·əs] *adj.* 1 Wildly hungry. 2 Extremely greedy. **—rav′en·ous·ly** *adv.*
ra·vine [rə·vēn′] *n.* A long, narrow, deep depression in the earth that has steep sides and was usually cut out by a flow of water; gorge.
rav·ing [rā′ving] 1 *adj.* Talking in a wild, confused way: a *raving* demagogue. 2 *adj.* Outstanding;

splendid: a *raving* success. **3** *n.* Wild, confused speech.
rav·i·o·li [rav′ē·ō′lē] *n.* A kind of pasta containing a filling, as of ground meat or cheese, usually served with a tomato sauce.
rav·ish [rav′ish] *v.* **1** To fill with strong emotion, especially delight. **2** To rape.
rav·ish·ing [rav′ish·ing] *adj.* Giving great delight; enchanting: a *ravishing* beauty.
raw [rô] *adj.* **1** Not cooked. **2** In a natural condition; not processed: *raw* sugar. **3** With no experience; untrained: a *raw* recruit. **4** Having the skin rubbed off; sore: The child's knees were *raw.* **5** Damp and chilling: *raw* weather. **6** *slang* Harsh or unfair: a *raw* deal. **—raw′ness** *n.*
raw·boned [rô′bōnd′] *adj.* Having little flesh covering the bones; gaunt.
raw·hide [rô′hīd′] *n.* **1** The untanned hide of cattle. **2** A whip made of a strip of this hide.
raw material Material in its natural condition; something that can be processed, treated, or manufactured to make it more useful or valuable.
ray[1] [rā] *n.* **1** A thin beam of light or other radiant energy. **2** A path taken by radiant energy. **3** Any of various forms of radiant energy, as gamma rays or X rays. **4** One of a group of lines coming from a common center and extending forever in one direction. **5** A part like this, as an arm of a starfish. **6** A faint gleam; trace: a *ray* of hope.
ray[2] [rā] *n.* A fish having a flat body, very broad fins, and a long, slender tail.

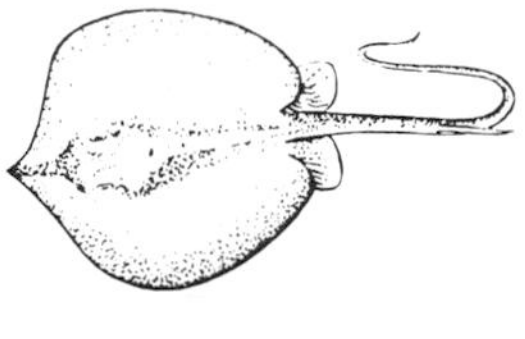
A typical ray

ray·on [rā′on′] *n.* **1** An artificial fiber made of cellulose dissolved in a chemical solution and squeezed into filaments. **2** Cloth, yarn, or thread made of rayon.
raze [rāz] *v.* **razed, raz·ing** To tear down, as a building; level to the ground.
ra·zor [rā′zər] *n.* A sharp cutting instrument used for shaving off hair, especially whiskers.
razz [raz] *v. slang* To make fun of with loud, scornful noises; heckle. ◆ *Razz* is a shortening of *raspberry,* a slang term for a jeering sound made by noisy fans at sports events.
Rb The symbol for the element rubidium.
rbi or **r.b.i.** run batted in.
RC or **R.C.** **1** Red Cross. **2** Roman Catholic.
RCAF or **R.C.A.F.** Royal Canadian Air Force.
rd. **1** (*often written* **Rd.**) road. **2** rod.
R.D. rural delivery.
RDA recommended daily allowance.
re [rā] *n.* In music, a syllable used to represent the second tone of a major scale or the fourth tone of a minor scale, or in a fixed system the tone D.
re- A prefix meaning: **1** Again, as in *redo.* **2** Back, as in *retract.* ◆ *Re-* meaning *again* is freely used in forming words. It is followed by a hyphen if the word formed would otherwise be spelled like an existing word with a different meaning. Since *recover* means to get back, the word meaning to cover again is written *re-cover.* Where no confusion would arise, *re-* as a prefix is usually joined to words directly, without a hyphen. However, many writers still prefer to put a hyphen between *re-* and a word beginning with a vowel, especially *e*: re-educate.
Re The symbol for the element rhenium.
reach [rēch] **1** *v.* To stretch one's hand or arm out or forth: How high can you *reach*?; I *reached* for the candy. **2** *v.* To stretch out or extend: *Reach* out your hand to him. **3** *v.* To touch or get hold of: Can you *reach* that book? **4** *v.* To hand over; pass: *Reach* me the wrench. **5** *n.* The act or power of reaching. **6** *n.* The distance over which a person or thing can reach: The top shelf is out of *reach.* **7** *n.* Range or scope; capacity: Higher mathematics is beyond my *reach.* **8** *v.* To go or extend: The ladder *reached* to the ceiling. **9** *n.* A stretch or expanse: the far *reaches* of Siberia. **10** *v.* To arrive at or come to: to *reach* a destination. **11** *v.* To get in touch with: You can *reach* me at home after 5 o'clock. **12** *v.* To influence or affect: The candidate's speech failed to *reach* the audience.
re·act [rē·akt′] *v.* **1** To act as the result of some thing, as a happening or stimulus: The horse *reacted* to the smell of smoke. **2** To act in turn or back and forth: Students and teachers *react* to one another. **3** To act in a contrary way or in opposition: to *react* against too much urging. **4** To take part in or undergo a chemical reaction.
re·ac·tion [rē·ak′shən] *n.* **1** An action in response to something, as a happening or stimulus. **2** Contrary, opposite, or back-and-forth action. **3** A tendency or trend toward an earlier idea or condition. **4** A chemical change. **5** Any change in an atomic nucleus.
re·ac·tion·ar·y [rē·ak′shən·er′ē] *adj., n., pl.* **re·ac·tion·ar·ies** **1** *adj.* Of, showing, or desiring a return to an earlier idea or condition, especially an out-of-date one. **2** *n.* A person opposed to political or social change.
re·ac·ti·vate [rē·ak′tə·vāt′] *v.* **re·ac·ti·vat·ed, re·ac·ti·vat·ing** To make active again.
re·ac·tive [rē·ak′tiv] *adj.* **1** Tending to react. **2** Of, having to do with, characterized by, or being a reaction: *reactive* vibrations after an explosion. **—re·ac·tiv·i·ty** [re′ak·tiv′ə·tē] *n.*
re·ac·tor [rē·ak′tər] *n.* **1** A person or thing that reacts. **2** An apparatus for the controlled release of atomic energy in which the chain reaction of nuclear fission is regulated by a moderator, such as layers of graphite.
read[1] [rēd] *v.* **read** [red], **read·ing** [rē′ding] **1** To get the meaning of (as a book, chart, or piece of music) by interpreting its printed or written symbols. **2** To say aloud the words of (something written): *Read* the letter to me. **3** To get information from written words: to *read* about the pioneers. **4** To study: to *read* law. **5** To have as its wording: The passage *reads* "principal," not "principle." **6** To use written language: Your speech *reads* well. **7** To guess, find, or tell hidden information in, from, or about: You can *read* my mind; to *read* palms; to *read* the future. **8** To interpret. **9** To register

R

a	add	**i**	it	**o͝o**	took	**oi**	oil
ā	ace	**ī**	ice	**o͞o**	pool	**ou**	pout
â	care	**o**	odd	**u**	up	**ng**	ring
ä	palm	**ō**	open	**û**	burn	**th**	thin
e	end	**ô**	order	**yo͞o**	fuse	**th**	this
ē	equal					**zh**	vision

ə = a in *above* e in *sicken* i in *possible* o in *melon* u in *circus*

and show: The speedometer *reads* 25 mph. **10** To note the indications of: to *read* a meter. **11** In computer technology, to obtain (information), as from a tape or a computer memory. **—read between the lines** To discover a meaning in addition to the open and obvious one. **—read into** To find possible hidden meaning or significance in.
read[2] [red] *adj.* Informed or educated by reading: often used in combination, as in *well-read.*
read·a·ble [rē′də·bəl] *adj.* **1** Clear enough to read; legible. **2** Interesting or fun to read.
read·er [rē′dər] *n.* **1** A person who reads. **2** A schoolbook used to teach reading.
read·i·ly [red′ə·lē] *adv.* **1** Quickly and easily. **2** Without objecting; willingly.
read·ing [rē′ding] *n.* **1** The act of a person who reads. **2** Something that is read or meant to be read. **3** An event at which something written is read aloud. **4** The amount measured and shown by a gauge or instrument. **5** An interpretation: a pianist's *reading* of a sonata.
re·ad·just [rē′ə·just′] *v.* **1** To adjust again. **2** To become accustomed again: to *readjust* to normal life after an illness.
read-on·ly memory [rēd′ōn′lē] A computer memory that the processor can read but not change, often used for permanently stored information such as the rules of arithmetic.
read·y [red′ē] *adj.* **read·i·er, read·i·est,** *v.* **read·ied, read·y·ing** **1** *adj.* Prepared for immediate use or action. **2** *v.* To make ready; prepare. **3** *adj.* On hand: *ready* money. **4** *adj.* Willing: *ready* to help. **5** *adj.* Likely; liable: *ready* to sink. **6** *adj.* Quick; prompt: a *ready* answer. **—read′i·ness** *n.*
read·y-made [red′ē·mād′] *adj.* Made up in a standard form in advance of any order; not made for one particular customer.
re·a·gent [rē·ā′jənt] *n.* A substance used as a test of the presence of any of certain chemicals with which it reacts characteristically.
real[1] [rēl *or* rē′əl] *adj.* **1** Existing, actual, or true; not imagined or invented: *real* life; the *real* reason. **2** Genuine: *real* pearls. **3** Made up of land, buildings, or other immovable or permanent property. **4** Adjusted to allow for inflation: She got a raise, but her *real* income remained about the same. ◆ *Real* is always an adjective. Its adverbial use in expressions like *real good* is nonstandard; to be strictly correct, use *really good.*
re·al[2] [rē′əl *or* rā·äl′] *n., pl.* **re·als** or **re·a·les** [rā·ä′·lās] A former Spanish silver coin.
real estate Land, including whatever is on or in it, as trees, houses, minerals, and crops.
re·al·ism [rē′əl·iz′əm] *n.* **1** A tendency to face facts and be practical. **2** In literature and art, the picturing of people and things as they are in real life. **—re′al·ist** *n.*
re·al·is·tic [rē′əl·is′tik] *adj.* **1** Having to do with or emphasizing what is real and practical: a *realistic* forecast. **2** Showing things in a lifelike way: a *realistic* story. **—re′al·is′ti·cal·ly** *adv.*
re·al·i·ty [rē·al′ə·tē] *n., pl.* **re·al·i·ties** **1** A being real; true condition; actual existence. **2** An actual person, thing, or fact: Our plan became a *reality.* **3** The real world of facts: to face *reality* after a vacation. **4** Artistic realism. **—in reality** In fact; really.
re·al·i·za·tion [rē′əl·i·zā′shən] *n.* **1** The act of realizing or the condition of being realized. **2** Something made real or actual. **3** A full, often sudden understanding or appreciation.
re·al·ize [rē′əl·īz′] *v.* **re·al·ized, re·al·iz·ing** **1** To understand or appreciate fully: I *realize* that you're ill. **2** To turn into actual fact or being: to *realize* a hope. **3** To sell (property or assets) for cash. **4** To get as a profit or return: The store *realized* $500 on the sale.
re·al·ly [rē′ə·lē *or* rē′lē] *adv.* **1** Actually or truly. **2** Honestly; indeed: *Really,* can't you behave?
realm [relm] *n.* **1** A kingdom. **2** A region or area: the *realm* of imagination.
real number Any rational or irrational number.
real time The actual time a computer takes to perform an operation that affects some process or activity going on at the same time.
re·al·tor [rē′əl·tər] *n.* A person whose work is to appraise, buy, and sell real estate.
re·al·ty [rē′əl·tē] *n.* Real estate.
ream[1] [rēm] *n.* **1** An amount of paper consisting of 480, 500, or 516 sheets. **2** (*pl.*) *informal* A great amount or number: *reams* of protests.
ream[2] [rēm] *v.* To enlarge or widen (a hole).
ream·er [rē′mər] *n.* **1** A tool used to enlarge or shape a hole. **2** A device for squeezing juice from fruit.

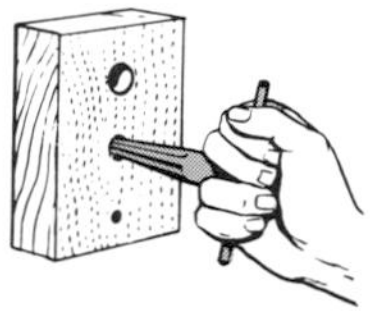
Reamer

re·an·i·mate [rē·an′ə·māt′] *v.* **re·an·i·mat·ed, re·an·i·mat·ing** To bring back to life; give fresh vigor to.
reap [rēp] *v.* **1** To cut down or gather in (grain); harvest (a crop). **2** To take a grain crop from, as a field. **3** To receive as a return: to *reap* the rewards of hard work. **—reap′er** *n.*
re·ap·pear [rē′ə·pir′] *v.* To appear again. **—re′ap·pear′ance** *n.*
re·ap·por·tion [rē′ə·pôr′shən] *v.* **1** To apportion or distribute again. **2** To make a new apportionment (def. 2) of: U.S. Congressional seats are *reapportioned* after every census. **—re′ap·por′tion·ment** *n.*
rear[1] [rir] **1** *n.* The part or space behind or in the back: the *rear* of the bus. **2** *adj.* At or in the back: *rear* windows. **3** *n.* The part of a military force that is farthest from the front.
rear[2] [rir] *v.* **1** To care for and train; bring up: to *rear* children. **2** To breed or raise: to *rear* animals. **3** To rise upon the hind legs, as a horse does. **4** To set up or build: to *rear* a tower. **5** To lift: Rebellion *reared* its head.
rear admiral A naval rank. In the U.S. Navy, a rear admiral is an officer ranking next above a captain and next below a vice admiral.
re·arm [rē·ärm′] *v.* **1** To arm again. **2** To arm with more modern weapons. **—re·ar′ma·ment** *n.*
re·ar·range [rē′ə·rānj′] *v.* **re·ar·ranged, re·ar·rang·ing** To arrange again or differently.
rear·view mirror [rir′vyo͞o′] A mirror placed so as to give a view of the area behind a vehicle.
rear·ward [rir′wərd] **1** *adj.* Toward, in, or at the back. **2** *adv.* Toward the rear; backward.
rea·son [rē′zən] **1** *n.* An explanation for something, as an action or belief: What is your *reason* for being late? **2** *n.* A motive or cause for an action or belief: Curiosity was my *reason* for asking. **3** *n.* The ability to think things through, have ideas, and reach conclusions: Human beings have *reason.* **4** *v.* To think in a logical, orderly way. **5** *v.* To argue or talk in a logical way meant to persuade: Try to *reason* with them. **6** *n.* Good judgment; common sense: They won't hear *reason.*

7 *n.* Sanity. **—by reason of** Because of. **—in reason** Within acceptable limits; reasonable. **—it stands to reason** It is logical or reasonable. ◆ *Reason, purpose,* and *motive* explain why people behave in certain ways. When your teacher asks why you did not do your homework, you should give a *reason,* such as "I was sick" or "I lost the assignment." The *purpose* of homework is to give you practice in learning by yourself, but your *motive* in doing it may simply be to get good grades.

rea·son·a·ble [rē′zən·ə·bəl] *adj.* 1 Having, using, or showing reason, fairness, or common sense; sensible: a *reasonable* person. 2 Moderate; fair: *reasonable* prices. 3 Not expensive. **—rea′son·a·ble·ness** *n.* **—rea′son·a·bly** *adv.*

rea·son·ing [rē′zən·ing] *n.* 1 The process of drawing a conclusion from a set of facts or premises. 2 Reasons; arguments.

re·as·sem·ble [rē′ə·sem′bəl] *v.* **re·as·sem·bled, re·as·sem·bling** 1 To put, bring, or call together again: *reassemble* a bicycle; *reassemble* the parliament. 2 To come together again: The class *reassembled* in the museum lobby.

re·as·sure [rē′ə·shŏŏr′] *v.* **re·as·sured, re·as·sur·ing** To give confidence back to; free from doubt or fear. **—re′as·sur′ance** *n.*

re·bate [rē′bāt′] *n.* A part returned out of a total amount paid, as a discount or refund.

reb·el *n.* or **re·bel** *v.* **re·belled, re·bel·ling** [*n.* reb′əl, *v.* ri·bel′] 1 *n.* A person who refuses to submit to authority and fights against it instead. 2 *adj. use: rebel* troops; a *rebel* army. 3 *v.* To rise up in active resistance, opposing authority: The American colonies *rebelled* against England. 4 *v.* To be filled with dislike or opposition: I *rebel* at the thought of cheating.

re·bel·lion [ri·bel′yən] *n.* 1 An armed uprising or revolt against a government. 2 An active struggle against authority or those in control.

re·bel·lious [ri·bel′yəs] *adj.* 1 Taking part in a rebellion. 2 Full of the disobedient spirit of a rebel. **—re·bel′lious·ly** *adv.*

re·birth [rē·bûrth′ *or* rē′bûrth′] *n.* 1 A new birth. 2 A new feeling or spirit; revival.

re·born [rē·bôrn′] *adj.* Having new vigor or spirit, as though born again.

re·bound [*v.* ri·bound′, *n.* rē′bound′] 1 *v.* To bounce back. 2 *n.* The act of springing or bouncing back: to catch a ball on the *rebound.*

re·buff [ri·buf′] 1 *n.* A sharp, rude rejection or refusal, as of a friendly offer or request. 2 *v.* To reject or refuse sharply or rudely; snub: to *rebuff* someone's unwelcome advice.

re·build [rē·bild′] *v.* **re·built, re·build·ing** 1 To build anew; reconstruct. 2 To make large changes in; reform or remodel.

re·buke [ri·byōōk′] *v.* **re·buked, re·buk·ing,** *n.* 1 *v.* To scold sharply; reprimand. 2 *n.* A strong statement of disapproval; sharp scolding.

re·bus [rē′bəs] *n.* A puzzle representing a word, phrase, or sentence by letters, numbers, or pictures.

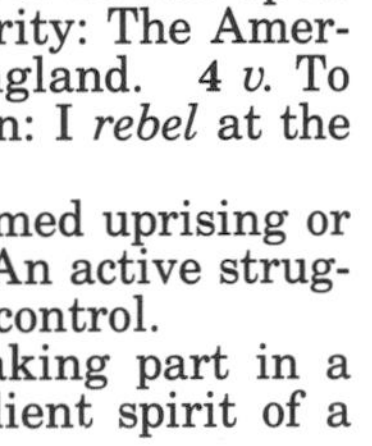

A rebus

re·but [ri·but′] *v.* **re·but·ted, re·but·ting** To contradict or disprove (as an argument or claim) by giving contrary evidence or proof.

re·but·tal [ri·but′(ə)l] *n.* 1 The act of rebutting. 2 A statement, speech, or argument that rebuts.

rec. 1 receipt. 2 record. 3 recording. 4 recreation.

re·cal·ci·trant [ri·kal′sə·trənt] *adj.* Stubbornly refusing to obey. **—re·cal′ci·trance** *n.*

re·call [*v.* ri·kôl′, *n.* ri·kôl′ *or* rē′kôl′] 1 *v.* To bring to mind again; remember: Can you *recall* that day? 2 *n.* A remembering; bringing back to mind: a *recall* even of the exact words. 3 *v.* To order to return or be returned; call back: The factory *recalled* a shipment of faulty merchandise. 4 *n.* A system by which public officials may be removed from office by vote of the people. 5 *v.* To take back; revoke: to *recall* an order. 6 *n.* The act of calling back or revoking.

re·cant [ri·kant′] *v.* To deny or give up publicly (as a belief or opinion). **—re′can·ta′tion** *n.*

re·cap [rē′kap′] *v.* **re·capped, re·cap·ping,** *n.* 1 *v.* To recapitulate; summarize: *recapping* the highlights of the game. 2 *n.* A recapitulation; summary.

re·ca·pit·u·late [rē′kə·pich′ōō·lāt′] *v.* **re·ca·pit·u·lat·ed, re·ca·pit·u·lat·ing** To review briefly; summarize; sum up. **—re′ca·pit′u·la′tion** *n.*

re·cap·ture [rē·kap′chər] *v.* **re·cap·tured, re·cap·tur·ing** 1 To capture again. 2 To get back through memory: to *recapture* past joys.

re·cast [rē·kast′] *v.* **re·cast, re·cast·ing** 1 To cast again or mold again. 2 To put in a different or better form: to *recast* a question.

recd. received.

re·cede [ri·sēd′] *v.* **re·ced·ed, re·ced·ing** 1 To move back; withdraw, as flood waters do. 2 To slant backward: a hairline that is *receding.*

re·ceipt [ri·sēt′] 1 *n.* A written acknowledgment, as of money paid or goods delivered. 2 *v.* To mark (as a bill) as having been paid. 3 *n.* The act of receiving or being received: On *receipt* of your note, I came at once. 4 *n.* (*usually pl.*) Money received, or the total amount received. 5 *n.* A recipe.

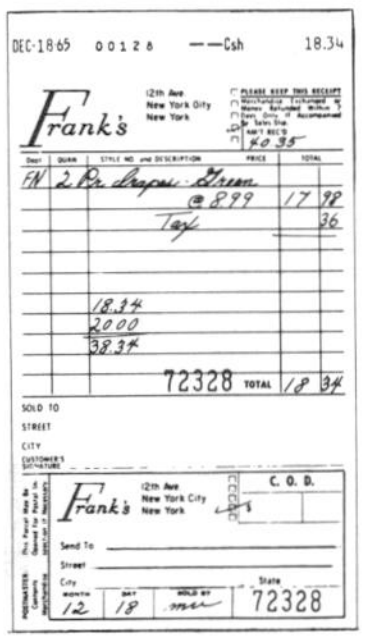
A receipt

re·ceiv·a·ble [ri·sē′və·bəl] *adj.* 1 That can be received or accepted. 2 Awaiting payment; due: the accounts *receivable* of a business.

re·ceive [ri·sēv′] *v.* **re·ceived, re·ceiv·ing** 1 To get or accept (something offered, given, or sent): to *receive* a package. 2 To be given, experience, or suffer: to *receive* a setback. 3 To gain knowledge of; learn: We *received* the news at noon. 4 To admit or welcome: to *receive* callers. 5 To welcome callers: The host *receives* on Fridays. 6 To carry or hold: These columns *receive* the weight of the house. 7 To convert (a transmitted signal) into a useful form, such as a sound or picture on television.

a	add	**i**	it	**ŏŏ**	took	**oi**	oil
ā	ace	**ī**	ice	**ōō**	pool	**ou**	pout
â	care	**o**	odd	**u**	up	**ng**	ring
ä	palm	**ō**	open	**û**	burn	**th**	thin
e	end	**ô**	order	**yōō**	fuse	**th̶**	this
ē	equal					**zh**	vision

ə = { a in *above* e in *sicken* i in *possible* / o in *melon* u in *circus* }

R

re·ceiv·er [ri·sē′vər] *n.* 1 A person who receives; recipient. 2 A person appointed by a court to manage the property of another until some official decision is made. 3 A device that converts an electrical signal into some useful form: a radio *receiver;* a telephone *receiver.*

re·ceiv·ership [ri·sē′vər·ship′] *n.* The condition of being managed by a receiver appointed by a court: a factory in *receivership.*

re·cent [rē′sənt] 1 *adj.* Of a time shortly before the present; not long past. 2 *n., adj.* (*written* **Recent**) Another name for HOLOCENE. **—re′cent·ly** *adv.*

re·cep·ta·cle [ri·sep′tə·kəl] *n.* A thing made to hold something else; container.

re·cep·tion [ri·sep′shən] *n.* 1 The act or way of receiving or being received: to be given a cool *reception.* 2 A party at which guests are formally greeted. 3 The clearness with which radio or television signals are received.

re·cep·tion·ist [ri·sep′shə·nist] *n.* A person employed in an office to greet callers, answer the telephone, and give general information.

re·cep·tive [ri·sep′tiv] *adj.* Able or willing to receive ideas, impressions, or suggestions. **—re′cep·tiv′i·ty** *n.*

re·cep·tor [ri·sep′tər] *n.* 1 A sense organ. 2 A nerve ending adapted to receive stimuli.

re·cess [*n.* ri·ses′ *or* rē′ses, *v.* ri·ses′] 1 *n.* [rē′ses] A short period of time during which work is stopped. 2 *v.* To take a recess or interrupt for a recess. 3 *n.* A hollow place: a small *recess* in the regular line of a wall. 4 *v.* To place in a recess: to *recess* a bookcase. 5 *v.* To make a recess in. 6 *n.* (*usually pl.*) A concealed inner place: the *recesses* of the mind.

re·ces·sion [ri·sesh′ən] *n.* 1 A slight drop in business activity; slight depression. 2 The act of receding or moving back; withdrawal.

re·ces·sion·al [ri·sesh′ən·əl] *n.* A hymn sung as the choir and clergy file out at the end of a church service.

re·ces·sive [ri·ses′iv] *adj.* 1 Tending to go back; receding. 2 Less active and less strong than an opposing hereditary character or trait.

re·charge [rē·chärj′] *v.* **re·charged, re·charg·ing** To refill with electricity: to *recharge* a battery.

re·cid·i·vism [ri·sid′ə·viz′əm] *n.* A tendency to return to a past manner or condition of behavior, especially to an undesirable or criminal behavior: the rate of *recidivism* among ex-convicts. **—re·cid′·i·vist** *n.*

rec·i·pe [res′ə·pē] *n.* 1 A set of directions for cooking or preparing something to eat. 2 A method for getting any desired result.

re·cip·i·ent [ri·sip′ē·ənt] *n.* A person or thing that receives: the *recipient* of an award.

re·cip·ro·cal [ri·sip′rə·kəl] 1 *adj.* Shared or given by both sides; mutual: *reciprocal* friendship. 2 *adj.* Given in exchange: a *reciprocal* baby-sitting arrangement. 3 *adj.* Marked by a mutual, balanced exchange: *reciprocal* motion; a *reciprocal* treaty. 4 *adj.* Expressing mutual relationship or action. *One another* in "They helped one another" is a reciprocal pronoun. 5 *n.* Either of two numbers whose product is 1. 5 is the *reciprocal* of 1/5. **—re·cip′ro·cal·ly** *adv.*

re·cip·ro·cate [ri·sip′rə·kāt′] *v.* **re·cip·ro·cat·ed, re·cip·ro·cat·ing** 1 To give and receive in exchange; interchange: We *reciprocated* favors. 2 To return equally: I admire her, and she *reciprocates* my respect. 3 To move backward and forward, as pistons in an engine do.

rec·i·proc·i·ty [res′ə·pros′ə·tē] *n.* 1 Mutual relationship, action, or exchange. 2 A mutual exchange of special trading privileges between two nations.

re·ci·sion [ri·sizh′ən] *n.* The act of rescinding or undoing; cancellation.

re·cit·al [ri·sīt′(ə)l] *n.* 1 The act of reciting or telling in great detail: a *recital* of one's woes. 2 A detailed statement. 3 A public performance in which musical works or dances are performed, usually by a soloist or pupils.

rec·i·ta·tion [res′ə·tā′shən] *n.* 1 The act of reciting. 2 A school exercise in which pupils are questioned orally on a lesson. 3 The reciting of a memorized piece before an audience. 4 A piece that is or is to be recited.

rec·i·ta·tive [res′ə·tə·tēv′] *n.* Words set to music in a style somewhat like speech, and accompanied by a series of chords.

re·cite [ri·sīt′] *v.* **re·cit·ed, re·cit·ing** 1 To answer questions orally on a lesson in school. 2 To say (something memorized or learned) before an audience. 3 To tell in great detail: to *recite* a tale of woe. **—re·cit′er** *n.*

reck [rek] *v.* 1 To care, heed, or mind. 2 To matter. ◆ This word is seldom used today.

reck·less [rek′lis] *adj.* Taking foolish risks; rash; careless: guilty of *reckless* driving. **—reck′less·ly** *adv.* **—reck′less·ness** *n.*

reck·on [rek′ən] *v.* 1 To figure by arithmetic; count; compute: *Reckon* the total amount owed. 2 To look upon as being; consider: I *reckon* you an honest individual. 3 *informal* To suppose. 4 To rely or depend: We *reckon* on your aid. **—reckon with** 1 To settle accounts with. 2 To take into account; consider.

reck·on·ing [rek′ən·ing] *n.* 1 The act of figuring; calculation. 2 A settlement of accounts; an answering for conduct: the day of *reckoning.* 3 A bill, as at a hotel. 4 Dead reckoning.

re·claim [ri·klām′] *v.* 1 To bring (as a swamp or desert) into a condition to support cultivation or life, as by draining or irrigating. 2 To get from used things or waste: to *reclaim* rubber. 3 To bring back from a bad state: to *reclaim* sinners. **—rec·la·ma·tion** [rek′lə·mā′shən] *n.*

re·cline [ri·klīn′] *v.* **re·clined, re·clin·ing** To lie down, lie back, or lean back.

re·cluse [ri·klo͞os′ *or* rek′lo͞os] *n.* A person who lives alone, shut away from the world.

rec·og·ni·tion [rek′əg·nish′ən] *n.* 1 The act of recognizing or knowing again. 2 The condition of being recognized: Many famous people wear dark glasses to avoid *recognition.* 3 Fame; great praise: The actor earned *recognition* for several fine performances. 4 A greeting; acknowledgment: a nod of *recognition.*

rec·og·niz·a·ble [rek′əg·nī′zə·bəl] *adj.* Capable of being recognized.

re·cog·ni·zance [ri·kog′nə·zəns *or* ri·kon′ə·zəns] *n.* 1 In law, a document that makes a person responsible for carrying out a certain act. 2 A sum of money usually deposited along with such a document. It is returned only after the act is carried out.

rec·og·nize [rek′əg·nīz′] *v.* **rec·og·nized, rec·og·niz·ing** 1 To be aware of, as someone or something previously known; know again: to *recognize* an apartment one had visited. **2** To know or identify, as if from previous acquaintance: to *recognize* an actor from a photograph. **3** To show appreciation or awareness of: to *recognize* an employee's hard work. **4** To perceive as true; realize: to *recognize* responsibilities. **5** To accept as true and valid and start to deal with: to *recognize* the government of a country. **6** To give formal permission to speak, as at a meeting.

re·coil [*v.* ri·koil′, *n.* ri·koil′ *or* rē′koil′] **1** *v.* To react suddenly, as to fear, pain, or danger, by leaping or shrinking back. **2** *n.* A leaping, shrinking, or springing back. **3** *v.* To spring back, as a gun that has just been fired.

rec·ol·lect [rek′ə·lekt′] *v.* To remember or recall to mind: to *recollect* one's childhood.

re-col·lect [rē′kə·lekt′] *v.* **1** To collect again, as things scattered. **2** To regain (one's self-control); pull (onself) together.

rec·ol·lec·tion [rek′ə·lek′shən] *n.* **1** The act of recollecting or remembering. **2** Something remembered. **3** Remembrance or memory.

re·com·bi·nant DNA [ri·kom′bə·nənt] DNA prepared in a laboratory by separating DNA from the genes of one organism and splicing or transplanting it to another organism.

re·com·bine [rē′kəm·bīn′] *v.* **re·com·bined, re·com·bin·ing** To combine in a new way.

rec·om·mend [rek′ə·mend′] *v.* **1** To praise as good, worthy, or desirable: to *recommend* a movie. **2** To be advantageous for or beneficial to: The seclusion of the lake *recommends* it to fishermen. **3** To advise; urge: to *recommend* a vacation. **4** To put in the care of; entrust: His doctor *recommended* him to a specialist.

rec·om·men·da·tion [rek′ə·men·dā′shən] *n.* **1** The act of recommending. **2** A being recommended. **3** Anything that recommends someone or something, as a favorable letter or statement. **4** A suggestion or advice.

rec·om·pense [rek′əm·pens′] *v.* **rec·om·pensed, rec·om·pens·ing,** *n.* **1** *v.* To pay or repay; reward: to *recompense* someone for work. **2** *n.* Payment or reward. **3** *v.* To make up for, as a loss.

rec·on·cile [rek′ən·sīl′] *v.* **rec·on·ciled, rec·on·cil·ing** **1** To bring back to friendship after a quarrel: Could you *reconcile* the two friends? **2** To settle or adjust, as a quarrel. **3** To make adjusted to; resign: to *reconcile* oneself to walking to school. **4** To make or show to be consistent; harmonize: Can you *reconcile* the way you act with what you tell us to do? **—rec′on·cile′ment** *n.*

rec·on·cil·i·a·tion [rek′ən·sil′ē·ā′shən] *n.* **1** The act of reconciling. **2** A being reconciled.

rec·on·dite [rek′ən·dīt′ *or* ri·kon′dīt′] *adj.* **1** Difficult to understand, as a complex mathematical formula. **2** Having to do with little-known matters: *recondite* learning.

re·con·di·tion [rē′kən·dish′ən] *v.* To overhaul; put back into good condition.

re·con·nais·sance [ri·kon′ə·səns] *n.* An investigation or scouting to get information, especially about an enemy's position, strength, or plans.

re·con·noi·ter [rē′kə·noi′tər *or* rek′ə·noi′tər] *v.* To examine or survey (as an area or position), especially to get military information.

re·con·sid·er [rē′kən·sid′ər] *v.* To consider or think about again, especially with the idea of changing one's mind.

re·con·struct [rē′kən·strukt′] *v.* To put (something) together again, usually as it was originally.

re·con·struc·tion [rē′kən·struk′shən] *n.* **1** The act of reconstructing. **2** Something that has been reconstructed. **3** (*written* **Reconstruction**) The bringing back into the Union of the seceded Southern states after the Civil War; also, the time during which this process took place, 1865-1877.

re·cord [*v.* ri·kôrd′, *n., adj.* rek′ərd] **1** *v.* To note down for future use: to *record* appointments. **2** *v.* To indicate; register, as a thermometer. **3** *n.* An official account, as of a trial. **4** *v.* To change (as sounds or images) into a form that can be stored for later reproduction, usually by electrical means. **5** *n.* A disk whose surface is cut in a long, spiral groove along which sound is stored for later reproduction on a phonograph. **6** *n.* Specific information concerning the action of a person or group: a good high school *record.* **7** *n.* The best listed achievement, as in some sport. **8** *adj.* More or better than what was formerly the best: a *record* snowfall. **—break a record** To do or be more or better than the best that has been recorded or achieved. **—off the record** Not meant for publication. **—on record** **1** Publicly declared. **2** Preserved in a record. ◆ *Record* comes from Latin roots meaning *back* and *heart* or *mind*, which combined to mean *back to mind* or *remember.*

re·cord·er [ri·kôr′dər] *n.* **1** A person or thing that records. **2** A public official with the power to enforce criminal law. **3** A musical instrument similar to a flute but played in a vertical position.

Recorder

re·cord·ing [ri·kôr′ding] *n.* **1** The process by which sound is recorded. **2** A phonograph record. **3** A tape recording.

record player A machine on which to play records; phonograph.

re·count[1] [ri·kount′] *v.* To tell in great detail, as a story or event.

re·count[2] [*v.* rē·kount′, *n.* rē′kount′] **1** *v.* To count again. **2** *n.* A second count: a *recount* of votes.

re·coup [ri·ko͞op′] *v.* **1** To win or earn back, as losses. **2** To pay back, as for a loss.

re·course [rē′kôrs *or* ri·kôrs′] *n.* **1** A turning to some person or thing, as for protection or help: to have *recourse* to a bank when one must borrow money. **2** The person or thing looked to for help.

re·cov·er [ri·kuv′ər] *v.* **1** To get back after losing; regain: to *recover* one's balance; to *recover* a lost wallet. **2** To make up for, as a loss. **3** To get well: to *recover* from a cold. **4** To restore (oneself), as to balance or health. **5** To make useful again: to *recover* eroded land.

re-cov·er [rē·kuv′ər] *v.* To cover again.

a	add	**i**	it	**o͝o**	took	**oi**	oil
ā	ace	**ī**	ice	**o͞o**	pool	**ou**	pout
â	care	**o**	odd	**u**	up	**ng**	ring
ä	palm	**ō**	open	**û**	burn	**th**	thin
e	end	**ô**	order	**yo͞o**	fuse	**t͟h**	this
ē	equal					**zh**	vision

ə = a in *above*, e in *sicken*, i in *possible*, o in *melon*, u in *circus*

R

re·cov·er·y [ri·kuv′ər·ē] *n., pl.* **re·cov·er·ies** 1 A coming back to health or a normal condition, as after sickness. 2 The finding of something lost or stolen.

recovery room A hospital room for the care of patients recovering from surgery or childbirth.

rec·re·ant [rek′rē·ənt] 1 *adj.* Unfaithful to something, as a cause or duty. 2 *adj.* Cowardly. 3 *n.* A person who is recreant.

rec·re·ate[1] [rek′rē·āt′] *v.* **rec·re·at·ed, rec·re·at·ing** To relax and amuse oneself; take recreation.

re·cre·ate[2] [rē′krē·āt′] *v.* **re·cre·at·ed, re·cre·at·ing** To create again, especially in the imagination: a dramatist who *recreates* scenes from childhood.

rec·re·a·tion [rek′rē·ā′shən] *n.* Amusement, relaxation, or play, such as gardening, hiking, music, reading, dancing, or sports. **—rec′re·a′tion·al** *adj.*

re·crim·i·nate [ri·krim′ə·nāt′] *v.* **re·crim·i·nat·ed, re·crim·i·nat·ing** To accuse (an accuser) in return.

re·crim·i·na·tion [ri·krim′ə·nā′shən] *n.* An accusation made in return for another accusation: The angry players kept shouting *recriminations* at one another.

re·cru·desce [rē′kroo͞·des′] *v.* **re·cru·desced, re·cru·desc·ing** To break out again after being inactive or dormant, as a disease.

re·cru·des·cence [rē′kroo͞·des′əns] *n.* A breaking out again, as of a disease, epidemic, crime, or violence. **—re′cru·des′cent** *adj.*

re·cruit [ri·kroo͞t′] 1 *v.* To enlist (people) for the armed services. 2 *n.* A newly enlisted member of the armed forces. 3 *v.* To cause to join a group or organization. 4 *n.* A new member of a group or organization. 5 *v.* To get, increase, or replenish: to *recruit* one's strength; to *recruit* help. **—re·cruit′·ment** *n.*

rec·tal [rek′təl] *adj.* Of, for, or having to do with the rectum: a *rectal* thermometer.

rec·tan·gle [rek′tang′gəl] *n.* A parallelogram whose angles are right angles.

rec·tan·gu·lar [rek·tang′gyə·lər] *adj.* Having the shape of a rectangle: a *rectangular* rug.

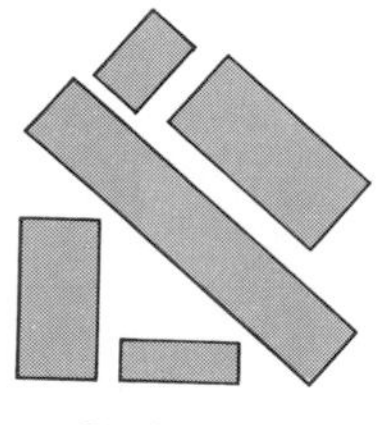
Rectangles

rec·ti·fier [rek′tə·fī′ər] *n.* 1 A person or thing that rectifies or makes right. 2 A device used to change an alternating electric current into a direct current.

rec·ti·fy [rek′tə·fī] *v.* **rec·ti·fied, rec·ti·fy·ing** 1 To correct or adjust: to *rectify* an error. 2 To change (an alternating electric current) into a direct current. 3 To refine by the process of distillation, as liquids. **—rec·ti·fi·ca·tion** [rek′tə·fə·kā′shən] *n.*

rec·ti·lin·e·ar [rek′tə·lin′ē·ər] *adj.* Forming, moving in, or composed of a straight line or lines.

rec·ti·tude [rek′tə·t(y)o͞od′] *n.* Honesty and goodness in principles and conduct; righteousness.

rec·tor [rek′tər] *n.* 1 In certain Christian churches, a clergyman who has charge of a parish. 2 A Roman Catholic priest in charge of a seminary or religious house. 3 The head of any of certain schools, colleges, and universities.

rec·to·ry [rek′tər·ē] *n., pl.* **rec·to·ries** A rector's house.

rec·tum [rek′təm] *n.* The lowest portion of the large intestine, connecting with the anus.

re·cum·bent [ri·kum′bənt] *adj.* Lying down, wholly or partly; reclining; leaning.

re·cu·per·ate [ri·k(y)o͞o′pə·rāt′] *v.* **re·cu·per·a·ted, re·cu·per·a·ting** To regain health or strength, as after being sick or fatigued. **—re·cu′per·a′tion** *n.*

re·cur [ri·kûr′] *v.* **re·curred, re·cur·ring** 1 To happen again, especially after a period of time. 2 To go back in thought or speech: The speaker *recurred* often to the same theme.

re·cur·rent [ri·kûr′ənt] *adj.* Happening or coming, especially repeatedly or at regular intervals: a *recurrent* thought. **—re·cur′rence** *n.*

re·cy·cle [rē·sī′kəl] *v.* **re·cy·cled, re·cy·cling** 1 To process (used or discarded things) in order to regain useful material: The city *recycles* garbage and extracts metals from it. 2 To use again: to *recycle* water.

red [red] *n., adj.* **red·der, red·dest** 1 *n.* The color of fresh blood. 2 *adj.* Having the color of fresh blood. 3 *adj.* (*usually written* **Red**) Of, having to do with, or professing radical or communistic doctrines. 4 *n.* (*written* **Red**) A radical or Communist. **—red′ness** *n.*

red·bird [red′bûrd′] *n.* 1 The cardinal bird. 2 The scarlet tanager.

red blood cell Another term for ERYTHROCYTE.

red-blood·ed [red′blud′id] *adj.* Vigourous; robust.

red·breast [red′brest′] *n.* A bird having a red breast, as the robin.

red·cap [red′kap′] *n. U.S.* A porter at a bus station, railroad station, or similar facility.

red·coat [red′kōt′] *n.* A British soldier during the American Revolution and the War of 1812.

red corpuscle Another term for ERYTHROCYTE.

Red Cross An international organization that cares for the sick and wounded in war and gives aid to victims of floods, earthquakes, and other disasters.

red deer 1 The kind of deer commonly found in Europe and Asia. 2 The white-tailed deer of America, when it is wearing its rust-colored summer coat.

red·den [red′(ə)n] *v.* 1 To make red, as by dyeing. 2 To blush; flush.

red·dish [red′ish] *adj.* Somewhat red.

re·dec·o·rate [rē·dek′ə·rāt′] *v.* **re·dec·o·rat·ed, re·dec·o·rat·ing** To decorate again, as by repainting walls and changing furnishings; refurbish.

re·ded·i·cate [rē·ded′ə·kāt′] *v.* **re·ded·i·cat·ed, re·ded·i·cat·ing** To dedicate anew or more earnestly: She *rededicated* herself to finding a cure for the disease.

re·deem [ri·dēm′] *v.* 1 To get back by paying a price, as something that has been pawned. 2 To pay off, as a bet or a promissory note. 3 To exchange (as coupons or stamps) for a premium or prize. 4 To fulfill, as an oath or promise. 5 To make amends for: The poor play was *redeemed* by skilled acting. 6 To rescue from sin.

re·deem·a·ble [ri·dē′mə·bəl] *adj.* 1 Capable of being redeemed. 2 That is to be redeemed in the future, as a bond.

re·deem·er [ri·dē′mər] *n.* 1 A person who redeems. 2 (*written* **The Redeemer**) Jesus Christ.

re·demp·tion [ri·demp′shən] *n.* 1 The act of redeeming. 2 The condition of being redeemed. 3 Salvation from sin.

re·demp·tive [ri·demp′tiv] *adj.* Of, having to do with, or causing redemption.

red-hand·ed [red′han′did] *adj.* In the act of committing a crime or before getting rid of evidence of having done it: a burglar caught *red-handed*.

red·head [red′hed′] *n.* A person with red hair.
red·head·ed [red′hed′id] *adj.* Having red hair.
red herring 1 Something brought up to draw attention away from a main issue. 2 Smoked herring.
red-hot [red′hot′] *adj.* 1 Glowing red from heat, as metal in a furnace. 2 Brand-new; fresh: *red-hot* news. 3 Angry or excited: a *red-hot* argument.
red-let·ter [red′let′ər] *adj.* Memorable; extraordinary: a *red-letter* day.
red·line [red′līn′] *v.* **red·lined, red·lin·ing** To discriminate against (a neighborhood) by refusing to make fair mortgage loans: a bank accused of *redlining* poor sections of the city.
red man A North American Indian.
re·do [rē·do͞o′] *v.* **re·did, re·done, re·do·ing** 1 To do over. 2 To redecorate.
red·o·lent [red′ə·lənt] *adj.* 1 Giving off a pleasant odor; fragrant. 2 Giving off a strong odor. 3 Suggestive or reminiscent: a story *redolent* of mystery. **—red′o·lence** *n.*
re·dou·ble [rē·dub′əl] *v.* **re·dou·bled, re·dou·bling** To make or become much greater; intensify: to *redouble* one's efforts.
re·doubt [ri·dout′] *n.* A small fort, enclosed all around, often standing alone to defend a hill or pass.
re·doubt·a·ble [ri·dou′tə·bəl] *adj.* Causing fear and dread: a *redoubtable* opponent.
re·dound [ri·dound′] *v.* To have an effect; return; contribute: The success of our graduates *redounds* to the credit of the school.
red pepper A hot, red pepper; cayenne.
re·dress [ri·dres′] 1 *v.* To set right; remedy: Their wrongs were *redressed.* 2 *n.* Correction or satisfaction, as for wrongs and injuries done.
red shift A shift toward red of the lines in the spectrum of a star, thought to happen because the star is moving away from the earth at an enormous speed.
red·skin [red′skin′] *n.* A North American Indian. ◆ This word is often considered offensive.
red·start [red′stärt′] *n.* 1 A small European warbler, with a rust-red breast and tail. 2 A fly-catching North American warbler.
red tape Too much attention to rules and small details, causing a great waste of time.
red tide Ocean water discolored by floating masses of reddish, plantlike, one-celled animals.
re·duce [ri·d(y)o͞os′] *v.* **re·duced, re·duc·ing** 1 To make less in size or amount: to *reduce* waste. 2 To express in the smallest possible numbers, as a fraction: 10/16 can be *reduced* to 5/8. 3 To lower or degrade: to *reduce* a captain to the rank of a lieutenant. 4 To subdue; conquer: to *reduce* an enemy installation. 5 To bring to a certain form or condition: Fire *reduced* the house to ashes; to *reduce* a person to tears. 6 To remove oxygen from, as a chemical compound. 7 To cause (an atom or radical) to undergo chemical reduction.
re·duc·i·ble [ri·d(y)o͞os′ə·bəl] *adj.* Capable of being reduced. **—re·duc′i·bil′i·ty** *n.*
re·duc·tion [ri·duk′shən] *n.* 1 The act of reducing. 2 The condition of being reduced. 3 Anything that has been reduced: This price is a great *reduction* from the former price. 4 The amount by which something is reduced: a 3% *reduction* in taxes. 5 A chemical change by which an atom or radical gains one or more electrons, thus becoming negatively charged and of lower valence. Whenever reduction occurs, there is simultaneous oxidation, since the electrons gained by one atom or radical have to be lost by a different atom or radical.
re·dun·dance [ri·dun′dəns] *n.* Redundancy.
re·dun·dancy [ri·dun′dən·sē] *n., pl.* **re·dun·dan·cies** 1 The condition of being redundant. 2 Something that is redundant. 3 The use of too many or of unnecessary words.
re·dun·dant [ri·dun′dənt] *adj.* 1 More than is needed; too much. 2 Using too many words to express an idea; wordy. "I suspect that you may perhaps be right" is a redundant sentence.
re·du·pli·cate [ri·d(y)o͞o′plə·kāt′] *v.* **re·du·pli·cat·ed, re·du·pli·cat·ing** To do again; repeat.
red·wing [red′wing′] *n.* 1 An American blackbird with bright scarlet patches on the wings of the male. 2 A European thrush with bright, reddish orange patches on the undersides of the wings.
red-winged blackbird [red′wingd′] The redwing of North America.
red·wood [red′wo͝od′] *n.* 1 A very tall evergreen tree of northern California, often 300 feet high. 2 The durable, reddish wood of this tree.

Redwood trees

re·ech·o or **re-ech·o** [rē·ek′ō] *n., pl.* **re·ech·oes** or **re-ech·oes,** *v.* **re·ech·oed** or **re-ech·oed, re·ech·o·ing** or **re-ech·o·ing** 1 *n.* An echo that is echoed or repeated. 2 *v.* To echo again or over and over.
reed [rēd] *n.* 1 Any of certain grasses having hollow stems and growing in wet places. 2 A musical instrument made from the hollow stem of a plant. 3 A thin, flat piece of wood, metal, or plastic in a musical instrument, as the clarinet, oboe, or reed organ. Air blown against a reed causes it to vibrate and produce a musical tone.
reed organ A keyboard organ with small metal reeds that produce the instrument's tones when they are vibrated by currents of air.
reed·y [rē′dē] *adj.* **reed·i·er, reed·i·est** 1 Full of reeds: a *reedy* swamp. 2 Like a reed: a tall, *reedy* child. 3 Having a sound like a reed instrument.
reef[1] [rēf] *n.* A ridge of sand, rocks, or coral at or near the surface of the water.
reef[2] [rēf] 1 *v.* To reduce or shorten (a sail) by folding or rolling part of it and fastening it down. 2 *n.* The part of the sail that can be taken in or let out.
reef·er [rē′fər] *n.* 1 A person who reefs. 2 A short

a	add	**i**	it	**o͝o**	took	**oi**	oil
ā	ace	**ī**	ice	**o͞o**	pool	**ou**	pout
â	care	**o**	odd	**u**	up	**ng**	ring
ä	palm	**ō**	open	**û**	burn	**th**	thin
e	end	**ô**	order	**yo͞o**	fuse	**t͟h**	this
ē	equal					**zh**	vision

ə = a in *above* e in *sicken* i in *possible* o in *melon* u in *circus*

R

coat made from a heavy material, worn usually by sailors.

reek [rēk] 1 *v.* To give off a strong, very unpleasant smell: to *reek* of tobacco. 2 *n.* A strong, offensive smell.

reel[1] [rēl] *n.* 1 A lively dance, chiefly Scottish or Irish. 2 The music for this dance.

reel[2] [rēl] *n., v.* 1 *n.* A round, spoollike device that turns or may be turned, and is used for winding things, as rope, wire, thread, film, or fishing line. 2 *v.* To wind on a reel, as fishing line, rope, or film. 3 *v.* To pull by winding line on a reel: to *reel* in a fish. 4 *n.* The amount wound on one reel, as of film or tape. **—reel off** To say or write quickly and easily: The student *reeled off* a long poem.

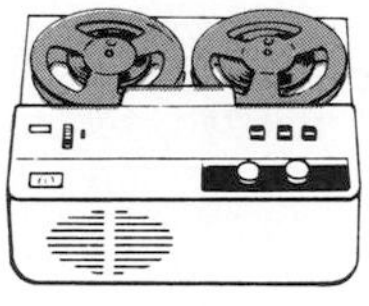
Reels of a tape recorder

reel[3] [rēl] *v.* 1 To sway from side to side; stagger: to *reel* down the street. 2 To be dizzy or giddy: My head is *reeling.* 3 To waver or fall back: The enemy *reeled* under the fierce frontal attack.

re·e·lect or **re-e·lect** [rē′i·lekt′] *v.* To elect again: They *reelected* the incumbent governor. **—re′e·lec′tion** or **re′-e·lec′tion** *n.*

re·en·force or **re-en·force** [rē′en·fôrs′] *v.* **re·en·forced** or **re-en·forced, re·en·forc·ing** or **re-en·forc·ing** Another spelling of REINFORCE. **—re′en·force′·ment** or **re′-en·force′ment** *n.*

re·en·ter or **re-en·ter** [rē·en′tər] *v.* To enter again: He *reentered* the room.

re·en·try or **re-en·try** [rē·en′trē] *n., pl.* **re·entries** or **re-en·tries** 1 The act of entering again. 2 The return of a rocket or spacecraft to the earth's atmosphere after it has been in orbit or at very high altitudes.

re·es·tab·lish or **re-es·tab·lish** [rē′ə·stab′lish] *v.* To establish again. **—re′es·tab′lish·ment** or **re′-es·tab′lish·ment** *n.*

ref [ref] *n. informal* A referee in a game.

ref. 1 referee. 2 reference. 3 referred. 4 refining. 5 reformation. 6 reformed. 7 refunding.

re·fec·to·ry [ri·fek′tər·ē] *n., pl.* **re·fec·to·ries** A room or hall for eating, especially in a monastery, convent, or college.

re·fer [ri·fûr′] *v.* **re·ferred, re·fer·ring** 1 To go for information or help: to *refer* to an encyclopedia. 2 To send for, as help, information, or treatment: The doctor *referred* her to an eye specialist. 3 To hand over or submit for consideration or settlement: The problem was *referred* to the principal. **—refer to** To make reference to; speak of.

ref·e·ree [ref′ə·rē′] *n., v.* **ref·e·reed, ref·e·ree·ing** 1 *n.* In certain sports, as boxing, basketball, or football, the person whose job is to see that the rules of the game are obeyed. 2 *n.* A person to whom anything is referred for a decision; arbitrator. 3 *v.* To observe and judge as a referee.

ref·er·ence [ref′ər·əns *or* ref′rəns] *n.* 1 The act of calling attention: No *reference* was made to the quarrel. 2 A statement, passage, or book to which attention is called: Further *references* are given at the end of the chapter. 3 Something that provides information or help: An encyclopedia is a book of *reference.* 4 *adj. use*: a *reference* book; a *reference* library. 5 Regard; relation: in *reference* to your second question. 6 A person who can be asked about another's character or qualifications for a job. 7 A statement or letter about a person's character or ability: Take your *references* with you when you go for an interview.

ref·er·en·dum [ref′ə·ren′dəm] *n., pl.* **ref·er·en·dums** or **ref·er·en·da** [ref′ə·ren′də] 1 The presentation to the people of a proposed bill so that they can vote to approve or reject it. 2 The vote in such a procedure.

re·fill [*v.* rē·fil′, *n.* rē′fil′] 1 *v.* To fill again. 2 *n.* A product used to replace the exhausted contents of a container: a *refill* for a tape dispenser. 3 *n.* Something provided again, as a second or subsequent filling of a medical prescription.

re·fine [ri·fīn′] *v.* **re·fined, re·fin·ing** 1 To make or become fine or pure; purify: to *refine* flour. 2 To make or become more polished or cultured: Practice *refined* her piano playing.

re·fined [ri·fīnd′] *adj.* 1 Free from impurities or unwanted substances: *refined* gold. 2 Free from vulgarity or coarseness; cultured.

re·fine·ment [ri·fīn′mənt] *n.* 1 The act or process of refining; purification. 2 Fineness, as of thought, taste, or language.

re·fin·er·y [ri·fī′nər·ē] *n., pl.* **re·fin·er·ies** A place where some crude material, as sugar or petroleum, is refined.

re·fit [rē·fit′] *v.* **re·fit·ted, re·fit·ting,** *n.* 1 *v.* To make fit or ready again, as by making repairs or replacing equipment. 2 *n.* The repair of damages or wear, as of a ship.

re·flect [ri·flekt′] *v.* 1 To throw or cast back (as heat, sound, or light): The white sand *reflects* the sun's rays. 2 To throw back an image of: The sailboat was *reflected* in the quiet lake. 3 To think; ponder: to *reflect* on the past. 4 To show or express: Newspapers *reflect* the opinions of their owners. 5 To cause as a result of one's actions or character: Your achievement *reflects* credit on your abilities. 6 To have an unfavorable effect upon: Poor conduct *reflects* seriously on one's school record. 7 To bring blame or discredit: Lying *reflects* on one's general character.

re·flec·tion [ri·flek′shən] *n.* 1 The bouncing back or off of light, sound, or other radiant energy when it strikes a surface or something that opposes its passage: An echo is caused by a *reflection* of sound. 2 Something reflected: I stared at my *reflection* in the mirror. 3 Meditation; serious thought. 4 A remark or comment made as a result of serious thought. 5 A suggestion of blame or reproach: Test scores are no *reflection* on intelligence.

re·flec·tive [ri·flek′tiv] *adj.* 1 Given to reflection or thought: a *reflective* person. 2 Reflecting: the *reflective* surface of a polished floor.

re·flec·tor [ri·flek′tər] *n.* 1 A polished surface for reflecting light, heat, or sound. 2 A telescope that transmits the image to the eyepiece from a mirror.

re·flex [rē′fleks′] 1 *n.* An action not controlled by the will, performed in response to the stimulation of a nerve or group of nerves, as a blink of the eye, a yawn, or a sneeze. 2 *adj.* Of or having to do with such an action: Shivering is a *reflex* action.

reflex angle An angle greater than a straight angle.

re·flex·ive [ri·flek′siv] 1 *adj.* Being a verb having an object that is identical with the subject. In "He dresses himself" *dresses* is a reflexive verb. 2 *adj.* Being a pronoun that is the object of a reflexive verb. In "She hurt herself" *herself* is a reflexive pronoun. 3 *n.* A reflexive verb or pronoun.

re·flux [rē′fluks′] *n.* A flowing back; ebb: the *reflux* of the tide.

re·for·est [rē·fôr′ist] *v.* To plant trees again in (an area). **—re′for·es·ta′tion** *n.*

re·form [ri·fôrm′] **1** *v.* To make better, as by correcting wrongs or abuses: to *reform* a city government. **2** *v.* To become or behave better; improve one's conduct: The poor student *reformed* and began studying. **3** *n.* A change for the better, as by the correction of wrongs or abuses. **4** *adj.* Of, having to do with, or favoring reform. **5** *adj.* (*written* **Reform**) Of, having to do with, or being a member of that branch of Judaism that attempts to reconcile historical Judaism with contemporary life, retaining only those laws and customs considered meaningful today.

ref·or·ma·tion [ref′ər·mā′shən] *n.* **1** The act of reforming. **2** The condition of being reformed. **3** (*written* **Reformation**) The religious and social movement in the 16th century in Europe that began as an effort to change or reform the Roman Catholic Church and ended with the founding of Protestantism.

re·form·a·to·ry [ri·fôr′mə·tôr′ē] *n., pl.* **re·form·a·to·ries,** *adj.* **1** *n.* An institution for the reformation and teaching of young lawbreakers. **2** *adj.* Tending or aiming to reform.

re·form·er [ri·fôr′mər] *n.* A person who brings about or tries to bring about reforms.

reform school A reformatory.

re·fract [ri·frakt′] *v.* To cause refraction. **—re·frac′tive** *adj.*

re·frac·tion [ri·frak′shən] *n.* A change in direction of a ray of light or other energy as it passes obliquely between media in which it has different wavelengths.

re·frac·tor [ri·frak′tər] *n.* A telescope that uses a second lens, not a mirror, to focus light rays.

re·frac·to·ry [ri·frak′tə·rē] *adj.* **1** Hard to control; obstinate: a *refractory* child. **2** Difficult to melt or work, as some metals or ores.

re·frain[1] [ri·frān′] *v.* To keep oneself back; abstain from action: to *refrain* from answering.

re·frain[2] [ri·frān′] *n.* A phrase in a poem or song repeated over and over, especially at the end of each stanza.

re·fresh [ri·fresh′] *v.* **1** To make fresh or vigorous again; revive: The cold drink *refreshed* us; to *refresh* one's memory about past events. **2** To become fresh again; revive.

re·fresh·ing [ri·fresh′ing] *adj.* **1** Tending to refresh or revive: a *refreshing* breeze. **2** Enjoyably unusual or novel: a *refreshing* movie.

re·fresh·ment [ri·fresh′mənt] *n.* **1** The act of refreshing. **2** The condition of being refreshed. **3** Something that refreshes, as food or drink. **4** (*pl.*) Food, drink, or both.

re·frig·er·ant [ri·frij′ər·ənt] *n.* A substance used for obtaining and maintaining a low temperature, as frozen carbon dioxide or ammonia.

re·frig·er·ate [ri·frij′ə·rāt′] *v.* **re·frig·er·at·ed, re·frig·er·at·ing** To keep or make cold. **—re·frig′er·a′·tion** *n.*

re·frig·er·a·tor [ri·frij′ə·rā′tər] *n.* A place, as a cabinet, room, or railroad car, for keeping foods fresh by means of ice, mechanical cooling, or other methods.

re·fu·el [rē·fyo͞o′əl *or* rē·fyo͞ol′] *v.* **re·fu·eled** or **re·fu·elled, re·fu·el·ing** or **re·fu·el·ling** **1** To fill again with fuel. **2** To take on a new supply of fuel.

ref·uge [ref′yo͞oj] *n.* **1** Shelter or protection from danger or distress. **2** A person or thing that shelters or protects. **3** A safe place.

ref·u·gee [ref′yo͝o·jē′ *or* ref′yo͝o·jē′] *n.* A person who flees from persecution or danger.

re·ful·gent [ri·ful′jənt] *adj.* Shining brilliantly; radiant. **—re·ful′gence** *n.*

re·fund [*v.* ri·fund′, *n.* rē′fund′] **1** *v.* To pay back (money): If you are not satisfied with our product, we will *refund* your money. **2** *n.* A repayment. **3** *n.* The amount refunded.

re·fur·bish [rē·fûr′bish] *v.* To brighten or freshen up; renovate or redecorate.

re·fus·al [ri·fyo͞o′zəl] *n.* **1** The act of refusing. **2** A choice of accepting or declining something before it is offered to someone else.

re·fuse[1] [ri·fyo͞oz′] *v.* **re·fused, re·fus·ing** To say that one will not take, agree to, give, allow, or do (something); decline: to *refuse* a helping of cake; to *refuse* to leave; to *refuse* permission.

ref·use[2] [ref′yo͞os] *n.* Worthless things; trash.

re·fute [ri·fyo͞ot′] *v.* **re·fut·ed, re·fut·ing** **1** To prove the untruth of: to *refute* an argument **2** To prove (a person) to be in the wrong. **—ref′u·ta′tion** *n.*

re·gain [ri·gān′] *v.* **1** To get possession of again; recover: to *regain* one's health. **2** To reach again; get back to: The tourists had to ask directions twice before they *regained* the street.

re·gal [rē′gəl] *adj.* **1** Of, belonging to, or fit for a monarch; royal. **2** Stately; splendid.

re·gale [ri·gāl′] *v.* **re·galed, re·gal·ing** To give pleasure or delight to; entertain: He *regaled* us with stories; Our hosts *regaled* us with a fine dinner.

re·ga·li·a [ri·gā′lē·ə *or* ri·gāl′yə] *n.pl.* **1** The symbols and emblems of royalty, as the crown and scepter. **2** The symbols and emblems of any society or order. **3** Fancy clothes; finery.

Regalia

re·gard [ri·gärd′] **1** *v.* To look at closely or attentively. **2** *n.* A look, especially a steady look. **3** *v.* To look on or think of in a certain way: I *regard* you as a friend. **4** *v.* To show consideration for; respect: to *regard* the opinion of others. **5** *n.* Consideration; respect. **6** *v.* To pay attention to; heed: Nobody *regarded* the warning. **7** *n.* Good opinion; esteem: a high *regard* for your ability. **8** *n.* (*pl.*) Good wishes; affection: My kindest *regards* to your family. **—in regard to** or **with regard to** In reference to; in relation to; about; concerning.

re·gard·ful [ri·gärd′fəl] *adj.* **1** Keeping in mind; attentive; observant: a teacher who is *regardful*

a	add	**i**	it	**o͝o**	took	**oi**	oil
ā	ace	**ī**	ice	**o͞o**	pool	**ou**	pout
â	care	**o**	odd	**u**	up	**ng**	ring
ä	palm	**ō**	open	**û**	burn	**th**	thin
e	end	**ô**	order	**yo͞o**	fuse	**th̶**	this
ē	equal					**zh**	vision

ə = a in *above*, e in *sicken*, i in *possible*, o in *melon*, u in *circus*

R

of everyone's right to an opinion. **2** Full of respect, regard, or consideration.

re·gard·ing [ri·gär′ding] *prep.* In reference to; in regard to; about; concerning.

re·gard·less [ri·gärd′lis] **1** *adj.* Having no consideration or concern; heedless: to act *regardless* of other people's feelings. **2** *adv. informal* In spite of everything; anyway. ◆ There is no such word as *irregardless. Regardless* already has the sense of "not" and doesn't need the negative prefix *ir-*.

re·gat·ta [ri·gat′ə *or* ri·gä′tə] *n.* A boat race, or a series of such races.

re·gen·cy [rē′jən·sē] *n., pl.* **re·gen·cies** **1** The government, office, or power of a regent or a group of regents. **2** The period of time during which a regent governs. **3** A group of regents.

re·gen·er·ate [ri·jen′ə·rāt′] *v.* **re·gen·er·at·ed, re·gen·er·at·ing** **1** To cause to become better morally or spiritually. **2** To make better by changing thoroughly. **3** To produce, generate, or form again, as a lost or damaged body part. **—re·gen′er·a′tion** *n.* **—re·gen·er·a·tive** [ri·jen′ər·ə·tiv] *adj.*

re·gent [rē′jənt] *n.* **1** A person who rules in the name and place of the sovereign: The duke served as *regent* until the queen was old enough to rule. **2** A member of a governing board, as of certain universities.

reg·gae [reg′ā] *n.* A kind of popular music that originated in Jamaica, characterized by elements of calypso, blues, and rock 'n' roll.

reg·i·cide [rej′ə·sīd′] *n.* **1** The act of killing a king. **2** A person who kills a king.

re·gime [ri·zhēm′] *n.* **1** A system of government. **2** A government in power. **3** A regimen.

ré·gime [rā·zhēm′] *n.* A regime.

reg·i·men [rej′ə·mən] *n.* A course of treatment as to diet or exercise, to improve health.

reg·i·ment [*n.* rej′ə·mənt, *v.* rej′ə·ment] **1** *n.* An army unit, larger than a battalion and smaller than a division, usually commanded by a colonel. **2** *v.* To require to follow one strict pattern of behavior. **—reg′i·men′tal** *adj.*

reg·i·men·tal [rej′ə·men′təl] **1** *adj.* Of or having to do with a regiment. **2** *n.(pl.)* The dress uniform of a particular regiment.

reg·i·men·ta·tion [rej′ə·men·tā′shən] *n.* **1** The act of forming into disciplined, uniform groups. **2** A putting under strict control.

re·gion [rē′jən] *n.* **1** An area of land, usually large; district: a southern *region*; a coal-mining *region*. **2** Any area, place, or space: the abdominal *region*; the *regions* of the sky.

re·gion·al [rē′jən·əl] *adj.* Of, having to do with, or in a region: a *regional* heat wave; a *regional* dialect. **—re′gion·al·ly** *adv.*

reg·is·ter [rej′is·tər] **1** *n.* An official record or list. **2** *n.* A book containing this. **3** *v.* To enter in a register: to *register* a birth. **4** *v.* To enter the name or names of in a register: to *register* students or voters. **5** *v.* To enter one's name in a register, as of voters or students; enroll. **6** *n.* A device for counting or recording: a cash *register*. **7** *v.* To indicate, as on a scale: The thermometer *registered* 70°. **8** *v.* To show; express: Her face *registered* surprise. **9** *v.* To cause (mail) to be recorded, by paying a fee, so as to ensure its delivery. **10** *n.* In music, the range, or a certain part of it, of a voice or instrument. **11** *n.* A device that can be opened or closed to admit heated or cooled air to a room.

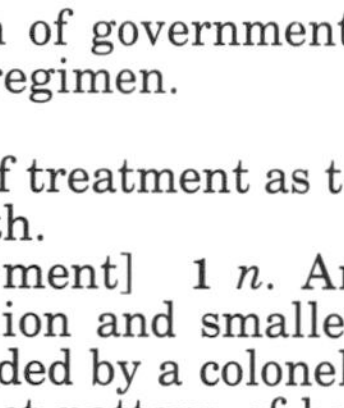

Cash register

registered nurse A trained nurse who has passed a registration test given by a state.

reg·i·strant [rej′is·trənt] *n.* A person who registers or who has registered.

reg·is·trar [rej′is·trär′] *n.* A keeper of a register or of records, especially in a college.

reg·is·tra·tion [rej′is·trā′shən] *n.* **1** The act of entering in a register. **2** An entry in a register. **3** The number of people registered.

reg·is·try [rej′is·trē] *n., pl.* **reg·is·tries** **1** A register (def. 1 and 2). **2** A place, such as an office, where a register or registers are kept. **3** The act of registering.

re·gress [*v.* ri·gres′, *n.* rē′gres] **1** *v.* To go back; return, as to a former condition. **2** *n.* An act or way of going back. **—re·gres′sion** *n.*

re·gres·sive [ri·gres′iv] *adj.* Going back or tending to go back, as to a former condition.

re·gret [ri·gret′] *v.* **re·gret·ted, re·gret·ting,** *n.* **1** *v.* To feel sorrow or grief about: to *regret* the loss of a friend; to *regret* having lost one's temper. **2** *n.* Sorrow or grief. **3** *n.* (*pl.*) A polite refusal of an invitation: We send our *regrets*.

re·gret·ful [ri·gret′fəl] *adj.* Feeling or showing regret. **—re·gret′ful·ly** *adv.*

re·gret·ta·ble [ri·gret′ə·bəl] *adj.* Causing regret or distress: a *regrettable* mistake.

reg·u·lar [reg′yə·lər] **1** *adj.* Even or symmetrical: a *regular* design; a *regular* heartbeat. **2** *adj.* Disciplined; orderly: My family leads a *regular* life. **3** *adj.* Usual; habitual: my *regular* seat; a store's *regular* customers. **4** *adj.* Always occurring at the same time: a *regular* meeting. **5** *adj.* In grammar, being inflected in a standard way. **6** *adj.* Of or belonging to the permanent army, whose members serve during peace as well as war. **7** *n.* A professional soldier; member of the regular army. **8** *adj.* Qualified to do a certain job: a *regular* nurse. **9** *adj. informal* Thorough; complete: a *regular* crook. **10** *adj. informal* Very pleasant; friendly: a *regular* guy. **—reg′u·lar·ly** *adv.*

reg·u·lar·i·ty [reg′yə·lar′ə·tē] *n., pl.* **reg·u·lar·i·ties** The condition or quality of being regular: A single hill broke the tiresome *regularity* of the plain.

reg·u·late [reg′yə·lāt′] *v.* **reg·u·lat·ed, reg·u·lat·ing** **1** To control according to certain rules: A police officer *regulates* traffic. **2** To adjust according to a standard: A thermostat *regulates* the heat in a building. **—reg′u·la′tor** *n.*

reg·u·la·tion [reg′yə·lā′shən] **1** *n.* The act of regulating. **2** *n.* The condition of being regulated. **3** *n.* A rule of conduct: school *regulations*. **4** *adj.* Done or made according to a rule or regulation. **5** *adj.* Usual, customary, or required: The scout is wearing the *regulation* uniform.

reg·u·la·to·ry [reg′yə·lə·tôr′ē] *adj.* Making regulations; regulating.

re·gur·gi·tate [ri·gûr′jə·tāt′] *v.* **re·gur·gi·tat·ed, re·gur·gi·tat·ing** **1** To rush or pour back. **2** To bring up partially digested food, as some birds do to feed their young. **3** To vomit. **—re·gur′gi·ta′tion** *n.*

re·ha·bil·i·tate [rē′hə·bil′ə·tāt′] *v.* **re·ha·bil·i·tat·ed, re·ha·bil·i·tat·ing** **1** To restore, as to good condition, health, or appearance: to *rehabilitate* a run-down neighborhood. **2** To restore, as to a former rank or privilege; reinstate. **—re′ha·bil′i·ta′tion** *n.*

re·hash [*v.* rē·hash′, *n.* rē′hash′] 1 *v.* To work into a new form; go over again: to *rehash* an old quarrel. 2 *n.* Something that has been rehashed: a *rehash* of an old play.

re·hears·al [ri·hûr′səl] *n.* 1 A practice session or performance to prepare for a public performance. 2 The act of rehearsing.

re·hearse [ri·hûrs′] *v.* **re·hearsed, re·hears·ing** 1 To practice or cause to practice in preparation for public performance: to *rehearse* a play; The conductor *rehearsed* the orchestra. 2 To tell in detail: I *rehearsed* my complaints to my friends.

Reich [rīk] *n.* A former name for Germany or its government. ◆ *Reich* is a German word meaning *empire* or *state.*

reign [rān] 1 *v.* To rule; govern, as a sovereign. 2 *n.* The period during which a sovereign rules: the *reign* of Elizabeth I. 3 *v.* To be everywhere; prevail: Silence *reigned* in the forest. 4 *n.* Controlling influence; power: a *reign* of terror.

re·im·burse [rē′im·bûrs′] *v.* **re·im·bursed, re·im·burs·ing** To pay back an amount that has been spent or lost: You will be *reimbursed* for your expenses. **—re′im·burse′ment** *n.*

rein [rān] 1 *n.* (*usually pl.*) A strap attached to the bit to control a horse or other animal while it is being ridden or driven. 2 *v.* To guide, control, or halt with or as if with reins: to *rein* in a horse; to *rein* in one's temper. 3 *n.* Any means of controlling or restraining. **—draw rein** To stop or slow down. **—give rein to** To free, as from control.

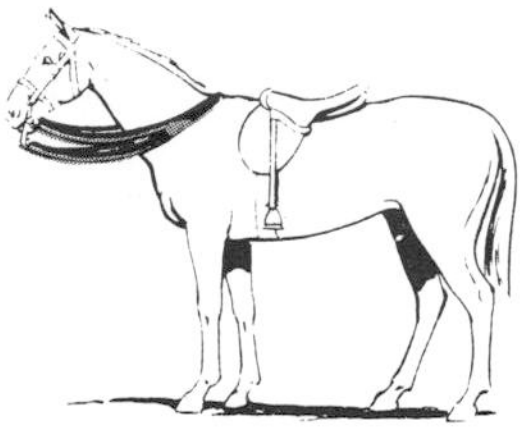

A horse's reins

re·in·car·nate [rē′in·kär′nāt′] *v.* **re·in·car·nat·ed, re·in·car·nat·ing** To provide (a soul) with a new body after death.

re·in·car·na·tion [rē′in·kär·nā′shən] *n.* 1 A belief that the soul may be reborn in a different body. 2 A new embodiment.

rein·deer [rān′dir′] *n., pl.* **rein·deer** A deer found in northern regions, having branching antlers in both sexes. It has been tamed for its milk and meat and is used to carry loads.

Reindeer

re·in·force [rē′in·fôrs′] *v.* **re·in·forced, re·in·forc·ing** 1 To give new force or strength to by adding something: to *reinforce* troops under attack; She *reinforced* her argument with facts. 2 To encourage (a person or animal) to behave in a certain way, as by giving a reward. 3 To encourage (certain behavior), as by giving a reward.

re·in·force·ment [rē′in·fôrs′mənt] *n.* 1 The act of reinforcing. 2 Anything that strengthens. 3 (*pl.*) Additional troops, aircraft, or ships.

re·in·state [rē′in·stāt′] *v.* **re·in·stat·ed, re·in·stat·ing** To put back into a former condition or situation. **—re′in·state′ment** *n.*

re·it·er·ate [rē·it′ə·rāt′] *v.* **re·it·er·at·ed, re·it·er·at·ing** To say or do again and again; repeat: to *reiterate* a request for a wage increase. **—re·it′er·a′tion** *n.*

re·ject [*v.* ri·jekt′, *n.* rē′jekt′] 1 *v.* To refuse to take, recognize, believe, or grant: to *reject* help. 2 *v.* To throw away as worthless; discard: to *reject* faulty machine parts. 3 *n.* A person or thing that has been rejected.

re·jec·tion [ri·jek′shən] *n.* 1 The act of rejecting. 2 The condition of being rejected. 3 A thing that is rejected.

re·joice [ri·jois′] *v.* **re·joiced, re·joic·ing** To be or make glad: I *rejoiced* at her good luck; The news *rejoiced* my heart.

re·joic·ing [ri·joi′sing] *n.* The feeling or expressing of joy.

re·join[1] [ri·join′] *v.* To answer; say in reply.

re·join[2] [rē·join′] *v.* 1 To join together again; reunite. 2 To come into company with again.

re·join·der [ri·join′dər] *n.* 1 An answer to a reply. 2 Any answer or reply.

re·ju·ve·nate [ri·jo͞o′və·nāt′] *v.* **re·ju·ve·nat·ed, re·ju·ve·nat·ing** To give new vigor or youthfulness to: The rest *rejuvenated* him. **—re·ju′ve·na′tion** *n.*

re·lapse [ri·laps′] *v.* **re·lapsed, re·laps·ing,** *n.* 1 *v.* To fall back into a former condition or state, as into illness after improving. 2 *n.* A falling back to a former state or condition after improving.

re·late [ri·lāt′] *v.* **re·lat·ed, re·lat·ing** 1 To tell about; narrate: to *relate* the important events of the Civil War. 2 To bring into connection or relation: to *relate* facts to events. 3 To refer; have to do with: The story *relates* to your grandparents.

re·lat·ed [ri·lā′tid] *adj.* 1 Connected; associated; linked: the recession and *related* problems. 2 Connected by blood or marriage: He is *related* to me on my mother's side.

re·la·tion [ri·lā′shən] *n.* 1 Connection, as in meaning, significance, or thought. 2 (*pl.*) Connections, as those between people, groups, or nations, brought about by personal, business, political, or other contacts. 3 Connection by descent or marriage; kinship. 4 A relative; kinsman. 5 An account; narration.

re·la·tion·ship [ri·lā′shən·ship′] *n.* 1 The condition of being related; connection; association. 2 Connection by blood or marriage; kinship. 3 A connection based on personal, business, political, or other contacts: the strained *relationship* of the superpowers.

rel·a·tive [rel′ə·tiv] 1 *adj.* Having to do with; relating: the facts *relative* to a situation. 2 *adj.* Having meaning only as related to something else: "High" is a *relative* term. 3 *adj.* Depending upon relation; comparative: the *relative* values of the dollar and the franc. 4 *n.* A person related to another by blood or marriage. 5 *adj.* In grammar, referring to an antecedent. 6 *n.* In grammar, a relative word, as *who* or *that.* **—relative to** In regard to; concerning; about.

a	add	**i**	it	**o͝o**	took	**oi**	oil
ā	ace	**ī**	ice	**o͞o**	pool	**ou**	pout
â	care	**o**	odd	**u**	up	**ng**	ring
ä	palm	**ō**	open	**û**	burn	**th**	thin
e	end	**ô**	order	**yo͞o**	fuse	**th̶**	this
ē	equal					**zh**	vision

ə = {a in *above* e in *sicken* i in *possible* / o in *melon* u in *circus*}

relative humidity A measure of how much water vapor is contained in the air at a given temperature, expressed as a percentage of the maximum that the air could contain at the same temperature.

rel·a·tive·ly [rel'ə·tiv·lē] *adv.* As compared with something else or with a standard; comparatively: a *relatively* small town; a *relatively* easy question.

relative pronoun A pronoun that refers back to an antecedent. In "The person who spoke was well informed," *who* is a relative pronoun referring to *person.*

rel·a·tiv·i·ty [rel'ə·tiv'ə·tē] *n.* 1 The quality or condition of being relative. 2 Either of two theories formulated by Albert Einstein explaining the relationship between matter, energy, space, and time. Some of the conclusions of **special relativity** are that mass and energy are equivalent and that mass and time are altered at speeds approaching the speed of light, which can never be exceeded. **General relativity** attempts to explain gravitation and other forms of accelerated motion.

re·lax [ri·laks'] *v.* 1 To avoid work or exercise; rest: to *relax* on a couch. 2 To make or become less tight or firm: The batter *relaxed* her grip on the bat; Tired muscles *relax* in a hot bath. 3 To make less severe or acute: to *relax* one's attention; to *relax* discipline. **—re'lax·a'tion** *n.*

re·lax·ant [ri·lak'sənt] *n.* A drug or other agent that relaxes, especially one that relaxes the muscles.

re·lay [*n.* rē'lā', *v.* ri·lā' *or* rē'lā'] 1 *n.* A fresh set, as of people or horses, to replace a tired set. 2 *n.* A relay race, or one of its laps. 3 *v.* To send onward by or as if by relays: to *relay* a message. 4 *n.* An electrical switch that is itself operated by electricity.

relay race A running or swimming race in which each member of a team races a certain distance and is then replaced by a teammate.

Relay race

re·lease [ri·lēs'] *v.* **re·leased, re·leas·ing,** *n.* 1 *v.* To set free: *Release* the sheep from the pen. 2 *n.* The act of setting free. 3 *n.* A being set free; liberation: *release* from worry. 4 *v.* To let go; discharge: to *release* air from a tire. 5 *n.* A spring, catch, or other device that releases or unfastens something, as a part of a machine. 6 *v.* To allow to be presented to the public: to *release* a motion picture. 7 *n.* Anything released to the public, as a motion picture or news story. 8 *n.* The act of giving up a claim. 9 *n.* The legal paper certifying this.

rel·e·gate [rel'ə·gāt'] *v.* **rel·e·gat·ed, rel·e·gat·ing** 1 To send off or assign, as to a less important position or place: to *relegate* a student to the last row. 2 To banish; exile. 3 To give over; assign, as a task or piece of business.

re·lent [ri·lent'] *v.* To become gentler or more compassionate: My friend finally *relented* and agreed to help me.

re·lent·less [ri·lent'lis] *adj.* 1 Without pity; unforgiving; harsh: a *relentless* enemy. 2 Continuing; persistent: a *relentless* noise. **—re·lent'less·ly** *adv.*

rel·e·vance [rel'ə·vəns] *n.* The condition of being relevant; pertinence.

rel·e·van·cy [rel'ə·vən·sē] *n.* Relevance.

rel·e·vant [rel'ə·vənt] *adj.* Connected with or having to do with the point or the matter at hand; pertinent; related: What the speaker said was not *relevant* to the discussion.

re·li·a·ble [ri·lī'ə·bəl] *adj.* Dependable; trustworthy: a *reliable* friend; a *reliable* report. **—re·li'a·bil'i·ty** *n.* **—re·li'a·bly** *adv.*

re·li·ance [ri·lī'əns] *n.* 1 Confidence; trust. 2 Dependence: a baby's *reliance* on its parents. 3 Something upon which one relies.

re·li·ant [ri·lī'ənt] *adj.* 1 Depending or relying. 2 Confident. 3 Self-reliant.

rel·ic [rel'ik] *n.* 1 Something remaining from what has disappeared or been destroyed: a *relic* of ancient Greece. 2 A memento connected with a saint or a saint's tomb.

re·lief [ri·lēf'] *n.* 1 Lessening of or freeing from something, as pain or difficulty. 2 Something that relieves: It's a *relief* to be home again. 3 Help in the form of money or food given to the needy. 4 Rest or freedom from work or duty. 5 A person who relieves another from a duty. 6 In architecture and sculpture, the raising of a figure, ornament, or other design element from a surface. 7 Something, as a figure or ornament, so raised. **—on relief** Receiving money from public funds, as when out of work.

Relief

relief map A map on which differences in height above sea level are shown by lines or colors, or by molding surface features, as hills, rivers, or valleys, in some solid material.

re·lieve [ri·lēv'] *v.* **re·lieved, re·liev·ing** 1 To lessen or ease: to *relieve* a headache. 2 To free (someone) from something unpleasant, as suffering, pain, or fear. 3 To help, as with food or money. 4 To substitute for and free from duty: to *relieve* a guard. 5 To make less dull and monotonous: to *relieve* a gray room with bright curtains.

re·li·gion [ri·lij'ən] *n.* 1 Belief in or worship of God or gods. 2 A particular system of belief or worship: the Jewish *religion.*

re·li·gi·os·i·ty [ri·lij'ē·os'ə·tē] *n.* 1 Devoutness; piety. 2 A pretense or show of being religious; excessive piety.

re·li·gious [ri·lij'əs] *adj., n., pl.* **re·li·gious** 1 *adj.* Of or having to do with religion: a *religious* holiday; *religious* training. 2 *adj.* Devout; pious: a *religious* person who observes many rites. 3 *n.* A member of a religious order; monk or nun. 4 *adj.* Conscientious; strict: to be *religious* about doing one's homework. **—re·li'gious·ly** *adv.*

re·lin·quish [ri·ling'kwish] *v.* To give up; let go; surrender: to *relinquish* a claim. **—re·lin'quish·ment** *n.*

rel·ish [rel'ish] 1 *n.* Appetizing flavor or taste. 2 *n.* Something eaten with or put on food to lend it flavor or zest, such as pickles or olives. 3 *n.* Appetite; liking: a *relish* for excitement. 4 *v.* To have an appetite for; like or enjoy.

re·live [rē·liv′] *v.* **re·lived, re·liv·ing** 1 To live again. 2 To experience again, especially in the imagination.

re·lo·cate [rē·lō′kāt′ *or* rē′lō·kāt′] *v.* **re·lo·cat·ed, re·lo·cat·ing** To move to another place.

re·luc·tant [ri·luk′tənt] *adj.* 1 Unwilling; not eager: My little brother is always *reluctant* to go to bed. 2 Expressing unwillingness: a *reluctant* answer. **—re·luc′tance** *n.* **—re·luc′tant·ly** *adv.*

re·ly [ri·lī′] *v.* **re·lied, re·ly·ing** To place trust or confidence: We can *rely* on their judgment.

REM The dreaming stage of sleep. ◆ Named for the *r*apid *e*ye *m*ovement that occurs in this stage.

re·main [ri·mān′] *v.* 1 To stay or continue in a place: The guests *remained* at the house; Nothing *remained* standing after the explosion. 2 To continue to be: The weather *remained* warm. 3 To be left: It *remains* to be proved.

re·main·der [ri·mān′dər] *n.* 1 Something, as a part, group, or number, left over; that which remains: We ate the *remainder* of the pie. 2 The part that is left over when a number cannot be evenly divided: 9 ÷ 4 = 2 with a *remainder* of 1.

re·mains [ri·mānz′] *n.pl.* 1 That which is left after a part has been destroyed or used up: the *remains* of a picnic lunch. 2 A dead body; corpse.

re·make [*v.* rē·māk′, *n.* rē′māk′] *v.* **re·made, re·mak·ing,** *n.* 1 *v.* To make again. 2 *n.* Something made again: a *remake* of an old movie.

re·mand [ri·mand′] 1 *v.* To order or send back, especially to jail to await trial. 2 *n.* An act of remanding.

re·mark [ri·märk′] 1 *v.* To mention or comment; say: Everyone *remarked* that the soup was delicious. 2 *n.* A brief comment: At the party, they made some amusing *remarks.* 3 *v.* To take particular notice of.

re·mark·a·ble [ri·mär′kə·bəl] *adj.* Worthy of notice; extraordinary; unusual: She has *remarkable* intelligence. **—re·mark′a·bly** *adv.*

re·me·di·a·ble [ri·mē′dē·ə·bəl] *adj.* Capable of being remedied or cured.

re·me·di·al [ri·mē′dē·əl] *adj.* Providing a remedy; intended to be used as a remedy.

rem·e·dy [rem′ə·dē] *n., pl.* **rem·e·dies,** *v.* **rem·e·died, rem·e·dy·ing** 1 *n.* Something that cures, relieves, or corrects: Aspirin is a *remedy* for headaches. 2 *v.* To heal or make right: to *remedy* poverty.

re·mem·ber [ri·mem′bər] *v.* 1 To bring back to the mind or memory: I never can *remember* telephone numbers. 2 To keep in mind carefully: to *remember* one's manners. 3 To mention as sending greetings: *Remember* me to your parents. 4 To bear in mind as worthy of a gift or reward: to *remember* someone in one's will.

re·mem·brance [ri·mem′brəns] *n.* 1 The act or power of remembering; memory: He had no *remembrance* of the occasion. 2 A keepsake; memento. 3 (*pl.*) Greetings; regards.

re·mind [ri·mīnd′] *v.* To cause to remember: I *reminded* the children that it was time to go.

re·mind·er [ri·mīn′dər] *n.* Something to help a person remember.

rem·i·nisce [rem′ə·nis′] *v.* **rem·i·nisced, rem·i·nisc·ing** To talk or think about the past, especially in a fond or dreamy way.

rem·i·nis·cence [rem′ə·nis′əns] *n.* 1 The act or practice of thinking or speaking about the past. 2 Something remembered from the past. 3 (*pl.*) An account of a person's past experiences.

rem·i·nis·cent [rem′ə·nis′ənt] *adj.* 1 Characterized by or given to reminiscence. 2 Causing memories of something previously known; suggestive: a song *reminiscent* of childhood.

re·miss [ri·mis′] *adj.* Careless about things needing attention; negligent; neglectful.

re·mis·sion [ri·mish′ən] *n.* 1 Forgiveness: *remission* of sins. 2 Release from a debt, duty, or the like. 3 Temporary lessening, as of a pain or fever.

re·mit [ri·mit′] *v.* **re·mit·ted, re·mit·ting** 1 To pardon; forgive: to *remit* sins. 2 To release someone from: to *remit* a debt or punishment. 3 To send (money) in payment. 4 To make less; slacken: to *remit* one's vigilance.

re·mit·tance [ri·mit′əns] *n.* 1 The act of sending money. 2 The money sent.

rem·nant [rem′nənt] *n.* 1 A short piece of cloth left over after the rest of a larger piece has been sold or used. 2 A remaining trace; vestige.

re·mod·el [rē·mod′(ə)l] *v.* **re·mod·eled** or **re·mod·elled, re·mod·el·ing** or **re·mod·el·ling** 1 To model again: to *remodel* a figure. 2 To make over, with changes of design or purpose: to *remodel* a house.

re·mon·strance [ri·mon′strəns] *n.* The act of remonstrating; protest.

re·mon·strate [ri·mon′strāt′] *v.* **re·mon·strat·ed, re·mon·strat·ing** To present and urge strong reasons in objecting or protesting: The principal *remonstrated* with the student about talking in class.

rem·o·ra [rem′ər·ə] *n.* A fish of warm seas that has a suction disk on its head with which it attaches itself to larger fishes and sometimes to ships. ◆ *Remora* comes from a Latin word meaning "delay." Sailors believed that these creatures slowed down their ships by catching rides on them.

re·morse [ri·môrs′] *n.* Great regret or anguish for something one has done; self-reproach.

re·morse·ful [ri·môrs′fəl] *adj.* Feeling remorse; full of self-reproach or guilt.

re·morse·less [ri·môrs′lis] *adj.* Without pity; cruel; having no compassion.

re·mote [ri·mōt′] *adj.* **re·mot·er, re·mot·est** 1 Distant: Greenland is a *remote* island. 2 From a distance, as by radio waves: *remote* guidance. 3 Distant in time: the *remote* future. 4 Distant in relationship: a *remote* cousin. 5 Not obvious; slight: a *remote* likeness. **—re·mote′ly** *adv.*

Remote control device

remote control Control of a machine or device from a distance, as by sending radio signals that activate or maneuver its parts: The Viking spacecraft performed

a	add	**i**	it	**o͝o**	took	**oi**	oil
ā	ace	**ī**	ice	**o͞o**	pool	**ou**	pout
â	care	**o**	odd	**u**	up	**ng**	ring
ä	palm	**ō**	open	**û**	burn	**th**	thin
e	end	**ô**	order	**yo͞o**	fuse	**th̶**	this
ē	equal					**zh**	vision

ə = a in *above*, e in *sicken*, i in *possible*, o in *melon*, u in *circus*

various experiments on Mars by *remote control.*

re·mount [*v.* rē·mount′, *n.* rē′mount′] **1** *v.* To mount again: When the horse was rested, the rider *remounted* and rode off. **2** *n.* A fresh horse for riding.

re·mov·al [ri·mōō′vəl] *n.* **1** The act of removing. **2** The condition of being removed. **3** Dismissal: *removal* from public office. **4** A changing of location: the *removal* of a corporation to another city.

re·move [ri·mōōv′] *v.* **re·moved, re·mov·ing,** *n.* **1** *v.* To take or move away: The typist *removed* everything from the desk. **2** *v.* To take off: to *remove* one's hat. **3** *v.* To get rid of: Using aluminum *removes* any danger of rust. **4** *v.* To dismiss: The mayor was *removed* from office. **5** *v.* To change location; move: to *remove* to another area. **6** *n.* A step or degree: A newspaper reader is at least one *remove* from witnessing events. **—re·mov′er** *n.*

re·moved [ri·mōōvd′] *adj.* Separated in relationship by a given number of generations: Your first cousin's child is your first cousin once *removed.*

re·mu·ner·ate [ri·myōō′nə·rāt′] *v.* **re·mu·ner·at·ed, re·mu·ner·at·ing** To pay; reward; compensate: The workers were well *remunerated* for their work.

re·mu·ner·a·tion [ri·myōō′nə·rā′shən] *n.* **1** The act of remunerating. **2** Payment; reward.

re·mu·ner·a·tive [ri·myōō′nə·rā′tiv *or* ri·myōō′nə·rə·tiv] *adj.* Profitable; paying: a *remunerative* job.

Re·mus [rē′məs] *n.* In Roman myths, the brother of Romulus. ◆ See ROMULUS.

Ren·ais·sance [ren′ə·säns′] *n.* **1** The great revival of art, literature, and learning that marked the 14th, 15th, and 16th centuries in Europe. **2** The period of this revival. **3** (*written* **renaissance**) Any revival or rebirth.

Renaissance architecture

re·nal [rē′nəl] *adj.* Of, having to do with, or near the kidneys.

Re·nas·cence [ri·nas′·əns *or* ri·nā′səns] *n.* **1** The Renaissance. **2** (*written* **renascence**) A new birth; revival or renewal.

re·nas·cent [ri·nas′ənt *or* ri·nā′sənt] *adj.* Appearing again with new life or vigor.

rend [rend] *v.* **rent** or **rend·ed, rend·ing** **1** To tear apart; split; break: to *rend* one's clothing; The silence was *rent* with cries. **2** To distress; grieve: Sorrow *rends* my heart.

ren·der [ren′dər] *v.* **1** To give, present, or submit: to *render* a bill for payment. **2** To provide or furnish: to *render* aid. **3** To give as due: to *render* obedience. **4** To perform; do: to *render* service; to *render* a song. **5** To give in return: to *render* good for evil. **6** To cause to be or become: The news *rendered* us helpless. **7** To surrender; give up: to *render* a fortress into enemy hands. **8** To translate: to *render* a French ballad into English. **9** To melt down: to *render* fat or lard.

ren·dez·vous [rän′dā·vōō′] *n., pl.* **ren·dez·vous,** *v.* **ren·dez·voused, ren·dez·vous·ing** **1** *n.* A meeting place. **2** *n.* A planned meeting or joining of troops or ships at a certain time and place. **3** *n.* Any meeting or appointment to meet. **4** *v.* To meet or cause to meet at a certain place or time. ◆ *Rendezvous* comes from two French words meaning *present yourself.*

ren·di·tion [ren·dish′ən] *n.* **1** A performance of a musical composition or a part in a play. **2** A translation from one language into another. **3** The act of rendering. **4** Something rendered.

ren·e·gade [ren′ə·gād′] *n.* A person who gives up faith, principles, or party to join the opposite side; traitor.

re·nege [ri·nig′] *v.* **re·neged, re·neg·ing** **1** In card games, to fail to follow suit when able and required by the rules to do so. **2** *informal* To fail to keep a promise.

re·new [ri·n(y)ōō′] *v.* **1** To make new or as if new again; restore: to *renew* one's health. **2** To begin again; resume: to *renew* a discussion. **3** To cause to continue in effect; extend: to *renew* a magazine subscription. **4** To replace with something new of the same sort: to *renew* the supply of oil.

re·new·al [ri·n(y)ōō′əl] *n.* **1** The act of renewing. **2** The condition of being renewed.

ren·net [ren′it] *n.* The dried extract from the stomach of a young calf. It contains rennin and is used in the manufacture of cheese.

ren·nin [ren′in] *n.* A yellowish substance with a slightly salty taste, obtained from rennet. It is an enzyme used to curdle milk.

re·nounce [ri·nouns′] *v.* **re·nounced, re·nounc·ing** **1** To give up, especially by formal statement: to *renounce* citizenship. **2** To refuse to acknowledge as one's own; disown: He *renounced* his wayward son. **—re·nounce′ment** *n.*

ren·o·vate [ren′ə·vāt′] *v.* **ren·o·vat·ed, ren·o·vat·ing** To make as good as new; repair; freshen: to *renovate* a house. **—ren′o·va′tion** *n.* **—ren′o·va′tor** *n.*

Renovations

re·nown [ri·noun′] *n.* Fame: She gained *renown* as an athlete.

re·nowned [ri·nound′] *adj.* Famous.

rent[1] [rent] **1** *n.* Money paid to a landlord or owner for the use of land, living quarters, or personal property. **2** *v.* To use in return for rent: We *rent* our home. **3** *v.* To grant the use of in return for rent. **4** *v.* To be available for a certain rental: The cabin *rents* for $140 a month. **—for rent** Available in return for rent. **—rent′er** *n.*

rent[2] [rent] **1** Past tense and past participle of REND. **2** *n.* A rip; tear.

rent·al [ren′təl] *n.* The amount of rent charged or paid: We paid a low *rental* for our summer house.

rent strike A refusal to pay rent by an organized group of tenants as a protest against something that their landlord is doing or not doing.

re·nun·ci·a·tion [ri·nun′sē·ā′shən] *n.* The act of renouncing or of giving up.

re·o·pen [rē·ō′pən] *v.* **1** To open again. **2** To start again; resume.

re·or·gan·ize [rē·ôr′gən·īz′] *v.* **re·or·gan·ized, re·or·gan·iz·ing** To organize again or in a different way: to *reorganize* a company. **—re′or·gan·i·za′tion** *n.*

Rep. **1** Representative. **2** Republican.

re·paid [ri·pād′] Past tense and past participle of REPAY.

re·pair[1] [ri·pâr′] **1** *v.* To restore to good or sound condition; mend. **2** *n.* (*often pl.*) A repairing: to make *repairs* about the house. **3** *n.* Condition resulting from proper repairing or from neglect: a car in good *repair*; a fence in poor repair. **4** *v.* To make up for, as a wrong.

re·pair[2] [ri·pâr′] *v.* To go: The group *repaired* to the garden.

re·pair·er [ri·pâr′ər] *n.* A person whose work is repairing, as appliances, automobiles, or furniture.

re·pair·man [ri·pâr′man′ *or* ri·pâr′mən] *n., pl.* **re·pair·men** [ri·pâr′men′ *or* ri·pâr′mən] A person whose work is making repairs; repairer.

rep·a·ra·ble [rep′ər·ə·bəl] *adj.* Capable of being repaired.

rep·a·ra·tion [rep′ə·rā′shən] *n.* **1** The act of making amends for wrong or injury. **2** (*usually pl.*) Money or goods exacted from losing nations to pay the winners for wartime damage.

rep·ar·tee [rep′ər·tē′ *or* rep′är·tā′] *n.* **1** A quick, witty reply. **2** Skill or quickness in replying.

re·past [ri·past′] *n.* A meal; food.

re·pa·tri·ate [rē·pā′trē·āt′] *v.* **re·pa·tri·at·ed, re·pa·tri·at·ing** To send back to one's own country, as a prisoner of war or a refugee. **—re·pa′tri·a′tion** *n.*

re·pay [ri·pā′] *v.* **re·paid, re·pay·ing** **1** To pay back: to *repay* a debt; Their kindness *repaid* us for all our work. **2** To pay back someone for: I *repaid* their efforts with thanks. **—re·pay′ment** *n.*

re·peal [ri·pēl′] **1** *v.* To revoke; cancel: to *repeal* a law. **2** *n.* The act of repealing.

re·peat [ri·pēt′] **1** *v.* To say again: to *repeat* a question. **2** *v.* To do again. **3** *n.* In music, something, as a passage, phrase, or section, that is repeated. **4** *v.* To tell to another: to *repeat* the details of a movie plot. **5** *v.* To recite from memory: to *repeat* a poem. **—repeat oneself** To say again what one has said before.

re·peat·ed [ri·pē′tid] *adj.* Said, done, or occurring again and again; frequent: my *repeated* absences. **—re·peat′ed·ly** *adv.*

re·peat·ing decimal [ri·pē′ting] A decimal in which a pattern is repeated without end. 7/11 can be expressed as the repeating decimal .636363 . . .

re·pel [ri·pel′] *v.* **re·pelled, re·pel·ling** **1** To force or drive back; repulse: to *repel* an attack. **2** To push or keep away, especially with invisible force: Like magnetic poles *repel* each other. **3** To resist mixing with, adhering to, or holding: This raincoat *repels* water. **4** To cause to feel distaste or disgust: That odor *repels* me. **5** To reject; refuse: to *repel* a suggestion.

re·pel·lent [ri·pel′ənt] **1** *adj.* That drives or keeps away or back: a *repellent* force. **2** *adj.* Disgusting; distasteful: *repellent* odor. **3** *n.* Something that repels, as a chemical that drives away insects.

re·pent [ri·pent′] *v.* **1** To feel sorrow or remorse about (something one has done or said): We *repented* not having invited everyone to the party. **2** To change one's mind about (something one has done) and come to regret it: I *repented* my hasty decision.

re·pent·ant [ri·pen′tənt] *adj.* Repenting or showing regret. **—re·pent′ance** *n.*

re·per·cus·sion [rē′pər·kush′ən] *n.* **1** An indirect effect or result of something: A decision of the Supreme Court may have *repercussions* all over the United States. **2** An echo; reverberation. **3** The action of springing back; recoil: the *repercussion* of a gun that has been fired.

rep·er·toire [rep′ər·twär′] *n.* A list, as of songs, plays, or operas, that a person or a group is prepared to perform.

rep·er·to·ry [rep′ər·tôr′ē] *n., pl.* **rep·er·to·ries** **1** Another word for REPERTOIRE. **2** A collection: a *repertory* of American folklore.

repertory theater A theater in which the same company of actors performs a number of different plays during a season.

rep·e·ti·tion [rep′ə·tish′ən] *n.* **1** The act of repeating. **2** Something repeated.

rep·e·ti·tious [rep′ə·tish′əs] *adj.* Full of repetition, especially in a useless or tiresome way. **—rep′e·ti′tious·ly** *adv.*

re·pet·i·tive [ri·pet′ə·tiv] *adj.* Full of repetition; repetitious.

re·pine [ri·pīn′] *v.* **re·pined, re·pin·ing** To complain; fret; be discontented.

re·place [ri·plās′] *v.* **re·placed, re·plac·ing** **1** To put back in place: to *replace* a card in a file. **2** To take the place of: Who can *replace* the class president? **3** To fill the place of: She *replaced* the light bulb with a new one.

re·place·ment [ri·plās′mənt] *n.* **1** The act of replacing. **2** The condition of being replaced. **3** A person or thing that replaces another: I'll work until you find a *replacement* for me.

re·play [*v.* rē·plā′, *n.* rē′plā′] **1** *v.* To play over: to *replay* a rained-out baseball game. **2** *n.* An act of playing over, as the playing on television of a videotape of something already presented or shown.

re·plen·ish [ri·plen′ish] *v.* To provide with a new supply; fill up again: to *replenish* the salad bowl. **—re·plen′ish·ment** *n.*

re·plete [ri·plēt′] *adj.* Completely filled; having a great supply of: a story *replete* with adventures. **—re·ple′tion** *n.*

rep·li·ca [rep′lə·kə] *n.* A duplicate or copy, as of a statue or painting, often made by the artist.

rep·li·cate [rep′lə·kāt′] *v.* **rep·li·cat·ed, rep·li·cat·ing** To repeat or redo exactly; duplicate: to *replicate* a scientific experiment.

re·ply [ri·plī′] *v.* **re·plied, re·ply·ing,** *n., pl.* **re·plies** **1** *v.* To give an answer or response. **2** *n.* An answer or response.

re·port [ri·pôrt′] **1** *v.* To give an account of; tell of: to *report* the day's happenings. **2** *n.* An accounting or telling of something, often formal or in writing: a news *report*; a book *report.* **3** *v.* To state; announce: The newspaper *reported* the event in detail. **4** *n.* An announcement or statement: a *report* of an accident. **5** *v.* To complain about, especially to an authority: to *report* a robbery to the police. **6** *v.* To present oneself: to *report* for service. **7** *n.* A rumor: *reports* of flying saucers. **8** *n.* An explosive sound: a gun's *report.* **9** *n.* Reputation: a person of good *report.*

a	add	**i**	it	**o͝o**	took	**oi**	oil
ā	ace	**ī**	ice	**o͞o**	pool	**ou**	pout
â	care	**o**	odd	**u**	up	**ng**	ring
ä	palm	**ō**	open	**û**	burn	**th**	thin
e	end	**ô**	order	**yo͞o**	fuse	**t͟h**	this
ē	equal					**zh**	vision

ə = a in *above*, e in *sicken*, i in *possible*, o in *melon*, u in *circus*

R

re·port·age [ri·pôr′tij *or* rep′ər·täzh′] *n.* 1 The reporting of news, as in publications or on television. 2 Something that is reported.
report card A report on a student's grades and behavior sent periodically to the student's parents or guardian.
re·port·ed·ly [ri·pôr′tid·lē] *adv.* According to report: The governor is *reportedly* about to resign.
re·port·er [ri·pôr′tər] *n.* A person who reports, especially one employed by a newspaper.
re·pose[1] [ri·pōz′] *n., v.* **re·posed, re·pos·ing** 1 *n.* Rest or sleep. 2 *v.* To lie at rest. 3 *v.* To lay or place in a position of rest: to *repose* oneself on the bed. 4 *n.* Quietness; calmness: a manner of great *repose.*
re·pose[2] [ri·pōz′] *v.* **re·posed, re·pos·ing** To place, as hope or confidence: The citizens *reposed* their trust in their leaders.
re·pos·i·to·ry [ri·poz′ə·tôr′ē] *n., pl.* **re·pos·i·to·ries** A place in which things may be stored for safekeeping.
re·pos·sess [rē′pə·zes′] *v.* To regain possession of; get back.
rep·re·hend [rep′ri·hend′] *v.* To express disapproval of; criticize. **—rep′re·hen′sion** *n.*
rep·re·hen·si·ble [rep′ri·hen′sə·bəl] *adj.* Deserving blame or rebuke.
rep·re·sent [rep′ri·zent′] *v.* 1 To be the symbol or expression of; stand for: The letters of the alphabet *represent* sounds of speech. 2 To be an example of; typify: Spending time with my friends *represents* a perfect evening. 3 To be an agent of; act and speak for: Two senators *represent* each state. 4 To depict; portray: The artist *represented* the child as having red hair. 5 To describe: He *represents* himself as a musician. 6 To act the part of: In the opera, members of the chorus *represent* villagers.
rep·re·sen·ta·tion [rep′ri·zen·tā′shən] *n.* 1 The act of representing. 2 The condition of being represented. 3 Anything that represents, as a picture, description, or symbol. 4 Representatives as a group: our *representation* in the state legislature. 5 (*often pl.*) A statement made against something or to bring about a change. **—rep′re·sen·ta′tion·al** *adj.*
rep·re·sen·ta·tive [rep′ri·zen′tə·tiv] 1 *adj.* Representing: lines *representative* of latitude. 2 *adj.* Serving as an illustration; typical: a *representative* sample. 3 *n.* A typical example: The mouse is a *representative* of the order of rodents. 4 *n.* A person chosen to represent others. 5 *n.* (*often written* **Representative**) In the U.S., a member of the House of Representatives or of a state legislature. 6 *adj.* Based on representation, as a government.
re·press [ri·pres′] *v.* 1 To hold back or down; check: to *repress* a desire to sneeze. 2 To put down or quell. **—re·pres′sion** *n.*
re·pres·sive [ri·pres′iv] *adj.* Capable of repressing or tending to repress: *repressive* acts. **—re·pres′·sive·ly** *adv.*
re·prieve [ri·prēv′] *n., v.* **re·prieved, re·priev·ing** 1 *n.* A temporary delay of an order to execute a person. 2 *n.* The official order for such a delay. 3 *v.* To give a reprieve to. 4 *n.* Temporary relief from any danger or trouble. 5 *v.* To give such relief to.
rep·ri·mand [rep′rə·mand′] 1 *n.* A severe or formal reproof. 2 *v.* To reprove sharply or formally.
re·print [*v.* rē·print′, *n.* rē′print′] 1 *v.* To print a new edition or copy of. 2 *n.* A reprinted edition or copy.
re·pri·sal [ri·prī′zəl] *n.* Any act of retaliation, especially one of force or violence by one nation against another.
re·prise [ri·prēz′] *n.* A repeated performance, as of a song, musical passage, or show.
re·proach [ri·prōch′] 1 *v.* To blame for some wrong: My parents *reproached* me for losing the car keys. 2 *n.* Blame: words of *reproach.* 3 *n.* Disgrace. 4 *n.* A cause of disgrace.
re·proach·ful [ri·prōch′fəl] *adj.* Filled with or expressing reproach: a *reproachful* lecture. **—re·proach′ful·ly** *adv.*
rep·ro·bate [rep′rə·bāt′] 1 *adj.* Wicked; depraved. 2 *n.* A wicked, dishonest person; scoundrel.
rep·ro·ba·tion [rep′rə·bā′shən] *n.* Disapproval; condemnation.
re·proc·ess [rē·pros′es] *v.* To cause to undergo a special process or treatment before reuse: *reprocessed* wool.
re·pro·duce [rē′prə·d(y)o͞os′] *v.* **re·pro·duced, re·pro·duc·ing** 1 To make a copy of. 2 To produce again: A phonograph *reproduces* music. 3 To produce offspring: Rabbits *reproduce* in great numbers.
re·pro·duc·tion [rē′prə·duk′shən] *n.* 1 The act of reproducing. 2 The process by which plants or animals produce others of their kind. 3 Something that is reproduced, as a copy of a picture.
re·pro·duc·tive [rē′prə·duk′tiv] *adj.* 1 Reproducing. 2 Of, having to do with, or for reproduction. **—re′pro·duc′tive·ly** *adv.*
re·proof [ri·pro͞of′] *n.* Words of blame; rebuke.
re·prove [ri·pro͞ov′] *v.* **re·proved, re·prov·ing** To find fault with; blame; rebuke.
rep·tile [rep′til *or* rep′tīl′] *n.* Any of a large class of cold-blooded, egg-laying animals, including extinct forms such as dinosaurs as well as snakes, alligators, lizard, and other modern forms.

A reptile

rep·til·i·an [rep·til′ē·ən] 1 *adj.* Of, having to do with, like, or characteristic of a reptile. 2 *n.* A reptile.
re·pub·lic [ri·pub′lik] *n.* A government in which the power is given to officials elected by and representing the people.
re·pub·li·can [ri·pub′li·kən] 1 *adj.* Of or having to do with a republic: *republican* government. 2 *n.* A person who supports a republic or this form of government. 3 *adj.* (*written* **Republican**) Of or having to do with the Republican Party. 4 *n.* (*written* **Republican**) A member or supporter of the Republican Party.
Republican Party One of the two major political parties of the U.S., founded in 1854.
re·pu·di·ate [ri·pyo͞o′dē·āt′] *v.* **re·pu·di·at·ed, re·pu·di·at·ing** 1 To refuse to accept as true or binding; reject: to *repudiate* an agreement. 2 To refuse to acknowledge or pay: to *repudiate* a debt. 3 To disown: to *repudiate* a family member. **—re·pu′di·a′tion** *n.*
re·pug·nant [ri·pug′nənt] *adj.* 1 Disgusting; offensive: Your suggestion was *repugnant* to me. 2 Contrary or opposed: deeds *repugnant* to one's conscience. **—re·pug′nance** *n.*

re·pulse [ri·puls′] *v.* **re·pulsed, re·puls·ing,** *n.* **1** *v.* To drive back; repel: to *repulse* an attacker. **2** *n.* The act of repulsing. **3** *n.* The condition of being repulsed. **4** *v.* To repel, as by coldness or discourtesy; reject. **5** *n.* Rejection; refusal.
re·pul·sion [ri·pul′shən] *n.* **1** The act of repulsing. **2** Aversion; disgust.
re·pul·sive [ri·pul′siv] *adj.* **1** Disgusting or horrifying. **2** Repelling: a *repulsive* force. **—re·pul′sive·ly** *adv.* **—re·pul′sive·ness** *n.*
rep·u·ta·ble [rep′yə·tə·bəl] *adj.* Well thought of; respected: a *reputable* doctor. **—rep′u·ta·bly** *adv.*
rep·u·ta·tion [rep′yə·tā′shən] *n.* **1** The general estimation in which a person or thing is held by others. **2** A good name: Scandal ruined the official's *reputation.* **3** Fame or renown.
re·pute [ri·pyōōt′] *n.* Reputation: people of good *repute.*
re·put·ed [ri·pyōō′tid] *adj.* Generally thought or supposed: the *reputed* leader of the conspirators. **—re·put′ed·ly** *adv.*
re·quest [ri·kwest′] **1** *v.* To ask for: to *request* an appointment. **2** *v.* To ask (a person) to do something. **3** *n.* The act of requesting; petition. **4** *n.* Something asked for: What is your *request*? **5** *n.* Demand: This book is in great *request.*
re·qui·em [rek′wē·əm *or* rē′kwē·əm] *n.* **1** (*often written* **Requiem**) A solemn Mass sung for a person or persons who have died. **2** Music written for parts of this Mass.
re·quire [ri·kwīr′] *v.* **re·quired, re·quir·ing** **1** To have need of: Children *require* plenty of sleep. **2** To order or insist upon: Formal dress is *required* at dinner.
re·quire·ment [ri·kwīr′mənt] *n.* **1** Something needed: Good eyesight is a *requirement* in driving a car. **2** Something demanded: *requirements* for entering college.
req·ui·site [rek′wə·zit] **1** *adj.* Necessary; indispensable. **2** *n.* A necessity; requirement.
req·ui·si·tion [rek′wə·zish′ən] **1** *n.* A formal request or demand, especially in writing: a *requisition* for new typewriters. **2** *v.* To make demands for or upon: to *requisition* supplies; to *requisition* farmers for grain. **3** *n.* The condition of being required or put to use.
re·quit·al [ri·kwit′(ə)l] *n.* Something done in return for a service or for a wrong.
re·quite [ri·kwīt′] *v.* **re·quit·ed, re·quit·ing** **1** To give or do something in return for: to *requite* a stranger's generosity. **2** To pay back: They never *requited* us for our effort.
re·route [rē·rōōt′ *or* rē·rout′] *v.* **re·rout·ed, re·rout·ing** To send or make go by another route, as mail or traffic.
re·run [*v.* rē·run′, *n.* rē′·run′] *v.* **re·ran, re·run, re·run·ning,** *n.* **1** *v.* To run again. **2** *v.* To show again: *rerun* a home movie. **3** *n.* A showing of a motion picture or television program that has already been presented.

Traffic being rerouted

re·sale [rē′sāl′ *or* rē·sāl′] *n.* The act of selling again.
re·scind [ri·sind′] *v.* To make void; repeal: to *rescind* a rule.
res·cue [res′kyōō] *v.* **res·cued, res·cu·ing,** *n.* **1** *v.* To save or free from, as from danger, capture, or harm. **2** *n.* A saving from danger or harm; deliverance: The firefighters came to our *rescue.* **—res′cu·er** *n.*
re·search [ri·sûrch′ *or* rē′sûrch′] **1** *n.* Careful, patient investigation and study: medical *research.* **2** *v.* To do research or research on. ◆ The verb *research* was derived from the noun, and although the verb form is not new, it was rarely used until recently.
re·sem·blance [ri·zem′bləns] *n.* Similarity; likeness: the *resemblance* between sisters.
re·sem·ble [ri·zem′bəl] *v.* **re·sem·bled, re·sem·bling** To be or look like.
re·sent [ri·zent′] *v.* To feel or show resentment at: to *resent* an insult.
re·sent·ful [ri·zent′fəl] *adj.* **1** Full of or tending to feel resentment. **2** Caused or characterized by resentment. **—re·sent′ful·ly** *adv.* **—re·sent′ful·ness** *n.*
re·sent·ment [ri·zent′mənt] *n.* Anger and ill will based on real or imagined wrong or injury.
res·er·va·tion [rez′ər·vā′shən] *n.* **1** The act of reserving. **2** A qualification or condition: The amended bill carried certain *reservations.* **3** A doubt or possible objection: I have one *reservation* about your plan. **4** A tract of government land reserved for a special purpose: an Indian *reservation.* **5** An agreement by which something, as a seat on a plane or a hotel room, is reserved in advance.
re·serve [ri·zûrv′] *v.* **re·served, re·serv·ing,** *n., adj.* **1** *v.* To hold back or set aside for special or future use. **2** *n.* Something reserved: a *reserve* of food. **3** *n.* The condition of being reserved: money kept in *reserve.* **4** *adj.* Kept in reserve: *reserve* troops. **5** *v.* To arrange for ahead of time; have set aside for someone's use: to *reserve* tickets. **6** *n.* Silence as to one's thoughts or feelings. **7** *n.* (*pl.*) Troops who live as civilians and train at certain times in order to be ready to enter the regular armed services in an emergency. **8** *n.* Government land reserved for a special purpose: a forest *reserve.*
re·served [ri·zûrvd′] *adj.* **1** Held in reserve or set apart, as for some person or purpose. **2** Keeping one's feelings, thoughts, and affairs to oneself. —**re·serv·ed·ly** [ri·zûr′vid·lē] *adv.*
re·ser·vist [ri·zûr′vist] *n.* A member of the military reserves.
res·er·voir [rez′ər·vwär′ *or* rez′ər·vwôr′] *n.* **1** A basin, either natural or constructed, for collecting and storing a large supply of water. **2** A container where some material, especially a liquid or gas, may be stored: an ink *reservoir* in a fountain pen. **3** Any large supply: a *reservoir* of facts.
re·side [ri·zīd′] *v.* **re·sid·ed, re·sid·ing** **1** To make one's home; live: We *reside* in New York. **2** To be or exist as a quality: It is in such action that real

R

a	add	**i**	it	**o͝o**	took	**oi**	oil
ā	ace	**ī**	ice	**ōō**	pool	**ou**	pout
â	care	**o**	odd	**u**	up	**ng**	ring
ä	palm	**ō**	open	**û**	burn	**th**	thin
e	end	**ô**	order	**yōō**	fuse	**th**	this
ē	equal					**zh**	vision

ə = { a in *above* e in *sicken* i in *possible* / o in *melon* u in *circus* }

courage *resides.* **3** To be vested: The power to make laws *resides* in Congress.

res·i·dence [rez′ə·dəns] *n.* **1** The place where a person lives. **2** The act or period of residing: a long *residence* in Denver.

res·i·den·cy [rez′ə·dən·sē] *n.* The period during which a physician receives advanced training in a specialty, usually while serving on the staff of a hospital.

res·i·dent [rez′ə·dənt] **1** *n.* A person who lives in a certain place, not a visitor. **2** *adj.* Living in a place, especially at one's place of work: The hotel has a *resident* physician.

res·i·den·tial [rez′ə·den′shəl] *adj.* **1** Of or suitable for homes: a *residential* area. **2** Of or having to do with residence: *residential* requirements for voting.

re·sid·u·al [ri·zij′o͞o·əl] *adj.* Left over; remaining.

res·i·due [rez′ə·d(y)o͞o′] *n.* The remainder after a part has been removed or treated: When coal is treated, certain tars are left as *residues.*

re·sign [ri·zīn′] *v.* **1** To give up (an office or position): The judge *resigned* because of poor health. **2** To give up; submit; yield: to *resign* oneself to one's fate.

res·ig·na·tion [rez′ig·nā′shən] *n.* **1** The act of resigning. **2** A written statement that one has resigned or intends to resign. **3** Patient acceptance: The losing side took the defeat with *resignation.*

re·signed [ri·zīnd′] *adj.* Patient and submissive: to be *resigned* to being ill. **—re·sign·ed·ly** [ri·zī′nid·lē] *adv.*

re·sil·ient [ri·zil′yənt] *adj.* **1** Springing back to a former shape or position: Rubber is *resilient.* **2** Able to bounce back, as from trouble or sorrow; buoyant: a *resilient* person. **—re·sil′ience** *n.*

res·in [rez′ən] *n.* **1** A gummy, brown or yellowish substance given off by certain plants, especially fir and pine trees, and used in turpentine, glue, and varnishes. **2** Any of a class of synthetic substances with similar properties, used in making plastics. **3** Rosin. **—res′in·ous** *adj.*

re·sist [ri·zist′] *v.* **1** To work or strive against; oppose: The workers *resisted* the new machinery. **2** To ward off; withstand: This cloth *resists* wrinkles. **3** To keep from: I can't *resist* a good joke.

re·sis·tance [ri·zis′təns] *n.* **1** The act of resisting: Cats offer *resistance* to being bathed. **2** The power of resisting: a metal's *resistance* to rust. **3** Any force tending to hinder motion. **4** The opposition given by a conductor to the passage of an electric current due to a change of electrical energy into heat.

re·sis·tant [ri·zis′tənt] *adj.* Offering resistance; resisting: a fabric *resistant* to wear.

re·sist·less [ri·zist′lis] *adj.* **1** Incapable of being resisted; irresistible. **2** Not resisting. **—re·sist′·less·ly** *adv.* **—re·sist′less·ness** *n.*

re·sis·tor [ri·zis′tər] *n.* A device used to offer resistance in an electrical current.

res·o·lute [rez′ə·lo͞ot′] *adj.* Determined or bold: *resolute* courage; *resolute* words. **—res′o·lute′ly** *adv.* **—res′o·lute′ness** *n.*

res·o·lu·tion [rez′ə·lo͞o′shən] *n.* **1** Something determined or decided upon, as a course of action: a New Year's *resolution* to exercise daily. **2** A formal expression of the feelings or will of an assembly: to adopt a *resolution* supporting the President's position. **3** Determination; firmness: A successful leader must act with *resolution.* **4** The separation of something into the parts that make it up. **5** A solving, as of a problem; solution.

re·solve [ri·zolv′] *v.* **re·solved, re·solv·ing,** *n.* **1** *v.* To decide or determine: I *resolved* to do better. **2** *n.* A firm determination: a *resolve* to stand up for one's rights. **3** *v.* To solve or make clear: to *resolve* a problem. **4** *v.* To end; remove: to *resolve* doubts. **5** *v.* To decide by vote: The class *resolved* to end the year with a picnic. **6** *v.* To change; convert: Calm discussion *resolved* itself into angry debate. **7** *v.* To separate or break up into parts: to *resolve* a chemical compound.

res·o·nance [rez′ə·nəns] *n.* **1** A resonant condition or quality. **2** The tendency of some things, as stretched strings, organ pipes, or certain electric circuits, to vibrate or allow vibrations most readily at their own natural rate. **3** The reinforcement of sound by vibrations within an enclosed space, as a room or musical instrument.

res·o·nant [rez′ə·nənt] *adj.* **1** Deep, rich, and full in tone or sound: a *resonant* voice. **2** Capable of making a sound more full and rich: the *resonant* wood used in a cello. **3** Reflecting or prolonging sound: a *resonant* wall.

re·sort [ri·zôrt′] **1** *v.* To turn for help; have recourse: He *resorted* to shouting so as to be heard. **2** *n.* A person, thing, or act from which one hopes to receive help or aid: Selling their house was their last *resort.* **3** *n.* The act of turning to a person or thing for help: A *resort* to angry words never settles a disagreement. **4** *v.* To go often: to *resort* to the country on weekends. **5** *n.* A place where people go for rest and recreation: a summer *resort.*

re·sound [ri·zound′] *v.* **1** To be filled with sound or echo back: The cave *resounded* with loud cries. **2** To make a loud sound: That night the bells *resounded.* **3** To be much talked about: News of the World Series *resounded.*

re·source [ri·sôrs′ *or* rē′sôrs′] *n.* **1** (*often pl.*) A supply of something that can be used or drawn on: natural *resources*; financial *resources*; *resources* of strength. **2** The ability to act usefully and well in an emergency or difficulty. **3** Something turned to for aid or support: A tired swimmer's *resource* is to float.

re·source·ful [ri·sôrs′fəl] *adj.* Skillful and imaginative in finding ways of doing things or of resolving difficulties. **—re·source′ful·ness** *n.*

re·spect [ri·spekt′] **1** *v.* To have or show high regard for; esteem; honor. **2** *n.* Honor and esteem. **3** *v.* To treat courteously or with consideration. **4** *n.* Courteous regard: to have *respect* for older people. **5** *n.* (*pl.*) An expression of regard or honor: to pay one's *respects.* **6** *n.* A point or detail; aspect: In what *respect* is adjustment necessary? **7** *n.* Reference or relation: Please write us with *respect* to your plans.

re·spect·a·ble [ri·spek′tə·bəl] *adj.* **1** Deserving respect; reputable: *respectable* conduct. **2** Fairly good; average: a *respectable* test score. **3** Fairly large or great: a *respectable* amount. **—re·spect′a·bil′i·ty** *n.* **—re·spect′a·bly** *adv.*

re·spect·ful [ri·spekt′fəl] *adj.* Showing respect; courteous. **—re·spect′ful·ly** *adv.* **—re·spect′ful·ness** *n.*

re·spect·ing [ri·spek′ting] *prep.* In relation to; regarding: a survey *respecting* population.

re·spec·tive [ri·spek′tiv] *adj.* Of or having to do with each of those mentioned or considered; particular: My mother and father went to their *respective* jobs. ◆ Be careful not to confuse *respective* with RESPECTFUL or RESPECTABLE.

re·spec·tive·ly [ri·spek′tiv·lē] *adv.* In the order given: Paris and London are, *respectively,* the capitals of France and Great Britain.

re·spell [rē·spel′] *v.* To spell again or in a different way, especially with the letters of a phonetic alphabet.

res·pi·ra·tion [res′pə·rā′shən] *n.* 1 Breathing. 2 The process by which a plant or animal takes in oxygen from the air and gives off carbon dioxide.

res·pi·ra·tor [res′pə·rā′tər] *n.* 1 A covering, often of gauze, worn over the mouth or nose as protection against breathing harmful substances. 2 A device for artificial respiration.

res·pi·ra·to·ry [res′pə·rə·tôr′ē *or* ri·spir′ə·tôr′ē] *adj.* Of or having to do with breathing.

re·spire [ri·spīr′] *v.* **re·spired, re·spir·ing** To inhale and exhale; breathe.

res·pite [res′pit] *n.* 1 A pause for rest: a *respite* from work. 2 A putting off or postponement, as of the carrying out of a sentence of death.

re·splen·dent [ri·splen′dənt] *adj.* Splendid; gorgeous. **—re·splen′dence** *n.*

re·spond [ri·spond′] *v.* 1 To give an answer or reply: Please *respond* to my letter. 2 To react; act as if in reply: My cold *responded* to treatment.

re·sponse [ri·spons′] *n.* 1 A reply or reaction. 2 Words in a service said or sung by a congregation or choir in reply to a member of the clergy.

re·spon·si·bil·i·ty [ri·spon′sə·bil′ə·tē] *n., pl.* **re·spon·si·bil·i·ties** 1 The condition of being responsible: The age of legal *responsibility* is 21. 2 A person or thing for which one is responsible: Their elderly parents are their greatest *responsibility.*

re·spon·si·ble [ri·spon′sə·bəl] *adj.* 1 Obliged to carry out or take care of, as a duty, trust, or debt. 2 Being the cause or reason; accountable: Warm weather is *responsible* for the crowded beaches. 3 Involving trust or important duties: a *responsible* job. 4 Reliable; trustworthy: a *responsible* mechanic. **—re·spon′si·bly** *adv.*

re·spon·sive [ri·spon′siv] *adj.* 1 Responding well; reacting, as with sympathy or interest: a *responsive* audience. 2 Expressing a response: a *responsive* wink. 3 Containing responses: a *responsive* prayer.

rest[1] [rest] 1 *v.* To sleep or be still or quiet. 2 *n.* Ease, sleep, or relaxation after work, strain, or effort. 3 *n.* A period of ease, sleep, or relaxation: I need an hour's *rest.* 4 *n.* A temporary stopping of work or activity to get over being tired. 5 *n.* A place for resting, as a shelter for travelers. 6 *v.* To give rest to: to *rest* one's feet. 7 *v.* To support or be supported; lean; lay or lie: The ladder *rested* against the barn; *Rest* your head on two pillows. 8 *n.* A support for something, as a footrest for the feet. 9 *v.* To be at ease or at peace; be tranquil: I won't *rest* until the test is over. 10 *n.* Freedom from worry or trouble; peace: Put your mind at *rest.* 11 *v.* To be or become inactive or without change: And there the matter *rests.* 12 *n.* A motionless state: The boulder came to *rest* only a yard away. 13 *v.* To lie in death; be dead. 14 *n.* The grave; death. 15 *n.* A pause or interval of silence, as in music or poetry. 16 *n.* A sign indicating such a pause and its duration. 17 *v.* To rely; depend: Our hope *rests* on you. 18 *v.* To belong or lie: The choice *rests* with me. 19 *v.* To be directed; remain: Everyone's eyes *rested* on me.

Musical rests

rest[2] [rest] *n.* 1 The part left over; remainder: The child threw the *rest* of the apple away. 2 (*used with plural verb*) The others: The *rest* are coming soon.

re·state [rē·stāt′] *v.* **re·stat·ed, re·stat·ing** To state again, or in different words. **—re·state′ment** *n.*

res·tau·rant [res′tər·ənt *or* res′tə·ränt′] *n.* A place where meals are sold and served to the public; public dining room.

res·tau·ra·teur [res′tər·ə·tûr′] *n.* A person who owns or runs a restaurant.

rest·ful [rest′fəl] *adj.* 1 Full of or giving rest: a *restful* trip. 2 Quiet; serene: a *restful* scene.

rest home A place where old or sick people are housed and cared for.

res·ti·tu·tion [res′tə·t(y)o͞o′shən] *n.* 1 The act of paying back or making amends for injury or loss to another. 2 A restoring of something that has been taken away or lost.

res·tive [res′tiv] *adj.* 1 Difficult to manage; unruly: a *restive* crowd. 2 Restless; uneasy.

rest·less [rest′lis] *adj.* 1 Unable to rest or be still; nervous; uneasy. 2 Not restful or relaxing: a *restless* sleep. 3 Never resting or still: *restless* waves. **—rest′less·ly** *adv.* **—rest′less·ness** *n.*

re·stor·a·tive [ri·stôr′ə·tiv] 1 *adj.* Tending or able to restore, especially health or consciousness. 2 *n.* Something that restores, as a medicine.

re·store [ri·stôr′] *v.* **re·stored, re·stor·ing** 1 To bring back to a former or original condition: to *restore* a painting. 2 To bring back; establish once more: Peace and order were *restored.* 3 To give back, as something lost or stolen; return: The deed to the farm was *restored* to the owners. 4 To put back in a former place or position: to *restore* a ruler to power. **—res·to·ra·tion** [res′tə·rā′shən] *n.*

re·strain [ri·strān′] *v.* To hold back; repress: to *restrain* a lively dog; to *restrain* one's anger.

re·straint [ri·strānt′] *n.* 1 The act of restraining: a *restraint* of trade. 2 A being restrained. 3 A thing that restrains: A leash on a dog is a *restraint.* 4 Self-control.

re·strict [ri·strikt′] *v.* To hold or keep within limits or bounds; confine.

re·strict·ed [ri·strik′tid] *adj.* 1 Limited; confined: A tiger's food is *restricted* to meat. 2 Not available or open to everybody: *restricted* information.

re·stric·tion [ri·strik′shən] *n.* 1 The act of restricting. 2 The condition of being restricted. 3 A thing that restricts: Taxes place *restrictions* on spending.

re·stric·tive [ri·strik′tiv] *adj.* 1 Restricting: a *re-*

a	add	**i**	it	**o͝o**	took	**oi**	oil		
ā	ace	**ī**	ice	**o͞o**	pool	**ou**	pout		
â	care	**o**	odd	**u**	up	**ng**	ring		
ä	palm	**ō**	open	**û**	burn	**th**	thin		
e	end	**ô**	order	**yo͞o**	fuse	**th̸**	this		
ē	equal					**zh**	vision		

ə = { a in *above* e in *sicken* i in *possible* / o in *melon* u in *circus* }

R

strictive tariff. 2 Describing a word, phrase, or clause, not set off by commas, that is essential to the meaning of a sentence. In "A car that won't run is of little use," *that won't run* is a restrictive clause.

rest room A room with toilets and washstands in a public building.

re·sult [ri·zult′] 1 *v.* To be an outcome or consequence; follow: Accidents can *result* from carelessness. 2 *n.* An outcome; consequence. 3 *n.* The outcome of a computation: The *result* of adding 20 and 20 is 40.

re·sul·tant [ri·zul′tənt] 1 *adj.* Resulting: the *resultant* snowdrift. 2 *n.* A result; consequence. 3 *n.* In physics, a force resulting from two or more forces acting at the same time.

re·sume [ri·zōōm′] *v.* **re·sumed, re·sum·ing** 1 To begin again after stopping: to *resume* work. 2 To take or occupy again: *Resume* your places in line.

rés·u·mé [rez′ōō·mā′ *or* rez′ōō·mā′] *n.* A summary, as of a story or of a person's experience and jobs.

re·sump·tion [ri·zump′shən] *n.* A beginning again after stopping: a *resumption* of work after vacation.

re·sur·gence [ri·sûr′jəns] *n.* A surging or rising again.

re·sur·gent [ri·sûr′jənt] *adj.* Rising or tending to rise again; reviving; renascent.

res·ur·rect [rez′ə·rekt′] *v.* 1 To bring back to life; raise from the dead. 2 To bring back into use or notice: to *resurrect* old clothes.

res·ur·rec·tion [rez′ə·rek′shən] *n.* 1 A rising from the dead. 2 A revival or renewal. **—the Resurrection** The rising of Jesus from the dead.

re·sus·ci·tate [ri·sus′ə·tāt′] *v.* **re·sus·ci·tat·ed, re·sus·ci·tat·ing** To bring or come back to life; revive from unconsciousness. **—re·sus′ci·ta′tion** *n.*

re·sus·ci·ta·tor [ri·sus′ə·tā′tər] *n.* A person or thing that resuscitates, especially a device used to force air into the lungs of a person whose normal breathing has failed.

re·tail [rē′tāl] 1 *v.* To sell in small quantities to the actual user. 2 *n.* The selling of goods to consumers in small quantities. 3 *v.* To be sold in small quantities: This shirt *retails* at $25. 4 *adj.* Selling or having to do with selling in small quantities: *retail* prices. 5 [ri·tāl′] *v.* To repeat, as gossip. **—at retail** At retail prices. **—re′tail·er** *n.*

re·tain [ri·tān′] *v.* 1 To keep; hold: elastic that *retains* its spring. 2 To keep in mind; remember. 3 To hire by paying a retainer.

re·tain·er[1] [ri·tā′nər] *n.* A fee paid beforehand to obtain services, especially those of a lawyer.

re·tain·er[2] [ri·tā′nər] *n.* A servant, especially to a person of high rank; attendant.

re·take [*v.* rē·tāk′, *n.* rē′tāk′] *v.* **re·took, re·tak·en, re·tak·ing,** *n.* 1 *v.* To take back or capture again: to *retake* a fort. 2 *v.* To photograph again. 3 *n.* Something, as a motion-picture or television scene, or part of a musical recording, done again.

re·tal·i·ate [ri·tal′ē·āt′] *v.* **re·tal·i·at·ed, re·tal·i·at·ing** To do something to get even, as for an injury or wrong; pay back like for like. **—re·tal′i·a′tion** *n.*

re·tal·i·a·to·ry [ri·tal′ē·ə·tôr′ē] *adj.* Done to pay back an injury or wrong.

re·tard [ri·tärd′] *v.* 1 To slow down; delay; hinder: Illness *retarded* our work. 2 To slow down the tempo of. **—re′tar·da′tion** *n.*

re·tard·ed [ri·tär′did] *adj.* Slow or backward in mental development or in school work.

retch [rech] *v.* To make an effort to vomit; go through the motions of vomiting.

re·tell [rē·tel′] *v.* **re·told, re·tell·ing** 1 To tell again. 2 To tell in a different way or form. 3 To count again; recount.

re·ten·tion [ri·ten′shən] *n.* 1 The act of retaining. 2 The condition of being retained. 3 The capacity to retain. 4 The ability to remember.

re·ten·tive [ri·ten′tiv] *adj.* 1 Able to retain or keep. 2 Able to remember things easily: a *retentive* mind.

ret·i·cent [ret′ə·sənt] *adj.* Saying little; not inclined to talk about what one thinks or feels; reserved. **—ret′i·cence** *n.*

re·tic·u·late [*v.* ri·tik′yə·lāt′, *adj.* ri·tik′yə·lit] *v.* **re·tic·u·lat·ed, re·tic·u·lat·ing,** *adj.* 1 *v.* To divide or be divided by crossing lines or veins. 2 *adj.* Having a netlike pattern of crossing lines or veins: a *reticulate* leaf.

ret·i·na [ret′ə·nə] *n.* The layer of cells at the back of the eyeball that is sensitive to light and receives images picked up by the lens.

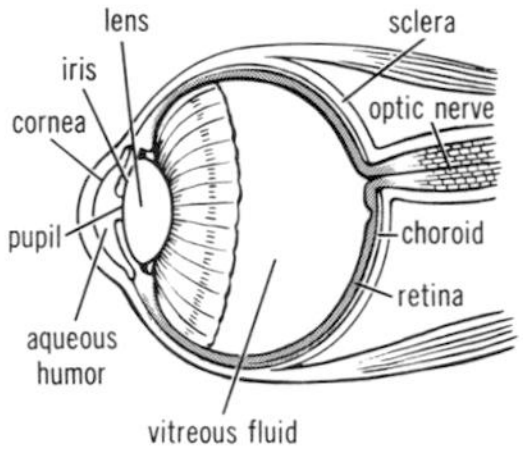

ret·i·nal [ret′ən·əl] *adj.* Of or having to do with the retina.

ret·i·nue [ret′ə·n(y)ōō′] *n.* A group of followers serving a person of high rank.

re·tire [ri·tīr′] *v.* **re·tired, re·tir·ing** 1 To withdraw or remove from a job, public life, or active service, often because of advancing age: They *retired* the admiral; The laborer *retired* at 65. 2 To go away, as for rest or privacy: to *retire* to a cottage. 3 To go to bed. 4 To fall back; retreat. 5 To pay off and withdraw from circulation: to *retire* bonds. **—re·tire′ment** *n.*

re·tir·ing [ri·tīr′ing] *adj.* Shy; modest.

re·took [rē·tŏŏk′] Past tense of RETAKE.

re·tort[1] [ri·tôrt′] 1 *v.* To reply sharply. 2 *n.* A sharp reply.

re·tort[2] [ri·tôrt′] *n.* A container with a bent tube for distilling or vaporizing chemicals by heat.

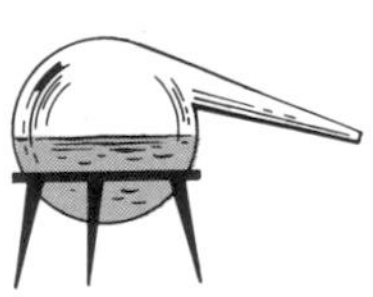

A retort

re·touch [rē·tuch′] *v.* To improve by adding new touches to: to *retouch* a sketch.

re·trace [ri·trās′] *v.* **re·traced, re·trac·ing** 1 To go back over: to *retrace* a path. 2 To trace the whole story of, from the beginning.

re·tract [ri·trakt′] *v.* 1 To draw back or in: The cat *retracted* its claws. 2 To take back; recant: to *retract* a confession. **—re·trac′tion** *n.*

re·trac·tile [ri·trak′til] *adj.* Capable of being drawn back or in.

re·tread [*v.* rē·tred′, *n.* rē′tred′] *v.* **re·tread·ed, re·tread·ing,** *n.* 1 *v.* To put a new tread on (a worn tire). 2 *n.* A retreaded tire.

re·treat [ri·trēt′] 1 *v.* To go back or backward; withdraw. 2 *n.* The act of retreating: the troop's *retreat.* 3 *n.* A signal for withdrawing. 4 *n.* A signal sounded at sunset when the flag is taken down: The bugle sounded *retreat.* 5 *n.* A quiet refuge: a *retreat* in the hills. **—beat a retreat** To turn back; flee.

re·trench [ri·trench′] *v.* To cut down or reduce (expenses). **—re·trench′ment** *n.*

re·tri·al [rē·trī′əl] *n.* A second or succeeding trial, as of a court case.

ret·ri·bu·tion [ret′rə·byōō′shən] *n.* Punishment given in return for a wrong a person has done.

re·trib·u·tive [ri·trib′yə·tiv] *adj.* Of, having to do with, or characterized by retribution.

re·triev·al [ri·trē′vəl] *n.* The act of retrieving or the condition of being retrieved.

re·trieve [ri·trēv′] *v.* **re·trieved, re·triev·ing** 1 To get back; regain: to *retrieve* a lost umbrella. 2 To get and bring back: The dog *retrieved* the newspaper. 3 To recover (information) from storage, especially by means of a computer. 4 To bring back to an improved condition: to *retrieve* one's good spirits. 5 To make up for; make amends for: to *retrieve* a blunder.

re·triev·er [ri·trē′vər] *n.* A dog bred and trained to retrieve game for hunters.

A typical retriever

retro- A prefix meaning: Back or backward, as in *retroactive.*

ret·ro·ac·tive [ret′rō·ak′tiv] *adj.* Having an effect on things that are already past: The new income tax rate is *retroactive* to January 1.

ret·ro·grade [ret′rə·grād′] *v.* **ret·ro·grad·ed, ret·ro·grad·ing,** *adj.* 1 *v.* To move backwards; retreat: The glacier is *retrograding.* 2 *adj.* Moving backward. 3 *v.* To go back to a less advanced stage of physical, intellectual, or moral development; deteriorate. 4 *adj.* Declining to or toward a worse condition; deteriorating.

ret·ro·gress [ret′rə·gres′] *v.* To go back or revert to an earlier or worse condition. **—ret′ro·gres′sion** *n.*

ret·ro·gres·sive [ret′rə·gres′iv] *adj.* Going or aiming backward; retrogressing.

ret·ro-rock·et [ret′rō·rok′it] *n.* A rocket fired to slow down or change the direction of a spacecraft, aircraft, or missile.

ret·ro·spect [ret′rə·spekt′] *n.* A viewing or consideration of past times or events: In *retrospect,* my taking this job was a good decision. **—ret′ro·spec′tion** *n.*

ret·ro·spec·tive [ret′rə·spek′tiv] 1 *adj.* Looking back on the past: a *retrospective* poem. 2 *n.* An exhibit of works done over a period of years by an artist or group. 3 *adj.* Applying to the past: a *retrospective* amnesty. **—ret′ro·spec′tive·ly** *adv.*

re·turn [ri·tûrn′] 1 *v.* To come or go back: to *return* home. 2 *v.* To bring, carry, send, or put back: to *return* a book. 3 *v.* To repay, especially in kind: to *return* a compliment. 4 *n.* The act of returning: a *return* home; the *return* of a pen. 5 *adj.* Of or for a return: a *return* ticket. 6 *n.* Something returned. 7 *adj.* Done in exchange: a *return* visit. 8 *v.* To answer; respond: "But I want to go!" the child *returned.* 9 *v.* To give or announce: to *return* a verdict. 10 *v.* To yield: to *return* a profit. 11 *n.* A yield; profit: a *return* of $100. 12 *n.* A formal or official report: an income tax *return.* 13 *n.* (*pl.*) A set of statistics that have been tabulated: election *returns.* **—in return** In exchange; as repayment: He did me a favor *in return.*

re·turn·ee [ri·tûr′nē′] *n.* A person who returns, as from military service abroad.

re·un·ion [rē·yōōn′yən] *n.* 1 The act of reuniting. 2 A gathering of people who have been apart from each other: a family *reunion.*

re·u·nite [rē′yōō·nīt′] *v.* **re·u·nit·ed, re·u·nit·ing** To bring or come together again.

rev [rev] *n., v.* **revved, rev·ving** *informal* 1 *n.* A revolution of an engine or motor. 2 *v.* To increase the speed of; step up: to *rev* up a car engine; a factory *revving* up production.

rev. 1 revenue. 2 reverse. 3 revised. 4 revolution.

Rev. Reverend.

re·val·u·ate [rē·val′yōō·āt′] *v.* **re·val·u·at·ed, re·val·u·at·ing** To set a new value for: to *revaluate* a currency.

re·vamp [rē·vamp′] *v.* To patch up or make over: to *revamp* an old coat.

re·veal [ri·vēl′] *v.* 1 To make known; disclose: to *reveal* a secret. 2 To make visible; show: The curtain opened to *reveal* a courtroom.

rev·eil·le [rev′i·lē] *n.* A signal by bugle or drum telling a group, as of soldiers or sailors, to wake up or to form ranks for the first time that day.

rev·el [rev′əl] *v.* **rev·eled** or **rev·elled, rev·el·ing** or **rev·el·ling** *n.* 1 *v.* To have noisy, boisterous fun. 2 *n.* Boisterous merrymaking. 3 *v.* To take delight: to *revel* in outdoor sports. **—rev′el·er** or **rev′el·ler** *n.*

rev·e·la·tion [rev′ə·lā′shən] *n.* 1 A making or becoming known. 2 Something made known, especially something surprising: Your knowledge of astronomy was a *revelation* to us. 3 An act of revealing the will or truth of God directly to human beings. 4 Something revealed to human beings by God. 5 (*written* **Revelation** or **Revelations**) The last book of the New Testament.

rev·el·ry [rev′əl·rē] *n., pl.* **rev·el·ries** Noisy or boisterous merrymaking.

re·venge [ri·venj′] *v.* **re·venged, re·veng·ing,** *n.* 1 *v.* To inflict something, as punishment or injury, in return for a wrong received: to *revenge* oneself for an insult. 2 *n.* The act of revenging. 3 *n.* The desire for or method of vengeance.

re·venge·ful [ri·venj′fəl] *adj.* 1 Desiring revenge. 2 Full of revenge: *revengeful* thoughts.

rev·e·nue [rev′ə·n(y)ōō′] *n.* 1 The income that a government receives, as from taxes and duties. 2 Income from any form of property.

re·ver·ber·ate [ri·vûr′bə·rāt′] *v.* **re·ver·ber·at·ed, re·ver·ber·at·ing** 1 To resound or echo back: The slam of the door *reverberated.* 2 To reflect or be reflected, as light or heat.

re·ver·ber·a·tion [ri·vûr′bə·rā′shən] *n.* A reflecting, as of sound waves, light, or heat.

re·vere [ri·vir′] *v.* **re·vered, re·ver·ing** To regard with reverence.

rev·er·ence [rev′ər·əns] *n., v.* **rev·er·enced, rev·er·enc·ing** 1 *n.* A feeling of great respect, often mingled with awe and affection. 2 *v.* To regard with respect and awe.

rev·er·end [rev′ər·ənd] *adj.* 1 Worthy of reverence. 2 (*written* **Reverend**) A title of respect used before the name of a clergyman: *Reverend* Henderson.

a	add	**i**	it	**o͝o**	took	**oi**	oil
ā	ace	**ī**	ice	**ōō**	pool	**ou**	pout
â	care	**o**	odd	**u**	up	**ng**	ring
ä	palm	**ō**	open	**û**	burn	**th**	thin
e	end	**ô**	order	**yōō**	fuse	**th**	this
ē	equal					**zh**	vision

ə = a in *above* e in *sicken* i in *possible* o in *melon* u in *circus*

rev·er·ent [rev′ər·ənt] *adj.* Feeling or showing reverence. **—rev′er·ent·ly** *adv.*
rev·er·en·tial [rev′ə·ren′shəl] *adj.* **1** Expressing or showing reverence. **2** Inspiring reverence.
rev·er·ie [rev′ər·ē] *n., pl.* **rev·er·ies** Distant and pleasant thoughts; daydreaming: lost in *reverie.*
re·ver·sal [ri·vûr′səl] *n.* The act or process of reversing or being reversed.
re·verse [ri·vûrs′] *adj., v.* **re·versed, re·vers·ing,** *n.* **1** *adj.* Turned, facing, or done backward or upside down: the *reverse* side of a rug; to do things in *reverse* order. **2** *v.* To turn upside down or inside out. **3** *n.* The back side: the *reverse* of a coin. **4** *v.* To turn or make go in the opposite direction. **5** *adj.* Causing backward movement: a *reverse* gear. **6** *n.* The gear, as in an automobile, that causes backward movement. **7** *n.* (*usually pl.*) A change for the worse; bad fortune: The business suffered *reverses* last season. **8** *v.* To change into something different or opposite: to *reverse* a decision. **9** *n.* Something directly opposite or contrary: The *reverse* of what you say is true.
re·vers·i·ble [ri·vur′sə·bəl] *adj.* **1** Carefully finished on both sides so that either side may be worn on the outside: a *reversible* coat. **2** Capable of going either forward or backward: a *reversible* chemical process.

A reversible coat

re·ver·sion [ri·vûr′zhən] *n.* **1** A return to or toward some former condition. **2** In law, the return of an estate to the owner or to the owner's heirs. **3** In law, the right of succession to an estate.
re·vert [ri·vûrt′] *v.* **1** To go or turn back, as to a former place, condition, or attitude. **2** In law, to return to the former owner or to the owner's heirs: The property *reverted* to the Adams family.
re·view [ri·vyōō′] **1** *v.* To go over or examine again: to *review* a lesson. **2** *v.* To think back on: to *review* the events of the past week. **3** *n.* The act of reviewing: a *review* of current events. **4** *v.* To look over carefully or inspect: to *review* a test paper. **5** *n.* A careful inspection or scrutiny. **6** *n.* A formal inspection, as of troops. **7** *n.* An article or essay discussing something, as a book, movie, or play. **8** *v.* To write such an article or essay on.
re·view·er [ri·vyōō′ər] *n.* A person who reviews movies, books, or plays, as for a newspaper.
re·vile [ri·vīl′] *v.* **re·viled, re·vil·ing** To attack with words of abuse or contempt; call bad names.
re·vise [ri·vīz′] *v.* **re·vised, re·vis·ing** **1** To read carefully so as to correct errors or make improvements and changes: to *revise* a textbook; to *revise* a manuscript. **2** To change: to *revise* a list of prices upward. **—re·vis′er** *n.*
re·vi·sion [ri·vizh′ən] *n.* **1** The act of revising. **2** Something that has been revised: This is a *revision* of an older spelling book.
re·vi·val [ri·vī′vəl] *n.* **1** A restoring or coming back to life, consciousness, or vigor. **2** A renewal of interest in something long neglected or forgotten: a *revival* of learning; a *revival* of an old moving picture. **3** A meeting for stirring up religious faith, usually by means of forceful and dramatic preaching.
re·vi·val·ist [ri·vī′vəl·ist] *n.* A person who conducts or promotes religious revivals.
re·vive [ri·vīv′] *v.* **re·vived, re·viv·ing** **1** To bring or come back to life or consciousness. **2** To give new strength or vigor to: The good news *revived* their hopes; Hot coffee *revived* the tired workers. **3** To bring back into use: to *revive* an old custom.
re·vo·ca·ble [rev′ə·kə·bəl *or* ri·vō′kə·bəl] *adj.* Capable of being revoked.
rev·o·ca·tion [rev′ə·kā′shən] *n.* A revoking, canceling, or repeal.
re·voke [ri·vōk′] *v.* **re·voked, re·vok·ing** To take back, cancel, or repeal, as a license, permit, or a law.
re·volt [ri·vōlt′] **1** *n.* An uprising against authority; rebellion or mutiny. **2** *v.* To rebel against authority. **3** *v.* To fill with disgust: This food *revolts* me. **4** *v.* To turn away in disgust: We *revolted* at the terrible odor.
re·volt·ing [ri·vōl′ting] *adj.* Disgusting.
rev·o·lu·tion [rev′ə·lōō′shən] *n.* **1** The overthrow of an established government by those formerly under its authority. **2** A great change, as in a condition or method: Aircraft have caused a *revolution* in travel. **3** Movement in a circle, ellipse, or other closed curve: the moon's *revolution* around the earth. **4** One complete circuit of such a movement. **5** Rotation on an axis.
rev·o·lu·tion·ar·y [rev′ə·lōō′shən·er′ē] *adj., n.* **rev·o·lu·tion·ar·ies** **1** *adj.* Of, having to do with, or causing a revolution or revolt. **2** *n.* A revolutionist. **3** *adj.* Rotating or revolving.
Revolutionary War The war for independence carried on by the 13 American colonies against Great Britain from 1775 to 1783.
rev·o·lu·tion·ist [rev′ə·lōō′shən·ist] *n.* A person who is in favor of or takes part in a revolution.
rev·o·lu·tion·ize [rev′ə·lōō′shən·īz′] *v.* **rev·o·lu·tion·ized, rev·o·lu·tion·iz·ing** To make a complete or extreme change in: This new type of train may *revolutionize* the railroads.
re·volve [ri·volv′] *v.* **re·volved, re·volv·ing** **1** To move in a circle or orbit around a center. **2** To spin around on an axis; rotate: The wheel *revolved* slowly. **3** To turn over in one's mind before making a decision, as a problem or plan.

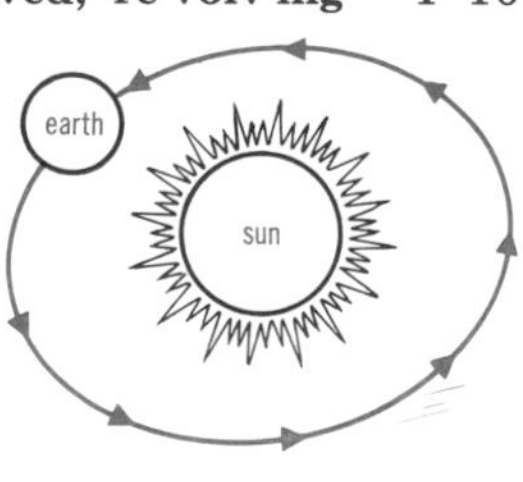

The earth revolves around the sun.

re·volv·er [ri·vol′vər] *n.* A type of pistol having a revolving cylinder with chambers to hold several cartridges that may be fired one after another without loading again.
re·vue [ri·vyōō′] *n.* A type of musical comedy made up of songs, dances, and skits that poke fun at current events and people.
re·vul·sion [ri·vul′shən] *n.* A sudden change of feeling, especially to one of disgust.
re·ward [ri·wôrd′] **1** *n.* Something given or done in return, especially a gift or prize for merit, service, or achievement. **2** *n.* Money offered for a service, as capturing a criminal or returning a lost article. **3** *v.* To give a reward to or for: to *reward* the dog with a pat; They *rewarded* our kindness with thanks.

re·wire [rē·wīr′] *v.* **re·wired, re·wir·ing** To put new electrical wiring in.
re·word [rē·wûrd′] *v.* To put into different words; say again in other words.
re·work [rē·wûrk′] *v.* To work on again; revise or reprocess.
re·write [rē·rīt′] *v.* **re·wrote, re·writ·ten** To write over again; revise: to *rewrite* a story.
Reyn·ard [ren′ərd *or* rā′nərd] *n.* A name for the fox in many old tales and poems.
R.F.D. rural free delivery.
Rh The symbol for the element rhodium.
rhap·sod·ic [rap·sod′ik] *adj.* **1** Of, having to do with, like, or characteristic of a rhapsody. **2** Full of unrestrained emotion or enthusiasm; rapturous.
rhap·so·dy [rap′sə·dē] *n., pl.* **rhap·so·dies** **1** A rapturous utterance, as of delight or excitement: The reviewer went into *rhapsodies* over the star's performance. **2** A piece of instrumental music irregular in form and full of emotion.

Rhea

rhe·a [rē′ə] *n.* A bird of South America that is like the ostrich, but smaller.
Rhen·ish [ren′ish] *adj.* Of or having to do with the Rhine River or the lands bordering it.
rhe·ni·um [rē′nē·əm] *n.* A heavy, silvery white metallic element with a high melting point.
rhe·o·stat [rē′ə·stat′] *n.* A device for regulating an electric current by increasing or decreasing the resistance.

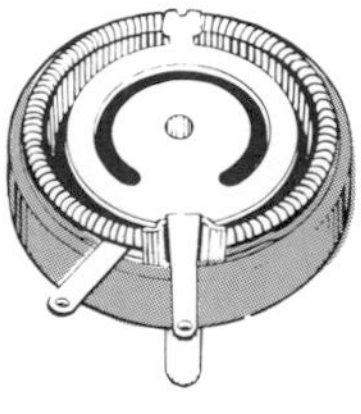
A rheostat

rhe·sus monkey [rē′səs] A pale brown, stocky monkey from India, widely used in medical experiments.
rhet·o·ric [ret′ə·rik] *n.* **1** The art of speaking or writing effectively. **2** The study of this art. **3** A book about it. **4** Extravagant or insincere language; bombast.
rhe·tor·i·cal [ri·tôr′i·kəl] *adj.* **1** Of or having to do with rhetoric. **2** Designed for showy oratorical effect: *rhetorical* phrases. **—rhe·tor′i·cal·ly** *adv.*
rhetorical question A question asked only for effect and not requiring an answer.
rhet·o·ri·cian [ret′ə·rish′ən] *n.* **1** A person who teaches or is an expert in rhetoric. **2** A person who speaks or writes eloquently. **3** A person who uses extravagant or insincere language.
rheum [ro͞om] *n.* A watery discharge from the nose and eyes, as during a cold. **—rheum′y** *adj.*
rheu·mat·ic [ro͞o·mat′ik] **1** *adj.* Of, having to do with, or caused by rheumatism: *rheumatic* pains. **2** *adj.* Having rheumatism. **3** *n.* A person who has rheumatism.
rheumatic fever A disease, usually affecting young people, marked by pain in the joints, fever, and often serious damage to the heart.
rheu·ma·tism [ro͞o′mə·tiz′əm] *n.* A painful inflammation and stiffness of the joints.
Rh factor [är′āch′] A substance that helps to produce antibodies and that is present in the red blood cells of most people. Blood containing it, called **Rh positive,** can cause dangerous reactions when transfused into a person with blood lacking it, called **Rh negative.** ◆ The *rh* in *Rh factor* refers to the *rhesus monkey*, in which the substance was first detected in 1940.
rhine·stone [rīn′stōn′] *n.* An imitation gem made of glass, cut and polished to look like a diamond.
rhi·no [rī′nō] *n., pl.* **rhi·nos** A rhinoceros.
rhi·noc·e·ros [rī·nos′ər·əs] *n., pl.* **rhi·noc·e·ros·es** or **rhi·noc·e·ros** A large, plant-eating mammal of Africa and Asia having one or two horns on its snout and a very thick hide. ◆ *Rhinoceros* comes from the Greek words for *nose* and *horn.*

Rhinoceros

rhi·zoid [ri′zoid′] *n.* One of the threadlike roots by which a moss or similar plant clings to a surface.
rhi·zome [rī′zōm′] *n.* A fleshy plant stem that grows horizontally under or along the ground and sends shoots and leaves upward and roots downward: To kill crabgrass, you must dig up its *rhizomes.*
rho [rō] *n.* The 17th letter of the Greek alphabet.
Rhode Island Red A breed of domestic chicken.
rho·di·um [rō′dē·əm] *n.* A hard, silvery white metallic element that occurs native and in ores associated with platinum.
rho·do·den·dron [rō′də·den′drən] *n.* An evergreen shrub that bears clusters of white, pink, or purple flowers.
rhom·boid [rom′boid′] *n.* A parallelogram having unequal adjacent sides.
rhom·bus [rom′bəs] *n., pl.* **rhom·bus·es** or **rhom·bi** [rom′bī′] A parallelogram whose sides are all equal, usually having two acute and two obtuse angles.

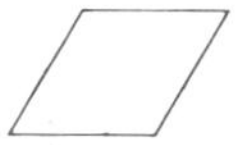
A rhombus

rhu·barb [ro͞o′bärb′] *n.* **1** A stout, coarse plant having large leaves. Its thick, acid stalks are cooked with sweetening and eaten. **2** *U.S. slang* A violent quarrel or dispute.
rhyme [rīm] *n., v.* **rhymed, rhym·ing** **1** *n.* A similarity of the final sounds of words, as *demand* and *unhand,* especially at the ends of lines of poetry. **2** *n.* A word whose sound matches another in this way: "Lake" is a *rhyme* for "rake." **3** *v.* To end in, or have lines ending in, matching sounds: "Hand" *rhymes* with "land"; These verses don't *rhyme.* **4** *v.* To use as a rhyme: Can "plot" be *rhymed* with "out"? **5** *n.* A verse having rhymed lines. **6** *v.* To make rhymes or verses.
rhyme·ster [rīm′stər] *n.* A bad poet.
rhythm [rith′əm] *n.* **1** Repetition, as of a beat, sound, accent, or motion, usually in a regular way:

a	add	**i**	it	**o͝o**	took	**oi**	oil
ā	ace	**ī**	ice	**o͞o**	pool	**ou**	pout
â	care	**o**	odd	**u**	up	**ng**	ring
ä	palm	**ō**	open	**û**	burn	**th**	thin
e	end	**ô**	order	**yo͞o**	fuse	**th**	this
ē	equal					**zh**	vision

ə = {a in *above* e in *sicken* i in *possible*
o in *melon* u in *circus*

Dance to the *rhythm* of the music. **2** The relative length and accent of musical sounds, or of the syllables in poetry. **3** A particular arrangement of lengths and stresses in music or poetry: march *rhythm.*

rhythm and blues Music with a strong beat and elements of the blues, developed and widely performed by black Americans.

rhyth·mic [ri*th*′mik] *adj.* Rhythmical.

rhyth·mi·cal [ri*th*′mə·kəl] *adj.* Of, having to do with, or having rhythm. **—rhyth′mi·cal·ly** *adv.*

RI Postal Service abbreviation of Rhode Island.

R.I. Rhode Island.

ri·a·ta or **re·a·ta** [rē·ä′tə] *n.* Another word for LARIAT.

rib [rib] *n., v.* **ribbed, rib·bing** **1** *n.* One of the long, curved bones attached in pairs to the backbone and enclosing the chest in humans and in many animals. **2** *n.* Something like a rib in shape or use, as one of the curved timbers in the framework of a boat. **3** *v.* To make or strengthen with ribs: to *rib* a boat. **4** *n.* A cut of meat containing a rib or ribs. **5** *n.* A ridge or raised stripe, as one in cloth or knitting. **6** *v.* To make or mark with ribs: to *rib* a sweater. **7** *n.* A vein of a leaf. **8** *v. slang* To make fun of; tease.

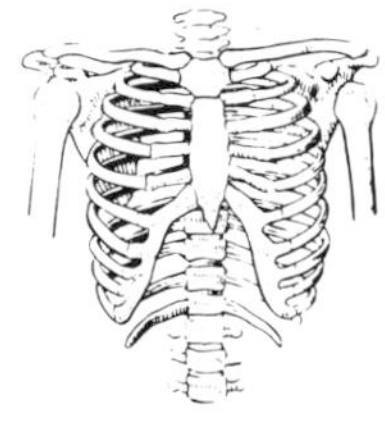

Ribs

rib·ald [rib′əld] *adj.* Using or having to do with crude language or vulgar humor: a *ribald* joke.

rib·ald·ry [rib′əl·drē] *n., pl.* **rib·ald·ries** Crude language or vulgar humor.

rib·bon [rib′ən] **1** *n.* A narrow strip of cloth with finished edges, often used for trimming. **2** *v.* To decorate with or make into ribbons. **3** *n.* Something like a ribbon, as the strip of inked cloth on a typewriter. **4** *n.* (*often pl.*) A narrow strip; shred: torn to *ribbons.*

rib cage The protective, enclosing structure formed by the ribs in the chest.

ri·bo·fla·vin [rī′bō·flā′vin *or* rī′bō·flā′vin] *n.* A member of the vitamin B complex, found in milk, leafy vegetables, egg yolk, and meat.

ri·bo·nu·cle·ic acid [rī′bō·n(y)ōō·klē′ik] A complex substance found in plant and animal cells, involved in building proteins.

ri·bose [rī′bōs′] *n.* A sugar that occurs in ribonucleic acid.

rice [rīs] *n., v.* **riced, ric·ing** **1** *n.* The starchy seeds of a grasslike plant, forming an important food throughout the world. **2** *n.* The plant itself, grown in warm climates. **3** *v.* To reduce (potatoes or other vegetables) to a form that looks something like rice by pressing them through a kitchen utensil that consists of a container with small holes in it.

rice·bird [rīs′bûrd′] *n.* A bird often found in rice fields, especially the bobolink of the southern U.S.

rice paper A thin paper made from the pith of an Asian tree.

rich [rich] *adj.* **1** Having a lot of money, goods, or property; wealthy. **2** *n.* Rich people: The *rich* donated money for the new hospital. **3** Valuable; costly; precious: *rich* fabrics. **4** Containing a great deal of such ingredients as butter, sugar, or eggs: a *rich* dessert. **5** Full and pleasant, as a tone, voice, or color. **6** Abundantly supplied: an area *rich* in coal. **7** Giving an abundant return; fruitful: *rich* soil. **8** *informal* Very funny or ridiculous: a *rich* joke. **—rich′ness** *n.*

rich·es [rich′iz] *n.pl.* **1** Much money or many valuable possessions; great wealth. **2** Things of great worth: The *riches* of fine recorded music are open to us all.

rich·ly [rich′lē] *adv.* **1** In a rich manner. **2** Fully; justly: a compliment *richly* deserved.

Rich·ter scale [rik′tər] A scale for expressing the magnitude of earthquakes, ranging from 1 to 10. ◆ The scale was named for Charles F. *Richter* (born 1900), an American scientist who proposed it.

rick [rik] *n.* A stack, as one of hay or straw, especially one covered for protection against rain.

rick·ets [rik′its] *n.* A disease of young children caused by a lack of vitamin D, resulting in softening and bending of the bones, especially of the legs.

rick·et·y [rik′it·ē] *adj.* **rick·et·i·er, rick·et·i·est** **1** Ready to collapse; not sturdy: a *rickety* old bridge. **2** Having or like rickets.

rick·rack [rik′rak′] *n.* Flat braid made in a zigzag form, used as trimming.

rick·shaw or **rick·sha** [rik′shô′] *n.* Another name for JINRICKSHA.

ric·o·chet [rik′ə·shā′] *v.* **ric·o·cheted** [rik′ə·shād′], **ric·o·chet·ing** [rik′ə·shā′ing] *n.* **1** *v.* To bounce or rebound from or off a surface: The bullet *ricocheted* off the wall. **2** *v.* To skip along a surface: The stone *ricocheted* across the water. **3** *n.* The action of ricocheting.

ri·cot·ta [ri·kot′ə] *n.* A soft, white Italian cheese that resembles cottage cheese.

rid [rid] *v.* **rid** or **rid·ded, rid·ding** To free, as from something unwanted: to *rid* a house of termites. **—be rid of** To be free of. **—get rid of** **1** To become free of. **2** To dispose of.

rid·dance [rid′(ə)ns] *n.* The clearing out or removal of something unpleasant. **—good riddance** A welcome relief or deliverance from an unwanted person or thing.

rid·den [rid′(ə)n] Past participle of RIDE.

rid·dle[1] [rid′(ə)l] *v.* **rid·dled, rid·dling,** *n.* **1** *v.* To make many holes in, as by shots. **2** *v.* To sift through a coarse sieve. **3** *n.* A coarse sieve. **4** *v.* To affect throughout; corrupt; permeate: The crew was *riddled* with potential mutineers.

rid·dle[2] [rid′(ə)l] *n., v.* **rid·dled, rid·dling** **1** *n.* A question or problem having a tricky or puzzling answer, as "What is black and white and red (read) all over?" "A newspaper." **2** *v.* To state or solve riddles. **3** *n.* A puzzling person or thing: Their behavior is a *riddle* to us all.

ride [rīd] *v.* **rode, rid·den, rid·ing,** *n.* **1** *v.* To sit on and guide the motion of (as a horse or bicycle). **2** *v.* To be carried along: to *ride* in a car. **3** *n.* A usually short trip made by being carried along, as on a horse or in a car. **4** *v.* To be supported on while moving: Our boat *rode* the waves. **5** *v.* To move or travel, often by mechanical means: This bus *rides* well; We *rode* for three days. **6** *v.* To cause to ride; transport: I'll *ride* you to the corner. **7** *v.* To dominate or control: to be *ridden* by fear. **8** *v. informal* To tease or pester. **9** *v. slang* To go on unchanged: Let the problem *ride* for a while. **10** *n.* A mechanical device, as at an amusement park, in which one rides for fun. **—ride out** To survive or endure successfully: The ship *rode out* a bad storm.

rid·er [rī′dər] *n.* 1 A person who rides. 2 Something added to a document, especially a clause added to a proposed law.
ridge [rij] *n., v.* **ridged, ridg·ing** 1 *n.* A long and narrow, raised strip: a cloth with *ridges.* 2 *n.* A long, usually narrow hill or range of hills. 3 *n.* The line where two sloping surfaces meet: the *ridge* of a roof. 4 *v.* To form into or provide with a ridge or ridges.
ridge·pole [rij′pōl′] *n.* The horizontal timber along the top of a sloping roof.

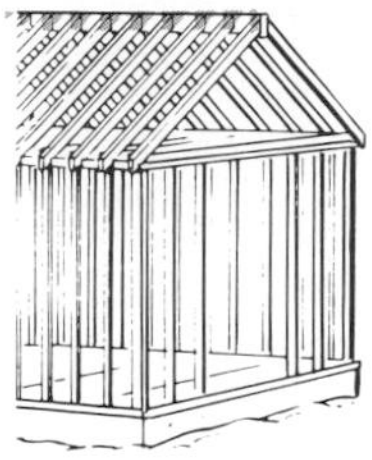
A ridgepole

rid·i·cule [rid′ə·kyo͞ol′] *n., v.* **rid·i·culed, rid·i·cul·ing** 1 *n.* Words or actions intended to make another person or thing seem foolish; mockery. 2 *v.* To make fun of; make a laughingstock of; mock.
ri·dic·u·lous [ri·dik′yə·ləs] *adj.* Deserving ridicule or laughter because of its absurdity or silliness. **—ri·dic′u·lous·ly** *adv.*
rife [rīf] *adj.* 1 Great in number or amount; abundant: Rumors were *rife.* 2 Filled; teeming: a sweater *rife* with holes.
riff·raff [rif′raf′] *n.* 1 Crude or common people; rabble. 2 Trash; rubbish.
ri·fle[1] [rī′fəl] *v.* **ri·fled, ri·fling** To search and rob: to *rifle* a mail sack; to *rifle* a desk.
ri·fle[2] [rī′fəl] *n., v.* **ri·fled, ri·fling** 1 *n.* A firearm having grooves that run in a spiral down the barrel, giving the bullet a spin as it is shot. 2 *v.* To make spiral grooves in.
ri·fle·man [rī′fəl·mən] *n., pl.* **ri·fle·men** [rī′fəl·mən] A person armed with or skilled in the use of a rifle.
rift [rift] 1 *n.* A split or crack; cleft. 2 *v.* To break open; split. 3 *n.* A stopping of or a break in a friendship, often only temporary.
rig [rig] *v.* **rigged, rig·ging,** *n.* 1 *v.* To fit (a ship) with sails and related gear. 2 *n.* The arrangement of sails and rigging on a ship. 3 *v.* To fit out; equip: to *rig* a car with a radio. 4 *v.* To build hurriedly or by makeshifts: to *rig* up a door from old boards. 5 *v. informal* To dress; clothe: The cast was *rigged* out in old-fashioned costumes. 6 *n. informal* A style of dress or costume. 7 *n. U.S. informal* A buggy or carriage with a horse or horses. 8 *v.* To control by fraud or dishonesty: to *rig* an election. **—rig′ger** *n.*
Ri·gel [rī′jəl *or* rī′gəl] *n.* One of the 20 brightest stars. It is in the constellation Orion.
rig·ging [rig′ing] *n.* 1 The ropes and cables that support a ship's mast and sails. 2 Apparatus; gear; equipment.

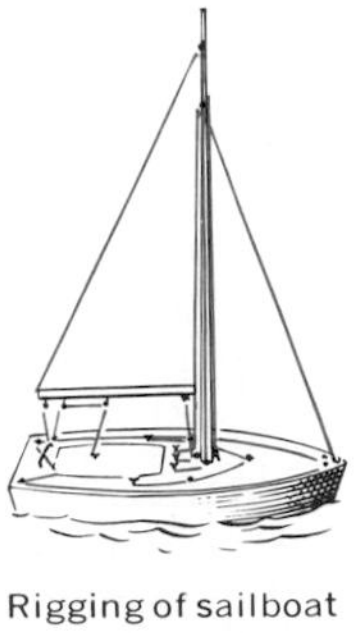
Rigging of sailboat

right [rīt] 1 *adj.* In agreement with law or morals; just; good: Confessing that I had broken the glass was the *right* thing to do. 2 *adv.* According to law or morals; justly: The firm acted *right* in dismissing the clerk. 3 *n.* Things that are lawful, moral, and just: Try to do *right,* not wrong. 4 *n.* A just and proper claim: the *right* to vote. 5 *n.* (*often pl.*) Something that may be claimed on just, moral, legal, or customary grounds: I demand my *rights.* 6 *v.* To correct; set right: to *right* a wrong. 7 *adj.* Conforming to truth or fact; correct; accurate: the *right* answer. 8 *adv.* According to truth or fact; correctly: to answer *right.* 9 *adj.* Conforming to standards or prevailing conditions; proper; suitable: *right* clothing for the party. 10 *adv.* Suitably; properly: to dress *right*; to do the job *right.* 11 *adv.* In good condition; orderly: to put things *right.* 12 *v.* To put in order; make neat or proper: to *right* a messy room. 13 *adj.* Of, on, related to, or indicating the side of the body that is toward the south when one faces east: the *right* hand. 14 *adv.* To or toward the right hand or side: Turn *right.* 15 *n.* The right side, direction, or hand. 16 *adj.* Nearer to the right side: Go through the *right* door. 17 *adj.* Holding one direction, as a line; straight; direct. 18 *adv.* In a straight line; directly: Go *right* to school. 19 *adv.* Precisely; exactly: Set it *right* here. 20 *adv.* Immediately: We'll leave *right* after lunch. 21 *adj.* Sound or healthy; well: to be in one's *right* mind. 22 *v.* To return to an upright or proper position: to *right* an overturned glass. 23 *adj.* Made to show or be worn outward: the *right* side of a fabric. 24 *adv.* Completely; all the way: The house burned *right* to the ground. 25 *adv.* (*written* **Right**) Exceedingly; very: used in titles: the *Right* Reverend. 26 *adj.* Conservative or reactionary in political views. 27 *n.* A person, group, or party having conservative or reactionary political views. **—by right** or **by rights** According to what is just, right, or proper; rightly. **—in the right** Not wrong. **—right away** or **right off** Without delay; immediately. **—to rights** *informal* In a proper condition: to put a room *to rights.*
right-an·gle [rīt′ang′gəl] *adj.* Right-angled.
right angle An angle measuring 90° and made by two lines that are straight up and down from each other. A square contains four right angles.

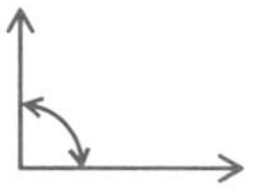
Right angle

right-an·gled [rīt′ang′gəld] *adj.* Having one or more right angles: a *right-angled* triangle.
right·eous [rī′chəs] *adj.* 1 Acting right; virtuous; upright: a *righteous* person. 2 Right according to morals or justice; fair: a *righteous* punishment. **—right′eous·ly** *adv.* **—right′eous·ness** *n.*
right·ful [rīt′fəl] *adj.* 1 Just and fair: a *rightful* claim. 2 According to morals or law: the *rightful* owner of the house. **—right′ful·ly** *adv.*
right-hand [rīt′hand′] *adj.* 1 On or toward the right side. 2 Made for use by or done with the right hand: a *right-hand* glove. 3 Chiefly depended on: the manager's *right-hand* assistant.
right-hand·ed [rīt′han′did] 1 *adj.* Using the right hand habitually and more easily than the left: a *right-handed* pitcher. 2 *adj.* Done with or made for use by the right hand: a *right-handed* putter. 3 *adj.* Turning or moving from left to right or in

a	add	**i**	it	**o͝o**	took	**oi**	oil
ā	ace	**ī**	ice	**o͞o**	pool	**ou**	pout
â	care	**o**	odd	**u**	up	**ng**	ring
ä	palm	**ō**	open	**û**	burn	**th**	thin
e	end	**ô**	order	**yo͞o**	fuse	**th**	this
ē	equal					**zh**	vision

ə = {a in *above* e in *sicken* i in *possible*
  o in *melon* u in *circus*}

a clockwise direction: a *right-handed* thread. **4** *adv.* With the right hand: to pitch *right-handed.*
right·ist [rī′tist] **1** *n.* A person with conservative or reactionary political opinions. **2** *adj.* Conservative or reactionary: *rightist* politics.
right·ly [rīt′lē] *adv.* **1** Correctly. **2** Honestly; justly; fairly. **3** Properly; fitly; aptly.
right of way **1** The legal right of a person to pass over the land of another. **2** The right to go or cross ahead of a person or vehicle, as at an intersection. **3** A strip of land occupied by a road, pipeline, power line, or other facility.
right triangle A triangle one of whose angles is a right angle.
right whale A kind of large whale, now nearly extinct, having a large head, plates of whalebone in the mouth, and no dorsal fin. ◆ Whalers gave these animals their name by considering them "the right whales" to hunt. They floated when killed and yielded much oil and whalebone.
right wing The conservative or reactionary members of a political party, governing group, or nation. **—right-wing** [rīt′wing′] *adj.*
rig·id [rij′id] *adj.* **1** Not giving or bending; stiff or firm: a *rigid* frame. **2** Fixed; unmoving. **3** Strict; unchanging: *rigid* regulations. **—ri·gid·i·ty** [ri·jid′ə·tē] *n.* **—rig′id·ly** *adv.*
rig·ma·role [rig′mə·rōl′] *n.* Confused or senseless talk or writing; nonsense; poppycock.
rig·or [rig′ər] *n.* **1** Strictness, carefulness, or severity: to punish with *rigor*; to think with *rigor.* **2** Harshness or discomfort: the *rigors* of living in tents.
rig·or mor·tis [rig′ər môr′tis] A temporary stiffening of the muscles that occurs after death.
rig·or·ous [rig′ər·əs] *adj.* **1** Very strict: a *rigorous* teacher. **2** Exact; precise: a *rigorous* science. **3** Harsh; severe: a *rigorous* winter. **—rig′or·ous·ly** *adv.*
rile [rīl] *v.* **riled, ril·ing** *informal* **1** To annoy or irritate. **2** To make (a liquid) muddy or unsettled by stirring up sediment.
rill [ril] *n.* A small stream or brook.
rim [rim] *n., v.* **rimmed, rim·ming** **1** *n.* An edge, margin, or border, usually of a round object. **2** *v.* To provide with a rim. **3** *v.* In various sports, to roll around the edge of (the basket or cup) without falling in.
rime[1] [rīm] *n., v.* **rimed, rim·ing** **1** *n.* A white frost formed from frozen fog or mist. **2** *v.* To cover or become covered with rime: The window *rimed* over; Mist and cold *rimed* the trees.
rime[2] [rīm] *n., v.* **rimed, rim·ing** Another spelling of RHYME.
rim·y [rī′mē] *adj.* **rim·i·er, rim·i·est** Covered with rime; frosty.
rind [rīnd] *n.* A skin or outer coating that may be peeled or removed, as of bacon or fruit.

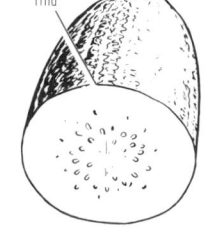

ring[1] [ring] *v.* **rang, rung, ring·ing,** *n.* **1** *v.* To make or cause to make the resonant sound of a bell: The bell *rang*; *Ring* the bell. **2** *n.* The sound made by a bell. **3** *n.* A sound similar to this: the *ring* of coins. **4** *v.* To announce or summon, as by sounding a bell: to *ring* in a New Year. **5** *v.* To be filled with sound; resound: The hall *rang* with music. **6** *v.* To have a sound or quality that suggests a certain character, as truth or falseness: Their story *rings* true. **7** *n.* A sound suggestive of something: the *ring* of truth. **8** *v.* To call by telephone: *Ring* me up. **9** *n.* A telephone call: Give me a *ring.* **10** *v.* To hear noises that are not there: My ears *ring* **—ring for** To call or summon by a bell: *Ring for* the nurse. **—ring up** To record (a sale) on a cash register.
ring[2] [ring] *n., v.* **ringed, ring·ing** **1** *n.* A circle or round loop. **2** *n.* A narrow circle, as one of metal or plastic, worn on a finger as an ornament, also used for such purposes as hanging curtains. **3** *v.* To put or make a ring around; enclose: The crowd *ringed* the speaker. **4** *n.* A group of persons or things in a circle: a *ring* of houses. **5** *v.* To form a circle: The children *ringed* about the exhibit. **6** *n.* A group of persons, often organized for some unlawful or evil purpose: a *ring* of smugglers. **7** *n.* A space set apart for a contest or show: a circus *ring.* **8** *n. informal* The sport of prize fighting. **9** *v.* To put a ring in the nose of (an animal, as a pig or bull). **10** *v.* In certain games, to throw a ring over (a peg or pin). **—run rings around** *informal* To do or be very much better than.

Antique ring

ring binder A loose-leaf notebook having rings in its metal spine that can be opened to hold punched sheets of paper.
ring·er[1] [ring′ər] *n.* **1** A person or thing that rings or makes a bell ring. **2** *slang* A contestant entered fraudulently in a competition. **3** *slang* A person or thing that closely resembles another.
ring·er[2] [ring′ər] *n.* **1** A person or thing that rings or encircles. **2** A horseshoe or other object thrown so as to encircle a peg or pin.
ring finger The third finger of the hand, especially the left hand, counting the index finger as the first.
ring·lead·er [ring′lē′dər] *n.* A person who leads a group, especially in some mischief or unlawful activity.
ring·let [ring′lit] *n.* **1** A long, spiral lock of hair; curl. **2** A small ring.
ring·mas·ter [ring′mas′tər] *n.* A person who supervises and sometimes introduces the acts in a circus ring.
ring·side [ring′sīd′] **1** *n.* The seats or space very close or next to a ring, as at a boxing match. **2** *adj.* Located at the ringside: a *ringside* seat.
ring·worm [ring′wûrm′] *n.* An infectious skin disease caused by a fungus, marked by scaly, discolored patches on the skin.
rink [ringk] *n.* An area or enclosure containing a surface of ice for skating or hockey or having a smooth, wooden floor for roller skating.
rinse [rins] *v.* **rinsed, rins·ing,** *n.* **1** *v.* To remove soap from by putting through clear water. **2** *v.* To wash lightly, as by dipping in water or by running water over or into. **3** *n.* A rinsing. **4** *n.* The water or solution used in rinsing.
ri·ot [rī′ət] **1** *n.* A violent disturbance made by a large group of people behaving in a wild, disorderly way. **2** *v.* To take part in a riot. **3** *n.* A brilliant and sometimes confusing display: a *riot* of colors. **4** *v.* To make merry in a wild, boisterous way. **5** *n. slang* A person or thing that is ex-

tremely funny: That comedian is a *riot.* **—read the riot act to** *informal* To scold or warn very bluntly and severely. **—run riot** 1 To act wildly. 2 To grow profusely, as vines. **—ri′ot·er** *n.*

ri·ot·ous [rī′ət·əs] *adj.* 1 Of, like, or having to do with a riot. 2 Causing or taking part in a riot. 3 Loud; uproarious; exuberant: *riotous* laughter. **—ri′ot·ous·ly** *adv.*

rip[1] [rip] *v.* **ripped, rip·ping,** *n.* 1 *v.* To tear or split apart: to *rip* a shirt; The blanket *ripped.* 2 *n.* A place, as in a garment, that is torn open. 3 *v.* To tear, pull, or remove in a rough way: to *rip* down a poster; to *rip* off clothes. 4 *v.* To saw (wood) in the direction of the grain. 5 *n.* A ripsaw. **—rip off** *slang* 1 To steal or steal from. 2 To exploit or deceive; swindle.

rip[2] [rip] *n.* 1 The rough water that results when conflicting tides or currents come together. 2 A rapid in a river.

R.I.P. may he (or she) rest in peace.

rip cord A cord pulled to open a parachute.

ripe [rīp] *adj.* **rip·er, rip·est** 1 Fully grown and ready to eat, as fruit or grain. 2 Ready to be used, as wine or cheese. 3 Fully developed; mature. 4 In full readiness; prepared: The men are *ripe* for mutiny. **—ripe′ness** *n.*

rip·en [rī′pən] *v.* To make or become ripe.

rip-off [rip′ôf′ *or* rip′of′] *n. slang* 1 A theft. 2 Something that exploits or deceives; swindle.

ri·poste [ri·pōst′] *n.* 1 In fencing, a quick return thrust that follows the successful parry of an opponent's lunge. 2 A quick and clever reply to a verbal attack; retort.

rip·ple [rip′əl] *v.* **rip·pled, rip·pling,** *n.* 1 *v.* To form into small waves: The water *rippled* as fish jumped; The wind *rippled* the lake. 2 *n.* A small wave or wavelike movement: the *ripple* of a summer breeze. 3 *n.* Any sound like that made by rippling.

Ripples

rip-roar·ing [rip′rôr′ing] *adj. informal* Lively and noisy; boisterous; riotous: a *rip-roaring* celebration.

rip·saw [rip′sô′] *n.* A saw having large teeth, used to cut wood in the direction of the grain.

Rip Van Winkle [rip van wing′kəl] In Washington Irving's story *Rip Van Winkle,* the hero, a man who wakes up after sleeping 20 years to find the world changed and himself forgotten.

rise [rīz] *v.* **rose, ris·en, ris·ing,** *n.* 1 *v.* To move upward; go to a higher position; ascend: The plane *rose* from the ground. 2 *n.* An upward movement; ascent: The balloon made a quick *rise.* 3 *v.* To incline upward: The ground *rises* here. 4 *n.* An upward incline or a small hill: a *rise* adjoining the plain. 5 *v.* To stand up after sitting or lying down. 6 *v.* To return to life or activity: to *rise* from the grave; to *rise* from sleep. 7 *v.* To become greater, as in force, strength, amount, value, or number: Prices *rose* alarmingly; The sound *rose* to a roar. 8 *v.* To swell up: Dough *rises.* 9 *n.* Increase: The noise made a sharp *rise.* 10 *v.* To move to a higher rank, status, fortune, or the like: to *rise* to the rank of colonel. 11 *n.* Advance or elevation, as in rank or status: a *rise* to power. 12 *v.* To appear over the horizon, as the sun or moon. 13 *v.* To revolt; rebel: The people *rose* against the tyrant. 14 *v.* To begin, as a river: This river *rises* in the mountains. 15 *n.* A beginning or place of beginning; origin. 16 *v.* To become elated or more cheerful: My spirits *rose.* **—give rise to** To cause to begin; bring about. **—rise to** To handle or deal with successfully: to *rise to* a difficult situation. ◆ *Rise* means to move upward. *Raise* means to cause to move upward. *Rise* does not take an object: The sun *rose. Raise* does take an object: Please *raise* your right hand. *Raise* is the word commonly used in the U.S. for an increase in pay. The British call such an increase a *rise.*

ris·en [riz′(ə)n] Past participle of RISE.

ris·er [rī′zər] *n.* 1 A person who rises, as from bed. 2 The vertical part of a step or stair.

ris·i·ble [riz′ə·bəl] *adj.* 1 Capable of or characterized by laughter: The human being is the *risible* animal. 2 Exciting laughter; laughable.

risk [risk] 1 *n.* A chance of meeting with harm or loss; danger; hazard. 2 *v.* To expose to a chance of injury or loss: to *risk* one's life; to *risk* one's money. 3 *v.* To take the risk of; chance: Will you *risk* being late?

risk·y [ris′kē] *adj.* **risk·i·er, risk·i·est** Full of risk; dangerous; hazardous: a *risky* mountain drive; a *risky* business deal.

ris·qué [ris·kā′] *adj.* Suggesting something improper or indecent: a *risqué* joke.

ri·tar·dan·do [rē′tär·dän′dō] *adj., adv., n., pl.* **ri·tar·dan·dos** 1 *adj.* In music, becoming gradually slower. 2 *adv.* Becoming gradually slow. 3 *n.* A gradual slowing down of tempo.

rite [rīt] *n.* 1 A formal, solemn, or religious ceremony performed in a set way. 2 The words or acts that make up such a ceremony.

rite of passage A ceremony or other event that marks a transition from one stage of a person's life to another, as from childhood to adulthood.

rit·u·al [rich′o͞o·əl] 1 *n.* A body or system of rites and ceremonies: to follow a set *ritual* in initiating new members. 2 *n.* A book in which rites or ceremonies are collected. 3 *adj.* Of, related to, or like a rite: a *ritual* act. **—rit′u·al·ly** *adv.*

rit·u·al·ism [rich′o͞o·əl·iz′əm] *n.* 1 The use or excessive use of rituals. 2 The study of rituals.

ritz·y [rit′sē] *adj.* **ritz·i·er, ritz·i·est** *slang* Elegant; fashionable; fancy: a *ritzy* hotel.

ri·val [rī′vəl] *n., v.* **ri·valed** or **ri·valled, ri·val·ing** or **ri·val·ling** 1 *n.* A person who tries to equal or outdo another, or who wants the same thing as another; competitor. 2 *adj. use*: a *rival* athlete. 3 *v.* To try to outdo or defeat; compete with: The teams *rivaled* each other for the championship. 4 *v.* To be the equal of: The teams *rival* each other in ability. ◆ *Rival* comes from a Latin word meaning *those living near the same stream.* They

a	add	**i**	it	**o͝o**	took	**oi**	oil
ā	ace	**ī**	ice	**o͞o**	pool	**ou**	pout
â	care	**o**	odd	**u**	up	**ng**	ring
ä	palm	**ō**	open	**û**	burn	**th**	thin
e	end	**ô**	order	**yo͞o**	fuse	**t͟h**	this
ē	equal					**zh**	vision

ə = a in *above*, e in *sicken*, i in *possible*, o in *melon*, u in *circus*

R

were "rivals" either because they lived on opposite banks or because they both depended on the same stream for water.

ri·val·ry [rī'vəl·rē] *n., pl.* **ri·val·ries** 1 The act of rivaling. 2 The condition of being a rival or rivals; competition: Their *rivalry* began the first time they played tennis together.

rive [rīv] *v.* **rived, rived** or **riv·en** [riv'ən], **riv·ing** To split apart by or with force: Lightning had *rived* the old pine in two.

riv·er [riv'ər] *n.* 1 A large, natural stream of water, usually fed by smaller streams and flowing to the sea, a lake, or other body of water. 2 Any large flow or stream: a *river* of glacial ice. ◆ *River* comes from a Latin word meaning *bank of a river.* In old French it came to mean the *stream.*

river basin The area of land drained by a river and its branches.

riv·er·bed [riv'ər·bed'] *n.* The ground over which a river flows or used to flow.

riv·er·head [riv'ər·hed'] *n.* The source of a river.

riv·er·side [riv'ər·sīd'] *n.* An area at the side of a river.

riv·et [riv'it] 1 *n.* A metal pin with a head at one end, used to fasten metal objects together. It is passed through a hole in both pieces and its headless end is hammered down, often while it is red hot. 2 *v.* To fasten with rivets. 3 *v.* To set or fix firmly: to *rivet* one's attention on the television set. **—riv'et·er** *n.*

riv·u·let [riv'yə·lit] *n.* A brook.

rm. 1 room. 2 (*usually written* **rms.**) rooms.

Rn The symbol for the element radon.

RN or **R.N.** 1 registered nurse. 2 Royal Navy.

RNA ribonucleic acid.

roach[1] [rōch] *n.* Another name for COCKROACH.

roach[2] [rōch] *n.* A European freshwater fish related to the carp, having a silvery white body, small mouth and large scales.

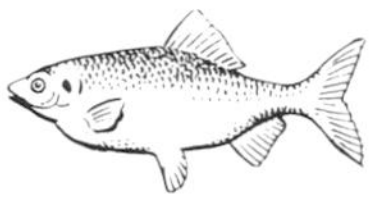
Roach

road [rōd] *n.* 1 An open way prepared for vehicles, persons, or animals to travel on from one place to another. 2 A way of reaching something, as a state, condition, or reward: the *road* to fame. 3 A railroad. 4 (*usually pl.*) A roadstead.

road·bed [rōd'bed'] *n.* The foundation on which railroad tracks are laid or a road is built.

road·block [rōd'blok'] *n.* 1 An obstruction in a road. 2 Any arrangement of people and materials for blocking passage, as of an enemy's troops.

road hog A person who drives a vehicle in or near the middle of a road, making it difficult for other drivers to pass.

road·run·ner [rōd'run'ər] *n.* A cuckoo of the plains of the western U.S., having a long tail, a shaggy crest, and legs adapted for very swift running.

road·side [rōd'sīd'] 1 *n.* The area along the side of a road. 2 *adj.* Located on the side of a road: a *roadside* restaurant.

road·stead [rōd'sted'] *n.* A sheltered place for ships to anchor offshore.

road·ster [rōd'stər] *n.* An automobile with no top, a single wide seat, and a rumble seat or large trunk.

road test 1 A test of a vehicle consisting of an actual drive on roads. 2 A test of a person's driving ability on the road, required for a driver's license.

road·way [rōd'wā'] *n.* A road, especially that part over which vehicles pass.

road·work [rōd'wûrk'] *n.* Physical training consisting of long outdoor runs.

roam [rōm] *v.* To wander around with no particular purpose. ◆ See WANDER.

roan [rōn] 1 *adj., n.* Reddish or yellowish brown heavily speckled with gray or white. 2 *n.* A horse having a color like this.

roar [rôr] 1 *v.* To give a loud, deep cry, as of anger or pain. 2 *n.* A loud, deep cry. 3 *v.* To make a loud noise, as the sea or a cannon. 4 *n.* A loud noise. 5 *v.* To shout or laugh loudly.

roast [rōst] 1 *v.* To cook (food) by the action of heat, as in an oven. 2 *n.* A roasted piece of meat or a piece of meat prepared to be roasted. 3 *adj.* Roasted: *roast* chicken. 4 *v.* To treat with heat: to *roast* an ore; to *roast* coffee. 5 *v.* To make or be very hot: We *roasted* in the sun. 6 *v. informal* To make fun of or criticize severely: The critic *roasted* the new novel.

roast·er [rōs'tər] *n.* 1 A pan or pot in which food is roasted. 2 Something to be roasted, as a chicken or young pig.

rob [rob] *v.* **robbed, rob·bing** 1 To seize money or property from, using force or the threat of force: to *rob* a cashier. 2 To take from by trickery or fraud; cheat: to *rob* a customer by overcharging. 3 To commit robbery. **—rob'ber** *n.*

rob·ber·y [rob'ər·ē] *n., pl.* **rob·ber·ies** The unlawful taking of property or money, as by stealth, force, or the threat of force.

robe [rōb] 1 *n.* A long, loose, flowing garment, usually worn over other clothing on special or ceremonial occasions or to show one's office or rank: a choir *robe*; a judge's *robes.* 2 *n.* Any long, loose, outer garment or gown. 3 *n.* A bathrobe. 4 *v.* To put a robe on; dress. 5 *n.* A blanket or covering for the lap.

Robe

rob·in [rob'in] *n.* 1 A large North American thrush having a gray back and rust-red breast. 2 A small European bird, common in England, with yellowish red cheeks and breast.

Robin Hood A legendary outlaw of medieval England, famed for his chivalry and daring, said to have robbed the rich to aid the poor.

ro·bot [rō'bot' *or* rō'bət] *n.* 1 A mechanical creature built to do work in the place of human beings. 2 A person who works dully and mechanically. ◆ *Robot* was probably first used of a mechanical creature in 1921 in the play *R.U.R.* (*Rossum's Universal Robots*) by the Czech playwright Karel Capek, but the word was based on a Czech word meaning *forced labor.*

ro·bust [rō·bust' *or* rō'bust] *adj.* 1 Strong; sturdy; vigorous: a *robust* athlete; *robust* plants. 2 Strong and rich, as in flavor: a *robust* stew. 3 Crude or rough: *robust* language.

roc [rok] *n.* In Arabian and Persian legend, an enormous and powerful bird of prey.

rock[1] [rok] *n.* 1 A large mass of stone or stony material. 2 A small piece of stone that can be picked up. **3** The hard, dense mass of minerals forming the earth's crust. **4** Something like a rock, as in strength or solidity.

rock[2] [rok] **1** *v.* To move or cause to move back and forth or from side to side; sway: to *rock* a boat. **2** *n.* A rocking or swaying movement. **3** *n.* Rock 'n' roll. **4** *v.* To disturb; upset: The news *rocked* the town. **5** *v.* To stun or daze: The blow *rocked* me.

rock-and-roll [rok′ən·rōl′] *n.* Another spelling of ROCK 'N' ROLL.

rock bottom The very bottom; lowest possible level: Prices hit *rock bottom.*

rock candy Pure sugar in clear, rocklike chunks.

rock crystal Transparent quartz, especially when colorless.

rock·er [rok′ər] *n.* **1** A person or thing that rocks. **2** One of the curved parts on which a cradle or rocking chair rocks. **3** A rocking chair.

rock·et [rok′it] **1** *n.* A machine that develops power and movement by burning its load of fuel and oxygen and forcing a stream of gases to the rear, used to propel fireworks, missiles, and space vehicles. **2** *v.* To move like or by a rocket.

rock·et·eer [rok′i·tir′] *n.* **1** A person who fires, rides in, or pilots a rocket. **2** A person whose work is concerned with or who is an expert in rocketry.

rock·et·ry [rok′it·rē] *n.* The science and techniques of designing, building, and flying rockets.

rocket ship A rocket-propelled spacecraft.

rock garden A flower garden grown on a rocky plot of land.

rocking chair A chair whose legs are set on curved rails, allowing it to rock back and forth.

rocking horse A toy horse mounted on rockers, large enough for a child to mount it and rock.

Rocking horse

rock 'n' roll [rok′ən·rōl′] A kind of popular music combining elements from blues and country music. It has a loud, steady beat and is often played with electronically amplified instruments.

rock salt Common salt in rocklike masses or large crystals.

rock wool A soft, fluffy material made from molten slag and rock, used as a packing and insulating material.

rock·y[1] [rok′ē] *adj.* **rock·i·er, rock·i·est** **1** Consisting of, full of, or like rocks. **2** Suggesting rock, as in hardness: a face with *rocky* features.

rock·y[2] [rok′ē] *adj.* **rock·i·er, rock·i·est** **1** Tending to rock or shake; unsteady. **2** *informal* Weak or dizzy; slightly sick.

Rocky Mountain sheep Another name for BIGHORN.

Rocky Mountain spotted fever An infectious disease characterized by muscular pain, high fever, and red to purple skin rash, caused by a germ transmitted by ticks.

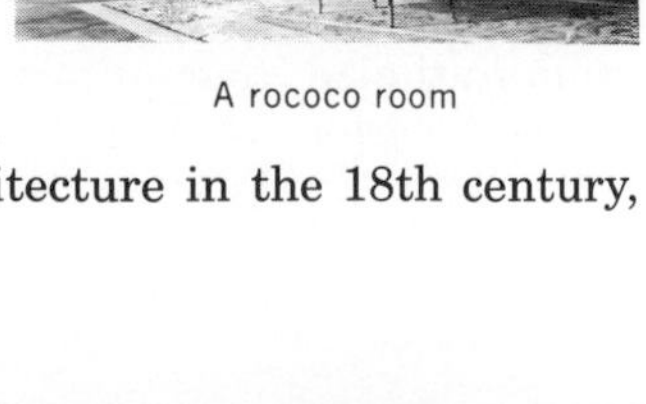
A rococo room

ro·co·co [rə·kō′kō] **1** *n.* The style of European art and architecture in the 18th century, marked by extremely fancy designs and decorations. **2** *n.* The formal, elegant style of European music in the 18th century. **3** *adj.* In or like the rococo style: a *rococo* painting; a *rococo* door.

rod [rod] *n.* **1** A straight, thin piece of wood, metal, or other hard material. **2** A thin stick used in beating someone as punishment. **3** The punishment given this way. **4** A unit of length equal to 5 1/2 yards. **5** A fishing rod. **6** A wand as a sign of power.

rode [rōd] Past tense of RIDE.

ro·dent [rōd′(ə)nt] *n.* Any of a group of mammals including mice, rats, squirrels, and beavers. They have very sharp front teeth that keep growing as they are worn down by gnawing.

ro·de·o [rō′dē·ō *or* rō·dā′ō] *n., pl.* **ro·de·os** **1** A public contest in which cowhands compete in various skills, as riding broncos or roping and throwing cattle. **2** A roundup (def. 1).

roe[1] [rō] *n., pl.* **roe** or **roes** A small, graceful deer of Europe and western Asia.

roe[2] [rō] *n.* The eggs of fishes.

roe·buck [rō′buk′] *n.* A male roe.

roent·gen [rent′gən] *n.* A unit for measuring X rays and gamma rays on the basis of their ionizing effect.

Roent·gen ray [rent′gən] Another name for X RAY.

rog·er [roj′ər] *interj.* A word used in two-way radio communications to indicate that a message has been received and understood.

rogue [rōg] *n.* **1** A dishonest and sneaky person; trickster; rascal. **2** A person who does innocent or playful mischief. **3** A fierce and dangerous animal, as an elephant, that lives apart from its herd.

ro·guer·y [rō′gər·ē] *n., pl.* **ro·guer·ies** **1** Conduct like that of a rogue. **2** A roguish act.

rogues' gallery A collection of pictures of known criminals kept by the police and shown to witnesses to help them to identify suspects in a crime.

ro·guish [rō′gish] *adj.* **1** Playfully mischievous. **2** Dishonest or sneaky. **—ro′guish·ly** *adv.* **—ro′guish·ness** *n.*

roil [roil] *v.* **1** To make muddy or unclear, as by stirring up material from the bottom: to *roil* a lake. **2** To irritate or make angry; rile.

roist·er [rois′tər] *v.* **1** To carry on loud merrymaking; revel. **2** To act in a bullying and boastful way; swagger. **—roist′er·er** *n.*

ROK Republic of (South) Korea.

Ro·land [rō′lənd *or* rō·län′] *n.* A legendary French warrior and hero of medieval epic poems.

role or **rôle** [rōl] *n.* **1** A part or character played by an actor. **2** A character or part that a person plays in life: one's *role* as a parent.

role model A person who serves as a model of how to behave in a particular role for another person to imitate.

a	add	**i**	it	**o͝o**	took	**oi**	oil
ā	ace	**ī**	ice	**o͞o**	pool	**ou**	pout
â	care	**o**	odd	**u**	up	**ng**	ring
ä	palm	**ō**	open	**û**	burn	**th**	thin
e	end	**ô**	order	**yo͞o**	fuse	**th**	this
ē	equal					**zh**	vision

ə = { a in *above* e in *sicken* i in *possible* / o in *melon* u in *circus* }

roll [rōl] **1** *v.* To move along a surface by turning over and over: The ball *rolled* five feet. **2** *n.* The act of rolling. **3** *n.* A rolling movement. **4** *v.* To move or be moved on wheels or rollers: The cart *rolled* away. **5** *n.* A roller, especially a cylinder rotating on a fixed axis. **6** *v.* To turn, wrap, or wind so as to make or become a ball or cylinder: *Roll* the yarn up; *Roll* it up in this newspaper. **7** *n.* Something rolled into the shape of a ball or cylinder: a *roll* of cloth. **8** *v.* To pass or go: Months *rolled* by; The clouds *rolled* by. **9** *v.* To make a deep, rumbling sound, as thunder. **10** *n.* A deep rumbling sound, as of thunder. **11** *v.* To strike (as a drum) with a series of rapid strokes. **12** *n.* The sound of a series of rapid strokes, as on a drum. **13** *v.* To say or utter with a trilling sound: to *roll* "r's." **14** *v.* To sway, rock, or move up and down or back and forth: The ship *rolled* in the storm; to *roll* one's eyes. **15** *v.* To move or appear to move in swells or billows, as a wave. **16** *n.* A swaying, rocking, or undulating movement: the *roll* of a ship; the *roll* of the sea. **17** *v.* To spread or flatten under a roller: to *roll* tin into sheets; Tar *rolls* easily. **18** *n.* A small, individually shaped piece of bread. **19** *n.* A list of names. **—roll in** *informal* **1** To arrive in large amounts or numbers. **2** To have and take great pleasure in: to *roll in* luxury. **—roll up** *informal* **1** To collect or accumulate. **2** To arrive, as a car.

roll call The calling out of a list of names so that each person present may reply to his or her name.

roll·er [rō′lər] *n.* **1** A person or thing that rolls. **2** Any of various cylindrical devices on which something is rolled or which is used to crush, press, smooth, or apply something: a window shade *roller*; a steam*roller*; a paint *roller*. **3** A long, swelling wave that breaks on a beach or shore line. **4** A canary that trills its song.

roller coaster *U.S.* A small railway with open cars that run over a series of sharp dips and curves, found in amusement parks.

roll·er-skate [rō′lər·skāt′] *v.* **roll·er-skat·ed, roll·er-skat·ing** To go on roller skates.

roller skate A skate having wheels instead of a runner, used on surfaces other than ice, as pavement.

A couple roller-skating

rol·lick·ing [rol′ik·ing] *adj.* Carefree and merry; light-hearted.

rolling mill **1** A factory for rolling metal into sheets or bars. **2** A machine for doing this.

rolling pin A cylinder, often of wood or plastic, with handles at the ends, used to roll out dough.

rolling stock All of the vehicles, as locomotives and cars, owned and operated by a railroad or bus company.

ro·ly-po·ly [rō′lē·pō′lē] *adj., n., pl.* **ro·ly-po·lies** **1** *adj.* Short and fat; pudgy; dumpy. **2** *n.* A roly-poly person or thing.

ROM READ-ONLY MEMORY.

Rom. **1** Roman. **2** (*usually written* **rom.**) roman (type). **3** Romania. **4** Romanian.

ro·maine [rō·mān′] *n.* A variety of lettuce with dark green leaves forming a long, narrow head.

Ro·man [rō′mən] **1** *adj.* Of, from, or belonging to ancient or modern Rome. **2** *n.* A person born or living in ancient or modern Rome. **3** *adj.* Of or belonging to the Roman Catholic Church. **4** *n.* (*pl., used with singular verb*) A book of the New Testament, written by Paul the Apostle. **5** *n.* The alphabet devised by the ancient Romans and used in writing Latin, and with modifications, English and most other modern western European languages. **6** *adj.* Of or in this alphabet. **7** *n.* (*usually written* **roman**) The common style of type or lettering, in which the letters are upright, not slanting. This sentence is in roman. **8** *adj.* (*usually written* **roman**) Of, having to do with, or printed in roman.

Roman Catholic **1** *adj.* Of, having to do with, or belonging to the Christian church that recognizes the Pope, the bishop of Rome, as its supreme head. **2** *n.* A member of this church.

ro·mance [*n.* rō·mans′ *or* rō′mans′, *v.* rō·mans′] *n.*, *v.* **ro·manced, ro·manc·ing** **1** *n.* A love affair. **2** *v. informal* To show or tell feelings of love to; woo. **3** *n.* Something fascinating, mysterious, or romantic, as an adventure, quality, or condition: the *romance* of faraway places. **4** *n.* A story or poem telling of heroism, adventure, or love, often based on medieval legends. **5** *n.* A fantastic falsehood. **6** *v.* To write, tell, or make up romances.

Romance language One of the languages that developed from Latin. French, Italian, Spanish, Portuguese, and Romanian are Romance languages.

Roman Empire The empire of ancient Rome, existing from 27 B.C. to A.D. 395.

Ro·man·esque [rō′mən·esk′] **1** *adj.* Of, having to do with, or indicating a style of architecture using rounded arches and vaults. It prevailed in Europe from the 5th to the 12th centuries. **2** *n.* The Romanesque style of art and architecture.

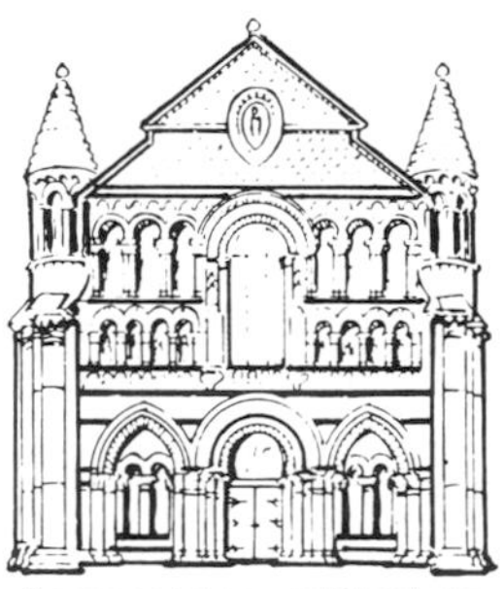
Romanesque architecture

Ro·ma·ni·an [rō·mā′nē·ən *or* rō·mān′yən] **1** *adj.* Of or from Romania. **2** *n.* A person born in or a citizen of Romania. **3** *n.* The language of Romania.

Roman nose A nose that slopes straight down from a projecting upper part.

Roman numerals The letters of the alphabet used by the ancient Romans as symbols to represent numbers. In this system I = 1, V = 5, X = 10, L = 50, C = 100, D = 500, M = 1,000.

ro·man·tic [rō·man′tik] **1** *adj.* Of, having to do with, or filled with romance. **2** *adj.* Having feelings and thoughts of love and romance: a *romantic* person. **3** *adj.* Suitable for courting or wooing: a *romantic* garden. **4** *adj.* Impractical or unrealistic. **5** *adj.* Of, relating to, or characterized by romanticism. **6** *n.* Someone romantic, as an artist or composer. **—ro·man′ti·cal·ly** *adv.*

ro·man·ti·cism [rō·man′tə·siz′əm] *n.* A movement in art, literature, and music of the late 18th and early 19th centuries. It was characterized by a revolt against rules, forms, and traditions and emphasized strong or lyric feelings, the imagination, nature, and often the supernatural and strange. **—ro·man′ti·cist** *n.*

ro·man·ti·cize [rō·man′tə·sīz′] *v.* **ro·man·ti·cized, ro·man·ti·ciz·ing** **1** To give a quality of adventure, heroism, or mystery to; make romantic: He *ro-*

manticizes his wartime exploits. **2** To think, talk, or act in a romantic way.

Rom·a·ny [rom′ə·nē *or* rō′mə·nē] *n., pl.* **Rom·a·nies,** *adj.* **1** *n.* A Gypsy. **2** *n.* The language spoken by the Gypsies. **3** *adj.* Of or having to do with the Gypsies or their language.

Ro·me·o [rō′mē·ō] *n.* In Shakespeare's play *Romeo and Juliet,* the hero, the lover of Juliet.

romp [romp] **1** *v.* To play in a rough, noisy way. **2** *n.* Rough, noisy play or frolic. **3** *n.* A child who romps.

romp·ers [rom′pərz] *n.pl.* An outer garment combining a shirt and short pants, worn by young children.

Rom·u·lus [rom′yə·ləs] *n.* In Roman myths, the founder and first ruler of Rome, who, along with his twin brother Remus, was nursed and raised by a wolf.

ron·do [ron·dō′] *n., pl.* **ron·dos** A musical composition or movement in which the principal theme, played at least three times, is alternated with contrasting themes.

rood [ro͞od] *n.* **1** A cross or crucifix. **2** A measure of area equal to 1/4 acre.

roof [ro͞of *or* ro͝of] **1** *n.* The top, outer covering of a building. **2** *n.* Something like this in form or use: the *roof* of the mouth. **3** *v.* To cover with or as if with a roof: Trees *roofed* the lane.

roof·ing [ro͞o′fing *or* ro͝of′ing] *n.* A material used for building roofs.

roof·top [ro͞of′top′ *or* ro͝of′top′] *n.* The roof of a building, especially the surface of a flat roof.

roof·tree [ro͞of′trē′] *n.* Another name for RIDGEPOLE.

rook[1] [ro͝ok] *n.* In chess, a castle-shaped piece that can move over any number of empty squares parallel to the edges of the board.

rook[2] [ro͝ok] **1** *n.* A crowlike bird of Europe that likes to nest in large colonies. **2** *n.* A cheat or trickster. **3** *v.* To cheat; swindle; defraud.

rook·er·y [ro͝ok′ər·ē] *n., pl.* **rook·er·ies** **1** A colony or breeding place of rooks. **2** A place where sea birds, seals, and other animals breed. **3** One or more shabby, crowded tenement houses.

rook·ie [ro͝ok′ē] *n. slang* **1** A new recruit, as one in the army or police. **2** A beginner or novice, as in a professional sport.

room [ro͞om *or* ro͝om] **1** *n.* Unoccupied or open space: There is lots of *room.* **2** *n.* A space enclosed by walls, as inside a building: a music *room.* **3** *v.* To occupy a room; lodge: We *roomed* together at college. **4** *n.* (*pl.*) Lodgings. **5** *n.* Everyone in a room: The *room* was shocked. **6** *n.* A chance, occasion, or opportunity: *room* for doubt.

room·er [ro͞o′mər *or* ro͝om′ər] *n.* A person who rents and occupies a room; lodger.

room·ette [ro͞o·met′] *n.* A small private sleeping room on a railroad train.

room·ful [ro͞om′fo͝ol′ *or* ro͝om′fo͝ol′] *n., pl.* **room·fuls** As much or as many as a room will hold.

rooming house *U.S.* A house for roomers.

room·mate [ro͞om′māt′ *or* ro͝om′māt′] *n.* One of two or more persons who rent and occupy the same lodgings.

room·y [ro͞o′mē′ *or* ro͝om′ē] *adj.* **room·i·er, room·i·est** Having a large amount of room. **—room′i·ness** *n.*

roost [ro͞ost] **1** *n.* A place, as a perch or ledge, where birds rest at night. **2** *n.* A building, as a hen house or barn, containing a perch or ledge where birds rest at night. **3** *v.* To sit or perch on or in a roost. **4** *v.* To come to rest; settle.

roost·er [ro͞os′tər] *n.* The adult male of the domestic fowl; cock.

Rooster

root[1] [ro͞ot *or* ro͝ot] **1** *n.* The part of a plant that grows into the earth, where it anchors the plant and takes up water and nourishment from the soil. **2** *v.* To put out roots and begin to grow, as a plant. **3** *n.* Any underground plant growth, as a bulb. **4** *n.* A rootlike part of an organ or structure: the *root* of a tooth; the *roots* of hair. **5** *v.* To fix or become fixed firmly: to be *rooted* to the spot. **6** *n.* A source or origin: Money is the *root* of evil. **7** *n.* (*pl.*) Ties to a place, community, or tradition. **8** *n.* A number that when multiplied by itself some number of times equals a specified number, or any quantity written under a radical sign: 2 is the fifth *root* of 32; $\sqrt{x-5}$ is a *root.* **9** *n.* A number that satisfies an equation when used in place of one of the unknowns: 2 and -2 are the *roots* of $x^2 - 4 = 0$. **10** *n.* A word or part of a word to which prefixes and suffixes are added to form other words, as *know* in *unknown* and *knowingly.* **—root up** or **root out** **1** To pull or tear up by or as if by the roots. **2** To destroy utterly: to *root out* crime.

root[2] [ro͞ot *or* ro͝ot] *v.* **1** To turn up or dig with the snout, as pigs. **2** To search about; rummage: to *root* through a drawer.

root[3] [ro͞ot] *v. U.S. informal* To cheer; shout encouragement. **—root′er** *n.*

root beer A carbonated drink made with yeast and the extracts of various roots.

root canal A narrow, pulp-filled cavity in the root of a tooth.

root hair Any of the fine, hairlike growths near the tip of the root of a plant. They help absorb nourishment.

root·less [ro͞ot′lis *or* ro͝ot′lis] *adj.* **1** Lacking roots. **2** Without ties to a home or community; not belonging anywhere.

root·let [ro͞ot′lit *or* ro͝ot′lit] *n.* A small root.

root·stock [ro͞ot′stok′ *or* ro͝ot′stok′] *n.* Another word for RHIZOME.

rope [rōp] *n., v.* **roped, rop·ing** **1** *n.* A thick, strong cord or line made by twisting tightly together several strands of fibers of such materials as hemp, cotton, or nylon. **2** *v.* To tie or fasten with or as if with rope. **3** *v.* To enclose, mark off, or divide with a rope: to *rope* off an entrance. **4** *n.* A number of things strung together in a line: a *rope* of beads. **5** *n.* A slimy or sticky thread or filament: a *rope* of syrup. **6** *n. U.S.* A lasso. **7** *v. U.S.* To catch with a lasso. **—know the ropes** To be familiar with a job or situation. **—the end of**

R

a	add	**i**	it	**o͝o**	took	**oi**	oil
ā	ace	**ī**	ice	**o͞o**	pool	**ou**	pout
â	care	**o**	odd	**u**	up	**ng**	ring
ä	palm	**ō**	open	**û**	burn	**th**	thin
e	end	**ô**	order	**yo͞o**	fuse	**th**	this
ē	equal					**zh**	vision

ə = a in *above*, e in *sicken*, i in *possible*, o in *melon*, u in *circus*

one's rope The limit of one's patience or endurance. **—rop'y** *adj.*

Roque·fort [rōk'fərt] *n.* A strong cheese with a blue mold in it, made in France: a trademark.

ro·sa·ry [rō'zə·rē] *n., pl.* **ro·sa·ries** 1 A series of prayers recited by Roman Catholics. 2 A string of beads for keeping count of the prayers recited. 3 A garden or bed of roses.

rose[1] [rōz] 1 *n.* Any of a group of shrubs having thorny stems and fragrant flowers. 2 *n.* The flower of such a shrub, occurring in a wide range of colors, chiefly red, pink, yellow, and white. 3 *n., adj.* Light, pinkish red. 4 *n.* Something that suggests a rose, as in color, form, or odor.

rose[2] [rōz] Past tense of RISE.

ro·sé [rō·zā'] *n.* A pink-colored, light wine.

ro·se·ate [rō'zē·it] *adj.* 1 Rose-colored; rosy. 2 Cheerful; optimistic.

rose·bud [rōz'bud'] *n.* The bud of a rose.

rose·bush [rōz'bo͝osh'] *n.* A rose-bearing shrub or vine.

rose-colored [rōz'kul'ərd] *adj.* 1 Of the color of a rose. 2 Optimistic; confident; cheerful. **—through rose-colored glasses** Optimistically or overoptimistically.

rose·mar·y [rōz'mâr'ē] *n., pl.* **rose·mar·ies** An evergreen shrub related to the mint, bearing blue flowers and fragrant leaves. It is used in cooking as a seasoning and in perfumes.

ro·sette [rō·zet'] *n.* An ornament or badge resembling a rose and often made of ribbon.

rose water A fragrant preparation made from water and the oil of rose petals, used as a toilet water and in cooking.

rose window A circular, stained-glass window with sections that radiate from the center.

rose·wood [rōz'wo͝od'] *n.* The hard, dark-colored, fragrant wood of certain tropical American trees.

Rosh Ha·sha·nah [rosh *or* rōsh hə·shä'nə] or **Rosh Ha·sho·nah** [hə·shō'nə] The Jewish New Year, celebrated in late September or early October.

ros·in [roz'ən] 1 *n.* A hard, yellowish substance extracted from crude turpentine, used on violin bows and on athletes' shoes or hands to prevent slipping. 2 *v.* To apply rosin to.

ros·ter [ros'tər] *n.* 1 A list of people and of their duties, as of police or soldiers. 2 Any list.

ros·trum [ros'trəm] *n., pl.* **ros·trums** or **ros·tra** [ros'·trə] A pulpit or platform from which speeches are given.

ros·y [rō'zē] *adj.* **ros·i·er, ros·i·est** 1 Like or having the color of a rose. 2 Bright or optimistic: a *rosy* outlook. **—ros'i·ness** *n.*

rot [rot] *v.* **rot·ted, rot·ting,** *n.* 1 *v.* To decay, spoil, or decompose: The dead leaves *rotted* in the field. 2 *v.* To fall to pieces; go to ruin: The old mansion *rotted* to the ground. 3 *v.* To cause decay, ruin, or rot in: Too much water *rots* plant roots. 4 *n.* The process of rotting. 5 *n.* A decayed or ruined condition. 6 *n.* Any of several diseases affecting plants or animals and caused by parasites. 7 *n. informal* Nonsense; rubbish.

rot. 1 rotating. 2 rotation.

Ro·tar·i·an [rō·târ'ē·ən] *n.* A member of the Rotary Club, an international organization of business and professional people.

ro·ta·ry [rō'tər·ē] *adj., n., pl.* **ro·ta·ries** 1 *adj.* Turning or built to turn around its axis, as a wheel. 2 *adj.* Having some important part that turns on its axis: a *rotary* press. 3 *n.* A traffic circle.

rotary engine 1 An engine in which all of the major moving parts rotate or travel in circles or other closed curves. A turbine is a rotary engine. 2 An internal-combustion engine in which a circle of cylinders revolves about a fixed crankshaft.

ro·tate [rō'tāt'] *v.* **ro·tat·ed, ro·tat·ing** 1 To turn or cause to turn on or as if on an axis. 2 To alternate in a definite order: In volleyball the players *rotate*; to *rotate* crops in a field. **—ro'ta·tor** *n.*

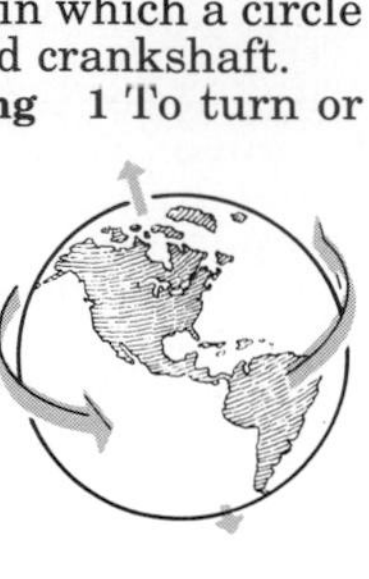
The earth rotates on its axis.

ro·ta·tion [rō·tā'shən] *n.* 1 The act or process of rotating. 2 A being rotated. 3 Change or alternation in some particular order; regular variation: *rotation* of crops.

ro·ta·to·ry [rō'tə·tôr'ē *or* rō'tə·tōr'ē] *adj.* Of, having to do with, causing, or characterized by rotation: *rotatory* muscles.

ROTC or **R.O.T.C.** Reserve Officers' Training Corps.

rote [rōt] *n.* A mechanical, unthinking repetition or way of doing something, especially in the phrase **by rote,** by simple memorization, without any interest in what one memorizes.

ro·ti·fer [rō'tə·fər] *n.* A microscopic water animal having at its head a ring of tiny waving hairs that help it to take in food and move.

ro·tis·se·rie [rō·tis'ər·ē] *n.* A device for roasting meat by rotating it slowly over a fire.

ro·to·gra·vure [rō'tə·grə·vyo͝or'] *n.* 1 A process of printing using engraved copper cylinders on which the pictures and printing to be reproduced are depressed instead of raised. 2 A section of a newspaper printed in such a way.

ro·tor [rō'tər] *n.* 1 The rotating part of a dynamo, turbine, or other generator of power. 2 The horizontal rotating blades of a helicopter.

Rotor of a helicopter

rot·ten [rot'(ə)n] *adj.* 1 Spoiled or decayed: *rotten* food. 2 Unpleasant; disagreeable: a *rotten* temper. 3 Untrustworthy; corrupt; dishonest: a *rotten* politician. 4 Liable to break or crack; rotted: *rotten* beams. 5 *informal* Bad or inferior in quality: a *rotten* novel. **—rot'ten·ness** *n.*

ro·tund [rō·tund'] *adj.* 1 Rounded out; plump: a *rotund* figure. 2 Full and resonant: a *rotund* voice. **—ro·tun'di·ty** *n.*

ro·tun·da [rō·tun'də] *n.* A circular building, room, or hall, usually having a dome on top.

A rotunda

rou·ble [ro͞o'bəl] *n.* Another spelling of RUBLE.

rou·é [ro͞o·ā'] *adj.* An immoral or dissolute man; rake.

rouge [ro͞ozh] *n., v.* **rouged, roug·ing** 1 *n.* A cosmetic used to color the cheeks or lips. 2 *n.* A preparation used to polish metal or glass. 3 *v.* To put or use rouge on.

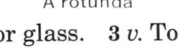

rough [ruf] 1 *adj.* Not smooth or even; bumpy; irregular: a *rough* sidewalk. 2 *adj.* Coarse or harsh to the touch: a *rough* cloth. 3 *v.* To make rough; roughen. 4 *adj.* Violent and rugged in action: *rough* sports. 5 *v.* To treat roughly or violently: Their team *roughed* up ours. **6** *adv.* In a rude or violent manner; roughly: They play *rough.* **7** *adj.* Stormy: *rough* seas. **8** *adj.* Lacking gentleness or courtesy; crude: a *rough* person. **9** *n.* A rude, loud, or disorderly person. **10** *adj.* Not easy or luxurious; hard; rugged: a *rough* life in the wilderness. **11** *adj.* Done or made quickly without much attention to small details: a *rough* drawing. **12** *adj.* Not polished or finished; crude: These jewels are in a *rough* state. **13** *v.* To make, cut, or sketch roughly: The architect *roughed* in the details of the drawing. **14** *adj. informal* Difficult; vexing: to give someone a *rough* time. **15** *n.* Any part of a golf course on which tall grass, bushes, or other vegetation grow. **—in the rough** In a crude or unpolished condition. **—rough it** To live, camp out, or travel in a rough manner without any luxuries or comforts. **—rough out** To make a sketchy first version of. **—rough′ness** *n.*

rough·age [ruf′ij] *n.* Any coarse substance, especially coarse, rough foods that help the movement of food through the intestines.

rough·en [ruf′ən] *v.* To make or become rough.

rough-hew [ruf′hyo͞o′] *v.* **rough-hewed, rough-hewn** or **rough-hewed, rough-hew·ing** To hew or shape roughly or irregularly; make crudely.

rough·house [ruf′hous′] *n., v.* **rough·housed, rough·hous·ing** **1** *n.* Rough, rowdy play. **2** *v.* To engage in rough, rowdy play.

rough·ly [ruf′lē] *adv.* **1** In a rough manner. **2** About; approximately: *Roughly* 100 schools were represented at the conference.

rough·neck [ruf′nek′] *n. U.S. slang* A rude or disorderly person; rowdy. ◆ *Roughneck* was formed by combining the words *rough* and *neck.*

rough·rid·er [ruf′rīd′ər] *n.* A person skilled at riding untrained horses.

rough·shod [ruf′shod′] *adj.* Shod with horseshoes having nails or sharp calks. **—ride roughshod over** To act toward (someone) in a very arrogant way, without any regard for the person's feelings or wishes.

rou·lette [ro͞o·let′] *n.* **1** A gambling game in which the players bet on which space of a rotating wheel a small ball will fall into. **2** A small notched disk that makes holes or marks in paper, as the holes between postage stamps.

Rou·ma·ni·an [ro͞o·mā′nē·ən *or* ro͞o·mān′yən] *adj., n.* Another spelling of ROMANIAN.

round [round] **1** *adj.* Having a shape or form that is like a circle, ball, or cylinder: a *round* table. **2** *adj.* Semicircular: a *round* arch. **3** *n.* Something round, as a globe, ring, or rung of a ladder. **4** *v.* To make or become round. **5** *adj.* Formed or moving in a circle: a *round* dance. **6** *n.* A round dance, as the polka. **7** *n.* Movement or motion that is circular or revolving. **8** *adv.* With a circular or rotating motion: The wheels turned *round.* **9** *prep.* So as to make a circle around: a belt *round* my waist. **10** *adj.* Returning to the point of departure: a *round* trip. **11** *v.* To travel or go around; make a circuit of: The ship *rounded* the cape at noon. **12** *adv.* So as to get to the other or opposite side of: to turn *round* the corner. **13** *n.* (*often pl.*) A route or circuit that ends where it began; beat: the watchman's *rounds.* **14** *adv.* So as to form a complete circuit or cycle of time: The holidays come *round* so slowly each year. **15** *adv.* On all sides: A crowd gathered *round.* **16** *prep.* On every side of: There were mountains *round* us. **17** *prep.* Toward every side of: He peered *round* him. **18** *prep.* To the people or places of: to travel *round* the country. **19** *adv.* From person to person or place to place: We have food enough to go *round*; We walked *round.* **20** *adv.* In a long or roundabout way: We walked *round* by the library on our way to school. **21** *adv.* In the vicinity or neighborhood: We stayed *round* all day but nothing happened. **22** *prep.* In, about, or near: to loaf *round* the drugstore. **23** *adv.* In the opposite direction: to turn *round.* **24** *adv.* In circumference: a log three feet *round.* **25** *n.* A series of actions or events, repeated more or less regularly: the daily *round* of life. **26** *n.* One of a series of actions performed together by many people: a *round* of applause. **27** *adj.* Large; ample: a good *round* fee. **28** *adj.* Plump: a baby's little *round* legs. **29** *adj.* Full; complete: a *round* ton. **30** *adj.* Full and rich; mellow: *round* tones. **31** *adj.* Formed or uttered with the lips rounded, as the vowel ō. **32** *v.* To utter (a vowel) with the lips in a rounded position. **33** *adj.* Bold; outspoken; frank: a *round* statement. **34** *adj.* Increased or decreased to the nearest unit, as ten or one hundred: 400 is a *round* number for 399. **35** *adj.* Quick; brisk: a *round* pace. **36** *n.* One of the divisions or units of a game or contest, as of a boxing match or golf match. **37** *n.* A short song in which each singer or group of singers begins to sing one after the other at a specified word or phrase in the song. **38** *n.* A firing of shots by a military company or squad in which each soldier fires once only; volley. **39** *n.* A single shot or unit of ammunition. **40** *n.* A cut of beef taken from the thigh. **41** *n.* The condition of being fully carved on all sides and standing apart from any background: The sculpture was in the *round.* **—round off** or **round out** **1** To make or become round or rounded. **2** To bring or come to completeness or perfection: The teacher *rounded out* the class hour with a brief summary. **3** To make into a round number. **—round up** **1** To collect (animals, as cattle) in a herd, as for driving to market. **2** *informal* To gather together; assemble: If you can *round up* four people, we can play ball. **—round′ness** *n.*

round·a·bout [round′ə·bout′] *adj.* Not direct, straight, or short: to go a *roundabout* way.

round dance **1** A type of folk dance in which the players form and dance in a circle. **2** A ballroom dance, as the waltz or polka, in which the couples whirl and circle around the room.

roun·de·lay [roun′də·lā′] *n.* **1** A song having a refrain that is often repeated. **2** A dance in which the dancers form or move in circles.

round·ers [roun′dərz] *n.pl.* (*used with singular verb*) An English game, somewhat like baseball, played with a bat and ball.

Round·head [round′hed′] *n.* A person who sup-

R

a add	**i** it	**o͝o** took	**oi** oil
ā ace	**ī** ice	**o͞o** pool	**ou** pout
â care	**o** odd	**u** up	**ng** ring
ä palm	**ō** open	**û** burn	**th** thin
e end	**ô** order	**yo͞o** fuse	**th** this
ē equal			**zh** vision

ə = a in *above*, e in *sicken*, i in *possible*, o in *melon*, u in *circus*

ported Parliament against the Royalists during the English Civil War (1642-1652). ◆ The Roundheads were so named because of their short-cropped hair.

round·house [round′hous′] *n.* 1 A large, round building for housing locomotives. It is built around a turntable in the center for switching or turning the locomotives around. 2 A cabin on the rear part of a ship's deck.

round·ish [roun′dish] *adj.* Somewhat round.

round·ly [round′lē] *adv.* 1 In a round manner, shape, or form. 2 Severely; vigorously: to be *roundly* beaten in the game. 3 Fully; thoroughly. 4 Frankly; bluntly: The principal spoke *roundly* to us all.

round number A number that is raised or lowered to the nearest unit, as ten, hundred, or thousand: 500 is a *round number* for 496.

round robin 1 A tournament in which each contestant plays every other contestant. 2 A document, as a protest or petition, having the signatures in a circle so as to conceal the identity of the first signer. 3 A letter circulated among the members of a group, each one signing and often adding to it before sending it on.

round-shoul·dered [round′shōl′dərd] *adj.* Having the upper back stooped or rounded and the shoulders bent forward.

Round Table 1 The table of King Arthur, made circular so that no knight could complain another was nearer the head of the table. 2 King Arthur and his knights. 3 (*written* **round table**) Any group that meets to discuss something.

round trip A trip to a place and back again, usually by the same route.

round·up [round′up′] *n. U.S.* 1 A bringing together of cattle scattered over a range, as for branding or inspection. 2 The cowhands, horses, and things used to do this. 3 *informal* A bringing together of persons or things for any purpose.

round·worm [round′wûrm′] *n.* Any of various threadlike worms, some of which, like the hookworm, are parasitic in the intestines of human beings.

rouse [rouz] *v.* **roused, rous·ing** 1 To wake up, as from sleep or indifference. 2 To stir up or excite: a crowd *roused* to fury.

roust·a·bout [rous′tə·bout′] *n.* A person who does unskilled work, as on a waterfront, on a ranch, or in a circus.

rout[1] [rout] 1 *v.* To defeat thoroughly. 2 *n.* A disastrous defeat. 3 *v.* To make flee or retreat in a disorderly way. 4 *n.* A disorderly retreat.

rout[2] [rout] *v.* 1 To dig or turn up with the snout: a pig *routing* for food. 2 To turn up or bring to view. 3 To hollow out or gouge, as with a scoop. 4 To drive or force out.

route [rōōt *or* rout] *n., v.* **rout·ed, rout·ing** 1 *n.* A road or course taken in traveling from one point to another. 2 *v.* To send by a certain way or course: to *route* goods through Chicago. 3 *n.* The territory routinely covered by a seller, as a newsboy or milkman.

rou·tine [rōō·tēn′] 1 *n.* A fixed, habitual way or method of doing something: My *routine* of exercises was always the same. 2 *adj.* Habitual; customary: a *routine* breakfast. 3 *adj.* Dull; uninspired: a *routine* job; a *routine* speech. —**rou·tine′·ly** *adv.*

rou·tin·ize [rōō·tē′nīz′ *or* rōōt′ən·īz′] *v.* **rou·tin·ized, rou·tin·iz·ing** To do in a fixed, habitual way; make a routine of.

roux [rōō] *n., pl.* **roux** [rōōz] A heated mixture of flour and fat, used to thicken gravies and soups.

rove [rōv] *v.* **roved, rov·ing** To roam or move about; wander: to *rove* over the farm; to *rove* the old section of town. ◆ See WANDER.

rov·er [rō′vər] *n.* 1 A person who roves; wanderer. 2 A pirate or pirate ship.

row[1] [rou] *n.* A noisy quarrel or disturbance.

row[2] [rō] 1 *v.* To propel (a boat) by using oars. 2 *v.* To carry or transport in a boat by using oars: We *rowed* our guests across the lake. 3 *n.* A trip in a rowboat. —**row′er** *n.*

A rowing team

row[3] [rō] *n.* An arrangement of things or persons in a line.

row·boat [rō′bōt′] *n.* A boat moved along by oars.

row·dy [rou′dē] *n., pl.* **row·dies,** *adj.* **row·di·er, row·di·est** 1 *n.* A rough, disorderly person; hoodlum. 2 *adj.* Rough, loud, and disorderly: a *rowdy* group. —**row′di·ness** or **row′·dy·ism** *n.*

row·el [rou′əl] *n.* A small wheel having spikes or teeth around it, as on a spur.

A rowel

row house One of a series of houses built side by side and connected by common walls.

row·lock [rō′lok′] *n.* Another word for OARLOCK.

roy·al [roi′əl] 1 *adj.* Of or for a king or queen: a *royal* hunting lodge. 2 *adj.* From or by a king or queen: a *royal* visit. 3 *adj.* Of or under the command of a king or queen: the *royal* guard. 4 *adj.* Like or good enough for a king or queen: a *royal* feast. 5 *n.* A sail next above the topgallant, used in a light breeze. —**roy′al·ly** *adv.*

roy·al·ist [roi′əl·ist] 1 *n.* A person who supports a king or queen or a monarchy. 2 *n.* (*written* **Royalist**) An American who supported British rule during the American Revolution. 3 *n.* (*written* **Royalist**) A supporter of the king against Parliament during the English Civil War (1642-1652). 4 *adj.* Of or having to do with royalists.

royal jelly A nutritious substance produced in the bodies of worker honeybees and fed briefly to young worker larvae and continuously to queen larvae.

roy·al·ty [roi′əl·tē] *n., pl.* **roy·al·ties** 1 A royal person. 2 Royal persons as a group: the vanishing *royalty* of Europe. 3 Royal rank, birth, or authority: *Royalty* today gives great influence to a king or queen but little power. 4 Something royal or regal, as a look, quality, or nature: *Royalty* shows in their bearing. 5 A share of the money earned, as by a song, play, invention, or novel. It is paid to the author or creator for the right to use, sell, or perform the work.

rpm or **r.p.m.** revolutions per minute.

rps or **r.p.s.** revolutions per second.

R.R. 1 railroad. 2 Right Reverend.

RSFSR or **R.S.F.S.R.** Russian Soviet Federated Socialist Republic.

RSV or **R.S.V.** Revised Standard Version (Bible).

r.s.v.p. or **R.S.V.P.** Please reply. ◆ *r.s.v.p.* is an abbreviation of the French phrase *Répondez s'il vous plaît,* which means *Please reply,* as to a letter.

rt. right.
RT 1 radio telephone. 2 room temperature.
rte. route.
Ru The symbol for the element ruthenium.
rub [rub] *v.* **rubbed, rub·bing,** *n.* 1 *v.* To move over the surface of with pressure or friction: to *rub* a sore muscle; The shoe *rubbed* my heel. 2 *v.* To move with friction; scrape: The cat *rubbed* against my leg. 3 *v.* To cause to move across a surface: to *rub* a towel over one's face. 4 *v.* To cause to become worn or sore from friction: This collar *rubs* my neck. 5 *v.* To apply or spread with pressure and friction: to *rub* polish on a table. 6 *v.* To do something, as clean, shine, or dry, by means of rubbing: I *rubbed* the wet dog with a towel. 7 *v.* To remove or be removed by rubbing; erase. 8 *n.* The act of rubbing. 9 *n.* Something that annoys or irritates, as a sarcastic remark. 10 *n.* A difficulty, doubt, or hindrance: There's the *rub.* **—rub down** To massage. **—rub it in** *slang* To remind someone often of his or her mistakes or faults. **—rub the wrong way** To annoy or irritate.
rub·ber[1] [rub′ər] *n.* 1 An elastic material made from the milky sap of certain tropical plants, or made artificially of chemicals. 2 Something made of rubber, as an elastic band, overshoe, or eraser. 3 *adj. use*: a *rubber* raincoat. 4 A person or thing that rubs.
rub·ber[2] [rub′ər] *n.* 1 In certain games, as bridge, a series of contests which ends when one player or team wins either two out of three or three out of five of the contests. 2 The odd contest that breaks a tie in such a series.
rubber band A band made of rubber that can be stretched, used to hold things together.
rub·ber·ize [rub′ər·īz′] *v.* **rub·ber·ized, rub·ber·iz·ing** To coat or cover with rubber.
rub·ber·neck [rub′ər·nek′] *slang* 1 *v.* To stare or gawk with undisguised curiosity. 2 *n.* A person who stares in this way. 3 *v.* To go on a sightseeing tour. 4 *n.* A sightseer; tourist.
rubber plant 1 Any of various plants that yield rubber. 2 A plant having large, shiny, leathery leaves, much used as a decorative house plant.
rub·ber-stamp [rub′ər·stamp′] *v.* 1 To mark with a rubber stamp. 2 To accept or approve in a routine way, without thought or question.
rubber stamp 1 A stamp made of rubber. When coated with ink, it prints dates, names, words, or images. 2 A person or group that accepts or approves the ideas and plans of others without much thought or without power to refuse.
rub·ber·y [rub′ə·rē] *adj.* Like rubber, as in elasticity.
rub·bish [rub′ish] *n.* 1 Trash, garbage, or refuse. 2 Nonsense: What they said was pure *rubbish.*
rub·ble [rub′əl] *n.* 1 Rough pieces of broken stone. 2 The masonry, as bricks and stones, of buildings that have been destroyed, as by earthquakes or bombings. 3 Masonry made of rubble.
rub·down [rub′doun′] *n.* A body massage.
ru·bel·la [ro͞o·bel′ə] *n.* Another word for GERMAN MEASLES.
ru·bi·cund [ro͞o′bə·kənd] *adj.* Reddish; rosy.
ru·bid·i·um [ro͞o·bid′ē·əm] *n.* A fairly abundant, faintly radioactive, very reactive metallic element with a low melting point.
ru·ble [ro͞o′bəl] *n.* The basic unit of money in the Soviet Union.
ru·bric [ro͞o′brik] *n.* 1 The part of any early manuscript or book that appears in red or in fancy type, as titles or first letters of a page. 2 A rule or direction for conducting religious ceremonies: the *rubrics* for the Mass.
ru·by [ro͞o′bē] *n., pl.* **ru·bies,** *adj.* 1 *n.* A rare and valuable jewel, having a clear, deep red color. 2 *n., adj.* Deep red.
ruck·sack [ruk′sak′] *n.* A knapsack, usually made of canvas.
ruck·us [ruk′əs] *n. U.S. slang* A noisy uproar.
rud·der [rud′ər] *n.* 1 A broad, flat, movable piece of wood or metal that is hinged to the rear of a boat or ship and is used to steer the vessel. 2 A similar device on an airplane. 3 Anything that guides or directs.

Rudder

rud·dy [rud′ē] *adj.* **rud·di·er, rud·di·est** 1 Tinged with red. 2 Having a healthy glow; rosy: a *ruddy* complexion. **—rud′di·ness** *n.*
rude [ro͞od] *adj.* **rud·er, rud·est** 1 Having no courtesy; impolite: a *rude* remark. 2 Unskillfully made or done; crude; rough: a *rude* little hut. 3 Not refined or educated; rustic; uncouth: the *rude* peasants. 4 Violent; harsh; savage: The storm broke with *rude* fury. 5 Vigorous; strong: *rude* health. **—rude′ly** *adv.* **—rude′ness** *n.*
ru·di·ment [ro͞o′də·mənt] *n.* 1 A first principle, rule, step, or stage in learning or doing something: the *rudiments* of French. 2 Something which is only partly developed or formed.
ru·di·men·ta·ry [ro͞o′də·men′tər·ē] *adj.* 1 Of or like a rudiment; beginning; elementary: a *rudimentary* knowledge of art. 2 Imperfectly developed; unformed: a *rudimentary* tail.
rue[1] [ro͞o] *n.* A small, bushy herb with bitter leaves that were once much used in medicine.
rue[2] [ro͞o] *v.* **rued, ru·ing** To feel sorrow or regret for: You'll *rue* your nasty temper.
rue·ful [ro͞o′fəl] *adj.* 1 Feeling or expressing sorrow, regret, or pity: with a *rueful* glance. 2 Causing sorrow, regret, or pity: a *rueful* tale.

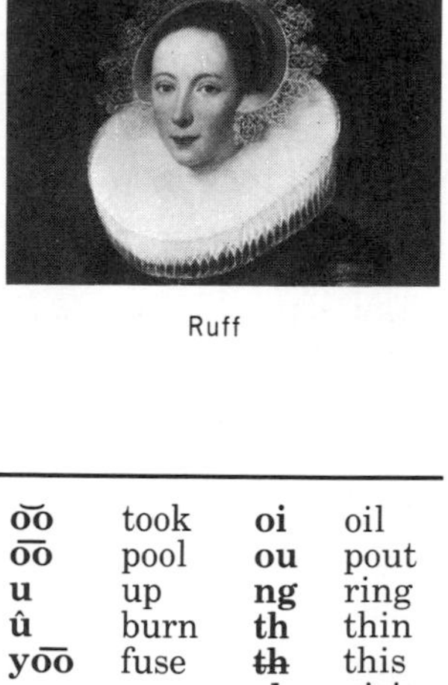
Ruff

ruff [ruf] *n.* 1 A wide, pleated, heavily starched collar worn in the 16th century. 2 A natural collar of feathers or hair

a	add	**i**	it	**o͝o**	took	**oi**	oil
ā	ace	**ī**	ice	**o͞o**	pool	**ou**	pout
â	care	**o**	odd	**u**	up	**ng**	ring
ä	palm	**ō**	open	**û**	burn	**th**	thin
e	end	**ô**	order	**yo͞o**	fuse	**t͟h**	this
ē	equal					**zh**	vision

ə = {a in *above* e in *sicken* i in *possible* / o in *melon* u in *circus*}

R

found around the necks of certain birds or animals. ◆ *Ruff* is a shortened form of RUFFLE.

ruffed grouse [ruft] A grouse of North America, often hunted for sport. It has a ruff of feathers on its neck.

ruf·fi·an [ruf′ē·ən *or* ruf′yən] **1** *n.* A brutal, cruel person; hoodlum. **2** *adj.* Recklessly brutal or cruel: to use *ruffian* behavior.

ruf·fle¹ [ruf′əl] *n., v.* **ruf·fled, ruf·fling** **1** *n.* A strip of material, as cloth or ribbon, that has been pleated on one edge, used for trimming. **2** *v.* To draw into folds or ruffles; gather: to *ruffle* the edge of cloth. **3** *v.* To put ruffles on: to *ruffle* a curtain. **4** *v.* To disturb or irritate; upset. **5** *n.* A feeling of irritation or uneasiness. **6** *n.* The cause of such feelings. **7** *v.* To disturb the smoothness or regularity of: The wind *ruffled* the lake. **8** *n.* A slight disturbance on a surface, as a ripple. **9** *v.* To raise (the feathers) in a ruff, as a bird does.

Ruffles

ruf·fle² *n.* A low, continuous beating of a drum that is not as loud as a roll.

rug [rug] *n.* **1** A covering for a floor or part of a floor, usually made of a heavy, durable material. **2** A robe to put over one's lap.

Rug·by [rug′bē] *n.* A type of football.

rug·ged [rug′id] *adj.* **1** Having a broken, irregular surface; rough; uneven: a *rugged* strip of land. **2** Strong and robust; sturdy: a *rugged* person. **3** Having strongly marked or wrinkled features: a *rugged*, handsome face. **4** Lacking refinement or culture; coarse: a *rugged* manner. **5** Not easy; harsh; stern: to lead a *rugged* life. **6** Stormy: a *rugged* night. **—rug′ged·ly** *adj.* **—rug′ged·ness** *n.*

ru·in [ro͞o′in] **1** *n.* (*often pl.*) The remains of something that has decayed or been destroyed: the *ruins* of bombed cities. **2** *n.* The destruction of the value or usefulness of something: the *ruin* of a promising career. **3** *n.* A condition of destruction or decay: *Ruin* was everywhere. **4** *v.* To destroy, demolish, or damage: The hail *ruined* the garden. **5** *n.* Something that causes destruction, decay, or downfall. **6** *v.* To make bankrupt or poor: The fire *ruined* the company.

ru·in·a·tion [ro͞o′in·ā′shən] *n.* **1** The act of ruining. **2** The condition of being ruined. **3** Something that ruins.

ru·in·ous [ro͞o′in·əs] *adj.* **1** Causing ruin and destruction: a *ruinous* rain. **2** Ruined; decayed; dilapidated: a *ruinous* condition. **—ru′in·ous·ly** *adv.* **—ru′in·ous·ness** *n.*

rule [ro͞ol] *n., v.* **ruled, rul·ing** **1** *n.* A direction, set of instructions, or a law that tells one the correct thing to do or the correct way to do it: the *rules* of a game; the *rules* of a religious order. **2** *v.* To decide or determine: The court *ruled* that the case be tried Tuesday. **3** *v.* To have authority or control over; govern: to *rule* a country; *Rule* your temper. **4** *n.* Government or reign; control: to be under the *rule* of a dictator. **5** *n.* A common or customary way of acting or thinking: It was my *rule* to rise early. **6** *n.* The usual or prevailing condition or thing: During this season rain is the *rule* instead of the exception. **7** *v.* To influence greatly; dominate: Desire for travel *ruled* her life. **8** *n.* A straight-edged instrument for measuring or drawing; ruler. **9** *v.* To mark with straight, usually parallel lines: to *rule* a notebook. **—as a rule** Ordinarily; usually. **—rule out** To eliminate from consideration; exclude: He has a perfect alibi so we can *rule* him *out* as a suspect.

rule of thumb **1** A rule, method, or judgment based on practical experience rather than on scientific knowledge. **2** A rough measurement.

rul·er [ro͞o′lər] *n.* **1** A person who rules or governs, as a king or queen. **2** A straight-edged instrument for use in measuring or in drawing lines.

rul·ing [ro͞o′ling] **1** *n.* The act of a person who rules or governs. **2** *adj.* Having power to rule or govern: a *ruling* monarch. **3** *n.* A decision or judgment, as of a court. **4** *adj.* Most important or powerful; predominant: a *ruling* passion.

rum [rum] *n.* **1** An alcoholic liquor made from fermented molasses or sugar cane. **2** Any alcoholic liquor.

Rum. **1** Rumania. **2** Rumanian.

Ru·ma·ni·an [ro͞o·mā′nē·ən *or* ro͞o·mān′yən] *adj., n.* Another spelling of ROMANIAN.

rum·ba [rum′bə] *n.* **1** A modern ballroom dance that is based on a dance of Cuban Negroes. **2** The music for this dance.

rum·ble [rum′bəl] *v.* **rum·bled, rum·bling,** *n.* **1** *v.* To make a low, heavy, rolling sound, as thunder. **2** *v.* To move or proceed with such a sound: The trucks *rumbled* off. **3** *n.* A low, heavy, rolling sound. **4** *n.* A seat or baggage compartment in the rear of a carriage. **5** *n.* A folding seat in the back of certain early automobiles, as a coupe. **6** *n. slang* A street fight, usually between gangs of teenagers.

rumble seat An uncovered, folding seat in the back of certain early automobiles.

Rumble seat

ru·men [ro͞o′mən] *n., pl.* **ru·mens** or **ru·mi·na** [ro͞o′mə·nə] The first of usually four chambers in the stomachs of animals that chew the cud, as sheep or cows. Food goes into the rumen first before being returned to the mouth for chewing.

ru·mi·nant [ro͞o′mə·nənt] **1** *n.* An animal that eats plants, chews the cud, and has a stomach containing a rumen. Deer, sheep, goats, cows, camels, and giraffes are all ruminants. **2** *adj.* Of, having to do with, or like such animals. **3** *adj.* Liking or given to quiet meditation; thoughtful.

ru·mi·nate [ro͞o′mə·nāt′] *v.* **ru·mi·nat·ed, ru·mi·nat·ing** **1** To chew the cud, as a cow. **2** To think or reflect; meditate. **—ru′mi·na′tion** *n.*

ru·mi·na·tive [ro͞o′mə·nā′tiv] *adj.* Tending to ruminate; meditative.

rum·mage [rum′ij] *v.* **rum·maged, rum·mag·ing,** *n.* **1** *v.* To search through (as a place or box) by turning things over in a disorderly manner; ransack: The robbers *rummaged* the house but found nothing. **2** *v.* To make a thorough search: We *rummaged* all through the attic. **3** *n.* A thorough search. **4** *n.* Things sold at a rummage sale.

rummage sale A sale of secondhand objects or other odds and ends, often for a charity.

rum·my [rum′ē] *n.* A card game in which points are

scored for three or four of a kind or sequences of three or more of the same suit.

ru·mor [ro͞o′mər] **1** *n.* A story or report that has not yet been proven true but is being told from person to person. **2** *n.* Common gossip or hearsay. **3** *v.* To tell or spread as a rumor.

rump [rump] *n.* **1** The round or fleshy upper part of the hindquarters of an animal. **2** A cut of beef from this area. **3** In human beings, the buttocks.

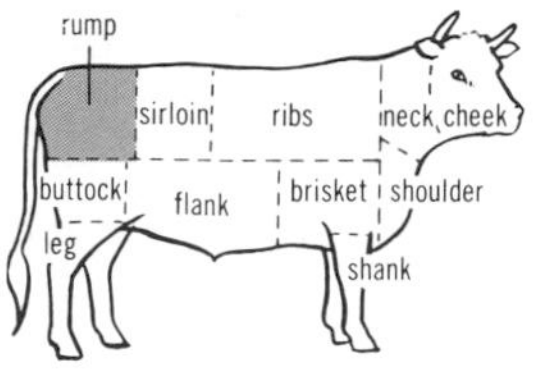

rum·ple [rum′pəl] *v.* **rum·pled, rum·pling,** *n.* **1** *v.* To wrinkle, mess, or crumple: to *rumple* one's clothes in packing. **2** *n.* A wrinkle or crease.

rum·pus [rum′pəs] *n. informal* A row or wrangle; disturbance.

run [run] *v.* **ran, run, run·ning,** *n.* **1** *v.* To move or go along by using steps that are faster than walking steps. **2** *v.* To move, go, or pass rapidly: A whisper *ran* through the crowd. **3** *v.* To take flight; flee: They *ran* for their very lives. **4** *n.* The act of running: They take a *run* each morning. **5** *n.* The movement or pace of running: The jogger broke into a *run.* **6** *v.* To make a journey or regular trips: We *ran* over to the island; This ship *runs* between New York and London. **7** *n.* A journey, trip, or route: Let's take a *run* up to Boston. **8** *v.* To go through or past: The ship *ran* the blockade. **9** *v.* To perform or accomplish by or as if by running: to *run* a race; to *run* an errand. **10** *v.* To flow or cause to flow: The wax *ran* down onto the table; to *run* water into a pan. **11** *n.* A flowing movement, as of a stream or liquid: the *run* of sap. **12** *n.* A stream or current. **13** *v.* To move (as the hand or eye) quickly or lightly: He *ran* his hand over the table. **14** *v.* To continue or extend in time or space: Our carnival *ran* only two nights; The wall *runs* to the edge of our property. **15** *v.* To come, bring, or pass into a specified place or condition: We *ran* out of breath; The well *ran* dry. **16** *n.* A continuous series of events, actions, or performances: The play had a long *run;* a *run* of good luck. **17** *n.* An unusually large number of demands, as by bank depositors or store customers. **18** *v.* To enter or take part in a race or contest: She *ran* for president of our class. **19** *n.* A course, direction, or tendency: the *run* of world events; the *run* of the grain in wood. **20** *v.* To climb or grow in long shoots: The ivy *ran* up the wall. **21** *n.* A period of continuous operation, as of a machine, or the amount of work done during this period. **22** *v.* To be or put in operation; work: The car *runs* well now; Don't *run* the machine too long. **23** *v.* To drive or force: I *ran* the car through the fence. **24** *v.* To direct or control; manage: to *run* a shop. **25** *v.* To have a certain price, size, or quality: The corn is *running* small this year. **26** *n.* A type, kind, or class: the ordinary *run* of readers. **27** *v.* To become torn by unraveling: Their stockings *ran.* **28** *n.* A rip or tear running up and down in knitted material: a *run* in my sweater. **29** *n.* A large enclosure for animals or poultry. **30** *n.* A mass migration or movement of animals, especially of fish to their spawning grounds. **31** *v.* To occur or return: An idea *ran* through his mind. **32** *v.* To be told or expressed: The story *runs* that you were sick. **33** *v.* To publish: to *run* an ad in the paper. **34** *v.* To become liable or expose oneself to; incur: to *run* a risk. **35** *v.* To suffer from (as a fever). **36** *v.* To give forth a discharge or flow: My nose is *running.* **37** *v.* To spread or mingle, as colors when wet. **38** *n.* The right to use or move about freely: We had the *run* of the place. **39** *n.* In baseball, a score made by a player's traveling around and touching all of the bases. **40** *n.* In music, a rapid series of notes. **41** *v.* To sew or stitch in a continuous line. **42** *v.* To mold, as from melted metal. **—a run for one's money** **1** Good, strong action or competition. **2** Satisfaction for the time, money, or effort spent. **—in the long run** At the final outcome or result; finally. **—on the run** Running away, retreating, or escaping. **—run across** To meet or find by chance. **—run away with** To be far better than all the others in: They *ran away with* all the games. **—run down** **1** To go after and overtake, as a fugitive. **2** To strike down while moving. **3** To stop working or operating, as a clock. **4** To make or become tired or ill, as from overwork. **5** To say bad or evil things about. **—run for it** To run so as to avoid or escape something. **—run foul of** **1** To hit or become tangled in: They *ran foul of* the hidden wires. **2** To get into trouble or conflict with: to *run foul of* the police. **—run in** **1** To include: *Run in* that sentence at the end. **2** *slang* To arrest and put in jail. **—run into** **1** To meet or find by chance. **2** To collide with. **—run off** **1** To make on a machine, as a typewriter or printing press: *Run off* 20 copies. **2** To decide (a tied race or game) by the outcome of extra play, as a race or game. **—run out** To come to an end, as supplies. **—run out of** To come to an end of one's supply of: We *ran out of* gasoline. **—run over** **1** To ride or drive over. **2** To overflow. **3** To rehearse or examine something quickly. **—run riot** **1** To act or behave wildly: The students *ran riot* after the game. **2** To be or grow in abundance: Poppies *ran riot* in the field. **—run through** **1** To spend or use wastefully. **2** To stab or pierce. **3** To read, rehearse, or examine rapidly. **—run up** **1** To produce or make quickly: to *run up* a shirt on a sewing machine. **2** To accumulate or grow rapidly: The company's debts kept *running up.* **3** To raise or rise quickly: *Run up* the flag.

run·a·bout [run′ə·bout′] *n.* A light, easy-to-drive vehicle, as an open carriage, a roadster, or a small motorboat.

run·a·round [run′ə·round′] *n. informal* Treatment, as of a request or inquiry, marked by evasions, delays, or misinformation.

run·a·way [run′ə·wā′] **1** *n.* A person or animal that runs away or flees, especially a horse of which the driver has lost control. **2** *adj.* Running away or escaping: a *runaway* prisoner. **3** *adj.* Easily

a	add	**i**	it	**o͝o**	took	**oi**	oil
ā	ace	**ī**	ice	**o͞o**	pool	**ou**	pout
â	care	**o**	odd	**u**	up	**ng**	ring
ä	palm	**ō**	open	**û**	burn	**th**	thin
e	end	**ô**	order	**yo͞o**	fuse	**th**	this
ē	equal					**zh**	vision

ə = { a in *above* e in *sicken* i in *possible* / o in *melon* u in *circus* }

won: a *runaway* race. **4** *adj.* Of or showing a rapid price rise. **5** *adj.* Brought about by running away: a *runaway* marriage.

run·back [run'bak'] *n.* In football, a run by a player who has caught a kickoff or punt or has intercepted a pass.

run·down [run'doun'] *n.* A brief report.

run-down [run'doun'] *adj.* **1** Physically weak, tired, or ill. **2** Falling apart or needing repair; dilapidated. **3** Stopped because not wound.

rune [ro͞on] *n.* **1** Any of the characters in an ancient alphabet used from about the 3rd to the 13th centuries in certain parts of northern Europe. **2** (*often pl.*) Ancient Norse stories or legends expressed in or as if in runes. **3** A secret or mysterious mark, spell, or saying. ◆ *Rune* comes from an Old English word meaning *mystery.*

rung[1] [rung] *n.* **1** A round crosspiece forming one of the steps on a ladder. **2** A crosspiece used in chairs to strengthen or support the legs or back. **3** A spoke of a wheel.

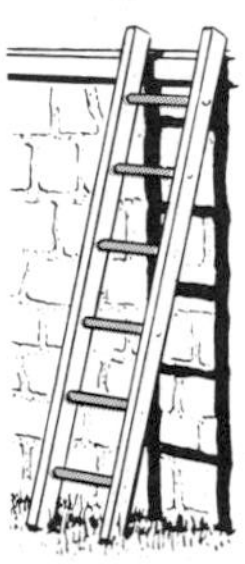
Rungs

rung[2] [rung] Past participle of RING[1].

ru·nic [ro͞o'nik] *adj.* Of, having to do with, or written in runes: a *runic* inscription.

run-in [run'in'] *n. informal* A disagreement, quarrel, or fight.

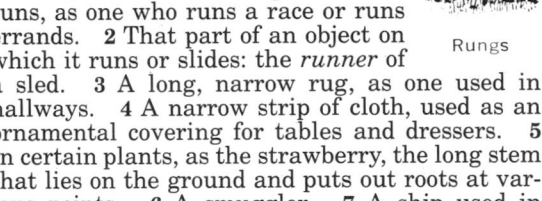

run·ner [run'ər] *n.* **1** A person who runs, as one who runs a race or runs errands. **2** That part of an object on which it runs or slides: the *runner* of a sled. **3** A long, narrow rug, as one used in hallways. **4** A narrow strip of cloth, used as an ornamental covering for tables and dressers. **5** In certain plants, as the strawberry, the long stem that lies on the ground and puts out roots at various points. **6** A smuggler. **7** A ship used in smuggling.

run·ner-up [run'ər·up'] *n., pl.* **run·ners-up** In a game or contest, a person or team finishing in second place.

run·ning [run'ing] **1** *n.* The act of a person or thing that runs. **2** *n.* A flow, as of a liquid. **3** *adj.* Moving or going rapidly. **4** *adj.* Flowing: *running* water. **5** *adj.* Sending out or discharging, as pus or saliva: a *running* sore. **6** *adj.* In operation; going: The driver had the engine *running*. **7** *adj.* Done or performed with a run: a *running* hop. **8** *adj.* Without a break; continuous: They talked for three hours *running*. **9** *adj.* Of or having to do with a trip or run: a train's *running* time. **—in the running** Still having a chance of winning. **—out of the running** No longer having any chance of winning.

running board A narrow board for stepping on at the side of an automobile or carriage.

running knot A knot made so that it slips along the rope, forming a noose that tightens when the rope is pulled.

running mate The candidate for the less important of two connected political offices. The candidate for the vice presidency is the running mate of the candidate for the presidency.

run·ny [run'ē] *adj.* **run·ni·er, run·ni·est** Tending to run or flow: a *runny* nose.

run·off [run'ôf'] *n.* **1** The part of the rainfall that is not absorbed directly by the soil but is drained off in rills or streams. **2** A special game or contest held to break a tie.

run-of-the-mill [run'əv·thə·mil'] *adj.* Not outstanding or unusual; ordinary. ◆ This expression first referred to articles made at a mill or factory and not sorted according to their quality.

run-on [run'on'] **1** *adj.* Continuing too long or without proper punctuation: a *run-on* sentence. **2** *adj.* Added at the end of a body of print without a break or the start of a new section. **3** *n.* Run-on printed matter. ◆ A *run-on entry word* in a dictionary is a word derived from an entry word simply by adding a suffix. It appears at the end of the entry without needing a definition of its own.

runt [runt] *n.* An unusually small animal, person, or plant.

run-through [run'thro͞o'] *n.* A quick review, rehearsal, or practice session.

runt·y [run'tē] *adj.* **runt·i·er, runt·i·est** Unusually small or underdeveloped.

run·way [run'wā'] *n.* **1** A track or path over or through which something runs. **2** A hard, roadlike surface for the takeoff and landing of aircraft.

Runway

ru·pee [ro͞o·pē'] *n.* The basic unit of money in certain countries, as India and Pakistan.

rup·ture [rup'chər] *n., v.* **rup·tured, rup·tur·ing** **1** *n.* The act of breaking apart. **2** *n.* The condition of being broken or torn apart: the *rupture* of a muscle. **3** *v.* To break apart; burst: to *rupture* a bodily organ. **4** *n.* The coming out of an organ of the body through a broken part in the surrounding wall of the cavity; hernia. **5** *v.* To cause to have or suffer from a rupture. **6** *n.* An ending of a friendship or of friendly relations.

ru·ral [ro͝or'əl] *adj.* Of or having to do with the country or with country people or things.

rural free delivery A free government service of delivering mail in rural districts.

ruse [ro͞oz] *n.* Some action or trick intended to deceive or mislead: a *ruse* to get out of the chore.

rush[1] [rush] **1** *v.* To move or go with great speed or haste: They *rushed* from the burning building. **2** *v.* To send with great speed or haste: *Rush* the package to us. **3** *v.* To act hastily without thinking or planning: to *rush* into a new job. **4** *v.* To do with haste or speed: to *rush* one's work; to *rush* through a lesson. **5** *v.* To make a sudden assault upon; attack: The audience *rushed* the rock group. **6** *n.* The act of rushing. **7** *n.* Great hurry or haste: Why is everyone in such a *rush*? **8** *adj.* Requiring haste or urgency: a *rush* order. **9** *n.* A sudden flocking of people to a new region or area, usually to acquire something, as land or gold. **10** *n.* A sudden or urgent press of traffic or business.

rush[2] [rush] *n.* Any of various grasslike plants growing in marshy ground and having round, strong, flexible stems that are often used in making baskets, mats, and seats of chairs.

rush hour A time when traffic or business is at its height.

rusk [rusk] *n.* **1** A bread or cake that has been made crisp and brown in an oven. **2** A light, sweetened bread or biscuit.

Russ. **1** Russia. **2** Russian.

rus·set [rus'it] **1** *n., adj.* Reddish or yellowish brown. **2** *n.* Coarse homemade cloth of this color. **3** *n.* A type of apple, greenish with brown spots.

Rus·sian [rush'ən] **1** *adj.* Of or from Russia. **2** *n.*

A person born in or a citizen of the Soviet Union or of the Russian empire. **3** *n.* The chief language of the Soviet Union.

Russian dressing A salad dressing made of mayonnaise, chili sauce or ketchup, and usually chopped pickles and seasonings.

Russian Orthodox Church An independent Christian church in the Soviet Union, governed by a patriarch. It is one of the Eastern Orthodox Churches and was the national religion of Russia under the czars.

Russian wolfhound Another term for BORZOI.

rust [rust] **1** *n.* The reddish or dark brown oxide formed on iron or steel surfaces that have been exposed to moist air. **2** *n., adj.* Reddish brown. **3** *n.* A fungus disease of plants that causes dark blotches on leaves and stems. **4** *v.* To become or cause to become coated with rust. **5** *v.* To make or become weakened or harmed through disuse: to allow one's talents to *rust.*

rus·tic [rus′tik] **1** *adj.* Of or having to do with the country; rural. **2** *n.* A country person of simple manners or character. **3** *adj.* Plain; simple: *rustic* clothes. **4** *adj.* Not polished or refined; awkward: *rustic* manners. **5** *adj.* Roughly and simply made, as of trees or branches: a *rustic* bridge.

rus·ti·cal [rus′ti·kəl] *adj.* Rustic. **—rus′ti·cal·ly** *adv.*

rus·ti·cate [rus′tə·kāt′] *v.* **rus·ti·cat·ed, rus·ti·cat·ing** To go or send to live in the country.

rus·tic·i·ty [rus·tis′ə·tē] *n., pl.* **rus·tic·i·ties** **1** The quality of being rustic. **2** A characteristic of country life or speech.

rus·tle [rus′(ə)l] *v.* **rus·tled, rus·tling,** *n.* **1** *v.* To move or cause to move with quick, small, rubbing sounds: The leaves *rustled* in the wind; He *rustled* the papers in his hand. **2** *n.* A rustling sound. **3** *v.* To steal (as cattle).

rus·tler [rus′lər] *n. U.S. informal* **1** A cattle or horse thief. **2** An energetic person.

rust·y [rus′tē] *adj.* **rust·i·er, rust·i·est,** *n.* **1** *adj.* Covered with or affected with rust: a *rusty* hinge. **2** *adj., n.* Reddish brown. **3** *adj.* Without skill or nimbleness, through lack of use or practice: The class is *rusty* in algebra. **4** *adj.* Dingy; faded; discolored: a *rusty* old satin pillow.

rut [rut] *n., v.* **rut·ted, rut·ting** **1** *n.* A sunken track in a road worn by the wheels of a vehicle, as an automobile. **2** *v.* To make a rut or ruts in: The trucks *rutted* the road. **3** *n.* A very settled, habitual, and monotonous way of acting or living. ◆ *Rut* may come from the older English word *route,* meaning *track of an animal.*

ru·ta·ba·ga [rōō′tə·bā′gə] *n.* A turnip having a large, yellowish, edible root.

Ruth [rōōth] *n.* **1** In the Bible, a widow who left her own people and went to live with her mother-in-law, Naomi. **2** The book of the Old Testament in which this story is told.

ru·the·ni·um [rōō·thē′nē·əm] *n.* A hard white metallic element found native along with platinum and in combination in various minerals, used as a catalyst and alloying element.

ruth·less [rōōth′lis] *adj.* Without pity, mercy, or compassion; cruel. **—ruth′less·ly** *adv.*

RV [är′vē′] *n., pl.* **RVs** A *R*ecreational *V*ehicle: A camper, motor home, or the like that is designed or outfitted for extended camping trips. **—RV park** A campground designed for RVs.

Rw. Rwanda.

Rwan·dan [rōō·än′dən] **1** *adj.* Of or from Rwanda. **2** *n.* A person born in or a citizen of Rwanda.

rwy. railway.

ry. or **Ry.** railway.

-ry Another form of the suffix -ERY.

rye [rī] *n.* **1** The grain or seeds of a cereal grass similar to wheat, used in the making of flour and whisky, and as a feed for livestock. **2** The plant from which these seeds or grains come.

R

a	add	**i**	it	**ŏŏ**	took	**oi**	oil
ā	ace	**ī**	ice	**ōō**	pool	**ou**	pout
â	care	**o**	odd	**u**	up	**ng**	ring
ä	palm	**ō**	open	**û**	burn	**th**	thin
e	end	**ô**	order	**yōō**	fuse	**th̶**	this
ē	equal					**zh**	vision

ə = a in *above*, e in *sicken*, i in *possible*, o in *melon*, u in *circus*

Ss

Early Phoenician (late 2nd millennium B.C.)

Phoenician (8th century B.C.)

Early Greek (9th-7th centuries B.C.)

Western Greek (6th century B.C.)

Classical Greek (403 B.C. onward)

Early Etruscan (8th century B.C.)

Monumental Latin (4th century B.C.)

Classical Latin

Uncial

Half uncial

Caroline minuscule

S is the nineteenth letter of the alphabet. The sign for it originated among Semitic people in the Near East, in the region of Palestine and Syria, probably in the middle of the second millennium B.C. Little is known about the sign until around 1000 B.C., when the Phoenicians began using it. They shaped it like our present-day *W*, named it *sin* or *shin*, and used it for the sibilant sounds *s* and *sh*.

When the Greeks adopted the Phoenician sign around the ninth century B.C., they confused the name with that of another Semitic sign called *samekh*. The sign for samekh became our *X* (see *X*), but the word *samekh* became *sigma*, the Greek name for the *s* sound. The Greeks also changed the shape of the letter.

As early as the eighth century B.C., the Etruscans adopted the Greek alphabet. It is from the Etruscans that the Romans took the sign for *S*. Eventually the Romans rounded it into the form we know today. Around the time of the Caesars, the Romans made the shape of the letter even more graceful. The model of the letter *S* found on the base of Trajan's column, erected in Rome in 114, is considered a masterpiece of letter design. A Trajan-style *majuscule*, or capital letter, *S* opens this essay.

The *minuscule*, or small letter, *s* developed gradually, between the third and the ninth centuries, in the handwriting that scribes used for copying books. Contributing to its shape—a smaller version of the uppercase letter—were the Roman *uncials* of the fourth to the eighth centuries, the *half uncials* of the fifth to the ninth centuries, and the *Caroline minuscules*, a script that evolved under the encouragement of Charlemagne (742-814). The Caroline minuscules were the principal handwriting system used on the medieval manuscripts of the ninth and tenth centuries. Between the seventeenth and nineteenth centuries, the English form of the minuscule was *ʃ*.

s or **S** [es] *n., pl.* **s's** or **S's** The 19th letter of the English alphabet.

s., s., S, or **S.** 1 south. 2 southern.

s. 1 scruple. 2 second. 3 shilling. 4 singular. 5 stere.

S The symbol for the element sulfur.

S. 1 Sabbath. 2 Saint. 3 Saturday. 4 Saxon. 5 (*sometimes written* S) school. 6 sea. 7 Sunday.

SA seaman apprentice.

S.A. 1 Salvation Army. 2 South Africa. 3 South America.

Sab. Sabbath.

Sab·bath [sab′əth] *n.* A day of the week set aside for rest and worship. Saturday is the Sabbath for Jews and some Christians. Sunday is the Sabbath for most Christians.

sab·bat·i·cal [sə·bat′i·kəl] 1 *adj.* Of, like, or for the Sabbath. 2 *n.* A time of rest, as the year's vacation some teachers get every seven years.

sa·ber [sā′bər] *n.* 1 A heavy cavalry sword with a curved blade. 2 In fencing, a light sword for thrusting or slashing.

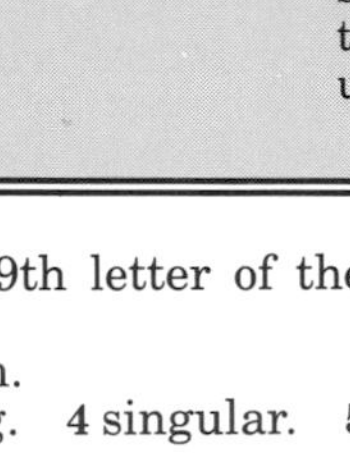

Sable

sa·ber-toothed tiger [sā′bər·to͞otht′] A large extinct animal with long, curved, upper canine teeth.

sa·ble [sā′bəl] 1 *n.* A slender animal found in northern Europe and Asia, valued for its fur. 2 *n.* The valuable fur of the sable. 3 *adj.* use: a *sable* coat. 4 *n.* (*usually pl.*) Garments made of sable. 5 *adj., n.* Black.

sa·bot [sab′ō] *n.* 1 A wooden shoe worn by French peasants. 2 A leather shoe with a wooden sole.

sab·o·tage [sab′ə·täzh′] *n., v.* **sab·o·taged, sab·o·tag·ing** 1 *n.* The destruction of a country's property, resources, or productive capacity by enemy agents in wartime. 2 *n.* Damage, as to machinery, tools, or products, by dissatisfied workers. 3 *v.* To damage or destroy by sabotage.

sab·o·teur [sab′ə·tûr′] *n.* A person who engages in sabotage.

sa·bra [sä′brə] *n.* A native-born Israeli.

sa·bre [sā′bər] *n.* Another spelling of SABER.

sac [sak] *n.* A pouch or baglike part in an animal or plant, often containing a fluid.

Sac [sak *or* sôk] *n., pl.* **Sac** or **Sacs** Another spelling of SAUK.

SAC [sak] Strategic Air Command.

sac·cha·rin [sak′ər·in] *n.* A very sweet substance made from coal tar. It is used as a substitute for sugar.

sac·cha·rine [sak′ər·in] 1 *adj.* Of or like sugar; sweet. 2 *adj.* Sickeningly sweet: a *saccharine* smile. 3 *n.* Saccharin.

sac·er·do·tal [sas′ər·dōt′(ə)l] *adj.* Of or having to do with a priest or the priesthood; priestly.

sa·chem [sā′chəm] *n.* The chief of a North American Indian tribe or of a group of allied tribes.

sa·chet [sa·shā′] *n.* A small, ornamental bag of perfumed powder, used for scenting clothing.

sack[1] [sak] 1 *n.* A bag, especially one of coarse

cloth, for holding articles, as food or grain. **2** *v.* To put into a sack. **3** *n.* The amount a sack will hold. **4** *n.* A short, loose jacket. **5** *v. slang* To dismiss (someone) from a job.

sack² [sak] **1** *v.* To rob or plunder (as a city or town) after capturing it during a war. **2** *v.* In football, to tackle the quarterback behind the line while he is trying to pass the ball. **3** *n.* The act of sacking.

sack³ [sak] *n.* A strong, dry, pale-colored wine of Spanish origin.

sack·cloth [sak'klôth'] *n.* **1** Coarse cloth used for making sacks. **2** Coarse cloth worn in penance or mourning.

sack·ful [sak'fŏŏl'] *n., pl.* **sack·fuls** As much as a sack will hold: a *sackful* of potatoes.

sack·ing [sak'ing] *n.* Coarse cloth used for making sacks.

sac·ra·ment [sak'rə·mənt] *n.* **1** Any of certain very holy rites in Christian churches, as baptism and communion. **2** (*usually written* **Sacrament**) Holy Communion. **—sac'ra·men'tal** *adj.*

sa·cred [sā'krid] *adj.* **1** Of, having to do with, or intended for religion or religious use: a *sacred* book; a *sacred* building. **2** Deserving reverence, honor, or respect: a *sacred* memory; a *sacred* vow. **3** Dedicated to a person or purpose: a church *sacred* to St. Peter. **—sa'cred·ness** *n.*

sacred cow A person or thing that cannot be criticized or challenged. ◆ This term comes from the traditional Hindu regard for cows as sacred animals.

sac·ri·fice [sak'rə·fīs'] *n., v.* **sac·ri·ficed, sac·ri·fic·ing** **1** *n.* The act of offering something, as the life of an animal or human being, to a god in worship or atonement. **2** *n.* The thing so offered. **3** *v.* To make an offering of (as an animal or human being) to a god. **4** *n.* A giving up of something cherished, usually for the sake of something else. **5** *n.* The thing which is given up: We made a *sacrifice* of our weekends to paint the house. **6** *v.* To give up (something) for someone or something else: I *sacrificed* a week's free time to help out at home. **7** *n.* Loss, as of profit or life: to sell at a *sacrifice*; The flood caused great *sacrifice* of life. **8** *v.* To sell at a loss. **9** *n.* In baseball, a bunt or fly that allows a runner to reach the next base although the batter is put out.

sacrifice fly In baseball, a fly ball that enables a base runner to score after it is caught.

sacrifice hit In baseball, a bunt that enables a runner to advance while the batter is being thrown out.

sac·ri·fi·cial [sak'rə·fish'əl] *adj.* Of, having to do with, or like a sacrifice.

sac·ri·lege [sak'rə·lij] *n.* An act of disrespect for anything sacred.

sac·ri·le·gious [sak'rə·lij'əs] *adj.* **1** Of, having to do with, or characterized by sacrilege. **2** Committing or having committed sacrilege. **—sac'ri·le'gious·ness** *n.*

sac·ris·tan [sak'ris·tən] *n.* A person having charge of the sacristy of a church.

sac·ris·ty [sak'ris·tē] *n., pl.* **sac·ris·ties** A room in a church for the sacred vessels and robes; vestry.

sac·ro·sanct [sak'rō·sangkt'] *adj.* Very sacred.

sa·crum [sā'krəm] *n., pl.* **sa·cra** [sā'krə] A triangular bone at the lower end of the spine. It forms a part of the pelvis.

sad [sad] *adj.* **sad·der, sad·dest** **1** Unhappy or depressed; sorrowful: to feel *sad*; a *sad* glance. **2** Causing sorrow or pity; distressing: a *sad* sight. **3** *informal* Not good enough. **—sad'ly** *adv.*

sad·den [sad'(ə)n] *v.* To make or become sad.

sad·dle [sad'(ə)l] *n., v.* **sad·dled, sad·dling** **1** *n.* A seat or pad for a rider, as on a horse or bicycle. **2** *v.* To put a saddle on: to *saddle* a horse. **3** *n.* A padded cushion for a horse's back, used as part of a harness or to support a pack. **4** *v.* To load, as with a burden or responsibility: to *saddle* (someone) with your troubles. **5** *n.* Something shaped like a saddle. **6** *n.* A cut of meat that includes the undivided hindquarters and both loins. **—in the saddle** In control.

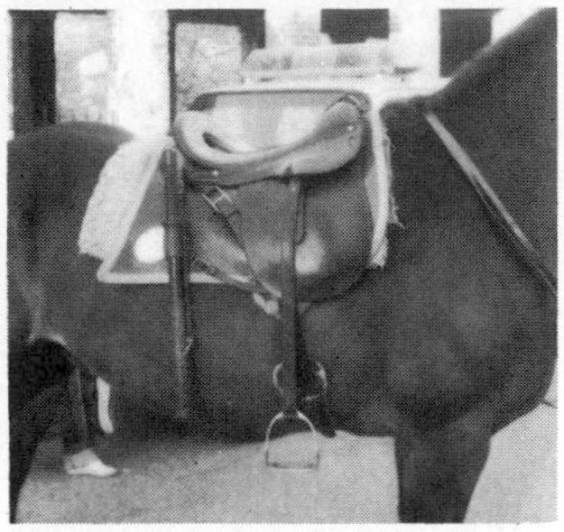

Saddle

sad·dle·bag [sad'(ə)l·bag'] *n.* One of a pair of pouches slung over a horse's back or attached to a saddle.

saddle horse A horse suitable for riding.

sad·dler [sad'lər] *n.* **1** A maker of saddles, harnesses, and other equipment for riding. **2** A saddle horse.

saddle shoe An oxford-style shoe in a light color with a dark band across the instep.

saddle soap A mild, oily soap used to clean and soften leather.

sad·ism [sā'diz'əm *or* sad'iz'əm] *n.* Enjoyment derived from being cruel to or inflicting pain on others.

sad·ist [sā'dist *or* sad'ist] *n.* A person who gets pleasure from being cruel to or inflicting pain on others. **—sa·dis·tic** [sə·dis'tik] *adj.*

sad·ness [sad'nis] *n.* A being sad.

sa·fa·ri [sə·fä'rē] *n., pl.* **sa·fa·ris** An expedition or journey, as for hunting, especially in eastern Africa.

safe [sāf] *adj.* **saf·er, saf·est,** *n.* **1** *adj.* Free or freed from danger or evil: *safe* from temptation; *safe* from thieves. **2** *adj.* Not injured; unharmed. **3** *adj.* Not risky; involving no loss: a *safe* investment. **4** *adj.* Trustworthy: a *safe* guide. **5** *adj.* Not likely to cause or do harm; careful: *safe* driving. **6** *n.* A strong metal box for protecting valuables. **7** *adj.* In baseball, having reached base without being put out. **—safe'ly** *adv.*

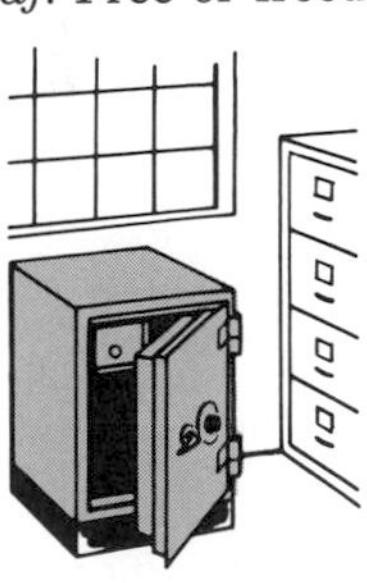

Safe

safe-con·duct [sāf'kon'dukt] *n.*

a	add	**i**	it	**ŏŏ**	took	**oi**	oil
ā	ace	**ī**	ice	**ōō**	pool	**ou**	pout
â	care	**o**	odd	**u**	up	**ng**	ring
ä	palm	**ō**	open	**û**	burn	**th**	thin
e	end	**ô**	order	**yōō**	fuse	**t͟h**	this
ē	equal					**zh**	vision

ə = a in *above* e in *sicken* i in *possible* o in *melon* u in *circus*

S

1 Protection given to a person passing through a hostile area, as in wartime. 2 A paper authorizing this.

safe·de·pos·it box [sāf'di·poz'it] A box for storing valuables, as in a bank vault.

safe·guard [sāf'gärd'] 1 *n.* A person or thing that protects one, as from danger, injury, or illness: a *safeguard* against infection. 2 *v.* To protect or guard.

safe·keep·ing [sāf'kē'ping] *n.* A keeping or being kept in safety: Important papers were left in the office for *safekeeping.*

safe·ty [sāf'tē] *n., pl.* **safe·ties,** *adj.* 1 *n.* Freedom from danger, risk, or injury. 2 *n.* A device or catch designed as a safeguard: the *safety* on a gun. 3 *adj.* Giving or designed to give safety: *safety* glass; a *safety* valve.

safety belt 1 A belt that goes aroung the waist and is fastened at both ends to a fixed object, used to prevent falling, worn by window cleaners, telephone installers, and others. 2 A seat belt.

safety glass Two sheets of glass having a film of transparent plastic between them that keeps them glued together and prevents shattering.

safety match A match that will light only when struck on a specially treated surface.

safety pin A pin whose point fastens within a protective guard, where it cannot prick.

safety razor A razor that has a metal guard for the blade, in order to prevent accidental cutting of the skin.

safety valve 1 A valve, as one in a steam boiler, that opens automatically to let out steam when the pressure mounts too high. 2 Any outlet for excess energy or emotion.

saf·flow·er [saf'lou'ər] *n.* 1 An Old World herb with spiny heads on orange or red flowers and seeds rich in oil. 2 Its flower heads, used as a dyestuff and to make medicine.

saf·fron [saf'rən] 1 *n.* A variety of crocus. 2 *n.* The dried, yellow-orange center parts of this flower, used in foods for coloring and seasoning. 3 *n., adj.* Bright yellow-orange.

S.Afr. South Africa.

sag [sag] *v.* **sagged, sag·ging,** *n.* 1 *v.* To bend or sink from weight or pressure, especially in the middle. 2 *n.* A place or part that sags: a *sag* in the roof. 3 *v.* To hang unevenly: The hem of your coat *sags.* 4 *v.* To lose strength; weaken, as from being tired: Our spirits *sagged.* 5 *v.* To go down, as in price or value.

sa·ga [sä'gə] *n.* 1 An ancient Scandinavian story of heroes and their deeds. 2 A long story or novel, often telling the history of a family.

sa·ga·cious [sə·gā'shəs] *adj.* Having or showing wisdom or shrewdness. —**sa·ga'cious·ly** *adv.*

sa·gac·i·ty [sə·gas'ə·tē] *n.* The quality of being sagacious; ready and accurate judgment; wisdom; shrewdness.

sag·a·more [sag'ə·môr'] *n.* A North American Indian chief, usually an Algonquin chief lower in rank than a sachem.

sage[1] [sāj] *adj.* **sag·er, sag·est,** *n.* 1 *adj.* Having or showing great wisdom and good judgment: a *sage* remark. 2 *n.* A person of great wisdom. —**sage'·ly** *adv.*

sage[2] [sāj] *n.* 1 An herb related to mint, with gray-green leaves, used as a seasoning in food. 2 Sagebrush.

sage·brush [sāj'brush'] *n.* A bitter herb or small shrub with white or yellow flowers, found on the dry plains of the western U.S.

Sag·it·tar·i·us [saj'i·târ'ē·əs] *n.* 1 A constellation in the Southern Hemisphere. 2 The ninth sign of the zodiac. 3 A person born under this sign.

sa·go [sā'gō] *n., pl.* **sa·gos** 1 Any of several varieties of palm trees. 2 A starch made from the soft pith of these palms, used to thicken foods, as puddings.

sa·gua·ro [sə·gwä'rō] *n.* A large desert cactus of the SW U.S.

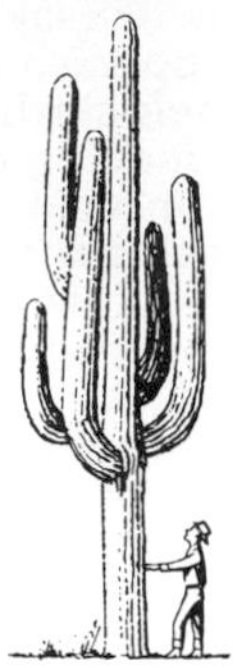

Saguaro

sa·hib [sä'ib] *n.* Master; sir: a title used in India and Pakistan for men of high rank, especially, formerly, for Europeans.

said [sed] 1 Past tense and past participle of SAY. 2 *adj.* In legal documents, mentioned before; named before: the *said* party.

sail [sāl] 1 *n.* A piece of strong cloth, as canvas, opened to catch the wind so as to make a ship or boat move on the water. 2 *n.* A boat or ship having sails. 3 *v.* To manage or steer a boat with sails: Can you *sail*? 4 *n.* A trip in a sailing ship or in any boat or ship. 5 *v.* To move forward by means of wind and sails: Does it *sail* well? 6 *v.* To travel over water in a ship or boat: to *sail* to Europe. 7 *v.* To begin a voyage over water: We *sail* at dawn. 8 *v.* To move across in a ship or boat: to *sail* the Great Lakes. 9 *n.* Something resembling a sail, as one of the broad arms of a windmill. 10 *v.* To move, glide, or float in the air: Clouds *sailed* by. 11 *v.* To move in a swift but dignified manner: to *sail* into a room. —**make sail** 1 To open a sail or sails to the wind. 2 To set out on a voyage. —**sail into** *informal* 1 To begin with energy: The students *sailed into* their studies. 2 To attack or scold: The manager *sailed into* me for not doing the work. —**set sail** To begin a voyage: to *set sail* for the Orient. —**under sail** With sails open to the wind. —**sail'a·ble** *adj.*

sail·boat [sāl'bōt'] *n.* A small boat moved by means of a sail or sails.

sail·cloth [sāl'klôth'] *n.* A closely woven canvas or other material suitable for sails.

sail·fish [sāl'fish'] *n., pl.* **sail·fish** or **sail·fish·es** Any of several ocean fishes having a long body, a spearlike snout, and a large fin on the back that looks like a sail.

Sailfish

sail·ing [sā'ling] *n.* 1 The activity or sport of operating a boat or ship, especially a sailboat. 2 The departure or time of departure of a ship from a port.

sail·or [sā'lər] *n.* 1 A person who is a member of a ship's crew: a *sailor* in the Navy. 2 A person traveling by ship or boat, rated by his or her resistance to seasickness: You're a fine *sailor*; but since I'm always sick, I'm a poor *sailor.* 3 A straw hat having a low, flat crown and a brim.

sail·plane [sāl'plān'] *n., v.* **sail·planed, sail·plan·ing** 1 *n.* A light, long-winged glider that can rise in upward air currents. 2 *v.* To fly a sailplane.

saint [sānt] *n.* 1 A very holy person, especially one who, after death, has been declared by the Roman Catholic Church to be worthy of veneration. 2 Any very good, patient, and unselfish person.

Saint Ber·nard [bər·närd′] A large dog having a thick, white and brown coat and a massive head, formerly used to rescue travelers lost in the snow in the Swiss Alps.

Saint Bernard

saint·ed [sān′tid] *adj.* 1 Officially declared a saint; canonized. 2 Very holy; saintly.
saint·hood [sānt′ho͝od′] *n.* The quality or condition of being a saint.
saint·ly [sānt′lē] *adj.* **saint·li·er, saint·li·est** Of, like, or fit for a saint. **—saint′li·ness** *n.*
Saint Patrick's Day March 17th, a day celebrated by the Irish in honor of their patron saint.
Saint Valentine's Day February 14th, the anniversary of the beheading of St. Valentine by the Romans, and also a day on which valentines are exchanged.
saith [seth] *v.* An old form of SAYS: used in the Bible and old poetry.
sake[1] [sāk] *n.* 1 Purpose, reason, or aim. 2 Welfare; interest; benefit: for your own *sake.*
sa·ke[2] or **sa·ki** [sä′kē] *n.* A Japanese wine made from fermented rice.
Sal. El Salvador.
sa·laam [sə·läm′] 1 *n.* A word that means *peace* in Arabic, used as a greeting. 2 *n.* A low bow with the palm of the right hand held to the forehead, used in parts of the Orient. 3 *v.* To make a salaam.
sal·a·ble [sā′lə·bəl] *adj.* Fit to be sold; wanted enough to attract buyers. **—sal′a·bil′i·ty** *n.*
sa·la·cious [sə·lā′shəs] *adj.* Arousing sexual feeling; lascivious; lewd.
sal·ad [sal′əd] *n.* A mixture of vegetables, usually uncooked and served with a dressing, as of oil, vinegar, and other ingredients. A salad can also be made with other foods, as chopped meat, fish, or fruit.
salad bar A counter in a restaurant where customers may help themselves to a variety of salads.
sal·a·man·der [sal′ə·man′dər] *n.* 1 A small lizard-like animal related to the frog, having a smooth, moist skin and living in damp places. 2 In myths, a lizard believed to live in fire.

Salamander

sa·la·mi [sə·lä′mē] *n., pl.* **sa·la·mis** A salted, spiced sausage, originally Italian.
sal·a·ried [sal′ər·ēd] *adj.* 1 Paid a salary, as a worker. 2 Providing a salary, as a job.
sal·a·ry [sal′ər·ē] *n., pl.* **sal·a·ries** A sum of money paid at regular times to professional and white-collar workers and to executives.
sale [sāl] *n.* 1 The act of selling property or goods for money. 2 A selling of goods at bargain prices: a *sale* on suits. 3 (*pl.*) Activities related to the promotion and selling of goods or services. 4 An auction. **—for sale** Offered or ready to be sold. **—on sale** Offered at bargain prices.
sale·a·ble [sā′lə·bəl] *adj.* Another spelling of SALABLE.
sales check [sālz] A piece of paper on which a store records certain information, as the items purchased by a particular customer and the price of the items.
sales·clerk [sālz′klûrk′] *n.* A person who sells goods in a store.
sales·man [sālz′mən] *n., pl.* **sales·men** [sālz′mən] 1 A person whose job is selling. 2 A man who sells goods or services.
sales·man·ship [sālz′mən·ship′] *n.* 1 Ability or skill in selling. 2 Techniques of selling.
sales·per·son [sālz′pûr′sən] *n.* A salesclerk.
sales representative An agent authorized to sell goods or services.
sales tax A tax based on the amount paid for goods bought, usually added to the price.
sales·wom·an [sālz′wo͝om′ən] *n., pl.* **sales·wom·en** [sālz′wim′in] 1 A salesclerk. 2 A woman who sells goods or services, often in a given territory.
sal·i·cyl·ic acid [sal′ə·sil′ik] A white, powdery compound used in making aspirin and as a food preservative.
sa·li·ent [sā′lē·ənt] *adj.* Standing out; easily seen or perceived: a *salient* feature in a landscape; the *salient* points of an argument.
sa·line [sā′līn′ *or* sā′lēn′] 1 *adj.* Of, like, or containing a salt, especially common salt: a *saline* solution. 2 *n.* A salt solution used by biologists and in medicine.
sa·lin·i·ty [sə·lin′ə·tē] *n., pl.* **sa·lin·i·ties** 1 The condition of being saline; saltiness. 2 The proportion of salt in something.
Salis·bur·y steak [sôlz′ber·ē *or* sôlz′brē] Hamburger, usually mixed with seasonings and formed into patties.
sa·li·va [sə·lī′və] *n.* The liquid produced by certain glands in the mouth; spit. It helps to prepare food for digestion.
sal·i·var·y [sal′ə·ver′ē] *adj.* Of or producing saliva: *salivary* glands.
sal·i·vate [sal′ə·vāt′] *v.* **sal·i·vat·ed, sal·i·vat·ing** To produce saliva. **—sal′i·va′tion** *n.*
Salk vaccine A vaccine against poliomyelitis, developed by Jonas E. Salk.
sal·low [sal′ō] *adj.* Of an unhealthy, yellowish color: said chiefly of the human skin.
sal·ly [sal′ē] *v.* **sal·lied, sal·ly·ing,** *n. pl.* **sal·lies** 1 *v.* To rush forth or go out suddenly and with energy. 2 *n.* A sudden rushing forth. 3 *n.* A little trip or excursion. 4 *n.* A witty remark.
salm·on [sam′ən] 1 *n.* Any of several food fishes having a delicate pink flesh. Salmon live in the Atlantic and Pacific Oceans and swim far up the coastal rivers when it is time to spawn. 2 *n., adj.* Reddish or pinkish orange.
Sa·lo·me [sə·lō′mē] *n.* In the Bible, a niece of Herod who persuaded him to give her the head of John the Baptist in return for her dancing.

Salmon

a	add	**i**	it	**o͝o**	took	**oi**	oil
ā	ace	**ī**	ice	**o͞o**	pool	**ou**	pout
â	care	**o**	odd	**u**	up	**ng**	ring
ä	palm	**ō**	open	**û**	burn	**th**	thin
e	end	**ô**	order	**yo͞o**	fuse	**th**	this
ē	equal					**zh**	vision

ə = { a in *above* e in *sicken* i in *possible* / o in *melon* u in *circus* }

S

sa·lon [sə·lon′] *n.* 1 A rather elaborate and formal room for entertaining guests. 2 A more or less regular meeting, as of artists, writers, and statesmen, in the home of a wealthy or prominent person. 3 A gallery for showing works of art. 4 A business offering some particular service: a beauty *salon.*

sa·loon [sə·lo͞on′] *n.* 1 A place where alcoholic drinks are sold; bar. 2 A large, often elaborate room, as the dining room of a ship.

sal·si·fy [sal′sə·fē] *n., pl.* **sal·si·fies** A plant with a white edible root that tastes like oysters.

sal soda [sal] Sodium carbonate used for washing and bleaching.

salt [sôlt] 1 *n.* A white crystalline compound, sodium chloride, found in all sea water and as a mineral in the earth. Formula: NaCl. It has many uses besides flavoring foods. 2 *adj.* Flavored with salt; salty: *salt* crackers. 3 *v.* To put salt on or in: to *salt* food; to *salt* ice. 4 *v.* To cure or preserve with salt: to *salt* meat. 5 *adj.* Cured or preserved with salt: *salt* pork. 6 *adj.* Containing salt: *salt* water. 7 *adj.* Growing in or overflowed by salt water: *salt* marshes. 8 *n.* In chemistry, a compound consisting of the negative ion of an acid and a metallic or other positive ion except that of hydrogen. 9 *n.* (*pl.*) A medicine used as a laxative. 10 *n.* (*pl.*) Smelling salts. 11 *n. informal* A sailor: an old *salt.* 12 *n.* Anything that gives zest, flavor, or sharpness to something: the *salt* of the writer's wit. 13 *v.* To add zest, fun, or flavor to: to *salt* one's speech with anecdotes. **—salt away** 1 To pack or preserve in salt. 2 *informal* To save or hoard, as money. **—salt down** To pack in salt for preserving. **—salt of the earth** The best, kindest, and truest people of the world. **—take with a grain of salt** To have doubts about the truthfulness of. **—worth one's salt** To be worth one's salary, board, or other measure of value.

SALT [sôlt] Strategic Arms Limitations Talks.

salt·box [sôlt′boks′] *n.* A house with two stories in front and a peaked roof that slopes down to one story in the rear.

salt·cel·lar [sôlt′sel′ər] *n.* A small container for salt, commonly either an open dish or a shaker, for use at the table. ◆ *Saltcellar* was formed by combining *salt* with *cellar.* The *cellar* part comes from the French word *salière*, which means *saltcellar* and which to English-speaking people sounded like *cellar* [sel′ər], the underground part of a building.

sal·tine [sôl·tēn′] *n.* A crisp, salty cracker.

salt lick A place, as a dried salt pond, where animals go to lick salt.

salt·pe·ter [sôlt′pē′tər] *n.* Any of several minerals that contain nitrates, used in gunpowder, fireworks, and fertilizers.

salt·shak·er [sôlt′shā′kər] *n.* A closed container with small holes in its top for sprinkling salt on food.

salt·wa·ter [sôlt′wô′tər] *adj.* Of or living in salt water: *saltwater* plants.

salt·y [sôl′tē] *adj.* **salt·i·er, salt·i·est** 1 Tasting of or containing salt. 2 Witty and spicy: a *salty* remark. **—salt′i·ness** *n.*

sa·lu·bri·ous [sə·lo͞o′brē·əs] *adj.* Good for the health; wholesome: *salubrious* air.

sal·u·tar·y [sal′yə·ter′ē] *adj.* 1 Useful; beneficial: *salutary* advice. 2 Healthful.

sal·u·ta·tion [sal′yə·tā′shən] *n.* 1 A saluting. 2 Any form of greeting. 3 The opening words of a letter, as *Dear Dr. Sanchez.*

sa·lu·ta·to·ri·an [sə·lo͞o′tə·tôr′ē·ən] *n. U.S.* In schools and colleges, the graduating student who receives the second highest honors and who delivers the salutatory at commencement.

sa·lu·ta·to·ry [sə·lo͞o′tə·tôr′ē] *n., pl.* **sa·lu·ta·to·ries,** *adj.* 1 *n.* An opening speech, as at a school commencement. 2 *adj.* Giving or expressing a greeting or welcome.

sa·lute [sə·lo͞ot′] *v.* **sa·lut·ed, sa·lut·ing,** *n.* 1 *v.* To recognize and honor (as a superior, leader, or flag) in some special way, as by raising the hand to the forehead or firing guns: to *salute* an army officer; to *salute* a ship carrying an admiral. 2 *v.* To make a salute: We *saluted* as we marched by. 3 *v.* To greet with a friendly sign of welcome or respect: Let's *salute* all our new members. 4 *n.* The act of saluting: The young lieutenant's *salute* was perfectly executed.

A salute

Sal·va·do·ran [sal′və·dôr′ən] 1 *adj.* Of or from El Salvador. 2 *n.* A person born in or a citizen of El Salvador.

Sal·va·do·ri·an [sal′və·dôr′ē·ən] *adj., n.* Salvadoran.

sal·vage [sal′vij] *v.* **sal·vaged, sal·vag·ing,** *n.* 1 *v.* To save, as from being wrecked, ruined, or burned: They *salvaged* the ship and its cargo; People *salvage* some strange things from a fire. 2 *n.* The saving of a ship or its cargo from loss or destruction. 3 *n.* The money paid for this. 4 *n.* The act of salvaging anything. 5 *n.* Something salvaged.

sal·va·tion [sal·vā′shən] *n.* 1 The condition of being saved or preserved, as from danger or evil. 2 Something that saves: The dog's barking was our *salvation* when the house caught fire. 3 In Christian belief, the saving of the soul from sin or from the punishment for sin.

Salvation Army A religious organization engaged in bringing Christianity and help to the poor or to those in trouble.

salve [sav] *n., v.* **salved, salv·ing** 1 *n.* A soothing or healing ointment, as for wounds, burns, or sores. 2 *n.* Anything that heals, soothes, or calms: Your kind words were a *salve* to our discouragement. 3 *v.* To soothe or calm.

sal·ver [sal′vər] *n.* A tray, as of silver.

sal·vo [sal′vō] *n., pl.* **sal·vos** or **sal·voes** 1 The firing of a number of guns at the same time to hit a target or give a salute. 2 An outburst, as of cheering: a *salvo* of applause.

SAM [sam] surface-to-air missile.

S.Am. South America.

sa·ma·ra [sam′ə·rə *or* sə·mâr′ə] *n.* A one-seeded fruit, as of a maple or elm, that has a winglike covering.

Sa·mar·i·tan [sə·mar′ə·tən] *n.* 1 A person born in or living in ancient Samaria. 2 A person like the Good Samaritan, who helps another in distress.

sa·mar·i·um [sə·mâr′ē·əm] *n.* A metallic element having several weakly radioactive isotopes, found in rare earths. ◆ See RARE-EARTH ELEMENT.

sam·ba [säm′bə] *n.* A Brazilian dance or the music for it.

same [sām] 1 *adj.* Being alike, identical, or equal in every way: Men and women should get the *same* wages for the *same* work. 2 *adj.* Being the very one or ones; identical: the *same* book I was talking about. 3 *adj.* Not different; unchanged: I haven't felt like the *same* person since I read that book. 4 *pron.* The same or identical person or thing. 5 *adv.* In like manner; equally: You must love them all the *same.* **—all the same** 1 Nevertheless; however. 2 Equally acceptable or unacceptable; of no importance: It's *all the same* to me. **—just the same** 1 Nevertheless; however. 2 Exactly alike or identical. ◆ When used as a pronoun, *same* always takes *the*: more of *the same* (not "more of same").

same·ness [sām′nis] *n.* 1 Lack of change or variety: There is a *sameness* in your writing. 2 A being alike or identical: a *sameness* in color.

S. Amer. South America.

sam·i·sen [sam′i·sen′] *n.* A Japanese guitarlike instrument, having three strings and played with a plectrum.

sa·mite [sā′mīt′ *or* sam′īt′] *n.* A rich fabric of silk often woven with gold or silver threads, used in the Middle Ages.

sa·miz·dat [sä′mēz·dät′] *n.* 1 The secret printing and distribution of writings banned by the government in the Soviet Union. 2 The writings printed and distributed in this way. ◆ *Samizdat* comes from a Russian compound word formed from the words for "self" and "publish."

Sa·mo·an [sə·mō′ən] 1 *adj.* Of or from Samoa. 2 *n.* A person born or living in Samoa. 3 *n.* The language of Samoa.

sam·o·var [sam′ə·vär′] *n.* A metal urn for heating water, as for making tea, widely used in Russia.

Samovar

Sam·o·yed [sam′ə·yed′] *n.* A strong dog with a thick, white coat, originally bred by herders in northern Russia.

sam·pan [sam′pan′] *n.* A small boat sculled with an oar or oars, having a flat bottom and sometimes a sail, used in China and Japan.

sam·ple [sam′pəl] *n., v.* **sam·pled, sam·pling** 1 *n.* A part or single piece that shows what the whole is like or is an example of quality: a *sample* of handwriting. 2 *adj. use*: a *sample* drawing. 3 *v.* To test or examine by samples: to *sample* a mince pie.

sam·pler [sam′plər] *n.* 1 A person who samples. 2 A piece of cloth covered with designs, mottoes, or words, done in fancy needlework.

sam·pling [sam′pling] *n.* 1 A small part of something or a number of items from a group chosen for examination in order to estimate the quality or nature of the whole. 2 The act or process of making such a selection.

Sam·son [sam′sən] *n.* In the Bible, a Hebrew judge of great strength.

Sam·u·el [sam′yo͞o·əl] *n.* 1 In the Bible, a Hebrew judge and prophet. 2 Either of two books of the Old Testament named for him.

sam·u·rai [sam′o͝o·rī′] *n., pl.* **sam·u·rai** 1 In the Japanese feudal system of former times, a soldier who was a member of the lower nobility. 2 A professional Japanese soldier.

san·a·to·ri·um [san′ə·tôr′ē·əm] *n., pl.* **san·a·to·ri·ums** or **san·a·to·ri·a** [san′ə·tôr′ē·ə] Another spelling of SANITARIUM.

San·cho Pan·za [san′chō pan′zə] *n.* In Cervantes' novel *Don Quixote*, the practical peasant who accompanies Don Quixote.

sanc·ti·fy [sangk′tə·fī] *v.* **sanc·ti·fied, sanc·ti·fy·ing** 1 To set apart as holy or for holy purposes; consecrate. 2 To free from sin; make holy. 3 To give approval or sanction to: a custom *sanctified* by long use. **—sanc′ti·fi·ca′tion** *n.*

sanc·ti·mo·ni·ous [sangk′tə·mō′nē·əs] *adj.* Pretending to be religious; insincerely righteous or holy. **—sanc′ti·mo′ni·ous·ly** *adv.*

sanc·tion [sangk′shən] 1 *n.* Final and official approval or confirmation of something: Does this rule have the *sanction* of the committee? 2 *v.* To approve officially; confirm; ratify: to *sanction* a new rule. 3 *v.* To permit or allow: How can you *sanction* all this noise? 4 *n.* (*usually pl.*) The steps or measures taken, usually by several nations, to force another nation to obey international law.

sanc·ti·ty [sangk′tə·tē] *n., pl.* **sanc·ti·ties** 1 Holiness; saintliness: the *sanctity* of a person's life. 2 The condition of being very sacred and solemn: the *sanctity* of a religious vow.

sanc·tu·ar·y [sangk′cho͞o·er′ē] *n., pl.* **sanc·tu·ar·ies** 1 A holy or sacred place, especially a church or the place in a church where the main altar is located. 2 A place where people or animals can find refuge and safety: a bird *sanctuary.* 3 Safety and peace: the *sanctuary* of a quiet library.

sanc·tum [sangk′təm] *n., pl.* **sanc·tums** or **sanc·ta** [sangk′tə] 1 A sacred place. 2 A private room where one is not to be disturbed.

sand [sand] 1 *n.* Particles of worn or broken rocks, larger than dust and smaller than gravel, most common in deserts and on beaches. 2 *n.* (*pl.*) Stretches of sandy beach or desert. 3 *v.* To sprinkle, cover, or fill with sand. 4 *v.* To smooth with sand or sandpaper.

san·dal [san′dəl] *n.* 1 A kind of shoe that usually consists of a sole held to the foot by straps. 2 A light, low-cut shoe with parts of the uppers cut out.

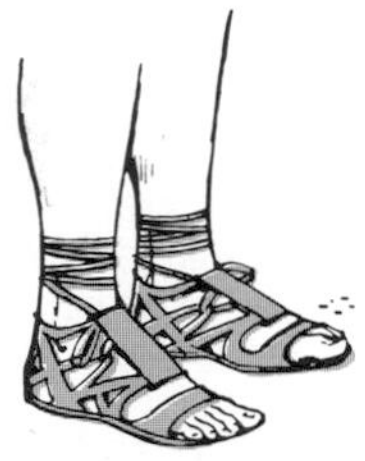
Greek sandals

san·dal·wood [san′dəl·wo͝od′] *n.* The hard, fragrant wood of certain East Indian trees. The wood is used for carvings and boxes and is burned as incense.

sand·bag [sand′bag′] *n., v.* **sand·bagged, sand·bag·ging** 1 *n.* A bag filled with sand, used as ballast in balloons or to build walls against a flood or enemy fire. 2 *v.* To fill or surround with sandbags. 3 *n.* A small bag filled with sand, used as a weapon. 4 *v.* To hit with a sandbag.

a	add	**i**	it	**o͝o**	took	**oi**	oil
ā	ace	**ī**	ice	**o͞o**	pool	**ou**	pout
â	care	**o**	odd	**u**	up	**ng**	ring
ä	palm	**ō**	open	**û**	burn	**th**	thin
e	end	**ô**	order	**yo͞o**	fuse	**t͟h**	this
ē	equal					**zh**	vision

ə = {a in *above* e in *sicken* i in *possible* / o in *melon* u in *circus*}

sand·bank [sand′bangk′] *n.* A mound, bar, or shoal made of sand.
sand·bar [sand′bär′] *n.* A ridge of sand, as in rivers or along beaches, formed by the action of currents or tides.
sand·blast [sand′blast′] 1 *n.* A fine stream of sand, propelled under steam or air pressure and used to clean, grind, or decorate hard surfaces. 2 *v.* To clean or engrave by means of a sandblast: to *sandblast* a building.
sand·box [sand′boks′] *n.* A low-walled enclosure filled with sand for children to play in.
sand dollar Any small, flat sea urchin having a circular shell.
sand·er [san′dər] *n.* A machine that smooths and polishes by means of a disk or belt of sandpaper or other rough material.
sand·lot [sand′lot′] *n.* 1 A vacant lot of the kind used by young people for unorganized sports. 2 *adj. use*: *sandlot* baseball.
sand·man [sand′man′] *n.* An imaginary person who is supposed to make children sleepy by putting sand in their eyes.
sand·pa·per [sand′pā′pər] 1 *n.* Heavy paper with sand glued on one side, used for smoothing and polishing. 2 *v.* To rub or polish with sandpaper.
sand·pi·per [sand′pī′pər] *n.* Any of certain small wading birds found in flocks on seashores.

Sandpiper

sand·stone [sand′stōn′] *n.* A rock composed mainly of sand, held together by silica, clay, and lime, used as a building material.
sand·storm [sand′stôrm′] *n.* A strong wind that blows great clouds of sand and dust before it.
sand·wich [sand′wich *or* san′·wich] 1 *n.* Two thin slices of bread with a filling, as meat or cheese, between them. 2 *v.* To place or squeeze between two objects: Our car was *sandwiched* between two large trucks. ◆ *Sandwich* is named after the fourth Earl of *Sandwich*, 1718–1792, who invented it in order to be able to eat without leaving the gambling table.
sand·y [san′dē] *adj.* **sand·i·er, sand·i·est** 1 Containing, covered with, or full of sand: a *sandy* beach. 2 Yellowish red: a *sandy* beard.
sane [sān] *adj.* **san·er, san·est** 1 Mentally healthy and sound; rational. 2 Reasonable and sensible: a *sane* rule. —**sane′ly** *adv.*
San·for·ized [san′fə·rīzd′] *adj.* Treated, as cloth, by a special process that prevents shrinking: a trademark.
sang [sang] Past tense of SING.
sang·froid [sän·frwä′] *n.* Coolness and composure, especially in tense situations. ◆ In French, *sangfroid* literally means "cold blood."
san·grí·a [sang·grē′ə] *n.* A cold drink whose ingredients include wine, fruit juice, and soda.
san·gui·nar·y [sang′gwə·ner′ē] *adj.* 1 Accompanied by bloodshed; bloody: a *sanguinary* murder. 2 Bloodthirsty.
san·guine [sang′gwin] *adj.* 1 Cheerful, confident, or hopeful; optimistic: a *sanguine* disposition. 2 Having a healthy, rosy color, as the skin; ruddy.
san·i·tar·i·um [san′ə·târ′ē·əm] *n., pl.* **san·i·tar·i·ums** or **san·i·tar·i·a** [san′ə·târ′ē·ə] A place where people having or recovering from certain illnesses, as tuberculosis, live and receive treatment.
san·i·tar·y [san′ə·ter′ē] *adj.* 1 Of or having to do with health or the preservation of health: *sanitary* measures. 2 Having or marked by great cleanliness: a *sanitary* container for food.
sanitary napkin A disposable pad worn to absorb menstrual flow.
san·i·ta·tion [san′ə·tā′shən] *n.* 1 The preservation of good health by sanitary methods and measures: Garbage disposal is a method of *sanitation.* 2 The act or result of making something sanitary.
san·i·tize [san′ə·tīz′] *v.* **san·i·tized, san·i·tiz·ing** To make sanitary, as by sterilizing.
san·i·ty [san′ə·tē] *n.* 1 The condition of having a sound, healthy mind. 2 Sensible moderation; reasonableness.
San Jo·se scale [san′hō·zā′] An insect that is destructive to various fruit trees.
sank [sangk] Past tense of SINK.
sans [sanz] *prep.* Without.
San·skrit or **San·scrit** [san′skrit′] *n.* The ancient, classical language of India, related to most European languages.
San·ta [san′tə] *n.* Santa Claus.
Santa Claus [klôz] A legendary, fat, jolly, old man with a white beard, supposed to bring presents to children at Christmas. ◆ *Santa Claus* comes from a Dutch dialect pronunciation of *Saint Nicholas*.
sap[1] [sap] *n.* 1 The juices that flow through a plant, bringing the materials necessary for growth to its cells. 2 *slang* A foolish person.
sap[2] [sap] *v.* **sapped, sap·ping** 1 To weaken by undermining: Termites can *sap* the foundation of a house. 2 To weaken or destroy gradually; impair or exhaust: Overwork *sapped* their strength.
sa·pi·ent [sā′pē·ənt] *adj.* Having great knowledge; wise. —**sa′pi·ence** *n.*
sap·ling [sap′ling] *n.* A young tree.
sap·o·dil·la [sap′ə·dil′ə] *n.* A large, tropical evergreen tree that bears brownish, edible fruit and has sap that yields chicle.
sa·pon·i·fy [sə·pon′ə·fī] *v.* **sa·pon·i·fied, sa·pon·i·fy·ing** To break up (a fat or oil) with an alkali to form a soap or glycerin. —**sa·pon·i·fi·ca·tion** [sə·pon′ə·fə·kā′shən] *n.*
sap·phire [saf′īr] 1 *n.* A valuable gem having a clear, deep blue color. 2 *adj., n.* Deep blue.
sap·py [sap′ē] *adj.* **sap·pi·er, sap·pi·est** 1 Full of sap; juicy. 2 *slang* Childish; silly.
sap·ro·phyte [sap′rə·fīt′] *n.* A plant that lives on dead or decaying organic matter, as certain bacteria or fungi.
sap·suck·er [sap′suk′ər] *n.* Any of several small black and white woodpeckers that damage orchard trees by drinking the sap.

Sapsucker

sap·wood [sap′wo͝od′] *n.* The moist, usually whitish wood that grows just under the bark of a tree and is the main conductor of sap.
Sar·a·cen [sar′ə·sən] *n.* 1 A Muslim, especially one during the Crusades. 2 Any Arab.
Sar·ah [sâr′ə] *n.* In the Bible, the mother of Isaac and the wife of Abraham.
sa·ran [sə·ran′] *n.* A plastic resin used in making a transparent wrapping material, fibers, pipes, and bristles.

sa·ra·pe [sə·rä′pē] *n.* Another spelling of SERAPE.

sar·casm [sär′kaz′əm] *n.* 1 A cutting, unpleasant remark that mocks or makes fun of something or someone. 2 The use of cutting or mocking language.

sar·cas·tic [sär·kas′tik] *adj.* 1 Mocking; taunting: a *sarcastic* smile. 2 Using sarcasm: a *sarcastic* person.

sar·co·ma [sär·kō′mə] *n., pl.* **sar·co·mas** or **sar·co·ma·ta** [sär·kō′mə·tə] A malignant tumor originating in connective tissue.

sar·coph·a·gus [sär·kof′ə·gəs] *n., pl.* **sar·coph·a·gus·es** or **sar·coph·a·gi** [sär·kof′ə·jī] A decorated stone coffin, usually placed in open view or in a large tomb.

Sarcophagus

sar·dine [sär·dēn′] *n.* A small, edible fish like the herring, commonly canned in oil.

sar·don·ic [sär·don′ik] *adj.* Bitterly scornful; mocking. —**sar·don′i·cal·ly** *adv.*

sar·gas·so [sär·gas′ō] *n.* An olive-brown seaweed with small air bladders on the stalks, found floating in great masses in warm seas.

sa·ri [sä′rē] *n., pl.* **sa·ris** A garment worn by the women of India and Pakistan. It consists of a long piece of cotton or silk cloth worn wound about the body, one end falling to the feet and the other crossed over the shoulder and sometimes over the head.

Sari

sa·rong [sə·rong′] *n.* A skirtlike garment of colored silk or cotton, worn by both sexes in Indonesia, Malaysia, and elsewhere.

sar·sa·pa·ril·la [sas′pə·ril′ə *or* sär′sə·pə·ril′ə] *n.* 1 The dried root of a tropical American plant of the lily family, used to flavor medicine and soft drinks. 2 A soft drink, flavored with this root.

sar·to·ri·al [sär·tôr′ē·əl] *adj.* 1 Having to do with a tailor or a tailor's work. 2 Having to do with clothes: *sartorial* splendor.

sash[1] [sash] *n., pl.* **sash·es** or **sash** A frame, as of a window, in which glass is set.

sash[2] [sash] *n.* A band, ribbon, or scarf worn around the waist or over the shoulder, often as part of a uniform or as a badge of honor.

sa·shay [sa·shā′] *v. informal* To walk in a swaggering or conspicuous way; strut.

Sask. Saskatchewan.

sass [sas] *informal* 1 *n.* Disrespectful speech; back talk. 2 *v.* To talk disrespectfully to.

sas·sa·fras [sas′ə·fras′] *n.* 1 A tall North American tree related to the laurel and having yellow flowers. 2 Its dried root, whose bark is used as a flavoring in candy and in medicine.

sas·sy [sas′ē] *adj.* **sas·si·er, sas·si·est** *informal* Saucy and impudent; impertinent: a *sassy* answer.

sat [sat] Past tense and past participle of SIT.

Sat. Saturday.

SAT Scholastic Aptitude Test.

Sa·tan [sā′tən] *n.* In the Bible, the Devil.

sa·tan·ic [sə·tan′ik] *adj.* 1 Of or having to do with Satan. 2 Very wicked; evil; fiendish.

satch·el [sach′əl] *n.* A small bag or case.

sate [sāt] *v.* **sat·ed, sat·ing** 1 To satisfy (a desire or appetite) completely. 2 To supply enough to fill too full or disgust; glut.

sa·teen [sa·tēn′] *n.* A cotton cloth woven so that it has a shiny look like satin.

sat·el·lite [sat′ə·līt′] *n.* 1 A celestial body that revolves in an orbit around a larger celestial body: The moon is a *satellite* of the earth. 2 An object launched by means of a rocket into an orbit around the earth or other celestial body. 3 A small nation that is controlled by and depends upon a greater, more powerful one. 4 A person who follows or copies someone more important.

sa·tia·ble [sā′shə·bəl] *adj.* Capable of being satisfied.

sa·ti·ate [sā′shē·āt′] *v.* **sa·ti·at·ed, sa·ti·at·ing** 1 To satisfy completely the appetite or desire of: The good dinner *satiated* us. 2 To make sick, disgusted, or annoyed, by giving or being given too much of something: The star was *satiated* by all the noise and the cheering crowds.

sa·ti·e·ty [sə·tī′ə·tē] *n.* The condition or feeling of having had too much of something.

sat·in [sat′ən] 1 *n.* A silk, cotton, rayon, or acetate fabric with a smooth glossy finish on one side. 2 *adj.* Of or like satin.

sat·in·wood [sat′(ə)n·wŏŏd′] *n.* 1 An East Asian tree having glossy, light brown wood used for veneers. 2 The wood of this or a similar tree.

sat·in·y [sat′(ə)n·ē] *adj.* Looking or feeling like satin; glossy and smooth.

sat·ire [sat′īr] *n.* 1 Sarcasm, irony, or humor used to expose and attack or ridicule human folly or vice. 2 A written composition that attacks folly or vice in this way.

sa·tir·ic [sə·tir′ik] *adj.* Satirical.

sa·tir·i·cal [sə·tir′i·kəl] *adj.* 1 Of, like, having, or using satire: a *satirical* writer. 2 Sarcastic: a *satirical* smile. —**sa·tir′i·cal·ly** *adv.*

sat·i·rist [sat′ə·rist] *n.* A person who writes or uses satire.

sat·i·rize [sat′ə·rīz′] *v.* **sat·i·rized, sat·i·riz·ing** To attack and make ridiculous by means of satire; criticize by means of mockery: to *satirize* the foolishness of humanity.

sat·is·fac·tion [sat′is·fak′shən] *n.* 1 The act of satisfying. 2 The condition of being satisfied. 3 Something that satisfies: It was a great *satisfaction* to win the race. 4 A making up for damage, a hurt, or injury, as by a payment: As *satisfaction*, the statesman demanded the newspaper print a complete retraction of the story. —**give satisfaction** 1 To satisfy. 2 To fight a duel with a person one has insulted.

a	add	**i**	it	**ŏŏ**	took	**oi**	oil
ā	ace	**ī**	ice	**ōō**	pool	**ou**	pout
â	care	**o**	odd	**u**	up	**ng**	ring
ä	palm	**ō**	open	**û**	burn	**th**	thin
e	end	**ô**	order	**yōō**	fuse	**th̸**	this
ē	equal					**zh**	vision

ə = a in *above*, e in *sicken*, i in *possible*, o in *melon*, u in *circus*

S

sat·is·fac·to·ry [sat′is·fak′tər·ē] *adj.* Giving satisfaction; good enough to meet needs or expectations. **—sat′is·fac′to·ri·ly** *adv.*

sat·is·fy [sat′is·fī] *v.* **sat·is·fied, sat·is·fy·ing** 1 To supply fully with what is wanted, expected, or needed: The meal *satisfied* them. 2 To free from doubt or worry; convince: The telegram *satisfied* us that they had arrived safely. 3 To give what is due to; pay, as a debt: The firm *satisfied* its creditors. 4 To fill the conditions or requirements of, as an equation.

sa·trap [sā′trap′ *or* sat′rap′] *n.* 1 In ancient Persia, a governor of a province. 2 Any minor, and often tyrannical, ruler.

sat·u·rate [sach′ə·rāt′] *v.* **sat·u·rat·ed, sat·u·rat·ing** 1 To soak thoroughly or fill completely: The rain *saturated* the soil. 2 To cause to absorb something, as a substance or influence, to the point where further additions cannot be taken in: to *saturate* a solution with salt; to *saturate* a people with propaganda.

sat·u·rat·ed [sach′ə·rā′tid] *adj.* 1 Incapable of holding or absorbing more of a substance or influence. 2 As pure as possible and containing no white: said about a color. 3 Fully soaked.

saturated fat Fat containing molecules that do not unite easily with other compounds. The solid fat in animal foods is saturated fat.

sat·u·ra·tion [sach′ə·rā′shən] *n.* 1 The act of saturating. 2 The condition of being saturated. 3 The degree of vividness or purity in a color, the less white in it, the more saturation.

Sat·ur·day [sat′ər·dē *or* sat′ər·dā′] *n.* The seventh day of the week.

Sat·urn [sat′ərn] *n.* 1 In Roman myths, the god of agriculture. 2 A planet of the solar system, second largest in size and sixth in distance from the sun.

sat·ur·na·li·a [sat′ər·nā′lē·ə] *n.pl.* 1 (*written* **Saturnalia**) In ancient Rome, a feast of Saturn held in December to celebrate the winter solstice. 2 Any season or period for wild parties and riotous revelry.

sat·ur·nine [sat′ər·nīn′] *adj.* Having a serious, often gloomy disposition or character.

sat·yr [sat′ər *or* sā′tər] *n.* In Greek myths, a minor woodland god, having a human form but pointed ears, goat's legs, and budding horns.

sauce [sôs] *n., v.* **sauced, sauc·ing** 1 *n.* A soft or liquid mixture, as a dressing or relish, served with food to add flavor. 2 *v.* To serve with or cook in a sauce: to *sauce* a fish. 3 *v.* To flavor or season, as with sauce. 4 *n.* A dish of fruit pulp stewed and sweetened: cranberry *sauce.* 5 *n. informal* Impudence. 6 *v. informal* To be saucy to.

sauce·pan [sôs′pan′] *n.* A metal or glass pot with a handle, used for cooking food.

sau·cer [sô′sər] *n.* 1 A small, round, shallow dish for holding a cup. 2 Something shaped like a saucer: a flying *saucer.*

sau·cy [sô′sē] *adj.* **sau·ci·er, sau·ci·est** 1 Too bold; impudent. 2 Lively with a dash of daring; pert: *saucy* wit. **—sau′ci·ness** *n.*

Saudi Arabian 1 Of or from Saudi Arabia. 2 A person born in or a citizen of Saudi Arabia.

sauer·bra·ten [sour′brät′·(ə)n] *n.* Beef that has been marinated in vinegar and spices before being cooked. ◆ *Sauerbraten* comes from two German words meaning *sour* and *to roast.*

sauer·kraut [sour′krout′] *n.* Shredded and salted cabbage fermented in its own juice.

Sauk [sôk] *n., pl.* **Sauk** or **Sauks** 1 A tribe of North American Indians once living in Michigan, Wisconsin, and Illinois, now in Iowa and Oklahoma. 2 A member of this tribe. 3 The language of this tribe.

Saul [sôl] *n.* In the Bible, the first king of Israel.

sau·na [sou′nə *or* sô′nə] *n.* 1 A bath taken in a closed, very hot room, usually with steam created by pouring water on heated stones. 2 A room for taking such a bath. 3 A bath taken in dry hot air. 4 A room or cabinet for taking such a bath.

saun·ter [sôn′tər] 1 *v.* To walk along in a slow, casual way; stroll. 2 *n.* A casual walk.

A gecko is a saurian.

sau·ri·an [sôr′ē·ən] *n.* Any of a group of reptiles with scaly bodies and usually with four limbs. This group is now restricted mainly to the lizards.

sau·sage [sô′sij] *n.* Finely chopped and highly seasoned meat, usually packed into a thin tube or skin, often of prepared animal intestine.

sau·té [sō·tā′] *v.* **sau·téed** [sō·tād′], **sau·té·ing** [sō·tā′·ing], *adj.* 1 *n.* To fry quickly in a little fat: to *sauté* onions. 2 *adj.* Fried quickly in this manner.

sau·terne [sō·tûrn′] *n.* A sweet white wine.

sav·age [sav′ij] 1 *adj.* Wild, untamed, and often fierce: *savage* beasts. 2 *adj.* Living in a wild condition; not civilized: *savage* tribes. 3 *n.* A person living in a wild or primitive condition. 4 *adj.* Cruel, vicious, and violent: a *savage* attack. 5 *n.* A brutal, fierce, or vicious person or animal. **—sav′age·ly** *adv.* **—sav′age·ness** *n.*

sav·age·ry [sav′ij·rē] *n., pl.* **sav·age·ries** 1 A savage or cruel quality. 2 A cruel, violent act. 3 A wild or savage condition.

sa·van·na or **sa·van·nah** [sə·van′ə] *n.* A grassy plain with few or no trees.

sa·vant [sə·vänt′ *or* sav′ənt] *n.* A learned person.

save[1] [sāv] *v.* **saved, sav·ing** 1 To rescue or preserve from danger, harm, or loss: to *save* a person from death; to *save* a life. 2 To free or deliver from sin or evil; redeem. 3 To keep from becoming tired, hurt, or damaged: *Save* your eyes by reading in a good light. 4 To prevent or spare: Your going *saves* us from having to go. 5 To keep from being spent, lost, or wasted: to *save* money, time, or energy. 6 To avoid expense, waste, or loss: You can *save* on clothes by making your own. 7 To set aside or reserve (as money) for future use: to *save* ten dollars each week; *Save* my seat. **—sav′er** *n.*

save[2] [sāv] *prep.* Except; but: They agree on every issue *save* one.

sav·ing [sā′ving] 1 *n.* Preservation from loss or danger. 2 *adj.* That saves, preserves, or rescues: The kitten's *saving* grace is its cuteness; a labor-*saving* device. 3 *n.* A reduction, as of effort, time, or waste: a *saving* of two hours. 4 *n.* A reduction of money spent: a *saving* of 10%. 5 *adj.* Avoiding needless waste; economical. 6 *n.* (*pl.*) Money saved and set aside for the future. 7 *prep.* With due respect for: *Saving* your presence, I must say what I think.

savings bank A bank that receives and pays interest on money that people deposit into it.

sav·ior [sāv′yər] *n.* 1 A person who saves, as from danger. 2 (*written* **Savior**) The Saviour.
Sav·iour [sāv′yər] *n.* 1 Jesus Christ. 2 (*written* **saviour**) A savior.
sa·vor [sā′vər] 1 *n.* The taste, smell, or flavor of something: the *savor* of roast beef. 2 *v.* To taste or experience with pleasure; relish. 3 *n.* A quality that is typical or that gives relish: My grandparents have continued to enjoy the *savor* of life. 4 *v.* To have a particular flavor or characteristic: The winner's speech *savored* of pride. 5 *v.* To give flavor to; season.
sa·vor·y[1] [sā′vər·ē] *adj.* 1 Pleasing to the sense of taste or smell: a *savory* meal. 2 Wholesome or respectable: a *savory* character.
sa·vor·y[2] [sā′vər·ē] *n., pl.* **sa·vor·ies** A fragrant herb related to mint, used for seasoning.
sav·vy [sav′ē] *n., v.* **sav·vied, sav·vy·ing** *slang* 1 *n.* Practical knowledge or understanding; know-how. 2 *v.* To understand.
saw[1] [sô] *n., v.* **sawed, sawed** or **sawn, saw·ing** 1 *n.* A tool used to cut, having a thin, flat blade with pointed teeth along or around its edge. 2 *n.* A machine for operating this tool. 3 *v.* To cut or be cut with a saw: to *saw* logs; This wood *saws* easily. 4 *v.* To fashion with a saw: to *saw* planks. 5 *v.* To cut or slice with the arms as if using a saw: to *saw* the air.
saw[2] [sô] *n.* A familiar saying; proverb. "All that glitters is not gold" is a saw.
saw[3] [sô] Past tense of SEE[1]: I *saw* you!
saw·buck [sô′buk′] *n.* 1 A frame with X-shaped ends for holding wood being sawed. 2 *slang* A ten-dollar bill.
saw·dust [sô′dust′] *n.* Fine, dustlike bits of wood that separate from wood when it is sawed.
saw·fish [sô′fish′] *n., pl.* **saw·fish** or **saw·fish·es** A large fish of warm seas having a long, flat snout with teeth along both sides.
saw·horse [sô′hôrs′] *n.* A frame on four legs, often one of a pair, used to hold wood being sawed.

Sawhorses

saw·mill [sô′mil′] *n.* A place where logs are sawed up by machines into planks or boards.
sawn [sôn] An alternative past participle of SAW[1].
saw·yer [sô′yər] *n.* A person who saws wood for a living, as in lumbering or in a sawmill.
sax [saks] *n. informal* A saxophone.
sax·i·frage [sak′sə·frij] *n.* Any of various plants found in rocky places and bearing clusters of white, pink, purple, or yellow flowers.
Sax·on [sak′sən] 1 *n.* A member or descendant of an old Germanic tribe. Groups of Saxons invaded England in the 5th and 6th centuries. 2 *adj.* Of or having to do with these people. 3 *n.* An Anglo-Saxon. 4 *adj.* Anglo-Saxon.

Saxophone

sax·o·phone [sak′sə·fōn′] *n.* A wind instrument having a single-reed mouthpiece, a conical metal body, and finger keys. **—sax′o·phon′ist** *n.*
say [sā] *v.* **said** [sed], **say·ing**, *n.* 1 *v.* To pronounce or utter; speak: "Yes," I *said.* 2 *n.* Right or turn to speak: Each student had a *say.* 3 *v.* To express in words; tell; state: The sign *says* "No parking." 4 *n.* An opinion or belief: What is your *say* in this matter? 5 *v.* To state positively or as an opinion: *Say* which you prefer. 6 *n.* The right to decide; authority: Our teacher has the final *say.* 7 *v.* To repeat or recite: to *say* one's prayers. 8 *v.* To suppose or assume: The basketball player is over six feet tall, I'd *say.* 9 *adv.* Approximately; about: to work for, *say*, an hour. 10 *adv.* For example: a great play, *say* "Hamlet." **—go without saying** To be so well understood that no discussion is needed. **—that is to say** In other words.
say·ing [sā′ing] *n.* 1 A phrase or proverb much repeated: as the *saying* goes. 2 Anything said.
says [sez] *v.* The third person singular form of SAY, in the present tense, used with *he, she, it,* and singular nouns: She *says* that she will go; The newspaper *says* that it will rain.
say-so [sā′sō′] *n., pl.* **say-sos** *informal* 1 An unsupported assertion that something is so: They won't believe this on my *say-so* alone. 2 The right or authority to make a decision: She listens to her advisers, but has the final *say-so* on policy.
Sb The symbol for the element antimony. ◆ The Latin word for antimony is *stibium.*
S.B. Bachelor of Science.
SBA Small Business Administration.
SbE south by east.
SbW south by west.
sc. 1 scale. 2 scene.
Sc The symbol for the element scandium.
Sc. 1 Scot. 2 Scotch. 3 Scotland. 4 Scottish.
SC 1 Postal Service abbreviation of South Carolina. 2 Security Council (United Nations).
S.C. 1 Signal Corps. 2 South Carolina. 3 Supreme Court.
scab [skab] *n., v.* **scabbed, scab·bing** 1 *n.* A crust that forms over a healing wound or sore. 2 *v.* To become covered with a scab. 3 *n.* A skin disease like mange that affects sheep. 4 *n.* A disease causing crustlike spots on plants. 5 *n. informal* A worker who takes the job of another worker who is on strike. 6 *v. informal* To act as a scab. **—scab′by** *adj.*
scab·bard [skab′ərd] *n.* A case or sheath to protect the blade of a weapon, as a sword or bayonet.

A scimitar and scabbard

sca·bies [skā′bēz′] *n.* A contagious skin ailment caused by tiny mites that get in and live as parasites under the skin. They cause intense itching.
scads [skadz] *n.pl. informal* A very large amount; lots.

S

a	add	**i**	it	**o͝o**	took	**oi**	oil
ā	ace	**ī**	ice	**o͞o**	pool	**ou**	pout
â	care	**o**	odd	**u**	up	**ng**	ring
ä	palm	**ō**	open	**û**	burn	**th**	thin
e	end	**ô**	order	**yo͞o**	fuse	**t͟h**	this
ē	equal					**zh**	vision

ə = {a in *above* e in *sicken* i in *possible* / o in *melon* u in *circus*}

scaf·fold [skaf′əld *or* skaf′ōld′] *n.* 1 A temporary structure put up to support workers and materials above the ground, as in building. 2 A raised platform for the hanging or beheading of criminals. 3 Any raised framework.

Scaffold

scaf·fold·ing [skaf′əl·ding] *n.* 1 A scaffold or system of scaffolds for workers. 2 Materials for making scaffolds. 3 Any framework.

scal·a·wag [skal′ə·wag′] *n.* 1 A native Southern white Republican just after the Civil War: a contemptuous term. 2 *informal* A worthless person; scamp.

scald [skôld] 1 *v.* To burn with hot liquid or steam: to *scald* one's arm. 2 *n.* A burn made in this way. 3 *v.* To cleanse or treat with boiling water: to *scald* cups. 4 *v.* To heat (a liquid, as milk) almost to the boiling point.

scale[1] [skāl] *n., v.* **scaled, scal·ing** 1 *n.* One of the thin, flat, usually overlapping plates of horny tissue that form a protective cover on the bodies of fishes and reptiles. 2 *n.* A thin part, piece, or layer like this: *scales* of paint. 3 *v.* To strip or clear of scales or a layer of scale: to *scale* fish. 4 *v.* To come off in scales. 5 *n.* A scale insect.

scale[2] [skāl] *n., v.* **scaled, scal·ing** 1 *n.* (*often pl.*) A balance or other device for weighing things: Are your *scales* accurate? 2 *v.* To weigh: The package *scaled* 15 pounds. 3 *n.* One of the two shallow pans, scoops, or cups for holding objects to be weighed in a balance. **—tip the scales** 1 To weigh: With full equipment, the firefighter *tips the scales* at 220 lbs. 2 To be a deciding factor: Her experience *tips the scales* in her favor. **—turn the scales** To determine or decide.

Scales

scale[3] [skāl] *n., v.* **scaled, scal·ing** 1 *n.* A series of lines and marks placed at regular intervals on an instrument for measuring various quantities or amounts: the *scale* on a yardstick. 2 *n.* Any system of such graduated lines or marks adapted for a special purpose: the Fahrenheit *scale*; a logarithmic *scale*. 3 *n.* A classification or scheme of different levels, ranks, or grades: a wage *scale*; the social *scale*. 4 *v.* To adjust according to a scale: to *scale* down expenses. 5 *n.* In music, a series of tones going up or down in order through the interval of an octave. 6 *v.* To go up, as by climbing a ladder: to *scale* a high wall. 7 *n.* A fixed proportion between the different parts of a map, model, or drawing, and the corresponding parts of what they represent: According to the *scale* of this map, one inch represents one mile. 8 *n.* Relative extent, size, or degree: We are in business on a small *scale*. 9 *n.* A system of writing numbers in terms of a base: the decimal *scale*.

scale insect Any of various small insects that feed on plants. The females are usually covered by a waxy, scalelike shield.

sca·lene [skā′lēn′ *or* skā·lēn′] *adj.* Having no two sides equal: a *scalene* triangle.

scal·lion [skal′yən] *n.* An onion having a long neck and a narrow bulb, as a young green onion.

scal·lop [skol′əp *or* skal′əp] 1 *n.* A small, soft-bodied sea animal with two shells ribbed in a fan pattern and hinged at the back and a strong muscle that is good to eat. 2 *n.* One of a series of semicircular curves along an edge, as for ornament. 3 *v.* To shape the edge of with scallops. 4 *v.* To bake in a casserole with bread crumbs and a sauce.

scalp [skalp] 1 *n.* The skin of the top and back of the head, usually covered with hair. 2 *n.* A part of this, formerly cut or torn away as a war trophy among certain North American Indians. 3 *v.* To cut or tear the scalp from.

scal·pel [skal′pəl] *n.* A small, pointed knife with a very sharp, thin blade, used in surgery.

scal·y [skā′lē] *adj.* **scal·i·er, scal·i·est** 1 Having a covering of scales: a *scaly* fish. 2 Scalelike. 3 Flaky, as stone.

scaly anteater Another name for PANGOLIN.

scam [skam] *n. slang* A fraud or swindle.

scamp[1] [skamp] *n.* A tricky, mischievous rascal.

scamp[2] [skamp] *v.* To perform (work) carelessly.

scam·per [skam′pər] 1 *v.* To run quickly or hastily. 2 *n.* A hurried run or departure.

scan [skan] *v.* **scanned, scan·ning,** *n.* 1 *v.* To pass the eyes over quickly: He *scanned* the newspaper to find the story. 2 *v.* To look or examine closely and carefully: The detective *scanned* every shred of evidence. 3 *v.* To separate (lines of verse) into rhythmic feet, as: "Thĕre wās/ăn ŏld wō/măn whŏ līved/ĭn ă shōe." 4 *v.* To sweep over (an object) with a moving camera or with a beam of light, electrons, X rays, or the like, so as to obtain multiple images that are then intergrated electronically. 5 *n.* An integrated image produced by scanning.

scan·dal [skan′dəl] *n.* 1 A shameful or shocking act or condition. 2 A person whose conduct is shocking. 3 Disgrace and shame resulting from bad conduct. 4 Gossip or reports that damage a person's reputation.

scan·dal·ize [skan′dəl·īz′] *v.* **scan·dal·ized, scan·dal·iz·ing** To shock or offend, as by conduct that is wrong or improper.

scan·dal·mong·er [skan′dəl·mung′gər] *n.* A person who spreads scandal and gossip.

scan·dal·ous [skan′dəl·əs] *adj.* 1 Causing scandal; disgraceful; shocking: *scandalous* conduct. 2 Spreading harmful gossip or scandal: *scandalous* reports. **—scan′dal·ous·ly** *adv.*

Scan·di·na·vi·an [skan′də·nā′vē·ən] 1 *adj.* Of or from Scandinavia. 2 *n.* A person born or living in Scandinavia. 3 *n.* A group of languages spoken in Scandinavia, including Danish, Icelandic, Norwegian, and Swedish.

scan·di·um [skan′dē·əm] *n.* A metallic element found in rare earths and differing from other rare-earth elements in having a much lower atomic weight. ◆ See RARE-EARTH ELEMENT.

scan·ner [skan′ər] *n.* 1 A person or thing that scans. 2 A device that sweeps a beam of radiation over a surface in order to search, map, or depict it. 3 A device for obtaining information to be stored, processed, or transmitted.

scan·sion [skan′shən] *n.* The division of lines of verse into feet; scanning of poetry.

scant [skant] 1 *adj.* Not quite sufficient or enough; meager: *scant* provisions. 2 *v.* To limit or restrict: Don't *scant* the family's food. 3 *adj.* Just short of the measure needed or mentioned: a *scant* two weeks. **—scant of** Without enough: We were *scant of* breath.

scant·y [skan′tē] *adj.* **scant·i·er, scant·i·est** 1 Not quite sufficient or barely enough; meager: a *scanty* supply. **2** Too small, as in size: a *scanty* curtain. **—scant′i·ly** *adv.* **—scant′i·ness** *n.*

scape·goat [skāp′gōt′] *n.* A person, group, or animal made to bear the blame for the sins or errors of others.

scape·grace [skāp′grās′] *n.* A rascal; scamp.

scap·u·la [skap′yə·lə] *n., pl.* **scap·u·las** or **scap·u·lae** [skap′yə·lē] The shoulder blade.

scar [skär] *n., v.* **scarred, scar·ring** **1** *n.* The mark left on the skin after the healing of a wound, burn, or sore. **2** *n.* A mark like this, as a scraped or scuffed place on furniture. **3** *v.* To mark or become marked with a scar. **4** *n.* The mental effect left by a painful experience.

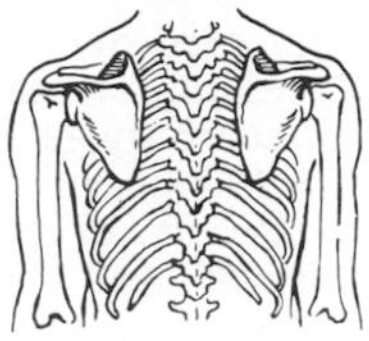
Scapulas

scar·ab [skar′əb] *n.* **1** A large black beetle considered sacred by the ancient Egyptians. **2** A charm or ornament representing this beetle.

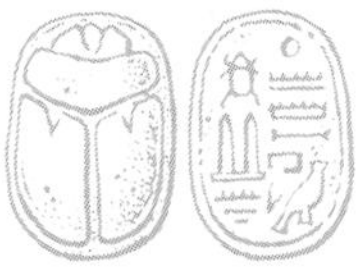
Scarab

scarce [skârs] *adj.* **scarc·er, scarc·est** Hard to find or get; not common; not plentiful: Coins were *scarce* last year. **—make oneself scarce** *informal* To go away or stay away. **—scarce′·ness** *n.*

scarce·ly [skârs′lē] *adv.* **1** Only just; barely: He *scarcely* felt the rain. **2** Surely not; hardly: You can *scarcely* ask us to accept that argument. ◆ See HARDLY.

scar·ci·ty [skâr′sə·tē] *n., pl.* **scar·ci·ties** The condition of being scarce; shortage; lack.

scare [skâr] *v.* **scared, scar·ing,** *n.* **1** *v.* To frighten or take fright: Ghost stories *scare* the children; Do you *scare* easily? **2** *n.* A feeling of alarm; sudden fright: You gave us a *scare.* **3** *v.* To get rid of by frightening: Our dog *scared* the stranger away. **—scare up** *informal* To get together in a hurry: to *scare up* a meal.

scare·crow [skâr′krō′] *n.* A crude image of a person, dressed in old clothes and propped up in a field to frighten birds away from crops.

Scarecrow

scare·mon·ger [skâr′mong′gər] *n.* A person who spreads alarming rumors.

scarf [skärf] *n., pl.* **scarfs** or **scarves** [skärvz] **1** A band or square of cloth worn about the head, neck, or shoulders for warmth or adornment. **2** A long strip of cloth used as a covering, as for tables or dressers.

scar·i·fy [skar′ə·fī′ *or* sker′ə·fī′] *v.* **scar·i·fied, scar·i·fy·ing** **1** To make shallow cuts in; scratch. **2** To criticize harshly or destructively. **3** To loosen or break up (topsoil).

scar·let [skär′lit] **1** *n., adj.* Brilliant red with a tinge of orange. **2** *n.* Cloth of this color.

scarlet fever A contagious disease chiefly affecting young people, marked by a sore throat, fever, and a scarlet rash.

scarlet tanager A North American bird, the male of which has brilliant red plumage with black wings and tail.

scarp [skärp] **1** *n.* A steep slope. **2** *v.* To cut to a steep slope. **3** *n.* The steep inside of a ditch surrounding a fortification.

scar·y [skâr′ē] *adj.* **scar·i·er, scar·i·est** *informal* **1** Easily frightened; timid: a *scary* child. **2** Causing fright.

scat[1] [skat] *v.* **scat·ted, scat·ting** To move or go away quickly.

scat[2] [skat] *n., v.* **scat·ted, scat·ting** **1** *n.* In jazz, improvised, meaningless syllables sung to a melody, usually with an instrumental accompaniment. **2** *v.* To sing scat.

scath·ing [skā′thing] *adj.* Painfully severe or bitter: *scathing* criticism. **—scath′ing·ly** *adv.*

scat·ter [skat′ər] **1** *v.* To throw about in various places; sprinkle: to *scatter* seed over a garden patch. **2** *n.* A scattering or sprinkling. **3** *v.* To go or drive away in different directions: to *scatter* enemy troops; The audience *scattered* for cover during the thunderstorm.

scat·ter·brained [skat′ər·brānd′] *adj.* Unable to think in an orderly way; flighty; giddy.

scat·ter·ing [skat′ər·ing] **1** *n.* A small number or amount spread out here and there: a *scattering* of votes. **2** *adj.* Spread out or coming at intervals: *scattering* drops of rain.

scatter rug A small rug used to cover only part of a floor.

scav·enge [skav′ənj] *v.* **scav·enged, scav·eng·ing** **1** To feed on dead things. **2** To search through (discarded material) for things to use, eat, or sell. **2** To find (something useful) while searching through discarded material.

scav·en·ger [skav′in·jər] *n.* **1** An animal that feeds on dead things, as the buzzard. **2** A person who searches through refuse or garbage for things that can be used or sold. **3** A street cleaner.

sce·nar·i·o [si·nâr′ē·ō *or* si·nä′rē·ō] *n., pl.* **sce·nar·i·os** Another word for SCREENPLAY.

sce·nar·ist [si·nâr′ist *or* si·när′ist] *n.* A person who writes screenplays; screenwriter.

scene [sēn] *n.* **1** A certain place and everything in it, as presented to view: a charming country *scene.* **2** The place in which an event occurs: the *scene* of the crime. **3** The place and time in which a play, story, motion picture, or the like, is set: The *scene* is London in 1944. **4** The scenery used to set the stage to represent a place, as in a play or motion picture: The *scene* represents a doctor's office. **5** A section of a play or motion picture, especially a division of an act: Act II, *scene* i. **6** A certain incident or event, as in a play or story: the rescue *scene.* **7** A show of anger or other embarrassing behavior: Don't make a *scene* in public. **—behind the scenes** **1** Out of sight backstage. **2** In secret. ◆ *Scene,* which comes from a Greek word meaning *tent* or *stage,* has broadened in meaning throughout the years. Now it often refers to actual places and events as well as to stage settings.

scen·er·y [sē′nər·ē] *n.* **1** The visible natural features of an outdoor area: woodland *scenery.* **2** The

a	add	**i**	it	**o͝o**	took	**oi**	oil
ā	ace	**ī**	ice	**o͞o**	pool	**ou**	pout
â	care	**o**	odd	**u**	up	**ng**	ring
ä	palm	**ō**	open	**û**	burn	**th**	thin
e	end	**ô**	order	**yo͞o**	fuse	**t͟h**	this
ē	equal					**zh**	vision

ə = { a in *above* e in *sicken* i in *possible* / o in *melon* u in *circus* }

painted backdrops and hangings that are used on a stage to represent various places or scenes.

sce·nic [sē′nik *or* sen′ik] *adj.* 1 Of or having to do with outdoor scenery: the *scenic* marvels of the Alps. 2 Having lovely or striking scenery: *scenic* areas. 3 Of stage scenery or lighting: the *scenic* effects of a play.

scent [sent] 1 *n.* An odor or smell, especially if pleasant: the *scent* of lilacs. 2 *n.* Perfume: to wear *scent.* 3 *v.* To make fragrant; perfume. 4 *n.* The sense of smell. 5 *n.* An odor by which a person or animal can be tracked: Bloodhounds picked up the missing child's *scent.* 6 *v.* To smell: The dogs *scented* a deer. 7 *n.* A trail or track leading to something sought: We are on the right *scent.* 8 *v.* To form a suspicion of: to *scent* a plot.

scep·ter [sep′tər] *n.* A staff or wand carried by a ruler as a sign of royal power.

Scepter

scep·tic [skep′tik] *n.* Another spelling of SKEPTIC.

scep·ti·cal [skep′ti·kəl] *adj.* Another spelling of SKEPTICAL.

scep·ti·cism [skep′tə·siz′əm] *n.* Another spelling of SKEPTICISM.

sch. or **Sch.** school.

sched·ule [skej′o͞ol] *n., v.* **sched·uled, sched·ul·ing** 1 *n.* A plan or program, as of things to be done: The touring company has a full *schedule.* 2 *n.* A list of the times when certain things are to take place; timetable: a TV *schedule.* 3 *n.* The time agreed upon in a plan: to be behind *schedule.* 4 *n.* A written or printed list giving details: a *schedule* of prices. 5 *v.* To place in or on a schedule: to *schedule* a meeting for 2:00 P.M. 6 *v.* To make a schedule of: In order not to waste time, you ought to *schedule* your work.

sche·mat·ic [skē·mat′ik] *adj.* Of, having to do with, or being a scheme or rough design: *schematic* drawings.

sche·ma·tize [skē′mə·tīz′] *v.* **sche·ma·tized, sche·ma·tiz·ing** 1 To form in or into a scheme; arrange systematically. 2 To represent in a scheme; diagram.

scheme [skēm] *n., v.* **schemed, schem·ing** 1 *n.* A plan or plot, especially if secret and sly or impractical: wicked or mad *schemes.* 2 *v.* To plan or plot, often secretly and slyly: The embezzler *schemed* to get the money. 3 *n.* An arrangement of something according to a plan or design: a color *scheme.* —**schem′er** *n.*

scher·zo [sker′tsō] *n., pl.* **scher·zos** or **scher·zi** [sker′·tsē] In music, a quick, playful movement, as of a sonata or symphony.

Schick test [shik] A test to find out if a person is susceptible to diphtheria, in which a small amount of diphtheria toxin is injected under the skin. ◆ The test was named for Béla Schick (1877-1967), a Hungarian-born U.S. pediatrician who developed it.

schism [siz′əm] *n.* A division into groups that are opposed to each other, especially a division within a church caused by disagreement in matters of belief.

schis·mat·ic [siz·mat′ik] 1 *adj.* Like, having to do with, or causing schism. 2 *n.* A person who brings about or takes part in a schism.

schist [shist] *n.* A rock, containing mica, that splits easily into flat layers.

schiz·oid [skit′soid′] 1 *adj.* Of, suffering from, or characteristic of schizophrenia. 2 *n.* A schizophrenic.

schiz·o·phre·ni·a [skit′sə·frē′nē·ə] *n.* A severe mental disorder in which a person confuses what is real and what is imaginary, with accompanying disturbances in behavior, thought, and emotion. ◆ *Schizophrenia* was coined by a Swiss psychiatrist in 1911 from two Greek words meaning "split" and "mind." He was referring to the fact that some schizophrenics seem cut off from their own selves.

schiz·o·phren·ic [skit′sə·fren′ik] 1 *adj.* Of or suffering from schizophrenia. 2 *n.* A person who suffers from schizophrenia.

schle·miel [shlə·mēl′] *n. slang* An inept or ineffectual person; bungler.

schlepp [shlep] *slang* 1 *v.* To carry with difficulty or in a clumsy way; lug; drag. 2 *v.* To move or go about, especially arduously. 3 *n.* A long or arduous trek or journey. 4 *n.* An unimportant, clumsy, or stupid person. —**schlep′per** *n.*

schlock [shlok] *slang* 1 *n.* Cheap or shoddy merchandise. 2 *adj.* Of poor quality.

schmaltz or **schmalz** [shmälts] *n. slang* Overly sentimental art or music. —**shmaltz′y** *adj.* ◆ *Schmaltz* was borrowed from Yiddish, in which it first meant "melted fat."

schnau·zer [shnou(t)′zər] *n.* A dog with a wiry gray coat, small ears, bushy eyebrows, and beardlike fur on its blunt muzzle. Schnauzers come in three sizes—miniature, standard, and giant.

schnit·zel [shnit′səl] *n.* A veal cutlet.

schol·ar [skol′ər] *n.* 1 A person who has learned a great deal through serious study. 2 A student who holds a scholarship. 3 A school pupil or student.

schol·ar·ly [skol′ər·lē] *adj.* 1 Devoted to serious study: a *scholarly* person. 2 Showing or requiring advanced knowledge: *scholarly* research; a *scholarly* book. 3 Of, like, or suiting a scholar.

schol·ar·ship [skol′ər·ship′] *n.* 1 A grant of money awarded to a student to help pay for his or her education. 2 Advanced learning or devotion to serious study. 3 The methods or quality of a student's study: poor *scholarship.*

scho·las·tic [skə·las′tik] *adj.* Of or having to do with scholars, education, or schools: *scholastic* excellence. —**scho·las′ti·cal·ly** *adv.*

school[1] [sko͞ol] 1 *n.* A place set up to teach students: grammar *school;* a cooking *school.* 2 *v.* To educate or teach: She was well *schooled* in the classics. 3 *n.* A schoolhouse or schoolroom. 4 *n.* Pupils and their teachers as a group: Our *school* gave $300 to the fund. 5 *n.* The period during which classes are taught: to keep a pupil in after *school.* 6 *n.* The training or instruction given at a school: *School* was hard for me. 7 *n.* A special division of a university: the medical *school.* 8 *n.* A group of persons whose ideas, beliefs, or methods are alike: an old-fashioned *school* of thought; a *school* of poets. 9 *v.* To train or teach: to *school* a dog to obey. 10 *n.* Anything that teaches, as experience or life: the *school* of hard knocks. ◆ *School* comes from a Greek word that means *spare time, leisure,* and *rest.* It also means *discussion* and *lecture,* because the ancient Greeks thought that spare time should be spent in learning.

school[2] [sko͞ol] *n.* A large number of fish or whales, swimming together; shoal.

school board A group of citizens responsible for directing a local public school system.

school·book [sko͞ol′bo͝ok′] *n.* A book which students study in school; textbook.

school·boy [sko͞ol′boi′] *n.* A boy who attends school.

school·girl [sko͞ol′gûrl′] *n.* A girl who attends school.

school·house [sko͞ol′hous′] *n.* The building in which the pupils of a school are taught.

school·ing [sko͞o′ling] *n.* Training or education, such as that received in a school.

school·mas·ter [sko͞ol′mas′tər] *n.* A person who teaches in a school or acts as its principal.

school·mate [sko͞ol′māt′] *n.* A person who is a pupil in the same school as someone else.

school·mis·tress [sko͞ol′mis′tris] *n.* A woman who teaches in a school or acts as its principal.

school·room [sko͞ol′ro͞om′] *n.* A room in which pupils are taught their lessons by a teacher.

school·teach·er [sko͞ol′tē′chər] *n.* A person whose profession is teaching in a school.

school·work [sko͞ol′wûrk′] *n.* Work assigned to a student in school.

school·yard [sko͞ol′yärd′] *n.* The grounds belonging to a school, especially those used to play in.

schoon·er [sko͞o′nər] *n.* A ship having two or more masts rigged with fore-and-aft sails.

Schooner

schot·tische [shot′ish] *n.* **1** A round dance similar to the polka, but somewhat slower. **2** Music for such a dance.

schwa [shwä] *n.* A weak vowel sound in a syllable that is not stressed in speech, as the *a* in "alone" or the *e* in "happen." Symbol: ə

sci. 1 science. 2 scientific.

sci·at·i·ca [sī·at′i·kə] *n.* Pain in the lower back, hips, or legs, caused by disturbances along the sciatic nerve.

sci·at·ic nerve [sī·at′ik] A nerve that extends from the hip down the back of the thigh, dividing near the knee into branches.

sci·ence [sī′əns] *n.* **1** Knowledge consisting of a systematic arrangement of facts and principles obtained through observation, experiment, and ordered thinking. **2** A branch of this kind of knowledge. Chemistry is a natural science, and civics is a social science. **3** Skill gained through study or practice: the *science* of swimming. ◆ *Science* comes from the Latin word for *knowing*.

science fiction A made-up, often fantastic adventure story or novel whose plot is built around either real or imaginary scientific developments.

sci·en·tif·ic [sī′ən·tif′ik] *adj.* **1** Of, having to do with, discovered by, or used in science. **2** Following the rules, principles, or methods of science. **—sci′en·tif′i·cal·ly** *adv.*

scientific method The procedures used by scientists to acquire knowledge, including observation, induction, experimentation, and the forming and testing of hypotheses.

scientific notation A means of expressing any very large or very small number as the product of that number between 1 and 10 and multiplied by a power of ten. Thus $35 = 3.5 \times 10^1$; $350 = 3.5 \times 10^2$; $0.35 = 3.5 \times 10^{-1}$; etc.

sci·en·tist [sī′ən·tist] *n.* A person expert in science or devoted to scientific study.

scim·i·tar or **scim·i·ter** [sim′ə·tər] *n.* A curved, short Oriental sword.

A scimitar and scabbard

scin·til·la [sin·til′ə] *n.* The tiniest bit or particle; trace; spark: not a *scintilla* of truth in the entire story.

scin·til·late [sin′tə·lāt′] *v.* **scin·til·lat·ed, scin·til·lat·ing** **1** To give off sparks or flashes of light. **2** To be sparkling or brilliant. **—scin′til·la′tion** *n.*

sci·on [sī′ən] *n.* **1** A child or descendant, as of an important family. **2** A twig or shoot of a plant, used for grafting; cion.

scis·sors [siz′ərz] *n.pl.* A cutting tool (also called a **pair of scissors**) having a pair of blades pivoted together so that their sharp edges close against each other.

scissors kick A swimming kick in which the legs are opened wide with the knees bent and then straightened and closed like scissors. It is used with the sidestroke.

scle·ra [skler′ə] *n.* A tough, opaque membrane that covers the surface of the eyeball except for the part covered by the cornea.

scle·ro·sis [sklə·rō′sis] *n., pl.* **scle·ro·ses** [sklə·rō′sēz] **1** An abnormal thickening or hardening of a body part, such as an artery. **2** A disease characterized by sclerosis.

scoff [skof *or* skôf] **1** *v.* To show scorn or mocking disbelief; jeer: to *scoff* at a theory. **2** *n.* A mocking or scornful remark. **—scoff′er** *n.*

scoff·law [skof′lô′ *or* skôf′lô′] *n.* A person who regularly violates a law or ignores orders to appear in court or pay fines.

scold [skōld] **1** *v.* To criticize sharply for faults. **2** *n.* A person who is always scolding.

sconce [skons] *n.* An ornamental wall bracket for holding a candle or other light.

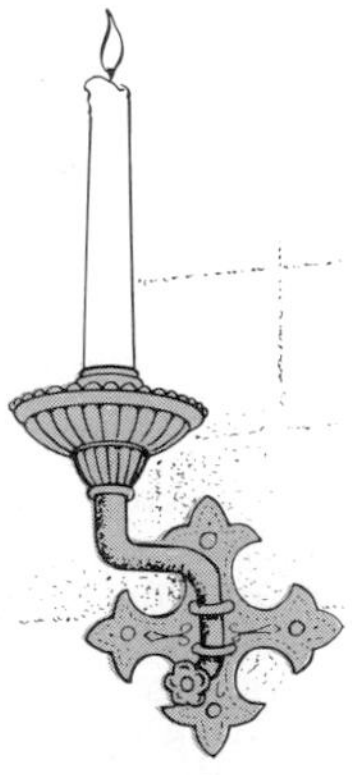
Sconce

scone [skōn] *n.* A round, flat cake or biscuit, usually eaten with butter.

scoop [sko͞op] **1** *n.* A tool like a little shovel or a deep, cuplike spoon, used to lift out portions of flour, sugar, ice cream, and the like. **2** *n.* The amount a scoop will hold: a *scoop* of ice cream. **3** *n.* The part of a dredge or power shovel that digs up and lifts mud, dirt, sand, or other material. **4** *v.* To lift out or up with or as if with a scoop: to *scoop up* handfuls of sand. **5** *n.* An act of scooping

S

a	add	**i**	it	**o͝o**	took	**oi**	oil
ā	ace	**ī**	ice	**o͞o**	pool	**ou**	pout
â	care	**o**	odd	**u**	up	**ng**	ring
ä	palm	**ō**	open	**û**	burn	**th**	thin
e	end	**ô**	order	**yo͞o**	fuse	**th̶**	this
ē	equal					**zh**	vision

ə = a in *above* e in *sicken* i in *possible* o in *melon* u in *circus*

or a scooping movement. **6** *v.* To hollow out, as by scooping: to *scoop* out a hollow. **7** *n.* A bowl-shaped hollow or hole. **8** *n. slang* A bit of information, as a news story, heard or published ahead of others. **9** *v. slang* To get and publish a news story before (a rival): One newspaper *scooped* all the others.

scoot [sko͞ot] *informal* **1** *v.* To go quickly; dart off. **2** *n.* A hurried darting off.

scoot·er [sko͞o′tər] *n.* A vehicle consisting of a footboard with a wheel at either end and steered by a handle in front.

scope [skōp] *n.* **1** The area covered; range; extent: the *scope* of a lesson. **2** Extent of understanding; grasp: a mind of limited *scope.* **3** Room or chance for expression or development: The job gave full *scope* to his talents.

-scope A combining form meaning: A device for viewing, observing, or examining, as in *microscope.*

-scopy A combining form meaning: Viewing, observation, or examination, as in *radioscopy.*

scorch [skôrch] **1** *v.* To burn just a little on the surface; singe: The hot iron *scorched* the cloth. **2** *n.* A slight burn on the surface of something. **3** *v.* To wither or shrivel by heat; dry up.

scorch·er [skôr′chər] *n.* **1** A person or thing that scorches. **2** *informal* An extremely hot day.

score [skôr] *n., v.* **scored, scor·ing** **1** *n.* The number of points won in a game or competition. **2** *n.* A record of points won: to keep *score.* **3** *v.* To keep such a record for: to *score* a tennis game. **4** *v.* To make (points or runs), as in a game: Our team *scored* a touchdown. **5** *v.* To win or attain, as a success. **6** *n.* A grade or mark made on a test: I got a *score* of 93. **7** *v.* To rate or grade: to *score* test papers. **8** *n.* A debt, wrong, or injury to be repaid or revenged: to settle old *scores.* **9** *n.* Reason, excuse, or account. **10** *v.* To mark with lines, cuts, or notches. **11** *n.* A cut or a similar line or mark. **12** *n.* A copy of a piece of music giving all the parts written for different instruments or voices. **13** *v.* To arrange (music) for an orchestra or instrument. **14** *n.* A set of twenty: a *score* of years. **15** *n.* (*pl.*) An indefinitely large number: *scores* of pigeons. **—scor′er** *n.* ◆ *Score* comes from an old Scandinavian word meaning *notch.* People once kept track of numbers or *scores* by cutting notches in a stick.

score·board [skôr′bôrd′] *n.* A large board, as at a stadium or in a gym, for displaying the score of a game and other information.

score·card [skôr′kärd′] *n.* A card for keeping score of a game.

score·keep·er [skôr′kē′pər] *n.* A person whose duty is to keep the official score during a game.

scorn [skôrn] **1** *n.* A feeling of despising someone or something as low, mean, or beneath one's notice; contempt. **2** *n.* An expression of contempt or disdain: My lip curled in *scorn.* **3** *v.* To treat with contempt; despise: to *scorn* a coward. **4** *v.* To refuse as being beneath one; disdain: to *scorn* an offer; They *scorned* to answer. **5** *n.* An object of contempt or disdain. ◆ See CONTEMPT.

scorn·ful [skôrn′fəl] *adj.* Full of or showing scorn: a *scornful* smile. **—scorn′ful·ly** *adv.*

Scor·pi·o [skôr′pē·ō′] *n.* **1** A constellation in the Southern Hemisphere that is thought to resemble a scorpion. **2** The eighth sign of the zodiac. **3** A person born under this sign.

scor·pi·on [skôr′pē·ən] *n.* A small animal related to the spider, having a lobster-like body and a long, curved tail with a poisonous sting.

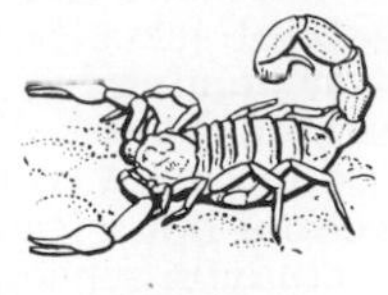

Scorpion

Scot [skot] *n.* A person born or living in Scotland.

scotch [skoch] *v.* **1** To put down or suppress, as by disproving; crush: *scotch* a rumor before it spreads. **2** To wound so as to cripple.

Scotch [skoch] **1** *adj.* Of or from Scotland. **2** *n.* (**the Scotch**) The people of Scotland. **3** *n.* The dialect of English spoken in Scotland. **4** *n.* Whisky made in Scotland. ◆ *Scotch, Scots,* and *Scottish* are all adjectives that refer to Scotland. *Scotch* is used for products of Scotland: *Scotch* tweed; *Scotch* whisky. *Scottish* and *Scots* are used when talking about the people of Scotland or the way they live.

Scotch·man [skoch′mən] *n., pl.* **Scotch·men** [skoch′mən] A Scot; Scotsman.

Scotch tape A kind of thin, usually clear adhesive tape used mostly on paper: a trademark.

Scotch·wom·an [skoch′wo͝om′ən] *n., pl.* **Scotch·wom·en** [skoch′wim′in] A woman who is Scottish.

scot-free [skot′frē′] *adj.* Without punishment or injury: The wrongdoer got off *scot-free.*

Scotland Yard The detective bureau of the London metropolitan police.

Scots [skots] **1** *adj.* Scottish: *Scots* law. **2** *n.* The dialect of English spoken in Scotland. ◆ See SCOTCH.

Scots·man [skots′mən] *n., pl.* **Scots·men** [skots′·mən] A Scot.

Scots·wom·an [skots′wo͝om′ən] *n., pl.* **Scots·wom·en** [skots′wim′in] A woman who is Scottish.

Scot·ti·cism [skot′ə·siz′əm] *n.* An expression characteristic of Scottish English.

Scot·tie [skot′ē] *n.* An informal name for SCOTTISH TERRIER.

Scot·tish [skot′ish] **1** *adj.* Of or from Scotland. **2** *n.* (**the Scottish**) The people of Scotland. **3** *n.* The Scotch dialect of English. ◆ See SCOTCH.

Scottish terrier A small terrier with short legs, a large head, and a wiry coat.

Scottish terrier

scoun·drel [skoun′drəl] *n.* A mean or dishonest person; rogue; villain.

scour[1] [skour] **1** *v.* To clean or brighten by washing and rubbing hard, as with sand or steel wool: to *scour* a pan. **2** *v.* To clean or clear, as by means of flowing water: to *scour* a drain. **3** *n.* The act of scouring: Give the pot a good *scour.* **4** *v.* To clean (wheat) before milling. **—scour′er** *n.*

scour[2] [skour] *v.* To go over or through every part of, usually with speed, as in making a search: Detectives *scoured* the area for clues.

scourge [skûrj] *n., v.* **scourged, scourg·ing** **1** *n.* A whip. **2** *v.* To whip severely; lash. **3** *v.* To punish or cause to suffer severely; afflict: A plague *scourged* the land. **4** *n.* A cause of great suffering or trouble, as war.

scout[1] [skout] **1** *n.* A soldier, plane, or ship sent out to observe and get information about the enemy. **2** *n.* Someone sent to find out about a rival or to locate persons worth hiring: a talent *scout* for motion pictures. **3** *v.* To observe or explore in order to obtain information: Two soldiers *scouted* the area ahead. **4** *v.* To search or hunt: to *scout* around for a campsite. **5** *n.* A boy scout or girl scout. **6** *n. slang* A friend: You're a good *scout.*

scout² [skout] *v.* To scorn and reject as absurd: They *scouted* the old-fashioned ideas.

scout·mas·ter [skout′mas′tər] *n.* The leader of a troop of Boy Scouts.

scow [skou] *n.* A large boat having a flat bottom and square ends, usually towed, used to carry such things as coal, oil, gravel, or garbage. ◆ *Scow* comes from a Dutch word.

scowl [skoul] **1** *v.* To lower the eyebrows and draw them together, as in anger or sullenness; frown. **2** *n.* A frowning look made in this way.

scrab·ble [skrab′əl] *v.* **scrab·bled, scrab·bling** **1** To scratch or grope about in a disorderly or frantic way: He *scrabbled* for a foothold on the steep slope. **2** To struggle painfully: to *scrabble* for a living as a tenant farmer. **3** To make or accumulate by or as if by scraping together: *scrabbling* together enough for a meal.

scrag [skrag] *n.* **1** A very thin, underfed creature. **2** The lean end of a neck of veal or mutton.

scrag·gly [skrag′lē] *adj.* **scrag·gli·er, scrag·gli·est** Rough, shaggy, or irregular.

scrag·gy [skrag′ē] *adj.* **scrag·gi·er, scrag·gi·est** **1** Rough; jagged: the *scraggy* mountain tops. **2** Very thin; scrawny; bony: the child's *scraggy* little legs.

scram [skram] *v.* **scrammed, scram·ming** *U.S. slang* To go away; get out.

scram·ble [skram′bəl] *v.* **scram·bled, scram·bling,** *n.* **1** *v.* To move or climb hastily, using the hands and feet: to *scramble* down a steep slope. **2** *n.* A hard walk or climb over rough land. **3** *v.* To struggle with others, as in trying to get something: to *scramble* for a place in front. **4** *n.* A struggle, often with pushing and shoving: a mad *scramble* for tickets. **5** *v.* To mix together in a confused way. **6** *v.* To distort (an electronic signal) in such a way that it is unintelligible to anyone without special receiving equipment. **7** *v.* To cook (eggs) by stirring mixed yolks and whites over heat. **—scram′bler** *n.*

scrap¹ [skrap] *n., adj., v.* **scrapped, scrap·ping** **1** *n.* A little piece or fragment; bit: *scraps* of food. **2** *n.* Useless material that has been thrown away. **3** *adj.* Made up of scrap: a *scrap* heap. **4** *v.* To throw away or abandon as no good: to *scrap* wrecked autos. **5** *n.* Pieces of old metal used in making new metal. **6** *v.* To break up into scrap. **7** *adj.* In broken pieces that have value only as material for making something new: *scrap* iron; *scrap* paper.

scrap² [skrap] *v.* **scrapped, scrap·ping,** *n. slang* **1** *v.* To fight; quarrel. **2** *n.* A noisy fight or disagreement. **—scrap′per** *n.*

scrap·book [skrap′bo͝ok′] *n.* A blank book for pictures, clippings, and other flat souvenirs.

scrape [skrāp] *v.* **scraped, scrap·ing,** *n.* **1** *v.* To rub (a surface) with or against something edged or rough, so as to take off something stuck on: to *scrape* plates before washing them. **2** *v.* To remove from a surface by rubbing with something sharp or rough: to *scrape* ice off a windshield. **3** *n.* A scraped spot. **4** *v.* To rub with a grating noise: to *scrape* fingernails across a blackboard. **5** *n.* A harsh, grating noise. **6** *v.* To draw the foot backward in bowing: to bow and *scrape.* **7** *n.* The act of scraping. **8** *v.* To gather gradually or by effort: They *scraped* up enough money to buy a stereo. **9** *v.* To get by barely, with trouble: Their neighbors just *scrape* by. **10** *n.* A difficult situation, especially one due to a rash or thoughtless act: The children got into one *scrape* after another. **11** *n. slang* A fight or quarrel.

scrap·er [skrā′pər] *n.* **1** A person who scrapes. **2** A device, especially a hand tool, for scraping off paint or other surface coatings.

scrap·ple [skrap′əl] *n.* Scraps of pork or other meat boiled with cornmeal and seasonings, set in a mold, and then sliced and fried.

scrap·py¹ [skrap′ē] *adj.* **scrap·pi·er, scrap·pi·est** Made of little pieces; fragmentary: *scrappy* information from here and there. **—scrap′pi·ness** *n.*

scrap·py² [skrap′ē] *adj.* **scrap·pi·er, scrap·pi·est** Eager to fight or compete energetically; aggressive. **—scrap′pi·ly** *adv.* **—scrap′pi·ness** *n.*

scratch [skrach] **1** *v.* To tear or mark the surface of with something sharp or rough: Briers *scratched* the hikers' arms. **2** *n.* A mark or cut made in this way: *scratches* on furniture. **3** *v.* To scrape lightly, as with the nails, to relieve itching: *Scratch* my back. **4** *n.* A slight flesh wound: It's only a *scratch.* **5** *v.* To rub with a grating or rasping noise: a dog *scratching* at the door. **6** *n.* A grating or rasping noise: the *scratch* of a match being struck. **7** *v.* To mark out with lines: to *scratch* out a word. **8** *v.* To withdraw an entrant from a competition. **9** *v.* To write awkwardly or hurriedly: to *scratch* off a reply. **10** *adj.* Used for quick notes: a *scratch* pad. **11** *adj.* Chosen or made by chance: a *scratch* team; a *scratch* shot. **12** *n.* The act of scratching. **—from scratch** From the beginning or from nothing: to begin again *from scratch.* **—up to scratch** *informal* In proper or fit condition: I don't feel *up to scratch.*

scratch·y [skrach′ē] *adj.* **scratch·i·er, scratch·i·est** **1** That scratches or irritates: a *scratchy* thicket; a *scratchy* wool sweater. **2** Making a scratching noise: a *scratchy* record. **3** Full of scratchlike marks: *scratchy* writing.

scrawl [skrôl] **1** *v.* To write in a hasty, clumsy, or careless way. **2** *n.* Rough or careless handwriting: I could not read your *scrawl.*

scraw·ny [skrô′nē] *adj.* **scraw·ni·er, scraw·ni·est** Lean and bony; skinny; thin.

scream [skrēm] **1** *v.* To utter a long, shrill cry, as in pain, terror, or surprise: to *scream* for help. **2** *v.* To make a loud noise like a scream: The train whistle *screamed.* **3** *n.* A loud, piercing cry or sound. **4** *v.* To shout with a shrill tone: Don't *scream* at me. **5** *n. U.S. slang* A person or situation causing shouts of laughter.

scream·ing [skrē′ming] *adj.* **1** Uttering screams.

a	add	**i**	it	**o͝o**	took	**oi**	oil
ā	ace	**ī**	ice	**o͞o**	pool	**ou**	pout
â	care	**o**	odd	**u**	up	**ng**	ring
ä	palm	**ō**	open	**û**	burn	**th**	thin
e	end	**ô**	order	**yo͞o**	fuse	**th**	this
ē	equal					**zh**	vision

ə = a in *above*, e in *sicken*, i in *possible*, o in *melon*, u in *circus*

S

2 Provoking screams or laughter: a *screaming* farce. **3** Startling: *screaming* colors.

screech [skrēch] **1** *v.* To scream or shriek in a harsh way: That singer is *screeching.* **2** *n.* A shrill, harsh cry or sound; shriek.

screech owl Any of several kinds of small owls that screech weirdly instead of hooting.

screech·y [skrē′chē] *adj.* **screech·i·er, screech·i·est** High-pitched and harsh; shrill: a *screechy* voice.

Screech owl

screen [skrēn] **1** *n.* A network of woven wires with small open spaces between them, as one used to cover doors or windows. **2** *n.* A covered frame or other partition used to separate, hide, protect, or ornament: The model changed costumes behind a *screen.* **3** *n.* Something that hides, shields, or separates, as a screen: a *screen* of shrubbery. **4** *v.* To hide, shield, or shelter with or as if with a screen: to *screen* a porch; Vines *screen* the window from view. **5** *n.* A smooth surface on which movies and TV shows are shown. **6** *v.* To exhibit (a movie) on a screen. **7** *n.* Motion pictures: a star of stage and *screen.* **8** *n.* A sieve used to separate little pieces (of gravel, ashes, and the like) from big ones. **9** *v.* To sift through such a sieve: to *screen* coal. **10** *v.* To examine in order to determine qualifications: to *screen* applicants for a scholarship.

screen·play [skrēn′plā′] *n.* The written plot and arrangement of incidents of a motion picture, including cast of characters and dialogue.

screen test A short film made to test an aspiring actor's ability or an actor's suitability for a role.

screen·writ·er [skrēn′rī′tər] *n.* A person who writes screenplays.

screw [skrōō] **1** *n.* A pointed fastener like a nail with a spiral ridge around its length. It is driven in by turning it. **2** *n.* A cylinder with a spiral ridge around it that fits into a socket with a matching spiral groove in its sides. **3** *v.* To attach or be attached with screws: to *screw* a bolt to a door; The towel rack *screws* to the wall. **4** *n.* A turn of or as of a screw: Give the lid a *screw.* **5** *v.* To turn or twist until tight: *Screw* the cap on the tube. **6** *v.* To twist out of the normal shape: to *screw* up one's mouth. **7** *v.* To gather for an effort or attempt: The student *screwed* up enough courage to submit a story to the paper. **8** *n.* Anything having the form of a screw. **9** *n.* A screw propeller. **—put the screws on** *slang* To use pressure or force on.

screw·ball [skrōō′bôl′] **1** *n.* In baseball, a pitched ball that curves in a direction opposite to a curve ball. **2** *n. slang* An eccentric or unpredictably funny person. **3** *adj.* Funny or eccentric; zany: a *screwball* movie.

screw·driv·er [skrōō′drī′vər] *n.* A tool that fits into the slot in the head of a screw to turn it.

screw propeller A hub having blades attached with their edges at an angle to the direction of rotation, like those of an electric fan, used to drive ships and some aircraft.

screw·y [skrōō′ē] *adj.* **screw·i·er, screw·i·est** *slang* **1** Insane; crazy. **2** Very unusual or eccentric; absurd.

scrib·ble [skrib′əl] *v.* **scrib·bled, scrib·bling,** *n.* **1** *v.* To write in a hasty or careless way: to *scribble* a note. **2** *v.* To make marks that mean nothing. **3** *n.* Writing or marks made by scribbling. **—scrib′·bler** *n.*

scribe [skrīb] *n., v.* **scribed, scrib·ing** **1** *n.* A person who copies manuscripts by hand, as was done before printing was invented. **2** *n.* A clerk or secretary. **3** *n.* A writer. **4** *n.* A teacher of the Jewish law in olden times.

scrib·er [skrī′bər] *n.* A pointed steel tool for making marks on metal and other hard surfaces.

scrim [skrim] *n.* A strong, loosely woven cotton or linen fabric.

scrim·mage [skrim′ij] *n., v.* **scrim·maged, scrim·mag·ing** **1** *n.* A rough, disorderly struggle. **2** *n.* In football, a play after the ball has been placed on the ground and snapped back. **3** *n.* In various sports, a practice session or unofficial game. **4** *v.* To engage in a scrimmage. **—line of scrimmage** In football, the imaginary line running across the field where the ball rests between opposing teams at the start of each play.

scrimp [skrimp] *v.* To limit spending by being very economical or stingy: to *scrimp* and save.

scrim·shaw [skrim′shô′] **1** *n.* The art of carving or engraving designs, often of nautical subjects, on ivory, bone, or shells. **2** *n.* An article made in this way, or such articles in general. **3** *v.* To carve or carve into scrimshaw.

scrip [skrip] *n.* **1** A piece of paper money less than a dollar, formerly issued in the U.S. **2** A document giving the holder the right to receive something else, as shares of stock.

script [skript] *n.* **1** Handwriting. **2** A printing type designed to imitate handwriting. **3** A copy of a play or dramatic role, for the use of actors.

scrip·tur·al [skrip′chər·əl] *adj.* (*usually written* **Scriptural**) Of, having to do with, found in, or according to the Scriptures: A *Scriptural* passage was the basis of the sermon.

Scrip·ture [skrip′chər] *n.* **1** (*often pl.*) The Bible or a passage from the Bible: Our minister often quotes the *Scriptures.* **2** (*written* **scripture**) Any writing considered sacred or authoritative.

scriv·en·er [skriv′ən·ər *or* skriv′nər] *n.* In olden days, a public clerk or scribe who prepared deeds, contracts, and other writings.

scrod [skrod] *n.* A young codfish split up for cooking.

scrof·u·la [skrof′yə·lə] *n.* Tuberculosis of the lymph glands, chiefly of the neck, marked by abscesses, inflammation, and swelling. **—scrof′u·lous** *adj.*

scroll [skrōl] *n.* **1** A roll of parchment or paper, especially one with writing on it. **2** An ornament like a partly unrolled scroll.

scroll saw A saw with a narrow blade for doing curved or irregular work.

scroll·work [skrōl′wûrk′] *n.* Decorative work, as in wood, characterized by spiral curves.

Scrooge [skrōōj] *n.* In Charles Dickens' story *A Christmas Carol,* the mean old miser.

scro·tum [skrō′təm] *n., pl.* **scro·tums** or **scro·ta** [skrō′tə] The pouch of skin that holds the testicles of a male mammal.

scrounge [skrounj] *v.* **scrounged, scroung·ing** *informal* **1** To forage; rummage. **2** To get or gather by searching hard or long: The boys *scrounged* up a can of old nails from the vacant lot. **3** To get by begging or pleading: *scrounge* a meal.

scrub¹ [skrub] *v.* **scrubbed, scrub·bing,** *n.* **1** *v.* To wash clean by rubbing hard: to *scrub* clothes. **2** *n.* The act of scrubbing.

scrub[2] [skrub] 1 *n.* Small, stunted trees or shrubs growing together. 2 *n.* Any small or inferior person or thing. 3 *adj.* Undersized or inferior: *scrub* oak or pine. 4 *n.* A player not on the regular team in sports. 5 *adj.* Of or involving such players: a *scrub* team.
scrub·ber [skrub′ər] *n.* A person or thing that scrubs, especially a device that removes impurities from a gas.
scrub·by [skrub′ē] *adj.* **scrub·bi·er, scrub·bi·est** 1 Undersized: a *scrubby* horse. 2 Covered with scrub or underbrush: *scrubby* ground.
scruff [skruf] *n.* The back part, or nape, of the neck or the loose skin that covers it.
scrump·tious [skrump′shəs] *adj. informal* Very pleasing, especially to the taste; delicious.

A puppy held by the scruff of its neck

scru·ple [skrōō′pəl] *n., v.* **scru·pled, scru·pling** 1 *n.* A feeling of doubt that holds someone back from doing what seems to be wrong: I have *scruples* about borrowing this record without asking. 2 *v.* To hesitate because of scruples: The pirates did not *scruple* to steal. 3 *n.* A small unit of weight used by druggists, equal to 20 grains.
scru·pu·lous [skrōō′pyə·ləs] *adj.* 1 Giving strict attention to what is right: a *scrupulous* parent. 2 Careful and exact: a *scrupulous* account of money spent. **—scru′pu·lous·ly** *adv.*
scru·ti·nize [skrōō′tə·nīz′] *v.* **scru·ti·nized, scru·ti·niz·ing** To look at closely; examine very carefully: to *scrutinize* every clue.
scru·ti·ny [skrōō′tə·nē] *n., pl.* **scru·ti·nies** A searching look or close, careful examination.
scu·ba [skōō′bə] 1 *n.* An apparatus for breathing underwater, worn on a diver's back. It is made up of a tank or tanks of compressed air connected by a hose to a mouthpiece. 2 *adj.* Of, having to do with, or using a scuba: *scuba* diving. ◆ *Scuba* is an acronym formed from the first letters of the words "*s*elf-*c*ontained *u*nderwater *b*reathing *a*pparatus."
scud [skud] *v.* **scud·ded, scud·ding,** *n.* 1 *v.* To move, run, or fly swiftly: clouds *scudding* before the wind. 2 *n.* Clouds or spray driven before the wind. 3 *n.* The act of scudding.
scuff [skuf] 1 *v.* To roughen or wear down the surface of, as by scraping: Don't *scuff* your shoes. 2 *v.* To drag or scrape the feet, as on the floor. 3 *n.* The act or sound of scuffing.
scuf·fle [skuf′əl] *v.* **scuf·fled, scuf·fling,** *n.* 1 *v.* To fight roughly or in a confused way: Tempers were short, and twice players *scuffled.* 2 *n.* A confused fight. 3 *v.* To shuffle the feet.
scull [skul] 1 *n.* A long oar worked from side to side over the rear of a boat. 2 *n.* A light, short oar, used in pairs by one person. 3 *v.* To propel (a boat) by a scull or sculls. 4 *n.* A light racing boat rowed with sculls. **—scull′er** *n.*
scul·ler·y [skul′ər·ē] *n., pl.* **scul·ler·ies** A room off a kitchen where vegetables are cleaned, pots and pans washed, and other tasks done.
scul·lion [skul′yən] *n.* A servant who washes dishes, pots, and kettles: seldom used today.
sculpt [skulpt] *v.* To sculpture.
sculp·tor [skulp′tər] *n.* An artist who creates sculpture out of stone, metal, wood, clay, or other material.
sculp·ture [skulp′chər] *n., v.* **sculp·tured, sculp·tur·ing** 1 *n.* The art of making figures or shapes, as by chiseling stone, casting molten metal, or modeling clay. 2 *n.* A work or works of art made in this manner. 3 *v.* To form or represent, as by carving or shaping: to *sculpture* a statue. 4 *v.* To beautify or decorate with sculpture. **—sculp′tur·al** *adj.*

Sculpture

scum [skum] *n., v.* **scummed, scum·ming** 1 *n.* A film of impure or foreign matter that forms upon the surface of a liquid. 2 *v.* To become covered with or form scum. 3 *v.* To take scum from; skim. 4 *n.* A vile or worthless person or group.
scum·my [skum′ē] *adj.* **scum·mi·er, scum·mi·est** 1 Covered with or like scum. 2 Low; vile.
scup [skup] *n., pl.* **scup** or **scups** A food fish of the porgy family, found along the Atlantic coast of the U.S.
scup·per [skup′ər] *n.* An opening along the side of a ship's deck, to let water run off.
scup·per·nong [skup′ər·nong′] *n.* A delicious yellowish green grape of the southern U.S.
scurf [skûrf] *n.* 1 Tiny scales of skin, shed as in dandruff. 2 Any scaly or flaky covering.
scur·ril·i·ty [skə·ril′ə·tē] *n., pl.* **scur·ril·i·ties** 1 Coarseness or vulgarity of language. 2 A coarse or vulgar remark.
scur·ri·lous [skûr′ə·ləs] *adj.* Vulgar and very coarse or abusive: *scurrilous* remarks. ◆ *Scurrilous* goes back to the Latin word for *buffoon* or *clown.*
scur·ry [skûr′ē] *v.* **scur·ried, scur·ry·ing,** *n., pl.* **scur·ries** 1 *v.* To run quickly or hastily; scamper. 2 *n.* The act or sound of scurrying.
scur·vy [skûr′vē] *n., adj.* **scur·vi·er, scur·vi·est** 1 *n.* A disease caused by a lack of vitamin C in the diet. It is marked by swollen and bleeding gums and great physical weakness. 2 *adj.* Nasty; mean; low: a *scurvy* trick.
scutch·eon [skuch′ən] *n.* A shield on whose surface there is a coat of arms; escutcheon.
scut·tle[1] [skut′(ə)l] *n.* A bucketlike container in which coal may be kept or carried.
scut·tle[2] [skut′(ə)l] *v.* **scut·tled, scut·tling** To run quickly; scamper; scurry.
scut·tle[3] [skut′(ə)l] *v.* **scut·tled, scut·tling,** *n.* 1 *v.* To sink (a ship) on purpose by making openings in it. 2 *n.* An opening with a lid or cover, as one in the deck or side of a ship.

a add	**i** it	**o͝o** took	**oi** oil
ā ace	**ī** ice	**ōō** pool	**ou** pout
â care	**o** odd	**u** up	**ng** ring
ä palm	**ō** open	**û** burn	**th** thin
e end	**ô** order	**yōō** fuse	**th** this
ē equal			**zh** vision

ə = {a in *above* e in *sicken* i in *possible* / o in *melon* u in *circus*}

S

scut·tle·butt [skut′(ə)l·but′] *n. informal* Rumor or gossip. ◆ This sense of *scuttlebutt* comes from an earlier sense: a *scuttlebutt* is a ship's water cask or drinking fountain where sailors meet and exchange gossip.
scuz·zy [skuz′ē] *adj.* **scuz·zi·er, scuz·zi·est** *slang* Dirty or shabby.
Scyl·la [sil′ə] *n.* In Greek myths, a sea monster with six heads living in a cave opposite the whirlpool of Charybdis. It represented a dangerous rock in the strait between Italy and Sicily. **—between Scylla and Charybdis** Between two dangers, where avoiding one means taking the risk of running into the other.
scythe [sīth] *n., v.* **scythed, scyth·ing** 1 *n.* A long, curved blade fixed at an angle to a long, bent handle and used to cut down grass or grain. 2 *v.* To cut with a scythe.

Scythe

SD Postal Service abbreviation of South Dakota.
S.D. South Dakota.
S. Dak. South Dakota.
se, s.e., SE, or **S.E.** 1 southeast. 2 southeastern.
Se The symbol for the element selenium.
sea [sē] *n.* 1 The large body of salt water that covers most of the earth's surface; ocean. 2 *adj. use*: a *sea* bird; a *sea* captain. 3 A large body of ocean water partly enclosed by land: the Aegean *Sea.* 4 A saltwater or freshwater lake: the *Sea* of Galilee; the Caspian *Sea.* 5 A wave: The ship floundered in heavy *seas.* 6 The swell or flow of the ocean or of its waves. 7 A very great amount or number: a *sea* of unanswered mail. **—at sea** 1 On the ocean. 2 At a loss; confused. **—follow the sea** To make one's living as a sailor. **—go to sea** 1 To become a sailor. 2 To take an ocean trip. **—put to sea** To start an ocean trip.
sea anchor An object, usually a canvas-covered frame, thrown overboard and towed behind a ship to keep the ship from drifting or to keep it heading into the wind.
sea anemone A sea animal having a tubelike body with a mouth at one end surrounded by brightly colored tentacles that look like flower petals.

Sea anemone

Sea·bee [sē′bē′] *n.* A member of the U.S. Navy construction crew assigned to building naval installations, especially in combat zones. ◆ *Seabee* comes from the initials of "*c*onstruction *b*attalion."
sea biscuit A hard bread or biscuit for use on sea voyages.
sea·board [sē′bôrd′] *n.* The land or region bordering on the sea; seacoast.
sea·coast [sē′kōst′] *n.* A coast that borders on the sea; seashore.
sea cow A manatee or a related large mammal that lives in the sea.
sea cucumber A sea animal with a flexible, cucumber-shaped body and tentacles around its mouth.
sea dog An old or experienced sailor.
sea·far·er [sē′fâr′ər] *n.* A sailor; mariner.
sea·far·ing [sē′fâr′ing] 1 *n.* Travel on the sea. 2 *adj.* Traveling by sea. 3 *n.* The occupation of a sailor. 4 *adj.* Working as a sailor.
sea·food [sē′fo͞od′] *n.* Fish or shellfish that are good to eat.
sea·girt [sē′gûrt′] *adj.* Surrounded by waters of the sea or ocean.
sea·go·ing [sē′gō′ing] *adj.* 1 Built for use on the ocean: a *seagoing* vessel. 2 Seafaring.
sea·gull A gull or large tern.
sea horse 1 A small, saltwater fish having a long slender tail and a head resembling that of a horse. 2 A mythical animal, half horse and half fish. 3 A walrus.

Sea gull

seal¹ [sēl] 1 *n.* An instrument or device for pressing a mark or design, especially an official one, into a soft material, such as wax or paper. 2 *n.* The mark or design made this way. 3 *v.* To mark with a seal, as to indicate official status or quality. 4 *n.* Something, as the paper or wax, that is marked with a seal and attached to something to indicate official status or quality. 5 *n.* A substance or device used to keep something firmly closed: the *seal* of an envelope; a *seal* on a door. 6 *v.* To fasten or close with or as if with a seal: to *seal* a letter; to *seal* a leak. 7 *n.* Something that confirms or makes certain. 8 *v.* To confirm or make certain: to *seal* a bargain with a handshake. 9 *n.* An ornamental stamp, as for greeting cards. **—seal′er** *n.*
seal² [sēl] 1 *n.* Any of various large, fish-eating sea mammals having flippers as limbs. Seals spend part of the time on land. 2 *n.* Fur or leather taken from a seal. 3 *v.* To hunt seals. **—seal′er** *n.*

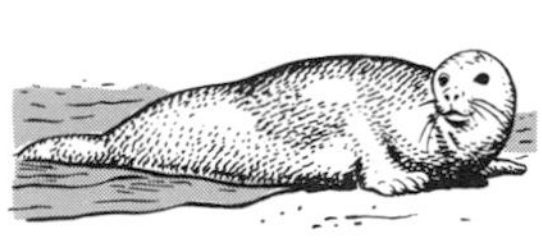
Seal

sea legs The ability to walk steadily on a rolling or pitching ship.
sea level The level of the surface of the ocean, halfway between high and low tide. Elevation of land is measured from sea level.
sealing wax A material that is soft when heated but becomes solid when it cools, as used for sealing papers and packages.
sea lion A very large seal of the Pacific coast of North America.
seal·skin [sēl′skin′] *n.* 1 The fur of a seal, especially when treated to remove the longer hairs and dyed brown or black. 2 A coat or other garment made of this fur.

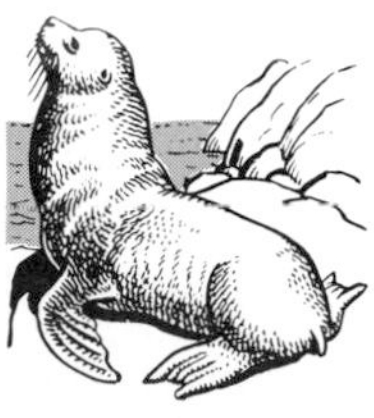
Sea lion

seam [sēm] 1 *n.* A line along which parts have been joined, especially the edges of two pieces of cloth sewn together. 2 *v.* To join by means of a seam. 3 *n.* A mark resembling a seam, as a scar or wrinkle. 4 *v.* To mark with wrinkles or scars, as the face. 5 *n.* A layer of rock or mineral; stratum.
sea·man [sē′mən] *n., pl.* **sea·men** [sē′mən] 1 A person whose work is to help with the sailing of a ship; sailor. 2 A person expert in managing a ship: John Paul Jones was a fine *seaman.* 3 An

enlisted person of low rank in a navy. **—sea′man·ship** *n.*
sea mew A gull, especially a European species.
seam·stress [sēm′stris] *n.* A woman skilled at sewing or earning her living by sewing.
seam·y [sē′mē] *adj.* **seam·i·er, seam·i·est** 1 Full of seams, as the wrong side of a garment. 2 Unpleasant or unattractive: Doctors often see the *seamy* side of life.
sé·ance [sā′äns′] *n.* 1 A meeting at which people try to communicate with the dead. 2 A session.
sea otter A rare, dark-brown otter of northern Pacific coastal waters that can grow to the size of a seal.
sea·plane [sē′plān′] *n.* An airplane designed and built to land on and take off from water.
sea·port [sē′pôrt′] *n.* 1 A harbor or port that ships can reach from the sea. 2 The city or town where it is located.
sea power 1 A nation whose navy is large and strong. 2 The naval strength of a nation.
sear [sir] 1 *v.* To wither; dry up: Sun and drought *seared* the lawn. 2 *adj.* Withered; dried up: used mostly in poems. 3 *v.* To burn the surface of; scorch: The heat *seared* the farmer's skin. 4 *v.* To make hard or insensitive: The experience had *seared* their feelings.
search [sûrch] 1 *v.* To look through or examine thoroughly: to *search* a closet for an overshoe; to *search* a captured prisoner for weapons. 2 *v.* To look very hard: to *search* for a cure. 3 *n.* The act of searching or examining. **—in search of** Looking for.
search·ing [sûr′ching] *adj.* 1 Investigating carefully and in detail: a *searching* inquiry. 2 Penetrating; observant: a *searching* glance.
search·light [sûrch′līt′] *n.* 1 A light with a powerful beam that can be moved about for searching or signaling. 2 The beam of such a light.
search warrant A document issued by a court allowing the police to search a house or building, as for stolen goods or papers.
sea·scape [sē′skāp′] *n.* A view or picture of the sea.
sea·shell [sē′shel′] The shell of a sea mollusk, as a clam or oyster.
sea·shore [sē′shôr′] *n.* Land that borders on the ocean.
sea·sick [sē′sik′] *adj.* Suffering from nausea, dizziness, or weakness caused by the motion of a ship at sea. **—sea′sick′ness** *n.*
sea·side [sē′sīd′] *n.* 1 The seashore, especially as a place for rest or amusement. 2 *adj. use*: a *seaside* hotel; a *seaside* resort.
sea snake Any of a large family of poisonous snakes, living in warm seas.
sea·son [sē′zən] 1 *n.* One of the four divisions of the year as determined by the earth's position with respect to the sun. The seasons are spring, summer, autumn, and winter. 2 *n.* Some particular part of the year: the planting *season*; the baseball *season.* 3 *v.* To make taste better by adding spices and herbs: to *season* a stew. 4 *v.* To add zest or interest to: to *season* a lecture with jokes. 5 *v.* To make fit for use by aging or drying, as wood. 6 *v.* To harden or make accustomed: to *season* troops for battle. **—in season** 1 Naturally ready for use; ripe: Apples are *in season* in the fall. 2 That can be legally caught or hunted, as game. **—in good season** Soon enough. **—out of season** Not in season.
sea·son·a·ble [sē′zən·ə·bəl] *adj.* 1 In keeping with the season; expected at that time of year. 2 Coming or done at the proper time.
sea·son·al [sē′zən·əl] *adj.* Having to do with or happening at a certain season or seasons: *seasonal* storms. **—sea′son·al·ly** *adv.*
sea·son·ing [sē′zən·ing] *n.* 1 Something added to food to improve its flavor. 2 An enlivening addition, as humor to a speech or lecture.
seat [sēt] 1 *n.* Something on which one sits, as a chair or stool. 2 *n.* The part of a piece of furniture on which one sits: the *seat* of a chair. 3 *v.* To cause to sit: to *seat* guests at the table. 4 *v.* To provide with seats: The theater *seats* 225 people. 5 *n.* The part of the body or of the clothes covering it on which one sits: the *seat* of one's pants. 6 *n.* A place where one has a right to sit: a *seat* for the play. 7 *n.* A manner of sitting, as on horseback. 8 *n.* Membership, as in a legislature or stock exchange: a *seat* in the Senate. 9 *n.* The place where something is located or established: the *seat* of government; the *seat* of a disease. 10 *n.* A place of residence; estate or mansion. **—be seated** 1 To sit. 2 To be sitting. 3 To be located or situated.
seat belt A strap attached to the seat of an airplane, automobile, or other vehicle that buckles about the waist in order to prevent or reduce injury by holding a person firmly seated.

seat·ing [sē′ting] *n.* 1 The act of providing with seats. 2 Fabric for upholstering seats. 3 The arrangement of seats, as in a room or auditorium: The *seating* was carefully planned.
SEATO [sē′tō] Southeast Asia Treaty Organization.
sea urchin A small sea animal whose body is enclosed in a round, spiny shell.
sea wall A wall built to keep waves from striking the shore and washing it away, or to serve as a breakwater.

Sea urchin

sea·ward [sē′wərd] 1 *adj.* Going toward the sea: a *seaward* trip. 2 *adj.* Coming from the sea, as a wind. 3 *adv.* In the direction of the sea: to fly *seaward.* 4 *n.* The direction toward the sea.
sea·wards [sē′wərdz] *adv.* Seaward.
sea·way [sē′wā′] *n.* 1 A route over the sea. 2 An inland waterway traveled by seagoing ships.
sea·weed [sē′wēd′] *n.* Any of the plants, especially algae, that grow in the ocean.

a	add	**i**	it	**o͝o**	took	**oi**	oil
ā	ace	**ī**	ice	**o͞o**	pool	**ou**	pout
â	care	**o**	odd	**u**	up	**ng**	ring
ä	palm	**ō**	open	**û**	burn	**th**	thin
e	end	**ô**	order	**yo͞o**	fuse	**th̶**	this
ē	equal					**zh**	vision

ə = a in *above*, e in *sicken*, i in *possible*, o in *melon*, u in *circus*

S

sea·wor·thy [sē′wûr′thē] *adj.* In fit condition for a sea voyage, as a ship.

se·ba·ceous [si·bā′shəs] *adj.* **1** Of, like, or having to do with fat. **2** Of or having to do with the sebaceous glands.

sebaceous gland Any of the small glands in the skin that secrete an oily fluid that lubricates and protects the hair and skin.

SEbE southeast by east.

SEbS southeast by south.

sec. **1** secant. **2** second. **3** secondary. **4** secretary. **5** section.

se·cant [sē′kant′] **1** *adj.* Cutting, especially into two parts. **2** *n.* In geometry, a straight line that cuts a given curve.

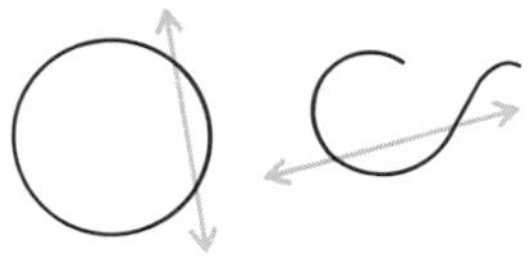

The red lines are secants.

se·cede [si·sēd′] *v.* **se·ced·ed, se·ced·ing** To withdraw from a union or association, especially a political or religious one: In 1860 and 1861, 11 Southern states *seceded.*

se·ces·sion [si·sesh′ən] *n.* **1** The act of seceding, especially from a political or religious association. **2** *U.S.* (*written* **Secession**) The withdrawal of the Southern states from the Union in 1860–1861, precipitating the Civil War. **—se·ces′sion·ist** *n.*

se·clude [si·klo͞od′] *v.* **se·clud·ed, se·clud·ing** **1** To remove and keep apart from others: to *seclude* oneself because of shyness. **2** To shut off, as from view; hide.

se·clu·sion [si·klo͞o′zhən] *n.* **1** The act of secluding. **2** The condition of being secluded; solitude. **3** A remote or hidden place.

sec·ond[1] [sek′ənd] *n.* **1** A unit of time that is equal to 1/60 of a minute. **2** A small amount of time: Wait a *second.* **3** A unit used in measuring angles, equal to 1/60 of a minute or 1/3600 of a degree.

sec·ond[2] [sek′ənd] **1** *adj.* (*sometimes written* **2nd** *or* **2d**) Coming next after the first: the *second* grade in school. **2** *adj.* Ranking next below the first or best: the *second* hitter on a baseball team. **3** *adv.* In the second position, place, or rank: to finish a race *second.* **4** *n.* The one next after the first: I was the *second* to arrive late. **5** *adj.* Being like someone who has gone before; another: a *second* Shakespeare. **6** *adj.* Playing or singing the lower or less important part: *second* soprano; *second* oboe. **7** *n.* (*pl.*) Articles of merchandise that have defects. **8** *n.* A person who supports or assists, as in a duel or boxing match. **9** *v.* To support or help in some way. **10** *v.* To announce support for or agreement with: to *second* a motion. **11** *adv.* As a second point; furthermore; secondly.

sec·on·dar·y [sek′ən·der′ē] *adj., n., pl.* **sec·on·dar·ies** **1** *adj.* Coming after that which is first or primary: *secondary* defenses; *secondary* education. **2** *adj.* Depending on or derived from what is primary or original: *secondary* sources; *secondary* colors. **3** *n.* A person or thing that is subordinate or secondary. **4** *n.* A nonmoving coil of wire, as in a transformer in which an electric current is induced. **5** *adj.* Of, related to, or indicating an induced current, as in a transformer. **—sec′on·dar′i·ly** *adv.*

secondary accent A mark (′) used to show where the secondary or weaker stress is placed in a word. In the word "secondary," the secondary accent is on the third syllable.

secondary school A high school.

secondary sex characteristic A characteristic that distinguishes males and females of the same species but does not have a direct purpose in reproduction. In human beings, facial hair, breast growth, and the pitch of the voice are secondary sex characteristics.

sec·ond-class [sek′ənd·klas′] **1** *adj.* Ranking next below first class: *second-class* travel accommodations; *second-class* mail. **2** *adj.* Of low quality; inferior: *second-class* goods. **3** *adv.* By or in second-class accommodations or mail: Magazines are mailed *second-class.*

second class The class of travel accommodations or mail that is next below first class.

Second Coming The return of Christ on Judgment Day, expected by some Christian denominations.

sec·ond-de·gree burn [sek′ənd·di·grē′] A burn of intermediate severity that causes blistering of the skin.

sec·ond-guess [sek′ənd·ges′] *v.* To make criticisms of (a person or a person's judgment) after an outcome is known: *second-guessing* a football coach.

sec·ond·hand [sek′ənd·hand′] **1** *adj.* Having been owned or used by someone else; not new: a *secondhand* radio. **2** *adj.* Received from another; not direct from the original source: *secondhand* information. **3** *adj.* Buying and selling goods that are not new: a *secondhand* furniture dealer. **4** *adv.* Not directly from the original source: to buy something *secondhand*; to hear news *secondhand.*

second hand On the face of a watch or clock, the hand that indicates the seconds.

second lieutenant A military rank. In the U.S. Army, a second lieutenant is the lowest-ranking commissioned officer, below a first lieutenant.

sec·ond·ly [sek′ənd·lē] *adv.* In the second place.

second nature A habit or quality of behavior that is acquired but becomes so fixed as to seem part of one's nature.

second person The form of a verb or pronoun that refers to the person or persons addressed. *You* and *yours* are in the second person.

sec·ond-rate [sek′ənd·rāt′] *adj.* Second, as in quality, size, rank, or importance: a *second-rate* song writer.

sec·ond-string [sek′ənd·string′] *adj.* Of, having to do with, or being a substitute rather than a regular: a *second-string* outfielder.

second thought A changed opinion; reconsideration: He impulsively agreed, then began to have *second thoughts.*

second wind Revived energy or stamina.

se·cre·cy [sē′krə·sē] *n.* **1** The condition or quality of being secret or hidden. **2** The habit of keeping secrets or the ability to do so.

se·cret [sē′krit] **1** *adj.* Kept from the view or knowledge of all but the persons concerned; hidden: a *secret* plot; a *secret* passageway. **2** *n.* Something not to be told. **3** *n.* Something that is not known or understood: the *secrets* of nature. **4** *adj.* Acting or having to do with hidden methods or ways: a *secret* agent; a *secret* society. **—in secret** **1** In a private or hidden place. **2** In privacy; without outsiders knowing. **—se′cret·ly** *adv.*

sec·re·tar·i·at [sek′rə·târ′ē·it] *n.* **1** The position of a secretary. **2** The place of business of a secretary. **3** An entire staff of secretaries; especially, a department headed by a governmental secretary.

sec·re·tar·y [sek′rə·ter′ē] *n., pl.* **sec·re·tar·ies** **1** A person whose duties involve writing letters and keeping records for a person, company, or other group. 2 An official who heads a government department: the *Secretary* of Defense. 3 A writing desk equipped with drawers and a bookcase. **—sec′re·tar′i·al** *adj.* ◆ *Secretary,* which comes from a Latin word meaning *secret,* originally meant *someone entrusted with a secret.* Now the word is much broader in meaning and may refer to stenographers as well as to high government officials.

Secretary

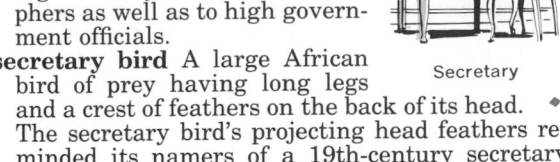

secretary bird A large African bird of prey having long legs and a crest of feathers on the back of its head. ◆ The secretary bird's projecting head feathers reminded its namers of a 19th-century secretary with quill pens thrust behind his ear.

sec·re·tar·y-gen·er·al [sek′rə·ter′ē·jen′ər·əl] *n., pl.* **sec·re·tar·ies-gen·er·al** An official who heads a large administrative staff, as of certain international organizations.

se·crete [si·krēt′] *v.* **se·cret·ed, se·cret·ing** 1 To keep from sight or knowledge; conceal; hide: to *secrete* a weapon. 2 To produce and give off (a secretion): The pituitary gland *secretes* hormones. **—se·cre′·tor** *n.*

se·cre·tion [si·krē′shən] *n.* 1 The process by which a gland produces a substance, as a hormone, that serves some special purpose in the function of the body. 2 The substance produced.

se·cre·tive *adj.* 1 [sē′krə·tiv *or* si·krē′tiv] Inclined to secrecy; tending to keep secrets. 2 [si·krē′tiv] Producing or causing secretion. **—se′cre·tive·ly** *adv.* **—se′cre·tive·ness** *n.*

se·cre·to·ry [si·krē′tə·rē] *adj.* Of, having to do with, promoting, or produced by secretion.

secret police A police force that operates in secret with the official purpose of tracking down foreign spies and saboteurs. Its actual purpose is more often to suppress and intimidate opponents of a government.

secret service 1 Secret investigation or spying done by a government. 2 (*written* **Secret Service**) A branch of the U.S. Treasury Department whose most important work is to find and arrest counterfeiters, and to guard the President and members of the President's immediate family.

secs. 1 seconds. 2 sections.

sect [sekt] *n.* A group of people who share the same beliefs or who follow the same leader or teacher, especially in religious matters.

sect. section.

sec·tar·i·an [sek·târ′ē·ən] 1 *adj.* Of, like, or devoted to a particular sect. 2 *n.* A member of a sect, especially if narrow-minded and blindly devoted.

sec·tar·i·an·ism [sek·târ′ē·ən·iz′·əm] *n.* The quality of being sectarian; division into sects.

sec·tion [sek′shən] 1 *n.* A separate part or division; portion: a *section* of a book; to cut a cake into *sections.* 2 *v.* To cut into parts or sections: to *section* a chicken. 3 *n.* A part of a city or community; district; area: a *residential* section. 4 *n.* A drawing or diagram of an object as it would look if cut through by a plane; cross section. 5 *n. U.S.* An area of land one mile square, making up 1/36 of a township.

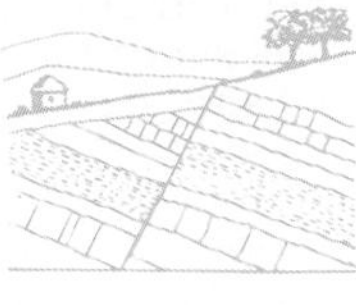
Section of the earth showing rock strata

sec·tion·al [sek′shən·əl] *adj.* 1 Of, related to, or like some particular area or its people; regional. 2 Made up of sections or separate parts: a *sectional* sofa. **—sec′tion·al·ly** *adv.*

sec·tion·al·ism [sek′shən·əl·iz′əm] *n.* An excessive interest or pride in the section or region of a country where one lives or where one was raised.

section gang A crew of workers who take care of a certain section of railroad track.

sec·tor [sek′tər] *n.* 1 A part of a circle bounded by an arc and two radii. 2 A section of a military area.

sec·u·lar [sek′yə·lər] *adj.* 1 Of or for the world rather than the church; not sacred or concerned with religion: *secular* art; *secular* education. 2 Not bound by monastic vows: *secular* clergy.

sec·u·lar·ize [sek′yə·lə·rīz′] *v.* **sec·u·lar·ized, sec·u·lar·iz·ing** To make separate from religion or the church: to *secularize* education. **—sec′u·lar·i·za′·tion** *n.*

se·cure [si·kyŏŏr′] *adj., v.* **se·cured, se·cur·ing** 1 *adj.* Not subject or exposed to danger or loss; safe: a *secure* fortress. 2 *v.* To make secure; protect; defend: *Secure* the gates! 3 *adj.* Free from fear or care: a *secure* childhood. 4 *adj.* Fixed or holding firmly in place: a *secure* fastening. 5 *v.* To fasten; make firm: to *secure* a rope. 6 *adj.* Certain; guaranteed: Your future success is *secure.* 7 *v.* To guarantee or ensure: to *secure* a loan. 8 *v.* To come to possess; get: to *secure* lodgings. 9 *v.* To bring about; effect. **—se·cure′ly** *adv.*

se·cur·i·ty [si·kyŏŏr′ə·tē] *n., pl.* **se·cur·i·ties** 1 The condition of being secure; freedom from danger, want, or fear. 2 A person or thing that secures or guarantees: A smoke alarm is a *security* against fire damage. 3 Something given or pledged as a guarantee for payment of money. 4 (*pl.*) Stocks or bonds: The safest place for *securities* is in the bank.

secy. or **sec′y.** secretary.

se·dan [si·dan′] *n.* 1 An enclosed automobile having two or four doors and front and back seats. 2 A sedan chair.

Sedan chair

sedan chair An enclosed chair carried on two poles extending forward and backward, used in the 17th and 18th centuries.

se·date [si·dāt′] *adj., v.* **se·dat·ed, se·dat·ing** 1 *adj.* Calm and steady in manner; composed. 2 *v.* To

a	add	**i**	it	**ŏŏ**	took	**oi**	oil
ā	ace	**ī**	ice	**ōō**	pool	**ou**	pout
â	care	**o**	odd	**u**	up	**ng**	ring
ä	palm	**ō**	open	**û**	burn	**th**	thin
e	end	**ô**	order	**yōō**	fuse	**t͟h**	this
ē	equal					**zh**	vision

ə = a in *above*, e in *sicken*, i in *possible*, o in *melon*, u in *circus*

calm with a sedative: The overexcited patient had to be *sedated.* **—se·date′ly** *adv.* **—se·date′ness** *n.* ◆ *Sedate* comes from a Latin word meaning *to make calm* and goes back to the word meaning *to sit.*

se·da·tion [si·dā′shən] *n.* **1** The act of sedating. **2** The condition of being sedated.

sed·a·tive [sed′ə·tiv] **1** *adj.* Having a soothing effect or relieving pain. **2** *n.* Something that soothes or relieves pain, as a medicine.

sed·en·tar·y [sed′ən·ter′ē] *adj.* **1** Requiring much sitting: A typist has a *sedentary* job. **2** Accustomed to much sitting: a *sedentary* person.

Se·der [sā′dər] *n., pl.* **Se·ders** or **Se·dar·im** [sə·där′·im] In Judaism, the feast in remembrance of the departure of the Israelites from Egypt, celebrated on the eve of the first day of Passover.

sedge [sej] *n.* Any of several coarse, grasslike plants that grow mainly in damp or swampy places.

sed·i·ment [sed′ə·mənt] *n.* **1** Matter that settles to the bottom of a liquid; dregs. **2** Small particles deposited by air or water.

sed·i·men·ta·ry [sed′ə·men′tər·ē] *adj.* **1** Of or like sediment. **2** Formed from sediment, as certain rocks.

sed·i·men·ta·tion [sed′ə·men·tā′shən] *n.* The accumulation or depositing of sediment.

se·di·tion [si·dish′ən] *n.* Speech or conduct that stirs up revolt against a government.

se·di·tious [si·dish′əs] *adj.* **1** Of or having to do with sedition. **2** Taking part in or guilty of sedition. **3** Stirring up revolt.

se·duce [si·d(y)o͞os′] *v.* **se·duced, se·duc·ing** To lead into wrongdoing; tempt: *Seduced* by their delicious flavor, I ate all the cookies. **—se·duc′er** *n.*

se·duc·tion [si·duk′shən] *n.* **1** The act of seducing. **2** Something that seduces; temptation.

se·duc·tive [si·duk′tiv] *adj.* Tempting or enticing; very attractive.

sed·u·lous [sej′o͞o·ləs] *adj.* Carefully attentive and hardworking; diligent. **—sed′u·lous·ly** *adv.*

see[1] [sē] *v.* **saw, seen, see·ing** **1** To be aware of or notice by means of the eyes: to *see* a dog. **2** To get images of things through the eyes: He can't *see* without glasses. **3** To grasp with the mind; understand: Now I *see* what you meant. **4** To find out; determine: Let's *see* how that works. **5** To have experience or knowledge of: The car has *seen* hard use. **6** To chance to meet: I *saw* them today. **7** To have a meeting or interview with: to *see* a dentist. **8** To visit with or receive as a visitor: We went to *see* our cousin; The mayor will *see* you now. **9** To attend as a spectator: to *see* a ball game. **10** To escort or accompany: I will *see* you home. **11** To take care; be sure: *See* that you do it right now! **12** To think hard: Let me *see*, where did I put my glasses? **—see about** **1** To find out about; investigate. **2** To take care of; attend to. **—see off** To say good-bye to at a place of departure. **—see out** To go with as far as an exit. **—see through** **1** To help or protect in a period of difficulty or danger. **2** To work or wait until something, as a job or difficulty, is ended. **3** To notice the falseness of; not be fooled by. **—see to** To take care of; attend to.

see[2] [sē] *n.* **1** The office, authority, or rank of a bishop. **2** The district under a bishop's rule. ◆ *See* comes from a Latin word meaning *seat.*

seed [sēd] *n., pl.* **seeds** or **seed,** *v.* **1** *n.* The embryo of a plant and food for its early growth. It is enclosed in a case or covering and is able to grow into a young plant under favorable conditions. **2** *v.* To plant seeds in: to *seed* a garden. **3** *v.* To remove the seeds from: to *seed* grapes. **4** *v.* To mature and produce seeds. **5** *n.* A small beginning from which something grows; source: the *seeds* of success. **6** *n.* Children and descendants; offspring: Abraham and his *seed.* **7** *v.* To scatter chemicals through (clouds) in an effort to produce rain. **—go to seed** **1** To develop and shed seed. **2** To become shabby; deteriorate. **—seed′er** *n.*

seed·bed [sēd′bed′] *n.* **1** A bed of soil prepared for planting seeds. **2** A place offering good conditions for growth or development: The Air Force was a *seedbed* for commercial airline pilots.

seed·case [sēd′kās′] *n.* The hollow, usually dry fruit containing the seeds of a plant; pod.

seed coat The protective outer covering of a seed.

seed·ling [sēd′ling] *n.* A young tree or plant, grown from a seed and not from a cutting.

seed money Money needed or used to start an enterprise.

seed pearl A very small, often irregularly shaped pearl, used as trimming on clothes or in jewelry.

seed·time [sēd′tīm′] *n.* **1** The season for planting crops. **2** A period of growth or development.

seed·y [sē′dē] *adj.* **seed·i·er, seed·i·est** **1** Full of seeds: *seedy* oranges. **2** Gone to seed. **3** Poor and ragged; shabby: a *seedy* bathrobe. **—seed′i·ly** *adv.* **—seed′i·ness** *n.*

see·ing [sē′ing] **1** *n.* The ability to see; sight. **2** *conj.* Considering; in view of the fact; because: *Seeing* that it's late, let's hurry. **3** *adj.* Having sight; able to see.

Seeing Eye A dog trained to lead a blind person: a trademark.

seek [sēk] *v.* **sought, seek·ing** **1** To go in search of; look for: to *seek* rare books. **2** To try to get or obtain: to *seek* wealth. **3** To attempt; try: They *seek* to win the championship. **—seek′er** *n.*

seem [sēm] *v.* **1** To have the appearance of being; look: The bridge *seems* safe. **2** To appear to oneself: I *seem* to smell gas. **3** To appear to be true or clear: It *seems* to be raining.

seem·ing [sē′ming] *adj.* Appearing to be true or real, but possibly false: the child's *seeming* innocence. **—seem′ing·ly** *adv.*

seem·ly [sēm′lē] *adj.* **seem·li·er, seem·li·est** Decent or proper; fitting; suitable. **—seem′li·ness** *n.*

seen [sēn] Past participle of SEE. ◆ *Seen* and *saw* are two forms of *see. Seen* is the past participle; it must be used with a form of *be* or *have*: I *have seen* him before. Do not use *seen* in place of the past form *saw* (as in "I seen him at the game").

seep [sēp] *v.* To soak through small spaces or openings; ooze: Water *seeped* into the cellar.

seep·age [sē′pij] *n.* **1** The act or process of seeping or oozing. **2** The fluid that seeps.

seer [sē′ər *or* sir] *n.* A person who foretells events; prophet.

seer·suck·er [sir′suk′ər] *n.* A thin fabric, as one of cotton or rayon, with a crinkled surface.

see·saw [sē′sô′] **1** *n.* A long board supported on a pivot at the center so that it can be made to move alternately up and down by persons at opposite ends. **2** *v.* To move up and down on a seesaw. **3** *v.* To move up and down or to and fro. **4** *adj.* Moving up and down or to and fro.

seethe [sēth] *v.* **seethed, seeth·ing** **1** To boil, or foam and bubble as if boiling. **2** To be excited or upset.

seg·ment [seg′mənt] 1 *n.* A part cut off or divided from the rest of something; section. 2 *v.* To cut or divide into segments. 3 *n.* A part of the interior of a circle bounded by an arc and a straight line. 4 *n.* A line segment. **—seg′men·ta′tion** *n.*
seg·men·tal [seg·men′təl] *adj.* Of, having to do with, or divided into segments.
se·go lily [sē′gō] A desert plant of western North America having bell-shaped flowers and an edible root. It is the state flower of Utah.
seg·re·gate [seg′rə·gāt′] *v.* **seg·re·gat·ed, seg·re·gat·ing** 1 To place apart from others; isolate: to *segregate* a sick animal. 2 To set apart and force to use separate facilities, as schools, housing, or parts of parks or buses, because of racial, religious, or social differences. 3 To regulate use of (as a school or park) so as to separate racial, religious, or ethnic groups. 4 To separate, as a small group from a large one or a liquid from a solid.
seg·re·ga·tion [seg′rə·gā′shən] *n.* 1 The act or process of segregating. 2 The practice of separating a racial or religious group from the rest of society, as in schools or housing. **—seg′re·ga′tion·ist** *n.*
se·gue [seg′wā′ *or* sā′gwā′] *v.* **se·gued, se·gue·ing,** *n.* 1 *v.* To move without a pause from one section or presentation to another, as in a musical performance. 2 *n.* A smooth transition without a pause.
sei·gneur [sēn·yûr′] *n.* In the Middle Ages, a feudal noble.
seine [sān] *n., v.* **seined, sein·ing** 1 *n.* A long fishnet hanging vertically in the water, having floats at the top and weights at the bottom. 2 *v.* To fish with such a net.

Seine

seis·mic [sīz′mik] *adj.* Of, having to do with, or caused by earthquakes: a severe *seismic* shock.
seis·mo·graph [sīz′·mə·graf′] *n.* An instrument that records the duration, direction, and intensity of earthquakes and other vibrations in the earth.
seis·mol·o·gy [sīz·mol′ə·jē] *n.* The study of earthquakes and other vibrations of the earth. **—seis′·mo·log′i·cal** *adj.* **—seis·mol′o·gist** *n.*
seize [sēz] *v.* **seized, seiz·ing** 1 To take hold of suddenly and with force; grab; snatch: to *seize* a sword. 2 To take prisoner; capture; arrest. 3 To take possession of by force: to *seize* a city. 4 To take possession of by right or authority. 5 To take quick advantage of: to *seize* a chance. 6 To strike or affect suddenly: to be *seized* with a fit of laughter. **—seize on** or **seize upon** To grab quickly.
sei·zure [sē′zhər] *n.* 1 The act of seizing. 2 A sudden, violent attack, as of a disease.
sel·dom [sel′dəm] *adv.* At widely separated times; rarely; not often. ◆ In formal writing, omit the *ever* from the informal expression *seldom ever.*
se·lect [si·lekt′] 1 *v.* To take in preference to another or others; choose: to *select* a record. 2 *adj.* Chosen for worth or high quality; choice. 3 *adj.* Very particular in choosing; exclusive.
se·lec·tee [si·lek′tē′] *n.* A person who is selected, especially a person drafted for military service.
se·lec·tion [si·lek′shən] *n.* 1 The act of selecting; choice. 2 A group of things from which to choose. 3 A thing chosen.
se·lec·tive [si·lek′tiv] *adj.* 1 Tending to select. 2 Of, related to, or characterized by selection. 3 Responding to a chosen frequency of radio waves and excluding others, as a radio receiver. **—se·lec·tiv·i·ty** [si·lek′tiv′ə·tē] *n.*
selective service A system of choosing people for required military service; draft.
se·lect·man [si·lekt′mən] *n., pl.* **se·lect·men** [si·lekt′mən] In New England, a member of a board of town officials elected yearly to run public affairs.
se·lec·tor [si·lek′tər] *n.* 1 A person who selects. 2 A switch or control used to choose different actions of a machine.

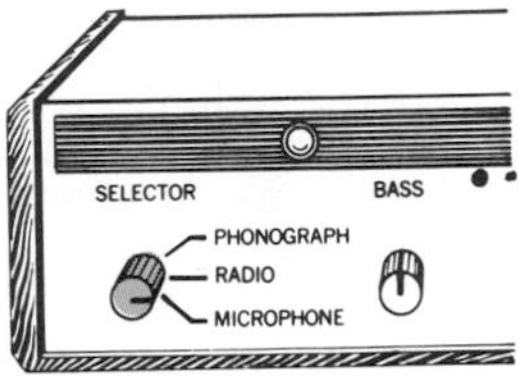

se·le·ni·um [si·lē′nē·əm] *n.* A gray, crystalline, nonmetallic element related to sulfur. Its electrical resistance changes under the influence of light.
self [self] *n., pl.* **selves** [selvz], *adj.* 1 *n.* One's own individual personality as distinct from others; one's own person: Today I am not my usual *self.* 2 *n.* One's own benefit or advantage: to put *self* first. 3 *adj.* Made of the same material as that with which it is used: The raincoat has a *self* belt.
self- A combining form meaning: 1 Of oneself, as in *self-criticism.* 2 By oneself, as in *self-educated.* 3 In or with oneself, as in *self-absorbed.* 4 To oneself, as in *self-injury.* 5 For oneself, as in *self-love.*
self-act·ing [self′ak′ting] *adj.* Capable of acting or operating by itself; automatic.
self-ad·dressed [self′ə·drest′] *adj.* Addressed to oneself.
self-ag·gran·diz·ing [self′ə·gran′dī′zing] *adj.* Acting or trying to increase one's own importance or power.
self-ap·point·ed [self′ə·poin′tid] *adj.* Appointed by oneself, with no other authorization and often without the abilities needed: a *self-appointed* critic.
self-as·ser·tion [self′ə·sûr′shən] *n.* The putting forward of oneself or one's ideas or claims.
self-as·sured [self′ə·shŏŏrd′] *adj.* Having confidence in one's own worth and abilities. **—self′-as·sur′ance** *n.*
self-cen·tered [self′sen′tərd] *adj.* Concerned mainly with oneself and often inconsiderate of others. **—self′-cen′tered·ness** *n.*
self-com·mand [self′kə·mand′] *n.* Full control of oneself and one's powers and feelings.
self-con·fi·dent [self′kon′fə·dənt] *adj.* Confident of

S

a add	**i** it	**ŏŏ** took	**oi** oil
ā ace	**ī** ice	**ōō** pool	**ou** pout
â care	**o** odd	**u** up	**ng** ring
ä palm	**ō** open	**û** burn	**th** thin
e end	**ô** order	**yōō** fuse	**th** this
ē equal			**zh** vision

ə = a in *above*, e in *sicken*, i in *possible*, o in *melon*, u in *circus*

oneself; self-assured. **—self′-con′fi·dence** *n.* **—self′-con′fi·dent·ly** *adv.*
self-con·scious [self′kon′shəs] *adj.* 1 So aware of how one appears to others that one is very embarrassed. 2 Showing such awareness or embarrassment: a *self-conscious* grin. **—self′-con′scious·ly** *adv.* **—self′-con′scious·ness** *n.*
self-con·tained [self′kən·tānd′] *adj.* 1 Containing everything it needs to operate or function: a *self-contained* phonograph; a *self-contained* community. 2 Not allowing one's thoughts and feelings to show. 3 Exercising self-control.
self-con·tra·dic·tion [self′kon′trə·dik′shən] *n.* 1 The act of contradicting oneself. 2 A statement or idea that has contradictory parts. **—self′con′·tra·dic′to·ry** *adj.*
self-con·trol [self′kən·trōl′] *n.* Control of one's emotions or actions.
self-de·feat·ing [self′di·fē′ting] *adj.* Harmful to one's or its own purposes or interest: Staying up all night to study for a test can be *self-defeating.*
self-de·fense [self′di·fens′] *n.* Defense of oneself or one's property.
self-de·ni·al [self′di·nī′əl] *n.* The giving up of things that are necessary or wanted.
self-de·ny·ing [self′di·nī′ing] *adj.* Practicing self-denial; unselfish.
self-de·struct [self′di·strukt′] *v.* To destroy itself: Without oil, a car engine will *self-destruct.*
self-de·struc·tive [self′di·struk′tiv] *adj.* Acting or tending to do harm to oneself.
self-de·ter·mi·na·tion [self′di·tûr′mə·nā′shən] *n.* 1 The right to make one's own decisions; free will. 2 The right of a people or country to choose its own form of government without outside interference.
self-dis·ci·pline [self′dis′ə·plin] *n.* Control of one's emotions or actions, often in order to improve oneself.
self-ed·u·cat·ed [self′ej′o͝o·kā′tid] *adj.* Educated by one's own effort, with little or no instruction in school; self-taught.
self-ef·fac·ing [self′i·fā′sing] *adj.* Tending to avoid the notice or attention of others; humble or shy.
self-em·ployed [self′im·ploid′] *adj.* Earning income from one's own business or profession rather than from an employer.
self-es·teem [self′ə·stēm′] *n.* 1 A good opinion of oneself. 2 Too good an opinion of oneself.
self-ev·i·dent [self′ev′ə·dənt] *adj.* Needing no evidence, proof, or explanation.
self-ex·plan·a·to·ry [self′ik·splan′ə·tôr′ē] *adj.* Easily understood without explanation; plain.
self-ex·pres·sion [self′ik·spresh′ən] *n.* Expression of one's feelings and thoughts, as in art.
self-gov·ern·ing [self′guv′ər·ning] *adj.* Having control over itself; not subject to an outside authority: a *self-governing* country.
self-gov·ern·ment [self′guv′ərn·mənt] *n.* The governing of an area by its own people.
self-help [self′help′] *n.* The act or an instance of taking care of or improving oneself.
self-im·age [self′im′ij] *n.* The mental picture that one has of oneself; one's idea of oneself.
self-im·por·tant [self′im·pôr′tənt] *adj.* Thinking too well of oneself; pompous or conceited. **—self′-im·por′tance** *n.*
self-im·prove·ment [self′im·pro͞ov′mənt] *n.* Action by oneself to improve one's condition, status, or prospects.
self-in·dul·gent [self′in·dul′jənt] *adj.* Satisfying one's own desires or whims. **—self′-in·dul′gence** *n.*
self-in·ter·est [self′in′tər·ist *or* self′in′trist] *n.* 1 Personal advantage or benefit. 2 Interest in or pursuit of personal advantage; selfishness.
self·ish [sel′fish] *adj.* 1 Caring mainly for oneself and hardly at all about others. 2 Showing or caused by an excessive care for oneself and disregard of others: a *selfish* action. **—self′ish·ly** *adv.* **—self′ish·ness** *n.*
self·less [self′lis] *adj.* Having little or no regard for self; unselfish. **—self′less·ly** *adv.*
self-made [self′mād′] *adj.* 1 Successful or rich because of one's own hard work. 2 Made by oneself.
self-pit·y [self′pit′ē] *n.* A feeling of pity for oneself.
self-por·trait [self′pôr′trit *or* self′pôr′trāt] *n.* A portrait of oneself made by oneself.
self-pos·sessed [self′pə·zest′] *adj.* Calm and in full control of one's emotions or actions.
self-pos·ses·sion [self′pə·zesh′ən] *n.* Full control over one's emotions or actions.
self-pres·er·va·tion [self′prez′ər·vā′shən] *n.* The act or instinct or keeping oneself alive or unharmed.
self-pro·pelled [self′prə·peld′] *adj.* Having within itself the means or power by which it moves: An automobile is a *self-propelled* vehicle.
self-re·li·ant [self′ri·lī′ənt] *adj.* Relying on one's own abilities, efforts, or judgment. **—self′-re·li′·ance** *n.*
self-re·spect [self′ri·spekt′] *n.* A proper sense of pride in or respect for oneself. **—self′-re·spect′ing** *adj.*
self-re·straint [self′ri·strānt′] *n.* Restraint of oneself; self-control.
self-right·eous [self′rī′chəs] *adj.* Believing one's own thoughts and actions to be more righteous than those of other people. **—self′-right′eous·ly** *adv.* **—self′-right′eous·ness** *n.*
self-ris·ing flour [self′rī′zing] *adj.* A commercially packaged mixture of flour, salt, and leaven.
self-rule [self′ro͞ol′] *n.* Self-government.
self-sac·ri·fice [self′sak′rə·fīs′] *n.* The sacrifice of oneself or one's needs or wants, usually because of duty or for the good of others. **—self′-sac′ri·fic′·ing** *adj.*
self·same [self′sām′] *adj.* Exactly the same; identical: to make the *selfsame* mistake again.
self-sat·is·fac·tion [self′sat′is·fak′shən] *n.* Satisfaction with oneself; conceit.
self-sat·is·fied [self′sat′is·fīd′] *adj.* Satisfied with oneself; conceited.
self-seek·ing [self′sē′king] 1 *adj.* Caring only about one's own gain or advancement; selfish. 2 *n.* The attitudes or actions of a self-seeking person. **—self′-seek′er** *n.*
self-ser·vice [self′sûr′vis] 1 *n.* The practice of having the patrons of a store or restaurant serve themselves. 2 *adj. use*: a *self-service* market.
self-styled [self′stīld′] *adj.* Called so by oneself: a *self-styled* musician.
self-suf·fi·cient [self′sə·fish′ənt] *adj.* 1 Able to supply everything needed without outside help. 2 Having great or too great confidence in oneself.
self-sup·port·ing [self′sə·pôr′ting] *adj.* Supporting oneself or itself without help.
self-sus·tain·ing [self′sə·stā′ning] *adj.* 1 Capable of sustaining oneself or itself without help. 2 Capable of maintaining itself after an initial input of energy: a *self-sustaining* nuclear reaction.

self-taught [self′tôt′] *adj.* Taught by oneself without formal instruction; self-educated.
self-will [self′wil′] *n.* Stubbornness in having one's own way; disregard for the wishes of others.
self-willed [self′wild′] *adj.* Tending to disregard the wishes of others; stubborn; obstinate.
self-wind·ing [self′wīn′ding] *adj.* Winding itself automatically, as a clock or watch.
sell [sel] *v.* **sold, sell·ing** 1 To give in exchange for money: to *sell* a house. 2 To deal in; offer for sale: Do you *sell* books? 3 To be on sale; be sold: Gold *sells* at a high price. 4 To help or influence the sale of: Advertising *sells* some products. 5 To betray for money or a reward: to *sell* one's honor. 6 *informal* To get approval from or for: They *sold* us on the scheme. **—sell out** 1 To sell one's complete stock of. 2 *slang* To betray (as a cause or person). **—sell′er** *n.*
sell·out [sel′out′] *n.* 1 The act of selling out: the *sellout* of his entire stock of T-shirts. 2 An entertainment or event for which all the tickets are sold. 3 *slang* A betrayal.
selt·zer [selt′sər] *n.* 1 A naturally bubbly mineral water. 2 Another name for SODA WATER.
sel·vage or **sel·vedge** [sel′vij] *n.* The edge of a woven fabric finished so as to prevent raveling.
selves [selvz] Plural of SELF.
Sem. 1 Semite. 2 Semitic.
se·man·tic [si·man′tik] *adj.* Of or related to the meanings of words.
se·man·ti·cist [si·man′ti·sist] *n.* An expert in the meaning of words.
se·man·tics [si·man′tiks] *n.* The study of the development of and the changes in the meanings of words. ◆ See -ICS.
sem·a·phore [sem′ə·fôr′] *n., v.* **sem·a·phored, sem·a·phor·ing** 1 *n.* A system of sending messages by holding the arms or flags in different positions. 2 *v.* To send (a message) by semaphore. 3 *n.* A tower with movable arms used to signal railroad trains.

Semaphore

sem·blance [sem′bləns] *n.* Likeness; outward appearance or show: a *semblance* of cleanliness.
se·men [sē′mən] *n.* The fluid that contains sperm, secreted by male animals.
se·mes·ter [si·mes′tər] *n.* 1 Either of the two parts of a school year, 17–20 weeks long; term. 2 Any term or session of instruction: Our summer school is divided into three *semesters*. ◆ *Semester* comes directly from the German.
semi- A prefix meaning: 1 Not fully; partly, as in *semiautomatic*. 2 Exactly half, as in *semicircle*. 3 Happening twice in the period of time mentioned, as in *semiannually*. ◆ See BI-.
sem·i·an·nu·al [sem′ē·an′yo͞o·əl] *adj.* Issued or happening twice a year. **—sem′i·an′nu·al·ly** *adv.*
sem·i·ar·id [sem′ē·âr′id] *adj.* Somewhat arid in climate; especially, having rainfall in the range of 10 to 20 inches per year.
sem·i·au·to·mat·ic [sem′ē·ô′tə·mat′ik] *adj.* 1 Partly automatic. 2 Firing once each time the trigger is pulled, without need of cocking or reloading: a *semiautomatic* rifle.
sem·i·cir·cle [sem′ē·sûr′kəl] *n.* A half circle.
sem·i·cir·cu·lar [sem′ē·sûr′kyə·lər] *adj.* Shaped like a half circle.
semicircular canal Any of three fluid-filled, looped tubes in the inner ear that act together to maintain the sense of balance.
sem·i·co·lon [sem′ē·kō′lən] *n.* A mark (;) of punctuation showing a separation that is greater than that shown by a comma but less than that shown by a period.
sem·i·con·duc·tor [sem′ē·kən·duk′tər] *n.* A material, such as silicon or germanium, that allows electricity to pass through it less easily than a conductor does but more easily than an insulator does. Semiconductors are used in transistors, integrated circuits, and other electronic devices.
sem·i·fi·nal [sem′ē·fī′nəl] 1 *n.* A round or match that is next to the last of a contest or competition. 2 *adj.* Of or having to do with such a round or match.
sem·i·fi·nal·ist [sem′ē·fī′nəl·ist] *n.* A contestant in a semifinal.
sem·i·month·ly [sem′ē·munth′lē] *adj.* Issued or taking place twice a month.
sem·i·nal [sem′ə·nəl] *adj.* 1 Of or containing semen or seed. 2 Being a source or having the potential to be a source; original; creative: one of the most *seminal* philosophers; a *seminal* idea.
sem·i·nar [sem′ə·när′] *n.* 1 A group of advanced students who do independent study in a specialized subject and meet to exchange information and results. 2 A meeting of such a group. 3 A conference for the exchange of information and opinion on a given subject.
sem·i·nar·i·an [sem′ə·nâr′ē·ən] *n.* A person who attends a seminary, especially a religious seminary.
sem·i·nar·y [sem′ə·ner′ē] *n., pl.* **sem·i·nar·ies** 1 A high school or school of higher education, especially a boarding school. 2 A school or college that trains ministers, priests, or rabbis.
Sem·i·nole [sem′ə·nōl′] *n., pl.* **Sem·i·nole** or **Sem·i·noles** 1 A tribe of North American Indians now living chiefly in Oklahoma but also in Florida. 2 A member of this tribe. 3 The language of this tribe.
sem·i·pre·cious [sem′ē·presh′əs] *adj.* Indicating gems, as jade, garnet, or opal, that are less valuable or rare than precious stones.
sem·i·pro [sem′ē·prō′] *adj., n. informal* Semiprofessional.
sem·i·pro·fes·sion·al [sem′ē·prə·fesh′ən·əl] 1 *adj.* Being a paid participant in an activity but not working full-time in it: a *semiprofessional* baseball player. 2 *adj.* Made up of such participants: *semiprofessional* baseball. 3 *n.* A semiprofessional person.
Sem·ite [sem′īt] *n.* A member of a group of peoples that includes the Hebrews, Arabs, and the ancient Assyrians and Babylonians.
Se·mit·ic [sə·mit′ik] *adj.* Of, having to do with, or like the Semites or their languages.
sem·i·tone [sem′ē·tōn′] *n.* The smallest interval of

a	add	**i**	it	**o͝o**	took	**oi**	oil
ā	ace	**ī**	ice	**o͞o**	pool	**ou**	pout
â	care	**o**	odd	**u**	up	**ng**	ring
ä	palm	**ō**	open	**û**	burn	**th**	thin
e	end	**ô**	order	**yo͞o**	fuse	**th̸**	this
ē	equal					**zh**	vision

ə = a in *above*, e in *sicken*, i in *possible*, o in *melon*, u in *circus*

the musical scale, as between a white key and an adjoining black key on a piano.

sem·i·trail·er [sem′ē·trā′lər] *n.* A truck trailer having wheels at the rear only, the forward part being supported by a truck tractor.

sem·i·trop·ical [sem′ē·trop′i·kəl] *adj.* Partly tropical: Louisiana has a *semitropical* climate.

sem·i·un·cial [sem′ē·un′shəl *or* sem′ē·un′she·əl *or* sem′ē·un′sē·əl] *n.* Another word for HALF UNCIAL.

sem·i·week·ly [sem′ē·wēk′lē] *adj.* Issued or happening twice weekly.

sem·o·li·na [sem′ə·lē′nə] *n.* The coarser particles of milled wheat, used for making spaghetti.

sen. or **Sen.** senator.

Sen. Senate.

sen·ate [sen′it] *n.* 1 A governing or lawmaking body. 2 (*written* **Senate**) The upper house of the Congress of the United States, or of the legislature of a state or other government.

sen·a·tor [sen′ə·tər] *n.* (*sometimes written* **Senator**) A member of a senate or a Senate.

sen·a·to·ri·al [sen′ə·tôr′ē·əl] *adj.* 1 Of, having to do with, or proper for a senator or senate. 2 Made up of senators. 3 Entitled to elect a senator: a *senatorial* district.

send [send] *v.* **sent, send·ing** 1 To cause or direct to go: *Send* them away. 2 To cause to be taken or transferred to another place: to *send* a telegram; The general *sent* more troops. 3 To cause to happen: Fate *sent* us the chance. 4 To issue; emit: The sun *sends* forth light. 5 To bring into a specific condition: The joke *sent* us into gales of laughter. **—send for** 1 To ask or order to come; summon. 2 To ask for; request; place an order for. **—send′er** *n.*

send-off [send′ôf′] *n.* A demonstration of affection or good wishes at the start of a trip or new venture.

Sen·e·ca [sen′ə·kə] *n., pl.* **Sen·e·ca** or **Sen·e·cas** 1 A tribe of North American Indians of western New York. It was the largest tribe of the Iroquois. 2 A member of this tribe. 3 The language of this tribe.

Sen·e·ga·lese [sen′ə·gə·lēz′] *adj., n., pl.* **Sen·e·ga·lese** 1 *adj.* Of or from Senegal. 2 *n.* A person born in or a citizen of Senegal.

sen·e·schal [sen′ə·shəl] *n.* In the residence of a medieval noble, an official in charge of the household; steward.

se·nile [sē′nīl′] *adj.* 1 Failing in body and mind because of old age. 2 Related to, caused by, or characteristic of old age: *senile* diseases.

se·nil·i·ty [si·nil′ə·tē] *n.* Mental and physical weakness caused by old age.

sen·ior [sēn′yər] 1 *adj.* Older, higher in rank, or longer in office. 2 *n.* The one who is older, higher in rank, or longer in office. 3 *n.* The older: written after the name of a father whose son has the same name, and usually abbreviated: John Snead. *Sr.* 4 *adj.* Of or during the final year of high school or college. 5 *n.* A student in the final year of high school or college.

senior high school A high school. In the U.S., it usually is made up of grades 10, 11, and 12.

sen·ior·i·ty [sēn·yôr′ə·tē] *n.* 1 Greater age, rank, or length of service. 2 Privileges or preference due to age, rank, or length of service.

sen·na [sen′ə] *n.* 1 The dried leaves of any of several plants related to the pea or bean, used as a laxative. 2 A plant having these leaves.

se·ñor [sā·nyôr′] *n., pl.* **se·ño·res** [sā·nyôr′ās] The male Spanish title of courtesy, equivalent to *Mr.*

se·ño·ra [sā·nyō′rä] *n.* The Spanish title of courtesy for a married woman, equivalent to *Mrs.*

se·ño·ri·ta [sā′nyō·rē′tä] *n.* The Spanish title of courtesy for an unmarried woman or girl, equivalent to *Miss.*

sen·sate [sen′sāt′] *adj.* Of, having to do with, perceiving, or perceived by the senses.

sen·sa·tion [sen·sā′shən] *n.* 1 The awareness of stimulation of any of the senses, as sight, smell, or touch: I have a *sensation* of coldness. 2 A feeling that comes from the mind or the emotions: a *sensation* of love. 3 Great interest or excitement: The movie caused a *sensation.* 4 Something that causes great interest or excitement.

sen·sa·tion·al [sen·sā′shən·əl] *adj.* 1 Causing great excitement or interest: a *sensational* play. 2 Designed to shock or startle: *sensational* news. 3 Of or having to do with the senses. **—sen·sa′·tion·al·ly** *adv.*

sen·sa·tion·al·ism [sen·sā′shən·əl·iz′əm] *n.* The use of material designed to attract an audience by shocking or startling it.

sense [sens] *n., v.* **sensed, sens·ing** 1 *n.* Any of the bodily or mental powers by which one is made aware of the world outside, as sight, hearing, touch, smell, or taste. 2 *n.* A feeling or awareness: a *sense* of fall in the air. 3 *v.* To become aware of: The deer *sensed* danger and ran. 4 *n.* (*often pl.*) Normal ability to think or reason clearly; sound or natural judgment: Chickens have little *sense*; to come to one's *senses.* 5 *n.* An awareness or understanding: a *sense* of right and wrong. 6 *n.* A meaning, as of a word. **—make sense** To mean something reasonable. **—in a sense** In a way.

sense·less [sens′lis] *adj.* 1 Without feeling or awareness; unconscious. 2 Stupid; foolish: a *senseless* prank. 3 Without purpose: *senseless* cruelty. **—sense′less·ly** *adv.* **—sense′less·ness** *n.*

sense organ A part of the body by which one receives sensations, as the eye, ear, or nose.

sen·si·bil·i·ty [sen′sə·bil′ə·tē] *n., pl.* **sen·si·bil·i·ties** 1 The capability or power of feeling or being aware: the *sensibility* of the eye to light. 2 (*often pl.*) Sensitive or delicate feelings: The off-key music hurt my *sensibilities*; to have a fine *sensibility* for art.

sen·si·ble [sen′sə·bəl] *adj.* 1 Having or showing wisdom or good judgment. 2 Capable of feeling or reacting; sensitive: *sensible* to heat. 3 Large enough to be noticed: a *sensible* difference of temperature. 4 Emotionally or mentally aware: to be *sensible* of a person's feelings. **—sen′si·bly** *adv.*

sen·si·tive [sen′sə·tiv] *adj.* 1 Capable of feeling, reacting, or appreciating quickly or easily: The ear is *sensitive* to sound; a *sensitive* thermometer; a film *sensitive* to light. 2 Easy to upset or make angry; touchy. 3 Extremely or abnormally susceptible: *sensitive* to changes in diet. 4 Tender or painful: a *sensitive* spot on the skin. **—sen′si·tive·ly** *adv.* **—sen′si·tive·ness** *n.*

sensitive plant Any of several plants of the mimosa family having leaflets that fold together when touched.

sen·si·tiv·i·ty [sen′sə·tiv′ə·tē] *n., pl.* **sen·si·tiv·i·ties** 1 The condition of being sensitive. 2 The degree to which something is sensitive.

sen·si·tize [sen′sə·tīz′] *v.* **sen·si·tized, sen′si·tiz·ing** To

make sensitive: This coating *sensitizes* the paper to light.
sen·sor [sen′sər] *n.* A device that reacts to a physical stimulus by recording it or transmitting an electrical impulse, used for automatic measurement or remote control: Seismic *sensors* on the moon detect the impact of meteorites.
sen·so·ry [sen′sər·ē] *adj.* Of or having to do with sensation: *sensory* nerves.
sen·su·al [sen′sho͞o·əl] *adj.* **1** Of or having to do with the body or the senses. **2** Indulging too much in bodily pleasures. **—sen·su·al·i·ty** [sen′·sho͞o·al′ə·tē] *n.* **—sen′su·al·ly** *adv.*
sen·su·ous [sen′sho͞o·əs] *adj.* **1** Coming from, having to do with, or appealing to the senses: a *sensuous* dance; *sensuous* enjoyment of music. **2** Enjoying the pleasures of the senses, especially in a delicate or refined way. **—sen′su·ous·ly** *adv.* **—sen′·su·ous·ness** *n.*
sent [sent] Past tense or past participle of SEND.
sen·tence [sen′təns] *n., v.* **sen·tenced, sen·tenc·ing** **1** *n.* In grammar, a word or group of words expressing a complete thought. **2** *n.* A final judgment, especially in a criminal case. **3** *n.* The punishment pronounced upon a person convicted of a crime. **4** *v.* To pass sentence upon; condemn.
sen·ten·tious [sen·ten′shəs] *adj.* **1** Using few words but expressing a good deal. **2** Habitually using proverbs or sayings in a dull, pompous, or moralizing way. **—sen·ten′tious·ly** *adv.*
sen·ti·ent [sen′shē·ənt] *adj.* Having awareness, sensations, and feelings: A stone is not a *sentient* thing.
sen·ti·ment [sen′tə·mənt] *n.* **1** A delicate or refined feeling. **2** An expression of such a feeling, especially in words. **3** A mental attitude toward a person, object, or idea, based on feeling instead of reason. **4** (*often pl.*) An attitude, opinion, or feeling: What are your *sentiments* about sports? **5** Feeling or emotion made too important, too obvious, or too much emphasized.
sen·ti·men·tal [sen′tə·men′təl] *adj.* **1** Having, showing, or appealing to very tender feelings: a *sentimental* song. **2** Acting on or influenced by feelings rather than logical thought: *sentimental* people. **3** Of or having to do with sentiment: to keep an old letter for *sentimental* reasons. **—sen′·ti·men′tal·ly** *adv.*
sen·ti·men·tal·ism [sen′tə·men′təl·iz′əm] *n.* Sentimentality. **—sen′ti·men′tal·ist** *n.*
sen·ti·men·tal·i·ty [sen′tə·men·tal′ə·tē] *n., pl.* **sen·ti·men·tal·i·ties** **1** A tendency to indulge in too much sentiment and to be too much influenced by it. **2** An expression of excessive or foolish emotion.
sen·ti·men·tal·ize [sen′tə·men′təl·īz] *v.* **sen·ti·men·tal·ized, sen·ti·men·tal·iz·ing** **1** To indulge in sentiment or sentimentality. **2** To represent or describe with sentiment or sentimentality: Some immigrants *sentimentalize* the country of their birth.
sen·ti·nel [sen′tə·nəl] *n.* A watcher or guard; sentry. **—stand sentinel** To keep watch; guard.
sen·try [sen′trē] *n., pl.* **sen·tries** A person, especially a soldier, assigned to guard an area against intruders and to look out for danger.

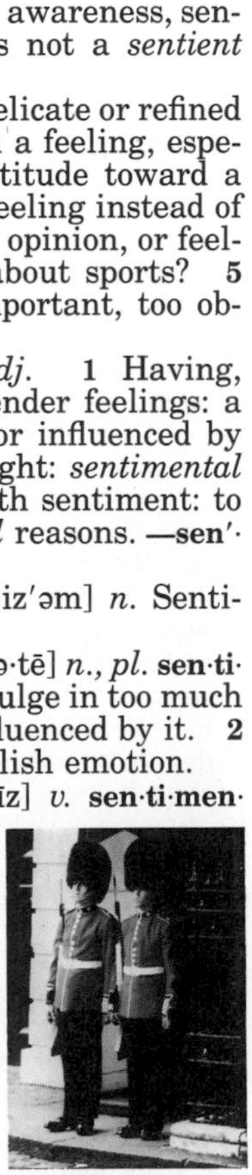

Sentries

sentry box A booth or other small shelter for a sentry standing guard.
se·pal [sē′pəl] *n.* One of the leaves that form the calyx surrounding the petals of a flower.

Sepals

sep·a·ra·ble [sep′ər·ə·bəl *or* sep′·rə·bəl] *adj.* That can be separated.
sep·a·rate [*v.* sep′ə·rāt′, *adj.* sep′·ər·it *or* sep′rit] *v.* **sep·a·rat·ed, sep·a·rat·ing,** *adj.* **1** *v.* To move apart; part: to *separate* a couple of dogs fighting: *Separate* the curtains. **2** *adj.* Not connected or joined; detached: The swimming pool is in a *separate* building. **3** *v.* To keep apart by being between; divide: The Hudson River *separates* New York City from New Jersey. **4** *v.* To divide into parts or groups: to *separate* water into oxygen and hydrogen; *Separate* knives from forks. **5** *v.* To take, go, or come apart; make or become disconnected or disunited: The team *separated* after the game. **6** *adj.* Existing or working as a unit distinct from others: the many *separate* parts that make up an engine. **7** *adj.* Not combined; distinct: two *separate* problems. **—sep′a·rate·ly** *adv.*
sep·a·ra·tion [sep′ə·rā′shən] *n.* **1** The act of separating or the condition of being separated. **2** An open space between things or parts; gap. **3** An arrangement in which a husband and wife live apart.
sep·a·ra·tist [sep′ər·ə·tist] *n.* A person who favors separation, as from a political or religious body.
sep·a·ra·tor [sep′ə·rā′tər] *n.* **1** Any device that separates things, as chaff from grain or cream from milk. **2** A person who separates.
se·pi·a [sē′pē·ə] **1** *adj., n.* Reddish brown. **2** *n.* A picture or photograph having a sepia color.
sep·sis [sep′sis] *n., pl.* **sep·ses** [sep′sēz′] A condition in which germs or their toxic products are present in the body; infection.
Sept. September.
Sep·tem·ber [sep·tem′bər] *n.* The ninth month of the year, having 30 days.
sep·tic [sep′tik] *adj.* **1** Of or caused by infection. **2** Causing infection; infectious.
sep·ti·ce·mi·a [sep′ti·sē′mē·ə] *n.* Another name for BLOOD POISONING.
septic tank A tank into which sewage drains to be destroyed by the action of bacteria.
sep·tum [sep′təm] *n., pl.* **sep·ta** [sep′tə] A dividing membrane or wall, as between two body cavities: A *septum* of cartilage separates the human nostrils.
sep·ul·cher or **sep·ul·chre** [sep′əl·kər] *n.* A burial place; grave; tomb.
se·pul·chral [si·pul′krəl] *adj.* **1** Of or having to do with a sepulcher. **2** Gloomy; dismal; sad.

a	add	**i**	it	**o͝o**	took	**oi**	oil
ā	ace	**ī**	ice	**o͞o**	pool	**ou**	pout
â	care	**o**	odd	**u**	up	**ng**	ring
ä	palm	**ō**	open	**û**	burn	**th**	thin
e	end	**ô**	order	**yo͞o**	fuse	**th**	this
ē	equal					**zh**	vision

ə = { a in *above* e in *sicken* i in *possible* / o in *melon* u in *circus* }

S

seq. 1 sequel. 2 sequence.

se·quel [sē′kwəl] *n.* 1 Something that follows, usually as a development of what went before. 2 A story that, though complete in itself, carries on from where a preceding story ended.

se·quence [sē′kwəns] *n.* 1 The coming of one thing after another in space or time: the *sequence* of the seasons. 2 The order or arrangement in which one thing comes after another: The correct *sequence* is for the youngest children to enter first. 3 A number of things following each other; series: a *sequence* of events.

se·quent [sē′kwənt] *adj.* Following in sequence.

se·ques·ter [si·kwes′tər] *v.* 1 To remove to a private or remote place; seclude: to *sequester* oneself in a quiet room; *sequestering* dangerous criminals. 2 To take over and keep, as enemy property in wartime. **—se′ques·tra′tion** *n.*

se·quin [sē′kwin] *n.* A small, shiny disk used as an ornamental trimming on clothing.

se·quoi·a [si·kwoi′ə] *n.* Either of two gigantic evergreen trees of the western United States. One is the redwood, the other is the big tree or giant sequoia. ◆ *Sequōia* comes from *Sequoyah,* 1770?–1843, a Cherokee Indian who invented the Cherokee alphabet.

se·ra [sir′ə] Alternate plural of SERUM.

se·ra·glio [si·ral′yō] *n.* That part of a Muslim house where the women and girls live; harem.

se·ra·pe [sə·rä′pē] *n.* A blanketlike outer garment worn in Latin America, especially in Mexico.

Serape

ser·aph [ser′əf] *n., pl.* **ser·aphs** or **ser·a·phim** [ser′ə·fim] An angel of the highest rank, having three pairs of wings.

se·raph·ic [si·raf′ik[*adj.* 1 Of or having to do with a seraph. 2 Like a seraph; angelic.

Serb [sûrb] *n.* A person born or living in Serbia.

Ser·bi·an [sûr′bē·ən] 1 *adj.* Of or from Serbia. 2 *n.* A person born or living in Serbia. 3 *n.* The language of Serbia; Serbo-Croatian.

Ser·bo-Cro·a·tian [sûr′bō·krō·ā′·shən] 1 *n.* A Slavic language spoken by the Serbs and Croats of Yugoslavia. 2 *adj.* Of or having to do with this language or its speakers.

sere [sir] *adj.* Dried or withered: used mostly in poems.

ser·e·nade [ser′ə·nād′] *n., v.* **ser·e·nad·ed, ser·e·nad·ing** 1 *n.* A song, usually one sung in the evening by a lover beneath a sweetheart's window. 2 *n.* The music for such a song. 3 *v.* To entertain with a serenade.

ser·en·dip·i·ty [ser′ən·dip′ə·tē] *n.* The act or knack of finding good things by accident. ◆ This word was coined in 1754 by the English writer Horace Walpole. He took it from the name of a Persian fairy tale, *The Three Princes of Serendip*, whose heroes "were always making discoveries . . . of things they were not in quest of."

se·rene [si·rēn′] *adj.* 1 Clear; fair; calm: a *serene* sky. 2 Peaceful; tranquil; unruffled; calm: a *serene* spirit. **—se·rene′ly** *adv.*

se·ren·i·ty [si·ren′ə·tē] *n.* 1 Peacefulness; repose. 2 Clearness; brightness.

serf [sûrf] *n.* 1 In feudal times, a person who could not leave the land he or she worked on, and who could be sold along with the land. 2 Any person treated like a slave.

serf·dom [sûrf′dəm] *n.* 1 The condition of being a serf. 2 The practice of having serfs.

serge [sûrj] *n.* A strong, woven fabric, usually of wool, having slanting lines or ridges on its surface, and used for clothing, as coats and suits.

ser·geant [sär′jənt] *n.* 1 A military rank. In the U.S. Army, a sergeant is a noncommissioned officer ranking above a corporal. 2 A police officer ranking next below a captain or sometimes below a lieutenant. ◆ *Sergeant* comes from an old French word meaning a *servant* or *attendant*, and this was the earliest meaning of the word in English. This meaning is still preserved in *sergeant at arms.*

sergeant at arms An officer whose main duty is to keep order in a legislative body or in certain courts or clubs. ◆ See SERGEANT.

sergeant major *pl.* **sergeants major** A military rank. In the U.S. Army or Marine Corps, a sergeant major is a noncommissioned officer of the highest rank.

se·ri·al [sir′ē·əl] 1 *adj.* Of, having to do with, or arranged in a series: *serial* numbers. 2 *n.* A story whose parts are presented one at a time in the issues of a newspaper or magazine. 3 *n.* A play presented in short, usually daily installments on television or radio. **—se′ri·al·ly** *adv.*

se·ri·al·ize [sir′ē·ə·līz′] *v.* **se·ri·al·ized, se·ri·al·iz·ing** To present in installments: The newspaper is *serializing* the book.

serial number A number given to a person or thing as a means of identification: Every typewriter has a *serial number.*

se·ries [sir′ēz] *n., pl.* **se·ries** 1 A number of people or things coming one after another in time or place: a *series* of visitors; a *series* of buildings. 2 A group of batteries or light bulbs so connected that the same electrical current flows through each of them in turn.

ser·if [ser′əf] *n.* Any of the short lines that extend from the ends of the main strokes of a printed letter.

se·ri·ous [sir′ē·əs] *adj.* 1 Grave; solemn; thoughtful: You look *serious* today. 2 Not joking; sincere: Are they *serious* about the trip? 3 Of great importance; weighty: a *serious* problem. 4 Likely to be harmful or dangerous: a *serious* accident; a *serious* illness. **—se′ri·ous·ly** *adv.* **—se′ri·ous·ness** *n.* ◆ *Serious, earnest,* and *sober* are all used to describe people. A *serious* person is not playful or silly but sets about acting or thinking with real purpose. An *earnest* person is more eager and shows more obvious sincerity. A *sober* person is apt to be more methodical and much less excitable than an *earnest* person. A *sober* person is generally more detached from circumstances and happenings than a *serious* person.

ser·mon [sûr′mən] *n.* 1 A religious talk, usually delivered by a member of the clergy as part of a church service. 2 A serious talk about how a person should act, think, and behave.

ser·mon·ize [sûr′mə·nīz′] *v.* **ser·mon·ized, ser·mon·iz·ing** 1 To deliver a sermon; preach. 2 To speak in a solemn, dogmatic way; lecture.

se·rous [sir′əs] *adj.* Having to do with, producing, or resembling serum.

ser·pent [sûr′pənt] *n.* 1 A snake, especially a large one. 2 An underhanded, treacherous person. 3 In the Bible, the devil; Satan.
ser·pen·tine [sûr′pən·tēn′ *or* sûr′pən·tīn′] 1 *adj.* Of or like a serpent. 2 *adj.* Curving; winding. 3 *adj.* Tricky; sly; subtle: *serpentine* reasoning. 4 *n.* A green, sometimes spotted mineral.
ser·rate [ser′āt′] *adj.* 1 Toothed or notched like a saw. 2 Having notched edges, as certain leaves.
ser·rat·ed [ser′ā·tid] *adj.* Serrate.
ser·ried [ser′ēd] *adj.* Crowded or close together: *serried* rows of soldiers.

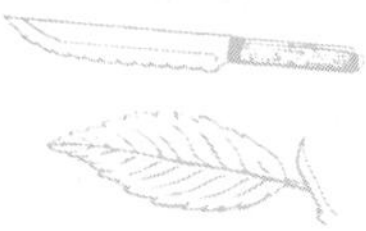
The knife and the leaf are serrate.

se·rum [sir′əm] *n., pl.* **se·rums** or **se·ra** [sir′ə] 1 The clear, slightly yellow part of an animal fluid that remains when the rest clots, especially this fluid in blood. 2 A liquid obtained from the blood of an animal that has been inoculated with a specific disease. This liquid is then used as an antitoxin against that disease. 3 Any similar fluid.
ser·val [sûr′vəl] *n.* An African wildcat having long legs and a yellow coat spotted with black.
ser·vant [sûr′vənt] *n.* 1 A person hired to work for another, especially one who assists with work in and around the house, as a maid or gardener. 2 A person who is a government official or holds a public office. 3 A person devoted to some cause: a *servant* of justice.
serve [sûrv] *v.* **served, serv·ing,** *n.* 1 *v.* To work or work for as a servant: The gardener has *served* for many years; The gardener *serves* the neighbors. 2 *v.* To promote the interest of; work for; aid; help: to *serve* one's country. 3 *v.* To obey and worship: to *serve* God. 4 *v.* To satisfy, be enough for, or be satisfactory: One package of food won't *serve* us all; This carton will *serve* as a bookcase. 5 *v.* To perform a duty or function: to *serve* as mayor; to *serve* on a jury. 6 *v.* To go through or put in (as a term of punishment): The convicted robber *served* four years in prison. 7 *v.* To do military or naval service for: to *serve* a certain country; to *serve* ten years. 8 *v.* To pass time in the armed forces: The soldier *served* loyally. 9 *v.* To furnish or provide: They *serve* the school with heat. 10 *v.* To help or wait on, as at table or in a store: to *serve* at dinner; Have you been *served*? 11 *v.* To bring or distribute: to *serve* dessert. 12 *v.* In a game, as tennis, to put (the ball) in play. 13 *v.* In tennis or other games, to put the ball in play. 14 *n.* In tennis or other games, the act or manner of serving. 15 *n.* A person's turn at serving, as in tennis. 16 *v.* To deliver or present: to *serve* a summons. 17 *v.* To be favorable: If the weather *serves*, we'll leave tomorrow. 18 *v.* To reward; deal with: It would *serve* you right if we didn't come to your party.
serv·er [sûr′vər] *n.* 1 A person who serves. 2 Something that is used in serving, as a tray.
ser·vice [sûr′vis] *n., v.* **ser·viced, ser·vic·ing** 1 *n.* Any work done or action performed for the benefit of another; assistance; benefit: to render *service* to a friend. 2 *n.* (*often pl.*) A useful work that does not produce a material object: the *services* of a doctor or lawyer. 3 *n.* The act of serving or the manner in which a person is served: The *service* in this store is excellent. 4 *n.* Something that benefits or aids the public as a whole: bus *service*; electric *service*. 5 *v.* To supply service to: One bus company *services* the whole city. 6 *n.* Employment in or a particular division of the government: civil *service*; the diplomatic *service*. 7 *n.* Any branch of the armed forces: to enlist in the *service*. 8 *adj.* Of or having to do with military service: *service* stripes. 9 *n.* A religious ceremony: to attend Sunday *service*. 10 *n.* The act, position, or condition of being a servant: to be in *service* with a large family. 11 *n.* A set of tableware for a specific purpose: a tea *service*. 12 *n.* The act of delivering or presenting something, as a summons or writ. 13 *n.* In a game, as tennis, the act or manner of serving a ball. 14 *adj.* Of, for, or having to do with service or servants: a *service* entrance. 15 *v.* To maintain or repair: to *service* a car. **—at one's service** Ready to do what is wanted: I'm *at your service*.
ser·vice·a·ble [sûr′vis·ə·bəl] *adj.* 1 Able to be of service; beneficial; useful. 2 Able to give long service; durable: a *serviceable* coat.
ser·vice·man [sûr′vis·man′] *n., pl.* **ser·vice·men** [sûr′vis·men′] 1 A member of one of the armed forces. 2 A servicer.
ser·vic·er [sûr′vis·ər] *n.* A person who takes care of, adjusts, or repairs such things as appliances, elevators, or cars.
service station 1 A place where drivers bring cars and trucks for gasoline, oil, greasing, or repairs. 2 A place for maintaining and repairing machines.
service stripe A stripe on the left sleeve of an enlisted person's uniform indicating a specified period of time the person has spent in the service.
ser·vice·wom·an [sûr′vis·wo͝om′in] *n., pl.* **ser·vice·wom·en** [sûr′vis·wim′in] A woman who is a member of the armed forces.
ser·vile [sûr′vīl′ *or* sûr′vəl] *adj.* 1 Without spirit or boldness; like a slave: always *servile* to the boss. 2 Of or appropriate for slaves or servants: a *servile* job. **—ser·vil·i·ty** [sûr·vil′ə·tē] *n.*
serv·ing [sûr′ving] *n.* 1 The act of one who serves. 2 A portion of food: two *servings*.
ser·vi·tor [sûr′və·tər] *n.* A servant or attendant.
ser·vi·tude [sûr′və·t(y)o͞od′] *n.* 1 Slavery. 2 Enforced labor as a punishment for crime.
ser·vo·mech·a·nism [sûr′vō·mek′ə·niz′əm] *n.* A mechanical device that automatically monitors and governs the performance of a machine, a part of which it is.
ses·a·me [ses′ə·mē] *n.* 1 A plant of the East Indies. 2 Its seeds, yielding a pale yellow oil and used as food. **—open sesame** A magic command, used originally by Ali Baba to open a door in a story from the *Arabian Nights*.
ses·sile [ses′īl′] *adj.* 1 Permanently attached; not free to move: Barnacles are *sessile* animals. 2 Having no stalk; attached directly at the base: a *sessile* leaf.
ses·sion [sesh′ən] *n.* 1 The meeting, as of a legis-

a	add	**i**	it	**o͝o**	took	**oi**	oil		
ā	ace	**ī**	ice	**o͞o**	pool	**ou**	pout		
â	care	**o**	odd	**u**	up	**ng**	ring		
ä	palm	**ō**	open	**û**	burn	**th**	thin		
e	end	**ô**	order	**yo͞o**	fuse	**th**	this		
ē	equal					**zh**	vision		

ə = {a in *above* e in *sicken* i in *possible* o in *melon* u in *circus*}

S

lative body, court, or class, to conduct its business: a morning *session* in the physics laboratory. **2** A series of such meetings. **3** Any meeting of two or more persons: I had a *session* with the principal this morning. **4** A division of a school year. **—in session** Meeting: Court is *in session*.

set [set] *v.* **set, set·ting,** *n., adj.* **1** *v.* To put in a certain place or position; place: I *set* my cup on a saucer. **2** *v.* To make or become hard, firm, or rigid: The gelatin has *set*; to *set* one's jaw. **3** *n.* The way in which a thing is placed or held: the stubborn *set* of a jaw. **4** *v.* To put in a certain condition: *Set* your mind at ease. **5** *v.* To put back in its proper position: to *set* a bone. **6** *v.* To put into position or condition for proper operation: to *set* a trap; to *set* a clock. **7** *v.* To place utensils and dishes on: to *set* a table. **8** *v.* To fix or establish; to *set* a time; to *set* a dance step. **9** *adj.* Fixed or established; deliberate: a *set* time; a *set* speech; a *set* action. **10** *adj.* Stubborn; obstinate: to be *set* in one's ways. **11** *v.* To present or provide so as to be copied: to *set* a bad example. **12** *v.* To direct: We *set* the course for Bermuda. **13** *v.* To place in a setting, as a gem. **14** *v.* To place (a hen) on eggs to hatch them. **15** *v.* To place (eggs) under a hen for hatching. **16** *v.* To sit on eggs, as a hen. **17** *v.* To provide or fit: to *set* words to music or music to words. **18** *v.* To create or arrange scenery for a play or other presentation: to *set* the stage for a jungle scene. **19** *n.* The scenery so created or arranged. **20** *v.* To go or pass below the horizon: The sun *set* yesterday at six o'clock. **21** *v.* In printing, to arrange (type) in proper order. **22** *v.* To start: I *set* the machine in motion. **23** *adj.* Ready; prepared: to be all *set*. **24** *adj.* Formed; built: a thick-*set* figure. **25** *n.* A group of persons or things that go or belong together: the jet *set*; a *set* of dishes. **26** *n.* The act of setting. **27** *n.* A being set. **28** *n.* The direction of a current or wind. **29** *n.* A group of six or more games making up part of a tennis match. **30** *n.* A number of different electrical or mechanical parts assembled for use: a radio *set*. **31** *n.* In mathematics, a collection of elements, points, or integers, having some characteristic in common: the *set* of all even numbers. **—set about** To start doing; begin. **—set against 1** To balance; compare. **2** To make unfriendly to. **—set apart** To put aside for a special purpose. **—set aside 1** To place apart or to one side. **2** To reject; dismiss. **—set back 1** To check. **2** To hinder or delay. **—set down 1** To place on a surface. **2** To write or print. **3** To consider. **4** To explain as caused by; attribute. **—set forth 1** To state or declare. **2** To start or begin, as a journey. **—set in 1** To begin to occur. **2** To blow or flow toward shore, as wind or tide. **—set off 1** To put apart. **2** To start or start to go. **3** To serve as a foil for; contrast with. **4** To cause to explode. **—set on** To urge to attack. **—set out 1** To present to view; display. **2** To plant. **3** To start something, especially a journey. **—set to 1** To start; begin. **2** To start fighting. **—set up 1** To place in an upright position. **2** To place in power or authority. **3** To construct, assemble, or build. **4** To found; establish. **5** To cause; start. **6** To cause to be heard: to *set up* a cry. **7** To claim to be: to *set* oneself *up* as an authority. **8** *informal* To make feel happy or encouraged: Our victory *set* us all *up*. **—set upon** To make an attack upon; assault. ◆ See SIT.

set·back [set′bak′] *n.* A reverse or check, as in progress or success: a business *setback*.

set·tee [se·tē′] *n.* **1** A long bench with a back. **2** A sofa large enough for two or three people.

set·ter [set′ər] *n.* **1** A person that sets: a *setter* of diamonds. **2** One of a breed of hunting dogs trained to point out game by standing rigid.

English setter

set theory The branch of mathematics dealing with sets.

set·ting [set′ing] *n.* **1** The act of a person or thing that sets. **2** The mounting that holds a gem. **3** The scene, time, or background, as of a play, motion picture, or novel: This book has a Civil War *setting*. **4** Any background or surroundings. **5** The music written for a poem or for other words. **6** The eggs on which a hen sits for hatching.

set·tle[1] [set′(ə)l] *v.* **set·tled, set·tling 1** To put in order; set to rights; arrange: to *settle* one's affairs. **2** To put firmly or comfortably in place: to *settle* oneself on a couch. **3** To free of disturbance; calm; quiet: to *settle* one's nerves. **4** To sink or cause to sink: The signpost *settled* in the mud. **5** To make or become clear: *Settle* the coffee; The coffee has *settled*. **6** To decide or determine: to *settle* on a plan. **7** To resolve or reconcile: to *settle* differences. **8** To pay, as a debt; satisfy, as a claim. **9** To establish a residence, as a home or colony, in: The English *settled* Virginia. **10** To take up residence; make a home: We *settled* in New York when I was ten. **11** To come to rest or as if to rest: A bee *settled* on the rose; Snow *settled* on the roof; A great sadness *settled* over me. **—settle down 1** To start living a regular, orderly life. **2** To become quiet or orderly. **—settle on** or **settle upon** To give (as money or property) to someone by a legal act.

set·tle[2] [set′(ə)l] *n.* A long wooden seat or bench with a high back.

set·tle·ment [set′(ə)l·mənt] *n.* **1** The act of settling. **2** A being settled. **3** An agreement or arrangement for settling: A *settlement* of the dock strike was reached today. **4** An area newly settled by people; colony. **5** A small community or village. **6** The transfer of something, as money or property, to another, as at marriage or divorce: to arrange for a property *settlement*. **7** The money, property, or other things thus transferred. **8** Payment: the *settlement* of a claim. **9** An institution offering services, as child care and educational courses, for the people of a poor neighborhood.

Settle

settlement house A settlement (def. 9).

set·tler [set′lər] *n.* **1** A person who settles, especially one who settles in a colony or new country. **2** A person or thing that settles something: a *settler* of labor disputes.

set·up [set′up′] *n. informal* The way in which something is organized or coordinated: You have to understand the *setup* to participate in an auction.

sev·en or **7** [sev′ən] *n., adj.* One more than six.

seven seas All the oceans of the world, by old tradition the North and South Atlantic, the North and South Pacific, the Indian, the Arctic, and the Antarctic oceans.

sev·en·teen or **17** [sev′ən·tēn′] *n., adj.* One more than sixteen.

sev·en·teenth or **17th** [sev′ən·tēnth′] **1** *adj.* Next after the sixteenth. **2** *n.* The seventeenth one. **3** *adj.* Being one of seventeen equal parts. **4** *n.* A seventeenth part.

sev·enth or **7th** [sev′ənth] **1** *adj.* Next after the sixth. **2** *n.* The seventh one. **3** *adj.* Being one of seven equal parts. **4** *n.* A seventh part.

sev·en·ti·eth or **70th** [sev′ən·tē·ith] **1** *adj.* Tenth in order after the sixtieth. **2** *n.* The seventieth one. **3** *adj.* Being one of seventy equal parts. **4** *n.* A seventieth part.

sev·en·ty or **70** [sev′ən·tē] *n., pl.* **sev·en·ties** or **70's,** *adj.* **1** *n., adj.* Ten more than sixty. **2** *n.* (*pl.*) The years between the age of 70 and the age of 80: My grandparents are in their *seventies.*

sev·en·ty-eight or **78** [sev′ən·tē·āt′] *n.* A phonograph record that plays at a speed of 78 revolutions per minute.

Seven Wonders of the World The seven works of human beings considered the most remarkable in the ancient world: the Egyptian pyramids, the hanging gardens of Babylon, the temple of Diana at Ephesus, the statue of Zeus by Phidias at Olympia, the mausoleum of King Mausolos at Halicarnassus, the Colossus of Rhodes, and the lighthouse of Alexandria.

sev·er [sev′ər] *v.* **1** To cut or break into two or more parts. **2** To separate. **3** To break off; end.

sev·er·al [sev′ər·əl *or* sev′rəl] **1** *adj.* Being more than two, yet not many: I read *several* books last week. **2** *n., pron.* More than two, yet not many: *Several* will come back shortly. **3** *adj.* Single; separate: After class, we all went our *several* ways. —**sev′er·al·ly** *adv.* ◆ See FEW.

sev·er·ance [sev′ər·əns *or* sev′rəns] *n.* **1** The act of severing. **2** A severed condition; separation; partition.

se·vere [si·vir′] *adj.* **se·ver·er, se·ver·est** **1** Strict; harsh: *severe* discipline; a *severe* criticism. **2** Extreme in degree or effects: a *severe* strain. **3** Serious and sober, as in manner or disposition. **4** Plain and simple in style or decoration: *severe* furniture. **5** Causing great distress, hardship, or damage: a *severe* snowstorm. —**se·vere′ly** *adv.*

se·ver·i·ty [si·ver′ə·tē] *n., pl.* **se·ver·i·ties** **1** Sternness; strictness: The *severity* of the punishment was too great. **2** Sharpness; harshness: the *severity* of the blizzard. **3** Simplicity and plainness: the *severity* of Puritan dress.

sew [sō] *v.* **sewed, sewed** or **sewn, sew·ing** **1** To make, mend, or fasten by using a needle and thread: to *sew* a garment; to *sew* up a rip. **2** To work with needle and thread: The whole class likes to *sew.* —**sew up** To conclude successfully: to *sew up* a deal. —**sew′er** *n.*

sew·age [sōō′ij] *n.* The waste matter which is carried off in sewers.

sew·er [sōō′ər] *n.* A pipe or drain, usually underground, to carry off dirty water, refuse, and other waste matter.

sew·er·age [sōō′ər·ij] *n.* **1** A systems of sewers. **2** The removal of waste by sewers. **3** Sewage.

sew·ing [sō′ing] *n.* **1** The act, business, or occupation of a person who sews. **2** The thing that is sewed; material on which a person is at work with needle and thread.

sewing machine A machine used for sewing.

sewn [sōn] An alternative past participle of SEW.

An old-fashioned sewing machine

sex [seks] *n.* **1** Either of two groups, male and female, into which human beings and many other living things are divided according to their functions in reproduction. **2** The character of being male or female. **3** Activities and feelings that have to do with the reproductive functions.

sex chromosome Either of two types of chromosomes, called X and Y, that determine the sex of an offspring in human beings, most animals, and some plants.

sex gland A gland in which male or female reproductive cells develop; testis or ovary.

sex·ism [sek′siz′əm] *n.* Discrimination and bias against one sex by the other. —**sex′ist** *adj., n.*

sex·tant [seks′tənt] *n.* **1** An instrument for measuring angular distance, as of a star or the sun, above the horizon, used in determining a ship's position. **2** A sixth part of a circle; a sector of 60°.

Sextant

sex·tet or **sex·tette** [seks·tet′] *n.* **1** A musical composition for six performers. **2** The six singers or players who perform such a composition. **3** Any group of six persons or things.

sex·ton [seks′tən] *n.* A janitor of a church, whose duties may include ringing the bell and digging graves.

sex·u·al [sek′shōō·əl] *adj.* **1** Of or having to do with sex or the sexes. **2** Of, involving, or designating reproduction in which male and female reproductive cells are united to form a fertilized egg or eggs. —**sex′u·al·ly** *adv.*

sex·u·al·i·ty [sek′shōō·al′ə·tē] *n.* **1** The condition of being male or female. **2** Sexual activity or feeling.

SF science fiction.

sgt. or **Sgt.** sergeant.

sgt. maj. or **Sgt. Maj.** sergeant major.

shab·by [shab′ē] *adj.* **shab·bi·er, shab·bi·est** **1** Threadbare; ragged, as from hard use or wear: *shabby* jeans. **2** Wearing threadbare, ragged clothing. **3** Dilapidated; run-down: a *shabby* neighborhood. **4** Mean or unfair: *shabby* treatment. —**shab′bi·ly** *adv.* —**shab′bi·ness** *n.*

Sha·bu·oth [shə·vōō′ōt′, shə·vōō′ōth′, *or* shə·vōō′·ōs′] *n.* A Jewish holiday commemorating the giving of the Ten Commandments to Moses.

a	add	**i**	it	**o͝o**	took	**oi**	oil
ā	ace	**ī**	ice	**ōō**	pool	**ou**	pout
â	care	**o**	odd	**u**	up	**ng**	ring
ä	palm	**ō**	open	**û**	burn	**th**	thin
e	end	**ô**	order	**yōō**	fuse	**t͟h**	this
ē	equal					**zh**	vision

ə = {a in *above* e in *sicken* i in *possible* / o in *melon* u in *circus*}

shack [shak] *n.* A small, crudely built, sometimes dilapidated house or cabin; shanty.

shack·le [shak′əl] *n., v.* **shack·led, shack·ling** **1** *n.* A metal ring or band, usually one of a pair joined by a chain, put around the wrist or ankle to restrain movement or prevent escape. **2** *n.* Anything that restrains or hinders: the *shackles* of poverty. **3** *v.* To restrain or hinder with or as if with a shackle.

Shackles

shad [shad] *n., pl.* **shad** A fish of the Atlantic coast, related to the herring and highly prized as food.

shade [shād] *n., v.* **shad·ed, shad·ing** **1** *n.* The darkness caused by something cutting off part of the light: the *shade* of a tree. **2** *n.* A slightly dark place, where sunshine is cut off: Let's sit in the *shade* where it's cool. **3** *v.* To screen or keep from a source of light; put in shade: A big tree *shades* our garden. **4** *v.* To make dim by cutting down light: to *shade* the light of a lamp. **5** *n.* A device that cuts off or reduces light: a window *shade*; a lamp *shade*. **6** *n.* A small difference, as of lightness or darkness, in a color: There are many *shades* of gray in that picture. **7** *v.* To give the effect of shadows or darkness in: to *shade* a figure in a drawing. **8** *n.* The dark part or parts, as those in a picture or drawing. **9** *v.* To change or vary by degrees: The sunset *shaded* from bright orange to blue. **10** *n.* A slight degree; small amount: There was a *shade* of laughter in your voice. **11** *n.* A small difference: many *shades* of meaning. **12** *n.* A spirit or ghost. **13** *n.* (*pl.*) The shadows and darkness that come after sunset.

shad·ing [shā′ding] *n.* **1** Protection against light or heat. **2** The lines, dots, or dark colors that show shadows, depth, or darkness in a picture or drawing. **3** A slight difference or variation: *shadings* of meaning.

shad·ow [shad′ō] **1** *n.* Partial darkness where light is cut off: a cat half hidden in *shadow.* **2** *n.* A dark figure or image cast on a surface by a body or object coming between the source of light and the surface: the *shadow* of a tree on the wall. **3** *v.* To make or cast a shadow or shadows upon: Trees *shadowed* the garden. **4** *n.* The shaded or dark portion of a picture. **5** *v.* To make shadows in a painting or picture. **6** *n.* Anything unreal or imaginary: Such "dangers" are just *shadows.* **7** *n.* A faint representation or indication: Only a *shadow* of greatness remains. **8** *n.* A very small amount; trace: a *shadow* of a doubt. **9** *n.* Gloom or unhappiness: The *shadow* of illness darkened these years. **10** *v.* To make sad or gloomy: Illness *shadowed* their happiness. **11** *v.* To follow closely or secretly; spy on. **12** *n.* A person who spies on or follows someone closely or secretly. **13** *n.* A ghost or spirit. **—in the shadow of** Very close or near to.

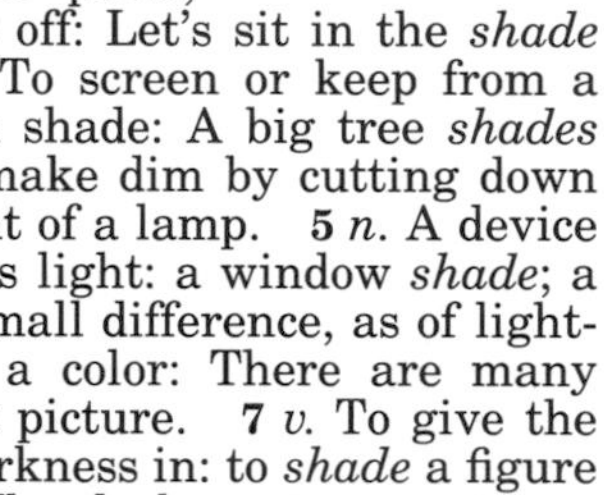
Shadow

shad·ow·box [shad′ō·boks′] *v.* To box with an imaginary opponent, especially as a training exercise.

shad·ow·y [shad′ō·ē] *adj.* **shad·ow·i·er, shad·ow·i·est** **1** Full of shade or shadows; dark; shady: a *shadowy* path in the woods. **2** Like a shadow in being unclear or dim: a *shadowy* recollection.

shad·y [shā′dē] *adj.* **shad·i·er, shad·i·est** **1** In the shade; shaded; sheltered: a *shady* spot in the forest. **2** Producing or giving shade: a *shady* beach umbrella. **3** *informal* Questionable as to honesty or legality: a *shady* character; a *shady* business firm. **—shad′i·ness** *n.*

shaft [shaft] *n.* **1** The long, narrow rod, as of an arrow or spear. **2** An arrow or spear. **3** Anything like an arrow or spear in appearance or effect: a *shaft* of light; *shafts* of ridicule. **4** A long handle, as of an ax or golf club. **5** The part of a column between its top and its base. **6** A slender column. **7** One of the two poles by which a horse is harnessed, as to a carriage or wagon. **8** In a machine, a rotating rod that transmits power. **9** A deep passage sunk into the earth, as the entrance to a mine. **10** A passage in the earth, as one for light, air, or water. **11** An opening through the floors of a building, as for an elevator.

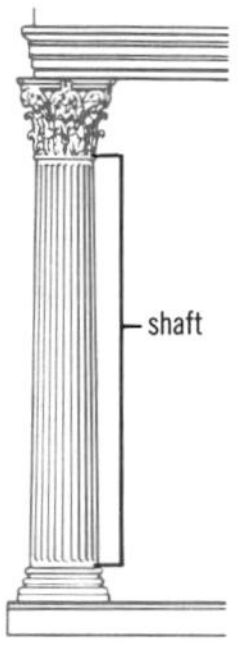

shag [shag] *n.* **1** A rough mass, as of hair or wool. **2** A long nap on cloth. **3** Cloth that has a rough or long nap.

shag·bark [shag′bärk′] *n.* A hickory tree with shaggy gray bark that peels off in long, narrow pieces.

shag·gy [shag′ē] *adj.* **shag·gi·er, shag·gi·est** **1** Having rough hair or wool: a *shaggy* animal. **2** Having a rough, fuzzy nap or surface: *shaggy* wool. **3** Rough and untidy: a *shaggy* haircut. **—shag′gi·ness** *n.*

shah [shä] *n.* A sovereign of Iran.

shake [shāk] *v.* **shook, shak·en, shak·ing,** *n.* **1** *v.* To move or cause to move back and forth, up and down, or from side to side with short, rapid movements. **2** *v.* To dislodge, force, or throw, by a shaking movement: She *shook* salt on her food; to *shake* a cat out of a tree. **3** *v.* To tremble or vibrate, or cause to tremble or vibrate: to *shake* from fear; to *shake* a door with a blow. **4** *v.* To weaken or disturb: to *shake* someone's determination. **5** *v. slang* To get rid of or away from: I tried to *shake* my pursuers. **6** *n.* The act of shaking. **7** *n.* A being shaken. **8** *n.* (*pl.*) A trembling, as from chills or fever. **—no great shakes** *informal* Of no great ability or excellence **—shake down** **1** To cause to fall by shaking. **2** To cause to settle; make compact. **3** *slang* To obtain money from in a dishonest way. **—shake hands** To clasp hands in greeting or agreement. **—shake off** To rid oneself of by or as if by shaking. **—shake up** **1** To shake, mix, or stir. **2** *informal* To shock or jar.

shak·er [shā′kər] *n.* **1** A person or thing that shakes. **2** A container for shaking something: a juice *shaker.* **3** (*written* **Shaker**) A member of a religious sect in the United States, so called because of trembling bodily motions made during their religious meetings.

shake-up [shāk′up′] *n.* A sudden, thorough change, as in a company or police department, often with the transfer or dismissal of high officials.

shak·o [shak′ō] *n., pl.* **shak·os** A kind of high, stiff military hat with an upright plume.

shak·y [shā′kē] *adj.* **shak·i·er, shak·i·est** 1 Continually shaking or trembling; weak; unsteady. 2 Not trustworthy; unreliable: a *shaky* business firm. **—shak′i·ness** *n.*

shale [shāl] *n.* A rock formed from hardened clay or mud. It splits easily into thin layers.

shall [shal] *v. Present tense for all subjects* **shall,** *past tense* **should** A helping verb used to express: 1 Things happening in the future: I *shall* be there tomorrow. 2 Determination, promise, threat, or command: They *shall* not pass; You *shall* have whatever you need; You *shall* pay for this. ◆ In ordinary usage in the U.S. today, *will* is used with all persons (*I, you, he, she, it, we, you, they*) both to indicate the future and to express determination or command. Traditionally, *shall* in the first person and *will* in the second and third indicate the future, and the reverse indicates determination; but this rule is observed only in very formal writing.

shal·lot [shə·lot′] *n.* A small vegetable resembling an onion, used as a seasoning.

shal·low [shal′ō] 1 *adj.* Having the bottom not far below the surface or top; not deep: a *shallow* pool. 2 *n.* (*usually pl.*) A shallow place in a body of water: We swam in the *shallows* of the river. 3 *adj.* Not wise or profound: a *shallow* thinker. 4 *v.* To make or become shallow. **—shal′low·ly** *adv.* **—shal′low·ness** *n.*

sha·lom [shä·lōm′] *interj.* A Hebrew word meaning "peace," used especially by Jews as a greeting and farewell.

shalt [shalt] A form of the verb SHALL, used with *thou*: seldom used today: Thou *shalt* not kill.

sham [sham] *n., adj., v.* **shammed, sham·ming** 1 *n.* Something not true; pretense; deception: That air of good nature is a *sham.* 2 *n.* A person who pretends or deceives. 3 *adj.* Pretended; false: *sham* grief. 4 *v.* To pretend: to *sham* illness.

sha·man [shä′mən *or* shā′mən] *n.* A kind of priest among native peoples in North America and Asia who calls on spirits to help him heal the sick and give advice. **—sha′man·ism** *n.*

sham·ble [sham′bəl] *v.* **sham·bled, sham·bling,** *n.* 1 *v.* To walk in a shuffling, unsteady manner. 2 *n.* A shuffling, unsteady walk.

sham·bles [sham′bəlz] *n.pl.* (*usually used with singular verb*) 1 A slaughterhouse. 2 Any place of execution or bloodshed. 3 A place in which there is great destruction or disorder: The living room was a *shambles* after the party.

shame [shām] *n., v.* **shamed, sham·ing** 1 *n.* A painful feeling of guilt caused by one's own or someone else's wrongdoing: to feel *shame* at having made such a mistake. 2 *v.* To cause to feel shame; make ashamed. 3 *n.* A person or thing that brings shame or disgrace. 4 *n.* A condition of dishonor or disgrace: The actions of the class brought *shame* to the school. 5 *v.* To bring shame upon; disgrace. 6 *n.* Something that brings regret or sorrow: What a *shame* you lost the game! 7 *v.* To force by causing a sense of shame: to *shame* someone into doing a favor. **—for shame!** You should be ashamed! **—put to shame** 1 To disgrace; make ashamed. 2 To do better than; surpass.

shame·faced [shām′fāst′] *adj.* 1 Showing shame in one's face; ashamed. 2 Modest; shy.

shame·ful [shām′fəl] *adj.* 1 Deserving or bringing shame; disgraceful. 2 Indecent. **—shame′ful·ly** *adv.*

shame·less [shām′lis] *adj.* 1 Done without shame. 2 Without modesty; brazen. **—shame′less·ly** *adv.*

sham·poo [sham·po͞o′] *n., v.* **sham·pooed, sham·poo·ing** 1 *n.* Any of various preparations, as of soap or oil, used to wash the hair and scalp. 2 *n.* The act or process of washing the hair. 3 *v.* To wash (the hair and scalp) with a shampoo. ◆ *Shampoo* comes from a Hindustani word meaning *to press* in the process of massaging.

sham·rock [sham′rok′] *n.* Any of several three-leaved plants resembling clover, accepted as the national emblem of Ireland. ◆ *Shamrock* comes from an Irish word meaning *small clover.*

shan·dy·gaff [shan′dē·gaf′] *n.* A drink of beer or ale mixed with ginger beer, ginger ale, or lemonade.

shang·hai [shang·hī′] *v.* **shang·haied, shang·hai·ing** 1 To drug and make unconscious in order to kidnap for service aboard a ship. 2 To cause to do something by force or trickery.

shank [shangk] *n.* 1 The part of the leg between the knee and the ankle. 2 The whole leg. 3 A cut of meat from the leg of an animal. 4 The part of a tool connecting the handle with the working part, as the stem of a drill.

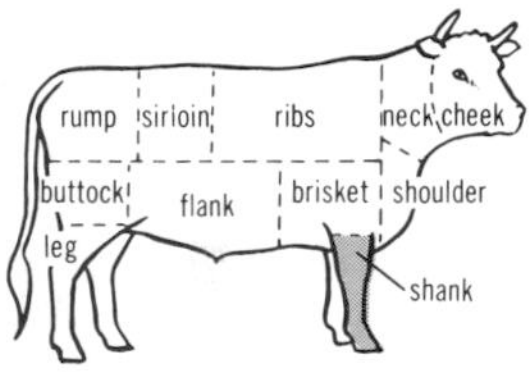

shan't [shant] Shall not: They *shan't* go to the movies with us.

shan·ty [shan′tē] *n., pl.* **shan·ties** A crude, hastily built shack or cabin.

shape [shāp] *n., v.* **shaped, shap·ing** 1 *n.* The outward form or outline of something: the *shape* of a building. 2 *v.* To give a shape to; mold; form. 3 *n.* A definite or developed form: to put an idea into *shape.* 4 *v.* To prepare; develop: to *shape* your ideas into a definite plan. 5 *v.* To become or develop: You have *shaped* up into a fine student. 6 *n.* Condition: The car's brakes were not in good *shape.* **—take shape** To have or take on a fixed form; become definite.

shape·less [shāp′lis] *adj.* 1 Having no definite shape. 2 Having an unattractive shape.

shape·ly [shāp′lē] *adj.* **shape·li·er, shape·li·est** Having a pleasing shape; well-formed.

shard [shärd] *n.* A broken piece of a brittle substance, as of a clay pot.

share[1] [shâr] *n., v.* **shared, shar·ing** 1 *n.* A single portion of something distributed among or contributed by several: my *share* of the ice cream; my *share* of the donation. 2 *v.* To divide and give out, each taking a part: to *share* the ice cream; to *share* the expense. 3 *n.* A part of something enjoyed or suffered in common: our *share* of the blame. 4 *v.*

a	add	**i**	it	**o͝o**	took	**oi**	oil
ā	ace	**ī**	ice	**o͞o**	pool	**ou**	pout
â	care	**o**	odd	**u**	up	**ng**	ring
ä	palm	**ō**	open	**û**	burn	**th**	thin
e	end	**ô**	order	**yo͞o**	fuse	**t͟h**	this
ē	equal					**zh**	vision

ə = {a in *above* e in *sicken* i in *possible*; o in *melon* u in *circus*}

To enjoy or suffer in common: The whole team *shared* the excitement of winning. **5** *v.* To own or use together: We *share* the telephone. **6** *n.* One of the equal parts into which the ownership or total stock of a company is divided. **7** *v.* To have a part or share: to *share* in the profits of a business deal. **—go shares** To take part equally.

share[2] [shâr] *n.* A plowshare.

share·crop·per [shâr′krop′ər] *n.* A farmer who lives on and farms land but does not own it and who gives the landowner a share of the crop as rent.

share·hold·er [shâr′hōl′dər] *n.* An owner of a share or shares of a company's stock; stockholder.

shark[1] [shärk] *n.* Any of various long-bodied marine fishes, some very large, that have hard, rough skins and very sharp teeth. Sharks eat other fish, and some kinds will attack humans.

Common shark

shark[2] [shärk] *n.* **1** A dishonest person; swindler. **2** *slang* A person who has great skill or ability in some special thing.

sharp [shärp] **1** *adj.* Having a keen edge or a fine point; able to cut or pierce. **2** *adj.* Coming to or having a point: a *sharp* peak. **3** *adj.* Turning or changing abruptly; not gradual: a *sharp* curve. **4** *adj.* Cutting; piercing; stinging: a *sharp* wind; a *sharp* blow. **5** *adj.* Affecting the mind or senses, as if by cutting or piercing: *sharp* pangs of remorse; a *sharp* taste or odor. **6** *adj.* Very keen and sensitive; acute: My dog has *sharp* vision and hearing. **7** *adj.* Attentive; watchful: Keep a *sharp* lookout. **8** *adj.* Eager; keen: a *sharp* appetite. **9** *adj.* Brisk; quick; active: *sharp* trading. **10** *adj.* Fiery; violent: a *sharp* debate. **11** *adj.* Harsh, irritable, or severe: a *sharp* answer. **12** *adj.* Quick-witted; clever; shrewd: a *sharp* bargainer. **13** *adj.* Not blurred; distinct; clear: a *sharp* outline. **14** *adj. slang* Attractive and excellent: You look *sharp*. **15** *adv.* In a sharp manner; sharply, keenly, or quickly: Look *sharp* now! **16** *adj.* Above the right, true pitch: That note was *sharp*. **17** *adv.* Above the right, true pitch: to sing *sharp*. **18** *n.* A sign (#) placed before a note to show that the note is raised a semitone above the natural pitch. **19** *n.* The note so altered. **20** *v.* To raise in pitch, as by a half tone. **21** *v.* To sing, play, or sound above the right pitch. **22** *adv.* Promptly; exactly. **—sharp′ly** *adv.* **—sharp′ness** *n.*

sharp·en [shär′pən] *v.* To make or become sharp or sharper. **—sharp′en·er** *n.*

sharp·shoot·er [shärp′shōō′tər] *n.* A skilled marksman, especially with the rifle.

sharp-sight·ed [shärp′sī′tid] *adj.* **1** Having keen eyesight. **2** Mentally quick and observant; alert.

sharp-wit·ted [shärp′wit′id] *adj.* Intelligent; keen; acute; clever.

shat·ter [shat′ər] *v.* **1** To break into pieces. **2** To damage; demolish; ruin.

shave [shāv] *v.* **shaved, shaved** or **shav·en, shav·ing,** *n.* **1** *v.* To cut (hair or beard) close to the skin with a razor: Did you *shave* yet?; to *shave* off a scraggly moustache. **2** *v.* To remove hair or beard from: The barber *shaved* me this morning. **3** *n.* The act or process of cutting off hair with a razor. **4** *v.* To trim closely, as if with a razor: to *shave* a lawn. **5** *v.* To cut thin slices from, as wood. **6** *v.* To touch or scrape in passing. **—close shave** A narrow escape.

shav·er [shā′vər] *n.* **1** A person or a thing that shaves. **2** *informal* A young person.

shav·ing [shā′ving] *n.* **1** The act of a person or thing that shaves. **2** A very thin piece shaved from anything.

Sha·vu·oth [shə·vōō′ōt′, shə·vōō′ōth′, *or* shə·vōō′·ōs′] *n.* Another spelling of SHABUOTH.

shawl [shôl] *n.* A wrap, as a square cloth or large scarf, worn over the head or shoulders.

Shaw·nee [shô·nē′] *n., pl.* **Shaw·nee** or **Shaw·nees** **1** A tribe of North American Indians now living in Oklahoma. **2** A member of this tribe. **3** The language of this tribe.

shay [shā] *n.* A two-wheeled, one-horse carriage for two persons; chaise. ◆ *Shay* comes from the word *chaise* [shāz], which was mistakenly thought to be a plural. The spelling was "Americanized" and *shay* was formed as the singular.

Shay

she [shē] *pron., pl.* **they,** *n., pl.* **shes** **1** *pron.* A female person or animal previously mentioned, or a thing usually spoken of as feminine, as a ship or machine: Grace said *she* would come to the party; When you see the sailboat, you'll agree *she* needs painting. **2** *pron.* Any female: *She* who listens learns. **3** *n.* A female person or animal: Is that dog a he or a *she*?

sheaf [shēf] *n., pl.* **sheaves** [shēvz] **1** A quantity of stalks of cut grain, as rye or wheat, bound together. **2** A collection of things that are tied or bound together, as papers.

shear [shir] *v.* **sheared, sheared** or **shorn, shear·ing** **1** To cut the hair or fleece from: to *shear* a sheep. **2** To cut or cut through, with or as if with shears: to *shear* wool. **3** To move or proceed as if by cutting: The arrow *sheared* through the air. **4** To take something away from; deprive: They *sheared* the tyrant of all power.

shears [shirz] *n.pl.* A large cutting tool similar to scissors (also called a **pair of shears**), worked by the crossing of its cutting edges.

sheath [shēth] *n., pl.* **sheaths** [shē<u>th</u>z *or* shēths] **1** A cover or case for a blade, as of a sword. **2** Any caselike covering, as that on the lower part of a blade of grass. **3** A close-fitting dress having a straight, narrow appearance.

sheathe [shē<u>th</u>] *v.* **sheathed, sheath·ing** **1** To put into a sheath. **2** To protect with a covering.

sheath·ing [shē′<u>th</u>ing] *n.* A close-fitting protective covering, especially the first layer of boards applied to the wall of a frame house.

sheave [shēv] *v.* **sheaved, sheav·ing** To gather into sheaves, as grain.

She·ba [shē′bə] *n.* The Old Testament name for a region of SW Arabia. *I Kings*, a book of the Old Testament, tells the story of the Queen of Sheba who visited Solomon to test his wisdom.

shed[1] [shed] *v.* **shed, shed·ding** **1** To pour forth or cause to pour forth: He *shed* tears over the loss. **2** To send forth; radiate: The moon *shed* its light. **3** To throw off without allowing to go through: An umbrella *sheds* rain. **4** To cast off (as hair or skin). **—shed blood** To kill. **—shed light on** To furnish information about.

shed² [shed] *n.* A small, low building, often with front or sides open.
she'd [shēd] 1 She had. 2 She would.
sheen [shēn] *n.* A glistening brightness; gloss; luster.
sheep [shēp] *n., pl.* **sheep** 1 A domesticated grazing animal related to the goat. It chews its cud and is bred in many varieties for its wool and meat. 2 The skin of a sheep, or anything made from it, as leather or parchment. 3 A meek, bashful, or timid person.

Sheep

sheep dog A dog trained to guard and control sheep, often a collie.
sheep·fold [shēp′fōld′] *n.* A place where sheep are kept at night; pen for sheep.
sheep·herd·er [shēp′hûr′dər] *n.* A person who tends a herd of sheep.
sheep·ish [shē′pish] *adj.* 1 Awkwardly shy, embarrassed, or abashed: a *sheepish* expression. 2 Foolish, meek, or timid, as a sheep. —**sheep′ish·ly** *adv.* —**sheep′ish·ness** *n.*
sheep's eyes [shēps] Bashful, amorous, often lovesick glances.
sheep·skin [shēp′skin′] *n.* 1 The skin of a sheep, or anything made of it, as leather or parchment. 2 A document written on parchment, as a diploma.
sheer¹ [shir] 1 *adj.* Complete; utter; absolute: *sheer* stupidity. 2 *adv.* Completely; utterly; absolutely. 3 *adj.* Very thin and fine: *sheer* fabrics. 4 *adj.* Sloping sharply; very steep: a *sheer* drop. 5 *adv.* Very steeply. —**sheer′ly** *adv.* —**sheer′ness** *n.*
sheer² [shir] 1 *v.* To turn or cause to turn aside from a course; swerve. 2 *n.* A turning aside from a course.
sheet¹ [shēt] 1 *n.* A large, lightweight piece of cloth, often of cotton, used on a bed in sets of two, one beneath the body and one as a cover. 2 *n.* A piece of paper. 3 *n.* A newspaper. 4 *n.* A piece of metal or other substance, hammered, rolled, or cut very thin. 5 *n.* A thin, broad piece: a *sheet* of ice. 6 *v.* To cover or provide with a sheet. 7 *n.* A broad, flat, often moving surface: a *sheet* of water; Rain fell in *sheets.*
sheet² [shēt] *n.* 1 A rope used to control the angle at which a sail is set. 2 (*pl.*) The spaces at either end of an open boat, called the **bow sheets** and the **stern sheets.**
sheet·ing [shē′ting] *n.* Any material in the form of sheets or that can be formed into sheets.
sheet lightning Lightning in sheetlike form, lighting up a broad area of the sky.
sheet metal Metal rolled and pressed into sheets.
sheet music Music printed on unbound sheets of paper, especially music for popular songs.
sheikh or **sheik** [shēk] *n.* The chief or head of an Arab tribe or family.
sheikh·dom or **sheik·dom** [shēk′dəm] *n.* An area ruled by a sheikh.
shek·el [shek′əl] *n.* 1 An ancient Hebrew unit of weight and money. 2 A coin having this weight.
shel·drake [shel′drāk′] *n.* 1 Any of several Old World ducks. 2 Another name for MERGANSER.
shelf [shelf] *n., pl.* **shelves** [shelvz] 1 A thin, flat piece of wood, metal, or other material, attached to a wall or supported by a frame and used to hold things. 2 Anything like a shelf, as a ledge or shoal. —**on the shelf** No longer in use.
shell [shel] 1 *n.* Any of various hard outer coverings, as the structure encasing a shellfish, the carapace of a turtle, the fragile outer coat of an egg, or the covering of a nut. 2 *v.* To remove from a shell: to *shell* peas. 3 *v.* To separate from the cob or husk: to *shell* corn. 4 *n.* Something that resembles a shell in appearance or in being hollow and light: a pie *shell.* 5 *n.* Tortoiseshell. 6 *n.* A framework with its interior removed, or one to be filled out or built upon: the *shell* of a house. 7 *n.* A very light, long, and narrow racing rowboat. 8 *n.* A cartridge for a rifle, shotgun, or hand gun. 9 *n.* A hollow metal projectile full of explosive, fired from cannon, mortars, and other weapons. 10 *v.* To fire shells at with a large gun; bombard: to *shell* a fort. —**shell out** *informal* To hand over, as money.

Shell

she'll [shēl] A contraction of: 1 She will: *She'll* be here soon. 2 She shall.
shel·lac [shə·lak′] *n., v.* **shel·lacked, shel·lack·ing** 1 *n.* A resinous material in the form of thin flakes. 2 *n.* A solution of this material in alcohol, used to coat and protect wood. 3 *v.* To cover with shellac: to *shellac* the floors. 4 *v. slang* To defeat badly.
shell·fire [shel′fīr′] *n.* The firing of shells.
shell·fish [shel′fish′] *n., pl.* **shell·fish** or **shell·fish·es** Any animal that lives in the water and has a shell, as an oyster.
shell shock A nervous condition resulting from long exposure to the strain of modern warfare.
shel·ter [shel′tər] 1 *n.* Something that covers or protects, as from danger or exposure to the weather. 2 *n.* The condition of being sheltered, covered, or protected. 3 *v.* To provide shelter or protection for. 4 *v.* To find shelter.
shelve [shelv] *v.* **shelved, shelv·ing** 1 To place on a shelf. 2 To postpone indefinitely; put aside: to *shelve* a project. 3 To provide or fit with shelves. 4 To slope gradually.
shelv·ing [shel′ving] *n.* 1 Shelves. 2 Material for shelves, as wood or metal.
she·nan·i·gans [shi·nan′ə·gənz] *n.pl. informal* Trickery; foolery; nonsense; mischief.
She·ol [shē′ōl] *n.* In the Old Testament, a place under the earth where the dead were believed to go.
shep·herd [shep′ərd] 1 *n.* A person who watches over and herds sheep. 2 *n.* A pastor or religious

a add	**i** it	**o͝o** took	**oi** oil
ā ace	**ī** ice	**o͞o** pool	**ou** pout
â care	**o** odd	**u** up	**ng** ring
ä palm	**ō** open	**û** burn	**th** thin
e end	**ô** order	**yo͞o** fuse	**th** this
ē equal			**zh** vision

ə = a in *above*, e in *sicken*, i in *possible*, o in *melon*, u in *circus*

S

leader. 3 *v.* To watch over, escort, or guide as a shepherd. **—the Good Shepherd** Jesus.

shep·herd·ess [shep′ərd·is] *n.* A woman or girl who watches over and herds sheep.

shepherd's pie A baked dish of meat in gravy, covered by a layer or bordered by a crust of mashed potatoes.

sher·bet [shûr′bit] *n.* 1 A frozen dessert made with such ingredients as water, milk, sugar, and fruit juice. 2 An Oriental drink made of sweetened fruit juice diluted with water. ◆ *Sherbet* comes from a Turkish word which comes from an Arabic word meaning *drink*.

sher·iff [sher′if] *n.* The leading law-enforcing official of a county.

sher·ry [sher′ē] *n., pl.* **sher·ries** 1 A strong wine of Spanish origin. 2 A wine made in imitation of this, as in California.

she's [shēz] A contraction of: 1 She is: *She's* here now. 2 She has: *She's* gone home.

Shet·land pony [shet′lənd] A small, hardy, shaggy breed of pony.

Shetland pony

shew [shō] *v.* **shewed, shewn, shew·ing** To show: seldom used today.

Shi·a [shē′ə] *n., pl.* **Shi·as,** *adj.* 1 *n.* The Persian branch of Islam. 2 *adj.* Of the Persian branch of Islam; Shiite. 3 *n.* A Muslim belonging to the Persian branch of Islam.

shib·bo·leth [shib′ə·lith] *n.* 1 A custom or use of language by which the members of a particular social class or profession may be distinguished: Dinner at eight is a cherished *shibboleth* of their family. 2 A pet phrase or watchword of a party.

shied [shīd] Past tense and past participle of SHY[1] or SHY[2].

shield [shēld] 1 *n.* A broad piece of armor, once commonly carried on the arm to fend off blows while fighting. 2 *n.* Anything that protects or defends, as a safety device that covers a dangerous machine part. 3 *v.* To protect or guard. 4 *n.* Anything resembling a shield, as a police badge.

Shield

shi·er [shī′ər] Comparative of SHY[1].

shi·est [shī′ist] Superlative of SHY[1].

shift [shift] 1 *v.* To change or move from one position or place to another: to *shift* one's weight; to *shift* responsibility; to *shift* gears. 2 *n.* A change of place, position, or direction: a *shift* in the wind; a *shift* of responsibility. 3 *n.* A group of workers: members of the night *shift*. 4 *n.* The working time of such a group: My *shift* is from 9 to 5. 5 *n.* A piece of trickery or deceit; dodge; evasion: I used many *shifts* to keep from doing my homework. **—shift for oneself** To provide for one's own needs; get along on one's own.

shift·less [shift′lis] *adj.* Showing a lack of energy or ambition; lazy.

shift·y [shif′tē] *adj.* **shift·i·er, shift·i·est** Using or expressing tricks, deception, or fraud: a *shifty* person; *shifty* eyes.

Shi·ite [shē′īt′] 1 *n.* A Muslim of the Shia branch of Islam. 2 *adj.* Of or having to do with the Shias.

shill [shil] *n.* A person who secretly helps a swindler while pretending to be an innocent onlooker or customer.

shil·le·lagh or **shil·la·lah** [shə·lā′lē] *n.* A club for striking blows; cudgel.

shil·ling [shil′ing] *n.* 1 A former British coin worth 1/20 pound. 2 The basic unit of money in Kenya, Somalia, Tanzania, and Uganda.

shil·ly-shal·ly [shil′ē·shal′ē] *v.* **shil·ly-shal·lied, shil·ly-shal·ly·ing,** *n., adj., adv.* 1 *v.* To keep changing one's mind; be unable to decide. 2 *n.* Indecision; hesitation. 3 *adj.* Undecided; hesitating. 4 *adv.* In an indecisive or hesitating manner.

shim·mer [shim′ər] 1 *v.* To shine with an unsteady, glimmering light. 2 *n.* A faint, unsteady light; glimmer; gleam. **—shim′mer·y** *adj.*

shim·my [shim′ē] *v.* **shim·mied, shim·my·ing,** *n., pl.* **shim·mies** 1 *v.* To vibrate or wobble, as an old automobile. 2 *n.* A shaking; vibration. 3 *n.* A dance popular in the 1920's, characterized by rapid shaking of the body. 4 *v.* To dance the shimmy.

shin [shin] *n., v.* **shinned, shin·ning** 1 *n.* The front part of the leg, below the knee. 2 *v.* To climb something, as a pole or rope, by gripping with the hands and legs: to *shin* up a mast.

shin·bone [shin′bōn′] *n.* Another word for TIBIA.

shin·dig [shin′dig′] *n. slang* A dance or noisy party.

shine [shīn] *v.* **shone** or **shined, shin·ing,** *n.* 1 *v.* To give off or reflect light: The stars are *shining*; The windows *shone* in the sunset. 2 *n.* The quality of being bright or shining; luster: the *shine* of clean hair. 3 *v.* To cause to shine: *Shine* your flashlight over here. 4 *v.* To be outstanding; excel: This group *shines* in spelling. 5 *v.* To brighten by rubbing or polishing: I *shined* my shoes. 6 *n.* A polish or gloss. 7 *n.* A polishing. 8 *v.* To be clearly visible: Happiness *shone* in their eyes. 9 *n.* Fair weather: in rain or *shine*. 10 *n.* informal A liking or fancy: to take a *shine* to someone.

shin·er [shī′nər] *n.* 1 A person or thing that shines. 2 *slang* A black eye from a blow.

shin·gle[1] [shing′gəl] *n., v.* **shin·gled, shin·gling** 1 *n.* A thin, tapering piece of wood or other material, as used to cover roofs. Shingles are laid in overlapping rows. 2 *v.* To cover (as a roof or building) with or as if with shingles. 3 *n.* A small signboard, as outside a doctor's office. 4 *n.* A short haircut. 5 *n.* To cut (the hair) in a shingle.

Shingles

shin·gle[2] [shing′gəl] *n.* Pieces of gravel, especially the coarse, water-worn gravel found on a beach.

shin·gles [shing′gəlz] *n.pl.* (*used with singular or plural verb*) A viral disease characterized by a skin rash along the course of an affected nerve and accompanied by pain.

shin·ing [shī′ning] *adj.* 1 Giving off or reflecting light; gleaming. 2 Distinguished; conspicuous: a *shining* example of courage.

shin·ny[1] [shin′ē] *v.* **shin·nied, shin·ny·ing** *informal*

To climb using one's arms and legs: to *shinny* up a pole.
shin·ny² [shin′ē] *n.* A game resembling hockey.
shin·splints [shin′splints′] *n.pl.* (*used with singular verb*) A painful straining of the muscles of the lower leg, often caused by running on hard surfaces.
Shin·to [shin′tō] *n.* A religion of Japan in which nature, heroes, and ancestors are worshiped.
Shin·to·ism [shin′tō·iz′əm] *n.* Shinto.
shin·y [shī′nē] *adj.* **shin·i·er, shin·i·est** Shining in appearance; bright; gleaming. **—shin′i·ness** *n.*
ship [ship] *n., v.* **shipped, ship·ping** 1 *n.* Any large vessel that moves through the water or in the air, driven by sails or engines, as a steamship, tanker, submarine, or airship. 2 *n.* A large sailing vessel with three masts carrying square sails on all three. 3 *v.* To put or go on board a ship. 4 *v.* To travel or go on a ship. 5 *v.* To transport (goods), as by ship or railroad. 6 *v.* To take in (water) over the side: Our sailboat *shipped* water during the squall. 7 *n.* The crew of a ship. 8 *v.* To take a job on a ship: to *ship* out as mate. 9 *v.* To hire and take aboard to work on a ship, as sailors. 10 *v.* To place in its proper position for use on a ship or boat: to *ship* a rudder. 11 *v. informal* To get rid of. **—when one's ship comes in** When one's fortune has been made or one's wishes have been granted.
-ship A suffix meaning: 1 The condition or quality of, as in *companionship.* 2 The office or rank of, as in *judgeship.* 3 The art or skill of, as in *marksmanship.*
ship biscuit Another name for HARDTACK.
ship·board [ship′bôrd′] 1 *n.* A ship, usually in the expression **on shipboard,** in or on a ship; aboard. 2 *adj.* Existing or happening on a ship: a *shipboard* romance.
ship·build·er [ship′bil′dər] *n.* A person who designs or builds ships. **—ship′build′ing** *n.*
ship·load [ship′lōd′] *n.* The quantity that a ship carries or can carry.
ship·mas·ter [ship′mas′tər] *n.* A person who commands a merchant ship.
ship·mate [ship′māt′] *n.* A sailor who serves with another on board the same ship.
ship·ment [ship′mənt] *n.* 1 Anything that is shipped. 2 The act of shipping.
ship·per [ship′ər] *n.* A person who ships goods.
ship·ping [ship′ing] *n.* 1 The act of shipping goods. 2 All the ships belonging to a country or port, or their tonnage.
ship·shape [ship′shāp′] *adj.* Orderly and neat, as on a ship; in good order.
ship·worm [ship′wûrm′] *n.* A clam with a long, wormlike body and two small shells with which it burrows into underwater wood, causing damage to ships and docks.
ship·wreck [ship′rek′] 1 *n.* The destruction of or damage to a ship at sea. 2 *v.* To wreck, as a vessel. 3 *n.* Scattered remains, as of a wrecked ship; wreckage. 4 *n.* Ruin; destruction: the *shipwreck* of one's hopes. 5 *v.* To ruin; destroy.
ship·yard [ship′yärd′] *n.* A place where ships are built or repaired.
shire [shīr] *n.* In Great Britain, a county: often used in county names, as *Devonshire.*
shirk [shûrk] *v.* To avoid doing (something that should be done) because of laziness or negligence: to *shirk* household chores. **—shirk′er** *n.*
shirr [shûr] 1 *v.* To draw (cloth) into three or more parallel rows of gathers. 2 *n.* Shirring. 3 *v.* To bake (eggs removed from the shell) in a buttered dish.
shirr·ing [shûr′ing] *n.* A drawing of material into three or more parallel rows of gathers.
shirt [shûrt] *n.* 1 A garment worn on the upper part of the body. 2 An undershirt. 3 A blouse. ◆ *Shirt* is a native English word, and *skirt* comes from an old Scandinavian word. Both originally meant *skirt* or *short garment.* The similarity of their older forms shows that they came originally from a common source.
shirt·ing [shûr′ting] *n.* Cloth for shirts.
shirt·waist [shûrt′wāst′] *n.* 1 A tailored blouse that looks something like a shirt. 2 A tailored dress having a bodice like a shirtwaist. 3 *adj. use*: a *shirtwaist* dress.
shish ke·bab or **shish ka·bob** or **shish ke·bob** [shish′kə·bob′] Chunks of seasoned meat cooked and served on skewers, often with onions and tomatoes.
Shi·va [shē′və] *n.* Another spelling of SIVA.
shiv·er¹ [shiv′ər] 1 *v.* To tremble, as with cold or fear; shake; quiver. 2 *n.* The act of shivering; trembling.
shiv·er² [shiv′ər] 1 *v.* To break suddenly into many pieces; shatter. 2 *n.* A splinter; sliver.
shiv·er·y [shiv′ər·ē] *adj.* 1 Shivering or inclined to shiver, as from fear or cold. 2 Causing shivers: a *shivery* wind.
shlock [shlok] *n., adj.* Another spelling of SCHLOCK.
shoal¹ [shōl] 1 *n.* A shallow place in any body of water. 2 *n.* A sandbar or bank under water which makes such a shallow place. 3 *v.* To make or become shallow. 4 *adj.* Shallow: *shoal* water.
shoal² [shōl] *n.* 1 A large group or multitude; throng. 2 A school of fish.
shoat [shōt] *n.* A young, weaned pig.
shock¹ [shok] 1 *n.* A violent jolt or blow; sudden impact: the *shock* of an explosion. 2 *v.* To shake by sudden collision; jar. 3 *n.* A sudden and severe upset of the mind or feelings, as in fright or great sorrow. 4 *v.* To disturb the feelings or mind of suddenly and violently; disgust or horrify: I was *shocked* by the story; The train wreck *shocked* the entire town. 5 *n.* The physical effects produced by the passing of a strong electric current through the body. 6 *v.* To give or receive an electric shock: The faulty lamp switch *shocked* the child. 7 *n.* A usually temporary state of bodily collapse, characterized by a sudden failure in blood circulation. It results from severe injuries, burns, or blood loss.
shock² [shok] 1 *n.* A number of bundles, as of grain or stalks of corn, stacked upright to dry in a field. 2 *v.* To gather (grain) into a shock or shocks.
shock³ [shok] *n.* A coarse, tangled mass, as of hair.

a	add	**i**	it	**o͝o**	took	**oi**	oil
ā	ace	**ī**	ice	**o͞o**	pool	**ou**	pout
â	care	**o**	odd	**u**	up	**ng**	ring
ä	palm	**ō**	open	**û**	burn	**th**	thin
e	end	**ô**	order	**yo͞o**	fuse	**t͟h**	this
ē	equal					**zh**	vision

ə = a in *above* e in *sicken* i in *possible* o in *melon* u in *circus*

S

shock ab·sorb·er [ab·sôr′bər] A device to lessen the shock of sudden bumps or jolts, as on the springs of automobiles.

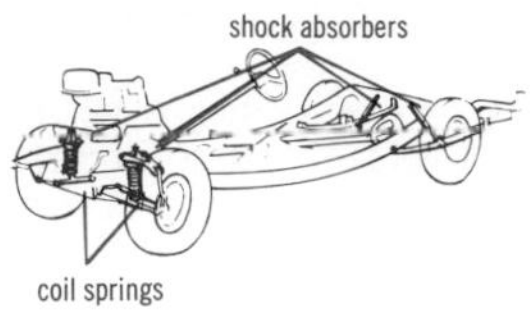

shock·ing [shok′ing] *adj.* **1** Causing an unpleasant surprise. **2** Disgusting; objectionable. **3** *informal* Very bad; terrible. **—shock′ing·ly** *adv.*

shock wave A violent disturbance in a fluid, especially air, that travels outward from a point of impact or explosion, often with destructive effects.

shod [shod] Past tense and past participle of SHOE: The blacksmith *shod* the horse.

shod·dy [shod′ē] *n., pl.* **shod·dies,** *adj.* **shod·di·er, shod·di·est** **1** *n.* A poor grade of wool made from used or waste wool. **2** *n.* Cloth woven from such wool. **3** *adj.* Made of or containing shoddy. **4** *adj.* Inferior; of poor quality: a *shoddy* piece of furniture. **5** *adj.* Mean; lowdown: a *shoddy* trick.

shoe [sho͞o] *n., v.* **shod, shoe·ing** **1** *n.* An outer covering, usually of leather, for the human foot. **2** *n.* Something like a shoe in position or use, as a horseshoe. **3** *v.* To furnish with shoes. **4** *n.* The part of a brake that presses on a wheel or drum to slow its turning. **—fill another's shoes** To take another's place or position. **—in another's shoes** In another's place or position.

A brake shoe

shoe·horn [sho͞o′hôrn′] *n.* A smooth, curved implement, as one of horn or metal, used to help slip on a shoe over the heel.

shoe·lace [sho͞o′lās′] *n.* A cord or lace for fastening a shoe.

shoe·mak·er [sho͞o′mā′kər] *n.* A person whose trade is making or repairing shoes.

shoe·string [sho͞o′string′] *n.* A shoelace. **—on a shoestring** With a small sum of money with which to begin: The successful executive began the business *on a shoestring.*

shoe·tree [sho͞o′trē′] *n.* A form put into a shoe to keep it in shape or to stretch it.

sho·far [shō′fär′ *or* shō′fər] *n., pl.* **sho·fars** or **sho·froth** [shō·frōt′ *or* shō·frōs′] A ram's horn made into a trumpet, sounded in Jewish synagogues at Rosh Hashanah and Yom Kippur.

shone [shōn] Past tense and past participle of SHINE.

shoo [sho͞o] *interj., v.* **shooed, shoo·ing** **1** *interj.* Be off! Go away! **2** *v.* To drive away, as by crying "shoo!": to *shoo* chickens away.

shook [sho͝ok] Past tense of SHAKE.

shoon [sho͞on] *n.pl.* Shoes: seldom used today.

shoot [sho͞ot] *v.* **shot, shoot·ing,** *n.* **1** *v.* To hit, wound, or kill with a bullet, arrow, or other weapon: to *shoot* a rabid animal. **2** *v.* To fire (a weapon): to *shoot* a rifle. **3** *v.* To send out or discharge from a weapon: to *shoot* bullets. **4** *v.* To go off; discharge: The pistol jammed and failed to *shoot.* **5** *n.* A shooting match or hunting party. **6** *v.* To direct or send forth suddenly, rapidly, or with force: The attorney *shot* questions at the suspect; to *shoot* out beams of light. **7** *v.* To move swiftly; rush: The children *shot* out of the bus; A meteor *shot* across the sky. **8** *v.* To pass over or through swiftly: to *shoot* rapids on a raft; A sharp pain *shot* up my leg. **9** *n.* A slide or passage down which things are slid or dropped; chute. **10** *v.* To film; make a photograph of: to *shoot* a street scene. **11** *v.* To score (a point) in certain games: to *shoot* baskets. **12** *v.* To play, as certain games: to *shoot* pool; to *shoot* nine holes of golf. **13** *v.* To put forth (as buds or leaves): Crocuses *shoot* up in the early spring. **14** *n.* A young bud, leaf, or branch. **15** *v.* To grow quickly: Children seem to *shoot* up several inches every year. **16** *v.* To mark with streaks of another color: The black scarf is *shot* with silver threads. **17** *v.* To jut out; project: The pier *shoots* out into the bay. **18** *v.* To slide (a door bolt) into place. **—shoot′er** *n.*

shooting star Another name for METEOR.

shop [shop] *n., v.* **shopped, shop·ping** **1** *n.* A place for the sale of retail goods; store. **2** *n.* A place for making or repairing things or for doing a certain kind of work: a carpentry *shop.* **3** *v.* To visit shops or stores to purchase or look at goods: We will *shop* for fall clothes this weekend. **—shop′per** *n.*

shop·keep·er [shop′kē′pər] *n.* A person who runs a shop or store.

shop·lift·er [shop′lif′tər] *n.* A person, pretending to be a shopper, who steals goods that are in a store to be sold. **—shop′lift′ing** *n.*

shop·ping [shop′ing] *n.* The act of buying goods at a shop or of looking in one or more shops for the goods one wants.

shopping center A group of stores and other facilities around or next to a parking lot, designed to serve the shopping needs of customers from a large surrounding area.

shop·talk [shop′tôk′] *n.* Conversation about one's work or special interest.

shop·worn [shop′wôrn′] *adj.* Dingy and soiled from having been on display so long at a shop.

shore¹ [shôr] *n.* The coast or land on the edge of an ocean, sea, lake, or large river.

shore² [shôr] *n., v.* **shored, shor·ing** **1** *n.* A beam or timber set as a prop under or against a wall or a boat in drydock. **2** *v.* To prop or support with shores: to *shore* up a rickety porch.

Shores

shore·line [shôr′līn′] *n.* The outline of a shore; line where the shore meets the water.

shore·ward [shôr′wərd] *adv., adj.* Toward the shore.

shorn [shôrn] An alternative past participle of SHEAR.

short [shôrt] **1** *adj.* Not having great length from end to end or from beginning to end; not long: a *short* piece of rope; a *short* vacation. **2** *adv.* So as to be not long: to have one's hair cut *short;* Cut your visit *short.* **3** *adj.* Below the average height: a *short* person. **4** *adj.* Rude and curt in manner: a *short* reply. **5** *adv.* In a rude or brief way: to answer *short.* **6** *adj.* Easily broken or crumbled: *short* bread. **7** *adj.* Not reaching a desired or required amount or measure: My account is *short* five dollars; Our oil supply is *short.* **8** *adv.* So as not to reach or extend to a certain point or condition: to fall *short.* **9** *n.* Anything that is short, as a brief movie run between showings of a main feature. **10** *n.* (*pl.*) Trousers with legs extending to or part way to the knees. **11** *n.* (*pl.*) Short pants worn as an undergarment. **12** *n.* A short circuit. **13** *adv.* Suddenly: The horse stopped *short* at the fence. **14**

adj. Relatively brief when sounded in speech, as the "i" in "hit." **—for short** As a short form; for the sake of brevity: An umpire is called ump *for short.* **—in short** Briefly. **—short of** **1** Not having a sufficient amount of: to be *short of* bread. **2** Less than: The boss wants nothing *short of* perfection. **3** On the near side of.

short·age [shôr′tij] *n.* A lack in the amount or number needed or desired; deficiency.

short·bread [shôrt′bred′] *n.* A thick, rich cookie made of flour, sugar, and shortening.

short·cake [shôrt′kāk′] *n.* A rich biscuit or layer cake filled or covered with berries or fruit.

short·change [shôrt′chānj′] *v.* **1** To give less than the right amount of change to. **2** To give less of something than is due; cheat.

short-cir·cuit [shôrt′sûr′kit] *v.* **1** To make a short circuit in. **2** To become a short circuit.

short circuit In an electric circuit, a path of low resistance that allows the current to bypass other circuit elements. Accidental short circuits are caused by faulty wiring or apparatus and can start fires.

short·com·ing [shôrt′kum′ing] *n.* A failure, weakness, or defect, as in one's character or behavior.

short·cut [shôrt′kut′] *n.* **1** A path or way between two places that is shorter than the regular way. **2** Any way of saving time, distance, or money.

short·en [shôr′tən] *v.* **1** To make or become short or shorter: to *shorten* the sleeves of a coat. **2** To make rich and crumbly, as pastry, by using a large proportion of shortening.

short·en·ing [shôr′tən·ing] *n.* **1** The act of a person who shortens. **2** A fat, such as butter or vegetable oil, used to make pastry rich.

short·fall [shôrt′fôl′] *n.* **1** A failure to reach a desired amount or goal. **2** The amount by which something falls short; deficiency or deficit: a *shortfall* in the state budget.

short·hand [shôrt′hand′] *n.* **1** A system of writing rapidly that uses symbols to stand for letters, words, or phrases. **2** Any writing made up of such symbols.

short·hand·ed [shôrt′han′did] *adj.* Not having enough workers or assistants.

short·horn [shôrt′hôrn′] *n.* A breed of cattle with short horns, originally from England.

short-lived [shôrt′līvd′ *or* shôrt′livd′] *adj.* Living or lasting only a short time.

short·ly [shôrt′lē] *adv.* **1** In a short time; quickly; soon: Come back *shortly.* **2** In few words; briefly. **3** Rudely; abruptly: I was annoyed and answered *shortly.*

short-range [shôrt′rānj′] *adj.* **1** Of or for short distances: *short-range* artillery fire. **2** Reaching only into the near future: *short-range* plans.

short·sight·ed [shôrt′sī′tid] *adj.* **1** Unable to see clearly at a distance; nearsighted. **2** Not preparing or planning for the future; lacking foresight. **—short′sight′ed·ly** *adv.* **—short′sight′ed·ness** *n.*

short·stop [shôrt′stop′] *n.* In baseball, an infielder whose position is between second and third base.

short story A short work of prose fiction.

short subject A short motion picture, often shown on the same program with a longer featured film.

short-tem·pered [shôrt′tem′pərd] *adj.* Easily angered; having a quick temper.

short·wave [shôrt′wāv′] *n., adj., v.* **short·waved, short·wav·ing** **1** *n.* A radio wave that is 60 meters or less in length. **2** *adj.* Indicating, operating by, or carried by shortwaves: a *shortwave* radio; a *shortwave* broadcast. **3** *v.* To transmit by shortwaves.

short-wind·ed [shôrt′win′did] *adj.* Breathing with difficulty or getting out of breath quickly.

Sho·sho·ne [shō·shō′nē] *n., pl.* **Sho·sho·nes** or **Sho·sho·ne** **1** Any of a group of North American Indian tribes formerly scattered over the Rocky Mountains region, now living in California, Idaho, Nevada, Utah, and Wyoming. **2** A member of any of these tribes. **3** A family of languages spoken by these tribes.

Sho·sho·ni [shō·shō′nē] *n., pl.* **Sho·sho·nis** or **Sho·sho·ni** Shoshone.

shot[1] [shot] *n., pl.* **shots** **1** The act of shooting, especially the discharge of a weapon: We heard *shots* down the street. **2** (*pl.* **shot**) A bullet or pellet of lead to be discharged from a gun. A shotgun usually fires a number of very small lead balls, or shot, at the same time. **3** A person who shoots; marksman: The officer is an excellent *shot.* **4** The distance that a bullet or other missile is or can be thrown. **5** A stroke in certain games, as billiards. **6** An attempt to hit, as by shooting: The first *shot* missed; a *shot* at the moon. **7** Any attempt or try: I had a *shot* at the trophy. **8** A cruel or unfriendly remark: His parting *shot* was, "You'll be sorry for this!" **9** A heavy metal ball which, in an athletic contest, is thrown overhand as far as possible. **10** A photograph, or a single scene recorded on motion picture film. **11** An injection by means of a hypodermic needle: a *shot* of penicillin. **—a long shot** Something, as a contestant or an attempt, that is not likely to succeed. **—not by a long shot** Not at all; not likely.

shot[2] [shot] **1** Past tense and past participle of SHOOT. **2** *adj.* Streaked or mixed with other colors: a sky *shot* with pink. **3** *adj. informal* Exhausted or ruined; worn-out.

shot·gun [shot′gun′] *n.* A gun with a smooth bore and either a single or double barrel, made to fire cartridges filled with small shot.

shot put **1** An athletic contest in which a shot is thrown, or put, for distance. **2** A single throw of the shot.

should [sho͝od] Past tense of SHALL, used chiefly, however, as a helping verb meaning: **1** Ought to: You *should* do your homework. **2** Were to: If I *should* go, he would go too. **3** Assuming that: *Should* our budget work out, we'll go on vacation next month. **4** Expect to: I *should* be home by noon. ◆ In American usage, either *should* or *would* may be used with the first person in such expressions as "I *should* be glad to come; We *would* be happy to do it." Some people think, however, that *should* with the first person sounds a bit more polite.

shoul·der [shōl′dər] **1** *n.* The part of the body to which a human's arm, an animal's foreleg, or a

a	add	**i**	it	**o͝o**	took	**oi**	oil
ā	ace	**ī**	ice	**o͞o**	pool	**ou**	pout
â	care	**o**	odd	**u**	up	**ng**	ring
ä	palm	**ō**	open	**û**	burn	**th**	thin
e	end	**ô**	order	**yo͞o**	fuse	**th**	this
ē	equal					**zh**	vision

ə = { a in *above* e in *sicken* i in *possible* / o in *melon* u in *circus* }

S

bird's wing is jointed. **2** *v.* To push with the shoulder: to *shoulder* a person out of the way. **3** *v.* To carry on the shoulder. **4** *v.* To undertake; bear: to *shoulder* one's responsibilities. **5** *n.* The section of a garment that fits over the shoulder. **6** *n.* A cut of meat consisting of the upper part of the foreleg of an animal: a *shoulder* of lamb. **7** *n.* Anything that is shaped like or sticks out like a shoulder: the *shoulder* of a mountain. **8** *n.* Either edge of a road. **—put one's shoulder to the wheel** To set to work with a strong effort. **—shoulder arms** To hold a rifle upright with the butt in one's hand and the barrel resting on the shoulder. **—shoulder to shoulder** In cooperation; working together. **—straight from the shoulder** *informal* Straightforwardly; frankly.

shoulder bag A bag, as of leather, plastic, or canvas, similar to a handbag but carried by a strap slung over the shoulder.

shoulder blade Either of two flat, triangular bones in the upper back; scapula.

shoulder strap **1** A strap worn on or over the shoulder to hold up a garment. **2** A strap of cloth marked with insignia of rank, worn by officers in the armed services.

should·n't [shŏŏd′(ə)nt] Should not.

shouldst [shŏŏdst] A form of the verb SHALL, used with *thou*: seldom used today.

shout [shout] **1** *n.* A sudden and loud outcry: a *shout* of anger; a *shout* of laughter. **2** *v.* To say or express with a shout: My neighbor *shouted* "Good morning" to me from across the street. **3** *v.* To cry out loudly: The children *shouted* with excitement when they saw the elephant. **—shout someone down** To drown out what someone is saying by shouting. **—shout′er** *n.*

shove [shuv] *v.* **shoved, shov·ing,** *n.* **1** *v.* To move by pushing from behind: to *shove* a stalled car. **2** *v.* To push hard against; jostle: to *shove* people in a crowd. **3** *n.* The act of shoving. **—shove off** **1** To push along or away, as a boat. **2** *informal* To go; start; leave: Let's *shove off* for home.

shov·el [shuv′əl] *n.*, *v.* **shov·eled** or **shov·elled, shov·el·ing** or **shov·el·ling** **1** *n.* A tool with a handle and a somewhat flattened scoop, used for lifting or moving things, as loose soil or coal. **2** *v.* To take up and move or heap up with a shovel. **3** *v.* To dig or clear with a shovel: to *shovel* a path through the snow. **4** *v.* To thrust into the mouth hastily and in large amounts: to *shovel* down food. **—shov′el·er** or **shov′el·ler** *n.*

Shovel

show [shō] *v.* **showed, shown** or **showed, show·ing,** *n.* **1** *v.* To cause or allow to see or be seen: He *showed* his feelings; They *showed* us their new kitten. **2** *v.* To be or become visible; appear: A light *showed* in the window. **3** *n.* The act of showing: a *show* of hands. **4** *n.* Anything shown or made apparent: a *show* of good faith. **5** *v.* To be seen easily; be obvious: Your happiness *shows* in your face. **6** *v.* To direct; guide: Please *show* us the way home. **7** *v.* To point out: A clock *shows* the time. **8** *v.* To explain; teach: The shop teacher *showed* me how to build a bench. **9** *v.* To give; bestow: to *show* mercy to someone. **10** *n.* An entertainment or exhibition: a TV *show*; an art *show.* **11** *n.* An elaborate display: a *show* of talent. **12** *n.* A false display: to make a great *show* of being sorry. **—for show** For effect; to attract notice. **—show off** **1** To try to attract too much attention to oneself or to one's accomplishments. **2** To display proudly: to *show off* one's birthday presents. **—show up** **1** To stand out: The poster will *show up* well on a white wall. **2** To expose, as faults. **3** *informal* To arrive.

show·boat [shō′bōt′] *n.* A boat, such as the old steamers on the Mississippi River, on which traveling troupes of actors and musicians give performances.

show business The businesses, arts, and occupations involved in putting on shows of all kinds; entertainment industry.

show·case [shō′kās′] *n.* A glass case for displaying and protecting articles, as in a store or museum.

show·down [shō′doun′] *n.* *informal* Anything, as an action, argument, or discussion, that tries to bring out into the open and settle some conflict or disputed issue: I had a *showdown* with my parents about an increase in my allowance.

show·er [shou′ər] **1** *n.* A brief fall of rain, hail, or sleet. **2** *v.* To sprinkle or wet with or as if with a shower. **3** *v.* To fall like a shower. **4** *n.* A large fall, as of tears or sparks. **5** *n.* An abundance; great amount: a *shower* of praise. **6** *v.* To send or pour out, like a shower; give: Grandparents like to *shower* affection on their grandchildren. **7** *v.* To give freely: Their friends *showered* gifts on the couple. **8** *n.* A shower bath. **9** *v.* To take a shower bath. **10** *n.* A party for giving gifts, as to a bride.

shower bath **1** A bath in which water is sprayed on the body from an overhead nozzle. **2** A device that provides such a bath.

show·ing [shō′ing] *n.* **1** An act of putting on view; presentation: five daily *showings* of a movie. **2** Performance, as in a contest: The team made a poor *showing* in the finals.

show·man [shō′mən] *n.*, *pl.* **show·men** [shō′mən] **1** A person who manages or produces a show. **2** Any person who does things in a showy or dramatic way. **—show′man·ship** *n.*

shown [shōn] An alternative past participle of SHOW.

show-off [shō′ôf′] *n.* *informal* **1** The act of showing off. **2** A person who shows off.

show·piece [shō′pēs′] *n.* Something displayed as an outstanding example of its kind.

show·room [shō′rōōm′ *or* shō′rŏŏm′] *n.* A room for displaying merchandise.

show·y [shō′ē] *adj.* **show·i·er, show·i·est** Making a great or brilliant display: *showy* flowers. **2** So gaudy and flashy as to be in poor taste: a *showy* fabric. **—show′i·ly** *adv.* **—show′i·ness** *n.*

shrank [shrangk] Past tense of SHRINK.

shrap·nel [shrap′nəl] *n.*, *pl.* **shrap·nel** **1** An artillery shell that explodes in the air and scatters a quantity of small metal balls. **2** Fragments scattered when a shell explodes.

shred [shred] *n.*, *v.* **shred·ded** or **shred, shred·ding** **1** *n.* A small, irregular strip torn or cut off: a *shred* of newspaper. **2** *n.* A bit; particle: The child hasn't a *shred* of self-consciousness. **3** *v.* To tear or cut into shreds.

shrew [shro͞o] *n.* 1 Any of various small mammals that look like mice. Shrews have long snouts and live mostly on insects. 2 A nagging, scolding person.

Shrew

shrewd [shro͞od] *adj.* Having sound, practical common sense; sharp; keen: a *shrewd* bargainer. **—shrewd'ly** *adv.* **—shrewd'ness** *n.* ◆ *Shrewd,* based on the Old English word for *shrew*, once meant *evil* or *wicked.* This meaning has softened over the years, and today a *shrewd* person is clever and sharp, and not necessarily evil.

shrew·ish [shro͞o'ish] *adj.* Like a shrew; ill-tempered; nagging.

shriek [shrēk] 1 *n.* A sharp, shrill outcry, scream, or sound. 2 *v.* To make such a sound: The animal *shrieked* in pain. 3 *v.* To say with a shriek: I *shrieked*, "Help me!"

shrift [shrift] *n.* The act of shriving or giving absolution. **—short shrift** Little or no mercy or delay, as in dealing with a person: The champion gave the challenger *short shrift*, and the match was soon over.

shrike [shrīk] *n.* A fierce bird with a hooked bill that feeds on insects and attacks other birds.

Shrike

shrill [shril] 1 *adj.* Having or making a high-pitched, piercing sound: a *shrill* whistle. 2 *v.* To make a high-pitched, piercing sound. **—shril'ly** *adj.* **—shrill'·ness** *n.*

shrimp [shrimp] *n.* 1 Any of several types of edible shellfish with long tails. 2 *slang* A small or unimportant person.

shrine [shrīn] *n.* 1 A place or object, as a tomb, chapel, or holy image, sacred to some holy person and often containing relics. 2 A place held in high honor because of the events or ideas connected with it: The Statue of Liberty is a *shrine* of freedom. ◆ In Old English *shrine* meant *a box* or *chest*. The word later came to be associated with sacred objects.

shrink [shringk] *v.* **shrank** or **shrunk, shrunk** or **shrunk·en, shrink·ing,** *n.* 1 *v.* To make or become smaller, as by drawing together or contracting: to *shrink* fabric before cutting; Sweaters often *shrink* when washed. 2 *v.* To make or become less; diminish: Too many demands on my time *shrink* my patience. 3 *v.* To draw back, as in disgust or fear: We *shrank* back from the edge of the cliff. 4 *n. slang* A headshrinker.

Statue of Liberty, a famous shrine

shrink·age [shringk'ij] *n.* 1 The act of shrinking; contraction. 2 The amount lost by such shrinking. 3 A decrease in value.

shrive [shrīv] *v.* **shrived** or **shrove, shriv·en** or **shrived, shriv·ing** 1 To receive the confession of and give absolution to. 2 To confess one's sins.

shriv·el [shriv'əl] *v.* **shriv·eled** or **shriv·elled, shriv·el·ing** or **shriv·el·ling** To contract into wrinkles; shrink and dry up: In the hot summer weather all of our plants *shriveled* up; Age had *shriveled* the man.

shriv·en [shriv'ən] Alternative past participle of SHRIVE.

shroud [shroud] 1 *n.* A garment for a dead person. 2 *n.* Anything that wraps up or conceals like such a garment: a *shroud* of mist. 3 *v.* To clothe or wrap in or as if in a shroud: The town is *shrouded* in darkness. 4 *n.* (*usually pl.*) Any of a set of ropes stretched from a masthead to a ship's side to brace the mast.

shrove [shrōv] Alternative past tense of SHRIVE.

Shrove Tuesday The day before Ash Wednesday.

shrub [shrub] *n.* A low, woody plant having many stems and branches springing from the base.

shrub·ber·y [shrub'ər·ē] *n., pl.* **shrub·ber·ies** A group of shrubs, as in a garden.

shrub·by [shrub'ē] *adj.* **shrub·bi·er, shrub·bi·est** 1 Covered with or full of shrubs. 2 Like a shrub.

shrug [shrug] *v.* **shrugged, shrug·ging,** *n.* 1 *v.* To draw up (the shoulders) to show an emotion, as doubt, dislike, or indifference. 2 *n.* The action of shrugging.

shrunk [shrungk] Alternative past tense and past participle of SHRINK.

shrunk·en [shrungk'ən] 1 Alternative past participle of SHRINK. 2 *adj.* Grown smaller and thinner; shriveled; withered: a *shrunken* old person.

shtick or **schtick** or **shtik** [shtik] *n. slang* 1 A routine used by a performer, especially one that causes laughter or attracts attention. 2 Any trait, talent, or way of behaving that is used to attract attention.

shuck [shuk] 1 *n.* A husk, shell, or pod: a corn *shuck*. 2 *v.* To remove the husks or shells from: to *shuck* oysters. 3 *v. informal* To take off, or cast off, as clothes.

shud·der [shud'ər] 1 *v.* To tremble or shake, as from fear or cold; shiver. 2 *n.* The act of shuddering; shivering.

shuf·fle [shuf'əl] *v.* **shuf·fled, shuf·fling,** *n.* 1 *v.* To drag (the feet) in walking or in a certain type of dancing. 2 *n.* A dragging of the feet in walking or dancing. 3 *v.* To mix the order of playing cards before a deal. 4 *n.* A mixing or changing of the order of playing cards. 5 *n.* A turn to shuffle cards. 6 *v.* To push about or mix together aimlessly: to *shuffle* papers on a desk. 7 *n.* An aimless pushing about or mixing together. 8 *v.* To act or speak in such a way as to deceive or mislead. 9 *n.* A misleading or deceiving action or speech.

shuf·fle·board [shuf'əl·bôrd'] *n.* A game in which large disks are slid, by means of a pronged pole, along a smooth surface toward numbered spaces.

shun [shun] *v.* **shunned, shun·ning** To keep clear of; avoid: to *shun* large crowds.

shunt [shunt] 1 *v.* To turn or move to one side or out of the way. 2 *v.* To put off on someone else, as a job. 3 *v.* To switch (a train or railroad car) from one track to another. 4 *n.* The act of shunt-

a	add	**i**	it	**o͝o**	took	**oi**	oil
ā	ace	**ī**	ice	**o͞o**	pool	**ou**	pout
â	care	**o**	odd	**u**	up	**ng**	ring
ä	palm	**ō**	open	**û**	burn	**th**	thin
e	end	**ô**	order	**yo͞o**	fuse	**t͟h**	this
ē	equal					**zh**	vision

ə = {a in *above* e in *sicken* i in *possible* / o in *melon* u in *circus*}

S

ing. 5 *n.* A railroad switch. 6 *v.* To divert or bypass, as an electric current or a circuit element. 7 *n.* In electricity, a circuit element, as a resistor or capacitor, connected in parallel with other elements in order to bypass part of the current.

shush [shush] 1 *interj.* Be silent; hush. 2 *v.* To demand silence from; hush.

shut [shut] *v.* **shut, shut·ting,** *adj.* 1 *v.* To bring into such a position as to close an opening: to *shut* a gate; to *shut* the lid of a box. 2 *v.* To be or become closed or in a closed position: This bureau drawer *shuts* easily. 3 *v.* To close something, as a door, window, or lid: to *shut* a trunk; to *shut* a beach house for the winter months. 4 *v.* To close and fasten securely, as with a lock or latch. 5 *v.* To close, fold, or bring together the parts of: to *shut* an umbrella. 6 *adj.* Fastened or closed: Keep the windows *shut* when it rains. **—shut down** 1 To keep from or stop operating for a time, as a factory. 2 To come down close: The fog *shut down* over the river. **—shut in** To keep from going outside; enclose. **—shut out** 1 To keep from coming in: The new building next door *shut out* the breeze from the ocean. 2 To keep (an opponent) from scoring in a game. **—shut up** 1 To close all the entrances to, as a house. 2 *informal* To stop talking or cause to stop talking. 3 To imprison or keep indoors.

shut·down [shut′doun′] *n.* The stopping of work or activity, as in a mine, factory, or place of business.

shut-in [shut′in′] 1 *n.* An invalid who is unable to go out of doors. 2 *adj.* Having to stay at home, as from illness.

shut·out [shut′out′] *n.* In sports, a game in which one side is kept from scoring.

shut·ter [shut′ər] *n.* 1 A hinged panel for covering a window. 2 A device on a camera that opens to admit light through the lens and closes rapidly. 3 A person or thing that shuts.

shut·tle [shut′(ə)l] *n., v.* **shut·tled, shut·tling** 1 *n.* A device used in weaving to carry a thread back and forth between the threads that run lengthwise. 2 *n.* The device for carrying the under thread back and forth in a sewing machine. 3 *n.* A plane, train, or bus that operates regularly between two nearby places. 4 *v.* To move back and forth like a shuttle.

shut·tle·cock [shut′(ə)l·kok′] *n.* A rounded piece of cork or other material with a crown of feathers. It is hit back and forth in the game of badminton.

shy[1] [shī] *adj.* **shi·er** or **shy·er, shi·est** or **shy·est,** *v.* **shied, shy·ing** 1 *adj.* Bashful or uncomfortable with people; ill at ease. 2 *adj.* Easily frightened or startled; timid: a *shy* wild bird. 3 *v.* To start suddenly aside, as in fear: The horse *shied* at the sound of an automobile's horn. 4 *v.* To draw back, as from fear: The child *shied* at going on the carnival ride. 5 *adj. slang* Short; lacking: I am still a few dollars *shy* of what I need to buy the gift. **—shy′ly** *adv.* **—shy′ness** *n.*

shy[2] [shī] *v.* **shied, shy·ing** To throw with a swift, sudden motion: to *shy* rocks.

Shy·lock [shī′lok′] *n.* In Shakespeare's *The Merchant of Venice*, the man who lent money with the agreement that if it was not paid back on time he was entitled to a pound of the borrower's flesh.

shy·ster [shī′stər] *n. slang* A dishonest lawyer or politician.

si [sē] *n.* Another name for TI.

Si The symbol for the element silicon.

Si·a·mese [sī′ə·mēz′ *or* sī′ə·mēs′] *adj., n., pl.* **Si·a·mese** Another word for THAI.

Siamese cat A blue-eyed cat of a slender, short-haired breed having a light tan or gray coat with a darker face, ears, paws, and tail.

Siamese twins Any pair of twins joined together from birth. A famous pair of the 19th century was born in Siam.

Sib. 1 Siberia. 2 Siberian.

Si·be·ri·an [sī·bir′ē·ən] 1 *adj.* Of or from Siberia. 2 *n.* A person born or living in Siberia.

sib·i·lant [sib′ə·lənt] 1 *adj.* Making or having a hissing sound. 2 *n.* A consonant produced with a hissing sound, such as the *s* and the *sh* in *swish.* **—sib′i·lance** *n.* **—sib′i·lant·ly** *adv.*

sib·ling [sib′ling] *n.* A brother or sister.

sib·yl [sib′əl] *n.* In ancient Greece and Rome, any of various women having the power to make prophecies under the inspiration of some god.

sic[1] [sik] *adv.* Thus; so. ◆ This Latin word is used in writing to show that a quoted word or phrase, though apparently or in fact a mistake, is given just as it is in the original.

sic[2] or **sick** [sik] *v.* **sicced** or **sicked, sic·cing** or **sick·ing** 1 To chase after or attack: used as a command to a dog. 2 To urge to attack; set: The guard *sicced* his dog on the intruders.

Si·cil·ian [si·sil′yən] 1 *adj.* Of or from Sicily. 2 A person born or living in Sicily. 3 The Italian dialect spoken in Sicily.

sick [sik] *adj.* 1 Having a disease or illness; ill: a *sick* child; *sick* with the measles. 2 *n. use*: Sick people: The *sick* need lots of rest and care. 3 Wanting to vomit; nauseated. 4 Of or used by sick people: *sick* leave from work. 5 Feeling disgust: The sight made people *sick.* 6 Tired, bored, or disgusted: I'm *sick* of telling you to be quiet. 7 Filled with longing: *sick* for home.

sick bay A room for the care of the sick or injured, especially on a ship.

sick·bed [sik′bed′] *n.* A bed on which a person lies sick.

sick·en [sik′ən] *v.* To make or become sick.

sick·en·ing [sik′ən·ing] *adj.* Causing disgust or making one sick at one's stomach.

sick·ish [sik′ish] *adj.* 1 Somewhat sick. 2 Slightly nauseating: a *sickish* perfume.

sick·le [sik′əl] *n.* A tool with a curved blade mounted on a short handle, used to cut tall grass or grain.

sick·le-cell anemia [sik′əl·sel′] A hereditary blood disorder in which red blood cells become sickle-shaped because they contain abnormal hemoglobin. It occurs mostly in Blacks.

sick·ly [sik′lē] *adj.* **sick·li·er, sick·li·est** 1 Often sick; unhealthy; frail: a *sickly* person. 2 Connected with or caused by poor health: a *sickly* complexion. 3 Faint; weak: to give someone a *sickly* smile. 4 Causing sickness or disgust: a *sickly* smell; *sickly* sentimentality. 5 Likely to lead to ill health: a *sickly* diet. **—sick′li·ness** *n.*

sick·ness [sik′nis] *n.* 1 The condition of being sick. 2 A particular disease or disorder; illness. 3 Vomiting; nausea.

sick pay Money paid to an employee for a period of absence from work because of illness.

side [sīd] *n., adj., v.,* **sid·ed, sid·ing** 1 *n.* Any of the bounding lines or surfaces of something: A rectangle has four *sides.* 2 *n.* Either of the two opposite surfaces of something thin and flat: the right and wrong *sides* of a rug. **3** *n.* One of the two surfaces of anything rectangular that is not the top, bottom, front, or back: the *side* of the building. **4** *n.* A particular surface of something: the rough *side* of a piece of sandpaper; the inner *side* of the arm. **5** *n.* Either the right or left half of the human body, especially the part between the armpit and hip. **6** *adj.* Of, at, or on one side: a *side* exit. **7** *adj.* Directed at some side: a *side* blow. **8** *n.* The space beside or near someone or something: The dog never left its master's *side.* **9** *adj.* Coming from one side: a *side* glance. **10** *n.* The left or right half of an animal slaughtered for food: a *side* of beef. **11** *n.* One of two or more opposite directions or places: the west *side* of town; the other *side* of the street. **12** *n.* A group of people who stand together against another group, as in a contest, a quarrel, or a set of beliefs. **13** *n.* A point of view; opinion: Let's hear your *side* of the story. **14** *v.* To support or to take the part of: The voters *sided* with the mayor on the tax issue. **15** *n.* A line of descent traced through one's mother or father: an aunt on my mother's *side.* **16** *n.* A particular quality of a person or thing: That story has a humorous *side.* **17** *adj.* Not first in importance: a *side* issue. **18** *n.* A slope, as of a mountain. **—side by side** Beside or next to each other: They walked *side by side.* **—take sides** To support or be in favor of a particular point of view.

side arm A weapon worn at the side, as a sword, pistol, or bayonet.

side·board [sīd′bôrd′] *n.* A piece of dining-room furniture with drawers and shelves, for silverware and table linen.

side·burns [sīd′bûrnz′] *n.pl.* The hair growing on the sides of a man's face in front of the ears.

side·car [sīd′kär′] *n.* A one-wheeled compartment attached to the side of a motorcycle for a passenger.

sid·ed [sī′did] *adj.* Having a certain number or special type of sides: used in combination, as in *four-sided.*

side effect An effect that occurs in addition to the main or desired effects, as of a drug: Upset stomach can be a *side effect* of aspirin.

side·kick [sīd′kik′] *n. slang* A steady friend or companion.

side·light [sīd′līt′] *n.* **1** A light coming from the side. **2** An incidental fact or bit of information: The book gave some *sidelights* on the explorer's character.

side·line [sīd′līn′] *n.* **1** One of the boundary lines at the sides of a football field, tennis court, or similar area. **2** (*usually pl.*) The area just outside these lines: The photographers stood on the *sidelines.* **3** A line of goods sold in addition to the main type of goods handled by a business. **4** A type of work carried on in addition to one's regular work.

side·long [sīd′lông′] **1** *adj.* Moving to one side: a *sidelong* motion. **2** *adv.* Toward the side; sideways: to glance *sidelong.*

si·de·re·al [sī·dir′ē·əl] *adj.* **1** Of or having to do with the stars. **2** Measured by means of the stars: *sidereal* parallax.

sidereal year The time that it takes the earth to travel once around the sun, starting and ending with the background of the fixed stars in exactly the same position. A sidereal year is 365 days, 6 hours, 9 minutes, and 9.54 seconds.

side·sad·dle [sīd′sad′(ə)l] **1** *n.* A saddle with one stirrup, for riding with both legs on the same side of the horse. **2** *adv.* With both legs on the same side: to ride *sidesaddle.*

side·show [sīd′shō′] *n.* A small show separated from a main show, as in a circus.

side·split·ting [sīd′split′ing] *adj.* Producing convulsive laughter; extremely funny.

side·step [sīd′step′] *v.* **side·stepped, side·step·ping** **1** To step to one side. **2** To avoid or postpone.

side·stroke [sīd′strōk′] *n.* A swimming stroke performed on one's side. The arms are swept forward and backward alternately, and the legs are lashed together in a scissors kick.

side·swipe [sīd′swīp′] *n., v.* **side·swiped, side·swip·ing** **1** *n.* A sweeping blow along the side. **2** *v.* To strike or collide with such a blow.

side·track [sīd′trak′] *v.* **1** To move to a siding, as a railroad train. **2** To turn away or distract from the main subject or line of action.

side·walk [sīd′wôk′] *n. U.S.* A path or pavement for walking along the side of a street.

side·ways [sīd′wāz′] **1** *adj.* From or toward one side: A crab walks *sideways.* **2** *adv.* With one side forward: Hold it *sideways.* **3** *adj.* Moving to or from one side: a *sideways* nod of the head.

side·wind·er [sīd′wīn′dər] *n.* A small rattlesnake of the deserts of the sw U.S. and Mexico that moves sideways with its body in a flattened S shape.

side·wise [sīd′wīz′] *adj., adv.* Sideways.

sid·ing [sī′ding] *n.* **1** A railroad track by the side of the main track, onto which cars may be switched. **2** A material, as overlapping boards, used to construct the outside walls of a house or building with a wooden frame.

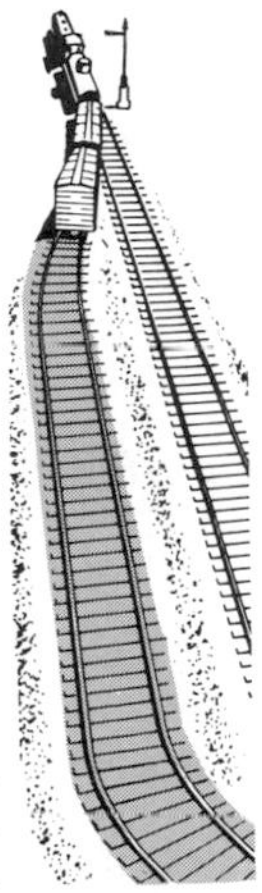
Siding

si·dle [sīd′(ə)l] *v.* **si·dled, si·dling** To move sideways, especially in a cautious or sly manner: The mail carrier *sidled* away from the growling dog.

siege [sēj] *n.* **1** The surrounding of a fortified place, town, or structure by a military force trying to capture it. **2** A steady and persistent attempt to win something. **3** The time during which one has a prolonged illness or difficulty: a *siege* of measles.

Sieg·fried [sēg′frēd′] *n.* In Germanic legends, a warrior who kills a dragon and thus gains a magic but accursed hoard of gold.

si·en·na [sē·en′ə] *n.* **1** A kind of clay containing oxides of iron and manganese, used as pigments in paints. The clay in its natural state (**raw sienna**) is yellowish-brown; when roasted (**burnt sienna**), it becomes reddish-brown. **2** A yellowish-brown or reddish-brown color.

S

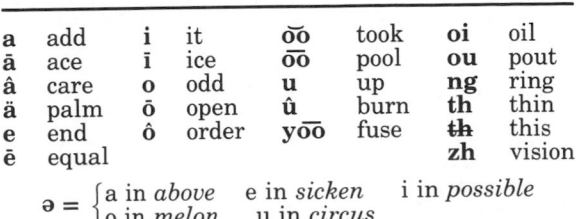

a	add	**i**	it	**o͝o**	took	**oi**	oil
ā	ace	**ī**	ice	**o͞o**	pool	**ou**	pout
â	care	**o**	odd	**u**	up	**ng**	ring
ä	palm	**ō**	open	**û**	burn	**th**	thin
e	end	**ô**	order	**yo͞o**	fuse	**th**	this
ē	equal					**zh**	vision

ə = { a in *above* e in *sicken* i in *possible* / o in *melon* u in *circus* }

si·er·ra [sē·er′ə] *n.* A mountain range or chain, especially one with a series of jagged peaks.

si·es·ta [sē·es′tə] *n.* In Spain and parts of Latin America, an afternoon nap.

sieve [siv] *n.* A utensil with holes in the bottom, used to separate solids too large to pass through from fine pieces or a liquid.

sift [sift] *v.* 1 To pass through a sieve or strainer in order to separate the fine parts from the coarse: to *sift* flour. 2 To scatter by or as if by passing through a sieve: to *sift* cinnamon and sugar on toast. 3 To use a sieve. 4 To pass or fall through or as if through a sieve: Sand *sifted* into our shoes. 5 To examine carefully or distinguish: to *sift* fact from fiction. **—sift′er** *n.*

sigh [sī] 1 *n.* To draw in and let out a deep, loud breath, as in sadness, weariness, or relief. 2 *v.* To make a sound like a sigh, as the wind does. 3 *n.* The act or sound of or as of sighing: to heave a *sigh* of relief. 4 *v.* To long; yearn: to *sigh* for one's youth. 5 *v.* To say with a sigh: I *sighed* "Goodbye."

sight [sīt] 1 *n.* The act of seeing: I remember my first *sight* of them. 2 *n.* The ability to see; vision: Owls have poor *sight* in the daytime. 3 *v.* To see; observe: to *sight* a whale. 4 *n.* That which is seen: The sea is a beautiful *sight.* 5 *n.* (*often pl.*) Things that are worth seeing: the *sights* of Paris. 6 *n.* The distance over or to which the sight reaches: The deer leaped out of *sight.* 7 *n.* (*often pl.*) A device, as on a gun or surveying instrument, used in aiming. 8 *v.* To look at or aim through sights. 9 *n.* An aim or observation taken with a telescope or other sighting device. 10 *n. informal* Something unusual or ugly to look at: The old, torn cap was a *sight.* 11 *n.* Point of view; estimation: In my *sight*, the research was thoroughly done. **—at sight** or **on sight** As soon as seen: to shoot *at sight*; to read music *at sight.* **—know by sight** To be familiar with the appearance of, although not acquainted with. **—not by a long sight** 1 Never; not at all. 2 Not nearly. ◆ See SITE.

sight·less [sīt′lis] *adj.* 1 Lacking sight; blind. 2 Invisible.

sight·ly [sīt′lē] *adj.* **sight·li·er, sight·li·est** Pleasing to look at; attractive. **—sight′li·ness** *n.*

sight-read [sīt′rēd′] *v.* **sight-read** [sīt′red′], **sight-read·ing** To read or perform without having prepared or studied in advance: to *sight-read* a French novel; to *sight-read* a piece of music.

sight·see·ing [sīt′sē′ing] *n.* The visiting of places of interest. **—sight′se′er** *n.*

sig·ma [sig′mə] *n.* The 18th letter of the Greek alphabet.

sign [sīn] 1 *n.* A symbol, object, or action that stands for something else: × is the *sign* for multiplication; He waved his hand as a *sign* of greeting. 2 *n.* A board or placard on which something is written to give information or warning: a street *sign*; a stop *sign.* 3 *n.* An indication, as of a state or condition: A fever is a *sign* of illness. 4 *n.* A gesture or action taking the place of speech: My neighbor made *signs* for me to come in. 5 *v.* To communicate by signs or signals: The teacher *signed* to me to go to the board. 6 *v.* To write one's signature or initials on: to *sign* a check. 7 *v.* To hire by getting the signature of on a contract: to *sign* a baseball player. 8 *n.* An indication associated with a number that it is positive or negative, as positive two (+2) or negative three (−3). **—sign off** In radio and television, to announce the close of a day's programs and cease broadcasting. **—sign up** 1 To enlist, as in the armed services. 2 To hire or be hired for a job. **—sign′er** *n.*

sig·nal [sig′nəl] *n., v.* **sig·naled** or **sig·nalled, sig·nal·ing** or **sig·nal·ling,** *adj.* 1 *n.* A sign agreed on as a way of sending a notice, warning, instruction, or other message: a *signal* of distress; a *signal* to announce lunch. 2 *v.* To make a signal or signals to: The driver ahead *signaled* me to pass. 3 *n.* An electric current or electromagnetic wave that varies in proportion to a sound or picture, as in a radio. 4 *v.* To make known by a signal: The factory whistle *signals* the end of the day's work. 5 *adj.* Used to signal. 6 *adj.* Outstanding; notable: a *signal* achievement.

sig·nal·ize [sig′nəl·īz′] *v.* **sig·nal·ized, sig·nal·iz·ing** To make noteworthy or remarkable: a deed *signalized* by great courage.

sig·nal·ly [sig′nəl·ē] *adv.* In a remarkable or noteworthy way: to fail *signally.*

sig·nal·man [sig′nəl·mən] *n., pl.* **sig·nal·men** [sig′·nəl·mən] A person whose job is to send signals, as on a ship or at a railway station.

sig·na·to·ry [sig′nə·tôr′ē] *adj., n., pl.* **sig·na·to·ries** 1 *adj.* Having signed a document: the *signatory* governments of a mutual defense treaty. 2 *n.* A signer of a document, especially a government bound with others in an agreement.

sig·na·ture [sig′nə·chər] *n.* 1 The name of a person written by himself or herself. 2 In music, a symbol placed at the beginning of a staff to show the key or time.

sign·board [sīn′bôrd′] *n.* A board on which a sign, direction, or advertisement is displayed.

sig·net [sig′nit] *n.* 1 A seal, especially one to make documents official. 2 A mark made by such a seal.

sig·nif·i·cance [sig·nif′ə·kəns] *n.* 1 The meaning; sense: We all understood the *significance* of what was said. 2 Importance; consequence: This is a matter of no *significance.*

sig·nif·i·cant [sig·nif′ə·kənt] *adj.* 1 Important; noteworthy: a *significant* scientific experiment. 2 Having or carrying a hidden meaning: a *significant* glance. **—sig·nif′i·cant·ly** *adv.*

sig·ni·fi·ca·tion [sig′nə·fə·kā′shən] *n.* 1 The act of signifying. 2 Meaning or sense.

sig·ni·fy [sig′nə·fī] *v.* **sig·ni·fied, sig·ni·fy·ing** 1 To make known by signs or words: to *signify* one's disapproval by saying "no." 2 To mean or express: In French, "oui" *signifies* "yes." 3 To be a sign or indication of: The wearing of purple traditionally *signifies* royalty.

sign language A way of communicating by means of signs, such as movements of the hands, instead of by speech. Deaf people often communicate in this way.

sign of the cross A gesture in which the hand traces a cross, usually by touching the forehead, chest, and each shoulder. Roman Catholics and some other Christians make the sign of the cross as a token of their faith or to invoke God's blessing.

si·gnor [sē·nyōr′] *n., pl.* **si·gnors** or **si·gno·ri** [sē·nyō′·rē] Signore.

si·gno·ra [sē·nyō′rä] *n., pl.* **si·gno·re** [sē·nyō′rā] The Italian title of courtesy for a married woman, equivalent to *Mrs.*

si·gno·re [sē·nyō′rā] *n., pl.* **si·gno·ri** [sē·nyō′rē] The

Italian title of courtesy for a man, equivalent to *Mr.* or *sir.*

si·gno·ri·na [sē′nyō·rē′nä] *n., pl.* **si·gno·ri·ne** [sē′nyō·rē′nā] The Italian title of courtesy for a girl or unmarried woman, equivalent to *Miss.*

sign·post [sīn′pōst′] *n.* A post bearing a sign on which directions or notices are given.

Sikh [sēk] *n.* A member of a monotheistic Hindu religious sect in India. —**Sikh′ism** *n.*

si·lage [sī′lij] *n.* Another word for ENSILAGE.

si·lence [sī′ləns] *n., v.* **si·lenced, si·lenc·ing** 1 *n.* Absence of sound or noise; stillness: the *silence* of the desert. 2 *n.* A time or condition of keeping still, without noise or talking: After a long *silence,* we began to speak. 3 *v.* To cause to be silent; make quiet: I *silenced* the parrot. 4 *v.* To put down; suppress: to *silence* rumors.

si·lenc·er [sī′lən·sər] *n.* 1 A person or thing that silences. 2 A device attached to the muzzle of a gun to muffle the sound when fired.

si·lent [sī′lənt] *adj.* 1 Not having or making any sound or noise; noiseless: a *silent* motor; the *silent* sea. 2 Not speaking; keeping silence: The students were *silent* while the teacher gave directions. 3 Not mentioned or spoken: a *silent* vowel; *silent* anger. 4 Taking no active part: a *silent* partner in a business. —**si′lent·ly** *adv.*

sil·hou·ette [sil′ōō·et′] *n., v.* **sil·hou·et·ted, sil·hou·et·ting** 1 *n.* A portrait in outline, cut out of black paper or drawn and filled in with a dark solid color. 2 *n.* The outline of a person or object seen against a light or a light background. 3 *v.* To cause to appear in silhouette: The moon *silhouetted* the tower against the sky.

Silhouette of Lincoln

sil·i·ca [sil′i·kə] *n.* A white or colorless, very hard silicon dioxide, the main ingredient of sand and quartz.

sil·i·cate [sil′i·kət] *n.* Any of various compounds containing silicon, a metal, and oxygen. Many minerals are silicates.

sil·i·con [sil′ə·kən] *n.* An abundant nonmetallic element related to carbon and very widely dispersed in the earth's crust in combination with oxygen as sand and rock.

sil·i·cone [sil′ə·kōn′] *n.* An organic chemical compound in which one or more carbon atoms have been replaced by silicon. It is used in synthetic waxes and rubbers.

silk [silk] 1 *n.* The very fine fiber spun by silkworms to form their cocoons. 2 *n.* Cloth, thread, or clothing made of this fiber. 3 *adj. use*: a *silk* scarf. 4 *n.* Any soft fiber like silk, such as a spider web, or the tassel on an ear of corn.

silk·en [sil′kən] *adj.* 1 Made of silk. 2 Like silk; smooth; glossy: *silken* curls.

silk·worm [silk′wûrm′] *n.* A caterpillar, the larva of any of certain moths, that spins silk to make its cocoon.

silk·y [sil′kē] *adj.* **silk·i·er, silk·i·est** Of or like silk; lustrous; soft; smooth: *silky* hair. —**silk′i·ness** *n.*

sill [sil] *n.* 1 The bottom of a door or window frame. 2 A beam at the base of a wall.

sil·ly [sil′ē] *adj.* **sil·li·er, sil·li·est** 1 Lacking good sense; foolish; stupid: a *silly* person; *silly* remarks. 2 *informal* Dazed or stunned, as by a blow: to be knocked *silly.* —**sil′li·ness** *n.*

si·lo [sī′lō] *n., pl.* **si·los** A tower in which feed, either ensilage or green fodder, is stored for cattle.

silt [silt] 1 *n.* Fine particles carried in or deposited by water. 2 *v.* To fill up or be filled with silt, as the mouth of a river. —**silt′y** *adj.*

Si·lur·i·an [si·lŏŏr′ē·ən *or* sī·lŏŏr′ē·ən] 1 *n.* The third geological period of the Paleozoic era. Rocks of this period yield fossils of the first land plants. 2 *adj.* Of the Silurian.

sil·van [sil′vən] *adj.* Another spelling of SYLVAN.

sil·ver [sil′vər] 1 *n.* A soft, white, metallic element that conducts heat and electricity very well. It is used in medicine, photography, and industry, and in making jewelry and coins. 2 *adj. use*: a *silver* bracelet; *silver* dollars. 3 *n.* Tableware, such as knives, forks, and spoons, usually made of silver. 4 *n.* Coins made of silver. 5 *adj.* Having the color of silver: *silver* moonlight. 6 *adj.* Marking a 25th anniversary: a *silver* wedding celebration.

sil·ver·fish [sil′vər·fish′] *n., pl.* **sil·ver·fish** or **sil·ver·fish·es** A wingless, silvery insect often found in damp basements and attics, where it feeds on wallpaper and other starchy materials.

silver plate Tableware and other utensils made of or coated with silver.

sil·ver·smith [sil′vər·smith′] *n.* A person whose work is to make things of silver.

sil·ver-tongued [sil′vər·tungd′] *adj.* Speaking smoothly and persuasively; eloquent.

sil·ver·ware [sil′vər·wâr′] *n.* Articles, especially table utensils, made of silver or of metal plated with silver or resembling silver.

sil·ver·y [sil′vər·ē] *adj.* 1 Like silver, as in color or luster: *silvery* moonlight. 2 Soft and clear in sound: *silvery* bells.

sim·i·an [sim′ē·ən] 1 *adj.* Of, related to, or like an ape or monkey. 2 *n.* An ape or monkey.

sim·i·lar [sim′ə·lər] *adj.* 1 Alike, but not completely the same: Bicycles and tricycles are *similar.* 2 Having corresponding angles equal, as two geometric figures. —**sim′i·lar·ly** *adv.*

sim·i·lar·i·ty [sim′ə·lar′ə·tē] *n., pl.* **sim·i·lar·i·ties** 1 The condition or quality of being similar; resemblance; likeness. 2 The point in which objects being compared are similar.

sim·i·le [sim′ə·lē] *n.* A figure of speech in which one thing is compared to another that is different in many ways, by the use of *as* or *like.* "The professor is as wise as an owl" is a simile.

si·mil·i·tude [si·mil′ə·t(y)ōōd′] *n.* Similarity; resemblance.

sim·mer [sim′ər] 1 *v.* To boil gently with a bubbling, humming sound. 2 *v.* To be or keep just below the boiling point. 3 *n.* The condition or process of simmering. 4 *v.* To be at the point of breaking out, as with rage. —**simmer down** 1 To reduce the liquid content of by boiling gently. 2 *informal* To calm down from a state of anger or excitement.

si·mo·ny [sī′mə·nē] *n.* The buying and selling of

S

a	add	**i**	it	**ŏŏ**	took	**oi**	oil
ā	ace	**ī**	ice	**ōō**	pool	**ou**	pout
â	care	**o**	odd	**u**	up	**ng**	ring
ä	palm	**ō**	open	**û**	burn	**th**	thin
e	end	**ô**	order	**yōō**	fuse	**t̶h̶**	this
ē	equal					**zh**	vision

ə = {a in *above* e in *sicken* i in *possible* / o in *melon* u in *circus*}

sacred things, as valued positions or advancement in the church.

si·moom [si·mo͞om′] *n.* A hot, dry wind of the deserts of northern Africa and sw Asia, full of sand and dust.

si·moon [si·mo͞on′] *n.* A simoom.

sim·per [sim′pər] **1** *v.* To smile in a silly, self-conscious way; smirk. **2** *v.* To say with a simper. **3** *n.* A silly, self-conscious smile.

sim·ple [sim′pəl] *adj.* **sim·pler, sim·plest** **1** Not complicated or complex; easy to understand or do: a *simple* puzzle. **2** Free from affectation; sincere: a *simple*, frank manner. **3** Feebleminded; silly. **4** Plain; not decorated: a *simple* wooden chair; This is the *simple* truth. **5** Low in rank; humble: a *simple* laborer. **6** Not divided or subdivided: a *simple* leaf.

simple fraction A fraction in which the numerator and the denominator are both integers. 1/2 and 12/17 are simple fractions.

sim·ple-heart·ed [sim′pəl·här′tid] *adj.* Having a warm, sincere heart; honest and open.

simple machine Any of six basic devices that help to do work. The simple machines are the inclined plane, the lever, the pulley, the screw, the wedge, and the wheel and axle.

sim·ple·mind·ed [sim′pəl·mīn′did] *adj.* **1** Having low intelligence; feebleminded. **2** Easily fooled or duped. **3** Stupid; foolish.

simple sentence A sentence made up of one independent clause and no dependent clauses. "The needle always points north" is a simple sentence.

sim·ple·ton [sim′pəl·tən] *n.* A weak-minded or foolish person.

sim·plic·i·ty [sim·plis′ə·tē] *n.* **1** The condition of being simple or free from difficulty. **2** The absence of affectation; sincerity. **3** An absence of decoration; plainness. **4** Lack of intelligence or good sense.

sim·pli·fi·ca·tion [sim′plə·fə·kā′shən] *n.* **1** The act of simplifying: The teacher's *simplification* of the math problem made it easy to understand. **2** Something that has been simplified.

sim·pli·fy [sim′plə·fī] *v.* **sim·pli·fied, sim·pli·fy·ing** To make more simple, plain, or easy.

sim·ply [sim′plē] *adv.* **1** In a simple or plain manner: a *simply* made meal; Try to explain the problem *simply*. **2** Really; absolutely: *simply* charming. **3** Merely; only; just: I am *simply* trying to save money.

sim·u·late [sim′yə·lāt′] *v.* **sim·u·lat·ed, sim·u·lat·ing** **1** To take on or have the appearance of; imitate: The stone in the ring *simulated* a ruby. **2** To make a show of; pretend: Actors are able to *simulate* grief. **—sim′u·la′tion** *n.*

si·mul·cast [sī′məl·kast′] *v.* **si·mul·cast** or **si·mul·cast·ed, si·mul·cast·ing,** *n.* **1** *v.* To broadcast (a program) over radio and television or over AM radio and FM radio at the same time. **2** *n.* A program that is simulcast.

si·mul·ta·ne·ous [sī′məl·tā′nē·əs] *adj.* Happening, done, or existing at the same time. **—si′mul·ta′ne·ous·ly** *adv.*, **—si′mul·ta′ne·ous·ness** *n.*

sin [sin] *n., v.* **sinned, sin·ning** **1** *n.* The breaking of a religious or divine law, especially when it is done deliberately. **2** *n.* A serious fault, wrong, or offense. **3** *v.* To commit a sin.

sin sine.

Si·nai [sī′nī] *n.* In the Bible, the mountain where Moses received the laws from God.

since [sins] **1** *prep.* During or throughout the time after: It has been raining *since* noon. **2** *conj.* Continuously from the time when: They have been busy *since* they came back. **3** *conj.* During the time after which: She has been working hard *since* she got home. **4** *conj.* Seeing that; because: You may have the books *since* I no longer need them. **5** *adv.* From a particular past time until now: The dog ran away last week and hasn't been seen *since*. **6** *adv.* At a time between a particular past time and the present: The original building was demolished last spring and has *since* been rebuilt. **7** *adv.* Before the present time; ago: Quill pens have long *since* been out of style. ◆ See BECAUSE.

sin·cere [sin·sir′] *adj.* **sin·cer·er, sin·cer·est** **1** Honest; faithful: You are a *sincere* friend. **2** Real; genuine: *sincere* regret. **—sin·cere′ly** *adv.*

sin·cer·i·ty [sin·ser′ə·tē] *n.* The quality or condition of being sincere, honest, or genuine.

Sind·bad or **Sin·bad** [sin′bad′] *n.* In the *Arabian Nights*, a merchant from Baghdad who goes on seven strange and perilous voyages.

sine [sīn] *n.* In a right triangle, the length of the side opposite an acute angle divided by the length of the hypotenuse. This quotient changes with the size of the angle.

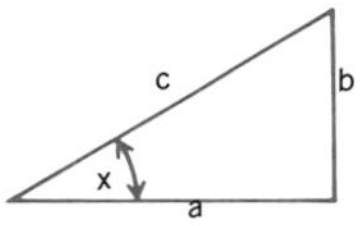

Sine $x = b/c$

si·ne·cure [sī′nə·kyo͝or′ *or* sin′ə·kyo͝or′] *n.* An office or position that requires little or no work, especially one which pays well.

si·ne qua non [sin′i kwä non′] An indispensable thing or condition. ◆ In Latin, *sine qua non* literally means *without which not.*

sin·ew [sin′yo͞o] *n.* **1** A band of tough, fibrous tissue attaching a muscle to some other bodily part, as a bone; tendon. **2** Strength or power. **3** Something that supplies strength or power.

sin·ew·y [sin′yo͞o·ē] *adj.* **1** Having sinews. **2** Strong, firm, or tough: a *sinewy* person. **3** Forceful; vigorous: a story written in a *sinewy* style.

sin·ful [sin′fəl] *adj.* Wicked; immoral; evil. **—sin′ful·ly** *adv.* **—sin′ful·ness** *n.*

sing [sing] *v.* **sang** or **sung, sung, sing·ing,** *n.* **1** *v.* To produce musical sounds with one's voice. **2** *v.* To utter the music of with the voice: to *sing* a song. **3** *n. informal* A gathering at which people sing songs together. **4** *v.* To bring into some condition by singing: to *sing* a child to sleep. **5** *v.* To tell or tell of in words of song or poetry: The minstrel *sang* of victory. **6** *v.* To speak of enthusiastically: They all *sang* their friend's praises. **7** *v.* To produce sounds like music, as a bird. **8** *v.* To make a sound like singing, as a teakettle or the wind. **9** *v.* To hum or buzz, as an arrow in flight. **—sing out** *informal* To call out loudly; shout.

sing. singular.

singe [sinj] *v.* **singed, singe·ing,** *n.* **1** *v.* To burn slightly; scorch. **2** *n.* A slight burn; scorch. **3** *v.* To remove hair or fuzz from by passing through a flame: to pluck and then *singe* a chicken. **4** *v.* To burn the ends of, as hair.

sing·er [sing′ər] *n.* **1** A person who sings, especially as a profession. **2** A bird that sings.

sin·gle [sing′gəl] *adj., n., v.* **sin·gled, sin·gling** **1** *adj.* One alone; separate; individual: Not a *single* star was visible. **2** *n.* A single person or thing. **3** *v.* To choose or select (one) from others: to *single* a student out. **4** *adj.* Unmarried. **5** *adj.* Designed for use by one person or family: a *single* bed; a *single* room; a *single* house. **6** *adj.* Between two individuals opposing each other: *single* combat. **7** *n.* (*pl.*) In a game, as tennis, a match having one player on each side. **8** *adj.* Having only one row of petals: said about flowers. **9** *n.* In baseball, a hit that enables the batter to reach first base safely. **10** *v.* To hit a single. **11** *adj.* Steadfast and not divided; sincere. **—sin′gle·ness** *n.*

People waiting in single file

sin·gle-breast·ed [sing′·gəl·bres′tid] *adj.* Having sides that close in front with little overlap and a single row of buttons: a *single-breasted* jacket.
single file An arrangement of persons or things one behind another in a single line.
sin·gle-hand·ed [sing′gəl·han′did] *adj.* Without assistance or help; by one's own efforts.
sin·gle-mind·ed [sing′gəl·mīn′did] *adj.* **1** Having only one purpose or aim in mind. **2** Sincere.
single parent A parent who lives with a child or children while the other parent does not.
sin·gle·tree [sing′gəl·trē′] *n.* A whiffletree.
sin·gly [sing′glē] *adv.* **1** One by one; one at a time. **2** Separately; alone. **3** Without aid.
sing·song [sing′sông′] **1** *adj.* Regular and monotonous in tone and beat, as rhythm or a voice reciting verse. **2** *n.* A way of speaking with a regular, boring rhythm and no expression.
sin·gu·lar [sing′gyə·lər] **1** *adj.* In grammar, being or indicating only one: a *singular* noun. **2** *n.* In grammar, the form that a word takes when it indicates only one: "Mouse" is the *singular* of "mice." **3** *adj.* Being the only one of its type; unique. **4** *adj.* Extraordinary; uncommon: a *singular* determination to win. **5** *adj.* Odd or peculiar: What *singular* behavior! **—sin′gu·lar·ly** *adv.*
sin·gu·lar·i·ty [sing′gyə·lar′ə·tē] *n., pl.* **sin·gu·lar·i·ties** **1** Singular nature, quality, or character. **2** Something uncommon or remarkable, as a habit or feature; peculiarity.
sin·is·ter [sin′is·tər] *adj.* **1** Threatening evil, trouble, or bad luck; ominous: There was something *sinister* about the old house. **2** Wrong, wicked, or evil: a *sinister* conspiracy. ◆ *Sinister* comes from a Latin word meaning *on the left*, which came to mean *unlucky* or *bad* because omens seen on the left were thought to be unfavorable.
sink [singk] *v.* **sank** or **sunk, sunk, sink·ing,** *n.* **1** *v.* To go or cause to go down beneath the surface: to *sink* in quicksand; The storm *sank* our boat. **2** *v.* To make by digging or excavating: to *sink* a mine shaft. **3** *v.* To penetrate; seep: The oil *sank* into the wood. **4** *v.* To go down or seem to go down gradually: The sun *sank*. **5** *v.* To drop, as to a lower level: He *sank* his head into his hands; She *sank* to her knees. **6** *v.* To lessen in force, volume, amount, or value: My voice *sank* to a whisper; Stocks are *sinking*. **7** *v.* To pass gradually into a certain condition: to *sink* into a coma. **8** *v.* To weaken and approach death: The patient is *sinking* fast. **9** *v.* To become hollow; cave in, as the cheeks. **10** *n.* A hollow where water collects. **11** *n.* A porcelain or metal basin with a drainpipe and faucets. **12** *n.* A place where filth collects or where wicked people gather: a *sink* of iniquity. **13** *n.* A cesspool or sewer. **14** *v.* To invest: The firm *sank* a million in that deal. **15** *v.* To ruin: If you tell, I'll be *sunk*. **—sink in** To be absorbed, fully understood, or wholly accepted by the mind.
sink·er [singk′ər] *n.* **1** A person or thing that sinks. **2** A weight for sinking a fishing line. **3** In baseball, a pitch that curves sharply downward as it approaches home plate.
sink·hole [singk′hōl′] *n.* A natural hollow or hole in the ground that connects with an underground passage.
sin·less [sin′lis] *adj.* Free from sin; innocent.
sin·ner [sin′ər] *n.* A person who has sinned.
Sino- A combining form meaning: Chinese, as in *Sino-American*.
sin·u·ous [sin′yo͞o·əs] *adj.* **1** Full of bends, curves, or turns; winding, as a snake: a *sinuous* path. **2** Not straightforward; morally crooked or devious. **—sin·u·os·i·ty** [sin′yo͞o·os′ə·tē] *n.* **—sin′u·ous·ly** *adv.*
si·nus [sī′nəs] *n.* An opening or cavity, especially any of the air-filled cavities in the bones of the skull that open into the nostrils.
si·nus·i·tis [sī′nə·sī′tis] *n.* Inflammation of a sinus or of the sinuses, especially of the skull.
-sion A suffix meaning: **1** The act of or the condition of being, as in *permission*. **2** The result of, as in *explosion*.
Siou·an [so͞o′ən] *n.* A family of North American Indian languages including those spoken by the Sioux, the Crow, and the Osage.
Sioux [so͞o] *n., pl.* **Sioux** **1** Any of a group of North American Indian tribes once living in the northern Great Plains, now living in Minnesota, Montana, Nebraska, North Dakota, and South Dakota. **2** A member of any of these tribes. **3** Any of the Siouan languages of these tribes.
sip [sip] *v.* **sipped, sip·ping,** *n.* **1** *v.* To drink in small swallows, a little bit at a time: to *sip* hot chocolate. **2** *n.* A very small drink; taste or swallow. **3** *n.* The act of sipping.
si·phon [sī′fən] **1** *n.* A bent tube used for drawing liquid up and over the edge of a container and carrying it to a lower level by means of air pressure and gravity. **2** *v.* To draw off by or pass through a siphon: to *siphon* off gasoline. **3** *n.* A bottle to hold carbonated water. When a valve is opened, pressure of gas in the bottle forces a stream of the liquid out through a tube. **4** *n.* A tubelike organ in

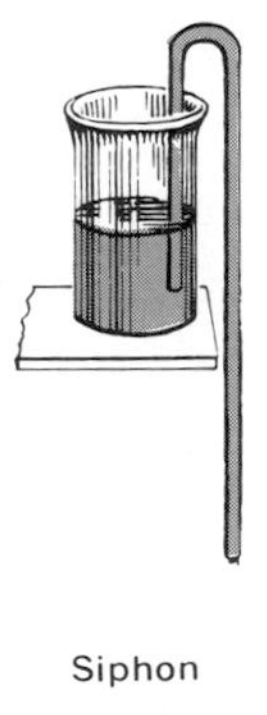
Siphon

a	add	**i**	it	**o͝o**	took	**oi**	oil
ā	ace	**ī**	ice	**o͞o**	pool	**ou**	pout
â	care	**o**	odd	**u**	up	**ng**	ring
ä	palm	**ō**	open	**û**	burn	**th**	thin
e	end	**ô**	order	**yo͞o**	fuse	**th**	this
ē	equal					**zh**	vision

ə = a in *above* e in *sicken* i in *possible* o in *melon* u in *circus*

clams and certain other animals, through which water is sucked in and expelled.

sir [sûr] *n.* **1** A respectful term of address for a man: May I help you, *sir*? **2** (*written* **Sir**) A title used before the given name or the full name of a knight or baronet: *Sir* Winston Churchill was knighted by Elizabeth II.

sire [sīr] *n., v.* **sired, sir·ing** **1** *n.* The male parent of a mammal, as a horse. **2** *v.* To father: a filly *sired* by a race horse. **3** *n.* A father or male ancestor: sometimes used in combination, as in *grandsire.* **4** *n.* A respectful form of address used when speaking to a king.

si·ren [sī′rən] *n.* **1** In Greek myths, one of the sea nymphs whose sweet singing lured sailors to destruction on the rocks. **2** A fascinating, dangerous woman. **3** A device that gives out a loud, piercing wail or whistle, used as a warning signal: the *siren* on a police car.

Sir·i·us [sir′ē·əs] *n.* The brightest star in the heavens. It is also called the Dog Star.

sir·loin [sûr′loin′] *n.* A cut of beef from the loin, especially the upper portion.

si·roc·co [si·rok′ō] *n., pl.* **si·roc·cos** **1** A hot, dry, dusty wind blowing from the African coast to Italy, Sicily, and Spain. **2** Any warm, sultry wind.

sir·rah [sir′ə] *n.* A term of address once used to show contempt or annoyance.

sir·up [sir′əp] *n.* Another spelling of SYRUP.

sis [sis] *n. informal* Sister.

si·sal [sī′səl] *n.* **1** A strong fiber used to make rope, obtained from the leaves of a West Indian plant. **2** The plant yielding this fiber.

sis·sy [sis′ē] *n., pl.* **sis·sies** *informal* A coward or weakling.

sis·ter [sis′tər] *n.* **1** A girl or woman having the same parents as another person of either sex. **2** A girl or woman associated with another or others, as through membership in a group or shared beliefs: *sisters* in the fight for suffrage. **3** A nun.

sis·ter·hood [sis′tər·ho͝od′] *n.* **1** The condition of being sisters. **2** A sisterly relationship. **2** A group of women joined together for some purpose, as work or fellowship.

sis·ter-in-law [sis′tər·in·lô′] *n., pl.* **sis·ters-in-law** **1** A sister of one's husband or wife. **2** The wife of one's brother or of one's wife's or husband's brother.

sis·ter·ly [sis′tər·lē] *adj.* **1** Of or like a sister. **2** Affectionate, kindly, or devoted: She has a *sisterly* feeling for me.

Sis·y·phus [sis′ə·fəs] *n.* In Greek myths, a king who was punished in Hades by having forever to push a stone to the top of a hill, from which it would always roll back down again.

sit [sit] *v.* **sat, sit·ting** **1** To rest with legs bent and the weight on the lower end of the body: to *sit* on a sofa; A cat *sat* on the sill. **2** To cause to sit; seat: I *sat* the baby in the high chair. **3** To occupy a seat: to *sit* in front. **4** To have or keep a seat upon: to *sit* a horse well. **5** To have a seat as a member of an assembly: to *sit* in Congress. **6** To hold a meeting or session, as a court. **7** To be or stay in a settled or inactive position: The car *sat* in the driveway overnight. **8** To baby-sit. **9** To pose, as for a portrait. **10** To perch or roost, as a bird. **11** To cover eggs in order to hatch them, as a hen. **12** To lie or press: Important decisions *sat* heavily on the president. **13** To be situated or located: The wind *sits* in the east. **14** To fit or suit: That hat *sits* well. **—sit down** To be seated. **—sit in** *U.S.* To join or take part, as in a game or discussion. **—sit on** or **sit upon** **1** To belong to (as a jury or commission) as a member. **2** To hold discussions about and look into carefully, as a case. **3** *informal* To suppress or squelch. **—sit out** **1** To sit or stay until the end of: to *sit out* a boring lecture. **2** To sit aside during: to *sit out* a dance. **—sit up** **1** To draw oneself up to or hold oneself in an upright sitting position. **2** To postpone going to bed. **—sit′ter** *n.* ◆ *Sit* and *set* both mean *to rest. Set* always takes an object, and its most common meaning is *to place*: I *set* the dishes down. *Sit* usually does not take an object: I *sat* down; *Sit* still. However, when *sit* means *to cause to sit,* it does take an object: The teacher *sat* him next to me.

si·tar [si·tär′] *n.* A stringed musical instrument of India, having a long neck and a rounded body.

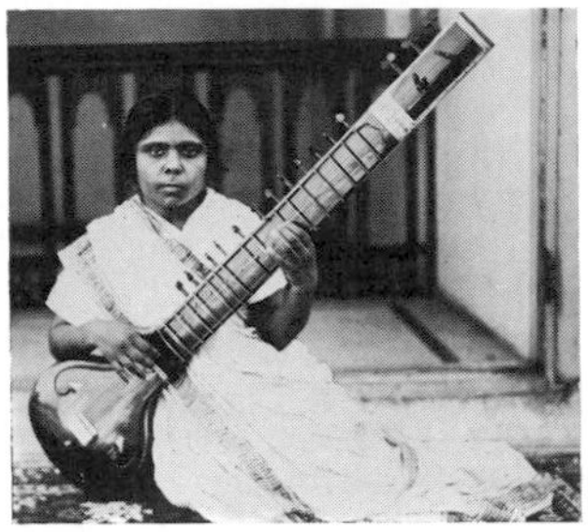
Sitar

sit·com [sit′kom′] *n. informal* A situation comedy.

site [sīt] *n.* **1** The place where something is or was situated: Jamestown is the *site* of the earliest English settlement here. **2** A plot of ground set apart for some special use: a *site* for a housing development. ◆ *Site* is a noun meaning *a place*: the *site* of the Hall of Fame. *Cite* is a verb meaning *to quote* or *mention*: The speaker *cited* several experts to prove the point. *Sight,* both a noun and verb, refers to one's ability to see or to something seen: the sense of *sight*; The lookout *sighted* a ship.

sit-in [sit′in′] *n.* A demonstration in which people sit down in a public place and refuse to move as a protest against a policy or condition they think unjust.

sit·ter [sit′ər] *n.* **1** A person who sits. **2** Another name for BABY-SITTER.

sit·ting [sit′ing] *n.* **1** The act or position of a person who sits. **2** A period during which one remains seated: to read a book in one *sitting*. **3** A session or term, as of a court. **4** A brooding upon eggs. **5** Another word for SETTING (def. 6).

sitting duck *informal* A person or thing that is easy to attack or criticize.

sitting room A living room or parlor.

sit·u·ate [sich′o͞o·wāt′] *v.* **sit·u·at·ed, sit·u·at·ing** To locate: The cottage was *situated* on a hill.

sit·u·at·ed [sich′o͞o·wāt′id] *adj.* **1** Having a location or position; located. **2** Located as to circumstances, especially financial circumstances: to be *well* situated because of an inheritance.

sit·u·a·tion [sich′o͞o·wā′shən] *n.* **1** A state of affairs brought about by a combination of circumstances: an unpleasant *situation.* **2** Position or location: the convenient *situation* of the supermarket. **3** A job: a *situation* as a travel agent.

situation comedy A television or radio series in which a continuing cast of characters is involved in a different humorous situation in each episode.

sit-up [sit′up′] *n.* An exercise for the abdominal muscles in which one lies on one's back and raises the trunk to a sitting position, then lies back again.

Si·va [shē′və *or* sē′və] *n.* In the Hindu religion, the god of destruction and regeneration.

six or **6** [siks] *n., adj.* One more than five. **—at sixes and sevens** Confused or disagreeing.

six-pack [siks′pak′] *n.* A container for holding six bottles or cans, sold as a unit.

six·pence [siks′pəns] *n.* A former British coin worth six pennies.

six-shooter [siks′sho͞o′tər] *n. informal* A revolver that can be fired six times before it has to be loaded again.

six·teen or **16** [siks′tēn′] *n., adj.* One more than fifteen.

six·teenth or **16th** [siks′tēnth′] **1** *adj.* Next after the fifteenth. **2** *n.* The sixteenth one. **3** *adj.* Being one of sixteen equal parts. **4** *n.* A sixteenth part.

sixth or **6th** [siksth] **1** *adj.* Next after the fifth. **2** *n.* The sixth one. **3** *adj.* Being one of six equal parts. **4** *n.* A sixth part.

sixth sense An ability to sense or suspect things not evident to the five senses; intuition.

six·ti·eth or **60th** [siks′tē·ith] **1** *adj.* Tenth in order after the fiftieth. **2** *n.* The sixtieth one. **3** *adj.* Being one of sixty equal parts. **4** *n.* A sixtieth part.

six·ty or **60** [siks′tē] *n., pl.* **six·ties** or **60′s,** *adj.* **1** *n., adj.* Ten more than fifty. **2** *n.* (*pl.*) The years between the age of 60 and the age of 70: a couple in their *sixties.*

siz·a·ble [sī′zə·bəl] *adj.* Fairly large: a *sizable* estate.

size[1] [sīz] *n., v.* **sized, siz·ing** **1** *n.* The amount of space which something occupies; physical proportions: the *size* and weight of a package. **2** *n.* Degree of largeness: Our club increased in *size* when new members joined. **3** *n.* One of a series of measures indicating the degree of largeness of certain goods or products: a *size* 6 shoe; my shirt *size.* **4** *v.* To arrange or classify according to size: to *size* fruit. **5** *n.* Bigness: We caught no fish of any *size.* **—of a size** Of the same size. **—size up** *informal* To form an estimate, judgment, or opinion of.

size[2] [sīz] *n., v.* **sized, siz·ing** **1** *n.* A thin, sticky, jellylike substance used to glaze paper or finish fabrics. **2** *v.* To treat with size.

size·a·ble [sī′zə·bəl] *adj.* Another spelling of SIZABLE.

sized [sīzd] *adj.* Of a given size: medium-*sized* helpings.

siz·zle [siz′(ə)l] *v.* **siz·zled, siz·zling,** *n.* **1** *v.* To give out a hissing sound when very hot, as frying bacon. **2** *n.* A hissing sound.

skate[1] [skāt] *n., v.* **skat·ed, skat·ing** **1** *n.* An ice skate. **2** *n.* A roller skate. **3** *v.* To glide or move on or as if on skates. **—skat′er** *n.*

skate[2] [skāt] *n., pl.* **skate** or **skates** A kind of fish with a flat body and broad fins.

skate·board [skāt′bôrd′] **1** *n.* An oblong board with four low wheels attached to the bottom, ridden in a standing or squatting position. **2** *v.* To ride on a skateboard. **—skate′board′er** *n.*

ske·dad·dle [ski·dad′(ə)l] *v.* **ske·dad·dled, ske·dad·dling** *informal* To run away or flee in a hurry; scram.

skein [skān] *n.* A quantity of something, as yarn or thread, wound into a long, loose coil.

skel·e·tal [skel′ə·təl] *adj.* Of, having to do with, forming, or resembling a skeleton.

skel·e·ton [skel′ə·tən] *n.* **1** The internal framework of bones and cartilage that supports the body of a human being or other vertebrate animal. **2** The external structure of hard material that covers and protects the body of a crustacean, insect, or certain other invertebrate animals. **3** An inner structure like a skeleton, as an outline of a written work or the framework of a house. **—skeleton in the closet** Some shameful fact that is kept hidden.

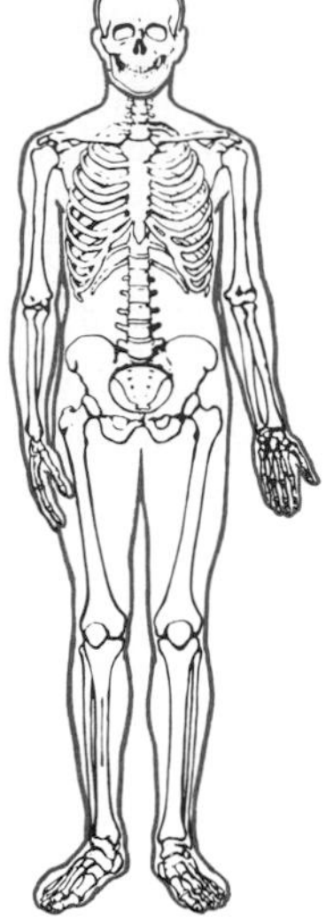
Human skeleton

skeleton key A key filed to a slender shape, used to open a number of different locks.

skep·tic [skep′tik] *n.* **1** A person who doubts or disbelieves things that many people accept as fact or truth. **2** A person who questions the fundamental doctrines of a religion.

skep·ti·cal [skep′ti·kəl] *adj.* **1** Not believing readily; inclined to question or doubt. **2** Showing doubt. **—skep′ti·cal·ly** *adv.*

skep·ti·cism [skep′tə·siz′əm] *n.* The tendency to question or doubt beliefs that others accept.

sketch [skech] **1** *n.* A rough, hasty, or unfinished drawing giving a general impression without full details. **2** *n.* A brief outline, as for a literary work. **3** *v.* To draw, outline, or describe in a sketch. **4** *v.* To make sketches. **5** *n.* A brief, light theatrical piece, as a scene in a revue.

sketch·book [skech′bo͝ok′] *n.* A book for sketching or drawing in.

sketch·y [skech′ē] *adj.* **sketch·i·er, sketch·i·est** Like a sketch; lacking detail or made up of a few essentials only; incomplete: a *sketchy* description.

skew [skyo͞o] **1** *v.* To twist, swerve, or slant. **2** *adj.* Lopsided or distorted. **3** *n.* A slant.

skew·er [skyo͞o′ər] **1** *n.* A long pin of wood or metal, thrust into food to hold it while roasting or broiling. **2** *v.* To run through or fasten with or as if with a skewer.

skew lines Lines in different planes that are not parallel and do not intersect.

ski [skē] *n., pl.* **skis,** *v.* **skied** [skēd], **ski·ing** **1** *n.* One of a pair of long runners of wood, metal, or plastic that are attached to the soles of boots for gliding over snow. **2** *v.* To travel on skis. **—ski′er** *n.*

skid [skid] *v.* **skid·ded, skid·ding,** *n.* **1** *v.* To slide sideways, as a car on an icy surface. **2** *n.* The act of skidding. **3** *v.* To slide instead of revolving, as

a add	**i** it	**o͝o** took	**oi** oil
ā ace	**ī** ice	**o͞o** pool	**ou** pout
â care	**o** odd	**u** up	**ng** ring
ä palm	**ō** open	**û** burn	**th** thin
e end	**ô** order	**yo͞o** fuse	**th** this
ē equal			**zh** vision

ə = a in *above*, e in *sicken*, i in *possible*, o in *melon*, u in *circus*

S

a wheel that does not turn although the vehicle is moving. **4** *n.* A device of metal or wood put under a wheel to keep it from turning. **5** *n.* One of a pair or group of logs or rails, used to support something or as a track on or down which to slide heavy objects. **6** *v.* To put, haul, or slide on skids. **—on the skids** *U.S. slang* Going rapidly down the road to ruin or failure.

skid row A shabby district of a city where vagrants and poor alcoholics live or gather.

skiff [skif] *n.* A light rowboat, sometimes having a small sail and a centerboard.

ski·ing [skē′ing] *n.* The act or sport of gliding over snow on skis.

ski jump **1** A jump made by a skier. **2** A steep skiing course for picking up speed in preparation for such a jump.

ski lift An apparatus for carrying skiers or sightseers up a mountainside. A typical ski lift has a circular, motor-driven cable from which seats are suspended.

skill [skil] *n.* **1** Ability developed by training or practice, enabling one to do something with ease or like an expert: She plays the violin with *skill.* **2** A specific art, craft, ability, or technique: Shorthand is an office *skill.*

skilled [skild] *adj.* **1** Having or showing skill; expert. **2** Having or requiring special ability or training: *skilled* workers; *skilled* labor.

skil·let [skil′it] *n.* A shallow cooking utensil used for frying foods.

skill·ful [skil′fəl] *adj.* Having or showing skill; expert; proficient. **—skill′ful·ly** *adv.*

An electric skillet

skim [skim] *v.* **skimmed, skim·ming** **1** To remove floating matter from the surface of (a liquid): to *skim* milk. **2** To remove in this way: to *skim* the cream from milk. **3** To move quickly and lightly over or near a surface; glide: skiers *skimming* over the snow. **4** To read hastily in glances, without reading every word. **5** To cover with a thin layer or film: a pond *skimmed* with ice.

skim·mer [skim′ər] *n.* **1** A person or thing that skims, as a shallow ladle for skimming liquids. **2** A sea bird that flies with its beak skimming the surface of the water to catch small fish and other food.

skim milk Milk from which the cream has been removed.

skimp [skimp] *v.* **1** To be very economical or stingy; scrimp: to *skimp* on carfare to buy books. **2** To put in or supply too little of: Don't *skimp* the sugar. **3** To do carelessly.

skimp·y [skim′pē] *adj.* **skimp·i·er, skimp·i·est** Hardly enough; meager; scanty: a *skimpy* meal.

skin [skin] *n., v.* **skinned, skin·ning** **1** *n.* The flexible outer protective tissue that covers the bodies of people and animals. **2** *n.* One's life: to save one's *skin.* **3** *n.* The pelt of a small animal. **4** *n.* A container for liquids made of animal skin. **5** *n.* An outside layer or covering resembling skin, as the rind of a fruit. **6** *v.* To tear or remove the skin of: I *skinned* my knee; to *skin* an onion. **7** *v. slang* To cheat or swindle. **—by the skin of one's teeth** By the narrowest of margins; barely.

skin-dive [skin′dīv′] *v.* **skin-dived** or **skin-dove, skin-dived, skin-div·ing** To engage in skin diving. **—skin diver**

skin diving Swimming under water by a swimmer wearing a face mask and foot fins, and sometimes breathing through a snorkel or from an air tank.

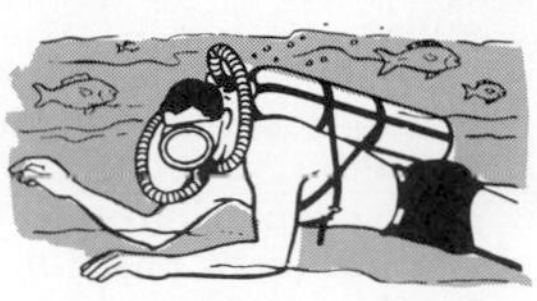

Skin diving

skin·flint [skin′flint′] *n.* A stingy person who is hard and mean where money is involved; miser; tightwad.

skin·ner [skin′ər] *n.* **1** A person who removes, treats, or deals in animal skins. **2** A driver of a team of draft animals.

skin·ny [skin′ē] *adj.* **skin·ni·er, skin·ni·est** Very thin or emaciated; lean.

skip [skip] *v.* **skipped, skip·ping,** *n.* **1** *v.* To move by stepping, hopping, and sliding on each foot in turn. **2** *n.* A light bound, spring, or hop. **3** *v.* To jump lightly over: to *skip* rope. **4** *v.* To bound along, ricochet from, or skim a surface. **5** *v.* To throw so as to cause a bounding, skimming movement: We *skipped* pebbles across the pool. **6** *v.* To pass from one point to another without going through what lies between: *Skip* from the third to the sixth stanza. **7** *v.* To pass over or leave out; omit: She *skipped* the second grade. **8** *n.* The act of passing over; omission. **9** *v. informal* To leave (a place) hurriedly: The crooks *skipped* town.

skip·per[1] [skip′ər] *n.* **1** The captain of a ship, especially a small vessel. **2** Any leader.

skip·per[2] [skip′ər] *n.* **1** A person or thing that skips. **2** Any of several stout-bodied butterflies that fly with quick, flitting movements.

skir·mish [skûr′mish] **1** *n.* A brief fight between small groups of troops. **2** *n.* Any minor conflict. **3** *v.* To take part in a skirmish.

skirt [skûrt] **1** *n.* The part of a garment, as a dress or robe, that hangs from the waist downward. **2** *n.* A separate garment that hangs from the waist. **3** *n.* A thing that hangs or covers like a skirt: a cloth *skirt* on a dressing table. **4** *n.* (*pl.*) The border or edge. **5** *v.* To go around, not through; pass along the edge of: The road *skirts* the park. ◆ See SHIRT.

ski run A trail down a slope suitable for skiing.

skit [skit] *n.* A short sketch, often comic, usually acted out, as for entertainment.

skit·ter [skit′ər] *v.* To move lightly and quickly over a surface; skim or skip.

skit·tish [skit′ish] *adj.* **1** Easily frightened; likely to shy, as a horse. **2** Shy or coy. **3** Lively, spirited, or frivolous. **4** Unreliable. **—skit′tish·ly** *adv.* **—skit′tish·ness** *n.*

skit·tles [skit′(ə)lz] *n.pl.* A game like ninepins, played with a ball or a sliding disk.

skoal [skōl] *interj.* Good health: used as a drinking toast.

skul·dug·ger·y or **skull·dug·ger·y** [skul·dug′ər·ē] *n., pl.* **skul·dug·ger·ies** or **skull·dug·ger·ies** A trick or trickery.

skulk [skulk] *v.* To move about, lurk, or hide in a stealthy, sneaky way. **—skulk′er** *n.*

skull [skul] *n.* The bony framework of the head of a vertebrate animal, enclosing the brain.

skull and crossbones A picture of a human skull over two crossed bones, used as a symbol of death, as a warning label on poison, and as an emblem on pirates' flags.

skull·cap [skul′kap′] *n.* A small cap without a brim, fitting snugly over the top of the head.

skunk [skungk] *n.* **1** A small, furry mammal of North America, usually black with white stripes on its back. It shoots out a liquid with a terrible smell when frightened or angry. **2** *informal* A hateful or contemptible person. ◆ *Skunk* comes from an Algonquian Indian word.

Skunk

skunk cabbage A plant found on swampy ground in eastern North America, having small, early-blooming flowers enclosed in bad-smelling, hoodlike spathes.

sky [skī] *n., pl.* **skies** **1** The region of the upper air that seems to arch over the earth. **2** (*often pl.*) The condition or appearance of the sky: cloudy *skies.* **3** Heaven. **—out of a clear blue sky** Without any warning. ◆ *Sky* comes from an old Scandinavian word meaning *cloud.*

sky blue A blue like the color of the sky.

sky·cap [skī′kap′] *n.* A porter at an airport.

sky·dive [skī′dīv′] *v.* **sky·dived** or **sky·dove** [skī′dōv′], **sky·dived, sky·div·ing** To jump from an aircraft and fall freely for a while before opening one's parachute. **—sky′div′er** *n.*

sky-high [skī′hī′] **1** *adv., adj.* Very high: garbage piled *sky-high* at a dump; *sky-high* gasoline prices. **2** *adv.* To pieces: blown *sky-high.*

sky·jack [skī′jak′] *v. informal* To take over (an airplane in flight) by force. **—sky′jack′er** *n.*

sky·lark [skī′lärk′] **1** *n.* A small European songbird that sings as it rises in flight. **2** *v.* To play or frolic in a lighthearted way.

sky·light [skī′līt′] *n.* A window in a roof or ceiling, letting in daylight from above.

sky·line [skī′līn′] *n.* **1** An outline or silhouette, as of city buildings, seen against the sky. **2** The line at which the earth or sea seems to meet the sky; horizon.

sky·rock·et [skī′rok′it] **1** *n.* A rocket, as in a fireworks display, that explodes high in the air with a burst of brilliant sparks. **2** *v.* To rise rapidly or suddenly: Costs *skyrocketed.*

sky·scrap·er [skī′skrā′pər] *n.* A very high building.

sky·ward [skī′wərd] *adv.* Towards the sky; upward.

sky·wards [skī′wərdz] *adv.* Skyward.

sky·writ·ing [skī′rī′ting] *n.* **1** The act of writing words in the sky by releasing trails of smoke or vapor from an airplane. **2** The words so written.

slab [slab] *n.* **1** A flat, broad, thick piece, as of stone or cheese: a *slab* of marble. **2** A rough outside piece cut off a log to square it before sawing it into lumber.

slack[1] [slak] **1** *adj.* Not tight, tense, or firm; loose or limp: a *slack* rope; a *slack* grip. **2** *n.* Something, as a part of a rope or a sail, that is slack or loose: Take up the *slack.* **3** *v.* To slacken: *Slack* the rope. **4** *adj.* Careless or negligent: *slack* service. **5** *adj.* Lacking activity; not busy: a *slack* season. **6** *n.* An inactive period, as in a business. **7** *n.* A halt in the strong flow of the tide or of a current of water. **8** *adj.* Slow, listless, or sluggish: a *slack* pace. **9** *adv.* In a slack manner. **—slack off** **1** To slow down or reduce effort. **2** To lessen or loosen. **—slack up** To slow down. **—slack′ly** *adv.* **—slack′ness** *n.*

slack[2] [slak] *n.* Coal particles and dirt remaining after more usable chunks of coal have been removed by screening.

slack·en [slak′ən] *v.* **1** To make or become less tight or firm; loosen: to *slacken* a sail. **2** To make or become slower, less active, or less forceful: to *slacken* one's efforts.

slack·er [slak′ər] *n.* A person who shirks duty or avoids military service in wartime.

slacks [slaks] *n.pl.* Long trousers, especially those worn for casual or sports wear.

slag [slag] *n.* **1** The cinderlike waste left after metals are separated from their ores by melting. **2** Loose, clinkerlike pieces of lava.

slain [slān] Past participle of SLAY.

slake [slāk] *v.* **slaked, slak·ing** **1** To satisfy, quench, or reduce in strength: to *slake* one's thirst by drinking deeply. **2** To cause (lime) to undergo a chemical change by mixing it with water or exposing it to moist air.

sla·lom [slä′ləm] *n.* In skiing, a race or a descent down a zigzag course laid out between posts and marked with flags.

Slalom

slam[1] [slam] *v.* **slammed, slam·ming,** *n.* **1** *v.* To close with force and a loud noise; shut loudly: to *slam* a door. **2** *v.* To put, throw, or hit with great force; bang: to *slam* down the phone. **3** *n.* The act or noise of slamming.

slam[2] [slam] *n.* In the game of bridge, the bid for and winning of all 13 tricks in a deal (**grand slam**) or of 12 tricks (**little slam** or **small slam**).

slan·der [slan′dər] **1** *n.* A false, spoken statement or report that harms another's reputation or prevents someone from continuing work. **2** *n.* The act of making such a statement publicly. **3** *v.* To make or spread false and damaging statements about; defame. **—slan′der·er** *n.* **—slan′der·ous** *adj.*

slang [slang] *n.* **1** An informal, often short-lived kind of language used in place of standard words for added vividness or humor. Some examples of slang are *dough* (money), *lid* (hat), *rip off* (steal), and *scuzzy* (dirty). **2** The special vocabulary of a certain group: army *slang.*

slang·y [slang′ē] *adj.* **slang·i·er, slang·i·est** Of, containing, or using a lot of slang.

slant [slant] **1** *v.* To slope, cause to slope, or move at an angle to the horizontal or the vertical; incline: handwriting that *slants* across the page; *Slant* the ladder. **2** *adj.* Sloping; oblique: *slant* eyes. **3** *n.* A slanting direction, surface, or line; slope: the *slant* of the river bank. **4** *n.* A point of view; attitude.

slant·ways [slant′wāz′] *adv.* Slantwise.

a	add	**i**	it	**o͝o**	took	**oi**	oil
ā	ace	**ī**	ice	**o͞o**	pool	**ou**	pout
â	care	**o**	odd	**u**	up	**ng**	ring
ä	palm	**ō**	open	**û**	burn	**th**	thin
e	end	**ô**	order	**yo͞o**	fuse	**th**	this
ē	equal					**zh**	vision

ə = { a in *above* e in *sicken* i in *possible* / o in *melon* u in *circus* }

S

slant·wise [slant′wīz′] *adv., adj.* At a slant.
slap [slap] *n., v.* **slapped, slap·ping** 1 *n.* A blow delivered with the open hand or with something flat. 2 *v.* To hit or strike with or as if with a slap. 3 *n.* The sound made by or as if by slapping. 4 *v.* To put or throw violently or carelessly: The customer *slapped* the money down.
slap·dash [slap′dash′] *adj.* Marked by careless haste; rushed and sloppy: The essay was a *slapdash* job the author didn't even proofread.
slap·stick [slap′stik′] *n.* Comedy full of horseplay in which the actors knock each other around to make people laugh.
slash [slash] 1 *v.* To cut with a long, sharp, sweeping stroke or strokes. 2 *v.* To strike with sweeping blows; whip or lash. 3 *n.* A sweeping cut or stroke. 4 *n.* A slit or gash. 5 *v.* To cut slits in, as a garment, so that ornamental material or lining will show. 6 *v.* To reduce sharply: to *slash* prices. 7 *v.* To criticize severely. 8 *n.* The act of slashing.
slat [slat] *n., v.* **slat·ted, slat·ting** 1 *n.* A thin, narrow strip of wood or metal. 2 *v.* To provide or make with slats: *Slat* this box to make a cage.
slate [slāt] *n., v.* **slat·ed, slat·ing** 1 *n.* A hard, fine-grained rock that splits easily into thin layers. 2 *n.* A thin piece of this rock, as one used as a roofing tile or one to be written on with chalk or a special pencil. 3 *v.* To cover (as a roof) with slate. 4 *n.* The dull, bluish gray color of slate. 5 *n.* A list arranged in advance, as a list of political candidates running for office. 6 *v.* To mark or select in advance: The technician was *slated* for a promotion. **—a clean slate** A record showing no bad behavior or poor performance in the past.
slat·tern [slat′ərn] *n.* A dirty, sloppy, or untidy woman. **—slat′tern·ly** *adj., adv.*
slaugh·ter [slô′tər] 1 *n.* The act of killing animals for market; butchering. 2 *v.* To butcher: to *slaughter* cattle. 3 *n.* The savage killing of human beings, especially killing on a large scale, as in war. 4 *v.* To kill brutally or savagely, especially in large numbers.
slaugh·ter·house [slô′tər·hous′] *n.* A place where animals are killed and cut up for food.
Slav [släv] *n.* A member of one of the peoples in eastern Europe that speak Slavic languages, including the Russians, Poles, Czechs, Slovaks, Bulgarians, and Serbians.
slave [slāv] *n., v.* **slaved, slav·ing** 1 *n.* A person owned by another like a piece of property. 2 *v.* To work as hard as a slave may be forced to; drudge; toil. 3 *n.* A person who works as hard as a slave does. 4 *n.* A person mastered or controlled by some habit, vice, influence, or desire: a *slave* to video games.
slave driver 1 A person in charge of slaves at work. 2 A harsh, demanding employer or supervisor.
slave·hold·er [slāv′hōl′dər] *n.* An owner of slaves. **—slave′hold′ing** *adj., n.*
slav·er[1] [slav′ər] 1 *v.* To drool. 2 *n.* Saliva dribbling from the mouth.
slav·er[2] [slā′vər] *n.* 1 A ship once used to transport people who were to be sold as slaves. 2 A person whose business is dealing in slaves.
slav·er·y [slā′vər·ē] *n.* 1 The practice of holding human beings as slaves. 2 The condition of being a slave: freed from *slavery.* 3 Hard labor like that of slaves; drudgery.
Slav·ic [slä′vik] 1 *n.* A group of eastern European languages including Russian, Polish, Czech, Slovak, and Bulgarian. 2 *adj.* Of or having to do with the Slavs or their languages.
slav·ish [slā′vish] *adj.* 1 Having or showing the humble, submissive spirit of a slave: *slavish* devotion. 2 Lacking independence of mind and originality: a *slavish* copy of another painting. **—slav′ish·ly** *adv.* **—slav′ish·ness** *n.*
slaw [slô] *n.* Coleslaw.
slay [slā] *v.* **slew, slain, slay·ing** To kill, especially by violence. **—slay′er** *n.*
slea·zy [slē′zē] *adj.* **slea·zi·er, slea·zi·est** 1 Of poor quality; flimsy or shoddy. 2 Cheap and disreputable: a *sleazy* row of bars. **—slea′zi·ness** *n.*
sled [sled] *n., v.* **sled·ded, sled·ding** 1 *n.* A vehicle on runners, used for carrying people or loads over snow and ice. 2 *v.* To carry by sled. 3 *n.* A small vehicle on runners, used for coasting on snow. 4 *v.* To ride on a sled.
sledge [slej] *n., v.* **sledged, sledg·ing** 1 *n.* A vehicle mounted on low runners for moving loads, especially over snow and ice. 2 *v.* To travel or carry on a sledge.
sledge hammer A large, heavy hammer, usually held and swung with both hands.
sleek [slēk] 1 *adj.* Smooth and glossy, as the coat of a horse that has been groomed. 2 *adj.* Having smooth, soft, shining hair, fur, or skin: *sleek* dogs. 3 *v.* To make sleek, as by smoothing or brushing; slick. 4 *adj.* Having elegance and style, as in appearance or design: the *sleek,* long lines of the boat. 5 *adj.* Insincerely smooth in manner; oily. **—sleek′ly** *adv.*
sleep [slēp] *n., v.* **slept, sleep·ing** 1 *n.* A natural condition or period when the eyes close and consciousness is wholly or partly lost so that the body and mind may rest. 2 *v.* To rest in sleep or be asleep; slumber. 3 *v.* To be in an inactive condition resembling sleep, as torpor, hibernation, or death. 4 *n.* A condition resembling sleep: the groundhog's winter *sleep.* **—go to sleep** 1 To fall asleep. 2 To become numb and then start to tingle because the blood is not circulating properly: My foot has *gone to sleep.* **—sleep off** To get rid of by sleep: to *sleep off* an irritable mood.
sleep·er [slē′pər] *n.* 1 A person or animal that sleeps. 2 A sleeping car. 3 *British* A tie that supports the rails of a railway track. 4 *U.S. informal* Something, as a play, motion picture, or book, that is unexpectedly successful.
sleeping bag A large bag with a warm lining, used for sleeping, especially out of doors.
sleeping car A railroad car with seats that open out into berths for passengers to sleep in.
sleeping sickness A disease marked by fever and abnormal sleepiness, especially a disease common in Africa, caused by the bite of a tsetse fly, and ending in prolonged sleep or death.
sleep·less [slēp′lis] *adj.* 1 Unable to sleep; wakeful. 2 Without sleep: a *sleepless* night.
sleep·walk·er [slēp′wô′kər] *n.* A person who walks while asleep. **—sleep′walk′ing** *n.*
sleep·y [slē′pē] *adj.* **sleep·i·er, sleep·i·est** 1 Ready to or about to go to sleep; drowsy. 2 Quiet, dull, and inactive: a *sleepy* country village. **—sleep′i·ly** *adv.* **—sleep′i·ness** *n.*
sleep·y·head [slē′pē·hed′] *n. informal* A drowsy or lazy person.
sleet [slēt] 1 *n.* A mixture of snow or hail and rain.

2 *n.* A thin coating of ice, as on a road. 3 *n.* A shower of partly frozen rain. 4 *v.* To pour or shower sleet. **—sleet′y** *adj.*

sleeve [slēv] *n.* 1 The part of a garment that fits over the arm. 2 A tube that fits over all or part of a shaft or another tube. **—laugh up one's sleeve** To be secretly amused. **—up one's sleeve** Hidden but readily available.

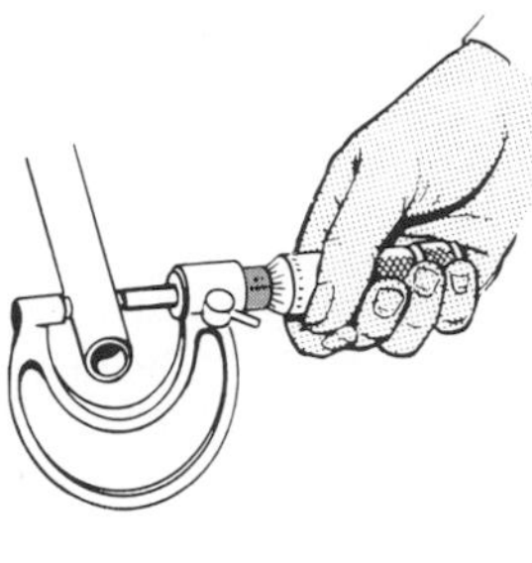

A micrometer sleeve

sleeve·less [slēv′lis] *adj.* Having no sleeves.

sleigh [slā] 1 *n.* A vehicle, usually drawn by a horse, with runners for use on snow and ice. 2 *v.* To ride or transport in a sleigh.

sleight [slīt] *n.* 1 Skill; dexterity. 2 Cunning; craft.

sleight of hand 1 Such skill in moving the hands that a spectator either fails to see some movements or is confused by them. 2 A trick or tricks done by a modern magician using this skill.

slen·der [slen′dər] *adj.* 1 Not very wide in proportion to the length or height; slim; thin: The greyhound is tall, *slender*, and fast. 2 Not large or strong; slight or weak: I won the race by a *slender* margin. 3 Small or inadequate: a *slender* income. **—slen′der·ness** *n.*

slept [slept] Past tense and past participle of SLEEP.

sleuth [slo͞oth] *n.* 1 A bloodhound. 2 *U.S. informal* A detective.

slew¹ [slo͞o] Past tense of SLAY.

slew² [slo͞o] *n. U.S. informal* A large number, crowd, or amount; lot.

slew³ [slo͞o] *v., n.* Another spelling of SLUE¹.

slice [slīs] *n., v.* **sliced, slic·ing** 1 *n.* A thin, broad piece cut off from a larger piece: a *slice* of meat. 2 *v.* To cut into slices: to *slice* a tomato. 3 *v.* To cut from a whole or larger piece: to *slice* off a piece of bread. 4 *v.* To cut with or as if with a sharp knife: The boat *sliced* through the waves. 5 *v.* To hit (as a golf ball) with a spin that makes it veer to the right if hit by a right-handed player. **—slic′er** *n.*

slick [slik] 1 *adj.* Smooth, glossy, or oily: *slick* hair. 2 *v.* To make smooth, glossy, or oily: to *slick* down hair with pomade. 3 *adj.* Slippery, as with oil or ice. 4 *n.* A smooth or slippery place, as a smooth place on a surface of water covered by a film of oil. 5 *adj.* Smart, clever, or tricky: That was a very *slick* answer. 6 *adj.* Smooth in manner but shallow or insincere: *slick* writing.

slick·er [slik′ər] *n.* 1 A waterproof overcoat, as of oilskin or plastic. 2 *informal* A clever, sly person.

slide [slīd] *v.* **slid** [slid], **slid** or **slid·den** [slid′(ə)n], **slid·ing** [slī′ding], *n.* 1 *v.* To pass or send over a surface with a smooth, slipping movement: to *slide* down the banisters. 2 *n.* An act of sliding. 3 *n.* A sliding part. 4 *n.* A smooth, slanting surface down which people or things may slide. 5 *v.* To slip: The soap *slid* from my hand. 6 *n.* The slipping of a mass, as of earth or snow, from a higher to a lower level. 7 *v.* To move easily, smoothly, gradually, or so as not to be noticed: We *slid* stealthily out of the room. 8 *v.* To continue without being acted on: Let the matter *slide.* 9 *n.* A small, transparent plate bearing a picture to be projected on a screen. 10 *n.* A small glass plate for holding an object to be examined under a microscope.

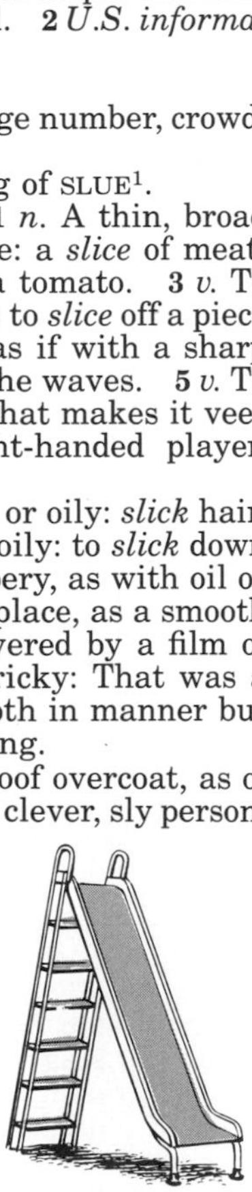

Slide

slide fastener Another name for a ZIPPER.

slide projector A device for projecting magnified images from slides onto a wall or screen.

slide rule A device that looks like a ruler with a strip in the center that slides, both marked with scales of logarithms, used for rapid calculation.

sliding door A door set in long grooves at top and bottom. It opens and closes by sliding sidewise on a track.

sli·er [slī′ər] Comparative of SLY.

sli·est [slī′ist] Superlative of SLY.

slight [slīt] 1 *adj.* Small in amount, degree, intensity, or importance; not great or serious: a *slight* headache. 2 *adj.* Slender or frail: to have a *slight* build. 3 *v.* To neglect as unimportant or show careless, rude, or scornful disregard for; ignore or snub: to *slight* a friend. 4 *n.* An act or omission showing a lack of courtesy or respect toward another; snub. **—slight′ly** *adv.*

slight·ing [slī′ting] *adj.* Showing a lack of respect or appreciation; belittling or insulting: *slighting* remarks.

sli·ly [slī′lē] *adv.* Another spelling of SLYLY.

slim [slim] *adj.* **slim·mer, slim·mest,** *v.* **slimmed, slim·ming** 1 *adj.* Slender or thin, as the human body. 2 *v.* To make or become thin or thinner: Exercise helped them *slim* down. 3 *adj.* Slight, small, or scant: a *slim* possibility; a *slim* attendance. **—slim′·ness** *n.* ◆ *Slim* comes from a Dutch word meaning *bad, crooked,* or *shifty.*

slime [slīm] *n.* Any soft, moist, sticky substance that clings and often soils, as muck.

slim·y [slī′mē] *adj.* **slim·i·er, slim·i·est** 1 Covered with or like slime. 2 Foul; filthy.

sling [sling] *n., v.* **slung, sling·ing** 1 *n.* A strap, as of leather, usually having a string attached to each end, for hurling a stone or other missile. 2 *n.* A slingshot. 3 *v.* To fling or hurl as if from a sling: to *sling* a pebble. 4 *n.* A rope, strap, or chain, used to lift, suspend, or move something, as a heavy object. 5 *v.* To place, hold, or move in a sling. 6 *v.* To hang loosely by means of a strap or rope: They *slung* the packs over the

Sling

a	add	**i**	it	**o͝o**	took	**oi**	oil
ā	ace	**ī**	ice	**o͞o**	pool	**ou**	pout
â	care	**o**	odd	**u**	up	**ng**	ring
ä	palm	**ō**	open	**û**	burn	**th**	thin
e	end	**ô**	order	**yo͞o**	fuse	**th**	this
ē	equal					**zh**	vision

ə = {a in *above* e in *sicken* i in *possible* / o in *melon* u in *circus*}

donkey's back. **7** *n.* A loop of cloth worn around the neck to support an injured arm.

sling·shot [sling′shot′] *n.* A weapon or toy for shooting things, as stones, made of an elastic strap attached to the prongs of a forked stick.

slink [slingk] *v.* **slunk, slink·ing** To move or creep in a sneaky, frightened, or guilty way.

slip[1] [slip] *v.* **slipped, slip·ping,** *n.* **1** *v.* To shift or fall accidentally out of place or out of the grasp: Don't let the scissors *slip*; The soap *slipped* out of my hand. **2** *v.* To slide accidentally and unexpectedly: I *slipped* and fell. **3** *n.* An act of slipping. **4** *v.* To worsen, fail, err, weaken, or drop: Your grades are *slipping*. **5** *v.* To move or put easily and smoothly; slide: to *slip* into a robe; *Slip* the collar on the dog. **6** *n.* An undergarment, usually the length of a dress. **7** *n.* A pillowcase. **8** *n.* *U.S.* A space for a ship between two wharves. **9** *v.* To come, go, or pass stealthily or unnoticed: The children *slipped* into the house; My friend *slipped* me a note. **10** *v.* To escape from; get away from: It *slipped* my mind. **11** *v.* To escape: That comment simply *slipped* out. **12** *n.* A lapse or error in speech, writing, or conduct: a *slip* of the tongue. **—give one the slip** To get away from someone cleverly. **—let slip** To say without intending to. **—slip up** *informal* To make a mistake.

slip[2] [slip] *n., v.* **slipped, slip·ping** **1** *n.* A small piece of paper, as for a note: a deposit *slip*. **2** *n.* A twig or shoot cut from a plant to be separately planted. **3** *v.* To cut a twig or shoot from: to *slip* a plant. **4** *n.* A slender young person: a *slip* of a child.

slip·cov·er [slip′kuv′ər] *n.* A fitted cloth cover, as for a chair, that is easily removed.

slip·knot [slip′not′] *n.* A knot that slides along a rope and loosens or tightens a loop.

Slipknot

slip-on [slip′on′] **1** *n.* A piece of clothing that is easily slipped on and taken off. **2** *adj.* Easily slipped on and off: a *slip-on* shoe.

slip·per [slip′ər] *n.* A low, light shoe that is easily slipped on or off the foot.

slip·per·y [slip′ər·ē] *adj.* **slip·per·i·er, slip·per·i·est** **1** Hard to hold or stand on because of a slick, greasy, or slimy surface. **2** Not reliable or trustworthy; tricky. **—slip′per·i·ness** *n.*

slip·shod [slip′shod′] *adj.* **1** Careless or slovenly, as work. **2** Shabby, as in appearance.

slip·stream [slip′strēm′] *n.* **1** A flow of air driven backward by the propellor of an aircraft. **2** An area of reduced air pressure and forward suction immediately behind a speeding ground vehicle.

slip·up [slip′up′] *n.* *informal* A mistake or blunder.

slit [slit] *n., v.* **slit, slit·ting** **1** *n.* A cut that is relatively long and straight. **2** *n.* A long, narrow opening. **3** *v.* To make a long cut in; slash. **4** *v.* To cut lengthwise into strips.

slith·er [sli*th*′ər] *v.* **1** To slide with an unsteady motion down or along a surface. **2** To glide like a snake.

sliv·er [sliv′ər] **1** *n.* A slender piece cut, split, or broken off lengthwise; splinter. **2** *v.* To cut, split, or break into slivers.

slob [slob] *n.* **1** A dirty, messy person. **2** A crude or uncultured person.

slob·ber [slob′ər] **1** *v.* To let liquid flow from the mouth; drool. **2** *n.* Liquid that is drooled. **3** *v.* To be gushy in showing one's feelings.

sloe [slō] *n.* **1** A small, sharp-tasting, plumlike fruit. **2** The shrub on which it grows.

slog [slog] *v.* **slogged, slog·ging,** *n.* **1** *v.* To move slowly and with difficulty: *slogging* through the mud. **2** *n.* A slow, hard march. **3** *v.* To keep working hard: to *slog* away at a problem until it is solved. **4** *n.* Hard, long, diligent work.

slo·gan [slō′gən] *n.* **1** An often-repeated phrase or motto, as one used in advertising or campaigning, to draw attention. **2** A battle cry.

sloop [slōōp] *n.* A sailing vessel with one mast, a mainsail, and at least one jib.

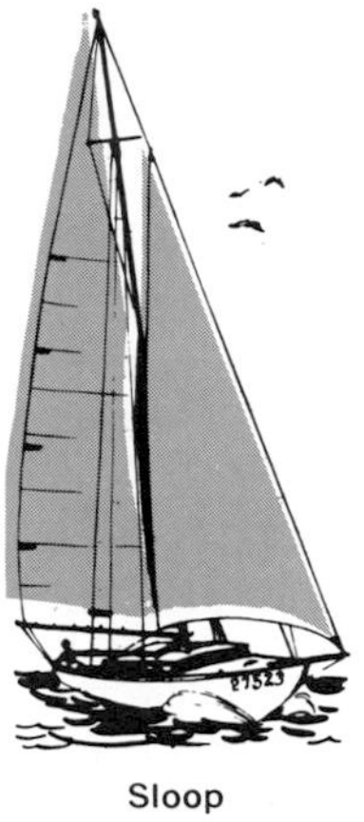
Sloop

slop [slop] *v.* **slopped, slop·ping,** *n.* **1** *v.* To splash or spill. **2** *n.* A puddle of splashed or spilled liquid. **3** *n.* Watery mud; slush. **4** *n.* (*often pl.*) Unappetizing, watery food. **5** *n.* (*pl.*) Waste food or swill fed to animals, as pigs. **6** *n.* (*often pl.*) Liquid waste to be thrown out. **—slop over** To overflow and splash.

slope [slōp] *v.* **sloped, slop·ing,** *n.* **1** *v.* To lie at an angle to the horizontal; slant: The ground *slopes* steeply here. **2** *n.* A piece of ground that slopes, as a snowy hillside down which people ski. **3** *n.* Any slanting surface or line. **4** *n.* The change in elevation of a line or plane per unit of horizontal distance. A hill that rises 10 feet in a horizontal distance of 100 feet has a slope of 10% or 1/10.

slop·py [slop′ē] *adj.* **slop·pi·er, slop·pi·est** **1** Wet and slushy enough to splash: a *sloppy* playing field. **2** *informal* Messy, careless, or untidy. **—slop′pi·ly** *adv.* **—slop′pi·ness** *n.*

slosh [slosh] *v.* To move, wade, or plod with splashes through water, mud, or slush.

slot [slot] *n., v.* **slot·ted, slot·ting** **1** *n.* A narrow opening or groove; slit: Put a dime in the *slot*. **2** *v.* To cut a slot in; groove.

sloth [slōth, slôth, *or* sloth] *n.* **1** Laziness. **2** A slow-moving mammal of South America that hangs upside down from tree branches by its claws and sleeps or dozes most of the day.

Sloth

sloth·ful [slōth′fəl, slôth′fəl, *or* sloth′fəl] *adj.* Lazy, sluggish, or indolent.

slot machine **1** A coin-operated vending machine. **2** A gambling device worked by inserting a coin and pulling a handle that spins a set of wheels.

slouch [slouch] **1** *v.* To stand, walk, or sit with a drooping of the head and shoulders and a slumping of the body. **2** *n.* A drooping of the head and shoulders. **3** *n.* An awkward, lazy, or incompetent person: She's no *slouch* at baseball.

slouch hat A hat having a wide, soft brim that bends easily downward.

slough[1] [slou *or* slōō] *n.* **1** A place of deep mud, mire, or stagnant water, as a bog or swamp. **2** A swampy, stagnant backwater or bayou.

slough[2] [sluf] **1** *n.* The outer skin of a snake, that has been or is about to be shed. **2** *v.* To cast off; shed: The serpent *sloughed* its skin; to *slough* off a bad habit. **3** *v.* To be cast off or shed: dead tissue that *sloughs*. **4** *n.* Something cast off like dead skin. **5** *v.* In certain card games, to discard (an unwanted card).

Slo·vak [slō′vak′] **1** *n.* A member of a Slavic people of eastern Czechoslovakia. **2** *n.* The Slavic language of the Slovaks. **3** *adj.* Of or having to do with the Slovaks or their language. **—Slo·va·ki·an** [slō·vä′kē·ən *or* slō·vak′ē·ən] *adj., n.*

Slo·vene [slō′vēn′] **1** *n.* A member of a Slavic people of NW Yugoslavia. **2** *n.* The Slavic language of the Slovenes. **3** *adj.* Of or having to do with the Slovenes or their language.

slov·en·ly [sluv′ən·lē] *adj.* **slov·en·li·er, slov·en·li·est** **1** Habitually untidy, messy, or dirty. **2** Lazily careless. **—slov′·en·li·ness** *n.*

slow [slō] **1** *adj.* Having a low rate of speed; not fast: a *slow* waltz. **2** *v.* To make, go, or become slow or slower: The bus *slowed* down. **3** *adj.* Taking a lot of time or more time than usual: a *slow* trip. **4** *adv.* In a slow or cautious manner or at a slow speed: Go *slow.* **5** *adj.* Behind the true time: The clock is *slow.* **6** *adj.* Hard to move fast on: a *slow* track. **7** *adj.* Not hastily moved: *slow* to anger. **8** *adj.* Not quick to learn: *slow* students. **9** *adj.* Lacking liveliness; dull or sluggish: a *slow* party. **10** *adj.* Inactive: Business is *slow.* **—slow′·ly** *adv.* **—slow′ness** *n.* ◆ In formal writing, use *slowly* (not *slow*) as an adverb: He drove *slowly.*

slow·down [slō′doun′] *n.* A slowing down, especially a deliberate slowing down of the rate of work or production.

slow motion A motion-picture technique by means of which filmed action is shown on the screen at a speed much slower than its true speed.

slow·poke [slō′pōk′] *n. informal* A person who works or moves at a very slow pace.

slow-wit·ted [slō′wit′id] *adj.* Slow, as in learning or calculating; stupid; dull.

sludge [sluj] *n.* **1** Slimy mud or icy slush. **2** Any muddy, slimy, or oily refuse or sediment.

slue[1] [slōō] *v.* **slued, slu·ing,** *n.* **1** *v.* To turn, twist, or swing to the side. **2** *n.* The act of sluing, or position after sluing.

slue[2] [slōō] *n.* A swamp or bog; slough.

slue[3] [slōō] *n.* Another spelling of SLEW[2].

slug[1] [slug] *n.* **1** A bullet or shot, usually round. **2** Any small piece or disk of metal, as one used as a counterfeit coin in machines.

slug[2] [slug] *n.* **1** A snaillike animal without a visible shell, often feeding on garden plants. **2** A smooth, creeping larva or caterpillar.

slug[3] [slug] *v.* **slugged, slug·ging,** *n. informal* **1** *v.* To hit hard, as with a baseball bat or fist. **2** *n.* A heavy blow. **—slug′ger** *n.*

slug·gard [slug′ərd] *n.* A lazy, idle person.

slug·gish [slug′ish] *adj.* **1** Not active or energetic; lazy or dull: The heat made us *sluggish.* **2** Moving very slowly: a *sluggish* brook. **—slug′gish·ly** *adv.* **—slug′gish·ness** *n.*

sluice [slōōs] *n., v.* **sluiced, sluic·ing** **1** *n.* An artificial channel for transporting water, equipped with a valve or gate to regulate the flow. **2** *n.* The gate that regulates the flow of water; sluice gate. **3** *n.* The water controlled by a sluice gate. **4** *v.* To draw out by or flow out from a sluice. **5** *n.* A trough through which water is run to separate gold, as from sand, or to float logs. **6** *v.* To wash (gold) out of sand, gravel, or dirt with water in a sluice.

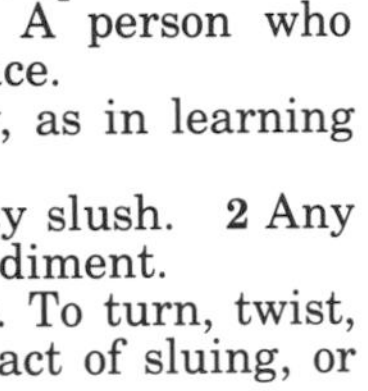

An opened and a closed sluice

sluice gate A gate, as in a dam, to control the flow of water through a sluice.

slum [slum] *n., v.* **slummed, slum·ming** **1** *n.* (*often pl.*) A shabby, dirty, run-down section of a city where the poor live crowded together. **2** *v.* To visit a slum or a slummy place, as out of curiosity.

slum·ber [slum′bər] **1** *v.* To sleep, especially lightly or quietly. **2** *n.* Sleep. **3** *v.* To be inactive. **4** *n.* A condition of inaction.

slum·ber·ous [slum′bər·əs] *adj.* **1** Sleepy; drowsy. **2** Causing or inviting sleep.

slum·brous [slum′brəs] *adj.* Slumberous.

slum·lord [slum′lôrd′] *n.* A person who owns and charges exhorbitant rentals for run-down housing in a slum area.

slum·my [slum′ē] *adj.* **slum·mi·er, slum·mi·est** Of, having to do with, or like a slum.

slump [slump] **1** *v.* To stand, walk, or sit with a drooping posture. **2** *v.* To fall suddenly or collapse: The sack *slumped* to the ground. **3** *n.* A fall or collapse. **4** *n.* A decline or period of decline, as in prices or business.

slung [slung] Past tense and past participle of SLING.

slunk [slungk] Past tense and past participle of SLINK.

slur [slûr] *v.* **slurred, slur·ring,** *n.* **1** *v.* To pronounce in an indistinct way, running together or passing over speech sounds: to *slur* "you all" and say "y'all." **2** *v.* To sing or play (two or more successive musical tones) so that there is no break between them. **3** *n.* A curved line (⌣ or ⌢) used in music to connect notes that are to be slurred. **4** *n.* A slurred pronunciation, sound, or set of notes. **5** *v.* To pass over lightly or hastily: to *slur* over a problem. **6** *v.* To speak of in an insulting way. **7** *n.* An insulting remark or insinuation.

slurp [slûrp] *v.* To eat or drink noisily.

slur·ry [slûr′ē] *n., pl.* **slur·ries** A thin mixture of an insoluble material, as earth, plaster, or rock, with water.

slush [slush] *n.* **1** Soft, sloppy material, as melting snow or soft mud. **2** Foolishly sentimental talk or writing. **3** Grease. **—slush′y** *adj.*

slush fund A fund raised to pay for some corrupt purpose, often political, as bribing an official.

slut [slut] *n.* **1** A dirty, sloppy, or untidy woman. **2** An immoral woman.

sly [slī] *adj.* **sli·er** or **sly·er, sli·est** or **sly·est** **1** Clever in a secret, stealthy, or sneaky way; artful in deceiving; cunning; crafty; wily: a *sly* old fox. **2** Hinting secret thoughts: a *sly* wink. **3** Playfully clever: *sly* wit. **—on the sly** Secretly. **—sly·ly** *adv.* **—sly′ness** *n.*

Sm The symbol for the element samarium.

smack[1] [smak] **1** *n.* A quick, sharp noise made by moving the lips apart, as in enjoyment over food.

a	add	**i**	it	**ŏŏ**	took	**oi**	oil
ā	ace	**ī**	ice	**ōō**	pool	**ou**	pout
â	care	**o**	odd	**u**	up	**ng**	ring
ä	palm	**ō**	open	**û**	burn	**th**	thin
e	end	**ô**	order	**yōō**	fuse	**th**	this
ē	equal					**zh**	vision

ə = a in *above*, e in *sicken*, i in *possible*, o in *melon*, u in *circus*

S

2 *v.* To make such a noise with: to *smack* one's lips. **3** *n.* A noisy kiss. **4** *n.* A loud slap or blow. **5** *v.* To slap noisily. **6** *adv. informal* Squarely: *smack* on the target.

smack² [smak] **1** *v.* To have a taste, flavor, or suggestion: That decision *smacks* of someone else's influence. **2** *n.* A faint but distinctive taste or flavor: a *smack* of curry. **3** *n.* A trace.

smack³ [smak] *n.* A small sailboat used chiefly for fishing, often having a well for live fish.

small [smôl] **1** *adj.* Not large in size or amount; little: a *small* town; a *small* price. **2** *adj.* Less large than the average: a *small* elephant. **3** *n.* The small or slender part: the *small* of the back. **4** *adj.* Soft and faint: a *small* voice. **5** *adj.* Not important or significant; trivial: *small* matters. **6** *adj.* Narrow, mean, or petty: *small* in spirit. — **feel small** To feel humiliated or ashamed: Their disapproval made me *feel small.* **—small′ness** *n.*

small arm A weapon, as a pistol or rifle, that can be carried and fired by hand.

small calorie Another name for CALORIE (def. 1).

small capital A printed letter that has the same form as a full-sized capital letter but is smaller. THESE ARE SMALL CAPITALS.

small change Coins of little value, as nickels, dimes, and quarters.

small fry **1** Small fish. **2** Young children. **3** Persons or things of minor or no significance.

small hours The early hours of the morning.

small intestine The longer and narrower portion of the intestine, leading from the stomach to the large intestine.

small·ish [smôl′ish] *adj.* Somewhat small.

small letter A letter that is not capitalized.

small-mind·ed [smôl′mīn′did] *adj.* Characterized by intolerant, selfish opinions or petty aims and hopes; narrow-minded; prejudiced.

small·pox [smôl′poks′] *n.* A highly contagious virus disease causing a high fever and skin eruptions that usually leave permanent scars.

small talk Casual, light conversation.

small-time [smôl′tīm′] *adj. informal* At a low level of achievement or importance; petty: a *small-time* entertainer.

smart [smärt] **1** *adj.* Quick in mind; intelligent; bright; clever. **2** *adj.* Keen or shrewd. **3** *adj.* Witty and quick but not deep: *smart* remarks. **4** *adj.* Sharp and stinging: a *smart* cuff on the ear. **5** *n.* A sharp, stinging sensation. **6** *v.* To experience or cause a stinging sensation: eyes *smarting* from smog; The cut *smarts.* **7** *v.* To feel hurt, sorry, irritated, or upset: I *smarted* over their rude remarks. **8** *adj.* Clean, neat, and trim in appearance. **9** *adj.* Fashionable; stylish: a *smart* outfit. **10** *adj.* Vigorous; brisk; lively: to move at a *smart* pace. **—smart′ly** *adv.* **—smart′ness** *n.*

smart al·eck [al′ik] A conceited person who is always trying to be clever and show how much he or she knows.

smart·en [smär′tən] *v.* To make or become more attractive, stylish, brisk, bright, or trim.

smash [smash] **1** *v.* To break into many pieces violently and noisily: to *smash* a glass against the wall; The vase fell and *smashed.* **2** *v.* To crush: to *smash* a rebellion. **3** *v.* To dash or hit violently; crash: The car *smashed* into a post. **4** *n.* The act or sound of smashing. **5** *n.* A wreck or crash resulting from a collision. **6** *v.* To wreck or destroy. **7** *n.* Ruin, failure, or disaster. **8** *n. informal* A great success; hit: The film is a box-office *smash.*

smash·ing [smash′ing] *adj. informal* Strikingly good or effective; wonderful: a *smashing* success.

smash·up [smash′up′] *n.* A damaging crash or collision; wreck.

smat·ter·ing [smat′ər·ing] *n.* A slight, surface knowledge: I have only a *smattering* of German.

smear [smir] **1** *v.* To spread, rub, or cover with a greasy, sticky, or dirty substance: to *smear* one's hands with paint. **2** *v.* To spread or apply in a thick layer or coating: to *smear* grease on an axle. **3** *v.* To blur or make indistinct: to *smear* the address on a letter. **4** *n.* A soiled spot or streak, caused by smearing. **5** *v.* To say bad or untruthful things about: The article *smeared* the candidate who was running against the governor. **6** *n.* A slanderous attack or accusation.

smear·y [smir′ē] *adj.* **smear·i·er, smear·i·est** **1** Characterized by or covered with smears. **2** Tending to cause smears.

smell [smel] *v.* **smelled** or **smelt, smell·ing,** *n.* **1** *v.* To perceive or be aware of by means of the nose and its special nerves: I can *smell* the lilacs. **2** *n.* The special sense by means of which odors are perceived: Bloodhounds track down lost people by *smell.* **3** *v.* To give off a particular odor or perfume: The field *smells* of clover. **4** *v.* To give off a bad odor: The garbage can *smells.* **5** *n.* The act of smelling: Have a *smell* of this cologne. **6** *n.* An odor: the *smell* of garlic. **—smell′er** *n.*

smelling salts An ammonia compound having a very strong or burning smell, used to relieve headaches or fainting spells.

smell·y [smel′ē] *adj.* **smell·i·er, smell·i·est** Having a bad odor.

smelt¹ [smelt] *n., pl.* **smelt** or **smelts** Any of various small, silvery fishes of the North Atlantic and Pacific oceans, used as food.

smelt² [smelt] *v.* **1** To melt (ore) in a furnace in order to obtain metal. **2** To obtain (metal) by melting away impurities in ore: to *smelt* tin.

smelt³ [smelt] An alternative past tense and past participle of SMELL.

smelt·er [smel′tər] *n.* **1** A place where ore is smelted. **2** A person whose work is smelting ore.

smid·gen [smij′ən] *n. informal* A very small amount; bit.

smile [smīl] *n., v.* **smiled, smil·ing** **1** *n.* A pleased, amused, or sometimes bitter or sarcastic expression of the face, made by raising up the corners of the mouth. **2** *v.* To have or give a smile: The baby *smiled.* **3** *v.* To express or show by means of a smile: We *smiled* our consent. **4** *n.* A pleasant look: the *smile* of spring.

smirch [smûrch] **1** *v.* To soil, as by contact with grime or dirt. **2** *n.* A dirty mark or stain. **3** *v.* To bring dishonor or disgrace on: to *smirch* a reputation.

smirk [smûrk] **1** *v.* To smile in a silly, self-satisfied, or affected manner. **2** *n.* Such a smile.

smite [smīt] *v.* **smote, smit·ten, smit·ing** **1** To strike or hit very hard: seldom used today. **2** To affect, impress, or attack powerfully and suddenly: The couple was *smitten* with love.

smith [smith] *n.* **1** A person who makes, shapes, or repairs something: often used in combination, as in lock*smith* or tin*smith.* **2** A blacksmith.

smith·er·eens [smith′ə·rēnz′] *n.pl.* Little fragments, bits, or pieces: blown to *smithereens.*

smith·y [smith'ē] *n., pl.* **smith·ies** 1 A blacksmith's shop or forge. 2 A blacksmith.

Smithy

smit·ten [smit'(ə)n] A past participle of SMITE.

smock [smok] 1 *n.* A loose outer garment worn over one's clothes to protect them from being soiled. 2 *v.* To ornament (a garment) with smocking.

smock·ing [smok'ing] *n.* Needlework in which the material is stitched into small pleats or gathers that look like a honeycomb.

smog [smog] *n.* A blend of smoke and fog.

smoke [smōk] *n., v.* **smoked, smok·ing** 1 *n.* The cloudlike mass of fine carbon particles arising from burning material, as coal or wood. 2 *n.* Any cloud or vapor that looks like smoke. 3 *v.* To give off smoke, especially too much smoke or in an undesired direction: That old stove *smokes.* 4 *v.* To inhale and exhale the smoke of: to *smoke* a pipe. 5 *n. informal* A cigarette, cigar, or pipeful of tobacco. 6 *n.* The act of smoking. 7 *v.* To cure or preserve (food) by treating it with smoke. 8 *v.* To force (someone) out of hiding with or as if with smoke.

smoke·house [smōk'hous'] *n.* A building or closed room where foods and other things, as hides, are hung and treated with smoke to preserve them.

smoke·jump·er [smōk'jum'pər] *n. informal* A person trained to parachute from an airplane to reach and fight forest fires.

smoke·less [smōk'lis] *adj.* Having or giving off little or no smoke: *smokeless* powder for guns.

smok·er [smō'kər] *n.* 1 A person or thing that smokes. 2 A railroad car where smoking is allowed. 3 A social gathering for men only.

smoke screen A dense cloud of smoke used to keep the enemy from seeing movements of troops, ships, or equipment.

smoke·stack [smōk'stak'] *n.* A chimney or funnel, as on a factory, ship, or locomotive, for carrying off smoke.

smok·y [smō'kē] *adj.* **smok·i·er, smok·i·est** 1 Giving out smoke, especially improperly or unpleasantly: a *smoky* furnace. 2 Mixed with or containing smoke: *smoky* air. 3 Of or like smoke in color, smell, or taste. 4 Made dark or dirty by smoke: *smoky* ceilings. **—smok'i·ly** *adv.* **—smok'i·ness** *n.*

smol·der [smōl'dər] *v.* 1 To burn slowly with smoke but no flame. 2 To exist but in a hidden or controlled state: Their anger *smoldered* for days, but they kept it hidden.

smooth [smo͞oth] 1 *adj.* Having a surface without any roughness or unevenness: *smooth* ice. 2 *v.* To make or become smooth on the surface: *Smooth* the ground around the plants; The wet cement *smoothed* easily. 3 *adj.* Without lumps: a *smooth* gravy. 4 *adj.* Free from bumps, shocks, or jolts: The pilot made a *smooth* landing. 5 *adj.* Calm and unruffled; pleasant; mild: a *smooth* disposition. 6 *adj.* Without any difficulties, annoyances, or troubles: the *smooth* course of a journey. 7 *v.* To make easy or less difficult: to *smooth* one's path to success. 8 *adj.* Not harsh or strong, as in taste or sound: a *smooth* cheese; a *smooth* voice. 9 *v.* To take away crudeness or awkwardness from; polish: to *smooth* a book report. 10 *adv.* In a smooth manner. **—smooth down** To calm, lull, or soothe. **—smooth over** To make seem less serious or unpleasant; minimize: I tried to *smooth over* my mistakes. **—smooth'ly** *adv.* **—smooth'ness** *n.*

smooth·bore [smo͞oth'bôr'] 1 *adj.* With no spiral grooves cut in the barrel. 2 *n.* A gun whose barrel does not have grooves cut inside it.

smor·gas·bord [smôr'gəs·bôrd'] *n.* A Scandinavian meal with a great variety of cheeses, meats, fish, and other foods set out as a buffet.

smote [smōt] Past tense of SMITE.

smoth·er [smuth'ər] 1 *v.* To prevent or be prevented from getting air to breathe; suffocate: The heat almost *smothered* us. We almost *smothered* in the heat. 2 *v.* To slow down or put out (a fire) with a covering that shuts out air. 3 *n.* A thick, choking cloud of dust or smoke. 4 *v.* To hide or suppress: to *smother* one's feelings. 5 *v.* To cover thickly and cook: to *smother* meat with vegetables.

smudge [smuj] *v.* **smudged, smudg·ing,** *n.* 1 *v.* To smear or soil: I *smudged* the paper. 2 *n.* A soiled spot; smear; stain. 3 *n.* A smoky fire used for driving away insects or preventing damage to crops by frost. **—smudg'y** *adj.*

smug [smug] *adj.* **smug·ger, smug·gest** 1 Very satisfied with oneself to the extent of irritating others. 2 Full of or showing great self-satisfaction: a *smug* look. **—smug'ly** *adv.* **—smug'ness** *n.*

smug·gle [smug'əl] *v.* **smug·gled, smug·gling** 1 To take (merchandise) into or out of a country without payment of lawful duties. 2 To bring in or take out secretly: We *smuggled* our dog into the hotel. 3 To engage in smuggling. **—smug'gler** *n.*

smut [smut] *n., v.* **smut·ted, smut·ting** 1 *n.* A bit of soot or other dirty substance. 2 *n.* A dirty mark, as one made by soot or smoke. 3 *v.* To blacken or stain, as with soot or smoke. 4 *n.* Any of various diseases of plants in which the diseased parts are replaced by a dusty black powder. 5 *n.* Dirty or vulgar language.

smut·ty [smut'ē] *adj.* **smut·ti·er, smut·ti·est** 1 Soiled or blackened with smut. 2 Having the disease smut: *smutty* corn. 3 Vulgar; obscene.

Sn The symbol for the element tin. ◆ The Latin word for tin is *stannum.*

snack [snak] 1 *n.* A light, hurried meal. 2 *n.* Anything eaten between meals. 3 *adj. use:* a *snack* bar. 4 *v.* To eat lightly, especially between meals.

snaf·fle [snaf'əl] *n.* A type of horse's bit that is jointed in the middle.

snag [snag] *n., v.* **snagged, snag·ging** 1 *n.* Anything that is sharp or jagged and on which things may be caught or torn. 2 *n.* The trunk or big branch of a tree caught fast in a river, bayou, or other

a	add	**i**	it	**o͝o**	took	**oi**	oil
ā	ace	**ī**	ice	**o͞o**	pool	**ou**	pout
â	care	**o**	odd	**u**	up	**ng**	ring
ä	palm	**ō**	open	**û**	burn	**th**	thin
e	end	**ô**	order	**yo͞o**	fuse	**th**	this
ē	equal					**zh**	vision

ə = { a in *above* e in *sicken* i in *possible*
o in *melon* u in *circus* }

body of water, by which boats are sometimes pierced. **3** *v.* To injure, destroy, tear, or catch on a snag: I *snagged* my shirt on a nail. **4** *n.* A tear or rip made by snagging. **5** *n.* An obstacle that is hidden or not expected: The new employee ran into many *snags* in that job. **6** *v. informal* To block or hinder. **7** *v.* To clear or rid of snags. ◆ *Snag* probably comes from an old Scandinavian word meaning *something sticking out,* as a short branch of a tree.

snag·gle·tooth [snag′əl·to͞oth′] *n., pl.* **snag·gle·teeth** [snag′əl·tēth′] An irregular, projecting, or broken tooth.

snail [snāl] *n.* **1** A small, slow-moving animal with a soft body and a spiral shell on its back into which it can pull itself. Some snails live on land, and some in water. **2** A slow or lazy person.

A typical snail

snake [snāk] *n., v.* **snaked, snak·ing** **1** *n.* Any of numerous kinds of scaly, legless reptiles with long, slim bodies and tapering tails. **2** *v.* To move, wind, or crawl like a snake. **3** *n.* An evil or unreliable person. **4** *n.* A long, flexible wire used to clean clogged drains or pipes.

snake·root [snāk′ro͞ot′] *n.* Any of several plants whose roots are believed to cure snakebites.

snake·skin [snāk′skin′] *n.* **1** The skin of a snake. **2** Leather made from this.

snak·y [snā′kē] *adj.* **snak·i·er, snak·i·est** **1** Of or like a snake; twisting or winding: a *snaky* path up a mountain. **2** Cunning; treacherous: a *snaky* person. **3** Full of snakes.

snap [snap] *v.* **snapped, snap·ping,** *n., adj.* **1** *v.* To make or cause to make a sharp, quick sound: to *snap* a whip; to *snap* one's fingers. **2** *n.* A sharp, quick sound: The guitar string broke with a *snap.* **3** *v.* To close, fasten, or fit into place with a click or a sharp, quick sound: The door *snapped* shut. **4** *n.* Any catch or fastener that closes with a snapping sound. **5** *v.* To try to bite or seize with the jaws: The dog *snapped* at me. **6** *n.* The act of snapping. **7** *v.* To seize or snatch quickly: The thief *snapped* up the wallet; to *snap* up bargains at a sale. **8** *v.* To break suddenly, as from strain or stress: The rubber band *snapped* when I stretched it. **9** *v.* To move or act with quick gestures: The soldier *snapped* to attention. **10** *n.* Brisk vigor and energy; vim. **11** *adj.* Made or done too quickly or without careful thought: a *snap* decision. **12** *v.* To speak sharply or irritably: "Stop that!" I *snapped.* **13** *v.* To sparkle; flash: My eyes *snapped* with anger. **14** *n.* A brief spell, as of cold weather. **15** *n.* A thin, crisp cookie: a chocolate *snap.* **16** *v.* To take a snapshot of: I *snapped* the star stepping off the plane. **17** *n. informal* Any task or duty that is easy to do: Scrambling eggs is a *snap.* **18** *adj. informal* Requiring little work; easy: a *snap* course. **19** *v.* In football, to put (the ball) in play from its position on the ground. **—snap one's fingers at** To be unimpressed by or unafraid of. **—snap out of it** **1** To recover quickly, as from an illness. **2** To recover one's senses, as after a fit of anger.

snap·drag·on [snap′drag′ən] *n.* A plant that has showy white, yellow, or purplish red flowers that grow on long spikes.

snap·per [snap′ər] *n.* **1** A person or thing that snaps. **2** A large food fish caught in the Gulf of Mexico, especially the **red snapper.** **3** A snapping turtle.

snapping turtle A large American turtle with strong, snapping jaws. It is used as a food.

snap·pish [snap′ish] *adj.* **1** Irritable and cross, especially in one's speech. **2** Apt to bite: a *snappish* dog. **—snap′pish·ly** *adv.* **—snap′pish·ness** *n.*

snap·py [snap′ē] *adj.* **snap·pi·er, snap·pi·est** **1** Snappishly irritable. **2** *informal* Energetic; brisk: a *snappy* salute. **3** *informal* Smart or stylish.

snap·shot [snap′shot′] *n.* A photograph made with a small camera, taken quickly.

snare[1] [snâr] *n., v.* **snared, snar·ing** **1** *n.* A noose that jerks tight, for catching small animals. **2** *n.* Anything that traps or tricks: The shady business deal was a *snare* for the unwary. **3** *v.* To trap or catch with or as if with a snare.

snare[2] [snâr] *n.* One of the cords or wires stretched across one of the heads of a snare drum.

snare drum A small drum with snares across the bottom head to make a rattling noise.

snarl[1] [snärl] **1** *v.* To growl, showing the teeth, as an angry or frightened dog or wolf. **2** *n.* A harsh, angry growl. **3** *v.* To say or express in an angry, growling tone: "Get out of here," the bully *snarled.*

snarl[2] [snärl] **1** *n.* A confused, tangled mess or condition, as of hair or yarn. **2** *v.* To put or get into such a condition: Long hair *snarls* easily; The wreck *snarled* traffic for blocks.

snatch [snach] *v.* To grab or take hold of suddenly, hastily, or eagerly. **2** *v.* To take or get when there is a chance: to *snatch* a few hours of sleep. **3** *n.* The act of snatching. **4** *n.* A brief period: a *snatch* of rest. **5** *n.* A small amount: *snatches* of distant music. **—snatch at** To attempt to grab swiftly and suddenly. **—snatch′er** *n.*

sneak [snēk] **1** *v.* To move, act, or go in a quiet, secret, often deceitful manner: The cat *sneaks* all over the house at night. **2** *v.* To bring, take, or put secretly or deceitfully: We *sneaked* the presents out of the closet. **3** *n.* A person who acts in a sly, secret manner. **4** *adj.* Stealthy; sly; secret: a *sneak* attack. ◆ Avoid the incorrect past form *snuck* (as in "I snuck up on him"). Use *sneaked.*

sneak·er [snē′kər] *n.* **1** A person who sneaks. **2** (*pl.*) *informal* Rubber-soled canvas shoes, worn especially for sports.

Sneakers

sneak·ing [snē′king] *adj.* **1** Secretly deceitful; mean; underhand: What a *sneaking* thing to do! **2** Kept hidden or secret; not yet expressed: I had a *sneaking* suspicion we'd go.

sneak·y [snē′kē] *adj.* **sneak·i·er, sneak·i·est** Showing or marked by dishonesty, meanness, or secrecy.

sneer [snir] **1** *n.* A look that shows dislike or contempt, made by slightly raising the upper lip. **2** *v.* To show dislike or contempt, as in speech or writing. **3** *n.* A mean or contemptuous remark.

sneeze [snēz] *v.* **sneezed, sneez·ing,** *n.* **1** *v.* To drive air out of the mouth and nose by a sudden, involuntary action when the nasal passages are irritated, as by a cold or dust. **2** *n.* The act of sneezing. **—not to be sneezed at** *informal* Not to be treated lightly.

snick·er [snik′ər] **1** *n.* A half-suppressed or smothered laugh, often used in making fun of someone. **2** *v.* To laugh in this way.

snide [snīd] *adj.* **snid·er, snid·est** Belittling or

wounding in a sarcastic or sly way; meanly critical.

sniff [snif] 1 *v.* To breathe in through the nose in short, audible breaths. 2 *v.* To smell or attempt to smell in this way: Our dog kept *sniffing* the ground. 3 *n.* The act or sound of sniffing. 4 *n.* Something smelled or inhaled by sniffing: a *sniff* of smoke. 5 *v.* To show or express dislike or contempt by or as if by sniffing.

snif·fle [snif'əl] *v.* **snif·fled, snif·fling,** *n.* 1 *v.* To breathe noisily through the nose, as when one has a bad head cold. 2 *v.* To sob or whimper. 3 *n.* The act or sound of sniffling. **—the sniffles** *informal* A cold in the head.

snig·ger [snig'ər] *n., v.* Another word for SNICKER.

snip [snip] *v.* **snipped, snip·ping,** *n.* 1 *v.* To cut or clip off with short, light strokes of the scissors. 2 *n.* The act of snipping. 3 *n.* A piece snipped off: a *snip* of cloth. 4 *n.* (*pl.*) Shears for cutting metal. 5 *n. informal* A young, often small or impudent person.

snipe [snīp] *n., pl.* **snipe** or **snipes,** *v.* **sniped, snip·ing** 1 *n.* Any of various long-billed birds that live in marshes or along the shore. 2 *v.* To hunt for snipe. 3 *v.* To shoot at enemies one at a time and from some hiding place.

Snipe

snip·er [snī'pər] *n.* A person who shoots at an enemy from some hiding place.

snip·pet [snip'it] *n.* 1 A small part, piece, or excerpt. 2 A small or young person; snip.

snip·py [snip'ē] *adj.* **snip·pi·er, snip·pi·est** *informal* 1 Impudent; insolent. 2 Brief; rude; curt.

snitch [snich] 1 *v.* To steal; pilfer. 2 *v.* To be an informer; tattle. 3 *n.* An informer; tattletale.

sniv·el [sniv'əl] *v.* **sniv·eled, sniv·el·ing** 1 To cry with sniffles. 2 To whine tearfully.

snob [snob] *n.* A person who looks down on anyone with less money or culture or lower social standing.

snob·ber·y [snob'ər·ē] *n., pl.* **snob·ber·ies** 1 A snobbish act. 2 The attitude of a snob.

snob·bish [snob'ish] *adj.* Of, having to do with, or like a snob. **—snob'bish·ly** *adv.* **—snob'bish·ness** *n.*

snood [sno͞od] *n.* A net worn at the back of the head to keep the hair in place.

snoop [sno͞op] *informal* 1 *v.* To look or pry into things that are none of one's business. 2 *n.* A person who snoops.

snoot·y [sno͞o'tē] *adj.* **snoot·i·er, snoot·i·est** *informal* 1 Haughtily disdainful or aloof; snobbish. 2 Characterized by snobbery; exclusive: a *snooty* neighborhood. ◆ *Snooty,* which means *looking down one's nose with disdain,* comes from *snoot,* a slang word for *snout* or *nose.*

snooze [sno͞oz] *v.* **snoozed, snooz·ing,** *n. informal* 1 *v.* To nap; doze. 2 *n.* A short nap.

snore [snôr] *v.* **snored, snor·ing,** *n.* 1 *v.* To breathe in sleep through the nose and open mouth with a hoarse, rough sound. 2 *n.* The sound of snoring.

snor·kel [snôr'kəl] *n.* 1 A tube extended from a submerged submarine to the surface in order to provide ventilation. 2 A similar tube attached to a skin diver's mask that makes breathing possible when a little under water.

snort [snôrt] 1 *v.* To force air violently and noisily through the nostrils. 2 *n.* The act or sound of snorting. 3 *v.* To express with a snort: "Humph!" I *snorted.* 4 *v.* To make a snorting sound: The engine *snorted* and stalled.

snout [snout] *n.* 1 The forward, projecting part of the head of many animals, usually including the nose and jaws: a hog's *snout.* 2 Something that resembles this. ◆ *Snout* is related to an Old English word meaning *to blow the nose.*

Snout

snow [snō] 1 *n.* Frozen water vapor in the air, usually falling in the form of small white flakes. 2 *v.* To fall as snow: It is *snowing.* 3 *v.* To cover, enclose, or obstruct with snow: The roads are all *snowed* under. 4 *n.* A fall of snow: two *snows* in November. 5 *n.* Anything resembling snow, especially a type of interference on a television screen.

snow·ball [snō'bôl'] 1 *n.* A small round mass of snow packed together for throwing. 2 *v.* To throw snowballs at. 3 *n.* A bush that has clusters of white flowers resembling snowballs. 4 *v.* To grow bigger fast, like a rolling snowball: The paper's circulation *snowballed.*

snow·bank [snō'bangk'] *n.* A large mound or drift of snow.

snow·bird [snō'bûrd'] *n.* 1 Any of various small grayish birds of North America commonly seen in flocks during the winter. 2 A bird of northern regions, the male of which in breeding seasons is snow-white with black markings.

snow-blind [snō'blīnd'] *adj.* Blinded temporarily by the glare of sunlight reflected from snow or ice. **—snow blindness**

snow·bound [snō'bound'] *adj.* Shut in or forced to stay in a place because of a heavy snow.

snow·capped [snō'kapt'] *adj.* Having a top covered with snow: *snowcapped* peaks.

snow·drift [snō'drift'] *n.* A snowbank or heap of snow drifted or blown together by the wind.

snow·drop [snō'drop'] *n.* A small European plant that blooms early in the spring and bears a single, white, drooping flower.

snow·fall [snō'fôl'] *n.* 1 A fall of snow. 2 The amount of snow that falls in any given period.

snow·flake [snō'flāk'] *n.* A small, feathery flake made of one or more crystals of snow.

snow leopard A large, long-tailed, wild cat of mountainous Asian regions, having grayish-white fur with black spots.

snow line The imaginary line on the sides of mountains above which there is perpetual snow.

a	add	**i**	it	**o͝o**	took	**oi**	oil
ā	ace	**ī**	ice	**o͞o**	pool	**ou**	pout
â	care	**o**	odd	**u**	up	**ng**	ring
ä	palm	**ō**	open	**û**	burn	**th**	thin
e	end	**ô**	order	**yo͞o**	fuse	**t͟h**	this
ē	equal					**zh**	vision

ə = { a in *above* e in *sicken* i in *possible* / o in *melon* u in *circus* }

snow·mak·er [snō′mā′kər] *n.* A machine for making artificial snow for ski slopes.
snow·man [snō′man′] *n., pl.* **snow·men** [snō′men′] A figure shaped out of snow and made to look like a person.
snow·mo·bile [snō′mō·bēl′] *n.* A motor vehicle moving on endless tracks, steered by short skis, for use on snow.
snow·plow [snō′plou′] *n.* Any of various devices for pushing or throwing snow off of an area, as a road or railroad track.
snow·shoe [snō′shōō′] *n., v.* **snow·shoed, snow·shoe·ing** 1 *n.* A network of leather thongs or strips set in a wooden frame and fastened on the foot in order to help a person walk on soft snow without sinking in. 2 *v.* To walk on snowshoes.
snowshoe rabbit A hare of northern North America having fur that is white in winter and brown in summer. Its large hind feet help it to run over deep snow.
snow·slide [snō′slīd′] *n.* An avalanche of snow.
snow·storm [snō′stôrm′] *n.* A storm with a heavy fall of snow.
snow·suit [snō′sōōt′] *n.* A warmly lined coverall garment worn by children in cold weather.
snow-white [snō′(h)wīt′] *adj.* White as fresh snow.
snow·y [snō′ē] *adj.* **snow·i·er, snow·i·est** 1 Full of snow: *snowy* streets. 2 Having a lot of snow: a *snowy* winter. 3 Like snow in whiteness or cleanliness: *snowy* linen.
snub [snub] *v.* **snubbed, snub·bing,** *n., adj.* 1 *v.* To treat with dislike or contempt, especially by paying no attention to; slight. 2 *n.* An act of snubbing someone; slight. 3 *v.* To stop or check (as a running rope), as by winding it around a post. 4 *n.* The act of snubbing a rope. 5 *adj.* Short and upturned: a *snub* nose.
snuff[1] [snuf] 1 *v.* To draw in or sniff (as air) through the nose. 2 *v.* To smell or sniff. 3 *n.* Tobacco ground into a fine powder and inhaled through the nostrils. **—up to snuff** *informal* In good condition; as good as usual.
snuff[2] [snuf] *v.* 1 To put out or extinguish, as a candle. 2 To trim off the burned part of (a candle wick). **—snuff out** 1 To put out; extinguish. 2 To bring to an end quickly or violently: The explosion *snuffed out* three lives.
snuff·box [snuf′boks′] *n.* A small box for carrying snuff.
snuf·fer [snuf′ər] *n.* An instrument something like a pair of scissors, used to extinguish candles and to trim their wicks.
snuf·fle [snuf′əl] *v.* **snuf·fled, snuf·fling,** *n.* 1 *v.* To breathe noisily, as when one has a cold. 2 *n.* The act or sound of snuffling. **—the snuffles** *informal* The sniffles.
snug [snug] *adj.* **snug·ger, snug·gest,** *adv.* 1 *adj.* Closely but comfortably covered or sheltered; cozy: The bears were *snug* in the cave all winter. 2 *adj.* Fitting closely; rather tight: Those pants are *snug.* 3 *adj.* Having room enough but not too much; compact: a *snug* little cabin. 4 *adv.* In a snug way: to fit *snug.* **—snug′ly** *adv.*
snug·gle [snug′əl] *v.* **snug·gled, snug·gling** To lie or hold close, as for comfort or warmth; cuddle: I *snuggled* the child in my arms; The puppies *snuggled* near the fire.
so[1] [sō] 1 *adj.* To this or that degree; to such a degree: The house has never been *so* quiet. 2 *adv.* In this or that manner: As the twig is bent, *so* is the tree inclined. 3 *adv.* Just as said or directed: Place your feet *so.* 4 *adv.* According to fact: That is not *so.* 5 *adv. informal* To an extreme degree; very: The jam is *so* good. 6 *adv. informal* Very much: I admire you *so.* 7 *pron.* About that; more or less: I'll stay a day or *so.* 8 *adv.* Most certainly; absolutely: You can *so* do it. 9 *conj.* Consequently; thus; therefore: You weren't there, *so* you can't be a witness. 10 *adv.* It seems that; apparently: *So* you like it here! 11 *interj.* Ah hah! Indeed!: *So*! That's what you've been up to. 12 *conj.* With the purpose that: They left early *so* they would arrive before dark. 13 *conj. informal* As a result of which: It started to snow, *so* they left early. **—so as** In order; for the purpose: He runs every day *so as* to keep in condition. ◆ *So, such,* and *such a* are used informally to make an adjective or noun following them stronger: The wall is *so* high; She has *such* intelligence; It was *such a* cold day. This use should be avoided in formal writing.
so[2] [sō] *n.* In music, another word for sol.
so. or **So.** 1 south. 2 southern.
soak [sōk] 1 *v.* To make completely wet by placing or keeping in a liquid. 2 *v.* To stay in a liquid until completely wet. 3 *v.* To suck up; absorb: Those towels will *soak* up the water. 4 *v.* To take in fully or quickly: to *soak* up knowledge. 5 *v.* To wet thoroughly; drench: The rain *soaked* my shoes. 6 *n.* The act of soaking.
so-and-so [sō′ən·sō′] *n., pl.* **so-and-sos** *informal* A person or thing whose name is not mentioned or can't be recalled.
soap [sōp] 1 *n.* A substance made from vegetable or animal fats mixed with an alkali. It is used with water for washing things clean. 2 *v.* To rub or treat with soap: to *soap* oneself. 3 *n. slang* A soap opera.
soap·box [sōp′boks′] *n.* An empty packing box or similar structure used as a platform for making informal speeches outdoors.
soap opera A daytime television or radio program that tells a continuing story usually filled with romance and melodrama. ◆ The first daytime serial dramas on radio were often sponsored by soap companies, so listeners began to call them *soap operas. Horse opera,* for a western drama, was a less successful nickname.
soap·stone [sōp′stōn′] *n.* A kind of rock that has a smooth surface with a soapy feel.
soap·suds [sōp′sudz′] *n.pl.* Water mixed with soap until it is foamy and forms suds.
soap·y [sō′pē] *adj.* **soap·i·er, soap·i·est** 1 Of, containing, or like soap or soapsuds. 2 Covered with soap or soapsuds: *soapy* hands.
soar [sôr] *v.* 1 To rise high into the air; fly high: The eagle *soared* effortlessly. 2 To rise sharply above the usual level: Prices *soared.* 3 To reach or approach something grand or lofty: The poet's imagination *soared.*
sob [sob] *v.* **sobbed, sob·bing,** *n.* 1 *v.* To weep with audible catches of the breath. 2 *v.* To utter with sobs: "I'm lost," the child *sobbed.* 3 *v.* To bring to a certain state or condition by sobbing: to *sob* oneself to sleep. 4 *v.* To make a sound like a sob, as the wind. 5 *n.* The act or sound of sobbing.
so·ber [sō′bər] 1 *adj.* Not drunk or intoxicated. 2 *adj.* Serious, calm, thoughtful, and well-balanced: a careful, *sober* study of air pollution. 3 *adj.* Solemn; grave: a *sober* look. 4 *adj.* Modest and quiet,

as in color or manner of dress. **5** *v.* To make or become sober. **—so′ber·ly** *adv.* ◆ See SERIOUS.
so·bri·e·ty [sō·brī′ə·tē] *n.* The condition or quality of being sober.
so·bri·quet [sō′bri·kā′] *n.* A nickname.
so-called [sō′kôld′] *adj.* Called or stated thus but usually not truthfully or correctly so: The *so-called* emergency was only a burned-out light.
soc·cer [sok′ər] *n.* A field game in which a round ball is propelled toward the opponents' goal by kicking or by striking with the body or head.
so·cia·ble [sō′shə·bəl] **1** *adj.* Liking to be with people; agreeable and pleasant in company; social. **2** *adj.* Full of pleasant conversation or companionship: a very *sociable* party. **3** *n.* A social. **—so′·cia·bil′i·ty** *n.* **—so′cia·bly** *adv.*
so·cial [sō′shəl] **1** *adj.* Liking or tending to live together in communities or in a society: Bees as well as people are *social* beings. **2** *adj.* Of or having to do with human beings as they live and act together in society: *social* life; *social* problems. **3** *adj.* Friendly and pleasant toward others; sociable. **4** *adj.* Of, having to do with, or promoting friendliness and companionship: a *social* club. **5** *adj.* Of or having to do with persons prominent in fashionable society: the *social* season. **6** *n.* An informal, friendly gathering, as of church members.
social climber A person who is trying to gain a higher social position.
so·cial·ism [sō′shəl·iz′əm] *n.* **1** The idea that the means of production and distribution, such as factories, railroads, and power plants, should be owned by the government or associations of workers and operated without private profit. **2** A political movement favoring putting this idea into practice more completely.
so·cial·ist [sō′shəl·ist] **1** *n.* A person who is in favor of socialism. **2** *n.* (*often written* **Socialist**) A person who is a member of a party that advocates socialism. **3** *adj.* Socialistic.
so·cial·is·tic [sō′shəl·is′tik] *adj.* **1** Of, having to do with, or practicing socialism. **2** Like or tending toward socialism: a *socialistic* belief.
so·cial·ite [sō′shə·līt′] *n.* A person who is socially prominent.
so·cial·ize [sō′shəl·īz′] *v.* **so·cial·ized, so·cial·iz·ing** **1** To manage or run according to socialistic principles. **2** To make more friendly, cooperative, or social. **3** To take part in social activities: to *socialize* on weekends. **—so′cial·i·za′tion** *n.*
so·cial·ly [sō′shə·lē] *adv.* **1** In a social manner: They live very *socially.* **2** With respect to society, a social group, or social activities: They are very much at ease *socially.*
social science A body of knowledge that deals with human society and people in their relation to other people, to the state, the family, or any social group or institution to which they belong. History, anthropology, sociology, economics, and politics are social sciences.
Social Security In the U.S., a system of payments to the aged, the unemployed, and certain others, supported by fees collected from employers and workers.
social studies In elementary and secondary schools, a course of study based on the social sciences.
social work Any of various services that attempt to improve the social conditions of a community, as by providing health clinics and aid to the poor.
social worker A person whose job is to do social work.
so·ci·e·tal [sə·sī′ə·təl] *adj.* Of or having to do with society: *societal* goals.
so·ci·e·ty [sə·sī′ə·tē] *n., pl.* **so·ci·e·ties** **1** All of the people living: *Society* benefits by these laws. **2** A group or body of persons living together in a particular place or at a particular time and having many things in common: a rural *society*; an ancient *society.* **3** A group of persons who join together for a common purpose or object: a medical *society.* **4** The fashionable or wealthy group of a country or city. **5** Fellowship or companionship: The people next door don't care too much for *society.*
Society of Friends A Christian religious group that does not believe in formal religious services and is against violence and war. Its members are also known as Quakers.
Society of Jesus The order of the Jesuits.
so·ci·ol·o·gy [sō′sē·ol′ə·jē *or* sō′shē·ol′ə·jē] *n.* The study of people living in groups or communities, past and present. Often using statistics, sociology deals with such matters as the family, marriage, education, religion, crime, and slums. **—so·ci·o·log·i·cal** [sō′sē·ə·loj′ə·kəl] *adj.* **—so′ci·ol′o·gist** *n.*
sock[1] [sok] *n.* A short stocking.
sock[2] [sok] *slang* **1** *v.* To strike or hit, especially with the fist. **2** *n.* A hard blow.
sock·et [sok′it] *n.* A hole, cavity, or hollow part that is made to receive and hold something: the *socket* for an electric bulb; the *socket* of the eye.
So·crat·ic [sə·krat′ik] *adj.* Of or having to do with Socrates, his philosophy, his followers, or his method of eliciting truth by questioning others.
sod [sod] *n., v.* **sod·ded, sod·ding** **1** *n.* The top layer of the earth, especially when covered with grass. **2** *n.* A piece of this layer held together by matted roots of grass and weeds. **3** *v.* To cover with pieces of sod.
so·da [sō′də] *n.* **1** Any of several compounds containing sodium, as baking soda for cooking. **2** Soda water. **3** A soft drink made of carbonated water and flavoring. **4** A drink made of ice cream, carbonated water, and flavoring.
soda fountain A counter at which soft drinks, ice cream, sundaes, and often other food are sold.
so·dal·i·ty [sō·dal′ə·tē] *n., pl.* **so·dal·i·ties** In the Roman Catholic Church, a society organized for devotional or charitable purposes.
soda water Water that is made to bubble or fizz by being charged with carbon dioxide gas.
sod·den [sod′(ə)n] *adj.* **1** Soaked with moisture: turf *sodden* with rain. **2** Heavy, doughy, or soggy, as poorly baked bread or biscuits.
so·di·um [sō′dē·əm] *n.* A soft, silver-white, very ac-

a	add	**i**	it	**o͝o**	took	**oi**	oil
ā	ace	**ī**	ice	**o͞o**	pool	**ou**	pout
â	care	**o**	odd	**u**	up	**ng**	ring
ä	palm	**ō**	open	**û**	burn	**th**	thin
e	end	**ô**	order	**yo͞o**	fuse	**th**	this
ē	equal					**zh**	vision

ə = { a in *above* e in *sicken* i in *possible* / o in *melon* u in *circus* }

S

tive metallic element that forms many compounds, the best known of which is common salt.

sodium ben·zo·ate [ben′zō·āt′] A white, powdery compound used chiefly as a food preservative.

sodium bicarbonate A white, crystalline compound used in medicine and cooking and commonly known as baking soda.

sodium carbonate A salt of carbonic acid, a white, powdery compound used in making soaps, bleaches, glass, and chemicals.

sodium chloride Common table salt.

sodium glu·ta·mate [glo͞o′tə·māt′] A white, crystalline compound used in cooking.

sodium hydroxide The hydroxide of sodium, found in lye and used in bleaching and in making soap and paper.

sodium nitrate The sodium salt of nitric acid, often used in fertilizers.

Sod·om [sod′əm] *n.* In the Bible, a city destroyed with the neighboring city, Gomorrah, because of the wickedness of the people.

so·fa [sō′fə] *n.* A long couch, upholstered and with raised arms at both ends and a back. ◆ *Sofa* comes from an Arabic word meaning *long bench* or *part of a floor raised to form a seat.*

Sofa

soft [sôft] 1 *adj.* Not hard or brittle; easily worked, shaped, cut, or pressed, usually without breaking: a *soft* dough; *soft* wood; *soft* metal. 2 *adj.* Smooth and delicate to the touch: *soft* skin. 3 *adj.* Not loud or harsh to the ear: *soft* music. 4 *adj.* Mild, gentle, and courteous: *soft* words; a *soft* manner. 5 *adj.* Tender, kind, and sympathetic: a *soft* heart. 6 *adj.* Not able to bear effort, hardship, or strain: *soft* muscles. 7 *adj. informal* Not hard or difficult to do or bear; easy: a *soft* job; a *soft* life. 8 *adj.* Not glaring, bright, or harsh: *soft* colors. 9 *adv.* In a soft manner; softly. 10 *adj.* Containing no alcohol: a *soft* drink. 11 *adj.* Describing the sound of *c* in *cent* and *g* in *gibe*, as opposed to the hard sound of *c* in *cord* or *g* in *good.* 12 *adj.* Free from certain salts, as water: Rain water is *soft* and easy to wash with. **—soft′ly** *adv.* **—soft′ness** *n.*

soft·ball [sôft′bôl′] *n.* 1 A variation of baseball, using a larger, softer ball and a smaller diamond. 2 The ball used in this game.

soft-boiled [sôft′boild′] *adj.* Boiled in the shell only long enough for the white to be set while the yolk remains soft.

soft coal Bituminous coal.

soft drink Any drink that does not contain alcohol, especially sweetened soda water, ginger ale, or cola.

sof·ten [sôf′ən] *v.* To make or become soft or softer: *Soften* the butter before using it; My heart *softened* when I saw them. **—sof′ten·er** *n.*

soft·heart·ed [sôft′här′tid] *adj.* Kind or merciful; sympathetic; compassionate; tender. **—soft′heart′·ed·ly** *adv.* **—soft′heart′ed·ness** *n.*

soft landing The landing of a spacecraft on a celestial body at a speed low enough to prevent damage to the vehicle or its contents.

soft shoulder Soft ground along the edge of a paved road.

soft-spo·ken [sôft′spō′kən] *adj.* Having a soft speaking voice.

soft spot A tendency to be especially generous or sympathetic.

soft·ware [sôft′wâr′] *n.* Programs, routines, and other written or printed information used in operating computers.

soft·wood [sôft′wo͝od′] *n.* 1 Any wood that can be cut or pierced comparatively easily, as pine wood. 2 Any tree, as the pine, that yields such wood.

soft·y [sôf′tē] *n., pl.* **soft·ies** *informal* A person who is weak, too sentimental, or too lenient.

sog·gy [sog′ē] *or* sôg′ē] *adj.* **sog·gi·er, sog·gi·est** 1 Soaked with water or moisture. 2 Heavy and moist: said of pastry. **—sog′gi·ness** *n.*

soil[1] [soil] *n.* 1 The ground in which plants grow; dirt; earth. 2 A country or land: one's native *soil.* 3 Anything thought of as a place for growth: Foods at room temperature are fertile *soil* for bacteria.

soil[2] [soil] 1 *v.* To make or become dirty: We *soiled* our clothes; This cloth *soils* easily. 2 *v.* To disgrace: to *soil* one's reputation. 3 *n.* A soiled spot or stain.

soi·ree or **soi·rée** [swä·rā′] *n.* A party or a reception given in the evening.

so·journ [*v.* sō′jûrn′ *or* sō·jûrn′, *n.* sō′jûrn′] 1 *v.* To stay or live for a time. 2 *n.* A stay or visit in a place. **—so′journ·er** *n.*

sol [sōl] *n.* In music, a syllable used to represent the fifth tone of a major scale or the seventh tone of a minor scale or, in a fixed system, the tone G.

Sol [sol] *n.* 1 The sun. 2 In ancient Roman myths, the god of the sun.

sol·ace [sol′is] *n., v.* **sol·aced, sol·ac·ing** 1 *n.* Comfort in times of unhappiness or trouble. 2 *n.* A person or thing that brings such comfort: Music is a *solace* when one is sad. 3 *v.* To comfort or cheer in unhappiness or trouble.

so·lar [sō′lər] *adj.* 1 Of, having to do with, or coming from the sun: the *solar* system; *solar* energy. 2 Measured by the movement of the earth around the sun: *solar* time. 3 Produced by, using, or having to do with energy derived from sunlight: a *solar* heating system; a *solar* collector.

solar battery A device that converts energy from the sun into electricity.

solar cell A semiconductor device that converts sunlight into electricity. A number of connected solar cells make a solar battery.

solar flare A sudden, flamelike outburst of gases from a small part of the sun's surface.

so·lar·i·um [sō·lâr′ē·əm] *n., pl.* **so·lar·i·a** [sō·lâr′ē·ə] or **so·lar·i·ums** A room or glass-enclosed porch where people can sun themselves.

solar panel A solar battery consisting of a number of connected solar cells.

solar plexus A large network of nerves just behind the stomach.

solar system The sun and the planets and other celestial bodies that revolve around it.

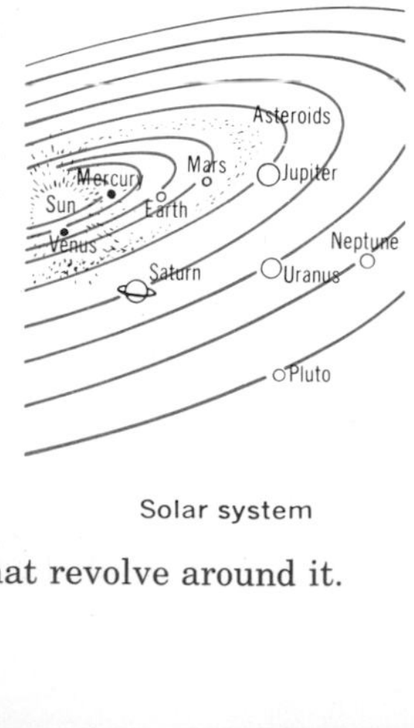

Solar system

solar wind The continuous flow of charged, high-speed atomic particles that radiates from the sun into outer space.

solar year Another name for TROPICAL YEAR.

sold [sōld] Past tense and past participle of SELL.

sol·der [sod′ər] 1 *n.* A metal or alloy that, when melted, can be used to join or mend metal parts or objects. 2 *v.* To join, mend, or work with solder: We *soldered* the pipes together.

sol·dier [sōl′jər] 1 *n.* Someone serving in the army, especially an enlisted person rather than a commissioned officer. 2 *n.* A person who is experienced or skillful in war. 3 *n.* A person who works hard for any cause: a *soldier* for equal rights. 4 *v.* To be a soldier. 5 *v.* To keep working or moving doggedly; press on.

sol·dier·ly [sōl′jər·lē] *adj.* Of or like a true soldier; brave: It was a *soldierly* thing to do.

soldier of fortune An adventurous, restless person who is willing to serve as a soldier for whoever will pay the most.

sol·dier·y [sōl′jər·ē] *n.* 1 Soldiers when thought of as a group. 2 Military training or skill.

sole¹ [sōl] *n., v.* **soled, sol·ing** 1 *n.* The bottom surface of the foot. 2 *n.* The bottom surface, as of a shoe, boot, or stocking. 3 *v.* To furnish with a sole: The shoemaker *soled* our shoes.

sole² [sōl] *n.* Any of various flatfish related to the flounder and much used as food.

sole³ [sōl] *adj.* 1 Being the only one: Here is the *sole* movie in town. 2 Only: Fishermen were the *sole* inhabitants of the island.

sol·e·cism [sol′ə·siz′əm] *n.* 1 A mistake in grammar or in the correct usage of words: "We have ate it" is a *solecism.* 2 Any social error or blunder.

sole·ly [sōl′lē] *adv.* 1 By oneself or itself alone; singly. 2 Only; exclusively: They lived *solely* for their children.

sol·emn [sol′əm] *adj.* 1 Majestic, impressive, and awe-inspiring: a very *solemn* ceremony. 2 Serious, grave, and earnest: a *solemn* expression. 3 Sacred; religious: a *solemn* day of thanksgiving. 4 Somber; gloomy: *solemn* colors. **—sol′emn·ly** *adv.*

so·lem·ni·ty [sə·lem′nə·tē] *n., pl.* **so·lem·ni·ties** 1 A serious or religious ceremony or service: Memorial Day *solemnities.* 2 A solemn or serious condition, quality, or feeling: the *solemnity* of a graduation address.

sol·em·nize [sol′əm·nīz′] *v.* **sol·em·nized, sol·em·niz·ing** 1 To perform in a legal, ceremonious way: to *solemnize* a marriage. 2 To observe with ceremony, as a religious holiday. 3 To make solemn or dignified. **—sol′em·ni·za′tion** *n.*

so·le·noid [sō′lə·noid′] *n.* A coil of wire that acts like a bar magnet when an electric current is flowing through it.

so·lic·it [sə·lis′it] *v.* To ask or ask for earnestly: to *solicit* a neighborhood for business; to *solicit* money for a charity. **—so·lic′i·ta′tion** *n.*

so·lic·i·tor [sə·lis′ə·tər] *n.* 1 A person who solicits, especially one who asks for donations of money. 2 A lawyer for an area, as a city, town, or state. 3 *British* A lawyer who can prepare cases or advise clients, but may plead cases in the lower courts only.

so·lic·i·tous [sə·lis′ə·təs] *adj.* 1 Full of concern, worry, or interest for someone or something: *solicitous* about someone's health. 2 Eager; desiring: *solicitous* to get approval. **—so·lic′i·tous·ly** *adv.*

so·lic·i·tude [sə·lis′ə·t(y)o͞od′] *n.* Concern, anxiety, or care for someone or something.

sol·id [sol′id] 1 *adj.* Not liquid or gaseous; not easily made to change shape or size; firm: Lava is *solid* after it cools. 2 *n.* Something firm and having a more or less definite shape that does not too easily change: Wood and ice are both *solids.* 3 *adj.* Having or dealing with length, width, and thickness: a *solid* figure; *solid* geometry. 4 *n.* A body having length, width, and thickness: A cone, cube, pyramid, and sphere are all *solids.* 5 *adj.* Not hollow, but filled with matter: This piece of wood is *solid* throughout. 6 *adj.* Containing only one element, as a color or metal: *solid* blue; *solid* gold. 7 *adj.* Strong; sound: The floor is not *solid*: *solid* opinions. 8 *adj.* Not frivolous, light, or fanciful; deep: a *solid* novel. 9 *adj.* Continuous; unbroken: a *solid* hour of study. 10 *adj.* Showing a united or unanimous spirit: The mayor had the *solid* support of the townspeople. **—sol′id·ly** *adv.* **—sol′id·ness** *n.*

sol·i·dar·i·ty [sol′ə·dar′ə·tē] *n.* The condition of being strongly united or in unison: The union supported the strike with *solidarity.*

solid geometry The branch of geometry that deals with figures having the three dimensions of length, width, and thickness.

so·lid·i·fy [sə·lid′ə·fī] *v.* **so·lid·i·fied, so·lid·i·fy·ing** 1 To make or become solid, hard, or compact. 2 To make or become strongly united. **—so·lid′i·fi·ca′·tion** *n.*

so·lid·i·ty [sə·lid′ə·tē] *n., pl.* **so·lid·i·ties** A solid state; firmness; hardness.

sol·id-state [sol′id·stāt′] *adj.* 1 Of or having to do with the physical properties of solid materials, especially crystalline solids: *solid-state* physics. 2 Of, having to do with, or using transistors or other semiconductor devices rather than electron tubes: a *solid-state* radio and stereo set.

so·lil·o·quize [sə·lil′ə·kwīz′] *v.* **so·lil·o·quized, so·lil·o·quiz·ing** To talk to oneself or to deliver a soliloquy.

so·lil·o·quy [sə·lil′ə·kwē] *n., pl.* **so·lil·o·quies** 1 The act of talking to oneself. 2 In a play, a speech in which an actor reveals personal thoughts to the audience, but not to the other actors.

sol·i·taire [sol′ə·târ′] *n.* 1 Any of several card games that can be played by one person. 2 A diamond or other gem set alone in a ring.

sol·i·tar·y [sol′ə·ter′ē] *adj.* 1 Living, being, or going alone: a *solitary* person. 2 Made, done, or passed alone: a *solitary* life. 3 Secluded or lonely: a *solitary* strip of beach. 4 Single; sole: Not a *solitary* soul was there.

sol·i·tude [sol′ə·t(y)o͞od′] *n.* 1 The condition of being away from others: At times everyone needs *solitude.* 2 A deserted or lonely place.

so·lo [sō′lō] *n., pl.* **so·los,** *adj., v.* **so·loed, so·lo·ing** 1

a	add	**i**	it	**o͝o**	took	**oi**	oil		
ā	ace	**ī**	ice	**o͞o**	pool	**ou**	pout		
â	care	**o**	odd	**u**	up	**ng**	ring		
ä	palm	**ō**	open	**û**	burn	**th**	thin		
e	end	**ô**	order	**yo͞o**	fuse	**t͟h**	this		
ē	equal					**zh**	vision		

ə = a in *above* e in *sicken* i in *possible* o in *melon* u in *circus*

S

n. A musical composition or passage for a single voice or instrument. 2 *adj.* Played or sung by a single voice or instrument. 3 *n.* A performance given by a single person without a partner or assistant: a dance *solo.* 4 *adj.* Done by a single person: a *solo* flight. 5 *adv.* Without another person; alone: to fly *solo.* 6 *v.* To fly an airplane alone, especially for the first time.

so·lo·ist [sō'lō·ist] *n.* A person who performs or sings a solo or solos.

Sol·o·mon [sol'ə·mən] *n.* A very wise king of Israel who lived in the 10th century B.C.

so·lon [sō'lən *or* sō'lon'] *n.* A wise lawmaker.

so long *informal* Good-bye. ◆ The first English speakers to say *so long,* in the middle 1800's, were probably shortening some such phrase as *so long as we are parted, may God be with you.* They might have been encouraged to do this by the existence of similar words of farewell in German (*so lange*) and Gaelic (*slán*).

sol·stice [sol'stis] *n.* Either of the two times in the year when the sun is at its furthest distance north or south of the equator. In the Northern Hemisphere, the **summer solstice** is about June 21 and the **winter solstice** is about December 22.

sol·u·bil·i·ty [sol'yə·bil'ə·tē] *n.* The ability of a particular substance to dissolve in another substance, especially in water.

sol·u·ble [sol'yə·bəl] *adj.* 1 Capable of being dissolved, especially in water. 2 Capable of being solved or explained: a *soluble* mystery.

sol·ute [sol'yōōt'] *n.* A substance dissolved in a solvent.

so·lu·tion [sə·lōō'shən] *n.* 1 The act or method of solving something, as a problem, difficulty, or doubt. 2 The answer to such a problem, difficulty, or doubt: Have you found the *solution* yet? 3 A mixture made by dissolving one substance in another, usually a liquid: Salt water is a *solution.* 4 The act of making such a mixture. 5 The condition of being dissolved: to hold salt in *solution.*

solution set The set of all the values that satisfy an equation or inequality.

solv·a·ble [sol'və·bəl] *adj.* Capable of being solved: a *solvable* problem.

solve [solv] *v.* **solved, solv·ing** To find or work out the answer or solution to: First we must *solve* the problem how to improve study habits.

sol·ven·cy [sol'vən·sē] *n.* The condition of being solvent.

sol·vent [sol'vənt] 1 *adj.* Capable of paying all debts: a *solvent* business. 2 *adj.* Capable of dissolving a substance: a *solvent* liquid. 3 *n.* A substance in which some other substance is or can be dissolved: Alcohol is a *solvent* for shellac.

Som. Somalia.

so·ma [sō'mə] *n.* The bodily substance of an organism exclusive of the germ plasm.

So·ma·li [sə·mä'lē] *adj., n., pl.* **So·ma·li** or **So·ma·lis** 1 *adj.* Of or from Somalia. 2 *n.* A person born in or a citizen of Somalia. 3 *n.* The language of Somalia. **—So·ma·li·an** [sə·mä'lē·ən *or* sə·mäl'yən] *adj., n.*

so·mat·ic [sō·mat'ik] *adj.* Of or having to do with the body: a *somatic* disease.

som·ber [som'bər] *adj.* 1 Having little light or brightness; dark: *somber* colors; a *somber* day. 2 Gloomy and melancholy; sad: You seem to be in a very *somber* mood today. **—som'ber·ly** *adv.* **—som'ber·ness** *n.*

som·bre·ro [som·brâr'ō] *n., pl.* **som·bre·ros** A hat having a very wide brim, much worn in Spain, Latin America, and the SW U.S. ◆ *Sombrero* means *hat* in Spanish. It comes from the Spanish word *sombra,* meaning *shade,* because the wide brim of the hat shades the face from the sun.

some [sum] 1 *adj.* Not definitely known as to quantity, number, or amount: *Some* people will not vote; The recipe calls for *some* milk. 2 *adj.* Not definitely known or recognized: *Some* people went by the window. 3 *pron.* An indefinite number, quantity, or amount: *Some* of the ink spilled. 4 *adv.* About: *Some* eighty people were present. 5 *adj. informal* Good, big, or otherwise notable: That was *some* cake!

-some[1] A suffix used to form adjectives and meaning: Characterized by or tending to be, as in *frolicsome* or *burdensome.*

-some[2] A suffix used to form nouns and meaning: A group consisting of, as in *threesome.*

some·bod·y [sum'bod'ē *or* sum'bəd·ē] *pron., n., pl.* **some·bod·ies** 1 *pron.* A person unknown or not named: *Somebody* went out the door. 2 *n.* A person of importance: That actor is a *somebody.*

some·day [sum'dā'] *adv.* At some future time.

some·how [sum'hou'] *adv.* In some way or in some manner not known or explained.

some·one [sum'wun'] *pron.* Some person; somebody.

some·place [sum'plās'] *adv.* Somewhere.

som·er·sault [sum'ər·sôlt'] 1 *n.* An acrobatic stunt in which a person either jumps or rolls completely over, turning heels over head, forward or backward. 2 *v.* To do a somersault.

Somersault

some·thing [sum'thing'] 1 *pron.* A thing not known, named, or understood: *Something* just flew in the window; Did you have *something* to say? 2 *n.* A person or thing of importance. 3 *adv.* Somewhat: now only in the phrase **something like**: The portrait looks *something like* me.

some·time [sum'tīm'] 1 *adv.* At some future time: We hope to go there *sometime.* 2 *adv.* At some time not stated or known: It will arrive *sometime* today. 3 *adj.* Former: a *sometime* student.

some·times [sum'tīmz'] *adv.* Now and then; at times; occasionally.

some·way [sum'wā'] *adv.* Somehow.

some·ways [sum'wāz'] *adv.* Someway.

some·what [sum'(h)wot'] 1 *adv.* To some degree or extent; rather; slightly: to feel *somewhat* sick. 2 *pron.* Something.

some·where [sum'(h)wâr'] *adv.* 1 In, at, or to some place not known or named: They go *somewhere* every summer. 2 In or at some point in time: She is *somewhere* in her twenties.

som·nam·bu·list [som·nam'byə·list] *n.* A person who walks while asleep. **—som·nam'bu·lism'** *n.*

som·no·lent [som'nə·lənt] *adj.* 1 Inclined to fall asleep; drowsy. 2 Bringing about sleep or drowsiness: a *somnolent* voice. **—som'no·lence** *n.*

son [sun] *n.* 1 A boy or man, considered in relation to either or both of his parents. 2 A boy or man regarded as related to something, as a country or cause, as a son is to a parent: the *sons* of liberty. **—the Son** Jesus Christ.

so·nar [sō′när′] *n.* A device that locates underwater objects by sending out high-frequency sound waves and picking up their echoes with a microphone.

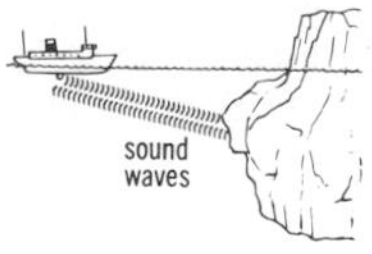

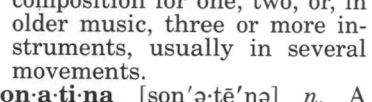

A ship locating an underwater hazard by sonar

so·na·ta [sə·nä′tə] *n.* A musical composition for one, two, or, in older music, three or more instruments, usually in several movements.
son·a·ti·na [son′ə·tē′nə] *n.* A short sonata.
song [sông] *n.* 1 A musical composition for one or more voices. 2 The act of singing. 3 A melodious sound: the *song* of a bird. 4 A poem, as a ballad, that can be sung or spoken. **—for a song** At a very low price.
song·bird [sông′bûrd′] *n.* Any bird that sings, as a canary or thrush.
song·smith [sông′smith′] A songwriter.
song sparrow A common songbird of North America, having brownish plumage and a white underside.
song·ster [sông′stər] *n.* 1 A person who sings. 2 A songbird. 3 A poet.
song·stress [sông′strəs] *n.* A woman who sings popular songs.
song thrush A European thrush, mostly brown above and white below, that produces a clear, musical song.
song·writ·er [sông′rī′tər] *n.* A person who writes lyrics or composes music for songs.
son·ic [son′ik] *adj.* 1 Of or having to do with sound. 2 Having a speed approaching that of sound.
sonic barrier A sharp increase in air resistance that occurs as an aircraft approaches the speed of sound.
sonic boom A disturbance of the atmosphere, heard as a loud clap of thunder, made by an airplane flying faster than the speed of sound.
son-in-law [sun′in·lô′] *n., pl.* **sons-in-law** The husband of one's daughter.
son·net [son′it] *n.* A poem of fourteen lines that rhyme according to a formal, fixed scheme.
so·nor·i·ty [sə·nôr′i·tē] *n., pl.* **so·nor·i·ties** 1 The state or quality of being sonorous; resonance. 2 A full, resonant sound.
so·no·rous [sə·nôr′əs *or* son′ər·əs] *adj.* 1 Loud and very full in sound; resonant: That organ has a *sonorous* tone. 2 Impressive, as in sound, effect, or style: a *sonorous* sentence.
soon [sōōn] *adv.* 1 At a time not far off; shortly: We go *soon* after dark. 2 Without delay; quickly: Send a doctor as *soon* as possible. 3 Early: We arrived at the party too *soon*. 4 With willingness or readiness: I would as *soon* eat four times a day as not.
soot [sŏŏt *or* sōōt] *n.* A black, powdery substance, mostly carbon, that rises in the air from the burning of a material, as wood, coal, or gas.
sooth [sōōth] 1 *n.* Truth: In *sooth*, I saw the monster. 2 *adj.* True; real. ◆ This word is no longer used.
soothe [sōōth] *v.* **soothed, sooth·ing** 1 To restore to a quiet or normal state; calm: We tried to *soothe* the frightened puppy. 2 To soften or relieve: to *soothe* someone's grief or pain. 3 To have a calming or relieving effect: Soft colors *soothe*.
sooth·ing [sōōth′ing] *adj.* Having a calming or relieving effect; comforting. **—sooth′ing·ly** *adv.*
sooth·say·er [sōōth′sā′ər] *n.* A person who claims to be able to tell what will happen or how things will turn out. **—sooth′say′ing** *n.*
soot·y [sŏŏt′ē *or* sōō′tē] *adj.* **soot·i·er, soot·i·est** 1 Covered with or blackened by soot. 2 Producing soot: soft, *sooty* coal. 3 Black, like soot.
sop [sop] *v.* **sopped, sop·ping,** *n.* 1 *v.* To dip or soak in a liquid: to *sop* bread in milk. 2 *n.* Any food softened in a liquid, as bread. 3 *v.* To wet or drench thoroughly; soak: Their clothes were *sopping* from the rain. 4 *v.* To take or soak up by absorption: The rags *sopped* up the water on the floor. 5 *n.* Something given to soothe, satisfy, or please someone, as a gift or bribe.
sop. soprano.
soph. sophomore.
soph·ism [sof′iz·əm] *n.* Clever but deceptive reasoning; sophistry.
soph·ist [sof′ist] *n.* 1 A person who argues cleverly but not always soundly or reasonably. 2 A thinker or philosopher.
so·phis·ti·cate [sə·fis′tə·kit *or* sə·fis′tə·kāt′] *n.* A sophisticated person.
so·phis·ti·cat·ed [sə·fis′tə·kā′tid] *adj.* 1 Cultured and well-educated: a *sophisticated* audience 2 Suited to the taste of sophisticated people, as a play or novel. 3 Wise and experienced in worldly things; lacking a natural simplicity: a *sophisticated* modern teenager. 4 Complicated or technologically advanced: a *sophisticated* machine. **—so·phis′ti·ca′tion** *n.*
soph·is·try [sof′is·trē] *n., pl.* **soph·is·tries** Argument or reasoning that at first seems correct but actually is false or misleading.
soph·o·more [sof′ə·môr′] *n.* In American high schools and colleges, a student in the second year.
soph·o·mor·ic [sof′ə·môr′ik] *adj.* 1 Of, having to do with, or characteristic of sophomores. 2 Self-assured but immature and superficially informed; cocky and overconfident.
sop·o·rif·ic [sop′ə·rif′ik] 1 *adj.* Causing or tending to cause sleep or drowsiness. 2 *n.* A drug or influence that causes sleep or drowsiness.
sop·ping [sop′ing] *adj.* Thoroughly wet; soaked through.
sop·py [sop′ē] *adj.* **sop·pi·er, sop·pi·est** 1 Soaked and softened with moisture; very wet: *soppy* shoes. 2 Rainy: *soppy* weather.
so·pran·o [sə·pran′ō] *adj., n., pl.* **so·pran·os** 1 *adj.* Having a high or the highest range, as a voice or instrument. 2 *n.* A soprano voice. 3 *n.* A singer with such a voice. 4 *adj.* Of or for a soprano voice. ◆ *Soprano* comes from an Italian word meaning *above.*
sor·cer·er [sôr′sər·ər] *n.* A wizard, conjurer, or magician.
sor·cer·ess [sôr′sər·is] *n.* A female wizard, conjurer, or magician; witch.

S

a	add	**i**	it	**ŏŏ**	took	**oi**	oil
ā	ace	**ī**	ice	**ōō**	pool	**ou**	pout
â	care	**o**	odd	**u**	up	**ng**	ring
ä	palm	**ō**	open	**û**	burn	**th**	thin
e	end	**ô**	order	**yōō**	fuse	**th**	this
ē	equal					**zh**	vision

ə = { a in *above* e in *sicken* i in *possible* o in *melon* u in *circus* }

sor·cer·y [sôr′sər·ē] *n., pl.* **sor·cer·ies** The use of magic or witchcraft, usually for some evil purpose.
sor·did [sôr′did] *adj.* 1 Filthy; dirty: a *sordid* area of the city. 2 Mean, selfish, or spiteful: *sordid* desires; a *sordid* argument.
sore [sôr] *adj.* **sor·er, sor·est,** *n.* 1 *adj.* Painful or tender to the touch: a *sore* finger. 2 *adj.* Having or feeling pain: We were *sore* after riding horseback. 3 *n.* A place on the body where the skin is broken, bruised, or inflamed. 4 *adj.* Full of sadness or grief: a *sore* heart. 5 *adj.* Arousing sad or painful feelings: The council's defeat in the last election is a *sore* point with the party. 6 *adj.* Extreme or severe: in *sore* need of money. 7 *adj. informal* Angry: Are you *sore* at me? **—sore′ly** *adv.* **—sore′ness** *n.*
sore·head [sôr′hed′] *n.* A person who is easily angered or offended.
sor·ghum [sôr′gəm] *n.* 1 A tall plant that looks rather like corn, is filled with a sweet juice, and is grown as food for livestock and to make syrup. 2 The sweet syrup made from sorghum.
so·ror·i·ty [sə·rôr′ə·tē] *n., pl.* **so·ror·i·ties** A social club for girls or women, often organized nationally and having local chapters in many schools, colleges, and universities.
sor·rel¹ [sôr′əl] *n.* A plant having sour, edible leaves, used in salads.
sor·rel² [sôr′əl] 1 *n., adj.* Reddish brown. 2 *n.* An animal of this color, especially a horse.
sor·row [sor′ō] 1 *n.* Sadness or distress of mind because of some loss or misfortune. 2 *n.* Any event that causes such sadness or distress. 3 *v.* To feel or show sorrow; grieve.
sor·row·ful [sor′ə·fəl] *adj.* Feeling, showing, or causing sorrow: a *sorrowful* person; a *sorrowful* event. **—sor′row·ful·ly** *adv.*
sor·ry [sor′ē] *adj.* **sor·ri·er, sor·ri·est** 1 Feeling sorrow or sadness; grieved: We were *sorry* to hear of the accident. 2 Feeling a mild regret: I am *sorry* you have to leave so early. 3 Arousing pity or ridicule: The muddy dog was a *sorry* spectacle.
sort [sôrt] 1 *n.* A kind or type; class: What *sort* of house in that? 2 *v.* To divide into groups according to quality or type: to *sort* eggs by size. **—of sorts** Just passable; not very good: an actor *of sorts.* **—out of sorts** *informal* 1 Mildly ill. 2 Grouchy. **—sort of** *informal* Somewhat; rather: That's *sort of* bad news. ◆ See KIND.
sor·tie [sôr′tē] *n.* 1 An attack from a besieged place against the besiegers. 2 A single military mission against an enemy by one plane.
S O S [es′ō′es′] *n.* 1 The radio signal of distress, used by ships and aircraft. 2 Any call for help.
so-so [sō′sō′] *adj.* Neither very good nor very bad.
sot [sot] *n.* A habitual drunkard.
sot·to vo·ce [sot′ō vō′chē] In a quiet voice; under one's breath. ◆ In Italian, *sotto voce* literally means *under the voice.*
sou [sōō] *n., pl.* **sous** A former French coin, worth 1/20 of a franc.
sou·bri·quet [sōō′bri·kā′] *n.* Another spelling of SOBRIQUET.
souf·flé [sōō·flā′] *n.* 1 A light, baked dish made fluffy with beaten egg whites combined with the yolks, often containing cheese, mushrooms, or other ingredients. 2 A similar dish made with sweet ingredients, served as a dessert.
sough [suf *or* sou] 1 *n.* A rustling sound, as of wind through trees. 2 *v.* To make such a sound.
sought [sôt] Past tense and past participle of SEEK.
soul [sōl] 1 *n.* A part of a person conceived of as being the essential self, within the body but not part of it and not dying with it. 2 *n.* Fervor or vitality: This music lacks *soul.* 3 *adj.* Of or having to do with American Blacks or their culture: *soul* food. 4 *n.* What is essential or vital: Justice is the *soul* of law. 5 *n.* A person thought of as being a fine example of a noble quality: the *soul* of generosity. 6 *n.* A person: Not a *soul* came.
soul·ful [sōl′fəl] *adj.* Expressing deep feeling: a *soulful* gaze.
soul·less [sōl′lis] *adj.* Without tender feelings; heartless.
sound¹ [sound] 1 *n.* Anything that can be heard. 2 *n.* Energy in the form of pressure waves that travel through air and other elastic materials, being audible when between 20 and 20,000 cycles per second in frequency. 3 *v.* To make a sound. 4 *v.* To cause to sound: *Sound* the bugle. 5 *v.* To pronounce; articulate: *Sound* your *t*'s. 6 *v.* To announce or signal: to *sound* an alarm. 7 *n.* Hearing distance; earshot: within *sound* of the sea. 8 *v.* To seem: The story *sounds* true.
sound² [sound] 1 *adj.* Healthy: a *sound* body. 2 *adj.* Without a weakness or defect: *sound* walls. 3 *adj.* True or correct: *sound* reasoning. 4 *adj.* Financially secure; solvent: a *sound* business. 5 *adj.* Not risky: a *sound* venture. 6 *adj.* Deep; unbroken: a *sound* sleep. 7 *adv.* Completely; deeply: *sound* asleep. 8 *adj.* Thorough: a *sound* beating. **—sound′ly** *adv.* **—sound′ness** *n.*
sound³ [sound] *n.* 1 A long, narrow channel connecting large bodies of water. 2 An inlet of the sea that divides an island from the mainland. 3 A bladder filled with air in the body of a fish by which it controls its equilibrium in the water.
sound⁴ [sound] *v.* 1 To measure the depth of (water) with a weight at the end of a line. 2 To determine (a depth) in such a way. 3 To make a deep, sudden dive, as a whale when harpooned. 4 To examine the views and attitudes of by questioning or consulting: to *sound* out a voter.
sound barrier Another name for SONIC BARRIER.
sound bite In politics, a catchy phrase or remark shown as a brief scene on a TV news broadcast.
sound·board [sound′bôrd′] *n.* A sounding board (def. 1).
sound box A hollow chamber in a musical instrument that increases the fullness and resonance of the tones produced.
sound·er [soun′dər] *n.* A device for taking soundings.
sound·ing [soun′ding] *n.* 1 A measurement of depth, as with a weight and line. 2 The depth so measured: a *sounding* of ten fathoms.
sounding board 1 A thin board in a musical instrument placed so as to vibrate with the tones produced and increase their loudness. 2 A structure placed above or behind a stage to reflect sounds toward the audience. 3 A means of spreading or testing ideas: She used the school newspaper as a *sounding board* for her views. 4 A person or group from whom one tries to get a reaction, as to an idea or plan.
sound·less [sound′lis] *adj.* Making no sound; silent. **—sound′less·ly** *adv.*
sound·proof [sound′prōōf′] 1 *adj.* That excludes or confines sound: a *soundproof* room. 2 *v.* To make soundproof.

sound track The part of a motion-picture film on which the sound is recorded.

sound wave An audible variation in the pressure of air or another material.

soup [sōōp] *n.* Liquid food made by boiling meat, vegetables, fish, or any mixture of them.

soup·y [sōō′pē] *adj.* **soup·i·er, soup·i·est** 1 Having a consistency like that of soup. 2 Very foggy or cloudy: *soupy* weather. 3 *informal* Overly sentimental; mawkish: a *soupy* sonnet.

sour [sour] 1 *adj.* Having a sharp, acid taste like that of vinegar, lemon juice, or spoiled milk. 2 *v.* To make or become sour. 3 *adj.* Unpleasant or disagreeable. 4 *adj.* Morose, crabbed, or disgusted. 5 *v.* To make bitter or disgusted. 6 *adj.* Too acid to grow crops on, as soil. **—sour′ly** *adv.* **—sour′ness** *n.*

source [sôrs] *n.* 1 The beginning of a stream or river, as a spring, lake, or glacier. 2 A person or thing from which something originates or comes.

sour·dough [sour′dō′] *n.* 1 Fermented dough used as a leaven for bread. 2 An old-time prospector in the Yukon or Alaska.

sour grapes A criticism or disparagement of something after one has failed to get it. ◆ *Sour grapes* refers to a fable by Aesop of the fox who, unable to reach some tasty-looking grapes, decided that they must be sour.

sou·sa·phone [sōō′zə·fōn′] *n.* A kind of large tuba designed to encircle the player's chest, used in marching bands.

souse [sous] *v.* **soused, sous·ing,** *n.* 1 *v.* To dip or steep in a liquid. 2 *v.* To pickle. 3 *n.* The act of sousing. 4 *n.* Something pickled, especially the feet and ears of a pig. 5 *n.* A liquid used in pickling; brine.

south [south] 1 *n.* The direction opposite north; one of the four main points of the compass. If you face the sun at sunrise, south is on your right. 2 *adj.* To, toward, or in the south; southern. 3 *adj.* Coming from the south: the *south* wind. 4 *adv.* In or toward the south; southward. **—south of** Farther south than: Utah is *south of* Idaho. **—the South** 1 The southern and southeastern U.S., especially the part south of the Mason-Dixon line, the Ohio River, and Missouri. 2 The Confederacy.

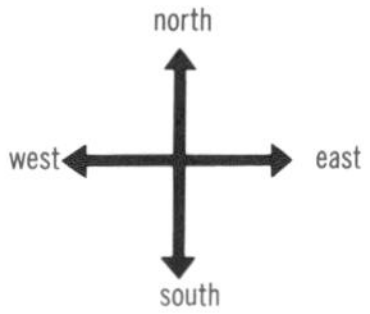

South African 1 Of or from South Africa. 2 A person born in or a citizen of South Africa.

South American 1 Of or from South America. 2 A person born or living in South America.

south by east The direction or compass point midway between south and south-southeast; 11 degrees 15 minutes east of due south.

south by west The direction or compass point midway between south and south-southwest; 11 degrees 15 minutes west of due south.

south·east [south′ēst′] 1 *n.* The direction midway between south and east. 2 *adj.* To, toward, or in the southeast. 3 *adj.* Coming from the southeast: a *southeast* wind. 4 *adv.* In or toward the southeast. **—southeast of** Farther southeast than: Pittsburgh is *southeast of* Detroit. **—the Southeast** The southeastern U.S.

southeast by east The direction or compass point midway between southeast and east-southeast; 11 degrees 15 minutes east of southeast.

southeast by south The direction or compass point midway between southeast and south-southeast; 11 degrees 15 minutes south of southeast.

south·east·er [south′ēs′tər] *n.* A gale or storm from the southeast.

south·east·er·ly [south′ēs′tər·lē] *adj., adv.* 1 Toward or in the southeast. 2 From the southeast.

south·east·ern [south′ēs′tərn] *adj.* 1 Of or from the southeast. 2 Toward or in the southeast: the *southeastern* part.

south·er·ly [suth′ər·lē] *adj.* 1 Toward the south. 2 From the south: a *southerly* wind.

south·ern [suth′ərn] *adj.* 1 Of or from the south. 2 Toward or in the south: the *southern* part. 3 (*sometimes written* **Southern**) Of or having to do with the South.

Southern Cross A southern constellation having four bright stars in the form of a cross.

south·ern·er [suth′ərn·ər] *n.* 1 A person born or living in the south. 2 (*often written* **Southerner**) A person born or living in the southern part of the U.S.

southern lights Another name for the AURORA AUSTRALIS.

south·ern·most [suth′ərn·mōst′] *adj.* Farthest south.

south·paw [south′pô′] *informal* 1 *n.* In baseball, a left-handed pitcher. 2 *n.* Any left-handed person. 3 *adj.* Left-handed.

South Pole 1 The southern end of the earth's axis; the southernmost point of the earth. 2 (*written* **south pole**) The end of a freely swinging magnet that points south.

south-southeast [south′south′ēst′] 1 *n.* The direction or compass point midway between south and southeast; 22 degrees 30 minutes east of due south. 2 *adj.* To, toward, or in the south-southeast. 3 *adv.* In or toward the south-southeast.

south-southwest [south′south′west′] 1 *n.* The direction or compass point midway between south and southwest; 22 degrees 30 minutes west of due south. 2 *adj.* To, toward, or in the south-southwest. 3 *adv.* In or toward the south-southwest.

south·ward [south′wərd] 1 *adv., adj.* To or toward the south. 2 *n.* A southward direction or location.

south·wards [south′wərdz] *adv.* Southward.

south·west [south′west′] 1 *n.* The direction midway between south and west. 2 *adj.* To, toward, or in the southwest: the *southwest* part. 3 *adj.* Coming from the southwest: a *southwest* wind. 4 *adv.* In or toward the southwest. **—southwest of** Farther southwest than: Kansas is *southwest of* Iowa. **—the Southwest** The southwestern U.S.

southwest by south The direction or compass point midway between southwest and south-southwest; 11 degrees 15 minutes south of southwest.

southwest by west The direction or compass point midway between southwest and west-southwest; 11 degrees 15 minutes west of southwest.

a	add	**i**	it	**ŏŏ**	took	**oi**	oil
ā	ace	**ī**	ice	**ōō**	pool	**ou**	pout
â	care	**o**	odd	**u**	up	**ng**	ring
ä	palm	**ō**	open	**û**	burn	**th**	thin
e	end	**ô**	order	**yōō**	fuse	**th**	this
ē	equal					**zh**	vision

ə = a in *above* e in *sicken* i in *possible* / o in *melon* u in *circus*

S

south·west·er [south′wes′tər] *n.* 1 A gale or storm from the southwest. 2 A waterproof hat, often of oilskin or canvas, with a broad brim behind to protect the neck.

Southwester

south·west·er·ly [south′wes′tər·lē] *adj., adv.* 1 Toward or in the southwest. 2 From the southwest.

south·west·ern [south′wes′tərn] *adj.* 1 Of or from the southwest. 2 Toward or in the southwest: the *southwestern* part.

sou·ve·nir [sōō′və·nir′] *n.* Something that is kept as a reminder of the past: I have many *souvenirs* from my travels.

sou·west·er [sou′wes′tər] *n.* Another spelling of SOUTHWESTER.

sov·er·eign [sov′rən] 1 *n.* A monarch; king or queen. 2 *adj.* Having supreme power: a *sovereign* ruler. 3 *adj.* Supreme; greatest: the *sovereign* good of the people. 4 *adj.* Free and independent: a *sovereign* nation. 5 *n.* A former British gold coin worth one pound.

sov·er·eign·ty [sov′rən·tē] *n., pl.* **sov·er·eign·ties** 1 Supreme authority or power. 2 The rank or status of a sovereign. 3 The condition of being independent and under self-government.

So·vi·et [sō′vē·et′] 1 *adj.* Of or having to do with the Soviet Union. 2 *n. (pl.)* The people or political leaders of the Soviet Union. 3 *n.* (*written* **soviet**) Any of various councils in the Soviet Union formed to govern villages, towns, and larger units. The highest legislative body is called the **Supreme Soviet.**

sow[1] [sō] *v.* **sowed, sown** or **sowed, sow·ing** 1 To plant (seed) in the ground so that it will grow. 2 To scatter seed over (land). 3 To spread about; implant: to *sow* suspicion. **—sow′er** *n.*

sow[2] [sou] *n.* A female hog.

soy [soi] *n.* 1 A sauce prepared from fermented and pickled soybeans, traditionally used on Chinese and Japanese foods. 2 A soybean.

soy·a [soi′ə] *n.* Soy.

soy·bean [soi′bēn′] *n.* 1 The edible seed of an Asian plant, widely grown also as a source of oil, flour, and other products. 2 The plant itself.

sp. 1 species. 2 spelling.

Sp. 1 Spain. 2 Spanish.

spa [spä] *n.* 1 A spring of mineral water. 2 A health resort having such a spring or springs.

space [spās] *n., v.* **spaced, spac·ing** 1 *n.* The region having an indefinite or boundless height, width, and depth, in parts of which all material things are located. 2 *n.* The region outside the earth's atmosphere; outer space. 3 *adj. use*: a *space* capsule; the *Space* Age. 4 *n.* The area or distance between two or more objects or points, or the area inside of something: a cupboard with lots of *space.* 5 *n.* A distance or period of time; interval. 6 *v.* To separate by spaces: to *space* chairs. 7 *v.* To put spaces between.

space·craft [spās′kraft′] *n., pl.* **space·craft** A vehicle, such as a rocket or artificial satellite, designed for research or travel in outer space.

space·man [spās′mən] *n., pl.* **space·men** [spās′mən] An astronaut.

space platform A space station.

space probe A spacecraft with instruments designed to collect information about outer space.

space·ship [spās′ship′] *n.* A spacecraft.

space shuttle A vehicle designed to be launched by rocket into orbit around the earth or to a rendezvous with a space station, and then to return to earth and land like an airplane.

space station A large artificial satellite placed in orbit around the earth, designed for use as a base for observation and research and as a launching site for spaceships.

space suit A pressurized suit equipped to make life and movement for the wearer possible in outer space.

space-time [spās′tīm′] *n.* Space with the added dimension of time, thought of as a system of four mathematical coordinates within which all physical objects and events can be located.

space walk A maneuver by an astronaut outside a spacecraft in space.

space·wom·an [spās′wŏŏm′ən] *n., pl.* **space·wom·en** [spās′wim′in] A woman who is an astronaut.

spac·ing [spā′sing] *n.* 1 The act of separating things so as to leave space between them. 2 The way spaces are arranged. 3 A space or spaces, as between words or lines in print.

spa·cious [spā′shəs] *adj.* 1 Having much space; large. 2 Vast; extensive.

spade[1] [spād] *n., v.* **spad·ed, spad·ing** 1 *n.* A tool resembling a shovel, but having a flatter blade. 2 *v.* To dig with a spade. **—call a spade a spade** To speak the plain truth.

spade[2] [spād] *n.* 1 A figure like this: ♠. 2 A playing card of the suit marked with black spades. 3 (*pl.*) The suit of cards so marked.

spa·dix [spā′diks] *n., pl.* **spa·di·ces** [spā′di·sēz′] A fleshy plant stalk bearing tiny flowers, usually enclosed in a spathe.

spa·ghet·ti [spə·get′ē] *n.* Long slender strings of flour paste, boiled as food.

spake [spāk] An alternative past tense of SPEAK: seldom used today: Thus *spake* Moses.

span[1] [span] *n., v.* **spanned, span·ning** 1 *n.* The greatest distance that the tips of the thumb and little finger can be spread apart, about 9 inches. 2 *v.* To measure by spans. 3 *v.* To stretch or extend across: The bridge *spans* the river. 4 *n.* The distance between the supports of an arch, bridge, or other structure. 5 *n.* An interval or distance: a *span* of a week.

span[2] [span] *n.* A team of two oxen or other beasts of burden harnessed together.

Span. Spanish.

span·gle [spang′gəl] *n., v.* **span·gled, span·gling** 1 *n.* A small bit of something sparkling, as metal or plastic, used as a decoration on cloth or jewelry. 2 *n.* Any small, sparkling object. 3 *v.* To decorate with or as if with spangles.

Span·iard [span′yərd] *n.* A person born in or a citizen of Spain.

span·iel [span′yəl] *n.* A small or medium-sized dog with large, drooping ears and usually long, silky hair.

A typical spaniel

Span·ish [span′ish] 1 *adj.* Of or from Spain. 2 *n.* **(the Spanish)** The people of Spain. 3 *n.* A Romance language spoken in Spain and Spanish America.

Span·ish-A·mer·i·can [span′ish·ə·mer′ə·kən] 1 *adj.* Of or having to do with Spanish America. 2 *adj.* Of or having to do with Spain and America.

3 *n.* A person born or living in Spanish America. **4** *n.* A person of Spanish or Spanish-American descent living in the U.S.

Spanish-American War A war between Spain and the U.S., fought in 1898.

Spanish moss A grayish-green air plant that grows in hanging masses on the branches of trees in the SE U.S. and the West Indies.

Spanish rice Rice cooked with tomatoes, onions, peppers, and seasonings.

spank [spangk] **1** *v.* To smack with the open hand or with an object, as a slipper. **2** *n.* A slap with the open hand or an object.

spank·ing [spang′king] **1** *n.* A series of slaps with the open hand or an object. **2** *adj.* Brisk; lively.

spar[1] [spär] *v.* **sparred, spar·ring** **1** To box, especially carefully and skillfully. **2** To argue; wrangle.

spar[2] [spär] *n., v.* **sparred, spar·ring** **1** *n.* Something, as a mast, yard, or boom, that supports or extends a sail. **2** *v.* To furnish (a ship) with spars.

spar[3] [spär] *n.* Any of various shiny, crystalline minerals that cleave easily.

spare [spâr] *adj.* **spar·er, spar·est,** *n., v.* **spared, spar·ing** **1** *adj.* Extra or available: *spare* parts. **2** *n.* An extra thing in reserve, as a tire. **3** *v.* To refrain from injuring or destroying: *Spare* that tree. **4** *v.* To free or relieve from something unpleasant or harmful: to *spare* a patient pain. **5** *v.* To part with; give up: to *spare* a dime. **6** *adj.* Scanty or lean: *spare* pickings; a *spare*, wiry person. **7** *v.* To refrain from using, or use in small amounts: to *spare* neither trouble nor expense. **8** *n.* In bowling, the knocking over of all the pins with two rolls of the ball. **—spare′ly** *adv.*

spare·rib [spâr′rib′] *n.* (*usually pl.*) A rib of pork without much meat on it.

spar·ing [spâr′ing] *adj.* Not wasteful or extravagant; frugal. **—spar′ing·ly** *adv.*

spark [spärk] **1** *n.* A small, glowing particle, as one thrown off by a fire or a hot material. **2** *n.* A short flash made by an electric current when it jumps across a gap. **3** *n.* Any bright point of light. **4** *v.* To give off sparks. **5** *v.* To activate or cause: to *spark* an investigation. **6** *n.* A faint trace; glimmer: a *spark* of hope.

spar·kle [spär′kəl] *v.* **spar·kled, spar·kling,** *n.* **1** *v.* To emit sparks or flashes. **2** *n.* A spark or flash. **3** *v.* To bubble, as soda water does. **4** *v.* To be witty and lively: The conversation *sparkled.*

spar·kler [spär′klər] *n.* **1** A thing that sparkles, as a gem. **2** A thin, rodlike type of fireworks that gives off sparks when lighted.

spar·kling [spär′kling] *adj.* **1** Emitting sparks. **2** Effervescent; bubbly. **3** Lively.

spark plug A device for igniting the fuel mixture in an internal combustion engine by an electric spark.

Sparrow

spar·row [spar′ō] *n.* **1** Any of several small finches. **2** A small bird, native to the Old World but now common worldwide, having brownish or grayish plumage and a black throat in the male.

sparse [spärs] *adj.* **spars·er, spars·est** Thinly scattered; not dense: *sparse* woods; a *sparse* population. **—sparse′ly** *adv.*

spar·si·ty [spär′sə·tē] *n., pl.* **spar·si·ties** A condition of being few in number or widely scattered: the *sparsity* of trees on the plains.

Spar·tan [spär′tən] **1** *adj.* Of or having to do with Sparta. **2** *n.* A person born or living in ancient Sparta. **3** *adj.* Like the Spartans in character; stern, self-denying, and courageous. **4** *n.* A person of Spartan character.

spasm [spaz′əm] *n.* **1** A sudden, involuntary contraction of a muscle or muscles. **2** Any sudden, brief burst of energy or activity.

spas·mod·ic [spaz·mod′ik] *adj.* Like a spasm; sudden, often intense, and irregular: a *spasmodic* twitch; *spasmodic* bursts of activity. **—spas·mod′i·cal·ly** *adv.*

spas·tic [spas′tik] **1** *adj.* Of, having to do with, or suffering from spasms: a *spastic* muscle. **2** *n.* A person who is afflicted with spasms of the muscles or has cerebral palsy.

spat[1] [spat] *n., v.* **spat·ted, spat·ting** **1** *n.* A small quarrel. **2** *v.* To have a small quarrel. **3** *n.* A slight blow; slap. **4** *v.* To slap.

spat[2] [spat] *n.* (*usually pl.*) A cloth covering for the ankle and instep, overlapping the shoe.

spat[3] [spat] Past tense and past participle of SPIT[1].

spat[4] [spat] *n., pl.* **spat** or **spats,** *v.* **spat·ted, spat·ting** **1** *n.* A young oyster or similar mollusk in the stage when it is developing its shell. **2** *v.* To spawn.

spate [spāt] *n.* **1** A sudden flood or rush: a *spate* of anger. **2** A large number occurring or appearing together: a *spate* of burglaries.

spathe [spāth] *n.* A leaflike plant part surrounding a flower spike or spadix, as in the calla lily and the skunk cabbage.

spa·tial [spā′shəl] *adj.* **1** Of, in, or having to do with space. **—spa′tial·ly** *adv.*

spat·ter [spat′ər] **1** *v.* To fall, scatter, or strike in drops or a shower: Rain *spattered* on the roof; Grease *spattered* the stove. **2** *v.* To stain or mark by or as if by spattering: to *spatter* a shirt with ink. **3** *n.* The act of spattering. **4** *n.* Something that has been spattered; splash: a *spatter* of mud.

spat·u·la [spach′o͝o·lə] *n.* A tool with a flat flexible blade, used in mixing, spreading, or lifting foods or mixing paints or drugs.

spat·u·late [spach′o͝o·lət] *adj.* Shaped like a spatula.

spav·in [spav′in] *n.* A disease in which the hock of a horse stiffens or swells, causing lameness.

spav·ined [spav′ind] *adj.* Lamed by spavin.

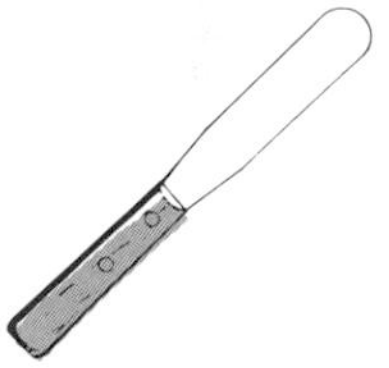
Spatula

spawn [spôn] **1** *n.* The eggs or new offspring of fishes or other water animals. **2** *v.* To deposit great numbers of eggs. **3** *n.* Offspring, especially in huge numbers. **4** *v.* To give rise to: The article *spawned* interest in the issue.

a	add	**i**	it	**o͝o**	took	**oi**	oil
ā	ace	**ī**	ice	**o͞o**	pool	**ou**	pout
â	care	**o**	odd	**u**	up	**ng**	ring
ä	palm	**ō**	open	**û**	burn	**th**	thin
e	end	**ô**	order	**yo͞o**	fuse	**th**	this
ē	equal					**zh**	vision

ə = { a in *above* e in *sicken* i in *possible* / o in *melon* u in *circus* }

S

spay [spā] *v.* To remove the ovaries of (a female animal).

SPCA or **S.P.C.A.** Society for the Prevention of Cruelty to Animals.

SPCC or **S.P.C.C.** Society for the Prevention of Cruelty to Children.

speak [spēk] *v.* **spoke** (or **spake**: seldom used today), **spo·ken, speak·ing** 1 To say words; talk. 2 To express or tell in this way: to *speak* one's ideas. 3 To make a speech. 4 To use or be able to use (a language) in speech: to *speak* Spanish. **—so to speak** One might say; to put it this way: I'm in a fog, *so to speak.* **—speak for** 1 To speak on behalf of. 2 To request. **—speak out** To speak openly or frankly. **—speak up** To make oneself heard. **—speak well for** To show favorably; recommend: His appearance *speaks well for* him.

speak·eas·y [spēk'ē'zē] *n., pl.* **speak·eas·ies** A place where alcoholic drinks are illegally sold, as during Prohibition in the U.S.

speak·er [spē'kər] *n.* 1 A person who speaks. 2 A person who gives a speech. 3 In certain legislative bodies, the chairperson: the *speaker* of the assembly. 4 A loudspeaker.

speak·er·ship [spē'kər·ship'] *n.* The position of speaker of a legislative body.

speak·ing [spē'king] *adj.* 1 Capable of speech. 2 Closely resembling an original; lifelike: a *speaking* likeness.

spear [spir] 1 *n.* A long pole with a pointed head at one end, used as a weapon in war or hunting. 2 *v.* To pierce or catch with a spear: to *spear* a fish. 3 *n.* A slender leaf or stalk.

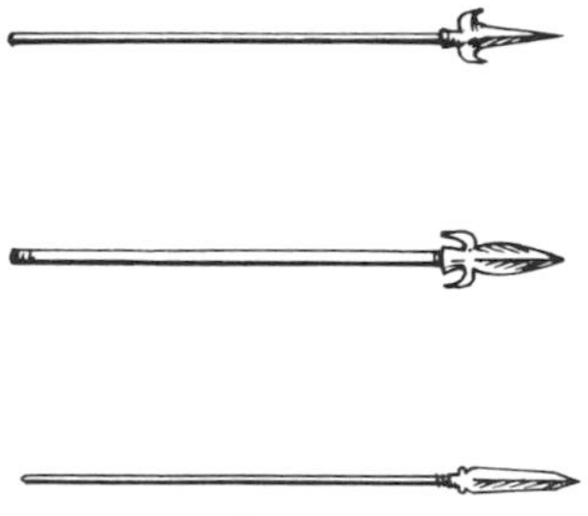

Spear

spear·head [spir'hed'] 1 *n.* The point of a spear. 2 *n.* The person or group that leads something, as a project or military attack. 3 *v.* To be first in or lead (as an attack).

spear·mint [spir'mint'] *n.* A plant, a common mint similar to peppermint.

spe·cial [spesh'əl] 1 *adj.* Of a particular kind; distinctive; out of the ordinary: Please do me a *special* favor. 2 *adj.* For a particular purpose or service: a *special* messenger; a *special* train to New York. 3 *n.* A person or thing selected for something special, as a duty or service. 4 *adj.* Intimate; close: a *special* friend.

special delivery Mail delivery at extra cost by a special messenger rather than the regular carrier.

spe·cial·ist [spesh'əl·ist] *n.* A person who specializes, especially a doctor who concentrates on one branch of medicine.

spe·cial·ize [spesh'əl·īz'] *v.* **spe·cial·ized, spe·cial·iz·ing** 1 To concentrate on one particular activity or subject. 2 To make or become fit for a particular use: to *specialize* a tool. **—spe·cial·i·za·tion** [spesh'ə·lə·zā'shən] *n.*

spe·cial·ly [spesh'ə·lē] *adv.* 1 Unusually; distinctively. 2 In a special way.

spe·cial·ty [spesh'əl·tē] *n., pl.* **spe·cial·ties** 1 Something special, as a study or occupation: Engineering is the *specialty* of this school. 2 The condition of being special or unusual. 3 A specially featured or outstanding thing: This restaurant makes a *specialty* of Chinese food.

spe·cie [spē'shē] *n.* Coined money; coin.

spe·cies [spē'shēz *or* spē'sēz] *n., pl.* **spe·cies** 1 A group of living things that are more or less alike and whose members can interbreed and produce fertile offspring: Leopards and lions are of different *species.* 2 Kind; sort; type.

spe·cif·ic [spi·sif'ik] 1 *adj.* Particular; definite. 2 *n.* Something specific, especially a medicine for a particular disease. 3 *adj.* In biology, of or having to do with a species. **—spe·cif'i·cal·ly** *adv.*

spec·i·fi·ca·tion [spes'ə·fə·kā'shən] *n.* 1 The act of specifying. 2 Something specified, as in a contract or plans. 3 (*usually pl.*) A specific description, as of types of materials or dimensions, to be used in manufacturing or building something.

specific gravity 1 A measure of the relative density of a solid or liquid, found by dividing its mass by the mass of an equal volume of water. 2 A measure of the relative density of a gas, found by dividing its mass by the mass of an equal volume of air or pure hydrogen.

specific heat The amount of heat in calories needed to raise the temperature of one gram of a substance by one degree centigrade. The specific heat of water is one calorie.

spec·i·fy [spes'ə·fī] *v.* **spec·i·fied, spec·i·fy·ing** 1 To indicate particularly; make definite. 2 To include in a set of specifications.

spec·i·men [spes'ə·mən] *n.* One person or thing of a group, or a small amount taken as a sample of a whole: a fine *specimen* of scouting; a blood *specimen.*

spe·cious [spē'shəs] *adj.* Seeming good, right, or true, but actually not so: a *specious* promise; *specious* reasoning.

speck [spek] 1 *n.* A tiny spot or stain: There is a *speck* of grease on my new jacket. 2 *v.* To mark or cover with specks. 3 *n.* A tiny particle.

speck·le [spek'əl] *n., v.* **speck·led, speck·ling** 1 *n.* A speck. 2 *v.* To mark with specks: The red fabric was *speckled* with gold. 3 *v.* To be scattered on like speckles: Islets *speckled* the horizon.

specs [speks] *n.pl. informal* 1 Spectacles; eyeglasses. 2 Specifications.

spec·ta·cle [spek'tə·kəl] *n.* 1 Something exhibited to the public, especially something grand and showy. 2 An unusual or painful sight: to be dressed so oddly as to make a *spectacle* of oneself. 3 (*pl.*) A pair of eyeglasses.

spec·tac·u·lar [spek·tak'yə·lər] 1 *adj.* Amazing to behold: a *spectacular* feat. 2 *adj.* Done on a grand scale: a *spectacular* film. 3 *n.* An imposing spectacle. **—spec·tac'u·lar·ly** *adv.*

spec·ta·tor [spek'tā·tər] *n.* A person who watches an event without taking part in it.

spec·ter [spek'tər] *n.* A ghost.

spec·tral [spek'trəl] *adj.* 1 Of or like a specter; ghostly. 2 Of or having to do with a spectrum or spectra.

spec·tro·graph [spek'trə·graf'] *n.* An instrument for photographing spectra.

spec·trom·e·ter [spek·trom'ə·tər] *n.* 1 A spectroscope that can measure the wavelengths of the spectra observed by it. 2 An instrument used in determining the index of refraction of substances.

spec·tro·scope [spek'trə·skōp'] *n.* An instrument that breaks light into spectra for observation.

spec·trum [spek'trəm] *n., pl.* **spec·tra** [spek'trə] 1

The rainbowlike band of color or pattern of lines seen when light from a source is separated according to wavelengths. The visible spectrum of the sun goes from red (long waves) to violet (short waves). **2** A continuous range of wavelengths.

spec·u·late [spek′yə·lāt′] *v.* **spec·u·lat·ed, spec·u·lat·ing** **1** To think seriously or wonderingly; form theories; conjecture: People *speculated* about living beings on Mars. **2** To invest money where there is a considerable risk of loss but the possibility of large profits. **—spec′u·la′tor** *n.*

spec·u·la·tion [spek′yə·lā′shən] *n.* **1** The act of speculating. **2** A theory; conjecture. **3** A risky investment of money.

spec·u·la·tive [spek′yə·lā′tiv *or* spek′yə·lə·tiv] *adj.* **1** Based on a guess: a *speculative* reply. **2** Inclined to speculate; reflective: a *speculative* thinker. **3** That is or involves a financial risk: *speculative* buying of stocks.

sped [sped] Past tense of SPEED.

speech [spēch] *n.* **1** The act of speaking; the saying of words. **2** The ability to speak: The child's *speech* was impaired. **3** A way of speaking that characterizes a person or group: educated *speech*; the *speech* of Mexican farm workers. **4** Something that is spoken, especially a public address or talk: The audience applauded the *speech.*

speech·less [spēch′lis] *adj.* **1** Lacking the power of speech. **2** Temporarily unable to speak, especially because of strong emotion: *speechless* with joy. **—speech′less·ly** *adv.* **—speech′less·ness** *n.*

speed [spēd] *n., v.* **sped, speed·ing** **1** *n.* The distance traveled per unit of time; rate: a *speed* of 4 miles an hour. **2** *n.* Any rate of progress or action: to read at a high *speed.* **3** *v.* To go or cause to go fast or faster: The train *sped* along; Fear *sped* us on. **4** *v.* To drive a motor vehicle faster than the law permits. **5** *n.* A gear of a motor vehicle: a sports car with four forward *speeds.* **6** *n.* Good luck: seldom used today. **7** *v.* To wish (a person) a successful journey. **8** *v.* To promote the success of. **—speed up** To accelerate. **—speed′i·ly** *adv.* ◆ *Speed* comes from the Old English word for *luck* or *prosperity.*

speed·boat [spēd′bōt′] *n.* A fast motorboat.

speed·er [spē′dər] *n.* A person or thing that speeds, especially a person who drives at reckless or illegal speeds.

speed·om·e·ter [spi·dom′ə·tər] *n.* An instrument that shows a driver at what speed the vehicle is traveling.

speed-read [spēd′rēd′] *v.* **speed-read** [spēd′red], **speed-read·ing** [spēd′rēd′ing] To engage in or practice speed-reading.

speed-read·ing [spēd′rēd′ing] *n.* A method of reading at a faster than normal speed that utilizes such techniques as skimming.

speed·up [spēd′up′] *n.* An increase in speed or rate of work.

speed·way [spēd′wā′] *n.* A road for vehicles traveling at high speed.

speed·well [spēd′wel′] *n.* A low-growing plant with clusters of small, usually bluish flowers.

speed·y [spē′dē] *adj.* **speed·i·er, speed·i·est** Swift; fast; rapid. **—speed′i·ly** *adv.*

spe·le·ol·o·gy [spē′lē·ol′ə·jē] *n.* The study or exploration of caves. **—spe′le·ol′o·gist** *n.*

spell¹ [spel] *v.* **spelled** or **spelt, spell·ing** **1** To name or write the letters of (a word) in their correct order. **2** To form or be the letters of: C-a-t *spells* cat. **3** To be equivalent to: Making the most of one's opportunities *spells* success. **—spell out** **1** To read with difficulty. **2** To indicate clearly: The leader *spelled out* the plans.

spell² [spel] *n.* **1** A word or words supposedly having magical power; charm. **2** An irresistible fascination or charm.

spell³ [spel] **1** *n.* An indefinite time. **2** *n.* A time characterized by something: a *spell* of drought. **3** *n.* A fit, as one of unconsciousness or weakness: a fainting *spell.* **4** *v.* To relieve temporarily of some work or duty: I will *spell* you at painting the woodwork. **5** *n.* Such a turn of duty.

spell·bind [spel′bīnd′] *v.* **spell·bound, spell·bind·ing** To hold under or as if under a spell; fascinate.

spell·bind·er [spel′bīn′dər] *n.* A speaker able to hold an audience spellbound.

spell·bind·ing [spel′bīn′ding] *adj.* Fascinating; enchanting.

spell·bound [spel′bound′] *adj.* Fascinated, as if bound by a spell.

spell·er [spel′ər] *n.* **1** A person who spells. **2** An elementary book of exercises in spelling.

spell·ing [spel′ing] *n.* **1** The act of naming or writing down in order the letters which spell a word. **2** The way a person spells.

spelling bee A gathering at which contestants compete in spelling words.

spelt [spelt] An alternative past tense and past participle of SPELL¹.

spe·lunk·er [spi·lung′kər] *n.* A person whose hobby is exploring caves.

spend [spend] *v.* **spent, spend·ing** **1** To exchange (money) for goods or services. **2** To use or use up: to *spend* time. **3** To pass or occupy: He *spent* his life helping others.

spend·thrift [spend′thrift′] **1** *n.* Someone who spends money wastefully or foolishly. **2** *adj. use*: a *spendthrift* person.

spent [spent] **1** Past tense and past participle of SPEND. **2** *adj.* Worn out or used up. **3** *adj.* Having lost its force: a *spent* bullet.

sperm [spûrm] *n., pl.* **sperm** or **sperms** **1** The fertilizing fluid of a male animal, containing fully matured reproductive cells. **2** One of these cells.

sper·ma·ce·ti [spûr′mə·set′ē] *n.* A waxy substance obtained from the oil of the sperm whale, used for making candles and ointments.

sper·mat·ic [spûr·mat′ik] *adj.* Of, having to do with, or containing sperm: *spermatic* fluid.

sper·mat·o·phyte [spûr·mat′ə·fīt′] *n.* Any seed-bearing plant.

sper·ma·to·zo·on [spûr′mə·tə·zō′ən] *n., pl.* **sper·ma·to·zo·a** [spûr′mə·tə·zō′ə] A reproductive cell of a male animal; sperm.

sperm oil A clear yellowish oil obtained from the sperm whale, once used as a fuel and now chiefly as a lubricant.

a	add	**i**	it	**o͝o**	took	**oi**	oil
ā	ace	**ī**	ice	**o͞o**	pool	**ou**	pout
â	care	**o**	odd	**u**	up	**ng**	ring
ä	palm	**ō**	open	**û**	burn	**th**	thin
e	end	**ô**	order	**yo͞o**	fuse	**t͟h**	this
ē	equal					**zh**	vision

ə = { a in *above* e in *sicken* i in *possible*
o in *melon* u in *circus* }

S

sperm whale A large, toothed whale of tropical waters, highly valued for its oil.

spew [spyo͞o] **1** *v.* To throw up; vomit: The volcano *spewed* ash and lava. **2** *n.* That which is spewed.

Sperm whale

sp.gr. specific gravity.

sphag·num [sfag′nəm] *n.* A grayish green moss that grows in swamps and bogs. Its decaying remains, compacted with other dead plants, form peat.

sphere [sfir] *n.* **1** A surface that has all its points the same distance from a particular point called its center; ball. **2** A range or scope: a *sphere* of activity. **3** A level of society; circle.

spher·i·cal [sfir′i·kəl] *adj.* **1** Shaped like a sphere; round; globular. **2** Of or having to do with a sphere or spheres.

spher·oid [sfir′oid′] *n.* An object shaped almost like a sphere.

sphinc·ter [sfing(k)′tər] *n.* A ring-shaped muscle at the opening of a body passage, contracting to keep it closed and relaxing to open it.

sphinx [sfingks] *n., pl.* **sphinx·es** or **sphin·ges** [sfin′·jēz] **1** In Egyptian myths, a monster with a lion's body and the head of a man, ram, or hawk. **2** A statue of a sphinx. **3** In Greek myths, a monster with wings, a woman's head, and a lion's body, who killed those who failed to guess its riddle. **4** A puzzling or mysterious person. **—the Sphinx** A huge sphinx with a man's head near Cairo, Egypt.

Sphinx

sphyg·mo·ma·nom·e·ter [sfig′mō·mə·nom′ə·tər] *n.* An instrument for measuring blood pressure.

spice [spīs] *n., v.* **spiced, spic·ing** **1** *n.* Any of various vegetable substances, as cloves or nutmeg, used to flavor food. **2** *v.* To season with spice. **3** *n.* Something that adds zest or interest. **4** *v.* To add zest or interest to: to *spice* a talk with jokes.

spick-and-span [spik′ən·span′] *adj.* **1** Neat and clean. **2** Brand new.

spic·y [spī′sē] *adj.* **spic·i·er, spic·i·est** **1** Flavored with spices. **2** Having a sharp taste or odor; pungent. **3** Lively or zestful. **—spic′i·ness** *n.*

spi·der [spī′dər] *n.* **1** A small animal with no wings, eight legs, and a body in two segments; type of arachnid. Many spiders spin webs and catch insects for food. **2** A frying pan with a long handle, sometimes having legs.

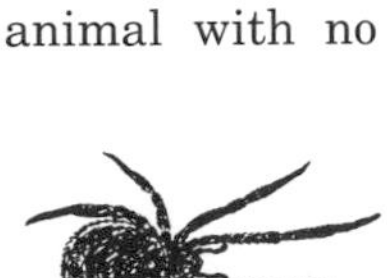
Black widow spider

spider monkey A monkey that uses its long limbs and prehensile tail to move among the trees in tropical American jungles.

spi·der·y [spī′dər·ē] *adj.* **1** Like a spider. **2** Thin; fine; delicate, like a spider's legs or web.

spied [spīd] Past tense and past participle of SPY.

spiel [spēl] *n. slang* A long, colorful speech intended to persuade listeners or potential customers.

spiff·y [spif′ē] *adj.* **spiff·i·er, spiff·i·est** *slang* Trim and stylish; good-looking; smart: *spiffy* clothes.

spig·ot [spig′ət] *n.* **1** A faucet. **2** A plug or valve to stop up the hole of a cask.

spike[1] [spīk] *n., v.* **spiked, spik·ing** **1** *n.* A very large nail. **2** *v.* To fasten, join, or pierce with a spike or spikes. **3** *n.* A sharp or pointed metal projection, as on the top of a fence or on the sole of certain shoes worn in sports. **4** *v.* To provide with spikes. **5** *v.* To pierce with or impale on a spike. **6** *v.* To put an end to; suppress; block: to *spike* a false rumor.

spike[2] [spīk] *n.* **1** An ear of grain. **2** A cluster of numerous flowers arranged closely on a long stalk.

spike·let [spīk′lit] *n.* A small spike of flowers, especially of a grass plant.

spike·nard [spīk′nərd] *n.* A fragrant and costly ointment used in ancient times.

spik·y [spī′kē] *adj.* **spik·i·er, spik·i·est** Having a sharp projecting point or points: the *spiky* top of the fence.

spile [spīl] *n.* **1** A supporting post; pile. **2** A plug for a cask or barrel.

spill[1] [spil] *v.* **spilled** or **spilt, spill·ing,** *n.* **1** *v.* To cause or allow to run out, slop, or fall: I *spilled* a glass of milk on the table. **2** *v.* To fall, run out, or flow: Milk *spilled* off the table; Water *spilled* over the dam. **3** *n.* The action of spilling. **4** *v.* To shed, as blood. **5** *v.* To cause to fall: The horse *spilled* its rider. **6** *n.* A fall; tumble: I took a bad *spill* on a waxed floor. **—spill the beans** *informal* To give away a secret.

spill[2] [spil] *n.* A thin strip of wood or rolled paper used for lighting lamps or fires.

spill·way [spil′wā′] *n.* A channel, as in a dam, to let surplus water run off.

spilt [spilt] An alternative past tense and past participle of SPILL[1].

Spillway

spin [spin] *v.* **spun, spin·ning,** *n.* **1** *v.* To draw out and twist (as cotton or flax) into thread. **2** *v.* To make fibers into (threads or yarn) by spinning. **3** *v.* To make something, as a web or cocoon, from secreted filaments. **4** *v.* To turn or whirl about; revolve; rotate: to *spin* a top. **5** *n.* A turning or whirling about. **6** *v.* To have a feeling of whirling: Excitement made my head *spin.* **7** *v.* To make up or relate (a story or tale). **8** *n.* A ride or drive, often for pleasure. **9** *v.* To move rapidly. **—spin′ner** *n.*

spin·ach [spin′ich] *n.* **1** A common herb with large, dark green leaves. **2** These leaves, eaten as a vegetable, usually cooked.

spi·nal [spī′nəl] *adj.* Of, in, or having to do with the spine.

spinal column The series of connected bones that form the main support of a vertebrate skeleton; backbone.

spinal cord The cord of nerve tissue inside the spinal column that with the brain forms the central nervous system.

spin·dle [spin′dəl] *n., v.* **spin·dled, spin·dling** **1** *n.* A rod on which thread is wound in spinning. **2** *n.* A rod or shaft that turns or on which something turns, as an axle. **3** *v.* To become long and slender, as a plant stalk. 4 *n.* A sharp-pointed rod or spike on which papers are kept by impaling them. 5 *v.* To impale or punch a hole in, as with a spindle: Do not *spindle* this card.

spin·dle-leg·ged [spin′dəl·leg′id *or* spin′dəl·legd′] *adj.* Having long, slender legs.

spin·dling [spind′ling] *adj.* Unusually tall and thin.

spin·dly [spind′lē] *adj.* **spin·dli·er, spin·dli·est** Spindling.

spin·drift [spin′drift′] *n.* Spray blown over the water from the crests of waves.

spine [spīn] *n.* 1 The spinal column; backbone. 2 The main support of something, as the back of a bound book. 3 A hard, pointed growth on a plant or animal, as a thorn on hawthorn or a porcupine's quill.

spine·less [spīn′lis] *adj.* 1 Having no spine or backbone. 2 Without spines. 3 Cowardly.

spin·et [spin′it] *n.* A small harpsichord or low upright piano.

spin·na·ker [spin′ə·kər] *n.* A large, bellying, triangular sail, often set on the other side of the mast from the mainsail of a racing yacht when sailing before the wind.

spin·ner·et [spin′ə·ret′] *n.* An organ, as of spiders and silkworms, by which fine thread is spun for webs or cocoons.

spin·ney [spin′ē] *n., pl.* **spin·neys** *British* A small wooded area; thicket.

spinning jenny An early type of spinning machine on which one person could spin several threads at once.

spinning wheel A device for spinning yarn or thread, consisting of a spindle rotated by a large wheel and operated by a treadle.

Spinning wheel

spin-off [spin′ôf′] *n.* Something derived from an earlier product, work, or enterprise: a successful TV series that led to several *spin-offs* starring characters who had minor roles in the first show.

spin·ster [spin′stər] *n.* An unmarried woman, especially one no longer young; old maid.

spin·y [spī′nē] *adj.* **spin·i·er, spin·i·est** 1 Like a spine. 2 Having spines; thorny.

spiny anteater Another name for ECHIDNA.

spiny lobster A crustacean that looks and tastes somewhat like a true lobster but has a spiny back and lacks enlarged claws.

spir·a·cle [spir′ə·kəl *or* spī′rə·kəl] *n.* An opening through which various animals breathe, as those on an insect's sides or the one on top of a whale's head.

spi·ral [spī′rəl] *n., adj., v.* **spi·raled** or **spi·ralled, spi·ral·ing** or **spi·ral·ling** 1 *n.* A curve traced by a point that moves in a plane and around a fixed center from which its distance continuously increases or decreases. 2 *n.* A curve resembling the thread of a screw; helix. 3 *adj.* Winding or curving like a spiral: a *spiral* staircase; a *spiral* path. 4 *v.* To take or cause to take a spiral path or form. **—spi′ral·ly** *adv.*

spire[1] [spīr] *n.* 1 The pointed top, as of a tower or steeple. 2 Something that looks like a spire, as a mountain peak.

spire[2] [spīr] *n.* 1 A spiral or coil. 2 A single turn of a spiral or coil. 3 The upper part of a spiral shell.

spi·ril·lum [spī·ril′əm] *n., pl.* **spi·ril·lums** or **spi·ril·la** [spī·ril′ə] Any of a group of active bacteria whose rodlike bodies are twisted into spirals.

spir·it [spir′it] 1 *n.* The life-giving force within a living thing; especially, a person's soul. 2 *n.* A divine being, such as God or an angel. 3 *n.* Any of various supernatural beings, as ghosts, goblins, or elves. 4 *adj. use*: the *spirit* world. 5 *n.* Energy; vitality; liveliness: a horse with *spirit.* 6 *n.* A person considered as a vital force: the moving *spirit* of the town. 7 *n.* (*pl.*) State of mind; mood: The news raised our *spirits.* 8 *n.* A widely held feeling or tendency: a *spirit* of rebellion. 9 *n.* Loyalty or devotion: school *spirit.* 10 *n.* Real intent rather than outward form: the *spirit* of the law. 11 *n.* (*pl.*) Strong alcoholic liquor. 12 *n.* (*pl.*) A concentrated substance drawn out or distilled from another: *spirits* of turpentine. 13 *n.* (*pl.*) A solution in alcohol: *spirits* of camphor. 14 *v.* To carry off secretly or mysteriously.

spir·it·ed [spir′it·id] *adj.* 1 Full of spirit; lively; vigorous: a *spirited* debate. 2 Having a specified kind of spirit or nature: a *mean-spirited* person. **—spir′it·ed·ly** *adv.* **—spir′it·ed·ness** *n.*

spirit lamp A lamp that burns alcohol or a similar fuel.

spir·it·less [spir′it·lis] *adj.* Lacking vigor, courage, or enthusiasm; listless.

spir·i·tu·al [spir′i·cho͞o·əl] 1 *adj.* Of, like, or having to do with the soul or spirit. 2 *adj.* Religious: a *spiritual* life or person; *spiritual* leaders. 3 *n.* A religious folk song originating among the Blacks of the southern U.S. **—spir·i·tu·al·i·ty** [spir′i·cho͞o·al′ə·tē] *n.* **—spir′i·tu·al·ly** *adv.*

spir·i·tu·al·ism [spir′i·cho͞o·əl·iz′əm] *n.* The belief that the spirits of the dead communicate with the living. **—spir′i·tu·al·ist** *n.*

spir·i·tu·al·ize [spir′i·cho͞o·ə·līz′] *v.* **spir·i·tu·al·ized, spir·i·tu·al·iz·ing** To make spiritual. **—spir·i·tu·al·i·za·tion** [spir′i·cho͞o·ə·lə·zā′shən] *n.*

spir·i·tu·ous [spir′i·cho͞o·əs] *adj.* Containing alcohol, especially distilled alcohol: *spirituous* liquors.

spi·ro·chete or **spi·ro·chaete** [spī′rə·kēt′] *n.* Any of a group of bacteria having flexible, corkscrew-shaped bodies.

spi·ro·gy·ra [spī′rə·jī′rə] *n.* A kind of algae commonly found in ponds.

spirt [spûrt] *n., v.* Another spelling of SPURT.

spit[1] [spit] *v.* **spat** or **spit, spit·ting,** *n.* 1 *v.* To blow or force out saliva or other matter from the mouth. 2 *n.* Spittle; saliva. 3 *n.* An act of spitting. 4 *v.* To throw out or utter violently: to *spit* out a reply. 5 *v.* To hiss or sputter, as does an angry cat. **—spit and image** or **spitting image** *informal* An exact likeness: She is the *spit and image* of her sister.

S

a	add	**i**	it	**o͝o**	took	**oi**	oil
ā	ace	**ī**	ice	**o͞o**	pool	**ou**	pout
â	care	**o**	odd	**u**	up	**ng**	ring
ä	palm	**ō**	open	**û**	burn	**th**	thin
e	end	**ô**	order	**yo͞o**	fuse	**th**	this
ē	equal					**zh**	vision

ə = a in *above* e in *sicken* i in *possible* o in *melon* u in *circus*

spit² [spit] *n., v.* **spit·ted, spit·ting** 1 *n.* A rod on which meat is speared and roasted. 2 *v.* To pierce with or as if with a spit. 3 *n.* A narrow point of land jutting from a shore.

spit·ball [spit′bôl′] *n.* 1 A little ball of moistened paper for throwing. 2 An illegal baseball pitch thrown with spit or sweat on the ball.

spite [spīt] *n., v.* **spit·ed, spit·ing** 1 *n.* Bitter resentment that leads to mean actions; ill will: The remark was made out of *spite.* 2 *v.* To show spite toward; try to hurt: It was said just to *spite* you. **—in spite of** Despite; notwithstanding: *In spite of* all their troubles, they were always cheerful.

spite·ful [spīt′fəl] *adj.* 1 Filled with spite. 2 Prompted by spite: a *spiteful* act. **—spite′ful·ly** *adv.* **—spite′ful·ness** *n.*

spit·fire [spit′fīr′] *n.* A quick-tempered, fiery person.

spit·tle [spit′(ə)l] *n.* The fluid secreted in the mouth; saliva; spit.

spit·toon [spi·to͞on′] *n.* A receptacle to spit into.

spitz [spits] *n.* A small stocky dog having a thick, usually white coat, a pointed muzzle, and a bushy tail that curls over the back.

splash [splash] 1 *v.* To dash or spatter about: to *splash* mud. 2 *v.* To spatter, wet, or soil in this way: to *splash* a coat with mud. 3 *n.* The act or noise of splashing. 4 *n.* A mark resulting from a splash. 5 *v.* To move with a splash or splashes: The diver *splashed* into the pool. 6 *n. informal* A striking impression or success, especially in the phrase **make a splash**: The book *made* quite *a splash.*

splash·down [splash′doun′] *n.* The landing of a spacecraft on water.

splash·y [splash′ē] *adj.* **splash·i·er, splash·i·est** 1 Marked by or as if by splashes; blotchy. 2 *informal* Sensational; showy: a *splashy* sports car.

splat·ter [splat′ər] 1 *v.* To spatter or splash. 2 *n.* A spatter or splash.

splay [splā] 1 *adj.* Spread out or broad, especially in an awkward or ungainly way: *splay* feet. 2 *v.* To spread outward; open. 3 *n.* A slanted surface or beveled edge. 4 *v.* To make something, as a doorway or window opening, with a splay.

spleen [splēn] *n.* 1 An oval organ near the stomach that has certain effects on the character of the blood. 2 Bad temper; spite; rage: to vent one's *spleen* on a poor dog. ◆ The *spleen* was once thought to be the source of bad temper, low spirits, and spite.

splen·did [splen′did] *adj.* 1 Brilliant or magnificent; glorious: a *splendid* view of the sea. 2 *informal* Very good; excellent: I'm in *splendid* health. **—splen′did·ly** *adv.*

splen·dor [splen′dər] *n.* Brilliance or magnificence.

splen·dor·ous or **splen·drous** [splen′·d(ə·)rəs] *adj.* Full of splendor; brilliant or magnificent.

sple·net·ic [spli·net′ik] *adj.* 1 Of or having to do with the spleen. 2 Bad-tempered.

splice [splīs] *v.* **spliced, splic·ing,** *n.* 1 *v.* To join by interlacing, twisting together, overlapping, or grafting, so that a neat joint results: to *splice* pieces of timber. 2 *n.* A joint or union made by splicing: a rope *splice.* **—splic′er** *n.*

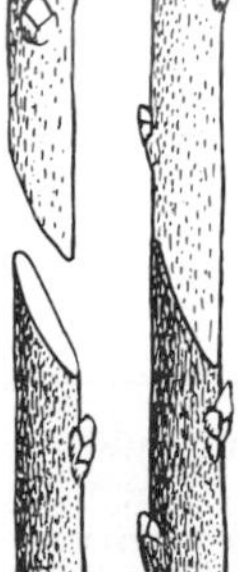

Two stems grafted by splicing

splint [splint] *n.* 1 A piece of wood or metal for holding the parts of a fractured bone in position. 2 A thin, flexible strip of wood, used for making baskets, chair bottoms, and other items. 3 A splinter.

splin·ter [splin′tər] 1 *n.* A thin, sharp piece of wood, glass, metal, or other material that has been split or torn off. 2 *v.* To split into thin, sharp fragments. **—splin′ter·y** *adj.*

split [split] *v.* **split, split·ting,** *n.* 1 *v.* To cut or break lengthwise or along the grain: to *split* logs; The rock *split* into two when it struck the ground. 2 *n.* A break or cleft. 3 *v.* To divide into shares: Let's *split* the cost. 4 *n.* The act of splitting. 5 *n.* A break in the unity of an organization. 6 *v.* To become divided or disunited: The club *split* on the proposal of higher dues. 7 *v.* To divide (one's vote or ballot) between political parties. 8 *n.* An acrobatic stunt in which one sits on the floor with the legs stretched in directly opposite directions. **—split hairs** To make overly fine or precise distinctions. **—split one's side** To laugh uproariously.

split infinitive An infinitive with a word or words placed between *to* and the verb, as in *to barely crawl* and *to more than equal.* ◆ Split infinitives are not grammatically incorrect, but most writers consider them clumsy and avoid them when an accurate and graceful alternative is available. *I expect to recover quickly* sounds and reads better than *I expect to quickly recover.*

split-lev·el [split′lev′əl] 1 *adj.* Having two or more floor levels that are separated by about half a story: a *split-level* house. 2 *n.* A split-level building.

split second An instant.

split·ting [split′ing] *adj.* Intense; piercing: a *splitting* headache.

splotch [sploch] 1 *n.* A spot, soil, or stain. 2 *v.* To spot or soil. **—splotch′y** *adj.*

splurge [splûrj] *n., v.* **splurged, splurg·ing** *informal* 1 *n.* An act of spending money lavishly or wastefully. 2 *v.* To spend money lavishly or wastefully. 3 *v.* To indulge oneself: to *splurge* on a complete new wardrobe.

splut·ter [splut′ər] 1 *v.* To make explosive sounds, one after the other; hiss; spit. 2 *v.* To speak quickly and incoherently, as from surprise or anger. 3 *n.* The sound of spluttering.

spoil [spoil] *v.* **spoiled** or **spoilt, spoil·ing,** *n.* 1 *v.* To lessen the quality, value, or usefulness of; damage or destroy: to *spoil* supper by overcooking it; to *spoil* film by exposing it to too much light. 2 *v.* To become damaged or rotten, as food: Milk *spoils* if not kept refrigerated. 3 *v.* To weaken or destroy the character of (a child) by giving in to his or her demands too often. 4 *n.* (*pl.*) Things seized and taken over by force; plunder; loot: the *spoils* of war. 5 *n.* (*pl.*) Public offices that people are appointed to as a reward for services to a victorious political party. **—be spoiling for** To have a great desire for.

spoil·age [spoi′lij] *n.* 1 The act or process of spoiling. 2 The condition of being spoiled. 3 Food or other material that has spoiled.

spoil·sport [spoil′spôrt′] *n.* Someone who spoils the pleasure of others.

spoils system The practice of a victorious political party of making appointment to public office a reward for service to the party.

spoilt [spoilt] An alternative past tense and past participle of SPOIL.

spoke[1] [spōk] **1** *n.* One of the rods or bars that connect the rim of a wheel to the hub. **2** *v.* To provide with spokes.

spoke[2] [spōk] Past tense of SPEAK.

spo·ken [spō′kən] **1** Past participle of SPEAK. **2** *adj.* Not written; said aloud. **3** *adj.* Speaking or said in a certain way: a *smooth-spoken* person.

spoke·shave [spōk′shāv′] *n.* A plane with a blade set between two handles; drawknife.

spokes·man [spōks′mən] *n., pl.* **spokes·men** [spōks′mən] A person who speaks on behalf of another or others.

spokes·per·son [spōks′pûr′sən] *n.* A person who speaks on behalf of another or other persons.

spokes·wom·an [spōks′wo͝om′ən] *n., pl.* **spokes·wom·en** [spōks′wim′in] A woman who speaks on behalf of another or other persons.

sponge [spunj] *n., v.* **sponged, spong·ing** **1** *n.* A simple water animal that lives in a colony with others of its kind. **2** *n.* Its dried skeleton or network of light, tough, elastic fibers, used in washing and cleaning because of its power to absorb water. **3** *n.* Any spongelike substance that is used as an absorbent. **4** *v.* To wipe, wet, or clean with a sponge. **5** *v. informal* To live or get things without cost or at the expense of others. **—spong′er** *n.*

Typical sponges

sponge cake A light cake made of beaten eggs, sugar, and flour, containing no shortening.

sponge rubber A porous, spongelike rubber used to fill cushions and pillows.

spong·y [spun′jē] *adj.* **spong·i·er, spong·i·est** Of or like a sponge; elastic and porous.

spon·sor [spon′sər] **1** *n.* A person who takes responsibility for some other person or for a thing, as a bill in a legislature. **2** *n.* A person who assumes responsibility for the welfare of some other person, especially in regard to religious instruction; godparent. **3** *n.* A business firm that pays for a radio or television program on which it advertises. **4** *v.* To act as a sponsor for. **—spon′·sor·ship** *n.*

spon·ta·ne·i·ty [spon′tə·nē′ə·tē] *n.* The quality or condition of being spontaneous.

spon·ta·ne·ous [spon·tā′nē·əs] *adj.* **1** Done naturally from impulse; not planned: a *spontaneous* dance. **2** Arising from or caused by inner forces with no outside cause. **—spon·ta′ne·ous·ly** *adv.*

spontaneous combustion The bursting into flame of a substance because of heat produced by rapid oxidation within the substance itself.

spoof [spo͞of] *informal* **1** *n.* A trick, joke, or humorous exaggeration. **2** *v.* To make mild fun of.

spook [spo͝ok] **1** *n. informal* A ghost. **2** *v. informal* To frighten; scare. **3** *n. slang* A spy.

spook·y [spo͞o′kē] *adj. informal* **spook·i·er, spook·i·est** **1** Ghostly. **2** Haunted.

spool [spo͞ol] **1** *n.* A cylinder of wood or metal with a rim at each end, on which thread, yarn, or wire is wound. **2** *v.* To wind on a spool.

spoon [spo͞on] **1** *n.* An implement with a small, shallow bowl at the end of a handle, used to lift, stir, or measure food or drink. **2** *v.* To lift up or out with a spoon.

spoon·bill [spo͞on′bil′] *n.* A long-legged wading bird with a long, flat, spoon-shaped bill.

Spoonbill

spoon·er·ism [spo͞o′nə·riz′əm] *n.* A mistake in speech in which sounds, usually initial sounds, in two or more words are transposed. ◆ *Spoonerism* was named for William A. Spooner (1844-1930), an English educator who occasionally amused students at Oxford University with such slips of the tongue. He is reported to have once said "God bless our queer old dean" when he meant "God bless our dear old queen."

spoon·ful [spo͞on′fo͝ol′] *n., pl.* **spoon·fuls** As much as a spoon will hold.

spoor [spo͝or] *n.* A track; trail, especially a footprint or other trace of a wild animal.

spo·rad·ic [spô·rad′ik] *adj.* Occurring here and there or now and then; occasional: *sporadic* bursts of applause. **—spo·rad′i·cal·ly** *adv.*

spo·ran·gi·um [spə·ran′jē·əm] *n., pl.* **spo·ran·gi·a** [spə·ran′jē·ə] A plant structure in which spores are produced, as in ferns and fungi.

spore [spôr] *n.* A small cell that can grow into a new plant or animal. Ferns, fungi, and algae reproduce by means of spores.

spore case A sporangium.

spor·ran [spôr′ən *or* spor′ən] *n.* A pouch, usually fur-covered, that is traditionally worn in front of a kilt by Scottish Highlanders.

sport [spôrt] **1** *n.* Anything generally amusing; pastime; play: It will be good *sport* to have a picnic. **2** *v.* To amuse oneself; play; frolic: Children like to *sport* in the water. **3** *n.* A game or contest, especially an outdoor or athletic game, as baseball, football, or track. **4** *adj.* For informal use: a *sport* coat. **5** *v. informal* To display or wear: to *sport* a new sweater. **6** *n.* A person thought of in reference to an ability to get along with others or to a sense of fair play: a good *sport*. **7** *n. informal* A person who lives a gay, lively life and is willing to take chances. **8** *n.* An animal or plant that shows a sudden, spontaneous difference from the normal type; mutation. **—in sport** or **for sport** In fun; for a joke. **—make sport of** To make fun of; mock.

sport·ing [spôr′ting] *adj.* **1** Related to, used in, or enjoying sports. **2** Observing the rules of fair play. **3** Interested in or betting on sports: a *sporting* person. **4** Involving the risk of loss or failure: a *sporting* chance.

spor·tive [spôr′tiv] *adj.* Of, having to do with, or fond of sport or play; playful; frolicsome.

sports [spôrts] *adj.* For informal use; casual: *sports* clothes.

a	add	**i**	it	**o͝o**	took	**oi**	oil
ā	ace	**ī**	ice	**o͞o**	pool	**ou**	pout
â	care	**o**	odd	**u**	up	**ng**	ring
ä	palm	**ō**	open	**û**	burn	**th**	thin
e	end	**ô**	order	**yo͞o**	fuse	**t͟h**	this
ē	equal					**zh**	vision

ə = { a in *above* e in *sicken* i in *possible* o in *melon* u in *circus* }

S

sports car A small, fast car, usually with two seats and often an open top.
sports·cast [spôrts′kast′] *n.* A television or radio broadcast of a sports event. **—sports′cast′er** *n.*
sports·man [spôrts′mən] *n., pl.* **sports·men** [spôrts′·mən] 1 A person who is active or interested in sports. 2 A person who believes in fair play.
sports·man·like [spôrts′mən·līk′] *adj.* 1 Having to do with sportsmen. 2 Abiding by the rules of fair play; honorable; generous.
sports·man·ship [spôrts′mən·ship′] *n.* Fair play or sportsmanlike conduct, especially in sports.
sports·wear [spôrts′wâr′] *n.* Clothing designed for sports and for informal wear.
sports·wom·an [spôrts′wo͝om′ən] *n., pl.* **sports·wom·en** [spôrts′wim′in] 1 A woman who is active or interested in sports. 2 A woman who believes in fair play.
sports·writ·er [spôrts′rī′tər] *n.* A journalist who writes about sports.
sport·y [spôr′tē] *adj.* **sport·i·er, sport·i·est** 1 Characteristic of a person who is a sport or who enjoys sports. 2 Casual; informal: *sporty* clothing. 3 Too informal or colorful; flashy. **—sport′i·ly** *adv.* **—sport′i·ness** *n.*
spot [spot] *n., v.* **spot·ted, spot·ting,** *adj.* 1 *n.* A small part of a surface that is different from the rest, as in color or feeling: a white dog with black *spots*; a sore *spot.* 2 *n.* A soiled place; stain. 3 *v.* To make or become marked or soiled with spots. 4 *n.* A stain or blemish on one's character or reputation. 5 *n.* A particular place or locality: a seaside *spot.* 6 *v.* To place; locate; station: to *spot* an usher at each exit. 7 *v. informal* To recognize; see. 8 *v. informal* To give (an advantage) to someone: We *spotted* them five points. 9 *adj.* Ready; on delivery: to pay *spot* cash. **—hit the spot** *slang* To fill a need or hunger. **—in a spot** *slang* In a difficult or embarrassing situation. **—on the spot** 1 At once; immediately. 2 At the very place. 3 *slang* In trouble or difficulty.
spot-check [spot′chek′] *v.* To make a random check.
spot check A random check or inspection.
spot·less [spot′lis] *adj.* Free from spots; very clean: *spotless* linens. **—spot′less·ly** *adv.*
spot·light [spot′līt′] *n.* 1 A circle of powerful light thrown on a stage to bring a performer into clearer view. 2 The lamp that produces such a light. 3 Public notice; center of attention: to be in the *spotlight.*
spot·ted [spot′id] *adj.* 1 Discolored in spots. 2 Marked with spots, as certain animals.
spot·ty [spot′ē] *adj.* **spot·ti·er, spot·ti·est** 1 Having many spots. 2 Uneven; not uniform in quality: *spotty* work.
spouse [spous *or* spouz] *n.* A husband or wife.
spout [spout] 1 *v.* To flow or pour out in large quantities and with force, as a liquid under pressure. 2 *n.* A stream or jet of liquid. 3 *v.* To throw out or discharge (a liquid): The volcano *spouted* lava. 4 *n.* A tube or channel from which liquid can flow. 5 *v. informal* To speak pompously for a long time.
sprain [sprān] 1 *n.* A violent twisting or straining of the ligaments around a joint. 2 *n.* The condition due to such an injury. 3 *v.* To cause a sprain in; wrench; twist: to *sprain* one's ankle.
sprang [sprang] An alternative past tense of SPRING: He *sprang* to his feet.
sprat [sprat] *n.* A small fish like the herring, found off the Atlantic coast of Europe.
sprawl [sprôl] 1 *v.* To sit or lie with the legs and arms stretched out in an ungraceful or relaxed way. 2 *v.* To be stretched out awkwardly or sloppily. 3 *v.* To spread out awkwardly or unevenly, as handwriting. 4 *n.* The act or position of sprawling: The puppy lay in a *sprawl.*
spray[1] [sprā] 1 *n.* Water or other liquid sent out in fine drops. 2 *n.* A device for sending out such fine drops, as an atomizer. 3 *n.* Anything resembling a spray of liquid: a *spray* of bullets. 4 *v.* To send out (a liquid) in fine drops: Atomizers *spray* perfume. 5 *v.* To apply spray to. **—spray′er** *n.*
spray[2] [sprā] *n.* A small branch of a tree or plant with its leaves and flowers or berries, either growing or cut off.
spray gun A device that resembles a gun and shoots out liquids such as paint or insecticides in a spray by means of air pressure.
spread [spred] *v.* **spread, spread·ing,** *n.* 1 *v.* To open or unfold to full width or extent, as wings or sails. 2 *v.* To extend or stretch out: The city *spread* out before us. 3 *n.* The limit to which something can extend or be spread, as a sail or a bird's wings. 4 *v.* To distribute, as over a surface: to *spread* papers on the floor. 5 *v.* To cover, as with a thin layer. 6 *n.* Something to spread on bread, crackers, or other food. 7 *v.* To move or force apart or farther apart: to *spread* one's fingers. 8 *v.* To extend over a period of time: to *spread* payments over six months. 9 *v.* To make or become more widely known or active: to *spread* rumors. 10 *n.* The act of spreading. 11 *v.* To set (as a table) for a meal. 12 *v.* To arrange or place on a table or other serving area: to *spread* a meal. 13 *n. informal* A meal, especially a lavish one; feast. 14 *n.* A cloth or covering for a bed.
spread·er [spred′ər] *n.* A person or thing that spreads, as a small knife for spreading butter.
spread·sheet [spred′shēt] *n., pl.* **spread·sheets** A type of computer program used in financial calculations and predictions. Such programs organize numerical data so users can see how a change in one factor might affect others.
spree [sprē] *n.* A lively time of unrestrained activity: a shopping *spree.*
spri·er [sprī′ər] Comparative of SPRY.
spri·est [sprī′ist] Superlative of SPRY.
sprig [sprig] *n.* A shoot or small branch of a tree or plant.
spright·ly [sprīt′lē] *adj.* **spright·li·er, spright·li·est** Brisk; gay; spirited: The young performers danced a *sprightly* jig. **—spright′li·ness** *n.*
spring [spring] *v.* **sprang** or **sprung, sprung, spring·ing,** *n.* 1 *v.* To move or rise suddenly and rapidly; leap; jump: The deer *sprang* across the creek. 2 *n.* A leaping up or forward suddenly; jump; bound. 3 *v.* To move suddenly, as by elastic reaction: The jaws of the trap *sprang* shut. 4 *n.* The quality of being elastic: the *spring* of a bow. 5 *v.* To cause to act, open, close, or snap suddenly: to *spring* a trap. 6 *n.* A device, as a coiled steel wire, that gives under pressure and returns to its normal shape when the pressure is taken away. 7 *v.* To become warped or bent, as the door of an automobile. 8 *v.* To come up or appear suddenly; begin to grow: New towns have *sprung* up. 9 *v.* To cause to happen, become known, or appear suddenly: to *spring* a surprise. 10 *v.* To originate; proceed, as from a source. 11 *n.* A source or origin. 12 *n.* The season of the year when plants

begin to grow again. It comes between winter and summer. **13** *adj. use: spring* weather. **14** *n.* A flow of water out of the ground. **—spring a leak** To develop a leak; begin to leak.

spring·board [spring′bôrd′] *n.* A flexible board that springs back into place, used by athletes and acrobats as an aid in tumbling, leaping, or diving.

spring·bok [spring′bok′] *n.* A small southern African gazelle that can leap high in the air.

Springbok

spring fever A lazy or yearning feeling that sometimes affects people when spring weather first arrives.

spring·tide [spring′·tīd′] *n.* The springtime.

spring tide The tide that comes at or shortly after the new or full moon when the rise and fall are greatest.

spring·time [spring′tīm′] *n.* The season of spring.

spring·y [spring′ē] *adj.* **spring·i·er, spring·i·est** Able to snap back; elastic.

sprin·kle [spring′kəl] *v.* **sprin·kled, sprin·kling,** *n.* **1** *v.* To scatter in small drops or particles. **2** *v.* To spray or cover by sprinkling: to *sprinkle* a salad with vinegar. **3** *v.* To fall or rain in scattered drops. **4** *n.* A falling in drops or particles. **5** *n.* A light rain. **6** *n.* A small amount.

sprin·kler [spring′klər] *n.* **1** A person or thing that sprinkles. **2** An outlet in a hose or pipe that releases water in a scattered spray. A **sprinkler system** in a building is a series of water pipes with outlets designed to open automatically and put out a fire.

sprin·kling [spring′kling] *n.* A small number or quantity: a *sprinkling* of snow on the ground.

sprint [sprint] **1** *n.* A short race run at top speed. **2** *v.* To run fast, as in a sprint. **—sprint′er** *n.*

sprit [sprit] *n.* On sailboats, a small pole, or spar, that reaches at a slant from a mast to support and spread a fore-and-aft sail.

sprite [sprīt] *n.* A fairy, elf, goblin, or similar creature.

sprit·sail [sprit′səl *or* sprit′sāl′] *n.* A sail held out by a sprit.

sprock·et [sprok′it] *n.* **1** One of a set of teeth, as on the rim of a wheel, for engaging with the links of a chain, as on a bicycle. **2** A wheel with such teeth.

sprout [sprout] **1** *v.* To put out shoots; begin to grow, as a plant. **2** *n.* A new shoot or bud on a plant. **3** *v.* To cause to sprout: This warm rain will *sprout* the seeds you planted.

spruce[1] [sprōōs] *n.* **1** One of various evergreen trees related to the pine, having leaves shaped like needles and bearing cones. **2** The soft wood of such a tree.

spruce[2] [sprōōs] *adj.* **spruc·er, spruc·est,** *v.* **spruced, spruc·ing** **1** *adj.* Neat; trim; smart; dapper. **2** *v.* To make (oneself) spruce.

sprung [sprung] Past participle and alternative past tense of SPRING.

spry [sprī] *adj.* **spri·er** or **spry·er, spri·est** or **spry·est** Quick and agile. **—spry′ly** *adv.*

spud [spud] *n.* **1** A tool like a spade with a narrow blade or prongs for digging out or cutting the roots of weeds. **2** *informal* A potato.

spume [spyōōm] *n., v.* **spumed, spum·ing** **1** *n.* Froth; foam; scum. **2** *v.* To foam; froth.

spu·mo·ni or **spu·mo·ne** [spōō·mō′nē] *n.* Italian ice cream consisting of several differently flavored layers containing bits of candied fruits and nuts.

spun [spun] Past tense and past participle of SPIN: The top *spun.*

spun glass Another name for FIBERGLASS.

spunk [spungk] *n. informal* Courage; pluck.

spunk·y [spungk′ē] *adj.* **spunk·i·er, spunk·i·est** *informal* Full of courage; spirited.

spun sugar Another name for COTTON CANDY.

spur [spûr] *n., v.* **spurred, spur·ring** **1** *n.* A device worn on a horseman's heel, having a point or a series of sharp points on a wheel. It is used to prick and urge on a horse. **2** *v.* To prick with spurs. **3** *n.* Anything that urges on or goads to action; incentive: The desire for fame was the *spur* that drove the young performer on. **4** *v.* To urge on; goad: A deadline *spurred* the crew to work harder. **5** *n.* A ridge sticking out from a mountain, or a line of mountains sticking out from a mountain range. **6** *n.* A sharp, stiff spine, as on the leg of a rooster. **7** *n.* A short branch running out from the main line of a railroad. **—on the spur of the moment** Hastily; on impulse; without planning. **—win one's spurs** To gain honor or distinction.

Spur

spu·ri·ous [spyŏŏr′ē·əs] *adj.* Not genuine; false; counterfeit: a *spurious* antique. **—spu′ri·ous·ly** *adv.* **—spu′ri·ous·ness.** *n.*

spurn [spûrn] *v.* **1** To reject with contempt; scorn: We *spurned* their attempts to be friendly. **2** To drive away, as by kicking.

spurt [spûrt] **1** *v.* To gush forth in a sudden stream or jet: Water *spurted* from the hose. **2** *n.* A sudden gush of liquid. **3** *v.* To make a sudden and extreme effort: Racers *spurt* near the finish line. **4** *n.* A sudden, brief burst of effort: I do my chores in *spurts.* ◆ *Spurt* was once spelled and pronounced *sprit.* Over the years the [r] and the [i] sounds were reversed, and the word came to be pronounced and spelled *spirt,* which later became *spurt.*

sput·nik [sput′nik *or* spŏŏt′nik] *n.* Any of several early artificial earth satellites launched by the Soviet Union. Sputnik I, launched on October 4, 1957, was the first space vehicle put into orbit around the earth. ◆ *Sputnik* comes from a Russian word meaning *traveling companion* or *satellite.*

sput·ter [sput′ər] **1** *v.* To make a series of spitting or hissing sounds. **2** *v.* To spit out particles of saliva or food from the mouth, as when speaking excitedly. **3** *v.* To speak in a confused, excited, or

a	add	**i**	it	**ŏŏ**	took	**oi**	oil
ā	ace	**ī**	ice	**ōō**	pool	**ou**	pout
â	care	**o**	odd	**u**	up	**ng**	ring
ä	palm	**ō**	open	**û**	burn	**th**	thin
e	end	**ô**	order	**yōō**	fuse	**th**	this
ē	equal					**zh**	vision

ə = { a in *above* e in *sicken* i in *possible* / o in *melon* u in *circus* }

S

angry way. **4** *n.* Confused, angry, or excited talk. **5** *n.* The act or sound of sputtering.

spu·tum [spyo͞o′təm] *n.* Saliva, often mixed with other matter coughed up from the lungs.

spy [spī] *n., pl.* **spies,** *v.* **spied, spy·ing** **1** *n.* A person employed by a government to discover military or other important secrets of an enemy country. **2** *n.* A person who watches others secretly. **3** *v.* To keep watch closely or secretly; act as a spy. **4** *v.* To catch sight of; see: We could *spy* the town from the hill. **5** *v.* To look for or find by careful or secret investigation: to *spy* out a hiding place.

spy·glass [spī′glas′] *n.* A small telescope.

sq. **1** squadron. **2** square.

squab [skwob] *n.* A young pigeon.

squab·ble [skwob′əl] *v.* **squab·bled, squab·bling** **1** *v.* To have a petty quarrel; wrangle. **2** *n.* A petty quarrel; wrangle: The youngsters had their *squabbles* but were really good friends. **—squab′·bler** *n.*

squad [skwod] *n.* **1** A small group of people organized to do something. **2** A small unit or group, as of soldiers or police officers. **3** A team.

squad car A car used by police for patrolling, equipped with a special kind of radio for communicating with headquarters.

squad·ron [skwod′rən] *n.* **1** In the U.S. Navy, a group or unit of vessels or aircraft. **2** In the U.S. Air Force, a unit of eight or more aircraft. **3** A unit of cavalry. **4** Any group of people organized to do something.

squal·id [skwol′id] *adj.* **1** Dirty and wretched from poverty or neglect: a *squalid* neighborhood. **2** Sordid; degraded: a *squalid* way of living.

squall[1] [skwôl] **1** *n.* A sudden, violent burst of wind, often accompanied by rain or snow. **2** *v.* To blow a squall; storm. **—squall′y** *adj.*

squall[2] [skwôl] **1** *v.* To cry loudly, as an angry child. **2** *n.* A loud, harsh, screaming cry.

squall·y [skwô′lē] *adj.* **squall·i·er, squall·i·est** Marked by sudden bursts of wind; gusty.

squal·or [skwol′ər] *n.* A squalid condition; filth, wretched poverty, or degradation.

squa·mous [skwā′məs] *adj.* Consisting of or covered with scales; scaly.

squan·der [skwon′dər] *v.* To spend (as money or time) wastefully.

square [skwâr] *n., adj., v.* **squared, squar·ing** **1** *n.* A flat figure having four equal sides and four right angles. **2** *n.* Any object, part, surface, or arrangement that has this shape. **3** *adj.* Being or resembling a square in shape: a *square* field. **4** *v.* To make square in form: to *square* a block of wood. **5** *v.* To mark off in squares: to *square* off a sheet of paper. **6** *v.* To shape or adjust so as to form or suggest a right angle: *Square* your shoulders. **7** *adj.* Forming a right angle: a *square* corner. **8** *n.* An instrument in the shape of an L or T, having one or more right angles that may be used to lay out or measure other right angles. **9** *adj.* Being the product of two lengths at right angles to one another and so representing area: A *square* mile is the area of a square one mile long and one mile wide. **10** *v.* To multiply (a number) by itself: 7 *squared* is 49. **11** *n.* The product of a number multiplied by itself: The *square* of 6 is 36. **12** *n.* An area in a city or town bounded on four sides by streets and often serving as a park. **13** *n.* An open area in a city or town formed by the intersection of several streets. **14** *adj.* Fair; just; honest: a *square* deal. **15** *adj.* Direct or straight. **16** *v.* To conform; agree: Your claim *squares* with the facts. **17** *v.* To make even; settle: to *square* accounts. **18** *adj.* Even; settled: Accounts between us are now *square.* **19** *adj. informal* Good and satisfying: said about a meal. **20** *n. slang* A person considered as a conformist or as one behind the times. **21** *adj. slang* Conventional or behind the times. **—on the square** **1** At right angles. **2** *informal* In a fair and honest manner. **—square off** To take a position for attack or defense. **—square oneself** *informal* To make up for something one did that was wrong: I tried to *square myself* for not arriving on time. **—square peg in a round hole** A person who does not fit in well. **—square′ly** *adv.* **—square′ness** *n.*

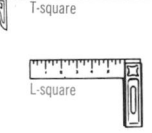

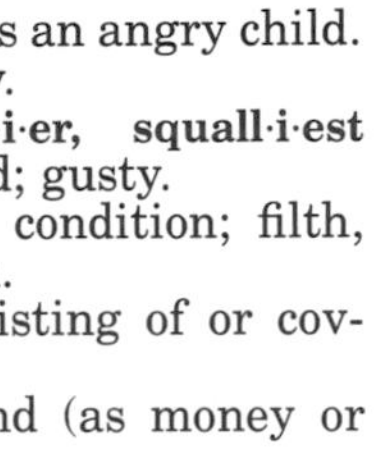

square dance *U.S.* A dance in which four couples form a square and then do various steps.

square knot A common double knot made by interlacing the ends of two cords, then interlacing them again in the opposite direction.

square measure A unit or system of units used to measure area.

square-rigged [skwâr′rigd′] *adj.* Fitted with four-cornered sails extended on yards fastened at the middle across the mast.

A square-rigged ship

square-rig·ger [skwâr′·rig′ər] *n.* A square-rigged ship.

square root The factor of a number which, multiplied by itself, gives the original number: The *square root* of 25 is 5.

squash[1] [skwosh] *n.* The fleshy, edible fruit of various trailing plants of the gourd family. ◆ *Squash* comes from an Algonquian Indian word.

squash[2] [skwosh] **1** *v.* To crush or become crushed into a pulp or soft mass. **2** *n.* A crushed mass. **3** *n.* The sudden fall of a heavy, soft, or bursting body, or the sound it makes. **4** *n.* The sound made by walking through ooze or mud. **5** *v.* To press or squeeze: So many people *squashed* into the auditorium that it became very hot and stuffy. **6** *v.* To put down; quell or suppress: to *squash* a revolt. **7** *n.* A game like tennis or handball, played on an indoor court with rackets and a ball.

squash·y [skwosh′ē] *adj.* **squash·i·er, squash·i·est** **1** Soft, moist, and mushy: *squashy* earth. **2** Easily squashed: a soft, *squashy* tomato.

squat [skwot] *v.* **squat·ted** or **squat, squat·ting,** *n., adj.* **1** *v.* To crouch and sit on one's heels, with the knees bent and the weight usually on the balls of the feet. **2** *v.* To sit on the ground with the legs drawn close to the body. **3** *n.* The act of squatting. **4** *n.* A squatting position. **5** *adj.* Crouching. **6** *adj.* Short and thick in shape. **7** *v.* To settle on a piece of land without owning it, paying for it, or having a right to it. **8** *v.* To settle on government land in accordance with laws that will eventually give title to it.

squat·ter [skwot′ər] *n.* **1** A person or animal that squats. **2** A person who settles on land without owning it, paying for it, or having a right to it.

squaw [skwô] *n.* An American Indian woman or wife. ◆ *Squaw* comes from an Algonquian Indian word meaning *woman.*
squawk [skwôk] 1 *v.* To give a shrill, harsh cry, as a parrot. 2 *n.* Such a shrill, harsh cry. 3 *v. slang* To complain or protest loudly. 4 *n. slang* A loud complaint or protest.
squeak [skwēk] 1 *n.* A thin, sharp, shrill sound. 2 *v.* To make a squeak, as a mouse or door. **—close squeak** or **narrow squeak** *informal* A narrow escape. **—squeak'y** *adj.*
squeal [skwēl] 1 *v.* To give a long, shrill, high-pitched cry, as a pig. 2 *n.* A cry like this. 3 *v. slang* To turn informer; tattle.
squeam·ish [skwē'mish] *adj.* 1 Easily made a little sick at the stomach. 2 Too easily disgusted or shocked; prudish. **—squeam'ish·ness** *n.*
squee·gee [skwē'jē] *n.* A tool with a handle and a crosspiece edged with rubber or leather, used to move a liquid over or off a surface, as in washing windows.

A squeegee

squeeze [skwēz] *v.* **squeezed, squeez·ing,** *n.* 1 *v.* To press hard upon or press together: to *squeeze* an orange. 2 *n.* A firm press. 3 *v.* To apply pressure: Don't *squeeze* so hard. 4 *v.* To yield to pressure: Wet cloth *squeezes* easily. 5 *v.* To push out by pressure: to *squeeze* juice from fruit; to *squeeze* contributions from the crowd. 6 *v.* To force or push; cram: Try to *squeeze* more into the suitcase. 7 *v.* To force one's way; push: to *squeeze* through a tight place. 8 *n.* The act of squeezing. 9 *v.* To hug; embrace. 10 *n.* A hug. **—squeez'er** *n.*
squelch [skwelch] *v. informal* To subdue or make silent, as with a crushing reply.
squib [skwib] *n.* 1 A small firework that explodes like a rocket after being thrown or rolled. 2 A broken firecracker that burns with a spitting sound. 3 A short speech or piece of writing that is witty and critical.
squid [skwid] *n., pl.* **squid** or **squids** A sea animal like the cuttlefish, but having a longer, thinner body, tail fins, and two of the ten arms around its mouth longer than the others.
squig·gle [skwig'əl] *n.* A short, irregularly twisting line or scrawl.
squint [skwint] 1 *v.* To look with half-closed eyes, as into bright light. 2 *n.* The act or habit of squinting. 3 *v.* To look sideways. 4 *n.* A hasty glance. 5 *v.* To be cross-eyed. 6 *n.* A cross-eyed condition.
squire [skwīr] *n., v.* **squired, squir·ing** 1 *n.* In England, a person who owns much land. 2 *n. U.S.* In small and rural areas, a title sometimes used for justices of the peace. 3 *n.* A young man who served as an attendant to a knight. 4 *n.* A person who escorts another person. 5 *v.* To escort (a person).
squirm [skwûrm] *v.* To bend and twist the body; wriggle, often from pain or nervousness.
squir·rel [skwûr'əl] *n.* 1 A small, furry animal that has a long bushy tail and sharp teeth and lives in trees. 2 The squirrel's fur.
squirt [skwûrt] 1 *v.* To come out or cause to come out in a thin stream or jet; spurt. 2 *v.* To wet by squirting: I *squirted* the flower beds with the hose. 3 *n.* A squirting or spurting. 4 *n.* A jet of liquid squirted out. 5 *n. informal* An impudent, usually young, person.
squish [skwish] *informal* 1 *v.* To crush or squash noisily. 2 *v.* To make a noise like that of mud being stepped on. 3 *n.* Such a noise.
Sr The symbol for the element strontium.
Sr. 1 senior. 2 Señor.
Sri Lan·kan [srē läng'kən] 1 Of or from Sri Lanka. 2 A person born in or a citizen of Sri Lanka.
SRO 1 single room occupancy. 2 standing room only.
S.S. steamship.
SSA Social Security Administration.
SSE south-southeast.
SSR or **S.S.R.** Soviet Socialist Republic.
SST supersonic transport.
SSW south-southwest.
st. or **St.** 1 statue. 2 strait. 3 street.
St. saint.
sta. or **Sta.** station.
stab [stab] *v.* **stabbed, stab·bing,** *n.* 1 *v.* To pierce or wound with a pointed weapon. 2 *v.* To thrust: to *stab* a pin into one's finger. 3 *v.* To give a wound or inflict pain with or as if with a pointed weapon: The insult *stabbed* like a dagger. 4 *n.* A thrust made with a pointed weapon. 5 *n.* A wound made by stabbing. 6 *n.* A sudden, sharp pain or feeling: a *stab* of conscience. 7 *n. informal* A try: to make a *stab* at painting pictures. **—stab in the back** To slander or injure in a treacherous or deceitful way. **—stab'ber** *n.*
sta·bil·i·ty [stə·bil'ə·tē] *n.* 1 A being stable; steadiness; balance. 2 Firmness of purpose or resolution. 3 Continued existence; permanence; durability.
sta·bi·lize [stā'bə·līz'] *v.* **sta·bi·lized, sta·bi·liz·ing** 1 To make firm or stable. 2 To keep steady; keep from changing: to *stabilize* prices. 3 To steady the motion of (an aircraft or ship) by means of a stabilizer. **—sta'bil·i·za'tion** *n.*
sta·bi·liz·er [stā'bə·lī'zər] *n.* 1 A person or thing that stabilizes. 2 A device or special construction to keep the motion of an aircraft or ship steady.
sta·ble[1] [stā'bəl] *adj.* **sta·bler, sta·blest** 1 Not easily moved or shaken; firm; fixed; steadfast. 2 Not changing; permanent; enduring. 3 Able to keep or to return to an original position.
sta·ble[2] [stā'bəl] *n., v.* **sta·bled, sta·bling** 1 *n.* A building set apart for sheltering and feeding horses or cattle. 2 *v.* To put or shelter in a stable: We made sure that the horses were *stabled* for the night. 3 *n.* A group of race horses belonging to a single owner.
stac·ca·to [stə·kä'tō] *adj., adv., n., pl.* **stac·ca·tos** 1 *adj.* Sounding for only part of its written value, as a musical note; cut short; disconnected. 2 *adv.* In a staccato manner: to play *staccato.* 3 *adj.*

a	add	**i**	it	**o͝o**	took	**oi**	oil		
ā	ace	**ī**	ice	**o͞o**	pool	**ou**	pout		
â	care	**o**	odd	**u**	up	**ng**	ring		
ä	palm	**ō**	open	**û**	burn	**th**	thin		
e	end	**ô**	order	**yo͞o**	fuse	**t͟h**	this		
ē	equal					**zh**	vision		

ə = {a in *above* e in *sicken* i in *possible*
 o in *melon* u in *circus*}

Using staccato notes. **4** *n.* A staccato style or passage.

stack [stak] **1** *n.* A large pile, as one of grain, hay, or straw, usually cone-shaped. **2** *n.* Any orderly pile or heap: a *stack* of coins. **3** *v.* To gather or place in a pile; pile up in a stack: to *stack* hay. **4** *n.* A group of rifles set upright and supporting one another. **5** *n.* (*pl.*) The part of a library where most of the books are shelved. **6** *n.* A chimney; smokestack. **7** *v.* To fix (playing cards) in advance in a secret and dishonest way: to lose at poker because the deck had been *stacked*. **—stack up 1** To add up. **2** To compare. **—stack′er** *n.*

sta·di·um [stā′dē·əm] *n., pl.* **sta·di·ums** or **sta·di·a** [stā′dē·ə] A structure with tiers of seats built around an open field, used for sports events and meetings.

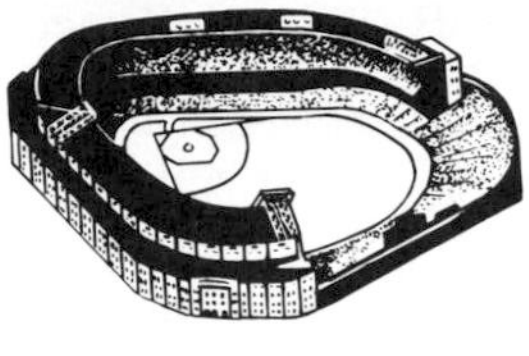

Stadium

staff [staf] *n., pl.* **staffs;** *for def. 1, also* **staves** [stāvz] **1** *n.* A stick or pole carried as an aid in walking or climbing, as a weapon, or as an emblem of authority. **2** *n.* Something that supports or maintains: Bread is the *staff* of life. **3** *n.* A group of people who work together under a manager or chief: the *staff* of a hotel. **4** *v.* To provide or supply with a staff, as of workers. **5** *n.* In music, the five horizontal lines and the spaces between them on which music is written.

stag [stag] **1** *n.* A fully grown male deer. **2** *n.* A person who attends a social event, as a party or dance, unaccompanied. **3** *adj.* For men only: a *stag* dinner.

stage [stāj] *n., v.* **staged, stag·ing 1** *n.* A raised platform, as that in a theater for the performance of plays, or that in an auditorium for the delivery of speeches and other presentations. **2** *n.* Acting as a profession; the occupation of an actor. **3** *n.* The drama; theater: writing for the *stage*. **4** *v.* To put or exhibit on the stage: to *stage* a play. **5** *n.* Any platform, as a dock or scaffold. **6** *n.* The field or plan of action of some notable event: to set the *stage* for war. **7** *v.* To carry on or conduct: to *stage* an investigation. **8** *n.* A stopping point on a journey. **9** *n.* The distance between two stopping points. **10** *n.* A stagecoach. **11** *n.* A step in a development or process: The adult *stage* of this larva is a moth. **12** *n.* Any of the propulsion units of a rocket vehicle, each firing after the one before it burns out and falls away. **—by easy stages** Traveling or acting without hurry and with many stops; slowly.

stage·coach [stāj′kōch′] *n.* A large coach drawn by horses and having a regular route from town to town for carrying passengers, mail, and packages.

Stagecoach

stage fright Nervousness about appearing before an audience.

stage·hand [stāj′·hand′] *n.* A worker in a theater who handles scenery and stage properties.

stage·struck [stāj′struk′] *adj.* Fascinated with the theater, especially with the hope of becoming an actor.

stage whisper A deliberately loud whisper, especially one on a stage that is meant to be heard by the audience but is supposed not to be heard by other actors.

stag·ger [stag′ər] **1** *v.* To walk or run unsteadily; sway; reel. **2** *v.* To cause to stagger. **3** *n.* A reeling or swaying motion: to run with a *stagger*. **4** *v.* To confuse or overwhelm, as by surprise or grief: The unexpected question *staggered* me. **5** *v.* To place in a zigzag arrangement. **6** *v.* To schedule so as to begin at different times: to *stagger* lunch hours. **—the staggers** (*used with singular verb*) **1** A disease of the nervous system in horses and some cattle, causing them to stagger and fall down. **2** Dizziness.

stag·nant [stag′nənt] *adj.* **1** Not flowing; motionless; still. **2** Stale and dirty because not moving or flowing: said about bodies of water: a *stagnant* pond. **3** Dull; sluggish. **—stag′nant·ly** *adv.*

stag·nate [stag′nāt′] *v.* **stag·nat·ed, stag·nat·ing** To make or become stagnant. **—stag·na′tion** *n.*

stag·y [stā′jē] *adj.* **stag·i·er, stag·i·est** Of or characteristic of the stage, especially in being artificial or exaggerated; theatrical: a *stagy* voice.

staid [stād] *adj.* Steady and sober; sedate.

stain [stān] **1** *n.* A spot of dirt or discoloration. **2** *v.* To make or become dirty or discolored; soil; spot. **3** *n.* A dye or pigment used to change the color of wood. **4** *v.* To color by the use of a dye or pigment. **5** *n.* A mark of disgrace or dishonor: a *stain* on one's reputation. **6** *v.* To taint by a wrong or dishonorable act; disgrace.

stained glass Glass bearing colored designs or pictures, used especially in church windows.

stain·less [stān′lis] *adj.* **1** With no stain; spotless. **2** That will not easily rust or tarnish: *stainless* steel.

stainless steel A steel alloyed with enough chromium to make it resist rusting and corrosion. It is used for kitchen utensils and appliances and as a building material.

stair [stâr] *n.* **1** A step or one of a series of steps, for going up or down from one level to another. **2** (*usually pl.*) A series of steps.

stair·case [stâr′kās′] *n.* A flight of stairs, including the supports and handrail.

stair·way [stâr′wā′] *n.* One or more flights of stairs.

stair·well [stâr′wel′] *n.* The vertical shaft of space that contains a stairway.

stake [stāk] *n., v.* **staked, stak·ing 1** *n.* A stick or post sharpened at one end for driving into the ground. **2** *v.* To fasten to or support by means of a stake: to *stake* tomatoes. **3** *v.* To mark the boundaries of with or as with stakes: Where did you *stake* out your claim? **4** *n.* A post to which a person is tied to be executed by being burned alive. **5** *n.* This method of execution: Joan of Arc was sentenced to the *stake*. **6** *n.* (*often pl.*) Something bet or risked, as money on a race. **7** *v.* To bet; wager. **8** *n.* (*often pl.*) A prize in any sort of contest. **9** *n.* An interest or share: a *stake* in a business. **10** *v. informal* To supply with money; finance. **—at stake** To be won or lost; in question. **—pull up stakes** To leave a place; move out.

sta·lac·tite [stə·lak′tīt′] *n.* A slender, tapering column of mineral matter, chiefly limestone, hanging like an icicle from the roof of a cave. It is formed by dripping water with lime in it.

sta·lag·mite [stə·lag′mīt′] *n.* A limestone column shaped like a cone rising from the floor of a cave.

Stalactites and stalagmites

stale [stāl] *adj.* **stal·er, stal·est,** *v.* **staled, stal·ing** 1 *adj.* Not fresh any longer; slightly changed or gone bad, as air or bread. 2 *adj.* Lacking interest because not new; worn out; trite: a *stale* joke. 3 *adj.* Poor in quality or condition, as from too much or too little activity: A boxer can become *stale* by breaking training for a long period of time. 4 *v.* To make or become stale. **—stale′ness** *n.*

stale·mate [stāl′māt′] *n., v.* **stale·mat·ed, stale·mat·ing** 1 *n.* In chess, a draw resulting from a position in which a player's king, not in check, would be put in check by any move the player made. 2 *n.* A draw like this, in which neither side can act effectively; standstill; deadlock. 3 *v.* To put into a deadlock or standstill.

stalk[1] [stôk] *n.* 1 A stem of a plant or any supporting or connecting part. 2 Any support that is like a stem.

stalk[2] [stôk] 1 *v.* To approach (as game or prey) secretly or stealthily. 2 *v.* To walk in a stiff, dignified, or angry manner: to *stalk* out of a room. 3 *n.* A stiff or angry walk. 4 *n.* The act of stalking. 5 *v.* To spread through: Famine *stalked* the land.

stalk·ing-horse [stô′king·hôrs′] *n.* 1 A horse trained to hide a hunter stalking game behind it. 2 A horselike figure used for the same purpose. 3 A candidate put forward to test the chances for or to conceal the reality of someone else's candidacy or to divide the real candidate's opposition.

stall[1] [stôl] 1 *n.* A compartment in a stable where a horse or cow is kept. 2 *v.* To place or keep in a stall. 3 *n.* A small place to show and sell things, as in a market or bazaar. 4 *n.* A seat, as in the orchestra of a theater or the choir of a church. 5 *v.* To stop or cause to stop, especially unintentionally: to *stall* the engine of a car. 6 *v.* To slow down, as an airplane, to the point where the pilot loses control.

stall[2] [stôl] *informal* 1 *v.* To delay, usually by not being direct or frank: to *stall* for time. 2 *v.* To put off or divert by not being direct or frank: to *stall* a teacher who is asking a question. 3 *n.* Something, as an argument or trick, used to put off or delay an action or decision.

stal·lion [stal′yən] *n.* A male horse that can be used for breeding.

Stamens

stal·wart [stôl′wərt] 1 *adj.* Strong and muscular; robust. 2 *adj.* Not giving in or yielding; resolute; determined. 3 *adj.* Brave; courageous. 4 *n.* A stalwart person, especially a loyal supporter, as of a political party or movement.

sta·men [stā′mən] *n.* The organ of a flower that bears the pollen, consisting of the anther and its stem.

stam·i·na [stam′ə·nə] *n.* Vitality; vigor; strength; endurance.

stam·i·nate [stam′ə·nit *or* stam′ə·nāt′] *adj.* 1 Having a stamen or stamens. 2 Having stamens but lacking pistils: *staminate* flowers.

stam·mer [stam′ər] 1 *v.* To pause, hesitate, and repeat the same sound without meaning to, in speaking. 2 *n.* The act of stammering. 3 *n.* Stammering speech: to speak with a *stammer.*

stamp [stamp] 1 *v.* To strike heavily with the sole of the foot: The dancer *stamped* the floor twice. 2 *v.* To bring down (the foot) heavily and noisily. 3 *v.* To walk with heavy, noisy footsteps. 4 *v.* To affect in some way by or as if by stamping; crush: to *stamp* a fire out; to *stamp* out all the opposition. 5 *n.* The act of stamping with or as if with the foot. 6 *n.* A die, block, or other device having a pattern, name, or design on it that can, by pressing, be transferred to another surface: a rubber *stamp.* 7 *v.* To print or form by using such a stamp: to *stamp* a design on cloth. 8 *v.* To make marks or figures on by means of a stamp: He *stamped* the paper with his name. 9 *n.* Something, as a pattern, official seal, or mark, made by stamping. 10 *n.* A device having sharp edges for cutting out articles in its own shape: That *stamp* cuts out squares of cloth. 11 *v.* To form or cut out by using such a stamp. 12 *n.* A small printed piece of paper attached to a letter, article, or package, to show that the proper fees or taxes have been paid. 13 *v.* To put a stamp or official seal on: to *stamp* a package. 14 *n.* A piece of paper similar to a postage stamp, given with certain purchases and later exchanged for various articles or premiums. 15 *v.* To mark or characterize: These pictures *stamp* the photographer as a person of talent. 16 *n.* Character, kind, or quality: I prefer books of a different *stamp.*

stam·pede [stam·pēd′] *n., v.* **stam·ped·ed, stam·ped·ing** 1 *n.* A sudden rushing off or flight through panic, as of a herd of cattle or horses. 2 *n.* Any sudden, impulsive rush, as of a crowd: the *stampede* to Alaska for gold. 3 *v.* To be part of or cause a stampede.

stamping ground One's customary or favorite place to be.

stance [stans] *n.* 1 A manner of standing; posture. 2 The position of a golfer's or batter's feet while the person makes a swing.

stanch[1] [stônch *or* stänch] 1 *v.* To stop or check the flow of: to *stanch* blood. 2 *v.* To stop or check the flow of blood from: to *stanch* a wound.

stanch[2] [stônch *or* stänch] *adj.* Another spelling of STAUNCH[1].

stan·chion [stan′shən] *n.* An upright bar that forms the main support of something.

stand [stand] *v.* **stood, stand·ing,** *n.* 1 *v.* To take or keep an upright position on one's feet: *Stand* up! 2 *v.* To be or place in an upright or erect position:

a	add	**i**	it	**o͝o**	took	**oi**	oil
ā	ace	**ī**	ice	**o͞o**	pool	**ou**	pout
â	care	**o**	odd	**u**	up	**ng**	ring
ä	palm	**ō**	open	**û**	burn	**th**	thin
e	end	**ô**	order	**yo͞o**	fuse	**t̶h̶**	this
ē	equal					**zh**	vision

ə = { a in *above* e in *sicken* i in *possible* / o in *melon* u in *circus* }

The tree used to *stand* here; *Stand* the baby up. **3** *n.* The act of standing. **4** *v.* To have a specified height when standing: The sunflower *stands* six feet tall. **5** *v.* To take a certain position: to *stand* aside. **6** *v.* To take on or have a definite opinion, position, or attitude: How do you *stand* on the new tax law? **7** *n.* An opinion, attitude, or position. **8** *v.* To be located; have position; lie: The house *stands* by the side of the road. **9** *n.* The place or position in which someone or something stands: a cab waiting at its *stand.* **10** *v.* To remain unchanged; hold good: My decision *stands.* **11** *v.* To be in a specific state or condition: We *stood* in fear of the consequences. **12** *v.* To be of a certain rank or class: I *stand* third in my class. **13** *v.* To stop or pause; halt. **14** *n.* A stop or halt, especially one made for putting up a defense. **15** *v.* To take a position for defense or offense: *Stand* and fight. **16** *v.* To put up with; endure; tolerate: I can't *stand* any more. **17** *v.* To withstand; resist, as wear or use. **18** *v.* To be subjected to; endure: to *stand* trial. **19** *n.* A small table on which things may be placed. **20** *n.* A rack or other piece of furniture on which things, as hats or canes, may be put. **21** *n.* A stall, booth, or counter where goods are sold. **22** *n.* A structure on which persons may sit or stand: a witness *stand.* **23** *v. informal* To pay for; bear the expense of: to *stand* a treat. **24** *v.* In sailing, to take or hold a course: The brig *stood* to the west. **25** *n.* A group of growing things, as plants or trees. **—stand a chance** To have a chance, as of success. **—stand by** **1** To stay near and be ready to help, operate, or begin. **2** To help; support. **3** To abide by; keep: *Stand by* your promise. **—stand clear** To remain at a safe distance. **—stand for** **1** To represent; symbolize. **2** To put up with; tolerate. **—stand off** To keep at a distance. **—stand out** **1** To stick out; be conspicuous or prominent. **2** To refuse to agree; remain in opposition. **—stand pat** To resist change. **—stand to reason** To be sensible or logical. **—stand up** **1** To stand erect. **2** To withstand, as wear or criticism. **3** *slang* To fail deliberately to keep an appointment with. **—stand up for** To side with; take the part of.

stan·dard [stan'dərd] **1** *n.* A flag, ensign, or banner used as the special emblem of a nation, group, or special cause. **2** *n.* Any established measure of size, quantity, quality, or value: a *standard* of weight. **3** *n.* Any type, model, or example for comparison; measure of excellence: a *standard* of conduct. **4** *adj.* Serving as a gauge or model: a *standard* weight. **5** *adj.* Of recognized excellence or authority: a *standard* author. **6** *adj.* Widely accepted; regularly used: *standard* equipment. **7** *adj.* Conforming to a level of language usage considered acceptable by educated speakers and writers. **8** *n.* An upright structure or support, as a column or pedestal.

stan·dard·ize [stan'dər·dīz'] *v.* **stan·dard·ized, stan·dard·iz·ing** To make to or regulate by a standard: Many of the schools *standardized* their requirements for graduation. **—stan'dard·i·za'tion** *n.*

standard of living The goods and services customarily enjoyed by or within the means of an individual or group.

standard time (*sometimes written* **Standard Time**) The official time of any place according to its location in one of 24 zones east or west of Greenwich, England. Eight such zones lie in or touch North America.

stand·by [stand'bī'] *n., pl.* **stand·bys** **1** A person or thing that can be depended on. **2** A person or thing that is ready to be used in case of need; substitute. **—on standby** **1** Ready to be used as a substitute or replacement. **2** Awaiting a place that might become available, as on an airplane flight.

stand·ee [stand'ē'] *n.* A person who stands, as in a theater or on a bus.

stand-in [stand'in'] *n.* A person who substitutes in some way for another person, especially a person who takes the place of an actor while lights or cameras are adjusted or put into place.

stand·ing [stan'ding] **1** *adj.* Remaining erect; upright. **2** *adj.* For regular or permanent use: a *standing* rule; a *standing* army. **3** *adj.* Begun while standing: a *standing* high jump. **4** *adj.* Not flowing; stagnant, as water. **5** *n.* Relative position or rank; repute: a person of low *standing.* **6** *n.* Time in which something goes on; duration: a custom of long *standing.*

stand·off·ish [stand'ôf'ish] *adj.* Unfriendly or reserved; aloof.

stand·pipe [stand'pīp'] *n.* A large, upright pipe or tank placed at a height and filled with water to provide pressure for a water system.

stand·point [stand'point'] *n.* A position from which things are seen or judged; point of view: From our *standpoint,* everything looks fine.

stand·still [stand'stil'] *n.* A stop; halt; rest.

stank [stangk] Past tense of STINK.

stan·nic [stan'ik] *adj.* Of or containing tin, especially with a valence of +4.

stan·nous [stan'əs] *adj.* Of, having to do with, or containing tin, especially with a valence of +2.

stan·za [stan'zə] *n.* A certain number of lines of verse grouped together according to a fixed plan to form a section of a poem.

sta·pes [stā'pēz'] *n., pl.* **sta·pes** or **sta·pe·des** [stə·pē'·dēz' *or* stā'pə·dēz'] Another word for STIRRUP BONE.

staph·y·lo·coc·cus [staf'ə·lō·kok'əs] *n., pl.* **staph·y·lo·coc·ci** [staf'ə·lō·kok'sī] or **staph·y·lo·coc·cus·es** Any of a group of bacteria, some of which cause boils and infect open wounds.

sta·ple[1] [stā'pəl] *n., v.* **sta·pled, sta·pling** **1** *n.* A U-shaped piece of metal with pointed ends driven into a surface to hold something, as a bolt, hook, or wire, in place. **2** *n.* A thin piece of wire usually shaped like a bracket ([), driven through paper, fabrics, or other material, as a fastening. **3** *v.* To fix or fasten by a staple or staples.

sta·ple[2] [stā'pəl] **1** *n.* A basic food or other ordinary item of household use, as flour and sugar. **2** *adj.* Regularly and constantly produced, used, or sold: *staple* foods. **3** *n.* The principal article produced or manufactured in a place or region: Tires are the *staple* of our town. **4** *adj.* Main; chief: a *staple* crop. **5** *n.* The carded or combed fiber of cotton, wool, or flax.

sta·pler [stā'plər] *n.* A device for driving in staples, especially a hand-punched device for fastening papers together with wire staples.

star [stär] *n., v.* **starred, star·ring** **1** *n.* Any of the many luminous bodies similar to the sun that are spread through space at vast distances from the earth. At night some are visible as apparently fixed points of light. ◆ Adj. *stellar.* **2** *n.* A planet or other heavenly body, considered in astrology as influencing one's fortune or destiny. **3** *n.* A figure with five or more radiating points (☆), used as an emblem or decoration. **4** *v.* To set or ornament with spangles or stars. **5** *n.* An asterisk (*). **6** *v.* To mark with an asterisk. **7** *n.* An actor who plays a leading part. **8** *v.* To play a leading part; be a star. **9** *n.* Anyone who is very prominent in a field: a sports *star.* **10** *v.* To show outstanding skill; be prominent: He *stars* on the tennis court. **11** *adj.* Prominent; brilliant.

star·board [stär′bərd] *n.* **1** The right-hand side of a ship, as one faces the front or bow. **2** *adj. use:* the *starboard* side. ◆ *Starboard* comes from an Old English word formed by combining *steor,* meaning *steering,* and *bord,* meaning *side of a ship.* Thus *steorbord* was the side of the ship used for steering.

starch [stärch] **1** *n.* A vegetable substance without taste or smell, produced by many plants. Potatoes contain a lot of starch. **2** *n.* A preparation of this substance used to stiffen clothes and to make paste. **3** *v.* To apply starch to; stiffen with or as if with starch. **4** *n.* A stiff, formal manner. **5** *n. informal* Vigor; energy.

starch·y [stär′chē] *adj.* **starch·i·er, starch·i·est** **1** Stiffened with starch. **2** Made of or combined with starch. **3** Stiff; formal: a *starchy* reply to my note.

star·dom [stär′dəm] *n.* The condition of being a star; fame as a performer.

stare [stâr] *v.* **stared, star·ing,** *n.* **1** *v.* To look steadily for some time, with the eyes wide open, as from surprise, curiosity, wonder, or bad manners. **2** *v.* To look at fixedly. **3** *n.* A fixed, intense gaze. **4** *v.* To stand out; be conspicuous; glare. **—stare down** To stare back at someone until the person looks away.

star·fish [stär′fish′] *n., pl.* **star·fish** or **star·fish·es** A small sea animal with a star-shaped body having five or more arms.

Starfish

star·gaze [stär′gāz′] *v.* **star·gaz·ed, star·gaz·ing** **1** To gaze at the stars. **2** To daydream. **—star′gaz′er** *n.*

stark [stärk] **1** *adj.* Barren; bleak: a *stark* stretch of land. **2** *adj.* Complete; utter; downright: *stark* indifference. **3** *adv.* Completely; utterly: *stark* naked; *stark* mad. **4** *adj.* Stiff or rigid, as in death. **—stark′ly** *adv.*

star·let [stär′lit] *n.* A young movie actress being publicized as a future star.

star·light [stär′līt′] *n.* The light given by a star or stars.

star·ling [stär′ling] *n.* A bird with an iridescent black body, short tail, and a yellow bill.

star·lit [stär′lit′] *adj.* Lighted by the stars.

Star of David [dā′vəd] A six-pointed star used as a symbol of Judaism.

star·ry [stär′ē] *adj.* **star·ri·er, star·ri·est** **1** Set with stars; full of stars. **2** Lighted by the stars. **3** Shining like the stars.

star·ry-eyed [stär′ē·īd′] *adj.* **1** Naively hopeful or trusting: a *starry-eyed* child. **2** Imaginative but impractical; visionary: *starry-eyed* schemes to save the world.

Stars and Stripes The flag of the U.S., with thirteen alternately red and white stripes and fifty white stars on a blue square.

star-span·gled [stär′spang′gəld] *adj.* Having many stars; spangled with stars.

Star-Spangled Banner **1** The flag of the U.S. **2** The national anthem of the U.S.

start [stärt] **1** *v.* To make a beginning; set out: We *started* on our trip today. **2** *v.* To begin; commence: The play *starts* at eight o'clock. **3** *v.* To set in motion or circulation; put into action: to *start* an engine; to *start* a rumor. **4** *v.* To set up: establish: to *start* a business. **5** *n.* The act of starting; beginning: to get an early *start.* **6** *n.* The time or place of starting: the *start* of a race. **7** *n.* Advantage or distance in advance at the outset: a *start* of five miles over the other cyclists. **8** *v.* To move or cause to move suddenly, as from fear or surprise: to make someone *start* by shouting. **9** *n.* A sudden, startled movement or feeling: to give a *start* at a noise. **10** *v.* To move suddenly with a spring, leap, or bound. **11** *v.* To make or become loose or warped. **—start in** To begin; undertake. **—start out** **1** To begin a journey. **2** To begin or commence anything: to *start out* on a new career. **—start up** **1** To rise or appear suddenly. **2** To begin or cause to begin operations, as an engine. **3** To begin or commence: The heat *started up* again at 7 o'clock.

start·er [stär′tər] *n.* **1** A person or thing that starts. **2** A person who gives the signal for the start of a race. **3** A person who sees that vehicles, as buses or trains, leave on schedule.

star·tle [stär′təl] *v.* **star·tled, star·tling,** *n.* **1** *v.* To frighten, surprise, or excite suddenly: You *startled* me. **2** *v.* To be frightened, surprised, or excited. **3** *n.* A sudden fright, surprise, or shock.

star·tling [stär′tling] *adj.* Causing abrupt and sharp surprise or fright; astonishing: a *startling* flash of lightning. **—star′tling·ly** *adv.*

star·va·tion [stär·vā′shən] *n.* **1** The act of starving. **2** The condition of being starved.

starve [stärv] *v.* **starved, starv·ing** **1** To grow weak or die from lack of food. **2** To make suffer or die from lack of food. **3** *informal* To be very hungry. **4** To bring to a certain condition by starving: to *starve* an enemy into surrender. **5** To suffer from lack or need: to *starve* for love. ◆ *Starve* once meant simply *to die,* but the meaning became limited to death caused by lack of food.

starve·ling [stärv′ling] **1** *n.* A person or animal that is starving. **2** *adj.* Starving; hungry.

stash [stash] *v. slang* To hide or conceal for storage and safekeeping.

state [stāt] *n., v.* **stat·ed, stat·ing** **1** *n.* The nature or condition of a person or thing: a *state* of excitement; mercury in a liquid *state.* **2** *n.* A frame of mind; mood: a *state* of happiness. **3** *n.* A very

a	add	**i**	it	**o͝o**	took	**oi**	oil
ā	ace	**ī**	ice	**o͞o**	pool	**ou**	pout
â	care	**o**	odd	**u**	up	**ng**	ring
ä	palm	**ō**	open	**û**	burn	**th**	thin
e	end	**ô**	order	**yo͞o**	fuse	**t͟h**	this
ē	equal					**zh**	vision

ə = {a in *above* e in *sicken* i in *possible* / o in *melon* u in *circus*}

grand or formal style of living or doing something; pomp: to be buried in *state.* **4** *adj. use*: a *state* dinner. **5** *n.* A nation: the French *state.* **6** *n.* (*often written* **State**) A group of people forming an organized political unit that is usually part of a larger federal government: the *State* of New York. **7** *adj. use*: *state* papers; a *state* job. **8** *n.* The territory of a state or nation: That law does not apply inside this *state.* **9** *v.* To set forth clearly in speech or writing; declare. **10** *v.* To fix; determine: to *state* a fee.

state·craft [stāt′kraft′] *n.* Skill in conducting affairs of a state or government.

stat·ed [stā′tid] *adj.* **1** Established; fixed; set: *stated* hours. **2** Declared; announced: *stated* reasons.

state·hood [stāt′hŏŏd′] *n.* The condition or status of being a state, especially of being one of the United States.

state·house [stāt′hous′] *n.* (*often written* **Statehouse**) A building in which a state legislature meets.

state·less [stāt′lis] *adj.* Lacking citizenship in any country: *stateless* refugees.

state·ly [stāt′lē] *adj.* **state·li·er, state·li·est** Dignified; imposing: a *stately* home. **—state′li·ness** *n.*

state·ment [stāt′mənt] *n.* **1** The act of stating. **2** Something that is stated: The conservationist made a *statement* to the press. **3** A report of an account, showing the amount of money owed or due: a bank's monthly *statement.*

state-of-the-art [stāt′əv·thē·ärt′] *adj.* Technically up-to-date at the time of manufacture: a *state-of-the-art* computer.

state of the art The current level of development of a device or technology that is steadily improving.

state·room [stāt′rōōm′] *n.* A private cabin on a ship or sleeping room on a train.

state·side [stāt′sīd′] **1** *adj.* Of or in the continental U.S.: *stateside* military duty. **2** *adv.* In, to, or toward the continental U.S.: returning *stateside* after a tour of duty abroad.

states·man [stāts′mən] *n., pl.* **states·men** [stāts′·mən] **1** A person who is skilled in government or diplomacy. **2** A wise political leader. **—states′·man·ship** *n.*

states' rights **1** The rights of state governments, as specified or implied by the U. S. Constitution. **2** The political belief that state governments should have greater power and the federal government less power.

states·wom·an [stāts′wŏŏm′ən] *n., pl.* **states·wom·en** [stāts′wim′in] **1** A woman who is skilled in government or diplomacy. **2** A woman who is a wise political leader.

state·wide [stāt′wīd′] *adj.* Throughout a state; a *statewide* search for the missing couple.

stat·ic [stat′ik] **1** *adj.* Not active, moving, or changing; at rest: *static* air. **2** *adj.* Of or having to do with bodies at rest or forces in equilibrium. **3** *adj.* Acting or pressing as weight but without moving: *static* pressure. **4** *adj.* Of, having to do with, or producing stationary electric charges: *Static* electricity is often produced by friction. **5** *n.* Electrical interference picked up by a radio or television set; noise.

stat·ics [stat′iks] *n.* The branch of physics that deals with bodies at rest and with forces balanced by equal and opposite forces. ◆ See -ICS.

sta·tion [stā′shən] **1** *n.* A place where a person or persons are located to perform some duty; assigned post: the guard's *station* before the palace. **2** *n.* A place, as a building or headquarters, occupied and used by a group working together: a *fire* station. **3** *v.* To assign or place in a certain spot or position. **4** *n.* A place, and usually a building, where trains or buses stop regularly and where passengers get on or off. **5** *n.* Social standing: a person of noble *station.* **6** *n.* The offices, studios, and technical equipment of a radio or television broadcasting unit.

sta·tion·ar·y [stā′shən·er′ē] *adj.* **1** Remaining in one place; fixed; not movable: *stationary* equipment. **2** Showing no change, as in character, condition, or size: a *stationary* civilization. ◆ *Stationary* (not moving) and *stationery* (writing materials) should not be confused. *Stationery* ends in *ery* and is used for *letters.*

sta·tion·er [stā′shən·ər] *n.* A person who sells such things as paper, envelopes, pens, pencils, and ink.

sta·tion·ery [stā′shən·er′ē] *n.* Materials used in writing, especially paper and envelopes for writing letters. ◆ See STATIONARY.

sta·tion·mas·ter [stā′shən·mas′tər] *n.* A person who supervises arrivals, departures, and other activities at a railroad station.

station wagon A closed automobile with rear seats that fold down or come out and a door that opens in the rear for loading.

Station wagon

sta·tis·tic [stə·tis′tik] **1** *adj.* Statistical. **2** *n.* A fact or item of information used in a statistical report or statement.

sta·tis·ti·cal [stə·tis′tə·kəl] *adj.* Of or having to do with statistics. **—sta·tis′ti·cal·ly** *adv.*

stat·is·ti·cian [stat′is·tish′ən] *n.* A person who is skilled in statistics.

sta·tis·tics [stə·tis′tiks] *n.pl.* **1** The science of collecting, arranging, and analyzing numerical data. **2** The numerical data collected: These *statistics* show how many people have taken up tennis. ◆ See -ICS.

sta·tor [stā′tər] *n.* The part of a motor or other rotary machine that does not move.

stat·u·ar·y [stach′ōō·er′ē] *n.* **1** Statues, as a group. **2** The art of making statues.

stat·ue [stach′ōō] *n.* A likeness, as of a person or animal, carved, molded, or cast of a substance such as marble, wood, clay, or bronze.

Statue of Liberty

stat·u·esque [stach′ōō·esk′] *adj.* Like a statue, as in grace, poise, dignity, or form.

stat·u·ette [stach′ōō·et′] *n.* A small statue.

stat·ure [stach′ər] *n.* **1** Natural height, as of a person. **2** Quality or status.

sta·tus [stā′təs *or* stat′əs] *n.* **1** State; condition: the *status* of the firm over the last year. **2** Position or rank: a person of high social *status.*

status quo [kwō] The condition in which a person or thing is at the present time.

stat·ute [stach′ōōt] *n.* A rule or law, especially a law passed by a legislature.

statute mile A standard mile, equal to 5,280 feet.

stat·u·to·ry [stach′ə·tôr′ē] *adj.* 1 Having to do with a statute. 2 Created by a statute.

staunch[1] [stônch *or* stänch] 1 *adj.* Firm and dependable; loyal: a *staunch* friend. 2 *adj.* Strongly and firmly built; sturdy. 3 *adj.* Watertight: a *staunch* ship. **—staunch′ly** *adv.* **—staunch′ness** *n.*

staunch[2] [stônch *or* stänch] *v.* Another spelling of STANCH[1].

stave [stāv] *n., v.* **staved** or **stove, stav·ing** 1 *n.* Any of the curved strips of wood or iron that together form the sides of a barrel, tub, or cask. 2 *v.* To furnish with staves. 3 *v.* To break in the staves of: to *stave* a barrel. 4 *v.* To break or make a hole in by crushing or smashing. 5 *n.* A musical staff. 6 *n.* A stanza or verse in a poem or song. 7 *n.* A rod or staff. **—stave off** To ward off; keep away. ◆ *Stave* was formed from the plural of *staff,* which is *staves.*

Staves

staves [stāvz] *n.* 1 A plural of STAFF. 2 The plural of STAVE.

stay[1] [stā] 1 *v.* To continue or remain, as in some certain place or condition: to *stay* indoors; to *stay* healthy. 2 *v.* To remain, as a guest or resident; dwell: to *stay* for a week at the seashore. 3 *v.* To remain for the duration of: to *stay* the night. 4 *n.* The act or time of staying; visit: a week's *stay* at the seashore. 5 *v.* To stop; check: to *stay* an impulse. 6 *v.* To put off; delay: to *stay* an execution. 7 *n.* A delay, as of an execution. 8 *v.* To satisfy temporarily: to *stay* the pangs of hunger. 9 *v.* To be able to keep going and last to the finish, as in a race.

stay[2] [stā] 1 *v.* To support, prop, or hold up: We *stayed* the weak limb with two poles. 2 *v.* To comfort or strengthen mentally or morally. 3 *n.* Something that gives support or serves as a prop. 4 *n.* A strip of plastic or metal, used to stiffen garments, as corsets or girdles.

stay[3] [stā] *n.* 1 A strong rope, often of wire, used to support and brace a mast or spar. 2 Any rope, chain, or wire used to steady or support something.

staying power Power to keep going when tired; endurance; stamina.

stay·sail [stā′səl *or* stā′sāl′] *n.* A sail, usually triangular, fastened on a stay.

stead [sted] *n.* Place of a person or thing taken by a substitute or, sometimes, by a successor: I could not baby-sit, so I sent my brother in my *stead.* **—stand in good stead** To be of good use.

stead·fast [sted′fast′] *adj.* Not moving or changing; constant: The children were *steadfast* in their devotion to the family. **—stead′fast′ly** *adv.*

stead·y [sted′ē] *adj.* **stead·i·er, stead·i·est,** *v.* **stead·ied, stead·y·ing** 1 *adj.* Stable in position; firmly supported; fixed: a *steady* shelf. 2 *adj.* Moving or acting regularly and without changes: a *steady* wind. 3 *adj.* Not easily disturbed or upset: *steady* nerves. 4 *adj.* Industrious; dependable; reliable: *steady* workers. 5 *adj.* Regular: a *steady* customer. 6 *v.* To make or become steady. **—stead′i·ly** *adv.* **—stead′i·ness** *n.*

steady state theory A theory in astronomy that the universe has always existed roughly as it is now and that its continuous expansion is made possible by the continuous creation of matter.

steak [stāk] *n.* 1 A slice of meat or fish, cooked or to be cooked, usually by broiling or frying. 2 Ground meat formed into a patty for cooking like a steak: hamburger *steak.*

steal [stēl] *v.* **stole, sto·len, steal·ing,** *n.* 1 *v.* To take from another without right or permission, and usually in a secret manner: to *steal* money from a bank. 2 *v.* To take, get, or win over, as by surprise, skill, or trickery: The speaker *stole* our hearts with charm and wit; The new singer *stole* the show. 3 *v.* To take, get, or do in a secret or concealed way: to *steal* a glance at someone. 4 *v.* To move or go secretly: to *steal* into a room. 5 *v.* In baseball, to gain (another base) by running during a pitch and beating the catcher's throw. 6 *n.* The act of stealing. 7 *n. informal* A bargain.

stealth [stelth] *n.* A manner of acting or doing something that is secret, furtive, or underhand.

stealth·y [stel′thē] *adj.* **stealth·i·er, stealth·i·est** Done in a secret, furtive, or underhand way: The burglar's movements were *stealthy.* **—stealth′i·ly** *adv.* ◆ *Stealthy, furtive,* and *underhand* all mean *done secretly.* Someone is *stealthy* who wants to escape notice, but a person is *furtive* who worries about being discovered: a *stealthy* hunter; a *furtive* thief. *Underhand* is usually applied to methods that are kept quiet because they are shady or dishonest: Rumor has it that the treasurer won the election by *underhand* means.

steam [stēm] 1 *n.* The gas or vapor into which water is changed by boiling. It is used for heating and, under pressure, as a source of energy. 2 *v.* To give off steam or vapor: The kettle is *steaming.* 3 *v.* To move or travel by the power of steam: The boat *steamed* up the river. 4 *v.* To treat with steam, as in softening, cooking, or cleaning. 5 *n.* The mist into which water vapor is condensed by cooling. 6 *v.* To become covered with condensed water vapor, as a window. 7 *n. informal* Vigor; force; speed: The players tired and ran out of *steam.* **—let off steam** *informal* To express pent-up emotions or opinions.

steam·boat [stēm′bōt′] *n.* A boat driven by steam, especially one used on a river.

steam chest The box or chest through which steam is delivered to an engine cylinder.

steam engine An engine driven by steam, especially one in which a piston is moved by the expanding force of steam under pressure.

steam·er [stē′mər] *n.* 1 Something, as a vehicle or engine, worked or driven by steam, as a steamship. 2 A container in which something is steamed: a *steamer* for vegetables. 3 A soft-shell clam cooked by steaming.

steam·fit·ter [stēm′fit′ər] *n.* A person who sets up or repairs steam pipes and boilers.

a	add	**i**	it	**o͝o**	took	**oi**	oil
ā	ace	**ī**	ice	**o͞o**	pool	**ou**	pout
â	care	**o**	odd	**u**	up	**ng**	ring
ä	palm	**ō**	open	**û**	burn	**th**	thin
e	end	**ô**	order	**yo͞o**	fuse	**th**	this
ē	equal					**zh**	vision

ə = { a in *above* e in *sicken* i in *possible*; o in *melon* u in *circus* }

S

steam·roll·er [stēm′rō′lər] *n.* 1 A machine driven by a steam, gasoline, or diesel engine, with heavy rollers that are used to pack down and level gravel, paving stones, and other materials. 2 Any power or force that crushes and overcomes whatever is in its way.

steam·ship [stēm′ship′] *n.* A large ship driven by steam.

steam shovel A machine for digging, originally operated by steam power, now by a gasoline or diesel engine.

Steamship

steam·y [stē′mē] *adj.* **steam·i·er, steam·i·est** Consisting of, like, or full of steam; misty.

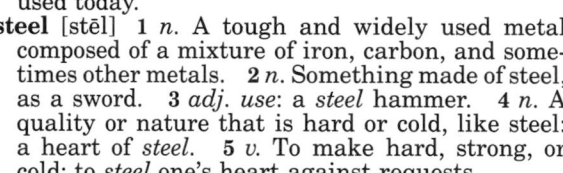

steed [stēd] *n.* A horse, especially a spirited war horse: seldom used today.

steel [stēl] 1 *n.* A tough and widely used metal composed of a mixture of iron, carbon, and sometimes other metals. 2 *n.* Something made of steel, as a sword. 3 *adj. use:* a *steel* hammer. 4 *n.* A quality or nature that is hard or cold, like steel: a heart of *steel.* 5 *v.* To make hard, strong, or cold: to *steel* one's heart against requests.

steel band A musical band consisting mainly of tuned percussion instruments made from empty oil barrels, originally developed in Trinidad.

steel engraving 1 The art and process of engraving on a steel plate. 2 The impression made from such a plate.

steel wool Steel fibers matted together for use in cleaning and polishing.

steel·work·er [stēl′wûr′kər] *n.* A person who works in a steel mill.

steel·works [stēl′wûrks′] *n.pl.* (*used with singular or plural verb*) A plant where steel is produced; steel mill.

steel·y [stē′lē] *adj.* **steel·i·er, steel·i·est** 1 Made of steel. 2 Like steel, as in strength, hardness, or coldness: a *steely* gaze.

steel·yard [stēl′yärd′] *n.* A weighing device made up of a scaled metal bar, a movable counterweight, and hooks. The object to be weighed is hung at the short end of the bar and the counterweight is moved along the long end until the bar is balanced.

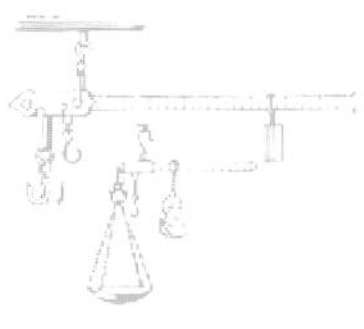

Modern and ancient steelyards

steep[1] [stēp] *adj.* 1 Having a sharp incline or slope: a *steep* hill. 2 *informal* High; excessive: a *steep* price. —**steep′ly** *adv.*

steep[2] [stēp] *v.* 1 To soak in a liquid: *Steep* the tea. 2 To absorb or involve completely; immerse: The student is *steeped* in history.

steep·en [stē′pən] *v.* To make or become steep or steeper.

stee·ple [stē′pəl] *n.* 1 A tall, usually tapering structure rising above a church tower; spire. 2 The entire tower of a church.

Steeplechase

stee·ple·chase [stē′pəl·chās′] *n.* A horse race over a course prepared with obstacles, as hedges, rails, and water jumps. ◆ *Steeplechase* was formed by combining *steeple* with *chase.* Church steeples were often used as landmarks or goals in races.

stee·ple·jack [stē′pəl·jak′] *n.* A person whose occupation is to climb steeples and other tall structures to inspect them or make repairs.

steer[1] [stir] *v.* 1 To direct the course of (a vessel or vehicle): I *steered* the car; I *steered* with one hand. 2 To be steered or guided: The car *steers* easily. 3 To set and follow; pursue: The captain *steered* a course for the island. 4 To direct; guide; control: The president *steered* the party to victory. —**steer clear of** To keep away from; avoid.

steer[2] [stir] *n.* A male of beef cattle, castrated usually before it is fully grown, especially one that is from two to four years old.

steer·age [stir′ij] *n.* The part of a passenger ship open to passengers paying the lowest fares. In former times it offered little or no comfort or privacy.

steering wheel A wheel turned by the driver or pilot of a vehicle, as a ship or airplane, to steer it.

steers·man [stirz′mən] *n., pl.* **steers·men** [stirz′mən] A person who steers a boat; helmsman.

steg·o·sau·rus [steg′ə·sôr′əs] *n.* Any of a genus of large dinosaurs with rows of bony plates along the back and tail.

stein [stīn] *n.* A beer mug.

ste·la [stē′lə] *n., pl.* **ste·lae** [stē′lē] An upright stone slab bearing a commemorative inscription or carving.

ste·le [stē′lē] *n., pl.* **ste·lae** [stē′lē] A stela.

stel·lar [stel′ər] *adj.* 1 Of or having to do with the stars. 2 Of, for, or by an important performer: a *stellar* part in a movie. 3 First-rate; excellent: a *stellar* performance.

St. El·mo's fire [sānt′ el′mōz] A flamelike light due to electricity produced in the atmosphere, sometimes seen on aircraft wings or the masts of ships.

stem[1] [stem] *n., v.* **stemmed, stem·ming** 1 *n.* The main body or stalk of a tree, shrub, or other plant, rising above the ground. 2 *n.* The slender growth that supports the fruit, flower, or leaf of a plant. 3 *v.* To remove the stems of or from. 4 *n.* Something that resembles a stem: a pipe *stem;* a watch *stem.* 5 *n.* The front part of a ship; bow; prow. 6 *n.* A line of descent from a particular ancestor. 7 *v.* To come or originate: My interest in the guitar *stemmed* from hearing these records. 8 *n.* The part of a word to which inflectional endings are added or which is itself changed by inflection: *Sing* is the *stem* of *sings, singing,* and *sung.*

stem[2] [stem] *v.* **stemmed, stem·ming** To stand firm or make progress against: to *stem* the tide.

stem[3] [stem] *v.* **stemmed, stem·ming** To stop, hold back, or dam up, as a current.

stench [stench] *n.* A foul odor; stink.

sten·cil [sten′səl] *n., v.* **sten·ciled** or **sten·cilled, sten·cil·ing** or **sten·cil·ling** 1 *n.* A sheet of paper or other material, in which patterns, letters, or words are cut out. When ink or paint is spread over the stencil, which is laid on a surface to be marked, it passes through the holes to the surface. 2 *n.* A decoration or the like produced by means of a stencil. 3 *v.* To mark with a stencil.

ste·nog·ra·pher [stə·nog′rə·fər] *n.* A person whose work is taking dictation, usually in shorthand, and typewriting.

sten·o·graph·ic [sten′ə·graf′ik] *adj.* Of, having to do with, or using stenography.

ste·nog·ra·phy [stə·nog′rə·fē] *n.* The art of writing in shorthand and of reading it.

sten·to·ri·an [sten·tôr′ē·ən] *adj.* Extremely loud.

step [step] *n., v.* **stepped, step·ping** **1** *n.* A movement made by lifting one foot and putting it down in a different place; one motion of a leg and foot as in walking or running. **2** *n.* The distance passed over in making such a movement: a short *step.* **3** *v.* To move by changing the position of the leg and foot: *Step* ahead! **4** *v.* To take (a step or pace): *Step* five paces to the rear. **5** *n.* Any short distance. **6** *v.* To walk a short distance: to *step* across the street. **7** *n.* A place on which to put the foot in going up or down, as a stair or a ladder rung. **8** *n.* A single action regarded as leading to something: the first *step* in our plan for reorganization. **9** *n.* A grade or rank: A lieutenant colonel is two *steps* above a captain. **10** *n.* The manner of stepping; walk; gait: a heavy *step.* **11** *n.* The sound of a footfall: I hear *steps* on the stairway. **12** *n.* A footprint; track. **13** *n.* A combination or a pattern of foot movements in dancing. **14** *v.* To perform the steps of: to *step* a square dance. **15** *v.* To move or act quickly or briskly: *Step* along, don't dawdle! **16** *v.* To move or pass into a situation or circumstance, as if in a single step: to *step* into a fortune. **17** *v.* To put or press the foot down: to *step* on an ant; to *step* on the brake. **18** *v.* To measure by taking steps: to *step* off five yards. **19** *n.* Something like a step, as a supporting framework: the *step* of a ship's mast. **20** *v.* To place the lower end of (a mast) in its step. **—in step** **1** Walking, dancing, marching, or moving in a way that fits a certain set rhythm. **2** *informal* In agreement or conformity. **—keep step** To remain in step while walking, marching, or moving. **—out of step** Not in step. **—step by step** By gradually advancing; gradually. **—step down** **1** To decrease gradually, or by steps or degrees. **2** To resign from an office or position. **—step up** To increase; raise. **—take steps** To do certain things in order to reach a desired end or result. **—watch one's step** To act with care; be careful.

step·broth·er [step′bruth′ər] *n.* The son of a person's stepmother or stepfather by a former marriage.

step·child [step′chīld′] *n., pl.* **step·chil·dren** [step′·chil′drən] The child of a person's husband or wife by a former marriage.

step·daugh·ter [step′dô′tər] *n.* A female stepchild.

step·fa·ther [step′fä′thər] *n.* The husband of a person's mother, but not that person's own father.

step·lad·der [step′lad′ər] *n.* A ladder with flat steps instead of rungs and often with a folding brace at the back.

step·moth·er [step′muth′ər] *n.* The wife of a person's father, but not that person's own mother.

step·par·ent [step′pâr′ənt] *n.* A stepmother or stepfather.

steppe [step] *n.* A vast, treeless plain, especially one of these areas in Soviet Europe and Asia.

stepped-up [stept′up′] *adj.* Increased, as in intensity or tempo; intensified; accelerated.

step·ping-stone [step′ing·stōn′] *n.* **1** A stone on which a person can step, as when crossing a stream. **2** A step or stage in the fulfillment of a goal: *stepping-stones* to fame.

step·sis·ter [step′sis′tər] *n.* The daughter of a person's stepmother or stepfather by a former marriage.

step·son [step′sun′] *n.* A male stepchild.

step-up [step′up′] *n.* An increase, as in size, amount, or rate of activity.

-ster A suffix meaning: A person who does or participates in something, as in *trickster* and *gangster.*

stere [stir] *n.* In the metric system, a unit of volume equal to one cubic meter.

ster·e·o [ster′ē·ō *or* stir′ē·ō] **1** *n.* A stereophonic system. **2** *adj.* Stereophonic. ◆ *Stereo* is a shortened form of *stereophonic.*

ster·e·o·phon·ic [ster′ē·ə·fon′ik] *adj.* Of or having to do with a sound reproduction system that uses two or more channels to receive, carry, and reproduce sound, so as to create the effect of different components of the sound coming from different directions.

ster·e·op·ti·con [ster′ē·op′ti·kon′ *or* stir′ē·op′ti·kon′] *n.* A device that projects pictures onto a screen by means of a powerful light; magic lantern.

ster·e·o·scope [ster′ē·ə·skōp′] *n.* A device through which one looks at two pictures of the same scene or object taken from slightly different angles. The image formed by the combined views no longer appears flat but seems to have depth and solidity.

ster·e·o·scop·ic [ster′ē·ə·skop′ik] *adj.* Of or having to do with a stereoscope.

ster·e·o·type [ster′ē·ə·tīp′ *or* stir′ē·ə·tīp′] *n., v.* **ster·e·o·typed, ster·e·o·typ·ing** **1** *n.* A metal plate used in printing. **2** *n.* A mental image or a way of thinking about a person, thing, or event that follows a conventional or fixed pattern and makes no allowances for individual differences. **3** *v.* To make a stereotype of.

ster·e·o·typed [ster′ē·ə·tīpt′ *or* stir′ē·ə·tīpt′] *adj.* **1** Of a conventional, fixed nature; hackneyed; trite; unoriginal. **2** Produced from a stereotype.

ster·ile [ster′əl] *adj.* **1** Unable to produce offspring or growth; barren: Mules are *sterile;* a *sterile* desert. **2** Free from harmful bacteria or germs: a *sterile* bandage. **—ste·ril′i·ty** *n.*

ster·il·ize [ster′əl·īz′] *v.* **ster·il·ized, ster·il·iz·ing** **1** To free from harmful bacteria or germs: to *sterilize* surgical instruments. **2** To deprive of the power of reproducing. **—ster′il·i·za′tion** *n.* **—ster′il·iz′er** *n.*

ster·ling [stûr′ling] **1** *n.* British money. **2** *adj.* Of British money: 20 pounds *sterling.* **3** *n.* Sterling silver. **4** *adj.* Of sterling silver. **5** *n.* An article or articles made of sterling silver. **6** *adj.* Excellent; genuine: a friend of *sterling* qualities.

sterling silver An alloy that is 92.5% pure silver.

stern[1] [stûrn] *adj.* **1** Harsh in nature or manner; strict; severe: a *stern* person; *stern* punishment. **2** Firm; fixed; unyielding: a *stern* resolve. **—stern′ly** *adv.*

stern[2] [stûrn] *n.* The rear part, as of a ship or boat.

a	add	**i**	it	**o͝o**	took	**oi**	oil
ā	ace	**ī**	ice	**o͞o**	pool	**ou**	pout
â	care	**o**	odd	**u**	up	**ng**	ring
ä	palm	**ō**	open	**û**	burn	**th**	thin
e	end	**ô**	order	**yo͞o**	fuse	**th**	this
ē	equal					**zh**	vision

ə = a in *above* e in *sicken* i in *possible* o in *melon* u in *circus*

S

ster·num [stûr′nəm] *n., pl.* **ster·na** [stûr′nə] or **ster·nums** The long, narrow bone in front of the chest to which most of the ribs are attached; breastbone.

ste·roid [ster′oid′] *n.* Any of numerous organic compounds that have a certain ringlike molecular structure and that are found in animals and plants. Some steroids are powerful hormones that control growth, metabolism, and sexual characteristics, and some are extracted or synthesized for use in drugs.

steth·o·scope [steth′ə·skōp′] *n.* A small, portable instrument by which doctors can hear sounds produced in the chest, especially in the lungs and heart. ◆ *Stethoscope* comes from two Greek words meaning, when translated freely, *chest watcher.*

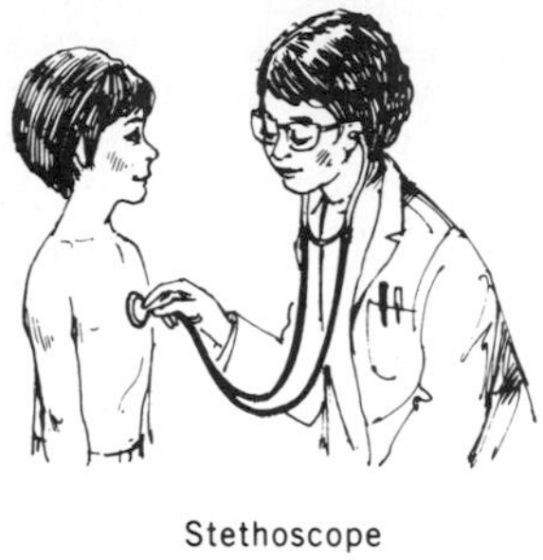

Stethoscope

ste·ve·dore [stē′və·dôr′] *n.* A person who works at loading or unloading a ship in port.

stew [st(y)o͞o] **1** *v.* To boil slowly and gently, usually for a long time. **2** *n.* Stewed food, especially a preparation of meat or fish and various vegetables, cooked together slowly. **3** *v. informal* To worry. **4** *n. informal* A state of worry or mental agitation.

stew·ard [st(y)o͞o′ərd] *n.* **1** A person who manages the property, finances, or other affairs of another person or persons. **2** A person in charge of provisions, staff, and equipment for a hotel, club, ship, or the like. **3** A servant on a ship, airplane, or other transport. ◆ *Steward* comes from an Old English word meaning *sty keeper.* Over the years stewards came to be entrusted with more respectable jobs.

stew·ard·ess [st(y)o͞o′ər·dis] *n.* A woman who aids passengers on a ship, airplane, or other transport.

stew·ard·ship [st(y)o͞o′ərd·ship′] *n.* **1** The position or work of a steward. **2** Careful management or protection: We left our garden to the *stewardship* of a neighbor.

stick [stik] *n., v.* **stuck, stick·ing** **1** *n.* A twig or branch cut or broken from a tree, bush, or similar plant. **2** *n.* Any long, slender piece of wood, as a cane, baton, or wand. **3** *n.* Anything like a stick in form: a *stick* of candy. **4** *n. informal* A stiff or dull person. **5** *n. (pl.) slang* A rural area: a cabin in the *sticks.* **6** *v.* To pierce or stab with a pin, knife, or other pointed instrument. **7** *v.* To fasten in place with or as with pins or nails: to *stick* a badge on a lapel. **8** *v.* To fasten to a surface by or as if by an adhesive substance: to *stick* on a stamp. **9** *v.* To put or thrust: He *stuck* his hand into his pocket. **10** *v.* To bring to a stop or halt: Our car was *stuck* in traffic. **11** *v. informal* To puzzle; baffle: The second question in the test really *stuck* me. **12** *v.* To hesitate: She *sticks* at nothing when her mind is made up. **13** *v.* To persist; persevere: to *stick* at one's job. **14** *v.* To be loyal or faithful: We must *stick* together. **—stick up** *slang* To hold up or rob.

stick·ball [stik′bôl′] *n.* A form of baseball played on city streets and playgrounds with a stick and a rubber ball.

stick·er [stik′ər] *n.* Something that is stuck onto a surface, as a gummed label or sign.

stick·le [stik′əl] *v.* **stick·led, stick·ling** To argue about or insist stubbornly.

stick·le·back [stik′əl·bak′] *n.* Any of various small fresh- or saltwater fishes of northern regions, having no scales, but sharp spines on the back. They are noted for the elaborate nests which the male builds for the female's eggs.

stick·ler [stik′lər] *n.* A person who demands that things be done in a certain, very precise way.

stick·pin [stik′pin′] *n.* An ornamental pin, often worn in a necktie.

stick shift An automobile gearshift that is operated by hand.

stick·up [stik′up′] *n. slang* A robbery; holdup.

stick·y [stik′ē] *adj.* **stick·i·er, stick·i·est** **1** That sticks as glue does: *sticky* syrup. **2** Covered with something that makes things stick: *sticky* hands. **3** Warm and humid: a *sticky* day. **—stick′i·ly** *adv.* **—stick′i·ness** *n.*

stiff [stif] *adj.* **1** Not easy to bend; not flexible; rigid: a *stiff* felt hat. **2** Moved with difficulty or with pain: *stiff* brakes; a *stiff* neck. **3** Not liquid or fluid in consistency; thick: a *stiff* varnish. **4** Not graceful or natural; formal: a *stiff* manner. **5** Strong or powerful: a *stiff* current. **6** Difficult; hard; arduous: a *stiff* test; a *stiff* climb. **7** Harsh; severe: a *stiff* penalty. **8** High; unreasonable: a *stiff* price. **—stiff′ly** *adv.* **—stiff′ness** *n.*

stiff·en [stif′ən] *v.* To make or become stiff or stiffer.

stiff-necked [stif′nekt′] *adj.* Not yielding; stubborn; obstinate.

sti·fle [stī′fəl] *v.* **sti·fled, sti·fling** **1** To keep back; suppress; repress: to *stifle* sobs. **2** To die or cause to die by suffocation. **3** To have difficulty in breathing.

stig·ma [stig′mə] *n., pl.* **stig·mas** or **stig·ma·ta** [stig·mä′tə *or* stig′mə·tə] **1** A mark or sign of disgrace or dishonor: Sitting in the corner used to be the *stigma* of disobedience in school. **2** The part of a pistil of a flower that receives pollen. **3** *(pl.)* Marks on the hands, feet, and the side, similar to the five wounds received by Jesus at the crucifixion. They are said to appear miraculously on certain persons.

stig·ma·tize [stig′mə·tīz′] *v.* **stig·ma·tized, stig·ma·tiz·ing** To describe or name as bad or disgraceful: Cheating on the test *stigmatized* the student.

stile [stīl] *n.* **1** A step, or series of steps, on each side of a fence or wall to aid in getting over it. **2** Another name for TURNSTILE.

Stile

sti·let·to [sti·let′ō] *n., pl.* **sti·let·tos** or **sti·let·toes** **1** A small dagger with a slender blade. **2** A small, sharp-pointed instrument for making eyelets in cloth that is to be embroidered.

still[1] [stil] **1** *adj.* Making no sound; silent. **2** *adj.* Free from disturbance; calm; peaceful. **3** *adj.* Without movement; motionless. **4** *v.* To become or make still: The applause suddenly *stilled*; The playwright *stilled* the applause of the audience. **5** *adv.* All the same; nevertheless: The soup, although salty, is *still* tasty. **6** *adv.* Even; yet: You can get *still* more if you try. **7** *conj.* Nevertheless; and yet: I like these pants; *still* I think the others fit better. **8** *adv.* Up to this or that time; yet: They are *still* here. **—still′ness** *n.*

still[2] [stil] *n.* An apparatus for distilling liquids, especially alcoholic liquors.
still·born [stil′bôrn′] *adj.* Dead at birth.
still life 1 In painting, the representation of inanimate objects, such as vases, fruits, and flowers. 2 (*pl.* **still lifes**) A picture of such a subject.
stilt [stilt] *n.* 1 One of a pair of long, slender poles made with a projection to support the foot some distance above the ground in walking. 2 A tall post or pillar used as a support for something, as for a dock or building. 3 Any of several long-legged, three-toed, wading birds.
stilt·ed [stil′tid] *adj.* Stiffly formal and dignified in manner; not natural or at ease.
stim·u·lant [stim′yə·lənt] 1 *n.* Something that stimulates or quickens the activity of the body or of a part of the body: Certain drugs are *stimulants.* 2 *n.* A stimulus or incentive. 3 *adj.* Serving or acting as a stimulant.
stim·u·late [stim′yə·lāt′] *v.* **stim·u·lat·ed, stim·u·lat·ing** 1 To rouse to activity or quickened action; excite; spur: to *stimulate* student interest. 2 To act as a stimulant. **—stim′u·la′tion** *n.*
stim·u·lus [stim′yə·ləs] *n., pl.* **stim·u·li** [stim′yə·lī] 1 Anything that rouses or stirs to action or greater effort. 2 Anything that rouses a part of the body to activity: Light is a *stimulus* to the optic nerve.
sting [sting] *v.* **stung, sting·ing,** *n.* 1 *v.* To pierce or prick painfully: The bee *stung* me. 2 *n.* The act of stinging. 3 *n.* The wound or the pain caused by a sting. 4 *n.* A sharp, pointed organ, as of a bee, able to inflict a painful and sometimes poisonous wound. 5 *v.* To suffer or cause to suffer a sharp pain: My fingers *stung* from the cold; The snow *stung* my face. 6 *v.* To cause to suffer mentally: I was *stung* with remorse. 7 *n.* Any sharp, painful sensation: the *sting* of remorse. 8 *v. slang* To overcharge; cheat.
sting·er [sting′ər] *n.* Something that stings, especially a sharp-pointed part, as of a bee or a scorpion, that inflicts a sting.
sting ray Any of several sea fishes having flat bodies, very broad side fins, and long, whiplike tails with sharp stingers that are capable of inflicting severe, often poisonous wounds.

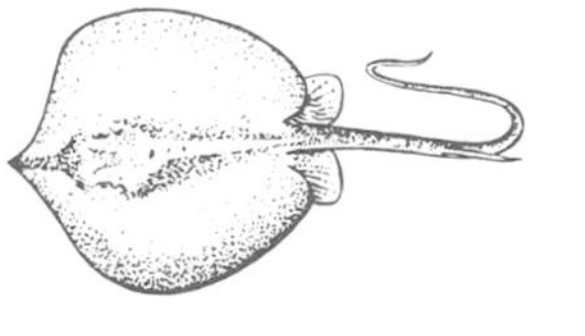
Sting ray

stin·gy [stin′jē] *adj.* **stin·gi·er, stin·gi·est** 1 Unwilling to spend or give; miserly. 2 Very small or scanty; meager. **—stin′·gi·ly** *adv.* **—stin′gi·ness** *n.*
stink [stingk] *n., v.* **stank** or **stunk, stunk, stink·ing** 1 *n.* A strong, foul odor; stench. 2 *v.* To have a strong, foul odor.
stink·er [stingk′ər] *n.* 1 A person or thing that stinks. 2 *informal* A nasty or offensive person.
stint [stint] 1 *v.* To limit, as in amount or share; be stingy with: Don't *stint* yourself. 2 *v.* To be saving or economical: Don't *stint* when it comes to feeding guests. 3 *n.* A task to be performed; share of work: Have you finished your *stint* in the office? 4 *n.* A stinting; limit: to give without *stint.*
sti·pend [stī′pend′] *n.* An allowance, salary, or pension, paid at regular intervals.
stip·ple [stip′əl] *v.* **stip·pled, stip·pling** To draw, paint, or engrave with dots or short strokes instead of lines.
stip·u·late [stip′yə·lāt′] *v.* **stip·u·lat·ed, stip·u·lat·ing** To specify as a condition of an agreement: They *stipulated* that the payments should be made quarterly. **—stip′u·la′tion** *n.*
stip·ule [stip′yo͞ol] *n.* One of a pair of small, leaflike growths at the base of the stem of a leaf.
stir [stûr] *v.* **stirred, stir·ring,** *n.* 1 *v.* To move around with a circular motion, as a fluid or group of dry particles, so as to mix thoroughly: *Stir* the soup; This paint *stirs* easily. 2 *n.* The act of stirring: Give the soup a *stir.* 3 *v.* To move or cause to move, especially slightly: The leaves *stirred*; The wind *stirred* the tall grass. 4 *v.* To move or cause to move energetically: Everyone was up and *stirring* around the house; We *stirred* ourselves to cook dinner. 5 *v.* To bring about; provoke: to *stir* up trouble. 6 *v.* To affect strongly; move with emotion: to *stir* an audience. 7 *n.* Excitement; agitation; interest: The speech provoked quite a *stir.*
stir-fry [stûr′frī′] *v.* **stir-fried, stir-fry·ing** To fry (sliced or diced food) quickly in oil while stirring constantly. This technique is widely used in Chinese cooking.
stir·ring [stûr′ing] *adj.* 1 Stimulating; inspiring: a *stirring* talk. 2 Lively; brisk; active.
stir·rup [stûr′əp *or* stir′əp] *n.* One of a pair of loops with flattened bases suspended by straps on each side of a saddle to support a rider's foot. They are made of wood, metal, or leather. ◆ *Stirrup* comes from an Old English word meaning *mounting rope.*
stirrup bone One of the three small bones of the middle ear. It looks like a stirrup and helps to transmit sound vibrations to the inner ear.
stitch [stich] 1 *n.* A single, complete movement of a threaded needle or other implement through fabric and back again, as in sewing or embroidery. 2 *n.* A single turn of thread or yarn around a needle or other implement, as in knitting or crocheting. 3 *n.* A loop or link made by stitching. 4 *n.* A peculiar or special arrangement of thread or threads in sewing or embroidery: the chain *stitch.* 5 *v.* To sew or join together with stitches. 6 *n.* A sharp, sudden pain, as in the side. 7 *n. informal* The smallest bit: Not a *stitch* of work was done today.
stoat [stōt] *n.* The ermine, especially in its brown summer coat.
stock [stok] 1 *n.* A quantity of something got or kept for use or sale; supply: a *stock* of food; a *stock* of shoes. 2 *n.* Livestock. 3 *v.* To furnish with livestock, as a farm, or with merchandise, as a store. 4 *v.* To lay in supplies or goods: to *stock* up on meat. 5 *v.* To keep for sale: This market *stocks* my favorite brand of cereal. 6 *adj.* Kept on hand, as for sale: a *stock* size. 7 *adj.* Commonly used; trite: a *stock* phrase. 8 *adj.* Employed in handling or caring for stocks of goods: a *stock* clerk. 9 *n.*

a	add	**i**	it	**o͝o**	took	**oi**	oil
ā	ace	**ī**	ice	**o͞o**	pool	**ou**	pout
â	care	**o**	odd	**u**	up	**ng**	ring
ä	palm	**ō**	open	**û**	burn	**th**	thin
e	end	**ô**	order	**yo͞o**	fuse	**th**	this
ē	equal					**zh**	vision

ə = {a in *above* e in *sicken* i in *possible*
o in *melon* u in *circus*

The ownership of a corporation divided into shares. **10** *n.* A share or shares of such ownership. **11** *n.* The trunk or main stem of a tree or other plant. **12** *n.* A line of family descent: They come from Dutch *stock.* **13** *n.* A related group or family of plants or animals. **14** *n.* The broth from boiled meat or fish, used in preparing soups and other foods. **15** *n.* (*pl.*) A wooden frame with holes for confining the ankles and often the wrists, formerly used in punishing petty offenders. **16** *n.* A part that serves as a handle or support, as the wooden part of a rifle. **17** *n.* A broad, stiffened band, formerly worn as a necktie. **—take stock** **1** To take an inventory. **2** To make a careful estimate or examination: January 1 is often a time to *take stock* of one's achievements and to make new resolutions.

stock·ade [sto·kād′] *n., v.* **stock·ad·ed, stock·ad·ing** **1** *n.* A series of posts or stakes, set upright in the earth to form a fence or barrier. **2** *n.* The area thus enclosed. **3** *v.* To surround or fortify with a stockade.

stock·bro·ker [stok′brō′kər] *n.* A person whose business is the buying and selling of stocks and bonds for others.

stock car A standard automobile adapted for racing.

stock company **1** An incorporated company that sells shares of stock. **2** A theatrical company that presents a series of plays.

stock exchange **1** A place where stocks and bonds are bought and sold. **2** A group of stockbrokers who deal in stocks and bonds.

stock·hold·er [stok′hōl′dər] *n.* A person who owns stock in a stock company.

stock·ing [stok′ing] *n.* A close-fitting, knitted or woven covering for the foot and leg.

stocking cap A knitted cap with a cone-shaped end often decorated with a tassel, worn for skiing, tobogganing, and other outdoor sports.

stock-in-trade [stok′ən·trād′] *n.* **1** The equipment needed to run a business or carry on a trade. **2** Something, as a skill, resource, or practice, characteristic of a particular person or group.

stock market **1** A stock exchange. **2** The buying and selling of stocks and bonds. **3** The lists of the prices of stocks and bonds.

stock·pile [stok′pīl′] *n., v.* **stock·piled, stock·pil·ing** **1** *n.* A reserve supply, as of scarce metals. **2** *v.* To accumulate a stockpile of.

stock·room [stok′rōōm′] *n.* A room where stocks of goods are stored.

stock-still [stok′stil′] *adj.* Still as a stock or post; motionless: I stood *stock-still.*

stock·y [stok′ē] *adj.* **stock·i·er, stock·i·est** Solidly built, thickset, and usually short.

stock·yard [stok′yärd′] *n.* A large yard with pens where livestock, as cattle, sheep, or pigs, are kept ready for shipping or slaughter.

stodg·y [stoj′ē] *adj.* **stodg·i·er, stodg·i·est** **1** Dull, stuffy, and commonplace: a *stodgy* speech. **2** Indigestible and heavy: a *stodgy* meal. **3** Overly conventional; old-fashioned; stuffy. **—stodg′i·ly** *adv.* **—stodg′i·ness** *n.*

sto·gie or **sto·gy** [stō′gē] *n., pl.* **sto·gies** A cheap cigar.

sto·ic [stō′ik] **1** *n.* A person who is calm and appears to be unaffected by either pleasure or pain. **2** *adj.* Unaffected by pleasure or pain. **—sto′i·cal** *adj.* **—sto′i·cal·ly** *adv.*

sto·i·cism [stō′ə·siz′əm] *n.* A calm indifference to either pleasure or pain.

stoke [stōk] *v.* **stoked, stok·ing** **1** To supply (a furnace) with fuel. **2** To stir up or tend (a fire or furnace).

stoke·hold [stōk′hōld′] *n.* The furnace room of a steamship.

stoke·hole [stōk′hōl′] *n.* **1** The opening in a furnace where coal is put in. **2** The space in front of the furnaces of a ship where the stokers stand to shovel in coal.

stok·er [stō′kər] *n.* **1** A person who supplies fuel to a furnace, as on a steamship or locomotive. **2** A device for feeding coal to a furnace.

stole[1] [stōl] *n.* **1** A long, narrow band of silk, linen, or other fabric, worn about the shoulders by members of the clergy. **2** A long scarf of fur or cloth, worn about the shoulders.

Stole

stole[2] [stōl] Past tense of STEAL.

sto·len [stō′lən] Past participle of STEAL.

stol·id [stol′id] *adj.* Having or showing little or no feeling; impassive; unemotional. **—stol′id·ly** *adv.*

sto·lid·i·ty [stə·lid′ə·tē] *n.* The condition of being stolid or unemotional; impassivity.

sto·lon [stō′lən] *n.* A plant stem that grows along the ground and takes root at its tip and nodes to form new plants; runner.

sto·ma [stō′mə] *n., pl.* **sto·ma·ta** [stō′mə·tə] **1** A very small opening or pore, as in the leaves of plants or in the walls of blood vessels. **2** A mouthlike opening in some worms.

stom·ach [stum′ək] **1** *n.* A pouchlike organ in the digestive tract that receives food when it is swallowed, partly digests it, and passes it on to the intestines. **2** *n.* The abdomen or belly. **3** *n.* A desire or inclination: I have no *stomach* for that kind of work. **4** *v.* To put up with; endure: I will not *stomach* mean talk.

sto·mach·ache [stum′ək·āk′] *n.* A pain in or near the stomach.

stom·ach·er [stum′ək·ər] *n.* A former article of dress, often embroidered or jeweled, worn over the breast and upper abdomen.

stomp [stomp] **1** *v.* To stamp. **2** *n.* A dance involving a heavy and lively step.

stone [stōn] *n., adj., v.* **stoned, ston·ing** **1** *n.* The hard mineral substance, not metal, of which rock is composed. **2** *adj.* Of or made of stone: a *stone* ax. **3** *v.* To cover or line with stone, as a well. **4** *n.* A small piece of rock, as a pebble. **5** *v.* To throw stones at or to kill with stones. **6** *n.* A jewel or gem. **7** *n.* A piece of stone shaped for a specific use, as a millstone or a gravestone. **8** *n.* A stony formation in the bladder or kidneys, causing illness and pain. **9** *n.* The hard seed or pit of certain fruits. **10** *v.* To remove the seeds or pits from. **11** *n., pl.* **stone** A unit of weight in Great Britain, equal to 14 pounds. **12** *adj.* Made of earthenware: a *stone* bottle.

Stone Age The earliest known period of human

culture, during which stone was used to make tools and weapons.
stone-blind [stōn′blīnd′] *adj.* Totally blind.
stone·cut·ter [stōn′kut′ər] *n.* A person or thing that cuts stone, especially a machine for smoothing or polishing.
stoned [stōnd] *adj. slang* Intoxicated from a drug or alcohol.
stone-deaf [stōn′def′] *adj.* Completely deaf.
Stone·henge [stōn′henj′] *n.* An arrangement of huge stones, now in ruins, erected in prehistoric times on a plain in southern England.
stone·ma·son [stōn′mā′sən] *n.* A person who cuts stones and builds structures with them.
stone·wall [stōn′wôl′] *v. slang* To refuse to give desired information to or cooperate with.
stone·ware [stōn′wâr′] *n.* A strong, heavy, opaque pottery.
stone·work [stōn′wûrk′] *n.* **1** Building or construction with stone as the main material. **2** Something made of stone.
ston·y [stō′nē] *adj.* **ston·i·er, ston·i·est** **1** Full of or covered by stones: a *stony* field. **2** Made of stone. **3** Hard as stone. **4** Like stone, as in hardness and coldness; unfeeling: a *stony* glance.
stood [stŏŏd] Past tense and past participle of STAND.
stooge [stōōj] *n.* **1** A weak-willed or corrupt person who is used to advance someone else's purposes; dupe; puppet. **2** Another name for STRAIGHT MAN.
stool [stōōl] *n.* **1** A backless and armless seat, high or low, for one person. **2** A low bench or rest for the feet, or for the knees in kneeling.
stool pigeon *slang* An informer or spy, especially for the police.
stoop[1] [stōōp] **1** *v.* To bend or lean the body forward and down; crouch. **2** *v.* To stand or walk with the upper part of the body always bent forward; slouch. **3** *n.* The act of stooping; slouch. **4** *v.* To lower or degrade oneself: to *stoop* to lying.
stoop[2] [stōōp] *n.* A small porch or platform at the entrance of a house.
stop [stop] *v.* **stopped, stop·ping,** *n.* **1** *v.* To come or bring to a halt: The clock *stopped* at noon; to *stop* an automobile. **2** *v.* To come or bring to an end: When the laughter *stopped*, the speaker continued; to *stop* a fight. **3** *v.* To prevent (someone) from doing something; hold back; restrain: They wanted to leave, but I *stopped* them. **4** *v.* To leave off, discontinue, or cease (something): to *stop* trying. **5** *v.* To block; obstruct; clog: The passage was *stopped* up with crates and boxes. **6** *v.* To fill in, cover, or close, as a hole. **7** *v.* To stay; visit; tarry; linger: to *stop* somewhere for a few minutes. **8** *n.* A halt or cessation: It was only a short *stop*. **9** *n.* The place where a stop is made: Where is the bus *stop*? **10** *n.* The act of stopping: Let's put a *stop* to the noise. **11** *n.* Something that stops: A *stop* for a door keeps it from slamming shut. **12** *n. British* A punctuation mark, as a period. **13** *n.* A knob on an organ by which the player can connect or disconnect a whole series of pipes.
stop·gap [stop′gap′] *n.* Something used to fill a need temporarily.
stop·light [stop′līt′] *n.* **1** A signal light, usually operated by electricity, that controls movement of traffic. **2** A red light on the rear of a motor vehicle that shines when the brakes are put on.
stop·o·ver [stop′ō′vər] *n.* A stop for a short period, especially one made while traveling and without paying additional fare, continuing the trip with the same ticket on a later train, bus, or other conveyance.
stop·page [stop′ij] *n.* **1** The act of stopping. **2** A being stopped. **3** An obstruction: a *stoppage* in a drain.
stop·per [stop′ər] **1** *n.* Something that stops up or closes, as a plug or cork. **2** *v.* To close with a stopper: to *stopper* a bottle.
stop·watch [stop′woch′] *n.* A watch that has a hand that can be started or stopped at will, used for timing races and other events.
stor·age [stôr′ij] *n.* **1** The act of storing. **2** A being stored. **3** A space for storing things. **4** A charge made for storing. **5** The part of a computer in which information can be saved until it is needed; computer memory.
storage battery A battery containing chemicals that can store up energy when an electric current is run through them and give up the energy as electricity when it is needed.
store [stôr] *n., v.* **stored, stor·ing** **1** *n.* A place where merchandise of any kind is kept for sale; shop. **2** *n.* Something that is laid up or put away for future need. **3** *v.* To put away for future need. **4** *n.* (*pl.*) Supplies, as of arms or clothing. **5** *v.* To furnish or supply; provide. **6** *n.* A large quantity of something; abundance: a *store* of knowledge. **7** *n.* A place where things are placed for safekeeping; storehouse; warehouse. **8** *v.* To place in a storehouse or warehouse. **—in store** In readiness; about to be used or to happen. **—set store by** To value or esteem; regard highly.
store·house [stôr′hous′] *n.* **1** A building in which goods are stored; warehouse. **2** A large or inexhaustible supply: a *storehouse* of ideas.
store·keep·er [stôr′kē′pər] *n.* A person who keeps a store or shop; shopkeeper.
store·room [stôr′rōōm′] *n.* A room in which things are stored, as supplies.
sto·rey [stôr′ē] *n., pl.* **sto·reys** Another spelling of STORY[2].
sto·ried[1] [stôr′ēd] *adj.* Famed in stories or in history; having a notable history: *storied* Greece.
sto·ried[2] [stôr′ēd] *adj.* Having or consisting of stories, as a building: a three-*storied* house.
stork [stôrk] *n.* Any of various large wading birds with long necks and long legs.

Stork

storm [stôrm] **1** *n.* A disturbance of the atmosphere, usually a strong wind accompanied by rain, snow, thunder, or lightning. **2** *n.* A heavy fall of rain, snow, or other precipitation. **3** *v.* To blow with violence; rain, snow, or hail heav-

S

a	add	**i**	it	**ŏŏ**	took	**oi**	oil
ā	ace	**ī**	ice	**ōō**	pool	**ou**	pout
â	care	**o**	odd	**u**	up	**ng**	ring
ä	palm	**ō**	open	**û**	burn	**th**	thin
e	end	**ô**	order	**yōō**	fuse	**th̸**	this
ē	equal					**zh**	vision

ə = a in *above* e in *sicken* i in *possible* o in *melon* u in *circus*

ily: It *stormed* all day. 4 *n.* A rapid flight or shower of objects, as of bullets or missiles. 5 *n.* A violent outburst: a *storm* of applause. 6 *n.* A violent attack or assault: We took the fort by *storm.* 7 *v.* To attack or assault: to *storm* a fort. 8 *v.* To be very angry; rage. 9 *v.* To move or rush with violence or rage: to *storm* about the room.

storm cellar An underground shelter for use during violent storms, as cyclones and tornadoes.

storm center The center or area of lowest pressure and comparative calm in a cyclone or hurricane.

storm petrel A small bird having a dusky black body, a forked or square tail, and long narrow wings. It can fly long distances over the ocean, and often stays at sea even in storms.

storm window An extra window outside the ordinary one as a protection against storms or for greater insulation against cold.

storm·y [stôr′mē] *adj.* **storm·i·er, storm·i·est** 1 Having or disturbed by a storm: *stormy* weather. 2 Violent; emotional: a *stormy* life.

sto·ry¹ [stôr′ē] *n., pl.* **sto·ries** 1 An account or tale of an event or series of events, whether real or made-up. 2 A fictional account or tale intended to entertain. 3 A version of the facts in a situation: a witness's *story.* 4 A news report or broadcast. 5 *informal* A lie.

sto·ry² [stôr′ē] *n., pl.* **sto·ries** A horizontal division in a building made up of the space between two successive floors.

sto·ry·book [stôr′ē·bo͝ok′] 1 *n.* A book of stories, especially for children. 2 *adj.* Of, having to do with, or occurring in a storybook.

sto·ry·tell·er [stôr′ē·tel′ər] *n.* A person who tells stories, especially to groups of children. **—sto′ry·tell′ing** *n., adj.*

stoup [sto͞op] *n.* 1 A basin for holy water at the entrance of a church. 2 A cup or tankard, or its contents: seldom used today.

stout [stout] 1 *adj.* Fat or thickset in body. 2 *adj.* Strong or firm in structure or material: a *stout* fortress. 3 *adj.* Determined; resolute: They put up a *stout* argument. 4 *adj.* Brave; courageous: *stout* warriors. 5 *n.* A strong, very dark, heavy ale or porter. **—stout′ly** *adv.* **—stout′ness** *n.*

stout·heart·ed [stout′här′tid] *adj.* Brave; courageous.

stove¹ [stōv] *n.* An apparatus that uses a fuel, as gas, oil, electricity, or coal, to create heat for warmth or cooking.

stove² [stōv] An alternative past tense and past participle of STAVE: The rock *stove* a hole in the bottom of the ship.

stove·pipe [stōv′pīp′] *n.* 1 A pipe to carry off smoke and gas from a stove to a chimney flue. 2 *informal* A tall silk hat.

stow [stō] *v.* 1 To arrange or pack in a neat, close way: to *stow* freight aboard a train. 2 To fill by packing: to *stow* a truck with goods. **—stow away** 1 To pack away; store. 2 To be a stowaway.

stow·a·way [stō′ə·wā′] *n.* A person who hides aboard a ship, train, or other transport, to travel without buying a ticket.

strad·dle [strad′(ə)l] *v.* **strad·dled, strad·dling,** *n.* 1 *v.* To stand, sit, or walk with the legs spread apart. 2 *v.* To have or put one leg on each side of: to *straddle* a chair. 3 *n.* The act of straddling. 4 *n.* A straddling position. 5 *v.* To seem to favor both sides of (as an issue or question).

Strad·i·var·i·us [strad′ə·vâr′ē·əs] *n., pl.* **Strad·i·var·i·i** [strad′ə·vâr′ē·ī′] A stringed instrument, especially a violin, made by Antonio Stradivari (1644-1737), an Italian violin maker.

strafe [strāf] *v.* **strafed, straf·ing** 1 To fire on (as ground troops) from a low-flying airplane: to *strafe* enemy troops. 2 To bombard heavily. ◆ *Strafe* comes from a German word meaning *to punish.*

strag·gle [strag′əl] *v.* **strag·gled, strag·gling** 1 To lag behind a group that one is traveling with. 2 To wander or stray, as from a road. 3 To be spread unevenly about: Flowers *straggled* all over the garden. **—strag′gler** *n.*

strag·gly [strag′lē] *adj.* **strag·gli·er, strag·gli·est** Scattered or spread out irregularly: *straggly* ivy growing on a wall.

straight [strāt] 1 *adj.* Extending in the same direction without curving; connecting two points in the shortest possible way: a *straight* road; a *straight* line. 2 *adj.* Not curly, as hair. 3 *adj.* In a row: five *straight* misses. 4 *adj.* Level: The picture on the wall isn't *straight.* 5 *adj.* Direct; without detours: a *straight* course. 6 *adj.* True, fair, or honest: a *straight* answer. 7 *adj.* In good condition or order: Is the room *straight*? 8 *adj.* Not smiling; composed: a *straight* face. 9 *adj.* Unmixed: a *straight* drink. 10 *adj.* Strictly following a particular party or policy: to vote a *straight* ticket. 11 *adv.* In a straight manner, line, or course: Stand *straight*; Go *straight* home. **—straight away** or **straight off** Without delay; at once; immediately.

straight angle An angle of 180°.

straight·a·way [strāt′ə·wā′] 1 *adj.* Having no curves or turns. 2 *n.* A straight road, path, or track. 3 *adv.* At once; immediately.

straight·edge [strāt′ej′] *n.* A bar of wood or metal with a straight edge for ruling lines.

straight·en [strāt′(ə)n] *v.* To make or become straight: *Straighten* the picture; The sapling *straightened* after the storm.

straight-faced [strāt′fāst′] *adj.* Showing no emotion, as amusement or displeasure.

straight·for·ward [strāt′fôr′wərd] 1 *adj.* Honest; frank. 2 *adj.* Going directly ahead. 3 *adv.* In a straight course. **—straight′for′ward·ly** *adv.*

straight man A member of a team of comedians who says things to which his or her partner makes funny replies.

straight razor A razor with a long steel blade hinged to a handle into which the blade folds when not in use, like a jackknife.

straight·way [strāt′wā′] *adv.* At once.

strain¹ [strān] 1 *v.* To use the full power of: to *strain* one's muscles. 2 *v.* To make a great effort: I *strained* to lift the weight. 3 *v.* To injure or damage by twisting or pulling: to *strain* an arm; to *strain* a hinge. 4 *n.* Damage or injury produced by straining. 5 *v.* To go beyond the proper limits of: to *strain* a rule. 6 *v.* To pour or squeeze (a liquid) through a sieve or strainer, so as to take out solid parts. 7 *v.* To pull or draw tight; stretch: to *strain* a new violin string. 8 *v.* To push or pull with great force: The dog *strained* at its collar. 9 *n.* Force or pressure: The *strain* broke the chain. 10 *n.* The act of straining. 11 *n.* A being strained. 12 *n.* Severe physical, mental, or emotional pressure: We have all been under a *strain.* 13 *v.* To hug tightly.

strain² [strān] *n.* 1 Line of heredity or descent; breed; race; stock. 2 An inborn or inherited quality, tendency, or character: a *strain* of nearsightedness in a family. **3** Tone, mood, or style: poetry with a *strain* of sadness. **4** (*often pl.*) A passage of music; melody; tune.

strained [strānd] *adj.* Made with effort; not natural; forced: a *strained* smile.

strain·er [strā'nər] *n.* Any of various devices having many small holes, used to strain things.

Strainer

strait [strāt] *n.* **1** A narrow body of water connecting two larger bodies of water. **2** (*often pl.*) A condition of trouble or distress: a family in pitiful *straits*.

strait·en [strāt'(ə)n] *v.* To make limited or restricted, now used especially in the phrase **in straitened circumstances,** without money; poor.

strait·jack·et [strāt'jak'it] *n.* **1** A strong canvas jacket, used to bind tightly the arms of a violent person. **2** A severe restraint.

strait·laced [strāt'lāst'] *adj.* Very strict about proper conduct, manners, or opinions.

strand[1] [strand] **1** *n.* A shore or beach. **2** *v.* To drive or run aground, as a ship. **3** *v.* To leave behind or in a helpless position: to be *stranded* on a desert island.

strand[2] [strand] **1** *n.* One of the threads, filaments, or wires twisted together to make a cord, rope, or cable. **2** *n.* Something like a cord, rope, or cable: a *strand* of pearls.

strange [strānj] *adj.* **strang·er, strang·est** **1** Not seen or heard of before; not familiar: A *strange* dog came to the door. **2** Peculiar or odd; not usual; remarkable: *strange* behavior. **3** Not at home or at ease: I felt *strange* when everybody spoke French. **4** Not accustomed or experienced: The clerk is *strange* to the new duties. **—strange'·ly** *adv.* **—strange'ness** *n.*

stran·ger [strān'jər] *n.* **1** A person who is unfamiliar or not known. **2** A foreigner. **3** A person who is not acquainted with and knows nothing about something or someone specified: The student was a *stranger* to mathematics.

stran·gle [strang'gəl] *v.* **stran·gled, stran·gling** **1** To kill by pressing on the windpipe to prevent breathing. **2** To block the breathing of; choke or suffocate: The smoke almost *strangled* the survivors. **3** To hold back or suppress: to *strangle* a sob. **—stran'gler** *n.*

stran·gu·la·tion [strang'gyə·lā'shən] *n.* **1** The act of strangling. **2** The condition of being strangled.

strap [strap] *n., v.* **strapped, strap·ping** **1** *n.* A long, narrow, flexible strip of leather or other material, usually having a buckle, for fastening about objects. **2** *n.* Any narrow strip that fastens or holds. **3** *v.* To fasten with a strap. **4** *v.* To beat with a strap. **5** *n.* A strop. **6** *v.* To sharpen on a strop.

strap·less [strap'lis] *adj.* Having no straps, especially shoulder straps.

strap·ping [strap'ing] *adj. informal* Large and muscular; robust.

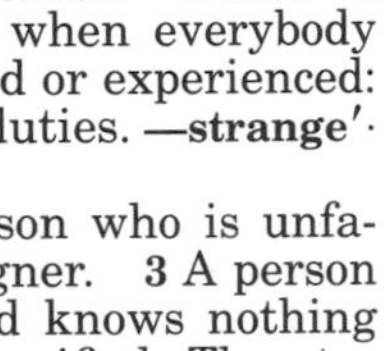
Rock strata

stra·ta [strā'tə *or* strat'ə] *n.pl.* Layers, beds, levels, or grades. Its singular form is STRATUM.

strat·a·gem [strat'ə·jəm] *n.* A trick or scheme used to outwit or deceive an enemy or opponent.

stra·te·gic [strə·tē'jik] *adj.* **1** Of or having to do with strategy. **2** Showing, used in, or important to strategy: a *strategic* move for winning the game. **3** Designed for attacks on an enemy's centers of power or population: *strategic* nuclear weapons; *strategic* bombers. **—stra·te'gi·cal·ly** *adv.*

strat·e·gist [strat'ə·jist] *n.* A person who is highly skilled in strategy.

strat·e·gy [strat'ə·jē] *n., pl.* **strat·e·gies** **1** The technique of planning and carrying on a war or a large part of a war. **2** The careful planning and directing of anything in order to gain some end: a boxer's *strategy*.

strat·i·fi·ca·tion [strat'ə·fə·kā'shən] *n.* Arrangement in or formation into layers or strata.

strat·i·fy [strat'ə·fī] *v.* **strat·i·fied, strat·i·fy·ing** To form into layers or strata; arrange in layers.

strat·o·sphere [strat'ə·sfir'] *n.* A layer of the atmosphere beginning about seven miles up, in which temperatures are more or less uniform and clouds are rare.

strat·o·spher·ic [strat'ə·sfir'ik] *adj.* Of, having to do with, or in the stratosphere.

stra·tum [strā'təm *or* strat'əm] *n., pl.* **stra·ta** or **stra·tums** A layer, bed, or level: a *stratum* of coal; the upper *stratum* of society.

stra·tus [strā'təs *or* strat'əs] *n., pl.* **stra·ti** [strā'tē *or* strat'ē] A low, foglike cloud that lies in a flat layer over a wide area.

straw [strô] **1** *n.* The dried stems or stalks of grains or other grasslike plants. **2** *n.* A single such dried stem. **3** *n.* A material woven from straw, used in making hats, baskets, and other items. **4** *adj.* Of or like straw: a *straw* mat. **5** *n.* A thin tube, as one of paper or glass, used to suck up a drink. **6** *adj.* Yellowish, as the color of straw. **7** *n.* Something almost worthless: I don't care a *straw* about going. **8** *adj.* Counting for nothing.

straw·ber·ry [strô'ber'ē] *n., pl.* **straw·ber·ries** **1** A small, red, tasty berry. **2** The stemless plant, related to the rose, on which this berry grows.

straw man **1** A figure resembling a person, made of straw. **2** An imaginary or weak opponent or position, set up for the purpose of being easily defeated or refuted. **3** A person used as a front for some questionable business or activity.

straw vote A vote with no official effect, taken to test opinion.

stray [strā] **1** *v.* To wander or turn away from what is correct, as a route, group, or place. **2** *n.* A person or a domestic animal that is wandering or lost. **3** *adj.* Having strayed; wandering or lost: a *stray* cat. **4** *v.* To turn away; leave off: to *stray* from honesty. **5** *adj.* Scattered about or occasional: a few *stray* trees.

streak [strēk] **1** *n.* A long, thin, and often uneven mark: a *streak* of lightning; a *streak* of dirt. **2** *v.* To mark or become marked with streaks: to *streak* a floor with dirt; That wet paint *streaks*. **3** *n.* A

S

a	add	**i**	it	**o͝o**	took	**oi**	oil
ā	ace	**ī**	ice	**o͞o**	pool	**ou**	pout
â	care	**o**	odd	**u**	up	**ng**	ring
ä	palm	**ō**	open	**û**	burn	**th**	thin
e	end	**ô**	order	**yo͞o**	fuse	**t͟h**	this
ē	equal					**zh**	vision

ə = a in *above* e in *sicken* i in *possible*; o in *melon* u in *circus*

small amount; trace: a *streak* of meanness. **4** *n.* A period of time; spell: a winning *streak.* **5** *n.* A layer or strip: a *streak* of coal. **6** *v.* To move, run, or travel at great speed.

streak·y [strē′kē] *adj.* **streak·i·er, streak·i·est** **1** Marked with or occurring in streaks. **2** Variable or uneven: a *streaky* concert, often bad but sometimes brilliant.

stream [strēm] **1** *n.* A small body of flowing water. **2** *n.* A continuous flow of a liquid or gas. **3** *v.* To flow out in a stream: Tears *streamed* from my eyes. **4** *v.* To pour out freely; gush: The tap *streamed* rusty water. **5** *n.* Any continuous passage or flow, as of people, light, or traffic. **6** *v.* To come out or pass by continuously and in large numbers: Hornets *streamed* from their nest. **7** *v.* To float with a waving movement, as a flag in a wind.

stream·er [strē′mər] *n.* **1** A long, ribbonlike flag. **2** Any long, narrow strip, as one of paper or cloth, with one end hanging loose: The ballroom was decorated with *streamers.*

stream·let [strēm′lit] *n.* A small stream.

stream·line [strēm′līn′] *n., v.* **stream·lined, stream·lin·ing** **1** *n.* A path taken by particles of a fluid, as gas, in flowing past an object when there is little or no turbulence. **2** *v.* To provide with a shape that will create minimum turbulence when passing through a gas or liquid: to *streamline* a motorboat. **3** *v.* To make more simple or efficient by removing unnecessary parts or stages: to *streamline* a production process.

stream·lined [strēm′līnd′] *adj.* **1** Designed to offer minimal resistance to motion through air or water: a *streamlined* airplane with swept-back wings. **2** Made efficient or compact by the removal of unnecessary parts or stages: a *streamlined* business operation.

street [strēt] *n.* **1** A public road in a city or town, usually with sidewalks and buildings on one or both sides. **2** A roadway for vehicles, usually between sidewalks. **3** *informal* The people who live, gather, or work on a particular street: The whole *street* came out to cheer the winner.

street·car [strēt′kär′] *n.* An electric car that runs on rails set into the street; trolley.

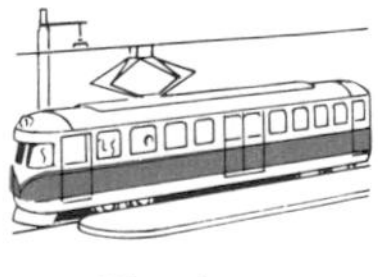

Streetcar

street·wise [strēt′wīz′] *adj.* Experienced in dealing with people and difficult situations in urban areas, especially as the result of having grown up in such an area.

strength [streng(k)th] *n.* **1** The quality of being strong; force or power, especially of the muscles. **2** The capacity of resisting a force without bending or breaking; toughness: the *strength* of steel. **3** Effectiveness or potency: the *strength* of a drug. **4** Intensity or concentration: the *strength* of a solution of ammonia. **5** Available numerical force: What is the army's full *strength*? **6** A person or thing that gives or represents strength.

strength·en [streng(k)′thən] *v.* To make or become strong or stronger.

stren·u·ous [stren′yōō·əs] *adj.* **1** Taking much effort or energy: Football is a *strenuous* sport. **2** Vigorously active: a *strenuous* athlete. **—stren′u·ous·ly** *adv.*

strep [strep] *adj. informal* Streptococcal.

strep·to·coc·cal [strep′tə·kok′əl] *adj.* Of, having to do with, caused by, or infected with streptococci: a *streptococcal* sore throat.

strep·to·coc·cus [strep′tə·kok′əs] *n., pl.* **strep·to·coc·ci** [strep′tə·kok′sī] One of a kind of ball-shaped bacteria grouped together in long chains. Some types cause disease.

strep·to·my·cin [strep′tō·mī′sin] *n.* A strong antibiotic obtained from a soil fungus. It is used to treat certain illnesses, as tuberculosis.

stress [stres] **1** *n.* A pressure or force that tends to change the shape of something; strain. **2** *v.* To apply such a force to: The weight *stressed* the beam. **3** *n.* The resistance of a body to outside forces. **4** *n.* In music or speech, special force or loudness given to a note or syllable; accent. **5** *v.* To give special accent to (a note or syllable). **6** *n.* Special weight or importance. **7** *v.* To give special weight or importance to: to *stress* science and mathematics. **8** *n.* Emotional or mental strain or tension.

stretch [strech] **1** *v.* To extend or be extended to full or normal size or beyond: The heavy weight *stretched* the rope. **2** *v.* To extend or be extended without breaking or losing elasticity: Rubber *stretches* easily. **3** *adj.* Capable of stretching easily so as to fit closely: said of clothing: *stretch* socks. **4** *n.* The ability to be extended in length or width without breaking or losing elasticity: Elastic may lose its *stretch.* **5** *v.* To reach or extend: to *stretch* out a hand in greeting. **6** *v.* To extend the body or a part of it, often to relieve stiffness: The cat *stretched.* **7** *v.* To cause to reach, as between two points: to *stretch* telegraph wires. **8** *n.* The act of stretching. **9** *n.* The condition of being stretched. **10** *v.* To strain or exert to the utmost: to *stretch* every nerve. **11** *v.* To go beyond the proper limits of; abuse: to *stretch* the truth. **12** *v.* To extend, as over an area or between two limits: The desert *stretches* for miles. **13** *n.* An extent or expanse, as of space or time: a *stretch* of forest; a *stretch* of luck. **14** *n.* Either of the straight parts of a racetrack, especially the one that includes the finish.

stretch·er [strech′ər] *n.* **1** A person or thing that stretches. **2** A thing used in stretching, as in making shoes larger or drying curtains. **3** A strip of canvas supported on poles, used to carry sick, injured, or dead persons.

strew [strōō] *v.* **strewed, strewed** or **strewn, strew·ing** **1** To throw about in a disorderly way; scatter: to *strew* bits of paper on the floor. **2** To cover by scattering or sprinkling: The table was *strewn* with magazines.

stri·at·ed [strī′āt·id] *adj.* Having small stripes or parallel grooves.

stri·a·tion [strī·ā′shən] *n.* **1** The condition of being striated. **2** One of a series of parallel stripes or grooves.

strick·en [strik′ən] **1** An alternative past participle of STRIKE. **2** *adj.* Strongly affected or overcome, as by a disaster or an illness. **3** *adj.* Wounded or hit, as by an arrow or bullet: a *stricken* animal.

strict [strikt] *adj.* **1** Following or enforcing rules exactly: a *strict* teacher. **2** Exact; precise: a *strict* account of what happened. **3** Rigidly enforced; allowing no exceptions or evasions: *strict* rules. **4** Complete; absolute: Pay *strict* attention. **—strict′ly** *adv.* **—strict′ness** *n.*

stric·ture [strik′chər] *n.* **1** An abnormal narrowing or closing off of a tube or duct in the body. **2** Severe criticism.

stride [strīd] *n., v.* **strode, strid·den** [strid′(ə)n], **strid·ing** **1** *n.* A long, sweeping step. **2** *n.* The distance covered by such a step. **3** *v.* To walk with long, sweeping steps: to *stride* along the lane. **4** *v.* To walk or cross with a stride or strides: to *stride* the floor; to *stride* over a brook. **5** *n.* (*often pl.*) An advance or achievement: to make great *strides* in science. **6** *v.* To sit or stand with one leg on either side of; straddle.

stri·dent [strīd′(ə)nt] *adj.* Harsh and noisy; grating: a *strident* shout. **—stri′dent·ly** *adv.*

strife [strīf] *n.* Any bitter or angry fight, quarrel, or conflict: *strife* among nations.

strike [strīk] *v.* **struck, struck** or **strick·en** [strik′ən], **strik·ing** *n.* **1** *v.* To make or cause to make forceful contact with; hit: The car *struck* the wall. **2** *v.* To come into forceful contact; hit: The cars *struck* together. **3** *v.* To hit with a blow: The fighter *struck* the punching bag. **4** *v.* To aim or deliver a blow or blows: The boxer *struck* about wildly. **5** *n.* The act of striking or hitting; blow. **6** *n.* In baseball, a pitch that the batter misses, allows to cross home plate between the shoulders and knees, or swings at and hits foul when having less than two strikes. **7** *n.* In bowling, the knocking down of all the pins with the first ball thrown. **8** *v.* To attack or assault: to *strike* the enemy. **9** *n.* An attack or assault, especially one made by air. **10** *v.* To remove: *Strike* it from the record. **11** *v.* To start burning; ignite, as a match. **12** *v.* To form, as by stamping or printing: to *strike* coins. **13** *v.* To indicate (the time) by the sound of a bell: The clock *struck* two. **14** *v.* To be indicated, as by the sound of a bell: Noon has *struck*. **15** *v.* To cause to sound, as by a blow: *Strike* a note on the piano. **16** *v.* To reach, come upon, or discover: The sound *struck* my ear; to *strike* oil. **17** *n.* A new or unexpected discovery, as of oil or ore. **18** *v.* To affect or overcome in a sudden or dramatic way: The listeners were *struck* speechless. **19** *v.* To occur to: An idea *strikes* me. **20** *v.* To give an impression to: The storekeeper *strikes* me as being honest. **21** *v.* To make an impression on: The idea *struck* their fancy. **22** *v.* To assume; take up: to *strike* an attitude. **23** *v.* To cause to enter suddenly: The thought *struck* fear into their hearts. **24** *v.* To lower or take down: to *strike* a tent. **25** *v.* To stop work, as a group, until some demands are met: The workers *struck* for better pay. **26** *n.* A stopping of work by a group of workers to make an employer meet their demands. **27** *v.* To agree upon: to *strike* a bargain. **28** *v.* To take a course; start: to *strike* for home. **—on strike** Not working because taking part in a strike. **—strike dumb** To astonish; amaze. **—strike home** **1** To deal an effective blow. **2** To have a strong effect. **—strike it rich** To suddenly become wealthy. **—strike off** To remove or take off, as from a list. **—strike out** **1** To cross out or erase. **2** To aim a blow or blows. **3** To make a start: to *strike out* on one's own. **4** In baseball, to put out or be put out as a result of three strikes. **—strike up** To start up; begin.

strike·break·er [strīk′brā′kər] *n.* A person who helps to make a strike fail by taking a striker's job. **—strike′break′ing** *n.*

strike·out [strīk′out′] *n.* In baseball, an out resulting from a batter's being charged with three strikes.

strik·er [strī′kər] *n.* **1** A person or thing that strikes. **2** An employee who is on strike.

strik·ing [strī′king] *adj.* Appealing strongly to the eye or to the imagination; impressive: the *striking* colors of the trees in autumn. **—strik′ing·ly** *adv.*

string [string] *n., v.* **strung, string·ing,** *adj.* **1** *n.* A cord thicker than thread, thinner than rope, used for tying and lacing. **2** *n.* Something else used for tying, as a strip of cloth or leather. **3** *n.* A group of things hung on a string: a *string* of beads. **4** *v.* To hang on or from a string: to *string* pearls. **5** *n.* A stringlike organ or part, as of a plant or animal. **6** *v.* To remove stringlike parts from: to *string* beans. **7** *v.* Cord of gut or wire for musical instruments. **8** *v.* To provide with strings: to *string* a harp. **9** *n.* (*pl.*) Stringed instruments, especially those played with a bow. **10** *adj.* Consisting of or meant to be played by such stringed instruments: a *string* trio. **11** *n.* A succession of things, acts, or events: a *string* of lakes; a *string* of lies. **12** *v.* To extend, stretch, or go, often in a line or series: to *string* a rope from the tree to the house. **13** *n.* (*usually pl.*) *informal* A condition, limitation, or restriction: a gift with no *strings* attached. **—pull strings** To use one's influence to gain an advantage. **—string along** *informal* To trick, deceive, or keep waiting. **—string along with** *informal* To go along or agree with.

string bean **1** A type of bean cultivated for its edible pod. **2** The pod itself. **3** *informal* Any very tall, thin person.

stringed instrument [stringd] An instrument played by plucking or, especially, by bowing its strings.

strin·gen·cy [strin′jən·sē] *n.* The quality or condition of being stringent.

strin·gent [strin′jənt] *adj.* **1** Closely binding; severe: *stringent* rules. **2** Limited or constricted: a test with a *stringent* time limit. **3** Characterized by or urging a scarcity of money or a difficulty in giving or receiving credit: a *stringent* economic policy. **—strin′gent·ly** *adv.*

string·er [string′ər] *n.* **1** A person or thing that strings. **2** A horizontal timber used to support or secure other parts of a structure.

string quartet **1** Four musicians playing stringed instruments together, usually two violins, a viola, and a cello. **2** A musical composition for such a group.

string tie A very narrow necktie, usually tied in a bow.

string·y [string′ē] *adj.* **string·i·er, string·i·est** **1** Suggesting a string or strings: a *stringy* plant; *stringy* hair. **2** Containing tough fibers or sinews: *stringy* meat. **3** Forming strings: *stringy* syrup. **4** Tall and wiry in build.

strip[1] [strip] *v.* **stripped, strip·ping** **1** To undress. **2** To remove the covering of: to *strip* a wire. **3** To

a	add	**i**	it	**o͝o**	took	**oi**	oil
ā	ace	**ī**	ice	**o͞o**	pool	**ou**	pout
â	care	**o**	odd	**u**	up	**ng**	ring
ä	palm	**ō**	open	**û**	burn	**th**	thin
e	end	**ô**	order	**yo͞o**	fuse	**t͟h**	this
ē	equal					**zh**	vision

ə = {a in *above* e in *sicken* i in *possible*; o in *melon* u in *circus*}

S

make bare or empty: to *strip* a theater of seats. **4** To remove; take away: to *strip* the wrapper from a package. **5** To deprive: The offender was *stripped* of all privileges. **6** To break or damage a part, as the teeth or thread, of: to *strip* gears; to *strip* a screw. **—strip down** To take apart for repair, as a motor. **—strip′per** *n.*

strip[2] [strip] *n.* A long, narrow piece of something, as cloth, wood, or land.

stripe[1] [strīp] *n., v.* **striped, strip·ing** **1** *n.* A line, band, or strip that is different, as in color or material, from what is on both sides of it. **2** *v.* To mark with a stripe or stripes. **3** *n.* Kind; sort: a person of that *stripe.* **4** *n.* A strip of material on the sleeve of a uniform, indicating rank or length of service.

stripe[2] [strīp] *n.* **1** A blow struck with a whip or rod. **2** The welt on the skin caused by this.

striped [strīpt] *adj.* Marked with stripes.

strip·ling [strip′ling] *n.* An adolescent boy; youth.

strive [strīv] *v.* **strove, striv·en** [striv′ən], **striv·ing** **1** To make a strong effort: to *strive* for good grades. **2** To contend, struggle, or fight: The two *strove* for the lead.

strode [strōd] Past tense of STRIDE.

stroke [strōk] *n., v.* **stroked, strok·ing** **1** *n.* The act of striking; blow or impact: a *stroke* with a whip; a *stroke* of lightning. **2** *n.* A blow or the sound of a blow of a striking mechanism, as of a clock. **3** *n.* A single movement, as of the hand, arm, or a tool: a tennis *stroke.* **4** *n.* A single mark, as of a pen or brush. **5** *n.* A sudden or dramatic event or action: a *stroke* of good luck. **6** *n.* A brilliant action; feat: a *stroke* of genius. **7** *n. informal* A portion or stint: The class hasn't done a *stroke* of work all day. **8** *n.* The bursting of a blood vessel in the brain. **9** *n.* One of a series of repeated motions: a *stroke* of a swimmer; a *stroke* of a machine. **10** *n.* The crew member who sets the rate of rowing for a crew. **11** *v.* To set the rate or tempo of rowing for: to *stroke* a crew. **12** *v.* To pass the hand over gently; pet. **13** *n.* A gentle rubbing or stroking movement.

stroll [strōl] **1** *v.* To walk in a slow, idle way. **2** *n.* A slow, idle walk. **3** *v.* To travel about; wander.

stroll·er [strō′lər] *n.* **1** A person who strolls. **2** A carriage in which a baby can sit upright.

strong [strông] *adj.* **1** Powerful or forceful: a *strong* wind; a *strong* person; a *strong* voice. **2** Solidly made or constituted; not easily destroyed, injured, or strained: *strong* walls. **3** Very potent or effective: a *strong* drug; a *strong* drink. **4** Having great ability: She is *strong* in mathematics. **5** Absorbing or compelling: a *strong* interest. **6** Resisting temptation and self-indulgence: a *strong* character. **7** Powerful or intense in its effect on the senses or mind: a *strong* odor; a *strong* suggestion. **8** Of a specified number: a group of members 500 *strong.* **—strong′ly** *adv.*

strong·box [strông′boks′] *n.* A sturdy box for storing money or valuables.

strong·hold [strông′hōld′] *n.* A fortified place; fortress.

stron·ti·um [stron′sh(ē·)əm *or* stron′tē·əm] *n.* A soft, very reactive metallic element that is chemically very similar to calcium.

strontium 90 A radioactive isotope of strontium that occurs as fallout from nuclear explosions. It is a hazard to health when cows graze where it has fallen because it is absorbed in bones and teeth like calcium and reaches humans through the cows' milk.

strop [strop] *n., v.* **stropped, strop·ping** **1** *n.* A strip, as one of leather or canvas, on which to sharpen a razor. **2** *v.* To sharpen on a strop.

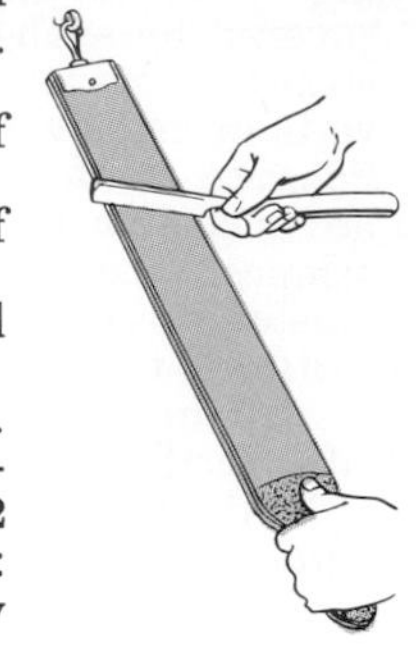

Strop

stro·phe [strō′fē] *n.* A division of a poem; stanza.

strove [strōv] Past tense of STRIVE.

struck [struk] Past tense and past participle of STRIKE.

struc·tur·al [struk′chər·əl] *adj.* **1** Of or having to do with structure: *structural* engineering. **2** Used or needed in construction: *structural* steel. **—struc′tur·al·ly** *adv.*

structural steel **1** Steel manufactured in the shapes of beams or girders, to be used in building. **2** An alloy of steel suitable for such use.

struc·ture [struk′chər] *n., v.* **struc·tured, struc·tur·ing** **1** *n.* Something that is constructed, as a building or machine. **2** *n.* The way in which something is constructed or put together: The *structure* of the cabin was sound. **3** *v.* To organize or put together: to *structure* a plan. **4** *n.* A part of an animal or plant: The eye is a delicate *structure.*

strug·gle [strug′əl] *n., v.* **strug·gled, strug·gling** **1** *n.* A violent effort or series of efforts. **2** *v.* To make violent efforts; strive. **3** *v.* To make one's way by violent efforts: to *struggle* through mud. **4** *n.* A flight or conflict. **5** *v.* To fight; battle.

strum [strum] *v.* **strummed, strum·ming,** *n.* **1** *v.* To play (as a stringed instrument or a tune) in a careless or unskillful way. **2** *n.* The act of strumming, or the sound made by such an act.

strum·pet [strum′pət] *n.* A prostitute.

strung [strung] Past tense of STRING.

strut [strut] *n., v.* **strut·ted, strut·ting** **1** *n.* A vain or pompous step or walk. **2** *v.* To walk in a vain or pompous way. **3** *n.* A rod or girder used to support or reinforce a structure. **4** *v.* To brace or support with struts.

strych·nine [strik′nin *or* strik′nīn′] *n.* A very poisonous drug, sometimes used in small doses as a stimulant.

stub [stub] *n., v.* **stubbed, stub·bing** **1** *n.* A short piece or end that is left after something is used up, torn out, or removed: the *stub* of a pencil; a check *stub.* **2** *n.* A stump, as of a tree or bush. **3** *n.* Something short or broad, as a pen with a wide point. **4** *v.* To strike (as one's toe) against something.

stub·ble [stub′əl] *n.* **1** The short stalks left in the ground after a crop has been cut. **2** Any short, stubby growth like this, as a short, bristly beard. **—stub′bly** *adj.*

stub·born [stub′ərn] *adj.* **1** Hard to persuade or convince; not giving in easily; obstinate. **2** Hard to handle or cure: a *stubborn* illness. **—stub′born·ly** *adv.* **—stub′born·ness** *n.* ◆ See OBSTINATE.

stub·by [stub′ē] *adj.* **stub·bi·er, stub·bi·est** **1** Short, stiff, and bristly: a *stubby* beard. **2** Short and thick: *stubby* fingers. **3** Full of stubs or stumps: *stubby* fields.

stuc·co [stuk′ō] *n., pl.* **stuc·cos** or **stuc·coes** *v.* **stuc·coed, stuc·co·ing** **1** *n.* A strong plaster or cement used to cover outside walls of a house or building.

2 *n.* A fine plaster used to decorate or ornament inside walls. 3 *v.* To apply stucco to.

stuck [stuk] Past tense and past participle of STICK.

stuck-up [stuk′up′] *adj. informal* Conceited, arrogant, or snobbish.

stud[1] [stud] *n., v.* **stud·ded, stud·ding** 1 *n.* A small knob, round-headed nail, or other projecting ornament used on a surface. 2 *v.* To set or decorate with studs: to *stud* a belt. 3 *n.* In building a wall, any of the vertical posts to which wallboards or laths are nailed. 4 *n.* A removable button, used to fasten shirts. 5 *v.* To be scattered or strewn over.

stud[2] [stud] *n.* 1 A collection of horses kept for breeding, riding, hunting, or racing. 2 A male animal kept for breeding purposes.

stu·dent [st(y)o͞od′(ə)nt] *n.* A person who studies, especially in a school or college.

stud·ied [stud′ēd] *adj.* Planned or deliberate; done on purpose: a *studied* insult.

stu·di·o [st(y)o͞o′dē·ō] *n., pl.* **stu·di·os** 1 The place where someone, especially an artist or musician, works or teaches. 2 A place in which films, recordings, or radio performances are made.

stu·di·ous [st(y)o͞o′dē·əs] *adj.* 1 Devoted to studying: a *studious* child. 2 Giving or showing serious attention: a *studious* expression; to be *studious* in pleasing others. **—stu′di·ous·ly** *adv.*

stud·y [stud′ē] *v.* **stud·ied, stud·y·ing,** *n., pl.* **stud·ies** 1 *v.* To attempt to learn, know, or understand: to *study* music; to *study* a crime. 2 *n.* The act of studying. 3 *n.* A branch of knowledge: the *study* of physics. 4 *n.* A room set aside for studying, reading, or writing. 5 *v.* To take classes in: to *study* dancing. 6 *n.* (*pl.*) Education or training: to do well in one's *studies.* 7 *v.* To examine with care: to *study* a plan to find its flaws. 8 *v.* To devote thought or attention; try: The guest *studies* to be polite. 9 *n.* Deep concentration or thought. 10 *n.* In art, a preliminary sketch or exercise. 11 *n.* A piece of music designed or played to develop a skill; étude. 12 *n.* A detailed examination or treatment of a subject: a *study* on butterflies.

stuff [stuf] 1 *n.* The basic substance from which something is made: What kind of *stuff* is that stew made of? 2 *n.* Basic character or quality: You are made of braver *stuff* than I. 3 *n.* Cloth; material. 4 *v.* To fill, pack, or block: to *stuff* a bag; to *stuff* a crack. 5 *v.* To fill with other food, as bread crumbs and seasoning: to *stuff* a turkey. 6 *v.* To fill the skin of (a dead bird or animal) in order to produce a lifelike appearance of the original. 7 *v.* To fill or cram with food. 8 *v.* To fill with faked votes: to *stuff* a ballot box. 9 *v.* To cram, jam, or shove: to *stuff* a handkerchief into a drawer. 10 *n. informal* A collection of objects or possessions. 11 *n.* Worthless things or ideas: *stuff* and nonsense.

stuffed shirt [stuft] *informal* A pompous person.

stuff·ing [stuf′ing] *n.* The material used to stuff something, as the down of a pillow, or the food used to stuff a turkey or roast.

stuff·y [stuf′ē] *adj.* **stuff·i·er, stuff·i·est** 1 Badly ventilated: a *stuffy* room. 2 Stopped up or causing difficult breathing: a *stuffy* nose. 3 *informal* Pompous and dull: a *stuffy* lecture. 4 *informal* Old-fashioned or stodgy. **—stuff′i·ness** *n.*

stul·ti·fy [stul′tə·fī′] *v.* **stul·ti·fied, stul·ti·fy·ing** 1 To cause to seem or be foolish or absurd. 2 To make useless, invalid, or futile.

stum·ble [stum′bəl] *v.* **stum·bled, stum·bling,** *n.* 1 *v.* To miss a step in walking or running; trip. 2 *v.* To move along in an unsteady way: The tired child *stumbled* up the stairs. 3 *v.* To speak or read in a halting way. 4 *v.* To find by accident: to *stumble* on a bargain. 5 *v.* To fall into wrongdoing or error. 6 *n.* The act of stumbling. 7 *n.* A misstep or blunder.

stumbling block Any obstacle or hindrance: Shyness is a *stumbling block* to making friends.

stump [stump] 1 *n.* The part of something that remains after the larger or principal part has been cut away, removed, or used up; stub: the *stump* of a tree; the *stump* of an arm. 2 *n.* A platform from which political speeches are made. 3 *v.* To go about (an area), making political speeches. 4 *v.* To walk in a stiff, heavy way. 5 *v. informal* To baffle or confuse: Your question certainly *stumps* me.

stump·y [stum′pē] *adj.* **stump·i·er, stump·i·est** 1 Short and thick; stubby. 2 Full of tree stumps: a *stumpy* field.

stun [stun] *v.* **stunned, stun·ning** 1 To make unconscious or unable to act: The blow *stunned* me. 2 To astonish or shock: The play *stunned* us, it was so forceful.

stung [stung] Past tense and past participle of STING.

stunk [stungk] A past tense and past participle of STINK.

stun·ning [stun′ing] *adj.* 1 Causing unconsciousness, astonishment, or shock: a *stunning* blow. 2 *informal* Extremely beautiful or stylish: a *stunning* costume.

stunt[1] [stunt] *v.* To stop the natural growth or development of: Lack of feed *stunted* the cattle.

stunt[2] [stunt] *informal* 1 *n.* A trick or show of skill; feat. 2 *v.* To perform a stunt or stunts, especially in an airplane.

stu·pe·fac·tion [st(y)o͞o′pə·fak′shən] *n.* 1 A stupefied state. 2 Amazement; astonishment.

stu·pe·fy [st(y)o͞o′pə·fī] *v.* **stu·pe·fied, stu·pe·fy·ing** 1 To dull the senses or capabilities of; stun: We were *stupefied* with exhaustion. 2 To amaze; astound.

stu·pen·dous [st(y)o͞o·pen′dəs] *adj.* Highly impressive or astonishing, especially because of overwhelming size. **—stu·pen′dous·ly** *adv.*

stu·pid [st(y)o͞o′pid] *adj.* 1 Not intelligent or bright; dull. 2 Showing or caused by a lack of intelligence or thought; senseless: a *stupid* mistake. 3 Dull; tedious; boring: a *stupid* play. **—stu′·pid·ly** *adj.*

stu·pid·i·ty [st(y)o͞o·pid′ə·tē] *n., pl.* **stu·pid·i·ties** 1 Lack of intelligence or understanding; dullness. 2 A foolish action or idea.

stu·por [st(y)o͞o′pər] *n.* A dazed state in which the power to feel, think, or act is lost or greatly lessened.

a	add	**i**	it	**o͝o**	took	**oi**	oil
ā	ace	**ī**	ice	**o͞o**	pool	**ou**	pout
â	care	**o**	odd	**u**	up	**ng**	ring
ä	palm	**ō**	open	**û**	burn	**th**	thin
e	end	**ô**	order	**yo͞o**	fuse	**th**	this
ē	equal					**zh**	vision

ə = a in *above* e in *sicken* i in *possible* o in *melon* u in *circus*

S

stur·dy [stûr′dē] *adj.* **stur·di·er, stur·di·est** 1 Vigorous; strong: a *sturdy* oak tree. 2 Not giving in or yielding; firm: a *sturdy* table; *sturdy* defense. **—stur′di·ly** *adv.* **—stur′di·ness** *n.*

stur·geon [stûr′jən] *n.* A large edible fish covered with bony plates, found in northern waters. It is valued as a source of caviar.

stut·ter [stut′ər] 1 *v.* To speak in a jerky, uneven way, often with hesitations or with the same sound repeated many times. 2 *n.* The action or habit of stuttering. **—stut′ter·er** *n.*

sty[1] [stī] *n., pl.* **sties** 1 A pen for hogs. 2 Any very filthy place.

sty[2] [stī] *n., pl.* **sties** An inflamed swelling of an oil gland on the edge of an eyelid.

sty·gi·an [stij′ē·ən] *adj.* 1 (*often written* **Stygian**) Of or having to do with the river Styx or the lower world of the dead. 2 Dark and gloomy.

style [stīl] *n., v.* **styled, styl·ing** 1 *n.* The method or manner in which something is done: a medieval *style* of architecture; an Oriental *style* of dress. 2 *n.* A distinctive or individual manner of expression, as in writing or painting: The novel shows *style.* 3 *n.* The current or fashionable manner or way of acting, dressing, or building: That suit is not in *style.* 4 *n.* A particular type, kind, or fashion: a new *style* of coat; an old *style* of car. 5 *v.* To design or fashion: to *style* clothes. 6 *n.* Luxury or elegance: to live in *style.* 7 *v.* To make consistent or correct in spelling and punctuation: to *style* a manuscript. 8 *n.* A stalk forming part of the pistil of a flower. 9 *n.* A stylus. 10 *v.* To name; call: New York City is *styled* the Big Apple.

styl·ish [stī′lish] *adj.* In current style or fashion; fashionable. **—styl′ish·ly** *adj.*

sty·list [stī′list] *n.* 1 A writer or other artist who cultivates a distinctive manner of expression. 2 A person who designs or recommends styles, as of hair arrangement or clothing.

sty·lis·tic [stī·lis′tik] *adj.* Of or having to do with style. **—sty·lis′ti·cal·ly** *adv.*

styl·ize [stī′līz′] *v.* **styl·ized, styl·iz·ing** 1 To put into or design according to a particular style or fashion. 2 To represent in a conventional rather than a realistic way: The heart on a playing card is *stylized.* **—styl·i·za·tion** [stī′lə·zā′shən] *n.*

sty·lus [stī′ləs] *n., pl.* **sty·lus·es** or **sty·li** [stī′lī] 1 A pointed tool, as one used for engraving or writing on wax. 2 The needle of a phonograph.

sty·mie [stī′mē] *v.* **sty·mied, sty·mie·ing** To bring to a standstill; impede completely; block: The plan to build a new school was *stymied* by lack of funds.

styp·tic [stip′tik] 1 *adj.* Causing the tissues to contract, especially so as to check bleeding. 2 *n.* A styptic substance, as alum.

sty·rene [stī′rēn′] *n.* A liquid hydrocarbon used in making plastics and resins.

Styx [stiks] *n.* In Greek myths, a river of the lower world. The dead had to pay Charon to ferry them across, to reach Hades.

sua·sion [swā′zhən] *n.* Persuasion. **—sua·sive** [swā′·siv *or* swā′ziv] *adj.*

suave [swäv] *adj.* Smoothly pleasant; urbane. **—suave′ly** *adv.* **—suave′ness** *n.* **—suav′i·ty** *n.*

sub [sub] *n., v.* **subbed, sub·bing** *informal* 1 *n.* A submarine. 2 *n.* A substitute. 3 *v.* To substitute: Who *subbed* for the regular shortstop?

sub- A prefix meaning: 1 Under; beneath; below, as in *subcutaneous.* 2 Almost; nearly; somewhat, as in *subtropical.* 3 Of a lower rank, grade, or class, as in *subhead.* 4 Being a division or part of, as in *subdivision.*

sub. 1 subject. 2 subscription. 3 substitute. 4 suburban. 5 subway.

sub·al·tern [sə·bôl′tərn] 1 *n.* In the British army, an officer ranking below a captain. 2 *adj.* Having a lower rank or position.

sub·a·tom·ic [sub′ə·tom′ik] *adj.* Located within or having dimensions smaller than an atom: *subatomic* particles.

sub·com·mit·tee [sub′kə·mit′ē] *n.* A small committee formed from a larger committee to do some special work.

sub·con·scious [sub·kon′shəs] 1 *n.* The part of one's mind that one is usually not aware of. 2 *adj.* In, of, or having to do with this part of the mind: a *subconscious* wish for power. **—sub·con′·scious·ly** *adv.* **—sub·con′scious·ness** *n.*

sub·con·tin·ent [sub′kon′tə·nənt] *n.* A large land mass that is part of a continent but that stands apart to a degree from the central land mass: India is a *subcontinent* of Asia.

sub·con·tract [*n.* sub′kon′trakt′, *v.* sub′kon′trakt′ *or* sub′kən·trakt′] 1 *n.* An agreement between a person who has already agreed to do some work and another person, whereby the second person agrees to do some or all of the work. 2 *v.* To make a subcontract for: The builder *subcontracted* the wiring of the house to an electrician. **—sub·con′·trac·tor** *n.*

sub·cu·ta·ne·ous [sub′kyōō·tā′nē·əs] *adj.* 1 Lying beneath the skin. 2 Applied or put in beneath the skin, as an injection.

sub·di·vide [sub′di·vīd′] *v.* **sub·di·vid·ed, sub·di·vid·ing** 1 To divide (a part) into smaller parts. 2 To divide (land) into building lots.

sub·di·vi·sion [sub′di·vizh′ən] *n.* 1 The act or process of subdividing. 2 Something produced by subdividing, especially a piece of land divided into building lots. 3 Any division of a division.

sub·due [sub·d(y)ōō′] *v.* **sub·dued, sub·du·ing** 1 To gain power over, as by force; conquer. 2 To overcome or hold back: to *subdue* a sneeze; to *subdue* rage. 3 To make (something, as a sound or color) less intense: I like *subdued* colors.

sub·fam·ily [sub′fam′ə·lē *or* sub′fam′lē] *n.* A subdivision of a family, as of plants, animals, or languages.

sub·head [sub′hed′] *n.* A secondary heading, as for a subdivision of a chapter or essay.

sub·hu·man [sub·hyōō′mən] *adj.* 1 Less than human, as in nature, form, or development. 2 Unfit for or unworthy of human beings: *subhuman* conditions in the mines.

subj. 1 subject. 2 subjective. 3 subjunctive.

sub·ject [*adj., n.* sub′jikt, *v.* səb·jekt′] 1 *adj.* Ruled or controlled by another or others: *subject* peoples. 2 *n.* A person who is under the power or influence of another, as of a monarch: *subjects* of the crown. 3 *v.* To bring under domination: The Mongols *subjected* part of Russia to their rule. 4 *adj.* Liable to have or be affected by: *subject* to disease; *subject* to criticism. 5 *v.* To make liable; expose: This behavior will *subject* you to punishment. 6 *v.* To force to endure: They were *subjected* to long hours of waiting. 7 *adj.* Dependent or contingent on something or someone: a plan *subject* to the approval of the boss. 8 *n.* The person, thing, act, idea, or field that one deals with, as in writing or painting: The old mill was the *subject* of the photograph. **9** *n.* A person or animal used in an experiment. **10** *n.* In grammar, the word, phrase, or clause about which something is said in a sentence. In "The boy bought a quart of ice cream," *boy* is the subject. **11** *n.* A musical theme. **12** *n.* A branch of learning or course of study. ◆ *Subject* comes from an old French word. It was originally spelled *sujet,* but was later changed to conform with the Latin word *subjectus,* from which the French word comes.

sub·jec·tion [səb·jek′shən] *n.* **1** The act of making subject: the *subjection* of a people. **2** The condition of being subjected.

sub·jec·tive [səb·jek′tiv] *adj.* **1** Of, related to, or coming from a person's emotions, prejudices, or interests, rather than from outside facts or evidence: a *subjective* opinion. **2** About or strongly influenced by one's feelings and thoughts: a *subjective* book. **3** In grammar, another word for NOMINATIVE. **—sub·jec′tive·ly** *adv.*

sub·jec·tiv·i·ty [sub′jek·tiv′ə·tē] *n.* The quality of coming from or being based on a person's own emotions, prejudices, or interests, rather than outside facts: the *subjectivity* of artistic taste.

subject matter Something that is being considered, discussed, studied, or written about.

sub·join [səb·join′] *v.* To add at the end or bottom; append.

sub·ju·gate [sub′jŏŏ·gāt′] *v.* **sub·ju·gat·ed, sub·ju·gat·ing** To bring under domination or control; conquer; subdue. **—sub′ju·ga′tion** *n.*

sub·junc·tive [səb·jungk′tiv] **1** *adj.* Of, having to do with, or being the mood of a verb that expresses an act or state not as actual but as wished, doubted, supposed, or depending on an unlikely condition. In "I wish you were here," *were* is subjunctive. **2** *n.* The subjunctive mood, or a verb form in this mood.

sub·king·dom [sub′king′dəm] *n.* A subdivision of a kingdom, as of plants or animals.

sub·lease [*n.* sub′lēs′, *v.* sub·lēs′] *n., v.* **sub·leased, sub·leas·ing** **1** *n.* A lease given to someone else by a person who rents the property. **2** *v.* To give or take a sublease of.

sub·let [*v.* sub·let′ *or* sub′let′, *n.* sub′let′] *v.* **sub·let, sub·let·ting,** *n.* **1** *v.* To rent (property one holds on a lease) to another. **2** *n.* Property, especially housing, that is sublet. **3** *v.* To give (part of the work that one has contracted to do) to another contractor.

sub·li·mate [sub′lə·māt′] *v.* **sub·li·mat·ed, sub·li·mat·ing** **1** To cause (a substance) to change from a solid to a gas and back again without passing through a liquid state. **2** To purify; refine. **3** To change the aim of (a psychological urge or drive) to a higher goal. **—sub′li·ma′tion** *n.*

sub·lime [sə·blīm′] *adj., v.* **sub·limed, sub·lim·ing** **1** *adj.* Inspiring awe or deep emotion; grand; noble; supreme: a *sublime* symphony. **2** *v.* To sublimate or be sublimated. **3** *v.* To change directly from a solid state into a vapor, as dry ice does. **—sub·lime′ly** *adv.* **—sub·lim·i·ty** [sə·blim′ə·tē] *n.*

sub·ma·chine gun [sub′mə·shēn′] A small machine gun fired from the shoulder or hip.

sub·ma·rine [*adj.* sub′mə·rēn′, *n.* sub′mə·rēn′] **1** *adj.* Existing, done, or operating beneath the surface of the sea: a *submarine* plant. **2** *n.* A ship designed to operate on or under the surface of the sea. **3** *adj.* Of or having to do with submarines.

sub·merge [səb·mûrj′] *v.* **sub·merged, sub·merg·ing** **1** To put or go into or under water or another liquid: to *submerge* a submarine; The walrus *submerged.* **2** To cover with water; inundate.

sub·merse [səb·mûrs′] *v.* **sub·mersed, sub·mers·ing** To submerge.

sub·mers·i·ble [səb·mûr′sə·bəl] *adj.* Capable of being submerged.

sub·mer·sion [səb·mûr′shən *or* səb·mûr′zhən] *n.* **1** The act of submerging. **2** A being submerged.

sub·mis·sion [səb·mish′ən] *n.* **1** The act of submitting or giving in. **2** The condition or quality of being submissive or humble. **3** The presenting of something, as for consideration or approval.

sub·mis·sive [səb·mis′iv] *adj.* Giving in or willing to give in to what is asked or demanded; obedient; docile. **—sub·mis′sive·ly** *adv.*

sub·mit [səb·mit′] *v.* **sub·mit·ted, sub·mit·ting** **1** To give up; yield to the authority, power, or will of another: The rebels finally *submitted.* **2** To present, as for decision, approval, or testing: to *submit* a budget.

sub·nor·mal [sub·nôr′məl] *adj.* **1** Below normal: *subnormal* temperatures. **2** Having less than normal mental ability; dull.

sub·or·bit·al [sub·ôr′bit·əl] *adj.* Making less than a full orbit, as of the earth: a *suborbital* flight of a spacecraft.

sub·or·der [sub′ôr′dər] *n.* A subdivision of an order, as of plants or animals.

sub·or·di·nate [*adj., n.* sə·bôr′də·nit, *v.* sə·bôr′də·nāt′] *adj., n., v.* **sub·or·di·nat·ed, sub·or·di·nat·ing** **1** *adj.* Being or belonging in an inferior position or class; secondary; minor. **2** *adj.* Under the authority or control of another: Privates are *subordinate* to sergeants. **3** *n.* A person who is subordinate to someone else. **4** *v.* To make subordinate. **—sub·or′di·na′tion** *n.*

subordinate clause Another term for DEPENDENT CLAUSE.

subordinating conjunction A conjunction that introduces a dependent clause.

sub·orn [sə·bôrn′] *v.* **1** To induce (a person) to commit a crime. **2** To induce (a person) to commit perjury. **—sub·or·na·tion** [sub′ôr·nā′shən] *n.* **—sub·orn′er** *n.*

sub·poe·na or **sub·pe·na** [sə(b)·pē′nə] *n., v.* **sub·poe·naed** or **sub·pe·naed, sub·poe·na·ing** or **sub·pe·na·ing** **1** *n.* An official order commanding a person to appear in or submit something to a court. **2** *v.* To summon or call for by a subpoena.

sub·scribe [səb·skrīb′] *v.* **sub·scribed, sub·scrib·ing** **1** To support or approve: to *subscribe* to the idea of equal justice for all. **2** To write (one's name) at the bottom of a document, often to show approval or agreement. **3** To agree to pay for and receive a number of issues of a newspaper, magazine, or other periodical. **4** To promise to pay or donate (a sum of money). **—sub·scrib′er** *n.*

a	add	**i**	it	**ŏŏ**	took	**oi**	oil
ā	ace	**ī**	ice	**ōō**	pool	**ou**	pout
â	care	**o**	odd	**u**	up	**ng**	ring
ä	palm	**ō**	open	**û**	burn	**th**	thin
e	end	**ô**	order	**yōō**	fuse	**th̶**	this
ē	equal					**zh**	vision

ə = a in *above* e in *sicken* i in *possible* o in *melon* u in *circus*

S

sub·script [sub′skript′] *n.* A number, letter, or other symbol, written below and to the right or left of a character, as $_2$ in H_2O.

sub·scrip·tion [səb·skrip′shən] *n.* **1** The act of subscribing. **2** Something, as approval, support, or money, given by subscribing. **3** An agreement to receive a number of issues of a newspaper, magazine, or other periodical.

sub·sec·tion [sub′sek′shən] *n.* A part of a section.

sub·se·quent [sub′sə·kwənt] *adj.* Following in time, place, or order: *Subsequent* events proved us wrong. **—sub′se·quent·ly** *adv.*

sub·serve [səb·sûrv′] *v.* **sub·served, sub·serv·ing** To help or further (as a cause, purpose, or action): to *subserve* justice.

sub·ser·vi·ence [səb·sûr′vē·əns] *n.* The condition or quality of being subservient.

sub·ser·vi·ent [səb·sûr′vē·ənt] *adj.* **1** Annoyingly polite; too eager to please: a *subservient* attendant. **2** Helping to further some purpose. **3** Subordinate. **—sub·ser′vi·ent·ly** *adv.*

sub·set [sub′set′] *n.* A set whose members are all included in another set: {x, y} and {x} are *subsets* of {x, y, z}.

sub·side [səb·sīd′] *v.* **sub·sid·ed, sub·sid·ing** **1** To become less violent or active: The storm *subsided.* **2** To sink to a lower level: The flood waters *subsided.* **—sub·si·dence** [səb·sīd′(ə)ns *or* sub′sə·dəns] *n.*

sub·sid·i·ar·y [səb·sid′ē·er′ē] *adj., n., pl.* **sub·sid·i·ar·ies** **1** *adj.* Giving aid or support, especially in a minor way: Even though these plans are *subsidiary,* they are very important. **2** *adj.* Of, like, or having to do with a subsidy. **3** *n.* A company owned and controlled by another company.

sub·si·dize [sub′sə·dīz′] *v.* **sub·si·dized, sub·si·diz·ing** To support or assist with a grant of money: States often *subsidize* hospitals.

sub·si·dy [sub′sə·dē] *n., pl.* **sub·si·dies** Financial aid given to a person or an enterprise by a government, a large corporation, or other group or individual.

sub·sist [səb·sist′] *v.* **1** To manage to stay alive: While lost in the woods, we *subsisted* on wild plants. **2** To exist or continue to exist.

sub·sis·tence [səb·sis′təns] *n.* **1** The act of subsisting. **2** Means of support; livelihood: One parent's salary was the family's only *subsistence.* **3** The minimum amount of food, clothing, and other essentials necessary to stay alive: They got a bare *subsistence* from farming.

sub·soil [sub′soil′] *n.* The layer of soil that is just below the surface soil.

sub·son·ic [sub·son′ik] *adj.* Of, having to do with, being, or moving at speeds less than the speed of sound.

sub·spe·cies [sub′spē′shēz *or* sub′spē′sēz] *n., pl.* **sub·spe·cies** A subdivision of a species of plants or animals.

sub·stance [sub′stəns] *n.* **1** The material of which anything is made or consists. **2** The main or essential idea or part; essence: The *substance* of the novel was given in a summary. **3** A solid or substantial quality or character: Your ideas have *substance.* **4** Material wealth or property.

sub·stan·dard [sub′stan′dərd] *adj.* Of a quality lower than the established standard or requirement; inferior: *substandard* housing.

sub·stan·tial [səb·stan′shəl] *adj.* **1** Of or having substance; actual; real: dangers far from imaginary but quite *substantial.* **2** Solid; strong; firm: a *substantial* foundation. **3** Large, as in amount or extent; considerable: *substantial* progress. **4** Wealthy and influential. **5** Having to do with the main points; essential. **—sub·stan′tial·ly** *adv.*

sub·stan·ti·ate [səb·stan′shē·āt′] *v.* **sub·stan·ti·at·ed, sub·stan·ti·at·ing** To establish as true by evidence; prove: to *substantiate* a claim. **—sub·stan′ti·a′tion** *n.*

sub·stan·tive [sub′stən·tiv] **1** *n.* A noun or any word or group of words acting as a noun in a sentence. **2** *adj.* Used as a noun. **3** *adj.* Expressing existence: "To be" is called the *substantive* verb. **4** *adj.* Independent in resources; self-supporting: a *substantive* country. **5** *adj.* Considerable in amount; substantial.

sub·sti·tute [sub′stə·t(y)o͞ot′] *n., v.* **sub·sti·tut·ed, sub·sti·tut·ing** **1** *n.* A person or thing that takes the place of someone or something else. **2** *v.* To be a substitute: An understudy *substituted* for the star. **3** *v.* To use (a person or thing) as a substitute: to *substitute* honey for sugar. **—sub′sti·tu′tion** *n.*

sub·stra·tum [sub·strā′təm *or* sub·strat′əm] *n., pl.* **sub·stra·ta** [sub·strā′tə *or* sub·strat′ə] or **sub·stra·tums** An underlying stratum or layer, as of earth or rock.

sub·ter·fuge [sub′tər·fyo͞oj′] *n.* A trick used to avoid something difficult or unpleasant.

sub·ter·ra·ne·an [sub′tə·rā′nē·ən] *adj.* **1** Located or happening under the earth: a *subterranean* pool. **2** Secret or hidden: a *subterranean* plot.

sub·ti·tle [sub′tīt′(ə)l] *n.* **1** A subordinate or explanatory title. **2** In foreign or silent films, a written translation or account of the words spoken, usually at the bottom of the screen.

sub·tle [sut′(ə)l] *adj.* **sub·tler, sub·tlest** **1** Having or showing a keen awareness, as of small points or differences: a *subtle* mind in legal matters. **2** Not direct or obvious; hard to see or understand: *subtle* differences in their arguments. **3** Cleverly or skillfully done or made: *subtle* work in gold. **4** Delicate: *subtle* colors. **5** Full of trickery or deceit; cunning; crafty: a *subtle* scheme for gaining power. **—sub′tly** *adv.*

sub·tle·ty [sut′(ə)l·tē] *n., pl.* **sub·tle·ties** **1** The condition or quality of being subtle. **2** Something that is subtle; a fine point or distinction.

sub·to·tal [sub′tōt′(ə)l] **1** *n.* The total of a series of numbers that forms part of a larger series. **2** *v.* To determine a subtotal for.

sub·tract [səb·trakt′] *v.* **1** To remove or take away, as a part from the whole. **2** To find the difference when one number is taken away from another number: If 5 is *subtracted* from 8, the difference is 3 (that is, $8 - 5 = 3$).

sub·trac·tion [səb·trak′shən] *n.* The act or process of subtracting.

sub·tra·hend [sub′trə·hend′] *n.* A number to be subtracted from another number.

sub·trop·i·cal [sub′trop′i·kəl] *adj.* Of, having to do with, or located in the regions near or bordering on the tropical zone.

sub·trop·ics [sub′trop′iks] *n.pl.* The subtropical regions.

sub·urb [sub′ûrb] *n.* **1** A place, as a town, village, or district, that is close to a large city. **2** (*pl.*) The area surrounding a large city.

sub·ur·ban [sə·bûr′bən] *adj.* Of, having to do with, or living in a suburb or the suburbs.

sub·ur·ban·ite [sə·bûr′bən·īt′] *n.* A person whose home is in a suburb.
sub·ur·bi·a [sə·bûr′bē·ə] *n.* 1 Suburbs in general. 2 Suburbanites or their way of life.
sub·ver·sion [səb·vûr′zhən] *n.* 1 The act of subverting. 2 The condition of being subverted.
sub·ver·sive [səb·vûr′siv] 1 *adj.* Tending to undermine or overthrow, as a government or law. 2 *n.* A person who uses subversive methods.
sub·vert [səb·vûrt′] *v.* 1 To overthrow completely, as a government. 2 To undermine the character or principles of; corrupt.
sub·way [sub′wā′] *n.* 1 An electric railroad that is mainly underground. 2 *adj. use*: a *subway* station. 3 Any underground passage.
suc·ceed [sək·sēd′] *v.* 1 To accomplish what is planned or intended; be successful: The attempt *succeeded.* 2 To follow next in order after: Wilson *succeeded* Taft as President.
suc·cess [sək·ses′] *n.* 1 A favorable or desired outcome; good results. 2 A person or thing that is successful: The party was a *success.* 3 The achievement of something desired, as wealth or fame.
suc·cess·ful [sək·ses′fəl] *adj.* 1 Reaching a favorable or desired outcome; achieving good results: a *successful* plan. 2 Having become wealthy or famous. **—suc·cess′ful·ly** *adv.*
suc·ces·sion [sək·sesh′ən] *n.* 1 A group of persons or things that follow one after another: a *succession* of victories. 2 The act of following in order after another: the *succession* of the new monarch. 3 The act or right of following another, as in an office or rank: The pretender's *succession* to the throne was challenged. 4 The order or plan by which something, as an office or rank, changes hands: The vice president is first in *succession* to the presidency. **—in succession** In order, one after another.
suc·ces·sive [sək·ses′iv] *adj.* Following in order without interruption; consecutive: our fifth *successive* victory. **—suc·ces′sive·ly** *adv.*
suc·ces·sor [sək·ses′ər] *n.* 1 A person or thing that comes after another. 2 A person who succeeds another, as on a throne or in office.
suc·cinct [sək·singkt′] *adj.* Made or expressed clearly and briefly, with no wasted words: a *succinct* statement. **—suc·cinct′ly** *adv.*
suc·cor [suk′ər] 1 *n.* Help or comfort given in danger or distress. 2 *n.* A person or thing that provides succor. 3 *v.* To comfort or help.
suc·co·tash [suk′ə·tash′] *n.* Kernels of corn and beans, usually lima beans, cooked together.
Suc·coth [sŏŏk′əs *or* sŏŏk′ōt] *n.* Another spelling of SUKKOTH.
suc·cu·lent [suk′yə·lənt] *adj.* 1 Full of juice; juicy: *succulent* fruit. 2 *adj.* Having fleshy leaves or stems that hold moisture: a *succulent* plant. 3 *n.* A succulent plant, as a cactus. **—suc′cu·lence** *n.*
suc·cumb [sə·kum′] *v.* 1 To give in or give way, as to force or persuasion. 2 To die.
such [such] 1 *adj.* Of that kind or the same kind: *Such* wit as this is rare. 2 *adj.* Of the type referred to: There is no *such* place. 3 *pron.* Such a person or thing: She was a chemist, and as *such* she excelled. 4 *adj.* So great, good, bad, or otherwise extreme: *Such* a heat wave! 5 *adj.* Not specified; some: The meeting will be held at *such* and *such* a place. **—as such** 1 As being what is indicated: A leader, *as such,* must take responsibility. 2 In itself: Discovery, *as such,* is its own incentive. **—such as** 1 For example. 2 Similar to. ◆ *Such* comes from an Old English word. See also SO.
such·like [such′līk′] 1 *adj.* Of a like kind; similar. 2 *pron.* A person or thing of the same kind.
suck [suk] 1 *v.* To draw into the mouth with the lips and tongue: A baby *sucks* milk through a nipple. 2 *v.* To draw fluid from with the mouth: to *suck* an orange. 3 *v.* To inhale, as air, or absorb, as liquid: A sponge *sucks* up water. 4 *v.* To hold in the mouth and lick or draw on with the mouth: to *suck* hard candy; Don't *suck* your thumb. 5 *n.* The act of sucking.
suck·er [suk′ər] *n.* 1 A person or thing that sucks. 2 A freshwater fish having thick and fleshy lips adapted for sucking in food. 3 A part or organ of the body with which certain animals suck or stick tight to things by suction. 4 A lollipop. 5 A shoot growing up from a root or underground stem of a plant. 6 *U.S. slang* A person who is easy to trick or cheat.
suck·le [suk′əl] *v.* **suck·led, suck·ling** 1 To feed with milk from the breast or udder; nurse. 2 To take milk from the breast by sucking.
suck·ling [suk′ling] *n.* A baby or young animal that is still feeding on its mother's milk.
su·crose [sōō′krōs′] *n.* Common sugar, as that extracted from sugar cane and sugar beets.
suc·tion [suk′shən] 1 *n.* The lowering of the pressure in an enclosure below that of the atmosphere, causing a liquid or gas to be forced in or a solid to be held fast. 2 *adj.*Working by suction. 3 *n.* The action of sucking.

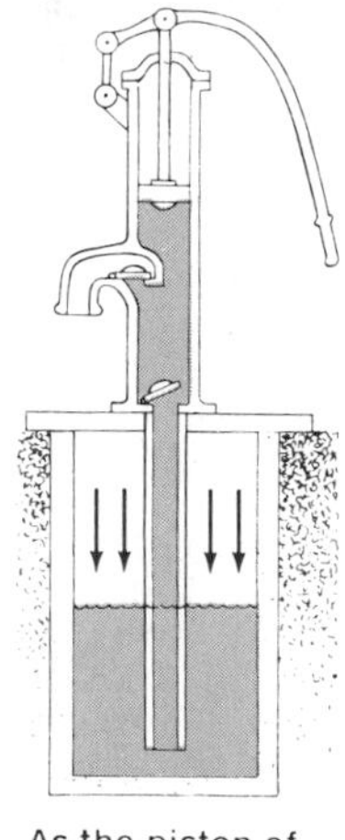
As the piston of the suction pump is raised, atmospheric pressure raises the water.

Su·da·nese [sōō′də·nēz′] *adj., n., pl.* **Su·da·nese** 1 *adj.* Of or from Sudan. 2 *n.* A person born in or a citizen of Sudan.
Su·dan·ic [sōō·dan′ik] *adj.* Of or from Sudan.
sud·den [sud′(ə)n] *adj.* 1 Happening quickly and without warning: a *sudden* storm. 2 Quickly made, done, or occurring: a *sudden* stop. 3 Causing or likely to cause surprise: a *sudden* curve in the highway ahead of us. **—all of a sudden** Without warning. **—sud′den·ly** *adv.* **—sud′den·ness** *n.*
suds [sudz] *n.pl.* Soapy water, or the bubbles and froth on its surface. **—suds′y** *adj.*
sue [sōō] *v.* **sued, su·ing** 1 To bring a lawsuit against (as a person, company, or group): The family *sued* the railroad for damages. 2 To ask, plead, or petition: The besieged city *sued* for peace.

a	add	**i**	it	**ŏŏ**	took	**oi**	oil
ā	ace	**ī**	ice	**ōō**	pool	**ou**	pout
â	care	**o**	odd	**u**	up	**ng**	ring
ä	palm	**ō**	open	**û**	burn	**th**	thin
e	end	**ô**	order	**yōō**	fuse	**th**	this
ē	equal					**zh**	vision

ə = a in *above* e in *sicken* i in *possible* o in *melon* u in *circus*

suede [swād] *n.* 1 Leather that has been rubbed to give it a soft nap like velvet. 2 *adj. use: suede* shoes. 3 A cloth resembling suede.

su·et [so͞o′it] *n.* The hard fat about the loins and kidneys of sheep and cattle. It is used in cooking, to feed birds, and to make tallow.

suf·fer [suf′ər] *v.* 1 To feel or endure (pain or distress). 2 To undergo, experience, or sustain: to *suffer* an injury. 3 To be harmed or get worse: If you don't get enough sleep, your work will *suffer.* 4 To allow; permit: The tyrant would not *suffer* them to depart. **—suf′fer·er** *n.*

suf·fer·ance [suf′ər·əns] *n.* Passive permission, given or implied by failure to forbid.

suf·fer·ing [suf′ər·ing] *n.* Pain, distress, anguish, or misery.

suf·fice [sə·fīs′] *v.* **suf·ficed, suf·fic·ing** 1 To be sufficient: I am wearing a jacket, but a sweater would *suffice.* 2 To be enough for; satisfy: Will a sandwich *suffice* you for lunch?

suf·fi·cien·cy [sə·fish′ən·sē] *n.* 1 An amount large enough to meet needs: a *sufficiency* of supplies. 2 The condition of being enough.

suf·fi·cient [sə·fish′ənt] *adj.* Equal to what is needed; enough; adequate: to have *sufficient* funds. **—suf·fi′cient·ly** *adv.*

suf·fix [*n.* suf′iks, *v.* suf′iks *or* sə·fiks′] 1 *n.* One or more syllables added on at the end of a word to make another word of different meaning or function, as *-ment, -ness, -ible, -ful, -ous,* or *-ly,* or to make an inflectional form, as *-ed, -ing,* or *-est.* 2 *v.* To add as a suffix.

suf·fo·cate [suf′ə·kāt′] *v.* **suf·fo·cat·ed, suf·fo·cat·ing** 1 To kill by depriving of air; smother; stifle. 2 To die from lack of air. 3 To have or cause difficulty in breathing, as because of stifling heat. **—suf′fo·ca′tion** *n.*

suf·fra·gan [suf′rə·gən] *n.* A bishop who is subordinate to another bishop.

suf·frage [suf′rij] *n.* 1 The right to vote. 2 A vote on some measure or for some candidate.

suf·fra·gette [suf′rə·jet′] *n.* Formerly, a woman who fought for women's right to vote.

suf·fra·gist [suf′rə·jist] *n.* A person who advocates extension of the right to vote, especially to women: a universal *suffragist.*

suf·fuse [sə·fyo͞oz′] *v.* **suf·fused, suf·fus·ing** To overspread, as with a fluid or color: A deep blush *suffused* his cheeks. **—suf·fu′sion** *n.*

sug·ar [sho͝og′ər] 1 *n.* Any of a class of carbohydrates, all with a more or less sweet taste. The sugar we commonly use for sweetening is sucrose, from sugarcane or sugar beets. Formula: $C_{12}H_{22}O_{11}$. 2 *v.* To form or produce sugar crystals: Fudge *sugars* if it is cooked too much. 3 *v.* To sweeten, cover, or coat with sugar. 4 *v.* To make agreeable or less distasteful, as by flattery: to *sugar* a refusal. ◆ *Sugar* comes from an Arabic word.

sugar beet A type of beet having a white root from which ordinary sugar is obtained.

sug·ar·cane [sho͝og′ər·kān′] *n.* A tall grass grown in tropical regions, having a solid, jointed stalk which is a major source of ordinary sugar.

sug·ar·coat [sho͝og′ər·kōt′] *v.* 1 To coat with sugar: to *sugarcoat* a pill. 2 To present (something unpleasant) in a way that makes it easier to accept: to *sugarcoat* a boring task by making a game out of it.

sug·ar·loaf [sho͝og′ər·lōf′] *n.* 1 A loaf-shaped mass of refined sugar. 2 Something shaped like a sugarloaf, as a mountain.

sugar maple A maple tree of eastern North America having sap that is made into maple syrup and maple sugar.

sug·ar·plum [sho͝og′ər·plum′] *n.* A small ball or flat oval of candy; bonbon.

sug·ar·y [sho͝og′ər·ē] *adj.* 1 Made of sugar or like sugar; sweet. 2 Too sweet; seeming sweet but not sincerely so: *sugary* compliments.

sug·gest [sə(g)·jest′] *v.* 1 To put forward as a proposal; propose: I *suggest* that we have a party. 2 To offer as a theory or imply as a possibility: Are you *suggesting* that it's time to leave? 3 To bring to mind by association or connection: The number of plants in the room *suggested* a greenhouse.

sug·gest·i·ble [sə(g)·jes′tə·bəl] *adj.* Readily adopting the suggestions of others; easily influenced by hints. **—sug·gest·i·bil·i·ty** [sə(g)·jes′tə·bil′ə·tē] *n.*

sug·ges·tion [sə(g)·jes′chən] *n.* 1 The act of suggesting: The date was changed at my *suggestion.* 2 Something suggested. 3 A touch, trace, or hint: a *suggestion* of spring in the air.

sug·ges·tive [sə(g)·jes′tiv] *adj.* 1 Giving or apt to give a suggestion or hint, often of something indecent. 2 Stimulating to thought.

su·i·cid·al [so͞o′ə·sī′dəl] *adj.* 1 Of or inclined to suicide: a *suicidal* mental patient. 2 Dangerous or destructive to oneself; foolhardy: a *suicidal* ski run down a sheer slope. **—su′i·cid′al·ly** *adv.*

su·i·cide [so͞o′ə·sīd′] *n.* 1 The act of killing oneself intentionally. 2 A person who kills himself or herself intentionally. 3 Ruin of one's own prospects or interests.

suit [so͞ot] 1 *n.* A matched set of garments, especially a jacket with trousers or a skirt. 2 *n.* An outfit or garment worn for a special purpose: a bathing *suit.* 3 *v.* To fulfill the needs of; be correct or fitting for: Dry soil *suits* some plants. 4 *v.* To make appropriate; adapt: *Suit* the speech to the audience. 5 *v.* To please or satisfy: That *suits* me fine. 6 *n.* One of the four sets of playing cards that make up a pack. Spades, hearts, diamonds, and clubs are suits. 7 *n.* A case brought to a court of law to settle a claim. 8 *n.* An appeal or petition. 9 *n.* The seeking of a person in marriage. **—follow suit** 1 To play a card whose suit matches that of the card led. 2 To do the same: I'll dive and you *follow suit.* **—suit yourself** Do whatever you like.

suit·a·ble [so͞o′tə·bəl] *adj.* Proper for the purpose or occasion; fitting. **—suit·a·bil·i·ty** [so͞o′tə·bil′ə·tē] *n.* **—suit′a·bly** *adv.*

suit·case [so͞ot′kās′] *n.* A boxlike container with a handle, used on trips to carry clothes and other items.

suite *n.* 1 [swēt] A set of connected rooms. 2 [swēt *or* so͞ot] A set of matching furniture to be used in the same room: a dining room *suite.* 3 [swēt] A set of related musical pieces, in former times always a series of dances. 4 [swēt] A group of attendants or followers; retinue.

suit·or [so͞o′tər] *n.* 1 A person who courts another. 2 A person who pleads or who sues.

su·ki·ya·ki [so͞o′kē·yä′kē *or* skē·yä′kē] *n.* A Japanese dish of thin-sliced meat and vegetables sautéed with seasonings.

Suk·koth [so͝ok′əs *or* so͝ok′ōt] *n.* A Jewish harvest festival celebrated for nine days in the fall. ◆ *Sukkoth* is a transliteration of a Hebrew word for *tabernacles*, the temporary shelters used by the ancient Hebrews during their wanderings in the wilderness. Today the festival is celebrated by eating meals in thatch-covered booths.

sul·fa drug [sul′fə] Any of a group of chemical compounds obtained from coal tar and used to treat various bacterial infections.

sul·fate [sul′fāt′] *n.* A salt of sulfuric acid.

sul·fide [sul′fīd′] *n.* A compound of sulfur and another element or radical.

sul·fur [sul′fər] *n.* A pale yellow, brittle, nonmetallic element, found both free and in compounds, some of which are essential constituents of living organisms. Sulfur burns with a blue flame, producing suffocating fumes.

sulfur dioxide A toxic chemical, normally a colorless but foul-smelling gas, used to make sulfuric acid and in bleaching, refrigeration, and food preservation.

sul·fu·ric [sul·fyŏŏr′ik] *adj.* Of, having to do with, derived from, or containing sulfur.

sulfuric acid A colorless, oily, and very corrosive liquid formed of sulfur, hydrogen, and oxygen.

sul·fur·ous [sul′fər·əs *or* sul·fyŏŏr′əs] *adj.* **1** Of, like, having to do with, derived from, or containing sulfur. **2** Like hell fire; fiery.

sulk [sulk] **1** *v.* To be sulky or sullen. **2** *n.* (*often pl.*) A sulky mood or humor.

sulk·y[1] [sul′kē] *adj.* **sulk·i·er, sulk·i·est** Sullenly cross or ill-humored. **—sulk′i·ly** *adv.*

sulk·y[2] [sul′kē] *n., pl.* **sulk·ies** A carriage with two wheels and a seat for one person.

Sulky

sul·len [sul′ən] *adj.* **1** Glumly silent and aloof because ill-humored or resentful. **2** Gloomy; dismal; somber: dark, *sullen* clouds. **—sul′len·ly** *adv.* **—sul′len·ness** *n.*

sul·ly [sul′ē] *v.* **sul·lied, sul·ly·ing** To soil or tarnish: to *sully* one's good name.

sul·phur [sul′fər] *n.* Another spelling of SULFUR.

sul·phu·ric [sul·fyŏŏr′ik] *adj.* Another spelling of SULFURIC.

sul·phur·ous [sul′fər·əs *or* sul·fyŏŏr′əs] *adj.* Another spelling of SULFUROUS.

sul·tan [sul′tən] *n.* The ruler of a Muslim country.

sul·tan·a [sul·tan′ə *or* sul·tä′nə] *n.* A sultan's wife, daughter, sister, or mother.

sul·tan·ate [sul′tən·āt′] *n.* The office, authority, reign, or territory of a sultan.

sul·try [sul′trē] *adj.* **sul·tri·er, sul·tri·est** **1** Uncomfortably hot, humid, and still, as weather. **2** Extremely hot: a *sultry* desert.

sum [sum] *n., v.* **summed, sum·ming** **1** *n.* The number or quantity reached by adding two or more other numbers or quantities: The *sum* of 7, 4, and 2 is 13. **2** *v.* To add into one total: to *sum* numbers. **3** *n.* An arithmetic problem. **4** *n.* The full amount; total; whole: the *sum* of human knowledge. **5** *n.* A particular amount, as of money: That's quite a *sum*. **—sum up** To review the main points of; present briefly.

su·mac or **su·mach** [sōō′mak′ *or* shōō′mak′] *n.* A shrub or small tree having clusters of small flowers and, later, of berries. Its leaves turn from green to bright red in autumn.

Su·me·ri·an [sōō·mer′ē·ən] **1** *adj.* Of or from Sumer. **2** *n.* A person who was born or lived in Sumer. **3** *n.* The language of Sumer.

sum·ma cum lau·de [sŏŏm′ə kŏŏm lou′də *or* sum′·ə kum lô′də] A Latin expression for "with highest praise," used on diplomas to indicate graduation with highest honors.

sum·ma·ri·ly [sə·mer′ə·lē *or* sum′ər·ə·lē] *adv.* Without ceremony or delay: *summarily* dismissed.

sum·ma·rize [sum′ə·rīz′] *v.* **sum·ma·rized, sum·ma·riz·ing** To make a summary of; sum up: to *summarize* a chapter.

sum·ma·ry [sum′ər·ē] *n., pl.* **sum·ma·ries,** *adj.* **1** *n.* A short statement presenting the main points. **2** *adj.* Presenting the main points in brief form: a *summary* paragraph. **3** *adj.* Done without ceremony or delay: a *summary* dismissal.

sum·ma·tion [sə·mā′shən] *n.* **1** The act of summing or totaling; addition. **2** A sum or total. **3** The last part of a speech that argues for something, as in a trial, in which facts or points are reviewed and a conclusion is expressed.

sum·mer [sum′ər] **1** *n.* The warmest season of the year, occurring between spring and autumn. **2** *adj. use: summer* sports; *summer* clothes. **3** *v.* To spend the summer: to *summer* at the beach.

sum·mer·house [sum′ər·hous′] *n., pl.* **sum·mer·hous·es** [sum′ər·hou′ziz] A small roofed structure providing shade during the summer, as in a garden or park.

sum·mer·time [sum′ər·tīm′] *n.* Summer.

sum·mer·y [sum′ər·ē] *adj.* Typical of or suitable for summer.

sum·mit [sum′it] *n.* **1** The highest point or level; top, as of a mountain. **2** The highest degree or level: the *summit* of human achievement.

summit meeting A meeting at which the heads of two or more governments talk and bargain in an attempt to settle international disputes.

sum·mon [sum′ən] *v.* **1** To send for or order to come. **2** To call together, as a legislature. **3** To order (a person) to appear in court. **4** To call into action; arouse: *Summon* up courage.

sum·mons [sum′ənz] *n., pl.* **sum·mons·es** **1** A request or order to appear at a given place or time. **2** A written order to appear in court.

sump [sump] *n.* A depression or reservoir for receiving water or draining off waste liquids.

sump·tu·ous [sump′chōō·əs] *adj.* Very expensive and luxurious; costly: a *sumptuous* feast.

sun [sun] *n., v.* **sunned, sun·ning** **1** *n.* The brilliant star around which the earth and other planets revolve and which provides them with light and heat. ◆ Adj., *solar.* **2** *n.* The light or heat radiated from the sun: This room gets a lot of *sun.* **3** *v.* To expose (oneself) to the light and heat of

a	add	**i**	it	**ŏŏ**	took	**oi**	oil
ā	ace	**ī**	ice	**ōō**	pool	**ou**	pout
â	care	**o**	odd	**u**	up	**ng**	ring
ä	palm	**ō**	open	**û**	burn	**th**	thin
e	end	**ô**	order	**yōō**	fuse	**t͟h**	this
ē	equal					**zh**	vision

ə = a in *above* e in *sicken* i in *possible* o in *melon* u in *circus*

S

the sun: Let's *sun* ourselves by the pool. **4** *n.* Any star like our sun that has planets revolving around it. **5** *n.* Anything brilliant and magnificent like the sun.
Sun. Sunday.
sun·bath [sun′bath′] *n.* Exposure of the body to sunlight or the rays of a sunlamp.
sun·bathe [sun′bāth′] *v.* **sun·bathed, sun·bath·ing** To take a sunbath. **—sun′bath′er** *n.*
sun·beam [sun′bēm′] *n.* A ray of sunlight.
sun·belt or **Sun·belt** [sun′belt′] *n.* A region that has a relatively warm climate, such as the southern and sw U.S.
sun·bon·net [sun′bon′it] *n.* A bonnet with a projecting brim and sometimes a ruffle in back, to shade the face and neck from the sun.
sun·burn [sun′bûrn′] *n., v.* **sun·burned** or **sun·burnt, sun·burn·ing** **1** *n.* A painful burn that makes the skin red and sore, caused by too much exposure to the sun. **2** *v.* To affect or be affected with sunburn: My back is *sunburned.*
sun·dae [sun′dē] *n.* A dish of ice cream served with crushed fruit, syrup, nuts, and other toppings.
Sun·day [sun′dē *or* sun′dā′] *n.* The first day of the week. It is the Christian day of rest and worship.
Sunday school A school that meets on Sundays, in which religious instruction is given.
sun·der [sun′dər] *v.* To break or split apart; separate or sever: a country *sundered* by war. **—in sunder** Into separate parts; apart.
sun·dew [sun′d(y)o͞o′] *n.* Any of several plants that trap and digest insects by means of sticky leaves.
sun·di·al [sun′dī′əl] *n.* An outdoor device that shows the time of day by means of the shadow cast by a pointer on a numbered dial.

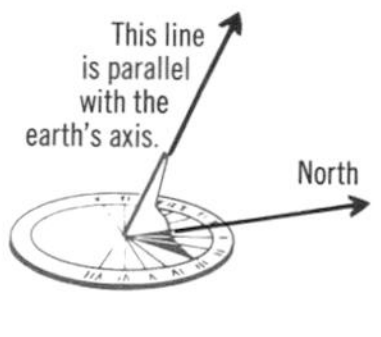

Sundial

sun·down [sun′doun′] *n. U.S.* Sunset.
sun·dries [sun′drēz] *n.pl.* Items or things too small or too numerous to be separately named.
sun·dry [sun′drē] *adj.* Various; several; miscellaneous: in *sundry* times and places.
sun·fish [sun′fish′] *n., pl.* **sun·fish** or **sun·fish·es** **1** A large ocean fish having a pancake-shaped body, two large fins, and a short tail. **2** A small North American freshwater fish.
sun·flow·er [sun′flou′ər] *n.* A tall plant with large, circular flowers that have a central dark disk surrounded by bright yellow rays.
sung [sung] Past participle and alternative past tense of SING.
sun·glass·es [sun′glas′iz] *n.pl.* Spectacles to protect the eyes from the glare of the sun, usually made with colored glass.
sunk [sungk] Past participle and alternative past tense of SINK.
sunk·en [sung′kən] *adj.* **1** Located beneath the surface or on the bottom of a body of water. **2** Lower than the surrounding level: *sunken* gardens. **3** Depressed or hollow: *sunken* cheeks.
sun·lamp [sun′lamp′] *n.* An electric lamp that gives off light with about the same range of wavelengths as sunlight, used for treating diseases and tanning the skin.
sun·less [sun′lis] *adj.* Lacking sun or sunlight; overcast or dark: *sunless* skies.
sun·light [sun′līt′] *n.* The light of the sun.
sun·lit [sun′lit′] *adj.* Lighted by the sun.
Sun·ni [so͝on′ē] *n., pl.* **Sun·nis,** *adj.* **1** *n.* The orthodox branch of Islam, consisting of most Muslims outside Iran. **2** *adj.* Of or having to do with this branch of Islam. **3** *n.* A Muslim belonging to the Sunni branch of Islam.
Sun·nite [so͝on′īt′] *n.* A Muslim of the Sunni branch of Islam.
sun·ny [sun′ē] *adj.* **sun·ni·er, sun·ni·est** **1** Filled with the light and warmth of the sun: a *sunny* afternoon. **2** Open or exposed to sunlight: a *sunny* patio. **3** Bright; cheery: a *sunny* smile.
sun·rise [sun′rīz′] *n.* **1** The appearing of the sun over the horizon. **2** The time when the sun rises. **3** The look of the sky at this time.
sun·set [sun′set′] *n.* **1** The disappearance of the sun below the horizon. **2** The time when the sun sets. **3** The look of the sky at this time.
sun·shade [sun′shād′] *n.* A shield from the sun, as a parasol or awning.
sun·shine [sun′shīn′] *n.* **1** The shining light of the sun. **2** The warmth of the sun's rays. **3** Brightness, cheerfulness, or happiness. **—sun′shin′y** *adj.*
sun·spot [sun′spot′] *n.* One of the dark spots that appear periodically on the surface of the sun, thought to be connected with magnetic disturbances.
sun·stroke [sun′strōk′] *n.* A sudden illness caused by staying too long in the hot sun.
sun·tan [sun′tan′] *n.* A tan skin color resulting from exposure to sunlight.
sun·up [sun′up′] *n. U.S.* Sunrise.
sup[1] [sup] *v.* **supped, sup·ping,** *n.* **1** *v.* To take (fluid food) in sips; sip. **2** *n.* A mouthful or taste of liquid or soft food.
sup[2] [sup] *v.* **supped, sup·ping** To eat supper.
su·per [so͞o′pər] **1** *n. informal* A superintendent of a building; janitor. **2** *n. informal* An actor with a small nonspeaking part; supernumerary. **3** *adj. slang* Extremely good; excellent: a *super* dancer.
super- A prefix meaning: **1** Above in position; over, as in *superstructure.* **2** Above or beyond; more than, as in *superhuman.* **3** Larger than or superior to others of its class, as in *superstar.* **4** Extremely or excessively, as in *superabundant.* **5** Extra, as in *supertax.*
su·per·a·bun·dant [so͞o′pər·ə·bun′dənt] *adj.* Much more than enough; extremely plentiful or excessive. **—su′per·a·bun′dance** *n.*
su·per·an·nu·at·ed [so͞o′pər·an′yo͞o·ā′tid] *adj.* **1** Retired because of age, especially with a pension. **2** Too old to be useful or efficient.
su·perb [so͞o·pûrb′] *adj.* **1** Grand; majestic; imposing: a *superb* dignity of manner. **2** Luxurious; elegant: a *superb* house. **3** Excellent; outstandingly good: The decorator has *superb* taste. **—su·perb′ly** *adv.*
su·per·car·go [so͞o′pər·kär′gō] *n., pl.* **su·per·car·goes** or **su·per·car·gos** An agent on board ship who is in charge of the cargo and its sale and purchase.
su·per·charge [so͞o′pər·chärj′] *v.* **su·per·charged, su·per·charg·ing** **1** To increase the power of (an internal-combustion engine) by forcing extra air and fuel into the cylinders under high pressure. **2** To fill heavily or excessively; overload.
su·per·charg·er [so͞o′pər·chär′jər] *n.* A pump or turbine that forces extra air and fuel into an internal-combustion engine.
su·per·cil·i·ous [so͞o′pər·sil′ē·əs] *adj.* Full of haughty contempt or indifference; too proud and disdainful; arrogant. **—su′per·cil′i·ous·ly** *adv.*

◆ *Supercilious* comes from a Latin word meaning *eyebrow.* A supercilious look often involves a raising of the eyebrows.

su·per·com·put·er [sōō′pər·kəm·pyōō′tər] *n.* The largest and most powerful type of computer.

su·per·con·duc·tiv·i·ty [sōō′pər·kon′dək·tiv′i·tē] *n.* The loss of all electrical resistance in certain metals and alloys at temperatures near absolute zero.

su·per·con·duc·tor [sōō′pər·kən·duk′tər] *n.* A metal or alloy that exhibits superconductivity. Zinc and lead are superconductors.

su·per·cool [sōō′pər·kōōl′] *v.* To cool below the freezing point without changing to a solid.

su·per·e·rog·a·to·ry [sōō′pər·i·rog′ə·tôr′ē] *adj.* Going beyond or being more than is needed or expected; superfluous.

su·per·fi·cial [sōō′pər·fish′əl] *adj.* 1 Of, on, or affecting only the surface: a *superficial* wound. 2 Not going past the surface or beyond the obvious; not deep or thorough; shallow or hasty: *superficial* understanding; a *superficial* search. 3 Not genuine: a *superficial* likeness. **—su·per·fi·ci·al·i·ty** [sōō′pər·fish′ē·al′ə·tē] *n.* **—su′per·fi′cial·ly** *adv.*

su·per·fine [sōō′pər·fīn′] *adj.* 1 Of very fine quality. 2 Of very fine texture or size: *superfine* sugar. 3 Too subtle or refined.

su·per·flu·i·ty [sōō′pər·flōō′ə·tē] *n., pl.* **su·per·flu·i·ties** 1 An amount greater than what is needed; excess. 2 An unnecessary thing.

su·per·flu·ous [sōō·pûr′flōō·əs] *adj.* More than is needed or called for; unnecessary: *superfluous* comments. **—su·per′flu·ous·ly** *adv.*

su·per·heat [*v.* sōō′pər·hēt′, *n.* sōō′pər·hēt′ *or* sōō′·pər·hēt′] 1 *v.* To heat to too high a temperature; overheat. 2 *v.* To heat (a liquid) above the normal boiling point without allowing vaporization. 3 *v.* To heat (steam or other vapor) so as to keep it from condensing. 4 *n.* The heat used or needed to superheat a vapor or liquid.

su·per·high·way [sōō′pər·hī′wā′] *n.* A divided highway for traffic moving at high speeds, generally having four or more traffic lanes.

su·per·hu·man [sōō′pər·(h)yōō′mən] *adj.* 1 Above or beyond the human; supernatural or divine. 2 Beyond the range of normal or ordinary human powers: to display *superhuman* strength.

su·per·im·pose [sōō′pər·im·pōz′] *v.* **su·per·im·posed, su·per·im·pos·ing** To place over, above, or on top of something else.

su·per·in·tend [sōō′pər·in·tend′] *v.* To be in charge of and direct; manage; supervise.

su·per·in·ten·dence [sōō′pər·in·ten′dəns] *n.* Direction and management; supervision.

su·per·in·ten·dent [sōō′pər·in·ten′dənt] *n.* 1 A person responsible for directing, managing, or supervising some work, organization, or department. 2 In parts of the U.S., a janitor.

su·pe·ri·or [sə·pir′ē·ər] 1 *adj.* Much better than the usual; extremely good; excellent. 2 *adj.* Conceited or disdainful because of a feeling of being better than others: Don't act so *superior.* 3 *adj.* Higher, as in rank, grade, or authority: a *superior* officer. 4 *adj.* Greater, as in size, power, or ability: The enemy was *superior* in numbers. 5 *n.* A person of greater authority or ability than another: The assistant vice president is my *superior* at work. 6 *n.* The head of a religious order or house, as a convent. **—superior to** 1 Better, larger, or more powerful than. 2 Above, as in rank. 3 Beyond the influence of; above giving in to.

su·pe·ri·or·i·ty [sə·pir′ē·ôr′ə·tē] *n.* The quality or condition of being superior.

su·per·la·tive [sə·pûr′lə·tiv *or* sōō·pûr′lə·tiv] 1 *adj.* Excellent in the highest degree: *superlative* work. 2 *adj.* In grammar, designating the form of an adjective or adverb used to express the highest or lowest quantity, quality, or relation. 3 *n.* The superlative degree of an adjective or adverb. *Greenest* and *most clearly* are superlatives of *green* and *clearly.* **—su·per′la·tive·ly** *adv.*

su·per·man [sōō′pər·man′] *n., pl.* **su·per·men** [sōō′·pər·men′] A man having superhuman powers.

su·per·mar·ket [sōō′pər·mär′kit] *n.* A large grocery store in which the customers select goods from the shelves and pay as they leave.

su·per·nal [sōō·pûr′nəl] *adj.* 1 Of or from the sky. 2 Of or from heaven or the heavens; celestial; heavenly. **—su·per′nal·ly** *adv.*

su·per·nat·u·ral [sōō′pər·nach′ər·əl] *adj.* 1 Outside the known laws or forces of nature: *supernatural* powers. 2 *n. use:* Supernatural things or events: tales of the *supernatural.*

su·per·nat·u·ral·ism [sōō′pər·nach′ər·ə·liz′əm] *n.* 1 The quality or state of being supernatural. 2 Belief in things such as ghosts and spirits that are outside the known laws or forces of nature.

su·per·no·va [sōō′pər·nō′və] *n., pl.* **su·per·no·vas** or **su·per·no·vae** [sōō′pər·nō′vē′] A rare celestial event in which a star explodes with an enormous release of energy, becoming very bright for a short time; very luminous nova.

su·per·nu·mer·ar·y [sōō′pər·n(y)ōō′mə·rer′ē] *adj., n., pl.* **su·per·nu·mer·ar·ies** 1 *adj.* Beyond a customary or necessary number; extra. 2 *n.* An extra person or thing. 3 *n.* An actor who plays a member of a crowd and has no lines.

su·per·pow·er [sōō′pər·pou′ər] *n.* A powerful nation that plays a dominant, competitive role in international affairs.

su·per·sat·u·rate [sōō′pər·sach′ə·rāt′] *v.* **su·per·sat·u·rat·ed, su·per·sat·u·rat·ing** To cause to absorb more of something than is normally possible: to *supersaturate* a solution with salt; to *supersaturate* a market with a product. **—su·per·sat·u·ra·tion** [sōō′pər·sach′ə·rā′shən] *n.*

su·per·script [sōō′pər·skript′] *n.* A character written or printed above and often to the side of a larger character, as the ³ in y^3.

su·per·scrip·tion [sōō′pər·skrip′shən] *n.* Something written on the outside or upper part of a thing, especially an address on a letter.

su·per·sede [sōō′pər·sēd′] *v.* **su·per·sed·ed, su·per·sed·ing** 1 To cause to be given up or set aside; displace: Buses have largely *superseded* streetcars. 2 To fill the position of; replace: The new teacher *supersedes* one who retired.

su·per·sen·si·tive [sōō′pər·sen′sə·tiv] *adj.* Very or unusually sensitive: seismographs that are *super-*

S

a	add	**i**	it	**o͝o**	took	**oi**	oil
ā	ace	**ī**	ice	**o͞o**	pool	**ou**	pout
â	care	**o**	odd	**u**	up	**ng**	ring
ä	palm	**ō**	open	**û**	burn	**th**	thin
e	end	**ô**	order	**yo͞o**	fuse	**t͟h**	this
ē	equal					**zh**	vision

ə = {a in *above* e in *sicken* i in *possible* / o in *melon* u in *circus*}

sensitive to vibrations. **—su′per·sen′si·tive·ly** *adv.* **—su′per·sen′si·tive·ness** *n.*

su·per·set [so͞o′pər·set′] *n.* A set that includes all the members of another set: {x,y,z} is a *superset* of {x,y}.

su·per·son·ic [so͞o′pər·son′ik] *adj.* Being or traveling faster than the speed of sound.

su·per·star [so͞o′pər·stär′] *n.* A very popular, much publicized, and usually highly paid star, as in the movies, television, or sports.

su·per·sti·tion [so͞o′pər·stish′ən] *n.* **1** The unreasoning fear or belief that many helpful and harmful supernatural forces exist and that certain actions will anger or pacify them. **2** A superstitious idea or practice: the *superstition* that walking under a ladder is unlucky.

su·per·sti·tious [so͞o′pər·stish′əs] *adj.* Of, based on, caused by, influenced by, or showing superstition. **—su′per·sti′tious·ly** *adv.*

su·per·struc·ture [so͞o′pər·struk′chər] *n.* **1** Any structure built upon another. **2** The part of a building above the foundation. **3** The part of a ship above the main deck.

su·per·tax [so͞o′pər·taks′] *n.* An extra tax in addition to the normal tax; surtax.

su·per·vene [so͞o′pər·vēn′] *v.* **su·per·vened, su·per·ven·ing** To happen as an additional or unexpected event. **—su·per·ven·tion** [so͞o′pər·ven′shən] *n.*

su·per·vise [so͞o′pər·vīz′] *v.* **su·per·vised, su·per·vis·ing** To oversee; direct and manage (as employees or a process).

su·per·vi·sion [so͞o′pər·vizh′ən] *n.* Direction or control; regulation; management.

su·per·vi·sor [so͞o′pər·vī′zər] *n.* **1** A person who oversees and directs others. **2** A worker in charge of other workers.

su·per·vi·so·ry [so͞o′pər·vī′zər·ē] *adj.* **1** Of or having to do with a supervisor or supervision. **2** Involving or limited to supervision.

su·pine [so͞o·pīn′] *adj.* **1** Lying on the back with the face upward. **2** Sluggishly inactive.

sup·per [sup′ər] *n.* An evening meal; last meal of the day.

sup·plant [sə·plant′] *v.* To take the place of, often unfairly: A tyrant *supplanted* the rightful king.

sup·ple [sup′əl] *adj.* **sup·pler** [sup′lər], **sup·plest** [sup′ləst] **1** Bending easily; flexible or limber: a *supple* body. **2** Able to adapt easily to new or different situations: a *supple* mind.

sup·ple·ment [*n.* sup′lə·mənt, *v.* sup′lə·ment′] **1** *n.* Something added, often to supply a lack: a food *supplement.* **2** *v.* To add to or provide what is lacking in: extra reading to *supplement* the textbook. **3** *n.* An extra section of a newspaper or book giving additional information: a yearly *supplement* to an encyclopedia.

sup·ple·men·tal [sup′lə·men′təl] *adj.* Supplementary; additional.

sup·ple·men·ta·ry [sup′lə·men′tər·ē] *adj.* Serving as an addition or to supply a lack.

supplementary angle Either of two angles whose sum is 180°.

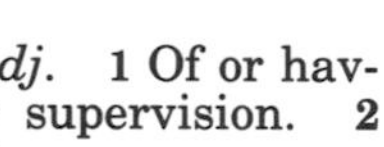

Angles *a* and *b* are supplementary.

sup·pli·ant [sup′lē·ənt] **1** *adj.* Asking earnestly and humbly; beseeching. **2** *n.* A person who begs or prays earnestly and humbly: The king agreed to listen to the entreaties of the *suppliants.*

sup·pli·cant [sup′lə·kənt] **1** *adj.* Asking humbly; beseeching. **2** *n.* A suppliant.

sup·pli·cate [sup′lə·kāt′] *v.* **sup·pli·cat·ed, sup·pli·cat·ing** To ask, entreat, or pray earnestly and humbly; beseech; implore.

sup·pli·ca·tion [sup′lə·kā′shən] *n.* An earnest prayer or entreaty.

sup·pli·ca·tor·y [sup′li·kə·tôr′ē] *adj.* Making an earnest and humble request; beseeching.

sup·ply[1] [sə·plī′] *v.* **sup·plied, sup·ply·ing,** *n., pl.* **sup·plies** **1** *v.* To furnish (what is needed or wanted); provide: to *supply* milk for a city. **2** *v.* To furnish (someone) with what is needed or wanted: to *supply* a class with paper. **3** *n.* An amount available for use; stock; store: a *supply* of fuel. **4** *n.* (*usually pl.*) Materials or goods kept on hand to be given out when needed: office *supplies.* **5** *n.* The act of supplying. **—sup·pli′er** *n.*

sup·ply[2] [sup′lē] *adv.* In a supple way.

sup·port [sə·pôrt′] **1** *v.* To bear the weight of; hold up or hold in place: Beams *support* the ceiling. **2** *v.* To provide the necessities of life for: We *support* five children. **3** *v.* To keep or tend to keep from failing; maintain: Oxygen *supports* burning. **4** *v.* To help prove the truth or correctness of: The evidence *supports* my theory. **5** *v.* To favor, help, or back: to *support* a candidate. **6** *n.* The act of supporting. **7** *n.* The state of being supported. **8** *n.* A person or thing that supports. **9** *v.* To endure or tolerate: I cannot *support* insolence. **—sup·port′er** *n.*

sup·port·a·ble [sə·pôr′tə·bəl] *adj.* Capable of being supported. **—sup·port′a·bly** *adv.*

sup·pose [sə·pōz′] *v.* **sup·posed, sup·pos·ing** **1** To assume as true, as for the sake of argument: *Suppose* the train is on time. **2** To imagine, think, believe, or guess: I *suppose* you're tired. **3** To expect or require: I'm *supposed* to be home by five. **4** To require as a necessary condition; imply: A gift *supposes* a giver.

sup·posed [sə·pōzd′] *adj.* Considered to be true or actual, often by mistake: your *supposed* honestly. **—sup·pos·ed·ly** [sə·pō′zid·lē] *adv.*

sup·po·si·tion [sup′ə·zish′ən] *n.* **1** The act of supposing. **2** Something supposed; assumption.

sup·pos·i·tor·y [sə·poz′ə·tôr′ē] *n., pl.* **sup·pos·i·tor·ies** A solid but readily melting piece of medication designed to be inserted into the rectum or some other body opening besides the mouth.

sup·press [sə·pres′] *v.* **1** To put down or end by force; crush: to *suppress* a rebellion. **2** To keep from getting out or becoming known; hold back: to *suppress* a sigh; to *suppress* news. **—sup·pres·sion** [sə·presh′ən] *n.*

sup·pres·sive [sə·pres′iv] *adj.* Serving or tending to suppress: The government took *suppressive* measures to close down opposition newspapers.

sup·pu·rate [sup′yə·rāt′] *v.* **sup·pu·rat·ed, sup·pu·rat·ing** To fester, or discharge pus.

sup·pu·ra·tion [sup′yə·rā′shən] *n.* **1** The formation or discharge of pus, as in a wound. **2** Pus.

su·pra·re·nal gland [so͞o′prə·rē′nəl] Another name for ADRENAL GLAND.

su·prem·a·cy [sə·prem′ə·sē] *n.* **1** Supreme power or authority. **2** The quality of being supreme.

su·preme [sə·prēm′] *adj.* **1** Highest in power or authority: *supreme* headquarters of the allied forces. **2** Highest, as in degree or quality; utmost: Shakespeare is the *supreme* English poet. **—su·preme′ly** *adv.*

Supreme Being God.

Supreme Court **1** The highest and final court of

appeal in the U.S., made up of nine justices. **2** The highest court in various states.

sur·cease [sûr′sēs′ *or* sər·sēs′] *n.* Cessation; end: seldom used today.

sur·charge [*n.* sûr′chärj′, *v.* sər·chärj′] *n., v.* **sur·charged, sur·charg·ing** **1** *n.* An extra charge over the regular rate. **2** *n.* An excessive charge or burden. **3** *v.* To charge extra, overcharge, or overload. **4** *n.* Something additional, as a new valuation, printed on a stamp. **5** *v.* To imprint a surcharge on (a stamp).

sur·cin·gle [sûr′sing′gəl] *n.* An encircling strap that holds a horse's saddle or pack in place; girth.

sur·coat [sûr′kōt′] *n.* An outer coat or garment, as a tunic worn by knights over armor.

Surcoat

surd [sûrd] *n.* An irrational number.

sure [shŏŏr] *adj.* **sur·er, sur·est,** *adv.* **1** *adj.* Free from doubt; certain; positive: I'm *sure* you'll succeed. **2** *adv. informal* Certainly; of course: *Sure,* I can go. **3** *adj.* Certain; destined; bound: You're *sure* to win. **4** *adj.* Bound to happen; inevitable: Victory seemed a *sure* thing. **5** *adj.* Not likely to fail: a *sure* shot. **6** *adj.* Dependable; reliable: a *sure* remedy. **7** *adj.* Secure; stable: a *sure* footing. **—to be sure** Certainly; undoubtedly. **—sure′ness** *n.* ◆ In speech or informal writing, *sure* may be used as an adverb: I *sure* wish you could come with us. In formal writing, use the adverb *surely.*

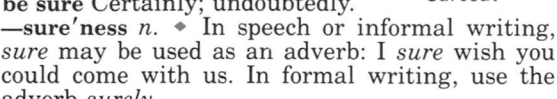

sure·fire [shŏŏr′fīr′] *adj. informal* Certain to succeed or win: a *surefire* method.

sure·foot·ed [shŏŏr′fŏŏt′id] *adj.* Not liable to slip, stumble, or fall: a *surefooted* burro.

sure·ly [shŏŏr′lē] *adv.* **1** Without doubt; certainly. **2** Securely; safely.

sure·ty [shŏŏr′(ə·)tē] *n., pl.* **sure·ties** **1** A person who takes responsibility for another's debt or action. **2** Security or guarantee against loss, damage, or failure to do something.

surf [sûrf] **1** *n.* The waves of the sea as they break on a beach, reef, or shoal. **2** *n.* The roar or foam of such waves. **3** *v.* To ride a surfboard.

sur·face [sûr′fis] *n., v.* **sur·faced, sur·fac·ing** **1** *n.* The outer part or face of any solid body, or the upper level of a liquid. **2** *adj. use*: *surface* activity. **3** *v.* To add a surface to; smooth: to *surface* a drive with asphalt. **4** *v.* To rise to the surface, as a submarine. **5** *n.* The outward part or appearance of a person or thing: They are always pleasant on the *surface.* **6** *adj. use*: a *surface* calm.

surface area The sum of the areas of the surfaces of a three-dimensional figure.

surf·board [sûrf′bôrd′] *n.* A long, narrow board, used in the water sport of surfing.

surf·cast·ing [sûrf′kas′ting] *n.* The sport of fishing along an open shore by casting a line into the surf. **—surf′cast′er** *n.*

sur·feit [sûr′fit] **1** *n.* Too much or an excess of something, as of food or drink. **2** *n.* The disgust felt by having too much of something. **3** *v.* To feed or supply with too much of something.

surf·ing [sûr′fing] *n.* The sport of riding waves, especially with a surfboard.

surge [sûrj] *n., v.* **surged, surg·ing** **1** *v.* To move or go with the strong rush of a wave: The crowd *surged* forward. **2** *n.* A surging or rushing movement: the rhythmic *surge* of the waves. **3** *n.* A strong, sudden increase or flow: a *surge* of energy.

sur·geon [sûr′jən] *n.* A doctor whose practice is largely limited to surgery.

surgeon general *pl.* **surgeons general** The chief medical officer of one of the armed services, or of the U.S. Public Health Service, or, in some states, of a state public health service.

sur·ger·y [sûr′jər·ē] *n.* **1** The branch of medical practice dealing with the repair or removal of diseased or injured organs or parts of the body. **2** An operation in which surgery is used. **3** A place or room where surgery is done.

sur·gi·cal [sûr′ji·kəl] *adj.* Of, having to do with, or used in surgery: a *surgical* mask.

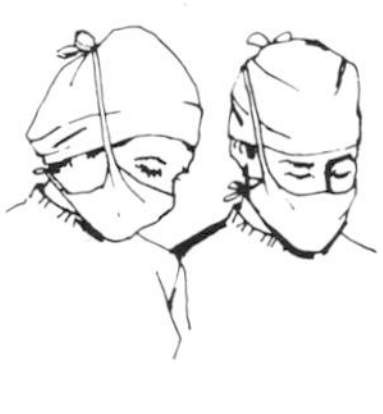
Surgical masks

Su·ri·nam·ese [sŏŏr′ə·nə·mēz′] *adj., n., pl.* **Su·ri·nam·ese** **1** *adj.* Of or from Suriname. **2** *n.* A person born in or a citizen of Suriname.

sur·ly [sûr′lē] *adj.* **sur·li·er, sur·li·est** Rude and ill-humored; cross; gruff. **—sur′li·ness** *n.*

sur·mise [sər·mīz′] *n., v.* **sur·mised, sur·mis·ing** **1** *n.* An opinion based on slight evidence; guess. **2** *v.* To form (such an opinion); guess.

sur·mount [sər·mount′] *v.* **1** To overcome (as difficulties or problems). **2** To reach the top or other side of (as an obstacle or mountain). **3** To be on or at the top of: A steeple *surmounted* the church.

sur·name [sûr′nām′] *n., v.* **sur·named, sur·nam·ing** **1** *n.* The name of a person's family; last name of a person: Some *surnames* are derived from professions, as Baker, Tanner, and Miller. **2** *n.* An added name; nickname: Philip IV was given the *surname* "the Fair." **3** *v.* To give a surname to. **4** *v.* To call or identify by a surname.

sur·pass [sər·pas′] *v.* **1** To be more, greater, or better than: Your playing *surpassed* our wildest hopes. **2** To go beyond the reach or powers of: The Acropolis *surpasses* all description.

sur·plice [sûr′plis] *n.* A loose, white garment with full sleeves, worn over a cassock by the clergy or choir of certain churches.

Surplices

sur·plus [sûr′plus′] **1** *n.* An amount above

a	add	**i**	it	**ŏŏ**	took	**oi**	oil
ā	ace	**ī**	ice	**ōō**	pool	**ou**	pout
â	care	**o**	odd	**u**	up	**ng**	ring
ä	palm	**ō**	open	**û**	burn	**th**	thin
e	end	**ô**	order	**yōō**	fuse	**th**	this
ē	equal					**zh**	vision

ə = a in *above*, e in *sicken*, i in *possible*, o in *melon*, u in *circus*

S

what is used or needed; something left over; excess. **2** *adj. use: surplus* food; *surplus* production.

sur·prise [sə(r)·prīz′] *v.* **sur·prised, sur·pris·ing,** *n.* **1** *v.* To strike with mild astonishment, as by being unexpected or unusual: The announcement *surprised* us all. **2** *n.* The condition of being surprised; astonishment. **3** *n.* Something that causes surprise: Their visit was a happy *surprise.* **4** *adj. use*: a *surprise* party. **5** *v.* To come upon suddenly or unexpectedly; take unawares: to *surprise* a thief. **6** *n.* The act of surprising: to take someone by *surprise.*

sur·pris·ing [sə(r)·prī′zing] *adj.* Causing surprise; unexpected: The fat man danced with *surprising* grace. **—sur·pris′ing·ly** *adv.*

sur·re·al·ism [sə·rē′əl·iz′əm] *n.* A movement in 20th-century art and literature stressing dreamlike, fantastic, and mysteriously symbolic imagery. **—sur·re′al·ist** *adj., n.*

sur·re·al·is·tic [sə·rē′ə·lis′tik] *adj.* **1** Of or having to do with surrealism: *surrealistic* paintings. **2** Having the mysterious or incongruous quality of a dream; fantastic. **—sur·re′al·is′ti·cal·ly** *adv.*

sur·ren·der [sə·ren′dər] **1** *v.* To give up, as to an enemy; yield. **2** *v.* To abandon or give up possession of: to *surrender* hope; to *surrender* a seat. **3** *n.* The act of surrendering.

sur·rep·ti·tious [sûr′əp·tish′əs] *adj.* Acting or done secretly and stealthily, so as to avoid notice: a *surreptitious* peek. **—sur′rep·ti′tious·ly** *adv.*

sur·rey [sûr′ē] *n.* A light carriage having two seats, four wheels, and often a flat, fringed top.

Surrey

sur·ro·gate [sûr′ə·gāt′ *or* sûr′ə·git] *n.* **1** A person having the authority to act in place of another; deputy. **2** A judge of a court whose duties include having charge of guardianships and settling estates.

sur·round [sə·round′] *v.* To enclose on all sides; envelop; encircle.

sur·round·ings [sə·roun′dingz] *n.pl.* The things or the conditions that surround a person or place; environment: pleasant *surroundings.*

sur·tax [sûr′taks′] **1** *n.* An extra or additional tax. **2** *v.* To charge with such a tax.

sur·veil·lance [sər·vā′ləns] *n.* **1** Close watch, as over a prisoner or suspect. **2** The act of watching or supervising closely.

sur·vey [*v.* sər·vā′, *n.* sûr′vā′] **1** *v.* To determine the area, boundaries, and shape of (land) by measurement and calculation. **2** *n.* The act or results of surveying. **3** *v.* To get an overall view of; look over as from a height: to *survey* the landscape. **4** *n.* A brief but thorough study or examination.

sur·vey·ing [sər·vā′ing] *n.* The methods or profession of measuring and mapping land.

sur·vey·or [sər·vā′ər] *n.* A person whose profession is surveying.

sur·viv·al [sər·vī′vəl] *n.* **1** The act or condition of surviving: Their *survival* depended on the skill of the pilot. **2** Something, as a custom or belief, that persists from a former time.

sur·vive [sər·vīv′] *v.* **sur·vived, sur·viv·ing** **1** To outlive or outlast: to *survive* a relative. **2** To live through: to *survive* a flood. **3** To remain alive or in existence.

sur·vi·vor [sər·vī′vər] *n.* A person or thing that survives: the *survivors* of the tornado.

sus·cep·ti·ble [sə·sep′tə·bəl] *adj.* Easily influenced, moved, or affected: Our *susceptible* sympathies were aroused. **—susceptible of** Capable of receiving, undergoing, or being influenced by: This testimony is *susceptible of* proof. **—susceptible to** Easily affected by; liable to; sensitive to: We are *susceptible to* colds; a child *susceptible to* the least criticism. **—sus·cep′ti·bil′i·ty** *n.*

su·shi [sōō′shē] *n.* A Japanese dish of cakes of rice topped with thin strips of raw fish or garnished, as with raw fish or vegetables, and wrapped in seaweed.

sus·pect [*v.* sə·spekt′, *n., adj.* sus′pekt′] **1** *v.* To believe that something or someone is bad, wrong, or guilty, without real proof: to *suspect* a bill to be counterfeit. **2** *n.* A person suspected of a crime or misdeed. **3** *v.* To have doubts about; mistrust: Do you *suspect* my motive? **4** *v.* To have a suspicion of; think possible: I *suspect* treachery. **5** *adj.* Arousing, open to, or viewed with suspicion: If shellfish is *suspect*, don't eat it.

sus·pend [sə·spend′] *v.* **1** To cause to hang down from a support: to *suspend* a bucket. **2** To cause to stop for a time; interrupt: to *suspend* business. **3** To put off for a time; delay action on: to *suspend* judgment until all the facts are in. **4** To bar or keep out for a time, as a punishment: The offending jockey may be *suspended.* **5** To hold in place as though supported: bits of dust *suspended* in the air.

sus·pend·ers [sə·spen′dərz] *n.pl.* A pair of straps worn over the shoulders for holding up the trousers.

sus·pense [sə·spens′] *n.* A condition or situation in which there is a good deal of doubt, worry, fear, or uncertainty about what is going to happen: a mystery play full of *suspense.*

sus·pen·sion [sə·spen′shən] *n.* **1** The act or result of suspending. **2** The condition of being suspended: Fog caused a *suspension* of flying. **3** A support from which something is hung. **4** The system of springs supporting the body of a car on the axles. **5** A mixture in which tiny solid particles stay suspended but not dissolved in a liquid or gas.

suspension bridge A bridge in which the roadway is hung from cables passing over towers and fastened at the ends.

Suspension bridge

sus·pi·cion [sə·spish′ən] *n.* **1** A feeling, thought, or idea, not based on real proof, that something is wrong. **2** The act of suspecting. **3** Consideration as a suspect: to be under *suspicion.* **4** The least bit; hint: a *suspicion* of onion in the soup.

sus·pi·cious [sə·spish′əs] *adj.* **1** Inclined to suspect; distrustful: a *suspicious* person. **2** Apt to arouse suspicion; questionable: a *suspicious* action. **3** Showing suspicion: a *suspicious* glance. **—sus·pi′cious·ly** *adv.* **—sus·pi′cious·ness** *n.*

sus·tain [sə·stān′] *v.* **1** To hold in position; support: Pillars *sustain* the porch roof. **2** To withstand or resist (as a force, pressure, or effect). **3** To undergo or suffer: to *sustain* an injury. **4** To keep up the courage or spirits of: The leader's calm *sustained* us when we got lost. **5** To keep in effect or in existence: The actor *sustained* the feeling of dread throughout the entire act. **6** To provide nourishment or necessities for: enough food to *sustain* life. **7** To uphold or establish as correct or fair: The court *sustained* the original verdict of guilty.

sus·te·nance [sus′tə·nəns] *n.* Something that maintains life or strength; nourishment; food.

su·tra [so͞o′trə] *n.* **1** An ancient Hindu precept or collection of precepts. **2** A Buddhist religious text that relates a conversation or speech of Buddha.

su·ture [so͞o′chər] *n., v.* **su·tured, su·tur·ing** **1** *n.* The sewing together of any parts or organs of the body or of the edges of a cut or wound. **2** *v.* To unite or bring together in this way. **3** *n.* The thread, catgut, or wire used in the stitches of this operation. **4** *n.* The line or edge along which two bones join together.

su·ze·rain [so͞o′zə·rin *or* so͞o′zə·rān′] *n.* **1** Formerly, a feudal lord. **2** A nation that controls the foreign affairs of another nation while giving it full freedom to manage its internal affairs.

su·ze·rain·ty [so͞o′zə·rən·tē *or* so͞o′zə·rān′tē] *n., pl.* **su·ze·rain·ties** The position or power of a suzerain.

svelte [svelt *or* sfelt] *adj.* **svelt·er, svelt·est** Slender and graceful; lithe. **—svelte′ly** *adv.* **—svelte′ness** *n.*

sw, s.w., SW, or **S.W.** **1** southwest. **2** southwestern.

swab [swob] *n., v.* **swabbed, swab·bing** **1** *n.* A wad of absorbent cotton or the like, often wound on the end of a small stick, used for cleaning out wounds and applying medication. **2** *v.* To clean or apply medication to with a swab: to *swab* a wound. **3** *n.* A mop for cleaning decks and floors. **4** *v.* To mop.

swad·dle [swod′(ə)l] *v.* **swad·dled, swad·dling** To wrap (an infant) with a long strip of linen or flannel.

swaddling clothes or **swaddling bands** Strips of cloth wound around an infant.

swag [swag] *n. slang* Property obtained by robbery or theft; plunder.

swag·ger [swag′ər] **1** *v.* To walk with a proud or insolent air; strut. **2** *v.* To boast; bluster. **3** *n.* A swaggering walk or manner.

Swa·hi·li [swä·hē′lē] *n.* A language of East Africa, used widely in African commerce and trade.

swain [swān] *n.* A young country boy, especially one who is courting: seldom used today.

swal·low¹ [swol′ō] *n.* A small bird having a short bill, long pointed wings, and a forked tail, noted for its swiftness in flight.

swal·low² [swol′ō] **1** *v.* To make the muscular action that causes (food or liquid) to pass from the mouth, through the throat and gullet, and into the stomach. **2** *n.* The act of swallowing. **3** *n.* The amount swallowed at one time. **4** *v.* To take in, as if by swallowing: The night *swallowed* them. **5** *v.* To hold in or conceal: to *swallow* tears; to *swallow* one's pride. **6** *v.* To endure or submit to: to *swallow* insults. **7** *v.* To take back: to *swallow* one's words. **8** *v. informal* To believe without question or criticism: Some people will *swallow* any old tale.

swal·low·tail [swol′ō·tāl′] *n.* A brightly colored butterfly, having two long tails or points on each hind wing.

swal·low-tailed coat [swol′ō·tāld′] A formal dress coat, having two long, tapering tails in the back.

swam [swam] The past tense of SWIM.

swa·mi [swä′mē] *n.* A Hindu religious teacher.

swamp [swomp] **1** *n.* An area of low, wet land; bog; marsh. **2** *v.* To drench with water or other liquid: The tidal wave *swamped* the coastal town. **3** *v.* To overwhelm; flood: *swamped* with invitations. **4** *v.* To fill or be filled with water; sink: The boat *swamped* in the surf. **—swamp′y** *adj.*

swamp·land [swomp′land′] *n.* An area or tract of land covered with swamps.

swan [swon] *n.* A large water bird with a long graceful neck and brilliant white feathers.

Swan

swan dive A dive performed with the back arched and the arms first extended sideways, then brought together in front of the head as the body enters the water headfirst.

swank [swangk] *adj. slang* Fashionable or stylish in a showy way: a *swank* neighborhood.

swank·y [swang′kē] *adj.* **swank·i·er, swank·i·est** *slang* Swank. **—swank′i·ly** *adv.* **—swank′i·ness** *n.*

swans·down or **swan's-down** [swonz′doun′] *n.* **1** The fine, soft feathers of a swan, used to make powder puffs and trimming for clothes. **2** A soft, thick cloth resembling this.

swan song **1** In legend, an exquisite song sung by a swan just before death. **2** The final creative work before death or retirement, as of an artist.

swap [swop] *v.* **swapped, swap·ping,** *n. informal* **1** *v.* To exchange (one thing for another); trade. **2** *n.* An exchange or trade; barter.

sward [swôrd] *n.* Land thickly covered with grass.

swarm [swôrm] **1** *n.* A large number of bees, accompanied by a queen, leaving a hive at one time in order to form a new colony. **2** *v.* To leave the hive in a swarm, as bees. **3** *n.* A hive of bees. **4** *n.* A large colony or group of insects or other small creatures: a *swarm* of flies. **5** *n.* A large crowd or throng: a *swarm* of commuters. **6** *v.* To collect, arrive, or move in great numbers: People *swarmed* to the show. **7** *v.* To fill or be filled, as with a large crowd: The platform *swarmed* with passengers.

swarth·y [swôr′thē] *adj.* **swarth·i·er, swarth·i·est** Having a dark complexion.

swash [swosh] **1** *v.* To move, wash, or splash noisily: The wind *swashed* the water against the rocks. **2** *n.* The splash of a liquid.

swash·buck·ler [swosh′buk′lər] *n.* **1** A swaggering, cocky, or boastful soldier or daredevil. **2** A novel or drama having to do with a swashbuckler.

swash·buck·ling [swosh′buk′ling] **1** *n.* The actions or manner of a swashbuckler. **2** *adj.* Of, like, or characterized by swashbuckling.

a	add	**i**	it	**o͝o**	took	**oi**	oil		
ā	ace	**ī**	ice	**o͞o**	pool	**ou**	pout		
â	care	**o**	odd	**u**	up	**ng**	ring		
ä	palm	**ō**	open	**û**	burn	**th**	thin		
e	end	**ô**	order	**yo͞o**	fuse	**th**	this		
ē	equal					**zh**	vision		

ə = a in *above* e in *sicken* i in *possible* o in *melon* u in *circus*

S

swas·ti·ka [swos′ti·kə] *n.* An ancient symbol, a cross with arms bent at right angles. One form of the swastika was adopted by the Nazis as their emblem.

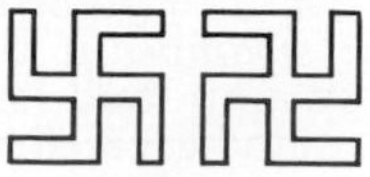

Swastika

swat [swot] *v.* **swat·ted, swat·ting,** *n.* **1** *v.* To hit with a sharp blow. **2** *n.* A quick, sharp blow. **—swat′·ter** *n.*

swatch [swoch] *n.* A sample piece of cloth or other material.

swath [swoth] *n.* **1** A row of cut grass or grain. **2** The space or width of one row of grass or grain, cut by any of various mowing devices. **3** Any broad strip: a *swath* of green lawn.

swathe [swāth *or* swāth] *v.* **swathed, swath·ing,** *n.* **1** *v.* To bind or wrap, as in cloth or bandages. **2** *n.* A wrapping or bandage for swathing. **3** *v.* To surround or envelop.

sway [swā] **1** *v.* To move or cause to move from side to side: The wind *swayed* the trees; The street sign *swayed* in the gale. **2** *v.* To lean or bend or cause to lean or bend: The flowers *swayed* to the ground. **3** *v.* To cause (as a person or opinion) to tend in a certain way; influence: What *swayed* you to accept the job? **4** *n.* Influence, control, or power: Nothing holds any *sway* over those children. **5** *v.* To change from one point of view or opinion to another. **6** *n.* The act of swaying.

sway·backed [swā′bakt′] *adj.* Having an abnormal sagging or inward curving of the back: a *swaybacked* horse.

SWbS southwest by south.

SWbW southwest by west.

swear [swâr] *v.* **swore, sworn, swear·ing** **1** To make a very solemn statement, with an appeal to God or to something held sacred, that something is true. **2** To promise or cause to promise solemnly: I *swore* I would not tell; We *swore* them to secrecy. **3** To use profanity; curse: I hate to hear you *swear.* **—swear by** **1** To appeal to (someone or something sacred) in taking an oath: I *swear by* heaven that I am innocent. **2** To have complete confidence in: They *swear by* those exercises to keep them healthy. **—swear in** To administer a legal oath to: The Chief Justice of the Supreme Court *swears in* the President of the U.S. **—swear off** *informal* To promise to give up: The dieter *swore off* cake.

swear·word [swâr′wûrd′] *n.* A word used in cursing; profane word.

sweat [swet] *v.* **sweat** or **sweat·ed, sweat·ing,** *n.* **1** *v.* To give off moisture through the pores of the skin; perspire: The athletes *sweated* during the hot weather. **2** *n.* The salty moisture given off through the pores of the skin. **3** *v.* To gather drops of moisture by condensation: The pitcher of ice water *sweated* in the hot kitchen. **4** *n.* The moisture formed on cold surfaces surrounded by warmer air. **5** *v. informal* To work or cause to work hard: We really *sweated* over that exam; The boss *sweated* the workers unmercifully. **6** *v.* To get rid of by sweating: to *sweat* away five pounds. **7** *v. informal* To suffer, worry, or be concerned: We *sweated* until we heard they were safe. **8** *n. informal* A condition of worry, hurry, or impatience: Don't get in a *sweat.* **—sweat out** To wait or work through anxiously or tediously.

sweat·band [swet′band′] *n.* **1** A band sewn around the inside of a hat or cap to protect it from sweat. **2** A band tied around the head or wrist to absorb sweat.

sweat·er [swet′ər] *n.* A garment for the upper part of the body, made in the form of a pullover or a jacket, with or without sleeves. ◆ *Sweater* comes from the word *sweat. Sweaters* were originally worn by athletes to make themselves sweat.

sweat gland Any of the glands, just below the skin, that secrete sweat.

sweat pants Cotton pants having a drawstring for tying at the waist and elastic cuffs at the ankles, worn especially by exercisers.

sweat shirt A heavy cotton pullover, usually having long sleeves, worn to soak up sweat.

sweat·shop [swet′shop′] *n.* A place where work is done under poor conditions, for very little pay, and for long hours.

sweat suit A matching outfit of sweat pants and a sweat shirt.

sweat·y [swet′ē] *adj.* **sweat·i·er, sweat·i·est** **1** Covered or wet with sweat. **2** Of or like sweat: a *sweaty* smell. **3** Causing sweat. **—sweat′i·ly** *adv.* **—sweat′i·ness** *n.*

Swede [swēd] *n.* A person born in or a citizen of Sweden.

Swed·ish [swē′dish] **1** *adj.* Of or from Sweden. **2** *n.* **(the Swedish)** The people of Sweden. **3** *n.* The language of Sweden.

sweep [swēp] *v.* **swept, sweep·ing,** *n.* **1** *v.* To clean with a broom or brush. **2** *v.* To collect, remove, or clear away with a broom or brush: Don't *sweep* the dirt under the rug. **3** *n.* The act or an instance of sweeping: He gave the floor a good *sweep.* **4** *n.* A chimney sweep. **5** *v.* To touch or brush: The monarch's train *swept* the ground. **6** *v.* To walk proudly or swiftly: They *swept* into the room. **7** *v.* To extend with a long line or curve: The road *sweeps* along the shore. **8** *n.* An open or unbroken area or stretch: a wide *sweep* of beach. **9** *n.* A long, sweeping stroke or movement: a *sweep* of an oar. **10** *v.* To take, remove, or carry along with a long, sweeping movement: I *swept* the pieces of the jigsaw puzzle onto the floor. **11** *v.* To move or put on, with an even, continuous motion: to *sweep* a cape over one's shoulders. **12** *n.* The range or area covered or reached by something: the great *sweep* of the beacon's light. **13** *n.* A curve or bend: the *sweep* of the scythe blade. **14** *v.* To move, pass, or go swiftly or with force: The train *swept* by; A great wave of joy *swept* through the crowd. **15** *v.* To pass over or through strongly or swiftly: We *swept* the sky with our eyes. **16** *v.* To move, carry, or bring, with force or strength: The flood *swept* the bridge away. **17** *n.* An easy victory or a series of victories. **18** *n.* A long, heavy oar. **19** *n.* A long pole pivoted on a post and having a bucket at one end, used to draw water from a well. **20** *v.* To drag the bottom of (as a body of water). **—sweep′er** *n.* ◆ *Sweep* was originally only a verb. Its use as a noun developed from its verb meanings.

sweep·ing [swē′ping] **1** *adj.* Moving or extending in a long line or curve or over a wide area: a *sweeping* glance. **2** *adj.* Covering or including many things; extensive: The board made *sweeping* reforms in the schools. **3** *n.* (*pl.*) Dirt or refuse that has been swept up.

sweep·stakes [swēp′stāks′] *n., pl.* **sweep·stakes** **1** A type of lottery, usually a horse race, in which all the money bet may be won by one or by a few of the bettors. **2** Any of various lotteries. **2** Any contest: a political *sweepstakes.*

sweet [swēt] **1** *adj.* Having an agreeable taste, like that of sugar, **2** *adj.* Containing sugar in some form: *sweet* fruit. **3** *n.* Something sweet, as a piece of candy. **4** *adj.* Not salty: *sweet* butter. **5** *adj.* Not spoiled or decaying; fresh: *sweet* cream. **6** *adj.* Agreeable or pleasant to the senses or the mind: *sweet* sounds. **7** *adj.* Having gentle, pleasing qualities: a *sweet* child. **8** *n.* A beloved person; darling. **9** *adv.* In a sweet manner. **—sweet′·ly** *adv.* **—sweet′ness** *n.*

sweet·bread [swēt′bred′] *n.* The pancreas or the thymus gland of a calf or other animal, used as food.

sweet·bri·er or **sweet·bri·ar** [swēt′brī′ər] *n.* A rose having very sharp, tough thorns and pink single flowers.

sweet corn A variety of corn having sweet, milky kernels, boiled or roasted as food.

sweet·en [swēt′(ə)n] *v.* To make or become sweet or sweeter.

sweet·en·er [swēt′(ə)n·ər] *n.* A substance, as sugar, added to food to make it sweeter.

sweet·en·ing [swēt′(ə)n·ing] *n.* **1** The act of making sweet. **2** Something that sweetens.

sweet flag A marsh plant having long, bladelike leaves and roots that yield a fragrant oil.

sweet·heart [swēt′härt′] *n.* A person whom one loves; lover.

sweet·meat [swēt′mēt′] *n.* (*usually pl.*) Something sweet to eat, as candy, candied fruits, or sugar-coated nuts.

sweet pea A climbing plant that has fragrant flowers of many colors.

sweet potato **1** A tropical vine having large, yellowish, sweet roots that are eaten as a vegetable. **2** The edible root of this plant.

sweet tooth *informal* A fondness for sweets.

sweet wil·liam or **sweet Wil·liam** [wil′yəm] A garden plant having clusters of showy, many-colored flowers.

swell [swel] *v.* **swelled, swelled** or **swol·len, swell·ing,** *n., adj.* **1** *v.* To increase or cause to increase, as in size, amount, or degree: A large deposit *swelled* my bank account. **2** *v.* To increase or cause to increase in loudness: The music *swelled* to a climax. **3** *n.* A gradual increase and then a decrease in the loudness of a sound. **4** *v.* To bulge or cause to bulge: Wind *swelled* the sails. **5** *v.* To rise or cause to rise, as land or water: The streams were *swollen* by rain. **6** *n.* The long, continuous body of a rolling wave. **7** *n.* A rise in the land. **8** *v.* To fill or become filled with some emotion: My heart *swelled* with sorrow. **9** *n.* The act of swelling. **10** *n.* A swollen condition. **11** *n. informal* A very fashionably dressed person. **12** *adj. slang* Very fine; excellent: It was a *swell* party.

swell·ing [swel′ing] *n.* **1** An increase, as in size or amount. **2** An enlargement or swollen part on the body, often due to an injury.

swel·ter [swel′tər] **1** *v.* To become weak and soaked with perspiration, from great heat. **2** *n.* A sweltering condition.

swel·ter·ing [swel′tər·ing] *adj.* **1** Extremely hot and humid: *sweltering* summer weather. **2** Overcome by or suffering from heat: the *sweltering* crowds. **—swel′ter·ing·ly** *adj.*

swept [swept] Past tense and past participle of SWEEP.

swept-back [swept′bak′] *adj.* Slanted rearward: the *swept-back* wings of a jet airplane.

swerve [swûrv] *v.* **swerved, swerv·ing,** *n.* **1** *v.* To turn or cause to turn aside from a course: We *swerved* our bicycles out of the car's way. **2** *n.* The act of swerving.

swift [swift] **1** *adj.* Moving or covering space very fast; rapid; quick: a *swift* train. **2** *adj.* Done, happening, or acting quickly: a *swift* change; a *swift* answer; a *swift* worker. **3** *n.* A bird that looks like a swallow and flies extremely fast. **—swift′ly** *adv.* **—swift′ness** *n.*

swig [swig] *n., v.* **swigged, swig·ging** *informal* **1** *n.* A big drink or swallow of something. **2** *v.* To drink greedily with big swallows.

Chimney swift

swill [swil] **1** *v.* To drink greedily or too much: They *swilled* soda. **2** *n.* Liquid food for animals, especially a mixture of liquid and solid food that is fed to pigs. **3** *n.* Partly liquid garbage.

swim[1] [swim] *v.* **swam, swum, swim·ming,** *n.* **1** *v.* To move through the water by using the arms, legs, fins, or the like. **2** *v.* To cause to swim: to *swim* a horse across a stream. **3** *v.* To cross by swimming: to *swim* the English Channel. **4** *v.* To take part in by swimming: to *swim* a race. **5** *n.* The act or distance of swimming: a refreshing *swim*; a long *swim*. **6** *v.* To move with a smooth, flowing motion: The clouds *swam* by. **7** *v.* To be in, covered with, or filled with a liquid: The peas *swam* in butter; Their eyes *swam* with tears. **—in the swim** In the place or places where the important or popular things are happening. **—swim′mer** *n.*

swim[2] [swim] *v.* **swam, swum, swim·ming,** *n.* **1** *v.* To be dizzy: The lights made my head *swim.* **2** *v.* To seem to whirl or spin: The entire house *swam* before my eyes as I fainted. **3** *n.* A sudden feeling of dizziness.

swim·mer·et [swim′ə·ret′] *n.* One of the small, paired appendages under the abdomen of a lobster, crab, or similar crustacean. They are used mainly for carrying eggs.

swim·ming [swim′ing] **1** *n.* The act of a person or thing that swims. **2** *adj.* Of or used for swimming: a *swimming* stroke; a *swimming* pool. **3** *adj.* Able to swim: a *swimming* bird.

swim·ming·ly [swim′ing·lē] *adv.* Easily, rapidly, and successfully: The work went *swimmingly.*

swimming pool An indoor or outdoor tank of water for swimming.

swim·suit [swim′sōōt′] *n.* A garment worn for swimming.

swin·dle [swin′dəl] *v.* **swin·dled, swin·dling,** *n.* **1** *v.* To cheat of money or property: The shopkeeper *swindled* us. **2** *v.* To get by cheating: to *swindle*

a	add	**i**	it	**ŏŏ**	took	**oi**	oil
ā	ace	**ī**	ice	**ōō**	pool	**ou**	pout
â	care	**o**	odd	**u**	up	**ng**	ring
ä	palm	**ō**	open	**û**	burn	**th**	thin
e	end	**ô**	order	**yōō**	fuse	**t͟h**	this
ē	equal					**zh**	vision

ə = a in *above*, e in *sicken*, i in *possible*, o in *melon*, u in *circus*

S

money out of someone. **3** *n.* An act or instance of swindling. **—swin′dler** *n.*

swine [swīn] *n., pl.* **swine** **1** A pig, hog, or boar. **2** A mean, greedy, or vicious person.

swine·herd [swīn′hûrd′] *n.* A person who takes care of pigs.

swing [swing] *v.* **swung, swung, swing·ing,** *n.* **1** *v.* To move or cause to move backward and forward, as something suspended. **2** *n.* A seat that hangs from ropes or chains and on which a person may move to and fro for recreation. **3** *v.* To move or cause to move in or with a sweeping motion: I *swung* the lasso over my head. **4** *n.* The curved or sweeping path of something that swings: the *swing* of a lasso. **5** *n.* A sweeping blow or stroke: to take a *swing* at the tree. **6** *v.* To walk with an even, swaying motion: The hikers *swung* off through the woods. **7** *v.* To move or hoist: They *swung* the mast into place. **8** *v.* To turn or cause to turn or pivot: We *swung* the gate shut. **9** *v.* To hang: *Swing* the lights from the ceiling. **10** *v. informal* To execute or be executed by hanging: Many criminals *swung* for their deeds. **11** *n.* The act, process, or manner of swinging. **12** *n.* Rhythmical movement or quality: Notice the *swing* of the dancers' shoulders; These poems have a great *swing* to them. **13** *n.* A type of jazz music having much improvisation and a strong, lively rhythm. **14** *v. informal* To play or sing (jazz music) in a lively, rhythmical style. **15** *v. informal* To bring to a successful conclusion; manage successfully: to *swing* a business deal. **—in full swing** At the height of activity or movement. ◆ *Swing* was originally a noun. Its use as a verb developed from its noun meanings.

swin·ish [swī′nish] *adj.* Of, like, or fit for swine; beastly; degraded; crude. **—swin′ish·ly** *adv.* **—swin′·ish·ness** *n.*

swipe [swīp] *v.* **swiped, swip·ing,** *n. informal* **1** *v.* To hit hard with a sweeping or swinging motion. **2** *n.* A hard, sweeping blow. **3** *v.* To steal.

swirl [swûrl] **1** *v.* To move or cause to move with a whirling or twisting motion: The water *swirled* down the drain. **2** *n.* A whirling motion. **3** *v.* To feel dizzy: My head *swirls* in the heat. **4** *n.* A curl or twist; spiral.

swish [swish] **1** *v.* To move or cause to move with a hissing or whistling sound: The arrow *swished* past; to *swish* a stick through the air. **2** *v.* To rustle: Their garments *swished* when they moved. **3** *n.* A hissing or rustling sound. **4** *n.* A movement that produces such a sound. ◆ *Swish* was formed in imitation of the sound [swish] that it describes.

Swiss [swis] *adj., n., pl.* **Swiss** **1** *adj.* Of or from Switzerland. **2** *n.* A person born in or a citizen of Switzerland.

Swiss cheese A pale yellow cheese with many large holes, made in or like that made in Switzerland.

Swiss steak A slice of beef pounded with flour and braised.

switch [swich] **1** *n.* A small, flexible stick or rod, used for whipping. **2** *v.* To whip or lash with or as if with a switch. **3** *n.* A blow or stroke given with or as if with a switch. **4** *v.* To move or whisk suddenly and sharply: The dog *switched* its tail against my legs. **5** *v.* To change: to *switch* plans. **6** *v.* To exchange: to *switch* hats. **7** *n.* A change or exchange. **8** *n.* A mechanism, usually consisting of a pair of movable rails, for shifting railroad cars from one track to another. **9** *v.* To shift to another track by means of a switch. **10** *n.* A device for making or breaking a connection in an electrical circuit. **11** *v.* To turn on or off with an electrical switch.

switch·blade [swich′blād′] *n.* A pocketknife having a blade that springs out from the handle when a button is pressed.

switch·board [swich′bôrd′] *n.* A panel having plugs and switches for connecting or disconnecting electrical circuits: a telephone *switchboard.*

switch-hit·ter [swich′hit′ər] *n.* A baseball player who bats either left-handed or right-handed, depending usually on the opposing pitcher.

switch·man [swich′mən] *n., pl.* **switch·men** [swich′·mən] A person whose job is to switch railroad cars.

switch·yard [swich′yärd′] *n.* An area where railroad cars are switched from one track to another and trains are assembled.

swiv·el [swiv′əl] *n., v.* **swiv·eled** or **swiv·elled, swiv·el·ing** or **swiv·el·ling** **1** *n.* A fastening device that permits anything attached to it, as a chain, to rotate or turn independently. **2** *n.* A support on which a gun can be rested and turned in any direction. **3** *v.* To turn on or as if on a swivel.

swivel chair A chair having a seat that turns on a swivel.

Swivel chair

swol·len [swō′lən] Alternative past participle of SWELL.

swoon [swo͞on] **1** *v.* To faint. **2** *n.* A faint.

swoop [swo͞op] **1** *v.* To drop or descend suddenly: The bird *swooped* down on its prey. **2** *v.* To take or seize suddenly: We *swooped* up the cake. **3** *n.* A sudden, swift, diving rush or attack, as of a hawk.

swop [swop] *v.* **swopped, swop·ping,** *n.* Another spelling of SWAP.

sword [sôrd] *n.* **1** A weapon consisting of a long blade fixed in a handle or hilt. **2** This weapon as the symbol of military force or of war: "The pen is mighter than the *sword.*"

sword·fish [sôrd′fish′] *n., pl.* **sword·fish** or **sword·fish·es** A large fish of the open sea, having a very long, pointed upper jawbone.

Swordfish

sword·play [sôrd′plā′] *n.* The act, art, or skill of using the sword, especially in fencing.

swords·man [sôrdz′mən] *n., pl.* **swords·men** [sôrdz′mən] A person skilled in the use of, or armed with a sword.

swore [swôr] Past tense of SWEAR.

sworn [swôrn] Past participle of SWEAR.

swum [swum] Past participle of SWIM.

swung [swung] Past tense and past participle of SWING.

syc·a·more [sik′ə·môr′] *n.* **1** A tree of North America having broad leaves and a bark that peels or flakes off easily. **2** A kind of maple tree of Europe and Asia. **3** A variety of fig tree of Egypt and Syria.

syc·o·phant [sik′ə·fənt] *n.* A person who uses flattery in order to gain advancement or favor.

syl·lab·ic [si·lab′ik] *adj.* **1** Of, having to do with, or containing a syllable or syllables. **2** Forming a separate syllable.

syl·lab·i·cate [si·lab′ə·kāt′] *v.* **syl·lab·i·cat·ed, syl·lab·i·cat·ing** To syllabify. **—syl·lab′i·ca′tion** *n.*

syl·lab·i·fy [si·lab'ə·fī] *v.* **syl·lab·i·fied, syl·lab·i·fy·ing** To divide into syllables. **—syl·lab·i·fi·ca·tion** [si·lab'ə·fə·kā'shən] *n.*

syl·la·ble [sil'ə·bəl] *n.* 1 A word or part of a word uttered in one single vocal impulse. "Spider" has two syllables; "run" has one syllable. 2 A part of a written word corresponding more or less to the spoken division, used to show how the word is pronounced or how it can best be hyphenated at the end of a line.

syl·la·bus [sil'ə·bəs] *n., pl.* **syl·la·bus·es** or **syl·la·bi** [sil'ə·bī'] A brief outline, as that explaining the main points of a course of study.

syl·lo·gism [sil'ə·jiz'əm] *n.* A method of argument or reasoning in which two statements are made, from which a conclusion is drawn in a third statement. Example: All water is wet. Rain is water. Therefore rain is wet.

sylph [silf] *n.* 1 An imaginary being supposed to live in the air. 2 Any slender, graceful young person.

syl·van [sil'vən] *adj.* 1 Of, having to do with, or living in a forest or wood. 2 Full of trees or forests: a *sylvan* countryside.

sym·bi·o·sis [sim'bī·ō'sis *or* sim'bē·ō'sis] *n., pl.* **sym·bi·o·ses** [sim'bī·ō'sēz *or* sim'bē·ō'sēz] The living together of two different kinds of organisms in a close association that is often but not necessarily helpful to each. A cow and the intestinal bacteria that help to digest the grass that the cow eats live in symbiosis. ◆ *Symbiosis* comes from a Greek word meaning *a living together.*

sym·bi·ot·ic [sim'bī·ot'ik *or* sim'bē·ot'ik] *adj.* Of, having to do with, or characterized by symbiosis. **—sym'bi·ot'i·cal·ly** *adv.*

sym·bol [sim'bəl] *n.* 1 Something chosen to stand for or represent something else. 2 A mark or sign used to indicate something, as a plus sign, a numeral, or a dollar sign.

sym·bol·ic [sim·bol'ik] *adj.* 1 Of, related to, or expressed by a symbol or symbols. 2 Serving as a symbol. **—sym·bol'i·cal·ly** *adv.*

sym·bol·i·cal [sim·bol'i·kəl] *adj.* Symbolic.

sym·bol·ism [sim'bəl·iz'əm] *n.* 1 The use of symbols to indicate or represent things, as in literature or art. 2 Any group or system of symbols: the *symbolism* of a mathematical equation.

sym·bol·ist [sim'bəl·ist] *n.* A person who uses symbols or is skilled in symbolism, as an artist or writer.

sym·bol·ize [sim'bəl·īz'] *v.* **sym·bol·ized, sym·bol·iz·ing** 1 To be a symbol of; represent; typify. 2 To represent by a symbol or symbols. 3 To use symbols.

sym·met·ric [si·met'rik] *adj.* Symmetrical.

sym·met·ri·cal [si·met'ri·kəl] *adj.* Having symmetry; well-balanced; regular: a *symmetrical* pattern. **—sym·met'ri·cal·ly** *adv.*

sym·me·try [sim'ə·trē] *n., pl.* **sym·me·tries** 1 A condition or arrangement in which each feature on one half of a figure, object, or arrangement has a matching feature in the other half. 2 Beauty or harmony resulting from a symmetrical or nearly symmetrical arrangement of parts. 3 The property that a geometric figure has if each of its points has a matching point on the opposite side of and equally distant from a point, line, or plane.

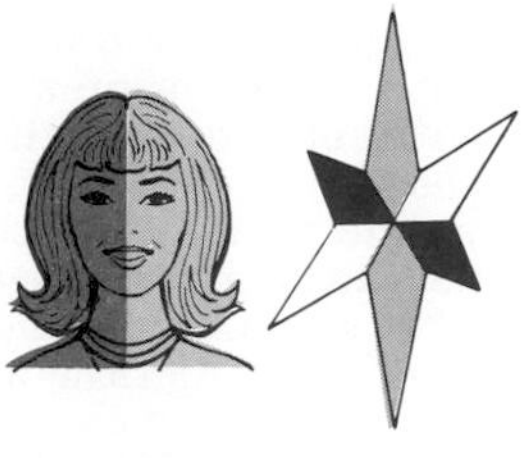
Two examples of symmetry

sym·pa·thet·ic [sim'pə·thet'ik] *adj.* 1 Feeling, expressing, or coming from sympathy: a *sympathetic* look. 2 Agreeable to one's tastes, opinions, or feelings; congenial: a *sympathetic* companion. 3 Showing approval; agreeable. **—sym'pa·thet'i·cal·ly** *adv.*

sym·pa·thize [sim'pə·thīz'] *v.* **sym·pa·thized, sym·pa·thiz·ing** 1 To share the feelings or ideas of another. 2 To feel or express sympathy or compassion: to *sympathize* with someone's sorrow. **—sym'pa·thiz'er** *n.*

sym·pa·thy [sim'pə·thē] *n., pl.* **sym·pa·thies** 1 The condition of being affected by another's state: to feel *sympathy* for a friend's pain. 2 A condition in which the thoughts, ideas, or feelings of one person are very much the same as those of another. 3 Loyalty, support, or agreement: Our *sympathies* were with the first plan.

sym·phon·ic [sim·fon'ik] *adj.* Having to do with or like a symphony or symphony orchestra.

sym·pho·ny [sim'fə·nē] *n., pl.* **sym·pho·nies** 1 A piece of music written to be played by a symphony orchestra and usually consisting of four movements. 2 A symphony orchestra. 3 Harmony or an agreeable blending, as of sounds or color.

symphony orchestra A large orchestra composed usually of strings, brasses, woodwinds, and percussion instruments.

sym·po·si·um [sim·pō'zē·əm] *n., pl.* **sym·po·si·ums** or **sym·po·si·a** [sim·pō'zē·ə] 1 A meeting for the discussion of a particular subject. 2 A collection of comments or opinions by several people on the same subject: A *symposium* on art was published in the magazine.

symp·tom [sim(p)'təm] *n.* A sign or indication of the existence of something, especially an indication of some bodily disease or disorder.

symp·to·mat·ic [sim(p)'tə·mat'ik] *adj.* Being, having to do with, or like a symptom: Fever and vomiting are *symptomatic* of the illness.

syn. 1 synonym. 2 synonymous. 3 synonymy.

syn·a·gogue [sin'ə·gôg'] *n.* 1 A place of meeting for Jewish worship and religious instruction. 2 A Jewish congregation.

syn·apse [sin'aps' *or* si·naps'] *n.* The point of contact between one neuron and another where a nervous impulse is transmitted.

syn·chro·nism [sing'krə·niz'əm] *n.* The fact or circumstance of happening at the same time; simultaneousness. **—syn'chro·nis'tic** *adj.*

syn·chro·nize [sing'krə·nīz'] *v.* **syn·chro·nized, syn·chro·niz·ing** 1 To adjust so as to move together or occur at the same time or speed: In films one must *synchronize* the action with the sound. 2

S

a	add	**i**	it	**o͝o**	took	**oi**	oil
ā	ace	**ī**	ice	**o͞o**	pool	**ou**	pout
â	care	**o**	odd	**u**	up	**ng**	ring
ä	palm	**ō**	open	**û**	burn	**th**	thin
e	end	**ô**	order	**yo͞o**	fuse	**th̶**	this
ē	equal					**zh**	vision

ə = a in *above*, e in *sicken*, i in *possible*, o in *melon*, u in *circus*

To cause (timepieces) to agree in keeping time. **—syn·chro·ni·za·tion** [sing′krə·nə·zā′shən] *n.*

syn·chro·nous [sing′krə·nəs] *adj.* Happening or moving at the same time or speed.

syn·chro·tron [sing′krə·tron′] *n.* A machine in which charged atomic particles are accelerated to very high speeds around a circular track by means of a varying magnetic field.

syn·cline [sing′klīn′] *n.* A sunken area or trough in layers of rock.

syn·co·pate [sing′kə·pāt′] *v.* **syn·co·pat·ed, syn·co·pat·ing** To play (music) with a rhythm in which the accented parts do not coincide with the normally strong beats.

syn·co·pa·tion [sing′kə·pā′shən] *n.* A condition in which the accented parts of a musical rhythm do not coincide with the normally strong beats.

synd. syndicate.

syn·di·cate [*n.* sin′də·kit, *v.* sin′də·kāt′] *n., v.* **syn·di·cat·ed, syn·di·cat·ing** 1 *n.* A group of people who have united in order to pursue business or another enterprise requiring a large sum of money. 2 *v.* To combine into or form a syndicate. 3 *n.* An agency that sells articles, stories, and other writings to a number of newspapers or magazines. 4 *v.* To sell (written material) for publication in many newspapers or magazines.

syn·di·ca·tion [sin′də·kā′shən] *n.* 1 The act of syndicating; sale for publication in many newspapers or magazines at once. 2 The condition of being syndicated.

syn·drome [sin′drōm′] *n.* A group of symptoms that, taken together, indicate the presence and the nature of a disease or disorder.

syn·er·gism [sī′nər·jiz′əm] *n.* Combined action that achieves more than the sum of actions taken separately: two drugs that act in *synergism.*

syn·er·gis·tic [sī′nər·jis′tik] *adj.* 1 Acting in synergism; working together cooperatively for added effect. 2 Of, having to do with, or like synergism. **—syn′er·gis′ti·cal·ly** *adv.*

syn·fu·el [sin′fyōō′əl] *n.* A fuel produced synthetically, especially one made by chemically treating coal, shale, or certain sands or sandstones.

syn·od [sin′əd] *n.* A regional council of a church, called together to discuss and act on church matters.

syn·o·nym [sin′ə·nim] *n.* A word having the same or almost the same meaning as another word: "Sure" and "certain" are *synonyms.*

syn·on·y·mous [si·non′ə·məs] *adj.* Alike or similar in meaning: "Glad" is *synonymous* with "happy."

syn·on·y·my [si·non′ə·mē] *n., pl.* **syn·on·y·mies** A list of synonyms, often with an explanation of their differences in meaning.

syn·op·sis [si·nop′sis] *n., pl.* **syn·op·ses** [si·nop′sēz′] A brief summary or outline, giving the main points, as of a story, book, or play.

syn·tac·tic [sin·tak′tik] *adj.* Of, having to do with, or following the rules of syntax. **—syn·tac′ti·cal·ly** *adv.*

syn·tax [sin′taks′] *n.* The arrangement and relationship of words in phrases and sentences.

syn·the·sis [sin′thə·sis] *n., pl.* **syn·the·ses** [sin′thə·sēz′] 1 The assembling or combining of separate parts into a whole: The *synthesis* of water is accomplished by chemically combining oxygen and hydrogen. 2 The whole that is formed in this way.

syn·the·size [sin′thə·sīz′] *v.* **syn·the·sized, syn·the·siz·ing** 1 To assemble, combine, or make by synthesis: to *synthesize* rubber. 2 To form or make a synthesis.

syn·the·siz·er [sin′thə·sī′zər] *n.* 1 A person or device that synthesizes. 2 An electronic device that can be made to produce and combine many kinds of sounds, used especially in music.

syn·thet·ic [sin·thet′ik] 1 *adj.* Of, having to do with, or using synthesis. 2 *adj.* In chemistry, produced artificially by synthesis rather than occurring naturally: *synthetic* gems. 3 *adj.* Not true or real: Their reasons for not going were *synthetic.* 4 *n.* Something synthetic: Many fabrics, such as rayon, are *synthetics.* **—syn·thet′i·cal·ly** *adv.*

syph·i·lis [sif′ə·lis] *n.* A venereal disease caused by a spirochete and typically progressing slowly but with ultimately severe or fatal effects. It is transmitted by sexual contact and also from an infected mother to her fetus.

syph·i·lit·ic [sif′ə·lit′ik] 1 *adj.* Of, having to do with, or suffering from syphilis. 2 *n.* A person suffering from syphilis.

sy·phon [sī′fən] *n., v.* Another spelling of SIPHON.

Syr. 1 Syria. 2 Syrian.

Syr·i·an [sir′ē·ən] 1 *adj.* Of or from Syria. 2 *n.* A person born in or a citizen of Syria.

sy·rin·ga [si·ring′gə] *n.* An ornamental shrub having fragrant, cream-colored flowers.

syr·inge [sə·rinj′ *or* sir′inj] *n., v.* **syr·inged, syr·ing·ing** 1 *n.* A device consisting of a tube with a rubber bulb or piston at one end for drawing in a liquid and then forcing it out in a fine stream. Syringes are used for injecting fluids into the body and cleaning wounds. 2 *v.* To cleanse or treat with a syringe. 3 *n.* A hypodermic syringe.

Hypodermic syringe

syr·inx [sir′ingks] *n., pl.* **sy·rin·ges** [sə·ring′gēz *or* sə·rin′jēz] or **syr·inx·es** Another word for PANPIPE.

syr·up [sir′əp] *n.* A thick, sweet liquid, as that made by boiling sugar with a liquid. **—syr′up·y** *adj.*

sys·tem [sis′təm] *n.* 1 A group of parts or things that are so related or that act together in such a way that they are considered as a whole: the solar *system*; a railroad *system*; the nervous *system.* 2 Any group of facts, concepts, or beliefs that are organized into an orderly plan: a *system* of teaching languages. 3 An orderly or organized method. 4 The entire body as a whole.

sys·tem·at·ic [sis′tə·mat′ik] *adj.* 1 Done according to, or having, a plan or system: a *systematic* course of study. 2 Orderly, methodical, and thorough: a *systematic* thinker; a *systematic* investigation. **—sys′tem·at′i·cal·ly** *adv.*

sys·tem·a·tize [sis′tə·mə·tīz′] *v.* **sys·tem·a·tized, sys·tem·a·tiz·ing** To make into a system; arrange in an orderly way. **—sys·tem·a·ti·za·tion** [sis′tə·mə·tə·zā′·shən] *n.* **—sys′tem·a·ti′zer** *n.*

sys·tem·ic [sis·tem′ik] *adj.* 1 Of or having to do with a system or systems. 2 Of, having to do with, or affecting the whole body: *systemic* disease.

systems analyst A specialist who studies a business to determine how it should be organized and how various operations can be done most efficiently through the use of data processing equipment.

sys·to·le [sis′tə·lē] *n.* The regular, periodic contraction of the heart, during which blood is pumped into the arteries. ◆ See DIASTOLE.

T is the twentieth letter of the alphabet. The sign for it originated among Semitic people in the Near East, in the region of Palestine and Syria, probably in the middle of the second millennium B.C. Little is known about the sign until around 1000 B.C., when the Phoenicians began using it. The Phoenicians named it *taw* and used it for the sound of the consonant *t*.

When the Greeks adopted the Phoenician sign around the ninth century B.C., they called it *tau* and used it also for the consonant sound *t*. At first they shaped it like an *X* but then soon gave it the characteristic T shape we know today.

As early as the eighth century B.C., the Etruscans adopted the Greek alphabet. It is from the Etruscans that the Romans took the sign for *T*. Around the time of the Caesars, the Romans made the shape of the letter more graceful. The model of the letter found on the base of Trajan's column, erected in Rome in 114, is considered a masterpiece of letter design. A Trajan-style *majuscule,* or capital letter, *T* can be found at the beginning of this essay.

The *minuscule,* or small letter, *t* developed gradually, between the third and ninth centuries, in the handwriting that scribes used for copying books. Contributing to its shape were the Roman *uncials* of the fourth to the eighth centuries and the *half uncials* of the fifth to the ninth centuries. The true ancestor of the lowercase *t*, however, was the script that evolved under the encouragement of Charlemagne (742-814). This letter was one of those known as the *Caroline minuscules,* which became the principal handwriting system used on the medieval manuscripts of the ninth and tenth centuries. In very early medieval manuscripts, the lowercase *t* had looked very much like a lowercase *c*. It became the practice among scribes, therefore, to extend the vertical stem somewhat beyond the horizontal stroke so that the two letters would not be confused.

Tt

Early Phoenician (late 2nd millennium B.C.)

Phoenician (8th century B.C.)

Early Greek (9th-7th centuries B.C.)

Western Greek (6th century B.C.)

Classical Greek (403 B.C. onward)

Early Etruscan (8th century B.C.)

Monumental Latin (4th century B.C.)

Classical Latin

Uncial

Half uncial

Caroline minuscule

t or **T** [tē] *n., pl.* **t's** or **T's** 1 The 20th letter of the English alphabet. 2 Anything shaped like the letter T: The two pencils formed a *T.* **—to a T** Exactly; precisely: to fit *to a T.*

t. 1 teaspoon(s). 2 ton(s).

T 1 technician. 2 temperature (absolute). 3 tension (surface). 4 time (of firing or launching).

T. 1 tablespoon. 2 territory. 3 Testament. 4 Thursday. 5 Tuesday.

Ta The symbol for the element tantalum.

tab [tab] *n.* 1 A small tag, flap, or loop, as on a garment or filing card. 2 An alphabetical guide, as on the side of a page in a book. 3 *informal* A bill or check, as for a meal in a restaurant. 4 A tabulator (def. 2). **—keep tabs on** To pay close attention to; watch carefully.

tab·ard [tab′ərd] *n.* 1 A knight's cloak with short sleeves worn over the armor and bearing a coat of arms. 2 A herald's short coat which is adorned with the lord's coat of arms.

Tabard

Ta·bas·co [tə·bas′kō] *n.* A spicy sauce made from hot peppers: a trademark.

tab·by [tab′ē] *n., pl.* **tab·bies** 1 A brown or gray cat with darker stripes. 2 Any cat which is kept as a pet, especially a female.

tab·er·nac·le [tab′ər·nak′əl] *n.* 1 A large temple or place of worship. 2 A small ornamental receptacle, usually resting on the altar and used to hold the Host or other holy objects. 3 (*written* **Tabernacle**) A curtained wooden framework used by the Jews as a portable place of worship while in the wilderness with Moses. 4 A tent or temporary shelter. 5 The human body as the temporary dwelling place of the soul.

ta·bla [tä′blə] *n.* A percussion instrument from India, consisting of two small hand drums of different sizes.

ta·ble [tā′bəl] *n., v.* **ta·bled, ta·bling** 1 *n.* A piece of furniture with a flat top that is held up by legs. 2 *v.* To put on a table: The players *tabled* the chess pieces. 3 *n.* A table prepared for a meal: The *table* was set for six. 4 *n.* The food served on a table. 5 *n.* The people seated at a table: Our *table* finished lunch first. 6 *v.* To put off, usually indefinitely, a discussion of: The committee *tabled*

a	add	**i**	it	**o͝o**	took	**oi**	oil
ā	ace	**ī**	ice	**o͞o**	pool	**ou**	pout
â	care	**o**	odd	**u**	up	**ng**	ring
ä	palm	**ō**	open	**û**	burn	**th**	thin
e	end	**ô**	order	**yo͞o**	fuse	**th̶**	this
ē	equal					**zh**	vision

ə = { a in *above* e in *sicken* i in *possible* / o in *melon* u in *circus* }

the bill. **7** *n.* A list of related numbers, facts, or items, arranged in some orderly way for reference: a *table* of contents; multiplication *table.* **8** *n.* A tableland; plateau. **9** *n.* A slab of stone, metal, or wood on which writing is carved; tablet: Roman laws were written on *tables.* **—turn the tables** To reverse conditions or relations: Their team had always beaten us, but today we *turned the tables.*

tab·leau [tab′lō] *n., pl.* **tab·leaux** [tab′lōz *or* tab′lō] or **tab·leaus** [tab′lōz] **1** A picture or scene. **2** A grouping of people dressed in costumes and posed to represent a scene: a *tableau* of Washington crossing the Delaware.

ta·ble·cloth [tā′bəl·klôth′] *n.* A cloth which covers a table, especially at meals.

ta·ble·land [tā′bəl·land′] *n.* A broad, flat, high region; plateau.

Tableland

table linen Cloth napkins and tablecloths.

table salt Sodium chloride, refined and ground for use as a food seasoning.

ta·ble·spoon [tā′bəl·spo͞on′] *n.* **1** A fairly large spoon for serving and measuring. **2** As much as a tablespoon will hold, equal to three teaspoons.

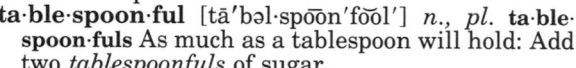

ta·ble·spoon·ful [tā′bəl·spo͞on′fo͝ol′] *n., pl.* **ta·ble·spoon·fuls** As much as a tablespoon will hold: Add two *tablespoonfuls* of sugar.

tab·let [tab′lit] *n.* **1** A pad of paper made by gluing many sheets together at one edge. **2** A thin sheet of metal, wood, or stone, with words or designs inscribed on it: They put up a *tablet* on the wall listing the names of those who had contributed to the building fund. **3** A small, flat disk or square, as of medicine or candy: a sleeping *tablet.*

table tennis A game resembling tennis, played on a table with small paddles and a small hollow ball; Ping-Pong.

Table tennis

ta·ble·ware [tā′bəl·wâr′] *n.* All the dishes, knives, forks, spoons, and other utensils used to eat a meal.

tab·loid [tab′loid′] *n.* A small-sized newspaper with short articles and many pictures. ◆ *Tabloid* was originally a trademark for a brand of tablets consisting of a number of drugs in condensed form.

ta·boo [tə·bo͞o′ *or* ta·bo͞o′] *n., pl.* **ta·boos,** *adj., v.* **ta·booed, ta·boo·ing** **1** *n.* A social or religious rule setting certain people or things apart as sacred or untouchable. **2** *v.* To forbid by taboo: Some religions *taboo* eating certain kinds of meat. **3** *adj.* Forbidden or protected by taboo. **4** *n.* A ban or prohibition. **5** *adj.* Prohibited by law: Selling alcohol to minors is *taboo* in most states.

ta·bor or **ta·bour** [tā′bər] *n.* A small drum once used with a pipe or fife.

ta·bu [tə·bo͞o′ *or* ta·bo͞o′] *n., pl.* **ta·bus,** *adj., v.* **ta·bued, ta·bu·ing** Another spelling of TABOO.

tab·u·lar [tab′yə·lər] *adj.* **1** Arranged in or having to do with tables or lists: a *tabular* account. **2** Having a flat surface.

tab·u·late [tab′yə·lāt′] *v.* **tab·u·lat·ed, tab·u·lat·ing** To arrange in a table or list: to *tabulate* the results. **—tab′u·la′tion** *n.*

tab·u·la·tor [tab′yə·lā′tər] *n.* **1** A person or machine that tabulates numbers or other data. **2** A key on a typewriter that sets automatic stops for paragraph indentations and columns.

ta·chom·e·ter [ta·kom′ə·tər] *n.* An instrument that measures the speed of a rotating engine shaft.

tach·y·car·di·a [tak′i·kär′dē·ə] *n.* An unusually fast heartbeat.

tach·y·on [tak′ē·on′] *n.* A hypothetical particle defined by physicists as able to travel faster than the speed of light.

tac·it [tas′it] *adj.* **1** Understood or meant without being said or spoken: a *tacit* agreement. **2** Silent; unspoken. **—tac′it·ly** *adv.*

tac·i·turn [tas′ə·tûrn′] *adj.* Not fond of speaking; usually silent or reserved. **—tac′i·tur′ni·ty** *n.* **—tac′·i·turn′ly** *adv.*

tack [tak] **1** *n.* A short nail having a sharp point and usually a flat head. **2** *v.* To attach with tacks. **3** *n.* A loose, temporary stitch used in sewing. **4** *v.* To sew with a tack: to *tack* on a sleeve; to *tack* a hem. **5** *v.* To add as something extra: The clerk *tacked* the sales tax onto the bill. **6** *v.* To sail into the wind by means of a zigzag course. **7** *n.* One straight reach of such a course, slanting into the wind. **8** *n.* The direction in which a boat sails in relation to the wind: A boat is on the starboard *tack* when the wind strikes it from the right. **9** *v.* To turn from one tack to the opposite: The sloop *tacked* to round the buoy. **10** *n.* A course of action or behavior: on the wrong *tack.*

tack·le [tak′əl] *n., v.* **tack·led, tack·ling** **1** *n.* The equipment used in work or sports; gear: fishing *tackle.* **2** *n.* A set of ropes and pulleys used to hoist or move objects: The movers were hoisting a piano to a second-story window by means of a *tackle.* **3** *v.* To grab, grapple with, or attack. **4** *v.* To try to solve or master; deal with: to *tackle* a problem. **5** *v.* To seize and stop, especially by forcing to the ground: In football, the defensive team tries to *tackle* the player with the ball. **6** *n.* The act of tackling. **7** *n.* In football, either of the two players stationed between a guard and an end. **—tack′ler** *n.*

tack·y[1] [tak′ē] *adj.* **tack·i·er, tack·i·est** Sticky; gummy: *tacky* fresh paint. **—tack′i·ness** *n.*

tack·y[2] [tak′ē] *adj.* **tack·i·er, tack·i·est** **1** Lacking style or taste; dowdy. **2** Showy; gaudy: *tacky* colors. **—tack′i·ness** *n.*

ta·co [tä′kō] *n., pl.* **ta·cos** A tortilla wrapped around a filling of meat, cheese, or vegetables and eaten like a sandwich.

tac·o·nite [tak′ə·nīt′] *n.* A hard sedimentary rock mined for its low-grade iron-ore content.

tact [takt] *n.* The ability to speak and behave so as not to hurt or offend others.

tact·ful [takt′fəl] *adj.* Showing or having tact: a *tactful* remark. **—tact′ful·ly** *adv.*

tac·tic [tak′tik] *n.* A device or maneuver used to achieve a specific goal.

tac·ti·cal [tak′ti·kəl] *adj.* **1** Of or concerning tactics: a *tactical* error. **2** Showing skill in handling a situation. **—tac′ti·cal·ly** *adv.*

tac·ti·cian [tak·tish′ən] *n.* An expert in tactics.

tac·tics [tak′tiks] *n.* **1** The science or art of moving and handling military, air, or naval forces against an enemy. **2** The art, technique, or means used to achieve one's goals; methods: campaign *tactics.* ◆ See -ICS.

tac·tile [tak′təl] *adj.* **1** Of or having to do with the sense of touch. **2** Capable of being felt by touch; tangible.

tact·less [takt′lis] *adj.* Having or showing no tact: a *tactless* remark. **—tact′less·ly** *adv.* **—tact′less·ness** *n.*

tad [tad] *n.* **1** *U.S. informal* A little child. **2** A little bit: This soup needs just a *tad* more salt.

tad·pole [tad′pōl′] *n.* A young frog or toad when it has a tail and gills and lives in water.

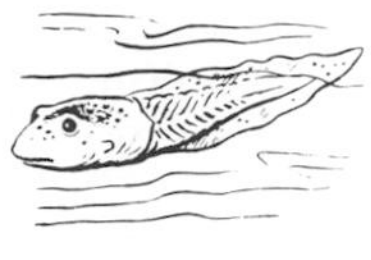
Tadpole

tae kwon do [tī kwon′ dō] A Korean martial art derived from karate.

taf·fe·ta [taf′ə·tə] *n.* A fine, stiff, glossy fabric woven from silk or rayon.

taff·rail [taf′rāl′ *or* taf′rəl] *n.* The rail around a ship's stern.

taf·fy [taf′ē] *n., pl.* **taf·fies** A candy made from sugar or molasses which is boiled and pulled into strands.

taffy pull A social gathering at which taffy is made.

tag[1] [tag] *n., v.* **tagged, tag·ging** **1** *n.* A piece of cardboard, paper, leather, or other material, tied or fastened to something as a label. **2** *v.* To fasten a tag or tags on: Please *tag* my suitcase. **3** *n.* A small loop or flap, as on a boot or zipper. **4** *n.* A hard tip at the end of a string, as on a shoelace. **5** *n.* The last line or two of a song, poem, or speech. **6** *v.* To follow closely: The younger children *tagged* after them.

tag[2] [tag] *n., v.* **tagged, tag·ging** **1** *n.* A game in which a child who is "it" chases and tries to touch another, who then becomes "it," and so on. **2** *v.* To touch (someone) with the hand as in tag or baseball.

Ta·ga·log [tə·gä′lôg′ *or* tə·gä′log′] *n., pl.* **Ta·ga·log** or **Ta·ga·logs** **1** *n.* A member of a native people of the northern Philippines. **2** *n.* The language of this people and the official language of the Philippines. **3** *adj.* Of the Tagalog, their language, or their culture.

tag·a·long [tag′ə·lông′] *n. informal* A person or animal that follows someone around.

tag sale A sale of used clothes or household items that are displayed in the seller's home or yard.

ta·hi·ni [tə·hē′nē] *n.* A thick sauce made from ground sesame seeds and spices.

Ta·hi·tian [tə·hē′shən] **1** *adj.* Of or from Tahiti. **2** *n.* A person born or living in Tahiti. **3** *n.* The language of Tahiti.

tai chi [tī′chē′ *or* tī′jē′] Tai chi chuan.

tai chi chuan [tī′chē′chwän′ *or* tī′jē′chwän′] A Chinese system of slow, fluid body movements and exercises intended to promote physical and spiritual well-being.

tai·ga [tī′gə] *n.* The forests of spruce and fir trees that grow just south of the Arctic parts of northern Asia, Europe, and North America.

tail [tāl] **1** *n.* The rear part of an animal, especially when it sticks out beyond the body. **2** *n.* Any extension that looks like an animal's tail: the *tail* of a comet. **3** *v.* To provide with a tail. **4** *n.* The rear or end part of something: the *tail* of a rocket. **5** *adj.* At the rear; last: the *tail* end of the year. **6** *n.* (*pl.*) The reverse side of a coin: heads or *tails.* **7** *v. informal* To follow in secret: The detective *tailed* the suspect. **8** *n.* (*pl.*) A kind of formal evening dress, including a swallow-tailed coat. **—tail off** To diminish or become less: The wind *tailed off.* **—turn tail** To avoid a dangerous or unpleasant situation by running away. **—tail′less** *adj.*

tail·board [tāl′bôrd′] *n.* Another word for TAILGATE.

tail·coat [tāl′kōt′] *n.* Another word for SWALLOW-TAILED COAT.

tail end The rearmost or final part: the *tail end* of a parade; the *tail end* of the movie.

tail·gate [tāl′gāt′] *n., v.* **tail·gat·ed, tail·gat·ing** **1** *n.* A hinged board or gate at the rear of a truck, wagon, or car. **2** *v. informal* To drive too closely behind for safety: The taxi *tailgated* the truck.

Tailgate

tail·light [tāl′līt′] *n.* A light, usually red, attached to the rear of a car, bicycle, or other vehicle.

tai·lor [tā′lər] **1** *n.* A person who makes or repairs outer clothing. **2** *v.* To work as a tailor: The people who *tailor* at that store do excellent alterations. **3** *v.* To make by tailoring: This shop will *tailor* suits and vests. **4** *v.* To make or adjust for a certain purpose: The budget was *tailored* to fit our income.

tail·piece [tāl′pēs′] *n.* A section or piece that is added at the end or that forms the end.

tail pipe A pipe through which exhaust gases are released, as at the rear of a car engine.

tail·race [tāl′rās′] *n.* The channel through which water leaving a water wheel flows.

tail·spin [tāl′spin′] *n.* An uncontrolled plunge of an airplane with its nose pointing down and its tail spinning.

tail wind A wind which blows in the same direction as the course of an airplane or ship.

taint [tānt] **1** *v.* To make or become spoiled or decayed: *tainted* food. **2** *v.* To contaminate morally; corrupt: The candidate's integrity was *tainted* by his association with hangers-on of questionable reputation. **3** *n.* A spot or mark caused by tainting.

Tai·wan·ese [tī′wə·nēz′] *adj., n., pl.* **Tai·wan·ese** **1** *adj.* Of or from Taiwan. **2** *n.* A person born in or a citizen of Taiwan.

take [tāk] *v.* **took, tak·en, tak·ing,** *n.* **1** *v.* To grasp: *Take* my hand. **2** *v.* To capture by force, charm, or skill; win: The army *took* the village; We were *taken* by the letter's direct manner. **3** *v.* To buy or subscribe to: We *take* a daily newspaper. **4** *v.* To steal or remove: Someone *took* my bike. **5** *v. slang* To cheat: They got *taken* on the deal. **6** *v.* To subtract or deduct: Five *taken* from ten is five. **7** *v.* To get from a source: lines *taken* from Shakespeare. **8** *v.* To occupy or rent: to *take* a seat; to *take* a room. **9** *v.* To hold or let in: The tank *takes* ten gallons. **10** *v.* To learn or find out by study or observation: The students *took* French; The doctor *took* my temperature. **11** *v.* To accept or receive: to *take* a chance; to *take* an offer. **12** *v.* To get for oneself; receive ownership of; assume: to *take* a spouse; to *take* office. **13** *v.* To undergo or

a	add	**i**	it	**o͝o**	took	**oi**	oil
ā	ace	**ī**	ice	**o͞o**	pool	**ou**	pout
â	care	**o**	odd	**u**	up	**ng**	ring
ä	palm	**ō**	open	**û**	burn	**th**	thin
e	end	**ô**	order	**yo͞o**	fuse	**th̸**	this
ē	equal					**zh**	vision

ə = { a in *above*   e in *sicken*   i in *possible*
  o in *melon*   u in *circus* }

submit to: to *take* a beating. **14** *v.* To become affected with or by: I *took* cold. **15** *v.* To become: They all *took* ill. **16** *v.* To begin to grow: The seeds *took* in the soil. **17** *v.* To catch hold: The fire *took* at last. **18** *v.* To receive and respond to: They *took* the bad news well. **19** *v.* To feel: They *take* pride in their son. **20** *v.* To understand: I *took* you to mean that you would not go. **21** *v.* To think of; consider: *Take* an example; Don't *take* life so seriously. **22** *v.* To use: *Take* two eggs for this recipe; Please *take* care. **23** *v.* To require or need: It *takes* money to go to college. **24** *v.* To eat or consume: Can the baby *take* solid food now? **25** *v.* To perform or make: to *take* a step. **26** *v.* To record, as by photographing or writing down: to *take* a picture; to *take* notes. **27** *v.* To be used with: This verb *takes* an object. **28** *v.* To aim or direct: to *take* a shot; to *take* a look. **29** *v.* To carry: *Take* your book with you. **30** *v.* To lead or escort: The road *takes* you to town; *Take* us to the movies. **31** *v.* To travel by: to *take* a taxi; to *take* the longer route. **32** *n.* The act of taking. **33** *n.* The amount or quantity taken at one time, as of money: The store's daily *take* was small. **—take after** 1 To look or be like; resemble. 2 *informal* To chase. **—take apart** To disassemble; dismantle. **—take back** To withdraw (something said). **—take down** 1 To write down: *Take down* this address. 2 To reduce the pride of; humble: We *took* them *down* a bit. **—take for** To mistake or think to be: Don't *take* me *for* a fool. **—take in** 1 To admit or receive: to *take in* roomers. 2 To include: The homework assignment *takes in* five pages. 3 *informal* To visit: to *take in* a show. 4 To make (clothing) smaller. 5 To notice or understand: to *take in* the situation. 6 *informal* To fool; trick: He was *taken in* by the swindler's lies. **—take off** 1 To remove: *Take off* your hat. 2 *informal* To imitate or mimic. 3 To leave the ground, as an airplane; depart. 4 *informal* To achieve great popularity: The new product *took off.* **—take on** 1 To accept, as a task, duty, or challenge. 2 To hire or employ. 3 *informal* To show violent emotion: Don't *take on* so! **—take over** To take the leadership or control of. **—take place** To happen. **—take to** 1 To grow fond of. 2 To go to: They *took to* the ship. **—take up** 1 To raise or lift. 2 To absorb (as moisture or gas). 3 To shorten or tighten. 4 To occupy or use, as space or time. 5 To begin to do, use, or study: to *take up* ballet. **—take up with** *informal* To become friends with. **—tak'er** *n.*

take·off [tāk'ôf'] *n.* 1 The rising from the ground, as of an aircraft or rocket. 2 *informal* An imitation of someone or something, usually meant to be funny.

Takeoff

take·out [tāk'out'] *adj.* Of, for, or being food that will not be eaten at the place of sale: a *takeout* counter.

take·over [tāk'ō'vər] *n.* The act of assuming control or ownership.

tak·ing [tā'king] 1 *n.* The act of a person who takes. 2 *n.* (*pl.*) Money collected or earned. 3 *adj.* Attractive; pleasing: *taking* ways.

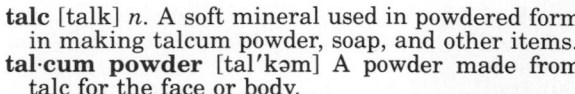

talc [talk] *n.* A soft mineral used in powdered form in making talcum powder, soap, and other items.

tal·cum powder [tal'kəm] A powder made from talc for the face or body.

tale [tāl] *n.* 1 A story; narrative or account of real or imaginary events. 2 A lie or fib. 3 A piece of gossip, usually harmful.

tale·bear·er [tāl'bâr'ər] *n.* A person who tells on another or gives away secrets. **—tale'bear'ing** *n.*

tal·ent [tal'ənt] *n.* 1 A natural ability to do something well; gift. 2 People with talent: We must encourage the local *talent.* 3 An ancient unit of weight or money. ◆ Contrast *talent* and *skill*: You are born with talents; you acquire or learn skills.

tal·ent·ed [tal'ən·tid] *adj.* Having natural aptitude or skill; gifted: a *talented* artist.

tal·is·man [tal'is·mən] *n., pl.* **tal·is·mans** 1 Something, as a ring or stone, bearing symbols believed to bring good luck. 2 Any magic charm.

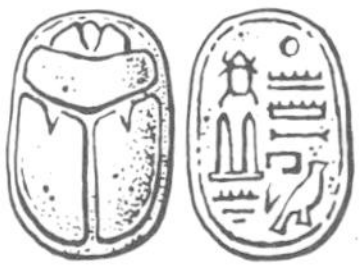
Talisman

talk [tôk] 1 *v.* To use spoken words; speak. 2 *n.* Speech; conversation: Can you hear the *talk* in the hall? 3 *v.* To communicate without spoken words: to *talk* by signs. 4 *v.* To use in speaking: They were *talking* French. 5 *n.* A special set of words or way of talking: baby *talk*; baseball *talk*. 6 *v.* To speak about; discuss: to *talk* politics. 7 *v.* To consult or confer: The teacher *talked* with the parents. 8 *n.* A conference: The world leaders held peace *talks*. 9 *v.* To make a speech; lecture. 10 *n.* A speech; lecture. 11 *n.* The person or thing spoken about: My appearance on TV was the *talk* of the party. 12 *v.* To persuade or affect by speaking: They *talked* us around to their way of thinking. 13 *v.* To gossip or spread rumors. 14 *n.* A rumor, report, or gossip: There is *talk* of a storm coming. **—talk back** To answer in a rude way. **—talk down to** To talk too simply to, thus showing no respect for the listener's ability to understand.

talk·a·tive [tôk'ə·tiv] *adj.* Liking to talk a lot or characterized by much talk: a *talkative* person.

talk·er [tô'kər] *n.* A person who talks, especially a great deal.

talk·ing-to [tô'king·to͞o'] *n., pl.* **talk·ing-tos** *informal* A scolding.

talk show A television or radio program in which famous people or experts are interviewed or participate in a discussion.

tall [tôl] *adj.* 1 Of more than average height; high: a *tall* mountain. 2 Having a certain height: six feet *tall.* 3 *informal* Not easy to believe; exaggerated: a *tall* story.

tal·low [tal'ō] *n.* The fat of certain animals, as of cows or sheep, used in making candles and soap.

tal·ly [tal'ē] *n., pl.* **tal·lies,** *v.* **tal·lied, tal·ly·ing** 1 *n.* A count, record, or score. 2 *n.* Anything on which scores or counts are kept. 3 *v.* To score: Our team *tallied* two goals. 4 *v.* To add: The scorekeeper *tallied* the results. 5 *v.* To match, correspond, or agree.

tal·ly·ho [tal'ē·hō'] *interj., n., pl.* **tal·ly·hos** 1 *interj.* A hunter's cry when a fox being chased is sighted. 2 *n.* A coach drawn by a team of four horses.

Tal·mud [tal'mo͝od'] *n.* A book containing and discussing certain early Jewish civil and religious laws.

tal·on [tal'ən] *n.* The claw of a bird or animal, especially of a bird that feeds on other animals.

ta·lus[1] [tā′ləs] *n., pl.* **ta·li** [tā′lī] The main bone of the ankle, connecting with the tibia and fibula at the ankle joint.
ta·lus[2] [tā′ləs] *n., pl.* **ta·lus·es** **1** A slope formed by an accumulation of rock fragments. **2** A pile of rock fragments at the bottom of a cliff or steep slope.
tam [tam] *n.* A tam-o'-shanter.
ta·ma·le [tə·mä′lē] *n.* A spicy Mexican food made from chopped meat, red peppers, and cornmeal, wrapped in corn husks and steamed.
tam·a·rack [tam′ə·rak′] *n.* A larch tree of North America or its wood.
tam·a·rind [tam′ə·rind′] *n.* **1** A tropical tree with hard yellow wood, yellow flowers, and brown pods. **2** The pods of the tamarind tree, used in cooking and medicine.
tam·a·risk [tam′ə·risk′] *n.* A low tree or shrub that grows in warm regions and has long, slender branches, scalelike leaves, and clusters of white or pink flowers.
tam·bour [tam′bo͝or′] *n.* A small, round, wooden frame in which fabric being embroidered is stretched.
tam·bou·rine [tam′bə·rēn′] *n.* A shallow drum with jingling metal disks in the sides, played by shaking or striking with the hand.

Tambourine

tame [tām] *adj.* **tam·er, tam·est,** *v.* **tamed, tam·ing** **1** *adj.* Wild by nature but made unafraid of people, gentler, and docile: *tame* deer. **2** *adj.* Used to being managed and cared for by people, as dogs, cats, and farm animals. **3** *v.* To make or become gentle, docile, and unafraid of people: The forest ranger *tamed* a bear cub; Seals *tame* quickly. **4** *v.* To bring under control; subdue: to *tame* a river; Nobody *tamed* that bronco. **5** *adj.* Not having much spirit or force: a *tame* discussion. **—tame′ly** *adv.* **—tame′ness** *n.* **—tam′er** *n.*
tame·less [tām′lis] *adj.* Untamed or too wild to tame. **—tame′less·ness** *n.*
tam-o'-shan·ter [tam′ə·shan′tər] *n.* A soft, round Scottish cap with a baggy top and often a pompon.
tamp [tamp] *v.* **1** To ram or pack down: The dentist *tamped* the filling in. **2** To fill (a hole containing explosives) with clay or sand, as in blasting.
tam·per[1] [tam′pər] *v.* **1** To interfere, as by mishandling or misusing, so as to damage or put out of working order: to *tamper* with a camera. **2** To have dealings, often accompanied by bribery or threats, in order to influence or corrupt: to *tamper* with a witness to a car accident.
tam·per[2] [tam′pər] *n.* **1** A person who tamps. **2** An instrument for tamping.
tam·pon [tam′pon′] *n.* A plug, as of cotton, inserted into a body cavity to absorb blood or secretions.
tan [tan] *n., adj.* **tan·ner, tan·nest,** *v.* **tanned, tan·ning** **1** *n., adj.* Yellowish brown. **2** *n.* A darkening of the skin caused by the sun. **3** *v.* To make or become tan, as by the sun: Sun and wind *tanned* us; You don't *tan* easily. **4** *n.* Tanbark. **5** *v.* To make (hides) into leather by treating with tannin. **6** *v. informal* To whip; thrash.
tan·a·ger [tan′ə·jər] *n.* Any of several small American birds related to the finch, as the scarlet tanager. The males are usually brightly colored.
tan·bark [tan′bärk′] *n.* The bark of certain trees, especially oak or hemlock, containing tannin. After the tannin is removed or used up, the bark is used to cover surfaces, as circus rings or racecourses.
tan·dem [tan′dəm] **1** *adv.* One in front of the other. **2** *n.* A team of two or more horses harnessed in single file. **3** *n.* A carriage having two wheels, pulled by a tandem of horses. **4** *n.* A bicycle with two or more seats, one in front of the other. It is also called a **tandem bicycle.**

Tandem

tang [tang] *n.* **1** A sharp, strong taste or flavor: Lemon has a *tang.* **2** A trace; hint. **3** A shank or prong, as on a tool or sword, that fits into a handle. **4** A tonguelike part, as of a belt buckle.
Tang [täng] A Chinese dynasty, 618–906, one of China's greatest periods of literature and art.
tan·ge·lo [tan′jə·lō′] *n., pl.* **tan·ge·los** A fruit that is a cross between a tangerine or mandarin orange and a grapefruit.
tan·gent [tan′jənt] **1** *adj.* Touching a curve at a particular point but not crossing it there. **2** *n.* A line that is tangent to a curve. **3** *n.* In a right triangle, the length of the short side opposite an acute angle divided by the length of the short side next to the acute angle. This quotient depends on the size of the angle. **—fly off on a tangent** or **go off on a tangent** To go suddenly from one course of action or line of thought to another.

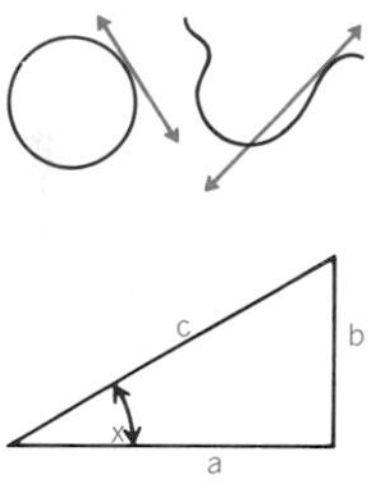

Illustration at top shows tangents in blue. In illustration below, tangent of $x = \frac{b}{a}$.

tan·gen·tial [tan·jen′shəl] *adj.* **1** Of, like, or along a tangent. **2** Connected only slightly or in one respect. **3** Departing from the topic; digressing: *tangential* comments.
tan·ger·ine [tan′jə·rēn′] *n.* **1** A small, juicy orange with a skin that is loose and easily removed. **2** A reddish orange color.
tan·gi·ble [tan′jə·bəl] **1** *adj.* Capable of being felt by the sense of touch: Still air is not *tangible.* **2** *adj.* Real; concrete; definite: no *tangible* cause for alarm. **3** *n.* (*pl.*) Material property; physical assets.
tan·gle [tang′gəl] *v.* **tan·gled, tan·gling,** *n.* **1** *v.* To twist or become twisted together into a confused mass: Don't *tangle* the wool; The ropes *tangled.* **2** *n.* A confused mass; snarl: I combed the *tangles* out of my hair. **3** *v.* To trap or hold as in a snare: Brambles *tangled* my ankles and tripped me. **4**

T

a	add	**i**	it	**o͝o**	took	**oi**	oil
ā	ace	**ī**	ice	**o͞o**	pool	**ou**	pout
â	care	**o**	odd	**u**	up	**ng**	ring
ä	palm	**ō**	open	**û**	burn	**th**	thin
e	end	**ô**	order	**yo͞o**	fuse	**t͟h**	this
ē	equal					**zh**	vision

ə = {a in *above* e in *sicken* i in *possible* / o in *melon* u in *circus*}

n. A state of confusion; disorder: If our plans do get in a *tangle,* we know what to do.

tan·go [tang′gō] *n., pl.* **tan·gos,** *v.* **tan·goed, tan·go·ing** 1 *n.* A slow, graceful dance that originated in Latin America. Its basic pattern is four short steps followed by a long glide. 2 *n.* A piece of music for this dance. 3 *v.* To dance the tango.

tang·y [tang′ē] *adj.* **tang·i·er, tang·i·est** Having a sharp, strong taste or flavor: a *tangy* hot sauce.

tank [tangk] *n.* 1 A large container used to store fluids: a gasoline *tank.* 2 An armored military vehicle which carries guns and moves on two endless metal belts. 3 A swimming pool.

Tank

tank·ard [tangk′ərd] *n.* A large drinking cup, usually having a handle and a hinged lid.

tank·er [tangk′ər] *n.* A cargo ship built to carry liquids, especially oil.

tank·ful [tangk′fo͝ol′] *n., pl.* **tank·fuls** As much as a tank can hold.

tank suit A woman's simple one-piece bathing suit with shoulder straps.

tank top A casual, sleeveless and collarless shirt that is pulled on over the head like an undershirt.

tan·ner [tan′ər] *n.* A person who makes leather out of hides by tanning.

tan·ner·y [tan′ər·ē] *n., pl.* **tan·ner·ies** A place where hides are tanned to make leather.

tan·nic [tan′ik] *adj.* Of, having to do with, or derived from tannin.

tannic acid Tannin.

tan·nin [tan′in] *n.* An acid obtained from oak bark and from parts of other plants, used in tanning, dyeing, and making ink, and in medicine.

tan·ning [tan′ing] *n.* 1 The technique or process of making leather from hides. 2 *informal* A whipping; thrashing.

tan·sy [tan′zē] *n., pl.* **tan·sies** An herb with small yellow flowers, a strong smell, and a bitter taste, once much used in medicine.

tan·ta·lite [tan′tə·līt′] *n.* A mineral, ranging in color from black to brownish red, that is the principal ore of tantalum.

tan·ta·lize [tan′tə·līz′] *v.* **tan·ta·lized, tan·ta·liz·ing** To torment by making something that one desires almost but never quite available: Mental pictures of cool waters *tantalized* the travelers in the desert. ◆ This word comes from the legend of TANTALUS.

tan·ta·lum [tan′tə·ləm] *n.* A gray, heavy, very hard, faintly radioactive metallic element, used in surgical appliances because it is resistant to corrosion by body fluids.

Tan·ta·lus [tan′tə·ləs] *n.* In Greek myths, a king who was punished by the gods by being immersed in cool water that receded when he bent to drink it and by having delicious fruit hanging above his head that rose out of reach when he stretched his arms to grasp it.

tan·ta·mount [tan′tə·mount′] *adj.* Having the same value or effect; equivalent: Not to help us is *tantamount* to being against us.

tan·trum [tan′trəm] *n.* A fit of rage or anger.

Tan·za·ni·an [tan′zə·nē′ən] 1 *adj.* Of or from Tanzania. 2 *n.* A person born in or a citizen of Tanzania.

Tao·ism [dou′iz′əm *or* tou′iz′əm] *n.* A philosophy originating in ancient China that teaches simplicity, harmony with nature, and the futility of action. It later added magical beliefs and practices and became a major religion. **—Tao′ist** *adj., n.*

tap[1] [tap] *n., v.* **tapped, tap·ping** 1 *n.* A light blow. 2 *v.* To touch or strike gently: He *tapped* the desk with his pen. 3 *v.* To give a light blow with: I *tapped* my hand against the door. 4 *v.* To make or produce by tapping: The telegraph *tapped* out the message.

tap[2] [tap] *n., v.* **tapped, tap·ping** 1 *n.* A faucet or spigot which regulates the flow of liquids: The gardener took water from the *tap.* 2 *n.* A plug or cork which stops up a hole in a cask. 3 *v.* To release the flow of liquid from, as by drilling or unstopping a hole: to *tap* a barrel. 4 *v.* To allow to pour out: to *tap* cider. 5 *v.* To open up to use: to *tap* resources. 6 *v.* To make a connection with, as by wires or pipes: to *tap* a gas line. 7 *n.* A connection in an electrical circuit or pipe. **—on tap** 1 Ready to be drawn from a cask: beer *on tap.* 2 *informal* Available; ready.

tap-dance [tap′dans′] *v.* **tap-danced, tap-danc·ing** To perform a tap dance. **—tap dancer.**

tap dance A dance accented by sharp taps on the floor with the dancer's heel or toe.

tape [tāp] *n., v.* **taped, tap·ing** 1 *n.* A narrow strip of cloth, paper, or other material, sometimes with one sticky side, used to bind, bandage, or hold things: adhesive *tape.* 2 *v.* To fasten or bind with tape: The trainer *taped* the horse's ankle. 3 *n.* A plastic strip coated with a magnetic material on which sounds and images can be recorded. 4 *v.* To record on tape: to *tape* a program for cable television. 5 *n.* A tape measure. 6 *v.* To measure with a tape. 7 *n.* The ribbon or string stretched above the finish line at a race.

tape deck An apparatus for recording and playing back magnetic tapes that usually lacks amplifiers and loudspeakers and must be connected to an audio system.

tape measure A cloth or metal tape marked off like a ruler and used to measure areas and distances.

ta·per [tā′pər] 1 *v.* To make or become smaller or thinner toward one end: The trousers *tapered* toward the cuffs; The carpenter *tapered* the stick. 2 *n.* A gradually tapering shape: the *taper* of the church's steeple. 3 *v.* To lessen gradually; diminish: The fire *tapered* off. 4 *n.* A long, slender candle. 5 *n.* A long wick coated with wax, used to light candles, gas lamps, and fires.

tape-re·cord [tāp′ri·kôrd′] *v.* To make a recording of on magnetic tape: She *tape-recorded* the rock concert.

tape recorder A machine that changes sound or video signals into magnetic patterns on a length of tape that can be played back later.

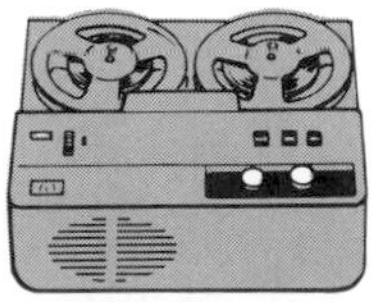
Tape recorder

tape recording A recording made on magnetic tape.

tap·es·try [tap′is·trē] *n., pl.* **tap·es·tries** A heavy ornamental cloth with designs or pictures woven into it, usually hung on a wall or used to cover furniture.

tape·worm [tāp′wûrm′] *n.* A long, ribbonlike worm that in its adult stage lives in the intestines of humans or animals.

tap·i·o·ca [tap′ē·ō′kə] *n.* A starchy substance obtained from the dried root of the cassava plant, used in puddings and to thicken liquids.

ta·pir [tā′pər] *n.* A large piglike animal with a long, flexible snout, living in tropical America and SE Asia.
tap·room [tap′ro͞om′] *n.* A bar or tavern.
tap·root [tap′ro͞ot′] *n.* A plant's main root growing downward.
taps [taps] *n.pl.* (*often used with a singular verb*) A military call sounded on a bugle or on a drum to signal the time to turn off the lights at night. It is often sounded at a military funeral or at memorial services.
tar[1] [tär] *n., v.* **tarred, tar·ring** 1 *n.* A dark, thick, gummy mixture of substances obtained from distilling wood or coal. 2 *v.* To cover with or as with tar. **—tar and feather** To cover (someone) with tar and feathers as a punishment.
tar[2] [tär] *n. informal* A sailor.
tar·an·tel·la [tar′ən·tel′ə] *n.* 1 A fast, lively dance that originated in southern Italy, in which couples whirl about in 6/8 time. 2 A piece of music for this dance.
ta·ran·tu·la [tə·ran′chə·lə] *n.* A large, hairy spider of southern Europe and the SW U.S. The bite of the U.S. variety is painful but not dangerous.
tar·di·ly [tär′də·lē] *adv.* 1 After the expected time; late. 2 At a slow pace; slowly.
tar·dy [tär′dē] *adj.* **tar·di·er, tar·di·est** 1 Late; delayed. 2 Moving slowly. **—tar′di·ness** *n.*
tare[1] [târ] *n.* 1 A weed mentioned in the Bible as growing among the wheat. 2 A kind of vetch grown to feed cattle, sometimes eaten by humans.
tare[2] [târ] *n.* The weight of the container or wrappings which is deducted from the total weight of something to determine the net weight.
tar·get [tär′git] *n.* 1 The object that one aims or shoots at, as with arrows, guns, or darts. 2 The object of criticism, attack, or attention: the *target* of all eyes.

Target

target date A date set or aimed for, as for the completion of a project.
tar·iff [tar′if] *n.* 1 A list of duties or taxes to be charged on imported or exported goods. 2 A duty or tax found on such a list: a *tariff* on perfume. 3 Any list of rates or prices.
tarn [tärn] *n.* A small mountain lake or pool.
tar·nish [tär′nish] 1 *v.* To dull the brightness of: Egg *tarnishes* silver. 2 *v.* To lose its brightness. 3 *n.* A loss of brightness. 4 *n.* A dull, discolored coating. 5 *v.* To stain or disgrace: to *tarnish* one's honor.
ta·ro [tär′ō *or* tar′ō] *n., pl.* **ta·ros** 1 A broad-leaved tropical plant that is widely cultivated for its starchy, edible tuber. 2 The tuber of this plant, cooked and eaten.
ta·rot [tar′ō] *n.* Any of a set of 22 playing cards with pictures on them, used in telling fortunes.
tar·pau·lin [tär·pô′lin *or* tär′pə·lin] *n.* A piece of canvas or other material that has been made waterproof, used to cover exposed objects.
tar·pon [tär′pon′ *or* tär′pən] *n., pl.* **tar·pon** or **tar·pons** A large, silvery game fish found off the West Indies and Florida.
tar·ra·gon [tar′ə·gon′] *n.* A plant with spicy, aromatic leaves that are used to flavor foods.
tar·ry[1] [tar′ē] *v.* **tar·ried, tar·ry·ing** 1 To stay for a while; linger. 2 To delay, wait, or be late.
tar·ry[2] [tär′ē] *adj.* **tar·ri·er, tar·ri·est** 1 Covered with tar: a *tarry* surface. 2 Of or like tar.
tar·sal [tär′səl] *adj.* Of or having to do with the ankle.
tar·si·er [tär′sē·ər *or* tär′sē·ā′] *n.* A small, tree-dwelling primate of the East Indies having large eyes and a long hairless tail.

Tarsier

tar·sus [tär′səs] *n., pl.* **tar·si** [tär′sī] The ankle, which in human beings consists of seven small bones.
tart[1] [tärt] *adj.* 1 Having a sharp, sour taste. 2 Sharp and biting in meaning or tone: a *tart* answer. **—tart′ly** *adv.* **—tart′·ness** *n.*
tart[2] [tärt] *n.* A small pastry shell filled with fruit or jam.
tar·tan [tär′tən] *n.* 1 A plaid woolen cloth worn by members of clans in the Scottish Highlands. Each clan has its own tartan. 2 Any plaid cloth.
tar·tar [tär′tər] *n.* 1 A hard mineral substance that forms on teeth. 2 A pinkish acid substance that is deposited in casks or barrels of wine. When purified, it is called cream of tartar.
Tar·tar [tär′tər] *n.* 1 A Tatar. 2 (*sometimes written* **tartar**) A person with a wild temper. 3 (*sometimes written* **tartar**) An unexpectedly formidable or intractable person.
tartar sauce Mayonnaise to which chopped pickles, onions, olives, and capers have been added, traditionally served with seafood.
Tar·ta·rus [tär′tə·rəs] *n.* In Greek myths, a region below Hades where the most wicked were punished.
task [task] 1 *n.* A piece of work to be done; duty: Your *task* is to water the plants. 2 *n.* A strain or exhausting burden: It is a *task* to climb to the top. 3 *v.* To put a strain on; burden: Practicing *tasked* my patience. **—take to task** To scold or lecture.
task force A temporary group, as of soldiers or sailors, under one leader and assigned to carry out some special mission.
task·mas·ter [task′mas′tər] *n.* A person who assigns tasks, especially burdensome ones.
task·mis·tress [task′mis′tris] *n.* A woman who assigns tasks, especially burdensome ones.
Tass [tas *or* täs] *n.* The official, government-controlled news agency of the Soviet Union.

a	add	**i**	it	**o͝o**	took	**oi**	oil
ā	ace	**ī**	ice	**o͞o**	pool	**ou**	pout
â	care	**o**	odd	**u**	up	**ng**	ring
ä	palm	**ō**	open	**û**	burn	**th**	thin
e	end	**ô**	order	**yo͞o**	fuse	**t͟h**	this
ē	equal					**zh**	vision

ə = a in *above* e in *sicken* i in *possible* o in *melon* u in *circus*

T

tas·sel [tas′əl] *n., v.* **tas·seled** or **tas·selled, tas·sel·ing** or **tas·sel·ling** 1 *n.* A hanging tuft of threads or cords, fastened together at the top. 2 *n.* Any similar object: There are *tassels* on corn. 3 *v.* To form into or provide with tassels. 4 *v.* To grow tassels: Corn *tassels* in summer. 5 *v.* To remove tassels from.

Tassel

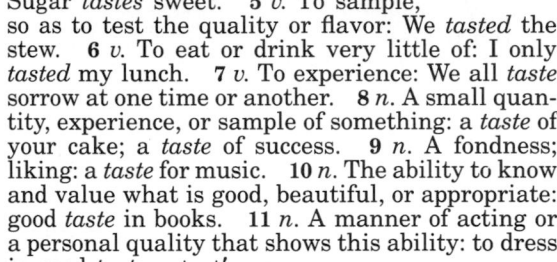

taste [tāst] *v.* **tast·ed, tast·ing,** *n.* 1 *v.* To experience or perceive the flavor of, by taking into the mouth or touching with the tongue. 2 *n.* The sense that perceives flavor: the sense of *taste.* 3 *n.* The sensation or flavor felt, as sweet, sour, salt, or bitter. 4 *v.* To have a certain flavor or quality: Sugar *tastes* sweet. 5 *v.* To sample, so as to test the quality or flavor: We *tasted* the stew. 6 *v.* To eat or drink very little of: I only *tasted* my lunch. 7 *v.* To experience: We all *taste* sorrow at one time or another. 8 *n.* A small quantity, experience, or sample of something: a *taste* of your cake; a *taste* of success. 9 *n.* A fondness; liking: a *taste* for music. 10 *n.* The ability to know and value what is good, beautiful, or appropriate: good *taste* in books. 11 *n.* A manner of acting or a personal quality that shows this ability: to dress in good *taste.* **—tast′er** *n.*

taste bud Any of the clusters of special cells inside the mouth, chiefly on the tongue, that are sensitive to taste.

taste·ful [tāst′fəl] *adj.* Having, showing, or conforming to good taste. **—taste′ful·ly** *adv.*

taste·less [tāst′lis] *adj.* 1 Having no flavor. 2 Lacking, or showing a lack of, good taste: *tasteless* behavior. **—taste′less·ly** *adv.*

tast·y [tās′tē] *adj.* **tast·i·er, tast·i·est** Having a good flavor; savory. **—tast′i·ness** *n.*

tat [tat] *v.* **tat·ted, tat·ting** To make lace by tatting.

ta·ta·mi [tə·tä′mē] *n.* A Japanese floor mat woven out of straw.

Ta·tar [tä′tər] *n.* Any of several Turkish or Mongolian peoples of central and western Asia and eastern Europe.

tat·ter [tat′ər] 1 *n.* A torn shred, as of cloth or paper; rag. 2 *n.* (*pl.*) Ragged clothing. 3 *v.* To tear into shreds.

tat·tered [tat′ərd] *adj.* Ragged; in tatters: a *tattered* shirt.

tat·ting [tat′ing] *n.* 1 The act or process of making lace by hand, by looping and knotting threads with a small shuttle. 2 The lace made in this way.

tat·tle [tat′(ə)l] *v.* **tat·tled, tat·tling,** *n.* 1 *v.* To tell tales or secrets; gossip. 2 *v.* To talk for the sake of talking; chatter. 3 *n.* Chatter or gossip. **—tat′·tler** *n.*

tat·tle·tale [tat′(ə)l·tāl′] *n.* A person who reveals secrets or who gossips; talebearer.

tat·too[1] [ta·tōō′] *v.* **tat·tooed, tat·too·ing,** *n., pl.* **tat·toos** 1 *v.* To mark (the skin) by pricking it with needles and inserting indelible pigment or by raising scars. 2 *v.* To draw on the skin in this way: A flag was *tattooed* on the sailor's arm. 3 *n.* A design or picture produced by tattooing.

tat·too[2] [ta·tōō′] *n., pl.* **tat·toos** 1 A steady rapping or drumming sound: to beat out a *tattoo* with one's foot. 2 A drum or bugle call used to signal the time at night for sailors and soldiers to return to their quarters.

tat·ty [tat′ē] *adj.* **tat·ti·er, tat·ti·est** Frayed; ragged; shabby: a *tatty* old sweater.

tau [tou *or* tô] *n.* The 19th letter of the Greek alphabet.

taught [tôt] Past tense and past participle of TEACH.

taunt [tônt] 1 *n.* A scornful, mocking, or sarcastic remark. 2 *v.* To insult, provoke, or make fun of with scornful, mocking, or sarcastic remarks.

taupe [tōp] *n., adj.* Deep, brownish gray.

Tau·rus [tôr′əs] *n.* 1 A constellation in the northern sky, thought of as shaped like a bull. 2 The second sign of the zodiac. 3 A person born under this sign.

taut [tôt] *adj.* 1 Stretched tight; not loose or slack. 2 Tense; strained. 3 Trim and neat. **—taut′ly** *adv.* **—taut′ness** *n.*

taut·en [tôt(ə)n] *v.* To make or become taut; stretch tight.

tau·tog [tô′tôg′ *or* tô′tog′] *n.* A dark green or blackish food fish found in the waters off the Atlantic coast of North America.

tau·tol·o·gy [tô·tol′ə·jē] *n., pl.* **tau·tol·o·gies** 1 A statement that is automatically true because it covers all possibilities, as "Either he will pass the math test or he will fail it." 2 Unnecessary repetition or redundancy, as in the statement "Unemployed people lack jobs." **—tau·to·log·i·cal** [tô′tə·loj′i·kəl] *adj.* **—tau′to·log′i·cal·ly** *adv.*

tav·ern [tav′ərn] *n.* 1 A place where people buy and drink whiskey, beer, and other beverages; bar. 2 An inn.

taw [tô] *n.* 1 A fancy marble to shoot marbles with. 2 A game of marbles. 3 The line from which players shoot when playing marbles.

taw·dry [tô′drē] *adj.* **taw·dri·er, taw·dri·est** Cheap and gaudy; showy. **—taw′dri·ness** *n.* ◆ *Tawdry* comes from *tawdry lace,* a ribbonlike ornament once worn around the neck. During the Middle Ages these ornaments were sold at *St. Audrey's* fair in England. At some point [sānt·ô′drē] became [sən·tô′drē]. This was shortened to [tô′drē], which came to be spelled *tawdry.*

taw·ny [tô′nē] *adj.* **taw·ni·er, taw·ni·est** Tan-colored; brownish yellow. **—tawn′i·ness** *n.*

tax [taks] 1 *n.* A charge paid by individuals or groups, as businesses, for support of government in a city, county, state, or nation. 2 *n.* A heavy strain or burden: A mile run puts a *tax* on one's endurance. 3 *v.* To put a tax on: to *tax* real estate; Running *taxed* their strength. 4 *v.* To accuse or blame: They *taxed* the driver with being reckless.

tax·a·ble [tak′sə·bəl] *adj.* That may be taxed; subject to taxation: *taxable* property.

tax·a·tion [tak·sā′shən] *n.* 1 The act of taxing. 2 The amount charged or paid in taxes.

tax evasion The intentional avoidance of taxes, especially by misstating one's taxable income or properties.

tax-ex·empt [taks′ig·zempt′] *adj.* Not taxable, or earning interest that is not taxable.

tax·i [tak′sē] *n., pl.* **tax·is,** *v.* **tax·ied, tax·i·ing** or **tax·y·ing** 1 *n.* A taxicab. 2 *v.* To ride in a taxi. 3 *v.* To move or cause to move slowly along the ground or water before a takeoff or after a landing.

tax·i·cab [tak′sē·kab′] *n.* An automobile hired to carry passengers. It usually has a meter that measures and shows the fare to be paid.

tax·i·der·my [tak′sə·dûr′mē] *n.* The art of stuffing and mounting the skins of dead animals, making them look alive. **—tax′i·der′mist** *n.*

tax·ing [tak'sing] *adj.* Exhausting; burdensome.
tax·on·o·mist [tak·son'ə·mist] *n.* A biologist who specializes in taxonomy.
tax·on·o·my [tak·son'ə·mē] *n.* The science of classifying animals and plants in related groups and subdivisions. **—tax·o·nom·ic** [tak'sə·nom'ik] *adj.* **—tax'o·nom'i·cal·ly** *adv.*
tax·pay·er [taks'pā'ər] *n.* A person who pays taxes or is subject to taxation.
tax shelter A financial investment or maneuver that reduces taxes on one's earnings.
tb, t.b., TB, or **T.B.** **1** tubercle bacillus. **2** tuberculosis.
Tb The symbol for the element terbium.
tba or **TBA** to be announced.
T-bone [tē'bōn'] *n.* A beefsteak cut from the tenderloin and loin and containing a small T-shaped bone.
tbs. or **tbsp.** tablespoon(s).
Tc The symbol for the element technetium.
td or **TD** touchdown.
TD or **T.D.** Treasury Department.
Te The symbol for the element tellurium.
tea [tē] *n.* **1** A drink made by soaking the dried leaves of an Asian shrub in hot water. **2** The dried leaves of this shrub. **3** The shrub bearing these leaves. **4** A late afternoon meal at which tea and light refreshments are served. **5** A reception or other social gathering in the late afternoon at which tea is served. **6** A tealike drink made from some other substance: beef *tea.* ◆ *Tea* comes from a Chinese word.
tea bag A small bag made of porous paper and containing ground tea leaves, dipped in hot water to make tea.
teach [tēch] *v.* **taught, teach·ing** **1** To help to learn: to *teach* a class of high school students. **2** To show how; train: The lifeguard *taught* us to swim. **3** To give lessons in; explain: to *teach* French. **4** To give lessons as a teacher: I started to *teach* last year. **5** To cause to understand through experience: Sickness *teaches* us to value health. ◆ *Learn* as a synonym for *teach*, as in *I'll learn you,* is not acceptable.
teach·a·ble [tē'chə·bəl] *adj.* Capable of being taught: a highly *teachable* pupil.
teach·er [tē'chər] *n.* A person who teaches, especially in a school.
teach-in [tēch'in'] *n.* An extended session of lectures and discussions on a controversial public issue, usually held on a college campus.
teach·ing [tē'ching] *n.* **1** The act or occupation of a teacher. **2** A doctrine; principle.
teaching machine A machine designed to present a step-by-step program of instruction and to check on a student's progress during lessons.
tea·cup [tē'kup'] *n.* **1** A cup for drinking tea. **2** A teacupful.
tea·cup·ful [tē'kup'fo͝ol'] *n., pl.* **tea·cup·fuls** The amount a teacup will hold.
tea·house [tē'hous'] *n., pl.* **tea·hous·es** [tē'hou'zəz] A restaurant serving tea and other light refreshments.
teak [tēk] *n.* **1** A large East Indian tree that has hard, heavy, durable wood. **2** The wood of this tree, used for furniture, ships, and other items.

Teakettle

tea·ket·tle [tē'ket'(ə)l] *n.* A covered kettle with a handle and a spout, used to boil water.
teak·wood [tēk'wo͝od'] *n.* The wood of the teak.
teal [tēl] *n., pl.* **teal** or **teals** **1** Any of several small, freshwater wild ducks with short necks. **2** A dark greenish blue.
team [tēm] **1** *n.* A set of two or more animals, as horses or mules, harnessed together. **2** *v.* To harness together in a team. **3** *n.* A group of people who work or play together as a unit: a baseball *team.* **4** *v.* To work or join together as a team: I *teamed* up with the rest of the class to play ball.
team·mate [tēm'māt'] *n.* Another member of the same team.
team·ster [tēm'stər] *n.* A person who drives a team or truck as an occupation.
team·work [tēm'wûrk'] *n.* The effective working together of members of a team or group; united effort: *Teamwork* is needed to win.
tea·pot [tē'pot'] *n.* A pot with a handle and spout, used to brew and serve tea.
tear[1] [târ] *v.* **tore, torn, tear·ing,** *n.* **1** *v.* To pull apart or rip by force: to *tear* a letter open. **2** *n.* A rip or hole: There's a *tear* in the mattress. **3** *v.* To make by tearing: You *tore* a hole in your shirt. **4** *v.* To become torn: cloth that *tears* easily. **5** *v.* To make one or more ragged wounds or deep scratches in: Briers *tore* my clothes. **6** *v.* To divide by fighting or disagreement: The committee was *torn* over the issue. **7** *v.* To distress greatly: a heart *torn* by grief. **8** *v.* To rush or move with great speed or force: The car *tore* around the corner. **9** *n.* The act of tearing. **—tear down** **1** To demolish; destroy. **2** To discredit, as a reputation. **—tear into** To attack fiercely.
tear[2] [tir] *n.* A drop of salty liquid in or shed from the eye, as in crying. **—in tears** Weeping.
tear·drop [tir'drop'] *n.* A tear.
tear·ful [tir'fəl] *adj.* **1** In tears; weeping: The child was *tearful.* **2** Causing tears; woeful: a *tearful* tale. **—tear'ful·ly** *adv.* **—tear'ful·ness** *n.*
tear gas [tir] A gas that irritates the eyes and temporarily blinds them with tears.
tear·jerk·er [tir'jûr'kər] *n. slang* A sad story, movie, or play that tends to make the audience cry.
tea·room [tē'ro͞om'] *n.* A restaurant serving light meals.
tease [tēz] *v.* **teased, teas·ing,** *n.* **1** *v.* To pick on or fool with (another) for fun, in order to annoy or provoke: It is dangerous to *tease* an unfriendly dog; I was only *teasing.* **2** *v.* To pester with demands or questions: The children *teased* their parents for new toys. **3** *n.* A person who teases. **4** *v.* To comb or straighten out, as wool or flax. **5** *v.* To scratch (cloth or other material) on the surface in order to raise a nap. **6** *v.* To comb (hair) in layers so that it stands out and is fluffy. **7** *n.* The act of teasing. **—teas'er** *n.* **—teas'ing·ly** *adv.*
tea·spoon [tē'spo͞on'] *n.* **1** A small spoon used to stir tea or other liquids. **2** A teaspoonful.

a	add	**i**	it	**o͝o**	took	**oi**	oil
ā	ace	**ī**	ice	**o͞o**	pool	**ou**	pout
â	care	**o**	odd	**u**	up	**ng**	ring
ä	palm	**ō**	open	**û**	burn	**th**	thin
e	end	**ô**	order	**yo͞o**	fuse	**th**	this
ē	equal					**zh**	vision

ə = a in *above*, e in *sicken*, i in *possible*, o in *melon*, u in *circus*

T

tea·spoon·ful [tē′spōōn′fōōl′] *n., pl.* **tea·spoon·fuls** The amount that a teaspoon will hold, equal to 1/3 of a tablespoon or 1 1/3 fluid drams.
teat [tēt] *n.* The nipple on a breast or udder.
tea·time [tē′tīm′] *n.* The time of day, usually late afternoon, when tea is served.
tech. 1 technical. 2 technology.
tech·ne·ti·um [tek·nē′shē·əm] *n.* An artificially produced radioactive metallic element.
tech·nic [tek′nik] 1 *n.* A technique. 2 *adj.* Technical.
tech·ni·cal [tek′ni·kəl] *adj.* 1 Of or having to do with mechanical or industrial skills or applied science: a *technical* school. 2 Of or having to do with special facts, ideas, or words of a particular art or science: "Patella" is a *technical* term for the kneecap. 3 Of or based on a strict application or interpretation of rules, laws, or definitions: Drinking coffee before the race was a *technical* violation of the ban on drugs. **—tech′ni·cal·ly** *adv.* **—tech′ni·cal·ness** *n.*
tech·ni·cal·i·ty [tek′ni·kal′ə·tē] *n., pl.* **tech·ni·cal·i·ties** 1 The state or quality of being technical. 2 A small, formal point or detail: *Technicalities* kept many from being eligible. 3 A technical detail, idea, or word known to a specialist in an art or science: the *technicalities* in a physics text.
tech·ni·cian [tek·nish′ən] *n.* A person skilled in the use of the instruments, machinery, or details of an art or science: a radio *technician.*
Tech·ni·col·or [tek′ni·kul′ər] *n.* A process for making motion pictures in color: a trademark.
tech·nique [tek·nēk′] *n.* 1 A way of or skill in handling something, whether tools, instruments, materials, or one's body, in an art, science, sport, craft, or the like: Both boxers and violinists need a great deal of *technique.* 2 A special method of doing something: a new printing *technique.*
technol. 1 technological. 2 technology.
tech·no·log·i·cal [tek′nə·loj′i·kəl] *adj.* Having to do with or resulting from technology. **—tech′no·log′i·cal·ly** *adv.*
tech·nol·o·gist [tek·nol′ə·jist] *n.* A person skilled in technology.
tech·nol·o·gy [tek·nol′ə·jē] *n., pl.* **tech·nol·o·gies** 1 The application of scientific and industrial skills to practical uses. 2 A body of technical methods, machines, or other products of applied science.
ted·dy bear [ted′ē] A stuffed toy shaped like a bear cub. ◆ *Teddy bear* celebrates President Theodore Roosevelt, nicknamed *Teddy.* The first teddy bears appeared after a cartoon was published showing him with a bear cub he had spared when hunting.
Te De·um [tē dē′əm *or* tā dā′əm] An ancient Christian hymn of praise to God, or its music.
te·di·ous [tē′dē·əs] *adj.* Long, dull, and tiresome: a *tedious* job. **—te′di·ous·ly** *adv.* **—te′di·ous·ness** *n.*
te·di·um [tē′dē·əm] *n.* The condition of being boring or monotonous.
tee [tē] *n., v.* **teed, tee·ing** 1 *n.* A small peg on which a golf ball may be placed for the first stroke in playing a hole. 2 *v.* To place (a golf ball) on a tee. 3 *n.* The area where a player must start to play a hole. 4 *n.* A mark aimed at in certain sports, as in curling. **—tee off** To strike a golf ball from a tee.
teem[1] [tēm] *v.* To be full and almost overflowing; abound: The hive *teems* with bees.
teem[2] [tēm] *v.* To pour out or down; rain hard.
teen [tēn] *n. informal* A teenager.
teen·age [tēn′āj′] *adj.* 1 Being in one's teens. 2 Of or for teenage people.
teen·aged [tēn′ājd′] *adj.* In one's teens.
teen·ag·er [tēn′ā′jər] *n.* A teenaged person.
teens [tēnz] *n.pl* 1 The numbers 13 through 19. 2 The years 13 through 19 in a person's lifetime or in a century.
teen·sy [tēn′sē] *adj. informal* **teen·si·er, teen·si·est** Very small; tiny.
teen·sy-ween·sy [tēn′sē·wēn′sē] *adj. informal* Tiny.
tee·ny [tē′nē] *adj. informal* **tee·ni·er, tee·ni·est** Very small; tiny.
teen·y·bop·per [tē′nē·bop′ər] *n. slang* A teenager, especially a girl, who follows teenage fads.
tee·ny-wee·ny [tē′nē·wē′nē] *adj. informal* Tiny.
tee·pee [tē′pē] *n.* Another spelling of TEPEE.
tee shirt Another spelling of T-SHIRT.
tee·ter [tē′tər] 1 *v.* To rock from side to side as if about to fall. 2 *n.* A teetering movement. 3 *n.* A seesaw. 4 *v.* To seesaw.
tee·ter-tot·ter [tē′tər·tot′ər] *n.* A seesaw.
teeth [tēth] Plural of TOOTH. **—in the teeth of** Directly against; in defiance of.
teethe [tēth] *v.* **teethed, teeth·ing** To cut or develop teeth, as babies do.
tee·to·tal·er [tē·tōt′(ə)l·ər] *n.* A person who does not drink alcoholic beverages.
Tef·lon [tef′lon′] *n.* A tough and durable synthetic plastic often used as a coating on cooking utensils to prevent food from sticking: a trademark.
teg·u·ment [teg′yə·mənt] *n.* Another word for INTEGUMENT.
tel. 1 telegram. 2 telegraph. 3 telephone.
tele- or **tel-** A combining form meaning: 1 Distant, as in *telegram.* 2 Telegraph, as in *teletypewriter.* 3 Television, as in *telecast.*
tel·e·cast [tel′ə·kast′] *n., v.* **tel·e·cast** or **tel·e·cast·ed, tel·e·cast·ing** 1 *n.* A program broadcast by television. 2 *v.* To broadcast by television. ◆ See TELEVISION.
tel·e·com·mu·ni·ca·tion [tel′ə·kə·myōō′nə·kā′shən] *n.* 1 Communication over long distances, as by telephone, telegraph, radio, or television. 2 (*usually written* **telecommunications**; *used with a singular verb*) The theory and practice of long-distance communications.
teleg. 1 telegram. 2 telegraph. 3 telegraphy.
tel·e·gram [tel′ə·gram′] *n.* A message sent by telegraph.
tel·e·graph [tel′ə·graf′] 1 *n.* A device for sending and receiving messages by means of a series of electrical or electromagnetic pulses. 2 *v.* To send (a message) by telegraph. 3 *v.* To send a message to, by telegraph. **—te·leg·ra·pher** [tə·leg′rə·fər] *n.*
tel·e·graph·ic [tel′ə·graf′ik] *adj.* Having to do with or sent by telegraph.
te·leg·ra·phy [tə·leg′rə·fē] *n.* The use or operation of a telegraphic system.
tel·e·mar·ket·ing [tel′ə·mär′kit·ing] *n.* The technique of selling or promoting a product by telephone calls to prospective customers.
tel·e·me·ter [tel′ə·mē′tər] 1 *n.* Any of various electronic devices for measuring and recording various quantities, as temperature, speed, or radiation, and then transmitting the data to distant points. 2 *v.* To measure and transmit (various quantities) by telemeter.
te·lem·e·try [tə·lem′ə·trē] *n.* The theory and practice of using telemeters.

tel·e·path·ic [tel′ə·path′ik] *adj.* Having to do with or sent by telepathy: a *telepathic* message. **—tel′e·path′i·cal·ly** *adv.*
te·lep·a·thy [tə·lep′ə·thē] *n.* Communication from one mind to another, apparently received without use of hearing, sight, or touch.
tel·e·phone [tel′ə·fōn′] *n., v.* **tel·e·phoned, tel·e·phon·ing** 1 *n.* A system for sending and receiving speech by electricity. 2 *n.* A device in this system that changes sounds to pulses in electric current and converts incoming pulses into sounds. 3 *v.* To call by telephone. 4 *v.* To send by telephone.
tel·e·phon·ic [tel′ə·fon′ik] *adj.* Having to do with or sent by the telephone.
te·le·pho·ny [tə·lef′ə·nē] *n.* The science and practice of sending sound over long distances, as by telephone or radio.
tel·e·pho·to lens [tel′ə·fō′tō] A camera lens used to make distant objects look nearer or larger.
Tel·e·Promp·Ter [tel′ə·promp′tər] *n.* A device that displays a moving script that prompts a television performer without being seen by the audience: a trademark.
tel·e·scope [tel′ə·skōp′] *n., v.* **tel·e·scoped, tel·e·scop·ing** 1 *n.* An instrument that uses lenses, and sometimes mirrors, to make far-off objects look nearer or larger. 2 *v.* To force or be forced into one another, like the sliding tubes of a folding telescope: The collision *telescoped* three cars. 3 *v.* To shorten, squeeze, or compress: The play *telescoped* the events of years into a single day. ◆ See TELEVISION.

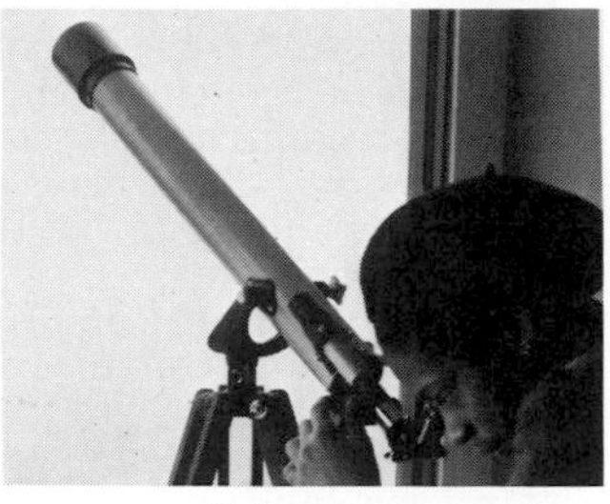

Telescope

tel·e·scop·ic [tel′ə·skop′ik] *adj.* 1 Of or having to do with a telescope. 2 Visible only through a telescope: a *telescopic* star. 3 Seen by or as if by a telescope. 4 Having parts that slide inside each other, like the sections of a telescope.
tel·e·thon [tel′ə·thon′] *n.* A long television program to raise money for a charity or publicly financed institution. ◆ *Telethon* is a blend of the words *television* and *marathon.*
Tel·e·type [tel′ə·tīp′] *n.* 1 A kind of teletypewriter: a trademark. 2 A message sent on a teletypewriter. Also written **teletype.**
tel·e·type·writ·er [tel′ə·tīp′rī′tər] *n.* A telegraph on which a message is sent from a typewriterlike keyboard and then is typed out automatically at its destination.
tel·e·vise [tel′ə·vīz′] *v.* **tel·e·vised, tel·e·vis·ing** To transmit by television. ◆ See TELEVISION.
tel·e·vi·sion [tel′ə·vizh′ən] *n.* 1 The devices and methods by which moving images, usually with sound, are changed into variations of an electromagnetic wave that travel through space or over cables to a receiver where the signals are recovered. 2 *adj. use*: a *television* set. 3 A television receiver. 4 The television industry. ◆ The combining form *tele-* comes from a Greek word meaning *far.* Thus *television* literally means *far or distant vision,* and *telescope* means *watcher from afar.* When there was a need for a verb with the meaning *to transmit by television, televise,* modeled after *television,* was created. *Telecast,* filling a similar need, was formed from *tele-* + *(broad)cast.*
Tel·ex [tel′eks′] 1 *n.* A system of teletypewriters interconnected through a telephone system: a trademark. 2 *n.* A typed message sent by such a system. 3 *v.* To communicate through a Telex system.
tell [tel] *v.* **told, tell·ing** 1 To say in words; utter: to *tell* a story. 2 To give facts to; inform: *Tell* me about the book. 3 To give information or description: The book *tells* about Japan. 4 To make known: to *tell* secrets. 5 To give away a secret or inform on someone: Please don't *tell.* 6 To show; indicate: Your face *told* how amused you were. 7 To distinguish or decide: I can't *tell* which dog is older. 8 To give an order to: *Tell* them to go. 9 *informal* To say to with force or emphasis: It's dangerous, I *tell* you! 10 To have a marked effect: TV debates *told* in our candidate's favor. 11 To count: All *told,* 19 chemicals were tested; to *tell* one's rosary beads while praying. **—tell off** 1 To count and set apart. 2 *informal* To scold severely. **—tell on** 1 To tire: The heat began to *tell on* them. 2 To inform on; bear tales about: A tattletale *tells on* others. **—tell time** To read the time shown on a clock or watch.
tell·er [tel′ər] *n.* 1 A person who tells: a *teller* of tales. 2 A person who counts and gives out or takes in money in a bank.
tell·ing [tel′ing] *adj.* Having a marked effect; effective: a *telling* speech.
tell·tale [tel′tāl′] 1 *n.* A person who informs on others or gives out secret or private information. 2 *adj.* Showing or revealing what is meant to be hidden: a *telltale* blush.
tel·lu·ri·um [te·lo͝or′ē·əm] *n.* A brittle crystalline element with some metallic properties, used in alloys.
te·mer·i·ty [tə·mer′ə·tē] *n.* Rash boldness.
temp. 1 temperature. 2 temporary.
tem·per [tem′pər] 1 *n.* A frame of mind; mood: in a good *temper.* 2 *n.* A tendency to become angry: to have a *temper.* 3 *n.* A rage: to fly into a *temper.* 4 *n.* Self-command; calmness: to lose one's *temper.* 5 *v.* To make less harsh or strong, as by adding something; moderate: to *temper* very hot coffee with ice. 6 *n.* The condition of something, as a metal or clay, regarding its hardness or elasticity. 7 *v.* To bring to the condition or temper desired by treating, as by heating and suddenly cooling (metal) or by moistening (clay).
tem·per·a·ment [tem′pər·ə·mənt] *n.* 1 The nature or emotional makeup of a person; disposition. 2 A sensitive, easily excited nature.
tem·per·a·men·tal [tem′prə·men′təl *or* tem′pər·ə·men′təl] *adj.* 1 Of or having to do with temper-

a	add	**i**	it	**o͝o**	took	**oi**	oil
ā	ace	**ī**	ice	**o͞o**	pool	**ou**	pout
â	care	**o**	odd	**u**	up	**ng**	ring
ä	palm	**ō**	open	**û**	burn	**th**	thin
e	end	**ô**	order	**yo͞o**	fuse	**th**	this
ē	equal					**zh**	vision

ə = {a in *above* e in *sicken* i in *possible* / o in *melon* u in *circus*}

T

ament. **2** Easily excited, irritated, or upset; sensitive. **—tem'per·a·men'tal·ly** *adv.*

tem·per·ance [tem'pər·əns] *n.* **1** The quality of being temperate; moderation. **2** The rule or practice of taking no alcoholic drinks.

tem·per·ate [tem'pər·it] *adj.* **1** Practicing or showing moderation or self-control in one's actions or in eating or drinking. **2** Moderate in temperature; mild: a *temperate* climate. **—tem'per·ate·ly** *adv.* **—tem'per·ate·ness** *n.*

temperate zone Either of two zones of the earth's surface. The **North Temperate Zone** lies between the tropic of Cancer and the Arctic Circle. The **South Temperate Zone** lies between the tropic of Capricorn and the Antarctic Circle.

tem·per·a·ture [tem'pər·ə·chər *or* tem'prə·chər] *n.* **1** The degree of heat or cold in a body or thing, as measured on some definite scale. **2** Excessive body heat; fever, especially in a human being. Normal heat for the human body is 98.6° F.

temperature-humidity index *U.S.* A number on a scale of 70 to 80 based on the humidity and temperature outdoors in warm weather. It suggests the degree of discomfort experienced by the average person, most people being comfortable when the index is 70, about half being uncomfortable at 75, and almost everyone experiencing discomfort at 80.

tem·pered [tem'pərd] *adj.* **1** Having a certain disposition: usually used in combination, as in *ill-tempered.* **2** Having the right degree of hardness and elasticity: *tempered* steel.

tem·pest [tem'pist] *n.* **1** A violent wind or storm. **2** A violent outburst or disturbance.

tem·pes·tu·ous [tem·pes'cho͞o·əs] *adj.* Stormy; violent; turbulent. **—tem·pes'tu·ous·ly** *adv.* **—tem·pes'tu·ous·ness** *n.*

Tem·plar [tem'plər] *n.* A member of a medieval military and religious order, the **Knights Templars,** founded by the Crusaders for the defense of Jerusalem and the protection of pilgrims.

tem·ple[1] [tem'pəl] *n.* **1** A stately building dedicated to the worship of a god or gods. **2** A church or synagogue. **3** (*written* **Temple**) Any of the three temples built one after the other by the Jews in ancient Jerusalem. **4** A building, usually of great beauty or size, that is devoted to some special purpose: a *temple* of the arts.

An ancient Greek temple

tem·ple[2] [tem'pəl] *n.* The flattened area extending back from the forehead on either side about as far as the ear.

tem·po [tem'pō] *n., pl.* **tem·pos** or **tem·pi** [tem'pē] **1** The relative speed at which a piece of music is played. **2** The pace or rate of activity: the fast *tempo* of city life.

tem·po·ral[1] [tem'pər·əl] *adj.* **1** Of or having to do with life on earth. **2** Of or having to do with time. **3** Temporary or passing. **4** Not sacred, religious, or ecclesiastic; secular; worldly.

tem·po·ral[2] [tem'pər·əl] *adj.* Of or near the temple or temples of the head: the *temporal* bones.

tem·po·rar·y [tem'pə·rer'ē] *adj.* Lasting or meant to be used for a short time only; not permanent. **—tem'po·rar'i·ly** *adv.*

tem·po·rize [tem'pə·rīz'] *v.* **tem·po·rized, tem·po·riz·ing** **1** To talk or act in an evasive or noncommital way so as to gain time or postpone making a decision. **2** To talk or act in a way that suits the time or circumstances.

tempt [tempt] *v.* **1** To try to persuade (a person) to do something wrong or foolish. **2** To attract or invite: The aroma *tempts* me. **3** To provoke or risk provoking: It is unwise to *tempt* fate.

temp·ta·tion [tem·tā'shən] *n.* **1** The act of tempting. **2** The condition of being tempted. **3** A tempting thing.

tempt·er [temp'tər] *n.* A person who tempts.

tempt·ing [temp'ting] *adj.* Having a strong appeal; attractive: a *tempting* display of food.

tempt·ress [temp'tris] *n.* A woman who tempts, especially a seductive woman.

tem·pu·ra [tem'pə·rə *or* tem·po͝or'ə] *n.* A Japanese dish of seafood or vegetables dipped in batter and fried.

ten or **10** [ten] *n., adj.* One more than nine.

ten·a·ble [ten'ə·bəl] *adj.* Capable of being believed, maintained, or defended: The theory that the earth is flat is no longer *tenable.* **—ten·a·bil·i·ty** [ten'ə·bil'ə·tē] *n.* **—ten'a·ble·ness** *n.* **—ten'a·bly** *adv.*

te·na·cious [ti·nā'shəs] *adj.* **1** Holding or grasping firmly: a *tenacious* grip. **2** Having parts that hold together well; cohesive, as a metal. **3** Clinging or sticky: a *tenacious* climbing plant. **4** Not forgetting; retentive: a *tenacious* memory. **—te·na'cious·ly** *adv.* **—te·na'cious·ness** *n.*

te·nac·i·ty [ti·nas'ə·tē] *n.* The condition or quality of being tenacious.

ten·an·cy [ten'ən·sē] *n., pl.* **ten·an·cies** **1** The condition of being a tenant. **2** The time during which one is a tenant.

ten·ant [ten'ənt] **1** *n.* A person who rents something, as land, a house, or an apartment, from another. **2** *n.* A dweller in any place; occupant. **3** *v.* To occupy or inhabit as a tenant.

tenant farmer A farmer who lives on and farms land owned by someone else and pays rent either in cash or in farm produce.

ten·ant·ry [ten'ən·trē] *n., pl.* **ten·ant·ries** **1** Another word for TENANCY. **2** The body of tenants on a landed estate.

Ten Commandments In the Bible, the set of laws given by God to Moses on Mount Sinai.

tend[1] [tend] *v.* To attend to; take care of; watch over: to *tend* a herd.

tend[2] [tend] *v.* **1** To be apt; have an inclination: the roof *tends* to leak. **2** To move or go in a certain direction: The road *tends* south.

ten·den·cy [ten'dən·sē] *n., pl.* **ten·den·cies** A leaning or inclination toward some condition or action: a *tendency* to rust; a *tendency* to argue.

ten·den·tious [ten·den'shəs] *adj.* Having a tendency to favor a particular point of view; biased: a *tendentious* reporter. **—ten·den'tious·ly** *adv.* **—ten·den'tious·ness** *n.*

ten·der[1] [ten'dər] *adj.* **1** Easily injured or damaged; delicate; sensitive: a *tender* plant. **2** Easily chewed or cut, as meat. **3** Young; immature: a *tender* age. **4** Kind and gentle; loving: *tender* care. **5** Easily moved; sympathetic; compassionate: a *tender* heart. **6** Painful if touched: a *tender* sore. **7** Likely to provoke strong feelings; touchy: a *tender* subject. **—ten'der·ly** *adv.* **—ten'der·ness** *n.*

ten·der[2] [ten'dər] **1** *v.* To offer, especially formally, or to present in payment: to *tender* a resignation. **2** *n.* An offer, especially a formal one. **3** *n.* Something offered as payment.

ten·der^{3} [ten′dər] *n.* **1** A boat used to carry passengers, supplies, and other things to and from a larger vessel. **2** A car that carries coal and water for a steam locomotive. **3** A person who tends.

Tender

ten·der·foot [ten′dər·fo͝ot′] *n., pl.* **ten·der·foots** or **ten·der·feet** [ten′dər·fēt′] **1** A person who is not used to a rugged, outdoor life. **2** Any inexperienced person. **3** A beginning boy scout. ◆ *Tenderfoot* comes from combining *tender* and *foot,* and first meant someone who got sore feet from hiking in the pioneer West.

ten·der·heart·ed [ten′dər·här′tid] *adj.* Easily moved to sympathy or compassion.

ten·der·ize [ten′də·rīz′] *v.* **ten·der·ized, ten·der·iz·ing** To make (tough meat) tender by pounding it or soaking it. **—ten·der·i·za·tion** [ten′də·rə·zā′shən] *n.* **—ten′der·iz′er** *n.*

ten·der·loin [ten′dər·loin′] *n.* The tender part of the loin of a cut of meat, as beef or pork.

ten·don [ten′dən] *n.* A tough band of tissue that connects a muscle to a bone.

ten·dril [ten′dril] *n.* **1** A thin, curling stem or growth by which a climbing plant attaches itself to something. **2** Anything that looks like this.

ten·e·ment [ten′ə·mənt] *n.* **1** An apartment house that is poorly built or maintained, usually overcrowded, and often in a slum. **2** A room or set of rooms for a single tenant or family.

ten·et [ten′it] *n.* An opinion, doctrine, or principle held to be true by a person or group.

ten·fold [*adj.* ten′fōld′, *adv.* ten′fōld′] **1** *adj.* Composed of ten parts. **2** *adj.* Ten times greater or more numerous. **3** *adv.* By ten times: to increase *tenfold.*

ten-gal·lon hat [ten′gal′ən] A hat with a large, soft crown and a wide brim, traditionally worn by cowboys.

Tenn. Tennessee.

Tennessee Valley Authority An agency of the U.S. government established in 1933 to control flooding and develop hydroelectric power and other resources in the Tennessee River basin.

ten·nis [ten′is] *n.* A game played by striking a ball back and forth with rackets over a net stretched between two equal areas.

ten·on [ten′ən] *n.* A projection on the end of a piece of wood or other material, for fitting into a mortise to form a joint.

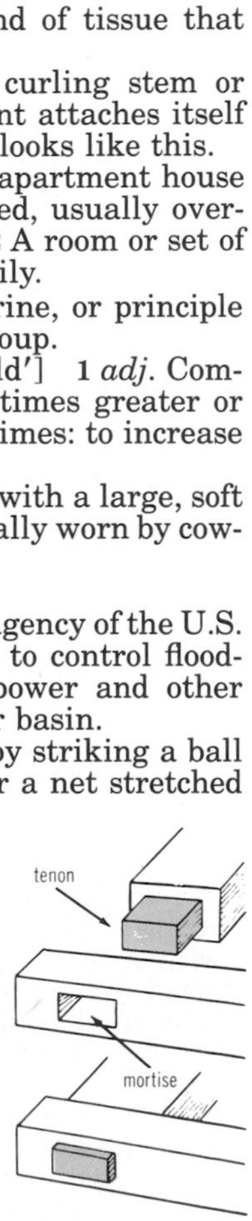

ten·or [ten′ər] *n.* **1** An adult male singing voice next higher than a baritone. **2** A person with such a voice. **3** The range of or a part for such a voice. **4** An instrument with such a range. **5** *adj. use*: a *tenor* saxophone. **6** The general course: the *tenor* of city life. **7** The main meaning or drift: The *tenor* of the review was very critical.

ten·pin [ten′pin′] *n.* **1** A pin with a long neck and a wide base, used in bowling. **2** *pl.* (*used with singular verb*) The game of bowling.

ten·rec [ten′rek′] *n.* Any of a number of small, often spiny, mammals that feed on insects.

tense^{1} [tens] *adj.* **tens·er, tens·est,** *v.* **tensed, tens·ing** **1** *adj.* Stretched tight; taut. **2** *adj.* Marked by, feeling, or causing nervous strain. **3** *v.* To make or become tense. **4** *adj.* Characterized by strain or suspense. **—tense′ly** *adv.* **—tense′ness** *n.*

tense^{2} [tens] *n.* **1** The property of a verb that indicates the time of the action or state of being expressed by the verb and whether the action or state of being is continuing or completed. **2** Any of the verb forms that illustrate this property, as the present tense and the future perfect tense.

ten·sile [ten′səl] *adj.* **1** Of or having to do with tension: *tensile* forces. **2** Capable of being drawn out without breaking.

tensile strength The greatest tension a material can withstand before it breaks apart.

ten·sion [ten′shən] *n.* **1** The act of stretching. **2** The condition of being stretched. **3** Mental strain; nervous anxiety. **4** Electrical potential; voltage.

ten·sor [ten′sər] *n.* A muscle that makes a part tense and firm.

tent [tent] **1** *n.* A shelter of canvas, skins, or other material, supported by poles and ropes. **2** *v.* To camp out or live in a tent.

ten·ta·cle [ten′tə·kəl] *n.* **1** A long, flexible outgrowth from the main body of an animal, as an octopus or squid, used for moving or for seizing prey. **2** A sensitive plant hair.

ten·ta·tive [ten′tə·tiv] *adj.* **1** Done or made as an experiment or for a short trial period; subject to change or revision; not final: a *tentative* agreement. **2** Hesitant; halfhearted: a *tentative* handshake. **—ten′ta·tive·ly** *adv.* **—ten′ta·tive·ness** *n.*

ten·ter [ten′tər] **1** *n.* A frame for stretching and drying cloth. **2** *v.* To stretch (cloth) in a frame.

ten·ter·hook [ten′tər·ho͝ok′] *n.* A sharp hook for holding cloth on a stretching frame. **—be on tenterhooks** To be in suspense; be nervous.

tenth or **10th** [tenth] **1** *adj.* Next after the ninth. **2** *n.* The tenth one. **3** *adj.* Being one of ten equal parts. **4** *n.* A tenth part.

ten·u·ous [ten′yo͞o·əs] *adj.* **1** Thin; slim; delicate: a *tenuous* web. **2** Weak; flimsy; unsubstantial: a *tenuous* idea. **3** Having slight density; rarefied, as a gas. **—ten′u·ous·ly** *adv.* **—ten′u·ous·ness** *n.*

ten·ure [ten′yər] *n.* **1** The act or right of holding something, as land or a position. **2** The conditions or manner of holding. **3** The time during which something is held. **4** The status of being a permanent member of a teaching faculty.

ten·ured [ten′yərd] *adj.* Having tenure: a *tenured* faculty member.

a	add	**i**	it	**o͝o**	took	**oi**	oil		
ā	ace	**ī**	ice	**o͞o**	pool	**ou**	pout		
â	care	**o**	odd	**u**	up	**ng**	ring		
ä	palm	**ō**	open	**û**	burn	**th**	thin		
e	end	**ô**	order	**yo͞o**	fuse	**th̶**	this		
ē	equal					**zh**	vision		

ə = {a in *above* e in *sicken* i in *possible* / o in *melon* u in *circus*}

T

te·pee [tē′pē] *n.* A cone-shaped tent used by some North American Indians. ◆ *Tepee* goes back to two North American Indian words meaning *used for dwelling.*

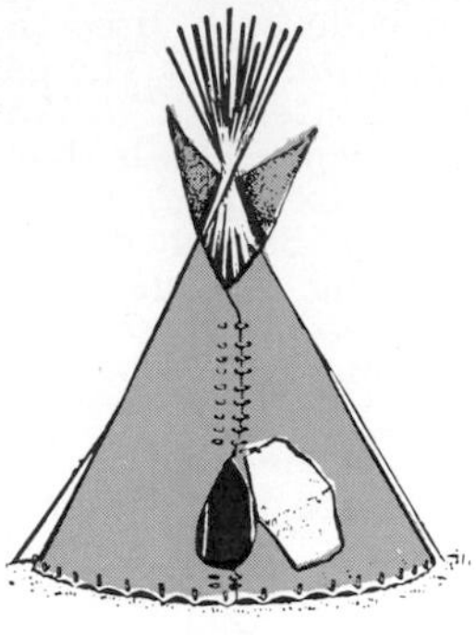
Tepee

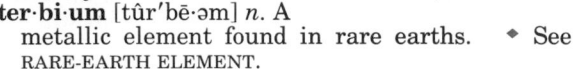

tep·id [tep′id] *adj.* Moderately warm; lukewarm.
ter. 1 terrace. 2 territory.
te·rat·o·gen [tə·rat′ə·jən] *n.* A chemical or other substance that can cause defects in a fetus. **—ter·at·o·gen·ic** [ter′ə·tə·jen′·ik] *adj.*
ter·bi·um [tûr′bē·əm] *n.* A metallic element found in rare earths. ◆ See RARE-EARTH ELEMENT.
ter·i·ya·ki [ter′ē·yä′kē] *n.* A Japanese dish of meat or shellfish that is marinated in soy sauce and then broiled or grilled.
term [tûrm] 1 *n.* A word or phrase having a certain meaning, especially in some particular field: a scientific *term*; to speak in vague *terms.* 2 *v.* To apply a term to; name or call: I *term* you a genius. 3 *n.* An established period of time, as one of the divisions of the school year. 4 *n.* (*pl.*) Mutual relations: to be on friendly *terms.* 5 *n.* (*pl.*) Agreement: to come to *terms.* 6 *n.* (*pl.*) Conditions or stipulations, as of a sale or contract. 7 *n.* The numerator or denominator of a fraction. 8 *n.* The parts of a mathematical expression that are added or subtracted, as ax^2, bx, and c in $ax^2 + bx - c$. **—in terms of** In comparison with; in relation to; with respect to.
term. 1 terminal. 2 terminate. 3 termination. 4 terminology.
ter·ma·gant [tûr′mə·gənt] *n.* A harsh, scolding person; shrew.
ter·mi·na·ble [tûr′mə·nə·bəl] *adj.* Capable of being ended, as a contract. **—ter′mi·na·ble·ness** *n.* **—ter′·mi·na·bly** *adv.*
ter·mi·nal [tûr′mə·nəl] 1 *adj.* Of, at, having to do with, or forming a limit or end. 2 *adj.* About to cause death: a *terminal* illness. 3 *n.* An end or limit. 4 *n.* The station at the end of a route, as of a train or bus. 5 *n.* Any of the points where electricity can enter or leave a device. 6 *n.* A device by means of which a user can enter data into a computer and receive data from it.
ter·mi·nate [tûr′mə·nāt′] *v.* **ter·mi·nat·ed, ter·mi·nat·ing** 1 To end; stop; finish: The road *terminates* there; to *terminate* a discussion. 2 To form the end of; bound: The field was *terminated* by a forest. **—ter′mi·na′tion** *n.*
ter·mi·nol·o·gy [tûr′mə·nol′ə·jē] *n.* The technical words and phrases of a trade, science, or art.
ter·mi·nus [tûr′mə·nəs] *n., pl.* **ter·mi·nus·es** or **ter·mi·ni** [tûr′mə·nī] 1 The final point or goal; end. 2 Either end of a railroad, bus, or airplane route.
ter·mite [tûr′mīt′] *n.* A small, pale insect that looks like a white ant. Termites are very destructive to things made of wood.
term paper A long written assignment that forms a major part of a student's work for a course.
tern [tûrn] *n.* A small, gull-like bird with a slender body, pointed wings, and forked tail.
terr. territory.
ter·race [ter′is] *n., v.* **ter·raced, ter·rac·ing** 1 *n.* A raised, level space, as of lawn, with one or more sloping sides. 2 *n.* One of a series of such spaces, as on a hill. 3 *v.* To form into or provide with a terrace or terraces. 4 *n.* A row of houses built on ground raised above a street, or the street on which such houses face. 5 *n.* A paved area adjoining a house; patio. 6 *n.* The flat roof of a house. 7 *n.* An open gallery or balcony.

Terrace

ter·ra-cot·ta [ter′ə·kot′ə] *n.* 1 A hard, reddish brown clay, used in sculpture and pottery and in building. 2 Brownish orange.
ter·ra fir·ma [ter′ə fûr′mə] Firm, solid ground.
ter·rain [tə·rān′] *n.* An area of land, especially as considered with respect to its use for military operations or some other purpose.
Ter·ra·my·cin [ter′ə·mī′sin] *n.* An antibiotic obtained from a mold that grows in the soil, effective against many different germs: a trademark.
ter·ra·pin [ter′ə·pin] *n.* Any of various edible North American turtles that live in fresh or partly salt water.
ter·rar·i·um [tə·râr′ē·əm] *n., pl.* **ter·rar·i·ums** or **ter·rar·i·a** [tə·râr′ē·ə] A transparent box in which small land animals or plants are grown and kept.
ter·raz·zo [tə·raz′ō *or* tə·rät′sō] *n.* A mosaic flooring of small pieces of stone, usually marble, embedded in cement and polished.
ter·res·tri·al [tə·res′trē·əl] 1 *adj.* Of, on, having to do with, or inhabiting the planet Earth. 2 *n.* An inhabitant of Earth. 3 *adj.* Living in or on the ground; not aquatic. 4 Earthly; worldly. **—ter·res′tri·al·ly** *adv.*
ter·ri·ble [ter′ə·bəl] *adj.* 1 Causing terror or awe: a *terrible* storm. 2 *informal* Unpleasant or inferior: a *terrible* book. **—ter′ri·ble·ness** *n.*
ter·ri·bly [ter′ə·blē] *adv.* 1 In a terrible way or manner. 2 *informal* Very: They're *terribly* nice.
ter·ri·er [ter′ē·ər] *n.* Any of various small, active dogs, formerly used to hunt burrowing animals.
ter·rif·ic [tə·rif′ik] *adj.* 1 *informal* Wonderful; splendid: a *terrific* book. 2 *informal* Extreme or very great: under *terrific* pressure. 3 Causing great terror or fear. **—ter·rif′i·cal·ly** *adv.*

Fox terrier

ter·ri·fy [ter′ə·fī] *v.* **ter·ri·fied, ter·ri·fy·ing** To fill with extreme fear; frighten greatly.
ter·ri·fy·ing [ter′ə·fī′ing] *adj.* Causing extreme fear: a *terrifying* explosion. **—ter′ri·fy′ing·ly** *adv.*
ter·ri·to·ri·al [ter′ə·tôr′ē·əl] 1 Of or having to do with a territory or territories. 2 Limited to or governed by a particular territory or region. **—ter′ri·to′ri·al·ly** *adv.*
territorial waters The areas of water over which a nation has jurisdiction, including inland waters and offshore waters usually to a distance of three miles from shore.
ter·ri·to·ry [ter′ə·tôr′ē] *n., pl.* **ter·ri·to·ries** 1 The geographical area ruled by a nation, state, or country. 2 A large division of a nation or country,

having a limited amount of self-government. **3** Any large area of land; region. **4** An area assigned for a special purpose: a salesman's *territory.*

ter·ror [ter′ər] *n.* **1** Great fear; extreme fright or dread. **2** A person or thing that causes such fear: Avalanches are the *terror* of mountain villages. **3** *informal* A person or thing that is annoying; nuisance.

ter·ror·ism [ter′ə·riz′əm] *n.* The use of violence and threats to frighten a people or a government into submission. **—ter′ror·ist** *n., adj.* **—ter′ror·is′tic** *adj.*

ter·ror·ize [ter′ə·rīz′] *v.* **ter·ror·ized, ter·ror·iz·ing** **1** To make very frightened; terrify. **2** To control or rule by threats and violence.

ter·ry [ter′ē] *n.* The loop of a pile fabric that has been left uncut.

terry cloth A thick, absorbent cotton cloth covered with small loops, used in making towels, bathrobes, and other items.

terse [tûrs] *adj.* **ters·er, ters·est** Short and to the point; concise. **—terse′ly** *adv.* **—terse′ness** *n.*

ter·tian [tûr′shən] **1** *adj.* Recurring every third day, or at 48-hour intervals: a *tertian* malarial attack. **2** *n.* A type of malaria in which severe symptoms recur about every 48 hours.

ter·ti·ar·y [tûr′shē·er′ē *or* tûr′shə·rē] *adj.* Of the third degree, rank, or class; third.

Ter·ti·ar·y [tûr′shē·er′ē] **1** *n.* The first geological period of the Cenozoic era, during which the world's principal mountain ranges were built up and mammals replaced reptiles as the dominant forms of life. **2** *adj.* Of the Tertiary.

test [test] **1** *n.* A trial, examination, or experiment to determine the nature, worth, or extent of something: a *test* of ore. **2** *n.* A series of questions or problems intended to measure something, as knowledge or skills. **3** *n.* A set of difficult conditions likened to a test; ordeal: Our new life was a severe *test.* **4** *v.* To subject (a person or thing) to a test. **5** *n.* A means of testing or judging; criterion. **6** *v.* To show certain properties or qualities when tested: The solution *tested* acid. **—test′er** *n.*

Test. Testament.

tes·ta·ment [tes′tə·mənt] *n.* **1** In law, one's will, used chiefly in the phrase **last will and testament.** **2** (*written* **Testament**) Either the Old Testament or the New Testament, but especially the New Testament.

tes·ta·men·ta·ry [tes′tə·men′tə·rē] *adj.* Of, having to do with, stated in, or given by a will.

tes·tate [tes′tāt′] *adj.* Having made a valid will.

tes·ta·tor [tes′tā·tər] *n.* Someone who makes a will or dies leaving a valid will.

test ban An international agreement not to test nuclear weapons, particularly in the atmosphere.

test-drive [test′drīv′] *v.* **test-drove** [test′drōv′], **test-driv·en** [test′driv′ən], **test-driv·ing** To try out (a motor vehicle) by driving it before buying it.

tes·tes [tes′tēz′] Plural of TESTIS.

tes·ti·cle [tes′ti·kəl] *n.* One of the two male sex glands in which the sperm is formed.

tes·ti·fy [tes′tə·fī] *v.* **tes·ti·fied, tes·ti·fy·ing** **1** To declare, especially under oath in a court. **2** To give evidence; bear witness: My eyes *testified* to my joy. **3** To give evidence of; indicate: The dog *testified* its distrust by a growl.

tes·ti·mo·ni·al [tes′tə·mō′nē·əl] *n.* **1** Something, as a letter or statement, praising or recommending a person or thing. **2** Something, as a token or statement, that gives praise or thanks; tribute.

tes·ti·mo·ny [tes′tə·mō′nē] *n., pl.* **tes·ti·mo·nies** **1** A declaration, especially before a court and under oath. **2** Evidence or proof. **3** An open statement of one's faith.

tes·tis [tes′tis] *n., pl.* **tes·tes** A gland in a male animal that produces reproductive cells.

test pilot A pilot who tests new aircraft designs by flying experimental models.

test tube A glass tube open at one end, and usually with a rounded bottom, used in making chemical tests.

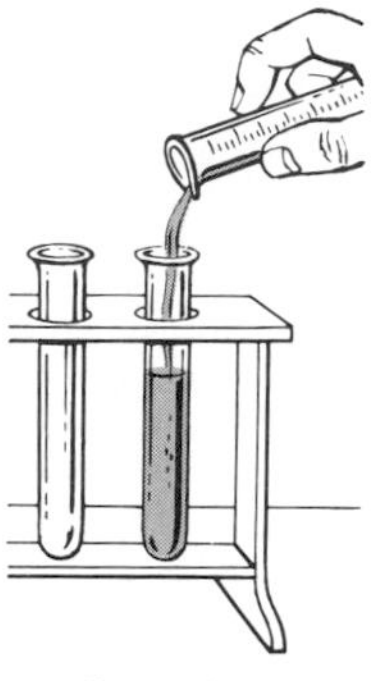

Test tubes

tes·ty [tes′tē] *adj.* **tes·ti·er, tes·ti·est** Easily made angry; touchy. **—tes′ti·ly** *adv.* **—tes′ti·ness** *n.*

Tet [tet] *n.* A three-day celebration of the Vietnamese New Year, beginning at the time of the first new moon after January 20.

tet·a·nus [tet′ə·nəs] *n.* A disease marked by stiffening and spasms of the muscles, especially of the neck and jaw, caused by a bacterium that enters the body through a wound.

tête-à-tête [tāt′ə·tāt′] **1** *n.* A private chat between two people. **2** *adj.* Private and confidential. **3** *adv.* Two together privately.

teth·er [teth′ər] **1** *n.* A rope or chain used to tie an animal so that it can range only so far. **2** *v.* To fasten or confine by a tether. **—at the end of one's tether** At the end of one's strength or resources.

tet·ra·he·dron [tet′rə·hē′drən] *n., pl.* **tet·ra·he·drons** or **tet·ra·he·dra** [tet′rə·hē′drə] *n.* A solid bounded by four triangular faces.

Teu·ton [t(y)o͞o′t(ə)n] *n.* **1** A member of an ancient German tribe. **2** A member of a group of northern European peoples, including the Dutch, the Scandinavians, and, especially, the Germans.

Teu·ton·ic [t(y)o͞o·ton′ik] *adj.* Of or having to do with the Germanic peoples of northern Europe, as the Germans, Dutch, and Swedes.

Tex. **1** Texan. **2** Texas.

text [tekst] *n.* **1** The main written or printed matter in a book or on a page, but not any notes, illustrations, or other material. **2** The original words of an author. **3** A quotation from the Bible, especially when used as the basis of a sermon. **4** A subject; topic. **5** A textbook.

text·book [tekst′bo͝ok′] *n.* A book used in the teaching of a subject, especially in a school.

tex·tile [teks′təl *or* teks′tīl′] **1** *n.* A woven fabric. **2** *adj.* Of or having to do with weaving or woven fabrics. **3** *adj.* Made by weaving.

tex·tu·al [teks′cho͞o·əl] *adj.* Having to do with, found in, or based on the text of a book.

a	add	**i**	it	**o͝o**	took	**oi**	oil
ā	ace	**ī**	ice	**o͞o**	pool	**ou**	pout
â	care	**o**	odd	**u**	up	**ng**	ring
ä	palm	**ō**	open	**û**	burn	**th**	thin
e	end	**ô**	order	**yo͞o**	fuse	**th**	this
ē	equal					**zh**	vision

ə = { a in *above* e in *sicken* i in *possible* o in *melon* u in *circus* }

T

tex·ture [teks′chər] *n.* 1 The arrangement of the threads of a woven fabric: Satin has a smooth *texture.* 2 The look or feel of the surface of any substance: the grainy *texture* of cement.

TGIF Thank God it's Friday.

-th A suffix used to form ordinal numbers: *tenth.* It is written *-eth* after vowels: *fortieth.*

Th The symbol for the element thorium.

Th. Thursday.

Thai [tī] 1 *adj.* Of or from Thailand. 2 *n.* A person born in or a citizen of Thailand. 3 *n.* The language of Thailand.

thal·a·mus [thal′ə·məs] *n., pl.* **thal·a·mi** [thal′ə·mī] An egg-shaped mass of nerve tissue in the central part of the brain under the cerebrum.

thal·li·um [thal′ē·əm] *n.* A soft, heavy metallic element that resembles lead. It is poisonous and suspected of causing cancer.

thal·lo·phyte [thal′ə·fīt′] *n.* Any of a group of primitive plants that do not have true roots, stems, or leaves, as fungi and algae.

thal·lus [thal′əs] *n., pl.* **thal·li** [thal′ī′] or **thal·lus·es** The plant body of a thallophyte, which lacks distinct leaves, roots, and stem.

than [t͟han *or* t͟hən] 1 *conj.* In comparison with: I am wiser *than* you. 2 *conj.* Except; but: no colors other *than* black and white. 3 *prep.* Compared to: a student *than* whom none was smarter. ◆ *Than* is sometimes confused with THEN. Always use *than* to make comparisons.

thane [thān] *n.* 1 In early England, a person who ranked above an ordinary freeman but below a noble. A thane held land of and performed military service for a lord or the monarch. 2 In early Scotland, a nobleman.

thank [thangk] *v.* 1 To express gratitude to; give thanks to. 2 To hold at fault; blame: You can *thank* yourself for this mess. **—thank you** I thank you; I am grateful to you.

thank·ful [thangk′fəl] *adj.* Feeling or expressing thanks; grateful. **—thank′ful·ly** *adv.* **—thank′ful·ness** *n.*

thank·less [thangk′lis] *adj.* 1 Not thankful; ungrateful. 2 Not likely to be appreciated: a *thankless* job. **—thank′less·ly** *adv.* **—thank′less·ness** *n.*

thanks [thangks] 1 *n.pl.* Gratitude or an expression of gratitude for something received, as a gift or favor. 2 *interj.* Thank you. **—thanks to** Because of; by virtue of.

thanks·giv·ing [thangks′giv′ing] *n.* 1 Expression of thanks, especially to God. 2 (*written* **Thanksgiving**) A holiday of thanksgiving in the U.S., usually held the fourth Thursday in November. It is more often called **Thanksgiving Day.**

that [t͟hat *or* t͟hət] *pron. & adj., pl.* **those** [t͟hōz], *adv., conj.* 1 *pron.* The person or thing mentioned or indicated: *That* is the one. 2 *adj.* Being the person or thing mentioned or indicated: *That* house is for sale. 3 *pron.* The person or thing indicated as different or farther away: Keep this, not *that.* 4 *adj.* Indicated as different or farther away: Do it this way, not *that* way. 5 *pron.* Who, whom, or which: I need a watch *that* runs. 6 *adv.* To that extent; so: You can't run *that* fast. 7 *conj. That* may be used to join a subordinate clause to its main clause. It can mean: **a** As a fact: I say *that* it is so. **b** As a result: I laughed so hard *that* I cried. **c** At which time; when: It was only yesterday *that* I saw them. **d** So that; in order that: I tell you *that* you may know. **e** Because: The teacher is angry *that* we are late. **f** I wish: O *that* we were there! ◆ Use *that* if the subordinate clause determines the meaning of the sentence: We live in a house *that* my father built. Use WHICH if the clause is a "side note": The house, *which* is painted white, has six rooms. **—in that** Because. ◆ See also THIS.

thatch [thach] 1 *n.* A covering of reeds, straw, or similar material, used on a roof. 2 *v.* To cover with or as with thatch. 3 *n.* Anything that resembles such a covering: a *thatch* of hair.

that'll [t͟hat′(ə)l] 1 That will. 2 That shall.

that's [t͟hats] That is.

thaw [thô] 1 *v.* To melt, as something frozen: Will the ice *thaw*?; The heat *thawed* the snow. 2 *v.* To get warm enough so that ice and snow will melt: It should *thaw* soon. 3 *n.* Weather that melts the snow of winter: a spring *thaw.* 4 *v.* To make or become less aloof or unfriendly. 5 *n.* The act of thawing. 6 *n.* A being thawed.

the [t͟hē *or* t͟hə] 1 *adj.* The definite article, used to modify nouns or noun phrases. It can mean: **a** That particular one or those particular ones here, mentioned, or understood: *the* house; *the* players. **b** That which is or those which are: *The* just will overcome *the* wicked. **c** Any one, and therefore all, of a kind, group, or species: *The* tiger is a fierce beast. **d** That well-known person, place, or thing: *the* Pope; *the* Statue of Liberty. **e** That particular one which is most outstanding: *the* game to see. **f** My, your, his, her, our, or their: a pat on *the* back; How is *the* family? 2 *adv.* By that much; by so much; to this extent: *the* more, *the* merrier.

the·a·ter or **the·a·tre** [thē′ə·tər] *n.* 1 A place built for the presentation of plays, films, and the like. 2 The arts and crafts involved in presenting plays. 3 A room arranged with rising rows of seats. 4 A place or area where something happens or is carried on: a *theater* of war.

the·at·ri·cal [thē·at′ri·kəl] 1 *adj.* Having to do with the theater or with dramatic performances. 2 *n.* (*pl.*) Dramatic performances, especially by amateurs. 3 *adj.* Suited to being presented on a stage: a *theatrical* novel. 4 *adj.* Artificial and dramatic: They dressed in a *theatrical* manner. 5 *n.* (*pl.*) Exaggerated actions or gestures, as if performed on stage. **—the·at·ri·cal·i·ty** [thē·at′ri·kal′ə·tē] *n.* **—the·at′ri·cal·ly** *adv.*

thee [t͟hē] *pron.* An old singular form of *you,* used as the object of a verb or preposition: seldom used today.

theft [theft] *n.* The act or crime of stealing.

their [t͟hâr] *pron.* A possessive form of *they*; belonging to them: *their* toys. ◆ Be careful when using the homophones *their,* THERE, and THEY'RE.

theirs [t͟hârz] *pron.* The one or ones belonging to or having to do with them: That house is *theirs.*

the·ism [thē′iz′əm] *n.* Belief in a god or gods. **—the′·ist** *n., adj.* **—the·is′tic** *adj.*

them [t͟hem *or* t͟həm] *pron.* The form of *they* used as the object of a verb or preposition: It belongs to *them*; Don't hurt *them*: ◆ *Them* is not an adjective. Use *these* or *those; these* things; *those* things.

the·mat·ic [thē·mat′ik] *adj.* Of or constituting a theme or themes. **—the·mat′i·cal·ly** *adv.*

theme [thēm] *n.* 1 A topic to be discussed in speech or writing. 2 A short composition, especially one written as a school assignment. 3 The subject in a piece of fiction or work of art. 4 The main melody of a piece of music. 5 A melody that identifies a radio or television program.

them·selves [t͟hem·selvz′ *or* t͟həm·selvz′] *pron.* 1 The ones that they really are; their very own selves. *Themselves* in this sense is used to refer back to the subject *they* or to make the *they* more emphatic: They helped *themselves*; They *themselves* did the work. 2 Their normal, healthy, usual, or proper condition: They weren't *themselves* then. ◆ Do not use *theirselves* in place of *themselves*. There is no such word as *theirselves*.

then [t͟hen] 1 *adv.* At that time: It was cold *then*. 2 *adj.* In or of that time: the *then* president. 3 *adv.* Soon or just afterward; next in space or time: You speak first; *then* it will be my turn. 4 *n.* The time mentioned or understood: I will be there by *then*. 5 *adv.* For that reason or by that means: If you succeed, *then* you'll be proud. 6 *adv.* In that case: If you won't do it, *then* I will. 7 *adv.* Also; besides: I like fruit, and *then* it's good for me. 8 *adv.* At another time: Now they're happy, *then* they're sad. **—then and there** At once; immediately.

thence [t͟hens] *adv.* 1 From that place. 2 From that time; after that time.

thence·forth [t͟hens′fôrth′] *adv.* From that time on; thereafter.

thence·for·ward [t͟hens′fôr′wərd] *adv.* 1 Thenceforth. 2 From that time or place forward.

the·oc·ra·cy [thē·ok′rə·sē] *n., pl.* **the·oc·ra·cies** 1 Government of a country by a group of people that claims a god as its ruler or by a church. 2 A country that is ruled in such a way.

the·o·crat·ic [thē′ə·krat′ik] *adj.* Having to do with or being a theocracy. **—the′o·crat′i·cal·ly** *adv.*

the·od·o·lite [thē·od′ə·līt′] *n.* An instrument used by surveyors to measure angles.

Theodolite

the·o·lo·gi·an [thē′ə·lō′jē·ən *or* thē′ə·lō′·jən] *n.* A person who is learned in theology.

the·o·log·i·cal [thē′ə·loj′i·kəl] *adj.* Of or having to do with theology. **—the′o·log′·i·cal·ly** *adv.*

the·ol·o·gy [thē·ol′ə·jē] *n., pl.* **the·ol·o·gies** 1 The study of God and religion. 2 A group of doctrines or beliefs set forth by a particular church or religious group.

the·o·rem [thē′ər·əm *or* thir′əm] *n.* 1 A proposition that can be proved or is taken to be true. 2 In mathematics, a proposition to be proved or one that has been proved or is taken to be true.

the·o·ret·ic [thē′ə·ret′ik] *adj.* Theoretical.

the·o·ret·i·cal [thē′ə·ret′i·kəl] *adj.* 1 Of, having to do with, or existing in theory. 2 Dealing best or easily with theory: a *theoretical* thinker. **—the′o·ret′i·cal·ly** *adv.*

the·o·re·ti·cian [thē′ər·ə·tish′ən] *n.* A theorist.

the·o·rist [thē′ər·ist] *n.* A person who theorizes.

the·o·rize [thē′ə·rīz′] *v.* **the·o·rized, the·o·riz·ing** To form or express a theory.

the·o·ry [thē′ə·rē *or* thir′ē] *n., pl.* **the·o·ries** 1 A set of principles suggested as an explanation of observed events, often supported or proved by its usefulness in making predictions: the *theory* of relativity. 2 The basic principles of a branch of science, mathematics, or the arts: the *theory* of numbers; the *theory* of music. 3 Knowledge, as distinguished from its practical use: In *theory*, you are correct. 4 An unsupported opinion.

ther·a·peu·tic [ther′ə·pyōō′tik] *adj.* 1 Having healing powers; curative. 2 Having to do with or used in the treatment of disease. **—ther′a·peu′ti·cal·ly** *adv.*

ther·a·peu·tics [ther′ə·pyōō′tiks] *n.pl.* The branch of medicine concerned with the treatment of disease. ◆ See -ICS.

ther·a·pist [ther′ə·pist] *n.* A person whose work is treating diseases and disabilities.

ther·a·py [ther′ə·pē] *n., pl.* **ther·a·pies** Treatment, as medication or exercise, meant to cure or correct diseases or disabilities.

there [t͟hâr] 1 *adv.* In, at, or about that place: Put it *there*. 2 *adv.* To, toward, or into that place: I'm going *there* now. 3 *adv.* At that stage or point of action or time: Begin *there*, please. 4 *n.* That place, stage, or point. 5 *adv.* In that matter: *There* I can't agree with you. 6 *interj.* An exclamation, as one of relief, triumph, or sympathy: *There*! It's over. ◆ *There* is used to introduce a verb, usually a form of the verb *be*, whose subject follows it: Once *there* were three bears; *There* ought to be a law. When used in this way, *there* is not stressed. However, when it is used to indicate place or time it receives a noticeable stress: Put the book *there*. The adverb *there* should never come before a noun, as in *that there house*. *That house there* is the proper order. *There* is used before a verb to point out or call attention to a thing: *There's* a good idea. *There* is also used to state general truths: *There's* no place like home.

there·a·bout [t͟hâr′ə·bout′] *adv.* Thereabouts.

there·a·bouts [t͟hâr′ə·bouts′] *adv.* Near that number, quantity, degree, place, or time.

there·af·ter [t͟hâr′af′tər] *adv.* After that time.

there·at [t͟hâr′at′] *adv.* 1 At that place; there. 2 At that time. ◆ This word is seldom used today.

there·by [t͟hâr′bī′ *or* t͟hâr′bī′] *adv.* 1 By means of that. 2 In connection with that.

there·for [t͟hâr′fôr′] *adv.* For this, that, it, or them: used mostly in legal documents.

there·fore [t͟hâr′fôr′] *adv., conj.* For this or that reason: I overslept; *therefore* I was late for work.

there·from [t͟hâr′frum′] *adv.* From that place; from there: used mostly in legal documents.

there·in [t͟hâr′in′] *adv.* 1 In that place or time. 2 In that matter or respect.

there·of [t͟hâr′uv′] *adv.* 1 Of it, them, or that. 2 From that source: seldom used today.

there·on [t͟hâr′on′] *adv.* Thereupon.

there's [t͟hârz] There is.

there·to [t͟hâr′tōō′] *adv.* 1 To that. 2 In addition; also. ◆ This word is seldom used today.

there·to·fore [t͟hâr′tə·fôr′] *adv.* Up to that time; before then: I had not seen it *theretofore*.

a	add	**i**	it	**ŏŏ**	took	**oi**	oil
ā	ace	**ī**	ice	**ōō**	pool	**ou**	pout
â	care	**o**	odd	**u**	up	**ng**	ring
ä	palm	**ō**	open	**û**	burn	**th**	thin
e	end	**ô**	order	**yōō**	fuse	**t͟h**	this
ē	equal					**zh**	vision

ə = a in *above* e in *sicken* i in *possible*
o in *melon* u in *circus*

T

there·un·der [thâr·un′dər] *adv.* Under that or it: Fill in the date and sign your name *thereunder.*
there·un·to [thâr′un·to͞o′] *adv.* Thereto.
there·up·on [thâr′ə·pon′] *adv.* 1 Upon this or that. 2 Just after, as a result of, or in response to that: I was insulted; *thereupon* I departed angrily.
there·with [thâr′with′ *or* thâr′with′] *adv.* 1 With this or that. 2 Immediately afterward. ◆ This word is seldom used today.
there·with·al [thâr′with·ôl′] *adv.* 1 With all this or that. 2 Besides. ◆ This word is seldom used today.
therm- or **thermo-** A combining form meaning: Heat, as in *thermostat.*
ther·mal [thûr′məl] 1 *adj.* Of, having to do with, using, or caused by heat. 2 *adj.* Hot or warm. 3 *n.* A rising current of warm air. **—ther′mal·ly** *adv.*
ther·mo·dy·nam·ic [thûr′mō·dī·nam′ik] *adj.* Of or having to do with thermodynamics. **—ther′mo·dy·nam′i·cal·ly** *adv.*
ther·mo·dy·nam·ics [thûr′mō·dī·nam′iks] *n.* The branch of physics dealing with heat and its relations to other forms of energy. ◆ See -ICS.
ther·mo·e·lec·tric [thûr′mō·i·lek′trik] *adj.* Of or having to do with electricity resulting from the action of heat.
ther·mo·e·lec·tric·i·ty [thûr′mō·i·lek′tris′ə·tē] *n.* Electricity resulting from the action of heat.
ther·mom·e·ter [thər·mom′ə·tər] *n.* An instrument for measuring temperature, often consisting of a sealed glass tube containing a liquid that rises or falls with changes of temperature. ◆ *Thermometer* comes from the Greek *thermo-*, meaning *heat* or *warmth*, and *meter*, a *measuring instrument.*

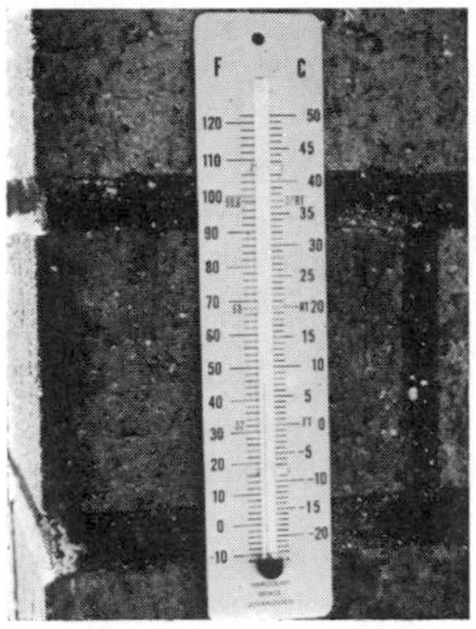
Thermometer

ther·mo·nu·cle·ar [thûr′mō·n(y)o͞o′klē·ər] *adj.* Of, related to, or using the fusion of atomic nuclei at high temperatures, as in stars or in a hydrogen bomb.
ther·mo·plas·tic [thûr′mə·plas′tik] 1 *adj.* Softening when heated and becoming hard again when cooled. 2 *n.* A thermoplastic substance.
Ther·mos bottle [thûr′məs] A bottle or jug for keeping liquids hot or cold by means of a vacuum surrounding an inner container: a trademark. Also written **thermos bottle.**
ther·mo·stat [thûr′mə·stat′] *n.* A device that automatically regulates temperature, as by turning a furnace on or off as required. ◆ *Thermostat* comes from *thermo-*, meaning *heat* or *warmth*, and another Greek word meaning *standing still.*
the·sau·rus [thə·sôr′əs] *n., pl.* **the·sau·ri** [thə·sôr′ī] or **the·sau·rus·es** A book that contains synonyms and antonyms arranged in categories.
these [thēz] *adj., pron.* Plural of THIS.
The·seus [thē′so͞os′ *or* thē′sē·əs] *n.* In Greek legends, a hero who killed the Minotaur.
the·sis [thē′sis] *n., pl.* **the·ses** [thē′sēz] 1 A proposition to be defended by argument. 2 A long, formal essay, as written by a candidate for a university degree.
thes·pi·an [thes′pē·ən] (*often written* **Thespian**) 1 *adj.* Of or having to do with the theater. 2 *n.* An actor or actress.
Thes·sa·lo·ni·ans [thes′ə·lō′nē·ənz] *n.pl.* (*used with singular verb*) Either of two books of the New Testament, each being of a letter from St. Paul to certain Christians in Greece.
the·ta [thā′tə *or* thē′tə] *n.* The eighth letter of the Greek alphabet.
The·tis [thē′tis] *n.* In Greek legends, a sea nymph who was the mother of Achilles.
thews [thyo͞oz] *n.pl.* 1 Muscles or sinews, especially strong ones. 2 Bodily strength; power.
they [thā] *pron.* 1 The plural of HE, SHE, or IT; the persons, things, or ideas understood or being talked about: The animals knew where *they* could find water; Our team knew what *they* had to do to win. 2 People in general: *They* say the climate here is nice.
they'd [thād] 1 They had. 2 They would.
they'll [thāl] They will.
they're [thâr] They are.
they've [thāv] They have.
T.H.I. temperature-humidity index.
thi·a·mine [thī′ə·mēn′ *or* thī′ə·min] *n.* A part of the vitamin B complex. It is necessary to human nutrition.
thick [thik] 1 *adj.* Having opposite surfaces rather far apart: a *thick* post. 2 *adj.* Measuring a certain amount between opposite surfaces: an inch *thick.* 3 *adj.* Built heavily: *thick* legs. 4 *adj.* Close together or having parts that are close together in space or time; dense: a *thick* forest; *thick* grass; a *thick* fog; a *thick* rain of blows. 5 *adv.* So as to be thick: Slice the bread *thick.* 6 *n.* The most crowded or thickest part: the *thick* of the battle. 7 *adj.* Dense and difficult to pour: *thick* oil. 8 *adj.* Hard to hear or understand; not distinct: a *thick* accent; a *thick* voice. 9 *adj.* Dull; stupid. 10 *adj. informal* Very friendly: Those two are *thick* as thieves. **—through thick and thin** Through both good times and difficult times. **—thick′ly** *adv.*
thick·en [thik′ən] *v.* 1 To make or become thick or thicker. 2 To make or become more complicated: The plot *thickens.*
thick·en·ing [thik′ə·ning] *n.* 1 A substance, as flour, added to a liquid to thicken it. 2 A thickened part or area.
thick·et [thik′it] *n.* A thick, dense growth, as of trees and bushes.
thick·head·ed [thik′hed′id] *adj.* Stupid.
thick·ness [thik′nis] *n.* 1 The condition or quality of being thick. 2 The measurement of a solid, other than its length or width. 3 A layer.
thick·set [thik′set′] *adj.* 1 Having a short, thick body; stout. 2 Set close together.
thick-skinned [thik′skind′] *adj.* 1 Having a thick skin. 2 Not bothered by insults or criticism.
thief [thēf] *n., pl.* **thieves** [thēvz] A person who steals, especially secretly and without using violence.
thieve [thēv] *v.* **thieved, thiev·ing** To steal.
thiev·er·y [thē′vər·ē] *n., pl.* **thiev·er·ies** The practice or act of thieving; theft.
thiev·ish [thē′vish] *adj.* 1 Of or like a thief. 2 Tending to steal.
thigh [thī] *n.* The part of the leg between the hip and the knee.
thigh·bone [thī′bōn′] *n.* Another word for FEMUR.
thim·ble [thim′bəl] *n.* A cap of metal, plastic, or other material, worn to protect the end of the finger that pushes the needle in sewing.
thin [thin] *adj.* **thin·ner, thin·nest,** *adv., v.* **thinned,**

thin·ning 1 *adj.* Having opposite surfaces rather close together: *thin* walls. 2 *adj.* Few and scattered or having parts or members that are few and scattered; not dense; sparse: a *thin* hedge; *thin* grass; a *thin* drizzle. 3 *adj.* Lacking in body, substance, richness, or force: a *thin* voice; *thin* blood; a *thin* excuse. 4 *adv.* So as to be thin: butter spread *thin.* 5 *adj.* Not fat or plump; lean; slender. 6 *adj.* Having a light texture and easy to pour; watery. 7 *v.* To make or become thin or thinner. **—thin'ly** *adv.* **—thin'ness** *n.*

thine [t͟hīn] *pron.* 1 The possessive case of THOU; an old singular form of YOURS. 2 A form of THY used before a word beginning with a vowel sound.

thing [thing] *n.* 1 An object, event, creature, act, or idea, thought of as separate from all others: A rose is a beautiful *thing*; What a nice *thing* to do. 2 A person or animal: used to show a feeling, as pity, affection, or contempt: "Oh, you poor *thing*!" 3 *(pl.)* Conditions; circumstances: *Things* have changed. 4 *(pl.)* Clothing; belongings: "Get your *things*." 5 A proper or fashionable act or manner of dress: used with *the*: Wearing bulky sweaters was *the thing* last year. ◆ *Thing* is a useful word because it can refer to almost any object, idea, or action. But avoid overworking *thing,* and choose a more specific word wherever possible.

think [thingk] *v.* **thought** [thôt], **think·ing** 1 To use the mind; have thoughts or ideas; reason: I want to *think* before I make a decision. 2 To have in the mind: *Think* happy thoughts. 3 To examine or solve in the mind. 4 To decide: *Think* what you ought to say about it. 5 To have a particular opinion or idea; believe; imagine: I *think* that you are right. 6 To regard or consider as being: I *think* the soup salty. 7 To plan or intend: I had *thought* to go today. 8 To expect: We had *thought* to see them here. 9 To remember: I never *thought* to leave the phone number. **—think about** To consider; ponder. **—think better of** 1 To decide against; reconsider: We *though better of* that plan. 2 To form a better opinion of. **think nothing of** To consider unimportant or easy to do. **—think of** 1 To bring to mind; recall. 2 To invent in the mind; imagine. 3 To have an opinion or attitude toward; regard. 4 To be considerate of: *Think of* our feelings. 5 To have concern: He *thinks* only *of* himself. **—think out** To work out, devise, or invent by thinking. **—think over** To ponder; consider. **—think twice** To consider carefully: I would *think twice* before leaving school. **—think up** To arrive at or invent by thinking. **—think'er** *n.*

think·a·ble [thing'kə·bəl] *adj.* 1 Capable of being thought about; comprehensible. 2 Possible; conceivable. **—think'a·ble·ness** *n.* **—think'a·bly** *adv.*

thin·ner [thin'ər] *n.* A liquid mixed with paint or varnish to make it easier to pour and brush on.

thin-skinned [thin'skind'] *adj.* 1 Having a thin skin. 2 Easily hurt or insulted; touchy.

third or **3rd** [thûrd] 1 *adj.* Next after the second. 2 *n.* The third one. 3 *adj.* Being one of three equal parts. 4 *n.* A third part. 5 *adv.* In the third order, rank, or place.

third-class [thûrd'klas'] 1 *adj.* Ranking next below second class. 2 *adv.* By or in third-class accommodations or mail.

third class The class of travel accommodations or mail that is next below second class.

third degree Harsh or brutal questioning by the police to make a prisoner confess.

third-de·gree burn [thûrd'di·grē'] A severe burn that destroys the outer layer of the skin and exposes nerve endings.

third·ly [thûrd'lē] *adv.* In the third place.

third person That form of a pronoun or verb used in referring to the person or thing spoken of. *He, she, it,* and *they* are in the third person.

third world or **Third World** 1 The poorer, economically undeveloped countries. 2 The minority groups within a country.

thirst [thûrst] 1 *n.* An uneasy feeling of dryness in the mouth and throat caused by a need to drink. 2 *n.* A bodily need for water. 3 *v.* To feel thirst. 4 *n.* A great longing or desire: a *thirst* for excitement. 5 *v.* To desire; long; yearn.

thirst·y [thûrs'tē] *adj.* **thirst·i·er, thirst·i·est** 1 Having or feeling thirst. 2 Very dry; parched: a *thirsty* garden. **—thirst'i·ly** *adv.* **—thirst'i·ness** *n.*

thir·teen or **13** [thûr'tēn'] *n., adj.* One more than twelve.

thir·teenth or **13th** [thûr'tēnth'] 1 *adj.* Next after the twelfth. 2 *n.* The thirteenth one. 3 *adj.* Being one of thirteen equal parts. 4 *n.* A thirteenth part.

thir·ti·eth or **30th** [thûr'tē·ith] 1 *adj.* Tenth in order after the twentieth. 2 *n.* The thirtieth one. 3 *adj.* Being one of thirty equal parts. 4 *n.* A thirtieth part.

thir·ty or **30** [thûr'tē] *n., pl.* **thir·ties** or **30's** 1 *n., adj.* Ten more than twenty. 2 *n.* *(pl.)* The years between the age of 30 and the age of 40.

thir·ty-sec·ond note [thûr'tē·sek'ənd] A musical note having a time value that is 1/32 of a whole note.

this [t͟his] *pron. & adj., pl.* **these** [t͟hēz], *adv.* 1 *pron.* The person or thing mentioned, indicated, or understood: *This* is the place I told you about. 2 *adj.* Being the person or thing mentioned, indicated, or understood: *This* house is for sale. 3 *pron.* The person or thing indicated as nearer than or in contrast with someone or something else: Keep *this,* not that. 4 *adj.* Being the one that is nearer or in contrast: Do it *this* way, not that way. 5 *pron.* The fact, idea, or statement about to be made clear: Listen to *this*! 6 *pron.* The present time: We should have returned before *this.* 7 *adv.* To this extent or degree: I didn't know things were *this* bad. ◆ *This* and *that* are often very similar in meaning. For instance, one could as well point something out by saying "Look at *this,*" as by saying "Look at *that.*" When they are used together, however, *this* refers to the thing closer in time or space, and *that* refers to the thing farther away. ◆ Avoid the nonstandard expressions *this here, that there, these here,* and *those there.*

this·tle [this'əl] *n.* A plant with prickly leaves, having flowers of purple or white.

a	add	**i**	it	**o͝o**	took	**oi**	oil
ā	ace	**ī**	ice	**o͞o**	pool	**ou**	pout
â	care	**o**	odd	**u**	up	**ng**	ring
ä	palm	**ō**	open	**û**	burn	**th**	thin
e	end	**ô**	order	**yo͞o**	fuse	**t͟h**	this
ē	equal					**zh**	vision

ə = a in *above* e in *sicken* i in *possible* / o in *melon* u in *circus*

T

this·tle·down [this′əl·doun′] *n.* The silky fluff from the dry, ripe flower of a thistle.
thith·er [thith′ər *or* thith′ər] *adv.* To or toward that place; in that direction.
tho [thō] *conj., adv.* Another spelling of THOUGH.
thole [thōl] *n.* A peg, usually one of four set closely together in pairs on each side of a boat, used to hold an oar in rowing. It is often called a **thole pin.**
Thom·as [tom′əs] *n.* In the Bible, an Apostle who at first doubted the resurrection of Jesus.
thong [thông] *n.* A narrow strip of leather, used as a whiplash or more often for tying or fastening.
Thor [thôr] *n.* In Norse myths, the god of war, thunder, and strength.
tho·rac·ic [thô·ras′ik] *adj.* Of, having to do with, or near the thorax.
tho·rax [thôr′aks] *n.* **1** The part of the body between the neck and the abdomen, enclosed by the ribs; chest. **2** The middle region of the body of an insect.

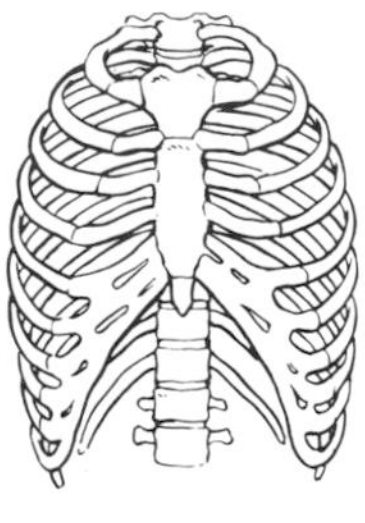
Thorax

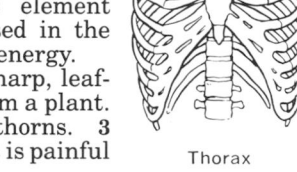

tho·ri·um [thôr′ē·əm] *n.* A gray, radioactive, metallic element that is sometimes used in the generation of atomic energy.
thorn [thôrn] *n.* **1** A sharp, leafless spine growing from a plant. **2** A plant that bears thorns. **3** A person or thing that is painful or annoying.
thorn·y [thôr′nē] *adj.* **thorn·i·er, thorn·i·est** **1** Full of thorns. **2** Sharp, as a thorn. **3** Causing trouble or annoyance.
thor·ough [thûr′ō] *adj.* **1** Complete and detailed in every respect: a *thorough* investigation. **2** Painstaking and careful: a *thorough* worker. **3** Utter; absolute; outright: a *thorough* idiot. **—thor′ough·ly** *adv.* **—thor′ough·ness** *n.*
thor·ough·bred [thûr′ō·bred′] **1** *adj.* Bred from pure stock, as an animal. **2** *n.* (*written* **Thoroughbred**) A distinct breed of racing or jumping horse, originally bred in England from three famous sires. **3** *n.* A thoroughbred animal. **4** *n.* A person of culture and breeding.
thor·ough·fare [thûr′ō·fâr′] *n.* **1** A roadway open to the public. **2** A highway.
thor·ough·go·ing [thûr′ə·gō′ing] *adj.* Thorough: a *thoroughgoing* search.
those [thōz] *adj., pron.* Plural of THAT: Whose are *those* books? *Those* are mine.
thou [thou] *pron.* An old singular form of YOU, used as the subject of a verb: seldom used today.
though [thō] **1** *conj.* Despite the fact that: *Though* it's hot, it's nice here. **2** *conj.* And yet; still; however: It's difficult, *though* not impossible. **3** *conj.* Even if: *Though* I could tell the secret, I would not. **4** *adv.* Nevertheless; however: I've never been skiing; I'd like to try it, *though.* **—as though** As if. ◆ *Though* is less formal than *although.*
thought[1] [thôt] *n.* **1** The act or process of using the mind; thinking. **2** The result of thinking; idea or judgment. **3** A way of thinking, as of a particular people or period: modern *thought.* **4** Consideration or attention: Give it some *thought.* **5** Intention or expectation: We gave up all *thought* of going. **6** A bit; small amount: Go a *thought* slower.
thought[2] [thôt] Past tense and past participle of THINK.
thought·ful [thôt′fəl] *adj.* **1** Full of or occupied with thought. **2** Showing or causing thought: a *thoughtful* book. **3** Considerate; attentive: a *thoughtful* gift. **—thought′ful·ly** *adv.* **—thought′ful·ness** *n.*
thought·less [thôt′lis] *adj.* **1** Without thought; careless. **2** Inconsiderate of others. **—thought′less·ly** *adv.* **—thought′less·ness** *n.*
thou·sand or **1000** [thou′zənd] *n., adj.* Ten times one hundred.
thou·sandth or **1000th** [thou′zəndth] **1** *adj.* Hundredth in order after the nine hundredth. **2** *n.* The thousandth one. **3** *adj.* Being one of a thousand equal parts. **4** *n.* A thousandth equal part.
Thra·cian [thrā′shən] **1** *n.* An inhabitant of Thrace. **2** *adj.* Of Thrace or its people.
thral·dom [thrôl′dəm] *n.* Another spelling of THRALLDOM.
thrall [thrôl] *n.* **1** Slavery or subjection; bondage. **2** Someone in this condition; slave.
thrall·dom [thrôl′dəm] *n.* Slavery; bondage.
thrash [thrash] *v.* **1** To beat with or as with something that is swung violently; whip. **2** To defeat soundly: The team *thrashed* its opponents. **3** To make or cause to make violent swinging or twisting movements: The fish *thrashed* about in the net. **4** To thresh (grain). **—thrash out** To settle by thorough discussion: to *thrash out* a problem in conference. **—thrash′er** *n.*
thrash·er [thrash′ər] *n.* An American songbird resembling a thrush and having a long tail.
thrash·ing [thrash′ing] *n.* A severe beating.
thread [thred] **1** *n.* A thin cord made of several strands of cotton, nylon, or other material, twisted together. **2** *v.* To pass a thread through the eye of (a needle). **3** *v.* To arrange or string on a thread: to *thread* beads. **4** *n.* Anything resembling a thread, as a fine strand or a thin beam of light. **5** *n.* The spiral groove cut into a screw or nut. **6** *v.* To cut such a thread on or in: to *thread* a hole. **7** *v.* To make (one's way) with care, as through a crowd. **8** *v.* To make one's way through: to *thread* a maze. **9** *n.* Something, as a series of events or a train of thought, that continues or runs through something else: the many *threads* of violence in the novel. **—thread′er** *n.*
thread·bare [thred′bâr′] *adj.* **1** So badly worn that the threads show, as a rug or garment. **2** Wearing threadbare clothing: a clean but *threadbare* person. **3** Commonplace or worn out; stale: *threadbare* humor.
thread·y [thred′ē] *adj.* **thread·i·er, thread·i·est** **1** Of or resembling a thread or threads; stringy. **2** Thin or weak: a *thready* pulse. **—thread′i·ness** *n.*
threat [thret] *n.* **1** A warning or a promise that one intends to hurt or punish another person or thing. **2** A sign or indication of something bad or unfavorable to come: a *threat* of rain.
threat·en [thret′(ə)n] *v.* **1** To make or utter a threat: My parents *threatened* to punish me if I did not behave. **2** To make a threat against: to *threaten* one's life. **3** To put in danger; menace: Fire *threatened* the hut. **4** To give a warning or sign of: The smoking volcano *threatened* another eruption.
three or **3** [thrē] *n., adj.* One more than two.
3-D three-dimensional.
three-di·men·sion·al [thrē′di·men′shən·əl] *adj.* **1** Having three dimensions, especially those of length, width, and depth. **2** Giving an illusion of

depth: A stereoscope creates a *three-dimensional* image of a picture.

three·fold [thrē′fōld′] 1 *adj.* Three times as great or as many: a *threefold* amount. 2 *adv.* So as to be three times as great or as many: to increase *threefold.* 3 *adj.* Made up of or having three parts: a *threefold* accusation.

three·score [thrē′skôr′] *n., adj.* Sixty.

three·some [thrē′səm] *n.* A group of three persons.

Three Wise Men Another name for the MAGI.

thren·o·dy [thren′ə·dē] *n., pl.* **thren·o·dies** An ode or song of sorrow for the dead; dirge.

thresh [thresh] *v.* 1 To beat or shake (ripened grain) to separate the seeds from the straw and husks. 2 To move or thrash about. **—thresh out** To thrash out.

thresh·er [thresh′ər] *n.* 1 A person or thing that threshes, especially a large machine for threshing. 2 A large shark of warm seas.

threshing machine A machine used on farms for separating grains or seeds from chaff.

thresh·old [thresh′(h)ōld′] *n.* 1 The bar of wood, stone, or other material, placed under a door. 2 The entrance or beginning of anything.

threw [thro͞o] Past tense of THROW.

thrice [thrīs] *adv.* Three times.

thrift [thrift] *n.* Care and economy in handling expenses; habit of saving.

thrift·less [thrift′lis] *adj.* Lacking thrift; wasteful. **—thrift′less·ly** *adv.* **—thrift′less·ness** *n.*

thrift shop A shop selling secondhand goods, often for a charity.

thrift·y [thrif′tē] *adj.* **thrift·i·er, thrift·i·est** 1 Careful about expenses; economical: a *thrifty* housekeeper. 2 Growing vigorously, as a plant. **—thrift′i·ly** *adv.* **—thrift′i·ness** *n.*

thrill [thril] 1 *v.* To feel or cause to feel great or tingling emotion or excitement. 2 *n.* A feeling of great excitement. 3 *n.* Something that causes such a feeling. 4 *v.* To vibrate or tremble. **—thrill′·ing·ly** *adv.*

thrill·er [thril′ər] *n.* A person or thing that thrills, especially a story, movie, or play that is full of suspense and excitement.

thrive [thrīv] *v.* **thrived** or **throve, thrived** or **thriv·en** [thriv′ən], **thriv·ing** 1 To prosper or be successful. 2 To grow vigorously; flourish.

thro′ or **thro** [thro͞o] *prep., adv., adj.* Other spellings of THROUGH.

throat [thrōt] *n.* 1 The upper part of the passage leading from the back of the mouth to the stomach and lungs. 2 The front part of the neck under the chin. 3 The voice. 4 Any narrow part or entrance: the *throat* of a vase. **—a lump in the throat** A difficulty in swallowing, usually due to a feeling, as when one tries not to cry.

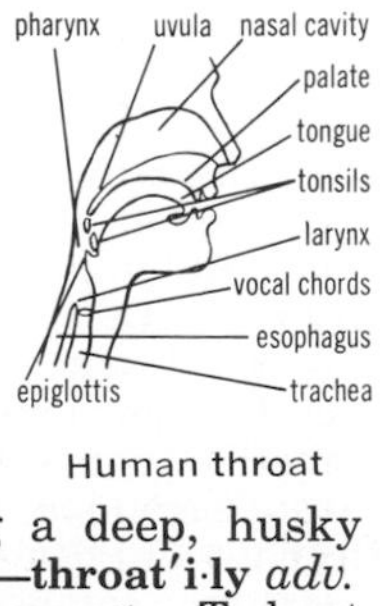

Human throat

throat·y [thrō′tē] *adj.* **throat·i·er, throat·i·est** Having or producing a deep, husky sound; guttural: a *throaty* voice. **—throat′i·ly** *adv.*

throb [throb] *v.* **throbbed, throb·bing,** *n.* 1 *v.* To beat or pulsate, especially rapidly or violently, as the heart from excitement. 2 *n.* A quick or strong beat or pulsation.

throe [thrō] *n.* 1 (*often pl.*) A violent pang or pain. 2 (*pl.*) A difficult struggle or ordeal: a country in the *throes* of civil war.

throm·bo·sis [throm·bō′sis] *n.* The formation or presence of a clot that blocks a blood vessel.

throne [thrōn] *n.* 1 The raised, often ornamented seat used by a monarch or high church official on important occasions. 2 The office or power of a monarch: to renounce a *throne.*

throng [throng] 1 *n.* A great crowd; multitude. 2 *v.* To move in or form a crowd. 3 *v.* To crowd into or around: The students *thronged* the street.

throt·tle [throt′(ə)l] *n., v.* **throt·tled, throt·tling** 1 *n.* A valve controlling the supply of steam to a steam engine or of fuel and air to an internal-combustion engine. 2 *n.* The lever or pedal that operates this valve. 3 *v.* To reduce or stop the flow of steam or fuel to (an engine). 4 *v.* To slow (an engine) in this way. 5 *v.* To strangle or choke. 6 *v.* To suppress; stop: to *throttle* objections.

through [thro͞o] 1 *prep., adv.* Into one side, end, or point, and out the other: The ball went *through* the window; The needle went right *through.* 2 *prep.* From one place to another or to all parts of: to ride *through* the streets; Odors spread *through* the house. 3 *adj.* Making few or no stops along its route: a *through* bus. 4 *adj.* Open; clear: a *through* route. 5 *prep.* During the whole time of: The students worked *through* the summer. 6 *adv.* To success or conclusion: to see something *through.* 7 *adj.* Finished; done: We're *through* for the day. 8 *prep.* To or at the end of: I'm *through* that ordeal. 9 *prep.* By way of: The dog left *through* the window. 10 *prep.* By means of, with the help of, or on account of: They succeeded *through* effort; I got the job *through* a friend. 11 *adv.* Completely; thoroughly: to be soaked *through.* ◆ *Through* goes back to the Old English word *thurh.* Eventually the [r] came to be pronounced before the vowel rather than after it.

through·out [thro͞o·out′] *adv., prep.* All through; all about: to search a house *throughout*; to travel *throughout* the nation.

through·way [thro͞o′wā′] *n.* Another spelling of THRUWAY.

throve [thrōv] A past tense of THRIVE.

throw [thrō] *v.* **threw, thrown, throw·ing,** *n.* 1 *v.* To cause to fly through the air by or as by a rapid motion of the arm; fling; hurl; toss. 2 *v.* To make or do by throwing: to *throw* a pitch. 3 *n.* An act of throwing. 4 *n.* The distance a thing is thrown. 5 *v.* To direct or cast: to *throw* a beam of light. 6 *v.* To cause to fall: The horse *threw* its rider. 7 *v.* To defeat in wrestling. 8 *v.* To put on or off carelessly: to *throw* on a coat. 9 *v.* To bring or put into a place or condition, often suddenly or violently: It *threw* us into panic; *Throw* water on the fire. 10 *v.* To connect or disconnect (as a switch, clutch, or motor) by moving a lever or other control. 11 *v. informal* To lose deliberately, as a game or prizefight. 12 A shawl or light blanket.

T

a	add	**i**	it	**o͝o**	took	**oi**	oil
ā	ace	**ī**	ice	**o͞o**	pool	**ou**	pout
â	care	**o**	odd	**u**	up	**ng**	ring
ä	palm	**ō**	open	**û**	burn	**th**	thin
e	end	**ô**	order	**yo͞o**	fuse	**th**	this
ē	equal					**zh**	vision

ə = {a in *above* e in *sicken* i in *possible* / o in *melon* u in *circus*}

—**throw away** 1 To cast off; discard. 2 To waste; squander. —**throw in** To add at no cost, often as an inducement to buy. —**throw off** 1 To rid oneself of; cast away. 2 To give off; emit. —**throw out** 1 To throw away; discard. 2 To offer casually: to *throw out* suggestions. 3 In baseball, to assist in putting out (a runner) by throwing the ball to a teammate who makes the play. —**throw over** 1 To overturn. 2 To discard. 3 To abandon or jilt. —**throw up** 1 To vomit. 2 To give up; release. 3 To build hurriedly. —**throw′er** *n.*

throw·back [thrō′bak′] *n.* 1 A return or reversion to some ancestral type or character. 2 An example of such reversion: a *throwback* to some Viking ancestor.

thrown [thrōn] Past participle of THROW.

throw rug Another term for SCATTER RUG.

thru [thro͞o] *prep., adv., adj.* Another spelling of THROUGH.

thrum [thrum] *v.* **thrummed, thrum·ming,** *n.* 1 *v.* To pluck on, as a guitar, especially idly. 2 *v.* To drum or tap idly with the fingers. 3 *n.* A monotonous drumming sound.

thrush [thrush] *n.* Any of a large group of songbirds, as the robin or bluebird.

Thrush

thrust [thrust] *v.* **thrust, thrust·ing,** *n.* 1 *v.* To push or shove with force or on sudden impulse: The child *thrust* the bouquet into my arms; to *thrust* someone aside roughly. 2 *n.* A sudden, forceful push or shove. 3 *v.* To stab or run through. 4 *v.* To force one's way, as into a crowd. 5 *n.* A propelling force, as produced by an airplane propeller, jet engine, or rocket.

thru·way [thro͞o′wā′] *n* A large superhighway.

thud [thud] *n., v.* **thud·ded, thud·ding** 1 *n.* A deep, dull sound, as of a heavy weight striking the floor. 2 *v.* To hit or fall on something with a thud.

thug [thug] *n.* A violent or brutal gangster or hoodlum.

thu·li·um [tho͞o′lē·əm] *n.* A metallic element occurring in rare earths. ◆ See RARE-EARTH ELEMENT.

thumb [thum] 1 *n.* The short, thick finger nearest the wrist. 2 *n.* The part of a glove or mitten that covers the thumb. 3 *v.* To handle, press, rub, or soil with the thumb: to *thumb* the pages of a book. 4 *v. informal* To ask for (a ride) by signaling with the thumb. —**thumbs down** *informal* No: a phrase or sign indicating disapproval or rejection. —**under the thumb of** Under the control or influence of.

thumb index A series of notches in the outer edges of the leaves of a book, making it easier to open at a desired section.

thumb·nail [thum′nāl′] 1 *n.* The nail of the thumb. 2 *adj.* Brief but giving important details: Write a *thumbnail* sketch of your life.

thumb·screw [thum′skro͞o′] *n.* 1 A screw made to be turned by the thumb and forefinger. 2 An instrument of torture for compressing thumbs.

thumb·tack [thum′tak′] *n.* A tack with a flat, broad head, easily pushed in by the thumb.

thump [thump] 1 *n.* A blow made with a blunt or heavy object. 2 *n.* The dull, heavy sound of a thump. 3 *v.* To beat or hit in such a way as to produce the sound of a thump. 4 *v.* To make a sound like a thump; pound; throb.

thun·der [thun′dər] 1 *n.* The sound that accompanies lightning, caused by the sudden heating and expansion of the air along the path of the electrical discharge. 2 *n.* Any loud, rumbling noise. 3 *v.* To make or give forth thunder or a sound like it. 4 *v.* To speak or express with a thundering sound: to *thunder* a warning.

thun·der·bolt [thun′dər·bōlt′] *n.* 1 A flash of lightning together with a clap of thunder. 2 Something very shocking and sudden.

thun·der·clap [thun′dər·klap′] *n.* 1 A loud crash of thunder. 2 Something sudden or violent.

thun·der·cloud [thun′dər·kloud′] *n.* A dark, heavy cloud highly charged with electricity.

thun·der·head [thun′dər·hed′] *n.* A rounded mass of cumulus cloud that often develops into a thundercloud.

thun·der·ing [thun′dər·ing] *adj.* 1 Of, related to, like, or accompanied by thunder. 2 *informal* Unusually great, large, or extreme.

thun·der·ous [thun′dər·əs] *adj.* Of or like thunder. —**thun′der·ous·ly** *adv.*

thun·der·show·er [thun′dər·shou′ər] *n.* A rain shower with thunder and lightning.

thun·der·storm [thun′dər·stôrm′] *n.* A storm with thunder and lightning.

thun·der·struck [thun′dər·struk′] *adj.* Amazed, astonished, shocked, or puzzled, as with fear or surprise: We were *thunderstruck* when the team lost.

Thur. or **Thurs.** Thursday.

Thurs·day [thûrz′dē *or* thûrz′dā′] *n.* The fifth day of the week.

thus [t͟hus] *adv.* 1 In this, that, or the following way: Do it *thus.* 2 To such a degree; so: *Thus* far your work seems to be improving. 3 Therefore; hence: *Thus* we knew they had arrived. ◆ Avoid the use of the term *thusly. Thus* is already an adverb; there's no reason to add *-ly* to it.

thwack [thwak] 1 *v.* To strike with something flat; whack. 2 *n.* A blow with something flat.

thwart [thwôrt] 1 *v.* To keep from doing or succeeding; foil; balk: Alert guards *thwarted* the prisoner's attempt to escape. 2 *adj.* Lying, moving, or extending across; transverse. 3 *n.* A seat extending across a boat for an oarsman. 4 *n.* A crosswise brace in a canoe.

thy [t͟hī] *adj.* An old singular form of YOUR: seldom used today.

thyme [tīm] *n.* A small plant related to mint, with fragrant leaves used as a seasoning.

thy·mus [thī′məs] *n.* A small glandular organ in the upper part of the chest, thought to help in immunizing the body against certain diseases.

thy·roid [thī′roid′] 1 *n.* A large gland situated in front of and on each side of the windpipe. It secretes hormones that regulate body growth and metabolism. 2 *adj.* Of or from the thyroid: a *thyroid* hormone.

thyroid cartilage The most prominent part of the larynx, composed of two sections of cartilage united in front to form the Adam's apple.

thyroid gland The thyroid.

thy·rox·ine or **thy·rox·in** [thī·rok′sēn′ *or* thī·rok′·sin] *n.* A thyroid hormone containing iodine.

thy·self [t͟hī·self′] *pron.* An old singular form of YOURSELF: seldom used today.

ti [tē] *n.* In music, a syllable used to represent the seventh tone of a major scale or the second tone of a minor scale, or in a fixed system the tone B.
Ti The symbol for the element titanium.
ti·ar·a [tē·âr'ə *or* tē·är'ə] *n.* **1** A semicircular band of jewels or flowers worn on the head on formal occasions. **2** The Pope's triple crown, worn on certain special occasions.
Ti·bet·an [ti·bet'ən] **1** *adj.* Of or from Tibet. **2** *n.* A person born or living in Tibet. **3** *n.* The language of Tibet.
tib·i·a [tib'ē·ə] *n., pl.* **tib·i·ae** [tib'ē·ē'] or **tib·i·as** The larger of the two bones that extend from the knee to the ankle; shinbone.

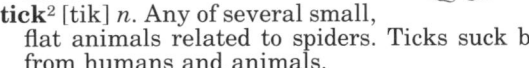

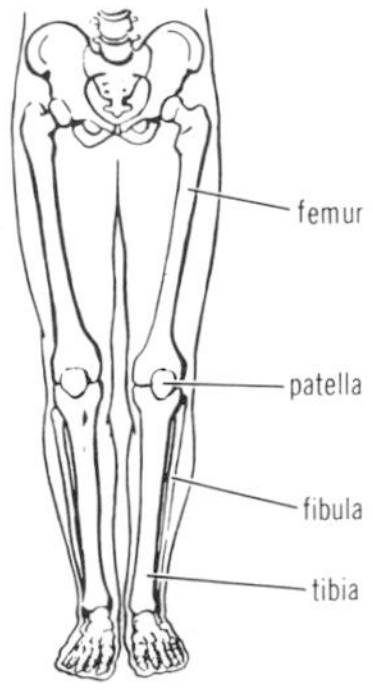

tic [tik] *n.* An involuntary twitch of a muscle, especially in the face.
tick[1] [tik] **1** *n.* A light sound, as that made by a watch, clock, or other mechanism. **2** *v.* To make a tick. **3** *v.* To indicate by ticking: to *tick* off seconds. **4** *n.* A mark, as a check or dash, used to check off items. **5** *v.* To mark with ticks: to *tick* off items.
tick[2] [tik] *n.* Any of several small, flat animals related to spiders. Ticks suck blood from humans and animals.
tick[3] [tik] *n.* The outer covering of a mattress or pillow, usually made of strong cloth.
tick·er [tik'ər] *n.* **1** An instrument that receives and prints stock prices, news, and other information on a tape. **2** *slang* The heart.
ticker tape The paper tape on which a ticker records stock prices.
tick·et [tik'it] **1** *n.* A card or slip which entitles the holder to certain privileges, as riding on a bus or train or entering a theater. **2** *n.* A label or tag: This *ticket* on the sweater gives its price, color, and size. **3** *v.* To put a ticket on; label. **4** *n.* A legal summons to appear in court, as for a traffic violation. **5** *n.* A list of candidates for nomination or election, supported by a party or group; slate.
tick·ing [tik'ing] *n.* A strong cotton or linen fabric, as that used for ticks and awnings.
tick·le [tik'əl] *v.* **tick·led, tick·ling,** *n.* **1** *v.* To touch or scratch so as to cause a laugh or twitch: The feathers *tickled* me. **2** *v.* To have such a sensation: My foot *tickles.* **3** *n.* The act of tickling. **4** *n.* The feeling produced by tickling. **5** *v. informal* To delight: I'm *tickled* to be going.
tick·lish [tik'lish] *adj.* **1** Sensitive to tickling. **2** Liable to be upset or easily offended: They are *ticklish* about their mistake. **3** Difficult; delicate: a *ticklish* situation.
tick·tack·toe or **tic-tac-toe** [tik'tak'tō'] *n.* A game in which two players taking turns each try to fill in a row of three X's or three O's in a grid formed by two intersecting double lines.
tid·al [tīd'(ə)l] *adj.* Of, having to do with, or caused by the tides: a *tidal* pool.
tidal wave **1** A high tide made higher by strong winds. **2** Another word for TSUNAMI. **3** A great surge: a *tidal wave* of support for the candidate.
tid·bit [tid'bit'] *n.* A choice bit, as of food or gossip.
tid·dle·dy·winks [tid'(ə)l·(d)ē·wingks'] *n.pl.* (*used with singular verb*) A game in which players try to flip small disks from a flat surface into a cup by pressing the edge of one disk with another disk.
tid·dly·winks [tid'lē·wingks'] *n.pl.* (*used with singular verb*) Another spelling of TIDDLEDYWINKS.
tide [tīd] *n., v.* **tid·ed, tid·ing** **1** *n.* The periodic rise and fall of the surface of an ocean or of waters connected with an ocean, caused by the attraction of the sun and moon. The tide rises and falls twice daily, or about every 12 hours. **2** *n.* Anything that rises and falls like the tide: the *tide* of our fortunes. **3** *n.* A tendency, current, or drift: the *tide* of events. **4** *v.* To give necessary help to: This money will *tide* you over until tomorrow. **—turn the tide** To change the course or outcome: One battle can *turn the tide* of a war.
tide·land [tīd'land'] *n.* Land covered and uncovered by the rise and fall of the tide.
tide·wa·ter [tīd'wô'tər] *n.* **1** Water influenced by the tide. **2** Any area, such as a seacoast, having such water. **3** *adj. use*: *tidewater* country.
ti·dings [tī'dingz] *n.pl.* Information; news.
ti·dy [tī'dē] *adj.* **ti·di·er, ti·di·est,** *v.* **ti·died, ti·dy·ing** **1** *adj.* Neat and orderly: a *tidy* desk. **2** *v.* To make tidy: to *tidy* a room. **3** *adj. informal* Fairly large: a *tidy* sum. **—ti'di·ly** *adv.* **—ti'di·ness** *n.*
tie [tī] *v.* **tied, ty·ing,** *n.* **1** *v.* To fasten, as by knotting cord or rope: to *tie* a bundle. **2** *v.* To lace up or tie a knot or bow in: to *tie* shoes; to *tie* a necktie. **3** *v.* To make or form, as a knot or bow. **4** *n.* A string, cord, or lace, with which something is tied. **5** *n.* A necktie. **6** *n.* Any bond or obligation: *ties* of affection. **7** *v.* To attach or bind: to be *tied* to one's family. **8** *n.* In music, a curved sign that indicates that two notes of the same pitch are to be played as one continuous tone. **9** *n.* A crossbar or beam to hold rails in place. **10** *v.* To make or become equal: Both of them *tied* for first place. **11** *n.* A contest in which neither side wins; draw: The game was a *tie.* **12** *n.* The score of such a contest. **—tie down** To hinder, restrict, or confine. **—tie up** **1** To fasten or tie tightly. **2** To block or hinder: to *tie up* traffic. **3** To keep busy or unavailable: We're *tied up* Monday.
tie-dye [tī'dī'] *v.* **tie-dyed, tie-dye·ing** To dye a pattern on (cloth) by first tying parts of the cloth so that those parts will not be exposed to the dye.
tier [tir] *n.* One of two or more rows that are placed one above another.

Two tiers of seats in a theater

tie-up [tī'up'] *n.* **1** A situation in which action or progress has been blocked. **2** *informal* A connection or relation.
tiff [tif] *n.* A minor quarrel.
ti·ger [tī'gər] *n.* A large, powerful, flesh-eating animal of the cat family. It has a tawny body with wavy black stripes and is found in the jungles of Asia.
tiger beetle A carnivorous, often

a	add	**i**	it	**o͝o**	took	**oi**	oil
ā	ace	**ī**	ice	**o͞o**	pool	**ou**	pout
â	care	**o**	odd	**u**	up	**ng**	ring
ä	palm	**ō**	open	**û**	burn	**th**	thin
e	end	**ô**	order	**yo͞o**	fuse	**t͟h**	this
ē	equal					**zh**	vision

ə = {a in *above* e in *sicken* i in *possible* / o in *melon* u in *circus*}

brightly colored beetle whose larva tunnels in the soil.
tiger cat 1 Any of various wild cats having markings on the coat, as the ocelot. 2 A domestic cat with a striped coat; tabby.
tiger lily A tall lily with orange flowers spotted with black.
tiger moth A striped or spotted moth.
tight [tīt] 1 *adj.* Firmly fixed or fastened in place; secure: a *tight* screw. 2 *adj.* Not letting anything, as air or water, in: a *tight* container. 3 *adj.* Taut: a *tight* wire. 4 *adv.* In a tight manner: to hold *tight*; to stop a bottle *tight*. 5 *adj.* Fitting closely or too closely: *tight* shoes. 6 *adj. informal* Difficult; troublesome: to be in a *tight* spot. 7 *adj.* Hard to get; scarce: *tight* money. 8 *adj. informal* Stingy. 9 *adj.* Very close; even: a *tight* contest. **—sit tight** To keep one's position without moving or acting. **—tight′ly** *adv.* **—tight′ness** *n.*
tight·en [tīt′(ə)n] *v.* To make or become tight or tighter: to *tighten* a knot.
tight·fist·ed [tīt′fis′tid] *adj.* Stingy.
tight-lipped [tīt′lipt′] *adj.* Unwilling to talk much or give away secrets.
tight·rope [tīt′rōp′] *n.* A rope or cable stretched tight above the ground, on which acrobats do balancing acts.
tights [tīts] *n.pl.* A tight garment usually covering the legs and body below the waist.
tight·wad [tīt′wod′] *n. U.S. informal* A person who hates to spend money; miser.
ti·gress [tī′gris] *n.* A female tiger.
tike [tīk] *n.* Another spelling of TYKE.
til·de [til′də] *n.* A pronunciation mark (~) showing certain special pronunciations. In Spanish it is placed over an "ñ" to show that the "n" is pronounced [ny], as in *señor.*
tile [tīl] *n., v.* **tiled, til·ing** 1 *n.* A thin, hard plate, often of baked clay, used to cover surfaces, as roofs and floors, or as an ornament. 2 *v.* To cover or provide with tiles. 3 *n.* A thin block, usually marked, and used in games. 4 *n.* A short pipe used as a drain.
til·ing [tī′ling] *n.* Tiles or a tile covering.
till[1] [til] 1 *prep., conj.* Until. 2 *prep.* Before: used with *not*: I can't go *till* noon.
till[2] [til] *v.* To work or cultivate (soil), as by plowing or hoeing. **—till′er** *n.*
till[3] [til] *n.* A place, as a drawer or tray, in which money or valuables are kept.
till·age [til′ij] *n.* 1 The cultivation of land. 2 Cultivated land.
till·er [til′ər] *n.* A bar or handle for turning the rudder in steering a boat.
tilt [tilt] 1 *v.* To incline at an angle; lean; tip: *Tilt* your head; The boat *tilted.* 2 *n.* Any inclination, slant, or slope. 3 *n.* A medieval sport in which two mounted knights, charging with lances, attempt to unseat each other; joust. 4 *v.* To practice this sport; joust. 5 *n.* A duel or confrontation. **—full tilt** Full speed or force.

A tilt

tilth [tilth] *n.* Another word for TILLAGE.
tim·ber [tim′bər] 1 *n.* Wood or a piece of wood suitable for use in building or carpentry. 2 *v.* To provide with timber. 3 *n.* Trees or their wood.
tim·bered [tim′bərd] *adj.* 1 Made of timber. 2 Covered with growing trees.
tim·ber·land [tim′bər·land′] *n.* Land covered with forests.
tim·ber·line [tim′bər·līn′] *n.* The line or height, as on a mountain or in arctic regions, above or beyond which trees do not grow.
timber wolf A large gray or brownish gray wolf of the forests of Canada and the northern U.S.

Timber wolf

tim·bre [tim′bər *or* tam′bər] *n.* The quality of a sound, aside from its pitch or loudness, that distinguishes it from another sound.
tim·brel [tim′brəl] *n.* An ancient tambourine.
time [tīm] *n., adj., v.* **timed, tim·ing** 1 *n.* An indefinite duration during which events and conditions occur in a sequence, proceeding from the past through the present to the future. 2 *n.* The particular moment, interval, or period in or during which something exists, happens, continues, or is done: the *time* of youth. 3 *n.* A definite or appointed moment, hour, day, or period: The *time* is 6:30; to serve *time* on a committee. 4 *n.* A system of reckoning or measuring passage of time: standard *time.* 5 *v.* To measure or record the speed or duration of: to *time* a race. 6 *n.* An occurrence or reoccurrence of some action or happening: the first *time*; three *times* at bat. 7 *adj.* Of or having to do with time: a *time* study. 8 *n.* (*often pl.*) A period of time having certain characteristics: modern *times*: the *time* of Galileo. 9 *n.* (*often pl.*) The conditions existing at any specific period of time: *Times* are hard today. 10 *v.* To choose or arrange the time or occasion for: We *timed* our arrival for noon. 11 *adj.* Set to operate at a certain time: a *time* lock. 12 *n.* A fitting moment: *time* to go. 13 *n.* Leisure: no *time* to read. 14 *n.* A person's experience or reaction: to have a good *time.* 15 *n.* In music or poetry, the tempo or rate of movement: waltz *time.* 16 *v.* To cause to match or correspond in tempo or rhythm: They *timed* their steps to the music. 17 *n.* The period during which a worker works or the pay given for this: to receive *time* and a half for overtime. **—against time** As quickly as possible, so as to finish at a certain time: to work *against time.*— **at the same time** However: *At the same time*, I don't think it'll work. **—at times** Sometimes; occasionally: *At times* our dog barks. **—behind the times** Old-fashioned. **—for the time being** For now; temporarily. **—from time to time** Now and then; occasionally. **—in no time** Right away; immediately. **—in time** 1 Before it is too late. 2 Eventually. 3 In the proper meter or tempo. **—make time** To go, work, or make rapidly. **—on time** 1 Not late; prompt. 2 Paid for or to be paid for in installments. **—take one's time** To proceed without hurrying. **—time after time** or **time and again** Repeatedly.
time bomb 1 A bomb that is or can be set to go off at a certain time. 2 A situation that threatens future disaster.
time capsule A container filled with objects of current interest, sealed, and stored (as in a cornerstone) for discovery in the future.

time card A card recording the starting and quitting times of an employee.

time clock A clock at a work place, designed to stamp employees' starting and quitting times on time cards inserted into it.

time exposure **1** Exposure of photographic film for a relatively long time. **2** A photograph made by such an exposure.

time-honored [tīm′on′ərd] *adj.* Followed or honored because of long use or existence: *time-honored* ways.

time·keep·er [tīm′kē′pər] *n.* **1** A person or thing that keeps time. **2** A person who times a race or other sports event. **3** A person who records the hours worked by employees.

time·less [tīm′lis] *adj.* **1** Having no ending; eternal. **2** Not limited to a certain time or era: *timeless* arguments as to the nature of truth. **3** Not changed or affected by time: the *timeless* beauty of a Greek temple.

time·ly [tīm′lē] *adj.* **time·li·er, time·li·est** Happening or coming at a good or suitable time: a *timely* letter. **—time′li·ness** *n.*

time-out [tīm′out′] *n.* In sports, a short recess not counted in the playing time of a game.

time·piece [tīm′pēs′] *n.* A watch or clock.

tim·er [tī′mər] *n.* **1** A timekeeper. **2** A stopwatch.

times [tīmz] *prep.* Multiplied by: What is four *times* four?

time-shar·ing [tīm′shâr′ing] *n.* A technique that enables a large number of users at terminals remote from a central computer to have simultaneous access to the computer.

time signature A sign on a musical staff that indicates the rhythm of the music that follows. The time signature is often a fraction (such as 3/4), with the numerator telling the number of beats to a measure (three), and the denominator giving the value of a note taking one beat (a quarter note).

time·ta·ble [tīm′tā′bəl] *n.* A schedule showing the time at which something happens, as the time of arrivals and departures for trains or buses.

time warp In science fiction, an interruption or reversal in the flow of time.

time·worn [tīm′wôrn′] *adj.* **1** Showing the effects of age or long exposure: a *timeworn* face. **2** Used too long or too much; stale: *timeworn* excuses.

time zone One of the 24 zones on the earth, within each of which a single standard time is used or followed. The time in any zone is an hour earlier or later than that in the next one.

tim·id [tim′id] *adj.* Fearful or shy. **—ti·mid·i·ty** [ti·mid′ə·tē] *n.* **—tim′id·ly** *adv.* **—tim′id·ness** *n.*

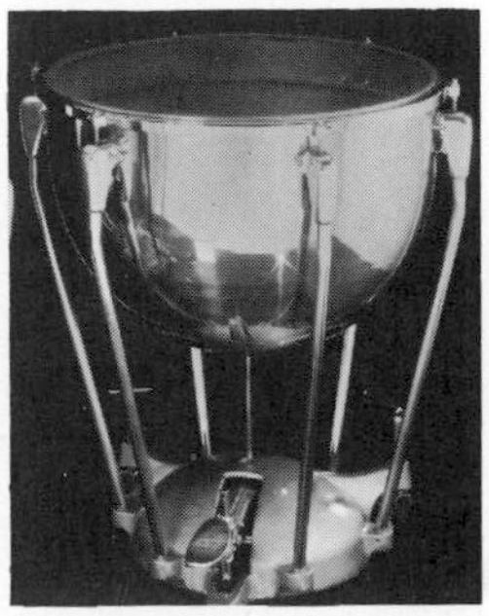

Timpani

tim·ing [tī′ming] *n.* The act or art of finding and then using the rhythm, tempo, or speed that will give the most effective result: A swimmer needs good *timing* in her strokes.

tim·or·ous [tim′ər·əs] *adj.* Fearful; timid.

tim·o·thy [tim′ə·thē] *n.* A perennial grass with long leaves and spikes, grown as fodder.

tim·pa·ni [tim′pə·nē] *n.pl.* (*used with singular or plural verb*) A set of kettledrums played as a unit in an orchestra or band. ◆ *Timpani* is the plural of *timpano*, the Italian word for *kettledrum.* The singular is not used in English.

tim·pa·nist [tim′pə·nist] *n.* A musician who plays the timpani.

tin [tin] *n., v.* **tinned, tin·ning** **1** *n.* A soft, white metallic element used in many alloys. **2** *adj. use*: *tin* alloys. **3** *n.* A container, vessel, or sheet of tin or tinplate. **4** *n.* A metal container; can. **5** *v.* To plate or cover with tin or an alloy of tin. **6** *v.* *British* To preserve in sealed cans; can.

tin can **1** A can made of tinplate or another corrosion-resistant material. **2** *slang* A destroyer (def. 2).

tinc·ture [tingk′chər] *n., v.* **tinc·tured, tinc·tur·ing** **1** *n.* A solution of medicine in alcohol: *tincture* of iodine. **2** *n.* A tinge of color; tint. **3** *n.* A slight additional flavor or quality: a *tincture* of sadness in a smile. **4** *v.* To give a slight tint or flavor to.

tin·der [tin′dər] *n.* Anything dry that will catch fire easily on contact with a spark.

tin·der·box [tin′dər·boks′] *n.* **1** A metal box for holding tinder and usually flint and steel. **2** Anything very flammable, explosive, or touchy.

tine [tīn] *n.* A spike or prong, as of a fork or antler.

tin·foil [tin′foil′] *n.* Thin metal sheeting sometimes made of tin but more often of a tin-lead alloy or aluminum, used as a wrapping material.

ting [ting] **1** *n.* A short, high-pitched, ringing sound. **2** *v.* To make or cause to make a ting.

tinge [tinj] *v.* **tinged, tinge·ing** or **ting·ing,** *n.* **1** *v.* To give a trace of color to: The cold *tinged* my face with red. **2** *n.* A trace of color. **3** *v.* To change or modify in some slight way: laughter *tinged* with tears. **4** *n.* A slight trace of something: a *tinge* of sadness.

tin·gle [ting′gəl] *v.* **tin·gled, tin·gling,** *n.* **1** *v.* To have or cause to have a prickly or slightly stinging feeling: to *tingle* with excitement; Winter *tingles* the skin. **2** *n.* Such a feeling.

tink·er [tingk′ər] **1** *n.* A person who travels about and mends pots, pans, and other utensils. **2** *v.* To mend or work as a tinker. **3** *v.* To work or repair in a clumsy way. **4** *v.* To putter; fuss: to *tinker* around the house.

tin·kle [ting′kəl] *n., v.* **tin·kled, tin·kling** **1** *n.* A slight, clear, metallic sound, as of a small bell. **2** *v.* To make or cause to make this sound.

tin·ner [tin′ər] *n.* **1** A person who works in a tin mine. **2** A tinsmith.

tin·ny [tin′ē] *adj.* **tin·ni·er, tin·ni·est** **1** Made of or containing tin. **2** Like tin in appearance. **3** Cheap or poor in quality: a *tinny* old car. **4** Having a thin sound, like that of tin being struck. **5** Tasting of tin, as food from a can. **—tin′ni·ly** *adv.* **—tin′ni·ness** *n.*

tin·plate [tin′plāt′] *n.* Sheet iron or steel plated with tin.

a	add	**i**	it	**o͝o**	took	**oi**	oil		
ā	ace	**ī**	ice	**o͞o**	pool	**ou**	pout		
â	care	**o**	odd	**u**	up	**ng**	ring		
ä	palm	**ō**	open	**û**	burn	**th**	thin		
e	end	**ô**	order	**yo͞o**	fuse	**th̶**	this		
ē	equal					**zh**	vision		

ə = {a in *above* e in *sicken* i in *possible* / o in *melon* u in *circus*}

T

tin-plate [tin′plāt′] *v.* **tin-plat·ed, tin-plat·ing** To coat or plate (iron or steel) with tin.
tin·sel [tin′səl] *n., v.* **tin·seled** or **tin·selled, tin·sel·ing** or **tin·sel·ling,** *adj.* **1** *n.* Very thin, glittering bits or strips of metal or foil, used as a decoration. **2** *v.* To decorate with tinsel. **3** *adj.* Made of or decorated with tinsel. **4** *n.* Anything cheap but showy in appearance. **5** *adj.* Cheap; showy: *tinsel* emotions. **6** *v.* To give a showy appearance to: to *tinsel* one's true feelings.
tin·smith [tin′smith′] *n.* A person who works with tin or tinplate.
tint [tint] **1** *n.* A slightly different shade of any one color. **2** *n.* Any pale or delicate color. **3** *n.* A slight trace or quality: a *tint* of worry in your voice. **4** *v.* To give a tint to.
tin·type [tin′tīp′] *n.* A positive photograph made directly on a thin iron plate by a special process.
tin·ware [tin′wâr′] *n.* Articles, such as kitchen utensils, made of tinplate.
ti·ny [tī′nē] *adj.* **ti·ni·er, ti·ni·est** Very small: *tiny* wrists.
-tion A suffix meaning: **1** The act or process of, as in *application.* **2** The condition of being, as in *completion.* **3** The result of, as in *connection.*
tip[1] [tip] *n., v.* **tipped, tip·ping** **1** *n.* The point or end of anything tapering: the *tip* of one's finger. **2** *n.* A piece or part made to form the end of anything: the gold *tip* of the pen. **3** *v.* To furnish or cover with a tip: to *tip* a cane with rubber. **4** *v.* To form the tip of.
tip[2] [tip] *n., v.* **tipped, tip·ping** **1** *n.* A small gift of money for service rendered. **2** *v.* To give a tip to: to *tip* a waiter. **3** *n.* A piece of helpful, expert, or secret information or advice: The coach gave us a *tip* on how to win. **4** *v.* To inform with a tip: to *tip* off the newspapers. **5** *v.* To hit lightly or glancingly: The batter *tipped* the pitch. **6** *n.* A light or glancing blow. **—tip′per** *n.*
tip[3] [tip] *v.* **tipped, tip·ping,** *n.* **1** *v.* To lean or cause to lean; tilt: The table is *tipping* slightly. **2** *v.* To raise slightly: to *tip* one's hat. **3** *n.* A slanting or inclined position; tilt. **4** *v.* To overturn or upset: to *tip* over a chair.
tip·pet [tip′it] *n.* **1** A scarf for the neck and shoulders, with ends hanging down in front. **2** Formerly, the long, narrow, hanging part of a hood, sleeve, or cape.
tip·ple [tip′əl] *v.* **tip·pled, tip·pling,** *n.* **1** *v.* To drink alcoholic liquor frequently. **2** *n.* Alcoholic liquor. **—tip′pler** *n.*
tip·ster [tip′stər] *n. informal* A person who gives or sells special information or advice, as on horse races or investments.
tip·sy [tip′sē] *adj.* **tip·si·er, tip·si·est** Somewhat drunk. **—tip′si·ly** *adv.* **—tip′si·ness** *n.*
tip·toe [tip′tō′] *n., v.* **tip·toed, tip·toe·ing** **1** *n.* The tip of a toe. **2** *v.* To walk softly on or as on one's toes. **—on tiptoe** **1** On the tips of the toes. **2** Eagerly: waiting *on tiptoe.* **3** Secretly or quietly.
tip·top [tip′top′] **1** *n.* The highest point. **2** *adj.* At the tiptop. **3** *adj. informal* Excellent; first-rate: in *tiptop* condition for the race.
ti·rade [tī′rād′ *or* tə·rād′] *n.* A long angry speech.
tire[1] [tīr] *v.* **tired, tir·ing** **1** To make or become weary or exhausted: The hike *tired* the scouts. **2** To make or become bored or impatient: The lecture *tired* us all.
tire[2] [tīr] *n.* A circular tube of rubber and cords, filled with air, used on a wheel of a car, bus, or other vehicle. A tire absorbs shock and provides traction.
tired [tīrd] *adj.* Weary; exhausted.
tire·less [tīr′lis] *adj.* Never tiring: a *tireless* worker. **—tire′less·ly** *adv.* **—tire′less·ness** *n.*
tire·some [tīr′səm] *adj.* Tedious; boring. **—tire′·some·ly** *adv.* **—tire′some·ness** *n.*
ti·ro [tī′rō] *n., pl.* **ti·ros** Another spelling of TYRO.
'tis [tiz] It is: used mostly in poems.
tis·sue [tish′o͞o] *n.* **1** In a plant or animal, a group of cells that are somewhat alike and perform a particular function: bone *tissue.* **2** A light, absorbent paper. **3** Tissue paper. **4** Any gauzelike fabric. **5** A group of things woven together; network: a *tissue* of myths.
tissue paper A very thin, soft paper for wrapping and protecting delicate articles.
tit[1] [tit] *n.* A titmouse, titlark, or any of certain other small birds.
tit[2] [tit] *n.* Another word for TEAT.
Ti·tan [tīt′(ə)n] *n.* **1** In Greek myths, one of a race of giant gods. **2** (*written* **titan**) A person of great size, strength, and skill.
Ti·ta·ni·a [ti·tā′nē·ə] *n.* Queen of the fairies, as in Shakespeare's play *A Midsummer Night's Dream.*
ti·tan·ic [tī·tan′ik] *adj.* Very great; huge.
ti·ta·ni·um [tī·tā′nē·əm] *n.* An abundant, strong, silvery gray metallic element used as an alloying element in steel.
tit·bit [tit′bit′] *n.* Another spelling of TIDBIT.
tit for tat Something of the same kind given in return: He insulted her, so she snubbed him, which was *tit for tat.*
tithe [tīth] *n., v.* **tithed, tith·ing** **1** *n.* A tax or offering of 10 percent of one's income to support a church. **2** *n.* A small or tenth part of anything. **3** *v.* To tax with a tithe: to *tithe* the entire parish. **4** *v.* To give or pay a tithe or a tenth part of: to *tithe* one's income.
tit·il·late [tit′ə·lāt′] *v.* **tit·il·lat·ed, tit·il·lat·ing** To tickle or excite pleasantly. **—tit′il·la′tion** *n.*
tit·lark [tit′lärk′] *n.* A pipit.
ti·tle [tīt′(ə)l] *n., v.* **ti·tled, ti·tling** **1** *n.* The name of something, as a book, play, or poem. **2** *v.* To give a title to; name: to *title* a new book. **3** *n.* A word or name showing one's rank, office, or profession: "Doctor" and "professor" are *titles,* as are the words "Mister," "Ms.," and "baker." **4** *n.* The right to own or possess a piece of property, as a house or car. **5** *n.* The deed or other document that is evidence of such a right. **6** *n.* In some sports, a championship: to play for the *title.*
ti·tled [tīt′(ə)ld] *adj.* Having a title, especially one of nobility.
title page The page of a book on which the title appears and usually the name of the author, the publisher, and the place of publication.
title role The character in a play, movie, or other presentation who is referred to in the title.
tit·mouse [tit′mous′] *n., pl.* **tit·mice** [tit′mīs′] A small, lively gray bird with a pointed crest.
tit·ter [tit′ər] **1** *v.* To laugh in a suppressed way, as from nervousness or in making fun; giggle; snicker. **2** *n.* Such a laugh.
tit·tle [tit′(ə)l] *n.* **1** A very small bit. **2** A small mark in writing, as the dot over an *i.*
tit·tle-tat·tle [tit′(ə)l·tat′(ə)l] *n., v.* **tit·tle-tat·tled, tit·tle-tat·tling** **1** *n.* Foolish talk or gossip. **2** *v.* To gossip. **3** *n.* A tattletale.
tit·u·lar [tich′o͞o·lər *or* tit′yə·lər] *adj.* **1** In name or

title only. **2** Of or having to do with a title. **3** Having a title.
tiz·zy [tiz′ē] *n., pl.* **tiz·zies** *slang* A condition of excitement or confusion; dither.
TKO or **T.K.O.** technical knockout.
Tl The symbol for the element thallium.
Tm The symbol for the element thulium.
tn. ton(s).
TN Postal Service abbreviation of Tennessee.
tng. training.
tnpk. turnpike.
TNT [tē′en·tē′] *n.* A toxic, flammable organic compound used as an explosive and in manufacturing other chemicals. ◆ *TNT* is an abbreviation of *trinitrotoluene.*
to [to͞o, *unstressed* tə] **1** *prep.* In the direction of: *to* the right. **2** *adv.* Toward something else; forward: Your sweater is wrong side *to.* **3** *prep.* As far as or until: Go *to* the end of the line; from Christmas *to* New Year's. **4** *prep.* In contact with; against; on: pinned *to* the wall. **5** *adv.* Shut; closed: Pull the door *to.* **6** *prep.* For the purpose of: They came *to* the rescue. **7** *prep.* In relation to; concerning: Your affairs are nothing *to* me. **8** *adv.* Into action or work: They fell *to* and ate. **9** *prep.* Resulting in: polished *to* a shine; *to* my surprise. **10** *prep.* Along with or accompanying: salt added *to* gravy. **11** *prep.* Agreeable with; for: *to* my liking. **12** *prep.* Compared with: a score of 15 *to* 14. **13** *prep.* In each: three feet *to* a yard. **14** *prep.* Belonging or used in connection with: the key *to* the door. **15** *adv.* Into consciousness: to come *to.* **16** *prep.* *To* is also used with an indirect object after a verb, as in "Give the book *to* me," or *to* can be used after a noun or adjective to indicate a particular viewpoint or condition, as in "They were always idols *to* me"; "They were not known *to* us," or to point out the receiver of an action, as in "The librarian gave a talk *to* the children." ◆ *To* is also used to indicate the infinitive and is often used in place of it: I don't know whether *to* go or *to* stay; They know a lot more than they seem *to.* **—to and fro** Back and forth.
toad [tōd] *n.* A small, tailless, froglike animal that lives chiefly on land.

A typical toad

toad·stool [tōd′sto͞ol′] *n.* Any mushroom with an umbrella-shaped top, especially a poisonous one.
toad·y [tō′dē] *n., pl.* **toad·ies,** *v.* **toad·ied, toad·y·ing** **1** *n.* A person who fawns on or flatters others to gain favors from them. **2** *v.* To act as a toady to (someone).
toast[1] [tōst] **1** *v.* To brown by heating: to *toast* slices of bread. **2** *n.* Toasted bread. **3** *v.* To make or become warm before a fire.
toast[2] [tōst] **1** *v.* To drink in honor of (a person or event). **2** *n.* The act of or a proposal for toasting. **3** *n.* Something, as a person, event, or sentiment, that is toasted: the *toast* of the town.
toast·er [tōs′tər] *n.* A device for making toast.
toaster oven A small electric oven convenient for toasting bread and heating up precooked foods.
toast·mas·ter [tōst′mas′tər] *n.* A person who gives toasts and introduces speakers at banquets.
to·bac·co [tə·bak′ō] *n., pl.* **to·bac·cos** or **to·bac·coes** **1** A plant with fragrant flowers and numerous large leaves. **2** The dried leaves of this plant, used for smoking and chewing.
to·bac·co·nist [tə·bak′ə·nist] *n.* A person who sells tobaccos and smokers' equipment.
To·ba·go·ni·an [tō′bə·gō′nē·ən] **1** *adj.* Of or from Tobago. **2** *n.* A person born or living in Tobago.
to·bog·gan [tə·bog′ən] **1** *n.* A long, narrow sled without runners, used for coasting. **2** *v.* To coast on a toboggan. **3** *v.* To move downward swiftly: Prices *tobogganed* yesterday. ◆ *Toboggan* comes from a French-Canadian word for *sleigh,* which in turn is from an Algonquian Indian word.
to·coph·er·ol [tō·kof′ə·rôl′] *n.* Any of several related organic compounds that make up vitamin E.
toc·sin [tok′sin] *n.* **1** An alarm signal given on a bell. **2** A bell used to give an alarm.
to·day [tə·dā′] **1** *n.* The present day, time, or age: *Today* is Monday. **2** *adv.* On or during the present day: We'll go *today.* **3** *adv.* Nowadays: *Today* horse-drawn carriages are rarely seen.
tod·dle [tod′(ə)l] *v.* **tod·dled, tod·dling** **1** *v.* To walk unsteadily and with short steps, as a little child. **2** *v.* To move along at a leisurely pace. **3** *n.* A slow or unsteady gait.
tod·dler [tod′lər] *n.* A young child who is just learning to walk.
tod·dy [tod′ē] *n., pl.* **tod·dies** A drink made with liquor, hot water, sugar, and lemon.
to-do [tə·do͞o′] *n., pl.* **to-dos** *informal* A fuss.
toe [tō] *n., v.* **toed, toe·ing** **1** *n.* One of the five parts at the end of a foot. **2** *n.* The portion of a shoe, sock, skate, or other foot covering that goes over the toes. **3** *v.* To touch with the toes: to *toe* the starting line. **4** *n.* Something like or suggesting a toe. **—on one's toes** Alert. **—toe the line** or **toe the mark** To follow strictly the rules or orders.
toed [tōd] *adj.* Having a certain kind or number of toes: often used in combination: a *three-toed* sloth.
toe·nail [tō′nāl′] *n.* The nail on a human toe.
tof·fee or **tof·fy** [tôf′ē] *n., pl.* **tof·fees** or **tof·fies** A kind of brittle taffy.
to·fu [tō′fo͞o′] *n.* Another word for BEAN CURD.
tog [tog *or* tôg] *n., v.* **togged, tog·ging** **1** *n.* (*pl.*) Clothing. **2** *v.* To dress, as for a special purpose: She was *togged* out for running.
to·ga [tō′gə] *n.* The loose outer garment worn in public by a citizen of ancient Rome.
to·geth·er [tə·geth′ər] *adv.* **1** With each other: to sing *together.* **2** Into union or contact with each other: Fasten the two sections *together.* **3** In the same place or at the same spot: Bring all the old books *together.* **4** At the same time; si-

Toga

a add	**i** it	**o͝o** took	**oi** oil
ā ace	**ī** ice	**o͞o** pool	**ou** pout
â care	**o** odd	**u** up	**ng** ring
ä palm	**ō** open	**û** burn	**th** thin
e end	**ô** order	**yo͞o** fuse	**th** this
ē equal			**zh** vision

ə = a in *above* e in *sicken* i in *possible* o in *melon* u in *circus*

multaneously: to sound the horns *together.* **5** In or into harmony or agreement: These colors go well *together.*

tog·gle [tog'(ə)l] *n., v.* **tog·gled, tog·gling** **1** *n.* A pin or rod inserted through a loop, chain link, or hole to prevent slippage, to fasten, or to provide a handle for twisting or tightening. **2** *v.* To provide or fasten with a toggle.

togs [togz or tôgz] *n.pl.* Clothes; outfit.

toil [toil] **1** *n.* Hard work; tiring labor. **2** *v.* To work hard. **3** *v.* To walk, go, or move with difficulty: to *toil* up the steps. **—toil'er** *n.*

toi·let [toi'lit] **1** *n.* A fixture with a seat atop a bowl in which bodily wastes can be flushed away. **2** *n.* A room with a toilet; bathroom. **3** *n.* The act or process of grooming oneself. **4** *adj.* Used in grooming: *toilet* articles.

toi·let·ry [toi'lit·rē] *n., pl.* **toi·let·ries** Any toilet article, as a comb or soap.

toi·lette [twä·let'] *n.* **1** The act of grooming oneself. **2** A person's dress or style of dress.

toilet water A scented liquid containing some alcohol, used after bathing or shaving.

toils [toilz] *n.pl.* Anything that traps or ensnares.

toil·some [toil'səm] *adj.* Demanding hard work; laborious: a *toilsome* duty.

toil·worn [toil'wôrn'] *adj.* Showing the effects of prolonged hard work: *toilworn* hands.

to·ken [tō'kən] **1** *n.* A visible sign or symbol: a *token* of love. **2** *adj.* Done or given merely to fulfill an obligation, and often in as small a way as possible: *token* payments; *token* integration. **3** *n.* A metal piece used in place of money, as for a fare. **4** *n.* Something given as a sign of friendship; memento; keepsake.

told [tōld] Past tense and past participle of TELL.

tol·er·a·ble [tol'ər·ə·bəl] *adj.* **1** Capable of being borne or put up with; bearable: a *tolerable* grief. **2** Neither good nor bad; fair: a *tolerable* performance. **—tol'er·a·bly** *adv.*

tol·er·ance [tol'ər·əns] *n.* **1** An attitude toward others which is fair and free from emotional bias regardless of differences in beliefs, customs, or race. **2** A similar attitude toward ideas and beliefs contrary to one's own. **3** The ability to withstand the action of a drug or poison without ill effects. **4** The ability to bear unpleasantness or pain; fortitude. **5** The range of allowable difference from an exact specification, as in the size of a manufactured product.

tol·er·ant [tol'ər·ənt] *adj.* Having or showing tolerance: a *tolerant* person; a *tolerant* attitude. **—tol'er·ant·ly** *adv.*

tol·er·ate [tol'ər·āt'] *v.* **tol·er·at·ed, tol·er·at·ing** **1** To allow to be or permit without opposition: to *tolerate* other beliefs. **2** To bear or endure: I can't *tolerate* spicy foods. **3** To have tolerance for a drug or poison.

tol·er·a·tion [tol'ə·rā'shən] *n.* Tolerance, especially in matters of religion.

toll[1] [tōl] *n.* **1** A charge, tax, or service fee, as on a bridge or turnpike. **2** An amount of suffering endured or lives lost: The earthquake took a heavy *toll* in deaths.

toll[2] [tōl] **1** *v.* To sound or cause to sound slowly and at regular intervals: The bell *tolled* all day. **2** *n.* The act or sound of tolling. **3** *v.* To announce by tolling, as the hour or a funeral.

toll·booth [tōl'bo͞oth'] *n.* A booth where tolls are paid, as on a turnpike.

toll·gate [tōl'gāt'] *n.* A gate on a bridge or road where tolls are paid.

Tol·tec [tōl'tek'] **1** *n.* A member of a nation of ancient Mexican Indians. **2** *adj.* Of or having to do with the Toltecs.

tol·u·ene [tol'yo͞o·ēn'] *n.* A liquid hydrocarbon compound similar to benzene, obtained from petroleum and other sources and used as a solvent, as a fuel additive, and in making other chemicals.

tom [tom] *n.* The male of certain animals, such as cats and turkeys.

tom·a·hawk [tom'ə·hôk'] **1** *n.* An axlike weapon used by North American Indians. **2** *v.* To strike or kill with a tomahawk. • *Tomahawk* goes back to an Algonquian Indian word meaning *he cuts.*

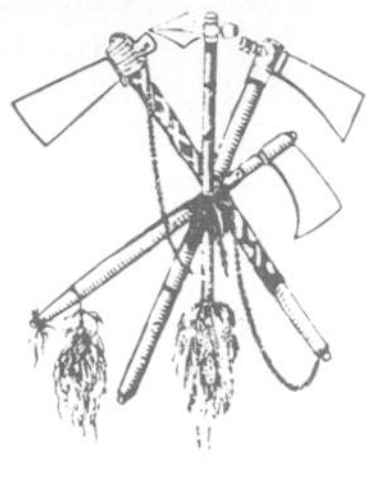

Tomahawks

to·ma·to [tə·mā'tō *or* tə·mä'tō] *n., pl.* **to·ma·toes** **1** The large, round, pulpy fruit of a perennial plant, yellow or red when ripe and widely used as a vegetable. **2** This plant.

tomb [to͞om] *n.* A place for the burial of the dead, as a vault or grave.

tom·boy [tom'boi'] *n.* A girl who behaves in ways traditionally associated with boys.

tomb·stone [to͞om'stōn'] *n.* A stone marking a person's burial place, usually inscribed with the person's name and dates of birth and death.

tom·cat [tom'kat'] *n.* A male cat.

tome [tōm] *n.* A large book; volume.

tom·fool [tom'fo͞ol'] **1** *n.* A very foolish or stupid person. **2** *adj.* Very stupid or foolish: a *tomfool* act.

tom·fool·er·y [tom'fo͞o'lər·ē] *n., pl.* **tom·fool·er·ies** Foolish behavior.

to·mo·gram [tō'mə·gram'] *n.* An X-ray photograph made by tomography.

to·mog·ra·phy [tō·mog'rə·fē] *n.* A diagnostic technique using X rays that show a cross section of the body clearly by blurring out the structures in front of and behind it. **—to·mo·graph·ic** [tō'mə·graf'ik] *adj.*

to·mor·row [tə·mor'ō *or* tə·môr'ō] **1** *n.* The next day after today. **2** *n.* Some time in the future. **3** *adv.* On or for tomorrow: We'll go *tomorrow.*

tom·tit [tom'tit'] *n.* Any of various small birds, as a titmouse or wren.

tom-tom [tom'tom'] *n.* A drum, originally of India and Africa, usually beaten with the hands.

ton [tun] *n.* A measure of weight, as the **short ton** of 2,000 pounds, used in the U.S. and Canada, the **long ton** of 2,240 pounds, used in England, or the **metric ton** of 1,000 kilograms.

to·nal [tō'nəl] *adj.* Of or having to do with a tone or tones, or with tonality.

to·nal·i·ty [tō·nal'ə·tē] *n., pl.* **to·nal·i·ties** **1** The tendency, in most music, for one tone to dominate and become central to all the others. **2** A key or scale in which this happens. **3** The general color scheme or tone of a painting.

tone [tōn] *n., v.* **toned, ton·ing** **1** *n.* A sound having a definite pitch. **2** *n.* A sound, especially in relation to its quality, volume, duration, or pitch: a harsh *tone*; a loud *tone*; a short *tone*; a high *tone.* **3** *n.* Any musical interval equal to the interval between do and re in a major scale: A is one *tone* above G. **4** *n.* A shade, hue, or tint: *tones* of red. **5** *n.* A manner of speech or writing that expresses a certain mood, style, or feeling: a warm *tone* of voice. **6** *n.* A certain style or character: the subdued *tone* of the room; the moral *tone* of a country. **7** *v.* To give a certain tone to. **8** *v.* To blend or harmonize. **9** *n.* Health or firmness, as of a muscle or organ: to lose muscle *tone* through lack of exercise. **—tone down** To soften the tone of. **—tone up** To make brighter, livelier, or stronger.

tone arm The part of a record player that holds the pickup and the stylus.

tone-deaf [tōn′def′] *adj.* Unable to distinguish between sounds of different pitch.

tong [tong *or* tông] *v.* To grasp, carry, or hold with tongs: to *tong* a burning log. **—tong′er** *n.*

Ton·gan [tong′gən] **1** *adj.* Of or from Tonga. **2** *n.* A person born in or a citizen of Tonga.

tongs [tongz *or* tôngz] *n.pl.* An implement for grasping or lifting objects, usually consisting of a pair of arms hinged or pivoted together.

tongue [tung] *n., v.* **tongued, tongu·ing** **1** *n.* The movable muscular organ in the mouth used in eating, in tasting, and in human speech. **2** *n.* An animal's tongue, as of beef, prepared as food. **3** *n.* The power or manner of speech: to lose one's *tongue*; a smooth *tongue.* **4** *n.* A language or dialect: the Greek *tongue.* **5** *n.* Anything resembling a tongue, as a slender projection of land or water, a strip of leather under the laces of a shoe, or a jet of flame. **6** *v.* To begin (a note or notes) by moving the tongue, as in playing certain wind instruments. **—hold one's tongue** To keep quiet. **—on the tip of one's tongue** **1** Ready to be said. **2** Almost but not quite remembered.

tongue-in-cheek [tung′in·chēk′] *adj.* Sarcastic in a playful way; humorously ironic.

tongue-tied [tung′tīd′] *adj.* **1** Unable to speak or move the tongue properly because the membrane connecting the bottom of the tongue to the mouth is too short. **2** Speechless or nearly so from an emotion, as shyness or embarrassment.

ton·ic [ton′ik] **1** *adj.* Giving, increasing, or restoring strength or energy; stimulating: A cold shower can have a *tonic* effect on the body. **2** *n.* Anything, as certain medicines, supposed to make a person feel better or more energetic. **3** *n.* In music, the keynote of a scale or key. **4** *adj.* Of or having to do with a keynote: a *tonic* chord.

to·night [tə·nīt′] **1** *n.* This present night or the night of this day. **2** *adv.* On or during this present night or the night of this day.

ton·nage [tun′ij] *n.* **1** The capacity of a ship expressed in terms of one ton per 100 cubic feet. A tonnage of 800 tons means 80,000 cubic feet of cargo space. **2** The total amount of shipping, as of a country or port, expressed in tons. **3** The total weight of any load in tons. **4** A shipping tax given at a rate per ton.

ton·sil [ton′səl] *n.* One of two oval masses of soft glandular tissue, one on each side of the throat at the back of the mouth.

ton·sil·lec·to·my [ton′sə·lek′tə·mē] *n., pl.* **ton·sil·lec·to·mies** A surgical operation in which the tonsils are removed.

ton·sil·li·tis [ton′sə·lī′tis] *n.* An inflammation and swelling of the tonsils.

ton·so·ri·al [ton·sôr′ē·əl] *adj.* Of or having to do with barbers: often used humorously.

ton·sure [ton′shər] *n.* **1** The shaving of all or part of the head, as of a priest or monk. **2** The part of the head left bare by tonsure.

To·ny [tō′nē] *n., pl.* **To·ny's** One of the awards given annually for notable achievements in the theater.

too [to͞o] *adv.* **1** In addition; also: I'm going *too.* **2** More than is necessary; excessively: *too* large. **3** Very: That's not *too* likely. **4** *informal* Indeed: You are *too* coming!

took [to͝ok] Past tense of TAKE.

tool [to͞ol] **1** *n.* An instrument, as a hammer, saw, or chisel, used for doing some kind of work by hand. **2** *n.* A similar instrument driven by a motor. **3** *v.* To make, shape, or ornament with a tool: to *tool* book covers. **4** *v.* To provide with tools. **5** *n.* A person or thing used to accomplish something: Words are a writer's *tools.* **6** *v. informal* To drive or ride a vehicle: I *tooled* along the highway. **7** *v.* To equip (a factory) with machinery for a certain kind of production.

toot [to͞ot] **1** *n.* A short note or blast, as on a horn or whistle. **2** *v.* To sound with short blasts: to *toot* a horn. **—toot′er** *n.*

tooth [to͞oth] *n., pl.* **teeth** [tēth] **1** One of the hard, white, bony parts in the mouth, used to bite and chew food, and in animals, often used as a weapon. **2** Something resembling a tooth in form or use, as one of the projecting points on a comb, fork, saw, or gearwheel. **3** Appetite; liking: used chiefly in the expression **sweet tooth,** a liking for sweet foods. **—tooth and nail** With all possible strength; fiercely. **—tooth′like′** *adj.*

tooth·ache [to͞oth′āk′] *n.* A pain in a tooth.

tooth·brush [to͞oth′brush′] *n.* A small brush for cleaning the teeth.

toothed [to͞otht *or* to͞ot͟hd] *adj.* **1** Having teeth or teeth of a certain kind: sharp-*toothed.* **2** Notched or indented: a *toothed* leaf.

tooth·less [to͞oth′lis] *adj.* Without teeth.

tooth·paste [to͞oth′pāst′] *n.* A paste used in cleaning the teeth.

tooth·pick [to͞oth′pik′] *n.* A small sliver, commonly of wood or plastic, used for removing particles of food from between the teeth.

tooth·some [to͞oth′səm] *adj.* Pleasant or tasty.

tooth·y [to͞o′thē] *adj.* **tooth·i·er, tooth·i·est** Having or showing prominent teeth: a *toothy* grin. **—tooth′i·ly** *adv.*

top[1] [top] *n., v.* **topped, top·ping,** *adj.* **1** *n.* The highest or uppermost part, side, or surface of anything: the *top* of the mountain; the *top* of the bookcase. **2** *n.* A lid or cover: a bottle *top.* **3** *v.* To form the top of: Snow *topped* the highest mountains. **4** *v.* To provide with a top: to *top* a bottle. **5** *v.* To reach or pass over the top of: to *top* a horse in gym. **6** *n.* The crown of the head. **7** *n.* The part of a plant that grows above the ground: carrot or beet *tops.* **8** *v.* To cut, trim, or remove the top of, as a plant or tree. **9** *adj.* Of, having to do with, or forming the top or upper part: the *top* layer of soil. **10** *n.* The highest degree, range, or rank:

a	add	**i**	it	**o͝o**	took	**oi**	oil
ā	ace	**ī**	ice	**o͞o**	pool	**ou**	pout
â	care	**o**	odd	**u**	up	**ng**	ring
ä	palm	**ō**	open	**û**	burn	**th**	thin
e	end	**ô**	order	**yo͞o**	fuse	**t͟h**	this
ē	equal					**zh**	vision

ə = {a in *above* e in *sicken* i in *possible*; o in *melon* u in *circus*}

the *top* of one's ambition; the *top* of one's profession. **11** *adj.* Highest or greatest in amount, degree, or rank: *top* authors; *top* speed. **12** *v.* To be or do more, greater, or better than: to *top* someone at tennis. **13** *v.* To be at or reach the top of: She *topped* the graduating class. **14** *n.* The highest pitch or volume: at the *top* of my voice. **15** *n.* The best or choicest part: the *top* of the crop. **16** *n.* A platform at the head of the lower section of a ship's mast. **—on top** **1** Very successful. **2** In a position of power or dominance. **—on top of** **1** Resting or pressing on from above. **2** In addition to. **3** *informal* In full control of. **—top off** To complete or finish with a final touch.

top² [top] *n.* A cone-shaped toy with a point on which it is made to spin.

to·paz [tō′paz′] *n.* A mineral found in the form of transparent or translucent crystals, yellow to brownish, that are valued as gems.

top·coat [top′kōt′] *n.* A lightweight overcoat.

top·flight [top′flīt′] *adj.* Superior; excellent: a *top-flight* performance.

top·gal·lant [tə·gal′ənt *or* top′gal′ənt] **1** *n.* The third section above the deck of a ship's mast, above the topmast. **2** *n.* The sail that belongs to this section. **3** *adj.* Having to do with this section.

top hat A hat for formal wear, having a tall, cylindrical crown and a narrow brim.

top-heavy [top′hev′ē] *adj.* **top-heav·i·er, top-heav·i·est** Having the top part heavier than the base; inclined to topple over.

to·pi·ar·y [tō′pē·er′ē] *adj., n., pl.* **to·pi·ar·ies** **1** *adj.* Of or having to do with the trimming of living shrubs or trees into decorative or animallike shapes. **2** *n.* Topiary work. **3** *n.* A topiary garden.

Topiary

top·ic [top′ik] *n.* A subject discussed in speech or in writing.

top·i·cal [top′i·kəl] *adj.* **1** Of or having to do with topics. **2** Having to do with a subject of current or local interest.

top·knot [top′not′] *n.* A crest of feathers or a knot of hair on top of the head.

top·mast [top′məst *or* top′mast′] *n.* The mast next above the lowest mast of a ship.

top·most [top′mōst′] *n.* Being at the very top: the *topmost* shelf of a bookcase.

top-notch [top′noch′] *adj. informal* First-rate; excellent.

top·o·graph·ic [top′ə·graf′ik] *adj.* Topographical.

top·o·graph·i·cal [top′ə·graf′i·kəl] *adj.* Of or having to do with topography; descriptive of an area or place. **—top′o·graph′i·cal·ly** *adv.*

to·pog·ra·phy [tə·pog′rə·fē] *n., pl.* **to·pog·ra·phies** **1** The physical features of a region or place, as mountains, rivers, roads, and parks. **2** The art of showing these on a map. **—to·pog′ra·pher** *n.*

to·pol·o·gy [tə·pol′ə·jē] *n.* **1** The history of the physical features of a region. **2** A branch of mathematics having to do with properties of geometric figures that are not changed by elastic distortion. **—to·po·log·i·cal** [top′ə·loj′i·kəl] *adj.* **—to′po·log′i·cal·ly** *adv.* **—to·pol′o·gist** *n.*

top·ping [top′ing] *n.* Something put on the top of a food, such as a garnish, sauce, or icing.

top·ple [top′əl] *v.* **top·pled, top·pling** **1** To push and cause to fall by its own weight: The child *toppled* the wobbly stack of blocks. **2** To fall over, as if from its own weight: The baby took a few steps and *toppled*.

tops [tops] *adj. informal* First-rate; outstanding: She's *tops* in her field.

top·sail [top′səl *or* top′sāl′] *n.* A sail set next above the lowest sail on a mast.

top secret Extremely confidential: a *top secret* government document.

top·side [top′sīd′] **1** *n.* The part of a ship's side above the waterline. **2** *n.* The part of a ship above the main deck. **3** *adj., adv.* On or to the upper parts of a ship.

top·soil [top′soil′] *n.* The surface or top layer of soil, usually more fertile than the soil beneath.

top·sy-tur·vy [top′sē·tûr′vē] **1** *adv.* Upsidedown. **2** *adv.* In great disorder. **3** *adj.* Turned upside-down or being in great disorder.

toque [tōk] *n.* A close-fitting, brimless hat.

Tor·ah [tôr′ə *or* tō′rə] *n.* In Judaism, the Pentateuch, or first five books of the Old Testament.

torch [tôrch] *n.* **1** A source of light, as a burning stick of wood that can be carried in the hand. **2** Anything that guides or sheds light. **3** A device that gives off a very hot flame, as a blowtorch. **4** *British* A flashlight.

torch·bear·er [tôrch′ber′ər] *n.* **1** A person who carries a torch. **2** A leader or inspirer.

torch·light [tôrch′līt′] *n.* The light of a torch or torches.

tore [tôr] Past tense of TEAR¹.

to·re·a·dor [tôr′ē·ə·dôr′] *n.* Another name for MATADOR.

to·re·ro [tə·râr′ō] *n., pl.* **to·re·ros** A matador or any of his assistants in a bullfight.

tor·ment [*n.* tôr′ment′, *v.* tôr·ment′] **1** *n.* Great bodily pain or mental agony. **2** *v.* To cause to suffer physically or mentally: My tight shoes *tormented* me. **3** *n.* A person or thing that torments. **4** *v.* To make miserable or annoyed: The patient *tormented* the hospital staff with repeated complaints. **—tor·men′tor** or **tor·men′ter** *n.*

torn [tôrn] Past participle of TEAR¹.

tor·na·do [tôr·nā′dō] *n., pl.* **tor·na·does** or **tor·na·dos** A violent, destructive, whirling wind, forming a funnel-shaped cloud that extends downward from a mass of cloud and moves along in a narrow path.

tor·pe·do [tôr·pē′dō] *n., pl.* **tor·pe·does** or **tor·pe·dos,** *v.* **tor·pe·doed, tor·pe·do·ing** **1** *n.* A large, underwater projectile that moves under its own power. It is shaped like a cigar and is filled with high explosives that blow up when it strikes a ship. **2** *v.* To damage or sink (a ship) with a torpedo.

torpedo boat A small, swift warship equipped with tubes for discharging torpedos.

tor·pid [tôr′pid] *adj.* **1** Not able to feel or move much, if at all, as a hibernating animal; dormant. **2** Sluggish; dull: The big meal made us all *torpid*.

tor·por [tôr′pər] *n.* The condition of being torpid or sluggish; stupor.

torque [tôrk] *n.* **1** A force acting in a way that tends to produce rotation. **2** The degree to which a force can make something rotate.

tor·rent [tôr′ənt] *n.* **1** A stream of water flowing with great speed and violence. **2** Any great or rapid flow: a *torrent* of tears; a *torrent* of words.

tor·ren·tial [tô·ren′shəl] *adj.* Of, like, or resulting from a torrent.

tor·rid [tôr′id] *adj.* Very hot; scorching; burning: a *torrid* climate.

tor·sion [tôr′shən] *n.* 1 The act of twisting. 2 A twisted condition. 3 The twisting of a body along the direction of its greatest length.

tor·so [tôr′sō] *n.* 1 The human body, apart from the head, arms, and legs; trunk. 2 A sculpture of a human trunk.

tort [tôrt] *n.* A wrongful act, excepting a breach of contract, for which the injured party may sue in a court of law.

tor·til·la [tôr·tē′yä] *n.* A round, flat Mexican bread made of coarse cornmeal baked on a sheet of iron or a slab of stone.

tor·toise [tôr′təs] *n., pl.* **tor·tois·es** or **tor·toise** 1 A turtle, especially one of the species that live entirely on land. 2 A slow-moving person or thing.

Tortoise

tor·toise·shell [tôr′təs·shel′] 1 *n.* A mottled brown translucent substance forming the shell of certain turtles, used to make combs and ornaments. 2 *n.* Any of several butterflies with mottled brown, orange, and black wings. 3 *adj.* Made of or resembling tortoiseshell, as in color. Also written **tortoise shell** and **tortoise-shell.**

tor·tu·ous [tôr′chōō·əs] *adj.* 1 Full of twists, turns, and windings: a *tortuous* mountain road. 2 Not straightforward; devious: a *tortuous* argument. —**tor′tu·ous·ly** *adv.* —**tor′tu·ous·ness** *n.* ◆ *Tortuous* and *torturous* both go back to the Latin word *tortus*, meaning *twisted.* Something *tortuous* has many twists or turns: a *tortuous* path. Something *torturous* often involves twisting part of the body to cause pain: a *torturous* punishment.

tor·ture [tôr′chər] *n., v.* **tor·tured, tor·tur·ing** 1 *n.* The infliction of great physical pain. 2 *n.* Great mental or physical suffering: the *torture* of an abcessed tooth; the *torture* of embarrassment. 3 *v.* To cause to suffer great pain. 4 *v.* To twist or turn the form or meaning of. —**tor′tur·er** *n.*

tor·tur·ous [tôr′chər·əs] *adj.* Extremely painful; causing torture. ◆ See TORTUOUS.

To·ry [tôr′ē] *n., pl.* **To·ries** 1 During the American Revolution, a colonist who was on the British side. 2 A member of an old British political party, officially named the **Conservative Party** since about 1832. 3 (*often written* **tory**) A person who is very conservative, especially in politics.

toss [tôs] 1 *v.* To throw or fling or be thrown or flung about: The wind *tossed* the treetops; The ships *tossed* in the stormy sea. 2 *v.* To throw lightly and easily with the hand: Please *toss* me an apple. 3 *v.* To lift with a quick motion, as the head. 4 *v.* To throw (a coin) into the air to decide something, the outcome depending on the side on which the coin falls. 5 *v.* To throw oneself from side to side; move about restlessly, as in sleep. 6 *n.* The act of tossing. —**toss off** 1 To drink all at once in one draft. 2 To do quickly and in an offhand manner.

toss-up or **toss·up** [tôs′up′] *n. informal* 1 The throwing up of a coin to decide something. 2 An even chance: It's a *toss-up* whether our team wins or not.

tot [tot] *n.* 1 A little child; toddler. 2 A small drink or portion of liquor.

to·tal [tōt′(ə)l] *n., adj., v.* **to·taled** or **to·talled, to·tal·ing** or **to·tal·ling** 1 *n.* The whole sum or amount; whole. 2 *adj. use*: the *total* amount. 3 *v.* To find the total of; add: to *total* a column of figures. 4 *v.* To come to or reach as a total: The bill *totaled* $26. 5 *adj.* Complete; absolute: The storm caused *total* destruction of the town. 6 *v. slang* To make a total wreck of; demolish.

to·tal·i·tar·i·an [tō·tal′ə·târ′ē·ən] 1 *adj.* Of or having to do with a type of government controlled exclusively by one political party and forbidding all other parties. 2 *n.* A person who advocates or practices totalitarianism. 3 *adj.* Despotic; authoritarian.

to·tal·i·tar·i·an·ism [tō·tal′ə·târ′ē·ə·niz′əm] *n.* 1 A totalitarian system of government. 2 Rigid control by a government over all aspects of human life.

to·tal·i·ty [tō·tal′ə·tē] *n., pl.* **to·tal·i·ties** The whole sum or quantity.

to·tal·ly [tōt′(ə)l·ē] *adv.* Completely; altogether.

tote [tōt] *v.* **tot·ed, tot·ing,** *n. informal* 1 *v.* To carry about on one's person, as a gun. 2 *v.* To haul; carry, as supplies. 3 *n.* A tote bag. —**tot′er** *n.*

tote bag A large bag with handles for carrying miscellaneous items.

to·tem [tō′təm] *n.* 1 An animal, plant, or other natural object thought by certain primitive peoples to be the ancestor or guardian spirit of the clan. 2 A carved or painted image of such an animal, plant, or object.

Totem pole

totem pole A tall pole carved or painted with symbols of totems by North American Indians, especially on the NW coast.

tot·ter [tot′ər] *v.* 1 To walk feebly and unsteadily: to *totter* across the room. 2 To shake or sway as if about to fall: People *totter* when they are dizzy.

tou·can [tōō′kan′] *n.* A large bird of tropical America with brightly colored plumage and a huge, thin-walled bill.

Toucan

touch [tuch] 1 *v.* To bring a bodily part, especially a finger, fingers, or the hand, into contact with; feel: to *touch* a statue. 2 *v.* To come into contact by hitting or striking lightly; tap: Whoever *touches* the tree trunk first wins the race. 3 *v.* To be in contact or in contact with: The two ends of the rope are almost *touching*; The car behind us is *touching* ours. 4 *n.* The act of touching:

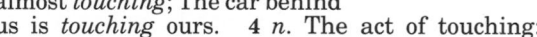

a	add	**i**	it	**ōō**	took	**oi**	oil
ā	ace	**ī**	ice	**ōō**	pool	**ou**	pout
â	care	**o**	odd	**u**	up	**ng**	ring
ä	palm	**ō**	open	**û**	burn	**th**	thin
e	end	**ô**	order	**yōō**	fuse	**th**	this
ē	equal					**zh**	vision

ə = { a in *above*, e in *sicken*, i in *possible*, o in *melon*, u in *circus* }

T

Some seed pods burst at a *touch.* **5** *n.* A being touched. **6** *n.* The sense by which the size, shape, and texture of outside objects are felt by any part of the body, especially the fingers. **7** *n.* The sensation one gets from touching something: Sandpaper has a rough *touch.* **8** *n.* Communication; connection: The two old friends had kept in *touch* since their school days. **9** *v.* To reach to; come up to: The paint roller *touched* the ceiling. **10** *v.* To handle or disturb: Don't *touch* an injured person before the doctor comes. **11** *v.* To handle, use, eat, or drink: After a big meal, I can never *touch* dessert. **12** *v.* To damage slightly: The tomato plants were *touched* by an early frost. **13** *v.* To stir the emotions of, especially to sympathy or gratitude: Your kind letter *touched* us all. **14** *v.* To talk briefly: The article *touched* on many topics. **15** *v.* To have to do with; concern: Our decisions *touch* your future plans. **16** *v.* To come up to; equal: My athletic abilities will never *touch* yours. **17** *v.* To occupy or concern oneself with; set about: You haven't *touched* your homework. **18** *n.* A small quantity; dash: a *touch* of garlic. **19** *n.* A slight attack or twinge: a *touch* of arthritis. **20** *n.* A slight detail or change, as that given to a story or picture. **21** *n.* A stroke, as with a pencil or brush. **22** *n.* The manner in which a musician presses the keys of a piano. **23** *n.* The distinctive manner or style of expression used by someone, as an artist or author. **—touch off** **1** To cause to explode. **2** To cause to happen or begin. **—touch up** To make small changes so as to improve.

touch-and-go [tuch′ən·gō′] *adj.* Uncertain; risky.

touch·back [tuch′bak′] *n.* A situation in football in which the ball is downed by a player behind his own goal line after the ball has been passed or kicked there by the opposing team. No points are awarded, and play resumes with the team in possession of the ball on its 20-yard line.

touch·down [tuch′doun′] *n.* In football, a play worth six points, ending with the ball in the possession of an attacking player over the opponent's goal line.

touched [tucht] *adj.* **1** Moved by sympathy, gratitude, or another tender emotion. **2** *informal* Somewhat unbalanced mentally.

touch football Football played without protective gear and employing tagging in place of tackling.

touch·ing [tuch′ing] **1** *adj.* Appealing to the emotions; moving. **2** *prep.* Concerning.

touch·stone [tuch′stōn′] *n.* **1** A dark, fine-grained stone once used to test the purity of gold or silver by the color of the streak left on the stone after rubbing it with the metal. **2** Anything by which the qualities of something are tested.

touch·y [tuch′ē] *adj.* **touch·i·er, touch·i·est** **1** Easily offended or hurt; irritable. **2** Calling for tact or skill. **—touch′i·ly** *adv.* **—touch′i·ness** *n.*

tough [tuf] **1** *adj.* Capable of withstanding great strain, pressure, or abuse without tearing or cracking: *tough* leather. **2** *adj.* Healthy and rugged; robust. **3** *adj.* Difficult to cut or chew: *tough* steak. **4** *adj.* Hard to do, play, or beat; difficult: Digging ditches is *tough* work; a *tough* team. **5** *adj.* Stern, severe, or demanding: a *tough* teacher; a *tough* law. **6** *adj.* Rough, rowdy, or dangerous: a *tough* neighborhood. **7** *n.* A rough, dangerous, or lawless person. **8** *adj.* Bitterly fought or played: a *tough* game. **9** *informal* Unfortunate: a *tough* break. **—tough′ly** *adv.* **—tough′ness** *n.*

tough·en [tuf′ən] *v.* To make or become tough.

tou·pee [tōō·pā′] *n.* A small wig to cover a bald spot on the head.

tour [tŏŏr] **1** *n.* A trip during which one visits a number of places for pleasure or to perform, as a theatrical company, musician, or athlete. **2** *n.* A walk or ramble through: a *tour* of a museum. **3** *v.* To make a tour of: to *tour* Ireland. **4** *v.* To make a tour: We *toured* for three months. **5** *v.* To take (a play or other presentation) on a tour.

tour de force [tŏŏr′də fôrs′] *pl.* **tours de force** [tŏŏr′ də fôrs′] A difficult thing accomplished by great skill or ingenuity.

tour·ism [tŏŏr′iz′əm] *n.* **1** The practice of traveling for pleasure. **2** The encouragement, guidance, or accommodation of tourists.

tour·ist [tŏŏr′ist] **1** *n.* A person who makes a tour for pleasure. **2** *adj. use*: *tourist* class.

tour·ma·line [tŏŏr′mə·lēn′ *or* tŏŏr′mə·lin] *n.* A mineral that occurs in various varieties and colors, of which transparent blues, pinks, reds, and greens are used as gems.

tour·na·ment [tŏŏr′nə·mənt *or* tûr′nə·mənt] *n.* **1** In medieval times, a contest in which mounted knights armed with lances tried to knock their opponents off their horses. **2** A series of matches in a sport or game involving many players: a chess *tournament.*

tour·ney [tŏŏr′nē *or* tûr′nē] *n., pl.* **tour·neys,** *v.* **tour·neyed, tour·ney·ing** **1** *n.* A tournament. **2** *v.* To take part in a tournament.

tour·ni·quet [tŏŏr′nə·kit] *n.* A device for stopping bleeding by closing a blood vessel, such as a bandage twisted tightly with a stick.

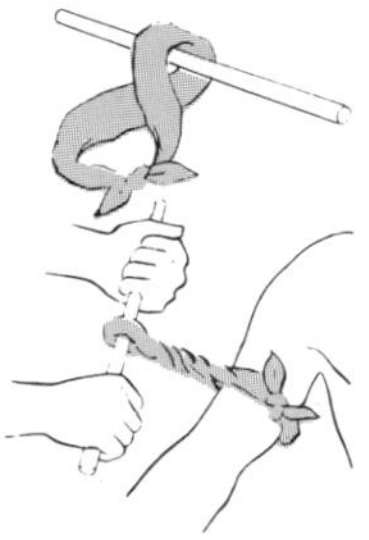
Tourniquet

tou·sle or **tou·zle** [tou′zəl] *v.* **tou·sled** or **tou·zled, tou·sling** or **tou·zling** To make untidy or disheveled; muss up: to *tousle* hair.

tout [tout] *informal* **1** *v.* To promote or publicize energetically. **2** *v.* To make exaggerated claims for. **3** *v.* To give or sell information about (race horses) to bettors. **4** *n.* A person who touts.

tow[1] [tō] *v.* To pull or drag by a rope or chain: to *tow* a wrecked car. **2** *n.* The act of towing. **3** *n.* A being towed: a tugboat with a barge in *tow.* **4** *n.* Something that is towed, as barges by a tugboat. **5** *n.* A rope or cable used in towing. **—take in tow** **1** To attach a line to, for towing. **2** To take under one's care; take charge of.

tow[2] [tō] *n.* Coarse, short fibers of flax or hemp ready for spinning.

to·ward [tôrd *or* tə·wôrd′] *prep.* **1** In the direction of; facing: to turn *toward* the door. **2** Near: *Toward* evening we went home. **3** In anticipation of; for: to save *toward* one's old age. **4** With respect to; regarding: to feel kindly *toward* animals. **5** Designed to result in.

to·wards [tôrdz *or* tə·wôrdz′] *prep.* Toward.

tow·boat [tō′bōt′] *n.* Another word for TUGBOAT.

tow·el [toul *or* tou′əl] *n., v.* **tow·eled** or **tow·elled, tow·el·ing** or **tow·el·ling** **1** *n.* A cloth or paper for drying anything by wiping. **2** *v.* To wipe or dry with a towel.

tow·er [tou′ər] **1** *n.* A tall but rather narrow structure, either standing alone or built as part of another building: a church *tower*; an observation *tower.* **2** *n.* A person, place, or thing that seems to give safety or security: During our trouble, my friend was a *tower* of strength. **3** *v.* To rise or stand high, like a tower: A giraffe *towers* over most other animals.

tow·er·ing [tou′ər·ing] *adj.* **1** Like a tower; lofty. **2** Great; outstanding: a *towering* genius. **3** Violent; furious: a *towering* rage.

Tower of London An 11th-century fortress in London, England, on the north bank of the Thames.

tow·head [tō′hed′] *n.* **1** A head of very blond or flaxen hair. **2** A person having such hair. **—tow′·head·ed** *adj.*

tow·hee [tō′(h)ē] *n.* A finch of eastern North America having black, white, and reddish plumage and a call that sounds like its name.

tow·line [tō′līn′] *n.* A cable or rope used for towing.

town [toun] *n.* **1** A large collection of homes and other buildings, usually larger than a village but smaller than a city. **2** The people who live in such a place: The whole *town* came to the fair. **3** A city: New York is a noisy *town.* **4** The business district of a city: Let's go to *town* and shop.

town crier In former times, an official who went about the streets calling out news or public announcements.

town hall A building containing the offices of the officials of a town, used for meetings and other town business.

town house **1** A house in town used by a person whose main residence is elsewhere. **2** Another name for ROW HOUSE.

town meeting A meeting of the qualified voters of a town, as in New England, to transact town business.

towns·folk [tounz′fōk′] *n.pl.* Townspeople.

town·ship [toun′ship′] *n.* **1** A division of a county that has certain powers of municipal government. **2** A unit or area in surveys of U.S. public lands, usually six miles square.

towns·man [tounz′mən] *n., pl.* **towns·men** [tounz′·mən] **1** A resident of a town. **2** A person who lives in one's town; fellow citizen.

towns·peo·ple [tounz′pē′pəl] *n.pl.* People who live in towns or in a particular town.

towns·wom·an [tounz′wo͝om′ən] *n., pl.* **towns·wom·en** [tounz′wim′in] **1** A woman who lives in a town. **2** A woman who lives in one's own town.

tow·path [tō′path′] *n.* A path along a river or canal, used by draft animals for towing boats.

tow·rope [tō′rōp′] *n.* A rope used for towing.

tox- or **toxi-** or **toxo-** A combining form meaning: Poisonous; poison, as in *toxemia.*

tox·e·mi·a [tok·sē′mē·ə] *n.* The presence of toxins in the blood. **—tox·e′mic** *adj.*

tox·ic [tok′sik] *adj.* **1** Of or caused by poison. **2** Poisonous. **—tox·ic·i·ty** [tok·sis′ə·tē] *n.*

tox·i·col·o·gy [tok′si·kol′ə·jē] *n.* The science dealing with poisonous substances and the prevention and treatment of poisoning. **—tox′i·col′o·gist** *n.*

tox·in [tok′sin] *n.* **1** Any of various poisons produced by certain bacteria and viruses and causing diseases. **2** A poison produced by a plant or animal, as snake venom.

tox·oid [tok′soid′] *n.* A toxin treated with chemicals so that it is nonpoisonous. It is often used in immunization.

toy [toi] **1** *n.* An article made to amuse a child; plaything. **2** *adj. use:* a *toy* tractor. **3** *n.* Any object of little importance or value. **4** *v.* To amuse oneself; fiddle; play: to *toy* with a rubber band. **5** *adj.* Of miniature size: a *toy* poodle.

tp. township.

tpk. turnpike.

tr. **1** transitive. **2** translated. **3** translation. **4** translator. **5** transpose. **6** treasurer. **7** treasury.

trace[1] [trās] *n., v.* **traced, trac·ing** **1** *n.* A mark, sign, or indication left by some person, animal, or past action or event: The Vikings left few *traces* of their voyage to North America; the *traces* left by an earthquake. **2** *v.* To follow the tracks or trail of: to *trace* an animal to its den. **3** *v.* To follow the course or development of: to *trace* the origin of a word. **4** *v.* To copy (a drawing) by placing a transparent sheet of paper over it and following the lines exactly. **5** *v.* To draw or mark out carefully with lines: to *trace* the plan of a building. **6** *n.* A small amount or indication: just a *trace* of onion in the salad. **—trace·a·ble** [trā′sə·bəl] *adj.*

trace[2] [trās] *n.* Either of two straps or chains that fasten a horse to the vehicle it pulls.

trace element A chemical element present or needed in very small quantities.

trac·er [trā′sər] *n.* **1** A person that traces. **2** A search for a thing or a person that has been lost or delayed. **3** A device for making copies by tracing. **4** An easily detected substance, such as a dye or a radioactive isotope, that is put into a system in order to trace the speed and course of a chemical or biological process within the system.

trac·er·y [trā′sər·ē] *n., pl.* **trac·er·ies** **1** A group of interlacing and branching lines forming an ornamental pattern, as in stonework or wood carving. **2** Any design resembling this: a *tracery* of frost on a window.

tra·che·a [trā′kē·ə] *n., pl.* **tra·che·ae** [trā′kē·ē′] or **tra·che·as** The windpipe. **—tra·che·al** [trā′kē·əl] *adj.*

tra·che·ot·o·my [trā′kē·ot′ə·mē] *n., pl.* **tra·che·ot·o·mies** A surgical incision into the trachea, usually to permit air to reach the lungs when the normal passage through the throat is blocked.

trac·ing [trā′sing] *n.* A copy made by following exactly the lines of the original on transparent paper placed over it.

track [trak] **1** *n.* A mark, trail, or series of footprints left by the passing of something: tire *tracks*; bear *tracks.* **2** *v.* To follow the tracks or trail of: to *track* a wild animal; to *track* down information. **3** *v.* To make footprints on: to *track* up the kitchen floor. **4** *v.* To make tracks with: to *track* mud on the carpet. **5** *n.* Any regular path or course. **6** *n.* Any kind of racecourse, as for people, horses, or automobiles. **7** *n.* Sports performed on such a course. **8** *adj. use:* a *track* meet. **9** *n.* A rail or pair of rails on which something may travel, especially the steel rails for railroads. **10** *n.* A course of action or thought followed to reach a

a	add	**i**	it	**o͝o**	took	**oi**	oil
ā	ace	**ī**	ice	**o͞o**	pool	**ou**	pout
â	care	**o**	odd	**u**	up	**ng**	ring
ä	palm	**ō**	open	**û**	burn	**th**	thin
e	end	**ô**	order	**yo͞o**	fuse	**t̶h̶**	this
ē	equal					**zh**	vision

ə = a in *above*, e in *sicken*, i in *possible*, o in *melon*, u in *circus*

T

goal: on the *track* of a new discovery. **11** *n.* Either of the endless metal belts on which a tank or bulldozer moves. **—in one's tracks** Right where one is; on the spot. **—keep track of** To keep in touch with, informed about, or aware of. **—lose track of** To fail to keep in touch with, informed about, or aware of: I *lost track of* the time. **—make tracks** *informal* To get away in a hurry.

track-and-field [trak′ən(d)·fēld′] *adj.* Being or having to do with athletic events that are performed on a track and the adjacent field, such as running, the pole vault, and the high jump.

track·less [trak′lis] *adj.* **1** Unmarked by trails or paths: a *trackless* desert. **2** Not running on tracks: a *trackless* trolley.

track meet A sports competition in track-and-field events.

tract[1] [trakt] *n.* **1** A large area, as of land or water. **2** An extensive region of the body made up of a system of parts or organs that perform some special function: the digestive *tract.*

tract[2] [trakt] *n.* A short treatise, especially a pamphlet on a religious topic.

tract·a·ble [trak′tə·bəl] *adj.* **1** Easily led or controlled; not stubborn; docile: a *tractable* animal. **2** Easily worked or shaped: Silver is a *tractable* metal. **—trac′ta·bil′i·ty** *n.* **—trac′ta·bly** *adv.*

tract house Any of a group of similar houses built on a tract of land.

trac·tion [trak′shən] *n.* **1** The act of pulling or drawing over a surface. **2** A being drawn or pulled. **3** The power used for such pulling or drawing. **4** The power to grip a surface and not slip while in motion: In the mud the tires lost *traction.* **5** Contraction, as of a muscle.

trac·tor [trak′tər] *n.* **1** A powerful, motor-driven vehicle used, as on farms, for pulling a plow or reaper. **2** A vehicle with a driver's cab and a powerful truck engine, used to pull large trailers.

Tractor

trade [trād] *n., v.* **trad·ed, trad·ing 1** *n.* A business or occupation, especially a specialized kind of work with the hands that requires training: the bricklaying *trade.* **2** *n.* The buying and selling of goods, at either wholesale or retail prices, within a country or between countries; commerce. **3** *v.* To engage in or carry on buying and selling: to *trade* in furs. **4** *n.* The people engaged in a particular kind of work: The new styles are the talk of the clothing *trade.* **5** *n.* Regular customers. **6** *v.* To buy or shop: to *trade* at a store. **7** *n.* An exchange of one thing for another; barter. **8** *v.* To exchange (one thing for another): I *traded* my old mitt for a new one. **9** *n.* (*usually pl.*) A trade wind. **—trade in** To give in exchange or as part payment: to *trade in* an old car on a new one. **—trade on** or **trade upon** To get advantage from; exploit: The children *trade on* their parents' fame. ◆ A *trade* usually involves skill with the hands, whereas a *profession* depends more on knowledge and judgment, and therefore requires a longer period of educational training. One speaks of a carpenter, barber, or plumber as having a *trade,* but of a doctor, lawyer, or teacher as belonging to a *profession.* See also OCCUPATION.

trade-in [trād′in′] *n.* Something given in exchange or as part payment for a purchase: Use your car as a *trade-in* on a new one.

trade·mark [trād′märk′] *n.* A name or symbol used to distinguish one maker's or seller's goods from those made or sold by others. Registered trademarks are the legal property of their owners.

trade name **1** The name given to a product, process, or service, by the company that deals in it. **2** The name of a business firm.

trade-off [trād′ôf′] *n.* **1** A choice among possible benefits or advantages, when having some prevents one from having others. **2** A giving up of one thing to gain another; calculated exchange.

trad·er [trā′dər] *n.* **1** A person who engages in trade. **2** A ship used in trade.

trade school A school in which students learn trades, as carpentry or plumbing.

trades·man [trādz′mən] *n., pl.* **trades·men** [trādz′·mən] **1** A person engaged in retail trade; shopkeeper. **2** A person engaged in a skilled trade; craftsman.

trade union Another name for LABOR UNION.

trade wind Either of two winds that blow continuously toward the equator, one from the northeast and the other from the southeast.

trading post A store in wild or unsettled country where trading and bartering are done.

trading stamp A printed stamp issued to a customer who has made a purchase, to be collected and redeemed for merchandise.

tra·di·tion [trə·dish′ən] *n.* **1** The passing down of customs, beliefs, and tales from one generation to the next. **2** A custom, belief, or set of practices passed down in this way.

tra·di·tion·al [trə·dish′ən·əl] *adj.* Of, handed down by, or following tradition: the *traditional* Fourth of July picnic. **—tra·di′tion·al·ly** *adv.*

tra·duce [trə·d(y)ōōs′] *v.* **tra·duced, tra·duc·ing** To say untrue things that damage the reputation of; slander. **—tra·duc′er** *n.*

traf·fic [traf′ik] *n., adj., v.* **traf·ficked, traf·fick·ing 1** *n.* The number or movement of things or people passing along a route: heavy *traffic*; slow *traffic.* **2** *adj.* Having to do with or directing traffic: a *traffic* jam; a *traffic* cop. **3** *n.* The business of buying and selling, especially when wrongful or illegal: *traffic* in stolen goods. **4** *v.* To engage in buying, selling, or trade, especially illegally. **5** *n.* The amount of freight or number of passengers carried by a transportation system. **6** *n.* Dealings: I have no *traffic* with dishonest merchants. **—traf′fick·er** *n.*

traffic circle *U.S.* An intersection where vehicles move around a central circle, counterclockwise, to get from one road to another.

traffic light A signal light that regulates the flow of traffic by alternating red and green lights symbolizing commands to stop and go.

tra·ge·di·an [trə·jē′dē·ən] *n.* **1** An actor who plays tragic heroes. **2** A writer of tragedies.

tra·ge·di·enne [trə·jē′dē·en′] *n.* An actress who plays tragic heroines.

trag·e·dy [traj′ə·dē] *n., pl.* **trag·e·dies 1** A serious play which ends sadly or disastrously. Shakespeare's *Julius Caesar* is a tragedy. **2** A sad or disastrous event. ◆ *Tragedy* once referred only to plays, but now it commonly refers to actual disasters as well: The destruction of the town by an earthquake was a terrible *tragedy.*

trag·ic [traj′ik] *adj.* **1** Of, like, or having to do with dramatic tragedy. **2** Causing or involving great suffering, injury, or unhappiness: a *tragic* accident. **—trag′i·cal·ly** *adv.*

trag·i·com·e·dy [traj′i·kom′ə·dē] *n., pl.* **trag·i·com·e·dies** A play with comic and tragic elements.

trail [trāl] **1** *v.* To drag or draw along behind: The cat's tail *trailed* in the grass. **2** *v.* To float or stream behind, as smoke or dust. **3** *n.* Anything that trails behind: a *trail* of bubbles. **4** *v.* To follow the track or scent of: to *trail* a deer. **5** *n.* A track or scent left by something that has passed: a bear's *trail.* **6** *n.* A path, as through a wood or wilderness. **7** *v.* To follow or lag behind, as in a race. **8** *v.* To grow along the ground in a creeping way, as ivy. **9** *v.* To become fainter: The thunder *trailed* off into a rumble.

trail·blaz·er [trāl′blā′zər] *n.* **1** A person who marks a trail by cutting blazes. **2** A person who leads the way in any field or project; pioneer.

trail·er [trā′lər] *n.* **1** A person, animal, or thing that trails. **2** A vehicle pulled by a car, truck, or tractor and equipped to carry goods or to serve as a home.

train [trān] **1** *n.* A line of railway cars coupled together and operated as a unit. **2** *n.* A group of attendants or servants, as those that follow a sovereign in a procession. **3** *n.* An extension of a dress skirt, trailing behind the wearer. **4** *n.* A line of vehicles, pack animals, or persons, traveling together: a wagon *train.* **5** *n.* A series or sequence of connected things: the valve *train* in an automobile engine; a *train* of thought. **6** *v.* To instruct, discipline, or drill for a special purpose: to *train* the students to take an exam; to *train* a dog to obey. **7** *v.* To bring up; rear: to *train* children properly. **8** *v.* To bring oneself to good physical condition by exercise and proper diet: to *train* for a boxing match. **9** *v.* To cause (a plant) to grow in a desired direction by bending or tying: to *train* ivy on a trellis. **10** *v.* To point or aim: to *train* the telescope on the moon.

train·ee [trā′nē′] *n.* A person who is being trained, as for a job; learner; apprentice.

train·er [trā′nər] *n.* **1** A person who trains. **2** A person who directs a course of physical training or who coaches athletes. **3** A person who trains animals, as for shows or circus acts.

train·ing [trā′ning] *n.* **1** Practical instruction needed to do or be something: driver *training.* **2** The process of being trained. **3** Good physical condition, or a program or regimen to keep one in condition: an athlete in *training.*

train·load [trān′lōd′] *n.* The amount that a freight or passenger train can carry.

train·man [trān′mən] *n., pl.* **train·men** [trān′mən] A person who is employed on a railroad train, especially a brakeman.

traipse [trāps] *v.* **traipsed, traips·ing** *informal* To walk about in an idle or aimless manner.

trait [trāt] *n.* A special feature or quality of one's character: Patience is a good *trait.*

trai·tor [trā′tər] *n.* A person who betrays friends, a cause, or an obligation, especially a person who betrays a country. ◆ *Traitor* comes from the Latin word *traditor,* meaning *a betrayer,* which in turn comes from *tradere,* meaning *to deliver* (into the hands of the enemy).

trai·tor·ous [trā′tər·əs] *adj.* Of or like a traitor or treason.

tra·jec·to·ry [trə·jek′tər·ē] *n., pl.* **tra·jec·to·ries** The curved path followed by a projectile or a comet in its flight.

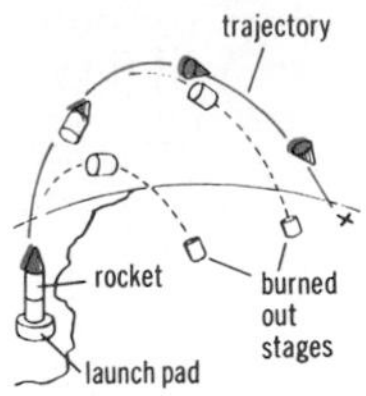

tram [tram] *n.* **1** A four-wheeled vehicle for carrying coal in coal mines. **2** *British* A streetcar. **3** A cable car.

tram·mel [tram′əl] *n., v.* **tram·meled** or **tram·melled, tram·mel·ing** or **tram·mel·ling** **1** *n.* (*usually pl.*) Anything that hinders freedom or activity: the *trammels* of financial obligations. **2** *v.* To hinder or restrict. **3** *n.* A shackle used in training horses. **4** *n.* A net for catching animals, as birds or fish. **5** *n.* A hook on which to hang pots over a fire in a fireplace.

tramp [tramp] **1** *n.* A homeless person who wanders around and begs for a living; vagrant. **2** *v.* To walk or wander, especially as a vagrant. **3** *n.* A long stroll or hike: a *tramp* along the beach. **4** *n.* A heavy tread; stamping. **5** *n.* The sound made by heavy walking or stamping. **6** *v.* To step or walk heavily: to *tramp* on someone's toes; to *tramp* up the steps. **7** *n.* A steamer that goes from port to port picking up freight wherever it can be found. **—tramp′er** *n.*

tram·ple [tram′pəl] *v.* **tram·pled, tram·pling,** *n.* **1** *v.* To walk heavily. **2** *v.* To walk or stamp on heavily, especially so as to crush or hurt: The runaway horse *trampled* the flower garden; to *trample* on someone's feeling of self-respect. **3** *n.* The act or sound of tramping. **—tram′pler** *n.*

tram·po·line [tram′pə·lēn′] *n.* A piece of strong net or canvas stretched on a frame, used as a springboard in tumbling.

Trampoline

tram·way [tram′wā′] *n.* **1** *British* The tracks for a streetcar. **2** An overhead cable or set of rails on which trams run.

trance [trans] *n.* **1** A condition between sleep and wakefulness brought on by illness, hypnosis, or other reasons, in which a person has no free choice to act or move. **2** A dreamlike state in which a person is completely absorbed in thought.

tran·quil [trang′kwil *or* tran′kwil] *adj.* Calm; serene: a *tranquil* evening; a *tranquil* mind. **—tran′quil·ly** *adv.* **—tran′quil·ness** *n.*

tran·quil·ize or **tran·quil·lize** [trang′kwə·līz′ *or* tran′kwə·līz′] *v.* **tran·quil·ized** or **tran·quil·lized, tran·quil·iz·ing** or **tran·quil·liz·ing** To make or become tranquil, especially to calm by administering a tranquilizer.

a	add	**i**	it	**o͝o**	took	**oi**	oil
ā	ace	**ī**	ice	**o͞o**	pool	**ou**	pout
â	care	**o**	odd	**u**	up	**ng**	ring
ä	palm	**ō**	open	**û**	burn	**th**	thin
e	end	**ô**	order	**yo͞o**	fuse	**t͟h**	this
ē	equal					**zh**	vision

ə = {a in *above* e in *sicken* i in *possible*; o in *melon* u in *circus*}

T

tran·quil·iz·er or **tran·quil·liz·er** [trang'kwə·lī'zər *or* tran'kwə·lī'zər] *n.* A kind of drug used to reduce tension or anxiety.

tran·quil·li·ty or **tran·quil·i·ty** [trang·kwil'ə·tē *or* tran·kwil'ə·tē] *n.* Calmness; serenity.

trans- A prefix meaning: Across, through, beyond, or on the other side of, as in *transcontinental*.

trans. 1 transaction. 2 transferred. 3 transitive. 4 translation. 5 transportation. 6 transpose.

trans·act [trans·akt' *or* tranz·akt'] *v.* To carry through; do: to *transact* business. **—trans·ac'tor** *n.*

trans·ac·tion [trans·ak'shən *or* tranz·ak'shən] *n.* 1 The act of transacting. 2 Something transacted, as a business deal. 3 (*pl.*) The reports or minutes of a formal meeting, often published.

trans·at·lan·tic [trans'ət·lan'tik] *adj.* 1 On the other side of the Atlantic Ocean. 2 Across or crossing the Atlantic Ocean: a *transatlantic* voyage.

tran·scend [tran·send'] *v.* 1 To go beyond; overstep the limits of: Your politeness *transcends* ordinary good manners. 2 To be superior to; excel: Her skill as a veterinary *transcends* that of the other trainees.

tran·scen·dence [tran·sen'dəns] *n.* The condition of being transcendent.

tran·scen·den·cy [tran·sen'dən·sē] *n.* Transcendence.

tran·scen·dent [tran·sen'dənt] *adj.* Going beyond what is usual; remarkable in every way; extraordinary: a *transcendent* experience. **—tran·scen'·dent·ly** *adv.*

tran·scen·den·tal [tran'sən·den'təl] *adj* 1 Transcendent. 2 Supernatural. **—tran'scen·den'tal·ly** *adv.*

trans·con·ti·nen·tal [trans'kon'tə·nen'təl] *adj.* Going from one side of the continent to the other: a *transcontinental* trip.

tran·scribe [tran·skrīb'] *v.* **tran·scribed, tran·scrib·ing** 1 To copy or recopy in handwriting or typewriting from an original or from shorthand notes. 2 To record (a radio or television program) for later use. **—tran·scrib'er** *n.*

tran·script [tran'skript'] *n.* A written or typewritten copy: a *transcript* of a school record.

tran·scrip·tion [tran·skrip'shən] *n.* 1 The act of transcribing. 2 A copy; transcript. 3 A radio or television performance that has been recorded for later use.

tran·sept [tran'sept'] *n.* Either of the arms at the sides of the nave of a church that is built in the form of a cross.

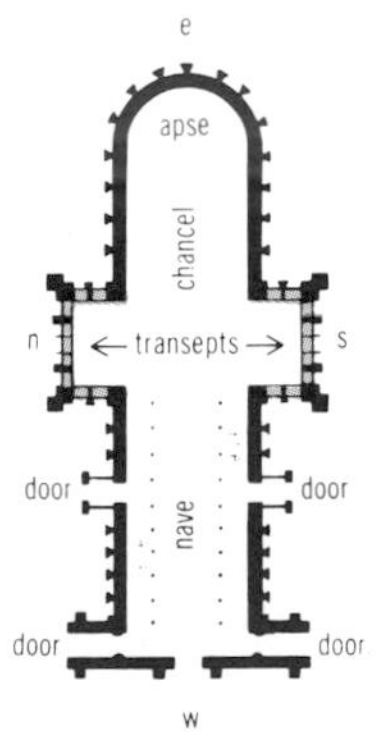

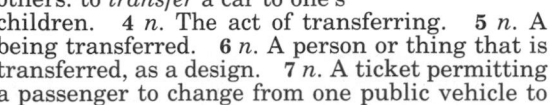

trans·fer [*v.* trans'fər *or* trans·fûr', *n.* trans'fər] *v.* **trans·ferred, trans·fer·ring,** *n.* 1 *v.* To move or send from one place or person to another: to *transfer* a book from a table to a shelf; She was *transferred* to another city to work. 2 *v.* To convey (a design or drawing) from one surface to another, as by specially prepared paper. 3 *v.* To make over the possession of to another or others: to *transfer* a car to one's children. 4 *n.* The act of transferring. 5 *n.* A being transferred. 6 *n.* A person or thing that is transferred, as a design. 7 *n.* A ticket permitting a passenger to change from one public vehicle to another without paying the full fare again. 8 *v.* To change from one public vehicle to another with such a ticket. **—trans·fer'rer** *n.*

trans·fer·a·ble [trans·fûr'ə·bəl] *adj.* Capable of being transferred.

trans·fer·ence [trans·fûr'əns] *n.* 1 The act of transferring. 2 A being transferred.

transfer RNA Ribonucleic acid that transports specific amino acids within a living cell to the location needed for the formation of a particular protein.

trans·fig·ur·a·tion [trans'fig·yə·rā'shən] *n.* 1 A change in appearance or form. 2 (*written* **Transfiguration**) In the New Testament, the supernatural change in Christ's appearance on the mountain.

trans·fig·ure [trans·fig'yər] *v.* **trans·fig·ured, trans·fig·ur·ing** 1 To change the form or appearance of. 2 To make exalted or glorious: Glittering ice *transfigured* the trees.

trans·fix [trans·fiks'] *v.* 1 To pierce through; impale: to *transfix* a shark with a harpoon. 2 To make motionless, as with horror or fear.

trans·form [trans·fôrm'] *v.* 1 To change the form or appearance of: Water can *transform* this desert into green and fertile fields. 2 To change the character or condition of: The basement has been *transformed* into a play room. 3 In electricity, to change the ratio of current to voltage, as of an alternating current.

trans·for·ma·tion [trans'fər·mā'shən] *n.* 1 The act of transforming. 2 A being transformed. 3 A radical change in appearance, character, condition, or form. 4 A change in the genetic makeup of a cell, especially a bacterial cell, by the introduction of a gene or genes from a different source.

trans·form·er [trans·fôr'mər] *n.* 1 A person or thing that transforms. 2 An electromagnetic device used in alternating current circuits to alter the ratio of current to voltage with very small loss of power.

trans·fuse [trans·fyōōz'] *v.* **trans·fused, trans·fus·ing** 1 To transfer (blood) from one person or animal to another. 2 To cause to pass from one person or thing to another; instill: My parents *transfused* their love of music into me.

trans·fu·sion [trans·fyōō'zhən] *n.* 1 The process or an instance of transfusing. 2 The injection of blood or another liquid into a vein or artery.

trans·gress [trans·gres'] *v.* 1 To break or violate, as a law or an oath. 2 To sin. 3 To pass beyond or over: The movie *transgresses* what is suitable viewing for children. **—trans·gres'sor** *n.*

trans·gres·sion [trans·gresh'ən] *n.* The act of transgressing, especially a sin or violation of a law.

tran·ship [tran·ship'] *v.* **tran·shipped, tran·ship·ping** Another spelling of TRANSSHIP. **—tran·ship'ment** *n.*

tran·sience [tran'shəns] *n.* The condition of being transient.

tran·sien·cy [tran'shən·sē] *n.* Transience.

tran·sient [tran'shənt] 1 *adj.* Passing away quickly; transitory: *transient* pain. 2 *adj.* Moving from place to place: a *transient* laborer. 3 *n.* A person who travels from place to place. 4 *n.* A person who stops briefly before moving on: a hotel for *transients*. **—tran'sient·ly** *adv.*

tran·sis·tor [tran·zis'tər] *n.* An electronic device made of a semiconductor, as germanium or silicon, with at least three electrodes. Transistors perform functions like those of electron tubes, being used in radios, television sets, computers, and other electronic equipment. ◆ *Transistor* is a blend of *trans(fer)* + *(res)istor.*

tran·sis·tor·ize [tran·zis′tə·rīz′] *v.* **tran·sis·tor·ized, tran·sis·tor·iz·ing** To design or make (an electronic device) with transistors.

transistor radio A compact radio equipped with transistors.

tran·sit [tran′sit] *n.* 1 The act of passing over or through; passage. 2 The act of carrying across or through; conveyance: We arrived while our new furniture was still in *transit.* 3 An instrument for measuring angles, used in surveying.

tran·si·tion [tran·zish′ən] *n.* The act or condition of changing from one form, place, or type of existence, to another: a *transition* from country to city life. **—tran·si′tion·al** *adj.* **—tran·si′tion·al·ly** *adv.*

tran·si·tive [tran′sə·tiv] *adj.* Taking or containing a direct object. In the sentence "I stubbed my toe," *stubbed* is a transitive verb and *stubbed my toe* is a transitive construction. **—tran′si·tive·ly** *adv.*

tran·si·to·ry [tran′sə·tôr′ē] *adj.* Existing for a short time only: *transitory* grief.

trans·late [trans·lāt′] *v.* **trans·lat·ed, trans·lat·ing** 1 To change (something spoken or written) into another language. 2 To explain in other words: Medical terms sometimes have to be *translated* for the lay reader. 3 To move or change to another place or condition: to *translate* promises into deeds. **—trans·lat·a·ble** [trans·lāt′ə·bəl] *adj.*

trans·la·tion [trans·lā′shən] *n.* 1 The act of translating. 2 Something that has been translated, especially a work translated into another language.

trans·la·tor [trans·lā′tər] *n.* A person who translates or interprets from one language to another.

trans·lit·er·ate [trans·lit′ə·rāt′] *v.* **trans·lit·er·at·ed, trans·lit·er·at·ing** To represent in the characters of another alphabet: to *transliterate* Russian words. **—trans·lit′er·a′tion** *n.*

trans·lu·cence [trans·lo͞o′səns] *n.* The condition of being translucent.

trans·lu·cen·cy [trans·lo͞o′sən·sē] *n.* Translucence.

trans·lu·cent [trans·lo͞o′sənt] *adj.* Allowing light to pass through, but blocking a view of objects on the other side: a *translucent* window. **—trans·lu′·cent·ly** *adv.*

trans·mi·grate [trans·mī′grāt′] *v.* **trans·mi·grat·ed, trans·mi·grat·ing** 1 To move to another place to live; migrate. 2 To pass to another body at death, as the soul is believed to do in certain religions. **—trans′mi·gra′tion** *n.*

trans·mis·si·ble [trans·mis′ə·bəl] *adj.* Capable of being transmitted. **—trans·mis′si·bil′i·ty** *n.*

trans·mis·sion [trans·mish′ən] *n.* 1 The act of transmitting or passing on. 2 Something that is transmitted. 3 The transfer of something, as power or electricity, from one point to another. 4 A device for this purpose, as the mechanism in an automobile that connects the engine and the driving wheels. 5 The passage through space of radio waves.

trans·mit [trans·mit′] *v.* **trans·mit·ted, trans·mit·ting** 1 To send or pass on from one person or place to another; transfer: to *transmit* a package by messenger; Dirty water *transmits* disease. 2 To pass on by means of heredity. 3 To send out (as messages or radio programs) by means of electricity or electromagnetic waves. 4 To cause (especially light or sound) to pass through a medium. ◆ The *-mit* in *transmit, emit,* and *permit* comes from the Latin word meaning *to send.* Thus *transmit* literally means *to send across,* or, more exactly, *from one place or person to another*: A walkie-talkie *transmits* messages. *Emit* means *to send out,* or *to give off or discharge*: Automobile exhausts *emit* fumes. *Permit* means *to send through* in the sense of letting go through or allowing. **—trans·mit′ta·ble** *adj.* **—trans·mit′tal** *n.*

trans·mit·ter [trans·mit′ər] *n.* 1 A person or thing that transmits. 2 A device in a radio or other communication system that sends out electrical signals in a form that corresponds to a message or picture being transmitted.

trans·mu·ta·tion [trans′myo͞o·tā′shən] *n.* 1 The conversion of a base metal to gold, as attempted by alchemists. 2 The conversion of one chemical element to another, as by atomic fission or radioactive decay.

trans·mute [trans·myo͞ot′] *v.* **trans·mut·ed, trans·mut·ing** 1 To change, as in nature, form, or quality. 2 To undergo or cause to undergo transmutation. **—trans·mut·a·ble** [trans·myo͞ot′ə·bəl] *adj.*

trans·o·ce·an·ic [trans′ō·shē·an′ik] *adj.* 1 Situated across the ocean. 2 Crossing the ocean: a *transoceanic* voyage.

tran·som [tran′səm] *n.* 1 A small window above a door or window, usually hinged to a horizontal crosspiece. 2 This crosspiece.

tran·son·ic [tran·son′ik] *adj.* Having to do with or moving at a speed about equal to the speed of sound in air.

transp. transportation.

trans·pa·cif·ic [trans′pə·sif′ik] *adj.* 1 Situated on the opposite side of the Pacific Ocean. 2 Crossing the Pacific Ocean: a *transpacific* flight.

trans·par·ence [trans·pâr′əns] *n.* The quality of being transparent.

trans·par·en·cy [trans·pâr′ən·sē] *n., pl.* **trans·par·en·cies** 1 The quality of being transparent. 2 A picture on a transparent substance, as glass, intended to be viewed by shining a light through it.

trans·par·ent [trans·pâr′ənt] *adj.* 1 So clear or sheer as to be easily seen through: *transparent* paper. 2 Easy to see or understand; obvious. **—trans·par′ent·ly** *adv.* **—trans·par′ent·ness** *n.*

tran·spi·ra·tion [tran′spə·rā′shən] *n.* 1 The process or an instance of transpiring. 2 The passage of water vapor containing waste products from living tissue through pores or membranes.

tran·spire [tran·spīr′] *v.* **tran·spired, tran·spir·ing** 1 To give off (waste products) in the form of moisture from the surface, as the human body does or as leaves do. 2 To become known. 3 *informal* To happen; occur.

trans·plant [trans·plant′] *v.* 1 To dig up (as a plant) from where it is growing and plant it again

a	add	**i**	it	**o͝o**	took	**oi**	oil		
ā	ace	**ī**	ice	**o͞o**	pool	**ou**	pout		
â	care	**o**	odd	**u**	up	**ng**	ring		
ä	palm	**ō**	open	**û**	burn	**th**	thin		
e	end	**ô**	order	**yo͞o**	fuse	**t͟h**	this		
ē	equal					**zh**	vision		

ə = a in *above*, e in *sicken*, i in *possible*, o in *melon*, u in *circus*

T

in another place. **2** To transfer (tissue or an organ) from one part of the body to another or from one person to another. **—trans′plan·ta′tion** *n.*

trans·port [*v.* trans·pôrt′, *n.* trans′pôrt′] **1** *v.* To carry or convey from one place to another. **2** *n.* The act of conveying from one place to another: Freight trains are used for the *transport* of many goods. **3** *n.* A ship used to carry troops and military supplies. **4** *n.* A vehicle used to carry passengers, mail, and equipment. **5** *v.* To carry away with strong emotion. **6** *n.* A strong emotion or feeling. **7** *v.* To send (criminals) to a penal colony, especially across the sea. **8** *n.* A mechanism that moves magnetic tape past a recording or sensing device, as on a tape recorder.

trans·por·ta·tion [trans′pər·tā′shən] *n.* **1** The act of transporting. **2** A being transported. **3** A means or system of transporting: air *transportation.* **4** A charge for transport; ticket or fare.

trans·pose [trans·pōz′] *v.* **trans·posed, trans·pos·ing** **1** To reverse the order or change the place of: If you *transpose* the letters in "but," you get "tub." **2** In music, to put in a different key. **—trans·pos′·a·ble** *adj.* **—trans·po·si·tion** [trans′pə·zish′ən] *n.*

trans·ship [trans·ship′] *v.* **trans·shipped, trans·ship·ping** To transfer (goods) from one carrier to another during shipment. **—trans·ship′ment** *n.*

trans-son·ic [tran·son′ik] *adj.* Another spelling of TRANSONIC.

tran·sub·stan·ti·a·tion [tran′səb·stan′shē·ā′shən] **1** In the Communion ceremony of some Christian churches, the change of the substance of the bread and wine into the body and blood of Christ, the bread and wine keeping unchanged their material qualities of taste and appearance. **2** A changing of anything into something different.

trans·ver·sal [trans·vûr′səl] **1** *adj.* Transverse. **2** *n.* A line intersecting a system of lines.

trans·verse [trans·vûrs′] *adj.* Lying or being across or from side to side: *transverse* braces.

trap [trap] *n., v.* **trapped, trap·ping** **1** *n.* A device for catching or snaring animals. **2** *n.* Any trick by which a person may be put off guard or deceived: The sale was a *trap* to attract customers. **3** *v.* To catch in a trap; ensnare: to *trap* beavers. **4** *v.* To set traps to catch game animals. **5** *n.* A device for hurling clay targets into the air for people to shoot at. **6** *n.* A U-shaped bend in a drainpipe to keep sewer gas from coming up. **7** *n.* A light, two-wheeled carriage suspended by springs. **8** *n.* A trap door. **9** *n.* (*pl.*) Percussion instruments, as drums and cymbals.

trap door A hinged or sliding door to cover an opening in a floor or roof.

tra·peze [tra·pēz′] *n.* A short swinging bar, suspended by two ropes, used by gymnasts.

tra·pe·zi·um [tra·pē′zē·əm] *n., pl.* **tra·pe·zi·ums** or **tra·pe·zi·a** [tra·pē′zē·ə] A quadrilateral having no two sides parallel.

trap·e·zoid [trap′ə·zoid′] *n.* A four-sided geometric figure having two sides parallel and the other two not parallel.

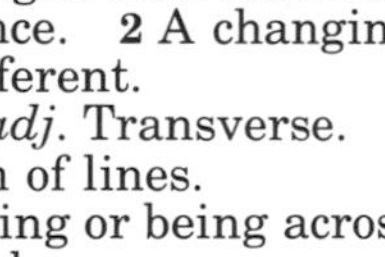

a and *b* are parallel, *c* and *d* are not.

trap·per [trap′ər] *n.* A person whose work is the trapping of fur-bearing animals.

trap·pings [trap′ingz] *n.pl.* **1** An ornamental covering or harness for a horse. **2** Very elaborate ornaments or garments.

trap·shoot·ing [trap′sho͞o′ting] *n.* The sport of shooting clay targets sent up from traps.

trash [trash] **1** *n.* Worthless things to be thrown out; rubbish. **2** *n.* Worthless ideas or writing; nonsense. **3** *n.* Worthless, disreputable people. **4** *v.* To throw away; get rid of. **5** *v. slang* To destroy (property) maliciously.

trash·y [trash′ē] *adj.* **trash·i·er, trash·i·est** Of poor quality; worthless: a *trashy* novel. **—trash′i·ness** *n.*

trau·ma [trô′mə *or* trou′mə] *n., pl.* **trau·mas** or **trau·ma·ta** [trô′mə·tə *or* trou′mə·tə] **1** A physical injury. **2** A severe emotional shock that has long-lasting psychological effects.

trau·mat·ic [trô·mat′ik *or* trou·mat′ik] *adj.* Of, constituting, or caused by a trauma: *traumatic* injuries; a *traumatic* experience. **—trau·mat′i·cal·ly** *adv.*

trav. **1** traveler. **2** travels.

trav·ail [trə·vāl′ *or* trav′āl] **1** *n.* Strenuous physical or mental labor; toil. **2** *v.* To work very hard. **3** *n.* The pains of childbirth. **4** *v.* To undergo the pains of childbirth. ◆ See TRAVEL.

trav·el [trav′əl] *v.* **trav·eled** or **trav·elled, trav·el·ing** or **trav·el·ling,** *n.* **1** *v.* To go from one place to another; make a journey or tour: to *travel* through France; to *travel* as a tourist. **2** *n.* The act of traveling. **3** *n.* (*pl.*) Journeys or trips. **4** *v.* To move or journey over, across, or through: to *travel* the open highway. **5** *v.* To be transmitted, as light or sound. **6** *v.* To move in a fixed path, as a piston. ◆ The word *travel* developed as another form of *travail,* one of whose meanings was *journey.*

trav·eled or **trav·elled** [trav′əld] *adj.* **1** Having made many journeys or travels. **2** Used much by travelers: a *traveled* highway.

trav·el·er or **trav·el·ler** [trav′(ə)·lər] *n.* **1** A person making a journey or tour. **2** A traveling salesman.

traveling salesman A person who travels from place to place taking orders on behalf of a wholesaler or manufacturer.

trav·e·logue or **trav·e·log** [trav′ə·lôg′ *or* trav′ə·log′] *n.* A lecture or film describing travels.

trav·erse [*v.* trə·vûrs′, *n., adj.* trav′ərs] *v.* **trav·ersed, trav·ers·ing,** *n., adj.* **1** *v.* To pass or travel over, across, or through: They *traversed* the glacier safely. **2** *n.* A part, as of a structure, placed across another part. **3** *adj.* Lying or being across; transverse. **4** *v.* To swing or turn (as a gun or telescope) to the right or left. **—trav′ers·a·ble** *adj.* **—trav′ers·er** *n.*

trav·es·ty [trav′is·tē] *n., pl.* **trav·es·ties,** *v.* **trav·es·tied, trav·es·ty·ing** **1** *n.* An imitation or burlesque of something serious, as a book, play, or speech, that makes it sound ridiculous. **2** *n.* Any careless or absurd treatment of something important: In countries having only one political party, elections are *travesties.* **3** *v.* To make (something serious) ridiculous by a comic imitation.

tra·vois trə·voi′ *or* trav′oi] *n., pl.* **tra·vois** [trə·voiz′ *or* trav′oiz] A simple vehicle without wheels once used by American Indians on the Great Plains. It consisted of two poles trailing from a draft animal with the load slung on a platform between them.

trawl [trôl] **1** *n.* A great fishing net shaped like a flattened bag and towed along the bottom of the ocean by a ship. **2** *n.* A long line having many short fishing lines fastened along it at intervals. It is held up by buoys. **3** *v.* To catch (fish) with a trawl.

trawl·er [trô′lər] *n.* A boat used in trawling.
tray [trā] *n.* A flat receptacle with a low rim, made of wood, metal, or other material, and used to carry or hold food or small articles.
treach·er·ous [trech′ər·əs] *adj.* 1 Likely to betray; disloyal; unreliable: a *treacherous* gossip. 2 Not as good or safe as it appears: a *treacherous* path. **—treach′er·ous·ly** *adv.* **—treach′er·ous·ness** *n.*
treach·er·y [trech′ər·ē] *n., pl.* **treach·er·ies** 1 Disloyal action; betrayal. 2 Treason.
trea·cle [trē′kəl] *n. British* Molasses.
tread [tred] *v.* **trod, trod·den** or **trod, tread·ing,** *n.* 1 *v.* To step or walk on, over, or along: We *trod* the boardwalk all morning. 2 *v.* To press with the feet; trample: The dog always *treads* on people's feet. 3 *v.* To make or form by tramping: to *tread* a path through the snow. 4 *v.* To do or accomplish in walking or in dancing: to *tread* a measure. 5 *n.* The act, manner, or sound of walking: A cat's *tread* is very soft. 6 *n.* The flat part of a step in a staircase. 7 *n.* The part of an automobile tire that touches the ground. **—tread water** (*past tense* **treaded**) In swimming, to keep the body erect and the head above water by moving the feet up and down as if walking.

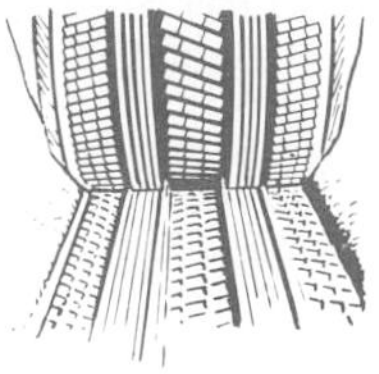
Tread

tread·le [tred′(ə)l] *n., v.* **tread·led, tread·ling** 1 *n.* A lever operated by the foot, usually to make the wheel of a machine rotate. 2 *v.* To work a treadle.

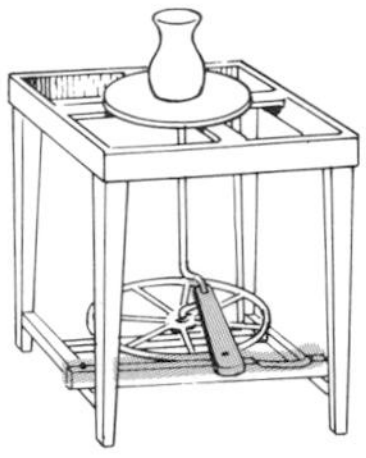
Treadle

tread·mill [tred′mil′] *n.* 1 A device turned by the walking motion of persons on steps around the rim of a large wheel. It was once used as a form of punishment for prisoners. 2 A somewhat similar device turned by the walking motion of persons or animals on a sloping, endless belt. 3 Any monotonous work or routine.
treas. 1 treasurer. 2 treasury.
trea·son [trē′zən] *n.* An act of betrayal, treachery, or breach of allegiance to one's country or sovereign.
trea·son·a·ble [trē′zən·ə·bəl] *adj.* Of or having to do with treason.
trea·son·ous [trē′zən·əs] *adj.* Treasonable.
treas·ure [trezh′ər] *n., v.* **treas·ured, treas·ur·ing** 1 *n.* Valuables stored up and carefully kept, especially money and jewels. 2 *n.* A person or thing that is regarded as valuable, rare, or very dear. 3 *v.* To set a high value upon; prize: We *treasure* a picture of our grandparents. 4 *v.* To store up or hoard as treasure.
treas·ur·er [trezh′ər·ər] *n.* An officer of a state, city, company, club, or other organization, who is in charge of its money.
treasure trove [trōv] 1 Something of value found and not claimed by its owner. 2 Any discovery of great value.
treas·ur·y [trezh′ər·ē] *n., pl.* **treas·ur·ies** 1 The place where the funds of a government, firm, or other organization are kept and paid out. 2 Funds; money: Can we pay for the party out of the club *treasury*? 3 (*written* **Treasury**) The department of the U.S. government that is in charge of the country's money. 4 Any collection of valuable or rare things, as in art or literature.
treat [trēt] 1 *v.* To act toward or deal with in a certain way: to *treat* one's parents with respect. 2 *v.* To look upon; consider: to *treat* the warning as a joke. 3 *v.* To try to cure or make better: The doctor *treated* my poison ivy. 4 *v.* To subject to some chemical or physical action in order to improve: wool *treated* against moths. 5 *v.* To discuss in writing or speaking: This book *treats* mountain climbing. 6 *v.* To pay for the entertainment, food, or drink of: to *treat* a friend to dinner. 7 *n.* The act of treating in such a way, or one's turn to treat. 8 *n.* Entertainment or refreshments paid for by another. 9 *n.* Anything that gives pleasure or satisfaction. 10 *v.* To arrange terms; negotiate. **—treat′er** *n.*
trea·tise [trē′tis] *n.* A generally long and detailed discussion of a subject in writing.
treat·ment [trēt′mənt] *n.* 1 The act, process, or way of treating a person or thing: The farm animals received good *treatment.* 2 The action taken or the materials used in treating something.
trea·ty [trē′tē] *n., pl.* **trea·ties** A formal agreement between two or more nations in reference to peace, commerce, or other matters.
tre·ble [treb′əl] *v.* **tre·bled, tre·bling,** *n., adj.* 1 *v.* To multiply by three; triple: The company's profits *trebled* in a year. 2 *adj.* Threefold; triple. 3 *adj.* Very high; soprano: the *treble* voices of children. 4 *n.* In music, the highest part; soprano. 5 *n.* A singer, instrument, or player taking the highest part. **—tre′bly** *adv.*
treble clef 1 A sign placed on a musical staff to indicate that the G above middle C is on the second line. 2 A musical staff with such a sign on it.
tree [trē] *n., v.* **treed, tree·ing** 1 *n.* A tall, woody plant, usually with a single trunk, having branches and leaves growing out at some distance above the ground. 2 *v.* To chase or drive up a tree: to *tree* a squirrel. 3 *n.* A pole or other piece of wood used for a special purpose: a hat *tree*; a shoe *tree.* 4 *n.* A diagram that looks like a tree, showing a family descent. **—up a tree** *informal* In a difficult or embarrassing situation.
tree fern A large tropical fern having a thick, woody stem with a crown of fronds at the top.
tree frog Any of numerous small frogs that live in trees and have sticky pads on their toes for clinging and climbing.
tre·foil [trē′foil′] *n.* 1 A plant, such as the clover, whose leaves are divided into three leaflets. 2 An ornament, especially in architecture, shaped like such a leaf.
trek [trek] *v.* **trekked, trek·king,** *n.* 1 *v.* To travel, especially slowly or laboriously. 2 *n.* A journey, especially a slow one. 3 *v.* In South Africa, to travel by ox wagon.

a	add	**i**	it	**o͝o**	took	**oi**	oil
ā	ace	**ī**	ice	**o͞o**	pool	**ou**	pout
â	care	**o**	odd	**u**	up	**ng**	ring
ä	palm	**ō**	open	**û**	burn	**th**	thin
e	end	**ô**	order	**yo͞o**	fuse	**t͟h**	this
ē	equal					**zh**	vision

ə = {a in *above* e in *sicken* i in *possible*; o in *melon* u in *circus*}

T

trel·lis [trel′is] *n.* A structure made of crossed strips, as of wood or metal, used as a screen or support for climbing plants.
trel·lis·work [trel′is·wûrk′] *n.* Another word for LATTICEWORK.
trem·a·tode [trem′ə·tōd′] *n.* A fluke or related parasitic flatworm.
trem·ble [trem′bəl] *v.* **trem·bled, trem·bling,** *n.* 1 *v.* To shake, as with agitation, fear, weakness, or cold. 2 *n.* The act of trembling. 3 *v.* To shake; quiver; vibrate: houses *trembling* after an explosion. 4 *v.* To feel anxious or afraid. **—trem′bler** *n.*
trem·bly [trem′blē] *adj.* Affected by trembling; tremulous.
tre·men·dous [tri·men′dəs] *adj.* 1 Dreadful; awful; overwhelming: a *tremendous* disaster. 2 *informal* Unusually large; enormous: a *tremendous* elephant. 3 *informal* Unusually great; wonderful: The book was *tremendous.* **—tre·men′dous·ly** *adv.*
trem·o·lo [trem′ə·lō′] *n., pl.* **trem·o·los** 1 A trembling effect produced in music by rapidly repeating a tone, varying the loudness of a tone, or alternating two tones. 2 A device on an organ for producing a tremolo.
trem·or [trem′ər] *n.* 1 A quick, vibrating movement; a shaking. 2 A quivering feeling, as of excitement, nervousness, or insecurity.
trem·u·lous [trem′yə·ləs] *adj.* 1 Affected by trembling; shaking: *tremulous* speech. 2 Showing fear; timid: a *tremulous* mouse. **—trem′u·lous·ly** *adj.* **—trem′u·lous·ness** *n.*
trench [trench] 1 *n.* A long, narrow opening that has been dug in the earth; ditch. 2 *n.* A long ditch with earth piled up in front, used by soldiers in battle to protect themselves from enemy fire. 3 *v.* To dig a trench in.
trench·an·cy [tren′chən·sē] *n.* The condition of being trenchant.
trench·ant [tren′chənt] *adj.* 1 Sharp and to the point; cutting; keen: a *trenchant* remark. 2 Forceful; effective: a *trenchant* argument for democracy. **—trench′ant·ly** *adv.*
trench coat A belted raincoat styled like those worn by military officers.
trench·er [tren′chər] *n.* A wooden platter for serving food.
trench·er·man [tren′chər·mən] *n., pl.* **trench·er·men** [tren′chər·mən] A person who eats heartily.
trench foot A foot disease resembling frostbite that results from long exposure to cold and wet.
trench mouth A painful bacterial infection of the mucous membrane of the mouth and gums. *Trench mouth* got its name from being epidemic among soldiers in the *trenches* in World War I.
trend [trend] 1 *n.* A general course or direction: new *trends* in men's sportswear. 2 *v.* To have or take a particular trend; tend.
trend·y [tren′dē] *adj. informal* **trend·i·er, trend·i·est** In keeping with the newest fashions; faddish.
trep·i·da·tion [trep′ə·dā′shən] *n.* 1 Fear; anxiety; dread. 2 A trembling.
tres·pass [tres′pəs *or* tres′pas′] 1 *v.* To enter or go without right on another's property. 2 *v.* To intrude; encroach: to *trespass* on another's privacy. 3 *n.* The act of trespassing. 4 *v.* To sin. 5 *n.* A sin or misdeed. **—tres′pas·ser** *n.*
tress [tres] *n.* (*usually pl.*) A lock of hair, especially long, loose hair: her silky *tresses.*
tres·tle [tres′əl] *n.* 1 A frame like a sawhorse used to hold up part of a table top or platform. 2 An open, braced framework used to support a road or railroad tracks.
trey [trā] *n.* A playing card, die, or domino with an indicated value of three.
trfd. transferred.
tri- A prefix meaning: 1 Having or containing three of something, as parts, groups, or atoms, as in *tricycle.* 2 Into three, as in *trisect.* 3 Occurring every three times, as in *triennial.* 4 Occurring three times within a period, as in *triweekly.*
tri·ad [trī′ad] *n.* A group of three, usually closely related persons or things.
tri·al [trī′əl *or* trīl] *n.* 1 The examination before a court of the charges made in a case in order to prove such charges either true or false. 2 The act of testing or proving by experience or use: the *trial* of a new vaccine. 3 An attempt or effort to do something; try: The contestant had three *trials* at hitting the mark. 4 *adj. use:* a *trial* shot at the moon. 5 A being tried or tested by difficulties, suffering, or the like: their hour of *trial.* 6 A cause of suffering, annoyance, or vexation: The children's behavior was a *trial* to their parents. **—on trial** In the process of being tried or tested.
trial and error A method of attacking a problem by trying different approaches and discarding those that do not work.
trial balloon An announcement of something being planned or considered, made in order to test public reaction.
tri·an·gle [trī′ang′gəl] *n.* 1 A plane figure having three sides and three angles. 2 Something shaped like this. 3 A musical instrument consisting of a metal bar bent into a triangle and sounded by being struck with a metal rod.
tri·an·gu·lar [trī·ang′gyə·lər] *adj.* Of, having to do with, or shaped like a triangle.
tri·an·gu·la·tion [trī·ang′gyə·lā′shən] *n.* 1 The division of a region into triangular sections by surveyors so that distances, directions, and locations in the region can be determined by trigonometry. 2 The finding of a position by measuring its bearings from two fixed points a known distance apart and then using trigonometry.
Tri·as·sic [trī·as′ik] 1 *n.* The earliest geological period of the Mesozoic era, during which many reptiles and the first known mammals appeared. 2 *adj.* Of the Triassic.
tri·ath·lon [trī·ath′län] *n.* An endurance race made up of three long-distance events: running, swimming, and bicycling.
trib. tributary.
trib·al [trī′bəl] *adj.* Of or having to do with a tribe or tribes. **—trib·al·ly** *adv.*
tribe [trīb] *n.* 1 A group of people, often a primitive people, having a leader and usually sharing the same customs, religious beliefs, and traditions. 2 A number of persons of any class or profession, taken together: the theatrical *tribe.* 3 A group of related plants or animals.
tribes·man [trībz′mən] *n., pl.* **tribes·men** [trībz′·mən] A member of a tribe.
trib·u·la·tion [trib′yə·lā′shən] *n.* 1 Misery; distress; suffering: the *tribulation* caused by war. 2 An instance of such misery or suffering.
tri·bu·nal [trī·byōō′nəl *or* tri·byōō′nəl] *n.* 1 A court or place of justice. 2 The seat set apart for judges, magistrates, or other officials.
trib·une[1] [trib′yōōn′] *n.* 1 In ancient Rome, an

official chosen by the common people to protect them against oppression. **2** Any person who defends the rights of the people.

tri·bune[2] [trib′yōōn′] *n.* A raised platform for a speaker.

trib·u·tar·y [trib′yə·ter′ē] *n., pl.* **trib·u·tar·ies** **1** *n.* A stream flowing into a larger stream or body of water. **2** *adj.* Bringing things, as supplies, to something larger: a *tributary* stream. **3** *n.* A person or state that pays tribute (def. 2). **4** *adj.* Paying tribute: a *tributary* nation.

trib·ute [trib′yōōt] *n.* **1** Something, as a speech, compliment, or gift, given to show admiration, gratitude, or respect. **2** Money or other payment given by one ruler or state to another as an act of submission or as the price of peace and protection. **3** Any enforced payment.

trice[1] [trīs] *n.* An instant, used only in the phrase **in a trice.**

trice[2] [trīs] *v.* **triced, tric·ing** To haul in or make secure with a rope: *Trice* the topgallant!

tri·ceps [trī′seps′] *n., pl.* **tri·ceps·es** [trī′sep′səz] or **tri·ceps** A large muscle at the back of the upper arm that extends from the shoulder blade to the elbow joint and has to do with extending the forearm.

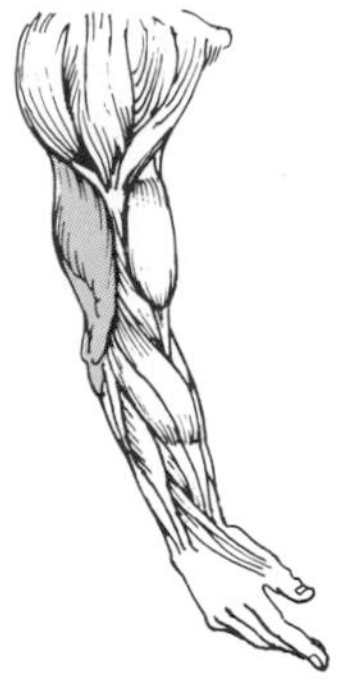
Triceps

tri·cer·a·tops [trī·ser′ə·tops′] *n.* A large plant-eating dinosaur that had a horn above each eye and one above the nose and a heavy horny plate covering the neck.

tri·chi·na [tri·kī′nə] *n., pl.* **tri·chi·nae** [tri·kī′nē] or **tri·chi·nas** A small roundworm that lives as a parasite in pigs and other animals.

trich·i·no·sis [trik′ə·nō′sis] *n.* A serious disease caused by trichinae in the body and marked by such symptoms as intestinal pain, diarrhea, and swollen muscles. Human beings can get trichinosis by eating infested pork that has not been cooked enough to kill the trichinae.

trick [trik] **1** *n.* Something done to fool, deceive, or outwit: After the performance, the magician said it was all a *trick.* **2** *v.* To deceive or cheat; fool: They *tricked* us by coming in the back door. **3** *n.* A malicious, injurious, or annoying act: a dirty *trick.* **4** *n.* A practical joke; prank. **5** *n.* A particular habit or manner: the *trick* of cracking one's knuckles. **6** *n.* A peculiar skill or knack: the *trick* of playing rapid scales on the piano. **7** *n.* An act of magic. **8** *adj.* Of, having to do with, or using tricks or trickery: a *trick* photograph. **9** *v.* To dress, usually in a fancy manner: The children were *tricked* out in old-fashioned costumes. **10** *n.* In card games, the whole number of cards played in one round. **11** *n.* A period of work, especially steering a ship. **—do the trick** *slang* To bring about the desired result.

trick·er·y [trik′ər·ē] *n., pl.* **trick·er·ies** The act of using tricks to cheat or deceive.

trick·le [trik′əl] *v.* **trick·led, trick·ling,** *n.* **1** *v.* To flow or cause to flow in a thin stream or drop by drop: Water *trickled* out of the spout. **2** *v.* To move slowly or bit by bit. **3** *n.* A thin stream or drip.

trick·ster [trik′stər] *n.* Someone who plays tricks; mischievous or dishonest person.

trick·y [trik′ē] *adj.* **trick·i·er, trick·i·est** **1** Likely to use or involve tricks; deceptive. **2** Calling for special skill or care: a *tricky* maneuver. **—trick′i·ly** *adv.* **—trick′i·ness** *n.*

tri·col·or [trī′kul′ər] **1** *adj.* Having three colors. **2** *n.* A flag having three colors. **3** *n.* (*sometimes written* **Tricolor**) The French flag.

tri·cot [trē′kō] *n.* **1** A plain, lightweight, knitted fabric usually of nylon or other synthetic fiber and used mostly for underwear. **2** A soft, ribbed fabric woven of wool or cotton and wool.

tri·cus·pid [trī·kus′pid] **1** *adj.* Having three cusps: a *tricuspid* molar. **2** *n.* A tooth with three cusps on the biting surface.

tri·cy·cle [trī′sik·əl] *n.* A three-wheeled vehicle, especially such a vehicle with pedals, used by children.

tri·dent [trīd′(ə)nt] **1** *n.* A three-pronged spear, as the one carried by the god of the sea in classical mythology. **2** *adj.* Having three teeth or prongs.

Trident

tried [trīd] **1** Past tense and past participle of TRY. **2** *adj.* Tested; trustworthy: a *tried* friendship. **—tried and true** Tested by experience and found to be good.

tri·en·ni·al [trī·en′ē·əl] **1** *adj.* Taking place every third year. **2** *n.* Something that takes place every third year. **3** *adj.* Lasting for three years. **—tri·en′ni·al·ly** *adv.*

tri·fle [trī′fəl] *n., v.* **tri·fled, tri·fling** **1** *n.* Anything of very little value or importance: a gift that was a mere *trifle.* **2** *n.* A small amount of money. **3** *v.* To act or deal with someone or something in a light, frivolous way: to *trifle* with a friendship. **4** *v.* To play; toy: to *trifle* with one's dinner. **5** *v.* To spend or waste in a worthless way, as time or money. **6** *n.* A rich dessert of cake soaked in flavorings and topped with custard, jam, and cream. **—tri′fler** *n.*

tri·fling [trī′fling] *adj.* **1** Lacking seriousness or importance; frivolous: a *trifling* conversation. **2** Lacking size, quantity, or value; trivial: a *trifling* sum. **—tri′fling·ly** *adv.*

trig [trig] *n., informal* Trigonometry.

trig. 1 trigonometric. 2 trigonometry.

trig·ger [trig′ər] **1** *n.* The lever or other device pressed by the finger to fire a gun. **2** *n.* Something that acts like a trigger in that it serves to begin some action or operation. **3** *v.* To begin; set off: An insult *triggered* the fight.

a	add	**i**	it	**ŏŏ**	took	**oi**	oil
ā	ace	**ī**	ice	**ōō**	pool	**ou**	pout
â	care	**o**	odd	**u**	up	**ng**	ring
ä	palm	**ō**	open	**û**	burn	**th**	thin
e	end	**ô**	order	**yōō**	fuse	**th**	this
ē	equal					**zh**	vision

ə = a in *above* e in *sicken* i in *possible* o in *melon* u in *circus*

T

tri·glyph [trī′glif′] *n.* An ornament repeated at intervals on a Doric frieze and consisting of a projecting rectangular block with vertical grooves.

trig·o·no·met·ric [trig′ə·nə·met′rik] *adj.* Of, having to do with, or occurring in trigonometry.

trig·o·nom·e·try [trig′ə·nom′ə·trē] *n.* The branch of mathematics that deals with the relations of the sides and angles of triangles. ◆ *Trigonometry* comes from two Greek words meaning *triangle measure.*

trill [tril] **1** *n.* In music, a rapid alternation of two tones either a tone or a semitone apart. **2** *n.* A sound like this, as that made by certain insects or birds. **3** *n.* A rapid vibration made by a speech organ, as in making the sound of *r* in some varieties of German. **4** *n.* The sound so made. **5** *v.* To sing, say, or play with a trill.

tril·lion [tril′yən] *n., adj.* **1** In the U.S., a thousand billion, written as 1,000,000,000,000. **2** In Great Britain, a million British billions, written as 1,000,000,000,000,000,000. **—tril·lionth** [tril′·yənth] *adj., n.*

tril·li·um [tril′ē·əm] *n.* Any of various plants related to the lily, having a stout stem bearing three leaves and a single flower with three petals.

tri·lo·bate [trī·lō′bāt′] *adj.* Having three lobes.

tri·lo·bite [trī′lə·bīt′] *n.* One of a group of extinct animals having long, flattened bodies divided lengthwise into three sections and enclosed in horny shells.

tril·o·gy [tril′ə·jē] *n., pl.* **tril·o·gies** A group of three plays or sometimes three novels or musical compositions, each complete in itself but making with the others a related series.

trim [trim] *v.* **trimmed, trim·ming,** *n., adj.* **trim·mer, trim·mest** **1** *v.* To put in or restore to order or good condition, as by clipping or pruning: to *trim* hair; to *trim* a rose bush. **2** *n.* A condition of fitness or order: The boxer had to get in *trim* before the fight. **3** *adj.* Being in good condition or order; neat, smart, or tidy: a *trim* uniform. **4** *v.* To remove by cutting: to *trim* away the lower branches of a tree. **5** *n.* The act of trimming, cutting, or clipping: The rose bush is in need of a *trim.* **6** *v.* To decorate; ornament: to *trim* a Christmas tree. **7** *n.* Decoration; ornament: the *trim* of a car. **8** *n.* Something used to ornament the inside of a building, as the moldings around doors or windows. **9** *adj.* Well built or designed: a *trim* figure; the *trim* lines of a car. **10** *v.* To adjust (sails) for sailing. **11** *v.* To balance (a ship, boat, or aircraft) by adjusting cargo or ballast. **12** *n.* The balancing of a boat, ship, or aircraft by such adjustment. **13** *n.* The fitness of a ship for sailing. **14** *v.* To act so as to appear to favor both sides in a quarrel or dispute. **15** *v. informal* To defeat: My opponent *trimmed* me in tennis. **—trim′ly** *adv.* **—trim′mer** *n.* **—trim′ness** *n.*

tri·mes·ter [trī·mes′tər] *n.* **1** A period of three months. **2** A school or college term consisting of a third of an academic year.

trim·ming [trim′ing] *n.* **1** Something used to decorate or ornament. **2** (*pl.*) The usual things that accompany a particular food or dish: turkey and all the *trimmings.* **3** (*pl.*) Something that is removed by trimming or cutting. **4** The act of a person who trims.

tri·month·ly [trī·munth′lē] *adj.* Occurring or appearing every three months.

Trin·i·dad·i·an [trin′ə·dad′ē·ən] **1** *adj.* Of or from Trinidad. **2** *n.* A person born or living in Trinidad.

tri·ni·tro·tol·u·ene [trī·nī′trō·tol′yə·wēn′] *n.* The chemical name for TNT.

trin·i·ty [trin′ə·tē] *n., pl.* **trin·i·ties** **1** Any union of three parts in one; trio. **2** (*written* **Trinity**) In Christian theology, the union in one God of three separate, divine persons, the Father, Son, and Holy Ghost.

trin·ket [tring′kit] *n.* **1** Any small ornament, as of jewelry. **2** Any small toy or object of little value.

tri·no·mi·al [trī·nō′mē·əl] **1** *adj.* Consisting of or containing three names or terms. **2** *n.* A mathematical expression containing three terms. **3** *n.* A taxonomic name for a plant or animal consisting of names for the genus, species, and subspecies or variety.

tri·o [trē′ō] *n., pl.* **tri·os** **1** A group of three. **2** A musical composition for three voices or three instruments. **3** A group of three persons who perform such a composition.

tri·ode [trī′ōd′] *n.* An electron tube having an anode, a cathode, and a third electrode in the form of a grid controlling the flow of electrons between the anode and cathode.

tri·ox·ide [trī·ok′sīd′] *n.* A compound with three atoms of oxygen and one other atom or radical in each molecule.

trip [trip] *n., v.* **tripped, trip·ping** **1** *n.* A journey or voyage. **2** *n.* A misstep or stumble. **3** *v.* To stumble or cause to stumble: I *tripped* on the doorstep. **4** *n.* The act of making a person stumble and fall. **5** *n.* A blunder; mistake. **6** *v.* To make or cause to make a blunder or mistake: I *tripped* on the first question. **7** *n.* A light, nimble step. **8** *v.* To move with light, nimble steps: Our guest *tripped* gracefully into the room.

tri·par·tite [trī·pär′tīt′] *adj.* **1** Made of or divided into three parts. **2** Agreed to or shared among three parties: a *tripartite* pact.

tripe [trīp] *n.* **1** A part of the stomach of an animal such as a deer, sheep, or cow, used for food. **2** *informal* Anything worthless; nonsense.

trip-ham·mer [trip′ham′ər] *n.* A very heavy hammer that is raised or tilted by power and then allowed to drop.

trip·le [trip′əl] *adj., n., v.* **trip·led, trip·ling** **1** *adj.* Consisting of three things or parts: a *triple* mirror. **2** *n.* A set or group of three. **3** *adj.* Three times as great or as many: We're carrying a *triple* load today. **4** *n.* A number or amount three times as great or as many. **5** *v.* To make or become three times as great or as many: We've *tripled* the load. **6** *n.* In baseball, a hit that enables the batter to reach third base. **7** *v.* In baseball, to hit a triple.

triple play A rare baseball play in which three outs are made.

trip·let [trip′lit] *n.* **1** A group of three of a kind. **2** One of three children born at one birth. **3** In music, a group of three equal notes played in the time usually given to two notes of the same type.

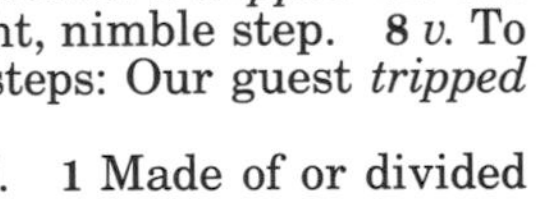

Triplet

triple time A musical rhythm consisting of three beats in a measure accented on the first beat.

trip·li·cate [*adj., n.* trip′lə·kit; *v.* trip′lə·kāt′] *adj., n., v.* **trip·li·cat·ed, trip·li·cat·ing** **1** *adj.* Consisting of three parts or copies: a *triplicate* form. **2** *n.* A set of or one of three identical things: Prepare this letter in *triplicate*. **3** *v.* To make three copies of or repeat three times. **—trip′li·ca′tion** *n.*

tri·ply [trip′(ə)·lē] *adv.* In three times the quantity or degree: *triply* compensated.

tri·pod [trī′pod′] *n.* **1** A three-legged stand for a camera, transit, or other instrument. **2** Anything that stands on three legs, as a stool, table, or pot.

trip·ping [trip′ing] *adj.* Light, nimble, and easy, as in action or movement. **—trip′ping·ly** *adv.*

trip·tych [trip′tik] *n.* **1** A picture on three hinged panels. **2** An ancient Roman writing tablet in three folding sections.

tri·reme [trī′rēm′] *n.* An ancient Greek or Roman warship with three rows of oars on each side.

tri·sect [trī′sekt′ *or* trī·sekt′] *v.* To divide into three parts, usually three equal parts. **—tri·sec·tion** *n.*

trite [trīt] *adj.* **trit·er, trit·est** Used so often as to be stale and dull; commonplace: "It never rains but it pours" is a *trite* saying. **—trite′ly** *adv.* **—trite′·ness** *n.*

trit·i·um [trit′ē·əm *or* trish′ē·əm] *n.* A rare radioactive isotope of hydrogen having a mass three times the mass of the common isotope of hydrogen and a half-life of about 12.5 years.

Tri·ton [trīt′(ə)n] n. In Greek myths, a sea god with a person's head and upper body and a dolphin's tail.

tri·umph [trī′əmf] **1** *n.* A victory or success of any kind: a *triumph* over setbacks. **2** *v.* To win a victory; be successful: The home team *triumphed* over the visitors. **3** *n.* Joy over victory or success: The contest winner let out a shout of *triumph.* **4** *v.* To be joyous over a victory.

tri·um·phal [trī·um′fəl] *adj.* **1** Of or having to do with a triumph. **2** Celebrating a triumph.

tri·um·phant [trī·um′fənt] *adj.* **1** Joyful over victory or success. **2** Victorious: The *triumphant* players marched by. **—tri·um′phant·ly** *adv.*

tri·um·vir [trī·um′vər] *n., pl.* **tri·um·virs** or **tri·um·vi·ri** [trī·um′və·rī] In ancient Rome, one of three officials who shared authority in certain public offices.

tri·um·vi·rate [trī·um′vər·it] *n.* **1** A group of three people who, together, are the heads of a government. **2** Government by such a group or the period during which they are in power. **3** Any group of three people; trio.

triv·et [triv′it] *n.* A three-legged stand for holding cooking pans in a fireplace or a hot dish on a table.

triv·i·a [triv′ē·ə] *n.pl.* Insignificant or unimportant matters: They talk of nothing but *trivia.*

triv·i·al [triv′ē·əl] *adj.* **1** Of little value or importance; insignificant: a *trivial* argument. **2** Ordinary; commonplace: a *trivial* mind.

triv·i·al·i·ty [triv′ē·al′ə·tē] *n., pl.* **triv·i·al·i·ties** **1** The quality of being trivial. **2** A trivial matter.

tri·week·ly [trī·wēk′lē] *adj., adv., n., pl.* **tri·week·lies** **1** *adj.* Taking place or appearing three times a week. **2** *adv.* Three times a week. **3** *adj.* Taking place or appearing every three weeks. **4** *adv.* Every three weeks. **5** *n.* A publication that is issued triweekly.

tro·che [trō′kē] *n.* A medicated lozenge.

tro·chee [trō′kē] *n.* A rhythmic unit in verse consisting of an accented syllable followed by an unaccented syllable.

trod [trod] Past tense and alternative past participle of TREAD: We *trod* country roads for hours.

trod·den [trod′(ə)n] Past participle of TREAD.

Tro·jan [trō′jən] **1** *n.* A native of ancient Troy. **2** *adj.* Of or having to do with ancient Troy or its people. **3** *n.* A person who works hard or is courageous: We worked like *Trojans.*

Trojan War In Greek legend, the ten-year war waged by the Greeks against the Trojans to recover Helen, wife of the king of Sparta, who had been abducted by Paris, a prince of Troy.

troll[1] [trōl] **1** *v.* To fish or fish for with a moving line and hook, as from a slowly moving boat: to *troll* in a quiet stream. **2** *v.* To sing in succession, as in a round. **3** *n.* In music, a round. **4** *v.* To sing loudly.

troll[2] [trōl] *n.* In folklore, a mischievous dwarf or a giant that lived underground or in caves.

trol·ley [trol′ē] *n., v.* **trol·leyed, trol·ley·ing** **1** *n.* A grooved metal wheel that conveys electric current from a wire to an electric vehicle, as to a trolley bus. **2** *n.* Another word for TROLLEY CAR. **3** *v.* To travel by trolley bus or trolley car. **4** *n.* Something, as a basket or case, hung from wheels that run along an overhead cable or rail. **5** *v.* To convey in such a basket.

trolley bus A bus run by electric current conveyed from two overhead wires by trolleys.

trolley car A vehicle for public transportation that runs on rails and is powered by electricity obtained from overhead wires through a trolley.

trol·lop [trol′əp] *n.* A slovenly or immoral woman.

trom·bone [trom·bōn′ *or* trom′bōn′] *n.* A brass instrument related to the trumpet, but larger and lower in pitch than the trumpet. A slide trombone changes notes by means of a sliding U-shaped tube. **—trom·bon′·ist** *n.*

Trombone

troop [trōōp] **1** *n.* A group or gathering of persons or animals: a *troop* of students. **2** *v.* To move along or gather as a troop or as a crowd: Our class *trooped* into the auditorium. **3** *n.* (*usually pl.*) A body of soldiers or soldiers as a group: The *troops* retreated. **4** *n.* A unit of Boy or Girl Scouts. **5** *n.* Another spelling of TROUPE.

troop·er [trōō′pər] *n.* **1** A member of a cavalry troop. **2** A mounted police officer. **3** A state police officer.

troop·ship [trōōp′ship′] *n.* A ship for carrying troops; transport.

trop. **1** tropic. **2** tropical.

tro·phy [trō′fē] *n., pl.* **tro·phies** Something representing victory or success, as a cup awarded for an athletic achievement or a weapon captured from an enemy.

a	add	**i**	it	**ŏŏ**	took	**oi**	oil
ā	ace	**ī**	ice	**ōō**	pool	**ou**	pout
â	care	**o**	odd	**u**	up	**ng**	ring
ä	palm	**ō**	open	**û**	burn	**th**	thin
e	end	**ô**	order	**yōō**	fuse	**t͟h**	this
ē	equal					**zh**	vision

ə = a in *above* e in *sicken* i in *possible* / o in *melon* u in *circus*

T

trop·ic [trop′ik] **1** *n.* (*pl.*) The hot, often humid region of the earth between the tropic of Cancer and the tropic of Capricorn. **2** *adj.* Of, having to do with, or located in the tropics; tropical.
trop·i·cal [trop′i·kəl] *adj.* Of, having to do with, or located in the tropics: a *tropical* climate.
tropical fish Any of various small, brightly colored fishes native to warm waters, often kept in aquariums.
tropical year The time between two consecutive vernal equinoxes. A tropical year is 365 days, 5 hours, 48 minutes, and 46 seconds.
tropic of Cancer An imaginary circle on the earth's surface about 23 1/2° north of the equator, the northern limit of the area on which the sun shines straight down a part of each year.
tropic of Capricorn An imaginary circle on the earth's surface about 23 1/2° south of the equator, the southern limit of the area on which the sun shines straight down a part of each year.
tro·pism [trō′piz·əm] *n.* An involuntary turning or movement of a plant or animal toward or away from a stimulus.
trop·o·sphere [trō′pə·sfir′] *n.* The region of the atmosphere extending from the earth's surface to the stratosphere. In this region there are marked changes of weather.
trot [trot] *n., v.* **trot·ted, trot·ting** **1** *n.* The gait of an animal, as a horse or mule, in which one front leg and the opposite hind leg are moved forward almost at the same time, then the other two, and so on. **2** *v.* To move or cause to move at a trot: to *trot* a horse. **3** *n.* A rapid but not too fast run: an easy *trot* across the field. **4** *v.* To move at such a pace.
troth [trôth] *n.* **1** A promise, especially a promise to marry. **2** Loyalty; fidelity. **3** Truth. ◆ This word is seldom used today.
trot·ter [trot′ər] *n.* **1** A horse that trots or is trained to trot. **2** The foot of a pig, sheep, or calf, prepared as food.
trou·ba·dour [trōō′bə·dôr′] *n.* One of a class of poets and musicians, usually of the noble class, who lived in southern France, northern Italy, and eastern Spain during the 12th and 13th centuries.
trou·ble [trub′əl] *n., v.* **trou·bled, trou·bling** **1** *n.* Distress, difficulty, worry, or suffering: times of *trouble.* **2** *v.* To make or become distressed, annoyed, worried, or ill: Did the noise *trouble* you? **3** *n.* Any difficulty, problem, or disturbance: Family *troubles* kept them busy. **4** *n.* Effort; inconvenience; pains: They went to lots of *trouble* to entertain us. **5** *v.* To put to extra work or inconvenience: Don't *trouble* yourself; I'll answer the phone myself. **6** *n.* A sick or diseased condition: lung *trouble.* **7** *v.* To stir up or disturb, as water.
trou·ble·mak·er [trub′əl·mā′kər] *n.* A person who causes trouble, disturbances, or problems.
trou·ble·shoot·er [trub′əl·shōō′tər] *n.* **1** A person skilled in locating and removing sources of trouble, as in machinery. **2** A person skilled in helping to settle diplomatic or political disputes.
trou·ble·some [trub′əl·səm] *adj.* Causing trouble; trying; disturbing: a *troublesome* illness.
trou·blous [trub′ləs] *adj.* **1** Turbulent; stormy. **2** Difficult; perplexing: a *troublous* decision. **—trou′blous·ly** *adv.* **—trou′blous·ness** *n.*
trough [trôf] *n.* **1** A long, narrow, open container for holding food or water for animals. **2** A long, narrow depression or hollow, as between ridges on land or waves at sea. **3** A gutter along or below the eaves of a house, for carrying off rainwater from the roof.
trounce [trouns] *v.* **trounced, trounc·ing** **1** To beat or thrash severely. **2** *informal* To defeat badly.
troupe [trōōp] *n., v.* **trouped, troup·ing** **1** *n.* A company of actors or other performers. **2** *v.* To travel and perform in a troupe. **—troup′er** *n.*
trou·sers [trou′zərz] *n.pl.* An outer garment covering the body from the waist to the ankles or knees, and divided so as to make a separate covering for each leg; pants.
trous·seau [trōō′sō *or* trōō·sō′] *n., pl.* **trous·seaux** [trōō′sōz *or* trōō·sōz′] or **trous·seaus** A bride's wardrobe, including her clothing and household linens.
trout [trout] *n., pl.* **trout** or **trouts** Any of various chiefly freshwater fish of Europe and North America related to the salmon but smaller, valued as game and food fishes.
trow [trō] *v.* To suppose; think; believe: seldom used today.
trow·el [trou′əl *or* troul] *n.* **1** A flat-bladed, sometimes pointed implement, used to smooth plaster or mortar. **2** A small, usually scoop-shaped implement, used in planting, potting, and digging around small plants.

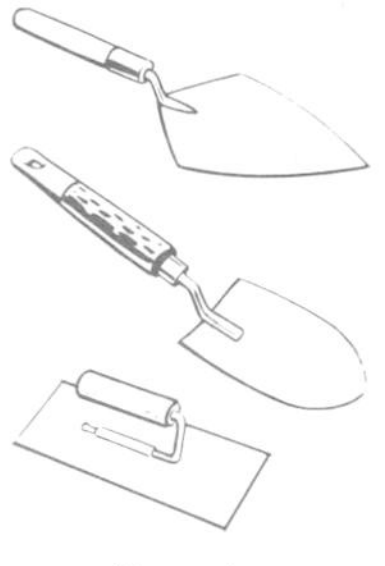
Trowels

troy weight [troi] A standard system of weights used by jewelers to weigh gems and precious metals. In this system, a grain is the same as in avoirdupois weight, and the pound contains 12 ounces, or 5,760 grains.
trp. troop(s).
tru·an·cy [trōō′ən·sē] *n., pl.* **tru·an·cies** **1** A truant condition. **2** An act of being truant.
tru·ant [trōō′ənt] **1** *n.* A person who is absent without permission from a duty or task, especially from school. **2** *adj.* Being absent in this manner: a *truant* student. **3** *adj.* Of or having to do with truants: a *truant* officer. **4** *adj.* Idle; lazy.
truce [trōōs] *n.* **1** A temporary stop in warfare or fighting by agreement of both sides. **2** A temporary relief or rest, as from pain.
truck[1] [truk] **1** *n.* Any of various motor vehicles for carrying heavy loads or freight. **2** *n.* A low frame or vehicle having two wheels at one end and handles at the other end, used for moving trunks, boxes, and other items. **3** *n.* A small, low, flat-topped vehicle on four wheels for moving heavy objects. **4** *v.* To carry (goods) on a truck. **5** *v.* To drive a truck. **6** *n.* A frame with usually two or more pairs of wheels, supporting an end of a railroad car or the like. **7** *n.* A small wheel.
truck[2] [truk] *n.* **1** Vegetables grown for sale at market. **2** *informal* Worthless articles; rubbish; trash. **3** *informal* Dealings: I'll have no *truck* with them.
truck·er [truk′ər] *n.* **1** A person who drives a truck. **2** An individual or business engaged in moving goods by truck.
truck farm A farm on which vegetables are grown for sale at market.
truck·ing [truk′ing] *n.* The business or activity of moving goods by truck.
truck·le [truk′əl] *v.* **truck·led, truck·ling** To yield or

give in weakly or too easily: The committee won't *truckle* to their demands.

truckle bed Another name for TRUNDLE BED.

truc·u·lence [truk′yə·ləns] *n.* The quality of being truculent.

truc·u·lent [truk′yə·lənt] *adj.* 1 Ferocious; savage; fierce. 2 Angry and aggressive; hostile; belligerent: A *truculent* moose barred our way. **—truc′·u·lent·ly** *adv.*

trudge [truj] *v.* **trudged, trudg·ing,** *n.* 1 *v.* To walk wearily or with great effort; plod: to *trudge* five miles. 2 *n.* A tiresome walk.

true [tro͞o] *adj.* **tru·er, tru·est,** *adv., v.* **trued, true·ing** or **tru·ing** 1 *adj.* Faithful to fact or reality; not false: a *true* story. 2 *adj.* Real or natural; genuine, not counterfeit: *true* gold. 3 *adj.* Faithful, as to promises or principles; loyal; steadfast: a *true* friend. 4 *adj.* Conforming to a standard type or pattern; accurate; exact: a *true* copy. 5 *adj.* Properly belonging to a class: not a *true* antelope. 6 *adj.* Placed, shaped, or fitted accurately: The door that sticks is not *true.* 7 *adv.* In a true and accurate manner: The wheel runs *true.* 8 *adj.* Lawful; legitimate: the *true* heir. 9 *v.* To make level or straight; align correctly. **—come true** To happen as desired, expected, or predicted. **—true′ness** *n.*

true-blue [tro͞o′blo͞o′] *adj.* Absolutely loyal.

true-life [tro͞o′līf′] *adj.* Corresponding to reality; true to life: a *true-life* soap opera.

truf·fle [truf′əl] *n.* Any of various fleshy underground fungi, highly valued as food.

tru·ism [tro͞o′iz·əm] *n.* A statement that is so widely known to be true that it does not need to be mentioned, such as: Ice is frozen water.

tru·ly [tro͞o′lē] *adv.* 1 In fact; really: Are those *truly* your statements? 2 Sincerely; genuinely: I *truly* like them. 3 Accurately; truthfully: The original design was *truly* reproduced.

trump [trump] 1 *n.* In various card games, a card of a suit which temporarily ranks above all other suits. 2 *n.* (*usually pl.*) This suit itself. 3 *v.* To play a trump. 4 *v.* To take with a trump: to *trump* your opponent's trick. **—trump up** To invent or concoct in order to deceive: I *trumped up* an excuse about having a headache.

trump·er·y [trum′pər·ē] *n., pl.* **trump·er·ies,** *adj.* 1 *n.* Something showy but worthless. 2 *n.* Nonsense. 3 *adj.* Showy but worthless.

trum·pet [trum′pit] 1 *n.* A brass instrument of high range with a flaring bell and a long, curved metal tube, whose pitch is varied by means of valves. 2 *v.* To blow a trumpet. 3 *n.* Something like a trumpet in shape. 4 *n.* A sound like that made by a trumpet. 5 *v.* To make a sound like that of a trumpet. 6 *v.* To proclaim by or as by a trumpet: to *trumpet* the news. **—trum′pet·er** *n.*

trumpet creeper A woody climbing vine of eastern North America having red trumpet-shaped flowers.

trun·cate [trung′kāt′] *v.* **trun·cat·ed, trun·cat·ing,** *adj.* 1 *v.* To shorten by cutting off a part. 2 *adj.* Having a flat end as if cut off: a *truncate* petal.

trun·ca·tion [trung·kā′shən] *n.* 1 The act of truncating. 2 A being truncated.

trun·cheon [trun′chən] *n.* 1 A police club; billy. 2 A short staff carried as an emblem of authority or privilege.

trun·dle [trun′dəl] *n., v.* **trun·dled, trun·dling** 1 *n.* A small wheel, as a caster. 2 *v.* To roll or propel as if by rolling. 3 *n.* A trundle bed.

trundle bed A bed with a very low frame resting on casters, so that it may be rolled under another bed.

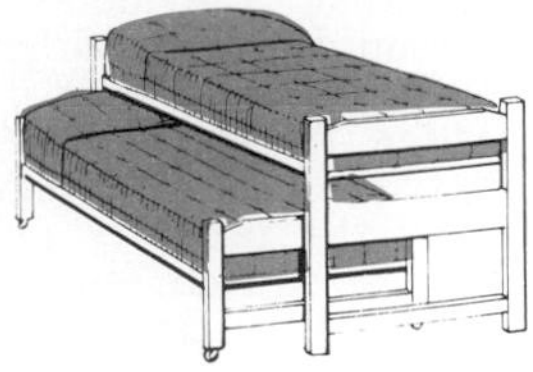
Trundle bed

trunk [trungk] *n.* 1 The main stem or stock of a tree, not including the limbs or roots. 2 The human body, apart from the head, neck, and limbs. 3 A main or central section of anything, as the main section of a nerve or blood vessel. 4 A long, flexible snout, as that of the elephant. 5 A large piece of luggage used for packing and carrying clothes, as for a journey. 6 A compartment of an automobile for storing luggage and other items. 7 (*pl.*) Very short pants or trousers, worn by swimmers and athletes.

trunk line The main line of a transportation, supply, or communication system: the *trunk line* of a railroad.

truss [trus] 1 *n.* A bandage or support for a hernia. 2 *n.* A braced framework or support, as for a roof. 3 *v.* To tie or bind; fasten.

trust [trust] 1 *n.* A confidence or belief in the strength, ability, or honesty of a person or thing: We had *trust* in our guide. 2 *n.* The person or thing in which confidence is put. 3 *v.* To have trust in; rely on: I *trusted* your answer. 4 *v.* To place trust: I *trust* in the experience of our mayor. 5 *n.* Something entrusted to a person's care; responsibility or duty: An aircraft's safety is a pilot's *trust.* 6 *n.* Custody; care: to give something to another's *trust.* 7 *v.* To commit something to the care of: I *trusted* my best friend with my favorite record. 8 *v.* To believe: I *trust* whatever you say. 9 *v.* To expect with confidence and hope: I *trust* the weather will improve tomorrow. 10 *n.* Confidence in the honesty or ability of a person or group to pay at a later date; credit: to sell something on *trust.* 11 *v.* To allow credit to: to *trust* someone for groceries. 12 *n.* Property held and managed by a group or an individual for the benefit of another. 13 *adj.* Held in trust: *trust* money. 14 *n.* A group of firms in a similar business that have united for the purpose of controlling production and prices. **—in trust** Given to another for care, safekeeping, or management but not to own: Money is *in trust* to send the children to college. **—trust to** To depend upon. ◆ *Trust, confidence,* and *faith* all describe a belief that someone or something is good, honest, or true. You have *trust* in someone if you believe in his or her goodness and honesty in actions and truthfulness in speech. *Confidence* is very similar to this and both rely heavily on evidence of things seen or heard. *Faith,* however, is more a feeling or emotion than either

a add	**i** it	**o͝o** took	**oi** oil
ā ace	**ī** ice	**o͞o** pool	**ou** pout
â care	**o** odd	**u** up	**ng** ring
ä palm	**ō** open	**û** burn	**th** thin
e end	**ô** order	**yo͞o** fuse	**th** this
ē equal			**zh** vision

ə = a in *above*, e in *sicken*, i in *possible*, o in *melon*, u in *circus*

T

of the other two and, as such, it does not depend on proof or evidence. One can have *faith* in a person or thing without really being able to explain why.

trus·tee [trus·tē′] *n.* 1 A person who holds property in trust. 2 One of a group of persons who hold in trust the property and manage the affairs of a college, church, foundation, or other organization.

trus·tee·ship [trus·tē′ship′] *n.* The office or duties of a trustee.

trust·ful [trust′fəl] *adj.* Inclined to trust or believe; trusting. **—trust′ful·ly** *adv.* **—trust′ful·ness** *n.*

trust fund Money or securities held in trust.

trust·ing [trus′ting] *adj.* Inclined to trust; trustful.

trust territory A territory, often a former colony, placed under the administration of a country by the United Nations.

trust·wor·thy [trust′wûr′thē] *adj.* Worthy of confidence; reliable: a *trustworthy* pilot. **—trust′wor′·thi·ly** *adv.* **—trust′wor′thi·ness** *n.*

trust·y [trus′tē] *adj.* **trust·i·er, trust·i·est,** *n., pl.* **trust·ies** 1 *adj.* Dependable; faithful; reliable. 2 *n.* A trustworthy person, especially a convict who has been found reliable and who is granted special privileges.

truth [tro͞oth] *n., pl.* **truths** [tro͞othz *or* tro͞oths] 1 The condition or quality of being true: That article is a lie; there is no *truth* in it. 2 Something, as a statement or belief, that is true: In the testimony of the witness, it is hard to separate the *truths* from the lies. 3 A theory, proposition, or principle that is accepted as fact: scientific *truths.* **—in truth** In fact; really.

truth·ful [tro͞oth′fəl] *adj.* 1 Habitually telling the truth: a *truthful* person. 2 Faithful to truth or to the facts: a *truthful* account. **—truth′ful·ly** *adv.* **—truth′ful·ness** *n.*

truth set Another term for SOLUTION SET.

try [trī] *v.* **tried, try·ing,** *n., pl.* **tries** 1 *v.* To make an attempt or an attempt at: *Try* the high dive now; You can do it if you *try.* 2 *v.* To test by using or doing: to *try* a new method; to *try* a new pen. 3 *v.* To put or subject to a hard test: to *try* one's patience. 4 *n.* The act of trying; effort; attempt: Let's have a *try* at our homework. 5 *v.* To determine the guilt or innocence of by judicial trial: to *try* someone for murder. 6 *v.* To examine or determine judicially: to *try* a case. 7 *v.* To put severe strain upon: This light *tries* my eyes. **—try and** *informal* To try to: *Try and* make the dance. **—try on** To put on a garment to test its fit and appearance. **—try out** 1 To attempt to qualify. 2 To test, as by use. ◆ *Try and* for *try to* is acceptable in informal English: *Try and* catch me! In formal speaking and writing it should be avoided.

try·ing [trī′ing] *adj.* Hard to endure; difficult: a *trying* person; a *trying* experience.

try·out [trī′out′] *n.* 1 A test of ability, as of an actor or an athlete. 2 A trial performance, as of a play, to discover its strengths and weaknesses.

tryp·sin [trip′sin] *n.* A digestive enzyme produced in the pancreas that breaks down proteins into amino acids.

try square An L-shaped carpenter's tool used to mark off and test right angles.

tryst [trist] *n.* 1 An appointment, as between sweethearts, to meet at a certain time and place. 2 The meeting place agreed upon. ◆ *Tryst* comes from an old French word for a *hunting station.*

t.s. or **T.S.** tensile strength (physics).

tsar [zär] *n.* Another spelling of CZAR.

tsa·ri·na [zä·rē′nə] *n.* Another spelling of CZARINA.

tset·se [(t)set′sē *or* tsēt′sē] *n.* A small, biting African fly that sucks the blood of cattle, horses, other animals, and humans. One kind transmits the parasite that causes sleeping sickness.

t.sgt. or **t/sgt, T.Sgt.** or **T/Sgt.** technical sergeant.

T-shirt [tē′shûrt′] *n.* 1 A collarless undershirt with short sleeves. 2 A similar shirt for outer wear.

tsp. teaspoon(s).

T square A T-shaped instrument for measuring or laying out right angles or parallel lines.

tsu·na·mi [tso͞o·nä′mē] *n.* A huge ocean wave caused by an undersea volcanic eruption or an undersea earthquake. ◆ *Tsunami* is the Japanese word for this kind of wave, which has often caused destruction along the coast of Japan.

TT 1 telegraphic transfer. 2 teletypewriter. 3 transit time. 4 tuberculin-tested.

Tu. Tuesday.

T.U. trade union.

tub [tub] *n., v.* **tubbed, tub·bing** 1 *n.* A broad, open container made of wood, metal, or other materials, used for various purposes, as for washing. 2 *n.* A bathtub. 3 *n.* *British* A bath taken in a tub. 4 *v.* To wash, bathe, or place in a tub. 5 *n.* The amount that a tub contains.

tu·ba [t(y)o͞o′bə] *n.* Any of several large brass instruments with a deep tone. Pitch is controlled by three, four, or sometimes five valves.

Tuba

tub·by [tub′ē] *adj.* **tub·bi·er, tub·bi·est** Short and stout; squat. **—tub′bi·ness** *n.*

tube [t(y)o͞ob] *n.* 1 A long, hollow pipe, as of metal or rubber, usually used to carry gas or liquids. 2 A cylinder of soft metal used to hold paints, toothpaste, creams, and the like. 3 Any long, tubelike part or organ: a bronchial *tube.* 4 A flexible, inflatable tube, usually of rubber, used inside an automobile tire. 5 An electron tube. 6 A tunnel or subway for cars, trains, or other vehicles. **—the tube** *informal* Television.

tu·ber [t(y)o͞o′bər] *n.* A short, thickened portion of an underground stem, as in the potato.

tu·ber·cle [t(y)o͞o′bər·kəl] *n.* 1 A small, rounded, humplike swelling, as on the roots of certain plants, on a bone, or on the surface of the skin. 2 One of the firm, rounded swellings, or knobs, caused in the body by tuberculosis and characteristic of it.

tu·ber·cu·lar [t(y)o͞o·bûr′kyə·lər] 1 *adj.* Of, having to do with, or affected with tuberculosis. 2 *n.* A person who has tuberculosis. 3 *adj.* Of, having, or like tubercles.

tu·ber·cu·lin [t(y)o͞o·bûr′kyə·lin] *n.* An extract containing substances produced by bacteria that cause tuberculosis, used in diagnosing this disease.

tu·ber·cu·lo·sis [t(y)o͞o·bûr′kyə·lō′sis] *n.* A disease caused by certain bacteria and marked by the formation of tubercles in various parts of the body. It chiefly affects the lungs, and is accompanied by a slow wasting away of strength and vitality. Tuberculosis is often called *TB.*

tu·ber·cu·lous [t(y)ōō·bûr'kyə·ləs] *adj.* Affected with or caused by tuberculosis. **—tu·ber'cu·lous·ly** *adv.*
tube·rose [t(y)ōōb'rōz'] *n.* A Mexican plant that has white, sweet-smelling flowers and grows offshoots from tubers on its roots.
tu·ber·ous [t(y)ōō'bər·əs] *adj.* **1** Of, like, or having tubers. **2** Having small, rounded knobs or swellings.
tub·ing [t(y)ōō'bing] *n.* **1** A series of tubes, as in a heating system. **2** A piece of tube. **3** Material for tubes.
tu·bu·lar [t(y)ōō'byə·lər] *adj.* **1** Having the shape of a tube. **2** Of or having to do with one or more tubes.
tu·bule [t(y)ōō'byōōl'] *n.* A tiny tube or minute channel.
tuck [tuk] **1** *v.* To fold or gather into folds so as to shorten. **2** *v.* To fold or push the loose edges or ends of (something) into place firmly: to *tuck* sheets under a mattress. **3** *v.* To wrap or cover snugly: to *tuck* in a baby. **4** *v.* To put or press into a close or hidden place: to *tuck* a handkerchief into a pocket. **5** *v.* To draw in, contract, or bring close to something else. **6** *n.* A fold stitched into a garment for a better fit or decoration. **7** *v.* To make tucks or folds in.
tuck·er[1] [tuk'ər] *n.* A covering, as of linen or lace, formerly worn over the neck and shoulders.
tuck·er[2] [tuk'ər] *v. informal* To make tired; exhaust.
Tu·dor [t(y)ōō'dər] **1** *n.* A royal family of England that reigned from 1485 to 1603. **2** *adj.* Of or like the architecture, poetry, or other art developed during the reigns of the Tudors.
Tues. Tuesday.
Tues·day [t(y)ōōz'dē *or* t(y)ōōz'dā'] *n.* The third day of the week.
tu·fa [t(y)ōō'fə] *n.* **1** A porous rock formed from material deposited by springs and streams. **2** Another word for TUFF.
tuff [tuf] *n.* A light, porous rock formed from compacted volcanic ash.
tuf·fet [tuf'ət] *n.* **1** A low seat; stool. **2** A cluster or clump, as of grass.
tuft [tuft] **1** *n.* A collection or bunch of small, flexible parts, as hair, grass, or feathers, growing or held together at the base and free at the opposite ends. **2** *v.* To cover or adorn with tufts. **3** *n.* A clump or knot, as a cluster of threads drawn tightly through a quilt, mattress, or upholstery to keep the stuffing in place. **4** *v.* To form tufts in (as in a mattress or quilt).
tug [tug] *v.* **tugged, tug·ging,** *n.* **1** *v.* To pull at with effort: to *tug* an oar; to *tug* at a chain. **2** *v.* To move by pulling with strength: The horse *tugged* the plow. **3** *n.* An act of tugging; violent pull. **4** *v.* To tow with a tugboat. **5** *n.* A tugboat. **6** *n.* A trace, part of a harness.
tug·boat [tug'bōt'] *n.* A small, strongly built boat used to tow ships and barges; tug.
tug of war A contest in which a number of persons at one end of a rope pull against a like number at the other end, each side trying to drag the other across a line marked between.
tu·i·tion [t(y)ōō·ish'ən] *n.* **1** The charge or payment for instruction in a school. **2** The act or business of teaching; instruction.
tu·lip [t(y)ōō'lip] *n.* A hardy plant related to the lily, grown from bulbs, and bearing large cup-shaped flowers in many colors.
tulip tree A tall, deciduous North American tree with lobed leaves and large greenish-yellow flowers resembling tulips.
tulle [tōōl] *n.* A fine, open-meshed, often stiffened material of silk, rayon, or other material, used for veiling and ballet costumes.
tum·ble [tum'bəl] *v.* **tum·bled, tum·bling,** *n.* **1** *v.* To roll, toss, or whirl about: The children *tumbled* on the lawn; to *tumble* clothes in a dryer. **2** *v.* To fall or cause to fall: to *tumble* down a staircase. **3** *v.* To perform acrobatic or gymnastic feats, as somersaults. **4** *n.* A fall or somersault. **5** *v.* To move quickly and awkwardly; stumble: The crowd *tumbled* out of the auditorium. **6** *v.* To throw into disorder or confusion. **7** *n.* A condition of disorder and confusion. **8** *n.* To experience a sharp drop or decline: Stock prices *tumbled* today.
tum·ble·down [tum'bəl·doun'] *adj.* Rickety, as if about to fall down or into pieces; dilapidated.
tum·bler [tum'blər] *n.* **1** A drinking glass without a stem. **2** An acrobat or gymnast. **3** A part of a lock that must be moved to a certain position, as by a key, before the lock can be opened.
tum·ble·weed [tum'bəl·wēd'] *n.* A plant that, when withered, breaks from its roots and is blown about by the wind, scattering its seed.
tum·brel or **tum·bril** [tum'bril] *n.* **1** A farmer's cart. **2** A cart which took prisoners to the guillotine during the French Revolution.
tu·mes·cence [t(y)ōō·mes'əns] *n.* A temporarily or moderately swollen condition.
tu·mes·cent [t(y)ōō·mes'ənt] *adj.* Somewhat swollen.
tu·mid [t(y)ōō'mid] *adj.* **1** Enlarged; swollen. **2** Pompous; turgid.
tum·my [tum'ē] *n., pl.* **tum·mies** *informal* The stomach. ◆ *Tummy* imitates the way a baby learning to talk might say *stomach.*
tu·mor [t(y)ōō'mər] *n.* **1** A swelling. **2** An abnormal growth of tissue in some part of the body, which may or may not become harmful.
tu·mult [t(y)ōō'məlt] *n.* **1** Commotion or noise, as that made by a loud, disorderly crowd. **2** Any violent agitation or disturbance.
tu·mul·tu·ous [t(y)ōō·mul'chōō·əs] *adj.* **1** Full of tumult; noisy and disorderly: a *tumultuous* reception for the astronaut. **2** Deeply disturbed; stormy: *tumultuous* feelings. **—tu·mul'tu·ous·ly** *adv.* **—tu·mul'tu·ous·ness** *n.*
tun [tun] *n.* **1** A large cask, especially for wine or beer. **2** A varying measure of capacity, usually equal to 252 gallons.
Tun. **1** Tunisia. **2** Tunisian.
tu·na [tōō'nə] *n., pl.* **tu·na** or **tu·nas** A large ocean food fish related to the mackerel.
tun·a·ble [t(y)ōō'nə·bəl] *adj.* Capable of being adjusted to a standard or correct musical pitch: a *tunable* piano. **—tun'a·bly** *adv.*

a	add	**i**	it	**ŏŏ**	took	**oi**	oil		
ā	ace	**ī**	ice	**ōō**	pool	**ou**	pout		
â	care	**o**	odd	**u**	up	**ng**	ring		
ä	palm	**ō**	open	**û**	burn	**th**	thin		
e	end	**ô**	order	**yōō**	fuse	**th̸**	this		
ē	equal					**zh**	vision		

ə = a in *above* e in *sicken* i in *possible* o in *melon* u in *circus*

tun·dra [tun′drə *or* to͝on′drə] *n.* A large, almost flat plain of the arctic regions, with no trees.
tune [t(y)o͞on] *n., v.* **tuned, tun·ing** 1 *n.* A melody or air, usually simple and easy to remember. 2 *n.* The condition of being at the proper musical pitch: out of *tune.* 3 *v.* To adjust the pitch of to a standard or correct pitch: to *tune* a violin. 4 *n.* Agreement; accord; harmony: These colors are not in *tune* with each other. **—change one's tune** To change one's manner, attitude, or approach. **—to the tune of** To the amount of: *to the tune of* $50. **—tune in** or **tune in on** To adjust a radio or television receiver so as to hear or see (a station or broadcast). **—tune out** 1 To adjust a radio or television set so as not to receive (a specific station or program). 2 *slang* To become inattentive or indifferent. **—tune up** 1 To bring (musical instruments) to a standard pitch. 2 To put in proper working order, as an engine.
tune·a·ble [t(y)o͞o′nə·bəl] *adj.* Another spelling of TUNABLE.
tune·ful [t(y)o͞on′fəl] *adj.* Full of melody; musical. **—tune′ful·ly** *adv.* **—tune′ful·ness** *n.*
tune·less [t(y)o͞on′lis] *adj.* Not tuneful; monotonous. **—tune′less·ly** *adv.*
tun·er [t(y)o͞o′nər] *n.* A person who tunes keyboard musical instruments.
tung·sten [tung′stən] *n.* A steel-gray, heavy metallic element, used in making electric light filaments and very hard steel alloys.
tu·nic [t(y)o͞o′nik] *n.* 1 In ancient Greece and Rome, a knee-length garment with or without sleeves, usually worn without a belt. 2 A modern outer garment, usually of hip length and gathered at the waist. 3 A close-fitting jacket, often worn as part of a uniform.
tun·ing fork [t(y)o͞o′ning] A two-pronged, metal instrument that sounds a fixed tone when struck.

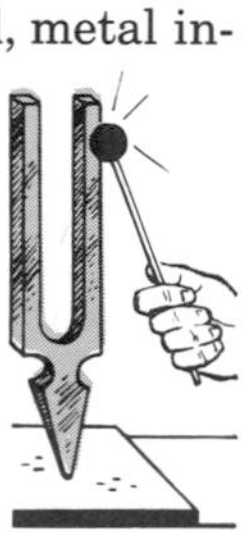
Tuning fork

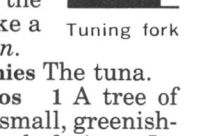

Tu·ni·sian [t(y)o͞o·nē′zhən] 1 *adj.* Of or from Tunisia. 2 *n.* A person born in or a citizen of Tunisia.
tun·nel [tun′əl] *n., v.* **tun·neled** or **tun·nelled, tun·nel·ing** or **tun·nel·ling** 1 *n.* A constructed underground passage, as for a railway. 2 *n.* Any passage under or through something, as the burrow of an animal. 3 *v.* To make a tunnel. **—tun′nel·er** or **tun′nel·ler** *n.*
tun·ny [tun′ē] *n., pl.* **tun·ny** or **tun·nies** The tuna.
tu·pe·lo [t(y)o͞o′pə·lō] *n., pl.* **tu·pe·los** 1 A tree of Asia and North America, bearing small, greenish-white flowers and dark blue or purple fruit. 2 Its tough wood.
tup·pence [tup′əns] *n.* Another spelling of TWOPENCE.
tur·ban [tûr′bən] *n.* 1 An oriental headdress consisting of a sash or shawl, twisted around the head or around a cap. 2 Any similar headdress.
tur·bid [tûr′bid] *adj.* 1 Cloudy or opaque; muddy: a *turbid* lake. 2 Mixed up; confused: *turbid* thinking. **—tur·bid·i·ty** [tûr·bid′ə·tē] *n.* **—tur′bid·ly** *adv.* **—tur′bid·ness** *n.*
tur·bine [tûr′bin *or* tûr′bīn′] *n.* A machine that changes the motion of a fluid, as steam, water, or gas, into rotary mechanical power by allowing the fluid to exert pressure on a series of vanes mounted on a rotating shaft.
tur·bo·jet [tûr′bō·jet′] *n.* An airplane propelled by a turbojet engine.
turbojet engine A jet engine in which a turbine supplies the power to compress the air that is taken in.
tur·bo·prop [tûr′bō·prop′] *n.* 1 An engine in which thrust is produced by a turbine-driven propeller as well as by a jet of hot exhaust gases. 2 An airplane propelled by such an engine.
tur·bot [tûr′bət] *n., pl.* **tur·bot** or **tur·bots** A large, flat-bodied European fish resembling the flounder and valued as food.
tur·bu·lence [tûr′byə·ləns] *n.* 1 The condition of being turbulent; agitation. 2 Irregular movement or disturbance in a liquid or a gas: Air *turbulence* made our plane trip bumpy. 3 Commotion; disorder: The meeting was marked by *turbulence.*
tur·bu·lent [tûr′byə·lənt] *adj.* 1 Being in violent agitation or commotion; disturbed; a *turbulent* sea. 2 Restless; disorderly; rebellious: a *turbulent* mob. **—tur′bu·lent·ly** *adv.*
tu·reen [t(y)o͞o·rēn′] *n.* A deep, covered dish, as for holding soup to be served at the table.
turf [tûrf] *n., pl.* **turfs** 1 The top level of the soil together with grass and other fine plants and their matted roots; sod. 2 A piece of this. 3 A piece of peat. 4 *slang* An area claimed and guarded as the private territory of an individual or a group. **—the turf** 1 A racetrack for horses. 2 Horse racing.
tur·gid [tûr′jid] *adj.* 1 Unnaturally puffed out; swollen. 2 Too fancy and pompous, as in choice of words or literary style: a *turgid* speech. **—tur·gid·i·ty** [tûr·jid′ə·tē] *n.* **—tur′gid·ly** *adv.* **—tur′gid·ness** *n.*
Turk [tûrk] *n.* 1 A person born in or a citizen of Turkey. 2 A member of a Turkic-speaking tribe or nation. 3 A Muslim.
Turk. 1 Turkey. 2 Turkish.
tur·key [tûr′kē] *n., pl.* **tur·keys** 1 A large American bird related to the pheasant, having a head without feathers and a spreading tail. 2 The turkey's flesh, used as food.

Turkey

turkey buzzard or **turkey vulture** A sooty black vulture with no feathers on its red head and neck, of North and South America.
Tur·kic [tûr′kik] 1 *adj.* Of or being a group of languages related to and including Turkish. 2 *adj.* Of Turkic-speaking people. 3 *n.* Turkic languages.
Turk·ish [tûr′kish] 1 *adj.* Of or from Turkey. 2 *n.* The language of Turkey.
Turkish towel A heavy, rough towel with a loose, uncut pile.
tur·mer·ic [tûr′mər·ik] *n.* 1 An Asian plant having a large, orange rhizome. 2 An orange powder prepared from the rhizome of this plant, used as a flavoring and coloring in food and as a dyestuff.
tur·moil [tûr′moil] *n.* A condition of great confusion or agitation; disturbance; tumult.
turn [tûrn] 1 *v.* To move or cause to move around or as around an axis; rotate: The key *turned* in the lock; to *turn* a wheel. 2 *n.* A rotation or revolution: the *turn* of a key. 3 *v.* To shift or swing part way around: He *turned* and ran. 4 *v.* To change or cause to change direction or position: The tide is *turning*; to *turn* a glass upside down.

5 *n.* A change of direction or position: a *turn* to the left. **6** *n.* The point where a change in direction occurs: a *turn* in a path. **7** *v.* To move so that the under part becomes the upper; reverse: to *turn* a page; to *turn* the soil. **8** *v.* To sprain or strain: to *turn* an ankle. **9** *v.* To shape in rounded form, as by turning on a lathe: to *turn* a chair leg. **10** *v.* To give graceful or finished form to: to *turn* a phrase. **11** *n.* A particular form or style: the *turn* of a phrase. **12** *v.* To perform by revolving: to *turn* cartwheels. **13** *v.* To change to something different, as a different form, condition, or color: to *turn* stocks into cash; The water *turned* into ice; My hair *turned* gray. **14** *v.* To change color: The leaves *turn* in autumn. **15** *n.* A change, as in condition or form: a *turn* for the better. **16** *v.* To make or become sour or rancid, as milk. **17** *v.* To make or become upset or nauseated; sicken: The odor *turned* my stomach. **18** *n.* To make or become disturbed, unsettled, or giddy: Compliments *turned* the child's head. **19** *v.* To change the direction or focus of (as thought or attention): Let's *turn* our attention to the next problem. **20** *v.* To change one's interest or attention: In later life, the lawyer *turned* to politics. **21** *n.* Direction; course: The talk took a serious *turn.* **22** *v.* To go around or to the other side of: to *turn* a corner. **23** *v.* To reach or pass beyond: My cousin *turned* 21 yesterday. **24** *v.* To depend; hinge: The council's decision *turns* on this afternoon's meeting. **25** *n.* The act of turning or changing. **26** *n.* The time of turning or changing: *turn* of the century. **27** *n.* A regular time or chance: It's my *turn* to play. **28** *n.* A deed performed: a good *turn*; a bad *turn.* **29** *n.* A short walk or drive: a *turn* in the park. **30** *n. informal* A shock or startling surprise: You gave us quite a *turn.* **—by turns** One after another; in succession. **—in turn** In the proper order or sequence. **—out of turn** Not in the proper order or sequence. **—take turns** To do something, one after another in proper order. **—to a turn** Just right; perfectly or exactly: The steak's done *to a turn.* **—turn against** To become or cause to become opposed or hostile to: Their former friends *turned against* them. **—turn down 1** To diminish, as the flow, volume, or intensity of: to *turn down* the gas. **2** To reject or refuse. **—turn in 1** To turn and enter: *Turn in* that side road. **2** To bend or incline inward: toes that *turn in.* **3** To hand over; deliver: *Turn in* your test papers. **4** *informal* To go to bed. **—turn loose** *informal* To set free; release. **—turn off 1** To cause to stop operating. **2** To make a turn and leave, as a road. **3** *slang* To make or become bored or unresponsive. **—turn on 1** To cause to operate, as a radio, a faucet, or an electric light. **2** To become hostile to or attack: to *turn on* one's friend. **3** *slang* To interest greatly; excite. **—turn out 1** To put out, as an electric light. **2** To put outside: They *turned* the dog *out* of the house. **3** To bend or incline outward. **4** To produce; make: The factory *turns out* a thousand cases an hour. **5** To come or go out: A large crowd *turned out* for the election. **6** To prove in the final result: You *turned out* to be a good student. **7** To dress or equip, especially in an elaborate way. **—turn over 1** To hand over; transfer or give. **2** To ponder or consider; think about. **—turn tail** To run away; flee. **—turn to 1** To set to work. **2** To go to for help. **—turn up 1** To find or be found. **2** To arrive. **3** To happen or occur. **4** To increase the flow, volume, or intensity of.

turn·buck·le [tûrn'buk'əl] *n.* A fastening device that can also loosen and tighten a cable. It consists of a hollow tube with threaded holes at the ends into which the two cable ends are screwed.

turn·coat [tûrn'kōt'] *n.* A person who goes over to the opposing side or party; traitor.

turn·er [tûr'nər] *n.* **1** An object or a person that turns something: a page *turner.* **2** A person who forms objects on a lathe.

turning point A point marked by an important change.

tur·nip [tûr'nip] *n.* **1** The round, white or yellow, fleshy root of a plant related to the cabbage. It is cooked and eaten as a vegetable. **2** The plant yielding this root.

turn·key [tûrn'kē'] *n., pl.* **turn·keys** A person who has charge of the keys of a prison; jailer.

turn·off [tûrn'ôf' *or* tûrn'of'] *n.* **1** An exit from a main road or turnpike. **2** *slang* Something boring or distasteful.

turn·out [tûrn'out'] *n.* **1** A group of people; gathering. **2** A quantity produced; output. **3** Equipment; outfit. **4** A manner or style of dress, especially an elaborate style. **5** A wide place in a narrow road where vehicles can pass one another.

turn·o·ver [tûrn'ō'vər] **1** *n.* The act of turning over; an upset, as of a vehicle. **2** *n.* The rate at which people, as employees or hospital patients, move on and are replaced. **3** *n.* A small pie made by filling half of a crust and turning the other half over on top. **4** *n.* The amount of business done during a given period. **5** *adj.* Capable of being turned over, folded down, or reversed.

turn·pike [tûrn'pīk'] *n.* **1** A highway on which there are tollgates. **2** A tollgate. ◆ *Turnpike* comes from an older English word, *turnpyke,* meaning a *spiked road barrier,* from the verb *turn* + *pike,* a medieval spear.

turn·stile [tûrn'stīl'] *n.* A gatelike device, having revolving, horizontal arms, set in an entrance or exit, used to control the passage or count the number of people passing through it.

turn·ta·ble [tûrn'tā'bəl] *n.* **1** A disk that rotates to turn a phonograph record. **2** A track on a revolving platform used to turn a locomotive around.

Turntable

tur·pen·tine [tûr'pən·tīn'] *n.* An oily liquid obtained from various cone-bearing trees, especially pines. It is used chiefly to thin paints and varnishes.

tur·pi·tude [tûr'pə·t(y)o͞od'] *n.* **1** Wickedness or baseness; depravity. **2** A base or wicked act.

tur·quoise [tûr'k(w)oiz'] **1** *n.* A sky-blue to greenish-blue mineral, some varieties of which, when

a	add	**i**	it	**o͝o**	took	**oi**	oil
ā	ace	**ī**	ice	**o͞o**	pool	**ou**	pout
â	care	**o**	odd	**u**	up	**ng**	ring
ä	palm	**ō**	open	**û**	burn	**th**	thin
e	end	**ô**	order	**yo͞o**	fuse	**t͟h**	this
ē	equal					**zh**	vision

ə = a in *above*, e in *sicken*, i in *possible*, o in *melon*, u in *circus*

T

highly polished, are used as gems. **2** *n., adj.* Light greenish blue.

tur·ret [tûr'it] *n.* **1** A rotating armed tower, large enough to contain powerful guns, forming a part of a warship, fort, tank, or airplane. **2** A small tower, often at the corner of a large building or castle. **3** A part of a lathe fitted with a device for holding various tools.

Turret

tur·ret·ed [tûr'it·id] *adj.* Having one or more turrets.

tur·tle [tûr'təl] *n.* A type of reptile that lives both on land and in the water and has a flat, oval body covered with a hard shell into which it can draw its four limbs, head, and tail. Certain turtles are valued as food.

tur·tle·dove [tûr'təl·duv'] *n.* A small wild dove having a black tail edged with white, and noted for its soft, mournful cooing.

tur·tle·neck [tûr'təl·nek'] *n.* **1** A high collar that fits snugly around the neck, usually turned over double. **2** A sweater or other garment with a turtleneck.

Tus·can [tus'kən] **1** *n.* A person born or living in Tuscany. **2** *n.* The standard language of Italy. **3** *n.* The dialect of Italian spoken in Tuscany. **4** *adj.* Of or having to do with Tuscans or Tuscany. **5** *adj.* Belonging to or resembling a plain Roman style of architecture derived from the Doric style.

tusk [tusk] *n.* A long, pointed, projecting tooth, generally one of a pair, as in the boar, walrus, or elephant.

Tusks

tusk·er [tus'kər] *n.* An animal with prominent tusks, as a wild boar or elephant.

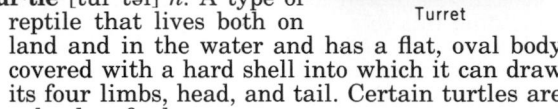

tus·sah [tus'ə] *n.* A coarse brown or yellow silk woven from fiber produced by a type of Asian silkworm.

tus·sle [tus'əl] *v.* **tus·sled, tus·sling,** *n.* **1** *v.* To fight or struggle roughly. **2** *n.* A rough struggle.

tus·sock [tus'ək] *n.* A clump of growing grass or the like.

tut [tut] *interj.* An exclamation, as of impatience, annoyance, disapproval, or disbelief.

tu·te·lage [t(y)ōō'tə·lij] *n.* **1** Protection, care, or patronage, as of a guardian. **2** Instruction.

tu·te·lar·y [t(y)ōō'tə·ler'ē] *adj.* **1** Protecting or guarding. **2** Having to do with a guardian.

tu·tor [t(y)ōō'tər] **1** *n.* A person who teaches another, usually privately. **2** *v.* To give or receive private instruction. **—tu·to·ri·al** [t(y)ōō·tôr'ē·əl] *adj.*

tut·ti-frut·ti [tōō'tē·frōō'tē] *adj.* Containing or flavored with a mixture of chopped, candied fruits. ◆ *Tutti-frutti* comes from the Italian words for *all fruits.*

tu·tu [tōō'tōō] *n.* A very short, many-layered skirt traditionally worn by ballerinas.

tux [tuks] *n.* An informal word for TUXEDO.

tux·e·do [tuk·sē'dō] *n., pl.* **tux·e·dos** **1** A formal jacket, usually black or in dark colors but without tails, worn at dances and formal dinners. **2** The suit of which such a jacket is part. ◆ *Tuxedo* was named after Tuxedo Park, New York, because the garment was first worn at a country club there.

TV or **T.V.** television.

TVA Tennessee Valley Authority.

TV dinner A frozen meal on a disposable foil tray requiring no preparation other than heating.

twad·dle [twod'(ə)l] *v.* **twad·dled, twad·dling,** *n.* **1** *v.* To talk foolishly. **2** *n.* Foolish, silly talk. **—twad'·dler** *n.*

twain [twān] *n., adj.* Two: used mostly in poems.

twang [twang] *n., v.* **twanged, twang·ing** **1** *n.* A sharp, vibrating sound, as of an instrument's string that has been plucked. **2** *v.* To make or cause to make such a sound. **3** *n.* Nasal speech or sound. **4** *v.* To speak or utter with a nasal sound.

'twas [twuz *or* twoz] It was.

tweak [twēk] **1** *v.* To pinch and twist sharply. **2** *n.* A twisting pinch: to give someone's nose a *tweak.*

tweed [twēd] *n.* **1** A woolen cloth with a rough texture, usually woven of yarns in two or more colors. **2** (*pl.*) Clothing made of tweed.

Twee·dle·dum and Twee·dle·dee [twēd'əl·dum' ən twēd'əl·dē'] Two persons or groups that are so alike that they are hard to tell apart.

tweet [twēt] **1** *n.* A thin, chirping note, as that of a young bird. **2** *v.* To make such a sound.

tweet·er [twē'tər] *n.* A small loudspeaker that reproduces high-pitched sounds in a hi-fi system.

tweez·ers [twē'zərz] *n.pl.* Small pincers for grasping and holding small objects.

twelfth or **12th** [twelfth] **1** *adj.* Next after the eleventh. **2** *n.* The twelfth one. **3** *adj.* Being one of twelve equal parts. **4** *n.* A twelfth part.

Twelfth Night The eve of Epiphany, or January 5.

twelve or **12** [twelv] *n., adj.* One more than eleven.

twelve·month [twelv'munth'] *n.* A year.

twen·ti·eth or **20th** [twen'tē·ith] **1** *adj.* Tenth in order after the tenth. **2** *n.* The twentieth one. **3** *adj.* Being one of twenty equal parts. **4** *n.* A twentieth part.

twen·ty or **20** [twen'tē] *n., pl.* **twen·ties** or **20's,** *adj.* **1** *n., adj.* One more than nineteen. **2** *n.* (*pl.*) The years between the age of 20 and the age of 30.

twen·ty-one [twen'tē·wun'] *n.* Another name for BLACKJACK (def. 4).

twice [twīs] *adv.* **1** Two times: She knocked *twice* and entered. **2** Two times as much; doubly: Once bitten, *twice* shy.

twice-told [twīs'tōld'] *adj.* Familiar because of many tellings: a *twice-told* tale.

twid·dle [twid'(ə)l] *v.* **twid·dled, twid·dling,** *n.* **1** *v.* To twirl or play with idly. **2** *n.* A gentle twirling, as of the fingers. **—twiddle one's thumbs** **1** To rotate one's thumbs idly around one another. **2** To pass time in doing nothing.

twig [twig] *n.* A shoot or small branch of a tree.

twi·light [twī'līt'] *n.* **1** The light in the sky just after sunset or just before sunrise. **2** *adj. use:* a *twilight* glow. **3** A period of decline: the *twilight* of ancient Rome.

twill [twil] **1** *n.* A weave which produces diagonal ribs or lines in cloth. **2** *n.* A cloth woven with such a weave. **3** *v.* To weave (cloth) in this way.

'twill [twil] It will.

twilled [twild] *adj.* Having woven diagonal ridges: a *twilled* fabric.

twin [twin] 1 *n.* One of two offspring born at the same time to the same mother. 2 *adj. use: twin* brothers. 3 *n.* One of two persons or things that are very much alike. 4 *adj. use: twin* chairs.

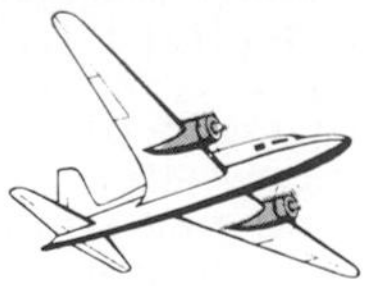
An airplane with twin engines

twine [twīn] *v.* **twined, twin·ing,** *n.* 1 *v.* To twist together: to *twine* threads. 2 *v.* To form by such twisting: to *twine* a wreath. 3 *n.* A string made up of two or more strands twisted together. 4 *v.* To coil or wind: Vines *twine* around the trunk. 5 *v.* To wind or meander, as a stream.

twinge [twinj] 1 *n.* A sharp, local, darting pain. 2 *n.* A mental, moral, or emotional pang: a *twinge* of grief. 3 *v.* To give or feel a twinge.

twin·kle [twing′kəl] *v.* **twin·kled, twin·kling,** *n.* 1 *v.* To shine with a sparkling light. 2 *n.* A flashing gleam of light; sparkle. 3 *v.* To be bright, as with amusement or happiness: Her eyes *twinkled.* 4 *n.* A sparkle of the eyes. 5 *v.* To move rapidly to and fro.

twin·kling [twing′kling] *n.* 1 A sparkle or gleam; twinkle. 2 A moment; instant.

twirl [twûrl] 1 *v.* To turn around rapidly; rotate; whirl. 2 *n.* A twirling motion; whirl. 3 *n.* A curl; twist; coil. **—twirl′er** *n.*

twist [twist] 1 *v.* To wind (as strands) around each other. 2 *v.* To form by such winding: to *twist* thread. 3 *v.* To force out of shape or place; wrench or sprain: to *twist* a wrist. 4 *v.* To turn or revolve: to *twist* a bracelet on an arm. 5 *v.* To curve or bend: The river *twisted* through the valley. 6 *n.* The act of twisting: a *twist* of the arm. 7 *n.* The condition of being twisted. 8 *n.* Something made by twisting: a bread *twist.* 9 *v.* To change the meaning of so as to mislead: Don't *twist* my story around. 10 *n.* A change, as in meaning or sense. 11 *n.* A strange or unexpected happening or development: a plot with many *twists.* 12 *n. informal* A new approach or way of doing something; gimmick.

twist·er [twis′tər] *n.* 1 A person or thing that twists. 2 *informal* A tornado.

twit [twit] *v.* **twit·ted, twit·ting,** *n.* 1 *v.* To taunt, tease, or annoy, as by reminding of a mistake or fault. 2 *n.* A taunt or reproach.

twitch [twich] 1 *v.* To move or pull with a sharp, quick jerk: I *twitched* the cloth off the table. 2 *n.* A sudden jerk or pull. 3 *n.* A sudden movement, not intended, of a part of the body.

twit·ter [twit′ər] 1 *v.* To utter light chirping notes, as a bird. 2 *n.* A series of light chirping notes. 3 *v.* To be excited; tremble. 4 *n.* An excited state.

twixt or **'twixt** [twikst] *prep.* Betwixt; between: used mostly in poems.

two or **2** [to͞o] *n., adj.* One more than one. **—in two** So as to be in two parts or pieces.

two bits *informal* Twenty-five cents.

two-by-four [to͞o′bī·fôr′] *n.* A piece of lumber actually measuring 1 5/8 inches by 3 3/8 inches.

two-edged [to͞o′ejd′] *adj.* 1 Having two edges, as a sword. 2 Having two meanings or effects, as an argument.

two-faced [to͞o′fāst′] *adj.* 1 Having two faces. 2 Dishonest; false; deceitful.

two-fisted [to͞o′fis′tid] *adj. informal* Vigorous; virile; aggressive.

two·fold [to͞o′fōld′] 1 *adj.* Made up of two parts. 2 *adj.* Two times as many or as great. 3 *adv.* So as to be two times as many or as great.

two·pence [tup′əns] *n.* A sum equal to two British pennies.

two·pen·ny [tup′ən·ē] *adj.* 1 Of the price or value of twopence. 2 Cheap; worthless.

two-ply [to͞o′plī′] *adj.* Made of two strands, layers, or thicknesses of material.

two·some [to͞o′səm] *n.* Two persons together; couple.

two-step [to͞o′step′] *n.* 1 A ballroom dance. 2 Music for such a dance, in march time.

two-time [to͞o′tīm′] *v.* **two-timed, two-tim·ing** *slang* 1 To be secretly unfaithful to. 2 To betray; double-cross. **—two′tim′er** *n.*

two-way [to͞o′wā′] *adj.* 1 Having or permitting movement in two directions: a *two-way* street. 2 Designed so as to send or receive messages: a *two-way* radio. 3 Having or allowing exchange or communication between two persons or groups: a *two-way* telephone conversation.

twp. township.

TX Postal Service abbreviation of Texas.

-ty[1] A suffix meaning: The condition of being, as in *sanity.*

-ty[2] A suffix meaning: Tens or times ten, as in *seventy.*

ty. or **Ty.** territory.

ty·coon [tī·ko͞on′] *n.* A wealthy and powerful industrial or business leader.

ty·ing [tī′ing] Present participle of TIE.

tyke [tīk] *n.* 1 *informal* A small child. 2 A mongrel dog; cur.

tym·pa·ni [tim′pə·nē] *n.pl.* Another spelling of TIMPANI.

tym·pan·ic [tim·pan′ik] *adj.* Of or relating to the eardrum or to a similar membrane.

tympanic membrane The eardrum.

tym·pa·nist [tim′pə·nist] *n.* Another spelling of TIMPANIST.

tym·pa·num [tim′pə·nəm] *n., pl.* **tym·pa·na** [tim′pə·nə] or **tym·pa·nums** 1 The middle ear. 2 The eardrum.

typ. 1 typographer. 2 typographical. 3 typography.

type [tīp] *n., v.* **typed, typ·ing** 1 *n.* A class, kind, or group of persons or things that have one or more characteristics in common: an outboard *type* of engine. 2 *n.* A person or thing displaying the characteristics common to a class or group; example: This building is a fine *type* of Byzantine architecture. 3 *v.* To be a model for; typify: Peter Pan *types* all the people who refuse to grow up. 4 *v.* To place in a class or group: The actor was usually *typed* to play a servant. 5 *v.* To find the type of; identify: to *type* a blood sample. 6 *n.* A piece of metal topped by a reversed letter, figure,

a	add	**i**	it	**o͝o**	took	**oi**	oil
ā	ace	**ī**	ice	**o͞o**	pool	**ou**	pout
â	care	**o**	odd	**u**	up	**ng**	ring
ä	palm	**ō**	open	**û**	burn	**th**	thin
e	end	**ô**	order	**yo͞o**	fuse	**t͟h**	this
ē	equal					**zh**	vision

ə = a in *above* e in *sicken* i in *possible* o in *melon* u in *circus*

T

or mark for use in printing. **7** *n.* A group of such pieces. **8** *n.* Printed or typewritten letters, figures, or marks. **9** *v.* To typewrite (something). ◆ *Type* is informal for *type of* (as in "that type program"). In formal writing, use *type of.*

type·script [tīp′skript′] *n.* A manuscript that has been typed.

type·set [tīp′set′] *v.* **type·set, type·set·ting** To set (matter to be printed) into type.

type·set·ter [tīp′set′ər] *n.* **1** A person who sets type. **2** A machine that sets type.

type·set·ting [tīp′set′ing] **1** *n.* The process of setting type. **2** *adj.* Having to do with setting type: *typesetting* instructions.

type·write [tīp′rīt′] *v.* **type·wrote, type·writ·ten, type·writ·ing** To write with a typewriter.

type·writ·er [tīp′rī′tər] *n.* A machine with a keyboard that produces printed characters by impressing type upon paper through an inked ribbon.

type·writ·ing [tīp′rī′ting] *n.* **1** The process of using a typewriter. **2** The printed characters made on paper with a typewriter.

ty·phoid [tī′foid′] **1** *adj.* Having to do with or resembling typhus. **2** *adj.* Having to do with or resembling typhoid fever. **3** *n.* Typhoid fever. **4** *n.* A disease affecting domestic animals and resembling typhoid fever.

typhoid fever An infectious disease caused by a bacterium found in infected food or water. It is marked by fever, diarrhea, red rash, and intestinal inflammation.

ty·phoon [tī·fo͞on′] *n.* A violent hurricane originating over tropical waters in the western Pacific and the China Seas.

ty·phus [tī′fəs] *n.* An acute, contagious disease caused by a germ carried by certain body lice or fleas. It is marked by high fever, skin eruptions, and extreme physical weakness.

typ·i·cal [tip′i·kəl] *adj.* **1** Having qualities or features common to the whole group or class: a *typical* American. **2** Being or having the essential features of a species, group, or class; characteristic: symptoms *typical* of measles. **—typ′i·cal·ly** *adv.*

typ·i·fy [tip′ə·fī] *v.* **typ·i·fied, typ·i·fy·ing** To be or serve as a type or example of: She *typifies* the students of our school.

typ·ist [tī′pist] *n.* A person who typewrites, especially one whose work is using a typewriter.

ty·po [tī′pō] *n., pl.* **ty·pos** *informal* A typographical error.

ty·pog·ra·pher [tī·pog′rə·fər] *n.* **1** A printer or typesetter. **2** A specialist in designing and arranging printed matter.

ty·po·graph·ic [tī′pə·graf′ik] *adj.* Of or used in typography.

ty·po·graph·i·cal [tī′pə·graf′i·kəl] *adj.* Typographic. **—ty′po·graph′i·cal·ly** *adv.*

ty·pog·ra·phy [tī·pog′rə·fē] *n.* **1** The art or process of setting type and printing from it. **2** The style and appearance of printed matter.

typw. **1** typewriter. **2** typewritten.

Tyr [tir] *n.* In Norse myths, the god of war and son of Odin.

ty·ran·nic [ti·ran′ik] *adj.* Tyrannical.

ty·ran·ni·cal [ti·ran′i·kəl] *adj.* Of or like a tyrant; harsh; cruel: a *tyrannical* manager. **—ty·ran′ni·cal·ly** *adv.*

tyr·an·nize [tir′ə·nīz′] *v.* **tyr·an·nized, tyr·an·niz·ing** **1** To rule as a tyrant. **2** To be cruel and harsh in treatment or rule.

ty·ran·no·saur [ti·ran′ə·sôr′] *n.* A huge, flesh-eating dinosaur that walked on its hind legs.

ty·ran·no·sau·rus [ti·ran′ə·sôr′əs] *n., pl.* **ty·ran·no·sau·rus·es** or **ty·ran·no·sau·ri** [ti·ran′ə·sôr′ī] Another name for TYRANNOSAUR.

tyr·an·nous [tir′ə·nəs] *adj.* Harsh; cruel; tyrannical.

tyr·an·ny [tir′ə·nē] *n., pl.* **tyr·an·nies** **1** Government in which a single ruler has absolute power. **2** Absolute power unfairly or cruelly used. **3** A cruel or tyrannical act.

ty·rant [tī′rənt] *n.* **1** A ruler having absolute power. **2** A ruler who exercises power cruelly or unfairly. **3** Any person who exerts power in such a way.

tyre [tīr] *n. British* A spelling of TIRE[2].

ty·ro [tī′rō] *n., pl.* **ty·ros** A beginner; novice: In photography I was only a *tyro.*

tzar [zär] *n.* Another spelling of CZAR.

tza·ri·na [zä·rē′nə] *n.* Another spelling of CZARINA.

tzet·ze [(t)set′sē] Another spelling of TSETSE.

U is the twenty-first letter of the alphabet. Its early history is the same as that for the letter *V.* The sign for both originated among Semitic people in the Near East, in the region of Palestine and Syria, probably in the middle of the second millennium B.C. Little is known about the sign until around 1000 B.C., when the Phoenicians began using it. The Phoenicians named it *waw* and used it for a *w*-like sound.

When the Greeks adopted the Phoenician sign around the ninth century B.C., they developed two signs of their own from it. The secondary form, called *digamma,* eventually became the letter *F* (see *F*). The Greeks used the main form for the vowel *upsilon,* which means "bare *U*" or "simple *U.*" *Upsilon* stood for the sounds of *u* and sometimes *y.*

As early as the eighth century B.C., the Etruscans adopted the Greek alphabet. It is from the Etruscans that the Romans took the letter. Both the Etruscans and the Romans, however, wrote the sign as *V.* To the Romans, the sign stood for the sounds of *u, v,* and *w.* The *w* sound later disappeared from Latin.

In early medieval times, a rounded U-shaped sign developed, but it, too, stood for the sounds of *u* and *v* indiscriminately. The V-shaped sign tended to be used when the letter was carved in stone; it appeared most often as a *majuscule,* or capital letter. Around the third to fifth centuries, *minuscules,* or lowercase letters, began to develop in the handwriting that scribes used for copying books. The U-shaped letter appeared most often there.

It was not until the fifteenth century that a distinction began to be made between *U* and *V.* More and more, *U* began to be used for the vowel sound, and *V* came to be thought of as the consonant. This distinction was not complete, however, until the seventeenth century. In general, the minuscule is just a smaller version of the majuscule.

Uu

Early Phoenician (late 2nd millennium B.C.)

Phoenician (8th century B.C.)

Early Greek (9th-7th centuries B.C.)

Western Greek (6th century B.C.)

Classical Greek (403 B.C. onward)

Early Etruscan (8th century B.C.)

Classical Etruscan (around 400 B.C.)

Monumental Latin (4th century B.C.)

Classical Latin

Roman uncial (4th-8th centuries)

Black-letter minuscule (15th century)

u or **U** [yōō] *n., pl.* **u's** or **U's** The 21st letter of the English alphabet.

u. or **U.** 1 uncle. 2 union. 3 unit. 4 university.

U The symbol for the element uranium.

UAE or **U.A.E.** United Arab Emirates.

U.A.R. United Arab Republic.

UAW or **U.A.W.** United Auto Workers.

u·biq·ui·tous [yōō·bik′wə·təs] *adj.* Existing, or seeming to exist, everywhere at once. **—u·biq′ui·tous·ly** *adv.* **—u·biq′ui·tous·ness** *n.*

u·biq·ui·ty [yōō·bik′wə·tē] *n.* The condition of being everywhere or in many places at once.

U-boat [yōō′bōt′] *n.* A German submarine.

u.c. or **U.C.** upper case (letters).

ud·der [ud′ər] *n.* A large, baglike organ of certain female animals, such as cows, in which milk is produced and from which it can be drawn in nursing and milking.

UFO or **U.F.O.** unidentified flying object.

u·fol·o·gy [yōō·fol′ə·jē] *n.* The study and pursuit of UFO's, or unidentified flying objects. **—u·fol·o·gist** [yōō·fol′ə·jist] *n.*

UFT or **U.F.T.** United Federation of Teachers.

Ug. Uganda.

U·gan·dan [yōō·gan′dən] 1 *adj.* Of or from Uganda. 2 *n.* A person born in or a citizen of Uganda.

ugh [ug *or* uk *or* u] *interj.* Any of various sounds expressing a negative feeling, as disgust or horror.

ug·li [ug′lē] *n., pl.* **ug·lis** or **ug·lies** A Jamaican citrus fruit, a cross between a grapefruit and a tangerine, having a wrinkled, splotched skin. ◆ *Ugli* may be from *ugly*, because of the fruit's unattractive appearance.

ug·li·fy [ug′lə·fī′] *v.* **ug·li·fied, ug·li·fy·ing** To make ugly.

ug·ly [ug′lē] *adj.* **ug·li·er, ug·li·est** 1 Very disagreeable in appearance: an *ugly* person. 2 *informal* Ill-tempered; quarrelsome; cross: Don't be *ugly* about sharing the candy. 3 Bad in nature or effect: an *ugly* cut; *ugly* rumors. 4 Horrible or disgusting: *ugly* sins. 5 Threatening: *ugly* weather. **—ug′li·ness** *n.* ◆ *Ugly* goes back to an old Scandinavian word meaning *fear.*

uhf or **u.h.f., UHF** or **U.H.F.** ultrahigh frequency.

UK or **U.K.** United Kingdom.

u·kase [yōō·kās′ *or* yōō·kāz′] *n.* An official decree, as one handed down by a czar of Russia.

U·krain·i·an [yōō·krā′nē·ən] 1 *adj.* Of or from the Ukraine. 2 *n.* A person born or living in the Ukraine. 3 *n.* The Slavic language spoken mainly in the Ukraine.

a	add	**i**	it	**o͝o**	took	**oi**	oil
ā	ace	**ī**	ice	**ōō**	pool	**ou**	pout
â	care	**o**	odd	**u**	up	**ng**	ring
ä	palm	**ō**	open	**û**	burn	**th**	thin
e	end	**ô**	order	**yōō**	fuse	**th̸**	this
ē	equal					**zh**	vision

ə = {a in *above* e in *sicken* i in *possible*; o in *melon* u in *circus*}

u·ku·le·le [(y)o͞o'kə·lā'lē] *n.* A small guitarlike musical instrument having four strings. ◆ *Ukulele* is also the Hawaiian word for *flea.* The link may be that guitars and fleas first reached Hawaii together, by the same ship.

Ukulele

-ular A suffix meaning: Of, having to do with, or resembling, as in *circular.*

ul·cer [ul'sər] *n.* 1 An open sore on an external or internal surface of the body. It usually contains pus, and is sometimes very painful. 2 A rotten or corrupting condition; evil: the *ulcer* of envy.

ul·cer·ate [ul'sə·rāt'] *v.* **ul·cer·at·ed, ul·cer·at·ing** To cause, form, or develop an ulcer or ulcers. **—ul'·cer·a'tion** *n.*

ul·cer·ous [ul'sər·əs] *adj.* 1 Like an ulcer. 2 Affected with an ulcer or ulcers.

ul·na [ul'nə] *n., pl.* **ul·nae** [ul'nē] or **ul·nas** 1 The thinner of the two bones of the forearm, on the same side as the little finger. 2 A corresponding bone in the foreleg of an animal.

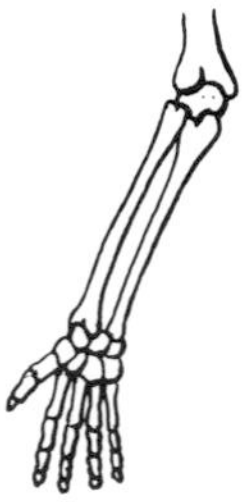
Ulna of the right arm

ul·ster [ul'stər] *n.* A very long, loose, heavy overcoat, sometimes belted at the waist.

ul·te·ri·or [ul·tir'ē·ər] *adj.* 1 Beneath what is shown or expressed; hidden: *ulterior* motives. 2 Lying beyond or on the farther side of some boundary: *ulterior* regions. 3 Following; future; further: *ulterior* measures.

ul·ti·ma [ul'tə·mə] *n.* The final syllable of a word.

ul·ti·mate [ul'tə·mit] 1 *adj.* Last, final, or eventual: the *ultimate* goal. 2 *adj.* Most distant in time or space; farthest or earliest: humanity's *ultimate* origins. 3 *adj.* Greatest or highest possible; maximum: the *ultimate* stress that a structure can bear. 4 *n.* Something ultimate: the *ultimate* in fashion. 5 *adj.* Basic, underlying, or fundamental: the *ultimate* facts of existence. 6 *n.* A fundamental or basic fact.

ul·ti·mate·ly [ul'tə·mit·lē] *adv.* In the end; at last; finally: *Ultimately,* we will win.

ul·ti·ma·tum [ul'tə·mā'təm *or* ul'tə·mä'təm] *n., pl.* **ul·ti·ma·tums** or **ul·ti·ma·ta** [ul'tə·mā'tə *or* ul'tə·mä'·tə] A final proposal, offer, or demand, to be refused only at the risk of force or punishment.

ul·tra [ul'trə] *adj.* Going beyond regular limits; immoderate; extreme: an *ultra* leftist.

ultra- A prefix meaning: 1 Beyond or above, as in *ultrasonic.* 2 Highly or extremely, as in *ultraconservative.*

ul·tra·con·ser·va·tive [ul'trə·kon·sûr'və·tiv] 1 *adj.* Highly conservative, as in politics. 2 *n.* A person who is ultraconservative.

ul·tra·high frequency [ul'trə·hī'] Any radio wave frequency between 300 and 3000 megahertz.

ul·tra·ma·rine [ul'trə·mə·rēn'] 1 *n.* A deep blue pigment. 2 *n., adj.* Deep blue. 3 *adj.* Beyond or across the sea.

ul·tra·son·ic [ul'trə·son'ik] *adj.* Indicating, operating by, or having to do with sound waves that are above the range of human hearing.

ul·tra·son·ics [ul'trə·son'iks] *n.* The study of the science and practical uses of ultrasonic sound waves. ◆ See -ICS.

ul·tra·vi·o·let [ul'trə·vī'ə·lit] 1 *adj.* Describing electromagnetic waves that are shorter than those of visible violet light and longer than X rays. 2 *n.* Ultraviolet radiation.

ultraviolet light Ultraviolet radiation.

U·lys·ses [yo͞o·lis'ēz'] *n.* The Latin name for ODYSSEUS.

um·bel [um'bəl] *n.* A flower cluster in which a number of flower stalks of almost equal length grow from the top of the main stem.

um·ber [um'bər] 1 *n.* A brown earth used as a pigment, either in its raw state or burnt. 2 *n., adj.* Yellowish brown or reddish brown.

um·bil·i·cal [um·bil'i·kəl] 1 *adj.* Of or having to do with the umbilicus. 2 *n.* A line from a spacecraft supplying oxygen to an astronaut on the outside. 3 *n.* A cable used before takeoff to carry power to a rocket or spacecraft.

umbilical cord The tough, ropelike tissue that connects a fetus with the placenta of its mother.

um·bil·i·cus [um·bil'i·kəs *or* um'bə·lī'kəs] *n., pl.* **um·bil·i·ci** [um·bil'i·sī', um'bə·lī'sī', um·bil'i·kī' *or* um'bə·lī'kī'] or **um·bil·i·cus·es** Another name for NAVEL.

um·bra [um'brə] *n., pl.* **um·bras** or **um·brae** [um'brē] 1 A shadow or dark area. 2 The part of the moon's or the earth's shadow that completely hides the sun or moon in an eclipse.

um·brage [um'brij] *n.* A feeling of resentment or offense, especially in the phrase **take umbrage**: I *took umbrage* at the remarks.

um·brel·la [um·brel'ə] *n.* A folding, ribbed frame covered with light cloth or plastic, used as a protection against rain or sun. ◆ *Umbrella* comes from an Italian word which literally means *a little shade,* because it gives protection from the sun.

umbrella tree An American magnolia tree that has clusters of large leaves at the ends of its branches, making it look like an open umbrella.

u·mi·ak [o͞o'mē·ak'] *n.* A large, open, Eskimo boat, made of skins drawn over a wooden frame.

Umiak

um·pire [um'pīr'] *n., v.* **um·pired, um·pir·ing** 1 *n.* An official who rules on the plays in a sports contest, as baseball. 2 *n.* A person called upon to settle a disagreement. 3 *v.* To act as umpire of: Our coach *umpired* the game. 4 *v.* To act as umpire.

ump·teen [ump'tēn'] *adj. informal* Of a large but unknown number. **—ump'teenth'** *adj.*

UMW or **U.M.W.** United Mine Workers.

un-[1] A prefix meaning: Not; the opposite of, as in *unfair.* ◆ *Un-*[1] is used to express the opposite or lack of something. It can be prefixed to many adjectives and adverbs, and sometimes to nouns: *unhappy, unadvisedly, uncertainty.*

un-[2] A prefix meaning: To do the opposite of, as in *unchain.* ◆ *Un-*[2] is used chiefly to reverse the action of verbs, as in *uncover, undo, unseat.*

UN or **U.N.** United Nations.

un·a·bashed [un'ə·basht'] *adj.* Not embarrassed or confused. **—un·a·bash·ed·ly** [un'ə·bash'id·lē] *adv.*

un·a·bat·ed [un'ə·bā'tid] *adj.* Not lessened: *unabated* noise.

un·a·ble [un·ā′bəl] *adj.* Lacking the necessary power or conditions; not able: *unable* to hear.

un·a·bridged [un′ə·brijd′] *adj.* 1 Not abridged; complete: an *unabridged* novel. 2 Being the largest and most comprehensive of its type: an *unabridged* dictionary.

un·ac·cent·ed [un·ak′sen·tid] *adj.* Not accented, as the *re* in the word *relent.*

un·ac·cep·ta·ble [un′ak·sep′tə·bəl] *adj.* Not good enough to be accepted or tolerated: *unacceptable* behavior.

un·ac·com·pa·nied [un′ə·kum′pə·nēd] *adj.* 1 Without a companion; alone. 2 Without musical accompaniment: an *unaccompanied* violin sonata.

un·ac·com·plished [un′ə·kom′plisht] *adj.* 1 Not done or finished. 2 Not skilled or talented.

un·ac·count·a·ble [un′ə·koun′tə·bəl] *adj.* 1 Impossible to explain: *unaccountable* rudeness. 2 Not responsible or liable to be called to account. **—un′ac·count′a·bly** *adv.*

un·ac·cus·tomed [un′ə·kus′təmd] *adj.* 1 Not accustomed; not used: *unaccustomed* to hardship. 2 Not familiar; strange: an *unaccustomed* sight.

un·ac·quaint·ed [un′ə·kwān′tid] *adj.* 1 Not known to one another: *unacquainted* neighbors. 2 Not familiar: I am *unacquainted* with her writings.

un·a·dap·ted [un′ə·dap′tid] *adj.* Not adapted; not fitting in.

un·a·dorned [un′ə·dôrnd′] *adj.* Without decoration; plain.

un·a·dul·ter·at·ed [un′ə·dul′tə·rā′tid] *adj.* With nothing added; unmixed: *unadulterated* milk.

un·ad·vis·ed·ly [un′əd·vī′zid·lē] *adv.* In a rash or unwise way: to act *unadvisedly.*

un·af·fect·ed[1] [un′ə·fek′tid] *adj.* Not changed or influenced: I was *unaffected* by the story.

un·af·fect·ed[2] [un′ə·fek′tid] *adj.* Natural, simple, and sincere. **—un′af·fect′ed·ly** *adv.*

un·a·fraid [un′ə·frād′] *adj.* Having or showing no fear; brave.

un·aid·ed [un·ā′did] *adj.* With no aid or help.

un·al·lied [un′ə·līd′] *adj.* 1 Not united or joined for a special purpose. 2 Not related: *unallied* subjects.

un·al·ter·a·ble [un·ôl′tər·ə·bəl] *adj.* Impossible to alter or change. **—un·al′ter·a·bly** *adv.*

un·al·tered [un·ôl′tərd] *adj.* Being the same; unchanged.

un·am·bi·tious [un′am·bish′əs] *adj.* 1 Indifferent to success. 2 Not requiring skill or effort: an *unambitious* plan. **—un′am·bi′tious·ly** *adv.*

un-A·mer·i·can [un′ə·mer′ə·kən] *adj.* Contrary to the character, customs, ideals, or interests of the U.S.: *un-American* activities.

un·a·mus·ing [un′ə·myo͞o′zing] *adj.* Not amusing or funny.

u·na·nim·i·ty [yo͞o′nə·nim′ə·tē] *n.* Total agreement: the *unanimity* of the jurors.

u·nan·i·mous [yo͞o·nan′ə·məs] *adj.* 1 In total agreement: We are *unanimous* in our approval of the plan. 2 Showing total agreement: a *unanimous* opinion or vote. **—u·nan′i·mous·ly** *adv.*

un·an·nounced [un′ə·nounst′] *adj.* Coming or happening without warning: an *unannounced* guest.

un·an·swer·a·ble [un·an′sər·ə·bəl] *adj.* 1 Not capable of being answered or disproved. 2 Not responsible. **—un·an′swer·a·bly** *adv.*

un·an·swered [un·an′sərd] *adj.* Not answered or replied to: *unanswered* letters.

un·ap·pe·tiz·ing [un·ap′ə·tī′zing] *adj.* Not appealing to the appetite or taste. **—un·ap′pe·tiz′ing·ly** *adv.*

un·ap·pre·ci·a·ted [un′ə·prē′shē·ā′tid] *adj.* Not appreciated or valued.

un·ap·pre·ci·a·tive [un′ə·prē′shə·tiv *or* un′ə·prē′·shē·ā′tiv] *adj.* Not having or showing appreciation; ungrateful.

un·ap·proach·a·ble [un′ə·prō′chə·bəl] *adj.* 1 Not easy to know or speak to; aloof: The judge seemed *unapproachable.* 2 Not capable of being reached: an *unapproachable* cliff. 3 Having no rival: *unapproachable* excellence.

un·ap·proved [un′ə·pro͞ovd′] *adj.* Not considered favorably; not accepted or approved.

un·armed [un·ärmd′] *adj.* 1 Not armed; without arms or weapons, especially a gun. 2 Without sharp prickles or points, as the spines or plates of some animals or plants.

un·a·shamed [un′ə·shāmd′] *adj.* 1 Not feeling guilt or shame. 2 Not embarrassed. **—un·a·sham·ed·ly** [un′ə·shā′mid·lē] *adv.*

un·asked [un·askt′] *adj.* 1 Not invited or summoned: arrived *unasked* for supper. 2 Not sought or asked for: *unasked* opinions.

un·as·sail·a·ble [un′ə·sāl′ə·bəl] *adj.* Too strong to be attacked or challenged: an *unassailable* fortress; an *unassailable* argument.

un·as·signed [un′ə·sīnd′] *adj.* Not assigned: *unassigned* reading for extra credit.

un·as·sum·ing [un′ə·so͞o′ming] *adj.* Not vain or conceited; modest. **—un′as·sum′ing·ly** *adv.*

un·at·tached [un′ə·tacht′] *adj.* 1 Not fastened or attached. 2 Not married or engaged.

un·at·tain·a·ble [un′ə·tān′ə·bəl] *adj.* Not capable of being reached or attained: an *unattainable* goal.

un·at·tempt·ed [un′ə·temp′tid] *adj.* Not attempted or tried.

un·at·tend·ed [un′ə·ten′did] *adj.* 1 Unaccompanied; alone. 2 Not attended to; undone: The farm work was left *unattended.*

un·at·trac·tive [un′ə·trak′tiv] *adj.* Not attractive or pleasing. **—un′at·trac′tive·ly** *adv.* **—un′at·trac′tive·ness** *n.*

un·au·thor·ized [un·ôth′ə·rīzd′] *adj.* 1 Without authority or power. 2 Without permission.

un·a·vail·a·ble [un′ə·vāl′ə·bəl] *adj.* Not available. **—un′a·vail′a·bil′i·ty** *n.*

un·a·vail·ing [un′ə·vā′ling] *adj.* Without success; useless: Their efforts were *unavailing.*

un·a·void·a·ble [un′ə·voi′də·bəl] *adj.* Not capable of being avoided or prevented: an *unavoidable* delay. **—un′a·void′a·bly** *adv.*

un·a·ware [un′ə·wâr′] 1 *adj.* Not aware; ignorant; unconscious: I was *unaware* of what was going on. 2 *adv.* Unawares: seldom used today.

un·a·wares [un′ə·wârz′] *adv.* In an unexpected way; by surprise; without warning: We came upon the deer *unawares.*

a add	**i** it	**o͝o** took	**oi** oil
ā ace	**ī** ice	**o͞o** pool	**ou** pout
â care	**o** odd	**u** up	**ng** ring
ä palm	**ō** open	**û** burn	**th** thin
e end	**ô** order	**yo͞o** fuse	**t͟h** this
ē equal			**zh** vision

ə = a in *above*, e in *sicken*, i in *possible*, o in *melon*, u in *circus*

U

un·bal·anced [un·bal′ənst] *adj.* 1 Not balanced: *unbalanced* weights; an *unbalanced* checkbook. 2 Mentally disturbed; not wholly sane.

un·bar [un·bär′] *v.* **un·barred, un·bar·ring** To remove the bar from; open: *Unbar* the door.

un·bear·a·ble [un·bâr′ə·bəl] *adj.* Impossible to tolerate or endure: *unbearable* pain. **—un·bear′a·bly** *adv.*

un·beat·a·ble [un·bē′tə·bəl] *adj.* Not capable of being beaten or surpassed: an *unbeatable* poker player.

un·beat·en [un·bēt′(ə)n] *adj.* 1 Not defeated. 2 Not traveled; not worn by footsteps, as a path. 3 Not shaped or mixed by beating.

un·be·com·ing [un′bi·kum′ing] *adj.* Not suitable, attractive, or proper; not becoming: *unbecoming* clothes; *unbecoming* conduct.

un·be·knownst [un′bi·nōnst′] *adj.* Unknown: *Unbeknownst* to us, the decision had already been made.

un·be·lief [un′bi·lēf′] *n.* Lack of belief or faith, especially a lack of religious belief.

un·be·liev·a·ble [un′bi·lē′və·bəl] *adj.* Not to be believed; incredible: an *unbelievable* explanation. **—un′be·liev′a·bly** *adv.*

un·be·liev·er [un′bi·lēv′ər] *n.* 1 A person who does not believe; skeptic. 2 A person who does not believe in a particular religion.

un·be·liev·ing [un′bi·lēv′ing] *adj.* Not believing; doubting; questioning.

un·bend [un·bend′] *v.* **un·bent, un·bend·ing** 1 To straighten: to *unbend* a wire hanger. 2 To relax, as after strain or formality: Once the party started, I *unbent* and had a good time.

un·bend·ing [un·ben′ding] *adj.* 1 Not bending easily. 2 Not yielding or compromising; firm.

un·bent [un·bent′] Past tense and past participle of UNBEND.

un·bi·ased or **un·bi·assed** [un·bī′əst] *adj.* Not prejudiced or partial; fair: an *unbiased* jury.

un·bid·den [un·bid′(ə)n] *adj.* Without having been asked, called, or invited: an *unbidden* guest.

un·bind [un·bīnd′] *v.* **un·bound, un·bind·ing** To release, as by untying; let loose.

un·blem·ished [un·blem′isht] *adj.* Without a mark or flaw: an *unblemished* record; *unblemished* skin.

un·blessed or **un·blest** [un·blest′] *adj.* 1 Not blessed. 2 Unholy; evil. 3 Unhappy; wretched.

un·blush·ing [un·blush′ing] *adj.* 1 Not blushing. 2 Shameless. **—un·blush′ing·ly** *adv.*

un·bolt [un·bōlt′] *v.* To unlock or open, as a door, by drawing back a bolt; unfasten.

un·bol·ted [un·bōl′tid] *adj.* Not fastened by bolts: an *unbolted* door.

un·born [un·bôrn′] *adj.* Not born, or yet to be born; to come; to be: *unborn* generations.

un·bos·om [un·bo͝oz′əm] *v.* To reveal, as one's thoughts or secrets. **—unbosom oneself** To tell one's thoughts, feelings, or troubles.

un·bound [un·bound′] 1 Past tense and past participle of UNBIND. 2 *adj.* Not bound in covers: an *unbound* book. 3 *adj.* Freed from bonds or fastenings: long, *unbound* hair.

un·bound·ed [un·boun′did] *adj.* 1 Without bounds or limits; very great: *unbounded* optimism. 2 Not restrained: *unbounded* freedom.

un·bowed [un·boud′] *adj.* Not bent or bowed down, as in defeat: a head bloody but *unbowed.*

un·break·a·ble [un·brāk′ə·bəl] *adj.* Not able to be broken: *unbreakable* dishes.

un·bri·dled [un·brīd′(ə)ld] *adj.* 1 Wearing no bridle: an *unbridled* horse. 2 Not held in or controlled: *unbridled* anger.

un·bro·ken [un·brō′kən] *adj.* 1 Not broken; whole; entire: an *unbroken* seal. 2 Not violated: an *unbroken* promise. 3 Going on without interruption: an *unbroken* series; *unbroken* sleep. 4 Not tamed or trained, as a horse.

un·buck·le [un·buk′əl] *v.* **un·buck·led, un·buck·ling** To undo the buckle or buckles of: to *unbuckle* the straps of a suitcase.

un·bur·den [un·bûr′dən] *v.* To free from a burden, fear, or worry.

un·bur·ied [un·ber′ēd] *adj.* Not buried.

un·burned [un·bûrnd′] *adj.* 1 Not burned or blackened. 2 Not yet set on fire: *unburned* leaves.

un·but·ton [un·but′(ə)n] *v.* To unfasten the button or buttons of (as on a coat or shirt).

un·called-for [un·kôld′fôr′] *adj.* Not necessary or asked for: an *uncalled-for* outburst.

un·can·celed [un·kan′səld] *adj.* 1 Not canceled; still in effect. 2 Not marked or used: an *uncanceled* postage stamp.

un·can·ny [un·kan′ē] *adj.* 1 Weird and mysterious; eerie: *uncanny* noises in the night. 2 So good as to seem beyond human powers: *uncanny* accuracy. **—un·can′ni·ly** *adv.*

un·cap [un·kap′] *v.* **un·capped, un·cap·ping** To take the cap off: to *uncap* a tube of toothpaste; to *uncap* a bottle.

un·caught [un·kôt′] *adj.* Not caught; still at large.

un·ceas·ing [un·sē′sing] *adj.* Never stopping or ending: *unceasing* noise; *unceasing* devotion.

un·cen·sored [un·sen′sərd] *adj.* Not censored by a government or other authority.

un·cer·e·mo·ni·ous [un′ser·ə·mō′nē·əs] *adj.* 1 Not very courteous; abrupt or rude. 2 Informal. **—un′cer·e·mo′ni·ous·ly** *adv.*

un·cer·tain [un·sûr′tən] *adj.* 1 Not certain; unsure; doubtful: They were *uncertain* of the answer. 2 Not capable of being known or predicted: The outcome is *uncertain.* 3 Not to be counted on; apt to change quickly: *uncertain* sunshine. 4 Capable of being misunderstood: I warned him in no *uncertain* terms. **—un·cer′tain·ly** *adv.*

un·cer·tain·ty [un·sûr′tən·tē] *n., pl.* **un·cer·tain·ties** 1 The condition of being uncertain; doubt. 2 Something uncertain.

un·chain [un·chān′] *v.* To release from a chain or chains; set free.

un·chal·lenged [un·chal′ənjd] *adj.* Not challenged or disputed.

un·change·a·ble [un·chān′jə·bəl] *adj.* Not changing or able to be changed. **—un·change′a·bly** *adv.*

un·changed [un·chānjd′] *adj.* Not changed.

un·chang·ing [un·chān′jing] *adj.* Not changing; remaining the same.

un·charged [un·chärjd′] *adj.* Without an electrical charge: an *uncharged* battery.

un·char·i·ta·ble [un·char′ə·tə·bəl] *adj.* Not kind or understanding; harsh in judging others.

un·chart·ed [un·chär′tid] *adj.* Not yet mapped or explored: *uncharted* mountains.

un·chaste [un·chāst′] *adj.* Not pure or virtuous; immoral. **—un·chaste′ly** *adv.*

un·checked [un·chekt′] *adj.* 1 Not held back or curbed: *unchecked* bleeding. 2 Not proven to be true or accurate: *unchecked* facts.

un·chewed [un·cho͞od′] *adj.* Not chewed: *unchewed* food.

un·chris·tian [un·kris′chən] *adj.* 1 Not Christian. 2 Contrary to Christian principles or teachings; not good or kind.

un·cial [un′shəl *or* un′shē·əl *or* un′sē·əl] 1 *n.* A style of handwriting in which the capital letters are somewhat rounded, used in Latin and Greek manuscripts copied between the fourth and the eighth century. 2 *n.* A letter in this style of handwriting. 3 *n.* A manuscript written in uncial. 4 *adj.* Of, having to do with, or written in uncial.

un·civ·il [un·siv′əl] *adj.* Not polite; rude.

un·civ·i·lized [un·siv′ə·līzd′] *adj.* 1 Not civilized; savage. 2 Not refined, as behavior.

un·clad [un·klad′] *adj.* Wearing no clothes; undressed.

un·claimed [un·klāmd′] *adj.* Not claimed, as by the rightful owner: an *unclaimed* parcel at the post office.

un·clasp [un·klasp′] *v.* 1 To undo the clasp of: to *unclasp* a necklace. 2 To free or be freed from a clasp or grasp.

un·class·i·fied [un·klas′ə·fīd′] *adj.* 1 Not belonging or assigned to a class 2 Available to the public; not secret: *unclassified* government documents.

un·cle [ung′kəl] *n.* 1 The brother of one's father or mother. 2 The husband of one's aunt. 3 (*written* **Uncle**) Uncle Sam.

un·clean [un·klēn′] *adj.* 1 Dirty; foul. 2 Not pure in a spiritual or religious sense.

un·clean·ly [*adj.* un·klen′lē, *adv.* un·klēn′lē] 1 *adj.* Dirty; unclean. 2 *adj.* Not pure. 3 *adv.* In an unclean way.

un·clear [un·klir′] *adj.* Not clear; not distinct or understandable: *unclear* instructions.

Uncle Sam [sam] The government or people of the U.S. personified as a tall, lean man with chin whiskers. ◆ The term *Uncle Sam* is said to be based on the nickname of *Samuel* Wilson, 1766-1854, a government official who approved meat barrels by stamping them *U.S.* during the War of 1812.

Uncle Sam

Uncle Tom [tom] *slang* A black person who humbles himself to please and gain the approval of whites. ◆ *Uncle Tom* comes from the name of a kind, faithful old slave in *Uncle Tom's Cabin,* a novel by Harriet Beecher Stowe.

un·cloak [un·klōk′] *v.* 1 To take off the coat or cloak of. 2 To expose; reveal.

un·clothed [un·klōt͟hd′] *adj.* Without clothes.

un·cloud·ed [un·klou′did] *adj.* Not clouded or darkened; clear.

un·coil [un·koil′] *v.* To unwind: to *uncoil* a rope; The snake *uncoiled.*

un·col·ored [un·kul′ərd] *adj.* Without color; colorless.

un·combed [un·kōmbd′] *adj.* Not combed.

un·com·fort·a·ble [un·kum′fər·tə·bəl *or* un·kumf′·tə·bəl] *adj.* 1 Not comfortable in body or mind. 2 Not allowing comfort or ease: an *uncomfortable* seat. **—un·com′fort·a·bly** *adv.*

un·com·mon [un·kom′ən] *adj.* 1 Not common or usual; rare. 2 Remarkable; outstanding. **—un·com′mon·ly** *adv.*

un·com·mu·ni·ca·tive [un′kə·myo͞o′nə·kə·tiv *or* un′kə·myo͞o′nə·kā′tiv] *adj.* Not willing to say much or to give much information; reserved.

un·com·plain·ing [un′kum·plā′ning] *adj.* Not complaining. **—un′com·plain′ing·ly** *adv.*

un·com·pli·ca·ted [un·kom′plə·kā′tid] *adj.* Not complicated; simple.

un·com·pli·men·ta·ry [un·kom′plə·men′tə·rē] *adj.* Not praising; critical; insulting.

un·com·pre·hend·ing [un·kom′prē·hen′ding] *adj.* Having or showing no understanding: an *uncomprehending* stare. **—un·com′pre·hend′ing·ly** *adv.*

un·com·pro·mis·ing [un·kom′prə·mī′zing] *adj.* Not yielding on any point; firm.

un·con·cealed [un′kən·sēld′] *adj.* Not hidden; open: *unconcealed* dislike.

un·con·cern [un′kən·sûrn′] *n.* Lack of interest or freedom from anxiety.

un·con·cerned [un′kən·sûrnd′] *adj.* Not interested, involved, or anxious.

un·con·di·tion·al [un′kən·dish′ən·əl] *adj.* Not limited by conditions; absolute: *unconditional* surrender. **—un′con·di′tion·al·ly** *adv.*

un·con·fined [un′kən·fīnd′] *adj.* 1 Not shut in or kept in. 2 Not limited.

un·con·firmed [un′kən·fûrmd′] *adj.* 1 Not verified or confirmed: an *unconfirmed* rumor. 2 Not approved or ratified: an *unconfirmed* pact. 3 Not a member of a church through confirmation.

un·con·gen·ial [un′kən·jēn′yəl] *adj.* 1 Not getting along well with others or with one another: *uncongenial* neighbors. 2 Not suited to one's nature or taste: an *uncongenial* climate. **—un′con·gen′ial·ly** *adv.*

un·con·quer·a·ble [un·kong′kər·ə·bəl] *adj.* Not capable of being conquered or defeated.

un·con·quered [un·kong′kərd] *adj.* Not conquered or beaten.

un·con·scion·a·ble [un·kon′shən·ə·bəl] *adj.* 1 Exceeding what is reasonable; excessive: an *unconscionable* delay. 2 Not restrained by conscience: an *unconscionable* liar.

un·con·scious [un·kon′shəs] *adj.* 1 Not able to feel and think; not conscious: The patient was *unconscious* during the operation. 2 Not aware; ignorant: *unconscious* of the plan. 3 Done or made without meaning to or realizing it: an *unconscious* imitation. **—the unconscious** The part of our mental life of which we are seldom or only briefly aware. **—un·con′scious·ly** *adv.* **—un·con′scious·ness** *n.*

un·con·sti·tu·tion·al [un′kon·sti·t(y)o͞o′shən·əl] *adj.* Contrary to the constitution of a nation or other organization. **—un·con·sti·tu·tion·al·i·ty** [un′kon·stə·t(y)o͞o′shə·nal′ə·tē] *n.*

a	add	**i**	it	**o͝o**	took	**oi**	oil
ā	ace	**ī**	ice	**o͞o**	pool	**ou**	pout
â	care	**o**	odd	**u**	up	**ng**	ring
ä	palm	**ō**	open	**û**	burn	**th**	thin
e	end	**ô**	order	**yo͞o**	fuse	**t͟h**	this
ē	equal					**zh**	vision

ə = {a in *above* e in *sicken* i in *possible* / o in *melon* u in *circus*}

un·con·strained [un'kən·strānd'] *adj.* 1 Not forced or compelled. 2 Not held back or restrained.
un·con·tam·i·nat·ed [un'kən·tam'ə·nā'tid] *adj.* Free from contamination; pure: *uncontaminated* water.
un·con·trol·la·ble [un'kən·trō'lə·bəl] *adj.* Not capable of being controlled. **—un'con·trol'la·bly** *adv.*
un·con·trolled [un'kən·trōld'] *adj.* Out of control; not checked: *uncontrolled* rage.
un·con·ven·tion·al [un'kən·ven'shən·əl] *adj.* Not conforming to accepted custom or established practice; out of the ordinary. **—un·con·ven·tion·al·i·ty** [un'kən·ven'shə·nal'ə·tē] *n.* **—un'con·ven'tion·al·ly** *adv.*
un·con·vinc·ing [un'kən·vin'sing] *adj.* Not convincing; not persuasive: an *unconvincing* argument.
un·cooked [un·kŏŏkt'] *adj.* Not cooked; raw: a dish of *uncooked* vegetables.
un·co·op·e·ra·tive [un'kō·op'ər·ə·tiv] *adj.* Not cooperative or helpful.
un·co·or·di·nat·ed [un'kō·ôr'də·nā'tid] *adj.* Not coordinated; not working together.
un·cork [un·kôrk'] *v.* To draw the cork from.
un·count·ed [un·koun'tid] *adj.* 1 Not counted. 2 Too many to count; countless; innumerable.
un·coup·le [un·kup'əl] *v.* **un·coup·led, un·coup·ling** To unfasten or disconnect: to *uncouple* the cars of a train.
un·couth [un·kōōth'] *adj.* Crude, rude, awkward, or clumsy: *uncouth* behavior; *uncouth* people.
un·cov·er [un·kuv'ər] *v.* 1 To take the cover or covering off of: to *uncover* a pot. 2 To make known; reveal: to *uncover* a scheme. 3 To raise or remove one's hat, as to show respect.
un·crit·i·cal [un·krit'i·kəl] *adj.* 1 Not finding fault. 2 Not making discriminating choices: an *uncritical* shopper.
un·cross [un·krôs'] *v.* To put back in a straight position: to *uncross* one's legs.
un·crowd·ed [un·krou'did] *adj.* Not crowded or pushed together.
un·crys·tal·lized [un·kris'tə·līzd'] *adj.* 1 Not formed into crystals. 2 Not yet definite: *uncrystallized* plans.
unc·tion [ungk'shən] *n.* 1 The act of applying oil or ointment to someone, often as part of a religious ceremony, as the rite of anointing the sick or the dying. 2 A substance used in anointing; oil or ointment. 3 Something that comforts or soothes, as flattery. 4 A deep feeling; earnestness; fervor. 5 A false or exaggerated earnestness of speech or manner, often used to arouse the fervor of others.
unc·tu·ous [ungk'chōō·əs] *adj.* 1 Like an ointment; oily, greasy, or soft. 2 Too smooth or too obviously persuasive, as in manner or speech.
un·cul·ti·vat·ed [un·kul'tə·vā'tid] *adj.* 1 Not cared for or tended: an *uncultivated* garden. 2 Not educated or cultured: an *uncultivated* mind.
un·cured [un·kyŏŏrd'] *adj.* 1 Not cured or made healthy. 2 Not preserved by smoking or salting: *uncured* pork.
un·curl [un·kûrl'] *v.* To straighten from a curled condition; unroll, untwist, or unwind.
un·cut [un·kut'] *adj.* 1 Not cut: *uncut* hair. 2 Not shortened or abridged: an *uncut* novel. 3 In a natural state before shaping and polishing: an *uncut* diamond.
un·dam·aged [un·dam'ijd] *adj.* Not damaged or hurt.
un·dat·ed [un·dā'tid] *adj.* Not marked with a date.
un·daunt·ed [un·dôn'tid] *adj.* Not discouraged or fearful: *undaunted* in the face of defeat.
un·de·bat·a·ble [un'di·bā'tə·bəl] *adj.* Not open to doubt or disagreement; certain.
un·de·ceive [un'di·sēv'] *v.* **un·de·ceived, un·de·ceiv·ing** To free from error or illusion, as by informing of the truth.
un·de·cid·ed [un'di·sī'did] *adj.* 1 Not having the mind made up: *undecided* about what to do. 2 Not yet settled or decided: Details are still *undecided.* **—un'de·cid'ed·ly** *adv.*
un·de·clared [un'di·klârd'] *adj.* Not announced formally: an *undeclared* war.
un·dec·o·rat·ed [un·dek'ə·rā'tid] *adj.* 1 Not made attractive with ornaments or new furnishings. 2 Not honored with a medal or ribbon: an *undecorated* hero.
un·de·feat·ed [un'di·fē'tid] *adj.* Not defeated or conquered: an *undefeated* army.
un·de·fend·ed [un'di·fen'did] *adj.* Not guarded or protected: an *undefended* city.
un·de·fined [un'di·fīnd'] *adj.* 1 Not defined or explained: *undefined* terms. 2 Not marked or bounded: an *undefined* territory.
un·de·livered [un'di·liv'ərd] *adj.* 1 Not distributed: *undelivered* mail. 2 Not given or spoken: an *undelivered* speech.
un·dem·o·crat·ic [un·dem'ə·krat'ik] 1 Not based on or following the principles of democracy. 2 Not treating all people the same way: an *undemocratic* prison system.
un·de·mon·stra·tive [un'di·mon'strə·tiv] *adj.* Not showing one's feelings, as of affection.
un·de·ni·a·ble [un'di·nī'ə·bəl] *adj.* Too true or good to be denied or questioned: *undeniable* excellence. **—un'de·ni'a·bly** *adv.*
un·de·pend·a·ble [un'di·pen'də·bəl] *adj.* Not dependable: an *undependable* worker.
un·der [un'dər] 1 *prep.* Beneath, so as to have something directly above: *under* the bed; *under* an umbrella. 2 *adv.* In or into a position below something: The wave knocked the child *under.* 3 *prep.* Lower than the surface of: *under* the ground. 4 *adj.* Lower, as in position: the *under* parts. 5 *prep.* Beneath the cover of: to wear a shirt *under* a sweater; The author writes *under* a pen name. 6 *adv.* So as to be covered or concealed: a desk snowed *under* with papers. 7 *prep.* Within the group or class of: That book is listed *under* adventure. 8 *prep.* Lower than or less than; below: a number *under* 100. 9 *adv.* Less: three pounds or *under.* 10 *prep.* Subject to the action, force, influence, or authority of: *under* pressure; *under* control; to serve *under* an officer. 11 *prep.* During the period or reign of: Rome *under* Caesar. 12 *prep.* Bound, controlled, or driven by: *under* oath; *under* orders; *under* sail. 13 *prep.* Because of: *under* the circumstances. **—go under** 1 To fail or collapse, as a business.
under- A prefix meaning: 1 Below in position; situated below or beneath, as in *underbrush.* 2 Below a surface or covering, as in *undershirt.* 3 Inferior in rank or importance, as in *undersecretary.* 4 Less than is usual or proper, as in *undervalue.*
un·der·a·chieve [un'dər·ə·chēv'] *v.* **un·der·a·chieved, un·der·a·chiev·ing** To perform at a lower level than expected, as in schoolwork. **—un'der·a·chiev'er** *n.* **—un'der·a·chieve'ment** *n.*

un·der·age [un′dər·āj′] *adj.* Not old enough, as to have certain legal rights and duties.

un·der·arm [un′dər·ärm′] 1 *adj.* Found or put under the arm or in the armpit: an *underarm* deodorant. 2 *n.* The armpit.

un·der·bel·ly [un′dər·bel′ē] *n., pl.* **un·der·bel·lies** The under surface of an animal's body.

un·der·bid [un′dər·bid′] *v.* **un·der·bid, un·der·bid·ding** To offer to accept a lower payment than (a rival bidder), as for doing work.

un·der·brush [un′dər·brush′] *n.* Small trees and shrubs growing under trees in the woods.

un·der·car·riage [un′dər·kar′ij] *n.* The framework supporting the body of a vehicle or other structure.

un·der·charge [*v.* un′dər·chärj′, *n.* un′dər·charj′]*v.* **un·der·charged, un·der·charg·ing,** *n.* 1 *v.* To charge too little: The clerk *undercharged* the customer. 2 *n.* A charge that is too small.

un·der·class [un′dər·klas′] *n.* A lower or oppressed social class.

un·der·clothes [un′dər·klō(t͟h)z′] *n.pl.* Garments worn next to the skin and covered by one's outer clothing; underwear.

un·der·cloth·ing [un′dər·klōt͟h′ing] *n.* Underclothes; underwear.

un·der·coat [un′dər·kōt′] *n.* 1 A growth of short hair, fur, or feathers covered by a longer growth. 2 A coat of paint or varnish applied to a surface before the final coat.

un·der·coat·ing [un′dər·kō′ting] *n.* A waterproof substance sprayed on the underside of a car or truck to prevent rust.

un·der·cov·er [un′dər·kuv′ər] *adj.* Acting or done in secret: an *undercover* investigator.

un·der·cur·rent [un′dər·kûr′ənt] *n.* 1 A current, as of water or air, below the surface or below another current. 2 An underlying or hidden feeling or attitude: We sensed an *undercurrent* of fear beneath their boasts.

un·der·cut [*v.* un′dər·kut′, *n.* un′dər·kut′] *v.* **un·der·cut, un·der·cut·ting,** *n.* 1 *v.* To cut under: to *undercut* a mass of coal to remove it. 2 *v.* To cut away a lower portion of: to *undercut* a carved design to make the upper part stand out. 3 *n.* The act or result of cutting under. 4 *v.* To work or sell for lower payment than (a rival).

un·der·de·vel·oped [un′dər·di·vel′əpt] *adj.* 1 Not properly or normally developed. 2 Not yet developed economically and industrially: an *underdeveloped* country.

un·der·dog [un′dər·dôg′] *n.* 1 A person or side expected to lose in a contest or fight. 2 A person who is oppressed by society or by those in power.

un·der·done [un′dər·dun′] *adj.* Not fully cooked; not cooked enough: *underdone* beef.

un·der·es·ti·mate [*v.* un′dər·es′tə·māt′, *n.* un′dər·es′tə·mit] *v.* **un·der·es·ti·mat·ed, un·der·es·ti·mat·ing,** *n.* 1 *v.* To judge to be less or lower than actually is the case: We *underestimated* the cost of the trip. 2 *n.* An estimate that is too low.

un·der·ex·pose [un′dər·ik·spōz′] *v.* **un·der·ex·posed, un·der·ex·pos·ing** To expose (a photographic film) to too weak a light or to enough light for too short a time.

un·der·feed [un′dər·fēd′] *v.* **un·der·fed, un·der·feed·ing** To provide with too little food.

un·der·foot [un′dər·fo͝ot′] *adv.* 1 Beneath the feet: The ground is very wet *underfoot.* 2 In the way: a pet always *underfoot.*

un·der·gar·ment [un′dər·gär′mənt] *n.* Any piece of underwear.

un·der·go [un′dər·gō′] *v.* **un·der·went, un·der·gone, un·der·go·ing** 1 To go through; experience: A person *undergoes* many changes growing from a child to an adult. 2 To be subjected to; endure or suffer: The athlete *underwent* having both ankles taped.

un·der·grad·u·ate [un′dər·graj′o͞o·it] *n.* 1 A college student who has not yet received a degree. 2 *adj. use*: an *undergraduate* course.

un·der·ground [*adv.* un′dər·ground′, *adj., n.* un′·dər·ground′] 1 *adv.* Beneath the surface of the ground: A subway runs *underground.* 2 *adj.* Situated, done, or operating beneath the surface of the ground: an *underground* passage. 3 *n.* A space or passage beneath the surface of the ground. 4 *adj.* Done in secret: *underground* revolutionary activity. 5 *adv.* In or into hiding or concealment: The patriots were forced to go *underground.* 6 *n.* A group secretly organized to work against the government or conquerors of their country.

un·der·growth [un′dər·grōth′] *n.* Underbrush.

un·der·hand [un′dər·hand′] 1 *adj.* Made with the hand lower than the elbow: an *underhand* throw. 2 *adv.* With an underhand motion: to throw a ball *underhand.* 3 *adj.* Sly and unfair or dishonest: to win by *underhand* methods. 4 *adv.* In a secret and sly manner. ◆ See STEALTHY.

un·der·hand·ed [un′dər·han′did] *adj.* Sly and unfair or dishonest; underhand. **—un′der·hand′ed·ly** *adv.*

un·der·lie [un′dər·lī′] *v.* **un·der·lay, un·der·lain, un·der·ly·ing** 1 To lie below or under: A layer of rock *underlies* the coal. 2 To be the basis or support of: What motives *underlie* your action?

un·der·line [un′dər·line′ *or* un′dər·līn′] *v.* **un·der·lined, un·der·lin·ing** 1 To draw a line beneath: to *underline* written words. 2 To emphasize: to *underline* spoken words by stressing them.

un·der·ling [un′dər·ling] *n.* A person inferior in rank and under the authority of others.

un·der·lip [un′dər·lip′] *n.* The lower lip.

un·der·ly·ing [un′dər·lī′ing] *adj.* 1 Lying under: an *underlying* layer. 2 Basic; fundamental; primary: *underlying* principles.

un·der·mine [un′dər·mīn′ *or* un′dər·mīn′] *v.* **un·der·mined, un·der·min·ing** 1 To dig a hole or passage under: to *undermine* a fortress. 2 To weaken by wearing away at the base: The river was *undermining* its high banks. 3 To weaken slowly or by sly means: The lies told to them *undermined* their faith in their leader.

un·der·most [un′dər·mōst′] 1 *adj.* Lowest. 2 *adv.* In the lowest place or position.

un·der·neath [un′dər·nēth′] 1 *prep.* Beneath; under; below: *underneath* the table. 2 *adv.* Beneath or on the underside: They picked it up to see what

a	add	**i**	it	**o͝o**	took	**oi**	oil
ā	ace	**ī**	ice	**o͞o**	pool	**ou**	pout
â	care	**o**	odd	**u**	up	**ng**	ring
ä	palm	**ō**	open	**û**	burn	**th**	thin
e	end	**ô**	order	**yo͞o**	fuse	**t͟h**	this
ē	equal					**zh**	vision

ə = {a in *above* e in *sicken* i in *possible* / o in *melon* u in *circus*}

U

was *underneath.* **3** *n.* The lower part or underside.

un·der·nour·ished [un′dər·nûr′isht] *adj.* Not getting enough food to stay healthy or to grow.

un·der·pants [un′dər·pants′] *n.pl.* An undergarment having either long or short legs.

un·der·pass [un′dər·pas′] *n.* A passage under an elevated roadway, bridge, or pedestrian pathway, as for a road.

Underpass

un·der·pay [un′dər·pā′] *v.* **un·der·paid, un·der·pay·ing** To pay (someone) too little or less than actually earned.

un·der·pin·ning [un′·dər·pin′ing] *n.* Supports or the foundation under a wall or building.

un·der·priv·i·leged [un′dər·priv′ə·lijd] *adj.* Lacking advantages and rights that everyone should have, usually because of being poor.

un·der·rate [un′dər·rāt′] *v.* **un·der·rat·ed, un·der·rat·ing** To rate too low; underestimate.

un·der·score [un′dər·skôr′] *v.* **un·der·scored, un·der·scor·ing** **1** To underline. **2** To emphasize.

un·der·sea [un′dər·sē′] **1** *adj.* Existing, carried on, or used below the surface of the sea. **2** *adv.* Beneath the surface of the sea.

un·der·seas [un′dər·sēz′] *adv.* Undersea.

un·der·sec·re·tar·y [un′dər·sek′rə·ter′ē] *n., pl.* **un·der·sec·re·tar·ies** In a government department, the official who ranks next below the secretary.

un·der·sell [un′dər·sel′] *v.* **un·der·sold, un·der·sell·ing** To sell at a lower price than.

un·der·shirt [un′dər·shûrt′] *n.* A garment, generally of cotton, worn beneath the shirt.

un·der·shoot [un′dər·sho͞ot′] *v.* **un·der·shot, un·der·shoot·ing** **1** To shoot a missile so that it fails to reach (the target). **2** To land an aircraft short of (the runway).

un·der·shot [un′dər·shot′] *adj.* **1** Moved by water flowing underneath: said about a water wheel. **2** Having the lower jaw or teeth sticking out past the upper when the mouth is shut.

Undershot water wheel

un·der·side [un′dər·sīd′] *n.* The lower or bottom side or surface.

un·der·signed [un′dər·sīnd′] *adj.* **1** Signed at or having one's signature at the bottom of a document. **2** *n. use*: The signer or signers of a document: The *undersigned* were witnesses.

un·der·sized [un′dər·sīzd′] *adj.* Of less than the normal or average size: an *undersized* fish.

un·der·skirt [un′dər·skûrt′] *n.* A petticoat or slip.

un·der·sold [un′dər·sōld′] Past tense and past participle of UNDERSELL.

un·der·staffed [un′dər·staft′] *adj.* Not having a staff large enough to do an adequate job: The post office is *understaffed.*

un·der·stand [un′dər·stand′] *v.* **un·der·stood, un·der·stand·ing** **1** To take in the meaning or purpose of; grasp with the mind: Do you *understand* the instructions? **2** To have been told or have the impression: We *understand* that there is a new teacher. **3** To think, take, or interpret: I *understood* the light to be a signal. **4** To accept as being agreed upon: It was *understood* that we would take turns. **5** To supply in thought when not expressed. In "My dog is bigger than yours," the word *is* is understood after *yours.* **6** To know well or appreciate: We *understand* modern art. **7** To know or be aware of the nature of, or be in sympathy with: They *understand* each other. **8** To have understanding or sympathy: My parents always *understand.*

un·der·stand·a·ble [un′dər·stan′də·bəl] *adj.* Capable of being understood.

un·der·stand·ing [un′dər·stan′ding] **1** *n.* A grasping of the essentials or meaning; knowledge: an *understanding* of mathematics. **2** *n.* The ability to take in meaning, to interpret, reason, and judge; intelligence. **3** *n.* Opinion or interpretation. **4** *n.* Insight or sympathy. **5** *adj.* Full of insight or sympathy: an *understanding* smile. **6** *n.* An informal agreement, as to marry. **7** *n.* A settlement of differences: The opposing sides came to an *understanding.*

un·der·state [un′dər·stāt′] *v.* **un·der·stat·ed, un·der·stat·ing** To describe or talk about as less than, or less important or colorful than, the actuality: The writer *understated* the book's success, calling it luck. **—un′der·state′ment** *n.*

un·der·stood [un′dər·sto͝od′] Past tense and past participle of UNDERSTAND.

un·der·stud·y [un′dər·stud′ē] *n., pl.* **un·der·stud·ies,** *v.* **un·der·stud·ied, un·der·stud·y·ing** **1** *n.* An actor who can take the place of another in a given role when necessary. **2** *v.* To study (a part) as an understudy. **3** *v.* To act as an understudy to (another actor).

un·der·take [un′dər·tāk′] *v.* **un·der·took, un·der·tak·en, un·der·tak·ing** **1** To take upon oneself; agree or promise to do: to *undertake* a task. **2** To engage in; start upon; begin: to *undertake* a journey.

un·der·tak·er [un′dər·tā′kər] *n.* A person whose business is to prepare dead people for burial and to manage and conduct funerals; mortician.

un·der·tak·ing [un′dər·tā′king *for defs. 1, 3,* un′·dər·tā′king *for def. 2*] *n.* **1** Something that a person promises or attempts to do, usually an important or difficult task. **2** The work or profession of an undertaker. **3** A pledge or promise.

un·der·tone [un′dər·tōn′] *n.* **1** A low sound, vocal tone, or whisper. **2** A soft or subdued shade of a color. **3** A color that is in back of and is seen through other colors: an *undertone* of red in this orange. **4** An emotional quality that is behind what a person says or does: an *undertone* of fear in your voice.

un·der·took [un′dər·to͝ok′] Past tense of UNDERTAKE.

un·der·tow [un′dər·tō′] *n.* A strong current under the surface of the water, as one flowing back out to sea or sideways along the beach while the surface current flows in to shore.

un·der·val·ue [un′dər·val′yo͞o] *v.* **un·der·val·ued, un·der·val·u·ing** To set too low a value upon: Don't *undervalue* your talents.

un·der·wa·ter [un′dər·wô′tər *or* un′dər·wo′tər] **1** *adj.* Found, done, or used beneath the surface of the water. **2** *adv.* Below the surface of water.

un·der·wear [un′dər·wâr′] *n.* Garments worn under one's outer clothes.

un·der·weight [un′dər·wāt′] **1** *adj.* Below the normal or proper weight. 2 *n.* Weight that does not come up to a standard or requirement.

un·der·went [un′dər·went′] Past tense of UNDERGO.

un·der·whelm [un′dər·(h)welm′] *v. slang* To fail to rouse, excite, or interest.

un·der·world [un′dər·wûrld′] *n.* 1 The part of society engaged in crime, especially organized criminals. 2 Hades, the kingdom of the dead.

un·der·write [un′dər·rīt′] *v.* **un·der·wrote, un·der·writ·ten, un·der·writ·ing** 1 To assume responsibility for or support, as with money: Business firms *underwrote* the opera's losses. 2 To issue (an insurance policy), assuming the risk for the property insured. 3 To agree to buy all or part of (an issue of stocks or bonds) that remains unsold. **—un′der·writ′er** *n.*

un·de·served [un′di·zûrvd′] *adj.* Not deserved: an *undeserved* high grade.

un·de·sir·a·ble [un′di·zīr′ə·bəl] 1 *adj.* Not desirable or pleasing; unwanted or objectionable. 2 *n.* An undesirable person.

un·de·tect·ed [un′di·tek′tid] *adj.* Not detected; unnoticed: an *undetected* disease.

un·de·terred [un′di·tûrd′] *adj.* Not prevented from doing something through fear: a criminal *undeterred* by the threat of jail.

un·de·vel·oped [un′di·vel′əpt] *adj.* Not yet developed: *undeveloped* muscles; *undeveloped* film.

un·did [un·did′] Past tense of UNDO.

un·dies [un′dēz] *n.pl. informal* Underwear.

un·dig·ni·fied [un·dig′nə·fīd′] *adj.* Lacking dignity: a stooped, *undignified* posture.

un·dim·in·ished [un′di·min′isht] *adj.* Not lessened in force or amount: an *undiminished* supply.

un·dis·ci·plined [un·dis′ə·plind] *adj.* Not disciplined or obedient; out of control.

un·dis·cov·ered [un′dis·kuv′ərd] *adj.* Not discovered or found: an *undiscovered* island.

un·dis·guised [un′dis·gīzd′] *adj.* Not disguised; plain to see: *undisguised* contempt.

un·dis·mayed [un′dis·mād′] *adj.* Not dismayed; not uneasy or alarmed: He was *undismayed* by his slow start.

un·dis·put·ed [un′dis·pyo͞o′tid] *adj.* Not opposed or challenged: an *undisputed* fact.

un·dis·tin·guished [un′dis·ting′gwisht] *adj.* Not distinguished or outstanding; commonplace.

un·dis·turbed [un′dis·tûrbd′] *adj.* Not disturbed or annoyed: Newborn kittens should be left *undisturbed.*

un·di·vid·ed [un′di·vī′did] *adj.* Not divided; complete; whole: her *undivided* attention.

un·do [un·do͞o′] *v.* **un·did, un·done, un·do·ing** 1 To loosen, untie, unfasten, or unwrap: to *undo* a clasp. 2 To cause to be as if never done; reverse or cancel: to try to *undo* a wrong that has been done. 3 To bring to ruin; destroy: The official was *undone* by greed.

un·dock [un·dok′] *v.* To break or undo the connection between; uncouple: to *undock* two freight cars.

un·do·ing [un·do͞o′ing] *n.* 1 Ruin or cause of ruin: Pride was their *undoing.* 2 The act of reversing or canceling what has been done. 3 The act of opening, untying, or unfastening.

un·done [un·dun′] 1 Past participle of UNDO. 2 *adj.* Not completed. 3 *adj.* Ruined. 4 *adj.* Untied; unfastened.

un·doubt·ed [un·dou′tid] *adj.* Not open to question; not doubted: *undoubted* superiority.

un·doubt·ed·ly [un·dou′tid·lē] *adv.* Without doubt; surely: You are *undoubtedly* right.

un·dra·mat·ic [un′drə·mat′ik] *adj.* Not dramatic; unexciting. **—un′dra·mat′i·cal·ly** *adv.*

un·dreamed [un·drēmd′] *adj.* Never even imagined or dreamed: marvels of technology that were *undreamed* of a hundred years ago.

un·dreamt [un·dremt′] *adj.* Undreamed.

un·dress [un·dres′] 1 *v.* To take off the clothes of: I *undressed* the baby. 2 *v.* To take one's clothes off. 3 *n.* Casual, informal clothes.

un·due [un·d(y)o͞o′] *adj.* 1 Not suitable; not proper. 2 Too much; excessive: *undue* severity.

un·du·lant [un′d(y)ə·lənt] *adj.* Moving or shaped in waves; wavy or rolling.

undulant fever A bacterial disease of cattle that can be transmitted to people through meat and milk. It is marked by fever, weakness, and joint pains.

un·du·late [un′d(y)ə·lāt′] *v.* **un·du·lat·ed, un·du·lat·ing** 1 To move or cause to move like a wave or in waves: The wheat *undulates* in the wind. 2 To have a wavy shape or appearance, as land full of hills.

un·du·la·tion [un′d(y)ə·lā′shən] *n.* 1 Movement in waves. 2 A wavy shape, outline, or appearence. 3 One of a series of waves or vibrations.

un·du·ly [un·d(y)o͞o′lē] *adv.* 1 More than is fitting or proper: *unduly* confident. 2 Unjustly or illegally: *unduly* influenced.

un·dy·ing [un·dī′ing] *adj.* Never dying or ending; everlasting: my *undying* gratitude.

un·earned [un·ûrnd′] *adj.* 1 Not earned or deserved: *unearned* privileges. 2 Not gained by work: Bank interest is *unearned* income.

un·earth [un·ûrth′] *v.* 1 To dig up from the ground: to *unearth* bones. 2 To discover by or as if by searching: to *unearth* the true facts.

un·earth·ly [un·ûrth′lē] *adj.* 1 Not of this earth; supernatural. 2 Weird and frightening.

un·eas·y [un·ē′zē] *adj.* **un·eas·i·er, un·eas·i·est** 1 Troubled; worried: *uneasy* about their safety. 2 Restless or nervous. 3 Not relaxed or natural; embarrassed; awkward: an *uneasy* laugh. 4 Not secure; unstable: an *uneasy* truce. **—un·eas′i·ly** *adv.* **—un·eas′i·ness** *n.*

un·ed·u·cat·ed [un·ej′o͝o·kā′tid] *adj.* 1 With little or no formal education. 2 Not trained or cultivated: an *uneducated* taste.

un·em·bar·rassed [un′im·bar′əst] *adj.* Not embarrassed or self-conscious.

un·e·mo·tion·al [un′i·mō′shə·nəl] *adj.* Showing little or no emotion or feeling. **—un′e·mo′tion·al·ly** *adv.*

un·em·ploy·a·ble [un′im·ploi′ə·bəl] 1 *adj.* Not fit to be employed, as because of poor health or lack of training. 2 *n.* An unemployable person.

un·em·ployed [un′im·ploid′] *adj.* 1 Without a job;

a	add	**i**	it	**o͝o**	took	**oi**	oil
ā	ace	**ī**	ice	**o͞o**	pool	**ou**	pout
â	care	**o**	odd	**u**	up	**ng**	ring
ä	palm	**ō**	open	**û**	burn	**th**	thin
e	end	**ô**	order	**yo͞o**	fuse	**th**	this
ē	equal					**zh**	vision

ə = a in *above*, e in *sicken*, i in *possible*, o in *melon*, u in *circus*

U

out of work. **2** *n. use*: People who have no jobs: to find work for the *unemployed.* **3** Not put to use: *unemployed* resources.

un·em·ploy·ment [un′im·ploi′mənt] *n.* The condition of being unemployed.

un·end·ing [un·end′ing] *adj.* Having or seeming to have no end; without limit: *unending* bad luck.

un·en·dur·a·ble [un′in·d(y)ŏŏr′ə·bəl] *adj.* Not able to be endured; unbearable: *unendurable* pain.

un·en·force·a·ble [un′in·fôr′sə·bəl] *adj.* Hard or impossible to enforce: *unenforceable* laws.

un·en·thu·si·as·tic [un′in·thōō′zē·as′tik] *adj.* Without enthusiasm.

un·e·qual [un·ē′kwəl] *adj.* **1** Not equal or balanced, as in size, strength, or ability. **2** Unfair: an *unequal* contest. **3** Not the same throughout; uneven: an *unequal* performance. **—unequal to** Lacking the ability or power needed for: The new employee was *unequal to* the demands of the job. **—un·e′qual·ly** *adv.*

un·e·qualed or **un·e·qualled** [un·ē′kwəld] *adj.* Having no equal; going beyond any other.

un·e·quiv·o·cal [un′i·kwiv′ə·kəl] *adj.* Not ambiguous or open to misunderstanding: an *unequivocal* refusal. **—un′e·quiv′o·cal·ly** *adv.*

un·err·ing [un·ûr′ing *or* un·er′ing] *adj.* Making no mistakes; free from error; exact; perfect: *unerring* accuracy. **—un·err′ing·ly** *adv.*

UNESCO [yōō·nes′kō] United Nations Educational, Scientific, and Cultural Organization.

un·e·ven [un·ē′vən] *adj.* **1** Not even, smooth, level, or equal: *uneven* floors; *uneven* margins. **2** Not equal or well matched: an *uneven* battle. **3** Changeable or varying, as in quality: *uneven* work. **4** Not capable of being divided by 2 without leaving a remainder. 7 is an uneven number. **—un·e′ven·ly** *adv.* **—un·e′ven·ness** *n.*

un·e·vent·ful [un′i·vent′fəl] *adj.* Without any interesting or important happenings: an *uneventful* day. **—un′e·vent′ful·ly** *adv.*

un·ex·ag·ger·at·ed [un′ig·zaj′ə·rā′tid] *adj.* Not exaggerated.

un·ex·am·pled [un′ig·zam′pəld] *adj.* Not like anything seen before or to be found elsewhere; unique: *unexampled* courtesy.

un·ex·celled [un′ik·seld′] *adj.* Not excelled or surpassed: an *unexcelled* tennis player.

un·ex·cep·tion·a·ble [un′ik·sep′shən·ə·bəl] *adj.* Not open to any criticism; beyond reproach; completely correct: *unexceptionable* conduct.

un·ex·cit·ed [un′ik·sī′tid] *adj.* Not excited; calm; composed.

un·ex·pect·ed [un′ik·spek′tid] *adj.* Coming or happening without warning; not expected: an *unexpected* shower. **—un′ex·pect′ed·ly** *adv.*

un·ex·plain·a·ble [un′ik·splān′ə·bəl] *adj.* Impossible to explain; inexplicable.

un·ex·plored [un′ik·splôrd′] *adj.* **1** Not explored: an *unexplored* island. **2** Not looked into or examined: an *unexplored* field of knowledge.

un·ex·posed [un′ik·spōzd′] *adj.* **1** Not revealed or uncovered: an *unexposed* crime. **2** Not yet exposed to light: an *unexposed* film.

un·fail·ing [un·fā′ling] *adj.* **1** Never lessening, running out, or stopping. **2** Certain; sure: an *unfailing* remedy. **—un·fail′ing·ly** *adv.*

un·fair [un·fâr′] *adj.* **1** Not fair, right, or just. **2** Dishonest. **—un·fair′ly** *adv.*

un·faith·ful [un·fāth′fəl] *adj.* **1** Breaking promises or ignoring duty; disloyal; faithless. **2** Not accurate, true, or exact: an *unfaithful* portrait. **—un·faith′ful·ness** *n.*

un·fal·ter·ing [un·fôl′tər·ing] *adj.* Not hesitating or wavering; firm; steadfast.

un·fa·mil·iar [un′fə·mil′yər] *adj.* **1** Not recognized or known; strange: an *unfamiliar* neighborhood. **2** Not acquainted or familiar: a stranger *unfamiliar* with local laws. **—un·fa·mil·i·ar·i·ty** [un′fə·mil′·ē·ar′ə·tē] *n.*

un·fash·ion·a·ble [un·fash′ə·nə·bəl] *adj.* Not in fashion; no longer stylish. **—un·fash′ion·a·bly** *adv.*

un·fast·en [un·fas′ən] *v.* To undo the fastenings of; unlatch; detach.

un·fath·om·a·ble [un·fath′əm·ə·bəl] *adj.* **1** Too deep to be measured, as seas. **2** Impossible to understand: an *unfathomable* mystery.

un·fath·omed [un·fath′əmd] *adj.* **1** Not measured in depth: *unfathomed* waters. **2** Not understood: *unfathomed* mysteries.

un·fa·vor·a·ble [un·fā′vər·ə·bəl] *adj.* Not favorable, helpful, encouraging, or approving. **—un·fa′vor·a·bly** *adv.*

un·fed [un·fed′] *adj.* Not fed.

un·feel·ing [un·fē′ling] *adj.* **1** Not sympathetic; hardhearted; cruel. **2** Not capable of feeling; insensate. **—un·feel′ing·ly** *adv.*

un·feigned [un·fānd′] *adj.* Not pretended; sincere; genuine: *unfeigned* admiration.

un·fin·ished [un·fin′isht] *adj.* **1** Not completed. **2** Lacking a particular finish, as not painted or not polished: *unfinished* furniture.

un·fit [un·fit′] *adj., v.* **un·fit·ted, un·fit·ting** **1** *adj.* Not fit, suitable, qualified, or in proper condition: stagnant water *unfit* for drinking. **2** *v.* To make unfit or not qualified: The bruises *unfit* the fruit for sale. **—un·fit′ness** *n.*

un·flag·ging [un·flag′ing] *adj.* Not weakening or failing; untiring: *unflagging* courage. **—un·flag′·ging·ly** *adv.*

un·flap·pa·ble [un·flap′ə·bəl] *adj.* Not easily embarrassed or upset. **—un·flap′pa·bil′i·ty** *n.* **—un·flap′pa·bly** *adv.*

un·flat·ter·ing [un·flat′ə·ring] *adj.* Not flattering or becoming: an *unflattering* remark; an *unflattering* dress.

un·fledged [un·flejd′] *adj.* **1** Not yet feathered, as a young bird. **2** Not mature; inexperienced.

un·flinch·ing [un·flin′ching] *adj.* Not shrinking, as from danger or pain; steadfast. **—un·flinch′ing·ly** *adv.*

un·fold [un·fōld′] *v.* **1** To open from a folded state; spread out: *Unfold* this sheet. **2** To open out, as a bud; develop. **3** To extend or be revealed: The valley *unfolded* before them. **4** To reveal or explain: The leader *unfolded* the plan.

un·forced [un·fôrst′] *adj.* **1** Done by one's own will; voluntary. **2** Not strained; effortless: an *unforced* laugh.

un·fore·seen [un′fôr·sēn′] *adj.* Not foreseen; not expected beforehand: *unforeseen* problems.

un·for·get·ta·ble [un′fər·get′ə·bəl] *adj.* Impossible to forget; memorable.

un·for·giv·a·ble [un′fər·giv′ə·bəl] *adj.* Not capable of being forgiven: an *unforgivable* crime.

un·formed [un·fôrmd′] *adj.* **1** Lacking a definite form; shapeless. **2** Not yet fully developed or matured.

un·for·tu·nate [un·fôr′chə·nit] **1** *adj.* Not fortunate or lucky: to be *unfortunate* in business. **2** *n.* An unlucky, poor, or outcast person. **3** *adj.* Not suitable or fitting: an *unfortunate* choice of words. **—un·for′tu·nate·ly** *adv.*

un·found·ed [un·foun′did] *adj.* Having no basis in fact; groundless: *unfounded* suspicions.

un·fre·quent·ed [un′fri·kwen′tid] *adj.* Hardly ever visited or frequented: an *unfrequented* part of town.

un·friend·ly [un·frend′lē] *adj.* 1 Showing ill will; not friendly or kind. 2 Not favorable.

un·fruit·ful [un·fro͞ot′fəl] *adj.* Not producing fruit, offspring, or good results; barren.

un·ful·filled [un′fo͝ol·fild′] *adj.* 1 Not performed, completed, or met: *unfulfilled* responsibilities. 2 Not brought into being: *unfulfilled* dreams.

un·furl [un·fûrl′] *v.* To spread out or open; unroll or unfold, as a sail or flag.

un·fur·nished [un·fûr′nisht] *adj.* 1 Not provided with furniture: an *unfurnished* house. 2 Not supplied: *unfurnished* with paper and pencils.

un·gain·ly [un·gān′lē] *adj.* Awkward; clumsy.

un·gen·er·ous [un·jen′ər·əs] *adj.* 1 Not generous; selfish. 2 Small or scanty: an *ungenerous* slice of cake. 3 Mean or narrow-minded. **—un·gen′er·ous·ly** *adv.*

un·god·ly [un·god′lē] *adj.* 1 Having no reverence for God. 2 Wicked; sinful. 3 *informal* Outrageous: at an *ungodly* hour.

un·gov·ern·a·ble [un·guv′ər·nə·bəl] *adj.* Hard or impossible to govern, control, or restrain: *ungovernable* anger. **—un·gov′ern·a·bly** *adv.*

un·grace·ful [un·grās′fəl] *adj.* Clumsy; awkward: an *ungraceful* walk. **—un·grace′ful·ly** *adv.* **—un·grace′ful·ness** *n.*

un·gra·cious [un·grā′shəs] *adj.* Not gracious or kind; impolite: an *ungracious* reply. **—un·gra′·cious·ly** *adv.* **—un·gra′cious·ness** *n.*

un·gram·mat·i·cal [un′grə·mat′i·kəl] *adj.* Not following the rules of grammar. **—un′gram·mat′i·cal·ly** *adv.*

un·grate·ful [un·grāt′fəl] *adj.* 1 Lacking gratitude; not thankful. 2 Not pleasant; disagreeable, as a task. **—un·grate′ful·ly** *adv.*

un·ground·ed [un·groun′did] *adj.* Having no basis in fact; without foundation: *ungrounded* complaints.

un·grudg·ing [un·gruj′ing] *adj.* 1 Not envious or resentful. 2 Given willingly: He gave people in trouble his *ungrudging* attention. **—un·grudg′ing·ly** *adv.*

un·guard·ed [un·gär′did] *adj.* 1 Not protected or defended: an *unguarded* entrance. 2 Not cautious or prudent; careless: an *unguarded* remark.

un·guent [ung′gwənt] *n.* An ointment or salve.

un·gu·late [ung′gyə·lit] 1 *adj.* Having hoofs, as the horse or cow. 2 *n.* A hoofed mammal.

un·hal·lowed [un·hal′ōd] *adj.* 1 Not consecrated or made holy: buried in *unhallowed* ground. 2 Evil; sinful.

un·hand [un·hand′] *v.* To stop holding with the hands; let go.

un·hap·py [un·hap′ē] *adj.* **un·hap·pi·er, un·hap·pi·est** 1 Not happy or content; sad, miserable, or dissatisfied. 2 Not lucky; unfortunate: *Unhappy* day! 3 Not suitable or appropriate: an *unhappy* remark. **—un·hap′pi·ly** *adv.* **—un·hap′pi·ness** *n.*

un·harmed [un·härmd′] *adj.* Not hurt or injured.

un·health·ful [un·helth′fəl] *adj.* Not good for one's health: an *unhealthful* climate. **—un·health′ful·ness** *n.*

un·health·y [un·hel′thē] *adj.* **un·health·i·er, un·health·i·est** 1 Not in good health; not well; sickly. 2 Harmful to the health or morals; not wholesome: an *unhealthy* climate; *unhealthy* influences.

un·heard [un·hûrd′] *adj.* 1 Not heard. 2 Not listened to or heeded. 3 Not given a hearing.

un·heard-of [un·hûrd′uv′] *adj.* Not ever heard of, done, or known before: *unheard-of* inventions.

un·heed·ing [un·hē′ding] *adj.* Not paying close attention.

un·help·ful [un·help′fəl] *adj.* 1 Not helpful. 2 Not useful or beneficial.

un·hes·i·tat·ing [un·hez′ə·tā′ting] *adj.* With no hesitation; prompt: an *unhesitating* rejection. **—un·hes′i·tat′ing·ly** *adv.*

un·hinge [un·hinj′] *v.* **un·hinged, un·hing·ing** 1 To take from the hinges or remove the hinges of: to *unhinge* a door. 2 To detach, separate, or remove. 3 To throw into disorder; unsettle: a mind *unhinged* by shock.

un·his·tor·i·cal [un·his·tôr′ə·kəl] *adj.* Never having happened or existed in the past.

un·hitch [un·hich′] *v.* To free from being attached or fastened; unfasten: to *unhitch* a tractor from a trailer.

un·ho·ly [un·hō′lē] *adj.* **un·ho·li·er, un·ho·li·est** 1 Not sacred or holy. 2 Wicked.

un·hook [un·ho͝ok′] *v.* 1 To unfasten by undoing a hook or hooks: to *unhook* a gate. 2 To become undone or loose from a hook. 3 To remove from a hook: to *unhook* a trout.

un·horse [un·hôrs′] *v.* **un·horsed, un·hors·ing** To knock or throw from a horse, as a knight.

un·hur·ried [un·hûr′ēd] *adj.* Not hurried; leisurely: an *unhurried* stroll. **—un·hur′ried·ly** *adv.*

un·hurt [un·hûrt′] *adj.* Without being hurt: He walked away *unhurt* from the plane crash.

uni- A prefix meaning: Having or consisting of one only, as in *unicellular.*

u·ni·cam·er·al [yo͞o′nə·kam′ər·əl] *adj.* Made up of only one legislative house or chamber.

UNICEF [yo͞o′nə·sef′] United Nations International Children's Emergency Fund.

u·ni·cel·lu·lar [yo͞o′nə·sel′yə·lər] *adj.* Consisting of a single cell, as a protozoan.

u·ni·corn [yo͞o′nə·kôrn′] *n.* An imaginary animal said to look like a horse with one long horn projecting from its forehead.

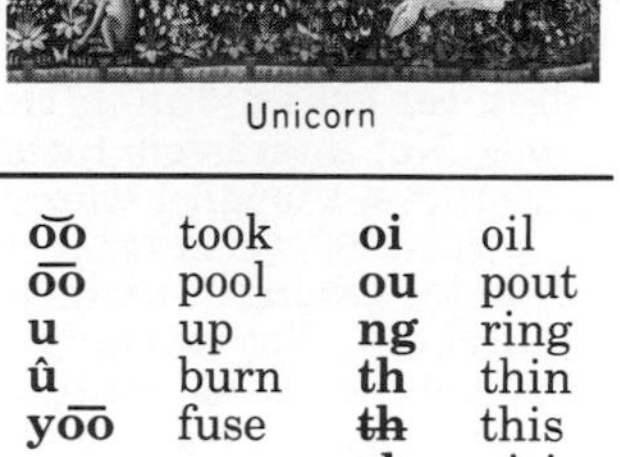
Unicorn

u·ni·cy·cle [yo͞o′nə·sī′·kəl] *n.* A vehicle made up of a single wheel and a seat above it for the rider, who pedals to make the wheel turn.

un·i·den·ti·fied [un′ī·den′tə·fīd′] *adj.* Not

a	add	**i**	it	**o͝o**	took	**oi**	oil
ā	ace	**ī**	ice	**o͞o**	pool	**ou**	pout
â	care	**o**	odd	**u**	up	**ng**	ring
ä	palm	**ō**	open	**û**	burn	**th**	thin
e	end	**ô**	order	**yo͞o**	fuse	**th**	this
ē	equal					**zh**	vision

ə = a in *above* e in *sicken* i in *possible* o in *melon* u in *circus*

named or known: The name "Jane Doe" is often given to an *unidentified* woman.

u·ni·fi·ca·tion [yo͞o′nə·fə·kā′shən] *n.* 1 The act of unifying. 2 A unified condition.

u·ni·form [yo͞o′nə·fôrm′] 1 *adj.* Always the same; not varying or changing: a canal of *uniform* depth. 2 *adj.* The same as one another; all alike: boxes *uniform* in shape. 3 *n.* A special kind of outfit worn by all members of a certain group. 4 *v.* To put into a uniform: to *uniform* a soldier. **—u′ni·form′ly** *adv.*

u·ni·form·i·ty [yo͞o′nə·fôr′mə·tē] *n.* The condition or quality of being uniform; sameness.

u·ni·fy [yo͞o′nə·fī′] *v.* **u·ni·fied, u·ni·fy·ing** To bring or come together into one; unite.

u·ni·lat·er·al [yo͞o′nə·lat′ər·əl] *adj.* On or by one side only: *unilateral* disarmament.

un·im·ag·i·na·ble [un′i·maj′ə·nə·bəl] *adj.* Impossible to imagine: *unimaginable* hardships.

un·i·mag·i·na·tive [un′i·maj′ə·nə·tiv] *adj.* Lacking or showing a lack of imagination: an *unimaginative* story. **—un′i·mag′i·na·tive·ly** *adv.*

un·im·peach·a·ble [un′im·pē′chə·bəl] *adj.* Not to be questioned or doubted; faultless: I got the information from an *unimpeachable* source.

un·im·por·tant [un′im·pôr′tənt] *adj.* 1 Not important or significant. 2 Trivial; petty.

un·im·pressed [un′im·prest′] *adj.* Not strongly or favorably affected: The play left the critics *unimpressed.*

un·im·pres·sive [un′im·pres′iv] *adj.* Not producing a strong impression: a man with an ordinary, *unimpressive* appearance.

un·in·cor·po·rat·ed [un′in·kôr′pə·rā′tid] *adj.* 1 Not taken in or included. 2 Not formed into a corporation.

un·in·flect·ed [un′in·flek′tid] *adj.* 1 Unvarying in tone; flat: an *uninflected* voice. 2 Not changed in grammatical form to show case, number, gender, or tense: The plural of "moose" is *uninflected.*

un·in·formed [un′in·fôrmd′] *adj.* 1 Not informed or told: I was *uninformed* of his departure. 2 Not having knowledge: *uninformed* about electronics.

un·in·hab·it·ed [un′in·hab′ə·tid] *adj.* Having no inhabitants: an *uninhabited* desert.

un·in·hib·it·ed [un′in·hib′ə·tid] *adj.* Not inhibited; not held back or checked: *uninhibited* laughter.

un·in·spired [un′in·spīrd′] *adj.* Showing no imagination or originality: a dull, *uninspired* piece of writing.

un·in·tel·li·gent [un′in·tel′ə·jənt] *adj.* Having little intelligence; stupid. **—un′in·tel′li·gent·ly** *adv.*

un·in·tel·li·gi·ble [un′in·tel′ə·jə·bəl] *adj.* Impossible to understand or follow: an *unintelligible* mumble. **—un′in·tel′li·gi·bly** *adv.*

un·in·ten·tion·al [un′in·ten′shə·nəl] *adj.* Not intentional; not deliberate: an *unintentional* snub. **—un′in·ten′tion·al·ly** *adv.*

un·in·ter·est·ed [un·in′tris·tid *or* un·in′tə·res′tid] *adj.* Not interested: I was fascinated by the book's pictures, though I was *uninterested* in the words. ◆ See DISINTERESTED.

un·in·ter·est·ing [un·in′tris·ting *or* un·in′tə·res′·ting] *adj.* Not catching or holding one's interest: an *uninteresting* meal; an *uninteresting* speaker. **—un·in′ter·est·ing·ly** *adv.*

un·in·ter·rup·ted [un′in·tə·rup′tid] *adj.* Without stopping; continuous: *uninterrupted* rain.

un·in·vit·ed [un′in·vī′tid] *adj.* Not invited or wanted: an *uninvited* guest.

un·in·vit·ing [un′in·vī′ting] *adj.* Not appealing or attractive: The raw liver looked *uninviting.*

un·ion [yo͞on′yən] *n.* 1 The act of joining together or uniting: Great Britain was formed by the *union* of Scotland with England and Wales. 2 The condition of being joined or united; combination. 3 An association, as of persons, nations, or states, united for a common purpose: the *Union* of Soviet Socialist Republics. 4 The joining of two persons in marriage. 5 Another name for LABOR UNION. 6 A device for connecting parts of machinery, as a coupling for pipes. **—the Union** 1 The United States. 2 The Federal government during the Civil War. ◆ *Union* goes back to the Latin word *unus,* meaning *one.*

un·ion·ist [yo͞on′yən·ist] *n.* 1 A person who favors or supports union or labor unions. 2 (*written* **Unionist**) A supporter of the Federal government during the Civil War. 3 A member of a labor union. **—un′ion·ism** *n.*

un·ion·ize [yo͞on′yən·īz′] *v.* **un·ion·ized, un·ion·iz·ing** 1 To cause to join or organize into a labor union: to *unionize* workers. 2 To put under union rules: to *unionize* a craft. **—un·ion·i·za·tion** [yo͞on′yən·ə·zā′shən] *n.*

union jack 1 A flag consisting of the symbol of union from a national flag, as a U.S. naval flag with 50 white stars on a blue field. 2 (*written* **Union Jack**) The flag of the United Kingdom.

Union Jack

u·nique [yo͞o·nēk′] *adj.* 1 Being the only one of its type; without an equal or like; singular: a *unique* gem. 2 Unusual, rare, or notable: a *unique opportunity.* **—u·nique′ly** *adv.* ◆ *Unique* is a strong word. Don't weaken it with qualifiers such as *rather* or *very.*

un·i·sex [yo͞o′ni·seks′] *adj.* Worn by or suitable for both males and females: *unisex* clothing.

u·ni·son [yo͞o′nə·sən] *n.* 1 Agreement in pitch, as among two or more voices or instruments. 2 Agreement. **—in unison** Sounding the same notes, speaking the same words, or making the same movements at the same time.

u·nit [yo͞o′nit] *n.* 1 A single person or thing, complete in itself but considered as part of a larger whole: The cell is the structural *unit* of animals and plants. 2 A group of persons or things thought of as being complete in itself: a military *unit.* 3 A part serving a special purpose: the cooling *unit* of a freezer. 4 A standard quantity used as a measure: An hour is a *unit* of time. 5 The smallest whole number; one.

U·ni·tar·i·an [yo͞o′nə·târ′ē·ən] *n.* A member of a Christian denomination that does not believe in the divinity of Jesus or in the Trinity and which emphasizes complete freedom of religious opinion. **—U′ni·tar′i·an·ism′** *n.*

u·ni·tar·y [yo͞o′nə·ter′ē] *adj.* Of, having to do with, or like a unit or units.

u·nite [yo͞o·nīt′] *v.* **u·nit·ed, u·nit·ing** 1 To join together so as to form a unit; combine: to *unite* two ingredients; The states *united* to form a nation. 2 To join together, as in action or interest.

u·nit·ed [yo͞o·nī′tid] *adj.* 1 Joined into one; combined: *united* voices. 2 Made or done by joint action of more than one. 3 In harmony and closely knit: a *united* family.
United Nations An organization made up of most of the world's nations, founded in 1945 to maintain international peace and security and work for economic and social betterment.
unit pricing A system of marking food products not only with total price but also with the price per pound, quart, or other unit of measure.
u·ni·ty [yo͞o′ni·tē] *n., pl.* **u·ni·ties** 1 The quality of being one or the power of acting as one; oneness: A regular team has greater *unity* than a group of new players. 2 A number that when multiplied by any other number gives that other number as the product. 3 Singleness, as of purpose. 4 In art and literature, the fitting together of parts so as to create a single effect. 5 Harmony; agreement.
univ. 1 universal. 2 universally. 3 (*often written* **Univ.**) university.
un·i·val·ent [yo͞o′ni·vā′lənt] *adj.* In chemistry, having a valance of one.
un·i·valve [yo͞o′ni·valv′] 1 *n.* A mollusk whose shell has a single part or valve, such as the snail. 2 *adj.* Having a single valve.
u·ni·ver·sal [yo͞o′nə·vûr′səl] *adj.* 1 Of, for, common to, or involving all: a *universal* practice. 2 Occurring everywhere: the *universal* desire for security. **—u·ni·ver·sal·i·ty** [yo͞o′nə·vər·sal′ə·tē] *n.*
U·ni·ver·sal·ist [yo͞o′nə·vûr′səl·ist] *n.* A member of a Christian church that believes that all souls will finally be saved.
universal joint A joint for coupling the end of a rotating shaft to the end of another that is at a slight angle to it.

A universal joint

u·ni·ver·sal·ly [yo͞o′nə·vûr′sə·lē] *adv.* 1 In all cases: *universally* valid. 2 Everywhere or by everyone: The movie was *universally* admired.
u·ni·verse [yo͞o′nə·vûrs′] *n.* The whole that is made up of everything that exists, including earth, sun, stars, planets, and outer space.
u·ni·ver·si·ty [yo͞o′nə·vûr′sə·tē] *n., pl.* **u·ni·ver·si·ties** An institution of higher learning, usually including a regular college or colleges as well as one or more schools for graduate or professional study, as in law or medicine.
un·just [un·just′] *adj.* Not fair or just. **—un·just′ly** *adv.*
un·jus·ti·fi·a·ble [un·jus′tə·fī′ə·bəl] *adj.* Not capable of being shown to be just or proper: an *unjustifiable* punishment. **—un·jus′ti·fi′a·bly** *adv.*
un·kempt [un·kempt′] *adj.* 1 Not combed. 2 Not clean, neat, or tidy: *unkempt* clothing.
un·kind [un·kīnd′] *adj.* Not kind, thoughtful, or sympathetic; mean, harsh, or cruel. **—un·kind′ly** *adv.* **—un·kind′ness** *n.*
un·know·a·ble [un·nō′ə·bəl] *adj.* Not capable of being known: The future is *unknowable.*
un·known [un·nōn′] *adj.* 1 Not known or not recognized: an *unknown* person. 2 Not yet discovered: an *unknown* quantity. 3 *n. use*: Something unknown, as persons or things: fear of the *unknown.*
un·la·beled or **un·la·belled** [un·lā′bəld] *adj.* Having no label or identification mark.
un·lace [un·lās′] *v.* **un·laced, un·lac·ing** To loosen or undo the laces of: to *unlace* boots.
un·latch [un·lach′] *v.* To open or unlock by lifting or releasing a latch: *Unlatch* the door.
un·law·ful [un·lô′fəl] *adj.* Not allowed by law; illegal. **—un·law′ful·ly** *adv.*
un·lead·ed [un·led′id] *adj.* Containing no lead: *Unleaded* gasoline causes less air pollution than regular gasoline.
un·learn [un·lûrn′] *v.* **un·learned** or **un·learnt, un·learn·ing** To forget or get rid of (something learned), as because it is wrong: to *unlearn* prejudices; to *unlearn* bad habits.
un·learn·ed *adj.* 1 [un·lûr′nid] Not educated; ignorant. 2 [un·lûrnd′] Not known by study or learning, as something known naturally: A baby's crying is an *unlearned* reaction.
un·leash [un·lēsh′] *v.* To let loose from or as if from a leash: to *unleash* a pet; The challenge *unleashed* all their energies.
un·leav·ened [un·lev′ənd] *adj.* Made without yeast or other leaven: *unleavened* bread.
un·less [un·les′] *conj.* In any event other than; except if: I'll come *unless* it snows.
un·let·tered [un·let′ərd] *adj.* 1 Not educated. 2 Unable to read or write; illiterate.
un·li·censed [un·lī′sənst] *adj.* 1 Without a license: an *unlicensed* dog. 2 Unauthorized.
un·light·ed [un·lī′tid] *adj.* 1 Not on fire; not lighted: an *unlighted* candle. 2 Dark: an *unlighted* hallway.
un·lik·a·ble [un·lī′kə·bəl] *adj.* Not easy to like.
un·like [un·līk′] 1 *adj.* Different from one another: *unlike* abilities. 2 *prep.* Not like or different from: It was *unlike* them to ask; Your watch is *unlike* mine.
un·like·ly [un·līk′lē] *adj.* 1 Not probable or likely. 2 Not likely to be successful.
un·lim·it·ed [un·lim′it·id] *adj.* Having no set limits: *unlimited* time; *unlimited* power.
un·lined [un·līnd′] *adj.* Having no lines or wrinkles: *unlined* paper; an *unlined* face.
un·load [un·lōd′] *v.* 1 To remove the load or cargo from: to *unload* a truck. 2 To remove (as cargo or passengers): to *unload* boxes. 3 To discharge a cargo. 4 To pour out onto another: *Unload* your story. 5 To remove the cartridges or other charge from (a weapon).
un·lock [un·lok′] *v.* 1 To unfasten or undo the lock of. 2 To lay open; reveal: Scientists *unlock* the secrets of life.
un·looked-for [un·lo͝okt′fôr′] *adj.* Unexpected.
un·loose [un·lo͞os′] *v.* **un·loosed, un·loos·ing** To set loose or set free; loosen or release.
un·loos·en [un·lo͞o′sən] *v.* To loose; unloose.
un·lov·a·ble [un·luv′ə·bəl] *adj.* Not worthy of affection or love.
un·loved [un·luvd′] *adj.* Not loved.

a	add	**i**	it	**o͝o**	took	**oi**	oil		
ā	ace	**ī**	ice	**o͞o**	pool	**ou**	pout		
â	care	**o**	odd	**u**	up	**ng**	ring		
ä	palm	**ō**	open	**û**	burn	**th**	thin		
e	end	**ô**	order	**yo͞o**	fuse	**th̸**	this		
ē	equal					**zh**	vision		

ə = { a in *above* e in *sicken* i in *possible* / o in *melon* u in *circus* }

U

un·luck·y [un·luk′ē] *adj.* **un·luck·i·er, un·luck·i·est** Marked by, having, or bringing bad luck; not lucky. **—un·luck′i·ly** *adv.*

un·man [un·man′] *v.* **un·manned, un·man·ning** 1 To cause to lose courage or strength: *unmanned* by terror. 2 To remove the crew from: to *unman* a ship.

un·man·age·a·ble [un·man′i·jə·bəl] *adj.* Incapable of being managed or controlled; unruly.

un·man·ly [un·man′lē] *adj.* 1 Effeminate; womanish. 2 Weak or cowardly: *unmanly* behavior. **—un·man′li·ness** *n.*

un·manned [un·mand′] *adj.* Having no crew: an *unmanned* aircraft.

un·man·ner·ly [un·man′ər·lē] *adj.* Lacking manners; rude.

un·mar·ried [un·mar′ēd] *adj.* Not married; single.

un·mask [un·mask′] *v.* 1 To remove a mask or disguise from: The guests *unmasked* themselves at midnight. 2 To remove one's mask or disguise: Everyone *unmasked* when the clock struck. 3 To reveal or disclose the truth about: The police *unmasked* the entire spy ring.

un·mean·ing [un·mē′ning] *adj.* 1 Having no meaning; senseless. 2 Showing no expression of intelligence or interest: an *unmeaning* stare.

un·meet [un·mēt′] *adj.* Not suitable or proper: seldom used today.

un·men·tion·a·ble [un·men′shən·ə·bəl] *adj.* Not suitable or proper for mention or discussion in polite conversation.

un·mer·ci·ful [un·mûr′sə·fəl] *adj.* Showing no mercy; cruel.

un·mer·it·ed [un·mer′i·tid] *adj.* Not earned or deserved: *unmerited* praise.

un·mind·ful [un·mīnd′fəl] *adj.* Not keeping in mind; inattentive; careless.

un·mis·tak·a·ble [un′mis·tā′kə·bəl] *adj.* That cannot be mistaken or misunderstood; clear: *unmistakable* directions. **—un′mis·tak′a·bly** *adv.*

un·mit·i·gat·ed [un·mit′ə·gā′tid] *adj.* 1 Not lessened or lightened: *unmitigated* sorrow. 2 Absolute; total: an *unmitigated* bore.

un·mor·al [un·môr′əl] *adj.* Not aware of or not involving right and wrong; neither moral nor immoral.

un·moved [un·mo͞ovd′] *adj.* 1 Not affected by feelings such as sympathy: The story left us *unmoved.* 2 Not changed in purpose, policy, or opinion: The boss was *unmoved* by all our arguments. 3 Not changed in position or place.

un·named [un·nāmd′] *adj.* 1 Having no name; nameless. 2 Unknown by name; anonymous.

un·nat·u·ral [un·nach′ər·əl] *adj.* 1 Not natural or normal; strange; abnormal. 2 Artificial; affected: an *unnatural* manner. 3 Very evil or shocking; inhuman: *unnatural* cruelty. **—un·nat′u·ral·ly** *adv.*

un·nec·es·sar·y [un·nes′ə·ser′ē] *adj.* Not required or necessary; needless. **—un·nec′es·sar′i·ly** *adv.*

un·need·ed [un·nē′did] *adj.* Not needed; unnecessary.

un·nerve [un·nûrv′] *v.* **un·nerved, un·nerv·ing** To cause to lose strength, firmness, self-control, or courage: The eerie quiet *unnerved* me.

un·no·tice·a·ble [un·nō′tis·ə·bəl] *adj.* Not noticeable or easily seen. **—un·no′tice·a·bly** *adv.*

un·no·ticed [un·nō′tist] *adj.* Not noticed; overlooked.

un·num·bered [un·num′bərd] *adj.* 1 Not given or marked with a number. 2 Too many to count; innumerable: the *unnumbered* stars of the Milky Way.

un·o·blig·ing [un′ə·blī′jing] *adj.* Refusing to do favors; unwilling to please.

un·ob·serv·a·ble [un′əb·zûr′və·bəl] *adj.* Not observable or readily seen.

un·ob·served [un′əb·zûrvd′] *adj.* 1 Not seen or noticed. 2 Not celebrated: an *unobserved* birthday. 3 Not obeyed: an *unobserved* rule.

un·ob·tain·a·ble [un′əb·tān′ə·bəl] *adj.* Not able to be obtained: In wartime many luxuries are *unobtainable.*

un·ob·tru·sive [un′əb·tro͞o′siv] *adj.* Not demanding notice; inconspicuous.

un·oc·cu·pied [un·ok′yə·pīd′] *adj.* 1 Not occupied; vacant: an *unoccupied* building. 2 Not held by troops. 3 Not working; unemployed. 4 Not busy; idle.

un·of·fi·cial [un′ə·fish′əl] *adj.* Not official. **—un′of·fi′cial·ly** *adv.*

un·o·pened [un·ō′pənd] *adj.* Not opened; shut or fastened: an *unopened* letter.

un·op·posed [un′ə·pōzd′] *adj.* Not opposed or resisted: His seizure of power was *unopposed.*

un·or·gan·ized [un·ôr′gə·nīzd′] *adj.* 1 Not organized: an *unorganized* political movement. 2 Not unionized: *unorganized* workers.

un·or·tho·dox [un·ôr′thə·doks′] *adj.* Not orthodox, conventional, or approved.

un·pack [un·pak′] *v.* 1 To open and take out the contents of: to *unpack* a trunk. 2 To take out from a box or other container: to *unpack* china. 3 To remove things from their containers: We *unpacked* all day long.

un·paid [un·pād′] *adj.* 1 Not yet paid or settled: an *unpaid* debt. 2 Working without pay: *unpaid* volunteers.

un·par·al·leled [un·par′ə·leld′] *adj.* Without parallel, equal, or match: an *unparalleled* success.

un·par·don·a·ble [un·pär′dən·ə·bəl] *adj.* Incapable of being pardoned or forgiven: *unpardonable* rudeness.

un·pa·tri·ot·ic [un·pā′trē·ot′ik] *adj.* Not patriotic; not showing love for one's country. **—un·pa′tri·ot′i·cal·ly** *adv.*

un·per·ceived [un′pər·sēvd′] *adj.* Not perceived; not observed or noticed.

un·per·fect·ed [un′pûr·fek′tid] *adj.* Not perfected.

un·picked [un·pikt′] *adj.* Not picked or gathered: *unpicked* fruit.

un·pin [un·pin′] *v.* **un·pinned, un·pin·ning** To unfasten or loosen by removing a pin or pins from: to *unpin* a hem.

un·pit·y·ing [un·pit′ē·ing] *adj.* Without pity; pitiless; cruel.

un·planned [un·pland′] *adj.* Not planned; spontaneous.

un·plant·ed [un·plan′tid] *adj.* Not planted: an *unplanted* field.

un·played [un·plād′] *adj.* Not played: *unplayed* music; *unplayed* games.

un·pleas·ant [un·plez′ənt] *adj.* Not pleasing; disagreeable; objectionable: *unpleasant* manners. **—un·pleas′ant·ly** *adv.* **—un·pleas′ant·ness** *n.*

un·plowed [un·ploud′] *adj.* Not plowed or made ready for planting: an *unplowed* field.

un·plug [un·plug′] *v.* **un·plugged, un·plug·ging** 1 To disconnect (an electrical appliance) by pulling out the plug from an outlet. 2 To remove a stopper or obstruction from: to *unplug* a drain.

un·po·et·ic [un′pō·et′ik] *adj.* 1 Not like or suitable for poetry or poets. 2 Not imaginative or beautiful.

un·po·et·i·cal [un′pō·et′i·kəl] *adj.* Unpoetic. —**un′·po·et′i·cal·ly** *adv.*

un·pol·ished [un·pol′isht] *adj.* 1 Not polished: *unpolished* shoes. 2 Not perfected: an *unpolished* musical performance.

un·pol·lut·ed [un′pə·lo͞o′tid] *adj.* Not polluted, as by automobile exhaust gases or industrial wastes: an *unpolluted* stream.

un·pop·u·lar [un·pop′yə·lər] *adj.* Not liked or approved of by a rather large number of people: an *unpopular* official; an *unpopular* idea. —**un·pop·u·lar·i·ty** [un·pop′yə·lar′ə·tē] *n.*

un·pop·u·lat·ed [un·pop′yə·lā′tid] *adj.* Having no inhabitants; without people: *unpopulated* areas of Outer Mongolia.

un·prac·ticed [un·prak′tist] *adj.* 1 Without practice or skill; not expert. 2 Not used often: an *unpracticed* skill.

un·prec·e·dent·ed [un·pres′ə·den′tid] *adj.* Having no precedent or earlier example; unheard-of: an *unprecedented* victory.

un·pre·dict·a·ble [un′pri·dik′tə·bəl] *adj.* Not able to be predicted or known in advance: an *unpredictable* outcome. —**un′pre·dict′a·ble·ness** *n.* —**un′·pre·dict′a·bly** *adv.*

un·prej·u·diced [un·prej′o͝o·dist] *adj.* Free from prejudice; fair; impartial.

un·pre·med·i·tat·ed [un′prē·med′ə·tā′tid] *adj.* Not premeditated; not planned in advance: an *unpremeditated* murder.

un·pre·pos·sess·ing [un′prē·pə·zes′ing] *adj.* Not creating a good first impression; unimpressive.

un·pre·ten·tious [un′pri·ten′shəs] *adj.* Not showy; simple; modest: an *unpretentious* cottage. —**un′·pre·ten′tious·ly** *adv.* —**un′pre·ten′tious·ness** *n.*

un·pre·vent·a·ble or **un·pre·vent·i·ble** [un′pri·ven′·tə·bəl] *adj.* Not capable of being prevented: an *unpreventable* tragedy.

un·prin·ci·pled [un·prin′sə·pəld] *adj.* Lacking moral principles; unscrupulous.

un·print·a·ble [un·prin′tə·bəl] *adj.* Not fit to be printed; too indecent or profane to be printed.

un·pro·fes·sion·al [un′prə·fesh′ən·əl] *adj.* Not according to professional standards or conduct: It is considered *unprofessional* for a doctor to advertise for patients.

un·prof·i·ta·ble [un·prof′it·ə·bəl] *adj.* Not bringing profit or gain. —**un·prof′i·ta·bly** *adv.*

un·prom·is·ing [un·prom′is·ing] *adj.* Not promising; not likely to succeed or please: an *unpromising* weather forecast.

un·pro·nounce·a·ble [un′prə·noun′sə·bəl] *adj.* Not easy to pronounce or pronounce properly.

un·pro·tect·ed [un′prə·tek′tid] *adj.* Not protected or sheltered.

un·proved [un·pro͞ovd′] *adj.* Not shown to be true or correct: an *unproved* accusation.

un·pro·voked [un′prə·vōkt′] *adj.* Without apparent cause; not provoked: an *unprovoked* attack.

un·pun·ished [un·pun′isht] *adj.* Not punished or held to account: an *unpunished* robbery; an *unpunished* criminal.

un·qual·i·fied [un·kwol′ə·fīd′] *adj.* 1 Not having the proper qualifications; unfit. 2 Without any limitation or restriction; absolute; entire: *unqualified* approval.

un·quench·a·ble [un·kwench′ə·bəl] *adj.* That cannot be quenched or extinguished: an *unquenchable* thirst; *unquenchable* enthusiasm.

un·ques·tion·a·ble [un·kwes′chən·ə·bəl] *adj.* Not to be doubted; absolutely certain: It was an *unquestionable* victory for us. —**un·ques′tion·a·bly** *adv.*

un·ques·tioned [un·kwes′chənd] *adj.* Not doubted or disputed.

un·qui·et [un·kwī′ət] *adj.* 1 Not still or quiet; agitated: the *unquiet* sea. 2 Uneasy or restless: *unquiet* times; an *unquiet* mind.

un·quote [un·kwōt′] *v.* **un·quot·ed, un·quot·ing** To close or end a quotation.

un·rav·el [un·rav′əl] *v.* **un·rav·eled** or **un·rav·elled, un·rav·el·ing** or **un·rav·el·ling** 1 To separate or pull apart the threads of (something knitted, woven, or tangled): The dog *unraveled* the sleeve of my sweater. 2 To solve, make clear, or explain: to *unravel* the plot of a mystery story. 3 To become unraveled.

un·reach·a·ble [un·rēch′ə·bəl] *adj.* Not able to be reached: Simon is *unreachable* by phone.

un·read [un·red′] *adj.* 1 Having read very little: The student was *unread* in history. 2 Not yet read: an *unread* book.

un·read·y [un·red′ē] *adj.* Not ready or prepared.

un·real [un·rēl′ *or* un·rē′əl] *adj.* Not real or actual; imaginary: Dreams are *unreal* things. —**un·re·al·i·ty** [un′rē·al′ə·tē] *n.*

un·re·al·is·tic [un′rē·ə·lis′tik] *adj.* 1 Not consistent with reality; not lifelike or probable: an *unrealistic* drama. 2 Not sensible or possible: *unrealistic* plans. —**un′re·al·is′ti·cal·ly** *adv.*

un·rea·son·a·ble [un·rē′zən·ə·bəl] *adj.* 1 Not reasonable or sensible: Your objection is *unreasonable.* 2 Greater than what is reasonable; excessive; exorbitant: an *unreasonable* salary. —**un·rea′son·a·bly** *adv.*

un·rea·son·ing [un·rē′zə·ning] *adj.* Not showing or governed by reason; irrational: *unreasoning* terror.

un·re·cep·tive [un′ri·sep′tiv] *adj.* Not receptive; unwilling to accept ideas or suggestions.

un·rec·og·niz·a·ble [un·rek′əg·nī′zə·bəl] *adj.* Not capable of being recognized or identified: The mask made him *unrecognizable.*

un·rec·og·nized [un·rek′əg·nīzd′] *adj.* 1 Not recognized or identified: The spy crossed the border *unrecognized.* 2 Not pointed out or appreciated: *unrecognized* good works. 3 Not accepted for full diplomatic relations: an *unrecognized* foreign government.

un·re·cord·ed [un′ri·kôr′did] *adj.* Not recorded or registered.

un·re·fined [un′ri·fīnd′] *adj.* 1 Not cleansed of impurities: *unrefined* gold. 2 Not cultured or polished; crude: an *unrefined* person.

un·re·gen·er·ate [un′ri·jen′ər·it] *adj.* 1 Wicked; sinful. 2 Not spiritually reborn; not reformed.

a	add	**i**	it	**o͝o**	took	**oi**	oil
ā	ace	**ī**	ice	**o͞o**	pool	**ou**	pout
â	care	**o**	odd	**u**	up	**ng**	ring
ä	palm	**ō**	open	**û**	burn	**th**	thin
e	end	**ô**	order	**yo͞o**	fuse	**th**	this
ē	equal					**zh**	vision

ə = a in *above*, e in *sicken*, i in *possible*, o in *melon*, u in *circus*

un·reg·is·tered [un·rej′is·tərd] *adj.* Not registered or recorded: an *unregistered* birth.

un·re·hearsed [un′ri·hûrst′] *adj.* Not rehearsed or practiced beforehand: an *unrehearsed* speech.

un·re·lent·ing [un′ri·len′ting] *adj.* 1 Not softened by kindness or pity; merciless: an *unrelenting* taskmaster. 2 Not relaxing or growing less: *unrelenting* efforts.

un·re·li·a·ble [un′ri·lī′ə·bəl] *adj.* Not to be relied on; not trustworthy. **—un′re·li′a·bil′i·ty** *n.* **—un′re·li′a·ble·ness** *n.* **—un′re·li′a·bly** *adv.*

un·re·mit·ting [un′ri·mit′ing] *adj.* Not letting up or stopping; constant: *unremitting* noise.

un·re·pent·ant [un′ri·pen′tənt] *adj.* Not repenting or showing regret.

un·re·port·ed [un′ri·pôr′tid] *adj.* Not reported or made known: *unreported* news; *unreported* income.

un·re·quit·ed [un′ri·kwī′tid] *adj.* Not returned in kind; not reciprocated: *unrequited* love.

un·re·served [un′ri·zûrvd′] *adj.* 1 Not limited; full; unqualified: *unreserved* approval. 2 Open, frank, and informal, as in manner or speech. 3 Not reserved, as for a particular person: *unreserved* seats. **—un·re·serv·ed·ly** [un′ri·zûr′vid·lē] *adv.*

un·rest [un·rest′] *n.* 1 Restlessness, especially of the mind. 2 Angry discontent or turmoil sometimes not far from rebellion.

un·re·strained [un′ri·strānd′] *adj.* Not held back or repressed: *unrestrained* laughter.

un·re·tent·ive [un′ri·ten′tiv] *adj.* Unable to remember things easily: an *unretentive* memory.

un·re·turned [un′ri·tûrnd′] *adj.* Not brought back: *unreturned* library books.

un·re·vealed [un′ri·vēld′] *adj.* Not shown or made known.

un·re·ward·ed [un′ri·wôr′did] *adj.* Not given a reward.

un·right·eous [un·rī′chəs] *adj.* Not righteous; wicked; sinful. **—un·right′eous·ness** *n.*

un·ripe [un·rīp′] *adj.* Not ripe or ready: *unripe* apples.

un·ri·valed or **un·ri·valled** [un·rī′vəld] *adj.* Having no rival or competitor; unequaled; matchless: the *unrivaled* beauty of the sea.

un·roll [un·rōl′] *v.* 1 To spread out or open (something rolled up). 2 To become opened or rolled out flat. 3 To show or reveal: The photograph album *unrolled* the whole history of the family.

un·ro·man·tic [un′rō·man′tik] *adj.* Not romantic: an ordinary, *unromantic* life.

UNRRA [un′rə] United Nations Relief and Rehabilitation Administration.

un·ruf·fled [un·ruf′əld] *adj.* 1 Not nervous, disturbed, or upset; calm. 2 Not disturbed; smooth: The lake was *unruffled.*

un·ruled [un·ro͞old′] *adj.* 1 Having no lines: *unruled* paper. 2 Not under control; unruly.

un·ru·ly [un·ro͞o′lē] *adj.* **un·ru·li·er, un·ru·li·est** Difficult to control or discipline; disobedient: an *unruly* child; an *unruly* class. **—un·ru′li·ness** *n.*

UNRWA United Nations Relief and Works Agency.

un·sad·dle [un·sad′(ə)l] *v.* **un·sad·dled, un·sad·dling** 1 To remove a saddle, as from a horse. 2 To throw from a saddle.

un·safe [un·sāf′] *adj.* Not safe: a rickety, *unsafe* bridge.

un·said [un·sed′] 1 Past tense and past participle of UNSAY. 2 *adj.* Not said; not spoken.

un·sal·a·ried [un·sal′ə·rēd] *adj.* Working without a salary; unpaid: an *unsalaried* government adviser.

un·san·i·tar·y [un·san′ə·ter′ē] *adj.* Not sanitary; unclean: *unsanitary* living conditions.

un·sat·is·fac·to·ry [un′sat·is·fak′tər·ē] *adj.* Not satisfactory; not meeting standards. **—un′sat·is·fac′·to·ri·ly** *adv.*

un·sat·is·fied [un·sat′is·fīd′] *adj.* Not satisfied; not supplied fully with what is wanted: *unsatisfied* customers.

un·sat·is·fy·ing [un·sat′is·fī′ing] *adj.* Not satisfying: a skimpy, *unsatisfying* meal.

un·sat·u·rat·ed [un·sach′ə·rā′tid] *adj.* 1 Able to absorb more of a substance, as a solution. 2 Of, characterized by, or being a chemical compound in which carbon atoms are joined by double or triple bonds: *unsaturated* fats.

un·sa·vor·y [un·sā′vər·ē] *adj.* 1 Having a disagreeable taste or odor. 2 Morally bad or offensive: an *unsavory* reputation.

un·say [un·sā′] *v.* **un·said, un·say·ing** To take back or retract (something said).

un·scarred [un·skärd′] *adj.* Not marked with a scar or scars.

un·scathed [un·skāthd′] *adj.* Not hurt or injured.

un·sched·uled [un·skej′o͞old] *adj.* Not on the schedule: The train made an *unscheduled* stop.

un·schol·ar·ly [un·skol′ər·lē] *adj.* Not scholarly or meeting standards of scholarship: an *unscholarly*, careless piece of research.

un·sci·en·tif·ic [un′sī·ən·tif′ik] *adj.* Not following the principles and methods of science. **—un′sci·en·tif′i·cal·ly** *adv.*

un·scram·ble [un·skram′bəl] *v.* **un·scram·bled, un·scram·bling** To make orderly, clear, or intelligible: Can you *unscramble* the puzzle?

un·scratched [un·skracht′] *adj.* Not marked or cut with something sharp: an *unscratched* table.

un·screw [un·skro͞o′] *v.* 1 To remove the screw or screws from: *Unscrew* the hinge. 2 To loosen or take off or out by turning, as a nut, a jar lid, or a light bulb.

un·scru·pu·lous [un·skro͞o′pyə·ləs] *adj.* Having no scruples, principles, or conscience; dishonest. **—un·scru′pu·lous·ly** *adv.*

un·seal [un·sēl′] *v.* 1 To break or take off the seal of; open: *Unseal* the letter, please. 2 To open (something tightly closed): No amount of teasing could *unseal* their lips.

un·search·a·ble [un·sûr′chə·bəl] *adj.* Not capable of being explored or explained: an *unsearchable* mystery. **—un·search′a·bly** *adv.*

un·sea·son·a·ble [un·sē′zən·ə·bəl] *adj.* 1 Not normal for or suited to the season: This cold weather is *unseasonable* for summer. 2 Not coming at the right time: July is an *unseasonable* time to sell skis. **—un·seas′on·a·ble·ness** *n.* **—un·seas′on·a·bly** *adv.*

un·seas·oned [un·sē′zənd] *adj.* 1 Without seasoning: *unseasoned* soup. 2 Not sufficiently aged or dried for use: *unseasoned* firewood. 3 Not fully trained or hardened: *unseasoned* troops.

un·seat [un·sēt′] *v.* 1 To throw (a rider) from a saddle. 2 To remove from office: to *unseat* a public official.

un·seem·ly [un·sēm′lē] *adj.* **un·seem·li·er, un·seem·li·est** 1 *adj.* Not proper or decent; unbecoming: *unseemly* behavior. 2 *adv.* In an improper or unseemly manner.

un·seen [un·sēn'] *adj.* 1 Not seen or noticed: The boy slipped out *unseen.* 2 Not to be seen; invisible.

un·self·ish [un·sel'fish] *adj.* Not selfish; generous in helping, giving to, or caring for others. **—un·self'·ish·ly** *adv.* **—un·self'ish·ness** *n.*

un·set·tle [un·set'(ə)l] *v.* **un·set·tled, un·set·tling** 1 To make or become confused, disturbed, or upset: The breakdown of the electric plants *unsettled* every activity in the city. 2 To make or become unsteady or unfixed.

un·set·tled [un·set'(ə)ld] *adj.* 1 Not orderly or calm; disturbed; confused. 2 Uncertain; changeable: *unsettled* weather. 3 Not yet decided or determined: The answer to that question is still *unsettled.* 4 Not lived in; unpopulated: an *unsettled* county in the West. 5 Not paid or disposed of, as a debt or estate.

un·shak·a·ble or **un·shake·a·ble** [un·shā'kə·bəl] *adj.* Not easy to weaken or upset: He showed *unshakable* courage in battle.

un·shak·en [un·shā'kən] *adj.* Not shaken or weakened: *unshaken* determination.

un·shav·en [un·shā'vən] *adj.* Not shaved: an *unshaven* beard.

un·sheathe [un·shēth'] *v.* **un·sheathed, un·sheath·ing** To take from or as if from a scabbard or sheath: The cat *unsheathed* its claws.

un·shod [un·shod'] *adj.* Not wearing shoes.

un·sight·ly [un·sīt'lē] *adj.* **un·sight·li·er, un·sight·li·est** Not pleasing to look at; ugly.

un·skilled [un·skild'] *adj.* 1 Having no special skill or training: an *unskilled* worker. 2 Requiring no special skills: *unskilled* work.

un·skill·ful or **un·skil·ful** [un·skil'fəl] *adj.* Lacking in skill; bungling; clumsy.

un·smil·ing [un·smī'ling] *adj.* Not smiling or accompanied with a smile: an *unsmiling* good-bye.

un·snap [un·snap'] *v.* **un·snapped, un·snap·ping** To undo the snap or snaps of; unfasten.

un·snarl [un·snärl'] *v.* To take the snarls out of; untangle.

un·so·cia·ble [un·sō'shə·bəl] *adj.* Preferring to be alone; not friendly. **—un·so'cia·ble·ness** *n.* **—un·so'·cia·bly** *adv.*

un·sold [un·sōld'] *adj.* Not sold: *unsold* goods.

un·solved [un·solvd'] *adj.* Not solved or worked out: an *unsolved* problem.

un·so·phis·ti·cat·ed [un'sə·fis'tə·kā'tid] *adj.* Not sophisticated; simple, natural, or innocent; inexperienced in worldly things.

un·sought [un·sôt'] *adj.* Not asked for or tried for: *unsought* publicity.

un·sound [un·sound'] *adj.* 1 Not solid or strong; weak: an *unsound* floor. 2 Not healthy: an *unsound* mind. 3 Not true, valid, or logical: an *unsound* argument. 4 Not deep or restful: an *unsound* sleep.

un·spar·ing [un·spâr'ing] *adj.* 1 Not sparing or stingy; generous; liberal: to be *unsparing* in one's efforts to help. 2 Showing no mercy; severe; harsh. **—un·spar'ing·ly** *adv.*

un·speak·a·ble [un·spē'kə·bəl] *adj.* 1 That cannot be expressed because it is so great; unutterable: *unspeakable* joy. 2 Extremely bad or objectionable: an *unspeakable* crime. **—un·speak'a·bly** *adv.*

un·spec·i·fied [un·spes'ə·fīd'] *adj.* Not specified; not made definite: an *unspecified* number of books.

un·spent [un·spent'] *adj.* Not spent or used up: *unspent* money; *unspent* energy.

un·spoiled [un·spoild'] *adj.* 1 Not damaged, marred, or rotten: The oranges from Florida arrived *unspoiled.* 2 Not harmed by too much indulgence: an *unspoiled* child.

un·spok·en [un·spō'kən] *adj.* Not spoken; left unsaid: an *unspoken* understanding.

un·sports·man·like [un·spôrts'mən·līk'] *adj.* Not abiding by the rules of fair play: It is *unsportsmanlike* to be a poor loser.

un·spot·ted [un·spot'id] *adj.* 1 Not having spots: The mountain lion has an *unspotted* coat. 2 Not disgraced or flawed: an *unspotted* reputation.

un·sta·ble [un·stā'bəl] *adj.* 1 Not stable, firm, or fixed; liable to shake or move: an *unstable* building. 2 Not emotionally steady; variable: an *unstable* person. 3 Easily decomposed, as a chemical compound.

un·stat·ed [un·stā'tid] *adj.* Not stated or made clear: an *unstated* purpose.

un·stead·y [un·sted'ē] *adj.* 1 Not steady or firm; shaky. 2 Not regular or constant; changeable: the machine's *unsteady* speed. **—un·stead'i·ly** *adv.* **—un·stead'i·ness** *n.*

un·stop [un·stop'] *v.* **un·stopped, un·stop·ping** 1 To remove a plug or cork from: to *unstop* a soda bottle. 2 To clear of an obstruction: to *unstop* a clogged drain.

un·strap [un·strap'] *v.* **un·strapped, un·strap·ping** To loosen or unfasten the strap or straps of.

un·stressed [un·strest'] *adj.* Not stressed in speech or accented in music: an *unstressed* syllable; an *unstressed* note.

un·string [un·string'] *v.* **un·strung, un·string·ing** 1 To remove from a string: to *unstring* beads. 2 To remove or slacken the strings of: to *unstring* a harp. 3 To make upset or nervous.

un·strung [un·strung'] *adj.* 1 Having the strings removed or loosened. 2 Nervous and upset; distressed.

un·stud·ied [un·stud'ēd] *adj.* Not affected or forced; natural: *unstudied* friendliness.

un·sub·stan·tial [un'səb·stan'shəl] *adj.* 1 Not substantial; lacking strength or solidity: an *unsubstantial* shack. 2 Not true or valid: *unsubstantial* claims. 3 Lacking material substance: an *unsubstantial* phantom.

un·suc·cess·ful [un'sək·ses'fəl] *adj.* 1 Failing to become wealthy or famous. 2 Not achieving a favorable or desired outcome: an *unsuccessful* attempt to climb Mount Everest. **—un'suc·cess'ful·ly** *adv.*

un·suit·a·ble [un·sōō'tə·bəl] *adj.* Not proper for the purpose or occasion: A party dress is *unsuitable* for horseback riding. **—un·suit'a·bly** *adv.*

un·suit·ed [un·sōō'tid] *adj.* Not fitted or adapted: My eyes are *unsuited* to watchmaking.

un·sul·lied [un·sul'ēd] *adj.* Not soiled or tarnished.

un·sung [un·sung'] *adj.* 1 Not yet sung. 2 Not

a	add	**i**	it	**ŏŏ**	took	**oi**	oil
ā	ace	**ī**	ice	**ōō**	pool	**ou**	pout
â	care	**o**	odd	**u**	up	**ng**	ring
ä	palm	**ō**	open	**û**	burn	**th**	thin
e	end	**ô**	order	**yōō**	fuse	**th**	this
ē	equal					**zh**	vision

ə = a in *above*, e in *sicken*, i in *possible*, o in *melon*, u in *circus*

U

honored or celebrated; obscure: *unsung* heroes and heroines.

un·sup·port·ed [un′sə·pôr′tid] *adj.* 1 Not provided with the necessities of life: *unsupported* children. 2 Not backed or helped: an *unsupported* candidate. 3 Not held up or kept in place by supports: an *unsupported* column. 4 Not confirmed or verified: *unsupported* evidence.

un·sure [un·shŏŏr′] *adj.* 1 Not certain; doubtful: an *unsure* future. 2 Not confident: Jake was *unsure* of his talent. 3 Not firm or stable: an *unsure* footing.

un·sur·passed [un′sər·past′] *adj.* Not surpassed or improved upon: His time for the mile run is *unsurpassed.*

un·sus·pect·ed [un′sə·spek′tid] *adj.* 1 Not viewed with suspicion. 2 Not thought of; unexpected: She fought back with *unsuspected* strength.

un·sus·pect·ing [un′sə·spek′ting] *adj.* Having no doubt or suspicion; trusting. **—un′sus·pect′ing·ly** *adv.*

un·sus·pi·cious [un′sə·spish′əs] *adj.* Not suspicious or questionable.

un·sweet·ened [un·swēt′(ə)nd] *adj.* Not sweetened; without added sugar.

un·sym·met·ri·cal [un′si·met′ri·kəl] *adj.* Not symmetrical or balanced; irregular. **—un′sym·met′ri·cal·ly** *adv.*

un·sym·pa·thet·ic [un′sim·pə·thet′ik] *adj.* Not feeling, showing, or arising from sympathy. **—un′sym·pa·thet′i·cal·ly** *adv.*

un·sys·tem·at·ic [un′sis·tə·mat′ik] *adj.* Not systematic; not orderly or methodical.

un·tact·ful [un·takt′fəl] *adj.* Not showing tact; tactless. **—un·tact′ful·ly** *adv.*

un·tal·ent·ed [un·tal′ən·tid] *adj.* Having no natural aptitude; not gifted.

un·tamed [un·tāmd′] *adj.* Not tamed; wild: an *untamed* monkey.

un·tan·gle [un·tang′gəl] *v.* **un·tan·gled, un·tan·gling** 1 To free from snarls or tangles: to *untangle* a fishing line. 2 To clear up or solve: to *untangle* a problem.

un·taught [un·tôt′] *adj.* 1 Not having been taught or educated; ignorant. 2 Known or learned without being taught; natural.

un·tax·a·ble [un·tak′sə·bəl] *adj.* Not taxable by the government: *untaxable* earnings.

un·ten·a·ble [un·ten′ə·bəl] *adj.* That cannot be proved or defended: *untenable* theories.

un·test·ed [un·tes′tid] *adj.* Not tested or tried out: *untested* theories.

un·thank·ful [un·thangk′fəl] *adj.* Not thankful; ungrateful.

un·think·a·ble [un·thing′kə·bəl] *adj.* Impossible to consider or believe; inconceivable: an *unthinkable* catastrophe.

un·think·ing [un·thing′king] *adj.* 1 Acting or done without thought: *unthinking* acceptance. 2 Not able to think: A worm is an *unthinking* creature. **—un·think′ing·ly** *adv.*

un·thought·ful [un·thôt′fəl] *adj.* Not thoughtful or considerate.

un·thought-of [un·thôt′uv′] *adj.* Not thought of; unexpected.

un·thrift·y [un·thrif′tē] *adj.* Careless about expenses; not economical.

un·ti·dy [un·tī′dē] *adj.* **un·ti·di·er, un·ti·di·est** Not orderly or neat; messy; careless; slovenly. **—un·ti′di·ly** *adv.* **—un·ti′di·ness** *n.*

un·tie [un·tī′] *v.* **un·tied, un·ty·ing** 1 To loosen or undo, as a knot. 2 To let loose; free: I *untied* the dog and let it run.

un·til [un·til′] 1 *prep.* Up to the time of; till: We will wait *until* midnight. 2 *conj.* To the time when: I'll remember that *until* I die. 3 *prep.* Before: The music doesn't begin *until* nine. 4 *conj.* Before: We couldn't leave *until* the car came. 5 *conj.* To the place or degree that: Walk east *until* you reach the river; We shouted *until* we were hoarse.

un·time·ly [un·tīm′lē] 1 *adj.* Coming or happening at a wrong or unsuitable time, as too early: an *untimely* death. 2 *adv.* Too soon or at any wrong time.

un·tir·ing [un·tīr′ing] *adj.* 1 Not tiring: *untiring* muscles. 2 Continuous; persistent: *untiring* attempts at success. **—un·tir′ing·ly** *adv.*

un·to [un′tōō] *prep.* To: seldom used today.

un·told [un·tōld′] *adj.* 1 Not told: a tale *untold.* 2 Not counted or measured: *Untold* millions were affected by the flood. 3 Too many or too much to be counted or measured: *untold* misery.

un·touch·a·ble [un·tuch′ə·bəl] 1 *adj.* Located or lying beyond a person's reach. 2 *adj.* Not to be touched; protected from being touched by rules. 3 *adj.* Protected or exempt from criticism or control. 4 *adj.* Unpleasant or dangerous to the touch. 5 *n.* In India, a member of the lowest caste, whose touch was formerly thought to defile anyone of a higher caste.

un·touched [un·tucht′] *adj.* 1 Not touched or handled. 2 Not tasted or eaten. 3 Not emotionally affected; unmoved: The homeless man's plight left them *untouched.*

un·to·ward [un·tôrd′] *adj.* 1 Unlucky; unfavorable; adverse: an *untoward* delay. 2 Stubborn; unruly; hard to manage: an *untoward* pupil.

un·trace·a·ble [un·trā′sə·bəl] *adj.* Not able to be identified or followed back to a source: A package with no return address is *untraceable.*

un·trained [un·trānd′] *adj.* Not trained or disciplined: an *untrained* worker.

un·trans·lat·a·ble [un′trans·lā′tə·bəl] *adj.* Not capable of being expressed adequately in another language: an *untranslatable* French phrase.

un·tried [un·trīd′] *adj.* 1 Not judged in a court of law: an *untried* killer. 2 Not tested or tried out: an *untried* typist.

un·trod [un·trod′] *adj.* Not traveled or explored: an *untrod* wilderness.

un·trod·den [un·trod′ən] *adj.* Untrod.

un·trou·bled [un·trub′əld] *adj.* 1 Free from worry or distress: an *untroubled* face. 2 Not stirred up: *untroubled* waters.

un·true [un·trōō′] *adj.* 1 Not true or correct; false. 2 Not loyal, constant, or faithful: an *untrue* servant. 3 Not level or upright: The walls slanted and the windows were *untrue.* **—un·tru′ly** *adv.*

un·truth [un·trōōth′] *n.* 1 Something that is not true, as a lie. 2 The fact, quality, or condition of not being true.

un·truth·ful [un·trōōth′fəl] *adj.* 1 Not truthful; untrue. 2 Inclined to tell lies: an *untruthful* person. **—un·truth′ful·ly** *adv.*

un·tu·tored [un·t(y)ōō′tərd] *adj.* 1 Untaught. 2 Simple; not sophisticated.

un·twine [un·twīn′] *v.* **un·twined, un·twin·ing** 1 To loosen or undo (something twined). 2 To become loosened or undone.

un·twist [un·twist′] *v.* To separate, unravel, or undo (something twisted): to *untwist* a rope.
un·used *adj.* 1 [un·yo͞ozd′] Not made use of or never having been used: *unused* machinery. 2 [un·yo͞ost′] Not accustomed: *unused* to hard work.
un·u·su·al [un·yo͞o′zho͞o·əl] *adj.* Not usual or ordinary; uncommon. **—un·u′su·al·ly** *adv.*
un·ut·ter·a·ble [un·ut′ər·ə·bəl] *adj.* Too great to be expressed by words: *unutterable* bliss. **—un·ut′ter·a·bly** *adv.*
un·ut·tered [un·ut′ərd] *adj.* Not spoken or mentioned: an *unuttered* wish.
un·van·quished [un·vang′kwisht] *adj.* Not overcome; undefeated: an *unvanquished* spirit.
un·var·nished [un·vär′nisht] *adj.* 1 Not varnished: *unvarnished* floors. 2 Not hidden under a false appearance: the *unvarnished* facts.
un·veil [un·vāl′] *v.* 1 To remove the veil or covering from so as to disclose to view; reveal: The artist *unveiled* the new pictures. 2 To remove a veil from one's face or person.
un·ver·i·fied [un·ver′ə·fīd′] *adj.* Not verified, checked, or confirmed: an *unverified* report.
un·voiced [un·voist′] *adj.* 1 Not spoken or stated: *unvoiced* opposition. 2 Produced without vibrating the vocal cords: *K* and *t* are *unvoiced* consonants.
un·war·rant·ed [un·wôr′ən·tid] *adj.* Not warranted or justified: his *unwarranted* suspicions.
un·war·y [un·wâr′ē] *adj.* Not careful or cautious; careless: an *unwary* shopper.
un·washed [un·wäsht′ *or* un·wôsht′] *adj.* Not washed; dirty.
un·wast·ed [un·wās′tid] *adj.* Not wasted; used or productive: *unwasted* efforts.
un·wav·er·ing [un·wā′və·ring] *adj.* Not wavering or failing: *unwavering* loyalty.
un·wed [un·wed′] *adj.* Not married.
un·wel·come [un·wel′kəm] *adj.* Not received with pleasure or gladness; not welcome: an *unwelcome* knock on the door.
un·well [un·wel′] *adj.* Not well; ailing; sick.
un·wept [un·wept′] *adj.* 1 Not grieved for; unmourned. 2 Not shed, as tears.
un·whole·some [un·hōl′səm] *adj.* 1 Not beneficial to health: an *unwholesome* climate. 2 Not good for one's morals or character: an *unwholesome* book. **—un·whole′some·ly** *adv.* **—un·whole′some·ness** *n.*
un·wield·y [un·wēl′dē] *adj.* Hard to handle or manage, usually because of size, weight, or shape; awkward: an *unwieldy* box.
un·will·ing [un·wil′ing] *adj.* 1 Not willing; reluctant: to be *unwilling* to go. 2 Done, said, or given against one's will: an *unwilling* consent. **—un·will′ing·ly** *adv.* **—un·will′ing·ness** *n.*
un·wind [un·wīnd′] *v.* **un·wound, un·wind·ing** 1 To loosen or undo (something wound up) by twisting or turning in the opposite direction. 2 To become unwound. 3 To relax.
un·wise [un·wīz′] *adj.* Showing a lack of wisdom, good sense, or sound judgment; foolish: It was an *unwise* thing to do. **—un·wise′ly** *adv.*
un·wit·ting [un·wit′ing] *adj.* 1 Not aware or knowing: The camera caught the *unwitting* models behaving naturally. 2 Not intentional or done on purpose: an *unwitting* benefit. **—un·wit′ting·ly** *adv.*
un·wont·ed [un·wun′tid *or* un·wôn′tid] *adj.* Not usual, customary, or habitual: an *unwonted* severity of manner.
un·work·a·ble [un·wûr′kə·bəl] *adj.* Not capable of being worked, operated, or carried out: an *unworkable* schedule.
un·world·ly [un·wûrld′lē] *adj.* 1 Involved with matters of the soul or spirit. 2 Not sophisticated; naive. **—un·world′li·ness** *n.*
un·wor·thy [un·wûr′t͟hē] *adj.* **un·wor·thi·er, un·wor·thi·est** 1 Not worthy or deserving: I feel *unworthy* of this honor. 2 Not proper or fit: a poor book, *unworthy* of its distinguished author. **—un·wor′·thi·ness** *n.*
un·wound [un·wound′] Past tense and past participle of UNWIND.
un·wrap [un·rap′] *v.* **un·wrapped, un·wrap·ping** 1 To take the wrapping from; open; undo: to *unwrap* a present. 2 To become unwrapped.
un·writ·ten [un·rit′(ə)n] *adj.* 1 Not written or in writing: an *unwritten* understanding between the two companies. 2 Traditional and customary, although not written or recorded: an *unwritten* law.
un·yield·ing [un·yēl′ding] *adj.* Not yielding; not giving way: *unyielding* determination.
un·yoke [un·yōk′] *v.* **un·yoked, un·yok·ing** 1 To set free from a yoke: to *unyoke* oxen. 2 To separate or disconnect. 3 To become unyoked.
up [up] *adv., prep., adj., v.* **upped, up·ping** 1 *adv.* In, on, or to a higher place, level, or position: The flag went *up*; Come on *up*. 2 *adv.* To or at a higher price: The bus fares went *up*. 3 *prep.* From a lower to a higher point or place of, on, or along: We ran *up* the side of the hill. 4 *adj.* Moving or directed upward or in a direction, position, or condition thought of as upward: The window blinds are *up*; The moon is *up*; The cost of living is *up*; an *up* grade. 5 *v. informal* To go, put, or lift up: We *upped* the end of the box. 6 *v. informal* To increase: The theater *upped* its prices. 7 *adv.* To or at a higher rank or station: to come *up* in the world. 8 *prep.* To a higher condition or rank on or in: to go *up* the social ladder. 9 *adv.* To or at a greater size or amount: to swell *up*. 10 *adv.* To or at a place that is regarded as higher: The sun came *up*; to go *up* north. 11 *prep.* To or at a point farther above, along, or toward the source of: The farm is *up* the road; We sailed *up* the river. 12 *adv.* To a later time or period: from the Middle Ages *up*. 13 *adv.* To a conclusion or source: Follow *up* this lead. 14 *adj.* At an end or close: The hour is *up*. 15 *adv.* In or to a vertical position: Get *up*. 16 *adj.* Out of bed: Are you *up* yet? 17 *adv.* So as to be compact, safe, or secure: Tie *up* the boxes. 18 *adv.* In or into a place of safekeeping: to lay *up* gold and riches. 19 *adv.* So as to be even or level with in time, space, or amount: Keep the records *up* to date. 20 *adv.* In or into view, discussion, or existence: Don't bring *up* that subject again. 21 *adv.* Completely; totally; wholly: The house burned *up*; to eat *up* the food.

a	add	**i**	it	**o͝o**	took	**oi**	oil
ā	ace	**ī**	ice	**o͞o**	pool	**ou**	pout
â	care	**o**	odd	**u**	up	**ng**	ring
ä	palm	**ō**	open	**û**	burn	**th**	thin
e	end	**ô**	order	**yo͞o**	fuse	**t͟h**	this
ē	equal					**zh**	vision

ə = { a in *above* e in *sicken* i in *possible* / o in *melon* u in *circus* }

U

22 *adj.* In baseball, at bat: Each team has been *up* three times. 23 *adv.* Apiece; alike: The score is 40 *up.* 24 *adj.* Running as a candidate: to be *up* for mayor. 25 *adj.* On trial: The suspect is *up* for murder. 26 *adj. informal* Going on; taking place: What's *up*? 27 *adj. informal* In an active or excited state: My temper is *up.* 28 *adv.* To a greater or higher degree, volume, intensity, or tension: Turn *up* the sound on the TV; The patient's blood pressure went *up.* **—up against** *informal* Face to face with: They will be *up against* many dangers. **—up on** *informal* Informed about: She reads the newspapers to be *up on* foreign affairs. **—ups and downs** Periods of happiness or good luck, followed by periods of unhappiness or bad luck: to have one's *ups and downs.* **—up to** 1 *informal* Doing or plotting: What are you *up to*? 2 Equal to or capable of: I'm not *up to* cleaning the house today. 3 Put before or left to for decision or action: It's *up to* you where we go; It's *up to* you to tell us. ◆ In informal speaking or writing, *up*, as an adverb, is often added to a verb without changing the meaning of the sentence, as in: The fire lit *up* the room; Please write *up* the report; I tore the letter *up.*

up-and-com·ing [up′ən·kum′ing] *adj.* Energetic and likely to succeed or gain advancement: an *up-and-coming* young doctor.

U·pa·ni·shad [o͞o·pän′i·shäd′] *n.* Any of a group of philosophical writings that form part of the basis of ancient Hinduism.

up·beat [up′bēt′] 1 *n.* An unaccented musical beat, usually the last beat of a measure. 2 *adj. informal* Full of good spirits or optimism.

up·braid [up·brād′] *v.* To scold, criticize, or rebuke: The child was *upbraided* for rudeness.

up·bring·ing [up′bring′ing] *n.* The care and training received by a person during childhood.

up-coun·try [up′kun′trē] 1 *n.* The inner part of a region, away from the sea. 2 *adj.* Of or located in the up-country: an *up-country* farm. 3 *adv.* Toward the interior: to travel *up-country.*

up·date [*v.* up′dāt′, *n.* up′dāt′] *v.* **up·dat·ed, up·dat·ing,** *n.* 1 *v.* To bring up to date: to *update* a dictionary. 2 *n.* An updating or a being updated. 3 *n.* A model, report, or version that has been made up-to-date.

up·draft [up′draft′] *n.* A current of air or gas that moves upward.

up·end [up·end′] *v.* To set or stand on end.

up·field [up′fēld′] *adj., adv.* In or into the part of the field toward which the team possessing the ball is headed: an *upfield* soccer kick.

up-front [up′frunt′] *adj. informal* 1 Honest; frank: He was *up-front* about his lack of experience. 2 Demanded in advance: an *up-front* payment.

up front Beforehand: The builders asked for full payment *up front.*

up·grade [*n.* up′grād′, *v.* up·grād′] *n., v.* **up·grad·ed, up·grad·ing** 1 *n.* An upward incline or slope. 2 *v.* To raise to a higher grade, rank, or quality: to *upgrade* a person's job. **—on the upgrade** 1 Improving: The class test scores are *on the upgrade.* 2 Rising: The number of automobile accidents is *on the upgrade.*

up·heav·al [up·hē′vəl] *n.* 1 A sudden or violent heaving or raising up, as of a portion of the earth's crust by an earthquake or volcanic action. 2 A violent disturbance or change: the terrible social *upheavals* caused by war.

up·held [up·held′] Past tense and past participle of UPHOLD.

up·hill [up′hil′] 1 *adv.* Up a hill: to walk *uphill.* 2 *adj.* Going up a hill; ascending: an *uphill* walk. 3 *adj.* Filled with difficulties: an *uphill* fight.

up·hold [up·hōld′] *v.* **up·held, up·hold·ing** 1 To keep from falling or sinking; hold up: These few columns *uphold* the entire roof. 2 To give aid or support to; agree with: The parents *upheld* the students in their desire for a better science laboratory. **—up·hold′er** *n.*

up·hol·ster [up·hōl′stər] *v.* To fit (as a sofa or chair) with springs, padding, and cushions, and then cover with fabric. **—up·hol′ster·er** *n.*

up·hol·ster·y [up·hōl′stər·ē *or* up·hōl′strē] *n., pl.* **up·hol·ster·ies** The springs, padding, cushions, and fabric with which furniture is upholstered.

up·keep [up′kēp′] *n.* 1 The maintaining of something in good condition. 2 The cost of this: the high *upkeep* of a house.

up·land [up′lənd *or* up′land′] *n.* 1 The higher parts or sections of a region or place. 2 *adj. use:* an *upland* town.

up·lift [*v.* up·lift′, *n.* up′lift′] 1 *v.* To raise or lift up. 2 *n.* The act of lifting or raising. 3 *v.* To raise or improve socially or morally. 4 *n.* Social or moral betterment, or the effort to secure it.

up·man·ship [up′mən·ship′] *n.* Another word for ONE-UPMANSHIP.

up·most [up′mōst′] *adj.* Uppermost.

up·on [ə·pon′] 1 *prep.* On. 2 *adv.* On: This paper has been written *upon.* ◆ *Upon* now differs little in use from *on.* However, when rest or support is indicated, *on* is preferred: The speaker stood *on* the platform. When movement into position is involved, *upon* is preferred: She jumped *upon* the horse.

up·per [up′ər] 1 *adj.* Higher than something else; being above: an *upper* story. 2 *adj.* Higher or farther inland in location or place: the *upper* valley. 3 *adj.* Higher in station, rank, or dignity: the *upper* middle class. 4 *n.* The part of a boot or shoe above the sole. **—on one's uppers** Having no money.

up·per·case [up′ər·kās′] *n., adj., v.* **up·per·cased, up·per·cas·ing** 1 *n.* In printing, capital letters. 2 *adj.* Of, indicating, or printed in capital letters. 3 *v.* To print in, set in, or change to capital letters. ◆ The words *uppercase* and *lowercase* come from the pair of vertical cases traditionally used by compositors for holding type. The upper one was for capital letters and the lower one for uncapitalized letters.

up·per-class [up′ər·klas′] *adj.* 1 Of or having to do with the upper class of society. 2 Of or having to do with the two higher classes in a secondary school or college.

upper class The people in a society who belong to the highest social and economic class.

up·per·cut [up′ər·kut′] *n., v.* **up·per·cut, up·per·cut·ting** 1 *n.* A punch in boxing delivered upward from below. 2 *v.* To hit (an opponent) with an uppercut.

upper hand A position of power, advantage, or control: In the debate the President clearly had the *upper hand.*

upper house The house of a two-house legislature that has fewer members. The United States Senate and the British House of Lords are upper houses.

up·per·most [up′ər·mōst′] 1 *adj.* Highest; top: the *uppermost* tip of the mast. 2 *adj.* Most important: Something to eat was our *uppermost* concern. 3 *adv.* To or in the highest or most important place: I placed new shoes *uppermost* among my needs.
up·pi·ty [up′i·tē] *adj. informal* Snobbish; arrogant.
up·raise [up·rāz′] *v.* **up·raised, up·rais·ing** To lift up; elevate: with swords *upraised.*
up·right [up′rīt′] 1 *adj.* Straight up; erect; in a vertical position: an *upright* post. 2 *n.* Something in a vertical position, as a mast or flagpole. 3 *n.* An upright piano. 4 *adv.* In an upright position; vertically: Gorillas sometimes stand *upright.* 5 *adj.* Just and honest: an *upright* person. **—up′·right′ly** *adv.* **—up′right′ness** *n.*
upright piano A piano smaller than a grand piano, having the strings arranged vertically in a rectangular case placed at right angles to the keyboard.

Upright piano

up·rise [up·rīz′] *v.* **up·rose, up·ris·en** [up·riz′ən], **up·ris·ing** 1 To get up; arise. 2 To rise up in revolt. 3 To go up to a higher position, as from below the horizon.
up·ris·ing [up′rī′zing] *n.* 1 The act of rising up. 2 A revolt: rebellion.
up·riv·er [up′riv′ər] *adv, adj.* To, toward or near a part of the river closer to its source: The campers headed *upriver.*
up·roar [up′rôr′] *n.* 1 A condition of violent agitation, disturbance, or noisy confusion: The news threw everyone into an *uproar.* 2 A loud and confused noise.
up·roar·i·ous [up·rôr′ē·əs] *adj.* 1 Making an uproar. 2 Loud and noisy. 3 Very funny. **—up·roar′·i·ous·ly** *adv.* **—up·roar′i·ous·ness** *n.*
up·root [up·ro͞ot′ *or* up·ro͝ot′] *v.* 1 To tear up by the roots. 2 To destroy completely: to *uproot* bad habits.
up·rose [up·rōz′] Past tense of UPRISE.
up·scale [up′skāl] *adj. informal* Of or for people who are affluent, well-educated, and stylish.
up·set [*v.* up·set′, *n.* up′set′, *adj.* up·set′ *or* up′set′] *v.* **up·set, up·set·ting,** *n., adj.* 1 *v.* To overturn or become overturned: to *upset* a vase of flowers; a table that *upsets* easily. 2 *n.* The act of upsetting. 3 *adj.* Tipped or turned over: an *upset* cup of coffee. 4 *v.* To disturb (something ordered or arranged): The weather *upset* our plans. 5 *v.* To make ill: Rich food *upsets* many people. 6 *v.* To disturb mentally: The bad news *upset* us all. 7 *adj.* Mentally or physically disturbed or ill: to be *upset* about something; an *upset* stomach. 8 *n.* A disturbed condition: a stomach *upset.* 9 *v.* To defeat (an opponent favored to win): The amateur team *upset* the professionals. 10 *n.* A defeat of an opponent favored to win.
up·shot [up′shot′] *n.* The final outcome or result.
up·side down [up′sīd′] 1 With the upper part or side down: We turned the table *upside down* to fix it. 2 In or into disorder: We turned the whole house *upside down* in order to find the papers.
up·si·lon [yo͞op′sə·lon′ *or* up′sə·lon′] *n.* The 20th letter of the Greek alphabet.
up·stage [up′stāj′] *adj., adv., v.* **up·staged, up·stag·ing** 1 *adj.* Of or having to do with the rear of a stage. 2 *adv.* Toward or at the rear of a stage. 3 *v.* To act so as to turn an audience's attention from (a fellow actor). 4 *v.* To call attention to oneself by interrupting or outdoing (someone).
up·stairs [up′stârz′] 1 *n.pl.* (*used with singular verb*) An upper story or stories, especially the part of a house above the ground floor. 2 *adj.* Of, having to do with, or located in an upper story: an *upstairs* bedroom. 3 *adv.* In, to, or toward an upper story: We ran *upstairs.*
up·stand·ing [up·stan′ding] *adj.* Honest and upright: a fine, *upstanding* citizen.
up·start [up′stärt′] *n.* 1 A person who has suddenly become wealthy or important, especially one who is conceited or arrogant. 2 Any forward, arrogant person impressed with his or her own importance: You young *upstart*!
up·state [up′stāt′] 1 *adj.* Of or having to do with the part of a state inland or north of a big city. 2 *adv.* To, in, or toward such an area: to go *upstate* by bus.
up·stream [up′strēm′] 1 *adv.* Toward or at the upper part or source of a stream; against the current. 2 *adj.* Of or having to do with the upper part of a stream: an *upstream* camp site.
up·surge [up′sûrj′] *n.* A sudden surging upward or increase: an *upsurge* in the stock market.
up·swing [up′swing′] *n.* 1 An upward movement or stroke: the *upswing* of a tennis racket. 2 An increase or rise: Car sales are on the *upswing.*
up·take [up′tāk′] *n.* 1 *informal* Understanding or awareness: In class the child was slow on the *uptake.* 2 A pipe or vent for drawing up smoke or gas, as from a mine.
up·tight [up′tīt′] *adj. slang* 1 Full of anxiety; nervous. 2 Angry; resentful. **—up′tight′ness** *n.*
up·time [up′tīm′] *n.* The period of time during which a computer or related piece of equipment is working or able to work.
up-to-date [up′tə·dāt′] *adj.* 1 Having the latest information or improvements: an *up-to-date* textbook. 2 Modern in manner, fashion, or style: an *up-to-date* coat.
up-to-the-min·ute [up′tə·t͟hə·min′it] *adj.* Extending up to the present; characterized by the inclusion of the most current information: listening to *up-to-the-minute* coverage of the Olympics.
up·town [up′toun′] *adv., adj.* To, toward, or in the upper section of a town or city: to move *uptown*; an *uptown* restaurant.
up·turn [*n.* up′tûrn′, *v.* up·tûrn′] 1 *n.* A change toward a better or improved condition: There was a slow *upturn* in the country's economy. 2 *v.* To turn up.
up·ward [up′wərd] 1 *adv.* In, to, or toward a higher point or place: to look *upward.* 2 *adj.* Going to-

a	add	**i**	it	**o͝o**	took	**oi**	oil
ā	ace	**ī**	ice	**o͞o**	pool	**ou**	pout
â	care	**o**	odd	**u**	up	**ng**	ring
ä	palm	**ō**	open	**û**	burn	**th**	thin
e	end	**ô**	order	**yo͞o**	fuse	**t͟h**	this
ē	equal					**zh**	vision

ə = {a in *above* e in *sicken* i in *possible* / o in *melon* u in *circus*}

U

ward a higher place: an *upward* slope. **3** *adv.* To or toward the source or origin: to trace a stream *upward.* **4** *adv.* To or toward a higher rank, amount, or age: *upward* from poverty; prices from $3.00 *upward*; The violinist had played from the age of ten *upward.* **5** *adv.* More; over: students 18 years old and *upward.* —**upward of** or **upwards of** More than: It cost *upwards of* $200.00. —**up'·ward·ly** *adv.*

upward mobility Movement or capacity for movement to a higher economic and social class.

up·wards [up'wərdz] *adv.* Upward.

up·wind [up'wind'] *adj., adv.* In the direction from which the wind is blowing.

Ur. Uruguay.

u·ra·ni·um [yōō·rā'nē·əm] *n.* A heavy, white, radioactive metallic element, used in the production of atomic energy.

U·ra·nus [yŏŏr'ə·nəs *or* yə·rā'nəs] *n.* **1** In Greek myths, the father of the Titans and Cyclopes. **2** A planet of the solar system, third largest in size and seventh in distance from the sun.

ur·ban [ûr'bən] *adj.* **1** Of, having to do with, or characteristic of a city: *urban* problems. **2** Living or located in a city: *urban* voters.

ur·bane [ûr·bān'] *adj.* Very refined and polite in behavior or manner; suave. —**ur·bane'ly** *adv.*

ur·ban·ite [ûr'bə·nīt'] *n.* A person who lives in a city.

ur·ban·i·ty [ûr·ban'ə·tē] *n., pl.* **ur·ban·i·ties** **1** The condition or quality of being urbane. **2** (*pl.*) Urbane acts or behavior.

ur·ban·ize [ûr'bə·nīz'] *v.* **ur·ban·ized, ur·ban·iz·ing** **1** To give the characteristics of a city to: to *urbanize* a suburb. **2** To give a city way of life to: to *urbanize* workers from rural areas. —**ur·ban·i·za·tion** [ûr'bə·nə·zā'shən] *n.*

ur·ban·ol·o·gy [ûr'bə·nol'ə·jē] *n.* The study of the problems of cities.

urban renewal A program to replace aged or deteriorated buildings with new, often publicly subsidized housing.

ur·chin [ûr'chin] *n.* **1** A young, mischievous child. **2** A poor, usually ragged child.

-ure A suffix meaning: **1** The act, process, or result of, as in *pressure.* **2** The condition of being, as in *pleasure.* **3** A group that, as in *legislature.* **4** The rank or office of, as in *prefecture.*

u·re·a [yōō·rē'ə] *n.* A substance found in urine and also made artificially. It is used in making plastics, fertilizers, and other items.

u·re·ter [yōō·rē'tər] *n.* The duct in the body by which urine passes from a kidney to the bladder.

u·re·thra [yōō·rē'thrə] *n., pl.* **u·re·thras** or **u·re·thrae** [yōō·rē'thrē] The canal by which urine is discharged from the bladder.

urge [ûrj] *v.* **urged, urg·ing,** *n.* **1** *v.* To drive or force forward: to *urge* the horses on. **2** *v.* To plead with or try to persuade (someone) to do something: We *urged* them to try our plan. **3** *v.* To recommend or advocate strongly: The citizen's group *urged* greater penalties for drunken driving. **4** *n.* A strong impluse or desire to do something: a sudden *urge* to take a walk.

ur·gen·cy [ûr'jən·sē] *n., pl.* **ur·gen·cies** **1** Urgent or pressing nature or character; need or demand for prompt action or attention: a matter of great *urgency.* **2** An insistent tone or manner: There was great *urgency* in the reporter's voice.

ur·gent [ûr'jənt] *adj.* **1** Needing or demanding prompt action or attention; pressing: an *urgent* need. **2** Pressing; insistent: an *urgent* appeal for funds. —**ur'gent·ly** *adv.*

u·ri·nal [yŏŏr'ə·nəl] *n.* **1** An upright wall fixture for men and boys to urinate into. **2** A container for urinating, used by bedridden patients.

u·ri·nal·y·sis [yŏŏr'ə·nal'ə·sis] *n., pl.* **u·ri·nal·y·ses** [yŏŏ'ə·nal'ə·sēz] A chemical analysis of urine in order to detect various diseases.

u·ri·nar·y [yŏŏr'ə·ner'ē] *adj.* Of or having to do with urine or the organs that produce or excrete it.

u·ri·nate [yŏŏr'ə·nāt'] *v.* **u·ri·nat·ed, u·ri·nat·ing** To pass or get rid of urine from the body.

u·rine [yŏŏr'in] *n.* A liquid containing body wastes, secreted by the kidneys, stored in the bladder, and then discharged from the body.

urn [ûrn] *n.* **1** A large vase, usually supported on a pedestal. It is used for flowers or plants and often for holding the ashes of a cremated body. **2** A receptacle having a faucet, used for the making and pouring of coffee or tea.

A coffee urn and an ornamental urn

Ur·sa Major [ûr'sə] A constellation of northern skies, containing the stars forming the Big Dipper. ◆ *Ursa* is the Latin word for *she-bear Ursa Major* means the Greater Bear, and *Ursa Minor* the Lesser (or Little) Bear.

Ursa Minor A constellation of northern skies, containing Polaris and the other stars that form the Little Dipper. ◆ See URSA MAJOR.

Ur·u·guay·an [yŏŏr'ə·gwā'ən *or* ŏŏr'ə·gwī'ən] **1** *adj.* Of or from Uruguay. **2** *n.* A person born in or a citizen of Uruguay.

us [us] *pron.* The form of *we* that serves as the object of a verb or of a preposition: They asked *us* what to do; Please talk to *us* again.

US or **U.S.** United States.

USA or **U.S.A.** **1** United States Army. **2** United States of America.

us·a·ble [yōō'zə·bəl] *adj.* **1** That can be used. **2** Ready or convenient to use. —**us'a·bil'i·ty** *n.* —**us'·a·ble·ness** *n.* —**us'a·bly** *adv.*

USAF or **U.S.A.F.** United States Air Force.

us·age [yōō'sij *or* yōō'zij] *n.* **1** The manner of using or treating a person or thing; use; treatment: Children give their play clothes a lot of hard *usage.* **2** The act of using. **3** A customary or habitual practice or way of doing something. **4** The customary way of using words or phrases.

usage note A note that tells how, where, when, or how often certain words are used or should be used. In this dictionary, usage notes are introduced by a colon or a blue or brown diamond.

USCG or **U.S.C.G.** United States Coast Guard.

USDA United States Department of Agriculture.

use [*v.* yōōz, *n.* yōōs] *v.* **used, us·ing,** *n.* **1** *v.* To employ or operate; put into action, service, or practice: to *use* a can opener; to *use* caution in crossing the street. **2** *v.* To consume or spend: to *use* all one's energy; to *use* up one's allowance. **3** *v.* To partake of: Do you *use* ketchup on your hamburger? **4** *n.* The act of using: the *use* of one's talents; Skills improve through *use.* **5** *n.* The condition of being used: Is that car still in *use*? **6** *n.* The right to use something: the *use* of a library book. **7** *n.*

Occasion, reason, or need to use something: I may have *use* for that later. **8** *n.* The ability to use something: to lose the *use* of one's leg. **9** *n.* The way or manner of using something: That is not the correct *use* of that word. **10** *n.* Advantage, profit, or usefulness: There is no *use* in being angry. **11** *v.* To behave toward; treat: We were *used* badly. **—have no use for** **1** To have no need of: I *have no use for* that rope now. **2** *informal* To want nothing to do with; dislike: I *have no use for* that person. **—used to** [yo͞os to͞o] **1** Familiar with or accustomed to by habit or practice: We are *used to* the cold by now. **2** Did at one time, did often, or did habitually in the past: We *used to* go there every summer. ◆ Be sure to add the *-d* to *use* in the expression *used to*. **—us'er** *n.*

use·a·ble [yo͞o'zə·bəl] *adj.* Another spelling of USABLE.

used [yo͞ozd] *adj.* That has had use or has belonged to another; secondhand: a *used* car.

use·ful [yo͞os'fəl] *adj.* Having a use; giving service; helpful; beneficial: a *useful* suggestion. **—use'ful·ly** *adv.* **—use'ful·ness** *n.*

use·less [yo͞os'lis] *adj.* Having no use; not helpful or beneficial; worthless: a *useless* old lawn mower. **—use'less·ly** *adv.* **—use'less·ness** *n.*

user-friendly [yo͞o'zər·frend'lē] *adj.* Of a computer or computer program, easy to understand and operate for people who are not computer experts.

ush·er [ush'ər] **1** *n.* A person who conducts people to their seats, as in a theater or church. **2** *v.* To lead, escort, or conduct, as to a seat. **—usher in** To lead in or announce the coming of: The rooster's crowing *ushered in* the morning.

ush·er·ette [ush'ə·ret'] *n.* A girl or woman who leads people to their seats, as in a church or theater.

USM or **U.S.M.** **1** United States Mail. **2** United States Mint.

USMA or **U.S.M.A.** United States Military Academy.

USMC or **U.S.M.C.** **1** United States Marine Corps. **2** United States Maritime Commission.

USN or **U.S.N.** United States Navy.

USNA or **U.S.N.A.** United States Naval Academy.

USO or **U.S.O.** United Service Organizations.

USPS or **U.S.P.S.** United States Postal Service.

USS or **U.S.S.** United States Ship, Steamer, or Steamship.

U.S.S. United States Senate.

USSR or **U.S.S.R.** Union of Soviet Socialist Republics.

usu. **1** usual. **2** usually.

u·su·al [yo͞o'zho͞o·əl] *adj.* Common or expected in the ordinary course of events; regular or normal: the *usual* childhood illnesses. **—as usual** In the regular or normal way. **—u'su·al·ly** *adv.* **—u'su·al·ness** *n.*

u·su·rer [yo͞o'zhər·ər] *n.* A person who lends money at a very high or illegal rate of interest.

u·su·ri·ous [yo͞o·zho͝or'ē·əs] *adj.* Practicing or having to do with usury. **—u·su'ri·ous·ly** *adv.* **—u·su'·ri·ous·ness** *n.*

u·surp [yo͞o·sûrp' *or* yo͞o·zûrp'] *v.* To seize and hold without legal right or by force. **—u·surp'er** *n.*

u·sur·pa·tion [yo͞o'sər·pā'shən *or* yo͞o'zər·pā'shən] *n.* The act of usurping.

u·su·ry [yo͞o'zhər·ē] *n., pl.* **u·su·ries** **1** The act or practice of lending money and charging a very high or illegal rate of interest. **2** A very high or illegal interest charged on a loan.

Ut. Utah.

UT Postal Service abbreviation of Utah.

u·ten·sil [yo͞o·ten'səl] *n.* A tool, implement, or container used to do or make something.

u·ter·us [yo͞o'tər·əs] *n., pl.* **u·ter·us·es** or **u·ter·i** [yo͞o'·tər·ī] The organ of female mammals in which the young develop before birth; womb.

u·til·i·tar·i·an [yo͞o·til'ə·târ'ē·ən] *adj.* **1** Having to do with utility. **2** Aiming for or possessing usefulness rather than beauty. **3** Concerned only with what is useful and practical.

u·til·i·ty [yo͞o·til'ə·tē] *n., pl.* **u·til·i·ties** **1** The quality or condition of being useful. **2** Something useful to the public, as gas, water, and electricity. **3** A company that provides services, as transportation, gas, and water, for the public.

u·til·ize [yo͞o'təl·īz'] *v.* **u·til·ized, u·til·iz·ing** To make good or profitable use of: The student has *utilized* all the resources of the library. **—u'ti·liz'a·ble** *adj.* **—u·til·i·za·tion** [yo͞o'təl·ə·zā'shən] *n.*

ut·most [ut'mōst] **1** *adj.* Greatest, highest, or largest, as in amount, degree or number: Use the *utmost* caution. **2** *adj.* Being at the farthest limit or point. **3** *n.* The greatest possible degree or the fullest extent: to play to the *utmost* of one's ability.

U·to-Az·tec·an [yo͞o'tō·az'tek'ən] **1** *n.* A large group of related Indian languages of North and Central America. **2** *n.* A member of a tribe that speaks any of these languages. **3** *adj.* Of or relating to this group of languages or its speakers.

u·to·pi·a [yo͞o·tō'pē·ə] *n.* **1** (*sometimes written* **Utopia**) An imaginary place having a perfect social and political life where complete happiness is enjoyed by all. **2** Any impractical plan for bringing perfect happiness and peace to all people.

u·to·pi·an or **U·to·pi·an** [yo͞o·tō'pē·ən] **1** *adj.* Of or resembling a utopia. **2** *adj.* Overly idealistic and impractical: a *utopian* plan to abolish money. **3** *n.* A person who believes in or tries to bring about a place with a perfect social and political life.

u·to·pi·an·ism or **U·to·pi·an·ism** [yo͞o·tō'pē·ə·niz'·əm] *n.* The vision and ideals of a utopian.

ut·ter¹ [ut'ər] *adj.* Complete; total: *utter* misery; *utter* darkness. **—ut'ter·ly** *adv.*

ut·ter² [ut'ər] *v.* To express, say, or give out in words or sounds: They *uttered* a cry of joy.

ut·ter·ance [ut'ər·əns] *n.* **1** The act of uttering or expressing in words or sounds; vocal expression: to give *utterance* to one's feelings. **2** Something uttered, spoken, or said. **3** The manner of speaking: a loud *utterance*.

ut·ter·most [ut'ər·mōst'] *adj., n.* Utmost: The teachers do their *uttermost* to encourage the students.

UV ultraviolet.

u·vu·la [yo͞o'vyə·lə] *n., pl.* **u·vu·las** or **u·vu·lae** [yo͞o'·vyə·lē] The small, fleshy portion of the soft palate that hangs down in the back of the mouth.

ux. wife (Latin *uxor*).

U

a add	**i** it	**o͝o** took	**oi** oil
ā ace	**ī** ice	**o͞o** pool	**ou** pout
â care	**o** odd	**u** up	**ng** ring
ä palm	**ō** open	**û** burn	**th** thin
e end	**ô** order	**yo͞o** fuse	**th̶** this
ē equal			**zh** vision

ə = a in *above*, e in *sicken*, i in *possible*, o in *melon*, u in *circus*

Vv

 **Early Phoenician (late 2nd millennium B.C.)**

 **Phoenician (8th century B.C.)**

 **Early Greek (9th-7th centuries B.C.)**

 **Western Greek (6th century B.C.)**

 **Classical Greek (403 B.C. onward)**

 **Early Etruscan (8th century B.C.)**

 **Classical Etruscan (around 400 B.C.)**

 **Monumental Latin (4th century B.C.)**

 **Classical Latin**

 **Roman uncial (4th-8th centuries)**

 **Black-letter minuscule (15th century)**

V is the twenty-second letter of the alphabet. From it are descended the letters *F, U, W,* and *Y.* The sign for *V* originated among Semitic people in the Near East, in the region of Palestine and Syria, probably in the middle of the second millennium B.C. Little is known about the sign until around 1000 B.C., when the Phoenicians began using it. They named it *waw* and used it for a *w*-like sound.

When the Greeks adopted the Phoenician sign around the ninth century B.C., they developed two signs of their own from it. The secondary form, called *digamma,* eventually became the letter *F* (see *F*). The Greeks used the main form for the vowel *upsilon,* which means "bare *U*" or "simple *U.*" *Upsilon* stood for the sound of *u* and sometimes *y.*

As early as the eighth century B.C., the Etruscans adopted the Greek alphabet. It is from the Etruscans that the Romans took the letter. Both the Etruscans and the Romans, however, wrote the sign as *V.* To the Romans, the sign stood for the sounds of *u, v,* and *w.* The *w* sound later disappeared from Latin.

In early medieval times, a rounded U-shaped sign developed, but it, too, stood for the sounds of *u* and *v* indiscriminately. The V-shaped sign tended to be used when the letter was carved in stone; it appeared most often as a *majuscule,* or capital letter. Around the third to fifth centuries, *minuscules,* or lowercase letters, began to develop in the handwriting that scribes used for copying books. The U-shaped letter appeared most often there.

It was not until the fifteenth century that a distinction began to be made between *U* and *V.* More and more, *U* began to be used for the vowel sound, and *V* came to be thought of as the consonant. This distinction was not complete, however, until the seventeenth century.

In general, the minuscule is just a smaller version of the majuscule.

v or **V** [vē] *n., pl.* **v's** or **V's** The 22nd letter of the English alphabet.

v. 1 valve. 2 verb. 3 verse. 4 versus. 5 voice. 6 voltage.

v. or **V.** 1 volt. 2 volume.

V The symbol for the element vanadium.

Va. Virginia.

VA 1 Veterans Administration. 2 Postal Service abbreviation of Virginia.

va·can·cy [vā'kən·sē] *n., pl.* **va·can·cies** 1 The condition of being vacant or empty; emptiness. 2 A vacant job or position that is to be filled. 3 A vacant place, as a house, office, or room, especially one that is for rent. 4 Emptiness of mind; lack of intelligence or interest.

va·cant [vā'kənt] *adj.* 1 Empty, unfilled, or unused: a *vacant* house; a *vacant* job; a *vacant* lot. 2 Being or appearing to be without thought, intelligence, or interest: a *vacant* look; a *vacant* mind. 3 Free, as from cares, work, or duties: a *vacant* moment. —**va'cant·ly** *adv.*

va·cate [vā'kāt'] *v.* **va·cat·ed, va·cat·ing** 1 To make vacant by leaving: They *vacated* the house. 2 To give up or quit: to *vacate* a position.

va·ca·tion [vā·kā'shən] 1 *n.* A period of time for rest or recreation, away from regular work, study, or duties. 2 *v.* To take a vacation. —**va·ca'tion·er** *n.* —**va·ca'tion·ist** *n.*

vac·ci·nate [vak'sə·nāt'] *v.* **vac·ci·nat·ed, vac·ci·nat·ing** To inoculate (a person or animal) with a vaccine to protect against certain diseases, especially smallpox.

vac·ci·na·tion [vak'sə·nā'shən] *n.* 1 The act of vaccinating. 2 The scar left by vaccinating.

vac·cine [vak·sēn' *or* vak'sēn'] *n.* 1 A substance made from the mild virus of cowpox and used for vaccination against the much more dangerous disease of smallpox. 2 Any similar preparation of weakened or dead viruses or bacteria used in vaccinations.

vac·il·late [vas'ə·lāt'] *v.* **vac·il·lat·ed, vac·il·lt·ing** 1 To change one's mind often; be indecisive; waver. 2 To sway back and forth. —**vac'il·la'tion** *n.* —**vac'·il·la'tor** *n.*

va·cu·i·ty [va·kyōō'ə·tē] *n., pl.* **va·cu·i·ties** 1 Emptiness. 2 An empty space; vacuum; void. 3 Idleness or emptiness of mind.

vac·u·ole [vak'yōō·ōl'] *n.* A small cavity in a cell containing air, fluid, or solid matter.

vac·u·ous [vak'yōō·əs] *adj.* 1 Having nothing inside; empty. 2 Without intelligence; stupid. 3 Without occupation or purpose; idle.

vac·u·um [vak'yōō(·ə)m] *n., pl.* **vac·u·ums**; *for defs. 1 and 2, also* **vac·u·a** [vak'yōō·ə], *v.* 1 *n.* A space completely empty of matter. 2 *n.* A portion of space, as in a thermos bottle, from which nearly all the air has been removed. 3 *v. informal* To use a vacuum cleaner on something, as a rug. 4 *n.* An informal name for VACUUM CLEANER. 5 *n.* A condition of being unaware of and isolated from outside events and influences.

vacuum bottle Another name for THERMOS BOTTLE.

vacuum cleaner A machine that cleans carpets and furnishings by sucking up the dirt.

vac·u·um-packed [vak′yo͞o(·ə)m·pakt′] *adj.* Packed with most of the air removed before sealing: *vacuum-packed* containers.
vacuum tube An electron tube in which the electrodes are separated by a vacuum.
vag·a·bond [vag′ə·bond′] 1 *n.* A wandering tramp. 2 *n.* A person without a settled home; wanderer. 3 *adj.* Wandering: The prospector lived a *vagabond* life. 4 *n.* A rascal.
va·gar·y [vā′gər·ē *or* və·gâr′ē] *n., pl.* **va·gar·ies** An odd or unexpected notion or act: the *vagaries* of a spoiled child.
va·gi·na [və·jī′nə] *n.* The canal leading to the uterus through which the fetus passes at birth.
vag·i·nal [vaj′ə·nəl] *adj.* Of or having to do with the vagina.
va·gran·cy [vā′grən·sē] *n., pl.* **va·gran·cies** The condition of being a vagrant.
va·grant [vā′grənt] 1 *n.* A person without a settled home or regular job; vagabond; tramp. 2 *adj.* Wandering about as a vagrant. 3 *adj.* Having a wandering course: a *vagrant* breeze.
vague [vāg] *adj.* **va·guer, va·guest** 1 Not definite, clear, precise, or distinct: *vague* ideas; a *vague* outline. 2 Not thinking clearly or stating thoughts precisely: a *vague* person. 3 Of uncertain authority or source: a *vague* rumor. **—vague′ly** *adv.* **—vague′ness** *n.*
vain [vān] *adj.* 1 Taking or showing too much pride in oneself, one's looks, or abilities. 2 Unsuccessful; useless: a *vain* attempt. 3 Having no worth or purpose; empty: *vain* chatter. **—in vain** 1 Without success or results: Our work was *in vain.* 2 In a manner that is not reverent or respectful: to pronounce the Lord's name *in vain.* ◆ *Vain* comes from a French word derived from the Latin word for *empty.*
vain·glo·ri·ous [vān′glôr′ē·əs] *adj.* Showing too much vanity or pride; boasting.
vain·glo·ry [vān′glôr′ē] *n.* Too much pride, boasting, or display.
val·ance [val′əns] *n.* 1 A drapery hanging from the edge of a bed, shelf, or canopy. 2 A short curtain or board, placed across the top of a window to hide the curtain rods or other fixtures.
vale [vāl] *n.* A valley: used mainly in poems.
val·e·dic·to·ri·an [val′ə·dik·tôr′ē·ən] *n.* The graduate, usually the one having the highest grades, who makes the farewell speech at graduation.
val·e·dic·to·ry [val′ə·dik′tər·ē] *adj., n., pl.* **val·e·dic·to·ries** 1 *adj.* Having to do with saying farewell. 2 *n.* A farewell speech.
va·lence [vā′ləns] *n.* A number indicating how many electrons per atom of an element can be or have been added or moved closer (negative valence) or subtracted or moved away (positive valence) in forming a compound.
Va·len·ciennes [və·len′sē·en(z)′] *n.* A fine handmade lace with a floral pattern, originally made in Valenciennes, France.
val·en·tine [val′ən·tīn′] *n.* 1 A card or gift sent on Saint Valentine's Day, February 14. 2 A sweetheart.
Valentine's Day Another name for SAINT VALENTINE'S DAY.
va·le·ri·an [və·lir′ē·ən] *n.* 1 Any of several herbs, as the heliotrope, whose roots are used in medicine as sedatives. 2 A drug made from such a root.
val·et [val′ā *or* val′it] *n.* A servant whose work is to look after the employer's clothing and help the employer dress.
Val·hal·la [val·hal′ə] *n.* In Norse myths, the hall where the souls of heroes who were killed in battle were feasted by Odin.
val·iant [val′yənt] *adj.* Having or showing courage; brave. **—val′iant·ly** *adv.*
val·id [val′id] *adj.* 1 Truthful, acceptable, or reasonable: a *valid* excuse. 2 Legally binding: a *valid* will. 3 Based on proper logic; sound: a *valid* conclusion.
val·i·date [val′ə·dāt′] *v.* **val·i·dat·ed, val·i·dat·ing** 1 To make valid; prove correct; verify: to *validate* an excuse. 2 To make legal: The official *validated* my ID card by stamping it. **—val′i·da′tion** *n.*
va·lid·i·ty [və·lid′ə·tē] *n.* The condition or quality of being valid.
va·lise [və·lēs′] *n.* A suitcase.
Val·kyr·ie [val·kir′ē] *n.* In Norse myths, one of the maidens who carry the souls of the heroes killed in battle to Valhalla.
val·ley [val′ē] *n., pl.* **val·leys** 1 A low area on the earth's surface, as between hills or mountains. 2 An area drained or watered by a river and its tributaries: the *valley* of the Hudson.
val·or [val′ər] *n.* Great courage or bravery, especially in war.
val·or·ous [val′ər·əs] *adj.* Having or showing valor; courageous; valiant. **—val′or·ous·ly** *adv.*
val·u·a·ble [val′y(o͞o·)ə·bəl] 1 *adj.* Being worth money or effort; having value. 2 *adj.* Being worth a great deal: a *valuable* painting. 3 *n.* (*usually pl.*) Something worth much money, as jewelry. 4 *adj.* Worthy of respect or esteem: a *valuable* friend.
val·u·ate [val′yo͞o·āt′] *v.* **val·u·at·ed, val·u·at·ing** To give a value to; evaluate.
val·u·a·tion [val′yo͞o·ā′shən] *n.* 1 The act of determining what something is worth: Would you make a *valuation* of these jewels? 2 The set or estimated value of something: The *valuation* of the jewels was very high.
val·ue [val′yo͞o] *n., v.* **val·ued, val·u·ing** 1 *n.* The relative worth, importance, or usefulness of a person or thing: Do you think education has more *value* than experience? 2 *v.* To place or rate as to worth, importance, or usefulness: to *value* fair play above winning. 3 *v.* To regard highly; prize: to *value* one's friends. 4 *n.* The worth of something in money or other exchangeable goods: What *value* would you place on your camera? 5 *v.* To determine or estimate the value of: They *valued* the old car at $800. 6 *n.* A fair return or exchange in service, goods, or money: This store gives excellent *value* for its prices. 7 *n.* (*pl.*) The beliefs, standards, principles, or ideals of a person or persons. 8 *n.* The meaning, quality, or effect, as of a word: the emotional *value* of certain

V

a add	**i** it	**o͝o** took	**oi** oil
ā ace	**ī** ice	**o͞o** pool	**ou** pout
â care	**o** odd	**u** up	**ng** ring
ä palm	**ō** open	**û** burn	**th** thin
e end	**ô** order	**yo͞o** fuse	**th** this
ē equal			**zh** vision

ə = a in *above*, e in *sicken*, i in *possible*, o in *melon*, u in *circus*

phrases. **9** *n.* In mathematics, a particular number or quantity represented by a variable.

val·ued [val′yo͞od] *adj.* Highly regarded; greatly esteemed.

val·ue·less [val′yo͞o·lis] *adj.* Having no value or merit; worthless.

valve [valv] *n.* **1** Any device that regulates or controls the flow of a fluid, as through a pipe. **2** One of the folds of tissue that control the flow of body fluids, as those which control the flow of blood to and from the heart. **3** In certain brass instruments, a device that allows the player to change the pitch by connecting additional lengths of tubing. **4** One of the two halves of the shell of an oyster, clam, or similar animal.

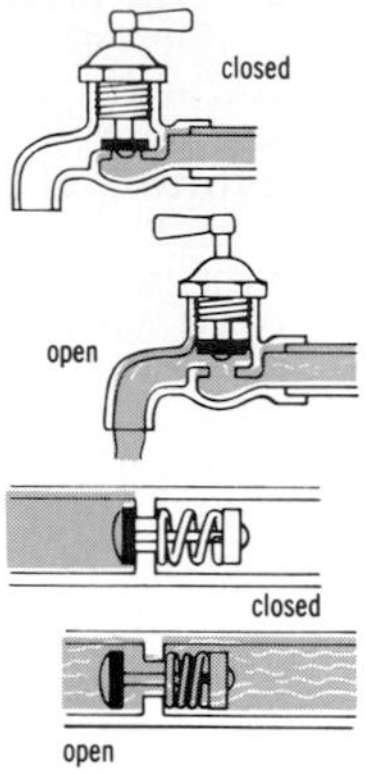

Valves

va·moose [va·mo͞os′] *v.* **va·moosed, va·moos·ing** *U.S. slang* To leave in a hurry.

vamp[1] [vamp] **1** *n.* The piece of leather forming the upper front part of a boot or shoe. **2** *v.* To repair or patch, as with a new vamp. **3** *n.* A musical accompaniment that is improvised. **4** *v.* To play an improvised musical accompaniment. **5** *v. informal* To make up as one goes along; improvise: to *vamp* up a story.

vamp[2] [vamp] *informal* **1** *n.* A woman who charms and entices men in order to get what she wants. **2** *v.* To use charm and enticements.

vam·pire [vam′pīr′] *n.* **1** In folk tales, a corpse that rises from its grave at night to suck the blood of sleeping people. **2** A bat of tropical America that sucks the blood of livestock, and sometimes of humans. It is often called the **vampire bat.**

van[1] [van] *n.* A vanguard.

van[2] [van] **1** *n.* A large, covered truck for moving furniture, livestock, and other items. **2** A motor vehicle like a small truck, having several seats for passengers and extra room for cargo.

va·na·di·um [və·nā′dē·əm] *n.* A rare, silver-white metallic element, used in steel alloys.

Van Al·len radiation [van al′ən] Rapidly-moving atomic particles held by the earth's magnetic field at the fringes of the atmosphere in two belts often called the **Van Allen belts.**

van·dal [van′dəl] **1** *n.* A person who commits vandalism. **2** *adj.* Willfully destructive. **3** *n.* (*written* **Vandal**) One of a Germanic people who invaded the western Roman Empire early in the fifth century and pillaged the city of Rome in 455.

van·dal·ism [van′də·liz′əm] *n.* Willful or ignorant destruction, as of art or beautiful things.

van·dal·ize [van′də·līz′] *v.* **van·dal·ized, van·dal·iz·ing** To damage (property) maliciously.

Van·dyke [van·dīk′] *n.* A short beard that comes to a point.

vane [vān] *n.* **1** A flat blade pivoted at the top of a spire, roof, or high place so that it will turn and point to the direction of the wind. **2** A blade, as on a waterwheel or electric fan.

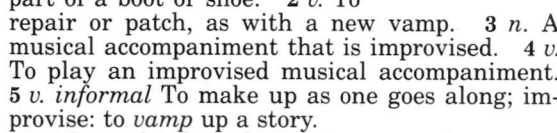

Vanes on waterwheel

van·guard [van′gärd′] *n.* **1** The advance troops of an army. **2** The leaders of any movement, as in art or culture.

va·nil·la [və·nil′ə] *n.* **1** A flavoring made from the seed pods of a climbing tropical orchid. **2** The seed pod or bean of this plant.

va·nil·lin [və·nil′in *or* van′ə·lin] *n.* A chemical compound found in vanilla beans and made synthetically, used in flavorings and perfumes.

van·ish [van′ish] *v.* **1** To disappear suddenly from sight. **2** To pass out of existence.

vanishing point **1** The place where receding parallel lines seem to meet, as on a perspective drawing. **2** A point at which something seems to disappear.

van·i·ty [van′ə·tē] *n., pl.* **van·i·ties** **1** Too much pride in oneself or in one's appearance; conceit. **2** Uselessness, emptiness, or worthlessness. **3** Something that is useless, empty, or worthless. **4** A dressing table.

vanity case A small bag or case used by women for keeping cosmetics and toilet articles.

vanity plates A set of personalized license plates, usually having a name or expression rather than a random group of letters and numbers.

van·quish [vang′kwish] *v.* To defeat or overcome: to *vanquish* an enemy; to *vanquish* fear.

van·tage [van′tij] *n.* Superiority or advantage, as over an opponent.

vantage point A position that offers a broad or commanding view.

vap·id [vap′id *or* vā′pid] *adj.* Lacking life or flavor; flat; dull: a *vapid* pudding; a *vapid* conversation.

va·por [vā′pər] *n.* **1** Moisture in the form of water droplets floating in the air as mist, fog, or steam. **2** The gas formed when a solid or liquid has been heated to a certain temperature: sodium *vapor.*

va·por·ize [vā′pə·rīz′] *v.* **va·por·ized, va·por·iz·ing** To change into or become vapor: A spray gun *vaporizes* insecticide; Water *vaporizes* when heated.

va·por·iz·er [vā′pə·rī′zər] *n.* A device that changes a liquid into a vapor, especially one used for moistening air or administering a medicine as a vapor to be inhaled.

va·por·ous [vā′pə·rəs] *adj.* **1** Containing or made of vapor. **2** Easily changing to vapor: a *vaporous* chemical. **3** Unclear; vague: *vaporous* images.

va·que·ro [vä·kā′rō] *n., pl.* **va·que·ros** A cowhand: a Spanish word used in the sw U.S.

var·i·a·ble [vâr′ē·ə·bəl] **1** *adj.* Likely or able to vary; changeable: *variable* weather. **2** *n.* Something that varies or is liable to change. **3** *n.* In mathematics, a number or quantity to which any of a set of values may be given. **—var·i·a·bil·i·ty** [vâr′ē·ə·bil′ə·tē] *n.*

var·i·ance [vâr′ē·əns] *n.* The condition of being variant or different; difference: Some *variance* between thermometers is to be expected. **—at variance** **1** Disagreeing; conflicting, as facts. **2** Arguing; quarreling.

var·i·ant [vâr′ē·ənt] **1** *adj.* Having or showing certain differences: "Grey" is a *variant* spelling of "gray." **2** *n.* Something different or variant, as in form or spelling: "Grey" is a *variant* of "gray."

var·i·a·tion [vâr′ē·ā′shən] *n.* **1** A varying or changing, as in degree or condition. **2** A changed or altered form. **3** The amount or range of change: a *variation* of 15 degrees. **4** A change, as in the rhythm or melodic pattern of a musical theme.

var·i·cel·la [var′ə·sel′ə] *n.* Another name for CHICKEN POX.

var·i·col·ored [vâr′i·kul′ərd] *adj.* Of various colors; marked with different colors.

var·i·cose [var′ə·kōs′] *adj.* Abnormally swollen or enlarged: *varicose* veins.
var·ied [vâr′ēd] *adj.* 1 Changed; altered: On Fridays our usual lunch is *varied.* 2 Having or made up of different things or parts: a *varied* menu. 3 Varicolored.
var·i·e·gat·ed [vâr′ē·ə·gā′tid] *adj.* 1 Spotted or streaked with different colors. 2 Having or showing differences, as in form, style, or variety: a *variegated* collection of flowers.
va·ri·e·ty [və·rī′ə·tē] *n.* 1 An absence of sameness; diversity: We all enjoy *variety* in our work. 2 A collection of different things; assortment: a *variety* of candies. 3 A class of things; sort; kind: a rose of a red *variety.*
variety show A show on stage, radio, or television that presents a series of unrelated acts by such performers as singers, dancers, comedians, and magicians.
va·ri·o·la [və·rī′ə·lə] *n.* Another name for SMALLPOX.
var·i·ous [vâr′ē·əs] *adj.* 1 Different from one another; of different kinds: *various* kinds of fruit. 2 More than one; several: *various* courses. **—var′i·ous·ly** *adv.* ◆ See FEW.
var·let [vär′lit] *n.* 1 A servant or page. 2 A knave; scoundrel. ◆ This word is seldom used today.
var·mint [vär′mənt] *n. informal* A person or animal that is troublesome or objectionable. ◆ *Varmint,* often used in rural parts of the U.S. and England, is a variation of the word *vermin.* Both words come from the Latin word meaning *worm.*
var·nish [vär′nish] 1 *n.* A solution of certain gums or resins, as those in alcohol or linseed oil, used to give a shiny coat to a surface. 2 *v.* To cover with varnish: to *varnish* floors. 3 *n.* The hard covering or surface made by varnish when it dries. 4 *n.* An outward show or appearance: a *varnish* of politeness. 5 *v.* To hide under a false appearance: to *varnish* the actual facts.
var·si·ty [vär′sə·tē] *n., pl.* **var·si·ties** The highest ranking team representing a school in an activity, as in football or debating.
var·y [vâr′ē] *v.* **var·ied, var·y·ing** 1 To make or become different in some way; change: The time of sunrise *varies* almost daily; The performer *varies* the program each week. 2 To be unlike; differ: These furs *vary* in quality. 3 To differ or deviate, as from the usual or normal: A six-toed cat *varies* from the common type.
vas·cu·lar [vas′kyə·lər] *adj.* Of, having to do with, or containing vessels or ducts to carry blood, lymph, or other body fluid.
vas def·er·ens [vas′ def′ə·renz′] *pl.* **va·sa def·er·en·tia** [vā′zə def′ə·ren′shē·ə] A tube in male vertebrate animals that carries sperm cells from the testes to the urethra.
vase [vās, vāz, *or* väz] *n.* An ornamental container often used for holding flowers.
vas·ec·to·my [va·sek′tə·mē] *n., pl.* **vas·ec·to·mies** A surgical operation in which part of the vas deferens is cut or removed so that a male will not be able to father children.
Vas·e·line [vas′ə·lēn′] *n.* A white or yellow jelly made from highly refined petroleum, used as a salve: a trademark. Also written **vaseline.**
vas·sal [vas′əl] 1 *n.* In feudalism, a person who held land and received protection from a noble to whom was owed, in return, military or other service. 2 *n.* Any person or country in the dependent position of a vassal. 3 *adj.* Of or like a vassal.
vas·sal·age [vas′əl·ij] *n.* 1 The condition of being a vassal. 2 The duties and obligations owed to a noble by a vassal. 3 Servitude.
vast [vast] *adj.* 1 Of very large size; enormous; huge: the *vast* ocean. 2 Very great: *vast* significance. **—vast′ly** *adv.* **—vast′ness** *n.*
vat [vat] *n., v.* **vat·ted, vat·ting** 1 *n.* A large tank or tub for storing or treating liquids. 2 *v.* To put into, store, or treat in a vat.
Vat. Vatican.
VAT value-added tax.
Vat·i·can [vat′i·kən] *n.* 1 The official residence of the pope in Vatican City, Italy. 2 The office or authority of the pope.
vau·de·ville [vôd′(ə·)vil *or* vōd′(ə·)vil] *n.* A type of theatrical show made up of unrelated acts, as songs, dances, skits, and trained animals.
vault[1] [vôlt] 1 *n.* An arched structure, as a ceiling or roof. 2 *v.* To cover with or as if with a vault. 3 *v.* To build in the form of a vault. 4 *n.* A room with an arched ceiling or roof. 5 *n.* Any vaultlike covering, as the sky. 6 *n.* A cellar or underground room. 7 *n.* A strongly protected place for keeping valuables, as in a bank. 8 *n.* A burial chamber.

Vault

vault[2] [vôlt] 1 *v.* To leap or leap over with the help of a pole or the hands. 2 *n.* A springing leap, as one made with the aid of a pole.
vaunt [vônt *or* vänt] 1 *v.* To speak boastfully. 2 *v.* To boast of. 3 *n.* A boast; bragging.
vb. 1 verb. 2 verbal.
VC or **V.C.** 1 Victoria Cross. 2 Vietcong.
VCR videocassette recorder.
VD or **V.D.** venereal disease.
veal [vēl] *n.* The flesh of a calf, used as food. ◆ *Veal* is from an Old French word for *calf.*
vec·tor [vek′tər] *n.* A line segment that begins at one specified point and ends at another. All vectors of the same length and direction are considered equivalent.
Ve·da [vā′də] *n.* Any of four collections of ancient Hindu sacred writings, including hymns, psalms, prayers, and forms of worship.
Ved·ic [vā′dik] *adj.* Of or having to do with the Vedas or with the time or language in which they were written.
veer [vir] 1 *v.* To shift or change direction. 2 *v.* 2 To change the course of: to *veer* a boat. 3 *n.* A change in direction; turn.
veg. 1 vegetable. 2 vegetation.

a	add	**i**	it	**o͝o**	took	**oi**	oil
ā	ace	**ī**	ice	**o͞o**	pool	**ou**	pout
â	care	**o**	odd	**u**	up	**ng**	ring
ä	palm	**ō**	open	**û**	burn	**th**	thin
e	end	**ô**	order	**yo͞o**	fuse	**th**	this
ē	equal					**zh**	vision

ə = a in *above* e in *sicken* i in *possible* / o in *melon* u in *circus*

Ve·ga [vē'gə *or* vā'gə] *n.* A very bright star in the constellation Lyra.

veg·an [vej'ən] *n.* An extreme vegetarian who eats no milk, eggs, or other foods derived from animals. **—veg'an·ism** *n.*

veg·e·ta·ble [vej'(ə·)tə·bəl] *n.* **1** A plant or part of a plant used as food, as corn, carrots, or lettuce. **2** Any plant. **3** *adj. use: vegetable* oil; the *vegetable* kingdom.

veg·e·tar·i·an [vej'ə·târ'ē·ən] **1** *n.* A person who eats mostly fruits and vegetables and no meat. **2** *adj.* Of, for, or having to do with vegetarians. **3** *adj.* Consisting only of fruits and vegetables: a *vegetarian* diet.

veg·e·tar·i·an·ism [vej'ə·târ'ē·ə·niz'əm] *n.* The beliefs or practices of vegetarians.

veg·e·tate [vej'ə·tāt'] *v.* **veg·e·tat·ed, veg·e·tat·ing** **1** To grow, as a plant. **2** To live sluggishly with little feeling, action, or thought.

veg·e·ta·tion [vej'ə·tā'shən] *n.* **1** Plant life: lush *vegetation.* **2** The act of vegetating.

veg·e·ta·tive [vej'ə·tā'tiv] *adj.* **1** Growing or capable of growing, as a plant. **2** Without much action, feeling, or thought: a *vegetative* existence.

ve·he·ment [vē'ə·mənt] *adj.* **1** Marked by strong feeling or passion; intense: a *vehement* outcry. **2** Acting with great force or energy; violent. **—ve'·he·mence** *n.* **—ve'he·ment·ly** *adv.*

ve·hi·cle [vē'ə·kəl] *n.* **1** Any device with wheels or runners used to carry something, as a car or spacecraft. **2** A means of expressing or making known: a *vehicle* for new ideas. **3** Oil or any other substance in which coloring matter is mixed to form paint.

ve·hic·u·lar [vē·hik'yə·lər] *adj.* **1** Having to do with vehicles: *vehicular* regulations. **2** Serving as a vehicle.

veil [vāl] **1** *n.* A piece of thin fabric, as net, worn to cover or adorn the face or head. **2** *v.* To cover with a veil. **3** *n.* Anything that hides or covers: a *veil* of smoke. **4** *v.* To hide or disguise. **—take the veil** To become a nun.

vein [vān] **1** *n.* One of the muscular, tubelike vessels that carry blood back to the heart. **2** *n.* One of the radiating ribs forming the framework of a leaf or of an insect's wings. **3** *n.* A deposit of ore or of a mineral substance, as found in the earth or rocks: a *vein* of iron; a *vein* of coal. **4** *n.* A colored strip or streak, as in marble. **5** *v.* To mark or ornament, as with veins. **6** *n.* A trait, mood, or quality: A *vein* of sadness ran through the book.

Veins

veld *or* **veldt** [velt *or* felt] *n.* In South Africa, open grassland with few shrubs or trees.

vel·lum [vel'əm] *n.* **1** Fine parchment, as used for expensive binding and printing. **2** Paper made to look like parchment.

ve·loc·i·pede [və·los'ə·pēd'] *n.* **1** An early type of bicycle or tricycle. **2** A child's tricycle.

ve·loc·i·ty [və·los'ə·tē] *n., pl.* **ve·loc·i·ties** **1** Speed or swiftness. **2** Rate of motion in a certain direction: a *velocity* of 50 mph.

ve·lour or **ve·lours** [və·lo͝or'] *n., pl.* **ve·lours** [və·lo͝orz'] A closely woven fabric, as one of cotton or wool, having a smooth, velvetlike surface.

vel·vet [vel'vit] **1** *n.* A cloth, as one of silk, rayon, or cotton, with a thick, smooth pile on one side. **2** *adj. use*: a *velvet* dress. **3** *adj.* Soft and smooth to the touch. ◆ *Velvet* goes back to a Latin word meaning *shaggy hair.*

vel·vet·een [vel'və·tēn'] *n.* A cotton fabric with a short, thick, velvetlike pile.

vel·vet·y [vel'və·tē] *adj.* **1** Soft and smooth to the touch, like velvet: a *velvety* cheek. **2** Smooth to the taste or ear: a *velvety* purée; a *velvety* voice.

ve·na ca·va [vē'nə kā'və] *pl.* **ve·nae ca·vae** [vē'nē kā'vē] Either of two large veins through which blood returns to the upper right chamber of the heart.

ve·nal [vē'nəl] *adj.* **1** Willing to give up honor or principles for money; capable of being bought or bribed. **2** Controlled or influenced by hope of gain or reward. **—ve·nal'i·ty** *n.*

ve·na·tion [ve·nā'shən *or* vē·nā'shən] *n.* The arrangement of veins, as in a leaf, an insect's wings, or a part of an animal's body.

vend [vend] *v.* **1** To sell. **2** To be a vender.

vend·er [ven'dər] *n.* A person who sells something, often out-of-doors or from door to door.

ven·det·ta [ven·det'ə] *n.* A feud or private warfare, often waged in revenge for murder.

vending machine A machine for selling candy, drinks, or other small items, operated by inserting coins or tokens.

ven·dor [ven'dər] *n.* Another spelling of VENDER.

ven·due [ven'd(y)o͞o'] *n.* A public auction.

ve·neer [və·nir'] **1** *n.* A thin layer, as of a valuable wood on a cheaper surface or ivory on piano keys. **2** *v.* To cover with a veneer. **3** *n.* An outward show; gloss: a *veneer* of politeness.

ven·er·a·ble [ven'ər·ə·bəl] *adj.* Worthy of respect, as because of age or good qualities: a *venerable* doctor.

ven·er·ate [ven'ə·rāt'] *v.* **ven·er·at·ed, ven·er·at·ing** To look upon with great respect or reverence; revere. **—ven'er·a'tion** *n.*

ve·ne·re·al disease [və·nir'ē·əl] Any of several diseases that are transmitted by sexual intercourse.

Ve·ne·tian [və·nē'shən] **1** *adj.* Of or from Venice. **2** *n.* A person born or living in Venice.

Venetian blind A flexible screen commonly hung over the interior of a window and consisting of overlapping horizontal slats that can be tilted. It may be raised or lowered by means of attached cords.

Venetian blind

Venez. Venezuela.

Ven·e·zue·lan [ven'ə·zwā'lən *or* ven'ə·zwē'lən] **1** *adj.* Of or from Venezuela. **2** *n.* A person born in or a citizen of Venezuela.

ven·geance [ven'jəns] *n.* Punishment inflicted in return for a wrong done; revenge. **—with a vengeance** **1** With great force or violence: The storm broke *with a vengeance.* **2** To an unusual extent; extremely.

venge·ful [venj'fəl] *adj.* Seeking or showing vengeance; vindictive: a *vengeful* nature; a *vengeful* action. **—venge'ful·ly** *adv.*

ve·ni·al [vē'nē·əl *or* vēn'yəl] *adj.* Easily pardonable or forgiven; minor: a *venial* sin.

ven·i·son [ven'ə·sən *or* ven'ə·zən] *n.* The flesh of the deer, used as food. ◆ *Venison*, derived from the French, ultimately goes back to the Latin word *venatus*, meaning *hunted.*

Venn diagram [ven] A diagram that uses circles or ellipses to represent sets and show relations between and operations on sets.

ven·om [ven′əm] *n.* 1 The poison secreted by certain snakes, spiders, or other animals. 2 Bitterness of feeling; malice; spite: to write with *venom.*

ven·om·ous [ven′əm·əs] *adj.* 1 Poisonous; able to secrete venom. 2 Full of spite; malicious: a *venomous* letter. **—ven′om·ous·ly** *adv.* **—ven′om·ous·ness** *n.*

ve·nous [vē′nəs] *adj.* Of, having to do with, or carried by the veins of the body: *venous* blood.

vent[1] [vent] 1 *n.* An opening, usually small, for gases or liquids to pass through. 2 *v.* To permit to escape from an opening. 3 *n.* A means of escape; outlet: a *vent* for one's energies. 4 *v.* To relieve or express freely: to *vent* one's rage by shouting. **—give vent to** To relieve or express freely: I *gave vent to* my feelings by writing the firm's president.

vent[2] [vent] *n.* A slit in a garment.

ven·ti·late [ven′tə·lāt′] *v.* **ven·ti·lat·ed, ven·ti·lat·ing** 1 To fill with fresh air or change the air in: to *ventilate* a room. 2 To make fresh or cool, as by a current of air: The sea breezes *ventilated* the entire house. 3 To examine and discuss openly and freely: to *ventilate* all one's complaints at a staff meeting.

ven·ti·la·tion [ven′tə·lā′shən] *n.* 1 The act of ventilating. 2 The condition of being ventilated. 3 A system by which fresh air is let in or circulated.

ven·ti·la·tor [ven′tə·lā′tər] *n.* A device or opening for changing the air, as in a room.

ven·tral [ven′trəl] *adj.* Of, near, on, or having to do with the belly or abdomen.

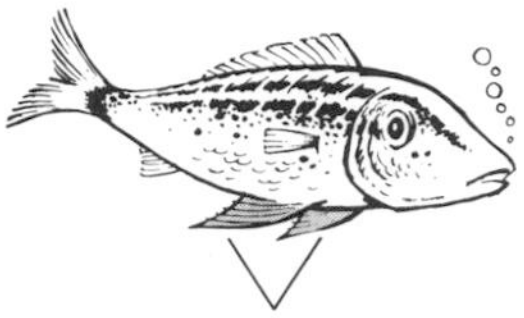

ventral fins

ven·tri·cle [ven′trə·kəl] *n.* One of the two lower chambers of the heart from which blood is pumped into the arteries. **—ven·tric·u·lar** [ven·trik′yə·lər] *adj.*

ven·tril·o·quism [ven·tril′ə·kwiz′əm] *n.* The art of speaking in such a way that the sounds seem to come from some source other than the person speaking. **—ven·tril′o·quist** *n.*

ven·tril·o·quize [ven·tril′ə·kwīz′] *v.* **ven·tril·o·quized, ven·tril·o·quiz·ing** To project one's voice to make it seem to come from some other source.

ven·ture [ven′chər] *v.* **ven·tured, ven·tur·ing,** *n.* 1 *v.* To expose to chance or risk; place in danger; hazard: to *venture* one's life. 2 *v.* To run the risk of; brave: to *venture* the unknown. 3 *n.* A risky or dangerous undertaking; risk, especially a business investment. 4 *v.* To dare: Nobody *ventured* to answer. 5 *v.* To say or put forward at the risk of being contradicted or denied: to *venture* a suggestion.

ven·ture·some [ven′chər·səm] *adj.* 1 Bold; daring. 2 Full of danger; risky.

ven·tur·ous [ven′chər·əs] *adj.* 1 Willing to take risks; adventurous. 2 Risky; dangerous.

ven·ue [ven′yo͞o] *n.* 1 The location in which a crime or other event resulting in legal action takes place. 2 The district in which a trial will be held.

Ve·nus [vē′nəs] *n.* 1 A planet of the solar system, sixth largest in size and second in distance from the sun. 2 In Roman myths, the goddess of love and beauty. Her Greek name was Aphrodite.

Ve·nus's-fly·trap [vē′nəs(·əz)·flī′trap′] *n.* A plant having leaves edged with spike like bristles that close instantly when touched by insects on which it feeds.

Venus's-fly trap

ver. 1 verse(s). 2 version.

ve·ra·cious [və·rā′·shəs] *adj.* 1 Truthful; honest. 2 True; accurate.

ve·rac·i·ty [və·ras′ə·tē] *n., pl.* **ve·rac·i·ties** 1 Truthfulness; honesty. 2 Truth.

ve·ran·da or **ve·ran·dah** [və·ran′də] *n.* A long, open, outdoor porch, usually roofed, along the outside of a building.

verb [vûrb] *n.* A word used to express action or a condition of being. Verbs change in form to express tense, person, and number. In "He was a teacher" and "We ran home," *was* and *ran* are verbs.

ver·bal [vûr′bəl] 1 *adj.* In or of words: a *verbal* picture of the falls. 2 *adj.* Concerned with words only rather than with the ideas they convey: *verbal* changes in a manuscript. 3 *adj.* Not written; spoken; oral: a *verbal* contract. 4 *adj.* Word for word; literal: a *verbal* translation. 5 *adj.* Formed from a verb: a *verbal* noun. 6 *adj.* Of or having to do with a verb. 7 *n.* A word formed from a verb that does the work of another part of speech in a sentence. Participles, gerunds, and infinitives are verbals. **—ver′bal·ly** *adv.*

ver·bal·ize [vûr′bə·līz′] *v.* **ver·bal·ized, ver·bal·iz·ing** To put into words: to *verbalize* one's hopes and fears. **—ver·bal·i·za·tion** [vûr′bə·lə·zā′shən] *n.*

ver·bat·im [vər·bā′tim] *adj., adv.* In exactly the same words: a *verbatim* account; The article repeated the speaker's remarks *verbatim.*

ver·be·na [vər·bē′nə] *n.* A plant grown for its clusters of showy red, pink, or white flowers.

ver·bi·age [vûr′bē·ij] *n.* The use of more words than are necessary for clearness.

ver·bose [vər·bōs′] *adj.* Using or containing an unnecessary number of words; wordy.

ver·bos·i·ty [vər·bos′ə·tē] *n., pl.* **ver·bos·i·ties** The use of too many words; wordiness.

ver·dant [vûr′dənt] *adj.* 1 Green: *verdant* plants. 2 Green with vegetation: *verdant* forests.

ver·dict [vûr′dikt] *n.* 1 The decision of a jury after a trial. 2 Any judgment or decision.

ver·di·gris [vûr′də·grēs′ *or* vûr′də·gris] *n.* A greenish coating that forms on the surface of copper, bronze, or brass after long exposure to air.

ver·dure [vûr′jər] *n.* The fresh greenness of growing plants, or the plants themselves.

V

a	add	**i**	it	**o͝o**	took	**oi**	oil		
ā	ace	**ī**	ice	**o͞o**	pool	**ou**	pout		
â	care	**o**	odd	**u**	up	**ng**	ring		
ä	palm	**ō**	open	**û**	burn	**th**	thin		
e	end	**ô**	order	**yo͞o**	fuse	**t̶h̶**	this		
ē	equal					**zh**	vision		

ə = {a in *above* e in *sicken* i in *possible*
     o in *melon* u in *circus*

verge [vûrj] *n., v.* **verged, verg·ing** 1 *n.* The edge of something; margin: at the garden's *verge.* 2 *n.* The point at which some action or condition is likely to occur: on the *verge* of failure. 3 *v.* To come near; border: *verging* on foolishness.
ver·i·fi·a·ble [ver′ə·fī′ə·bəl] *adj.* Capable of being verified or shown to be true or accurate.
ver·i·fi·ca·tion [ver′ə·fə·kā′shən] *n.* 1 The act of verifying. 2 The condition of being verified.
ver·i·fy [ver′ə·fī′] *v.* **ver·i·fied, ver·i·fy·ing** 1 To prove to be true or accurate; confirm: to *verify* a report. 2 To test or check the accuracy or truth of: to *verify* a list of prices.
ver·i·ly [ver′ə·lē] *adv.* In truth; certainly; really: seldom used today.
ver·i·si·mil·i·tude [ver′ə·si·mil′ə·t(y)ōōd′] *n.* The quality of seeming to be true or real.
ver·i·ta·ble [ver′ə·tə·bəl] *adj.* Authentic; true: a *veritable* monster. —**ver′i·ta·bly** *adv.*
ver·i·ty [ver′ə·tē] *n., pl.* **ver·i·ties** 1 Correctness; truth. 2 A true statement; fact.
ver·mi·cel·li [vûr′mə·chel′ē *or* vûr′mə·sel′ē] *n.* A very thin spaghetti.
ver·mi·form [vûr′mə·fôrm′] *adj.* Shaped like a worm.
vermiform appendix Another name for the APPENDIX (def. 2).
ver·mil·ion or **ver·mil·lion** [vər·mil′yən] 1 *n.* A brilliant red pigment. 2 *n., adj.* Bright red.
ver·min [vûr′min] *n., pl.* **ver·min** 1 Insects and small animals harmful or troublesome to humans, as flies, grasshoppers, mice, rats, and lice. 2 A harmful or unpleasant person. ◆ See VARMINT.
ver·min·ous [vûr′mə·nəs] *adj.* Full of or characterized by vermin.
ver·mouth [vər·mōōth′] *n.* A white wine flavored with herbs.
ver·nac·u·lar [vər·nak′yə·lər] 1 *n.* The language that is common to or most often heard in a particular place or locality. 2 *adj.* In, belonging to, or using language that is common to a particular place or region. 3 *n.* The common, everyday speech of the people. 4 *adj.* In or using common, everyday speech or language: a *vernacular* writer. 5 *n.* The vocabulary or jargon that is used by a certain group.
ver·nal [vûr′nəl] *adj.* Of, like, or having to do with spring.
ver·ni·er [vûr′nē·ər] *n.* 1 A small scale that slides along a longer scale and gives finer measurements. 2 A device that makes fine adjustments in an instrument. 3 Any of several small engines mounted on a rocket to adjust the speed, course, or attitude of the rocket.
ver·sa·tile [vûr′sə·til *or* vûr′sə·tīl′] *adj.* 1 Able to do many things well: a *versatile* person. 2 Having many uses: a *versatile* tool. —**ver′sa·til′i·ty** *n.*
verse [vûrs] *n.* 1 The type of writing that uses regular meter and often rhyme; poetry. 2 A particular kind of poetry or poem: iambic *verse.* 3 A poem. 4 A stanza or single line of a poem. 5 A short, numbered division of a chapter of the Bible.
versed [vûrst] *adj.* Educated, experienced, or skilled: a person well *versed* in science.
ver·si·fi·ca·tion [vûr′sə·fə·kā′shən] *n.* 1 The writing of poetry. 2 The structure of a poem with regard to certain elements, as rhyme and meter.
ver·si·fy [vûr′sə·fī′] *v.* **ver·si·fied, ver·si·fy·ing** 1 To compose verses. 2 To tell about in verse. —**ver′·si·fi′er** *n.*
ver·sion [vûr′zhən] *n.* 1 A description or account, usually from one person's point of view: the driver's *version* of the accident. 2 A translation from one language into another, especially such a translation of the Bible. 3 A particular adaptation of something: a movie *version* of a hit Broadway play.
ver·sus [vûr′səs] *prep.* 1 Against: the home team *versus* the visitors. 2 Rather than; in contrast to: theory *versus* practice.
ver·te·bra [vûr′tə·brə] *n., pl.* **ver·te·brae** [vûr′tə·brē] or **ver·te·bras** One of the bones forming the spinal column.

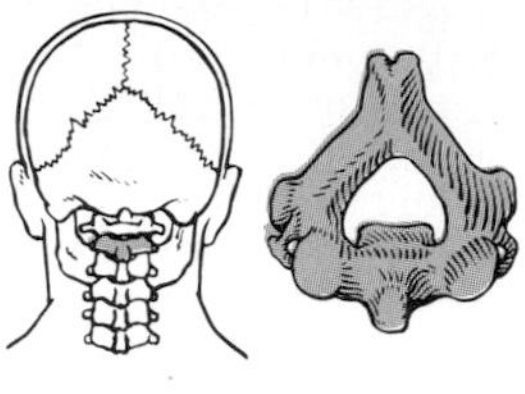
The second vertebra of the neck, shown in place and from above.

ver·te·bral [vûr′tə·brəl] *adj.* Of, consisting of, or having to do with vertebrae.
ver·te·brate [vûr′tə·brāt′ *or* vûr′tə·brit] 1 *adj.* Having a spinal column or backbone. 2 *n.* Any of a group of animals with backbones, as fish, reptiles, amphibians, birds, and mammals.
ver·tex [vûr′teks′] *n., pl.* **ver·tex·es** or **ver·ti·ces** [vûr′tə·sēz′] 1 The highest point; point farthest from the base; apex: the *vertex* of a pyramid. 2 The intersection of any two sides of a polygon or the point where several lines meet.
ver·ti·cal [vûr′ti·kəl] 1 *adj.* Straight up and down; making right angles with horizontal lines: a *vertical* column of figures. 2 *n.* Something vertical, as a line or plane. —**ver′·ti·cal·ly** *adv.*

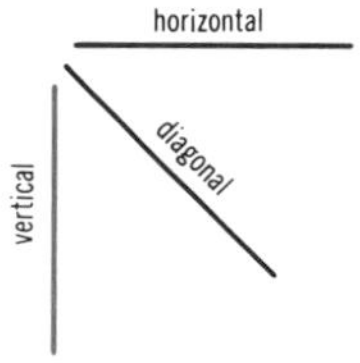

vertical angle Either of two angles with the same vertex on opposite sides of intersecting lines.
ver·ti·go [vûr′ti·gō′] *n.* A feeling of dizziness.
verve [vûrv] *n.* High spirits; enthusiasm; energy.
ver·y [ver′ē] *adv., adj.* **ver·i·er, ver·i·est** 1 *adv.* To or in a high degree; extremely; exceedingly: *very* weak; *very* generous. 2 *adv.* In fact; truly: the *very* same color. 3 *adj.* Actual or true: the *very* truth. 4 *adj.* Same; identical: my *very* words. 5 *adj.* Bare; mere: The *very* idea of going made us happy. 6 *adj.* Exact; absolute: the *very* middle of the night. 7 *adj.* Exactly suitable or right: the *very* hammer we needed. 8 *adj.* Total; unqualified: the *very* horror of it. —**the very** Even the: *The very* stones cry out. ◆ *Very* comes from the Latin word meaning *true,* and originally this is what the word meant in English: I am the *very* model of a modern major general. *Very* is now a much more general term used to intensify or strengthen the word that follows it: *very* lazy; *very* excited; the *very* truth. ◆ To avoid overworking *very,* use more precise words: *exhausted* (very tired), *ancient* (very old), *furious* (very angry), etc.
very high frequency Any radio wave frequency between 30 and 300 megahertz.
very low frequency The frequency range or radio waves from 3 to 30 kilohertz.
ves·i·cle [ves′i·kəl] *n.* 1 A small bladderlike sac or cavity in the body, containing liquid. 2 A blister on the skin.
ves·per [ves′pər] 1 *adj.* Of vespers or the evening. 2 *n.* A bell that announces vespers. 3 *n.* The evening star.

ves·pers [ves'pərz] *n.pl.* (*used with a singular or plural verb*) 1 (*sometimes written* **Vespers**) In certain churches, a service of worship held in the late afternoon or evening. 2 (*sometimes written* **Vespers**) The prayers said or sung at this service.

ves·sel [ves'(ə)l] *n.* 1 A hollow container, as a bowl, pitcher, or vat. 2 A ship or boat larger than a rowboat. 3 A tube, duct, or canal for carrying a body fluid: a blood *vessel.*

vest [vest] 1 *n.* A sleeveless garment, often worn over a shirt and under a suit coat. 2 *v.* To dress (oneself), especially in church vestments. 3 *v.* To give (authority, rights, ownership, or the like) to some person or persons: The right to build roads is *vested* in local government. 4 *v.* To give authority or ownership to: The court *vested* the landlord with the right to sell the property.

Ves·ta [ves'tə] *n.* The ancient Roman goddess of the hearth and the hearth fire.

ves·tal [ves'təl] *n.* 1 A priestess who kept the sacred fire burning in the temple of Vesta; often called a **vestal virgin.** 2 A virgin.

vest·ed [ves'tid] *adj.* 1 Put absolutely in the possession of a person or persons; not contingent on anything; settled: *vested* powers. 2 Dressed or robed, especially in church vestments.

ves·ti·bule [ves'tə·byo͞ol'] *n.* 1 An entrance hall or lobby. 2 The enclosed passageway between the connected cars of a passenger train.

ves·tige [ves'tij] *n.* 1 A trace or mark left by something absent, lost, or gone: In the caves we saw *vestiges* of prehistoric people. 2 A part or organ that is small or useless but which once had a use or function in ancestors of the organism: A human's appendix is a *vestige.*

ves·tig·i·al [ves·tij'ē·əl] *adj.* Of, like, or being a vestige: a *vestigial* part.

vest·ment [vest'mənt] *n.* A garment, especially any of various garments worn by the clergy in religious services.

vest-pock·et [vest'pok'it] *adj.* Made small enough to fit into the pocket of a vest: a *vest-pocket* dictionary.

ves·try [ves'trē] *n., pl.* **ves·tries** 1 A room in a church where vestments and altar linens are kept. 2 A room in a church used for Sunday school, meetings, and other gatherings. 3 In certain churches, a group of people who take care of the business affairs of a parish.

ves·try·man [ves'trē·mən] *n., pl.* **ves·try·men** [ves'trē·mən] A member of a vestry.

ves·try·wom·an [ves'trē·wo͝om'ən] *n., pl.* **ves·try·wom·en** [ves'trē·wim'in] A woman who is a member of a vestry.

ves·ture [ves'chər] *n.* Garments; clothing.

vet[1] [vet] *n., v.* **vet·ted, vet·ting** 1 *n.* An informal word for VETERINARIAN. 2 *v.* To treat medically, as a veterinarian or doctor would.

vet[2] [vet] *n.* An informal word for VETERAN.

vet. 1 veteran. 2 veterinary.

vetch [vech] *n.* A climbing vine related to the pea, grown as food for animals, as cattle or sheep.

vet·er·an [vet'ər·ən *or* vet'rən] *n.* 1 A former member of the armed forces. 2 A person who has had much experience in doing something: a *veteran* at shortstop. 3 *adj. use:* a *veteran* actor.

Veterans Day A U.S. national holiday honoring veterans of the armed forces, celebrated on November 11 or sometimes instead on the fourth Monday of October.

vet·er·i·nar·i·an [vet'ər·ə·nâr'ē·ən *or* vet'rə·nâr'ē·ən] A doctor who treats animals.

vet·er·i·nar·y [vet'ər·ə·ner'ē *or* vet'rə·ner'ē] *n., pl.* **vet·er·i·nar·ies,** *adj.* 1 *n.* A veterinarian. 2 *adj.* Having to do with the diseases of animals and their treatment.

ve·to [vē'tō] *n., pl.* **ve·toes,** *v.* **ve·toed, ve·to·ing** 1 *n.* The right of a chief executive, as a president or governor, to reject a bill already passed by a legislature. 2 *v.* To use the veto on: to *veto* a new bill. 3 *n.* The official document containing and giving reasons for a veto. 4 *v.* To forbid or prohibit with authority: Our teacher *vetoed* the picnic. 5 *n.* The act of vetoing.

veto power A power possessed by the chief executive, as of a state or nation, to prevent a bill passed by the legislature from becoming law. Usually it can, however, be overridden.

vex [veks] *v.* 1 To irritate or annoy: The delay *vexed* us. 2 To trouble or afflict.

vex·a·tion [vek·sā'shən] *n.* 1 The act of vexing. 2 The condition of being vexed: Their *vexation* at us was brief. 3 A person or thing that vexes.

vex·a·tious [vek·sā'shəs] *adj.* Troublesome; annoying.

VFW or **V.F.W.** Veterans of Foreign Wars.

vhf or **v.h.f., VHF** or **V.H.F.** very high frequency.

v.i. 1 intransitive verb. 2 (Latin *vide infra*) see below.

VI Postal Service abbreviation of Virgin Islands.

V.I. Virgin Islands.

vi·a [vī'ə *or* vē'ə] *prep.* By way of: He went to Asia *via* Europe. ◆ In informal usage *via* can refer to the means of travel as well as to the route: We went *via* train. *Via* means *way* in Latin.

vi·a·ble [vī'ə·bəl] *adj.* 1 Capable of living and growing, as a newborn infant or seed. 2 Practical; workable: It is a good, *viable* plan.

vi·a·duct [vī'ə·dukt'] *n.* A bridgelike structure, especially one that carries a roadway or railroad over a ravine or other roadway.

Viaduct

vi·al [vī'əl] *n.* A small bottle for liquids.

vi·and [vī'ənd] *n.* 1 An article of food. 2 (*pl.*) Food, especially choice or expensive food.

vibes [vībz] *n.pl.* 1 *informal* A vibraphone. 2 *slang* A distinctive emotional atmosphere; vibrations.

vi·brant [vī'brənt] *adj.* 1 Having vibrations; vibrating; pulsing. 2 Full of energy; vigorous: a *vibrant* personality. 3 Full, deep, and resonant: *vibrant* tones.

vi·bra·phone [vī'brə·fōn'] *n.* A musical percussion

a	add	**i**	it	**o͝o**	took	**oi**	oil
ā	ace	**ī**	ice	**o͞o**	pool	**ou**	pout
â	care	**o**	odd	**u**	up	**ng**	ring
ä	palm	**ō**	open	**û**	burn	**th**	thin
e	end	**ô**	order	**yo͞o**	fuse	**th**	this
ē	equal					**zh**	vision

ə = a in *above*, e in *sicken*, i in *possible*, o in *melon*, u in *circus*

instrument similar to a xylophone. It has metal bars and resonators that produce a vibrato.

vi·brate [vī′brāt′] *v.* **vi·brat·ed, vi·brat·ing** 1 To move back and forth rapidly; quiver: The drum *vibrates* when it is struck. 2 To sound or echo: The note *vibrated* on the ear. 3 To be moved; thrill: to *vibrate* with emotion.

vi·bra·tion [vī·brā′shən] *n.* 1 A rapid or quivering motion from side to side. 2 A motion from side to side from a position of equilibrium; oscillation. 3 (*pl.*) *informal* A distinctive emotional atmosphere or response that can be sensed.

vi·bra·to [vi·brä′tō *or* vē·brä′tō] *n., pl.* **vi·bra·tos** In music, a trembling effect give to a tone by rapid but very small changes in pitch.

vi·bra·tor [vī′brā′tər] *n.* Something that vibrates, especially an electrically operated device used to massage parts of the body.

vi·bur·num [vī·bûr′nəm] *n.* Any of various shrubs related to honeysuckle, having small flowers.

vic·ar [vik′ər] *n.* 1 In the Church of England, a parish priest who receives only a salary and not tithes. 2 In the Episcopal Church, a cleric in charge of a chapel or mission. 3 In the Roman Catholic Church, a representative of a bishop or the Pope. 4 Any substitute or deputy.

vic·ar·age [vik′ər·ij] *n.* 1 The residence of a vicar. 2 The salary and the duties of a vicar.

vi·car·i·ous [vī·kâr′ē·əs] *adj.* 1 Experienced or felt as if one person were doing or feeling what is actually being done or felt by another: While watching the player's home run, the rest of the team felt a *vicarious* excitement. 2 Done or suffered by one person acting as a substitute for another: a *vicarious* sacrifice. **—vi·car′i·ous·ly** *adv.*

vice[1] [vīs] *n.* Another spelling of VISE.

vice[2] [vīs] *n.* 1 An evil or immoral habit: Cheating is a *vice.* 2 Bad or wicked behavior.

vice[3] [vīs] *adj.* Ranking next below another officer and acting on occasion in that officer's place: a *vice* premier; the *vice* chairperson.

vice admiral In the U.S. Navy, an officer ranking next below an admiral.

vice-pres·i·den·cy [vīs′prez′ə·dən·sē] *n.* The office or term of a vice president.

vice president An officer ranking below a president and acting, on occasion, in the president's place.

vice·roy [vīs′roy′] *n.* 1 A person who rules a country, colony, or province as the deputy of a sovereign. 2 An orange and black American butterfly that resembles the monarch but is smaller.

vi·ce ver·sa [vī′sə vûr′sə *or* vīs′ vûr′sə] The same action or idea reversed; the other way around: We visit them and *vice versa.*

vi·chys·soise [vish′ē·swäz′ *or* vē′shē·swäz′] *n.* A thick soup made of puréed potatoes and leeks, usually served cold.

vi·cin·i·ty [vi·sin′ə·tē] *n., pl.* **vi·cin·i·ties** 1 A region nearby; neighborhood: We live in the *vicinity* of the school. 2 Nearness in space; proximity.

vi·cious [vish′əs] *adj.* 1 Spiteful or mean: *vicious* lies. 2 Violent or fierce: a *vicious* blow. 3 Having many vices; wicked. 4 Dangerous or likely to attack, as an animal. 5 Severe; intense: a *vicious* storm. **—vi′cious·ly** *adv.* **—vi′cious·ness** *n.*

vicious circle A situation in which solving a problem raises a new problem, and each successive solution raises another, until one comes back to the original problem.

vi·cis·si·tude [vi·sis′ə·t(y)o͞od′] *n.* (*often pl.*) Any of the sudden, unexpected changes, whether good or bad, that occur during a person's life or career.

vic·tim [vik′tim] *n.* 1 A person or animal that is killed, injured, or made to suffer: a war *victim.* 2 A person who is swindled or tricked.

vic·tim·ize [vik′tə·mīz′] *v.* **vic·tim·ized, vic·tim·iz·ing** 1 To make a victim of. 2 To cheat or take advantage of.

vic·tim·less [vik′tim·lis] *n.* Having no victim: Some people consider gambling a *victimless* crime.

vic·tor [vik′tər] *n.* The winner, as of a battle, war, struggle, or contest.

vic·to·ri·a [vik·tôr′ē·ə] *n.* A low, four-wheeled carriage with a folding top, a raised driver's seat in front, and a rear seat for two people.

Victoria

Vic·to·ri·an [vik·tôr′ē·ən] 1 *adj.* Of or having to do with the time during which Queen Victoria reigned. 2 *adj.* Outwardly proper, stuffy, and conventional, as conduct during those years seems to us to have been. 3 *n.* A person who lived during Victoria's reign.

vic·to·ri·ous [vik·tôr′ē·əs] *adj.* 1 Having gained a victory; winning. 2 Of or related to victory.

vic·to·ry [vik′tər·ē] *n., pl.* **vic·to·ries** The overcoming of an enemy, opponent, or difficulty; triumph.

vict·ual [vit′(ə)l] *v.* **vict·ualed** or **vict·ualled, vict·ual·ing** or **vict·ual·ling** To provide with food.

vict·uals [vit′(ə)lz] *n.pl.* Food. ◆ *Victual,* the singular form, goes back to the Latin word *victualis,* meaning *of food.* In older English it was spelled *vittle,* but more recent writers changed its spelling to conform with the original Latin. However, people kept on pronouncing it [vit′(ə)l].

vi·cu·ña [vi·ko͞on′yə *or* vi·kyo͞o′nə] *n.* 1 An animal from the high Andes, related to the llama and alpaca, with soft, valuable wool. 2 Cloth made from this wool.

Vicuna

vid·e·o [vid′ē·ō] 1 *adj.* Having to do with television, especially the picture part of a broadcast. 2 *n.* A short film that goes with the music of a popular song.

vid·e·o·cas·sette [vid′ē·ō·kə·set′] *n.* A videotape enclosed in a cassette.

videocassette recorder A machine that can be connected to a television set in order to record broadcasts or play back prerecorded videotapes.

vid·e·o·disc [vid′ē·ō·disk′] *n.* A disk used for recording and playing back images and sounds on television screens.

vid·e·o·phone [vid′ē·ō·fōn′] *n.* A telephone set with a screen that allows people to see each other as they talk.

vid·e·o·tape [vid′ē·ō·tāp′] *n., v.* **vid·e·o·taped, vid·e·o·tap·ing** 1 *n.* A special magnetic tape on which the sound and image of television performances are recorded for later broadcasting. Programs on home television sets can also be recorded on videotape. 2 *v.* To record on videotape.

vie [vī] *v.* **vied, vy·ing** To compete or strive: They *vied* for the prize; to *vie* with a rival.

Vi·en·nese [vē'ə·nēz'] 1 *adj.* Of or from Vienna. 2 *n.* A person born or living in Vienna.

Viet. 1 Vietnam. 2 Vietnamese.

Vi·et·nam·ese [vē·et'nə·mēz' *or* vyet'nä·mēz'] *adj., n., pl.* **Vi·et·nam·ese** 1 *adj.* Of or from Vietnam. 2 *n.* A person born in or a citizen of Vietnam. 3 *n.* The language of Vietnam.

view [vyōō] 1 *n.* The act of seeing or inspecting; examination: a close *view.* 2 *v.* To look at carefully; examine; inspect: The anthropologist *viewed* the ancient jug for a long time. 3 *v.* To look at; see: Come and *view* the sunset. 4 *n.* The distance or range of one's vision; sight: Have the mountains come into *view?* 5 *n.* That which is seen: a beautiful *view.* 6 *n.* A picture, drawing, or other image of something seen: The artist painted a *view* of the bay. 7 *v.* To think of or consider: We *viewed* the situation with alarm. 8 *n.* An opinion or judgment: Are these your *views* on the subject? 9 *n.* A mental impression or idea: I have not yet formed a clear *view* of the situation. **—in view** 1 In range of vision. 2 Under consideration. 3 As a goal or end. **—in view of** On account of; considering. **—on view** Set up so as to be seen by the public. **—with a view to** With the aim or hope of.

view·er [vyōō'ər] *n.* 1 A person who views something, especially one who watches television. 2 Any of several devices used for looking at photographic slides. 3 A part of an instrument, such as a microscope, through which one looks.

view·find·er [vyōō'fīn'dər] *n.* A device on a camera that lets the photographer see the image the camera will take.

view·point [vyōō'point'] *n.* 1 A position from which one looks at or considers something, as an object or situation. 2 A mental attitude or conviction.

vig·il [vij'əl] *n.* 1 The act of staying awake in order to observe or protect; watch: a *vigil* at the bedside of a sick person. 2 The day or eve before a holy day. 3 (*pl.*) Religious services on such a day or eve.

vig·i·lant [vij'ə·lənt] *adj.* Alert to possible danger; watchful. **—vig'i·lance** *n.* **—vig'i·lant·ly** *adv.*

vig·i·lan·te [vij'ə·lan'tē] *n.* A member of a group who, without authority, take upon themselves the punishment of crime and the keeping of order.

vi·gnette [vin·yet'] *n.* 1 A short description or picture in words written with charm and style. 2 A photograph or drawing with a background that shades off gradually at the edges.

vig·or [vig'ər] *n.* Active strength or force of mind or body; healthy energy.

vig·or·ous [vig'ər·əs] *adj.* 1 Full of vigor; robust; energetic. 2 Performed with vigor: a *vigorous* job of cleaning. **—vig'or·ous·ly** *adv.*

vi·king [vī'king] *n.* (*often written* **Viking**) One of the Scandinavian warriors who raided the coasts of Europe from the eighth to the tenth centuries.

vile [vīl] *adj.* **vil·er, vil·est** 1 Very unpleasant; bad: *vile* weather. 2 Disgusting; horrible: a *vile* stink. 3 Evil; low; depraved: *vile* abuse; *vile* language. 4 Degrading; humiliating; lowly: to serve in a *vile* position.

vil·i·fy [vil'ə·fī] *v.* **vil·i·fied, vil·i·fy·ing** To speak or write to or about with slander or abuse; revile.

vil·la [vil'ə] *n.* A large, luxurious house, as one in the country or at the seashore.

vil·lage [vil'ij] *n.* 1 A collection of houses in the country, smaller than a town but larger than a hamlet. 2 The people of a village.

vil·lag·er [vil'ij·ər] *n.* A person who lives in a village.

vil·lain [vil'ən] *n.* 1 A wicked or evil person, especially a wicked character in a novel or play. 2 A villein. ◆ *Villain* comes from an old French word for farm servant. In those days farm workers had the reputation of being rude, coarse people, and the word *villain* finally came to mean *a scoundrel* or *evil person.*

vil·lain·ous [vil'ən·əs] *adj.* Very bad; wicked.

vil·lain·y [vil'ən·ē] *n., pl.* **vil·lain·ies** 1 The quality of being wicked. 2 Wicked behavior or a wicked act: their many *villainies.*

vil·lein [vil'ən] *n.* In the Middle Ages, a peasant who was regarded legally as a freeman to all but the noble to whom the peasant was bound as a serf.

vil·lus [vil'əs] *n., pl.* **vil·li** [vil'ī'] One of the hairlike structures growing out of certain membranes, as of the small intestine, where they aid in digestion.

vim [vim] *n.* Force or vigor; energy; spirit.

vin·di·cate [vin'də·kāt'] *v.* **vin·di·cat·ed, vin·di·cat·ing** 1 To clear of accusation, blame, or suspicion of wrongdoing: The trial *vindicated* the defendant. 2 To defend successfully against challenge or attack; justify: Historians have *vindicated* the general's actions.

vin·di·ca·tion [vin'də·kā'shən] *n.* 1 The act of vindicating. 2 A being vindicated. 3 Justification; defense.

vin·dic·tive [vin·dik'tiv] *adj.* Moved by or showing a mean desire for punishment or revenge. **—vin·dic'tive·ly** *adv.* **—vin·dic'tive·ness** *n.*

vine [vīn] *n.* 1 A plant with a weak stem that grows along the ground or climbs by twining around or clasping a support. 2 A grapevine.

vin·e·gar [vin'ə·gər] *n.* An acid liquid obtained by fermenting certain fluids, as cider or wine, used to preserve or flavor foods. ◆ *Vinegar* comes from two old French words meaning *sour wine.*

vin·e·gar·y [vin'ə·g(ə·)rē] *adj.* 1 Full of or like vinegar: a *vinegary* taste. 2 Unpleasant or bad-tempered; sour: a *vinegary* personality.

vine·yard [vin'yərd] *n.* An area where grapevines are planted.

vin·tage [vin'tij] 1 *n.* A season's crop of grapes in a certain district. 2 *n.* The wine made from it. 3 *adj.* Of the highest quality: *vintage* wine. 4 *n.* The harvesting of a vineyard. 5 *n.* The year or period of origin or manufacture: a sports car of 1930 *vintage*; a joke of ancient *vintage.*

vint·ner [vint'nər] *n.* *British* A wine merchant.

vi·nyl [vī'nəl] *n.* A plastic used in making phonograph records, combs, floor coverings, and other items.

V

a	add	**i**	it	**ŏŏ**	took	**oi**	oil
ā	ace	**ī**	ice	**ōō**	pool	**ou**	pout
â	care	**o**	odd	**u**	up	**ng**	ring
ä	palm	**ō**	open	**û**	burn	**th**	thin
e	end	**ô**	order	**yōō**	fuse	**th**	this
ē	equal					**zh**	vision

ə = a in *above* e in *sicken* i in *possible* o in *melon* u in *circus*

vi·ol [vī′əl] *n.* Any of a group of old musical instruments usually having six strings and played with a bow. Viols were the forerunners of the violin family.

vi·o·la [vē·ō′lə] *n.* An instrument similar to the violin, but larger and lower in pitch.

vi·o·late [vī′ə·lāt′] *v.* **vi·o·lat·ed, vi·o·lat·ing** 1 To break or fail to follow, as a law, rule, or agreement: to *violate* a city ordinance. 2 To treat in a disrespectful or sacrilegious way: Vandals *violated* the cemetery. 3 To break in upon; disturb: to *violate* a home. **—vi′o·la′tor** *n.*

vi·o·la·tion [vī′ə·lā′shən] *n.* 1 The act of violating. 2 The condition of being violated. 3 An instance of breaking a law, rule, or regulation: fined for a traffic *violation.*

vi·o·lence [vī′ə·ləns] *n.* 1 Unrestrained and often destructive force; intensity; fury: the *violence* of the hurricane; the *violence* of uncontrolled rage. 2 Rough, harmful, or destructive use of force: crimes of *violence.* 3 Injury or damage caused by a failure to respect: Denying personal beliefs can do *violence* to one's conscience.

vi·o·lent [vī′ə·lənt] *adj.* 1 Acting with or showing rough, harmful, or destructive force: a *violent* eruption. 2 Resulting from unusual force: a *violent* death. 3 Showing or resulting from extremely strong feelings: *violent* words. 4 Intense, extreme, or severe: a *violent* headache. **—vi′o·lent·ly** *adv.*

vi·o·let [vī′ə·lit] 1 *n.* A small plant bearing flowers that are usually bluish purple but sometimes yellow or white. 2 *n.* The flower of this plant. 3 *n., adj.* Bluish purple.

vi·o·lin [vī′ə·lin′] *n.* A musical instrument with a wooden body and four strings, played with a bow. The **violin family** of instruments includes the violin, viola, and cello.

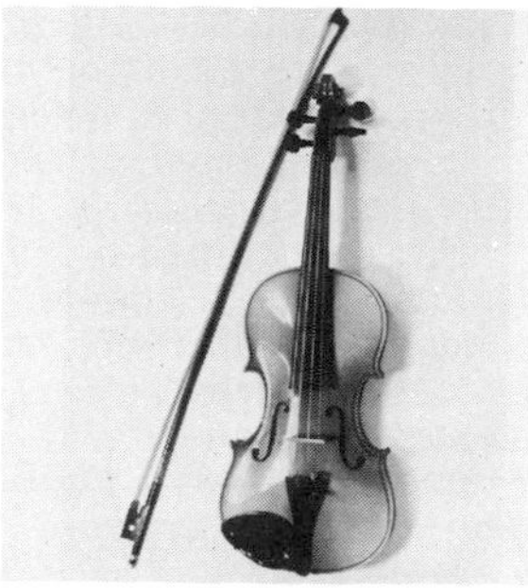
Violin

vi·o·lin·ist [vī′ə·lin′ist] *n.* A violin player.

vi·ol·ist [vē·ō′list] *n.* A person who plays the viola.

vi·o·lon·cel·lo [vī′ə·lən·chel′ō] *n., pl.* **vi·o·lon·cel·los** Another name for a CELLO.

VIP or **V.I.P.** very important person.

vi·per [vī′pər] *n.* 1 Any of various poisonous snakes. 2 A treacherous or spiteful person.

vi·per·ous [vī′pə·rəs] *adj.* 1 Of or like a viper. 2 Wicked, treacherous, and spiteful: a *viperous* plot.

vi·ra·go [vi·rä′gō *or* vī·rā′gō] *n., pl.* **vi·ra·goes** or **vi·ra·gos** A quarrelsome, ill-tempered woman.

vi·ral [vī′rəl] *adj.* Caused by or having to do with a virus: a *viral* infection.

vir·e·o [vir′ē·ō] *n., pl.* **vir·e·os** A small, grayish green songbird that eats insects.

vir·gin [vûr′jin] 1 *n.* A person who has never had sexual intercourse. 2 *adj.* Of, being, or suiting a virgin. 3 *adj.* Chaste; modest. 4 *adj.* Not yet or not previously touched or used: a *virgin* forest. 5 *adj.* Not dirtied; pure: *virgin* snow. **—the Virgin** The Virgin Mary. **—vir′gin·al** *adj.*

vir·gin·al [vûr′jin·əl] *n.* (*often pl.*) A small, rectangular harpsichord having no legs.

Virginia creeper A North American climbing vine that bears tiny flowers, blue-black berries, and leaves with five leaflets.

Virginia reel A lively American folk dance performed by two facing lines of dancers.

vir·gin·i·ty [vər·jin′ə·tē] *n.* The condition of being a virgin or of being virgin.

Virgin Mary Mary, the mother of Jesus.

Vir·go [vûr′gō] *n.* 1 A constellation near the celestial equator, thought to resemble a girl. 2 The sixth sign of the zodiac. 3 A person born under this sign.

vir·ile [vir′əl *or* vir′īl′] *adj.* 1 Having the characteristics of adult manhood; masculine. 2 Having vigor and strength; manly. 3 Forceful.

vi·ril·i·ty [və·ril′ə·tē] *n.* 1 Manhood or masculinity. 2 Vigor, strength, or force.

vi·rol·o·gy [vi·rol′ə·jē] *n.* The scientific study of viruses and viral diseases. **—vi·rol′o·gist** *n.*

vir·tu·al [vûr′chōō·əl] *adj.* Being (the thing specified) in effect, though not in name or in fact: a *virtual* certainty. **—vir′tu·al·ly** *adv.*

vir·tue [vûr′chōō] *n.* 1 Moral excellence; right living; morality; goodness. 2 A particular type of moral excellence. 3 A good quality or feature: They explained the *virtues* of the new policy. 4 Purity; chastity. 5 Effectiveness: a medicine of great *virtue.* **—by virtue of** or **in virtue of** Because of or by means of.

vir·tu·os·i·ty [vûr′chōō·os′ə·tē] *n.* The skill or technical mastery of a virtuoso, as in music.

vir·tu·o·so [vûr′chōō·ō′sō] *n., pl.* **vir·tu·o·sos** or **vir·tu·o·si** [vûr′chōō·ō′sē] An artist who displays dazzling skill or technique in performance, especially in performing music.

vir·tu·ous [vûr′chōō·əs] *adj.* Having or showing virtue; good or pure. **—vir′tu·ous·ly** *adv.*

vir·u·lent [vir′(y)ə·lənt] *adj.* 1 Extremely harmful, infectious, or poisonous: a *virulent* ulcer. 2 Full of bitter hate or spite. **—vir′u·lence** *n.* **—vir′u·lent·ly** *adv.*

vi·rus [vī′rəs] *n.* 1 Any of a class of tiny particles smaller than bacteria, capable of multiplying only in certain living cells and causing various diseases in humans, animals, and plants. Influenza, colds, and measles are among the illnesses caused by viruses. 2 A malfunction in a computer system that can spread from one machine to another, damaging or destroying files and records.

vi·sa [vē′zə] *n.* A mark of approval made on a passport by an official of a foreign country, giving the bearer special permission to visit that country.

vis·age [viz′ij] *n.* The face or expression of the face of a person: a frowning *visage.*

vis·cer·a [vis′ər·ə] *n.pl.* The internal organs of the body, as the intestines, stomach, heart, and lungs.

vis·cer·al [vis′ər·əl] *adj.* 1 Of or having to do with the viscera. 2 Felt or arising from deep within a person; profound or instinctive: an unexplainable, *visceral* reaction.

vis·cid [vis′id] *adj.* 1 Sticky, thick, and hard to pour. 2 Having a sticky surface.

vis·cose [vis′kōs′] *n.* A thick, honeylike substance chemically prepared from cellulose and used in the making of rayon and cellophane.

vis·cos·i·ty [vis·kos′ə·tē] *n., pl.* **vis·cos·i·ties** The condition, quality, or degree of being viscous: oils of differing *viscosities.*

vis·count [vī′kount′] *n.* A noble who ranks below an earl or count and above a baron.

vis·count·ess [vī′koun′tis] *n.* 1 The wife or widow

of a viscount. 2 A woman holding a rank equal to that of a viscount.
vis·cous [vis′kəs] *adj.* 1 Sticky; adhesive. 2 Thick and hard to pour, as certain oils.
vise [vīs] *n.* A clamp having two jaws that can be closed together with a screw, used to grasp and hold objects as they are worked on.

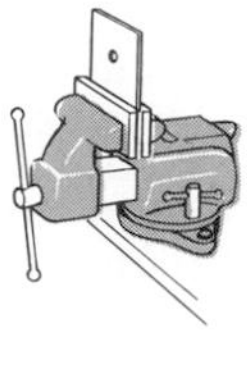
Vise

Vish·nu [vish′no͞o] *n.* One of the three chief Hindu gods, considered to be the preserver.
vis·i·bil·i·ty [viz′ə·bil′ə·tē] *n.* 1 The condition of being visible. 2 The distance to which objects can be clearly seen under given weather conditions: *visibility*, one mile.
vis·i·ble [viz′ə·bəl] *adj.* 1 Capable of being seen: No star was *visible.* 2 Apparent; evident: There was no *visible* motive for their actions.
vis·i·bly [viz′ə·blē] *adv.* In a noticeable way; evidently; plainly: The student was *visibly* uneasy.
Vis·i·goth [viz′ə·goth′] *n.* One of the western Goths that sacked Rome in 410.
vi·sion [vizh′ən] *n.* 1 The ability to see; sense of sight: Glasses sharpen one's *vision.* 2 A sight of something imagined or spiritually revealed, seen in the mind, in a dream, or in a trancelike state: a *vision* of an ideal world. 3 Insight; imagination. 4 The ability to look ahead into the future; foresight: Leaders should be people of *vision.* 5 A very beautiful or pleasing sight.
vi·sion·ar·y [vizh′ən·er′ē] *adj., n., pl.* **vi·sion·ar·ies** 1 *adj.* Being, like, or in a vision; not real; imaginary. 2 *adj.* Likely to daydream or have visions. 3 *n.* A person who has visions. 4 *adj.* Idealistic but not practical: *visionary* schemes. 5 *n.* A person full of impractical ideas, ideals, or schemes; dreamer.
vis·it [viz′it] 1 *v.* To go or come to see (a person, persons, or a place). 2 *v.* To stay with (a person) or in (a place) as a temporary guest. 3 *n.* The act or time of visiting: long *visits.* 4 *v.* To send or come upon; inflict or afflict: to *visit* one's anger on the disobedient; They were *visited* by an epidemic of yellow fever.
vis·i·tant [viz′ə·tənt] *n.* 1 A visitor. 2 A migratory bird that stops at a place for a short time.
vis·i·ta·tion [viz′ə·tā′shən] *n.* 1 The act of visiting; visit. 2 An official inspection. 3 A punishment or reward thought to come from God or from a god: a *visitation* of famine.
vis·i·tor [viz′ə·tər] *n.* A person who visits.
vi·sor [vī′zər] *n.* 1 Something that shades the eyes, as the projecting part of a cap. 2 The movable part of a helmet that shields the face.

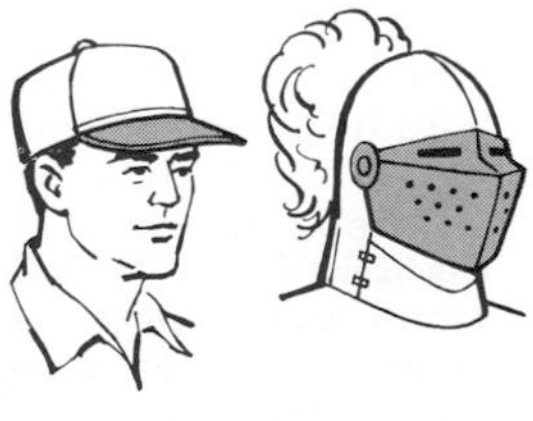
Visors

vis·ta [vis′tə] *n.* 1 A view, especially one shut in at the sides and reaching into a distance: A walk lined with high hedges provided a *vista* of the sea. 2 A long mental view of past events or events to come: The discovery opened up new *vistas* to the scientist.
VISTA [vis′tə] *n.* Volunteers in Service to America.
vis·u·al [vizh′o͞o·əl] *adj.* 1 Of, having to do with, or serving the sense of sight. 2 Capable of being seen; visible. **—vis′u·al·ly** *adv.*
visual aid An instructional aid, as a map, diagram, picture, or filmstrip, that appeals mainly to the sense of sight.
vis·u·al·ize [vizh′o͞o·əl·īz′] *v.* **vis·u·al·ized, vis·u·al·iz·ing** To form a mental image of; see in the mind.
vi·tal [vīt′(ə)l] *adj.* 1 Of or having to do with life or human lives: *vital* energy; *vital* statistics. 2 Necessary or essential to life: The lungs are *vital* organs. 3 Lively and energetic: a *vital* personality. 4 Having great or essential importance: a *vital* question. 5 Dangerous, fatal, or ruinous: a *vital* error. **—vi′tal·ly** *adv.*
vi·tal·i·ty [vī·tal′ə·tē] *n., pl.* **vi·tal·i·ties** 1 Physical or mental energy; vigor; liveliness: a person of great *vitality.* 2 The capacity to live or to continue living and grow. 3 The capacity to endure or survive: the *vitality* of a new government.
vi·tal·ize [vīt′(ə)l·īz′] *v.* **vi·tal·ized, vi·tal·iz·ing** To give life, energy, or vigor to.
vi·tals [vīt′(ə)lz] *n.pl.* 1 The parts or organs necessary to life, as the lungs, heart, and brain. 2 The essential parts of anything.
vi·ta·min [vī′tə·min] *n.* Any of a group of organic substances found in most natural foodstuffs and required, usually in very small amounts, for the proper health of the body.
vitamin A A vitamin needed for growth and good vision, formed from carotene and other plant pigments and stored in the livers of fish and mammals.
vitamin B 1 Another name for THIAMINE. 2 Another name for VITAMIN B COMPLEX.
vitamin B_1 Another name for THIAMINE.
vitamin B_2 Another name for RIBOFLAVIN.
vitamin B_6 Another name for PYRIDOXINE.
vitamin B_{12} A vitamin needed for growth and for blood-cell formation, a complex compound of cobalt found in liver and yeast and produced by certain bacteria.
vitamin B complex A diverse group of vitamins that are soluble in water, including thiamine, riboflavin, niacin, biotin, vitamin B_{12}, and others.
vitamin C A vitamin found in certain foods, as citrus fruits, tomatoes, and green leafy vegetables; ascorbic acid. A lack of it causes scurvy.
vitamin D A vitamin that helps the growth of bones and teeth, found in cod-liver oil, milk, and other foods. A lack of it causes rickets.
vitamin E Any of a group of substances found in vegetable oils, lack of which has caused sterility in experiments with rats. Nutritionists accept vitamin E as being important in the human diet, but its function has not yet been determined.
vitamin G Another name for RIBOFLAVIN.
vitamin H Another name for BIOTIN.
vi·ti·ate [vish′ē·āt′] *v.* **vi·ti·at·ed, vi·ti·at·ing** 1 To spoil or weaken the goodness, purity, or effectiveness of: Excessive fermentation *vitiates* a fine wine.

V

a	add	**i**	it	**o͝o**	took	**oi**	oil
ā	ace	**ī**	ice	**o͞o**	pool	**ou**	pout
â	care	**o**	odd	**u**	up	**ng**	ring
ä	palm	**ō**	open	**û**	burn	**th**	thin
e	end	**ô**	order	**yo͞o**	fuse	**t͟h**	this
ē	equal					**zh**	vision

ə = a in *above*, e in *sicken*, i in *possible*, o in *melon*, u in *circus*

milk. 2 To make void; cancel: Fraud *vitiates* a contract. **—vi'ti·a'tion** *n.*

vit·re·ous [vit'rē·əs] *adj.* Of, having to do with, made from, or like glass: *vitreous* china.

vitreous humor The transparent, jellylike substance between the lens and retina of the eye.

vit·ri·fy [vit'rə·fī] *v.* **vit·ri·fied, vit·ri·fy·ing** To change into glass or a glassy substance through the action of heat.

vit·ri·ol [vit'rē·ōl' *or* vit'rē·əl] *n.* 1 Sulfuric acid. 2 A sulfate of a heavy metal, as **green vitriol,** iron sulfate; **blue vitriol,** copper sulfate; and **white vitriol,** zinc sulfate.

vit·ri·ol·ic [vit'rē·ol'ik] *adj.* 1 Of, derived from, or like vitriol. 2 Painfully sharp, cutting, or sarcastic: a *vitriolic* letter.

vi·tu·per·ate [vī·t(y)o͞o'pə·rāt'] *v.* **vi·tu·per·at·ed, vi·tu·per·at·ing** To attack with harsh words; scold severely. **—vi·tu'per·a'tion** *n.* **—vi·tu·per·a·tive** [vī·t(y)o͞o'pər·ə·tiv] *adj.*

vi·va [vē'və] *interj.* A cry that means "long live," used before a name to express approval or admiration.

vi·va·cious [vi·vā'shəs *or* vī·vā'shəs] *adj.* Full of life and spirit; lively by nature: a *vivacious* personality. **—vi·va'cious·ly** *adv.* **—vi·va'cious·ness** *n.*

vi·vac·i·ty [vi·vas'ə·tē *or* vī·vas'ə·tē] *n.* Liveliness; animation.

vi·var·i·um [vi·vâr'ē·əm] *n., pl.* **vi·var·i·ums** or **vi·var·i·a** [vi·vâr'ē·ə] An enclosed place for keeping land animals and plants for observation.

viv·id [viv'id] *adj.* 1 Very bright or strong; intense: *vivid* orange. 2 Creating clear, lifelike, or original images in the mind: a *vivid* account of an adventure; a *vivid* imagination. 3 Full of life or seeming very much alive: a *vivid* character in a book. **—viv'id·ly** *adv.*

viv·i·fy [viv'ə·fī] *v.* **viv·i·fied, viv·i·fy·ing** 1 To give life to. 2 To make vivid.

vi·vip·a·rous [vī·vip'ər·əs] *adj.* Bringing forth live young and not eggs, as most mammals do.

viv·i·sect [viv'ə·sekt'] *v.* To perform vivisection on (a living animal).

viv·i·sec·tion [viv'ə·sek'shən] *n.* Biological or medical experimentation that involves surgery and other procedures carried out on living animals.

viv·i·sec·tion·ist [viv'ə·sek'shə·nist] *n.* A person who practices vivisection or believes in its usefulness.

vix·en [vik'sən] *n.* 1 A female fox. 2 An ill-tempered, quarrelsome person; shrew.

viz or **viz.** (Latin *videlicet*) namely.

vi·zier or **vi·zir** [vi·zir'] *n.* A high official of a Muslim country, as a minister of state.

vi·zor [vī'zər] *n.* Another spelling of VISOR.

vlf or **v.l.f., VLF** or **V.L.F.** very low frequency.

VMD or **V.M.D.** Doctor of Veterinary Medicine.

vocab. vocabulary.

vo·cab·u·lar·y [vō·kab'yə·ler'ē] *n., pl.* **vo·cab·u·lar·ies** 1 The total number of words that a person knows and can use. 2 The set of words used by a certain group or in a special field or activity: the *vocabulary* of jazz. 3 All the words of a language. 4 A list of words, usually arranged in alphabetical order, together with their meanings.

vo·cal [vō'kəl] *adj.* 1 Of, having to do with, or made by the voice: *vocal* sounds. 2 Capable of speaking or uttering sounds; having a voice. 3 Open in expressing one's opinions; outspoken: a highly *vocal* critic. **—vo'cal·ly** *adv.*

vocal cords Either of two pairs of folds of membrane that stick out into the throat. The lower pair can be made to vibrate and produce voice sounds when air from the lungs passes between them.

vo·cal·ic [vō·kal'ik] *adj.* 1 Containing mostly vowels: Hawaiian is a *vocalic* language. 2 Of or pronounced as a vowel: The letter "y" is sometimes *vocalic.*

vo·cal·ist [vō'kəl·ist] *n.* A singer.

vo·cal·ize [vō'kəl·īz'] *v.* **vo·cal·ized, vo·cal·iz·ing** To sing, speak, or make vocal sounds.

vo·ca·tion [vō·kā'shən] *n.* 1 A profession, career, or trade, especially the one a person chooses or for which a person is best suited; calling. 2 A call to or fitness for a certain career, especially the religious life. ◆ See OCCUPATION.

vo·ca·tion·al [vō·kā'shən·əl] *adj.* Having to do with an occupation or trade, or the choice of one: *vocational* guidance; a *vocational* school.

vo·cif·er·ous [vō·sif'ər·əs] *adj.* Making or marked by a loud outcry; clamorous; noisy: a *vociferous* baseball fan; *vociferous* protests.

vod·ka [vod'kə] *n.* An alcoholic liquor, originally from Russia, made from grain or potatoes.

vogue [vōg] *n.* 1 Style; fashion: Vests are back in *vogue.* 2 Popular acceptance; popularity: Science fiction enjoyed a great *vogue* then.

voice [vois] *n., v.* **voiced, voic·ing** 1 *n.* The sound made through the mouth of a person or animal, especially the sound made by human beings in speaking or singing. 2 *v.* To utter or produce with a sound made by vibration of the vocal cords. 3 *n.* The ability to make vocal sounds: to lose one's *voice.* 4 *n.* The quality or character of one's vocal sound: a melodious *voice.* 5 *n.* The ability to sing. 6 *n.* The condition of the vocal organs as it affects one's singing ability: to be in poor *voice.* 7 *n.* Something thought of as like the human voice or speech: the *voice* of the wind; the *voice* of experience. 8 *n.* In music, a part, as for a single singer or instrument. 9 *v.* To express in words; utter: A committee member *voiced* an objection. 10 *n.* Expression, as in words: to give *voice* to one's ideas. 11 *n.* The right to express an opinion, preference, or judgment; vote or say: We had no *voice* in the selection of the winner. 12 *n.* Expressed opinion, preference, or judgment: One juror's *voice* was for acquittal. 13 *n.* In grammar, the property of a verb that indicates whether it expresses an action performed by its subject or upon its subject.

voice box Another name for LARYNX.

voiced [voist] *adj.* 1 Having a certain kind of voice: used in combination: a hoarse-*voiced* man. 2 Uttered with the vibration of the vocal cords: The "th" in *thy* is *voiced*; in *thigh* it is not *voiced.*

voice·less [vois'lis] *adj.* 1 Having no voice, speech, or vote. 2 Produced or uttered without vibration of the vocal cords: *P, t,* and *s* are *voiceless* consonants.

voice-o·ver [vois'ō'vər] *n.* The voice of a speaker who is not seen during a motion picture or television program.

voice·print [vois'print'] *n.* The characteristics of a person's voice recorded graphically as a means of identification.

voice recognition The ability of a computer to recognize and decipher human speech.

void [void] 1 *adj.* Without legal force or effect; invalid: The permit had expired and was *void.* 2 *v.*

To take away the legal force or effect of; cancel; annul: to *void* a contract. **3** *adj.* Not occupied; empty; vacant: a *void* space. **4** *n.* An empty space or gap: to fill a *void.* **5** *n.* An empty condition or feeling: My friend's departure left a *void* in my life. **6** *v.* To send out; discharge: to *void* urine. **7** *v.* To empty out; make vacant. **8** *adj.* Entirely lacking; destitute: an action *void* of reason.

voile [voil] *n.* A type of fine, sheer cloth.

vol. **1** volcano. **2** volume. **3** volunteer.

vol·a·tile [vol′ə·təl *or* vol′ə·tīl′] *adj.* **1** Evaporating quickly at ordinary temperatures, as gasoline or ether. **2** Fickle; changeable: a *volatile* person. —**vol·a·til·i·ty** [vol′ə·til′ə·tē] *n.*

vol·can·ic [vol·kan′ik] *adj.* **1** Of, produced by, or thrown up from a volcano: a *volcanic* eruption; *volcanic* ash. **2** Like a volcano; apt to erupt violently; explosive: *volcanic* anger.

vol·ca·no [vol·kā′nō] *n., pl.* **vol·ca·noes** or **vol·ca·nos** **1** An opening in the earth's crust from which hot gases, lava, and ashes are thrown up, forming a cone-shaped hill or mountain with a central crater. **2** The hill or mountain itself.

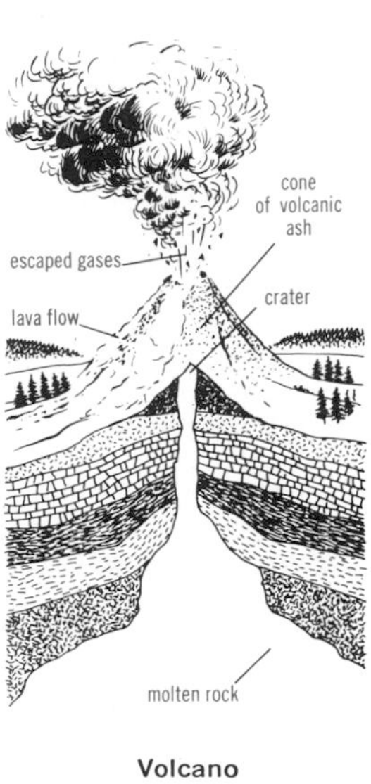

Volcano

vole [vōl] *n.* A small rodent resembling a mouse or rat, having a stocky body and a short tail.

vo·li·tion [vō·lish′ən *or* və·lish′ən] *n.* The act or power of exercising one's own will in choosing or deciding; will: I left of my own *volition.*

vol·ley [vol′ē] *n., pl.* **vol·leys,** *v.* **vol·leyed, vol·ley·ing** **1** *n.* The shooting or firing of a number of weapons at the same moment. **2** *v.* To shoot or fire or be shot or fired in a volley. **3** *n.* A shower of things shot off at the same time, as bullets or questions. **4** *v.* To hit or return (a tennis ball) before it bounces. **5** *n.* The hitting of a tennis ball before it touches the ground.

vol·ley·ball [vol′ē·bôl′] *n.* **1** A game in which two teams on either side of a high net strike a large ball with the hands in an attempt to send the ball over the net without letting it touch the ground. **2** The large ball itself.

volt [vōlt] *n.* A unit for measuring the difference of potential between two points in a circuit. If a resistance of one ohm carries a current of one ampere, one volt is developed across its terminals.

volt·age [vōl′tij] *n.* Electromotive force expressed in volts: high *voltage.*

vol·ta·ic cell [vol·tā′ik *or* vōl·tā′ik] A cell that produces electricity by chemical action.

volt·me·ter [vōlt′mē′tər] *n.* An instrument used to measure voltage.

vol·u·ble [vol′yə·bəl] *adj.* Talking a great deal or with great ease; talkative. —**vol·u·bil·i·ty** [vol′yə·bil′ə·tē] *n.* —**vol′u·bly** *adv.*

vol·ume [vol′yəm *or* vol′yo͞om] *n.* **1** A book. **2** A book that is part of a set of two or more books. **3** The measure of the space inside a closed figure of three dimensions: A box 3 feet by 3 feet by 3 feet has a *volume* of 27 cubic feet. **4** A quantity or amount: to do a larger *volume* of business. **5** Fullness of sound or tone; loudness: Turn down the *volume* of the TV.

vol·u·met·ric [vol′yŏŏ·met′rik] *adj.* Having to do with the measurement of volume.

vo·lu·mi·nous [və·lo͞o′mə·nəs] *adj.* **1** Being enough or writing enough to fill whole books: *voluminous* letters; a *voluminous* writer. **2** Of great bulk or size: a *voluminous* cape.

vol·un·tar·y [vol′ən·ter′ē] *adj.* **1** Given, made, or done by one's own will or choice; not compelled: a *voluntary* donation. **2** Acting by one's own choice or without a guarantee of reward: a *voluntary* group of hospital workers. **3** Done on purpose; not accidental. **4** Supported by charitable contributions: a *voluntary* hospital. **5** Under the control of the will: The action of the heart is not *voluntary.* —**vol′un·tar′i·ly** *adv.*

vol·un·teer [vol′ən·tir′] **1** *n.* A person who offers, out of free will or choice, to do some service, as military service. **2** *adj. use: volunteer* firefighters. **3** *v.* To offer without being asked or compelled to do so: to *volunteer* advice; She *volunteered* to go. **4** *v.* To offer oneself or one's services: to *volunteer* for extra duty.

vo·lup·tu·ar·y [və·lup′cho͞o·er′ē] *n., pl.* **vo·lup·tu·ar·ies** A person who is devoted to luxury and the pleasures of the senses.

vo·lup·tu·ous [və·lup′cho͞o·əs] *adj.* **1** Delighting the senses: *voluptuous* music. **2** Devoted to the pleasures of the senses: a *voluptuous* life. —**vo·lup′tu·ous·ness** *n.*

vol·vox [vol′voks′] *n.* Any of a group of protozoans that form spherical colonies.

vom·it [vom′it] **1** *v.* To throw up (matter that has been eaten or swallowed), as when sick at the stomach. **2** *n.* Matter that is thrown up from the stomach in this way. **3** *v.* To send or come forth in a way that suggests vomiting: The volcano *vomited* smoke.

voo·doo [vo͞o′do͞o] *n., pl.* **voo·doos** **1** A religion of African origin, characterized by belief in magic and the use of charms and witchcraft. **2** A person who practices this religion. ◆ *Voodoo* comes from an African word. See also MAGIC.

voo·doo·ism [vo͞o′do͞o·iz′əm] *n.* **1** The religion of voodoo. **2** Belief in or practice of voodoo.

vo·ra·cious [vô·rā′shəs *or* və·rā·shəs] *adj.* **1** Eating with great appetite; greedy; ravenous. **2** Taking a great deal of something without getting enough: a *voracious* reader. —**vo·ra′cious·ly** *adv.* —**vo·rac·i·ty** [vô·ras′ə·tē *or* və·ras′ə·tē] *n.*

vor·tex [vôr′teks′] *n., pl.* **vor·tex·es** or **vor·ti·ces** [vôr′tə·sēz′] A whirling current, as in water or air, usually spiraling in toward a center and tending to drag things with it; whirlpool or whirlwind.

vo·ta·ry [vō′tər·ē] *n., pl.* **vo·ta·ries** **1** A person

a add	**i** it	**o͝o** took	**oi** oil
ā ace	**ī** ice	**o͞o** pool	**ou** pout
â care	**o** odd	**u** up	**ng** ring
ä palm	**ō** open	**û** burn	**th** thin
e end	**ô** order	**yo͞o** fuse	**th** this
ē equal			**zh** vision

ə = {a in *above* e in *sicken* i in *possible* / o in *melon* u in *circus*}

bound by a vow or promise, as a nun or priest. 2 A person devoted to some particular worship, pursuit, or study: a *votary* of art.

vote [vōt] *n., v.* **vot·ed, vot·ing** 1 *n.* A formal expression of opinion, preference, or choice, made by those individuals who have a say in a group decision or election. 2 *n.* The means by which a voter expresses a choice, as a ballot or raised hand: to tally *votes.* 3 *v.* To cast a vote: to *vote* against a proposal; to *vote* for a candidate. 4 *n.* The right to vote: to be granted the *vote.* 5 *n.* The number of votes cast: a light *vote.* 6 *n.* Votes thought of as a group or bloc: the farm *vote.* 7 *n.* The result of an election: The candidate won by a *vote* of 20 to 12. 8 *v.* To decide, elect, defeat, grant, or bring into effect by a vote: Let's *vote* on it; Congress *voted* a tax cut. 9 *v. informal* To declare by general agreement: The critics *voted* the show a success.

vot·er [vō′tər] *n.* A person who votes or who has the right to vote.

vo·tive [vō′tiv] *adj.* Done, given, made, or lit to fulfill a vow or as an act of worship or devotion: a *votive* light.

vouch [vouch] *v.* To give a guarantee; give assurance: I'll *vouch* for the accuracy of the timer.

vouch·er [vou′chər] *n.* 1 A paper or other piece of evidence that serves to prove something, as a receipt showing that a bill was paid. 2 A person who vouches for someone or something.

vouch·safe [vouch′sāf′] *v.* **vouch·safed, vouch·saf·ing** To grant or give, often as though doing a kindness to an inferior.

vow [vou] 1 *n.* A solemn promise to God. 2 *n.* Any solemn promise or pledge: marriage *vows.* 3 *v.* To make a vow, as one to give, do, or get: to *vow* one's loyalty. 4 *v.* To promise or declare earnestly; swear: We *vowed* to return as soon as possible.

vow·el [vou′əl] *n.* 1 A speech sound made when the breath is not blocked by the teeth, tongue, or lips in the way that it is when a consonant is pronounced. 2 *adj. use: Cat* has one *vowel* sound. 3 A letter representing such a sound, as *a, e, i, o, u,* and sometimes *y,* as in *sky.*

voy·age [voi′ij] *n., v.* **voy·aged, voy·ag·ing** 1 *n.* A journey by water, especially by sea. 2 *n.* Any journey, as one through air or space: a *voyage* in a spaceship. 3 *v.* To travel on a voyage or voyages. **—voy′a·ger** *n.*

voy·a·geur [voi′ə·zhûr′ *or* vwä′yä·zhûr′] *n.* One of the woodsmen, boatmen, or scouts employed by fur companies to transport workers and supplies to and from remote stations, especially in Canada.

VP or **V.P.** vice president.

vs. versus.

v.s. (Latin *vide supra*). see above.

v.t. transitive verb.

Vt. Vermont.

VT 1 vacuum tube. 2 Postal Service abbreviation of Vermont.

VTOL vertical takeoff and landing.

VTR videotape recorder.

Vul·can [vul′kən] *n.* In Roman myths, the god of fire and the forge.

vul·can·ite [vul′kə·nīt′] *n.* A hard, tough, vulcanized rubber.

vul·can·ize [vul′kən·īz′] *v.* **vul·can·ized, vul·can·iz·ing** To treat (rubber) with chemicals, usually combining it with sulfur and heating it, to increase its strength and elasticity and improve other physical properties. **—vul·can·i·za·tion** [vul′kən·ə·zā′shən] *n.*

vul·gar [vul′gər] *adj.* 1 Lacking refinement or good taste; low, crude, or coarse: *vulgar* language; *vulgar* clothes. 2 Of, like, or having to do with the common people: Dante wrote poetry in the *vulgar* tongue, Italian, instead of in the literary language, Latin. ◆ *Vulgar* comes from a Latin word meaning *the common people.*

vul·gar·ism [vul′gə·riz′əm] *n.* A word, phrase, or expression that is not used by educated people. *That ain't no good* is a vulgarism.

vul·gar·i·ty [vul·gar′ə·tē] *n., pl.* **vul·gar·i·ties** 1 The quality of being vulgar or crude. 2 Something vulgar, as an action or remark.

vul·gar·ize [vul′gə·rīz′] *v.* **vul·gar·ized, vul·gar·iz·ing** 1 To make vulgar. 2 To simplify and popularize.

Vulgar Latin The form of Latin spoken by the common people of ancient Rome. Vulgar Latin eventually developed into the various Romance languages.

Vul·gate [vul′gāt′] *n.* A Latin version of the Bible, translated in the fourth century by St. Jerome, now revised and used as the authorized version by the Roman Catholic Church.

vul·ner·a·ble [vul′nər·ə·bəl] *adj.* 1 Capable of being hurt, injured, or wounded: the *vulnerable* human body; a person who is *vulnerable* to criticism. 2 Open to attack; without sufficient defenses: The fort was located in a *vulnerable* position. **—vul·ner·a·bil·i·ty** [vul′nər·ə·bil′ə·tē] *n.*

vul·pine [vul′pīn′] *adj.* Of or resembling a fox.

vul·ture [vul′chər] *n.* 1 A large bird, usually with a naked head, that feeds mostly on decaying flesh. It is related to eagles and hawks. 2 A savagely greedy person.

Vulture

vul·va [vul′və] *n., pl.* **vul·vae** [vul′vē] or **vul·vas** The external parts of the female genital organs.

vy·ing [vī′ing] Present participle of VIE.

W is the twenty-third letter of the alphabet. Its early history is the same as that for the letter *V*. The sign for both originated among Semitic people in the Near East, in the region of Palestine and Syria, probably in the middle of the second millennium B.C. Little is known about the sign until around 1000 B.C., when the Phoenicians began using it. They named it *waw* and used it for a *w*-like sound.

When the Greeks adopted the Phoenician sign around the ninth century B.C., they developed two signs of their own from it. The secondary form, called *digamma*, was used by Western Greeks for the *w* sound; this sound had disappeared from Eastern Greek dialects. The Greeks used the main form for the vowel *upsilon*, which stood for the sounds of *u* and sometimes *y*.

As early as the eighth century B.C., the Etruscans adopted the Greek alphabet. They used the Greek digamma for the sounds of *v* or *w* and combined it with *H* to approximate the sound of *f*. They used the Greek upsilon for the sound of *u*. It was from the Etruscans that the Romans took their alphabet. In time, the Greek digamma sign became *F* (see *F*) in Latin. The Greek upsilon, written as *V* in both Etruscan and Latin, was used by the Romans for the sounds of *u*, *v*, and *w*. But the *w* sound later disappeared from Latin. No sign was thus available for expressing the *w* sound in English.

The Roman alphabet reached Ireland and England in the sixth and seventh centuries. In seventh-century Old English manuscripts, the *w* sound was represented by a native character, ƿ, called the *wen*, or *wynn*. Norman scribes after the conquest of England (1066) dropped the wen, preferring to double one of their own letters for the *w* sound. Thus, they invented the "double *u*."

Both *majuscule*, or capital letter, and *minuscule*, or small letter, developed. Those from the fifteenth century were quite elaborate.

W w

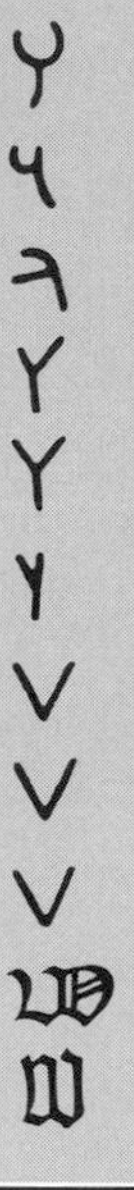

Early Phoenician (late 2nd millennium B.C.)
Phoenician (8th century B.C.)
Early Greek (9th-7th centuries B.C.)
Western Greek (6th century B.C.)
Classical Greek (403 B.C. onward)
Early Etruscan (8th century B.C.)
Classical Etruscan (around 400 B.C.)
Monumental Latin (4th century B.C.)
Classical Latin
Black-letter majuscule (15th century)
Black-letter minuscule (15th century)

w or **W** [dub′əl·yo͞o′] *n., pl.* **w's** or **W's** The 23rd letter of the English alphabet.
w, w., W, or **W.** **1** watt. **2** west. **3** western.
w. **1** warden. **2** week(s). **3** weight. **4** width. **5** word. **6** work.
W The symbol for the element tungsten. ◆ A former name for tungsten was *wolfram.*
W. **1** Wales. **2** Wednesday. **3** Welsh.
WA Postal Service abbreviation of Washington.
wab·ble [wob′əl] *v.* **wab·bled, wab·bling,** *n.* Another spelling of WOBBLE.
Wac [wak] *n.* A member of the Women's Army Corps.
WAC or **W.A.C.** Women's Army Corps.
wack·o [wak′ō] *n., pl.* **wack·os** *slang* A crazy or very eccentric person.
wack·y [wak′ē] *adj.* **wack·i·er, wack·i·est** *slang* Crazy or foolish. **—wack′i·ly** *adv.* **—wack′i·ness** *n.*
wad [wod] *n., v.* **wad·ded, wad·ding** **1** *n.* A small, compact mass: a *wad* of gum. **2** *v.* To press into a wad: to *wad* paper. **3** *n.* A thin plug to hold the charge in place in a gun or cartridge. **4** *v.* To stuff or pack tightly with wadding for protection, as valuables. **5** *n.* A tight bundle, as of paper money. **6** *n. informal* Great wealth.
wad·ding [wod′ing] *n.* Soft material used for padding or stuffing.
wad·dle [wod′(ə)l] *v.* **wad·dled, wad·dling,** *n.* **1** *v.* To sway from side to side in walking. **2** *n.* A clumsy, swaying walk, like that of a duck.
wade [wād] *v.* **wad·ed, wad·ing** **1** To walk through water, mud, or anything that hinders one's progress. **2** To cross (a stream, pond, or other body of water) by wading. **3** To proceed with much labor and difficulty: to *wade* through a textbook. **—wade in** or **wade into** *informal* To attack or begin energetically or vigorously.
wad·er [wā′dər] *n.* **1** A person who wades. **2** Any bird with long legs that wades in water in search of food. **3** (*pl.*) High, waterproof boots for wading.
wa·di [wä′dē] *n., pl.* **wa·dis** An intermittent stream or riverbed in the Middle East that is dry except during the rainy season.
Waf [waf] *n.* A member of the Women in the Air Force.
WAF or **W.A.F.** Women in the Air Force.
wa·fer [wā′fər] *n.* **1** A thin, crisp biscuit. **2** A small, flat piece of candy. **3** A small, flat disk of unleavened bread used in the Holy Communion service of some churches. **4** A small, adhesive disk used for sealing letters, documents, and other items. **5** A thin disk of silicon or other semicon-

a	add	**i**	it	**o͝o**	took	**oi**	oil		
ā	ace	**ī**	ice	**o͞o**	pool	**ou**	pout		
â	care	**o**	odd	**u**	up	**ng**	ring		
ä	palm	**ō**	open	**û**	burn	**th**	thin		
e	end	**ô**	order	**yo͞o**	fuse	**th̶**	this		
ē	equal					**zh**	vision		

ə = {a in *above*, e in *sicken*, i in *possible*, o in *melon*, u in *circus*

ductor prepared for use as an electronic component.

waf·fle[1] [wof'əl *or* wô'fəl] *n.* A batter cake, crisper than a pancake, baked between two metal plates that have rows of knobs on them.

waf·fle[2] [wof'əl *or* wô'fəl] *v.* **waf·fled, waf·fling** To avoid expressing a frank opinion or answer; be evasive.

waffle iron Hinged plates for baking waffles.

waft [wäft *or* waft] **1** *v.* To carry or move gently through air or over water: The scent of flowers *wafted* in. **2** *n.* A sound, smell, or puff, as of smoke, borne by the air. **3** *n.* A puff of breeze.

Waffle iron

wag[1] [wag] *v.* **wagged, wag·ging,** *n.* **1** *v.* To swing back and forth or up and down: The dog *wags* its tail. **2** *v.* To move busily in producing speech: Tongues will *wag.* **3** *n.* The act or motion of wagging.

wag[2] [wag] *n.* A person who likes to make jokes.

wage [wāj] *v.* **waged, wag·ing,** *n.* **1** *v.* To engage in; carry on: to *wage* war. **2** *n.* (*often pl.*) Money paid for the services of an employee. **3** *n.* (*often pl. and used with a singular verb*) Payment; reward: The *wages* of sin is death.

wage earner A salaried employee.

wa·ger [wā'jər] **1** *n.* A bet. **2** *v.* To bet.

wag·ger·y [wag'ər·ē] *n., pl.* **wag·ger·ies** **1** The actions, manner, or behavior of a wag. **2** A joke or amusing comment.

wag·gish [wag'ish] *adj.* **1** Inclined to make jokes; playful. **2** Comical; droll: a *waggish* grin. **—wag'·gish·ly** *adv.* **—wag'gish·ness** *n.*

wag·gle [wag'əl] *v.* **wag·gled, wag·gling,** *n.* **1** *v.* To move in quick, jerking motions: to *waggle* a finger. **2** *n.* A waggling movement. **—wag'gly** *adj.*

wag·on [wag'ən] *n.* **1** Any of various large vehicles, drawn by animals and used mainly to carry freight. **2** Any small vehicle with wheels that is pulled by hand.

Wagon

wag·on·er [wag'ən·ər] *n.* A person whose work is driving wagons.

waif [wāf] *n.* A homeless, lost, or abandoned creature, especially a child or a pet.

wail [wāl] **1** *n.* A long, high cry, as of pain or grief. **2** *n.* A sound that is like this, as that of the wind. **3** *v.* To make or utter a wail.

wain [wān] *n.* A large farm wagon: seldom used today.

wain·scot [wān'skət *or* wān'skōt' *or* wān'skot'] *n., v.* **wain·scot·ed** or **wain·scot·ted, wain·scot·ing** or **wain·scot·ting** **1** *n.* A facing for the walls inside a room, usually of wooden panels. **2** *n.* The lower part of an inside wall when finished differently from the rest of the wall. **3** *v.* To cover with wainscot.

wain·scot·ing or **wain·scot·ting** [wān'skōt'ing *or* wān'skot'ing *or* wān'skət'ing] *n.* Material for a wainscot, especially wooden panels.

wain·wright [wān'rīt'] *n.* A person who constructs and repairs wagons: seldom used today.

waist [wāst] *n.* **1** The part of the body below the ribs and above the hips. **2** The part of a garment that covers the body from the neck or shoulders to the waist. **3** A blouse. **4** A waistband. **5** The middle of something, especially if narrower than the rest of it.

waist·band [wāst'band'] *n.* A band circling the waist, as of a skirt or pair of trousers.

waist·coat [wes'kət *or* wāst'kot'] *n. British* A man's vest.

waist·line [wāst'līn'] *n.* **1** The line thought of as being around the waist. **2** The line at which the skirt of a dress meets the waist.

wait [wāt] **1** *v.* To remain or stay until something happens: to *wait* for the bus to come; The car is *waiting.* **2** *n.* Time spent in waiting. **3** *n.* The act of waiting. **4** *v.* To remain temporarily neglected or undone: That will have to *wait* until tomorrow. **5** *v.* To act as a waiter or waitress. **6** *v. informal* To put off; postpone. **—in waiting** In attendance, as upon a monarch. **—lie in wait** To remain hidden in order to make a surprise attack. **—wait on** or **wait upon** **1** To act as a servant or waiter to. **2** To pay a respectful visit to. ◆ In writing, avoid using *wait on* in place of *wait for:* I'm *waiting for* [not *on*] a friend.

wait·er [wā'tər] *n.* A person who serves food and drink at tables, as in restaurants.

waiting list A list of persons waiting their turn, as for an appointment or a vacant apartment.

waiting room A room for persons who are waiting, as for a train, doctor, or dentist.

wait·ress [wā'tris] *n.* A female who serves food and drink at tables, as in restaurants.

waive [wāv] *v.* **waived, waiv·ing** **1** To give up voluntarily, as a claim, right, or privilege. **2** To put aside; postpone; delay.

waiv·er [wā'vər] *n.* **1** The voluntary giving up, as of a right or claim. **2** A written declaration of this.

wake[1] [wāk] *v.* **woke** or **waked, waked** or **wo·ken, wak·ing,** *n.* **1** *v.* To stop or cause to stop sleeping; awake. **2** *v.* To become alert or aware: I finally *woke* to the demands of the situation. **3** *v.* To make or become active or aroused: to *wake* memories of the past. **4** *n.* A watch kept over a dead person through the night before burial.

wake[2] [wāk] *n.* **1** The trail of turbulent water left by a moving vessel. **2** The path or course over which any person or thing has passed: The fire left chaos in its *wake.* **—in the wake of** Following closely or resulting from.

wake·ful [wāk'fəl] *adj.* **1** Unable to sleep. **2** Without sleep. **3** Alert; watchful. **—wake'ful·ness** *n.*

wak·en [wā'kən] *v.* To wake.

wale [wāl] *n., v.* **waled, wal·ing** **1** *n.* A stripe raised on the skin by a blow; welt. **2** *v.* To raise wales on, as with a whip. **3** *n.* A ridge on the surface of cloth. **4** *v.* To weave (cloth) with ridges or ribs.

walk [wôk] **1** *v.* To move on foot at a normal rate. When a person walks, one foot is always touching the ground. **2** *v.* To pass through, over, or along, by walking: to *walk* the path to school. **3** *n.* The act of walking: a morning *walk.* **4** *n.* The distance walked, or the time taken by one who walks: a five-mile *walk*; a three-hour *walk.* **5** *n.* A manner of walking; gait. **6** *n.* A pathway, usually paved, intended for walking. **7** *v.* To cause or allow (a horse, dog, or other animal) to walk. **8** *v.* To go with on a walk: I'll *walk* you home. **9** *v.* In baseball, to reach or allow to reach first base as a result of the pitching of four balls. **10** *n.* In baseball, an instance of walking. **11** *n.* Manner or station: various *walks* of life.

walk·er [wôk′ər] *n.* 1 A person or animal that walks. 2 A lightweight circular frame on wheels that supports a very young child who is learning to walk. 3 A lightweight frame used by a convalescent or disabled person for support when walking.

Walker

walk·ie-talk·ie [wô′·kē·tô′kē] *n.* A radio transmitter and receiver that one person can carry.
walk-in [wôk′in′] 1 *adj.* Large enough for a person to walk into: a *walk-in* closet. 2 *n.* Something, as a closet, that is large enough for a person to walk into. 3 *adj.* Entered directly from the street: a *walk-in* apartment. 4 *n.* A person who has come for service, as to a dentist or doctor, without an appointment.
walk·ing stick [wô′king] 1 A staff or cane carried in the hand. 2 An insect having long, slender legs and body. It resembles a twig.
walk-on [wôk′on′] *n.* A small part without spoken lines in a theatrical performance.
walk·out [wôk′out′] *n. informal* A workers' strike.
walk·o·ver [wôk′ō′vər] *n.* An easy victory in a race or contest.
walk-up [wôk′up′] *n.* 1 An office or apartment located above the ground level in a building that has no elevator: a fifth-floor *walk-up.* 2 A multistoried building that has no elevator.
walk·way [wôk′wā′] *n.* A passageway or lane for walkers.
wall [wôl] 1 *n.* An upright structure built to enclose or divide a space, especially one side of a room or building. 2 *v.* To provide, surround, or protect, with or as if with a wall. 3 *v.* To divide, fill, or block with a wall: to *wall* up a door; to *wall* off an area. 4 *n.* Something that suggests a wall: a *wall* of flame. 5 *n.* The side of any cavity, vessel, or receptacle: the *wall* of a furnace. **—off the wall** *slang* 1 Crazy; zany. 2 Highly unlikely or unconventional. **—up the wall** *slang* Into a state of great distress or frustration.
wal·la·by [wol′ə·bē] *n., pl.* **wal·la·bies** or **wal·la·by** Any of various small kangaroos.
wall·board [wôl′bôrd′] *n.* Any of various materials manufactured in large panels for use instead of plaster or wood for walls and ceilings.
wal·let [wol′it] *n.* A small folding case, usually of leather, for holding paper money, personal papers, and other items.
wall·eye [wôl′ī′] *n.* 1 An eye that turns out toward the side of the face. 2 An eye in which the iris is white or light-colored. 3 A large, staring eye. 4 A walleyed pike.
wall·eyed [wôl′īd′] *adj.* 1 Having the pupils of the eyes turned out to the sides so that a great amount of the white shows. 2 Having eyes with white or light-colored irises. 3 Having large, staring eyes, as certain fishes.
walleyed pike A freshwater food and game fish of eastern North America that has large, staring eyes.
wall·flow·er [wôl′flou′ər] *n.* 1 A garden plant having fragrant yellow, orange, or red flowers. 2 *informal* A person who cannot attract partners for dancing at a party and therefore sits by the wall.
Wal·loon [wo·lo͞on′] *n.* 1 A member of a French-speaking people of Celtic descent who live in Belgium and NE France. 2 The dialect of France spoken by the Walloons.
wal·lop [wol′əp] *informal* 1 *n.* A hard blow. 2 *v.* To strike with a wallop. 3 *v.* To beat soundly.
wal·low [wol′ō] 1 *v.* To roll or tumble about; flounder, as in mud or water: Pigs *wallow* in mud. 2 *n.* A muddy place where animals like to wallow. 3 *v.* To indulge or debase oneself: to *wallow* in filth; to *wallow* in luxury.
wall·pa·per [wôl′pā′pər] *n.* Paper specially prepared and printed in colors and designs, for covering walls and ceilings of rooms.
Wall Street 1 A street that runs through the financial district of New York City. 2 Powerful financial interests located in New York City.
wal·nut [wôl′nut′] 1 *n.* A large, edible nut with its seed divided in halves. 2 *n.* The tree it grows on. 3 *n.* The wood of this tree, used to make furniture. 4 *adj., n.* Dark brown.
wal·rus [wôl′rəs *or* wol′rəs] *n., pl.* **wal·rus·es** or **wal·rus** A large, seallike animal of the arctic, having two long tusks in the upper jaw.

Walrus

waltz [wôlts] 1 *n.* A smooth, flowing dance for couples, done to music in triple time. 2 *v.* To dance a waltz. 3 *n.* Music for a waltz.
wam·pum [wom′pəm] *n.* 1 Small beads made of polished shells, usually cylindrical in shape, often worked into belts and bracelets, once used as money or ceremonial pledges by North American Indians. 2 *informal* Money. ◆ *Wampum* comes from an Algonquian Indian word meaning *white string (of beads).*
wan [won] *adj.* **wan·ner, wan·nest** 1 Pale or faint, as from being ill or very tired. 2 Showing illness or fatigue. **—wan′ly** *adv.* **—wan′ness** *n.*
wand [wond] *n.* A thin stick or rod, as one used to do magic tricks.
wan·der [won′dər] *v.* 1 To move or travel about in an aimless or leisurely way; roam. 2 To stray: to *wander* off course. 3 To take an irregular, twisting route: The stream *wanders* by. 4 To become confused or irrational: The mind of an elderly person sometimes *wanders.* **—wan′der·er** *n.* ◆ *Wander, rove,* and *roam* all mean to move about with no fixed destination. To *wander* is to move about aimlessly, as if lost, but *roam* and *rove* sug-

a	add	**i**	it	**o͝o**	took	**oi**	oil
ā	ace	**ī**	ice	**o͞o**	pool	**ou**	pout
â	care	**o**	odd	**u**	up	**ng**	ring
ä	palm	**ō**	open	**û**	burn	**th**	thin
e	end	**ô**	order	**yo͞o**	fuse	**th**	this
ē	equal					**zh**	vision

ə = a in *above* e in *sicken* i in *possible* / o in *melon* u in *circus*

gest movement over a large area, with a purpose, although it may be indefinite.

wan·der·lust [won'dər·lust'] *n.* A strong impulse or desire to travel about or wander.

wane [wān] *v.* **waned, wan·ing,** *n.* 1 *v.* To grow progressively less or smaller, as in size or brightness: The moon *waned.* 2 *v.* To decline or decrease gradually; draw to an end. 3 *n.* The action of waning. **—on the wane** Decreasing; fading out.

wan·gle [wang'gəl] *v.* **wan·gled, wan·gling,** *n. informal* 1 *v.* To get or accomplish by sly or irregular means: to *wangle* an invitation to a party. 2 *n.* An act of wangling.

want [wont *or* wônt] 1 *v.* To feel a desire or wish for: We *want* to go home; Do you *want* a glass of milk? 2 *n.* Something required or desired: to have few *wants.* 3 *v.* To need or lack: This food *wants* salt. 4 *n.* A lack or scarcity; need: They failed for *want* of planning. 5 *n.* Poverty; need: to be in *want.* 6 *v.* To be very poor or needy. 7 *v.* To wish to see or speak to: Did you *want* me? 8 *v.* To seek in order to arrest: The suspect is *wanted* for armed robbery.

want ad A brief advertisement placed in a newspaper or magazine, offering or seeking something; classified advertisement.

want·ing [won'ting *or* wôn'ting] *adj.* 1 Not at hand; missing; lacking: There is one volume *wanting* in our encyclopedia. 2 Not up to standard: The work was found *wanting.*

wan·ton [won'tən] *adj.* 1 Brutal or destructive without reason or purpose: *wanton* murder; *wanton* mischief. 2 Playful in an unrestrained manner: a *wanton* child. 3 Immoral; lewd. **—wan'ton·ly** *adv.* **—wan'ton·ness** *n.*

wap·i·ti [wop'ə·tē] *n., pl.* **wap·i·tis** or **wap·i·ti** The elk of North America.

Wapiti

war [wôr] *n., v.* **warred, war·ring** 1 *n.* Conflict between the armed forces of nations or states, especially on a large scale. 2 *n.* Any condition of conflict or enmity: a *war* on poverty. 3 *v.* To carry on a war.

War between the States The American Civil War.

war·ble [wôr'bəl] *v.* **war·bled, war·bling,** *n.* 1 *v.* To sing with trills or runs, as some birds. 2 *v.* To make a liquid, murmuring sound, as a stream. 3 *n.* A bird's song, or a sound like it.

war·bler [wôr'blər] *n.* 1 A person or thing that warbles. 2 Any of several songbirds.

war·bon·net [wôr'bon'it] *n.* A North American Indian ceremonial headdress, often covered with upright eagle feathers.

war crime Any of various acts, as torture of prisoners or genocide, that are considered to be violations of the written or unwritten conventions of warfare. **—war criminal**

ward [wôrd] *n.* 1 A large room in a hospital, usually equipped to care for six or more patients. 2 A political division of a city. 3 A young person who is in the charge of a guardian or of a court of law. **—ward off** To repel; turn aside: to *ward off* a thrust; to *ward off* an illness.

-ward A suffix meaning: Toward; in the direction of, as in *homeward.*

war·den [wôr'dən] *n.* 1 The chief officer of a prison. 2 Someone who guards an area or enforces regulations: a fire *warden.* ◆ *Warden* and *guardian* come from an old French word meaning *to guard.*

ward·er [wôr'dər] *n.* A keeper; guard; watchman.

ward·robe [wôrd'rōb'] *n.* 1 A personal supply of clothing. 2 A collection of costumes, as in a theater. 3 A cabinet or other storage place for clothing or costumes.

-wards Another form of -WARD.

ware [wâr] *n.* 1 Manufactured goods of a stated kind: often used in combination: *kitchenware; glassware.* 2 (*pl.*) Items for sale; goods. 3 Pottery; earthenware.

ware·house [wâr'hous'] *n.* A storehouse for goods or merchandise.

war·fare [wôr'fâr'] *n.* Fighting; war; conflict.

war·head [wôr'hed'] *n.* The front end of a torpedo, missile, or the like, which carries the explosive.

war-horse [wôr'hôrs'] *n.* 1 A horse used in battle. 2 *informal* A person with long experience in some competitive or strenuous activity; veteran.

war·i·ly [wâr'ə·lē] *adv.* With care; cautiously.

war·i·ness [wâr'ə·nis] *n.* Caution; care.

war·like [wôr'līk'] *adj.* 1 Fit and ready for war; liking war: *warlike* troops. 2 Threatening war. 3 Of or having to do with war.

war·lock [wôr'lok'] *n.* A male witch; sorcerer.

war·lord [wôr'lôrd'] *n.* A military leader who rules the territory in which he operates.

warm [wôrm] 1 *adj.* Moderately or comfortably hot. 2 *v.* To make or become warm. 3 *adj.* Giving or keeping in warmth: *warm* gloves. 4 *adj.* Suggestive of warmth: *warm* colors. 5 *adj.* Affectionate, kind, or enthusiastic: a *warm* greeting; a *warm* smile. 6 *v.* To fill with good feeling: It *warms* my heart. 7 *adj.* Excited; passionate: a *warm* discussion. 8 *v.* To make or become passionate or enthusiastic: to *warm* to a subject. **—warm up** 1 To warm. 2 To exercise or operate, in preparation for activity or use: The pitcher *warmed up* before the game. **—warm'ly** *adv.*

warm-blood·ed [wôrm'blud'id] *adj.* 1 Having a constant warm body temperature regardless of surroundings, as mammals and birds. 2 Full of passionate feeling; fervent; ardent.

warm front The boundary between a moving mass of warm air and the cold air it displaces.

warm·heart·ed [wôrm'här'tid] *adj.* Kind; affectionate.

warm·ing pan [wôr'ming] A closed metal pan with a long handle, containing hot coals or water, used in former times to warm a bed.

war·mon·ger [wôr'mung'gər *or* wôr'mong'gər] *n.* A person who advocates or tries to bring about war.

warmth [wôrmth] *n.* The condition or feeling of being warm.

warm-up [wôrm'up'] 1 *n.* An act or period of exercising or operating in preparation for activity or use. 2 *adj.* Of or for warming up: *warm-up* exercises before a race.

warn [wôrn] *v.* 1 To make aware of possible harm or danger; put on guard; caution. 2 To inform; give notice in advance: The bell *warned* of the train's approach.

warn·ing [wôr'ning] *n.* 1 A notice of danger: a storm *warning.* 2 Something that warns or reproves: a *warning* from the principal.

War of 1812 The war between the U.S. and Great Britain, lasting from 1812 to 1815.

War of Independence The American Revolution.

warp [wôrp] **1** *v.* To turn or twist out of shape. **2** *n.* A bend or twist, as in a plank. **3** *v.* To make evil or immoral; corrupt. **4** *v.* To move (a vessel) by hauling on a rope fastened to a pier or anchor. **5** *n.* The threads that run along the length of a fabric, crossed by the woof.

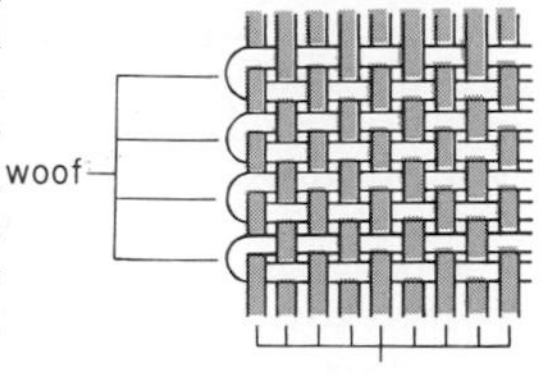

warp

war·path [wôr′path′] *n.* The road to battle taken by American Indians, especially in the phrase **on the warpath,** meaning: **1** Making war, or eager to make war. **2** Ready for a fight; furious.

war·plane [wôr′plān′] *n.* An airplane designed for use in combat.

war·rant [wôr′ənt *or* wor′ənt] **1** *n.* A legal paper giving authority to arrest, search, or seize. **2** *n.* Something that is a guarantee, proof, or confirmation of something else: Wanting a victory is no *warrant* of having one. **3** *n.* A reason or justification for an action or belief: You have no *warrant* to think that it was a deliberate act. **4** *v.* To be sufficient grounds for; justify: The situation *warrants* bold action.

warrant officer An officer in the armed forces who ranks below commissioned officers and above enlisted people.

war·ran·ty [wôr′ən·tē *or* wor′ən·tē] *n., pl.* **war·ran·ties** **1** Something that guarantees, authorizes, or justifies something else; warrant. **2** A usually written guarantee that the product being sold belongs to the person selling it and that it is as described to the buyer.

war·ren [wôr′ən *or* wor′ən] *n.* **1** A place where rabbits live and breed. **2** An enclosure for small game. **3** Any crowded place where people live.

war·ri·or [wôr′ē·ər *or* wor′ē·ər] *n.* A person engaged in or experienced in war; soldier.

war·ship [wôr′ship′] *n.* Any ship used in naval combat.

wart [wôrt] *n.* **1** A small, hard lump growing on the skin. **2** A similar growth on a plant.

wart hog An African wild hog having wartlike knobs on the face and large tusks in both jaws.

war·time [wôr′tīm′] *n.* A time of war.

wart·y [wôr′tē] *adj.* **wart·i·er, wart·i·est** Having or resembling warts: *warty* growths.

war·y [wâr′ē] *adj.* **war·i·er, war·i·est** Watchful and suspicious; very careful; cautious.

was [wuz *or* woz] A form of the verb BE. It shows past time, and is used with *I, he, she, it,* or singular nouns: I *was* born in May.

wash [wôsh *or* wosh] **1** *v.* To free of dirt or other unwanted material by the action of a liquid, as water, and usually a soap. **2** *v.* To wash clothes. **3** *n.* An amount, as of clothing, washed at one time. **4** *v.* To wash oneself: *Wash* before you eat. **5** *v.* To pass water over or through (gravel, earth, ore, or other material) in order to obtain something: to *wash* sand for gold. **6** *v.* To carry away, move, or remove by the action of water: *Wash* that dirt off; The sea *washed* the boat ashore. **7** *v.* To be carried or worn away, moved, or removed by the action of water: All the color *washed* out. **8** *v.* To withstand washing without damage: Will this shirt *wash*? **9** *n.* The act, process, or an instance of washing: the weekly *wash.* **10** *v.* To flow over or against: Waves *washed* the shore. **11** *n.* The breaking or the sound of the breaking of waves against a shore. **12** *v.* To apply a thin layer of paint, color, or metal to: to *wash* a copper pan with tin. **13** *n.* Something used in coating or washing: a *wash* of color; a *wash* of tin. **14** *n.* Liquid or semiliquid garbage; swill. **15** *n.* The eddies or currents produced in the air or water, as by an airplane, rocket, or boat. **16** *n.* A shallow part, as of a river or bay. **17** *n.* Material such as mud or silt collected and deposited by flowing water. **—wash one's hands of** To end all connection with; have nothing more to do with. **—wash up** **1** To wash oneself. **2** To wash the dishes and utensils after a meal.

Wash. Washington.

wash·a·ble [wôsh′ə·bəl *or* wosh′ə·bəl] *adj.* Capable of being washed without damage.

wash-and-wear [wôsh′ən·wâr′ *or* wosh′ən·wâr′] *adj.* Treated so as to require no ironing after being washed: a *wash-and-wear* shirt.

wash·ba·sin [wôsh′bā′sən *or* wosh′bā′sən] *n.* A washbowl.

wash·board [wôsh′bôrd′ *or* wosh′bôrd′] *n.* A board or frame having a ridged surface on which to rub clothes while washing them.

wash·bowl [wôsh′bōl′ *or* wosh′bōl′] *n.* A wide, shallow bowl or sink used to hold water for washing one's hands and face.

wash·cloth [wôsh′klôth′ *or* wosh′klôth′] *n.* A small cloth used for washing the body.

washed-out [wôsht′out′ *or* wosht′out′] *adj.* **1** Pale or faded in color. **2** Exhausted; listless.

washed-up [wôsht′up′ *or* wosht′up′] *adj.* **1** *informal* Tired or exhausted. **2** *slang* Failed; finished: a *washed-up* prizefighter.

wash·er [wôsh′ər *or* wosh′ər] *n.* **1** A person or thing that washes. **2** A washing machine. **3** A flat ring, often of metal or rubber. It takes pressure and stops leaking.

Washer

wash·er·wom·an [wôsh′ər·wo͝om′ən *or* wosh′ər·wo͝om′ən] *n., pl.* **wash·er·wom·en** [wôsh′ər·wim′in *or* wosh′ər·wim′in] A woman who earns her living by washing other people's clothes and linens; laundress.

wash·ing [wôsh′ing *or* wosh′ing] *n.* **1** The act of a person or thing that washes. **2** A group of things washed or to be washed at a certain time. **3** Something obtained by washing: a *washing* of ore. **4** A thin coat of metal.

washing machine A machine for washing laundry.

Washington's Birthday February 22, George Washington's birthday, now usually observed as a holiday on the third Monday in February.

a	add	**i**	it	**o͝o**	took	**oi**	oil
ā	ace	**ī**	ice	**o͞o**	pool	**ou**	pout
â	care	**o**	odd	**u**	up	**ng**	ring
ä	palm	**ō**	open	**û**	burn	**th**	thin
e	end	**ô**	order	**yo͞o**	fuse	**th**	this
ē	equal					**zh**	vision

ə = a in *above* e in *sicken* i in *possible* o in *melon* u in *circus*

wash·out [wôsh′out′ *or* wosh′out′] *n.* 1 The washing away, as of earth, a road, or a path, by flowing water. 2 The break or gap made by it. 3 *slang* A complete failure.
wash·rag [wôsh′rag′ *or* wosh′rag′] *n.* Washcloth.
wash·room [wôsh′ro͞om′ *or* wosh′ro͞om′] *n.* A room equiped with sinks and toilets.
wash·stand [wôsh′stand′ *or* wosh′stand′] *n.* 1 A bowl with pipes and faucets for washing the hands and face. 2 A stand to hold a basin and pitcher for washing the hands and face.
wash·tub [wôsh′tub′ *or* wosh′tub′] *n.* A tub in which laundry is washed by hand.
was·n't [wuz′ənt *or* woz′ənt] Was not.
wasp [wosp *or* wôsp] *n.* Any of various stinging insects related to bees and ants.
WASP or **Wasp** [wosp *or* wôsp] *n.* A white Anglo-Saxon Protestant.
wasp·ish [wos′pish *or* wôs′pish] *adj.* 1 Like a wasp. 2 Easily made angry; irritable; irascible. **—wasp′ish·ly** *adv.* **—wasp′ish·ness** *n.*
was·sail [wos′əl *or* wo·sāl′] 1 *n.* An ancient party at which toasts were drunk. 2 *n.* The liquor prepared for such a festivity. 3 *v.* To take part in a wassail. 4 *v.* To drink the health of; toast. **—was′·sail·er** *n.*
wast [wost] An old form of WAS, used with *thou.*
wast·age [wās′tij] *n.* Something that is lost, as by wear or waste.
waste [wāst] *v.* **wast·ed, wast·ing,** *n.* 1 *v.* To use, spend, or let pass to no good purpose or advantage: to *waste* fuel; to *waste* a chance. 2 *v.* To destroy or consume utterly: Insects *wasted* the crops. 3 *v.* To make or become less vigorous or strong: to *waste* away from disease. 4 *n.* An act of wasting: Seeing that movie was a *waste* of time. 5 *n.* The condition of being wasted. 6 *n.* A barren or desolate region; wilderness. 7 *adj. use*: a *waste* plain. 8 *n.* Something to be thrown away as not usable or wanted. 9 *adj. use*: *waste* gases; *waste* scrap. 10 *n.* Cotton threads used in bunches to wipe machinery and soak up oil. **—lay waste** To destroy utterly. **—wast′er** *n.*
waste·bas·ket [wāst′bas′kit] *n.* A container for paper scraps and other waste.
waste·ful [wāst′fəl] *adj.* Tending to waste things, as food, money, or materials. **—waste′ful·ly** *adv.* **—waste′ful·ness** *n.*
waste·land [wāst′land′] *n.* A barren, desolate area.
waste·pa·per [wāst′pā′pər] *n.* Paper thrown away as used or useless.
wast·ing [wā′sting] *adj.* Characterized by a slow and gradual deterioration. **—wast′ing·ly** *adv.*
wast·rel [wā′strəl] *n.* 1 A wasteful person. 2 An idle good-for-nothing.
watch [woch] 1 *v.* To look or look at; observe: to *watch* a play; Just sit and *watch.* 2 *v.* To wait or look expectantly or alertly: *Watch* for the signal. 3 *v.* To keep in one's care; guard. 4 *v.* To pay attention or keep informed about: to *watch* an actor's rise to fame. 5 *v.* To remain awake, as in tending a sick person through the night. 6 *n.* The act of watching: The shepherds keep *watch* over the flocks. 7 *n.* One or more persons set to watch; guard. 8 *n.* A period of duty for a guard. 9 *n.* One of the sections of a ship's crew that are on duty by turns. 10 *n.* A period of duty for a ship's watch. 11 *n.* A small timepiece made to be worn on the wrist or carried in the pocket. **—watch out** To be on guard; take care. **—watch′er** *n.*
watch·band [woch′band′] *n.* A leather, metal, or plastic strap that fastens a watch on the wrist.
watch·dog [woch′dôg′] *n.* A dog kept to guard a building or other property.
watch·ful [woch′fəl] *adj.* Watching carefully; alert; vigilant. **—watch′ful·ly** *adv.* **—watch′ful·ness** *n.*
watch·mak·er [woch′mā′kər] *n.* A person who makes and repairs watches. **—watch′mak′ing** *n.*
watch·man [woch′mən] *n., pl.* **watch·men** [woch′·mən] *n.* A person who keeps watch, as one hired to guard a building at night.
watch·tow·er [woch′tou′ər] *n.* A tower from which a person may keep watch.
watch·word [woch′wûrd′] *n.* 1 A password. 2 A rallying cry or slogan.
wa·ter [wô′tər *or* wot′ər] 1 *n.* A liquid compound of hydrogen and oxygen that freezes at 0° C (32° F) and boils at 100° C (212° F). Formula: H_2O. It falls from clouds and covers nearly 75 percent of the earth by seas, lakes, and other bodies. It is needed by all living things. 2 *v.* To give water to: to *water* livestock. 3 *v.* To make moist or wet by water, as by sprinkling or soaking. 4 *v.* To drink or take in water. 5 *v.* To weaken or dilute with water: to *water* vinegar. 6 *n.* Any body of water, as a lake, river, or ocean. 7 *n.* (*usually pl.*) Still, flowing, or moving water, as of a lake, river, or ocean: the *waters* of the Hudson. 8 *n.* A liquid like or containing water: soda *water*; toilet *water.* 9 *n.* Any of the body fluids that resemble water, as saliva or tears. 10 *v.* To secrete or discharge one of these fluids: The eyes *water* when irritated; The smell made my mouth *water.* 11 *n.* The clarity or luster of a gem: a pearl of the first *water.* 12 *n.* A wavy sheen put on some fabrics or metals. 13 *v.* To put a wavy sheen on. **—hold water** To be acceptable or effective: That story doesn't *hold water.*
water bird A wading or swimming bird, or one usually found near water.
wa·ter·borne [wô′tər·bôrn′ *or* wot′ər·bôrn′] *adj.* 1 Supported by water; afloat. 2 Transported by ship or boat.
wa·ter·buck [wôt′ər·buk′ *or* wo′tər·buk′] *n.* A large African antelope with long horns, generally found close to water.
water buffalo A powerful buffalo of India, Africa, and the Philippines, having very wide curving horns. It is used to pull heavy loads.

Water buffalo

water bug Any of various insects that live on or near water.
water chestnut 1 A grasslike aquatic plant native to Asia. 2 The tasty underwater stem of this plant, used in Oriental cooking.
water clock An ancient instrument for measuring time by a regulated flow of water.
water closet A toilet.
wa·ter·col·or [wô′tər·kul′ər *or* wot′ər·kul′ər] *n.* 1 A color for painting made ready for use by mixing with water. 2 A painting done in such colors.
water cooler A device for storing, cooling, and dispensing drinking water.

wa·ter·course [wô′tər·kôrs′ *or* wot′ər·kôrs′] *n.* **1** A stream of water; river; brook. **2** A channel for, or made by, water.
wa·ter·craft [wô′tər·kraft′ *or* wot′ər·kraft′] *n., pl.* **wa·ter·craft** **1** Any vehicle designed to travel across water, as a canoe, sailboat, or steamship. **2** Skill in activities relating to water, as sailing and swimming.
wa·ter·cress [wô′tər·kres′ *or* wot′ər·kres′] *n.* A creeping plant that grows in water, having leaves that are used in salads.
wa·ter·fall [wô′tər·fôl′ *or* wot′ər·fôl′] *n.* A stream falling from a high place, as from a cliff.
wa·ter·fowl [wô′tər·foul′ *or* wot′ər·foul′] *n., pl.* **wa·ter·fowls** or **wa·ter·fowl** A water bird, especially a bird that swims.
wa·ter·front [wô′tər·frunt′ *or* wot′ər·frunt′] *n.* An area next to a body of water, especially a part of a city that contains docks and other facilities for ships.
water gap A break in a mountain ridge through which a stream flows.
water hole A small pond or pool of water, especially one from which animals drink.
wa·ter·ing can [wô′tər·ing *or* wot′ər·ing] A container having a handle and a long spout, used to water plants.
watering place **1** A source of drinking water. **2** A resort that is near water or mineral springs.
water lily A water plant having large floating leaves and bright, showy flowers.
wa·ter·line [wô′tər·līn′] *n.* **1** The line where the surface of the water meets the side of a ship or boat. **2** One of the lines marked on a ship's hull to measure how far its load lowers it in the water.
wa·ter·logged [wô′tər·lôgd′ *or* wot′ər·logd′] *adj.* Flooded or soaked with water: a *waterlogged* boat; a *waterlogged* sponge.
water main A large pipe for carrying water, especially underground.
wa·ter·man [wô′tər·mən *or* wot′ər·mən] *n., pl.* **wa·ter·men** [wô′tər·mən *or* wot′ər·mən] A person who works on or operates a boat.
wa·ter·mark [wô′tər·märk′ *or* wot′ər·märk′] *n.* **1** A mark showing the height to which water has risen. **2** A faint mark or design impressed on paper as it is being made.
wa·ter·mel·on [wô′tər·mel′ən *or* wot′ər·mel′ən] *n.* A large melon with a thick rind, many seeds, and a very juicy pink pulp.
water mill A mill driven by running water.
water moccasin A large, heavy, dark-colored, poisonous snake of the southern U.S.
water of crystallization Water that is combined with another compound in a crystal and that is necessary for the maintenance of the crystal structure.
water polo A water game in which two teams of swimmers try to pass or carry a large ball across opposite goal lines.
water power Power obtained from flowing or falling water and used to drive machinery.
wa·ter·proof [wô′tər·pro͞of′ *or* wot′ər·pro͞of′] **1** *adj.* Allowing no water to penetrate or enter. **2** *v.* To make waterproof. **3** *n.* A waterproof fabric. —**wa′·ter·proof′ness** *n.*
water rat **1** A rat or ratlike animal that makes its home on the banks of streams or ponds. **2** A muskrat.
wa·ter-re·pel·lent [wô′tər·ri·pel′ənt *or* wot′ər·ri·pel′ənt] *adj.* Having a surface that repels water but that is not completely waterproof.
wa·ter·shed [wô′tər·shed′ *or* wot′ər·shed′] *n.* **1** The region from which a river drains its water. **2** A ridge separating two such regions.
wa·ter-ski [wô′tər·skē′ *or* wot′ər·skē′] *n., v.* **wa·ter-skied, wa·ter-ski·ing** **1** *n.* One of a pair of skilike runners on which one glides over water while being towed by a motorboat. **2** *v.* To travel on water-skis. —**wa′ter-ski′er** *n.*

Waterskiing

water snake Any of several snakes that live in fresh water and are not poisonous.
wa·ter·spout [wô′tər·spout′ *or* wot′ər·spout′] *n.* **1** A whirling storm, often similar to a tornado, occurring over a large body of water and carrying a good deal of water vapor and spray, mostly in its lower part. **2** A pipe that carries off water, as from a roof.
water strid·er [strī′dər] A type of insect having long middle and hind legs adapted for darting over the surface of water.
water table The upper limit of the underground zone that is saturated with water.
wa·ter·tight [wô′tər·tīt′ *or* wot′ər·tīt′] *adj.* **1** Closing so tightly that no water can leak in or out. **2** Having no weak point; foolproof.
water tower **1** A large, elevated tank for storing water. **2** A firefighting apparatus that raises water in a vertical pipe to the upper parts of tall buildings.
water vapor Water in gaseous form.
wa·ter·way [wô′tər·wā′ *or* wot′ər·wā′] *n.* A body of water, as a river, channel, or canal, used as a means of travel.
wa·ter·wheel [wô′tər·(h)wēl′ *or* wot′ər·(h)wēl′] *n.* A wheel turned by moving water, used to provide power.
water wings An inflatable, bouyant device that provides support to a person learning to swim.
wa·ter·works [wô′tər·wûrks′ *or* wot′ər·wûrks′] *n. pl.(often used with a singular verb)* **1** The system that supplies water to a community. **2** A pumping station in such a system.
wa·ter·y [wô′tər·ē *or* wot′ər·ē] *adj.* **1** Of water. **2** Like water; thin or liquid. **3** Brimming with water: *watery* eyes. **4** Diluted with too much water: *watery* tea.
WATS Wide-Area Telephone Service.
watt [wot] *n.* A unit of power equal to about 0.7377 foot-pounds per second, or the electrical equiva-

a	add	**i**	it	**o͝o**	took	**oi**	oil
ā	ace	**ī**	ice	**o͞o**	pool	**ou**	pout
â	care	**o**	odd	**u**	up	**ng**	ring
ä	palm	**ō**	open	**û**	burn	**th**	thin
e	end	**ô**	order	**yo͞o**	fuse	**th**	this
ē	equal					**zh**	vision

ə = {a in *above*, e in *sicken*, i in *possible*, o in *melon*, u in *circus*}

lent of this, the power developed in one ohm by a current of one ampere. ◆ The unit *watt* is named after James *Watt*.

wat·tage [wot′ij] *n.* 1 Electric power as measured in watts. 2 The number of watts of electrical power needed to operate an appliance.

watt-hour [wot′our′] *n.* A unit of energy, most commonly used with electricity, equal to the power of one watt acting for one hour, or 3,600 joules.

wat·tle [wot′(ə)l] *n., v.* **wat·tled, wat·tling** 1 *n.* A frame of rods or twigs woven together to make fences, roofs, and other structures. 2 *v.* To weave or twist, as twigs, into a network. 3 *v.* To form by intertwining twigs. 4 *n.* A fold of flesh, often brightly colored, hanging from the throat or neck of chickens, turkeys, and some reptiles.

wave [wāv] *v.* **waved, wav·ing,** *n.* 1 *v.* To move or cause to move back and forth or with a fluttering motion. 2 *v.* To wave something, especially the hand, as in giving a signal. 3 *n.* The act of waving. 4 *n.* A disturbance consisting of a peak followed by a dip that travels across the surface of a liquid. 5 *n.* Any energy, as light or sound, that exists in the form of pulses or alternations of one kind or another. 6 *n.* A single such pulse or alternation. 7 *n.* Something that seems to travel or pass like a wave: a *wave* of protest; a tropical heat *wave.* 8 *v.* To form into a series of ridges and dips: to *wave* one's hair. 9 *n.* One of a series of wide curves or ridges in the hair.

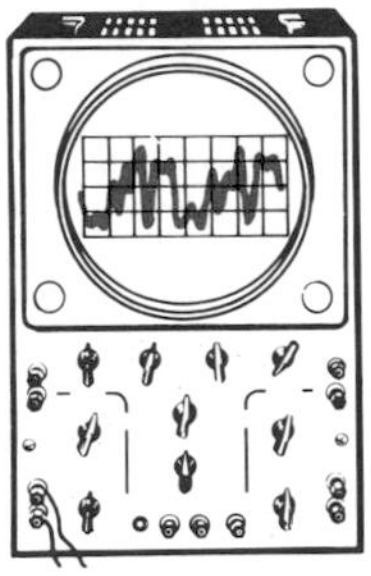

Sound wave from an oboe shown on an oscilloscope

Wave [wāv] *n.* A woman who is a member of the U.S. Navy. ◆ *Wave* is an acronym based on the name *Women Accepted for Volunteer Emergency Service,* a military group organized during World War II.

wave·length [wāv′leng(k)th′] *n.* The distance between corresponding parts of successive waves. —**be on the same wavelength** To share or understand another person's feelings and ideas.

wave·let [wāv′lət] *n.* A small wave; ripple.

wa·ver [wā′vər] *v.* 1 To move one way and the other; sway; flutter. 2 To be uncertain or undecided. 3 To show signs of falling back or giving way; falter.

WAVES Women Accepted for Volunteer Emergency Service (Navy).

wav·y [wā′vē] *adj.* **wav·i·er, wav·i·est** Full of, or like, waves: *wavy* hair; a *wavy* pattern. —**wav′i·ness** *n.*

wax[1] [waks] 1 *n.* Any of various dense, fatty substances occurring in plants and animals and also made artificially. 2 *n.* Beeswax. 3 *n.* A substance like wax, as paraffin, which is used in making candles, polishes, and other items. 4 *v.* To coat or treat with a wax or polish: to *wax* a floor.

wax[2] [waks] *v.* 1 To increase gradually, as in size, brightness, or effect: The moon is *waxing.* 2 To become: to *wax* poetic.

wax bean A kind of string bean having yellow pods.

waxed paper Another term for WAX PAPER.

wax·en [wak′sən] *adj.* 1 Made of wax: *waxen* flowers. 2 Having the whitish or yellowish color of wax: a *waxen* complexion.

wax myrtle A shrub of eastern North America that has small berries coated with a waxlike substance that is used in making sweet-smelling candles.

wax paper Paper that has been treated with wax or paraffin to make it waterproof.

wax·wing [waks′wing′] *n.* A bird having soft, brown feathers except for the wings, which are tipped with red or yellow.

wax·work [waks′wûrk′] *n.* 1 A usually lifesize figure of a person, made of wax. 2 (*pl.*) A place where wax figures of famous or notorious persons are exhibited.

wax·y [wak′sē] *adj.* **wax·i·er, wax·i·est** 1 Like wax, as in color or texture. 2 Of, containing, or covered with wax. —**wax′i·ness** *n.*

way [wā] *n.* 1 A manner or method: We were greeted in a polite *way*; an unusual *way* of doing things. 2 A specific point; a particular: This report needs adjustment in two *ways.* 3 A path, track, or course: The guide knew the *way* through the swamp. 4 Room for passage: Make *way* for the parade. 5 Direction or vicinity: It's over that *way.* 6 Distance or expanse: a long *way* between towns. 7 Route from one place to another: Show me the *way* to your house. 8 Behavior, habits, or practices: the *ways* of vacationers. 9 Desire or will: to have one's own *way.* 10 *informal* Condition, as of health: You're in a fine *way.* —**by the way** In connection with that; incidentally. —**by way of** 1 For the purpose of: to pack a tent *by way of* shelter. 2 On a route through or past: *by way of* the North Pole. —**out of the way** 1 Removed or settled, as an obstacle or problem. 2 Odd or unusual. 3 Wrong; improper. 4 Remote or secluded. —**under way** Moving; making progress: Let's get *under way.* ◆ Use *way,* not *ways,* to refer to distance: It's a long *way* to Chicago.

way·far·er [wā′fâr′ər] *n.* A person who journeys; traveler. —**way′far′ing** *adj., n.*

way·lay [wā′lā′ *or* wā′lā′] *v.* **way·laid, way·lay·ing** 1 To attack from ambush, as in order to rob. 2 To stop to question or speak to.

-ways A suffix meaning: In a (specified) manner, direction, or position, as in *sideways.*

way·side [wā′sīd′] *n.* 1 The side or edge of a road or highway. 2 *adj. use:* a *wayside* inn.

way station A small station between major stops on a route, especially on a railroad line.

way·ward [wā′wərd] *adj.* 1 Insisting on what one wishes; willful; disobedient. 2 Irregular and unsteady; capricious. —**way′ward·ly** *adv.* —**way′·ward·ness** *n.*

way·worn [wā′wôrn′] *adj.* Weary from traveling.

W.B. Weather Bureau.

WbN west by north.

WbS west by south.

w.c. 1 water closet. 2 without charge.

WCTU or **W.C.T.U.** Women's Christian Temperance Union.

wd. 1 wood. 2 word.

WD or **W.D.** War Department.

we [wē] *pron.* The persons speaking or writing; I and one or more others. ◆ A monarch speaking formally or a person writing formally will often use *we* instead of *I* in order to sound more solemn or impersonal: *We* are not amused.

weak [wēk] *adj.* 1 Lacking in strength or effectiveness: to be *weak* after a long illness; a *weak* character; a *weak* protest. 2 Lacking the ability to withstand strain or wear: The bridge collapsed because of *weak* construction. 3 Without the usual strength or force: *weak* coffee; a *weak* heart.

4 Lacking or not strong in something specified: to be *weak* in reading.

weak·en [wē'kən] *v.* To make or become weak or weaker.

weak·fish [wēk'fish'] *n., pl.* **weak·fish** or **weak·fish·es** A food fish found along the Atlantic coastal waters of the U.S.

weak-kneed [wēk'nēd'] *adj.* Lacking courage or determination; timid.

weak·ling [wēk'ling] *n.* A feeble person or animal.

weak·ly [wēk'lē] *adj.* **weak·li·er, weak·li·est,** *adv.* 1 *adj.* Sickly; feeble; weak. 2 *adv.* In a weak or feeble way.

weak-mind·ed [wēk'mīn'did] *adj.* 1 Lacking strength of mind or will. 2 Mentally deficient.

weak·ness [wēk'nis] *n.* 1 The condition or quality of being weak. 2 A fault or flaw: a *weakness* in a foundation. 3 A liking that is hard to resist: a *weakness* for cakes or pies.

weal[1] [wēl] *n.* Welfare or sound condition: the *weal* of the community: seldom used today.

weal[2] [wēl] *n.* A mark on the skin, as from a blow; welt.

wealth [welth] *n.* 1 An abundance of personal property; riches. 2 Anything of value, as products or natural resources: the *wealth* of a nation. 3 An abundance: a *wealth* of golden hair.

wealth·y [wel'thē] *adj.* **wealth·i·er, wealth·i·est** Having wealth; rich.

wean [wēn] *v.* 1 To accustom (a young mammal) to food other than its mother's milk. 2 To cause (someone) gradually to give up a habit or dependence: to *wean* oneself from candy.

weap·on [wep'ən] *n.* 1 Any tool, device, or part of the body used in fighting or killing, as a pistol or the claws of a cat. 2 Anything used for attack or defense: the *weapon* of wit.

wear [wâr] *v.* **wore, worn, wear·ing,** *n.* 1 *v.* To have or carry (a garment or ornament) on the person. 2 *n.* Clothing; apparel: children's *wear*: often used in combination: foot*wear*. 3 *n.* The act of wearing: clothing for formal *wear*. 4 *n.* The condition of being worn: clothing in constant *wear*. 5 *n.* Capability for being used or worn: the *wear* left in a car. 6 *v.* To withstand use or friction: a rug that *wears* well. 7 *v.* To weaken, tire out, or deteriorate by much use: The farmer was *worn* by years of hard work; to *wear* a coat threadbare. 8 *n.* The destructive effect, as of work, use, or time. 9 *v.* To make (a hole or groove) by or as if by rubbing. 10 *v.* To remove material from by friction: to *wear* away rock. 11 *v.* To pass in a dull way: The hours *wore* on. 12 *v.* To exhibit; display: to *wear* a smile. —**wear down** To break down or overcome by repeated effort. —**wear off** To lessen gradually: My headache *wore off*. —**wear out** 1 To wear until no longer suitable for use: to *wear out* one's shoes. 2 To tire out; exhaust: The heat *wore* the players *out*. —**wear'a·ble** *adj.* —**wear'er** *n.*

wear and tear Damage or loss that occurs as a result of ordinary use.

wear·ing [wâr'ing] *adj.* 1 Designed to be worn: *wearing* apparel. 2 Causing fatigue; tiring: a *wearing* experience.

wea·ri·some [wir'ē·səm] *adj.* Causing fatigue; tiresome; tedious. —**wea'ri·some·ly** *adv.*

wea·ry [wir'ē] *adj.* **wea·ri·er, wea·ri·est,** *v.* **wea·ried, wea·ry·ing** 1 *adj.* Tired; fatigued: to be *weary* after work. 2 *adj.* Discontented or bored: *weary* of this job. 3 *adj.* Causing weariness or boredom: a *weary* task; a dull, *weary* lecture. 4 *v.* To make or become weary. —**wea'ri·ly** *adv.* —**wea'ri·ness** *n.*

wea·sel [wē'zəl] *n.* A small, slender animal with brownish fur that preys on smaller animals and birds.

Weasel

weath·er [weth'ər] 1 *n.* The condition of the atmosphere with respect to certain factors, as temperature, moisture, and winds: cold, rainy *weather*. 2 *v.* To expose to the action of the weather. 3 *v.* To undergo changes from exposure to the weather: lumber that has *weathered*. 4 *v.* To pass through successfully: to *weather* a crisis. 5 *adj.* That is toward the wind; windward. 6 *v.* To pass to the windward of. —**under the weather** *informal* Somewhat ill; out of sorts.

weath·er-beat·en [weth'ər·bēt'(ə)n] *adj.* Toughened or worn by exposure to the weather.

weather bureau An office that collects information about weather in order to make predictions, issue storm warnings, and keep records.

weath·er·cock [weth'ər·kok'] *n.* A weather vane shaped like a cock.

weath·er·glass [weth'ər·glas'] *n.* 1 A simple device to show changes in atmospheric pressure. 2 Any barometer.

weath·er·ing [weth'ər·ing] *n.* Changes, especially in rock or soil, brought about by exposure to the weather.

weath·er·man [weth'ər·man'] *n., pl.* **weath·er·men** [weth'ər·men'] A person who reports on and makes predictions about weather conditions.

weath·er·proof [weth'ər·proof'] 1 *adj.* Capable of withstanding exposure to severe weather conditions without being damaged. 2 *v.* To make weatherproof.

weather station A place where observations of the weather are made and recorded daily.

weath·er-strip [weth'ər·strip'] *v.* **weath·er-stripped, weath·er-strip·ping** To seal or fit with weather stripping.

weather stripping A strip of material, as felt, plastic, or metal, that is fitted around the edges of doors and windows to prevent wind and cold air from entering.

weather vane A vane that turns with the wind and shows in which direction it is blowing.

weave [wēv] *v.* **wove** (or **weaved** for def. 10), **wov·en** or **wove** (or **weaved** for def. 10), **weav·ing,** *n.* 1 *v.* To form or produce by interlacing threads, strands, or strips: to *weave* a fabric; to *weave* a

a	add	**i**	it	**o͝o**	took	**oi**	oil
ā	ace	**ī**	ice	**o͞o**	pool	**ou**	pout
â	care	**o**	odd	**u**	up	**ng**	ring
ä	palm	**ō**	open	**û**	burn	**th**	thin
e	end	**ô**	order	**yo͞o**	fuse	**th**	this
ē	equal					**zh**	vision

ə = a in *above*, e in *sicken*, i in *possible*, o in *melon*, u in *circus*

W

basket. **2** *v.* To interlace (threads, grass, or other materials) in weaving something. **3** *v.* To work at weaving, as at a loom. **4** *n.* A particular method or pattern of weaving. **5** *v.* To become woven or interlaced. **6** *v.* To make by combining details or elements: to *weave* a tale. **7** *v.* To combine so as to make a whole: to *weave* ideas together. **8** *v.* To twist into, about, or through something else. **9** *v.* To make (a web), as a spider. **10** *v.* To move in a twisting or zigzag path. **—weav′er** *n.*

weav·er·bird [wē′vər·bûrd′] *n.* Any of various small birds of Africa, southern Asia, and Australia that build nests of interwoven twigs and grasses.

web [web] *n., v.* **webbed, web·bing** **1** *n.* Something woven, as from threads or strips, especially a whole piece of cloth woven or being woven. **2** *n.* A mesh or network, as that woven by a spider: a *web* of cables; a *web* of falsehoods. **3** *n.* A fold of skin connecting the toes of various water birds, frogs, otters, and other animals. **4** *v.* To connect, cover, or surround with a web.

webbed [webd] *adj.* **1** Formed like or having a web. **2** Having the toes united by folds of skin.

web·bing [web′ing] *n.* **1** A woven strip of strong fiber, as that used in upholstery. **2** Any structure or material forming a web.

web-foot·ed [web′fŏŏt′id] *adj.* Having the toes connected by a fold of skin.

wed [wed] *v.* **wed·ded, wed·ding** **1** To marry. **2** To unite; combine.

we'd [wēd] **1** We had. **2** We would. **3** We should.

Wed. Wednesday.

wed·ded [wed′id] *adj.* **1** Married. **2** Joined. **3** United by devotion: to be *wedded* to one's music.

wed·ding [wed′ing] *n.* **1** The ceremony or celebration of a marriage. **2** A special anniversary of a marriage: a golden *wedding*.

Webfooted birds

wedge [wej] *n., v.* **wedged, wedg·ing** **1** *n.* A tapering piece of wood, metal, or other material, that can be forced into a narrow opening to split something apart or secure movable parts. **2** *v.* To split or secure with or as if with a wedge. **3** *n.* Anything shaped like a wedge: a *wedge* of cake. **4** *n.* A small beginning or opening, as for changes or new plans. **5** *v.* To crowd or squeeze (people or things) into a small or confined place.

Wedg·wood [wej′wŏŏd′] *n.* A type of fine English pottery typically decorated with white figures in relief on a blue or green background: a trademark.

wed·lock [wed′lok′] *n.* The condition or relation of being married; matrimony.

Wednes·day [wenz′dē *or* wenz′dā′] *n.* The fourth day of the week. ◆ See WODEN.

wee [wē] *adj.* **we·er, we·est** Very small; tiny.

weed [wēd] **1** *n.* Any useless or unsightly plant, especially one that grows abundantly and tends to crowd out cultivated plants. **2** *v.* To remove weeds from (a garden, lawn, or other area). **3** *v.* To eliminate as useless, inadequate, or harmful: to *weed* out outgrown clothes. **—weed′er** *n.*

weeds [wēdz] *n.pl.* The black clothes worn by people in mourning.

weed·y [wē′dē] *adj.* **weed·i·er, weed·i·est** **1** Full of weeds. **2** Of, like, or characteristic of a weed. **3** Tall and thin; spindly: a *weedy* young man.

week [wēk] *n.* **1** A period of seven days, especially such a period beginning with Sunday. **2** The days or time within a week devoted to work: The office has a 35-hour *week*.

week·day [wēk′dā′] *n.* Any day of the week except Sunday, or except Saturday and Sunday.

week·end [wēk′end′] *n.* Saturday and Sunday, or the time from Friday evening to the following Monday morning.

week·ly [wēk′lē] *adv., adj., n., pl.* **week·lies** **1** *adv.* Once a week. **2** *adj.* Done, occurring, or computed once a week or by the week: a *weekly* wash; a *weekly* wage. **3** *n.* A publication issued once a week.

ween [wēn] *v.* To suppose; guess; fancy: seldom used today.

weep [wēp] *v.* **wept, weep·ing** **1** To show grief or other strong emotion by shedding tears. **2** To shed: to *weep* hot tears. **3** To mourn: The town *wept* for the lost child. **4** To release (a liquid, as sap) slowly; ooze. **—weep′er** *n.*

weep·ing willow [wē′ping] *n.* A willow tree with slim, drooping branches, native to China but widely cultivated.

weep·y [wē′pē] *adj.* **weep·i·er, weep·i·est** **1** Tending to cry easily. **2** Causing tears; pitiful or sentimental. **—weep′i·ly** *adv.* **—weep′i·ness** *n.*

wee·vil [wē′vəl] *n.* Any of various small beetles whose larvae destroy cotton, grain, nuts, and other plants.

weft [weft] *n.* Another name for WOOF.

weigh [wā] *v.* **1** To determine the weight of, as by using a scale. **2** To have as weight: That rock *weighs* a ton. **3** To measure (a substance or an amount) by weight: to *weigh* out five pounds of potatoes. **4** To consider carefully: to *weigh* an offer; to *weigh* one's words. **5** To bend or press down by weight; burden: The load *weighed* down the car. **6** To bear down; be a burden: Cares *weighed* upon one's mind. **7** To have influence or be of importance: A good education will *weigh* in your favor. **8** To raise (an anchor) in preparation for sailing: to *weigh* anchor.

weight [wāt] **1** *n.* The heaviness of a thing; the amount a thing weighs: The *weight* of the package is six pounds. **2** *n.* The force with which a thing presses downward, equal to its mass multiplied by the acceleration of gravity. **3** *n.* A piece of metal of known heaviness used as a standard in weighing on a balance. **4** *v.* To add weight to; make heavier. **5** *n.* A unit or system for measuring weight: troy *weight*; avoirdupois *weight*. **6** *n.* A load or burden. **7** *n.* Something like a load; burden: the *weight* of responsibility. **8** *v.* To put a load or burden on. **9** *n.* Influence or significance: Your ideas carry *weight*.

weight·less [wāt′lis] *adj.* Having no weight: Objects inside a space capsule in orbit are *weightless*. **—weight′less·ly** *adv.* **—weight′less·ness** *n.*

weight·y [wā′tē] *adj.* **weight·i·er, weight·i·est** **1** Of great importance, influence, or significance: *weighty* discussions; *weighty* problems. **2** Difficult to bear; burdensome. **3** Heavy. **—weight′i·ly** *adv.* **—weight′i·ness** *n.*

weir [wir] *n.* **1** A small dam placed in a stream. **2** A fence, as one of stakes, set in a stream in order to trap fishes.

weird [wird] *adj.* **1** Strange in an unearthly or supernatural way; eerie. **2** *informal* Peculiar; odd: a *weird* idea. **—weird′ly** *adv.* **—weird′ness** *n.*

weird·o [wir'dō] *n., pl.* **weird·os** *slang* A very peculiar or bizarre person or thing.

wel·come [wel'kəm] *adj., v.* **wel·comed, wel·com·ing,** *n., interj.* 1 *adj.* Received with joy or gladness: a *welcome* visitor; a *welcome* relief. 2 *v.* To greet gladly or receive with pleasure. 3 *n.* The act of welcoming: a warm *welcome.* 4 *adj.* Under no obligation for anything given, as kindness or gifts: You are *welcome.* 5 *adj.* Freely given the possession or use of something: You're *welcome* to the book. 6 *interj.* An exclamation expressing greeting: *Welcome,* friend. 7 *v.* To accept with calmness, pleasure, or courage: to *welcome* an opinion. **—wear out one's welcome** To impose upon a person so much that one is no longer welcome.

weld [weld] 1 *v.* To unite (pieces of metal) by softening with heat and pressing together. 2 *v.* To be welded or capable of being welded. 3 *n.* A joint or seam formed by welding pieces of metal. 4 *v.* To join closely; unite: The coach *welded* them into a unit. **—weld'er** *n.*

wel·fare [wel'fâr'] *n.* 1 The condition of being healthy, prosperous, and happy; well-being. 2 Organized efforts by a community or group of people to give money and aid to those who are poor and in need. 3 *adj. use*: *welfare* workers.

welfare state A state or community in which the government assumes responsibility for the health and prosperity of its citizens.

wel·kin [wel'kin] *n.* The heavens; sky: seldom used today. **—make the welkin ring** To make a loud, resounding sound.

well[1] [wel] 1 *n.* A hole or shaft dug or drilled into the earth to reach a deposit, as of water, petroleum, or gas. 2 *n.* A natural spring of water. 3 *v.* To rise or pour forth, as water from a spring: Blood *welled* up from the wound. 4 *n.* A container holding a supply of a liquid: a *well* for ink. 5 *n.* A source of continuing supply: a *well* of information. 6 *n.* A vertical opening through the floors of a building: an elevator *well.*

well[2] [wel] *adv., & adj.* **bet·ter, best,** *interj.* 1 *adv.* In a good, proper, favorable, or satisfying way: The team plays *well*; to eat *well.* 2 *adj.* In good health: Are you *well*? 3 *adv.* To a considerable or large extent or degree: *well* over six feet: I knew them *well.* 4 *adv.* Thoroughly; completely: Wash your hands *well.* 5 *adv.* Properly; rightly; fairly: We can't *well* refuse the offer. 6 *adj.* Satisfactory, fortunate, or wise: All is *well*; It is *well* you called early. 7 *interj.* A mild expression, as of surprise, doubt, or relief. 8 *interj.* A word used just to introduce the next remark: *Well,* I'm tired. **—as well** 1 Also; in addition. 2 With equal effect: You might *as well* go. **—as well as** In addition to being: strong *as well as* fast. ◆ See GOOD.

we'll [wēl] 1 We will. 2 We shall.

well-ad·vised [wel'əd·vīzd'] *adj.* Showing good judgment; wise; prudent: You would be *well-advised* to give up smoking.

well-ap·point·ed [wel'ə·poin'tid] *adj.* Well furnished or equipped: a *well-appointed* room.

well-bal·anced [wel'bal'ənst] *adj.* 1 Having the right amount or proportion of everything: a *well-balanced* diet. 2 Sensible; sane.

well-be·haved [wel'bi·hāvd'] *adj.* Showing or characterized by good manners and proper social conduct.

well-be·ing [wel'bē'ing] *n.* The condition of being healthy, prosperous, and happy; welfare.

well·born [wel'bôrn'] *adj.* Of good birth or ancestry; coming from a distinguished family.

well-bred [wel'bred'] *adj.* Polite and refined; having good manners.

well-de·fined [wel'di·fīnd'] *adj.* 1 Clearly and unambiguously stated: *well-defined* regulations. 2 Having distinct boundaries or edges: *well-defined* muscles.

well-done [wel'dun'] *adj.* 1 Done well; properly executed. 2 Thoroughly cooked.

well-fa·vored [wel'fā'vərd] *adj.* Attractive; good-looking. **—well'-fa'vored·ness** *n.*

well-fed [wel'fed'] *adj.* 1 Plump. 2 Properly fed.

well-fixed [wel'fikst'] *adj. informal* Being in a secure financial position; well-off.

well-found·ed [wel'foun'did] *adj.* Based on fact or sound evidence: a *well-founded* theory.

well-groomed [wel'grōōmd'] *adj.* Neat in appearance: a *well-groomed* person.

well-ground·ed [wel'groun'did] *adj.* 1 Thoroughly acquainted with the basic facts and theories in a particular field. 2 Based on sound logic or solid evidence; well-founded.

well-heeled [wel'hēld'] *adj. informal* Wealthy; rich.

well-in·formed [wel'in·fôrmd'] *adj.* 1 Having correct and up-to-date information about a subject. 2 Having wide general knowledge.

well-known [wel'nōn'] *adj.* 1 Widely known: a *well-known* fact. 2 Famous: a *well-known* author.

well-made [wel'mād'] *adj.* Constructed carefully and soundly: a *well-made* toy; a *well-made* plot.

well-man·nered [wel'man'ərd] *adj.* Having good manners; courteous.

well-mean·ing [wel'mē'ning] *adj.* 1 Having good intentions. 2 Done with good intentions.

well-nigh [wel'nī'] *adv.* Very nearly; almost.

well-off [wel'ôf'] *adj.* 1 Being in a good or favorable condition; fortunate. 2 Wealthy.

well-read [wel'red'] *adj.* Having a wide knowledge of books and literature; having read much.

well-rounded [wel'roun'did] *adj.* 1 Informed, skilled, or interested in many different subjects or areas. 2 Made up of or dealing with many different subjects or areas: a *well-rounded* education.

well-spo·ken [wel'spō'kən] *adj.* 1 Speaking effectively or courteously. 2 Expressed well: some *well-spoken* words on a touchy subject.

well·spring [wel'spring'] *n.* 1 The source of a stream or spring; fountainhead. 2 A source of continual supply: a *wellspring* of inspiration.

well-tak·en [wel'tā'kən] *adj.* Proper; justifiable; pertinent; apt: a speech with *well-taken* points.

well-timed [wel'tīmd'] *adj.* Occurring or done at a suitable or fortunate moment; timely.

well-thought-of [wel'thôt'uv' *or* wel'thôt'ov'] *adj.* Having a good reputation; held to be of value.

well-to-do [wel'tə·dōō'] *adj.* Well supplied with material comforts; prosperous; rich.

a	add	**i**	it	**ŏŏ**	took	**oi**	oil		
ā	ace	**ī**	ice	**ōō**	pool	**ou**	pout		
â	care	**o**	odd	**u**	up	**ng**	ring		
ä	palm	**ō**	open	**û**	burn	**th**	thin		
e	end	**ô**	order	**yōō**	fuse	**th**	this		
ē	equal					**zh**	vision		

ə = a in *above*, e in *sicken*, i in *possible*, o in *melon*, u in *circus*

well-wish·er [wel′wish′ər] *n.* A person who wishes health, happiness, or success to another.
well-worn [wel′wôrn′] *adj.* 1 Having been worn or used a lot. 2 Having been used or said too often; trite: a *well-worn* phrase.
Welsh [welsh] 1 *adj.* Of or from Wales. 2 *n.* (**the Welsh**) The people of Wales. 3 *n.* The Celtic language of Wales.
Welsh cor·gi [kôr′gē] A dog native to Wales that has short legs, a long body, and a foxlike head.

Welsh corgi

Welsh·man [welsh′·mən] *n., pl.* **Welsh·men** [welsh′mən] A person born or living in Wales.
Welsh rabbit Melted cheese cooked in cream or milk, often with ale or beer added, and served hot on toast or crackers.
Welsh rarebit Welsh rabbit.
Welsh·wom·an [welsh′wo͝om′ən] *n., pl.* **Welsh·wom·en** [welsh′wim′in] A woman born in or living in Wales.
welt [welt] 1 *n.* A strip of leather or other material that reinforces the seam between the upper part of a shoe and the sole. 2 *v.* To supply with a welt or welts. 3 *n.* A stripe raised on the skin by a blow. 4 *v. informal* To whip so as to raise welts.
wel·ter [wel′tər] 1 *v.* To roll about; wallow. 2 *n.* A rolling movement, as of waves. 3 *v.* To lie or be soaked in some fluid. 4 *n.* A commotion; turmoil. 5 *n.* A large, confused mass; jumble.
wel·ter·weight [wel′tər·wāt′] *n.* A boxer or wrestler who weighs between 136 and 147 pounds.
wen [wen] *n.* A harmless tumor on the skin, often on the face or scalp.
wench [wench] *n.* 1 A young woman or girl: considered humorous or derogatory. 2 A female servant; maid: seldom used today.
wend [wend] *v.* To go or proceed on (one's way).
went [went] Past tense of GO.
wept [wept] Past tense of WEEP.
were [wûr] A form of the verb BE, in the past tense, used with *you, we, they,* and plural nouns. *Were* is also used as the subjunctive with all persons to express wishing or supposing.
we're [wir] We are.
weren't [wûrnt *or* wûr′ənt] Were not.
were·wolf [wir′wo͝olf′ *or* wâr′wo͝olf′] *n., pl.* **were·wolves** [wir′wo͝olvz′ *or* wâr′wo͝olvz′] In folk tales, a person who has been changed, or who is able to change, into a wolf.
wert [wûrt] An old form of WERE, used with *thou.*
Wes·ley·an [wes′lē·ən *or* wez′lē·ən] 1 *n.* A follower of the church founded by John Wesley; Methodist. 2 Of or having to do with John Wesley or the Methodist Church.
west [west] 1 *n.* The direction opposite east; one of the four main points of the compass. If you face the sun at sunset, you are facing west. 2 *adj.* To, toward, or in the west; western. 3 *adj.* Coming from the west: the *west* wind. 4 *adv.* In or toward the west; westward. 5 *n.* Any place or region in the western part of a specified area or lying west of a specified point. **—the West** 1 The countries west of Asia and Turkey, especially the countries of North America, South America, and Europe; Occident. 2 The Western Hemisphere. 3 The western part of the U.S., especially the part west of the Mississippi River. **—west of** Farther west than: Chicago is *west of* New York.

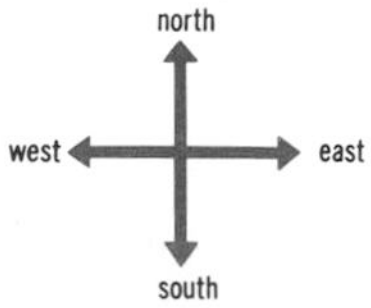

west·bound [west′bound′] *adj.* Heading west: a *westbound* airliner.
west by north The direction or compass point midway between west and west-northwest; 11 degrees 15 minutes north of due west.
west by south The direction or compass point midway between west and west-southwest; 11 degrees 15 minutes south of due west.
wes·ter [wes′tər] 1 *v.* To turn, move, or shift westward. 2 *n.* A wind or storm from the west.
west·er·ly [wes′tər·lē] *adj., adv., n., pl.* **west·er·lies** 1 *adj.* In or of the west. 2 *adj., adv.* Toward or from the west. 3 *n.* A strong wind or storm blowing in from the west.
west·ern [wes′tərn] 1 *adj.* Of, to, or in the west. 2 *adj.* From the west: a *western* breeze. 3 *adj.* (*often written* **Western**) Of, referring to, or like the West. 4 *n.* A movie, story, radio show, or TV program about the life of cowhands or pioneer days in the western U.S.
west·ern·er [wes′tər·nər] *n.* 1 A person born or living in the west. 2 (*usually written* **Westerner**) A person born or living in the West, especially in the western U.S.
west·ern·ize [wes′tər·nīz′] *v.* **west·ern·ized, west·ern·iz·ing** To adopt or cause to adopt the ways or characteristics of Europe and North America: Attempts have been made to *westernize* the Japanese diet.
west·ern·most [wes′tərn·mōst′] *adj.* Farthest west.
Western Samoan 1 Of or from Western Samoa. 2 A person born in or a citizen of Western Samoa.
West German 1 Of or from West Germany. 2 A person born in or a citizen of West Germany.
West Indian 1 Of or from the West Indies. 2 A person born or living in the West Indies.
West·min·ster Abbey [west′min′stər] A large church in London where British kings and queens are crowned and many notable people are buried.
west-northwest [west′nôrth′west′] 1 *n.* The direction or compass point midway between west and northwest; 22 degrees 30 minutes north of due west. 2 *adj.* To, toward, or in the west-northwest. 3 *adv.* In or toward the west-northwest.
west-southwest [west′south′west′] 1 *n.* The direction or compass point midway between west and southwest; 22 degrees 30 minutes south of due west. 2 *adj.* To, toward, or in the west-southwest. 3 *adv.* In or toward the west-southwest.
west·ward [west′wərd] 1 *adj., adv.* Toward the west. 2 *n.* A westward direction or location.
west·wards [west′wərdz] *adv.* Westward.
wet [wet] *adj.* **wet·ter, wet·test,** *v.* **wet** or **wet·ted, wet·ting,** *n.* 1 *adj.* Covered, soaked, or moist with water or another liquid: *wet* laundry. 2 *v.* To make or become wet: to *wet* a washcloth; The doll *wets.* 3 *adj.* Not yet dry: *wet* paint. 4 *n.* Water or moisture. 5 *adj.* Rainy: the *wet* season. 6 *n.* Rainy weather: I caught cold out in the *wet.* 7 *adj. informal* Permitting the sale of alcoholic beverages: a *wet* county. **—wet′ly** *adv.* **—wet′ness** *n.*

wet blanket *informal* A person or thing that spoils people's fun or enthusiasm.
wet cell A voltaic cell in which the electrolyte is in liquid form.
wet suit A close-fitting suit, as of rubber, worn by divers and swimmers to hold in their body heat.
we've [wēv] We have.
whack [(h)wak] *informal* **1** *v.* To hit with a sharp, loud blow. **2** *n.* A sharp blow that makes a loud noise, or the noise itself. **3** *n.* A try. **—out of whack** *informal* Not working properly.
whack·y [(h)wak'ē] *adj.* **whack·i·er, whack·i·est** Another spelling of WACKY. **—whack'i·ly** *adv.* **—whack'i·ness** *n.*
whale[1] [(h)wāl] *n., v.* **whaled, whal·ing** **1** *n.* A mammal that lives in the ocean and resembles a gigantic fish. Whales have a thick layer of blubber under a smooth skin, and this blubber is a source of oil. **2** *v.* To hunt for whales.

Whale

whale[2] [(h)wāl] *v.* **whaled, whal·ing** *informal* To strike or beat; thrash.
whale·boat [(h)wāl'bōt'] *n.* A long, deep rowboat, sharp at both ends, first used in whaling but now used as a coast-guard boat for rescue.
whale·bone [(h)wāl'bōn'] *n.* **1** The horny, elastic substance hanging from the upper jaw of toothless whales in long, narrow plates with frayed, bristly inner edges. These bristly plates strain out of the water the tiny sea animals that such whales eat. **2** A strip of whalebone, once used to stiffen corsets and other items.
whal·er [(h)wā'lər] *n.* A person employed or a ship used in whaling.
whal·ing [(h)wā'ling] *n.* The industry of hunting, catching, and killing whales.
wharf [(h)wôrf] *n., pl.* **wharves** [(h)wôrvz] or **wharfs** A structure, usually a platform, built along or out from a shore, alongside which ships or boats may lie to load or unload.
wharf·age [(h)wôr'fij] *n.* **1** The use of a wharf to moor, load, or unload a ship or to store cargo. **2** The fee for using a wharf.
what [(h)wot *or* (h)wut] **1** *pron.* Which thing, things, action, condition, type, or class: I don't know *what* to do; *What* are you holding in your hand? **2** *adj.* Which or which type of: *What* refreshments shall we bring? **3** *pron.* That or those which: I know *what* I want to buy. **4** *pron.* Anything that; whatever: Wear *what* you choose. **5** *adj.* Whatever or whichever; any that: Choose *what* story you would like to hear. **6** *conj. informal* That: I do not doubt but *what* they will come. **7** *interj.* An exclamation of surprise, annoyance, or disbelief: *What*! They didn't come? **8** *adv.* In which specific way: *What* does it matter if we take a later train? **9** *pron., adj.* How much: *What* did it cost?; *What* difference does it make? **10** *adj.* How great or surprising: *What* a shame! *What* talent! **11** *adv.* In part; partly: *What* with the heat and *what* with the noise, we couldn't sleep. **—and what not** And other things that need not be mentioned. **—what for** For what reason; why: *What* did you do that *for*? **—what if** What would happen if; suppose that. **—what's what** *informal* The real situation or state of affairs. ◆ Do not use *what* to mean *that*: The book *that* [not *what*] I told you about.
what·e'er [(h)wot'âr' *or* (h)wut'âr'] *pron., adj.* Whatever: used mostly in poems.
what·ev·er [(h)wot'ev'ər *or* (h)wut'ev'ər] **1** *pron.* Anything that or all that: Do *whatever* you can. **2** *adj.* Any or all: *Whatever* games they play, they win. **3** *pron.* No matter what: *Whatever* happens, don't be afraid. **4** *pron. informal* What: used in questions for added emphasis: *Whatever* is the matter? **5** *adj.* Of any type, character, or kind: to have no plans *whatever*.
what·not [(h)wot'not' *or* (h)wut'not'] *n.* A set of shelves to hold ornaments, figurines, and other small items.
what's [(h)wots *or* (h)wuts] What is.
what·so·ev·er [(h)wot'sō·ev'ər *or* (h)wut'sō·ev'ər] *pron., adj.* Whatever.
wheal [(h)wēl] *n.* **1** A ridge raised on the skin by a lashing blow; welt. **2** A small, itching swelling on the skin.
wheat [(h)wēt] *n.* **1** The grain of a cereal plant, out of which flour is made. **2** The plant bearing this grain on dense spikes at the top.
wheat·en [(h)wēt'(ə)n] *adj.* Of, having to do with, or made of wheat.
wheat germ The nutritious embryo of wheat grains, often separated out before milling and used as a food supplement.
whee·dle [(h)wēd'(ə)l] *v.* **whee·dled, whee·dling** **1** To coax or persuade by flattering in a sweet and gentle way: We *wheedled* them into staying. **2** To obtain by wheedling: They managed to *wheedle* the information out of me. **—whee'dler** *n.*
wheel [(h)wēl] **1** *n.* A circular framework or disk that is attached to a central axle, on which it turns. **2** *v.* To turn on or as if on an axis; rotate, revolve, or pivot: I *wheeled* around and went back. **3** *n.* Anything round or going around like a wheel. **4** *v.* To move on wheels or in a wheeled vehicle: to *wheel* a baby in a carriage. **5** *n.* Something having a wheel as its distinctive feature, as a steering wheel or spinning wheel. **6** *n. informal* A bicycle. **7** *n.* (*pl.*) The forces that direct motion or control activity: the *wheels* of industry. **—at the wheel** **1** Driving or steering a car, boat, or other conveyance. **2** In control; in charge.
wheel·bar·row [(h)wēl'bar'ō] *n.* A boxlike vehicle ordinarily having one wheel and two handles, used for moving small loads.
wheel·base [(h)wēl'bās'] *n.* The distance in inches between the central points of the front and rear axles of an automobile, truck, or other vehicle.
wheel·chair or **wheel chair** [(h)wēl'châr'] *n.* A chair mounted on large wheels, for the use of sick or injured people.

a	add	**i**	it	**o͝o**	took	**oi**	oil
ā	ace	**ī**	ice	**o͞o**	pool	**ou**	pout
â	care	**o**	odd	**u**	up	**ng**	ring
ä	palm	**ō**	open	**û**	burn	**th**	thin
e	end	**ô**	order	**yo͞o**	fuse	**t͟h**	this
ē	equal					**zh**	vision

ə = a in *above*, e in *sicken*, i in *possible*, o in *melon*, u in *circus*

W

wheel·house [(h)wēl′hous′] *n.* An enclosure on a ship containing the steering wheel.

wheel·wright [(h)wēl′rīt′] *n.* A person who makes or repairs wheels, carriages, and wagons.

wheeze [(h)wēz] *v.* **wheezed, wheez·ing,** *n.* 1 *v.* To breathe hard with a husky, whistling sound, as with a chest cold. 2 *n.* A wheezing sound. 3 *v.* To make such a sound. 4 *n. informal* A joke, especially one that is old or widely known. —**wheez′er** *n.*

wheez·y [(h)wē′zē] *adj.* **wheez·i·er, wheez·i·est** Wheezing or making a wheezing sound: a *wheezy* laugh. —**wheez′i·ly** *adv.* —**wheez′i·ness** *n.*

whelk [(h)welk] *n.* A large sea mollusk with a spiral shell. One kind of whelk is edible.

whelm [(h)welm] *v.* To overwhelm.

whelp [(h)welp] 1 *n.* One of the young of a dog, wolf, lion, or other beast; puppy or cub. 2 *v.* To give birth to (young).

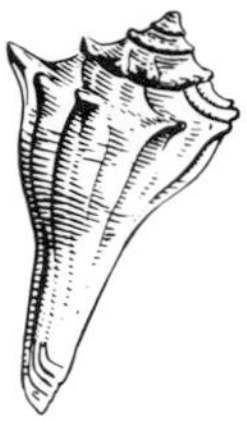
Whelk

when [(h)wen] 1 *adv., conj.* At what or which time: *When* did you arrive?. 2 *pron.* What or which time: Until *when* will the meeting last? 3 *conj.* At which: the time *when* dinner is served. 4 *conj.* After which; and then: We had just eaten *when* you called. 5 *conj.* As soon as: I laughed *when* I heard the joke. 6 *conj.* Whenever: We play inside *when* it rains. 7 *conj.* During or at the time that; while: *when* you were a baby. 8 *conj.* Although: The children walk *when* they might ride. 9 *conj.* Considering that; if: How can I go *when* I have no money? ◆ Do not use *is when* for *means that* in writing a definition (as in "S.R.O. is when all the tickets are sold and there is standing room only").

whence [(h)wens] 1 *adv., conj.* From what place, source, or cause: *Whence* does this stranger come? 2 *conj.* From or out of which place, source, or cause: Find the place *whence* these sounds arise.

when·e'er [(h)wen′âr′] *adv., conj.* Whenever: used mostly in poems.

when·ev·er [(h)wen′ev′ər] 1 *adv.* When: used for emphasis: *Whenever* will this speech end? 2 *conj.* At whatever time: We'll begin *whenever* you're ready. 3 *conj.* Every time: It hurts *whenever* I yawn.

when·so·ev·er [(h)wen′sō·ev′ər] *adv., conj.* At whatever time; whenever: seldom used today.

where [(h)wâr] 1 *adv.* At or in what place: *Where* is my book? 2 *conj.* At which place: Let's go home *where* we can relax. 3 *adv., conj.* To what place: *Where* are you going? 4 *adv.* From what place, source, or cause: *Where* did you get that idea? 5 *pron.* What place: *Where* did you come from? 6 *conj.* The place in which: The bear passed near *where* we were parked. 7 *adv.* At, in, or to which: The place *where* it happened is the place *where* we are going. 8 *conj.* To, at, or in the place to which or in which: Put it *where* I told you to. 9 *adv.* In what way or respect; how: *Where* does it concern us? 10 *conj.* With the condition that: D = VT *where* D is distance, V is velocity, and T is time. ◆ In writing, do not use *where* in place of *that* (as in "I read where taxes will increase next year").

where·a·bouts [(h)wâr′ə·bouts′] 1 *n.pl.* (*often used with singular verb*) The place where a person or thing is: Their present *whereabouts* is unknown. 2 *adv.* Near or at what place; about where.

where·as [(h)wâr′az′] *conj.* 1 Because of the fact that; since: *Whereas* everyone helped with dinner, it was hardly any work. 2 And on the other hand; while: Heat causes metals to expand, *whereas* cold causes them to contract.

where·at [(h)wâr′at′] 1 *conj.* At which or for which reason. 2 *adv.* At what: *Whereat* are you angry? ◆ This word is seldom used today.

where·by [(h)wâr′bī′] *adv., conj.* By means of which; through which: a treaty *whereby* both nations agreed to a common defense.

where·fore [(h)wâr′fôr′] 1 *adv.* For what reason; why: seldom used today: *Wherefore* do you doubt me? 2 *conj.* For which reason; therefore: seldom used today. 3 *n.* A cause or reason: all the whys and *wherefores* of the verdict.

where·from [(h)wâr′frum′ *or* (h)wâr′from′] *conj.* From which: seldom used today.

where·in [(h)wâr′in′] *adv., conj.* 1 In what particular or regard: *Wherein* is the error? 2 In which: a home *wherein* joy dwells.

where·of [(h)wâr′uv′ *or* (h)wâr′ov′] *adv., conj.* Of or about what, which, or whom: They seem to know *whereof* they speak.

where·on [(h)wâr′on′] *adv., conj.* On what or on which: seldom used today.

where·so·ev·er [(h)wâr′sō·ev′ər] *adv., conj.* In or to whatever place; wherever: seldom used today: *Wheresoever* you go, I will follow.

where·to [(h)wâr′to͞o′] 1 *adv.* To what place or end: *Whereto* is this leading? 2 *conj.* To which or to whom: the place *whereto* you hasten. ◆ This word is seldom used today.

where·up·on [(h)wâr′ə·pon′] 1 *conj.* At which; after which: The family finished dinner, *whereupon* the children cleared the table. 2 *adv.* Upon what or which; whereon: seldom used today.

wher·ev·er [(h)wâr′ev′ər] 1 *conj.* In, at, or to whatever place: Sit *wherever* you like. 2 *adv. informal* Where: used in questions for added emphasis: *Wherever* did you find that book?

where·with [(h)wâr′with′ *or* (h)wâr′with′] *conj., adv.* With which or with what: seldom used today.

where·with·al [*n.* (h)wâr′with·ôl′, *adv.* (h)wâr′with·ôl′] 1 *n.* Whatever is needed to do a certain thing, especially the necessary money: Do they have the *wherewithal* to go on vacation? 2 *adv.* With which or with what: no longer used.

wher·ry [(h)wer′ē] *n., pl.* **wher·ries** A light, fast rowboat.

whet [(h)wet] *v.* **whet·ted, whet·ting,** *n.* 1 *v.* To sharpen, as a knife or tool, by rubbing. 2 *n.* The act of whetting. 3 *v.* To make more keen or eager: to *whet* one's appetite.

wheth·er [(h)weth′ər] *conj.* 1 If it is true or probable that: Tell me *whether* or not you are going. 2 Either: *Whether* by luck or hard work, the plan will succeed. 3 In either case if: *Whether* it rains or snows, the roads become slippery. ◆ Omit the unecessary *as to* from *as to whether.* ◆ See IF.

whet·stone [(h)wet′stōn′] *n.* A stone on which to sharpen knives, axes, and other edged tools.

whew [(h)wo͞o *or* (h)wyo͞o] *interj.* A word that expresses amazement, relief, discomfort, or other reaction.

whey [(h)wā] *n.* The clear, watery liquid left when the curd is separated from milk, as in making cheese.

which [(h)wich] 1 *adj., pron.* What one or ones out of a number of things or people: *Which* song is your favorite? **2** *pron.* The one or those ones that: You may have several, so choose *which* you prefer. **3** *pron.* That: the song *which* we sang. **4** *pron.* The thing or things just mentioned: a song with *which* I am familiar; The party, which was held outdoors, was fun. ◆ *Which* refers to things, *who* to people, and *that* to either people or things.

which·ev·er [(h)wich′ev′ər] **1** *pron.* Any one or ones that: Select three colors, *whichever* you prefer. **2** *adj.* Any: Wear *whichever* outfit you choose. **3** *adj.* No matter which: *Whichever* route you take, you'll have to cross the river.

which·so·ev·er [(h)wich′sō·ev′ər] *pron., adj.* Whichever: seldom used today.

whiff [(h)wif] **1** *n.* A slight puff, as of air or smoke. **2** *n.* A slight smell borne on a puff of air. **3** *v.* To blow, move, or sniff in whiffs.

whif·fle·tree [(h)wif′əl·trē′] *n.* A crossbar in front of a wagon, to which the ends of the traces of a harness are fastened.

Whig [(h)wig] *n.* **1** A member of an old British political party, opposed to the Tories and later known as the **Liberal Party.** **2** An American colonist who supported the Revolutionary War against England. **3** A member of a political party in the U.S. during the middle 1800's that was formed to oppose the Democratic Party.

while [(h)wīl] *n., v.* **whiled, whil·ing,** *conj.* **1** *n.* Any period of time, especially a short period: Rest a *while.* **2** *v.* To cause (time) to pass lightly and pleasantly: to *while* away a summer's afternoon. **3** *conj.* During the time that; as long as: *While* I was in school, I wore glasses. **4** *conj.* Although: *While* I am certainly able to go, I don't choose to. **5** *conj.* Whereas: This tree is short, *while* that one is tall: *While* is widely used with this meaning, although in traditional usage *whereas* is preferred. **—the while** At the same time. **—worth one's while** Worth time, effort, trouble, or expense.

whi·lom [(h)wī′ləm] **1** *adj.* Former: Our *whilom* friends turned against us. **2** *adv.* Formerly. ◆ This word is seldom used today.

whilst [(h)wīlst] *conj. British* While.

whim [(h)wim] *n.* A sudden notion, desire, or fancy having no special cause.

whim·per [(h)wim′pər] **1** *v.* To cry with low, mournful, broken sounds: The abandoned puppy *whimpered* all night. **2** *n.* A low, broken, whining cry. **—whimp′er·er** *n.*

whim·sey [(h)wim′zē] *n., pl.* **whim·seys** Another spelling of WHIMSY.

whim·si·cal [(h)wim′zi·kəl] *adj.* **1** Full of whims, caprices, curious ideas, or fanciful notions. **2** Odd, quaint, or fanciful, often in an amusing way. **—whim′si·cal·ly** *adv.*

whim·si·cal·i·ty [(h)wim′zi·kal′ə·tē] *n., pl.* **whim·si·cal·i·ties** **1** The quality of being whimsical. **2** A whimsical idea or act.

whim·sy [(h)wim′zē] *n., pl.* **whim·sies** **1** A sudden, fanciful or curious notion or desire. **2** Quaint, fanciful humor, as in a story.

whine [(h)wīn] *v.* **whined, whin·ing,** *n.* **1** *v.* To make a low, wailing sound or cry. **2** *v.* To complain, beg, or plead in a tiresome or childish way. **3** *n.* The act or sound of whining. **—whin′er** *n.*

whin·ny [(h)win′ē] *n., pl.* **whin·nies,** *v.* **whin·nied, whin·ny·ing** **1** *n.* A gentle neigh made by a horse. **2** *v.* To neigh in a low or gentle way.

whip [(h)wip] *n., v.* **whipped** or **whipt, whip·ping** **1** *n.* An instrument for striking or beating, consisting of a lash attached to a handle. **2** *v.* To strike with or as if with a whip; beat. **3** *v. U.S. informal* To defeat. **4** *n.* A stroke, blow, or lashing motion made with or as if with a whip. **5** *n.* A leader in a legislature who directs other members of a party. **6** *v.* To move or pull quickly and suddenly: to *whip* out a revolver. **7** *v.* To thrash about: pennants *whipping* in the wind. **8** *v.* To beat to a froth: to *whip* egg whites. **9** *n.* A dessert containing cream or egg whites beaten to a froth: apricot *whip.*

whip·cord [(h)wip′kôrd′] *n.* **1** A strong, braided or twisted cord, used especially to make whips. **2** A tough cloth that has a diagonally ribbed surface.

whip hand The controlling or dominating position; advantage: She has the *whip hand* in these negotiations.

whip·lash [(h)wip′lash′] *n.* **1** The lash of a whip. **2** An injury to the neck that is a result of a sudden jerk of the head backward or forward. Whiplash can happen to a person in a vehicle that is struck from the rear or front.

whip·per·snap·per [(h)wip′ər·snap′ər] *n.* A person, especially a young one, who thinks highly of himself or herself and shows disrespect for older or more important people.

whip·pet [(h)wip′it] *n.* A swift breed of dog very much like a small greyhound, used in racing.

Whippet

whip·ping [(h)wip′ing] *n.* A beating with or as if with a whip.

whip·ple·tree [(h)wip′əl·trē′] *n.* Another spelling of WHIFFLETREE.

whip·poor·will [(h)wip′ər·wil′] *n.* A small bird of North America that is active at night and gives a call which sounds like its name.

whipt [(h)wipt] A past tense and past participle of WHIP.

whir [(h)wûr] *v.* **whirred, whir·ring,** *n.* **1** *v.* To fly, move, or whirl with a hum or buzz: The engine, idling, *whirred* softly. **2** *n.* Such a sound: the *whir* of a bird's wings.

whirl [(h)wûrl] **1** *v.* To turn very fast with a circular motion; spin rapidly: The cowboy *whirled* the lasso. **2** *v.* To carry along with a revolving motion: The wind *whirled* the dust into the air. **3** *n.* A turning motion: the *whirl* of propellers. **4** *n.* Something whirling, as a cloud of dust. **5** *v.* To move or go swiftly: The bicycles *whirled* past. **6** *v.* To have the feeling of spinning: My mind *whirls* when I think of outer space. **7** *n.* A short drive or run; spin. **8** *n.* A giddy or confused condition: My head was in a *whirl.* **9** *n.* A rapid series, as of events or parties. **10** *n. informal* A try.

a	add	**i**	it	**o͝o**	took	**oi**	oil
ā	ace	**ī**	ice	**o͞o**	pool	**ou**	pout
â	care	**o**	odd	**u**	up	**ng**	ring
ä	palm	**ō**	open	**û**	burn	**th**	thin
e	end	**ô**	order	**yo͞o**	fuse	**th**	this
ē	equal					**zh**	vision

ə = a in *above*, e in *sicken*, i in *possible*, o in *melon*, u in *circus*

W

whirl·i·gig [(h)wûr′lə·gig′] *n.* 1 A toy that spins, as a top. 2 A merry-go-round. 3 Something that is always whirling or changing. 4 A whirling motion.

Whirligig

whirl·pool [(h)wûrl′·pōōl′] *n.* A rapidly whirling current of water, usually spiraling in toward a depressed center and tending to drag things down with it.

whirl·wind [(h)wûrl′wind′] *n.* A funnel-shaped column of air whirling rapidly, with an upward spiral motion.

whirr [(h)wûr] *v., n.* Another spelling of WHIR.

whish [(h)wish] 1 *v.* To move or cause to move with a soft, hissing sound, as of rushing air. 2 *n.* A soft, hissing sound.

whisk [(h)wisk] 1 *v.* To sweep or brush with light motions: to *whisk* away flies. 2 *v.* To move quickly and softly: The snake *whisked* into the grass. 3 *n.* A light, sweeping motion: a *whisk* of a horse's tail. 4 *n.* A whisk broom. 5 *n.* A small wire instrument used in cooking for whipping cream, eggs, and other foods to a froth.

whisk broom A small, short-handled broom for brushing clothing, furniture, and other items.

whisk·er [(h)wis′kər] *n.* 1 (*pl.*) The hair that grows on the sides of a person's face. 2 A single hair in a person's beard. 3 One of the long, stiff hairs on the sides of the mouth of cats, rats, and other animals. —**whisk′ered** *adj.*

whis·key or **whis·ky** [(h)wis′kē] *n., pl.* **whis·kies** or **whis·keys** An alcoholic liquor made by distilling certain fermented grains, as rye, barley, or corn.

whis·per [(h)wis′pər] 1 *v.* To speak, say, or tell in a soft, low tone. 2 *n.* The act of whispering. 3 *n.* A soft, low voice, tone, sound, or utterance. 4 *v.* To tell privately, as a secret or rumor. 5 *n.* A hint, rumor, or suggestion: not a *whisper* of scandal. 6 *v.* To murmur or rustle: The waves *whispered* on the sand. 7 *n.* A low, rustling sound; murmur. —**whis′per·er** *n.*

whist [(h)wist] *n.* A card game for two pairs of partners. It was the forerunner of bridge.

whis·tle [(h)wis′(ə)l] *v.* **whis·tled, whis·tling,** *n.* 1 *v.* To make a shrill, piping sound by forcing the breath through the teeth or through pursed lips. 2 *n.* The act of whistling. 3 *v.* To produce (a tune or melody) by whistling. 4 *n.* A device for producing a shrill tone by forcing air or steam through a pipe or tube with a narrow opening. 5 *v.* To blow or sound a whistle. 6 *v.* To move with a whistling sound: The wind *whistled* through the cracked window. 7 *n.* Any whistling sound: the *whistle* of a boiling kettle. —**whis′tler** *n.*

whit [(h)wit] *n.* The least or slightest bit: I was not one *whit* ashamed.

white [(h)wīt] *n., adj.* **whit·er, whit·est,** *v.* **whit·ed, whit·ing** 1 *n.* The opposite of black; the lightest of all colors. White is the color of the margins on this page. 2 *adj.* Having the color white. 3 *v.* To make white; whiten or bleach. 4 *n.* A white paint or pigment. 5 *n.* (*sometimes pl.*) White clothes: Nurses wear *white*; a sailor's summer *whites.* 6 *n.* The white or light-colored part, as that of an egg or the eye. 7 *adj.* Light in color: the *white* meat of a turkey. 8 *adj.* Having a light-colored skin, as a Caucasian. 9 *n.* A person having light-colored skin; Caucasian. 10 *adj.* Pale; bloodless: to turn *white* with terror. 11 *adj.* Silvery, as with age: *white* hair. —**white′ness** *n.*

white ant Another name for TERMITE.

white blood cell Another term for LEUKOCYTE.

white·cap [(h)wīt′kap′] *n.* A wave with a crest of foam.

white-col·lar [(h)wīt′kol′ər] *adj.* Of, doing, or having to do with jobs that call for relatively formal dress, as in offices, rather than manual work clothes or uniforms.

white corpuscle Another term for LEUKOCYTE.

white dwarf Any of a class of very dense, faint stars that can be as small as the earth.

white elephant A possession that is of little use and is expensive or bothersome to keep, store, or take care of.

white feather A mark of cowardice.

white·fish [(h)wīt′fish′] *n., pl.* **white·fish** or **white·fish·es** A fish with whitish or silvery sides, found in lakes, and eaten as food.

white flag A white flag or cloth shown as a sign of truce or surrender.

white gold An alloy of gold and a white metal. White gold looks like platinum.

white heat 1 The temperature at which a substance glows white-hot. 2 A state of intense activity or excitement; fervor.

white-hot [(h)wīt′hot′] *adj.* 1 So hot that it gives off a bright, white light: *white-hot* metal. 2 Full of fervor or excitement; zealous; fervid.

White House, the 1 The official residence of the President of the United States, in Washington, D.C. 2 The executive branch of the United States government.

white knight A rescuer, especially a corporation that saves another company from an unwanted takeover attempt.

white lie An unimportant lie, often told in order to be polite or kind.

white matter The portion of the brain and spinal cord made up chiefly of nerve fibers.

whit·en [(h)wīt′(ə)n] *v.* To make or become white; bleach.

white oak 1 A large oak tree of eastern North America having leaves with rounded lobes. 2 The strong, light-colored wood of this tree.

white paper An official government report on a subject.

white pepper A hot seasoning prepared by grinding the dried, hulled, unripe berries of the pepper plant.

white pine 1 A pine tree of eastern North America that has five needles to a cluster and brown, slender cones. 2 The wood of this tree.

white-tailed deer [(h)wīt′tāld′] A deer of North America having a reddish-brown summer coat and a bushy tail that is white on the undersurface.

white tie 1 A white bow tie that is worn with men's most formal evening clothes. 2 Men's most formal evening clothes.

white·wall [(h)wīt′wôl′] *n.* An automobile tire that has a wide white stripe on its outer side.

white·wash [(h)wīt′wäsh′ *or* (h)wīt′wôsh′] 1 *n.* A mixture of lime and water used for whitening walls, fences, and other structures. 2 *v.* To coat with whitewash. 3 *v.* To cover up, hide, or gloss over the bad things about: to *whitewash* a scandal. **4** *n.* A covering up of mistakes or faults. **5** *n.* Something that covers up mistakes or faults. **6** *v. informal* In sports, to defeat (an opponent) without allowing the opponent to score.

whith·er [(h)wi*th*′ər] *adv., conj.* To what or which place; where: used mostly in poems.

whit·ing[1] [(h)wīt′ing] *n.* Any of various fishes found in the ocean and used for food.

whit·ing[2] [(h)wīt′ing] *n.* A pure white, powdered chalk, used in making whitewash, putty, and silver polish.

whit·ish [(h)wīt′ish] *adj.* Somewhat white.

Whit·sun·day [(h)wit′sun′dē *or* (h)wit′sən·dā′] *n.* The seventh Sunday after Easter; Pentecost.

Whit·sun·tide [(h)wit′sən·tīd′] *n.* The week that begins with Whitsunday, especially the first three days.

whit·tle [(h)wit′(ə)l] *v.* **whit·tled, whit·tling** **1** To cut or shave bits from (wood or a stick). **2** To make by whittling: to *whittle* a toy horse. **3** To reduce gradually: to *whittle* down taxes.

whiz or **whizz** [(h)wiz] *v.* **whizzed, whiz·zing,** *n., pl.* **whiz·zes** **1** *v.* To make a hissing or humming sound while passing through the air. **2** *n.* A whizzing sound. **3** *v.* To move or pass with such a sound. **4** *n. slang* A skillful person; expert.

who [ho͞o] *pron.* **1** Which or what person or persons: *Who* is coming to the party?; I don't know *who* the author is. **2** That: The neighbor *who* has the big dog is nice. **3** Whoever: *Who* delays, pays. ◆ *Who* is often used in place of *whom*: I saw him there. *Who* did you see? But be sure to use *whom* with prepositions (as in *to whom*).

WHO World Health Organization.

whoa [(h)wō] *interj.* Stop! Stand still! ◆ This word is used as a command to a horse.

who'd [ho͞od] **1** Who would. **2** Who had.

who·ev·er [ho͞o·ev′ər] *pron.* **1** Any person who: *Whoever* wants a cookie may have one. **2** No matter who: *Whoever* comes, don't let anyone in. **3** Who: used in questions for added emphasis: *Whoever* is making all that noise?

whole [hōl] **1** *adj.* Having all parts or components; complete: I have a *whole* set of Shakespeare's plays. **2** *n.* All of the parts making up a thing: The *whole* of my check was spent on a vacation. **3** *adj.* With no part left out or left over; entire: to spend the *whole* night pacing the floor. **4** *n.* An organization of parts that make a complete thing; system: The players in a string quartet make up a *whole*. **5** *adj.* Not broken; intact: not a *whole* cup and saucer in the house. **6** *adj.* Not divided or cut into pieces. **7** *adj.* Not injured or hurt; sound of body. **8** *adj.* Being an integer, not a fraction. **—on the whole** Taking everything into consideration. **—whole′ness** *n.*

whole·heart·ed [hōl′här′tid] *adj.* Earnest; hearty: my *wholehearted* support. **—whole′heart′ed·ly** *adv.* **—whole′heart′ed·ness** *n.*

whole note A note in music having a time value equal to twice that of a half note.

Whole notes

whole number An integer.

whole·sale [hōl′sāl′] *n., adj., adv., v.* **whole·saled, whole·sal·ing** **1** *n.* The selling of goods in large quantities, especially to retail stores for resale to the public. **2** *adj.* Of, having to do with, or engaged in this method of selling goods: *wholesale* prices; a *wholesale* druggist. **3** *adv.* In bulk or quantity and at lower prices: to buy goods *wholesale*. **4** *v.* To sell or be sold wholesale. **5** *adj.* Made or done on a large scale: a *wholesale* outbreak of flu. **—whole′sal′er** *n.*

whole·some [hōl′səm] *adj.* **1** Beneficial to the health; healthful: *wholesome* air and food. **2** Favorable to the development of the mind or charactor: *wholesome* entertainment. **—whole′·some·ly** *adv.* **—whole′some·ness** *n.*

whole step An interval of a musical scale consisting of two adjacent semitones.

whole tone Another term for WHOLE STEP.

whole wheat Made of the entire grain of the wheat, including the bran: *whole wheat* flour.

who'll [ho͞ol] **1** Who will. **2** Who shall.

whol·ly [hō′lē] *adv.* Completely; totally: *wholly* deaf; I don't *wholly* agree.

whom [ho͞om] *pron.* The form of WHO used as the object of a verb or preposition: *Whom* did you visit?; To *whom* am I speaking? See WHO.

whom·ev·er [ho͞om′ev′ər] *pron.* The form of WHOEVER used as object of a verb or preposition.

whom·so·ev·er [ho͞om′sō·ev′ər] *pron.* The form of WHOSOEVER used as object of a verb or preposition.

whoop [h(w)o͞op *or* h(w)o͝op] **1** *n.* A loud cry, as of excitement or surprise. **2** *v.* To make loud cries. **3** *n.* The loud drawing in of the breath, as after a series of coughs in whooping cough. **4** *v.* To make such a sound. **—whoop it up** **1** To have a noisy good time. **2** To arouse enthusiasm.

whooping cough A contagious disease of childhood in which there are violent fits of coughing ending in whoops.

whooping crane A large, long-legged North American crane that has a whooplike call.

whop·per [(h)wop′ər] *n. informal* Something large or remarkable, especially a big lie.

whop·ping [(h)wop′ing] *adj. informal* Very large.

whorl [(h)wûrl *or* (h)wôrl] *n.* An arrangement of things in the form of a circle, as leaves coming from the same point on a stem, a turn of a spiral shell, or curves in the pattern of a fingerprint.

who's [ho͞oz] **1** Who is. **2** Who has.

whose [ho͞oz] *pron.* The possessive form of WHO or WHICH: *Whose* coat is this?; a cat *whose* whiskers are white. ◆ Don't confuse *whose* with *who's*. *Whose* is a possessive; *who's* is a contraction.

who·so·ev·er [ho͞o′sō·ev′ər] *pron.* Any person whatever; who; whoever.

why [(h)wī] *adv., n., pl.* **whys** **1** *adv.* For what cause, purpose, or reason: *Why* are you wearing dark glasses? **2** *adv.* The reason or cause for which: I don't know *why* they went. **3** *adv.* Because of which; for which: I know no reason *why* they went. **4** *n.* A reason or cause: the *whys* and wherefores of the case. **5** *interj.* A word used to express sur-

a	add	**i**	it	**o͝o**	took	**oi**	oil		
ā	ace	**ī**	ice	**o͞o**	pool	**ou**	pout		
â	care	**o**	odd	**u**	up	**ng**	ring		
ä	palm	**ō**	open	**û**	burn	**th**	thin		
e	end	**ô**	order	**yo͞o**	fuse	***th***	this		
ē	equal					**zh**	vision		

ə = {a in *above* e in *sicken* i in *possible* / o in *melon* u in *circus*}

prise or hesitation or to gain time: *Why*, there's the key I lost yesterday.

WI Postal Service abbreviation of Wisconsin.

W.I. 1 West Indian. 2 West Indies.

wick [wik] *n.* A band of loosely woven or twisted fibers in a lamp or candle that draws up fuel, which burns on it when lighted.

wick·ed [wik′id] *adj.* 1 Evil; sinful; depraved: a *wicked* act. 2 Playfully mischievous; naughty: a *wicked* prank. 3 *informal* Severe or painful: a *wicked* wind; a *wicked* toothache. **—wick′ed·ly** *adv.* **—wick′ed·ness** *n.*

wick·er [wik′ər] 1 *n.* A pliant young branch or twig, as of osier. 2 *n.* Such branches or twigs woven into a kind of fabric used in making baskets, light furniture, and other items. 3 *adj. use*: a *wicker* chair. 4 *n.* Objects made of wicker.

wick·er·work [wik′ər·wûrk′] *n.* 1 Branches or twigs woven into a kind of fabric; wicker. 2 Objects made of wicker.

wick·et [wik′it] *n.* 1 A small door or gate near or within a larger one. 2 A small window, often partly covered by a grating, as one where tickets are sold. 3 In croquet, any of the wire arches through which the ball must be hit. 4 In cricket, either of two groups of sticks which one side tries to hit with the ball.

wick·i·up [wik′ē·up′] *n.* A cone-shaped hut used by certain North American Indians, consisting of a frame of wooden poles covered by matting, brush, or bark.

wide [wīd] *adj.* & *adv.* **wid·er, wid·est** 1 *adj.* Extending far from side to side; broad: a *wide* river. 2 *adj.* Extending far in every direction; vast: a *wide* area. 3 *adj.* Having a certain width: a table 36 inches *wide*. 4 *adj.* Large in range or content; including many or much: a *wide* selection of ties. 5 *adj., adv.* Far distant from the target or goal: to fall *wide* of the mark. 6 *adj.* Very far or fully open: *wide* eyes. 7 *adv.* Fully or almost fully: Open the window *wide*. 8 *adv.* To a great distance: She wandered far and *wide*. **—wide′ly** *adv.* **—wide′ness** *n.*

wide-a·wake [wīd′ə·wāk′] *adj.* 1 Fully awake. 2 Alert, attentive, and watchful.

wide-eyed [wīd′īd′] *adj.* With the eyes wide open, as in wonder or surprise.

wid·en [wīd′(ə)n] *v.* To make or become wide or wider.

wide·spread [wīd′spred′] *adj.* 1 Spread wide, as wings. 2 Spreading over, happening in, or affecting a wide area: a *widespread* rumor.

wid·geon [wij′ən] *n., pl.* **wid·geon** or **wid·geons** A wild freshwater duck with brown or gray feathers.

wid·ow [wid′ō] 1 *n.* A woman whose husband is dead, and who has not married again. 2 *v.* To make a widow of.

wid·ow·er [wid′ō·ər] *n.* A man whose wife is dead, and who has not married again.

wid·ow·hood [wid′ō·ho͝od′] *n.* The condition or time of being a widow.

widow's peak A V-shaped point made by the hairline just above the middle of the forehead.

width [width] *n.* 1 The size of something, as measured from one side to the other; wideness; breadth. 2 A piece of something, as cloth, having a certain width.

width·wise [width′wīz′] *adv.* Across the width; from side to side.

wield [wēld] *v.* 1 To hold and use (a weapon or tool); handle: to *wield* a knife. 2 To hold and use (authority, power, or the like).

wie·ner [wē′nər] *n. U.S.* A sausage made of beef and pork; frankfurter or a shorter sausage.

wie·ner·wurst [wē′nər·wûrst′] *n.* A wiener.

wife [wīf] *n., pl.* **wives** [wīvz] A woman to whom a man is married; married woman.

wife·ly [wīf′lē] *adj.* **wife·li·er, wife·li·est** Of, like, or fitting for a wife.

wig [wig] *n.* A covering of hair for the head, used to hide one's own hair, cover baldness, or complete a costume.

wig·gle [wig′əl] *v.* **wig·gled, wig·gling,** *n.* 1 *v.* To move or twist from side to side: The dog *wiggled* its nose; The snake *wiggled* under the fence. 2 *n.* A wiggling motion.

wig·gler [wig′lər] *n.* 1 A person or thing that wiggles. 2 The larva of a mosquito.

wig·gly [wig′lē] *adj.* **wig·gli·er, wig·gli·est** 1 Wiggling or tending to wiggle: a *wiggly* snake. 2 Full of twists and bends: a *wiggly* road.

wight [wīt] *n.* A person; creature: seldom used today.

wig·wag [wig′wag′] *v.* **wig·wagged, wig·wag·ging,** *n.* 1 *v.* To send (a message) by moving small flags or lights, according to a code. 2 *n.* The action or method of sending messages in this way. **—wig′·wag′ger** *n.*

wig·wam [wig′wom′] *n.* A hut in the shape of a cone or dome built by North American Indians, and consisting of a framework of poles covered by bark, hides, or other materials.

Wigwam

wild [wīld] 1 *adj.* Living in the fields, plains, or forests; not tamed or domesticated: *wild* dogs. 2 *adj.* Growing in a natural state; not cultivated: *wild* flowers. 3 *adj.* Not lived in or used by civilized people: *wild* country. 4 *n.* (*usually pl.*) Uninhabited or uncultivated country: the Arctic *wilds*. 5 *adj.* Savage or primitive; uncivilized: *wild* tribes in the jungle. 6 *adj.* Not controlled or restrained, and often unruly or disorderly: a *wild* crowd; a *wild* dance; *wild* with delight. 7 *adj.* Fantastic or odd: a *wild* story. 8 *adj.* Violent or turbulent: a *wild* sea. 9 *adj.* Missing the intended target by a large amount: a *wild* throw. 10 *adv.* In a wild way: to run *wild*. **—wild′·ly** *adv.* **—wild′ness** *n.*

wild boar A wild hog of Europe, Asia, and Africa, having a dark coat and short tusks.

wild·cat [wīld′kat′] *n., v.* **wild·cat·ted, wild·cat·ting,** *adj.* 1 *n.* A wild animal related to the domestic cat, but somewhat larger. It is also called a lynx. 2 *n.* A person who is always ready to quarrel or fight. 3 *n.* A successful oil well drilled in an area thought not to contain oil. 4 *v.* To drill for oil in an area not known to contain it. 5 *n.* A risky business venture. 6 *adj.* Likely to fail; risky: a *wildcat* investment. 7 *adj.* Made, done, or carried on without official permission; unauthorized: a *wildcat* strike. **—wild′cat′ter** *n.*

wil·de·beest [wil′də·bēst′ *or* vil′də·bēst′] *n., pl.* **wil·de·beests** or **wil·de·beest** Another word for GNU.

wil·der·ness [wil′dər·nis] *n.* A region that is not cultivated or lived in.

wild·fire [wīld′fīr′] *n.* A rapidly spreading fire that is hard to control or put out.

wild flower or **wild·flow·er** [wīld′flou′ər] *n.* An uncultivated flowering plant or its flower.

wild·fowl or **wild fowl** [wīld′foul′] *n., pl.* **wild·fowl** or **wild·fowls** or **wild fowl** or **wild fowls** A wild duck, pheasant, or other game bird.

wild-goose chase [wīld′go͞os′] A hopeless or futile pursuit or undertaking.

wild·life [wīld′līf′] *n.* Animals and plants in their natural or wild state.

wild pitch In baseball, a pitch that the catcher cannot reasonably be expected to catch and that allows a runner to advance.

Wild West The western U.S. during the early pioneer period.

wild·wood [wīld′wo͝od′] *n.* A forest in its natural state.

wile [wīl] *n., v.* **wiled, wil·ing** **1** *n.* A trick or scheme to deceive or entice: *wiles* that hook a fish. **2** *v.* To coax or lure by wiles.

wi·li·ness [wī′lē·nis] *n.* The condition or quality of being wily.

will[1] [wil] *v. Present tense for all subjects* **will,** *past tense* **would** A helping verb used to express: **1** Things happening in the future: I *will* ride there; They said they *would* come. **2** Capability: *Will* the plan work?; It certainly *will.* **3** Willingness: Why *will* you not tell the truth? **4** Custom or habit: They *will* get upset over trifles. **5** A command: You *will* come when I call you. ◆ See SHALL.

will[2] [wil] *n., v.* **willed, will·ing** **1** *n.* The power that the mind has to make choices and decisions and select acts to carry them out: a person of strong *will.* **2** *n.* Something chosen or decided upon; desire or wish: What is your *will*? **3** *v.* To choose or decide: Elections show what the people *will*; Do as you *will.* **4** *n.* Strong determination or self-control: With her *will*, she'll succeed. **5** *v.* To control or bring about by the exercise of the will. **6** *n.* The way a person feels toward another: to show good *will.* **7** *n.* A legal document telling how a person wishes his or her wealth and property to be disposed of after his or her death. **8** *v.* To give by means of a will: to *will* money to a child. **—at will** As one wishes.

will·ful or **wil·ful** [wil′fəl] *adj.* **1** Insisting on having one's own way: a *willful* child. **2** Done on purpose; deliberate: *willful* damage; a *willful* action. **—will′ful·ness** or **wil′ful·ness** *n.*

will·ful·ly or **wil·ful·ly** [wil′fəl·ē] *adv.* **1** On purpose. **2** In a stubborn or obstinate way.

will·ing [wil′ing] *adj.* **1** Ready or disposed; prepared: We are *willing* to do the task. **2** Cheerfully meeting demands and requirements: a *willing* worker. **3** Gladly given or done: *willing* service. **—will′ing·ly** *adv.* **—will′ing·ness** *n.*

will-o'-the-wisp [wil′ə·th̶ə·wisp′] *n.* **1** A flickering light seen over marshes and swamps at night. **2** Anything that misleads by luring one on but staying out of reach.

wil·low [wil′ō] *n.* **1** One of a group of trees and shrubs having smooth branches, thin flexible twigs which hang down, and long narrow leaves. **2** The wood of one of these trees.

wil·low·y [wil′ō·ē] *adj.* **1** Full of willows: a *willowy* bank. **2** Slender or supple: a *willowy* dancer.

will·pow·er [wil′pou′ər] *n.* The strength of mind needed to carry out plans and achieve one's goals; self-control.

wil·ly-nil·ly [wil′ē·nil′ē] *adv.* Whether one wants to or not: We must pay the bill *willy-nilly.*

wilt[1] [wilt] *v.* To lose or cause to lose freshness, energy, or vitality; make or become limp: Dryness *wilted* the grass; My shirt *wilted* in the heat.

wilt[2] [wilt] A form of the verb WILL used with *thou*: seldom used today.

wi·ly [wī′lē] *adj.* **wi·li·er, wi·li·est** Full of or using wiles; sly; cunning.

wim·ple [wim′pəl] *n.* A cloth wrapped around the head and neck, exposing only the face. It is now worn only by nuns.

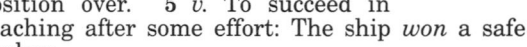

Nun wearing a wimple

win [win] *v.* **won, win·ning,** *n.* **1** *v.* To be victorious in (a game, contest, war, or other struggle): to *win* a game; The home team *won.* **2** *n.* An instance of winning; victory. **3** *v.* To get by effort or hard work: to *win* fame and fortune. **4** *v.* To get the good will or favor of: The argument *won* the opposition over. **5** *v.* To succeed in reaching after some effort: The ship *won* a safe harbor.

wince [wins] *v.* **winced, winc·ing,** *n.* **1** *v.* To shrink or draw back, as from a blow or a pain; flinch. **2** *n.* The act of wincing.

winch [winch] *n.* A machine for lifting or pulling, consisting of a drum onto which a rope or cable is wound by a hand crank or by a motor.

wind[1] [wind] **1** *n.* A movement or current of air of any speed. **2** *n.* Air that carries some scent: The dogs got *wind* of the fox. **3** *n.* The power of breathing; breath. **4** *v.* To make short of breath: The long run *winded* the racers. **5** *n.* Idle or useless talk: That's a lot of *wind.* **6** *n.* (*pl.*) Wind instruments, as in an orchestra. **—get wind of** To find out about; discover. **—in the wind** In progress or about to happen.

wind[2] [wīnd] *v.* **wound, wind·ing,** *n.* **1** *v.* To coil or pass (thread, rope, or the like) around itself or around something else: to *wind* thread. **2** *v.* To coil or twine, as around some central object: The rope *winds* on this drum. **3** *v.* To cover with something by coiling: to *wind* a spool with thread. **4** *v.* To make (a machine, as a clock) go by coiling a spring or raising a weight. **5** *v.* To run or move in a turning, twisting course; meander: The road *winds* through town. **6** *n.* A winding; turn or twist. **—wind up** **1** To coil onto a reel, drum, or other central object. **2** To bring to an end. **3** To put in readiness for action; excite or arouse. **4** To move the arm and body in preparation for pitching a ball.

wind·bag [wind′bag′] *n. informal* A talkative person who says nothing important or interesting.

a	add	**i**	it	**o͝o**	took	**oi**	oil
ā	ace	**ī**	ice	**o͞o**	pool	**ou**	pout
â	care	**o**	odd	**u**	up	**ng**	ring
ä	palm	**ō**	open	**û**	burn	**th**	thin
e	end	**ô**	order	**yo͞o**	fuse	**th̶**	this
ē	equal					**zh**	vision

ə = a in *above* e in *sicken* i in *possible* o in *melon* u in *circus*

W

wind·break [wind′brāk′] *n.* Something, as a line of trees, used to break the force of the wind.
Wind·break·er [wind′brā′kər] *n.* A short jacket made of wind-resistant material: a trademark.
wind·burn [wind′bûrn′] *n.* Redness and irritation of the skin caused by exposure to wind. **—wind′·burned′** *adj.*
wind-chill factor [wind′chil′] A temperature that is a measure of how cold the air feels to human skin, taking into account the chilling effect of the wind as well as the actual air temperature.
wind·fall [wind′fôl′] *n.* 1 An unexpected lucky event or profit. 2 Something blown down by the wind, especially ripe fruit.
wind·flow·er [wind′flou′ər] *n.* Another name for ANEMONE.
wind·ing [wīn′ding] 1 *n.* The act of a person or thing that winds. 2 *n.* A bend or turn or a series of them. 3 *adj.* Having or making bends or turns. 4 *n.* Something that is wound about an object.
wind·ing sheet [wīn′ding] A sheet that in former times was wrapped around a corpse.
wind instrument [wind] An instrument whose sound is produced by a stream of air, especially air from the player's breath.
wind·jam·mer [wind′jam′ər] *n.* A ship with sails.
wind·lass [wind′ləs] *n.* A device for hauling or lifting; winch.

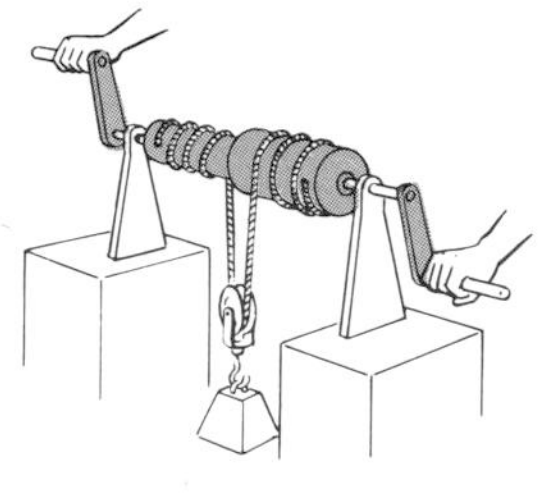
Windlass

wind·mill [wind′mil′] *n.* A machine that gets its power from a set of vanes turned by the wind. It is used especially to pump water.
win·dow [win′dō] *n.* 1 An opening in the side of a building to let in light and air. 2 The frame and panes of glass used to close such an opening. 3 An opportunity, during a limited time, to do something. 4 On a computer screen, a separate viewing area giving different information from the rest of the screen. ◆ *Window* comes from two Scandinavian words meaning *wind* and *eye*.
window box A long, narrow box for growing plants and flowers on the sill or ledge of a window.
window dressing 1 The process or art of exhibiting merchandise in store windows. 2 The merchandise so exhibited. 3 Anything used to make something appear more attractive or more desirable than it really is.
win·dow·pane [win′dō·pān′] *n.* A sheet of glass used in a window.
win·dow-shop [win′dō·shop′] *v.* **win·dow-shopped, win·dow-shop·ping** To look at the goods shown in store windows without buying them. **—win′dow-shop′per** *n.*
win·dow·sill [win′dō·sil′] *n.* The horizontal structural part that extends across the bottom of a window opening.
wind·pipe [wind′pīp′] *n.* The passage that connects the throat to the lungs; trachea.
wind·row [wind′rō′] *n.* A long ridge of hay raked together to be piled into haystacks.
wind·shield [wind′shēld′] *n.* A sheet of glass or plastic in front of the driver and riders in a vehicle, plane, or boat to block off wind and rain.
wind sock A conical sleeve open at both ends, mounted on a pivot so that the big end points to the direction of the wind.
Wind·sor [win′zər] *n.* The name of the royal family of Great Britain since 1917.
Windsor Castle A castle in southern England, residence of the British sovereign.
wind·storm [wind′stôrm′] *n.* A strong wind with little or no rain.
wind tunnel A large cylindrical structure in which models of aircraft, rockets, and boats are tested with measured, artificially-made winds.
wind·up [wīnd′up′] *n.* 1 An ending or closing; conclusion. 2 The movements of the arm and body made in preparation for pitching a baseball.
wind vane Another name for WEATHER VANE.
wind·ward [wind′wərd] 1 *n.* The direction or side facing the wind. 2 *adj.* Moving toward or located on the side facing the wind: a *windward* shore. 3 *adv.* In the direction from which the wind is blowing; into the wind.
wind·y [win′dē] *adj.* **wind·i·er, wind·i·est** 1 Having or exposed to much wind. 2 Making dull, pompous talk. **—wind′i·ly** *adv.* **—wind′i·ness** *n.*
wine [wīn] 1 *n.* Grape juice fermented so that it contains alcohol. 2 *n.* A similar drink made from the juice of any fruit or plant. 3 *n., adj.* Deep, purplish red. **—wine and dine** To entertain or treat.
wine·press [wīn′pres′] *n.* A vat in which juice is pressed from grapes.
Wine·sap [wīn′sap′] A dark-red apple with very white flesh.
wing [wing] 1 *n.* One of a pair of parts, or set of two pairs, that a bird, bat, or insect extends and moves in order to fly. 2 *n.* Something like a wing in shape, position, or use: an airplane *wing.* 3 *v.* To cause to be rapid or go quickly: Hope *winged* our steps. 4 *v.* To damage the wing or arm of, as with a bullet or arrow. 5 *n.* Something sticking out to the side from the main part: a *wing* of a house; the *wings* of a stage. 6 *n.* A group holding extreme views, as in a political organization: the left *wing.* 7 *n.* Either the right or left section of an army or fleet. **—on the wing** 1 In flight. 2 In motion; hardly stopping: had a quick lunch *on the wing.* **—take wing** To fly away. **—under one's wing** Under one's protection. **—wing′like** *adj.*
wing case Either of a pair of hardened, modified forewings that cover and protect the flying wings of a beetle.
winged [wingd *or* wing′id] *adj.* 1 Having wings. 2 Passing swiftly; fast; rapid.
wing·less [wing′lis] *adj.* Having no wings, or having incompletely developed wings.
wing·span [wing′span′] *n.* Another word for WINGSPREAD.
wing·spread [wing′spred′] *n.* The distance between the tips of a pair of fully extended wings.
wink [wingk] 1 *v.* To close and open (the eyes, or especially one eye) rapidly, often as a sign or hint. 2 *n.* The act of winking. 3 *n.* A hint or sign given by winking. 4 *v.* To give off light in short flashes; twinkle. 5 *n.* A short time; instant: They'll be here in a *wink.* **—wink at** To pretend not to see: to *wink at* a prank.
win·ner [win′ər] *n.* A person or thing that wins.
win·ning [win′ing] 1 *adj.* Successful, especially in competition. 2 *n.* The act of a person or thing that wins. 3 *n.* (*pl.*) Something won, especially money won, as by gambling. 4 *adj.* Charming; attractive; winsome. **—win′ning·ly** *adv.*

win·now [win′ō] *v.* **1** To blow away the chaff from (grain). **2** To blow off (chaff) from grain. **3** To sift out; separate: A reporter must *winnow* facts from hearsay. **—win′now·er** *n.*

win·some [win′səm] *adj.* Having a charming, attractive appearance or manner. **—win′some·ly** *adv.* **—win′some·ness** *n.*

win·ter [win′tər] **1** *n.* The coldest season of the year, occurring between autumn and spring. **2** *adj. use*: *winter* sports; a *winter* coat. **3** *v.* To pass the winter: to *winter* in the tropics. **4** *v.* To feed or care for during the winter: to *winter* animals.

win·ter·green [win′tər·grēn′] *n.* **1** A small evergreen plant whose oval leaves yield an aromatic oil. **2** The oil from this plant, used as a flavoring.

win·ter·ize [win′tə·rīz′] *v.* **win·ter·ized, win·ter·iz·ing** To equip or prepare (as an engine or automobile) for winter.

win·ter·time [win′tər·tīm′] *n.* The winter season.

win·try [win′trē] *adj.* **win·tri·er, win·tri·est** Of or like winter; cold; frosty. **—win′tri·ness** *n.*

wipe [wīp] *v.* **wiped, wip·ing,** *n.* **1** *v.* To rub, usually with a soft or absorbent material: to *wipe* a table dry. **2** *v.* To apply or remove by rubbing lightly: to *wipe* on polish; to *wipe* off grease. **3** *v.* To clean or dry by or as if by rubbing: to *wipe* one's shoes on a doormat; to *wipe* the dishes. **4** *v.* To move along or across; cause to rub: to *wipe* your hand across your brow. **5** *n.* The act of wiping. **—wipe out** To destroy completely, as by killing. **—wip′er** *n.*

wire [wīr] *n., v.* **wired, wir·ing** **1** *n.* Metal that has been drawn into a slender rod, strand, or thread. **2** *n.* Such metal covered with insulation, used to carry electricity. **3** *v.* To fasten with wire: to *wire* a box shut. **4** *v.* To equip with wires for carrying electricity: to *wire* a radio. **5** *n.* A telegraph system: to signal by *wire.* **6** *v. informal* To telegraph or telegraph to: to *wire* a message; to *wire* a senator. **7** *n. informal* A telegram. **—pull wires** To use hidden influence.

wire·haired [wīr′hârd′] *adj.* Having thick, stiff hairs: a *wirehaired* terrier.

wire·less [wīr′lis] **1** *adj.* Having no wires; operating without a connection by wire. **2** *n. British* Radio. **3** *n. British* A telegram sent by radio. **4** *v. British* To send a telegram by radio.

wire service An agency that gathers news and pictures of current events and supplies them by telegraph or telephone to such customers as newspapers and television stations.

wire·tap [wīr′tap′] *v.* **wire·tapped, wire·tap·ping,** *n.* **1** *v.* To make a secret connection with (a telephone or telegraph line) so as to overhear messages. **2** *n.* A secret connection of this kind. **3** *n.* A concealed electronic device that is used in wiretapping.

wire·worm [wīr′wûrm′] *n.* The stiff, wiry larva of certain beetles, some of which destroy plant roots.

wir·ing [wīr′ing] *n.* A system of wires used to carry an electric current.

wir·y [wīr′ē] *adj.* **wir·i·er, wir·i·est** **1** Like wire; thin and stiff. **2** Slender, but tough and strong: a *wiry* prize-fighter. **—wir′i·ness** *n.*

Wis. or **Wisc.** Wisconsin.

wis·dom [wiz′dəm] *n.* **1** Good judgment and knowledge of what is true or right, based on experience. **2** Accumulated knowledge or learning: the *wisdom* of the ancients.

wisdom tooth The last tooth on either side of the upper or lower jaw in humans, usually appearing between the 17th and 22nd year.

wise[1] [wīz] *adj.* **wis·er, wis·est** **1** Having or showing wisdom: to act in a *wise* manner; to be *wiser* as a result of study. **2** *U.S. slang* Offensively bold and arrogant: a *wise* guy. **—wise to** *informal* Aware of: I'm *wise to* your tricks. **—wise′ly** *adv.*

wise[2] [wīz] *n.* Way, manner, or method: Those tricks are in no *wise* clever.

-wise A combining form meaning: **1** In a certain manner, as in *likewise.* **2** In a certain direction or position, as in *clockwise.* **3** In regard to or with reference to, as in *moneywise.* ◆ This suffix is overworked and should be used carefully.

wise·a·cre [wīz′ā′kər] *n.* A person who claims or pretends to be very wise.

wise·crack [wīz′krak′] *slang* **1** *n.* A short, witty remark, often disrespectful or mocking. **2** *v.* To make a wisecrack or wisecracks.

wish [wish] **1** *v.* To want, desire, or be glad to have: We *wish* to make sure. **2** *n.* A desire or hope to do, get, have, be, or experience something: a *wish* to travel. **3** *v.* To have or express a desire or craving: We *wished* for a solution to the problem. **4** *n.* Something hoped or wished for: We got our *wish.* **5** *v.* To want or desire (something) for someone: I *wish* you luck. **6** *n.* The expression of a wish: My parents send their best *wishes.* **7** *v.* To request or command: I *wish* you to be quiet.

wish·bone [wish′bōn′] *n.* In many birds, a forked bone located in front of the breastbone.

wish·ful [wish′fəl] *adj.* Having, showing, or founded on a wish or desire: *wishful* thinking. **—wish′ful·ly** *adv.* **—wish′ful·ness** *n.*

wish·y-wash·y [wish′ē·wôsh′ē *or* wish′ē·wosh′ē] *adj.* **1** Weak, thin, or diluted, as watered soup. **2** Without strength, character, or decisiveness: a *wishy-washy* person who can't make decisions.

wisp [wisp] *n.* **1** A small bunch, as of hay or hair. **2** A small bit: a *wisp* of vapor. **3** A frail or slight person or thing: a *wisp* of a child. **—wisp′y** *adj.*

wist [wist] Past tense and past participle of WIT[2].

wis·tar·i·a [wis·târ′ē·ə] *n.* Another spelling of WISTERIA.

wis·ter·i·a [wis·tir′ē·ə] *n.* Any of various climbing vines related to the bean and having clusters of blue, purple, or white flowers.

wist·ful [wist′fəl] *adj.* **1** Wishful; longing. **2** Thoughtful; pensive. **—wist′ful·ly** *adv.* **—wist′ful·ness** *n.*

wit[1] [wit] *n.* **1** The ability to say or write clever, intelligent, and amusing things: The critic's *wit* was sharp but constructive. **2** A person who has this ability: The critic was a true *wit.* **3** (*pl.*) The ability to perceive and understand: a person of quick *wits.* **4** (*pl.*) Mental balance: to be frightened out of one's *wits.* **—at one's wit's end** Not able to know what to do, say, or think.

a add	**i** it	**o͝o** took	**oi** oil
ā ace	**ī** ice	**o͞o** pool	**ou** pout
â care	**o** odd	**u** up	**ng** ring
ä palm	**ō** open	**û** burn	**th** thin
e end	**ô** order	**yo͞o** fuse	**th** this
ē equal			**zh** vision

ə = a in *above* e in *sicken* i in *possible* o in *melon* u in *circus*

W

wit² [wit] *v.* **wist, wit·ting** To learn or know: seldom used today. **—to wit** That is to say; namely: I told two people; *to wit*, my father and mother.

witch [wich] *n.* 1 A woman supposed to have magical powers, especially the power to work evil. 2 Any mean or ugly old woman; hag.

witch·craft [wich′kraft′] *n.* 1 The supernatural power of a witch or warlock. 2 The use of this power. ◆ See MAGIC.

witch doctor Among certain primitive people, a person thought to be able to work magic or to keep witchcraft from working; medicine man.

witch·er·y [wich′ər·ē] *n., pl.* **witch·er·ies** 1 The power to charm; fascination. 2 Witchcraft.

witch hazel 1 A shrub of the U.S. and Canada, having pliant branches and small, yellow flowers. 2 A liquid preparation made from the bark and leaves of this shrub, used as a soothing, cooling lotion for the skin.

witch-hunt [wich′hunt′] *n.* An investigation supposedly undertaken to uncover subversion, but whose actual purpose or effect is to persecute political dissenters.

witch·ing [wich′ing] *adj.* 1 Charming; fascinating. 2 Of or suitable for witchery.

with [wit͟h or with] *prep.* 1 In the company of: We went *with* the others. 2 Having or exhibiting: a hat *with* a feather. 3 By adding, having, or containing: a pillowcase trimmed *with* lace. 4 As a member or associate of: The science teacher has been *with* the school for years. 5 Among: to be counted *with* the others. 6 In the course of; during: One forgets *with* time. 7 So as to be separated from: to do away *with* luxuries. 8 Against: to fight *with* someone. 9 In the opinion of: That is all right *with* me. 10 Because of: to be faint *with* hunger. 11 In charge or in possession of: Leave the key *with* the janitor. 12 By means or aid of: to write *with* a pencil. 13 In spite of: *With* all the money in the world, one can't buy health. 14 At the same time as: They woke up *with* the sunrise. 15 In the same direction as: to drift *with* the crowd. 16 In regard to; in the case of: I am pleased *with* them. 17 Onto; to: Join this tube *with* that one. 18 Into: Mix the water *with* the flour. 19 In proportion to: Fame grows *with* good deeds. 20 In support of: This district voted *with* the other party. 21 Of the same opinion as: I'm *with* you there! 22 Compared or contrasted to: Consider this book *with* that one. 23 Immediately after; following: *With* that, the meeting was ended. 24 Having received or been granted: *With* my parents' consent, I left. 25 As well as: I can cook *with* the best of them.

with·al [wit͟h·ôl′ *or* with·ôl′] *adv.* In addition; besides: seldom used today.

with·draw [wit͟h·drô′ *or* with·drô′] *v.* **with·drew, with·drawn, with·draw·ing** 1 To take away or remove: The board *withdrew* support for the project. 2 To take back: to *withdraw* a statement. 3 To move or go back or away: They *withdrew* from the room. 4 To resign or retire; leave: to *withdraw* from the committee.

with·draw·al [wit͟h·drô′əl *or* with·drô′əl] *n.* The act or process of withdrawing.

with·drawn [wit͟h·drôn′ *or* with·drôn′] 1 Past participle of WITHDRAW. 2 *adj.* Very quiet and reserved, as if in deep thought.

with·drew [wit͟h·dro͞o′ *or* with·dro͞o′] Past tense of WITHDRAW.

withe [with *or* wit͟h *or* wīt͟h] *n.* A long twig, usually of willow, that bends easily and can be used to tie things together.

with·er [wit͟h′ər] *v.* 1 To become or cause to become limp, dry, or lifeless: Drought *withered* the crop. 2 To lose force or vitality; weaken: Once halted, the rebellion soon *withered*. 3 To make timid or ashamed: She *withered* him with a scornful glance.

with·ers [wit͟h′ərz] *n.pl.* The highest part of the back of a horse, deer, ox, or other animal, located between the shoulder blades.

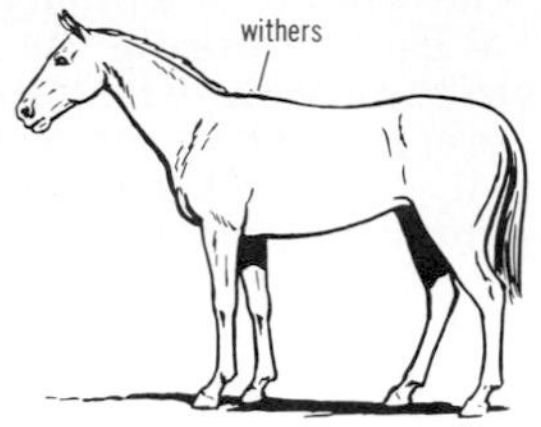

with·hold [with·hōld′ *or* wit͟h·hōld′] *v.* **with·held, with·hold·ing** 1 To hold back; restrain: Please *withhold* all queries. 2 To refuse to grant or give: My parents *withheld* their permission.

withholding tax A portion of an employee's wages deducted by the employer and given to the government as payment of income tax.

with·in [wit͟h·in′ *or* with·in′] 1 *adv.* In, on, or to the inner part: Paths lead *within*. 2 *adv.* Indoors: Go *within* at once. 3 *n.* An inner part or place: trouble from *within*. 4 *prep.* In the inner part or parts of; inside: *within* the house. 5 *prep.* In the limits or range of; not farther than: *within* a mile of here. 6 *prep.* In the reach, limit, or scope of; not beyond: *within* my power.

with·out [wit͟h·out′ *or* with·out′] 1 *prep.* Not having, doing, or making; lacking; with no: coffee *without* sugar; to get in *without* paying. 2 *prep.* Free from: *without* fear. 3 *adv.* In, on, or to the outer part: Smoke passed *without*. 4 *prep.* In, on, at, or to the outside of: *Without* the harbor, the storm raged. 5 *adv.* Outdoors; outside a building: It was cold *without*. 6 *n.* An outer part or place: to get help from *without*. 7 *prep.* On, at, to, or toward the outside of: *without* the city.

with·stand [with·stand′ *or* wit͟h·stand′] *v.* **with·stood, with·stand·ing** To stand up against; oppose; resist: to *withstand* hard use.

wit·less [wit′lis] *adj.* Lacking in wit or intelligence; stupid; foolish. **—wit′less·ly** *adv.* **—wit′less·ness** *n.*

wit·ness [wit′nis] 1 *n.* A person who has seen or knows something and can give evidence concerning it: a *witness* to the murder. 2 *v.* To see or know by personal experience: to *witness* an accident. 3 *n.* A person who, under oath, gives evidence in a court of law. 4 *n.* A person who is present, as at a transaction or ceremony, and who then signs a document stating or proving that the event actually took place: a *witness* to a marriage. 5 *v.* To act as a witness of: They *witnessed* the signing of my contract. 6 *n.* Evidence; proof; testimony: giving false *witness*. 7 *v.* To give evidence of; show: Your grin *witnessed* your satisfaction. **—bear witness** To be or serve as evidence or proof of something: Our happy faces *bore witness* to our victory.

wit·ted [wit′id] *adj.* Having a certain kind of wit: often used in combination, as in *quick-witted*.

wit·ti·cism [wit′ə·siz′əm] *n.* A witty saying.

wit·ty [wit′ē] *adj.* **wit·ti·er, wit·ti·est** Full of or having wit; clever or amusing: a *witty* person. **—wit′ti·ly** *adv.* **—wit′ti·ness** *n.*

wives [wīvz] Plural of WIFE.

wiz·ard [wiz′ərd] *n.* 1 A man thought to have magical powers; sorcerer. 2 *informal* Any very clever or skillful person.
wiz·ard·ry [wiz′ərd·rē] *n.* 1 Magic. 2 Skill so great that it seems magical.
wiz·ened [wiz′ənd] *adj.* Shrunken and dried up; withered: *wizened* cheeks.
wk. 1 week. 2 work.
wks. weeks.
WNW west-northwest.
wo [wō] *n., pl.* **wos** Woe: seldom used today.
wob·ble [wob′əl] *v.* **wob·bled, wob·bling,** *n.* 1 *v.* To move or sway or cause to move or sway unsteadily: The top *wobbled* as it slowed down. 2 *n.* An unsteady, wobbling motion. 3 *v.* To be uncertain or undecided. **—wob′bly** *adj.*
Wo·den [wōd′(ə)n] *n.* The Old English name for Odin, the chief Norse god. Wednesday is named for Woden.
woe [wō] *n.* 1 Great sorrow; grief. 2 Terrible trouble; calamity; disaster.
woe·be·gone or **wo·be·gone** [wō′bi·gôn′ *or* wō′bi·gon] *adj.* Overcome with or showing woe or sadness.
woe·ful or **wo·ful** [wō′fəl] *adj.* 1 Full of woe; sad; mournful. 2 Causing woe; pitiful: a *woeful* lack of food. 3 Of very poor quality. **—woe′ful·ly** or **wo′ful·ly** *adv.* **—woe′ful·ness** or **wo′ful·ness** *n.*
wok [wok] *n.* A bowl-shaped metal pan used for frying and steaming Oriental food.
woke [wōk] A past tense of WAKE[1]: I *woke* early.
wo·ken [wō′kən] A past participle of WAKE[1]: She had already *woken* up.
wold [wōld] *n.* A tract of open upland, often hilly or rolling.
wolf [wo͝olf] *n., pl.* **wolves** [wo͝olvz] *v.* 1 *n.* Any of a group of wild animals related to the dog. Wolves usually hunt in packs and prey on other animals. 2 *n.* Any ravenous, greedy, or cruel person or thing. 3 *v.* To eat in a greedy manner; gulp down; devour. **—cry wolf** To give a false alarm. **—keep the wolf from the door** To keep from being hungry or needy. **—wolf′ish** *adj.*

Wolf

wolf·hound [wo͝olf′hound′] *n.* A large dog of any of several breeds originally trained to catch and kill wolves.
wolf·ram [wo͝ol′frəm] *n.* Another name for TUNGSTEN.
wol·ver·ine [wo͝ol′və·rēn′] *n.* A strong, heavily built, carnivorous animal of North American forests, related to the weasel.
wolves [wo͝olvz] The plural of WOLF.
wom·an [wo͝om′ən] *n., pl.* **wom·en** [wim′in] 1 An adult human female. 2 Women as a group. 3 A female attendant or servant.
wom·an·hood [wo͝om′ən·ho͝od′] *n.* 1 The condition of being a woman. 2 Women as a group. 3 The traits or qualities of women.
wom·an·ish [wo͝om′ən·ish] *adj.* Like or for a woman.
wom·an·kind [wo͝om′ən·kīnd′] *n.* Women as a group.
wom·an·like [wo͝om′ən·līk′] *adj.* Characteristic of or suitable for a woman; womanly.
wom·an·ly [wo͝om′ən·lē] *adj.* 1 Becoming to or fit for a woman: a *womanly* voice. 2 Having qualities becoming to or fit for a woman: a *womanly* person. **—wom′an·li·ness** *n.*
womb [wo͞om] *n.* The organ of female mammals in which the young develop before birth; uterus.
wom·bat [wom′bat′] *n.* An Australian animal that looks like a small bear. The female carries her young in a pouch outside her body.
wom·en [wim′in] Plural of WOMAN.
wom·en·folk [wim′in·fōk′] *n.pl. informal* 1 Women as a group. 2 The female members of a family or community.
wom·en·folks [wim′in·fōks′] *n.pl. informal* Womenfolk.
women's rights 1 Legal, political, social, and economic rights for women equal to those held by men. 2 A political movement in support of women's rights.
won [wun] Past tense and past participle of WIN.
won·der [wun′dər] 1 *n.* A feeling of curiosity and surprise; astonishment: We looked with *wonder* at the falling star. 2 *n.* Something strange or unusual that makes one have such a feeling. 3 *v.* To be filled with wonder or awe; marvel: We *wondered* at the sight of the huge falls. 4 *v.* To be doubtful or curious about something; want to know: I *wonder* what the painting was sold for. 5 *v.* To feel surprise.
won·der·ful [wun′dər·fəl] *adj.* 1 Causing wonder or awe. 2 Unusually good; excellent: a *wonderful* concert. **—won′der·ful·ly** *adv.* **—won′der·ful·ness** *n.*
won·der·land [wun′dər·land′] *n.* A place, usually imaginary, filled with wonders.
won·der·ment [wun′dər·mənt] *n.* 1 Wonder; awe. 2 Great surprise; astonishment.
won·drous [wun′drəs] 1 *adj.* Wonderful; marvelous. 2 *adv.* Surprisingly; unusually: seldom used today. **—won′drous·ly** *adv.* **—won′drous·ness** *n.*
wont [wônt *or* wōnt *or* wunt] 1 *adj.* Accustomed; used: They are *wont* to relax after dinner. 2 *n* Ordinary or accustomed practice or habit: It is their *wont* to walk five miles every day.
won't [wōnt] Will not: I simply *won't* go.
wont·ed [wôn′tid *or* wōn′tid *or* wun′tid] *adj.* Habitual; accustomed: to leave at one's *wonted* hour.
woo [wo͞o] *v.* 1 To seek the love or affection of, especially in order to marry; court. 2 To try to obtain; seek: to *woo* fortune. 3 To seek the favor of: Politicians *woo* the public. **—woo′er** *n.*
wood [wo͝od] 1 *n.* The hard substance found beneath the bark of a tree or shrub. 2 *n.* This hard substance cut for use in building and as fuel. 3 *adj. use*: a *wood* pail. 4 *n.* (*pl.*) Woodwinds in an orchestra. 5 *n.* (*often pl.*) A large group of growing trees; forest. 6 *adj.* Living or growing in

a	add	**i**	it	**o͝o**	took	**oi**	oil
ā	ace	**ī**	ice	**o͞o**	pool	**ou**	pout
â	care	**o**	odd	**u**	up	**ng**	ring
ä	palm	**ō**	open	**û**	burn	**th**	thin
e	end	**ô**	order	**yo͞o**	fuse	**th̶**	this
ē	equal					**zh**	vision

ə = a in *above* e in *sicken* i in *possible* o in *melon* u in *circus*

W

woods: a *wood* flower. **—out of the woods** Clear of doubts, difficulties, or danger.
wood alcohol A poisonous alcohol distilled from wood or made artificially, used as a fuel, solvent, and antifreeze.
wood·bine [wŏŏd′bīn′] *n.* Any of several climbing plants, as the common honeysuckle of Europe or the Virginia creeper.
wood carving 1 The activity or art of shaping objects of wood with sharp-edged hand tools. 2 An object carved out of wood. **—wood-car·ver** [wŏŏd′kär′vər] *n.*
wood·chuck [wŏŏd′chuk′] *n.* A chunky animal, a marmot of North America, having coarse brown fur and a short tail. It can climb and swim and sleeps in its burrow all winter; groundhog. ◆ *Woodchuck* comes from the word *we-jack*, of a North American Indian language. The Indian word sounded strange to English-speaking settlers, and they substituted the more familiar sounds of *wood* and *chuck*.

Woodchuck

wood·cock [wŏŏd′kok′] *n., pl.* **wood·cock** or **wood·cocks** A small American bird with a long bill and short legs.
wood·craft [wŏŏd′kraft′] *n.* 1 Skill in things having to do with life in the woods, as hunting or camping. 2 Skill in woodworking.
wood·cut [wŏŏd′kut′] *n.* 1 A block of wood on which a picture or design has been cut. 2 A print made from such a block.
wood·ed [wŏŏd′id] *adj.* Covered with trees or woods: *wooded* hills.
wood·en [wŏŏd′(ə)n] *adj.* 1 Made of wood. 2 Awkward and stiff: a *wooden* pose. 3 Dull; stupid: a *wooden* look. **—wood′en·ly** *adv.*
wood·land [wŏŏd′lənd *or* wŏŏd′land′] 1 *n.* Land covered with woods. 2 *adj.* Belonging to, growing in, or living in the woods.
wood louse *pl.* **wood lice** Any of numerous very small animals with flat oval bodies, usually found under old logs and decaying wood.
wood·man [wŏŏd′mən] *n., pl.* **wood·men** [wŏŏd′·mən] Another spelling of WOODSMAN.
wood nymph In Greek and Roman myths, any of many nymphs who dwelt in and were guardians of the forests.
wood·peck·er [wŏŏd′pek′ər] *n.* Any of a group of birds having strong claws, stiff tail feathers, and a sharp bill for drilling holes in trees and wood in search of insects.
wood·pile [wŏŏd′pīl′] *n.* A pile of wood, especially of wood cut or split in sizes for burning in a fireplace, stove, or campfire.
wood pulp Ground-up wood that has been chemically processed, used especially in the manufacture of paper.
wood·shed [wŏŏd′shed′] *n.* A shed for storing firewood.
woods·man [wŏŏdz′mən] *n., pl.* **woods·men** [wŏŏdz′·mən] 1 A person who lives or works in the woods. 2 A person skilled in woodcraft.
woods·y [wŏŏd′zē] *adj.* **woods·i·er, woods·i·est** Of or like the woods: a *woodsy* smell.
wood tar A thick, syrupy, black fluid obtained by the destructive distillation of wood and used in making pitch, preservatives, and medicines.
wood thrush A large thrush of North American woods, noted for its clear, sweet song.
wood·wind [wŏŏd′wind′] 1 *n.* Any of a group of wind instruments made mainly of wood and sounded by a player's breath passing through a reed or striking a sharp edge, as oboes, bassoons, clarinets, and flutes. 2 *adj.* Of or for these instruments: a *woodwind* player or part. 3 *n.* (*pl.*) The woodwind section of an orchestra.
wood·work [wŏŏd′wûrk′] *n.* Something made of wood, especially the doors, moldings, and stairways of a house or room.
wood·work·ing [wŏŏd′wûr′king] *n.* The act, art, or work of forming things of wood.
wood·y [wŏŏd′ē] *adj.* **wood·i·er, wood·i·est** 1 Of, like, or containing wood. 2 Covered with trees: a *woody* tract of land. **—wood′i·ness** *n.*
woof [wŏŏf *or* wōōf] *n.* 1 In weaving, the threads that are carried from side to side across the fixed threads of the warp in a loom; weft. 2 A fabric, or the texture of a fabric.
woof·er [wŏŏf′ər] *n.* A loudspeaker designed to reproduce sounds of relatively low frequencies, usually used in conjunction with a tweeter or other loudspeaker that produces higher frequencies.
wool [wŏŏl] *n.* 1 The soft, curly hair obtained from the fleece of sheep and some related animals. 2 Yarn, cloth, or clothes made of wool. 3 *adj. use*: a *wool* suit. 4 A fibrous substance resembling wool. **—pull the wool over one's eyes** To trick or deceive one.
wool·en [wŏŏl′ən] 1 *adj.* Made of wool. 2 *n.* (*pl.*) Cloth or garments made of wool. 3 *adj.* Having to do with wool, its manufacture, or its sale: the *woolen* industry.
wool·gath·er·ing [wŏŏl′ga*th*′ər·ing] *n.* Daydreaming, idle reverie, or absentmindedness.
wool·len [wŏŏl′ən] *adj., n.* Another spelling of WOOLEN.
wool·ly [wŏŏl′ē] *adj.* **wool·li·er, wool·li·est,** *n., pl.* **wool·lies** 1 *adj.* Made of, covered with, or like wool. 2 *n.* (*often pl.*) A woolen garment, especially heavy or woolen underwear. 3 *adj.* Not clear, definite, or precise; fuzzy: *woolly* thinking. 4 *adj.* Rough and exciting: The old West was wild and *woolly.* **—wool′li·ness** *n.*
woolly bear The caterpillar of certain moths, having a body covered with long, soft hairs.
wool·y [wŏŏl′ē] *adj.* **wool·i·er, wool·i·est,** *n., pl.* **wool·ies** Another spelling of WOOLLY.
wooz·y [wōōz′ē *or* wŏŏz′ē] *adj.* **wooz·i·er, wooz·i·est** 1 Dazed and confused; stunned. 2 Slightly nauseated; queasy. **—wooz′i·ly** *adv.* **—wooz′i·ness** *n.*
Worces·ter·shire sauce [wŏŏs′tər·shir] A spicy sauce made of vinegar, soy sauce, and other flavorings: a trademark.
word [wûrd] 1 *n.* A spoken sound or group of sounds having a definite meaning. 2 *n.* The letters or characters used in writing or printing such a sound or sounds. 3 *adj. use*: a *word* game. 4 *v.* To write or express in words: How did you *word* the telegram? 5 *n.* (*usually pl.*) Conversation; talk: a person of few *words.* 6 *n.* A brief remark or statement: a *word* of warning. 7 *n.* A piece of news or information: Send me *word* when you arrive. 8 *n.* A command, signal, or direction: Give the *word* to start. 9 *n.* (*pl.*) An angry quarrel: They had *words.* 10 *n.* A promise: to keep one's *word.* **—be as good as one's word** To keep one's promises. **—by word of mouth** By means of speech rather than writing; orally. **—eat one's words** To take back or publicly regret something

one has said. **—in a word** Briefly; in short. **—mince words** To avoid coming to the point; be evasive. **—take one at one's word** To take seriously what a person says and to act accordingly. **—take the words out of one's mouth** To say what another person was just about to say. **—the Word** The Bible. **—word for word** Using exactly the same words.

word·book [wûrd′bo͝ok′] *n.* A collection of words, as a vocabulary or dictionary.

word·ing [wûr′ding] *n.* The way in which something is said, especially in writing; choice and arrangement of words: awkward *wording.*

word·less [wûrd′lis] *adj.* 1 Not speaking; mute. 2 Not expressed in words: a scowl that was a *wordless* protest. **—word′less·ly** *adv.* **—word′less·ness** *n.*

word processing A system for producing and editing printed material, such as letters and business reports, very quickly and efficiently through the use of computers. Word processing equipment usually consists of a keyboard; a display terminal; disk, diskette, or tape storage; and a high-speed printer. **—word processor**

word square A square of letters that spell the same series of words when read across or down.

word·y [wûr′dē] *adj.* **word·i·er, word·i·est** Using or having more words than is necessary. **—word′i·ness** *n.*

wore [wôr] Past tense of WEAR.

work [wûrk] *n., v.* **worked** (or **wrought**: used in metalwork), **work·ing,** *adj.* 1 *n.* Any labor or effort, whether physical or mental, that is intended to accomplish something. 2 *v.* To exert oneself either physically or mentally in order to accomplish something; labor; toil. 3 *v.* To cause or bring about: to *work* a miracle. 4 *n.* What one does to earn a living; occupation, profession, or trade. 5 *v.* To be employed; have a position or job. 6 *adj.* Of, having to do with, or used for work: *work* clothes. 7 *n.* A place of employment: My parents are at *work.* 8 *n.* (*pl., usually used with a singular verb*) A factory: The gas *works* is on fire. 9 *v.* To cause to do work: The boss *works* us too hard. 10 *n.* Something written, painted, or composed; a creation of the imagination: the *works* of Beethoven. 11 *n.* A job, chore, or task. 12 *n.* A person's manner of working or the quality of the work: slow, careful *work.* 13 *v.* To cause to function or be productive; operate: to *work* a machine; to *work* a mine. 14 *v.* To perform properly; operate: This machine *works.* 15 *n.* (*pl.*) The machinery or inner moving parts of something: the *works* of a watch. 16 *n.* A righteous deed: Jane Addams' good *works* live on. 17 *v.* To come or cause to come to some specified condition: The bolts *worked* loose; to *work* oneself into a passion. 18 *v.* To make or achieve by effort: She *worked* her way through college. 19 *v.* To make, shape, or prepare by toil, skill, or manipulation: I *worked* the copper into a bowl. 20 *v.* To solve: to *work* a puzzle. 21 *v.* To be effective; succeed: Our plan *worked* well. 22 *v.* To ferment or cause to ferment: The heat caused the juice to *work.* 23 *v.* To carry on some activity in: to *work* a stream for trout. 24 *n.* In physics, the transfer of energy from one body or system to another. 25 *n.* (*pl.*) *slang* The whole of anything; everything: I sold the *works.* **—shoot the works** *slang* To risk everything in one try or attempt. **—work in** To insert or be inserted. **—work off** To get rid of. **—work on** To try to influence or persuade. **—work out** 1 To make its way out or through. 2 To accomplish, solve, or develop. 3 To come to some outcome or result. 4 *informal* To have a workout. **—work up** 1 To excite; arouse. 2 To form, shape, or develop. 3 To go or move up; advance.

work·a·ble [wûr′kə·bəl] *adj.* Capable of being worked, put into operation, or carried out: a *workable* plan; in *workable* condition. **—work′a·bil′i·ty** *n.* **—work′a·ble·ness** *n.*

work·a·day [wûrk′ə·dā′] *adj.* 1 Of, related to, or fit for working days. 2 Commonplace; ordinary: a *workaday* type of story.

work·a·hol·ic [wûr′kə·hôl′ik] *n.* A person who has a compulsion to work.

work·bench [wûrk′bench′] *n.* A heavy, strong table on which work is done, as by a carpenter.

work·book [wûrk′bo͝ok′] *n.* 1 A book based on a course of study, with problems and exercises that a student works out directly on the pages. 2 A book of instructions for running a machine.

work·day [wûrk′dā′] *n.* 1 A day on which work is done, usually not a holiday or Sunday. 2 The part (in hours) of a day spent in work.

work·er [wûr′kər] *n.* 1 A person who works. ◆ *Worker* is now freely attached to other words as in *steelworker, houseworker, metalworker,* and so on. 2 Any of a class of bees, ants, wasps, or termites unable to produce offspring but doing the work of a hive or colony.

work·horse [wûrk′hôrs′] *n.* 1 A horse used for pulling loads rather than for riding or racing. 2 A person who works very hard.

work·house [wûrk′hous′] *n.* 1 A prison where criminals who commit minor crimes are kept and made to work. 2 *British* A poorhouse where the inmates are made to work.

work·ing [wûr′king] 1 *adj.* Engaged in work or some employment. 2 *adj.* Of, having to do with, or used in work: Monday is a *working* day; *working* shoes. 3 *n.* The act or operation of a person or thing that works: the *working* of nature. 4 *adj.* Enough for use or action: a *working* knowledge of French; a *working* majority. 5 *n.* (*usually pl.*) The part of a mine or quarry where excavation is going on or has gone on.

working class The class of people who earn wages, especially from industrial or manual labor.

work·ing·man [wûr′king·man′] *n., pl.* **work·ing·men** [wûr′king·men′] A person who works, especially one who does hard, manual labor.

working papers Legal documents issued by the government granting an alien or a minor the right to get a job.

work·load [wûrk′lōd′] *n.* 1 The amount of work to be performed in a given period of time by a worker or group of workers. 2 The amount of work that a machine is capable of performing in a given period of time.

a	add	**i**	it	**o͝o**	took	**oi**	oil
ā	ace	**ī**	ice	**o͞o**	pool	**ou**	pout
â	care	**o**	odd	**u**	up	**ng**	ring
ä	palm	**ō**	open	**û**	burn	**th**	thin
e	end	**ô**	order	**yo͞o**	fuse	**th̶**	this
ē	equal					**zh**	vision

ə = a in *above* e in *sicken* i in *possible* o in *melon* u in *circus*

work·man [wûrk′mən] *n., pl.* **work·men** [wûrk′·mən] A workingman.
work·man·like [wûrk′mən·līk′] *adj.* Done with care and skill.
work·man·ship [wûrk′mən·ship′] *n.* 1 The art or skill of a craftsman. 2 The quality of work done. 3 Something produced by work.
work·men's compensation [wûrk′mənz] Payments that an employer or an insurance company is legally required to make to a worker who has been injured on a job.
work·out [wûrk′out′] *n. informal* 1 A session of athletic activity for exercise, practice, or training. 2 Any vigorous activity.
work·room [wûrk′rōōm′ *or* wûrk′rŏŏm′] *n.* A room where work is done, especially manual work.
work·shop [wûrk′shop′] *n.* 1 A building or room where work is carried on. 2 A group of people who work on or study together some special project or subject: a drama *workshop.*
work·ta·ble [wûrk′tā′bəl] *n.* A table used for working and for holding tools and materials, as by a carpenter.
world [wûrld] *n.* 1 The earth. 2 A division or part of the earth: the Old *World.* 3 The universe; cosmos. 4 A division or section of things on or of the earth: the animal and plant *worlds.* 5 A definite group of people having common interests or characteristics: the *world* of sports; the music *world.* 6 The people of the earth; humanity: The *world* knew little of our town. 7 The people, places, and things of public or social life: They fled from the *world* and lived on a remote island. 8 A division of time or history: the modern *world.* 9 A great deal or quantity; large amount: Your help made a *world* of difference. **—for all the world** In every respect; exactly.
world-class [wûrld′klas′] *adj.* Of the highest ranking or ability: a *world-class* tennis player.
world·ly [wûrld′lē] *adj.* **world·li·er, world·i·est** 1 Of or having to do with the world or earthly existence rather than with religious or spiritual things. 2 Caring a great deal for and knowing a lot about the things of this world: an experienced, *worldly* person. **—world′li·ness** *n.*
world·ly-wise [wûrld′lē·wīz′] *adj.* Experienced in practical affairs and in dealing with people; sophisticated.
world power A nation powerful enough to act in and affect world affairs.
World Series A series of baseball games played at the end of the season between the winning teams of the National League and the American League.
world war A war involving most or all of the leading nations of the world.
World War I A war between France, Great Britain, Russia, the United States, and other nations on one side, and Germany, Austria-Hungary, and other countries on the other side. It lasted from 1914 to 1918.
World War II A war between France, Great Britain, the Soviet Union, the United States, and other countries on one side, and Germany, Italy, Japan, and other nations on the other side. It lasted from 1939 to 1945.
world-wear·y [wûrld′wir′ē] *adj.* Tired of life and material pleasures. **—world′-wear′i·ness** *n.*
world·wide [wûrld′wīd′] *adj.* Extended throughout the world: a *worldwide* conflict.
worm [wûrm] 1 *n.* A small, creeping animal having a long, soft, slender body and no legs. 2 *n.* Any creeping animal like a worm. 3 *n.* (*pl.*) A disease due to the presence of parasitic worms in the body. 4 *v.* To get the worms out of: to *worm* a puppy. 5 *n.* Something like a worm in appearance or movement, as the spiral thread of a screw. 6 *n.* A mean, groveling, contemptible person. 7 *v.* To get by stealthy or indirect ways or methods: to *worm* a secret out of someone. **—worm one's way** 1 To crawl or creep stealthily: to *worm one's way* through underbrush. 2 To advance stealthily or guilefully; insinuate: to *worm one's way* into a job.
worm-eat·en [wûrm′ēt′(ə)n] *adj.* 1 Pierced or gnawed by worms: a *worm-eaten* apple. 2 Old, worn-out, or antiquated.
worm gear A toothed wheel turned by a revolving screw.
worm·hole [wûrm′hōl′] *n.* A hole made by the passage of a worm.
worm·wood [wûrm′wŏŏd′] *n.* 1 Any of several European herbs or shrubs having a strong smell and bitter taste. 2 Something that causes feelings of bitterness or unpleasantness.
worm·y [wûr′mē] *adj.* **worm·i·er, worm·i·est** 1 Having worms. 2 Spoiled by worms. **—worm′i·ness** *n.*
worn [wôrn] 1 Past participle of WEAR. 2 *adj.* Damaged or affected by much use or wear: a *worn* suit. 3 *adj.* Tired, as from worry, anxiety, or illness: a *worn* face.
worn-out [wôrn′out′] *adj.* 1 Used until it has no further usefulness. 2 Very tired; exhausted.
wor·ri·some [wûr′ē·səm] *adj.* 1 Causing worry or anxiety. 2 Often worrying; given to worry.
wor·ry [wûr′ē] *v.* **wor·ried, wor·ry·ing,** *n., pl.* **wor·ries** 1 *v.* To be or cause to be uneasy in the mind; feel or make anxious: You must not *worry* any longer; You *worry* me. 2 *n.* A feeling of anxiety, vexation, or uneasiness: to be filled with *worry.* 3 *n.* Something that causes such a feeling: Debts were *worries.* 4 *v.* To bother; pester. 5 *v.* To pull, tear, or shake with the teeth, as a dog does. ◆ *Worry* comes from an Old English word meaning *to choke* or *strangle.* **—wor′ri·er** *n.*
wor·ry·wart [wûr′ē·wôrt′] *n. informal* A person who worries too much.
worse [wûrs] 1 Comparative of BAD, BADLY, and ILL. 2 *adj.* More harmful, evil, unpleasant, or faulty: A *worse* deed I can't imagine. 3 *adj.* More ill; less well: The patient is *worse* today. 4 *adv.* In a worse way or degree: The team played *worse* than usual. 5 *n.* Something more unsatisfactory or evil: There is even *worse* to come.
wors·en [wûr′sən] *v.* To make or become worse.
wor·ship [wûr′ship] *n., v.* **wor·shiped** or **wor·shipped, wor·ship·ing** or **wor·ship·ping** 1 *n.* Respect, honor, or love given to God or something held sacred. 2 *n.* A prayer or rite showing such feeling. 3 *v.* To express such feeling to, by a prayer or rite. 4 *v.* To participate in a church service: They *worship* every Sunday. 5 *n.* Great love or admiration for someone or something. 6 *v.* To love or admire a great deal: to *worship* one's parents. 7 *n. British* A title of honor used in addressing persons of rank or station: your *worship.* **—wor′ship·er** or **wor′ship·per** *n.*
wor·ship·ful [wûr′ship·fəl] *adj.* 1 Giving or feeling worship. 2 *British* Worthy of respect.
worst [wûrst] 1 Superlative of BAD, BADLY, and ILL. 2 *adj.* Most harmful, evil, unpleasant, or faulty: the *worst* performance of all. 3 *adv.* In the worst

way or degree: Today the chorus sang *worst* of all. **4** *n.* That which is worst: The *worst* that can happen is a scolding. **5** *v.* To defeat; vanquish: They *worsted* us badly. **—at worst** Under the most unfavorable circumstances. **—if worst comes to worst** If the worst or most awful thing actually happens. **—in the worst way** *slang* Very much.

wors·ted [wŏŏs′tid *or* wûr′stid] *n.* **1** A yarn spun from long strands of wool. **2** Cloth woven with this yarn, having a firm surface and no nap. **3** *adj. use*: a *worsted* suit.

worth [wûrth] **1** *n.* Any quality or qualities that can make a person or thing valuable, desirable, or useful: a teacher of great *worth.* **2** *prep.* Deserving of: a place *worth* a visit. **3** *n.* The value of anything in money or other exchangeable goods: a car of little *worth.* **4** *prep.* Equal in value to; exchangeable for: a job *worth* $20,000. **5** *n.* The amount of something to be had for a specific sum: ten cents *worth* of candy. **6** *n.* Wealth: What is the firm's *worth*? **7** *prep.* Having money or possessions amounting to.

worth·less [wûrth′lis] *adj.* Having no worth, value, or usefulness: a *worthless* good-for-nothing. **—worth′less·ly** *adv.* **—worth′less·ness** *n.*

worth·while [wûrth′(h)wīl′] *adj.* Having enough value or importance to be worth the effort, time, or money involved: a *worthwhile* trip.

wor·thy [wûr′t͟hē] *adj.* **wor·thi·er, wor·thi·est,** *n., pl.* **wor·thies** **1** *adj.* Having worth, value, or merit: a *worthy* charity. **2** *adj.* Fit or suitable for; deserving: courage *worthy* of our praise. **3** *n.* A person of great worth or prominence. **—wor′thi·ly** *adv.* **—wor′thi·ness** *n.*

wot [wot] Present tense of WIT[2]: formerly used with singular nouns or with *I, he, she,* or *it,* as in "God *wot,*" which means "God knows."

would [wŏŏd] Past tense of WILL, used chiefly, however, as a helping verb to express: **1** Desire or inclination: those who *would* ban noisy scooters. **2** Something depending on a condition contrary to the actual one: We *would* go if we were able. **3** Determination: The child *would* not speak. **4** Preference: We *would* have you succeed rather than fail. **5** Request: *Would* you give us a call? **6** Custom or habit: We *would* ride together every day. **7** Doubt or uncertainty: It *would* seem to be wrong. ◆ See SHOULD.

would-be [wŏŏd′bē′] *adj.* **1** Desiring or pretending to be: a *would-be* poet. **2** Intended to be: The *would-be* jokes annoyed us all.

would·n't [wŏŏd′(ə)nt] Would not.

wouldst [wŏŏdst] *v.* A form of the verb WOULD, used with *thou*: seldom used today.

wound[1] [wōōnd] **1** *n.* A hurt or injury caused by something piercing, cutting, or tearing through the skin. **2** *v.* To injure by penetrating through the skin. **3** *n.* Any hurt to the feelings or pride. **4** *v.* To injure the feelings or pride of.

wound[2] [wound] Past tense and past participle of WIND[2]: I *wound* the clock last night.

wove [wōv] Past tense and alternative past participle of WEAVE.

wo·ven [wō′vən] Alternative past participle of WEAVE.

wow [wou] *informal* **1** *interj.* An exclamation of wonder, pleasure, or enthusiasm. **2** *n.* A great success. **3** *v.* To please or impress greatly.

wpm or **w.p.m.** words per minute.

wrack [rak] *n.* **1** Ruin and destruction, especially in the phrase **wrack and ruin.** **2** Seaweed or other vegetation washed ashore by the sea.

wraith [rāth] *n.* **1** A ghostlike image of a person, seen shortly before or shortly after death. **2** Any ghost or specter.

wran·gle [rang′gəl] *v.* **wran·gled, wran·gling,** *n.* **1** *v.* To argue or quarrel noisily or angrily. **2** *n.* An angry or noisy quarrel. **3** *v. U.S.* To herd or round up (horses).

wran·gler [rang′glər] *n.* **1** A person who wrangles. **2** *U.S.* A person who herds livestock; cowhand.

wrap [rap] *v.* **wrapped** or **wrapt** [rapt], **wrap·ping,** *n.* **1** *v.* To surround and cover by something folded or wound about: The waiter *wrapped* the rolls in a napkin. **2** *v.* To wind or fold about something: I *wrapped* a towel around my head. **3** *v.* To cover with paper or the like and tie or fasten: to *wrap* a box. **4** *n.* An outer cloak or garment. **5** *v.* To blot out or conceal; envelop: The city was *wrapped* in smoke. **—keep under wraps** To keep secret or hidden. **—wrapped up in** **1** Clothed or enveloped by. **2** Exclusively interested or involved in; engrossed in.

wrap·per [rap′ər] *n.* **1** Something used to cover or protect, as a paper wrapped around a magazine before mailing. **2** A dressing gown. **3** A person or thing that wraps.

wrap·ping [rap′ing] *n.* (*often pl.*) A covering in which something is wrapped.

wrapt [rapt] An alternative past tense and past participle of WRAP.

wrap-up [rap′up′] *n. informal* A concluding summary, especially of a news or sports broadcast.

wrath [rath] *n.* Great or violent anger; rage.

wrath·ful [rath′fəl] *adj.* Extremely angry; feeling or showing wrath. **—wrath′ful·ly** *adv.* **—wrath′ful·ness** *n.*

wreak [rēk] *v.* **1** To give free expression to (a malevolent emotion). **2** To inflict (vengeance or punishment). **3** To cause: *wreak* havoc.

wreath [rēth] *n., pl.* **wreaths** [rēt͟hz] **1** A ring of flowers or leaves woven together. **2** Any curled or spiral shape, as of smoke.

wreathe [rēt͟h] *v.* **wreathed, wreath·ing** **1** To form into a wreath: to *wreathe* flowers. **2** To decorate or encircle with or as if with wreaths: to *wreathe* a window at Christmas. **3** To cover or envelop: a face *wreathed* in smiles.

wreck [rek] **1** *v.* To undergo or cause to undergo ruin, damage, or destruction: The storm *wrecked* the ship. **2** *v.* To tear down: to *wreck* a building. **3** *n.* Something that has been ruined, damaged, or destroyed: a *wreck* on the side of the road. **4** *n.* Destruction, ruin, or loss: The storm led to the *wreck* of many ships. **5** *v.* To change, frustrate, or put an end to: The rain *wrecked* our plans. **6** *n.* A person who is physically, mentally, or morally in a very bad condition.

W

a	add	**i**	it	**ŏŏ**	took	**oi**	oil
ā	ace	**ī**	ice	**ōō**	pool	**ou**	pout
â	care	**o**	odd	**u**	up	**ng**	ring
ä	palm	**ō**	open	**û**	burn	**th**	thin
e	end	**ô**	order	**yōō**	fuse	**t͟h**	this
ē	equal					**zh**	vision

ə = {a in *above* e in *sicken* i in *possible*; o in *melon* u in *circus*}

wreck·age [rek′ij] *n.* 1 The act of wrecking. 2 A wrecked condition. 3 The remains or fragments of a wreck.

wreck·er [rek′ər] *n.* 1 A person or thing that causes destruction, damage, or frustration. 2 A person whose occupation is tearing down old structures, as buildings or bridges. 3 A person, train, car, or machine that clears away wrecks.

wren [ren] *n.* Any of numerous small songbirds, having a short, sometimes upturned tail.

wrench [rench] 1 *v.* To twist or pull violently or with force: to *wrench* a knife from someone's hand. 2 *n.* A violent twist: Give the lid a *wrench* and it will come off. 3 *v.* To twist, so as to cause a sprain or injury: I *wrenched* my shoulder. 4 *n.* A sprain or injury caused by a sharp or violent twist or pull. 5 *n.* Any of various tools for holding or turning bolts, nuts, or pipe. 6 *n.* Any sudden grief or pain: It gave us a *wrench* to say good-bye. 7 *v.* To distort the original meaning or character of.

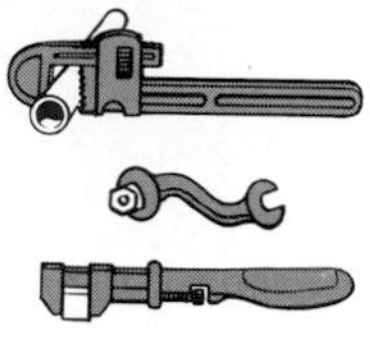

Wrenches

wrest [rest] *v.* 1 To pull or force away by violent twisting or wringing: to *wrest* a weapon from one's grasp. 2 To seize by violence: to *wrest* power from a ruler. 3 To twist (words) into meanings not intended. 4 To gain or get by toil and effort: to *wrest* a living from barren soil.

wres·tle [res′(ə)l] *v.* **wres·tled, wres·tling,** *n.* 1 *v.* To engage in wrestling. 2 *v.* To engage in a wrestling contest with. 3 *n.* The act of wrestling. 4 *v.* To struggle, as for mastery or a solution: to *wrestle* with a problem. 5 *n.* Any hard struggle. —**wres′tler** *n.*

wres·tling [res′ling] *n.* A sport or exercise in which each of two unarmed contestants tries to throw or force the other to the ground or into a certain position on the ground.

wretch [rech] *n.* 1 A vile or wicked person. 2 An unfortunate or miserable person.

wretch·ed [rech′id] *adj.* 1 Very unhappy, miserable, or dejected. 2 Causing discomfort, misery, or grief: *wretched* surroundings. 3 Mean, wicked, or bad: a *wretched* criminal. 4 Poor, worthless, or unsatisfactory: a *wretched* movie. —**wretch′ed·ly** *adv.* —**wretch′ed·ness** *n.*

wri·er [rī′ər] The comparative of WRY.

wri·est [rī′əst] The superlative of WRY.

wrig·gle [rig′əl] *v.* **wrig·gled, wrig·gling,** *n.* 1 *v.* To twist or squirm: After an hour all the children were *wriggling* in their chairs. 2 *v.* To move or proceed by twisting or crawling: The worm *wriggled* across my hand. 3 *n.* A wriggling motion. 4 *v.* To escape or get out of something in a sneaky, sly manner: to *wriggle* out of an unpleasant situation. —**wrig′gly** *adj.*

wrig·gler [rig′lər] *n.* 1 A person or thing that wriggles. 2 The larva of a mosquito.

wright [rīt] *n.* A person who builds, writes, or creates: used chiefly in combination, as in *shipwright.*

wring [ring] *v.* **wrung** [rung], **wring·ing,** *n.* 1 *v.* To squeeze or twist, usually to get water out of something: to *wring* wet clothes. 2 *v.* To squeeze or press out, usually by twisting: to *wring* water out of a bathing suit. 3 *v.* To get or acquire by force, violence, or threats: to *wring* an answer out of someone. 4 *v.* To press and twist (the hands) together: I *wrung* my hands. 5 *v.* To make sad; torment: The unhappy situation *wrung* our hearts. 6 *n.* The act of wringing.

wring·er [ring′ər] *n.* A person or thing that wrings, especially a device that wrings water out of wet laundry.

wrin·kle [ring′kəl] *n., v.* **wrin·kled, wrin·kling** 1 *n.* A small ridge, crease, or fold on a surface: *wrinkles* on one's skin. 2 *v.* To make a wrinkle or wrinkles in: to *wrinkle* a shirt. 3 *v.* To become wrinkled: a face *wrinkled* with laughter.

wrist [rist] *n.* The joint that connects the hand and the forearm.

wrist·band [rist′band′] *n.* 1 The part of a sleeve that covers the wrist; cuff. 2 A strap for a wrist watch.

wrist·watch [rist′woch′] *n.* A watch on a band or bracelet worn on the wrist.

writ [rit] 1 A past tense and past participle of WRITE: seldom used today. 2 *n.* An order written and issued by a court of law commanding the person to whom it is issued to do or not to do something. 3 *n.* Something written, now chiefly used in **Holy Writ,** meaning the Bible.

write [rīt] *v.* **wrote, writ·ten, writ·ing** 1 To make or form (letters, words, or numbers) on a surface, usually with a pen or pencil. 2 To make or put down the letters, words, or numbers of: *Write* your phone number in this space. 3 To cover or fill with writing: to *write* ten pages every day. 4 To tell or tell something to by writing, usually by writing a letter: I *wrote* that I would be home soon; They *wrote* us every day. 5 To be the author or composer of: to *write* a song. 6 To be a writer: It is hard work to *write* for a living. 7 To produce a specified quality of writing: This author *writes* very well. 8 To draw up or draft by writing: to *write* a check or a will. 9 To show or make visible: Fear was *written* on your face. —**write down** To put into writing. —**write off** 1 To cancel. 2 To give up as lost or failed. —**write out** 1 To put into writing. 2 To write in full or complete form. —**write up** To describe in writing.

write-in [rīt′in′] *n.* A vote cast by writing in the name of a candidate whose name does not appear on the ballot.

writ·er [rī′tər] *n.* A person who writes, especially a person who writes for a living.

write-up [rīt′up′] *n. informal* A written description, record, or account of something.

writhe [rīth] *v.* **writhed, writh·ing** 1 To twist or distort the body or part of the body, as in pain. 2 To suffer mentally from embarrassment, shame, sorrow, or other painful emotion.

writ·ing [rī′ting] *n.* 1 The act of a person who writes. 2 Anything written or expressed in letters, especially a literary composition. 3 Handwriting: I can't read this *writing.* 4 Written form: Your order must be in *writing.* 5 The art or profession of a writer.

writ·ten [rit′(ə)n] Past participle of WRITE.

wrong [rông] 1 *adj.* Not right, moral, just, or lawful: It is *wrong* to cheat. 2 *adj.* Not correct or true: a *wrong* estimate. 3 *adj.* Not suitable, fit, or proper: the *wrong* clothes. 4 *n.* Something that is wrong, especially an evil or unjust act: I did the group a *wrong.* 5 *v.* To do something that is wrong, evil, or unjust to: You *wrong* their generosity by saying that. 6 *adj.* Not working or acting properly: Something is *wrong* with the lock. 7

adj. Not desired or intended: to take a *wrong* road. **8** *adv.* In a wrong direction or place: You turned *wrong*. **9** *adv.* In a wrong, incorrect, or unsatisfactory manner: to answer *wrong*. **10** *n.* The condition of being wrong: to be in the *wrong*. **11** *adj.* Intended or made to be turned under, inward, or so as not to be seen: the *wrong* side of the cloth. **—go wrong** 1 To turn out badly or unsatisfactorily. **2** To do things that are not right, good, or just. **—in the wrong** 1 In error; mistaken. **2** At fault. **—wrong′ly** *adv.*

wrong·do·ing [rông′do͞o′ing] *n.* The doing of something evil or wicked. **—wrong′do′er** *n.*

wrong·ful [rông′fəl] *adj.* Not right, just, or lawful; wrong. **—wrong′ful·ly** *adv.* **—wrong′ful·ness** *n.*

wrong·head·ed [rông′hed′id] *adj.* Stubbornly wrong, as in one's ideas, judgments, or opinions. **—wrong′head′ed·ly** *adv.* **—wrong′head′ed·ness** *n.*

wrote [rōt] Past tense of WRITE.

wroth [rôth] *adj.* Angry; furious: seldom used today.

wrought [rôt] **1** A past tense and past participle of WORK. **2** *adj.* Beaten or hammered into shape by tools: *wrought* gold. **3** *adj.* Formed or fashioned: a delicately *wrought* clock. **—wrought up** Excited; agitated: to get *wrought up* over trifles.

wrought iron Iron with little carbon in it, that can be easily forged or hammered into various shapes but is very strong and hard to break or crack.

Wrought iron fence

wrung [rung] Past tense and past participle of WRING: Have you *wrung* the clothes dry?

wry [rī] *adj.* **wri·er, wri·est** **1** Bent, twisted, or turned to one side: a *wry* smile. **2** Grim, bitter, or ironic: Your comments are full of *wry* humor. **—wry′ly** *adv.* **—wry·ness** *n.*

WSW west-southwest.

wt. weight.

WV Postal Service abbreviation of West Virginia.

W.Va. West Virginia.

WWI or **W.W.I** World War I.

WWII or **W.W.II** World War II.

WY Postal Service abbreviation of Wyoming.

Wyo. Wyoming.

a	add	**i**	it	**o͝o**	took	**oi**	oil
ā	ace	**ī**	ice	**o͞o**	pool	**ou**	pout
â	care	**o**	odd	**u**	up	**ng**	ring
ä	palm	**ō**	open	**û**	burn	**th**	thin
e	end	**ô**	order	**yo͞o**	fuse	**th**	this
ē	equal					**zh**	vision

ə = a in *above*, e in *sicken*, i in *possible*, o in *melon*, u in *circus*

Xx

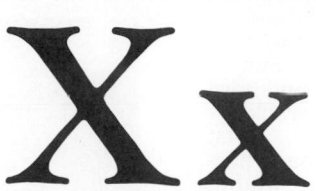

Early Phoenician (late 2nd millennium B.C.)

Phoenician (8th century B.C.)

Eastern Greek (6th century B.C.)

Western Greek (6th century B.C.)

Classical Greek (403 B.C. onward)

Monumental Latin (4th century B.C.)

Classical Latin

Uncial

Half uncial

Caroline minuscule

X is the twenty-fourth letter of the alphabet. The sign for it may have originated among Semitic people in the Near East, in the region of Palestine and Syria, probably in the middle of the second millennium B.C. Little is known about the sign until around 1000 B.C., when the Phoenicians began using it. They called it *samekh* and used it, along with three other letters, for the sibilant *s* sound.

When the Greeks adopted the Phoenician alphabet around the ninth century B.C., they had no use for all the Semitic letters for *s* sounds. Eastern Greeks used the sign for *samekh*—but not its name, which became the Greek *sigma*—for the sound *ks*. They renamed the sign *xi*. The Eastern Greeks had a second sign, an *X*—which had no counterpart in the Semitic script—to stand for the *kh* sound. This sign came to be called *chi*. Western Greeks, on the other hand, had only one sign. They had no *kh* sound. They used *X* for the *ks* sound.

As early as the eighth century B.C., the Etruscans adopted the Greek alphabet. However, they had no *ks* sound. The Romans, who in general took the alphabet from the Etruscans, adopted *X* directly from the Western Greeks. Around the time of the Caesars, the Romans made the shapes of letters more graceful. The model of *X* found on the base of Trajan's column, erected in Rome in 114, is considered a masterpiece of letter design. A Trajan-style *majuscule,* or capital letter, *X* opens this essay.

The *minuscule,* or small letter, *x* developed as a smaller version of the large letter, between the third and the ninth centuries, in the handwriting that scribes used for copying books. Contributing to its development were the Roman *uncials* of the fourth to the eighth centuries, the *half uncials* of the fifth to the ninth centuries, and the *Caroline minuscules,* a script that evolved under the encouragement of Charlemagne (742-814). The Caroline minuscules were used on the medieval manuscripts of the ninth and tenth centuries.

x or **X** [eks] *n., pl.* **x's** or **X's** [ek′siz] **1** The 24th letter of the English alphabet. **2** An unknown quantity, factor, or result. **3** (*usually written* **X**) The Roman numeral for ten. **4** A mark shaped like an X, representing the signature of a person who cannot write. **5** A mark used in maps and diagrams to direct attention, as to a place or a figure. **6** A symbol meaning "times" or "by."

X **1** Christ. **2** Christian. **3** extra.

X-axis [eks′ak′sis] *n., pl.* **X-ax·es** [eks′ak′sēz] On a graph, the axis that extends most usually from the left of the figure to the right; the axis of abscissas.

X chromosome One of the paired chromosomes that determine sex in animals and plants.

Xe The symbol for the element xenon.

xe·bec [zē′bek] *n.* A small, three-masted vessel, formerly used by Algerian pirates in the Mediterranean Sea.

xe·non [zē′non′] *n.* A colorless, odorless, practically inert gaseous element found in traces in the atmosphere.

xen·o·pho·bi·a [zen′ə·fō′bē·ə] *adj.* An abnormal fear of strangers, foreigners, and things and ideas that are strange or foreign. **—xen·o·pho·bic** [zen′·ə·fō′bik] *adj.*

xe·ric [zir′ik] *adj.* Of, having to do with, or adapted to a very dry environment.

xe·rog·ra·phy [zi·rog′rə·fē] *n.* A way of making photocopies by using light, heat, and a powdered pigment instead of liquid solutions. **—xe·ro·graph·ic** [zir′ə·graf′ik] *adj.* **—xe′ro·graph′i·cal·ly** *adv.*

xe·ro·phyte [zir′ə·fīt′] *n.* A plant adapted to growing and surviving in a dry environment.

Xe·rox [zir′oks] **1** *n.* A machine or process for making photocopies using xerography: a trademark. **2** *n.* A copy made by a Xerox machine: a trademark. **3** *v.* To photocopy on a Xerox machine.

xi [zī *or* sī] *n.* The 14th letter of the Greek alphabet.

XL **1** extra large. **2** extra long.

X·mas [kris′məs *or* eks′məs] *n.* Christmas. ◆ The *X* in *Xmas* stands for the Greek letter *chi*, which is the first letter of *Christ* when written in Greek. *X* has been used as a symbol for *Christ* for hundreds of years, but *Xmas* should be avoided in formal writing.

Xn Christian.

Xnty Christianity.

X-ray [eks′rā′] **1** *adj.* Producing, using, or having to do with X rays: an *X-ray* machine. **2** *v.* To examine, photograph, or treat with X rays.

X ray **1** Electromagnetic radiation of very short wavelength and high energy. The ability of X rays to penetrate solids makes them useful in medical diagnosis and treatment and in inspecting machine parts. **2** A picture made with X rays: an X ray of the chest. ◆ The term *X ray* is a translation from the German. X rays were so named because their nature was unknown.

xy·lem [zī′ləm] *n.* The woody tissue of a plant, found in the stems or trunk.

xy·lo·phone [zī′lə·fōn′] *n.* A musical instrument having wooden bars of different sizes that are sounded by being struck with mallets.

Yy

Y is the twenty-fifth letter of the alphabet. Its early history is the same as that for the letter *V.* The sign for both originated among Semitic people in the Near East, in the region of Palestine and Syria, probably in the middle of the second millennium B.C. Little is known about the sign until around 1000 B.C., when the Phoenicians began using it. They named it *waw* and used it for a *w*-like sound.

When the Greeks adopted the Phoenician sign around the ninth century B.C., they developed two signs of their own from it. The secondary form, called *digamma,* eventually became the letter *F* (see *F*). The Greeks used the main form for the vowel *upsilon,* which means "bare *U*" or "simple *U*." *Upsilon* stood for the sound of *u* and sometimes *y.*

As early as the eighth century B.C., the Etruscans adopted the Greek alphabet, and they used the Greek upsilon as their vowel *u.* It is from the Etruscans that the Romans took the letter. Both the Etruscans and the Romans, however, wrote the sign as *V.* To the Romans, the sign stood for the sounds of *u, v,* and *w.* The *w* sound later disappeared from Latin.

The Romans had no use for a *Y* sign until after they had conquered Greece in 146 B.C. Then many Greek words began to enter the Latin language, and the Romans needed a *Y* sign to use in some of these words. The Romans borrowed the upsilon sign as written by the Greeks. They used it for the sounds *u, ue,* and *y.* In the Greek words, these sounds quickly began to sound like our present-day *i* [ī], a sound that *y* often has today. The sign adopted by the Romans became our *majuscule,* or capital letter, *Y.*

In time, a *minuscule,* or small letter, appeared. The small letter is essentially a smaller version of the majuscule except that the stem extends below the line. As a help to readers, early English scribes often used the minuscule *y* instead of *i,* especially when the undotted *i* (see *I*) occurred near an *m* or *n* or *u.*

Early Phoenician (late 2nd millennium B.C.)
Phoenician 8th century B.C.)
Early Greek (9th-7th centuries B.C.)
Western Greek (6th century B.C.)
Classical Greek (403 B.C. onward)
Early Etruscan (8th century B.C.)
Classical Etruscan (around 400 B.C.)
Monumental Latin (4th century B.C.)
Classical Latin
Roman capital (4th-5th centuries)
Anglo-Saxon minuscule (8th-9th centuries)

y or **Y** [wī] *n., pl.* **y's** or **Y's** [wīz] **1** The 25th letter of the English alphabet. **2** Anything shaped like Y: a *Y* in the road.

y. **1** yard(s). **2** year(s).

Y The symbol for the element yttrium.

Y or **Y.** **1** Young Men's Christian Association. **2** Young Men's Hebrew Association. **3** Young Women's Christian Association. **4** Young Women's Hebrew Association.

-y[1] A suffix meaning: **1** Having the quality of or full of, as in *snowy.* **2** Resembling or like, as in *summery.* **3** Somewhat; rather, as in *chilly.* **4** Inclined to; apt to, as in *sleepy.*

-y[2] A suffix meaning: **1** The quality or state of being, as in *victory.* **2** The act, action, or activity of, as in *entreaty.*

-y[3] A suffix meaning: **1** Little; small, as in *kitty.* **2** Dear, as in *aunty* or *Billy.*

yacht [yot] **1** *n.* A vessel for racing or for private cruising for pleasure. **2** *v.* To cruise, race, or sail in a yacht.

yacht·ing [yot′ing] *n.* The sport of sailing or racing a yacht.

yachts·man [yots′mən] *n., pl.* **yachts·men** [yots′·mən] A person who owns or sails a yacht.

yack [yak] *v. slang* Another spelling of YAK.[2]

yack·e·ty-yak [yak′i·tē·yak′] *v.* **yack·e·ty-yakked, yack·e·ty-yak·king** *slang* Another word for YAK.[2]

ya·hoo [yä′hōō′ *or* yā′hōō′] *n., pl.* **ya·hoos** A brutish or crude person.

Yah·weh [yä′wā] or **Yah·veh** [yä′vā] *n.* The name of the God of the ancient Hebrews.

yak[1] [yak] *n.* A large ox with long hair, found in Tibet and central Asia, often used as a beast of burden.

Yak

yak[2] [yak] *v.* **yakked, yak·king** *slang* To talk on and on without stopping.

y'all [yôl] *Southern U.S.* You-all.

yam [yam] *n.* **1** The fleshy, edible root of any of several vines growing mostly in warm regions. **2** The vine having such a root. **3** A variety of sweet potato.

yam·mer [yam′ər] *v. informal* To complain or speak persistently.

yang [yang] *n.* In Chinese cosmic philosophy, the active male principle.

yank [yangk] *informal* **1** *v.* To jerk or pull suddenly. **2** *n.* A sudden, sharp pull; jerk.

a	add	**i**	it	**o͝o**	took	**oi**	oil
ā	ace	**ī**	ice	**o͞o**	pool	**ou**	pout
â	care	**o**	odd	**u**	up	**ng**	ring
ä	palm	**ō**	open	**û**	burn	**th**	thin
e	end	**ô**	order	**yo͞o**	fuse	**t͟h**	this
ē	equal					**zh**	vision

ə = {a in *above* e in *sicken* i in *possible* / o in *melon* u in *circus*}

Yank [yangk] *n. informal* A Yankee.
Yan·kee [yang′kē] 1 *n.* A person born or living in New England. 2 *n.* A person born or living in the northern U.S. 3 *n.* A person born in or a citizen of the U.S.; American: chiefly a foreign usage. 4 *adj.* Of or having to do with a Yankee or Yankees.
yap [yap] *n., v.* **yapped, yap·ping** 1 *n.* A bark or yelp. 2 *v.* To bark or yelp.
yard[1] [yärd] *n.* 1 A measure of length equal to 3 feet, or 36 inches, or 0.914 meter. 2 A long, slender pole set crosswise on a mast and used to support sails.
yard[2] [yärd] *n.* 1 A piece of ground next to or around a residence, church, school, or other building. 2 An enclosed area used for some specific work: often used in combinaton, as in *shipyard.* 3 An area with tracks where cars are stored and trains made up.
yard·age [yär′dij] *n.* The amount or length of something, expressed in yards.
yard·arm [yärd′ärm′] *n.* Either end of a yard that supports a sail.
yard goods Cloth that is sold by the yard.
yard·mas·ter [yärd′mas′tər] *n.* A person in charge of a railroad yard.
yard·stick [yärd′stik′] *n.* 1 A measuring stick a yard in length. 2 Any standard of comparison.
yar·mul·ke [yä(r)′mə(l)·kə] *n.* A skull cap worn by many Jewish men and boys.
yarn [yärn] *n.* 1 Any spun strand, natural or synthetic, prepared for use in weaving and knitting. 2 An adventure story, especially one that is made up.
yar·row [yar′ō] *n.* Any of several hardy perennial plants having narrow, fernlike leaves, clusters of small flowers, and a sharp smell.

Yarmulke

yat·a·ghan [yat′ə·gan′] *n.* A Turkish sword with a double curve to the blade and no handle guard.
yaw [yô] 1 *v.* To turn or move out of its course, as a ship when struck by a heavy sea. 2 *n.* A movement away from a straight course.
yawl [yôl] 1 *n.* A sailboat with a mainmast near the bow and a shorter mast very near the stern. 2 A ship's boat, rowed by oars.
yawn [yôn] 1 *v.* To open the mouth wide, usually in a way that cannot be controlled, with a long intake of breath, as when one is sleepy or bored. 2 *n.* The act of yawning: I tried to stifle a *yawn.* 3 *v.* To be or stand wide open, as a cave.
yawp [yôp] 1 *n.* A loud, sharp cry. 2 *v.* To make a loud, sharp cry.
yaws [yôz] *n.pl.* A contagious disease of the tropics, marked by skin eruptions.

Yawl

Y-ax·is [wī′ak′sis] *n., pl.* **Y-ax·es** [wī′ak′sēz] On a graph, the axis that is most usually vertical; axis of ordinates.
Yb The symbol for the element ytterbium.
Y chromosome One of the paired chromosomes that determine sex in animals and plants.
y·clept or **y·cleped** [i·klept′] *adj.* Called; named: seldom used today.
yd. 1 yard. 2 (*usually written* **yds.**) yards.
ye[1] [yē] *pron.* You: seldom used today.
ye[2] [t͟hē] *adj.* The: a mistaken form resulting from the substitution of the character *y* for the character that represented the sound [t͟h] in the Old English alphabet: seldom used today.
yea [yā] 1 *adv.* Yes: seldom used today. 2 *adv.* In reality; indeed. 3 *n.* An affirmative vote or voter.
yeah [ye′ə, yā′ə, *or* ya′ə] *adv. informal* Yes.
year [yir] *n.* 1 The period of time in which the earth completes one revolution around the sun, consisting of 365 or, in leap year, 366 days, divided into 12 months, beginning January 1 and ending December 31. 2 A period of 12 months starting at any time: a *year* from now. 3 A period of time, usually less than a year, given over to some special work or activity: the school *year.* 4 (*pl.*) Age: My grandparents are active for their *years.* **—year after year** Every year.
year·book [yir′bo͝ok′] *n.* 1 A book published annually presenting information about the previous year. 2 A book published to commemorate the members and activities of a high school or college graduating class.
year·ling [yir′ling] 1 *n.* An animal between one and two years old. 2 *adj.* A year old: a *yearling* filly.
year·ly [yir′lē] 1 *adj.* Happening, done, or appearing once a year: a *yearly* visit. 2 *adv.* Once a year; annually: They pay us a visit *yearly.* 3 *adj.* Of, for, or lasting for a year: a *yearly* income.
yearn [yûrn] *v.* 1 To have an earnest desire; long. 2 To be deeply moved; feel sympathy.
yearn·ing [yûr′ning] *n.* An earnest desire; deep longing.
year-round [yir′round′] 1 *adj.* Available or occurring throughout the year: a *year-round* sport. 2 *adv.* Throughout the year: She plays tennis *year-round.*
yeast [yēst] *n.* 1 A substance formed by the clumping together of certain tiny fungi in a thick, frothy, yellow mass. It is used to make bread rise and in the brewing of beer. 2 A cake of this substance mixed with flour or meal.
yegg [yeg] *n. slang* A thief, especially a burglar who robs safes.
yel. yellow.
yell [yel] 1 *v.* To shout; scream; roar. 2 *n.* A sharp, loud cry or scream. 3 *v.* To cheer. 4 *n.* A rhythmic cheer, made up of a series of words or nonsense syllables and shouted by a group, as at a football game.
yel·low [yel′ō] 1 *n.* The color of ripe lemons or of sunflowers. 2 *adj.* Of or having this color. 3 *v.* To make or become yellow. 4 *n.* Any paint or dye having such a color. 5 *adj.* Having a yellowish complexion. 6 *n.* The yolk of an egg. 7 *adj. informal* Cowardly. **—yel′low·ness** *n.*
yellow fever An infectious disease of warm countries caused by a virus transmitted to humans by the bite of certain mosquitoes. It is marked by fever, vomiting, and a yellowing of the skin.
yel·low·ham·mer [yel′ō·ham′ər] *n.* A bird like the bunting, the male of which has bright yellow plumage.
yel·low·ish [yel′ō·ish] *adj.* Somewhat yellow.

yellow jack 1 The yellow flag raised on a ship in quarantine. 2 Yellow fever.

yellow jacket Any of various wasps having bright yellow markings on the body.

Yellow jacket

yelp [yelp] 1 *n.* A sharp, shrill cry or bark. 2 *v.* To utter or express by a yelp.

Yem. Yemen.

Yem·e·ni [yem'ə·nē] 1 *adj.* Of or from the Yemen Arab Republic. 2 *adj.* Of or from the People's Democratic Republic of Yemen. 3 *n.* A person born in or a citizen of the Yemen Arab Republic. 4 *n.* A person born in or a citizen of the People's Democratic Republic of Yemen.

Yem·en·ite [yem'ə·nīt'] *n.* 1 A person born in or a citizen of the Yemen Arab Republic. 2 A person born in or a citizen of the People's Democratic Republic of Yemen.

yen[1] [yen] *n., pl.* **yen** The basic unit of money in Japan.

yen[2] [yen] *informal* An intense longing; strong desire; urge.

yen·ta [yen'tə] *n. slang* A nosy gossip.

yeo·man [yō'mən] *n., pl.* **yeo·men** [yō'mən] 1 In the U.S. Navy or Coast Guard, a petty officer who performs clerical duties. 2 *British* A person who cultivates his or her own farm.

yeo·man·ry [yō'mən·rē] *n.* Yeomen as a class; farmers who cultivate their own land.

yep [yep] *adv. informal* Yes.

yes [yes] *adv., n., pl.* **yes·es** or **yes·ses** 1 *adv.* As you say; truly; just so. 2 *adv.* And in addition; moreover: The store has a large selection, *yes*, and inexpensive too. 3 *n.* An affirmative reply: The invitation got three *yeses* and two noes. 4 *n.* A vote in favor of something.

ye·shi·va or **ye·shi·vah** [yə·shē'və] *n.* 1 A Jewish school that offers religious and secular education. 2 A Jewish school for the study of the Talmud.

yes-man [yes'man'] *n., pl.* **yes-men** [yes'men'] *informal* A person who always voices agreement with the opinions and suggestions of superiors.

yes·ter·day [yes'tər·dē *or* yes'tər·dā'] 1 *n.* The day before today. 2 *adv.* On the day before today. 3 *n.* The near past. 4 *adv.* In the near past.

yes·ter·night [yes'tər·nīt'] 1 *n.* Last night. 2 *adv.* In or during the preceding night. ◆ This word is used mostly in poems.

yes·ter·year [yes'tər·yir'] 1 *n.* Last year. 2 *adv.* In or during the preceding year. ◆ This word is used mostly in poems.

yet [yet] 1 *adv.* Up to the present time; so far: They haven't called me *yet*. 2 *adv.* At the present time; now: Don't go *yet*. 3 *adv.* Now as previously; still: I can hear the song *yet*. 4 *adv.* Sometime; eventually: The plan will succeed *yet*. 5 *adv.* After all the time passed away: Aren't you ready *yet*? 6 *adv.* In addition; still: We have to go a mile *yet*. 7 *adv.* Even; still: a *yet* higher price. 8 *adv.* Nevertheless; however: It was hot, *yet* not unpleasant. 9 *conj.* Nevertheless; but: I ask as a friend, *yet* you will not help. —**as yet** Up to now.

ye·ti [yet'ē] *n., pl.* **yet·is** A large, hairy, humanlike creature supposed to live in the Himalayas.

yew [yo͞o] *n.* 1 Any of various evergreen trees having flat, slender needles, a berrylike fruit, and a hard, fine-grained wood. 2 The wood of the yew.

Yew

Yid·dish [yid'ish] 1 *n.* A Germanic language written in Hebrew letters and spoken by many Jews in central and eastern Europe and by Jewish immigrants in other places. 2 *adj.* Of or having to do with Yiddish; written or spoken in Yiddish.

yield [yēld] 1 *v.* To give forth; produce: The field will *yield* a good crop. 2 *n.* The amount yielded; product; result. 3 *v.* To give up, as to superior power; surrender: to *yield* a fortress. 4 *v.* To grant or concede: to *yield* consent. 5 *v.* To give way, as to pressure or force. 6 *v.* To assent; consent: to *yield* to persuasion. 7 *v.* To give place: I *yield* to no one.

yield·ing [yēl'ding] *adj.* Willing or likely to yield; submissive.

yin [yin] *n.* In Chinese cosmic philosophy, the passive female principle.

yip·pee [yip'ē] *interj.* An expression used to express joy or triumph.

YMCA or **Y.M.C.A.** Young Men's Christian Association.

YMHA or **Y.M.H.A.** Young Men's Hebrew Association.

YOB or **Y.O.B.** year of birth.

yo·del [yōd'(ə)l] *v.* **yo·deled** or **yo·delled, yo·del·ing** or **yo·del·ling,** *n.* 1 *v.* To sing in the form of a warble, by changing one's voice rapidly back and forth from its natural tone to a shrill falsetto, as is done in the Swiss mountains. 2 *n.* The act or sound of yodeling. 3 *n.* A melody sung by yodeling. —**yo'·del·er** or **yo'del·ler** *n.*

yo·ga [yō'gə] *n.* 1 A Hindu system of mystical philosophy and meditation in which the individual human spirit seeks union with that of the universe. 2 A related system of exercises which help to attain physical and mental well-being. ◆ *Yoga* comes from a Hindustani word derived from a Sanskrit word meaning *union*.

yo·gi [yō'gē] *n., pl.* **yo·gis** A person who practices yoga or who follows the yoga philosophy.

yo·gurt or **yo·ghurt** [yō'gərt] *n.* A thick milk food made by the addition of bacteria to curdled milk. ◆ *Yogurt* comes from a Turkish word.

a	add	**i**	it	**o͝o**	took	**oi**	oil
ā	ace	**ī**	ice	**o͞o**	pool	**ou**	pout
â	care	**o**	odd	**u**	up	**ng**	ring
ä	palm	**ō**	open	**û**	burn	**th**	thin
e	end	**ô**	order	**yo͞o**	fuse	**th**	this
ē	equal					**zh**	vision

ə = a in *above* e in *sicken* i in *possible* o in *melon* u in *circus*

Y

yoke [yōk] *n., v.* **yoked, yok·ing** 1 *n.* A curved, wooden frame with attachments used to join together two animals, as oxen. 2 *v.* To attach (an animal): to *yoke* an ox to a plow. 3 *n., pl.* **yoke** A pair of animals, as oxen, joined by a yoke. 4 *n.* Any of various yokelike devices, as a frame fitted to a person's shoulders for carrying a bucket hung at each end. 5 *v.* To put a yoke upon. 6 *v.* To join or unite: to be *yoked* in marriage. 7 *n.* Something that binds or connects; bond: the *yoke* of love. 8 *n.* A force or influence that holds people in submission or bondage. 9 *n.* A fitted part of a garment, usually over the shoulders or hips.

Yoke

yoke·fel·low [yōk′fel′ō] *n.* 1 Either of a pair of animals joined by a yoke. 2 A fellow worker.

yo·kel [yō′kəl] *n.* A simple or naive country person: usually considered offensive.

yolk [yōk] *n.* The yellow portion of an egg.

Yom Kip·pur [yom′ kip′ər *or* yōm′ ki·po͝or′] A Jewish holiday marked by prayer and fasting for 24 hours; Day of Atonement.

yon [yon] *adj., adv.* Yonder: seldom used today.

yon·der [yon′dər] 1 *adj.* Being at a distance, but in sight. 2 *adv.* In or to that place; there.

yore [yôr] *n.* Time long past. **—of yore** Of long ago.

Yorkshire pudding A batter cake baked in the drippings of roasting meat.

you [yo͞o] *pron., pl.* **you** 1 The person or persons addressed: *You* are right; I'll see *you* tomorrow. 2 Any person; one: *You* learn by trying.

you-all [yo͞o′ôl′ *or* yôl] You all. ◆ The expression *you-all*, sometimes pronounced [yôl], is especially common in the American South. It has the meaning of the plural *you*. "How are *you-all*?" means "How are you and your family?"

you'd [yo͞od] 1 You had. 2 You would.

you'll [yo͞ol] 1 You will. 2 You shall.

young [yung] *adj.* **young·er** [yung′gər], **young·est** [yung′gist], *n.* 1 *adj.* Being in the early period of life, growth, or development; not old: a *young* child; The night is still *young*. 2 *n. use*: Young people: The *young* are often foolhardy. 3 *n.* Offspring, especially of animals: The lions fed their *young*. 4 *adj.* Of or having to do with youth or early life; fresh; vigorous: My grandparents have *young* ideas. 5 *adj.* Inexperienced; immature: You are a little *young* to read that book. 6 *adj.* Younger than another person having the same name or title; junior: *young* Fred, not Fred, senior. **—with young** With child; pregnant.

young·ish [yung′ish] *adj.* Rather young.

young·ling [yung′ling] 1 *n.* A young person, animal, or plant. 2 *adj.* Young. ◆ This word is seldom used today.

young·ster [yung′stər] *n.* A child or young person.

your [yôr *or* yo͝or] *pron.* A possessive form of YOU used before the thing possessed: *your* hat.

you're [yo͝or *or* yôr] You are. ◆ Don't confuse the contraction *you're* with the possessive *your*.

yours [yôrz *or* yo͝orz] *pron.* A possessive form of YOU used standing alone: My bike is lighter than *yours*. ◆ *Yours* is often used with another word at the end of a letter to form a polite closing, as in "Sincerely *yours*."

your·self [yôr·self′ *or* yo͝or·self′] *pron., pl.* **your·selves** [yôr·selvz′ *or* yo͝or·selvz′] 1 The one that you really are; your very own self. *Yourself* in this sense is used to refer back to the subject *you* or to make *you* more emphatic: You help *yourself*; You *yourselves* must do it. 2 Your normal, usual, or proper self: Be *yourself* instead of pretending!

youth [yo͞oth] *n., pl.* **youths** [yo͞oths *or* yo͞o*th*z] 1 The period of time when one is young; part of life between childhood and adulthood. 2 The condition or quality of being young: My grandparents are still full of *youth*. 3 The early period of being or development: during the *youth* of a nation. 4 A young man. 5 (*often used with a plural verb*) Young people as a group: The *youth* of that community are very well educated.

youth·ful [yo͞oth′fəl] *adj.* 1 Having youth; being still young. 2 Having the quality of youth; fresh; vigorous: a *youthful* outlook on life. 3 Of, having to do with, or proper for youth: a *youthful* wardrobe.

you've [yo͞ov] You have.

yowl [youl] 1 *n.* A loud, prolonged, wailing cry; howl. 2 *v.* To make such a sound; howl; yell.

yo-yo [yō′yō′] *n., pl.* **yo-yos,** *v.* 1 *n.* A wheellike toy with a string about it in a deep groove. The yo-yo spins up and down the string which is held and manipulated by the operator's hand. 2 *v. informal* To change positions repeatedly; vacillate.

yr. 1 year. 2 younger. 3 your.

yrs. 1 years. 2 yours.

YT or **Y.T.** Yukon Territory.

yt·ter·bi·um [i·tûr′bē·əm] *n.* A metallic element occurring in rare earths. ◆ See RARE-EARTH ELEMENT.

yt·tri·um [it′rē·əm] *n.* A metallic element found in rare earths and differing from other rare-earth elements in having a much lower atomic weight. ◆ See RARE-EARTH ELEMENT.

yu·an [yo͞o·än′] *n., pl* **yu·an** or **yu·ans** The basic unit of money in the People's Republic of China.

yuc·ca [yuk′ə] *n.* Any of various plants of the southern U.S. and Mexico having long pointed leaves and clusters of white bell-shaped flowers growing on a tall stalk.

Yug. 1 Yugoslavia. 2 Yugoslavian.

Yugo. 1 Yugoslavia. 2 Yugoslavian.

Yu·go·slav [yo͞o′gō·släv′] 1 *adj.* Of or from Yugoslavia. 2 *n.* A person born in or a citizen of Yugoslavia.

yule [yo͞ol] *n.* (*often written* **Yule**) Christmas time, or the feast of Christmas.

yule log A large log burned on Christmas eve.

yule·tide [yo͞ol′tīd′] *n.* (*often written* **Yuletide**) Christmas time.

yum·my [yum′ē] *adj.* **yum·mi·er, yum·mi·est** *informal* Delicious; tasty.

yup [yup] *adv. slang* Another word for YES.

yup·pie [yup′ē] *n. informal* A young adult who is thought to be very concerned about making money, getting ahead in business, and keeping up with the latest trends in clothing, food, home furnishings, and so on. ◆ *Yuppie* comes from the phrase *Y*oung *U*rban *P*rofessional.

yurt [yûrt] *n.* A dome-shaped tent made of skins, used by nomads in central Asia.

YWCA or **Y.W.C.A.** Young Women's Christian Association.

YWHA or **Y.W.H.A.** Young Women's Hebrew Association.

Z is the twenty-sixth letter of the alphabet. The sign for it originated among Semitic people in the Near East, in the region of Palestine and Syria, probably in the middle of the second millennium B.C. Little is known about the sign until around 1000 B.C., when the Phoenicians began using it. The Phoenicians named the sign *zayin* and used it for the sound of the consonant *z*.

When the Greeks adopted the Phoenician sign around the ninth century B.C., they called it *zeta* and made its shape more regular—a straight vertical line with a crossbar at the top and bottom. It was not until classical times that the Greek sign was written with a slanted line between the crossbars, like our present-day *Z*. Like the Phoenicians, the Greeks used the sign for the sound of *z*. The Greek *z* sound differed from our *z* sound, however. In fact, it probably varied somewhat from place to place, depending on local dialects.

As early as the eighth century B.C., the Etruscans adopted the Greek sign, using it for the *z* sound but shaping the letter crudely, as the early Greeks had shaped it. It was from the Etruscans that the Romans took the sign, but they soon dropped it because their language had no *z* sound. Therefore, the Romans did not need a *z* sign.

After the Romans conquered Greece in 146 B.C., however, they realized that they needed the sign again. Many Greek words came into the Latin language at the time, and a *Z* sign was needed in some of these words. The Romans reintroduced the letter, putting it at the end of the alphabet. (Originally, it had been in seventh place; that place had been given to the letter *G*.) The Romans did not take over all the Greek *z* sounds, however, but only one—the one that we still use today. The sign they reintroduced is the one we know; it is still our *majuscule*, or capital letter, *Z*.

In time, a *minuscule*, or small letter, appeared. The small letter is essentially a smaller version of the majuscule.

Zz

Early Phoenician (late 2nd millennium B.C.)

Phoenician (8th century B.C)

Early Greek (9th-7th centuries B.C.)

Western Greek (6th century B.C.)

Classical Greek (403 B.C. onward)

Early Etruscan (8th century B.C.)

Classical Etruscan (around 400 B.C.)

Classical Latin

Roman capital (4th-5th centuries)

Anglo-Saxon minuscule (8th-9th centuries)

z or **Z** [zē] *n., pl.* **z's** or **Z's** The 26th letter of the English alphabet.

z. or **Z.** 1 zero. 2 zone.

Za·ir·e·an [zä·ir′ē·ən] 1 *adj.* Of or from Zaire. 2 *n.* A person born in or a citizen of Zaire.

Zam·bi·an [zam′bē·ən] 1 *adj.* Of or from Zambia. 2 *n.* A person born in or a citizen of Zambia.

za·ny [zā′nē] *adj.* **za·ni·er, za·ni·est,** *n., pl.* **za·nies** 1 *adj.* Odd and funny: a *zany* movie. 2 *n.* An odd, funny person. 3 *n.* A fool; simpleton.

zap [zap] *v.* **zapped, zap·ping,** *n. slang* 1 *v.* To destroy quickly: to *zap* bugs. 2 *n.* A quick destructive attack. **—zap′per** *n.*

zeal [zēl] *n.* Great interest and devotion, as when working for a cause; enthusiasm.

zeal·ot [zel′ət] *n.* A person who displays too much zeal or enthusiasm; fanatic.

zeal′ot·ry [zel′ə·trē′] *n., pl.* **zeal·ot·ries** Excessive zeal; fanatical devotion.

zeal·ous [zel′əs] *adj.* Filled with or caused by zeal. **—zeal′ous·ly** *adv.*

Zebra

ze·bra [zē′brə] *n.* Any of several African animals related to horses, with dark stripes on white or buff coats.

zebra crossing A pedestrian crosswalk marked with white or yellow stripes.

ze·bu [zē′byōō] *n.* A domesticated ox of Asia and Africa, having a hump on the shoulders, a large dewlap, and short, curved horns.

Zebu

Zech·a·ri·ah [zek′ə·rī′ə] *n.* 1 In the Bible, a Hebrew prophet of the 6th century B.C. 2 A book of the Old Testament named after him.

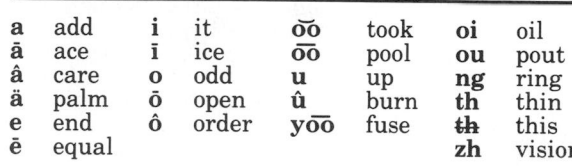

zed [zed] *n. British* The letter z.

Zen [zen] *n.* A Japanese Buddhist sect that believes in enlightenment through meditation and intuition rather than through study of scriptures.

ze·nith [zē′nith] *n.* 1 The point in the sky directly overhead. 2 The highest or most important point; acme; peak: At the time of her election, the prime minister was at the *zenith* of her career.

a	add	**i**	it	**o͝o**	took	**oi**	oil		
ā	ace	**ī**	ice	**o͞o**	pool	**ou**	pout		
â	care	**o**	odd	**u**	up	**ng**	ring		
ä	palm	**ō**	open	**û**	burn	**th**	thin		
e	end	**ô**	order	**yo͞o**	fuse	**t͟h**	this		
ē	equal					**zh**	vision		

ə = {a in *above* e in *sicken* i in *possible*; o in *melon* u in *circus*}

zeph·yr [zef′ər] *n.* **1** The west wind. **2** Any soft, gentle wind. **3** A soft, lightweight yarn.

zep·pe·lin [zep′ə·lin] *n.* A large dirigible having a rigid, cigar-shaped body. ◆ The *zeppelin* was named after Count von Zeppelin, 1838–1917, who designed it.

Zeppelin

ze·ro [zir′ō *or* zē′rō] *n., pl.* **ze·ros** or **ze·roes,** *adj.* **1** *n.* The numeral or symbol 0; cipher; naught. **2** *n.* The number which, when added to any other number, gives that other number as their sum. **3** *n.* Nothing. **4** *n.* The point on a scale, as of a thermometer, from which something is measured. **5** *n.* The lowest point: The bad news made my hopes hit *zero.* **6** *adj.* Of or at zero. **—zero in on 1** To concentrate firepower on. **2** To focus attention on. ◆ *Zero* and *cipher* go back to the same Arabic word.

zero gravity The weightless condition of an object that is not subject to any net gravitational force or that has such a force counterbalanced by an opposite force.

zero hour The time set for a military operation or other important event to begin.

zest [zest] *n.* **1** A quality of excitement or enjoyment: A surprise gift added *zest* to my birthday party. **2** Keen enjoyment; great pleasure: to read with *zest.* **3** The thin outer part of an orange or lemon rind, used as flavoring.

zest·ful [zest′fəl] *adj.* Full of zest or enthusiasm: *zestful* enjoyment. **—zest′ful·ly** *adv.*

ze·ta [zā′tə *or* zē′tə] *n.* The sixth letter of the Greek alphabet.

Zeus [zōōs] *n.* In Greek myths, the supreme god, ruling all other gods. He was called Jupiter by the Romans.

zig·gu·rat [zig′ə·rat′] *n.* An ancient Mesopotamian temple in the shape of a stepped pyramid.

zig·zag [zig′zag′] *n., adj., adv., v.* **zig·zagged, zig·zag·ging 1** *n.* A series of short, sharp turns or angles. **2** *n.* Something having such angles or turns, as a path or pattern. **3** *adj.* Of or having short sharp turns or angles. **4** *adv.* In a zigzag manner. **5** *v.* To move in or form a zigzag.

zilch [zilch] *n. slang* Nothing; zero.

zil·lion [zil′yən] *n. informal* A very large number: *zillions* of flies.

Zim·ba·bwe·an [zim·bä′bwā·ən] **1** *adj.* Of or from Zimbabwe. **2** *n.* A person born in or a citizen of Zimbabwe.

zinc [zingk] *n., v.* **zinced** or **zincked, zinc·ing** or **zinck·ing 1** *n.* A bluish white, metallic element, used in making alloys, for coating metals, in medicine, and as an electrode in electric batteries. **2** *v.* To coat or cover with zinc; galvanize.

zinc oxide A white or yellowish powdery compound used in paints, rubber, and cosmetics.

zinc white A white paint or pigment that contains zinc oxide.

zing [zing] **1** *n.* A short, high-pitched, humming or buzzing sound. **2** *v.* To make or move with such a sound.

zing·er [zing′ər] *n. slang* A clever remark or response.

zin·ni·a [zin′ē·ə] *n.* Any of several North American plants having brightly colored, showy flowers with many petals like rays.

Zion [zī·ən] *n.* **1** The Jewish people. **2** A poetic word for the original, actual, or ideal homeland of the Jewish people. **3** Heaven.

Zi·on·ism [zī′ən·iz′əm] *n.* A movement for the reestablishment of a Jewish nation in Palestine and, after 1948, for the emigration of Jews to Israel. —**Zi′on·ist** *adj., n.*

zip [zip] *n., v.* **zipped, zip·ping 1** *n.* A sharp, hissing sound, as of a bullet passing through the air. **2** *v.* To travel with such a sound. **3** *n. informal* Energy; vitality; vim. **4** *v. informal* To move or act with energy and speed. **5** *v.* To fasten with a zipper. ◆ The word *zip* was formed in imitation of the kind of sound made by something moving very fast.

zip-code [zip′kōd′] *v.* **zip-cod·ed, zip-cod·ing** To place a zip code on or assign a zip code to.

zip code or **Zip code** [zip] A numerical code made up by the U.S. Postal Service to aid in the distribution of domestic mail. A separate zip code is assigned to each delivery area and is part of the address on mail to that area. ◆ *Zip* code comes from Z(ONE) I(MPROVEMENT) P(LAN).

zip·per [zip′ər] *n.* A fastener having two rows of interlocking teeth that may be joined or separated by a sliding device.

zip·py [zip′ē] *adj.* **zip·pi·er, zip·pi·est** Energetic; brisk; snappy.

zir·con [zûr′kon′] *n.* A crystalline mineral, some clear varieties of which are used as jewels.

zir·co·ni·um [zər·kō′nē·əm] *n.* A grayish white metallic element very resistant to corrosion.

zith·er [zith′ər] *n.* A musical instrument having 30 to 40 strings stretched across a flat resonant board. It is played by plucking the strings.

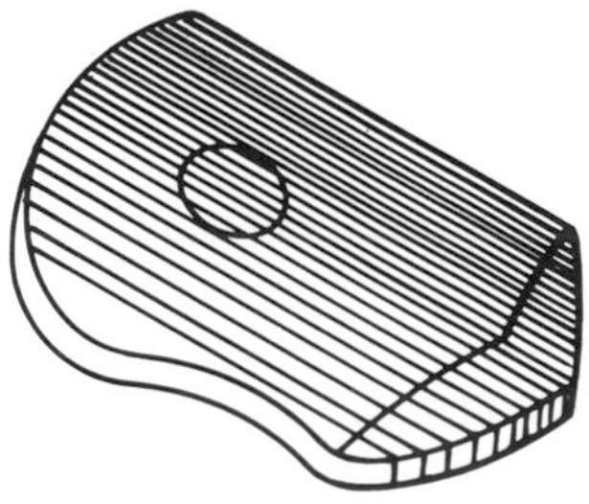

Zither

zlo·ty [zlô′tē] *n., pl.* **zlo·tys** or **zlo·ty** The basic unit of money in Poland.

Zn The symbol for the element zinc.

zo·di·ac [zō′dē·ak′] *n.* **1** An imaginary belt in the sky along which the sun appears to travel. It is divided into twelve sections, each of which is named after a different constellation. **2** A diagram or chart representing this belt and its signs, used in astrology.

zo·di·a·cal [zō·dī′ə·kəl] *adj.* Of or having to do with the zodiac.

zom·bie or **zom·bi** [zom′·bē] *n., pl.* **zom·bies** or **zom·bis 1** A supernatural power believed by some West Indian natives to enter a dead body and make it move and act. **2** A dead body brought back to physical life in this way.

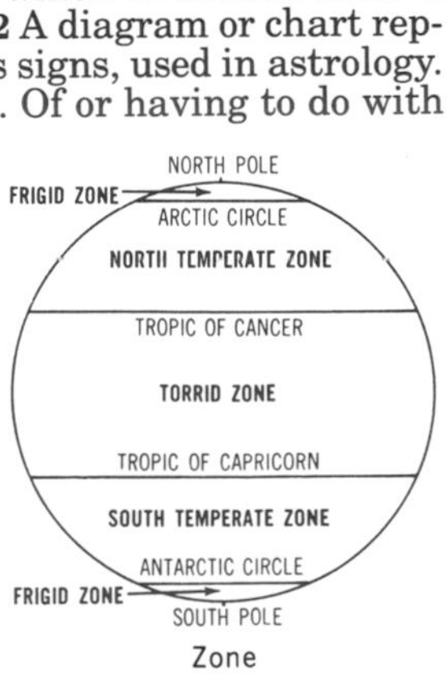

Zone

zon·al [zō′nəl] *adj.* Of or divided into zones.

zone [zōn] *n., v.* **zoned, zon·ing 1** *n.* Any of the five divisions of the earth's surface, each bounded by parallels of latitude and named for the climate most frequently found in the division. **2** *n.* An area set apart from nearby areas for some special reason or purpose: a war *zone*; a no-parking *zone*. **3** *n.* Any of the areas around a particular mailing point, set up by the post office to determine parcel post rates for packages mailed from that particular point. **4** *n.* A section of a city set apart by law for a certain use: a residential *zone*; a business *zone*. **5** *n.* A section of a city to which a number is assigned to aid in the distribution of mail. **6** *v.* To divide into zones. **7** *n.* A belt or girdle: seldom used today. **8** *v.* To surround or encircle with a zone or belt. ◆ *Zone* goes back to a Greek word meaning *belt* or *girdle*, which is what the word once meant in English.

zoo [zo͞o] *n., pl.* **zoos** A park or garden in which wild animals are kept and shown to the public.

zool. **1** zoological. **2** zoology.

zo·o·log·i·cal [zō′ə·loj′i·kəl] *adj.* **1** Of or having to do with zoology. **2** Of or having to do with animals.

zoological garden Another name for ZOO.

zo·ol·o·gy [zō·ol′ə·jē] *n.* The science that has to do with animals and their classification, structure, and development. **—zo·ol′o·gist** *n.*

zoom [zo͞om] **1** *v.* To make a low-pitched but loud humming sound. **2** *v.* To move with such a sound. **3** *v.* To climb sharply in an airplane. **4** *v.* To move rapidly upward or downward. **5** *v.* In TV and motion pictures, to make the subject being pictured appear rapidly larger or smaller while keeping it in focus by means of a zoom lens. **6** *n.* The act of zooming. **7** *n.* A zooming sound. **8** *n.* Another name for ZOOM LENS.

zoom lens A camera lens whose focal length can be rapidly and continuously changed so that an image growing larger or smaller can be kept in focus.

zo·ri [zôr′ē] *n., pl.* **zo·ris** A flat Japanese sandal.

Zo·ro·as·tri·an [zôr′ō·as′trē·ən] **1** *n.* A person who follows the religion of Zoroastrianism. **2** *adj.* Of or having to do with the religion of Zoroastrianism or its followers.

Zo·ro·as·tri·an·ism [zôr′ō·as′trē·ən·iz′əm] *n.* The religious system of the ancient Persians, founded by Zoroaster.

zounds [zoundz] *interj.* A mild oath used to express surprise or anger: seldom used today.

Zr The symbol for the element zirconium.

zuc·chi·ni [zo͞o·kē′nē] *n., pl.* **zuc·chi·ni** or **zuc·chi·nis** A squash with long, narrow, dark-green fruits that ripen in the summer.

Zu·lu [zo͞o′lo͞o] *n., pl.* **Zu·lus** or **Zu·lu,** *adj.* **1** *n.* A member of a people in SE Africa. **2** *n.* The Bantu language of this people. **3** *adj.* Of or having to do with the Zulus or their language.

Zu·ni or **Zu·ñi** [zo͞o′nē *or* zo͞o′nyē] *n., pl.* **Zu·ni** or **Zu·nis** or **Zu·ñi** or **Zu·ñis** **1** A member of a tribe of North American Indians living in pueblos in New Mexico. **2** The language of this tribe.

zwie·back [zwī′bak′, zwē′bäk′, *or* swī′bäk′] *n.* A kind of biscuit or bread baked in a loaf and later sliced and toasted in an oven.

zy·gote [zī′gōt′] *n.* An egg cell after its fertilization by the male germ cell.

a	add	**i**	it	**o͝o**	took	**oi**	oil
ā	ace	**ī**	ice	**o͞o**	pool	**ou**	pout
â	care	**o**	odd	**u**	up	**ng**	ring
ä	palm	**ō**	open	**û**	burn	**th**	thin
e	end	**ô**	order	**yo͞o**	fuse	**th̸**	this
ē	equal					**zh**	vision

ə = { a in *above* e in *sicken* i in *possible* / o in *melon* u in *circus* }

Z

Customary Weights and Measures

LINEAR MEASURE

				Metric Equivalent
		1 inch (in.)	=	2.5400 centimeters (cm)
12 inches	=	1 foot (ft)	=	30.48 centimeters
3 feet	=	1 yard (yd)	=	0.9144 meter (m)
5½ yards or 16½ feet	=	1 rod (rd)	=	5.0292 meters
40 rods	=	1 furlong (fur)	=	201.168 meters
8 furlongs or 1,760 yards or 5,280 feet	=	1 mile (mi)	=	1.6093 kilometers (km) or 1609.347 meters
3 miles	=	1 league	=	4.8280 kilometers

SQUARE MEASURE

		1 square inch (sq in.)	=	6.4516 sq centimeters (cm^2)
144 square inches	=	1 square foot (sq ft)	=	929.03 sq centimeters
9 square feet	=	1 square yard (sq yd)	=	0.8361 sq meter (m^2)
30¼ square yards	=	1 square rod (sq rd)	=	25.293 sq meters
160 square rods or 4,840 square yards or 43,560 square feet	=	1 acre (A)	=	0.4047 hectare (ha)
640 acres	=	1 square mile (sq mi)	=	258.9998 hectares

CUBIC MEASURE

		1 cubic inch (cu in.)	=	16.387 cu centimeters (cm^3)
1,728 cubic inches	=	1 cubic foot (cu ft)	=	0.0283 cu meter (m^3)
27 cubic feet	=	1 cubic yard (cu yd)	=	0.7646 cu meter
128 cubic feet	=	1 cord (cd)	=	3.625 cu meters

LIQUID MEASURE

		1 gill (gi)	=	0.1183 liter (l)
4 gills	=	1 pint (pt)	=	0.4732 liter
2 pints	=	1 quart (qt)	=	0.9463 liter
4 quarts	=	1 gallon (gal)	=	3.7853 liters

DRY MEASURE

		1 pint (pt)	=	0.5506 liter (l)
2 pints	=	1 quart (qt)	=	1.1012 liters
8 quarts	=	1 peck (pk)	=	8.8096 liters
4 pecks	=	1 bushel (bu)	=	35.2383 liters
3.28 bushels	=	1 barrel (bbl)	=	115.62 liters

LINEAR MEASURE

						Customary Equivalent	
millimeter	=	0.001	meter	=	0.03937	inch
centimeter	=	0.01	meter	=	0.3937	inch
decimeter	=	0.1	meter	=	3.937	inches
meter	=	1.0	meter	=	39.37	inches
decameter	=	10.0	meters	=	10.93	yards
hectometer	=	100.0	meters	=	328.08	feet
kilometer	=	1,000.0	meters	=	0.6214	miles

SQUARE MEASURE

square centimeter	=	.0001	square meter	=	.155	sq inch
centare	=	1.0	square meter	=	10.764	sq feet
hectare	=	10,000.0	square meters	=	2.471	acres
square kilometer	=	1,000,000.0	square meters	=	.3861	sq miles

CAPACITY

milliliter	=	0.001	liter	=	0.034	fluid ounce
centiliter	=	0.01	liter	=	0.338	fluid ounce
deciliter	=	0.1	liter	=	3.38	fluid ounces
liter	=	1.0	liter	=	1.05	liquid quarts
decaliter	=	10.0	liters	=	0.284	bushel
hectoliter	=	100.0	liters	=	2.837	bushels
kiloliter	=	1,000.0	liters	=	264.18	gallons

MASS (WEIGHT)

milligram	=	0.001	gram	=	0.0154	grain
centigram	=	0.01	gram	=	0.1543	grain
decigram	=	0.1	gram	=	1.543	grains
gram	=	1.0	gram	=	15.43	grains
decagram	=	10.0	grams	=	0.3527	ounce avoirdupois
hectogram	=	100.0	grams	=	3.527	ounces avoirdupois
kilogram	=	1,000.0	grams	=	2.2	pounds avoirdupois
metric ton	=	1,000,000.0	grams	=	2,204.6	pounds avoirdupois

TABLE OF SYMBOLS

+	plus	$\sqrt{49}$	square root: square root of forty-nine
−	minus	$^{+}4$	positive four
×	times	$^{-}4$	negative four
÷, $\overline{)}$	divided by	$\lvert 4^{-} \rvert$	absolute value
=	is equal to	(2.5)	ordered pair: (× = 2, y = 5)
≠	is not equal to	∟	right angle
>	is greater than	∠ XYZ	angle XYZ
<	is less than	°	degree
≤	is less than or equal to	.B	point B
≥	is greater than or equal to	$\overline{CD}$	line segment with endpoints C and D
≈	is approximately equal to	$\overrightarrow{CD}$	ray CD with endpoint C
~	is similar to	$\overleftrightarrow{CD}$	line through points C and D
≅	is congruent to	∥	is parallel to
3 r7	three remainder seven	⊥	is perpendicular to
$14\underline{.8}$	decimal point: fourteen and eight-tenths	△XYZ	triangle XYZ
$0.\overline{39}$	repeating decimal: 0.393939 . . .	π	pi (appriximately 3.14 or $\frac{22}{7}$)
. . .	pattern continues without end	P(E)	probability of event E
20%	percent: twenty percent	3!	the factorial of 3: 3×2×1
8.2	ratio: eight to two	¢	cent sign
6^2	six to the second power or six squared	$	dollar sign
6^3	six to the third power or six cubed		

Perimeter (*P*) of a:

rectangle = 2 × the length + 2 × the width
$P = 2l + 2w$

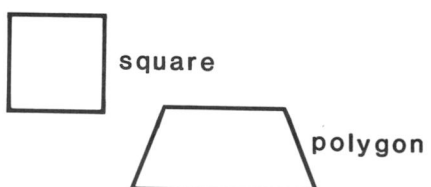

rectangle

square = 4 × the side
$P = 4s$

square

polygon = the sum of the sides
$P = a + b + c + d$

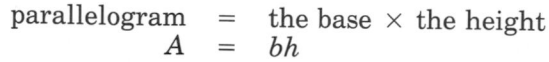

polygon

Circumference (*C*) of a:

circle = π × the diameter
$C = \pi d = 2\pi r$

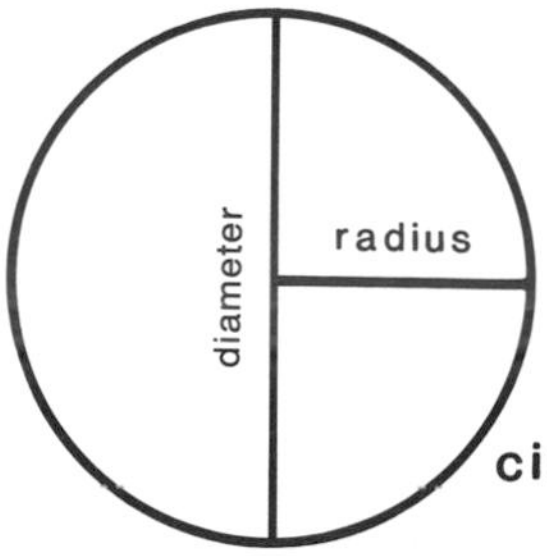

circle

Area (*A*) of a:

rectangle = the length × the width
$A = lw$

square = a side × a side
$A = s \times s = s^2$

parallelogram = the base × the height
$A = bh$

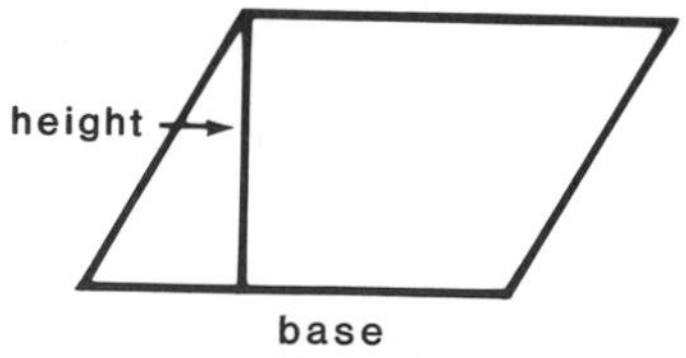

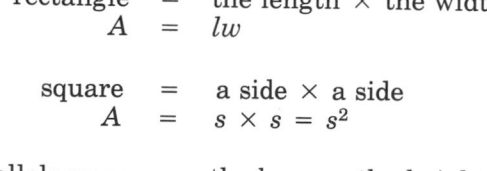

parallelogram

triangle $= \frac{1}{2} \times$ the base $\times$ the height
$A = \frac{1}{2} bh$

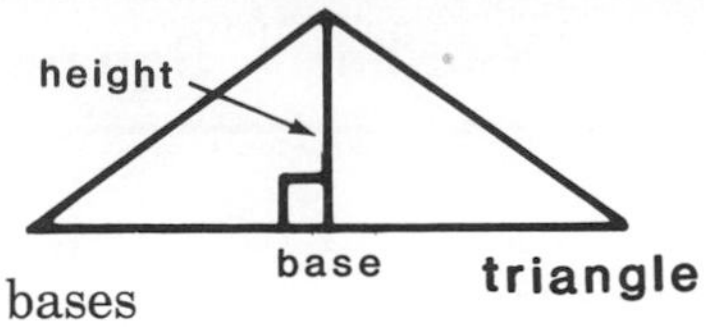

trapezoid $= \frac{1}{2} \times$ the height $\times$ the sum of the bases
$A = \frac{1}{2} h\,(a + b)$

circle $= \pi \times$ the radius squared
$A = \pi r^2$

Surface Area (S) of a:

rectangular prism = the sum of the area of its faces

pyramid = the area of the base $+ \frac{1}{2} \times$ the slant height $\times$ the perimeter of the base
S the area of the base $+ \frac{1}{2} lp$

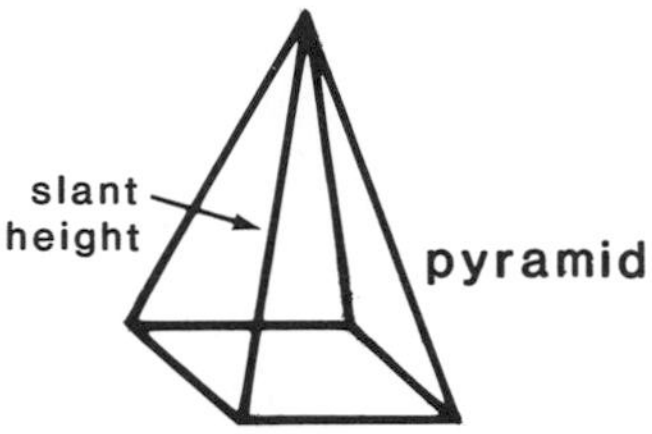

cylinder $= 2\pi \times$ the radius $\times$ (the radius + the height)
$S = 2\pi r\,(r + h)$

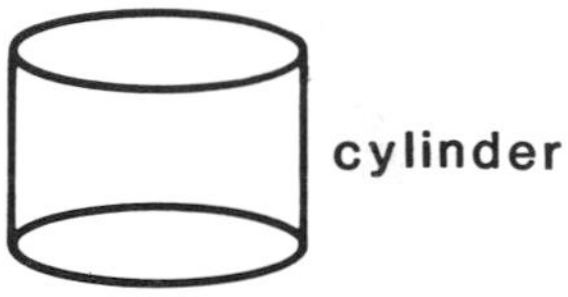

cone = area of base $+ \pi \times$ radius $\times$ slant height
$S = \pi r^2 + \pi rl = \pi r\,(r + l)$

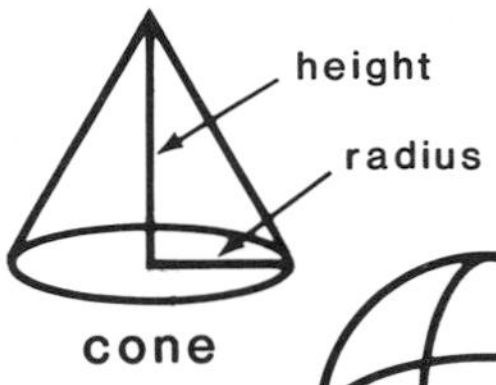

sphere $= 4\pi \times$ the radius squared
$S = 4\pi r^2$

Volume (V) of a:

prism = the area of the base $\times$ the height
$V = Bh = l \times w \times h$

rectangular prism = the length $\times$ the width $\times$ the height
$V = lwh$

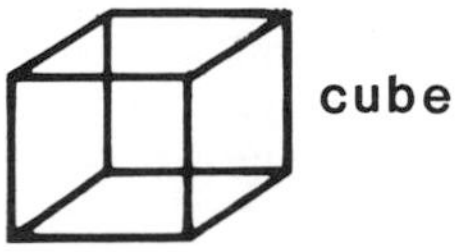

pyramid $= \frac{1}{3} \times$ the area of the base $\times$ the height
$V = \frac{1}{3} Bh$

cylinder = the area of the base $\times$ the height
$V = Bh = \pi r^2 h$

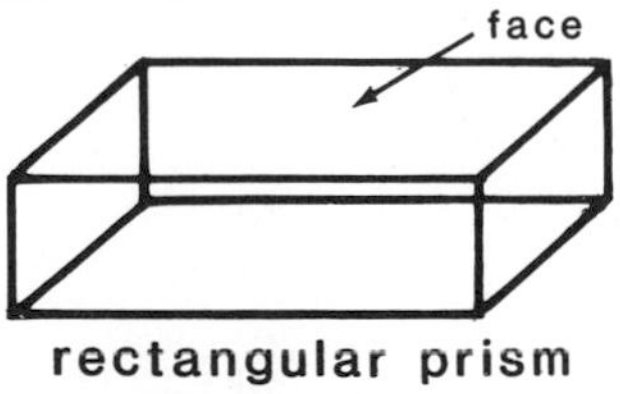

cone $= \frac{1}{3} \times$ the area of the base $\times$ the height
$V = \frac{1}{3} Bh = \frac{1}{3} \pi r^2 h$

sphere $= \frac{4}{3} \times \pi \times$ 4 to the third power
$V = \frac{4}{3} \pi r^3$

Table of Square Roots

Number	Square Root	Number	Square Root
1	1	51	7.141
2	1.414	52	7.211
3	1.732	53	7.280
4	2	54	7.348
5	2.236	55	7.416
6	2.449	56	7.483
7	2.646	57	7.550
8	2.828	58	7.616
9	3	59	7.681
10	3.162	60	7.746
11	3.317	61	7.810
12	3.464	62	7.874
13	3.606	63	7.937
14	3.742	64	8
15	3.873	65	8.062
16	4	66	8.124
17	4.123	67	8.185
18	4.243	68	8.246
19	4.359	69	8.307
20	4.472	70	8.367
21	4.583	71	8.426
22	4.690	72	8.485
23	4.796	73	8.544
24	4.899	74	8.602
25	5	75	8.660
26	5.099	76	8.718
27	5.196	77	8.775
28	5.295	78	8.832
29	5.385	79	8.888
30	5.477	80	8.944
31	5.568	81	9
32	5.659	82	9.055
33	5.745	83	9.110
34	5.831	84	9.165
35	5.916	85	9.220
36	6	86	9.274
37	6.083	87	9.327
38	6.164	88	9.381
39	6.245	89	9.434
40	6.325	90	9.487
41	6.403	91	9.539
42	6.481	92	9.592
43	6.557	93	9.644
44	6.633	94	9.695
45	6.708	95	9.747
46	6.782	96	9.798
47	6.856	97	9.849
48	6.928	98	9.899
49	7	99	9.950
50	7.071	100	10

Roman Numerals

1 — I	17 — XVII	60 — LX
2 — II	18 — XVIII	70 — LXX
3 — III	19 — XIX	80 — LXXX
4 — IV	20 — XX	90 — XC
5 — V	21 — XXI	100 — C
6 — VI	22 — XXII	200 — CC
7 — VII	23 — XXIII	400 — CD
8 — VIII	24 — XXIV	500 — D
9 — IX	25 — XXV	900 — CM
10 — X	26 — XXVI	1,000 — M
11 — XI	27 — XXVII	5,000 — $\overline{V}$
12 — XII	28 — XXVIII	10,000 — $\overline{X}$
13 — XIII	29 — XXIX	50,000 — $\overline{L}$
14 — XIV	30 — XXX	100,000 — $\overline{C}$
15 — XV	40 — XL	500,000 — $\overline{D}$
16 — XVI	50 — L	1,000,000 — $\overline{M}$

Large Numbers

million	1,000,000	(6 zeros)
billion	1,000,000,000	(9 zeros)
trillion	1,000,000,000,000	(12 zeros)
quadrillion	1,000,000,000,000,000	(15 zeros)
quintillion	1,000,000,000,000,000,000	(18 zeros)
sextillion	1,000,000,000,000,000,000,000	(21 zeros)
septillion	1,000,000,000,000,000,000,000,000	(24 zeros)
octillion	1,000,000,000,000,000,000,000,000,000	(27 zeros)
nonillion	1,000,000,000,000,000,000,000,000,000,000	(30 zeros)
decillion	1,000,000,000,000,000,000,000,000,000,000,000	(33 zeros)

Celsius and Fahrenheit Temperature Scales

Two kinds of temperature scales are in common use. The Celsius scale has the freezing point of water at 0° and its boiling point at 100°. It is used in science everywhere, and for all purposes throughout much of the world. The Fahrenheit scale has the freezing point of water at 32° and the boiling point at 212°. Not used in science, it is customary for other purposes, such as weather reports, in the United States.

To change a Fahrenheit reading to Celsius, subtract 32 from the Fahrenheit reading and multiply by $\frac{5}{9}$.

To change a Celsius reading to Fahrenheit, multiply the Celsius reading by $\frac{9}{5}$ and add 32.

	Celsius	Fahrenheit
Freezing point of water	0° C	32° F
Boiling point of water	100° C	212° F
Normal body temperature	37° C	98.6° F

Bodies of the Solar System

	Mean distance from sun in millions of		Diameter in	
	kilometers	miles	kilometers	miles
Sun			1,392,000	865,000
Moon			3,470	2,160
Mercury	58	36.2	4,865	3,050
Venus	107.5	67.2	12,100	7,520
Earth	149.7	92.9	12,756	7,926
Mars	227.8	141.5	6,760	4,200
Jupiter	778.4	483.5	142,700	88,700
Saturn	1,426	886	120,860	75,100
Uranus	2,868	1,782	51,000	31,620
Neptune	4,486	2,793	49,000	36,380
Pluto	5,915	3,676	2,300	1,426

Tables of Chemical Elements

Chemical Element	Symbol	Atomic No.	Chemical Element	Symbol	Atmoic No.
Actinium	Ac	89	Neon	Me	10
Aluminum	Al	13	Neptunium	Np	93
Americium	Am	95	Nickel	Ni	28
Antimony *(stibium)*	Sb	51	Niobium	Nb	41
Argon	Ar	18	Nitrogen	N	7
Arsenic	As	33	Nobelium	No	102
Astatine	At	85	Osmium	Os	76
Barium	Ba	56	Oxygen	O	8
Berkelium	Bk	97	Palladium	Pd	46
Beryllium	Be	4	Phosphorus	P	15
Bismuth	Bi	83	Platinum	Pt	78
Boron	B	5	Plutonium	Pu	94
Bromine	Br	35	Polonium	Po	84
Cadmium	Cd	48	Potassium *(kalium)*	K	19
Calcium	Ca	20	Praseodymium	Pr	59
Californium	Cf	98	Promethium	Pm	61
Carbon	C	6	Protactinium	Pa	91
Cerium	Ce	58	Radium	Ra	88
Cesium	Cs	55	Radon	Rn	86
Chlorine	Cl	17	Rhenium	Re	75
Chromium	Cr	24	Rhodium	Rh	45
Cobalt	Co	27	Rubidium	Rb	37
Copper *(cuprum)*	Cu	29	Ruthenium	Ru	44
Curium	Cm	96	Samarium	Sm	62
Dysprosium	Dy	66	Scandium	Sc	21
Einsteinium	Es	99	Selenium	Se	34
Erbium	Er	68	Silicon	Si	14
Europium	Eu	63	Silver *(argentum)*	Ag	47
Fermium	Fm	100	Sodium *(natrium)*	Na	11
Fluorine	F	9	Strontium	Sr	38
Francium	Fr	87	Sulfur	S	16
Gadolinium	Gd	64	Tantalum	Ta	73
Gallium	Ga	31	Technetium	Tc	43
Germanium	Ge	32	Tellurium	Te	52
Gold *(aurum)*	Au	79	Terbium	Tb	65
Hafnium	Hf	72	Thallium	Tl	81
Helium	He	2	Thorium	Th	90
Holmium	Ho	67	Thulium	Tm	69
Hydrogen	H	1	Tin *(stannum)*	Sn	50
Indium	In	49	Titanium	Ti	22
Iodine	I	53	Tungsten *(wolfram)*	W	74
Iridium	Ir	77	Uranium	U	92
Iron *(ferrum)*	Fe	26	Vanadium	V	23
Krypton	Kr	36	Xenon	Xe	54
Lanthanum	La	57	Ytterbium	Yb	70
Lawrencium	Lw	103	Yttrium	Y	39
Led *(plumbum)*	Pb	82	Zinc	Zn	30
Lithium	Li	3	Zirconium	Zr	40
Lutetium	Lu	71	(not official)	Ung	104
Magnesium	Mg	12	(not official)	Unp	105
Manganese	Mn	25	(not official)	Unh	106
Mendelevium	Md	101	(not official)	Uns	107
Mercury *(hydrargyrum)*	Hg	80	(not isolated)		108
Molybdenum	Mo	42	(not official)	Une	109
Neodymium	Nd	60			

Chart of Indo-European Languages

About half of all of the people in the world speak an Indo-European language, and Indo-European languages are spoken natively by people on all continents of the world. All of the Indo-European languages are descendants of a language spoken several thousand years ago by a small group of people living, probably, somewhere in central Europe. The Indo-European branch to which English belongs is Germanic. Germanic was spoken two thousand years ago mostly in the forests of Scandinavia and what is now Germany. About A.D. 450 some of the Germanic-speaking tribes invaded and conquered Great Britain and established there the variety of Germanic that became English. From England, English has of course spread over much of the world.

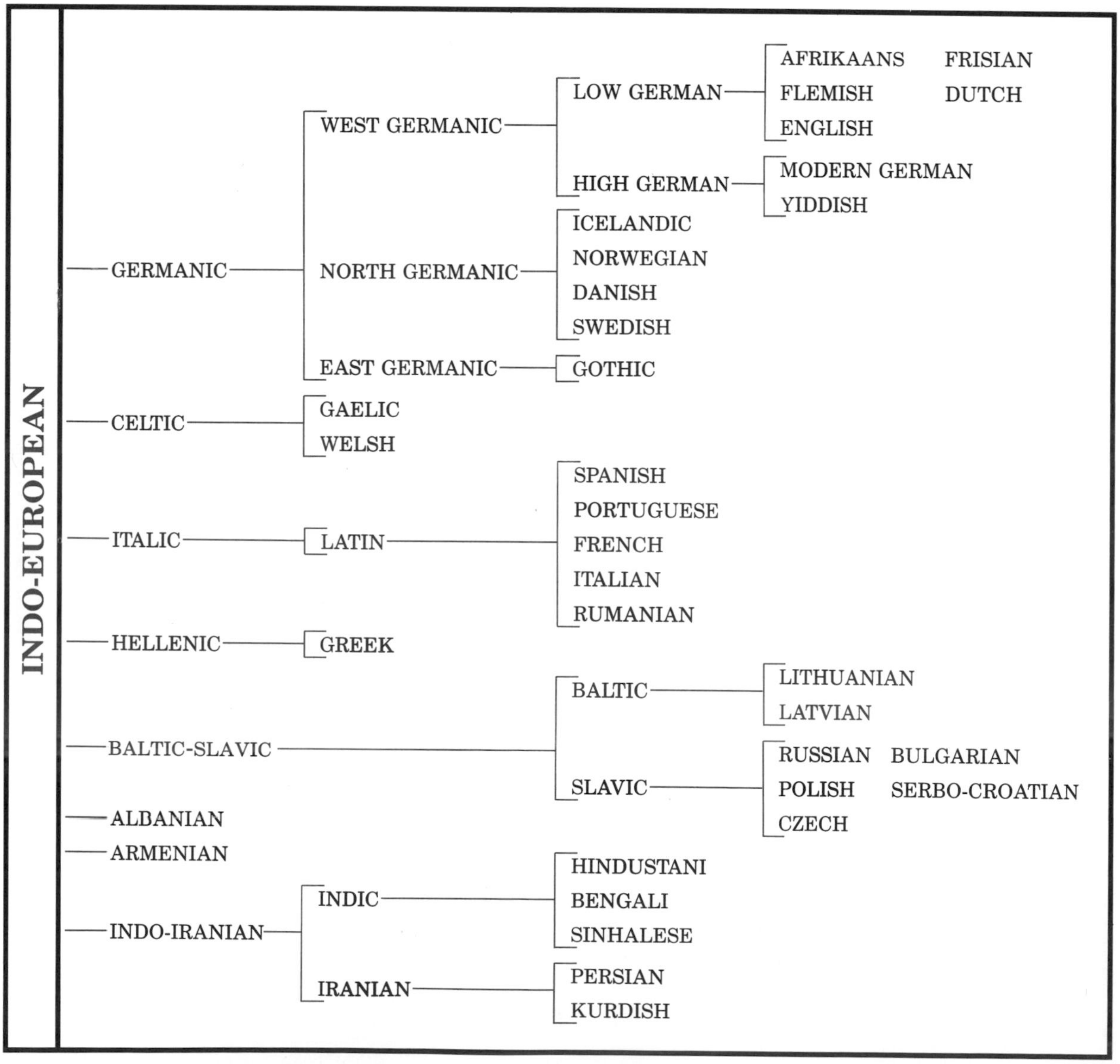

capitalize	add something	add quotation marks	take something away	make a lowercase letter
make a period	add a comma	spell correctly	indent the paragraph	transpose

The Lion and the Mouse

One day, a lion was taking an afternoon Nap in some tall grass. Suddenly, he felt something touch his left front paw. Opening a sleepy eye, he saw a small mouse attempting to make its way around him. Quick as a flash, the lion siezed the mouse and opened his great jaws to receive the squirming tidbit.

"Oh, please, sir," cried the mouse. "do not make me your lunch!"

"Lunch!" exclaimed the lion. "You're enough for a snack."

"Spare me, then, mighty lion and perhaps someday I can be of service to you," replied hopefully the mouse.

"You—of service to me?" laughed the lion. That is absurd! However, you have made me laugh, and that is a rare thing nowadays I will let you go.

The mouse thanked the lion and scampered off.

A few months later, the mouse was nibbling peacefully on some grain when a loud roar shock the ground.

"My goodness, said the startled Mouse. "That sounds like my friend, the lion."

Sounds of a struggle led the mouse to a clearing. There was the lion, caught in a net that was held to the ground by ropes The lion was thrashing about so wildly that mouse was afraid to approach him.

"Lion, listen to me!" cried the mouse. "If you quiet down a bit, I can gnaw on the ropes and set your free."

The lion lay still and mouse bit through the Ropes. Soon the lion was free. He thanked the mouse and bounded off through the grass.

The lion had learned a lesson: The smallest freind can be the best freind when one is in need.

Periods

Place a period at the end of a declarative or an imperative sentence.

It is raining. Take an umbrella.

Place a period after most abbreviations.

Oct. U.S.A. Wed.

Do not place a period after abbreviations of organizations, agencies, or postal service abbreviations of state names.

NATO IL MI

Place a period after an initial.

William H. Taft A. R. Lofft

Place a period after each number or letter in an outline.

I. Purebred dogs
   A. Working dogs
      1. Siberian husky

Commas

Place a comma between the day and the year in a date. If the year is followed by more words in the sentence, place a comma after the year.

On May 7, 1984, I went to my school reunion.

Use a comma between the city and the state in an address. In a sentence, put commas after the street address, between the city and state, and at the end of the address.

We live at 14 Park Place, Forestdale, Illinois.

Place a comma after the salutation of a friendly letter or a social note and after the closing of any letter.

Dear Laura, Sincerely yours, Your friend,

Place commas after every element but the last in a series.

We ordered eggs, toast, and juice.

Place a comma before the coordinating conjunctions **or, and,** or **but** in a compound sentence.

Marion studied to be a doctor, and Robert studied to be a lawyer.

Use commas to set off a noun in direct address.

Claire, take your sister to school.

Place a comma after the words **yes** and **no,** after mild interjections, after most dependent clauses, and after long introductory prepositional phrases or participial phrases.

Yes, I found your keys.

Wonderful, I think I'll do that.

Because I made supper, we were able to leave early.

Having completed his work, he read a book.

Use a comma to set off quoted words from the rest of a sentence unless a question mark or exclamation point is needed.

"I think," said Harry, "that I will go to the beach."

Use commas to set off transitional expressions.

These books, however, are very helpful.

Use commas after two introductory prepositional phrases and to set off most appositives.

In the town, there is a fountain. We visited Laura, a friend of mine.

Quotation Marks

Place quotation marks around the exact words of a direct quotation. If the quotation is divided into two parts by other words, place quotation marks around the quoted words only.

"I will come," he replied, "or I will send my daughter."

If there are several sentences in a direct quotation, do not close the quotation until after the last sentence.

"I need one. I will buy it tomorrow," he said.

Always place commas and periods inside the closing quotation marks. Place question marks and exclamation points inside the closing quotation marks if the quotation itself is a question or an exclamation.

The professor said, "Your exam will be on Friday."
"Wow, that was a perfect dive!" she exclaimed.
"Where did I put my book?" he asked.
Did Laura say, "I'll be there at five"?

Apostrophes

Use an apostrophe for possessive nouns but not for possessive pronouns.

Lewis's Fluffy's girls' people's
his its theirs yours

Use an apostrophe to form contractions of pronouns and verbs and to form contractions of verbs and the adverb **not.**

I'm she'd shouldn't won't

Use an apostrophe and underlining to form the plurals of letters.

You spell that word with two <u>e</u>'s.

Question Marks and Exclamation Points

Place a question mark at the end of an interrogative sentence.

Have you heard the weather report?

Place an exclamation point at the end of an exclamatory sentence and after a strong interjection.

How frightened I am! Oh no! Let's find shelter.

Semicolons and Colons

Use semicolons to separate items in a series in which commas have already been used.

I visited London, England; Paris, France; and Lima, Peru.

A semicolon can also be used to take the place of a comma and coordinating conjunction in a compound sentence.

Ned liked watercolors; I prefer oil paints.

Use a colon after the salutation of a business letter.

Dear Mr. Johnson: Dear Senator Field:

Place a colon between the hour and the minute in the time of day.

6:05 A.M. 9:30 P.M.

Use a colon before a list or series of items, especially when the list follows expressions such as **the following** or **as follows.**

We must order the following: brushes, canvas, and paint.

Presidents of the United States

Name	Born	Died	Native State	Political Party	Served	Age at Inauguration
George Washington	1732	1799	Virginia	Federalist	1789–1797	57
John Adams	1735	1826	Massachusetts	Federalist	1797–1801	61
Thomas Jefferson	1743	1826	Virginia	Democratic-Republican	1801–1809	57
James Madison	1751	1836	Virginia	Democratic-Republican	1809–1817	57
James Monroe	1758	1831	Virginia	Democratic-Republican	1817–1825	58
John Quincy Adams	1767	1848	Massachusetts	Democratic-Republican	1825–1829	57
Andrew Jackson	1767	1845	South Carolina	Democrat	1829–1837	61
Martin Van Buren	1782	1862	New York	Democrat	1837–1841	54
William H. Harrison[1]	1773	1841	Virginia	Whig	1841–1841	68
John Tyler	1790	1862	Virginia	Whig	1841–1845	51
James K. Polk	1795	1849	North Carolina	Democrat	1845–1849	49
Zachary Taylor[1]	1784	1850	Virginia	Whig	1849–1850	64
Millard Fillmore	1800	1874	New York	Whig	1850–1853	50
Franklin Pierce	1804	1869	New Hampshire	Democrat	1853–1857	48
James Buchanan	1791	1868	Pennsylvania	Democrat	1857–1861	65
Abraham Lincoln[2]	1809	1865	Kentucky	Republican	1861–1865	52
Andrew Johnson	1808	1875	North Carolina	Democrat	1865–1869	56
Ulysses S. Grant	1822	1885	Ohio	Republican	1869–1877	46
Rutherford B. Hayes	1822	1893	Ohio	Republican	1877–1881	54
James A. Garfield[2]	1831	1881	Ohio	Republican	1881–1881	49

[1] *Died in office* [2] *Assassinated* [3] *Resigned*

Name	Born	Died	Native State	Political Party	Served	Age at Inauguration
Chester A. Arthur	1830	1886	Vermont	Republican	1881–1885	50
Grover Cleveland	1837	1908	New Jersey	Democrat	1885–1889	47
Benjamin Harrison	1833	1901	Ohio	Republican	1889–1893	55
Grover Cleveland	1837	1908	New Jersey	Democrat	1893–1897	55
William McKinley[2]	1843	1901	Ohio	Republican	1897–1901	54
Theodore Roosevelt	1858	1919	New York	Republican	1901–1909	42
William H. Taft	1857	1930	Ohio	Republican	1909–1913	51
Woodrow Wilson	1856	1924	Virginia	Democrat	1913–1921	56
Warren G. Harding[1]	1865	1923	Ohio	Republican	1921–1923	55
Calvin Coolidge	1872	1933	Vermont	Republican	1923–1929	51
Herbert C. Hoover	1874	1964	Iowa	Republican	1929–1933	54
Franklin D. Roosevelt[1]	1882	1945	New York	Democrat	1933–1945	51
Harry S Truman	1884	1972	Missouri	Democrat	1945–1953	60
Dwight D. Eisenhower	1890	1969	Texas	Republican	1953–1961	62
John F. Kennedy[2]	1917	1963	Massachusetts	Democrat	1961–1963	43
Lyndon B. Johnson	1908	1973	Texas	Democrat	1963–1969	55
Richard M. Nixon[3]	1913		California	Republican	1969–1974	56
Gerald R. Ford	1913		Nebraska	Republican	1974–1977	61
Jimmy Carter	1924		Georgia	Democrat	1977–1981	52
Ronald Reagan	1911		Illinois	Republican	1981–1989	69
George Bush	1924		Massachusetts	Republican	1989–	65

[1] *Died in office* [2] *Assassinated* [3] *Resigned*

Vice Presidents of the United States

Name	Served	President
John Adams	1789–1797	George Washington
Thomas Jefferson	1797–1801	John Adams
Arron Burr	1801–1805	Thomas Jefferson
George Clinton[1]	1805–1812	Thomas Jefferson, James Madison
Elbridge Gerry[1]	1813–1814	James Madison
Daniel D. Tompkins	1817–1825	James Monroe
John C. Calhoun[2]	1825–1832	John Quincy Adams, Andrew Jackson
Martin Van Buren	1833–1837	Andrew Jackson
Richard M. Johnson	1837–1841	Martin Van Buren
John Tyler[3]	1841	William H. Harrison
George M. Dallas	1845–1849	James K. Polk

[1] *Died in office* [2] *Resigned to become U.S. Senator* [3] *Succeeded to Presidency upon death of the President* [4] *Resigned, charged with tax evasion* [5] *Succeeded to Presidency on the President's resignation*

Vice Presidents of the United States

Name	Served	President
Millard Fillmore[3]	1849–1850	Zachary Taylor
William R. King[1]	1853	Franklin Pierce
John C. Breckinridge	1857–1861	James Buchanan
Hannibal Hamlin	1861–1865	Abraham Lincoln
Andrew Johnson[3]	1865	Abraham Lincoln
Schuyler Colfax	1869–1873	Ulysses S. Grant
Henry Wilson[1]	1873–1875	Ulysses S. Grant
William A. Wheeler	1877–1881	Rutherford B. Hayes
Chester A. Arthur[3]	1881	James A. Garfield
Thomas A. Hendricks[1]	1885	Grover Cleveland
Levi P. Morton	1889–1893	Benjamin Harrison
Adlai E. Stevenson	1893–1897	Grover Cleveland
Garret A. Hobart[1]	1897–1899	William McKinley
Theodore Roosevelt[3]	1901	William McKinley
Charles W. Fairbanks	1905–1909	Theodore Roosevelt
James S. Sherman[1]	1909–1912	William H. Taft
Thomas R. Marshall	1913–1921	Woodrow Wilson
Calvin Coolidge[3]	1921–1923	Warren G. Harding
Charles G. Dawes	1925–1929	Calvin Coolidge
Charles Curtis	1929–1933	Herbert C. Hoover
John N. Garner	1933–1941	Franklin D. Roosevelt
Henry A. Wallace	1941–1945	Franklin D. Roosevelt
Harry S Truman[3]	1945	Franklin D. Roosevelt
Alben W. Barkley	1949–1953	Harry S Truman
Richard M. Nixon	1953–1961	Dwight D. Eisenhower
Lyndon B. Johnson[3]	1961–1963	John F. Kennedy
Hubert H. Humphrey	1965–1969	Lyndon B. Johnson
Spiro T. Agnew[4]	1969–1973	Richard M. Nixon
Gerald R. Ford[5]	1973–1974	Richard M. Nixon
Nelson A. Rockefeller	1974–1977	Gerald R. Ford
Walter F. Mondale	1977–1981	Jimmy Carter
George Bush	1981–1989	Ronald Reagan
J. Danforth (Dan) Quayle	1989	George Bush

[1] *Died in office* [2] *Resigned to become U.S. Senator* [3] *Succeeded to Presidency upon death of the President* [4] *Resigned, charged with tax evasion* [5] *Succeeded to Presidency on the President's resignation*

When in the Course of human events, it becomes necessary for one people to dissolve the political bands which have connected them with another, and to assume among the powers of the earth, the separate and equal station to which the Laws of Nature and of Nature's God entitle them, a decent respect to the opinions of mankind requires that they should declare the causes which impel them to the separation.

We hold these truths to be self-evident, that all men are created equal, that they are endowed by their Creator with certain unalienable Rights, that among these are Life, Liberty and the pursuit of Happiness. That to secure these rights, Governments are instituted among Men, deriving their just powers from the consent of the governed. That whenever any Form of Government becomes destructive of these ends, it is the Right of the People to alter or to abolish it, and to institute new Government, laying its foundation on such principles and organizing its powers in such form, as to them shall seem most likely to effect their Safety and Happiness. Prudence, indeed, will dictate that Governments long established should not be changed for light and transient causes; and accordingly all experience hath shewn, that mankind are more disposed to suffer, while evils are sufferable, than to right themselves by abolishing the forms to which they are accustomed. But when a long train of abuses and usurpations, pursuing invariably the same Object evinces a design to reduce them under absolute Despotism, it is their right, it is their duty, to throw off such Government, and to provide new Guards for their future security. Such has been the patient sufferance of these Colonies; and such is now the necessity which constrains them to alter their former Systems of Government. The history of the present King of Great Britain is a history of repeated injuries and usurpations, all having in direct object the establishment of an absolute Tyranny over these States. To prove this, let Facts be submitted to a candid world.

He has refused his Assent to Laws, the most wholesome and necessary for the public good.

He has forbidden his Governors to pass Laws of immediate and pressing importance, unless suspended in their operation till his Assent should be obtained; and when so suspended, he has utterly neglected to attend to them.

He has refused to pass other Laws for the accommodation of large districts of people, unless those people would relinquish the right of Representation in the Legislature, a right inestimable to them and formidable to tyrants only.

He has called together legislative bodies at places, unusual, uncomfortable, and distant from the depository of their public Records, for the sole purpose of fatiguing them into compliance with his measures.

He has dissolved Representative Houses repeatedly, for opposing with manly firmness his invasions on the rights of the people.

He has refused for a long time, after such dissolutions, to cause others to be elected; whereby the Legislative powers, incapable of Annihilation, have returned to the People at large for their exercise; the State remaining in the mean time exposed to all the dangers of invasion from without, and convulsions within.

He has endeavoured to prevent the population of these States; for that purpose obstructing the Laws for Naturalization of Foreigners; refusing to pass others to encourage their migration hither, and raising the conditions of new Appropriations of Lands.

He has obstructed the Administration of Justice, by refusing his Assent to Laws for establishing Judiciary powers.

He has made Judges dependent on his Will alone, for the tenure of their offices, and the amount and payment of their salaries.

He has erected a multitude of New Offices, and sent hither swarms of Officers to harass our people, and eat out their substance.

He has kept among us, in times of peace, Standing Armies without the Consent of our legislatures.

He has affected to render the Military independent of and superior to the Civil Power.

He has combined with others to subject us to a jurisdiction foreign to our constitution, and unacknowledged by our laws; giving his Assent to their Acts of pretended Legislation:

For quartering large bodies of armed troops among us:

For protecting them, by a mock Trial, from punishment for any Murders which they should commit on the Inhabitants of these States:

For cutting off our Trade with all parts of the world:

For imposing Taxes on us without our Consent:

For depriving us in many cases, of the benefits of Trial by Jury:

For transporting us beyond Seas to be tried for pretended offences:

For abolishing the free System of English Laws in a neighbouring Province, establishing therein an Arbitrary government, and enlarging its Boundaries so as to render it at once an example and fit instrument for introducing the same absolute rule into these Colonies:

For taking away our Charters, abolishing our most valuable Laws and altering fundamentally the Forms of our Governments:

For suspending our own Legislatures, and declaring themselves invested with power to legislate for us in all cases whatsoever.

He has abdicated Government here, by declaring us out of his Protection and waging War against us.

He has plundered our seas, ravaged our Coasts, burnt our towns, and destroyed the lives of our people.

He is at this time transporting large Armies of foreign Mercenaries to compleat the works of death, desolation and tyranny, already begun with circumstances of Cruelty & perfidy scarcely paralleled in the most barbarous ages, and totally unworthy the Head of a civilized nation.

He has constrained our fellow Citizens taken Captive on the high Seas to bear Arms against their Country, to become the executioners of their friends and Brethren, or to fall themselves by their Hands.

He has excited domestic insurrections amongst us, and has endeavoured to bring on the inhabitants of our frontiers, the merciless Indian Savages, whose known rule of warfare, is an undistinguished destruction of all ages, sexes and conditions.

In every stage of these Oppressions We have Petitioned for Redress in the most humble terms: Our repeated Petitions have been answered only by repeated injury. A Prince, whose character is thus marked by every act which may define a Tyrant, is unfit to be the ruler of a free people.

Nor have We been wanting in attentions to our British brethren. We have warned them from time to time of attempts by their legislature to extend an unwarrantable jurisdiction over us. We have reminded them of the circumstances of our emigration and settlement here. We have appealed to their native justice and magnanimity, and we have conjured them by the ties of our common kindred to disavow these usurpations, which, would inevitably interrupt our connections and correspondence. They too have been deaf to the voice of justice and consanguinity. We must, therefore, acquiesce in the necessity, which denounces our Separation, and hold them, as we hold the rest of mankind, Enemies in War, in Peace Friends.

WE, THEREFORE, the Representatives of the United States of America, in General Congress, Assembled, appealing to the Supreme Judge of the world for the rectitude of our intentions, do, in the Name, and by Authority of the good People of these Colonies, solemnly publish and declare, That these United Colonies are, and of Right ought to be **FREE AND INDEPENDENT STATES**; that they are Absolved from all Allegiance to the British Crown, and that all political connections between them and the State of Great Britain, is and ought to be totally dissolved; and that as Free and Independent States, they have full Power to levy War, conclude Peace, contract Alliances, establish Commerce, and to do all other Acts and Things which Independent States may of right do. And for the support of this Declaration, with a firm reliance on the protection of Divine Providence, we mutually pledge to each other our Lives, our Fortunes, and our sacred Honor.

Signed by order and in behalf of the Congress.

(actual signature of John Hancock, a signer of the Declaration)

Signers of the Declaration of Independence

NEW YORK
William Floyd
Philip Livingston
Francis Lewis
Lewis Morris

NEW JERSEY
Richard Stockton
John Witherspoon
Francis Hopkinson
John Hart
Abraham Clark

SOUTH CAROLINA
Edward Rutledge
Thomas Heyward, Jr.
Thomas Lynch, Jr.
Arthur Middleton

NEW HAMPSHIRE
Josiah Bartlett
William Whipple
Matthew Thornton

GEORGIA
Button Gwinnett
Lyman Hall
George Walton

VIRGINIA
George Wythe
Richard Henry Lee
Thomas Jefferson
Benjamin Harrison
Thomas Nelson, Jr.
Francis Lightfoot Lee
Carter Braxton

NORTH CAROLINA
William Hooper
Joseph Hewes
John Penn

PENNSYLVANIA
Robert Morris
Benjamin Rush
Benjamin Franklin
John Morton
George Clymer
James Smith
George Taylor
James Wilson
George Ross

DELAWARE
Caesar Rodney
George Read
Thomas McKean

MASSACHUSETTS-BAY
Samuel Adams
John Adams
Robert Treat Paine
Elbridge Gerry

MARYLAND
Samuel Chase
William Paca
Thomas Stone
Charles Carroll
of Carrollton

RHODE ISLAND
Stephen Hopkins
William Ellery

CONNECTICUT
Roger Sherman
Samuel Huntington
William Williams
Oliver Wolcott

Note: *In 1776, the Declaration of Independence complained of many injustices actually experienced by colonists at the hands of the British king and government. In 1789, Americans wanted guarantees that their own new government could never repeat such injustices. Notice how many of them are covered in the Bill of Rights, which follows here. It became part of our Constitution in 1791.*

Bill of Rights

Amendment 1

Congress shall make no law respecting an establishment of religion, or prohibiting the free exercise thereof; or abridging the freedom of speech, or of the press; or the right of the people peaceably to assemble, and to petition the Government for a redress of grievances.

Amendment 2

A well-regulated Militia, being necessary to the security of a free State, the right of the people to keep and bear Arms, shall not be infringed.

Amendment 3

No Soldier shall, in time of peace be quartered in any house, without the consent of the Owner, nor in time of war, but in a manner to be prescribed by law.

Amendment 4

The right of the people to be secure in their persons, houses, papers, and effects, against unreasonable searches and seizures, shall not be violated, and no Warrants shall issue, but upon probable cause, supported by Oath or affirmation, and particularly describing the place to be searched, and the persons or things to be seized.

Amendment 5

No person shall be held to answer for a capital, or otherwise infamous crime, unless on a presentment or indictment of a Grand Jury, except in cases arising in the land or naval forces, or in the Militia, when in actual service in time of War or public danger; nor shall any person be subject for the same offence to be twice put in jeopardy of life or limb; nor shall be compelled in any criminal case to be a witness against himself, nor be deprived of life, liberty, or property, without due process of law; nor shall private property be taken for public use, without just compensation.

Amendment 6

In all criminal prosecutions, the accused shall enjoy the right to a speedy and public trial, by an impartial jury of the State and district wherein the crime shall have been committed, which district shall have been previously ascertained by law, and to be informed of the nature and cause of the accusation; to be confronted with the witnesses against him; to have compulsory process for obtaining witnesses in his favor, and to have the Assistance of Counsel for his defence.

Amendment 7

In Suits at common law, where the value in controversy shall exceed twenty dollars, the right of trial by jury shall be preserved, and no fact tried by a jury, shall be otherwise re-examined in any Court of the United States, than according to the rules of the common law.

Amendment 8

Excessive bail shall not be required, nor excessive fines imposed, nor cruel and unusual punishments inflicted.

Amendment 9

The enumeration in the Constitution, of certain rights, shall not be construed to deny or disparage others retained by the people.

Amendment 10

The powers not delegated to the United States by the Constitution, nor prohibited by it to the States, are reserved to the States respectively, or to the people.

Chief Justices of the United States Supreme Court

NAME	YEARS SERVED	NAME	YEARS SERVED
John Jay	1789-1795	Edward White	1910-1921
John Rutledge	1795	William H. Taft	1921-1930
Oliver Ellsworth	1796-1800	Charles E. Hughes	1930-1941
John Marshall	1801-1835	Harlan F. Stone	1941-1946
Roger B. Taney	1836-1864	Fred M. Vinson	1946-1953
Salmon P. Chase	1864-1873	Earl Warren	1953-1969
Morrison R. Waite	1874-1888	Warren E. Burger	1969-1986
Melville W. Fuller	1888-1910	William H. Rehnquist	1986-

Major Supreme Court Decisions

The following cases are among the landmark decisions made by the Supreme Court.

Marbury v. Madison (1803)	The Supreme Court has the power of judicial review. It can declare a law unconstitutional.
McCulloch v. Maryland (1819)	The Constitution gives the federal government implied powers that are necessary to carry out expressed powers.
Dartmouth College v. Woodward (1819)	The Constitution protects contracts against infringement by the states.
Gibbons v. Ogden (1824)	States may not make laws in areas where federal powers are enumerated in the Constitution. The federal government has the power to control interstate commerce.
Charles River Bridge v. Warren Bridge (1837)	Private property interests, unless explicitly protected by grant or charter, cannot impede improvements for the public benefit.
Dred Scott v. Sandford (1857)	Blacks could not be citizens. Congress could not prohibit slavery in United States territories. This decision was overturned by the 13th and 14th amendments.
Ex Parte Milligan (1866)	Civilians cannot be tried in military courts if civilian courts are available. Martial rule is confined to the locality of actual war.
Plessy v. Ferguson (1896)	"Separate but equal" public accommodations for Blacks and whites are constitutional. This decision was overturned by Brown v. Board of Education of Topeka, Kansas (1954).
Schenck v. United States (1919)	Freedom of speech may not be restricted unless the speech results in a "clear and present danger" that the government has the duty to prevent.

Powell v. Alabama (1932)	A person on trial for his or her life who cannot afford to hire a lawyer must be provided with a lawyer by the state.
Korematsu v. United States (1944)	The United States government had the right to remove persons of Japanese ancestry from areas of the country open to attack by the Japanese during World War II.
Brown v. Board of Education (1954)	Separate but equal facilities for Blacks in public schools violate the constitutional requirement for equal protection of the law.
Mapp v. Illinois (1961)	It is not permissible to use evidence obtained by unlawful means in a criminal trial.
Baker v. Carr (1962)	Federal courts can hear cases challenging unfair election districting.
Gideon v. Wainwright (1963)	The state must provide a lawyer for a defendant in a criminal case who cannot afford legal counsel.
Escobedo v. Illinois (1964)	A confession cannot be used as evidence if the person accused of the crime has been denied permission to see a lawyer.
Reynolds v. Sims (1964)	The rule of "one person, one vote" applies to the United States House of Representatives and both houses of state legislatures. Election district lines must be drawn to create districts nearly equal in population.
Heart of Atlanta, Inc. v. United States (1964)	The Civil Rights Act of 1964, which banned racial discrimination in public accommodations such as hotels and restaurants, is constitutional.
Miranda v. Arizona (1966)	A person accused of a crime must be informed of his or her constitutional rights before being questioned.
United States v. Nixon (1974)	The President's right of executive privilege does not extend to evidence needed in a criminal trial.
Regents of the University of California v. Bakke (1978)	College and universities may not use quotas to establish racial balance. Race can be considered as a "plus" factor when considering applicants.
Fitzgerald v. Nixon (1982)	No President of the United States may be held liable for any official action taken while in office. This immunity applies only to civil suits, not to criminal prosecution or other kinds of judicial action.

State	Capital	Admitted to The Union	State Flower	State Bird	State Nickname
Alabama	Montgomery	Dec. 14, 1819	Camellia	Yellowhammer	Cotton State
Alaska	Juneau	Jan. 3, 1959	Forget-me-not	Willow ptarmigan	Last Frontier
Arizona	Phoenix	Feb. 14, 1912	Saguaro cactus	Cactus wren	Grand Canyon State
Arkansas	Little Rock	June 15, 1836	Apple blossom	Mockingbird	Land of Opportunity
California	Sacramento	Sept. 9, 1850	Golden poppy	California valley quail	Golden State
Colorado	Denver	Aug. 1, 1876	Rocky Mountain columbine	Lark bunting	Centennial State
Connecticut	Hartford	Jan. 9, 1788*	Mountain laurel	American robin	Nutmeg State or Constitution State
Delaware	Dover	Dec. 7, 1787*	Peach blossom	Blue hen chicken	Diamond State or First State
Florida	Tallahassee	Mar. 3, 1845	Orange blossom	Mockingbird	Sunshine State
Georgia	Atlanta	Jan. 2, 1788*	Cherokee rose	Brown thrasher	Empire State of the South
Hawaii	Honolulu	Aug. 21, 1959	Hibiscus	Nene (Hawaiian goose)	Aloha State
Idaho	Boise	July 3, 1890	Syringa	Mountain bluebird	Gem State
Illinois	Springfield	Dec. 3, 1818	Native violet	Cardinal	Prairie State
Indiana	Indianapolis	Dec. 11, 1816	Peony	Cardinal	Hoosier State
Iowa	Des Moines	Dec. 28, 1846	Wild rose	Eastern goldfinch	Hawkeye State
Kansas	Topeka	Jan. 29, 1861	Sunflower	Western meadowlark	Sunflower State
Kentucky	Frankfort	June 1, 1792	Goldenrod	Kentucky cardinal	Bluegrass State
Louisiana	Baton Rouge	Apr. 30, 1812	Magnolia	Eastern brown pelican	Pelican or Creole State
Maine	Augusta	Mar. 15, 1820	Pine cone and tassel	Chickadee	Pine Tree State
Maryland	Annapolis	Apr. 28, 1788*	Black-eyed Susan	Baltimore oriole	Old Line State or Free State
Massachusetts	Boston	Feb. 6, 1788*	Mayflower	Chickadee	Bay State
Michigan	Lansing	Jan. 26, 1837	Apple blossom	Robin	Wolverine State
Minnesota	St. Paul	May 11, 1858	Pink and white lady's-slipper	Common loon	Gopher State
Mississippi	Jackson	Dec. 10, 1817	Magnolia	Mockingbird	Magnolia State
Missouri	Jefferson City	Aug. 10, 1821	Hawthorn	Bluebird	Show Me State

State	Capital	Admitted to The Union	State Flower	State Bird	State Nickname
Montana	Helena	Nov. 8, 1889	Bitterroot	Western meadowlark	Treasure State
Nebraska	Lincoln	Mar. 1, 1867	Goldenrod	Western meadowlark	Cornhusker State
Nevada	Carson City	Oct. 31, 1864	Sagebrush (unofficial)	Mountain bluebird (unofficial)	Sagebrush State
New Hampshire	Concord	June 21, 1788*	Purple lilac	Purple finch	Granite State
New Jersey	Trenton	Dec. 18, 1787*	Purple violet	Eastern goldfinch	Garden State
New Mexico	Santa Fe	Jan. 6, 1912	Yucca	Road runner	Land of Enchantment
New York	Albany	Jan. 26, 1788*	Rose	Bluebird (unofficial)	Empire State
North Carolina	Raleigh	Nov. 21, 1789*	Dogwood	Cardinal	Tar Heel State
North Dakota	Bismarck	Nov. 2, 1889	Wild prairie rose	Western meadowlark	Flickertail State or Sioux State
Ohio	Columbus	Mar. 1, 1803	Scarlet carnation	Cardinal	Buckeye State
Oklahoma	Oklahoma City	Nov. 16, 1907	Mistletoe	Scissor-tailed flycatcher	Sooner State
Oregon	Salem	Feb. 14, 1859	Oregon grape	Western meadowlark	Beaver State
Pennsylvania	Harrisburg	Dec. 12, 1787*	Mountain laurel	Ruffed grouse	Keystone State
Rhode Island	Providence	May 29, 1790*	Violet (unofficial)	Rhode Island Red	Little Rhody
South Carolina	Columbia	May 23, 1788*	Carolina yellow jessamine	Carolina wren	Palmetto State
South Dakota	Pierre	Nov. 2, 1889	American pasque-flower	Ringnecked pheasant	Coyote State
Tennessee	Nashville	June 1, 1796	Iris	Mockingbird	Volunteer State
Texas	Austin	Dec. 29, 1845	Bluebonnet	Mockingbird	Lone Star State
Utah	Salt Lake City	Jan. 4, 1896	Sego lily	Sea gull	Beehive State
Vermont	Montpelier	Mar. 4, 1791	Red clover	Hermit thrush	Green Mountain State
Virginia	Richmond	June 25, 1788*	Dogwood	Cardinal	Old Dominion
Washington	Olympia	Nov. 11, 1889	Coast rhododendron	Willow goldfinch	Evergreen State
West Virginia	Charleston	June 20, 1863	Rhododendron	Cardinal	Mountain State
Wisconsin	Madison	May 29, 1848	Violet	Robin	Badger State
Wyoming	Cheyenne	July 10, 1890	Indian paintbrush	Meadowlark	Equality State

* *One of the thirteen original states*

20th Century Political Leaders

UNITED STATES

NAME OF LEADER	YEARS SERVED
William McKinley	1897-1901
Theodore Roosevelt	1901-1909
William H. Taft	1909-1913
Woodrow Wilson	1913-1921
Warren G. Harding	1921-1923
Calvin Coolidge	1923-1929
Herbert C. Hoover	1929-1933
Franklin D. Roosevelt	1933-1945
Harry S Truman	1945-1953
Dwight D. Eisenhower	1953-1961
John F. Kennedy	1961-1963
Lyndon B. Johnson	1963-1969
Richard M. Nixon	1969-1974
Gerald R. Ford	1974-1977
Jimmy Carter	1977-1981
Ronald Reagan	1981-1989
George Bush	1989-

GREAT BRITAIN

NAME OF LEADER	YEARS SERVED
Marquess of Salisbury	1895-1902
Arthur J. Balfour	1902-1905
Henry Campbell-Bannerman	1905-1908
Herbert H. Asquith	1908-1916
David Lloyd George	1916-1922
Andrew Bonar Law	1922-1923
Stanley Baldwin	1923-1924
James Ramsay MacDonald	1924-1924
Stanley Baldwin	1924-1929
James Ramsay MacDonald	1929-1935
Stanley Baldwin	1935-1937
Neville Chamberlain	1937-1940
Winston Churchill	1940-1945
Clement R. Attlee	1945-1951
Winston Churchill	1951-1955
Anthony Eden	1955-1957
Harold Macmillan	1957-1963
Alexander Douglas-Home	1963-1964
Harold Wilson	1964-1970
Edward Heath	1970-1974
Harold Wilson	1974-1976
James Callaghan	1976-1979
Margaret Thatcher	1979-

FRANCE

NAME OF LEADER	YEARS SERVED
Émile Loubet	1899-1906
Clement Armand Fallières	1906-1913
Raymond Poincaré	1913-1920
Paul E. L. Deschanel	1920-1920
Alexandre Millerand	1920-1924
Gaston Doumergue	1924-1931
Paul Doumer	1931-1932
Albert Lebrun	1932-1940
Henri Philippe Pétain (Vichy government)	1940-1944
Charles de Gaulle	1944-1946
Félix Gouin	1946-1946
Georges Bidault	1946-1947
Vincent Auriol	1947-1954
René Coty	1954-1959
Charles de Gaulle	1959-1969
Georges Pompidou	1969-1974
Valéry Giscard d'Estaing	1974-1981
François Mitterand	1981-

U.S.S.R.

NAME OF LEADER	YEARS SERVED
Czar Nicholas II	1894-1917
Prince Georgi Lvov	1917-1917
Alexander Kerensky	1917-1917
Nikolai Lenin	1917-1924
Aleksei Rykov	1924-1930
Vyacheslav Molotov	1930-1941
Joseph Stalin	1941-1953
Georgi M. Malenkov	1953-1955
Nikolai A. Bulganin	1955-1958
Nikita S. Khrushchev	1958-1964
Leonid I. Brezhnev	1964-1982
Yuri Andropov	1982-1984
Konstantin U. Chernenko	1984-1985
Mikhail S. Gorbachev	1985-

UNITED STATES

NAME OF LEADER	YEARS SERVED
William McKinley	1897-1901
Theodore Roosevelt	1901-1909
William H. Taft	1909-1913
Woodrow Wilson	1913-1921
Warren G. Harding	1921-1923
Calvin Coolidge	1923-1929
Herbert C. Hoover	1929-1933
Franklin D. Roosevelt	1933-1945
Harry S Truman	1945-1953
Dwight D. Eisenhower	1953-1961
John F. Kennedy	1961-1963
Lyndon B. Johnson	1963-1969
Richard M. Nixon	1969-1974
Gerald R. Ford	1974-1977
Jimmy Carter	1977-1981
Ronald Reagan	1981-1989
George Bush	1989-

ITALY

NAME OF LEADER	YEARS SERVED
Giuseppe Saracco	1900-1901
Giuseppe Zanardelli	1901-1903
Giovanni Gioletti	1903-1905
Alessandro Fortis	1905-1906
Giovanni Gioletti	1906-1909
Sidney, Baron Sonnino	1909-1910
Luigi Luzzatti	1910-1911
Giovanni Gioletti	1911-1914
Antonio Salandra	1914-1916
Paolo Boselli	1916-1917
Vittorio Emmanuele Orlando	1917-1919
Francesco Nitti	1919-1920
Giovanni Gioletti	1920-1921
Ivanoe Bonomi	1921-1921
Benito Mussolini	1922-1943
Pietro Badoglio	1943-1944
Ivanoe Bonomi	1944-1945
Alcide de Gasperi	1945-1953
Giuseppe Pella	1953-1954
Mario Scelba	1954-1955
Antonio Segni	1955-1957
Adone Zoli	1957-1958
Amintore Fanfani	1958-1959
Antonio Sequi	1959-1960
Amintore Fanfani	1960-1963
Aldo Moro	1964-1968
Mariano Rumor	1968-1970
Emilio Colombo	1970-1972
Giulio Andreotti	1972-1973
Mariano Rumor	1973-1974
Aldo Moro	1974-1976
Giulio Andreotti	1976-1978
Francesco Cossiga	1979-1980
Arnaldo Forlani	1980-1981
Giovanni Spadolini	1981-1982
Amintore Fanfani	1982-1983
Bettino Craxi	1983-1987
Giovanni Goria	1987-1988
Ciriaco De Mita	1988-

GERMANY

NAME OF LEADER	YEARS SERVED
Emperor William II	1888-1918
Friedrich Ebert	1919-1925
Paul von Hindenburg	1925-1934
Adolf Hitler	1934-1945
Karl Doenitz	1945-1945

WEST GERMANY

(Military Occupation) 1945-1949

Konrad Adenauer	1949-1963
Ludwig Erhard	1963-1966
Kurt George Kiesinger	1966-1969
Willy Brandt	1969-1974
Helmut Schmidt	1974-1982
Helmut Kohl	1982-

EAST GERMANY

(Military Occupation) 1945-1949

Wilhelm Pieck	1949-1960
Walter Ulbricht	1960-1973
Willi Stoph	1973-1976
Erich Honecker	1976-

UNITED STATES

NAME OF LEADER	YEARS SERVED
William McKinley	1897-1901
Theodore Roosevelt	1901-1909
William H. Taft	1909-1913
Woodrow Wilson	1913-1921
Warren G. Harding	1921-1923
Calvin Coolidge	1923-1929
Herbert C. Hoover	1929-1933
Franklin D. Roosevelt	1933-1945
Harry S Truman	1945-1953
Dwight D. Eisenhower	1953-1961
John F. Kennedy	1961-1963
Lyndon B. Johnson	1963-1969
Richard M. Nixon	1969-1974
Gerald R. Ford	1974-1977
Jimmy Carter	1977-1981
Ronald Reagan	1981-1989
George Bush	1989-

SPAIN

NAME OF LEADER	YEARS SERVED
King Alfonso XIII	1886-1931
Niceto Alcalá Zamora y Torres	1931-1936
Manuel Azaña	1936-1939
Francisco Franco	1939-1975
King Juan Carlos	1975-

CANADA		MEXICO	
NAME OF LEADER	YEARS SERVED	NAME OF LEADER	YEARS SERVED
Wilfrid Laurier	1896-1911	Porfirio Diaz	1876-1911
Robert L. Borden	1911-1920	Francisco I. Madero	1911-1913
		Victoriano Huerta	1913-1914
		Venustiano Carranza	1914-1920
Arthur Meighen	1920-1921	Alvaro Obregón	1920-1924
W. L. Mackenzie King	1921-1926		
Arthur Meighen	1926-1926	Plutarco Elias Calles	1924-1928
W. L. Mackenzie King	1926-1930	Emilio Portes Gil	1928-1930
Richard B. Bennett	1930-1935	Pascual Ortiz Rubio	1930-1932
		Abelardo L. Rodriguez	1932-1934
W. L. Mackenzie King	1935-1948	Lázaro Cárdenas	1934-1940
		Manuel Avila Camacho	1940-1946
Louis S. St. Laurent	1948-1957	Miguel Alemán Valdés	1946-1952
		Adolfo Ruiz Cortines	1952-1958
John Diefenbaker	1957-1963	Adolfo Lopez Mateos	1958-1964
Lester B. Pearson	1963-1968		
		Gustavo Diaz Ordaz	1964-1970
Pierre E. Trudeau	1968-1979		
		Luis Echeverría Alvarez	1970-1976
		Jose Lopez Portillo	1976-1982
Charles Joseph Clark	1979-1980		
Pierre E. Trudeau	1980-1984		
John Turner	1984-1984		
Martin Brian Mulroney	1984-	Miguel de la Madrid Hurtado	1982-

20th Century Political Leaders

UNITED STATES	
NAME OF LEADER	YEARS SERVED
William McKinley	1897-1901
Theodore Roosevelt	1901-1909
William H. Taft	1909-1913
Woodrow Wilson	1913-1921
Warren G. Harding	1921-1923
Calvin Coolidge	1923-1929
Herbert C. Hoover	1929-1933
Franklin D. Roosevelt	1933-1945
Harry S Truman	1945-1953
Dwight D. Eisenhower	1953-1961
John F. Kennedy	1961-1963
Lyndon B. Johnson	1963-1969
Richard M. Nixon	1969-1974
Gerald R. Ford	1974-1977
Jimmy Carter	1977-1981
Ronald Reagan	1981-1989
George Bush	1989-

JAPAN	
NAME OF LEADER	YEARS SERVED
Emperor Meiji	1867-1912
Emperor Taisho	1912-1926
Emperor Hirohito	1926-1989
Emperor Akinito	1989-
(*Figureheads after World War II*)	
(Postwar Premiers)	
Shigeru Yoshida	1946-1947
Tetsu Katayama	1947-1948
Hitoshi Ashida	1948-1948
Shigeru Yoshida	1948-1954
Ichirō Hatoyama	1954-1956
Tanzan Ishibashi	1956-1957
Nobusuke Kishi	1957-1960
Hayato Ikeda	1960-1964
Eisaku Satō	1964-1972
Kakuei Tanaka	1972-1974
Takeo Miki	1974-1976
Takeo Fukuda	1976-1978
Masayoshi Ohira	1978-1980
Zenko Suzuki	1980-1982
Yasuhiro Nakasone	1982-1987
Noboru Takeshita	1987-1989
Sousuke Uno	1989-1989
Toshiki Kaifu	1989-

CHINA

NAME OF LEADER	YEARS SERVED
Emperor Zaidian	1875-1908
Empress Zi Xi	1898-1908
Emperor Puyi	1908-1912
Sun Yat-sen	1912-1912
Yuan Shikai	1912-1916
Li Yuanhong	1916-1917
Sun Yat-sen (Canton Administration)	1917-1925
(Disorders)	1926-1927
Chiang Kai-shek (President in Nanking)	1928-1931
Lin Sen	1932-1943
(War with Japan)	1937-1945
Chiang Kai-shek (Nationalists)	1945-1949
Mao Zedong (Communists)	1945-1949
Mao Zedong (Communist Party Chairman)	1949-1976
Zhou Enlai (Premier)	1949-1976
Hua Guofeng	1976-1980
Deng Xiaoping	1977-1987
Zhao Ziyang	1980-
Yang Shangkun (President)	1988-
Li Peng (Premier)	1987-

INDIA

(In 1757 the British East India Company gained control of India. In 1858 the British government took over control and maintained it until 1947. During the latter part of British rule, Mohandas K. Gandhi became a leader of the Indian independence movement. India became an independent nation on August 15, 1947. A close associate of Gandhi, Jawaharlal Nehru, became India's first prime minister.)

NAME OF LEADER	YEARS SERVED
Pandit Jawaharlal Nehru	1947-1964
Lal Bahadur Shastri	1964-1966
Indira Gandhi (daughter of Jawaharlal Nehru)	1966-1977
Morarji R. Desai	1977-1979
Charan Singh	1979-1980
Indira Gandhi	1980-1984
Rajiv Gandhi	1984-

UNITED STATES

NAME OF LEADER	YEARS SERVED
William McKinley	1897-1901
Theodore Roosevelt	1901-1909
William H. Taft	1909-1913
Woodrow Wilson	1913-1921
Warren G. Harding	1921-1923
Calvin Coolidge	1923-1929
Herbert C. Hoover	1929-1933
Franklin D. Roosevelt	1933-1945
Harry S Truman	1945-1953
Dwight D. Eisenhower	1953-1961
John F. Kennedy	1961-1963
Lyndon B. Johnson	1963-1969
Richard M. Nixon	1969-1974
Gerald R. Ford	1974-1977
Jimmy Carter	1977-1981
Ronald Reagan	1981-1989
George Bush	1989-

ISRAEL

(Beginning in the mid-1800's, increasing numbers of European Jews settled in Palestine, which was then part of the Ottoman Empire. After World War I, Palestine came under British control. Following Word War II, the United Nations recommended dividing Palestine into a Jewish state and an Arab state. On May 14, 1948, the Jews established the independent state of Israel.)

NAME OF LEADER	YEARS SERVED
David Ben-Gurion	1948-1953
Moshe Sharett	1953-1955
David Ben-Gurion	1955-1963
Levi Eshkol	1963-1969
Golda Meir	1969-1974
Yitzhak Rabin	1974-1977
Menachem Begin	1977-1983
Yitzhak Shamir	1983-

EGYPT

NAME OF LEADER	YEARS SERVED
(Under British rule)	1882-1922
King Ahmed Fuad	1922-1936
King Farouk	1936-1956
Mohammed Naguib	1952-1954
Gamal Abdel Nasser	1954-1970
Anwar el-Sadat	1970-1981
Hosni Mubarak	1981-

UNITED NATIONS

(The United Nations is an international organization estblished after World War II to work for peace and the betterment of humanity. The chief official of the organization is the Secretary-General.)

NAME OF LEADER	YEARS SERVED
Trygve Lie	1946-1953
Dag Hammarskjöld	1953-1961
U Thant	1961-1972
Kurt Waldheim	1972-1982
Javiere Perez de Cuellar	1982-

Members of the United Nations

Date of Entry	Member
1946	Afghanistan
1955	Albania
1962	Algeria
1976	Angola
1981	Antigua and Barbuda
1945	Argentina
1945	Australia
1955	Austria
1973	Bahamas
1971	Bahrain
1974	Bangladesh
1966	Barbados
1945	Belgium
1981	Belize
1960	Benin
1971	Bhutan
1945	Bolivia
1966	Botswana
1945	Brazil
1984	Brunei Darussalam
1955	Bulgaria
1948	Burma
1962	Burundi
1945	Byelorussian SSR
1955	Cambodia (now: Kampuchea)
1960	Cameroon, United Republic of
1945	Canada
1975	Cape Verde
1960	Central African Republic
	(Ceylon: see Sri Lanka)
1960	Chad
1945	Chile
1945	China[1]
1945	Colombia
1975	Comoros
1960	Congo, People's Republic of the
	(Congo, Democratic Republic of the: see Zaire)
1945	Costa Rica
1945	Cuba
1960	Cyprus
1945	Czechoslovakia
	(Dahomey: see Benin)
1945	Denmark
1977	Djibouti
1978	Dominica
1945	Dominican Republic
1945	Ecuador
1945	Egypt[2]
1945	El Salvador
1968	Equatorial Guinea

Date of Entry	Member
1945	Ethiopia
1970	Fiji
1955	Finland
1945	France
1960	Gabon
1965	Gambia
1973	German Democratic Republic (East)
1973	Germany, Federal Republic of (West)
1957	Ghana
1945	Greece
1974	Grenada
1945	Guatemala
1958	Guinea
1974	Guinea-Bissau
1966	Guyana
1945	Haiti
1945	Honduras
1955	Hungary
1946	Iceland
1945	India
1950	Indonesia
1945	Iran
1945	Iraq
1955	Ireland
1949	Israel
1955	Italy
1960	Ivory Coast
1962	Jamaica
1956	Japan
1955	Jordan
1963	Kenya
1963	Kuwait
1955	Laos
1945	Lebanon
1966	Lesotho
1945	Liberia
1955	Libya
1945	Luxembourg
1960	Madagascar
1964	Malawi
1957	Malaysia[3]
1965	Maldives
1960	Mali
1964	Malta
1961	Mauritania
1968	Mauritius
1945	Mexico
1961	Mongolia
1956	Morocco
1975	Mozambique

Date of Entry	Member
1955	Nepal
1945	Netherlands
1945	New Zealand
1945	Nicaragua
1960	Niger
1960	Nigeria
1945	Norway
1971	Oman
1947	Pakistan
1945	Panama
1975	Papua-New Guinea
1945	Paraguay
1945	Peru
1945	Philippines
1945	Poland
1955	Portugal
1971	Qatar
1955	Romania
1962	Rwanda
1983	Saint Kitts-Nevis
1979	Saint Lucia
1980	Saint Vincent and the Grenadines
1976	Samoa (Western)
1975	São Tomé e Principe
1945	Saudi Arabia
1960	Senegal
1976	Seychelles
1961	Sierra Leone
1965	Singapore[3]
1978	Solomon Islands
1960	Somalia
1945	South Africa
1955	Spain
1955	Sri Lanka (Ceylon)
1956	Sudan
1975	Suriname
1968	Swaziland
1946	Sweden
1945	Syria[2]
1961	Tanzania[4]
1946	Thailand
1960	Togo
1962	Trinidad and Tobago
1956	Tunisia
1945	Turkey
1962	Uganda
1945	Ukrainian SSR
1945	Union of Soviet Socialist Republics
1971	United Arab Emirates
1945	United Kingdom of Great Britain and Northern Ireland
1945	United States of America
1960	Upper Volta (now Burkina-Faso)
1945	Uruguay
1981	Vanuatu
1945	Venezuela
1977	Vietnam
1947	Yemen
1967	Yemen, People's Democratic Republic of
1945	Yugoslavia
1960	Zaire (Democratic Republic of the Congo)
1964	Zambia
1980	Zimbabwe

[1] *China's original United Nations membership went to Chiang Kai-shek's nationalist republic, soon only on the island of Taiwan. In 1971, the UN General Assembly voted to transfer all rights to the People's Republic of China, expelled Chiang Kai-shek's representatives, and installed those of the People's Republic.*

[2] *Egypt and Syria were original members of the United Nations. In 1958 they joined to form the United Arab Republic and kept only a single membership. In 1961, however, Syria withdrew from the union and resumed both its independence and its separate membership. In 1971, Egypt changed its official name from United Arab Republic to Arab Republic of Egypt.*

[3] *The Federation of Malaya joined the United Nations in 1957. After taking in Singapore and two other states, it changed its name to Malaysia in 1963. In 1965, Singapore became an independent state and a United Nations member.*

[4] *Tanganyika joined the United Nations in 1961, Zanzibar in 1963. In 1964, they united to form a new republic, which continued as a single member, soon given a new name, United Republic of Tanzania.*

Nobel Prize for Peace

The following is a list of winners of the Nobel Prize for Peace. There were no awards given in the years not listed.

1901	Jean Henri Dunant	Swiss
	Frédéric Passy	French
1902	Élie Ducommun	Swiss
	Charles Albert Gobat	Swiss
1903	William R. Cremer	British
1904	The Institute of International Law	
1905	Bertha von Suttner	Austrian
1906	Theodore Roosevelt	American
1907	Ernesto T. Moneta	Italian
	Louis Renault	French
1908	Klas Pontus Arnoldson	Swedish
	Fredrik Bajer	Danish
1909	Auguste M.F. Beernaert	Belgian
	Paul d'Estournelles	French
1910	The International Peace Bureau	
1911	Tobias M.C. Asser	Dutch
	Alfred H. Fried	Austrian
1912	Elihu Root	American
1913	Henri Lafontaine	Belgian
1917	The International Red Cross	
1919	Woodrow Wilson	American
1920	Léon Bourgeois	French
1921	Karl Hjalmar Branting	Swedish
	Christian Louis Lange	Norwegian
1922	Fridtjof Nansen	Norwegian
1925	Austen Chamberlain	British
	Charles G. Dawes	American
1926	Aristide Briand	French
	Gustav Stresemann	German
1927	Ferdinand Buisson	French
	Ludwig Quidde	German
1929	Frank Billings Kellogg	American
1930	Nathan Söderblom	Swedish
1931	Jane Addams	American
	Nicholas Murray Butler	American
1933	Norman Angell	British
1934	Arthur Henderson	British
1935	Carl von Ossietzky	German
1936	Carlos Saavedra Lamas	Argentine
1937	Edgar Algernon Robert Cecil	British
1938	The International Office for Refugees	
1944	The International Red Cross	
1945	Cordell Hull	American
1946	John R. Mott	American
	Emily G. Balch	American
1947	The Friends Service Council and the American Friends Service Committee	
1949	John Boyd Orr	British
1950	Ralph J. Bunche	American
1951	Léon Jouhaux	French
1952	Albert Schweitzer	French
1953	George C. Marshall	American
1954	Office of the United Nations High Commissioner for Refugees	
1957	Lester B. Pearson	Canadian
1958	Dominique Georges Pire	Belgian
1959	Philip Noel-Baker	British
1960	Albert John Luthuli	African
1961	Dag Hammarskjöld	Swedish
1962	Linus Pauling	American
1963	The International Committee of the Red Cross and The League of Red Cross Societies	
1964	Martin Luther King, Jr.	American
1965	United Nations Children's Fund	
1968	René Cassin	French
1969	International Labor Organization	
1970	Norman E. Borlaug	American
1971	Willy Brandt	German
1973	Henry A. Kissinger	American
	Le Duc Tho	North Vietnamese
1974	Sean MacBride	Irish
	Eisaku Sato	Japanese
1975	Andrei D. Sakharov	Russian
1976	Mairead Corrigan	Irish
	Betty Williams	Irish
1977	Amnesty International	
1978	Menachem Begin	Israeli
	Anwar el-Sadat	Egyptian
1979	Mother Teresa of Calcutta	Albanian-Indian
1980	Adolfo Perez Esquivel	Argentine
1981	U.N. High Comm. for Refugees	
1982	Alva Myrdal	Swedish
	Alfonso Garcia Robles	Mexican
1983	Lech Walesa	Poland
1984	Bishop Desmond Tutu	Africa
1985	International Physicians for the Prevention of Nuclear War	U.S.
1986	Elie Wiesel	Romanian, U.S.
1987	Oscar Arias Sanchez	Costa Rica
1988	The United Nations peacekeeping forces	

Each state has jurisdiction over the holidays it observes. Most states observe federal legal holidays. Many states observe other holidays as well. When a holiday falls on a Saturday or Sunday, it is usually observed on the preceding Friday or the following Monday.

The following are the federal legal public holidays.

New Year's Day	January 1
Dr. Martin Luther King, Jr. Day	3rd Monday in January
President's Day (Washington's birthday [Feb. 16] and Lincoln's birthday [Feb. 12] are now celebrated together)	3rd Monday in February
Memorial Day	Last Monday in May (In some states, May 31)
Independence Day	July 4
Labor Day	1st Monday in September
Columbus Day	2nd Monday in October
Veterans Day	November 11
Thanksgiving Day	Thursday in the last full week in November.
Christmas Day	December 25

Forms of Address

Forms of address are the appropriate way to speak or write to someone. In these examples Thomas Jones and Carol Smith are used as representative names.

President
The President
The White House
Washington, D.C. 20500
Dear Mr. or Madam President:

Vice President
The Vice President
United States Senate
Washington, D.C. 20510
Dear Mr. or Madam Vice President:

Chief Justice of the Supreme Court
The Chief Justice of the United States
Supreme Court Building
Washington, D.C. 20543
Dear Mr. or Madam Chief Justice:

Associate Justice of the Supreme Court
Dear Mr. or Madam Justice:
or Dear Mr. or Madam Justice Jones:

United States Senator
The Honorable Thomas Jones
The Honorable Carol Smith
United States Senate
Washington, D.C. 20510
Dear Senator: or Dear Senator Smith

United States Representatives
The Honorable Carol Smith
The Honorable Thomas Jones
House of Representatives
Washington, D.C. 20515
Dear Ms. Smith or Dear Mr. Jones:
or Dear Representative Smith

For years people set their clocks to match local sun time, generally using the clock that the watchmaker or jeweler kept in a store window as a measure of correctness. This system caused little difficulty until the railroads came. Schedules were difficult to maintain when the conductor of an eastbound and a westbound train relied on watches set by local sun time at each one's starting place. Confusion and sometimes wrecks resulted.

In 1883 the railroads in the United States and Canada agreed to operate on a system of standard time. Under this system, the United States, Canada, and eventually the world were divided into zones, each with an average width of 15° of longitude. Within any zone, all points are on the same time. Adjacent zones are an hour apart. The United States has six time zones: Eastern, Central, Mountain, Pacific, Yukon-Alaska, and Hawaii.

United States Time Zones

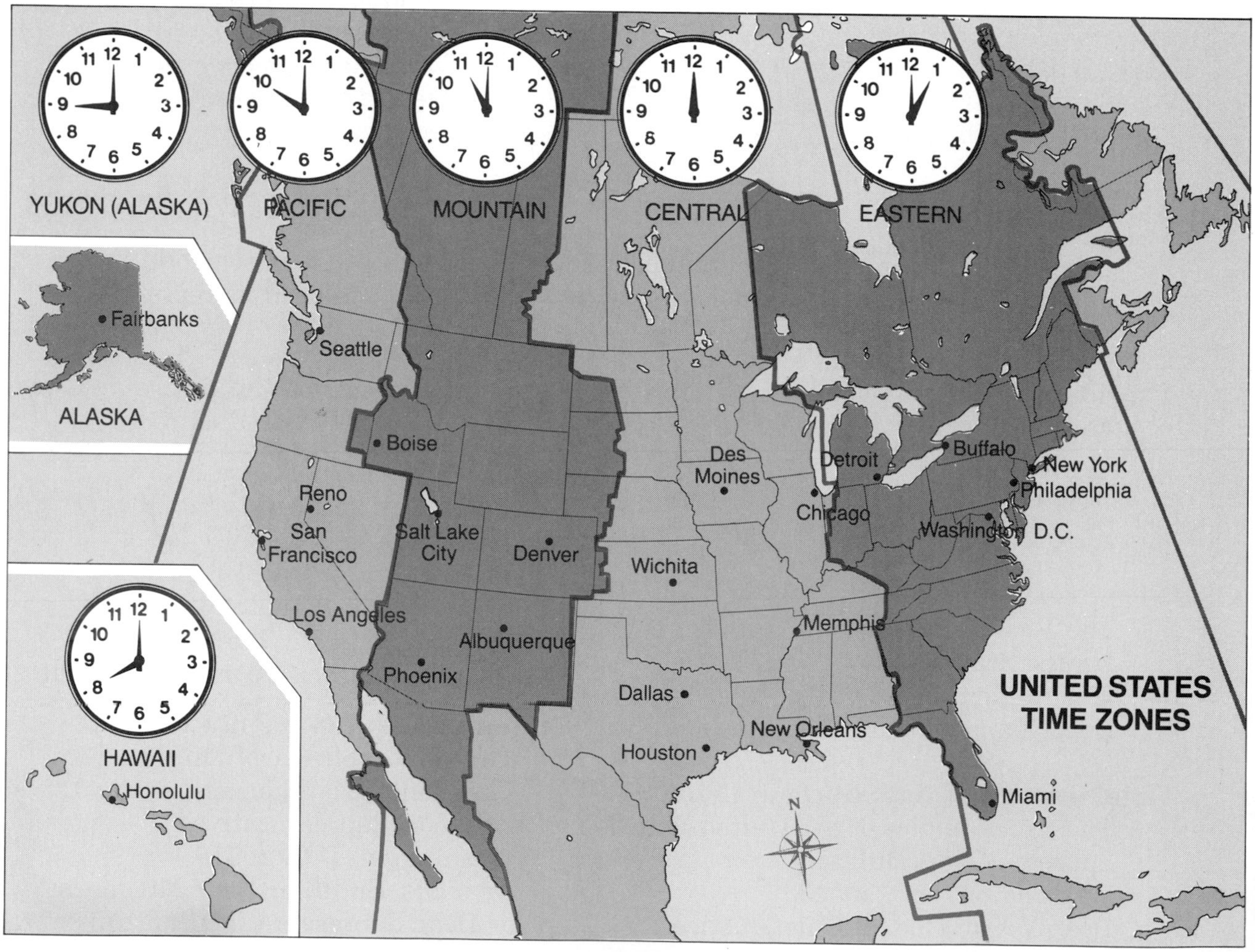

Kobo Abe

Ralph Abernathy

Abigail Adams

John Adams

A

Aaron, Hank, 1934-, U.S. baseball player who set lifetime home run record.
Abbott, Edith, 1876-1957, U.S. social reformer and author, sister of Grace Abbott.
—**Grace,** 1878-1939, U.S. social reformer.
—**Robert,** 1868-1940, U.S. journalist, founder of largest chain of black newspapers.
Abdul Baha, 1844-1921, Persian religious leader.
Abdul-Jabbar, Kareem (Lewis Alcindor), 1947-, U.S. basketball player.
Abe, Kobo, 1924-, Japanese author.
Abelard, Peter, 1079-1142, French philosopher and theologian.
Abernathy, Ralph David, 1926-, U.S. clergyman and civil rights leader.
Acheson, Dean, 1893-1971, U.S. secretary of state, 1949-1953.
Adams, Abigail Smith, 1744-1818, U.S. social and political writer, wife of John Adams.
—**Ansel,** 1902-1984 U.S. photographer.
—**Henry Brooks,** 1838-1918, U.S. historian and philosopher.
—**John,** 1735-1826, U.S. statesman and 2nd president of the U.S., 1797-1801.
—**John Quincy,** 1767-1848, U.S. statesman and 6th president of the U.S., 1825-1829. He was the son of John and Abigail Adams.
—**Samuel,** 1722-1803, American patriot, signer of the Declaration of Independence.
Adamson, Joy, 1910-1980, naturalist and conservationist active in Africa, born in Austria.
Addams, Jane, 1860-1935, U.S. social reformer and pacifist.
Addison, Joseph, 1672-1719, English author.
Adenauer, Konrad, 1876-1967, first chancellor of West Germany, 1949-1963.
Adler, Alfred, 1870-1937, Austrian psychiatrist.
Adler, Mortimer, 1902-, U.S. educator and philosopher.
Aeschylus, 525-456 B.C., Greek writer of tragic plays.
Aesop, 620?-560? B.C., Greek writer whose collection of fables has been popular for over two thousand years.
Agassiz, Louis, 1807-1873, U.S. naturalist born in Switzerland.
Agee, James, 1909-1955, U.S. author.
Aguinaldo, Emilio, 1869-1964, Philippine patriot and statesman.
Aiken, Conrad, 1889-1973, U.S. writer.
Ailey, Alvin, 1931-, U.S. dancer and choreographer.
Albert of Saxe-Coburg-Gotha, Prince, 1819-1861, husband of Queen Victoria of Great Britain.
Alcott, Louisa May, 1832-1888, U.S. author.
Aldrin, Edwin ("Buzz"), 1930-, U.S. astronaut, second person on the moon.
Alexander the Great, 356-323 B.C., king of Macedonia and conqueror of a vast empire.

Jane Addams

Konrad Adenauer

Emilio Aguinaldo

Louisa May Alcott

Luis Alvarez

Roald Amundsen

Marian Anderson

Maya Angelou

Alfred the Great, 849-899, king of the West Saxons, 871-899.
Alger, Horatio, 1832-1899, U.S. author of novels for boys.
Ali, Muhammad (Cassius Marcellus Clay, Jr.), 1942-, U.S. boxer. Won the heavyweight boxing championship four times.
Allen, Ethan, 1738-1789, American patriot and soldier.
—Florence, 1884-1966, U.S. jurist.
—Richard, 1760-1831, U.S. religious leader.
—Woody, 1935-, U.S. motion-picture director, writer, and actor.
Allende Gossens, Salvador, 1908-1973, Chilean statesman and president, 1970-1973.
Alvarez, Luis, 1911-1988, U.S. Nobel Prize-winning physicist.
Ampère, André Marie, 1775-1836, French physicist.
Amundsen, Roald, 1872-1928, Norwegian explorer who discovered the South Pole in 1911.
Anaximander, 611-547? B.C., Greek philosopher and astronomer.
Andersen, Hans Christian, 1805-1875, Danish writer of fairy tales.
Anderson, Marian, 1902-, U.S. singer.
—Maxwell, 1888-1959, U.S. playwright.
—Philip Warren, 1923-, U.S. physicist.
—Sherwood, 1876-1941, U.S. author.
Andrea del Sarto, 1486-1531, Italian painter.
Andropov, Yuri, 1914-1984, Soviet statesman.
Angelico, Fra, 1387-1455, Italian painter.
Angelou, Maya, 1928-, U.S. author.
Anne, 1665-1714, queen of Great Britain and Ireland, 1702-1714.
Anne of Cleves, 1515-1557, fourth wife of Henry VII of England.
Anthony, Susan B., 1820-1906, U.S. social reformer and women's suffragist.
Antony, Mark, 83?-30 B.C., Roman general and political leader.
Apgar, Virginia, 1909-1974, U.S. physician who developed a system for rating the condition of newborn infants.
Appleseed, Johnny, 1775?-1845, U.S. pioneer. His real name was John Chapman.
Aquinas, Thomas, 1225?-1274, Italian monk, famous philosopher, and Christian theologian; made a saint.
Arafat, Yasir, 1929-, Arab leader of the Palestine Liberation Organization.
Archimedes, 287?-212 B.C., Greek mathematician and inventor.
Arendt, Hannah, 1906-1975, U.S. political scientist and author born in Germany.
Aristophanes, 445?-385? B.C., Greek comic poet.
Aristotle, 384-322 B.C., Greek philosopher, a pupil of Plato.
Armstrong, Louis ("Satchmo"), 1900-1971, U.S. jazz musician.
—Neil, 1930-, U.S. astronaut, first person to step on the moon.

Susan B. Anthony

Hannah Arendt

Louis Armstrong

Neil Armstrong

Arthur Ashe

Isaac Asimov

John Jacob Astor

John James Audubon

Arnold, Benedict, 1741-1801, American general in the Revolutionary War, who became a traitor.
—Henry Harley, 1886-1950, U.S. military leader, first Air Force Commander.
—Matthew, 1822-1888, English poet and critic.
Arp, Jean, 1887-1966, French sculptor and painter.
Arthur Chester A., 1829-1886, 21st president of the U.S., 1881-1885.
Ashe, Arthur, 1943-, U.S. tennis player.
Asimov, Isaac, 1920-, U.S. author born in the U.S.S.R.
Astaire, Fred, 1899-1987, U.S. dancer and actor.
Astor, John Jacob, 1763-1848, U.S. fur trader and financier born in Germany.
—Viscountess, born Nancy Witcher Langhorne, 1879-1964, first woman member of the British Parliament, 1919-1945.
Atahualpa, 1500?-1533, Inca king of Peru, killed by Pizarro.
Attila, 406?-453, barbaric king of the Huns.
Attucks, Crispus, 1723?-1770, American black patriot killed during the Boston Massacre.
Auden, W(ysten) H(ugh), 1907-1973, U.S. author born in Great Britain.
Audubon, John James, 1785-1851, U.S. naturalist and artist born in Haiti, famous for his study and paintings of birds.
Augustine, Saint, 354-430, Christian philosopher and church father, born in Roman Africa.
Augustus Caesar, 63 B.C.-A.D. 14, first Roman emperor, 27 B.C.-A.D. 14.
Austen, Jane, 1775-1817, English novelist.
Austin, Stephen, 1793-1836, U.S. pioneer who founded an American colony in Texas.
Avogadro, Amadeo, 1776-1856, Italian physicist.
Axis Sally, 1902-, broadcaster of Nazi propaganda during World War II, born in United States. Her real namd is Mildred Gillars.
Ayckbourn, Alan, 1939-, English playwright.

B

Babbage, Charles, 1792-1871, English mathematician. Invented the first computer.
Bach, Johann Sebastian, 1685-1750, German composer.
Bacon, Francis, 1561-1626, English philosopher, statesman, and essayist.
—Roger, 1214?-1292?, English philosopher and scientist. Founded experimental science.
Baden-Powell, Sir Robert, 1857-1941, British soldier, founder of the Boy Scout movement.
Baez, Joan, 1941-, U.S. folk singer and civil rights activist.
Bagehot, Walter, 1826-1877, English social scientist.
Bagnold, Enid, 1889-1981, English writer.

Jane Austen

Johann Sebastian Bach

Francis Bacon

Enid Bagnold

George Balanchine

Vasco De Balboa

James Baldwin

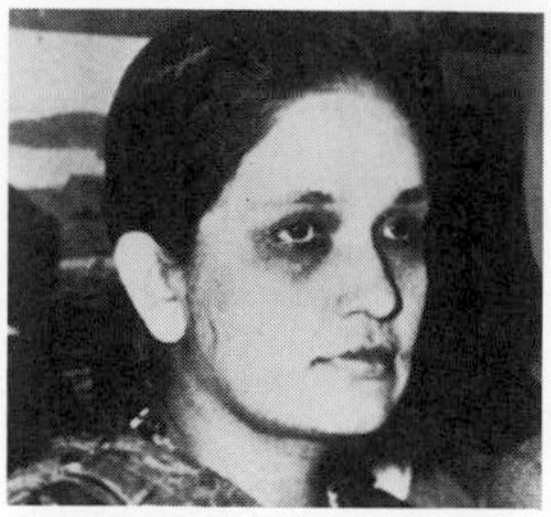
Sirimavo Bandaranaike

Balanchine, George, 1904-1983, U.S. choreographer born in Russia.
Balboa, Vasco de, 1475-1517, Spanish explorer.
Balch, Emily, 1867-1961, U.S. economist and sociologist.
Baldwin, James, 1924-1988, U.S. author.
Balzac, Honoré de, 1799-1850, French author.
Bandaranaike, Sirimavo, 1916-, Sri Lankan stateswoman, world's first woman prime minister, 1960-1965; 1970-1977.
Banneker, Benjamin, 1731-1806, U.S. scientist and writer.
Banting, Sir Frederick Grant, 1891-1941, Canadian physician who contributed to the discovery of insulin.
Bañuelos, Romana Acosta, 1925-, U.S. businesswoman and government official.
Baraka, Imamu Amiri, 1934-, born LeRoi Jones, U.S. poet and playwright.
Barnard, Christiaan, 1923-, South African surgeon; performed first human heart transplant.
Barnum, Phineas Taylor, 1810-1891, U.S. circus owner and showman.
Barrymore, Ethel, 1879-1959, U.S. actress, and her brothers **John,** 1882-1942, and **Lionel,** 1878-1954, U.S. actors.
Bartók, Béla, 1881-1945, Hungarian composer.
Barton, Clara, 1821-1912, U.S. founder of the American Red Cross.
Baruch, Bernard, 1870-1965, U.S. financier and presidential advisor.
Baryshnikov, Mikhail, 1948-, Russian ballet dancer and choreographer, living in the U.S.
Basho, Matsuo, 1644-1694, Japanese poet.
Basie, Count (William), 1904-1984, U.S. jazz pianist and bandleader.
Batista y Zaldívar, Fulgencio, 1901-1973, Cuban military and political leader.
Baudelaire, Charles, 1821-1867, French poet.
Beach, Amy, 1867-1944, U.S. composer and pianist.
Beard, Charles, 1874-1948, U.S. historian.
—Mary, 1876-1958, U.S. historian and feminist.
Beatles, The, English musical group, 1960-1970. The members were **John Lennon,** 1940-1980, **Paul McCartney,** 1942-, **George Harrison,** 1943-, and **Ringo Starr,** 1940-.
Beatrix, 1938-, queen of the Netherlands, 1980-.
Beauregard, Pierre, 1818-1893, Confederate general in U.S. Civil War.
Beauvoir, Simone de, 1908-, French author.
Becket, Saint Thomas à, 1118?-1170, Archbishop of Canterbury, 1162-1170.
Beckett, Samuel, 1906-, Irish author.
Bede, Saint, 673-735, English theologian and historian. Also the **Venerable Bede.**
Beethoven, Ludwig van, 1770-1827, German composer.
Begin, Menachem, 1913-, prime minister of Israel 1977-1983, born in Poland.
Bell, Alexander Graham, 1847-1922, U.S. scientist born in Scotland, inventor of the telephone.
Bellow, Saul, 1915-, U.S. author.

Romana Bañuelos

Clara Barton

Charles Beard

Alexander Graham Bell

Sarah Bernhardt

Mary McLeod Bethune

Otto von Bismarck

Elizabeth Blackwell

Benèt, Stephen Vincent, 1898-1943, U.S. poet and author.
Ben-Gurion, David, 1886-1973, Israeli statesman. Frist prime minister of Israel, 1949-1953; also 1955-1963.
Benny, Jack, 1894-1974, U.S. comedian.
Bergman, Ingmar, 1918-, Swedish motion-picture director.
Berkeley, George, 1685-1753, Irish philosopher and clergyman.
Berlin, Irving, 1888-, U.S. songwriter.
Bernhardt, Sarah, 1844-1923, born Rosine Bernard, French actress.
Bernstein, Leonard, 1918-, U.S. composer and conductor.
Besant, Annie Wood, 1847-1933, British religious philosopher and writer, political and social activist.
Bethune, Mary McLeod, 1875-1955, U.S. educator.
Bettelheim, Bruno, 1903-, U.S. psychologist, born in Austria.
Bickerdyke, Mary Ann, 1817-1901, U.S. Civil War nurse.
Binet, Alfred, 1857-1911, French psychologist.
Birdseye, Clarence, 1886-1956, U.S. inventor.
Birney, Alice McLellan, 1858-1907, U.S. educator; founder of the National Congress of Parents and Teachers (PTA).
Bishop, Elizabeth, 1911-1971, U.S. poet.
Bismarck, Otto von, 1815-1898, chancellor of the German empire, 1871-1890.
Black Hawk, 1767-1838, American Indian leader.
Black, Hugo, 1886-1971, U.S. jurist; justice of the U.S. Supreme Court, 1937-1971.
Blackwell, Elizabeth, 1821-1910, first woman physician in U.S., born in England.
Blake, William, 1757-1827, English poet, artist, and mystic.
Bloomer, Amelia, 1818-1894, U.S. social reformer.
Blow, Susan, 1843-1916, U.S. educator.
Bly, Nellie, 1867-1922, U.S. journalist and advocate of women's rights. Her real name was Elizabeth Cochrane Seaman.
Boadicea, ?-A.D. 62, queen of the Iceni, an ancient tribe of Britain.
Boccaccio, Giovanni, 1313-1375, Italian author.
Bohr, Niels, 1885-1962, Nobel Prize-winning Danist physicist.
Boleyn, Anne, 1507-1536, second wife of Henry VIII of England, mother of Queen Elizabeth I.
Bolívar, Simon, 1783-1830, Venezuelan general.
Bonaparte, Napoleon See NAPOLEON I.
Bonheur, Rosa, 1822-1899, French painter.
Bonnard, Pierre, 1867-1947, French painter and graphic artist.
Bontemps, Arna, 1902-1973, U.S. poet and writer.
Boone, Daniel, 1735?-1820, U.S. frontiersman in Kentucky and Missouri.
Booth, Evangeline Cory, 1865-1950, English and U.S. leader of the Salvation Army, daughter of William Booth.
—John Wilkes, 1838-1865, U.S. actor, assassin of Abraham Lincoln.

Nellie Bly

Simon Bolívar

Napoleon Bonaparte

Daniel Boone

Jorge Luis Borges

Nadia Boulanger

Margaret Bourke-White

Johannes Brahms

Booth, William, 1829-1912, British founder of the Salvation Army.
Borges, Jorge Luis, 1899-1986, Argentine author, poet, and essayist.
Borgia, Cesare, 1475?-1507, Italian cardinal and military figure, brother of Lucrezia Borgia.
—Lucrezia, 1480-1519, Italian aristocrat and patron of the arts, sister of Cesare.
Bosch, Hieronymus, 1450?-1516, Dutch painter.
Boswell, James, 1740-1795, Scottish diarist and biographer of Samuel Johnson.
Botticelli, Sandro, 1444?-1510, Italian painter.
Boulanger, Nadia, 1887-1979, French composer and music teacher.
Bourke-White, Margaret, 1906-1972, U.S. photographer.
Bradbury, Ray, 1920-, U.S. author of science fiction.
Braddock, Edward, 1695-1755, British general in the French and Indian War.
Bradford, William, 1590-1657, second British governor of the Pilgrim colony in Massachusetts.
Bradstreet, Anne, 1612?-1672, American poet born in England.
Brady, Mathew, 1823?-1896, U.S. photographer who chronicled the Civil War.
Bragg, Braxton, 1817-1876, Confederate general during the U.S. Civil War.
Brahms, Johannes, 1833-1897, German composer.
Brandeis, Louis, 1856-1941, U.S. jurist; justice of the U.S. Supreme Court, 1916-1939.
Brandt, Willy, 1913-, West German politicial leader, chancellor, 1969-1974.
Braque, Georges, 1882-1963, French painter.
Brecht, Bertolt, 1898-1956, German playwright.
Breckinridge, Sophonisba, 1866-1948, U.S. lawyer, educator, author, and social worker.
Brezhnev, Leonid, 1906-1982, Soviet statesman.
Bridger, James, 1804-1991, U.S. frontier scout.
Brontë, The family name of three English sisters who were writers: **Anne,** 1820-1849; **Charlotte,** 1816-1855; **Emily,** 1818-1848.
Brooke, Edward, 1919-, U.S. legislator.
Brooks, Gwendolyn, 1917-, U.S. novelist and poet; first Black to win the Pulitzer Prize.
Brown, John, 1800-1859, U.S. abolitionist.
—William Wells, 1815-1885, U.S. novelist and dramatist.
Browning, Elizabeth Barrett, 1806-1861, English poet, wife of Robert Browning.
—Robert, 1812-1889, English poet.
Bruce, Blanche K., 1841-1884, U.S. legislator; first Black to serve a full term as a U.S. senator.
—Robert the, 1274-1329, king of Scotland, 1306-1329.
Brueghel, Pieter, 1525?-1569, Flemish painter.
Bruke, Selma, 1908-, U.S. sculptor. She did the profile for the Franklin D. Roosevelt dime.
Brutus, Marcus, 85?-42 B.C., Roman politician who helped kill Julius Ceasar.
Bryan, William Jennings, 1860-1925, U.S. politician.

Gwendolyn Brooks

Elizabeth Barrett Browning

Robert Browning

Blanche Bruce

Pearl Buck

Ralph Bunche

Richard Byrd

George Gordon Byron

Bryant, William Cullen, 1794-1878, U.S. poet and newspaper editor.
Buchanan, James, 1791-1868, 15th president of the U.S. 1857-1861.
Buck, Pearl, 1892-1973, U.S. novelist.
Buddha, 563?-483 B.C., religious leader of India, founder of Buddhism.
Buffalo Bill, 1846-1917, U.S. army scout and showman. His real name was William F. Cody.
Bunche, Ralph, 1904-1971, U.S. diplomat instrumental in setting up the United Nations.
Burbank, Luther, 1849-1926, U.S. horticulturist; bred new types of flowers, fruits, and vegetables.
Burdett-Coutts, Angela, 1814-1906, English philanthropist.
Burgoyne, John, 1722-1792, British general and playwright.
Burke, Edmund, 1729-1797, British statesman.
—Martha Jane See CALAMITY JANE.
Burnett, Elizabeth, 1849-1924, U.S. writer born in England.
Burney, Fanny, 1752-1840, English novelist and diarist.
Burns, Robert, 1759-1796, Scottish poet.
Burr, Aaron, 1756-1836, U.S. political leader, 3rd Vice President (1801-1805).
Bush, George Herbert Walker, 1924-, 41st U.S. President, 1989-.
Butler, Josephine, 1828-1906, British social reformer.
Byrd, Richard E., 1888-1957, U.S. explorer.
Byron, George Gordon, 1788-1824, English poet.

C

Cabot, John, 1450?-1498, English explorer born in Italy, father of Sebastian Cabot.
—Sebastian, 1467?-1557, English explorer born in Italy.
Cabrini, Saint Frances Xavier ("Mother Cabrini"), 1850-1917, U.S. religious leader born in Italy.
Caesar, Julius, 100-44 B.C., Roman general, statesman, and historian; assassinated.
Calamity Jane, 1852?-1903, U.S. frontier heroine and sharpshooter. Her real name was Martha Jane Burke (or Burk).
Calder, Alexander, 1898-1976, U.S. sculptor.
Caldwell, Sarah, 1928-, U.S. conductor and opera company director.
—Taylor, 1900-, U.S. author.
Calhoun, John C., 1782-1850, U.S. politician; vice president of the U.S., 1825-1832.
Callas, Maria, 1923-1977, U.S. opera singer.
Calvin, John, 1509-1564, French Protestant reformer.
Camus, Albert, 1913-1960, French author and philosopher.

Mother Cabrini

Julius Caesar

Calamity Jane

Sarah Caldwell

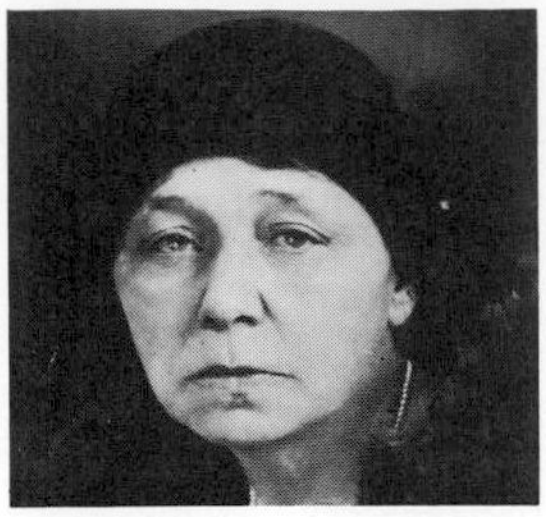
Hattie Caraway

Rachel Carson

Jimmy Carter

George Washington Carver

Cañas, José Simeon, 1767-1838, Central American educator, leader in independence movement.
Cannon, Annie, 1863-1964, U.S. astronomer.
Capone, Al(phonse), 1899?-1947, U.S. gangster; controlled the Chicago underworld in the 1920s.
Capote, Truman, 1924-1984, U.S. author.
Capra, Frank, 1897- U.S. film director.
Caravaggio, Michelangelo da, 1569?-1609, Italian painter.
Caraway, Hattie, 1878-1950, U.S. legislator; first woman elected to the U.S. senate, 1931-1945.
Cardozo, Benjamin, 1870-1938, U.S. jurist; justice of the U.S. Supreme Court, 1932-1938.
Carlota, 1840-1927, empress of Mexico, 1864-1867.
Carlyle, Thomas, 1795-1881, Scottish author.
Carnegie, Andrew, 1835-1919, U.S. industrialist and philanthropist born in Scotland.
Carroll, Lewis, 1832-1898, British mathematician and author of *Alice in Wonderland.* His real name was Charles Lutwidge Dodgson.
Carson, Christopher (Kit), 1809-1868, U.S. frontier scout.
—Rachel, 1907-1964, U.S. marine biologist and author.
Carter, James Earl (Jimmy), Jr., 1924-, 39th president of the U.S., 1977-1981.
Caruso, Enrico, 1873-1921, Italian operatic tenor.
Carver, George Washington, 1864-1943, U.S. botanist and chemist.
Casals, Pablo, 1876-1973, Spanish cellist, composer, and conductor.
Cassatt, Mary, 1845-1926, U.S. painter.
Castro, Fidel, 1927-, Cuban revolutionary leader and premier, 1959-.
Cather, Willa Sibert, 1873-1947, U.S. author.
Catherine de Medici, 1519-1589, queen of France, wife of King Henry II.
Catherine the Great, 1729-1796, empress of Russia, 1762-1796; born in Germany.
Cato, Marcus Porcius, 234-149 B.C., Roman statesman. Also **Cato the Elder.**
Catt, Carrie Chapman, 1859-1947, U.S. suffragist, founder of the League of Women Voters.
Catton, Bruce, 1899-1978, U.S. historian.
Cavell, Edith, 1865-1915, British nurse and patriot executed by the Germans in Belgium during World War I.
Caxton, William, 1422-1491, first English printer.
Cellini, Benevenuto, 1500-1571, Italian sculptor and goldsmith.
Celsius, Anders, 1701-1744, Swedish astronomer.
Cervantes, Miguel de, 1547-1616, Spanish writer, author of *Don Quixote.*
Cézanne, Paul, 1839-1906, French painter.
Chagall, Marc, 1887-1985, French painter born in Russia.
Champlain, Samuel de, 1567-1635, French explorer who founded Quebec.
Chaplin, Charles Spencer (Charlie), 1889-1977, English motion-picture actor and director.
Charlemagne, 742-814, king of the Franks, emperor of the Holy Roman Empire, 800-814.

Willa Cather

Catherine the Great

Carrie Chapman Catt

Edith Cavell

Mary Ellen Chase

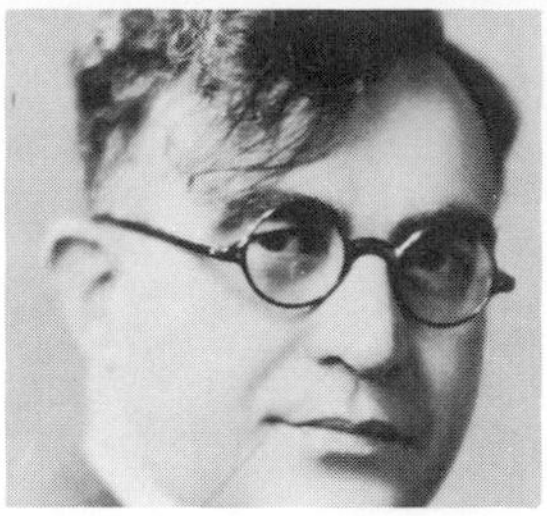
Carlos Chávez

Chiang Kai-shek

Julia Child

Charles, Prince of Wales, 1948-, son of Queen Elizabeth II and heir to the throne of Great Britain.
Charles I, 1600-1649, king of England, Scotland, and Ireland, 1625-1649; executed for treason.
Charles II, 1630-1685, king of England, Scotland, and Ireland, 1660-1685; son of Charles I.
Charles V, 1500-1558, Holy Roman emperor, 1519-1556; also king of Spain, 1516-1556, as Charles I.
Charles Martel, 689?-741, king of the Franks and grandfather of Charlemagne.
Chase, Mary Ellen, 1887-1973, U.S. educator and author.
Châtelet, Gabrielle du, 1707-1749, French mathematician and physicist.
Chaucer, Geoffrey, 1340?-1400, English poet, author of *The Canterbury Tales*.
Chávez, Carlos, 1899-1978, Mexican composer and conductor.
—Cesar, 1927-, Mexican-American union organizer and social activist.
Cheever, John, 1912-1982, U.S. short-story writer and novelist.
Chekhov or **Chekov, Anton Pavlovich,** 1860-1904, Russian playwright and short-story writer.
Cheops, Egyptian king of the fourth dynasty (about 2900 B.C.), builder of the largest of the pyramids.
Chernenko, Konstantin U., 1911-1985, Soviet statesman.
Chomsky, Noam, 1928-, U.S. linguist.
Chiang Kai-shek, 1887-1975, president of the Republic of China (Taiwan), 1948-1975.
Child, Julia, 1912-, U.S. cooking expert and author.
Chisholm, Jesse, 1805-1868, U.S. scout. He laid out the Chisholm Trail.
—Shirley, 1924-, U.S. legislator; first black woman elected to Congress.
Claudius I, 10 B.C.-A.D. 54, emperor of Rome.
Chopin, Frédéric, 1810-1849, Polish composer and pianist who lived in France.
Chou En-lai See ZHOU ENLAI.
Christ, Jesus SEE JESUS.
Christie, Dame Agatha, 1891-1976, English author of mysteries.
Churchill, Sir Winston, 1874-1965, British statesman and prime minister, 1940-1945, 1951-1955.
Cicero, Marcus Tullius, 106-43 B.C., Roman statesman, orator, and author.
Clark, Kenneth, 1903-1983, English art critic and writer.
—Kenneth Bancroft, 1914-, U.S. psychologist and educator.
—William, 1770-1838, U.S. explorer with Meriwether Lewis.
Clemente, Roberto, 1934-1972, Puerto Rican baseball player.
Clay, Henry, 1772-1852, U.S. statesman.
Clemens, Samuel Langhorne See TWAIN, MARK.
Cleopatra, 69-30 B.C., last queen of ancient Egypt.
Cleveland, (Stephen) Grover, 1837-1908, 22nd and 24th president of the U.S., 1885-1889 and 1893-1897.
Clinton, De Witt, 1769-1828, U.S. politician.

Shirley Chisholm

Agatha Christie

Winston Churchill

Kenneth B. Clark

Cochise

Jacqueline Cochran

Colette

Joan Cooney

Cochise, 1812?-1874, American Indian chief.
Cochran, Jacqueline, 1912-1980, U.S. businesswoman and pilot.
Cody, William F. See BUFFALO BILL.
Coleridge, Samuel Taylor, 1772-1834, English poet.
Colette, Sidonie Gabrielle Claudine, 1873-1954, French novelist.
Columbus, Christopher, 1451?-1506, Italian explorer who discovered America for Spain in 1492.
Commager, Henry Steele, 1902-, U.S. historian.
Confucius, 551-478? B.C., Chinese philosopher.
Conrad, Joseph, 1857-1924, English author.
Constable, John, 1776-1837, English painter.
Constantine the Great, 280?-337, Roman emperor, 306-337.
Cook, Captain James, 1728-1779, British navigator and explorer.
Coolidge, Calvin, 1872-1933, 30th president of the U.S., 1923-1929.
Cooney, Joan Ganz, 1929-, U.S. television producer, originator of *Sesame Street*.
Cooper, James Fenimore, 1789-1851, U.S. novelist.
Copernicus, Nicolaus, 1473-1543, Polish astronomer.
Copland, Aaron, 1900-, U.S. composer.
Corbin, Margaret, 1751-1800, American heroine of the Revolutionary War.
Corday, Charlotte, 1768-1793, French revolutionary patriot.
Cornwallis, Charles, 1738-1805, British general and political leader.
Coronado, Francisco, 1510-1554, Spanish explorer.
Corot, Jean-Baptiste Camille, 1796-1875, French painter.
Cortés or **Cortez, Hernando,** 1485-1547, Spanish conqueror of Mexico.
Courbet, Gustave, 1819-1877, French painter.
Cousteau, Jacques-Yves, 1910-, French author and undersea explorer.
Coward, Noël, 1899-1973, English actor, playwright, and composer.
Cowper, William, 1731-1800, English poet.
Crandall, Prudence, 1803-1890, U.S. educator.
Crane, (Harold) Hart, 1899-1932, U.S. poet.
—Stephen, 1871-1900, U.S. novelist and short-story writer.
Crazy Horse, 1849?-1877, American Indian chief who defeated Custer at Little Bighorn.
Crockett, Davy, 1786-1836, U.S. frontiersman and legislator.
Cromwell, Oliver, 1599-1658, British general, statesman, and ruler of England, 1653-1658.
Crowfoot, 1830-1890, American Indian chief.
Cullen, Countee, 1903-1946, U.S. poet.
Cummings, E(dward) E(stlin), 1894-1962, U.S. poet and playwright.
Curie, Marie, 1867-1934, French scientist born in Poland, wife of Pierre Curie.
—Pierre, 1859-1906, French scientist.

Nicholaus Copernicus

Hernando Cortés

Marie Curie

Pierre Curie

Salvador Dali

Leonardo da Vinci

Benjamin Davis

Dorothy Day

Custer, George Armstrong, 1839-1876, U.S. army general killed at the Little Bighorn.
Cyrus, died 529 B.C., king of Persia who made it an empire. He was called **Cyrus the Great.**

D

Da Gama, Vasco, 1469?-1524, Portuguese sea captain and explorer.
Dali, Salvador, 1904-1989, Spanish surrealist painter.
Dante Alighieri, 1265-1321, Italian poet, author of the *Divine Comedy.*
Danton, George Jacques, 1759-1794, French revolutionary leader.
Dare, Virginia, 1587?-1587?, first child of English parents born in America.
Darío, Rubén, 1867-1916, Nicaraguan poet.
Darius I, 558?-486? B.C., king of Persia.
Darrow, Clarence, 1857-1938, U.S. lawyer.
Darwin, Charles Robert, 1809-1882, British naturalist.
Daumier, Honoré, 1808-1879, French artist.
David, Jacques-Louis, 1748-1825, French painter.
da Vinci, Leonardo, 1452-1519, Italian painter, sculptor, and architect. Pioneer in biology, geology, engineering, and military science.
Davis, Benjamin, O., Jr., 1912-, U.S. military officer; first black Air Force general.
—Jefferson, 1808-1889, U.S. statesman and president of the Confederacy.
Day, Dorothy, 1897-1980, U.S. social worker and journalist.
Dayan, Moshe, 1915-1981, Israeli military and political leader.
Debs, Eugene Victor, 1855-1926, U.S. Socialist leader.
Debussy, Claude, 1862-1918, French composer.
Defoe, Daniel, 1660?-1731, English writer.
De Forest, Lee, 1873-1961, U.S. inventor.
Degas, Edgar, 1834-1917, French artist.
de Gaulle, Charles, 1890-1970, French general and president of France, 1945-1946, 1959-1969.
de Kooning, Willem, 1904-, U.S. painter born in the Netherlands.
Delacroix, Eugène, 1798-1863, French painter.
Delany, Martin, 1812-1885, U.S. physician, journalist, and abolitionist.
Deloria, Ella C., 1888-1971, U.S. linguist.
—Vine, Jr., 1933-, U.S. author.
De Mille, Agnes, 1906?-, U.S. choreographer.
—Cecil B., 1881-1959, U.S. motion-picture producer and director.
Descartes, René, 1596-1650, French philosopher and mathematician.
de Soto, Hernando, 1500?-1542, Spanish explorer; European discoverer of the Mississippi River.
De Valera, Eamon, 1882-1975, Irish political leader.

Charles de Gaulle

Vine Deloria, Jr.

Agnes De Mille

Hernando de Soto

Emily Dickinson

Babe Didrikson

Walt Disney

Helen Gahagan Douglas

Dewey, John, 1859-1952, U.S. philosopher and educator.
Diana, Princess of Wales, 1961-, wife of Prince Charles of Great Britain.
Dickens, Charles, 1812-1870, English novelist.
Dickinson, Emily, 1830-1886, U.S. poet.
Didion, Joan, 1934-, U.S. author.
Didrikson, Mildred Ella ("Babe"), 1914-1956, U.S. athlete.
Diefenbaker, John George, 1895-1979, prime minister of Canada, 1957-1963.
Diem, Ngo Dinh, 1901-1963, president of South Vietnam, 1955-1963. He was assassinated.
DiMaggio, Joe, 1914-, U.S. baseball player.
Dinesen, Isak, 1885-1962, Danish author. Her real name was Baroness Karen Blixen.
Diogenes, 412-323 B.C., Greek philosopher.
Disney, Walter Elias (Walt), 1901-1966, U.S. cartoonist and film producer.
Disraeli, Benjamin, 1804-1881, British politician and author; prime minister, 1868 and 1874-1880.
Dix, Dorothea, 1802-1887, U.S. social reformer.
Dodge, Mary Elizabeth, 1831-1905, U.S. author.
Dodgson, Charles Lutwidge See CARROLL, LEWIS.
Donatello, 1386?-1466, Italian sculptor.
Donne, John, 1573?-1631, English poet.
Doolittle, Hilda (H.D.), 1886-1961, U.S. poet.
Dos Passos, John, 1896-1970, U.S. author.
Dostoevski, Feodor, 1821-1881, Russian novelist.
Douglas, Helen Gahagan, 1900-1980, U.S. politician, actress, and author.
—Stephen A., 1813-1861, U.S. politician.
Douglass, Frederick, 1817-1895, U.S. author, abolitionist, and editor.
Doyle, Sir Arthur Conan, 1859-1930, English writer and creator of Sherlock Holmes.
Drake, Sir Francis, 1540-1596, English navigator, the first Englishman to sail around the world.
Draper, Ruth, 1884-1956, U.S. monologist.
Dreiser, Theodore, 1871-1945, U.S. novelist.
Drew, Charles, 1904-1950, U.S. physicist.
Dreyfus, Alfred, 1859-1935, French army officer imprisoned for treason in 1894, but later pardoned.
Dryden, John, 1631-1700, English poet.
Du Barry, Marie Jeanne Bécu, 1746?-1793, French countess, mistress of Louis XV.
Du Bois, Shirley, 1907-1977, U.S. novelist, dramatist, and composer; wife of W. E. B. Du Bois.
—W(illiam) E(dward) B(urghardt), 1868-1963, U.S. historian and educator; one of the founders of the NAACP.
Duchamp, Marcel, 1887-1968, French painter.
Dumas, Alexandre, 1802-1870, and his son **Alexandre,** 1924-1895, French authors.
du Maurier, Daphne, 1907-, English author.
Dunbar, Paul Laurence, 1872-1906, U.S. poet and novelist.
Duncan, Isadora, 1878-1927, U.S. dancer.
Dunham, Katherine, 1912-, U.S. dancer, choreographer, and anthropologist.
Duniway, Abigail, 1834-1915, U.S. pioneer of the West and suffragist.

Frederick Douglass

Alfred Dreyfus

W. E. B. Du Bois

Isadora Duncan
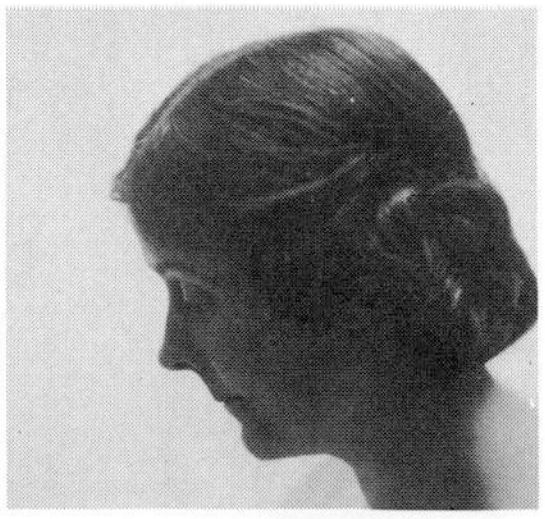

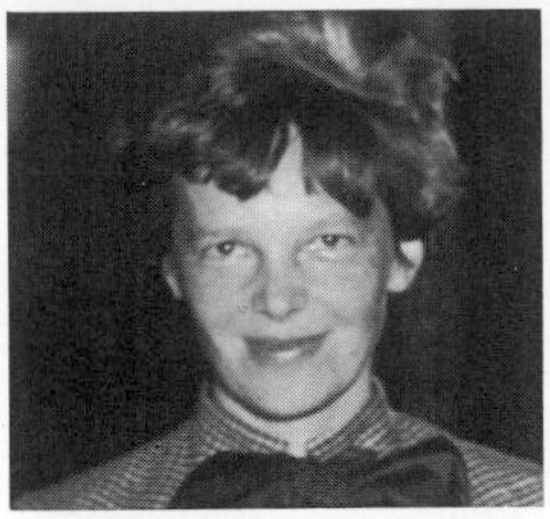
Amelia Earhart

Charles Eastman

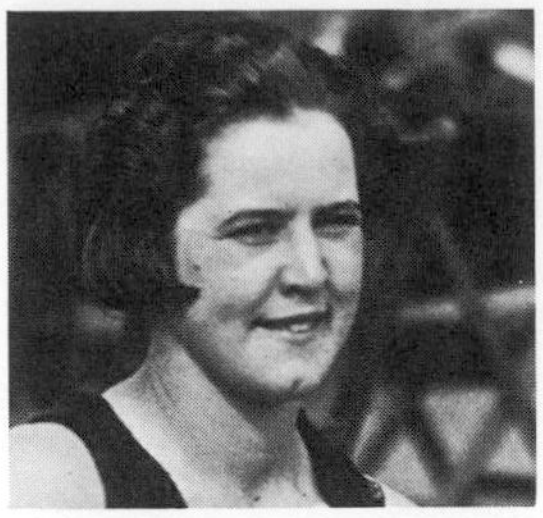
Gertrude Ederle

Alfred Einstein

Dürer, Albrecht, 1471-1528, German painter and engraver.
Du Sable, Jean Baptiste, 1745-1818, U.S. explorer born in Haiti.
Duse, Eleonora, 1859-1924, Italian actress.
Dylan, Bob, 1941-, U.S. singer and songwriter.

E

Earhart, Amelia, 1897-1937, U.S. aviator, first woman to fly across the Atlantic.
Earp, Wyatt, 1848-1929, lawman and gunfighter in the American West.
Eastman, Charles Alexander, 1858-1939, U.S. physician and author.
—George, 1854-1932, U.S. inventor.
Eddy, Mary Baker, 1821-1910, U.S. religious leader and founder of Christian Science.
Ederle, Gertrude, 1907?-, U.S. swimmer, first woman to swim the English Channel.
Edison, Thomas Alva, 1847-1931, U.S. inventor.
Edward VII, 1841-1910, king of Great Britain and Ireland, 1901-1910.
Edward VIII, 1894-1972, British king, 1936. He abdicated and became the Duke of Windsor.
Edwards, Jonathan, 1703-1758, U.S. theologian and preacher in colonial America.
Einstein, Albert, 1879-1955, U.S. physicist born in Germany.
Eisenhower, Dwight David, 1890-1969, U.S. general and 34th president of the U.S., 1953-1961.
Eleanor of Aquitaine, 1122?-1204, queen of France and England.
El Greco, 1548?-1614, Spanish painter born in Crete.
Elijah, Hebrew prophet who lived during the ninth century B.C.
Eliot George, 1819-1880, English novelist. Her real name was Mary Ann Evans.
—T(homas) S(tearns), 1888-1965, English poet and critic born in the U.S.
Elizabeth I, 1533-1603, queen of England, 1558-1603.
Elizabeth II, 1926-, queen of Great Britain and Northern Ireland, 1952-.
Ellington, Edward Kennedy ("Duke"), 1899-1974, U.S. composer, pianist, and bandleader.
Ellison Ralph, 1914-, U.S. novelist.
Emerson, Ralph Waldo, 1803-1882, U.S. philosopher and writer.
Engels, Friedrich, 1820-1895, German socialist and author.
Erasmus, Desiderius, 1466?-1536, Dutch scholar and humanist.
Ericson, Leif, 980?-1025?, Norwegian navigator who is believed to have landed in North America.
Eric the Red, 950?-1003?, Norwegian navigator, discoverer of Greenland about 982.

Dwight D. Eisenhower

El Greco

Duke Ellington
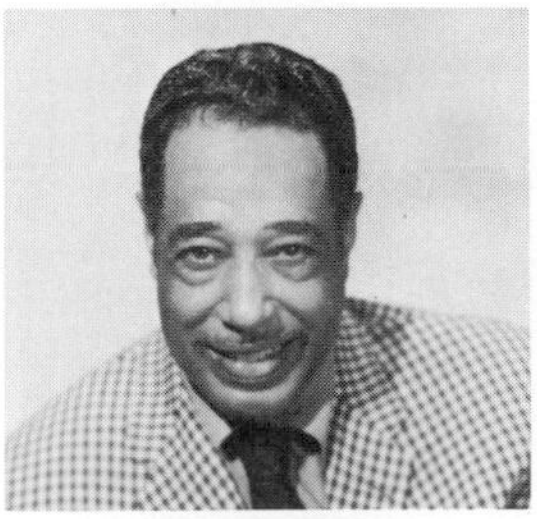

Ralph Waldo Emerson

Medgar Evers

Michael Faraday

Fanny Farmer

Edna Ferber

Euclid, third century B.C. Greek mathematician who wrote a famous book on geometry.
Euripides, 480?-406? B.C., Greek writer of tragic plays.
Evers, Medgar, 1925-1963, U.S. civil rights activist, assassinated.

F

Fahrenheit, Gabriel Daniel, 1686-1736, German physicist.
Faraday, Michael, 1791-1867, British chemist and physicist.
Farmer, Fanny, 1857-1915, U.S. cooking expert, educator, and author of cookbooks.
Farragut, David Glasgow, 1801-1870, U.S. naval commander.
Farrell, James T., 1904-1979, U.S. novelist.
Farrar, Margaret, 1897-1984, U.S. editor.
Faulkner, William, 1897-1962, U.S. novelist.
Fellini, Federico, 1920-, Italian film director.
Ferber, Edna, 1887-1968, U.S. novelist and playwright.
Ferdinand V, 1452-1516, king of Castile. His marriage to Isabella I of Aragon united Spain.
Fermi, Enrico, 1901-1954, U.S. nuclear physicist born in Italy.
Ferraro, Geraldine A., 1935-, U.S. politician and first female to be a Vice-Presidential candidate.
Fielding, Henry, 1707-1754, English novelist and dramatist.
Fillmore, Millard, 1800-1874, 13th president of the U.S., 1850-1853.
FitzGerald, Edward, 1809-1893, English author and translator.
Fitzgerald, Ella, 1918-, U.S. jazz singer.
—F. Scott, 1896-1940, U.S. novelist and short-story writer.
Flagstad, Kirsten, 1895-1962, Norwegian opera singer.
Flaubert, Gustave, 1821-1880, French author.
Fleming, Alexander, 1881-1955, British scientist, discoverer of penicillin.
Foch, Ferdinand, 1851-1929, French general in World War I.
Fonteyn, Dame Margot, 1917-, English ballet dancer.
Forbes, Esther, 1891-1967, U.S. historian and novelist.
Ford, Gerald Rudolph, 1913-, 38th president of the U.S., 1974-1977.
—Henry, 1863-1947, U.S. automobile manufacturer.
—Henry II, 1917-1987, U.S. business leader, grandson of Henry Ford.
—John, 1895-1973, U.S. film director.
Forster, E(dward) M(organ), 1879-1970, English novelist, essayist and critic.

Kirsten Flagstad

Alexander Fleming

Margot Fonteyn

Gerald Ford

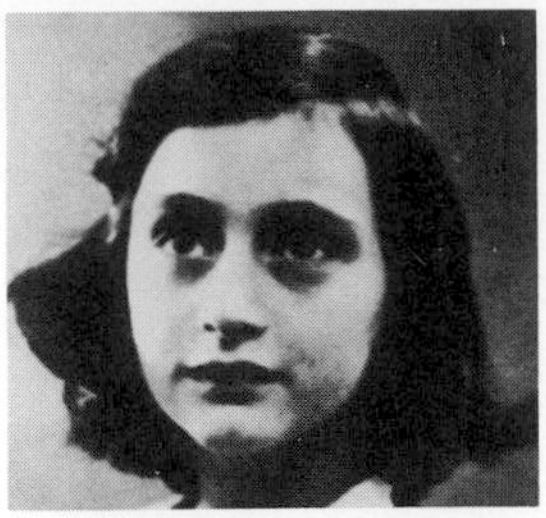
Anne Frank

Benjamin Franklin

Anna Freud

Sigmund Freud

Foster, Stephen Collins, 1826-1864, U.S. songwriter.
Francis Ferdinand, 1863-1914, Austrian archduke, assassinated.
Francis of Assisi, 1182?-1226, Italian friar and saint. He founded the Franciscan order in 1209.
Franco, Francisco, 1892-1975, dictator of Spain, 1936-1975.
Frank Anne, 1929-1945, Dutch girl who wrote *The Diary of Anne Frank.*
Frankenthaler, Helen, 1928-, U.S. abstract painter.
Franklin, Benjamin, 1706-1790, American patriot, writer, and scientist.
Frazier, E(dward) Franklin, 1894-1962, U.S. historian and sociologist.
Freeman, Mary Eleanor Wilkins, 1852-1930, U.S. writer.
Freud, Anna, 1895-1982, English psychoanalyst born in Austria, daughter of Sigmund Freud.
—Sigmund, 1856-1939, Austrian physician and founder of psychoanalysis.
Friedan, Betty, 1921-, U.S. feminist and author.
Friedman, Milton, 1912-, U.S. economist.
Frietchie, Barbara, 1766-1862, U.S. Civil War heroine.
Fromm, Erich, 1900-1980, U.S. psychoanalyst and author.
Frost, Robert Lee, 1875-1963, U.S. poet.
Fuentes, Carlos, 1928-, Mexican writer.
Fuller, Margaret, 1810-1850, U.S. author, journalist, and reformer.
—R(ichard) Buckminster, 1895-, U.S. architect and engineer.
Fulton, Robert, 1765-1815, U.S. inventor.

G

Gagarin, Yuri, 1934-1968, Russian astronaut, first human to travel in space.
Gainsborough, Thomas, 1727-1788, English painter.
Galbraith, John Kenneth, 1908-, U.S. economist and public official.
Galileo Galilei, 1564-1642, Italian astronomer and physicist.
Gall, 1840-1894, American Indian chief who fought at the Battle of the Little Bighorn.
Gallatin, Albert, 1761-1849, U.S. statesman and financier born in Switzerland.
Galsworthy, John, 1867-1933, English author.
Gamio, Manuel, 1883-1960, Mexican anthropologist and archaeologist.
Gandhi, Indira, 1917-1984, first woman premier of India; assassinated.
—Mohandas K., 1869-1948, Indian nationalist and spiritual leader, widely known as **Mahatma Gandhi;** assassinated.

Betty Friedan

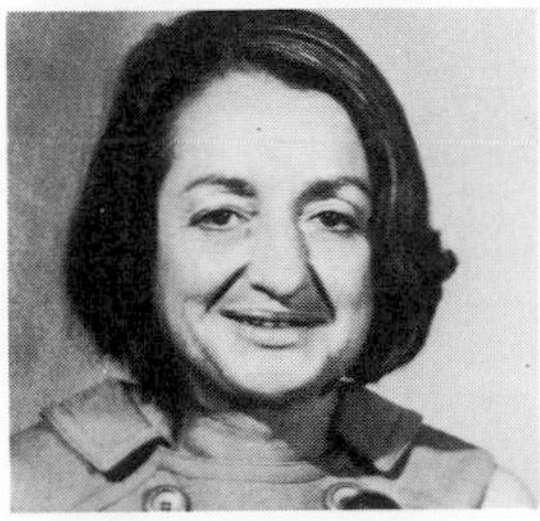

Yuri Gagarin

Galileo

Mahatma Gandhi

Gabriel García Marquez

William Lloyd Garrison

Marcus Garvey

Geronimo

Garbo, Greta, 1905-, Swedish-American film actress.
García Lorca, Federico, 1899-1936, Spanish poet and dramatist.
García Marquez, Gabriel José, 1928-, Colombian novelist.
Garfield, James A., 1831-1881, 20th president of the U.S., 1881. He was assassinated.
Garibaldi, Guiseppe, 1807-1882, Italian patriot.
Garland, Hamlin, 1860-1940, U.S. author.
Garrick, David, 1717-1779, English actor.
Garrison, William Lloyd, 1805-1879, U.S. editor and abolitionist.
Garvey, Marcus, 1887-1940, Jamaican black nationalist, led a back-to-Africa movement.
Gauguin, Paul, 1848-1903, French painter.
Genghis Khan, 1162-1227, Mongol conqueror.
George I, 1660-1727, king of Great Britain and Ireland, 1714-1727.
George II, 1683-1760, king of Great Britain and Ireland, 1727-1760.
George III, 1738-1820, king of Great Britain and Ireland, 1760-1820.
George IV, 1762-1830, regent, 1811-1820, then king of Great Britain and Ireland, 1820-1830.
George V, 1865-1936, king of Great Britain and Ireland, 1910-1936.
George VI, 1895-1952, king of Great Britain and Northern Ireland, 1936-1952.
Geronimo, 1829-1909, American Indian chief.
Gershwin, George, 1898-1937, U.S. composer.
Getty, J(ean) Paul, 1892-1976, U.S. business executive.
Giacometti, Alberto, 1901-1966, Swiss sculptor.
Gibbon, Edward, 1737-1794, English historian.
Gibson, Althea, 1927-, U.S. tennis player.
—Charles Dana, 1867-1944, U.S. illustrator.
Gide, André 1869-1951, French author.
Gilbert, Sir William S., 1836-1911, English poet and collaborator with Sir Arthur Sullivan on comic operettas.
Ginsberg, Allen, 1926-, U.S. poet.
Giotto, 1266?-1337, Italian painter, architect, and sculptor.
Giovanni, Nikki, 1943-, U.S. poet.
Gladstone, William Ewart, 1809-1898, British statesman, leader of the Liberal Party who served four times as prime minister.
Glenn, John, 1921-, U.S. astronaut and politician; first American to orbit the earth.
Goddard, Robert Hutchings, 1882-1945, U.S. scientist and rocket pioneer.
Goethals, George W., 1858-1928, U.S. engineer.
Goethe, Johann Wolfgang von, 1749-1832, German author.
Gogol, Nikolai, 1809-1852, Russian author.
Goldman, Emma, 1869-1940, U.S. advocate of anarchism born in Russia.
Goldsmith, Oliver, 1730-1774, English author born in Ireland.
Gompers, Samuel, 1850-1924, U.S. leader of early labor unions.

George Gershwin

Althea Gibson

Nikki Giovanni

George Goethals

Francisco de Goya

Martha Graham

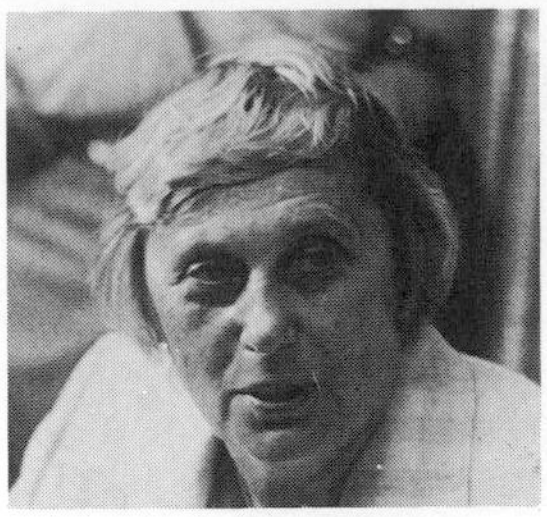
Ella Grasso

Hetty Green

Goodall, Jane, 1934-, British zoologist.
Goodman, Benny, 1909-, U.S. clarinetist and band leader.
Gorbachev, Mikhail S., 1931-, Soviet Statesman. General Secretary of the Communist Party 1985-.
Gorky, Maxim, 1868-1936, Russian author.
Goya, Francisco de, 1746-1828, Spanish painter.
Graham, Katharine, 1917-, U.S. publisher.
—Martha, 1893-, U.S. choreographer and dance company founder and director.
Grant, Ulysses Simpson, 1822-1885, U.S. Civil War general; 18th president of the U.S., 1869-1877.
Grasso, Ella Tambussi, 1919-1981, U.S. politician; first elected woman governor.
Gray, Thomas, 1716-1771, English poet.
Greeley, Horace, 1811-1872, U.S. newspaper editor.
Green, Henrietta (Hetty), 1834-1916, U.S. financier.
Grey, Lady Jane, 1537-1554, queen of England 1553; executed for treason.
Grieg, Edvard, 1843-1907, Norwegian composer.
Griffith, D(avid) W(ark), 1875-1948, U.S. film director.
Grimm, Jakob, 1785-1863, and his brother **Wilhelm,** 1786-1859, German philologists.
Grofé, Ferde, 1892-1972, U.S. conductor.
Gromyko, Andrei, 1909-, Soviet diplomat and political leader.
Gropius, Walter, 1883-1969, German architect.
Guggenheim, Simon, 1867-1941, U.S. industrialist, philanthropist, and politician.
Guinan, Mary Louise ("Texas"), 1884-1933, U.S. entertainer and businesswoman.
Gutenberg, Johann, 1400?-1468?, German printer, the first European to print with moveable type.
Gutierrez, José Angel, 1944-, Mexican-American leader of civil rights movement.

H

Hadrian, 76-138, Roman emperor who established a unified law code.
Hahn, Otto, 1879-1968, German chemist, developed process of nuclear fission.
Haile Selassie, 1891-1975, emperor of Ethiopia.
Hale, Nathan, 1755-1776, American patriot hanged as a spy by the British.
Haley, Alex, 1921-, U.S. author.
Hals, Frans, 1580-1666, Dutch portrait painter.
Hamilton, Alexander, 1757-1804, U.S. statesman, first secretary of the treasury.
—Alice, 1869-1970, U.S. physician, social reformer; first woman on faculty of Harvard University.
—Edith, 1867-1963, U.S. author and scholar, born in Germany.
Hammarskjöld, Dag, 1905-1961, Swedish statesman and U.N. official.
Hammerstein, Oscar, 1895-1960, U.S. composer.

Texas Guinan

José Gutierrez

Haile Selassie

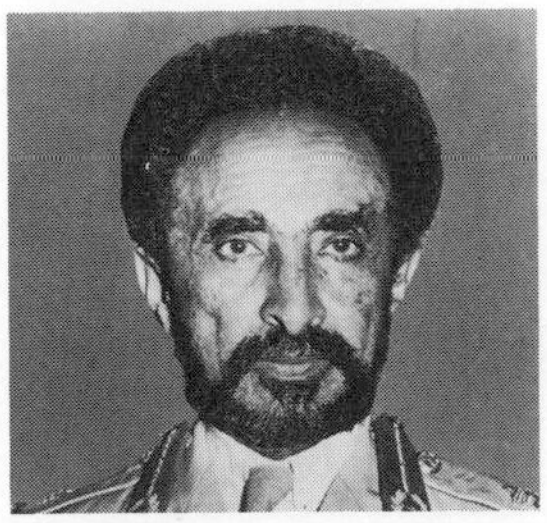

Alexander Hamilton

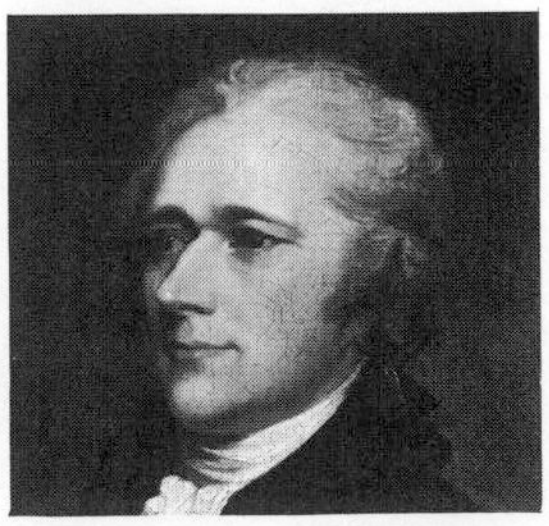

W. C. Handy

Lorraine Hansberry

Warren G. Harding

Patricia Harris

Hammurabi, 18th century B.C. or earlier, king of Babylon who issued a famous code of laws.
Hancock, John, 1737-1793, American patriot, first signer of the Declaration of Independence.
Handel, George Frederick, 1685-1759, English composer born in Germany.
Handy, W(illiam) C(hristopher), 1873-1958, U.S. musician and composer.
Hanna, Mark, 1837-1904, U.S. politician and businessman.
Hannibal, 247-183 B.C., Carthaginian general.
Hansberry, Lorraine, 1930-1965, U.S. playwright.
Harding, Warren Gamaliel, 1865-1923, 29th president of the U.S., 1921-1923; died in office.
Hardy, Thomas, 1840-1928, English novelist and poet.
Hargreaves, James, 1720?-1778, English inventor.
Harper, Frances E., 1825-1911, U.S. writer, lecturer, and abolitionist.
Harris, Joel Chandler, 1848-1908, U.S. writer; author of the *Uncle Remus Stories*.
—Patricia, 1924-1985, U.S. diplomat and government official.
Harrison, Benjamin, 1833-1901, 23rd president of the U.S., 1889-1893; grandson of W. H. Harrison.
—William Henry, 1773-1841, 9th president of the U.S., for one month in 1841.
Harte, Bret, 1836-1902, U.S. author of short stories about the West.
Harvey, William, 1578-1657, British physician and anatomist.
Hastie, William Henry, 1904-1976, U.S. jurist; first black judge to serve on the U.S. Court of Appeals.
Hathaway, Anne, 1557?-1623, wife of William Shakespeare.
Hawthorne, Nathaniel, 1804-1864, U.S. novelist and short-story writer.
Haydn, Franz Joseph, 1732-1809, Austrian composer.
Hayes, Helen, 1900-, U.S. actress.
—Rutherford Birchard, 1822-1893, 19th president of the U.S., 1877-1881.
Hearst, William Randolph, 1863-1951, U.S. newspaper and magazine publisher.
Hegel, G(eorg) W(ilhelm) F(reidrich), 1770-1831, German philosopher.
Heidegger, Martin, 1889-1976, German philosopher.
Heifetz, Jascha, 1901-1987, U.S. violinist born in Russia.
Heinlein, Robert A., 1907-, U.S. author of science fiction.
Hellman, Lillian, 1905-1984, U.S. playwright.
Hemingway, Ernest, 1899-1961, U.S. novelist and short-story writer.
Henry, Marguerite, 1902-, U.S. author.
—O. See O. HENRY.
—Patrick, 1736-1799, American statesman and public speaker.
Henry II, 1133-1189, king of England, 1154-1189.
— 1519-1559, king of France, 1547-1559.
Henry IV, 1553-1610, king of France, 1589-1610.

William Hastie

Helen Hayes

William Randolph Hearst

Ernest Hemingway

Matthew Henson

Barbara Hepworth

Myra Hess

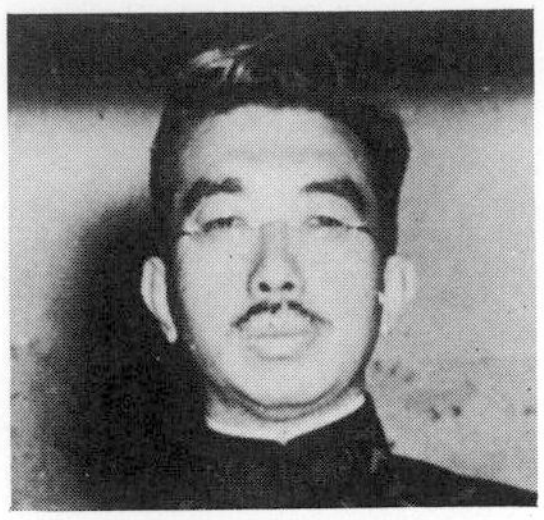
Hirohito

Henry V, 1387-1422, king of England, 1413-1422.
Henry VII, 1457-1509, king of England, 1485-1509.
Henry VIII, 1491-1547, king of England, 1509-1547.
Henson, Matthew A., 1866-1955, explorer and author.
Hepworth, Dame Barbara, 1903-1975, English sculptor.
Herod, 73?-4 B.C., king of Judea, 37-4 B.C.
Herodotus, 484?-425 B.C., Greek historian.
Hesiod, 8th century? B.C., Greek poet.
Hess, Dame Myra, 1890-1965, English pianist.
Hesse, Herman, 1877-1962, German novelist and poet.
Hiawatha, 16th-century American Indian chief.
Hickok, James Butler ("Wild Bill"), 1837-1876, U.S. frontier scout and lawman.
Hidalgo y Costilla, Miguel, 1753-1811, Mexican priest and leader of the independence movement.
Hillary, Sir Edmund, 1919-, New Zealand mountain climber and explorer.
Hirohito, 1901-1989, emperor of Japan, 1926-1989.
Hiroshige, Ando, 1797-1858, Japanese artist.
Hitler, Adolf, 1889-1945, dictator of Nazi Germany, 1933-1945, born in Austria.
Hobbes, Thomas, 1588-1679, English philosopher.
Ho Chi Minh, 1890-1969, Vietnamese Communist revolutionist and president of North Vietnam, 1954-1969.
Hodgkin, Dorothy, 1910-, British chemist born in Egypt; Nobel Prize winner, 1974.
Hogarth, William, 1697-1764, English painter and engraver.
Hokinson, Helen, 1899?-1945, U.S. cartoonist.
Holbein, Hans, 1465-1524, and his son **Hans,** 1497?-1543, German painters.
Holiday, Billie, 1915-1959, U.S. jazz singer.
Holmes, Oliver Wendell, 1809-1894, U.S. writer, father of Oliver Wendell Holmes Jr.
—Oliver Wendell, Jr., 1841-1935, U.S. jurist; justice of the U.S. Supreme Court, 1902-1932.
Homer, Greek epic poet who lived in about the ninth century B.C.; author of the *Iliad* and the *Odyssey*.
—Winslow, 1836-1910, U.S. painter.
Hoover, Herbert, 1874-1964, 31st president of the U.S., 1929-1933.
—J(ohn) Edgar, 1895-1972, U.S. director of the Federal Bureau of Investigation (1924-1972).
Hopkins, Gerard Manley, 1844-1889, English poet.
Hooper, Edward, 1882-1967, U.S. painter.
—Grace, 1906-, U.S. mathematician and computer specialist.
Horace (Quintus Horatius Flaccus), 65 B.C.-8 B.C., Latin poet.
Horney, Karen, 1885-1952, U.S. psychoanalyst born in Germany.
Houdini, Harry, 1874-1926, U.S. magician and escape artist.
Housman, A(lfred) E(dward), 1859-1936, English poet.

Ho Chi Minh

Helen Hokinson

Herbert Hoover

Karen Horney
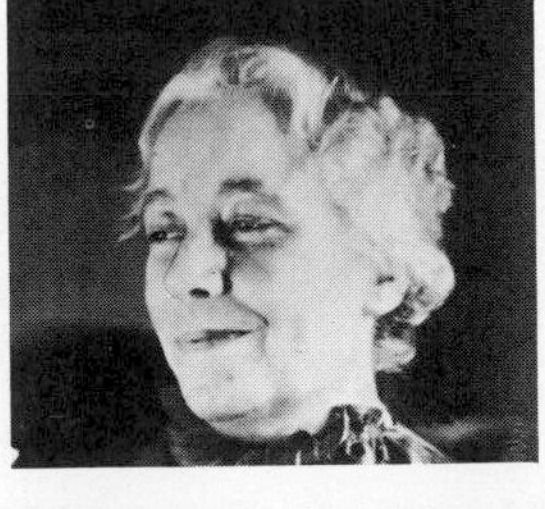

Samuel Houston

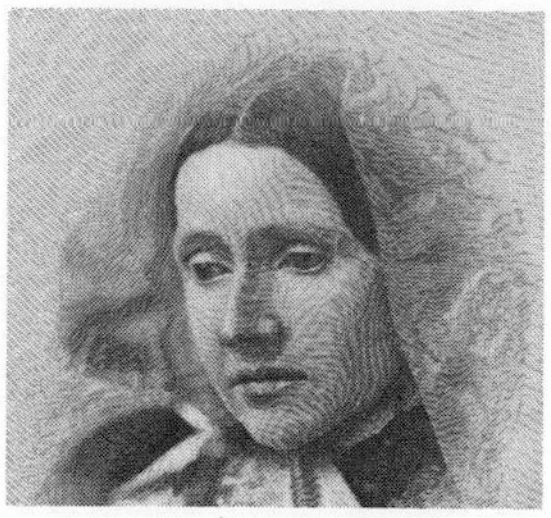
Julia Ward Howe

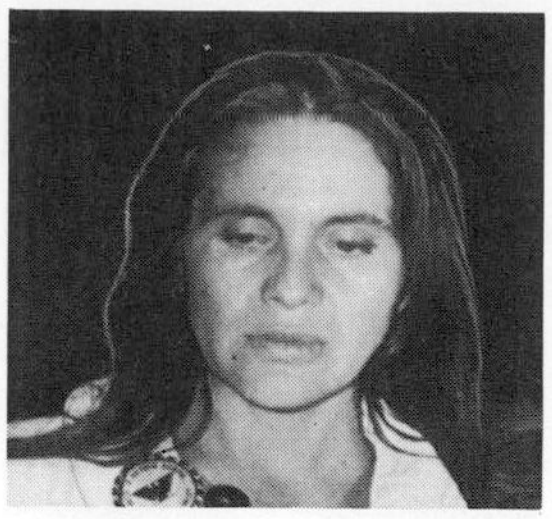
Delores Huerta

Victor Hugo

Houston, Samuel, 1793-1863, U.S. general and statesman.
Howe, Julia Ward, 1819-1910, U.S. writer and social reformer.
Hudson, Henry, 1572?-1611, English explorer and sea captain.
Huerta, Delores, 1930-, Mexican-American labor organizer and social reformer.
Hughes, Charles Evans, 1862-1948, U.S. statesman and jurist; justice of the U.S. Supreme Court, 1930-1941.
—Howard Robard, 1905-1976, U.S. business executive and aviator.
—Langston, 1902-1967, U.S. poet and author.
Hugo, Victor, 1802-1885, French poet, novelist, and dramatist.
Humphrey, Hubert Horatio, 1911-1978, U.S. legislator; Vice President, 1965-1969.
Hurston, Zora Neale, 1901-1980, U.S. educator, novelist,and playwright.
Husted, Marjorie ("Betty Crocker"), 1892?-1986, U.S. home economics executive.
Hutchinson, Anne, 1591?-1643, American religious leader in Massachusetts and Rhode Island, born in England.
Huxley, Aldous, 1894-1963, England author, grandson of Thomas Henry Huxley.
—Thomas Henry, 1825-1895, English biologist and proponent of Darwinism.

I

Ibsen, Henrik, 1828-1906, Norwegian playwright.
Ichikawa, Fusae, died 1981, Japanese feminist and suffragist.
Ingres, Jean Auguste Dominique, 1780-1867, French painter.
Inness, George, 1825-1894, U.S. painter.
Ionesco, Eugene, 1912-, French playwright.
Irving, Washington, 1783-1859, U.S. writer and humorist.
Isabella I, 1451-1504, queen of Castille and Aragon; sponsor of Christopher Columbus.
Isaiah Hebrew prophet who lived during the eighth century B.C.
Isherwood, Christopher, 1904-, English author.
Iturbi, José, 1895-1980, Spanish pianist and conductor.
Ivan III, 1440-1505, Russian ruler who defeated the Tartars. Also **Ivan the Great.**
Ivan IV, 1530-1584, first czar of Russia, 1547-1584. Also **Ivan the Terrible.**

J

Jackson, Andrew, 1767-1845, 7th president of the U.S., 1829-1837.

Marjorie Husted

Fusae Ichikawa

Isabella I

Ivan the Terrible

Henry James

William James

Thomas Jefferson

Jiang Zing

—**Helen Hunt,** 1830-1885, U.S. historian and advocate of American Indian rights.
—**Jesse,** 1941-, U.S. clergyman and civil rights activist.
—**Mahalia,** 1911-1972, U.S. gospel singer.
—**Thomas Jonathan ("Stonewall"),** 1824-1863, Confederate general in the Civil War.
James Henry, 1843-1916, U.S. writer and critic, active in England; brother of William James.
—**Jesse,** 1847-1882, U.S. bank robber and outlaw.
—**William,** 1842-1910, U.S. philosopher and psychologist.
James I, 1566-1625, king of England, 1603-1625.
Jay, John, 1745-1829, U.S. jurist; first chief justice of the U.S. Supreme Court, 1789-1795.
Jeanne d'Arc The French spelling of JOAN OF ARC.
Jefferson, Thomas, 1743-1826, American statesman, writer, and philosopher; 3rd president of the U.S., 1801-1809.
Jenner, Edward, 1749-1823, English physician; discovered vaccination.
—**Sir William,** 1815-1898, English physician.
Jesus, 4? B.C.-A.D. 29, the person whose life, teachings, and death are the basis of Christianity.
Jewett, Sarah Orne, 1849-1909, U.S. novelist and short-story writer.
Jiang Zing, 1914-, Chinese revolutionary and political leader, wife of Mao Zedong.
Joan of Arc, 1412?-1431, French heroine, martyr, and saint who led the French army against the English in 1429.
John, 1167-1216, king of England, 1199-1216. He signed the Magna Carta in 1215.
John Paul II, 1920-, pope, 1978-.
Johnson, Andrew, 1808-1875, 17th president of the U.S., 1865-1869.
—**Charles S.,** 1893-1956, U.S. educator and sociologist.
—**Claudia ("Lady Bird"),** 1912-, U.S. businesswoman, wife of Lyndon Baines Johnson.
—**Ellen,** 1829-1899, U.S. prison reformer.
—**(Emily) Pauline,** 1861-1913, Canadian poet.
—**Georgia,** 1886-1966, U.S. author.
—**James Weldon,** 1871-1938, U.S. poet.
—**Lyndon Baines,** 1908-1973, 36th president of the U.S., 1963-1969.
—**Samuel,** 1709-1784, English lexicographer, poet, and writer.
John the Baptist, 5 B.C.-A.D. 30, prophet who baptized Jesus, his cousin.
Joliet, Louis, 1645-1700, French-Canadian explorer in America.
Jones, John Paul, 1747-1792, American naval commander in the Revolutionary War.
—**Mary Harris ("Mother"),** 1830-1930, U.S. labor organizer born in Ireland.
Jonson, Ben, 1572-1637, English dramatist and poet.
Joplin, Scott, 1869-1917, U.S. composer noted for ragtime.
Jordan, Barbara, 1936-, U.S. legislator and educator.

Lady Bird Johnson

Lyndon B. Johnson

John Paul Jones

Scott Joplin

Chief Joseph

Benito Juárez

Kamehameha I

Helen Keller

Jordan, Vernon E., Jr., 1935-, U.S. lawyer and civil rights activist.
Joseph, Chief, 1840?-1904, American Indian chief.
Josephine, 1763-1814, empress of France, wife of Napoleon Bonaparte.
Joyce, James, 1882-1941, Irish author.
Juan Carlos I, 1938-, king of Spain, 1975-.
Juárez, Benito, 1806-1872, Mexican political leader.
Juliana, 1909-, queen of the Netherlands, 1948-1980.
Jung, Carl, 1875-1961, Swiss psychiatrist.
Justinian I, 482-565, Byzantine lawgiver and emperor, 527-565.

K

Kafka, Franz, 1883-1924, Austrian author born in Czechoslovakia.
Kamehameha I, 1758?-1819, king of Hawaii.
Kandinsky, Wassily, 1866-1944, Russian painter.
Kant, Immanuel, 1724-1804, German philosopher.
Keats, John, 1795-1821, English poet.
Keller, Helen, 1880-1968, U.S. educator.
Kelly, Grace, 1929-1982, Princess Consort of Monaco. U.S. film star.
Kennedy, John Fitzgerald, 1917-1963, 35th president of the U.S., 1961-1963; assassinated.
Kennedy, Robert Francis, 1925-1968, U.S. politician; brother of John F. Kennedy; assassinated.
Kenny, Elizabeth ("Sister"), 1886-1952, Australian nurse; developed treatment for poliomyelitis.
Kenyon, Dame Kathleen M., 1906-1978, British archaeologist; discoverer of Biblical Jericho.
Kepler, Johannes, 1571-1630, German astronomer.
Kerensky, Alexander, 1881-1970, Russian revolutionary leader.
Kerouac, Jack, 1922-1969, U.S. writer.
Key, Francis Scott, 1779-1843, U.S. author of the Star-Spangled Banner.
Keynes, John Maynard, 1883-1946, English economist.
Khomeini, Ruhollah 1900-1989, Iranian religious and political leader.
Khrushchev, Nikita, 1894-1971, Soviet statesman and premier, 1958-1964.
King, Coretta Scott, 1927-, U.S. civil rights leader, wife of Martin Luther King, Jr.
—Martin Luther, Jr., 1929-1968, U.S. civil rights leader; assassinated.
Kipling, Rudyard, 1865-1936, English writer and poet.
Kirkpatrick, Jeane, 1926-, U.S. diplomat, first U.S. woman ambassador to the United Nations.
Kissinger, Henry Alfred, 1923-, U.S. secretary of state, 1973-1977.
Klee, Paul, 1879-1940, Swiss painter.

John F. Kennedy

Robert Kennedy

Kathleen Kenyon

Martin Luther King, Jr.

Thaddeus Kosciusko

Juanita Kreps

Marquis de Lafayette

Selma Lagerlöf

Kokoschka, Oskar, 1886-1980, Austrian painter and writer.

Kosciusko, Thaddeus, 1746-1817, Polish patriot who aided the Americans during the Revolutionary war.

Kreps, Juanita M., 1921-, U.S. public official.

Kubrick, Stanley, 1928-, American motion-picture director.

Ku K'ai-Chih, 345?-406?, Chinese painter.

Kurosawa, Akira, 1910, Japanese film director.

L

Lafayette, Marquis de, 1757-1834, French general who fought in the Revolutionary war.

La Follette, Belle Case, 1859-1931, U.S. journalist and social reformer, wife of Robert La Follette.

—Robert M., 1855-1925, U.S. political reformer, leader of the Progressive Party.

Lafontant, Jewell, 1922-, U.S. jurist, diplomat, and founding member of CORE (Congress of Racial Equality).

Lagerlöf, Selma, 1858-1940, Swedish author, first woman to receive a Nobel Prize for literature.

Lamb, Charles, 1775-1834, English critic and essayist.

Landers, Ann, 1918-, U.S. newspaper columnist. Her real name is Esther Pauline Friedman.

Lange, Dorothea, 1895-1965, U.S. photographer.

Lanier, Sidney, 1842-1881, U.S. poet.

Lao-tse or **Lao-tzu,** 604?-531 B.C., Chinese philosopher; founder of Taoism.

La Salle, Sieur de, 1643-1687, born René Robert Cavelier, French explorer of America.

Lathrop, Julia Clifford, 1858-1932, U.S. government official and social reformer.

—Rose Hawthorne, 1851-1926, U.S. founder of an order of nursing nuns; biographer of her father, Nathaniel Hawthorne.

Laurencin, Marie, 1885-1956, French painter.

Lawrence, D(avid) H(erbert), 1885-1930, English novelist and poet.

—T(homas) E(dward), 1888-1935, British author and soldier known as Lawrence of Arabia.

Lazarus, Emma, 1849-1887, U.S. poet.

Leakey, Louis S. B., 1903-1972, British anthropologist born in Kenya, husband of Mary N. Leakey and father of Richard E. Leakey.

—Mary N., 1913-, British anthropologist, mother of Richard E. Leakey.

—Richard E., 1944-, British anthropologist.

Lear, Edward, 1812-1888, English humorist and artist.

Le Corbusier, 1887-1965, French architect.

Lee, Henry, 1756-1818, American Revolutionary leader, known as "Light-horse Harry Lee." Father of Robert E. Lee.

—Robert E., 1807-1870, U.S. army officer; commander in chief of the Confederate army.

Louis Leakey

Mary Leakey

Richard Leakey

Robert E. Lee

Nikolai Lenin

Liliuokalani

Abraham Lincoln

Jenny Lind

Lee, Tsung Dao, 1926-, U.S. physicist, born in China.
Leech, Margaret K., 1893-1974, U.S. historian.
Leeuwenhoek, Anton van, 1632-1723, Dutch naturalist; early user of the microscope.
Le Guin, Ursula K., 1929-, U.S. writer of science fiction.
Leibniz, Gottfried Wilhelm, Baron von, 1646-1716, German philosopher and mathematician.
L'Engle, Madeleine, 1918-, U.S. author.
Lenin, V. I. (Nikolai), 1870-1924, Russian revolutionary leader.
Leonardo See DA VINCI.
Lessing, Doris, 1919-, British author born in Persia and raised in Rhodesia.
Leví-Strauss, Claude, 1908-, French anthropologist and leading exponent of structuralism.
Lewis, C(live) S(taples), 1898-1963, English author.
—John L., 1880-1969, U.S. labor leder.
—Meriwether, 1774-1809, U.S. explorer with William Clark.
—Sinclair, 1885-1951, U.S. novelist.
Lie, Trygvie, 1896-1968, Norwegian diplomat and first Secretary-General of the U.N.
Liliuokalani, 1839-1917, born Lydia Kamekeha, queen of Hawaii, 1891-1893.
Lincoln, Abraham, 1809-1865, 16th president of the U.S., 1861-1865. He was assassinated.
—Mary Todd, 1818-1882, wife of Abraham Lincoln.
Lind, Jenny, 1820-1887, Swedish soprano.
Lindbergh, Anne Morrow, 1906-, U.S. author, wife of Charles Lindbergh.
—Charles Augustus, 1902-1974, U.S. aviator who made the first solo flight across the Atlantic.
Lin Yutang, 1895-1976, U.S. author and philosopher, born in China.
Li Po, 700?-762, Chinese poet.
Liszt, Franz, 1811-1886, Hungarian composer.
Liu Shao-chi, 1900?-1973, Chinese statesman.
Lloyd George, David, 1863-1945, British statesman; prime minister of Great Britain, 1916-1922.
Locke, Alain, 1886-1954, U.S. scholar.
—John, 1632-1704, English philosopher.
Lockwood, Belva Ann, 1830-1917, U.S. lawyer and suffragist.
London, Jack, 1876-1916, U.S. author.
Longfellow, Henry Wadsworth, 1807-1882, U.S. poet.
Longworth, Alice Roosevelt, 1884-1980, U.S. socialite and hostess, daughter of Theodore Roosevelt.
Louis, Joe, 1914-1981, U.S. heavyweight boxing champion.
Louis Napoleon, 1808-1873, emperor of France, 1852-1870; nephew of Napoleon I. Also **Napoleon III.**
Louis XIV, 1638-1715, king of France, 1643-1715.
Louis XVI, 1754-1793, king of France, 1774-1792. He ws guillotined during the French Revolution.
Low, Juliette Gordon, 1860-1927, U.S. founder of the Girl Scouts of America.

Anne Morrow Lindbergh

Charles Lindbergh

Henry Wadsworth Longfellow

Alice Roosevelt Longworth

Amy Lowell

Claire Boothe Luce

Martin Luther

Douglas MacArthur

Lowell, Amy, 1874-1925, U.S. poet.
—James Russell, 1819-1891, U.S. poet and editor.
Lucas, George, 1944-, U.S. motion-picture producer and director.
Luce, Claire Boothe, 1903-1987, U.S. playwright, member of Congress, and diplomat.
—Henry, 1898-1967, U.S. magazine publisher and editor.
Lucretius, 99?-55? B.C., Roman poet and philosopher.
Luther, Martin, 1483-1546, German monk and leader in the Reformation and formation of Protestant Churches.

M

MacArthur, Douglas, 1880-1964, U.S. general.
Machiavelli, Niccolò, 1469-1527, Italian statesman and political theorist.
MacLeish, Archibald, 1892-1982, U.S. poet and dramatist.
Madison, Dolley, 1768-1849, U.S. hostess, wife of James Madison.
—James, 1751-1836, 4th president of the U.S., 1809-1817.
Magellan, Ferdinand, 1480?-1521, Portuguese navigator in the service of Spain. He led the first expedition to sail around the world.
Mahler, Gustav, 1860-1911, Austrian composer.
Mahomet See MUHAMMAD.
Mailer, Norman, 1923-, U.S. author.
Malamud, Bernard, 1914-1986, U.S. author.
Malcolm X (Malcolm Little), 1925-1965, U.S. black nationalist; assassinated.
Manet, Edouard, 1832-1883, French painter.
Manley, Mary, 1663-1724, first English woman journalist.
Mann, Horace, 1796-1859, U.S. philosopher and educator.
—Thomas, 1875-1955, German author.
Mansa Musa, died 1337, ruler of the Mali Empire in Africa, 1312-1337.
Mao Tse-tung See MAO ZEDONG.
Mao Zedong, 1893-1976, Chinese Communist revoluationary and political leader of People's Republic of China, 1949-1976.
Marat, Jean Paul, 1743-1793, French revolutionist born in Switzerland; assassinated by Charlotte Corday.
Marceau, Marcel, 1923-, French mime.
Marconi, Guglielmo, 1874-1937, Italian inventor who developed the wireless telegraph.
Marco Polo See POLO, MARCO.
Marcos, Ferdinand, 1917-, Philippine president (1965-1986).
Marcus Aurelius, 121-180, Roman emperor and philosopher.
Margaret of Anjou, 1430-1482, queen of Henry VI of England.

Dolley Madison

James Madison

Ferdinand Magellan

Mao Zedong

Marie Antoinette

Thurgood Marshall

Maria Martínez

Mary, Queen of Scotts

Maria Theresa, 1717-1780, Austrian archduchess and Holy Roman empress.

Marie Antoinette, 1755-1793, queen of France, 1774-1792, guillotined during the French Revolution; wife of Louis XVI.

Mark Twain See TWAIN, MARK.

Marquette, (Père) Jacques, 1637-1675, French Jesuit Missionary who explored the Great Lakes and Mississippi valley.

Marshall George Catlett, 1880-1959, U.S. general, diplomat, and statesman.

—John, 1755-1835, U.S. jurist; chief justice of the U.S. Supreme Court, 1801-1835.

—Thurgood, 1908-, U.S. jurist; first black justice of the U.S. Supreme Court, 1967-.

Martí, Jose, 1853-1895, Cuban patriot.

Martínez, Maria Montoya, 1887-1980, Mexican potter, known as **Maria the Potter.**

Marx, Karl, 1818-1883, German philosopher and Communist theoretician.

Mary I, 1516-1558, queen of England, 1553-1558. She was also known as **Mary Tudor** or **Bloody Mary.**

Mary II, 1662-1694, queen of England, 1688-1694.

Mary, Queen of Scots, 1542-1587, queen of Scotland, 1542-1567, beheaded by order of Queen Elizabeth I.

Masaccio, 1401?-1429?, Italian painter.

Masefield, John, 1878-1967, English poet.

Massasoit, 1580?-1661, American Indian chief.

Masters, Edgar Lee, 1869-1950, U.S. poet.

Mather, Cotton, 1663-1728, and his father, **Increase Mather,** 1639-1723, religious leaders in colonial America.

Matisse, Henri, 1869-1954, French painter.

Matthews, Marjorie S., 1916-, U.S. clergywoman; first woman elected bishop of a major denomination.

Maugham, W(illiam) Somerset, 1874-1965, English author.

Maupassant, Guy de, 1850-1893, French author.

Maximilian, 1832-1867, emperor of Mexico, 1864-1867.

McAuliffe, Christa, 1949-1986, U.S. teacher; first private citizen to fly in the space shuttle. Killed in the *Challenger* explosion.

McCarthy, Mary, 1912-, U.S. author.

McClung, Nellie, 1873-1951, Canadian feminist and author.

McCormick, Cyrus, 1809-1884, U.S. inventor.

McCullers, Carson, 1917-1967, U.S. novelist.

McKinley, William, 1843-1901, 25th president of the U.S., 1897-1901, assassinated.

McPhereson, Aimee Semple, 1890-1944, U.S. evangelist born in Canada.

Mead, Margaret, 1901-1978, U.S. anthropologist and author.

Meany, George, 1894-1980, U.S. labor leader.

Medici, the name of an influential family in Florence, Italy: **Catherine de,** 1519-1589, virtual ruler of France, 1559-1589; **Cosimo de,** 1389-1464, financier, political leader, and art patron;

Massasoit

Henri Matisse

Marjorie Matthews

Margaret Mead

Golda Meir

Felix Mendelssohn

Michelangelo

John Milton

Lorenzo de, 1449-1492, political leader on whom Machiavelli based his book *The Prince*.
Meir, Golda, 1898-1978, first woman premier of Israel, 1969-1974, born in Russia.
Mellon, Andrew, 1855-1937, U.S. financier.
Melville, Herman, 1819-1891, U.S. novelist.
Mencken, Henry L(ouis), 1880-1956, U.S. critic and journalist.
Mendel, Gregor Johann, 1822-1884, Austrian botanist, formulated laws of genetics.
Mendeleev, Dmitri Ivanovich, 1834-1907, Russian chemist who devised the table of elements.
Mendelssohn, Felix, 1809-1847, German composer.
Meredith, James, 1933-, U.S. civil rights activist.
Mesta, Perle, 1891-1975, U.S. diplomat.
Michelangelo Buonarroti, 1475-1564, Italian sculptor, painter, architect, and poet.
Millay, Edna St. Vincent, 1892-1950, U.S. poet.
Miller, Arthur, 1915-, U.S. playwright.
Milton, John, 1608-1674, English poet and essayist.
Miró, Joan, 1893-1983, Spanish painter.
Mistral, Gabriela, 1889-1957, Chilean poet and educator.
Mitchell Maria, 1818-1889, U.S. astronomer; discovered Mitchell's comet.
Mitterand, François Maurice, 1916-, French politician, president of French, 1981-.
Modigliani, Amedeo, 1884-1920, Italian painter.
Mohammed See MUHAMMAD.
Mohammed Reza Pahlavi, 1919-1980, shah of Iran, 1941-1979.
Molière, 1622-1673, French comic dramatist and actor. His real name was Jean Baptiste Poquelin.
Momaday, N. Scott, 1934-, U.S. author.
Mondale, Walter Frederick, 1928-, U.S. legislator, vice president 1977-1981.
Mondrian, Piet, 1872-1944, Dutch painter.
Monet, Claude, 1840-1926, French painter.
Monroe, Harriet, 1860-1936, U.S. poet.
—James, 1758-1831, 5th president of the U.S., 1817-1825.
—Marilyn, 1926-1962, U.S. motion-picture actress.
Montaigne, Michel, 1533-1592, French essayist.
Montessori, Maria, 1870-1952, Italian educator, developed a special method for teaching children.
Montezuma or Moctezuma, 1480?-1520, Aztec emperor of Mexico (1502-1520).
Moore, Marianee, 1887-1972, U.S. poet.
More, Sir Thomas, 1478-1535, English author and statesman.
Morgan, Sir Henry, 1635?-1688, British pirate.
—J(ohn) P(ierpont), 1837-1913, U.S. financier.
Morse, Samuel F. B., 1791-1872, U.S. artist and inventor who made the first telegraph.
Moses, Anna Mary, 1860-1961, U.S. painter. She is known as **Grandma Moses.**
Mother Teresa, 1910-, winner of the Nobel Peace Prize for her work with the poor.
Motley, Constance Baker, 1921-, U.S. jurist; first black woman to become a federal judge.

Gabriela Mistral

Maria Mitchell

N. Scott Momaday

Constance Baker Motley

Bess Myerson

Ralph Nader

Nefertiti

Pablo Neruda

Mott, Lucretia, 1793-1880, U.S. abolitionist and pioneer for equal rights for women.
Mozart, Wolfgang Amadeus, 1756-1791, Austrian composer.
Mubarak, Hosni, 1928-, Egyptian politican, president of Egypt, 1981-.
Muhammad, 570?-632, Arabian founder of Islam and its chief prophet.
—Elijah (Elijah Poole), 1897-1975, U.S. black nationalist leader.
Muir, John, 1838-1914, U.S. naturalist.
Mulroney, (Martin) Brian, 1939-, Canadian Political leader.
Murphy, Audie, 1924-1971, U.S. soldier; most-decorated World War II hero.
Murrow, Edward R., 1908-1965, U.S. broadcast journalist.
Mussolini, Benito, 1883-1945, Italian Fascist dictator, premier, 1922-1943; executed.
Myerson, Bess, 1924-, U.S. consumer advocate and government official.

N

Nabokov, Vladimir, 1899-1977, Russian author.
Nader, Ralph, 1934-, U.S. lawyer, author, and consumer advocate.
Napoleon I, 1769-1821, French military leader and conqueror; emperor, 1804-1815.
Napoleon III See LOUIS NAPOLEON.
Nash, Ogden, 1902-1971, U.S. humorist and poet.
Nasser, Gamal Abdul, 1918-1970, Egyptian statesman, president of the United Arab Republic, 1958-1970.
Nast, Thomas, 1840-1902, U.S. political cartoonist born in Germany.
Nation, Carry, 1846-1911, U.S. advocate of temperance.
Nefertiti, queen of ancient Egypt, 1367-1350 B.C.
Nehru, Jawaharlal, 1899-1964, Indian nationalist leader, first prime minister, 1947-1964.
Nelson, Horatio, 1758-1805, English naval hero.
Nero, 37-68, emperor of Rome, 54-68.
Neruda, Pablo, 1904-1973, Chilean poet.
Nevelson, Louise, 1900-1988, U.S. sculptor.
Newton, Sir Isaac, 1642-1727, British philosopher and mathematician.
Nicholas II, 1868-1918, czar of Russia, 1894-1917.
Nietzsche, Friedrich Wilhelm, 1844-1900, German philosopher.
Nightingale, Florence, 1820-1910, English nurse and hospital reformer born in Italy.
Nijinsky, Waslaw, 1890-1950, Russian ballet dancer.
Nin Anaïs, 1903-1977, U.S. author born in France.
Nixon, Richard Milhous, 1913-, 37th president of the U.S., 1969-1974. He resigned.
Nobel, Alfred Bernhard, 1833-1896, Swedish chemist, philanthropist, and inventor.
Noguchi, Isamu, 1904, U.S. sculptor.

Louise Nevelson
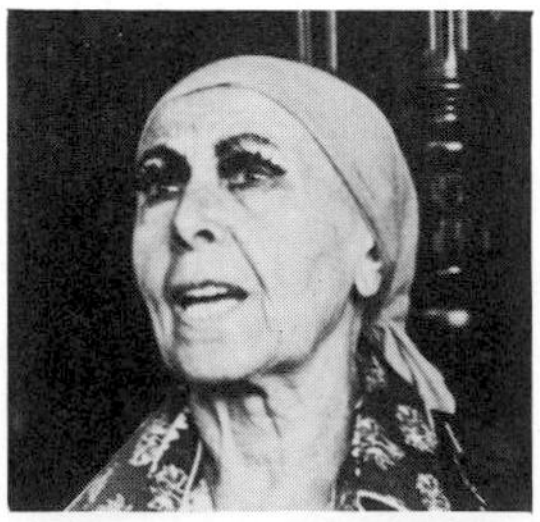

Richard Nixon

Alfred Nobel

Isamu Noguchi

Annie Oakley

Sandra Day O'Connor

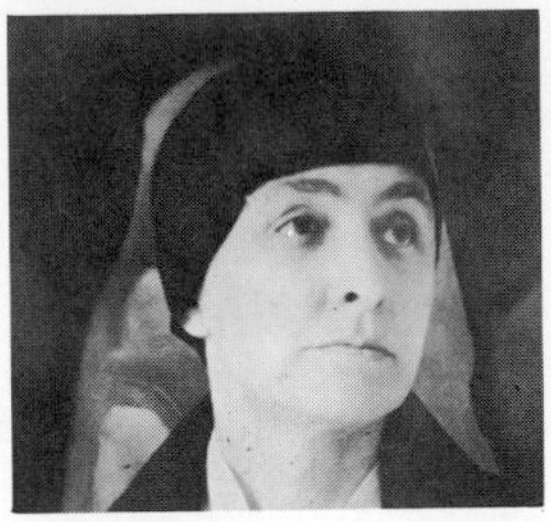
Georgia O'Keeffe

Eugene O'Neill

Nostradamus, 1503-1566, French astrologer and physician.

O

Oakley, Annie, 1860-1926, U.S. sharpshooter. Her real name was Phoebe Anne Oakley Mozee.
Oates, Joyce Carol, 1938-, U.S. author.
O'Connor, Flannery, 1925-1964, U.S. author.
—Sandra Day, 1930-, U.S. jurist; first woman justice of the U.S. Supreme Court.
Offenbach, Jacques, 1819-1880, French composer.
O'Hair, Madelyn Murray, 1919-, U.S. reformer.
O'Hara, John, 1905-1970, U.S. author.
O. Henry The pen name of William Sydney Porter, 1862-1910, U.S. short-story writer.
O'Higgins, Bernardo, 1778-1842, Chilean statesman and soldier.
Ohm, Georg Simon, 1787-1854, German physicist.
O'Keeffe, Georgia, 1887-1986, U.S. artist.
Olivier, Laurence, 1907-, English actor.
Omar Khayyam, 1050?-1123?, Persian poet.
Onassis, Jacqueline (Kennedy), 1929-, U.S. former First Lady; widow of President John F. Kennedy.
O'Neill, Eugene, 1888-1953, U.S. playwright.
Orozco, José Clemente, 1883-1949, Mexican painter.
Orwell, George (Eric Arthur Blair), 1903-1950, English author, born in India.
Osceola, 1804?-1838, American Indian chief.
Otis, James, 1725-1783, American patriot in Revolutionary War.
Owens, Jesse, 1913-1980, U.S. Olympic Athlete.

P

Paganini, Niccolo, 1782-1840, Italian violinist.
Paine, Thomas, 1737-1809, U.S. political writer, born in England.
Pandit, Vijaya Lakshmi, 1900-, Indian diplomat, first woman president of U.N. General Assembly.
Pankhurst Emmeline, 1858-1928, British suffragist.
Park Chung Hee, 1917-1979, South Korean leader, president of South Korea, 1963-1979.
Parker, Dorothy, 1893-1967, U.S. poet and writer.
—Ely Samuel, 1828-1895, first American Indian appointed Commissioner of Indian Affairs.
Parkman, Francis, 1823-1893, U.S. historian.
Parks, Rosa Lee, 1913-, U.S. civil rights activist.
Pascal, Blaise, 1623-1662, French philosopher and mathematician.
Pasternak, Boris, 1890-1960, Russian author.

José Orozco

Jesse Owens

Vijaya Lakshmi Pandit

Ely Samuel Parker

Louis Pasteur

Anna Pavlova

I. M. Pei

Frances Perkins

Pasteur, Louis, 1822-1895, French chemist.
Paul, ?-A.D. 67?, Christian apostle, missionary, and saint.
Pauling, Linus Carl, 1901-, U.S. chemist.
Pavlov, Ivan, 1849-1936, Russian physiologist.
Pavlova, Anna, 1882-1931, Russian ballet dancer.
Paz, Octavio, 1914-, Mexican poet and essayist.
Peale, Norman Vincent, 1898-, U.S. clergyman.
Peary, Robert, 1856-1920, U.S. explorer who discovered the North Pole.
Pei, I(eoh) M(ing), 1917-, U.S. architect born in China.
Penn, William, 1644-1718, English religious leader, the founder of Pennsylvania Colony.
Pepys, Samuel, 1633-1703, English public official and author of the most famous English diary.
Pérez de Cuéllar, Javier, 1920-, Peruvian diplomat and UN official.
Pericles, died 429 B.C., Athenian statesman, orator, and general.
Perkins, Frances, 1882-1965, U.S. social worker and government offical; first woman appointed to a cabinet-level position.
Perón, Eva, 1919-1952, Argentine social reformer, first wife of Juan Perón.
—Juan Domingo, 1895-1974, Argentine politician; president of Argentina, 1946-1955, 1973-1974.
—María Estela (Isabel) Martínez de, 1931-, president of Argentina, 1974-1976, second wife of Juan Perón.
Perry, Oliver Hazard, 1785-1819, U.S. naval officer and hero during the War of 1812.
Peter, ?-A.D. 64?, Christian apostle and Saint, considered to be the first pope. Also **Simon Peter.**
Peter I, 1672-1725, Russian ruler and reformer. Also **Peter the Great.**
Phillip II, 382-336 B.C., king of Macedon.
Piaget, Jean, 1896-1980, Swiss child psychologist.
Picasso, Pablo, 1881-1973, Spanish painter and sculptor, active in France.
Pierce, Franklin, 1804-1869, 14th president of the U.S., 1853-1857.
Pilate, Pontius, Roman procurator of Judea, 26-36?, who condemned Jesus to be crucified.
Pinter, Harold, 1930-, English dramatist.
Pirandello, Luigi, 1867-1936, Italian author.
Pitcher, Molly, 1754-1832, American Revolutionary War hero. Her real name was Mary Ludwig.
Pitseolak, Peter, 1902-1973, Canadian Innuit artist and historian.
Pizarro, Francisco, 1478?-1541, Spanish conqueror of Incas in Peru.
Planck, Max, 1858-1947, German Physicist.
Plath, Sylvia, 1932-1963, U.S. poet.
Plato, 437?-346? B.C., Greek philosopher.
Pocahontas, 1595?-1617, American Indian princess. She is said to have saved Captain John Smith from death.
Poe, Edgar Allan, 1809-1849, U.S. poet, critic, and short-story writer.

Pablo Picasso

Peter Pitseolak

Francisco Pizarro

Pocahontas

Emily Post

Beatrix Potter

Marcel Proust

Joseph Pulitzer

Polk, James Knox, 1795-1849, 11th president of the U.S., 1845-1849.
Pollock, Jackson, 1912-1956, U.S. artist.
Polo, Marco, 1254?-1324?, Venetian traveler who wrote about his travels in Asia.
Pompadour, Marquise de, 1721-1764, born Jeanne Poisson, prominent member of the court of Louis XV.
Ponce de León, Juan, 1460?-1521, Spanish explorer who discovered Florida, 1513.
Pontiac, 1720?-1760, American Indian chief.
Porter, Katherine Anne, 1890-1980, U.S. novelist and short-story writer.
Post, Emily, 1873?-1960, U.S. columnist and author of books on etiquette.
Potter, Beatrix, 1866-1943, English author and illustrator.
Powell, Adam Clayton, 1908-1972, U.S. legislator.
Powhatan, 1550?-1618, American Indian chief, father of Pocahontas.
Presley, Elvis, 1935-1977, U.S. popular singer.
Priestley, Joseph, 1733-1804, Enlgish chemist.
Porkofiev, Sergei Sergeevich, 1891-1953, Russian and Soviet composer.
Proust, Marcel, 1871-1922, French author.
Ptolemy Greek mathematician and astronomer who lived in Egypt, in the second century A.D.
Pulitzer, Joseph, 1847-1911, U.S. newspaper publisher born in Hungary. He established the Pulitzer Prize.
P'u-yi, 1906-1967, last emperor of China, 1908-1912.

Q

Quanah, 1845-1911, American Indian chief.
Quarles, Benjamin, 1904-, U.S. historian, educator, and author.
Quezon, Manuel Luis, 1878-1944, Philippine statesman, president of the Philippines, 1935-1944.

R

Rabelais, Francois, 1494?-1553, French humorist.
Rachmaninoff, Sergei, 1873-1943, Russian composer, conductor, and pianist.
Raleigh, Sir Walter, 1552?-1618, English colonizer, courtier, and poet.
Ramses II, 1301?-1225 B.C., Egyptian pharaoh 1290-1225 B.C.
Rand, Ayn, 1905-1982, U.S. author born in Russia.
Randolph, A. Philip, 1889-1979, U.S. labor leader.
Rankin, Jeannette, 1883-1973, U.S. legislator; first woman member of the U.S. Congress.

Manuel Luis Quezon

Walter Raleigh

A. Philip Randolph

Jeannette Rankin

Ronald Reagan

Red Jacket

Walter Reed

Hiram Revels

Raphael, 1483-1520, Italian painter.
Rasputin, Grigori, 1872?-1916, Russian holy man and courtier.
Rauschenberg, Robert, 1925-, U.S. painter.
Ravel, Maurice, 1875-1937, French composer.
Rawlings, Marjorie Kinnan, 1896-1953, U.S. author.
Rayburn, Samuel (Sam), 1882-1961, U.S. legislator; member of U.S. Congress 47 years.
Reagan, Ronald, 1911-, 40th president of the U.S., 1981-1989.
Red Cloud, 1822-1909, American Indian chief.
Red Jacket, 1750?-1830, American Indian leader and orator.
Reed, Walter, 1851-1902, U.S. Army doctor who helped discover a way of controlling typhoid and yellow fever.
Rembrandt, 1606-1669, Dutch painter and etcher.
Renoir, Pierre Auguste, 1840-1919, French painter.
Resnik, Judith, 1949-1986, U.S. engineer and astronaut; killed in the *Challenger* explosion.
Revels, Hiram, 1822-1901, U.S. politican; first Black to serve as a U.S. Senator, 1870-1871.
Revere, Paul, 1735-1818, American patriot and silversmith, warned colonists that the British troops were coming.
Reynolds, Sir Joshua, 1723-1792, English portrait painter.
Rhee, Syngman, 1875-1965, South Korean statesman, first president of South Korea, 1948-1960.
Richard I, 1157-1199, king of England, 1189-1199. He was called **Richard the Lion-Hearted.**
Richard II, 1367-1400, king of England, 1377-1399.
Richard III, 1452-1485, king of England, 1483-1485.
Richardson, Samuel, 1689-1761, English novelist.
Richelieu, 1585-1642, French duke, cardinal, and statesman. He was prime minister of France, 1624-1642.
Rickenbacker, Eddie, 1890-1973, U.S. pilot, World War I hero, and airline executive.
Rickover, Hyman, 1900-1986, U.S. naval officer.
Ride, Sally, 1951-, U.S. physicist; first U.S. woman astronaut in space.
Rimsky-Korsakov, 1844-1908, Russian composer.
Rinehart, Mary Roberts, 1876-1958, U.S. author of mysteries.
Rivera, Diego, 1886-1957, Mexican artist.
Robb, Inez, 1901-1979, U.S. journalist.
Robbins, Jerome, 1918-, U.S. choreographer.
Robeson, Paul LeRoy, 1898-1976, U.S. actor, singer, and social activist.
Robespierre, Maximilien François Marie Isidore de, 1758-1794, French revolutionary leader.
Robinson, Edwin Arlington, 1869-1935, U.S. poet.
—Jack Roosevelt (Jackie), 1919-1972, U.S. athlete; first Black to play major league baseball.
Rockefeller, David, 1915-, U.S. businessman, and his brother **Nelson A.,** 1908-1979, U.S. politician and philanthropist; sons of John D. Rockefeller, Jr.
—John D., 1839-1937, and his son **John D., Jr.,** 1874-1960, U.S. industrialists and philanthropists.

Paul Revere

Sally Ride

Jackie Robinson

John D. Rockefeller

Auguste Rodin

Will Rogers

Eleanor Roosevelt

Franklin D. Roosevelt

Rockne, Knute, 1881-1931, U.S. football coach.
Rockwell, Norman, 1894-1978, U.S. artist.
Rodgers, Richard, 1902-1979, U.S. composer.
Rodin, Auguste, 1840-1917, French sculptor.
Roentgen, Wilhelm, 1845-1923, German physicist who discovered X rays.
Rogers, Will, 1879-1935, U.S. humorist.
Roget, Peter, 1779-1869, English lexicographer.
Romanov, Mikhail, 1596-1645, czar of Russia, 1613-1645; founder of the Romanov dynasty.
Rommel, Erwin, 1891-1944, German general in World War II.
Roosevelt, Eleanor, 1884-1962, U.S. lecturer, writer, and diplomat, wife of Franklin Delano Roosevelt.
—Franklin Delano, 1882-1945, U.S. statesman, 32nd president of the U.S., 1933-1945; died in office.
—Theodore, 1858-1919, U.S. army officer and statesman, 26th president of the U.S., 1901-1909.
Ross, Betsy, 1752-1836, American patriot. She was said to have made the first U.S. flag.
Rostand, Edmond, 1868-1918, French dramatist.
Roth, Philip, 1933-, U.S. author.
Rousseau, Jean Jacques, 1712-1778, French philosopher and author born in Switzerland.
Rubens, Peter, 1577-1640, Flemish painter.
Rubenstein, Helena, 1882?-1965, U.S. businesswoman born in Poland.
Rubinstein, Arthur, 1887-1982, U.S. pianist, born in Poland.
Rudkin, Maragaret, 1897-1967, U.S. businesswoman.
Russell, Bertrand, 1872-1970, Welsh philosopher and mathematician.
Rustin, Bayard, 1910-1987, U.S. civil rights leader.
Ruth, Babe (George Herman Ruth), 1895-1948, U.S. baseball player who set the season home run record in 1927.
Rutherford, Sir Ernest, 1871-1937, British physicist born in New Zealand.

S

Saarinen, Eero, 1910-1961, U.S. architect, born in Finland.
Sabin, Albert Bruce, 1906-, U.S. doctor, developed oral vaccine to combat poliomyelitis.
Sacajawea, 1787-1812, American Indian guide and interpreter who accompanied the Lewis and Clark expedition.
Sackville-West, Victoria, 1892-1962, English author.
Sadat, Anwar el-, 1918-1981, Egyptian statesman, president of Egypt, 1970-1981; assassinated.
Sagan, Carl, 1934-, U.S. astronomer, author, and educator.

Margaret Rudkin

Bayard Rustin

Eero Saarinen

Anwar el Sadat

Jonas Salk

Dorothy Schiff

Albert Schweitzer

Mother Seton

Sakharov, Andrei, 1921-, Soviet physicist.
Salinger, J(erome) D(avid), 1919-, U.S. author.
Salk, Jonas Edward, 1914-, U.S. physician and medical researcher; developed a vaccine for polio.
Sampson, Deborah, 1760-1827, American patriot who, disguised as a man, fought in the Revolutionary war.
Samuelson, Paul, 1915-, U.S. economist.
Sand, George, 1804-1876, French writer. Her real name ws Amandine Dudevant.
Sandburg, Carl, 1878-1967, U.S. poet.
Sanger, Margaret, 1883-1966, U.S. social worker, promoted birth control education.
Santa Anna, Antonio López de, 1795-1876, Mexican military and political leader.
Sargent, John Singer, 1856-1925, U.S. painter.
Saroyan, William, 1908-1981, U.S. author.
Satre, Jean Paul, 1905-1980, French philosopher, playwright, and novelist.
Schiff, Dorothy, 1903-, U.S. newspaper publisher.
Schiller, Johann Friedrich von, 1759-1805, German playwright and poet.
Schlafly, Phyllis, 1924-, U.S. opponent of women's rights movement.
Schlesigner, Arthur, 1888-1965, and his son, **Arthur, Jr.,** 1917-, U.S. historians.
Schubert, Franz, 1797-1828, Austrian composer.
Schultz, Charles, 1922-, U.S. cartoonist.
Schumann, Robert, 1810-1856, German composer.
Schweitzer, Albert, 1875-1965, French philosopher and medical missionary in Africa.
Scott, Dred, 1795-1858, U.S. Slave whose suit to gain his freedom was denied in a controversial U.S. Supreme Court decision.
Scott, Sir Walter, 1771-1832, Scottish author.
Sendak, Maurice, 1928-, U.S. illustrator and author of children's books.
Sennett, Mack, 1884-1960, U.S. director of early motion pictures, born in Canada.
Sequoya, 1770?-1843, American Indian who devised an alphabet for writing the Cherokee language.
Serra, Junípero, 1713-1784, Spanish missionary active in Mexico and California.
Seton, Saint Elizabeth Anne, 1774-1821, U.S. religious leader and Roman Catholic saint.
Seurate, Georges, 1859-1891, French painter.
Seward, William Henry, 1801-1872, U.S. statesman.
Sexton, Anne, 1928-1974, U.S. poet.
Seymour, Jane, 1509?-1537, queen of England as 3rd wife of Henry VIII.
Shakespeare, William, 1564-1616, English poet and dramatist.
Shange, Ntosake, 1948-, U.S. poet, novelist, and playwright.
Shaw, George Bernard, 1856-1950, British dramatist and critic born in Ireland.
Shelley, Mary Wollstonecraft, 1797-1851, English author, wife of P. B. Shelley.
—Percy Bysshe, 1792-1822, English poet.
Shepard, Alan, 1923-, first U.S. astronaut in space.

William Shakespeare

Ntosake Shange

George Bernard Shaw

Alan Shepard

Dimitri Shostakovich

Sitting Bull

Margaret Chase Smith

Ch'ing-ling Soong

Sheridan, Philip Henry, 1831-1888, U.S. cavalry general in the Civil War.
—Richard Brinsley, 1751-1816, British playwright and statesman born in Ireland.
Sherman, William Tecumseh, 1820-1891, U.S. general in the Civil War.
Shostakovich, Dimitri, 1906-1975, Soviet composer.
Sibelius, Jean, 1865-1975, Finnish composer.
Silko, Leslie Marmon, 1948-, U.S. author.
Sills, Beverly, 1929-, U.S. singer and opera company director.
Simon, Neil, 1927-, U.S. playwright.
Sinclair, Upton, 1878-1968, U.S. author and social reformer.
Singer, Isaac Bashevis, 1904-, U.S. author, born in Poland.
Siqueiros, David Alfaro, 1898-1974, Mexican painter and muralist.
Sitting Bull, 1834?-1890, American Indian chief.
Skinner, B(urrhus) F(rederic), 1904-, U.S. psychologist.
Smith, Adam, 1723-1790, Scottish economist.
—Bessie, 1894-1937, U.S. blues singer and song writer.
—John, 1580-1631, English explorer and colonist in Virginia, 1608-1609.
—Joseph, 1805-1844, U.S. religious leader, founder of the Mormon Church.
—Margaret Chase, 1897-, U.S. legislator, first woman elected to both houses of Congress.
Socrates, 469?-399 B.C., Greek philospher and teacher, chief person in the dialogues of Plato.
Solon, 638?-559?, B.C., Athenian lawgiver.
Solzhenitsyn, Alexander, 1918, Soviet writer living in the U.S.
Soong, Ch'ing-ling, 1890-1981, Chinese stateswoman; wife of Sun Yat-sen.
—Mei-ling, 1898-, Chinese stateswoman, wife of Chiang Kai-shek.
Sophocles, 496?-406 B.C., Greek tragic dramatist.
Sousa, John Philip, 1854-1932, U.S. composer.
Spencer, Herbert, 1820-1903, English philosopher.
Spenser, Edmund, 1552?-1599, English poet.
Spielberg, Steven, 1947-, U.S. motion-picture director.
Spinoza, Baruch, 1632-1677, Dutch philospher.
Spotted Tail, 1823?-1881, American Indian leader.
Squanto, 1580-1622, American Indian who helped the Pilgrims in Massachusetts.
Staël, Germaine de, 1766-1817, French historian, critic, and essayist.
Stalin, Joseph, 1879-1953, Soviet statesman; dictator, 1927-1953.
Standish, Miles, 1584?-1656, English colonist; military leader of the Pilgrims.
Stanton, Elizabeth Cady, 1815-1902, U.S. early leader of the women's rights movement.
Starr, Belle, 1848-1889, U.S. outlaw.
St. Denis, Ruth, 1877?-1968, U.S. choreographer.
Stein, Gertrude, 1874-1964, U.S. author active in France.

John Philip Sousa

Joseph Stalin

Elizabeth Cady Stanton

Gertrude Stein

Gloria Steinem

Charles Steinmetz

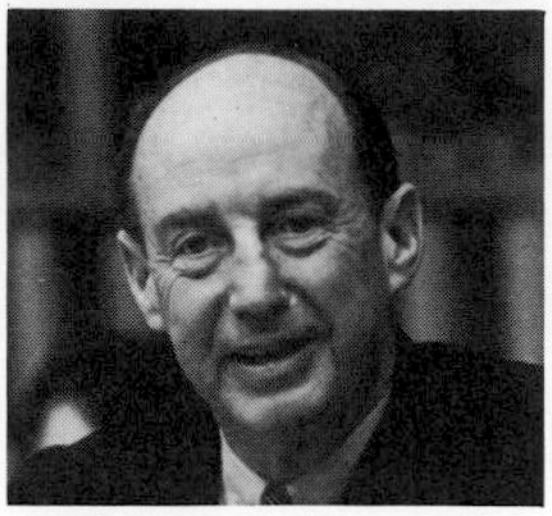
Adlai Stevenson

Harriet Beecher Stowe

Steinbeck, John, 1902-1968, U.S. author.
Steinem, Gloria, 1935-, U.S. feminist and author.
Steinmetz, Charles, 1865-1923, U.S. electrical engineer born in Germany.
Stevens, Wallace, 1879-1955, U.S. poet.
Stevenson, Adlai, 1900-1965, U.S. statesman.
—Robert Louis, 1850-1894, Scottish author.
Stieglitz, Alfred, 1864-1946, U.S. photographer.
St. John, Adela Rogers, 1894-, U.S. journalist, lecturer, and author.
Stokowski, Leopold, 1882-1977, U.S. conductor, born in England.
Stone, Lucy, 1818-1893, early leader of women's rights movement.
Stowe, Harriet Beecher, 181-1896, U.S. writer; author of *Uncle Tom's Cabin.*
Strachey, Lytton, 1880-1932, English biographer.
Strauss, Johann, 1804-1849, and his son **Johann,** 1825-1899, Austrian composers.
—Richard, 1864-1949, German composer.
Stravinsky, Igor, 1882-1971, U.S. composer born in Russia.
Strindberg, August, 1849-1912, Swedish author.
Stuart, Gilbert, 1755-1828, U.S. artist.
Stuyvesant, Peter, 1610?-1672, Dutch governor of colonial New York (New Netherland).
Sukarno, 1901-1970, president of the Republic of Indonesia, 1945-1967.
Sullivan, Anne, 1867-1936, U.S. educator; tutor of and companion to Helen Keller.
—Sir Arthur, 1842-1900, English composer and collaborator with Sir William Gilbert on comic operettas.
Sun Yat-sen, 1865-1925, Chinese revolutionary.
Sutherland, Dame Joan, 1926-, Australian opera singer.
Swift, Jonathan, 1667-1745, British writer and clergyman born in Ireland.
Szilard, Leo, 1898-1964, U.S. physicist born in Hungary.
Szold, Henrietta, 1860-1945, U.S. Zionist leader and founder of Hadassah.

T

Tabei, Junko, 1940-, Japanese mountain climber, first woman to climb Mt. Everest.
Taft, William Howard, 1857-1930, 27th president of the U.S., 1909-1913; chief justice of the U.S. Supreme Court, 1921-1930.
Tagore, Sir Rabindranath, 1861-1941, Indian poet and author.
Tallchief, Maria, 1925-, U.S. ballerina.
Talleyrand, Charles Maurice de, 1754-1838, French statesman and diplomat.
Tarbell, Ida, 1857-1944, U.S. author.
Takington, Booth, 1869-1946, U.S. novelist and dramatist.

Sun Yat-sen

Junko Tabei

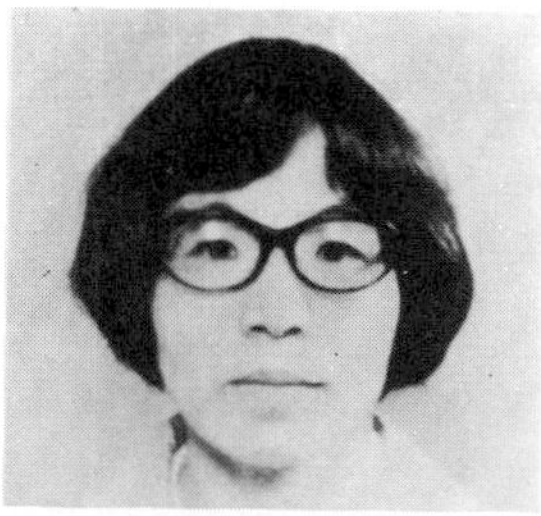

William Howard Taft

Maria Tallchief

Valentina Tereshkova

Margaret Thatcher

Dorothy Thompson

Jim Thorpe

Taylor Zachary, 1784-1850, U.S. general and 12th president of the U.S., 1849-1850.
Tchaikovsky, Peter Ilych, 1840-1893, Russian composer.
Teasdale, Sara, 1884-1933, U.S. poet.
Tecumseh, 1768?-1813, American Indian chief.
Teller, Edward, 1908-, U.S. physicist, born in Hungary.
Tennyson, Alfred, 1809-1892, English poet known as **Alfred, Lord Tennyson.**
Tereshkova, Valentina, 1937-, russian cosmonaut, first woman in space.
Terry, Ellen, 1848-1928, English actress.
Thackereay, William Makepeace, 1811-1863, English novelist.
Thant, U, 1909-1974, Burmese UN official.
Thatcher, Margarete, 1925-, British stateswoman, first woman prime minister of Great Britain.
Theodora 502?-548, Byzantine empress, wife of Justinian I.
Theresa of Avila, 1515-1582, Spanish nun and Roman Catholic saint.
Thomas, Dylan, 1914-1953, Welsh poet.
—Martha Carey, 1857-1935, U.S. educator and suffragist.
Thompson, Dorothy, 1894-1961, U.S. journalist and author.
Thoreau, Henry David, 1817-1862, U.S. author and philosopher.
Thorndike, Edward, 1874-1949, U.S. educational psychologist.
Thorpe, Jim, 1888-1953, U.S. Olympic athlete.
Thucydides, 4460?-400? B.C., Greek historian.
Thurber, James, 1894-1961, U.S. humorist.
Tintoretto, 1518-1594, Venetian painter.
Titian, 1477-1576, Italian painter.
Tito, 1892-1980, born Josip Broz, Yugoslav marshal and statesman; president of Yugoslavia, 1953-1980.
Tojo Hideki, 1884-1948, Japanese military leader.
Tokyo Rose, 1916-, born Iva D'Aquino in the U.S. She broadcast Japanese propaganda to U.S. troops during World War II.
Tolkien, J(ohn) R(onald) R(evel), 1892-1973, English author.
Tolstoy, Leo, 1828-1919, Russian author.
Torquemada, Tomás de, 1420-1498, Spanish cleric; a leader of the Spanish Inquisition.
Toscanini, Arturo, 1867-1957, Italian conductor.
Toulouse-Lautrec, Henri de, 1864-1901, French painter.
Trotsky, Leon, 1879-1940, Russian revolutionary and Soviet leader; assassinated.
Trudeau, Pierre Elliott, 1919-, Canadian statesman, prime minister of Canada, 1968-1979; 1980-1984.
Truman, Harry S, 1884-1972, 33rd president of the U.S., 1945-1953.
Truth, Sojourner, 1797-1883, U.S. abolitionist and social reformer.
Tubman, Harriet, 1823-1913, U.S. abolitionist and spy for the Union during the Civil War.
Tuchman, Barbara, 1912-1989, U.S. historian.

Marshal Tito

Leo Tolstoy

Harry S Truman

Sojourner Truth

Tutankhamen

Mark Twain

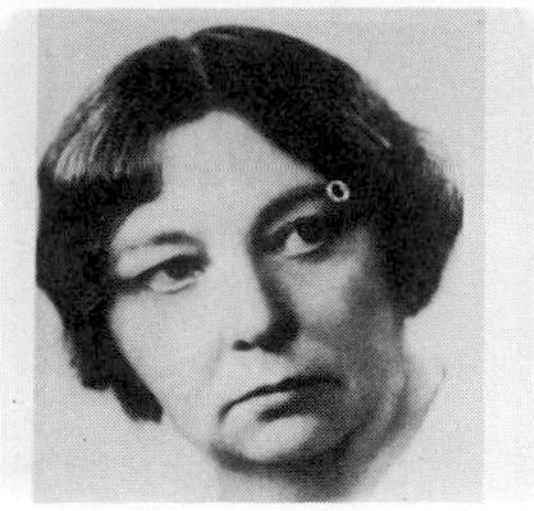
Sigrid Undset

Vincent van Gogh

Turgenev, Ivan Sergeevich, 1818-1883, Russian author.
Turner, Joseph M. W., 1775-1851, English painter.
—Nat, 1800-1831, U.S. slave leader.
Tutankhamen Egyptian king of the 14th century B.C. His tomb was discovered in 1922.
Tutu, Desmond, 1931-, South African clergyman and civil rights leader.
Twain, Mark, 1835-1910, U.S. humorist and novelist. His real name was Samuel Clemens.
Tyler, John, 1790-1862, 10th president of the U.S., 1841-1845.

U

Undset, Sigrid, 1882-1949, Norwegian author.
Updike, John, 1932-, U.S. author.
Utamaro, Kitagawa, 1753-1806, Japanese artist.

V

Van Buren, Martin, 1782-1862, 8th president of the U.S., 1837-1841.
Vanderbuilt, Cornelius, 1794-1877, U.S. railroad magnate.
van Eyck, Jan, 1370?.-1440, Flemish painter.
van Gogh, Vincent, 1853-1890, Dutch painter.
Velázquez, Diego, 1599-1660, Spanish painter.
Verdi, Giuseppe, 1813-1901, Italian composer.
Vergil, 70-19 B.C., Roman poet who wrote the *Aeneid.*
Verne, Jules, 1828-1905, French author.
Vespucci, Amerigo, 1451-1512, Italian explorer for whom America was named.
Victoria, 1819-1901, queen of Great Britain and Ireland, 1837-1901.
Virgil Another spelling of VERGIL.
Voltaire, 1694-1778, French author and philosopher. His real name was François Marie Arouet.
von Braun, Werner, 1912-1977, U.S. rocket engineer, born in Germany.

W

Wagner, Richard, 1813-1883, German composer of operas.
Walesa, Lech, 1943-, Polish labor leader.
Walker, Alice, 1944-, U.S. author.
—Mary Edwards, 1832-1919, U.S. physician and feminist.

Diego Velázquez

Queen Victoria

Voltaire

Richard Wagner

Barbara Ward

Mercy Otis Warren

George Washington

Martha Washington

Walters, Barbara, 1931-, U.S. broadcast journalist.
Ward, Barbara (Lady Jackson), 1914-1981, English economicst and author.
Warhol, Andy, 1928-1987, U.S. artist.
Warren, Earl, 1891-1974, U.S. jurist; chief justice of the U.S. Supreme Court, 1953-1969.
—Mercy Otis, 1728-1814, American patriot, pamphleteer, playwright, and historian; sister of James Otis.
—Robert Penn, 1905-, U.S. author and critic.
Washington, Booker T., 1856-1915, U.S. educator.
—George, 1732-1799, 1st president of the U.S., 1789-1797; commander in chief of American troops in Revolutionary War.
—Martha, 1731-1802, wife of George Washington.
Wassermann, August von, 1866-1925, German physician and bacteriologist.
Waters, Ethel, 1900-1977, U.S. actress and singer.
Watt, James, 1736-1819, Scottish inventor.
Waugh, Evelyn, 1903-1966, English author.
Wayne, John, 1906-1979, U.S. motion-picture actor.
Weaver, Robert C., 1907-, U.S. government official, author, and educator; first Black appointed to a cabinet-level position. He served as secretary of the Department of Housing and Urban Development.
Webb, Beatrice, 1858-1943, British economist and socialist reformer, wife of Sydney Webb.
—Sydney, 1859-1947, British economist and socialist reformer.
Webster, Daniel, 1782-1852, U.S. statesman and orator.
—Noah, 1758-1843, U.S. lexicographer.
Weizmann, Chaim, 1874-1952, first president of Israel, 1949-1952, born in Russia.
Welles, Orson, 1915-1985, U.S. motion-picture director and actor.
Wellington, Duke of, 1769-1852, British general and statesman; defeated Napoleon at Waterloo.
Wells, H(erbert) G(eorge), 1866-1946, English author.
Welty, Eudora, 1909-, U.S. novelist and short-story writer.
Wesley, John, 1703-1791, British clergyman, founder of Methodism.
West, Dame Rebecca, 1892-1983, English author, journalist, and feminist.
—Jessamyn, 1907-1984, U.S. author.
Westinghouse, George, 1846-1914, U.S. inventor.
Westmoreland, William, 1914-, U.S. general in the Vietnam War.
Wharton, Edith, 1862-1937, U.S. novelist.
Wheatley, Phyllis, 1753?-1784, U.S. poet born in Africa.
Whistler, James Abbott McNeil, 1834-1903, U.S. painter and etcher.
White, E(lwyn) B(rooks), 1899-, U.S. author.
Whitman, Walt, 1819-1892, U.S. Poet.
Whitney, Eli, 1765-1825, U.S. inventor of the cotton gin.
Whittier, John Greenleaf, 1807-1892, U.S. poet.

Robert Weaver

Noah Webster

Edith Wharton

Walt Whitman

Oscar Wilde

Queen Wilhelmina

Roy Wilkins

Victoria Woodhull

Wiggin, Kate, 1856-1923, U.S. author and educator.

Wilde, Oscar, 1854-1900, British playwright and author born in Ireland.

Wilder, Laura Ingalls, 1867-1957, U.S. author.

—Thornton, 1897-1975, U.S. novelist and playwright.

Wilhelmina, 1880-1962, queen of the Netherlands, 1890-1948; abdicated.

Wilkins, Roy, 1901-1981, U.S. civil rights leader.

Willard, Emma, 1787-1870, U.S. educator who advocated higher education for woman.

William I, 1027?-1087, Duke of Normandy who invaded England in 1066 and was king of England, 1066-1087. He was called **William the Conqueror**.

William II, 1057?-1100, second Norman king of England, 1087-1100, son of William I.

Williams, Elizabeth, 1943-, Irish pece worker.

—Roger, 1603?-1683, British clergyman in New England. He founded Rhode Island.

—Thomas Lanier ("Tennessee") 1911-1983, U.S. playwright.

—Ted, 1918, U.S. baseball player.

—William Carlos, 1883-1963, U.S. poet.

Wilson, Harold, 1916-, British statesman; prime minister of Great Britain, 1964-1970; 1974-1976.

—Woodrow, 1856-1924, U.S. statesman, 28th president of the U.S., 1913-1921.

Winnemuca, Sarah, 1844?-1893, U.S. social reformer who sought fair treatment for American Indians.

Wodehouse, (Sir) P(elham) G(renville), 1881-1975, English author.

Wolfe, Thomas, 1900-1938, U.S. author.

—Tom (Thomas Kennerly Wolfe, Jr.), 1931-, U.S. author.

Wollstonecraft, Mary SeeSHELLEY, MARY WOLLSTONECRAFT.

Wood, Grant, 1891-1942, U.S. artist.

Woodhull, Victoria, 1838-1927, U.S. businesswoman and journalist; first woman to run for president of the U.S.

Woodson, Carter, 1875-1950, U.S. historian.

Woolf, Virginia, 1882-1941, English novelist.

Wordsworth, William, 1770-1850, English poet.

Wren, Sir Christopher, 1632-1723, English architect.

Wright, Frances, 1795-1852, U.S. journalist, lecturer, social reformer, and abolitionist.

—Frank Lloyd, 1869-1959, U.S. architect.

—Orville, 1871-1948, and his brother **Wilbur,** 1867-1912, U.S. pioneers in aviation who built and flew an airplane in 1903, the first successful flight.

—Richard, 1908-1960, U.S. novelist.

Wu, Chien-Shiung, 1912-, U.S. nuclear physicist, born in China.

Wu Tao-tzy 8th century Chinese painter.

Wycliff, John, 1324?-1384, Enlgish religious reformer. He translated the Bible into English.

Wyeth, Andrew, 1917-, and his father, **N.C. Wyeth,** 1882-1945, and son, **Jamie Wyeth,** 1946-, U.S. artists.

Virginia Woolf

Frank Lloyd Wright

Richard Wright

Chien-Shiung Wu

Rosalyn Yalow

Chen Ning Yang

William Butler Yeats

Andrew Young

X

Xavier, Saint Francis, 1506-1552, Spanish missionary in the Orient.
Xenophon, 435?-355? B.C., Greek historian and soldier.
Xerxes I, 519?-465? B.C., king of Persia, 486?-465? B.C.

Y

Yale, Elihu, 1649-1721, English merchant and college benefactor, born in America.
Yalow, Rosalyn Sussman, 1921-, U.S. medical physicist.
Yang, Chen Ning, 1922-, U.S. physicist, born in China.
Yeager, Charles, 1923-, U.S. pilot who was the first to fly faster than the speed of sound.
Yeats, William Butler, 1865-1939, Irish poet and playwright.
Yee, Chiang, 1903?-1977, Chinese author and poet.
Yevtushenko, Yevgeny Aleksandrovich, 1933-, Soviet poet.
Young, Andrew, 1932-, U.S. politician and civil rights activist.
—Brigham, 1801-1877, U.S. Mormon leader.
—Ella Flagg, 1845-1918, U.S. educator.
—Whitney M., Jr., 1921-1971, U.S. civil rights leader, author, and educator.
Yukawa, Hideki, 1907-1981, Japanese physicist.

Z

Zaharias, Babe Didrikson See DIDRIKSON, MILDRED ELLA.
Zapata, Emiliano, 1879-1919, Mexican revolutionary leader.
Zenger, John Peter, 1697-1746, journalist in colonial America, born in Germany.
Zeppelin, Ferdinand von, 1838-1917, German aircraft designer.
Zhao Ziyang, 1919-, Chinese political leader; premier of China, 1980-.
Zhou Enlai, 1898-1976, Chinese political leader.
Zola, Émile, 1840-1902, French author.
Zoroaster 6th- or 7th-century B.C., Persian religious leader, founder of Zoroastrianism.
Zwingli, Huldreich or **Ulrich,** 1484-1531, Swiss religious reformer.

Whitney M. Young, Jr.

Hideki Yukawa

Emiliano Zapata

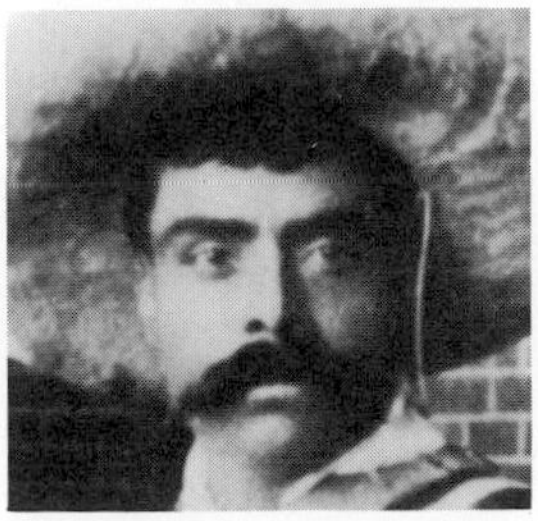

Zhou Enlai

Geographical Section

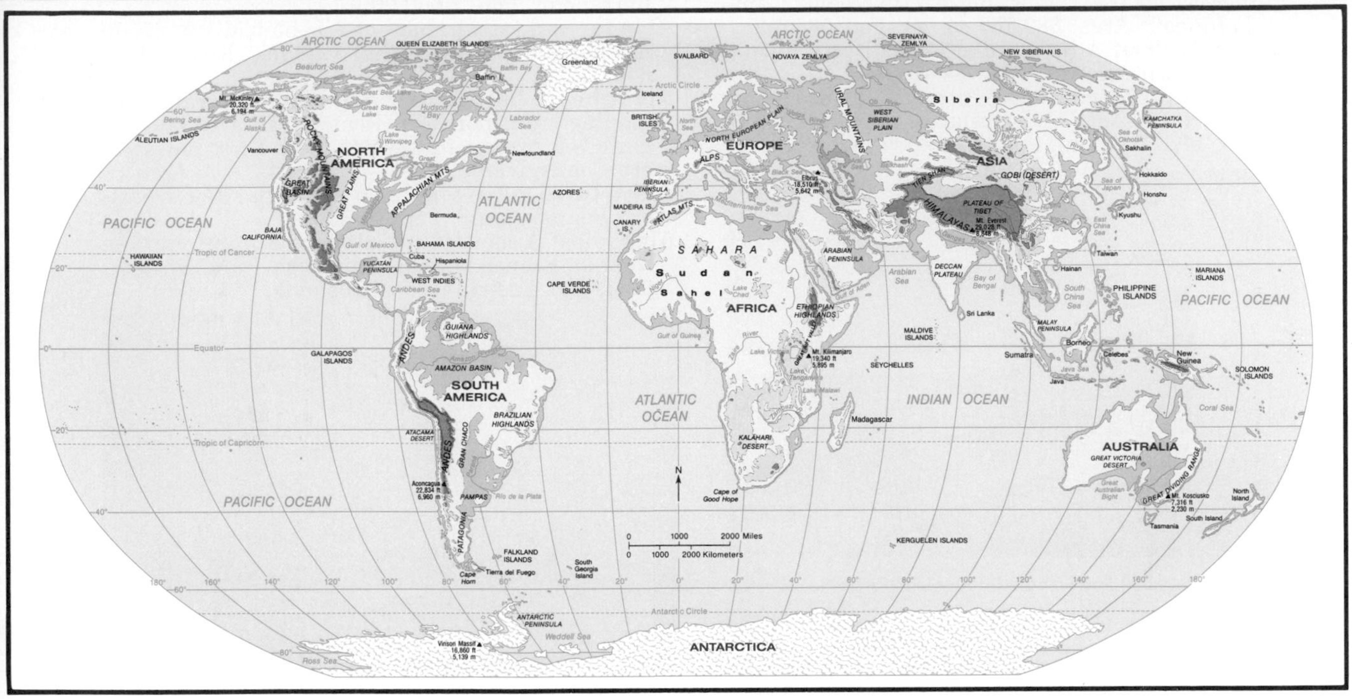

A

A·ba·dan [ä'bä·dän'] A city in SW Iran. Pop. 301,000.

Ab·er·deen [ab'ər·dēn'] A major port in NE Scotland, on the North Sea. Pop. 217,000.

Ab·i·djan [ab'i·jän'] The capital and chief port of the Ivory Coast. Pop. 1,100,000.

A·bu Dha·bi [ä'bo͞o dä'bē] The capital of the United Arab Emirates, on the SE Persian Gulf. Pop. 537,000.

Ab·ys·sin·i·a [ab'ə·sin'ē·ə] An old name for ETHIOPIA.

A·ca·pul·co [ak'ə·po͞ol'kō] A port and resort on the Pacific coast of southern Mexico. Pop. 465,000.

Ac·cra [ak'rə *or* ə·krä'] The capital and chief port of Ghana, on the Gulf of Guinea. Pop. 1,400,000.

A·con·ca·gua [ä'kông·kä'gwä] The highest mountain in the Western Hemisphere, in the Andes mountains in western Argentina. Height, 22,831 ft.

Ad·dis Ab·a·ba [ad'is ab'ə·bə] The capital and largest city of Ethiopia. Pop. 1,423,000.

Ad·e·laide [ad'ə·lād'] A city in southern Australia, on an inlet of the Indian Ocean. Pop. 993,000.

A·den [ā'dən *or* ä'dən] The capital of the People's Democratic Republic of Yemen, a major port on the Gulf of Aden. Pop. 320,000.

Aden, Gulf of The SW arm of the Arabian Sea, between southern Arabia and Somalia.

Ad·i·ron·dacks [ad'ə·ron'daks] A mountain range in NE New York. Also **Adirondack Mountains.**

A·dri·at·ic Sea [ā'drē·at'ik] An arm of the Mediterranean that separates Italy from Yugoslavia and Albania.

Ae·ge·an Sea [i·jē'ən] An arm of the Mediterranean that lies between Greece and Turkey.

Af·ghan·i·stan [af·gan'ə·stan'] A country in SW Asia bordered by the Soviet Union, China, Pakistan, and Iran. Capital, Kabul. Area, 250,000 sq. mi. Pop. 17,375,000.

Af·ri·ca [af'ri·kə] The second largest continent, in the Eastern Hemisphere south of Europe. Area, 11,714,000 sq. mi. Pop. 645,300,000.

A·ga·na [ä·gä'nyä] The capital and chief port of Guam. Pop. 2,119.

The Taj Majal, in Agra, was built by an Indian shah.

A·gra [ä'grə] A city in northern India, site of the Taj Mahal. Pop. 770,000.

A·guas·ca·lien·tes [ä'gwä·skäl·yen'tās] A city in central Mexico. Pop. 360,000.

Ah·mad·a·bad or **Ah·med·a·bad** [äm'əd·ə·bäd'] A city in western India. Pop. 2,548,000.

Ak·ron [ak'rən] A city in NE Ohio. Pop. 225,000.

Al·a·bam·a [al'ə·bam'ə] A state of the SE U.S., on the Gulf of Mexico. Capital, Montgomery. Area, 51,609 sq. mi. Pop. 4,090,000.

A·las·ka [ə·las′kə] A state of the U.S. in NW North America, on the Pacific and Arctic oceans. Capital, Juneau. Area, 589,757 sq. mi. Pop. 535,000.

Alaska, Gulf of A broad inlet of the North Pacific off southern Alaska.

Al·ba·ni·a [al·bā′nē·ə] A country in SE Europe, on the Adriatic south of Yugoslavia. Capital, Tirane. Area, 11,100 sq. mi. Pop. 3,248,000.

State buildings on the South Mall in Albany

Al·ba·ny [ôl′bə·nē] The capital of New York, in the eastern part on the Hudson. Pop. 97,000.

Al·bert [al′bərt], **Lake** A lake through which the upper Nile flows, between Uganda and NE Zaire.

Al·ber·ta [al·bûr′tə] A province in western Canada. Capital, Edmonton. Area, 255,285 sq. mi. Pop. 2,375,300.

San Felipe de Neri, oldest church in Albuquerque

Al·bu·quer·que [al′bə·kûr′kē] The largest city in New Mexico, in the central part. Pop. 367,000.

A·lep·po [ə·lep′ō] A city and ancient trading center in NW Syria. Pop. 977,000.

A·leu·tian Islands [ə·lo͞o′shən] A chain of volcanic islands of SW Alaska, about 1,200 mi. long. Also **the Aleutians.**

Al·ex·an·der Archipelago [al′ig·zan′dər] A large group of islands along the coast of SE Alaska.

Al·ex·an·dri·a [al′ig·zan′drē·ə] The chief port of Egypt, on the Mediterranean northwest of Cairo. It was an ancient capital of Egypt, founded by Alexander the Great. Pop. 2,893,000.

Al·ge·ri·a [al·jir′ē·ə] A country in NW Africa, on the Mediterranean. Capital, Algiers. Area, 919,591 sq. mi. Pop. 25,063,000.

Al·giers [al·jirz′] The capital of Algeria, on the Mediterranean. Pop. 2,000,000.

Al·la·ha·bad [al′ə·hə·bad′ *or* ä′lə·hä·bäd′] A city in northern India, on the Ganges River. Pop. 642,000.

Al·le·ghe·ny [al′ə·gā′nē] **1** A mountain range extending from northern Pennsylvania to SW Virginia. **2** A river in western New York and western Pennsylvania.

Al·len·town [al′ən·toun′] An industrial city in eastern Pennsylvania. Pop. 104,000.

Alps [alps] A mountain system of Europe, curving from SE France through northern Italy, Switzerland, and Austria into Yugoslavia.

The city of Strasbourg in Alsace-Lorraine

Al·sace-Lor·raine [al′sās·lô·rān′ *or* äl·zäs·lô·ren′] A region of NE France that was once part of Germany.

Al·tai Mountains [al·tī′ *or* äl·tī′] A mountain range mostly in NW China and SW Mongolia.

Am·a·ril·lo [am′ə·ril′ō] A city in NE Texas. Pop. 166,000.

The Amazon winds through the jungles of South America.

Am·a·zon [am′ə·zon′] The longest river in South America, flowing from the Andes in Peru eastward across northern Brazil to the Atlantic.

A·mer·i·ca [ə·mer′i·kə] **1** The lands in the Western Hemisphere, including North America, Central America, South America, and the West Indies. **2** The United States.

American Samoa The eastern islands of Samoa in the south central Pacific, a U.S. territory. Capital, Pago Pago. Area, 76 sq. mi. Pop. 37,000.

Amiens [äm·yan′] A city of northern France on the Somme River. Pop. 137,000.

Am·man [ä·män′ *or* a·man′] The capital of Jordan, in the NW part of the country. Pop. 972,000.

Am·rit·sar [am·rit′sər] An industrial city in NW India, holy city of the Sikhs. Pop. 589,000.

An old section of Amsterdam reflected in a canal

Am·ster·dam [am′stər·dam′] The official capital of the Netherlands, in the western part near the Ijsselmeer. Pop. 679,000.

A·mu Dar·ya [ä′mōō där′yä] A river of central Asia that forms part of the boundary between the Soviet Union and Afghanistan.

A·mur [ä·mŏŏr′] A river of eastern Asia that forms part of the Chinese-Soviet border during its 1,800-mile course to the Pacific.

An·a·heim [an′ə·hīm′] A city in SW California. Pop. 241,000.

An·a·to·li·a [an′ə·tō′lē·ə] Another name for ASIA MINOR. Also **Anatolian Peninsula.**

An·chor·age [ang′kər·ij] The largest city in Alaska, in the southern part on an inlet of the Gulf of Alaska. Pop. 236,000.

An·des [an′dēz] A mountain system in western South America, the longest mountain range in the world, extending from Panama to Cape Horn.

St. Julian, Andorra

An·dor·ra [an·dôr′ə] **1** A country in the eastern Pyrenees between Spain and France. Capital, Andorra. Area, 175 sq. mi. Pop. 52,000. **2** The capital of Andorra. Pop. 15,600.

Angel Falls The highest waterfall in the world, in SE Venezuela. Height, 3,212 ft.

An·go·la [ang·gō′lə] A country in SW Africa, on the Atlantic. Capital, Luanda. Area, 481,354 sq. mi. Pop. 8,971,000.

An·go·ra [ang·gôr′a] An old name for ANKARA.

An·jou [an′jōō] A region of western France, in the Loire valley.

An·ka·ra [ang′kər·ə] The capital of Turkey, in the central part. Formerly *Angora.* Pop. 2,316,400.

The U.S. Naval Academy in Annapolis

An·nap·o·lis [ə·nap′ə·lis] The capital of Maryland, site of the United States Naval Academy. Pop. 32,000.

An·na·pur·na [an′ə·pŏŏr′nə] A mountain in the Himalayas in northern Nepal. Height, 26,504 ft.

Ann Ar·bor [an′ är′bər] A city in SE Michigan, the site of the University of Michigan. Pop. 108,000.

An·ta·na·na·ri·vo [an′tə·nan′ə·rē′vō] The capital of Madagascar. Formerly *Tananarive.* Pop. 663,000.

Ant·arc·tic [ant·är(k)′tik] The south polar region.

Penguins thrive in areas touched by Antarctic sea currents.

Ant·arc·ti·ca [ant·är(k)′ti·kə] An ice-covered continent mostly within the Antarctic Circle. The South Pole is near its center. Area, 5,100,000 sq. mi.

Antarctic Circle An imaginary circle at about 66° 33′ south latitude, south of which the sun cannot be seen in the depth of winter. It is the boundary of the south frigid zone.

An·tie·tam [an·tē′təm] A creek in western Maryland, the site of a Civil War battle.

An·ti·gua and Bar·bu·da [an·tē′g(w)ə ənd bär·bōō′də] An island country of the West Indies, in the northern Leeward Islands. Capital, St. John's. Area, 171 sq. mi. Pop. 100,000.

An·til·les [an·til′ēz] A chain of islands that separates the Caribbean Sea from the Atlantic Ocean. Cuba, Hispaniola, Jamaica, and Puerto Rico are called the **Greater Antilles.** The smaller islands extending southeast from Puerto Rico are the **Lesser Antilles.**

An·ti·och [an′tē·ok′] An ancient city in southern Turkey, near the Syrian border. Pop. 85,000.

Ant·werp [an′twərp] A seaport in northern Belgium. Pop. 483,000.

Ap·en·nines [ap′ə·nīnz′] A mountain range that extends the length of Italy.

A·pi·a [ä′pē·ä] The capital of Western Samoa. Pop. 35,000.

Ap·pa·la·chi·an Mountains [ap′ə·lā′chē·ən *or* ap′·ə·lā′chən] A mountain system of eastern North America, extending from SE Canada to Alabama. Also **the Appalachians.**

Appalachian Trail The world's largest continuous trail, running 1,995 miles through the Appalachian Mountains from Maine to Georgia.

Ap·pi·an Way [ap′ē·ən] A highway south of Rome, built by the ancient Romans and still partly in use today.

Ap·po·mat·tox [ap′ə·mat′əks] A village in central Virginia where Lee surrendered to Grant in 1865, ending the Civil War.

A·ra·bi·a [ə·rā′bē·ə] A large desert peninsula of SW Asia, between the Red Sea and the Persian Gulf.

Arabian Sea The part of the Indian Ocean between Arabia and India.

Ar·a·gon [ar′ə·gon′] A former powerful kingdom in NE Spain.

Ar·al Sea [ar′əl] A large saltwater lake in the SW Soviet Union, east of the Caspian Sea.

Ar·a·rat [ar′ə·rat′] A mountain in extreme eastern Turkey. Height, 16,946 ft.

Ar·ca·di·a [är·kā′dē·ə] A mountain region in ancient Greece remembered for the simple, pastoral life led by its inhabitants.

Arch·an·gel [ärk′ān′jəl] Another name for ARKHANGELSK.

Arc·tic [är(k)′tik] The region about the North Pole, including the far northern parts of Eurasia and North America.

Arctic Archipelago A large group of islands in northern Canada between the Canadian mainland and Greenland.

Arctic Circle An imaginary circle at about 66° 33′ north latitude, north of which the sun cannot be seen in the depth of winter. It is the boundary of the north frigid zone.

Arctic Ocean The ocean surrounding the North Pole.

Avenida 9 de Julio in Buenos Aires, named for the Argentine day of independence, is the widest street in the world.

Ar·gen·ti·na [är′jən·tē′nə] A nation in SE South America, on the Atlantic. Capital, Buenos Aires. Area, 1,072,163 sq. mi. Pop. 32,600,000.

Remains of Pueblo Indian homes in Canyon de Chelly, Arizona

Ar·i·zo·na [ar′ə·zō′nə] A state in the SW U.S. Capital, Phoenix. Area, 113,909 sq. mi. Pop. 3,390,000.

Ar·kan·sas [är′kən·sô′] **1** A state in the south central U.S. Capital, Little Rock. Area, 53,104 sq. mi. Pop. 2,388,000. **2** A river that flows southeast from Colorado through Arkansas into the Mississippi.

Ar·khan·gelsk [är·kän′gelsk] A city on the NW coast of the Soviet Union. Also *Archangel.* Pop. 416,000.

Tomb of the Unknown Soldier, Arlington

Ar·ling·ton [är′ling·tən] A county in northern Virginia, site of Arlington National Cemetery.

Ar·me·ni·a [är·mē′nē·ə *or* är·mēn′yə] An ancient country in SW Asia, now divided between the Soviet Union, Turkey, and Iran. The Soviet part is a constituent republic of the Soviet Union.

A·sia [ā′zhə] The largest continent of the world, in the Eastern Hemisphere north of the equator. It is separated from Europe by the Ural Mountains. Area, 17,012,000 sq. mi. Pop. 3,057,400,000.

Asia Minor A peninsula in western Asia, bounded by the Black, Aegean, and Mediterranean seas.

As·syr·i·a [ə·sir′ē·ə] An ancient empire of SW Asia, in what is now Iraq.

A·sun·ción [ä·sōōn·syôn′] The capital and largest city of Paraguay. Pop. 730,000.

As·wan High Dam [as′wän] A large dam on the Nile, forming Lake Nasser in southern Egypt.

The Acropolis of Athens

Ath·ens [ath′ənz] The capital of Greece, in the SE part. Ancient Athens was the center of Greek culture and art. Pop. 3,027,000.
At·lan·ta [at·lan′tə] The capital of Georgia, in the NW part of the state. Pop. 422,000.
At·lan·tic [at·lan′tik] The ocean extending from the Arctic to the Antarctic between the Americas and Europe and Africa.
Atlantic City A resort city on the SE coast of New Jersey. Pop. 40,000.

Atlas Mountains rising behind Marrakesh, Morocco

At·las Mountains [at′ləs] A mountain range in NW Africa, mostly in Morocco and Algeria.
At·ti·ca [at′i·kə] The region surrounding Athens in ancient and modern Greece.
Auck·land [ôk′land] A city and seaport in northern New Zealand. Pop. 890,000.
Augs·burg [ôgz′bûrg′] An industrial and historic city in southern West Germany. Pop. 245,600.
Au·gus·ta [ô·gus′tə] The capital of Maine, in the SW part of the state. Pop. 22,000.
Ausch·witz [oush′vits] A city in southern Poland, site of an infamous Nazi concentration camp. It is now called *Oswiecim.*
Austin [ôs′tən] The capital of Texas, in the central part of the state on the Colorado River. Pop. 467,000.
Aus·tral·a·sia [ôs′trə·lā′zhə] The lands of the SW Pacific, including Australia, New Zealand, New Guinea, and other nearby islands.

Ayers Rock in Australia, the largest monolith in the world

Aus·tral·ia [ôs′trāl′yə] **1** An island continent southeast of Asia. **2** A country including this continent and Tasmania. Capital, Canberra. Area, 2,967,909 sq. mi. Pop. 16,500,000.
Aus·tri·a [ôs′trē·ə] A country in central Europe. Capital, Vienna. Area, 32,374 sq. mi. Pop. 7,555,000.
Aus·tri·a-Hun·ga·ry [ôs′trē·ə·hung′gə·rē] A former monarchy in central Europe, broken up at the end of World War I.
A·von [ā′vən *or* av′ən] A river in central England. Stratford, the birthplace of William Shakespeare, lies on this river.
A·zer·bai·jan [äz′ər·bī·jän′] A region and constituent republic of the SW Soviet Union, on the western shore of the Caspian Sea.
A·zores [ā′zôrz *or* ə·zôrz′] An island group of Portugal in the North Atlantic. Area, 905 sq. mi. Pop. 273,000.
A·zov [ä·zôf′ *or* az′ôf′], **Sea of** An inland sea in the SW Soviet Union, north of and connected to the Black Sea.

B

Bab·y·lon [bab′ə·lən *or* bab′ə·lon′] The capital of ancient Babylonia, on the Euphrates River.
Bab·y·lo·ni·a [bab′ə·lō′nē·ə] An ancient empire of Mesopotamia that was at its height from 1800 to 1500 B.C.
Bad·lands [bad′landz′] A region in SW South Dakota known for its barren, eroded landscape.
Baf·fin Island [baf′in] An island northeast of Hudson Bay, part of Canada's Northwest Territories. Area, 195,927 sq. mi.

Kadhimain Mosque, Baghdad

Bagh·dad or **Bag·dad** [bag′dad′] The capital of Iraq, on the Tigris River. Pop. 3,500,000.

Ba·ha·mas [bə·hä′məz] An island country in the North Atlantic northeast of Cuba. Capital, Nassau. Area, 5,380 sq. mi. Pop. 240,000.

Bah·rain [bä·rān′] An island country in the Persian Gulf east of Saudi Arabia. Capital, Manama. Area, 240 sq. mi. Pop. 483,000.

Bai·kal [bī·kôl′], **Lake** A very deep freshwater lake in the SE Soviet Union. Area, 12,160 sq. mi.

Ba·ku [bä·ko͞o′] A city of the SW Soviet Union, in Azerbaijan on the Caspian Sea. Pop. 1,722,000.

Bal·e·ar·ic Islands [bal′ē·ar′ik] An island group of Spain in the western Mediterranean. Area, 1,936 sq. mi. Pop. 685,000.

Ba·li [bä′lē] An island in southern Indonesia east of Java. Area, 2,905 sq. mi. Pop. 2,470,000.

Bal·kan States [bôl′kən] The countries of the **Balkan Peninsula** in SE Europe: Albania, Bulgaria, Greece, Romania, Yugoslavia, and part of Turkey. Also **the Balkans.**

Bal·tic Sea [bôl′tik] An inland sea in northern Europe between Sweden and the Soviet Union.

Baltic States Latvia, Lithuania, and Estonia, all now constituent republics of the Soviet Union.

Bal·ti·more [bôl′tə·môr′] A city in northern Maryland, on upper Chesapeake Bay. Pop. 753,000.

Ba·ma·ko [bä′mä·kō′] The capital and largest city of Mali, on the Niger River. Pop. 800,000.

The banks of the Ganges River in Banaras

Ba·na·ras [bə·när′əs] A city in NE India, on the Ganges. Also *Benares, Varanasi.* Pop. 800,000.

Ban·dung [bän′do͝ong] A city of Indonesia, in Java near Jakarta. Pop. 1,602,000.

Ban·ga·lore [bang′gə·lôr′] A city in central southern India. Pop. 2,482,500.

A Thai temple in the Royal Palace grounds, Bangkok

Bang·kok [bang′kok′] The capital and largest city of Thailand, on the Chao Phraya River. Pop. 5,175,000.

Ban·gla·desh [bäng′glə·desh′ *or* bang′glə·desh′] A country in southern Asia, bordered by India and Burma. Formerly *East Pakistan.* Capital, Dacca. Area, 55,126 sq. mi. Pop. 112,757,000.

Ban·gui [bäng·gē′] The capital of the Central African Republic, on the Ubangi River. Pop. 474,000.

Ban·jer·ma·sin [bän′jər·mä′sin] A port city in Indonesia, in SE Borneo. Pop. 395,000.

Ban·jul [bän′jo͞ol *or* ban·jo͞ol′] The capital and chief port of Gambia. Formerly *Bathurst.* Pop. 44,000.

Bar·ba·dos [bär·bā′dōz *or* bär·bā′dos] The easternmost island and nation of the West Indies. Capital, Bridgetown. Area, 166 sq. mi. Pop. 300,000.

Bar·ba·ry [bär′bər·ē] A north African coastal region on the Mediterranean between Egypt and the Atlantic Ocean. It was formerly called the **Barbary States** and used as a base by pirates.

Bar·ce·lo·na [bär′sə·lō′nə] A Mediterranean port city on the NE coast of Spain. Pop. 1,753,000.

Ba·rents Sea [bar′ənts] The part of the Arctic Ocean northeast of Scandinavia.

Bar·ran·qui·lla [bär′ən·kēl′yə] A city and port in northern Colombia, on the Magdalena River. Pop. 1,120,000.

Bar·row [bar′ō], **Point** The northernmost point in the U.S., in Alaska on the Arctic Ocean.

Ba·sel [bä′zəl] A city in NW Switzerland, on the Rhine River. Pop. 175,000.

Bas·ra [bäs′rə] A city in southern Iraq, on the Shatt-al-Arab. Pop. 335,000.

Ba·su·to·land [bə·so͞o′tō·land′] An old name for LESOTHO.

Ba·taan [bə·tan′ *or* bə·tän′] A peninsula on the Philippine island of Luzon, site of a World War II battle.

Bath [bath] A city and resort in SW England. Pop. 84,000.

Bat·on Rouge [bat′ən ro͞ozh′] The capital of Louisiana, in the south central part of the state on the Mississippi. Pop. 241,000.

Ba·var·i·a [bə·vâr′ē·ə] A state in southern West Germany. Area, 27,239 sq. mi. Pop. 10,994,000.

Beau·fort Sea [bō′fərt] Part of the Arctic Ocean off NE Alaska and NW Canada.

Bech·u·a·na·land [bech′o͞o·ä′nə·land′] An old name for BOTSWANA.

The Temple of Heaven in Beijing

Bei·jing [bā′jing′] The capital of the People's Republic of China, in the NE part of the country. Also *Peiping, Peking.* Pop. 9,330,000.

Bei·rut [bā·ro͞ot′] The capital and chief port of Lebanon, on the Mediterranean. Pop. 750,000.

Be·lém [be·lem′] A city in northern Brazil, near the mouth of the Amazon. Pop. 780,000.

Bel·fast [bel′fast′] The capital and largest city of Northern Ireland, on the east coast. Pop. 303,000.

Belgian Congo An old name for ZAIRE.

Bel·gium [bel′jəm] A country in NW Europe, on the North Sea. Capital, Brussels. Area, 11,781 sq. mi. Pop. 9,909,000.

Bel·grade [bel′grād′] The capital and largest city of Yugoslavia, on the Danube. Pop. 1,250,000.

Be·lize [bə·lēz′] A small nation east of Guatemala, on the Caribbean. Formerly *British Honduras.* Capital, Belmopan. Area, 8,867 sq. mi. Pop. 179,400.

Bel·mo·pan [bel′mō·pän′] The capital of Belize, in the central part of the country. Pop. 5,000.

Be·lo Ho·ri·zon·te [bə′lō hô·rē·zôn′tī] A city in eastern Brazil. Pop. 2,122,000.

Be·lo·rus·sia [b(y)el′ō·rush′ə] Another spelling of BYELORUSSIA.

Be·na·res [bə·när′əs] Another name for BANARAS.

Ben·gal [ben(g)·gôl′] A region of southern Asia, divided in 1947 between India and Pakistan. The Pakistani territory became the country of Bangladesh.

Bengal, Bay of The part of the Indian Ocean between India on the west and Burma and Thailand on the east.

Ben·gha·zi [ben·gä′zē] A city in NE Libya, on the Mediterranean. Pop. 400,000.

Be·nin [be·nēn′] A country in western Africa, on the Gulf of Guinea west of Nigeria. Formerly *Dahomey.* Capital, Porto-Novo. Area, 43,484 sq. mi. Pop. 4,550,000.

Ben Nev·is [ben nē′vis *or* ben nev′is] The highest mountain in Great Britain, in the Grampians of western Scotland. Height, 4,406 ft.

Ber·gen [bûr′gən] A city of SW Norway, on an inlet of the North Sea. Pop. 209,000.

Ber·ing Sea [bâr′ing *or* bir′ing] The part of the North Pacific between Alaska and Siberia.

Bering Strait The narrow waterway that connects the Bering Sea to the Arctic Ocean.

Berke·ley [bûrk′lē] A city in west central California, on San Francisco Bay. Pop. 104,000.

The center of downtown West Berlin

Ber·lin [bûr·lin′] A city in east central Germany, the former capital of Germany. It is now divided into East Berlin, the capital of East Germany, and West Berlin, a part of West Germany. Pop. 3,095,000.

Ber·mu·da [bər·myōō′də] A group of British islands in the western part of the North Atlantic. Area, 21 sq. mi. Pop. 58,000.

Bern or **Berne** [bûrn] The capital of Switzerland, in the west central part. Pop. 137,000.

Beth·a·ny [beth′ə·nē] In the New Testament, a village near Jerusalem.

Beth·le·hem [beth′li·hem′ *or* beth′lē·əm] An ancient town now in Jordan, southwest of Jerusalem. It was the birthplace of Jesus.

Bhu·tan [bōō·tän′] A small country in the Himalayas, between India and Tibet. Capital, Thimbu. Area, 18,147 sq. mi. Pop. 1,538,000.

Bi·a·fra [bē·ä′frə] A region in SE Nigeria that declared its independence in 1967 and was rejoined to Nigeria in 1970.

Bi·ki·ni [bi·kē′nē] An atoll in the Marshall Islands of the western Pacific. It was the site of U.S. nuclear bomb tests.

Bil·ba·o [bil·bä′ō] A city in northern Spain on the Bay of Biscay. Pop. 435,000.

Bi·o·ko [bē·ō′kō] An island of Equatorial Guinea in the Gulf of Guinea. Area, 778 sq. mi.

Bir·ming·ham 1 [bûr′ming·əm] A leading manufacturing city in central England. Pop. 1,008,000. 2 [bûr′ming·ham′] The largest city in Alabama, in the north central part. Pop. 278,000.

Bis·cay [bis′kā], **Bay of** A large, open bay of the North Atlantic, west of France and north of Spain.

Bis·marck [biz′märk] The capital of North Dakota, in the southern part on the Missouri River. Pop. 45,000.

Bis·sau [bi·sou′] The capital and chief port of Guinea-Bissau. Pop. 112,000.

Black Forest A mountainous forest region in southern West Germany.

Black Hills A mountain range in SW South Dakota and NE Wyoming.

Black Sea A large inland sea north of Turkey and south of the Soviet Union.

Bloem·fon·tein [blōōm′fon·tān′] The judicial capital of South Africa, in the central part of the country. Pop. 231,000.

Blue Nile A tributary of the Nile, flowing 1000 miles through northern Ethiopia and eastern Sudan.

A view along the Skyline Drive in the Blue Ridge Mountains

Blue Ridge Mountains A SE range of the Appalachians, extending from Pennsylvania to Georgia.

Bo·go·tá [bō′gə·tä′] The capital of Colombia, in the central part of the country. Pop. 4,208,000.

Bo·he·mia [bō·hē′mē·ə] A historic region of western Czechoslovakia.

Boi·se [boi′sē *or* boi′zē] The capital of Idaho, in the SW part of the state. Pop. 108,000.

Bo·liv·i·a [bə·liv′ē·ə] A landlocked country in west central South America. Capitals, Sucre and La Paz. Area, 424,165 sq. mi. Pop. 6,876,000.

Bo·lo·gna [bə·lōn′yə] A city in northern Italy. Pop. 433,000.

Bom·bay [bom·bā′] A large city of western India, on the Arabian Sea. Pop. 8,227,300.

Bonn [bon] The capital of West Germany, in the NW part on the Rhine. Pop. 298,800.

Bo·phu·tha·tswa·na [bō′po͞o·tät·swä′nä] A group of districts in northern South Africa that South Africa has declared an independent black homeland. Capital, Mmabatho. Area, 15,610 sq. mi. Pop. 1,740,000.
Bor·deaux [bôr·dō′] A city in SW France on the Garonne River. Pop. 212,000.
Bor·ne·o [bôr′nē·ō] The third largest island in the world, in the Malay Archipelago on the equator. It is divided between Indonesia, Malaysia, and Brunei. Area, 287,023 sq. mi. Pop. 5,153,000.
Bos·po·rus [bos′pər·əs] A strait near Istanbul that divides the European part of Turkey from the Asian part.

Old houses on Commonwealth Avenue, Boston

Bos·ton [bô′stən *or* bos′tən] The capital of Massachusetts, in the eastern part on the Atlantic. Pop. 574,000.
Bot·swa·na [bot·swä′nə] A landlocked country in southern Africa. Formerly *Bechuanaland.* Capital, Gaborone. Area, 231,805 sq. mi. Pop. 1,300,000.
Boul·der Dam [bōl′dər] An old name for HOOVER DAM.
Brah·ma·pu·tra [brä′mə·p(y)o͞o′trə] A river that flows from the Himalayas in Tibet through NE India and Bangladesh to the Bay of Bengal.
Bran·den·burg [bran′dən·bürg′] A former province of Prussia, now part of Poland and East Germany.
Bra·sí·lia [brə·zil′yə] The capital of Brazil, a recently built city in the central part of the country. Pop. 1,550,000.
Bra·zil [brə·zil′] The largest country in South America, on the Atlantic. Capital, Brasília. Area, 3,386,488 sq. mi. Pop. 149,900,000.
Bra·zos [braz′əs] A river that flows southeast through Texas to the Gulf of Mexico.
Braz·za·ville [brä′zə·vēl′ *or* braz′ə·vil′] The capital of the Congo, in the south on the Congo River. Pop. 595,000.
Brem·en [brem′ən *or* brā′mən] An important port in northern West Germany, on the Weser River. Pop. 530,000.
Bre·mer·ha·ven [brā′mər·hä′fən] A city in northern West Germany, on the North Sea. Pop. 133,000.
Bren·ner [bren′ər] A pass through the Alps that links Italy and Austria.
Bres·lau [bres′lou] The German name for WROCLAW.
Bridge·port [brij′pôrt′] A city in SW Connecticut, on Long Island Sound. Pop. 142,000.
Bridge·town [brij′toun′] The capital and chief port of Barbados. Pop. 8,000.
Bris·bane [briz′bən *or* briz′bān′] A major port in eastern Australia, on the Pacific. Pop. 1,196,000.
Bris·tol [bris′təl] A city in SW England. Pop. 391,000.
Bristol Channel An inlet of the Atlantic between southern Wales and SE England.
Bri·tain [brit′(ə)n] Great Britain.

Totems in Vancouver, British Columbia

British Columbia A province of SW Canada with a long coastline on the Pacific. Capital, Victoria. Area, 366,255 sq. mi. Pop. 2,883,000.
British Commonwealth of Nations An association formed of the United Kingdom, its colonies, and nations that were formerly its colonies, such as Canada, Australia, and India.
British Guiana An old name for GUYANA.
British Honduras An old name for BELIZE.
British Isles Great Britain, Ireland, and the nearby smaller islands.

A 16th-century castle on the Mavenne River in Brittany

Brit·ta·ny [brit′(ə)n·ē] A historic region of NW France.
Brno [bûr′nō] A manufacturing city in central Czechoslovakia. Pop. 385,000.
Bronx [brongks] One of the five boroughs that make up New York City. Also **The Bronx.** Pop. 1,194,000.
Brook·lyn [bro͝ok′lin] One of the five boroughs that make up New York City. Pop. 2,293,000.
Bru·nei [bro͞o·nī′] An independent sultanate on the

NW coast of Borneo. Capital, Bandar Seri Begawan. Area, 2,226 sq. mi. Pop. 282,000.

One of the most beautiful streets in Brussels

Brus·sels [brus′əlz] The capital of Belgium, in the central part. Pop. 976,000.

Bu·cha·rest [b(y)o͞o′kə·rest′] The capital of Romania, in the southern part. Pop. 1,976,000.

Bu·da·pest [bo͞o′də·pest′] The capital of Hungary, in the north central part on the Danube. Pop. 2,076,000.

Bue·nos Ai·res [bwā′nəs ī′riz] The capital of Argentina, in the eastern part on the Río de la Plata. Pop. 3,000,000.

Buf·fa·lo [buf′ə·lō′] A city in western New York, on Lake Erie. Pop. 325,000.

Bu·jum·bu·ra [bo͞o′jo͞om·bo͞o′rä] The capital of Burundi, a port on Lake Tanganyika. Pop. 273,000.

Bul·gar·i·a [bul·gâr′ē·ə *or* bo͝ol·gâr′ē·ə] A country in SE Europe, along the Black Sea. Capital, Sofia. Area, 42,858 sq. mi. Pop. 9,037,000.

Bull Run [bo͝ol′ run′] A stream in NE Virginia, the site of two Confederate victories in the Civil War.

Bun·ker Hill [bung′kər] A hill in Boston, Massachusetts. Near it, on Breed's Hill, the first major battle of the American Revolution was fought.

Bur·gun·dy [bûr′gən·dē] A region in eastern France that at one time was a kingdom.

Bur·ki·na Faso [bo͝or·kē′nə·fä′sō] A landlocked country in western African, between Ghana and Mali. Capital, Ouagadougou. Area, 105,869 sq. mi. Pop. 7,980,000.

A temple in Mandalay, Burma

Bur·ma [bûr′mə] A country in SE Asia, between Bangladesh and Thailand. Capital, Rangoon. Area, 261,790 sq. mi. Pop. 40,500,000.

Bu·run·di [bo͞o·ro͞on′dē *or* bə·run′dē] A landlocked country in central Africa, northwest of Tanzania. Capital, Bujumbura. Area, 10,747 sq. mi. Pop. 5,233,000.

Bye·lo·rus·sia [b(y)el′ō·rush′ə] A region and constituent republic of the western Soviet Union.

By·zan·ti·um [bi·zan′shē·əm *or* bi·zan′tē·əm] An ancient city that became Constantinople, the capital of the Byzantine Empire. This city is now called *Istanbul.*

C

Ca·bin·da [kə·bin′də] A small territory of Angola north of and separated from the rest of the country, on the Atlantic between Zaire and Congo.

Cá·diz [kə·diz′ *or* kā′diz] A port in southern Spain, on the Atlantic. Pop. 158,000.

Cai·ro [kī′rō] The capital of Egypt, in the NE part on the Nile. Pop. 12,560,000.

Ca·lais [ka·lā′] A city in northern France, on the Strait of Dover. Pop. 100,000.

Cal·cut·ta [kal·kut′ə] A major city in eastern India, on the Ganges delta. Pop. 9,194,000.

Cal·ga·ry [kal′gə·rē] A city in SW Alberta, Canada. Pop. 672,000.

Ca·li [kä′lē] A city in western Colombia. Pop. 1,654,000.

Cal·i·for·nia [kal′ə·fôrn′yə] A state in the western U.S., on the Pacific. Capital, Sacramento. Area, 158,693 sq. mi. Pop. 27,700,000.

California, Gulf of An inlet of the North Pacific between the main part of Mexico and Lower California.

Cal·la·o [kä·yä′ō] The chief port of Peru, on the Pacific near Lima. Pop. 520,000.

Cal·va·ry [kal′və·rē] The place near ancient Jerusalem where Jesus was crucified.

Cam·bo·di·a [kam·bō′dē·ə] Another name for KAMPUCHEA.

St. John's College at Cambridge, England

Cam·bridge [kām′brij] **1** A city in Massachusetts near Boston, the site of Harvard University. Pop. 95,000. **2** A city in east central England, the site of Cambridge University. Pop. 102,000.

Cam·den [kam′dən] A city in SW New Jersey, on the Delaware River opposite Philadelphia. Pop. 85,000.

Cam·er·oon or **Cam·er·oun** [kam′ə·ro͞on′] A country in west central Africa, on the Gulf of Guinea southeast of Nigeria. Capital, Yaoundé. Area, 183,569 sq. mi. Pop. 10,874,000.

Quebec City viewed across the St. Lawrence River, Canada

Can·a·da [kan′ə·də] A large country in northern North America. Capital, Ottawa. Area, 3,851,809 sq. mi. Pop. 25,700,000.

Canal Zone A strip of land across central Panama that was formerly governed by the U.S. for the operation of the Panama Canal.

Ca·nar·y Islands [kə·nâr′ē] An island group belonging to Spain, near the NW coast of Africa. Area, 2,808 sq. mi. Pop. 1,445,000.

The launch of a space shuttle at Cape Canaveral

Ca·nav·er·al [kə·nav′ər·əl], **Cape** A cape on the eastern coast of Florida where U.S. missiles are tested and spacecraft are launched.

Can·ber·ra [kan′bər·ə *or* kan′ber′ə] The capital of Australia, in the SE part of the country. Pop. 281,000.

Cannes [kan(z)] A resort city in SE France, on the Mediterranean. Pop. 73,000.

Can·ter·bur·y [kan′tər·ber′ē] A historic city in SE England, known for its cathedral. Pop. 127,000.

Can·ton [kan′ton′ *or* kan′ton′] A city in southern China, a river port near the South China Sea. Also called *Guangzhou.* Pop. 5,550,000.

Cape Bret·on Island [bret′ən] An island of SE Canada that forms the NE part of the province of Nova Scotia. Area, 3,970 sq. mi.

Cape Town or **Cape·town** [kāp′toun′] The legislative capital of the Republic of South Africa, in the SW part on the Atlantic. Pop. 1,912,000.

Cape Verde [vûrd] A country consisting of a group of islands in the North Atlantic off the west coast of Africa. Capital, Praia. Area, 1,557 sq. mi. Pop. 339,000.

Ca·pri [kə·prē′ *or* kä′prē] An island belonging to Italy, in the Bay of Naples. Area, 5 sq. mi.

Ca·ra·cas [kə·rä′kəs] The capital of Venezuela, near the Caribbean coast. Pop. 3,247,000.

Car·diff [kär′dif] The chief city and port of Wales. Pop. 282,000.

Car·ib·be·an Sea [kar′ə·bē′ən *or* kə·rib′ē·ən] The part of the North Atlantic between the West Indies and Central and South America.

Stalactites and stalagmites in the Carlsbad Caverns

Carls·bad Caverns National Park [kärlz′bad′] A park in SE New Mexico, known for its limestone caves.

Car·o·li·na [kar′ə·lī′nə] One of the original English colonies in North America, divided in 1729 into North Carolina and South Carolina.

Car·o·line Islands [kar′ə·līn] A large island group in the western Pacific north of New Guinea, administered by the U.S. Also **the Carolines.**

Car·pa·thi·an Mountains [kär·pā′thē·ən] A range of mountains mostly in southern Poland, eastern Czechoslovakia, and Romania. Also **the Carpathians.**

Car·son City [kär′sən] The capital of Nevada, in the western part of the state. Pop. 32,000.

Car·ta·ge·na [kär′tə·jē′nə] **1** A city in NW Colombia on the Caribbean. Pop. 560,000. **2** A Mediterranean port in SE Spain. Pop. 173,000.

Roman ruins of Carthage in Tunisia

Car·thage [kär′thij] An ancient city and state on the Mediterranean coast of Africa, near present-day Tunis. It was destroyed by Rome in 146 B.C.

Cas·a·blan·ca [kas'ə·blang'kə *or* kä'sə·bläng'kə] The largest city and chief port of Morocco, on the Atlantic. Pop. 2,158,400.

Cas·cade Mountains [kas·kād'] A range of volcanic peaks in northern California, Oregon, and Washington. Also **the Cascades.**

Cas·pi·an Sea [kas'pē·ən] The largest saltwater lake in the world. It lies between SE Europe and SW Asia.

Cas·tile [kas·tēl'] A region and former kingdom in north central Spain.

Cas·tries [kas·trē' *or* kas'trēz] The capital and chief port of St. Lucia, in the West Indies. Pop. 47,000.

Cat·a·li·na Island [kat'ə·lē'nə] A resort island off the coast of SW California.

Cat·a·lo·ni·a [kat'ə·lō'nē·ə] A historic region in NE Spain.

Ca·ta·nia [kə·tän'yə] A city and port of eastern Sicily. Pop. 372,000.

Ca·thay [ka·thā'] An old name for CHINA.

Cats·kill Mountains [kat'skil'] A range of low mountains in SE New York. Also **the Catskills.**

Cau·ca·sus [kô'kə·səs] A mountain range in the SW Soviet Union, between the Black Sea and the Caspian Sea.

Cay·enne [kī·en' *or* kā·en'] The capital and chief port of French Guiana. Pop. 38,000.

Cay·man Islands [kī·män' *or* kā'mən] British island group in the West Indies, south of Cuba.

Cedar Rapids [sē'dər] A city in eastern Iowa. Pop. 108,000.

Cel·e·bes [sel'ə·bēz] A large island in central Indonesia, on the equator. Also *Sulawesi.*

Central African Republic A landlocked country in central Africa, north of the equator. Capital, Bangui. Area, 240,535 sq. mi. Pop. 2,990,000.

Central America The southernmost part of North America, including all the countries from Guatemala to Panama.

Cey·lon [si·lon'] Another name for SRI LANKA.

A village in Chad. Villagers raise such crops as cotton, sorghum, rice, cassava, and beans.

Chad [chad] A landlocked country in north central Africa. Capital, Ndjamena. Area, 495,800 sq. mi. Pop. 5,250,000.

Chad, Lake A lake on the border between Chad and Nigeria.

Cham·pagne [shäm·pän'yə] A region and former province in NE France.

Cham·plain [sham·plān'], **Lake** A lake between NE New York and NW Vermont, extending into Canada.

Chang [chäng] Another name for the YANGTZE.

Chang·chun [chäng'chōōn'] A city in NE China, south of Harbin. Pop. 1,600,000.

Channel Islands A group of British islands in the English Channel, off the coast of Normandy.

Cha·pul·te·pec [chə·pōōl'tə·pek'] A hill in Mexico City, site of a U.S. victory in the Mexican War.

Charleston, South Carolina, is famous for its historic homes.

Charles·ton [chärl'stən] **1** The capital of West Virginia, in the western part. Pop. 64,000. **2** A port city in SE South Carolina. Pop. 70,000.

Char·lotte [shär'lət] The largest city in North Carolina, in the south central part. Pop. 352,000.

Char·lotte A·ma·li·e [shär'lət ä·mäl'yə] The capital and chief port of the U.S. Virgin Islands, on St. Thomas. Pop. 53,000.

Char·lotte·town [shär'lət·toun'] The capital of the Canadian province of Prince Edward Island. Pop. 17,000.

The Gothic cathedral of Chartres

Char·tres [shärt] A city in northern France near Paris. Pop. 41,000.

Chat·ta·noo·ga [chat'ə·nōō'gə] An industrial city in SE Tennessee. Pop. 169,600.

Chen·du or Cheng·tu [chung'dōō'] A city in SW China, capital of the Sichuan province. Pop. 3,900,000.

Ches·a·peake Bay [ches'ə·pēk'] An inlet of the Atlantic extending north between the Virginia and Maryland coasts and the Delmarva Peninsula.

Chey·enne [shī·an' *or* shī·en'] The capital of Wyoming, in the SE part of the state. Pop. 47,000.

Chi·ca·go [shi·kä'gō *or* shi·kô'gō] A city in NE Illinois, on Lake Michigan. Pop. 3,010,000.

Chi·chén It·zá [chē·chen′ēt·sä′] An ancient Mayan city in Yucatán, SE Mexico.
Chi·hua·hua [chi·wä′wä] A city in northern Mexico. Pop. 407,000.
Chil·e [chil′ē] A long, narrow country on the SW coast of South America. Capital, Santiago. Area, 292,258 sq. mi. Pop. 12,866,000.

The Great Wall of China

Chi·na [chī′nə] **1** The most populous country in the world, occupying east central Asia. Also **Communist China, People's Republic of China.** Capital, Beijing. Area, 3,691,523 sq. mi. Pop. 1,069,628,000. **2** Another name for TAIWAN.
China Sea A part of the western Pacific along the eastern coast of Asia, divided into the **East China Sea,** between Taiwan and Japan, and the **South China Sea,** between Taiwan and Malaysia.
Chis·holm Trail [chiz′əm] An old route followed by cattle drivers from San Antonio to Wichita.
Chit·ta·gong [chit′ə·gông′] A city in SE Bangladesh near the Bay of Bengal. Pop. 1,388,500.
Chong·qing [chŏŏng′ching′] A city in south central China, on the Yangtze River. Also *Chungking.* Pop. 6,300,000.
Chung·king [chŏŏng′king′] Another name for CHONGQING.
Cin·cin·na·ti [sin′sə·nat′ē] A city in SW Ohio, on the Ohio River. Pop. 370,000.
Cis·kei [sis′kī′] A district in South Africa that has been declared an independent black homeland.
Ciu·dad Juá·rez [sē′ōō·däd′ (h)wä′res] A city in northern Mexico, on the Rio Grande opposite El Paso, Texas. Pop. 567,000.
Cleve·land [klēv′lənd] A city in NE Ohio, on Lake Erie. Pop. 536,000.
Cod [kod], **Cape** A peninsula projecting into the Atlantic from SE Massachusetts.
Co·logne [kə·lōn′] A city in western West Germany, on the Rhine. Pop. 914,000.
Co·lom·bi·a [kə·lum′bē·ə] A country in NW South America. Capital, Bogotá. Area, 439,737 sq. mi. Pop. 31,821,000.
Co·lom·bo [kə·lum′bō] The capital and chief port of Sri Lanka. Pop. 1,262,000.
Col·o·rad·o [kol′ə·rad′ō *or* kol′ə·rä′dō] **1** A state in the west central U.S. Capital, Denver. Area, 104,247 sq. mi. Pop. 3,300,000. **2** A river of the SW U.S. that rises in the Rocky Mountains and flows west and south into the Gulf of California.
Colorado Springs A city in central Colorado near Pikes Peak. It is the site of the U.S. Air Force Academy. Pop. 273,000.
Co·lum·bi·a [kə·lum′bē·ə] **1** The capital and largest city of South Carolina, in the central part. Pop. 100,000. **2** A river that rises in SW Canada and flows through Washington into the Pacific.
Co·lum·bus [kə·lum′bəs] **1** A city in Georgia, on the western boundary of the state. Pop. 181,000. **2** The capital of Ohio, in the central part. Pop. 566,000.
Communism, Mount The highest mountain in the Soviet Union, in the Pamirs of south central Asia. Also *Garmo Peak.* Height, 24,590 ft.
Com·o·ros [kom′ə·rōz′] An island nation in the Indian Ocean, between the African mainland and Madagascar. Capital, Moroni. Area, 838 sq. mi. Pop. 428,000.
Con·a·kry [kon′ə·krē] The capital and chief port of Guinea. Pop. 656,000.
Con·cep·ción [kôn·sep·syôn′] A city in central Chile, near the Pacific coast. Pop. 218,000.
Con·cord [kong′kərd] **1** The capital of New Hampshire, in the south central part. Pop. 30,000. **2** A town in NE Massachusetts, scene of a Revolutionary War battle. Pop. 16,000.
Confederate States of America A league of eleven southern states that seceded from the U.S. in 1860 and 1861.
Con·go [kong′gō] **1** A long river of central Africa flowing through Zaire into the Atlantic. Also *Zaire River.* **2** A country in west central Africa, west of the lower Congo River. Capital, Brazzaville. Area, 132,047 sq. mi. Pop. 2,300,000. **3** An old name for ZAIRE.
Con·nect·i·cut [kə·net′i·kət] A state in the NE U.S., on Long Island Sound. Capital, Hartford. Area, 5,009 sq. mi. Pop. 3,215,000.
Con·stan·ti·no·ple [kon′stan·tə·nō′pəl] An old name for ISTANBUL.
Continental Divide The high ridge of the Rocky Mountains that separates rivers flowing to the east from those flowing to the west.
Co·pen·ha·gen [kō′pən·hā′gən *or* kō′pən·hä′gən] The capital and largest city of Denmark. Pop. 635,000.
Cór·do·ba [kôrd′ə·bə] A city in central Argentina, on the Rio Primero. Pop. 1,000,000.

The Convent of St. Vlacherna in Corfu

Cor·fu [kôr′f(y)ōō] An island off the NW coast of Greece. Area, 227 sq. mi.

Cor·inth [kôr′inth] An ancient city in Greece, noted for its art and luxurious living.
Cork [kôrk] A city in southern Ireland, on an inlet of the Atlantic. Pop. 142,000.

St. Mawes on the picturesque coast of Cornwall

Corn·wall [kôrn′wôl′] A county in SW England.
Cor·pus Chris·ti [kôr′pəs kris′tē] A major port city in SE Texas, on **Corpus Christi Bay,** an inlet of the Gulf of Mexico. Pop. 264,000.
Cor·si·ca [kôr′si·kə] A French island in the Mediterranean, off the NW coast of Italy. Area, 3,367 sq. mi.
Cos·ta Ri·ca [kos′tə rē′kə *or* kô′stə rē′kə] A country in Central America between Nicaragua and Panama. Capital, San José. Area, 19,575 sq. mi. Pop. 2,922,000.
Co·to·pax·i [kō′tə·pak′sē] One of the highest active volcanoes in the world, in the Andes in Ecuador. Height, 19,347 ft.
Cov·en·try [kuv′ən·trē] A city in central England. Pop. 310,000.
Crater Lake National Park A park in SW Oregon, site of Crater Lake, the deepest lake in the U.S.
Crete [krēt] A large island in SE Greece, in the eastern Mediterranean.
Cri·me·a [krī·mē′ə] A peninsula in the SW Soviet Union, on the north coast of the Black Sea.
Cro·a·tia [krō·ā′shə] A former kingdom, now a region of Yugoslavia.
Cu·ba [kyōō′bə] An island country in the Caribbean, south of Florida. Capital, Havana. Area, 44,218 sq. mi. Pop. 10,580,000.
Cum·ber·land Gap [kum′bər·lənd] A pass through the Appalachian Mountains where Virginia, Kentucky, and Tennessee come together.
Cu·ra·çao [k(y)ŏŏr′ə·sou′ *or* k(y)ŏŏr′ə·sō′] An island in the Netherlands Antilles, in the Caribbean off NW Venezuela.
Cuz·co or **Cus·co** [kōō′skō] A city in southern Peru that was the capital of the Incas. Pop. 182,000.
Cy·prus [sī′prəs] An island country in the eastern Mediterranean, south of Turkey. Capital, Nicosia. Area, 3,572 sq. mi. Pop. 696,000.
Czech·o·slo·va·ki·a [chek′ə·slə·vä′kē·ə] A country in east central Europe. Capital, Prague. Area, 49,371 sq. mi. Pop. 15,661,000.

D

Dac·ca [dak′ə] Another name for DHAKA.
Da·chau [dä′kou] A city in SW West Germany, site of a Nazi concentration camp. Pop. 34,000.
Da·ho·mey [də·hō′mē] An old name for BENIN.
Da·kar [dä·kär′] The capital and chief port of Senegal. It is the westernmost city in Africa. Pop. 975,000.
Dal·las [dal′əs] The second largest city in **Texas,** in the NE part. Pop. 1,004,000.

The Omayad Mosque in Damascus

Da·mas·cus [də·mas′kəs] The capital of Syria, one of the oldest cities in the world. Pop. 1,292,000.
Dan·ube [dan′yōōb] A long river flowing from SW West Germany southeastward into the Black Sea.
Dan·zig [dan′sig] The German name for GDANSK.
Dar·da·nelles [där′də·nelz′] A narrow strait connecting the Sea of Marmara with the Aegean Sea. It was once called the *Hellespont.*
Dar es Sa·laam [där′ es sə·läm′] The capital and chief port of Tanzania. Pop. 1,400,000.
Dar·ling [där′ling] The longest river in Australia, in the SE part of the country.
Dav·en·port [dav′ən·pôrt′] A city in eastern Iowa, on the Mississippi. Pop. 103,000.
Day·ton [dā′tən] A city in SW Ohio. Pop. 179,000.
Dead Sea A salt lake on Israel and Jordan's boundary. It is the lowest point on earth.

Dawn from Zabriskie Point in Death Valley

Death Valley A desert valley in eastern California. It contains the lowest point in the Western Hemisphere (282 ft. below sea level).
Del·a·ware [del′ə·wâr′] **1** A state in the eastern U.S., on the Atlantic. Capital, Dover. Area, 2,057 sq. mi. Pop. 644,000. **2** A river separating Pennsylvania and Delaware from New York and New Jersey.

The Jami Masjid Mosque in Delhi

Del·hi [del′ē] A city in northern India, once the capital. Pop. 5,729,300.
Del·mar·va Peninsula [del·mär′və] A peninsula on the east coast of the U.S., between Chesapeake Bay and the Atlantic.
Den·mark [den′märk′] A small country in northern Europe, between the North Sea and the Baltic Sea. Capital, Copenhagen. Area, 16,619 sq. mi. Pop. 5,074,000.
Den·ver [den′vər] The capital of Colorado, in the central part. Pop. 505,000.
Des Moines [də moin′] The capital and largest city of Iowa, in the central part. Pop. 192,000.
De·troit [di·troit′] A city in SE Michigan. Pop. 1,086,000.
Devil's Island A small island off the coast of French Guiana that was once a penal colony.
Dev·on [dev′ən] A county in SW England.
Dha·ka [dak′ə] The capital of Bangladesh, in the eastern part of the country. Pop. 4,470,000.
District of Columbia The U.S. federal district, an area between Virginia and Maryland that is wholly occupied by the capital city of Washington. Area, 69 sq. mi.
Dja·kar·ta [jə·kär′tə] Another spelling of JAKARTA.
Dji·bou·ti [ji·boo͞′tē] **1** A small, desert country on the eastern coast of Africa, between the Red Sea and the Gulf of Aden. Capital, Djibouti. Area, 8,494 sq. mi. Pop. 470,000. **2** The capital of Djibouti, a port on the Gulf of Aden. Pop. 250,000.
Dne·pro·pe·trovsk [dyne′prō·pe·trôfsk′] A major industrial city in the Soviet Union, in the eastern Ukraine. Pop. 1,100,000.
Dnie·per [nē′pər *or* dyne′per] A river in the European Soviet Union that flows south and west into the Black Sea.
Dnies·ter or **Dnestr** [nē′stər *or* dnyes′ter] A river in the European Soviet Union, flowing southeast into the Black Sea.
Do·ha [dō′hə *or* dō′hä] The capital of Qatar, on the Persian Gulf. Pop. 250,000.
Dom·i·ni·ca [dom′ə·nē′kə *or* də·min′ə·kə] An island country in the West Indies, in the Leeward Islands south of Guadeloupe. Capital, Roseau. Area, 290 sq. mi. Pop. 94,000.
Do·min·i·can Republic [də·min′i·kən] A country in the West Indies, on the eastern part of Hispaniola. Capital, Santo Domingo. Area, 18,700 sq. mi. Pop. 7,307,000.
Don [don] A river of the European Soviet Union flowing into the Sea of Azov.
Don·etsk [də·netsk′] A city in SW Soviet Union in the Ukraine, on the Kalmius River. Pop. 1,081,000.
Dor·set [dôr′sit] A county in southern England.
Do·ver [dō′vər] **1** The capital of Delaware, in the central part. Pop. 24,000. **2** A city of SE England on the **Strait of Dover,** the narrowest part of the English Channel. Pop. 34,000.
Dres·den [drez′dən] A city in East Germany, on the Elbe. Pop. 520,000.
Dub·lin [dub′lin] The capital of the Republic of Ireland, on the east coast. Pop. 550,000.
Du·luth [də·loo͞th′] A port in NE Minnesota on Lake Superior. Pop. 93,000.
Dur·ban [dûr′bən] A city in eastern South Africa, on the Indian Ocean coast. Pop. 975,000.
Dur·ham [dûr′əm] A city in NE North Carolina. Pop. 114,000.
Düs·sel·dorf [do͞os′əl·dôrf′] A city in western West Germany, on the Rhine. Pop. 561,000.
Dutch Guiana An old name for SURINAME.
Dutch West Indies Another name for the NETHERLANDS ANTILLES.

E

East Berlin The capital of East Germany. Pop. 1,216,000.

More than 600 statues have been found on Easter Island.

East·er Island [ēs′tər] A South Pacific island governed by Chile, known for its huge statues.
Eastern Hemisphere The half of the earth that lies east of the Atlantic Ocean, including Eurasia, Africa, and Australia.
East Germany The NE part of Germany, now a separate country called the *German Democratic Republic*. Capital, East Berlin. Area, 41,800 sq. mi. Pop. 16,740,000.
East Indies Another name for the MALAY ARCHIPELAGO.
East Pakistan An old name for BANGLADESH.
Ec·ua·dor [ek′wə·dôr′] A country in NW South America, bordering on the Pacific. Capital, Quito. Area, 106,000 sq. mi. Pop. 10,375,000.
Ed·in·burgh [ed′(ə)n·bûr′ō] The capital of Scotland, in the SE part on the Firth of Forth. Pop. 439,000.
Ed·mon·ton [ed′mən·tən] The capital of Alberta, Canada. Pop. 785,000.

The Sphinx at Giza, Egypt

E·gypt [ē′jipt] A country in NE Africa, on the Mediterranean and Red seas. Capital, Cairo. Area, 386,662 sq. mi. Pop. 54,503,000.

Ei·re [âr′ə] The Irish Gaelic name for the Republic of Ireland.

El·ba [el′bə] An island off the west coast of Italy, where Napoleon was exiled in 1814 and 1815.

El·be [el′bə *or* elb] A river in central Europe, flowing into the North Sea.

El·brus [el′brōōs′], **Mount** The highest mountain in Europe, in the Caucasus Mountains in the SW Soviet Union. Height, 18,481 ft.

Elles·mere Island [elz′mir] A large island northwest of Greenland, part of the Northwest Territories of Canada. Area, 82,119 sq. mi. Pop. 120.

El Pas·o [el pas′ō] A city in western Texas, on the Mexican border. Pop. 492,000.

El Sal·va·dor [el sal′və·dôr′] The smallest country in Central America, on the Pacific southeast of Guatemala. Capital, San Salvador. Area, 8,124 sq. mi. Pop. 5,548,000.

Eng·land [ing′glənd] The largest and southernmost division of the island of Great Britain, one of the four countries in the United Kingdom of Great Britain and Northern Ireland. Area, 50,366 sq. mi. Pop. 47,190,000.

English Channel A strait between England and France, connecting the North Sea with the North Atlantic.

Equatorial Guin·ea [gin′ē] A small nation near the equator in west central Africa. Capital, Malabo. Area, 10,830 sq. mi. Pop. 389,000.

E·rie [ir′ē] A city in NW Pennsylvania, on Lake Erie. Pop. 115,000.

Erie, Lake The fourth largest and southernmost of the Great Lakes. Area, 9,940 sq. mi.

Erie Canal A historic waterway in New York State, connecting Albany and Buffalo.

Er·i·tre·a [er′i·trē′ə] A region in northern Ethiopia along the Red Sea.

Es·sen [es′ən] A city in West Germany, in the Ruhr valley. Pop. 618,000.

Es·to·ni·a [es·tō′nē·ə] A constituent republic of the NW Soviet Union, on the Baltic. It was once an independent country.

E·thi·o·pi·a [ē′thē·ō′pē·ə] A country in eastern Africa, on the Red Sea. Formerly *Abyssinia.* Capital, Addis Ababa. Area, 454,900 sq. mi. Pop. 47,700,000.

Et·na [et′nə] A volcano in eastern Sicily. Height, 10,902 ft.

E·tru·ri·a [i·trōōr′ē·ə] An ancient country in what is now west central Italy.

Eu·phra·tes [yōō·frā′tēz] A river in SW Asia that flows from eastern Turkey through Syria and Iraq to the Shatt-al-Arab near the Persian Gulf.

Eur·a·sia [yōō·rā′zhə] The body of land making up Europe and Asia.

Eu·rope [yōōr′əp] A continent that is east of the North Atlantic and west of the Ural Mountains and the Black Sea. Area, 4,063,000 sq. mi. Pop. 676,000,000.

Ev·er·est [ev′ər·ist], **Mount** The highest mountain in the world, in the Himalayas on the border between Tibet and Nepal. Height, 29,028 ft.

Ev·er·glades [ev′ər·glādz′] A swampy region in southern Florida, partly reserved as a national park.

F

Faer·oe Islands [fâr′ō] A group of Danish islands in the North Atlantic between Iceland and Great Britain. Area, 540 sq. mi. Pop. 46,000.

Fair·banks [fâr′bangks′] A city in central Alaska. Pop. 23,000.

Falk·land Islands [fôk′lənd] A group of islands in the South Atlantic, east of southern Argentina. They are administered by Great Britain but also claimed by Argentina. Also **the Falklands.** Area, 4,618 sq. mi. Pop. 2,045.

Far East The countries of eastern Asia.

Federal Republic of Germany The official name for WEST GERMANY.

Fertile Crescent A crescent-shaped region in the Middle East from the Nile delta to the upper Euphrates and Tigris and along those rivers to their mouth. It supported various ancient civilizations.

Fez [fez] A city in northern Morocco. Pop. 852,000.

Fi·ji [fē′jē] An island country in the South Pacific, north of New Zealand. Capital, Suva. Area, 7,055 sq. mi. Pop. 758,000.

Fin·land [fin′lənd] A country in northern Europe, on the Baltic Sea. Capital, Helsinki. Area, 130,130 sq. mi. Pop. 4,990,000.

Finland, Gulf of An inlet of the Baltic Sea between southern Finland and the NW Soviet Union.

Flan·ders [flan′dərz] A historic region of northern France and western Belgium.

Flint [flint] A city in Michigan. A major automobile-manufacturing center. Pop. 159,600.

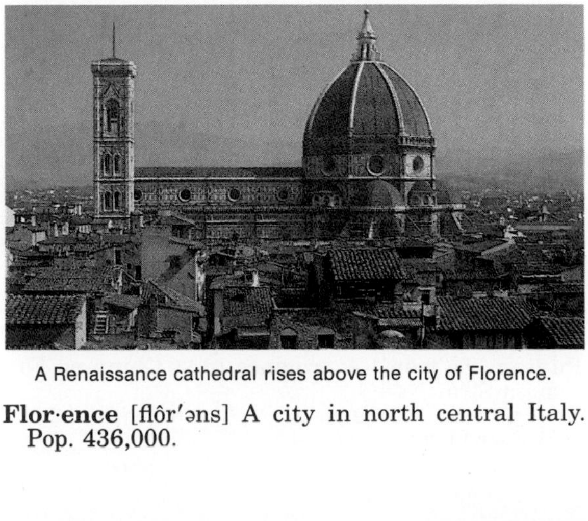

A Renaissance cathedral rises above the city of Florence.

Flor·ence [flôr′əns] A city in north central Italy. Pop. 436,000.

Flor·i·da [flôr′i·də] A state in the SE U.S., mainly on a peninsula between the Gulf of Mexico and the Atlantic. Capital, Tallahassee. Area, 58,560 sq. mi. Pop. 12,023,000.

For·mo·sa [fôr·mō′sə] Another name for TAIWAN.

Formosa Strait A strait between China and Taiwan.

For·ta·le·za [fôr′tə·lā′zə] A city in NE Brazil on the Atlantic. Pop. 1,900,000.

Fort-de-France [fôr′də·fräns′] The capital of Martinique. Pop. 100,000.

Forth [fôrth], **Firth of** An inlet of the North Sea off SE Scotland.

Fort-La·my [fôr′lä·mē′] An old name for NDJAMENA.

Fort Lau·der·dale [lô′dər·dāl′] A resort city in SE Florida, on the Atlantic near Miami. Pop. 149,000.

Fort Wayne [wān] A city in NE Indiana. Pop. 173,000.

Fort Worth [wûrth] A city in NE Texas, just west of Dallas. Pop. 430,000.

France [frans] A country in western Europe. Capital, Paris. Area (including Corsica), 211,208 sq. mi. Pop. 55,813,000.

Frank·fort [frangk′fərt] The capital of Kentucky, in the north central part. Pop. 26,000.

Frank·furt [frangk′fərt] A city in south central West Germany, on the Main River. Pop. 593,000.

Fra·ser [frā′zər] A river that flows mostly southward through British Columbia, Canada.

Fred·er·ic·ton [fred′(ə)rik·tən] The capital of the Canadian province of New Brunswick. Pop. 45,000.

Free·town [frē′toun′] The capital and chief port of Sierra Leone. Pop. 469,000.

French Gui·a·na [gē·an′ə *or* gē·än′ə] A region on the NE coast of South America, administered as a part of France. Capital, Cayenne. Area, 35,135 sq. mi. Pop. 92,000.

French West Indies Seven scattered islands in the eastern West Indies that belong to France, including Guadeloupe and Martinique. Pop. 664,000.

Fres·no [frez′nō] A city in central California. Pop. 285,000.

Fri·sian Islands [frizh′ən *or* frē′zhən] Several groups of islands in the North Sea scattered along the coasts of northern Netherlands, NW West Germany, and SW Denmark.

Japan's Mount Fuji seen in the summer

Fu·ji [fōō′jē], **Mount** The highest mountain in Japan, in southern Honshu. Height, 12,388 ft.

Fu·jian [fōō′jyän′] A province in SE China on Formosa Strait.

Fu·ji·ya·ma [fōō′jē·yä′mə] Another name for MOUNT FUJI.

Fu·ku·o·ka [fōō′kōō·ō′kə] A city and port in Japan. Pop. 1,160,400.

Fu·na·fu·ti [f(y)ōō′nə·f(y)ōō′tē] An atoll in the western Pacific, the capital of Tuvalu. Pop. 2,800.

Fun·dy [fun′dē], **Bay of** An inlet of the Atlantic between Nova Scotia and New Brunswick, known for its high tides.

G

Ga·bon [gä·bôn′] A country in west central Africa, on the equator. Capital, Libreville. Area, 103,347 sq. mi. Pop. 1,110,000.

Ga·bo·ro·ne [gä′bə·rō′nē] The capital of Botswana, in the SE part of the country. Pop. 96,000.

Fantastic lizards called iguanas thrive in the Galapagos.

Ga·lá·pa·gos Islands [gə·lä′pə·gōs′] An island group in the eastern Pacific, west of and belonging to Ecuador.

Gal·i·lee [gal′ə·lē′] A region in northern Israel.

Galilee, Sea of A freshwater lake in NE Israel.

Gal·lip·o·li [gə·lip′ə·lē] A peninsula in European Turkey, between the Aegean Sea and the Dardanelles.

Gam·bi·a [gam′bē·ə] A small country in western Africa, on the Atlantic. Also **the Gambia.** Capital, Banjul. Area, 4,361 sq. mi. Pop. 840,000.

Gan·ges [gan′jēz] A river in northern India flowing 1,500 miles southeast to the Bay of Bengal.

Gar·mo Peak [gär′mō] Another name for MOUNT COMMUNISM.

Gar·y [gâr′ē *or* gar′ē] A steel-producing city in NW Indiana. Pop. 137,000.

Perce Rock, Bonaventure Island, on the Gaspé Peninsula

Gas·pé Peninsula [gas·pā′] A peninsula in SE Quebec, Canada, on the south side of the lower St. Lawrence River.

Gaul [gôl] An ancient country of western Europe, roughly comprising modern-day France and Belgium.

Ga·za [gä'zə *or* gaz'ə] The chief city of the Gaza Strip. Pop. 1,608,000.

Gaza Strip A densely populated strip of land along the eastern Mediterranean northeast of Sinai, administered by Israel since 1967.

Gdansk [gə·dänsk'] A city in northern Poland on the Vistula River. Formerly *Danzig*. Pop. 469,000.

Ge·ne·va [jə·nē'və] A city in SW Switzerland, on the **Lake of Geneva.** Pop. 161,000.

Gen·o·a [jen'ō·ə] A seaport in NW Italy. Pop. 738,000.

George·town [jôrj'toun'] The capital of Guyana, a port on the Atlantic. Pop. 170,000.

The Governor's Mansion in Atlanta, Georgia

Geor·gia [jôr'jə] **1** A state in the SE U.S. Capital, Atlanta. Area, 58,876 sq. mi. Pop. 6,225,000. **2** A region and constituent republic of the SW Soviet Union, on the Black Sea.

German Democratic Republic The official name for EAST GERMANY.

Ger·ma·ny [jûr'mə·nē] A historic region and former country of western Europe, divided into East Germany and West Germany following World War II.

Get·tys·burg [get'iz·bûrg' *or* get'ēz·bûrg'] A town in southern Pennsylvania, scene of an important Civil War battle (July 1-3, 1863).

Gha·na [gä'nə] A country in western Africa on the Gulf of Guinea. Capital, Accra. Area, 92,100 sq. mi. Pop. 14,786,000.

Ghent [gent] A port city in western Belgium. Pop. 234,300.

Gi·bral·tar [ji·brôl'tər] A British colony, fortress, and naval base on a huge rock at the southern tip of Spain. Area, 2.5 sq. mi. Pop. 33,000.

Gibraltar, Strait of A waterway connecting the North Atlantic Ocean and the Mediterranean Sea.

Gil·e·ad [gil'ē·əd] A mountainous region of ancient Palestine, east of the Jordan River.

Gi·za [gē'zə] A city in northern Egypt where the Sphinx and pyramids are located. Pop. 1,670,800.

Glas·gow [glas'gō *or* glas'kō] A major port in SW Scotland. Pop. 733,000.

Glen·dale [glen'dāl'] A city in California, northeast of Los Angeles. Pop. 154,000.

Go·a [gō'ə] A former Portuguese province on the west coast of India.

Go·bi [gō'bē] A large desert in southern Mongolia and northern China.

God·win Aus·ten [god'win ô'stən]; **Mount** Another name for K2.

Golden Gate A strait connecting San Francisco Bay and the North Pacific.

Gol·go·tha [gol'gə·thə] Another name for CALVARY.

Good Hope, Cape of A cape at the SW tip of Africa.

Gor·ki or **Gor·ky** [gôr'kē] A city in the western Soviet Union, on the Volga east of Moscow. Pop. 1,409,000.

Gö·te·borg [yoo͞'tə·bôr'yə] A major port on the SW coast of Sweden. Pop. 430,000.

Gram·pi·an Mountains [gram'pē·ən] A mountain range in central Scotland. Also **the Grampians.**

The Alhambra, a Moorish palace and citadel in Granada

Gra·na·da [grə·nä'də] A city in SE Spain that was the capital of a Moorish kingdom in medieval times. Pop. 214,000.

Grand Banks A fishing ground off the SE coast of Newfoundland.

The Grand Canyon has colorful walls and rock formations.

Grand Canyon A large gorge formed by the Colorado River in NW Arizona.

Grand Cou·lee [koo͞'lē] A dam on the Columbia River, in NE Washington.

Grand Rapids A city in SW Michigan. Pop. 187,000.

Great Barrier Reef A chain of coral formations 1,260 miles long, off the NE coast of Australia.

Great Bear Lake The largest lake in Canada, in the western Northwest Territories.

Great Bri·tain [brit'(ə)n] **1** A large island off the western coast of Europe, the main island of the United Kingdom. It contains England, Scotland, and Wales. **2** Another name for the UNITED KINGDOM.

Great Lakes A chain of five large lakes in east central North America, on the border between the U.S. and Canada. They are Lakes Superior, Michigan, Huron, Erie, and Ontario.

Great Plains A sloping plateau in central North America just east of the Rocky Mountains.

Great Salt Lake A salt lake in NW Utah.

Great Slave Lake The deepest lake in North America, in the SW Northwest Territories of Canada.

Great Smoky Mountains A range of the Appalachians on the border between North Carolina and Tennessee.

The lions of Delos, Greece, date from the 7th century B.C.

Greece [grēs] A country in SE Europe, including the southern part of the Balkan Peninsula and many islands in the Aegean Sea. Capital, Athens. Area, 50,944 sq. mi. Pop. 10,100,000.

Green·land [grēn′lənd] An island belonging to Denmark in the North Atlantic, northeast of Canada. It is the largest island in the world. Area, 840,000 sq. mi. Pop. 56,000.

Greens·bor·o [grēnz′bûr′ō] A city in north central North Carolina. Pop. 177,000.

The Royal Observatory in Greenwich

Green·wich [gren′ich] A borough of eastern London, England. The meridian at 0° longitude passes through the Royal Observatory there.

Gre·na·da [gri·nā′də] An island country in the SE West Indies, north of Venezuela. Capital, St. George's. Area, 133 sq. mi. Pop. 111,000.

Gren·a·dines [gren′ə·dēnz] A chain of small islands in the West Indies.

Gua·da·la·ja·ra [gwä′də·lə·hä′rə] A city in west central Mexico. Pop. 3,000,000.

Gua·dal·ca·nal [gwä′dəl·kə·nal] One of the Solomon Islands, the site of a battle between American and Japanese forces in World War II.

Gua·de·loupe [gwä′də·lo͞op′] Two islands in the eastern West Indies that are administered as a part of France. Area, 687 sq. mi. Pop. 335,000.

Guam [gwäm] An island territory of the U.S. in the western Pacific. Area, 209 sq. mi. Pop. 116,000.

Guang·dong [gwäng′dông′] A province in SE China on the South China Sea.

Guang·zhou [gwäng′jō′] Another name for CANTON.

Guan·tá·na·mo Bay [gwän·tä′nə·mō′] The site of a U.S. naval base on the SE coast of Cuba.

Gua·te·ma·la [gwä′tə·mä′lə] A country in Central America, south of Mexico. Capital, Guatemala City. Area, 42,000 sq. mi. Pop. 9,112,000.

Guatemala City The capital of Guatemala, in the southern part of the country. Pop. 1,250,000.

Guay·a·quil [gwī′ə·kēl′] The chief port and largest city of Ecuador. Pop. 1,573,000.

Guern·sey [gûrn′zē] One of the Channel Islands of Great Britain, in the English Channel.

Gui·an·a [gē·an′ə *or* gē·ä′nə] A coastal region of NE South America, including Guyana, Suriname, and French Guiana.

Guin·ea [gin′ē] A country in western Africa, on the Atlantic between Guinea-Bissau and Sierra Leone. Capital, Conakry. Area, 94,926 sq. mi. Pop. 6,532,000.

Guinea, Gulf of A wide inlet of the Atlantic formed by the bend in the western coast of Africa.

Guin·ea-Bis·sau [gin′ē·bi·sou′] A small country in western Africa, on the Atlantic between Senegal and Guinea. Formerly *Portuguese Guinea.* Capital, Bissau. Area, 13,948 sq. mi. Pop. 929,000.

Gulf States Florida, Alabama, Mississippi, Louisiana, and Texas, the states bordering on the Gulf of Mexico.

Gulf Stream The warm ocean current that flows out of the Gulf of Mexico and northward along the eastern coast of the U.S., then in a northeasterly direction toward Europe.

Guy·an·a [gī·an′ə] A country in northern South America, on the Atlantic. Formerly *British Guiana.* Capital, Georgetown. Area, 83,000 sq. mi. Pop. 807,000.

H

Haar·lem [här′ləm] A city in the Netherlands, west of Amsterdam. Pop. 149,000.

Hague [hāg], **The** The seat of government of the Netherlands, on the SW coast. Pop. 443,500.

Hai·fa [hī′fə] The chief port of Israel, on the Mediterranean. Pop. 223,000.

Hai·nan [hī′nan′] An island of southern China, in the South China Sea east of Vietnam.

Hai·ti [hā′tē] A country in the West Indies, on the western part of Hispaniola. Capital, Port-au-Prince. Area, 10,714 sq. mi. Pop. 6,216,000.

Hal·i·fax [hal′ə·faks′] The capital of the Canadian province of Nova Scotia, a major port on the Atlantic. Pop. 296,000.

Ham·burg [ham′bûrg] A large port city in northern West Germany, on the Elbe. Pop. 1,576,000.

Ham·il·ton [ham′əl·tən] **1** The capital of Bermuda. Pop. 3,000. **2** A manufacturing city in SE Ontario, Canada, on Lake Ontario. Pop. 557,000.

Ham·mond [ham′ənd] An industrial city in the NW corner of Indiana, on Lake Michigan. Pop. 94,000.

Hamp·ton [hamp′tən] A city in SE Virginia, on Chesapeake Bay. Pop. 126,000.

Hampton Roads A channel in SE Virginia at the mouth of three rivers on Chesapeake Bay. It was the site of the Civil War battle between the *Monitor* and the *Merrimac.*

Ha·noi [ha·noi′] The capital of Vietnam, in the northern part. Pop. 2,570,900.

Han·o·ver [han′ō′vər] A city in northern West Germany. Pop. 506,000.

Ha·ra·re [hə·rä′rē] The capital and largest city of Zimbabwe. Formerly *Salisbury.* Pop. 730,000.

Har·bin [här′bin] An important city and river port in NE China. Pop. 3,730,000.

Har·lem [här′ləm] A black and Hispanic community of upper Manhattan in New York City.

Har·pers Ferry [här′pərz] A village in NE Virginia on the Potomac. It was the site of John Brown's raid on a federal arsenal in 1859.

Har·ris·burg [har′is·bûrg′] The capital of Pennsylvania, in the SE part of the state. Pop. 53,000.

Hart·ford [härt′fərd] The capital of Connecticut, in the central part on the Connecticut River. Pop. 138,000.

Has·tings [hā′stingz] A city in SE England on the Strait of Dover, near the site of a battle (1066) at which the Normans defeated the Saxons. Pop. 74,000.

Hat·ter·as [hat′ər·əs], **Cape** A cape that projects into the North Atlantic on a barrier island of NE North Carolina.

Ha·van·a [hə·van′ə] The capital of Cuba, a port on the NW coast. Pop. 2,014,000.

Hotels and apartments line Waikiki Beach, Honolulu, Hawaii.

Ha·wai·i [hə·wī′ē *or* hə·wä′ē] **1** A state of the western U.S. composed of the **Hawaiian Islands** in the central Pacific. Capital, Honolulu. Area, 6,450 sq. mi. Pop. 1,085,000. **2** The largest and southeasternmost island of the Hawaiian Islands.

Heb·ri·des [heb′ri·dēz′] The islands off the west coast of Scotland. Area, 2,596 sq. mi. Pop. 44,000.

Hel·en·a [hel′ə·nə] The capital of Montana, in the west central part of the state. Pop. 23,000.

Hel·las [hel′əs] The Greek name for GREECE.

Hel·les·pont [hel′is·pont′] The ancient name for the DARDANELLES.

Hel·sin·ki [hel′sing′kē] The capital of Finland, in the southern part of the country. Pop. 488,000.

Hen·an [hen′än′] A province in eastern China.

Hi·a·le·ah [hī′ə·lē′ə] A city in SE Florida, site of the Hialeah Park Race Course. Pop. 145,300.

High·lands [hī′ləndz] A mountainous region comprising most of Scotland north of Glasgow and Edinburgh.

Many Himalayan peaks are snow-covered from November to May.

Hi·ma·la·yas [him′ə·lā′əz *or* hi·mäl′yəz] A range of mountains between Tibet and India containing the highest mountains in the world. Also **Himalaya Mountains.**

Hin·du Kush [hin′do͞o ko͝osh′] A mountain range in central Asia, mainly in NE Afghanistan.

Hi·ro·shi·ma [hir′ō·shē′mə *or* hi·rō′shi·mə] A city in SW Japan where the first atomic bomb used in warfare was dropped by the U.S. on August 6, 1945. Pop. 1,044,000.

His·pan·io·la [his′pən·yō′lə] A large island in the West Indies divided between Haiti and the Dominican Republic.

Ho·bart [hō′bərt] A city of Australia on the SE coast of Tasmania. Pop. 180,000.

Ho Chi Minh City [hō′ chē′ min′] A city in SE Vietnam. Formerly *Saigon,* the capital of South Vietnam. Pop. 3,450,000.

Hok·kai·do [ho·kī′dō] The northernmost and second largest of the main islands of Japan.

Hol·land [hol′ənd] Another name for the NETHERLANDS.

Hol·ly·wood [hol′ē·wo͝od′] An area in Los Angeles, California, that is regarded as the center of the U.S. movie industry.

Holy Land Palestine.

Ho·nan [hō′nan′ *or* hō′nän′] Another spelling of HENAN.

Hon·du·ras [hon·d(y)o͝or′əs] A country in Central America between Guatemala and Nicaragua. Capital, Tegucigalpa. Area, 43,277 sq. mi. Pop. 4,800,000.

Hong Kong has a large, busy harbor.

Hong Kong [hong′ kong′] A British colony on the SE coast of China. Capital, Victoria. Area, 403 sq. mi. Pop. 5,590,000.

Ho·ni·a·ra [hō′nē·är′ə] The capital of the Solomon Islands, on the island of Guadalcanal. Pop. 15,000.

Ho·no·lu·lu [hon′ə·lo͞o′lo͞o] The capital of Hawaii, on the island of Oahu. Pop. 373,000.

Hon·shu [hon′shōō] The largest island of Japan.

Hood [hŏŏd], **Mount** An extinct volcano in the Cascades in NW Oregon. Height, 11,235 ft.

Hoover Dam and powerhouse on the Colorado River

Hoo·ver Dam [hōō′vər] A dam on the Colorado River between Arizona and Nevada. Formerly *Boulder Dam.*

Hor·muz [hôr′muz′ *or* hôr·mōōz′], **Strait of** A strait connecting the Persian Gulf and the Gulf of Oman.

Horn [hôrn], **Cape** A cape on an island at the southern tip of South America.

Hous·ton [hyōō′stən] The largest city of Texas in the SE part. Pop. 1,729,000.

Huang [hwäng] Another name for the YELLOW RIVER.

Hud·son [hud′sən] A river in eastern New York, flowing south to the Atlantic at New York City.

Hudson Bay A large inlet of the Atlantic in NE Canada between the Northwest Territories and Quebec.

Hu·nan [hōō′nän′] A province in SE China.

Hun·ga·ry [hung′gə·rē] A landlocked country in central Europe. Capital, Budapest. Area, 35,919 sq. mi. Pop. 10,571,000.

Hun·ting·ton Beach [hun′ting·tən] A city in SW California, on the Pacific. Pop. 184,000.

Hunts·ville [hunts′vil′] A city in northern Alabama. Pop. 163,000.

Huron [hyŏŏr′ən *or* hyŏŏr′on′], **Lake** The second largest of the Great Lakes, between Michigan and Ontario, Canada. Area, 23,010 sq. mi.

Hwang Ho [hwäng′ hō′] Another name for the YELLOW RIVER.

Hy·der·a·bad [hī′dər·ə·bäd′ *or* hī′dər·ə·bad′] **1** A city in south central India. Pop. 2,545,000. **2** A city in SE Pakistan, on the Indus. Pop. 795,000.

I

I·ba·dan [ē·bäd′ən] A city in SW Nigeria near Lagos. Pop. 1,060,000.

I·be·ri·a [ī·bir′ē·ə] A peninsula of SW Europe occupied by Spain and Portugal. Also **Iberian Peninsula.**

Ice·land [īs′lənd] A country occupying a large island in the North Atlantic east of Greenland. Capital, Reykjavík. Area, 39,769 sq. mi. Pop. 251,000.

I·da·ho [ī′də·hō′] A state in the NW U.S. Capital, Boise. Area, 83,557 sq. mi. Pop. 998,000.

Ijs·sel·meer [ī′səl·mâr′] A freshwater lake in NW Netherlands, separated from the North Sea by a dike.

Il·i·um [il′ē·əm] Another name for TROY.

I·llam·pu [ē·yäm′pōō] A mountain in the Andes in western Bolivia. Height, 21,490 ft.

Il·li·nois [il′ə·noi′] A state in the central U.S., touching on Lake Michigan. Capital, Springfield. Area, 56,400 sq. mi. Pop. 11,590,000.

In·de·pend·ence [in′di·pen′dəns] A city in western Missouri, east of Kansas City. Pop. 113,000.

In·di·a [in′dē·ə] **1** A country in southern Asia between the Arabian Sea and the Bay of Bengal. Capital, New Delhi. Area, 1,269,346 sq. mi. Pop. 824,700,000. **2** A large peninsula or subcontinent of southern Asia that includes India, Pakistan, and Bangladesh.

In·di·an·a [in′dē·an′ə] A state in the east central U.S., between Illinois and Ohio. Capital, Indianapolis. Area, 36,291 sq. mi. Pop. 5,531,000.

In·di·an·ap·o·lis [in′dē·ə·nap′ə·lis] The capital of Indiana, in the central part. Pop. 720,000.

Indian Ocean An ocean east of Africa, west of Australia, and south of Asia.

In·dies [in′dēz] **1** The East Indies. **2** The West Indies.

In·do·chi·na [in′dō·chī′nə] A peninsula of SE Asia east of India and south of China and including the Malay Peninsula.

The Barong dance performed in Bali, Indonesia

In·do·ne·sia [in′də·nē′zhə] A country of SE Asia that includes over 13,500 islands of the Malay Archipelago and the western part of New Guinea. Capital, Jakarta. Area, 788,425 sq. mi. Pop. 182,400,000.

In·dus [in′dəs] A river rising in Tibet, flowing through Pakistan, emptying into Arabian Sea.

Io·ni·a [ī·ō′nē·ə] A colony of ancient Greece on the western coast of Asia Minor.

I·o·ni·an Sea [ī·ō′nē·ən] Part of the Mediterranean Sea between Italy and Greece.

I·o·wa [ī′ə·wə] A state in the central U.S. Capital, Des Moines. Area, 56,290 sq. mi. Pop. 2,834,000.

I·ran [i·ran′ *or* ē·rän′] A country in SW Asia with coastlines on the Persian Gulf and the Caspian Sea. Formerly *Persia.* Capital, Teheran. Area, 636,296 sq. mi. Pop. 51,900,000.

I·raq [i·rak′ *or* ē·räk′] A country in SW Asia between Iran and Saudi Arabia. Capital, Baghdad. Area, 167,925 sq. mi. Pop. 17,610,000.

Ire·land [īr′lənd] **1** A large island in the North Atlantic, the westernmost of the British Isles. It contains the country of Ireland and the smaller Northern Ireland in the northeast. **2** A country occupying most of this island. Capital, Dublin. Area, 27,136 sq. mi. Pop. 3,734,000.

Irish Sea The part of the North Atlantic separating Ireland from Great Britain.

Ir·kutsk [ir·ko͞otsk′] A city in the SE Soviet Union near Lake Baikal. Pop. 609,000.
Ir·ra·wad·dy [ir′ə·wod′ē] A river flowing 1,250 miles through Burma into the Bay of Bengal.
Is·lam·a·bad [is·läm′ə·bäd′] The capital of Pakistan, in the northern part. Pop. 201,000.
Is·ra·el [iz′rē·əl] A country in SW Asia, on the Mediterranean Sea. Capital, Jerusalem. Area, 8,019 sq. mi. Pop. 4,477,000.

The Blue Mosque in Istanbul

Is·tan·bul [is′tan·bo͞ol *or* is′täm·bo͞ol′] A city in NW Turkey, on both sides of the Bosporus. Formerly *Constantinople*. Pop. 5,858,600.
It·a·ly [it′ə·lē] A country in southern Europe that includes the **Italian Peninsula** and the islands of Sardinia and Sicily. Capital, Rome. Area, 116,314 sq. mi. Pop. 57,439,000.
Ith·a·ca [ith′ə·kə] A small island near the west coast of Greece, said to have been the home of Odysseus.
Ivory Coast A country in western Africa, on the Gulf of Guinea west of Ghana. Capital, Abidjan. Area, 124,504 sq. mi. Pop. 11,798,000.
Iz·mir [iz′mir] A city in western Turkey, on the Aegean Sea. Formerly *Smyrna*. Pop. 2,316,800.

J

Jack·son [jak′sən] The capital of Mississippi, in the central part. Pop. 208,000.
Jack·son·ville [jak′sən·vil′] The largest city in Florida, in the NE part. Pop. 610,000.
Jaf·fa [jaf′ə] An ancient city in Israel that became part of Tel Aviv in 1950.

The Parliament Building in Jakarta

Ja·kar·ta [jə·kär′tə] The capital and largest city of Indonesia, on the NW coast of Java. Formerly *Batavia*. Pop. 7,636,000.
Ja·mai·ca [jə·mā′kə] An island country in the West Indies, in the Caribbean south of Cuba. Capital, Kingston. Area, 4,244 sq. mi. Pop. 2,473,000.
James·town [jāmz′toun′] A restored village in SE Virginia. It was the first permanent English settlement in America (1607).
Ja·pan [jə·pan′] A country of eastern Asia made up of four large and many smaller islands east of the mainland. Capital, Tokyo. Area, 145,834 sq. mi. Pop. 123,235,000.
Japan, Sea of An arm of the Pacific Ocean between Japan and Korea and the Soviet Union.
Ja·va [jä′və *or* jav′ə] The most populous island of Indonesia, south of Borneo. Area, 52,000 sq. mi. Pop. 75,000,000.
Jef·fer·son City [jef′ər·sən] The capital of Missouri, in the south central part. Pop. 34,000.
Jer·i·cho [jer′ə·kō′] A village near the Dead Sea in a disputed area between Israel and Jordan, site of an important ancient city.
Jer·sey [jûr′zē] The largest of the Channel Islands of Great Britain. Area, 45 sq. mi.
Jersey City A city in NE New Jersey. Pop. 219,000.

The sacred Dome of the Rock in Jerusalem

Je·ru·sa·lem [jə·ro͞o′sə·ləm] An ancient city of Palestine that is the capital of modern Israel. The eastern portion of the city was seized by Israel from Jordan in 1967. Pop. 468,400.
Jiang·su [jē·äng′so͞o′] A province in eastern China on the Yellow Sea.
Jid·da [jid′də] A city in west central Saudi Arabia on the Red Sea. Pop. 1,210,000.
Jo·han·nes·burg [jō·han′is·bûrg′] A city in NE South Africa. Pop. 1,609,000.
Jor·dan [jôr′dən] **1** A country in SW Asia between Saudi Arabia and Israel. Capital, Amman. Area, 37,378 sq. mi. Pop. 3,500,000. **2** A river that flows south through NE Israel and NW Jordan into the Dead Sea.
Juá·rez [(h)wä′res] Another name for CIUDAD JUÁREZ.
Ju·de·a or **Ju·dae·a** [jo͞o·dē′ə] The southern part of ancient Palestine.
Ju·neau [jo͞o′nō′] The capital of Alaska, in the SE part on an inlet of the Pacific. Pop. 20,000.
Jung·frau [yo͝ong′frou′] A mountain in the Alps of south central Switzerland. Height, 13,653 ft.
Jut·land [jut′lənd] A peninsula of northern Europe occupied by Denmark and northern West Germany.

K

K2 [kā′to͞o′] The second highest mountain in the world, in the NW Himalayas on the border between Pakistan and China. Also *Mt. Godwin Austen*. Height, 28,250 ft.

Ka·bul [kä'bo͝ol] The capital and largest city of Afghanistan, in the eastern part. Pop. 915,000.

Ka·la·ha·ri Desert [kä'lə·här'ə] An arid desert area in SW Africa. Area, 200,000 sq. mi.

Kal·a·ma·zoo [kal'ə·mə·zo͞o'] A city in SW Michigan. Pop. 80,000.

Ka·li·nin·grad [kə·lē'nin·grad'] A city in the western Soviet Union, on the Baltic. Pop. 394,000.

Kam·chat·ka Peninsula [kam·chat'kə] A peninsula of the extreme eastern Soviet Union, between the Bering Sea and the Sea of Okhotsk.

Kam·pa·la [käm·pä'lə] The capital and largest city of Uganda, on Lake Victoria. Pop. 459,000.

Temples in the jungle ruins of Angkor Wat, Kampuchea

Kam·pu·che·a [kam'po͞o·chē'ə] A country in SE Asia between Vietnam and Thailand. Also *Cambodia*. Capital, Phnom Penh. Area, 69,898 sq. mi. Pop. 6,750,000.

Kan·chen·jun·ga [kän'chən·jo͝ong'gə] The third highest mountain in the world, in the Himalayas on the Nepal-Sikkim border. Height, 28,208 ft.

Kan·pur [kän'pòòr] A city in north central India on the Ganges River. Pop. 1,639,100.

Kan·sas [kan'zəs] A state in the central U.S. Capital, Topeka. Area, 82,264 sq. mi. Pop. 2,476,000.

Kansas City 1 A city in western Missouri. Pop. 441,000. 2 A city in NE Kansas. Pop. 161,000.

Ka·ra·chi [kə·rä'chē] A city in southern Pakistan on the Arabian Sea. Pop. 5,208,100.

Ka·ri·ba [kə·rē'bə], **Lake** A lake on the boundary between Zambia and Zimbabwe.

Mogul Gardens in the Vale of Kashmir, one of India's most beautiful areas

Kash·mir [kash'mir' *or* kash·mir'] A mountainous region in northern India and NE Pakistan.

Ka·tan·ga [kə·tang'gə *or* kə·täng'gə] A region in SE Zaire that sought independence in the 1960's.

Kat·man·du [kat'man·do͞o'] The capital and largest city of Nepal. Pop. 393,500.

Ka·to·wi·ce [kä'tə·vēt'sə] An industrial city in southern Poland. Pop. 394,600.

Kau·nas [kou'näs] A city of the western Soviet Union, in Lithuania. Pop. 417,000.

Ka·zakh·stan [kə·zäk'stan'] A vast region and constituent republic of the central Soviet Union, between the Caspian Sea and China.

Ka·zan [kə·zän'] A historic Tatar city, in the western Soviet Union on the Volga River. Pop. 1,068,000.

Kent [kent] A county in SE England.

Horses feeding on Kentucky bluegrass

Ken·tuck·y [kən·tuk'ē] A state in the east central U.S. Capital, Frankfort. Area, 40,395 sq. mi. Pop. 3,729,000.

Ken·ya [ken'yə *or* kēn'yə] A country in east central Africa, on the Indian Ocean. Capital, Nairobi. Area, 224,961 sq. mi. Pop. 23,450,000.

Kenya, Mount A mountain in Kenya near the equator. Height, 17,058 ft.

Key West A city in Florida.

Khar·kov [kär'kôf *or* kär'kôv] A city in the western Soviet Union, in the NE Ukraine. Pop. 1,567,000.

Khar·toum [kär·to͞om'] The capital of Sudan, in the NE part on the Nile. Pop. 476,000.

Khy·ber Pass [kī'bər] A mountain pass connecting Pakistan and Afghanistan.

Kiel [kēl] A city in northern West Germany. Pop. 245,000.

Ki·ev [kē'ef *or* kē'ev] A city of the western Soviet Union, the capital of the Ukraine. Pop. 2,495,000.

Ki·ga·li [kē·gä'lē] The capital of Rwanda, in the central part of the country. Pop. 150,000.

Mount Kilimanjaro is an extinct volcano.

Kil·i·man·ja·ro [kil'ə·mən·jär'ō], **Mount** The highest mountain in Africa, in NE Tanzania. Height, 19,340 ft.

Kim·ber·ley [kim'bər·lē] A city and diamond-mining center in central South Africa. Pop. 145,000.

Kings·ton [kingz'tən *or* king'stən] The capital and chief port of Jamaica. Pop. 132,000.

Kings·town [kingz′toun′] The capital of Saint Vincent and the Grenadines. Pop. 34,000.
Kin·sha·sa [kin·shä′sə] The capital and largest city of Zaire, in the western part on the Congo River. Formerly *Leopoldville.* Pop. 2,653,500.
Kir·ghi·zi·a or **Kir·gi·zi·a** [kir·gē′z(h)ē·ə] A region and constituent republic of the south central Soviet Union, on the Chinese border.
Ki·ri·ba·ti [kir′ə·bas′] A country consisting of many islands in the central Pacific south of Hawaii. Capital, Tarawa. Area, 278 sq. mi. Pop. 65,000.
Kitch·e·ner [kich′ə·nər] A city in southern Ontario, Canada. Pop. 311,000.
Kit·ty Hawk [kit′ē hôk′] A village in NE North Carolina, the site of Wilbur and Orville Wright's first successful airplane flight (1903).
Klon·dike [klon′dīk′] An area in the Yukon Territory where gold was discovered in 1896.
Knox·ville [noks′vil′] A city in eastern Tennessee. Pop. 173,000.
Ko·be [kō′bē] A city on the southern coast of Honshu in Japan. Pop. 1,410,000.
Ko·di·ak [ko′dē·ak′] An island in southern Alaska in the Gulf of Alaska. Area 3,465 sq. mi.
Ko·ly·ma [kə·lē′mə] A river of the extreme eastern Soviet Union, flowing about 1,335 miles north to the Arctic Ocean.
Ko·re·a [kə·rē′ə *or* kô·rē′ə] A peninsula in eastern Asia, south of NE China. It is divided into two countries, North Korea and South Korea. Also **Korean Peninsula.**
Krak·a·to·a [krak′ə·tō′ə] A small island in Indonesia between Sumatra and Java. It was the site of an enormous volcanic explosion in 1883.
Kra·kow [krak′ou *or* krä′ko͝of] A city in south central Poland on the Vistula River. Pop. 740,000.
Kua·la Lum·pur [kwä′lə lo͝om′po͝or′] The capital and largest city of Malaysia, on the Malay Peninsula. Pop. 1,000,000.
Kurd·i·stan [kûr′di·stan′] A region in eastern Turkey, NE Iraq, and NW Iran.
Ku·ril Islands [k(y)o͝or′ēl′ *or* k(y)o͝o·rēl′] A group of islands in the extreme eastern Soviet Union, in the Pacific northeast of Japan. Area, 3,960 sq. mi.
Ku·wait [ko͞o·wāt′] **1** A country in SW Asia, on the Persian Gulf between Iraq and Saudi Arabia. Capital, Kuwait. Area, 7,780 sq. mi. Pop. 2,000,000. **2** The capital and chief port of Kuwait. Pop. 61,000.
Kwang·tung [kwang′tung′ *or* kwäng′to͝ong′] Another spelling of GUANGDONG.

Kyoto's Golden Pavilion is situated on a small lake.

Kyo·to [kyō′tō] A city on southern Honshu in Japan. Pop. 1,479,000.
Kyu·shu [kyo͞o′sho͞o] The southernmost main island of Japan.

L

Lab·ra·dor [lab′rə·dôr′] **1** A peninsula of eastern Canada between the Atlantic and Hudson Bay. **2** The eastern part of this peninsula, forming the mainland territory of Newfoundland province, Canada.
Lac·e·dae·mon [las′i·dē′mən] Another name for SPARTA.
Lad·o·ga [lä′də·gə], **Lake** A lake in the NW Soviet Union near Leningrad.
La·gos [lā′gäs *or* lä′gōs] The capital and largest city of Nigeria, in the SW part. Pop. 1,097,000.
La·hore [lə·hôr′] A city in eastern Pakistan. Pop. 2,952,700.
Lake District An area in NW England noted for its scenic beauty.
La Man·cha [lä män′chə] An arid region in south central Spain.
Lan·chow [län′jō′] Another spelling of LANZHOU.
Land's End A cape at the SW tip of England.
Lan·sing [lan′sing] The capital of Michigan, in the south central part. Pop. 129,000.
Lan·zhou [län′jō′] A city in north central China. Pop. 1,350,000.
La·os [lous *or* lä′ōs] A country in SE Asia, in Indochina west of Vietnam. Capital, Vientiane. Area, 91,429 sq. mi. Pop. 4,080,000.
La Paz [lä päs′] The administrative capital of Bolivia, in the western part. Pop. 992,000.

Lapp children in native costumes at Hammerfest, Norway.

Lap·land [lap′land′] A region of northern Norway, northern Sweden, northern Finland, and the extreme NW Soviet Union.
La Pla·ta [lä plä′tä] **1** A city in eastern Argentina on the Río de la Plata. Pop. 561,000. **2** See RÍO DE LA PLATA.
Las Ve·gas [läs vā′gəs] A resort city in SE Nevada. Pop. 192,000.
Latin America The countries in the Western Hemisphere south of the U.S.
Lat·vi·a [lat′vē·ə] A constituent republic of the NW Soviet Union, on the Baltic. It was once an independent country.
Lau·ren·tian Mountains [lô·ren′shən] A mountain range in southern Quebec, Canada.
Lau·sanne [lō·zan′] A city in western Switzerland, on Lake Geneva. Pop. 137,000.
La·val [lə·val′] A city near Montreal in southern Quebec. Pop. 284,000.
Leb·a·non [leb′ə·nən] A country of SW Asia, on the Mediterranean north of Israel. Capital, Beirut. Area, 4,015 sq. mi. Pop. 2,852,000.
Leeds [lēdz] A city in north central England. Pop. 711,000.

Lee·ward Islands [lē′wərd] The islands of the NE West Indies from the Virgin Islands to Dominica. Also **the Leewards.**

Le Havre [lə hä′vrə] A city in northern France on the English Channel. Pop. 255,000.

Leip·zig [līp′sig *or* līp′sik] A city in south central East Germany. Pop. 554,000.

Le·na [l(y)e′nə *or* lē′nə] A river in the eastern Soviet Union, rising near Lake Baikal and flowing about 3,000 miles northward to the Arctic Ocean.

The beautiful Pushkin Palace is in a suburb of Leningrad.

Len·in·grad [len′in·grad′] A city in the NW Soviet Union, at the eastern end of the Gulf of Finland. Formerly *St. Petersburg.* Pop. 4,904,000.

Le·o·pold·ville [lē′ə·pōld·vil′] An old name for KINSHASA.

Les·bos [lez′bos] An island of Greece, in the Aegean Sea off the western coast of Turkey.

Le·so·tho [lə·sō′tō] A country surrounded by South Africa. Formerly *Basutoland.* Capital, Maseru. Area, 11,720 sq. mi. Pop. 1,681,000.

Le·vant [lə·vant′] The countries on the eastern Mediterranean, between western Greece and western Egypt.

Lex·ing·ton [lek′sing·tən] **1** A town in NE Massachusetts where the first battle of the American Revolution was fought on April 19, 1775. **2** A city in north central Kentucky. Pop. 213,000.

Lha·sa [lä′sə *or* las′ə] A city in SW China, the capital of Tibet. Pop. 80,000.

Li·be·ri·a [lī·bir′ē·ə] A country in western Africa, on the Atlantic between Sierra Leone and Ivory Coast. It was founded in 1847 by freed slaves from the U.S. Capital, Monrovia. Area, 43,000 sq. mi. Pop. 2,554,000.

Li·bre·ville [lē′brə·vil′] The capital of Gabon, on the Gulf of Guinea. Pop. 235,000.

Lib·ya [lib′ē·ə] A country in northern Africa, on the Mediterranean west of Egypt. Capital, Tripoli. Area, 679,362 sq. mi. Pop. 4,270,000.

Liech·ten·stein [lik′tən·stīn′] A small country in south central Europe between Switzerland and Austria. Capital, Vaduz. Area, 61 sq. mi. Pop. 30,000.

Li·ege [lē·ezh′] A city in western Belgium. Pop. 202,000.

Lille [lēl] An industrial city in northern France. Pop. 175,000.

Li·long·we [lē·lông′wā] The capital of Malawi, in the west central part. Pop. 103,000.

Li·ma [lē′mə] The capital and largest city of Peru, in the west central part. Pop. 5,331,000.

Lin·coln [ling′kən] The capital of Nebraska, in the SE part. Pop. 183,000.

Lis·bon [liz′bən] The capital of Portugal, in the SW part on the Tagus River. Pop. 1,154,000.

Lith·u·a·ni·a [lith′o͞o·ā′nē·ə] A constituent republic of the NW Soviet Union, on the Baltic. It was once an independent country.

Little America A U.S. base in Antarctica.

Little Big Horn A river in NW Wyoming and southern Montana, near the site of General Custer's defeat by the Sioux Indians (1876).

Little Rock The capital and largest city in Arkansas, in the central part. Pop. 181,000.

Liv·er·pool [liv′ər·po͞ol′] A seaport in NW England. Pop. 492,000.

Lodz [lo͞oj] A city in central Poland. Pop. 848,000.

Loire [lwär] The longest river in France, rising in the SE and flowing northwest into the Bay of Biscay.

Lom·bar·dy [lom′bər·dē] A region of northern Italy.

Lo·mond [lō′mənd], **Loch** A lake in central Scotland.

Lo·mé [lô·mā′] The capital of Togo, on the Gulf of Guinea. Pop. 300,000.

London's historic Big Ben and Houses of Parliament

Lon·don [lun′dən] **1** The capital of the United Kingdom, in SE England. Pop. 6,767,000. **2** A city in SE Ontario, Canada, between Lake Huron and Lake Erie. Pop. 342,000.

Lon·don·der·ry [lun′dən·der′ē] A city in NW Northern Ireland. Pop. 97,000.

Long Beach A port city in southern California. Pop. 396,000.

The lighthouse at Montauk Point, Long Island

Long Island A large island of SE New York, separated from Connecticut by **Long Island Sound.**

Los An·ge·les [lôs an′jə·ləs *or* lôs an′jə·lēz′] A city in SW California, on the Pacific. Pop. 3,259,000.

Lou·i·si·an·a [lo͞o·ē′zē·an′ə *or* lo͞o′ə·zē·an′ə] A state in the south central U.S., on the Gulf of Mexico. Capital, Baton Rouge. Area, 48,523 sq. mi. Pop. 4,461,000.

Lou·is·ville [lo͞o′ē·vil′] The largest city in Kentucky, in the NW part on the Ohio River. Pop. 286,000.
Lou·ren·ço Mar·ques [lō·ren′sō mär′kes] An old name for MAPUTO.
Low Countries The Netherlands, Belgium, and Luxembourg.
Lower California A long peninsula of NW Mexico, just south of California.
Low·lands [lō′lәndz] The less mountainous regions of southern and eastern Scotland.
Lu·an·da [lo͞o·an′dә] The capital and largest city of Angola, in the NW part on the Atlantic. Pop. 960,000.
Lub·bock [lub′әk] A city in NW Texas. Pop. 186,000.
Lu·bum·ba·shi [lo͞o′bo͝om·bä′shē] A city in SE Zaire. Pop. 544,000.
Lü·da [lo͞o′dä′] A city in NE China, on the Yellow Sea. Pop. 1,630,000.
Lu·sa·ka [lo͞o·sä′kә] The capital and largest city of Zambia, in the south central part. Pop. 538,000.
Lux·em·bourg or **Lux·em·burg** [lûk′sәm·bûrg′] **1** A country in western Europe, between Belgium, France, and West Germany. Capital, Luxembourg. Area, 998 sq. mi. Pop. 379,000. **2** The capital and largest city of Luxembourg. Pop. 83,000.

The Court of Ramses II in the Temple of Luxor

Lux·or [luk′sôr] A city in central Egypt, on part of the site of ancient Thebes. Pop. 138,000.
Lu·zon [lo͞o·zon′] The largest and northernmost of the main Philippine Islands.
Lvov [lә·vôf′] A city in the western Soviet Union, in the western Ukraine. Pop. 767,000.
Lyd·i·a [lid′ē·ә] An ancient kingdom in western Asia Minor.
Ly·on [lē·ōn′] A city in SE France. Pop. 410,000.

M

Ma·cao [ma·kou′] A peninsula and several islands on the southern coast of China that form an overseas province of Portugal. Area, 6 sq. mi. Pop. 427,000.
Mac·e·don [mas′ә·don′] An ancient country north of Greece that became a leading world power under Alexander the Great.
Mac·e·do·ni·a [mas′ә·dō′nē·ә] **1** A historic region of SE Europe, divided among Bulgaria, Greece, and Yugoslavia. **2** Another name for MACEDON.

Machu Picchu stands on a mountain about 8,000 feet high.

Ma·chu Pic·chu [mä′cho͞o pēk′cho͞o] An ancient city of the Incas in SE Peru near Cuzco.
Mac·ken·zie [mә·ken′zē] A river in NW Canada that flows from Great Slave Lake to the Beaufort Sea.
Mack·i·nac [mak′ә·nô′], **Straits of** A waterway connecting Lake Michigan and Lake Huron.
Ma·con [mā′kәn] A city in central Georgia. Pop. 118,000.
Mad·a·gas·car [mad′ә·gas′kәr] An island country off the east coast of Africa, south of the equator. Formerly the *Malagasy Republic*. Capital, Antananarivo. Area, 226,658 sq. mi. Pop. 11,100,000.
Ma·dei·ra [mә·dir′ә] **1** A group of Portuguese islands in the North Atlantic, west of Morocco. **2** The largest island of this group. Area, 285 sq. mi.
Mad·i·son [mad′ә·sәn] The capital of Wisconsin, in the south central part. Pop. 176,000.
Ma·dras [mә·dras′ *or* mә·dräs′] A city in SE India on the Bay of Bengal. Pop. 4,289,300.

The National Palace in Madrid

Ma·drid [mә·drid′] The capital and largest city of Spain, in the central part. Pop. 3,159,000.
Mag·de·burg [mag′dә·bûrg′] A historic city in East Germany, on the Elbe River. Pop. 289,000.
Ma·gel·lan [ma·jel′әn], **Strait of** The channel separating the South American mainland and Tierra del Fuego.
Maine [mān] A state in the NE U.S., on the Atlantic. Capital, Augusta. Area, 33,215 sq. mi. Pop. 1,187,000.
Ma·jor·ca [mә·jôr′kә *or* mә·yôr′kә] The largest of the Balearic Islands of Spain. Area, 1,405 sq. mi.
Ma·ka·lu [muk′ә·lo͞o′] A mountain in the Himalayas in NE Nepal. Height, 27,824 ft.
Ma·la·bo [mä·lä′bō] The capital of Equatorial Guinea, a port on Bioko Island in the Gulf of Guinea. Pop. 37,000.

Mál·a·ga [mal′ə·gə] A port and resort on the southern coast of Spain, east of Gibraltar. Pop. 505,000.
Mal·a·gas·y Republic [mal′ə·gas′ē] An old name for MADAGASCAR.
Ma·la·wi [mə·lä′wē] A landlocked country near the SE coast of Africa. Formerly *Nyasaland.* Capital, Lilongwe. Area, 45,757 sq. mi. Pop. 7,900,000.
Malawi, Lake Another name for LAKE NYASA.
Ma·lay·a [mə·lā′ə] The Malay Peninsula.
Ma·lay Archipelago [mə·lā′ *or* mā′lā′] A large group of islands between SE Asia and Australia, including Sumatra, Borneo, Java, Celebes, and many smaller islands. Sometimes New Guinea and the Philippines are considered part of it.
Malay Peninsula A peninsula of SE Asia, divided between Malaysia and Thailand.
Ma·lay·sia [mə·lā′zhə] A country in SE Asia consisting of the southern Malay Peninsula and northern Borneo. Capital, Kuala Lumpur. Area, 127,316 sq. mi. Pop. 17,000,000.
Mal·dives [môl′dīvz′] A country consisting of a chain of islands in the Indian Ocean, south of India. Capital, Male. Area, 115 sq. mi. Pop. 200,000.
Ma·le [mä′lā] The capital of Maldives. Pop. 46,344.
Ma·li [mä′lē] A landlocked country in NW Africa, south of Algeria. Capital, Bamako. Area, 478,767 sq. mi. Pop. 8,700,000.
Mal·mö [mal′mō] A Baltic seaport in southern Sweden. Pop. 230,000.
Mal·ta [môl′tə] A country made up of a group of islands in the Mediterranean south of Sicily. Capital, Valetta. Area, 122 sq. mi. Pop. 400,000.
Man [man], **Isle of** A British island in the Irish Sea north of Wales. Area, 221 sq. mi.
Ma·na·gua [mä·nä′gwä] The capital of Nicaragua, in the western part. Pop. 682,000.
Ma·na·ma [mə·nam′ə] The capital of Bahrain, on the Persian Gulf. Pop. 150,000.
Ma·naus [mə·nous′] A city in NW Brazil, on the Rio Negro near the Amazon. Pop. 613,100.
Man·ches·ter [man′ches′tər *or* man′chə·stər] **1** A city in NE England. Pop. 450,000. **2** A city in southern New Hampshire. Pop. 91,000.
Man·chu·ri·a [man·cho͝or′ē·ə] A region in NE China.

The skyline of Manhattan provides breathtaking views when approached by air.

Man·hat·tan [man·hat′ən *or* mən·hat′ən] An island of SE New York in the Hudson River. It is one of the boroughs of New York City. Area, 31 sq. mi. Pop. 1,478,000.

The Chinese Pavilion in Rizal Park, Manila

Ma·nil·a [mə·nil′ə] The capital and chief city of the Philippines, on Luzon. Pop. 1,728,000.
Man·i·to·ba [man′i·tō′bə] A province in central Canada. Capital, Winnipeg. Area, 251,000 sq. mi. Pop. 1,050,000.
Mann·heim [män′hīm′] A river port in SW West Germany. Pop. 295,000.
Ma·pu·to [mə·po͞o′tō] The capital of Mozambique, in the southern part on the Indian Ocean. Pop. 882,800.
Mar·a·cai·bo [mar′ə·kī′bō] A port city in NW Venezuela. Pop. 1,295,000.
Mar·a·thon [mar′ə·thon′] A plain near Athens, Greece, where the Athenians defeated the Persians in 490 B.C.
Mar·i·an·a Islands [mar′ē·an′ə] An island group in the western Pacific east of the Philippines, administered by the U.S. Also **the Marianas.**
Maritime Provinces The Canadian provinces of New Brunswick, Nova Scotia, and Prince Edward Island.
Mar·ma·ra [mär′mər·ə], **Sea of** A sea that separates the Asian and European parts of Turkey and connects the Aegean Sea and the Black Sea.
Marne [märn] A river in NE France, the site of two major battles in World War I.
Mar·que·sas Islands [mär·kā′zəs] An island group of France in the South Pacific, due west of Peru.
Mar·ra·kesh or **Mar·ra·kech** [mə·rä′kesh *or* mar′·ə·kesh′] A city in central Morocco. Pop. 550,000.

Marseilles is the second largest city in France.

Mar·seilles or **Mar·seille** [mär·sā′] A seaport in SE France. Pop. 868,000.
Mar·shall Islands [mär′shəl] A U.S.-administered island group in the central Pacific, in Micronesia. Also **the Marshalls.**
Mar·ti·nique [mär′ti·nēk′] A French island in the eastern West Indies. Area, 425 sq. mi. Pop. 300,000.

Mar·y·land [mer′ə·lənd] A state in the eastern U.S. on Chesapeake Bay and the Atlantic. Capital, Annapolis. Area, 9,837 sq. mi. Pop. 4,535,000.

Ma·se·ru [mäz′ə·ro͞o′] The capital of Lesotho. Pop. 80,200.

Ma·son-Dix·on line [mā′sən·dik′sən] The boundary between Pennsylvania and Maryland, thought of as dividing the North from the South.

Marblehead, Massachusetts, an old city northeast of Boston

Mas·sa·chu·setts [mas′ə·cho͞o′sits] A state in the NE U.S. on the Atlantic. Capital, Boston. Area, 8,257 sq. mi. Pop. 5,885,000.

Mat·ter·horn [mat′ər·hôrn′] A mountain in the Alps on the Swiss-Italian border. Height, 14,692 ft.

Mau·na Ke·a [mou′nə kē′ə] A volcano on the island of Hawaii north of Mauna Loa. Height, 13,796 ft.

Mau·na Lo·a [mou′nə lō′ə] An active volcano on the island of Hawaii. Height, 13,677 ft.

Mau·ri·ta·ni·a [môr′i·tā·nē·ə] A country in NW Africa on the Atlantic. Capital, Nouakchott. Area, 397,956 sq. mi. Pop. 2,100,000.

Mau·ri·tius [mô·rish′əs *or* mô·rish′ē·əs] An island nation east of Madagascar, in the Indian Ocean. Capital, Port Louis. Area, 789 sq. mi. Pop. 1,100,000.

Mba·bane [(ə)m·bä′bän′ *or* em′bə·bän′] The capital of Swaziland. Pop. 40,000.

Mc·Kin·ley [mə·kin′lē], **Mount** The highest mountain in North America, in south central Alaska. Height, 20,320 ft.

The courtyard of Al-Masjid al Haram mosque in Mecca

Mec·ca [mek′ə] A city in Saudi Arabia, the birthplace of Muhammad and a holy city of Islam. Pop. 463,000.

Me·del·lín [med′ə·lin *or* mə·dà′lin] A city in west central Colombia. Pop. 2,069,000.

Me·di·a [mē′dē·ə] An ancient country of SW Asia, in present-day NW Iran.

Me·di·na [mə·dē·nə] A Muslim holy city in Saudi Arabia. Muhammad is buried there. Pop. 198,000.

Med·i·ter·ra·ne·an Sea [med′i·tə·rā′nē·ən] A great inland sea between Europe, Asia, and Africa.

Me·kong [mā′kong′] A river in SE Asia that rises in Tibet and flows SE through Indochina to the South China Sea.

Mel·a·ne·sia [mel′ə·nē·zhə] The islands of the western Pacific that lie south of the equator from New Guinea eastward through Fiji.

Mel·bourne [mel′bərn] A large seaport in SE Australia. Pop. 2,931,900.

Mem·phis [mem′fis] **1** A city in SW Tennessee, on the Mississippi. Pop. 653,000. **2** An ancient Egyptian city on the Nile south of Cairo.

Mé·ri·da [mer′i·də *or* mā′rē·thä′] A city on the Yucatán Peninsula in Mexico. Pop. 424,000.

Me·sa [mà′sə] A city in south central Arizona. Pop. 251,400.

Me·sa·bi Range [mə·sä′bē] A chain of mountains in NE Minnesota, once a major source of iron ore.

A 12th-century cliff dwelling, Mesa Verde National Park

Me·sa Verde National Park [mā′sə vûrd′(ē)] A park in SW Colorado containing the ruins of cliff dwellings built by Indians centuries ago.

Me·shed [mə·shed′] A city in NE Iran. Pop. 2,038,000.

Mes·o·po·ta·mi·a [mes′ə·pə·tā′mē·ə] A historic region in SW Asia between the Tigris and Euphrates rivers, part of modern Iraq.

Mes·si·na [mə·sē′nə] A city in NE Sicily on the **Strait of Messina,** which separates mainland Italy from Sicily. Pop. 269,000.

Gracious architecture abounds in Mexico's capital city.

Mex·i·co [mek′si·kō] A country in southern North America, south of the U.S. Capital, Mexico City. Area, 761,605 sq. mi. Pop. 88,087,000.

Mexico City The capital of Mexico, in the south central part. Pop. 18,000,000.

Mexico, Gulf of A part of the North Atlantic nearly enclosed by the U.S., Mexico, and Cuba.

Mi·am·i [mī·am′ē] A city in SE Florida on an inlet of the Atlantic. Pop. 374,000.

Mich·i·gan [mish′ə·gən] A state in the north central U.S. Capital, Lansing. Area, 58,216 sq. mi. Pop. 9,200,000.

Michigan, Lake The third largest of the Great Lakes, between Michigan and Wisconsin. Area, 22,400 sq. mi.

Mi·cro·ne·sia [mī′krə·nē′zhə] A large group of islands in the western Pacific north of the equator.

Middle East A region of NE Africa and SW Asia, including the countries from Libya to Afghanistan.

Middle West A region of the U.S. that includes Ohio, Indiana, Michigan, Illinois, Wisconsin, Minnesota, Iowa, and Missouri.

Mid·east [mid′ēst′] The Middle East.

Mid·way Islands [mid′wā′] An island group of the U.S., in the central Pacific west of Hawaii.

Mid·west [mid′west′] The Middle West.

Mi·lan [mi·lan′] A city in northern Italy. Pop. 1,535,000.

Mil·wau·kee [mil·wô′kē] A city in SE Wisconsin, on Lake Michigan. Pop. 605,100.

Min·da·nao [min′də·nou′] The second largest and southernmost of the main Philippine Islands.

Min·ne·ap·o·lis [min′ē·ap′ə·lis] A city in eastern Minnesota, on the Mississippi River. Pop. 357,000.

Min·ne·so·ta [min′i·sō′tə] A state in the north central U.S. Capital, St. Paul. Area, 84,063 sq. mi. Pop. 4,246,000.

Minsk [minsk] A city in the western Soviet Union, the capital of Byelorussia. Pop. 1,510,000.

An antebellum home in Natchez, Mississippi

Mis·sis·sip·pi [mis′i·sip′ē] **1** A state in the SE U.S. Capital, Jackson. Area, 47,716 sq. mi. Pop. 2,625,000. **2** A river in the central U.S., flowing about 2,330 miles from northern Minnesota to the Gulf of Mexico.

Mis·sou·ri [mi·zoor′e *or* mi·zoor′ə] **1** A state in the central U.S. Capital, Jefferson City. Area, 69,686 sq. mi. Pop. 5,103,000. **2** The longest river of the U.S., flowing 2,714 miles from the Rockies in SW Montana to the Mississippi in eastern Missouri.

Mo·bile [mō′bēl′ *or* mō·bēl′] A city in SW Alabama on an inlet of the Gulf of Mexico. Pop. 203,000.

Mog·a·di·shu [mog′ə·dish′o͞o] The capital and chief port of Somalia, in the southern part on the Indian Ocean. Pop. 700,000.

Mo·ja·ve Desert [mō·hä′vē] A desert in SE California.

Mol·da·vi·a [mol·dā′vē·ə] A region divided between NE Romania and the Soviet Union. The Soviet part is a constituent republic of the SW Soviet Union.

Mo·lo·kai [mō′lō·kī′] An island of Hawaii east of Oahu.

Mo·luc·cas [mə·luk′əz] An island group in Indonesia between Celebes and New Guinea. Formerly *Spice Islands*.

Mom·ba·sa [mom·bä′sə] A seaport in SE Kenya. Pop. 401,000.

Monaco is one of the world's smallest countries.

Mon·a·co [mon′ə·kō *or* mə·nä′kō] A tiny country on the SE coast of France. Capital, Monaco. Area, .58 sq. mi. Pop. 29,000.

Mon·go·li·a [mon(g)·gō′lē·ə] **1** A region in east central Asia divided between the Mongolian People's Republic and northern China. **2** A country in east central Asia between the eastern Soviet Union and northern China. It includes most of the region of Mongolia. Also **Mongolian People's Republic.** Capital, Ulan Bator. Area, 604,250 sq. mi. Pop. 2,000,000.

Mo·non·ga·he·la [mə·non′gə·hē′lə] A river in West Virginia and Pennsylvania that joins the Allegheny at Pittsburgh to form the Ohio River.

Mon·ro·vi·a [mən·rō′vē·ə] The capital of Liberia, on the Atlantic. Pop. 400,000.

Mon·tan·a [mon·tan′ə] A state in the NW U.S. Capital, Helena. Area, 147,138 sq. mi. Pop. 809,000.

Mont Blanc [mont blangk′ *or* môn blän′] The highest peak in the Alps, on the French-Italian border. Height, 15,771 ft.

Mon·te Car·lo [mon′tē kär′lō] A district in Monaco known for its gambling casino. Pop. 13,000.

Mon·te·ne·gro [mon′tə·nē′grō] A historic region in southern Yugoslavia.

Mon·ter·rey [mon′tə·rā′] A city in NE Mexico. Pop. 2,700,000.

Mon·te·vi·de·o [mon′tə·vi·dā′ō] The capital of Uruguay, on the Río de la Plata. Pop. 1,325,000.

Mont·gom·er·y [mont·gum′(ə)rē] The capital of Alabama, in the central part. Pop. 194,000.

Mont·pel·ier [mont·pēl′yər] The capital of Vermont, in the central part. Pop. 8,241.

Mont·re·al or **Mont·ré·al** [mon′trē·ôl′ *or* môn′·rā·äl′] The largest city in Canada, in southern Quebec on the St. Lawrence River. Pop. 2,922,000.

The abbey of Mont Saint Michel, built in the 12th century

Mont-Saint-Mi·chel [môn·san·mē·shel′] A small island off the NW coast of France, noted for its Gothic abbey church.

Mo·roc·co [mə·rok′ō] A country in NW Africa on the Atlantic and the Mediterranean. Capital, Rabat. Area, 172,414 sq. mi. Pop. 25,380,000.

Mo·ro·ni [mə·rō′nē] The capital and chief port of the Comoros in the Indian Ocean. Pop. 26,000.

Characteristic onion domes of the Kremlin in Moscow

Mos·cow [mos′kou *or* mos′kō] The capital of the Soviet Union, in the western part of the country. Pop. 8,714,000.

Mo·zam·bique [mō′zəm·bēk′] A country in SE Africa, on the Indian Ocean. Capital, Maputo. Area, 302,330 sq. mi. Pop. 15,259,000.

Muk·den [mo͝ok′den′] Another name for SHENYANG.

Mu·nich [myo͞o′nik] A city in SE West Germany. Pop. 1,270,000.

Mur·mansk [mo͝or·mansk′] A city in the NW Soviet Union, on an inlet of the Barents Sea. Pop. 432,000.

Mur·ray [mûr′ē] A river in SE Australia.

Mus·cat [mus′kat′] The capital of Oman, in the northern part on the Gulf of Oman. Pop. 85,000.

My·ce·nae [mī·sē′nē] An ancient Greek city in the NE Peloponnesus, powerful in prehistoric times.

N

Na·ga·sa·ki [nä·gə·sä′kē] A city on the west coast of Kyushu, Japan, destroyed by an atomic bomb dropped by the U.S. on August 9, 1945. Pop. 450,000.

Na·go·ya [nä·gō′yä] A city in southern Honshu, Japan. Pop. 2,116,400.

Nag·pur [näg′po͝or] A city in central India. Pop. 1,300,000.

Cheetahs in Kenya's Nairobi Park

Nai·ro·bi [nī·rō′bē] The capital of Kenya, in the south central part. Pop. 959,000.

Na·mib·i·a [nə·mib′ē·ə] A region in SW Africa south of Angola, controlled by South Africa. Also *South-West Africa.* Area, 318,099 sq. mi. Pop. 1,700,000.

Nan·jing [nän′jying′] A city in east central China, on the Yangtze. Pop. 4,560,000.

Nan·king [nan′king′] Another spelling of NANJING.

Nantes [nants *or* nänt] A city in western France on the Loire River. Pop. 237,800.

Nan·tuck·et [nan·tuk′it] A resort island and former whaling center off the SE coast of Massachusetts.

A view of Naples with Mount Vesuvius in the background

Na·ples [nā′pəlz] A city in SW Italy on the **Bay of Naples,** an inlet of the Mediterranean. Pop. 1,207,000.

Nash·ville [nash′vil′] The capital of Tennessee, in the central part. Pop. 473,700.

Nas·sau [nas′ô] The capital and largest city of the Bahamas. Pop. 140,000.

Nationalist China Another name for TAIWAN.

Na·u·ru [nä·o͞o′ro͞o] An island country in the western Pacific, just south of the equator. Area, 8 sq. mi. Pop. 8,100.

Naz·a·reth [naz′ər·əth *or* naz′ə·rith] The town in northern Israel where Jesus spent his childhood.

Ndja·me·na [ən·jä'mā·nä] The capital and largest city of Chad, in the SW part. Pop. 512,000.

Near East The Middle East, sometimes including the Balkans.

Ne·bras·ka [nə·bras'kə] A state in the central U.S. Capital, Lincoln. Area, 77,227 sq. mi. Pop. 1,549,000.

Neg·ev [neg'ev] A desert that covers the southern half of Israel.

Ne·pal [nə·pôl' *or* nə·päl'] A country between India and Tibet, in the Himalayas. Capital, Katmandu. Area, 54,362 sq. mi. Pop. 18,300,000.

The Netherlands is noted for its beautiful tulip fields.

Neth·er·lands [neth'ər·ləndz] A country in NW Europe, on the North Sea. Also *Holland.* Capital, Amsterdam. Seat of government, The Hague. Area, 15,892 sq. mi. Pop. 14,700,000.

Netherlands Antilles Six scattered islands in the West Indies that belong to the Netherlands.

Ne·vad·a [nə·vad'ə *or* nə·vä'də] A state in the western U.S. Capital, Carson City. Area, 110,540 sq. mi. Pop. 1,007,000.

New·ark [n(y)ōō'ərk] A city in NE New Jersey. Pop. 316,000.

New Britain An island in the western Pacific belonging to Papua New Guinea. Area, 14,000 sq. mi.

New Bruns·wick [brunz'wik] A province in SE Canada northeast of Maine. Capital, Fredericton. Area, 28,354 sq. mi. Pop. 710,500.

New Cal·e·do·ni·a [kal'i·dō'ne·ə] An island belonging to France, in the SW Pacific north of New Zealand. Area, 6,223 sq. mi.

New·cas·tle [n(y)ōō'kas'əl] A seaport in NE England. Pop. 281,000.

New Del·hi [del'ē] The capital of India, in the northern part of the country adjacent to Delhi. Pop. 302,000.

New England The NE part of the U.S., including Maine, New Hampshire, Vermont, Massachusetts, Rhode Island, and Connecticut.

New·found·land [n(y)ōō'fənd·lənd *or* n(y)ōō'fənd·land'] **1** A large island off the SE coast of Canada, between the Gulf of St. Lawrence and the North Atlantic. **2** A province of SE Canada that includes this island and Labrador on the mainland. Capital, St. John's. Area, 158,185 sq. mi. Pop. 568,000.

New Guin·ea [gin'ē] A large island just north of Australia. The eastern part is the mainland of Papua New Guinea, and the western part belongs to Indonesia. Area, 307,000 sq. mi.

New Hamp·shire [ham(p)'shər] A state in the NE U.S. Capital, Concord. Area, 9,304 sq. mi. Pop. 1,057,000.

New Ha·ven [hā'vən] A city in southern Connecticut, the site of Yale University. Pop. 123,000.

New Heb·ri·des [heb'ri·dēz'] An old name for VANUATU.

New Jer·sey [jûr'zē] A state in the eastern U.S., on the Atlantic. Capital, Trenton. Area, 7,836 sq. mi. Pop. 7,672,000.

New Mexico A state in the SW U.S., bordering on Mexico. Capital, Santa Fe. Area, 121,666 sq. mi. Pop. 1,500,000.

New Or·le·ans [ôr'lē·ənz, ôr'lənz, *or* ôr·lēnz'] A port city in SE Louisiana, on the Mississippi near its mouth. Pop. 554,000.

New·port [n(y)ōō'pôrt'] A resort city in SE Rhode Island, on the Atlantic. Pop. 30,000.

Newport News [n(y)ōōz'] A seaport in SE Virginia near Hampton Roads. Pop. 162,000.

New South Wales A state in SE Australia.

New York [yôrk] **1** A state in the NE U.S. Capital, Albany. Area, 49,576 sq. mi. Pop. 17,825,000. **2** A city in SE New York at the mouth of the Hudson River. It is the largest city in the U.S. Also *New York City.* Pop. 7,263,000.

New Zea·land [zē'lənd] A country on two main islands in the SW Pacific southeast of Australia. Capital, Wellington. Area, 102,883 sq. mi. Pop. 3,300,000.

Niagara Falls is a major U.S. tourist attraction.

Ni·ag·a·ra [nī·ag'(ə)rə] A river that flows along the U.S.-Canadian border from Lake Erie to Lake Ontario, passing over **Niagara Falls,** two broad scenic waterfalls.

Nia·mey [nyä·mā'] The capital and largest city of Niger, in the SW part. Pop. 350,000.

Nic·a·ra·gua [nik'ə·rä'gwə] **1** A country in Central America south of Honduras, with coastlines on the Pacific and the Caribbean. Capital, Managua. Area, 50,193 sq. mi. Pop. 3,600,000. **2** The largest lake in Central America, in SW Nicaragua.

Nice [nēs] A resort city in SE France, on the Mediterranean. Pop. 331,000.

Nic·o·si·a [nik'ə·sē'ə] The capital of Cyprus, in the central part. Pop. 164,000.

Ni·ger [nī'jər] **1** A country in NW Africa, between Nigeria and Algeria. Capital, Niamey. Area, 489,191 sq. mi. Pop. 7,200,000. **2** A river of western Africa that flows about 2,600 miles from Guinea to the Gulf of Guinea in Nigeria.

Ni·ge·ri·a [nī·jir′ē·ə] A country in western Africa, on the Gulf of Guinea north of the equator. Capital, Lagos. Area, 356,669 sq. mi. Pop. 111,900,000.

The Nile is responsible for Egypt's rich farmland.

Nile [nīl] The longest river in the world, flowing about 4,100 miles from Lake Victoria in central Africa northward to the Mediterranean in Egypt. It is called the **White Nile** in southern and central Sudan.

Nin·e·veh [nin′ə·və] An ancient city on the Tigris River, capital of Assyria.

Nip·pon [ni·pon′ *or* nip′on] The Japanese name for JAPAN.

Ni·u·e [nē·ōō′ā] An island belonging to New Zealand, in the south central Pacific south of Samoa. Area, 100 sq. mi. Pop. 2,500.

Nor·folk [nôr′fək] The largest city in Virginia, in the SE part on the Atlantic. Pop. 275,000.

Rouen, in Normandy, where Joan of Arc was burned at the stake

Nor·man·dy [nor′mən·dē] A region and former province of northern France, on the English Channel.

North America The northern continent of the Western Hemisphere, including Canada, the U.S., Mexico, and Central America.

North Carolina A state in the SE U.S., on the Atlantic. Capital, Raleigh. Area, 52,586 sq. mi. Pop. 6,413,000.

North Da·ko·ta [də·kō′tə] A state in the north central U.S., bordering Canada. Capital, Bismarck. Area, 70,665 sq. mi. Pop. 672,000.

Northern Hemisphere The half of the earth north of the equator.

Northern Ireland A part of the United Kingdom occupying the NE corner of the island of Ireland. Capital, Belfast. Area, 5,462 sq. mi. Pop. 1,568,000.

Northern Territory A territory in north central Australia.

North Island The northern island of the two main islands of New Zealand. Area, 44,280 sq. mi.

North Ko·re·a [kə·rē′ə *or* kô·rē′ə] A country occupying the northern part of the Korean peninsula. Capital, Pyongyang. Area, 46,540 sq. mi. Pop. 21,964,000.

North Pole The northernmost point on the earth, a point near the middle of the Arctic Ocean.

North Sea The part of the North Atlantic between Great Britain and northern Europe.

North·um·bri·a [nôr·thum′brē·ə] An ancient Anglo-Saxon kingdom in central Great Britain.

North Vietnam See VIETNAM.

Northwest Passage A water route from the Atlantic to the Pacific along the northern coast of North America. Long sought by explorers, it proved impractical.

Northwest Territories A vast, largely undeveloped region in northern Canada, including the Arctic Archipelago. Capital, Yellowknife. Area, 1,304,903 sq. mi. Pop. 52,300.

Northwest Territory A former territory of the U.S., established in 1787. It later became the states of Illinois, Indiana, Michigan, Ohio, Wisconsin, and part of Minnesota.

Geirangerfjord, on the west coast of Norway

Nor·way [nôr′wā′] A Scandinavian country of northern Europe, west of Sweden. Capital, Oslo. Area, 128,181 sq. mi. Pop. 4,200,000.

Nouak·chott [nwäk′shot′] The capital of Mauritania, on the Atlantic. Pop. 400,000.

No·va Sco·tia [nō′və skō′shə] A province of SE Canada. Capital, Halifax. Area, 21,425 sq. mi. Pop. 873,500.

Nov·go·rod [nôv′gə·rəd] A city in the NW Soviet Union near Leningrad. Pop. 228,000.

No·vo·kuz·netsk [nô′vō·kōōz·n(y)etsk′] A city in the central Soviet Union. Pop. 589,000.

No·vo·si·birsk [nō′vō·si·birsk′] A manufacturing city in the central Soviet Union. Pop. 1,400,000.

Nu·bi·a [n(y)ōō′bē·ə] An ancient African region and kingdom in southern Egypt and northern Sudan.

Nu·kua·lo·fa [nōō'kwa·lô'fə] The capital and chief port of Tonga. Pop. 29,000.

Nuremberg, one of the oldest cities in Germany

Nu·rem·berg [n(y)ŏŏr'əm·bûrg'] A historic city in southern West Germany. Pop. 467,000.

Ny·as·a [nī·as'ə], **Lake** A large lake in SE Africa between Malawi, Mozambique, and Tanzania. Also *Lake Malawi.*

Ny·as·a·land [nī·as'ə·land'] An old name for MALAWI.

O

O·a·hu [ō·ä'hōō] The most populous island of Hawaii, the site of Pearl Harbor and Honolulu.

Oak·land [ōk'lənd] A city in western California, on San Francisco Bay opposite San Francisco. Pop. 357,000.

Oak Ridge [ōk'rij'] A city in eastern Tennessee, the site of an atomic research center. Pop. 28,000.

Oa·xa·ca [wä·hä'kä] A city of south central Mexico. Pop. 157,000.

Ob [ob *or* ôb] A river of the central Soviet Union, flowing 2,300 miles north to the Arctic Ocean.

O·ce·an·i·a [ō'shē·an'ē·ə] The islands of the central and south Pacific, including Melanesia, Micronesia, and Polynesia, and sometimes the Malay Archipelago and Australasia.

O·der [ō'dər] A river rising in Czechoslovakia and flowing through Poland and East Germany to the Baltic.

O·des·sa [ō·des'ə] A city in the SW Soviet Union, on the Black Sea. Pop. 1,132,000.

O·hi·o [ō·hī'ō] **1** A state of the east central U.S., on Lake Erie. Capital, Columbus. Area, 41,222 sq. mi. Pop. 10,784,000. **2** A river flowing from SW Pennsylvania southwest to the Mississippi.

O·jos del Sa·la·do [ō'hōz del sə·lä'dō] A mountain in the Andes on the Argentina-Chile border. Height, 22,572 ft.

O·kee·cho·bee [ō'kē·chō'bē], **Lake** A lake in southern Florida.

O·khotsk [ō·kotsk'], **Sea of** A part of the North Pacific between the eastern Soviet mainland and Kamchatka Peninsula.

O·ki·na·wa [ō'kə·nä'wə] An island of Japan, the largest of the Ryukyus, south of Kyushu.

O·kla·ho·ma [ō'klə·hō'mə] A state in the south central U.S. Capital, Oklahoma City. Area, 69,919 sq. mi. Pop. 3,272,000.

Oklahoma City The capital of Oklahoma, in the central part. Pop. 446,100.

Ol·du·vai Gorge [ôl'dōō·vī'] A canyon in northern Tanzania where fossils of early hominids have been found.

Old World The Eastern Hemisphere, including Europe, Asia, and Africa.

O·lym·pi·a [ō·lim'pē·ə] **1** In ancient Greece, a plain where the Olympic games were held. **2** The capital of Washington, at the south end of Puget Sound. Pop. 24,000.

O·lym·pus [ō·lim'pəs], **Mount** The highest mountain in Greece, regarded in Greek myths as the home of the gods. Height, 9,570 ft.

O·ma·ha [ō'mə·hô *or* ō'mə·hä'] A city in eastern Nebraska on the Missouri River. Pop. 349,300.

O·man [ō·män'] A country in eastern Arabia on the Arabian Sea. Capital, Muscat. Area, 82,030 sq. mi. Pop. 1,400,000.

Oman, Gulf of An inlet of the Arabian Sea between Oman and SE Iran.

Omsk [omsk] A city in the central Soviet Union. Pop. 1,044,000.

On·tar·i·o [on·târ'ē·ō] A province in Canada between Hudson Bay and the Great Lakes. Capital, Toronto. Area, 412,582 sq. mi. Pop. 9,113,500.

Ontario, Lake The easternmost and smallest of the Great Lakes. Area, 7,540 sq. mi.

Oporto processes and exports port wines.

O·por·to [ō·pôr'tō] A city in NW Portugal on the Atlantic. Also *Pôrto.* Pop. 1,500,000.

O·ran [ô·rän'] A city in NW Algeria on the Mediterranean. Pop. 663,000.

Or·e·gon [ôr'ə·gən *or* ôr'ə·gon'] A state in the NW U.S., on the Pacific. Capital, Salem. Area, 96,981 sq. mi. Pop. 2,724,000.

O·ri·ent [ôr'ē·ənt], **the** The countries east of Europe.

O·ri·no·co [ôr'ə·nō'kō] A river in Venezuela, flowing into the Atlantic.

Ork·ney Islands [ôrk'nē] A group of islands off the northern coast of Scotland. Area, 376 sq. mi.

Or·lan·do [ôr·lan'dō] A resort city in central Florida. Pop. 146,000.

Or·lé·ans [ôr·lā·än'] A city in northern France on the Loire. Pop. 106,000.

O·sa·ka [ō·sä'kə] A city on the southern coast of Honshu, Japan. Pop. 2,648,000.

Os·lo [oz'lō *or* os'lō] The capital and largest city of Norway, in the SE part. Pop. 450,000.

Os·wie·cim [ôsh′vē·en′səm] The Polish name for AUSCHWITZ.

Stately buildings add to Ottawa's beauty.

Ot·ta·wa [ot′ə·wə] The capital of Canada, in SE Ontario. Pop. 819,000.

Oua·ga·dou·gou [wä′gə·dōō′gōō] The capital of Burkina Faso, in the central part. Pop. 236,000.

Ox·ford [oks′fərd] A city in SE England, the site of Oxford University. Pop. 116,000.

Ozark Mountains [ō′zärk] A low mountain range extending from southern Illinois across Arkansas to NE Oklahoma. Also **the Ozarks.**

P

Pa·cif·ic [pə·sif′ik] The world's largest ocean, extending from the Arctic to the Antarctic between the Americas and Asia and Australia.

Pacific Islands, Trust Territory of the Several groups of islands in the western Pacific north and northeast of Papua New Guinea, including the Carolines, the northern Marianas, and the Marshalls. They are administered by the U.S. under a mandate from the United Nations. Pop. 140,000.

Pad·u·a [paj′ōō·ə *or* pad′yōō·ə] A historic city in northern Italy, west of Venice. Pop. 225,000.

A cable car takes visitors across Pago Pago Bay.

Pa·go Pa·go [päng′(g)ō päng′(g)ō *or* pä′gō pä′gō] The capital of American Samoa. Pop. 3,100.

Pak·i·stan [pak′i·stan *or* pä′ki·stan′] A country in southern Asia, west of India. Capital, Islamabad. Area, 310,404 sq. mi. Pop. 107,500,000.

Pa·la·wan [pə·lä′wän′] A long, narrow island in the SW Philippines. Area, 4,550 sq. mi.

Pa·ler·mo [pä·lâr′mō] A port city in NW Sicily. Pop. 706,000.

Pal·es·tine [pal′i·stīn′] A historic region in SW Asia extending from the eastern coast of the Mediterranean to or beyond the Jordan River, now divided between Israel and Jordan.

Pa·mirs [pə·mirz′] A region of high mountains in the south central Soviet Union and adjacent parts of northern Afghanistan, northern Pakistan, and western China. Also **Pamir.**

Pam·plo·na [pam·plō′nə] A city in northern Spain. Pop. 183,000.

Pan·a·ma [pan′ə·mä′] The southernmost country of Central America. Capital, Panama City. Area, 29,209 sq. mi. Pop. 2,300,000.

Panama, Gulf of A wide inlet of the Pacific formed by the bend in the southern coast of Panama.

The Miraflores locks of the Panama Canal

Panama Canal A ship canal across Panama connecting the Atlantic and Pacific oceans.

Panama Canal Zone Another name for the CANAL ZONE.

Panama City The capital of Panama, on the Gulf of Panama. Pop. 439,000.

Papal States Land in central Italy over which the popes had civil authority from 756 to 1870.

Pap·u·a New Guin·ea [pap′(y)ōō·ə n(y)ōō gin′ē] A country in the western Pacific occupying the eastern half of New Guinea and islands to the east. Capital, Port Moresby. Area, 178,260 sq. mi. Pop. 3,700,000.

Par·a·guay [par′ə·gwā *or* pär′ə·gwī′] **1** A landlocked country in central South America. Capital, Asunción. Area, 157,048 sq. mi. Pop. 4,400,000. **2** A river flowing about 1,500 miles through western Brazil and central Paraguay to the Paraná.

Par·a·mar·i·bo [par′ə·mar′ə·bō′] The capital of Suriname, near the Atlantic. Pop. 180,000.

Pa·ra·ná [par′ə·nä′] A river that flows south through southern Brazil, along the Paraguay border, and through NE Argentina to the Río de la Plata.

Qi·qi·har [chē′chē′här′] A city in NE China. Pop. 1,260,000.
Que·bec or **Qué·bec** [kwi·bek′ *or* kā′bek′] **1** A province of eastern Canada. Capital, Quebec. Area, 594,860 sq. mi. Pop. 6,540,300. **2** The capital of Quebec, a port on the St. Lawrence River. Pop. 625,000.
Queens [kwēnz] One of the five boroughs of New York City. Pop. 1,923,000.
Queens·land [kwēnz′land′ *or* kwenz′lənd] A state of NE Australia.
Que·zon City [kā′sôn′] A city on Luzon in the Philippines. Pop. 1,326,000.
Qui·to [kē′tō] The capital of Ecuador, in the northern part near the equator. Pop. 1,137,000.

R

Ra·bat [rä·bät′] The capital of Morocco, in the northern part on the Atlantic. Pop. 843,000.
Rai·nier [rə·nir′ *or* rā·nir′], **Mount** A mountain in west central Washington. Height, 14,410 ft.
Ra·leigh [rô′lē *or* rä′lē] The capital of North Carolina, in the central part of the state. Pop. 180,500.

The Shwedagon Pagoda and Golden Temple in Rangoon

Ran·goon [rang·gōōn′] The capital and largest city of Burma, on the delta of the Irrawaddy. Pop. 2,300,000.
Ra·wal·pin·di [rä′wəl·pin′dē] A city in northern Pakistan. Pop. 795,000.
Re·ci·fe [rə·sē′fe] A city in NE Brazil, on the Atlantic. Pop. 1,290,000.
Red River **1** A river that flows eastward along the Oklahoma-Texas border and through Louisiana to the Mississippi. **2** A river that flows northward along the Minnesota-North Dakota border and into Lake Winnipeg in Manitoba. **3** A river of southern China and northern Vietnam, flowing into the Gulf of Tonkin.
Red Sea A long, narrow sea between NE Africa and Arabia. It is connected to the Mediterranean by the Suez Canal.
Reg·gio di Ca·la·bri·a [rā′j(ē)ō dē kä·lä′brē·ä] A city in southern Italy on the Strait of Messina. Also **Reggio.** Pop. 179,000.
Reg·gio nell'E·mi·lia [rā′j(ē)ō nel′lā·mē′lyä] A city in north central Italy. Also **Reggio.** Pop. 130,000.
Re·gi·na [ri·jī′nə] The capital of Saskatchewan, Canada, in the southern part. Pop. 187,000.
Reims [rēmz *or* ranz] A historic city in northern France, noted for its cathedral. Pop. 182,000.
Ré·un·ion [rā′ōō·nyôn′] An island belonging to France in the Indian Ocean southwest of Mauritius. Area, 970 sq. mi. Pop. 565,000.
Rey·kja·vík [rā′kyə·vēk′] The capital of Iceland, on an inlet of the SW coast. Pop. 89,000.
Rheims [rēmz *or* ranz] Another spelling of REIMS.

Germany's Rhine Valley is studded with castles.

Rhine [rīn] A river flowing northward from SE Switzerland through western West Germany and the Netherlands to the North Sea.
Rhode Island [rōd] A state in the NE U.S., on the Atlantic. Capital, Providence. Area, 1,214 sq. mi. Pop. 986,000.
Rhodes [rōdz] An island of Greece, in the Aegean off the SW coast of Turkey. Area, 545 sq. mi.
Rho·de·sia [rō·dē′zhə] An old name for ZIMBABWE.
Rhône or **Rhone** [rōn] A river in SW Switzerland and SE France, flowing to the Mediterranean.
Rich·mond [rich′mənd] The capital of Virginia, in the eastern part. Pop. 218,000.
Ri·ga [rē′gə] A city in the NW Soviet Union, in Latvia on the Baltic. Pop. 900,000.

Rio de Janeiro, second largest city in South America

Ri·o de Ja·nei·ro [rē′ō dā zhə·nâr′ō] A city in SE Brazil, the former national capital, on an inlet of the Atlantic. Pop. 5,615,100.
Rí·o de la Pla·ta [rē′ō de lä plä′tä] A wide river estuary between eastern Argentina and southern Uruguay.
Ri·o Grande [rē′ō grand′ *or* rē′ō gran′dē] A river that rises in SW Colorado and forms the Texas-Mexico border as it flows to the Gulf of Mexico.

Ri·o Ne·gro [rē′ō nā′grō] A river that flows 1,400 miles from eastern Colombia to the Amazon in NW Brazil.

Riv·er·side [riv′ər·sīd′] A city in SW California. Pop. 197,000.

Riv·i·er·a [riv′ē·âr′ə] A resort area along the Mediterranean coast of SE France, Monaco, and NW Italy.

Ri·yadh [rē·yäd′] The capital of Saudi Arabia, in the central part of the country. Pop. 1,230,000.

Ro·a·noke [rō′ə·nōk′] A city in SW Virginia. Pop. 102,000.

Roch·es·ter [roch′es′tər *or* roch′i·stər] A city in western New York, near Lake Ontario. Pop. 236,000.

Rock·y Mountains [rok′ē] The main mountain system of western North America, extending from northern Alaska to northern Mexico. Also **the Rockies.**

Ro·ma·nia [rō·mā′nē·ə *or* rō·mān′yə] A country in SE Europe, with a short coastline on the Black Sea. Capital, Bucharest. Area, 91,699 sq. mi. Pop. 23,000,000.

Ruins of the Forum, center of life in ancient Rome

Rome [rōm] The capital of Italy, in the west central part on the Tiber. It was the capital of the ancient Roman Empire. Pop. 2,827,000.

Ross Ice Shelf [rôs *or* ros] A broad area of glacial ice that fills the southern part of the Ross Sea off Antarctica.

Ross Sea A broad inlet of the South Pacific off the coast of Antarctica south of New Zealand.

Ros·tock [ros′tok] A city in East Germany near the Baltic. Pop. 246,000.

Ros·tov [rə·stôf′ *or* ro·stôv′] A city in the SW Soviet Union, near the Sea of Azov. Pop. 1,004,000.

Rot·ter·dam [rot′ər·dam′] A city in SW Netherlands, a major port on the Rhine delta. Pop. 571,000.

Rou·en [ro͞o·än′] A city in northern France, site of the burning of Joan of Arc. Pop. 120,000.

Rou·ma·ni·a [ro͞o·mā′nē·ə *or* ro͞o·mān′yə] Another spelling of ROMANIA.

Rub′ al Kha·li [ro͝ob′ äl kä′lē] A desert in southern Arabia.

Ru·bi·con [ro͞o′bi·kon′] A river in north central Italy, the ancient boundary between Gaul and Italy. By crossing it into Italy in 49 B.C., Julius Caesar deliberately started civil war.

Ru·dolf [ro͞o′dolf′], **Lake** A lake in northern Kenya and southern Ethiopia. Also *Lake Turkana.*

Rug·by [rug′bē] A city in central England, site of a famous school for boys founded in 1567.

Ruhr [ro͝or] **1** A river of western West Germany, flowing west into the Rhine River. **2** An industrial and coal-mining region in the Ruhr valley.

Ru·ma·ni·a [ro͞o·mā′nē·ə *or* ro͞o·mān′yə] Another spelling of ROMANIA.

Mount Rushmore, a national memorial to four presidents

Rush·more [rush′môr′], **Mount** A mountain in western South Dakota on which are carved the faces of Presidents Washington, Jefferson, Lincoln, and Theodore Roosevelt. Height, 6,200 ft.

Rus·sia [rush′ə] **1** A former empire that became the Soviet Union in 1917. **2** An informal name for the UNION OF SOVIET SOCIALIST REPUBLICS (Soviet Union). **3** The largest constituent republic of the Soviet Union, a vast region that extends from eastern Europe to the Pacific and occupies three fourths of the area of the nation.

Rwan·da [ro͞o·än′də] A landlocked country in east central Africa, just south of the equator. Capital, Kigali. Area, 10,169 sq. mi. Pop. 5,340,000.

Ryu·kyu Islands [ryo͞o′kyo͞o] An island group of southern Japan that stretches between Taiwan and Kyushu. Area, 1,205 sq. mi. Pop. 1,179,800.

S

Saar [sär *or* zär] A coal-producing region in western West Germany. Also **Saarland.**

Sa·bah [sä′bä′] A state of Malaysia in NE Borneo.

Sac·ra·men·to [sak′rə·men′tō] **1** The capital of California, in the north central part on the Sacramento River. Pop. 324,000. **2** A river in northern California.

Sa·har·a [sə·hâr′ə *or* sə·här′ə] The world's largest desert, stretching across northern Africa.

Sai·gon [sī′gon′] An old name for HO CHI MINH CITY.

Saint Au·gus·tine [sānt′ ô′gəs·tēn′] The oldest U.S. city, on the NE coast of Florida. Pop. 12,000.

Saint George's [sānt′ jôr′jəz] The capital and chief port of Grenada. Pop. 9,000.

Saint George's Channel A strait between SW Wales and Ireland.

Saint He·le·na [sānt′ hə·lē′nə] A British island in the South Atlantic off the SW coast of Africa where Napoleon lived in exile from 1815 to his death in 1821. Area, 47 sq. mi. Pop. 5,900.

Saint Helens, Mount [sānt hel′ənz] An active volcano in SW Washington state in the Cascade Mountain range. It erupted violently in 1980.

Saint John's [sānt′ jonz′] 1 The capital of the province of Newfoundland, Canada, a port on the SE coast. Pop. 162,000. 2 The capital of Antigua and Barbuda. Pop. 30,000.

Saint Kitts-Nev·is [sānt kits′nē′vis] A nation composed of three islands in the NE West Indies, in the Leewards. Capital, Basseterre. Area, 104 sq. mi. Pop. 47,000.

Saint Law·rence [sānt′ lôr′əns] A river of SE Canada, flowing from Lake Ontario northeast to the Gulf of St. Lawrence.

Saint Lawrence, Gulf of An inlet of the North Atlantic off the shores of New Brunswick, western Newfoundland, and SE Quebec.

Saint Lawrence Seaway A system of canals along the St. Lawrence River which, with the river, provides a channel for ships from the Great Lakes to the North Atlantic.

Saint Lou·is [sānt′ lo͞o′is] A city in eastern Missouri, on the Mississippi River. Pop. 426,300.

Saint Lu·cia [sānt′ lo͞o′shə] An island country of the SE West Indies, in the Windward Islands south of Martinique. Capital, Castries. Area, 238 sq. mi. Pop. 100,000.

Saint Paul [sānt′ pôl′] The capital of Minnesota, in the SE part of the state. Pop. 264,000.

Saint Pe·ters·burg [sānt′ pē′tərz·bûrg′] 1 An old name for LENINGRAD. 2 A city in western Florida, on Tampa Bay. Pop. 239,500.

Saint Pi·erre and Mi·que·lon [san pē·âr′ and mē·klôn′] Two French islands in the North Atlantic off southern Newfoundland. Area, 93 sq. mi.

Saint Thom·as [sānt′ tom′əs] One of the U.S. Virgin Islands. Area, 32 sq. mi.

Saint Vin·cent and the Gren·a·dines [sānt′ vin′·sənt, ənd thə gren′ə·dēnz′] An island country in the SE West Indies, in the Windward Islands west of Barbados. Capital, Kingstown. Area, 150 sq. mi. Pop. 100,000.

Sa·kha·lin [sak′ə·lēn′] An island of the extreme eastern Soviet Union, in the Pacific north of Japan. Area, 24,560 sq. mi.

Sa·lem [sā′ləm] The capital of Oregon, in the NW part of the state. Pop. 89,000.

Salis·bur·y [sôlz′ber′ē] An old name for HARARE.

Sa·lo·ni·ka [sə·lon′i·kə *or* sal′ə·nē′kə] A port city in northern Greece. Also *Thessaloníki.* Pop. 406,000.

Salt Lake City The capital of Utah, in the northern part of the state. Pop. 158,000.

Sal·va·dor [sal′və·dôr′] 1 The oldest city in Brazil, on the eastern coast. Pop. 1,812,000. 2 Another name for EL SALVADOR. Pop. 5,480,000.

Sal·ween [sal′wēn′] A river, 1,750 miles long, in Tibet and Burma.

Salzburg, a city famous for its music festivals

Salz·burg [sôlz′bûrg′ *or* zälts′bo͝ork′] A city in western Austria. Pop. 139,000.

Sa·mar·i·a [sə·mâr′ē·ə] A city and region in ancient Palestine, in what is now NW Jordan.

Sam·ar·kand [sam′ər·kand′] A city in the south central Soviet Union. Pop. 388,000.

Sa·mo·a [sə·mō′ə] An island group in Polynesia in the south central Pacific, divided between American Samoa and Western Samoa.

Sa·mos [sā′mos′] An island of Greece, in the Aegean off western Turkey. Area, 171 sq. mi.

Sa·n'a [sä·nä′] The capital of the Yemen Arab Republic, in the central part. Pop. 427,000.

San An·to·ni·o [san′ an·tō′nē·ō] A city in south central Texas. Pop. 914,500.

San Ber·nar·di·no [san′ bûr′nə·dē′nō] A city in southern California. Pop. 139,000.

San Di·e·go [san′ dē·ā′gō] A port city and naval base in SW California. Pop. 1,015,200.

Sand·wich Islands [san(d)′wich′] An old name for the HAWAIIAN ISLANDS.

San Francisco with the Golden Gate Bridge

San Fran·cis·co [san′ frən·sis′kō] A city in west central California, a port on San Francisco Bay. Pop. 750,000.

San Francisco Bay An inlet of the North Pacific off west central California.

San Jo·se [san′ hō·zā′] A city in west central California, southeast of San Francisco. Pop. 712,100.

San Jo·sé [san′ hō·zā′] The capital and largest city of Costa Rica, in the central part. Pop. 278,500.

An old section of San Juan

San Juan [san′ (h)wän′] The capital and largest city of Puerto Rico, on the NE coast. Pop. 435,000.

San Ma·ri·no [san′ mə·rē′nō] 1 A tiny country located within northern Italy. Capital, San Marino. Area, 24 sq. mi. Pop. 22,000. 2 The capital of San Marino. Pop. 4,400.

San Sal·va·dor [san sal′və·dôr′] **1** The capital and largest city of El Salvador. Pop. 453,000. **2** An island in the central Bahamas where Columbus first landed in the New World. Area, 60 sq. mi.

San·ta An·a [san′tə an′ə] A city in northern El Salvador. Pop. 135,000.

San·ta Cruz de Te·ne·rife [san′tə krōōz′ də ten′ə·rif′] A port city in the western Canary Islands. Pop. 191,000.

San·ta Fe [san′tə fā′] **1** The capital of New Mexico, in the north central part of the state. Pop. 49,000. **2** A city in NE Argentina. Pop. 290,000.

Santa Fe Trail An old wagon route that extended from Independence, Missouri, to Santa Fe, New Mexico, in use from about 1821 to 1880.

San·tan·der [sän′tän·der′] A city in northern Spain on the Bay of Biscay. Pop. 180,000.

San·ti·a·go [san′tē·ä′gō] The capital and largest city of Chile, in the central part. Pop. 4,834,000.

San·ti·a·go de Cu·ba [san′tē·ä′gō də k(y)ōō′bə] A city on the SE coast of Cuba. Pop. 358,000.

San·to Do·min·go [san′tō də·ming′gō] The capital of the Dominican Republic, a port on the Caribbean coast. It was the first city established by Europeans in the New World. Pop. 1,700,000.

San·tos [san′təs] A city and port in SE Brazil. Pop. 441,000.

São Fran·cis·co [sou′ frən·sis′kō] A river in eastern Brazil, flowing northeast to the Atlantic.

Unusual buildings form Sao Pāulo's modern skyline.

São Pau·lo [sou′ pou′lō] The largest city in South America, in SE Brazil. Pop. 10,099,000.

São To·mé [sou′ tōō·mā′] **1** An island in the Gulf of Guinea, the southern island of São Tomé and Príncipe. **2** The capital of São Tomé and Príncipe, on São Tomé Island. Pop. 35,000.

São Tomé and Prín·ci·pe [prin′si·pē] Two islands that form a country in the Gulf of Guinea off the west coast of Africa, just north of the equator. Capital, São Tomé. Area, 372 sq. mi. Pop. 114,000.

Sap·po·ro [sə·pôr′ō] A city in SW Hokkaido, Japan. Pop. 1,543,000.

Sar·a·gos·sa [sar′ə·gos′ə] A city in NE Spain. Pop. 591,000.

Sa·ra·je·vo [sar′ə·yā′vō] A city in central Yugoslavia. The assassination of the Archduke Ferdinand of Austria in this city on June 14, 1914, led to the outbreak of World War I.

Sa·ra·tov [sä·rä′tôf] A city in the western Soviet Union on the lower Volga River. Pop. 918,000.

Sa·ra·wak [sə·rä′wä(k)] A region of Malaysia in NW Borneo.

Sar·din·i·a [sär·din′ē·ə] A large island of Italy, west of the mainland and south of Corsica.

Sar·gas·so Sea [sär·gas′ō] A large area of the North Atlantic northeast of the West Indies.

Sas·katch·e·wan [sas·kach′ə·won′] A province of south central Canada, bordering on Montana and North Dakota. Capital, Regina. Area, 251,000 sq. mi. Pop. 1,010,000.

Sa·u·di Arabia [sä·ōō′dē *or* sou′dē] A country that occupies most of the Arabian Peninsula. Capital, Riyadh. Area, 830,000 sq. mi. Pop. 14,200,000.

Sault Sainte Ma·rie Canals [sōō′ sānt′mə·rē′] Three canals that bypass rapids in the waterway connecting Lakes Superior and Huron. Also *Soo Canals.*

Sa·van·nah [sə·van′ə] A city in eastern Georgia near the Atlantic. Pop. 147,000.

Sax·o·ny [sak′sə·nē] **1** A region and former duchy in northern West Germany. **2** A region and former duchy in southern East Germany.

Scan·di·na·vi·a [skan′də·nā′vē·ə] **1** The region of NW Europe occupied by Sweden, Norway, and Denmark, sometimes including Finland and Iceland. **2** The peninsula of NW Europe containing Norway and Sweden. Also **Scandinavian Peninsula.**

Remains of the Castle Eilean Donan, Loch Alsh, Scotland

Scot·land [skot′lənd] A division of the United Kingdom occupying the northern part of Great Britain and adjacent island groups. Area, 30,416 sq. mi. Pop. 5,131,000.

Scyth·i·a [sith′ē·ə] An ancient region of central Eurasia, roughly from the NW coast of the Black Sea east to the borders of China.

Se·at·tle [sē·at′(ə)l] A city in NW Washington, on Puget Sound. Pop. 486,200.

Seine [sān *or* sen] A river in northern France, flowing northwest to the English Channel.

Se·ma·rang [sə·mär′äng] A port city in north central Java, Indonesia. Pop. 1,269,000.

Sen·e·gal [sen′ə·gôl′] **1** A country in extreme western Africa, on the Atlantic south of Mauritania. Capital, Dakar. Area, 75,750 sq. mi. Pop. 7,000,000. **2** A river in western Africa that forms part of the Mauritania-Senegal border on its 1000-mile northwesterly course to the Atlantic.

Seoul [sōl] The capital and largest city of South Korea, in the NW part. Pop. 9,600,000.

Ser·bi·a [sûr′bē·ə] A constituent republic in SE Yugoslavia. It was once an independent kingdom.

Ser·en·get·i [ser′ən·get′ē] A plain in northern Tanzania noted for its wildlife.

Se·vas·to·pol [sə·vas′tə·pōl′] A city in the SW Soviet Union, in the Crimea on the Black Sea. Pop. 350,000.

Se·ville [sə·vil′] A historic city in SW Spain. Pop. 646,000.

Sew·ard Peninsula [sōō′ərd] A peninsula in western Alaska on the Bering Strait.

Sey·chelles [sā·shel(z)′] An island country in the western Indian Ocean, north of Madagascar. Capital, Victoria. Area, 171 sq. mi. Pop. 67,000.

Shan·dong [shän′dông′] A province in NE China on the Yellow Sea.

Shang·hai [shang′hī′] The largest city in China, on the east central coast at the mouth of the Yangtze. Pop. 11,940,000.

Shan·non [shan′ən] A river in western Ireland that flows southwest to the Atlantic.

Shan·tung [shan′tung′ *or* shän′tōōng′] Another spelling of SHANDONG.

Shas·ta [shas′tə], **Mount** A mountain of the Cascades in northern California. Height, 14,162 ft.

Shatt-al-Ar·ab [shät′äl·är′əb] A river in SE Iraq formed by the confluence of the Tigris and the Euphrates.

Shef·field [shef′ēld′] An industrial city in north central England. Pop. 539,000.

Shen·an·do·ah [shen′ən·dō′ə] A river that flows to the Potomac through a scenic wooded valley in northern Virginia and NW West Virginia.

Shen·yang [shun′yäng′] A city in NE China. Also *Mukden*. Pop. 4,210,000.

Sher·wood Forest [shûr′wŏŏd′] A forest in central England, famous as the home of Robin Hood and his men.

Shi·ko·ku [shē′kō·kōō′] An island of southern Japan between Honshu and Kyushu.

Shi·raz [shē·räz′] A city in SW Iran. Pop. 848,000.

Shreve·port [shrēv′pôrt′] A city in NW Louisiana. Pop. 220,400.

Si·am [sī·am′] An old name for THAILAND.

Si·an [shē′än′] Another spelling of XI′AN.

Si·be·ri·a [sī·bir′ē·ə] A vast region of the Soviet Union, from the Ural Mountains to the Pacific.

Si·chuan [sōō′chwän′] A province in south central China.

The Temple at Selinunte, one of the landmarks of Sicily

Sic·i·ly [sis′ə·lē] A large island of southern Italy off the SW tip of the mainland. Area, 9,926 sq. mi.

Si·er·ra Le·one [sē·er′ə lē·ōn′] A country in western Africa, on the Atlantic between Guinea and Liberia. Capital, Freetown. Area, 27,699 sq. mi. Pop. 4,000,000.

Si·er·ra Ma·dre [sē·er′ə mä′drā] Any of three mountain ranges in Mexico. **Sierra Madre del Sur** [del sōōr′] is in the south, along the Pacific coast. **Sierra Madre Oc·ci·den·tal** [ok′sə·den·täl′] is in the northwest, along the Pacific coast. **Sierra Madre Or·ien·tal** [ôr′yen·täl′] is in the northeast, inland from the Gulf of Mexico.

Lake Tahoe in the Sierra Nevada, California

Si·er·ra Ne·vad·a [sē·er′ə nə·vä′də] A mountain range in eastern California.

Sik·kim [sik′im] A state of NE India in the Himalayas between Bhutan and Nepal. It was once an independent kingdom.

Si·le·sia [si·lē′zhə *or* sī·lē′zhə] A region in SW Poland and northern Czechoslovakia.

Si·nai [sī′nī′] A peninsula in NE Egypt, bordering Israel.

Sinai, Mount A mountain in southern Sinai, believed to be where Moses received the Ten Commandments. Height, 7,500 ft.

Sin·ga·pore [sing′(g)ə·pôr′] **1** An island country in SE Asia, at the southern tip of the Malay Peninsula. Capital, Singapore. Area, 238 sq. mi. Pop. 2,700,000. **2** The capital and chief port of Singapore. Pop. 2,500,000.

Sin·kiang [sing′kyang′ *or* shin′jyäng′] A region in NW China between Tibet and Mongolia.

Skop·lje [skôp′lā′ *or* skôp′yā′] A city in SE Yugoslavia. Pop. 507,000.

Slo·va·ki·a [slō·vä′kē·ə] The region comprising the eastern part of Czechoslovakia.

Slo·ve·ni·a [slō·vē′nē·ə] A region and constituent republic of NW Yugoslavia.

Smyr·na [smûr′nə] Another name for IZMIR.

So·fi·a [sō′fē·ə *or* sō·fē′ə] The capital of Bulgaria, in the western part. Pop. 1,115,000.

Sol·o·mon Islands [sol′ə·mən] **1** An island group of the western Pacific east of New Guinea, divided between Papua New Guinea and the independent Solomon Islands. Also **the Solomons. 2** A country comprising the SE part of this group. Capital, Honiara. Area, 11,500 sq. mi. Pop. 300,000.

So·ma·li·a [sō·mä′lē·ə *or* sə·mäl′yə] A country in eastern Africa, on the Gulf of Aden and the Indian Ocean. Capital, Mogadishu. Area, 246,201 sq. mi. Pop. 8,000,000.

Soo Canals [sōō] Another name for the SAULT SAINTE MARIE CANALS.

South, the The SE and south central U.S., especially the 11 states that joined the confederacy.

South Africa A country in southern Africa, with coastlines on the South Atlantic and Indian oceans. Capitals, Cape Town (legislative), Pretoria (administrative), Bloemfontein (judicial). Area, 471,445 sq. mi. Pop. 35,100,000.

South America The southern continent of the Western Hemisphere.

South·amp·ton [south·(h)amp′tən] A city in southern England on the English Channel. Pop. 208,000.

South Australia A state in south central Australia.

South Bend A city in north central Indiana. Pop. 107,000.

A cypress garden in South Carolina

South Carolina A state in the SE U.S., on the Atlantic. Capital, Columbia. Area, 31,055 sq. mi. Pop. 3,425,000.

South China Sea A sea touching SE China, the Philippines, Malaysia, and Vietnam.

The Needles, Black Hills National Forest, South Dakota

South Da·ko·ta [də·kō′tə] A state in the north central U.S. Capital, Pierre. Area, 77,047 sq. mi. Pop. 709,000.

Southern Hemisphere The half of the earth south of the equator.

Southern Yemen See YEMEN, PEOPLE'S DEMOCRATIC REPUBLIC OF.

South Island The southern island of the two main islands of New Zealand. Area, 58,092 sq. mi.

South Ko·re·a [kə·rē′ə *or* kô·rē′ə] A country in eastern Asia occupying the southern part of the Korean peninsula. Capital, Seoul. Area, 38,004 sq. mi. Pop. 45,240,000.

South Pole The southernmost point on the earth, a point near the middle of Antarctica.

South Seas The parts of the oceans south of the equator, especially the South Pacific.

South Vietnam A former country incorporated into Vietnam in 1975.

South-West Africa Another name for NAMIBIA.

Soviet Russia Russia (def. 3).

Soviet Union Another name for the UNION OF SOVIET SOCIALIST REPUBLICS.

So·we·to [sə·wē′tō] A city in NE South Africa, near Johannesburg. Pop. 602,000.

A building by architect Antonio Gaudi in Barcelona, Spain

Spain [spān] A country in SW Europe, occupying most of the Iberian Peninsula. Capital, Madrid. Area, 194,885 sq. mi. Pop. 39,000,000.

Spanish America The countries south of the U.S. in which Spanish is spoken.

Spanish Main The northern coast of South America on the Caribbean Sea, in the days of sailing ships and pirates.

Spanish Sahara An old name for WESTERN SAHARA.

Spar·ta [spär′tə] A city in ancient Greece known for its military power.

Spice Islands An old name for the MOLUCCAS.

Spo·kane [spō·kan′] A city in eastern Washington. Pop. 173,000.

Spring·field [spring′fēld′] **1** The capital of Illinois, in the central part. Pop. 100,000. **2** A city in SW Massachusetts. Pop. 149,000. **3** A city in SW Missouri. Pop. 139,000.

Sri Lan·ka [srē läng′kə] An island country off the SE coast of India. Formerly *Ceylon.* Capital, Colombo. Area, 25,332 sq. mi. Pop. 16,600,000.

Sta·lin·grad [stä′lin·grad′] An old name for VOLGOGRAD.

Stat·en Island [stat′ən] An island that forms one of the boroughs of New York City. Area, 64 sq. mi. Pop. 375,000.

Stock·holm [stok′hō(l)m] The capital of Sweden, in the SE part on the Baltic. Pop. 1,409,000.

Stock·ton [stok′tən] A city in central California. Pop. 184,000.

Stras·bourg [sträs′bûrg] A city in NE France near the West German border. Pop. 253,000.

Strat·ford-up·on-A·von [strat′fərd·ə·pon·ā′vən *or* ā′von] A city in central England, the birthplace of William Shakespeare. Also **Stratford-on-Avon.**

Stutt·gart [s(h)to͝ot′gärt′] A city in southern West Germany. Pop. 564,000.

Su·cre [so͞o′krā] The official capital of Bolivia, in the central part of the country. Pop. 80,000.

Su·dan [so͞o·dan′] **1** A country in NE Africa, south of Egypt. Capital, Khartoum. Area, 967,500 sq. mi. Pop. 24,000,000. **2** A region of northern Africa, between the North Atlantic and the Upper Nile and south of the Sahara.

Su·ez [so͞o·ez′ *or* so͞o′ez] A city in NE Egypt at the southern end of the Suez Canal. Pop. 254,000.

Suez Canal A canal in NE Egypt that connects the Red and Mediterranean seas.

Su·la·we·si [so͞o′lə·wä′sē] Another name for CELEBES.

Su·ma·tra [so͞o·mä′trə] A large island of western Indonesia. Area, 166,789 sq. mi.

Su·mer [so͞o′mər] An ancient country of Mesopotamia, later a part of Babylonia.

Sum·ter [sum(p)′tər], **Fort** A fort in the harbor of Charleston, South Carolina. Confederate batteries attacked this fort on April 12, 1861, opening the Civil War.

Sun·da Islands [so͝on′də *or* sun′də] The western islands of the Malay Archipelago, including the **Greater Sunda Islands** (Sumatra, Borneo, Celebes, and Java) and the **Lesser Sunda Islands** (those from Bali to Timor). Also **the Sundas.**

Su·pe·ri·or [sə·pir′ē·ər], **Lake** The largest and westernmost of the Great Lakes. Area, 31,820 sq. mi.

Su·ri·nam [so͝or′ə·nam′] Another spelling of SURINAME.

Su·ri·na·me [so͝or′ə·nä′mə] A country on the northern coast of South America. Formerly *Dutch Guiana.* Capital, Paramaribo. Area, 63,037 sq. mi. Pop. 400,000.

Sur·rey [sûr′ē] A county in SE England, south of London.

Sus·que·han·na [sus′kwə·han′ə] A river in New York, Pennsylvania, and Maryland, flowing south to Chesapeake Bay.

Su·va [so͞o′və] The capital and largest city of Fiji. Pop. 69,000.

Su·wan·nee [sə·wä′nē] A river that flows through SE Georgia and northern Florida to the Gulf of Mexico.

Sval·bard [sväl′bär′] A group of Norwegian islands in the Arctic Ocean, north of Scandinavia.

Sverd·lovsk [sverd·lôfsk′] A city in the west central Soviet Union, in the Urals. Pop. 1,315,000.

Swa·zi·land [swä′zē·land′] A landlocked country in SE Africa. Capital, Mbabane. Area, 6,704 sq. mi. Pop. 700,000.

A section of Stockholm, Sweden, on Lake Malaren

Swe·den [swē′dən] A country in NW Europe, on the Baltic east of Norway. Capital, Stockholm. Area, 173,732 sq. mi. Pop. 8,400,000.

Switz·er·land [swit′sər·lənd] A mountainous country in west central Europe. Capital, Bern. Area, 15,941 sq. mi. Pop. 6,600,000.

The Opera House in Sydney, a strikingly dramatic building

Syd·ney [sid′nē] A city in SE Australia on an inlet of the Tasman Sea. Pop. 3,430,000.

Syr·a·cuse [sir′ə·kyo͞os′] **1** A city in central New York. Pop. 161,000. **2** A city in SE Sicily, Italy, that was an important Greek colony in ancient times. Pop. 123,000.

Syr·i·a [sir′ē·ə] A country in SW Asia, on the eastern Mediterranean south of Turkey. Capital, Damascus. Area, 71,498 sq. mi. Pop. 11,300,000.

Szcze·cin [shchet′sēn′] A city in NW Poland, on the Oder near the Baltic. Pop. 392,000.

Sze·chwan [se′chwän′] Another spelling of SICHUAN.

T

Ta·briz [tä·brēz′] A city in NW Iran. Pop. 571,000.

Ta·co·ma [tə·kō′mə] A city on Puget Sound in west central Washington. Pop. 159,000.

Ta·dzhik·i·stan [tä·jik′i·stan′] A region and constituent republic of the south central Soviet Union, bordering on Afghanistan and China.

Tae·gu [tī′go͞o′] A city in SE South Korea. Pop. 2,030,000.

Ta·gus [tā′gəs] A river that flows through central Spain and Portugal to the Atlantic.

Tahiti's natural beauty and warm climate are legendary.

Ta·hi·ti [tə·hē′tē] A French island of Polynesia in the South Pacific. Area, 402 sq. mi.

Ta·hoe [tä′hō], **Lake** A lake in the Sierra Nevada on the border between California and Nevada.

Tai·pei [tī·pä′ *or* tī′bä′] The capital and largest city of Taiwan, in the northern part of the country. Pop. 2,534,000.

Tai·wan [tī′wän′] An island country off the SE coast of mainland China. Also *Formosa, Nationalist China, Republic of China.* Capital, Taipei. Area, 13,885 sq. mi. Pop. 19,800,000.

Tal·la·has·see [tal′ə·has′ē] The capital of Florida, in the NW part of the state. Pop. 119,000.

Tal·linn [tal′in *or* tä′lin] A city in the NW Soviet Union on the Gulf of Finland. It is the capital of Estonia. Pop. 478,000.

Tam·pa [tam′pə] A city in western Florida, a major port on **Tampa Bay,** an inlet of the Gulf of Mexico. Pop. 278,000.

Ta·nan·a·rive [tə·nan′ə·rēv′] An old name for ANTANANARIVO.

Tan·gan·yi·ka [tan(g)′gən·yē′kə] A region and former British colony in eastern Africa, now part of Tanzania.

Tanganyika, Lake A long lake in central Africa, between Zaire and Tanzania.

Tan·gier [tan·gir′] A seaport in northern Morocco, at the western end of the Mediterranean. Pop. 304,000.

Dry grasslands in Tanganyika, a part of Tanzania

Tan·za·ni·a [tan′zə·nē′ə] A country in east central Africa, on the Indian Ocean. Capital, Dar es Salaam. Area, 364,900 sq. mi. Pop. 24,300,000.

Ta·ran·to [tä′rən·tō] A city in SE Italy, on the Ionian Sea. Pop. 248,000.

Tash·kent [täsh·kent′] The largest city in the Asian part of the Soviet Union, north of Afghanistan. Pop. 2,077,000.

Tas·ma·ni·a [taz·mā′nē·ə] An island and state of Australia, southeast of the mainland.

Tas·man Sea [taz′mən] The part of the South Pacific between Australia and New Zealand.

Tbi·li·si [tə·bil′i·sē *or* tə·blē′sē] A city in the SW Soviet Union. Pop. 1,174,000.

Te·gu·ci·gal·pa [tā·go͞o′sē·gäl′pä] The capital of Honduras, in the central part. Pop. 571,000.

Te·he·ran or **Teh·ran** [tā′ə·rän′ *or* tā′ə·ran′] The capital of Iran, in the northern part of the country. Pop. 6,038,000.

Tel A·viv [tel′ ə·vēv′] A city in western Israel, on the Mediterranean. Pop. 320,000.

Ten·nes·see [ten′i·sē′] **1** A state in the SE U.S. Capital, Nashville. Area, 42,244 sq. mi. Pop. 4,855,000. **2** A river in the SE U.S. that flows for 650 miles in an arc through eastern and western Tennessee and western Kentucky to the Ohio River.

Te·noch·ti·tlan [tā·nôch′tē·tlän′] The capital of the ancient Aztecs, on the site of modern Mexico City.

Tex·as [tek′səs] A state in the south central U.S. Capital, Austin. Area, 267,338 sq. mi. Pop. 16,789,000.

Thai·land [tī′land′] A country in SE Asia, between Burma and Kampuchea. Formerly *Siam.* Capital, Bangkok. Area, 198,457 sq. mi. Pop. 54,700,000.

Henley-on-Thames, a small town near London

Thames [temz] A river in southern England, flowing through London into the North Sea.

Temple ruins in Luxor, the modern-day name of Thebes

Thebes [thēbz] **1** A city in ancient Egypt, famous for its temples and tombs. **2** A city in ancient Greece, northwest of Athens.

Ther·mop·y·lae [thər·mop′ə·lē] A mountain pass in east central Greece where, in 480 B.C., a small force of Spartans resisted the Persian army for three days.

Thes·sa·lo·ní·ki [thes′ə·lô·nē′kē] The Greek name for SALONIKA.

Thes·sa·ly [thes′ə·lē] A region of north central Greece.

Thim·bu [t(h)im′bo͞o] The capital of Bhutan, in the western part of the country. Pop. 15,500.

Thousand Islands A group of many small islands in the St. Lawrence River between New York and Canada, just east of Lake Ontario.

Thrace [thrās] A region and ancient country of the eastern Balkan Peninsula, north of the Aegean.

Thunder Bay A city in SW Ontario, Canada, on Lake Superior. Pop. 122,000.

Tian·jin [tyän′jin′] A city in northern China, southeast of Beijing. Pop. 5,400,000.

Tian Shan [tyän′ shän′] A mountain range in NW China and the south central Soviet Union.

The Castle of St. Angelo on the Tiber

Ti·ber [tī′bər] A river in central Italy flowing through Rome.

Prayer flags fly in front of the Potala, monastery of the Dalai Lama in Lhasa, Tibet, now a museum for tourists.

Ti·bet [ti·bet′] A region of high mountains and plateaus in SW China, north of India. Tibet was once an independent country.

Tien Shan [tyen′ shän′] Another spelling of TIAN SHAN.

Tien·tsin [tyen′tsin′] Another spelling of TIANJIN.

Tier·ra del Fue·go [tyer′ə del fwā′gō] A large island and many smaller islands at the southern end of South America, divided between Chile and Argentina.

Ti·gris [tī′gris] A river in SW Asia flowing from eastern Turkey through Iraq to the Shatt-al-Arab near the Persian Gulf.

Ti·jua·na [tē′ə·wä′nə] A city in extreme NW Mexico, on the U.S. border. Pop. 496,000.

Tim·buk·tu [tim′buk·to͞o′] A town in central Mali that flourished as a center of trade and learning from the 13th to the 16th century.

Ti·mor [tē′môr′ *or* tē·môr′] An island in southern Indonesia, southeast of Celebes.

Ti·ra·ne or **Ti·ra·na** [ti·rä′nə] The capital of Albania, in the central part. Pop. 206,000.

Ti·rol [tə·rōl′, tir′ōl′, *or* tī′rōl′] Another spelling of TYROL.

To·ba·go [tə·bā′gō] A small island northeast of Trinidad, with which it forms Trinidad and Tobago. Area, 116 sq. mi.

To·go [tō′gō] A country in western Africa, on the Gulf of Guinea between Ghana and Benin. Capital, Lomé. Area, 21,622 sq. mi. Pop. 3,300,000.

Kabuki dancers in a Tokyo theater

To·ky·o [tō′kē·ō] The capital of Japan, in eastern Honshu on **Tokyo Bay,** an inlet of the Pacific. Pop. 8,355,000.

To·le·do [tə·lē′dō] **1** A city in NW Ohio on Lake Erie. Pop. 340,000. **2** A historic city in central Spain. Pop. 56,000.

Ton·ga [tong′gə] An island country in the SW Pacific, in Polynesia south of Samoa. Capital, Nukualofa. Area, 270 sq. mi. Pop. 108,000.

Ton·kin [ton′kin′ *or* tong′kin′], **Gulf of** An arm of the South China Sea off northern Vietnam and southern China.

To·pe·ka [tə·pē′kə] The capital of Kansas, in the NE part of the state. Pop. 119,000.

The dramatically modern City Hall of Toronto

To·ron·to [tə·ron′tō] The capital of the province of Ontario, Canada, on Lake Ontario. Pop. 3,427,000.

Tra·fal·gar [trə·fal′gər], **Cape** A cape on the SW coast of Spain, where the British fleet under Horatio Nelson defeated the French and Spanish in October, 1805.

Trans·kei [trans′kī′] A group of districts in SE South Africa that South Africa has declared an independent black homeland. Capital, Umtata. Area, 16,675 sq. mi. Pop. 3,000,000.

Trans·vaal [trans·väl′] A province in NE South Africa.

Tran·syl·va·ni·a [tran′sil·vā′nē·ə] A region in west central Romania.

Tren·ton [tren′tən] The capital of New Jersey, in the west central part on the Delaware River. Pop. 92,000.
Tri·este [trē·est′] A city in NE Italy, on an inlet of the Adriatic. Pop. 239,000.
Trin·i·dad [trin′i·dad′] An island off NE Venezuela, part of Trinidad and Tobago.
Trin·i·dad and To·ba·go A country consisting of two islands off the NE coast of Venezuela. Capital, Port of Spain. Area, 1,980 sq. mi. Pop. 1,300,000.
Trip·o·li [trip′ə·lē] The capital of Libya, on the Mediterranean. Pop. 587,000.
Troy [troi] An ancient city in NW Asia Minor, near the Dardanelles. It figures in many ancient Greek and medieval legends. Also *Ilium.*
Tsing·tao [tsing′tou′] Another name for QINGDAO.
Tuc·son [tōō′son] A city in SE Arizona. Pop. 359,000.
Tul·sa [tul′sə] A city in NE Oklahoma. Pop. 374,000.
Tu·nis [t(y)ōō′nis] The capital of Tunisia, in the northern part on the Mediterranean. Pop. 1,000,000.

A small town market in Tunisia

Tu·ni·sia [t(y)ōō·nē′zhə] A country in northern Africa, on the Mediterranean east of Algeria. Capital, Tunis. Area, 63,170 sq. mi. Pop. 7,700,000.
Tu·rin [t(y)ŏŏ′rin] A city in NW Italy. Pop. 1,050,000.
Tur·ka·na (tər·kan′ə), **Lake** Another name for LAKE RUDOLF.
Tur·ke·stan [tûr′kə·stan′] A region of central Asia mostly between the southern Caspian Sea and China.

Mount Ararat, Turkey

Tur·key [tûr′kē] A country in SW Asia and SE Europe, between the Black and Mediterranean seas. Capital, Ankara. Area, 301,382 sq. mi. Pop. 52,900,000.
Turk·men·i·stan [tûrk·men′i·stan′] A constituent republic of the south central Soviet Union, bordering on Iran and Afghanistan.
Tu·va·lu [tōō′və·lōō′] An island country in the SW Pacific east of the Solomons. Capital, Funafuti. Area, 10 sq. mi. Pop. 9,000.
Tyre [tīr] An important city in ancient Phoenicia, on the Mediterranean in present-day Lebanon.

The farming village of Hofer in the Austrian Tyrol

Tyr·ol [tə·rōl′, tir′ōl′, *or* tī′rōl′] A region in the Alps of western Austria and northern Italy.
Tyr·rhe·ni·an Sea [ti·rē′nē·ən] The part of the Mediterranean between the Italian mainland and Corsica, Sardinia, and Sicily.

U

U·gan·da [yōō·gan′də *or* ōō·gän′də] A country in east central Africa, on Lake Victoria and the equator. Capital, Kampala. Area, 91,134 sq. mi. Pop. 16,400,000.
U·kraine [yōō·krān′ *or* yōō′krān′] A region and constituent republic of the SW Soviet Union, on the Black Sea.
U·lan Ba·tor [ōō′län bä′tôr] The capital of the Mongolian People's Republic, in the north central part. Pop. 500,000.
Ul·ster [ul′stər] A former province of Ireland, now forming Northern Ireland and part of the Republic of Ireland.
Union of Soviet Socialist Republics The largest country in the world, in eastern Europe and northern Asia. It is a union of 15 constituent republics. Also *Soviet Union.* Capital, Moscow. Area, 8,603,000 sq. mi. Pop. 286,000,000.
United Arab E·mir·ates [i·mir′əts] A country in eastern Arabia formed by a union of sheikdoms on the southern Persian Gulf. Capital, Abu Dhabi. Area, 32,000 sq. mi. Pop. 1,500,000.
United Kingdom A country made up of England, Scotland, Wales, and Northern Ireland. It is called in full the **United Kingdom of Great Britain and Northern Ireland.** Also *Great Britain.* Capital, London. Area, 94,217 sq. mi. Pop. 57,100,000.
United States of America A country in North America, a federal republic of 50 states, the District of Columbia, and Puerto Rico. All of the states lie between Canada and Mexico except for Hawaii in the central Pacific and Alaska in NW North America. Also **United States.** Capital, Washington, D.C. Area, 3,615,211 sq. mi. Pop. 246,100,000.

Upper Vol·ta [vol′tə *or* vōl′tə] Another name for BURKINA FASO.

Ur [ûr] An ancient city on the Euphrates in southern Babylonia, in present-day southern Iraq.

U·ral [yo͝or′əl] A river in the west central Soviet Union, flowing into the Caspian Sea.

Ural Mountains A mountain system in the west central Soviet Union, the traditional boundary between Europe and Asia. Also **the Urals.**

U·ru·guay [yo͝or′ə·gwā′ *or* o͞or′ə·gwī′] A country in SE South America, on the Atlantic and the Río de la Plata. Capital, Montevideo. Area, 68,536 sq. mi. Pop. 3,000,000.

Rock formations, Bryce National Park, Utah

U·tah [yo͞o′tô *or* yo͞o′tä] A state in the western U.S. Capital, Salt Lake City. Area, 84,916 sq. mi. Pop. 1,680,000.

U·trecht [yo͞o′trekt′] A city in the central Netherlands, on the Rhine. Pop. 229,000.

Ux·mal [o͞osh·mal′] Site of the ruins of an ancient Mayan city in Yucatán, SE Mexico.

Uz·bek·i·stan [o͞oz·bek′i·stan′] A constituent republic of the Soviet Union, southeast of the Aral Sea.

V

Va·duz [vä′do͞ots, vä·doots′, *or* fä·do͞ots′] The capital of Liechtenstein, on the Rhine. Pop. 5,000.

Va·len·ci·a [və·len′s(h)e·ə *or* və·len′shə] **1** A city in eastern Spain on the Mediterranean. Pop. 752,000. **2** A city in northern Venezuela. Pop. 616,000.

Val·let·ta [və·let′ə] The capital and chief port of Malta. Pop. 15,000.

Valley Forge [fôrj] A village of SE Pennsylvania, winter headquarters of the Continental Army (1777–1778).

Val·pa·rai·so [val′pə·rī′zō] A city in central Chile, a major port on the Pacific. Pop. 278,000.

Van·cou·ver [van·ko͞o′vər] A city in SW British Columbia, Canada, on the Pacific opposite Vancouver Island. Pop. 1,380,000.

Vancouver Island A large island of SW British Columbia, Canada. Area, 12,408 sq. mi.

Va·nu·a·tu [vä′no͞o·ä′to͞o] A country consisting of a group of islands in the SW Pacific north of New Zealand. Formerly *New Hebrides*. Capital, Vila. Area, 5,700 sq. mi. Pop. 200,000.

Va·ra·na·si [və·rä′nə·sē] Another name for BANARAS.

The Church of Saint Peter in Vatican City

Vat·i·can City [vat′i·kən] An independent papal state within Rome. It is the center of the Roman Catholic Church. Area, 108 acres. Pop. 1,000.

Ven·da [ven′də] A group of districts in NE South Africa that South Africa has declared an independent black homeland. Capital, Thohoyandou.

Ven·e·zue·la [ven′ə·zwā′lə] A country on the northern coast of South America. Capital, Caracas. Area, 352,145 sq. mi. Pop. 19,246,000.

A view along the Grand Canal of Venice

Ven·ice [ven′is] A city in NE Italy built on over 100 small islands in a lagoon at the NW end of the Adriatic. Pop. 340,000.

Ver·a·cruz [ver′ə·kro͞oz′] A city in southern Mexico, on the Gulf of Mexico east of Mexico City. Pop. 305,000.

Verde [vûrd], **Cape** A peninsula on the Atlantic coast of Senegal, forming the westernmost point of Africa.

Ver·mont [vər·mont′] A state in the NE U.S. Capital, Montpelier. Area, 9,609 sq. mi. Pop. 548,000.

The Palace of Versailles

Ver·sailles [ver·sī′] A city in northern France, near Paris. The site of a palace built by Louis XIV. The treaty ending World War I was signed here in 1919.

Ve·su·vi·us [və·sōō′vē·əs], **Mount** An active volcano near Naples, Italy. Height, 4,190 ft.

Vi·chy [vish′ē *or* vē′she′] A city in central France, the seat of the government during World War II. Pop. 32,000.

Vic·to·ri·a [vik·tôr′ē·ə] **1** A state in SE Australia. **2** The capital of British Columbia, Canada, a port on SE Vancouver Island. Pop. 256,000. **3** The capital of Hong Kong. Pop. 1,027,000. **4** The capital of the Seychelles. Pop. 23,000.

Victoria, Lake The largest lake in Africa, in the east central part of the continent with coastlines in Kenya, Uganda and Tanzania.

Victoria Falls A large waterfall in the Zambesi River between Zambia and Zimbabwe.

The world famous Spanish Court Riding School of Vienna

Vi·en·na [vē·en′ə] The capital of Austria, in the NE part. Pop. 1,550,000.

Vien·tiane [vyen·tyän′] The capital of Laos, on the Mekong River. Pop. 377,000.

Viet·nam or **Viet Nam** [vyet′nam′ *or* vyet′näm′] A country in SE Asia, on the South China Sea. It was formerly divided into North Vietnam and South Vietnam. Capital, Hanoi. Area, 128,402 sq. mi. Pop. 66,708,000.

Vi·la [vē′lə] The capital of Vanuatu. Pop. 15,000.

Vil·ni·us [vil′nē·əs′] A city in the western Soviet Union, the capital of Lithuania. Pop. 566,000.

Vir·gin·ia [vûr·jin′yə] A state in the eastern U.S., on the Atlantic and Chesapeake Bay. Capital, Richmond. Area, 40,817 sq. mi. Pop. 5,909,000.

Virginia Beach A city in SE Virginia on the Atlantic. Pop. 333,000.

Vir·gin Islands [vûr′jin] An island group in the West Indies east of Puerto Rico. Three of the islands in the southwest are the **Virgin Islands of the United States,** a U.S. territory. The rest make up the **British Virgin Islands.**

Vi·sa·yan Islands [və·sī′ən] The islands in the Philippines between Mindanao and Luzon. Also **the Visayans.**

Vis·tu·la [vis′chə·lə] A river in Poland, flowing northward into the Baltic Sea.

Vla·di·vos·tok [vlad′ə·vos′tok *or* vlä′di·vos·tok′] A port city in the extreme SE Soviet Union, on the Sea of Japan. Pop. 615,000.

Vol·ga [vol′gə] The longest river in Europe, flowing 2,300 mi. east and south through the western part of the Soviet Union, to the Caspian Sea.

Vol·go·grad [vol′gə·grad′] A city in the SE Soviet Union, on the lower Volga. Formerly *Stalingrad.* Pop. 974,000.

Vol·ta [väl′tə *or* vōl′tə] A river system in western Africa. The **Black Volta** and the **White Volta** both rise in Upper Volta and flow southward to central Ghana. There they join to form the **Volta,** which flows southward through the artificial **Lake Volta** into the Gulf of Guinea.

Vosges [vōzh] A mountain range in NE France.

W

Wa·bash [wô′bash′] A river in the east central U.S. that forms part of the Indiana-Illinois border as it flows to the Ohio River.

Wai·ki·ki [wī′ki·kē′] A beach and resort section of Honolulu, Hawaii.

Wake Island [wāk] A small U.S. island in the northern Pacific west of Hawaii. Area, 3 sq. mi.

Wal·den Pond [wôl′dən] A pond near Concord, Massachusetts, where Henry David Thoreau lived.

Harlech Castle in Wales

Wales [wālz] A division of the United Kingdom, in SW Great Britain west of England. Area, 8,017 sq. mi. Pop. 2,790,000.

War·ren [wôr'ən *or* wor'ən] A city in SE Michigan. Pop. 150,000.
War·saw [wôr'sô] The capital and largest city of Poland, in the east central part of the country. Pop. 1,659,000.
War·wick·shire [wor'ik·shir *or* wor'ik·shər] A county in central England.

The Jefferson Memorial in Washington, D.C.

Wash·ing·ton [wash'ing·tən *or* wô'shing·tən] **1** A state in the NW U.S. on the Pacific. Capital, Olympia. Area, 68,192 sq. mi. Pop. 4,409,000. **2** The capital of the U.S., in the District of Columbia. Pop. 626,000.
Washington, Mount The highest of the White Mountains in New Hampshire. Height, 6,288 ft.
Wa·ter·bur·y [wô'tər·ber'ē] A city in west central Connecticut. Pop. 102,000.
Wa·ter·loo [wô'tər·lōō' *or* wot'ər·lōō'] A town in central Belgium where Napoleon was defeated in 1815. Pop. 18,000.
Wed·dell Sea [wə·del' *or* wed'(ə)l] A broad inlet of the South Atlantic off the coast of Antarctica.
Wei·mar [vī'mär' *or* wī'mär'] A city in SW East Germany where the republic was established that ruled Germany from 1919 to 1933. Pop. 63,000.
Wel·land Canal [wel'ənd] A ship canal connecting Lakes Ontario and Erie just west of the Niagara River in SE Ontario, Canada.
Wel·ling·ton [wel'ing·tən] The capital of New Zealand, on the southern coast of North Island. Pop. 1,037,000.
West Berlin The part of the city of Berlin politically associated with West Germany. Pop. 1,879,000.
Western Australia A state of western Australia.
Western Hemisphere The half of the earth that lies west of the Atlantic Ocean, including North America and South America.
Western Sahara A region and former Spanish territory in NW Africa, now forming the southern part of Morocco. Formerly *Spanish Sahara.*
Western Samoa An island country comprising the western part of the Samoa islands in the South Pacific. Capital, Apia. Area, 1,133 sq. mi. Pop. 200,000.
West Germany The western and southern part of Germany, now a separate country called the *Federal Republic of Germany.* Capital, Bonn. Area, 96,000 sq. mi. Pop. 61,200,000.
West In·dies [in'dēz] The many islands between North and South America, separating the North Atlantic from the Caribbean Sea. They are divided into the Bahamas and the Antilles.
West I·ri·an [ir'ē·än'] The western part of the island of New Guinea, administered by Indonesia.

West Point has been a U.S. military post since 1802.

West Point The U.S. Military Academy, in SE New York on the Hudson.
West Virginia A state in the eastern U.S. Capital, Charleston. Area, 24,181 sq. mi. Pop. 1,897,000.
White·horse [(h)wīt'hôrs'] The capital of Yukon Territory, Canada, in the southern part. Pop. 18,000.
White Mountains A range of the Appalachians in north central New Hampshire.
White Russia Another name for BYELORUSSIA.
Whit·ney [(h)wit'nē], **Mount** A peak in the Sierra Nevada in eastern California. Height, 14,495 ft.
Wich·i·ta [wich'i·tô'] A city in south central Kansas. Pop. 289,000.
Wight [wīt], **Isle of** An island off the southern coast of England, in the English Channel near Southampton. Area, 147 sq. mi.

Restored homes in Williamsburg

Wil·liams·burg [wil'yəmz·bûrg'] A historic town in eastern Virginia with a restored colonial district.
Wilt·shire [wilt'shir *or* wilt'shər] A county in southern England.
Wind·sor [win'zər] A city in southern Ontario, Canada, opposite Detroit. Pop. 254,000.
Wind·ward Islands [wind'wərd] The islands of the SE West Indies from Martinique to Grenada. Also **the Windwards.**
Win·ni·peg [win'ə·peg'] The capital of Manitoba, Canada, in the southern part. Pop. 672,000.
Winnipeg, Lake A large lake in southern Manitoba, Canada.

Win·ston-Sa·lem [win′stən·sā′ləm] A city in NW North Carolina. Pop. 148,000.

Taliesin East, home of Frank Lloyd Wright, in Spring Green, Wisconsin

Wis·con·sin [wis·kon′sən] A state in the north central U.S. Capital, Madison. Area, 56,154 sq. mi. Pop. 4,807,000.

Woods, Lake of the A lake mostly in SW Ontario, Canada, and partly in northern Minnesota.

Worces·ter [wo͝os′tər] A city in east central Massachusetts. Pop. 158,000.

Wro·claw [vrôt′släf′] A city in SW Poland on the Oder River. Formerly *Breslau.* Pop. 637,000.

Wu·han [wo͞o′hän′] A city in east central China on the Yangtze. Pop. 4,250,000.

Wy·o·ming [wī·ō′ming] A state in the west central U.S. Capital, Cheyenne. Area, 97,914 sq. mi. Pop. 490,000.

X

Xi'·an [shē′än′] A city in central China. Pop. 2,820,000.

Xin·jiang [shēn′jyäng′] Another spelling of SINGKIANG.

Xi·zang [shē′tsäng′] Another name for TIBET.

Y

Ya·kutsk [yä·ko͞otsk′] A city in the eastern Soviet Union, on the Lena River in Siberia. Pop. 184,000.

Yal·ta [yôl′tə] A city in the SW Soviet Union, in the Crimea on the Black Sea. Pop. 85,000.

Ya·lu [yä′lo͞o] A river rising in NE China, flowing along the Manchuria-North Korea border, and emptying into the Yellow Sea.

Yang·tze [yang′sē *or* yäng′tsē′] The longest river of Asia, flowing about 3,450 miles across central China to the East China Sea. Also *Chang.*

Ya·oun·dé [yä·o͞on·dā′] The capital of Cameroon, in the south central part. Pop. 583,000.

Yel·low·knife [yel′ō·nīf′] The capital of the Northwest Territories, Canada, on Great Slave Lake. Pop. 11,000.

Yellow River A river that flows across northern China to the Yellow Sea. Also *Huang* or *Hwang Ho.*

Yellow Sea An inlet of the North Pacific between Korea and China.

A buffalo on the Firehole River, Yellowstone National Park

Yel·low·stone National Park [yel′ō·stōn′] The largest and oldest U.S. national park, largely in NW Wyoming.

Yem·en [yem′ən], **People's Democratic Republic of** A country in southern Arabia on the Arabian Sea. Also *Southern Yemen.* Capital, Aden. Area, 111,075 sq. mi. Pop. 2,400,000.

Yemen Arab Republic A country in southern Arabia on the Red Sea. Capital, San'a. Area, 75,290 sq. mi. Pop. 6,530,000.

Ye·re·van [ye·re·vän′] A city in the SW Soviet Union near the Turkish border. It is the capital of Armenia. Pop. 1,168,000.

Yo·ko·ha·ma [yō′kə·hä′mə] A port city on SE Honshu, Japan. Pop. 2,993,000.

Yon·kers [yong′kərz] A city in SE New York, on the Hudson north of New York City. Pop. 186,000.

The Cathedral of York in Yorkshire is one of the finest churches in England.

York·shire [yôrk′shir *or* york′shər] A former county of NE England.

York·town [yôrk′toun′] A town in SE Virginia where a large British force surrendered in 1781, concluding the Revolutionary War.

Yo·sem·i·te National Park [yō·sem′i·tē] A national park in east central California. A section of the park, **Yosemite Valley,** is noted for its waterfalls.

Youngs·town [yungz′toun′] A steel-producing center in NE Ohio. Pop. 105,000.

The Mayan monuments of Chichén Itzá in the Yucatán

Yu·ca·tán [yo͞o′kə·tan′] A peninsula of SE Mexico and NW Central America.

Medieval Dubrovnik, Yugoslavia, a major tourist attraction

Yu·go·sla·vi·a [yo͞o′gō·slä′vē·ə] A country in SE Europe, on the Adriatic Sea. Capital, Belgrade. Area, 98,766 sq. mi. Pop. 23,600,000.
Yu·kon [yo͞o′kon′] A river that flows from southern Yukon Territory, Canada, across central Alaska to the Bering Sea.
Yukon Territory A territory in NW Canada. Capital, Whitehorse. Area, 207,076 sq. mi. Pop. 23,500.
Yun·nan [yo͞o′nän′] A province in southern China bordering on Vietnam, Laos, and Burma.

Z

Za·greb [zä′greb] A city in NW Yugoslavia. Pop. 765,000.
Za·ire [zä·ir′] **1** A country in central Africa, on the equator. Formerly *Belgian Congo*. Capital, Kinshasa. Area, 905,568 sq. mi. Pop. 33,300,000. **2** Another name for the CONGO River.

Victoria Falls in the Zambezi River

Zam·be·zi or **Zam·be·si** [zam·bē′zē] A river in southern Africa, flowing into the Indian Ocean in central Mozambique.
Zam·bi·a [zam′bē·ə] A landlocked country in south central Africa. Capital, Lusaka. Area, 290,586 sq. mi. Pop. 7,500,000.
Zan·zi·bar [zan′zə·bär′] An island of Tanzania in the Indian Ocean off the NE coast. It was once an independent sultanate. Area, 640 sq. mi.
Zim·ba·bwe [zim·bä′bwā] A landlocked country in south central Africa. Formerly *Rhodesia*. Capital, Harare. Area, 150,800 sq. mi. Pop. 9,700,000.
Zi·on [zī′ən] **1** A hill in Jerusalem, the site of the ancient Jewish Temple. **2** Israel.
Zui·der Zee [zī′dər zē′] A former shallow inlet of the North Sea in the NW Netherlands, now partly drained and turned into the Ijsselmeer.
Zu·lu·land [zo͞o′lo͞o·land′] A region in NE South Africa along the Indian Ocean.

Old houses on the Limmat River in Zurich

Zu·rich [zo͝or′ik] A city in NE Switzerland. Pop. 349,500.

Maps (Contents)

The World

Robinson Projection

GREENLAND (DEN.)
ALASKA (U. S.)
CANADA
NORTH AMERICA
UNITED STATES
PACIFIC OCEAN
ATLANTIC OCEAN
MIDWAY ISLANDS (U. S.)
Tropic of Cancer
See inset below
MEXICO
HAWAII (U. S.)
VENEZUELA
GUYANA
SURINAME
FRENCH GUIANA (FR.)
COLOMBIA
Equator
GALAPAGOS ISLANDS (ECUADOR)
ECUADOR
SOUTH AMERICA
PERU
BRAZIL
WESTERN SAMOA
AMERICAN SAMOA (U. S.)
TONGA
FRENCH POLYNESIA (FR.)
BOLIVIA
PARAGUAY
Tropic of Capricorn
EASTER ISLAND (CHILE)
CHILE
URUGUAY
ARGENTINA
PACIFIC OCEAN
FALKLAND ISLANDS (U.K.)
Antarctic Circle
80°
60°
40°
20°
0°
20°
40°
60°
80°
180°
160°
140°
120°
100°
80°
60°
40°

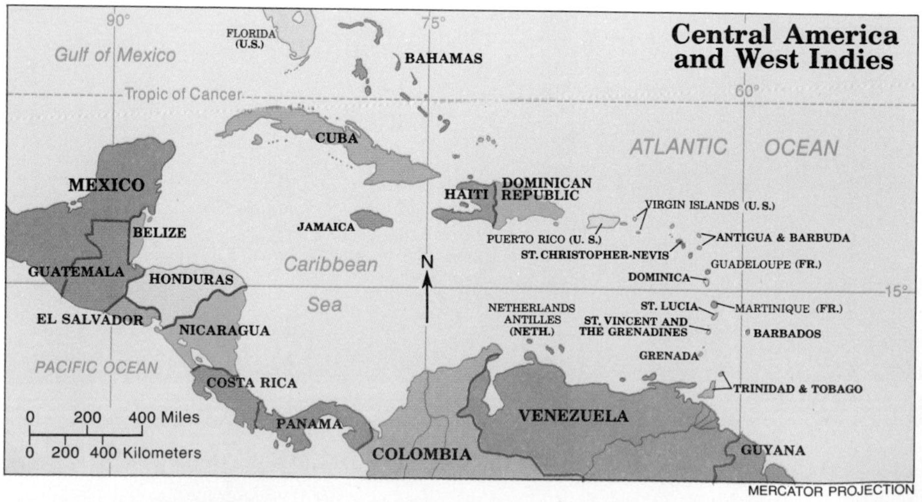

Central America and West Indies
90°
75°
60°
15°
Gulf of Mexico
FLORIDA (U.S.)
BAHAMAS
Tropic of Cancer
CUBA
ATLANTIC OCEAN
MEXICO
HAITI
DOMINICAN REPUBLIC
VIRGIN ISLANDS (U. S.)
BELIZE
JAMAICA
PUERTO RICO (U. S.)
ANTIGUA & BARBUDA
ST. CHRISTOPHER-NEVIS
GUADELOUPE (FR.)
Caribbean Sea
N
GUATEMALA
HONDURAS
DOMINICA
NETHERLANDS ANTILLES (NETH.)
ST. LUCIA
MARTINIQUE (FR.)
ST. VINCENT AND THE GRENADINES
BARBADOS
EL SALVADOR
NICARAGUA
GRENADA
PACIFIC OCEAN
COSTA RICA
TRINIDAD & TOBAGO
0 200 400 Miles
0 200 400 Kilometers
PANAMA
VENEZUELA
COLOMBIA
GUYANA
MERCATOR PROJECTION

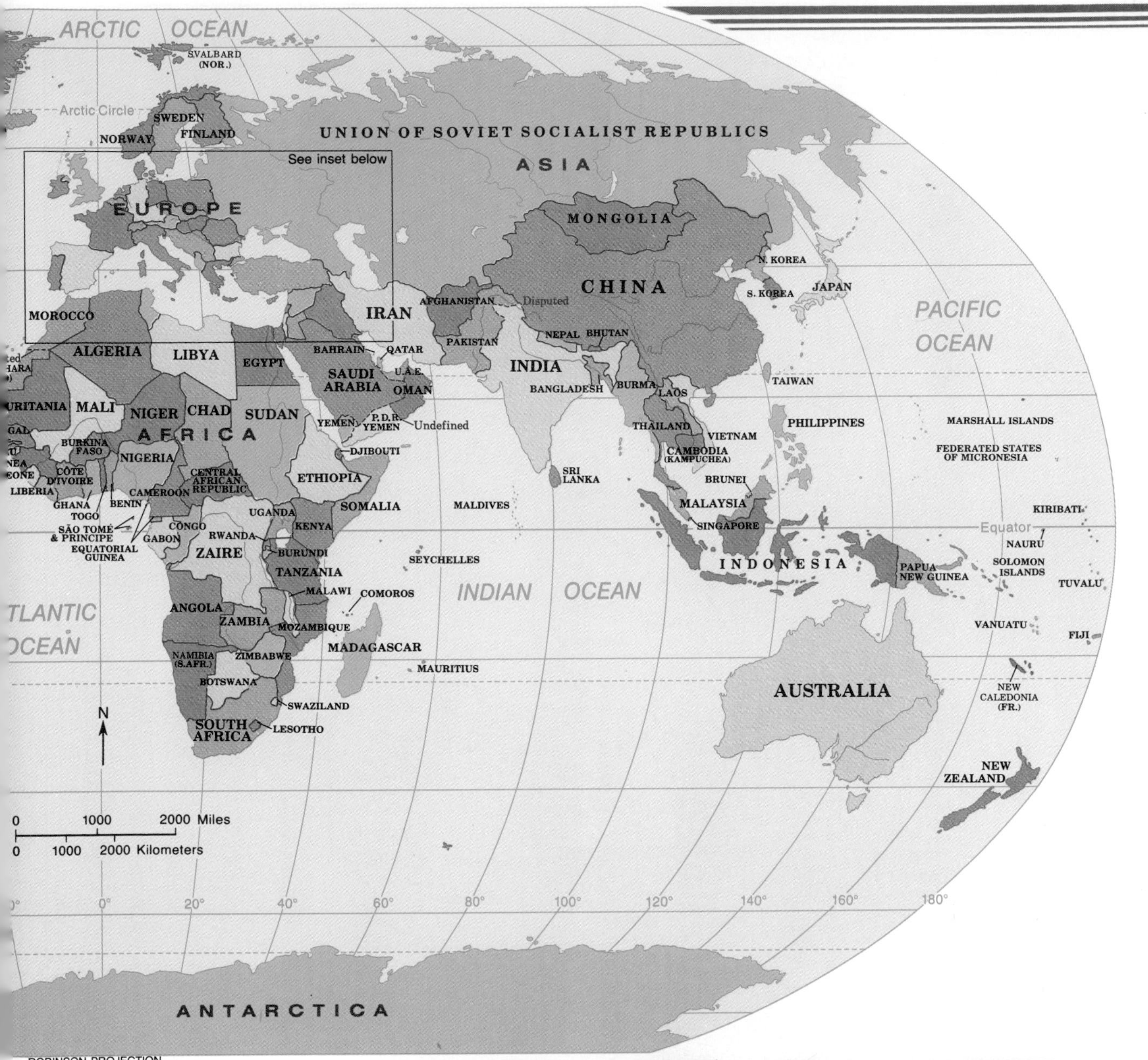

ROBINSON PROJECTION

Abbreviation Country

DEN.	**–DENMARK**
FR.	**–FRANCE**
NETH.	**–NETHERLANDS**
NOR.	**–NORWAY**
PORT.	**–PORTUGAL**
SWITZ.	**–SWITZERLAND**
S. AFR.	**–SOUTH AFRICA**
U.A.E.	**–UNITED ARAB EMIRATES**
U.K.	**–UNITED KINGDOM**
U.S.	**–UNITED STATES**

MERCATOR PROJECTION

North America

Azimuthal Equal Area Projection

ASIA
ARCTIC OCEAN
CHUKCHI SEA
Bering Strait
BERING SEA
BEAUFORT SEA
BROOKS RANGE
QUEEN ELIZABETH ISLANDS
GREENLAND
(Icecap—always frozen)
ICELAND
Denmark Strait
ARCTIC CIRCLE
PARRY ISLANDS
BANKS ISLAND
VICTORIA ISLAND
BAFFIN BAY
BAFFIN ISLAND
Davis Strait
Yukon River
ALASKA (U.S.A.)
Fairbanks
ALASKA RANGE
Anchorage
KODIAK ISLAND
MACKENZIE MOUNTAINS
Mackenzie River
Great Bear Lake
Great Slave Lake
Hudson Strait
HUDSON BAY
ALEXANDER ARCHIPELAGO
Juneau
COAST MOUNTAINS
ROCKY MOUNTAINS
Peace River
Lake Athabasca
QUEEN CHARLOTTE ISLANDS
CANADA
Athabasca River
Churchill River
Nelson River
Edmonton
Saskatchewan River
Lake Winnipeg
NEWFOUNDLAND
St. John's
ANTICOSTI ISLAND
GULF OF ST. LAWRENCE
VANCOUVER ISLAND
Vancouver
Victoria
Calgary
Regina
Winnipeg
Thunder Bay
Lake Superior
Quebec
St. Lawrence River
Halifax
Seattle
Montreal
Ottawa
Columbia River
MOUNTAINS
PACIFIC OCEAN
Portland
CASCADE RANGE
Snake River
Missouri River
GREAT PLAINS
Minneapolis
Lake Michigan
Lake Huron
Toronto
Lake Ontario
Boston
Hudson River
ATLANTIC OCEAN
Detroit
Lake Erie
New York
Philadelphia
Chicago
Cleveland
Great Salt Lake
GREAT BASIN
Platte River
Omaha
Washington
San Francisco
COAST RANGES
SIERRA NEVADA
Denver
Kansas City
Ohio River
Norfolk
APPALACHIAN
Arkansas River
St. Louis
BERMUDA
Colorado River
UNITED STATES OF AMERICA
Memphis
COLORADO PLATEAU
OZARK PLATEAU
Los Angeles
Albuquerque
Atlanta
Phoenix
Red River
Birmingham
Mississippi
El Paso
Dallas
Jacksonville
Ciudad Juárez
Rio Grande
Houston
New Orleans
THE BAHAMAS
Chihuahua
SIERRA MADRE OCCIDENTAL
SIERRA MADRE ORIENTAL
Miami
TROPIC OF CANCER
GULF OF CALIFORNIA
GULF OF MEXICO
Monterrey
Havana
VIRGIN ISLANDS
CUBA
HAITI
DOMINICAN REPUBLIC
San Juan
PUERTO RICO
MEXICO
León
Guadalajara
Port-au-Prince
Santo Domingo
JAMAICA
Kingston
Mexico City
Puebla
BELIZE
Belmopan
Acapulco
CARIBBEAN SEA
GUATEMALA
Guatemala
HONDURAS
Tegucigalpa
San Salvador
EL SALVADOR
NICARAGUA
Managua
San José
Panamá
COSTA RICA
PANAMA
SOUTH AMERICA
EQUATOR
ELEVATION in meters
OVER 2000
1000 - 2000
200 - 1000
0 - 200
HAWAII (U.S.A.)
KAUAI
NIIHAU
OAHU
Honolulu
MOLOKAI
LANAI
MAUI
KAHOOLAWE
HAWAII
0 100 miles
0 100 kilometers
0 400 miles
0 400 kilometers
GUADELOUPE
DOMINICA
MARTINIQUE
GRENADA
BARBADOS
TRINIDAD AND TOBAGO
0 600 miles
0 600 kilometers

Azimuthal Equal Area Projection

Canada

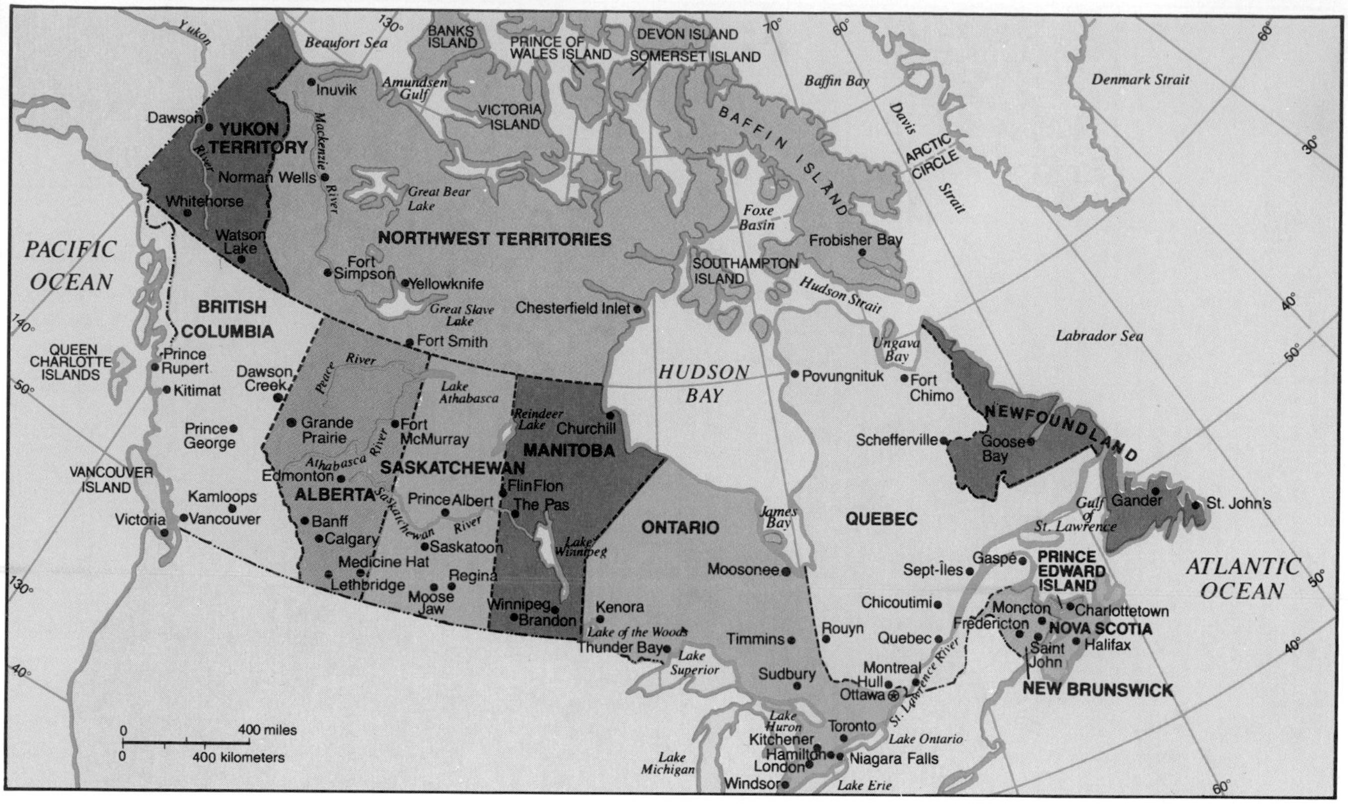
Yukon
Beaufort Sea
BANKS ISLAND
PRINCE OF WALES ISLAND
DEVON ISLAND
SOMERSET ISLAND
Baffin Bay
Denmark Strait
Inuvik
Amundsen Gulf
VICTORIA ISLAND
Dawson
YUKON TERRITORY
Mackenzie River
BAFFIN ISLAND
Davis Strait
ARCTIC CIRCLE
Norman Wells
Great Bear Lake
Whitehorse
Watson Lake
NORTHWEST TERRITORIES
Foxe Basin
Frobisher Bay
PACIFIC OCEAN
Fort Simpson
Yellowknife
SOUTHAMPTON ISLAND
Hudson Strait
BRITISH COLUMBIA
Great Slave Lake
Chesterfield Inlet
Fort Smith
Ungava Bay
Labrador Sea
QUEEN CHARLOTTE ISLANDS
Prince Rupert
Kitimat
Dawson Creek
Peace River
Lake Athabasca
HUDSON BAY
Povungnituk
Fort Chimo
Reindeer Lake
Churchill
NEWFOUNDLAND
Prince George
Grande Prairie
Fort McMurray
MANITOBA
Schefferville
Goose Bay
VANCOUVER ISLAND
Edmonton
Athabasca River
SASKATCHEWAN
Flin Flon
The Pas
Kamloops
ALBERTA
Prince Albert
Saskatchewan River
Vancouver
Victoria
Banff
Calgary
Saskatoon
ONTARIO
James Bay
QUEBEC
Gulf of St. Lawrence
Gander
St. John's
Lake Winnipeg
Medicine Hat
Regina
Lethbridge
Moose Jaw
Moosonee
Sept-Îles
Gaspé
PRINCE EDWARD ISLAND
ATLANTIC OCEAN
Winnipeg
Brandon
Kenora
Chicoutimi
Moncton
Charlottetown
Lake of the Woods
Thunder Bay
Rouyn
Fredericton
NOVA SCOTIA
Timmins
Quebec
Saint John
Halifax
Lake Superior
Sudbury
Montreal
St. Lawrence River
Hull
Ottawa
NEW BRUNSWICK
Lake Huron
Toronto
Kitchener
Lake Ontario
Hamilton
Niagara Falls
London
Lake Michigan
Windsor
Lake Erie
400 miles
400 kilometers

Azimuthal Equal Area Projection

Mexico

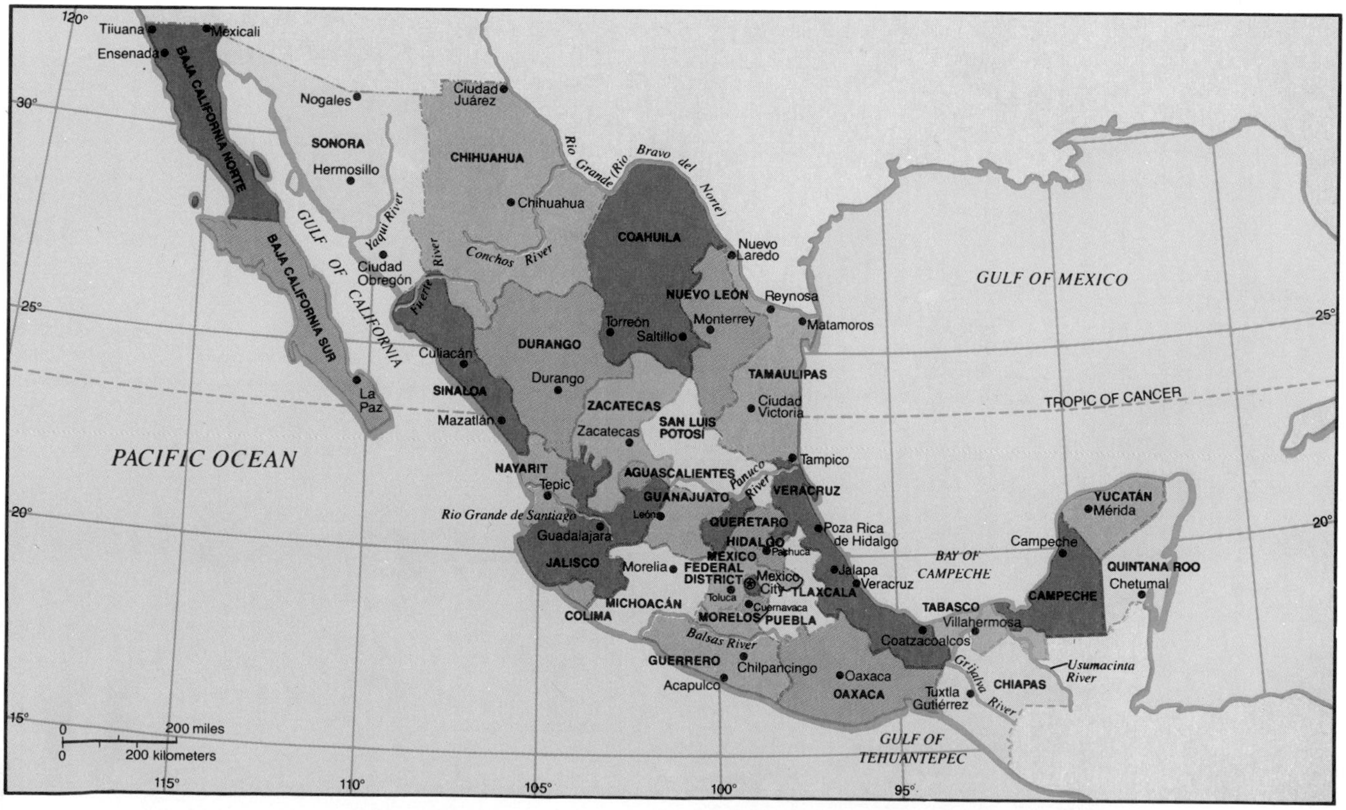
Tijuana
Mexicali
Ensenada
BAJA CALIFORNIA NORTE
Ciudad Juárez
Nogales
SONORA
CHIHUAHUA
Hermosillo
Rio Grande (Rio Bravo del Norte)
Chihuahua
GULF OF CALIFORNIA
Yaqui River
COAHUILA
BAJA CALIFORNIA SUR
Ciudad Obregón
Conchos River
Nuevo Laredo
GULF OF MEXICO
Fuerte River
NUEVO LEÓN
Reynosa
Torreón
Monterrey
Saltillo
Matamoros
DURANGO
Culiacán
TAMAULIPAS
La Paz
SINALOA
Durango
Ciudad Victoria
TROPIC OF CANCER
ZACATECAS
SAN LUIS POTOSÍ
Mazatlán
Zacatecas
PACIFIC OCEAN
Tampico
NAYARIT
AGUASCALIENTES
Panuco River
Tepic
GUANAJUATO
VERACRUZ
YUCATÁN
León
Mérida
Rio Grande de Santiago
QUERÉTARO
Poza Rica de Hidalgo
Campeche
Guadalajara
HIDALGO
Pachuca
BAY OF CAMPECHE
JALISCO
MÉXICO
QUINTANA ROO
Morelia
FEDERAL DISTRICT
Mexico City
Jalapa
Veracruz
Chetumal
Toluca
TLAXCALA
CAMPECHE
MICHOACÁN
Cuernavaca
TABASCO
COLIMA
MORELOS
PUEBLA
Villahermosa
Balsas River
Coatzacoalcos
GUERRERO
Chilpancingo
Grijalva River
Usumacinta River
Oaxaca
Acapulco
OAXACA
Tuxtla Gutiérrez
CHIAPAS
GULF OF TEHUANTEPEC
200 miles
200 kilometers

United States*

Albers Equal Area Projection

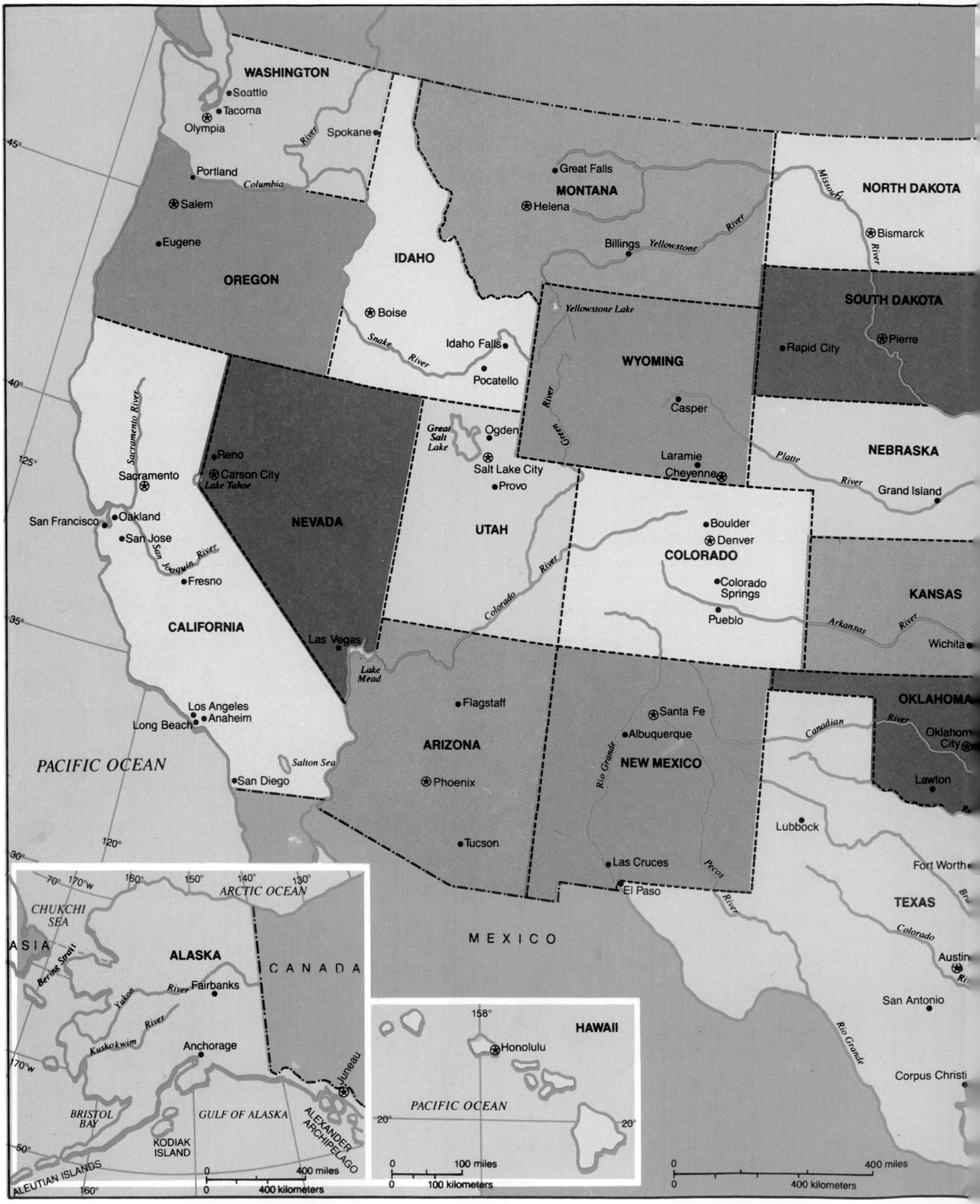

* To understand the relative locations of Alaska and Hawaii as well as the vast distances separating them from the rest of the United States, see the map on pages 1076–77.

South America

Azimuthal Equal Area Projection

CARIBBEAN SEA
Barranquilla
Cartagena
Maracaibo
Lake Maracaibo
Caracas
Valencia
Port of Spain
TRINIDAD AND TOBAGO
VENEZUELA
Ciudad Bolívar
Georgetown
Paramaribo
Cayenne
GUYANA
SURINAME
FRENCH GUIANA
Medellín
Bogotá
Cali
Magdalena River
Orinoco River
COLOMBIA
Rio Negro
MARAJÓ ISLAND
EQUATOR
Quito
ECUADOR
Guayaquil
Manaus
Amazon River
Belém
Marañón River
Fortaleza
Madeira River
Tapajoz River
Xingu River
Tocantins River
PERU
Ucayali River
BRAZIL
Recife
São Francisco River
Callao
Lima
Cuzco
Salvador
Lake Titicaca
BOLIVIA
La Paz
Brasília
Goiânia
Sucre
PACIFIC OCEAN
Paraná River
Belo Horizonte
Paraguay River
PARAGUAY
Campinas
Nova Iguaçu
Rio de Janeiro
São Paulo
Santos
TROPIC OF CAPRICORN
Curitiba
Asunción
Tucumán
Salado River
CHILE
ATLANTIC OCEAN
Uruguay River
Pôrto Alegre
Córdoba
Rosario
URUGUAY
Montevideo
Valparaiso
Santiago
Buenos Aires
La Plata
Rio de la Plata
Concepción
ARGENTINA
0 1000 miles
0 1000 kilometers
FALKLAND ISLANDS
Punta Arenas
Strait of Magellan
TIERRA DEL FUEGO
CAPE HORN
SOUTH GEORGIA
80°
60°
50°
40°
10°N
0°
10°S
20°
30°
40°
50°
100°
90°
70°
30°
20°

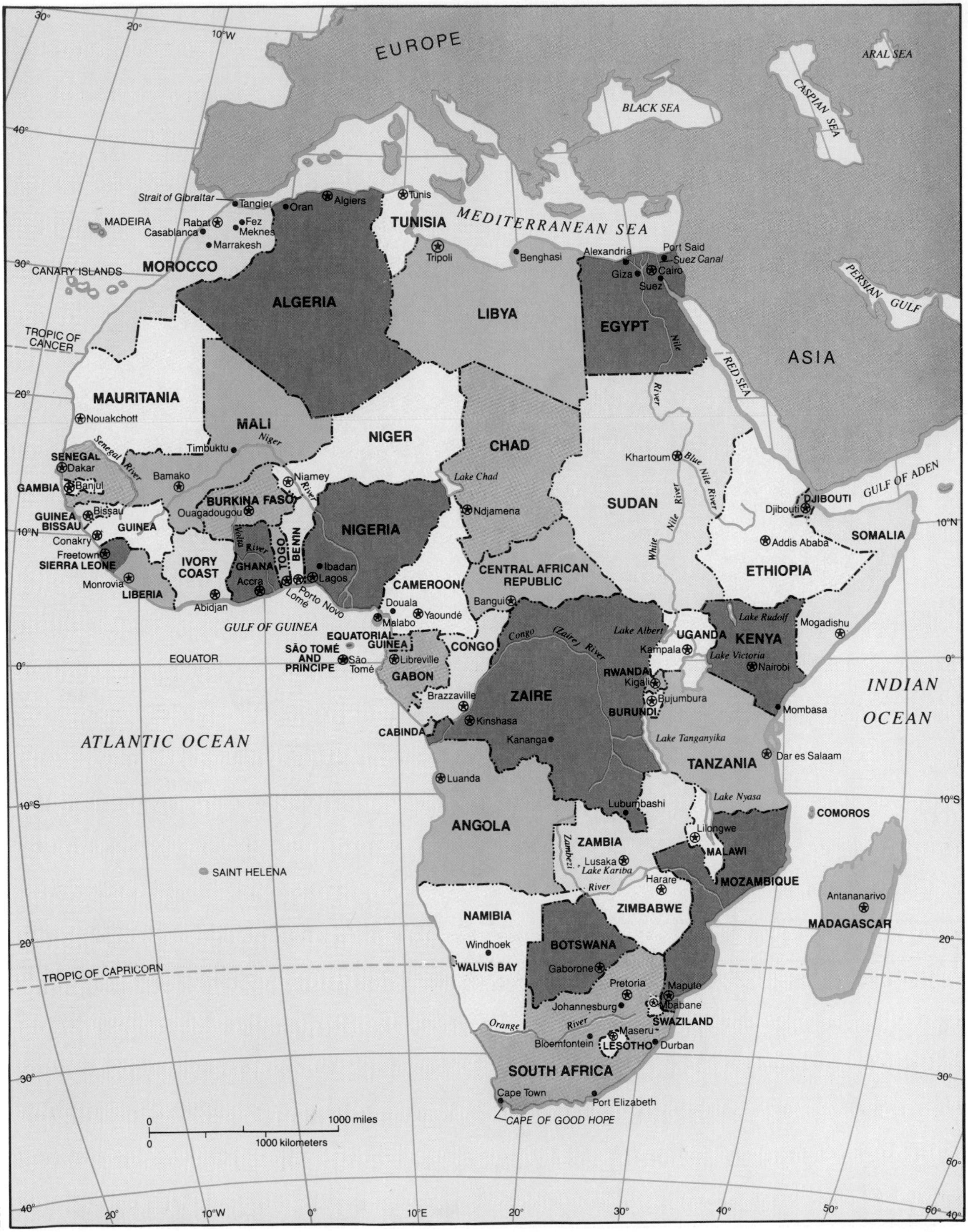
EUROPE
ARAL SEA
BLACK SEA
CASPIAN SEA
Strait of Gibraltar
Tangier
Oran
Algiers
Tunis
MADEIRA
Rabat
Fez
Meknes
Casablanca
Marrakesh
TUNISIA
MEDITERRANEAN SEA
Tripoli
Benghasi
Alexandria
Port Said
Suez Canal
Giza
Cairo
Suez
CANARY ISLANDS
MOROCCO
ALGERIA
LIBYA
EGYPT
Nile
PERSIAN GULF
TROPIC OF CANCER
RED SEA
ASIA
MAURITANIA
Nouakchott
MALI
Niger
NIGER
CHAD
Timbuktu
SENEGAL
Dakar
Senegal River
Bamako
Niamey
Niger River
Lake Chad
Khartoum
Blue Nile River
GAMBIA
Banjul
BURKINA FASO
Ouagadougou
NIGERIA
Ndjamena
SUDAN
White Nile River
DJIBOUTI
Djibouti
GULF OF ADEN
GUINEA-BISSAU
Bissau
GUINEA
Conakry
Freetown
SIERRA LEONE
Monrovia
LIBERIA
IVORY COAST
Abidjan
Volta River
GHANA
Accra
TOGO
BENIN
Lomé
Porto Novo
Ibadan
Lagos
CAMEROON
Douala
Malabo
Yaoundé
CENTRAL AFRICAN REPUBLIC
Bangui
Addis Ababa
SOMALIA
ETHIOPIA
Lake Rudolf
KENYA
Mogadishu
GULF OF GUINEA
EQUATORIAL GUINEA
SÃO TOMÉ AND PRINCIPE
São Tomé
Libreville
GABON
CONGO
Congo (Zaire) River
Lake Albert
UGANDA
Kampala
Lake Victoria
Nairobi
EQUATOR
RWANDA
Kigali
BURUNDI
Bujumbura
Brazzaville
ZAIRE
Kinshasa
Mombasa
INDIAN OCEAN
ATLANTIC OCEAN
CABINDA
Kananga
Lake Tanganyika
TANZANIA
Dar es Salaam
Luanda
Lubumbashi
Lake Nyasa
COMOROS
ANGOLA
Lilongwe
ZAMBIA
Zambezi River
Lusaka
Lake Kariba
MALAWI
SAINT HELENA
Harare
MOZAMBIQUE
Antananarivo
MADAGASCAR
NAMIBIA
ZIMBABWE
Windhoek
BOTSWANA
WALVIS BAY
Gaborone
TROPIC OF CAPRICORN
Pretoria
Maputo
Johannesburg
Mbabane
Orange River
SWAZILAND
Maseru
Bloemfontein
LESOTHO
Durban
SOUTH AFRICA
Cape Town
Port Elizabeth
CAPE OF GOOD HOPE
0 1000 miles
0 1000 kilometers
30°
20°
10°W
40°
30°
20°
10°N
0°
10°S
20°
30°
40°
20°
10°W
0°
10°E
20°
30°
40°
50°
60°
10°N
0°
10°S
20°
30°
60°
40°

Europe

Azimuthal Equal Area Projection

45°
60°
BARENTS SEA
Murmansk
WHITE SEA
Arkhangelsk
Lake Onega
Lake Ladoga
UNION OF SOVIET SOCIALIST REPUBLICS
Perm
ASIA
Rostov
Gorki
Volga River
Kazan
Moscow
Kuybyshev
Saratov
Don River
Kiev
Kharkov
Dnieper River
Ural River
Volgograd
Dnepropetrovsk
Donetsk
Odessa
SEA OF AZOV
Astrakhan
ARAL SEA
BLACK SEA
CASPIAN SEA
Tbilisi
Baku
Yerevan
CYPRUS
0
1000 miles
0
1000 kilometers

Asia

Robinson Projection

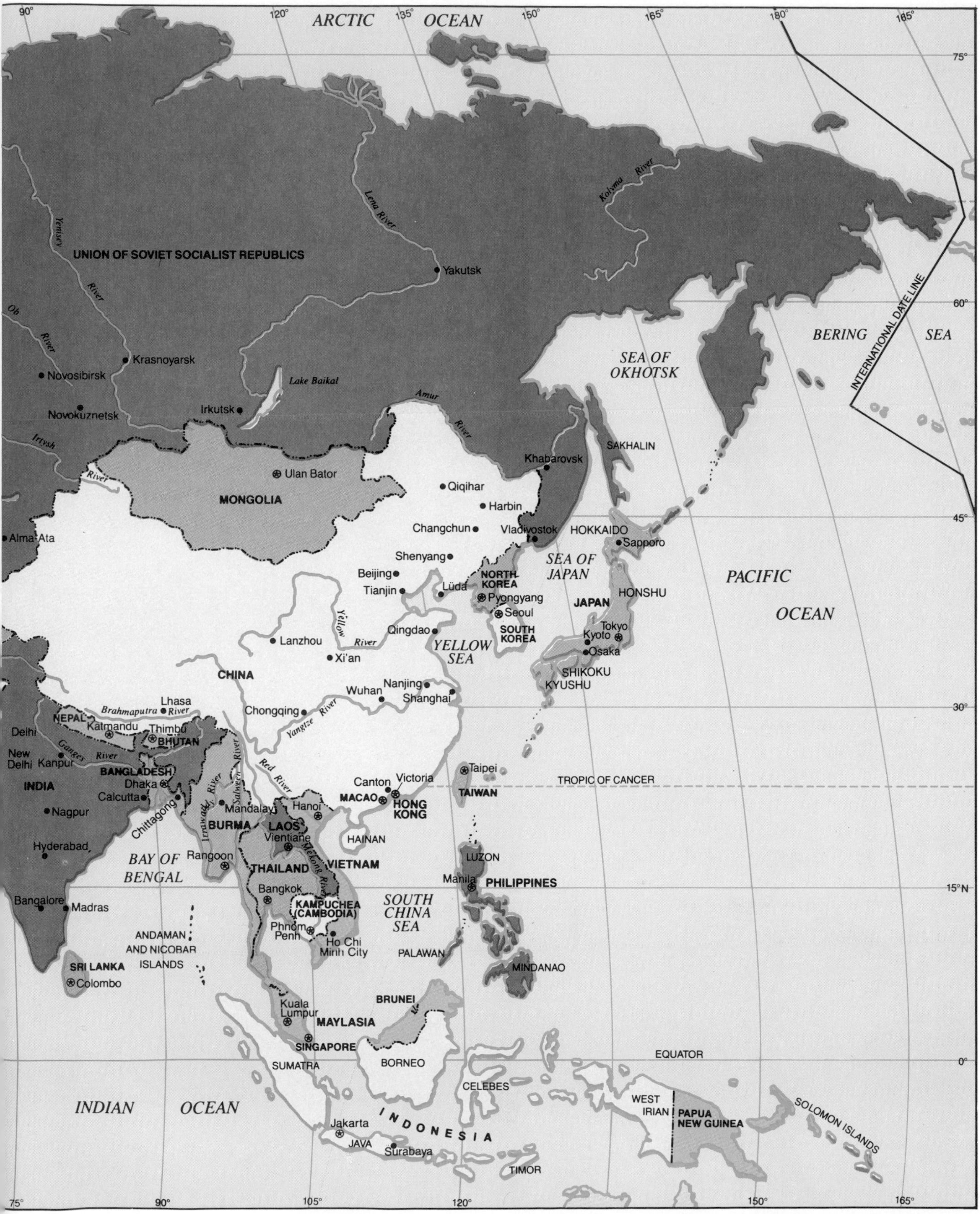
ARCTIC OCEAN
UNION OF SOVIET SOCIALIST REPUBLICS
Yakutsk
Krasnoyarsk
Novosibirsk
Novokuznetsk
Irkutsk
Lake Baikal
Yenisey River
Ob River
Irtysh River
Lena River
Kolyma River
Amur River
SEA OF OKHOTSK
BERING SEA
INTERNATIONAL DATE LINE
SAKHALIN
Khabarovsk
MONGOLIA
Ulan Bator
Qiqihar
Harbin
Changchun
Vladivostok
HOKKAIDO
Sapporo
Alma-Ata
Shenyang
Beijing
Tianjin
Lüda
NORTH KOREA
Pyongyang
Seoul
SOUTH KOREA
SEA OF JAPAN
JAPAN
HONSHU
PACIFIC OCEAN
Tokyo
Kyoto
Osaka
SHIKOKU
KYUSHU
Qingdao
YELLOW SEA
Yellow River
Lanzhou
Xi'an
CHINA
Nanjing
Wuhan
Shanghai
Lhasa
Brahmaputra River
Chongqing
Yangtze River
NEPAL
Katmandu
Thimbu
BHUTAN
Delhi
New Delhi
Kanpur
Ganges River
INDIA
BANGLADESH
Dhaka
Calcutta
Chittagong
Red River
Salween River
Irrawaddy River
Mandalay
BURMA
Hanoi
LAOS
Vientiane
Canton
Victoria
MACAO
HONG KONG
HAINAN
Taipei
TAIWAN
TROPIC OF CANCER
Nagpur
Hyderabad
BAY OF BENGAL
Rangoon
THAILAND
VIETNAM
Mekong River
LUZON
Manila
PHILIPPINES
Bangkok
KAMPUCHEA (CAMBODIA)
SOUTH CHINA SEA
Bangalore
Madras
Phnom Penh
Ho Chi Minh City
ANDAMAN AND NICOBAR ISLANDS
PALAWAN
MINDANAO
SRI LANKA
Colombo
BRUNEI
Kuala Lumpur
MAYLASIA
SINGAPORE
SUMATRA
BORNEO
EQUATOR
CELEBES
INDIAN OCEAN
INDONESIA
WEST IRIAN
PAPUA NEW GUINEA
SOLOMON ISLANDS
Jakarta
JAVA
Surabaya
TIMOR
90°
120°
135°
150°
165°
180°
165°
75°
60°
45°
30°
15°N
0°
75°
90°
105°
120°
150°
165°

Australia and New Zealand

Mercator Projection

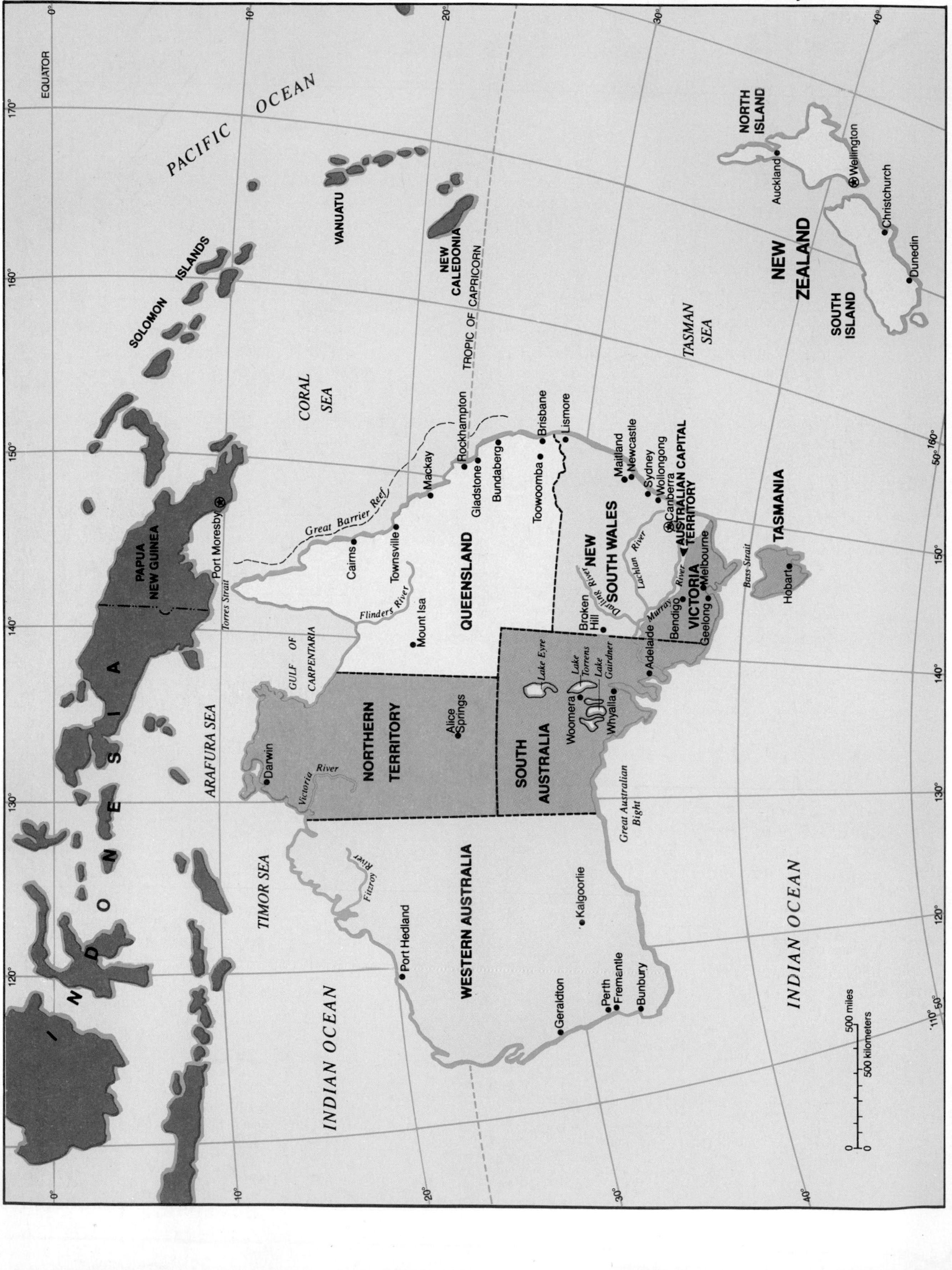

EQUATOR
PACIFIC OCEAN
SOLOMON ISLANDS
VANUATU
NEW CALEDONIA
TROPIC OF CAPRICORN
CORAL SEA
TASMAN SEA
NORTH ISLAND
SOUTH ISLAND
NEW ZEALAND
Auckland
Wellington
Christchurch
Dunedin
PAPUA NEW GUINEA
Port Moresby
Torres Strait
I N D O N E S I A
ARAFURA SEA
TIMOR SEA
GULF OF CARPENTARIA
Great Barrier Reef
Cairns
Townsville
Mackay
Rockhampton
Gladstone
Bundaberg
Brisbane
Lismore
Toowoomba
Flinders River
Mount Isa
QUEENSLAND
NORTHERN TERRITORY
Darwin
Victoria River
Alice Springs
SOUTH AUSTRALIA
Lake Eyre
Lake Torrens
Lake Gairdner
Woomera
Whyalla
Adelaide
Broken Hill
Darling River
Lachlan River
Murray River
NEW SOUTH WALES
Maitland
Newcastle
Sydney
Wollongong
Canberra
AUSTRALIAN CAPITAL TERRITORY
VICTORIA
Bendigo
Melbourne
Geelong
Bass Strait
TASMANIA
Hobart
Great Australian Bight
WESTERN AUSTRALIA
Fitzroy River
Port Hedland
Kalgoorlie
Geraldton
Perth
Frementle
Bunbury
INDIAN OCEAN
INDIAN OCEAN
500 miles
500 kilometers
0
0

C
D
E
F
G
H
I
J